Carolyn W. Lima
John A. Lima

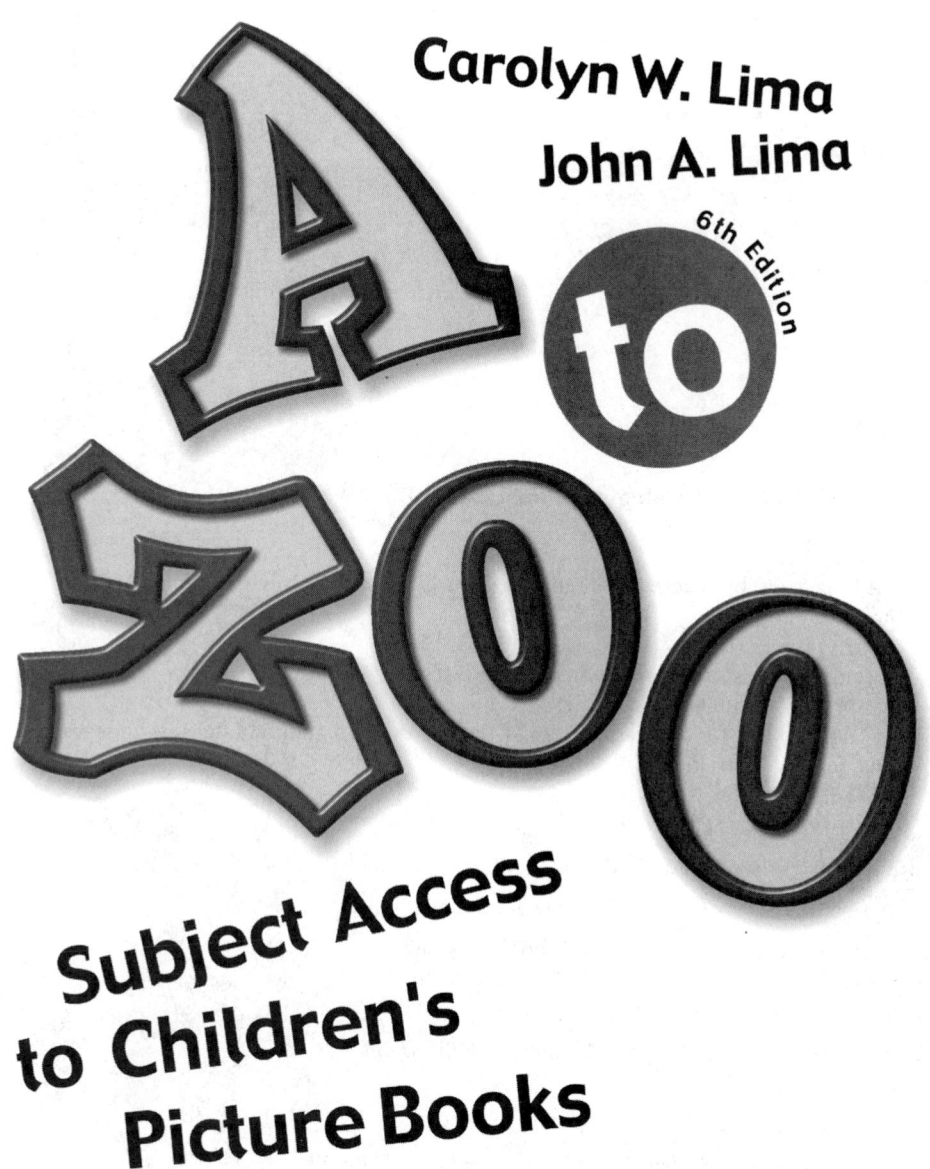

6th Edition

A to ZOO

Subject Access
to Children's
Picture Books

Bowker-Greenwood
Westport, Connecticut • London

Library of Congress Cataloging-in-Publication Data

Lima, Carolyn W.
   A to zoo : subject access to children's picture books / Carolyn W. Lima and John A.
Lima—6th ed.
      p. cm.
   Includes bibliographical references and indexes.
   ISBN 0–313–32069–1 (alk. paper)
   1. Picture books for children—Indexes. 2. Children's literature, English—Indexes. I.
Lima, John A. II. Title.
   Z1037 .L715 2001
   011.62—dc21   2001037398

British Library Cataloguing in Publication Data is available.

Library of Congress Catalog Card Number: 2001037398
ISBN: 0–313–32069–1

First published in 2001

Bowker-Greenwood, 88 Post Road West, Westport, CT 06881
An imprint of Greenwood Publishing Group, Inc.
www.greenwood.com

Printed in the United States of America

The paper used in this book complies with the
Permanent Paper Standard issued by the National
Information Standards Organization (Z39.48–1984).

10 9 8 7 6 5 4 3 2 1

A to Zoo is a trademark of Reed Properties, Inc., used under license.

Dedication

To the loving memory of my father, Herbert Efton Womack,
who taught me the value of storytelling.

Contents

Preface

The picture book, long a source of delight and learning for young readers, continues to gain importance over the years with the increasing emphasis on early childhood education and the growing need for supervised child care for working mothers. Teachers, librarians, and parents are finding the picture book an important learning and entertainment tool. Choosing the right book for a particular situation can be time-consuming and frustrating without some guidance. Many responsible professionals and parents have neither the time nor the materials to develop an intimate familiarity with the field. Rather than simply choosing the first title that appears to treat a specific subject from among the many thousands of books available, the user can now confidently identify a book that will cover the desired subject, using this sixth edition of *A to Zoo: Subject Access to Children's Picture Books*. The only comprehensive guide of its kind, *A to Zoo* has nearly 23,000 titles cataloged under more than 1,200 subjects.

Originally, the titles in *A to Zoo* were based on the San Diego (California) Public Library's collection of picture books for children. But recent editions of *A to Zoo* have outgrown even this large and versatile collection, which remains typical of the best and most carefully chosen children's work and was acquired over more than a century. In an effort to ensure that the most up-to-date information is included in this edition of *A to Zoo*, the authors consulted many sources. Other public and university library collections, review copies from various publishers, published reviews, and the authors' personal searches of titles and literature provided an information base. The authors read nearly every book to determine subject information and suitability. Out-of-print titles are included because school and public library collections consist mostly of out-of-print materials.

The picture book, as broadly defined within the scope of this book, is a fiction or nonfiction title with illustrations occupying as much or more space than the text and with text, vocabulary, or concepts suitable for preschool through grade two. It is noted, however, that picture books appeal to a wider audience; adults, older children, and others often find picture books enjoyable, useful, and informative.[1]

The "Introduction: Genesis of the English-Language Picture Book" has been updated, and recent sources and reference works have been added to the list of suggested titles for further reading. Developments of historical proportions have not been discerned in the few years since the fifth edition was published (1998). Some trends, however, still seem evident: mechanical and "pop-up" books remain prolific; attention to the very young reader is reflected in a large number of "board books"—books with cardboard pages designed for tiny tots; and there is a continued trend toward picture books of a serious nature, bearing a message or lesson, designed to accomplish some social purpose other than mere entertainment of the young reader. Indeed, nonfiction is becoming more and more available for younger and younger readers.[2] Others have noted[3] the new graphic trends in children's picture books, including the treatment of black as an actual color, the spatial relations of objects, and the use of technologies that lend new life to collages and other media. Two examples of black-and-white books that have recaptured interest in that "color" combination are *Jumanji* and *The Garden of Abdul Gasazi*, both by Chris Van Allsburg.[4]

Recent trends in education, particularly for illiterate or second-language students emphasize picture books—once relegated to children's use only—as a beginning for adults because of the controlled vocabulary and concepts.[5] Indeed, one publication[6] makes note of "crossover" books, one book with two markets, such as picture books that also appeal to adults. Graeme Base's books *Animalia* and *The Sign of the Seahorse* are prominent examples. A large number of classics continue to be reissued, some with new illustrations; and a significant trend is the continually improved quality of art work in picture books. Such artists as Barry Moser, William Joyce, Chris Van Allsburg, Thomas Locker, and, very recently, Thomas Kincaid, have contributed to the improvement of picture books and to the acceptance of picture books as quality literature and art.

One other trend of note: the picture book has joined the realm of the e-book. More than one hundred virtual picture books can now be purchased and read or viewed in cyberspace at www.ipicturebooks.com.[7]

HOW TO USE THIS BOOK

A to Zoo can be used to obtain information about children's picture books in two ways: to learn the titles, authors, and illustrators of books on a particular subject, such as "dragons" or "weddings"; or to ascertain the subject (or subjects) when only the title, author and title, or illustrator and title are known. For example, if the title *The Sugaring-Off Party* is known, this volume will enable the user to discover that *The Sugaring-Off Party* is written by Jonathan London, illustrated by Gilles Pelletier, and published by Dutton in 1995, and that it also concerns Family life—grandmothers, Food, Foreign lands—Canada, and Trees.

For ease and convenience of reference use, *A to Zoo* is divided into five sections:

> Subject Headings
> Subject Guide
> Bibliographic Guide
> Title Index
> Illustrator Index

SUBJECT HEADINGS: This section contains an alphabetical list of the subjects cataloged in this book. The subject headings reflect the established terms used commonly in public libraries, originally based on questions asked by parents and teachers and then modified and adapted by librarians. To facilitate reference use, and because subjects are requested in a variety of terms, the list of subject headings contains numerous cross-references. Subheadings are arranged alphabetically under each general topic, for example:

Animals (general topic)
Animals—anteaters (subheading)
Animals—antelopes (subheading)
Animals—apes *see* Animals—gorillas; Animals—monkeys (cross-reference)

SUBJECT GUIDE: This guide to nearly 23,000 picture books for preschool children through second graders is cataloged under more than 1,200 subjects. The guide reflects the arrangement in the Subject Headings, alphabetically arranged by subject heading and subheading. Many books, of course, relate to more than one subject, and this comprehensive list provides a means of identifying all those books that may contain any information or material on a particular subject.

If, for example, the user wants books on crabs (crustaceans), the Subject Headings section will show that Crustaceans is a subject classification. A look in the Subject Guide reveals that under Crustaceans there are 28 titles listed alphabetically by author.

BIBLIOGRAPHIC GUIDE: Each book is listed with full bibliographic information. This section is arranged alphabetically by author, or by title when the author is unknown, or by uniform (classic) title. Each entry contains bibliographic information in order: author, title, illustrator, publisher and date of publication, miscellaneous notes when given, International Standard Book Number (ISBN), and subjects, listed according to the alphabetical classification in the Subject Headings section. Where ISBNs appear they probably indicate entries new to the third and subsequent editions, and are the library binding edition or the next best quality edition available. However, many older books have been given ISBNs retrospectively, and where these were available, the entries have been updated.

The user can consult the Bibliographic Guide to find complete data on each of the 28 titles listed in the Subject Guide under the subject of Crustaceans, as for example:

Knutson, Barbara. *Why the crab has no head: an African tale* ill. by author. Carolrhoda Books, 1987. ISBN 0-87614-322-2. Subj: Behavior—boasting. Crustaceans. Folk and fairy tales. Foreign lands—Africa. Foreign lands—Zaire.

In the case of joint authors, the second author is listed in alphabetical order, followed by the book title and the name of the primary author or main entry. The user can then locate the first-named author for complete bibliographic information. For example:

Stoker, Wayne. *I can be a welder* (Lillegard, Dee)

Bibliographic information for this title will be found in the Bibliographic Guide section under "Lillegard, Dee."

Titles for an author who is both a single author and a joint author are interfiled alphabetically. Where the author is not known, the entry is listed alphabetically by title with complete bibliographic information following the same format as given above.

Library of Congress conventions regarding the cataloged name of the author(s) have been followed in this edition. Thus, books published under the name "Aliki" are listed in alphabetical order under Aliki; a cross-reference with the name "Brandenberg, Aliki" refers the user to the name preferred.

TITLE INDEX: This section contains an alphabetical list of all titles in the book with authors in parentheses, followed by the page number of the full listing in the Bibliographic Guide, such as:

> *Albert's story* (Long, Claudia), 1018

If a title has no known author, the name of the illustrator is given if available. When multiple versions of the same title are listed, the illustrator's name is given with the author's name (when known) in parentheses:

> *The night before Christmas*, ill. by Michael Foreman (Moore, Clement C.), 1080
> *The night before Christmas*, ill. by Gyo Fujikawa (Moore, Clement C.), 1080

ILLUSTRATOR INDEX: This section contains an alphabetical list of illustrators with titles and authors, followed by the page number of the full listing in the Bibliographic Guide, for example:

> Glasser, Judy. *Albert's story* (Long, Claudia), 1018

Titles listed under an illustrator's name appear in alphabetical sequence. When the author is the same as the illustrator the author's name is not repeated.

Notes

1. Hearne, Betsy Gould, and Deborah Stevenson. *Choosing Books for Children: A Commonsense Guide.* Urbana, Ill.: Univ. of Illinois Press, 1999.

2. Horning, Kathleen T. *From Cover to Cover: Evaluating and Reviewing Children's Books.* New York: HarperCollins, 1997.

3. Hale, Robert D. *Horn Book Magazine* (May/June 1994), p. 356.

4. Silvey, Anita. *Horn Book Magazine* (Sept./Oct. 1994), p. 516.

5. Ammon, Bette D., and Gale W. Sherman. *Worth a Thousand Words: An Annotated Guide to Picture Books for Older Readers.* Englewood, Colo.: Libraries Unlimited, 1996.

6. *Publishers Weekly* (Nov. 23, 1992), p. 38.

7. Maughan, Shannon. *Publishers Weekly* (Jan. 29, 2001), pp. 30–32.

Acknowledgments

The authors wish to express their thanks for the assistance provided by many people in bringing this book together. Special thanks to our editors, first at R. R. Bowker and then at Greenwood Press; Nancy Bucenec of Bowker for her patience and confidence, and Lynn Malloy of Greenwood for her expertise and assistance in taking over this project and making it work. Special thanks also to Catherine Barr, Julia C. Miller, and Chris McNaull, who did much work on the database, sorting, and typesetting for both this and the previous edition.

We also wish to thank many publishers for providing review copies of their picture books, especially HarperCollins; Harcourt Brace; Firefly Books; Little, Brown; Crowell; Lothrop; Lippincott; Holiday House, Greenwillow and Morrow; and Hyperion Books.

Introduction
Genesis of the English-Language Picture Book

Each year increasing numbers of children's books are published, each one touched in some way by those that preceded it. Consumer awareness is on the rise, books are being mass marketed, and the Internet is being used to market, promote, and even display children's books.[1] But how or by what path did the unique genre known as children's picture books arrive at this present and prolific state? Certainly, to imagine a time when children's books did not exist takes more than a little effort.

Probably the roots of what we know as children's literature lie in the stories and folktales told and retold through the centuries in every civilization since human beings first learned to speak. These stories were narrated over and over as a sort of oral history, literature, and education.[2] But they were not intended, either primarily or exclusively, for children. It was only through the passing years, as the children who were part of any audience responded with interest and delight to these tales and as adults found less leisure time in an increasingly busy world, that the stories and folktales came to be regarded as belonging to the world of the child. These were repeated or retold often by traveling storytellers. Some tales were written down, printed, and spread throughout England and Europe. In the nineteenth century, the brothers Grimm (Jacob and Wilhelm) invited storytellers to their home to narrate the folktales of Germany, and to collect them and refine them. They altered stories to make them more acceptable for children or for adults who were concerned about what children read and heard, creating a stylistic ideal for fairy tales "more proper and prudent for bourgeois audiences."[3]

Book art or book illustration began with manuscripts—handwritten on parchment or other materials, rolled or scrolled, and later loosely bound into books—that were illuminated or "decorated in lively, vigorous and versatile styles."[4] In time, these decorations—some realistic, some intricate, some imaginative—took on the technological advances of other art forms, notably stained glass, and color was introduced to illustrated texts.[5] The children's books that existed in the Middle Ages, before the invention of movable type, were rarely intended to amuse the reader. They were, instead, mostly instructional and moralizing. Monastic teachers, writing essentially for the children of wealthy families, usually wrote in Latin and "began the tradition of didacticism that was to dominate children's books for hundreds of years."[6] Children's books of that day frequently followed either the rhymed format or the question-and-answer format, both attributed to Aldhelm, abbot of Malmesbury.[7] An early encyclopedia, thought to be the work of Anselm (1033–1109), archbishop of Canterbury, addressed such subjects as "manners and customs, natural science, children's duties, morals, and religious precepts."[8] The books were intended for instruction and indoctrination in the principles of moral and religious belief and behavior,[9] an intent that persisted even after the invention of movable type. Indeed, "children were not born to live happy but to die holy, and true education lay in preparing the soul to meet its maker."[10]

Perhaps the first printed book that was truly intended for children, other than elementary Latin grammar texts, was the French *Les Contenances de la Table*, on the courtesies and manners of dining.[11] Printed and illustrated children's books in Europe followed the invention of printing in the fifteenth century. Those first books were printed in lowercase letters, and "blank spaces were left on the page for initials and marginal decorations to be added in color by hand. In general, the effect was the same as in manuscript.[12] Some well-known and important artists of the time did the illustrations, using woodcuts, engravings, and lithographic processes.[13] This combination of pictures and printed text, still with the intent of teaching and incorporating the earlier but persistent dedication to moral and religious education, finally resulted in what is often assumed to be the first real children's picture book in 1657—the *Orbis Pictus of John Amos Comenius*.[14] The simple idea of this Czech author was that a child could be taught most quickly by naming and showing the object at the same time, a seventeenth-century ABC! Noted for its many illustrations, the book contained the seeds of future children's publications, softening somewhat the earlier "harshness with which, in the unsympathetic age, the first steps of learning were always associated.[15]

In the English language, children's books followed a parallel pattern. William Caxton, England's first printer, was responsible for printing many books that, although intended for adults, were often adopted by children as their own. One, *Æsop's Fables* (about 1484), featured woodcut illustrations and is an early "milestone" in the history of children's literature.[16] His stories, the first for English children in their own language, gave the lessons of "The Fox and the Grapes" and "The Tortoise and the Hare" to children of the fifteenth century and all who followed thereafter.

Nearly 200 years later, American authors and books in English for American children began to appear. Like English publications before them, these books reflected a basic profile of moral and religious education. American John Cotton's *Spiritual Milk for Boston Babes* (1646) was not an especially easy text for the young minds that had to master its Puritan lessons. Later came similar books such as *Pilgrim's Progress* by John Bunyan (1678), *The New England Primer* with its rhyming alphabet (1691), and *Divine and Moral Songs for Children* by Isaac Watts (1715).

In the early eighteenth century, a significant movement began in English children's books with the publication of *Robinson Crusoe* by Daniel Defoe (1715), a narrative that delighted children as well as adults. This innovation, utilizing children's books to carry more intricate messages, perhaps aimed at adults as well as older children, reflected a growing sophistication of society and perhaps some shifting of purely religious or moral bases toward political morality. An all-time favorite with young readers, *Gulliver's Travels* by Jonathan Swift, published in 1726, illustrates this dual thrust. This work, embellished with a wit and rather pointed sarcasm that is sure to escape the young, nonetheless delighted children with the inhabitants of mythical lands and has survived through the years. Perhaps the ultimate development of this trend is found in Lewis Carroll's *Alice's Adventures in Wonderland* (1865), which manages to be perfectly palatable and interesting to children, yet contains subtle lessons for adult society. Although based on earlier plays and vignettes that had been written only for the purpose of entertainment and use of imagination, *Alice*, and other books of the time, began to reflect a change in society's view of children and of reading materials suitable for children.

The English translation of *Tales of Mother Goose* by Charles Perrault in 1729 made moral lessons for young readers less didactic, but it was 1744 that "saw the real foundation of something today everywhere taken for granted—the production of books for children's enjoyment."[17] This book from a small bookstall in London was *A Little Pretty Pocket-Book*, "now famous as the first book for children published by John Newbery."[18] It may indeed be the first book recognizing children as people with intelligence and human needs, notably the need for humor and entertainment.[19]

For the next 20 years or so, Newbery published well-illustrated and inexpensive little books for young readers. Soon other books designed especially for children followed this trend. Pictures became an essential and integral component, somewhat downplaying the soul-saving educational harshness of earlier books and promoting amusement and enlightened education. Thomas Bewick's first book specifically intended for children, *A Pretty Book of Pictures for Little Masters and Misses, or Tommy Trip's History of Beasts and Birds*, was published in 1779 and represented a major stride in the refinement of woodcuts used for book illustration. Bewick "developed better tools for this work, made effective use of the white line, and carried the woodcut to a high level of artistic achievement."[20] His efforts and those of his brother John had a more lasting effect on illustrators and illustrations for children's books. As a result of Bewick's contributions, "artists of established reputations began to sign their pictures for children's books."[21]

Some talented artists lovingly produced children's books with special artistic achievement, although their principal skills were directed toward adults. For example, William Blake, an artist and poet of considerable renown, published *Songs-of-Innocence* in 1789.[22] An engraver, he produced this "first great original picture book" using etched plates in which the garlands and scrolls of his own original design were lovingly engraved and hand-colored after printing.[23]

Some efforts were also great commercial successes. When John Harris published, in 1805, *The Comic Adventures of Old Mother Hubbard and her Dog*, by "S.C.M." [Sarah Catherine Martin], he sold some 10,000 copies in a few months. Within a year, twenty editions had been issued. Adults as well as children enjoyed the humor of Old Mother Hubbard.[24] The serious business of writing and illustrating children's books was now respectable and worthwhile, and those books had a feeling of class. But such loving dedication as that of William Blake and others did not long enjoy a singular place in publishing history. Commercialism soon entered the scene and, although some very dedicated people in America and England alike continued to develop books for children, some hackwork also appeared. "Publishers, realizing that children formed a new and somewhat undiscriminating market, were quick to take advantage of the fact. Having chosen a suitable title, and having available some spare woodcut blocks that might be sufficiently relevant for a juvenile book, a publisher would commission a story or series of tales to be woven around the illustrations. One of the results of this was that illustrations of different proportions might be used in the same story, while on other occasions it was clear that the pictures were by different hands. Sometimes the inclusion of a picture was obviously forced. A good example occurs in one of the editions of *Goody Two-Shoes*," attributed to Oliver Goldsmith.[25]

Fortunately, under the guidance of innovative and bold publishers, carefully designed works, crafted with an eye toward the complete and final unit and with special consideration for the means of production, appeared in the field of children's picture books. Beautiful printing became the mark of publishers such as Edmund Evans, printer and artist in his own right, who with his special skill in color engraving published the works of Walter Crane, Randolph Caldecott, and Kate Greenaway. The work of the three great English picture-book artists of the nineteenth century represents the best to be found in picture books for children in any era; the strength of design and richness of color and detail of Walter Crane's pictures; the eloquence, humor, vitality, and movement of Randolph Caldecott's art; and the tenderness, dignity, and grace of the very personal interpretation of Kate Greenaway's enchanted land of childhood."[26]

These three were indeed great names in the history of children's picture books. The first nursery picture books of Walter Crane, an apprentice wood engraver, were *Sing a Song for Sixpence, The House That Jack Built, Dame Trot and Her Comical Cat,* and *The History of Cock Robin and Jenny Wren,* published by the firm of Warne in 1865 and 1866. Crane was one of the first of the modern illustrators who believe that text and illustrations should be in harmony, forming a complete unit. Randolph Caldecott, who began drawing at age six, could make animals come alive on a page. During his short life (1846–1886), he illustrated numerous books for children, producing fine examples of fun and good humor including *The Diverting History of John Gilpin* and *The Babes in the Wood.* His preeminence in the art of the children's picture book has been acknowledged by many more recent artists, and is certainly a seminal factor in the establishment of the English style as a standard by which to measure picture book art.[27]

Kate Greenaway's simple verses made an appropriate accompaniment to her lovely drawings. *Under the Window* was her first picture book, published by Routledge in 1878. Everywhere in her books are the flowers she so loved. She is probably best known for her *Almanacs,* published between 1883 and 1897. Like Crane, Caldecott, and Greenaway, the works of Britain's Beatrix Potter became well known to American children. Potter, a self-taught artist specializing in animals with charming characteristics, produced a number of tales for young children, the best known being *The Tale of Peter Rabbit* (1901), which presented the illustrations as an integral part of the story and marked a pivotal point in the development of the modern picture book in Europe. The excellence of the growing children's book field in England eclipsed the technologically inferior American product, virtually driving American efforts from the marketplace until nearly 15 years after World War I.[28]

Meanwhile, the books of such English artists as L. Leslie Brooke, Arthur Rackham, Edmund Dulac, Charles Folkard, and others continued the tradition of excellence through the first three decades of the twentieth century. Despite the superior English publications, "a self-conscious and systematic concern for children and the books they read had been growing in the United States."[29] Children's libraries and children's librarians appeared around the turn of the century. In 1916, the Bookshop for Boys and Girls was founded in Boston.[30] In 1924 the Bookshop published *The Horn Book Magazine,* "the first journal in the world to be devoted to the critical appraisal of children's books."[31] Another publication, *Junior Libraries,* made its appearance in 1954; this periodical later became *School Library Journal,* published by R. R. Bowker. In this area, the Americans were ten years ahead of Europeans.

Publishers and editors were becoming more and more oriented toward children's literature. In 1919, Macmillan established a Children's Book Department separate from its adult publishing line; other publishing houses began to do the same. Children's Book Week was instituted, an idea that started with Franklin K. Mathiews and was supported by Frederic G. Melcher. A landmark in children's book publishing was established in the United States in 1922 when Melcher, then chief editor of *Publishers Weekly,* proposed at the 1921 American Library Association meeting that a medal be awarded each year for the year's most distinguished contribution to American literature for children written by an American citizen or resident and published in the United States. Named for John Newbery, the medal was first awarded to Hendrik Willem van Loon for *The Story of Mankind.*

Melcher, who was always aware of the significance of books in the lives of children, later proposed the establishment of a similar award for picture books, named in honor of Randolph Caldecott, whose pictures still delight today's children. Since 1938, the Caldecott Medal has been awarded annually by an awards committee of the American Library Association's Association for Library Service to Children to the illustrator of the most distinguished American picture book for children published in the United States during the preceding year. Again, the recipient must reside in or be a citizen of the United States.

The end of the 1920s marked the newly emerging prominence of the modern children's picture book in America. Mainly imported from Europe until that time, children's picture books now began to be published in America. William Nicholson's *Clever Bill* (1927) was followed the next year by one of the most successful picture books of all time, *Millions of Cats* by Wanda Gág. The near perfect marriage of the rhythmic prose and flowing movement of her dramatic black-and-white illustrations presents a simple, direct story with a folk flavor. This title is still included in the repertoire of today's storytellers and continues to be taken from the shelves by young readers; it ushered in the "Golden Thirties" of children's book publishing.[32]

By 1930, many publishers had set up separate editorial departments expressly for the purpose of publishing children's materials. The White House Conference on Child Health and Protection was held that year to study the plight of the child.[33] Improved technologies accelerated and economized book production. The stage was set for the modern picture book with its profuse illustration. Until this time there were only a few great children's books, illustrated with pictures that were largely an extension of the text. "Yet in a very few years, in respect to the books for the younger children, the artist has attained a place of equal importance with the writer."[34]

The period between World War I and World War II saw many authors and illustrators collaborate on picture books. Their talents and varied backgrounds contributed immensely to the changes in the picture book in America, which truly came into its own in this period of lower production costs. The "Golden Thirties" and the 1940s produced a spectacular number and variety of profusely illustrated books for young children.[35] Many of the new authors and illustrators then beginning their careers in this developing field have continued to keep their places in the hearts of children: such familiar names as Marjorie Flack, Maud and Miska Petersham, Ingri and Edgar d'Aulaire, Ludwig Bemelmans, Theodor Geisel (Dr. Seuss), Marcia Brown, Feodor Rojankovsky, James Daugherty, Robert Lawson, Marguerite de Angeli, Virginia Lee Burton, Robert McCloskey, and many, many more.

The war years affected the progress of children's picture books with shortages of materials, poor quality paper, narrow margins, inferior bindings, and less color and illustration. However, the postwar years began a boom in children's publishing, adding to the list of talented authors and illustrators such names as Maurice Sendak, Brian Wildsmith, Trina Schart Hyman, Paul Galdone, Leo Politi, Ezra Jack Keats, Gyo Fujikawa, Arnold Lobel, and so many more.

Through the years many factors have contributed to the growth, even explosion, of children's picture books: society's changing attitudes toward the child; the development of children's libraries, awards, councils, and studies; increasing interest in children's reading on the part of publishers, educators, and literary critics; changing technologies; and the development of American artists and authors. More recently, new directions in publishing—challenging the library as the principal outlet for children's books, seeking consumer markets, and applying modern marketing strategies—have affected the nature of the children's picture book.[36] Children's books, including picture books, have found a natural marketing presence on the Internet; the Web features publishers' sites, promotions, information on individual books, and even sample pages.[37] Today the picture book is a part of growing up, a teaching tool, an entertainment medium, a memory to treasure. Perhaps only imagination and the talent of the artist and author can define its limits.

Emphasizing the value of good materials and the quality of art as an essential standard of good picture books, some have recognized the late twentieth century as the "day of the artist" in children's books.[38] Others have noted the graphic trends in children's picture books, including the treatment of black as an actual color, the spatial relations of objects, and the use of technologies that lend new life to collages and other media.[39] Some have noted the coming of age of children's books as an art form.[40] Certainly, some of the modern trends give one pause. Spectacular color, shading, and texture are all very evident today, along with broader subject perspectives, picture books that are aimed more at older children (and adults) than at the traditional audience, and a generally higher level of sophistication. More mechanical books (pop-ups) reminiscent of the Victorian age are reappearing, as are gimmicks, and the trading on the familiarity of existing themes.[41]

Many old favorites are being reissued, often showcasing a new illustrator's talents. Many collections or compendiums of an author's or illustrator's works are being published, often in large formats with 60 to 120 or more pages, straining the definition and concept of "picture book." At times, these appear in what can only be called a large "coffee-table" format; impressive but hardly "child-friendly." Other trends include the large number of "board" books and other unusual formats, and the development of themes that emphasize reality, such as everyday situations, misbehavior or mischievous behavior, and multicultural or multi-ethnic experiences.

Professionalism, curiosity on all subjects, and freedom of expression have brought the children's picture book into the twenty-first century with a bewildering array of materials from which to choose. Imaginary animals of the past and future line the shelves with the cats, dogs, horses, and dolphins of the modern day. Fantasy lands compete with tales of spaceships and astronauts; dreams of the future can be found alongside the realities of the past; picture books of all kinds for all kinds of children—and adults—to enjoy!

For the teacher, librarian, or parent who wishes to open this fantastic world of color and imagination for the child, some tool is necessary that will provide access to the great number of possibilities for enjoyment in the picture book field today. *A to Zoo: Subject Access to Children's Picture Books* is designed with just this purpose in mind. For those interested in exploring more deeply the world of children's publishing and the children's picture book, a list of suggested titles for further reading begins on page xxii.

Notes

1. Rosen, Judith. "Children's Books Make Strong Internet Showing," *Publishers Weekly*, 244:2 (Jan. 13, 1997): p. 32.

2. Hewins, Caroline M. "The History of Children's Books (1988)," in *Children and Literature: Views and Reviews*, comp. by Virginia Haviland. New York: Lothrop, 1974, p. 30.

3. Zipes, Jack, tr. "Once There Were Two Brothers Named Grimm," in *The Complete Fairy Tales of the Brothers Grimm*. New York: Bantam, 1992, pp. xvii–xxxi.

4. MacCann, Donnarae, and Olga Richard. *The Child's First Books: A Critical Study of Pictures and Texts*. New York: Wilson, 1973, p. 11.

5. Ibid.

6. Sutherland, Zena. *Children and Books*, 9th ed. New York: Longman, 1997, p. 42.

7. Ibid.

8. Ibid.

9. Ibid.

10. Hürlimann, Bettina. *Three Centuries of Children's Books in Europe*, tr. and ed. by Brian Alderson. London: Oxford Univ. Press, 1967, p. xii.

11. Sutherland, op. cit., p. 42.

12. MacCann and Richard, op. cit., p. 11.

13. Ibid.

14. Hürlimann, op. cit., pp. 127–129.

15. Freeman, Ruth Sunderlin. *Children's Picture Books, Yesterday and Today*. Watkins Glen, N.Y.: Century House, 1967, p. 12.

16. Sutherland, op. cit., pp. 42, 122, 170.

17. John Newbery, *Little Pretty Pocket-Book: A Facsimile*. London: Oxford Univ. Press, 1966, p. 2.

18. Ibid., p. 3.

19. Ibid., p. 2.

20. Sutherland, op. cit., p. 123.

21. Ibid.

22. Ibid., p. 138.

23. Alderson, Brian. *Sing a Song for Sixpence: The English Picture Book Tradition and Randolph Caldecott.* Cambridge, England: Cambridge Univ. Press, 1986, p. 46.

24. Ibid., pp. 49–51.

25. Whalley, Joyce Irene. *Cobwebs to Catch Flies: Illustrated Books for the Nursery and Schoolroom 1700–1900.* Berkeley: Univ. of California Press, 1975, p. 14.

26. Alderson, op. cit., p. 8.

27. Viguers, Ruth Hill. "Introduction," in Kate Greenaway, *The Kate Greenaway Treasury.* Cleveland: World, 1967, p. 13.

28. Bader, Barbara. *American Picturebooks from Noah's Ark to the Beast Within.* New York: Macmillan, 1976, p. 7.

29. Viguers, loc. cit., p. 39.

30. Ibid.

31. Ibid.

32. Sutherland, op. cit., p. 127.

33. Wilkin, Binnie Tate. *Survival Themes in Fiction for Children and Young People.* Metuchen, N.J.: Scarecrow, 1978, p. 21.

34. Meigs, Cornelia, et al. *A Critical History of Children's Literature,* Rev. ed. New York: Macmillan, 1969, p. 649.

35. Ibid., p. 402.

36. Elleman, Barbara. "Current Trends in Literature for Children," *Library Trends* 35: 3 (Winter 1987): p. 421.

37. Rosen, Judith, "Children's Books Make Strong Internet Showing," *Publishers Weekly* 244:2 (Jan. 13, 1997): p. 32.

38. Sutherland, op. cit., p. 147.

39. Hale, Robert D. "Musings," *Horn Book Magazine* 70:3 (May/June 1994): p. 356.

40. Hearne, Betsy Gould. *Choosing Books for Children: A Commonsense Guide.* Urbana: Univ. of Illinois Press, 1999, p. 29.

41. Elleman, loc. cit., pp. 415, 421.

Further Reading

Alderson, Brian. *The Brothers Grimm: Popular Folk Tales.* London: Victor Gollancz Ltd., 1978.

———. *Looking at Picture Books 1973.* Chicago: Children's Book Council, 1974.

*———. *Sing a Song for Sixpence: The English Picture Book Tradition and Randolph Caldecott.* Cambridge, England: Cambridge Univ. Press, 1986.

Ammon, Bette D., and Gale W. Sherman. *Worth a Thousand Words: An Annotated Guide to Picture Books for Older Readers.* Englewood, Colo.: Libraries Unlimited, 1996.

Andersson, Theodore. *A Guide to Family Reading in Two Languages: The Preschool Years.* Wheaton, Md.: National Clearinghouse for Bilingual Education, 1981.

Arbuthnot, May Hill, et al. *The Arbuthnot Anthology of Children's Literature,* 4th ed. Glenview, Ill.: Scott, Foresman, 1976.

*Bader, Barbara. *American Picturebooks from Noah's Ark to the Beast Within.* New York: Macmillan, 1976.

Barchilon, Jacques, and Henry Pettit. *The Authentic Mother Goose Fairy Tales and Nursery Rhymes.* Athens, Ohio: Swallow Press, 1960.

Barr, John. *Illustrated Children's Books.* London; Dover, N.H.: British Library, 1986.

Barry, Florence V. *A Century of Children's Books.* London: Methuen, 1922.

Bauer, Caroline Feller. *Read for the Fun of It: Active Programming with Books for Children.* New York: Wilson, 1992.

Beyond Words: Picture Books for Older Readers and Writers, ed. by Susan Benedict and Lenore Carlisle. Portsmouth, N.H.: Heinemann, 1992.

Bingham, Jane, ed. *Writers for Children.* New York: Scribner's, 1987.

*———, and Grayce Scholt, eds. *Fifteen Centuries of Children's Literature: An Annotated Chronology of British and American Works in Historical Context.* Westport, Conn.: Greenwood Press, 1980.

Bland, David. *A History of Book Illustration,* 2nd ed. London: Faber & Faber, 1969.

———. *The Illustration of Books.* London: Faber & Faber, 1962.

Bodger, Joan. *How the Heather Looks.* New York: Viking, 1965.

Bottigheimer, Ruth B. *Grimms' Bad Girls and Bold Boys.* New Haven, Conn.: Yale Univ. Press, 1987.

* Indicates especially recommended titles in this reading list.

Braun, Saul. "Sendak Raises the Shade on Childhood." *New York Times Magazine* (June 7, 1970): 34+.

Bush, Margaret A. *Children's Literature: A Guide to Reference Services and Monographs.* Englewood, Colo.: Libraries Unlimited, 1988.

Butler, Dorothy. *Babies Need Books.* New York: Atheneum, 1980.

Butler, Francelia, and Richard W. Robert, eds. *Reflections on Literature for Children.* Hamden, Conn.: Shoe String Press, 1984.

————. *Triumphs of the Spirit in Children's Literature.* Hamden, Conn.: Library Professional Publications, 1986.

Carroll, Frances Laverne, and Mary Meacham. *Exciting, Funny, Scary, Short, Different, and Sad Books Kids Like About Animals, Science, Sports, Families, Songs, and Other Things.* Chicago: American Library Association, 1984.

Children's Book Illustration and Design, ed. by Julie Cummins. New York: Library of Applied Design, PBC International, 1991.

Cianciola, Patricia. *Illustrations in Children's Books,* 2nd ed. Dubuque, Iowa: William C. Brown, 1976.

————. *Picture Books for Children,* 3rd ed. Chicago: American Library Association, 1990.

Clay, Marie. "Introduction." In *Cushla and Her Books,* by Dorothy Butler, Boston: Horn Book, 1980.

————, and Dorothy Butler. *Reading Begins at Home,* 2nd ed. Exeter, N.H.: Heinemann, 1987.

Comenius, John Amos. *The Orbis Pictus of John Amos Comenius.* Detroit: Singing Tree, 1968.

Crouch, Marcus. *Treasure Seekers and Borrowers: Children's Books in Britain 1900–1960.* London: Library Association, 1962.

Dahl, Svend. *Dahl's History of the Book,* 3rd English ed. Ed. by Bill Katz. Metuchen, N.J.: Scarecrow Press, 1995.

Dalby, Richard. *The Golden Age of Children's Book Illustrations.* London: M. O'Mara Books, 1991.

Daniel, Eloise. *A Treasury of Books for Family Enjoyment: Books for Children from Infancy to Grade 2.* Pontiac, Mich.: Blue Engine Press, 1983.

Darling, Richard L. *The Rise of Children's Book Reviewing in America, 1865–1881.* New York: R. R. Bowker, 1968.

Darrell, Margery, ed. *Once Upon a Time: The Fairy-Tale World of Arthur Rackham.* New York: Viking, 1972.

*Darton, F. J. H. *Children's Books in England: Five Centuries of Social Life,* 3rd ed. Ed. by Brian Alderson. New York: Cambridge Univ. Press, 1982.

Datlow, Ellen, and Terri Windling, eds. *Snow White and Blood Red.* New York: Morrow, 1993.

Day, Alexandra; Cooper Edens; and Welleran Poltarnees. *Children from the Golden Age, 1880–1930.* San Diego: Green Tiger Press, 1987.

*Delamar, Gloria T. *Mother Goose: From Nursery to Literature.* Jefferson, N.C.: McFarland, 1987.

Demers, Patricia, ed. *A Garland from the Golden Age: Children's Literature from 1850–1900.* New York: Oxford Univ. Press, 1984.

————, and Gordon Moyles, eds. *From Instruction to Delight: An Anthology of Children's Literature to 1850.* New York: Oxford Univ. Press, 1982.

Duvoisin, Roger. "Children's Book Illustration: The Pleasure and Problems." *Top of the News* 22 (Nov. 1965): 30.

Earle, Alice Morse. *Child Life in Colonial Days.* New York: Macmillan, 1899.

Eckenstein, Lina. *Comparative Studies in Nursery Rhymes.* London: Duckworth, 1906; Detroit: Singing Tree, 1968.

Egoff, Sheila A.; G. T. Stubbs; and L. F. Ashley, eds. *Only Connect: Readings on Children's Literature,* 2nd ed. New York: Oxford Univ. Press, 1980.

————. *Worlds Within: Children's Fantasy from the Middle Ages to Today.* Chicago: American Library Association, 1988.

Ellis, Alec. *A History of Children's Reading and Literature.* Elmsford, N.Y.: Pergamon Press, 1968.

Estes, Glen, ed. *American Writers for Children Since 1960.* Detroit: Gale, 1987.

Ettlinger, John R. T., and Diana L. Spirt. *Choosing Books for Young People,* Vol. 2. Phoenix: Oryx, 1987.

Eyre, Frank. *British Children's Books in the Twentieth Century.* New York: Dutton, 1973.

————. *Twentieth Century Children's Books.* Cambridge, Mass.: Robert Bentley, 1953.

Fiction, Folklore, Fantasy and Poetry for Children, 1976–1985, 2 vols. New York: R. R. Bowker, 1986.

Field, Louise F. *The Child and His Book: Some Account of the History and Progress of Children's Literature in England.* Detroit: Singing Tree, 1968.

Fisher, Margery Turner. *Intent upon Reading: A Critical Appraisal of Modern Fiction for Children.* Leicester, England: Brockhampton Press, 1961.

————. *Who's Who in Children's Books: A Treasury of the Familiar Characters of Childhood.* New York: Holt, 1975.

Fox, Geoffrey Percival, et al., eds. *Writers, Critics, and Children: Articles from Children's Literature in Education.* New York: Agathon Press, 1976.

Freeman, Judy. *More Books Kids Will Sit Still For.* New Providence, N.J.: R. R. Bowker, 1995.

*Freeman, Ruth Sunderlin, *Children's Picture Books, Yesterday and Today*. Watkins Glen, N.Y.: Century House, 1967.

Galinsky, Ellen, and Judy David. *The Preschool Years: Family Strategies That Work—From Experts and Parents*. New York: Times Books, 1988.

*Gillespie, John T. *Best Books for Children: Preschool Through the Middle Grades*, 7th ed. Westport, Conn.: Bowker-Greenwood 2001.

Gillespie, Margaret C., and John W. Connor. *Creative Growth Through Literature for Children and Adolescents*. Columbus, Ohio: Merrill, 1975.

Gottlieb, Gerald. *Early Children's Books and Their Illustration*. Boston: Godine, 1975.

Green, Percy B. *A History of Nursery Rhymes*. Detroit: Singing Tree, 1968.

Green, Roger Lancelyn. *Tellers of Tales: British Authors of Children's Books from 1800 to 1964*. New York: Watts, 1965.

*Greenaway, Kate. *The Kate Greenaway Treasury*. Cleveland: World, 1967.

Halsey, Rosalie V. *Forgotten Books of the American Nursery*. Detroit: Singing Tree, 1969.

Harrison, Barbara G., and Gregory Maguire. *Innocence and Experience: Essays and Conversations on Children's Literature*. New York: Lothrop, 1987.

*Haviland, Virginia, comp. *Children and Literature: Views and Reviews*. New York: Lothrop, 1974.

———. *Children's Literature: A Guide to Reference Sources*. Washington, D.C.: Library of Congress, 1966; first supplement, 1972.

*Hearne, Betsy Gould, with Deborah Stevenson. *Choosing Books for Children: A Commonsense Guide*. Urbana, Ill.: Univ. of Illinois Press, 1999.

Hendrickson, Linnea. *Children's Literature: A Guide to the Criticism*. Boston: G. K. Hall, 1987.

Horning, Kathleen T. *From Cover to Cover: Evaluating and Reviewing Children's Books*. New York: HarperCollins Children's Books, 1997.

Huber, Miriam Blanton. *Story and Verse for Children*, 3rd ed. New York: Macmillan, 1965.

*Hürlimann, Bettina. *Three Centuries of Children's Books in Europe*. Ed. and tr. by Brian Alderson. London: Oxford Univ. Press, 1967; Cleveland: World, 1968.

Inglis, Fred. *The Promise of Happiness*. New York: Cambridge Univ. Press, 1981.

James, Philip. *Children's Books of Yesterday*. Ed. by C. Geoffrey Holme. London and New York: Studio, 1933; Detroit: Gale, 1976.

Jan, Isabelle. *On Children's Literature*. Ed. by Catherine Storr. New York: Schocken Books, 1974.

Katz, Bill, ed. *A History of Book Illustration: 29 Points of View*. Metuchen, N.J.: Scarecrow Press, 1994.

Katz, Lillian G., ed. *Current Topics in Early Childhood Education*, Vol. 6. Norwood, N.J.: Ablex, 1986.

Kiefer, Monica. *American Children Through Their Books, 1700–1835*. Philadelphia: Univ. of Pennsylvania Press, 1948, 1970.

Klemin, Diana. *The Art of Art for Children's Books*. Greenwich, Conn.: Murton Press, 1966, 1982.

———. *The Illustrated Book*. Greenwich, Conn.: Murton Press, 1970, 1983.

Lanes, Selma G. "The Art of Maurice Sendak: A Diversity of Influences Inform an Art for Children," *Artforum* IX (May 1971): 70–73.

Leif, Irving P. *Children's Literature: A Historical and Contemporary Bibliography*. Troy, N.Y.: Whitston, 1977.

Lewis, John. *The Twentieth Century Book: Its Illustration and Design*. New York: Van Nostrand Reinhold, 1967.

Linder, Leslie L. *The Art of Beatrix Potter*, 6th rev. ed. London: Warne, 1972.

*Lipson, Eden Ross. *The New York Times Parent's Guide to the Best Books for Children*, 3rd ed. Three Rivers Press, 2000.

Lukens, Rebecca J. *A Critical Handbook of Children's Literature*, 2nd ed. Glenview, Ill.: Scott, Foresman, 1981.

Lynn, Ruth Nadelman. *Fantasy Literature for Children and Young Adults: An Annotated Bibliography*, 4th ed. New Providence, N.J.: R. R. Bowker, 1995.

Lystad, Mary. *From Dr. Mather to Dr. Seuss: Two Hundred Years of American Books for Children*. Cambridge, Mass.: Schenkman, 1980.

*MacCann, Donnarae, and Olga Richard. *The Child's First Books*. New York: Wilson, 1973.

MacCann, Donnarae, and Gloria Woodard, eds. *The Black American in Books for Children: Readings in Racism*, 2nd ed. Metuchen, N.J.: Scarecrow Press, 1985.

MacDonald, Margaret Read. *The Storyteller's Sourcebook: A Subject, Title, and Motif Index to Folklore Collections for Children*. Detroit: Neal-Schuman Publishers, Inc., in association with Gale Research Co., 1982.

MacDonald, Ruth K. *Dr. Seuss*. Boston: Twayne, 1988.

*McTigue, Bernard, ed. *A Child's Garden of Delights: Pictures, Poems, and Stories for Children from the Collection of the New York Public Library*. New York: Abrams, 1987.

Mahoney, Ellen, and Leah Wilcox. *Ready, Set, Read: Best Books to Prepare Preschoolers*. Metuchen,

N.J.: Scarecrow, 1985.

Mahony, Bertha E.; Latimer, Louise P.; and Folmsbee, Beulah, comps. *Illustrators of Children's Books, 1744–1945*. Boston: Horn Book, 1947.

Marantz, Sylvia S. *Artists of the Page: Interviews with Children's Book Illustrators*. Jefferson, N.C.: McFarland, 1992.

———. *Picture Books for Looking and Learning: Awakening Visual Perceptions Through the Art of Children's Books*. Phoenix, Ariz.: Oryx Press, 1992.

——— and Kenneth A. Marantz. *The Art of Children's Picture Books*. New York: Garland Pub., 1995.

Martin, Douglas. *The Telling Line: Essays on Fifteen Contemporary Book Illustrators*. New York: Delacorte Press, 1990.

Maughan, Shannon. "A Revolution Waiting to Happen?" *Publishers Weekly* 248:5 (Jan. 29, 2001): 30+.

Meacham, Mary. *Information Sources in Children's Literature*. New York: Macmillan, 1953; rev. ed., 1969.

Monson, Diane L., ed. *Adventuring with Books: A Booklist for Pre-K–Grade 6*. Urbana, Ill.: NCTE, 1985.

Moore, Anne Carroll. *My Roads to Childhood*. Boston: Horn Book, 1961.

Moransee, Jesse R., ed. *Children's Prize Books*. Ridgewood, N.J.: K. G. Saur, 1983.

Muir, Percy. *English Children's Books, 1600–1900*. New York: Praeger, 1969.

*Newbery, John. *A Little Pretty Pocket-Book: A Facsimile*. London: Oxford Univ. Press, 1966.

*Nodelman, Perry. *Words About Pictures: The Narrative Art of Children's Picture Books*. Athens, Ga.: Univ. of Georgia Press, 1989.

Norby, Shirley, and Gregory Ryan. *Famous Illustrators of Children's Literature*. Minneapolis, Minn.: T.S. Denison, 1992.

Opie, Iona, and Peter Opie. *A Family Book of Nursery Rhymes*. New York: Oxford Univ. Press, 1964.

———. *A Nursery Companion*. New York: Oxford Univ. Press, 1964.

———. *The Oxford Dictionary of Nursery Rhymes*. New York: Oxford Univ. Press, 1951.

Oppenheim, Joanne F., et al. *Choosing Books for Kids*. New York: Ballantine, 1986.

The Original Mother Goose's Melody, As First Issued by John Newbery, of London, about A.D. 1760. Reproduced in facsimile from the edition as reprinted by Isaiah Thomas of Worcester, Mass., about A.D. 1785, with introductory notes by William H. Whitmore. Detroit: Singing Tree, 1969.

Paterson, Katherine. *The Spying Heart: More Thoughts on Reading and Writing Books for Children*. New York: Dutton, 1988.

*Pellowski, Anne. *The Family Storytelling Handbook*. New York: Watson-Guptill, 1963.

Potter, Beatrix. *Beatrix Potter: The V and A Collection*. London: Warne, 1986.

Prentice, Jeffrey, and Bettina Bird. *Dromkeen: A Journey into Children's Literature*. New York: Henry Holt, 1988.

Preschool Services and Parent Education Committee, Association for Library Service to Children. *Opening Doors for Preschool Children and Their Parents*, 2nd ed. Chicago: American Library Association, 1981.

Richard, Olga. "The Visual Language of the Picture Book." *Wilson Library Bulletin* (Dec. 1969).

Roback, Diane, ed. "Arnold Lobel's Three Years with Mother Goose." *Publishers Weekly* 230: 8 (Aug. 22, 1986).

Roberts, Ellen E. M. *The Children's Picture Book*. Cincinnati, Ohio: Writer's Digest, 1981, 1987.

Roberts, Patricia L. *Counting Books Are More Than Numbers: An Annotated Action Bibliography*. Hamden, Conn.: Library Professional Publications, 1990.

Rosenbach, Abraham S. W. *Early American Children's Books by A. S. W. Rosenbach, with Bibliographical Descriptions of the Books in His Private Collection*. Foreword by A. Edward Newton. Portland, Maine: Southworth Press, 1933.

Russell, David L. *Literature for Children: A Short Introduction*, 3rd ed. White Plains, N.Y.: Longman, 1997.

Sadker, Myra, and David Miller Sadker. *Now Upon a Time: A Contemporary View of Children's Literature*. New York: Harper, 1977.

Salway, Lance, ed. *A Peculiar Gift*. New York: Penguin, 1976.

San Diego Museum of Art Staff, eds. *Dr. Seuss from Then to Now*. New York: Random House, 1987.

Sendak, Maurice. *Caldecott & Co.: Notes on Books and Pictures*. New York: Farrar, Straus & Giroux, 1988.

———. "Mother Goose's Garnishings." *Book Week* Fall Children's Issue (Oct. 31, 1965): 5, 38–40; also printed in Haviland, *Children and Literature*, pp. 188–195.

Senick, Gerald J., ed. *Children's Literature Review*, Vols. 12, 13. Detroit: Gale, 1987.

Smith, Dora V. *Fifty Years of Children's Books, 1910–1960*. Urbana, Ill.: NCTE, 1963.

*Smith, Elva S. *The History of Children's Literature: A Syllabus with Selected Bibliographies*, rev. and enlarged by Margaret Hodges and Susan Stein-first. Chicago: American Library Association, 1980.

Stott, Jon. *Children's Literature from A to Z: A Guide for Parents and Teachers.* New York: McGraw-Hill, 1984.

Sutherland, Zena, ed. *The Best in Children's Books: The University of Chicago Guide to Children's Literature, 1979–1984.* Chicago: Univ. of Chicago Press, 1986.

*———. *Children and Books,* 9th ed. New York: Longman, 1997.

Targ, William, ed. *Bibliophile in the Nursery.* Metuchen, N.J.: Scarecrow, 1969.

Taylor, Ina. *The Art of Kate Greenaway: A Nostalgic Portrait of Childhood.* Gretna, La.: Pelican Pub. Co., 1991.

*Taylor, Judy. *Beatrix Potter: Artist, Storyteller and Countrywoman.* London: Warne, 1986.

——— et al. *Beatrix Potter, 1866–1943: The Artist and Her World.* London: Warne, 1987.

Thomas, Katherine Elwes. *The Real Personages of Mother Goose.* New York: Lothrop, 1930.

Thomson, Susan Ruth, ed. *Kate Greenaway: A Catalogue of the Kate Greenaway Collection, Rare Book Room, Detroit Public Library.* Detroit: Wayne State Univ. Press, 1977.

Thwaite, Mary. *From Primer to Pleasure in Reading,* 2nd ed. London: The Library Association, 1972.

Townsend, John Rowe. *Written for Children: An Outline of English-Language Children's Literature,* 3rd rev. ed. New York: Harper, 1988.

Very Best of Children's Book Illustration, comp. by the Society of Illustrators. Cincinnati, Ohio: North Light Books, 1993.

Viguers, Ruth Hill; Marcia Dalphin; and Bertha Mahony Miller, comps. *Illustrators of Children's Books, 1946–1956.* Boston: Horn Book, 1958.

Vries, Leonard de. *A Treasury of Illustrated Children's Books: Early Nineteenth-Century Classics from* the Osborne Collection. New York: Abbeville Press, 1989.

Warner, Marina. *From the Beast to the Blonde: On Fairy Tales and Their Tellers.* New York: Farrar, Straus and Giroux, 1995.

Weitenkampf, Frank. *The Illustrated Book.* Cambridge, Mass.: Harvard Univ. Press, 1938.

Welch, D'Alte A. *A Bibliography of American Children's Books Printed Prior to 1821.* Worcester, Mass.: American Antiquarian Society, 1972.

*Whalley, Joyce Irene. *Cobwebs to Catch Flies: Illustrated Books for the Nursery and Schoolroom 1700–1900.* Berkeley, Calif.: Univ. of California Press, 1975.

——— and Tessa Rose Chester. *The Bright Stream: A History of Children's Book Illustration.* Boston: D. R. Godine, 1994, c1988.

White, Burton L. *Educating the Infant and Toddler.* Lexington, Mass.: Lexington Bks., 1987.

White, Dorothy M. Neal. *Books Before Five.* New York: Oxford Univ. Press, 1954.

White, Mary Lou. *Adventuring with Books: A Booklist for Pre-K–Grade 6.* Chicago: American Library Association, 1981.

———. *Children's Literature: Criticism and Response.* Columbus, Ohio: Merrill, 1976.

*Wilkin, Binnie Tate. *Survival Themes in Fiction for Children and Young People.* Metuchen, N.J.: Scarecrow, 1978.

Williams, Helen E. *Books by African-American Authors and Illustrators for Children and Young Adults.* Chicago: American Library Association, 1991.

Wilson, Elizabeth L. *Books Children Love.* Westchester, Ill.: Good News, 1987.

Winkel, Lois, and Sue Kimmel. *Mother Goose Comes First: An Annotated Guide to the Best Books and Recordings for Your Preschool Child.* New York: Henry Holt, 1990.

*Zipes, Jack, tr. *The Complete Fairy Tales of the Brothers Grimm.* New York: Bantam, 1992.

Subject Headings

Main headings, subheadings, and cross-references are arranged alphabetically and provide a quick reference to the subjects used in the Subject Guide section, where author and title names appear under appropriate headings.

Aardvarks *see* Animals – aardvarks
ABC books
Abnaki Indians *see* Indians of North America – Abnaki
Abused children *see* Child abuse
Acadians *see* Ethnic groups in the U.S. – Acadians
Accidents
Accordion books *see* Format, unusual
Accountants *see* Careers – accountants
Acrobats *see* Careers – acrobats
Activities
Activities – babysitting
Activities – baking
Activities – ballooning
Activities – bargaining *see* Activities – trading
Activities – bartering *see* Activities – trading
Activities – bathing
Activities – cooking
Activities – dancing
Activities – digging
Activities – drawing
Activities – driving
Activities – eating *see* Food
Activities – flying
Activities – gardening *see* Gardens, gardening
Activities – jumping
Activities – knitting
Activities – making things
Activities – painting *see also* Careers – artists; Careers – painters
Activities – photographing
Activities – picnicking
Activities – playing
Activities – reading
Activities – running
Activities – sewing
Activities – shopping *see* Shopping
Activities – singing
Activities – storytelling
Activities – swapping *see* Activities – trading
Activities – swinging
Activities – talking
Activities – trading
Activities – traveling
Activities – vacationing

Activities – walking
Activities – weaving
Activities – whistling
Activities – working
Activities – writing
Actors *see* Careers – actors
ADD *see* Handicaps – ADD
Adoption
Aerialists *see* Careers – aerialists
Afghanistan *see* Foreign lands – Afghanistan
Africa *see* Foreign lands – Africa
African Americans *see* Ethnic groups in the U.S. – African Americans
Aged *see* Old age
AIDS *see* Illness – AIDS
Airplane pilots *see* Careers – airplane pilots
Airplanes, airports
Airports *see* Airplanes, airports
Alaska
Albatrosses *see* Birds – albatrosses
Alcoholism *see* Illness – alcoholism
Aleuts *see* Indians of North America – Aleuts
Algonquian Indians *see* Indians of North America – Algonquian
Aliens
Allergies *see* Illness – allergies
Alligators *see* Reptiles – alligators, crocodiles
Alphabet books *see* ABC books
Alzheimer's *see* Illness – Alzheimer's
Amazon *see* Foreign lands – Amazon
Ambition *see* Character traits – ambition
American Indians *see* Indians of Central America; Indians of North America; Indians of South America
Amish *see* Ethnic groups in the U.S. – Amish
Amphibians *see* Frogs and toads; Reptiles
Anasazi Indians *see* Indians of North America – Anasazi
Anatomy
Anatomy – ears
Anatomy – eyes

Anatomy – faces
Anatomy – feet
Anatomy – hands
Anatomy – heads
Anatomy – legs
Anatomy – mouths
Anatomy – noses
Anatomy – skeletons
Anatomy – skin
Anatomy – tails
Anatomy – teeth *see* Teeth
Anatomy – thumbs *see* Thumb sucking
Anatomy – toes
Angels
Anger *see* Emotions – anger
Animals *see also* Birds; Frogs and toads; Reptiles
Animals – aardvarks
Animals – anteaters
Animals – antelopes
Animals – apes *see* Animals – baboons; Animals – chimpanzees; Animals – gorillas; Animals – monkeys
Animals – armadillos
Animals – babies
Animals – baboons
Animals – badgers
Animals – bandicoots
Animals – bats
Animals – bears
Animals – beavers
Animals – bison *see* Animals – buffaloes
Animals – bobcats
Animals – brush wolves *see* Animals – coyotes
Animals – buffaloes
Animals – bulls, cows
Animals – bushbabies
Animals – camels
Animals – caribou *see* Animals – reindeer
Animals – cats
Animals – cheetahs
Animals – chimpanzees
Animals – chipmunks
Animals – cougars
Animals – cows *see* Animals – bulls, cows
Animals – coyotes
Animals – deer
Animals – dislike of *see* Behavior – animals, dislike of

Animals – dogs
Animals – dolphins
Animals – donkeys
Animals – dormice
Animals – elephant seals
Animals – elephants
Animals – elk
Animals – endangered animals
Animals – ferrets
Animals – foxes
Animals – gerbils
Animals – giraffes
Animals – goats
Animals – gorillas
Animals – groundhogs
Animals – guinea pigs
Animals – hamsters
Animals – hedgehogs
Animals – hippopotamuses
Animals – horses, ponies
Animals – hyenas
Animals – jackals
Animals – jaguars
Animals – kangaroos
Animals – kindness to animals
    see Character traits – kindness
    to animals
Animals – koalas
Animals – lemmings
Animals – lemurs
Animals – leopards
Animals – lions
Animals – llamas
Animals – lynx
Animals – manatees
Animals – mice
Animals – migration see
    Migration
Animals – minks
Animals – moles
Animals – mongooses
Animals – monkeys
Animals – moose
Animals – mountain lions see
    Animals – cougars
Animals – mules
Animals – muskrats
Animals – octopuses see
    Octopuses
Animals – opossums see Animals
    – possums
Animals – orangutans
Animals – otters
Animals – oxen
Animals – pack rats
Animals – pandas
Animals – panthers see Animals
    – leopards
Animals – pigs
Animals – polar bears
Animals – porcupines
Animals – porpoises see Animals
    – dolphins
Animals – possums
Animals – prairie dogs
Animals – prairie wolves see
    Animals – coyotes
Animals – pumas see Animals –
    cougars
Animals – rabbits
Animals – raccoons
Animals – rats
Animals – reindeer
Animals – rhinoceros

Animals – salamanders see
    Reptiles – salamanders
Animals – sea lions
Animals – seals
Animals – sheep
Animals – shrews
Animals – skunks
Animals – sloths
Animals – slugs
Animals – snails
Animals – snow leopards see
    Animals – leopards
Animals – sponges
Animals – squirrels
Animals – tapirs
Animals – tigers
Animals – walruses
Animals – warthogs
Animals – water buffaloes
Animals – weasels
Animals – whales
Animals – wildebeests
Animals – wolves
Animals – wombats
Animals – woodchucks see
    Animals – groundhogs
Animals – worms
Animals – yaks
Animals – zebras
Antarctic see Foreign lands –
    Antarctic
Antarctica see Foreign lands –
    Antarctic
Anteaters see Animals –
    anteaters
Antelopes see Animals –
    antelopes
Anti-violence see Violence,
    nonviolence
Ants see Insects – ants
Apache see Indians of North
    America – Apache
Apes see Animals – baboons;
    Animals – chimpanzees;
    Animals – gorillas; Animals –
    monkeys
Appearance see Character traits
    – appearance
April Fools' Day see Holidays –
    April Fools' Day
Aprons see Clothing – aprons
Aquariums
Arab Americans see Ethnic
    groups in the U.S. – Arab
    Americans
Arabia see Foreign lands –
    Arabia
Archaeologists see Careers –
    archaeologists
Archery see Sports – archery
Architects see Careers –
    architects
Arctic see Foreign lands – Arctic
Argentina see Foreign lands –
    Argentina
Arguing see Behavior – fighting,
    arguing
Arithmetic see Counting,
    numbers
Armadillos see Animals –
    armadillos
Armenia see Foreign lands –
    Armenia
Art

Artists see Careers – artists
Asia see Foreign lands – Asia
Asian Americans see Ethnic
    groups in the U.S. – Asian
    Americans
Assertiveness see Character traits
    – assertiveness
Asthma see Illness – asthma
Astrology see Zodiac
Astronauts see Careers –
    astronauts; Space and space
    ships
Astronomers see Careers –
    astronomers
Astronomy
Athabascan Indians see Indians
    of North America –
    Athabascan
Aunts see Family life – aunts,
    uncles
Australia see Foreign lands –
    Australia
Australian aborigines
Austria see Foreign lands –
    Austria
Authors see Careers – authors
Authors, children see Children
    as authors
Autism see Handicaps – autism
Automobiles
Autumn see Seasons – fall
Award winning books see
    Caldecott award books;
    Caldecott award honor books
Aztec Indians see Indians of
    North America – Aztec

Babies see also Animals – babies;
    Birds – babies
Babies, new see Family life – new
    sibling
Baboons see Animals – baboons
Babysitting see Activities –
    babysitting
Bad day see Behavior – bad day
Badgers see Animals – badgers
Bakers see Careers – bakers
Bali see Foreign lands – Bali
Ballerinas see Ballet; Careers –
    dancers
Ballet
Ballooning see Activities –
    ballooning
Balloons see Toys – balloons
Balls see Toys – balls
Bandicoots see Animals –
    bandicoots
Barbers see Careers – barbers
Bargaining see Activities –
    trading
Barns
Barons see Royalty
Bartering see Activities – trading
Baseball see Sports – baseball
Bashfulness see Character traits
    – shyness
Basketball see Sports –
    basketball
Bathing see Activities – bathing
Bats see Animals – bats
Bavaria see Foreign lands –
    Austria; Foreign lands –
    Germany

Beaches *see* Sea and seashore
Bears *see* Animals – bears
Beasts *see* Monsters
Beauty shops
Beavers *see* Animals – beavers
Beds *see* Furniture – beds
Bedtime
Bees *see* Insects – bees
Beetles *see* Insects – beetles
Beggars *see* Careers – beggars
Behavior
Behavior – animals, dislike of
Behavior – bad day
Behavior – boasting
Behavior – boredom
Behavior – bullying
Behavior – carelessness
Behavior – collecting things
Behavior – disbelief
Behavior – dissatisfaction
Behavior – fidgeting
Behavior – fighting, arguing
Behavior – forgetfulness
Behavior – gossip
Behavior – greed
Behavior – growing up
Behavior – hiding
Behavior – hiding things
Behavior – hurrying
Behavior – imitation
Behavior – indifference
Behavior – losing things
Behavior – lost
Behavior – lying
Behavior – messy
Behavior – misbehavior
Behavior – mistakes
Behavior – misunderstanding
Behavior – nagging
Behavior – name calling
Behavior – naughty *see* Behavior
  – misbehavior
Behavior – needing someone
Behavior – potty training *see*
  Toilet training
Behavior – running away
Behavior – saving things
Behavior – secrets
Behavior – seeking better things
Behavior – sharing
Behavior – solitude
Behavior – stealing
Behavior – talking to strangers
Behavior – tardiness
Behavior – toilet training *see*
  Toilet training
Behavior – trickery
Behavior – unnoticed, unseen
Behavior – wishing
Behavior – worrying
Being different *see* Character
  traits – being different
Belize *see* Foreign lands – Belize
Bible *see* Religion
Bicycling *see* Sports – bicycling
Bigotry *see* Prejudice
Birds
Birds – albatrosses
Birds – babies
Birds – blackbirds
Birds – bluejays
Birds – boobys
Birds – buzzards
Birds – canaries

Birds – cardinals
Birds – chickens
Birds – cockatoos
Birds – condors
Birds – cormorants
Birds – cranes
Birds – crows
Birds – cuckoos
Birds – dodos
Birds – doves
Birds – ducks
Birds – eagles
Birds – egrets
Birds – emus
Birds – falcons
Birds – flamingos
Birds – geese
Birds – guinea fowl
Birds – hawks
Birds – herons
Birds – hornbills
Birds – humming birds
Birds – ibis
Birds – larks
Birds – loons
Birds – macaws
Birds – magpies
Birds – mockingbirds
Birds – nightingales
Birds – ostriches
Birds – owls
Birds – parakeets, parrots
Birds – peacocks, peahens
Birds – pelicans
Birds – penguins
Birds – pigeons
Birds – plovers
Birds – puffins
Birds – quail
Birds – ravens
Birds – robins
Birds – sandpipers
Birds – seagulls
Birds – sparrows
Birds – spoonbills
Birds – storks
Birds – swallows
Birds – swans
Birds – toucans
Birds – turkeys
Birds – vultures
Birds – wood-hoopoe
Birds – woodpeckers
Birds – wrens
Birth
Birthdays
Bison *see* Animals – buffaloes
Black Americans *see* Ethnic
  groups in the U.S. – African
  Americans
Black Carib *see* Indians of
  Central America – Black
  Carib
Blackbirds *see* Birds – blackbirds
Blackfoot Indians *see* Indians of
  North America – Blackfoot
Blackouts *see* Power failure
Blindness *see* Handicaps –
  blindness; Senses – seeing
Blizzards *see* Weather – blizzards
Blocks *see* Toys – blocks
Bluejays *see* Birds – bluejays
Board books *see* Format,
  unusual – board books

Boasting *see* Behavior – boasting
Boat builders *see* Careers – boat
  builders
Boats, ships
Bobcats *see* Animals – bobcats
Bombs *see* Weapons
Boobys *see* Birds – boobys
Boogy man *see* Monsters
Books *see* Activities – reading;
  Libraries
Boots *see* Clothing – boots;
  Clothing – shoes
Boredom *see* Behavior –
  boredom
Borneo *see* Foreign lands –
  Borneo
Botswana *see* Foreign lands –
  Botswana
Bowling *see* Sports – bowling
Boxing *see* Sports – boxing
Bravery *see* Character traits –
  bravery
Brazil *see* Foreign lands – Brazil
Bridges
Brothers *see* Family life; Family
  life – brothers; Sibling rivalry
Brownies *see* Mythical creatures
  – elves
Brush wolf *see* Animals – coyotes
Bubbles
Buffaloes *see* Animals –
  buffaloes
Bugs *see* Insects
Buildings
Bulldozers *see* Machines
Bulls *see* Animals – bulls, cows
Bullying *see* Behavior – bullying
Bumble bees *see* Insects – bees
Bungee Indians *see* Indians of
  North America – Bungee
Burglars *see* Crime
Burma *see* Foreign lands –
  Burma
Burros *see* Animals – donkeys
Bus drivers *see* Careers – bus
  drivers
Buses
Bushbabies *see* Animals –
  bushbabies
Butchers *see* Careers – butchers
Butterflies *see* Insects –
  butterflies, caterpillars
Buzzards *see* Birds – buzzards

Cab drivers *see* Careers – taxi
  drivers
Cable cars, trolleys
Cabs *see* Taxis
Cafés *see* Restaurants
Caldecott award books
Caldecott award honor books
Cambodia *see* Foreign lands –
  Cambodia
Cambodian Americans *see*
  Ethnic groups in the U.S. –
  Cambodian Americans
Camels *see* Animals – camels
Cameroon *see* Foreign lands –
  Cameroon
Camps, camping
Canada *see* Foreign lands –
  Canada
Canaries *see* Birds – canaries

Cancer *see* Illness – cancer
Canoes and canoeing
Caps *see* Clothing – hats
Cardboard page books *see* Format, unusual – board books
Cardinals *see* Birds – cardinals
Careers
Careers – accountants
Careers – acrobats
Careers – actors
Careers – aerialists
Careers – airplane pilots
Careers – archaeologists
Careers – architects
Careers – artists *see also* Activities – painting; Careers – painters
Careers – astronauts
Careers – astronomers
Careers – authors
Careers – bakers
Careers – barbers
Careers – beggars
Careers – boat builders
Careers – bus drivers
Careers – butchers
Careers – cab drivers *see* Careers – taxi drivers
Careers – carpenters
Careers – chefs, cooks
Careers – clockmakers
Careers – coaches
Careers – composers
Careers – construction workers
Careers – custodians, janitors
Careers – dancers
Careers – dentists
Careers – detectives
Careers – doctors
Careers – electricians
Careers – engineers
Careers – entertainers
Careers – explorers
Careers – farmers
Careers – firefighters
Careers – fishermen
Careers – forest rangers *see* Careers – park rangers
Careers – fortune tellers
Careers – garbage collectors *see* Careers – sanitation workers
Careers – geologists
Careers – handymen
Careers – hatters
Careers – housekeepers
Careers – illustrators
Careers – inventors
Careers – janitors *see* Careers – custodians, janitors
Careers – journalists
Careers – judges
Careers – lawyers
Careers – librarians
Careers – lifeguards
Careers – lumberjacks
Careers – magicians
Careers – mail carriers *see* Careers – postal workers
Careers – mechanics
Careers – migrant workers
Careers – military
Careers – miners
Careers – models

Careers – museum workers
Careers – musicians
Careers – nuns
Careers – nurses
Careers – opera singers
Careers – organists
Careers – painters *see also* Activities – painting; Careers – artists
Careers – paleontologists
Careers – park rangers
Careers – peddlers
Careers – photographers
Careers – physicians *see* Careers – doctors
Careers – plasterers
Careers – plumbers
Careers – police officers
Careers – postal workers
Careers – preachers
Careers – printers
Careers – puppeteers
Careers – race car drivers
Careers – railroad engineers
Careers – ranchers
Careers – rangers *see* Careers – park rangers
Careers – sailors *see* Careers – military; Sailors
Careers – salesmen
Careers – sanitation workers
Careers – school principals
Careers – scientists
Careers – seamstresses
Careers – shepherds
Careers – sheriffs
Careers – shoemakers
Careers – sign painters
Careers – singers
Careers – soldiers *see* Careers – military
Careers – storekeepers
Careers – tailors
Careers – taxi drivers
Careers – teachers
Careers – telephone operators
Careers – toy makers
Careers – train engineers *see* Careers – railroad engineers
Careers – truck drivers
Careers – veterinarians
Careers – waiters, waitresses
Careers – waitresses *see* Careers – waiters, waitresses
Careers – welders
Careers – whalers
Careers – window cleaners
Careers – woodcarvers
Careers – writers
Careers – zoo keepers
Carelessness *see* Behavior – carelessness
Caribbean Islands *see* Foreign lands – Caribbean Islands
Caribou *see* Animals – reindeer
Carnivals *see* Fairs
Carousels *see* Merry-go-rounds
Carpenters *see* Careers – carpenters
Carrier *see* Indians of North America – Carrier
Cars *see* Automobiles
Castles

Caterpillars *see* Insects – butterflies, caterpillars
Cats *see* Animals – cats
Cave drawings *see* Petroglyphs
Cavemen
Caves
Central America *see* Foreign lands – Central America
Cerebral palsy *see* Handicaps – cerebral palsy
Chairs *see* Furniture – chairs
Chameleons *see* Reptiles – chameleons
Chanukah *see* Holidays – Hanukkah
Character traits
Character traits – ambition
Character traits – appearance
Character traits – assertiveness
Character traits – being different
Character traits – bravery
Character traits – cleanliness
Character traits – cleverness
Character traits – clumsiness
Character traits – completing things
Character traits – compromising
Character traits – conceit
Character traits – confidence
Character traits – courage *see* Character traits – bravery
Character traits – cruelty to animals *see* Character traits – kindness to animals
Character traits – curiosity
Character traits – flattery
Character traits – foolishness
Character traits – fortune *see* Character traits – luck
Character traits – freedom
Character traits – generosity
Character traits – helpfulness
Character traits – honesty
Character traits – incentive *see* Character traits – ambition
Character traits – individuality
Character traits – kindness
Character traits – kindness to animals
Character traits – laziness
Character traits – littleness *see* Character traits – smallness
Character traits – loyalty
Character traits – luck
Character traits – meanness
Character traits – optimism
Character traits – orderliness
Character traits – ostracism *see* Character traits – being different
Character traits – patience
Character traits – perseverance
Character traits – persistence
Character traits – practicality
Character traits – pride
Character traits – questioning
Character traits – responsibility
Character traits – selfishness
Character traits – shyness
Character traits – smallness
Character traits – stubbornness
Character traits – vanity

Character traits – willfulness
Cheerleading
Cheetahs *see* Animals – cheetahs
Chefs *see* Careers – chefs, cooks
Cherokee Indians *see* Indians of North America – Cherokee
Cherubs *see* Angels
Cheyenne (Sioux) Indians *see* Indians of North America – Cheyenne (Sioux)
Chickasaw Indians *see* Indians of North America – Chickasaw
Chicken pox *see* Illness – chicken pox
Chickens *see* Birds – chickens
Child abuse
Children as authors
Children as illustrators
Chile *see* Foreign lands – Chile
Chimpanzees *see* Animals – chimpanzees
China *see* Foreign lands – China
Chinese Americans *see* Ethnic groups in the U.S. – Asian Americans; Ethnic groups in the U.S. – Chinese Americans
Chinese New Year *see* Holidays – Chinese New Year
Chinook Indians *see* Indians of North America – Chinook
Chipmunks *see* Animals – chipmunks
Chippewa *see* Indians of North America – Chippewa
Chol Indians *see* Indians of North America – Chol
Christmas *see* Holidays – Christmas
Chumash Indians *see* Indians of North America – Chumash
Cinco de Mayo *see* Holidays – Cinco de Mayo
Circular tales
Circus
City
Clallam Indians *see* Indians of North America – Clallam
Cleanliness *see* Character traits – cleanliness
Cleverness *see* Character traits – cleverness
Clockmakers *see* Careers – clockmakers
Clocks, watches
Clothing
Clothing – aprons
Clothing – boots
Clothing – coats
Clothing – costumes
Clothing – dresses
Clothing – gloves, mittens
Clothing – hats
Clothing – neckties
Clothing – pajamas
Clothing – pants
Clothing – shirts
Clothing – shoes
Clothing – socks
Clothing – sweaters
Clouds *see* Weather – clouds
Clowns, jesters
Clubs, gangs
Clumsiness *see* Character traits – clumsiness

Coaches *see* Careers – coaches
Coats *see* Clothing – coats
Cockatoos *see* Birds – cockatoos
Cockroaches *see* Insects – cockroaches
Codes *see* Secret codes
Cold *see* Concepts – cold and heat; Illness – cold (disease); Weather – cold
Cold and heat *see* Concepts – cold and heat
Cold (disease) *see* Illness – cold (disease)
Collecting things *see* Behavior – collecting things
Colombia *see* Foreign lands – Colombia
Color *see* Concepts – color
Columbus Day *see* Holidays – Columbus Day
Comanche Indians *see* Indians of North America – Comanche
Communication
Communities, neighborhoods
Competition *see* Sibling rivalry
Completing things *see* Character traits – completing things
Composers *see* Careers – composers
Compromising *see* Character traits – compromising
Computers
Conceit *see* Character traits – conceit
Concepts
Concepts – cold and heat
Concepts – color
Concepts – counting *see* Counting, numbers
Concepts – distance
Concepts – in and out
Concepts – left and right
Concepts – measurement
Concepts – opposites
Concepts – perspective
Concepts – self *see* Self-concept
Concepts – shape
Concepts – size
Concepts – speed
Concepts – up and down
Concepts – weight
Condors *see* Birds – condors
Confidence *see* Character traits – confidence
Conservation *see* Ecology
Construction workers *see* Careers – construction workers
Contests
Cooking *see* Activities – cooking
Cooks *see* Careers – bakers; Careers – chefs, cooks
Coquelle *see* Indians of North America – Coquelle
Cora *see* Indians of North America – Cora
Coral Islands *see* Foreign lands – South Sea Islands
Cormorants *see* Birds – cormorants
Costa Rica *see* Foreign lands – Costa Rica

Costumes *see* Clothing – costumes
Couches, sofas *see* Furniture – couches, sofas
Cougars *see* Animals – cougars
Counting, numbers
Countries, foreign *see* Foreign lands
Country
Courage *see* Character traits – bravery
Cousins *see* Family life – cousins
Cowboys
Cows *see* Animals – bulls, cows
Coyotes *see* Animals – coyotes
Crabs *see* Crustaceans
Cradles *see* Furniture – cradles
Crafts *see* Activities – making things
Cranes (birds) *see* Birds – cranes
Creation
Creatures *see* Monsters; Mythical creatures
Cree Indians *see* Indians of North America – Cree
Creek Indians *see* Indians of North America – Creek
Creeks *see* Rivers
Crickets *see* Insects – crickets
Crime
Criminals *see* Crime; Prisons
Crippled *see* Handicaps – physical handicaps
Crocodiles *see* Reptiles – alligators, crocodiles
Crow Indians *see* Indians of North America – Crow
Crows *see* Birds – crows
Cruelty to animals *see* Character traits – kindness to animals
Crustaceans
Crying *see* Emotions
Cuckoos *see* Birds – cuckoos
Cumulative tales
Curiosity *see* Character traits – curiosity
Currency *see* Money
Custodians *see* Careers – custodians, janitors
Cycles *see* Motorcycles; Sports – bicycling
Czechoslovakia *see* Foreign lands – Czechoslovakia
Czechoslovakian Americans *see* Ethnic groups in the U.S. – Czechoslovakian Americans

Dakota (Sioux) Indians *see* Indians of North America – Dakota (Sioux)
Damselflies *see* Insects – damselflies
Dancers *see* Careers – dancers
Dancing *see* Activities – dancing; Ballet
Daniel *see* Religion – Daniel
Dark *see* Night
Darkness – fear *see* Emotions – fear
Daughters *see* Family life – daughters
David and Goliath *see* Religion – David

Dawn *see* Morning
Day
Day of the Dead *see* Holidays – Day of the Dead
Days of the week, months of the year
Deafness *see* Anatomy – ears; Handicaps – deafness; Senses – hearing
Death
Deer *see* Animals – deer
Delaware Indians *see* Indians of North America – Delaware
Demons *see* Devil; Monsters
Denmark *see* Foreign lands – Denmark
Dentists *see* Careers – dentists
Department stores *see* Stores
Desert
Detective stories *see* Problem solving
Detectives *see* Careers – detectives
Devil
Diabetes *see* Illness – diabetes
Dictionaries
Diggers *see* Machines
Digging *see* Activities – digging
Diners *see* Restaurants
Dinosaurs
Disbelief *see* Behavior – disbelief
Disguises
Dissatisfaction *see* Behavior – dissatisfaction
Distance *see* Concepts – distance
Divali *see* Holidays – Divali
Diving *see* Sports – skin diving
Divorce
Doctors *see* Careers – doctors
Dodos *see* Birds – dodos
Dogs *see* Animals – dogs
Dolls *see* Toys – dolls
Dolphins *see* Animals – dolphins
Donkeys *see* Animals – donkeys
Dormice *see* Animals – dormice
Doves *see* Birds – doves
Down and up *see* Concepts – up and down
Down syndrome *see* Handicaps – Down syndrome
Dragonflies *see* Insects – dragonflies
Dragons
Drawing *see* Activities – drawing
Drawing games *see* Games
Dreams
Dressers *see* Furniture – dressers
Dresses *see* Clothing – dresses
Driving *see* Activities – driving
Droughts *see* Weather – droughts
Drug addiction *see* Illness – drug addiction
Ducks *see* Birds – ducks
Dutch Americans *see* Ethnic groups in the U.S. – Dutch Americans
Dwarfs, midgets
Dwellings *see* Buildings; Homes, houses
Dying *see* Death

Eagles *see* Birds – eagles

Ears *see* Anatomy – ears; Handicaps – deafness; Senses – hearing
Earth
Earthquakes
East Indian Americans *see* Ethnic groups in the U.S. – East Indian Americans
Easter *see* Holidays – Easter
Eating *see* Food
Ecology
Ecuador *see* Foreign lands – Ecuador
Education *see* School
Eggs
Egrets *see* Birds – egrets
Egypt *see* Foreign lands – Egypt
Egyptian language *see* Hieroglyphics
El Salvador *see* Foreign lands – El Salvador
Elderly *see* Old age
Electricians *see* Careers – electricians
Elephant seals *see* Animals – elephant seals
Elephants *see* Animals – elephants
Elevators, escalators
Elk *see* Animals – elk
Elves *see* Mythical creatures – elves
Embarrassment *see* Emotions – embarrassment
Emergencies *see* Hospitals
Emotions
Emotions – anger
Emotions – embarrassment
Emotions – envy, jealousy
Emotions – fear
Emotions – grief
Emotions – happiness
Emotions – hate
Emotions – jealousy *see* Emotions – envy, jealousy
Emotions – loneliness
Emotions – love
Emotions – sadness
Emotions – unhappiness *see* Emotions – happiness; Emotions – sadness
Emperors *see* Royalty – emperors
Emus *see* Birds – emus
Endangered animals *see* Animals – endangered animals
Engineered books *see* Format, unusual – toy and movable books
Engineers *see* Careers – engineers
England *see* Foreign lands – England
Entertainers *see* Careers – entertainers
Entertainment *see* Theater
Envy *see* Emotions – envy, jealousy
Escalators *see* Elevators, escalators
Eskimos
Estonia *see* Foreign lands – Estonia

Ethiopia *see* Foreign lands – Ethiopia
Ethnic groups in the U.S.
Ethnic groups in the U.S. – Acadians
Ethnic groups in the U.S. – African Americans
Ethnic groups in the U.S. – Amish
Ethnic groups in the U.S. – Arab Americans
Ethnic groups in the U.S. – Asian Americans
Ethnic groups in the U.S. – Black Americans *see* Ethnic groups in the U.S. – African Americans
Ethnic groups in the U.S. – Cambodian Americans
Ethnic groups in the U.S. – Chinese Americans
Ethnic groups in the U.S. – Czechoslovakian Americans
Ethnic groups in the U.S. – Dutch Americans
Ethnic groups in the U.S. – East Indian Americans
Ethnic groups in the U.S. – French Americans
Ethnic groups in the U.S. – German Americans
Ethnic groups in the U.S. – Greek Americans
Ethnic groups in the U.S. – Hispanic Americans
Ethnic groups in the U.S. – Hmong Americans
Ethnic groups in the U.S. – Irish Americans
Ethnic groups in the U.S. – Italian Americans
Ethnic groups in the U.S. – Japanese Americans
Ethnic groups in the U.S. – Korean Americans
Ethnic groups in the U.S. – Lebanese Americans
Ethnic groups in the U.S. – Lithuanian Americans
Ethnic groups in the U.S. – Mexican Americans
Ethnic groups in the U.S. – Pakistani Americans
Ethnic groups in the U.S. – Polish Americans
Ethnic groups in the U.S. – Puerto Rican Americans
Ethnic groups in the U.S. – Russian Americans
Ethnic groups in the U.S. – Shakers
Ethnic groups in the U.S. – Vietnamese Americans
Etiquette
Europe *see* Foreign lands – Europe
Evening *see* Twilight
Exercise *see* Health and fitness – exercise
Experiments *see* Science
Explorers *see* Careers – explorers
Eye glasses *see* Glasses

Eyes *see* Anatomy – eyes;
   Handicaps – blindness;
   Senses – seeing

Fables *see* Folk and fairy tales
Faces *see* Anatomy – faces
Fairies
Fairs
Fairy tales *see* Folk and fairy tales
Falcons *see* Birds – falcons
Fall *see* Seasons – fall
Families *see* Family life
Family life
Family life – aunts, uncles
Family life – brothers *see also*
   Family life; Family life –
   brothers and sisters; Sibling
   rivalry
Family life – brothers and sisters
Family life – cousins
Family life – daughters
Family life – fathers
Family life – grandfathers
Family life – grandmothers
Family life – grandparents
Family life – great-grandparents
Family life – mothers
Family life – new sibling
Family life – only child
Family life – parents
Family life – sisters *see also*
   Family life; Family life –
   brothers and sisters; Sibling
   rivalry
Family life – sons
Family life – step families
Family life – stepchildren *see*
   Divorce; Family life – step
   families
Family life – stepparents *see*
   Divorce; Family life – step
   families
Farmers *see* Careers – farmers
Farms
Fathers *see* Family life – fathers
Father's Day *see* Holidays –
   Father's Day
Fear *see* Emotions – fear
Feeling *see* Senses – touching
Feelings *see* Emotions
Feet *see* Anatomy – feet
Ferrets *see* Animals – ferrets
Fidgeting *see* Behavior –
   fidgeting
Fighting *see* Behavior – fighting,
   arguing
Fiji *see* Foreign lands – Fiji
Fingers *see* Anatomy – hands
Finishing things *see* Character
   traits – completing things
Finland *see* Foreign lands –
   Finland
Fire
Fire engines *see* Careers –
   firefighters; Trucks
Firefighters *see* Careers –
   firefighters
Fireflies *see* Insects – fireflies
Fires
Fish
Fish – sharks
Fishermen *see* Careers –
   fishermen

Fishing *see* Sports – fishing
Fitness *see* Health and fitness
Flamingos *see* Birds – flamingos
Flattery *see* Character traits –
   flattery
Fleas *see* Insects – fleas
Flies *see* Insects – flies
Floods *see* Weather – floods
Flowers
Flowers – roses
Flying *see* Activities – flying
Fog *see* Weather – fog
Fold out books *see* Format,
   unusual – toy and movable
   books
Folk and fairy tales
Food
Foolishness *see* Character traits –
   foolishness
Football *see* Sports – football
Foreign lands
Foreign lands – Afghanistan
Foreign lands – Africa
Foreign lands – Amazon
Foreign lands – Antarctic
Foreign lands – Arabia
Foreign lands – Arctic
Foreign lands – Argentina
Foreign lands – Armenia
Foreign lands – Asia
Foreign lands – Australia
Foreign lands – Austria
Foreign lands – Bali
Foreign lands – Bavaria *see*
   Foreign lands – Austria;
   Foreign lands – Germany
Foreign lands – Belize
Foreign lands – Borneo
Foreign lands – Botswana
Foreign lands – Brazil
Foreign lands – Burma
Foreign lands – Cambodia
Foreign lands – Cameroon
Foreign lands – Canada
Foreign lands – Caribbean
   Islands
Foreign lands – Central
   America
Foreign lands – Chile
Foreign lands – China
Foreign lands – Colombia
Foreign lands – Congo
   (Democratic Republic)
Foreign lands – Costa Rica
Foreign lands – Czechoslovakia
Foreign lands – Denmark
Foreign lands – Ecuador
Foreign lands – Egypt
Foreign lands – El Salvador
Foreign lands – England
Foreign lands – Estonia
Foreign lands – Ethiopia
Foreign lands – Europe
Foreign lands – Fiji
Foreign lands – Finland
Foreign lands – France
Foreign lands – French Guiana
Foreign lands – Galapagos
   Islands
Foreign lands – Galilee
Foreign lands – Gambia
Foreign lands – Germany
Foreign lands – Ghana

Foreign lands – Gilbert Islands
   see Foreign lands – South Sea
   Islands
Foreign lands – Greece
Foreign lands – Greenland
Foreign lands – Guatemala
Foreign lands – Guyana
Foreign lands – Haiti
Foreign lands – Himalayas
Foreign lands – Holland
Foreign lands – Hungary
Foreign lands – Iceland
Foreign lands – India
Foreign lands – Indonesia
Foreign lands – Iran
Foreign lands – Iraq
Foreign lands – Ireland
Foreign lands – Israel
Foreign lands – Italy
Foreign lands – Jamaica
Foreign lands – Japan
Foreign lands – Kenya
Foreign lands – Korea
Foreign lands – Korea (North)
Foreign lands – Kurdistan
Foreign lands – Laos
Foreign lands – Lapland
Foreign lands – Latin America
Foreign lands – Latvia
Foreign lands – Lebanon
Foreign lands – Liberia
Foreign lands – Madagascar
Foreign lands – Malaysia
Foreign lands – Mali
Foreign lands – Martinique
Foreign lands – Mexico
Foreign lands – Middle East
Foreign lands – Mongolia
Foreign lands – Morocco
Foreign lands – Namibia
Foreign lands – Nepal
Foreign lands – Netherlands *see*
   Foreign lands – Holland
Foreign lands – New Guinea
Foreign lands – New Zealand
Foreign lands – Nicaragua
Foreign lands – Nigeria
Foreign lands – Norway
Foreign lands – Pakistan
Foreign lands – Palestine
Foreign lands – Panama
Foreign lands – Persia
Foreign lands – Peru
Foreign lands – Philippines
Foreign lands – Poland
Foreign lands – Portugal
Foreign lands – Puerto Rico
Foreign lands – Romania
Foreign lands – Russia
Foreign lands – Rwanda
Foreign lands – Sahara Desert
Foreign lands – Scandinavia
Foreign lands – Scotland
Foreign lands – Serbia
Foreign lands – Siam *see*
   Foreign lands – Thailand
Foreign lands – Siberia
Foreign lands – South Africa
Foreign lands – South America
Foreign lands – South Sea
   Islands
Foreign lands – Soviet Union
Foreign lands – Spain
Foreign lands – Sri Lanka

Foreign lands – Sudan
Foreign lands – Suriname
Foreign lands – Sweden
Foreign lands – Switzerland
Foreign lands – Taiwan
Foreign lands – Tanzania
Foreign lands – Thailand
Foreign lands – Tibet
Foreign lands – Trinidad
Foreign lands – Turkey
Foreign lands – Tyrol
Foreign lands – Ukraine
Foreign lands – Uzbekistan
Foreign lands – Vatican City
Foreign lands – Venezuela
Foreign lands – Vietnam
Foreign lands – Wales
Foreign lands – West Indies
Foreign lands – Zaire
Foreign lands – Zanzibar
Foreign languages
Forest rangers *see* Careers –
  park rangers
Forest, woods
Forgetfulness *see* Behavior –
  forgetfulness
Format, unusual
Format, unusual – board books
Format, unusual – toy and
  movable books
Fortune *see* Character traits –
  luck
Fortune tellers *see* Careers –
  fortune tellers
Fourth of July *see* Holidays –
  Fourth of July
Foxes *see* Animals – foxes
France *see* Foreign lands –
  France
Freedom *see* Character traits –
  freedom
French Americans *see* Ethnic
  groups in the U.S. – French
  Americans
French Guiana *see* Foreign lands
  – French Guiana
Friendship
Frogs and toads
Frontier life *see* U.S. history –
  frontier and pioneer life
Furniture
Furniture – beds
Furniture – chairs
Furniture – couches, sofas
Furniture – cradles
Furniture – dressers
Furniture – tables

Galapagos Islands *see* Foreign
  lands – Galapagos Islands
Galilee *see* Foreign lands –
  Galilee
Gambia *see* Foreign lands –
  Gambia
Games
Gangs *see* Clubs, gangs
Garage sales, rummage sales
Garbage collectors *see* Careers –
  sanitation workers
Gardens, gardening
Geese *see* Birds – geese
Gender roles
Genealogy

Generosity *see* Character traits –
  generosity
Geography
Geologists *see* Careers –
  geologists
Gerbils *see* Animals – gerbils
German Americans *see* Ethnic
  groups in the U.S. – German
  Americans
Germany *see* Foreign lands –
  Germany
Ghana *see* Foreign lands –
  Ghana
Ghosts
Giants
Gifts
Gilbert Islands *see* Foreign lands
  – South Sea Islands
Giraffes *see* Animals – giraffes
Glasses
Gloves *see* Clothing – gloves,
  mittens
Gnats *see* Insects – gnats
Gnomes *see* Mythical creatures –
  gnomes
Goats *see* Animals – goats
Goblins *see* Mythical creatures –
  goblins
Golf *see* Sports – golf
Gorillas *see* Animals – gorillas
Gossip *see* Behavior – gossip
Grammar *see* Language
Grandfathers *see* Family life –
  grandfathers; Family life –
  grandparents
Grandmothers *see* Family life –
  grandmothers; Family life –
  grandparents
Grandparents *see* Family life –
  grandfathers; Family life –
  grandmothers; Family life –
  grandparents
Grasshoppers *see* Insects –
  grasshoppers
Great-grandparents *see* Family
  life – great-grandparents
Great Plains Indians *see* Indians
  of North America – Great
  Plains
Greece *see* Foreign lands –
  Greece
Greed *see* Behavior – greed
Greek Americans *see* Ethnic
  groups in the U.S. – Greek
  Americans
Greenland *see* Foreign lands –
  Greenland
Grief *see* Emotions – grief
Griffins *see* Mythical creatures –
  griffins
Grocery stores *see* Shopping;
  Stores
Groundhog Day *see* Holidays –
  Groundhog Day
Groundhogs *see* Animals –
  groundhogs
Growing up *see* Behavior –
  growing up
Guatemala *see* Foreign lands –
  Guatemala
Guinea fowl *see* Birds – guinea
  fowl
Guinea pigs *see* Animals –
  guinea pigs

Guns *see* Weapons
Guy Fawkes Day *see* Holidays –
  Guy Fawkes Day
Guyana *see* Foreign lands –
  Guyana
Gymnastics *see* Sports –
  gymnastics
Gypsies

Habits *see* Thumb sucking
Haida Indians *see* Indians of
  North America – Haida
Hair
Haiti *see* Foreign lands – Haiti
Halloween *see* Holidays –
  Halloween
Hamsters *see* Animals –
  hamsters
Handicaps
Handicaps – ADD
Handicaps – autism
Handicaps – blindness
Handicaps – cerebral palsy
Handicaps – deafness
Handicaps – Down syndrome
Handicaps – mental handicaps
Handicaps – physical handicaps
Hands *see* Anatomy – hands
Handymen *see* Careers –
  handymen
Hanukkah *see* Holidays –
  Hanukkah
Happiness *see* Emotions –
  happiness
Hares *see* Animals – rabbits
Hate *see* Emotions – hate
Hats *see* Clothing – hats
Hatters *see* Careers – hatters
Hawaii
Hawks *see* Birds – hawks
Heads *see* Anatomy – heads
Health and fitness
Health and fitness – exercise
Hearing *see* Handicaps –
  deafness; Senses – hearing
Heat *see* Concepts – cold and
  heat
Heavy equipment *see* Machines
Hedgehogs *see* Animals –
  hedgehogs
Helicopters
Helpfulness *see* Character traits
  – helpfulness
Hens *see* Birds – chickens
Herons *see* Birds – herons
Hibernation
Hiccups
Hiding *see* Behavior – hiding
Hiding things *see* Behavior –
  hiding things
Hieroglyphics
Hiking *see* Sports – hiking
Himalayas *see* Foreign lands –
  Himalayas
Hinduism *see* Religion –
  Hinduism
Hippopotamuses *see* Animals –
  Hippopotamuses
Hispanic Americans *see* Ethnic
  groups in the U.S. – Hispanic
  Americans

Hmong Americans *see* Ethnic groups in the U.S. – Hmong Americans
Hobby horses *see* Toys – rocking horses
Hockey *see* Sports – hockey
Hogs *see* Animals – pigs
Hohokam Indians *see* Indians of North America – Hohokam
Holidays
Holidays – April Fools' Day
Holidays – Chanukah *see* Holidays – Hanukkah
Holidays – Chinese New Year
Holidays – Christmas
Holidays – Cinco de Mayo
Holidays – Columbus Day
Holidays – Day of the Dead
Holidays – Divali
Holidays – Easter
Holidays – Father's Day
Holidays – Fourth of July
Holidays – Groundhog Day
Holidays – Guy Fawkes Day
Holidays – Halloween
Holidays – Hanukkah
Holidays – Independence Day *see* Holidays – Fourth of July
Holidays – Juneteenth
Holidays – Kwanzaa
Holidays – Mardi Gras *see* Mardi Gras
Holidays – May Day
Holidays – Memorial Day
Holidays – Mother's Day
Holidays – New Year's
Holidays – Passover
Holidays – Purim
Holidays – Ramadan
Holidays – Rosh Hashanah
Holidays – St. Patrick's Day
Holidays – Sukkot
Holidays – Thanksgiving
Holidays – Valentine's Day
Holidays – Washington's Birthday
Holidays – Yom Kippur
Holland *see* Foreign lands – Holland
Holocaust
Homeless
Homes, houses
Homosexuality
Honesty *see* Character traits – honesty
Honey bees *see* Insects – bees
Hope
Hopi Indians *see* Indians of North America – Hopi
Hornbills *see* Birds – hornbills
Hornets *see* Insects – hornets
Horses *see* Animals – horses, ponies
Horses, rocking *see* Toys – rocking horses
Hospitals
Hotels
Housekeepers *see* Careers – housekeepers
Houses *see* Homes, houses
Huichol Indians *see* Indians of North America – Huichol
Humming birds *see* Birds – humming birds

Humor
Hungary *see* Foreign lands – Hungary
Hungry
Hunting *see* Sports – hunting
Huron Indians *see* Indians of North America – Huron
Hurricanes *see* Weather – hurricanes
Hurrying *see* Behavior – hurrying
Hyenas *see* Animals – hyenas
Hygiene

Ibis *see* Birds – ibis
Ice skating *see* Sports – ice skating
Iceland *see* Foreign lands – Iceland
Identity *see* Self-concept
Iguanas *see* Reptiles – iguanas
Illness
Illness – AIDS
Illness – alcoholism
Illness – allergies
Illness – Alzheimer's
Illness – asthma
Illness – cancer
Illness – chicken pox
Illness – cold (disease)
Illness – diabetes
Illness – drug addiction
Illness – measles
Illness – mental illness
Illness – mumps
Illness – muscular dystrophy
Illness – tonsillectomy
Illusions, optical *see* Optical illusions
Illustrators *see* Careers – illustrators
Illustrators, children *see* Children as illustrators
Imaginary friends *see* Imagination – imaginary friends
Imagination
Imagination – imaginary friends
Imitation *see* Behavior – imitation
Immigrants
Immigration
Imps *see* Mythical creatures – imps
In and out *see* Concepts – in and out
Incas *see* Indians of South America – Incas
Incentive *see* Character traits – ambition
Independence Day *see* Holidays – Fourth of July
India *see* Foreign lands – India
Indians, American *see* Indians of Central America; Indians of North America; Indians of South America
Indians of Central America – Black Carib
Indians of Central America – Maya
Indians of North America

Indians of North America – Abnaki
Indians of North America – Aleuts
Indians of North America – Algonquian
Indians of North America – Anasazi
Indians of North America – Apache
Indians of North America – Athabascan
Indians of North America – Aztec
Indians of North America – Blackfoot
Indians of North America – Bungee
Indians of North America – Carrier
Indians of North America – Cherokee
Indians of North America – Cheyenne (Sioux)
Indians of North America – Chickasaw
Indians of North America – Chinook
Indians of North America – Chippewa
Indians of North America – Chol
Indians of North America – Chumash
Indians of North America – Clallam
Indians of North America – Comanche
Indians of North America – Coquelle
Indians of North America – Cora
Indians of North America – Cree
Indians of North America – Creek
Indians of North America – Crow
Indians of North America – Dakota (Sioux)
Indians of North America – Delaware
Indians of North America – Great Plains
Indians of North America – Haida
Indians of North America – Hohokam
Indians of North America – Hopi
Indians of North America – Huichol
Indians of North America – Huron
Indians of North America – Inuit
Indians of North America – Inuk
Indians of North America – Iroquois
Indians of North America – Karok
Indians of North America – Kato

Indians of North America –
  Kutenai
Indians of North America –
  Lakota (Sioux)
Indians of North America –
  Lenape
Indians of North America –
  Maidu
Indians of North America –
  Micmac
Indians of North America –
  Missisauga
Indians of North America –
  Miwok
Indians of North America –
  Modoc
Indians of North America –
  Mohawk
Indians of North America –
  Muskogee
Indians of North America –
  Nanticoke
Indians of North America –
  Narragansett
Indians of North America –
  Navajo
Indians of North America – Nez
  Perce
Indians of North America –
  Nishnawbe
Indians of North America –
  Nisqually
Indians of North America –
  Nobscusset
Indians of North America –
  Ojibwa
Indians of North America –
  Paiute
Indians of North America –
  Papago
Indians of North America –
  Pawnee
Indians of North America –
  Penobscot
Indians of North America –
  Pima
Indians of North America –
  Potawatomi
Indians of North America –
  Powhaton
Indians of North America –
  Pueblo
Indians of North America –
  Seminole
Indians of North America –
  Seneca
Indians of North America –
  Shawnee
Indians of North America –
  Shoshone
Indians of North America –
  Siksika
Indians of North America –
  Sioux
Indians of North America –
  Southwest
Indians of North America –
  Taino
Indians of North America –
  Tarascan
Indians of North America –
  Tewa
Indians of North America –
  Tlingit

Indians of North America –
  Tohono O'Odham
Indians of North America –
  Tsimshian
Indians of North America – Twa
Indians of North America – Ute
Indians of North America –
  Wampanoag
Indians of North America –
  Windigos
Indians of North America –
  Yana
Indians of North America –
  Yupik
Indians of North America –
  Zapotec
Indians of North America –
  Zuni
Indians of South America
Indians of South America –
  Incas
Indians of South America –
  Quechua
Indians of South America –
  Yanomamo
Indifference *see* Behavior –
  indifference
Individuality *see* Character traits
  – individuality
Indonesia *see* Foreign lands –
  Indonesia
Indonesian Archipelago *see*
  Foreign lands – South Sea
  Islands
Insects
Insects – ants
Insects – bees
Insects – beetles
Insects – butterflies, caterpillars
Insects – caterpillars *see* Insects
  – butterflies, caterpillars
Insects – cockroaches
Insects – crickets
Insects – damselflies
Insects – dragonflies
Insects – fireflies
Insects – fleas
Insects – flies
Insects – gnats
Insects – grasshoppers
Insects – hornets
Insects – lady birds *see* Insects –
  ladybugs
Insects – ladybugs
Insects – lice
Insects – lightning bugs *see*
  Insects – fireflies
Insects – mosquitoes
Insects – moths
Insects – praying mantis
Insects – wasps
Interracial marriage *see*
  Marriage, interracial
Inuit Indians *see* Indians of
  North America – Inuit
Inuk *see* Indians of North
  America – Inuk
Inventions
Inventors *see* Careers – inventors
Iran *see* Foreign lands – Iran
Iraq *see* Foreign lands – Iraq
Ireland *see* Foreign lands –
  Ireland

Irish Americans *see* Ethnic
  groups in the U.S. – Irish
  Americans
Iroquois *see* Indians of North
  America – Iroquois
Islam *see* Religion – Islam
Islands
Israel *see* Foreign lands – Israel
Italian Americans *see* Ethnic
  groups in the U.S. – Italian
  Americans
Italy *see* Foreign lands – Italy

Jackals *see* Animals – jackals
Jackets *see* Clothing – coats
Jaguars *see* Animals – jaguars
Jails *see* Prisons
Jamaica *see* Foreign lands –
  Jamaica
Janitors *see* Careers –
  custodians, janitors
Japan *see* Foreign lands – Japan
Japanese Americans *see* Ethnic
  groups in the U.S. – Asian
  Americans; Ethnic groups in
  the U.S. – Japanese
  Americans
Jealousy *see* Emotions – envy,
  jealousy
Jesters *see* Clowns, jesters
Jewelry
Jewish culture
Jewish culture – Passover
Jobs *see* Careers
Jokes *see* Riddles
Jonah *see* Religion – Jonah
Journalists *see* Careers –
  journalists
Judges *see* Careers – judges
Jumping *see* Activities – jumping
Jumping rope *see* Sports –
  jumping rope
Juneteenth *see* Holidays –
  Juneteenth
Jungle

Kangaroos *see* Animals –
  kangaroos
Karate *see* Sports – karate
Karok Indians *see* Indians of
  North America – Karok
Kato *see* Indians of North
  America – Kato
Kelpies *see* Mythical creatures –
  kelpies
Kenya *see* Foreign lands – Kenya
Khans *see* Royalty – khans
Kindness *see* Character traits –
  kindness
Kindness to animals *see*
  Character traits – kindness to
  animals
Kings *see* Royalty – kings
Kissing
Kites
Knights
Knitting *see* Activities – knitting
Koala bears *see* Animals – koalas
Komodo dragons *see* Reptiles –
  Komodo dragons
Korea *see* Foreign lands – Korea

Korea (North) *see* Foreign lands
– Korea (North)
Korean Americans *see* Ethnic
groups in the U.S. – Asian
Americans; Ethnic groups in
the U.S. – Korean Americans
Kurdistan *see* Foreign lands –
Kurdistan
Kutenai Indians *see* Indians of
North America – Kutenai
Kwanzaa *see* Holidays – Kwanzaa

Lady birds *see* Insects – ladybugs
Ladybugs *see* Insects – ladybugs
Lakes, ponds
Lakota (Sioux) Indians *see*
Indians of North America –
Lakota (Sioux)
Lambs *see* Animals – sheep
Language
Language, foreign *see* Foreign
languages
Languages
Laos *see* Foreign lands – Laos
Lapland *see* Foreign lands –
Lapland
Larks *see* Birds – larks
Latin America *see* Foreign lands
– Latin America
Latvia *see* Foreign lands – Latvia
Laundry
Law *see* Careers – judges;
Careers – lawyers; Careers –
police officers; Crime;
Prisons
Lawyers *see* Careers – lawyers
Laziness *see* Character traits –
laziness
Lebanese Americans *see* Ethnic
groups in the U.S. –
Lebanese Americans
Lebanon *see* Foreign lands –
Lebanon
Left and right *see* Concepts –
left and right
Left-handedness
Legends *see* Folk and fairy tales
Legs *see* Anatomy – legs
Lemmings *see* Animals –
lemmings
Lemurs *see* Animals – lemurs
Lenape *see* Indians of North
America – Lenape
Leopards *see* Animals – leopards
Leprechauns *see* Mythical
creatures – leprechauns
Letters, cards
Liberia *see* Foreign lands –
Liberia
Librarians *see* Careers –
librarians
Libraries
Lice *see* Insects – lice
Lifeguards *see* Careers –
lifeguards
Lighthouses
Lightning bugs *see* Insects –
fireflies
Lights
Lions *see* Animals – lions
Lithuanian Americans *see*
Ethnic groups in the U.S. –
Lithuanian Americans

Little people
Littleness *see* Character traits –
smallness
Lizards *see* Reptiles – lizards
Llamas *see* Animals – llamas
Lobsters *see* Crustaceans
Loneliness *see* Emotions –
loneliness
Loons *see* Birds – loons
Losing things *see* Behavior –
losing things
Lost *see* Behavior – lost
Love *see* Emotions – love
Loyalty *see* Character traits –
loyalty
Luck *see* Character traits – luck
Lullabies
Lumberjacks *see* Careers –
lumberjacks
Lying *see* Behavior – lying
Lynx *see* Animals – lynx

Macaws *see* Birds – macaws
Machines
Madagascar *see* Foreign lands –
Madagascar
Magic
Magicians *see* Careers –
magicians
Magpies *see* Birds – magpies
Maidu Indians *see* Indians of
North America – Maidu
Mail *see* Careers – postal
workers; Letters, cards; Post
office
Mail carriers *see* Careers – postal
workers; Letters, cards; Post
office
Making things *see* Activities –
making things
Malaysia *see* Foreign lands –
Malaysia
Mali *see* Foreign lands – Mali
Manatees *see* Animals –
manatees
Manners *see* Etiquette
Maps
Mardi Gras
Marionettes *see* Puppets
Markets *see* Stores
Marriage, interracial
Marriages *see* Weddings
Martinique *see* Foreign lands –
Martinique
Masks
Math *see* Counting, numbers
Maya Indians *see* Indians of
Central America – Maya
Mazes
Meanness *see* Character traits –
meanness
Measles *see* Illness – measles
Measurement *see* Concepts –
measurement
Mechanical men *see* Robots
Mechanics *see* Careers –
mechanics
Memorial Day *see* Holidays –
Memorial Day
Memories, memory
Menehunes *see* Mythical
creatures – menehunes

Mental handicaps *see* Handicaps
– mental handicaps
Mental illness *see* Illness –
mental illness
Mermaids *see* Mythical creatures
– mermaids, mermen
Mermen *see* Mythical creatures –
mermaids, mermen
Merry-go-rounds
Messy *see* Behavior – messy
Metamorphosis
Mexican Americans *see* Ethnic
groups in the U.S. – Hispanic
Americans; Ethnic groups in
the U.S. – Mexican
Americans
Mexico *see* Foreign lands –
Mexico
Mice *see* Animals – mice
Micmac Indians *see* Indians of
North America – Micmac
Middle Ages
Middle East *see* Foreign lands –
Middle East
Migrant workers *see* Careers –
migrant workers
Migration
Military *see* Careers – military
Mimes *see* Clowns, jesters
Miners *see* Careers – miners
Minks *see* Animals – minks
Minorities *see* Ethnic groups in
the U.S.
Mirages *see* Optical illusions
Mirrors
Misbehavior *see* Behavior –
misbehavior
Missions
Missisauga *see* Indians of North
America – Missisauga
Mist *see* Weather – fog
Mistakes *see* Behavior – mistakes
Misunderstanding *see* Behavior
– misunderstanding
Mittens *see* Clothing – gloves,
mittens
Miwok Indians *see* Indians of
North America – Miwok
Mockingbirds *see* Birds –
mockingbirds
Models *see* Careers – models
Modoc Indians *see* Indians of
North America – Modoc
Mohawk Indians *see* Indians of
North America – Mohawk
Moles *see* Animals – moles
Money
Mongolia *see* Foreign lands –
Mongolia
Mongooses *see* Animals –
mongooses
Monitor lizards *see* Reptiles –
monitor lizards
Monkeys *see* Animals – monkeys
Monsters
Monsters – vampires
Months of the year *see* Days of
the week, months of the year
Moon
Moose *see* Animals – moose
Mopeds *see* Motorcycles
Morning
Morocco *see* Foreign lands –
Morocco

Moses *see* Religion – Moses
Mosquitoes *see* Insects – mosquitoes
Mother Goose *see* Nursery rhymes
Mothers *see* Family life – mothers
Mother's Day *see* Holidays – Mother's Day
Moths *see* Insects – moths
Motorcycles
Mountain climbing *see* Sports – mountain climbing
Mountain lions *see* Animals – cougars
Mountains
Mouths *see* Anatomy – mouths
Moving
Mules *see* Animals – mules
Multi-ethnic *see* Ethnic groups in the U.S.
Multiple birth children *see* Multiple births – sextuplets; Multiple births – triplets; Multiple births – twins
Multiple births – sextuplets
Multiple births – triplets
Multiple births – twins
Mummies
Mumps *see* Illness – mumps
Muppets *see* Puppets
Muscular dystrophy *see* Illness – muscular dystrophy
Museum workers *see* Careers – museum workers
Museums
Music
Musical instruments *see* Music
Musicians *see* Careers – musicians
Muskogee Indians *see* Indians of North America – Muskogee
Muskrats *see* Animals – muskrats
Mystery stories
Mythical creatures
Mythical creatures – aliens *see* Aliens
Mythical creatures – elves
Mythical creatures – gnomes
Mythical creatures – goblins
Mythical creatures – griffins
Mythical creatures – imps
Mythical creatures – kelpies
Mythical creatures – leprechauns
Mythical creatures – menehunes
Mythical creatures – mermaids, mermen
Mythical creatures – ogres
Mythical creatures – Pegasus
Mythical creatures – phoenix
Mythical creatures – pixies
Mythical creatures – pooka spirit
Mythical creatures – sandman
Mythical creatures – selkies
Mythical creatures – trolls
Mythical creatures – unicorns
Mythical creatures – werewolves

Nagging *see* Behavior – nagging

Name calling *see* Behavior – name calling
Names
Namibia *see* Foreign lands – Namibia
Nanticoke Indians *see* Indians of North America – Nanticoke
Napping *see* Sleep
Narragansett *see* Indians of North America – Narragansett
Native Americans *see* Eskimos; Indians of Central America; Indians of North America; Indians of South America
Nativity *see* Religion – nativity
Nature
Naughty *see* Behavior – misbehavior
Navajo Indians *see* Indians of North America – Navajo
Neckties *see* Clothing – neckties
Needing someone *see* Behavior – needing someone
Neighborhoods *see* Communities, neighborhoods
Nepal *see* Foreign lands – Nepal
Netherlands *see* Foreign lands – Holland
New Guinea *see* Foreign lands – New Guinea
New Year's *see* Holidays – New Year's
New Zealand *see* Foreign lands – New Zealand
Nez Perce Indians *see* Indians of North America – Nez Perce
Nicaragua *see* Foreign lands – Nicaragua
Nigeria *see* Foreign lands – Nigeria
Night
Nightingales *see* Birds – nightingales
Nightmares *see* Bedtime; Monsters; Mythical creatures – goblins; Night; Sleep
Nishnawbe Indians *see* Indians of North America – Nishnawbe
Nisqually *see* Indians of North America – Nisqually
No text *see* Wordless
Noah *see* Religion – Noah
Nobscusset *see* Indians of North America – Nobscusset
Noise, sounds
North Pole *see* Foreign lands – Arctic
Norway *see* Foreign lands – Norway
Noses *see* Anatomy – noses; Senses – smelling
Numbers *see* Counting, numbers
Nuns *see* Careers – nuns
Nursery rhymes
Nursery school *see* School
Nurses *see* Careers – nurses

Oceans *see* Sea and seashore
Octopuses

Odors *see* Senses – smelling
Ogres *see* Mythical creatures – ogres
Oil
Ojibwa Indians *see* Indians of North America – Ojibwa
Old age
Olympics *see* Sports – Olympics
Only child *see* Family life – only child
Opera singers *see* Careers – opera singers
Opossums *see* Animals – possums
Opposites *see* Concepts – opposites
Optical illusions
Optimism *see* Character traits – optimism
Orangutans *see* Animals – orangutans
Orderliness *see* Character traits – orderliness
Organists *see* Careers – organists
Orphans
Ostracism *see* Character traits – being different
Ostriches *see* Birds – ostriches
Otters *see* Animals – otters
Outer space *see* Space and spaceships
Owls *see* Birds – owls
Oxen *see* Animals – oxen

Pack rats *see* Animals – pack rats
Painters *see* Activities – painting; Careers – artists
Painting *see* Activities – painting
Paiute Indians *see* Indians of North America – Paiute
Pajamas *see* Clothing – pajamas
Pakistan *see* Foreign lands – Pakistan
Paleontologists *see* Careers – paleontologists
Palestine *see* Foreign lands – Palestine
Panama *see* Foreign lands – Panama
Pandas *see* Animals – pandas
Panthers *see* Animals – leopards
Pants *see* Clothing – pants
Papago Indians *see* Indians of North America – Papago
Paper
Parades
Parakeets *see* Birds – parakeets, parrots
Park rangers *see* Careers – park rangers
Parks
Parrots *see* Birds – parakeets, parrots
Participation
Parties
Passover *see* Holidays – Passover
Patience *see* Character traits – patience
Pawnee Indians *see* Indians of North America – Pawnee
Peacocks, peahens *see* Birds – peacocks, peahens
Peddlers *see* Careers – peddlers

Pegasus *see* Mythical creatures –
Pegasus
Pelicans *see* Birds – pelicans
Pen pals
Penguins *see* Birds – penguins
Penobscot Indians *see* Indians of
North America – Penobscot
Perseverance *see* Character traits
– perseverance
Persia *see* Foreign lands – Persia
Persistence *see* Character traits –
persistence
Perspective *see* Concepts –
perspective
Peru *see* Foreign lands – Peru
Petroglyphs
Petroleum *see* Oil
Pets
Pharaohs *see* Royalty – pharaohs
Philippines *see* Foreign lands –
Philippines
Phoenix *see* Mythical creatures –
phoenix
Photographers *see* Careers –
photographers
Photography *see* Activities –
photographing
Physical handicaps *see*
Handicaps – physical
handicaps
Physicians *see* Careers – doctors
Piano
Picnics *see* Activities – picnicking
Picture puzzles
Pigeons *see* Birds – pigeons
Pigs *see* Animals – pigs
Pilgrims
Pilots *see* Careers – airplane
pilots
Pima *see* Indians of North
America – Pima
Pioneer life *see* U.S. history –
frontier and pioneer life
Pirates
Pixies *see* Mythical creatures –
pixies
Planes *see* Airplanes, airports
Planets
Plants
Plasterers *see* Careers –
plasterers
Playing *see* Activities – playing
Plays *see* Theater
Plovers *see* Birds – plovers
Plumbers *see* Careers –
plumbers
Poems
Poetry
Poland *see* Foreign lands –
Poland
Polar bears *see* Animals – polar
bears
Police officers *see* Careers –
police officers
Polish Americans *see* Ethnic
groups in the U.S. – Polish
Americans
Poltergeists *see* Ghosts
Ponds *see* Lakes, ponds
Ponies *see* Animals – horses,
ponies
Pooka spirit *see* Mythical
creatures – pooka spirit
Poor *see* Homeless; Poverty

Pop-up books *see* Format,
unusual – toy and movable
books
Porcupines *see* Animals –
porcupines
Porpoises *see* Animals –
dolphins
Portugal *see* Foreign lands –
Portugal
Possums *see* Animals – possums
Post office
Postal workers *see* Careers –
postal workers
Potawatomi *see* Indians of North
America – Potawatomi
Potty training *see* Toilet training
Poverty
Power failures
Powhaton Indians *see* Indians of
North America – Powhaton
Practicality *see* Character traits –
practicality
Prairie dogs *see* Animals –
prairie dogs
Prairie wolves *see* Animals –
coyotes
Praying mantis *see* Insects –
praying mantis
Preachers *see* Careers –
preachers
Prehistoric man *see* Cavemen
Prejudice
Pride *see* Character traits – pride
Princes *see* Royalty – princes
Princesses *see* Royalty –
princesses
Printers *see* Careers – printers
Prisons
Problem solving
Progress
Proverbs
Pueblo Indians *see* Indians of
North America – Pueblo
Puerto Rican Americans *see*
Ethnic groups in the U.S. –
Hispanic Americans; Ethnic
groups in the U.S. – Puerto
Rican Americans
Puerto Rico *see* Foreign lands –
Puerto Rico
Puffins *see* Birds – puffins
Pumas *see* Animals – cougars
Punchball *see* Sports –
punchball
Puppeteers *see* Careers –
Puppeteers
Puppets
Purim *see* Holidays – Purim
Puzzles *see also* Picture puzzles;
Rebuses; Riddles

Quail *see* Birds – quail
Quechua *see* Indians of South
America – Quechua
Queens *see* Royalty – queens
Questioning *see* Character traits
– questioning
Quicksand *see* Sand
Quilts

Rabbits *see* Animals – rabbits

Raccoons *see* Animals –
raccoons
Race car drivers *see* Careers –
race car drivers
Racing *see* Sports – racing
Radio
Railroad engineers *see* Careers –
railroad engineers
Railroads *see* Trains
Rain *see* Weather – rain
Rainbows *see* Weather –
rainbows
Rajahs *see* Royalty – rajahs
Ramadan *see* Holidays –
Ramadan
Ranchers *see* Careers – ranchers
Rangers *see* Careers – park
rangers
Rats *see* Animals – rats
Ravens *see* Birds – ravens
Reading *see* Activities – reading
Rebuses
Reindeer *see* Animals – reindeer
Religion
Religion – Daniel
Religion – David
Religion – Hinduism
Religion – Islam
Religion – Jonah
Religion – Moses
Religion – Nativity
Religion – Noah
Remembering
Repetitive stories *see* Cumulative
tales
Reptiles
Reptiles – alligators, crocodiles
Reptiles – chameleons
Reptiles – crocodiles *see* Reptiles
– alligators, crocodiles
Reptiles – iguanas
Reptiles – Komodo dragons
Reptiles – lizards
Reptiles – monitor lizards
Reptiles – salamanders
Reptiles – snakes
Reptiles – turtles, tortoises
Responsibility *see* Character
traits – responsibility
Rest *see* Sleep
Restaurants
Rhinoceros *see* Animals –
rhinoceros
Rhyming text
Riddles
Right and left *see* Concepts – left
and right
Riots
Rivers
Roads
Robbers *see* Crime
Robins *see* Birds – robins
Robots
Rock climbing *see* Sports – rock
climbing
Rockets *see* Space and space
ships
Rocking chairs *see* Furniture –
chairs
Rocking horses *see* Toys –
rocking horses
Rocks
Rodeos

Roller skating *see* Sports – roller skating

Romania *see* Foreign lands – Romania

Roosters *see* Birds – chickens

Rosh Hashanah *see* Holidays – Rosh Hashanah

Royalty

Royalty – emperors

Royalty – khans

Royalty – kings

Royalty – pharaohs

Royalty – princes

Royalty – princesses

Royalty – queens

Royalty – rajahs

Royalty – sultans

Royalty – tsars

Rummage sales *see* Garage sales, rummage sales

Running *see* Activities – Running

Running away *see* Behavior – running away

Russia *see* Foreign lands – Russia

Russian Americans *see* Ethnic groups in the U.S. – Russian Americans

Rwanda *see* Foreign lands – Rwanda

Sadness *see* Emotions – sadness

Safety

Sahara Desert *see* Foreign lands – Sahara Desert

Sailing *see* Sports – sailing

Sailors

Saint Patrick's Day *see* Holidays – St. Patrick's Day

St. Patrick's Day *see* Holidays – St. Patrick's Day

Salamanders *see* Reptiles – salamanders

Salesmen *see* Careers – salesmen

Sand

Sandcastles *see* Sand

Sandman *see* Mythical creatures – sandman

Sandpipers *see* Birds – sandpipers

Sandstorms *see* Weather – sandstorms

Sanitation workers *see* Careers – sanitation workers

Santa Claus

Saving things *see* Behavior – saving things

Scandinavia *see* Foreign lands – Scandinavia

Scarecrows

School

School – first day

School principals *see* Careers – school principals

Science

Scientists *see* Careers – scientists

Scotland *see* Foreign lands – Scotland

Scuba diving *see* Sports – skin diving

Sea and seashore

Sea lions *see* Animals – sea lions

Sea serpents *see* Monsters; Mythical creatures

Seagulls *see* Birds – seagulls

Seahorses *see* Crustaceans

Seals *see* Animals – seals

Seamstresses *see* Careers – seamstresses

Seashore *see* Sea and seashore

Seasons

Seasons – fall

Seasons – spring

Seasons – summer

Seasons – winter

Secret codes

Secrets *see* Behavior – secrets

Seeds

Seeing *see* Anatomy – eyes; Glasses; Handicaps – blindness; Senses – seeing

Seeking better things *see* Behavior – seeking better things

Self-concept

Self-esteem *see* Self-concept

Self-image *see* Self-concept

Self-reliance *see* Character traits – confidence

Selfishness *see* Character traits – selfishness

Selkies *see* Mythical creatures – selkies

Seminole Indians *see* Indians of North America – Seminole

Seneca Indians *see* Indians of North America – Seneca

Senses

Senses – hearing

Senses – seeing

Senses – smelling

Senses – tasting

Senses – touching

Serbia *see* Foreign lands – Serbia

Sewing *see* Activities – sewing

Sex instruction

Sex roles

Sextuplets *see* Multiple births – sextuplets

Shadows

Shakers *see* Ethnic groups in the U.S. – Shakers

Shakespeare

Shape *see* Concepts – shape

Shaped books *see* Format, unusual

Sharing *see* Behavior – sharing

Sharks *see* Fish – sharks

Shawnee Indians *see* Indians of North America – Shawnee

Sheep *see* Animals – sheep

Shells *see* Sea and seashore

Shepherds *see* Careers – shepherds

Sheriffs *see* Careers – sheriffs

Ships *see* Boats, ships

Shirts *see* Clothing – shirts

Shoemakers *see* Careers – shoemakers

Shoes *see* Clothing – shoes

Shopping

Shops *see* Stores

Shoshone Indians *see* Indians of North America – Shoshone

Shows *see* Theater

Shrews *see* Animals – shrews

Shrimp *see* Crustaceans

Shyness *see* Character traits – shyness

Siam *see* Foreign lands – Thailand

Siberia *see* Foreign lands – Siberia

Sibling rivalry

Siblings *see* Family life – brothers; Family life – brothers and sisters; Family life – sisters

Sickness *see* Health and fitness; Illness

Sight *see* Anatomy – eyes; Glasses; Handicaps – blindness; Senses – seeing

Sign painters *see* Careers – sign painters

Siksika Indians *see* Indians of North America – Siksika

Singers *see* Careers – singers

Singing *see* Activities – singing

Sioux Indians *see* Indians of North America – Cheyenne (Sioux); Indians of North America – Dakota (Sioux); Indians of North America – Lakota (Sioux); Indians of North America – Sioux

Sisters *see* Family life; Family life – brothers and sisters; Family life – sisters; Sibling rivalry

Size *see* Concepts – size

Skateboarding *see* Sports – skateboarding

Skating *see* Sports – ice skating; Sports – hockey; Sports – roller skating

Skeletons *see* Anatomy – skeletons

Skiing *see* Sports – skiing

Skin *see* Anatomy – skin

Skin diving *see* Sports – skin diving

Skunks *see* Animals – skunks

Sky

Slavery

Sledding *see* Sports – sledding

Sleep

Sleepovers

Sleight-of-hand *see* Magic

Sloths *see* Animals – sloths

Slugs *see* Animals – slugs

Smallness *see* Character traits – smallness

Smelling *see* Anatomy – noses; Senses – smelling

Snails *see* Animals – snails

Snakes *see* Reptiles – snakes

Snow *see* Weather – blizzards; Weather – snow

Snow plows *see* Machines

Snowmen

Soccer *see* Sports – soccer

Society Islands *see* Foreign lands – South Sea Islands

Socks *see* Clothing – socks

Sofas *see* Furniture – couches, sofas

Soldiers *see* Careers – military

Soldiers, toy *see* Toys – soldiers

Solitude *see* Behavior – solitude

Songs

Sons *see* Family life – sons
Sorcerers *see* Wizards
Sounds *see* Noise, sounds
South Africa *see* Foreign lands – South Africa
South America *see* Foreign lands – South America
South Pole *see* Foreign lands – Antarctic
South Sea Islands *see* Foreign lands – South Sea Islands
Southwest Indians *see* Indians of North America – Southwest
Soviet Union *see* Foreign lands – Russia; Foreign lands – Soviet Union
Space and space ships
Spain *see* Foreign lands – Spain
Sparrows *see* Birds – sparrows
Special Olympics *see* Sports – Special Olympics
Spectacles *see* Glasses
Speech *see* Language
Speed *see* Concepts – speed
Spelunking *see* Caves
Spiders
Split page books *see* Format, unusual
Sponges *see* Animals – sponges
Spooks *see* Ghosts; Mythical creatures – goblins
Spoonbills *see* Birds – spoonbills
Sports
Sports – archery
Sports – baseball
Sports – basketball
Sports – bicycling
Sports – bowling
Sports – boxing
Sports – camping *see* Camps, camping
Sports – fishing
Sports – football
Sports – golf
Sports – gymnastics
Sports – hiking
Sports – hockey
Sports – hunting
Sports – ice skating
Sports – jumping rope
Sports – karate
Sports – mountain climbing
Sports – Olympics
Sports – punchball
Sports – racing
Sports – rock climbing
Sports – roller skating
Sports – sailing
Sports – skateboarding
Sports – skiing
Sports – skin diving
Sports – sledding
Sports – soccer
Sports – Special Olympics
Sports – surfing
Sports – swimming
Sports – T-ball
Sports – Tae Kwon Do
Sports – wrestling
Sportsmanship
Spring *see* Seasons – spring
Squirrels *see* Animals – squirrels
Stage *see* Theater
Stars

Stealing *see* Behavior – stealing; Crime
Steam shovels *see* Machines
Steamrollers *see* Machines
Step families *see* Divorce; Family life – step families
Stepchildren *see* Divorce; Family life – step families
Stepparents *see* Divorce; Family life – step families
Stones *see* Rocks
Storekeepers *see* Careers – storekeepers
Stores
Stories in rhyme *see* Rhyming text
Storks *see* Birds – storks
Storms *see* Weather – storms
Storytelling *see* Activities – storytelling
Strangers *see* Behavior – talking to strangers
Streams *see* Rivers
Streets *see* Roads
String
Stubbornness *see* Character traits – stubbornness
Sukkot *see* Holidays – Sukkot
Sullivan Islands *see* Foreign lands – South Sea Islands
Sultans *see* Royalty – sultans
Summer *see* Seasons – summer
Sun
Superstition
Surfing *see* Sports – surfing
Suriname *see* Foreign lands – Suriname
Swallows *see* Birds – swallows
Swamps
Swans *see* Birds – swans
Swapping *see* Activities – trading
Sweaters *see* Clothing – sweaters
Sweden *see* Foreign lands – Sweden
Swimming *see* Sports – swimming
Swinging *see* Activities – swinging
Switzerland *see* Foreign lands – Switzerland

T-ball *see* Sports – T-ball
Tables *see* Furniture – tables
Tae Kwon Do *see* Sports – Tae Kwon Do
Tailors *see* Careers – tailors
Tails *see* Anatomy – tails
Taiwan *see* Foreign lands – Taiwan
Talking *see* Activities – talking
Talking to strangers *see* Behavior – talking to strangers
Tall tales
Tanzania *see* Foreign lands – Tanzania
Tapirs *see* Animals – tapirs
Tarascan Indians *see* Indians of North America – Tarascan
Tardiness *see* Behavior – tardiness
Tasting *see* Senses – tasting

Taxi drivers *see* Careers – taxi drivers
Taxis
Teachers *see* Careers – teachers
Teasing *see* Behavior – bullying
Teddy bears *see* Toys – bears
Teeth
Telephone
Telephone operators *see* Careers – telephone operators
Television
Telling stories *see* Activities – storytelling
Telling time *see* Clocks, watches; Time
Temper tantrums *see* Emotions – anger
Textless *see* Wordless
Thailand *see* Foreign lands – Thailand
Thanksgiving *see* Holidays – Thanksgiving
Theater
Thumb sucking
Thunder *see* Weather – storms; Weather – thunder
Tibet *see* Foreign lands – Tibet
Tigers *see* Animals – tigers
Time
Tin soldiers *see* Toys – soldiers
Tlingit Indians *see* Indians of North America – Tlingit
Toads *see* Frogs and toads
Toes *see* Anatomy – toes
Toilet training
Tongue twisters
Tonsillectomy *see* Illness – tonsillectomy
Tools
Tornadoes *see* Weather – Tornadoes
Tortoises *see* Reptiles – turtles, tortoises
Toucans *see* Birds – toucans
Touching *see* Senses – touching
Towns *see* City
Toy and movable books *see* Format, unusual – toy and movable books
Toy makers *see* Careers – toy makers
Toys
Toys – balloons
Toys – balls
Toys – bears
Toys – blocks
Toys – dolls
Toys – hobby horses *see* Toys – rocking horses
Toys – pandas *see* Toys – bears
Toys – rocking horses
Toys – soldiers
Toys – teddy bears *see* Toys – bears
Toys – tin soldiers *see* Toys – soldiers
Toys – trains
Tractors
Trading *see* Activities – trading
Traffic, traffic signs
Train engineers *see* Careers – railroad engineers
Trains

Trains, toy *see* Toys – trains
Transportation
Traveling *see* Activities – traveling
Trees
Trickery *see* Behavior – trickery
Tricks *see* Magic
Trinidad *see* Foreign lands – Trinidad
Trolleys *see* Cable cars, trolleys
Trolls *see* Mythical creatures – trolls
Truck drivers *see* Careers – truck drivers
Trucks
Tsars *see* Royalty – tsars
Tsimshian Indians *see* Indians of North America – Tsimshian
Tsunamis
Turkey *see* Foreign lands – Turkey
Turkeys *see* Birds – turkeys
Turtles *see* Reptiles – turtles, tortoises
TV *see* Television
Twa *see* Indians of North America – Twa
Twilight
Tyrol *see* Foreign lands – Tyrol

U.S. history
U.S. history – frontier and pioneer life
Ukraine *see* Foreign lands – Ukraine
Umbrellas
Uncles *see* Family life – aunts, uncles
Unhappiness *see* Emotions – happiness; Emotions – sadness
UNICEF
Unicorns *see* Mythical creatures – unicorns
Unnoticed *see* Behavior – unnoticed, unseen
Unseen *see* Behavior – unnoticed, unseen
Unusual format *see* Format, unusual
Up and down *see* Concepts – up and down
Ute Indians *see* Indians of North America – Ute
Uzbekistan *see* Foreign lands – Uzbekistan

Vacationing *see* Activities – vacationing
Vacuum cleaners *see* Machines
Valentine's Day *see* Holidays – Valentine's Day
Values
Vampires *see* Monsters
Vanity *see* Character traits – vanity
Vatican City *see* Foreign lands – Vatican City

Venezuela *see* Foreign lands – Venezuela
Veterinarians *see* Careers – veterinarians
Vietnam *see* Foreign lands – Vietnam
Vietnamese Americans *see* Ethnic groups in the U.S. – Asian Americans; Ethnic groups in the U.S. – Vietnamese Americans
Violence, nonviolence
Volcanoes
Vultures *see* Birds – vultures

Waiters *see* Careers – waiters, waitresses
Waitresses *see* Careers – waiters, waitresses
Wales *see* Foreign lands – Wales
Walking *see* Activities – walking
Walruses *see* Animals – walruses
Wampanoag Indians *see* Indians of North America – Wampanoag
War
Warthogs *see* Animals – warthogs
Washing machines *see* Machines
Washington's Birthday *see* Holidays – Washington's Birthday
Wasps *see* Insects – wasps
Watches *see* Clocks, watches
Water
Water buffaloes *see* Animals – water buffaloes
Weapons
Weasels *see* Animals – weasels
Weather
Weather – blizzards
Weather – clouds
Weather – cold
Weather – droughts
Weather – floods
Weather – fog
Weather – hurricanes
Weather – mist *see* Weather – fog
Weather – rain
Weather – rainbows
Weather – sandstorms
Weather – snow
Weather – storms
Weather – thunder
Weather – tornadoes
Weather – wind
Weaving *see* Activities – weaving
Weddings
Weekdays *see* Days of the week, months of the year
Weight *see* Concepts – weight
Welders *see* Careers – welders
Werewolves *see* Mythical creatures – werewolves
West *see* U.S. history
West Indies *see* Foreign lands – West Indies
Whalers *see* Careers – whalers
Whales *see* Animals – whales

Wheels
Whistling *see* Activities – whistling
Wildebeests *see* Animals – wildebeests
Willfulness *see* Character traits – willfulness
Wind *see* Weather – wind
Windigos Indians *see* Indians of North America – Windigos
Windmills
Window cleaners *see* Careers – window cleaners
Wings
Winter *see* Seasons – winter
Wishing *see* Behavior – wishing
Witches
Wizards
Wolves *see* Animals – wolves
Wombats *see* Animals – wombats
Woodcarvers *see* Careers – woodcarvers
Woodchucks *see* Animals – groundhogs
Wood-hoopoe *see* Birds – wood-hoopoe
Woodpeckers *see* Birds – woodpeckers
Woods *see* Forest, woods
Word games *see* Language
Wordless
Words *see* Language
Working *see* Activities – working; Careers
World
Worms *see* Animals – worms
Worrying *see* Behavior – worrying
Wrecking machines *see* Machines
Wrens *see* Birds – wrens
Wrestling *see* Sports – wrestling
Writers *see* Careers – writers
Writing *see* Activities – writing
Writing letters *see* Letters, cards

Yaks *see* Animals – yaks
Yana Indians *see* Indians of North America – Yana
Yanomamo Indians *see* Indians of South America – Yanomamo
Yom Kippur *see* Holidays – Yom Kippur
Yupik *see* Indians of North America – Yupik

Zaire *see* Foreign lands – Zaire
Zanzibar *see* Foreign lands – Zanzibar
Zapotec Indians *see* Indians of North America – Zapotec
Zebras *see* Animals – zebras
Zodiac
Zookeepers *see* Careers – zoo keepers
Zoos
Zuni Indians *see* Indians of North America – Zuni

Subject Guide

This is a subject-arranged guide to picture books. Under appropriate subject headings and subheadings, titles appear alphabetically by author name, or by title when author is unknown. Complete bibliographic information for each title cited will be found in the Bibliographic Guide.

Aardvarks *see* Animals – aardvarks

ABC books

A is for alphabet
ABCDEFGHIJKLMNOPQRSTUVWXYZ in English and Spanish
Abrons, Mary. *For Alice a palace*
Ackerman, Karen. *Flannery Row*
Ada, Alma Flor. *Gathering the sun*
Alda, Arlene. *Arlene Alda's ABC*
Alexander, Anne (Anna Barbara Cooke). *ABC of cars and trucks*
Allington, Richard L. *Letters*
Andersen, Karen Born. *An alphabet in five acts*
Anglund, Joan Walsh. *A is for always*
Anno, Mitsumasa. *Anno's alphabet*
  Anno's magical ABC
Argent, Kerry. *Animal capers*
Arnosky, Jim. *Mouse numbers and letters*
  Mouse writing
Asch, Frank. *The alphabet zoo*
  Little Devil's ABC
Ashley Bryan's abc of African American poetry
Ashton, Elizabeth Allen. *An old-fashioned ABC book*
Aylesworth, Jim. *The folks in the valley*
  Old Black Fly
Azarian, Mary. *A farmer's alphabet*
Babson, Jane F. *Babson's bestiary*
Baker, Alan. *Black and White Rabbit's ABC*
Balian, Lorna. *Humbug potion*
Balog, James. *James Balog's animals A to Z*
Bannatyne-Cugnet, Jo. *A prairie alphabet*
Barry, Katharina. *A is for anything*
Barry, Robert E. *Animals around the world*
Base, Graeme. *Animalia*
Baskin, Leonard. *Hosie's alphabet*
Bayer, Jane. *A my name is Alice*
Beller, Janet. *A-B-C-ing*
Bender, Robert. *The A to Z beastly jamboree*
Berenstain, Stan. *The Berenstains' B book*

Berger, Terry. *Ben's ABC day*
Bernhard, Durga. *Alphabeasts*
Bishop, Ann. *Riddle-iculous rid-alphabet book*
Black, Floyd. *Alphabet cat*
Blake, Quentin. *Quentin Blake's ABC*
Bond, Jean Carey. *A is for Africa*
Bond, Michael. *Paddington's ABC*
Borlenghi, Patricia. *From albatross to zoo*
Bourke, Linda. *Eye count*
Bove, Linda. *Sign language ABC with Linda Bove*
Bowen, Betsy. *Antler, bear, canoe*
Boxer, Devorah. *26 ways to be somebody else*
Boynton, Sandra. *A is for angry*
Bridwell, Norman. *Clifford's ABC*
Brown, Judith Gwyn. *Alphabet dreams*
Brown, Marcia. *All butterflies*
  Peter Piper's alphabet
Brown, Margaret Wise. *Sleepy ABC*
Brown, Ruth. *Alphabet times four*
Bruce, Lisa. *Oliver's alphabets*
Bruchac, Joseph. *Many nations*
Bruna, Dick. *B is for bear*
Brunhoff, Laurent de. *Babar's ABC*
Brusca, María Cristina. *When jaguars ate the moon*
Budd, Lillian. *The pie wagon*
Budney, Blossom. *N is for nursery school*
Bullard, Lisa. *Not enough beds!*
Bunting, Jane. *My first ABC*
Burningham, John. *First steps*
  John Burningham's ABC
Burnstein, Chaya M. *The Jewish kids' Hebrew-English wordbook*
Burton, Jane. *ABC*
Burton, Marilee Robin. *Aaron awoke*
Calmenson, Stephanie. *ABC*
  It begins with an A
Carlson, Nancy L. *ABC, I like me!*
Chandra, Deborah. *A is for Amos*
Chaplin, Susan Gibbons. *I can sign my ABCs*
Chardiet, Bernice. *C is for circus*
Charles, Donald. *Shaggy dog's animal alphabet*
Charlip, Remy. *Handtalk*
Chase, Catherine. *An alphabet book*
  Baby mouse learns his ABC's
Chess, Victoria. *Alfred's alphabet walk*
Chial, Debra. *M is for Minnesota*
A child's picture English-Hebrew dictionary
Chin-Lee, Cynthia. *A is for Asia*
Chouinard, Roger. *The amazing animal alphabet book*
Chwast, Seymour. *Alphabet parade*

Still another alphabet book

Cleary, Beverly. *The hullabaloo ABC*, ill. by Ted Rand

The hullabaloo ABC, ill. by Earl Thollander

Cleaver, Elizabeth. *ABC*

Coats, Laura Jane. *Alphabet garden*

Cohen, Nora. *From apple to zipper*

Cohen, Peter Zachary. *Authorized autumn charts of the Upper Red Canoe River country*

Coletta, Irene. *From A to Z*

Conran, Sebastian. *My first ABC book*

Cooney, Barbara. *A garland of games and other diversions*

Cousins, Lucy. *Maisy's ABC*

Cox, Lynn. *Crazy alphabet*

Cremins, Robert. *My animal ABC*

Crews, Donald. *We read*

Crowther, Robert. *The most amazing hide-and-seek alphabet book*

My pop-up surprise ABC

Cushman, Doug. *The ABC mystery*

Daleo, Morgan Simone. *A spirited alphabet*

Darling, Kathy (Mary Kathleen). *ABC cats*

ABC dogs

Amazon A B C

Dauphin, Francine Legrand. *A French A. B. C.*

DeLage, Ida. *ABC Christmas*

ABC Easter bunny

ABC fire dogs

ABC Halloween witch

ABC pigs go to market

ABC pirate adventure

ABC Santa Claus

ABC triplets at the zoo

Delaunay, Sonia. *Sonia Delaunay's alphabet*

Demarest, Chris L. *The cowboy ABC*

De Mejo, Oscar. *Oscar de Mejo's ABC*

Demi. *Demi's find the animals A B C*

The peek-a-boo ABC

Dodd, Lynley. *The minister's cat: ABC*

Domanska, Janina. *A was an angler*

Doolittle, Eileen. *The ark in the attic*

Doubilet, Anne. *Under the sea from A to Z*

Downie, Jill. *Alphabet puzzle*

Dragonwagon, Crescent. *Alligator arrived with apples*

Dreamer, Sue. *Circus ABC*

Drucker, Malka. *A Jewish holiday ABC*

Duke, Kate. *The guinea pig ABC*

Duvoisin, Roger Antoine. *A for the ark*

Eastman, P. D. (Philip D.). *The alphabet book*

Edens, Cooper. *An ABC of fashionable animals*

Edwards, Michelle. *Alef-bet*

Edwards, Pamela Duncan. *The wacky wedding*

Ehlert, Lois. *Eating the alphabet*

Eichenberg, Fritz. *Ape in cape*

Elliot, David. *An alphabet of rotten kids!*

Elting, Mary. *Q is for duck*

Emberley, Ed (Edward Randolph). *Ed Emberley's ABC*

Ernst, Lisa Campbell. *The letters are lost!*

Falls, C. B. (Charles Buckles). *ABC book*

Farber, Norma. *As I was crossing Boston Common*

Feelings, Muriel. *Jambo means hello*

Feldman, Judy. *The alphabet in nature*

Ferguson, Don. *Winnie the Pooh's A to Zzzz*

Fife, Dale. *Adam's ABC*

Fisher, Leonard Everett. *The ABC exhibit*

Floyd, Lucy. *Agatha's alphabet, with her very own dictionary*

Ford, Juwanda G. *K is for Kwanzaa*

Freeman, Don. *Add-a-line alphabet*

Fujikawa, Gyo. *Gyo Fujikawa's A to Z picture book*

Gabler, Mirko. *The alphabet soup*

Gág, Wanda. *ABC bunny*

Gantz, David. *The genie bear with the light brown hair word book*

Gardner, Beau. *Have you ever seen . . . ?*

Garten, Jan. *The alphabet tale*

Geringer, Laura. *The cow is mooing anyhow*

Gerstein, Mordicai. *The absolutely awful alphabet*

Glyman, Caroline A. *Learning your ABC's of nutrition*

Goennel, Heidi. *Heidi's zoo*

Golding, Kim. *Alphababies*

Good, Phyllis Pellman. *Plain Pig's ABCs*

Greenaway, Kate. *A apple pie*

Gretz, Susanna. *Teddy bears ABC*

Grimes, Nikki. *C is for city*

Groening, Maggie. *Maggie Simpson's alphabet book*

Grossbart, Francine. *A big city*

Grover, Max. *The accidental zucchini*

Gundersheimer, Karen. *A B C, say with me*

Gunning, Monica. *The two Georges*

Hague, Kathleen. *Alphabears*

Hallinan, P. K. (Patrick K.). *When I grow up*

Hansen, Biruta Akerbergs. *Parading with piglets*

Harada, Joyce. *It's the ABC book*

Harness, Cheryl. *Midnight in the cemetery*

Harrison, Ted. *A northern alphabet*

Hausman, Bonnie. *A to Z, do you ever feel like me?*

Hausman, Gerald. *Turtle Island ABC*

Hawkins, Colin. *Busy ABC*

Hayward, Linda. *Alphabet School*

D is for doll

Heller, Nicholas. *Goblins in green*

Hepworth, Catherine. *ANTics! an alphabetical anthology*

Hill, Susan. *Simba's A-Z*

Hillman, Priscilla. *A Merry-Mouse Christmas A B C*

Hindley, Judy. *Crazy ABC*

Hoban, Tana. *A B See!*

26 letters and 99 cents

Hobbie, Holly. *Toot and Puddle, Puddle's ABC*

Hoberman, Mary Ann. *Nuts to you and nuts to me*

Hoguet, Susan Ramsay. *I unpacked my grandmother's trunk*

Holabird, Katharine. *The little mouse ABC*

Holl, Adelaide. *The ABC of cars, trucks and machines*

Hooper, Patricia. *A bundle of beasts*

Hopkins, Lee Bennett. *April, bubbles, chocolate*

Horenstein, Henry. *A is for – ?*

Arf! beg! catch!

Howard-Gibbon, Amelia Frances. *An illustrated comic alphabet*

Howland, Naomi. *ABCDrive!*

Hubbard, Woodleigh Marx. *C is for curious*

Hudson, Wade. *Afro-bets kids I'm gonna be*

Hughes, Langston. *The sweet and sour animal book*

Hughes, Shirley. *Alfie's ABC*

Lucy and Tom's A.B.C.

Hyman, Trina Schart. *A little alphabet*

Ilsley, Velma. *A busy day for Chris*

M is for moving

Inkpen, Mick. *Kipper's A to Z*

Ipcar, Dahlov. *I love my anteater with an A*

Isadora, Rachel. *ABC pop!*

City seen from A to Z

J. Paul Getty Museum. *A is for artist*

Pratt, Kristin Joy. *A fly in the sky*
   A swim through the sea
Reed, Lynn Rowe. *Pedro, his perro, and the alphabet*
   sombrero
Reeves, James. *Ragged Robin*
Ressmeyer, Roger. *Astronaut to zodiac*
Rey, H. A. (Hans Augusto). *Curious George learns the*
   alphabet
   Look for the letters
Rice, James. *Cajun alphabet*
Roe, Richard. *Animal ABC*
Rojankovsky, Feodor. *ABC, an alphabet of many*
   things
   Animals in the zoo
Rosario, Idalia. *Idalia's project ABC*
Rosen, Michael J. (1954-). *Avalanche*
Rosenberg, Liz. *A big and little alphabet*
Ruben, Patricia. *Apples to zippers*
Rubin, Cynthia Elyce. *ABC Americana from the*
   National Gallery of Art
Ryden, Hope. *Wild animals of Africa ABC*
Sabuda, Robert. *ABC Disney*
Sabuda, Robert James. *The Christmas alphabet*
Samton, Sheila White. *Amazing Aunt Agatha*
Sanders, Marilyn. *What's your name?*
Sandved, Kjell Bloch. *The butterfly alphabet*
Sardegna, Jill. *K is for kiss good night*
Scarry, Richard. *Richard Scarry's ABC word book*
Schnur, Steven. *Autumn*
The Sea World alphabet book
Sendak, Maurice. *Alligators all around*
Sesame Street. *The Sesame Street book of letters*
Seuss, Dr. *Dr. Seuss's ABC*
   Hooper Humperdink . . . ? Not him!
Shannon, George. *Tomorrow's alphabet*
Shelby, Anne. *Potluck*
Shepard, E. H. (Ernest Howard). *Winnie-the-Pooh's*
   ABC
Shuttlesworth, Dorothy Edwards. *ABC of buses*
Sierra, Judy. *There's a zoo in room 22*
Silverman, Maida. *Bunny's ABC*
Simpson, Gretchen Dow. *Gretchen's ABC*
Slate, Joseph. *Miss Bindergarten gets ready for kinder-*
   garten
Sloat, Teri. *From letter to letter*
   Patty's pumpkin patch
Smith, William Jay. *Puptents and pebbles*
Snow, Alan. *The monster book of ABC sounds*
Staake, Bob. *My little ABC book*
Steiner, Charlotte. *ABC*
Stevenson, James. *Grandpa's great city tour*
Stock, Catherine. *Alexander's midnight snack*
Stutson, Caroline. *Prairie primer A to Z*
Tapahonso, Luci. *Navajo ABC*
Testa, Fulvio. *A long trip to Z*
Thornhill, Jan. *Wildlife ABC*
The Timbertoes ABC alphabet book
Tobias, Tobi. *A world of words*
Tryon, Leslie. *Albert's alphabet*
Tucker, Sian. *A is for astronaut*
Turner, Priscilla. *Among the odds and evens*
Van Allsburg, Chris. *The Z was zapped*
Viorst, Judith. *The Alphabet from Z to A*
Waber, Bernard. *An anteater named Arthur*
Walters, Marguerite. *The city-country ABC*
Walton, Rick. *So many bunnies*
Watson, Clyde. *Applebet*
Watson, Nancy Dingman. *What does A begin with?*
Wethered, Peggy. *Touchdown Mars!*

Wilbur, Richard. *The disappearing alphabet*
Wild, Robin. *The bears' ABC book*
Williams, Garth. *The big golden animal ABC*
Williams, Laura E. *ABC kids*
Wilner, Isabel. *A garden alphabet*
Wilson, Barbara Ker. *ABC et = and 123*
Wojtowycz, David. *David Wojtowycz presents Animal*
   ABC
Wolf, Janet. *Adelaide to Zeke*
Yolen, Jane. *All in the woodland early*
   Elfabet

Abnaki Indians *see* Indians of North America
– Abnaki

Abused children *see* Child abuse

Acadians *see* Ethnic groups in the U.S. – Acadians

Accidents

Biro, Val. *Gumdrop and the steamroller*
Brown, Marc Tolon. *D. W. thinks big, a board book*
Carlson, Nancy L. *Arnie and the new kid*
Carrick, Carol. *The accident*
French, Vivian. *Oh no, Anna!*
Harder, Dan (Dan Wymbs). *Colliding with Chris*
Hindley, Judy. *The big red bus*
How Raggedy Ann got her candy heart
Hurd, Thacher. *Santa Mouse and the ratdeer*
Keeshan, Robert. *Itty Bitty Kitty makes a big splash*
Lawson, Julie. *Emma and the silk train*
Loewen, Nancy. *Emergencies*
McPhail, David M. *Big brown bear*
Marzollo, Jean. *What's the matter with Mother Goose?*
Mattern, Joanne. *Safety in public places*
O'Connor, Jane. *Nina, Nina ballerina*
Perrow, Angeli. *Captain's castaway*
Polacco, Patricia. *In Enzo's splendid gardens*
Porter, Sue. *Parsnip and the runaway tractor*
Rand, Gloria. *Baby in a basket*
Rylant, Cynthia. *Silver packages*
Weller, Frances Ward. *The angel of Mill Street*

Accordion books *see* Format, unusual

Accountants *see* Careers – accountants

Acrobats *see* Careers – acrobats

Activities

Accorsi, William. *Short short short stories*
Ahlberg, Allan. *Me and my friend*
Alborough, Jez. *Can you jump like a kangaroo?*
Alderson, Sue Ann. *Bonnie McSmithers is at it again!*
Aliki. *Overnight at Mary Bloom's*
Allard, Harry. *The Stupids step out*
Allington, Richard L. *Feelings*
   Hearing
   Looking
   Smelling
   Tasting
   Touching
Andre, Evelyn M. *Places I like to be*
Anno, Mitsumasa. *All in a day*

Arnold, Caroline. *How do we have fun?*

Asch, Frank. *The alphabet zoo*
  Gia and the one hundred dollars worth of bubblegum

Aylesworth, Jim. *Wake up, little children*

Azarian, Mary. *A farmer's alphabet*

Baird, Anne. *The guppies of Hilly Dale House*

Bantock, Nick. *Runners, sliders, bouncers, climbers*

Behrens, June. *Can you walk the plank?*

Beller, Janet. *A-B-C-ing*

Bender, Robert. *The A to Z beastly jamboree*

Beni, Ruth. *Sir Baldergog the great*

Benjamin, Alan. *Busy bunnies*

Bennett, Jill. *Days are where we live and other poems*

Bowie, C. W. *Busy toes*

Boyd, Lizi. *The not-so-wicked stepmother*

Brandenberg, Franz. *Otto is different*

Brann, Esther. *A book for baby*

Brown, Elinor. *The little story book*

Brown, Margaret Wise. *The little fur family*

Brown, Ruth. *Our cat Flossie*

Bryant, Dean. *Here am I*

Bulla, Clyde Robert. *Daniel's duck*

Bundey, Nikki. *In the park*
  In the snow
  In the water

Bunting, Jane. *My first word book*

Burdekin, Harold. *A child's grace*

Burningham, John. *Skip trip*
  Sniff shout
  Wobble pop

Calmenson, Stephanie. *The kindergarten book*
  Meet Penny
  Meet Timmy

Carle, Eric. *From head to toe*

Carlson, Nancy L. *Arnie goes to camp*
  Bunnies and their hobbies
  Look out kindergarten, here I come!

Carr, Jan. *Frozen noses*

Cartlidge, Michelle. *The bear's bazaar*
  A mouse's diary

Carton, Lonnie Caming. *Mommies*

Cauley, Lorinda Bryan. *Clap your hands*

Chernoff, Goldie Taub. *Clay-dough, play-dough*
  Just a box?
  Pebbles and pods
  Puppet party

Chorao, Kay. *Peekaboo! Was it you?*

Cole, Joanna. *Fun on wheels*, ill. by Whitney Darrow
  Fun on wheels, ill. by Don Gauthier

Costa, Nicoletta. *The grown-up dog*

Cote, Nancy. *Flip-flops*

Creighton, Jill. *One day there was nothing to do*

Crews, Nina. *A high, low, near, far, loud, quiet story*

Crume, Marion W. *Let me see you try*
  Listen!
  What do you say?

Curtiss, A. B. *In the company of bears*

Dahl, Tessa. *The same but different*

Davies, Kay. *My balloon*
  My mirror

Day, Alexandra. *Boswell wide-awake*

Delton, Judy. *I'm telling you now*

Denim, Sue. *Make way for Dumb Bunnies*

Denslow, Sharon Phillips. *Night owls*

Dinosaurs and monsters

Dodds, Siobhan. *Words and pictures*

Dunn, Phoebe. *Busy, busy toddlers*

Dwight, Laura. *We can do it!*

Edwards, Richard. *Fly with the birds*

Ehrlich, Amy. *Bunnies all day long*

Ernst, Lisa Campbell. *Sam Johnson and the blue ribbon quilt*

Erskine, Jim. *Bert and Susie's messy tale*

Facklam, Margery. *So can I*

Fair, Sylvia. *The bedspread*

Falconer, Ian. *Olivia*

Faunce-Brown, Daphne. *Snuffles' house*

Flournoy, Valerie. *The best time of day*

Foord, Jo. *The book of babies*

Ford, Miela. *Watch us play*

Freeman, Don. *The day is waiting*

Fujikawa, Gyo. *My favorite thing*
  Surprise! Surprise!

Gentieu, Penny. *Baby! Talk!*

George, Jean Craighead. *Morning, noon, and night*

Gibbons, Gail. *The missing maple syrup sap mystery*

Giff, Patricia Reilly. *Ronald Morgan goes to camp*

Giovanni, Nikki. *The genie in the jar*

Gipson, Morrell. *Hello, Peter*

Gliori, Debi. *Mr. Bear babysits*

Goennel, Heidi. *My day*
  Sometimes I like to be alone
  While I am little

Gomi, Taro. *My friends*
  Seeing, saying, doing, playing

Good, Merle. *Amos and Susie*

Goor, Ron. *In the driver's seat*

Gore, Sheila. *My shadow*

Gove, Doris. *My mother talks to trees*

Grambling, Lois G. *Daddy will be there*

Grejniec, Michael. *Good morning, good night*

Haddon, Mark. *At home*
  At playgroup
  In the garden
  On vacation

Hafner, Marylin. *A year with Molly and Emmett*

Hallinan, P. K. (Patrick K.). *I'm glad to be me*
  Just being alone

Hanly, Shelia. *Toddler's book of fun things to do*

Harper, Piers. *If you love a bear*

Hawkins, Colin. *Busy ABC*

Heiligman, Deborah. *On the move*

Helldorfer, M. C. (Mary Claire). *Carnival*

Henley, Claire. *At the zoo*

Hennessy, B. G. (Barbara G.). *Busy Dinah Dinosaur*

Hest, Amy. *How to get famous in Brooklyn*

Hines, Anna Grossnickle. *What can you do in the rain?*
  What can you do in the snow?
  What can you do in the sun?
  What can you do in the wind?

Holzenthaler, Jean. *My feet do*
  My hands can

Hooks, William H. *How do you make a bubble?*

Hubbard, Woodleigh Marx. *2 is for dancing*

Hughes, Shirley. *Bouncing*

Hynard, Julia. *Percival's party*

Hynard, Stephen. *Snowy the rabbit*

Ingman, Bruce. *A night on the tiles*

Isadora, Rachel. *Babies*
  Friends

Iverson, Diane. *Discover the seasons*

Jabar, Cynthia. *Bored blue? Think what you can do!*

Jennings, Sharon. *When Jeremiah found Mrs. Ming*

Jensen, Helen Zane. *When Panda came to our house*

Johnson, Paul Brett. *The pig who ran a red light*

Jonas, Ann. *When you were a baby*

Kaufman, Curt. *Hotel boy*

Kelley, True. *Look, baby! Listen, baby! Do, baby!*
Kilroy, Sally. *Busy babies*
Kitchen, Bert. *Somewhere today*
Koller, Jackie French. *Bouncing on the bed*
Konigsburg, E. L. (Elaine Lobl). *Amy Elizabeth explores Bloomingdale's*
Krasilovsky, Phyllis. *The very little boy*
Krementz, Jill. *Katharine goes to nursery school*
Kunhardt, Edith. *Which one would you choose?*
    Which pig would you choose?
Kunnas, Mauri. *The nighttime book*
Lachner, Dorothea. *Smoky's special Easter present*
Lavis, Steve. *Jump!*
Lawson, Carol. *Teddy bear, teddy bear*
Lawston, Lisa. *Can you hop?*
Leavy, Una. *Harry's stormy night*
Leblanc, Anne. *Benjamin's busy day*
Leedy, Loreen. *A dragon Christmas*
Leonard, Marcia. *Busy babies*
Lester, Alison. *Celeste sails to Spain*
    Clive eats alligators
    Tessa snaps snakes
    Yikes!
Le-Tan, Pierre. *The afternoon cat*
Liatsos, Sandra Olson. *Bicycle riding and other poems*
Lilly, Kenneth. *Animal builders*
    Animal climbers
    Animal jumpers
    Animal runners
    Animal swimmers
Lionni, Leo. *Let's make rabbits*
Loomis, Christine. *At the laundromat*
Lyon, George Ella. *A sign*
MacDonald, Amy. *Let's do it*
    Let's try
McKié, Roy. *Snow*
MacKinnon, Debbie. *My day: I can do it!*
McMillan, Bruce. *Step by step*
McNaughton, Colin. *Autumn*
    Winter
McPhail, David M. *A bug, a bear, and a boy*
    A girl, a goat, and a goose
    Those can-do pigs
McQuade, Jacqueline. *Good times with Teddy Bear*
Maestro, Betsy. *Busy day*
Mainwaring, Jane. *My feather*
Maitland, Barbara. *My bear and me*
Mangin, Marie-France. *Suzette and Nicholas and the seasons clock*
Martin, David. *Piggy and Dad*
Masks and puppets
Mazer, Anne. *Watch me*
Milios, Rita. *Yo soy = I am*
Miller, Margaret. *Every day*
    Happy days
Moncure, Jane Belk. *Now I am five!*
    Now I am four!
    Now I am three!
Monfried, Lucia. *Dishes all done*
Moser, Barry. *Tucker Pfeffercorn*
Most, Bernard. *A pair of protoceratops*
    A trio of triceratops
Motyka, Sally Mitchell. *An ordinary day*
Munsch, Robert N. *Up, up, down!*
Myers, Arthur. *Kids do amazing things*
Nelson, Brenda. *Mud for sale*
Neumeier, Marty. *Action alphabet*
Noble, Trinka Hakes. *The day Jimmy's boa ate the wash*

Noll, Sally. *Jiggle wiggle prance*
Numeroff, Laura Joffe. *Chimps don't wear glasses*
    If you take a mouse to the movies
O'Brien, Anne Sibley. *Come play with us*
O'Brien, Claire. *Sam's sneaker search*
Ormerod, Jan. *Who's whose?*
Oxenbury, Helen. *I can*
    Tom and Pippo's day
Paradis, Susan. *My Daddy*
Parish, Peggy. *I can - can you?*
Pelham, David. *Worms wiggle*
Peyo. *What do smurfs do all day?*
Pirotta, Saviour. *Little bird*
Pitcher, Caroline. *Animals*
    Cars and boats
Pizer, Abigail. *Harry's night out*
Pluckrose, Henry Arthur. *Join it!*
Pomerantz, Charlotte. *Serena Katz*
Ray, Karen. *Sleep song*
Reasoner, Charles. *Who pretends?*
Regan, Dian Curtis. *Daddies*
Rice, Eve. *Aren't you coming too?*
Rockwell, Anne F. *In our house*
Rockwell, Harlow. *I did it*
    Look at this
Rosenberry, Vera. *Run, jump, whiz, splash*
Ross, H. L. *Not counting monsters*
Ross, Tony. *Treasure of Cozy Cove*
Rubel, Nicole. *Me and my kitty*
Rukeyser, Muriel. *More night*
Sage, Chris. *That's mine, that's yours*
Samuels, Barbara. *Duncan and Dolores*
Schindel, John. *Busy penguins*
Schweninger, Ann. *Summertime*
Senisi, Ellen B. *Hurray for pre-K!*
Shields, Carol Diggory. *Day by day a week goes round*
Simon, Francesca. *Toddler time*
Simon, Norma. *I'm busy, too*
    What do I do?
Siomades, Lorianne. *Kangaroo and cricket*
Spetter, Jung-Hee. *Lily and Trooper's winter*
Stevenson, James. *Rolling Rose*
Stickland, Paul. *A child's book of things*
Stock, Catherine. *Halloween monster*
Taberski, Sharon. *Morning, noon, and night*
Tafuri, Nancy. *Do not disturb*
Takeshita, Fumiko. *The park bench*
Thompson, Carol. *Baby days*
Thomson, Ruth. *My bear: I can . . . can you?*
Thorne, Jenny. *My uncle*
Türk, Hanne. *The rope skips Max*
Uff, Caroline. *Lulu's busy day*
Van Laan, Nancy. *People, people, everywhere*
Vasiliu, Mircea. *What's happening?*
Voake, Charlotte. *First things first*
Vulliamy, Clara. *Wide awake*
Walsh, Melanie. *Do donkeys dance?*
Warnick, Elsa. *Bedtime*
Weiss, Nicki. *On a hot, hot day*
Wellington, Monica. *All my little ducklings*
    Night city
Wells, Rosemary. *Night sounds, morning colors*
What we do
Williams, Jenny (Jennifer). *Playtime 1 2 3*
Williams, Sam. *The baby's word book*
Winn, Chris. *Archie's acrobats*
    Helping
Winteringham, Victoria. *Penguin day*
Wood, Audrey. *King Bidgood's in the bathtub*

Yolen, Jane. *Elfabet*
Zalben, Jane Breskin. *Oliver and Alison's week*
Ziefert, Harriet. *Baby Ben's busy book*
  Baby Ben's noisy book
  Bear's busy morning
  Piggety Pig from morn 'til night
  A polar bear can swim
Zimelman, Nathan. *How the second grade got
  $8,205.50 to visit the Statue of Liberty*
Zolotow, Charlotte (Shapiro). *Wake up and good-
  night*

Activities – babysitting

Abel, Ruth. *The new sitter*
Anderson, Peggy Perry. *Time for bed, the babysitter
  said*
Berenstain, Stan. *The Berenstain bears and the sitter*
Berman, Linda. *The goodbye painting*
Blaustein, Muriel. *Baby Mabu and Auntie Moose*
Brown, Marc Tolon. *Arthur babysits*
Bush, Timothy. *Benjamin McFadden and the robot
  babysitter*
Carlson, Natalie Savage. *Marie Louise's heyday*
Carrick, Carol. *The climb*
Cazet, Denys. *Big shoe, little shoe*
Chalmers, Mary. *Be good, Harry*
Christelow, Eileen. *Jerome and the Witchcraft kids*
  Jerome the babysitter
Cole, William. *What's good for a three-year-old?*
Crowley, Arthur. *Bonzo Beaver*
Day, Alexandra. *Carl makes a scrapbook*
  Carl pops up
  Carl's afternoon in the park
  Carl's birthday
  Carl's Christmas
  Follow Carl!
  Good dog, Carl
Finfer, Celentha. *Grandmother dear*
Gliori, Debi. *Mr. Bear babysits*
Gordon, Margaret. *Frogs' holiday*
Greenberg, Barbara. *The bravest babysitter*
Gretz, Susanna. *Roger takes charge!*
Grimes, Nikki. *Someone's baby-sitting*
Harris, Robie H. *Don't forget to come back*
Hellard, Susan. *Eleanor and the babysitter*
Hest, Amy. *Nannies for hire*
Himmelman, John. *J.J. versus the babysitter*
Hindley, Judy. *Mrs. Mary Malarky's seven cats*
Hines, Anna Grossnickle. *Grandma gets grumpy*
Hughes, Shirley. *An evening at Alfie's*
  George the babysitter
Hurd, Edith Thacher. *Hurry, hurry!*
  Stop, stop
Impey, Rose. *Joe's café*
Johnson, Angela. *Shoes like Miss Alice's*
Johnson, Dolores. *What kind of baby-sitter is this?*
Johnson, Doug. *Never babysit the hippopotamuses!*
Joyce, William. *George shrinks*
Keller, Holly. *Geraldine and Mrs. Duffy*
  What Alvin wanted
Lawson, Annetta. *The lucky yak*
Loomis, Christine. *My new baby-sitter*
McAllister, Angela. *The babies of Cockle Bay*
McCourt, Lisa. *Chicken soup for little souls: The never-
  forgotten doll*
McCully, Emily Arnold. *The grandma mix-up*
Martin, C. L. G. *The dragon nanny*
Miranda, Anne. *Baby-sit*

Moore, Lilian. *Little Raccoon and no trouble at all*
Mueller, Virginia. *Monster and the baby*
Nelson, Nan Ferring. *My day with Anka*
Newberry, Clare Turlay. *T-Bone, the baby-sitter*
Nilsson, Ulf. *Little sister rabbit*
Olofsdotter, Marie. *Frej the fearless*
Ovenell-Carter, Julie. *Adam's daycare*
Paterson, Bettina. *Bun and Mrs. Tubby*
Paton, Priscilla. *Howard and the sitter surprise*
Puner, Helen Walker. *The sitter who didn't sit*
Quackenbush, Robert M. *Henry babysits*
Rayner, Mary. *Mr. and Mrs. Pig's evening out*
Richardson, Jean. *Thomas's sitter*
Rubel, Nicole. *Uncle Henry and Aunt Henrietta's hon-
  eymoon*
Schick, Eleanor. *Peter and Mr. Brandon*
Sendak, Maurice. *Outside over there*
Simon, Francesca. *The Topsy-Turvies*
Steel, Danielle. *Max and the baby sitter*
Sykes, Julie. *Robbie Rabbit and the little ones*
Teague, Mark. *Baby tamer*
Tsutsui, Yoriko. *Anna in charge*
Van den Honert, Dorry. *Demi the baby sitter*
Van Laan, Nancy. *Mama rocks, Papa sings*
Viorst, Judith. *The good-bye book*
Waggoner, Karen. *The lemonade babysitter*
Wahl, Jan. *Peter and the troll baby*
Wardlaw, Lee. *Saturday night jamboree*
Watson, Jane Werner. *My friend the babysitter*
Watson, Pauline. *Curley Cat baby-sits*
Wells, Rosemary. *Max's dragon shirt*
  Shy Charles
  Stanley and Rhoda
Weninger, Brigitte. *Will you mind the baby, Davy?*
Williams, Barbara. *Jeremy isn't hungry*
Winthrop, Elizabeth. *Bear and Mrs. Duck*
  Bear and Roly-Poly
  Bear's Christmas surprise
Yolen, Jane. *Baby Bear's bedtime book*
Young, Ruth. *My baby-sitter*
Zweifel, Frances W. *Animal baby-sitters*

Activities – baking

Hooper, Meredith. *A cow, a bee, a cookie, and me*
Macdonald, Maryann. *Hedgehog bakes a cake*
McKissack, Patricia C. *Messy Bessey's holidays*
Moon, Nicola. *Alligator tails and crocodile cakes*

Activities – ballooning

Adams, Adrienne. *The great Valentine's Day balloon
  race*
Appelt, Kathi. *Elephants aloft*
Bansemer, Roger. *Rachael's splendifilous adventure*
Bynum, Janie. *Altoona Baboona*
Calhoun, Mary. *Hot-air Henry*
Coerr, Eleanor. *The big balloon race*
  Curious George and the hot air balloon
Delacre, Lulu. *Nathan's balloon adventure*
DeLage, Ida. *The old witch gets a surprise*
Gibbons, Gail. *Flying*
Goffe, Toni. *Toby's animal rescue service*
Haseley, Dennis. *Horses with wings*
Hayes, Sarah. *The grumpalump*
Johnson, Neil. *Fire and silk*
Lenssen, Ann. *A rainbow balloon*
McPhail, David M. *Henry Bear's park*
Mott, Evelyn Clarke. *Balloon ride*

Peppé, Rodney. *The mice and the flying basket*
Quin-Harkin, Janet. *Benjamin's balloon*
Rogers, Paul Patrick. *What can you see?*
Wade, Alan. *I'm flying!*
Wallner, Alexandra. *The first air voyage in the United States*
Wegen, Ron. *The balloon trip*
Wildsmith, Brian. *Bear's adventure*

Activities – bargaining *see* Activities – trading

Activities – bartering *see* Activities – trading

Activities – bathing

Alborough, Jez. *Bare bear*
Allen, Pamela. *Mr. Archimedes' bath*
Ambrus, Victor G. *The Sultan's bath*
Anderson, Lena. *Bunny bath*
Anderson, Peggy Perry. *To the tub*
Arnold, Tedd. *No more water in the tub!*
Aulaire, Ingri Mortenson d'. *Children of the north-lights*
Bethell, Jean. *Bathtime*
Blocksma, Mary. *Rub-a-dub-dub*
Brouillard, Anne. *The bathtub prima donna*
Burningham, John. *Time to get out of the bath, Shirley*
Buxbaum, Susan Kovacs. *Splash!*
Capucilli, Alyssa Satin. *Bathtime for Biscuit*
Carlstrom, Nancy White. *Jesse Bear's tra-la tub*
Cartlidge, Michelle. *Good night, Teddy*
Conrad, Pam. *The Tub People*
Cottle, Joan. *Emily's shoes*
DeFelice, Cynthia C. *Casey in the bath*
Demarest, Chris L. *My blue boat*
Dickens, Lucy. *Dirty Henry*
Dodds, Siobhan. *Ting-a-ling!*
Dowling, Paul. *You need a bath, Mustard*
Edwards, Frank B. *Mortimer Mooner stopped taking a bath*
  Troubles with bubbles
Faulkner, Matt. *The amazing voyage of Jackie Grace*
Goodman, Joan Elizabeth. *Bernard's bath*
Hall, Derek. *Elephant bathes*
Hazen, Barbara Shook. *The me I see*
Hedderwick, Mairi. *Katie Morag and the two grand-mothers*
Henkes, Kevin. *Clean enough*
Hughes, Shirley. *Bathwater's hot*
Inkpen, Mick. *Kipper's bathtime*
Jackson, Ellen B. *The bear in the bathtub*
Janovitz, Marilyn. *Is it time?*
Johansen, K. V. (Krista V.). *Pippin takes a bath*
Jonell, Lynne. *Mommy go away!*
Josephs, Rhoda. *The baby bubble book*
Kopper, Lisa. *Daisy knows best*
Kroll, Steven. *The pigrates clean up*
Kudrna, C. Imbior. *To bathe a boa*
Lindbloom, Steven. *Let's give kitty a bath!*
Lindgren, Barbro. *Sam's bath*
McDonald, Megan. *Bedbugs*
McDonnell, Flora. *I love boats*
Mackinnon, Debbie. *Daniel's duck*
McLeod, Emilie Warren. *One snail and me*
McNeal, Tom. *The dog who lost his Bob*
McPhail, David M. *Andrew's bath*
Manushkin, Fran. *Bubblebath!*
Meister, Cari. *Tiny's bath*

Miller, Margaret. *Where's Jenna?*
Nayer, Judy. *Bath*
Nomura, Takaaki. *Grandpa's town*
Pallotta, Jerry. *The dory story*
Paterson, Diane. *The bathtub ocean*
Pryor, Ainslie. *The baby blue cat and the dirty dog brothers*
Reavin, Sam. *Hurray for Captain Jane!*
Ripley, Catherine. *Why is soap so slippery?*
Roffey, Maureen. *Bathtime*
Sayre, April Pulley. *Splish! splash! animal baths*
Schotter, Roni. *Captain Bob sets sail*
Shott, Steve (Stephen). *Bathtime*
Slangerup, Erik Jon. *Dirt Boy*
Slate, Joseph. *The mean, clean, giant canoe machine*
Spohn, Kate. *Piglet's bath*
Stevens, Kathleen. *The beast in the bathtub*
Stuart, Chad. *The Ballymara flood*
Sutherland, Harry A. *Dad's car wash*
Sykes, Julie. *I don't want to take a bath!*
Thompson, Richard. *Effie's bath*
Varekamp, Marjolein. *Little Sam takes a bath*
Wabbes, Marie. *Rose's bath*
Watanabe, Shigeo. *I can take a bath!*
Weeks, Sarah. *Splish splash*
Wells, Rosemary. *Max's bath*
Willis, Jeanne. *The tale of Georgie Grub*
Wilson, Sarah. *Uncle Albert's flying birthday*
Wood, Audrey. *King Bidgood's in the bathtub*
Woodruff, Elvira. *Tubtime*
Yolen, Jane. *No bath tonight*
Ziefert, Harriet. *Harry takes a bath*
Zion, Gene. *Harry, the dirty dog*

Activities – cooking

Abolafia, Yossi. *A fish for Mrs. Gardenia*
Adinolfi, JoAnn. *Tina's diner*
Andersen, H. C. (Hans Christian). *The nightingale*, ill. by Christopher Santoro
Armstrong, Jennifer. *Little Salt Lick and the Sun King*
Axelrod, Amy. *Pigs in the pantry*
Bastin, Marjolein. *Vera in the kitchen*
Beck, Andrea. *Elliot bakes a cake*
Beil, Karen Magnuson. *A cake all for me!*
Blundell, Tony. *Beware of boys*
Brink, Carol Ryrie. *Goody O'Grumpity*
Brown, Marcia. *Skipper John's cook*
Brunhoff, Laurent de. *Babar learns to cook*
Bunting, Eve (Anne Evelyn). *Barney the Beard*
Cauley, Lorinda Bryan. *The bake-off*
  Pease porridge hot
Chandra, Deborah. *Miss Mabel's table*
Christelow, Eileen. *Don't wake up Mama!*
Cocca-Leffler, Maryann. *Wednesday is spaghetti day*
Cooper, Helen (Helen F.). *Pumpkin soup*
Cousins, Lucy. *Maisy makes gingerbread*
Cunliffe, John. *The king's birthday cake*
Czernecki, Stefan. *The sleeping bread*
Da Rif, Andrea. *The blueberry cake that little fox baked*
Darling, Abigail. *Teddy bears' picnic cookbook*
Darling, Benjamin. *Valerie and the silver pear*
De Paola, Tomie (Thomas Anthony). *Pancakes for breakfast*
  The popcorn book
  Things to make and do for Valentine's Day
De Regniers, Beatrice Schenk. *Sam and the impossible thing*

Devlin, Wende. *Old Black Witch!*
  Old Witch and the polka-dot ribbon
  Old Witch rescues Halloween
Dodds, Siobhan. *Grandpa Bud*
Dooley, Norah. *Everybody bakes bread*
Douglass, Barbara. *The chocolate chip cookie contest*
Dragonwagon, Crescent. *This is the bread I baked for Ned*
Edwards, Frank B. *Is the spaghetti ready?*
Edwards, Pamela Duncan. *Four famished foxes and Fosdyke*
  Warthogs in the kitchen
English, Karen. *Just right stew*
Ernst, Lisa Campbell. *Little Red Riding Hood*
Everitt, Betsy. *Mean soup*
Falwell, Cathryn. *Feast for ten*
Feder, Harriet K. *What can you do with a bagel?*
Florian, Douglas. *A chef*
Gabler, Mirko. *The alphabet soup*
Geeslin, Campbell. *How Nanita learned to make flan*
Gelsanliter, Wendy. *Dancin' in the kitchen*
Gibbons, Gail. *The too-great bread bake book*
Gilchrist, Theo E. *Halfway up the mountain*
Goldin, Barbara Diamond. *Cakes and miracles*
Greenberg, Melanie Hope. *My father's luncheonette*
Gregory, Valiska. *Riddle soup*
Gretz, Susanna. *Teddybears cookbook*
Harris, Lee. *Never let your cat make lunch for you*
Heath, Amy. *Sofie's role*
Hill, Eric. *Spot bakes a cake*
Hippely, Hilary Horder. *A song for Lena*
Hoban, Lillian. *Arthur's Christmas cookies*
Hoopes, Lyn Littlefield. *The unbeatable bread*
Jacobs, Laurie A. *So much in common*
Kahl, Virginia. *The Duchess bakes a cake*
Kidd, Richard. *Monsieur Thermidor*
Krasilovsky, Phyllis. *The man who cooked for himself*
  The man who entered a contest
Krensky, Stephen. *The pizza book*
Lasker, Joe. *Lentil soup*
Latimer, Jim. *James Bear's pie*
Lemerise, Bruce. *Sheldon's lunch*
Leonard, Marcia. *Food is fun!*
Levitin, Sonia. *Nobody stole the pie*
Lindman, Maj. *Flicka, Ricka, Dicka bake a cake*
Lindsey, Treska. *When Batistine made bread*
Long, Earlene. *Johnny's egg*
Loomis, Christine. *In the diner*
Maccarone, Grace. *Pizza party*
MacDonald, Elizabeth. *Miss Poppy and the honey cake*
  Mr. Badger's birthday pie
Mayer, Marianna. *Marcel the pastry chef*
Meddaugh, Susan. *Hog-eye*
Meijer, Marie. *The bake-a-cake book*
Miller, Alice P. *The mouse family's blueberry pie*
Moss, Marissa. *Mel's diner*
Murphy, Stuart J. *A fair bear share*
Myers, Edward. *Forri the baker*
Nelson, Nan Ferring. *My day with Anka*
Nixon, Joan Lowery. *Beats me, Claude*
Nolen, Jerdine. *In my momma's kitchen*
Oxenbury, Helen. *It's my birthday*
Parker, Nancy Winslow. *Love from Aunt Betty*
Patron, Susan. *Burgoo stew*
Pelham, David. *Sam's pizza*
Petie, Haris. *The seed the squirrel dropped*
Powell, Jillian. *Eggs*

Priceman, Marjorie. *How to make an apple pie and see the world*
Reiser, Lynn. *Cherry pies and lullabies*
Rice, Eve. *Benny bakes a cake*
Rockwell, Anne F. *The Mother Goose cookie-candy book*
Root, Phyllis. *Turnover Tuesday*
Rotner, Shelley. *Hold the anchovies!*
Rylant, Cynthia. *The cookie-store cat*
  Mr. Putter and Tabby bake the cake
Schwalje, Marjory. *Mr. Angelo*
Shecter, Ben. *The big stew*
Shiefman, Vicky. *Sunday potatoes, Monday potatoes*
Shohet, Marti. *Market days*
Speed, Toby. *Brave potatoes*
  Hattie baked a wedding cake
Spohn, Kate. *Ruth's bake shop*
Stevens, Janet. *Cook-a-doodle-doo!*
Swendson, Patsy. *The potluck adventures of Mrs. Marmalade*
Tomchek, Ann Heinrichs. *I can be a chef*
Tornborg, Pat. *The Sesame Street cookbook*
Torres, Leyla. *Saturday sancocho*
Tzannes, Robin. *Sanji and the baker*
Ungerer, Tomi. *Zeralda's ogre*
Wagner, Karen. *Chocolate chip cookies*
Wallace, Nancy Elizabeth. *Apples, apples, apples*
Wallis, Diz. *Pip's adventure*
Wayne-von-Königslöw, Andrea. *Bing and Chutney*
Wellington, Monica. *Mr. Cookie Baker*
Wells, Rosemary. *Bunny cakes*
Willard, Nancy. *The high rise glorious skittle skat roarious sky pie angel food cake*
Wilson-Kelly, Becky. *Mother Grumpy's dog biscuits*
Yee, Paul. *Roses sing on new snow*
Young, Miriam Burt. *The sugar mouse cake*
Zweifel, Frances W. *The Make-Something Club*

Activities – dancing

Ackerman, Karen. *Song and dance man*
Allen, Pamela. *Bertie and the bear*
Ambrus, Victor G. *The seven skinny goats*
Ancona, George. *Dancing is*
  Let's dance!
Andersen, H. C. (Hans Christian). *The red shoes*
Asch, Frank. *Moondance*
  Moongame
Auch, Mary Jane. *Hen lake*
  Peeping Beauty
Babbitt, Natalie. *Nellie, a cat on her own*
Baron, Alan. *Red Fox dances*
Baumgardner, Mary Alice. *Alexandra, keeper of dreams*
Bell, Anthea. *Swan Lake*
Berger, Barbara Helen. *The jewel heart*
Bianco, Margery Williams. *The hurdy-gurdy man*
Blocksma, Mary. *The best dressed bear*
Bornstein, Ruth Lercher. *The dancing man*
Bottner, Barbara. *Messy*
  Myra
Boynton, Sandra. *Barnyard dance!*
Brighton, Catherine. *Nijinsky*
Bunting, Eve (Anne Evelyn). *The day before Christmas*
Burstein, Fred. *The dancer*
Cazet, Denys. *Dancing*
Charlot, Martin. *Felisa and the magic tikling bird*
Chevance, Audrey. *Tutu*

Childress, Mark. *Joshua and Bigtooth*
Clayton, Elaine. *Ella's trip to the museum*
Cox, David. *Ayu and the perfect moon*
Daly, Niki. *Papa Lucky's shadow*
Deetlefs, Rene. *Tabu and the dancing elephants*
De Paola, Tomie (Thomas Anthony). *Oliver Button is a sissy*
Dickens, Lucy. *Dancing class*
Edelman, Elaine. *Boom-de-boom*
Edwards, Pamela Duncan. *Honk!*
Esbensen, Barbara Juster. *Dance with me*
Evans, Richard Paul. *The dance*
Eversole, Robyn Harbert. *The magic house*
Fern, Eugene. *Pepito's story*
Fonteyn, Margot, Dame. *Coppélia*
French, Vivian. *One ballerina two*
Gallwey, Kay. *Dancing Daisy*
Gauch, Patricia Lee. *Bravo, Tanya*
   Dance, Tanya
   Presenting Tanya, the Ugly Duckling
   Tanya and Emily in a dance for two
   Tanya and the magic wardrobe
   Tanya steps out
Gelsanliter, Wendy. *Dancin' in the kitchen*
Geringer, Laura. *Molly's new washing machine*
Getz, Arthur. *Humphrey, the dancing pig*
Goble, Paul. *Star boy*
Graves, Keith. *Frank was a monster who wanted to dance*
Gray, Libba Moore. *My mama had a dancing heart*
Greene, Carol. *Katherine Dunham*
Grimm, Jacob. *The twelve dancing princesses*, ill. by Kinuko Y. Craft
   The twelve dancing princesses, ill. by Anne Dalton
   The twelve dancing princesses, ill. by Dennis Hockerman
   The twelve dancing princesses, ill. by Errol Le Cain
   The twelve dancing princesses, ill. by Gerald McDermott
   The twelve dancing princesses, ill. by Jane Ray
   The twelve dancing princesses, ill. by Uri Shulevitz
   The twelve dancing princesses, ill. by Suçie Stevenson
Hampshire, Susan. *Rosie's ballet slippers*
Hazen, Barbara Shook. *Turkey in the straw*
Hesse, Karen. *Come on, rain*
Hoban, Russell. *Charlie Meadows*
   The dancing tigers
Hobbs, Will. *Beardream*
Hoffmann, E. T. A. *The nutcracker*, ill. by Francesca Crespi
   The nutcracker, ill. by Carolyn Ewing
   The nutcracker, ill. by Rachel Isadora
   The nutcracker, ill. by Joanna Isles
   The nutcracker, ill. by Maurice Sendak
   The nutcracker, ill. by Lisbeth Zwerger
   The nutcracker ballet, ill. by Vladimir Vasil'evich Vagin
Holabird, Katharine. *Angelina and the princess*
   Angelina ballerina
   Angelina dances
   Angelina on stage
Hurd, Edith Thacher. *I dance in my red pajamas*
Inkpen, Mick. *Wibbly Pig can dance!*
Isadora, Rachel. *Lili at ballet*
   Lili on stage
   Max
   My ballet class
   My ballet diary

   Opening night
Jabar, Cynthia. *Shimmy shake earthquake*
Jennings, Linda M. *Coppelia*
   Crispin and the dancing piglet
   The sleeping beauty
Jonas, Ann. *Color dance*
Jones, Bill T. *Dance*
Kingsland, Robin. *Bus stop bop*
Komaiko, Leah. *Aunt Elaine does the dance from Spain*
Kraus, Robert. *Dance, Spider, dance!*
Kroll, Virginia L. *Can you dance, Dalila?*
Kuklin, Susan. *Going to my ballet class*
Landström, Olof. *Boo and Baa in a party mood*
La Prise, Larry. *The hokey pokey*
Lasky, Kathryn. *The solo*
   Starring Lucille
Lattimore, Deborah Nourse. *Punga the goddess of ugly*
Lee, Jeanne M. *Silent lotus*
Lemaître, Pascal. *Zelda's secret*
Lemieux, Margo. *The fiddle ribbon*
Lewison, Wendy Cheyette. *I wear my tutu everywhere!*
   Ten little ballerinas
Lifton, Betty Jean. *Tell me a real adoption story*
Lillegard, Dee. *The Big Bug Ball*
London, Jonathan. *Who bop*
Loredo, Elizabeth. *Boogie Bones*
McCoy, Karen Kawamoto. *Bon Odori dancer*
McKissack, Patricia C. *Mirandy and brother wind*
McLerran, Alice. *The ghost dance*
McMullan, Kate (Hall). *Noel the first*
   Nutcracker Noel
Maiorano, Robert. *A little interlude*
Marshall, James. *The Cut-Ups carry on*
   George and Martha encore
   Swine lake
Martin, Bill (William Ivan). *Barn dance!*
Martin, Nora. *The stone dancers*
Mathers, Petra. *Sophie and Lou*
Mayer, Mercer. *The queen always wanted to dance*
Medearis, Angela Shelf. *Dancing with the Indians*
Medina, Nina. *Have you ever noticed that rabbits don't sing?*
Mellor, Corinne. *Bruce the balding moose*
Moers, Hermann. *Annie's dancing day*
Morris, Ann. *Little ballerinas*
Nelson, Esther L. *Holiday singing and dancing games*
Norman, Philip Ross. *Dancing dogs*
O'Connor, Jane. *Nina, Nina and the copycat ballerina*
   Nina, Nina ballerina
   Nina, Nina, star ballerina
Ormerod, Jan. *Emily dances*
Oxenbury, Helen. *The dancing class*
Palazzo-Craig, Janet. *Ballet dancer*
Pancheri, Jan. *The twelve poodle princess*
Paxton, Tom. *Engelbert the elephant*
Pinkney, Andrea Davis. *Alvin Ailey*
Pulver, Robin. *Alicia's tutu*
Quin-Harkin, Janet. *Peter Penny's dance*
Raczek, Linda Theresa. *The night the grandfathers danced*
Richardson, Jean. *The bear who went to the ballet*
   Clara's dancing feet
   The sleeping beauty
Riddell, Chris. *The bear dance*
Rose, Emma. *Ballet magic*

Satterfield, Barbara. *The story dance*
Schaefer, Jackie Jasina. *Miranda's day to dance*
Scheffrin-Falk, Gladys. *Another celebrated dancing bear*
Schertle, Alice. *Bill and the google-eyed goblins*
Schick, Eleanor. *I have another language*
Schroeder, Alan. *Ragtime Tumpie*
Schumaker, Ward. *Dance!*
Shannon, George. *April showers*
 Dancing the breeze
Shields, Carol Diggory. *Saturday night at the dinosaur stomp*
Simon, Carly. *Amy the dancing bear*
Smith, Cynthia Leitich. *Jingle dancer*
Sorine, Stephanie Riva. *Our ballet class*
Stapler, Sarah. *Cordellia, dance!*
Stickland, Paul. *Dinosaur stomp!*
Sutton, Jane. *What should a hippo wear?*
Taylor, Ann. *Baby dance*
Tilden, Ruth. *Sophie's dance class*
Tompert, Ann. *Savina, the gypsy dancer*
Turner, Nancy Byrd. *When young Melissa sweeps*
Waboose, Jan Bourdeau. *Firedancers*
Walton, Rick. *Dance, pioneer, dance!*
 Noah's square dance
Wardlaw, Lee. *Saturday night jamboree*
Warner, Sunny. *Madison finds a line*
Waters, Kate. *Lion dancer*
Wayne-von-Königslöw, Andrea. *Bing and Chutney*
Welch, Willy. *Dancing with Daddy*
Westman, Barbara. *Dancing dogs*
Whittington, Mary K. *Carmina, come dance!*
Wilkes, Larry. *The king's egg dance*
Wolkstein, Diane. *Bouki dances the Kokioko*
Wood, Audrey. *Little Penguin's tale*
Wright, Jill. *The old woman and the Willy Nilly Man*
Yee, Wong Herbert. *The Officers' Ball*
Ziefert, Harriet. *Dancing*

Activities – digging

Agard, John. *Dig away two-hole Tim*
Aliki. *Digging up dinosaurs*
Ayres, Pam. *When dad fills in the garden pond*
Baynton, Martin. *Fifty gets the picture*
Brown, Margaret Wise. *The diggers*
Cleary, Beverly. *The real hole*
Crowther, Robert. *Dump trucks and diggers*
Duke, Kate. *Archaeologists dig for clues*
Gibbons, Gail. *Tunnels*
Harrison, Troon. *Don't dig so deep, Nicholas!*
Hoban, Tana. *Dig, drill, dump, fill*
Krauss, Ruth. *A hole is to dig*
Kumin, Maxine W. *Speedy digs downside up*
Paraskevas, Betty. *Maggie and the Ferocious Beast, the big carrot*
Perkins, Al. *The digging-est dog*
Rawlins, Donna. *Digging to China*
Rex, Michael. *Who digs?*
Royston, Angela. *Diggers and dump trucks*

Activities – drawing

Asch, Frank. *Monkey face*
Berlan, Kathryn Hook. *Andrew's amazing monsters*
Bornstein, Ruth Lercher. *That's how it is when we draw*
Carle, Eric. *Draw me a star*
Engel, Diana. *The shelf-paper jungle*

Fain, Moira. *Snow day*
Greenblat, Rodney Alan. *Thunder Bunny*
Hamsa, Bobbie. *Fast-draw Freddie*
Hoban, Russell. *Monsters*
Inkpen, Mick. *Wibbly Pig makes pictures*
Jennings, Linda M. *Franklin's neighborhood*
Kamish, Daniel. *The night scary beasties popped out of my head*
Kleven, Elisa. *The paper princess*
Kroll, Steven. *Patches*
Levine, Arthur A. *The boy who drew cats*
Littlesugar, Amy. *Josiah True and the art maker*
McClintock, Barbara. *The fantastic drawings of Danielle*
McPhail, David M. *Drawing lessons from a bear*
 Moony B. Finch, fastest draw in the West
Moss, Marissa. *Regina's big mistake*
Nikola-Lisa, W. *Can you top that?*
Poydar, Nancy. *Cool Ali*
Russo, Marisabina. *Under the table*
Thomson, Ruth. *Drawing*
Van Allsburg, Chris. *Bad day at Riverbend*
Wallner, Alexandra. *Beatrix Potter*
Wilson, April. *April Wilson's magpie magic*

Activities – driving

Aylesworth, Jim. *Through the night*
Gibbons, Faye. *Mama and me and the Model-T*
Greenfield, Eloise. *Kia Tanisha drives her car*

Activities – eating *see* Food

Activities – flying

Aardema, Verna. *Jackal's flying lesson*
Abolafia, Yossi. *Yanosh's Island*
Adoff, Arnold. *Flamboyan*
Allard, Harry. *The Stupids take off*
Allen, Laura Jean. *Where is Freddy?*
Anderson, Joan. *Harry's helicopter*
Anderson, Lonzo. *Mr. Biddle and the birds*
Arabian Nights. *The flying carpet*
Arvetis, Chris. *Why does it fly?*
Aulaire, Ingri Mortenson d'. *Wings for Per*
Ayal, Ora. *The adventures of Chester the chest*
Ayres, Becky Hickox. *Victoria flies high*
Balian, Lorna. *Wilbur's space machine*
Bang, Molly. *Goose*
Benchley, Nathaniel. *The flying lessons of Gerald Pelican*
Berger, Melvin. *How do airplanes fly?*
Blathwayt, Benedict. *Tangle and the silver bird*
Borden, Louise. *Goodbye, Charles Lindbergh*
Bradfield, Roger (Jolly Roger). *The flying hockey stick*
Breathed, Berkeley. *A wish for wings that work*
Brenner, Barbara A. *The flying patchwork quilt*
Brimner, Larry Dane. *If dogs had wings*
Brock, Emma Lillian. *Surprise balloon*
Brown, Marc Tolon. *Wings on things*
Brown, Margaret Wise. *Streamlined pig*
Bruna, Dick. *The happy apple*
 Miffy goes flying
Buchanan, Heather S. *George Mouse learns to fly*
Buckingham, Simon. *Alec and his flying bed*
Cherry, Lynne. *The armadillo from Amarillo*
Clearman, Deborah. *The goose's tale*
Collicott, Sharleen. *Seeing stars*

Collins, Pat Lowery. *Tomorrow, up and away!*
Corbalis, Judy. *Porcellus, the flying pig*
Crebbin, June. *Fly by night*
Crews, Donald. *Flying*
Dabcovich, Lydia. *Ducks fly*
Demarest, Chris L. *Lindbergh*
Dorros, Arthur. *Abuela*
Drawson, Blair. *Flying Dimitri*
Dunbar, Joyce. *Baby bird*
Duvoisin, Roger Antoine. *Petunia takes a trip*
Erlbruch, Wolf. *Mrs. Meyer, the bird*
Florian, Douglas. *Airplane ride*
Foreman, Michael. *The little reindeer*
Fort, Patrick. *Redbird*
French, Vivian. *Little Ghost*
Gay, Michel. *Bibi takes flight*
Gerrard, Roy. *Jocasta Carr, movie star*
Gibbons, Gail. *Flying*
Gorbachev, Valeri. *The Fool of the world and the flying ship*
Gramatky, Hardie. *Loopy*
Gregorowski, Christopher. *Fly, eagle, fly!*
Hays, Hoffman Reynolds. *Charley sang a song*
Hill, Eric. *Up there*
Hoban, Russell. *Ace Dragon Ltd.*
Hughes, Shirley. *Up and up*
Jackson, Carolyn. *The flying ark*
James, J. Alison. *Eucalyptus wings*
Jenny, Anne. *The fantastic story of King Brioche the First*
Jeschke, Susan. *Perfect the pig*
Johnson, Neil. *Fire and silk*
Johnson, Paul Brett. *The cow who wouldn't come down*
Joyce, William. *Santa calls*
Jukes, Mavis. *I'll see you in my dreams*
Kaufmann, John. *Flying giants of long ago*
King, Christopher L. *The boy who ate the moon*
Kleven, Elisa. *The paper princess*
Kojima, Naomi. *The flying grandmother*
Krauss, Ruth. *I can fly*
Kuskin, Karla. *Just like everyone else*
Lang, Andrew. *The flying ship*
Liddell, Janice. *Imani and the Flying Africans*
Lies, Brian. *Hamlet and the enormous Chinese dragon kite*
Lindbergh, Reeve. *Nobody owns the sky*
Lindgren, Barbro. *Shorty takes off*
Lobato, Arcadio. *Paper bird*
McConnachie, Brian. *Flying boy*
McDermott, Gerald. *Coyote*
McKee, David. *Elmer and the wind*
  Elmer takes off
McPhail, David M. *First flight*
Maizlish, Lisa. *The ring*
Metaxas, Eric. *The fool and the flying ship*
Mills, Lauren A. *Fairy wings*
Munsch, Robert N. *Angela's airplane*
Murphy, Pat. *Pigasus*
Myers, Bernice. *The flying shoes*
Myers, Christopher A. *Wings*
Myers, Walter Dean. *How Mr. Monkey saw the whole world*
Nones, Eric Jon. *Angela's wings*
Osborne, Mary Pope. *Moonhorse*, ill. by David McPhail
  Moonhorse, ill. by S. M. Saelig
Pacovská, Kveta. *Flying*

Peet, Bill (William Bartlett). *The kweeks of Kookatumdee*
  Merle the high flying squirrel
Pinkney, J. Brian. *The adventures of sparrowboy*
Pirotta, Saviour. *Little bird*
Pomerantz, Charlotte. *Flap your wings and try*
Potok, Chaim. *The sky of now*
Priestley, Alice. *Someone is reading this book*
Provensen, Alice. *The glorious flight*
Ransome, Arthur. *The fool of the world and the flying ship*
Rigby, Rodney. *Hello, this is your penguin speaking*
Ringgold, Faith. *Tar Beach*
Ross, Pat. *Your first airplane trip*
Ryan, Pam Muñoz. *Amelia and Eleanor go for a ride*
Ryder, Joanne. *Rainbow wings*
Schomp, Virginia. *If you were a . . . pilot*
Schulz, Walter A. *Will and Orv*
Schumacher, Claire. *Nutty's birthday*
Scruton, Clive. *Pig in the air*
Scuderi, Lucia. *To fly*
Seibold, J. Otto. *Mr. Lunch takes a plane ride*
  Penguin dreams
Simont, Marc. *The goose that almost got cooked*
Smith, Lane. *Flying Jake*
Spurr, Elizabeth. *Mrs. Minetta's car pool*
Stadler, John. *Three cheers for hippo!*
Stevenson, James. *Grandpa's great city tour*
Taylor, Judy. *Dudley goes flying*
Testa, Fulvio. *The paper airplane*
Titus, Eve. *Anatole over Paris*
Trez, Denise. *Maila and the flying carpet*
Uhlberg, Myron. *Flying over Brooklyn*
Ungerer, Tomi. *Adelaide*
  The Mellops go flying
Valens, Evans G. *Wingfin and Topple*
Walter, Mildred Pitts. *Brother to the wind*
Ward, Helen. *The king of the birds*
Waterton, Betty. *Orff, 27 dragons (and a snarkel)*
Watson, Clyde. *Midnight moon*
Wende, Philip. *Bird boy*
West, Ian. *Silas, the first pig to fly*
Wheeling, Lynn. *When you fly*
Wiesner, David. *Tuesday*
Wolkstein, Diane. *The cool ride in the sky*
  The magic wings
Woodruff, Elvira. *The wing shop*
Yolen, Jane. *Wings*
Young, Miriam Burt. *If I flew a plane*

Activities – gardening *see* Gardens, gardening

Activities – jumping

Akass, Susan. *Number nine duckling*
Bright, Robert. *My hopping bunny*
Cain, Sheridan. *Look out for the big bad fish!*
Cole, Joanna. *Norma Jean, jumping bean*
Easton, Violet. *Elephants never jump*
Esbensen, Barbara Juster. *Jumping day*
Lyne, Alice. *A, my name is . . .*
Most, Bernard. *The very boastful kangaroo*
Murphy, Stuart J. *Ready, set, hop!*
Powell, Jillian. *Jumpers*
Scruggs, Afi. *Jump rope magic*
Stephens, Karen. *Jumping*

Activities – knitting

Anholt, Catherine. *Tom's rainbow walk*
Blackwood, Mary. *Derek the knitting dinosaur*
Hilton, Nette. *The long red scarf*
Hissey, Jane. *Jolly Tall*
Holl, Adelaide. *Mrs. McGarrity's peppermint sweater*
Laurin, Anne. *Little things*
Lecher, Doris. *Angelita's magic yarn*
Martinez, Ruth. *Mrs. McDockerty's knitting*
Smee, Nicola. *The Tusk Fairy*
Storr, Catherine (Cole). *Hugo and his grandma*
Wild, Margaret. *Mr. Nick's knitting*
Ziefert, Harriet. *With love from Grandma*

Activities – making things

Ahlberg, Allan. *Miss Brick, the builder's baby*
Arnold, Tedd. *The simple people*
Balterman, Lee. *Girders and cranes*
Bartels, Alice L. *The grandmother doll*
The big Peter Rabbit book
Blocksma, Mary. *Easy-to-make spaceships that really fly*
Blos, Joan W. *The grandpa days*
Boucher, Jerry. *Fire truck nuts and bolts*
Calder, Lyn. *Walt Disney's Alice's tea party*
Crowley, Michael. *New kid on Spurwick Ave.*
Curtis, Neil. *How paper is made*
Dalmais, Anne-Marie. *And may the best animal win!*
Petey the puppy
Day, Alexandra. *Carl makes a scrapbook*
De Paola, Tomie (Thomas Anthony). *Things to make and do for Valentine's Day*
Ehlert, Lois. *Hands*
Engel, Diana. *The little lump of clay*
Falwell, Cathryn. *Nicky and Alex*
Flint, Russ. *Let's build a house*
Florian, Douglas. *A potter*
Fox, Perla. *The Wooodles*
Gibbons, Gail. *How a house is built*
Ginsburg, Mirra. *Clay boy*
Gliori, Debi. *New big house*
Graham, Thomas. *Mr. Bear's chair*
Grossman, Bill. *The banging book*
Hall, Donald. *Lucy's Christmas*
Halperin, Wendy Anderson. *Once upon a company*
Himmelman, John. *The day-off machine*
The great leaf blast-off
Hindley, Judy. *The little train*
Hoban, Tana. *Construction zone*
Huff, Vivian. *Let's make paper dolls*
Hughes, Shirley. *The big concrete lorry*
Inkpen, Mick. *Wibbly Pig can make a tent*
Iverson, Diane. *Discover the seasons*
Johnson, Angela. *Those building men*
Kiser, Kevin. *Buzzy Widget*
Kiser, SuAnn. *The birthday thing*
Kreye, Walter. *The giant from the little island*
Kroll, Steven. *Will you be my valentine?*
Kuklin, Susan. *From head to toe*
Kunhardt, Edith. *Danny's Christmas star*
Lanteigne, Helen. *The seven chairs*
Leedy, Loreen. *A dragon Christmas*
Lohf, Sabine. *Things I can make with buttons*
Things I can make with cloth
Things I can make with cork
Things I can make with paper
Lopshire, Robert. *How to make snop snappers and other fine things*

Lum, Kate. *What! cried Granny*
McCain, Becky R. (Becky Ray). *Grandmother's dreamcatcher*
Martin, Jacqueline Briggs. *Good times on Grandfather Mountain*
Maurer-Mathison, Diane V. *Make your own spectacular Valentines*
Miller, Cameron. *Woodlore*
Miller, Margaret. *I can make it!*
Moon, Nicola. *Lucy's picture*
Moss, Marissa. *Knick knack paddywack*
Neitzel, Shirley. *The house I'll build for the wrens*
Oates, Eddie Hershel. *Making music*
Parker, Steve. *I wonder why tunnels are round*
Pfanner, Louise. *Louise builds a boat*
Louise builds a house
Pilkey, Dav. *The Silly Gooses build a house*
Radford, Derek. *Harry builds a house*
Ransom, Candice F. *The promise quilt*
Ray, Mary Lyn. *Basket moon*
Rockwell, Anne F. *What we like*
Rosenberg, Liz. *The scrap doll*
Rumford, James. *The cloudmakers*
Sohi, Morteza E. *Look what I did with a leaf!*
Swinburne, Stephen R. *Swallows in the birdhouse*
Tafuri, Nancy. *Counting to Christmas*
Thelen, Gerda. *The toy maker*
Thomson, Ruth. *Printing*
The Rainforest Indians
Tryon, Leslie. *Albert's alphabet*
Vainio, Pirkko. *The dream house*
Wallace, John. *Building a house with Mr. Bumble*
Weller, Frances Ward. *Matthew Wheelock's wall*
Wood, Audrey. *The flying dragon room*
Ziefert, Harriet. *Before I was born*
Zweifel, Frances W. *The Make-Something Club*

Activities – painting *see also* Careers – artists; Careers – painters

Adams, Adrienne. *The Easter egg artists*
Agee, Jon. *The incredible painting of Felix Clousseau*
Asch, Frank. *Bread and honey*
Baker, Alan. *Benjamin's portrait*
Black and White Rabbit's ABC
White Rabbit's color book
Bang, Molly. *Tye May and the magic brush*
Bassède, Francine. *George paints his house*
Becker, Edna. *Nine hundred buckets of paint*
Beim, Jerrold. *Jay's big job*
Bond, Michael. *Paddington's art exhibit*
Bromhall, Winifred. *Mary Ann's first picture*
Carrick, Donald. *Morgan and the artist*
Catalanotto, Peter. *The painter*
Coats, Laura Jane. *Marcella and the moon*
Craven, Carolyn. *What the mailman brought*
Day, Marie. *Quennu and the cave bear*
Decker, Dorothy W. *Stripe visits New York*
Demi. *Liang and the magic paintbrush*
De Paola, Tomie (Thomas Anthony). *The legend of the Indian paintbrush*
Dionetti, Michelle V. *Painting the wind*
Duvoisin, Roger Antoine. *The house of four seasons*
Ernst, Lisa Campbell. *Hamilton's art show*
Flanagan, Alice K. *The Wilsons, a house-painting team*
Florian, Douglas. *A painter*
Freeman, Don. *The chalk box story*
Helldorfer, M. C. (Mary Claire). *Cabbage Rose*

Hest, Amy. *Jamaica Louise James*
Himmelman, John. *Ellen and the goldfish*
Hurd, Thacher. *Art dog*
Johnston, Tony. *Pages of music*
Kessler, Leonard P. *Mr. Pine's purple house*
Kidd, Richard. *Almost famous Daisy!*
Leaf, Margaret. *Eyes of the dragon*
Leonard, Marcia. *Paintbox penguins*
Lindsay, Elizabeth. *A letter for Maria*
McClintock, Barbara. *The fantastic drawings of Danielle*
McPhail, David M. *Big brown bear*
    Lorenzo
    Something special
Martin, Charles E. *For rent*
Menter, Ian. *The Albany Road mural*
Miller, Warren. *Pablo paints a picture*
Molarsky, Osmond. *A sky full of kites*
Morris, Jill. *The boy who painted the sun*
Muller, Robin. *The magic paintbrush*
Nerlove, Miriam. *Flowers on the wall*
    If all the world were paper
Nez, Redwing T. *Forbidden talent*
Pinkwater, Daniel Manus. *The big orange splot*
Pittman, Helena Clare. *Still-life stew*
Rinder, Lenore. *A big mistake*
Rogers, Paul (Patrick). *Don't blame me!*
Romanelli, Serena. *Little Bobo saves the day*
Roth, Roger. *The sign painter's dream*
Rylant, Cynthia. *All I see*
Sharratt, Nick. *The time it took Tom*
Silsbe, Brenda. *Just one more color*
Skorpen, Liesel Moak. *We were tired of living in a house*
Spier, Peter. *Oh, were they ever happy!*
Tamar, Erika. *The garden of happiness*
Thomas, Abigail. *Pearl paints*
Thomson, Ruth. *Painting*
Voigt, Hannelore. *Not now, Sara!*
Wabbes, Marie. *Rose's picture*
Walsh, Ellen Stoll. *Mouse paint*
Walsh, Jill Paton. *Pepi and the secret names*
Walsh, Melanie. *Ned's rainbow*
Weisgard, Leonard. *Mr. Peaceable paints*
Williams, Karen Lynn. *Painted dreams*
Ziefert, Harriet. *Elemenopeo*

Activities – photographing

Brimner, Larry Dane. *Max and Felix*
Castle, Caroline. *Grandpa Baxter and the photographs*
Hest, Amy. *Weekend girl*
Johnson, Dinah. *All around town*
Levinson, Riki. *I go with my family to Grandma's*
McClintock, Barbara. *The fantastic drawings of Danielle*
McPhail, David M. *Pig Pig and the magic photo album*
Manushkin, Fran. *The perfect Christmas picture*
Marshall, Janet Perry. *My camera*
Morrow, Barbara. *Edward's portrait*
Seguin-Fontes, Marthe. *A wedding book*
Swinburne, Stephen R. *Guess whose shadow?*
Talley, Linda. *Jackson's plan*
Tison, Annette. *Animal hide-and-seek*
Türk, Hanne. *Snapshot Max*
Villarejo, Mary. *The tiger hunt*
Vincent, Gabrielle. *Smile, Ernest and Celestine*
Watts, Mabel (Pizzey). *Weeks and weeks*
Willard, Nancy. *Simple pictures are best*

Wyllie, Stephen. *Snappity snap*

Activities – picnicking

Alborough, Jez. *It's the bear*
Asch, Frank. *Sand cake*
Benjamin, Alan. *A change of plans*
Berger, Terry. *The turtles' picnic and other nonsense stories*
Binnamin, Vivian. *The case of the anteater's missing lunch*
Bishop, Bonnie. *Ralph rides away*
Bowden, Joan Chase. *The Ginghams and the backward picnic*
Bratton, John. *The teddy bears' picnic*, ill. by Renate Kozikowski
Brown, Ruth. *The picnic*
Browne, Eileen. *Where's that bus?*
Brunhoff, Laurent de. *Babar's picnic*
Bunting, Eve (Anne Evelyn). *Someday a tree*
Butler, Dorothy. *Higgledy, piggledy, hobbledy hoy*
Butterworth, Nick. *All together now!*
    The rescue party
Capucilli, Alyssa Satin. *Biscuit's picnic*
Cauley, Lorinda Bryan. *Treasure hunt*
Chalmers, Mary. *Here comes the trolley*
    Mr. Cat's wonderful surprise
Christelow, Eileen. *Five little monkeys sitting in a tree*
Christian, Mary Blount. *Go west, swamp monsters*
Claverie, Jean. *The picnic*
Darling, Abigail. *Teddy bears' picnic cookbook*
Daugherty, James Henry. *The picnic*
Delton, Judy. *On a picnic*
Denton, Kady MacDonald. *The picnic*
Dickinson, Mary. *Alex's outing*
Dubanevich, Arlene. *Pig William*
Dunham, Meredith. *Picnic*
Du Quette, Keith. *Ripping day for a picnic*
Ernst, Lisa Campbell. *Up to ten and down again*
Ets, Marie Hall. *In the forest*
Freschet, Berniece. *The ants go marching*
Gackenbach, Dick. *Claude has a picnic*
Garland, Sarah. *Having a picnic*
Gliori, Debi. *Mr. Bear's picnic*
Goldstone, Bruce. *The beastly feast*
Goodall, John S. *The surprise picnic*
Gordon, Margaret. *Wilberforce goes on a picnic*
Graham, Bob. *Libby, Oscar and me*
Graham, Thomas. *Mr. Bear's boat*
Hayes, Sarah. *This is the bear and the picnic lunch*
Hest, Amy. *Weekend girl*
Higham, Jon Atlas. *Aardvark's picnic*
Hill, Eric. *Spot's first picnic*
Hines, Anna Grossnickle. *Come to the meadow*
    The greatest picnic in the world
Hurd, Edith Thacher. *No funny business*
Ichikawa, Satomi. *Nora's surprise*
Inkpen, Mick. *Picnic*
Iwamura, Kazuo. *The fourteen forest mice and the spring meadow picnic*
Kasza, Keiko. *The pigs' picnic*
Keller, Holly. *Henry's Fourth of July*
Kennedy, Jimmy. *The teddy bears' picnic*, ill. by Alexandra Day
    The teddy bears' picnic, ill. by Michael Hague
    The teddy bears' picnic, ill. by Prue Theobalds
Killingback, Julia. *Busy Bears' picnic*
King, Bob. *Sitting on the farm*
Knox-Wagner, Elaine. *The oldest kid*

Kroll, Steven. *It's Groundhog Day!*
Lathrop, Dorothy Pulis. *Who goes there?*
Lewis, J. Patrick. *The la-di-da hare*
Little, Jean. *Once upon a golden apple*
London, Jonathan. *Let's go, Froggy!*
Losi, Carol A. *The 512 ants on Sullivan Street*
McCully, Emily Arnold. *Picnic*
MacGregor, Marilyn. *Helen the hungry bear*
Maestro, Betsy. *The perfect picnic*
Mahy, Margaret. *The rattlebang picnic*
Maris, Ron. *In my garden*
Marshall, Edward. *Three by the sea*
Matje, Martin. *Celeste*
Miranda, Anne. *Pignic*
Morton, Christine. *Picnic farm*
Naylor, Phyllis Reynolds. *The picnic*
Numeroff, Laura Joffe. *What mommies do best*
Polacco, Patricia. *Picnic at Mudsock Meadow*
Prater, John. *Once upon a picnic*
Radlauer, Ruth Shaw. *Molly*
   Molly goes hiking
Rappus, Gerhard. *When the sun was shining*
Robertson, Lilian. *Picnic woods*
Rodgers, Richard. *A real nice clambake*
Roffey, Maureen. *Mealtime*
Rogers, Paul (Patrick). *Lily's picnic*
Rowinski, Kate. *L. L. Bear's island adventure*
Samton, Sheila White. *On the river*
Saunders, Susan. *Charles Rat's picnic*
   Fish fry
Scarry, Richard. *My first word book*
Schroeder, Binette. *Tuffa and the picnic*
Shapiro, Arnold L. *Square*
Spetter, Jung-Hee. *Lily and Trooper's spring*
Szekeres, Cyndy. *Ladybug, ladybug, where are you?*
Taylor, Judy. *Sophie and Jack*
Tether, Graham. *Skunk and possum*
Thomas, Jane Resh. *Celebration!*
Tsutsui, Yoriko. *Before the picnic*
Vaës, Alain. *The porcelain pepper pot*
Van Stockum, Hilda. *A day on skates*
Vincent, Gabrielle. *Ernest and Celestine's picnic*
Waddell, Martin. *Mimi and the picnic*
Wasmuth, Eleanor. *The picnic basket*
Watson, Clyde. *Hickory stick rag*
The weekend
Westcott, Nadine Bernard. *The giant vegetable garden*
Weston, Martha. *Bea's four bears*
Wheeler, Cindy. *Marmalade's picnic*
Wood, Joyce. *Grandmother Lucy goes on a picnic*
Woodson, Jacqueline. *We had a picnic this Sunday past*
Yeoman, John. *The bear's water picnic*
Yolen, Jane. *Picnic with Piggins*

Activities – playing

Adam, Barbara. *The big, big box*
Adorjan, Carol Madden. *I can! Can you?*
Agee, Jon. *Ellsworth*
Ahlberg, Allan. *Me and my friend*
Ahlberg, Janet. *Funnybones*
   Playmates
Alberts, Nancy Markham. *No toys on Sunday*
Alborough, Jez. *Hide and seek*
Alexander, Martha G. *Blackboard Bear*
   Good night, Lily
   I'll be the horse if you'll play with me

Lily and Willy
Where's Willy?
Willy's boot
Aliki. *Overnight at Mary Bloom's*
Allen, Pamela. *I wish I had a pirate suit*
Allen, Robert. *Ten little babies play*
Arnold, Caroline. *How do we have fun?*
   Playtime for zoo animals
   Splashtime for zoo animals
Arnosky, Jim. *Watching foxes*
Artis, Vicki Kimmel. *Pajama walking*
Asch, Frank. *Rebecka*
Aulaire, Ingri Mortenson d'. *Children of the north-lights*
Ayal, Ora. *Ugbu*
Bailey, Debbie. *The playground*
Baillie, Allan. *Drac and the gremlin*
Bang, Molly. *One fall day*
   Yellow ball
Baron, Alan. *Little Pig's bouncy ball*
Batchelor, Louise. *Whoops!*
Bauer, Helen. *Good times at the park*
Baugh, Dolores M. *Slides*
   Swings
Benét, William Rose. *Timothy's angels*
Bergman, Donna. *Timmy Green's blue lake*
Berkowitz, Linda. *Alfonse, where are you?*
Berry, Holly. *Busy Lizzie*
Best, Cari. *Last licks*
   Taxi! Taxi!
Bethell, Jean. *Playmates*
Blegvad, Lenore. *Rainy day Kate*
Blizzard, Gladys S. *Come look with me*
Bogacki, Tomasz. *Cat and mouse in the snow*
Bonsall, Crosby Newell. *And I mean it, Stanley*
Bottner, Barbara. *Bootsie Barker bites*
Boyd, Lizi. *Willy and the cardboard boxes*
Bram, Elizabeth. *Saturday morning lasts forever*
Breeze, Lynn. *This little baby's morning*
Breinburg, Petronella. *Doctor Shawn*
Brinckloe, Julie. *Playing marbles*
Brown, Myra Berry. *First night away from home*
Brown, Ruth. *Our puppy's vacation*
Browne, Anthony. *Things I like*
Bruna, Dick. *Miffy at the playground*
   Miffy's dream
Buck, Nola. *Oh, cats!*
   Sid and Sam
Buckley, Helen Elizabeth. *"Take care of things," Edward said*
Burningham, John. *Where's Julius?*
Burns, Maurice. *Go ducks, go!*
Burstein, Fred. *Whispering in the park*
Butterworth, Nick. *When we play together*
Cabban, Vanessa. *Bertie and Small and the fast bike ride*
Carlstrom, Nancy White. *Heather hiding*
Carrier, Lark. *Scout and Cody*
Carroll, Ruth. *Where's the bunny?*
Cartlidge, Michelle. *Pippin and Pod*
   Teddy's friends
Caseley, Judith. *The noisemakers*
Cauley, Lorinda Bryan. *Clap your hands*
Chichester Clark, Emma. *More!*
Chorao, Kay. *Annie and cousin Precious*
Christian, Mary Blount. *The sand lot*
Cimarusti, Marie Torres. *Peek-a-moo*
Coffelt, Nancy. *Good night, Sigmund*
Cole, William. *What's good for a four-year-old?*

What's good for a six-year-old?
Cooney, Nancy Evans. *Chatter-box Jamie*
Cousins, Lucy. *Maisy goes to the playground*
Creighton, Jill. *Maybe a monster*
Crews, Nina. *Snowball*
Dahlbäck-Lutteman, Helena. *My sister Lotta and me*
Dale, Penny. *All about Alice*
Day, Alexandra. *Carl goes to daycare*
   Follow Carl!
DeLage, Ida. *Frannie's flower*
De Paola, Tomie (Thomas Anthony). *Katie, Kit and cousin Tom*
Derby, Sally. *My steps*
Dickens, Lucy. *At the beach*
   Our day
   Outside
   Playtime
Donaldson, Joan. *The real pretend*
Donovan, Mary Lee. *Won't you come and play with me?*
Doyle, Charlotte Lackner. *You can't catch me*
Dubowski, Cathy East. *Snug Bug's play day*
Duke, Kate. *The playground*
Eaton, Deborah. *The rainy day grump*
Emecheta, Buchi. *Nowhere to play*
Ets, Marie Hall. *Play with me*
Falwell, Cathryn. *Nicky and Alex*
   Nicky and grandpa
   Where's Nicky?
Fitzhugh, Louise. *Bang, bang, you're dead*
Ford, Christine. *Snow!*
Ford, Miela. *Follow the leader*
   Mom and me
   My day in the garden
French, Vivian. *Little Ghost*
Fujikawa, Gyo. *That's not fair!*
Gebert, Warren. *The old ball and the sea*
George, Jean Craighead. *Snow bear*
Gibbons, Gail. *Playgrounds*
Gliori, Debi. *Mr. Bear says peek-a-boo*
   The snowchild
Goffstein, M. B. (Marilyn Brooke). *Our snowman*
Greenfield, Eloise. *Big friend, little friend*
   My doll, Keshia
Gretz, Susanna. *Duck takes off*
   Teddy bears stay indoors
Gundersheimer, Karen. *Find cat, wear hat*
   Splish splash bang crash!
Hallinan, P. K. (Patrick K.). *Let's play as a team*
Hallworth, Grace. *Down by the river*
Halpern, Shari. *What shall we do when we all go out?*
Hann, Jacquie. *Follow the leader*
Hartman, Gail. *For sand castles or seashells*
Haus, Felice. *Beep! Beep! I'm a jeep*
Havill, Juanita. *Jamaica Tag-Along*
Hawkins, Colin. *Dip, dip, dip*
   One finger, one thumb
   Oops-a-Daisy
   Where's bear?
Henderson, Kathy. *Bounce, bounce, bounce*
Hendrickson, Karen. *Baby and I can play*
   Fun with toddlers
Henkes, Kevin. *Oh!*
   A weekend with Wendell
Henley, Claire. *Playtime*
Hill, Eric. *Spot and friends play*
   Spot at play
   Spot goes to the beach
   Spot goes to the park

Spot sleeps over
   Spot's walk in the woods
Hillert, Margaret. *Play ball*
   What is it?
Hines, Anna Grossnickle. *Bethany for real*
   It's just me, Emily
   Keep your old hat
   They really like me!
Hines-Stephens, Sarah. *Bean's games*
Hirschi, Ron. *A time for playing*
Hissey, Jane. *Jolly snow*
Hoffman, Phyllis. *We play*
Houghton, Eric. *The backwards watch*
   The crooked apple tree
Hru, Dakari. *The magic moonberry jump ropes*
Hubbell, Patricia. *Pots and pans*
Hughes, Shirley. *Alfie's feet*
   Playing
Hulme, Joy N. *Bubble trouble*
Hutchins, H. J. (Hazel J.). *Norman's snowball*
Ichikawa, Satomi. *Isabela's ribbons*
   Let's play
   Suzanne and Nicholas in the garden
Impey, Rose. *Joe's café*
Inkpen, Mick. *Kipper's playtime*
   Kipper's snowy day
   Swing!
   Wibbly Pig can dance!
   Wibbly Pig can make a tent
Jackson, Ellen B. *Monsters in my mailbox*
Jakob, Donna. *My new sandbox*
   Tiny toes
Jaramillo, Raquel. *Ride, baby, ride!*
Jensen, Patricia. *The mess*
Jewell, Nancy. *Try and catch me*
Johnson, Mildred D. *Wait, skates!*
Kasza, Keiko. *Dorothy and Mikey*
Keats, Ezra Jack. *Skates*
   The snowy day
   The snowy day (a board book)
Keeping, Charles. *Willie's fire-engine*
Kennedy, Kim. *Napoleon*
Kent, Jack. *Joey*
Keown, Elizabeth. *Emily's snowball*
Kline, Suzy. *Don't touch!*
Knutson, Kimberley. *Muddigush*
Kobayashi, Yuji. *Miss Josephine's secret walk*
Krahn, Fernando. *Robot-bot-bot*
Kraus, Robert. *Come out and play, little mouse*
   Springfellow
Krauss, Ruth. *I can fly*
Krementz, Jill. *Lily goes to the playground*
Krupp, Robin Rector. *Get set to wreck!*
Kvasnosky, Laura McGee. *One, two, three, play with me!*
Lacome, Julie. *I'm a jolly farmer*
   Ruthie's big old coat
Lakin, Pat (Patricia). *Play*
Landa, Norbert. *Rabbit and chicken play hide and seek*
LaRochelle, David. *The evening king*
Lasky, Kathryn. *Pond year*
Lebrun, Claude. *Little Brown Bear learns to share*
Lenski, Lois. *Let's play house*
Leonard, Marcia. *Dress-up*
   Hop, skip, run
Lester, Alison. *Alice and Aldo*
Lewis, Kim. *Floss*
Lewison, Wendy Cheyette. *Mud*

Lindgren, Barbro. *Rosa*
  The wild baby goes to sea
Lipkind, William. *Sleepyhead*
London, Jonathan. *Puddles*
Loomis, Christine. *Cowboy bunnies*
Lopshire, Robert. *New tricks I can do!*
Luenn, Nancy. *Otter play*
McCarthy, Ruth. *Katie and the smallest bear*
McCord, David. *Every time I climb a tree*
McCully, Emily Arnold. *First snow*
MacDonald, Amy. *Let's go*
  Let's play
  Let's pretend
McGuirk, Leslie. *Tucker flips!*
McKee, David. *Elmer in the snow*
MacKinnon, Debbie. *Let's play: I can do it!*
  What am I?
McLerran, Alice. *Roxaboxen*
McMillan, Bruce. *Play day*
McNulty, Faith. *When a boy wakes up in the morning*
McPhail, David M. *Pig Pig rides*
Maestro, Betsy. *Harriet at play*
Major, Beverly. *Playing sardines*
Manushkin, Fran. *The best toy of all*
  Swinging and swinging
Marino, Dorothy. *Edward and the boxes*
Marshall, James. *Three up a tree*
Martin, David. *Lizzie and her friend*
  Lizzie and her puppy
Mayers, Patrick. *Just one more block*
Mayper, Monica. *Oh snow*
Medearis, Angela Shelf. *Here comes the snow*
  We play on a rainy day
Meeks, Esther K. *The hill that grew*
Merriam, Eve. *Boys and girls, girls and boys*
Meryl, Debra. *Baby's peek-a-boo album*
Miller, Margaret. *Let's play!*
  Playtime
  Water play
Miller, Virginia. *In a minute!*
Miranda, Anne. *Baby walk*
Mitchell, Cynthia. *Halloweena Hecatee*
  Playtime
Moffett, Martha A. *A flower pot is not a hat*
Morgan-Vanroyen, Mary. *Wild Rosie*
Morozumi, Atsuko. *Playing*
Morris, Ann. *Play*
Moss, Elaine. *Polar*
Moss, Marissa. *Want to play?*
Mueller, Virginia. *A playhouse for Monster*
Munsch, Robert N. *Mud puddle*
Murphy, Jill. *All for one*
Narahashi, Keiko. *Is that Josie?*
Naylor, Phyllis Reynolds. *King of the playground*
Neitzel, Shirley. *I'm taking a trip on my train*
Newcome, Zita. *Toddlerobics*
Nikola-Lisa, W. *Bein' with you this way*
Nobisso, Josephine. *Hot-cha-cha!*
Northway, Jennifer. *Get lost, Laura!*
Offen, Hilda. *The sheep made a leap*
O'Malley, Kevin. *The box*
Oppenheim, Joanne. *James will never die*
Oram, Hiawyn. *In the attic*
Ormerod, Jan. *Midnight pillow fight*
  The saucepan game
Owen, Annie. *Playtime duck*
Oxenbury, Helen. *All fall down*
  Clap hands
  Grandma and Grandpa

  Playing
  Say goodnight
  Tickle, tickle
  Tom and Pippo and the dog
Packard, Mary. *Bubble trouble*
  Where is Jake?
Paré, Roger. *Summer days*
Paschkis, Julie. *Play all day*
Paul, Ann Whitford. *Hello toes! Hello feet!*
Pearson, Susan. *That's enough for one day!*
Pfister, Marcus. *Chris and Croc*
Pirani, Felix. *Abigail at the beach*
Pocock, Rita. *Annabelle and the big slide*
Pollock, Penny. *Water is wet*
Poydar, Nancy. *Snip, snip . . . snow!*
Pragoff, Fiona. *It's fun to be one*
  It's great to be two
Priest, Robert. *The old pirate of Central Park*
Pringle, Laurence P. *Octopus hug*
Quinlan, Patricia. *Emma's sea journey*
Raebeck, Lois. *Who am I?*
Raney, Ken. *Stick horse*
Reid, Rob. *Wave goodbye*
Reiser, Lynn. *Best friends think alike*
Ring, Elizabeth. *Some stuff*
Roche, Harriet. *Pete's puddles*
Rockwell, Anne F. *At the beach*
  I play in my room
  My back yard
Roddie, Shen. *Toes are to tickle*
Rogers, Fred. *Making friends*
Rosner, Ruth. *Arabba gah zee, Marissa and Me!*
Russ, Lavinia. *Alec's sand castle*
Russo, Marisabina. *The big brown box*
  The line up book
  Where is Ben?
Sato, Satoru. *I wish I had a big, big tree*
Schaefer, Carole Lexa. *Snow pumpkin*
Sendak, Maurice. *Maurice Sendak's Really Rosie*
  The sign on Rosie's door
Shearer, Marilyn J. *I like to play*
Shirotani, Hideo. *Let's play*
Shott, Steve (Stephen). *Playtime*
Siddals, Mary McKenna. *I'll play with you*
Silverman, Erica. *Follow the leader*
Simon, Charnan. *Mud!*
Simon, Francesca. *Calling all toddlers*
Snyder, Zilpha Keatley. *Come on, Patsy*
Spetter, Jung-Hee. *Lily and Trooper's fall*
  Lily and Trooper's spring
  Lily and Trooper's summer
Standon, Anna. *Three little cats*
Steig, William. *Pete's pizza*
  Toby, where are you?
Steiner, Charlotte. *Kiki's play house*
  Look what Tracy found
Steptoe, John. *Baby says*
Stevenson, Robert Louis. *Where go the boats?*
Stevenson, Suçie. *Do I have to take Violet?*
Stine, Jovial Bob. *Pork and beans*
Stinson, Kathy. *The dressed up book*
Swanson-Natsues, Lyn. *Days of adventure*
Thompson, Richard. *Jenny's neighbours*
Thwaites, Lyndsay. *Super Adam and Rosie Wonder*
Todd, Kathleen. *Snow*
Tompert, Ann. *Just a little bit*
Townson, Hazel. *What on earth . . . ?*
Trimble, Marcia. *Malinda Martha and her stepping stones*

Turkle, Brinton. *Obadiah the Bold*
Turner, Ann Warren. *Let's be animals*
Turner, Charles. *The turtle and the moon*
Udry, Janice May. *Mary Ann's mud day*
Vasiliu, Mircea. *A day at the beach*
Veldkamp, Tjibbe. *22 orphans*
Vigna, Judith. *Boot weather*
Viorst, Judith. *Sunday morning*
Vulliamy, Clara. *Bang and shout*
    Boo baby boo!
Waber, Bernard. *Ira sleeps over*
Waddell, Martin. *Squeak-a-lot*
Wahl, Jan. *Push Kitty*
Wallace, John. *Little Bean's friend*
Walsh, Jill Paton. *Connie came to play*
Wasmuth, Eleanor. *An alligator day*
Watanabe, Shigeo. *Daddy, play with me!*
    I can build a house!
    I can ride it!
    I'm the king of the castle!
Wells, Rosemary. *A lion for Lewis*
Williams, Sherley Anne. *Girls together*
Williams, Sophy. *Nana's garden*
Winn, Chris. *Playing*
Winter, Jeanette. *Cowboy Charlie*
Winthrop, Elizabeth. *Bunk beds*
    That's mine
Wood, Audrey. *The Tickleoctopus*
Wood, Jakki. *Dads are such fun*
Yee, Patrick. *Let's play*
Yim, Natasha. *Otto's rainy day*
Yolen, Jane. *Before the storm*
Young, Miriam Burt. *Jellybeans for breakfast*
Ziefert, Harriet. *Baby Ben's go-go book*
    Come out, Jessie!
    Lewis the fire fighter
    Strike four!
Zimelman, Nathan. *Walls are to be walked*
Ziner, Feenie. *Counting carnival*
Zinnemann-Hope, Pam. *Let's play ball, Ned*
Zolotow, Charlotte (Shapiro). *The park book*
    The white marble

Activities – reading

Aliki. *How a book is made*
Allington, Richard L. *Reading*
Anholt, Catherine. *Come back, Jack!*
Asch, Frank. *Dear brother*
    Moonbear's books
Austin, Virginia. *Say please*
Baggette, Susan K. *Jonathan goes to the library*
Baker, Betty. *Worthington Botts and the steam machine*
Bank Street College of Education. *People read*
Barasch, Lynne. *Rodney's inside story*
Bauer, Caroline Feller. *Too many books!*
Baumgart, Klaus. *The little green dragon steps out*
Black, Irma (Simonton). *The little old man who could not read*
Bloom, Becky. *Wolf*
Bogart, Jo Ellen. *Jeremiah learns to read*
Bradby, Marie. *More than anything else*
Brillhart, Julie. *Story hour - starring Megan!*
Brimner, Larry Dane. *Aggie and Will*
Brown, Marc Tolon. *Arthur's really helpful word book*
Browne, Anthony. *I like books*
Browne, Eileen. *No problem*
Bruna, Dick. *I can read*
    I can read difficult words

I can read more
Bunting, Eve (Anne Evelyn). *The Wednesday surprise*
Caseley, Judith. *Sophie and Sammy's library sleepover*
Christian, Mary Blount. *The bookstore mouse*
Cohen, Miriam. *When will I read?*
Collins, Pat Lowery. *Don't tease the guppies*
DiFiori, Lawrence. *My first book*
Duvoisin, Roger Antoine. *Petunia*
Feiffer, Jules. *Meanwhile . . .*
Fox, Mem. *A bedtime story*
Friskey, Margaret (Margaret Richards). *Mystery of the gate sign*
Funk, Tom (Thompson). *I read signs*
Furtado, Jo. *Sorry, Miss Folio!*
Giff, Patricia Reilly. *The beast in Ms. Rooney's room*
Gile, John. *Oh, how I wished I could read!*
Gillham, Bill. *The early words picture book*
Goor, Ron. *Signs*
Grifalconi, Ann. *Electric Yancy*
Haley, Gail E. *Dream peddler*
Hallinan, P. K. (Patrick K.). *Just open a book*
Heller, Nicholas. *A book for Woody*
Herman, Gail. *Fievel's big showdown*
Hoban, Lillian. *Arthur's prize reader*
Hoban, Tana. *I read signs*
    I read symbols
    I walk and read
Holl, Adelaide. *Most-of-the-time Maxie*
Holleyman, Sonia. *Mona the vampire*
Hopkins, Lee Bennett. *Good books, good times*
Huff, Barbara A. *Once inside the library*
Hurd, Edith Thacher. *Johnny Lion's book*
Hutchins, H. J. (Hazel J.). *Nicholas at the library*
Hutchins, Pat. *The tale of Thomas Mead*
Johnson, Dolores. *Papa's stories*
Johnston, Tony. *Amber on the mountain*
Krensky, Stephen. *Breaking into print*
Kuskin, Karla. *Watson, the smartest dog in the U.S.A.*
Lattimore, Deborah Nourse. *The sailor who captured the sea*
Levinson, Nancy Smiler. *Clara and the bookwagon*
Lexau, Joan M. *Olaf reads*
Lillegard, Dee. *Sitting in my box*
Little, Jean. *Gruntle Piggle takes off*
    Once upon a golden apple
Lyon, George Ella. *Book*
McDonald, Megan. *Lucky star*
McGill, Alice. *Molly Bannaky*
McLenighan, Valjean. *One whole doughnut, one doughnut hole*
McPhail, David M. *Edward and the pirates*
    Fix-it
    Santa's book of names
Maestro, Betsy. *Harriet reads signs and more signs*
Marshall, James. *Wings*
Meddaugh, Susan. *Hog-eye*
Meister, Cari. *Tiny goes to the library*
Miller, William. *Richard Wright and the library card*
Minsberg, David. *The book monster*
Mora, Pat. *Tomás and the library lady*
Most, Bernard. *There's an ant in Anthony*
O'Neill, Catharine. *Mrs. Dunphy's dog*
Ormerod, Jan. *Reading*
Ormondroyd, Edward. *Broderick*
Pearson, Susan. *That's enough for one day!*
Polacco, Patricia. *Aunt Chip and the great Triple Creek dam affair*
    Thank you, Mr. Falker
Porazinska, Janina. *The enchanted book*

Purdy, Carol. *Least of all*
Radlauer, Ruth Shaw. *Molly at the library*
Rahaman, Vashanti. *Read for me, Mama*
Rau, Dana Meachen. *The secret code*
Seuss, Dr. *I can read with my eyes shut*
Sharmat, Marjorie Weinman. *My mother never listens to me*
Steer, Dougald. *Just one more story*
Stewart, Sarah. *The library*
Stortz, Diane M. *Barnaby Mouse, detective, and the mystery of the big book*
Viorst, Judith. *The good-bye book*
Wells, Rosemary. *Read to your bunny*
Wiesner, David. *Free fall*
Williams, Suzanne. *Library Lil*
Zemach, Kaethe. *The character in the book*

Activities – running

Adoff, Arnold. *I am the running girl*
Greenfield, Eloise. *Kia Tanisha*

Activities – sewing

Armstrong, Jennifer. *Pockets*
Brown, Craig McFarland. *Patchwork farmer*
Hoffman, Christine. *Sewing by hand*
Hopkinson, Deborah. *Sweet Clara and the freedom quilt*
Kuskin, Karla. *Patchwork island*
Leonard, Marcia. *Violet and the pirates*
Ransom, Candice F. *The promise quilt*
Sabuda, Robert James. *The Blizzard's robe*
Shea, Pegi Deitz. *The whispering cloth*
Wallner, Alexandra. *Betsy Ross*
Warner, Sunny. *The magic sewing machine*
Woolf, Virginia. *Nurse Lugton's curtain*
Yolen, Jane. *Old Dame Counterpane*

Activities – shopping *see* Shopping

Activities – singing

Allamand, Pascale. *The pop rooster*
Aroner, Miriam. *The kingdom of singing birds*
Auch, Mary Jane. *Bantam of the opera*
Birdseye, Tom. *She'll be comin' round the mountain*
Brouillard, Anne. *The bathtub prima donna*
Buck, Nola. *Sid and Sam*
Cazet, Denys. *Dancing*
Cowley, Joy. *Singing down the rain*
Czernecki, Stefan. *The singing snake*
Dodds, Dayle Ann. *Sing, Sophie!*
Downey, Lynn. *Sing, Henrietta! Sing!*
Fleming, Candace. *Westward ho, Carlotta!*
Fowler, Susi Gregg. *Fog*
Goble, Paul. *I sing for the animals*
Gold, Julie. *From a distance*
Goss, Linda. *The frog who wanted to be a singer*
Grigg, Carol. *The singing snow bear*
Himmelman, John. *Simpson Snail sings*
Hirschi, Ron. *A time for singing*
Jewell, Nancy. *Sailor song*
Kraus, Robert. *Screamy Mimi*
Latimer, Jim. *James Bear and the goose gathering*
Lucado, Max. *Alabaster's song*
McCully, Emily Arnold. *The orphan singer*
Peterson, Jeanne Whitehouse. *My mama sings*
Saul, Carol P. *Peter's song*

Sikundar, Sylvia. *Forest singer*
Stenmark, Victoria. *The singing chick*
Sundgaard, Arnold. *The bear who loved Puccini*
Taylor, Ann. *Baby dance*
Wahl, Jan. *The singing geese*

Activities – storytelling

Ahlberg, Janet. *It was a dark and stormy night*
Brutschy, Jennifer. *Just one more story*
De Paola, Tomie (Thomas Anthony). *The Prince of the Dolomites*
Dwyer, Mindy. *Coyote in love*
Farley, Carol J. *Mr. Pak buys a story*
Foreman, Michael. *Grandfather's pencil and the room of stories*
Hest, Amy. *The babies are coming!*
Lester, Helen. *Help! I'm stuck!*
Le Tord, Bijou. *God's little seeds*
Lewin, Ted. *The storytellers*
McDonald, Megan. *Tundra mouse*
O'Malley, Kevin. *Velcome*
Paton, Priscilla. *Howard and the sitter surprise*
Reiser, Lynn. *Little clam*
Rochelle, Belinda. *Jewels*
Schwartz, Amy. *Some babies*
Simms, Laura. *Rotten teeth*
Slate, Joseph. *Story time for Little Porcupine*
Van Leeuwen, Jean. *The tickle stories*
Walsh, Ellen Stoll. *Jack's tale*
Watts, Jeri Hanel. *Keepers*
Yolen, Jane. *Miz Berlin walks*

Activities – swapping *see* Activities – trading

Activities – swinging

Anderson, Robin. *Sinabouda Lily*
Baugh, Dolores M. *Swings*
Manushkin, Fran. *Swinging and swinging*
Marks, Marcia Bliss. *Swing me, swing tree*

Activities – talking

Ziefert, Harriet. *Talk, baby!*

Activities – trading

Andersen, H. C. (Hans Christian). *The old man is always right*
Burdick, Margaret. *Bobby Otter and the blue boat*
Bushey, Jerry. *The barge book*
Chorao, Kay. *The cherry pie baby*
Davidson, Jill A. *And that's what happened to little Lucy*
De Regniers, Beatrice Schenk. *Was it a good trade?*
Dick Whittington and his cat. *Dick Whittington*, ill. by Edward Ardizzone
   Dick Whittington, ill. by Antony Maitland
   Dick Whittington and his cat, ill. by Marcia Brown
   Dick Whittington and his cat, ill. by Kurt Werth
Edwards, Pamela Duncan. *Livingstone Mouse*
Fowler, Susi Gregg. *I'll see you when the moon is full*
Gill, Bob. *A balloon for a blunderbuss*
Hale, Irina. *The lost toys*
Hirsh, Marilyn. *The pink suit*
Hughes, Shirley. *David and dog*
   Dogger
Inkpen, Mick. *Penguin small*

Kimmel, Eric A. *Onions and garlic*
Langstaff, John M. *The swapping boy*
Levine, Abby. *Ollie knows everything*
Lichtveld, Noni. *I lost my arrow in a kankan tree*
McAllister, Angela. *Matepo*
McKay, Lawrence. *Caravan*
Shannon, George. *The Piney Woods peddler*
Stroyer, Poul. *It's a deal*
Suen, Anastasia. *Window music*
Torres, Leyla. *Saturday sancocho*
Watts, Mabel (Pizzey). *Something for you, something for me*

Activities – traveling

Aardema, Verna. *Traveling to Tondo*
Aksakov, Sergei. *The scarlet flower*
Anderson, Scoular. *MacPelican's American adventure*
Arnold, Caroline. *How do we travel?*
Axelrod, Amy. *Pigs on the move*
Aylesworth, Jim. *My sister's rusty bike*
Ball, Duncan. *Jeremy's tail*
Ballard, Robin. *When we get home*
Bansemer, Roger. *Rachael's splendifilous adventure*
Barklem, Jill. *The high hills*
Barracca, Debra. *Maxi, the star*
Bate, Lucy. *How Georgina drove the car very carefully from Boston to New York*
Baum, Louis. *JuJu and the pirate*
Beatty, Hetty Burlingame. *Moorland pony*
Bemelmans, Ludwig. *Quito express*
Billout, Guy. *By camel or by car*
Blech, Dietlind. *Hello Irina*
Bolognese, Don. *A new day*
Borchers, Elisabeth. *Dear Sarah*
Brandenberg, Franz. *Everyone ready?*
Brann, Esther. *'Round the world*
Bridgman, Elizabeth. *How to travel with grownups*
  Nanny bear's cruise
Brisson, Pat. *Kate on the coast*
  Magic carpet
  Your best friend, Kate
Bröger, Achim. *Bruno takes a trip*
Bromhall, Winifred. *Johanna arrives*
Brown, Don. *Alice Ramsey's grand adventure*
Brown, Laurie Krasny. *Dinosaurs travel*
Brown, Marc Tolon. *Arthur meets the president*
Brown, Margaret Wise. *Three little animals*
Brown, Tricia. *The city by the bay*
Bruna, Dick. *The sailor*
Brunhoff, Jean de. *The travels of Babar*
Brutschy, Jennifer. *Just one more story*
Buchanan, Heather S. *George Mouse's covered wagon*
Buffett, Jimmy. *The jolly mon*
Bunting, Eve (Anne Evelyn). *Ducky*
  A picnic in October
  The traveling men of Ballycoo
Bursik, Rose. *Amelia's fantastic flight*
Butler, Dorothy. *A happy tale*
  My brown bear Barney
Cabban, Vanessa. *Bertie and Small and the brave sea journey*
Caines, Jeannette. *Just us women*
Calmenson, Stephanie. *Zip, whiz, zoom!*
Carle, Eric. *The rooster who set out to see the world*
  Rooster's off to see the world
Cech, John. *My grandmother's journey*
Chalmers, Mary. *Here comes the trolley*
Chwast, Seymour. *Tall city, wide country*

Coerr, Eleanor. *The Josefina story quilt*
Conway, Celeste. *Where is Papa now?*
Cooney, Barbara. *Miss Rumphius*
Coy, John. *Night driving*
Cummings, Pat. *My aunt came back*
Czernecki, Stefan. *Zorah's magic carpet*
Davis, Maggie S. *The best way to Ripton*
Day, Edward C. *John Tabor's ride*
De Beer, Hans. *Little polar bear, take me home!*
Demarest, Chris L. *My little red car*
Demi. *The adventures of Marco Polo*
Denslow, Sharon Phillips. *Riding with Aunt Lucy*
Denton, Terry. *Home is the sailor*
Derby, Sally. *The mouse who owned the sun*
DeSaix, Deborah Durland. *In the back seat*
Diller, Harriett. *Grandaddy's highway*
Dugan, Barbara. *Leaving home with a pickle jar*
Eisenstein, Marilyn. *Periwinkle isn't Paris*
Ekker, Ernest A. *What is beyond the hill?*
Fairclough, Chris. *Take a trip to China*
  Take a trip to England
  Take a trip to Holland
  Take a trip to Israel
  Take a trip to Italy
  Take a trip to West Germany
Feldman, Barbara. *Going, going*
Field, Rachel Lyman. *A road might lead to anywhere*
Fox, Mem. *Possum magic*
Gackenbach, Dick. *With love from Gran*
Gans, Roma. *How do birds find their way?*
Gantschev, Ivan. *The train to Grandma's*
Garay, Luis. *The long road*
Gay, Michel. *Night ride*
Gerrard, Roy. *Jocasta Carr, movie star*
  Wagons west!
Gikow, Louise. *Follow that Fraggle!*
Gomi, Taro. *Bus stop*
Goodall, John S. *Paddy goes traveling*
Grahame, Kenneth. *The open road*
  The wind in the willows
Gray, Genevieve. *How far, Felipe?*
Greenblat, Rodney Alan. *Thunder Bunny*
Greene, Carla. *A motor holiday*
Gretz, Susanna. *Teddy bears take the train*
Haley, Patrick. *The little person*
Hammerschmid, Carl A. *The go away doll*
Handford, Martin. *Find Waldo now*
  The great Waldo search
  Where's Waldo?
  Where's Waldo? In Hollywood
  Where's Waldo now?
  Where's Waldo? The fantastic journey
  Where's Waldo? The wonder book
Hannan, Peter. *Sillyville or bust*
Harrison, Troon. *Lavender Moon*
Harvey, Brett. *Cassie's journey*
Hayashi, Akiko. *Aki and the fox*
Heckman, Philip. *The moon is following me*
Heuck, Sigrid. *Who stole the apples?*
Hobbie, Holly. *Toot and Puddle*
  Toot and Puddle, I'll be home for Christmas
Holabird, Katharine. *Alexander and the magic boat*
Houk, Randy. *Chessie, the travelin' man*
Howard, Elizabeth Fitzgerald. *The train to Lulu's*
Howland, Naomi. *ABCDrive!*
Hughes, Shirley. *Abel's moon*
Hurd, Thacher. *Hobo dog*
Isadora, Rachel. *No, Agatha!*
  Over the green hills

Isele, Elizabeth. *Pooks*
Jacobs, Leland B. (Leland Blair). *Is somewhere always far away?*, ill. by John E. Johnson
  Is somewhere always far away?, ill. by Jeff Kaufman
Janosch. *The trip to Panama*
Jonas, Ann. *Round trip*
Joosse, Barbara M. *Lewis and papa*
Kalman, Maira. *Sayonara, Mrs. Kackleman*
Karmi, Giora. *And Shira imagined*
Kay, Verla. *Covered wagons, bumpy trails*
Kellogg, Steven (Stephen). *Johnny Appleseed*
Kesselman, Wendy Ann. *There's a train going by my window*
Kessler, Leonard P. *Mrs. Pine takes a trip*
Kidd, Richard. *Almost famous Daisy!*
Kilroy, Sally. *On the road*
Knapp, Jennifer. *The go go dogs*
Koralek, Jenny. *Night ride to Nanna's*
Krementz, Jill. *Jamie goes on an airplane*
  A visit to Washington, D.C.
Lasky, Kathryn. *The Gates of the Wind*
Leedy, Loreen. *Blast off to Earth!*
Leighton, Maxinne Rhea. *An Ellis Island Christmas*
Lenski, Lois. *Davy goes places*
Leonard, Marcia. *Bye-bye, Baby-boo*
Lester, Alison. *The journey home*
Leventhal, Debra. *What is your language?*
Levitin, Sonia. *Nine for California*
Lewin, Hugh. *Jafta - the journey*
Lewis, Thomas P. *Clipper ship*
Liddell, Janice. *Imani and the Flying Africans*
Lindbergh, Reeve. *Johnny Appleseed*
Lobel, Anita. *Away from home*
Locker, Thomas. *Sailing with the wind*
Lodge, Bernard. *Cloud Cuckoo Land (and other odd spots)*
London, Jonathan. *Moshi moshi*
Lööf, Jan. *Uncle Louie's fantastic sea voyage*
Loomis, Christine. *We're going on a trip*
Lyndon, Kerry Raines. *A birthday for Blue*
Lyon, George Ella. *A regular rolling Noah*
  A traveling cat
McAllister, Angela. *Jessie's journey*
McCarty, Peter. *Little bunny on the move*
McCormack, John E. *Rabbit travels*
McDonald, Megan. *The night Iguana left home*
McKay, Lawrence. *Caravan*
  Journey home
McKissack, Patricia C. *Big bug book of places to go*
McToots, Rudi. *The kid's book of games for cars, trains and planes*
Maestro, Betsy. *Ferryboat*
Mahy, Margaret. *A busy day for a good grandmother*
  The three-legged cat
Manson, Christopher. *Two travelers*
Marshak, S. (Samuil). *The pup grew up!*
Martin, C. L. G. *The blueberry train*
Martin, Charles E. *Sam saves the day*
May, Charles Paul. *High-noon rocket*
Meddaugh, Susan. *Maude and Claude go abroad*
Miller, Edna. *Mousekin takes a trip*
Milton, Nancy. *The giraffe that walked to Paris*
Moss, Marissa. *In America*
Munro, Roxie. *The inside-outside book of Washington, D.C.*
Nayer, Judy. *The happy little engine*
Neitzel, Shirley. *The bag I'm taking to Grandma's*
Nixon, Joan Lowery. *If you say so, Claude*
Nordqvist, Sven. *Willie in the big world*

Oechsli, Helen. *Fly away!*
O'Kelley, Mattie Lou. *Moving to town*
Ormerod, Jan. *Miss Mouse takes off*
Owen, Annie. *Bumper to bumper*
Patz, Nancy. *Gina Farina and the Prince of Mintz*
Peters, Lisa Westberg. *This way home*
Petty, Kate. *On a plane*
Piers, Helen. *Is there room on the bus?*
Pinkney, Gloria Jean. *The Sunday outing*
Poulin, Stéphane. *Travels for two*
Priceman, Marjorie. *How to make an apple pie and see the world*
Quackenbush, Robert M. *Henry's world tour*
Quattlebaum, Mary. *Underground train*
Rabe, Berniece. *A smooth move*
Raney, Ken. *Stick horse*
Robbins, Ken. *City/country*
Roberts, Bethany. *Camel caravan*
Rogers, Fred. *Going on an airplane*
Rose, Gerald. *PB takes a holiday*
Rosenberg, Liz. *Grandmother and the runaway shadow*
Rosenblum, Richard. *Journey to the golden land*
Rumford, James. *The Island-below-the-star*
Rush, Ken. *Friday's journey*
Rylant, Cynthia. *The relatives came*
  Tulip sees America
Salter, Mary Jo. *The moon comes home*
Say, Allen. *Grandfather's journey*
Schneider, Howie. *No dogs allowed*
Schories, Pat. *Mouse around*
Schulz, Charles M. *Bon voyage, Charlie Brown (and don't come back!!)*
Seuss, Dr. *I had trouble getting to Solla Sollew*
Sharratt, Nick. *Mrs. Pirate*
Sheldon, Dyan. *Love, your bear, Pete*
Slater, Teddy. *The fabulous fish from Lake Wiggawalla*
Slavin, Bill. *The cat came back*
Smith, Barry. *The first voyage of Christopher Columbus*
Smith, Maggie (Margaret C.). *Counting our way to Maine*
Smyth, Gwenda. *A pet for Mrs. Arbuckle*
Sorensen, Henri. *New Hope*
Steel, Danielle. *Freddie's trip*
Steger, Hans-Ulrich. *Traveling to Tripiti*
Stevenson, Harvey. *Grandpa's house*
Stevenson, James. *All aboard!*
  Are we almost there?
Storm, Theodor. *Little Hobbin*
Suben, Eric. *Pigeon takes a trip*
Tapio, Pat Decker. *The lady who saw the good side of everything*
Tews, Susan. *Lizard sees the world*
Tomlinson, Theresa. *Little stowaway*
Trevelyan, Kathy. *Don't be surprised!*
Türk, Hanne. *Max packs*
Turner, Ann Warren. *Nettie's trip south*
Tzannes, Robin. *Sanji and the baker*
Ungerer, Tomi. *Adelaide*
Valfre, Edward. *Backseat buckaroo*
Van Leeuwen, Jean. *Across the wide dark sea*
Vevers, Gwynne. *Animals that travel*
Waddell, Martin. *Small Bear lost*
Walters, Virginia. *Are we there yet, Daddy?*
Watson, Mary. *The butterfly seeds*
Whitcher, Susan. *Something for everyone*
Wiesmüller, Dieter. *The adventures of Marco and Polo*

Wild, Margaret. *Going home*
Willard, Nancy. *The voyage of the Ludgate Hill*
Willis, Jeanne. *Earth mobiles as explained by Professor Xargle*
Wood, Audrey. *Silly Sally*
Woodtor, Dee. *Big meeting*
Wright, Courtni Crump. *Wagon train*
Yee, Paul. *Let's eat*
Ziefert, Harriet. *A car trip for mole and mouse*
　　Keeping daddy awake on the way home from the beach

Activities – vacationing

Adams, Adrienne. *The Easter egg artists*
Ahlberg, Allan. *Skeleton crew*
Bemelmans, Ludwig. *Hansi*
Berenstain, Stan. *The Berenstain bears and too much vacation*
Best, Cari. *Montezuma's revenge*
Blades, Ann. *Back to the cabin*
Bond, Michael. *Paddington at the seaside*
Bornstein, Ruth Lercher. *I'll draw a meadow*
Brandenberg, Franz. *A fun weekend*
Briggs, Raymond. *Father Christmas goes on holiday*
Bright, Robert. *Georgie and the noisy ghost*
Brisson, Pat. *Kate on the coast*
　　Your best friend, Kate
Brown, Marc Tolon. *Arthur's family vacation*
Brown, Ruth. *Our puppy's vacation*
Brunhoff, Laurent de. *Babar's cousin, that rascal Arthur*
　　Babar's mystery
Buchanan, Heather S. *George Mouse's covered wagon*
Carlstrom, Nancy White. *The moon came too*
Carrick, Carol. *The washout*
Chall, Marsha Wilson. *Up north at the cabin*
Cole, Joanna. *The Clown-Arounds go on vacation*
Dalmais, Anne-Marie. *Henry the hedgehog*
De Paola, Tomie (Thomas Anthony). *Strega Nona takes a vacation*
Dodd, Lynley. *Schnitzel von Krumm forget-me-not*
Du Bois, William Pène. *Otto and the magic potatoes*
Duvoisin, Roger Antoine. *Petunia takes a trip*
Everton, Macduff. *El circo magico modelo*
Fatio, Louise. *The happy lion's vacation*
Florian, Douglas. *A summer day*
Gili, Phillida. *Fanny and Charles*
Goodall, John S. *Paddy Pork's holiday*
Goyder, Alice. *Holiday in Catland*
Graham, Bob. *Greetings from Sandy Beach*
Haddon, Mark. *On vacation*
Hale, Kathleen. *Orlando and the water cats*
Hänel, Wolfram. *Mia the beach cat*
Hayward, Linda. *Grover's summer vacation*
Hill, Eric. *Spot goes on holiday*
Joyce, William. *Dinosaur Bob*
Kellogg, Steven (Stephen). *Ralph's secret weapon*
Kessler, Leonard P. *Are we lost, daddy?*
Khalsa, Dayal Kaur. *My family vacation*
Lawson, Julie. *Midnight in the mountains*
Lazard, Naomi. *What Amanda saw*
Lester, Alison. *Magic beach*
Lindman, Maj. *Snipp, Snapp, Snurr and the red shoes*
Lippman, Peter. *The Know-It-Alls take a winter vacation*
Loomis, Christine. *We're going on a trip*
McPhail, David M. *Emma's pet*
　　Emma's vacation
Maestro, Betsy. *The pandas take a vacation*

Marshall, James. *George and Martha 'round and 'round*
Martin, Charles E. *Sam saves the day*
Maynard, Bill. *Santa's time off*
Meddaugh, Susan. *Martha calling*
Monfried, Lucia. *The Daddies Boat*
Murdocca, Sal (Salvatore). *Lucy takes a holiday*
Murphy, Stuart J. *The best vacation ever*
Nethery, Mary. *Hannah and Jack*
Newton, Patricia Montgomery. *Vacation surprise*
Njeng, Pierre Yves. *Vacation in the village*
Noll, Sally. *Lucky morning*
Pohrt, Tom. *Having a wonderful time*
Rand, Gloria. *The cabin key*
Rockwell, Anne F. *On our vacation*
Rodda, Emily. *Yay!*
Roffey, Maureen. *I spy on vacation*
Samuels, Barbara. *Aloha, Dolores*
Schneider, Howie. *No dogs allowed*
Shea, Pegi Deitz. *Bungalow fungalow*
Steel, Danielle. *Freddie's trip*
Stevenson, James. *The Sea View Hotel*
Tafuri, Nancy. *The brass ring*
Thomson, Ruth. *Peabody all at sea*
Tobias, Tobi. *At the beach*
Valfre, Edward. *Vacationers from outer space*
Van Leeuwen, Jean. *Touch the sky summer*
Wallace, Karen. *City pig*
Weiss, Nicki. *Weekend at Muskrat Lake*
Williams, Jay. *The city witch and the country witch*
Ziefert, Harriet. *Pushkin minds the bundle*

Activities – walking

Ackerman, Karen. *Walking with Clara Belle*
Alexander, Martha G. *Where does the sky end, Grandpa?*
Arnosky, Jim. *Crinkleroot's guide to walking in wild places*
　　Outdoors on foot
Aylesworth, Jim. *Siren in the night*
Bax, Martin. *Edmond went far away*
Berry, Christine. *Mama went walking*
Bodsworth, Nan. *A nice walk in the jungle*
Brown, Margaret Wise. *Four fur feet*
Buchanan, Joan. *It's a good thing*
Buckley, Helen Elizabeth. *Grandfather and I*
Bullock, Kathleen. *It chanced to rain*
Davidson, Jill A. *And that's what happened to little Lucy*
De Regniers, Beatrice Schenk. *Going for a walk*
Dowling, Paul. *Where are you going, Jimmy?*
Edwards, Pamela Duncan. *The worrywarts*
Falwell, Cathryn. *Nicky loves daddy*
　　Nicky's walk
Florian, Douglas. *Nature walk*
George, Lindsay Barrett. *In the woods*
Greenfield, Karen R. *Sister Yessa's story*
Hill, Eric. *The park*
　　Spot's first walk
Hindley, Judy. *Funny walks*
　　Into the jungle
Hoban, Tana. *I walk and read*
Hubbell, Patricia. *Sidewalk trip*
Johnson, D. B. (Donald B.). *Henry hikes to Fitchburg*
Jonas, Ann. *The trek*
　　Watch William walk
Kingman, Lee. *Peter's long walk*
Klein, Leonore. *Henri's walk to Paris*

Komaiko, Leah. *Great Aunt Ida and her Great Dane, Doc*
Krupinski, Loretta. *Into the woods*
Lenski, Lois. *I went for a walk*
Lewis, Kim. *One summer day*
Lobe, Mira. *The snowman who went for a walk*
London, Jonathan. *Wiggle, waggle*
Luenn, Nancy. *Squish!*
McNaughton, Colin. *Walk rabbit walk*
Manuel, Lynn. *The night the moon blew kisses*
Oxenbury, Helen. *Our dog*
Pearson, Susan. *Silver morning*
Pfister, Marcus. *Penguin Pete and Little Tim*
Radlauer, Ruth Shaw. *Molly*
    Molly goes hiking
Ray, Deborah Kogan. *The cloud*
Rockwell, Anne F. *Willy can count*
Sarton, May. *A walk through the woods*
Sharmat, Marjorie Weinman. *Burton and Dudley*
Shirotani, Hideo. *Let's take a walk = Vamos a caminar*
Showers, Paul. *The listening walk*
Smalls-Hector, Irene. *Jonathan and his mommy*
Stevenson, James. *Rolling Rose*
Stynes, Barbara White. *Walking with mama*
Thomas, Ianthe. *Walk home tired, Billy Jenkins*
Thompson, Richard. *I have to see this*
Tobias, Tobi. *The dawdlewalk*
Türk, Hanne. *Rainy day Max*
Turner, Ethel. *Walking to school*
Tworkov, Jack. *The camel who took a walk*
Viorst, Judith. *Try it again, Sam*
Watanabe, Shigeo. *I can take a walk!*
Williams, David. *Walking to the creek*
Williams, Sue. *I went walking*
Wood, Joyce. *Grandmother Lucy goes on a picnic*
Yolen, Jane. *Miz Berlin walks*
Zolotow, Charlotte (Shapiro). *One step, two . . . Say it!*
    The summer night

Activities – weaving

Bang, Molly. *Dawn*
Blood, Charles L. *The goat in the rug*
Bodkin, Odds. *The crane wife*
Castaneda, Omar S. *Abuela's weave*
Chanin, Michael. *Chief's blanket*
Coombs, Patricia. *Tilabel*
Czernecki, Stefan. *Zorah's magic carpet*
Duncan, Lois. *The magic of Spider Woman*
Ernst, Lisa Campbell. *Nattie Parsons' good-luck lamb*
Gill, Janet. *Basket Weaver and Catches Many Mice*
Heyer, Marilee. *The weaving of a dream*
Keo, Ena. *The crane wife*
Khan, Rukhsana. *The roses in my carpets*
Kherdian, David. *The golden bracelet*
Lattimore, Deborah Nourse. *The dragon's robe*
Le Tord, Bijou. *Picking and weaving*
London, Jonathan. *The village basket weaver*
Medearis, Angela Shelf. *Seven spools of thread*
Murphy, Shirley Rousseau. *Wind child*
Oughton, Jerrie. *The magic weaver of rugs*
Radley, Gail. *The spinner's gift*
San Souci, Robert D. *The enchanted tapestry*
    A weave of words
Trân-Khánh-Tuyê. *The little weaver of Thái-Yên Village*
Tseng, Grace. *White tiger, blue serpent*

Yagawa, Sumiko. *The crane wife*

Activities – whistling

Alexander, Anne (Anna Barbara Cooke). *I want to whistle*
Ambrus, Victor G. *The three poor tailors*
Bason, Lillian. *Pick a raincoat, pick a whistle*
Blackwood, Gladys Rourke. *Whistle for Cindy*
Honeycutt, Natalie. *Whistle home*
Keats, Ezra Jack. *Whistle for Willie*
Watts, Bernadette. *The Christmas bird*

Activities – working

Ackerman, Karen. *By the dawn's early light*
    When mama retires
Ahlberg, Allan. *Mrs. Wobble the waitress*
Alda, Arlene. *Sonya's mommy works*
Allen, Jeffrey. *Mary Alice, operator number 9*
Altman, Linda Jacobs. *Amelia's road*
Ardizzone, Edward. *Paul, the hero of the fire*
Arkin, Alan. *Tony's hard work day*
Asch, Frank. *Good lemonade*
Aylesworth, Jim. *Shenandoah Noah*
Bach, Othello. *Lilly, Willy and the mail-order witch*
Barber, Barbara E. *Saturday at the new you*
Bartoletti, Susan Campbell. *Silver at night*
Barton, Byron. *Machines at work*
Basso, Bill. *The top of the pizzas*
Beim, Jerrold. *Jay's big job*
Bethell, Jean. *Three cheers for Mother Jones!*
Blance, Ellen. *Monster gets a job*
Bond, Michael. *Paddington cleans up*
Brooks, Ben. *Lemonade parade*
Buehner, Caralyn. *A job for Wittilda*
Bunting, Eve (Anne Evelyn). *A day's work*
Burke, Timothy. *Tugboats in action*
Burton, Virginia Lee. *Mike Mulligan and his steam shovel*
Butterworth, Nick. *When there's work to do*
Caple, Kathy. *The purse*
Carle, Eric. *Walter the baker*
Civardi, Anne. *Things people do*
Clark, Ann Nolan. *The little Indian basket maker*
    The little Indian pottery maker
Claverie, Jean. *Working*
Cole, Babette. *The trouble with dad*
Dahl, Roald. *The giraffe and the pelly and me*
DeGross, Monalisa. *Granddaddy's street songs*
Delaney, Ned. *Terrible things could happen*
Delton, Judy. *Hired help for Rabbit*
    My mother lost her job today
Duke, Kate. *Clean-up day*
Dumbleton, Mike. *Dial-a-croc*
Dupasquier, Philippe. *A busy day at the garage*
Eisenberg, Phyllis Rose. *You're my Nikki*
Euvremer, Teryl. *Sun's up*
Fleischman, Paul. *The animal hedge*
Florian, Douglas. *People working*
    A potter
Gág, Wanda. *Gone is gone*
Gallo, Giovanni. *The lazy beaver*
Garland, Michael. *Circus girl*
Gibbons, Gail. *Deadline!*
    Zoo
Goffstein, M. B. (Marilyn Brooke). *An actor*
    A writer
Goodall, John S. *Paddy Pork*

Grossman, Patricia. *The night ones*
Haley, Gail E. *Two bad boys*
Hall, Donald. *The ox-cart man*
Harper, Anita. *How we work*
Harvey, Brett. *My prairie year*
Hautzig, Deborah. *It's not fair!*
Hazen, Barbara Shook. *Mommy's office*
Heide, Florence Parry. *The day of Ahmed's secret*
Heine, Helme. *Merry-go-round*
Henderson, Kathy. *In the middle of the night*
Hoban, Julia. *Buzby to the rescue*
Hoban, Russell. *Charlie the tramp*
Horvath, Betty F. *Jasper makes music*
Joseph, Lynn. *Jasmine's parlour day*
Killingback, Julia. *Monday is washing day*
Komaiko, Leah. *A million moms and mine*
    On Sally Perry's farm
Krahn, Fernando. *Robot-bot-bot*
Kroll, Steven. *Howard and Gracie's luncheonette*
Lasker, Joe. *Mothers can do anything*
Leiner, Katherine. *Both my parents work*
Lewis, Kim. *Floss*
Lindsey, Treska. *When Batistine made bread*
Lockwood, Primrose. *Cissy Lavender*
London, Jonathan. *Hip cat*
Look, Lenore. *Love as strong as ginger*
Loomis, Christine. *Rush hour*
Love, Ann. *Fishing*
Lyon, David. *The biggest truck*
Lyon, George Ella. *Mama is a miner*
McCunn, Ruthanne L. *Pie-Biter*
McGowen, Tom (Thomas). *The only glupmaker in the U.S. Navy*
McPhail, David M. *Annie and Co.*
    Pig Pig gets a job
Maestro, Betsy. *Harriet at work*
Marshall, James. *Fox on the job*
Maynard, Joyce. *New house*
Medearis, Angela Shelf. *Picking peas for a penny*
Merriam, Eve. *Mommies at work*
Mitchell, Joyce Slayton. *My mommy makes money*
Modesitt, Jeanne. *Lunch with Milly*
Morris, Ann. *Work*
Nethery, Mary. *Hannah and Jack*
100 words about working
Paterson, Diane. *Soap and suds*
Paulsen, Gary. *Worksong*
Peterson, Cris. *Horsepower*
Petrides, Heidrun. *Hans and Peter*
Pilkey, Dav. *The paperboy*
Pryor, Bonnie. *The dream jar*
Puner, Helen Walker. *Daddys, what they do all day*
Purdy, Carol. *Least of all*
Quinlan, Patricia. *My dad takes care of me*
Rodriguez, Anita. *Jamal and the angel*
Rose, Deborah Lee. *Meredith's mother takes the train*
Ross, Jessica. *Ms. Klondike*
Rylant, Cynthia. *Mr. Griggs' work*
Sandberg, Inger. *Come on out, Daddy!*
San Souci, Robert D. *The hired hand*
Sathre, Vivian. *On Grandpa's farm*
Shipton, Jonathan. *Busy! Busy! Busy!*
Simon, Norma. *I'm busy, too*
Singer, Marilyn. *Chester, the out-of-work dog*
Skurzynski, Gloria. *Martin by himself*
Spinelli, Eileen. *Night shift daddy*
Stolz, Mary Slattery. *Zekmet, the stone carver*
Türk, Hanne. *Raking leaves with Max*
Turner, Nancy Byrd. *When young Melissa sweeps*

Valens, Amy. *Jesse's day care*
Waber, Bernard. *Lyle at the office*
Williams, Sherley Anne. *Working cotton*
Wittmann, Patricia. *Go ask Giorgio!*
Ye, Ting-xing. *Three monks, no water*
Yee, Wong Herbert. *Hamburger Heaven*
Yeoman, John. *The wild washerwomen*

Activities – writing

Aliki. *Communication*
Allington, Richard L. *Writing*
Arnosky, Jim. *Mouse writing*
Brown, Marc Tolon. *Arthur writes a story*
Caseley, Judith. *Dear Annie*
Cech, John. *The southernmost cat*
Cobb, Vicki. *Writing it down*
Cronin, Doreen. *Click, clack, moo*
Dewey, Jennifer Owings. *Stories on stone*
Fain, Moira. *Snow day*
Felt, Sue. *Rosa-too-little*
Foreman, Michael. *Grandfather's pencil and the room of stories*
Greenblat, Rodney Alan. *Thunder Bunny*
Greene, Carol. *Margaret Wise Brown, author of Goodnight moon*
Harrison, Joanna. *Dear bear*
Heide, Florence Parry. *The day of Ahmed's secret*
Hoban, Lillian. *Arthur's pen pal*
Hughes, Shirley. *Abel's moon*
Joslin, Sesyle. *Dear dragon*
Kraus, Robert. *The adventures of Wise Old Owl*
Krauss, Ruth. *I write it*
Lattimore, Deborah Nourse. *The sailor who captured the sea*
Leedy, Loreen. *The Furry News*
    Messages in the mailbox
Lockwood, Primrose. *Cissy Lavender*
Miles, Miska. *The pointed brush . . .*
Nixon, Joan Lowery. *If you were a writer*
Oakley, Graham. *The diary of a church mouse*
Rylant, Cynthia. *Best wishes*
Schotter, Roni. *Nothing ever happens on 90th Street*
Seuss, Dr. *I can write!*
Spurr, Elizabeth. *The long, long letter*

Actors *see* Careers – actors

ADD *see* Handicaps – ADD

Adoption

Banish, Roslyn. *A forever family*
Bawden, Nina. *Princess Alice*
Bloom, Suzanne. *A family for Jamie*
Brodzinsky, Anne Braff. *The mulberry bird*
Bunin, Catherine. *Is that your sister?*
Caines, Jeannette. *Abby*
Chapman, Noralee. *The story of Barbara*
Cole, Joanna. *How I was adopted: Samantha's story*
Curtis, Jamie Lee. *Tell me again about the night I was born*
D'Antonio, Nancy. *Our baby from China*
Fisher, Iris L. *Katie-Bo*
Fowler, Susi Gregg. *When Joel comes home*
Freudberg, Judy. *Susan and Gordon adopt a baby*
Gabel, Susan L. *Where the sun kisses the sea*
Ginsburg, Mirra. *We adopted you, Benjamin Koo*

Girard, Linda Walvoord. *Adoption is for always*
Greenberg, Judith E. *Adopted*
Hess, Edith. *Peter and Susie find a family*
Hutchins, Pat. *Our baby is best*
Kasza, Keiko. *A mother for Choco*
Keller, Holly. *Horace*
Koehler, Phoebe. *The day we met you*
Kroll, Virginia L. *Beginnings*
Lapsley, Susan. *I am adopted*
Livingston, Carole. *"Why was I adopted?"*
London, Jonathan. *A koala for Katie*
McCully, Emily Arnold. *My real family*
McCutcheon, John. *Happy adoption day!*
MacKay, Jed. *The big secret*
Milgram, Mary. *Brothers are all the same*
Miller, Kathryn Ann. *Did my first mother love me?*
Molnar-Fenton, Stephan. *An Mei's strange and won-drous journey*
Mora, Pat. *Pablo's tree*
Nixon, Joan Lowery. *That's the spirit, Claude*
  You bet your britches, Claude
Peacock, Carol Antoinette. *Mommy far, Mommy near*
Pellegrini, Nina. *Families are different*
Rogers, Fred. *Adoption*
Rondell, Florence. *The family that grew*
Rosen, Michael J. (1954-). *Bonesy and Isabel*
Rosenberg, Maxine B. *Being adopted*
Say, Allen. *Allison*
Schnitter, Jane. *William is my brother*
Sobol, Harriet Langsam. *We don't look like our mom and dad*
Stanek, Muriel. *My little foster sister*
Stein, Sara Bonnett. *The adopted one*
Stein, Stephanie. *Lucy's feet*
Turner, Ann Warren. *Through moon and stars and night skies*
Udry, Janice May. *Theodore's parents*
Voake, Charlotte. *Mrs. Goose's baby*
Wasson, Valentina Pavlovna. *The chosen baby*

Aerialists *see* Careers – aerialists

Afghanistan *see* Foreign lands – Afghanistan

Africa *see* Foreign lands – Africa

African Americans *see* Ethnic groups in the U.S. – African Americans

Aged *see* Old age

AIDS *see* Illness – AIDS

Airplane pilots *see* Careers – airplane pilots

Airplanes, airports

Bagwell, Richard. *This is an airport*
Baker, Donna. *I want to be a pilot*
Barton, Byron. *Airplanes*
  Airport
Baumann, Kurt. *The paper airplane*
Berger, Melvin. *How do airplanes fly?*
Brenner, Anita. *I want to fly*
Brown, Don. *Ruth Law thrills a nation*
Brown, Margaret Wise. *Streamlined pig*

Browne, Eileen. *No problem*
Browne, Gerard. *The aircraft lift-the-flap book*
Buchanan, Heather S. *George Mouse learns to fly*
Bunting, Eve (Anne Evelyn). *Fly away home*
Bursik, Rose. *Amelia's fantastic flight*
Butler, Dorothy. *A happy tale*
Cave, Ron. *Airplanes*
Cotler, Joanna. *Sky above earth below*
Crews, Donald. *Flying*
Demarest, Chris L. *Lindbergh Plane*
Duchess of York. *Budgie at Bendick's Point*
  Budgie the little helicopter
Emberley, Ed (Edward Randolph). *Cars, boats, and planes*
Floca, Brian. *Five trucks*
Florian, Douglas. *Airplane ride*
Fort, Patrick. *Redbird*
Gay, Michel. *Bibi takes flight*
  Little plane
Gibbons, Gail. *Flying*
Gramatky, Hardie. *Loopy*
Ingoglia, Gina. *The big book of real airplanes*
Joseph, Lynn. *Fly, Bessie, fly*
Krementz, Jill. *Jamie goes on an airplane*
Lenski, Lois. *The little airplane*
Lindbergh, Reeve. *Nobody owns the sky*
Loomis, Christine. *We're going on a trip*
McPhail, David M. *First flight*
Magee, Doug. *Let's fly from A to Z*
Mantegazza, Giovanna. *Look inside an airplane*
Morgan, Allen. *Matthew and the midnight pilot*
Munsch, Robert N. *Angela's airplane*
Nolan, Dennis. *Wizard McBean and his flying machine*
O'Donnell, Peter. *Dizzy*
Oechsli, Helen. *Fly away!*
Olschewski, Alfred. *We fly*
Ormerod, Jan. *Miss Mouse takes off*
Pallotta, Jerry. *The airplane alphabet book*
Petty, Kate. *On a plane*
Planes
Potter, Tony. *See how it works: planes*
Provensen, Alice. *The glorious flight*
Rand, Gloria. *Salty takes off*
Richards, Jon. *Jetliners*
Rockwell, Anne F. *Planes*
Rogers, Fred. *Going on an airplane*
Ross, Pat. *Your first airplane trip*
Royston, Angela. *Planes*
Ryan, Pam Muñoz. *Amelia and Eleanor go for a ride*
Schulz, Charles M. *Snoopy's facts and fun book about planes*
Schulz, Walter A. *Will and Orv*
Seibold, J. Otto. *Mr. Lunch takes a plane ride*
Seymour, Peter S. *Pilots*
Siebert, Diane. *Plane song*
Spier, Peter. *Bored - nothing to do!*
Testa, Fulvio. *The paper airplane*
Thompson, Brenda. *Famous planes*
Ungerer, Tomi. *The Mellops go flying*
Wheeling, Lynn. *When you fly*
Wilson-Max, Ken. *Little red plane*
Young, Miriam Burt. *If I flew a plane*
Zaffo, George J. *The book of real airplanes*
  The giant nursery book of things that go

Airports *see* Airplanes, airports

Alaska

Blake, Robert J. *Akiak*
Boyle, Doe. *Gray wolf pup*
Carlstrom, Nancy White. *Midnight dance of the snow-shoe hare*
   Raven and river
Dixon, Ann. *The blueberry shoe*
Fowler, Susi Gregg. *Circle of thanks*
Griese, Arnold A. *Anna's Athabaskan summer*
Magdanz, James S. *Go home, river*
Martin, Rafe. *The eagle's gift*
Miller, Debbie S. *A caribou journey*
Nicolai, Margaret. *Kitaq goes ice fishing*
Rand, Gloria. *Baby in a basket*
   Prince William
   Salty sails north
   Salty takes off
Schoenherr, John. *Bear*
Seibert, Patricia. *Mush!*

Albatrosses *see* Birds – albatrosses

Alcoholism *see* Illness – alcoholism

Aleuts *see* Indians of North America – Aleuts

Algonquian Indians *see* Indians of North America – Algonquian

Aliens

Camp, Lindsay. *Why?*
Kirk, Daniel. *Hush, little alien*
Layton, Neal. *Smile if you're human*
McNaughton, Colin. *Here come the aliens!*
McPhail, David M. *Tinker and Tom and the Star Baby*
Mooser, Stephen. *Funnyman meets the monster from outer space*
Pinkwater, Daniel Manus. *Guys from space*
Pryor, Bonnie. *Mr. Munday and the space creatures*
Rix, Jamie. *The last chocolate cookie*
Rosen, Michael (1946-). *Mission Ziffoid*
Shields, Carol Diggory. *Martian rock*
Valfre, Edward. *Vacationers from outer space*
Weston, Martha. *Space guys!*
Whatley, Bruce. *Captain Pajamas*
Willis, Jeanne. *The long blue blazer*
Wood, Audrey. *The Christmas adventure of Space Elf Sam*
Ziegler, Ursina. *Squaps the moonling*

Allergies *see* Illness – allergies

Alligators *see* Reptiles – alligators, crocodiles

Alphabet books *see* ABC books

Alzheimer's *see* Illness – Alzheimer's

Amazon *see* Foreign lands – Amazon

Ambition *see* Character traits – ambition

American Indians *see* Indians of Central America; Indians of North America; Indians of South America

Amish *see* Ethnic groups in the U.S. – Amish

Amphibians *see* Frogs and toads; Reptiles

Anasazi Indians *see* Indians of North America – Anasazi

Anatomy

Allen, Robert. *Ten little babies eat*
Anholt, Catherine. *One, two, three, count with me*
Arnold, Tedd. *Parts*
Artell, Mike. *Legs*
Barner, Bob. *Dem bones*
Blegvad, Lenore. *This is me*
Boynton, Sandra. *Horns to toes and in between*
Brown, Laurie Krasny. *What's the big secret?*
Campbell, Rod. *It's mine*
Caputo, Robert. *More than just pets*
Carle, Eric. *From head to toe*
   My very first book of heads and tails
Castle, Sue. *Face talk, hand talk, body talk*
Cho, Shinta. *The gas we pass*
Clark, Sue. *Bodies*
Cole, Brock. *The giant's toe*
Cole, Joanna. *The magic school bus inside the human body*
   Your insides
Cummings, Phil. *Goodness gracious!*
Elkin, Benjamin. *Gillespie and the guards*
Facklam, Margery. *But not like mine*
Faulkner, Keith. *This is me*
Hazen, Barbara Shook. *The me I see*
Hindley, Judy. *Eyes, nose, fingers and toes*
Hirschmann, Linda. *In a lick of a flick of a tongue*
Hooks, William H. *Read-a-rebus*
Jackson, Ellen B. *The book of slime*
Jeram, Anita. *Bill's belly button*
Kates, Bobbi Jane. *We're different, we're the same*
Kelley, True. *Look, baby! Listen, baby! Do, baby!*
Kilroy, Sally. *Babies' bodies*
Krauss, Ruth. *Eyes, nose, fingers, toes*
MacKinnon, Debbie. *All about me*
Manning, Mick. *My body, your body*
Markle, Sandra. *Outside and inside alligators*
   Outside and inside bats
   Outside and inside you
Martin, Bill (William Ivan). *Here are my hands*
Moon, Nicola. *At the beginning of a pig*
Munsch, Robert N. *Good families don't*
My body
Nanao, Jun. *Contemplating your bellybutton*
Pluckrose, Henry Arthur. *Fur and feathers*
   Paws and claws
Rauzon, Mark J. *Feet, flippers, hooves, and hands*
Rothman, Joel. *This can lick a lollipop*
Rotner, Shelley. *The body book*
Royston, Angela. *My body*
Schoen, Mark. *Bellybuttons are navels*
Sharmat, Marjorie Weinman. *Helga high-up*
Shott, Steve (Stephen). *Look at me*
Showers, Paul. *A drop of blood*
   How you talk
   You can't make a move without your muscles

Singer, Marilyn. *The one and only me*
Smallman, Clare. *Outside in*
Stinson, Kathy. *The bare naked book*
Waxman, Stephanie. *What is a girl? What is a boy?*
Willis, Jeanne. *The boy who lost his bellybutton*

Anatomy – ears

Bolliger, Max. *The rabbit with the sky blue ears*
Davison, Martine. *Robby visits the doctor*
Greenway, Shirley. *Here's ears*
Irbinskas, Heather. *How Jackrabbit got his very long ears*
Perkins, Al. *The ear book*
Rauzon, Mark J. *Eyes and ears*
Rowe, Jeannette. *Whose ears?*
Showers, Paul. *Ears are for hearing*

Anatomy – eyes

Bailey, Jill. *Eyes*
Naylor, Phyllis Reynolds. *Jennifer Jean, the Cross-Eyed Queen*
Patterson, Elizabeth Burman. *Whose eyes are these?*
Rauzon, Mark J. *Eyes and ears*
Seuss, Dr. *The eye book*
Showers, Paul. *Look at your eyes*
Thomson, Ruth. *Eyes*
Worthy, Judith. *Eyes*

Anatomy – faces

Anno, Mitsumasa. *Anno's faces*
Brenner, Barbara A. *Faces, faces, faces*
Butterworth, Nick. *Making faces*
Clark, Sue. *Faces*
Emberley, Ed (Edward Randolph). *Ed Emberley's crazy mixed-up face game*
Intrater, Roberta Grobel. *Two eyes, a nose, and a mouth*
Isaacs, Gwynne L. *Baby face*
Miller, Margaret. *Baby faces*
Pienkowski, Jan. *Faces*
Rotner, Shelley. *Faces*
Yep, Laurence. *The city of dragons*
Yudell, Lynn Deena. *Make a face*

Anatomy – feet

Aliki. *My feet*
Bailey, Jill. *Feet*
Blanchard, Arlene. *Sounds my feet make*
Chase, Catherine. *Feet*
Goor, Ron. *All kinds of feet*
Hamm, Diane Johnston. *How many feet in the bed?*
Holzenthaler, Jean. *My feet do*
Machotka, Hana. *What neat feet!*
Morgenstern, Constance. *Good night, feet*
Neidigh, Sherry. *Creatures at my feet*
Paul, Ann Whitford. *Hello toes! Hello feet!*
Rauzon, Mark J. *Feet, flippers, hooves, and hands*
Rowe, Jeannette. *Whose feet?*
Schertle, Alice. *My two feet*
Schubert, Ingrid. *Little big feet*
Seuss, Dr. *The foot book*
Waller, Barrett. *New feet for old*
Walton, Rick. *My two hands, my two feet*
Weiss, Leatie. *Funny feet!*

Anatomy – hands

Aliki. *My hands*
Baer, Edith. *The wonder of hands*
Blume, Karin. *My new friends*
Calmenson, Stephanie. *Kinderkittens, show-and-tell*
Ehlert, Lois. *Hands*
Holzenthaler, Jean. *My hands can*
Kroll, Virginia L. *Hands!*
Perkins, Al. *Hand, hand, fingers, thumb*
Price, Hope Lynne. *These hands*
Rauzon, Mark J. *Feet, flippers, hooves, and hands*
Ryder, Joanne. *My father's hands*
Walton, Rick. *My two hands, my two feet*

Anatomy – heads

Bishop, Claire Huchet. *The man who lost his head*
Miller, Margaret. *What's on my head?*

Anatomy – legs

Greenway, Shirley. *Legs and all*
Mead, Katherine. *How spiders got eight legs*

Anatomy – mouths

Bailey, Jill. *Mouths*

Anatomy – noses

Bailey, Jill. *Noses*
Bentley, Nancy. *I've got your nose!*
Boujon, Claude. *The fairy with the long nose*
Brown, Marc Tolon. *Arthur's nose*
Caple, Kathy. *The biggest nose*
Dubov, Christine Salac. *Aleksandra, where is your nose?*
Faulkner, Keith. *The long-nosed pig*
Fazzi, Maura. *The circus of mystery*
Hawcock, David. *Whose nose?*
Hutton, Warwick. *The nose tree*
Johnston, Tony. *The badger and the magic fan*
Krüss, James. *Johnny Longnose*
Machotka, Hana. *Breathtaking noses*
Moncure, Jane Belk. *What your nose knows!*
Ormerod, Jan. *This little nose*
Perkins, Al. *The nose book*
Rowe, Jeannette. *Whose nose?*

Anatomy – skeletons

Ahlberg, Allan. *The black cat*
    Dinosaur dreams
    The ghost train
    Mystery tour
    The pet shop
    Skeleton crew
Ahlberg, Janet. *Funnybones*
Balestrino, Philip. *The skeleton inside you*
Esbensen, Barbara Juster. *Sponges are skeletons*
Faulkner, Keith. *Basil Rattlebones*
Gross, Ruth Belov. *A book about your skeleton*
Johnston, Tony. *The ghost of Nicholas Greebe*
    Soup bone
Loredo, Elizabeth. *Boogie Bones*
McDonald, Megan. *The bone keeper*
McMullan, Kate (Hall). *Skeletons! Skeletons! All about bones*

Spohn, David. *Nate's treasure*
Stevenson, James. *The most amazing dinosaur*
Villoldo, Alberto. *Skeleton woman*

Anatomy – skin

Grossman, Bill. *The bear whose bones were Jezebel Jones*
Hawcock, David. *Whose coat?*
Kipling, Rudyard. *How the rhinoceros got his skin*
Machotka, Hana. *Outstanding outsides*
Pluckrose, Henry Arthur. *Skin, shell and scale*
Sandeman, Anna. *Skin, teeth, and hair*
Showers, Paul. *Your skin and mine*

Anatomy – tails

Greenway, Shirley. *A tale of tails*
Gregg, Andy. *Great Rabbit and the long-tailed Wildcat*
Machotka, Hana. *Terrific tails*

Anatomy – teeth *see* Teeth

Anatomy – thumbs *see* Thumb sucking

Anatomy – toes

Bowie, C. W. *Busy toes*
Dubov, Christine Salac. *Aleksandra, where are your toes?*
Elias, Joyce. *Whose toes are those?*
Hawkins, Colin. *This little pig*
Jakob, Donna. *Tiny toes*
Paul, Ann Whitford. *Hello toes! Hello feet!*

Angels

Absolutely angels
Aichinger, Helga. *The shepherd*
Andersen, H. C. (Hans Christian). *The red shoes*
Arnold, Mary. *The fussy angel*
Benét, William Rose. *Timothy's angels*
Brown, Abbie Farwell. *The Christmas angel*
Brown, Ruth. *The shy little angel*
Clements, Andrew. *Bright Christmas*
Collington, Peter. *The angel and the soldier boy*
Cowen-Fletcher, Jane. *Baby angels*
Downes, Belinda. *Every little angel's handbook*
Garland, Michael. *Angel cat*
Greenfield, Eloise. *Angels*
Greeson, Janet. *The stingy baker*
Gregory, Valiska. *Looking for angels*
Hoffman, Mary. *An angel just like me*
Ives, Penny. *The golden angel*
    The snow angel
Kavanaugh, James J. *The crooked angel*
Knight, Hilary. *Angels and berries and candy canes*
Krahn, Fernando. *A funny friend from heaven*
Lathrop, Dorothy Pulis. *An angel in the woods*
Lester, Julius. *What a truly cool world*
Lucado, Max. *Alabaster's song*
McAllister, Angela. *The snow angel*
Martin, Judith. *The tree angel*
Marzollo, Jean. *Snow angel*
Myers, Walter Dean. *Brown angels*
    Glorious angels
Paterson, Katherine. *The angel and the donkey*
Pittman, Helena Clare. *The angel tree*
Prose, Francine. *The angel's mistake*
    Dybbuk

Ragz, M. M. *Lost little angel*
Rodriguez, Anita. *Jamal and the angel*
Rylant, Cynthia. *Dog Heaven*
Safran, Sheri. *The musical cherub*
    The painted cherub
Sawyer, Ruth. *The Christmas Anna angel*
Shannon, Mark. *The acrobat and the angel*
Stone, Phoebe. *What night do the angels wander?*
Tangvald, Christine Harder. *Hey, Mr. Angel!*
Tazewell, Charles. *The littlest angel*
Thomas, Kathy. *The angel's quest*
Turner, Ann Warren. *Angel hide and seek*
Vainio, Pirkko. *The Christmas angel*
Wallace, Ian. *Morgan the magnificent*
Weller, Frances Ward. *The angel of Mill Street*
Willard, Nancy. *The high rise glorious skittle skat roarious sky pie angel food cake*
Zimelman, Nathan. *The star of Melvin*

Anger *see* Emotions – anger

Animals *see also* Birds; Frogs and toads; Reptiles

Aardema, Verna. *Princess Gorilla and a new kind of water*
    Rabbit makes a monkey of lion
    Traveling to Tondo
    The vingananee and the tree toad
    What's so funny, Ketu?
    Who's in Rabbit's house?
    Why mosquitoes buzz in people's ears
Abisch, Roz. *The clever turtle*
Abolafia, Yossi. *Fox tale*
Ackerman, Karen. *This old house*
Ada, Alma Flor. *Dear Peter Rabbit*
    The unicorn of the west
Adler, David A. *The carsick zebra and other riddles*
Adlerman, Dan. *Africa calling*
Æsop. *Animal fables from Æsop*
    The lion and the mouse and other Æsop fables
    Seven fables from Æsop
Agee, Jon. *Dmitri the astronaut*
Agell, Charlotte. *To the island*
Ahlberg, Allan. *Big bad pig*
Aitken, Amy. *Kate and Mona in the jungle*
    Wanda's circus
Akass, Susan. *Number nine duckling*
Albert, Richard E. *Alejandro's gift*
Alborough, Jez. *Beaky*
    Can you jump like a kangaroo?
    Can you peck like a hen?
    Clothesline
    Duck in the truck
    Hide and seek
    There's something at the mail slot
    Watch out! Big Bro's coming!
Alda, Arlene. *Pig, horse, or cow, don't wake me now*
    Sheep, sheep, sheep, help me fall asleep
Aldridge, Josephine Haskell. *The best of friends*
    A possible tree
Alexander, Martha G. *Pigs say oink*
Aliki. *My visit to the aquarium*
    My visit to the zoo
    Wild and woolly mammoths
Allamand, Pascale. *The animals who changed their colors*
    The camel who left the zoo
Allan, Jonathan. *Two by two by two*

Allard, Harry. *Bumps in the night*
Allen, Gertrude E. *Everyday animals*
Allen, Jeffrey. *Mary Alice, operator number 9*
 Nosey Mrs. Rat
Allen, Jonathan. *A bad case of animal nonsense*
Allen, Linda. *Mrs. Simkin's bed*
Allen, Marjorie N. *One, two, three – ah-choo!*
Allen, Martha Dickson. *Real life monsters*
Allen, Pamela. *Mr. Archimedes' bath*
 Who sank the boat?
Allen, Robert. *The zoo book*
Alphabestiary
Amery, H. *At the zoo*
 The farm picture book
 The zoo picture book
Ancona, George. *Handtalk zoo*
Andersen, H. C. (Hans Christian). *The emperor's*
 new clothes, ill. by Robert Byrd
Anderson, Laurie Halse. *Ndito runs*
Anderson, Lena. *Bunny story*
 Tick-tock
Andreae, Giles. *Rumble in the jungle*
Anholt, Catherine. *Chaos at Cold Custard Farm*
 A kiss like this
 Twins, two by two
Animal 123's
Anno, Mitsumasa. *Anno's animals*
 Anno's masks
Aoki, Hisako. *Santa's favorite story*
Apperley, Dawn. *In the jungle*
Apple, Margot. *Blanket*
Applebaum, Stan. *Going my way?*
Archambault, John. *Counting sheep*
Argent, Kerry. *Animal capers*
Ariane. *Animal stories*
Armour, Richard Willard. *Animals on the ceiling*
 Have you ever wished you were something else?
Arnold, Caroline. *Five nests*
 Mealtime for zoo animals
 Mother and baby zoo animals
 Noisytime for zoo animals
 Playtime for zoo animals
 Sleepytime for zoo animals
 Splashtime for zoo animals
 A walk by the seashore
 A walk in the desert
 A walk in the woods
 A walk on the Great Barrier Reef
 A walk up the mountain
Arnold, Katya. *The adventures of Snowwoman*
 Meow!
Arnold, Tedd. *Sounds*
Arnosky, Jim. *Crinkleroot's guide to knowing animal*
 habitats
 Crinkleroot's 25 mammals every child should know
 Every autumn comes the bear
 I see animals hiding
Artell, Mike. *Legs*
Aruego, José. *Look what I can do*
 We hide, you seek
Arvetis, Chris. *Why does it fly?*
 Why is it dark?
Asbjørnsen, P. C. (Peter Christen). *The man who*
 kept house
Asch, Frank. *Barnyard lullaby*
 Bread and honey
 I can blink
 I can roar
 Monkey face

 Moonbear's dream
Ashabranner, Brent. *I'm in the zoo, too*
Ashforth, Camilla. *Calamity*
Asimov, Isaac. *Animals of the Bible*
Atwell, Debby. *Humphrey Thud*
Atwood, Margaret. *Anna's pet*
Auch, Mary Jane. *The nutquacker*
Aulaire, Ingri Mortenson d'. *Animals everywhere*
 Children of the northlights
Austin, Margot. *A friend for Growl Bear*
Austin, Virginia. *Say please*
Axworthy, Anni. *Guess what I am*
 Guess what I'll be
Aylesworth, Jim. *The good-night kiss*
 One crow
B. B. Blacksheep and Company
Babson, Jane F. *Babson's bestiary*
Backovsky, Jan. *Trouble in Paradise*
Bahr, Robert. *Blizzard at the zoo*
Bailey, Jill. *Eyes*
 Feet
 Mouths
 Noses
Baillie, Marilyn. *Side by side*
Baker, Alan. *Gray Rabbit's one, two, three*
 Two tiny mice
 Where's mouse?
Baker, Betty. *Sonny-Boy Sim*
Baker, Eugene H. *Bicycles*
 Fire
 Home
 Outdoors
 School
 Water
Baker, Jeffrey J. W. *Patterns of nature*
Baker, Laura Nelson. *The friendly beasts*
Ballart, Elisabet. *Let's count*
Balmer, Helen. *Jungle adventure*
Balog, James. *James Balog's animals A to Z*
Bancroft, Henrietta. *Animals in winter*
Bandes, Hanna. *Sleepy river*
Bang, Betsy. *The old woman and the red pumpkin*
 The old woman and the rice thief
Bang, Molly. *Delphine*
Banks, Merry. *Animals of the night*
Bannon, Laura. *The best house in the world*
 Little people of the night
 Red mittens
 The scary thing
Bantock, Nick. *Runners, sliders, bouncers, climbers*
Barasch, Marc Ian. *No plain pets!*
Barbosa, Rogério Andrade. *African animal tales*
Barbot, Daniel. *A bicycle for Rosaura*
Bare, Colleen Stanley. *Who comes to the water hole?*
Baron, Alan. *Little Pig's bouncy ball*
 Red Fox dances
Barrett, Judi. *Animals should definitely not act like peo-*
 ple
 Animals should definitely not wear clothing
 Snake is totally tail
Barry, Robert E. *Animals around the world*
Barton, Byron. *Zoo animals*
Baruch, Dorothy. *Kappa's tug-of-war with the big*
 brown horse
Base, Graeme. *Animalia*
 My grandma lived in Gooligulch
Baskin, Leonard. *Hosie's zoo*
Bason, Lillian. *Castles and mirrors and cities of sand*
Bassett, Lisa. *A clock for Beany*

Bateman, Robert. *Safari*
Bates, Ivan. *All by myself*
Batherman, Muriel. *Animals live here*
Battles, Edith. *What does the rooster say, Yoshio?*
Bauer, Marion Dane. *If you were born a kitten*
    Sleep, little one, sleep
Baugh, Dolores M. *Let's see the animals*
Baumann, Hans. *Chip has many brothers*
Bax, Martin. *Edmond went far away*
Bayer, Jane. *A my name is Alice*
Bayley, Nicola. *One old Oxford ox*
Baylor, Byrd. *Desert voices*
    We walk in sandy places
Beach, Stewart. *Good morning, sun's up!*
Beck, Andrea. *Elliot bakes a cake*
Becker, Bonny. *Tickly prickly*
Beifuss, John. *Armadillo Ray*
Beil, Karen Magnuson. *A cake all for me!*
Beim, Jerrold. *Eric on the desert*
Belling the cat and other stories
Belloc, Hilaire. *The bad child's book of beasts*
    The bad child's book of beasts, and more beasts for
      worse children
    The bad child's pop-up book of beasts
    More beasts for worse children
Bellville, Rod. *Large animal veterinarians*
Belpré, Pura. *Dance of the animals*
Bemelmans, Ludwig. *Rosebud*
Bender, Robert. *The A to Z beastly jamboree*
Bendick, Jeanne. *Why can't I?*
Bennett, David. *One cow moo moo*
Bennett, Jill. *Animal fair*
Berends, Polly Berrien. *I heard said the bird*
Berger, Melvin. *Prehistoric mammals*
Berger, Terry. *The turtles' picnic and other nonsense*
    stories
Berkowitz, Linda. *Alfonse, where are you?*
Bernhard, Durga. *Alphabeasts*
Bernhard, Emery. *How Snowshoe Hare rescued the*
    sun
Bernstein, Joanne E. *Creepy crawly critter riddles*
Bernstein, Margery. *Coyote goes hunting for fire*
    The first morning
Berson, Harold. *I'm bored, Ma!*
    Why the jackal won't speak to the hedgehog
Bester, Roger. *Guess what?*
Bethell, Jean. *Bathtime*
    Playmates
Bible, Charles. *Hamdaani*
Bible. Old Testament. Noah. *Noah and the ark*, ill.
    by Pauline Baynes
    Noah and the ark, ill. by Jim Cummins
Bierhorst, John. *Doctor Coyote*
The big Peter Rabbit book
Binzen, Bill. *Alfred goes house hunting*
Birchmore, Daniel A. *Pilly, Polly, and Wee*
Biro, Val. *Gumdrop and the farmyard caper*
    Gumdrop and the great sausage caper
Bischhoff-Miersch, Andrea. *Do you know the differ-*
    ence?
Bishop, Roma. *Animals*
    My first pop-up book of prehistoric animals
    On a safari
Black, Charles C. *The royal nap*
Blake, Quentin. *Zagazoo*
Blathwayt, Benedict. *Tangle and the silver bird*
Bloom, Becky. *Mr. Cuckoo*
    Wolf
Blough, Glenn O. *Who lives in this meadow?*

Bodsworth, Nan. *Monkey business*
Bogacki, Tomasz. *I hate you! I like you!*
Bograd, Larry. *Egon*
Bohdal, Susi. *1,2,3, what do you see?*
    Tom cat
Bolliger, Max. *Noah and the rainbow*
Bond, Felicia. *Tumble bumble*
Bonfils, Bolette. *Peter joins the circus*
Bonino, Louise. *The cozy little farm*
Bonning, Tony. *Another fine mess*
Boon, Emilie. *1 2 3 how many animals can you see?*
    Peterkin's very own garden
    Peterkin's wet walk
Borden, Beatrice Brown. *Wild animals of Africa*
Borg, Inga. *Plupp builds a house*
Borlenghi, Patricia. *From albatross to zoo*
Bottner, Barbara. *Zoo song*
Bourgeois, Paulette. *Franklin and the thunderstorm*
    Franklin rides a bike
    Franklin's class trip
    Franklin's secret club
    Too many chickens
Bowden, Miriam. *The adventure of Paz in the land of*
    numbers
Bowen, Betsy. *Tracks in the wild*
Bowman, Peter. *I wish I were big*
Boyd, Lizi. *Lulu Crow's garden*
Boyd, Selma. *I met a polar bear*
Boynton, Sandra. *A is for angry*
    Barnyard dance!
    The going to bed book
    Good night, good night
    Moo, baa, lalala
Bozylinsky, Hannah Heritage. *Lala Salama*
Bradman, Tony. *See you later, alligator*
Brandenberg, Franz. *Aunt Nina and her nephews*
    and nieces
    Cock-a-doodle-doo
Brasch, Kate. *Prehistoric monsters*
Breebaart, Joeri. *When I die, will I get better?*
Breeze, Lynn. *Baby's animals*
Brennan, John. *Zoo day*
Brenner, Barbara A. *Ostrich feathers*
Brent, Isabelle. *Noah's ark*
Brett, Jan. *Annie and the wild animals*
    Armadillo rodeo
    Berlioz the bear
    The hat
Brice, Tony. *Baby animals*
Brierley, Louise. *King Lion and his cooks*
Brimner, Larry Dane. *Dinosaurs dance*
Bro, Marguerite (Harmon). *The animal friends of*
    Peng-u
Brock, Emma Lillian. *Nobody's mouse*
    Surprise balloon
Brooke, L. Leslie (Leonard Leslie). *Johnny Crow's*
    garden
    Johnny Crow's new garden
    Johnny Crow's party
Brooks, Alan. *Frogs jump*
Brown, Andrew. *Armored animals*
    Dangerous animals
Brown, Craig McFarland. *My barn*
Brown, Ken (Ken James). *Mucky Pup*
Brown, Marc Tolon. *Arthur and the true Francine*
    Arthur goes to camp
    Arthur's April fool
    Arthur's Christmas
    Arthur's eyes

Duck in the pond
Elephant in the jungle
Cartwright, Ann. *Norah's ark*
Caseley, Judith. *Mickey's class play*
Casey, Patricia. *Beep! Beep! Oink! Oink! animals in the city*
Cluck cluck
Cassedy, Sylvia. *Red dragonfly on my shoulder*
Cassidy, Dianne. *Circus animals*
Castle, Caroline. *Herbert Binns and the flying tricycle*
Catalanotto, Peter. *Mr. Mumble*
Catchpole, Clive. *Deserts*
Grasslands
Jungles
Mountains
Cathon, Laura E. *Tot Botot and his little flute*
Cauley, Lorinda Bryan. *The animal kids*
The bake-off
Causley, Charles. *"Quack!" said the billy-goat*
Cave, Kathryn. *Out for the count*
Cazet, Denys. *Are there any questions?*
The duck with squeaky feet
Frosted glass
Lucky me
Mother night
Never spit on your shoes
Nothing at all
Sunday
Cech, John. *Django*
Cecil, Laura. *Noah and the space ark*
Chalmers, Audrey. *Hundreds and hundreds of pancakes*
Chalmers, Mary. *A Christmas story*
Easter parade
Chapman, Cheryl. *Pass the fritters, critters*
Charles, Donald. *Calico Cat at the zoo*
Shaggy dog's animal alphabet
Chase, Catherine. *Noah's ark*
Chen, Tony. *Animals showing off*
Cherry, Lynne. *The great kapok tree*
Who's sick today?
Chichester Clark, Emma. *Little Miss Muffet's count-along surprise*
Chicken Little. *Chicken Licken*, ill. by Jutta Ash
Chicken Licken, ill. by Gavin Bishop
Chicken Little, ill. by Sally Hobson
Henny Penny, ill. by Emily Bolam
Henny Penny, ill. by Stephen Butler
Henny Penny, ill. by Paul Galdone
Henny Penny, ill. by William Stobbs
Henny-Penny, ill. by Jane Wattenberg
The sky is falling
The story of Chicken Licken
Chinery, Michael. *Desert animals*
Grassland animals
Cho, Shinta. *The gas we pass*
Chocolate, Deborah M. Newton. *Imani in the belly*
Chorao, Kay. *Carousel round and round*
Lemon moon
Number one number fun
Chottin, Ariane. *A home for Little Turtle*
Chouinard, Roger. *The amazing animal alphabet book*
One magic box
Christelow, Eileen. *Glenda Feathers casts a spell*
Olive and the magic hat
The robbery at the diamond dog diner
Christensen, Gardell Dano. *Mrs. Mouse needs a house*

Christiana, David. *White nineteens*
Christmas in the stable, ill. by Beverly K. Duncan
Chukovskii, Kornei Ivanovich. *Telephone*
Chwast, Seymour. *Mr. Merlin and the turtle*
The twelve circus rings
Cimarusti, Marie Torres. *Peek-a-moo*
Clément, Claude. *The hungry duckling*
Clement, Rod. *Just another ordinary day*
Clewes, Dorothy. *Henry Hare's boxing match*
The wild wood
Climo, Shirley. *The cobweb Christmas*
The little red ant and the great big crumb
Clymer, Ted. *The horse and the bad morning*
Coats, Laura Jane. *Ten little animals*
Coatsworth, Elizabeth. *A peaceable kingdom, and other poems*
Cober, Alan E. *Cober's choice*
Cock Robin. *The courtship, merry marriage, and feast of Cock Robin and Jenny Wren*
Who killed Cock Robin?, ill. by William Stobbs
Coffey, Maria. *A cat in a kayak*
Cohen, Caron Lee. *Pigeon, pigeon*
Colby, C. B. (Carroll Burleigh). *Who lives there?*
Who went there?
Cole, Babette. *Tarzanna!*
Cole, Joanna. *Animal sleepyheads*
Evolution
It's too noisy
Large as life daytime animals
Large as life nighttime animals
Cole, Michael. *Head in the sand*
Cole, Sheila. *The hen that crowed*
When the tide is low
Cole, William. *I went to the animal fair*
A zooful of animals
Coleman, Michael. *Lazy Ozzie*
Collard, Sneed B. *Creepy creatures*
Collicott, Sharleen. *Seeing stars*
Toestomper and the caterpillars
Collins, Pat Lowery. *Tomorrow, up and away!*
Colman, Hila. *Watch that watch*
Cone, Molly. *Squishy, misty, damp & muddy*
Conklin, Gladys. *I caught a lizard*
Conrad, Pam. *Animal lingo*
Animal lullabies
Cooper, Ann (Ann C.). *In the forest*
Cooper, Helen (Helen F.). *Pumpkin soup*
Cooper, Melrose. *Pets!*
Cooper, Susan. *Matthew's dragon*
Coplans, Peta. *Spaghetti for Suzy*
Corey, Dorothy. *A shot for baby bear*
Will it ever be my birthday?
Cormack, M. Grant. *Animal tales from Ireland*
Cortesi, Wendy W. *Explore a spooky swamp*
Cosgrove, Margaret. *Wintertime for animals*
Cousins, Lucy. *Country animals*
Farm animals
Garden animals
Happy birthday, Maisy
Katy Cat and Beaky Boo
Maisy dresses up
Maisy's bedtime
Maisy's pool
Noah's ark
Pet animals
What can rabbit hear?
What can rabbit see?
Coville, Bruce. *Sarah's unicorn*
Cowcher, Helen. *Rain forest*

Cowley, Stewart. *Down Ladybug Lane*
  In dragonfly forest
  In songbird jungle
  On Butterfly Farm
  What's that sound?
Coxe, Molly. *Whose footprints?*
Craig, M. Jean. *Spring is like the morning*
Craighead, Charles. *The eagle and the river*
Craver, Mike. *Beaver ball at the bug club*
Crawford, Ron. *Pet?*
Crawford, Sheryl Ann. *The baby who changed the world*
Crebbin, June. *Cows in the kitchen*
Creighton, Jill. *One day there was nothing to do*
Cremins, Robert. *My animal ABC*
  My animal Mother Goose
Crimi, Carolyn. *Don't need friends*
Cristini, Ermanno. *In the pond*
  In the woods
Cross, Genevieve. *A trip to the yard*
Crowe, Robert L. *Tyler Toad and the thunder*
Crowther, Robert. *Animal rap!*
  Animal snap!
  Who lives in the country?
  Who lives in the garden?
Croxford, Vera. *All kinds of animals*
Crump, Donald J. *Creatures small and furry*
Cummings, Pat. *Carousel*
Curle, Jock J. *The four good friends*
Curry, Peter. *Animals*
Cushman, Doug. *The ABC mystery*
  The mystery of the monkey's maze
Cutler, Ivor. *The animal house*
  Herbert
Cuyler, Margery. *The biggest, best snowman*
  That's good! that's bad!
Czernecki, Stefan. *The singing snake*
Dahl, Roald. *The enormous crocodile*
  The giraffe and the pelly and me
Dale, Penny. *Daisy Rabbit's tree house*
  The elephant tree
Dalmais, Anne-Marie. *And may the best animal win!*
  The Elephant's airplane and other machines
Daly, Kathleen N. *Today's biggest animals*
  Unusual animals
Damjan, Mischa. *The big squirrel and the little rhinoceros*
Darling, Kathy (Mary Kathleen). *Amazon A B C*
  Arctic babies
  Desert babies
  Pecos Bill finds a horse
  Rain forest babies
  Seashore babies
Davenier, Christine. *Leon and Albertine*
Davidson, Jill A. *And that's what happened to little Lucy*
Davis, Douglas F. *There's an elephant in the garage*
Davis, Katie (Katie I.). *Who hops?*
Davis, Lee. *The lifesize animal opposites book*
Davol, Marguerite W. *Batwings and the curtain of night*
  How snake got his hiss
Davoll, Barbara. *Dusty Mole, private eye*
Day, Alexandra. *The Christmas we moved to the barn*
  Helping the animals
  Helping the flowers and trees
  Helping the night
  Helping the sun
Day, David. *King of the woods*

Day, Marie. *Dragon in the rocks*
DeBoer, Jesslyn. *Getting ready for Christmas*
De Groat, Diane. *Happy Birthday to you, you belong in a zoo*
  Roses are pink, your feet really stink
  Trick or treat, smell my feet
DeLage, Ida. *ABC triplets at the zoo*
  Good morning, lady
Delamare, David. *The Christmas secret*
Delessert, Etienne. *The endless party*
Delton, Judy. *The perfect Christmas gift*
Demarest, Chris L. *Farmer Nat*
  Kitman and Willy at sea
Demi. *A Chinese zoo*
  Demi's basket of books
  Demi's Christmas surprise
  Demi's count the animals 1-2-3
  Demi's dragons and fantastic creatures
  Demi's find the animals A B C
  Demi's opposites
  Find Demi's baby animals
  Find Demi's sea creatures
  Three little elephants
Demuth, Patricia Brennan. *Ornery morning*
Denim, Sue. *The Dumb Bunnies go to the zoo*
Dennard, Deborah. *Do cats have nine lives?*
  Travis and the better mousetrap
Dennis, Suzanne E. *Answer me that*
Dennis, Wesley. *Flip*
Denton, Terry. *Home is the sailor*
De Paola, Tomie (Thomas Anthony). *Bill and Pete to the rescue*
  Country farm
  The hunter and the animals
  Jingle, the Christmas clown
  Noah and the ark
De Posadas Mane, Carmen. *Mister North Wind*
De Regniers, Beatrice Schenk. *Going for a walk*
  It does not say meow!
  May I bring a friend?
De Zutter, Hank. *Who says a dog goes bow-wow?*
DiFiori, Lawrence. *Baby animals*
Dijs, Carla. *Are you my daddy?*
  Are you my mommy?
  Mommy, would you love me if . . . ?
Dionetti, Michelle V. *The day Eli went looking for bear*
Dixon, Ann. *The blueberry shoe*
Dodd, Lynley. *Find me a tiger*
  Wake up, bear
Dodds, Dayle Ann. *Do bunnies talk?*
Dodds, Siobhan. *Charles Tiger*
  Elizabeth Hen
Domanska, Janina. *What do you see?*
Domestic animals
Donaldson, Julia. *The gruffalo*
Donohue, Dorothy. *Big and little on the farm*
Dowling, Paul. *Happy birthday, Owl*
  Where are you going, Jimmy?
  You need a bath, Mustard
Dragonwagon, Crescent. *Alligator arrived with apples*
  Alligators and others all year long!
Dryden, Emma. *Good morning - good night*
Du Bois, William Pène. *Bear circus*
  Bear party
Dubov, Christine Salac. *Oink! and other sounds*
Duff, Maggie (Margaret K.). *Dancing turtle*
Duffy, Dee Dee (Deborah). *Barnyard tracks*
Duke, Kate. *Aunt Isabel tells a good one*

If you walk down this road
Dunbar, Joyce. *Baby bird*
   Eggday
Duncan, Riana. *A nutcracker in a tree*
   When Emily woke up angry
Dunn, Judy. *The animals of Buttercup Farm*
Dunn, Phoebe. *Baby's animal friends*
Dunphy, Madeleine. *Here is the Arctic winter*
   Here is the tropical rain forest
Dunrea, Olivier. *Deep down underground*
Du Quette, Keith. *Hotel Animal*
   Ripping day for a picnic
Durant, Alan. *Mouse party*
   Snake supper
Durrell, Julie. *Mouse tails*
Duvoisin, Roger Antoine. *A for the ark*
   The crocodile in the tree
   Jasmine
   Our Veronica goes to Petunia's farm
   Petunia
   Petunia and the song
   Petunia, beware!
   Petunia takes a trip
   Petunia, the silly goose
   Petunia's treasure
Easter babies
Easton, Violet. *Elephants never jump*
Edens, Cooper. *An ABC of fashionable animals*
Edwards, Pamela Duncan. *The grumpy morning*
   Some smug slug
   The worrywarts
Edwards, Richard. *The forest child*
   Moon frog
Egan, Tim. *The blunder of the Rogues*
   Friday night at Hodges' café
   Metropolitan cow
Ehrlich, Amy. *Lucy's winter tale*
   Parents in the pigpen, pigs in the tub
Eichenberg, Fritz. *Dancing in the moon*
Elborn, Andrew. *Noah and the ark and the animals*
Elias, Joyce. *Whose toes are those?*
Elkin, Benjamin. *Why the sun was late*
Elting, Mary. *Q is for duck*
Emberley, Barbara. *One wide river to cross*
Emberley, Ed (Edward Randolph). *Animals*
Enderle, Judith (Ann) Ross. *A pile of pigs*
   Six snowy sheep
   Upstairs
Erickson, Russell E. *Warton's Christmas eve adventure*
Ernst, Lisa Campbell. *Hamilton's art show*
Ets, Marie Hall. *Another day*
   Beasts and nonsense
   Elephant in a well
   In the forest
   Just me
   Mister Penny
   Mister Penny's circus
   Play with me
Euvremer, Teryl. *The thieves of Peck's pocket*
Evans, Eva Knox. *Sleepy time*
   Where do you live?
Facklam, Margery. *But not like mine*
   I eat dinner
   I go to sleep
   Only a star
   So can I
Falda, Dominique. *The treasure chest*
Farber, Norma. *All those mothers at the manger*
   As I was crossing Boston Common

   How the hibernators came to Bethlehem
   How the left-behind beasts built Ararat
   How to ride a tiger
   When it snowed that night
   Without wings, mother, how can I fly?
Farm animals [Macmillan, 1991]
Farm animals, photos sel. by Debby Slier
Farm house
Farris, Pamela J. *Young Mouse and Elephant*
Faulkner, Keith. *My pets*
   The wide-mouthed frog
Fay, Hermann. *My zoo*
Fearnley, Jan. *Little Robin's Christmas*
Feczko, Kathy. *Umbrella parade*
Feldman, Eve B. *Animals don't wear pajamas*
Fiddle-i-fee, ill. by Diane Stanley
Fife, Dale. *The little park*
Finzel, Julia. *Large as life*
Fischer, Hans. *The birthday*
Fischetto, Laura. *Inside Noah's ark*
   The jungle is my home
Fisher, Aileen Lucia. *Anybody home?*
   Do bears have mothers too?
   We went looking
   Where does everyone go?
Flack, Marjorie. *Ask Mr. Bear*
Flanders, Michael. *Creatures great and small*
Fleming, Denise. *Barnyard banter*
   Count!
   In the small, small pond
   Where once there was a wood
Fletcher, Elizabeth. *What am I?*
Floca, Brian. *The frightful story of Harry Walfish*
Flora, James. *The day the cow sneezed*
Florian, Douglas. *At the zoo*
   Beast feast
   A bird can fly
   In the swim
Foreman, Michael. *Look! Look!*
   Panda and the bushfire
Fournier, Catharine. *The coconut thieves*
Fowler, Allan. *Cubs and colts and calves and kittens*
   Hard-to-see animals
Fowler, Richard. *Cat's cake*
   Cat's car
   Happy birthday, Mouse!
   Little Chick's big adventure
   Mr. Little's noisy car
   Mr. Little's noisy fire engine
   Mr. Little's noisy truck
Fowler, Susi Gregg. *Circle of thanks*
Fox, Charles Philip. *Mr. Stripes the gopher*
Fox, Mem. *Hattie and the fox*
   Time for bed
   Wombat divine
   Zoo-looking
Francis, Frank. *The magic wallpaper*
Frascino, Edward. *My cousin the king*
Freedman, Russell. *Farm babies*
   Hanging on
   Tooth and claw
   When winter comes
Freeman, Don. *Add-a-line alphabet*
French, Fiona. *Anancy and Mr. Dry-Bone*
French, Vivian. *Little Tiger goes shopping*
Freschet, Berniece. *Owl in the garden*
   Where's Henrietta's hen?
Friedrich, Priscilla. *The wishing well in the woods*
The friendly beasts, ill. by Sarah Chamberlain

Frith, Michael K. *Some of us walk, some fly, some swim*
A frog he would a-wooing go (folk-song). *Frog went a-courtin'*, ill. by Feodor Rojankovsky
The frog went a-courting, adapt. and ill. by Dominic Catalano
Froggie went a courting, ill. by Marjorie Priceman
Froggie went a-courting, ill. by Chris Conover
Mr. Frog went a-courting
Wendy Watson's frog went a-courting
From King Boggen's hall to nothing-at-all
Fromm, Lilo. *Muffel and Plums*
Fuchshuber, Annegert. *Two peas in a pod*
Fussenegger, Gertrud. *Noah's ark*
Futamata, Eigoro. *How not to catch a mouse*
Gackenbach, Dick. *Supposes*
Gaffney, Michael. *Secret forests*
Galdone, Paul. *Cat goes fiddle-i-fee*
Gambill, Henrietta D. *Little Christmas animals*
Gammell, Stephen. *Once upon MacDonald's farm*
Ganeri, Anita. *Animal hideaways*
The hunt for food
Gantos, Jack (John, Jr.). *The perfect pal*
Gardam, Catharine. *The animals' Christmas*
Gardner, Beau. *Can you imagine . . . ?*
Guess what?
Garelick, May. *Look at the moon*, ill. by Barbara Garrison
Look at the moon, ill. by Leonard Weisgard
Garland, Sarah. *Billy and Belle*
Garrett, Ann. *What's for lunch?*
Garten, Jan. *The alphabet tale*
Gauch, Patricia Lee. *Noah*
Gay, Michel. *Bibi's birthday surprise*
Night ride
Gay, Zhenya. *Look!*
Geis, Jacqueline. *Where the buffalo roam*
Geisert, Arthur. *After the flood*
The ark
George, Jean Craighead. *Morning, noon, and night*
George, Lindsay Barrett. *Around the pond*
In the woods
George, William T. *Christmas at Long Pond*
Fishing at Long Pond
Geraghty, Paul. *The great green forest*
Over the steamy swamp
Stop that noise!
Gerber, Carole. *Arctic dreams*
Geringer, Laura. *The cow is mooing anyhow*
Gerrard, Roy. *Mik's mammoth*
Gershator, Phillis. *When it starts to snow*
Gerstein, Mordicai. *The absolutely awful alphabet*
Daisy's garden
Noah and the great flood
William, where are you?
Gervais, Bernadette. *Voyage under the stars*
Gibbons, Gail. *Nature's green umbrella*
Prehistoric animals
Say woof!
Zoo
Giffard, Hannah. *Hens say cluck*
Striped zebra
Gilbert, Suzie. *Hawk Hill*
Ginsburg, Mirra. *The fox and the hare*
Mushroom in the rain
Gipson, Morrell. *Whose tracks are these?*
Gleeson, Brian. *The tiger and the Brahmin*
Gliori, Debi. *Mr. Bear says, "Are you there, Baby Bear?"*
Goble, Paul. *The great race of the birds and animals*

Godard, Alex. *Idora*
Godwin, Laura. *Little white dog*
Goennel, Heidi. *Heidi's zoo*
If I were a penguin . . .
Goffe, Toni. *Toby's animal rescue service*
Goffin, Josse. *Yes*
Goffstein, M. B. (Marilyn Brooke). *Natural history*
Goldsmith, Howard. *Sleepy little owl*
Goldstone, Bruce. *The beastly feast*
Gomi, Taro. *Guess who?*
My friends
Santa through the window
Goode, Diane. *The little book of farm friends*
Goode, Molly. *Mama loves*
Goodhart, Pippa. *Noah makes a boat*
Row, row, row your boat
Goodspeed, Peter. *A rhinoceros wakes me up in the morning*
Goor, Ron. *All kinds of feet*
Gorbachev, Valeri. *Where is the apple pie?*
Gordon, Shirley. *Grandma zoo*
Grabianski, Janusz. *Grabianski's wild animals*
Graham, Bob. *First there was Frances*
Graham, John. *A crowd of cows*
I love you, mouse
Grahame, Kenneth. *The open road*
The wind in the willows
The wind in the willows
The wind in the willows
The wind in the willows
Gray, Libba Moore. *Is there room on the feather bed?*
Greaves, Margaret. *The naming*
Greeley, Valerie. *Animals*
Farm animals
Field animals
Pets
Where's my share?
White is the moon
Zoo animals
Greenaway, Shirley. *Forests*
Jungles
Greene, Ellin. *The legend of the cranberry*
Greene, Rhonda Gowler. *Barnyard song*
Greenfield, Karen R. *Sister Yessa's story*
Greenway, Shirley. *Animal homes: burrows*
Can you see me?
Color me bright
Here's ears
How big am I?
How do I move?
Legs and all
A tale of tails
Two's company . . .
What do I eat?
Where do I live?
Whose baby am I?
Gregory, Valiska. *When stories fell like shooting stars*
Gretz, Susanna. *Duck takes off*
Frog, duck, and rabbit
Frog in the middle
Rabbit rambles on
Greydanus, Rose. *Animals at the zoo*
Griffith, Helen V. *Grandaddy's place*
How many candles?
Grimes, Nikki. *Minnie's new friend*
Grimm, Jacob. *The Bremen town band*
The Bremen town musicians, ill. by Donna Diamond

The Bremen town musicians, ill. by Janina Doman-ska
The Bremen town musicians, ill. by Paul Galdone
The Bremen town musicians, ill. by David Johnson
Bremen town musicians, ill. by Josef Palecek
The Bremen town musicians, ill. by Ilse Plume
The Bremen town musicians, ill. by Janet Stevens
The Bremen town musicians, ill. by Bernadette Watts
Little Red Riding Hood, ill. by John S. Goodall
The musicians of Bremen, ill. by John Segal
The musicians of Bremen, ill. by Svend Otto S
The musicians of Bremen, ill. by Martin Ursell
The traveling musicians of Bremen
Groening, Maggie. *Maggie Simpson's book of animals*
Grossman, Bill. *The bear whose bones were Jezebel Jones*
Grosvenor, Donna. *Zoo babies*
Gryspeerdt, Rebecca. *Counting friends*
Guarino, Deborah. *Is your mama a llama?*
Gullikson, Sandy. *Trouble for breakfast*
Gundersheimer, Karen. *Colors to know*
Guthrie, Donna. *Nobiah's well*
Haas, Irene. *A summertime song*
Haley, Gail E. *Noah's ark*
Hall, Donald. *Andrew the lion farmer*
Hall, Malcolm. *CariCATures*
Halpern, Shari. *My river*
Hamanaka, Sheila. *I look like a girl*
Hamberger, John. *The day the sun disappeared*
Hamilton, Virginia. *Jaguarundi*
Hamm, Diane Johnston. *Rock-a-bye farm*
Han, Oki S. *Kongi and Potgi*
Hands, Hargrave. *Duckling sees*
Little lamb sees
Hanna, Jack. *Jungle Jack Hanna's safari adventure*
The petting zoo
Hannant, Judith Stuller. *The doorknob collection of pets and pals*
Hansen, Biruta Akerbergs. *Parading with piglets*
Harris, Joel Chandler. *Jump!*
Jump again!
Harris, Susan. *Creatures that look alike*
Harrison, David Lee. *The animals' song*
Wake up, sun!
Harrison, Sarah. *In granny's garden*
Harrison, Troon. *Don't dig so deep, Nicholas!*
Harter, Debbie. *Walking through the jungle*
Hartman, Gail. *As the crow flies*
As the roadrunner runs
Hartmann, Wendy. *One sun rises*
Haseley, Dennis. *The cave of snores*
Haubensak-Tellenbach, Margrit. *The story of Noah's ark*
Hausman, Gerald. *How Chipmunk got tiny feet*
Hawcock, David. *Whose coat?*
Whose home?
Whose nose?
Hawkins, Colin. *Max and the magic word*
Where's my mommy?
Hawkinson, John. *Robins and rabbits*
Hayes, Ann. *Meet the Marching Smithereens*
Meet the orchestra
Hayes, Sarah. *The grumpalump*
Hayles, Karen. *What is stuck*
Haywood, Carolyn. *Hello, star*
Hazelaar, Cor. *Zoo dreams*
Hazen, Barbara Shook. *Where do bears sleep?*, ill. by Mary Morgan-Vanroyen
Where do bears sleep?, ill. by Ian E. Staunton

Heatwole, Marsha. *Jambo, watoto!*
Heiligman, Deborah. *On the move*
Heine, Helme. *Friends*
Friends go adventuring
Mollywoop
Three little friends: the alarm clock
Three little friends: the racing cart
Three little friends: the visitor
Hellard, Susan. *Time to get up*
Hellen, Nancy. *Animals of the jungle*
Circle farm
A visit to the farm
A visit to the zoo
Heller, Nicholas. *Mathilda the dream bear*
Heller, Ruth. *Animals born alive and well*
How to hide a gray treefrog and other amphibians
How to hide a polar bear
How to hide an octopus
Helweg, Hans. *Farm animals*
Henderson, Kathy. *Counting farm*
I can be a rancher
Hendra, Sue. *Oliver's wood*
Hendrick, Mary Jean. *If anything ever goes wrong at the zoo*
Henkes, Kevin. *Chrysanthemum*
Oh!
Henley, Claire. *At the zoo*
Dinnertime
Farm day
In the ocean
Jungle day
Playtime
Quack, quack
Henley, Karyn. *Hatch!*
Hennessy, B. G. (Barbara G.). *Eeney, Meeney, Miney, Mo*
Herriot, James. *Only one woof*
Hersom, Kathleen. *The copycat*
Hess, Paul. *Farmyard animals*
Polar animals
Rainforest animals
Safari animals
Heuck, Sigrid. *Who stole the apples?*
Higham, Jon Atlas. *Aardvark's picnic*
Hightower, Susan. *Twelve snails to one lizard*
Hill, Eric. *Spot at play*
Spot at the fair
Spot counts from 1 to 10
Spot goes to the farm
Spot on the farm
Spot's favorite baby animals
Hill, Susan. *Simba's A-Z*
Himmelman, John. *Amanda and the magic garden*
A guest is a guest
Montigue on the high seas
Hindley, Judy. *Funny walks*
Into the jungle
One by one
Ten bright eyes
Hines, Anna Grossnickle. *I'll tell you what they say*
Miss Emma's wild garden
Hippely, Hilary Horder. *Adventure on Klickitat Island*
The Hippopotamus's birthday and other poems about animals and birds
Hirschi, Ron. *Faces in the forest*
Fall
Forest
Loon lake

Karlin, Nurit. *I see, you saw*
Kastner, Jill. *Barnyard big top*
Kasza, Keiko. *A mother for Choco*
   When the elephant walks
Katz, Bobbi. *The creepy crawly book*
Kaufmann, John. *Flying giants of long ago*
Keats, Ezra Jack. *Pet show!*
Keller, Holly. *Furry*
   That's mine, Horace
   Too big
   Will it rain?
Kelley, True. *Look again at funny animals*
Kellogg, Steven (Stephen). *Aster Aardvark's alphabet adventures*
   Chicken Little
Kemp, Anthea. *Mr. Percy's magic greenhouse*
Kemp, Moira. *Lift-the-flap chick*
   Lift-the-flap kitten
Kennaway, Adrienne. *Little elephant's walk*
Kennedy, X. J. *The beasts of Bethlehem*
Kent, Jack. *Joey runs away*
   Little Peep
Kepes, Juliet. *Five little monkeys*
Kerins, Tony (Anthony). *The brave ones*
Kessler, Brad. *Brer Rabbit and Boss Lion*
Kessler, Ethel. *Are there hippos on the farm?*
   Do baby bears sit in chairs?
   Is there an elephant in your kitchen?
Kessler, Leonard P. *The big mile race*
   Do you have any carrots?
Kharms, Daniil. *The story of a boy named Will, who went sledding down the hill*
Kherdian, David. *The animal*
   The cat's midsummer jamboree
Kidd, Richard. *Monsieur Thermidor*
Kilroy, Sally. *Animal noises*
   Babies' zoo
Kimmel, Eric A. *Anansi and the moss-covered rock*
   Anansi and the talking melon
   I took my frog to the library
   The rooster's antlers
King, Bob. *Sitting on the farm*
Kingman, Lee. *Peter's long walk*
Kipling, Rudyard. *The elephant's child*, ill. by Louise Brierley
   The elephant's child, ill. by Lorinda Bryan Cauley
   The elephant's child, ill. by Tim Raglin
   The elephant's child, ill. by John A. Rowe
   How the camel got his hump, ill. by Quentin Blake
   How the camel got his hump, ill. by Tim Raglin
   The miracle of the mountain
Kirn, Ann. *Beeswax catches a thief*
Kitchen, Bert. *And so they build*
   Animal alphabet
   Animal numbers
   Pig in a barrow
   Somewhere today
   Tenrec's twigs
   When hunger calls
Knight, Bertram T. *Working at a zoo*
Knowles, Sheena. *Edward the emu*
Knüppel, Helga. *The adventures of Christabel Crocodile*
Knutson, Barbara. *How the guinea fowl got her spots*
Kobayashi, Robert. *Maria Mazaretti loves spaghetti*
Kobayashi, Yuji. *Miss Josephine's secret walk*
Koch, Michelle. *Hoot, howl, hiss*
Koelling, Caryl. *Animal mix and match*
Koide, Tan. *May we sleep here tonight?*

Kolar, Bob. *Stomp, stomp!*
Koller, Jackie French. *Fish fry tonight*
   Mole and Shrew step out
Komori, Atsushi. *Animal mothers*
Koopmans, Loek. *The woodcutter's mitten*
Koralek, Jenny. *The friendly fox*
Koscielniak, Bruce. *Euclid Bunny delivers the mail*
Krahn, Fernando. *The biggest Christmas tree on earth*
Kramer, Anthony Penta. *Numbers on parade*
Kraus, Robert. *The adventures of Wise Old Owl*
   Animal families
   Buggy Bear cleans up
   Ella the bad speller
   Good morning, Miss Gator
   Here comes Tardy Toad
   How Spider saved Easter
   Klunky Monkey, new kid in class
   Robert Kraus' a sunny day in Babytown
   Springfellow's parade
   Squirmy's big secret
   The three friends
   Wise Old Owl's Christmas adventure
Krauze, Andrzej. *What's so special about today?*
Kroll, Steven. *It's Groundhog Day!*
   Queen of the May
Kroll, Virginia L. *Lunching and munching*
   Sweet Magnolia
Krüss, James. *3 X 3*
Kubler, Susanne. *The three friends*
Kuchalla, Susan. *Baby animals*
Kuhn, Dwight. *Hungry little frog*
Kuklin, Susan. *Taking my dog to the vet*
Kulling, Monica. *Waiting for Amos*
Kunhardt, Edith. *I'm going to be a vet*
Kuskin, Karla. *The animals and the ark*
   James and the rain
   Roar and more
   Something sleeping in the hall
Kvasnosky, Laura McGee. *Pink, red, blue, what are you?*
Kwitz, Mary DeBall. *When it rains*
Lacome, Julie. *Garden*
   Seashore
   Walking through the jungle
Lady Eden's School. *Just how stories*
Laird, Elizabeth. *The day the ducks went skating*
   The day Veronica was nosy
Lake, Mary Dixon. *The royal drum*
Langstaff, John M. *Over in the meadow*
Lapp, Eleanor. *The mice came in early this year*
Lass, Bonnie. *Who took the cookies from the cookie jar?*
Lathrop, Dorothy Pulis. *Who goes there?*
Latimer, Jim. *James Bear and the goose gathering*
   Moose and friends
   When moose was young
Laurencin, Geneviève. *I wish I were*
Lavies, Bianca. *Lily pad pond*
   Tree trunk traffic
Lavis, Steve. *Cock-a-doodle-doo*
   Jump!
Layton, Neal. *Smile if you're human*
Lazard, Naomi. *What Amanda saw*
Lee, Jeanne M. *I once was a monkey*
   Toad is the uncle of heaven
Leedy, Loreen. *Fraction action*
   The Furry News
   The great trash bash
   Mission – addition
   There's a frog in my throat

Sea shapes
McDonnell, Flora. *I love animals*
  Splash!
McFall, Gardner. *Naming the animals*
McGee, Marni. *The quiet farmer*
MacGill-Callahan, Sheila. *When Solomon was king*
Machotka, Hana. *Breathtaking noses*
  Outstanding outsides
  Terrific tails
  What do you do at a petting zoo?
  What neat feet!
McKee, David. *Elmer's friends*
  I can too!
  The sad story of Veronica who played the violin
  Zebra's hiccups
MacKeen, Leslie Ann. *Who can fix it?*
McKié, Roy. *Noah's ark*
MacLeod, Elizabeth. *I heard a little baa*
McLeod, Emilie Warren. *One snail and me*
McNally, Darcie. *In a cabin in a wood*
McNaught, Harry. *Baby animals*
McNaughton, Colin. *If dinosaurs were cats and dogs*
McNeer, May Yonge. *Little Baptiste*
McPhail, David M. *Andrew's bath*
  Animals A to Z
  The day the dog said, "Cock-a-doodle doo!"
  Edward in the jungle
  Farm morning
  The Glerp
  The great race
  Lorenzo
  The party
  The puddle
  Where can an elephant hide?
McQuade, Jacqueline. *At the petting zoo with Teddy Bear*
Madgwick, Wendy. *Animaze!*
Mado, Michio. *The animals*
Maestro, Giulio. *Leopard is sick*
  One more and one less
Maestro, Marco. *Geese find the missing piece*
Mahy, Margaret. *Boom Baby boom, boom*
  The Christmas tree tangle
  17 kings and 42 elephants
  Simply delicious!
  A summery Saturday morning
  When the king rides by
Mallory, Kenneth. *Families of the deep blue sea*
Mann, Peggy. *King Laurence, the alarm clock*
Manning, Linda. *Animal hours*
Manning, Mick. *My body, your body*
Manson, Christopher. *A farmyard song*
Manushkin, Fran. *My Christmas safari*
Margret and H. A. Rey's Curious George and the puppies
Mari, Iela. *Eat and be eaten*
Maris, Ron. *Bernard's boring day*
  Better move on, frog!
  Ducks quack
  Frogs jump
  I wish I could fly
  In my garden
  Runaway rabbit
Marks, Burton. *Animals*
Marsh, T. J. *Way out in the desert*
Marshall, Edward. *Fox all week*
Marshall, James. *Four little troubles*
  Hey, diddle, daddle
  Willis

Marshall, Janet Perry. *A honey of a day*
  My camera
Martin, Bill (William Ivan). *Chicken Chuck*
  Polar bear, polar bear, what do you hear?
Martin, C. L. G. *Down Dairy Farm Road*
Martin, Francesca. *Clever Tortoise*
  The honey hunters
Martin, Rafe. *Will's mammoth*
Marzollo, Jean. *Home sweet home*
  I spy little animals
  Mama, Mama
  Papa, papa
  Pretend you're a cat
  Sun song
  Ten cats have hats
  What's the matter with Mother Goose?
Massie, Diane Redfield. *The baby beebee bird*
Mathers, Petra. *A cake for Herbie*
Mathews, Judith. *Nathaniel Willy, scared silly*
Mathis, Melissa Bay. *Animal house*
Maxner, Joyce. *Nicholas Cricket*
Mayer, Marianna. *Beauty and the beast*
  The Brambleberrys animal alphabet
  The Brambleberrys animal book of big and small shapes
  The Brambleberrys animal book of colors
  The Brambleberrys animal book of counting
  The little jewel box
Mayer, Mercer. *Appelard and Liverwurst*
  What do you do with a kangaroo?
Mayne, William. *Come, come to my corner*
Meddaugh, Susan. *The best place*
Medearis, Angela Shelf. *Barry and Bennie*
Meeker, Clare Hodgson. *Who wakes rooster?*
Meeks, Esther K. *Friendly farm animals*
  Something new at the zoo
Meeuwissen, Tony. *Remarkable animals*
Mellor, Corinne. *Bruce the balding moose*
Melmed, Laura Krauss. *I love you as much . . .*
Mendoza, George. *Need a house? Call Ms. Mouse*
  Traffic jam
Merriam, Eve. *The birthday cow*
  Goodnight to Annie, ill. by Carol Schwartz
  What in the world?
  Where is everybody?
Metaxas, Eric. *The birthday ABC*
Michels, Tilde. *Who's that knocking at my door?*
Michelson, Richard. *Animals that ought to be*
Miklowitz, Gloria D. *The zoo that moved*
Miles, Miska. *Noisy gander*
  Sylvester Jones and the voice in the forest
Miller, Edna. *Mousekin's Thanksgiving*
Miller, J. P. (John Parr). *Farmer John's animals*
Miller, Jane. *Farm noises*
  Seasons on the farm
Miller, Margaret. *I love colors*
Miller, Ruth. *I went to the bay*
Millhouse, Nicholas. *Blue-footed booby*
Minarik, Else Holmelund. *Am I beautiful?*
  The little girl and the dragon
Miranda, Anne. *Does a mouse have a house?*
  To market, to market
Miryam. *The happy man and his dump truck*
Mitchell, Adrian. *Our mammoth*
  Twice my size
Mizumura, Kazue. *If I were a cricket . . .*
Modesitt, Jeanne. *Lunch with Milly*
  The night call
  Vegetable soup

Moffatt, Judith. *Who stole the cookies?*
Mogensen, Jan. *Teddy's birthday bugle*
Mollel, Tololwa M. (Tololwa Marti). *Dume's roar*
  The king and the tortoise
  Rhinos for lunch and elephants for supper
  To dinner, for dinner
Moncure, Jane Belk. *Riddle me a riddle*
Monsell, Mary Elise. *Underwear!*
Moon, Nicola. *At the beginning of a pig*
Moore, Elaine. *Grandma's house*
Moore, John. *Granny Stickleback*
Moore, Karen Ann. *The baby king*
Mora, Emma. *Animals of the forest*
Mora, Pat. *Delicious hullabaloo = Pachanga deliciosa*
  Listen to the desert = Oye al desierto
  The race of toad and deer
  This big sky
Morehead, Debby. *A special place for Charlee*
Moreton, Daniel. *La Cucaracha Martina*
Morgan, Michaela. *Edward gets a pet*
Morley, Carol. *Farmyard song*
Morozumi, Atsuko. *One gorilla*
Morpurgo, Michael. *Wombat goes walkabout*
Morris, Ann. *The animal book*
Morris, Linda Lowe. *Morning milking*
Morrison, Sean. *Is that a happy hippopotamus?*
Morse, Samuel French. *All in a suitcase*
Morton, Christine. *Picnic farm*
Moser, Erwin. *The crow in the snow and other bedtime stories*
Moser, Madeline. *Ever heard of an aardwolf?*
Moses, Amy. *At the zoo*
Most, Bernard. *Catbirds and dogfish*
  Cock-a-doodle-moo!
  The cow that went oink
  Dinosaur cousins?
  Peek-a-moo!
  Row, row, row your goat
  Zoodles
Mother Goose. *Hey diddle diddle*, ill. by Marilyn Janovitz
  Hey diddle, diddle, ill. by Moira Kemp
  Hickory, dickory, dock, ill. by Suzanne Duranceau
  Pat-a-cake, ill. by Marilyn Janovitz
Mozelle, Shirley. *The pig is in the pantry, the cat is on the shelf*
Mudd-Ruth, Maria. *The ultimate ocean book*
Mullins, Edward S. *Animal limericks*
Munari, Bruno. *Animals for sale*
  Bruno Munari's zoo
  The elephant's wish
  Who's there? Open the door
Munsch, Robert N. *Alligator baby*
Munsterberg, Peggy. *Beastly banquet*
Murdocca, Sal (Salvatore). *Tuttle's shell*
Murphy, Mary. *My puffer train*
Murphy, Stuart J. *Animals on board*
Murray, Marjorie Dennis. *The stars are waiting*
Musicant, Elke. *The night vegetable eater*
Mwenye Hadithi. *Crafty chameleon*
  Lazy lion
  Tricky tortoise
My first book of baby animals
Myers, Bernice. *The flying shoes*
Myers, Walter Dean. *The story of the three kingdoms*
Nail, James T. *Whose tracks are these?*
Nakabayashi, Ei. *The rainy day puddle*
Nakano, Hirotaka. *Elephant blue*
Nakatani, Chiyoko. *The zoo in my garden*

Narahashi, Keiko. *Is that Josie?*
Nash, Ogden. *Custard the dragon*
Nathan, Cheryl. *Bugs and beasties ABC*
  The long and the short of it
Nayer, Judy. *Jungle life*
  Night animals
  Sea creatures
Naylor, Phyllis Reynolds. *The picnic*
Neidigh, Sherry. *Creatures at my feet*
Nerlove, Miriam. *I made a mistake*
Neugebauer, Charise. *Santa's gift*
Newcome, Zita. *Rosie goes exploring*
Newton, Patricia Montgomery. *The frog who drank the waters of the world*
Nichol, B. P. *Once*
Nichols, Grace. *Asana and the animals*
Nicholson, Nicholas B. A. *Little girl in a red dress with cat and dog*
Nikola-Lisa, W. *Can you top that?*
  No babies asleep
Nilsén, Anna. *Let's all hang and dangle*
  Where are Percy's friends?
  Where is Percy's dinner?
Noble, Kate. *Bubble gum*
  Oh look, it's a nosserus
Noll, Sally. *Jiggle wiggle prance*
  Lucky morning
Norman, Charles. *The hornbean tree and other poems*
Norman, Philip Ross. *A mammoth imagination*
Novak, Matt. *Mr. Floop's lunch*
Numeroff, Laura Joffe. *The Chicken sisters*
  Chimps don't wear glasses
Nye, Naomi Shihab. *Lullaby raft*
Nygaard, Elizabeth. *Snake alley band*
Obligado, Lilian. *Faint frogs feeling feverish and other terrifically tantalizing tongue twisters*
O'Brien, Claire. *Sam's sneaker search*
O'Donnell, Elizabeth Lee. *Winter visitors*
O'Donnell, Peter. *Carnegie's excuse*
  Moonlit journey
Offen, Hilda. *As quiet as a mouse*
  A fox got my socks
  The sheep made a leap
Old MacDonald had a farm. *E I E I O*
  Old MacDonald, ill. by Rosemary Wells
  Old MacDonald had a farm, ill. by Holly Berry
  Old MacDonald had a farm, ill. by Lorinda Bryan Cauley
  Old MacDonald had a farm, ill. by Mel Crawford
  Old MacDonald had a farm, ill. by Tracey English
  Old MacDonald had a farm, ill. by David Frankland
  Old MacDonald had a farm, ill. by Abner Graboff
  Old MacDonald had a farm, ill. by Nancy Hellen
  Old MacDonald had a farm, ill. by Carol Jones
  Old MacDonald had a farm, ill. by Tracey Campbell Pearson
  Old MacDonald had a farm, ill. by Robert M. Quackenbush
  Old MacDonald had a farm, ill. by Glen Rounds
  Old MacDonald had a farm, ill. by Jessica Souhami
  Old MacDonald had a farm, ill. by William Stobbs
  Old MacDonald had a farm, ill. by Prue Theobalds
Oppenheim, Joanne. *"Not now!" said the cow*
  "Uh-oh!" said the crow
  You can't catch me!
Oppenheim, Shulamith Levey. *What is the full moon full of?*
Oram, Hiawyn. *Badger's bad mood*

Badger's bring something party
Mole's moon
Ormerod, Jan. *Joe can count*
  Ms. MacDonald has a class
  When we went to the zoo
Ostheeren, Ingrid. *Jonathan Mouse, detective*
Otto, Carolyn. *What color is camouflage?*
Over in the Grasslands
Over in the meadow, ill. by Paul Galdone
Over in the meadow, ill. by Ezra Jack Keats
Owen, Roy. *My night forest*
Oxenbury, Helen. *Friends*
  It's my birthday
  Monkey see, monkey do
  Pippo gets lost
  729 curious creatures
  729 merry mix-ups
Pack, Robert. *Then what did you do?*
Pacovská, Kveta. *Flying*
Palazzo, Tony (Anthony D.). *Animal babies*
  Animals 'round the mulberry bush
Palazzo-Craig, Janet. *Little Danny Dinosaur*
Pallotta, Jerry. *The dory story*
Palmer, Mary Babcock. *No-sort-of-animal*
Paraskevas, Betty. *Junior Kroll and Company*
Paré, Roger. *Animal capers*
  Circus days
  Play time
  Summer days
Park, W. B. *Bakery business*
  The costume party
Parker, Nancy Winslow. *Working frog*
Parnall, Peter. *Alfalfa Hill*
  Winter barn
Parsons, Alexandra. *Amazing mammals*
Partridge, Jenny. *Colonel Grunt*
  Grandma Snuffles
  Hopfellow
  Mr. Squint
  Peterkin Pollensnuff
Paschkis, Julie. *So happy/So sad*
Patent, Dorothy Hinshaw. *Bold and bright, black-and-white animals*
Paterson, Bettina. *My first wild animals*
Paterson, Diane. *If I were a toad*
Patterson, Elizabeth Burman. *Whose eyes are these?*
Patterson, Geoffrey. *The lion and the gypsy*
Paul, Jan S. *Hortense*
Paul, Korky. *Winnie in winter*
Paxton, Tom. *Belling the cat and other Æsop fables*
  Going to the zoo
Payne, Joan Balfour. *The stable that stayed*
Peaceable kingdom
Pearce, Q. L. *In the African grasslands*
  In the desert
Peek, Merle. *The balancing act*
  Mary wore her red dress and Henry wore his green sneakers
Peet, Bill (William Bartlett). *The ant and the elephant*
  Cock-a-doodle Dudley
  Farewell to Shady Glade
  The gnats of knotty pine
  No such things
Pelham, David. *A is for animals*
  Crawlies creep
  Worms wiggle
Peppé, Rodney. *Little circus*

Percy, Graham. *24 strange little animals in a haunted house*
Peters, Lisa Westberg. *The hayloft*
Peters, Sharon. *Animals at night*
Peterson, Esther Allen. *Frederick's alligator*
Pevear, Richard. *Mister Cat-and-a-Half*
Peyo. *The Smurfs and their woodland friends*
Pfister, Marcus. *Hopper hunts for spring*
  How Leo learned to be king
Phillips, Mildred. *And the cow said, "moo"!*
Piatti, Celestino. *Celestino Piatti's animal ABC*
Pienkowski, Jan. *Farm*
  Homes
  Zoo
Piers, Helen. *Is there room on the bus?*
  Who's in my bed?
Pilkey, Dav. *The Moonglow Roll-O-Rama*
Pinkwater, Daniel Manus. *Rainy morning*
Pirotta, Saviour. *Little bird*
Pitcher, Caroline. *Animals*
Pittman, Helena Clare. *Once when I was scared*
Pizer, Abigail. *It's a perfect day*
Plante, Patricia. *The turtle and the two ducks*
Please, Mr. Crocodile!
Pluckrose, Henry Arthur. *Fur and feathers*
  Paws and claws
  Skin, shell and scale
Pomerantz, Charlotte. *The birthday letters*
Poole, Valerie. *Obadiah Coffee and the music contest*
Porter, Sue. *One potato*
Porter-Gaylord, Laurel. *I love my daddy because . . .*
  I love my mommy because . . .
Potter, Beatrix. *Appley Dapply's nursery rhymes*
  Cecily Parsley's nursery rhymes
  Ginger and Pickles
  More tales from Beatrix Potter
  Peter Rabbit's ABC
  The tale of Jemima Puddle-Duck and other farmyard tales
  The tale of Peter Rabbit and other stories
  A treasury of Peter Rabbit and other stories
  Yours affectionately, Peter Rabbit
Pouyanne, Rési. *What I see hidden by the pond*
Powell, Consie. *A bold carnivore*
Powell, Jillian. *Jumpers*
Powzyk, Joyce Ann. *Tasmania*
Prater, John. *On top of the world*
Pratt, Kristin Joy. *A fly in the sky*
Prelutsky, Jack. *Beneath a blue umbrella*
  The pack rat's day and other poems
Price, Mathew. *Do you see what I see?*
  Don't worry, Alfie
Price-Thomas, Brian. *The magic ark*
Provensen, Alice. *Our animal friends at Maple Hill Farm*
  The year at Maple Hill Farm
Pryor, Bonnie. *Greenbrook farm*
The pudgy book of farm animals
Purcell, John Wallace. *African animals*
Quackenbush, Robert M. *Pete Pack Rat*
Rankin, Joan. *You're somebody special, Walliwigs!*
Raschka, Christopher. *Moosey Moose*
Raskin, Ellen. *And it rained*
  Who, said Sue, said whoo?
Rathmann, Peggy. *Good night, Gorilla*
Rauzon, Mark J. *Eyes and ears*
  Feet, flippers, hooves, and hands
Rayner, Shoo. *My first picture joke book*
Reasoner, Charles. *Who drives this?*

Reddix, Valerie. *Millie and the mudhole*
Reeves, Mona Rabun. *I had a cat*
Reider, Katja. *Snail started it!*
Reidy, Hannah. *Crazy creature contrasts*
Reiser, Lynn. *Little clam*
 Night thunder and the Queen of the Wild Horses
Rex, Michael. *Who digs?*
Rey, H. A. (Hans Augusto). *Tit for tat*
 Where's my baby?
Rey, Margret (Margret Elisabeth Waldstein). *Billy's picture*
Rice, Eve. *Sam who never forgets*
Rich, Scharlotte. *Who made the wild woods?*
Richardson, John. *Ten bears in a bed*
Richter, Mischa. *Quack?*
Riddell, Chris. *Bird's new shoes*
Riddle, Tohby. *The great escape from City Zoo*
Riley, Linda Capus. *Elephants swim*
Roberts, Bethany. *Valentine mice!*
Robinson, Irene Bowen. *Picture book of animal babies*
Robinson, W. W. (William Wilcox). *On the farm*
Rockwell, Anne F. *Big bad goat*
 The good llama
 Honk honk!
 Poor Goose
 Root-a-toot-toot
Roddie, Shen. *Animal stew*
Roe, Richard. *Animal ABC*
Roffey, Maureen. *I spy at the zoo*
Rogers, Paul (Patrick). *Quacky Duck*
Rojankovsky, Feodor. *Animals in the zoo*
 Animals on the farm
 The great big animal book
 The great big wild animal book
Root, Phyllis. *Moon tiger*
 One duck stuck
 One windy Wednesday
Roscoe, William. *The butterfly's ball and the grasshopper's feast*
Rose, Anne K. *Spider in the sky*
Rose, Gerald. *Trouble in the ark*
Rosen, Michael (1946-). *How the animals got their colors*
 Little rabbit Foo Foo
Rosen, Michael J. (1954-). *All eyes on the pond*
 With a dog like that, a kid like me . . .
Rosenberg, Liz. *A big and little alphabet*
Ross, Eileen. *The Halloween showdown*
Rotner, Shelley. *Pick a pet*
Roughsey, Dick. *The giant devil-dingo*
Rounds, Glen. *Washday on Noah's ark*
Rowan, James P. *I can be a zoo keeper*
Rowe, Jeannette. *Whose ears?*
 Whose feet?
 Whose nose?
Rowe, John A. *Smudge*
Rowinski, Kate. *L. L. Bear's island adventure*
Royston, Angela. *Baby animals*
 Jungle animals
 Night-time animals
 Sea animals
 Small animals
Runcie, Jill. *Cock-a-doodle-doo*
Rupprecht, Siegfried P. *The tale of the vanishing rainbow*
Ruschak, Lynette. *The counting zoo*
Rusling, Albert. *The mouse and Mrs. Proudfoot*
Russell, Solveig Paulson. *What good is a tail?*
Rutherford, Meg. *Animal poems*

Ryan, Pam Muñoz. *Armadillos sleep in dugouts*
Ryder, Joanne. *Fog in the meadow*
 A house by the sea
 The night flight
Rylant, Cynthia. *Night in the country*
Sabuda, Robert James. *The movable Mother Goose*
Sadler, Marilyn. *Elizabeth, Larry, and Ed*
Sage, Angie. *Monkeys in the jungle*
Saleh, Harold J. *Even tiny ants must sleep*
Samton, Sheila White. *Ten tiny monsters*
San Diego Zoological Society. *Families*
 A visit to the zoo
Sandberg, Inger. *Nicholas' favorite pet*
San Souci, Robert D. *Two bear cubs*
Santore, Charles. *A stowaway on Noah's Ark*
Sasso, Sandy Eisenberg. *A prayer for the earth*
Saunders, Dave. *Snowtime*
 Ten times better
Savage, Stephen. *Making tracks*
Sayre, April Pulley. *Home at last*
 If you should hear a honey guide
 Splish! splash! animal baths
Scarry, Richard. *Is this the house of Mistress Mouse?*
 Pie rats ahoy!
 Richard Scarry's animal nursery tales
 Richard Scarry's great big mystery book
 Richard Scarry's mix or match storybook
 Richard Scarry's Postman Pig and his busy neighbors
Schaefer, Carole Lexa. *Down in the woods at sleepytime*
Schaefer, Jackie Jasina. *Miranda's day to dance*
Scharer, Niko. *Emily's house*
Schatz, Letta. *The extraordinary tug-of-war*
Scheidl, Gerda Marie. *Can we help you, Saint Nicholas?*
Schertle, Alice. *Advice for a frog and other poems*
Schick, Eleanor. *A surprise in the forest*
Schindler, Regina. *The bear's cave*
Schlein, Miriam. *Sleep safe, little whale*
Schmid, Eleonore. *Farm animals*
Schongut, Emanuel. *Look kitten*
Schrecker, Judie. *Santa's new reindeer*
Schumacher, Claire. *King of the zoo*
 Nutty's birthday
 Tim and Jim
Schumaker, Ward. *Dance!*
Schwartz, David M. *If you hopped like a frog*
Schweitzer, Iris. *Hilda's restful chair*
Scruton, Clive. *Mary's pets*
Seignobosc, Françoise. *The big rain*
 The story of Colette
Selberg, Ingrid. *Nature's hidden world*
Selkowe, Valrie M. *Spring green*
Selsam, Millicent E. *All kinds of babies*
 A first look at kangaroos, koalas and other animals with pouches
 A first look at seashells
 Hidden animals
 How to be a nature detective
 Keep looking!
 Night animals
Sendak, Maurice. *Very far away*
Seuling, Barbara. *Winter lullaby*
Seuss, Dr. *Mr. Brown can moo! Can you?*
 Would you rather be a bullfrog?
Severn, Jeffrey. *George and his giant shadow*
Sewall, Marcia. *Animal song*
Seymour, Peter S. *Animals in disguise*
Seymour, Tres. *I love my buzzard*

Shapiro, Arnold L. *Who says that?*
Sharmat, Marjorie Weinman. *Bartholomew the bossy*
   Taking care of Melvin
   The 329th friend
   Walter the wolf
Sheppard, Jeff. *Splash, splash*
Shields, Carol Diggory. *Colors*
Short, Mayo. *Andy and the wild ducks*
Showers, Paul. *Sleep is for everyone*
Sierra, Judy. *There's a zoo in room 22*
Simmons, Jane. *Daisy says Coo!*
   Daisy's favorite things
Simon, Carly. *Midnight farm*
Simon, Francesca. *But what does the hippopotamus say?*
Simon, Mina Lewiton. *If you were an eel, how would you feel?*
Simon, Paul. *At the zoo*
Simon, Seymour. *Animal fact - animal fable*
Simple gifts
Singer, Isaac Bashevis. *Why Noah chose the dove*
Singer, Marilyn. *Turtle in July*
Siomades, Lorianne. *Kangaroo and cricket*
   My box of color
Siracusa, Catherine. *No mail for Mitchell*
Skaar, Grace Marion. *What do the animals say?*
Skofield, James. *Crow moon, worm moon*
Skorpen, Liesel Moak. *All the Lassies*
Slate, Joseph. *Miss Bindergarten gets ready for kindergarten*
   Who is coming to our house?
Sloat, Teri. *Farmer Brown goes round and round*
   Rib-ticklers
   There was an old lady who swallowed a trout
   The thing that bothered Farmer Brown
Slobodkin, Louis. *Friendly animals*
   Melvin, the moose child
   Our friendly friends
Slobodkina, Esphyr. *The wonderful feast*
Small, David. *George Washington's cows*
   Imogene's antlers
Smith, Donald. *Who's wearing my baseball cap?*
   Who's wearing my bow tie?
   Who's wearing my sneakers?
   Who's wearing my sunglasses?
Smith, Janice Lee. *Wizard and Wart in trouble*
Smith, Jim. *The frog band and the onion seller*
   The frog band and the owlnapper
   Nimbus the explorer
Smith, Lane. *The big pets*
Smith, Mavis. *Fred, is that you?*
Smith, Roger. *How the animals saved the ark and put two and two together*
Smith, William Jay. *Birds and beasts*
Sneed, Brad. *Lucky Russell*
Snyder, Dick. *One day at the zoo*
   Talk to me tiger
Solotareff, Grégoire. *Never trust an ogre*
Souhami, Jessica. *No dinner!*
Sowler, Sandie. *Amazing animal disguises*
   Amazing armored animals
Spence, Robert, III. *Clickety clack*
Spier, Peter. *Gobble, growl, grunt*
   Noah's ark
   The pet store
Spilka, Arnold. *Little birds don't cry*
Spohn, David. *Nate's treasure*
Stadler, John. *Animal café*
   Cat is back at bat

   Gorman and the treasure chest
   One seal
Stafford, William. *The animal that drank up sound*
Staines, Bill. *All God's critters got a place in the choir*
Stanley, Sanna. *Monkey Sunday*
Staub, Leslie. *Bless this house*
Stehr, Frédéric. *Quack-quack*
Steig, William. *Sylvester and the magic pebble*
   Toby, where are you?
Steinmetz, Leon. *Clocks in the woods*
Stenmark, Victoria. *The singing chick*
Stern, Maggie. *Acorn magic*
Stevens, Carla. *Hooray for pig!*
   Pig and the blue flag
   Stories from a snowy meadow
Stevens, Harry. *Fat mouse*
   Parrot told snake
Stevens, Janet. *Animal fair*
   Cook-a-doodle-doo!
   Old bag of bones
Stevenson, James. *Clams can't sing*
   Don't make me laugh
   Happy Valentine's Day, Emma!
   Heat wave at Mud Flat
   Mr. Hacker
   The most amazing dinosaur
   National worm day
   No need for Monty
   A village full of valentines
   We can't sleep
   Which one is Whitney?
   Yard sale
Stevenson, Suçie. *I forgot*
Stobbs, William. *Animal pictures*
Stockdale, Susan. *Some sleep standing up*
Stoddard, Sandol. *Bedtime mouse*
Stoeke, Janet Morgan. *Hide and seek*
Stojic, Manya. *Rain*
Stratemeyer, Clara Georgeanna. *Pepper*
Strete, Craig Kee. *How the Indians bought the farm*
   The lost boy and the monster
Struppi
Supraner, Robyn. *Sam Sunday and the mystery at the Ocean Beach Hotel*
Sutton, Jane. *What should a hippo wear?*
Swartz, Nancy Sohn. *In our image*
Sweet, Melissa. *Fiddle-i-fee*
Swendson, Patsy. *The potluck adventures of Mrs. Marmalade*
Swinburne, Stephen R. *Water for one, water for everyone*
Sykes, Julie. *Dora's eggs*
   I don't want to take a bath!
   Smudge
Szekeres, Cyndy. *Long ago*
Tafuri, Nancy. *The barn party*
   Counting to Christmas
   Do not disturb
   I love you, little one
   Junglewalk
   My friends
   Rabbit's morning
   This is the farmer
   Where we sleep
   Who's counting?
Takao, Yuko. *A winter concert*
Talley, Linda. *Jackson's plan*
Tanaka, Beatrice. *The chase*
Taylor, Harriet Peck. *Two days in May*

Weiss, Nicki. *Dog boy cap skate*
  Where does the brown bear go?
  Where does the brown bear go? A board book
Welber, Robert. *Goodbye, hello*
Welch, Willy. *Dancing with Daddy*
Wellington, Monica. *Bunny's first snowflake*
  Bunny's rainbow day
Wells, Rosemary. *Hazel's amazing mother*
Weninger, Brigitte. *The elf's hat*
  Merry Christmas, Davy!
West, Colin. *Go tell it to the toucan*
  I brought my love a tabby cat
  One day in the jungle
  "Pardon?" said the giraffe
West, Judy. *Have you got my purr?*
Westcott, Nadine Bernard. *There's a hole in the
    bucket*
Whippo, Walt. *Little white duck*
Whitfield, Susan. *The animals of the Chinese zodiac*
Whitney, Dorothy B. *Creatures of an exceptional kind*
Whybrow, Ian. *Parcel for Stanley*
  Quacky quack-quack!
Wiesner, William. *Noah's ark*
Wilds, Kazumi Inose. *Hajime in the North Woods*
Wildsmith, Brian. *Animal games*
  Animal homes
  Animal shapes
  Animal tricks
  Goat's trail
  Professor Noah's spaceship
  Python's party
  What the moon saw
  Wild animals
Willard, Nancy. *The voyage of the Ludgate Hill*
Williams, Garth. *The big golden animal ABC*
Williams, Jenny (Jennifer). *Ride a cockhorse*
Williams, Sue. *I went walking*
  Let's go visiting
Willis, Jeanne. *The boy who lost his bellybutton*
  Sloth's shoes
Wilner, Isabel. *A garden alphabet*
Wilson, Sarah. *Love and kisses*
Winch, Madeleine. *Come by chance*
Windham, Sophie. *Noah's ark*
Winter, Jeanette. *The girl and the moon man*
Winters, Kay. *Wolf watch*
Wiseman, Bernard. *Doctor Duck and Nurse Swan*
  Little new kangaroo
  Tails are not for painting
Wojtowycz, David. *Animal antics from 1 to 10*
  David Wojtowycz presents Animal ABC
Wolcott, Patty. *Eeeeeek!*
Wolf, Jake. *Daddy, could I have an elephant?*
Wolfe, Art. *1, 2, 3 moose*
Wolff, Ashley. *A year of beasts*
Wolkstein, Diane. *Little Mouse's painting*
Wood, A. J. *Amazing animals*
Wood, Audrey. *Little Penguin's tale*
  The napping house
  The napping house wakes up
  Silly Sally
Wood, Douglas. *Old Turtle*
Wood, Jakki. *Across the big blue sea*
  Dads are such fun
  Fiddle-i-fee
  Moo moo, brown cow
Wood, Jenny. *The animal kingdom*
Wood, John Norris. *Jungles*
Woolf, Virginia. *Nurse Lugton's curtain*

Wormell, Christopher. *Blue Rabbit and friends*
Wormell, Mary. *Hilda Hen's happy birthday*
  Why not?
Worthington, Phoebe. *Teddy bear farmer*
Worthy, Judith. *Eyes*
Wundrow, Deanna. *Jungle drum*
Wyler, Rose. *Puddles and ponds*
Wyllie, Stephen. *The great race*
  Snappity snap
Yabuuchi, Masayuki. *Animals sleeping*
  Whose baby?
  Whose footprints?
Yaccarino, Dan. *Deep in the jungle*
  An octopus followed me home
Yee, Wong Herbert. *Eek! There's a mouse in the house*
  Fireman Small
  Fireman Small, fire down below
  Fireman Small to the rescue
  Hamburger Heaven
  Mrs. Brown went to town
  The Officers' Ball
Yen, Clara. *Why rat comes first*
Yep, Laurence. *Tiger woman*
Ylla. *Animal babies*
Yolen, Jane. *Dragon night and other lullabies*
  How beastly!
  An invitation to the butterfly ball
  Jane Yolen's Old MacDonald songbook
  Nocturne
  Picnic with Piggins
  Piggins
  Welcome to the icehouse
  Welcome to the sea of sand
Yoshi. *Who's hiding here?*
Yoshida, Toshi. *Elephant crossing*
  Rhinoceros mother
Young animals in the zoo
Young domestic animals
Young, Ruth. *Who says moo?*
Youngs, Betty. *Pink pigs in mud*
Youngs, Betty Ferrell. *One panda*
Zabar, Abbie. *Fifty-five friends*
Zadrzynska, Ewa. *The Peaceable Kingdom*
Zalben, Jane Breskin. *Basil and Hillary*
  Norton's nighttime
Ziefert, Harriet. *All clean!*
  All gone!
  Animal music
  Animals of the Bible
  Baby Ben's bow-wow book
  Cock-a-doodle-doo!
  Cow in the house
  Dancing
  Happy birthday, Grandpa!
  I swapped my dog
  Listen! Piggety Pig
  Oh, what a noisy farm!
  On our way to the barn
  On our way to the zoo
  A polar bear can swim
  Run! Run!
Zoehfeld, Kathleen Weidner. *What lives in a shell?*
  What's alive?
Zoll, Max Alfred. *Animal babies*
Zolotow, Charlotte (Shapiro). *The sleepy book,* ill. by
    Vladimir Bobri
  The sleepy book, ill. by Ilse Plume
  Wake up and goodnight
Zoo animals, (Imported Pubs., 1983)

Zoo animals, (Macmillan, 1991)
Zweifel, Frances W. *Animal baby-sitters*

Animals – aardvarks

Brown, Marc Tolon. *Arthur babysits*
  Arthur goes to school
  Arthur lost and found
  Arthur meets the president
  Arthur tricks the tooth fairy
  Arthur writes a story
  Arthur's baby
  Arthur's birthday
  Arthur's chicken pox
  Arthur's computer disaster
  Arthur's family vacation
  Arthur's first sleepover
  Arthur's neighborhood
  Arthur's new puppy
  Arthur's new puppy (board book)
  Arthur's nose
  Arthur's pet business
  Arthur's really helpful word book
  Arthur's TV trouble
  Arthur's underwear
  D. W., go to your room!
  D. W. rides again!
  D. W., the picky eater
  D. W. thinks big, a board book
  D. W.'s lost blankie
  Glasses for D. W.
  Marc Brown's Boat book
  The true Francine
Caple, Kathy. *Inspector Aardvark and the perfect cake*
Higham, Jon Atlas. *Aardvark's picnic*
Kellogg, Steven (Stephen). *Aster Aardvark's alphabet adventures*
Lindbergh, Reeve. *The awful aardvarks go to school*
  The awful Aardvarks shop for school
Mwalimu. *Awful aardvark*
Schaffer, Libor. *Arthur sets sail*

Animals – anteaters

Binnamin, Vivian. *The case of the anteater's missing lunch*
Brown, Marc Tolon. *D. W. all wet*
  D. W. flips!
Hall, Malcolm. *The friends of Charlie Ant Bear*
Hellard, Susan. *Eleanor and the babysitter*
Waber, Bernard. *An anteater named Arthur*

Animals – antelopes

Jensen, Patricia. *Be careful, Little Antelope*
Lacapa, Michael. *Antelope Woman*

Animals – apes *see* Animals – baboons; Animals – chimpanzees; Animals – gorillas; Animals – monkeys

Animals – armadillos

Allard, Harry. *The cactus flower bakery*
Beifuss, John. *Armadillo Ray*
Brett, Jan. *Armadillo rodeo*
Cherry, Lynne. *The armadillo from Amarillo*
Kipling, Rudyard. *The beginning of the armadillos*, ill. by Lorinda Bryan Cauley
  The beginning of the armadillos, ill. by Charles Keeping
Lewis, Robin Baird. *Aunt Armadillo*
Monsell, Mary Elise. *Armadillo*
Patton, Don. *Armadillos*
Saunders, Susan. *Charles Rat's picnic*
Simon, Sidney B. *The armadillo who had no shell*
Singer, Marilyn. *Archer Armadillo's secret room*

Animals – babies

Alexander, Martha G. *When the new baby comes, I'm moving out*
Aliki. *At Mary Bloom's*
Arbeit, Eleanor Werner. *Mrs. Cat hides something*
Arnold, Caroline. *Mother and baby zoo animals*
Bauer, Marion Dane. *If you were born a kitten*
Blake, Quentin. *Zagazoo*
Brandenberg, Franz. *Aunt Nina and her nephews and nieces*
Brown, Andrew. *Baby animals*
Brown, Craig McFarland. *In the spring*
Burton, Jane. *Caper the kid*
  Dizzie the pony
  Fancy the fox
  Ginger the kitten
  Gipper the guinea pig
  Hoppy the toad
  Jack the puppy
  Pacer, the pony
  Surfer the seal
Calmenson, Stephanie. *Kinderkittens, who took the cookie from the cookie jar?*
Cartlidge, Michelle. *Baby mice at home*
Chwast, Seymour. *Traffic jam*
Coats, Lucy. *One hungry baby*
Cole, Joanna. *A calf is born*
Darling, Kathy (Mary Kathleen). *Desert babies*
Donohue, Dorothy. *Big and little on the farm*
Fleming, Denise. *Mama cat has three kittens*
Fuchshuber, Annegert. *Two peas in a pod*
George, Jean Craighead. *Look to the north*
Goode, Molly. *Mama loves*
Grindley, Sally. *Little Elephant Thunderfoot*
  Polar Star
Hamsa, Bobbie. *Animal babies*
Hellard, Susan. *Baby lemur*
Henley, Claire. *I'm a baby, too!*
Hindley, Judy. *The best thing about a puppy*
Hirschi, Ron. *A time for babies*
James, Betsy. *Tadpoles*
Jensen, Patricia. *Be patient, Little Chick*
Kaizuki, Kiyonori. *A calf is born*
Kopper, Lisa. *Daisy knows best*
  I'm a baby, you're a baby
Kroll, Virginia L. *Motherlove*
Landa, Norbert. *Cubs*
  Kittens
  Puppies
Lewis, Kim. *Just like Floss*
  Little Baa
  Little calf
  Little lamb
  Little puppy
Lilly, Kenneth. *Baby animals*
London, Jonathan. *Baby whale's journey*
  Snuggle wuggle
MacDonald, Elizabeth. *Dilly-Dally and the nine secrets*

McGeorge, Constance W. *Boomer's big surprise*
McMullan, Kate (Hall). *If you were my bunny*
Marsh, T. J. *Way out in the desert*
Miller, Margaret. *Me and my bear*
Otto, Carolyn. *Our puppies are growing*
Partis, Joanne. *Stripe*
Plummer, David. *Counting kittens*
Porter, Sue. *Parsnip*
    Parsnip and the pink blanket
    Parsnip and the runaway tractor
Radcliffe, Theresa. *Bashi, elephant baby*
Ryan, Pam Muñoz. *A pinky is a baby mouse, and other baby animal names*
Slepian, Jan. *Lost moose*
Tafuri, Nancy. *I love you, little one*
Tildes, Phyllis Limbacher. *Baby animals black and white*
Walters, Catherine. *Are you there, Baby Bear?*
Ward, Jennifer. *Somewhere in the ocean*
Wolfe, Art. *Northwest animal babies*
Wormell, Mary. *Why not?*
Wright, Cliff. *Santa's ark*
Yolen, Jane. *Off we go!*

Animals – baboons

Banks, Kate (Katherine A.). *Baboon*
Ching. *The baboon's umbrella*
Field, Susan. *The sun, the moon, and the silver baboon*
Noble, Kate. *Bubble gum*
Olaleye, Isaac. *Bitter bananas*

Animals – badgers

Baker, Betty. *Partners*
Brewster, Patience. *Two bushy badgers*
Carlstrom, Nancy White. *No nap for Benjamin Badger*
Cox, Paul. *The case of the botched book*
    The great eucalyptus mystery
    The riddle of the floating island
Hoban, Russell. *A baby sister for Frances*
    A bargain for Frances
    Bedtime for Frances
    Best friends for Frances
    A birthday for Frances
    Bread and jam for Frances
Johnston, Tony. *The badger and the magic fan*
Liersch, Anne. *A house is not a home*
MacDonald, Elizabeth. *Mr. Badger's birthday pie*
Oram, Hiawyn. *Badger's bad mood*
    Badger's bring something party
Potter, Beatrix. *The tale of Mr. Tod*
Silverman, Erica. *Warm in winter*
Tompert, Ann. *Badger on his own*
Varley, Susan. *Badger's parting gifts*
Wells, Rosemary. *Hazel's amazing mother*

Animals – bandicoots

Argent, Kerry. *Wombat and Bandicoot*

Animals – bats

Appelt, Kathi. *Bats on parade*
Berman, Ruth. *Squeaking bats*
Cannon, Annie. *The bat in the boot*
Cannon, Janell. *Stellaluna*
    Stellaluna: a pop-up book and mobile

Carlson, Natalie Savage. *Spooky and the wizard's bats*
Davol, Marguerite W. *Batwings and the curtain of night*
Dragonwagon, Crescent. *Bat in the dining room*
Freeman, Don. *Hattie the backstage bat*
Glaser, Linda. *Beautiful bats*
Hoban, Russell. *Lavina bat*
Horowitz, Ruth. *Bat time*
Jarrell, Randall. *A bat is born*
McMullan, Kate (Hall). *Batty riddles*
Maestro, Betsy. *Bats*
Markle, Sandra. *Outside and inside bats*
Medearis, Angela Shelf. *Barry and Bennie*
Mollel, Tololwa M. (Tololwa Marti). *A promise to the sun*
Quackenbush, Robert M. *Batbaby*
    Batbaby finds a home
Ungerer, Tomi. *Rufus*

Animals – bears

Alborough, Jez. *Ice cream bear*
    It's the bear
    My friend bear
    Where's my teddy?
Alderson, Sue Ann. *Wherever bears be*
Alexander, Martha G. *And my mean old mother will be sorry, Blackboard Bear*
    Blackboard Bear
    I sure am glad to see you, Blackboard Bear
    We're in big trouble, Blackboard Bear
    You're a genius, Blackboard Bear
Alexander, Sally Hobart. *Maggie's whopper*
Allen, Pamela. *Bertie and the bear*
Ambrus, Victor G. *Never laugh at bears*
Amoit, Pierre. *Bijou, the little bear*
Andreae, Giles. *Love is a handful of honey*
Anglund, Joan Walsh. *Cowboy and his friend*
    The cowboy's Christmas
Arnosky, Jim. *Every autumn comes the bear*
Asch, Frank. *Bear shadow*
    Bear's bargain
    Bread and honey
    Good night, Baby Bear
    Goodbye house
    Happy birthday, moon!
    Just like daddy
    Milk and cookies
    Moonbear
    Moonbear's books
    Moonbear's canoe
    Moonbear's dream
    Moonbear's friend
    Moonbear's pet
    Mooncake
    Moondance
    Moongame
    Popcorn
    Sand cake
    Skyfire
Austin, Margot. *A friend for Growl Bear*
Bach, Alice. *Millicent the magnificent*
    The smartest bear and his brother Oliver
    Warren Weasel's worse than measles
Bailey, Linda. *Gordon Loggins and the three bears*
Baker, Jill. *Basil of Bywater Hollow*
Barrett, John M. *The bear who slept through Christmas*
    The Easter bear
Barto, Emily Newton. *Chubby bear*

Bartoli, Jennifer. *Snow on bear's nose*
Bassett, Lisa. *Beany and Scamp*
  Beany wakes up for Christmas
  A clock for Beany
Beck, Martine. *Rescue of Brown Bear and White Bear*
  The wedding of Brown Bear and White Bear
Bellows, Cathy. *The Grizzly sisters*
Benton, Robert. *Don't ever wish for a 7-foot bear*
Berenstain, Stan. *After the dinosaurs*
  The bear detectives
  Bears in the night
  Bears on wheels
  The Berenstain bears and mama's new job
  The Berenstain bears and the bad dream
  The Berenstain bears and the bad habit
  The Berenstain bears and the big road race
  The Berenstain bears and the double dare
  The Berenstain bears and the ghost of the forest
  The Berenstain bears and the messy room
  The Berenstain bears and the missing dinosaur bone
  The Berenstain bears and the missing honey
  The Berenstain bears and the prize pumpkin
  The Berenstain bears and the sitter
  The Berenstain bears and the slumber party
  The Berenstain bears and the spooky old tree
  The Berenstain bears and the trouble with friends
  The Berenstain bears and the truth
  The Berenstain bears and the week at grandma's
  The Berenstain bears and the wild, wild honey
  The Berenstain bears and too much birthday
  The Berenstain bears and too much junk food
  The Berenstain bears and too much TV
  The Berenstain bears and too much vacation
  The Berenstain bears blaze a trail
  The Berenstain bears' Christmas tree
  The Berenstain bears' counting book
  The Berenstain bears don't pollute anymore
  The Berenstain bears forget their manners
  The Berenstain bears get in a fight
  The Berenstain bears get stage fright
  The Berenstain bears get the gimmies
  The Berenstain bears go out for the team
  The Berenstain bears go to camp
  The Berenstain bears go to school
  The Berenstain bears go to the doctor
  The Berenstain bears in the dark
  The Berenstain bears learn about strangers
  The Berenstain bears meet Santa Bear
  The Berenstain bears' moving day
  The Berenstain bears no girls allowed
  The Berenstain bears on the moon
  The Berenstain bears ready, set, go!
  The Berenstain bears' science fair
  The Berenstain bears trick or treat
  The Berenstain bears' trouble at school
  The Berenstain bears' trouble with money
  The Berenstain bears' trouble with pets
  The Berenstain bears visit the dentist
  The Berenstains' B book
  He bear, she bear
  Inside outside upside down
  Old hat, new hat
Berman, Ruth. *Fishing bears*
Bird, E. J. *How do bears sleep?*
Bishop, Claire Huchet. *Twenty-two bears*
Bittner, Wolfgang. *Wake up, Grizzly!*
Blackstone, Stella. *Bear in a square*
  Bear on a bike
Blathwayt, Benedict. *Bear's adventure*

Blocksma, Mary. *The best dressed bear*
Bodnar, Judit Z. *Tale of a tail*
Boegehold, Betty. *Bear underground*
Boehm, Arlene P. *Jack in search of Art*
Bond, Michael. *Paddington and the knickerbocker rainbow*
  Paddington at the circus
  Paddington at the fair
  Paddington at the palace
  Paddington at the seaside
  Paddington at the tower
  Paddington at the zoo
  Paddington Bear, ill. by R. W. Alley
  Paddington Bear, ill. by John Lobban
  Paddington Bear and the Busy Bee Carnival
  Paddington Bear and the Christmas surprise
  Paddington cleans up
  Paddington's ABC
  Paddington's art exhibit
  Paddington's colors
  Paddington's garden
  Paddington's lucky day
  Paddington's 1 2 3
  Paddington's opposites
Boon, Emilie. *Belinda's balloon*
Bowden, Joan Chase. *The bear's surprise party*
Bradman, Tony. *A bad week for the three bears*
Brandenberg, Franz. *A fun weekend*
Brenner, Barbara A. *Two orphan cubs*
Brett, Jan. *Berlioz the bear*
Bridgman, Elizabeth. *Nanny bear's cruise*
Bright, Robert. *Me and the bears*
Brimner, Larry Dane. *Country Bear's good neighbor*
  Country Bear's surprise
Brinckloe, Julie. *Gordon's house*
Browne, Anthony. *Bear goes to town*
  Bear hunt
  The little bear book
Bunting, Eve (Anne Evelyn). *The Valentine bears*
Butterfield, Moira. *Brown, fierce, and furry*
Cahill, Chris. *Bear magic*
Caple, Kathy. *Fox and bear*
Carleton, Barbee Oliver. *Benny and the bear*
Carlstrom, Nancy White. *Better not get wet, Jesse Bear*
  Guess who's coming, Jesse Bear
  Happy birthday, Jesse Bear!
  How do you say it today, Jesse Bear?
  It's about time, Jesse Bear
  Jesse Bear, what will you wear?
  Jesse Bear's tra-la tub
  Jesse Bear's tum-tum tickle
  Jesse Bear's wiggle-jiggle jump-up
  Jesse Bear's yum-yum crumble
  Let's count it out, Jesse Bear
  What a scare, Jesse Bear!
Carmichael, Clay. *Bear at the beach*
Carson, Jo. *The great shaking*
Cartlidge, Michelle. *Bear in the forest*
  The bear's bazaar
  Bears on the go
  Teddy trucks
Cauley, Lorinda Bryan. *Treasure hunt*
Chambless, Jane. *Tucker and the bear*
Cherry, Lynne. *Grizzly bear*
Chevalier, Christa. *The little bear who forgot*
Christian, Peggy. *Chocolate, a glacier grizzly*
Compton, Joanne. *Sody Sallyratus*
Cooper, Helen (Helen F.). *The bear under the stairs*
Crespi, Francesca. *Little Bear and the oompah-pah*

Crewe, Sabrina. *The bear*
Dabcovich, Lydia. *Sleepy bear*
Dalmais, Anne-Marie. *The Best bedtime stories of*
    Mother Bear
Davis, Aubrey. *Sody salleratus*
Day, Alexandra. *Boswell wide-awake*
    Frank and Ernest
    Frank and Ernest on the road
    Frank and Ernest play ball
Day, Marie. *Quennu and the cave bear*
De Beer, Hans. *Bernard Bear's amazing adventure*
Degen, Bruce. *Jamberry*
DeLage, Ida. *The old witch and the snores*
Delton, Judy. *Bear and Duck on the run*
    Brimhall comes to stay
    Brimhall turns detective
    Brimhall turns to magic
    The elephant in Duck's garden
    No time for Christmas
    A pet for Duck and Bear
    Rabbit finds a way
    Two good friends
Dennis, Morgan. *Burlap*
De Regniers, Beatrice Schenk. *How Joe the bear and*
    Sam the mouse got together
Dodd, Lynley. *Wake up, bear*
Dorian, Marguerite. *When the snow is blue*
Dowling, Paul. *You need a bath, Mustard*
Dubois, Claude K. *He's my jumbo!*
    Looking for Ginny
Dunbar, Joyce. *A cake for Barney*
Duvoisin, Roger Antoine. *Snowy and Woody*
Edwards, Richard. *Copy me, Copycub*
Edwards, Roberta. *Anna Bear's first winter*
Falk, Barbara Bustetter. *Grusha*
Fatio, Louise. *The happy lion and the bear*
Flack, Marjorie. *Ask Mr. Bear*
Fleishman, Seymour. *Too hot in Potzburg*
Fleming, Denise. *Time to sleep*
Flory, Jane. *The bear on the doorstep*
Foreman, Michael. *Moose*
Fox, Mem. *Sleepy bears*
Freeman, Don. *Bearymore*
Gage, Wilson. *Cully Cully and the bear*
Galdone, Joanna. *The little girl and the big bear*
Gammell, Stephen. *Wake up, bear . . . It's Christmas!*
Gantschev, Ivan. *Otto the bear*
    RumpRump
Gantz, David. *The genie bear with the light brown hair*
    word book
George, Jean Craighead. *The grizzly bear with the*
    golden ears
Gerstein, Mordicai. *Anytime Mapleson and the hun-*
    gry bears
Gifford, Kathie Lee. *Giff the scaredy bear*
    Giff's big game
Gilks, Helen. *Bears*
Ginsburg, Mirra. *Two greedy bears*
Gliori, Debi. *Mr. Bear babysits*
    Mr. Bear says, "Are you there, Baby Bear?"
    Mr. Bear says peek-a-boo
    Mr. Bear's new baby
    Mr. Bear's picnic
    Willie Bear and the Wish Fish
Goldman, Dara. *There's no such thing!*
Goldstein, Bobbye S. *Bear in mind*
Gordon, Margaret. *Wilberforce goes on a picnic*
    Wilberforce goes to a party
Gordon, Sharon. *Christmas surprise*

Graham, Thomas. *Mr. Bear's boat*
    Mr. Bear's chair
Greaves, Margaret. *Little Bear and the Papagini circus*
Gregory, Valiska. *Through the mickle woods*
Greydanus, Rose. *Bedtime story*
    Climb aboard
Grimm, Jacob. *The bear and the kingbird*
    Rose Red and the bear prince
    Snow White and Rose Red, ill. by Adrienne Adams
    Snow-White and Rose-Red, ill. by Barbara Cooney
    Snow White and Rose Red, ill. by John Wallner
    Snow White and Rose Red, ill. by Bernadette Watts
Grindley, Sally. *What are friends for?*
    What will I do without you?
Grossman, Bill. *The bear whose bones were Jezebel Jones*
Guilfoile, Elizabeth. *Nobody listens to Andrew*
Hague, Kathleen. *Calendarbears*
    Ten little bears
Hamsa, Bobbie. *Your pet bear*
Hansen, Carla. *Barnaby Bear builds a boat*
    Barnaby Bear visits the farm
Hanson, Mary Elizabeth. *Snug*
Harper, Piers. *If you love a bear*
Harrison, Joanna. *Dear bear*
Hawkins, Colin. *Dip, dip, dip*
    I'm not sleepy!
    One finger, one thumb
    Oops-a-Daisy
    Where's bear?
Hayes, Geoffrey. *Christmas in Puttyville*
    Patrick and his grandpa
    Patrick and Ted
    The secret inside
Heine, Helme. *Prince Bear*
Heller, Nicholas. *Mathilda the dream bear*
Hellsing, Lennart. *The wonderful pumpkin*
Heuck, Sigrid. *Pony and Bear are friends*
Hill, Eric. *At home*
    Baby Bear's bedtime
    Good morning, baby bear
    My pets
    Up there
Hillert, Margaret. *The three bears*
Hirschi, Ron. *Where are my bears?*
Hobbs, Will. *Beardream*
    Howling Hill
Hoff, Syd. *Bernard on his own*
    Grizzwold
Hol, Coby. *Tippy Bear and little Sam*
    Tippy Bear goes to a party
    Tippy Bear hunts for honey
    Tippy Bear's Christmas
Holl, Adelaide. *Small Bear builds a playhouse*
    Small Bear solves a mystery
Hooks, William H. *Snowbear Whittington, an*
    Appalachian Beauty and the Beast
Isenberg, Barbara. *The adventures of Albert, the run-*
    ning bear
    Albert the running bear gets the jitters
    Albert the running bear's exercise book
Isherwood, Shirley. *The band over the hill*
Jackson, Ellen B. *The bear in the bathtub*
Janice. *Little Bear marches in the St. Patrick's Day*
    parade
    Little Bear's Christmas
    Little Bear's New Year's party
    Little Bear's pancake party
    Little Bear's Sunday breakfast
    Little Bear's Thanksgiving

Wild, Robin. *The bears' ABC book*
   The bears' counting book
Wildsmith, Brian. *Bear's adventure*
   The lazy bear
Williams, Leslie. *A bear in the air*
Winter, Paula. *The bear and the fly*
Winthrop, Elizabeth. *Bear and Mrs. Duck*
   Bear's Christmas surprise
Wiseman, Bernard. *Christmas with Morris and Borris*
   Morris and Boris at the circus
   Morris has a birthday party!
Wood, Audrey. *Oh my baby bear!*
Wood, Jakki. *One bear with bees in his hair*
Woodman, Allen. *The bear who came to stay*
Yee, Patrick. *Baby bear*
Yee, Wong Herbert. *Big black bear*
Yektai, Niki. *Bears at the beach*
   Bears in pairs
Yeoman, John. *The bear's water picnic*
Ylla. *Two little bears*
Yolen, Jane. *Baby Bear's bedtime book*
   The three bears holiday rhyme book
   The three bears rhyme book
Yulya. *Bears are sleeping*
Zalben, Jane Breskin. *Beni's first Chanukah*
   Beni's first wedding
   Happy Passover, Rosie
   Leo and Blossom's Sukkah
Ziefert, Harriet. *Bear all year*
   Bear gets dressed
   Bear goes shopping
   Bear's busy morning
Zimnik, Reiner. *The bear on the motorcycle*
Zirbes, Laura. *How many bears?*

Animals – beavers

Barr, Cathrine. *Little Ben*
Bernstein, Margery. *How the sun made a promise and kept it*
Bowen, Vernon. *The lazy beaver*
Carlson, Nancy L. *Take time to relax*
   A visit to grandma's
Chottin, Ariane. *Beaver gets lost*
Crowley, Arthur. *Bonzo Beaver*
Dabcovich, Lydia. *Busy beavers*
Gallo, Giovanni. *The lazy beaver*
George, William T. *Beaver at Long Pond*
Gibson, Kari Smalley. *Mooki's secret*
Hamsa, Bobbie. *Your pet beaver*
Himmelman, John. *The Clover County carrot contest*
   The day-off machine
   The great leaf blast-off
   The super camper caper
Hoban, Russell. *Charlie the tramp*
Hodge, Deborah. *Beavers*
Kalas, Sybille. *The beaver family book*
MacDonald, Amy. *Little Beaver and the echo*
Minarik, Else Holmelund. *Percy and the five houses*
Pryor, Bonnie. *The beaver boys*
Sheehan, Angela. *The beaver*
Tresselt, Alvin R. *The beaver pond*

Animals – bison *see* Animals – buffaloes

Animals – bobcats

Hodge, Deborah. *Wild cats*
Rockwell, Anne F. *A bear, a bobcat and three ghosts*

Animals – brush wolves *see* Animals – coyotes

Animals – buffaloes

Baker, Olaf. *Where the buffaloes begin*
Esbensen, Barbara Juster. *The great buffalo race*
Glasscock, Sarah. *My prairie summer*
Goble, Paul. *Her seven brothers*
   The return of the buffaloes
Grimsdell, Jeremy. *Kalinzu*
Kershen, L. Michael (Lloyd Michael). *Why buffalo roam*
Latimer, Jim. *Snail and Buffalo*
McCarthy, Bobette. *Buffalo girls*
Midge, Tiffany. *Buffalo*
Roop, Peter. *The buffalo jump*
Stilz, Carol Curtis. *Grandma Buffalo, May, and me*
Wittmann, Patricia. *Buffalo Thunder*

Animals – bulls, cows

Aliki. *Milk from cow to carton*
Allen, Pamela. *Belinda*
Asch, Frank. *Oats and wild apples*
Babcock, Chris. *No moon, no milk!*
Barker, Melvern J. *Country fair*
Bulla, Clyde Robert. *Dandelion Hill*
Carlson, Natalie Savage. *Time for the white egret*
Carrick, Donald. *The deer in the pasture*
   Milk
Choldenko, Gennifer. *Moonstruck*
Climo, Shirley. *The Irish Cinderlad*
Cole, Babette. *Supermoo!*
Cole, Joanna. *A calf is born*
Coulter, Hope Norman. *Uncle Chuck's truck*
Cronin, Doreen. *Click, clack, moo*
Cushman, Jerome. *Marvella's hobby*
Dennis, Wesley. *Flip and the cows*
Dreier, Ted. *Moozie's kind adventure*
Drescher, Henrik. *Looking for Santa Claus*
Dubanevich, Arlene. *Calico cows*
Du Bois, William Pène. *Elisabeth, the cow ghost*
Ericsson, Jennifer A. *No milk!*
Ernst, Lisa Campbell. *When Bluebell sang*
Ets, Marie Hall. *The cow's party*
Forrester, Victoria. *The magnificent moo*
   Poor Gabriella
Fox, Mem. *Because of the bloomers*
Gibbons, Gail. *Yippee-yay!*
Glass, Andrew. *Chickpea and the talking cow*
Gomi, Taro. *Spring is here*
Greene, Ellin. *Billy Beg and his bull*
Greenstein, Elaine. *Emily and the crows*
Hader, Berta Hoerner. *The story of Pancho and the bull with the crooked tail*
Hancock, Sibyl. *Old Blue*
Harrison, David Lee. *When cows come home*
Herriot, James. *Blossom comes home*
Jackson, Woody. *Counting cows*
Johnson, Paul Brett. *The cow who wouldn't come down*
Johnston, Tony. *The bull and the fire truck*
   The promise
Kaizuki, Kiyonori. *A calf is born*
Kent, Jack. *Mrs. Mooley*
Ketteman, Helen. *Bubba the cowboy prince*
Kirby, David K. *Cows are going to Paris*
Koch, Dorothy Clarke. *When the cows got out*

Kovalski, Maryann. *Queen Nadine*
Krasilovsky, Phyllis. *The cow who fell in the canal*
Kroll, Virginia L. *The Christmas cow*
Laden, Nina. *When Pigasso met Mootisse*
Leaf, Munro. *The story of Ferdinand the bull*
Lent, Blair. *Pistachio*
Le Tord, Bijou. *A brown cow*
Lewis, Kim. *Little calf*
Lindgren, Astrid. *A calf for Christmas*
Ling, Mary. *Calf*
Lowell, Susan. *Little Red Cowboy Hat*
Macaulay, David. *Black and white*
MacFarland, Cynthia. *Cows in the parlor*
Martin, Bill (William Ivan). *White Dynamite and Curly Kidd*
Mathews, Judith. *There's nothing to d-o-o-o!*
Meeks, Esther K. *The curious cow*
Merrill, Jean. *Tell about the cowbarn, Daddy*
Milgrim, David. *Cows can't fly*
Miranda, Anne. *Cownting*
Moers, Hermann. *Camomile heads for home*
Morck, Irene. *Tyler's new boots*
Morris, Linda Lowe. *Morning milking*
Most, Bernard. *Moo-ha!*
   Peek-a-moo!
Nikola-Lisa, W. *Wheels go round*
Pellowski, Michael. *Clara joins the circus*
Peterson, Cris. *Extra cheese, please!*
Poskanzer, Susan Cornell. *Dairy farmer*
Royston, Angela. *Cow*
Schertle, Alice. *How now, brown cow?*
Scruton, Clive. *Circus cow*
Sewall, Marcia. *The wee, wee mannie and the big, big coo*
Speed, Toby. *Two cool cows*
Talley, Carol. *Clarissa*
Thomas, Patricia. *"There are rocks in my socks!" said the ox to the fox*
Weidt, Maryann N. *Daddy played music for the cows*
Whishaw, Iona. *Henry and the cow problem*
Whybrow, Ian. *Parcel for Stanley*
Wiseman, Bernard. *Morris the moose*
   Oscar is a mama
Wright, Dare. *Look at a calf*
Ziefert, Harriet. *Cow in the house*

Animals – bushbabies

Kennaway, Adrienne. *Bushbaby*

Animals – camels

Bailey, Donna. *Camels*
Coatsworth, Elizabeth. *Song of the camels*
Eduar, Gilles. *Dream journey*
Goodenow, Earle. *The last camel*
Hamsa, Bobbie. *Your pet camel*
Kipling, Rudyard. *How the camel got his hump*, ill. by Quentin Blake
   How the camel got his hump, ill. by Tim Raglin
Lewin, Betsy. *What's the matter, Habibi?*
McKee, David. *The day the tide went out and out and out*
Oppenheim, Shulamith Levey. *The hundredth name*
Parker, Nancy Winslow. *The Christmas camel*
Peet, Bill (William Bartlett). *Pamela Camel*
Roberts, Bethany. *Camel caravan*
Rubinetti, Donald. *Cappy the lonely camel*
Simon, Francesca. *Camels don't ski*

Thury, Frederick. *The last straw*
Tworkov, Jack. *The camel who took a walk*
Wells, Rosemary. *Abdul*

Animals – caribou see Animals – reindeer

Animals – cats

Abercrombie, Barbara. *Charlie Anderson*
   Michael and the cats
Adam, Barbara. *The big, big box*
Æsop. *Town mouse, country mouse*, ill. by Jan Brett
Aggs, Patrice. *The visitor*
Ahlberg, Allan. *The black cat*
Alcantara, Ricardo. *Dog and cat*
Alexander, Lloyd. *The house Gobbaleen*
Aliki. *Tabby*
Allen, Jeffrey. *Up the steps, down the slide*
Allen, Jonathan. *My cat*
   Purple sock, pink sock
Allen, Pamela. *My cat Maisie*
Althea. *Jeremy Mouse and cat*
Ambrus, Victor G. *Grandma, Felix, and Mustapha Biscuit*
Amoore, Susannah. *Motley the cat*
Anderson, Douglas. *Let's draw a story*
Apple, Margot. *Brave Martha*
Arbeit, Eleanor Werner. *Mrs. Cat hides something*
Archambault, John. *A beautiful feast for a big king cat*
Armitage, Ronda. *The lighthouse keeper's catastrophe*
Armstrong, Jennifer. *Chin Yu Min and the ginger cat*
Arnold, Katya. *Meow!*
Asare, Meshack. *Cat . . . in search of a friend*
Astley, Judy. *When one cat woke up*
Aulaire, Ingri Mortenson d'. *Foxie, the singing dog*
Averill, Esther. *The fire cat*
Axworthy, Anni. *Along came Toto*
Aylesworth, Jim. *McGraw's Emporium*
   Mother Halverson's new cat
Baba, Noboru. *Eleven cats and a pig*
   Eleven cats and albatrosses
   Eleven cats in a bag
   Eleven hungry cats
Babbitt, Natalie. *Nellie, a cat on her own*
Bahous, Sally. *Sitti and the cats*
Baker, Barbara. *Digby and Kate*
   Digby and Kate again
Baker, Keith. *Cat tricks*
Baker, Leslie A. *The antique store cat*
   Paris cat
   The third-story cat
Balian, Lorna. *Amelia's nine lives*
   Leprechauns never lie
Ballard, Robin. *Cat and Alex and the magic flying carpet*
Barbaresi, Nina. *Firemouse*
Barber, Antonia. *Catkin*
   The mousehole cat
Bare, Colleen Stanley. *Critter, the class cat*
   To love a cat
Barnes-Murphy, Rowan. *Numbers*
Barrows, Marjorie Wescott. *Fraidy cat*
Barton, Byron. *The wee little woman*
Bascom, Joe. *Malcolm Softpaws*
   Malcolm's job
Bassède, Francine. *George paints his house*
Bayley, Nicola. *Crab cat*
   Elephant cat

Parrot cat
Polar bear cat
Spider cat
Beecroft, John. *What? Another cat!*
Beisner, Monika. *Catch that cat!*
Berg, Jean Horton. *The O'Learys and friends*
 The wee little man
Bernhard, Durga. *What's Maggie up to?*
Bernhard, Josephine Butkowska. *Lullaby*
Berson, Harold. *Raminagrobis and the mice*
Bible. Old Testament. Jonah. *Jonah*, ill. by Kurt
 Mitchell
Bingham, Mindy. *Minou*
Birnbaum, Abe. *Green eyes*
Black, Floyd. *Alphabet cat*
Blegvad, Lenore. *Mr. Jensen and cat*
 Mittens for kittens and other rhymes about cats
Boegehold, Betty. *In the castle of cats*
 Pawpaw's run
 Three to get ready
Bogacki, Tomasz. *Cat and mouse in the night*
 Cat and mouse in the snow
Bohdal, Susi. *Tom cat*
Bonners, Susan. *Why does the cat do that?*
Bonsall, Crosby Newell. *The amazing the incredible*
 super dog
 Listen, listen!
Borton, Lady. *Fat chance!*
Boyd, Lizi. *Baby play*
Boynton, Sandra. *Chloë and Maude*
Bradman, Tony. *A goodnight kind of feeling*
Brandenberg, Franz. *Aunt Nina and her nephews*
 and nieces
 Aunt Nina's visit
 No school today!
 A robber! A robber!
 What's wrong with a van?
Brenner, Barbara A. *Where's that cat?*
Brent, Isabelle. *Cameo cats*
Brett, Jan. *Annie and the wild animals*
 Comet's nine lives
Brewster, Patience. *Ellsworth and the cats from Mars*
Bright, Robert. *Miss Pattie*
Brown, Marc Tolon. *The cloud over Clarence*
Brown, Marcia. *Felice*
Brown, Margaret Wise. *House of a hundred windows*
 Night and day
 A pussycat's Christmas, ill. by Anne Mortimer
 Pussycat's Christmas, ill. by Helen Stone
 Sneakers
 When the wind blew
Brown, Myra Berry. *Benjy's blanket*
Brown, Ruth. *Copycat*
 Our cat Flossie
Bruna, Dick. *Kitten Nell*
Bryan, Ashley. *The cat's purr*
Buck, Nola. *Oh, cats!*
Buck, Pearl S. (Pearl Sydenstricker). *The Chinese*
 story teller
Buckmaster, Henrietta. *Lucy and Loki*
Bulla, Clyde Robert. *Valentine cat*
Burch, Robert. *Joey's cat*
Burns, Theresa. *You're not my cat*
Burton, Jane. *Ginger the kitten*
 Kitten
Butterworth, Nick. *Jasper's beanstalk*
 Jingle bells
 Just like Jasper
Byrd, Robert. *Marcella was bored*

Calder, S. J. *If you were a cat*
Calhoun, Mary. *Audubon cat*
 Blue-ribbon Henry
 Cross-country cat
 Henry the sailor cat
 High-wire Henry
 Hot-air Henry
 The nine lives of Homer C. Cat
 Tonio's cat
 The witch of Hissing Hill
 The witch who lost her shadow
 Wobble the witch cat
Calmenson, Stephanie. *Kinderkittens, show-and-tell*
 Kinderkittens, who took the cookie from the cookie jar?
Cameron, Alice. *The cat sat on the mat*
Cameron, John. *If mice could fly*
Cameron, Polly. *The cat who thought he was a tiger*
Campbell, Rod. *Misty's mischief*
Caple, Kathy. *Starring Hillary*
Capucilli, Alyssa Satin. *Happy birthday, Biscuit!*
Carle, Eric. *Have you seen my cat?*
Carlson, Nancy L. *Arnie and the skateboard gang*
 Arnie goes to camp
Carlson, Natalie Savage. *Spooky and the bad luck*
 raven
 Spooky and the ghost cat
 Spooky and the witch's goat
 Spooky and the wizard's bats
 Spooky night
Carlstrom, Nancy White. *What does the rain play?*
Carroll, Ruth. *Old Mrs. Billups and the black cats*
Carter, Anne. *Bella's secret garden*
Carter, Noelle. *Where's my squishy ball?*
Cartlidge, Michelle. *Teddy's cat*
Casey, Patricia. *My cat Jack*
Cass, Joan E. *The cat thief*
 The cats go to market
Cassedy, Sylvia. *The best cat suit of all*
Cate, Rikki. *A cat's tale*
Cazet, Denys. *Are there any questions?*
 Good morning, Maxine!
 Never spit on your shoes
Cech, John. *The southernmost cat*
Cecil, Mirabel. *Lottie's cats*
Chalmers, Audrey. *Fancy be good*
Chalmers, Mary. *Be good, Harry*
 Boots finds a house
 The cat who liked to pretend
 Come to the doctor, Harry
 George Appleton
 Merry Christmas, Harry
 Mr. Cat's wonderful surprise
 Take a nap, Harry
 Throw a kiss, Harry
Chapman, Jean. *Moon-Eyes*
Charles, Donald. *Calico Cat at school*
 Calico Cat at the zoo
 Calico Cat meets bookworm
 Calico Cat's exercise book
 Calico Cat's year
 Time to rhyme with Calico Cat
Chenery, Janet. *Pickles and Jake*
Cherry, Lynne. *Archie, follow me*
Chittum, Ida. *The cat's pajamas*
Choi, Yangsook. *New cat*
Chorao, Kay. *Ida and Betty and the secret eggs*
 Knock at the door and other baby action rhymes
Chottin, Ariane. *Little Mouse's rescue*
Christian, Mary Blount. *Scarabee, the witch's cat*

Chwast, Seymour. *Traffic jam*
Cleary, Beverly. *Two dog biscuits*
Clements, Andrew. *Temple cat*, ill. by Kate Kiesler
  Temple cat, ill. by Alan Marks
Cleveland-Peck, Patricia. *City cat, country cat*
Coats, Laura Jane. *City cat*
Coatsworth, Elizabeth. *The giant golden book of cat stories*
Cocca-Leffler, Maryann. *Wednesday is spaghetti day*
Coffelt, Nancy. *The dog who cried woof*
  Good night, Sigmund
Coffey, Maria. *A cat in a kayak*
  A seal in the family
Cohen, Caron Lee. *Whiffle Squeek*
Cohn, Norma. *Brother and sister*
Cole, Joanna. *My new kitten*
Collington, Peter. *My darling kitten*
Cook, Bernadine. *Looking for Susie*
Coombs, Patricia. *The magician and McTree*
Cooper, Helen (Helen F.). *Pumpkin soup*
Cooper, Jacqueline. *Angus and the Mona Lisa*
Coplans, Peta. *Cat and dog*
Corrin, Ruth. *Mister cat*
Costa, Nicoletta. *The birthday party, a board book*
  Dressing up
  A friend comes to play
  The missing cat
  Molly and Tom, the birthday party
Cousins, Lucy. *Katy Cat and Beaky Boo*
Cowley, Stewart. *Five little kittens*
Coxon, Michèle. *The cat who lost his purr*
Craft, Ruth. *Carrie Hepple's garden*
Crawford, Phyllis. *The blot*
Cretan, Gladys Yessayan. *Lobo and Brewster*
Crozat, François. *I am a little cat*
Daily, Don. *The twelve days of Christmas cats*
Dalmais, Anne-Marie. *Best bedtime stories of Mother Cat*
  Kelly the kitten
Damjan, Mischa. *The little prince and the tiger cat*
Darling, Kathy (Mary Kathleen). *ABC cats*
Dauer, Rosamond. *The 300 pound cat*
Daugherty, Charles Michael. *Wisher*
Davis, Douglas F. *There's an elephant in the garage*
Day, Nancy Raines. *A kitten's year*
Deeter, Catherine. *Seymour Bleu*
Degen, Bruce. *Aunt Possum and the pumpkin man*
DeJong, David Cornel. *Looking for Alexander*
DeLage, Ida. *The old witch and the wizard*
Demarest, Chris L. *Kitman and Willy at sea*
  The lunatic adventure of Kitman and Willy
Demi. *So soft kitty*
Dennis, Morgan. *Skit and Skat*
De Paola, Tomie (Thomas Anthony). *Bonjour, Mister Satie*
  Katie, Kit and cousin Tom
  Kit and Kat
De Regniers, Beatrice Schenk. *Cats cats cats*
  Everyone is good for something
  Picture book theater
  So many cats!
Desimini, Lisa. *I am running away today*
Dick Whittington and his cat. *Dick Whittington*, ill. by Edward Ardizzone
  Dick Whittington, ill. by Antony Maitland
  Dick Whittington and his cat, ill. by Marcia Brown
  Dick Whittington and his cat, ill. by Kurt Werth
Dillon, Eilis. *The cats' opera*
Disher, Garry. *Switch cat*

Diska, Pat. *Andy says . . . Bonjour!*
Dodd, Lynley. *Hairy Maclary from Donaldson's dairy*
  Hairy Maclary, Scattercat
  Hairy Maclary's caterwaul caper
  Hairy Maclary's showbusiness
  The minister's cat: ABC
  Slinky Malinki
  Slinky Malinki catflaps
  Slinky Malinki, open the door
Doherty, Berlie. *Paddiwak and cozy*, ill. by Alison Bartlett
  Paddiwak and cozy, ill. by Teresa O'Brien
Douglas, Michael. *Round, round world*
Dowling, Paul. *Are you sleepy, Puff?*
Drake, John. *The beginning of the river*
Driscoll, Laura. *The bravest cat!*
Dubanevich, Arlene. *Tom's tail*
Duvoisin, Roger Antoine. *Veronica and the birthday present*
Ehlert, Lois. *Feathers for lunch*
  Top cat
Eisler, Colin. *Cats know best*
Eliot, T. S. (Thomas Stearns). *Mr. Mistoffelees with Mungojerrie and Rumpelteazer*
Elzbieta. *Brave Babette and sly Tom*
Emberley, Michael. *Ruby*
Ernst, Lisa Campbell. *The rescue of Aunt Pansy*
Ets, Marie Hall. *Mr. T. W. Anthony Woo*
Evans, Eva Knox. *That lucky Mrs. Plucky*
Evans, Mark. *Kitten*
Farjeon, Eleanor. *Cats*
  Cats sleep anywhere., ill. by Mary Price Jenkins
  Cats sleep anywhere, ill. by Anne Mortimer
The fat cat, ill. by Jack Kent
Fatio, Louise. *Marc and Pixie and the walls in Mrs. Jones's garden*
Faunce-Brown, Daphne. *Snuffles' house*
Feder, Jane. *Beany*
Fehlner, Paul. *Dog and cat*
Field, Eugene. *The gingham dog and the calico cat*, ill. by Janet Street
  The gingham dog and the calico cat, ill. by Johanna Westerman
Fischer-Nagel, Heiderose. *A kitten is born*
Fish, Hans. *Pitschi, the kitten who always wanted to do something else*
Flack, Marjorie. *Angus and the cat*
  William and his kitten
Fleming, Denise. *Mama cat has three kittens*
Flory, Jane. *We'll have a friend for lunch*
Foreman, Michael. *Cat and canary*
  Cat in the manger
Forrester, Victoria. *The magnificent moo*
Fowler, Richard. *Cat's story*
Frascino, Edward. *My cousin the king*
  Nanny Noony and the dust queen
  Nanny Noony and the magic spell
French, Vivian. *Christmas kitten*
Freschet, Berniece. *Furlie Cat*
Fujikawa, Gyo. *Shags finds a kitten*
Funakoshi, Canna. *One morning*
Gág, Flavia. *Chubby's first year*
Gág, Wanda. *Millions of cats*
Galdone, Paul. *King of the cats*
Gantos, Jack (John, Jr.). *Back to school for Rotten Ralph*
  Happy birthday, Rotten Ralph
  Not so Rotten Ralph
  Rotten Ralph

Keats, Ezra Jack. *Hi, cat!*
  Kitten for a day
  Pssst! doggie
Keens-Douglas, Richardo. *The Miss Meow pageant*
Keeshan, Robert. *Itty Bitty Kitty*
  Itty Bitty Kitty makes a big splash
Keillor, Garrison. *Cat, you better come home*
Keller, Holly. *A bed full of cats*
Kellogg, Steven (Stephen). *A rose for Pinkerton*
  Tallyho, Pinkerton!
Kemp, Moira. *Lift-the-flap kitten*
Kent, Lorna. *No, no, Charlie Rascal!*
Kerr, Judith. *Mog and bunny*
  Mog's Christmas
Ketteman, Helen. *Grandma's cat*
Kettner, Christine. *An ordinary cat*
Khalsa, Dayal Kaur. *The snow cat*
Kherdian, David. *The cat's midsummer jamboree*
  Country cat, city cat
Killilea, Marie (Marie Lyons). *Newf*
Kimmel, Eric A. *Ten suns*
King, Deborah. *Cloudy*
King-Smith, Dick. *A mouse called Wolf*
Kinsey-Warnock, Natalie. *Wilderness cat*
Kitamura, Satoshi. *Captain Toby*
Knotts, Howard. *The summer cat*
  The winter cat
Kocí, Marta. *Katie's kitten*
Koehler, Phoebe. *Making room*
Koenig, Marion. *The tale of fancy Nancy*
  The wonderful world of night
Komoda, Beverly. *Simon's soup*
Koontz, Robin Michal. *Chicago and the cat*
  Chicago and the cat, the camping trip
  Chicago and the cat, the family reunion
  Pussycat ate the dumplings
Koralek, Jenny. *Cat and Kit*
Krahn, Fernando. *Catch that cat!*
Krasilovsky, Phyllis. *Scaredy cat*
Kraus, Robert. *Big Squeak, Little Squeak*
  Come out and play, little mouse
Krensky, Stephen. *Fraidy Cats*
Kroll, Steven. *Branigan's cat and the Halloween ghost*
  It's April Fools' Day!
Kunhardt, Dorothy. *Kitty's new doll*
Kunhardt, Edith. *Pat the cat*
Kuskin, Karla. *The upstairs cat*
Kyte, Dennis. *Mattie and Cataragus*
Lachner, Dorothea. *Look out, Cinder!*
Landa, Norbert. *Kittens*
Landalf, Helen. *The secret night world of cats*
Landshoff, Ursula. *Cats are good company*
Lansdown, Brenda. *Galumph*
Larrick, Nancy. *Cats are cats*
Laskowski, Jerzy. *Master of the royal cats*
Lasson, Robert. *Orange Oliver*
Lawrence, John. *Rabbit and pork*
Lear, Edward. *Of pelicans and pussycats*
  The owl and the pussy cat, ill. by Ian Beck
  The owl and the pussycat, ill. by Jan Brett
  The owl and the pussycat, ill. by Lorinda Bryan
    Cauley
  The owl and the pussy-cat, ill. by Barbara Cooney
  The owl and the pussycat, ill. by Emma Crosby
  The owl and the pussy-cat, ill. by William Pène Du
    Bois
  The owl and the pussycat, ill. by Lori Farbanish
  The owl and the pussy-cat, ill. by Gwen Fulton
  The owl and the pussycat, ill. by Paul Galdone

  The owl and the pussy-cat, ill. by Elaine Muis
  The owl and the pussycat, ill. by Erica Rutherford
  The owl and the pussycat, ill. by Janet Stevens
  The owl and the pussycat, ill. by Louise Voce
  The owl and the pussy-cat, ill. by Colin West
  The owl and the pussy-cat, ill. by Owen Wood
Le Guin, Ursula K. *A visit from Dr. Katz*
Leman, Jill. *Ten little pussy cats*
Lent, Blair. *Ruby and Fred*
Leonard, Marcia. *The kitten twins*
  Violet and the pirates
Leslie, Amanda. *Play kitten play*
Le-Tan, Pierre. *The afternoon cat*
Levine, Arthur A. *The boy who drew cats*
Levitin, Sonia. *All the cats in the world*
Lewin, Betsy. *Cat count*
Lewis, J. Patrick. *The Fat-Cats at sea*
Lewis, Naomi. *The stepsister*
Lexau, Joan M. *Come here, cat*
Lillie, Patricia. *Jake and Rosie*
Lindbloom, Steven. *Let's give kitty a bath!*
Lindgren, Barbro. *Sam's ball*
Lindman, Maj. *Flicka, Ricka, Dicka and the three kit-
  tens*
Lipkind, William. *Russet and the two reds*
  The two reds
The little book of cats
Little Robin Redbreast
Lively, Penelope. *The cat, the crow, and the banyan
  tree*
Livermore, Elaine. *Find the cat*
  Three little kittens lost their mittens
Livingston, Myra Cohn. *Cat poems*
Lloyd, David. *Cat and dog*
Lobel, Anita. *One lighthouse, one moon*
Lobel, Arnold. *The rose in my garden*
  Whiskers and rhymes
Lockwood, Primrose. *Cat boy!*
London, Jonathan. *Hip cat*
Luttrell, Ida. *Mattie's little possum pet*
Lyon, George Ella. *A traveling cat*
MacArthur-Onslow, Annette Rosemary. *Minnie*
McBratney, Sam. *The dark at the top of the stairs*
McClintock, Barbara. *The battle of Luke and Long-
  nose*
McCully, Emily Arnold. *Four hungry kittens*
McGurn, Patty. *Me and Marie*
Macken, JoAnn Early. *Cats on Judy*
MacKinnon, Debbie. *Ken's kitten*
  My kitty!
McLerran, Alice. *I want to go home*
McMillan, Bruce. *Kitten can . . .*
McMullan, Kate (Hall). *Kitty riddles*
  No no Jo
McPhail, David M. *Great cat*
McQuade, Jacqueline. *Good times with Teddy Bear*
Macsolis. *Baile de luna*
Mahurin, Tim. *Jeremy Kooloo*
Mahy, Margaret. *The Christmas tree tangle*
  The three-legged cat
Maitland, Barbara. *The bookstore ghost*
Malkovych, Ivan. *The cat and the rooster*
Mandry, Kathy. *The cat and the mouse and the mouse
  and the cat*
Mantegazza, Giovanna. *The cat*
Manuel, Lynn. *Lucy Maud and the Cavendish cat*
Maris, Ron. *My book*
Mark, Jan. *Fun with Mrs. Thumb*
  Fur

Martin, Ann M. *Leo the Magnificat*
Martin, David. *Lizzie and her kitty*
Martinez, Ruth. *Mrs. McDockerty's knitting*
Marzollo, Jean. *Christmas cats*
   Thanksgiving cats
   Uproar on Hollercat Hill
   Valentine cats
Maschler, Fay. *T. G. and Moonie go shopping*
   T. G. and Moonie have a baby
   T. G. and Moonie move out of town
Matthias, Catherine. *I love cats*
Mayer, Mercer. *The great cat chase*
Mayne, William. *Pandora*
   The patchwork cat
   Tibber
Meddaugh, Susan. *Too short Fred*
Merriam, Eve. *The birthday door*
   Where's that cat?
Metaxas, Eric. *Puss in boots*
   The white cat
Micklethwait, Lucy. *Spot a cat*
Micucci, Charles. *A little night music*
Miller, Edna. *Patches finds a new home*
Miller, Virginia. *Be gentle!*
Minarik, Else Holmelund. *Cat and dog*
   It's spring!
Modell, Frank. *Seen any cats?*
Mole, John. *Copy cat*
Moncure, Jane Belk. *The talking tabby cat*
Monks, Lydia. *The cat barked?*
Monson, A. M. *Wanted . . . best friend*
Moore, Inga. *Six dinner Sid*
Moore, Lilian. *See my lovely poison ivy, and other*
   verses about witches, ghosts and things
Mooser, Stephen. *The fat cat*
Mora, Pat. *A birthday basket for Tía*
Morris, Ann. *Hello Peter = Bonjour, Rémy*
Moskin, Marietta D. *Lysbet and the fire kittens*
Mother Goose. *Cats by Mother Goose*
   Hickory dickory dock, ill. by Doug Cushman
   Hickory dickory dock, ill. by Marilyn Janovitz
   Kitten rhymes
   The three little kittens, ill. by Lorinda Bryan Cauley
   The three little kittens, ill. by Paul Galdone
   The three little kittens, ill. by Dorothy Stott
   The three little kittens, ill. by Shelley Thornton
Mott, Evelyn Clarke. *Cool cat*
The moving adventures of Old Dame Trot and her comi-
   cal cat
Murphey, Sara. *The animal hat shop*
Murphy, Chuck. *Black cat, white cat*
Namioka, Lensey. *The loyal cat*
Nethery, Mary. *Hannah and Jack*
   Orange cat goes to market
Newberry, Clare Turlay. *April's kittens*
   The kittens' ABC
   Marshmallow
   Pandora
   Percy, Polly and Pete
   Smudge
   T-Bone, the baby-sitter
   Widget
Newman, Lesléa. *Cats, cats, cats*
Newton, Jill. *Cat-fish*
Nicoll, Helen. *Meg and Mog*
   Meg at sea
   Meg on the moon
   Meg's eggs
   Mog's box

Nightingale, Sandy. *Cat's knees and bee's whiskers*
Noll, Sally. *Surprise!*
Nones, Eric Jon. *Wendell*
Nordqvist, Sven. *Festus and Mercury go camping*
   Festus and Mercury: ruckus in the garden
   Festus and Mercury wishing to go fishing
   The fox hunt
   Pancake pie
Norman, Philip Ross. *Dancing dogs*
Northrup, Mili. *The watch cat*
Oakley, Graham. *The church cat abroad*
   The church mice and the moon
   The church mice and the ring
   The church mice at bay
   The church mice spread their wings
   The church mouse
   The diary of a church mouse
Oana, Kay D. *Shasta and the shebang machine*
Oates, Joyce Carol. *Come meet Muffin!*
Obrist, Jürg. *Fluffy*
Okimoto, Jean Davies. *Blumpoe the grumpoe meets*
   Arnold the cat
Olson, Arielle North. *Noah's cats and the devil's fire*
Oppenheim, Joanne. *Do you like cats?*
   No way, Slippery Slick!
Oram, Hiawyn. *Just Dog*
Ormerod, Jan. *Come back, kittens*
   Kitten day
   The saucepan game
Otto, Margaret Glover. *The little brown horse*
Palazzo-Craig, Janet. *Muffy and Fluffy*
Panek, Dennis. *Catastrophe Cat*
   Catastrophe Cat at the zoo
Paré, Roger. *A friend like you*
Parish, Peggy. *The cats' burglar*
   Scruffy
Parker, Nancy Winslow. *Puddums, the Cathcarts'*
   orange cat
Passen, Lisa. *Grammy and Sammy*
Pearson, Tracey Campbell. *The storekeeper*
Peet, Bill (William Bartlett). *Jennifer and Josephine*
Peppé, Rodney. *Cat and mouse*
   The color catalog
Perrault, Charles. *Puss in boots*, ill. by Marcia Brown
   Puss in boots, ill. by Lorinda Bryan Cauley
   Puss in boots, ill. by Jean Claverie
   Puss in boots, ill. by Andrea Da Rif
   Puss in boots, ill. by Stasys Eidrigevicius
   Puss in boots, ill. by Hans Fischer
   Puss in boots, ill. by Paul Galdone
   Puss in boots, retold and ill. by John S. Goodall
   Puss in boots, retold and ill. by Gail E. Haley
   Puss in boots, ill. by Giuliano Lunelli
   Puss in boots, ill. by Fred Marcellino [pub. by Far-
     rar, 1990]
   Puss in boots, ill. by Fred Marcellino [pub. by Far-
     rar, 1998]
   Puss in boots, ill. by Julia Noonan
   Puss in boots, ill. by Tony Ross
   Puss in boots, ill. by William Stobbs
   Puss in boots, ill. by Yan Thomas
   Puss in boots, ill. by Alain Vaës
   Puss in boots, ill. by Barry Wilkinson
Peters, Lisa Westberg. *The hayloft*
Petersen-Fleming, Judy. *Kitten training and critters,*
   too!
Pevear, Richard. *Mister Cat-and-a-Half*
Pfloog, Jan. *Kittens*
Pilkey, Dav. *Dragon's fat cat*

When cats dream
Pinkwater, Daniel Manus. *The phantom of the lunch wagon*
  Roger's umbrella
Pittman, Helena Clare. *Miss Hindy's cats*
Pizer, Abigail. *Harry's night out*
  Nosey Gilbert
Plummer, David. *Counting kittens*
Pohrt, Tom. *Having a wonderful time*
Polacco, Patricia. *Mrs. Katz and Tush*
  Tikvah means hope
Polette, Nancy. *The little old woman and the hungry cat*
Politi, Leo. *Lito and the clown*
Polushkin, Maria. *Here's that kitten*
  Kitten in trouble
  Who said meow?, ill. by Giulio Maestro
  Who said meow?, ill. by Ellen Weiss
Pomerantz, Charlotte. *The ballad of the long-tailed rat*
  Buffy and Albert
Potter, Beatrix. *The pie and the patty-pan*
  Rolly-polly pudding
  The sly old cat
  The story of Miss Moppet
  The tale of Tom Kitten
Poulin, Stéphane. *Can you catch Josephine?*
  Have you seen Josephine?
Powell, Roxanne Dyer. *Cat, mouse and moon*
Price, Mathew. *Patch finds a friend*
Priceman, Marjorie. *My nine lives / by Clio*
Pringle, Laurence P. *Naming the cat*
Pryor, Ainslie. *The baby blue cat and the dirty dog brothers*
  The baby blue cat and the smiley worm doll
  The baby blue cat who said no
  Puppies and kittens
Purdy, Carol. *Mrs. Merriwether's musical cat*
Rankin, Joan. *The little cat and the greedy old woman*
Rathmann, Peggy. *Ruby the copycat*
Redies, Rainer. *The cats' party*
Reiser, Lynn. *Bedtime cat*
  Dog and cat
Richard, Françoise. *On Cat Mountain*
Ridlon, Marcia. *Kittens and more kittens*
Robertus, Polly M. *The dog who had kittens*
Robinson, Thomas P. *Buttons*
Rockwell, Anne F. *Space vehicles*
  The way to Captain Yankee's
Roffey, Maureen. *Here, kitty kitty!*
Rohmann, Eric. *The cinder-eyed cats*
Rose, Agatha. *Hide-and-seek in the yellow house*
Ross, Eileen. *The Halloween showdown*
Ross, George Maxim. *When Lucy went away*
Ross, Tony. *I want a cat*
  Treasure of Cozy Cove
Rowinski, Kate. *Cats in the dark*
Rubel, Nicole. *Me and my kitty*
  Sam and Violet are twins
  Sam and Violet go camping
Rylant, Cynthia. *The cookie-store cat*
  Mr. Putter and Tabby bake the cake
  Mr. Putter and Tabby pick the pears
  Mr. Putter and Tabby pour the tea
  Mr. Putter and Tabby walk the dog
Samuels, Barbara. *Aloha, Dolores*
  Duncan and Dolores
Sanderson, Ruth. *Papa Gatto*
San Souci, Robert D. *The white cat*

Sara. *Across town*
Saul, Carol P. *Barn cat*
Say, Allen. *Allison*
Scamell, Ragnhild. *Solo plus one*
Schachner, Judith Byron. *The Grannyman*
Schaffer, Marion. *I love my cat!*
Schatz, Letta. *Whiskers, my cat*
Schertle, Alice. *I am the cat*
  That Olive!
Schilling, Betty. *Two kittens are born*
Scruton, Clive. *Scaredy cat*
Seguin-Fontes, Marthe. *The cat's surprise*
Seidler, Rosalie. *Grumpus and the Venetian cat*
Seignobosc, Françoise. *Minou*
Selsam, Millicent E. *A first look at cats*
  How kittens grow
Seuss, Dr. *The cat in the hat*
  The cat in the hat comes back!
Shaw, Richard. *The kitten in the pumpkin patch*
Siekkinen, Raija. *Mister King*
Silverman, Erica. *Mrs. Peachtree and the Eighth Avenue cat*
Simmie, Lois. *Mister got to go/No cats allowed*
Simmonds, Posy. *Fred*
Simon, Norma. *Cats do, dogs don't*
  Mama cat's year
  Oh, that cat!
  Where does my cat sleep?
Siomades, Lorianne. *Three little kittens*
Skaar, Grace Marion. *Nothing but (cats) and all about (dogs)*
  The very little dog
Slate, Joseph. *Lonely Lula cat*
Slavin, Bill. *The cat came back*
Sloan, Carolyn. *Carter is a painter's cat*
Slobodkin, Louis. *Colette and the princess*
Slobodkina, Esphyr. *Billy, the condominium cat*
  Pinky and the petunias
Smart, Christopher. *For I will consider my cat Jeoffry*
Smyth, Gwenda. *A pet for Mrs. Arbuckle*
Sneed, Brad. *Lucky Russell*
Snow, Alan. *The truth about cats*
Soto, Gary. *Chato and the party animals*
  Chato's kitchen
Spanner, Helmut. *I am a little cat*
Spier, Peter. *Little cats*
Spohn, Kate. *Clementine's winter wardrobe*
Stadler, John. *The cats of Mrs. Calamari*
Standon, Anna. *Three little cats*
Stanley, Diane. *Captain Whiz-Bang*
  A country tale
  Siegfried
Steel, Danielle. *Max and the baby sitter*
Steig, William. *Solomon the rusty nail*
Stein, Sara Bonnett. *Cat*
Steiner, Charlotte. *Kiki and Muffy*
Stephens, Helen. *I'm too busy*
  What about me?
Stern, Peter. *Floyd, a cat's story*
Stevens, Cat. *Teaser and the firecat*
Stevens, Janet. *My big dog*
Stock, Catherine. *Sampson the Christmas cat*
Stoddard, Sandol. *My very own special particular private and personal cat*
Stone, Bernard. *The charge of the mouse brigade*
Stratemeyer, Clara Georgeanna. *Pepper*
Sturgis, Matthew. *Tosca's surprise*
Sumiko. *Kittymouse*
Sutton, Eve. *My cat likes to hide in boxes*

Sykes, Julie. *This and that*
Szekeres, Cyndy. *Suppertime for Frieda Fuzzypaws*
Taber, Anthony. *Cats' eyes*
Tan, Amy. *The Chinese Siamese cat*
Tapio, Pat Decker. *The lady who saw the good side of everything*
Taylor, Mark. *The case of the missing kittens*
Teague, Mark. *The trouble with the Johnsons*
Thayer, Jane. *The cat that joined the club*
Thompson, Harwood. *The witch's cat*
Thornhill, Jan. *Wild in the city*
Tiller, Ruth. *Cats vanish slowly*
Titus, Eve. *Anatole and the cat*
    The kitten who couldn't purr
Tufts, Mary L. *The wee kitten who sucked her thumb*
Turkle, Brinton. *Do not open*
Turnbull, Ann. *The tapestry cats*
Uchida, Yoshiko. *The two foolish cats*
Udry, Janice May. *"Oh no, cat!"*
Ungerer, Tomi. *Flix*
    No kiss for mother
Untermeyer, Louis. *The kitten who barked*
Unwin, Pippa. *Tomcat takes a walk*
Vagin, Vladimir Vasil'evich. *Here comes the cat!*
Vainio, Pirkko. *The dream house*
Van Haeringen, Annemarie. *The cats' tale*
Van Horn, William. *Harry Hoyle's giant jumping bean*
Vesey, A. *Merry Christmas, Thomas!*
Viorst, Judith. *The tenth good thing about Barney*
Voake, Charlotte. *Ginger*
    Tom's cat
Waber, Bernard. *Lyle at Christmas*
    Mice on my mind
    Rich cat, poor cat
Waddell, Martin. *Who do you love?*
Wagner, Jenny. *John Brown, Rose and the midnight cat*
Wahl, Jan. *Dracula's cat*
    Dracula's cat and Frankenstein's dog
    My cat Ginger
    Push Kitty
Waite, Judy. *Mouse, look out!*
Wallace-Brodeur, Ruth. *Goodbye, Mitch*
Wallis, Diz. *Pip's adventure*
Ward, Cindy. *Cookie's week*
Wardlaw, Lee. *The tales of Grandpa Cat*
Warner, Sunny. *Madison finds a line*
Watson, Pauline. *Curley Cat baby-sits*
Watson, Wendy. *Happy Easter day!*
Weihs, Erika. *Count the cats*
Weilerstein, Sadie Rose. *K'tonton's Yom Kippur kitten*
Welch, Martha McKeen. *Will that wake mother?*
Wellington, Monica. *Night city*
    Squeaking of art, the mice go to the museum
Wells, Rosemary. *Yoko*
West, Judy. *Have you got my purr?*
Westell, Kerry. *Amanda's book*
Wethered, Peggy. *Touchdown Mars!*
Wezel, Peter. *The naughty bird*
Wheeler, Cindy. *Marmalade's Christmas present*
    Marmalade's nap
    Marmalade's picnic
    Marmalade's snowy day
    Marmalade's yellow leaf
Whitmore, Adam. *Max in America*
    Max in Australia
    Max in India

    Max leaves home
Whitney, Alma Marshak. *Leave Herbert alone*
Whittle, Emily. *Sailor cats*
Whybrow, Ian. *Parcel for Stanley*
Wijngaard, Juan. *Cat*
Wild, Margaret. *Big cat dreaming*
    The very best of friends
Wild, Robin. *Spot's dogs and the alley cats*
Wilkon, Piotr. *The brave little kittens*
    Rosie the cool cat
Willis, Jeanne. *Earth tigerlets as explained by Professor Xargle*
Wilson, Joyce Lancaster. *Tobi*
Withers, Carl. *The tale of a black cat*
Wolff, Ashley. *Only the cat saw*
Wood, Jakki. *Moo moo, brown cow*
Wooding, Sharon L. *The painter's cat*
Wormell, Mary. *Why not?*
Wright, Betty Ren. *The cat next door*
    Pet detectives!
Wright, Dare. *The doll and the kitten*
    The lonely doll learns a lesson
    Look at a kitten
Wright, Josephine Lord. *Cotton Cat and Martha Mouse*
Wynne-Jones, Tim. *Zoom upstream*
Yashima, Mitsu. *Momo's kitten*
Yeoman, John. *Mouse trouble*
Ylla. *I'll show you cats*
Young, Ed (Edward). *Cat and Rat*
    Up a tree
Young, James. *Penelope and the pirates*
Ziefert, Harriet. *Elemenopeo*
    Nicky upstairs and down
    Nicky's Christmas surprise
    Nicky's friends
    No, no, Nicky!
    Wee G.
    Where's the cat?
Zimelman, Nathan. *The great adventure of Wo Ti*
    Mean Murgatroyd and the ten cats

Animals – cheetahs

Adamson, Joy. *Pippa the cheetah and her cubs*
Camp, Lindsay. *Keeping up with Cheetah*
Conklin, Gladys. *Cheetahs, the swift hunters*
Heatwole, Marsha. *Jambo, watoto!*
Irvine, Georgeanne. *Sasha the cheetah*
Milton, Joyce. *Big cats*
Morrison, Taylor. *Cheetah*

Animals – chimpanzees

Blaustein, Muriel. *Jim chimp's story*
Browne, Anthony. *I like books*
    Things I like
    Willy and Hugh
    Willy the champ
    Willy the dreamer
    Willy the wimp
    Willy the wizard
Hoban, Lillian. *Arthur's back to school day*
    Arthur's Christmas cookies
    Arthur's funny money
    Arthur's great big Valentine
    Arthur's pen pal
    Arthur's prize reader
Hurd, Edith Thacher. *The mother chimpanzee*

Parish, Peggy. *Jumper goes to school*

Animals – chipmunks

Angelo, Valenti. *The acorn tree*
Berenstain, Michael. *Peat Moss and Ivy and the birthday present*
   Peat Moss and Ivy's backyard adventure
Conger, Marion. *The chipmunk that went to church*
Haas, Jessie. *Chipmunk!*
Moore, Lilian. *Little Raccoon and no trouble at all*
Price, Dorothy E. *Speedy gets around*
Ryder, Joanne. *Chipmunk song*
Stevenson, James. *Wilfred the rat*
Williams, Barbara. *Chester Chipmunk's Thanksgiving*

Animals – cougars

Anderson, C. W. (Clarence Williams). *Blaze and the mountain lion*
Gregg, Andy. *Great Rabbit and the long-tailed Wildcat*
Hodge, Deborah. *Wild cats*
Milton, Joyce. *Big cats*

Animals – cows *see* Animals – bulls, cows

Animals – coyotes

Aardema, Verna. *Borreguita and the coyote*
Baker, Betty. *And me, coyote!*
   Partners
Baylor, Byrd. *Coyote cry*
   Moon song
Bernstein, Margery. *Coyote goes hunting for fire*
Bierhorst, John. *Doctor Coyote*
Carey, Valerie Scho. *Quail song*
Carrick, Carol. *Two coyotes*
Cornette. *Purple coyote*
Covault, Ruth M. *Pablo and Pimienta*
De Montaño, Martha Kreipe. *Coyote in love with a star*
Dwyer, Mindy. *Coyote in love*
French, Fiona. *Lord of the animals*
Goble, Paul. *Iktomi and the ducks*
Hausman, Gerald. *Coyote walks on two legs*
Johnston, Tony. *The tale of Rabbit and Coyote*
Levy, Elizabeth. *Cleo and the coyote*
London, Jonathan. *At the edge of the forest*
   Fire race
Lowell, Susan. *The three little javelinas*
Lund, Jillian. *Two cool coyotes*
McDermott, Gerald. *Coyote*
Nunes, Susan Miho. *Coyote dreams*
Pohrt, Tom. *Coyote goes walking*
Sage, James. *Coyote makes man*
Stevens, Janet. *Old bag of bones*
Taylor, Harriet Peck. *Coyote and the laughing butterflies*

Animals – deer

Aragon, Jane Chelsea. *Salt hands*
   Winter harvest
Arnosky, Jim. *All about deer*
   Deer at the brook
Asch, Frank. *Oats and wild apples*
Bare, Colleen Stanley. *Never grab a deer by the ear*
Bemelmans, Ludwig. *Parsley*
Boegehold, Betty. *Small Deer's magic tricks*

Buff, Mary (Marsh). *Dash and Dart*
   Forest folk
Carrick, Donald. *The deer in the pasture*
   Harold and the great stag
Eberle, Irmengarde. *Fawn in the woods*
Frankel, Bernice. *Half-As-Big and the tiger*
Helldorfer, M. C. (Mary Claire). *Night of the white stag*
Henderson, Kathy. *Disney's Bambi: the winter trail*
Hodge, Deborah. *Deer, moose, elk and caribou*
Hodges, Margaret. *The golden deer*
Holmes, Efner Tudor. *Deer in the hollow*
Ikeda, Daisaku. *Kanta and the deer*
Lindman, Maj. *Snipp, Snapp, Snurr and the reindeer*
Oates, Joyce Carol. *Come meet Muffin!*
Prusski, Jeffrey. *Bring back the deer*
San Souci, Daniel. *In the moonlight mist*
Schlein, Miriam. *Deer in the snow*
Taylor, Harriet Peck. *Two days in May*
Troughton, Joanna. *Mouse-Deer's market*

Animals – dislike of *see* Behavior – animals, dislike of

Animals – dogs

Adoff, Arnold. *The return of Rex and Ethel*
Agee, Jon. *Ellsworth*
Alcantara, Ricardo. *Dog and cat*
Alexander, Martha G. *Bobo's dream*
   Maggie's moon
Allen, Jeffrey. *The secret life of Mr. Weird*
Allen, Jonathan. *My dog*
Allen, Pamela. *Bertie and the bear*
Aller, Susan B. *Emma and the night dogs*
Ambler, C. Gifford (Christopher Gifford). *Ten little foxhounds*
Anderson, Douglas. *Let's draw a story*
Anholt, Laurence. *The new puppy*
Annett, Cora. *The dog who thought he was a boy*
Ardizzone, Edward. *Tim's friend Towser*
Argueta, Manlio. *The magic dogs of the volcanoes*
Armstrong, Jennifer. *Little Salt Lick and the Sun King*
Arnold, Katya. *Meow!*
Asch, Frank. *The last puppy*
   Rebecca
Auch, Mary Jane. *Bird dogs can't fly*
Aulaire, Ingri Mortenson d'. *Foxie, the singing dog*
Axworthy, Anni. *Along came Toto*
Aylesworth, Jim. *The bad dream*
Bacon, Ethel. *To see the moon*
Baker, Barbara. *Digby and Kate*
   Digby and Kate again
Baker, Charlotte. *Little brother*
Baker, Jeannie. *Home in the sky*
Baker, Margaret. *A puppy called Spinach*
Barasch, Lynne. *Old friends*
Bare, Colleen Stanley. *Sammy, dog detective*
   To love a dog
Barner, Bob. *Elevator escalator book*
Baron, Alan. *Little Pig's bouncy ball*
Barr, Cathrine. *Hound dog's bone*
Barracca, Debra. *Maxi, the hero*
   Maxi, the star
   A taxi dog Christmas
Barracca, Sal. *The adventures of taxi dog*
Barton, Byron. *Jack and Fred*

Where's Al?
Bastin, Marjolein. *A little dog for Vera*
Batherman, Muriel. *Some things you should know about my dog*
Battles, Edith. *The terrible terrier*
Bauer, Steven. *The strange and wonderful tale of Robert McDoodle*
Baumann, Kurt. *Piro and the fire brigade*
Baumgart, Klaus. *Don't be afraid, Tommy*
Baylor, Byrd. *Coyote cry*
Baynes, Pauline. *How dog began*
Beim, Lorraine. *The little igloo*
Belting, Natalia Maree. *Verity Mullens and the Indian*
Bemelmans, Ludwig. *Madeline's rescue*
Benchley, Peter. *Jonathan visits the White House*
Berends, Polly Berrien. *Ladybug and dog and the night walk*
Berenstain, Stan. *The Berenstain bears on the moon*
Beresford, Elisabeth. *Snuffle to the rescue*
Bertrand, Cécile. *Let's pretend!*
Best, Cari. *Montezuma's revenge*
Bettina (Bettina Ehrlich). *Pantaloni*
Bingham, Mindy. *My way Sally*
Biro, Val. *Gumdrop and the secret switches*
Black, Irma (Simonton). *Big puppy and little puppy*
Blackwood, Gladys Rourke. *Whistle for Cindy*
Blake, Quentin. *Mrs. Armitage and the big wave*
Blake, Robert J. *Akiak*
Blegvad, Lenore. *Hark! Hark! The dogs do bark, and other poems about dogs*
Bliss, Corinne Demas. *That dog Melly!*
Blocksma, Mary. *The pup went up*
Rub-a-dub-dub
Boland, Janice. *A dog named Sam*
Bolognese, Elaine. *The sleepy watchdog*
Bonsall, Crosby Newell. *The amazing the incredible super dog*
And I mean it, Stanley
Listen, listen!
Who's afraid of the dark?
Bontemps, Arna Wendell. *The fast sooner hound*
Bornstein, Ruth Lercher. *I'll draw a meadow*
Jim
Bottner, Barbara. *Horrible Hannah*
Bowden, Joan Chase. *Boo and the flying flews*
Boyd, Lizi. *Black dog red house*
Boynton, Sandra. *Doggies*
Bradford, Ann. *The mystery of the blind writer*
The mystery of the missing dogs
Brenner, Barbara A. *A dog I know*
Brett, Jan. *Comet's nine lives*
The first dog
The trouble with trolls
Bridgman, Elizabeth. *A new dog next door*
Bridwell, Norman. *Clifford counts bubbles*
Clifford goes to Hollywood
Clifford's ABC
Clifford's good deeds
Clifford's Halloween
Bright, Robert. *Georgie and the little dog*
Brimner, Larry Dane. *Dinosaurs dance*
If dogs had wings
Bröger, Achim. *Francie's paper puppy*
Brown, Ken (Ken James). *Mucky Pup*
Mucky Pup's Christmas
Brown, Marc Tolon. *Arthur's new puppy*
Arthur's new puppy (board book)
Arthur's pet business

Brown, Margaret Wise. *Big dog, little dog*
The country noisy book
Don't frighten the lion
The indoor noisy book
The quiet noisy book
The seashore noisy book
The summer noisy book
The winter noisy book
Brown, Ruth. *The ghost of Greyfriar's Bobby*
I don't like it!
Our puppy's vacation
Browne, Anthony. *Voices in the park*
Bruna, Dick. *Snuffy*
Snuffy and the fire
Bryan, Dorothy. *Friendly little Jonathan*
Just Tammie!
Buck, Pearl S. (Pearl Sydenstricker). *The Chinese story teller*
Buckley, Helen Elizabeth. *Josie's Buttercup*
Buckmaster, Henrietta. *Lucy and Loki*
Bunting, Eve (Anne Evelyn). *Ghost's hour, spook's hour*
Jane Martin, dog detective
Burningham, John. *Cannonball Simp*
Courtney
The dog
Burton, Jane. *Jack the puppy*
Puppy
Bushey, Jeanne. *A sled dog for Moshi*
Calhoun, Mary. *High-wire Henry*
Houn' dog
Mrs. Dog's own house
Calmenson, Stephanie. *Fido*
Rosie, a visiting dog's story
Shaggy, waggy dogs (and others)
Campbell, Rod. *Henry's busy day*
Capucilli, Alyssa Satin. *Bathtime for Biscuit*
Biscuit
Biscuit finds a friend
Biscuit's picnic
Happy birthday, Biscuit!
Hello, Biscuit!
Carlson, Nancy L. *Harriet and the garden*
Harriet and the roller coaster
Harriet and Walt
Harriet's Halloween candy
Harriet's recital
Poor Carl
Carrick, Carol. *The accident*
Ben and the porcupine
The foundling
Lost in the storm
Carrier, Lark. *Scout and Cody*
Carroll, Ruth. *What Whiskers did*
Where's the bunny?
Carter, Debby L. *Clipper*
Cartlidge, Michelle. *Doggy days*
Catalanotto, Peter. *Dylan's day out*
Cazet, Denys. *Frosted glass*
Saturday
Chalmers, Audrey. *Hector and Mr. Murfit*
Chapman, Cheryl. *Snow on snow on snow*
Charles, Donald. *Shaggy dog's birthday*
Shaggy dog's Halloween
Shaggy dog's tall tale
Time to rhyme with Calico Cat
Charlton, Nancy Lee. *Derek's dog days*
Chase, Catherine. *Pete, the wet pet*
Chenery, Janet. *Pickles and Jake*

Chorao, Kay. *Annie and cousin Precious*
 The cherry pie baby
Christelow, Eileen. *The five-dog night*
 Gertrude, the bulldog detective
 Not until Christmas, Walter!
Christian, Mary Blount. *The green thumb thief*
 No dogs allowed, Jonathan!
Ciardi, John. *Scrappy, the pup*
Clayton, Elaine. *Pup in school*
Cleary, Beverly. *Two dog biscuits*
Clement, Rod. *Frank's great museum adventure*
Coffelt, Nancy. *The dog who cried woof*
 Dogs in space
Cohen, Caron Lee. *Bronco dogs*
 Three yellow dogs
Cohen, Miriam. *Jim's dog Muffins*
Cole, Babette. *Dr. Dog*
Cole, Joanna. *Monster and Muffin*
 My puppy is born
Cole, William. *Have I got dogs!*
Cook, Marion B. *Waggles and the dog catcher*
Coontz, Otto. *The quiet house*
Copeland, Eric. *Milton, my father's dog*
Coplans, Peta. *Cat and dog*
Costa, Nicoletta. *The clever dog*
 The grown-up dog
 The naughty puppy
 The new puppy
Cowley, Stewart. *Hide-and-seek puppies*
Cretan, Gladys Yessayan. *Lobo and Brewster*
Crimi, Carolyn. *Don't need friends*
Crozat, François. *I am a little dog*
Cullen, Lynn. *The mightiest heart*
Curious George and the puppies
Cuyler, Margery. *Freckles and Jane*
 Freckles and Willie
 Shadow's baby
Czarnecki, Lois R. *The six wrinkled Woos*
Dale, Penny. *Wake up, Mr. B.!*
Dale, Ruth Bluestone. *Benjamin . . . and Sylvester*
 also
Dalmais, Anne-Marie. *Petey the puppy*
Daly, Kathleen N. *The Giant little Golden Book of dogs*
Daly, Maureen. *Patrick visits the library*
Damjan, Mischa. *Atuk*
Darling, Kathy (Mary Kathleen). *ABC dogs*
Day, Alexandra. *Carl goes shopping*
 Carl goes to daycare
 Carl makes a scrapbook
 Carl pops up
 Carl's afternoon in the park
 Carl's birthday
 Carl's Christmas
 Carl's masquerade
 Follow Carl!
 Good dog, Carl
 Paddy's pay-day
De Beer, Hans. *Little polar bear and the husky pup*
DeLage, Ida. *ABC fire dogs*
 What does a witch need?
Delaney, Ned. *Bad dog!*
Delton, Judy. *I'll never love anything ever again*
Demi. *Fuzzy wuzzy puppy*
Denchfield, Nick. *Desmond the dog*
 Desmond the dog, a wag-the-tail pop-up book
Denison, Carol. *A part-time dog for Nick*
Dennis, Morgan. *Burlap*
 The pup himself
 The sea dog

 Skit and Skat
Dickens, Lucy. *Dirty Henry*
DiSalvo-Ryan, DyAnne. *A dog like Jack*
Dodd, Lynley. *A dragon in a wagon*
 Hairy Maclary from Donaldson's dairy
 Hairy Maclary, Scattercat
 Hairy Maclary, sit
 Hairy Maclary's bone
 Hairy Maclary's caterwaul caper
 Hairy Maclary's rumpus at the vet
 Hairy Maclary's showbusiness
 Schnitzel von Krumm forget-me-not
 Schnitzel von Krumm's basketwork
Domanska, Janina. *Spring is*
Doughtie, Charles. *Gabriel Wrinkles, the bloodhound*
 who couldn't smell
Dowling, Paul. *Jimmy's snowy book*
Drescher, Joan E. *Max and Rufus*
Du Bois, William Pène. *Giant Otto*
 Otto and the magic potatoes
 Otto at sea
 Otto in Africa
 Otto in Texas
Dubowski, Cathy East. *A cake for Jake*
Dumas, Philippe. *Laura, Alice's new puppy*
 Laura and the bandits
 Laura loses her head
 Laura on the road
Dunn, Judy. *The little puppy*
Dunrea, Olivier. *Fergus and Bridey*
Dupré, Ramona Dorrel. *Too many dogs*
Duvoisin, Roger Antoine. *Day and night*
Eagle, Ellen. *Gypsy's cleaning day*
Eastman, P. D. (Philip D.). *Go, dog, go!*
Edwards, Pamela Duncan. *Ed and Fred Flea*
Ehrlich, Amy. *Maggie and Silky and Joe*
Ellwand, David. *Alfred's camera*
Enderle, Judith (Ann) Ross. *Francis, the earthquake*
 dog
Enell, Trinka. *Roll over, Rosie*
Erickson, Phoebe. *Just follow me*
Erlbruch, Wolf. *Leonard*
Ernst, Lisa Campbell. *Duke, the Dairy Delight dog*
 Ginger jumps
 Walter's tail
Ets, Marie Hall. *Mr. T. W. Anthony Woo*
Evans, Katie. *Hunky Dory ate it*
Evans, Mark. *Puppy*
Falwell, Cathryn. *P.J. & Puppy*
Fanelli, Sara. *The doggy book*
Fechner, Amrei. *I am a little dog*
Fehlner, Paul. *Dog and cat*
Feiffer, Jules. *Bark, George*
Ferns, Ronald. *Osbert and Lucy*
Field, Eugene. *The gingham dog and the calico cat*, ill.
 by Janet Street
 The gingham dog and the calico cat, ill. by Johanna
 Westerman
Fischer-Nagel, Heiderose. *A puppy is born*
Fisher, Aileen Lucia. *I like weather*
Flack, Marjorie. *Angus and the cat*
 Angus and the ducks
 Angus lost
Flather, Lisa. *Ten silly dogs*
Foster, Sally. *A pup grows up*
Fox, Mem. *Night noises*
Francia, Silvia. *Roberta's vacation*
Freeman, Don. *Ski pup*
Frith, Michael K. *I'll teach my dog 100 words*

Fujikawa, Gyo. *Millie's secret*
   Shags finds a kitten
Furchgott, Terry. *Phoebe and the hot water bottles*
Gackenbach, Dick. *A bag full of pups*
   Barker's crime
   Beauty, brave and beautiful
   Claude and Pepper
   Claude has a picnic
   Claude the dog
   The dog and the deep dark woods
   Dog for a day
   Pepper and all the legs
   What's Claude doing?
Gág, Wanda. *Nothing at all*
Gannett, Ruth Stiles. *Katie and the sad noise*
Geoghegan, Adrienne. *Dogs don't wear glasses*
Gerrard, Roy. *Jocasta Carr, movie star*
Gerson, Corinne. *Good dog, bad dog*
Gerstein, Mordicai. *The new creatures*
Ghigna, Charles. *Good dogs/Bad dogs*
Gibbons, Gail. *Dogs*
Giff, Patricia Reilly. *Good luck, Ronald Morgan*
Gikow, Louise. *Follow that Fraggle!*
Gliori, Debi. *The snow lambs*
Goennel, Heidi. *My dog*
Goldsmith, Howard. *Little lost dog*
Golembe, Carla. *Annabelle's big move*
Goode, Diane. *Mama's perfect present*
Goodspeed, Peter. *Hugh and Fitzhugh*
Gordon, Sharon. *What a dog!*
Graeber, Charlotte Towner. *Nobody's Dog*
Graham, Amanda. *Who wants Arthur?*
Graham, Bob. *Benny*
   Libby, Oscar and me
Graham, Margaret Bloy. *Benjy and his friend Fifi*
   Benjy and the barking bird
   Benjy's boat trip
   Benjy's dog house
Gray, Nigel. *The dog show*
Green, Phyllis. *Bagdad ate it*
Green-Armytage, Stephen. *Dudley, the little terrier that could*
Gregoire, Caroline. *Uglypuss*
Gregory, Nan. *How Smudge came*
Gregory, Valiska. *The oatmeal cookie giant*
   Riddle soup
   Sunny side up
   Terribly wonderful
Gretz, Susanna. *Teddy bears at the seaside*
Griffith, Helen V. *Alex and the cat*
   Alex remembers
   Dream meadow
   Mine will, said John
   More Alex and the cat
   Pluck's dreams
Grimm, Jacob. *The horse, the fox, and the lion*
Grindley, Sally. *Four black puppies*
Gwynne, Fred. *Easy to see why*
Haas, Jessie. *Busybody Brandy*
Hains, Harriet. *My new puppy*
Hall, Donald. *I am the dog, I am the cat*
Hamberger, John. *Hazel was an only pet*
   The lazy dog
Hansard, Peter. *Wag, wag, wag*
Harper, Isabelle. *My dog Rosie*
   Our new puppy
Harriott, Ted. *Coming home*
Harrison, Troon. *The dream collector*
Harsh, Fred. *Alfie*

Hausherr, Rosmarie. *My first puppy*
Hawkins, Colin. *Tog the dog*
Hayes, Sarah. *This is the bear and the bad little girl*
   This is the bear and the picnic lunch
Hazelaar, Cor. *Dogs everywhere*
Hazen, Barbara Shook. *Digby*
   Fang
   The new dog
   Stay, Fang
Heine, Helme. *Mr. Miller, the dog*
Heller, Nicholas. *Happy birthday, Moe dog*
Hendry, Diana. *Dog Donovan*
Henkes, Kevin. *Circle dogs*
Herman, Gail. *My dog talks*
   Otto the cat
   The puppy who went to school
   What a hungry puppy!
Herriot, James. *Only one woof*
Hesse, Karen. *Lester's dog*
Hewett, Joan. *Rosalie*
Hill, Eric. *Puppy love*
   Spot and friends dress up
   Spot and friends play
   Spot at home
   Spot at play
   Spot at the fair
   Spot bakes a cake
   Spot counts from 1 to 10
   Spot goes on holiday
   Spot goes to a party
   Spot goes to school
   Spot goes to the beach
   Spot goes to the circus
   Spot goes to the farm
   Spot goes to the park
   Spot in the garden
   Spot looks at colors
   Spot looks at opposites
   Spot looks at shapes
   Spot looks at weather
   Spot on the farm
   Spot sleeps over
   Spot visits his grandparents
   Spot visits the hospital
   Spot's baby sister
   Spot's big book of colors, shapes and numbers; El libro grande de Spot
   Spot's big book of colours, shapes, and numbers
   Spot's big book of words; El libro grande de las palabras de Spot
   Spot's favorite baby animals
   Spot's favorite colors
   Spot's favorite numbers
   Spot's favorite words
   Spot's first Christmas
   Spot's first Easter
   Spot's first 1, 2, 3 frieze
   Spot's first picnic
   Spot's first walk
   Spot's first words
   Spot's magical Christmas
   Spot's toy box
   Spot's walk in the woods
Hillert, Margaret. *What is it?*
Himmelman, John. *The talking tree*
Hindley, Judy. *The best thing about a puppy*
Hines, Anna Grossnickle. *I'll tell you what they say*
Hoban, Lillian. *The laziest robot in zone one*
Hoban, Russell. *The stone doll of Sister Brute*

Hoberman, Mary Ann. *One of each*
Hoff, Syd. *Barkley*
   Lengthy
Holmes, Efner Tudor. *Carrie's gift*
Honeycutt, Natalie. *Whistle home*
Hooks, William H. *A dozen dizzy dogs*
   Where's Lulu?
Hopkins, Lee Bennett. *A dog's life*
Horenstein, Henry. *Arf! beg! catch!*
Howard, Arthur. *Cosmo zooms*
Howard, Ellen. *Murphy and Kate*
Howe, James. *Creepy-crawly birthday*
   Rabbit-Cadabra!
   Scared silly
Hurd, Edith Thacher. *The black dog who went into the woods*
   Little dog, dreaming
Hurd, Thacher. *Art dog*
   Hobo dog
Hürlimann, Bettina. *Barry*
Ingman, Bruce. *Lost property*
Inkiow, Dimiter. *Me and Clara and Snuffy the dog*
Inkpen, Mick. *Arnold*
   Butterfly
   Hissss!
   Honk!
   Kipper
   Kipper's A to Z
   Kipper's bathtime
   Kipper's bedtime
   Kipper's birthday
   Kipper's book of colors
   Kipper's book of counting
   Kipper's book of numbers
   Kipper's book of opposites
   Kipper's book of weather
   Kipper's Christmas Eve
   Kipper's playtime
   Kipper's snacktime
   Kipper's snowy day
   Kipper's toybox
   Meow!
   Picnic
   Splosh!
   Swing!
   Thing
   Where, oh where, is Kipper's bear?
Ipcar, Dahlov. *Black and white*
Isele, Elizabeth. *Pooks*
Iwamura, Kazuo. *Ton and Pon*
   Ton and Pon
Iwasaki, Chihiro. *What's fun without a friend?*
Jacka, Martin. *Waiting for Billy*
Janice. *Angélique*
   Mr. and Mrs. Button's wonderful watchdogs
Janovitz, Marilyn. *Bowl patrol!*
Jeram, Anita. *It was Jake*
Jessell, Camilla. *The puppy book*
Joerns, Consuelo. *Oliver's escape*
Johansen, K. V. (Krista V.). *Pippin takes a bath*
Johnson, Crockett. *The blue ribbon puppies*
   Terrible terrifying Toby
Johnson, David. *Oh, that Nuzzle!*
Johnson, Diana F. *Princesa and Friskie*
Johnson, Janet P. *How Mr. Dog got tame*
Johnson, Paul Brett. *Lost*
Johnston, Tony. *The ghost of Nicholas Greebe*
Jonas, Ann. *Watch William walk*
Jonell, Lynne. *It's my birthday, too!*

Jones, Rebecca C. *The biggest, meanest, ugliest dog in the whole wide world*
Joosse, Barbara M. *Better with two*
   Nugget and Darling
Jordan, June. *Kimako's story*
Kahl, Virginia. *Away went Wolfgang*
   Maxie
Kanome, Kayoko. *Little Mop lost*
Keats, Ezra Jack. *Kitten for a day*
   My dog is lost!
   Pssst! doggie
   Skates
   Whistle for Willie
Keller, Holly. *Goodbye, Max*
Kelley, Anne. *Daisy's discovery*
Kellogg, Steven (Stephen). *Best friends*
   Give the dog a bone
   A penguin pup for Pinkerton
   Pinkerton, behave!
   Prehistoric Pinkerton
   A rose for Pinkerton
   Tallyho, Pinkerton!
Kemp, Moira. *Lift-the-flap puppy*
Kennedy, Kim. *Napoleon*
Keyser, Marcia. *Roger on his own*
Khalsa, Dayal Kaur. *I want a dog*
Killilea, Marie (Marie Lyons). *Newf*
Kimmel, Eric A. *Sirko and the wolf*
Kimmelman, Leslie. *Frannie's fruits*
Kimura, Yasuko. *Fergus and the sea monster*
King, Deborah. *Sirius and Saba*
King-Smith, Dick. *Puppy love*
Kirk, Daniel. *Moondogs*
Kitamura, Satoshi. *Lily takes a walk*
Knapp, Jennifer. *The go go dogs*
Kocí, Marta. *Blackie and Marie*
Koehler, Phoebe. *Making room*
Komaiko, Leah. *Great Aunt Ida and her Great Dane, Doc*
Kopczynski, Anna. *Jerry and Ami*
Kopper, Lisa. *Daisy knows best*
   Daisy thinks she is a baby
Kovalski, Maryann. *Brenda and Edward*
Kraus, Robert. *The detective of London*
   Ludwig the dog who snored symphonies
Kroll, Steven. *Don't get me in trouble*
   The magic rocket
   Oh, Tucker!
   Woof, woof!
Kumin, Maxine W. *What color is Caesar?*
Kunhardt, Edith. *Pat the puppy*
Kuskin, Karla. *City dog*
   Watson, the smartest dog in the U.S.A.
Lacome, Julie. *Funny business*
   I'm a jolly farmer
Laird, Elizabeth. *The day Patch stood guard*
Lamm, C. Drew. *Anniranni and Mollymishi, the wild-haired doll*
Lamont, Priscilla. *Out to lunch*
Landa, Norbert. *Puppies*
Lane, Judith. *Buster, where are you?*
Laskowski, Jerzy. *Master of the royal cats*
Lathrop, Dorothy Pulis. *Puppies for keeps*
Lawlor, Laurie. *Second-grade dog*
Leaf, Munro. *Noodle*
Lebentritt, Julia. *The Kooken*
Leemis, Ralph. *Smart dog*
Leichman, Seymour. *Shaggy dogs and spotty dogs and shaggy and spotty dogs*

Lemberg, Stephen H. *Scaredy dog*
Lenski, Lois. *Davy and his dog*
  Debbie and her dolls
  A dog came to school
Lent, Blair. *Ruby and Fred*
Leonard, Marcia. *Get the ball, Slim*
  Laura Jean the yard sale queen
Lerman, Rory S. *Charlie's checklist*
Leslie, Amanda. *Play puppy play*
Levine, Evan. *Not the piano, Mrs. Medley!*
Levinson, Riki. *Country dawn to dusk*
Levy, Elizabeth. *Cleo and the coyote*
Lewis, Kim. *First snow*
  Floss
  Just like Floss
  Little puppy
Lewis, Thomas P. *Call for Mr. Sniff*
  Mr. Sniff and the motel mystery
Lewison, Wendy Cheyette. *My new puppy*
Lexau, Joan M. *The dog food caper*
  Go away, dog, ill. by Crosby Newell Bonsall
  Go away, dog, ill. by Paul Meisel
  I'll tell on you
Lidz, Jane. *Zak, the one-of-a-kind dog*
Lillegard, Dee. *My yellow ball*
Lindenbaum, Pija. *Boodil, my dog*
Lindgren, Barbro. *Rosa*
  Sam's bath
  Sam's wagon
  The wild baby gets a puppy
Lindman, Maj. *Flicka, Ricka, Dicka and a little dog*
  Snipp, Snapp, Snurr and the seven dogs
  Snipp, Snapp, Snurr and the yellow sled
Lipkind, William. *Even Steven*
  Finders keepers
Livingston, Myra Cohn. *Dog poems*
Lloyd, David. *Cat and dog*
Lockwood, Primrose. *One winter's night*
Lohans, Alison. *Sundog rescue*
London, Jonathan. *Shawn and Keeper and the birthday party*
  Shawn and Keeper: show-and-tell
Lopshire, Robert. *New tricks I can do!*
  Put me in the zoo
Lorenz, Lee. *Hugo and the spacedog*
Low, Joseph. *My dog, your dog*
Ludwig, Warren. *Good morning, Granny Rose*
Luttrell, Ida. *Mattie's little possum pet*
Lyon, George Ella. *Ada's pal*
McCutcheon, Marc. *Grandfather's Christmas camp*
McGeorge, Constance W. *Boomer goes to school*
  Boomer's big day
  Boomer's big surprise
McGough, Roger. *Until I met Dudley*
McGuirk, Leslie. *Tucker flips!*
Machetanz, Sara. *A puppy named Gia*
McKinley, Robin. *Rowan*
MacKinnon, Debbie. *Pippa's puppy*
MacLachlan, Patricia. *Three names*
McLean, Janet. *Dog tales*
McMullan, Kate (Hall). *Puppy riddles*
McNeal, Tom. *The dog who lost his Bob*
Mahy, Margaret. *Making friends*
Manushkin, Fran. *Walt Disney's one hundred one dalmations*
Marie, Geraldine. *The magic box*
Markoe, Merrill. *The day my dogs became guys*
Marshak, S. (Samuil). *In the van*
  The pup grew up!

Marshall, James. *Miss Dog's Christmas Speedboat*
Martin, Charles E. *Dunkel takes a walk*
Martin, David. *Lizzie and her puppy*
Martin, Sarah Catherine. *The comic adventures of Old Mother Hubbard and her dog*
  Old Mother Hubbard
  Old Mother Hubbard and her dog, ill. by Lisa Amoroso
  Old Mother Hubbard and her dog, ill. by Paul Galdone
  Old Mother Hubbard and her dog, ill. by Evaline Ness
  Old Mother Hubbard and her wonderful dog
Martinez, Ruth. *Mrs. McDockerty's knitting*
Mason, Jane B. *The wee puppy who wouldn't go to sleep*
Masurel, Claire. *No, no, Titus!*
  Ten dogs in the window
Mathers, Petra. *Theodor and Mr. Balbini*
Mayer, Mercer. *A boy, a dog, a frog and a friend*
  A boy, a dog and a frog
Meddaugh, Susan. *Martha and Skits*
  Martha blah blah
  Martha calling
  Martha speaks
  Martha walks the dog
  The witches' supermarket
Meister, Cari. *Tiny goes to the library*
  Tiny's bath
  When Tiny was tiny
Micklethwait, Lucy. *Spot a dog*
Miles, Miska. *Show and tell . . .*
  Somebody's dog
Milgrim, David. *Dog brain*
  Why Benny barks
Mills, Lauren A. *The dog prince*
Minarik, Else Holmelund. *Cat and dog*
Modell, Frank. *Skeeter and the computer*
  Tooley! Tooley!
Monks, Lydia. *The cat barked?*
Moore, Elaine. *Roly-poly puppies*
Moore, Inga. *Little dog lost*
Morris, Terry Nell. *Lucky puppy! Lucky boy!*
Moss, Marissa. *Knick knack paddywack*
Mostacchi, Massimo. *A dog's best friend*
Mother Goose. *Baa baa, black sheep*, ill. by Marilyn Janovitz
Mott, Evelyn Clarke. *Hot dog*
Moyer, Marshall M. *Rollo Bones, canine hypnotist*
Muller, Robin. *Little Wonder*
Murdocca, Sal (Salvatore). *Lucy takes a holiday*
Murphy, Mary. *Here comes spring, and summer and fall and winter*
  I feel happy, and sad, and angry, and glad
  You smell and taste and feel and see and hear
Murphy, Stuart J. *Get up and go!*
  Henry the fourth
Myers, Walter Dean. *The blues of Flats Brown*
Myller, Rolf. *A very noisy day*
Nakatani, Chiyoko. *The day Chiro was lost*
Nayer, Judy. *Tricky puppies*
Newberry, Clare Turlay. *Barkis*
Nichol, Barbara. *Biscuits in the cupboard*
Nilsén, Anna. *Where are Percy's friends?*
  Where is Percy's dinner?
Norman, Philip Ross. *Dancing dogs*
Novak, Matt. *The Pillow War*
Oakley, Graham. *The church mice and the ring*

O'Brien, John (1953-). *Mother Hubbard's Christmas*
  Sam and Spot
Okimoto, Jean Davies. *A place for Grace*
O'Neill, Catharine. *Mrs. Dunphy's dog*
Oram, Hiawyn. *Just Dog*
Ormerod, Jan. *Come back, puppies*
Osborne, Mary Pope. *Molly and the prince*
Osofsky, Audrey. *My buddy*
Ostheeren, Ingrid. *The blue monster*
  The new dog
Ottley, Matt. *What Faust saw*
Otto, Carolyn. *Our puppies are growing*
Overbeck, Cynthia. *Rusty the Irish setter*
Oxenbury, Helen. *Our dog*
  Tom and Pippo and the dog
Pancheri, Jan. *The twelve poodle princess*
Pape, D. L. (Donna Lugg). *Doghouse for sale*
Paraskevas, Betty. *Hoppy and Joe*
  A very Kroll Christmas
Parker, Nancy Winslow. *Cooper, the McNallys' big
  black dog*
  Poofy loves company
Patent, Dorothy Hinshaw. *Maggie, a sheep dog*
Paterson, Katherine. *Celia and the sweet, sweet water*
Paul, Ann Whitford. *Hello toes! Hello feet!*
Pearson, Tracey Campbell. *The howling dog*
Peet, Bill (William Bartlett). *The Whingdingdilly*
Perkins, Al. *The digging-est dog*
Perrow, Angeli. *Captain's castaway*
Petersen-Fleming, Judy. *Puppy training and critters,
  too!*
Pfloog, Jan. *Puppies*
Phillips, Joan. *My new boy*
Piers, Helen. *Puppy's ABC*
Pilkey, Dav. *The Hallo-wiener*
Pinkwater, Daniel Manus. *Aunt Lulu*
Pizer, Abigail. *Charlie the puppy*
  Nosey Gilbert
Politi, Leo. *Emmet*
  The nicest gift
Polushkin, Maria. *Who said meow?*, ill. by Giulio
  Maestro
  Who said meow?, ill. by Ellen Weiss
Pomerantz, Charlotte. *The outside dog*
Porte, Barbara Ann. *Harry's dog*
Potter, Beatrix. *The pie and the patty-pan*
Powell, Consie. *Old dog Cora and the Christmas tree*
Prather, Ray. *Double dog dare*
Price, Mathew. *Patch and the rabbits*
  Patch finds a friend
Pryor, Ainslie. *The baby blue cat and the dirty dog
  brothers*
Pulver, Robin. *Homer and the house next door*
Puppies and kittens
Rand, Gloria. *Aloha, Salty!*
  Salty dog
  Salty sails north
  Salty takes off
Ranville, Myralene. *Tex*
Rascal. *Socrates*
Raschka, Christopher. *Can't sleep*
Rathmann, Peggy. *Officer Buckle and Gloria*
Rayner, Mary. *Marathon and Steve*
Reed, Lynn Rowe. *Pedro, his perro, and the alphabet
  sombrero*
Reiser, Lynn. *Any kind of dog*
  Dog and cat
Reneaux, J. J. *Why Alligator hates Dog*

Rey, Margret (Margret Elisabeth Waldstein). *Pret-
  zel*
  Pretzel and the puppies
Rice, Eve. *Benny bakes a cake*
  Papa's lemonade and other stories
Robertus, Polly M. *The dog who had kittens*
Robins, Joan. *Addie meets Max*
Rockwell, Anne F. *Fire engines*
  Hugo at the park
  Hugo at the window
  When Hugo went to school
  Willy runs away
Roffey, Maureen. *Quick, catch Dan!*
Rogers, Paul Patrick. *What can you see?*
Rose, Gerald. *Scruff*
Rose, Mitchell. *Norman*
Rosen, Michael J. (1954-). *Avalanche*
  Bonesy and Isabel
  The dog who walked with God
  With a dog like that, a kid like me . . .
Ross, Tony. *This old man*
  Towser and the terrible thing
Rotenberg, Lisa. *Rodeo pup*
Round, Graham. *Hangdog*
Rowand, Phyllis. *George*
  George goes to town
Ruby-Spears Enterprises. *The puppy's new adventures*
Rylant, Cynthia. *The bookshop dog*
  Dog Heaven
  Mr. Putter and Tabby walk the dog
  Tulip sees America
Saltzberg, Barney. *Cromwell*
Sandberg, Inger. *Nicholas' favorite pet*
San Souci, Robert D. *The Hobyahs*
Sarrazin, Johan. *Tootle*
Saunders, Susan. *Wales' tale*
Saxon, Charles D. *Don't worry about Poopsie*
Scheidl, Gerda Marie. *Pickle and Patch*
Schneider, Elisa. *The merry-go-round dog*
Schneider, Howie. *No dogs allowed*
Schroeder, Binette. *Tuffa and her friends*
  Tuffa and the bone
  Tuffa and the ducks
  Tuffa and the picnic
  Tuffa and the snow
Schulman, Janet. *The great big dummy*
Schulz, Charles M. *Snoopy's facts and fun book about
  boats*
  Snoopy's facts and fun book about farms
  Snoopy's facts and fun book about houses
  Snoopy's facts and fun book about nature
  Snoopy's facts and fun book about planes
  Snoopy's facts and fun book about seashores
  Snoopy's facts and fun book about seasons
  Snoopy's facts and fun book about trucks
Schwartz, Amy. *Oma and Bobo*
Schweninger, Ann. *Autumn days*
  Summertime
  Wintertime
Scott, Sally. *Little Wiener*
  There was Timmy!
Seeber, Dorothea P. *A pup just for me . . . A boy just
  for me*
Seibert, Patricia. *Mush!*
Seibold, J. Otto. *Mr. Lunch borrows a canoe*
Seligson, Susan. *The amazing Amos and the greatest
  couch on earth*
  Amos ahoy
  Amos camps out

Winthrop, Elizabeth. *I'm the Boss!*
Wirth, Beverly. *Margie and me*
Wittbold, Maureen. *Mending Peter's heart*
Wold, Jo Anne. *Well! Why didn't you say so?*
Wood, Leslie. *A dog called Mischief*
Wright, Betty Ren. *Pet detectives!*
Yeoman, John. *Old Mother Hubbard's dog dresses up*
   Old Mother Hubbard's dog learns to play
   Old Mother Hubbard's dog needs a doctor
   Old Mother Hubbard's dog takes up sport
Yolen, Jane. *Nocturne*
Yorinks, Arthur. *Harry and Lulu*
   Hey, Al
Ziefert, Harriet. *A dozen dogs*
   I swapped my dog
   Pushkin meets the bundle
   Pushkin minds the bundle
   Sam and Lucy
   Sleepy dog
   Where's the dog?
Zimelman, Nathan. *Mean Murgatroyd and the ten cats*
Zion, Gene. *Harry, the dirty dog*
   No roses for Harry
Zolotow, Charlotte (Shapiro). *The old dog*
   The poodle who barked at the wind

Animals – dolphins

Anderson, Lonzo. *Arion and the dolphins*
Bailey, Donna. *Dolphins*
Behrens, June. *Whales of the world*
Chottin, Ariane. *The curious little dolphin*
Cousteau Society. *Dolphins*
DeSaix, Frank. *The girl who danced with dolphins*
Fowler, Allan. *Friendly dolphins*
Gordon, Sharon. *Dolphins and porpoises*
Jacka, Martin. *Waiting for Billy*
Lilly, Kenneth. *Animals of the ocean*
McKenna, Virginia. *Back to the blue*
Nakatani, Chiyoko. *Fumio and the dolphins*
Orstadius, Brita. *The dolphin journey*
Winton, Tim. *The deep*
Wood, Audrey. *The rainbow bridge*

Animals – donkeys

Æsop. *The miller, his son and their donkey*, ill. by Roger Antoine Duvoisin
   The miller, his son and their donkey, ill. by Eugen Sopko
Bates, H. E. (Herbert Ernest). *Achilles and Diana*
   Achilles the donkey
Berger, Barbara Helen. *The donkey's dream*
Bettina (Bettina Ehrlich). *Cocolo comes to America*
   Cocolo's home
   Piccolo
Brown, Katherine. *The Small One*
Brown, Marcia. *Tamarindo!*
Brown, Margaret Wise. *Little Donkey close your eyes*
Calhoun, Mary. *Old man Whickutt's donkey*
Clark, Elizabeth. *Father Christmas and the donkey*
Cohen, Barbara. *The donkey's story*
Crawford, Sheryl Ann. *The baby who changed the world*
Daugherty, Sonia (Medvedeva). *Vanka's donkey*
DeVajay, Szabolcs. *The animals' gift*
Devlin, Wende. *Cranberry summer*
Dumas, Philippe. *Lucy, a tale of a donkey*

   The story of Edward
Duvoisin, Roger Antoine. *Donkey-donkey*
Evans, Katherine. *The man, the boy and the donkey*
Gramatky, Hardie. *Bolivar*
Gray, Genevieve. *How far, Felipe?*
Grimm, Jacob. *The donkey prince*
Grindley, Sally. *Why is the sky blue?*
Hale, Irina. *Donkey's dreadful day*
Hol, Coby. *Niki's little donkey*
Hurd, Edith Thacher. *Under the lemon tree*
Jensen, Patricia. *Little Donkey learns to help*
La Fontaine, Jean de. *The miller, the boy and the donkey*, adapt. and ill. by Brian Wildsmith
McCrea, James. *The king's procession*
Maris, Ron. *Hold tight, bear!*
Morpurgo, Michael. *Jo-Jo the melon donkey*
Ness, Evaline. *Josefina February*
Oppenheim, Joanne. *Donkey's tale*
Oppenheim, Shulamith Levey. *Yanni rubbish*
Quintero-Spongberg, Emily. *Hannibal and the king*
Raphael, Elaine. *Donkey and Carlo*
   Donkey, it's snowing
Seignobosc, Françoise. *Chouchou*
Showalter, Jean B. *The donkey ride*
Silver, Jody. *Isadora*
Steig, William. *Farmer Palmer's wagon ride*
   Sylvester and the magic pebble
Tangvald, Christine Harder. *The Rinky Dinky Donkey*
Van Woerkom, Dorothy. *Donkey Ysabel*
Wildsmith, Brian. *A Christmas story*
Winter, Paula. *Sir Andrew*
Young, Ed (Edward). *Donkey trouble*

Animals – dormice

Alexander, Sue. *Dear Phoebe*
Dale, Elizabeth. *How long?*
De Beer, Hans. *Bernard Bear's amazing adventure*
Ezra, Mark. *The sleepy dormouse*
Fuchshuber, Annegert. *Giant story – Mouse tale*
Ravilious, Robin. *Two in a pocket*
San José, Christine. *Sleeping Beauty*

Animals – elephant seals

Bare, Colleen Stanley. *Elephants on the beach*

Animals – elephants

Alborough, Jez. *Esther's trunk*
Allen, Judy. *Elephant*
Allinson, Beverley. *Effie*
Ambrus, Victor G. *Mishka*
Appelt, Kathi. *Elephants aloft*
Backstein, Karen. *The blind men and the elephant*
Balian, Lorna. *Elephant?*
Barner, Bob. *Elephant facts*
Barry, David. *The Rajah's rice*
Bates, Ivan. *All by myself*
Berry, James. *Don't leave an elephant to go and chase a bird*
Bishop, Ann. *The Ella Fannie elephant riddle book*
Blumberg, Rhoda. *Jumbo*
Bohman, Nils Axel Erik. *Jim, Jock and Jumbo*
Bos, Burny. *Ollie the elephant*
Boynton, Sandra. *If at first . . .*
Brown, Ken (Ken James). *Nellie's knot*
Brunhoff, Jean de. *Babar and Father Christmas*

On the town
Through the year with Harriet
Where is my friend?
Manson, Christopher. *Two travelers*
Martin, Bill (William Ivan). *Smoky Poky*
Mayer, Mercer. *Ah-choo*
Melmed, Laura Krauss. *Jumbo's lullaby*
Miranda, Anne. *The elephant at the Waldorf*
Mitra, Annie. *Tusk! Tusk!*
Mogensen, Jan. *The tiger's breakfast*
Moser, Erwin. *Wilma the elephant*
Murphy, Jill. *All in one piece*
Five minutes' peace
A piece of cake
A quiet night in
Nakano, Hirotaka. *Elephant blue*
Noble, Kate. *The blue elephant*
O'Donnell, Peter. *Dizzy*
Oscar
Offen, Hilda. *Elephant pie*
Paterson, Bettina. *Bun and Mrs. Tubby*
Bun's birthday
Patz, Nancy. *No thumpin' no bumpin' no rumpus tonight!*
Pumpernickel tickle and mean green cheese
Paxton, Tom. *Engelbert the elephant*
Pearce, Philippa. *Emily's own elephant*
Peek, Merle. *The balancing act*
Peet, Bill (William Bartlett). *The ant and the elephant*
Ella
Encore for Eleanor
Percy, Graham. *Elephants never forget*
Perkins, Al. *Tubby and the lantern*
Tubby and the Poo-Bah
Petersham, Maud. *The circus baby*
Pluckrose, Henry Arthur. *Elephants*
Price, Mathew. *Dumbo*
Propp, James. *Tuscanini*
Quigley, Lillian Fox. *The blind men and the elephant*
Radcliffe, Theresa. *Bashi, elephant baby*
Richardson, Judith Benét. *The way home*
Riddell, Chris. *The trouble with elephants*
Rogers, Edmund. *Elephants*
Sadler, Marilyn. *Alistair's elephant*
Saxe, John Godfrey. *The blind men and the elephant*
Schlein, Miriam. *Elephant herd*
Schwartz, Amy. *How to catch an elephant*
Schwartz, Roslyn. *Rose and Dorothy*
Seuss, Dr. *Horton hatches the egg*
Horton hears a Who!
Sheppard, Jeff. *The right number of elephants*
Simont, Marc. *How come elephants?*
Slobodkina, Esphyr. *Pezzo the peddler and the circus elephant*
Smath, Jerry. *But no elephants*
Elephant goes to school
Steig, William. *Doctor De Soto goes to Africa*
An eye for elephants
Stock, Catherine. *Alexander's midnight snack*
Talbot, John. *Pins and needles*
Tompert, Ann. *Just a little bit*
Tresselt, Alvin R. *Smallest elephant in the world*
Velthuijs, Max. *Crocodile's masterpiece*
Vries, Anke de. *My elephant can do almost anything*
Wahl, Jan. *Hello, elephant*
Ward, Nanda Weedon. *The elephant that ga-lumped*
Wayne-von-Königslöw, Andrea. *Bing and Chutney*
Weedn, Flavia. *The elephant prince*

Weinberg, Lawrence. *The Forgetful Bears meet Mr. Memory*
Weisgard, Leonard. *Silly Willy Nilly*
Weiss, Leatie. *My teacher sleeps in school*
Wells, H. G. (Herbert George). *The adventures of Tommy*
Westcott, Nadine Bernard. *Peanut butter and jelly*
Williamson, Hamilton. *Little elephant*
Yee, Patrick. *Little Buddy meets Bobo*
Ylla. *The little elephant*
Yoshida, Toshi. *Elephant crossing*
Young, Ed (Edward). *Seven blind mice*
Young, Miriam Burt. *If I rode an elephant*

Animals – elk

Hausman, Gerald. *The story of Blue Elk*
Hodge, Deborah. *Deer, moose, elk and caribou*

Animals – endangered animals

Ackerman, Diane. *Monk seal hideaway*
Aliki. *My visit to the zoo*
Allen, Judy. *Eagle*
Elephant
Panda
Seal
Tiger
Whale
Balog, James. *James Balog's animals A to Z*
Cowcher, Helen. *Tigress*
Cromie, William J. *Steven and the green turtle*
Davis, Maggie S. *A garden of whales*
Dobson, David. *Can we save them?*
Fowler, Allan. *The biggest animal on land*
Greene, Carol. *Reading about the gray wolf*
Reading about the peregrine falcon
Reading about the river otter
Hall, Derek. *Baby animals*
Hamilton, Virginia. *Jaguarundi*
Havill, Juanita. *Sato and the elephants*
Heinz, Brian J. *The wolves*
Hirschi, Ron. *Where are my bears?*
Where are my prairie dogs and black-footed ferrets?
Where are my puffins, whales, and seals?
Where are my swans, whooping cranes, and singing loons?
Jenkins, Priscilla Belz. *Falcons nest on skyscrapers*
Jonas, Ann. *Aardvarks, disembark!*
Kalman, Benjamin. *Animals in danger*
Lee, Sandra. *Giant pandas*
London, Jonathan. *Condor's egg*
McFarlane, Sheryl. *Eagle dreams*
Mullins, Patricia. *V for vanishing*
Paladino, Catherine. *Our vanishing farm animals*
Raffi. *Baby beluga*
Sackett, Elisabeth. *Danger on the African grassland*
Danger on the Arctic ice
Schertle, Alice. *Advice for a frog and other poems*
Steele, Philip. *The blue whale*
The giant panda
Turbak, Gary. *Mountain animals in danger*
Ocean animals in danger
Weeks, Sarah. *Crocodile smile*

Animals – ferrets

Hirschi, Ron. *Where are my prairie dogs and black-footed ferrets?*

London, Jonathan. *Phantom of the prairie*

Animals – foxes

Abolafia, Yossi. *Fox tale*
Æsop. *The raven and the fox*
  Three Æsop fox fables
Ambrus, Victor G. *Country wedding*
Anderson, Paul S. *Red fox and the hungry tiger*
Anno, Mitsumasa. *Anno's Æsop*
Arnosky, Jim. *Watching foxes*
Auch, Mary Jane. *Peeping Beauty*
Ayers, Rebecca Hickox. *Zorro and Quwi*
Baron, Alan. *Red Fox dances*
Barr, Cathrine. *Hound dog's bone*
Baynton, Martin. *Fifty and the fox*
Beck, Ian. *Five little ducks*
Bemelmans, Ludwig. *Welcome home!*
Bergman, Donna. *City fox*
Berson, Harold. *Henry Possum*
  Joseph and the snake
Bingham, Mindy. *My way Sally*
Blyler, Allison. *Finding foxes*
Bodnar, Judit Z. *Tale of a tail*
  A wagonload of fish
Bonning, Tony. *Another fine mess*
Brown, Marcia. *The neighbors*
Brown, Margaret Wise. *Fox eyes*
Brutschy, Jennifer. *The winter fox*
Buck, Pearl S. (Pearl Sydenstricker). *The little fox in
  the middle*
Bunting, Eve (Anne Evelyn). *Box, fox, ox, and the
  peacock*
  Red fox running
Burningham, John. *Harquin*
Burton, Jane. *Fancy the fox*
  Trill the fox cub
Calhoun, Mary. *Houn' dog*
Caple, Kathy. *Fox and bear*
Carroll, Ruth. *What Whiskers did*
Carter, Anne. *Ruff leaves home*
Chaucer, Geoffrey. *Chanticleer and the fox*
Christelow, Eileen. *Henry and the red stripes*
Conover, Chris. *Mother Goose and the sly fox*
Cox, Judy. *Rabbit pirates*
Cunningham, Julia. *The vision of François the fox*
Davis, Lavinia (Riker). *Roger and the fox*
Delton, Judy. *Duck goes fishing*
Domanska, Janina. *The best of the bargain*
DuBois, Ivy. *Mother fox*
Edwards, Pamela Duncan. *Four famished foxes and
  Fosdyke*
Ehlert, Lois. *Mole's hill*
  Moon rope
Enderle, Judith (Ann) Ross. *What would Mama do?*
Fatio, Louise. *The red bantam*
Firmin, Peter. *Basil Brush and the windmills*
Fox, Charles Philip. *A fox in the house*
The fox went out on a chilly night
French, Vivian. *Red Hen and Sly Fox*
Giffard, Hannah. *Red Fox*
  Red Fox on the move
Ginsburg, Mirra. *Across the stream*
  The fox and the hare
  Mushroom in the rain
  Two greedy bears
Gliori, Debi. *No matter what*
Grimm, Jacob. *The golden bird*, ill. by Isabelle Brent
  The golden bird, ill. by Sandro Nardini

The horse, the fox, and the lion
Mrs. Fox's wedding
Grindley, Sally. *Silly Goose and Dizzy Duck play hide-
  and-seek*
What are friends for?
What will I do without you?
Guzzo, Sandra E. *Fox and Heggie*
Hartley, Deborah. *Up north in the winter*
Havard, Christian. *The fox, playful prowler*
Hayes, Sarah. *Nine ducks nine*
Hayward, Linda. *All stuck up*
Hogrogian, Nonny. *One fine day*
Houck, Eric L. *Rabbit surprise*
Hurd, Edith Thacher. *Under the lemon tree*
Hutchins, Pat. *Rosie's walk*
  Rosie's walk, a board book
Isami, Ikuyo. *The fox's egg*
Jacobson, Jennifer Richard. *Moon sandwich mom*
Janovitz, Marilyn. *Little Fox*
Kent, Jack. *Silly goose*
Komaiko, Leah. *Fritzi Fox flew in from Florida*
Koralek, Jenny. *The friendly fox*
Kraus, Robert. *All my chickens*
Kvasnosky, Laura McGee. *Zelda and Ivy*
  Zelda and Ivy and the boy next door
  Zelda and Ivy one Christmas
Langston, Laura. *The fox's kettle*
Latimer, Jim. *The fox under first base*
Leverich, Kathleen. *The hungry fox and the foxy duck*
Lifton, Betty Jean. *The many lives of Chio and Goro*
Lindgren, Astrid. *The tomten and the fox*
Ling, Mary. *Fox*
Lionni, Leo. *In the rabbitgarden*
Lipkind, William. *The Christmas bunny*
  The little tiny rooster
Livermore, Elaine. *Follow the fox*
London, Jonathan. *Gray fox*
  Ice Bear and Little Fox
McBratney, Sam. *I'll always be your friend*
McDermott, Gerald. *The fox and the stork*
McKissack, Patricia C. *Flossie and the fox*
Malkovych, Ivan. *The cat and the rooster*
Marshall, Edward. *Fox all week*
  Fox and his friends
  Fox at school
  Fox in love
  Fox on wheels
Marshall, James. *Fox on the job*
  Rapscallion Jones
  Wings
Marston, Elsa. *The fox maiden*
Mayne, William. *A house in town*
Meddaugh, Susan. *Maude and Claude go abroad*
Miles, Miska. *The fox and the fire*
Miller, Edward. *Frederick Ferdinand Fox*
Nikola-Lisa, W. *The dancin' fox*
Nordqvist, Sven. *The fox hunt*
Numeroff, Laura Joffe. *What daddies do best*
Palatini, Margie. *Zoom Broom*
Pevear, Richard. *Mister Cat-and-a-Half*
Potter, Beatrix. *The tale of Mr. Tod*
Preston, Edna Mitchell. *Squawk to the moon, little
  goose*
Rankin, Joan. *Wow! It's great being a duck*
Riordan, James. *Little Bunny Bobkin*
Roach, Marilynne K. *Dune fox*
Rockwell, Anne F. *Big boss*
Sara. *The rabbit, the fox, and the wolf*

Schami, Rafik. *Albert and Lila*
Schlein, Miriam. *The four little foxes*
Selsam, Millicent E. *A first look at dogs*
Sharmat, Marjorie Weinman. *The best Valentine in the world*
Small, David. *Eulalie and the hopping head*
Steig, William. *Doctor De Soto*
   Roland, the minstrel pig
Szekeres, Cyndy. *Good night, Sammy*
Taylor, Harriet Peck. *Ulaq and the northern lights*
Tejima, Keizaburo. *Fox's dream*
Thomas, Patricia. *"There are rocks in my socks!" said the ox to the fox*
Threadgall, Colin. *Proud rooster and the fox*
The three little pigs. *The three little pigs and the fox*
Tompert, Ann. *Grandfather Tang's story*
   Little Fox goes to the end of the world
Turner, Ann Warren. *Hedgehog for breakfast*
Varga, Judy. *The mare's egg*
Wallace, Karen. *Red fox*
Walsh, Ellen Stoll. *You silly goose*
Walt Disney Productions. *Tod and Copper*
   Tod and Vixey
Watson, Clyde. *Father Fox's feast of songs*
   Tom Fox and the apple pie
   Valentine foxes
Watson, Wendy. *Tales for a winter's eve*
Weil, Lisl. *Gillie and the flattering fox*
Wells, Rosemary. *Don't spill it again, James*
Westwood, Jennifer. *Going to Squintum's*
Wiese, Kurt. *The dog, the fox and the fleas*
Wilhelm, Hans. *More bunny trouble*
Wyllie, Stephen. *Dinner with fox*

Animals – gerbils

Petty, Kate. *Gerbils*
Roth, Susan L. *Cinnamon's day out*

Animals – giraffes

Aggs, Patrice. *The visitor*
Bailey, Donna. *Giraffes*
Brenner, Barbara A. *Mr. Tall and Mr. Small*
Brunhoff, Laurent de. *Serafina the giraffe*
Bush, John. *The giraffe who got in a knot*
Collier, Mary Jo. *The king's giraffe*
Cooke, Ann. *Giraffes at home*
Doughtie, Charles. *High Henry . . . the cowboy who was too tall to ride a horse*
Duvoisin, Roger Antoine. *Periwinkle*
George, Jean Craighead. *Giraffe trouble*
Godard, Alex. *Idora*
Hamsa, Bobbie. *Your pet giraffe*
Irvine, Georgeanne. *Georgie the giraffe*
Le Guin, Ursula K. *Solomon Leviathan's nine hundred and thirty-first trip around the world*
Lemaître, Pascal. *Emily the giraffe*
Milton, Nancy. *The giraffe that walked to Paris*
Rey, H. A. (Hans Augusto). *Cecily G and the nine monkeys*
Riches, Judith. *Giraffes have more fun*
Sharmat, Marjorie Weinman. *Helga high-up*
Weedn, Flavia. *The enchanted tree*

Animals – goats

Ada, Alma Flor. *Jordi's star*
Allamand, Pascale. *The little goat in the mountains*

Ambrus, Victor G. *The seven skinny goats*
   The three poor tailors
Asbjørnsen, P. C. (Peter Christen). *Billy goats Gruff*, ill. by Wendy Edelson
   Billy goats Gruff, ill. by Susan Hellard
   The three billy goats Gruff, ill. by Tim Arnold
   The three billy goats Gruff, ill. by Robert Bender
   The three billy goats Gruff, ill. by Marcia Brown
   The three billy goats Gruff, ill. by Stephen Carpenter
   Three billy goats Gruff, ill. by Tom Dunnington
   The three billy goats Gruff, ill. by Paul Galdone
   The three billy goats Gruff, ill. by David Jorgensen
   The three billy goats Gruff, ill. by Dennis Kendrick
   The three billygoats Gruff, ill. by Eric Kincaid
   The three billy goats Gruff, ill. by Jonathan Langley
   The three billy goats Gruff, ill. by Loretta Lustig
   The three billy goats Gruff, ill. by Thomas Newbury
   The three billy goats Gruff, ill. by Lilian Obligado
   The three billy goats Gruff, ill. by Ed Parker
   The three billy goats Gruff, ill. by Heidi Petach
   The three billy goats Gruff, ill. by Laura Rader
   The three billy goats Gruff, ill. by Glen Rounds
   The three billy goats Gruff, ill. by Janet Stevens
   The three billy goats Gruff, ill. by William Stobbs
   The three billy goats Gruff, ill. by Svend Otto S
   The truth about three billy goats Gruff
Berson, Harold. *Balarin's goat*
Blood, Charles L. *The goat in the rug*
Bornstein, Ruth Lercher. *Of course a goat*
Burton, Jane. *Caper the kid*
Carigiet, Alois. *Anton the goatherd*
Carlson, Natalie Savage. *Spooky and the witch's goat*
Chandoha, Walter. *A baby goat for you*
Chiefari, Janet. *Kids are baby goats*
Chottin, Ariane. *Little Goat's new horns*
Damjan, Mischa. *The wolf and the kid*
Daudet, Alphonse. *The brave little goat of Monsieur Séguin*
Dunn, Judy. *The little goat*
Emberley, Rebecca. *Three cool kids*
Fletcher, Elizabeth. *The little goat*
Gage, Wilson. *Mrs. Gaddy and the fast-growing vine*
Grimm, Jacob. *Nanny goat and the seven little kids*
   The wolf and the seven kids, ill. by Kinuko Y. Craft
   The wolf and the seven little kids, ill. by Svend Otto S
   The wolf and the seven little kids, ill. by Martin Ursell
Hillert, Margaret. *The three goats*
Hoff, Syd. *Happy birthday, Henrietta!*
Hooks, William H. *The Gruff brothers*
Jacobs, Laurie A. *So much in common*
Kessler, Cristina. *One night*
Kimmel, Eric A. *One Eye, Two Eyes, Three Eyes*
Kinsey-Warnock, Natalie. *The summer of Stanley*
Kroll, Steven. *The goat parade*
Leaf, Munro. *Gordon, the goat*
Lewis, J. Patrick. *The night of the goat children*
Lipkind, William. *Billy the kid*
McPhail, David M. *A girl, a goat, and a goose*
Mahy, Margaret. *The queen's goat*
Mills, Alan. *The hungry goat*
Morris, Ann. *700 kids on Grandpa's farm*
Pizer, Abigail. *Hattie the goat*
Rappus, Gerhard. *When the sun was shining*
Royston, Angela. *The goat*
Sattler, Helen Roney. *No place for a goat*
Seignobosc, Françoise. *Biquette, the white goat*

Springtime for Jeanne-Marie
Sharmat, Mitchell. *Gregory, the terrible eater*
Siddiqui, Ashraf. *Bhombal Dass, the uncle of lion*
Slobodkin, Louis. *The polka-dot goat*
   Up high and down low
Suhl, Yuri. *The Purim goat*
Tompert, Ann. *The hungry black bag*
Tudor, Tasha. *Corgiville fair*
Watson, Nancy Dingman. *The birthday goat*
Wildsmith, Brian. *Goat's trail*
Wolkstein, Diane. *The banza*
Ziefert, Harriet. *Pumpkin Pie*

Animals – gorillas

Aardema, Verna. *Princess Gorilla and a new kind of water*
Browne, Anthony. *Gorilla*
   Voices in the park
   Willy and Hugh
   Willy the champ
   Willy the wimp
Buehner, Caralyn. *The escape of Marvin the ape*
Conklin, Gladys. *Little apes*
Delton, Judy. *On a picnic*
George, Jean Craighead. *Gorilla gang*
Hall, Derek. *Gorilla builds*
Harrison, David Lee. *Detective Bob and the great ape escape*
Hazen, Barbara Shook. *The gorilla did it!*
   Gorilla wants to be the baby
Hoff, Syd. *Julius*
Howe, James. *The day the teacher went bananas*
Kessler, Ethel. *Is there a gorilla in the band?*
Krahn, Fernando. *The great ape*
Layton, Neal. *Smile if you're human*
Meyers, Susan. *The truth about gorillas*
Morozumi, Atsuko. *My friend gorilla*
   One gorilla
Most, Bernard. *There's an ape behind the drape*
Palatini, Margie. *Ding dong ding dong*
Schertle, Alice. *The gorilla in the hall*
Selsam, Millicent E. *A first look at monkeys*
Weller, Frances Ward. *The closet gorilla*
Zimelman, Nathan. *Positively no pets allowed*

Animals – groundhogs

Balian, Lorna. *A garden for a groundhog*
Bang, Molly. *Goose*
Bond, Felicia. *Wake up, Vladimir*
Cohen, Carol L. *Wake up, groundhog!*
Coombs, Patricia. *Tilabel*
Delton, Judy. *Groundhog's Day at the doctor*
Glass, Marvin. *What happened today, Freddy Groundhog?*
Hamberger, John. *This is the day*
Jensen, Patricia. *Go to sleep, little groundhog*
Johnson, Crockett. *Will spring be early or will spring be late?*
Kesselman, Wendy Ann. *Time for Jody*
Koscielniak, Bruce. *Geoffrey Groundhog predicts the weather*
Levine, Abby. *Gretchen Groundhog, it's your day!*
Lewin, Betsy. *Groundhog day*
McNulty, Faith. *Woodchuck*
Palazzo, Tony (Anthony D.). *Waldo the woodchuck*
Stanovich, Betty Jo. *Hedgehog adventures*
Tompert, Ann. *Nothing sticks like a shadow*

Watson, Wendy. *Has winter come?*

Animals – guinea pigs

Ayers, Rebecca Hickox. *Zorro and Quwi*
Bare, Colleen Stanley. *Guinea pigs don't read books*
Brooks, Andrea. *The guinea pigs' adventure*
Burton, Jane. *Dazy the guinea pig*
   Gipper the guinea pig
Cooper, Patrick. *Never trust a squirrel*
Duke, Kate. *Bedtime*
   Clean-up day
   The guinea pig ABC
   Guinea pigs far and near
   The playground
   What bounces?
Evans, Mark. *Guinea pigs*
King-Smith, Dick. *I love guinea pigs*
Kroll, Steven. *Patches*
Mayne, William. *Barnabas walks*
Meade, Holly. *John Willy and Freddy McGee*
Meshover, Leonard. *The guinea pigs that went to school*
Miller, Michaela. *Guinea pigs*
Potter, Beatrix. *The tale of Tuppeny*
Pursell, Margaret Sanford. *Polly the guinea pig*
Shannon, Margaret. *Gullible's troubles*
Ziefert, Harriet. *Where's the guinea pig?*

Animals – hamsters

Ambrus, Victor G. *Grandma, Felix, and Mustapha Biscuit*
Baker, Alan. *Benjamin and the box*
   Benjamin bounces back
   Benjamin's balloon
   Benjamin's book
   Benjamin's dreadful dream
   Benjamin's portrait
Blacker, Terence. *Herbie Hamster, where are you?*
Blegvad, Lenore. *The great hamster hunt*
Brandenberg, Franz. *The hit of the party*
Brook, Judy. *Hector and Harriet the night hamsters*
Claude-Lafontaine, Pascale. *Monsieur Bussy, the celebrated hamster*
Gregory, Valiska. *A valentine for Norman Noggs*
Leonard, Marcia. *Hannah the hamster hunter*
Norac, Carl. *Hello, sweetie pie*
   I love you so much
Petty, Kate. *Hamsters*
Rathmann, Peggy. *10 minutes till bedtime*
Vaës, Alain. *The wild hamster*
Watts, Barrie. *Hamster*

Animals – hedgehogs

Berson, Harold. *Why the jackal won't speak to the hedgehog*
Brett, Jan. *Christmas trolls*
   The hat
Brook, Judy. *Tim mouse goes down the stream*
   Tim mouse visits the farm
Cartwright, Ann. *The winter hedgehog*
Dalmais, Anne-Marie. *Henry the hedgehog*
Domanska, Janina. *The best of the bargain*
Flot, Jeannette B. *Princess Kalina and the hedgehog*
Guzzo, Sandra E. *Fox and Heggie*
Holden, Edith. *The hedgehog feast*
McClure, Gillian. *Prickly pig*

Macdonald, Maryann. *Hedgehog bakes a cake*
  Rabbit's birthday kite
Millais, Raoul. *Elijah and Pin-Pin*
Myller, Lois. *No! No!*
Pfister, Marcus. *The happy hedgehog*
Potter, Beatrix. *The tale of Mrs. Tiggy-Winkle*
Ruck-Pauquèt, Gina. *Little hedgehog*
Schubert, Ingrid. *Bear's eggs*
Stanovich, Betty Jo. *Hedgehog adventures*
Stewart, Paul. *The birthday presents*
  A little bit of winter
Stott, Rowena. *The hedgehog feast*
Turner, Ann Warren. *Hedgehog for breakfast*
Waddell, Martin. *The happy hedgehog band*
Yeoman, John. *The bear's water picnic*

Animals – hippopotamuses

Alexander, Sue. *Ellsworth and Millicent*
  What's wrong now, Millicent?
Allen, Frances Charlotte. *Little hippo*
Bennett, Rainey. *The secret hiding place*
Bohman, Nils Axel Erik. *Jim, Jock and Jumbo*
Bos, Claire. *Maurice the hippo*
Boynton, Sandra. *But not the hippopotamus*
  Hester in the wild
  Hippos go berserk
Brown, Marcia. *How, hippo!*
Calmenson, Stephanie. *The birthday hat*
  Where is Grandma Potamus?
Camp, Lindsay. *Keeping up with Cheetah*
Caple, Kathy. *The coolest place in town*
Cole, Babette. *Nungu and the hippopotamus*
Croswell, Volney. *How to hide a hippopotamus*
Dijs, Carla. *Pretend you're a hippo*
Duvoisin, Roger Antoine. *Lonely Veronica*
  Our Veronica goes to Petunia's farm
  Veronica
  Veronica and the birthday present
  Veronica's smile
Flanders, Michael. *The hippopotamus song*
Grejniec, Michael. *Albert's nap*
Heide, Florence Parry. *The bigness contest*
Hill, Eric. *Spot's baby sister*
Jacobs, Laurie A. *So much in common*
Jenkin-Pearce, Susie. *Percy Short and Cuthbert*
Johnson, Doug. *Never babysit the hippopotamuses!*
Kasza, Keiko. *Dorothy and Mikey*
Kishida, Eriko. *The hippo boat*
Kraus, Robert. *Musical Max*
Lasher, Faith B. *Hubert Hippo's world*
Lee, Hector Viveros. *I had a hippopotamus*
Leemis, Ralph. *Mister Momboo's hat*
Leonard, Marcia. *Swimming in the sand*
Lewin, Betsy. *Chubbo's pool*
  Hip, hippo, hooray!
McCarthy, Bobette. *Happy hiding hippos*
  Ten little hippos
MacDonald, Maryann. *Little Hippo gets glasses*
  Little Hippo starts school
Mahy, Margaret. *The boy who was followed home*
Mantegazza, Giovanna. *The hippopotamus*
Marshall, James. *George and Martha*
  George and Martha back in town
  George and Martha encore
  George and Martha one fine day
  George and Martha rise and shine
  George and Martha 'round and 'round
  George and Martha, tons of fun

Martin, Bill (William Ivan). *The happy hippopotami*
Mayer, Marianna. *Marcel the pastry chef*
Mayer, Mercer. *Hiccup*
  Oops
Minarik, Else Holmelund. *Am I beautiful?*
Morgan, Michaela. *Helpful Betty solves a mystery*
  Helpful Betty to the rescue
Most, Bernard. *Hippopotamus hunt*
Mwenye Hadithi. *Hot hippo*
Neugebauer, Charise. *The real winner*
Panek, Dennis. *Matilda Hippo has a big mouth*
Parker, Nancy Winslow. *Love from Uncle Clyde*
Patz, Nancy. *To Annabella Pelican from Thomas Hip-*
  popotamus
Paxton, Tom. *The jungle baseball game*
Pouyanne, Thérèse. *The hippo*
Radford, Derek. *Harry at the garage*
Raschka, Christopher. *The blushful hippopotamus*
Shipton, Jonathan. *How to be a happy hippo*
Slobodkin, Louis. *Hustle and bustle*
Stadler, John. *Three cheers for hippo!*
Sugita, Yutaka. *Helena the unhappy hippopotamus*
Sutton, Jane. *What should a hippo wear?*
Taylor, Judy. *Sophie and Jack*
  Sophie and Jack help out
Thaler, Mike. *Hippo lemonade*
  It's me, hippo!
  There's a hippopotamus under my bed
  What could a hippopotamus be?
Tyler, Linda Wagner. *Waiting for mom*
  When daddy comes home
Waber, Bernard. *"You look ridiculous," said the rhi-*
  noceros to the hippopotamus
Wahl, Jan. *Old Hippo's Easter egg*
Wharton, Thomas. *Hildegard sings*
Woychuk, Denis. *The other side of the wall*
  Pirates
Yee, Wong Herbert. *The Officers' Ball*
Young, Miriam Burt. *Please don't feed Horace*
Ziefert, Harriet. *Harry takes a bath*

Animals – horses, ponies

Aarle, Thomas Van. *Don't put your cart before the*
  horse race
All the pretty little horses
Anderson, C. W. (Clarence Williams). *Billy and*
  Blaze
  Blaze and the forest fire
  Blaze and the gray spotted pony
  Blaze and the gypsies
  Blaze and the Indian cave
  Blaze and the lost quarry
  Blaze and the mountain lion
  Blaze and Thunderbolt
  Blaze finds forgotten roads
  Blaze finds the trail
  Blaze shows the way
  The crooked colt
  Linda and the Indians
  Lonesome little colt
  A pony for Linda
  A pony for three
  The rumble seat pony
Arundel, Jocelyn. *Shoes for Punch*
Asch, Frank. *Goodnight horsey*
Ayers, Rebecca Hickox. *Per and the Dala horse*
Baker, Betty. *Three fools and a horse*
Baker, Karen Lee. *Seneca*

Balet, Jan B. *Five Rollatinis*
Barr, Cathrine. *A horse for Sherry*
Barrett, Lawrence Louis. *Twinkle, the baby colt*
Beatty, Hetty Burlingame. *Bucking horse*
    Little Owl Indian
    Moorland pony
Bemelmans, Ludwig. *Madeline in London*
Blech, Dietlind. *Hello Irina*
Boegehold, Betty. *A horse called Starfire*
Bowden, Joan Chase. *A new home for Snow Ball*
Brett, Jan. *Fritz and the beautiful horses*
Brimner, Larry Dane. *Cowboy up!*
Burningham, John. *Humbert, Mister Firkin and the Lord Mayor of London*
Burton, Jane. *Dizzie the pony*
    Pacer, the pony
Callan, Elizabeth Koda. *Good luck pony*
Chan, Chin-Yi. *Good luck horse*
Chandler, Edna Walker. *Pony rider*
Chandra, Deborah. *A is for Amos*
Charmatz, Bill. *The Troy St. bus*
Choldenko, Gennifer. *Moonstruck*
Christiansen, Candace. *The ice horse*
Climo, Lindee. *Clyde*
Coerr, Eleanor. *Chang's paper pony*
Cohen, Caron Lee. *The mud pony*
Cole, Babette. *Babette Cole's ponies*
    Winni Allfours
Cole, Joanna. *Riding Silver Star*
Collington, Peter. *The midnight circus*
Couture, Susan Arkin. *The biggest horse I ever did see*
Cox, David. *Tin Lizzie and Little Nell*
Cretien, Paul D. *Sir Henry and the dragon*
Cummings, W. T. (Walter Thies). *The kid*
Damrell, Liz. *With the wind*
Darling, Kathy (Mary Kathleen). *Pecos Bill finds a horse*
Demi. *The hallowed horse*
Dennis, Wesley. *Flip and the cows*
    Flip and the morning
    Tumble, the story of a mustang
Doherty, Berlie. *Snowy*
Dragonwagon, Crescent. *Margaret Ziegler is horse-crazy*
Duncan, Lois. *Horses of dreamland*
Ehrlich, Amy. *Emma's new pony*
Elborn, Andrew. *Noah and the ark and the animals*
Ets, Marie Hall. *Mr. Penny's race horse*
Fain, James W. *Rodeos*
Farley, Walter. *Black stallion*
Fatio, Louise. *Anna, the horse*
Felton, Harold W. *Pecos Bill and the mustang*
Fregosi, Claudia. *The happy horse*
Friskey, Margaret (Margaret Richards). *Indian Two Feet and his horse*
Frost, Robert. *The runaway*
Garbutt, Bernard. *Roger, the rosin back*
Gaston, Susan. *New boots for Salvador*
Glass, Andrew. *The sweetwater run*
Goble, Paul. *Adopted by the eagles*
    The gift of the sacred dog
    The girl who loved wild horses
Grabianski, Janusz. *Horses*
Greaves, Margaret. *The star horse*
Greenfield, Eloise. *On my horse*
Greydanus, Rose. *Horses*
Grimm, Jacob. *The horse, the fox, and the lion*
Gross, Ruth Belov. *The girl who wouldn't get married*
Haas, Jessie. *Getting ready to drive a horse and cart*

    No foal yet
    Sugaring
Hasler, Eveline. *Martin is our friend*
Hawkinson, John. *Where the wild apples grow*
Heilbroner, Joan. *Robert the rose horse*
Herman, R. A. (Ronnie Ann). *Pal the pony*
Herriot, James. *Bonny's big day*
Herzig, Alison Cragin. *Bronco busters*
Heuck, Sigrid. *Pony and Bear are friends*
Hirschi, Ron. *What is a horse?*
    Where do horses live?
Hoban, Russell. *The rain door*
Hoberman, Mary Ann. *Mr. and Mrs. Muddle*
Hoff, Syd. *Chester*
    The horse in Harry's room
Hoffman, Mary. *Clever Katya*
Hol, Coby. *Henrietta saves the show*
Honda, Tetsuya. *Wild horse winter*
Inkiow, Dimiter. *Me and Clara and Baldwin the pony*
Ipcar, Dahlov. *One horse farm*
    World full of horses
Jacka, Martin. *Waiting for Billy*
James, Shirley Kerby. *Going to a horse farm*
Jauck, Andrea. *Assateague*
Jeffers, Susan. *All the pretty horses*
Karim, Roberta. *Mandy Sue Day*
Keeping, Charles. *Molly o' the moors*
Kessler, Ethel. *Is there a horse in your house?*
King, Deborah. *Custer*
Kinsey-Warnock, Natalie. *The wild horses of Sweetbriar*
Kraus, Robert. *Springfellow*
    Springfellow's parade
Krauss, Ruth. *Charlotte and the white horse*
Krum, Charlotte. *The four riders*
La Farge, Phyllis. *Joanna runs away*
Lasell, Fen. *Michael grows a wish*
Le Guin, Ursula K. *A ride on the red mare's back*
Lester, Julius. *Black cowboy, wild horses*
Ling, Mary. *Foal*
Lobel, Arnold. *Lucille*
Locker, Thomas. *The mare on the hill*
London, Jonathan. *If I had a horse*
    Mustang canyon
London, Sara. *Firehouse Max*
Low, Alice. *David's windows*
McGinley, Phyllis. *The horse who lived upstairs*
McMillan, Bruce. *Gletta the foal*
Marshall, James. *Hey, diddle, daddle*
Martin, Bill (William Ivan). *Chicken Chuck*
Martin, Jacqueline Briggs. *The finest horse in town*
Mayer, Marianna. *The black horse*
Medearis, Angela Shelf. *The zebra-riding cowboy*
Meeks, Esther K. *Playland pony*
Metaxas, Eric. *The gardener's apprentice*
Miles, Miska. *Friend of Miguel*
Mullins, Patricia. *One horse waiting for me*
Nelson, S. D. *Gift horse*
Osborne, Mary Pope. *Moonhorse*, ill. by David McPhail
    Moonhorse, ill. by S. M. Saelig
Otsuka, Yuzo. *Suho and the white horse*
Otto, Margaret Glover. *The little brown horse*
Paterson, A. B. (Andrew Barton). *Mulga Bill's bicycle*
Patterson, Geoffrey. *The naughty boy and the strawberry horse*
Peet, Bill (William Bartlett). *Cowardly Clyde*
Pender, Lydia. *Barnaby and the horses*

Peterson, Cris. *Horsepower*
Peterson, Jeanne Whitehouse. *Sometimes I dream horses*
Pitcher, Caroline. *Run with the wind*
Pluckrose, Henry Arthur. *Horses*
Porter, Sue. *Parsnip and the pink blanket*
Primavera, Elise. *Basil and Maggie*
Rabinowitz, Sandy. *A colt named mischief*
    What's happening to Daisy?
Richards, Jane. *A horse grows up*
Robbins, Sandra. *The firefly star*
Rosenberg, Liz. *The carousel*
Rounds, Glen. *Once we had a horse*
    The strawberry roan
Royston, Angela. *The pony*
Saville, Lynn. *Horses in the circus ring*
Scheidl, Gerda Marie. *Pickle and Patch*
Scott, Ann Herbert. *Someday rider*
Sewall, Marcia. *Ridin' that strawberry roan*
Sewell, Helen Moore. *Peggy and the pony*
Slobodkina, Esphyr. *The wonderful feast*
Sonberg, Lynn. *A horse named Paris*
Springer, Nancy. *Music of their hooves*
Steers, Billy. *Tractor Mac*
Sutton, Elizabeth Henning. *A pony for keeps*
Thayer, Jane. *Andy and the runaway horse*
    The horse with the Easter bonnet
Thompson, Vivian Laubach. *The horse that liked sandwiches*
Tinkelman, Murray. *Cowgirl*
Van Camp, Richard. *What's the most beautiful thing you know about horses?*
Ward, Lynd. *The silver pony*
Watson, Esther (Pearl). *The adventures of Jules and Gertie*
Wells, Rosemary. *Abdul*
Winthrop, Elizabeth. *The little humpbacked horse*
Wondriska, William. *The stop*
Wright, Dare. *Look at a colt*
Yeoman, John. *The young performing horse*
Yolen, Jane. *Sky dogs*
Young, Ed (Edward). *The lost horse*
Young, Miriam Burt. *If I rode a horse*
Zimnik, Reiner. *The proud circus horse*
Zolotow, Charlotte (Shapiro). *I have a horse of my own*

Animals – hyenas

Grimsdell, Jeremy. *Kalinzu*
Kimmel, Eric A. *Anansi and the magic stick*
Prelutsky, Jack. *The mean old mean hyena*

Animals – jackals

Aardema, Verna. *Jackal's flying lesson*
Alexander, Sue. *Peacocks are very special*

Animals – jaguars

Brusca, María Cristina. *When jaguars ate the moon*
Cowcher, Helen. *Jaguar*
Hamilton, Virginia. *Jaguarundi*
Milton, Joyce. *Big cats*
Ryder, Joanne. *Jaguar in the rain forest*

Animals – kangaroos

Braun, Kathy. *Kangaroo and kangaroo*
Bridges, Margaret Park. *Will you take care of me?*
Brown, Margaret Wise. *Young kangaroo*
Chottin, Ariane. *Little Kangaroo finds his way*
Cole, Joanna. *Norma Jean, jumping bean*
Hague, Michael. *The perfect present*
Hamsa, Bobbie. *Your pet kangaroo*
Harper, Anita. *It's not fair!*
Hurd, Edith Thacher. *The mother kangaroo*
Johnson, Crockett. *Upside down*
Katz, Avner. *The little pickpocket*
Kent, Jack. *Joey*
    Joey runs away
Kipling, Rudyard. *The sing-song of old man kangaroo*
Leonard, Marcia. *Counting kangaroos*
McKee, David. *Elmer and the kangaroo*
Most, Bernard. *The very boastful kangaroo*
Murphy, Stuart J. *Too many kangaroo things to do!*
Pape, D. L. (Donna Lugg). *Where is my little Joey?*
Payne, Emmy. *Katy no-pocket*
Sanchez, Jose Louis Garcia. *Kangaroo*
Schlein, Miriam. *Big talk*, ill. by Joan Auclair
    Big talk, ill. by Laura Lydecker
Selig, Sylvie. *Kangaroo*
Stonehouse, Bernard. *Kangaroos*
Townsend, Anita. *The kangaroo*
Ungerer, Tomi. *Adelaide*
Vaughan, Marcia Kapok. *Snap!*
Wiseman, Bernard. *Little new kangaroo*

Animals – kindness to animals *see* Character traits – kindness to animals

Animals – koalas

Armitage, Ronda. *Harry hates shopping!*
Bassett, Lisa. *Koala Christmas*
Bowden, Miriam. *The adventure of Paz in the land of numbers*
Broome, Errol. *The smallest koala*
Cox, Paul. *The case of the botched book*
    The great eucalyptus mystery
    The riddle of the floating island
Du Bois, William Pène. *Bear circus*
    Bear party
Fox, Mem. *Koala Lou*
Gelman, Rita Golden. *A koala grows up*
Hellard, Susan. *Eleanor and the babysitter*
Irvine, Georgeanne. *Sydney the koala*
Krings, Antoon. *Oliver's bicycle*
    Oliver's pool
    Oliver's strawberry patch
Levens, George. *Kippy the koala*
London, Jonathan. *A koala for Katie*
Nobisso, Josephine. *For the sake of a cake*
Quackenbush, Robert M. *I don't want to go, I don't know how to act*
Ruck-Pauquèt, Gina. *Oh, that koala!*
Snyder, Dick. *One day at the zoo*
Sotzek, Hannelore. *A koala is not a bear!*
Walsh, Grahame L. *Didane the koala*

Animals – lemmings

Steig, Jeanne. *Consider the lemming*

Animals – lemurs

Chichester Clark, Emma. *Lunch with Aunt Augusta*
Hellard, Susan. *Baby lemur*

Animals – leopards

Aardema, Verna. *Half-a-ball-of-kenki*
Cherry, Lynne. *Snow leopard*
Ipcar, Dahlov. *Stripes and spots*
Irvine, Georgeanne. *Lindi the leopard*
Keller, Holly. *Brave Horace*
    Horace
Kepes, Juliet. *Run little monkeys, run, run, run*
Kipling, Rudyard. *How the leopard got his spots*, ill. by
    Caroline Ebborn
    How the leopard got his spots, ill. by Lori
    Lohstoeter
Livermore, Elaine. *Looking for Henry*
McDonald, Mary Ann. *Leopards*
Maestro, Giulio. *Leopard is sick*
Milton, Joyce. *Big cats*
Mollel, Tololwa M. (Tololwa Marti). *To dinner, for
    dinner*
Radcliffe, Theresa. *The snow leopard*
Robertson, Janet. *Oscar's spots*
Souhami, Jessica. *The leopard's drum*

Animals – lions

Aardema, Verna. *The lonely lioness and the ostrich
    chicks*
Adamson, Joy. *Elsa*
    Elsa and her cubs
Æsop. *Androcles and the lion*, ill. by Janusz Grabian-
    ski
    Androcles and the lion, ill. by Dennis Nolan
    Androcles and the lion, ill. by Robert Rayevsky
    Androcles and the lion, ill. by Janet Stevens
    The lion and the mouse, ill. by Carol Jones
    The lion and the mouse, ill. by Lisa McCue
    The lion and the mouse, ill. by Gerald Rose
    The lion and the mouse, ill. by Bernadette Watts
    The lion and the mouse, ill. by Ed Young
Allen, Pamela. *A lion in the night*
Anholt, Catherine. *A kiss like this*
Balet, Jan B. *Ned and Ed and the lion*
Bannerman, Helen. *The story of the teasing monkey*
Belloc, Hilaire. *Jim, who ran away from his nurse,
    and was eaten by a lion*
Bible. Old Testament. Daniel. *Daniel in the lions'
    den*, ill. by Leon Baxter
    Daniel in the lions' den, ill. by Jim Cummins
    Daniel in the lions' den, ill. by Diana Mayo
Bohman, Nils Axel Erik. *Jim, Jock and Jumbo*
Brenner, Barbara A. *Lion and Lamb*
Bridges, William. *Lion Island*
Brown, Margaret Wise. *The sleepy little lion*
Cabrera, Jane. *Rory and the lion*
Chichester Clark, Emma. *The story of Horrible Hilda
    and Henry*
Cottringer, Anne. *Ella and the naughty lion*
Daugherty, James Henry. *Andy and the lion*
    The picnic
Davies, Andrew. *Poonam's pets*
Davis, Douglas F. *The lion's tail*
Day, Nancy Raines. *The lion's whiskers*
Delton, Judy. *On a picnic*
Demarest, Chris L. *Clemens' kingdom*
Devlin, Wende. *Aunt Agatha, there's a lion under the
    couch!*
Du Bois, William Pène. *Lion*
Fatio, Louise. *The happy lion*
    The happy lion and the bear

    The happy lion in Africa
    The happy lion roars
    The happy lion's quest
    The happy lion's rabbits
    The happy lion's treasure
    The happy lion's vacation
    The three happy lions
Fechner, Amrei. *I am a little lion*
Ford, Miela. *Watch us play*
Freeman, Don. *Dandelion*
Galdone, Paul. *Androcles and the lion*
Gay, Zhenya. *I'm tired of lions*
George, Jean Craighead. *Giraffe trouble*
Gliori, Debi. *A lion at bedtime*
Goodhart, Pippa. *Row, row, row your boat*
Greaves, Margaret. *Sarah's lion*
Grimm, Jacob. *The horse, the fox, and the lion*
Hancock, Joy Elizabeth. *The loudest little lion*
Hawkins, Mark. *A lion under her bed*
Hill, Susan. *Simba's A-Z*
Hoban, Russell. *The rain door*
Hodges, Margaret. *St. Jerome and the lion*
Hurd, Edith Thacher. *Johnny Lion's bad day*
    Johnny Lion's book
    Johnny Lion's rubber boots
Jensen, Patricia. *Gentle Little Lion*
Kasza, Keiko. *The mightiest*
Kishida, Eriko. *The lion and the bird's nest*
Kleven, Elisa. *The lion and the little red bird*
La Fontaine, Jean de. *The lion and the rat*
MacDonald, Suse. *Nanta's lion*
McKean, Thomas. *Hooray for Grandma Jo!*
Mahy, Margaret. *A lion in the meadow*
Makower, Sylvia. *Samson's breakfast*
Mann, Peggy. *King Laurence, the alarm clock*
Michael, Emory H. *Androcles and the lion*
Michel, Anna. *Little wild lion cub*
Milton, Joyce. *Big cats*
Moers, Hermann. *Evie to the rescue!*
    Hugo's baby brother
Mollel, Tololwa M. (Tololwa Marti). *Dume's roar*
Montenegro, Laura Nyman. *Sweet Tooth*
Mostacchi, Massimo. *The beast and the boy*
Mwenye Hadithi. *Lazy lion*
Ness, Evaline. *Fierce*
Newberry, Clare Turlay. *Herbert the lion*
Peet, Bill (William Bartlett). *Eli*
    Hubert's hair-raising adventures
    Randy's dandy lions
Pfister, Marcus. *How Leo learned to be king*
Pitcher, Caroline. *The time of the lion*
Pluckrose, Henry Arthur. *Lions and tigers*
Presencer, Alain. *Roaring lion tales*
Scheffler, Ursel. *Be brave, little lion!*
Schneider, Antonie. *Luke the Lionhearted*
Siddiqui, Ashraf. *Bhombal Dass, the uncle of lion*
Siepmann, Jane. *The lion on Scott Street*
Skorpen, Liesel Moak. *If I had a lion*
Stephenson, Dorothy. *How to scare a lion*
Stewart, Elizabeth Laing. *The lion twins*
Townsend, Kenneth. *Felix, the bald-headed lion*
Varga, Judy. *Miss Lollipop's lion*
Waber, Bernard. *A lion named Shirley Williamson*
Wagener, Gerda. *Leo the lion*
Wolf, Gita. *The very hungry lion*
Yaccarino, Dan. *Deep in the jungle*
Yee, Patrick. *Baby lion*
Yoshida, Toshi. *Young lions*
Zelinsky, Paul O. *The lion and the stoat*

Zimelman, Nathan. *Treed by a pride of irate lions*

Animals – llamas

Alexander, Ellen. *Llama and the great flood*
Guarino, Deborah. *Is your mama a llama?*
Rockwell, Anne F. *The good llama*

Animals – lynx

Bonners, Susan. *Hunter in the snow*
Hodge, Deborah. *Wild cats*
London, Jonathan. *Let the lynx come in*

Animals – manatees

Cousteau Society. *Manatees*
Harms, John, II. *The saving of Sly Manatee*
Houk, Randy. *Chessie, the travelin' man*

Animals – mice

Æsop. *The country mouse and the city mouse*
  The lion and the mouse, ill. by Carol Jones
  The lion and the mouse, ill. by Lisa McCue
  The lion and the mouse, ill. by Gerald Rose
  The lion and the mouse, ill. by Bernadette Watts
  The lion and the mouse, ill. by Ed Young
  The town mouse and the country mouse, ill. by
    Lorinda Bryan Cauley
  The town mouse and the country mouse, ill. by
    Helen Craig
  The town mouse and the country mouse, ill. by Paul
    Galdone
  The town mouse and the country mouse, ill. by Tom
    Garcia
  The town mouse and the country mouse, ill. by Janet
    Stevens
  The town mouse and the country mouse, ill. by
    Bernadette Watts
  Town mouse, country mouse, ill. by Jan Brett
  Town mouse, country mouse, ill. by Carol Jones
Albert, Shirley. *Doll party*
Alborough, Jez. *Watch out! Big Bro's coming!*
Aliki. *At Mary Bloom's*
Allen, Laura Jean. *Rollo and Tweedy and the case of
  the missing cheese*
Allen, Linda. *The mouse bride*
Althea. *Jeremy Mouse and cat*
Angelo, Nancy Carolyn Harrison. *Camembert*
Angelo, Valenti. *The candy basket*
Aragon, Jane Chelsea. *The major and the mousehole
  mice*
Archambault, John. *A beautiful feast for a big king
  cat*
Arnosky, Jim. *Mouse numbers and letters*
  Mouse writing
Asch, Frank. *Dear brother*
Augarde, Steve (Stephen). *Barnaby Shrew, Black
  Dan and . . . the mighty wedgwood*
Aylesworth, Jim. *The completed hickory dickory dock*
  Two terrible frights
Baehr, Patricia. *Mouse in the house*
Baker, Alan. *Two tiny mice*
  Where's mouse?
Balian, Lorna. *Mother's Mother's Day*
Balzano, Jeanne. *The wee moose*
Barbaresi, Nina. *Firemouse*
Barkan, Joanne. *Whiskerville bake shop*

Whiskerville firehouse
Whiskerville post office
Whiskerville school
Barklem, Jill. *Autumn story*
  The big book of Brambly Hedge
  The high hills
  The secret staircase
  Spring story
  Summer story
  Winter story
Barner, Bob. *Which way to the Revolution?*
Barnes-Murphy, Rowan. *Numbers*
Barrows, Marjorie Wescott. *Muggins' big balloon*
  Muggins Mouse
  Muggins takes off
  *The Rand McNally book of favorite Muggins Mouse
    stories*
Bastin, Marjolein. *A little dog for Vera*
  My name is Vera
  Vera and her friends
  Vera dresses up
  Vera in the kitchen
  Vera the mouse
  Vera's special hobbies
Belpré, Pura. *Pérez and Martina*
Benjamin, A. H. *It could have been worse*
Berson, Harold. *A moose is not a mouse*
  Raminagrobis and the mice
Bible. Old Testament. Jonah. *Jonah*, ill. by Kurt
  Mitchell
Boegehold, Betty. *Pippa Mouse*
  Pippa pops out!
Bogacki, Tomasz. *Cat and mouse in the night*
  Cat and mouse in the snow
Bond, Felicia. *The Halloween performance*
  The Halloween play
Boyd, Lizi. *Mouse in a house*
Boynton, Sandra. *If at first . . .*
Brady, Irene. *Wild mouse*
Brady, Susan. *Find my blanket*
Brandenberg, Franz. *Everyone ready?*
  Six new students
Brenner, Barbara A. *Mr. Tall and Mr. Small*
Bright, Robert. *Georgie and the runaway balloon*
Brook, Judy. *Tim mouse goes down the stream*
  Tim mouse visits the farm
Brown, Palmer. *Something for Christmas*
Buchanan, Heather S. *Emily Mouse saves the day*
  Emily Mouse's beach house
  Emily Mouse's first adventure
  Emily Mouse's garden
  George and Matilda Mouse and the floating school
  George and Matilda Mouse and the moon rocket
  George Mouse learns to fly
  George Mouse's covered wagon
  George Mouse's first summer
  George Mouse's riverboat band
Bullock, Kathleen. *A surprise for Mitzi Mouse*
Bunting, Eve (Anne Evelyn). *The Mother's Day mice*
Burningham, John. *Trubloff*
Burton, Katherine. *One gray mouse*
Butler, Stephen. *The mouse and the apple*
Butterworth, Nick. *Jingle bells*
Cameron, Alice. *The cat sat on the mat*
Cameron, John. *If mice could fly*
Cantieni, Benita. *Little Elephant and Big Mouse*
Carle, Eric. *Do you want to be my friend?*
Carlson, Nancy L. *Look out kindergarten, here I come!*
Carlstrom, Nancy White. *I'm not moving, mama!*

Carter, Noelle. *I'm a little mouse*
    Where's my squishy ball?
Cartlidge, Michelle. *Baby mice at home*
    Fairy letters
    A house for Lily Mouse
    Michelle Cartlidge's book of words
    Mouse birthday
    Mouse Christmas
    Mouse in the house
    Mouse letters
    Mouse theater
    Mouse time
    A mouse's diary
    Mouse's scrapbook
    Pippin and Pod
Castle, Caroline. *Herbert Binns and the flying tricycle*
Charles, Donald. *Calico Cat's exercise book*
Chase, Catherine. *Baby mouse goes shopping*
    Baby mouse learns his ABC's
    The mouse in my house
Choi, Yangsook. *New cat*
Chorao, Kay. *Cathedral mouse*
Chottin, Ariane. *Little Mouse's rescue*
Christensen, Gardell Dano. *Mrs. Mouse needs a house*
Christian, Mary Blount. *The bookstore mouse*
Claret, Maria. *Melissa Mouse*
Coombs, Patricia. *Mouse Café*
Cousins, Lucy. *Count with Maisy*
    Happy birthday, Maisy
    Maisy at the farm
    Maisy dresses up
    Maisy goes swimming
    Maisy goes to bed
    Maisy goes to school
    Maisy goes to the playground
    Maisy makes gingerbread
    Maisy's ABC
    Maisy's bedtime
    Maisy's colors
    Maisy's pool
    Maisy's pop-up playhouse
Coxe, Molly. *6 sticks*
Craig, Helen. *Charlie and Tyler at the seashore*
Cressey, James. *Max the mouse*
Cunningham, Julia. *A mouse called Junction*
Currey, Anna. *Tickling tigers*
Cushman, Doug. *Mouse and Mole and the Christmas walk*
Dalmais, Anne-Marie. *Best bedtime stories of Mother Mouse*
    Molly and Mimi the mouse twins
Dauer, Rosamond. *Bullfrog grows up*
Daugherty, James Henry. *The picnic*
Delacre, Lulu. *Nathan and Nicholas Alexander*
    Nathan's balloon adventure
    Nathan's fishing trip
Delaney, Ned. *Two strikes, four eyes*
Delessert, Etienne. *How the mouse was hit on the head by a stone and so discovered the world*
Demarest, Chris L. *Kitman and Willy at sea*
    The lunatic adventure of Kitman and Willy
Dennard, Deborah. *Travis and the better mousetrap*
De Paola, Tomie (Thomas Anthony). *Charlie needs a cloak*
Derby, Sally. *The mouse who owned the sun*
De Regniers, Beatrice Schenk. *How Joe the bear and Sam the mouse got together*
    Picture book theater

Dominguez, Angel. *Diary of a Victorian mouse*
Donaldson, Julia. *The gruffalo*
Doty, Roy. *Old-one-eye meets his match*
Dubanevich, Arlene. *Tom's tail*
Duke, Kate. *Aunt Isabel makes trouble*
    Aunt Isabel tells a good one
Dupré, Judith. *The mouse bride*
Durant, Alan. *Mouse party*
Durrell, Julie. *Mouse tails*
Edwards, Pamela Duncan. *Livingstone Mouse*
Elzbieta. *Brave Babette and sly Tom*
Emberley, Michael. *Ruby*
Engel, Diana. *Eleanor, Arthur, and Claire*
    Gino Badino
Ernst, Lisa Campbell. *The rescue of Aunt Pansy*
Esbensen, Barbara Juster. *The dream mouse*
Ets, Marie Hall. *Mr. T. W. Anthony Woo*
Ezra, Mark. *The sleepy dormouse*
Farris, Pamela J. *Young Mouse and Elephant*
Félix, Monique. *The further adventures of the little mouse trapped in a book*
    The story of a little mouse trapped in a book
Field, Rachel Lyman. *A road might lead to anywhere*
Fisher, Aileen Lucia. *The house of a mouse*
    Sing, little mouse
Fleming, Denise. *Lunch*
Forward, Toby. *Ben's Christmas carol*
Fowler, Richard. *Happy birthday, Mouse!*
Freeman, Don. *The guard mouse*
    Norman the doorman
Freeman, Lydia. *Pet of the Met*
Freschet, Berniece. *Bear mouse*
    Bernard of Scotland Yard
Futamata, Eigoro. *How not to catch a mouse*
Gackenbach, Dick. *The perfect mouse*
Gág, Wanda. *Snippy and Snappy*
Gantz, David. *The genie bear with the light brown hair word book*
Garland, Michael. *The mouse before Christmas*
Gay, Marie-Louise. *Moonbeam on a cat's ear*
Geraghty, Paul. *Look out, Patrick!*
    Stop that noise!
Ghigna, Charles. *Mice are nice*
Gifford, Kathie Lee. *Moochie's surprise*
Gili, Phillida. *Fanny and Charles*
Ginsburg, Mirra. *Four brave sailors*
Goodall, John S. *Creepy castle*
    Naughty Nancy goes to school
Gordon, Margaret. *The supermarket mice*
Goundaud, Karen Jo. *A very mice joke book*
Graham, John. *I love you, mouse*
Greaves, Margaret. *The mice of Nibbling Village*
Greene, Carol. *A computer went a-courting*
Grimm, Jacob. *Godfather Cat and Mousie*
    Little Red Riding Hood, ill. by John S. Goodall
Gundersheimer, Karen. *1, 2, 3, play with me*
    Shapes to show
Hale, Irina. *Chocolate mouse and sugar pig*
Hale, Linda. *The glorious Christmas soup party*
Hall, Malcolm. *And then the mouse . . .*
Harris, Leon A. *The great diamond robbery*
    The great picture robbery
Hawkinson, John. *The old stump*
Hazen, Barbara Shook. *The Fat Cats, Cousin Scraggs and the monster mice*
Hellings, Colette. *Too little, too big*
Henkes, Kevin. *Chester's way*
    Lilly's purple plastic purse
    Owen

McKissack, Patricia C. *Who is coming?*
Margret and H. A. Rey's Curious George and the puppies
Martin, David. *Monkey business*
   Monkey trouble
Martin, Rafe. *The monkey bridge*
Mathiesen, Egon. *Oswald, the monkey*
Meshover, Leonard. *The monkey that went to school*
Metaxas, Eric. *The monkey people*
Moore, Inga. *Fifty red night-caps*
Morgan, Michaela. *Helpful Betty to the rescue*
Myers, Walter Dean. *How Mr. Monkey saw the whole world*
Olds, Helen Diehl. *Miss Hattie and the monkey*
Oxenbury, Helen. *Tom and Pippo and the dog*
   Tom and Pippo go shopping
   Tom and Pippo in the garden
   Tom and Pippo on the beach
   Tom and Pippo see the moon
   Tom and Pippo's day
P'an, Ts'ai-ying. *Monkey creates havoc in heaven*
Paxton, Tom. *The jungle baseball game*
Preston, Edna Mitchell. *Monkey in the jungle*
Reitveld, Jane Klatt. *Monkey island*
Rey, H. A. (Hans Augusto). *Cecily G and the nine monkeys*
   Curious George
   Curious George gets a medal
   Curious George learns the alphabet
   Curious George rides a bike
   Curious George takes a job
   The original Curious George
Rey, Margret (Margret Elisabeth Waldstein). *Curious George flies a kite*
   Curious George goes to the hospital
Rockwell, Anne F. *The stolen necklace*
Rowe, John A. *Monkey trouble*
San Souci, Robert D. *Pedro and the monkey*
Schubert, Dieter. *Where's my monkey?*
Selsam, Millicent E. *A first look at monkeys*
Shi, Zhang Xiu. *Monkey and the white bone demon*
Slobodkina, Esphyr. *Caps for sale*
Souhami, Jessica. *Rama and the demon king*
Stanley, Sanna. *Monkey Sunday*
Suba, Susanne. *The monkeys and the pedlar*
Teleki, Geza. *Aerial apes*
Temple, Frances. *Tiger soup*
Thaler, Mike. *Moonkey*
Van Laan, Nancy. *So say the little monkeys*
Wiesmüller, Dieter. *The adventures of Marco and Polo*
Williamson, Hamilton. *Monkey tale*
Wolkstein, Diane. *The cool ride in the sky*
Woodruff, Elvira. *Mrs. McCloskey's monkeys*
Yee, Patrick. *Baby monkey*
Young, Ed (Edward). *Monkey King*

Animals – moose

Alexander, Martha G. *Even that moose won't listen to me*
Allen, Jonathan. *Mucky moose*
Bourgeois, Paulette. *Franklin's new friend*
Brown, Marc Tolon. *Moose and goose*
Bunting, Eve (Anne Evelyn). *A turkey for Thanksgiving*
Carlstrom, Nancy White. *Moose in the garden*
Foreman, Michael. *Moose*
Freschet, Berniece. *Moose baby*

Hodge, Deborah. *Deer, moose, elk and caribou*
Hoff, Syd. *Santa's moose*
Kasperson, James. *Little brother moose*
Kelley, True. *Buggly Bear's hiccup cure*
Latimer, Jim. *Going the moose way home*
   Moose and friends
   When moose was young
McNeer, May Yonge. *My friend Mac*
Marshall, James. *The guest*
Mellor, Corinne. *Bruce the balding moose*
Numeroff, Laura Joffe. *If you give a moose a muffin*
Palatini, Margie. *Moosetache*
Prøysen, Alf. *Mrs. Pepperpot and the moose*
Raschka, Christopher. *Moosey Moose*
Seuss, Dr. *Thidwick, the big-hearted moose*
Slepian, Jan. *Lost moose*
Slobodkin, Louis. *Melvin, the moose child*
Stadler, John. *The ballad of Wilbur and the moose*
Stapler, Sarah. *Spruce the moose cuts loose*
Stern, Maggie. *Acorn magic*
Wiseman, Bernard. *Christmas with Morris and Borris*
   Morris and Boris at the circus
   Morris has a birthday party!
   Morris the moose

Animals – mountain lions *see* Animals – cougars

Animals – mules

Beatty, Hetty Burlingame. *Droopy*
Brown, Kathryn. *Muledred*
Sharmat, Marjorie Weinman. *Hooray for Father's Day!*
Snyder, Anne. *The old man and the mule*
Zemach, Margot. *Jake and Honeybunch go to heaven*

Animals – muskrats

Arnosky, Jim. *Come out, muskrats*
Hoban, Russell. *Harvey's hideout*
Savageau, Cheryl. *Muskrat will be swimming*
Wilson, Sarah. *Muskrat, muskrat, eat your peas!*

Animals – octopuses *see* Octopuses

Animals – opossums *see* Animals – possums

Animals – orangutans

Carrick, Carol. *Banana beer*
Cherry, Lynne. *Orangutan*
Grindley, Sally. *Little Sibu*
Romanelli, Serena. *Little Bobo saves the day*

Animals – otters

Allen, Laura Jean. *Ottie and the star*
Berger, Barbara Helen. *A lot of otters*
Boyle, Doe. *Otter on his own*
Burdick, Margaret. *Bobby Otter and the blue boat*
Carlstrom, Nancy White. *Swim the silver sea, Joshie Otter*
Cousteau Society. *Otters*
Greene, Carol. *Reading about the river otter*
Hall, Derek. *Otter swims*
Harshman, Terry Webb. *Porcupine's pajama party*
Hoban, Lillian. *Big Little Otter*

Hoban, Russell. *Emmet Otter's jug-band Christmas*
Luenn, Nancy. *Otter play*
Shaw, Evelyn S. *Sea otters*
Sheehan, Angela. *The otter*
Simms, Laura. *Moon and Otter and Frog*
Tompert, Ann. *Little Otter remembers and other stories*
Wisbeski, Dorothy Gross. *Pícaro, a pet otter*

Animals – oxen

Bunting, Eve (Anne Evelyn). *Box, fox, ox, and the peacock*
DeVajay, Szabolcs. *The animals' gift*
Emberley, Barbara. *The story of Paul Bunyan*
Hong, Lily Toy. *How the ox star fell from heaven*

Animals – pack rats

Miller, Edna. *Pebbles, a pack rat*
Quackenbush, Robert M. *Pete Pack Rat*
Van Horn, William. *Harry Hoyle's giant jumping bean*

Animals – pandas

Allen, Judy. *Panda*
Cabrera, Jane. *Panda Big and Panda Small*
Calmenson, Stephanie. *Dinner at the Panda Palace*
Conover, Chris. *Sam Panda and Thunder Dragon*
Dunbar, Joyce. *Gander's pond*
  The secret friend
Foreman, Michael. *Dad! I can't sleep*
  Look! Look!
  Panda and the bunyips
  Panda and the bushfire
  Panda's puzzle, and his voyage of discovery
  Surprise! Surprise!
Granfield, Linda. *The legend of the panda*
Greaves, Margaret. *Once there were no pandas*
Grosvenor, Donna. *Pandas*
Hall, Derek. *Panda climbs*
Hoban, Tana. *Panda, panda*
Hoffman, Mary. *Animals in the wild: panda*
Jensen, Helen Zane. *When Panda came to our house*
Kraus, Robert. *Milton the early riser*
Lee, Sandra. *Giant pandas*
Leedy, Loreen. *Pingo the plaid panda*
Maestro, Betsy. *The pandas take a vacation*
Mayer, Marianna. *The Brambleberrys animal book of colors*
Owen, Annie. *Hungry panda*
Pluckrose, Henry Arthur. *Bears*
Rigby, Shirley Lincoln. *Smaller than most*
Steele, Philip. *The giant panda*
Stimson, Joan. *Big Panda, Little Panda*
Wild, Margaret. *Tom goes to kindergarten*

Animals – panthers *see* Animals – leopards

Animals – pigs

Allard, Harry. *There's a party at Mona's tonight*
Anholt, Catherine. *Truffles in trouble*
  Truffles is sick
Aruego, José. *Rockabye crocodile*
Asch, Frank. *Ziggy Piggy and the three little pigs*
Augarde, Steve (Stephen). *Pig*
Axelrod, Amy. *Pigs in the pantry*
  Pigs on a blanket

Pigs on the ball
Pigs on the move
Pigs will be pigs
Aylesworth, Jim. *Hanna's hog*
Ayres, Becky Hickox. *Victoria flies high*
Ayres, Pam. *Piggo and the nosebag*
  Piggo has a train ride
Baldner, Gaby. *Joba and the wild boar*
Baron, Alan. *Little Pig's bouncy ball*
Beil, Karen Magnuson. *A cake all for me!*
Berson, Harold. *Truffles for lunch*
Bianchi, John. *Swine snafu*
Bishop, Claire Huchet. *The truffle pig*
Blake, Jon. *Wriggly Pig*
Blegvad, Lenore. *This little pig-a-wig and other rhymes about pigs*
Bloom, Suzanne. *We keep a pig in the parlor*
Boegehold, Betty. *You are much too small*
Boland, Janice. *Annabel*
  Annabel again
Bond, Felicia. *Mary Betty Lizzie McNutt's birthday*
  Poinsettia and her family
  Poinsettia and the firefighters
Boynton, Sandra. *Hester in the wild*
Brand, Millen. *This little pig named Curly*
Brimner, Larry Dane. *Nana's hog*
Brock, Emma Lillian. *Pig with a front porch*
Brown, Judith Gwyn. *Max and the truffle pig*
Brown, Ken (Ken James). *Mucky Pup's Christmas*
Brown, Marc Tolon. *Perfect pigs*
Browne, Anthony. *Piggybook*
Bruna, Dick. *Poppy Pig goes to market*
Calhoun, Mary. *The witch's pig*
Calmenson, Stephanie. *Never take a pig to lunch and other funny poems about animals*
Caple, Kathy. *The wimp*
Carlson, Nancy L. *Louanne Pig in making the team*
  Louanne Pig in the mysterious valentine
  Louanne Pig in the perfect family
  Witch lady
Cazet, Denys. *Mud baths for everyone*
Christelow, Eileen. *The great pig escape*
  Mr. Murphy's marvelous invention
Cibula, Matt S. *Slumgullion, the executive pig*
Cole, Brock. *Nothing but a pig*
Coontz, Otto. *Starring Rosa*
Corbalis, Judy. *Porcellus, the flying pig*
Craig, Helen. *The night of the paper bag monsters*
  Susie and Alfred in a busy day in town
  Susie and Alfred in the knight, the princess and the dragon
  A welcome for Annie
Cushman, Doug. *Once upon a pig*
Dalmais, Anne-Marie. *Best bedtime stories of Mother Pig*
Davenier, Christine. *Leon and Albertine*
Davis, Maggie S. *The rinky-dink café*
Degen, Bruce. *Sailaway home*
DeLage, Ida. *ABC pigs go to market*
Denslow, Sharon Phillips. *Riding with Aunt Lucy*
Dubanevich, Arlene. *Pig William*
  The piggest show on earth
  Pigs at Christmas
  Pigs in hiding
Dunbar, Joyce. *The pig who wished*
Dunrea, Olivier. *Eddy B, pigboy*
Dyke, John. *Pigwig*
  Pigwig and the pirates
Edwards, Frank B. *Melody Mooner stayed up all night*

Mortimer Mooner stopped taking a bath
Enderle, Judith (Ann) Ross. *A pile of pigs*
Eriksson, Ake. *Joel, Jasper, and Julia*
Ernst, Lisa Campbell. *The prize pig surprise*
Erskine, Jim. *Bert and Susie's messy tale*
Falconer, Ian. *Olivia*
Faulkner, Keith. *The long-nosed pig*
Fischetto, Laura. *All pigs on deck*
Gackenbach, Dick. *Harvey, the foolish pig*
  Hurray for Hattie Rabbit!
  The pig who saw everything
Galdone, Paul. *The amazing pig*
Geisert, Arthur. *Oink*
  Oink oink
  Pigs from 1 to 10
Getz, Arthur. *Humphrey, the dancing pig*
Gibbons, Gail. *Pigs*
Gikow, Louise. *Bye-bye, pacifier*
Gliori, Debi. *A present for Big Pig*
Good, Phyllis Pellman. *Plain Pig's ABCs*
Goodall, Jane. *Dr. White*
Goodall, John S. *The adventures of Paddy Pork*
  The ballooning adventures of Paddy Pork
  Paddy goes traveling
  Paddy Pork
  Paddy Pork's holiday
  Paddy to the rescue
  Paddy under water
  Paddy's evening out
  Paddy's new hat
Gralley, Jean. *Hogula, dread pig of night*
Gray, Nigel. *Little pig's tale*
  Pigs can't fly
Gretz, Susanna. *It's your turn, Roger*
  Roger loses his marbles!
  Roger takes charge!
Grossman, Bill. *Tommy at the grocery store*
Guthrie, Donna. *This little pig stayed home*
Hale, Irina. *Chocolate mouse and sugar pig*
Hammar, Asa. *Fit for pigs*
Haswell, Peter. *Pog*
  Pog climbs Mount Everest
Hauptmann, Tatjana. *A day in the life of Petronella Pig*
Hawkins, Colin. *Mig the pig*
  This little pig
Heine, Helme. *The pigs' wedding*
Hellard, Susan. *This little piggy*
Heller, Nicholas. *A book for Woody*
  Woody
Hiskey, Iris. *Cassandra who?*
Hoban, Lillian. *Mr. Pig and family*
  Mr. Pig and Sonny too
Hobbie, Holly. *Toot and Puddle*
  Toot and Puddle, a present for Toot
  Toot and Puddle, I'll be home for Christmas
  Toot and Puddle, Puddle's ABC
  Toot and Puddle, you are my sunshine
Hoff, Syd. *Happy birthday, Henrietta!*
Hofstrand, Mary. *Albion pig*
  By the sea
Hutchins, Pat. *Little pink pig*
Inkpen, Mick. *Arnold*
  Gumboot's chocolatey day
  If I had a pig
  Kipper's A to Z
  Wibbly Pig can dance!
  Wibbly Pig can make a tent
  Wibbly Pig is upset

Wibbly Pig likes bananas
Wibbly Pig makes pictures
Wibbly Pig opens his presents
Jackson, Ellen B. *Boris the boring boar*
Jacobs, Joseph. *The three sillies*, ill. by Kathryn Hewitt
  The three sillies, ill. by Steven Kellogg
Jennings, Linda M. *Crispin and the dancing piglet*
  Tom's tail
Jeschke, Susan. *Perfect the pig*
Johnson, Angela. *Julius*
Johnson, Paul Brett. *A perfect pork stew*
  The pig who ran a red light
Johnston, Tony. *Farmer Mack measures his pig*
Jolley, Mike. *Grunter, a pig with an attitude!*
Kasza, Keiko. *The pigs' picnic*
Keller, Holly. *Geraldine and Mrs. Duffy*
  Geraldine first
  Geraldine's baby brother
  Geraldine's big snow
  Geraldine's blanket
  Merry Christmas, Geraldine
Kent, Jack. *Piggy Bank Gonzalez*
King-Smith, Dick. *All pigs are beautiful*
  The spotty pig
Kiser, SuAnn. *The hog call to end all!*
Korth-Sander, Irmtraut. *Will you be my friend?*
Koscielniak, Bruce. *Hector and Prudence*
  Hector and Prudence - all aboard!
Kranendonk, Anke. *Just a minute*
Krause, Ute. *Pig surprise*
Kroll, Steven. *The pigrates clean up*
  Pigs in the house
Laden, Nina. *When Pigasso met Mootisse*
Laird, Donivee Martin. *The three little Hawaiian pigs and the magic shark*
Laird, Elizabeth. *The day Sidney ran off*
Lasky, Kathryn. *Starring Lucille*
Lawrence, John. *Rabbit and pork*
Leonard, Marcia. *Birthday in a bathtub*
Lester, Helen. *Me first*
Levine, Abby. *You push, I ride*
Lewis, Bobby. *Home before midnight*
Lies, Brian. *Hamlet and the enormous Chinese dragon kite*
Lindgren, Barbro. *Benny's had enough*
Ling, Mary. *Pig*
The Little book of pigs
Little, Jean. *Gruntle Piggle takes off*
Lobel, Arnold. *Small pig*
  A treeful of pigs
Lorenz, Lee. *A weekend in the country*
Lowell, Susan. *The three little javelinas*
Luttrell, Ida. *Milo's toothache*
McClenathan, Louise. *The Easter pig*
MacDonald, Allan. *The pig in a wig*
MacDonald, Elizabeth. *Miss Poppy and the honey cake*
McNaughton, Colin. *Boo!*
  Little boo!
  Little goal!
  Little oops!
  Little suddenly!
  Oomph!
  Oops!
  Preston's goal!
  Shh! (Don't tell Mr. Wolf!)
  Suddenly!
  Yum!

McPhail, David M. *Big Pig and Little Pig*
   Pig Pig and the magic photo album
   Pig Pig gets a job
   Pig Pig goes to camp
   Pig Pig grows up
   Pig Pig rides
   Pigs ahoy
   Pigs aplenty, pigs galore!
   Those can-do pigs
McQueen, Lucinda. *Tidy pig*
Maestro, Betsy. *The guessing game*
Marshall, James. *Portly McSwine*
   Swine lake
   Yummers!
   Yummers too
Martin, David. *Five little piggies*
   Piggy and Dad
Martin, Jacqueline Briggs. *The water gift and the pig of the pig*
Martinez, Ruth. *Mrs. McDockerty's knitting*
Mathews, Louise. *The great take-away*
Mayne, William. *Lady Muck*
Meddaugh, Susan. *Hog-eye*
Miles, Miska. *This little pig*
Miranda, Anne. *Pignic*
   To market, to market
Moon, Cliff. *Pigs on the farm*
Moore, Inga. *The truffle hunter*
Morley, Carol. *A spider and a pig*
Most, Bernard. *Oink-ha!*
   Z-Z-Zoink!
Mother Goose. *This little pig*, ill. by Leonard Lubin
   This little pig went to market, ill. by L. Leslie Brooke
   This little piggy
Munsch, Robert N. *Pigs*
Murphy, Pat. *Pigasus*
Nayer, Judy. *Pig in a wig*
Newton, Patricia Montgomery. *Vacation surprise*
Newton-John, Olivia. *A pig tale*
Nightingale, Sandy. *Pink pigs aplenty*
Novak, Matt. *Jazzbo and Googy*
Numeroff, Laura Joffe. *If you give a pig a pancake*
Offen, Hilda. *Nice work, little wolf!*
Ostheeren, Ingrid. *Fabian Youngpig sails the world*
Oxenbury, Helen. *Pig tale*
Palatini, Margie. *Piggie pie*
Paraskevas, Betty. *The ferocious beast with the polka-dot hide*
   Maggie and the Ferocious Beast, the big scare
Patterson, Geoffrey. *A pig's tale*
Peck, Robert Newton. *Hamilton*
Peet, Bill (William Bartlett). *Chester the worldly pig*
Pizer, Abigail. *Penelope pig*
Plourde, Lynn. *Pigs in the mud in the middle of the rud*
Pomerantz, Charlotte. *The piggy in the puddle*
Potter, Beatrix. *The tale of Little Pig Robinson*
   The tale of Pigling Bland
Pryor, Bonnie. *Amanda and April*
   Merry Christmas, Amanda and April
Rayner, Mary. *Garth Pig and the ice cream lady*
   Mr. and Mrs. Pig's evening out
   Mrs. Pig gets cross and other stories
   Mrs. Pig's bulk buy
   One by one
   Ten pink piglets
Reddix, Valerie. *Millie and the mudhole*
Robb, Laura. *Snuffles and snouts*

Root, Phyllis. *Mrs. Potter's pig*
Ross, Tony. *The enchanted pig*
Roth, Carol. *Ten dirty pigs / Ten clean pigs*
Royston, Angela. *The pig*
Samton, Sheila White. *Frogs in clogs*
Saul, Carol P. *Peter's song*
Scarry, Richard. *Mr. Frumble's worst day ever*
   Pig Will and Pig Won't
   Pig Will and Pig Won't
   Richard Scarry's Peasant Pig and the terrible dragon
Schaffer, Libor. *Arthur sets sail*
Schami, Rafik. *Albert and Lila*
Schotter, Roni. *That extraordinary pig of Paris*
Schwartz, Mary. *Spiffen*
Scieszka, Jon. *The true story of the three little pigs by A. Wolf, as told to Jon Scieszka*
Scruton, Clive. *Pig in the air*
Sharmat, Mitchell. *The seven sloppy days of Phineas Pig*
Shecter, Ben. *Partouche plants a seed*
Slate, Joseph. *The mean, clean, giant canoe machine*
Snow, Alan. *Oink!*
Spohn, Kate. *Piglet's bath*
Stadler, John. *The ballad of Wilbur and the moose*
Steer, Dougald. *Just one more story*
Steig, William. *The amazing bone*
   Farmer Palmer's wagon ride
   Roland, the minstrel pig
   Zeke Pippin
Stepto, Michele. *Snuggle Piggy and the magic blanket*
Stevens, Carla. *Hooray for pig!*
   Pig and the blue flag
Stine, Jovial Bob. *Pork and beans*
Stobbs, William. *This little piggy*
Teague, Mark. *Pigsty*
Tharlet, Eve. *Little pig, big trouble*
Thompson, Carol. *Piggy goes to bed*
The three little pigs. *The original three little pigs re-told*, ill. by Jonathan Smith
   The story of the three little pigs, ill. by L. Leslie Brooke
   The story of the three little pigs, ill. by William Stobbs
   Three little pigs [Facsimile ed]
   The three little pigs, ill. by Val Biro
   The three little pigs, ill. by Gavin Bishop
   The three little pigs, ill. by Erik Blegvad
   The three little pigs, ill. by Caroline Bucknall
   The three little pigs, ill. by Stephen Cartwright
   The three little pigs, ill. by Lorinda Bryan Cauley
   The three little pigs, ill. by Jean Claverie
   The three little pigs, ill. by Doug Cushman
   The three little pigs, ill. by William Pène Du Bois
   The three little pigs, ill. by Paul Galdone
   The three little pigs, ill. by Madelaine Gill
   The three little pigs, ill. by Steven Kellogg
   The three little pigs, ill. by David McPhail
   The three little pigs, ill. by James Marshall
   The three little pigs, ill. by Paul Meisel
   The three little pigs, ill. by Rodney Peppé
   The three little pigs, ill. by Edda Reinl
   The three little pigs, ill. by John Wallner
   The three little pigs, ill. by Irma Wilde
   The three little pigs, ill. by Margot Zemach
   The three little pigs and the big bad wolf
   The three little pigs and the fox
   The three pigs, ill. by Tony Ross
   Who's at the door?
Tripp, Wallace. *The tale of a pig*

Tyler, Linda Wagner. *The sick-in-bed birthday book*
Ungerer, Tomi. *Christmas eve at the Mellops*
  The Mellops go diving for treasure
  The Mellops go flying
  The Mellops go spelunking
  The Mellops strike oil
Uttley, Alison. *The Christmas box*
  Sam Pig and the dragon
  Sam Pig and the hurdy-gurdy man
  Sam Pig and the wind
Van der Meer, Ron. *Pigs at home*
Van Leeuwen, Jean. *More tales of Oliver Pig*
Van Nutt, Julia. *The mystery of Mineral Gorge*
  Pignapped!
  Pumpkins from the sky?
Varekamp, Marjolein. *Little Sam takes a bath*
Vernon, Tannis. *Little Pig and the blue-green sea*
Wabbes, Marie. *Rose is hungry*
  Rose is muddy
  Rose's bath
  Rose's picture
Waddell, Martin. *The pig in the pond*
Waechter, Friedrich Karl. *Three is company*
Wagner, Karen. *Silly Fred*
Wahl, Jan. *Mrs. Owl and Mr. Pig*
Waldron, Jan L. *Angel Pig and the hidden Christmas*
  John Pig's Halloween
Walker, Barbara K. (Barbara Kerlin). *Pigs and pirates*
Wallace, Karen. *City pig*
Watson, Pauline. *Wriggles, the little wishing pig*
Wayne-von-Königslöw, Andrea. *Bing and Chutney*
Weiss, Ellen. *Pigs in space*
Wells, Rosemary. *The little lame prince*
West, Ian. *Silas, the first pig to fly*
West, Keith. *Little Pig's special day*
Weston, Martha. *Peony's rainbow*
  Tuck in the pool
Wheeler, Cindy. *Rose*
White, Carolyn. *Whuppity Stoorie*
Wild, Margaret. *Old Pig*
Wild, Robin. *Little Pig and the big bad wolf*
Wilhelm, Hans. *Oh, what a mess*
Winthrop, Elizabeth. *Sloppy kisses*
Wiseman, Bernard. *Don't make fun!*
Wondriska, William. *Mr. Brown and Mr. Gray*
Wood, David. *Piggies*
Yee, Wong Herbert. *Fireman Small*
  Fireman Small, fire down below
  Fireman Small to the rescue
  Hamburger Heaven
Yeoman, John. *The bear's water picnic*
Yolen, Jane. *Picnic with Piggins*
  Piggins
Zakhoder, Boris Vladimirovich. *How a piglet crashed the Christmas party*
Zalben, Jane Breskin. *Basil and Hillary*
Ziefert, Harriet. *Let's go! Piggety Pig*
  No more! Piggety Pig
  Piggety Pig from morn 'til night

Animals – polar bears

Adinolfi, JoAnn. *The Egyptian polar bear*
Alborough, Jez. *Bare bear*
  Running Bear
Aulaire, Ingri Mortenson d'. *East of the sun and west of the moon*
Bishop, Adela. *The Christmas polar bear*

Briggs, Raymond. *The bear*
Curtiss, A. B. *In the company of bears*
Dabcovich, Lydia. *The polar bear son*
Dasent, George W. *East o' the sun, west o' the moon*
De Beer, Hans. *Ahoy there, little polar bear*
  Little polar bear
  Little polar bear and the brave little hare
  Little polar bear and the husky pup
  Little polar bear finds a friend
  Little polar bear, take me home!
Dickens, Lucy. *Go fish*
Duvoisin, Roger Antoine. *Snowy and Woody*
Ford, Miela. *Follow the leader*
  Mom and me
George, Jean Craighead. *Snow bear*
Grigg, Carol. *The singing snow bear*
Grindley, Sally. *Polar Star*
Hall, Derek. *Polar bear leaps*
Harlow, Joan Hiatt. *Shadow bear*
Heinz, Brian J. *Nanuk, lord of the ice*
Heller, Ruth. *How to hide a polar bear*
Inkpen, Mick. *Penguin small*
Kern, Noris. *I love you with all my heart*
Lesser, Carolyn. *Great crystal bear*
Lilly, Kenneth. *Animals of the ocean*
London, Jonathan. *Ice Bear and Little Fox*
Newton, Jill. *Polar bear scare*
Pinkwater, Daniel Manus. *At the Hotel Larry*
  Bongo Larry
  Young Larry
Pluckrose, Henry Arthur. *Bears*
Rose, Gerald. *PB takes a holiday*
Ryder, Joanne. *White bear, ice bear*
Wahl, Jan. *"I remember," cried Grandma Pinky*
Wild, Margaret. *Thank you, Santa*
Wouters, Anne. *This book is for us*
  This book is too small
Ylla. *Polar bear brothers*

Animals – porcupines

Annett, Cora. *When the porcupine moved in*
Carrick, Carol. *Ben and the porcupine*
Harshman, Terry Webb. *Porcupine's pajama party*
Joly, Fanny. *Mr. Fine, porcupine*
Lester, Helen. *A porcupine named Fluffy*
Lies, Brian. *Hamlet and the enormous Chinese dragon kite*
Lipson, Beth Weiner. *Benjamin's perfect solution*
Massie, Diane Redfield. *Tiny pin*
Morgan-Vanroyen, Mary. *Benjamin's bugs*
Pfister, Marcus. *Where is my friend?*
The porcupine
Schlein, Miriam. *Lucky porcupine!*
Slate, Joseph. *Story time for Little Porcupine*
Stren, Patti. *Hug me*
Thomas, Patricia. *The one and only, super-duper, golly-whopper, jim-dandy, really-handy clock-tock-stopper*

Animals – porpoises *see* Animals – dolphins

Animals – possums

Berson, Harold. *Henry Possum*
Burch, Robert. *Joey's cat*
Carlson, Natalie Savage. *Marie Louise's heyday*
Conford, Ellen. *Eugene the brave*
  Impossible, possum

Just the thing for Geraldine
Cushman, Doug. *Possum stew*
Degen, Bruce. *Aunt Possum and the pumpkin man*
DeLage, Ida. *Good morning, lady*
Dodd, Lynley. *The apple tree*
Fontenot, Mary Alice. *Tah-Tye*
Fox, Mem. *Possum magic*
Freschet, Berniece. *Possum baby*
Glaser, Linda. *Keep your socks on, Albert!*
Hoban, Russell. *Nothing to do*
Hunter, Anne. *Possum and the peeper*
    Possum's harvest moon
Hurd, Thacher. *Mama don't allow*
Kasza, Keiko. *Don't laugh, Joe*
Keller, Holly. *Henry's Fourth of July*
Lipson, Beth Weiner. *Benjamin's perfect solution*
Luttrell, Ida. *Mattie's little possum pet*
Swendson, Patsy. *The potluck adventures of Mrs. Marmalade*
Taylor, Mark. *Old Blue, you good dog you*
Tether, Graham. *Skunk and possum*
Van Laan, Nancy. *Possum come a-knocking*
Winthrop, Elizabeth. *Potbellied possums*
Young, James. *Everyone loves the moon*

Animals – prairie dogs

Baylor, Byrd. *Amigo*
Casey, Denise. *The friendly prairie dog*
Hirschi, Ron. *Where are my prairie dogs and black-footed ferrets?*
Luttrell, Ida. *Lonesome Lester*

Animals – prairie wolves *see* Animals – coyotes

Animals – pumas *see* Animals – cougars

Animals – rabbits

Adams, Adrienne. *The Christmas party*
    The Easter egg artists
    The great Valentine's Day balloon race
Adler, David A. *Bunny rabbit rebus*
Æsop. *The hare and the frogs*
    The hare and the tortoise, ill. by Paul Galdone
    The hare and the tortoise, ill. by Carol Jones
    The hare and the tortoise, ill. by Gerald Rose
    The hare and the tortoise, ill. by Helen Ward
    The hare and the tortoise, ill. by Peter Weevers
    The tortoise and the hare
Anderson, Lena. *Bunny bath*
    Bunny box
    Bunny fun
    Bunny party
    Bunny story
    Bunny surprise
Anderson, Lonzo. *Two hundred rabbits*
Annett, Cora. *When the porcupine moved in*
Arnosky, Jim. *Rabbits and raindrops*
Baby's first book of colors
Baker, Alan. *Black and White Rabbit's ABC*
    Brown Rabbit's shape book
    Gray Rabbit's one, two, three
    Little Rabbit's first number book
    White Rabbit's color book
Balian, Lorna. *Humbug rabbit*
Barasch, Lynne. *Rodney's inside story*

Barrett, John M. *The Easter bear*
Bartoli, Jennifer. *In a meadow, two hares hide*
Barton, Byron. *Jack and Fred*
Bate, Lucy. *Little rabbit's loose tooth*
Baumann, Hans. *The hare's race*
Becker, John Leonard. *Seven little rabbits*
Benjamin, Alan. *Busy bunnies*
Bergström, Gunilla. *Is that a monster, Alfie Atkins?*
Berson, Harold. *Pop! goes the turnip*
Bianco, Margery Williams. *The velveteen rabbit*, ill. by Allen Atkinson
    The velveteen rabbit, ill. by Michael Green
    The velveteen rabbit, ill. by Michael Hague
    The velveteen rabbit, ill. by David Jorgensen
    The velveteen rabbit, ill. by William Nicholson
    The velveteen rabbit, ill. by Ilse Plume
    The velveteen rabbit, ill. by S. D. Schindler
    The velveteen rabbit, ill. by Tien
Bishop, Adela. *The Easter wolf*
Bishop, Gavin. *Little Rabbit and the sea*
Blake, Jon. *You're a hero, Daley B.!*
Blau, Judith. *Bunny Mitten's book*
Boelts, Maribeth. *Little Bunny's cool tool set*
    Little Bunny's pacifier plan
    Little Bunny's preschool countdown
Bolliger, Max. *The rabbit with the sky blue ears*
Bonfils, Bolette. *Peter joins the circus*
Bornstein, Ruth Lercher. *Indian bunny*
    Rabbit's good news
Bourguignon, Laurence. *A friend for Tiger*
Bowden, Joan Chase. *The bouncy baby bunny*
    Bouncy baby bunny finds his bed
    Little grey rabbit
Boyd, Lizi. *Bunny hop*
Boyle, Doe. *Summer coat, winter coat*
Brewster, Patience. *Rabbit Inn*
Bright, Robert. *My hopping bunny*
Brophy, Nannette. *The color of my fur*
Brown, Marc Tolon. *The bionic bunny show*
    One, two buckle my shoe
    What do you call a dumb bunny? and other rabbit riddles, games, jokes and cartoons
Brown, Marcia. *The neighbors*
Brown, Margaret Wise. *The golden egg book*
    Goodnight moon
    Little chicken
    The runaway bunny
    The whispering rabbit
Browne, Eileen. *Where's that bus?*
Bruna, Dick. *Miffy*
    Miffy at the beach
    Miffy at the playground
    Miffy at the seaside
    Miffy at the zoo
    Miffy goes flying
    Miffy goes to school
    Miffy in the hospital
    Miffy in the snow
    Miffy's bicycle
    Miffy's birthday
    Miffy's dream
Brutschy, Jennifer. *The winter fox*
Bryant, Donna. *My rabbit Roberta*
Bullock, Kathleen. *Rabbits are coming*
Burningham, John. *The rabbit*
Burton, Jane. *Freckles the rabbit*
Cahill, Chris. *Bunny magic*
Cain, Sheridan. *Why so sad, Brown Rabbit?*
Caldwell, Mary. *Morning, rabbit, morning*

Calmenson, Stephanie. *One red shoe (the other's blue!)*
  Wanted
Campbell, Alison. *Are you asleep, rabbit?*
Capucilli, Alyssa Satin. *Peekaboo bunny*
Carlson, Nancy L. *Bunnies and their hobbies*
  Bunnies and their sports
  Loudmouth George and the big race
  Loudmouth George and the cornet
  Loudmouth George and the fishing trip
  Loudmouth George and the new neighbors
  Loudmouth George and the sixth-grade bully
Carlstrom, Nancy White. *Kiss your sister, Rose Marie*
  Midnight dance of the snowshoe hare
  Who gets the sun out of bed?
Carrick, Carol. *A rabbit for Easter*
Carroll, Ruth. *What Whiskers did*
  Where's the bunny?
Carter, Anne. *Bella's secret garden*
Cartlidge, Michelle. *Bunny's birthday*
Cazet, Denys. *Big shoe, little shoe*
  Christmas moon
  December 24th
  You make the angels cry
Chadwick, Tim. *Cabbage moon*
Chalmers, Mary. *Come for a walk with me*
  Kevin
Chandoha, Walter. *A baby bunny for you*
Christelow, Eileen. *Henry and the dragon*
  Henry and the red stripes
Claret, Maria. *The chocolate rabbit*
Cleveland, David. *The April rabbits*
Coatsworth, Elizabeth. *Pika and the roses*
Cocca-Leffler, Maryann. *Missing: one stuffed rabbit*
Coldrey, Jennifer. *The world of rabbits*
Compton, Joanne. *Little Rabbit's Easter surprise*
Cosgrove, Stephen (Edward). *Sleepy time bunny*
Cousins, Lucy. *What can Pinky hear?*
  What can Pinky see?
  What can rabbit hear?
  What can rabbit see?
Cowley, Stewart. *Little bunny*
  Little lost rabbit
Cox, Judy. *Rabbit pirates*
Cross, Genevieve. *My bunny book*
Dale, Penny. *Daisy Rabbit's tree house*
Dalmais, Anne-Marie. *Betsy the bunny*
Darling, Kathy (Mary Kathleen). *The Easter bunny's secret*
De Beer, Hans. *Little polar bear and the brave little hare*
Delacre, Lulu. *Peter Cottontail's Easter book*
DeLage, Ida. *ABC Easter bunny*
  Am I a bunny?
  A bunny ride
  Bunny school
Delton, Judy. *Brimhall turns detective*
  Brimhall turns to magic
  Hired help for Rabbit
  Rabbit finds a way
  Rabbit goes to night school
  Three friends find spring
Demi. *Fleecy bunny*
  Little bitty bunny
Denim, Sue. *The Dumb Bunnies*
  The Dumb Bunnies' Easter
  The Dumb Bunnies go to the zoo
  Make way for Dumb Bunnies
Dennis, Lynne. *Raymond Rabbit's early morning*

De Paola, Tomie (Thomas Anthony). *Too many Hopkins*
Dodds, Dayle Ann. *Do bunnies talk?*
Dorsky, Blanche. *Harry, a true story*
Doucet, Sharon Arms. *Why Lapin's ears are long and other stories of the Louisiana bayou*
Dowling, Paul. *You can do it, Rabbit*
Doyle, Charlotte Lackner. *Where's Bunny's mommy?*
Du Bois, William Pène. *The hare and the tortoise and the tortoise and the hare*
Dunbar, Joyce. *Lollopy*
  Tell me something happy before I go to sleep
Dunn, Judy. *The little rabbit*
Dutton, Sandra. *The cinnamon hen's autumn day*
Dyjak, Elisabeth. *Bertha's garden*
Easterling, Bill. *Prize in the snow*
Ehrlich, Amy. *Bunnies all day long*
  Bunnies and their grandma
  Bunnies at Christmastime
  Bunnies on their own
Elzbieta. *Jon-Jon and Annette*
Ernst, Lisa Campbell. *Miss Penny and Mr. Grubbs*
Evans, Mark. *Rabbit*
Fatio, Louise. *The happy lion's rabbits*
Ferns, Ronald. *Osbert and Lucy*
Fisher, Aileen Lucia. *Listen, rabbit*
  Rabbits, rabbits
Flory, Jane. *The bear on the doorstep*
Friskey, Margaret (Margaret Richards). *Mystery of the gate sign*
Gackenbach, Dick. *Hattie be quiet, Hattie be good*
  Hattie rabbit
  Hurray for Hattie Rabbit!
  Mother Rabbit's son Tom
Gág, Wanda. *ABC bunny*
Galdone, Paul. *A strange servant*
Gay, Michel. *Rabbit express*
Gay, Zhenya. *Small one*
Geringer, Laura. *Molly's new washing machine*
Gill, Madelaine. *The spring hat*
Ginsburg, Mirra. *The fox and the hare*
Gorbachev, Valeri. *Nicky and the big, bad wolves*
Gordon, Sharon. *Easter Bunny's lost egg*
Green, Adam. *The funny bunny factory*
Greenblat, Rodney Alan. *Thunder Bunny*
Greene, Carol. *The insignificant elephant*
Gretz, Susanna. *Rabbit food*
  Rabbit rambles on
Greydanus, Rose. *Climb aboard*
Grindley, Sally. *Why is the sky blue?*
Grossman, Virginia. *Ten little rabbits*
Hands, Hargrave. *Bunny sees*
Hayward, Linda. *All stuck up*
  Hello, house!
  Sunny Day Bunny
Heine, Helme. *Superhare*
Henkes, Kevin. *Bailey goes camping*
Herford, Oliver. *The most timid in the land*
Heyward, Du Bose. *The country bunny and the little gold shoes*
Hide-and-seek bunnies
Ho, Minfong. *Brother Rabbit*
Hoban, Lillian. *Harry's song*
Hoban, Tana. *Where is it?*
Hogrogian, Nonny. *Carrot cake*
Hooks, William H. *Rough, tough, Rowdy*
  Three rounds with rabbit
Hooper, Meredith. *Tom's rabbit*
Houck, Eric L. *Rabbit surprise*

Peters, Sharon. *Ready, get set, go!*
  Stop that rabbit
Petty, Kate. *Rabbits*
Pfister, Marcus. *Hang on, Hopper!*
  Hopper
  Hopper hunts for spring
  Hopper's treetop adventure
Pizer, Abigail. *Loppylugs*
Poole, Valerie. *Obadiah Coffee and the music contest*
Porter, Sue. *My little rabbit tale*
Posey, Lee. *Night rabbits*
Potter, Beatrix. *The complete adventures of Peter Rabbit*
  Peter Rabbit's one two three
  The story of fierce bad rabbit
  The tale of Benjamin Bunny
  The tale of Mr. Tod
  The tale of Peter Rabbit, ill. by Margot Apple
  The tale of Peter Rabbit, ill. by Beatrix Potter
  The tale of the Flopsy Bunnies
  Where's Peter Rabbit?
Price, Mathew. *Patch and the rabbits*
The pudgy bunny book
Quackenbush, Robert M. *First grade jitters*
  Funny bunnies
  Funny bunnies on the run
Ratnett, Michael. *Marmaduke and the scary story*
Ratz de Tagyos, Paul. *A coney tale*
Rey, Margret (Margret Elisabeth Waldstein). *Spotty*
Riordan, James. *Little Bunny Bobkin*
Roberts, Bethany. *Waiting-for-Christmas stories*
  Waiting-for-Papa stories
  Waiting-for-spring stories
Rosen, Michael (1946-). *Little rabbit Foo Foo*
Roth, Carol. *Little Bunny's sleepless night*
Rowe, John A. *Rabbit moon*
Ryder, Joanne. *Hello, first grade*
Rylant, Cynthia. *Bunny bungalow*
Sadler, Marilyn. *It's not easy being a bunny*
Sara. *The rabbit, the fox, and the wolf*
Schlein, Miriam. *Little Rabbit, the high jumper*
Schotter, Roni. *Bunny's night out*
Schweninger, Ann. *Birthday wishes*
  Christmas secrets
  Halloween surprises
  The hunt for rabbit's galosh
  Off to school!
  Valentine friends
Selby, Jennifer. *Beach bunny*
Seuss, Dr. *The eye book*
Sharmat, Marjorie Weinman. *Thornton, the worrier*
Silverman, Erica. *Warm in winter*
Silverman, Maida. *Bunny's ABC*
Smith, Barry. *Grandma Rabbitty's visit*
Smith, Cara Lockhart. *Twenty-six rabbits run riot*
Solotareff, Grégoire. *Don't call me little bunny*
Sonnenschein, Harriet. *Harold's hideaway thumb*
  Harold's runaway nose
Spelman, Cornelia. *When I feel angry*
Spier, Peter. *Little rabbits*
Steig, William. *Solomon the rusty nail*
Steiner, Charlotte. *My bunny feels soft*
Steiner, Jörg. *Rabbit Island*
Stevens, Janet. *Tops and bottoms*
Stevenson, James. *Monty*
Stevenson, Suçie. *Christmas eve*
  Do I have to take Violet?
Stewart, Paul. *The birthday presents*
  A little bit of winter

Sykes, Julie. *Robbie Rabbit and the little ones*
Szekeres, Cyndy. *Cyndy Szekeres' learn to count, funny bunnies*
  Hide-and-seek duck
  I can count 100 bunnies, and so can you!
Tafuri, Nancy. *Rabbit's morning*
  Will you be my friend?
Tarrant, Graham. *Rabbits*
Taylor, Shirley. *The cross in the egg*
Tejima, Keizaburo. *Ho-limlim*
Thomas, Patricia. *The one and only, super-duper, golly-whopper, jim-dandy, really-handy clock-tock-stopper*
Tidd, Louise Vitellaro. *The best pet yet*
Tompert, Ann. *Nothing sticks like a shadow*
Tresselt, Alvin R. *The rabbit story,* ill. by Carolyn Ewing
  Rabbit story, ill. by Leonard Weisgard
Trez, Denise. *Rabbit country*
Tripp, Wallace. *My Uncle Podger*
Troughton, Joanna. *How rabbit stole the fire*
Van Emst, Charlotte. *Little Rabbit's big day*
Van Woerkom, Dorothy. *Harry and Shelburt*
Velthuijs, Max. *Little Man to the rescue*
Vozar, David. *M. C. Turtle and the hip hop hare*
Wabbes, Marie. *Good night, Little Rabbit*
  Happy birthday, Little Rabbit
  It's snowing, Little Rabbit
  Little Rabbit's garden
Waddell, Martin. *We love them*
Wahl, Jan. *Carrot nose*
  Doctor Rabbit's foundling
  The five in the forest
  Rabbits on roller skates!
Wallace, John. *Tiny Rabbit goes to a birthday party*
Wallace, Nancy Elizabeth. *Apples, apples, apples*
  Paperwhite
  Rabbit's bedtime
  Snow
  Tell-a-bunny
Walton, Rick. *One more bunny*
Watson, Carol. *Rabbit*
Watson, Wendy. *The bunnies' Christmas eve*
  Lollipop
Watts, Barrie. *Rabbit*
Watts, Bernadette. *Harvey Hare, postman extraordinaire*
  Harvey Hare's Christmas
Wayland, April Halprin. *To Rabbittown*
Weil, Lisl. *The candy egg bunny*
Welch, Willy. *Grumpy Bunnies*
Wellington, Monica. *Bunny's first snowflake*
  Bunny's rainbow day
  Night rabbits
Wells, Rosemary. *Bunny cakes*
  Bunny money
  Emily's first 100 days of school
  First tomato
  Hooray for Max
  The island light
  Max and Ruby's Midas
  Max cleans up
  Max's bath
  Max's bedtime
  Max's birthday
  Max's breakfast
  Max's chocolate chicken
  Max's Christmas
  Max's dragon shirt

Max's first word
Max's new suit
Max's ride
Max's toys
Morris's disappearing bag
Moss pillows
Read to your bunny
Weninger, Brigitte. *Happy birthday, Davy*
Merry Christmas, Davy!
What's the matter, Davy?
Why are you fighting, Davy?
Will you mind the baby, Davy?
Whybrow, Ian. *Parcel for Stanley*
Wiese, Kurt. *Happy Easter*
Wild, Margaret. *Rosie and Tortoise*
Wilhelm, Hans. *Bunny trouble*
More bunny trouble
Williams, Garth. *The rabbits' wedding*
Wolf, Ann. *The rabbit and the turtle*
Wolf, Winfried. *The Easter bunny*
Wood, Douglas. *Rabbit and the moon*
Wormell, Christopher. *Blue Rabbit and friends*
Worth, Bonnie. *Peter Cottontail's surprise*
Wyllie, Stephen. *White Rabbit builds a dream house*
Yee, Patrick. *Bedtime for Rosie Rabbit*
Little Buddy meets Bobo
Rosie Rabbit's colors
Rosie Rabbit's numbers
Rosie Rabbit's opposites
Rosie Rabbit's shapes
Winter rabbit
Zakhoder, Boris Vladimirovich. *Rosachok*
Zalben, Jane Breskin. *Miss Violet's shining day*
Ziefert, Harriet. *Breakfast time!*
Bye-bye, daddy!
Good morning, sun!
Happy birthday, Grandpa!
Happy Easter, Grandma!
Let's get dressed!
Rabbit and Hare divide an apple
Zolotow, Charlotte (Shapiro). *The bunny who found Easter*
Mr. Rabbit and the lovely present

Animals – raccoons

Arnosky, Jim. *Raccoons and ripe corn*
Bellows, Cathy. *The royal raccoon*
Bradford, Ann. *The mystery at Misty Falls*
The mystery of the missing raccoon
Brown, Margaret Wise. *Wait till the moon is full*
Burdick, Margaret. *Sara Raccoon and the secret place*
Calmenson, Stephanie. *Come to my party*
Cummings, Pat. *Petey Moroni's Camp Runamok diary*
Duvoisin, Roger Antoine. *Petunia, I love you*
Freschet, Berniece. *Five fat raccoons*
Hoban, Lillian. *The case of the two masked robbers*
Here come raccoons
Johnson, Donna Kay. *Brighteyes*
Leedy, Loreen. *The race*
Leonard, Marcia. *Alphabet bandits*
Lewison, Wendy Cheyette. *Where is Sammy's smile?*
McPhail, David M. *Henry Bear's Christmas*
Something special
Stanley: Henry Bear's friend
Miklowitz, Gloria D. *Save that raccoon!*
Miles, Miska. *The raccoon and Mrs. McGinnis*
Moore, Lilian. *Little Raccoon and no trouble at all*
Little Raccoon and the outside world

Little Raccoon and the thing in the pool
Morgan, Allen. *Molly and Mr. Maloney*
Neugebauer, Charise. *The real winner*
Noguere, Suzanne. *Little raccoon*
St. George, Judith. *The Halloween pumpkin smasher*
Sharmat, Marjorie Weinman. *The 329th friend*
Steiner, Barbara (Annette). *But not Stanleigh*
Thayer, Jane. *The clever raccoon*
Wells, Rosemary. *Timothy goes to school*
Yoko
Whelan, Gloria. *A week of raccoons*
Young, James. *Everyone loves the moon*
Zweifel, Frances W. *The Make-Something Club*

Animals – rats

Annixter, Jane. *Brown rats, black rats*
Augarde, Steve (Stephen). *Barnaby Shrew, Black Dan and . . . the mighty wedgwood*
Barnaby Shrew goes to sea
Bartos-Hoppner, Barbara. *The pied piper of Hamelin*
Baynton, Martin. *Fifty saves his friend*
Bellows, Cathy. *Four fat rats*
Berson, Harold. *The rats who lived in the delicatessen*
Bianchi, John. *The lab rats of Doctor Eclair*
Biro, Val. *The pied piper of Hamelin*
Black, Floyd. *Alphabet cat*
Browning, Robert. *The pied piper of Hamelin*, ill. by Patricia and Robin DeWitt
The pied piper of Hamelin, ill. by Kate Greenaway
The pied piper of Hamelin, ill. by Anatoly Ivanov
The pied piper of Hamelin, ill. by Errol Le Cain
The pied piper of Hamelin, ill. by Drahos Zak
Bryan, Ashley. *The cat's purr*
Cohen, Barbara. *The chocolate wolf*
Cole, Babette. *Hurray for Ethelyn*
Three cheers for Errol!
Cook, Joel. *The rat's daughter*
Cressey, James. *Fourteen rats and a rat-catcher*
Crimi, Carolyn. *Don't need friends*
Cunningham, Julia. *A mouse called Junction*
Doty, Roy. *Old-one-eye meets his match*
Emberley, Rebecca. *Three cool kids*
Erickson, Russell E. *Warton and the traders*
Harris, Marian. *Tuesday in Arizona*
Hearn, Michael Patrick. *The porcelain cat*
Hoban, Russell. *Flat cat*
Hurd, Thacher. *Mystery on the docks*
Johnston, Tony. *Sparky and Eddie, trouble with rats*
Karlin, Nurit. *The fat cat sat on the mat*
Kasza, Keiko. *The rat and the tiger*
Knüppel, Helga. *Christabel Crocodile's birthday egg*
Kouts, Anne. *Kenny's rat*
La Fontaine, Jean de. *The lion and the rat*
Lager, Claude. *A tale of two rats*
Latimer, Jim. *The Irish piper*
Lester, Helen. *Hooway for Wodney Wat*
McNaughton, Colin. *The rat race*
Mayer, Mercer. *The pied piper of Hamelin*
Meddaugh, Susan. *Cinderella's rat*
Miles, Miska. *Wharf rat*
Moore, Inga. *Aktil's big swim*
Oakley, Graham. *The church mice adrift*
Peppé, Rodney. *The mice and the clockwork bus*
The mice and the flying basket
Pomerantz, Charlotte. *The ballad of the long-tailed rat*
Potter, Beatrix. *The sly old cat*
Root, Phyllis. *Sam, who was swallowed by a shark*

Ross, Tony. *The pied piper of Hamelin*
Rowe, John A. *Smudge*
Saunders, Susan. *Charles Rat's picnic*
Schiller, Barbara. *The white rat's tale*
Sharmat, Marjorie Weinman. *Mooch the messy*
Snow, Alan. *The monster book of ABC sounds*
Stevenson, James. *The most amazing dinosaur Wilfred the rat*
Van Woerkom, Dorothy. *The rat, the ox and the zodiac*
Walt Disney Productions. *Walt Disney's The adventures of Mr. Toad*
Young, Ed (Edward). *Cat and Rat*
Zemach, Kaethe. *The beautiful rat*

Animals – reindeer

Bernhard, Emery. *Reindeer*
Brett, Jan. *The wild Christmas reindeer*
Cleaver, Elizabeth. *The enchanted caribou*
Foreman, Michael. *The little reindeer*
Haywood, Carolyn. *How the reindeer saved Santa*
Hodge, Deborah. *Deer, moose, elk and caribou*
Hoff, Syd. *Where's Prancer?*
Janovitz, Marilyn. *What could be keeping Santa?*
Jessell, Tim. *Amorak*
May, Robert Lewis. *Rudolph the red-nosed reindeer*
Miller, Debbie S. *A caribou journey*
Okrend, Elise. *Blintzes for Blitzen*
Owens, Mary Beth. *A caribou alphabet*
Schrecker, Judie. *Santa's new reindeer*
Wright, Cliff. *Santa's ark*

Animals – rhinoceros

Ardizzone, Edward. *Diana and her rhinoceros*
Brunhoff, Laurent de. *Babar's battle*
Bush, John. *The cross-with-us rhinoceros*
Cazet, Denys. *Great-Uncle Felix*
George, Jean Craighead. *Rhino romp*
Heine, Helme. *The boxer and the princess*
Johnson, Louise. *Malunda*
Kipling, Rudyard. *How the rhinoceros got his skin*
Maestro, Giulio. *Just enough Rosie*
Mammano, Julie. *Rhinos who skateboard*
Noble, Kate. *Oh look, it's a nosserus*
O'Malley, Kevin. *Bud*
Palmer, Todd Starr. *Rhino and Mouse*
Sackett, Elisabeth. *Danger on the African grassland*
Sis, Peter. *Rainbow Rhino*
Standon, Anna. *The singing rhinoceros*
Yoshida, Toshi. *Rhinoceros mother*

Animals – salamanders *see* Reptiles – salamanders

Animals – sea lions

Hamsa, Bobbie. *Your pet sea lion*
Olds, Elizabeth. *Plop plop ploppie*
Schreiber, Georges. *Bambino the clown*
Tafuri, Nancy. *Follow me!*

Animals – seals

Ackerman, Diane. *Monk seal hideaway*
Allen, Judy. *Seal*
Barr, Cathrine. *Sammy seal ov the sircus*
Bos, Claire. *Webster's wardrobe*

Burton, Jane. *Surfer the seal*
Cherry, Lynne. *Seal*
Coffey, Maria. *A seal in the family*
Cooper, Susan. *The Selkie girl*
Cousteau Society. *Seals*
Duran, Bonté. *The adventures of Arthur and Edmund*
Foreman, Michael. *Seal surfer*
Freeman, Don. *The seal and the slick*
Gerstein, Mordicai. *The seal mother*
Hirschi, Ron. *Where are my puffins, whales, and seals?*
Hoff, Syd. *Sammy the seal*
Kessler, Ethel. *Are there seals in the sandbox?*
Lilly, Kenneth. *Animals of the ocean*
McClure, Gillian. *Selkie*
MacGill-Callahan, Sheila. *The seal prince*
Sackett, Elisabeth. *Danger on the Arctic ice*
Yolen, Jane. *Greyling*

Animals – sheep

Aardema, Verna. *Borreguita and the coyote*
Alborough, Jez. *The grass is always greener*
Alda, Arlene. *Sheep, sheep, sheep, help me fall asleep*
Baird, Anne. *The Christmas lamb*
Ballart, Elisabet. *Let's count*
Beskow, Elsa Maartman. *Pelle's new suit*
Blanchard, Arlene. *The naughty lamb*
Brenner, Barbara A. *Lion and Lamb*
Brown, Margaret Wise. *Little lost lamb*
Butterworth, Nick. *The lost sheep*
Carlstrom, Nancy White. *Ten Christmas sheep*
Carrick, Carol. *Valentine*
Cazzola, Gus. *The bells of Santa Lucia*
Clayton, Gordon. *Lamb*
Coe, Lloyd. *Charcoal*
Dalmais, Anne-Marie. *Best bedtime stories of Mother Sheep*
Demi. *Fleecy lamb*
  Little baby lamb
De Paola, Tomie (Thomas Anthony). *Charlie needs a cloak*
  Haircuts for the Woolseys
Duncan, Jane. *Brave Janet Reachfar*
Dunn, Judy. *The little lamb*
Enderle, Judith (Ann) Ross. *Six creepy sheep*
  Six sandy sheep
Ernst, Lisa Campbell. *Nattie Parsons' good-luck lamb*
Eversole, Robyn Harbert. *Red berry wool*
Fleetwood, Jenni. *While shepherds watched*
Galdone, Paul. *Little Bo-Peep*
Ginsburg, Mirra. *The strongest one of all*
Gliori, Debi. *The snow lambs*
Gordon, Jeffie Ross. *Six sleepy sheep*
Grejniec, Michael. *When I open my eyes*
Hale, Sarah Josepha Buell. *Mary had a little lamb*
  Mary had a little lamb, ill. by Tomie de Paola
  Mary had a little lamb, photos. by Bruce McMillan
  Mary had a little lamb, ill. by Salley Mavor
  Mary had a little lamb, ill. by Ann Schweninger
  Mary had a little lamb, ill. by Suzanne Vasilak
Heck, Elisabeth. *The black sheep*
Hedderwick, Mairi. *Katie Morag and the two grandmothers*
Helldorfer, M. C. (Mary Claire). *Daniel's gift*
Ichikawa, Satomi. *Nora's surprise*
Inkpen, Mick. *If I had a sheep*
Ipcar, Dahlov. *The land of flowers*
Johnston, Tony. *Three little bikers*
Kiser, Kevin. *Sherman the sheep*

Kitamura, Satoshi. *Sheep in wolves' clothing*
   When sheep cannot sleep
Kraus, Robert. *Strudwick, a sheep in wolf's clothing*
Landström, Olof. *Boo and Baa at sea*
   Boo and Baa in a party mood
   Boo and Baa in windy weather
   Boo and Baa on a cleaning spree
Levine, Arthur A. *Sheep dreams*
Lewis, Kim. *Emma's lamb*
   First snow
   Little Baa
   Little lamb
   The shepherd boy
Lewis, Robin Baird. *Friska, the sheep that was too small*
London, Jonathan. *At the edge of the forest*
Lunn, Janet Louise Swoboda. *Amos's sweater*
McCully, Emily Arnold. *My real family*
   Speak up, Blanche!
McGee, Barbara. *Counting sheep*
MacGregor, Marilyn. *On top*
McMullan, Kate (Hall). *Sheepish riddles*
Mallat, Kathy. *Seven stars, more!*
Mendoza, George. *Alphabet sheep*
   Silly sheep and other sheepish rhymes
Mills, Claudia. *One small lost sheep*
Mother Goose. *Baa baa, black sheep*, ill. by Marilyn Janovitz
   Baa, baa, black sheep, ill. by Moira Kemp
Novak, Matt. *While the shepherd slept*
O'Brien, Mary. *Counting sheep to sleep*
Oram, Hiawyn. *Where are you hiding, little lamb?*
Patent, Dorothy Hinshaw. *Maggie, a sheep dog*
Peet, Bill (William Bartlett). *Buford the little bighorn*
Porter, Sue. *Parsnip*
   Parsnip and the pink blanket
   Parsnip and the runaway tractor
Rogers, Paul (Patrick). *Sheepchase*
Royston, Angela. *The sheep*
Russell, Betty. *Run sheep run*
Ryder, Joanne. *Beach party*
Sanders, Scott R. (Scott Russell). *Warm as wool*
Shaw, Nancy (Nancy E.). *Sheep in a jeep*
   Sheep in a shop
   Sheep on a ship
   Sheep out to eat
   Sheep take a hike
   Sheep trick or treat
Sloat, Teri. *Farmer Brown shears his sheep*
Slobodkin, Louis. *Up high and down low*
Snyder, Zilpha Keatley. *The changing maze*
Steiner, Charlotte. *Red Ridinghood's little lamb*
Strete, Craig Kee. *Big thunder magic*
Sundgaard, Arnold. *The lamb and the butterfly*
Trapani, Iza. *Mary had a little lamb*
Wallace, Barbara Brooks. *Argyle*
Weiss, Ellen. *Clara the fortune-telling chicken*
Wellington, Monica. *The sheep follow*
Widman, Christine. *The star grazers*
Wild, Jocelyn. *Florence and Eric take the cake*
Zalben, Jane Breskin. *Pearl plants a tree*
   Pearl's eight days of Chanukah
   Pearl's marigolds for grandpa

Animals – shrews

Augarde, Steve (Stephen). *Barnaby Shrew, Black Dan and . . . the mighty wedgwood*
   Barnaby Shrew goes to sea

Goodall, John S. *Shrewbettina's birthday*
Koller, Jackie French. *Mole and Shrew*
   Mole and Shrew are two
   Mole and Shrew step out
Olsen, Alfa-Betty. *Gabby the shrew*

Animals – skunks

De Regniers, Beatrice Schenk. *A special birthday party for someone very special*
Fair, David. *The fabulous four skunks*
Gray, Libba Moore. *Is there room on the feather bed?*
Hoban, Brom. *Skunk Lane*
Jones, Chuck. *William the backwards skunk*
Latimer, Jim. *James Bear's pie*
Reeves, Mona Rabun. *The spooky eerie night noise*
Schlein, Miriam. *What's wrong with being a skunk?*
Schoenherr, John. *The barn*
Tether, Graham. *Skunk and possum*
Wells, Rosemary. *Fritz and the mess fairy*

Animals – sloths

Knight, Hilary. *Sylvia the sloth*
Sharmat, Mitchell. *Sherman is a slowpoke*
Turnbull, Ann. *Too tired*
Willis, Jeanne. *Sloth's shoes*

Animals – slugs

Edwards, Pamela Duncan. *Some smug slug*
Raschka, Christopher. *Sluggy Slug*

Animals – snails

Byars, Betsy Cromer. *The lace snail*
Cutler, Jane. *Mr. Carey's garden*
Greenberg, David (David T.). *Slugs*
Hightower, Susan. *Twelve snails to one lizard*
Himmelman, John. *Simpson Snail sings*
Jackson, Ellen B. *The precious gift*
Janovitz, Marilyn. *Look out, bird!*
Latimer, Jim. *Snail and Buffalo*
Lord, John Vernon. *Mr. Mead and his garden*
McAllister, Angela. *Snail's birthday problem*
Marshall, James. *The guest*
O'Hagan, Caroline. *It's easy to have a snail visit you*
Oleson, Jens. *Snail*
Reider, Katja. *Snail started it!*
Rockwell, Anne F. *The story snail*
Ryder, Joanne. *Snail in the woods*
   The snail's spell
Stadler, John. *Hooray for snail!*
   Snail saves the day
Ungerer, Tomi. *Snail, where are you?*

Animals – snow leopards *see* Animals – leopards

Animals – sponges

Esbensen, Barbara Juster. *Sponges are skeletons*

Animals – squirrels

Alexander, Sue. *There's more . . . much more*
Angelo, Valenti. *The acorn tree*
Ashabranner, Brent. *I'm in the zoo, too*
Bare, Colleen Stanley. *Busy, busy squirrels*

Tree squirrels

Bassett, Lisa. *Beany and Scamp*
  Beany wakes up for Christmas
Browne, Eileen. *Tick-tock*
  Where's that bus?
Buff, Mary (Marsh). *Hurry, Skurry and Flurry*
Carey, Valerie Scho. *Harriet and William and the terrible creature*
Carter, Anne. *Scurry's treasure*
Chottin, Ariane. *Beaver gets lost*
Coldrey, Jennifer. *The world of squirrels*
Collins, Pat Lowery. *Tomorrow, up and away!*
Cooper, Helen (Helen F.). *Pumpkin soup*
Cooper, Patrick. *Never trust a squirrel*
Crane, Donn. *Flippy and Skippy*
DeLage, Ida. *The squirrel's tree party*
Drummond, Violet H. *Phewtus the squirrel*
Earle, Olive L. *Squirrels in the garden*
Ehlert, Lois. *Nuts to you!*
Ernst, Lisa Campbell. *Squirrel Park*
Falda, Dominique. *The treasure chest*
Grindley, Sally. *What will I do without you?*
James, Simon. *The wild woods*
Jensen, Patricia. *Little Squirrel's special nest*
Jones, Penelope. *I didn't want to be nice*
Kroll, Steven. *The squirrels' Thanksgiving*
Lane, Margaret. *The squirrel*
McBratney, Sam. *Just one!*
Miller, Edna. *Scamper*
Mills, Joyce C. *Gentle Willow*
Oxford Scientific Films. *Grey squirrel*
Peet, Bill (William Bartlett). *Merle the high flying squirrel*
Peterson, Hans. *Erik has a squirrel*
Pfister, Marcus. *Hopper's treetop adventure*
Potter, Beatrix. *The tale of Squirrel Nutkin*
  The tale of Timmy Tiptoes
Quackenbush, Robert M. *Batbaby*
Ryden, Hope. *The raggedy red squirrel*
Schmid, Eleonore. *The squirrel and the moon*
Schumacher, Claire. *Nutty's birthday*
  Nutty's Christmas
Shannon, George. *Heart to heart*
  The surprise
Sharmat, Marjorie Weinman. *Attila the angry*
  Sophie and Gussie
  The trip
Stage, Mads. *The lonely squirrel*
Stern, Maggie. *The missing sunflowers*
Stevenson, James. *Wilfred the rat*
Waldron, Kathleen Cook. *Loon Lake fishing derby*
Yeoman, John. *The bear's water picnic*
Young, Miriam Burt. *Miss Suzy's Easter surprise*
Zion, Gene. *The meanest squirrel I ever met*
Zweifel, Frances W. *Bony*
  The Make-Something Club

Animals – tapirs

Maestro, Giulio. *The tortoise's tug of war*

Animals – tigers

Adams, Richard (Richard Newbold). *The tyger voyage*
Allen, Judy. *Tiger*
Anderson, Paul S. *Red fox and the hungry tiger*
Baker, Keith. *Who is the beast?*
Bannerman, Helen. *The story of Little Babaji*

The story of little black Sambo
Barrows, Marjorie Wescott. *Timothy Tiger*
Blake, William. *The tyger*
Blaustein, Muriel. *Bedtime, Zachary!*
  Make friends, Zachary!
Bourguignon, Laurence. *A friend for Tiger*
Butterfield, Moira. *Fast, strong, and striped*
Canning, Kate. *A painted tale*
Choi, Yangsook. *The sun girl and the moon boy*
Cowcher, Helen. *Tigress*
Currey, Anna. *Tickling tigers*
De Beer, Hans. *Little polar bear, take me home!*
Dines, Glen. *A tiger in the cherry tree*
Dodds, Siobhan. *Charles Tiger*
Domanska, Janina. *Why so much noise?*
Edwards, Roland. *Tigers*
Egan, Tim. *Friday night at Hodges' café*
Farber, Norma. *How to ride a tiger*
Fenner, Carol. *Tigers in the cellar*
Frankel, Bernice. *Half-As-Big and the tiger*
French, Vivian. *Little Tiger finds a friend*
  Little Tiger goes shopping
  Tiger and the new baby
  Tiger and the temper tantrum
Gleeson, Brian. *The tiger and the Brahmin*
Hall, Derek. *Tiger runs*
Hewett, Joan. *Tiger, tiger, growing up*
Hoban, Russell. *The dancing tigers*
Hoffman, Mary. *Animals in the wild: tiger*
Ipcar, Dahlov. *Stripes and spots*
Justice, Jennifer. *The tiger*
Kasza, Keiko. *The rat and the tiger*
Kepes, Juliet. *Cock-a-doodle-doo*
Kraus, Robert. *Leo the late bloomer*
  Little Louie the baby bloomer
Lester, Julius. *Sam and the tigers*
Lewis, Sharon. *Tiger!*
Milton, Joyce. *Big cats*
O'Donnell, Peter. *Carnegie's excuse*
Offen, Hilda. *Good girl, Gracie Growler!*
Palecek, Libuse. *Brave as a tiger*
Parkison, Jami. *Amazing Mallika*
Partis, Joanne. *Stripe*
Paul, Anthony. *The tiger who lost his stripes*
Pluckrose, Henry Arthur. *Lions and tigers*
Prelutsky, Jack. *The terrible tiger*
Rockwell, Anne F. *Big boss*
Root, Phyllis. *Moon tiger*
Rose, Gerald. *The tiger-skin rug*
Round, Graham. *Hangdog*
Seuss, Dr. *I can lick 30 tigers today and other stories*
Sykes, Julie. *I don't want to take a bath!*
  Little Tiger's big surprise
Taylor, Mark. *Henry explores the jungle*
Temple, Frances. *Tiger soup*
Tseng, Grace. *White tiger, blue serpent*
Tworkov, Jack. *The camel who took a walk*
Villarejo, Mary. *The tiger hunt*
Wahl, Jan. *Tiger watch*
Wallace, Karen. *Imagine you are a tiger*
Wersba, Barbara. *Do tigers ever bite kings?*
Whitney, Alex. *Once a bright red tiger*
Winters, Kay. *Tiger trail*
Wolkstein, Diane. *The banza*
Wolski, Slawomir. *Tiger cat*
Xiong, Blia. *Nine-in-one Grr! Grr!*

Animals – walruses

Bridges, William. *Ookie, the walrus who likes people*
Hoff, Syd. *Walpole*
Stevenson, James. *Winston, Newton, Elton, and Ed*

Animals – warthogs

Edwards, Pamela Duncan. *Warthogs in the kitchen*
Hazen, Barbara Shook. *Wally the worry-warthog*

Animals – water buffaloes

Gobhai, Mehlli. *Lakshmi, the water buffalo who wouldn't*

Animals – weasels

Bach, Alice. *Warren Weasel's worse than measles*
Blake, Jon. *You're a hero, Daley B.!*
Ernst, Lisa Campbell. *Zinnia and Dot*
Ezra, Mark. *The sleepy dormouse*
Hallensleben, Georg. *Pauline*
Holder, Heidi. *Crows*
Lobel, Arnold. *Mouse soup*
Mathews, Louise. *Cluck one*
Zelinsky, Paul O. *The lion and the stoat*

Animals – whales

Allen, Judy. *Whale*
Appelbaum, Neil. *Is there a hole in your head?*
Archambault, John. *The birth of a whale*
Armitage, Ronda. *The lighthouse keeper's rescue*
Armour, Richard Willard. *Sea full of whales*
Baumann, Kurt. *The story of Jonah*
Behrens, June. *Whales of the world*
    Whalewatch!
Bellamy, David. *How green are you?*
Benchley, Nathaniel. *The deep dives of Stanley Whale*
Bible. Old Testament. Jonah. *The Book of Jonah*
    Jonah, ill. by Kurt Mitchell
    Jonah and the great fish, ill. by Leon Baxter
    Jonah and the great fish, ill. by Jim Cummins
Borovsky, Paul. *The fish that wasn't*
Bulla, Clyde Robert. *Jonah and the great fish*
Cech, John. *The southernmost cat*
Clark, Harry. *The first story of the whale*
Climo, Shirley. *The adventure of Walter*
Conklin, Gladys. *Journey of the gray whales*
Cousteau Society. *Whales*
Davies, Nicola. *Big blue whale*
Davis, Maggie S. *A garden of whales*
Day, Edward C. *John Tabor's ride*
Drummond, Allan. *Moby Dick*
Dunbar, Joyce. *Indigo and the whale*
Duvoisin, Roger Antoine. *The Christmas whale*
Engle, Joanna. *Cap'n kid goes to the South Pole*
Fowler, Allan. *The biggest animal ever*
    Friendly dolphins
Franklin, Kristine L. *The gift*
French, Vivian. *Whale journey*
Gerstein, Mordicai. *Jonah and the two great fish*
Gibbons, Gail. *Whales*
Grigg, Carol. *The singing snow bear*
Haiz, Danah. *Jonah's journey*
Hanze. *Yann and the whale*
Hayles, Karen. *What is stuck*
Hennessy, B. G. (Barbara G.). *Meet Winslow whale*

Himmelman, John. *Ibis*
Hirschi, Ron. *Where are my puffins, whales, and seals?*
Hudson, Eleanor. *A whale of a rescue*
Hurd, Edith Thacher. *What whale? Where?*
Hutton, Warwick. *Jonah and the great fish*
If you ever meet a whale
James, Simon. *Dear Mr. Blueberry*
    My friend whale
Johnston, Johanna. *Whale's way*
Johnston, Tony. *Whale song*
King, Patricia. *Mable the whale*
Le Guin, Ursula K. *Solomon Leviathan's nine hundred and thirty-first trip around the world*
Lent, Blair. *John Tabor's ride*
Lewis, Paul Owen. *Storm boy*
Lewis, Sharon. *Orca! the killer whale*
Lilly, Kenneth. *Animals of the ocean*
Lobato, Arcadio. *The greatest treasure*
London, Jonathan. *Baby whale's journey*
McAllister, Angela. *The whales' tale*
McCloskey, Robert. *Bert Dow, deep-water man*
McDermott, Beverly Brodsky. *Jonah*
McFarlane, Sheryl. *Waiting for the whales*
McMillan, Bruce. *Going on a whale watch*
Maestro, Giulio. *The tortoise's tug of war*
Metaxas, Eric. *The boy and the whale*
Nobisso, Josephine. *Shh! the whale is smiling*
O'Neill, Alexis. *Loud Emily*
Patterson, Geoffrey. *Jonah and the whale*
Pfister, Marcus. *Rainbow fish and the big blue whale*
Pitcher, Caroline. *The snow whale*
Pluckrose, Henry Arthur. *Whales*
Postgate, Oliver. *Noggin and the whale*
Raffi. *Baby beluga*
Raschka, Christopher. *Whaley Whale*
Roy, Ronald. *A thousand pails of water*
Ryder, Joanne. *Winter whale*
Rylant, Cynthia. *The whales*
Schlein, Miriam. *Sleep safe, little whale*
Selsam, Millicent E. *A first look at whales*
Sheldon, Dyan. *The whales' song*
Siberell, Anne. *Whale in the sky*
Sis, Peter. *An ocean world*
Stansfield, Ian. *The legend of the whale*
Steele, Philip. *The blue whale*
Steiner, Barbara (Annette). *The whale brother*
Strange, Florence. *Rock-a-bye whale*
Thorne, Jenny. *Jonah and the whale*
Tokuda, Wendy. *Humphrey the lost whale*
Watanabe, Yuichi. *Wally the whale who loved balloons*
Whales
Williams, Marcia. *Jonah and the whale*
Wilson, Bob. *Stanley Bagshaw and the twenty-two ton whale*
Wilson, Lynn. *Baby whale*
Wood, Audrey. *Little Penguin's tale*

Animals – wildebeests

Berliner, Franz. *Wildebeest*

Animals – wolves

Allen, Jonathan. *Mucky moose*
Ambrus, Victor G. *Country wedding*
Asch, Frank. *Ziggy Piggy and the three little pigs*
Baynes, Pauline. *How dog began*
Berman, Ruth. *Watchful wolves*
Bishop, Adela. *The Easter wolf*

Blades, Ann. *Mary of mile 18*
Bloom, Becky. *Wolf*
Blundell, Tony. *Beware of boys*
Boyle, Doe. *Gray wolf pup*
Bradman, Tony. *Look out, he's behind you*
Brett, Jan. *The first dog*
Bruna, Dick. *Dick Bruna's Little Red Riding Hood*
Bunting, Eve (Anne Evelyn). *On Call Back Mountain*
Cohen, Barbara. *The chocolate wolf*
Curti, Anna. *Seasons*
Damjan, Mischa. *Atuk*
   The wolf and the kid
Daudet, Alphonse. *The brave little goat of Monsieur Séguin*
Delaney, A. *The gunnywolf*
De Marolles, Chantal. *The lonely wolf*
De Regniers, Beatrice Schenk. *Red Riding Hood*
Dinardo, Jeffrey. *The wolf who cried boy*
Douzou, Olivier. *Wolf's lunch*
Dyjak, Elisabeth. *Bertha's garden*
Ernst, Lisa Campbell. *Little Red Riding Hood*
Evans, Katherine. *The boy who cried wolf*
Firmin, Peter. *Chicken stew*
Friskey, Margaret (Margaret Richards). *Indian Two Feet and the wolf cubs*
Gackenbach, Dick. *Harvey, the foolish pig*
Gay, Michel. *The Christmas wolf*
George, Jean Craighead. *Look to the north*
Goble, Paul. *The friendly wolf*
Gorbachev, Valeri. *Nicky and the big, bad wolves*
Greene, Carol. *Reading about the gray wolf*
Grimm, Jacob. *Little red cap*
   Little Red Riding Hood, ill. by Frank E. Aloise
   Little Red Riding Hood, ill. by Gwen Connelly
   Little Red Riding Hood, ill. by Paul Galdone
   Little Red Riding Hood, ill. by John S. Goodall
   Little Red Riding Hood, ill. by Trina Schart Hyman
   Little Red Riding Hood, ill. by Mireille Levert
   Little Red Riding Hood, ill. by Jean-François Martin
   Little Red Riding Hood, ill. by David M. McPhail
   Little Red Riding Hood, ill. by Bernadette Watts
   Nanny goat and the seven little kids
   The wolf and the seven kids, ill. by Kinuko Y. Craft
   The wolf and the seven little kids, ill. by Svend Otto S
   The wolf and the seven little kids, ill. by Martin Ursell
Gunthrop, Karen. *Adam and the wolf*
Guthrie, Donna. *This little pig stayed home*
Harper, Wilhelmina. *The gunniwolf*
Hawkins, Colin. *What time is it, Mr. Wolf?*
Hayward, Linda. *Hello, house!*
Heinz, Brian J. *The wolves*
Hobbs, Will. *Howling Hill*
Hoffman, Alice. *Fireflies*
Jackson, Ellen B. *Boris the boring boar*
Janovitz, Marilyn. *Can I help?*
   Is it time?
Jessell, Tim. *Amorak*
Johnson, Janet P. *How Mr. Dog got tame*
Jones, Carol. *What's the time, Mr. Wolf?*
Kasza, Keiko. *The wolf's chicken stew*
Kimmel, Eric A. *Sirko and the wolf*
Kitamura, Satoshi. *Sheep in wolves' clothing*
Kraus, Robert. *Strudwick, a sheep in wolf's clothing*
Lester, Helen. *Tacky the penguin*

Lewis, Robin Baird. *Friska, the sheep that was too small*
London, Jonathan. *The eyes of Gray Wolf*
   Red wolf country
Lowell, Susan. *Little Red Cowboy Hat*
McClure, Gillian. *What's the time, Rory Wolf?*
MacDonald, Elizabeth. *The wolf is coming!*
McDonald, Megan. *The bone keeper*
McNaughton, Colin. *Oomph!*
   Oops!
   Preston's goal!
   Shh! (Don't tell Mr. Wolf!)
   Suddenly!
   Yum!
McPhail, David M. *A wolf story*
Marshall, James. *Red Riding Hood*
   Swine lake
Meddaugh, Susan. *The best place*
   Hog-eye
Morris, Ann. *The Little Red Riding Hood rebus book*
Murphy, Jim. *The call of the wolves*
Offen, Hilda. *Nice work, little wolf!*
Palatini, Margie. *Piggie pie*
Parish, Peggy. *Granny, the baby and the big gray thing*
Peck, Robert Newton. *Hamilton*
Pinkwater, Daniel Manus. *Wolf Christmas*
Porter, Sue. *Little Wolf and the giant*
Prokofiev, Sergei Sergeievitch. *Peter and the wolf*, ill. by Reg Cartwright
   Peter and the wolf, ill. by Warren Chappell
   Peter and the wolf, ill. by Barbara Cooney
   Peter and the wolf, ill. by Julia Gukova
   Peter and the wolf, ill. by Frans Haacken
   Peter and the wolf, ill. by Alan Howard
   Peter and the wolf, ill. by Charles Mikolaycak
   Peter and the wolf, ill. by Jörg Müller
   Peter and the wolf, ill. by Josef Palecek
   Peter and the wolf, ill. by Kozo Shimizu
   Peter and the wolf, retold and ill. by Vladimir Vagin
   Peter and the wolf, ill. by Erna Voigt
Prusski, Jeffrey. *Bring back the deer*
Rayner, Mary. *Garth Pig and the ice cream lady*
   Mr. and Mrs. Pig's evening out
Rockwell, Anne F. *Romulus and Remus*
   The wolf who had a wonderful dream
Ross, Gayle. *How Turtle's back was cracked*
Ross, Tony. *The boy who cried wolf*
   Stone soup
Roth, Susan L. *Kanahena*
Sara. *The rabbit, the fox, and the wolf*
Scamell, Ragnhild. *Who likes Wolfie?*
Schick, Alice. *Just this once*
Scieszka, Jon. *The true story of the three little pigs by A. Wolf, as told to Jon Scieszka*
Selsam, Millicent E. *A first look at dogs*
Sharmat, Marjorie Weinman. *Walter the wolf*
Sheehan, Patty. *Shadow and the ready time*
Souhami, Jessica. *No dinner!*
Stevenson, Harvey. *Big scary wolf*
Storr, Catherine (Cole). *Clever Polly and the stupid wolf*
Sweeten, Sami. *Wolf*
The three little pigs. *The original three little pigs retold*, ill. by Jonathan Smith
   The story of the three little pigs, ill. by L. Leslie Brooke
   The story of the three little pigs, ill. by William Stobbs

Three little pigs [Facsimile ed]
The three little pigs, ill. by Val Biro
The three little pigs, ill. by Gavin Bishop
The three little pigs, ill. by Erik Blegvad
The three little pigs, ill. by Caroline Bucknall
The three little pigs, ill. by Stephen Cartwright
The three little pigs, ill. by Lorinda Bryan Cauley
The three little pigs, ill. by Jean Claverie
The three little pigs, ill. by Doug Cushman
The three little pigs, ill. by William Pène Du Bois
The three little pigs, ill. by Paul Galdone
The three little pigs, ill. by Madelaine Gill
The three little pigs, ill. by Steven Kellogg
The three little pigs, ill. by David McPhail
The three little pigs, ill. by James Marshall
The three little pigs, ill. by Paul Meisel
The three little pigs, ill. by Rodney Peppé
The three little pigs, ill. by Edda Reinl
The three little pigs, ill. by John Wallner
The three little pigs, ill. by Irma Wilde
The three little pigs, ill. by Margot Zemach
The three little pigs and the big bad wolf
The three pigs, ill. by Tony Ross
Who's at the door?
Vozar, David. *Yo, hungry wolf!*
Wild, Robin. *Little Pig and the big bad wolf*
Winters, Kay. *Wolf watch*
Wyllie, Stephen. *Dinner with fox*
Young, Ed (Edward). *Lon Po Po*
Ziefert, Harriet. *Little Red Riding Hood*

Animals – wombats

Argent, Kerry. *Happy birthday wombat!*
  Wombat and Bandicoot
Cushman, Doug. *The mystery of King Karfu*
Elks, Wendy. *Charles B. Wombat and the very strange
  thing*
Fox, Mem. *Wombat divine*
Morpurgo, Michael. *Wombat goes walkabout*

Animals – woodchucks *see* Animals – groundhogs

Animals – worms

Ahlberg, Janet. *The little worm book*
Barwin, Gary. *The racing worm brothers*
Demi. *Where is Willie Worm?*
Glaser, Linda. *Wonderful worms*
Hayward, Linda. *The city worm and the country worm*
Kraus, Robert. *Squirmy's big secret*
Lindgren, Barbro. *A worm's tale*
O'Callahan, Jay. *Herman and Marguerite*
O'Hagan, Caroline. *It's easy to have a worm visit you*
Raschka, Christopher. *Wormy Worm*
San Souci, Robert D. *Two bear cubs*
Scarry, Richard. *Richard Scarry's busy houses*
Thayer, Jane. *Andy and the wild worm*
Wong, Herbert H. *Our earthworms*

Animals – yaks

Lawson, Annetta. *The lucky yak*

Animals – zebras

Cousins, Lucy. *Za-Za's baby brother*
Goodall, Daphne Machin. *Zebras*

McKee, David. *Zebra's hiccups*
Mwenye Hadithi. *Greedy zebra*
Padt, Maartje. *Shanti*
Peet, Bill (William Bartlett). *Zella, Zack, and Zodiac*

Antarctic *see* Foreign lands – Antarctic

Antarctica *see* Foreign lands – Antarctic

Anteaters *see* Animals – anteaters

Antelopes *see* Animals – antelopes

Anti-violence *see* Violence, nonviolence

Ants *see* Insects – ants

Apache *see* Indians of North America – Apache

Apes *see* Animals – baboons; Animals – chimpanzees; Animals – gorillas; Animals – monkeys

Appearance *see* Character traits – appearance

April Fools' Day *see* Holidays – April Fools' Day

Aprons *see* Clothing – aprons

Aquariums

Aliki. *My visit to the aquarium*
Binnamin, Vivian. *The case of the mysterious mermaid*
Calder, S. J. *If you were a fish*
Collins, Pat Lowery. *Don't tease the guppies*
Curious George goes to the aquarium

Arab Americans *see* Ethnic groups in the U.S. – Arab Americans

Arabia *see* Foreign lands – Arabia

Archaeologists *see* Careers – archaeologists

Archery *see* Sports – archery

Architects *see* Careers – architects

Arctic *see* Foreign lands – Arctic

Argentina *see* Foreign lands – Argentina

Arguing *see* Behavior – fighting, arguing

Arithmetic *see* Counting, numbers

Armadillos *see* Animals – armadillos

Armenia *see* Foreign lands – Armenia

Art

Agee, Jon. *The incredible painting of Felix Clousseau*
Anderson, Douglas. *Let's draw a story*
Angelo, Nancy Carolyn Harrison. *Camembert*
Angelou, Maya. *My painted house, my friendly chicken, and me*
Anholt, Laurence. *Camille and the sunflowers*
Auch, Mary Jane. *Eggs mark the spot*
Baker, Jeannie. *Grandmother*
Baylor, Byrd. *When clay sings*
Blizzard, Gladys S. *Come look with me*
  Come look with me
Boehm, Arlene P. *Jack in search of Art*
Bond, Michael. *Paddington's art exhibit*
Bornstein, Ruth Lercher. *That's how it is when we draw*
Borten, Helen. *Do you see what I see?*
  A picture has a special look
Brent, Isabelle. *Cameo cats*
Brett, Jan. *The first dog*
Bröger, Achim. *Francie's paper puppy*
Bromhall, Winifred. *Mary Ann's first picture*
Brown, Laurie Krasny. *Visiting the art museum*
Browne, Anthony. *Bear goes to town*
  Bear hunt
  The little bear book
Bulla, Clyde Robert. *Daniel's duck*
Canning, Kate. *A painted tale*
Carle, Eric. *Hello, red fox*
Carmack, Lisa Jobe. *Philippe in Monet's garden*
Carrick, Donald. *Morgan and the artist*
Catalanotto, Peter. *The painter*
Cazet, Denys. *Frosted glass*
The Christmas story
Clayton, Elaine. *Ella's trip to the museum*
Cober, Alan E. *Cober's choice*
Cohen, Miriam. *No good in art*
Collins, Pat Lowery. *I am an artist*
Craig, Helen. *Susie and Alfred in the knight, the princess and the dragon*
Decker, Dorothy W. *Stripe visits New York*
Deeter, Catherine. *Seymour Bleu*
De Mejo, Oscar. *Oscar de Mejo's ABC*
De Paola, Tomie (Thomas Anthony). *The art lesson*
  Bonjour, Mister Satie
Dewey, Jennifer Owings. *Stories on stone*
Dionetti, Michelle V. *Painting the wind*
  Thalia Brown and the blue bug
Edens, Cooper. *An ABC of fashionable animals*
Elliott, Dan. *Ernie's little lie*
Emberley, Ed (Edward Randolph). *Ed Emberley's big green drawing book*
  Ed Emberley's big orange drawing book
  Ed Emberley's big purple drawing book
  Ed Emberley's crazy mixed-up face game
  Ed Emberley's drawing book
Emberley, Michael. *More dinosaurs!*
Emberley, Rebecca. *Drawing with numbers and letters*
Ernst, Lisa Campbell. *Hamilton's art show*
Everett, Gwen. *Li'l Sis and Uncle Willie*
Feldman, Eve B. *Birthdays!*
Fifield, Flora. *Pictures for the palace*
Florian, Douglas. *A painter*
  A potter
Freeman, Don. *Norman the doorman*
Galli, Letizia. *Mona Lisa*
Gardner, Jane Mylum. *Henry Moore*
Gibbons, Gail. *The art box*

Goffstein, M. B. (Marilyn Brooke). *An artist*
  Artists' helpers enjoy the evening
Green, Marion. *The magician who lived on the mountain*
Hammond, Anna. *This home we have made*
Harris, Leon A. *The great picture robbery*
Haskins, Jim (James). *The Statue of Liberty*
Hughes, Langston. *The sweet and sour animal book*
Hurd, Edith Thacher. *Wilson's world*
Hurd, Thacher. *Art dog*
Ingoglia, Gina. *The art class*
Isadora, Rachel. *ABC pop!*
Isom, Joan Shaddox. *The first starry night*
J. Paul Getty Museum. *A is for artist*
Johnson, Crockett. *Harold and the purple crayon*
  A picture for Harold's room
Johnson, Ryerson. *Kenji and the magic geese*
Johnston, Tony. *The last snow of winter*
Kesselman, Wendy Ann. *Emma*
Kidd, Richard. *Almost famous Daisy!*
Kilroy, Sally. *Copycat drawing book*
Lehan, Daniel. *This is not a book about dodos*
Lessac, Frané. *Caribbean canvas*
Le Tord, Bijou. *A bird or two*
Lionni, Leo. *Let's make rabbits*
Littlesugar, Amy. *Josiah True and the art maker*
  Marie in fourth position
Lobato, Arcadio. *Paper bird*
MacDonald, Elizabeth. *John's picture*
MacGill-Callahan, Sheila. *And still the turtle watched*
McPhail, David M. *The magical drawings of Moony B. Finch*
Maestro, Betsy. *The story of the Statue of Liberty*
Massey, Ed. *Milton*
Mayers, Florence Cassen. *Egyptian art from the Brooklyn Museum*
  The Museum of Fine Arts, Boston
  The Museum of Modern Art, New York
Mayhew, James. *Katie and the Mona Lisa*
  Katie meets the Impressionists
Mendoza, George. *Henri Mouse*
Menter, Ian. *The Albany Road mural*
Micklethwait, Lucy. *Spot a cat*
  Spot a dog
Miller, Thomas Patton. *Can a coal scuttle fly?*
Moon, Nicola. *Lucy's picture*
Moss, Marissa. *Regina's big mistake*
Nez, Redwing T. *Forbidden talent*
Nicholson, Nicholas B. A. *Little girl in a red dress with cat and dog*
Peet, Bill (William Bartlett). *Encore for Eleanor*
Pilkey, Dav. *When cats dream*
Pinkwater, Daniel Manus. *The bear's picture*
Pittman, Helena Clare. *Still-life stew*
Porte, Barbara Ann. *Chickens! Chickens!*
Rauch, Hans-Georg. *The lines are coming*
Rey, Margret (Margret Elisabeth Waldstein). *Billy's picture*
Ringgold, Faith. *Dinner at Aunt Connie's house*
Rubin, Cynthia Elyce. *ABC Americana from the National Gallery of Art*
Rylant, Cynthia. *All I see*
Scheidl, Gerda Marie. *The moon man*
Schick, Eleanor. *Art lessons*
Seuss, Dr. *I can draw it myself*
Sharon, Mary Bruce. *Scenes from childhood*
Simpson, Gretchen Dow. *Gretchen's ABC*
Steiner, Barbara (Annette). *The whale brother*
Sullivan, Charles. *Numbers at play*

Thomas, Abigail. *Pearl paints*
Thomson, Ruth. *Drawing*
  Painting
  Printing
Türk, Hanne. *Max the artlover*
Tusa, Tricia. *Bunnies in my head*
  Stay away from the junkyard!
Villarejo, Mary. *The art fair*
Voigt, Hannelore. *Not now, Sara!*
Wabbes, Marie. *Rose's picture*
Waddell, Martin. *Alice the artist*
Wallner, Alexandra. *Beatrix Potter*
Weitzman, Jacqueline Preiss. *You can't take a balloon into the Metropolitan Museum*
  You can't take a balloon into the National Gallery
Wellington, Monica. *Squeaking of art, the mice go to the museum*
Williams, Vera B. *Cherries and cherry pits*
Winter, Jeanette. *Cowboy Charlie*
Winter, Jonah. *Diego*
Wolf, Janet. *The best present is me*
Wooding, Sharon L. *The painter's cat*
Zadrzynska, Ewa. *The Peaceable Kingdom*
Zelinsky, Paul O. *The lion and the stoat*
Zelver, Patricia. *The wonderful Towers of Watts*

Artists *see* Careers – artists

Asia *see* Foreign lands – Asia

Asian Americans *see* Ethnic groups in the U.S. – Asian Americans

Assertiveness *see* Character traits – assertiveness

Asthma *see* Illness – asthma

Astrology *see* Zodiac

Astronauts *see* Careers – astronauts; Space and space ships

Astronomers *see* Careers – astronomers

Astronomy

Carpenter, Mary-Chapin. *Halley came to Jackson*
Crew, Gary. *Bright star*
Dussling, Jennifer. *Stars*
Gibbons, Gail. *The planets*
  Stargazers
Hirst, Robin. *My place in space*
Jones, Brian. *Space*
Leedy, Loreen. *Postcards from Pluto*
Markoe, Merrill. *The day my dogs became guys*
Ressmeyer, Roger. *Astronaut to zodiac*
Rosen, Sidney. *Where's the big dipper?*
Sis, Peter. *Starry messenger*

Athabascan Indians *see* Indians of North America – Athabascan

Aunts *see* Family life – aunts, uncles

Australia *see* Foreign lands – Australia

Australian aborigines

Lester, Alison. *Ernie dances to the didgeridoo*

Austria *see* Foreign lands – Austria

Authors *see* Careers – authors

Authors, children *see* Children as authors

Autism *see* Handicaps – autism

Automobiles

Aldag, Kurt. *Some things never change*
Alexander, Anne (Anna Barbara Cooke). *ABC of cars and trucks*
Aulaire, Ingri Mortenson d'. *The two cars*
Baugh, Dolores M. *Trucks and cars to ride*
Biro, Val. *Gumdrop and the birthday surprise*
  Gumdrop and the farmyard caper
  Gumdrop and the great sausage caper
  Gumdrop and the secret switches
  Gumdrop and the steamroller
  Gumdrop at the zoo
  Gumdrop beats the clock
  Gumdrop catches a cold
  Gumdrop finds a friend
  Gumdrop finds a ghost
  Gumdrop floats away
  Gumdrop gets a lift
  Gumdrop gets his wings
  Gumdrop goes to school
  Gumdrop has a birthday
  Gumdrop in double trouble
  Gumdrop is the best
  Gumdrop on the Brighton run
  Gumdrop races a train
  Gumdrop, the adventures of a vintage car
Brandenberg, Franz. *What's wrong with a van?*
Bridwell, Norman. *Clifford's good deeds*
Broekel, Ray. *I can be an auto mechanic*
Brown, Don. *Alice Ramsey's grand adventure*
Buller, Jon. *Toad on the road*
Burningham, John. *Mr. Gumpy's motor car*
  Slam bang
Caines, Jeannette. *Just us women*
Campbell, Rod. *Funwheels with moving parts!*
Cars and trucks
Cars and trucks and other vehicles
Cartlidge, Michelle. *Bears on the go*
Cave, Ron. *Automobiles*
Coy, John. *Night driving*
Cummings, W. T. (Walter Thies). *Miss Esta Maude's secret*
Demarest, Chris L. *My little red car*
DeSaix, Deborah Durland. *In the back seat*
DiFiori, Lawrence. *If I had a little car*
Dupasquier, Philippe. *A busy day at the garage*
Emberley, Ed (Edward Randolph). *Cars, boats, and planes*
Ets, Marie Hall. *Little old automobile*
Feldman, Barbara. *Going, going*
Florian, Douglas. *An auto mechanic*
Fowler, Richard. *Cat's car*
  Mr. Little's noisy car
Gay, Michel. *Little auto*
Gibbons, Faye. *Mama and me and the Model-T*

Gibbons, Gail. *Fill it up!*
Giffard, Hannah. *Fast car*
Greenblat, Rodney Alan. *Uncle Wizzmo's new used car*
Greene, Carla. *A motor holiday*
Greenfield, Eloise. *Kia Tanisha drives her car*
Greve, Andreas. *Christopher's dream car*
Hannan, Peter. *Sillyville or bust*
Holl, Adelaide. *The ABC of cars, trucks and machines*
Howland, Naomi. *ABCDrive!*
Hurd, Thacher. *Zoom City*
Janosch. *The magic auto*
Jordan, Jennifer. *Albert goes to town*
Kirk, Daniel. *Lucky's twenty-four hour garage*
Kirk, David. *Miss Spider's new car*
Koralek, Jenny. *Night ride to Nanna's*
Lenski, Lois. *The little auto*
Leslie, Amanda. *Let's look inside the red car*
Löfgren, Ulf. *The traffic stopper that became a grand-mother visitor*
Loomis, Christine. *We're going on a trip*
Maccarone, Grace. *Cars! Cars! Cars!*
MacKeen, Leslie Ann. *Who can fix it?*
McPartland, Suzy. *Zoom, car, zoom*
Mahy, Margaret. *The rattlebang picnic*
Mantegazza, Giovanna. *Look inside a car*
Marshall, James. *The Cut-Ups crack up*
Mendoza, George. *Traffic jam*
Miranda, Anne. *Beep! beep!*
  Vroom, chugga, vroom-vroom
Mitgutsch, Ali. *From rubber tree to tire*
Murphy, Stuart J. *Beep beep, vroom vroom!*
Nayer, Judy. *The happy little engine*
Newton, Laura P. *William the vehicle king*
Nilsén, Anna. *Drive your car*
Osborne, Victor. *Rex, the most special car in the world*
Owen, Annie. *Bumper to bumper*
Oxenbury, Helen. *The car trip*
Parish, Herman. *Good driving, Amelia Bedelia*
Patron, Susan. *Dark cloud strong breeze*
Peet, Bill (William Bartlett). *Jennifer and Josephine*
Peppé, Rodney. *Little wheels*
Petrie, Catherine. *Hot Rod Harry*
Pinkwater, Daniel Manus. *Tooth-gnasher superflash*
Pitcher, Caroline. *Cars and boats*
Potter, Tony. *See how it works: cars*
Radford, Derek. *Harry at the garage*
Reasoner, Charles. *Who drives this?*
Robbins, Ken. *City/country*
Rockwell, Anne F. *Cars*
Royston, Angela. *Cars*
Rylant, Cynthia. *Tulip sees America*
Scarry, Huck. *On the road*
Scarry, Richard. *The great big car and truck book*
Spier, Peter. *Bill's service station*
Spurr, Elizabeth. *Mrs. Minetta's car pool*
Steel, Danielle. *Freddie's trip*
Stobbs, William. *A car called beetle*
Walters, Virginia. *Are we there yet, Daddy?*
Wilkinson, Sylvia. *Automobiles*
  I can be a race car driver
Wood, Tim. *Motor racing*
Young, Miriam Burt. *If I drove a car*
Ziefert, Harriet. *A car trip for mole and mouse*
  Where's daddy's car?

Autumn *see* Seasons – fall

Award winning books *see* Caldecott award books; Caldecott award honor books

Aztec Indians *see* Indians of North America – Aztec

Babies *see also* Animals – babies; Birds – babies

Ahlberg, Allan. *Miss Brick, the builder's baby*
  Mockingbird
Ahlberg, Janet. *The baby's catalogue*
  Bye-bye, baby
  Peek-a-boo!
Alexander, Martha G. *Nobody asked me if I wanted a baby sister*
Aliki. *Welcome, little baby*
Allen, Pamela. *A lion in the night*
Allen, Robert. *Ten little babies count*
  Ten little babies dress
  Ten little babies eat
  Ten little babies play
Ancona, George. *It's a baby!*
Andry, Andrew C. *Hi, new baby*
  How babies are made
Anglund, Joan Walsh. *Baby brother*
  How many days has Baby to play?
  Love is a baby
Anholt, Catherine. *Aren't you lucky!*
  Here come the babies
  Toddlers
  What makes me happy?
  When I was a baby
Appelt, Kathi. *Someone's come to our house*
Arnstein, Helene S. *Billy and our new baby*
Asch, Frank. *Baby in the box*
  Starbaby
Auch, Mary Jane. *Monster brother*
Baby's words
Baird, Anne. *Baby socks*
  Kiss, kiss
Baker, Charlotte. *Little brother*
Baker, Gayle. *Special delivery*
Ballard, Robin. *When I am a sister*
Banish, Roslyn. *Let me tell you about my baby*
Bendick, Jeanne. *What made you you?*
Berends, Polly Berrien. *I heard said the bird*
Birdseye, Tom. *Waiting for baby*
Blackstone, Stella. *Baby high, baby low*
Bogart, Jo Ellen. *Daniel's dog*
Bolognese, Don. *A new day*
Bond, Rebecca. *Just like a baby*
Boyd, Lizi. *Baby play*
  Baby's journal
  Sam is my half brother
Bradman, Tony. *Billy and the baby*
  This little baby
Brann, Esther. *A book for baby*
Breeze, Lynn. *Baby's animals*
  Baby's clothes

Baby's food
Baby's toys
This little baby goes out
This little baby's bedtime
This little baby's morning
Brice, Tony. *Baby animals*
Brooks, Robert B. *So that's how I was born*
Brown, Craig McFarland. *In the spring*
Brown, Marc Tolon. *Arthur's baby*
Browne, Anthony. *The big baby*
  Changes
Buck, Nola. *Hey, little baby!*
  How a baby grows
Bunting, Eve (Anne Evelyn). *Our teacher's having a baby*
  Twinnies
Burningham, John. *Avocado baby*
  The baby
Busy baby
Byars, Betsy Cromer. *Go and hush the baby*
Byers, Rinda M. *Mycca's baby*
Byrne, David. *Stay up late*
Carlson, Nancy L. *Poor Carl*
Carlstrom, Nancy White. *Kiss your sister, Rose Marie*
Carter, Alden R. *Big brother Dustin*
Caseley, Judith. *Mama, coming and going*
  Silly baby
Cazet, Denys. *Dancing*
Chaffin, Lillie D. *Tommy's big problem*
Charlip, Remy. *Sleepytime rhyme*
Chess, Victoria. *Poor Esmé*
Chorao, Kay. *Baby's Christmas treasury*
  The baby's good morning book
  The cherry pie baby
  Knock at the door and other baby action rhymes
Christenson, Larry. *The wonderful way that babies are made*
Clarke, Gus. *Along came Eric*
Clifton, Lucille. *Everett Anderson's nine months long*
Coats, Lucy. *One hungry baby*
Cohn, Janice I. *Molly's rosebush*
Cole, Babette. *Mommy laid an egg!*
Cole, Joanna. *How you were born*
  I'm a big brother
  I'm a big sister
  The new baby at your house
Collins, Pat Lowery. *Waiting for baby Joe*
Cooke, Trish. *So much*
Cooper, Helen (Helen F.). *Little monster did it!*
Corey, Dorothy. *Will there be a lap for me?*
Cottringer, Anne. *Ella and the naughty lion*
Cowen-Fletcher, Jane. *Baby angels*
Curtis, Jamie Lee. *Tell me again about the night I was born*
  When I was little
Cutler, Jane. *Darcy and Gran don't like babies*
Cuyler, Margery. *Shadow's baby*
Dahl, Tessa. *Babies, babies, babies*
Davis, Jennifer. *Before you were born*
Day, Alexandra. *Carl's masquerade*
Dedieu, Thierry. *Baby clown*
Delacre, Lulu. *Good times with baby*
De Paola, Tomie (Thomas Anthony). *The baby sister*
  Baby's first Christmas
Dilley, Becki. *Sixty fingers, sixty toes*
Douglass, Ann. *Baby science*
Dragonwagon, Crescent. *Wind Rose*

Drescher, Henrik. *The strange appearance of Howard Cranebill, Jr.*
Driscoll, Debbie. *Baby comes home*
Dunn, Phoebe. *Baby's animal friends*
  Busy, busy toddlers
  I'm a baby!
Edelman, Elaine. *I love my baby sister (most of the time)*
Falwell, Cathryn. *Nicky and Alex*
  Nicky and grandpa
  Nicky loves daddy
  Nicky, 1-2-3
  Nicky's walk
  We have a baby
  Where's Nicky?
Ferguson, Alane. *That new pet!*
Fisher, Iris L. *Katie-Bo*
Foord, Jo. *The book of babies*
Foreman, Michael. *Ben's baby*
Foulds, Elfrida Vipont. *The elephant and the bad baby*
Fowler, Susi Gregg. *When Joel comes home*
Franklin, Jonathan. *Don't wake the baby*
Frasier, Debra. *On the day you were born*
French, Vivian. *Tiger and the new baby*
Fujikawa, Gyo. *Ten little babies*
Galbraith, Kathryn Osebold. *Roommates*
  Waiting for Jennifer
Garland, Sarah. *All gone!*
  Billy and Belle
  Oh, no!
  Polly's puffin
Gauch, Patricia Lee. *Christina Katerina and the great bear train*
Geddes, Anne. *Shapes*
Gelbard, Jane. *My bye-bye bottle book*
  My dressing book
  My eating book
  My sharing book
Gentieu, Penny. *Baby! Talk!*
  Grow! babies!
Gerstein, Mordicai. *The gigantic baby*
Gewing, Lisa. *Mama, daddy, baby and me*
Gikow, Louise. *Baby Kermit's Christmas*
  Bye-bye, pacifier
Gill, Joan. *Hush, Jon!*
Girard, Linda Walvoord. *You were born on your very first birthday*
Gliori, Debi. *Mr. Bear's new baby*
  New big sister
Golding, Kim. *Alphababies*
Gorog, Judith. *Zilla Sasparilla and the mud baby*
Graham, Bob. *Crusher is coming!*
Graham, Richard. *Jack and the monster*
Green, Jen. *Our new baby*
Greenberg, Barbara. *The bravest babysitter*
Greenberg, Judith E. *Adopted*
Greenfield, Eloise. *She come bringing me that little baby girl*
  Sweet baby coming
Greenfield, Monica. *The baby*
Grimes, Nikki. *Baby's bedtime*
Haarhoff, Dorian. *Desert December*
Hains, Harriet. *My baby brother*
Hamilton-Merritt, Jane. *Our new baby*
Hamm, Diane Johnston. *Rock-a-bye farm*
Hanson, Joan. *I don't like Timmy*
Harper, Anita. *It's not fair!*
Hathorn, Libby (Elizabeth). *Freya's fantastic surprise*
Hayes, Sarah. *Eat up, Gemma*

Hayward, Linda. *Baby Moses*
Hazen, Barbara Shook. *Why couldn't I be an only kid like you, Wigger?*
Heap, Sue. *Cowboy Baby*
Hedderwick, Mairi. *Katie Morag and the tiresome Ted*
Hello, baby
Helmering, Doris Wild. *We're going to have a baby*
Henderson, Kathy. *The baby dances*
　The baby's book of babies
　Bumpety bump
　Newborn
Hendrickson, Karen. *Baby and I can play*
　Fun with toddlers
Henley, Claire. *I'm a baby, too!*
Herter, Jonina. *Eighty-eight kisses*
Hesse, Karen. *Lavender*
Hest, Amy. *The babies are coming!*
　In the rain with Baby Duck
　Nannies for hire
　Off to school, Baby Duck
　You're the boss, Baby Duck
Hiatt, Fred. *Baby talk*
Hill, Susan. *King of kings*
Hines, Anna Grossnickle. *Big like me*
Hirsh, Marilyn. *Leela and the watermelon*
　Where is Yonkela?
Hobson, Laura Z. *"I'm going to have a baby!"*
Hoffman, Mary. *Henry's baby*
Hoffman, Phyllis. *Baby's first year*
Hoffman, Rosekrans. *Sister Sweet Ella*
Hol, Coby. *Tippy Bear and little Sam*
Holabird, Katharine. *Angelina's baby sister*
Holland, Viki. *We are having a baby*
Horowitz, Ruth. *Mommy's lap*
Horton, Barbara Savadge. *What comes in spring?*
Hubbell, Patricia. *Wrapping paper romp*
Hudson, Cheryl Willis. *Animal sounds for baby*
　Good morning baby
　Good night baby
Hughes, Shirley. *Angel Mae*
　Being together
Hush little baby. *Hush little baby*, ill. by Aliki
　Hush little baby, ill. by Shari Halpern
　Hush little baby, ill. by Jeanette Winter
　Hush little baby, ill. by Margot Zemach
Hutchins, Pat. *Our baby is best*
　Where's the baby?
Hutton, Warwick. *Moses in the bulrushes*
Ife, Elaine. *Moses in the bulrushes*
Intrater, Roberta Grobel. *Peek-a-boo!*
　Smile!
Isaacs, Gwynne L. *Baby face*
Isadora, Rachel. *Babies*
　I hear
　I see
Jam, Teddy. *Night cars*
Jaramillo, Raquel. *Ride, baby, ride!*
Jarrell, Mary. *The knee baby*
Josephs, Rhoda. *The baby bubble book*
Keats, Ezra Jack. *Peter's chair*
Keller, Holly. *Geraldine's baby brother*
　What Alvin wanted
Kelley, True. *Look, baby! Listen, baby! Do, baby!*
Kilroy, Sally. *Babies' bodies*
　Baby colors
　Busy babies
Kleven, Elisa. *A monster in the house*
Knight, Joan. *Opal in the closet*
Knight, Margy Burns. *Welcoming babies*

Knowlton, Laurie Lazzaro. *The Nativity*
Koehler, Phoebe. *The day we met you*
　Making room
Komaiko, Leah. *Where can Daniel be?*
Kopper, Lisa. *Daisy knows best*
　Daisy thinks she is a baby
　I'm a baby, you're a baby
　Ten little babies
Krasilovsky, Phyllis. *The very little boy*
　The very little girl
Kraus, Robert. *Big brother*
　Robert Kraus' a sunny day in Babytown
　Robert Kraus' Babytown express
　Robert Kraus' meet the babies
　Robert Kraus' welcome to Babytown
Kroll, Virginia L. *She is born*
Kunhardt, Edith. *Where's Peter?*
Lagerlöf, Selma. *The changeling*
Lakin, Pat (Patricia). *Don't touch my room*
Langstaff, Nancy. *A tiny baby for you*
Lasky, Kathryn. *A baby for Max*
　Baby love
Lawrence, Michael (Michael C.). *Baby loves*
Leonard, Marcia. *Babies help out*
　Busy babies
　Bye-bye, Baby-boo
　Night-night, Baby-boo
　Peek-a-boo, baby!
　What's that, Baby-boo?
　Where's Baby-boo?
Leuck, Laura. *My baby brother has ten tiny toes*
Levi, Dorothy Hoffman. *A very special sister*
Levine, Abby. *What did mommy do before you?*
Levinson, Riki. *Me baby!*
Levitin, Sonia. *Taking charge*
Lewison, Wendy Cheyette. *Baby has a boo-boo*
　Bye-bye, baby
　Don't wake the baby!
　Our new baby
　Uh oh, baby
　Where's baby?
Lexau, Joan M. *Finders keepers, losers weepers*
Lindgren, Astrid. *I want a brother or sister*
Lippman, Sidney. *A you're adorable*
Livingston, Myra Cohn. *B is for baby*
McAllister, Angela. *The babies of Cockle Bay*
Maccarone, Grace. *Baby visits grandma and grandpa*
　Baby's toys
MacGregor, Marilyn. *Baby takes a trip*
MacKinnon, Debbie. *Baby's first year*
　Find my boots!
MacLachlan, Patricia. *All the places to love*
McMillan, Bruce. *Step by step*
McMullan, Kate (Hall). *If you were my bunny*
　Papa's song
Mahy, Margaret. *Boom Baby boom, boom*
　A busy day for a good grandmother
Malecki, Maryann. *Mom and dad and I are having a baby!*
Mantegazza, Giovanna. *Look how a baby grows*
Manushkin, Fran. *Baby*
　Baby, come out!
　Little rabbit's baby brother
Mario, Heidi Stetson. *I'd rather have an iguana*
Marzollo, Jean. *Do you know new?*
Mazer, Anne. *The No-Nothings and their baby*
Medearis, Angela Shelf. *Bye-bye, babies!*
　Eat, babies, eat!
Melmed, Laura Krauss. *The rainbabies*

Miller, Margaret. *At my house*
  Baby faces
  I love colors
  In my room
  My first words: me and my clothes
  Now I'm big
  Time to eat
Mills, Lauren A. *The goblin baby*
Miranda, Anne. *Baby talk*
  Baby walk
Monfried, Lucia. *Baby's world*
Moon, Nicola. *Something special*
Moore, Julia. *While you sleep*
Morris, Ann. *The baby book*
Moses, Will. *Silent night*
Mueller, Virginia. *Monster and the baby*
Munsch, Robert N. *Alligator baby*
Murdocca, Sal (Salvatore). *Baby wants the moon*
Murphy, Jill. *The last noo-noo*
Nanao, Jun. *Contemplating your bellybutton*
Nayer, Judy. *Bath*
  Games
  Rhymes
  Toys
Naylor, Phyllis Reynolds. *The baby, the bed, and the rose*
Newberry, Clare Turlay. *Cousin Toby*
  T-Bone, the baby-sitter
Nikola-Lisa, W. *No babies asleep*
O'Book, Irene. *Maybe my baby*
O'Brien, John (1953-). *Poof!*
Offen, Hilda. *Good girl, Gracie Growler!*
Old, Wendie C. *Stacy had a little sister*
Oppenheim, Shulamith Levey. *Waiting for Noah*
Ormerod, Jan. *Bend and stretch*
  Dad's back
  Just like me
  Making friends
  Messy baby
  Mom's home
  101 things to do with a baby
  Our Ollie
  Rock-a-baby
  The saucepan game
  Silly goose
  Sleeping
  This little nose
  Young Joe
Osofsky, Audrey. *Dreamcatcher*
Overend, Jenni. *Welcome with love*
Oxenbury, Helen. *All fall down*
  Clap hands
  I can
  I hear
  I see
  I touch
  Playing
  Say goodnight
  Tickle, tickle
Parish, Peggy. *Granny, the baby and the big gray thing*
Patent, Dorothy Hinshaw. *Babies!*
Pearson, Susan. *When baby went to bed*
Politi, Leo. *Rosa*
Polushkin, Maria. *Baby brother blues*
Pragoff, Fiona. *It's fun to be one*
  It's great to be two
Pryor, Bonnie. *Greenbrook farm*
The pudgy book of babies
Pursell, Margaret Sanford. *A look at birth*

Rand, Gloria. *Baby in a basket*
Reader, Dennis. *Butterfingers*
Rheingrover, Jean Sasso. *Veronica's first year*
Rice, Eve. *What Sadie sang*
Richards, Kitty. *Merry Christmas, Rugrats!*
Rigby, Shirley Lincoln. *Smaller than most*
Rippon, Penelope. *My day*
Robins, Joan. *My brother, Will*
Rockwell, Anne F. *Long ago yesterday*
  Once upon a time this morning
Rockwell, Lizzy. *Hello baby!*
Roddie, Shen. *Hatch, egg, hatch!*
  Toes are to tickle
Rogers, Fred. *The new baby*
Root, Phyllis. *Mrs. Potter's pig*
  What Baby wants
Rosenberg, Liz. *Window, mirror, moon*
Rosenberg, Maxine B. *Mommy's in the hospital having a baby*
Ross, Christine. *Lily and the present*
Ross, Katharine (1950-). *When you were a baby*
Russo, Marisabina. *Hannah's baby sister*
  Waiting for Hannah
Sage, Chris. *Happy baby*
  Sleepy baby
  The trouble with babies
Scheffler, Ursel. *Taking care of Sister Bear*
Schick, Eleanor. *Peggy's new brother*
Schlein, Miriam. *Laurie's new brother*
Schwartz, Amy. *A teeny, tiny baby*
Sendak, Maurice. *Outside over there*
Shapp, Martha. *Let's find out about babies*
Shea, Pegi Deitz. *I see me!*
Sheffield, Margaret. *Before you were born*
  Where do babies come from?
Shields, Carol Diggory. *I wish my brother was a dog*
Showers, Paul. *Before you were a baby*
Slepian, Jan. *Lost moose*
Smith, Peter. *Jenny's baby brother*
Steel, Danielle. *Max's new baby*
Stein, Sara Bonnett. *Oh, baby!*
  That new baby
Steptoe, John. *Baby says*
Stevenson, James. *Rolling Rose*
  Worse than Willy!
Stimson, Joan. *Big Panda, Little Panda*
Stuve-Bodeen, Stephanie. *Mama Elizabeti*
Tafuri, Nancy. *The ball bounced*
  My friends
Taylor, Ann. *Baby dance*
Thayer, Jane. *Gus and the baby ghost*
Thomas, Iolette. *Janine and the new baby*
Thomas, Joyce Carol. *You are my perfect baby*
Thompson, Carol. *Baby days*
Titherington, Jeanne. *Baby's boat*
  Baby's boat, a board book
  A place for Ben
Tucker, Sian. *At home*
  Going out
  My clothes
  My toys
Van der Beek, Deborah. *Superbabe!*
Van Laan, Nancy. *Mama rocks, Papa sings*
Vigna, Judith. *Couldn't we have a turtle instead?*
Voake, Charlotte. *Mr. Davies and the baby*
Vulliamy, Clara. *Bang and shout*
  Blue hat, red coat
  Boo baby boo!
  Ellen and Penguin and the new baby

Good night, baby
Yum yum
Waddell, Martin. *When the teddy bears came*
Wahl, Jan. *Mabel ran away with the toys*
The sleepytime book
Wattenberg, Jane. *Mrs. Mustard's baby faces*
Watts, Bernadette. *David's waiting day*
Wayne-von-Königslöw, Andrea. *That's my baby?*
Wellington, Monica. *Baby at home*
Baby in a buggy
Baby in a car
Wells, Rosemary. *McDuff and the baby*
Max cleans up
Weninger, Brigitte. *Will you mind the baby, Davy?*
West, Keith. *Little Pig's special day*
Weston, Martha. *Bad baby brother*
What do babies do?
What do toddlers do?
Whybrow, Ian. *A baby for Grace*
Wilds, Kazumi Inose. *Hajime in the North Woods*
Wilhelm, Hans. *It's too windy!*
Wilkes, Angela. *See how I grow*
Wilkowski, Susan. *Baby's Bris*
Williams, Barbara. *Jeremy isn't hungry*
Williams, Sam. *The baby's word book*
Williams, Susan. *Poppy's first year*
Williams, Vera B. *"More more more," said the baby*
Willis, Jeanne. *Earthlets as explained by Professor Xargle*
What did I look like when I was a baby?
Wilner, Isabel. *The baby's game book*
Winter, Susan. *A baby just like me*
Wishinsky, Frieda. *Oonga boonga*, ill. by Suçie Stevenson
Oonga boonga, ill. by Carol Thompson
Yee, Wong Herbert. *A drop of rain*
Young, Ruth. *My blanket*
The new baby
Ziefert, Harriet. *Baby Ben's bow-wow book*
Baby Ben's busy book
Baby Ben's go-go book
Baby Ben's noisy book
Before I was born
Breakfast time!
Bye-bye, daddy!
Getting ready for new baby
Good morning, sun!
Let's get dressed!
Pushkin meets the bundle
Pushkin minds the bundle
Talk, baby!
Waiting for baby
Zolotow, Charlotte (Shapiro). *But not Billy*
Do you know what I'll do?

Babies, new *see* Family life – new sibling

Baboons *see* Animals – baboons

Babysitting *see* Activities – babysitting

Bad day *see* Behavior – bad day

Badgers *see* Animals – badgers

Bakers *see* Careers – bakers

Bali *see* Foreign lands – Bali

Ballerinas *see* Ballet; Careers – dancers

Ballet

Auch, Mary Jane. *Hen lake*
Peeping Beauty
Baumgardner, Mary Alice. *Alexandra, keeper of dreams*
Bell, Anthea. *Swan Lake*
Berger, Barbara Helen. *The jewel heart*
Brighton, Catherine. *Nijinsky*
Burstein, Fred. *The dancer*
Chevance, Audrey. *Tutu*
De Paola, Tomie (Thomas Anthony). *Oliver Button is a sissy*
Edwards, Pamela Duncan. *Honk!*
Eversole, Robyn Harbert. *The magic house*
The firebird, ill. by Reg Cartwright
The firebird, ill. by Francesca Crespi
The firebird, ill. by Demi
The firebird, adapt. and ill. by Rachel Isadora
The firebird, ill. by Moira Kemp
The firebird, ill. by Kris Waldherr
The firebird, ill. by Boris Zvorykin
Fonteyn, Margot, Dame. *Coppélia*
French, Vivian. *One ballerina two*
Gallwey, Kay. *Dancing Daisy*
Gauch, Patricia Lee. *Bravo, Tanya*
Dance, Tanya
Presenting Tanya, the Ugly Duckling
Tanya and Emily in a dance for two
Tanya and the magic wardrobe
Tanya steps out
Gray, Libba Moore. *My mama had a dancing heart*
Greaves, Margaret. *Petrushka*
Hampshire, Susan. *Rosie's ballet slippers*
Hoffmann, E. T. A. *The nutcracker*, ill. by Francesca Crespi
The nutcracker, ill. by Carolyn Ewing
The nutcracker, ill. by Rachel Isadora
The nutcracker, ill. by Joanna Isles
The nutcracker, ill. by Maurice Sendak
The nutcracker, ill. by Lisbeth Zwerger
The nutcracker ballet, ill. by Vladimir Vasil'evich Vagin
Holabird, Katharine. *Angelina and the princess*
Angelina ballerina
Angelina dances
Angelina on stage
Isadora, Rachel. *Lili at ballet*
Lili on stage
Max
My ballet class
My ballet diary
Jennings, Linda M. *Coppelia*
The sleeping beauty
Kroll, Virginia L. *Can you dance, Dalila?*
Kuklin, Susan. *Going to my ballet class*
Lasky, Kathryn. *Starring Lucille*
Lemaître, Pascal. *Zelda's secret*
Lewison, Wendy Cheyette. *I wear my tutu everywhere!*
Ten little ballerinas
Littlesugar, Amy. *Marie in fourth position*
McMullan, Kate (Hall). *Noel the first*
Nutcracker Noel

Maiorano, Robert. *A little interlude*
Marshall, James. *Swine lake*
Moers, Hermann. *Annie's dancing day*
Morris, Ann. *Little ballerinas*
O'Connor, Jane. *Nina, Nina and the copycat ballerina*
   Nina, Nina ballerina
   Nina, Nina, star ballerina
Oxenbury, Helen. *The dancing class*
Palazzo-Craig, Janet. *Ballet dancer*
Pulver, Robin. *Alicia's tutu*
Richardson, Jean. *The bear who went to the ballet*
   Clara's dancing feet
   The sleeping beauty
Rose, Emma. *Ballet magic*
Sorine, Stephanie Riva. *Our ballet class*
Tilden, Ruth. *Sophie's dance class*
Ziefert, Harriet. *Dancing*

Ballooning *see* Activities – ballooning

Balloons *see* Toys – balloons

Balls *see* Toys – balls

Bandicoots *see* Animals – bandicoots

Barbers *see* Careers – barbers

Bargaining *see* Activities – trading

Barns

Atwell, Debby. *Barn*
Brown, Craig McFarland. *My barn*
Brown, Margaret Wise. *Big red barn*, ill. by Felicia Bond
   Big red barn, ill. by Rosella Hartman
Carrick, Carol. *The old barn*
Climo, Lindee. *Chester's barn*
High, Linda Oatman. *Barn savers*
Johnston, Tony. *The barn owls*
Lindbergh, Reeve. *Benjamin's barn*
Martin, Bill (William Ivan). *Barn dance!*
Merrill, Jean. *Tell about the cowbarn, Daddy*
Miles, Miska. *The raccoon and Mrs. McGinnis*
Oppenheim, Joanne. *"Uh-oh!" said the crow*
Parnall, Peter. *Winter barn*
Schoenherr, John. *The barn*
Sewell, Helen Moore. *Blue barns*
Tafuri, Nancy. *The barn party*
Yolen, Jane. *Raising Yoder's barn*

Barons *see* Royalty

Bartering *see* Activities – trading

Baseball *see* Sports – baseball

Bashfulness *see* Character traits – shyness

Basketball *see* Sports – basketball

Bathing *see* Activities – bathing

Bats *see* Animals – bats

Bavaria *see* Foreign lands – Austria; Foreign lands – Germany

Beaches *see* Sea and seashore

Bears *see* Animals – bears

Beasts *see* Monsters

Beauty shops

Barber, Barbara E. *Saturday at the new you*

Beavers *see* Animals – beavers

Beds *see* Furniture – beds

Bedtime

Alda, Arlene. *Sheep, sheep, sheep, help me fall asleep*
Alexander, Martha G. *Good night, Lily*
Allison, Diane Worfolk. *In window eight, the moon is late*
Anderson, Lena. *Bunny box*
   Bunny story
Anderson, Peggy Perry. *Time for bed, the babysitter said*
Anholt, Catherine. *Twins, two by two*
Appelt, Kathi. *Bayou lullaby*
   Cowboy dreams
Apple, Margot. *Blanket*
   Brave Martha
Archambault, John. *Counting sheep*
Arnold, Tedd. *No jumping on the bed!*
Asch, Frank. *Good night, Baby Bear*
   Goodnight horsey
   Milk and cookies
Asher, Sandy. *Princess Bee and the royal good-night story*
Ashforth, Camilla. *Horatio's bed*
Auch, Mary Jane. *Monster brother*
Aylesworth, Jim. *The good-night kiss*
   Teddy bear tears
   Tonight's the night
Baird, Anne. *No sheep*
Ballard, Robin. *When we get home*
Bang, Molly. *One fall day*
   Ten, nine, eight
   Wiley and the hairy man
Banks, Kate (Katherine A.). *And if the moon could talk*
Barasch, Lynne. *Rodney's inside story*
Barrett, Judi. *I hate to go to bed*
Bauer, Marion Dane. *Sleep, little one, sleep*
Baum, Louis. *I want to see the moon*
Beckman, Kaj. *Lisa cannot sleep*
Bedtime
Berenstain, Stan. *Bears in the night*
   The Berenstain bears and the slumber party
Berridge, Celia. *Grandmother's tales*
Berry, Holly. *Busy Lizzie*
Bertrand, Lynne. *Dragon naps*
Blaustein, Muriel. *Bedtime, Zachary!*
Blocksma, Mary. *Did you hear that?*
Bond, Felicia. *Poinsettia and the firefighters*
Bottner, Barbara. *There was nobody there*
Bowden, Joan Chase. *Bouncy baby bunny finds his bed*

Bowers, Kathleen Rice. *At this very minute*
Bowman, Peter. *Goodnight, teddy bear*
Boyd, Lizi. *Sweet dreams, Willy*
Boynton, Sandra. *Dinosaur's binkit*
  The going to bed book
  Good night, good night
Bozylinsky, Hannah Heritage. *Lala Salama*
Brandenberg, Franz. *Aunt Nina, good night*
Breeze, Lynn. *This little baby's bedtime*
Brown, Margaret Wise. *A child's good night book*
  Goodnight moon
  Little Donkey close your eyes
  Sleepy ABC
  The sleepy men
Buchholz, Quint. *Sleep well, little bear*
Bullard, Lisa. *Not enough beds!*
Bunting, Eve (Anne Evelyn). *No nap*
Burleigh, Robert. *It's funny where Ben's train takes him*
Butler, John. *While you were sleeping*
Butterworth, Nick. *When it's time for bed*
Calhoun, Mary. *While I sleep*
Callen, Larry. *Dashiel and the night*
Calmenson, Stephanie. *All aboard the goodnight train*
Cameron, Ann. *Harry (the monster)*
Camp, Lindsay. *The biggest bed in the world*
Campbell, Alison. *Are you asleep, rabbit?*
Capucilli, Alyssa Satin. *Biscuit*
Carlstrom, Nancy White. *Northern lullaby*
  Swim the silver sea, Joshie Otter
Carpenter, Mary-Chapin. *Dreamland*
Cartlidge, Michelle. *Good night, Teddy*
Caseley, Judith. *Slumber party!*
Catalanotto, Peter. *Christmas always . . .*
Cave, Kathryn. *Out for the count*
Cazet, Denys. *I'm not sleepy*
  Mother night
  Night lights
Chevalier, Christa. *Spence and the sleepytime monster*
Chislett, Gail. *Whump*
Chorao, Kay. *Lemon moon*
Christelow, Eileen. *Five little monkeys jumping on the bed*
  Henry and the dragon
Cleary, Beverly. *Petey's bedtime story*
Clise, Michele Durkson. *Ophelia's bedtime book*
Coats, Lucy. *One hungry baby*
Coatsworth, Elizabeth. *Good night*
Cole, Joanna. *Sweet dreams, Clown-Arounds!*
Cole, William. *Frances face-maker*
Compton, Kenn. *Granny Greenteeth and the noise in the night*
Corddry, Thomas I. *Kibby's big feat*
Cosgrove, Stephen (Edward). *Sleepy time bunny*
Count in the dark with Glo Worm
Cousins, Lucy. *Maisy goes to bed*
  Maisy's bedtime
Dahl, Roald. *Dirty beasts*
Dale, Penny. *Bet you can't*
  Ten out of bed
  Ten play hide-and-seek
Dalmais, Anne-Marie. *The Best bedtime stories of Mother Bear*
  Best bedtime stories of Mother Cat
  Best bedtime stories of Mother Hen
  Best bedtime stories of Mother Mouse
  Best bedtime stories of Mother Pig
  Best bedtime stories of Mother Sheep

Damjan, Mischa. *How do Dinosaurs say goodnight?*
Davis, Katie (Katie I.). *I hate to go to bed!*
Davol, Marguerite W. *Batwings and the curtain of night*
Denton, Kady MacDonald. *Granny is a darling*
De Paola, Tomie (Thomas Anthony). *Fight the night*
  Pajamas for Kit
Dowling, Paul. *Are you sleepy, Puff?*
  Splodger
Dubowski, Cathy East. *Snug Bug*
Duke, Kate. *Aunt Isabel tells a good one*
  Bedtime
Dunbar, Joyce. *Tell me something happy before I go to sleep*
Edwards, Frank B. *Melody Mooner stayed up all night*
Emberley, Ed (Edward Randolph). *Go away, big green monster!*
Engel, Diana. *Circle song*
Engvick, William. *Lullabies and night songs*
Eriksson, Eva. *Hocus-pocus*
Erskine, Jim. *Bedtime story*
Facklam, Margery. *I go to sleep*
Feldman, Eve B. *Animals don't wear pajamas*
Foreman, Michael. *Dad! I can't sleep*
Foster, Karen Sharp. *Good night my little chicks = Buenas noches mis pollitos*
Fox, Mem. *A bedtime story*
  Time for bed
Fox, Siv Cedering. *The blue horse and other night poems*
Freedman, Sally. *Devin's new bed*
Gackenbach, Dick. *Poppy the panda*
Galouchko, Annouchka. *Shô and the demons of the deep*
Garland, Sherry. *Goodnight, cowboy*
Gay, Marie-Louise. *Moonbeam on a cat's ear*
Gerstein, Mordicai. *Bedtime, everybody!*
  William, where are you?
Ginsburg, Mirra. *Asleep, asleep*
  Which is the best place?
Gliori, Debi. *A lion at bedtime*
  When I'm big
Goffstein, M. B. (Marilyn Brooke). *Sleepy people*
Goldsmith, Howard. *Sleepy little owl*
Goode, Diane. *I hear a noise*
Goodman, Joan Elizabeth. *Bernard's nap*
Goodspeed, Peter. *A rhinoceros wakes me up in the morning*
Gorbachev, Valeri. *Nicky and the big, bad wolves*
Gordon, Jeffie Ross. *Two badd babies*
Graff, Nancy Price. *In the hush of the evening*
Grambling, Lois G. *Night sounds*
Greenberg, Dan. *The bed who ran away from home*
Greenleaf, Ann. *No room for Sarah*
Gregory, Valiska. *Kate's giants*
Gretz, Susanna. *Hide-and-seek*
  I'm not sleepy
  Ready for bed
  Too dark!
Greydanus, Rose. *Bedtime story*
Grimes, Nikki. *Baby's bedtime*
Grindley, Sally. *Knock, knock! Who's there?*
Hamm, Diane Johnston. *How many feet in the bed?*
  Rock-a-bye farm
Hancock, Joy Elizabeth. *The loudest little lion*
Harley, Bill. *Nothing happened*
Harris, Dorothy Joan. *Goodnight Jeffrey*
Harshman, Marc. *All the way to morning*

Night counting
Sleepy, sleepy
Morris, Terry Nell. *Good night, dear monster!*
Morris, Winifred. *What if the shark wears tennis shoes?*
Mother Goose. *Hush-a-bye baby*
Mueller, Virginia. *Monster can't sleep*
Munsch, Robert N. *Mortimer*
Muntean, Michaela. *Kermit and Robin's scary story*
Murphy, Jill. *A quiet night in*
What next, baby bear!
Murray, Marjorie Dennis. *The stars are waiting*
Namm, Diane. *Bunny's bedtime*
Nichol, B. P. *Once*
Nixon, Joan Lowery. *Will you give me a dream?*
Nobisso, Josephine. *Shh! the whale is smiling*
O'Brien, Mary. *Counting sheep to sleep*
O'Donnell, Elizabeth Lee. *Sing me a window*
Ogburn, Jacqueline K. *Noise lullaby*
O'Keefe, Susan Heyboer. *Good night, God bless*
Oppenheim, Joanne. *The story book prince*
Oppenheim, Shulamith Levey. *What is the full moon full of?*
Orgel, Doris. *Little John*
Ormerod, Jan. *Moonlight*
Otto, Carolyn. *Dinosaur chase*
Owen, Annie. *Goodnight bear!*
Owen, Roy. *My night forest*
Oxenbury, Helen. *Good night, good morning*
Packard, Mary. *We are monsters*
Paul, Ann Whitford. *Everything to spend the night . . . from A to Z*
Pearson, Susan. *When baby went to bed*
Pedersen, Judy. *When night time comes near*
Petersham, Maud. *Off to bed*
Pfister, Marcus. *I see the moon*
Piers, Helen. *Who's in my bed?*
Pierson, Judith Patterson. *The always moon*
Plath, Sylvia. *The bed book*
Plotz, Helen. *A week of lullabies*
Plourde, Lynn. *Wild child*
Pomerantz, Charlotte. *All asleep*
Posy
Preston, Edna Mitchell. *Monkey in the jungle*
Pryor, Ainslie. *The baby blue cat who said no*
Quackenbush, Robert M. *Batbaby*
Raschka, Christopher. *Can't sleep*
Rathmann, Peggy. *10 minutes till bedtime*
Ray, Karen. *Sleep song*
Rees, Mary. *Ten in a bed*
Reiser, Lynn. *Bedtime cat*
Little clam
Night thunder and the Queen of the Wild Horses
Rice, Eve. *Goodnight, goodnight*
Richardson, John. *Ten bears in a bed*
Richter, Mischa. *To bed, to bed!*
Riddell, Chris. *Mr. Underbed*
Ripley, Catherine. *Why do stars twinkle?*
Roberts, Bethany. *Waiting-for-Christmas stories*
Robison, Deborah. *No elephants allowed*
Rockwell, Anne F. *Buster and the bogeyman*
Rogers, Paul (Patrick). *Somebody's sleepy*
Rohmann, Eric. *The cinder-eyed cats*
Rosen, Michael (1946-). *Under the bed*
Rosenberg, Liz. *Adelaide and the night train*
Roth, Carol. *Ten dirty pigs / Ten clean pigs*
Roth, Susan L. *Night-time numbers*
Russo, Marisabina. *Why do grownups have all the fun?*

Rydell, Katy. *Wind says good night*
Sage, James. *To sleep*
Saltzberg, Barney. *It must have been the wind*
Sanromán, Susana. *Señora Reganoña*
Sardegna, Jill. *K is for kiss good night*
Schaefer, Carole Lexa. *Down in the woods at sleepy-time*
Schertle, Alice. *Goodnight, Hattie, my dearie, my dove*
Schindel, John. *Who are you?*
Schlein, Miriam. *Sleep safe, little whale*
Schneider, Nina. *While Susie sleeps*
Schotter, Roni. *Bunny's night out*
Schreier, Joshua. *Luigi's all-night parking lot*
Schubert, Ingrid. *There's a crocodile under my bed!*
Schwartz, Amy. *Some babies*
Sharmat, Marjorie Weinman. *Go to sleep, Nicholas Joe*
Goodnight, Andrew. Goodnight, Craig
Shepperson, Rob. *The sandman*
Shipton, Jonathan. *In the night*
Showers, Paul. *Sleep is for everyone*
Silverman, Erica. *Follow the leader*
Simmons, Jane. *Go to sleep, Daisy*
Simms, Laura. *The squeaky door*
Simon, Carly. *Midnight farm*
Skorpen, Liesel Moak. *Outside my window*
Slate, Joseph. *The star rocker*
Smee, Nicola. *Finish the story, dad*
Smith, Edward Biko. *A lullaby for Daddy*
Smith, Robert Paul. *Nothingatall, nothingatall, nothingatall*
Spinelli, Eileen. *When Mama comes home tonight*
Where is the night train going?
Staub, Leslie. *Bless this house*
Steer, Dougald. *Just one more story*
Steiner, Charlotte. *The sleepy quilt*
Stevens, Kathleen. *The beast in the bathtub*
Stevenson, Harvey. *Big scary wolf*
Stevenson, James. *We can't sleep*
What's under my bed?
Stock, Catherine. *Alexander's midnight snack*
Stoddard, Sandol. *Bedtime for bear*
Bedtime mouse
Turtle time
Stone, Kazuko G. *Goodnight Twinklegator*
Storm, Theodor. *Little Hobbin*
Strahl, Rudi. *Sandman in the lighthouse*
Strand, Mark. *The planet of lost things*
Sugita, Yutaka. *Good night 1, 2, 3*
Sussman, Susan. *Hippo thunder*
Sutherland, Harry A. *Dad's car wash*
Swados, Elizabeth. *Lullaby*
Swain, Ruth Freeman. *Bedtime!*
Sweeney, Jacqueline. *Katie and the night noises*
Tafuri, Nancy. *What the sun sees / What the moon sees*
Takamado no Miya Hisako. *Katie and the dream-eater*
Taylor, Livingston. *Pajamas*
Thomas, Shelley Moore. *Good night, Good Knight*
Putting the world to sleep
Titherington, Jeanne. *Baby's boat*
Baby's boat, a board book
A child's prayer
Tobias, Tobi. *Chasing the goblins away*
Trez, Denise. *Good night, Veronica*
Trottier, Maxine. *Dreamstones*
Türk, Hanne. *Goodnight Max*
Twining, Edith. *Sandman*
Van Leeuwen, Jean. *The tickle stories*

Velthuijs, Max. *Frog is frightened*
Viorst, Judith. *My mama says there aren't any zombies, ghosts, vampires, creatures, demons, monsters, fiends, goblins, or things*
Vulliamy, Clara. *Good night, baby*
Wabbes, Marie. *Good night, Little Rabbit*
Waber, Bernard. *Bearsie Bear and the surprise sleep-over party*
   Ira sleeps over
Waddell, Martin. *Can't you sleep, Little Bear?*
   Night night Cuddly Bear
   Who do you love?
Wahl, Jan. *Humphrey's bear*
   The sleepytime book
Wallace, Nancy Elizabeth. *Rabbit's bedtime*
Walsh, Melanie. *Hide and sleep*
Walty, Margaret. *Rock-a-bye baby*
Warnick, Elsa. *Bedtime*
Watson, Clyde. *Fisherman lullabies*
   Midnight moon
Weir, Alison. *Peter, good night*
Weiss, Nicki. *Where does the brown bear go?*
   Where does the brown bear go? A board book
Wells, Rosemary. *Goodnight Max*
   Max's bedtime
Westcott, Nadine Bernard. *Going to bed*
Whishaw, Iona. *Henry and the cow problem*
Whiteside, Karen. *Lullaby of the wind*
Whitman, Candace. *The night is like an animal*
Wiesner, David. *Free fall*
Willis, Jeanne. *The monster bed*
Winthrop, Elizabeth. *Bunk beds*
   Maggie and the monster
Wood, Audrey. *Moonflute*
   Oh my baby bear!
   Sweet dream pie
Yaccarino, Dan. *Good night, Mr. Night*
Yee, Patrick. *Bedtime for Rosie Rabbit*
Yolen, Jane. *Baby Bear's bedtime book*
   Dragon night and other lullabies
   The lullaby songbook
   Moon ball
Zalben, Jane Breskin. *Norton's nighttime*
Ziefert, Harriet. *Clara Ann Cookie go to bed!*
   Good night everyone!
   I want to sleep in your bed!
   I won't go to bed!
   Moonride
   Say good night!
Zinnemann-Hope, Pam. *Time for bed, Ned*
Zolotow, Charlotte (Shapiro). *Flocks of birds*
   The sleepy book, ill. by Vladimir Bobri
   The sleepy book, ill. by Ilse Plume
   The summer night
   Wake up and goodnight
   When the wind stops
   Who is Ben?

Bees *see* Insects – bees

Beetles *see* Insects – beetles

Beggars *see* Careers – beggars

Behavior

Armitage, Ronda. *Harry hates shopping!*

Arnold, Tedd. *Mother Goose's words of wit and wisdom*
Babbitt, Lorraine. *Pink like the geranium*
Beim, Jerrold. *The swimming hole*
Belloc, Hilaire. *The bad child's book of beasts*
Berenstain, Stan. *The Berenstain bears' trouble at school*
Bertrand, Cécile. *Mr. and Mrs. Smith have only one child, but what a child!*
Blake, Jon. *Wriggly Pig*
Blundell, Tony. *Joe on Sunday*
Bluthenthal, Diana Cain. *Matilda the moocher*
Boegehold, Betty. *Three to get ready*
Bond, Felicia. *Poinsettia and her family*
Bonners, Susan. *Why does the cat do that?*
Brown, Marc Tolon. *The true Francine*
Brown, Ruth. *Copycat*
Buehner, Caralyn. *I did it, I'm sorry*
Bunting, Eve (Anne Evelyn). *My backpack*
Butler, Geoff. *The hangashore*
Carle, Eric. *The grouchy ladybug*
Carlson, Nancy L. *Life is fun*
Caseley, Judith. *The noisemakers*
Caudill, Rebecca. *Contrary Jenkins*
Cecil, Ivon. *Kirby Kelvin and the not laughing lessons*
Cibula, Matt S. *What's up with you, Taquandra Fu?*
Cole, Joanna. *Don't tell the whole world*
Cuetara, Mittie. *Terrible Teresa and other very short stories*
Cuneo, Diane. *Mary Louise loses her manners*
Curious George and the hot air balloon
Curious George and the puppies
Curious George goes to a movie
Cyrus, Kurt. *Slow train to Oxmox*
Delton, Judy. *I'm telling you now*
Egan, Tim. *Metropolitan cow*
Elliot, David. *An alphabet of rotten kids!*
Erickson, Karen. *Do I have to go home?*
Ets, Marie Hall. *Bad boy, good boy*
   Play with me
Falconer, Ian. *Olivia*
Foreman, Michael. *The angel and the wild animal*
French, Vivian. *Lazy Jack*
   Tiger and the temper tantrum
Gackenbach, Dick. *Hattie be quiet, Hattie be good*
Gaeddert, LouAnn Bigge. *Noisy Nancy Norris*
Gambill, Henrietta D. *Self-control*
Gray, Nigel. *The grocer's daughter*
Greaves, Margaret. *Sarah's lion*
Grimes, Nikki. *Someone's baby-sitting*
Grindley, Sally. *I don't want to!*
Gwynne, Fred. *Easy to see why*
Hannan, Peter. *The battle of Sillyville*
Hanson, Mary Elizabeth. *Snug*
Harber, Frances. *The brothers' promise*
Harris, Robie H. *Don't forget to come back*
Haugaard, Erik Christian. *Princess Horrid*
Hautzig, Deborah. *Little Witch's bad dream*
Hayward, Linda. *A day in the life of Oscar the Grouch*
Hazen, Barbara Shook. *The new dog*
Himmelman, John. *Wanted: perfect parents*
Hines, Anna Grossnickle. *Mean old Uncle Jack*
Hoban, Russell. *Dinner at Alberta's*
Hogrogian, Nonny. *Carrot cake*
Hood, Susan. *The new kid*
Horvath, Betty F. *Be nice to Josephine*
Hutchins, Pat. *Tidy Titch*
Ikeda, Daisaku. *The princess and the moon*
Inwald, Robin. *Cap it off with a smile*

Irbinskas, Heather. *How Jackrabbit got his very long ears*
Jackson, Jean. *Thorndike and Nelson*
James, Betsy. *Tadpoles*
Jeram, Anita. *Birthday happy, Contrary Mary*
  Contrary Mary
Johnson, Paul Brett. *The pig who ran a red light*
Johnston, Marianne. *Dealing with anger*
Jolley, Mike. *Grunter, a pig with an attitude!*
Kasza, Keiko. *Don't laugh, Joe*
Keller, Holly. *The new boy*
  That's mine, Horace
Kerr, Phyllis Forbes. *I tricked you*
Kettner, Christine. *An ordinary cat*
Lakin, Pat (Patricia). *A good sport*
Lester, Helen. *Me first*
  Tacky in trouble
Lester, Julius. *Albidaro and the mischievous dream*
Livingston, Myra Cohn. *Higgledy-Piggledy*
Low, Joseph. *Don't drag your feet . . .*
  My dog, your dog
Luttrell, Ida. *Ottie Slockett*
MacDonald, Suse. *Peck, slither and slide*
Markoe, Merrill. *The day my dogs became guys*
Masurel, Claire. *No, no, Titus!*
Meyer, Eleanor Walsh. *The keeper of ugly sounds*
Mills, Lauren A. *The dog prince*
Morgan-Vanroyen, Mary. *Gentle Rosie*
  Wild Rosie
Myller, Lois. *No! No!*
Naylor, Phyllis Reynolds. *Sweet strawberries*
O'Callahan, Jay. *Orange cheeks*
Pace, David. *Shouting Sharon*
Panek, Dennis. *Matilda Hippo has a big mouth*
Parker, Nancy Winslow. *Puddums, the Cathcarts' orange cat*
Parr, Todd. *Do's and don'ts*
Paterson, Diane. *Wretched Rachel*
Patterson, Geoffrey. *The naughty boy and the strawberry horse*
Pfister, Marcus. *How Leo learned to be king*
  Milo and the magical stones
Pilkey, Dav. *The Silly Gooses*
Quackenbush, Robert M. *I don't want to go, I don't know how to act*
Reider, Katja. *Snail started it!*
Remkiewicz, Frank. *Greedyanna*
Ringi, Kjell (Arne Sorensen). *The winner*
Rotner, Shelley. *The A.D.D. book for kids*
Scarry, Richard. *Pig Will and Pig Won't*
  Pig Will and Pig Won't
Shannon, David. *A bad case of stripes*
  The rain came down
Sharmat, Marjorie Weinman. *Scarlet Monster lives here*
Spelman, Cornelia. *When I feel angry*
Stevenson, James. *Don't make me laugh*
Stover, Jo Ann. *If everybody did*
Supraner, Robyn. *Would you rather be a tiger?*
Svendsen, Carol. *Hulda*
Swain, Ruth Freeman. *Bedtime!*
Swope, Sam. *The Araboolies of Liberty Street*
Tabor, Nancy (Maria Grande). *Bottles break*
Teague, Mark. *Baby tamer*
Thomas, Karen. *The good thing . . . the bad thing*
Van Laan, Nancy. *A mouse in my house*
Waggoner, Karen. *The lemonade babysitter*
Wahl, Jan. *Little Johnny Buttermilk*
Wahl, Robert. *Pyxx*

Walker, Alice. *Finding the green stone*
Wittels, Harriet. *Things I hate!*
Yaccarino, Dan. *If I had a robot*

Behavior – animals, dislike of

Bemelmans, Ludwig. *Madeline and the bad hat*
Kay, Helen. *An egg is for wishing*
Udry, Janice May. *Alfred*

Behavior – bad day

Alborough, Jez. *Running Bear*
Andrews, F. Emerson (Frank Emerson). *Nobody comes to dinner*
Baker, Alan. *Benjamin's portrait*
Balzola, Asun. *Munia and the day things went wrong*
Berenstain, Stan. *The Berenstain bears get in a fight*
Birdseye, Tom. *A regular flood of mishap*
Demuth, Patricia Brennan. *Ornery morning*
Duncan, Jane. *Janet Reachfar and Chickabird*
Everitt, Betsy. *Mean soup*
Fernandes, Eugenie. *A difficult day*
Fujikawa, Gyo. *Sam's all-wrong day*
Gammell, Stephen. *Is that you, winter?*
Giff, Patricia Reilly. *Today was a terrible day*
Griffith, Helen V. *Nata*
Haywood, Carolyn. *Santa Claus forever!*
Hoban, Russell. *The sorely trying day*
Hurd, Thacher. *Mystery on the docks*
  Santa Mouse and the ratdeer
Johnston, Deborah. *Mathew Michael's beastly day*
Keith, Eros. *Bedita's bad day*
Kline, Suzy. *Ooops!*
Krahn, Fernando. *Here comes Alex Pumpernickel!*
Lexau, Joan M. *I should have stayed in bed*
Martin, Jane Read. *Now everybody really hates me*
  Now I will never leave the dinner table
Miller, Virginia. *I love you just the way you are*
Morris, Ann. *Eleanora Mousie's gray day*
Oram, Hiawyn. *Badger's bad mood*
Oxenbury, Helen. *The car trip*
Prater, John. *The perfect day*
Robins, Joan. *Addie's bad day*
Rockwell, Anne F. *No! No! No!*
Scarry, Richard. *Mr. Frumble's worst day ever*
Shannon, George. *Laughing all the way*
Simon, Charnan. *The good bad day*
Simon, Francesca. *Spider school*
Smath, Jerry. *Mr. Digby's bad day*
Sondheimer, Ilse. *The boy who could make his mother stop yelling*
Van Leeuwen, Jean. *Too hot for ice cream*
Viorst, Judith. *Alexander and the terrible, horrible, no good, very bad day*
Vreeken, Elizabeth. *One day everything went wrong*
Wells, Rosemary. *Unfortunately Harriet*

Behavior – boasting

Augarde, Steve (Stephen). *Barnaby Shrew, Black Dan and . . . the mighty wedgwood*
Bonsall, Crosby Newell. *The amazing the incredible super dog*
  Mine's the best
Browne, Anthony. *Look what I've got!*
Butterworth, Nick. *My dad is awesome*
  My grandpa is amazing
Carlson, Nancy L. *Loudmouth George and the big race*

Loudmouth George and the cornet
Loudmouth George and the fishing trip
Loudmouth George and the new neighbors
Loudmouth George and the sixth-grade bully
Collins, Pat Lowery. *My friend Andrew*
Currey, Anna. *Tickling tigers*
Diot, Alain. *Better, best, bestest*
Duvoisin, Roger Antoine. *See what I am*
Ellentuck, Shan. *A sunflower as big as the sun*
Farris, Pamela J. *Young Mouse and Elephant*
Gretz, Susanna. *Rabbit rambles on*
Harshman, Marc. *Uncle James*
Hayes, Joe. *A spoon for every bite*
Johnston, Tony. *Farmer Mack measures his pig*
Kajpust, Melissa. *The peacock's pride*
Kepes, Juliet. *The story of a bragging duck*
Knutson, Barbara. *Why the crab has no head*
Lopshire, Robert. *I am better than you*
Lund, Doris Herold. *You ought to see Herbert's house*
May, Kara. *Big brave brother Ben*
Miller, Moira. *The moon dragon*
Miller, Warren. *The goings on at Little Wishful*
Oppenheim, Joanne. *You can't catch me!*
Parker, Kristy. *My dad the magnificent*
Pavey, Peter. *I'm Taggarty Toad*
Peterson, Esther Allen. *Frederick's alligator*
Raphael, Elaine. *Turnabout*
Ross, Gayle. *How Turtle's back was cracked*
Schindler, Regina. *The bear's cave*
Schlein, Miriam. *Big talk*, ill. by Joan Auclair
  Big talk, ill. by Laura Lydecker
Schwartz, Amy. *Her Majesty, Aunt Essie*
Simmonds, Posy. *The chocolate wedding*
Slater, Teddy. *The cow that could tap dance*
  The fabulous fish from Lake Wiggawalla
Yolen, Jane. *Little Mouse and Elephant*

Behavior – boredom

Alexander, Martha G. *We never get to do anything*
Anholt, Catherine. *Come back, Jack!*
Ayal, Ora. *The adventures of Chester the chest*
Berson, Harold. *I'm bored, Ma!*
Christelow, Eileen. *Five little monkeys with nothing to do*
Creighton, Jill. *One day there was nothing to do*
Delton, Judy. *My mom hates me in January*
Duvoisin, Roger Antoine. *Veronica's smile*
Eriksson, Eva. *One short week*
Geoghegan, Adrienne. *There's a wardrobe in my monster!*
Hannan, Peter. *Sillyville or bust*
Henkes, Kevin. *Once around the block*
Hoban, Russell. *Nothing to do*
Ichikawa, Satomi. *Nora's roses*
Jennings, Sharon. *When Jeremiah found Mrs. Ming*
Krauss, Ruth. *A good man and his good wife*
Lawlor, Laurie. *Second-grade dog*
McConnachie, Brian. *Lily of the forest*
McGovern, Ann. *Nicholas Bentley Stoningpot III*
McKee, David. *Elmer again*
McLaughlin, Lissa. *Why won't winter go?*
Maris, Ron. *Bernard's boring day*
Meroux, Felix. *The prince of the rabbits*
Modarressi, Mitra. *The parent thief*
Noble, Trinka Hakes. *Meanwhile back at the ranch*
Oram, Hiawyn. *In the attic*
Raskin, Ellen. *Nothing ever happens on my block*
Reit, Seymour. *The king who learned to smile*

Seymour, Tres. *Too quiet for these old bones*
Spier, Peter. *Bored - nothing to do!*
Stevenson, James. *There's nothing to do!*
Szekeres, Cyndy. *Toby!*
Thayer, Jane. *Mr. Turtle's magic glasses*
Watts, Marjorie-Ann. *Crocodile medicine*

Behavior – bullying

Alexander, Martha G. *I sure am glad to see you, Blackboard Bear*
  Move over, Twerp
Berquist, Grace. *The boy who couldn't roar*
Bible. Old Testament. David. *David and the giant*
Bottner, Barbara. *Bootsie Barker bites*
Boyd, Lizi. *Bailey the big bully*
Browne, Anthony. *Willy the champ*
Bryant, Bernice. *Follow the leader*
Caple, Kathy. *The wimp*
Carlson, Nancy L. *Loudmouth George and the sixth-grade bully*
Cauley, Lorinda Bryan. *The trouble with Tyrannosaurus Rex*
Cazet, Denys. *Mud baths for everyone*
Chapman, Carol. *Herbie's troubles*
Charlton, Elizabeth. *Terrible tyrannosaurus*
Christelow, Eileen. *Jerome camps out*
Clayton, Elaine. *Pup in school*
Cohen, Miriam. *Tough Jim*
Cole, Babette. *Hurray for Ethelyn*
Cole, Joanna. *Don't call me names!*
Collicott, Sharleen. *Toestomper and the caterpillars*
De Paola, Tomie (Thomas Anthony). *Katie, Kit and cousin Tom*
  Kit and Kat
Dodd, Lynley. *Hairy Maclary, Scattercat*
Freschet, Berniece. *Furlie Cat*
Gretz, Susanna. *Roger takes charge!*
Henkes, Kevin. *Chester's way*
Hooks, William H. *Rough, tough, Rowdy*
Isenberg, Barbara. *Albert the running bear gets the jitters*
Janice. *Angélique*
Johnston, Marianne. *Dealing with bullying*
Karas, G. Brian. *Home on the bayou*
Kasza, Keiko. *The rat and the tiger*
Keats, Ezra Jack. *Goggles*
Kroll, Steven. *It's April Fools' Day!*
Lagercrantz, Rose. *Brave little Pete of Geranium Street*
Laurencin, Geneviève. *I wish I were*
Lester, Helen. *Hooway for Wodney Wat*
Liersch, Anne. *A house is not a home*
Little, Jean. *Jess was the brave one*
McCain, Becky R. (Becky Ray). *Nobody knew what to do*
McMullan, Kate (Hall). *Hey, Pipsqueak!*
Mahy, Margaret. *Beaten by a balloon*
Marton, Jirina. *Flowers for mom*
Meddaugh, Susan. *Martha walks the dog*
Minarik, Else Holmelund. *The little girl and the dragon*
Modarressi, Mitra. *The beastly visits*
Morimoto, Junko. *The two bullies*
Mwenye Hadithi. *Crafty chameleon*
  Tricky tortoise
Naylor, Phyllis Reynolds. *King of the playground*
Nickle, John. *The ant bully*
Passen, Lisa. *Fat, fat Rose Marie*
Peet, Bill (William Bartlett). *Big bad Bruce*

Pinkney, J. Brian. *The adventures of sparrowboy*
Rayner, Mary. *Crocodarling*
Roche, P. K. (Patrick K.). *Plaid bear and the rude rabbit gang*
Shipton, Jonathan. *No biting, horrible crocodile!*
Staunton, Ted. *Taking care of Crumley*
Taylor, Scott. *Dinosaur James*
Waddell, Martin. *Yum, yum, yummy*
Wagner, Jenny. *Amy's monster*
Wilhelm, Hans. *Tyrone the horrible*

Behavior – carelessness

Aliki. *Keep your mouth closed, dear*
Biro, Val. *Gumdrop gets a lift*
Bottner, Barbara. *Messy*
Brett, Jan. *Comet's nine lives*
Brown, Marc Tolon. *The cloud over Clarence*
Brunhoff, Laurent de. *Babar's little girl*
Buchanan, Joan. *It's a good thing*
Carrick, Carol. *A rabbit for Easter*
Chislett, Gail. *The rude visitors*
Claret, Maria. *The chocolate rabbit*
Cleary, Beverly. *Lucky Chuck*
De Paola, Tomie (Thomas Anthony). *The quicksand book*
   Strega Nona's magic lessons
Gackenbach, Dick. *Binky gets a car*
Gantos, Jack (John, Jr.). *Aunt Bernice*
Haas, Jessie. *Chipmunk!*
Harris, Robie H. *Messy Jessie*
Ilsley, Velma. *The pink hat*
Kline, Suzy. *Ooops!*
Koscielniak, Bruce. *Euclid Bunny delivers the mail*
Mayer, Mercer. *Oops*
Moskin, Marietta D. *Lysbet and the fire kittens*
Novak, Matt. *Elmer Blunt's open house*
Oram, Hiawyn. *Reckless Ruby*
Panek, Dennis. *Catastrophe Cat*
Pender, Lydia. *Barnaby and the horses*
Reader, Dennis. *Butterfingers*
Roberts, Sarah. *Ernie's big mess*
Serfozo, Mary. *Dirty Kurt*
Sommers, Tish. *Bert and the broken teapot*

Behavior – collecting things

Bauer, Caroline Feller. *Too many books!*
Beim, Lorraine. *Lucky Pierre*
Bram, Elizabeth. *Woodruff and the clocks*
Braun, Kathy. *Kangaroo and kangaroo*
Carlstrom, Nancy White. *The moon came too*
Cleary, Beverly. *Janet's thingamajigs*
Couture, Susan Arkin. *The block book*
Enderle, Judith (Ann) Ross. *Good junk*
Engel, Diana. *Josephina, the great collector*
Evans, Eva Knox. *That lucky Mrs. Plucky*
Gans, Roma. *Let's go rock collecting*
   Rock collecting
Geringer, Laura. *A three hat day*
Greenblat, Rodney Alan. *Aunt Ippy's museum of junk*
Hayward, Linda. *Ernie and Bert's summer project*
Heller, Nicholas. *Ten old pails*
Heyduck-Huth, Hilde. *The starfish*
   The strawflower
Horse, Harry. *A friend for Little Bear*
Johnson, Pamela. *A mouse's tale*
Krasilovsky, Phyllis. *The woman who saved things*
Lewis, Naomi. *The butterfly collector*

Lillie, Patricia. *When this box is full*
McDonald, Megan. *Insects are my life*
Penner, Fred. *Proud*
Pfeffer, Wendy. *Marta's magnets*
Tusa, Tricia. *Stay away from the junkyard!*
Van Horn, William. *Harry Hoyle's giant jumping bean*
Weil, Lisl. *To sail a ship of treasures*
Westell, Kerry. *Amanda's book*
Zelver, Patricia. *The wonderful Towers of Watts*

Behavior – disbelief

Alexander, Martha G. *Even that moose won't listen to me*
Brisson, Pat. *Wanda's roses*
Cole, Brock. *The king at the door*
Gunthrop, Karen. *Adam and the wolf*
Jackson, Ellen B. *Ants can't dance*
Norman, Howard A. *The owl-scatterer*
Turner, Ann Warren. *Nettie's trip south*
Waber, Bernard. *Do you see a mouse?*

Behavior – dissatisfaction

Alexander, Sue. *Ellsworth and Millicent*
   What's wrong now, Millicent?
Aliki. *The twelve months*
   The wish workers
Allen, Jeffrey. *The secret life of Mr. Weird*
Asch, Frank. *Monkey face*
Balet, Jan B. *The king and the broom maker*
Bauer, Steven. *The strange and wonderful tale of Robert McDoodle*
Bentley, Nancy. *I've got your nose!*
Best, Cari. *Montezuma's revenge*
Brewster, Patience. *Nobody*
Brock, Emma Lillian. *Pig with a front porch*
Brothers, Aileen. *Sad Mrs. Sam Sack*
Butterworth, Nick. *Jasper's beanstalk*
Byars, Betsy Cromer. *The groober*
Chapman, Carol. *The tale of Meshka the Kvetch*
Clymer, Ted. *The horse and the bad morning*
Coffey, Maria. *A cat in a kayak*
Cole, Babette. *King Change-A-Lot*
Cronin, Doreen. *Click, clack, moo*
Crowley, Arthur. *The boogey man*
Cushman, Doug. *Nasty Kyle the crocodile*
Dale, Ruth Bluestone. *Benjamin . . . and Sylvester also*
Day, Shirley. *Waldo's back yard*
Duvoisin, Roger Antoine. *Petunia, beware!*
Elborn, Andrew. *Bird Adalbert*
Ets, Marie Hall. *The cow's party*
Fish, Hans. *Pitschi, the kitten who always wanted to do something else*
Fowler, Richard. *Cat's cake*
Gackenbach, Dick. *Mother Rabbit's son Tom*
Gay, Zhenya. *I'm tired of lions*
Getz, Arthur. *Humphrey, the dancing pig*
Hautzig, Deborah. *It's not fair!*
Hazen, Barbara Shook. *The Fat Cats, Cousin Scraggs and the monster mice*
Heide, Florence Parry. *Oh, grow up!*
Herman, Gail. *Flower girl*
Hest, Amy. *The mommy exchange*
Hille-Brandts, Lene. *The little black hen*
Hoban, Lillian. *Stick-in-the-mud turtle*
Jenkin-Pearce, Susie. *Percy Short and Cuthbert*
Johnson, Evelyne. *The cow in the kitchen*

Jolin, Dominique. *It's not fair!*
Keats, Ezra Jack. *Jennie's hat*
McDermott, Gerald. *The stonecutter*
MacDonald, Margaret Read. *The old woman who lived in a vinegar bottle*
McDonald, Megan. *The night Iguana left home*
McGinley, Phyllis. *The horse who lived upstairs*
Massie, Diane Redfield. *Walter was a frog*
May, Kara. *Creepy crawly caterpillar*
Meddaugh, Susan. *The best place*
Milstein, Linda Breiner. *Amanda's perfect hair*
Newton, Jill. *Cat-fish*
Nightingale, Sandy. *The witch's spell*
O'Donnell, Elizabeth Lee. *Maggie doesn't want to move*
Olsen, Alfa-Betty. *Gabby the shrew*
Olujic, Grozdana. *Rose of Mother-of-Pearl*
Oram, Hiawyn. *Jenna and the troublemaker*
Palatini, Margie. *Good as Goldie*
Palmer, Mary Babcock. *No-sort-of-animal*
Peet, Bill (William Bartlett). *The caboose who got loose*
   The luckiest one of all
   The Whingdingdilly
Price, Roger. *The last little dragon*
Roberts, Bethany. *Camel caravan*
Roth, Carol. *Little Bunny's sleepless night*
Russo, Marisabina. *Why do grownups have all the fun?*
Sadler, Marilyn. *It's not easy being a bunny*
Sarnoff, Jane. *That's not fair*
Sharmat, Marjorie Weinman. *Grumley the grouch*
Simon, Francesca. *Camels don't ski*
Testa, Fulvio. *Never satisfied*
Turnage, Sheila. *Trout the magnificent*
Waller, Barrett. *New feet for old*
Weedn, Flavia. *The ragged peddler*
White, Linda Arms. *Too many pumpkins*
Wiesner, William. *Turnabout*
Yaccarino, Dan. *Deep in the jungle*
Yaffe, Alan. *The magic meatballs*
Zakhoder, Boris Vladimirovich. *Rosachok*
Zolotow, Charlotte (Shapiro). *It's not fair*

Behavior – fidgeting

Carlson, Nancy L. *Sit still!*

Behavior – fighting, arguing

Alexander, Martha G. *I'll be the horse if you'll play with me*
Bassett, Jeni. *The chicks' trick*
Beim, Lorraine. *Two is a team*
Berry, Joy Wilt. *Fighting*
Boegehold, Betty. *The fight*
Bruchac, Joseph. *The great ball game*
Bunting, Eve (Anne Evelyn). *Box, fox, ox, and the peacock*
Burdett, Lois. *Macbeth for kids*
   Romeo and Juliet for kids
Burningham, John. *Mr. Gumpy's outing*
Burton, Jane. *Animals fighting*
Christian, Mary Blount. *The sand lot*
Dayton, Mona. *Earth and sky*
Ernst, Lisa Campbell. *Zinnia and Dot*
Field, Eugene. *The gingham dog and the calico cat*, ill. by Janet Street
   The gingham dog and the calico cat, ill. by Johanna Westerman

Foreman, Michael. *The two giants*
Gekiere, Madeleine. *The frilly lily and the princess*
Gilchrist, Theo E. *Halfway up the mountain*
Goffin, Josse. *Who is the boss?*
Grimes, Nikki. *Someone's fighting*
Harvey, Amanda. *Stormy weather*
Hoban, Russell. *Harvey's hideout*
   The sorely trying day
   Tom and the two handles
Hodges, Margaret. *The kitchen knight*
Holabird, Katharine. *Alexander and the dragon*
Hooks, William H. *Peach boy*
Lasker, Joe. *A tournament of knights*
Levitin, Sonia. *Who owns the moon?*
Lionni, Leo. *It's mine!*
McBratney, Sam. *I'm sorry*
McFarland, Lyn Rossiter. *The pirate's parrot*
McKee, David. *Tusk tusk*
   Two monsters
Martin, Francesca. *The honey hunters*
Merriam, Eve. *Fighting words*
Minarik, Else Holmelund. *No fighting, no biting!*
Novak, Matt. *The Pillow War*
Pfister, Marcus. *Rainbow fish and the big blue whale*
Rose, Gerald. *Trouble in the ark*
St. Germain, Sharon. *The terrible fight*
Sharmat, Marjorie Weinman. *I'm not Oscar's friend any more*
   Rollo and Juliet . . . forever!
   Sometimes mama and papa fight
Shute, Linda. *Momotaro, the peach boy*
Slobodkin, Louis. *Hustle and bustle*
Steadman, Ralph. *The bridge*
Stevenson, James. *Are we almost there?*
Tusa, Tricia. *Sisters*
Udry, Janice May. *Let's be enemies*
   Thump and Plunk, ill. by Geoffrey Hayes
   Thump and Plunk, ill. by Ann Schweninger
Venable, Alan. *The checker players*
Waggoner, Karen. *Dad Gummit and Ma Foot*
Wallis, Diz. *Battle of the beasts*
Weninger, Brigitte. *Why are you fighting, Davy?*
White, Kathryn (Kathryn Ivy). *When they fight*
Widman, Christine. *Housekeeper of the wind*
Williams, Arlene. *Dragon soup*
Winthrop, Elizabeth. *That's mine*
Yorinks, Arthur. *Oh, brother*
Zolotow, Charlotte (Shapiro). *The quarreling book*
   The unfriendly book

Behavior – forgetfulness

Alexander, Sue. *Witch, Goblin and sometimes Ghost*
Aliki. *Use your head, dear*
Arnold, Tedd. *Ollie forgot*
Birdseye, Tom. *Soap! Soap! Don't forget the soap!*
Brown, Ken (Ken James). *Nellie's knot*
Cole, Joanna. *Aren't you forgetting something, Fiona?*
Copp, James (Andrew James). *Martha Matilda O'Toole*
De Paola, Tomie (Thomas Anthony). *Strega Nona*
Dines, Glen. *A tiger in the cherry tree*
Dodd, Lynley. *Schnitzel von Krumm forget-me-not*
Domanska, Janina. *Palmiero and the ogre*
Fox, Mem. *Wilfrid Gordon McDonald Partridge*
Galdone, Joanna. *Gertrude, the goose who forgot*

Galdone, Paul. *The magic porridge pot*
Guthrie, Donna. *Grandpa doesn't know it's me*
Hale, Irina. *The lost toys*
Hutchins, Pat. *Don't forget the bacon!*
King-Smith, Dick. *Farmer Bungle forgets*
MacGregor, Ellen. *Theodor Turtle*
Marshak, S. (Samuil). *The absentminded fellow*
Miles, Miska. *Chicken forgets*
Nikly, Michelle. *The perfume of memory*
Parish, Peggy. *Be ready at eight*
Patz, Nancy. *Pumpernickel tickle and mean green cheese*
Rogers, Paul (Patrick). *Forget-me-not*
Schatell, Brian. *The McGoonys have a party*
Schweninger, Ann. *The hunt for rabbit's galosh*
Stevenson, Sucie. *I forgot*
Sutherland, Colleen. *Jason goes to show-and-tell*
Van Allsburg, Chris. *The stranger*
Wahl, Jan. *"I remember," cried Grandma Pinky*
Weinberg, Lawrence. *The Forgetful Bears*
    The Forgetful Bears meet Mr. Memory
Weisgard, Leonard. *Silly Willy Nilly*
Wild, Margaret. *Remember me*

Behavior – gossip

Allen, Jeffrey. *Nosey Mrs. Rat*
Andersen, H. C. (Hans Christian). *It's perfectly true!*
Berson, Harold. *The thief who hugged a moonbeam*
Brenner, Barbara A. *Good news*
Chicken Little. *Chicken Licken*, ill. by Jutta Ash
    Chicken Licken, ill. by Gavin Bishop
    Chicken Little, ill. by Sally Hobson
    Henny Penny, ill. by Emily Bolam
    Henny Penny, ill. by Stephen Butler
    Henny Penny, ill. by Paul Galdone
    Henny Penny, ill. by William Stobbs
    Henny-Penny, ill. by Jane Wattenberg
    The sky is falling
    The story of Chicken Licken
Holl, Adelaide. *The runaway giant*
Hutchins, Pat. *The surprise party*
Kraus, Robert. *Mert the blurt*
Love, Ann. *The prince who wrote a letter*
Mantinband, Gerda. *Blabbermouths*
Stevens, Harry. *Parrot told snake*
Varga, Judy. *The monster behind Black Rock*
Zolotow, Charlotte (Shapiro). *The hating book*

Behavior – greed

Aardema, Verna. *Sebgugugu the glutton*
Afanas'ev, Aleksandr N. *Salt*
Aliki. *The eggs*
Allen, Pamela. *Hidden treasure*
Andersen, H. C. (Hans Christian). *The woman with the eggs*
Angelo, Valenti. *The candy basket*
Arnold, Caroline. *The terrible Hodag*
Aulaire, Ingri Mortenson d'. *Don't count your chicks*
Aylesworth, Jim. *Mary's mirror*
Barker, Inga-Lil. *Why teddy bears are brown*
Bascom, Joe. *Malcolm Softpaws*
Battles, Edith. *The terrible terrier*
    The terrible trick or treat
Bellows, Cathy. *Four fat rats*
Berenstain, Stan. *The Berenstain bears get the gimmies*
Berson, Harold. *Larbi and Leila*
    The rats who lived in the delicatessen
Bohdal, Susi. *The magic honey jar*

Bolliger, Max. *The golden apple*
Bonsall, Crosby Newell. *It's mine! A greedy book*
Borovsky, Paul. *Nico*
Brenner, Barbara A. *Ostrich feathers*
Brown, Marcia. *The bun*
Buckley, Richard. *The greedy python*
Bunting, Eve (Anne Evelyn). *The man who could call down owls*
Carlson, Nancy L. *Harriet's Halloween candy*
Carter, Anne. *Bella's secret garden*
Chichester Clark, Emma. *More!*
Christian, Mary Blount. *The devil take you, Barnabas Beane!*
Coco, Eugene Bradley. *The wishing well*
Cooper, Susan. *The silver cow*
Corbalis, Judy. *The cuckoo bird*
Dauer, Rosamond. *The 300 pound cat*
De Paola, Tomie (Thomas Anthony). *Andy (that's my name)*
Edwards, Pamela Duncan. *Ed and Fred Flea*
Ernst, Lisa Campbell. *The prize pig surprise*
Evans, Katherine. *The maid and her pail of milk*
Faulkner, William J. *Brer Tiger and the big wind*
Forward, Toby. *Ben's Christmas carol*
Gackenbach, Dick. *Barker's crime*
Gantschev, Ivan. *The moon lake*
Gerson, Mary-Joan. *Why the sky is far away*
Gifaldi, David. *The boy who spoke colors*
Ginsburg, Mirra. *Two greedy bears*
Green, Phyllis. *Bagdad ate it*
Gregory, Valiska. *When stories fell like shooting stars*
Grimm, Jacob. *The fisherman and his wife*, ill. by Eleanor Hubbard
    The fisherman and his wife, ill. by Monika Laimgruber
    The fisherman and his wife, ill. by Alan Marks
    The fisherman and his wife, ill. by Laurinda Spear
    The fisherman and his wife, ill. by Margot Tomes
    The fisherman and his wife, ill. by Margot Zemach
    The golden bird, ill. by Isabelle Brent
    The golden bird, ill. by Sandro Nardini
    Mother Holly
    One gift deserves another
Hausman, Gerald. *Coyote walks on two legs*
Henwood, Simon. *A piece of luck*
Hewitt, Kathryn. *King Midas and the golden touch*
Heyer, Carol. *Robin Hood*
Ishii, Momoko. *The tongue-cut sparrow*
Jacobs, Joseph. *Hudden and Dudden and Donald O'Neary*
Kennedy, Richard. *The lost kingdom of Karnica*
Kimmel, Eric A. *Onions and garlic*
Kinter, Judith. *King of magic, man of glass*
Kismaric, Carole. *The rumor of Pavel and Paali*
Krudop, Walter Lyon. *The man who caught fish*
Kuskin, Karla. *What did you bring me?*
Lewis, J. Patrick. *The tsar and the amazing cow*
Lionni, Leo. *The biggest house in the world*
Lorenz, Lee. *Pinchpenny John*
Luenn, Nancy. *Miser on the mountain*
Lussert, Anneliese. *The farmer and the moon*
Luttrell, Ida. *The star counters*
McClenathan, Louise. *My mother sends her wisdom*
McKissack, Patricia C. *King Midas and his gold*
McLenighan, Valjean. *Three strikes and you're out*
Mahy, Margaret. *Rooms for rent*
Manson, Christopher. *Here begins the tale of the marvellous blue mouse*
Mark, Jan. *The Midas touch*

Marshall, James. *Yummers too*
Matsutani, Miyoko. *How the withered trees blossomed*
Mayne, William. *Lady Muck*
Mollel, Tololwa M. (Tololwa Marti). *The flying tortoise*
Muller, Robin. *The magic paintbrush*
Mwenye Hadithi. *Greedy zebra*
Obrist, Jürg. *The miser who wanted the sun*
Paraskevas, Betty. *The ferocious beast with the polka-dot hide*
Peet, Bill (William Bartlett). *Kermit the hermit*
    The kweeks of Kookatumdee
Peppé, Rodney. *The mice and the flying basket*
Perkins, Al. *King Midas and the golden touch*
Porter, David Lord. *Mine!*
Roffey, Maureen. *Look, there's my hat!*
Rohmer, Harriet. *The invisible hunters*
Ross, Tony. *The greedy little cobbler*
Sanderson, Ruth. *Papa Gatto*
Sanfield, Steve. *Just rewards, or, Who is that man in the moon and what's he doing up there anyway?*
San Souci, Robert D. *The enchanted tapestry*
Schroeder, Alan. *The stone lion*
Selway, Martina. *Greedyguts*
Shibano, Tamizo. *The old man who made the trees bloom*
Solotareff, Grégoire. *Never trust an ogre*
Stadler, John. *Animal café*
Stage, Mads. *The greedy blackbird*
Stewig, John Warren. *King Midas*
Storr, Catherine (Cole). *King Midas*
Tompert, Ann. *The hungry black bag*
Waddell, Martin. *Yum, yum, yummy*
Wells, Rosemary. *The little lame prince*
    Max and Ruby's Midas
Winthrop, Elizabeth. *That's mine*
Yep, Laurence. *Tiger woman*

Behavior – growing up

Alexander, Sue. *Dear Phoebe*
Aliki. *I'm growing!*
Allison, Alida. *The toddler's potty book*
Anholt, Catherine. *When I was a baby*
Anholt, Laurence. *Billy and the big new school*
Appell, Clara. *Now I have a daddy haircut*
Ardizzone, Edward. *Paul, the hero of the fire*
Aseltine, Lorraine. *First grade can wait*
Aulaire, Ingri Mortenson d'. *Too big*
Balzola, Asun. *Munia and the red shoes*
Barrett, Judi. *I hate to take a bath*
    I'm too small, you're too big
Bat-Ami, Miriam. *Sea, salt, and air*
Baumgart, Klaus. *Don't be afraid, Tommy*
Boelts, Maribeth. *Little Bunny's pacifier plan*
Bogot, Howard. *I'm growing*
Bolliger, Max. *The magic bird*
Bonnici, Peter. *The festival*
Borden, Louise. *Albie the lifeguard*
Bourgeois, Paulette. *Big Sarah's little boots*
Brentano, Clemens. *Schoolmaster Whackwell's wonderful sons*
Brinckloe, Julie. *Fireflies!*
Bromhall, Winifred. *Bridget's growing day*
Brown, Margaret Wise. *Another important book*
Brown, Myra Berry. *Benjy's blanket*
Bruchac, Joseph. *A boy called Slow*
Bruna, Dick. *I can dress myself*
Bryant, Bernice. *Follow the leader*

Buck, Nola. *Hey, little baby!*
Buckley, Kate. *Love notes*
Bulla, Clyde Robert. *Dandelion Hill*
Burton, Jane. *Caper the kid*
    Dizzie the pony
    Fancy the fox
    Ginger the kitten
    Gipper the guinea pig
    Hoppy the toad
    Jack the puppy
    Pacer, the pony
    Snowy, the barn owl
    Surfer the seal
    Taddy the toad
Cannon, Janell. *Verdi*
Carle, Eric. *My very first book of growth*
Carrier, Lark. *Scout and Cody*
Carter, Dorothy (Dorothy A.). *Wilhe'mina Miles after the stork night*
Caseley, Judith. *Annie's potty*
Chaffin, Lillie D. *Tommy's big problem*
Ciardi, John. *Scrappy, the pup*
Civardi, Anne. *Potty time*
Clayton, Gordon. *Lamb*
Cleary, Beverly. *The growing-up feet*
    Janet's thingamajigs
Coats, Laura Jane. *Mr. Jordan in the park*
Cobb, Vicki. *Feeding yourself*
    Getting dressed
Cohen, Miriam. *Jim meets the thing*
Cole, Joanna. *Your new potty*
Cooke, Trish. *When I grow bigger*
Cooney, Nancy Evans. *The blanket that had to go*
    Donald says thumbs down
Corey, Dorothy. *Tomorrow you can*
Curtis, Jamie Lee. *When I was little*
Dauer, Rosamond. *Bullfrog grows up*
Delton, Judy. *The best mom in the world*
DeLuise, Dom. *Charlie the caterpillar*
De Paola, Tomie (Thomas Anthony). *Katie's good idea*
Douglass, Ann. *Baby science*
Drescher, Joan E. *I'm in charge!*
Ernst, Kathryn F. *Danny and his thumb*
Esbensen, Barbara Juster. *Who shrank my grandmother's house?*
Faison, Eleanora. *Becoming*
Fassler, Joan. *Don't worry dear*
    The man of the house
Felt, Sue. *Rosa-too-little*
Fontenot, Mary Alice. *Tah-Tye*
Fox, Mem. *Shoes from grandpa*
Freedman, Sally. *Devin's new bed*
Fribourg, Marjorie G. *Ching-Ting and the ducks*
Galbraith, Kathryn Osebold. *Roommates*
Garelick, May. *Just my size*
Gelbard, Jane. *My bye-bye bottle book*
    My dressing book
    My eating book
    My sharing book
Gentieu, Penny. *Grow! babies!*
George, Jean Craighead. *Look to the north*
Gikow, Louise. *Bye-bye, pacifier*
Goennel, Heidi. *When I grow up . . .*
    While I am little
Gould, Deborah. *Aaron's shirt*
Graham, Bob. *The red woolen blanket*
Grifalconi, Ann. *Flyaway girl*
Grimes, Nikki. *It's raining laughter*

Something on my mind
Grindley, Sally. *Little Sibu*
Hale, Irina. *Small big bad boy*
Hall, Derek. *Elephant bathes*
  Gorilla builds
  Polar bear leaps
Hanson, Joan. *I won't be afraid*
Harris, Robie H. *I hate kisses*
Hayes, Geoffrey. *Patrick and Ted*
Heide, Florence Parry. *Oh, grow up!*
Heitler, Susan M. (Susan McCrensky). *David decides, no more thumb-sucking*
Hellard, Susan. *Baby lemur*
Henderson, Kathy. *The baby dances*
Henkes, Kevin. *Owen*
Hines, Anna Grossnickle. *All by myself*
  Big like me
Ho, Minfong. *The two brothers*
Hoban, Brom. *Skunk Lane*
Hoban, Lillian. *Big Little Otter*
Hobbs, Will. *Howling Hill*
Hoffman, Phyllis. *Baby's first year*
Hopkins, Lee Bennett. *Through our eyes*
Horn, Peter. *When I grow up –*
Horner, Althea J. *Little big girl*
Howard, Arthur. *When I was five*
Howard, Ellen. *The big seed*
Iverson, Genie. *I want to be big*
Jenkin-Pearce, Susie. *Boris's big ache*
Jensen, Patricia. *Be patient, Little Chick*
  Gentle Little Lion
Johnson, Crockett. *We wonder what will Walter be?*
  When he grows up
Jonas, Ann. *When you were a baby*
Joosse, Barbara M. *Fourth of July*
Kandoian, Ellen. *Maybe she forgot*
Keller, Holly. *Jacob's tree*
Kessler, Cristina. *One night*
Khalsa, Dayal Kaur. *I want a dog*
Kirk, Daniel. *Bigger*
Klinting, Lars. *Regal the golden eagle*
Koralek, Jenny. *Cat and Kit*
Krasilovsky, Phyllis. *The very little boy*
  The very little girl
Kraus, Robert. *Leo the late bloomer*
Krauss, Ruth. *The growing story*
Krensky, Stephen. *Children of the wind and water*
Lakin, Pat (Patricia). *Growing up*
Lebrun, Claude. *Little Brown Bear does not want to eat*
  Little Brown Bear learns to share
Lester, Alison. *When Frank was four*
Levine, Abby. *What did mommy do before you?*
Lexau, Joan M. *I hate red rover*
Lindgren, Barbro. *Sam's potty*
London, Jonathan. *Old salt, young salt*
Maccarone, Grace. *My tooth is about to fall out*
McCully, Emily Arnold. *The ballot box battle*
MacDonald, Amy. *Cousin Ruth's tooth*
MacKinnon, Debbie. *Baby's first year*
McPhail, David M. *Pig Pig grows up*
Marshak, S. (Samuil). *The pup grew up!*
Martin, C. L. G. *The blueberry train*
Mason, Jane B. *Hello, two-wheeler!*
Massie, Diane Redfield. *Tiny pin*
Mayer, Marianna. *The prince and the pauper*
Meddaugh, Susan. *Martha and Skits*
Meister, Cari. *When Tiny was tiny*
Miller, Virginia. *On your potty!*

Moers, Hermann. *Camomile heads for home*
  Little Ben
Moncure, Jane Belk. *Now I am five!*
  Now I am four!
  Now I am three!
Mordvinoff, Nicolas. *Coral Island*
Moss, Thylias. *I want to be*
Munsch, Robert N. *Andrew's loose tooth*
  I have to go!
Murphy, Jill. *The last noo-noo*
Nelson, S. D. *Gift horse*
Newberry, Clare Turlay. *Percy, Polly and Pete*
Noll, Sally. *I have a loose tooth*
  That bothered Kate
Nordlicht, Lillian. *I love to laugh*
Once I was . . .
Otto, Carolyn. *Our puppies are growing*
Packard, Mary. *When I am big*
Parish, Peggy. *I can - can you?*
Pellowski, Anne. *Stairstep farm*
Pinkwater, Daniel Manus. *Young Larry*
Pitcher, Caroline. *Run with the wind*
Poulin, Stéphane. *My mother's loves*
Power, Barbara. *I wish Laura's mommy was my mommy*
Reichmeier, Betty. *Potty time!*
Rogers, Fred. *Going to the potty*
Rosman, Steven M. *Deena the damselfly*
Ross, Anna. *I did it!*
  I have to go
Ross, Katharine (1950-). *When you were a baby*
Ross, Tony. *I want my potty*
Schertle, Alice. *Maisie*
Schlein, Miriam. *Billy, the littlest one*
  Herman McGregor's world
  When will the world be mine?
Schwartz, Amy. *Begin at the beginning*
Scott, Ann Herbert. *Someday rider*
Scuderi, Lucia. *To fly*
Sharmat, Marjorie Weinman. *Bartholomew the bossy*
Shavick, Andrea. *You'll grow soon, Alex*
Sheehan, Patty. *Shadow and the ready time*
Sis, Peter. *Madlenka*
Slepian, Jan. *Emily just in time*
Smith, Robert Paul. *When I am big*
Snyder, Zilpha Keatley. *Come on, Patsy*
Solomon, Chuck. *Moving up from kindergarten to first grade*
Sonnenschein, Harriet. *Harold's hideaway thumb*
Stanley, Diane. *Captain Whiz-Bang*
Stevenson, James. *Higher on the door*
  I meant to tell you
Stimson, Joan. *Big Panda, Little Panda*
Strub, Susanne. *Lulu goes swimming*
  Lulu on her bike
Svend Otto S (Svend Otto Sorensen). *The giant fish and other stories*
Turkle, Brinton. *Obadiah the Bold*
Waber, Bernard. *You're a little kid with a big heart*
Waddell, Martin. *Once there were giants*
Wallace, Karen. *Imagine you are a tiger*
Watts, Barrie. *Mouse*
Waxman, Stephanie. *What is a girl? What is a boy?*
Weiss, Nicki. *Barney is big*
Welber, Robert. *Goodbye, hello*
Wells, Rosemary. *Timothy goes to school*
Wilhelm, Hans. *I lost my tooth!*
Wilkes, Angela. *See how I grow*
Willis, Jeanne. *What did I look like when I was a baby?*

Willis, Val. *Silly little chick*
Winters, Kay. *Tiger trail*
　Wolf watch
Wittman, Sally. *A special trade*
Wood, Audrey. *Oh my baby bear!*
Yoshida, Toshi. *Young lions*
Young, Helen. *A throne for Sesame*
Young, Ruth. *My potty chair*
Zagone, Theresa. *No nap for me*
Zagwÿn, Deborah Turney. *The pumpkin blanket*
Zimelman, Nathan. *If I were strong enough . . .*
Zolotow, Charlotte (Shapiro). *But not Billy*
　Do you know what I'll do?
　I like to be little
　May I visit?
　Someone new
　When I have a son

Behavior – hiding

Adler, David A. *Hiding from the Nazis*
Ahlberg, Allan. *Master Salt the sailor's son*
Alborough, Jez. *Hide and seek*
Aldis, Dorothy (Keeley). *Hiding*
Apperley, Dawn. *In the jungle*
Arnosky, Jim. *I see animals hiding*
Aruego, José. *We hide, you seek*
Asch, Frank. *Moongame*
Bernhard, Durga. *Alphabeasts*
Blacker, Terence. *Herbie Hamster, where are you?*
Blake, Quentin. *Cockatoos*
Blanchard, Arlene. *The naughty lamb*
Brutschy, Jennifer. *Celeste and Crabapple Sam*
Burns, Kate. *In the snow*
Chorao, Kay. *Kate's box*
Cole, Michael. *Head in the sand*
Dale, Penny. *Ten play hide-and-seek*
Dodd, Lynley. *Find me a tiger*
Dubanevich, Arlene. *Pigs in hiding*
Ganeri, Anita. *Animal hideaways*
Gerstein, Mordicai. *William, where are you?*
Gomi, Taro. *Where's the fish?*
Greene, Carol. *Where is that cat?*
Gretz, Susanna. *Hide-and-seek*
Greydanus, Rose. *My secret hiding place*
Heller, Ruth. *How to hide a butterfly*
　How to hide a polar bear
Hughes, Shirley. *Hiding*
Hulse, Gillian. *Morris, where are you?*
Humphries, Tudor. *Hiding*
Hutchins, Pat. *Titch and Daisy*
Koralek, Jenny. *The cobweb curtain*
Kudrna, C. Imbior. *To bathe a boa*
Livermore, Elaine. *Looking for Henry*
McCarthy, Bobette. *Happy hiding hippos*
McClung, Robert. *How animals hide*
McNaughton, Colin. *Shh! (Don't tell Mr. Wolf!)*
McPhail, David M. *Where can an elephant hide?*
Major, Beverly. *Playing sardines*
Matus, Greta. *Where are you, Jason?*
Milios, Rita. *Sneaky Pete*
Mintzberg, Yvette. *Sally, where are you?*
Nims, Bonnie Larkin. *Where is the bear in the city?*
Oppenheim, Shulamith Levey. *The lily cupboard*
Oram, Hiawyn. *Where are you hiding, little lamb?*
Oxford Scientific Films. *Danger colors*
　Hide and seek
Polacco, Patricia. *The butterfly*
Price, Mathew. *Where's Alfie?*

Raschka, Christopher. *Whaley Whale*
Santore, Charles. *A stowaway on Noah's Ark*
Schertle, Alice. *Jeremy Bean's St. Patrick's Day*
　That Olive!
Sowler, Sandie. *Amazing animal disguises*
Steig, William. *Toby, where are you?*
Stoeke, Janet Morgan. *Hide and seek*
Szekeres, Cyndy. *Hide-and-seek duck*
Tulloch, Richard. *Danny in the toybox*
Unwin, Pippa. *The great zoo hunt!*
Vigna, Judith. *The hiding house*
Walsh, Ellen Stoll. *Mouse paint*
Walsh, Melanie. *Hide and sleep*
Warren, Cathy. *Springtime bears*
Wood, John Norris. *Jungles*
　Oceans
Ziefert, Harriet. *Where's the cat?*
　Where's the dog?
　Where's the guinea pig?
　Where's the turtle?
Zion, Gene. *Hide and seek day*

Behavior – hiding things

Allen, Pamela. *Hidden treasure*
Bason, Lillian. *Those foolish Molboes!*
Baylor, Byrd. *Your own best secret place*
Brady, Susan. *Find my blanket*
Croswell, Volney. *How to hide a hippopotamus*
Demi. *Demi's find the animals A B C*
Henwood, Simon. *A piece of luck*
Ivory, Lesley Anne. *The birthday cat*
Micklethwait, Lucy. *Spot a cat*
　Spot a dog
Modesitt, Jeanne. *Little Bunny's Easter surprise*
Wood, Leslie. *A dog called Mischief*

Behavior – hurrying

Alda, Arlene. *Hurry Granny Annie*
Biro, Val. *Gumdrop beats the clock*
Gomi, Taro. *First comes Harry*
Greydanus, Rose. *Willie the slowpoke*
Hurd, Edith Thacher. *Hurry, hurry!*
Myers, Bernice. *It happens to everyone*
Pfister, Marcus. *Wake up, Santa Claus!*
Steiner, Charlotte. *What's the hurry, Harry?*
Thoreau, Henry D. *What befell at Mrs. Brooks's*

Behavior – imitation

Allamand, Pascale. *The animals who changed their colors*
Aruego, José. *Look what I can do*
Asch, Frank. *Just like daddy*
Barrett, Judi. *Animals should definitely not act like people*
　Animals should definitely not wear clothing
Bendick, Jeanne. *Why can't I?*
Blake, Quentin. *Zagazoo*
Blakeley, Peggy. *What shall I be tomorrow?*
Buckmaster, Henrietta. *Lucy and Loki*
Calhoun, Mary. *The nine lives of Homer C. Cat*
Canning, Kate. *A painted tale*
Cauley, Lorinda Bryan. *The animal kids*
Charlton, Elizabeth. *Terrible tyrannosaurus*
Clewes, Dorothy. *Henry Hare's boxing match*
Cole, Brock. *Nothing but a pig*
Farber, Norma. *There goes feathertop!*

Gauch, Patricia Lee. *Dance, Tanya*
Graham, Amanda. *Who wants Arthur?*
Hallinan, P. K. (Patrick K.). *Where's Michael?*
Heine, Helme. *Mr. Miller, the dog*
Hersom, Kathleen. *The copycat*
Inkpen, Mick. *Kipper*
Jones, Chuck. *William the backwards skunk*
Kellogg, Steven (Stephen). *A rose for Pinkerton*
Kent, Jack. *The once-upon-a-time dragon*
Lavis, Steve. *Jump!*
Marzollo, Jean. *Pretend you're a cat*
Mole, John. *Copy cat*
Moore, Inga. *Fifty red night-caps*
Munsch, Robert N. *Stephanie's ponytail*
Newcome, Zita. *Animal fun*
Noll, Sally. *That bothered Kate*
Numeroff, Laura Joffe. *If you give a mouse a cookie*
O'Connor, Jane. *Nina, Nina and the copycat ballerina*
Ostheeren, Ingrid. *I'm the real Santa Claus!*
Packard, Mary. *When I am big*
Rathmann, Peggy. *Ruby the copycat*
Riddell, Chris. *Bird's new shoes*
Ross, Christine. *Lily and the bears*
Saltzberg, Barney. *The yawn*
Schwartz, Amy. *Bea and Mr. Jones*
Shields, Carol Diggory. *I am really a princess*
Van Caster, Nancy. *An alligator lives in Benjamin's house*

Behavior – indifference

Blos, Joan W. *Old Henry*
Dubanevich, Arlene. *Pig William*
Hogrogian, Nonny. *The hermit and Harry and me*
Kroll, Steven. *Will you be my valentine?*
Roy, Ronald. *Three ducks went wandering*
Sendak, Maurice. *Pierre*
Sharmat, Marjorie Weinman. *I don't care*
Watts, Mabel (Pizzey). *The day it rained watermelons*

Behavior – losing things

Abolafia, Yossi. *A fish for Mrs. Gardenia*
Ackerman, Karen. *Araminta's paint box*
Ahlberg, Allan. *Mystery tour*
Amoss, Berthe. *What did you lose, Santa?*
Ardizzone, Edward. *The little girl and the tiny doll*
Armitage, Ronda. *The lighthouse keeper's catastrophe*
Ayer, Jacqueline. *Nu Dang and his kite*
Baker, Alan. *Where's mouse?*
Baker, Leslie A. *Paris cat*
Banks, Kate (Katherine A.). *Peter and the talking shoes*
Bannon, Laura. *Red mittens*
Barrows, Marjorie Wescott. *The funny hat*
Bassett, Lisa. *Beany and Scamp*
Birdseye, Tom. *Airmail to the moon*
Blos, Joan W. *Hello, shoes!*
Bond, Michael. *Paddington at the zoo*
Bottner, Barbara. *Big boss! Little boss!*
Bowden, Joan Chase. *Who took the top hat trick?*
Boyle, Constance. *The story of little owl*
Brett, Jan. *The mitten*
Bromhall, Winifred. *Middle Matilda*
Brown, Marc Tolon. *D. W.'s lost blankie*
Burningham, John. *The blanket*
Carter, Noelle. *Where's my squishy ball?*
Chorao, Kay. *Maudie's umbrella*

Molly's lies
Molly's Moe
Coman, Carolyn. *Losing things at Mr. Mudd's*
Coombs, Patricia. *The lost playground*
Craft, Ruth. *The day of the rainbow*
Davidson, Amanda. *Teddy in the garden*
Denton, Terry. *The school for laughter*
Dixon, Ann. *The blueberry shoe*
Dodds, Siobhan. *Charles Tiger*
Dornbusch, Erica. *Finding Kate's shoes*
Dunrea, Olivier. *The trow-wife's treasure*
Eagle, Ellen. *Gypsy's cleaning day*
Ellwand, David. *Alfred's camera*
Eriksson, Eva. *The tooth trip*
Ernst, Lisa Campbell. *Stella Louella's runaway book*
Feiffer, Jules. *I lost my bear*
Garland, Sarah. *Polly's puffin*
Gay, Michel. *Little shoe*
Gillerlain, Gayle. *Reverend Thomas's false teeth*
Guthrie, Donna. *Grandpa doesn't know it's me*
Haddon, Mark. *Gilbert's gobstopper*
Handford, Martin. *Where's Waldo?*
   Where's Waldo? The wonder book
Harranth, Wolf. *The flute concert*
Hassett, John. *Junior*
Havill, Juanita. *Jamaica's find*
Hayes, Sarah. *A bad start for Santa*
Hayward, Linda. *The case of the missing Duckie*
Herman, Gail. *What a hungry puppy!*
Hines, Anna Grossnickle. *Moompa, Toby, and Bomp*
Hissey, Jane. *Little Bear lost*
Hoff, Syd. *Arturo's baton*
Hutchins, H. J. (Hazel J.). *Leanna builds a genie trap*
   Norman's snowball
Ichikawa, Satomi. *The first bear in Africa!*
Ingman, Bruce. *Lost property*
Inkpen, Mick. *Billy's beetle*
   Where, oh where, is Kipper's bear?
Jeram, Anita. *Bill's belly button*
Johnson, B. J. *My blanket Burt*
Jonas, Ann. *Where can it be?*
Kay, Helen. *One mitten Lewis*
Keenen, George. *The preposterous week*
Keller, Holly. *A bed full of cats*
Kelley, Anne. *Daisy's discovery*
Kellogg, Steven (Stephen). *The mystery of the magic green ball*
   The mystery of the missing red mitten
Ketteman, Helen. *I remember papa*
Kroll, Steven. *Patches*
Lakin, Pat (Patricia). *Trash and treasure*
Lewis, Kim. *First snow*
Lewison, Wendy Cheyette. *Where's my teddy?*
Lexau, Joan M. *Finders keepers, losers weepers*
Livermore, Elaine. *Lost and found*
   Three little kittens lost their mittens
London, Jonathan. *Let's go, Froggy!*
Lyon, George Ella. *Basket*
McCourt, Lisa. *Chicken soup for little souls: The never-forgotten doll*
MacDonald, Amy. *Cousin Ruth's tooth*
McGinley, Phyllis. *Lucy McLockett*
McKean, Thomas. *Hooray for Grandma Jo!*
McKee, David. *Elmer and the lost teddy*
MacKinnon, Debbie. *Billy's boots*
   Cathy's cake
   Ken's kitten
   Meg's monkey
McNeely, Jeannette. *Where's Izzy?*

Marcus, Susan. *The missing button adventure*
Marks, Alan. *Nowhere to be found*
Marshak, S. (Samuil). *The pup grew up!*
Martin, Jacqueline Briggs. *Bizzy Bones and the lost quilt*
Morgan, Allen. *Matthew and the midnight money van*
Mother Goose. *The three little kittens*, ill. by Lorinda Bryan Cauley
 The three little kittens, ill. by Paul Galdone
 The three little kittens, ill. by Dorothy Stott
 The three little kittens, ill. by Shelley Thornton
Munari, Bruno. *Jimmy has lost his cap*
Murdocca, Sal (Salvatore). *Tuttle's shell*
Murrow, Liza Ketchum. *Good-bye, Sammy*
O'Brien, Anne Sibley. *Where's my truck?*
O'Brien, Claire. *Sam's sneaker search*
Oxenbury, Helen. *Pippo gets lost*
Parr, Letitia. *A man and his hat*
Porter, Sue. *Parsnip and the pink blanket*
Poydar, Nancy. *Busy Bea*
Precek, Katharine Wilson. *Penny in the road*
Price, Mathew. *Do you see what I see?*
Pryor, Ainslie. *The baby blue cat and the smiley worm doll*
 The baby blue cat and the whole batch of cookies
Rabe, Berniece. *Where's Chimpy?*
Rogers, Jean. *Runaway mittens*
Rogers, Paul (Patrick). *Forget-me-not*
Ryder, Eileen. *Winston's new cap*
Schubert, Dieter. *Where's my monkey?*
Scott, C. Anne (Cynthia Anne). *Old Jake's skirts*
Sharmat, Marjorie Weinman. *The trip*
Siomades, Lorianne. *Three little kittens*
Smith, Barry. *Cumberland Road*
Sonnenschein, Harriet. *Harold's runaway nose*
Stadler, John. *One seal*
Teague, Mark. *The Lost and found*
Upham, Elizabeth. *Little brown bear loses his clothes*
Wallace, John. *Little Bean's friend*
Walsh, Jill Paton. *Lost and found*
Weninger, Brigitte. *What's the matter, Davy?*
West, Judy. *Have you got my purr?*
White, Florence Meiman. *How to lose your lunch money*
Whybrow, Ian. *Sammy and the dinosaurs*
Yorinks, Arthur. *Christmas in July*
Zander, Hans. *My blue chair*
Ziefert, Harriet. *Good night, Jessie!*
Zinnemann-Hope, Pam. *Find your coat, Ned*

Behavior – lost

Alexander, Liza. *Ernie gets lost*
Allen, Laura Jean. *Where is Freddy?*
Aller, Susan B. *Emma and the night dogs*
Anderson, C. W. (Clarence Williams). *Blaze finds forgotten roads*
 Blaze finds the trail
Anderson, Scoular. *MacPelican's American adventure*
Ayer, Jacqueline. *Little Silk*
Bacheller, Irving. *Lost in the fog*
Baker, Leslie A. *Paris cat*
Balian, Lorna. *Amelia's nine lives*
Barklem, Jill. *Autumn story*
Bartoli, Jennifer. *Snow on bear's nose*
Barton, Byron. *Where's Al?*
Bassett, Lisa. *Beany and Scamp*
Belting, Natalia Maree. *Verity Mullens and the Indian*

Bemelmans, Ludwig. *Madeline and the gypsies*
Beni, Ruth. *Sir Baldergog the great*
Benjamin, Alan. *Ribtickle Town*
Bergen, Lara Rice. *Washington Irving's Rip Van Winkle*
Berger, Barbara Helen. *A lot of otters*
Berson, Harold. *Henry Possum*
Boegehold, Betty. *Pawpaw's run*
Bograd, Larry. *Lost in the store*
Bolliger, Max. *Sandy at the children's zoo*
Bornstein, Ruth Lercher. *Annabelle Jim*
Bothwell, Jean. *Paddy and Sam*
Brewster, Patience. *Ellsworth and the cats from Mars*
Brown, Jane Clark. *Whonk, and whonk again*
Brown, Judith Gwyn. *Max and the truffle pig*
Brown, Marc Tolon. *Arthur lost and found*
Brown, Marcia. *Tamarindo!*
Brown, Margaret Wise. *Little lost lamb*
 Three little animals
Bruna, Dick. *Snuffy*
Brunhoff, Laurent de. *Babar's little girl*
Buffett, Jimmy. *Trouble dolls*
Bunting, Eve (Anne Evelyn). *Jane Martin, dog detective*
Butterworth, Nick. *The lost sheep*
Calmenson, Stephanie. *Where is Grandma Potamus?*
Carigiet, Alois. *Anton the goatherd*
Carle, Eric. *Have you seen my cat?*
Carrick, Carol. *The highest balloon on the common*
 Left behind
Carter, Anne. *Ruff leaves home*
Carter, Noelle. *I'm a little mouse*
Cartlidge, Michelle. *Pippin and Pod*
Chottin, Ariane. *Beaver gets lost*
Cocca-Leffler, Maryann. *Missing: one stuffed rabbit*
Cohen, Miriam. *Lost in the museum*
Cole, Joanna. *The Clown-Arounds go on vacation*
Corddry, Thomas I. *Kibby's big feat*
Cowley, Stewart. *Little lost rabbit*
Cummings, Betty Sue. *Turtle*
Dalmais, Anne-Marie. *Betsy the bunny*
Daly, Niki. *The boy on the beach*
De Beer, Hans. *Little polar bear*
 Little polar bear, take me home!
Deetlefs, Rene. *Tabu and the dancing elephants*
Delaney, Ned. *Bad dog!*
Demas, Corinne. *The littlest matryoshka*
Drummond, Violet H. *Phewtus the squirrel*
Dubanevich, Arlene. *Calico cows*
Enderle, Judith (Ann) Ross. *Where are you, little Zack?*
Erickson, Phoebe. *Just follow me*
Escudie, René. *Paul and Sebastian*
Farber, Norma. *Where's Gomer?*
Flack, Marjorie. *Angus lost*
Fletcher, Elizabeth. *The little goat*
Fowler, Richard. *Little Chick's big adventure*
Francis, Frank. *The magic wallpaper*
Gantschev, Ivan. *The Christmas teddy bear*
Gay, Michel. *Take me for a ride*
Gay, Zhenya. *Small one*
George, Jean Craighead. *Rhino romp*
Gliori, Debi. *Mr. Bear says, "Are you there, Baby Bear?"*
Goble, Paul. *The friendly wolf*
Goldsmith, Howard. *Little lost dog*
Goode, Diane. *Where's our mama?*

Grimm, Jacob. *Hansel and Gretel*, ill. by Winslow P. Pels

Grimsdell, Jeremy. *Kalinzu*

Grossman, Bill. *Tommy at the grocery store*

Guilfoile, Elizabeth. *Have you seen my brother?*

Guthrie, Donna. *Grandpa doesn't know it's me*

Hader, Berta Hoerner. *Lost in the zoo*

Hamm, Diane Johnston. *Laney's lost momma*

Hardy, Tad. *Lost cat*

Hassett, John. *Junior*

Hawkins, Colin. *Tog the dog*

Hayes, Sarah. *This is the bear*

Henderson, Kathy. *Disney's Pooh's grand adventure: the search for Christopher Robin*

Henkes, Kevin. *Sheila Rae, the brave*

Hill, Eric. *Where's Spot?*

Hines, Anna Grossnickle. *Don't worry, I'll find you*

Hirsh, Marilyn. *Where is Yonkela?*

Hoban, Lillian. *The laziest robot in zone one*

Hobbs, Will. *Howling Hill*

Hoff, Syd. *Bernard on his own*

Hutchins, Pat. *Where's the baby?*

Irving, Washington. *Rip Van Winkle*, ill. by John Howe

   Rip Van Winkle, ill. by Thomas Locker

   Rip Van Winkle, ill. by Peter Wingham

Jaques, Faith. *Tilly's rescue*

Jeram, Anita. *Bunny, my Honey*

Joerns, Consuelo. *The foggy rescue*

   The forgotten bear

Johnson, Paul Brett. *Lost*

Jonas, Ann. *Two bear cubs*

Kanome, Kayoko. *Little Mop lost*

Keats, Ezra Jack. *My dog is lost!*

Kemp, Moira. *Lift-the-flap chick*

Kessler, Leonard P. *Are we lost, daddy?*

Kinsey-Warnock, Natalie. *The bear that heard crying*

Knüppel, Helga. *The adventures of Christabel Crocodile*

   Christabel Crocodile's birthday egg

Kocí, Marta. *Katie's kitten*

Komaiko, Leah. *Where can Daniel be?*

Kovalski, Maryann. *Brenda and Edward*

Krause, Ute. *Nora and the great bear*

Lane, Judith. *Buster, where are you?*

Lears, Laurie. *Ian's walk*

Levine, Abby. *Ollie knows everything*

Lewis, J. Patrick. *The Christmas of the reddle moon*

Lisker, Sonia O. *Lost*

Livermore, Elaine. *Follow the fox*

Lobel, Arnold. *Uncle Elephant*

London, Jonathan. *Ali, child of the desert*

Lubell, Winifred. *Rosalie, the bird market turtle*

Maccarone, Grace. *The class trip*

McCloskey, Robert. *Blueberries for Sal*

McCully, Emily Arnold. *Picnic*

McKee, David. *Elmer and Wilbur*

McPhail, David M. *Lost*

Maisner, Heather. *Find Mouse in the house*

Maris, Ron. *Are you there, bear?*

Marks, Alan. *Nowhere to be found*

Martin, Jacqueline Briggs. *Bizzy Bones and Moose-mouse*

Marzollo, Jean. *Snow angel*

Mathews, Judith. *There's nothing to d-o-o-o!*

   Tuti, Blue Horse, and the Nipnope Man

Melmed, Laura Krauss. *Little Oh*

Mendoza, George. *Alphabet sheep*

Miles, Miska. *This little pig*

Miller, M. L. *The enormous snore*

Modell, Frank. *Tooley! Tooley!*

Moers, Hermann. *Annie's dancing day*

Mogensen, Jan. *Lost and found Teddy*

   When Teddy woke early

Morley, Carol. *A spider and a pig*

Morpurgo, Michael. *Wombat goes walkabout*

Moser, Erwin. *Wilma the elephant*

Nakatani, Chiyoko. *The day Chiro was lost*

Naylor, Phyllis Reynolds. *Ducks disappearing*

Nims, Bonnie Larkin. *Where is the bear?*

Oates, Joyce Carol. *Come meet Muffin!*

Offen, Hilda. *Elephant pie*

Olsen, Ib Spang. *Cat alley*

Parenteau, Shirley. *I'll bet you thought I was lost*

Paul, Jan S. *Hortense*

Peet, Bill (William Bartlett). *Ella*

Politi, Leo. *The nicest gift*

Ragz, M. M. *Lost little angel*

Rand, Gloria. *Willie takes a hike*

Remkiewicz, Frank. *The last time I saw Harris*

Rey, Margret (Margret Elisabeth Waldstein). *Curious George goes to the hospital*

Rubel, Nicole. *It came from the swamp*

Sauer, Julia Lina. *Mike's house*

Saxon, Charles D. *Don't worry about Poopsie*

Scheffler, Ursel. *Taking care of Sister Bear*

Schertle, Alice. *Little Frog's song*

Schneider, Antonie. *Luke the Lionhearted*

Schumacher, Claire. *Tim and Jim*

Seignobosc, Françoise. *Minou*

   Springtime for Jeanne-Marie

Shortall, Leonard W. *Andy, the dog walker*

Simmons, Jane. *Come along, Daisy!*

Singer, Marilyn. *Chester, the out-of-work dog*

Slepian, Jan. *Lost moose*

Slobodkin, Louis. *Yasu and the strangers*

Smith, Cara Lockhart. *Twenty-six rabbits run riot*

Standon, Anna. *Little duck lost*

Stevenson, James. *Howard*

Taylor, Mark. *The case of the missing kittens*

   Henry the castaway

   Henry the explorer

Titherington, Jeanne. *Where are you going, Emma?*

Tokuda, Wendy. *Humphrey the lost whale*

Trimble, Patti. *Lost!*

Trottier, Maxine. *Dreamstones*

Tsutsui, Yoriko. *Anna in charge*

Turnbull, Ann. *Rob goes a-hunting*

Vincent, Gabrielle. *Where are you, Ernest and Celestine?*

Vreeken, Elizabeth. *The boy who would not say his name*

Waddell, Martin. *Sailor Bear*

   Small Bear lost

Ward, Heather Patricia. *I promise I'll find you*

Ward, Nick. *Farmer George and the lost chick*

Watanabe, Shigeo. *Where's my daddy?*

Waters, Tony. *Sailor's bride*

Wells, Rosemary. *McDuff comes home*

   Max's dragon shirt

Wold, Jo Anne. *Well! Why didn't you say so?*

Ylla. *Two little bears*

Young, Evelyn. *The tale of Tai*

Ziefert, Harriet. *Wee G.*

Behavior – lying

Æsop. *Wolf! Wolf!*

Belloc, Hilaire. *Matilda who told lies and was burned to death*
Berenstain, Stan. *The Berenstain bears and the truth*
Brown, Marc Tolon. *Arthur and the true Francine*
Chorao, Kay. *Molly's lies*
Cohen, Miriam. *Liar, liar, pants on fire!*
Collodi, Carlo. *The adventures of Pinocchio*
   Pinocchio
Diakité, Baba Wagué. *The hunterman and the crocodiles*
Dinardo, Jeffrey. *The wolf who cried boy*
Elliott, Dan. *Ernie's little lie*
Elzbieta. *Dikou the little troon who walks at night*
Evans, Katherine. *The boy who cried wolf*
Gackenbach, Dick. *Crackle, Gluck and the sleeping toad*
Helena, Ann. *The lie*
Jeram, Anita. *It was Jake*
Lexau, Joan M. *Finders keepers, losers weepers*
Lloyd, David. *The ridiculous story of Gammer Gurton's needle*
Parsons, Virginia. *Pinocchio and Gepetto*
Pearson, Kit. *The singing basket*
Ross, Tony. *The boy who cried wolf*
Saltzberg, Barney. *Phoebe and the spelling bee*
Sharmat, Marjorie Weinman. *A big fat enormous lie*
Turkle, Brinton. *The adventures of Obadiah*

Behavior – messy

Jensen, Patricia. *The mess*
McKissack, Patricia C. *Ada, la desordenada*
   Messy Bessey
   Messy Bessey's closet
Riley, Linnea Asplind. *Mouse mess*

Behavior – misbehavior

Adams, Lisa K. *Dealing with teasing*
Agard, John. *Dig away two-hole Tim*
Ahlberg, Allan. *Monkey do!*
Alexander, Martha G. *We're in big trouble, Blackboard Bear*
Allard, Harry. *Miss Nelson is back*
   Miss Nelson is missing!
Anderson, Peggy Perry. *Out to lunch*
Archambault, John. *A beautiful feast for a big king cat*
Arnold, Tedd. *Huggly takes a bath*
   No jumping on the bed!
   The signmaker's assistant
Asch, Frank. *Moonbear's dream*
Ashforth, Camilla. *Monkey tricks*
Ashley, Bernard. *Dinner ladies don't count*
Auer, Martin. *Now, now Markus*
Baba, Noboru. *Eleven cats and a pig*
   Eleven cats and albatrosses
   Eleven cats in a bag
   Eleven hungry cats
Baker, Alan. *Benjamin's book*
   Benjamin's dreadful dream
Baker, Margaret. *A puppy called Spinach*
Baumann, Kurt. *The story of Jonah*
Baumgart, Klaus. *Anna and the little green dragon*
Beech, Caroline. *Peas again for lunch*
Beim, Jerrold. *The taming of Toby*
Belloc, Hilaire. *Jim, who ran away from his nurse, and was eaten by a lion*
   Matilda who told lies and was burned to death

Bellows, Cathy. *The Grizzly sisters*
Bemelmans, Ludwig. *Madeline and the bad hat*
Berenstain, Stan. *The Berenstain bears and the truth*
Berridge, Celia. *Hannah's temper*
Berry, Joy Wilt. *Being destructive*
   Being selfish
   Disobeying
   Fighting
   Throwing tantrums
   Whining
Birchman, David F. *Jigsaw Jackson*
Biro, Val. *Gumdrop goes to school*
Blake, Robert J. *Yudonsi*
Blaustein, Muriel. *Baby Mabu and Auntie Moose*
   Bedtime, Zachary!
Boland, Janice. *A dog named Sam*
Boyd, Lizi. *Half wild and half child*
Bradman, Tony. *The bad babies' book of colors*
   The bad babies' counting book
   A bad week for the three bears
   Michael
Brown, Ken (Ken James). *Mucky Pup's Christmas*
Brown, Marc Tolon. *Arthur's computer disaster*
   Arthur's first sleepover
Brown, Margaret Wise. *Sneakers*
Browne, Eileen. *Tick-tock*
Brunhoff, Laurent de. *Babar's cousin, that rascal Arthur*
Calhoun, Mary. *The goblin under the stairs*
Campbell, Rod. *Henry's busy day*
   Misty's mischief
Carlson, Nancy L. *How to lose all your friends*
Carr, Jan. *The nature of the beast*
Cartlidge, Michelle. *Pippin and Pod*
Chalmers, Audrey. *Fancy be good*
Chapman, Carol. *Herbie's troubles*
Chess, Victoria. *Alfred's alphabet walk*
Chichester Clark, Emma. *The story of Horrible Hilda and Henry*
Childress, Mark. *Joshua and the big bad blue crabs*
Christelow, Eileen. *Five little monkeys jumping on the bed*
   Five little monkeys sitting in a tree
   Jerome and the Witchcraft kids
Christian, Mary Blount. *Go west, swamp monsters*
Claverie, Jean. *The party*
Cohen, Miriam. *Starring first grade*
Cole, Babette. *Bad habits! or, The taming of Lucretzia Crum*
   Tarzanna!
Cole, William. *That pest Jonathan*
Colette, Sidonie Gabrielle. *The boy and the magic*
Collington, Peter. *Little pickle*
Collins, Pat Lowery. *Taking care of Tucker*
Collodi, Carlo. *The adventures of Pinocchio*
   Pinocchio
Cooper, Helen (Helen F.). *Little monster did it!*
Costa, Nicoletta. *The naughty puppy*
   The new puppy
Couture, Susan Arkin. *Melanie Jane*
Cowley, Stewart. *The naughty ducklings*
Craig, Helen. *A welcome for Annie*
Crebbin, June. *Cows in the kitchen*
Crowley, Arthur. *The boogey man*
Dauer, Rosamond. *My friend, Jasper Jones*
David, Lawrence. *The good little girl*
Day, Alexandra. *Carl's birthday*
De Groat, Diane. *Roses are pink, your feet really stink*
Delaney, A. *The gunnywolf*

Delaney, Ned. *Bad dog!*
　Rufus the doofus
Denchfield, Nick. *Desmond the dog*
　Desmond the dog, a wag-the-tail pop-up book
Dodd, Lynley. *Hairy Maclary's rumpus at the vet*
　Slinky Malinki, open the door
Douglass, Barbara. *Good as new*
Dowling, Paul. *Splodger*
Eastman, P. D. (Philip D.). *Are you my mother?*
Enright, Elizabeth. *Zeee*
Faulkner, Keith. *The monster in my bathroom*
　The monster in my toybox
Flack, Marjorie. *The story about Ping*
Floca, Brian. *The frightful story of Harry Walfish*
Froment, Eugène. *The story of a round loaf*
Gackenbach, Dick. *Pepper and all the legs*
Gág, Wanda. *The sorcerer's apprentice*
Galbraith, Kathryn Osebold. *Katie did!*
Gantos, Jack (John, Jr.). *Happy birthday, Rotten Ralph*
　Not so Rotten Ralph
　Rotten Ralph
　Rotten Ralph's rotten romance
　Wedding bells for Rotten Ralph
　Worse than Rotten Ralph
Garland, Sarah. *Oh, no!*
Geisert, Arthur. *Oink*
　Oink oink
Gerson, Corinne. *Good dog, bad dog*
Gerstein, Mordicai. *Stop those pants!*
Ghigna, Charles. *Good cats/Bad cats*
　Good dogs/Bad dogs
Gliori, Debi. *Mr. Bear babysits*
Goodall, John S. *Naughty Nancy*
　Naughty Nancy goes to school
Gordon, Margaret. *Wilberforce goes to a party*
Graham, Bob. *Has anyone here seen William?*
Grindley, Sally. *Four black puppies*
Gullikson, Sandy. *Trouble for breakfast*
Harper, Wilhelmina. *The gunniwolf*
Havill, Juanita. *Jamaica and the substitute teacher*
　Magic fort
Hawkes, Kevin. *Then the troll heard the squeak*
Hayes, Sarah. *Bad egg*
Hedderwick, Mairi. *Katie Morag and the big boy cousins*
　Katie Morag and the tiresome Ted
　Katie Morag delivers the mail
Helmer, Marilyn. *Mr. McGratt and the ornery cat*
Henkes, Kevin. *A weekend with Wendell*
Heo, Yumi. *The green frogs*
Hill, Eric. *Spot visits the hospital*
　Spot's first picnic
Hiller, Catherine. *Argentaybee and the boonie*
Hilton, Nette. *Prince Lachlan*
Himmelman, John. *Amanda and the witch switch*
Hirsh, Marilyn. *Deborah the dybbuk*
Hoban, Russell. *How Tom beat Captain Najork and his hired sportsmen*
Hodeir, André. *Warwick's 3 bottles*
Hogan, Inez. *About Nono, the baby elephant*
Hort, Lenny. *The boy who held back the sea*
Hughes, Shirley. *The snow lady*
Humphries, Tudor. *Hiding*
Hutchins, Pat. *Three-star Billy*
　Where's the baby?
Inkiow, Dimiter. *Me and Clara and Baldwin the pony*
　Me and Clara and Snuffy the dog
　Me and my sister Clara

Jeffers, Susan. *Wild Robin*
Jeram, Anita. *It was Jake*
Johnston, Tony. *Lorenzo the naughty parrot*
Joosse, Barbara M. *The thinking place*
Keller, Beverly. *When mother got the flu*
Keller, Holly. *A bear for Christmas*
Kellogg, Steven (Stephen). *Prehistoric Pinkerton*
Kent, Jack. *The scribble monster*
Kent, Lorna. *No, no, Charlie Rascal!*
Kline, Suzy. *Don't touch!*
Koenig, Marion. *The wonderful world of night*
Kranendonk, Anke. *Just a minute*
Krasilovsky, Phyllis. *The man who entered a contest*
Kraus, Robert. *Boris bad enough*
Krause, Ute. *Pig surprise*
Kroll, Steven. *Otto*
　Pigs in the house
Langreuter, Jutta. *Little Bear and the big fight*
Lattimore, Deborah Nourse. *Punga the goddess of ugly*
Leach, Norman. *My wicked stepmother*
Leaf, Munro. *A flock of watchbirds*
Levinson, Riki. *Touch! Touch!*
Lexau, Joan M. *I'll tell on you*
Lieberman, Syd. *The wise shoemaker of Studena*
Lillie, Patricia. *One very, very quiet afternoon*
Lindbergh, Reeve. *The awful aardvarks go to school*
　The awful Aardvarks shop for school
　The day the goose got loose
Lindgren, Barbro. *The wild baby*
Lipkind, William. *Nubber bear*
Lippman, Peter. *The Know-It-Alls go to sea*
　The Know-It-Alls help out
　The Know-It-Alls mind the store
　The Know-It-Alls take a winter vacation
Littlewood, Valerie. *The season clock*
Lobel, Arnold. *Prince Bertram the bad*
London, Jonathan. *Shawn and Keeper: show-and-tell*
Lorimer, Janet. *The biggest bubble in the world*
Luttrell, Ida. *Mattie and the chicken thief*
McBratney, Sam. *The caterpillow fight*
McGuire, Richard. *What goes around comes around*
McNaughton, Colin. *Captain Abdul's pirate school*
McPhail, David M. *Andrew's bath*
Mahiri, Jabari. *The day they stole the letter J*
Mahy, Margaret. *The boy with two shadows*
Malloy, Judy. *Bad Thad*
Manning, Linda. *Dinosaur days*
Margret and H. A. Rey's Curious George and the puppies
Marshall, Edward. *Fox and his friends*
　Fox on wheels
Marshall, James. *The Cut-Ups*
　The Cut-Ups at Camp Custer
　The Cut-Ups crack up
　The Cut-Ups cut loose
　Fox on the job
　George and Martha back in town
Martin, David. *Monkey trouble*
Marzollo, Jean. *Uproar on Hollercat Hill*
Mayer, Mercer. *Appelard and Liverwurst*
Mazer, Anne. *The Fixits*
Milgrim, David. *Dog brain*
Moremen, Grace E. *No, no, Natalie*
Morgan, Allen. *Molly and Mr. Maloney*
Moss, Marissa. *Who was it?*
Mozelle, Shirley. *The pig is in the pantry, the cat is on the shelf*
Munsch, Robert N. *Angela's airplane*

Good families don't
Moira's birthday
Murphy, Jill. *All in one piece*
Myller, Lois. *No! No!*
Nones, Eric Jon. *Wendell*
Oana, Kay D. *Shasta and the shebang machine*
Obrist, Jürg. *Bear business*
O'Kelley, Mattie Lou. *Circus!*
Oldfield, Pamela. *Melanie Brown climbs a tree*
Olson, Helen Kronberg. *The strange thing that happened to Oliver Wendell Iscovitch*
O'Malley, Kevin. *Carl caught a flying fish*
Oram, Hiawyn. *Ned and the Joybaloo*
Oxenbury, Helen. *The car trip*
The important visitor
Parker, Nancy Winslow. *Cooper, the McNallys' big black dog*
Poofy loves company
Parsons, Virginia. *Pinocchio and Gepetto*
Partis, Joanne. *Stripe*
Paterson, Diane. *Soap and suds*
Paton, Priscilla. *Howard and the sitter surprise*
Pearson, Tracey Campbell. *The howling dog*
Sing a song of sixpence
Polushkin, Maria. *Kitten in trouble*
Potter, Beatrix. *The complete adventures of Peter Rabbit*
The tale of Benjamin Bunny
The tale of Peter Rabbit, ill. by Margot Apple
The tale of Peter Rabbit, ill. by Beatrix Potter
The tale of two bad mice
The two bad mice
Where's Peter Rabbit?
Poulin, Stéphane. *Can you catch Josephine?*
Prater, John. *"No!" said Joe*
On Friday something funny happened
You can't catch me!
Preston, Edna Mitchell. *Horrible Hepzibah*
Squawk to the moon, little goose
Provensen, Alice. *Punch in New York*
Quackenbush, Robert M. *Mouse feathers*
Rabinowitz, Sandy. *A colt named mischief*
Rappus, Gerhard. *When the sun was shining*
Rice, Eve. *Benny bakes a cake*
Richardson, Jean. *Thomas's sitter*
Robison, Deborah. *Your turn, doctor*
Rockwell, Anne F. *The boy who wouldn't obey*
Honk honk!
Ross, Tony. *Oscar got the blame*
Rovetch, Lissa. *Trigwater did it*
Rubel, Nicole. *Goldie's nap*
Ruck-Pauquèt, Gina. *Oh, that koala!*
Russo, Marisabina. *Under the table*
Sadler, Marilyn. *Alistair's elephant*
Sandberg, Inger. *Dusty wants to help*
Nicholas' red day
Sarrazin, Johan. *Tootle*
Say, Allen. *Allison*
Schatell, Brian. *Farmer Goff and his turkey Sam*
Schroeder, Binette. *Tuffa and the picnic*
Schumacher, Claire. *King of the zoo*
Schwartz, Amy. *Camper of the week*
Sendak, Maurice. *Where the wild things are*
Shannon, David. *David goes to school*
No, David!
Sharratt, Nick. *The time it took Tom*
Sherrow, Victoria. *There goes the ghost*
Simmonds, Posy. *The chocolate wedding*
Simmons, Steven J. *Alice and Greta's color magic*

Greta's revenge
Small, David. *Paper John*
Smith, Barry. *A child's guide to bad behavior*
Smith, Cara Lockhart. *Twenty-six rabbits run riot*
Smith, Janice Lee. *The monster in the third dresser drawer and other stories about Adam Joshua*
Solotareff, Grégoire. *Don't call me little bunny*
Standon, Anna. *Three little cats*
Stevenson, James. *Worse than the worst*
Stevenson, Suçie. *Jessica the blue streak*
Sykes, Julie. *Robbie Rabbit and the little ones*
Tharlet, Eve. *Little pig, big trouble*
Tierney, Hanne. *Where's your baby brother, Becky Bunting?*
Trapani, Iza. *Mary had a little lamb*
Van Allsburg, Chris. *The garden of Abdul Gasazi*
Veldkamp, Tjibbe. *22 orphans*
Vigna, Judith. *Anyhow, I'm glad I tried*
She's not my real mother
Vincent, Gabrielle. *Breakfast time, Ernest and Celestine*
Waddell, Martin. *Amy said*
Wade, Barrie. *Little monster*
Wahl, Jan. *Little Eight John*
Wallace, Ian. *Morgan the magnificent*
The sparrow's song
Ward, Cindy. *Cookie's week*
Ward, Nick. *Giant*
Ward, Sally G. *Charlie and Grandma*
Watanabe, Yuichi. *Wally the whale who loved balloons*
Watson, Wendy. *Lollipop*
We wish you a merry Christmas
Weilerstein, Sadie Rose. *K'tonton's Yom Kippur kitten*
Wells, Rosemary. *Fritz and the mess fairy*
Good night, Fred
Hazel's amazing mother
White, Florence Meiman. *How to lose your lunch money*
Wild, Margaret. *Toby*
Willard, Nancy. *The well-mannered balloon*
Williams, Barbara. *Whatever happened to Beverly Bigler's birthday?*
Wiseman, Bernard. *Don't make fun!*
Wood, Audrey. *Elbert's bad word*
Woodruff, Elvira. *Mrs. McCloskey's monkeys*
Wright, Jill. *The old woman and the jar of ums*
Yee, Wong Herbert. *Big black bear*
Yeoman, John. *The wild washerwomen*
Zemach, Margot. *Jake and Honeybunch go to heaven*
Zemke, Deborah. *The shadow of Matilda Hunt*
Ziefert, Harriet. *Strike four!*

Behavior – mistakes

Aliki. *Jack and Jake*
Becker, Bonny. *The Christmas crocodile*
Boehm, Arlene P. *Jack in search of Art*
Boyd, Selma. *The how: making the best of a mistake*
Brandenberg, Franz. *No school today!*
Brett, Jan. *Armadillo rodeo*
Bridwell, Norman. *Clifford's good deeds*
Burdett, Lois. *Twelfth night*
Chevalier, Christa. *Spence makes circles*
Cohen, Peter Zachary. *Olson's meat pies*
Cowley, Joy. *Big moon tortilla*
Cresswell, Helen. *Two hoots and the king*
Two hoots in the snow
Demi. *The leaky umbrella*

Erickson, Karen. *No one is perfect*
Gág, Wanda. *Gone is gone*
Galdone, Paul. *Obedient Jack*
Geringer, Laura. *Molly's new washing machine*
Hoban, Julia. *Buzby to the rescue*
Hoff, Syd. *Henrietta, the early bird*
Inkpen, Mick. *Kipper's birthday*
Jacobs, Joseph. *Hereafterthis*
Lexau, Joan M. *It all began with a drip, drip, drip*
Lindbergh, Reeve. *If I'd known then what I know now*
Lipson, Beth Weiner. *Benjamin's perfect solution*
McFarland, Lyn Rossiter. *The pirate's parrot*
Martin, Rafe. *Foolish rabbit's big mistake*
Medearis, Angela Shelf. *Poppa's new pants*
Pilkey, Dav. *The Silly Gooses build a house*
Prager, Annabelle. *The baseball birthday party*
Prose, Francine. *The angel's mistake*
Rinder, Lenore. *A big mistake*
Root, Phyllis. *Contrary bear*
Rowe, John A. *Monkey trouble*
Spinelli, Eileen. *Somebody loves you, Mr. Hatch*
Springstubb, Tricia. *The magic guinea pig*
Stoeke, Janet Morgan. *Minerva Louise at the fair*
Waber, Bernard. *Nobody is perfick*
Walker, Barbara K. (Barbara Kerlin). *New patches for old*
Wiseman, Bernard. *Tails are not for painting*
Yee, Wong Herbert. *A drop of rain*

Behavior – misunderstanding

Allard, Harry. *The Stupids die*
Baron, Alan. *Little Pig's bouncy ball*
Berg, Jean Horton. *The O'Learys and friends*
Berson, Harold. *Kassim's shoes*
Boyd, Lizi. *The not-so-wicked stepmother*
Bryant, Sara Cone. *Epaminondas and his auntie*
Bush, John. *The cross-with-us rhinoceros*
Carrick, Carol. *Old Mother Witch*
Catalanotto, Peter. *Mr. Mumble*
Cohen, Barbara. *Make a wish, Molly*
Demuth, Patricia Brennan. *Max, the bad-talking parrot*
Dickinson, Mike. *My dad doesn't even notice*
Donaldson, Joan. *The real pretend*
Ericsson, Jennifer A. *No milk!*
Gackenbach, Dick. *Arabella and Mr. Crack King Wacky*
Harper, Jo. *Prairie dog pioneers*
Hopkins, Lee Bennett. *I loved Rose Ann*
Knight, Joan. *Bon appetit, Bertie!*
Komaiko, Leah. *Earl's too cool for me*
Kraus, Robert. *Ladybug, ladybug!*
Krause, Ute. *Pig surprise*
Lionni, Leo. *Fish is fish*
McClintock, Marshall. *A fly went by*
Mayer, Marianna. *The prince and the pauper*
Morgan, Michaela. *Helpful Betty to the rescue*
Nixon, Joan Lowery. *Bigfoot makes a movie*
Nordqvist, Sven. *Porker finds a chair*
Polushkin, Maria. *Mother, Mother, I want another*
Roberts, Sarah. *Bert and the missing mop mix-up*
Schatell, Brian. *The McGoonys have a party*
Shannon, David. *The rain came down*
Sharmat, Marjorie Weinman. *Gila monsters meet you at the airport*
Simmons, Jane. *Ebb and Flo and the greedy gulls*
Stoeke, Janet Morgan. *A hat for Minerva Louise*

Minerva Louise
Minerva Louise at school
Turner, Ann Warren. *Hedgehog for breakfast*
Tusa, Tricia. *Chicken*
Waber, Bernard. *Funny, funny Lyle*
Wild, Jocelyn. *Florence and Eric take the cake*
Wiseman, Bernard. *Morris has a birthday party!*
Morris the moose
Wold, Jo Anne. *Well! Why didn't you say so?*
Yorinks, Arthur. *Company's coming*
Young, Ed (Edward). *Donkey trouble*
Zemke, Deborah. *The way it happened*

Behavior – nagging

Dickinson, Mary. *Alex's outing*
Mahy, Margaret. *Mrs. Discombobulous*
Stalder, Valerie. *Even the devil is afraid of a shrew*

Behavior – name calling

Merriam, Eve. *Fighting words*
Waber, Bernard. *But names will never hurt me*

Behavior – naughty *see* Behavior – misbehavior

Behavior – needing someone

Aardema, Verna. *The lonely lioness and the ostrich chicks*
Ahlberg, Janet. *Bye-bye, baby*
Asare, Meshack. *Cat . . . in search of a friend*
Asher, Sandy. *Princess Bee and the royal good-night story*
Austin, Margot. *A friend for Growl Bear*
Axworthy, Anni. *Along came Toto*
Billam, Rosemary. *Fuzzy rabbit*
Bingham, Mindy. *Minou*
Biro, Val. *Gumdrop gets a lift*
Bulla, Clyde Robert. *The stubborn old woman*
Cain, Sheridan. *Why so sad, Brown Rabbit?*
Chichester Clark, Emma. *I love you, Blue Kangaroo!*
Collins, Pat Lowery. *Taking care of Tucker*
Corey, Dorothy. *Will there be a lap for me?*
You go away
Coxon, Michèle. *The cat who lost his purr*
Crimi, Carolyn. *Don't need friends*
David, Lawrence. *The good little girl*
Farber, Norma. *The boy who longed for a lift*
Fine, Anne. *Poor Monty*
Gauch, Patricia Lee. *Christina Katerina and the time she quit the family*
Graeber, Charlotte Towner. *Nobody's Dog*
Guilfoile, Elizabeth. *Nobody listens to Andrew*
Hassett, John. *Cat up a tree*
Hawkins, Colin. *Where's my mommy?*
Hayes, Sarah. *Mary Mary*
Herriot, James. *Blossom comes home*
Hippely, Hilary Horder. *The crimson ribbon*
Hughes, Richard. *Gertrude's child*
Hughes, Shirley. *Alfie gives a hand*
Jacobs, Kate. *A sister's wish*
Jensen, Patricia. *Little Donkey learns to help*
Jeschke, Susan. *Lucky's choice*
Keats, Ezra Jack. *Louie's search*
Kent, Jack. *There's no such thing as a dragon*
Kiser, Kevin. *Buzzy Widget*
Lewis, Kim. *Emma's lamb*

Lindgren, Barbro. *Andrei's search*
Livermore, Elaine. *Follow the fox*
Lobel, Anita. *A birthday for the princess*
McCormick, Wendy. *Daddy, will you miss me?*
McGinnis, Lila Sprague. *If Daddy only knew me*
McLerran, Alice. *The mountain that loved a bird*
McPhail, David M. *Emma's pet*
   Great cat
Mayer, Mercer. *Whinnie the lovesick dragon*
Morris, Terry Nell. *Lucky puppy! Lucky boy!*
Moser, Erwin. *Wilma the elephant*
Munsch, Robert N. *Millicent and the wind*
Olsen, Ib Spang. *The grown-up trap*
Oppenheim, Joanne. *On the other side of the river*
Paraskevas, Betty. *The tangerine bear*
Peet, Bill (William Bartlett). *Zella, Zack, and Zodiac*
Ranville, Myralene. *Tex*
Rayner, Mary. *Crocodarling*
Roberts, Sarah. *I want to go home!*
Rodell, Susanna. *Dear Fred*
Schindel, John. *Dear Daddy*
Schubert, Dieter. *Where's my monkey?*
Scott, Ann Herbert. *On mother's lap*
   Sam
Seeber, Dorothea P. *A pup just for me . . . A boy just*
   for me
Sendak, Maurice. *Very far away*
Singer, Marilyn. *Pickle plan*
Skorpen, Liesel Moak. *Charles*
Stehr, Frédéric. *Quack-quack*
Strauss, Gwen. *The night shimmy*
Sugita, Yutaka. *Helena the unhappy hippopotamus*
Tennyson, Noel. *The lady's chair and the ottoman*
Thompson, Colin (Colin Edward). *Unknown*
Tokuda, Wendy. *Humphrey the lost whale*
Tompert, Ann. *Will you come back for me?*
Vigna, Judith. *Mommy and me by ourselves again*
Wells, Rosemary. *McDuff moves in*
   Noisy Nora
Wilhelm, Hans. *Schnitzel's first Christmas*
Wolde, Gunilla. *Betsy and the chicken pox*
Wyeth, Sharon Dennis. *Always my dad*

Behavior – potty training *see* Toilet training

Behavior – running away

Ackerman, Karen. *Bingleman's midway*
Adoff, Arnold. *Where wild Willie?*
Ahlberg, Allan. *Monkey do!*
Alexander, Martha G. *And my mean old mother will*
   be sorry, Blackboard Bear
Allamand, Pascale. *The camel who left the zoo*
Baker, Leslie A. *The antique store cat*
   The third-story cat
Barrett, Lawrence Louis. *Twinkle, the baby colt*
Barton, Byron. *The wee little woman*
Bates, H. E. (Herbert Ernest). *Achilles the donkey*
Bauer, Steven. *The strange and wonderful tale of*
   Robert McDoodle
Belloc, Hilaire. *Jim, who ran away from his nurse,*
   and was eaten by a lion
Bond, Felicia. *Wake up, Vladimir*
Brimner, Larry Dane. *Elliot Fry's good-bye*
Brown, Margaret Wise. *The runaway bunny*
Brunhoff, Jean de. *The story of Babar, the little ele-*
   phant
Burton, Virginia Lee. *Choo choo*
Byrd, Robert. *Marcella was bored*

Carlson, Natalie Savage. *Runaway Marie Louise*
Carroll, Ruth. *What Whiskers did*
Charles, Veronika Martenova. *The crane girl*
Christelow, Eileen. *The great pig escape*
Christian, Mary Blount. *Go west, swamp monsters*
Clayton, Elaine. *The yeoman's daring daughter and*
   the princes in the tower
Clements, Andrew. *Temple cat*, ill. by Kate Kiesler
   Temple cat, ill. by Alan Marks
Clifton, Lucille. *My brother fine with me*
Cohen, Barbara. *The chocolate wolf*
Coombs, Patricia. *Lisa and the grompet*
Davy's scary journey
Desimini, Lisa. *I am running away today*
Dumas, Philippe. *Lucy, a tale of a donkey*
DuPasquier, Philippe. *The great escape*
Duvoisin, Roger Antoine. *The missing milkman*
Edwards, Pamela Duncan. *Barefoot*
Egan, Tim. *Metropolitan cow*
Eisenstein, Marilyn. *Periwinkle isn't Paris*
Elzbieta. *Dikou and the mysterious moon sheep*
   Dikou and the Snively Snoak
Farber, Norma. *The boy who longed for a lift*
   Return of the shadows
Ferns, Ronald. *Osbert and Lucy*
Freeman, Don. *Beady Bear*
French, Vivian. *It's a go-to-the-park day*
Gackenbach, Dick. *Claude and Pepper*
Galbraith, Richard. *Reuben runs away*
Gianni, Peg. *Alex, the amazing juggler*
The gingerbread boy. *Gingerbread baby*, ill. by Jan
   Brett
   The gingerbread boy, ill. by Emily Bolam
   The gingerbread boy, ill. by Scott Cook
   The gingerbread boy, ill. by Richard Egielski
   The gingerbread boy, ill. by Paul Galdone
   The gingerbread boy, ill. by Joan Elizabeth Good-
   man
   The gingerbread boy, ill. by William Curtis
   Holdsworth
   The gingerbread man, ill. by Megan Lloyd
   The gingerbread man, ill. by Barbara McClintock
   The gingerbread man, ill. by Gerald Rose
   The pancake boy
   Whiff, sniff, nibble and chew
Goodall, John S. *The adventures of Paddy Pork*
Gray, Nigel. *I'll take you to Mrs. Cole!*
   Running away from home
Greenberg, Dan. *The bed who ran away from home*
Greene, Graham. *The little train*
Hale, Irina. *Chocolate mouse and sugar pig*
Hamilton, Morse. *My name is Emily*
Hanson, Joan. *I'm going to run away*
Hayward, Linda. *The runaway Christmas toy*
Heck, Elisabeth. *The black sheep*
Heller, Nicholas. *Up the wall*
Heller, Wendy. *Clementine and the cage*
Herman, Gail. *Teddy bear for sale*
Hillert, Margaret. *The little runaway*
Hoban, Russell. *A baby sister for Frances*
Hooks, William H. *The rainbow ribbon*
Howe, James. *Bunnicula escapes!*
Hughes, Richard. *Gertrude's child*
Hyman, Robin. *Casper and the rainbow bird*
Isenberg, Barbara. *The adventures of Albert, the run-*
   ning bear
Jeschke, Susan. *Lucky's choice*
Joerns, Consuelo. *Oliver's escape*
Johnson, Dolores. *Seminole diary*

Johnson, Jane. *Today I thought I'd run away*
Keller, Holly. *Maxine in the middle*
Kent, Jack. *Joey runs away*
Kimmel, Eric A. *The runaway tortilla*
Kimmelman, Leslie. *The runaway latkes*
Kiser, SuAnn. *The catspring somersault flying one-handed flip-flop*
Knight, Hilary. *Where's Wallace?*
Kraus, Robert. *Where are you going, little mouse?*
La Farge, Phyllis. *Joanna runs away*
Langner, Nola. *By the light of the silvery moon*
Lasker, Joe. *The do-something day*
Lindgren, Barbro. *Benny's had enough*
Lisowski, Gabriel. *Roncalli's magnificent circus*
Lobel, Arnold. *The man who took the indoors out*
    Small pig
McClure, Gillian. *Fly home McDoo*
McConnachie, Brian. *Lily of the forest*
McCully, Emily Arnold. *My real family*
MacDonald, Maryann. *Rosie runs away*
McKissack, Patricia C. *Who is coming?*
McNeal, Tom. *The dog who lost his Bob*
McPhail, David M. *Stanley: Henry Bear's friend*
Maris, Ron. *Runaway rabbit*
Marol, Jean-Claude. *Vagabul escapes*
Martín Larrañaga, Ana. *Woo!*
Mayne, William. *Pandora*
Meade, Holly. *John Willy and Freddy McGee*
Miles, Miska. *This little pig*
Modarressi, Mitra. *The parent thief*
Mogensen, Jan. *Teddy runs away*
Moore, Inga. *Little dog lost*
Mora, Jo. *Budgee Budgee Cottontail*
Mostacchi, Massimo. *The beast and the boy*
    A dog's best friend
Moyer, Marshall M. *Rollo Bones, canine hypnotist*
Munsch, Robert N. *Aaron's hair*
Oakley, Graham. *Hetty and Harriet*
O'Donnell, Elizabeth Lee. *Maggie doesn't want to move*
Parker, Nancy Winslow. *The crocodile under Louis Finneberg's bed*
Patterson, Geoffrey. *A pig's tale*
Paxton, Tom. *Jennifer's rabbit*
Pearson, Susan. *Saturday, I ran away*
Peet, Bill (William Bartlett). *Pamela Camel*
Pittaway, Margaret. *The rainforest children*
Pizer, Abigail. *Loppylugs*
Poulin, Stéphane. *Have you seen Josephine?*
Prater, John. *You can't catch me!*
Ravilious, Robin. *The runaway chick*
Robins, Joan. *Addie runs away*
Rockwell, Anne F. *Willy runs away*
Rogers, Paul (Patrick). *Sheepchase*
Rosen, Michael (1946-). *Crow and Hawk*
Roth, Susan L. *Cinnamon's day out*
Schneider, Antonie. *Luke the Lionhearted*
Seligman, Dorothy Halle. *Run away home*
Sendak, Maurice. *Very far away*
Sharmat, Marjorie Weinman. *Rex*
Singer, Marilyn. *Archer Armadillo's secret room*
Slangerup, Erik Jon. *Dirt Boy*
Steig, William. *Zeke Pippin*
Stevens, Janet. *My big dog*
Svend Otto S (Svend Otto Sorensen). *Taxi dog*
Sykes, Julie. *I don't want to take a bath!*
Van Laan, Nancy. *Little baby Bobby*
Vernon, Tannis. *Little Pig and the blue-green sea*
Voake, Charlotte. *Ginger*

Waber, Bernard. *Bernard*
    A lion named Shirley Williamson
Wahl, Jan. *Mabel ran away with the toys*
Whitmore, Adam. *Max leaves home*
Wilkon, Piotr. *Rosie the cool cat*
Wooding, Sharon L. *The painter's cat*
Woolaver, Lance. *From Ben Loman to the sea*
Wright, Dare. *Edith and Mr. Bear*
Yep, Laurence. *The city of dragons*
Yolen, Jane. *The girl who loved the wind*
Yorinks, Arthur. *Hey, Al*
Ziefert, Harriet. *Sam and Lucy*
Zimnik, Reiner. *The bear on the motorcycle*
    The proud circus horse
Zion, Gene. *Harry, the dirty dog*
Zolotow, Charlotte (Shapiro). *Big sister and little sister*

Behavior – saving things

Calhoun, Mary. *The traveling ball of string*
Ciardi, John. *John J. Plenty and Fiddler Dan*
Delton, Judy. *Penny wise, fun foolish*
Foster, Doris Van Liew. *A pocketful of seasons*
Mayne, William. *The patchwork cat*

Behavior – secrets

Aardema, Verna. *What's so funny, Ketu?*
Allard, Harry. *Miss Nelson has a field day*
Auerbach, Marjorie. *King Lavra and the barber*
Bahr, Amy C. *Sometimes it's ok to tell secrets*
Bang, Molly. *Dawn*
Barklem, Jill. *The secret staircase*
Baylor, Byrd. *Your own best secret place*
Beisner, Monika. *Secret spells and curious charms*
Brandenberg, Franz. *A secret for grandmother's birthday*
Brighton, Catherine. *Five secrets in a box*
Christelow, Eileen. *The robbery at the diamond dog diner*
Cole, Joanna. *Don't tell the whole world*
Compton, Kenn. *Happy Christmas to all!*
Coombs, Patricia. *The magician and McTree*
Cummings, W. T. (Walter Thies). *Miss Esta Maude's secret*
Davis, Maggie S. *Grandma's secret letter*
Emberley, Rebecca. *My mother's secret life*
Galbraith, Kathryn Osebold. *Waiting for Jennifer*
Giff, Patricia Reilly. *I love Saturday*
Gretz, Susanna. *Frog in the middle*
Guthrie, Donna. *One hundred and two steps*
Hayes, Sarah. *This is the bear*
Heide, Florence Parry. *The day of Ahmed's secret*
Hest, Amy. *In the rain with Baby Duck*
Hines, Anna Grossnickle. *The secret keeper*
Hughes, Shirley. *Sally's secret*
Krahn, Fernando. *The secret in the dungeon*
Lakin, Pat (Patricia). *Don't forget*
Lemaître, Pascal. *Zelda's secret*
Lifton, Betty Jean. *The secret seller*
Naylor, Phyllis Reynolds. *Keeping a Christmas secret*
Olofsdotter, Marie. *Frej the fearless*
Oppenheim, Shulamith Levey. *The hundredth name*
Pevear, Richard. *Our king has horns!*
Polacco, Patricia. *The butterfly*
Prose, Francine. *You never know*
Rappaport, Doreen. *The long-haired girl*
Riggio, Anita. *Secret signs*

Russell, Pamela. *Do you have a secret?*
San Souci, Robert D. *The snow wife*
Senisi, Ellen B. *Secrets*
Theroux, Phyllis. *Serefina under the circumstances*
Thomson, Peggy. *The king has horse's ears*
Wadsworth, Ginger. *Tomorrow is Daddy's birthday*
Willis, Val. *The secret in the matchbox*
Zemke, Deborah. *The way it happened*

Behavior – seeking better things

Abolafia, Yossi. *Yanosh's Island*
Alborough, Jez. *The grass is always greener*
Allen, Jeffrey. *The secret life of Mr. Weird*
Altman, Linda Jacobs. *Amelia's road*
Bradby, Marie. *More than anything else*
Brandenberg, Franz. *What's wrong with a van?*
Buckley, Richard. *The foolish tortoise*
Carmichael, Clay. *Bear at the beach*
Carter, Anne. *The fisherwoman*
Carter, Penny. *A new house for the Morrisons*
Chichester Clark, Emma. *More!*
Climo, Lindee. *Clyde*
Cole, Brock. *Nothing but a pig*
Cummings, W. T. (Walter Thies). *The kid*
Damjan, Mischa. *The clown said no*
Demarest, Chris L. *Benedict finds a home*
Gackenbach, Dick. *Little bug*
Gage, Wilson. *Mrs. Gaddy and the fast-growing vine*
Gantschev, Ivan. *Where is Mr. Mole?*
Ganz, Yaffa. *The story of Mimmy and Simmy*
Giff, Patricia Reilly. *Next year I'll be special*
Hamilton, Virginia. *Jaguarundi*
Heilbroner, Joan. *Tom the TV cat*
Hopkinson, Deborah. *Sweet Clara and the freedom quilt*
Ivanov, Anatoly. *Ol' Jake's lucky day*
Jennings, Linda M. *Crispin and the dancing piglet*
Joly-Berbesson, Fanny. *Marceau Bonappetit*
Keillor, Garrison. *Cat, you better come home*
Kent, Jack. *Joey runs away*
Kraus, Robert. *Where are you going, little mouse?*
Kwon, Holly H. *The moles and the mireuk*
Lasky, Kathryn. *Sea swan*
Le Guin, Ursula K. *Solomon Leviathan's nine hundred and thirty-first trip around the world*
Lindgren, Astrid. *My nightingale is singing*
Lionni, Leo. *Tillie and the wall*
Lopshire, Robert. *I want to be somebody new!*
McCunn, Ruthanne L. *Pie-Biter*
McKee, David. *The hill and the rock*
Mahy, Margaret. *The man whose mother was a pirate*
Marshall, James. *Rapscallion Jones*
Miller, Moira. *Oscar Mouse finds a home*
Moore, Inga. *The truffle hunter*
Nixon, Joan Lowery. *If you say so, Claude*
Pittaway, Margaret. *The rainforest children*
Rose, Anne K. *As right as right can be*
Stanley, Diane. *A country tale*
Watts, Bernadette. *St. Francis and the proud crow*
Williams, Vera B. *A chair for my mother*
Yorinks, Arthur. *Bravo, Minski*

Behavior – sharing

Albert, Burton. *Mine, yours, ours*
Allan, Jonathan. *Two by two by two*
Allan, Nicholas. *The bird*
Azaad, Meyer (Mahmud). *Half for you*

Banks, Kate (Katherine A.). *The bird, the monkey, and the snake in the jungle*
Beim, Jerrold. *The smallest boy in the class*
Berliner, Franz. *Wildebeest*
Bernard, Robin. *Juma and the honey-guild*
Boelts, Maribeth. *Little Bunny's cool tool set*
Brett, Jan. *Christmas trolls*
Brownridge, William Roy. *The final game*
Buckley, Helen Elizabeth. *Moonlight kite*
Caudill, Rebecca. *A pocketful of cricket*
Cleveland-Peck, Patricia. *City cat, country cat*
Cohen, Miriam. *Don't eat too much turkey!*
Corey, Dorothy. *Everybody takes turns*
    We all share
Croll, Carolyn. *Too many babas*
Curry, Jane Louise. *The Christmas knight*
Davis, Aubrey. *The enormous potato*
Davis, Gibbs. *The other Emily*
Delacre, Lulu. *Nathan and Nicholas Alexander*
DeLage, Ida. *Beware! Beware! A witch won't share*
De Lynam, Alicia Garcia. *It's mine!*
Demarest, Chris L. *Morton and Sidney*
Devlin, Wende. *Cranberry Christmas*
Dowling, Paul. *Meg and Jack's new friends*
Dubois, Claude K. *He's my jumbo!*
Dubowski, Cathy East. *Snug Bug's play day*
Dunbar, Joyce. *Gander's pond*
Ehlert, Lois. *Top cat*
Ets, Marie Hall. *The cow's party*
Flory, Jane. *The unexpected grandchildren*
Forest, Heather. *Stone soup*
Forward, Toby. *Ben's Christmas carol*
Fox, Mem. *Feathers and fools*
French, Vivian. *Little Tiger goes shopping*
Gackenbach, Dick. *Claude the dog*
Galdone, Paul. *The magic porridge pot*
Gantschev, Ivan. *Where the moon lives*
Gelbard, Jane. *My sharing book*
Gervais, Bernadette. *Voyage under the stars*
Gikow, Louise. *Jim Henson's Muppets in What's fair is fair*
Glaser, Linda. *The borrowed Hanukkah latkes*
Goldin, Barbara Diamond. *Just enough is plenty*
Gould, Deborah. *Brendan's best-timed birthday*
Gretz, Susanna. *It's your turn, Roger*
Grosz, Peter. *The special gifts*
Hallinan, P. K. (Patrick K.). *Let's care about sharing!*
Heuck, Sigrid. *Who stole the apples?*
Hoberman, Mary Ann. *One of each*
Holder, Heidi. *Carmine the crow*
Hooker, Ruth. *Sara loves her big brother*
Houston, John A. *The bright yellow rope*
Hughes, Monica. *A handful of seeds*
Hutchins, Pat. *The doorbell rang*
    It's my birthday!
Jakob, Donna. *My new sandbox*
Johnston, Tony. *Mole and Troll trim the tree*
Kadono, Eiko. *Grandpa's soup*
Karon, Jan. *Miss Fannie's hat*
Kasza, Keiko. *The rat and the tiger*
Keats, Ezra Jack. *Peter's chair*
Klein, Norma. *Visiting Pamela*
Koehler, Phoebe. *Making room*
Lacoe, Addie. *Just not the same*
Lakin, Pat (Patricia). *Don't touch my room*
    Growing up
Lebrun, Claude. *Little Brown Bear does not want to eat*
    Little Brown Bear learns to share

Lesikin, Joan. *Down the road*
Lester, Helen. *The wizard, the fairy and the magic chicken*
Lindgren, Barbro. *Sam's car*
   Sam's cookie
Littledale, Freya. *The farmer in the soup*
Luttrell, Ida. *Three good blankets*
McAllister, Angela. *The battle of Sir Cob and Sir Filbert*
Maccarone, Grace. *Sharing time troubles*
Macdonald, Maryann. *Rosie and the poor rabbits*
Maiorano, Robert. *A little interlude*
Masurel, Claire. *Christmas is coming*
Mills, Lauren A. *The rag coat*
Munsch, Robert N. *We share everything!*
Murphy, Stuart J. *Give me half!*
Noble, June. *Two homes for Lynn*
Novak, Matt. *Mr. Floop's lunch*
O'Brien, Anne Sibley. *I want that!*
O'Connor, Jane. *Kate skates*
Oram, Hiawyn. *Mine!*
Ormerod, Jan. *101 things to do with a baby*
Palazzo-Craig, Janet. *Muffy and Fluffy*
Parkinson, Kathy. *The enormous turnip*
Paterson, Bettina. *Bun's birthday*
Peck, Jan. *The giant carrot*
Pfister, Marcus. *The rainbow fish*
Pinkwater, Daniel Manus. *Doodle flute*
Porte, Barbara Ann. *Harry's visit*
Rankin, Joan. *The little cat and the greedy old woman*
Rathmann, Peggy. *Officer Buckle and Gloria*
Riddell, Chris. *Ben and the bear*
Ring, Elizabeth. *Some stuff*
Rosen, Michael (1946-). *This is our house*
Russo, Marisabina. *The big brown box*
Rylant, Cynthia. *Birthday presents*
Sage, Chris. *That's mine, that's yours*
Sawyer, Ruth. *The remarkable Christmas of the cobbler's sons*
Sharmat, Marjorie Weinman. *The trip*
Sherman, Ivan. *I do not like it when my friend comes to visit*
Siomades, Lorianne. *A place to bloom*
Smalls-Hector, Irene. *Because you're lucky*
Smith, Wendy. *The lonely, only mouse*
Spinelli, Eileen. *Thanksgiving at Tappletons'*
Spurr, Elizabeth. *The biggest birthday cake in the world*
Stadler, John. *Gorman and the treasure chest*
Stage, Mads. *The greedy blackbird*
Stanek, Muriel. *My little foster sister*
Stewart, Paul. *The birthday presents*
Swartz, Nancy Sohn. *In our image*
Turkle, Brinton. *Rachel and Obadiah*
Vigna, Judith. *The hiding house*
Vincent, Gabrielle. *Bravo, Ernest and Celestine!*
   Ernest and Celestine's patchwork quilt
Waber, Bernard. *Bernard*
Wahl, Jan. *Mrs. Owl and Mr. Pig*
Wallner, Alexandra. *An Alcott family Christmas*
Walsh, Jill Paton. *Connie came to play*
Watson, Clyde. *Tom Fox and the apple pie*
Watts, Mabel (Pizzey). *Something for you, something for me*
Weninger, Brigitte. *Merry Christmas, Davy!*
Weston, Martha. *Bea's four bears*
Wezel, Peter. *The good bird*
Wilson, Christopher Bernard. *Hobnob*
Winthrop, Elizabeth. *That's mine*

Wolff, Ferida. *The emperor's garden*
Wright, Josephine Lord. *Cotton Cat and Martha Mouse*
Yolen, Jane. *Spider Jane*
Ziefert, Harriet. *Me, too! Me, too!*
   Rabbit and Hare divide an apple
Zolotow, Charlotte (Shapiro). *The new friend*

Behavior – solitude

Alborough, Jez. *Cuddly Dudley*
Bennett, Rainey. *The secret hiding place*
Bulla, Clyde Robert. *Keep running, Allen!*
Burdick, Margaret. *Sara Raccoon and the secret place*
Carrick, Carol. *Sleep out*
Dragonwagon, Crescent. *Katie in the morning*
   When light turns into night
Ehrlich, Amy. *The everyday train*
Goennel, Heidi. *Sometimes I like to be alone*
Hall, Donald. *The man who lived alone*
Hallinan, P. K. (Patrick K.). *Just being alone*
Hayes, Geoffrey. *Bear by himself*
Henkes, Kevin. *All alone*
Huck, Charlotte S. *Secret places*
Keller, Beverly. *Pimm's place*
Keyser, Marcia. *Roger on his own*
Luttrell, Ida. *Lonesome Lester*
Morris, Jill. *The boy who painted the sun*
Reesink, Marijke. *The princess who always ran away*
Schertle, Alice. *In my treehouse*
Stubbs, Joanna. *Happy Bear's day*
Sweetland, Nancy. *God's quiet things*
Tresselt, Alvin R. *I saw the sea come in*
Yezback, Steven A. *Pumpkinseeds*

Behavior – stealing

Ada, Alma Flor. *The gold coin*
Ahlberg, Janet. *Jeremiah in the dark wood*
Alborough, Jez. *It's the bear*
Aylesworth, Jim. *Hanna's hog*
Barr, Cathrine. *Hound dog's bone*
Barton, Byron. *The wee little woman*
Brennan, Patricia D. *Hitchety hatchety up I go!*
Brett, Jan. *Christmas trolls*
Carlson, Nancy L. *Arnie and the stolen markers*
   Loudmouth George and the sixth-grade bully
Cass, Joan E. *The cat thief*
Cate, Rikki. *A cat's tale*
Christian, Mary Blount. *The doggone mystery*
   The green thumb thief
Cohn, Janice I. *"Why did it happen?"*
Cole, Joanna. *The secret box*
Collington, Peter. *The angel and the soldier boy*
Cooper, Jacqueline. *Angus and the Mona Lisa*
De Gerez, Toni. *Louhi, witch of North Farm*
De Paola, Tomie (Thomas Anthony). *Bill and Pete go down the Nile*
Devlin, Wende. *Cranberry Halloween*
Dodd, Lynley. *The apple tree*
Dyke, John. *Pigwig*
Enderle, Judith (Ann) Ross. *Nell Nugget and the cow caper*
Euvremer, Teryl. *The thieves of Peck's pocket*
Fagan, Cary. *Gogol's coat*
Farmer, Nancy. *Runnery granary*
Fine, Edith Hope. *Under the lemon moon*
The firebird, ill. by Reg Cartwright
The firebird, ill. by Francesca Crespi

The firebird, ill. by Demi
The firebird, adapt. and ill. by Rachel Isadora
The firebird, ill. by Moira Kemp
The firebird, ill. by Kris Waldherr
The firebird, ill. by Boris Zvorykin
Foulds, Elfrida Vipont. *The elephant and the bad baby*
Freschet, Berniece. *Owl in the garden*
Ginsburg, Mirra. *Striding slippers*
Goodall, John S. *Paddy to the rescue*
Hare, Norma Q. *Mystery at mouse house*
Helldorfer, M. C. (Mary Claire). *The darling boys*
Hennessy, B. G. (Barbara G.). *The missing tarts*
Hogrogian, Nonny. *Rooster brother*
Hooks, William H. *The rainbow ribbon*
Kimmel, Eric A. *The tale of Ali Baba and the forty thieves*
Kroll, Steven. *Amanda and the giggling ghost*
Moffatt, Judith. *Who stole the cookies?*
Moore, Inga. *Fifty red night-caps*
Murphy, Pat. *Pigasus*
My first Raggedy Ann, Raggedy Ann's wishing pebble
Pyle, Howard. *The Swan Maiden*
Ross, Tony. *Hugo and the man who stole colors*
Tompert, Ann. *The hungry black bag*
Yolen, Jane. *Piggins*

Behavior – talking to strangers

Bahr, Amy C. *It's ok to say no*
Berenstain, Stan. *The Berenstain bears learn about strangers*
Boegehold, Betty. *Hurray for Pippa!*
Bradman, Tony. *Look out, he's behind you*
Bruna, Dick. *Dick Bruna's Little Red Riding Hood*
Chlad, Dorothy. *Strangers*
Choi, Yangsook. *The sun girl and the moon boy*
Conover, Chris. *Mother Goose and the sly fox*
Davoll, Barbara. *Dusty Mole, private eye*
De Regniers, Beatrice Schenk. *Red Riding Hood*
Emberley, Michael. *Ruby*
Ernst, Lisa Campbell. *Little Red Riding Hood*
Girard, Linda Walvoord. *Who is a stranger, and what should I do?*
Grimm, Jacob. *Little red cap*
  Little Red Riding Hood, ill. by Frank E. Aloise
  Little Red Riding Hood, ill. by Gwen Connelly
  Little Red Riding Hood, ill. by Paul Galdone
  Little Red Riding Hood, ill. by John S. Goodall
  Little Red Riding Hood, ill. by Trina Schart Hyman
  Little Red Riding Hood, ill. by Mireille Levert
  Little Red Riding Hood, ill. by Jean-François Martin
  Little Red Riding Hood, ill. by David M. McPhail
  Little Red Riding Hood, ill. by Bernadette Watts
Hooks, William H. *The monster from the sea*
Joyce, Irma. *Never talk to strangers*
Keller, Irene. *Benjamin Rabbit and the stranger danger*
Marshall, James. *Red Riding Hood*
Meyer, Linda D. *Safety zone*
Morris, Ann. *The Little Red Riding Hood rebus book*
Petty, Kate. *Being careful with strangers*
Potter, Beatrix. *The tale of Little Pig Robinson*
Raschka, Christopher. *Elizabeth imagined an iceberg*
Vogel, Carole Garbuny. *The dangers of strangers*
Wood, Audrey. *Heckedy Peg*
Ziefert, Harriet. *Little Red Riding Hood*

Behavior – tardiness

Axelrod, Amy. *Pigs on a blanket*
Boyd, Selma. *I met a polar bear*
Burningham, John. *John Patrick Norman McHennessy - the boy who was always late*
Dalmais, Anne-Marie. *Danny the duck*
Edwards, Pamela Duncan. *The grumpy morning*
Grossman, Bill. *The guy who was five minutes late*
Herman, Gail. *Ice cream soup*
Hines, Anna Grossnickle. *What Joe saw*
Hutchins, Pat. *Little pink pig*
Johns, Linda. *Sarah's secret plan*
Kraus, Robert. *Here comes Tardy Toad*
Lamont, Priscilla. *Out to lunch*
O'Donnell, Peter. *Carnegie's excuse*
Sykes, Julie. *Hurry, Santa!*
Teague, Mark. *The secret shortcut*
Tidd, Louise Vitellaro. *I'll do it later*
Wallace-Brodeur, Ruth. *Home by five*
Willis, Jeanne. *Sloth's shoes*

Behavior – toilet training see Toilet training

Behavior – trickery

Aardema, Verna. *Anansi finds a fool*
  Borreguita and the coyote
  Jackal's flying lesson
  Rabbit makes a monkey of lion
Abolafia, Yossi. *Fox tale*
Æsop. *Three Æsop fox fables*
  Wolf! Wolf!
Alexander, Lloyd. *The house Gobbaleen*
Allard, Harry. *There's a party at Mona's tonight*
Althea. *Jeremy Mouse and cat*
Annett, Cora. *When the porcupine moved in*
Aylesworth, Jim. *Hanna's hog*
Baron, Alan. *Red Fox dances*
Bartos-Hoppner, Barbara. *The pied piper of Hamelin*
Berry, James. *Don't leave an elephant to go and chase a bird*
Bingham, Mindy. *My way Sally*
Biro, Val. *The pied piper of Hamelin*
Bishop, Gavin. *Maui and the sun*
Boegehold, Betty. *Small Deer's magic tricks*
Bowden, Joan Chase. *Strong John*
Brown, Marc Tolon. *Arthur tricks the tooth fairy*
Brown, Marcia. *The blue jackal*
Browning, Robert. *The pied piper of Hamelin*, ill. by Patricia and Robin DeWitt
  The pied piper of Hamelin, ill. by Kate Greenaway
  The pied piper of Hamelin, ill. by Anatoly Ivanov
  The pied piper of Hamelin, ill. by Errol Le Cain
  The pied piper of Hamelin, ill. by Drahos Zak
Burdett, Lois. *Twelfth night*
Calhoun, Mary. *The pixy and the lazy housewife*
Carey, Valerie Scho. *The devil and mother Crump*
  Quail song
Carrick, Carol. *Norman fools the tooth fairy*
Chicken Little. *Chicken Licken*, ill. by Jutta Ash
  Chicken Licken, ill. by Gavin Bishop
  Chicken Little, ill. by Sally Hobson
  Henny Penny, ill. by Emily Bolam
  Henny Penny, ill. by Stephen Butler
  Henny Penny, ill. by Paul Galdone
  Henny Penny, ill. by William Stobbs
  Henny-Penny, ill. by Jane Wattenberg
  The sky is falling

The story of Chicken Licken
Christelow, Eileen. *Jerome the babysitter*
   Olive and the magic hat
   The robbery at the diamond dog diner
Cohen, Caron Lee. *Sally Ann Thunder Ann Whirlwind Crockett*
Cox, Judy. *Rabbit pirates*
Craig, Helen. *A welcome for Annie*
Cushman, Doug. *Possum stew*
DeFelice, Cynthia C. *Clever crow*
De Paola, Tomie (Thomas Anthony). *The unicorn and the moon*
DeSpain, Pleasant. *The dancing turtle*
Dinardo, Jeffrey. *The wolf who cried boy*
Dines, Glen. *Gilly and the wicharoo*
Domanska, Janina. *The best of the bargain*
Duff, Maggie (Margaret K.). *Dancing turtle*
Duvoisin, Roger Antoine. *Petunia, I love you*
Elkin, Benjamin. *Gillespie and the guards*
Euvremer, Teryl. *Triple whammy*
Evans, Katherine. *The boy who cried wolf*
Gage, Wilson. *The crow and Mrs. Gaddy*
Galdone, Paul. *A strange servant*
Goble, Paul. *Iktomi and the buffalo skull*
   Iktomi and the buzzard
   Iktomi and the coyote
   Iktomi and the ducks
Goldman, Dara. *There's no such thing!*
Grimm, Jacob. *The horse, the fox, and the lion*
Han, Oki S. *Sir Whong and the golden pig*
Hausman, Gerald. *Coyote walks on two legs*
Hayward, Linda. *All stuck up*
   Hello, house!
Helldorfer, M. C. (Mary Claire). *Jack, Skinny Bones, and the golden pancakes*
Isenberg, Barbara. *Albert the running bear gets the jitters*
Jennings, Michael. *Robin Goodfellow and the giant dwarf*
Johnson, Paul Brett. *A perfect pork stew*
Johnston, Tony. *Alice Nizzy Nazzy, the Witch of Santa Fe*
   The badger and the magic fan
Joyce, James. *The cat and the devil*
Kellogg, Steven (Stephen). *Chicken Little*
Kimmel, Eric A. *Anansi and the moss-covered rock*
   Anansi and the talking melon
   Anansi goes fishing
   Baba Yaga
Kitamura, Satoshi. *Sheep in wolves' clothing*
Kraus, Robert. *Come out and play, little mouse*
   The king's trousers
   Strudwick, a sheep in wolf's clothing
Latimer, Jim. *The Irish piper*
   James Bear and the goose gathering
Luenn, Nancy. *Song for the ancient forest*
McAfee, Annalena. *The visitors who came to stay*
McDermott, Gerald. *Raven*
   Tim O'Toole and the wee folk
   Zomo the rabbit
MacDonald, Amy. *Please, Malese!*
MacDonald, Margaret Read. *Pickin' peas*
Magnus, Erica. *The boy and the devil*
Mahy, Margaret. *The great white man-eating shark*
Manson, Christopher. *Here begins the tale of the marvellous blue mouse*
Mayer, Marianna. *The black horse*
Mayer, Mercer. *The pied piper of Hamelin*
Mirkovic, Irene. *The greedy shopkeeper*

Mogensen, Jan. *The tiger's breakfast*
Mollel, Tololwa M. (Tololwa Marti). *Ananse's feast*
   The flying tortoise
   Shadow dance
Mora, Pat. *The race of toad and deer*
Muller, Robin. *Mollie Whuppie and the giant*
Munsch, Robert N. *Mmm, cookies!*
Nikola-Lisa, W. *The dancin' fox*
Nordqvist, Sven. *The fox hunt*
O'Callahan, Jay. *Tulips*
Oppenheim, Joanne. *Mrs. Peloki's substitute*
Oram, Hiawyn. *Baba Yaga and the wise doll*
Parker, Nancy Winslow. *The crocodile under Louis Finneberg's bed*
Potter, Beatrix. *The pie and the patty-pan*
   The story of Miss Moppet
Rockwell, Anne F. *The gollywhopper egg*
Root, Phyllis. *Aunt Nancy and Old Man Trouble*
Ross, Tony. *The boy who cried wolf*
San Souci, Robert D. *Feathertop*
Shannon, Margaret. *Gullible's troubles*
Smith, Mavis. *A snake mistake*
Snyder, Dianne. *The boy of the three-year nap*
Souhami, Jessica. *No dinner!*
Steig, William. *Solomon the rusty nail*
Stevens, Janet. *Tops and bottoms*
Stevenson, James. *Emma*
   Fried feathers for Thanksgiving
Strete, Craig Kee. *How the Indians bought the farm*
Szekeres, Cyndy. *Suppertime for Frieda Fuzzypaws*
Temple, Frances. *Tiger soup*
Thayer, Jane. *The clever raccoon*
Turkle, Brinton. *Do not open*
Ungerer, Tomi. *The beast of Monsieur Racine*
Varga, Judy. *The mare's egg*
Wegen, Ron. *Billy Gorilla*
Wild, Robin. *Spot's dogs and the alley cats*
Wildsmith, Brian. *Python's party*
Wolf, Gita. *The very hungry lion*
Wolkstein, Diane. *Bouki dances the Kokioko*
Wright, Jill. *The old woman and the Willy Nilly Man*
Yep, Laurence. *The man who tricked a ghost*
Yerxa, Leo. *A fish tale, or, The little one that got away*
Young, Ed (Edward). *Monkey King*
Zemach, Harve. *The tricks of Master Dabble*
Zimelman, Nathan. *The great adventure of Wo Ti*

Behavior – unnoticed, unseen

Bishop, Bonnie. *No one noticed Ralph*
Jones, Diana Wynne. *Yes, dear*
Kroll, Steven. *The candy witch*
Krudop, Walter Lyon. *Something is growing*
Levinson, Riki. *Me baby!*
Mwenye Hadithi. *Crafty chameleon*
Scott, Ann Herbert. *Hi!*
Udry, Janice May. *How I faded away*

Behavior – wishing

Aliki. *The wish workers*
Allen, Pamela. *I wish I had a pirate suit*
   A lion in the night
Ayer, Jacqueline. *A wish for little sister*
Baker, Betty. *My sister says*
Baruch, Dorothy. *I would like to be a pony and other wishes*
Bentley, Nancy. *I've got your nose!*
Benton, Robert. *Don't ever wish for a 7-foot bear*

Beresford, Elisabeth. *Jack and the magic stove*
Berson, Harold. *Truffles for lunch*
Bodsworth, Nan. *Monkey business*
Bos, Burny. *Ollie the elephant*
Bowman, Peter. *I wish I were big*
Brandenberg, Franz. *I wish I was sick, too!*
Breathed, Berkeley. *A wish for wings that work*
Brenner, Barbara A. *Rosa and Marco and the three wishes*
Brett, Jan. *Fritz and the beautiful horses*
Bright, Robert. *Me and the bears*
Bruchac, Joseph. *Gluskabe and the four wishes*
Bruna, Dick. *The happy apple*
Buehner, Caralyn. *Fanny's dream*
Bush, John. *The fish who could wish*
Bush, Timothy. *Benjamin McFadden and the robot babysitter*
Butcher, Julia. *The sheep and the rowan tree*
Carlstrom, Nancy White. *Wishing at dawn in summer*
Chapman, Carol. *Barney Bipple's magic dandelions*
Chess, Victoria. *Poor Esmé*
Christensen, Jack. *The forgotten rainbow*
Clifton, Lucille. *Three wishes*, ill. by Stephanie Douglas
    Three wishes, ill. by Michael Hays
Coco, Eugene Bradley. *The wishing well*
Cole, Joanna. *Mixed-up magic*
Coopersmith, Jerome. *A Chanukah fable for Christmas*
Damjan, Mischa. *The big squirrel and the little rhinoceros*
Daugherty, Charles Michael. *Wisher*
Davis, Karen. *Star light, star bright*
Demi. *The stonecutter*
Dragonwagon, Crescent. *Coconut Diana, maybe*
Dunbar, Joyce. *The pig who wished*
Duncan, Lois. *The longest hair in the world*
Dupré, Rick. *The wishing chair*
Elborn, Andrew. *Bird Adalbert*
Erlbruch, Wolf. *Leonard*
Fox, Mem. *Possum magic*
Friedrich, Priscilla. *The wishing well in the woods*
Fuchshuber, Annegert. *The wishing hat*
Gackenbach, Dick. *Hattie rabbit*
Gliori, Debi. *Willie Bear and the Wish Fish*
Greaves, Margaret. *The star horse*
Greenberg, Polly. *Oh, Lord, I wish I was a buzzard*
Griffith, Helen V. *Emily and the enchanted frog*
Haas, Irene. *The Maggie B*
Haddon, Mark. *Toni and the tomato soup*
Hale, Irina. *Small big bad boy*
Harshman, Marc. *A little excitement*
Heller, Nicholas. *Woody*
Hermes, Patricia. *When snow lay soft on the mountain*
Himmelman, John. *Amanda and the witch switch*
Hines, Anna Grossnickle. *Moon's wish*
Hoban, Lillian. *It's really Christmas*
Howe, James. *I wish I were a butterfly*
Hru, Dakari. *Joshua's Masai mask*
Iwasaki, Chihiro. *The birthday wish*
Jacobs, Kate. *A sister's wish*
Jaffe, Rona. *Last of the wizards*
Janosch. *Just one apple*
Kay, Helen. *An egg is for wishing*
Kent, Jack. *Knee-high Nina*
Kojima, Naomi. *The flying grandmother*
Kovalski, Maryann. *Pizza for breakfast*

Krauss, Ruth. *Mama, I wish I was snow. Child, you'd be very cold*
Krensky, Stephen. *A good knight's sleep*
Kreye, Walter. *The giant from the little island*
Lasell, Fen. *Michael grows a wish*
Laurencin, Geneviève. *I wish I were*
Leemis, Ralph. *Smart dog*
Lewis, J. Patrick. *At the wish of the fish*
Lillegard, Dee. *My yellow ball*
Littledale, Freya. *The snow child*
Lobato, Arcadio. *Just one wish*
McAllister, Angela. *The Christmas wish*
    Sleepy Ella
McClintock, Barbara. *Molly and the magic wishbone*
McKee, David. *The monster and the teddy bear*
McKissack, Patricia C. *King Midas and his gold*
Maris, Ron. *I wish I could fly*
Mark, Jan. *The Midas touch*
Mayer, Marianna. *The spirit of the blue light*
Mike, Jan M. *Juan Bobo and the horse of seven colors*
Mitra, Annie. *Penguin moon*
Modesitt, Jeanne. *Mama, if you had a wish*
Mollel, Tololwa M. (Tololwa Marti). *Big boy*
Munari, Bruno. *The elephant's wish*
Munsch, Robert N. *Millicent and the wind*
    Wait and see
Murphy, Mary. *Caterpillar's wish*
My first Raggedy Ann, Raggedy Ann's wishing pebble
Myers, Bernice. *Sidney Rella and the glass sneaker*
Orbach, Ruth. *Please send a panda*
Osborne, Mary Pope. *Moonhorse*, ill. by David McPhail
    Moonhorse, ill. by S. M. Saelig
Ostheeren, Ingrid. *Coriander's Easter adventure*
Paterson, Diane. *If I were a toad*
Perkins, Al. *King Midas and the golden touch*
Pfister, Marcus. *Make a wish, Honey Bear!*
Polacco, Patricia. *Luba and the wren*
Power, Barbara. *I wish Laura's mommy was my mommy*
Prater, John. *The gift*
Proimos, James. *Joe's wish*
Pulver, Robin. *Alicia's tutu*
Ratnett, Michael. *Jenny's bear*
Recknagel, Friedrich. *Meg's wish*
Reed, Kit. *When we dream*
Riddell, Chris. *The wish factory*
Rodriguez, Anita. *Jamal and the angel*
Rosen, Winifred. *Henrietta and the day of the iguana*
Sachs, Marilyn. *Fleet-footed Florence*
Schweninger, Ann. *Birthday wishes*
Seignobosc, Françoise. *Jeanne-Marie counts her sheep*
Seuss, Dr. *I wish that I had duck feet*
    Please try to remember the first of Octember!
Sewell, Helen Moore. *Peggy and the pony*
Shecter, Ben. *The discontented mother*
Shepard, Aaron. *The gifts of Wali Dad*
Shields, Carol Diggory. *I wish my brother was a dog*
Shimin, Symeon. *I wish there were two of me*
Simon, Norma. *I wish I had my father*
Stevenson, James. *The wish card ran out!*
Storr, Catherine (Cole). *King Midas*
Tan, Amy. *The moon lady*
Thaler, Mike. *Hippo lemonade*
Tobias, Tobi. *Jane wishing*
Tornqvist, Rita. *The Christmas carp*
Turkle, Brinton. *Do not open*
Turnbull, Ann. *The tapestry cats*
Varga, Judy. *Janko's wish*

Vigna, Judith. *I wish my daddy didn't drink so much*
Waber, Bernard. *You're a little kid with a big heart*
Watson, Pauline. *Wriggles, the little wishing pig*
Weisgard, Leonard. *Who dreams of cheese?*
Willard, Nancy. *The marzipan moon*
Williams, Barbara. *Someday, said Mitchell*
Williams, Suzanne. *My dog never says please*
Wolkstein, Diane. *The magic wings*
Wood, Audrey. *Jubal's wish*
Wooding, Sharon L. *Arthur's Christmas wish*
Wooldridge, Connie Nordhielm. *Wicked Jack*
Zemach, Margot. *The three wishes*
Zimelman, Nathan. *To sing a song as big as Ireland*
Zolotow, Charlotte (Shapiro). *Someday*

Behavior – worrying

Benedek, Elissa P. *The secret worry*
Boelts, Maribeth. *Little Bunny's preschool countdown*
Brown, Marc Tolon. *Arthur's underwear*
Carlson, Nancy L. *What if it never stops raining?*
Delton, Judy. *The elephant in Duck's garden*
    On a picnic
Devlin, Wende. *Cranberry Easter*
Edwards, Pamela Duncan. *The worrywarts*
Erlbruch, Wolf. *Mrs. Meyer, the bird*
Gackenbach, Dick. *Where are Momma, Poppa, and Sister June?*
Gorog, Judith. *Zilla Sasparilla and the mud baby*
Greene, Carol. *The golden locket*
Gross, Alan. *Sometimes I worry . . .*
    What if the teacher calls on me?
Hanson, Regina. *The tangerine tree*
Hazen, Barbara Shook. *Wally the worry-warthog*
Heide, Florence Parry. *Timothy Twinge*
Herman, Charlotte. *My mother didn't kiss me goodnight*
Komaiko, Leah. *Where can Daniel be?*
Lasky, Kathryn. *Lunch bunnies*
Lerner, Harriet Goldhor. *What's so terrible about swallowing an apple seed?*
Levitin, Sonia. *A piece of home*
    A single speckled egg
Lindenbaum, Pija. *Else-Marie and her seven little daddies*
MacDonald, Maryann. *Sam's worries*
Magorian, Michelle. *Who's going to take care of me?*
Marshall, James. *Portly McSwine*
Segal, Lore. *The story of old Mrs. Brubeck and how she looked for trouble and where she found him*
Sewall, Marcia. *The cobbler's song*
Sharmat, Marjorie Weinman. *Lucretia the unbearable*
    Thornton, the worrier
Tyler, Linda Wagner. *Waiting for mom*
Waddell, Martin. *Mimi's Christmas*
Williams, Marcia. *Not a worry in the world*

Being different *see* Character traits – being different

Belize *see* Foreign lands – Belize

Bible *see* Religion

Bicycling *see* Sports – bicycling

Bigotry *see* Prejudice

Birds

Aardema, Verna. *Jackal's flying lesson*
Ada, Alma Flor. *The malachite palace*
Adoff, Arnold. *Birds*
Alborough, Jez. *Beaky*
Alexander, Martha G. *Out! Out! Out!*
Aliki. *My visit to the zoo*
    The wish workers
Allred, Mary. *Grandmother Poppy and the funny-looking bird*
Anderson, Lonzo. *Mr. Biddle and the birds*
Anholt, Laurence. *Billy and the big new school*
Arnold, Caroline. *Five nests*
Arnosky, Jim. *Crinkleroot's 25 birds every child should know*
    Mouse writing
Aroner, Miriam. *The kingdom of singing birds*
Asch, Frank. *Baby Bird's first nest*
    Bear's bargain
    Moonbear
    Moonbear's dream
    Moonbear's pet
    Mooncake
Ash, Jutta. *Wedding birds*
Ayer, Jacqueline. *A wish for little sister*
Azaad, Meyer (Mahmud). *Half for you*
Bailey, Jill. *Eyes*
    Feet
    Mouths
Baker, Jeffrey J. W. *Patterns of nature*
Bancroft, Henrietta. *Animals in winter*
Bang, Betsy. *Tuntuni the tailor bird*
Banks, Kate (Katherine A.). *The bird, the monkey, and the snake in the jungle*
Barber, Antonia. *The enchanter's daughter*
Bash, Barbara. *Urban roosts*
Baskin, Leonard. *Hosie's aviary*
Baum, Willi. *Birds of a feather*
Beisert, Heide Helene. *Poor fish*
Berends, Polly Berrien. *I heard said the bird*
Berliner, Franz. *Miserable Marabou*
Bernard, Robin. *Juma and the honey-guild*
Bernhard, Durga. *What's Maggie up to?*
Borden, Beatrice Brown. *Wild animals of Africa*
Boyle, Constance. *Little Owl and the weed*
Bright, Robert. *Georgie and the baby birds*
Brillhart, Julie. *The dino expert*
Brock, Emma Lillian. *The birds' Christmas tree*
Brodzinsky, Anne Braff. *The mulberry bird*
Browne, Philippa-Alys. *A gaggle of geese*
Browne, Vee. *Monster birds*
Bruchac, Joseph. *The great ball game*
Bruna, Dick. *The little bird*
    Little bird tweet
Brunhoff, Laurent de. *Babar's visit to Bird Island*
Burstein, Fred. *Anna's rain*
Burton, Robert. *The egg*
Cannon, Janell. *Stellaluna*
    Stellaluna: a pop-up book and mobile
Chönz, Selina. *Florina and the wild bird*
Christelow, Eileen. *The robbery at the diamond dog diner*
Climo, Shirley. *King of the birds*
Coatsworth, Elizabeth. *Under the green willow*
Colby, C. B. (Carroll Burleigh). *Who lives there?*

Who went there?
Cole, Michael. *Head in the sand*
Conklin, Gladys. *If I were a bird*
Cortesi, Wendy W. *Explore a spooky swamp*
Cousins, Lucy. *Portly's hat*
Cowley, Stewart. *"Tweet, tweet, tweet"*
Cristini, Ermanno. *In the woods*
Cronin, Doreen. *Click, clack, moo*
Cross, Diana Harding. *Some birds have funny names*
Cross, Genevieve. *A trip to the yard*
Cutler, Ivor. *Doris*
Dalmais, Anne-Marie. *The butterfly book of birds*
Damjan, Mischa. *Goodbye little bird*
Darby, Gene. *What is a bird?*
Darling, Kathy (Mary Kathleen). *Arctic babies*
Day, David. *King of the woods*
Delaney, Ned. *A worm for dinner*
Demarest, Chris L. *Benedict finds a home*
Dobson, Clive. *Fred's TV*
Dodd, Lynley. *Slinky Malinki, open the door*
Dunbar, Joyce. *Baby bird*
    Eggday
Eastman, P. D. (Philip D.). *Are you my mother?*
    Flap your wings
Egan, Tim. *Distant Feathers*
Ehlert, Lois. *Cuckoo: a Mexican folktale = Cucú: un cuento folklórico mexicano*
    Feathers for lunch
Elbling, Peter. *Aria*
Elborn, Andrew. *Bird Adalbert*
Elzbieta. *Brave Babette and sly Tom*
Erlbruch, Wolf. *Mrs. Meyer, the bird*
Fender, Kay. *Odette!*
Fisher, Aileen Lucia. *We went looking*
Fitzsimons, Cecilia. *My first birds*
Flanders, Michael. *Creatures great and small*
Fleming, Candace. *When Agnes caws*
Flora. *Feathers like a rainbow*
Florian, Douglas. *On the wing*
Fowler, Allan. *It could still be a bird*
Freeman, Don. *Fly high, fly low*
French, Fiona. *The blue bird*
Freschet, Berniece. *The little woodcock*
    Owl in the garden
Friskey, Margaret (Margaret Richards). *Birds we know*
Fujita, Tamao. *The boy and the bird*
Gans, Roma. *How do birds find their way?*
    Hummingbirds in the garden
    When birds change their feathers
Ginsburg, Mirra. *The old man and his birds*
Givens, Janet Eaton. *Just two wings*
Goble, Paul. *The great race of the birds and animals*
Goode, Molly. *Mama loves*
Greeley, Valerie. *Where's my share?*
Greene, Ellin. *Ling-li and the phoenix fairy*
Grimm, Jacob. *The bear and the kingbird*
    The golden bird, ill. by Isabelle Brent
    The golden bird, ill. by Sandro Nardini
Hader, Berta Hoerner. *Mister Billy's gun*
Hague, Kathleen. *The legend of the Veery bird*
Haley, Gail E. *Birdsong*
Hautzig, Deborah. *Get well, Granny Bird*
Hawkinson, Lucy (Ozone). *Birds in the sky*
Heller, Ruth. *How to hide a parakeet and other birds*
    How to hide a whip-poor-will and other birds
Helweg, Hans. *Farm animals*
Henley, Claire. *Quack, quack*

Hindley, Judy. *Ten bright eyes*
Hines, Anna Grossnickle. *Miss Emma's wild garden*
Hirschi, Ron. *Faces in the forest*
    What is a bird?
    Where do birds live?
    Who lives in . . . the forest?
Hoban, Lillian. *No, no, Sammy Crow*
Hoban, Tana. *A children's zoo*
Hooks, William H. *Feed me!*
Hurd, Edith Thacher. *Look for a bird*
Ipcar, Dahlov. *Bright barnyard*
    "The song of the day birds" and "The song of the night birds"
Janovitz, Marilyn. *Look out, bird!*
Jenny, Anne. *The fantastic story of King Brioche the First*
John, Naomi. *Roadrunner*
Johnson, Angela. *Mama bird, baby birds*
Johnston, Tony. *The old lady and the birds*
Jonas, Ann. *Bird talk*
Kamal, Aleph. *The bird who was an elephant*
Kantrowitz, Mildred. *When Violet died*
Kasza, Keiko. *A mother for Choco*
Kaufmann, John. *Birds are flying*
    Flying giants of long ago
Kellogg, Steven (Stephen). *Aster Aardvark's alphabet adventures*
Kimmel, Eric A. *The birds' gift*
Kishida, Eriko. *The lion and the bird's nest*
Kleven, Elisa. *The lion and the little red bird*
Krauss, Ruth. *The happy egg*
Kroll, Virginia L. *Sweet Magnolia*
Kuchalla, Susan. *Birds*
Kumin, Maxine W. *Mittens in May*
Langton, Jane. *The queen's necklace*
Lavis, Steve. *Jump!*
Lent, Blair. *Ruby and Fred*
Lifton, Betty Jean. *Joji and the Amanojaku*
    Joji and the dragon
    Joji and the fog
Lionni, Leo. *Inch by inch*
    Tico and the golden wings
Lobato, Arcadio. *Paper bird*
Lubell, Winifred. *Rosalie, the bird market turtle*
Lyfick, Warren. *The little book of fowl jokes*
McCauley, Jane R. *Baby birds and how they grow*
McLerran, Alice. *The mountain that loved a bird*
McPhail, David M. *Farm morning*
Mallat, Kathy. *Brave bear*
Marshak, S. (Samuil). *The merry starlings*
Martchenko, Michael. *Bird feeder banquet*
Massie, Diane Redfield. *The baby beebee bird*
Mathers, Petra. *Lottie's new friend*
Mayer, Marianna. *The little jewel box*
Mayer, Mercer. *Two moral tales*
Mazzola, Frank. *Counting is for the birds*
Mead, Alice. *Billy and Emma*
Meddaugh, Susan. *Tree of birds*
Meeker, Clare Hodgson. *A tale of two rice birds*
Millhouse, Nicholas. *Blue-footed booby*
Mitchell, Adrian. *Twice my size*
Mollel, Tololwa M. (Tololwa Marti). *A promise to the sun*
    Song bird
Most, Bernard. *Zoodles*
Munari, Bruno. *Bruno Munari's zoo*
    Tic, Tac and Toc
Myers, Christopher A. *Sparrows*

Neitzel, Shirley. *The house I'll build for the wrens*
Nesbit, Edith. *Cockatoucan*
Ness, Evaline. *Pavo and the princess*
Norman, Charles. *The hornbean tree and other poems*
Oana, Kay D. *Robbie and the raggedy scarecrow*
O Huigin, Sean. *King of the birds*
Okimoto, Jean Davies. *No dear, not here*
Olds, Elizabeth. *Feather mountain*
Oppenheim, Joanne. *Have you seen birds?*
Paraskevas, Betty. *Junior Kroll and Company*
Parnall, Peter. *Alfalfa Hill*
Parsons, Alexandra. *Amazing birds*
Paulsen, Gary. *Canoe days*
Pearson, Susan. *Lenore's big break*
Pearson, Tracey Campbell. *The purple hat*
Pedersen, Judy. *The tiny patient*
Peet, Bill (William Bartlett). *The kweeks of Kooka-tumdee*
   The pinkish, purplish, bluish egg
Peters, Lisa Westberg. *This way home*
Pirotta, Saviour. *Little bird*
Pomerantz, Charlotte. *Flap your wings and try*
Postgate, Oliver. *Noggin the king*
Potter, Beatrix. *The tale of Jemima Puddle-Duck and other farmyard tales*
Powell, Consie. *A bold carnivore*
Pratt, Kristin Joy. *A fly in the sky*
Ringgold, Faith. *Bonjour, Lonnie*
Rockwell, Anne F. *Honk honk!*
   Our yard is full of birds
Rohmann, Eric. *Time flies*
Rose, Gerald. *The bird garden*
Rossetti, Christina Georgina. *Fly away, fly away over the sea*
Rowe, John A. *Smudge*
Rylant, Cynthia. *The bird house*
Sayre, April Pulley. *If you should hear a honey guide*
Scamell, Ragnhild. *Who likes Wolfie?*
Schumacher, Claire. *Alto and Tango*
Scuderi, Lucia. *To fly*
Seidler, Rosalie. *Grumpus and the Venetian cat*
Selsam, Millicent E. *A first look at bird nests*
   A first look at owls, eagles and other hunters of the sky
Seuss, Dr. *Horton hatches the egg*
   Thidwick, the big-hearted moose
Seymour, Tres. *The gulls of the Edmund Fitzgerald*
Shulevitz, Uri. *What is a wise bird like you doing in a silly tale like this*
Simmons, Al. *Counting feathers*
Simple gifts
Sis, Peter. *Rainbow Rhino*
Smith, Lane. *Flying Jake*
Smith, William Jay. *Birds and beasts*
Snoopy on wheels
Stage, Mads. *The greedy blackbird*
Stanley, Diane. *Birdsong lullaby*
Stone, A. Harris. *The last free bird*
Tafuri, Nancy. *Will you be my friend?*
Taylor, Sydney. *Mr. Barney's beard*
Thornhill, Jan. *Wild in the city*
Troughton, Joanna. *How the birds changed their feathers*
Tusa, Tricia. *Maebelle's suitcase*
Twinem, Neecy. *In the air*
Van den Berg, Marinus. *The three birds*
Van Fleet, Matthew. *Fuzzy yellow ducklings*
Van Laan, Nancy. *The big fat worm*
Varley, Dimitry. *The whirly bird*
Velthuijs, Max. *Frog is frightened*

   The painter and the bird
Vyner, Sue. *The stolen egg*
Waechter, Friedrich Karl. *Three is company*
Wallis, Diz. *Battle of the beasts*
Walsh, Grahame L. *The goori goori bird*
Ward, Helen. *The king of the birds*
Watts, Barrie. *Bird's nest*
Watts, Bernadette. *The Christmas bird*
Weatherill, Stephen. *The very first Lucy Goose book*
West, Colin. *Have you seen the crocodile?*
Wezel, Peter. *The good bird*
   The naughty bird
Wildsmith, Brian. *Brian Wildsmith's birds*
Williams, Julie Stewart. *And the birds appeared*
Wolff, Ashley. *A year of birds*
Wood, A. J. *Beautiful birds*
Wood, Audrey. *Little Penguin's tale*
Yolen, Jane. *Bird watch*
   Spider Jane
Yoshida, Toshi. *Rhinoceros mother*
Ziefert, Harriet. *Happy Easter, Grandma!*
Zirkel, Lynn. *The shell dragon*
Zolotow, Charlotte (Shapiro). *Flocks of birds*

Birds – albatrosses

Cousteau Society. *Albatross*
Hoff, Syd. *Albert the albatross*

Birds – babies

Asch, Frank. *Baby Bird's first nest*

Birds – blackbirds

Duff, Maggie (Margaret K.). *Rum pum pum*
Murphy, Pat. *Pigasus*

Birds – bluejays

Angelo, Valenti. *The acorn tree*
Margolis, Richard J. *Big bear, spare that tree*
Newton, Patricia Montgomery. *The frog who drank the waters of the world*

Birds – boobys

Lewin, Betsy. *Booby hatch*

Birds – buzzards

Goble, Paul. *Iktomi and the buzzard*
Myers, Walter Dean. *How Mr. Monkey saw the whole world*
Sandburg, Helga. *Anna and the baby buzzard*
Wolkstein, Diane. *The cool ride in the sky*

Birds – canaries

Chase, Jan Brinckerhoff. *The golden song*
Foreman, Michael. *Cat and canary*
Freeman, Don. *Quiet! There's a canary in the library*
Heller, Wendy. *Clementine and the cage*
Nones, Eric Jon. *Canary prince*
Schneider, Antonie. *Good-bye, Vivi!*

Birds – cardinals

Galinsky, Ellen. *The baby cardinal*
Maloney, Peter. *Redbird at Rockefeller Center*

Preller, James. *Cardinal and sunflower*

Birds – chickens

Ada, Alma Flor. *The rooster who went to his uncle's
wedding*
Allamand, Pascale. *The pop rooster*
Allard, Harry. *I will not go to market today*
Allen, Pamela. *Fancy that!*
Ambrus, Victor G. *The little cockerel*
Auch, Mary Jane. *Bantam of the opera*
The Easter egg farm
Eggs mark the spot
Hen lake
Peeping Beauty
Aulaire, Ingri Mortenson d'. *Don't count your chicks*
Foxie, the singing dog
Back, Christine. *Chicken and egg*
Barber, Antonia. *Gemma and the baby chick*
Barbot, Daniel. *A bicycle for Rosaura*
Bassett, Jeni. *The chicks' trick*
Belpré, Pura. *Santiago*
Berkowitz, Linda. *Alfonse, where are you?*
Berquist, Grace. *Speckles goes to school*
Bishop, Adela. *The Easter wolf*
Bishop, Ann. *Chicken riddle*
Bond, Felicia. *Christmas in the chicken coop*
Bourgeois, Paulette. *Too many chickens*
Bourke, Linda. *Ethel's exceptional egg*
Boutwell, Edna. *Red rooster*
Brothers, Aileen. *Jiffy, Miss Boo and Mr. Roo*
Brown, Margaret Wise. *Little chicken*
Burton, Jane. *Chester the chick*
Chick
Carle, Eric. *The rooster who set out to see the world*
Rooster's off to see the world
Casey, Patricia. *Cluck cluck*
Quack quack
Cazet, Denys. *Lucky me*
Chaucer, Geoffrey. *Chanticleer and the fox*
Chicken Little. *Chicken Licken*, ill. by Jutta Ash
Chicken Licken, ill. by Gavin Bishop
Chicken Little, ill. by Sally Hobson
Henny Penny, ill. by Emily Bolam
Henny Penny, ill. by Stephen Butler
Henny Penny, ill. by Paul Galdone
Henny Penny, ill. by William Stobbs
Henny-Penny, ill. by Jane Wattenberg
The sky is falling
The story of Chicken Licken
Chukovskii, Kornei Ivanovich. *Good morning, chick*
Coerr, Eleanor. *The Josefina story quilt*
Coldrey, Jennifer. *The world of chickens*
Cole, Joanna. *A chick hatches*
Cole, Sheila. *The hen that crowed*
Conrad, Pam. *The rooster's gift*
Cousins, Lucy. *Hen on the farm*
Cowley, Stewart. *Little chick*
Dabcovich, Lydia. *Mrs. Huggins and her hen Han-
nah*
Dalmais, Anne-Marie. *Best bedtime stories of Mother
Hen*
Davenier, Christine. *Leon and Albertine*
Delaney, Ned. *Cosmic chickens*
Demi. *Cuddly chick*
Little chick chick
Denslow, Sharon Phillips. *Hazel's circle*
Dodds, Siobhan. *Elizabeth Hen*
Dumas, Philippe. *Caesar, cock of the village*

Dutton, Sandra. *The cinnamon hen's autumn day*
Edwards, Dorothy. *A wet Monday*
Edwards, Michelle. *Chicken Man*
Ehrhardt, Reinhold. *Kikeri*
Ernst, Lisa Campbell. *Zinnia and Dot*
Fatio, Louise. *The red bantam*
Firmin, Peter. *Chicken stew*
Foster, Karen Sharp. *Good night my little chicks =
Buenas noches mis pollitos*
Fowler, Richard. *Little Chick's big adventure*
Fox, Mem. *Hattie and the fox*
French, Vivian. *Red Hen and Sly Fox*
Freschet, Berniece. *Where's Henrietta's hen?*
Froissart, Bénédicte. *Uncle Henry's dinner guests*
Ginsburg, Mirra. *Across the stream*
The chick and the duckling
The golden goose, ill. by William Stobbs
Graeber, Jean B. *Bantie and her chicks*
Graham, Bob. *Queenie, one of the family*
Groves-Raines, Antony. *The tidy hen*
Hader, Berta Hoerner. *Cock-a-doodle doo*
Halperin, Wendy Anderson. *When chickens grow
teeth*
Hamilton, Morse. *The black hen, or, The under-
ground inhabitants*
Hariton, Anca. *Egg story*
Hartelius, Margaret A. *The chicken's child*
Hawkins, Colin. *Jen the hen*
Heine, Helme. *Mollywoop*
The most wonderful egg in the world
Three little friends: the alarm clock
Three little friends: the racing cart
Three little friends: the visitor
Hille-Brandts, Lene. *The little black hen*
Hoban, Julia. *Quick chick*
Hoff, Syd. *Happy birthday, Henrietta!*
Henrietta, circus star
Henrietta goes to the fair
Henrietta, the early bird
Henrietta's Halloween
Merry Christmas, Henrietta!
Houselander, Caryll. *Petook*
Hutchins, Pat. *Rosie's walk*
Rosie's walk, a board book
Isami, Ikuyo. *The fox's egg*
Jackson, Jacqueline. *Chicken ten thousand*
Jaynes, Ruth M. *Three baby chicks*
Jensen, Patricia. *Be patient, Little Chick*
Kasza, Keiko. *The wolf's chicken stew*
Kellogg, Steven (Stephen). *Chicken Little*
Kemp, Moira. *Lift-the-flap chick*
Kent, Jack. *Little Peep*
Kepes, Juliet. *Cock-a-doodle-doo*
Kimmel, Eric A. *The rooster's antlers*
The valiant red rooster
Kraus, Robert. *All my chickens*
Kwitz, Mary DeBall. *Little chick's breakfast*
Little chick's story
Landa, Norbert. *Rabbit and chicken count eggs*
Rabbit and chicken find a box
Rabbit and chicken play hide and seek
Rabbit and chicken play with colors
Lane, Megan Halsey. *Something to crow about*
Legg, Gerald. *From egg to chicken*
Leslie, Amanda. *Are chickens stripy?*
Lester, Helen. *The revenge of the magic chicken*
The wizard, the fairy and the magic chicken
Lewison, Wendy Cheyette. *The rooster who lost his
crow*

Lexau, Joan M. *Crocodile and hen*
Lifton, Betty Jean. *The many lives of Chio and Goro*
Lind, Mecka. *Cackle goes a-courting*
Lindman, Maj. *Flicka, Ricka, Dicka and the big red hen*
Lipkind, William. *The little tiny rooster*
The little red hen. *The cock, the mouse and the little red hen*
    The little red hen, ill. by Byron Barton
    The little red hen, ill. by Emily Bolam
    The little red hen, ill. by Janina Domanska
    The little red hen, ill. by Paul Galdone
    The little red hen, ill. by Dennis Hockerman
    Little red hen, ill. by Norman Messenger
    The little red hen, ill. by Mel Pekarsky
    The little red hen, ill. by William Stobbs
    The little red hen, ill. by Margot Zemach
    The Little Red Hen makes a pizza
Little Tuppen
Littlefield, William. *The whiskers of Ho Ho*
Lloyd, Megan. *Chicken tricks*
Lobel, Anita. *King Rooster, Queen Hen*
Lobel, Arnold. *How the rooster saved the day*
Luttrell, Ida. *Mattie and the chicken thief*
McConnachie, Brian. *Elmer and the chickens vs. the big league*
McCrea, Lilian. *Mother hen*
McCue, Lisa. *The little chick*
McKelvey, David. *Bobby the mostly silky*
McMullan, Kate (Hall). *Chickie riddles*
Malkovych, Ivan. *The cat and the rooster*
Marshall, James. *Wings*
Martin, Bill (William Ivan). *Chicken Chuck*
Martin, David. *Little Chicken Chicken*
Mathers, Petra. *Lottie's new beach towel*
    Maria Theresa
Mathews, Louise. *Cluck one*
Meeker, Clare Hodgson. *Who wakes rooster?*
Miles, Miska. *Chicken forgets*
Min, Laura. *Mrs. Sato's hens*
Mollel, Tololwa M. (Tololwa Marti). *Kele's secret*
Most, Bernard. *Cock-a-doodle-moo!*
Mueller, Virginia. *In the morning*
Murphey, Sara. *The animal hat shop*
Myers, Bernice. *The millionth egg*
Nordqvist, Sven. *Festus and Mercury go camping*
Numeroff, Laura Joffe. *The Chicken sisters*
Oakley, Graham. *Hetty and Harriet*
O'Neill, Mary. *Big red hen*
Otto, Margaret Glover. *The little brown horse*
Peet, Bill (William Bartlett). *Cock-a-doodle Dudley*
Polushkin, Maria. *The little hen and the giant*
Pomerantz, Charlotte. *Here comes Henny*
Poole, Amy Lowry. *How the rooster got his crown*
Porte, Barbara Ann. *Chickens! Chickens!*
Provensen, Alice. *My little hen*
Pursell, Margaret Sanford. *Jessie the chicken*
Rankin, Joan. *You're somebody special, Walliwigs!*
Ravilious, Robin. *The runaway chick*
Reiser, Lynn. *The surprise family*
Rockwell, Anne F. *The wonderful eggs of Furicchia*
Roddie, Shen. *Hatch, egg, hatch!*
    Help, Mama, help!
Ross, Tony. *Stone soup*
Royston, Angela. *The hen*
Rubel, Nicole. *Goldie*
    Goldie's nap
Scarry, Richard. *Egg in the hole*
Schami, Rafik. *Albert and Lila*

Scheffler, Ursel. *Stop your crowing, Kasimir!*
Selsam, Millicent E. *Egg to chick*
Sharmat, Marjorie Weinman. *Hooray for Mother's Day!*
Sherman, Nancy. *Gwendolyn and the weathercock*
    Gwendolyn the miracle hen
Snow, Alan. *Cluck!*
Sondergaard, Arensa. *Biddy and the ducks*
Stenmark, Victoria. *The singing chick*
Stevens, Janet. *Cook-a-doodle-doo!*
Stoeke, Janet Morgan. *A hat for Minerva Louise*
    Hide and seek
    Minerva Louise
    Minerva Louise at school
    Minerva Louise at the fair
Sykes, Julie. *Dora's eggs*
Threadgall, Colin. *Proud rooster and the fox*
The three little pigs. *The three little pigs and the fox*
Tripp, Valerie. *Sillyhen's big surprise*
Tusa, Tricia. *Chicken*
Van Horn, Grace. *Little red rooster*
Van Woerkom, Dorothy. *Something to crow about*
Voake, Charlotte. *Mrs. Goose's baby*
Waber, Bernard. *How to go about laying an egg*
Wallace, Karen. *My hen is dancing*
Walton, Rick. *Dumb clucks!*
Ward, Nick. *Farmer George and the lost chick*
Weil, Lisl. *Gillie and the flattering fox*
Weiss, Ellen. *Clara the fortune-telling chicken*
Williams, Garth. *The chicken book*
Willis, Val. *Silly little chick*
Wormell, Mary. *Hilda Hen's happy birthday*
    Hilda Hen's search

Birds – cockatoos

Blake, Quentin. *Cockatoos*
Cummings, W. T. (Walter Thies). *Wickford of Beacon Hill*
Pershall, Mary K. *Hello, Barney!*

Birds – condors

London, Jonathan. *Condor's egg*

Birds – cormorants

Bunting, Eve (Anne Evelyn). *Magic and the night river*

Birds – cranes

Bang, Molly. *Dawn*
    The paper crane
Bodkin, Odds. *The crane wife*
Charles, Veronika Martenova. *The crane girl*
Coerr, Eleanor. *Sadako*
Hirschi, Ron. *Where are my swans, whooping cranes, and singing loons?*
Keller, Holly. *Grandfather's dream*
Keo, Ena. *The crane wife*
Laurin, Anne. *Perfect crane*
Owens, Mary Beth. *Counting cranes*
The peasant's pea patch
Yagawa, Sumiko. *The crane wife*

Birds – crows

Armstrong, Jennifer. *King crow*

Boyd, Lizi. *Lulu Crow's garden*
Cunningham, David. *A crow's journey*
DeFelice, Cynthia C. *Clever crow*
DeLage, Ida. *The old witch and the crows*
Dillon, Jana. *Jeb Scarecrow's pumpkin patch*
Frascino, Edward. *Nanny Noony and the magic spell*
Freeman, Don. *Cyrano the crow*
Gage, Wilson. *The crow and Mrs. Gaddy*
Goble, Paul. *Crow chief*
Greenstein, Elaine. *Emily and the crows*
Guy, Ginger Foglesong. *Black crow, black crow*
Hale, Irina. *The naughty crow*
Harsh, Fred. *Alfie*
Hazelton, Elizabeth Baldwin. *Sammy, the crow who remembered*
Holder, Heidi. *Carmine the crow*
  Crows
Hyman, Robin. *Casper and the rainbow bird*
Latimer, Jim. *James Bear's pie*
Lionni, Leo. *Six crows*
Lively, Penelope. *The cat, the crow, and the banyan tree*
McDermott, Gerald. *Coyote*
Marion, Jeff Daniel. *Hello, Crow*
Oppenheim, Joanne. *"Not now!" said the cow*
Orgel, Doris. *Two crows counting*
Rosen, Michael (1946-). *Crow and Hawk*
Rowe, John A. *Baby Crow*
Schami, Rafik. *The crow who stood on his beak*
Van Laan, Nancy. *Rainbow crow*

Birds – cuckoos

Bloom, Becky. *Mr. Cuckoo*
Corbalis, Judy. *The cuckoo bird*
Ehlert, Lois. *Cuckoo: a Mexican folktale = Cucú: un cuento folklórico mexicano*

Birds – dodos

Lehan, Daniel. *This is not a book about dodos*
Mathers, Petra. *Dodo gets married*

Birds – doves

Æsop. *The ant and the dove*
Agostinelli, Maria Enrica. *On wings of love*
Baker, Keith. *The dove's letter*
Freeman, Don. *The turtle and the dove*
Peet, Bill (William Bartlett). *The pinkish, purplish, bluish egg*
Potter, Beatrix. *The tale of the faithful dove*
Sage, James. *The boy and the dove*
Singer, Isaac Bashevis. *Why Noah chose the dove*
Wells, Rosemary. *The language of doves*
Wolff, Ashley. *The bells of London*

Birds – ducks

Akass, Susan. *Number nine duckling*
Alborough, Jez. *Duck in the truck*
Allen, Jeffrey. *Mary Alice, operator number 9*
  Mary Alice returns
Andersen, H. C. (Hans Christian). *The ugly duckling*, ill. by Adrienne Adams
  The ugly duckling, ill. by Lorinda Bryan Cauley
  The ugly duckling, ill. by Troy Howell
  The ugly duckling, ill. by Tadasu Izawa and Shigemi Hijikata
  The ugly duckling, ill. by Monika Laimgruber
  The ugly duckling, ill. by Johannes Larsen
  The ugly duckling, ill. by Thomas Locker
  The ugly duckling, ill. by Alan Marks
  The ugly duckling, ill. by Josef Palecek
  The ugly duckling, ill. by Jerry Pinkney
  The ugly duckling, ill. by Maria Ruis
  The ugly duckling, ill. by Daniel San Souci
  The ugly duckling, ill. by Robert Van Nutt
  The ugly duckling, ill. by Bernadette Watts
  The ugly little duck, ill. by Peggy Perry Anderson
Arnosky, Jim. *All night near the water*
Auch, Mary Jane. *The nutquacker*
Barnhart, Peter. *The wounded duck*
Bassède, Francine. *George paints his house*
Baumgardner, Mary Alice. *Alexandra, keeper of dreams*
Beck, Ian. *Five little ducks*
Bedard, Michael. *Sitting ducks*
Benjamin, A. H. *A duck so small*
Blocksma, Mary. *Where's that duck?*
Bothwell, Jean. *Paddy and Sam*
Boyd, Lizi. *The not-so-wicked stepmother*
Brown, Margaret Wise. *The duck*
  The golden egg book
Bunting, Eve (Anne Evelyn). *Happy birthday, dear duck*
Burton, Jane. *Dabble the duckling*
Cain, Sheridan. *Why so sad, Brown Rabbit?*
Capucilli, Alyssa Satin. *Biscuit finds a friend*
Cartlidge, Michelle. *Duck in the pond*
Caseley, Judith. *Mickey's class play*
Casey, Patricia. *Quack quack*
Cazet, Denys. *The duck with squeaky feet*
Clément, Claude. *The hungry duckling*
Coats, Laura Jane. *Marcella and the moon*
Conover, Chris. *Six little ducks*
Cooper, Helen (Helen F.). *Pumpkin soup*
Cowley, Stewart. *The naughty ducklings*
  Curious George and the dump truck
Dabcovich, Lydia. *Ducks fly*
Dalmais, Anne-Marie. *Danny the duck*
  Davy's scary journey
Delton, Judy. *Bear and Duck on the run*
  Duck goes fishing
  The elephant in Duck's garden
  The perfect Christmas gift
  A pet for Duck and Bear
  Three friends find spring
  Two good friends
Demi. *Downy duckling*
  Little lucky ducky
Dreier, Ted. *Moozie's kind adventure*
Dunn, Judy. *The little duck*
Duvoisin, Roger Antoine. *Two lonely ducks*
Egan, Tim. *Friday night at Hodges' café*
Ellis, Anne Leo. *Dabble Duck*
Enderle, Judith (Ann) Ross. *Where are you, little Zack?*
Flack, Marjorie. *Angus and the ducks*
  The story about Ping
Freschet, Berniece. *Wood duck baby*
Fribourg, Marjorie G. *Ching-Ting and the ducks*
Friskey, Margaret (Margaret Richards). *Seven diving ducks*
Gantschev, Ivan. *Where the moon lives*
Garland, Sarah. *Having a picnic*
Garland, Sherry. *Why ducks sleep on one leg*
Georgiady, Nicholas P. *Gertie the duck*

Gerstein, Mordicai. *Follow me!*
Gibson, Betty. *The story of Little Quack*
Ginsburg, Mirra. *Across the stream*
    The chick and the duckling
Goble, Paul. *Iktomi and the ducks*
Goldin, Augusta. *Ducks don't get wet*
Gordon, Gaelyn. *Duckat*
Grahame, Kenneth. *Duck song*
Gretz, Susanna. *Duck takes off*
Grindley, Sally. *Silly Goose and Dizzy Duck play hide-and-seek*
Hader, Berta Hoerner. *Cock-a-doodle doo*
Hayes, Sarah. *Nine ducks nine*
Herman, Gail. *The littlest duckling*
Hest, Amy. *Baby Duck and the bad eyeglasses*
    In the rain with Baby Duck
    Off to school, Baby Duck
    You're the boss, Baby Duck
Hillert, Margaret. *The funny baby*
Hurd, Edith Thacher. *Last one home is a green pig*
Hutchins, H. J. (Hazel J.). *One duck*
Ichikawa, Satomi. *Nora's duck*
Inkpen, Mick. *Gumboot's chocolatey day*
Isenbart, Hans-Heinrich. *A duckling is born*
Janice. *Angélique*
Jeram, Anita. *All together now*
    Bunny, my Honey
Jonas, Ann. *Watch William walk*
Joyce, William. *Bently and egg*
Kepes, Juliet. *The story of a bragging duck*
Laird, Elizabeth. *The day the ducks went skating*
Leverich, Kathleen. *The hungry fox and the foxy duck*
Lloyd, David. *Duck*
Loomis, Jennifer A. *A duck in a tree*
Lorenz, Lee. *A weekend in the country*
Lunn, Janet Louise Swoboda. *Duck cakes for sale*
McCloskey, Robert. *Make way for ducklings*
MacDonald, Elizabeth. *Dilly-Dally and the nine secrets*
Mackinnon, Debbie. *Daniel's duck*
Mamin-Sibiryak, D. N. *Grey Neck*
Mathers, Petra. *A cake for Herbie*
Matje, Martin. *Celeste*
Mendoza, George. *Were you a wild duck, where would you go?*
Miles, Miska. *Noisy gander*
Moore, Sheila. *Samson Svenson's baby*
Naylor, Phyllis Reynolds. *Ducks disappearing*
Nethery, Mary. *Mary Veronica's egg*
Otto, Carolyn. *Ducks, ducks, ducks*
Owen, Annie. *Playtime duck*
Paparone, Pamela. *Five little ducks*
Paterson, Katherine. *The tale of the Mandarin ducks*
Peters, Lisa Westberg. *Cold little duck, duck, duck*
Pizer, Abigail. *Percy the duck*
Pomerantz, Charlotte. *One duck, another duck*
Potter, Beatrix. *The tale of Jemima Puddle-Duck*
Quackenbush, Robert M. *Henry babysits*
    Henry's world tour
Rankin, Joan. *Wow! It's great being a duck*
Reiser, Lynn. *The surprise family*
Richter, Mischa. *Eric and Matilda*
    Quack?
Rogers, Paul (Patrick). *Quacky Duck*
Root, Phyllis. *One duck stuck*
Roy, Ronald. *Three ducks went wandering*
Saunders, Dave. *Snowtime*
Scamell, Ragnhild. *Solo plus one*
Schroeder, Binette. *Tuffa and the ducks*

Scruton, Clive. *Bubble and squeak*
Seignobosc, Françoise. *Springtime for Jeanne-Marie*
Sewell, Helen Moore. *Blue barns*
Shannon, George. *Laughing all the way*
    Shapes
Shaw, Evelyn S. *Nest of wood ducks*
Sheehan, Angela. *The duck*
Simmons, Jane. *Come along, Daisy!*
    Daisy and the egg
    Daisy says Coo!
    Daisy's day out
    Daisy's favorite things
    Go to sleep, Daisy
    Sizes
Smith, Mavis. *Fred, is that you?*
Snow, Alan. *Quack!*
Sondergaard, Arensa. *Biddy and the ducks*
Spier, Peter. *Little ducks*
Standon, Anna. *Little duck lost*
Stehr, Frédéric. *Quack-quack*
Stevenson, James. *Howard*
    Monty
Stott, Dorothy. *Little Duck's bicycle ride*
    Too much
Szekeres, Cyndy. *Hide-and-seek duck*
Tafuri, Nancy. *Have you seen my duckling?*
Thiele, Colin. *Farmer Schulz's ducks*
Tryon, Leslie. *Albert's alphabet*
    Albert's birthday
    Albert's Christmas
    Albert's Halloween
Tudor, Bethany. *Samuel's tree house*
    Skiddycock Pond
Turska, Krystyna. *The woodcutter's duck*
Udry, Janice May. *Thump and Plunk*, ill. by Geoffrey Hayes
Van Laan, Nancy. *Shingebiss*
Velthuijs, Max. *Frog in love*
Verboven, Agnes. *Ducks like to swim*
Waddell, Martin. *Farmer Duck*
Wahl, Jan. *Old Hippo's Easter egg*
Watts, Barrie. *Duck*
Wellington, Monica. *All my little ducklings*
Wells, Rosemary. *The itsy-bitsy spider*
Whippo, Walt. *Little white duck*
Whybrow, Ian. *Parcel for Stanley*
Wijngaard, Juan. *Duck*
Wildsmith, Brian. *The little wood duck*
Winthrop, Elizabeth. *Bear and Mrs. Duck*
    Bear's Christmas surprise
Withers, Carl. *The wild ducks and the goose*
Wright, Dare. *Edith and the duckling*

Birds – eagles

Allen, Judy. *Eagle*
Bernhard, Emery. *Eagles*
    Spotted Eagle and Black Crow
Craighead, Charles. *The eagle and the river*
Foreman, Michael. *Moose*
Gibbons, Gail. *Soaring with the wind*
Goble, Paul. *Adopted by the eagles*
Gregorowski, Christopher. *Fly, eagle, fly!*
Hausman, Gerald. *Eagle boy*
Klinting, Lars. *Regal the golden eagle*
McFarlane, Sheryl. *Eagle dreams*
Martin, Rafe. *The eagle's gift*
Mason, Jane B. *River day*
Melville, Herman. *Catskill eagle*

Morrison, Gordon. *Bald eagle*
Paraskevas, Betty. *On the day the tall ships sailed*

Birds – egrets

Carlson, Natalie Savage. *Time for the white egret*

Birds – emus

Knowles, Sheena. *Edward the emu*

Birds – falcons

Greene, Carol. *Reading about the peregrine falcon*
Jenkins, Priscilla Belz. *Falcons nest on skyscrapers*

Birds – flamingos

Carlstrom, Nancy White. *Fish and flamingo*
Damjan, Mischa. *The fake flamingos*
Keller, Holly. *Island baby*
McCloskey, Kevin. *Mrs. Fitz's flamingos*
Rossetti, Christina Georgina. *What is pink?*
Walsh, Ellen Stoll. *For Pete's sake*
Zoll, Max Alfred. *A flamingo is born*

Birds – geese

Asch, Frank. *MacGooses's grocery*
Auch, Mary Jane. *Bird dogs can't fly*
Bacheller, Irving. *Lost in the fog*
Bang, Molly. *Goose*
Berkowitz, Linda. *Alfonse, where are you?*
Braun, Trudi. *My goose Betsy*
Brenner, Barbara A. *Good news*
Brown, Marc Tolon. *Moose and goose*
Bunting, Eve (Anne Evelyn). *Goose dinner*
Burningham, John. *Borka*
Cauley, Lorinda Bryan. *The goose and the golden coins*
Chandoha, Walter. *A baby goose for you*
Clearman, Deborah. *The goose's tale*
Conover, Chris. *Mother Goose and the sly fox*
Day, Betsy. *Stefan and Olga*
Deedy, Carmen Agra. *Agatha's feather bed*
Delton, Judy. *On a picnic*
Demarest, Chris L. *Honk!*
Dunbar, Joyce. *Gander's pond*
    The secret friend
Duvoisin, Roger Antoine. *Petunia*
    Petunia and the song
    Petunia, beware!
    Petunia, I love you
    Petunia takes a trip
    Petunia, the silly goose
    Petunia's Christmas
    Petunia's treasure
Enderle, Judith (Ann) Ross. *What would Mama do?*
Fox, Mem. *Boo to a goose*
Freeman, Don. *Will's quill*
Galdone, Joanna. *Gertrude, the goose who forgot*
George, Lindsay Barrett. *William and Boomer*
Gervais, Bernadette. *Voyage under the stars*
Grindley, Sally. *Silly Goose and Dizzy Duck play hide-and-seek*
Holmes, Efner Tudor. *Amy's goose*
Houston, James. *Kiviok's magic journey*
Ichikawa, Satomi. *Nora's surprise*
Illyés, Gyula. *Matt the gooseherd*

Inkpen, Mick. *Honk!*
Johnson, Ryerson. *Kenji and the magic geese*
Kalas, Sybille. *The goose family book*
Kasperson, James. *Little brother moose*
Kent, Jack. *Silly goose*
King, Deborah. *The flight of the snow geese*
Koch, Dorothy Clarke. *Gone is my goose*
Lasell, Fen. *Fly away goose*
Latimer, Jim. *James Bear and the goose gathering*
Lears, Laurie. *Waiting for Mr. Goose*
Le Tord, Bijou. *Good wood bear*
Lindbergh, Reeve. *The day the goose got loose*
Low, Joseph. *Benny rabbit and the owl*
    Boo to a goose
McBratney, Sam. *Just you and me*
McPhail, David M. *A girl, a goat, and a goose*
Mahy, Margaret. *A summery Saturday morning*
Manning, Mick. *Honk! honk!*
Mother Goose. *The golden goose book*, ill. by L. Leslie Brooke
Oram, Hiawyn. *Gerda the goose*
Pilkey, Dav. *The Silly Gooses*
    The Silly Gooses build a house
Pizer, Abigail. *Nosey Gilbert*
Polacco, Patricia. *I can hear the sun*
    Rechenka's eggs
Preston, Edna Mitchell. *Squawk to the moon, little goose*
Rockwell, Anne F. *Poor Goose*
Root, Phyllis. *Grandmother Winter*
Rossiter, Nan Parson. *The way home*
Ryder, Joanne. *Catching the wind*
Sanfield, Steve. *The girl who wanted a song*
Sansone, Adele. *The little green goose*
Saunders, Dave. *Snowtime*
Schoenherr, John. *Rebel*
Schubert, Ingrid. *Bear's eggs*
Sewell, Helen Moore. *Blue barns*
Simont, Marc. *The goose that almost got cooked*
Stevens, Kathleen. *Aunt Skilly and the stranger*
Strand, Keith. *Grandfather's Christmas tree*
Voake, Charlotte. *Mrs. Goose's baby*
Wahl, Jan. *The singing geese*
Walsh, Ellen Stoll. *You silly goose*
Weatherill, Stephen. *The very first Lucy Goose book*
Zeman, Ludmila. *The first red maple leaf*
Zijlstra, Tjerk. *Benny and his geese*

Birds – guinea fowl

Knutson, Barbara. *How the guinea fowl got her spots*

Birds – hawks

Baylor, Byrd. *Hawk, I'm your brother*
Bliss, Corinne Demas. *Matthew's meadow*
Gilbert, Suzie. *Hawk Hill*
Houk, Randy. *Rico's hawk*
Rosen, Michael (1946-). *Crow and Hawk*

Birds – herons

Owen, Roy. *The ibis and the egret*

Birds – hornbills

Shepard, Steve. *Elvis Hornbill, international business bird*

Birds – humming birds

Allard, Harry. *The hummingbirds' day*
Czernecki, Stefan. *The hummingbird's gift*
Hausman, Gerald. *Doctor Bird*
Ryder, Joanne. *Dancers in the garden*

Birds – ibis

Owen, Roy. *The ibis and the egret*

Birds – larks

Czernecki, Stefan. *The singing snake*

Birds – loons

Hassett, John. *Junior*
Hirschi, Ron. *Loon lake*
　Where are my swans, whooping cranes, and singing loons?
London, Jonathan. *Loon Lake*
Martin, Jacqueline Briggs. *Washing the willow tree loon*

Birds – macaws

Mead, Alice. *Billy and Emma*

Birds – magpies

Wilson, April. *April Wilson's magpie magic*

Birds – mockingbirds

Ryder, Joanne. *Mockingbird morning*

Birds – nightingales

Andersen, H. C. (Hans Christian). *The emperor and the nightingale*, ill. by Meilo So
　The emperor and the nightingale, ill. by James Watling
　The emperor's nightingale, ill. from the Disney arcives
　The emperor's nightingale, ill. by Georges Lemoine
　The nightingale, ill. by Harold Berson
　The nightingale, ill. by Nancy Ekholm Burkert
　The nightingale, ill. by Alison Claire Darke
　The nightingale, ill. by Demi
　The nightingale, ill. by Beni Montresor
　The nightingale, ill. by Josef Palecek
　The nightingale, ill. by Regolo Ricci
　The nightingale, ill. by Christopher Santoro
　The nightingale, ill. by Lisbeth Zwerger
Chase, Catherine. *The nightingale and the fool*
Maugham, W. Somerset (William Somerset). *Princess September and the nightingale*
Moore, Inga. *Rose and the nightingale*

Birds – ostriches

Aardema, Verna. *The lonely lioness and the ostrich chicks*
Burton, Marilee Robin. *Oliver's birthday*
Delton, Judy. *Penny wise, fun foolish*
Peet, Bill (William Bartlett). *Zella, Zack, and Zodiac*
Ylla. *Look who's talking*

Birds – owls

Æsop. *Town mouse, country mouse*, ill. by Jan Brett
Beifuss, John. *Armadillo Ray*
Bennett, Rainey. *After the sun goes down*
Bernhard, Emery. *The girl who wanted to hunt*
Boyle, Constance. *The story of little owl*
Bright, Robert. *Georgie to the rescue*
Bunting, Eve (Anne Evelyn). *The man who could call down owls*
Burton, Jane. *Buffy the barn owl*
　Snowy, the barn owl
Carey, Mary. *The owl who loved sunshine*
Coleman, Michael. *Lazy Ozzie*
Crebbin, June. *Fly by night*
Cresswell, Helen. *Two hoots and the king*
　Two hoots in the snow
DeLage, Ida. *The old witch and the crows*
Delton, Judy. *Duck goes fishing*
Dowling, Paul. *Happy birthday, Owl*
Duvoisin, Roger Antoine. *Day and night*
Eastman, P. D. (Philip D.). *Sam and the firefly*
Flower, Phyllis. *Barn owl*
Foster, Doris Van Liew. *Tell me, Mr. Owl*
Freschet, Berniece. *Owl in the garden*
Funazaki, Yasuko. *Baby owl*
Gantschev, Ivan. *Where is Mr. Mole?*
Gates, Frieda. *Owl eyes*
Goldsmith, Howard. *Sleepy little owl*
Goodenow, Earle. *The owl who hated the dark*
Harshman, Terry Webb. *Porcupine's pajama party*
Hendra, Sue. *Oliver's wood*
Hissey, Jane. *Hoot*
Hoban, Russell. *Charlie Meadows*
Hoopes, Lyn Littlefield. *My own home*
Houk, Randy. *Ruffle, Coo and Hoo Doo*
Hutchins, Pat. *Good night owl*
Johnston, Tony. *The barn owls*
Kirn, Ann. *I spy*
Kraus, Robert. *The adventures of Wise Old Owl*
　Owliver
　Wise Old Owl's canoe trip adventure
　Wise Old Owl's Christmas adventure
Lamm, C. Drew. *Screech Owl at Midnight Hollow*
Lear, Edward. *The owl and the pussy cat*, ill. by Ian Beck
　The owl and the pussycat, ill. by Jan Brett
　The owl and the pussycat, ill. by Lorinda Bryan Cauley
　The owl and the pussy-cat, ill. by Barbara Cooney
　The owl and the pussy-cat, ill. by Emma Crosby
　The owl and the pussy-cat, ill. by William Pène Du Bois
　The owl and the pussy-cat, ill. by Lori Farbanish
　The owl and the pussy-cat, ill. by Gwen Fulton
　The owl and the pussy-cat, ill. by Paul Galdone
　The owl and the pussy-cat, ill. by Elaine Muis
　The owl and the pussy-cat, ill. by Erica Rutherford
　The owl and the pussy-cat, ill. by Janet Stevens
　The owl and the pussy-cat, ill. by Louise Voce
　The owl and the pussycat, ill. by Colin West
　The owl and the pussy-cat, ill. by Owen Wood
Leonard, Marcia. *Little owl leaves the nest*
Lionni, Leo. *Six crows*
Lobel, Arnold. *Owl at home*
London, Jonathan. *The owl who became the moon*
McDonald, Megan. *Whoo-oo is it?*
McGuire, Leslie. *Baby night owl*
McKeever, Katherine. *A family for Minerva*

Maschler, Fay. *T. G. and Moonie go shopping*
  T. G. and Moonie have a baby
  T. G. and Moonie move out of town
Most, Bernard. *Z-Z-Zoink!*
Nicoll, Helen. *Meg at sea*
  Meg's eggs
Norman, Howard A. *The owl-scatterer*
O'Malley, Kevin. *Who killed Cock Robin?*
Panek, Dennis. *Detective Whoo*
Pfister, Marcus. *The sleepy owl*
Piatti, Celestino. *The happy owls*
Potter, Beatrix. *The tale of Squirrel Nutkin*
Schären, Beatrix. *Tillo*
Schoenherr, John. *The barn*
Shles, Larry. *Moths and mothers, feathers and fathers*
Slobodkin, Louis. *Wide-awake owl*
Smith, Jim. *The frog band and the owlnapper*
Tejima, Keizaburo. *Owl lake*
Thaler, Mike. *Owley*
Tompert, Ann. *Badger on his own*
Waddell, Martin. *Owl babies*
Wahl, Jan. *Mrs. Owl and Mr. Pig*
Wildsmith, Brian. *The owl and the woodpecker*
Yolen, Jane. *Owl moon*

Birds – parakeets, parrots

Asch, Frank. *George's store*
Augarde, Steve (Stephen). *Barnaby Shrew, Black Dan and . . . the mighty wedgwood*
Banchek, Linda. *Snake in, snake out*
Baum, Louis. *JuJu and the pirate*
Best, Cari. *Top banana*
Bishop, Bonnie. *No one noticed Ralph*
  Ralph rides away
Blegvad, Lenore. *The parrot in the garret and other rhymes about dwellings*
Bradford, Ann. *The mystery of the tree house*
Cressey, James. *Pet parrot*
Demuth, Patricia Brennan. *Max, the bad-talking parrot*
Dragonwagon, Crescent. *Coconut*
Fox, Mem. *Tough Boris*
Gál, László. *The parrot*
Gordon, Sharon. *Pete the parakeet*
Graham, Bob. *Pete and Roland*
Graham, Margaret Bloy. *Benjy and the barking bird*
Hamsa, Bobbie. *Polly wants a cracker*
Heller, Ruth. *How to hide a parakeet and other birds*
Holman, Felice. *Victoria's castle*
Houk, Randy. *Ruffle, Coo and Hoo Doo*
Hyman, Robin. *Casper and the rainbow bird*
Johnston, Tony. *Little wild parrot*
  Lorenzo the naughty parrot
Lester, Helen. *Princess Penelope's parrot*
McDermott, Gerald. *Papagayo, the mischief maker*
McFarland, Lyn Rossiter. *The pirate's parrot*
Mahy, Margaret. *The horrendous hullabaloo*
Meddaugh, Susan. *Martha walks the dog*
Potter, Stephen. *Squawky, the adventures of a clasper-choice*
Rankin, Joan. *You're somebody special, Walliwigs!*
Remkiewicz, Frank. *The last time I saw Harris*
Steig, William. *Wizzil*
Zacharias, Thomas. *But where is the green parrot?*
Zusman, Evelyn. *The Passover parrot*

Birds – peacocks, peahens

Alan, Sandy. *The plaid peacock*
Alexander, Sue. *Peacocks are very special*
Auch, Mary Jane. *Hen lake*
Bunting, Eve (Anne Evelyn). *Box, fox, ox, and the peacock*
Daniel, Doris Temple. *Pauline and the peacock*
Fox, Mem. *Feathers and fools*
Hamberger, John. *The peacock who lost his tail*
Kajpust, Melissa. *The peacock's pride*
Kepes, Juliet. *The seed that peacock planted*
Peet, Bill (William Bartlett). *The spooky tail of Prewitt Peacock*
Polacco, Patricia. *Just plain Fancy*
Schami, Rafik. *The crow who stood on his beak*
Wittman, Sally. *Pelly and Peak*
  Plenty of Pelly and Peak

Birds – pelicans

Benchley, Nathaniel. *The flying lessons of Gerald Pelican*
Crane, Alan. *Pepita bonita*
Freeman, Don. *Come again, pelican*
Hewett, Joan. *Fly away free*
Jenkin-Pearce, Susie. *Percy Short and Cuthbert*
Lear, Edward. *Of pelicans and pussycats*
  The pelican chorus, ill. by Harold Berson
  The pelican chorus and the quangle wangle's hat, ill. by Kevin W. Maddison
O'Reilly, Edward. *Brown pelican at the pond*
Patz, Nancy. *To Annabella Pelican from Thomas Hippopotamus*
Wildsmith, Brian. *Pelican*
Wittman, Sally. *Pelly and Peak*
  Plenty of Pelly and Peak

Birds – penguins

Alborough, Jez. *Cuddly Dudley*
Arrhenius, Peter. *The Penguin Quartet*
Benson, Patrick. *Little penguin*
Breathed, Berkeley. *A wish for wings that work*
Bright, Robert. *Which is Willy?*
Chester, Jonathan. *Splash!*
Coldrey, Jennifer. *Penguins*
Cousins, Lucy. *Portly's hat*
Cousteau Society. *Penguins*
Fatio, Louise. *Hector and Christina*
  Hector penguin
Faulkner, Keith. *The puzzled penguin*
Gay, Michel. *Bibi takes flight*
  Bibi's birthday surprise
Geraghty, Paul. *Solo*
Gibbons, Gail. *Penguins!*
Hamsa, Bobbie. *Your pet penguin*
Hogan, Paula Z. *The penguin*
Howe, Caroline Walton. *Counting penguins*
Inkpen, Mick. *Penguin small*
Johnston, Johanna. *Penguin's way*
Kellogg, Steven (Stephen). *A penguin pup for Pinkerton*
Kessler, Ethel. *Is there a penguin at your party?*
Knüppel, Helga. *Christabel Crocodile's birthday egg*
Leonard, Marcia. *Paintbox penguins*
Lester, Helen. *Tacky and the Emperor*
  Tacky in trouble
  Tacky the penguin

Three cheers for Tacky
Lilly, Kenneth. *Animals of the ocean*
McMillan, Bruce. *Puffins climb, penguins rhyme*
Mitra, Annie. *Penguin moon*
Murphy, Mary. *My puffer train*
Please be quiet!
Nichols, Cathy. *Tuxedo Sam*
O'Donnell, Peter. *Pinkie goes south*
Perlman, Janet. *The Emperor Penguin's new clothes*
Pfister, Marcus. *Penguin Pete and Little Tim*
Rigby, Rodney. *Hello, this is your penguin speaking*
Schindel, John. *Busy penguins*
Seibold, J. Otto. *Penguin dreams*
Sheehan, Angela. *The penguin*
Shields, Carol Diggory. *Martian rock*
Somme, Lauritz. *The penguin family book*
Stevenson, James. *Winston, Newton, Elton, and Ed*
Walker, Jane. *Ten little penguins*
Weiss, Leatie. *Funny feet!*
Wiesmüller, Dieter. *The adventures of Marco and Polo*
Winteringham, Victoria. *Penguin day*
Wood, Audrey. *Little Penguin's tale*
Yee, Patrick. *Baby penguin*

Birds – pigeons

Allan, Nicholas. *The bird*
Baker, Jeannie. *Home in the sky*
Millicent
Benchley, Nathaniel. *Walter the homing pigeon*
Erdrich, Louise. *Grandmother's pigeon*
Kingman, Lee. *Pierre Pigeon*
Kurtz, Jane. *Only a pigeon*
McClure, Gillian. *Fly home McDoo*
Peet, Bill (William Bartlett). *Fly, Homer, fly*
Shulman, Milton. *Prep, the little pigeon of Trafalgar Square*
Suben, Eric. *Pigeon takes a trip*
Wells, Rosemary. *The language of doves*

Birds – plovers

De Paola, Tomie (Thomas Anthony). *Bill and Pete*
Bill and Pete go down the Nile
Bill and Pete to the rescue

Birds – puffins

Drew, Patricia. *Spotter Puff*
Hall, Pam. *On the edge of the eastern ocean*
Hirschi, Ron. *Where are my puffins, whales, and seals?*
Lawson, Annetta. *The lucky yak*
Lewis, Naomi. *Puffin*
McMillan, Bruce. *Nights of the pufflings*
Puffins climb, penguins rhyme

Birds – quail

Carey, Valerie Scho. *Quail song*
Troughton, Joanna. *The quail's egg*

Birds – ravens

Æsop. *The raven and the fox*
Aiken, Joan. *Arabel and Mortimer*
Carlstrom, Nancy White. *Raven and river*
Dixon, Ann. *How raven brought light to people*

Grimm, Jacob. *The seven ravens*, ill. by Felix Hoffmann
The seven ravens, ill. by Lisbeth Zwerger
Luenn, Nancy. *Song for the ancient forest*
McDermott, Gerald. *Raven*

Birds – robins

Calder, S. J. *If you were a bird*
Cock Robin. *The courtship, merry marriage, and feast of Cock Robin and Jenny Wren*
Who killed Cock Robin?, ill. by William Stobbs
Fearnley, Jan. *Little Robin's Christmas*
Flack, Marjorie. *The restless robin*
Hawkinson, John. *Robins and rabbits*
Jenkins, Priscilla Belz. *A nest full of eggs*
Kent, Jack. *Round Robin*
Kraus, Robert. *The first robin*
Little Robin Redbreast
O'Malley, Kevin. *Who killed Cock Robin?*
Rockwell, Anne F. *My spring robin*
Stern, Elsie-Jean. *Wee Robin's Christmas song*
Tresselt, Alvin R. *Hi, Mister Robin*

Birds – sandpipers

Hurd, Edith Thacher. *Sandpipers*
Mendoza, George. *The scribbler*

Birds – seagulls

Armitage, Ronda. *The lighthouse keeper's lunch*
Carrick, Carol. *Beach bird*
Melanie
Duvoisin, Roger Antoine. *Snowy and Woody*
Hoff, Syd. *The lighthouse children*
Ness, Evaline. *Do you have the time, Lydia?*
Paraskevas, Betty. *Hoppy and Joe*
Pursell, Margaret Sanford. *Shelley the sea gull*
Simmons, Jane. *Ebb and Flo and the greedy gulls*
Turkle, Brinton. *Thy friend, Obadiah*

Birds – sparrows

Cowley, Joy. *The video shop sparrow*
Crabtree, Judith. *The sparrow's story at the king's command*
Fregosi, Claudia. *The pumpkin sparrow*
Gerstein, Mordicai. *Prince Sparrow*
Ishii, Momoko. *The tongue-cut sparrow*
Myers, Christopher A. *Sparrows*
Ostheeren, Ingrid. *Jonathan Mouse and the baby bird*
Selden, George. *Sparrow socks*
Wallace, Ian. *The sparrow's song*

Birds – spoonbills

Guiberson, Brenda Z. *Spoonbill swamp*

Birds – storks

Berliner, Franz. *Miserable Marabou*
Bos, Burny. *Prince Valentino*
Brown, Margaret Wise. *Wheel on the chimney*
Damjan, Mischa. *The fake flamingos*
Drescher, Henrik. *The strange appearance of Howard Cranebill, Jr.*
Gantschev, Ivan. *Journey of the storks*
McDermott, Gerald. *The fox and the stork*

Birds – swallows

Politi, Leo. *Song of the swallows*
Swinburne, Stephen R. *Swallows in the birdhouse*

Birds – swans

Andersen, H. C. (Hans Christian). *The ugly duck-ling*, ill. by Adrienne Adams
   The ugly duckling, ill. by Lorinda Bryan Cauley
   The ugly duckling, ill. by Troy Howell
   The ugly duckling, ill. by Tadasu Izawa and Shigemi Hijikata
   The ugly duckling, ill. by Monika Laimgruber
   The ugly duckling, ill. by Johannes Larsen
   The ugly duckling, ill. by Thomas Locker
   The ugly duckling, ill. by Alan Marks
   The ugly duckling, ill. by Josef Palecek
   The ugly duckling, ill. by Jerry Pinkney
   The ugly duckling, ill. by Maria Ruis
   The ugly duckling, ill. by Daniel San Souci
   The ugly duckling, ill. by Robert Van Nutt
   The ugly duckling, ill. by Bernadette Watts
   The ugly little duck, ill. by Peggy Perry Anderson
   The wild swans, ill. by Angela Barrett
   The wild swans, ill. by Susan Jeffers
Auer, Martin. *Now, now Markus*
Bell, Anthea. *Swan Lake*
Canfield, Jane White. *Swan cove*
Clément, Claude. *The painter and the wild swans*
Day, David. *The swan children*
DeChristopher, Marlowe. *Greencoat and the swanboy*
Edwards, Pamela Duncan. *Honk!*
Fox, Mem. *Feathers and fools*
Gantschev, Ivan. *Where the moon lives*
Grimm, Jacob. *The six swans*, ill. by Dorothée Duntze
   The six swans, ill. by Daniel San Souci
   The six swans, ill. by Margot Tomes
Hillert, Margaret. *The funny baby*
Hirschi, Ron. *Where are my swans, whooping cranes, and singing loons?*
Hogan, Paula Z. *The black swan*
Lemberg, Stephen H. *Scaredy dog*
Lewis, Naomi. *Swan*
MacGill-Callahan, Sheila. *The children of Lir*
Pyle, Howard. *The Swan Maiden*
Seabrooke, Brenda. *The swan's gift*
   Swan flyway
Tejima, Keizaburo. *Swan sky*
Willington, Monica. *Seasons of swans*

Birds – toucans

McKee, David. *Two can toucan*

Birds – turkeys

Arnosky, Jim. *All about turkeys*
Balian, Lorna. *Sometimes it's turkey*
Bunting, Eve (Anne Evelyn). *A turkey for Thanksgiving*
Cowley, Joy. *Gracias, the Thanksgiving turkey*
Kraus, Robert. *How Spider saved Turkey*
Kroll, Steven. *One tough turkey*
Morgan, Allen. *Matthew and the midnight ball game*
   Matthew and the midnight turkeys
Nikola-Lisa, W. *The dancin' fox*
Pilkey, Dav. *'Twas the night before Thanksgiving*

Pollock, Penny. *The turkey girl*
Schatell, Brian. *Farmer Goff and his turkey Sam*
   Sam's no dummy, Farmer Goff
Wickstrom, Sylvie (Sylvie Kantrovitz). *Turkey on the loose!*

Birds – vultures

Allard, Harry. *Crash helmet*
Duvoisin, Roger Antoine. *Petunia, I love you*
Peet, Bill (William Bartlett). *Eli*
Ungerer, Tomi. *Orlando, the brave vulture*
Wolkstein, Diane. *The cool ride in the sky*

Birds – wood-hoopoe

Kroll, Virginia L. *Wood-hoopoe Willie*

Birds – woodpeckers

Tejima, Keizaburo. *Woodpecker forest*
Wildsmith, Brian. *The owl and the woodpecker*

Birds – wrens

Brock, Emma Lillian. *Mr. Wren's house*
Cock Robin. *The courtship, merry marriage, and feast of Cock Robin and Jenny Wren*
   Who killed Cock Robin?, ill. by William Stobbs
O'Malley, Kevin. *Who killed Cock Robin?*
Polacco, Patricia. *Luba and the wren*
Ravilious, Robin. *Two in a pocket*

Birth

Alexander, Sue. *One more time, Mama*
Andry, Andrew C. *Hi, new baby*
   How babies are made
Archambault, John. *The birth of a whale*
Baker, Gayle. *Special delivery*
Banish, Roslyn. *Let me tell you about my baby*
Berry, James. *Celebration song*
Brooks, Robert B. *So that's how I was born*
Brown, Craig McFarland. *In the spring*
Burton, Jane. *Chick*
   Kitten
   Puppy
Carrick, Carol. *In the moonlight, waiting*
Carter, Dorothy (Dorothy A.). *Wilhe'mina Miles after the stork night*
Christenson, Larry. *The wonderful way that babies are made*
Clayton, Gordon. *Lamb*
Cole, Babette. *Mommy laid an egg!*
Cole, Joanna. *A calf is born*
   How you were born
   My puppy is born
Corrin, Ruth. *Mister cat*
Dahl, Tessa. *Babies, babies, babies*
Davis, Jennifer. *Before you were born*
Farber, Norma. *All those mothers at the manger*
Fischer-Nagel, Heiderose. *A kitten is born*
   A puppy is born
Foreman, Michael. *Seal surfer*
Fox, Mem. *Sophie*
Frasier, Debra. *On the day you were born*
Fuchshuber, Annegert. *Two peas in a pod*
Girard, Linda Walvoord. *You were born on your very first birthday*

Gliori, Debi. *New big sister*
Haas, Jessie. *No foal yet*
Hariton, Anca. *Egg story*
Helldorfer, M. C. (Mary Claire). *Silver Rain Brown*
Hobson, Laura Z. *"I'm going to have a baby!"*
Horton, Barbara Savadge. *What comes in spring?*
Isenbart, Hans-Heinrich. *A duckling is born*
Jarrell, Randall. *A bat is born*
Jessell, Camilla. *The kitten book*
 The puppy book
Kaizuki, Kiyonori. *A calf is born*
MacLachlan, Patricia. *All the places to love*
Mantegazza, Giovanna. *Look how a baby grows*
Manushkin, Fran. *Baby, come out!*
Mark, Jan. *Fur*
Nanao, Jun. *Contemplating your bellybutton*
Oppenheim, Shulamith Levey. *Waiting for Noah*
Overend, Jenni. *Welcome with love*
Padt, Maartje. *Shanti*
Pringle, Laurence P. *Everybody has a bellybutton*
Pursell, Margaret Sanford. *A look at birth*
Rabinowitz, Sandy. *What's happening to Daisy?*
Rockwell, Lizzy. *Hello baby!*
Roddie, Shen. *Hatch, egg, hatch!*
Rosenberg, Maxine B. *Mommy's in the hospital having a baby*
Russo, Marisabina. *Waiting for Hannah*
Schilling, Betty. *Two kittens are born*
Selsam, Millicent E. *Egg to chick*
Sheffield, Margaret. *Before you were born*
 Where do babies come from?
Showers, Paul. *Before you were a baby*
Sykes, Julie. *Dora's eggs*
 This and that
Taylor, Kim. *Frog*
Watts, Barrie. *Duck*
 Rabbit
Willington, Monica. *Seasons of swans*

Birthdays

Abrons, Mary. *For Alice a palace*
Alexander, Sue. *World famous Muriel*
Aliki. *June 7!*
 Use your head, dear
Amoss, Berthe. *It's not your birthday*
Anderson, C. W. (Clarence Williams). *Billy and Blaze*
Anderson, Lena. *Stina's visit*
Anholt, Catherine. *Snow fairy and the spaceman*
Annett, Cora. *The dog who thought he was a boy*
Argent, Kerry. *Happy birthday wombat!*
Armitage, Ronda. *The bossing of Josie*
Arnold, Caroline. *Everybody has a birthday*
Arthur, Catherine. *My sister's silent world*
Asch, Frank. *Happy birthday, moon!*
Ashley, Bernard. *Dinner ladies don't count*
Ayer, Jacqueline. *A wish for little sister*
Balan, Bruce. *Pie in the sky*
Bannon, Laura. *Manuela's birthday*
Barbot, Daniel. *A bicycle for Rosaura*
Barklem, Jill. *Spring story*
Barrett, Judi. *Benjamin's 365 birthdays*
Bassett, Lisa. *A clock for Beany*
Bauer, Helen. *Good times at the park*
Bauer, Steven. *The strange and wonderful tale of Robert McDoodle*
Baum, Arline. *Opt*
Beck, Andrea. *Elliot bakes a cake*

Bell, Norman. *Linda's airmail letter*
Bemelmans, Ludwig. *Madeline in London*
Benchley, Peter. *Jonathan visits the White House*
Berenstain, Michael. *Peat Moss and Ivy and the birthday present*
Berenstain, Stan. *The Berenstain bears and too much birthday*
Beskow, Elsa Maartman. *Peter in Blueberry Land*
 Peter's adventures in Blueberry Land
Best, Cari. *Three cheers for Catherine the Great!*
Bible, Charles. *Jennifer's new chair*
Billam, Rosemary. *Fuzzy rabbit*
Biro, Val. *Gumdrop has a birthday*
Blocksma, Mary. *Grandma Dragon's birthday*
Bond, Felicia. *Mary Betty Lizzie McNutt's birthday*
Borden, Louise. *A. Lincoln and me*
Borovsky, Paul. *The fish that wasn't*
Bourgeois, Paulette. *Postal workers*
Boynton, Sandra. *Birthday monsters!*
Bradman, Tony. *The bad babies' book of colors*
Brandenberg, Franz. *Aunt Nina and her nephews and nieces*
 A secret for grandmother's birthday
Brillhart, Julie. *When daddy came to school*
Brimner, Larry Dane. *Country Bear's surprise*
Bromhall, Winifred. *Mary Ann's first picture*
Brown, Marc Tolon. *Arthur's birthday*
Brown, Margaret Wise. *The golden birthday book*
Brown, Tricia. *Hello, amigos!*
Browne, Anthony. *Gorilla*
Browne, Eileen. *No problem*
Bruna, Dick. *Miffy's birthday*
 Tilly and Tess
Brunhoff, Laurent de. *Babar's birthday surprise*
 Serafina the giraffe
Buntain, Ruth Jaeger. *The birthday story*
Bunting, Eve (Anne Evelyn). *Flower garden*
 Happy birthday, dear duck
 The robot birthday
 The Wednesday surprise
Burton, Marilee Robin. *Oliver's birthday*
Calmenson, Stephanie. *The birthday hat*
 Come to my party
 Zip, whiz, zoom!
Capucilli, Alyssa Satin. *Happy birthday, Biscuit!*
Carle, Eric. *Hello, red fox*
 The secret birthday message
Carlstrom, Nancy White. *Happy birthday, Jesse Bear!*
Carrick, Carol. *Paul's Christmas birthday*
Cartlidge, Michelle. *Bunny's birthday*
 Mouse birthday
Caseley, Judith. *Slumber party!*
 Three happy birthdays
Cazet, Denys. *December 24th*
 A fish in his pocket
Chalmers, Mary. *A hat for Amy Jean*
Charles, Donald. *Shaggy dog's birthday*
Charlip, Remy. *Handtalk birthday*
Chichester Clark, Emma. *Little Miss Muffet's count-along surprise*
Christelow, Eileen. *Don't wake up Mama!*
Clark, Gus. *How many days to my birthday?*
Clifton, Lucille. *Don't you remember?*
Cocca-Leffler, Maryann. *Ice-cold birthday*
Cohen, Barbara. *Make a wish, Molly*
Cole, Babette. *Babette Cole's beastly birthday book*
Cole, William. *What's good for a three-year-old?*
Cooke, Trish. *So much*
Corey, Dorothy. *Will it ever be my birthday?*

Lewis, Thomas P. *Call for Mr. Sniff*
Lexau, Joan M. *Go away, dog*, ill. by Crosby Newell Bonsall
  Go away, dog, ill. by Paul Meisel
  Me day
Lindman, Maj. *Flicka, Ricka, Dicka bake a cake*
  Snipp, Snapp, Snurr and the red shoes
Lishak, Anthony. *Row your boat*
Little, Lessie Jones. *I can do it by myself*
Livingston, Myra Cohn. *Birthday poems*
Lobe, Mira. *Christoph wants a party*
Lobel, Anita. *A birthday for the princess*
Lodge, Bernard. *Mouldylocks*
London, Jonathan. *Shawn and Keeper and the birthday party*
Lopez, Loretta. *The birthday swap*
Lorian, Nicole. *A birthday present for Mama*
Lowrey, Janette Sebring. *Six silver spoons*
Lundell, Margo. *Teddy bear's birthday*
Lyndon, Kerry Raines. *A birthday for Blue*
McAllister, Angela. *The enchanted flute*
  Snail's birthday problem
McCourt, Lisa. *Chicken soup for little souls: The never-forgotten doll*
  Della Splatnuk birthday girl
McCue, Lisa. *Corduroy's party*
MacDonald, Elizabeth. *Mr. Badger's birthday pie*
MacDonald, Maryann. *Rabbit's birthday kite*
McKee, David. *King Rollo and the birthday*
  Prince Peter and the teddy bear
MacKinnon, Debbie. *Cathy's cake*
  Find my cake!
McKissack, Patricia C. *Messy Bessey and the birthday overnight*
McNeill, Janet. *The giant's birthday*
Madrigal, Antonio Hernandez. *Erandi's braids*
Marie, Geraldine. *The magic box*
Martin, Bill (William Ivan). *Fire! Fire! said Mrs. McGuire*
Martin, David. *Monkey business*
Merriam, Eve. *The birthday door*
Metaxas, Eric. *The birthday ABC*
Miklowitz, Gloria D. *Bearfoot boy*
Miles, Miska. *Mouse six and the happy birthday*
Miller, Margaret. *My birthday*
Minarik, Else Holmelund. *Little Bear*
Miranda, Anne. *Cownting*
  Monster math
Modarressi, Mitra. *The dream pillow*
Modell, Frank. *Ice cream soup*
Mogensen, Jan. *Teddy's birthday bugle*
Moon, Grace Purdie. *One little Indian*
Mora, Pat. *A birthday basket for Tía*
  Pablo's tree
  Uno, dos, tres = One, two, three
Morice, Dave. *The happy birthday handbook*
Mother Goose. *Pat-a-cake*, ill. by Marilyn Janovitz
Mueller, Virginia. *Monster's birthday hiccups*
Munari, Bruno. *The birthday present*
Munsch, Robert N. *Moira's birthday*
  Wait and see
Murphy, Stuart J. *Too many kangaroo things to do!*
Myers, Bernice. *Charlie's birthday present*
Myller, Rolf. *How big is a foot?*
Myrick, Jean Lockwood. *Ninety-nine pockets*
Ness, Evaline. *Josefina February*
Nightingale, Sandy. *I'm a little monster*
Nixon, Joan Lowery. *When I am eight*

Noble, Trinka Hakes. *Jimmy's boa and the big splash birthday bash*
Noll, Sally. *Surprise!*
O'Donnell, Elizabeth Lee. *Patrick's day*
Oppenheim, Shulamith Levey. *Waiting for Noah*
Ostheeren, Ingrid. *The blue monster*
Owen, Annie. *Bumper to bumper*
Oxenbury, Helen. *The birthday party*
  It's my birthday
Parish, Peggy. *Be ready at eight*
  Scruffy
  Snapping turtle's all wrong day
Park, W. B. *Bakery business*
Parker, Nancy Winslow. *Love from Uncle Clyde*
Paterson, Bettina. *Bun's birthday*
Patz, Nancy. *No thumpin' no bumpin' no rumpus tonight!*
Pearson, Susan. *Happy birthday, Grampie*
Peek, Merle. *Mary wore her red dress and Henry wore his green sneakers*
Peppé, Rodney. *The kettleship pirates*
Perkins, Al. *Tubby and the lantern*
Peters, Sharon. *Happy birthday*
Peterson, Esther Allen. *Penelope gets wheels*
Pfister, Marcus. *Make a wish, Honey Bear!*
Pittman, Helena Clare. *A dinosaur for Gerald*
Polacco, Patricia. *Some birthday!*
Pomerantz, Charlotte. *The half-birthday party*
  You're not my best friend anymore
Prager, Annabelle. *The surprise party*
  The pudgy fingers counting book
Quin-Harkin, Janet. *Helpful Hattie*
Radlauer, Ruth Shaw. *Breakfast by Molly*
Reed, Lynn Rowe. *Pedro, his perro, and the alphabet sombrero*
Rice, Eve. *Benny bakes a cake*
Robins, Joan. *Addie's bad day*
Rockwell, Anne F. *Happy birthday to me*
  Hugo at the window
Rodda, Emily. *Power and glory*
Roffey, Maureen. *Mealtime*
Rollings, Susan. *New shoes, red shoes*
Root, Phyllis. *Gretchen's grandma*
Russo, Marisabina. *Only six more days*
Rylant, Cynthia. *Birthday presents*
Saltzberg, Barney. *The Flying Garbanzos*
Samuels, Barbara. *Happy birthday, Dolores*
Sandberg, Inger. *Nicholas' favorite pet*
Sawicki, Norma Jean. *Something for mom*
Schneider, Antonie. *The birthday bear*
Schumacher, Claire. *Nutty's birthday*
Schweninger, Ann. *Birthday wishes*
Seuss, Dr. *Happy birthday to you!*
  Hooper Humperdink . . . ? Not him!
Sewell, Helen Moore. *Birthdays for Robin*
Shannon, George. *The surprise*
Sherrow, Victoria. *Wilbur waits*
Shimin, Symeon. *A special birthday*
Singer, Marilyn. *Minnie's Yom Kippur birthday*
Sis, Peter. *Going up!*
Smith, Wendy. *Say hello, Tilly*
Soto, Gary. *Chato and the party animals*
Spurr, Elizabeth. *The biggest birthday cake in the world*
Stapler, Sarah. *Spruce the moose cuts loose*
Steiner, Charlotte. *Birthdays are for everyone*
Steptoe, John. *Birthday*
Stevenson, Suçie. *I forgot*
Stewart, Paul. *The birthday presents*

Stock, Catherine. *The birthday present*
Supraner, Robyn. *Sam Sunday and the mystery at the Ocean Beach Hotel*
Sutton, Elizabeth Henning. *A pony for keeps*
Tafuri, Nancy. *The barn party*
Theroux, Phyllis. *Serefina under the circumstances*
Thomas, Naturi. *Uh-oh! It's Mama's birthday!*
Trimble, Patti. *What day is it?*
Tryon, Leslie. *Albert's birthday*
Türk, Hanne. *Happy birthday Max*
Turnbull, Ann. *The tapestry cats*
Tyler, Linda Wagner. *The sick-in-bed birthday book*
Uchida, Yoshiko. *Sumi's special happening*
Van der Beek, Deborah. *Alice's blue cloth*
Vigna, Judith. *Mommy and me by ourselves again*
    My two uncles
Wabbes, Marie. *Happy birthday, Little Rabbit*
Waber, Bernard. *Lyle and the birthday party*
Wadsworth, Ginger. *Tomorrow is Daddy's birthday*
Wallace, John. *Tiny Rabbit goes to a birthday party*
Wallace, Nancy Elizabeth. *Tell-a-bunny*
Wardlaw, Lee. *Bow-wow birthday*
Watanabe, Shigeo. *It's my birthday*
Watson, Nancy Dingman. *The birthday goat*
    Tommy's mommy's fish, ill. by Aldren Auld Watson
    Tommy's mommy's fish, ill. by Thomas Aldren Dingman Watson
Weeks, Sarah. *Happy birthday, Frankie*
Weiss, Ellen. *Mokey's birthday present*
Wells, Rosemary. *Max's birthday*
Weninger, Brigitte. *Happy birthday, Davy*
West, Colin. *Go tell it to the toucan*
White, Linda Arms. *Comes a wind*
Whittington, Mary K. *The patchwork lady*
Wickstrom, Sylvie (Sylvie Kantrovitz). *Mothers can't get sick*
Willard, Nancy. *The high rise glorious skittle skat roarious sky pie angel food cake*
    The marzipan moon
Williams, Barbara. *Whatever happened to Beverly Bigler's birthday?*
Williams, Vera B. *Something special for me*
Willis, Jeanne. *Sloth's shoes*
Wilson, Sarah. *Uncle Albert's flying birthday*
Wormell, Mary. *Hilda Hen's happy birthday*
Worth, Bonnie. *Peter Cottontail's surprise*
Yaroshevskaya, Kim. *Little Kim's doll*
Yashima, Taro. *Umbrella*
Yezerski, Thomas. *Queen of the world*
Yolen, Jane. *Picnic with Piggins*
Ziefert, Harriet. *Happy birthday, Grandpa!*
    Surprise!
Zimelman, Nathan. *Once when I was five*
Zolotow, Charlotte (Shapiro). *Mr. Rabbit and the lovely present*

Bison *see* Animals – buffaloes

Black Americans *see* Ethnic groups in the U.S. – African Americans

Black Carib *see* Indians of Central America – Black Carib

Blackbirds *see* Birds – blackbirds

Blackfoot Indians *see* Indians of North America – Blackfoot

Blackouts *see* Power failure

Blindness *see* Handicaps – blindness; Senses – seeing

Blizzards *see* Weather – blizzards

Blocks *see* Toys – blocks

Bluejays *see* Birds – bluejays

Board books *see* Format, unusual – board books

Boasting *see* Behavior – boasting

Boat builders *see* Careers – boat builders

Boats, ships

Agell, Charlotte. *The sailor's book*
Ahlberg, Allan. *Skeleton crew*
Alexander, Anne (Anna Barbara Cooke). *Boats and ships from A to Z*
Allan, Jonathan. *Two by two by two*
Allen, Pamela. *Who sank the boat?*
Amoss, Berthe. *Old Hannibal and the hurricane*
Anderson, Joan. *Sally's submarine*
Anderson, Lonzo. *Arion and the dolphins*
Ardizzone, Edward. *Little Tim and the brave sea captain*
    Ship's cook Ginger
    Tim all alone
    Tim and Charlotte
    Tim and Ginger
    Tim and Lucy go to sea
    Tim in danger
    Tim to the rescue
    Tim's friend Towser
    Tim's last voyage
Augarde, Steve (Stephen). *Barnaby Shrew goes to sea*
Baker, Betty. *My sister says*
Barton, Byron. *Boats*
Bate, Norman. *What a wonderful machine is a submarine*
Beck, Ian. *Emily and the golden acorn*
Benjamin, Alan. *A change of plans*
Berenstain, Michael. *The ship book*
Bible. Old Testament. Noah. *Noah and the ark*, ill. by Pauline Baynes
    Noah and the ark, ill. by Jim Cummins
Blake, Robert J. *Spray*
Bolliger, Max. *Noah and the rainbow*
Brent, Isabelle. *Noah's ark*
Bridgman, Elizabeth. *Nanny bear's cruise*
Brown, Jane Clark. *Whonk, and whonk again*
Brown, Judith Gwyn. *The happy voyage*
Brown, Marc Tolon. *Marc Brown's Boat book*
Brown, Marcia. *Skipper John's cook*
Brown, Rick. *Who built the ark?*
Bruna, Dick. *The sailor*
Buchanan, Heather S. *George Mouse's riverboat band*
Burchard, Peter. *The Carol Moran*
Burdett, Lois. *Twelfth night*

Burke, Timothy. *Tugboats in action*
Burningham, John. *Mr. Gumpy's outing*
Bushey, Jerry. *The barge book*
Calhoun, Mary. *Euphonia and the flood*
   Henry the sailor cat
Campbell, Ann. *Let's find out about boats*
Carrick, Carol. *The washout*
Carryl, Charles E. (Charles Edward). *A capital ship*
   The walloping window-blind, ill. by Jim LaMarche
   The walloping window blind
Carter, Katharine. *Ships and seaports*
Chalmers, Mary. *Boots finds a house*
Chase, Catherine. *Noah's ark*
Cohen, Peter Zachary. *Authorized autumn charts of*
   the Upper Red Canoe River country
Conrad, Pam. *The lost sailor*
Conway, Celeste. *Where is Papa now?*
Cousins, Lucy. *Noah's ark*
Crews, Donald. *Harbor*
   Sail away
Day, Alexandra. *River parade*
Deedy, Carmen Agra. *The secret of Old Zeb*
DeLage, Ida. *Pilgrim children on the Mayflower*
Delessert, Etienne. *The endless party*
Demarest, Chris L. *My blue boat*
   Ship
Demi. *The magic boat*
Dennis, Morgan. *The sea dog*
Denton, Terry. *Home is the sailor*
De Paola, Tomie (Thomas Anthony). *Four stories*
   for four seasons
   Noah and the ark
DeRubertis, Barbara. *Columbus Day*
Devlin, Harry. *The walloping window blind*
Diller, Harriett. *The waiting day*
Doherty, Berlie. *Snowy*
Domanska, Janina. *I saw a ship a-sailing*
Dorros, Arthur. *Pretzels*
Du Bois, William Pène. *Otto at sea*
Dunrea, Olivier. *Fergus and Bridey*
Dupasquier, Philippe. *Dear Daddy . . .*
   Jack at sea
Duvoisin, Roger Antoine. *A for the ark*
Elborn, Andrew. *Noah and the ark and the animals*
Elting, Mary. *The big book of real boats and ships*
Emberley, Ed (Edward Randolph). *Cars, boats, and*
   planes
Farber, Norma. *How the left-behind beasts built Ararat*
   Where's Gomer?
Faulkner, Matt. *The amazing voyage of Jackie Grace*
Figley, Marty Rhodes. *Noah's wife*
Fischetto, Laura. *All pigs on deck*
   Inside Noah's ark
Flack, Marjorie. *The boats on the river*
Flora, James. *Fishing with dad*
Foreman, Michael. *Jack's fantastic voyage*
French, Fiona. *Rise and shine*
Fry, Christopher. *The boat that mooed*
Fussenegger, Gertrud. *Noah's ark*
Garland, Sherry. *My father's boat*
Gauch, Patricia Lee. *Noah*
Gay, Michel. *Little boat*
Gedin, Birgitta. *The little house from the sea*
Geisert, Arthur. *After the flood*
   The ark
Gerrard, Roy. *Sir Francis Drake*
Gerstein, Mordicai. *Noah and the great flood*
Gibbons, Gail. *Boat book*
Ginsburg, Mirra. *Four brave sailors*

Goffstein, M. B. (Marilyn Brooke). *My Noah's ark*
Gomboli, Mario. *Look inside a ship*
Goodall, John S. *Jacko*
Goodhart, Pippa. *Noah makes a boat*
   Row, row, row your boat
Gorbachev, Valeri. *The Fool of the world and the fly-*
   ing ship
Graham, Lorenz B. *God wash the world and start*
   again
Graham, Margaret Bloy. *Benjy's boat trip*
Graham, Thomas. *Mr. Bear's boat*
Gramatky, Hardie. *Little Toot*
   Little Toot and the Loch Ness monster
   Little Toot on the Mississippi
   Little Toot on the Thames
   Little Toot through the Golden Gate
Greene, Carol. *Sunflower Island*
Haas, Irene. *The Maggie B*
Halak, Glenn. *A grandmother's story*
Haley, Gail E. *Noah's ark*
Hansen, Carla. *Barnaby Bear builds a boat*
Harness, Cheryl. *Mark Twain and the queens of the*
   Mississippi
Haubensak-Tellenbach, Margrit. *The story of Noah's*
   ark
Hayward, Linda. *Noah's ark*
Helldorfer, M. C. (Mary Claire). *Sailing to the sea*
Henderson, Kathy. *The little boat*
Henrioud, Charles. *Mr. Noah and the animals*
Hest, Amy. *A sort-of sailor*
Hewitt, Kathryn. *Two by two*
Hillert, Margaret. *The yellow boat*
Hogrogian, Nonny. *Noah's ark*
Holabird, Katharine. *Alexander and the magic boat*
Hooper, Meredith. *Tom's rabbit*
Hoopes, Lyn Littlefield. *Half a button*
Hunt, Jonathan. *Leif's saga*
Hurd, Edith Thacher. *What whale? Where?*
Hutton, Warwick. *Noah and the great flood*
Ife, Elaine. *Noah and the ark*
Isadora, Rachel. *No, Agatha!*
Janisch, Heinz. *Noah's ark*
Joerns, Consuelo. *The foggy rescue*
Johnson, Pamela. *A mouse's tale*
Jonas, Ann. *Aardvarks, disembark!*
Kellogg, Steven (Stephen). *The island of the skog*
   Mike Fink
Kovacs, Deborah. *Moonlight on the river*
Kroll, Steven. *The pigrates clean up*
Kuskin, Karla. *The animals and the ark*
Landström, Olof. *Boo and Baa at sea*
Lang, Andrew. *The flying ship*
Lenski, Lois. *Mr. and Mrs. Noah*
Leonard, Marcia. *Violet and the pirates*
Le Tord, Bijou. *Noah's trees*
Lewin, Ted. *Amazon boy*
   Nilo and the tortoise
Lewis, J. Patrick. *The boat of many rooms*
   The Fat-Cats at sea
Lewis, Thomas P. *Clipper ship*
Lindman, Maj. *Sailboat time*
Lippman, Peter. *The Know-It-Alls go to sea*
Litowinsky, Olga. *Boats for bedtime*
Locker, Thomas. *Sailing with the wind*
London, Jonathan. *Old salt, young salt*
Lööf, Jan. *Uncle Louie's fantastic sea voyage*
Ludwig, Warren. *Old Noah's elephants*
Maass, Robert. *Tugboats*
MacBeth, George. *Noah's journey*

McCarthy, Bobette. *Dreaming*
McCaughrean, Geraldine. *The story of Noah and the ark*
McCloskey, Robert. *Bert Dow, deep-water man*
McCully, Emily Arnold. *The pirate queen*
McDonnell, Flora. *I love boats*
MacGill-Callahan, Sheila. *To capture the wind*
McGovern, Ann. *Nicholas Bentley Stoningpot III*
McGowan, Alan. *Sailing ships*
McKié, Roy. *Noah's ark*
McMillan, Bruce. *Going on a whale watch*
McPhail, David M. *Pigs ahoy!*
Maestro, Betsy. *Big city port*
  Ferryboat
Mahy, Margaret. *Sailor Jack and the twenty orphans*
Marshall, James. *Speedboat*
Marston, Elsa. *Cynthia and the runaway gazebo*
Martin, Charles E. *Noah's ark*
Meddaugh, Susan. *Maude and Claude go abroad*
Mee, Charles L. *Noah*
Mendoza, George. *The alphabet boat*
Metaxas, Eric. *The fool and the flying ship*
  Stormalong, the legendary sea captain
Miles, Miska. *No, no, Rosina*
Miller, Ruth. *I went to the bay*
Mills, Judith Christine. *The stonehook schooner*
Modarressi, Mitra. *The parent thief*
Monfried, Lucia. *The Daddies Boat*
Morgan, Allen. *Nicole's boat*
Most, Bernard. *Row, row, row your goat*
Nakawatari, Harutaka. *The sea and I*
O'Hearn, Michael. *Hercules the harbor tug*
Olson, Arielle North. *Noah's cats and the devil's fire*
O'Neill, Alexis. *Loud Emily*
Ostheeren, Ingrid. *Fabian Youngpig sails the world*
Palazzo, Tony (Anthony D.). *Noah's ark*
Pallotta, Jerry. *The dory story*
Paraskevas, Betty. *On the day the tall ships sailed*
Partridge, Jenny. *Hopfellow*
Peppé, Rodney. *The kettleship pirates*
Perkins, Al. *Tubby and the Poo-Bah*
Pfanner, Louise. *Louise builds a boat*
Pitcher, Caroline. *Cars and boats*
Potter, Beatrix. *The tale of Little Pig Robinson*
Priest, Robert. *The old pirate of Central Park*
Rand, Gloria. *Aloha, Salty!*
  Salty dog
  Salty sails north
Ransome, Arthur. *The fool of the world and the flying ship*
Rassmus, Jens. *Farmer Enno and his cow*
Reavin, Sam. *Hurray for Captain Jane!*
Reesink, Marijke. *The golden treasure*
Rettich, Margret. *The voyage of the jolly boat*
Rockwell, Anne F. *Boats*
  Ferryboat ride!
Rohmann, Eric. *The cinder-eyed cats*
Root, Phyllis. *Sam, who was swallowed by a shark*
Rose, Gerald. *Trouble in the ark*
Rotner, Shelley. *Boats afloat*
Round, Graham. *Hangdog*
Rounds, Glen. *Washday on Noah's ark*
Royston, Angela. *Ships and boats*
Rubel, Nicole. *Uncle Henry and Aunt Henrietta's honeymoon*
Rumford, James. *The Island-below-the-star*
Samton, Sheila White. *Jenny's journey*
San Souci, Robert D. *Brave Margaret*
Santore, Charles. *A stowaway on Noah's Ark*

Sasso, Sandy Eisenberg. *A prayer for the earth*
Scarry, Richard. *Pie rats ahoy!*
Schaefer, Lola M. *Tugboats*
Schaffer, Libor. *Arthur sets sail*
Schulz, Charles M. *Snoopy's facts and fun book about boats*
Seibold, J. Otto. *Mr. Lunch borrows a canoe*
Seymour, Tres. *The gulls of the Edmund Fitzgerald*
Shaw, Nancy (Nancy E.). *Sheep on a ship*
Shecter, Ben. *If I had a ship*
Shortall, Leonard W. *Tod on the tugboat*
Singer, Isaac Bashevis. *Why Noah chose the dove*
Sis, Peter. *Ship ahoy!*
Slawski, Wolfgang. *Captain Jonathan sails the sea*
Smith, Barry. *The first voyage of Christopher Columbus*
Smith, Elmer Boyd. *The story of Noah's ark*
Smith, Roger. *How the animals saved the ark and put two and two together*
Spier, Peter. *Noah's ark*
Spooner, J. B. *The story of the little Black Dog*
Stevenson, James. *The stowaway*
Stevenson, Jocelyn. *Jim Henson's Muppets at sea*
Surany, Anico. *Ride the cold wind*
Swift, Hildegarde Hoyt. *The little red lighthouse and the great gray bridge*
Tagore, Rabindranath. *Paper boats*
Taylor, Mark. *Henry the castaway*
Thomson, Ruth. *Peabody all at sea*
Thorne, Jenny. *Noah's ark*
Titherington, Jeanne. *Baby's boat*
  Baby's boat, a board book
Trapani, Iza. *Row, row, row your boat*
Tudor, Bethany. *Skiddycock Pond*
Twining, Edith. *Sandman*
Van Allsburg, Chris. *The wreck of the Zephyr*
Van Leeuwen, Jean. *Across the wide dark sea*
Venable, Alan. *The checker players*
Vernon, Tannis. *Little Pig and the blue-green sea*
Waddell, Martin. *Sailor Bear*
Walton, Rick. *Noah's square dance*
Waters, Tony. *Sailor's bride*
Webb, Clifford. *The story of Noah*
Wiesner, William. *Noah's ark*
Willard, Nancy. *The voyage of the Ludgate Hill*
Williams, Vera B. *Three days on a river in a red canoe*
Windham, Sophie. *Noah's ark*
Winter, Jeanette. *The Christmas tree ship*
Wood, Jakki. *Across the big blue sea*
Young, James. *Penelope and the pirates*
Young, Miriam Burt. *If I sailed a boat*
Young, Ruth. *Daisy's taxi*
Zaffo, George J. *The giant nursery book of things that go*
Ziefert, Harriet. *My sister says nothing ever happens when we go sailing*

Bobcats *see* Animals – bobcats

Bombs *see* Weapons

Boobys *see* Birds – boobys

Boogy man *see* Monsters

Books *see* Activities – reading; Libraries

Boots *see* Clothing – boots; Clothing – shoes

Boredom *see* Behavior – boredom

Borneo *see* Foreign lands – Borneo

Botswana *see* Foreign lands – Botswana

Bowling *see* Sports – bowling

Boxing *see* Sports – boxing

Bravery *see* Character traits – bravery

Brazil *see* Foreign lands – Brazil

Bridges

Buckley, Helen Elizabeth. *The leftover bridge*
Carlisle, Norman. *Bridges*
Hunter, Ryan Ann. *Cross a bridge*
Lobel, Anita. *Sven's bridge*
McCully, Emily Arnold. *Crossing the new bridge*
Neville, Emily Cheney. *The bridge*
Oppenheim, Joanne. *On the other side of the river*
Steadman, Ralph. *The bridge*
Swift, Hildegarde Hoyt. *The little red lighthouse and the great gray bridge*
Yagelski, Robert. *The day the lifting bridge stuck*

Brothers *see* Family life; Family life – brothers; Family life – brothers and sisters; Sibling rivalry

Brownies *see* Mythical creatures – elves

Brush wolf *see* Animals – coyotes

Bubbles

Anastasio, Dina. *Baby Piggy and giant bubble*
Bridwell, Norman. *Clifford counts bubbles*
De Paola, Tomie (Thomas Anthony). *The bubble factory*
   Strega Nona takes a vacation
Edwards, Frank B. *Troubles with bubbles*
Hooks, William H. *How do you make a bubble?*
Hulme, Joy N. *Bubble trouble*
Inkpen, Mick. *Thing*
Josephs, Rhoda. *The baby bubble book*
Lorimer, Janet. *The biggest bubble in the world*
Manushkin, Fran. *Bubblebath!*
Mayer, Mercer. *Bubble bubble*
O'Connor, Jane. *Benny's big bubble*
Packard, Mary. *Bubble trouble*
Schubert, Ingrid. *The magic bubble trip*
Woodruff, Elvira. *Show and tell*
   Tubtime
Zager, Karen. *Bubbles*

Buffaloes *see* Animals – buffaloes

Bugs *see* Insects

Buildings

Balterman, Lee. *Girders and cranes*
Barkan, Joanne. *Whiskerville bake shop*
   Whiskerville firehouse
   Whiskerville post office
   Whiskerville school
Bunting, Eve (Anne Evelyn). *Night of the gargoyles*
Cooper, Elisha. *Building*
Czernecki, Stefan. *The cricket's cage*
Gibbons, Gail. *Up goes the skyscraper!*
Henri, Adrian. *The postman's palace*
Hunter, Ryan Ann. *Into the sky*
Merriam, Eve. *Bam, bam, bam*
Numeroff, Laura Joffe. *What daddies do best*
Otto, Carolyn. *Pioneer church*
Parker, Steve. *I wonder why tunnels are round*
Pluckrose, Henry Arthur. *Walls*
Reasoner, Charles. *The big busy building*
Rex, Michael. *Who builds?*
Tarsky, Sue. *The busy building book*
Zelver, Patricia. *The wonderful Towers of Watts*

Bulldozers *see* Machines

Bulls *see* Animals – bulls, cows

Bullying *see* Behavior – bullying

Bumble bees *see* Insects – bees

Bungee Indians *see* Indians of North America – Bungee

Burglars *see* Crime

Burma *see* Foreign lands – Burma

Burros *see* Animals – donkeys

Bus drivers *see* Careers – bus drivers

Buses

Blance, Ellen. *Monster on the bus*
Brown, Marc Tolon. *Arthur lost and found*
Browne, Eileen. *Where's that bus?*
Cole, Joanna. *The magic school bus in the time of the dinosaurs*
   The magic school bus inside a beehive
   The magic school bus lost in the solar system
   The magic school bus on the ocean floor
Cossi, Olga. *Gus the bus*
Crews, Donald. *School bus*
Demarest, Chris L. *Bus*
Denslow, Sharon Phillips. *Bus riders*
Foreman, Michael. *The perfect present*
Fuller, Ted. *Barney the bus*
Giffard, Hannah. *Red bus*
Gomi, Taro. *Bus stop*
Hellen, Nancy. *Bus stop*
Hindley, Judy. *The big red bus*
Hirst, Robin. *My place in space*
Jewell, Nancy. *Bus ride*
Kilroy, Sally. *On the road*
Kingsland, Robin. *Bus stop bop*
Kovalski, Maryann. *The wheels on the bus*
McMahon, Patricia. *Listen for the bus*
Matthias, Catherine. *Out the door*
Muntean, Michaela. *The very bumpy bus ride*
Nichols, Paul. *Big Paul's school bus*
Peppé, Rodney. *The mice and the clockwork bus*

Piers, Helen. *Is there room on the bus?*
Shuttlesworth, Dorothy Edwards. *ABC of buses*
Wolcott, Patty. *Double-decker, double-decker, double-decker bus*
Young, Miriam Burt. *If I drove a bus*
Zelinsky, Paul O. *The wheels on the bus*
Ziefert, Harriet. *Jason's bus ride*

Bushbabies *see* Animals – bushbabies

Butchers *see* Careers – butchers

Butterflies *see* Insects – butterflies, caterpillars

Buzzards *see* Birds – buzzards

Cab drivers *see* Careers – taxi drivers

Cable cars, trolleys

Burton, Virginia Lee. *Maybelle, the cable car*
Caen, Herb. *The cable car and the dragon*
Chalmers, Mary. *Here comes the trolley*
Gramatky, Hardie. *Sparky*
McMillan, Bruce. *Grandfather's trolley*
Taniuchi, Kota. *Trolley*

Cabs *see* Taxis

Cafés *see* Restaurants

Caldecott award books

Aardema, Verna. *Why mosquitoes buzz in people's ears*
Ackerman, Karen. *Song and dance man*
Alger, Leclaire Gowans. *Always room for one more*
Aulaire, Ingri Mortenson d'. *Abraham Lincoln*
Bemelmans, Ludwig. *Madeline's rescue*
Brown, Marcia. *Once a mouse . . .*
Brown, Margaret Wise. *The little island*
Bunting, Eve (Anne Evelyn). *Smoky night*
Burton, Virginia Lee. *The little house*
Cendrars, Blaise. *Shadow*
Chaucer, Geoffrey. *Chanticleer and the fox*
De Regniers, Beatrice Schenk. *May I bring a friend?*
Emberley, Barbara. *Drummer Hoff*
Ets, Marie Hall. *Nine days to Christmas*
Field, Rachel Lyman. *Prayer for a child*
A frog he would a-wooing go (folk-song). *Frog went a-courtin'*, ill. by Feodor Rojankovsky
Goble, Paul. *The girl who loved wild horses*
Grimm, Jacob. *Rapunzel*, ill. by Paul O. Zelinsky
Hader, Berta Hoerner. *The big snow*
Haley, Gail E. *A story, a story*
Hall, Donald. *The ox-cart man*
Handforth, Thomas. *Mei Li*
Hodges, Margaret. *Saint George and the dragon*
Hogrogian, Nonny. *One fine day*
Keats, Ezra Jack. *The snowy day*

The snowy day (a board book)
Lawson, Robert. *They were strong and good*
Lipkind, William. *Finders keepers*
Lobel, Arnold. *Fables*
Macaulay, David. *Black and white*
McCloskey, Robert. *Make way for ducklings*
   Time of wonder
McCully, Emily Arnold. *Mirette on the high wire*
McDermott, Gerald. *Arrow to the sun*
Martin, Jacqueline Briggs. *Snowflake Bentley*
Milhous, Katherine. *The egg tree*
Mosel, Arlene. *The funny little woman*
Musgrove, Margaret. *Ashanti to Zulu*
Ness, Evaline. *Sam, Bangs, and moonshine*
Perrault, Charles. *Cinderella*, ill. by Marcia Brown
Petersham, Maud. *The rooster crows*
Politi, Leo. *Song of the swallows*
Provensen, Alice. *The glorious flight*
Ransome, Arthur. *The fool of the world and the flying ship*
Rathmann, Peggy. *Officer Buckle and Gloria*
Robbins, Ruth. *Baboushka and the three kings*
St. George, Judith. *So you want to be president?*
Sendak, Maurice. *Where the wild things are*
Spier, Peter. *Noah's ark*
Steig, William. *Sylvester and the magic pebble*
Taback, Simms. *Joseph had a little overcoat*
Thurber, James. *Many moons*, ill. by Louis Slobodkin
Tresselt, Alvin R. *White snow, bright snow*
Udry, Janice May. *A tree is nice*
Van Allsburg, Chris. *Jumanji*
   The polar express
Ward, Lynd. *The biggest bear*
Wiesner, David. *Tuesday*
Yolen, Jane. *Owl moon*
Yorinks, Arthur. *Hey, Al*
Young, Ed (Edward). *Lon Po Po*
Zemach, Harve. *Duffy and the devil*

Caldecott award honor books

Alger, Leclaire Gowans. *All in the morning early*
Andersen, H. C. (Hans Christian). *The ugly duckling*, ill. by Jerry Pinkney
Armer, Laura Adams. *The forest pool*
Artzybasheff, Boris. *Seven Simeons*
Baker, Olaf. *Where the buffaloes begin*
Bang, Molly. *The grey lady and the strawberry snatcher*
   Ten, nine, eight
   When Sophie gets angry – really, really angry . . .
Bartone, Elisa. *Peppe the lamplighter*
Baskin, Leonard. *Hosie's alphabet*
Baylor, Byrd. *The desert is theirs*
   Hawk, I'm your brother
   The way to start a day
   When clay sings
Belting, Natalia Maree. *The sun is a golden earring*
Bemelmans, Ludwig. *Madeline*
Birnbaum, Abe. *Green eyes*
Brown, Marcia. *Henry fisherman*
   Skipper John's cook
   Stone soup
Brown, Margaret Wise. *A child's good night book*
   Little lost lamb
   Wheel on the chimney
Buff, Mary (Marsh). *Dash and Dart*
Cathon, Laura E. *Tot Botot and his little flute*

Caudill, Rebecca. *A pocketful of cricket*
Chan, Chin-Yi. *Good luck horse*
A child's calendar
Clark, Ann Nolan. *In my mother's house*
Crews, Donald. *Freight train*
  Truck
Cronin, Doreen. *Click, clack, moo*
Dalgliesh, Alice. *The Thanksgiving story*
Daugherty, James Henry. *Andy and the lion*
Davis, Lavinia (Riker). *Roger and the fox*
  The wild birthday cake
Dayrell, Elphinstone. *Why the sun and the moon live in the sky*
De Angeli, Marguerite. *The book of nursery and Mother Goose rhymes*
  Yonie Wondernose
De Paola, Tomie (Thomas Anthony). *Strega Nona*
Dick Whittington and his cat. *Dick Whittington and his cat*, ill. by Marcia Brown
Domanska, Janina. *If all the seas were one sea*
Du Bois, William Pène. *Bear party*
  Lion
Ehlert, Lois. *Color zoo*
Eichenberg, Fritz. *Ape in cape*
Elkin, Benjamin. *Gillespie and the guards*
Emberley, Barbara. *One wide river to cross*
Ets, Marie Hall. *In the forest*
  Just me
  Mister Penny
  Mr. Penny's race horse
  Mr. T. W. Anthony Woo
  Play with me
Falconer, Ian. *Olivia*
Feelings, Muriel. *Jambo means hello*
  Menjo means one
Fish, Helen Dean. *Four and twenty blackbirds*
Flack, Marjorie. *The boats on the river*
Fleming, Denise. *In the small, small pond*
Ford, Lauren. *The ageless story*
The fox went out on a chilly night
Freeman, Don. *Fly high, fly low*
Gág, Wanda. *Nothing at all*
Goffstein, M. B. (Marilyn Brooke). *Fish for supper*
Goudey, Alice E. *The day we saw the sun come up*
  Houses from the sea
Graham, Al. *Timothy Turtle*
Grifalconi, Ann. *The village of round and square houses*
Grimm, Jacob. *The Bremen town musicians*, ill. by Ilse Plume
  Hansel and Gretel, ill. by Paul O. Zelinsky
  Little Red Riding Hood, ill. by Trina Schart Hyman
  Snow White and the seven dwarfs, ill. by Wanda Gág
Hader, Berta Hoerner. *Cock-a-doodle doo*
  The mighty hunter
Henkes, Kevin. *Owen*
Ho, Minfong. *Hush!*
Hodges, Margaret. *The wave*
Hogrogian, Nonny. *The contest*
Holbrook, Stewart. *America's Ethan Allen*
Holling, Holling C. (Holling Clancy). *Paddle-to-the-sea*
The house that Jack built. The house that Jack built, ill. by Antonio Frasconi
Isaacs, Anne. *Swamp Angel*
Isadora, Rachel. *Ben's trumpet*
Johnson, Stephen T. *Alphabet city*

Jonas, Ann. *Holes and peeks*
Jones, Jessie Mae Orton. *Small rain*
Joslin, Sesyle. *What do you say, dear?*
Keats, Ezra Jack. *Goggles*
Kepes, Juliet. *Five little monkeys*
Kimmel, Eric A. *Hershel and the Hanukkah goblins*
Kingman, Lee. *Pierre Pigeon*
Krauss, Ruth. *The happy day*
  A very special house
Leaf, Munro. *Wee Gillis*
Lester, Julius. *John Henry*
Lionni, Leo. *Alexander and the wind-up mouse*
  Frederick
  Inch by inch
  Swimmy
Lipkind, William. *The two reds*
Little old lady who swallowed a fly. There was an old lady who swallowed a fly, ill. by Simms Taback
Lobel, Arnold. *Frog and Toad are friends*
  On Market Street
Low, Joseph. *Mice twice*
Macaulay, David. *Castle*
  Cathedral
McCloskey, Robert. *Blueberries for Sal*
  One morning in Maine
McDermott, Gerald. *Anansi the spider*
  Raven
MacDonald, Suse. *Alphabatics*
McGinley, Phyllis. *All around the town*
  The most wonderful doll in the world
McKissack, Patricia C. *Mirandy and brother wind*
Minarik, Else Holmelund. *Little Bear's visit*
Moss, Lloyd. *Zin! zin! zin! A violin*
Mother Goose. *Mother Goose*, ill. by Tasha Tudor
  Mother Goose and nursery rhymes, ill. by Philip Reed
  The three jovial huntsmen, ill. by Susan Jeffers
Myers, Walter Dean. *Harlem*
Newberry, Clare Turlay. *April's kittens*
  Barkis
  Marshmallow
  T-Bone, the baby-sitter
Olds, Elizabeth. *Feather mountain*
Peet, Bill (William Bartlett). *Bill Peet: an autobiography*
Pelletier, David. *The graphic alphabet*
Perrault, Charles. *Puss in boots*, ill. by Marcia Brown
  Puss in boots, ill. by Fred Marcellino [pub. by Farrar, 1990]
Petersham, Maud. *An American ABC*
Pilkey, Dav. *The paperboy*
Pinkney, Andrea Davis. *Duke Ellington*
Politi, Leo. *Juanita*
  Pedro, the angel of Olvera Street
Preston, Edna Mitchell. *Pop Corn and Ma Goodness*
Raschka, Christopher. *Yo! Yes?*
Reyher, Rebecca (Hourwich). *My mother is the most beautiful woman in the world*
Ringgold, Faith. *Tar Beach*
Rohmann, Eric. *Time flies*
Ryan, Cheli Durán. *Hildilid's night*
Rylant, Cynthia. *The relatives came*
  When I was young in the mountains
San Souci, Robert D. *The faithful friend*
  The talking eggs
Sawyer, Ruth. *The Christmas Anna angel*
  Journey cake, ho!
Say, Allen. *Grandfather's journey*
Scheer, Julian. *Rain makes applesauce*

Schick, Eleanor. *The little school at Cottonwood Corners*
Schlein, Miriam. *When will the world be mine?*
Schreiber, Georges. *Bambino the clown*
Scieszka, Jon. *The Stinky Cheese Man and other fairly stupid tales*
Sendak, Maurice. *In the night kitchen*
   Outside over there
Seuss, Dr. *Bartholomew and the Oobleck*
   If I ran the zoo
   McElligot's pool
Shannon, David. *No, David!*
Shulevitz, Uri. *Snow*
   The treasure
Sis, Peter. *Starry messenger*
Sleator, William. *The angry moon*
Snyder, Dianne. *The boy of the three-year nap*
Steig, William. *The amazing bone*
Steptoe, John. *Mufaro's beautiful daughters*
   The story of jumping mouse
Stevens, Janet. *Tops and bottoms*
Stewart, Sarah. *The gardener*
Tafuri, Nancy. *Have you seen my duckling?*
Thayer, Ernest Lawrence. *Casey at the bat*, ill. by Christopher Bing
The three bears. *Goldilocks and the three bears*, ill. by James Marshall
Titus, Eve. *Anatole*
   Anatole and the cat
Tom Tit Tot. *Tom Tit Tot*
Tresselt, Alvin R. *Hide and seek fog*
   Rain drop splash
Tudor, Tasha. *1 is one*
Turkle, Brinton. *Thy friend, Obadiah*
Udry, Janice May. *The moon jumpers*
Van Allsburg, Chris. *The garden of Abdul Gasazi*
Wheeler, Opal. *Sing in praise*
   Sing Mother Goose
Wiese, Kurt. *Fish in the air*
   You can write Chinese
Wiesner, David. *Free fall*
   Sector 7
Willard, Nancy. *A visit to William Blake's inn*
Williams, Sherley Anne. *Working cotton*
Williams, Vera B. *A chair for my mother*
   "More more more," said the baby
Wisniewski, David. *Golem*
Wood, Audrey. *King Bidgood's in the bathtub*
Yashima, Taro. *Crow boy*
   Seashore story
   Umbrella
Yolen, Jane. *The emperor and the kite*
Young, Ed (Edward). *Seven blind mice*
Zemach, Harve. *The judge*
Zemach, Margot. *It could always be worse*
Zion, Gene. *All falling down*
Zolotow, Charlotte (Shapiro). *Mr. Rabbit and the lovely present*
   The storm book

Cambodia *see* Foreign lands – Cambodia

Cambodian Americans *see* Ethnic groups in the U.S. – Cambodian Americans

Camels *see* Animals – camels

Cameroon *see* Foreign lands – Cameroon

Camps, camping

Armitage, Ronda. *One moonlit night*
Bauer, Marion Dane. *When I go camping with Grandma*
Berenstain, Stan. *The Berenstain bears go to camp*
Blaustein, Muriel. *Make friends, Zachary!*
Boynton, Sandra. *Hester in the wild*
Brillhart, Julie. *When Daddy took us camping*
Brown, Marc Tolon. *Arthur goes to camp*
   Arthur's first sleepover
Brown, Myra Berry. *Pip camps out*
Bunting, Eve (Anne Evelyn). *I don't want to go to camp*
Carrick, Carol. *Sleep out*
Chesworth, Michael. *Archibald Frisby*
Christelow, Eileen. *Jerome camps out*
Cummings, Pat. *Petey Moroni's Camp Runamok diary*
   Curious George goes camping
Delton, Judy. *My mom made me go to camp*
Giff, Patricia Reilly. *Ronald Morgan goes to camp*
Gould, Deborah. *Camping in the Temple of the Sun*
Graham, Bob. *Greetings from Sandy Beach*
Hannan, Peter. *Escape from Camp Wannabarf*
Hayward, Linda. *Elmo goes to day camp*
Henkes, Kevin. *Bailey goes camping*
Himmelman, John. *Lights out!*
   The super camper caper
Hoff, Syd. *Danny and the dinosaur go to camp*
Inkpen, Mick. *Wibbly Pig can make a tent*
Johnson, Paul Brett. *Lost*
Koontz, Robin Michal. *Chicago and the cat, the camping trip*
Leonard, Marcia. *My camp-out*
London, Jonathan. *The waterfall*
Lyon, George Ella. *A day at damp camp*
McCully, Emily Arnold. *Monk camps out*
McCutcheon, Marc. *Grandfather's Christmas camp*
McPhail, David M. *Pig Pig goes to camp*
Maestro, Betsy. *Camping out*
Marino, Dorothy. *Buzzy Bear goes camping*
Marshall, James. *The Cut-Ups at Camp Custer*
Mayer, Mercer. *Just me and my dad*
   You're the scaredy cat
Maynard, Joyce. *Camp-out*
Nordqvist, Sven. *Festus and Mercury go camping*
Osofsky, Audrey. *My buddy*
Peters, Sharon. *Fun at camp*
Price, Dorothy E. *Speedy gets around*
Robins, Joan. *Addie runs away*
Roche, P. K. (Patrick K.). *Webster and Arnold go camping*
Rockwell, Anne F. *The night we slept outside*
   On our vacation
Rubel, Nicole. *Sam and Violet go camping*
Schulman, Janet. *Camp Kee Wee's secret weapon*
Schwartz, Amy. *Camper of the week*
Schwartz, Henry. *How I captured a dinosaur*
Seligson, Susan. *Amos camps out*
Shulevitz, Uri. *Dawn*
Spohn, David. *Starry night*
Stern, Maggie. *Acorn magic*
Stock, Catherine. *Sophie's knapsack*
Tafuri, Nancy. *Do not disturb*
Thompson, Vivian Laubach. *Camp-in-the-yard*
Warren, Cathy. *The ten-alarm camp-out*
Weiss, Nicki. *Battle day at Camp Delmont*
Williams, Vera B. *Three days on a river in a red canoe*
Wolff, Ashley. *Stella and Roy go camping*

Yolen, Jane. *The giants go camping*

Canada *see* Foreign lands – Canada

Canaries *see* Birds – canaries

Cancer *see* Illness – cancer

Canoes and canoeing

Asch, Frank. *Moonbear's canoe*
Baker, Sanna Anderson. *Mississippi going north*
Kraus, Robert. *Wise Old Owl's canoe trip adventure*
London, Jonathan. *Loon Lake*
Mason, Jane B. *River day*
Paulsen, Gary. *Canoe days*

Caps *see* Clothing – hats

Cardboard page books *see* Format, unusual – board books

Cardinals *see* Birds – cardinals

Careers

Aitken, Amy. *Ruby!*
Arnold, Caroline. *What is a community?*
   Who keeps us safe?
   Who works here?
Azaad, Meyer (Mahmud). *Half for you*
Baker, Eugene H. *I want to be a computer operator*
Bank Street College of Education. *People read*
Barber, Barbara E. *Saturday at the new you*
Bauer, Caroline Feller. *My mom travels a lot*
Berenstain, Stan. *The Berenstain bears and mama's new job*
Bond, Michael. *Paddington Bear and the Christmas surprise*
Boxer, Devorah. *26 ways to be somebody else*
Brandenberg, Alexa. *I am me!*
Brentano, Clemens. *Schoolmaster Whackwell's wonderful sons*
Brott, Ardyth. *Jeremy's decision*
Butterworth, Nick. *Busy people*
Calmenson, Stephanie. *Fido*
Civardi, Anne. *Things people do*
Davis, Gary. *Working at a TV station*
Dupasquier, Philippe. *Dear Daddy . . .*
Florian, Douglas. *People working*
Freeman, Don. *The night the lights went out*
Gibbons, Gail. *Emergency!*
   Farming
   Fill it up!
   The pottery place
Goffstein, M. B. (Marilyn Brooke). *An actor*
Greenberg, Melanie Hope. *My father's luncheonette*
Greene, Carol. *I can be a baseball player*
Grossman, Patricia. *The night ones*
Hallinan, P. K. (Patrick K.). *When I grow up*
Halperin, Wendy Anderson. *Once upon a company*
Harper, Anita. *How we work*
Harris, Steven Michael. *This is my trunk*
Hazen, Barbara Shook. *Mommy's office*
Ipcar, Dahlov. *I like animals*
Jensen, Patricia. *Kitty's special job*
Ketteman, Helen. *Shoeshine Whittaker*

Kherdian, David. *The golden bracelet*
Klein, Norma. *Girls can be anything*
Kraus, Robert. *Owliver*
Krensky, Stephen. *How Santa got his job*
   How Santa lost his job
Kroll, Steven. *Howard and Gracie's luncheonette*
Lasker, Joe. *Mothers can do anything*
Lenski, Lois. *Lois Lenski's big book of Mr. Small*
Le-Tan, Pierre. *Timothy's dream book*
Liebman, Daniel. *I want to be a cowboy*
MacKinnon, Debbie. *What am I?*
McNaughton, Colin. *Yum!*
McPhail, David M. *Pig Pig gets a job*
Matthias, Catherine. *I can be a computer operator*
Mayer, Mercer. *Little Monster at work*
Merriam, Eve. *Mommies at work*
Miller, Margaret. *Who uses this?*
   Whose hat?
Mitchell, Joyce Slayton. *My mommy makes money*
Moore, Elaine. *Good morning, city*
Morris, Ann. *Work*
Morrison, Bill. *Louis James hates school*
Myers, Bernice. *The gold watch*
Nichols, Paul. *Big Paul's school bus*
Nolen, Jerdine. *Raising dragons*
O'Book, Irene. *Maybe my baby*
Oliver, Dexter. *I want to be . . .*
100 words about working
Oppenheim, Joanne. *On the other side of the river*
Oppenheim, Shulamith Levey. *Yanni rubbish*
Paulsen, Gary. *Worksong*
Portnoy, Mindy Avra. *Ima on the Bima*
Puner, Helen Walker. *Daddys, what they do all day*
Ray, Mary Lyn. *Basket moon*
Reasoner, Charles. *Who drives this?*
Robinson, Aminah Brenda Lynn. *A street called home*
Rockwell, Anne F. *Career day*
Rowan, James P. *I can be a zoo keeper*
Rowe, Jeanne A. *City workers*
Sandberg, Inger. *Come on out, Daddy!*
Scarry, Richard. *Richard Scarry's busiest people ever*
   Richard Scarry's Postman Pig and his busy neighbors
Seignobosc, Françoise. *What do you want to be?*
Sesame Street. *The Sesame Street book of people and things*
Shank, Ned. *The sanyasin's first day*
Sharmat, Marjorie Weinman. *I'm Santa Claus and I'm famous*
Shepard, Steve. *Elvis Hornbill, international business bird*
Stevenson, James. *Sam the Zamboni man*
Stewart, Robert S. *The daddy book*
Thaler, Mike. *What could a hippopotamus be?*
Upton, Pat. *Who does this job?*
Williams, Barbara. *I know a salesperson*
Wittmann, Patricia. *Go ask Giorgio!*

Careers – accountants

Hudson, Wade. *Jamal's busy day*
Lasky, Kathryn. *Marven of the Great North Woods*

Careers – acrobats

Saltzberg, Barney. *The Flying Garbanzos*

Careers – actors

Gerrard, Roy. *Jocasta Carr, movie star*
Krementz, Jill. *A very young actress*
Littlesugar, Amy. *Tree of hope*
McCully, Emily Arnold. *Zaza's big break*
McKissack, Patricia C. *Paul Robeson*
Philpot, Graham. *Fabulous fairy tale follies*

Careers – aerialists

McCully, Emily Arnold. *Mirette and Bellini cross Niagara Falls*

Careers – airplane pilots

Adler, David A. *A picture book of Amelia Earhart*
Baker, Donna. *I want to be a pilot*
Barton, Byron. *Airport*
Behrens, June. *I can be a pilot*
Borden, Louise. *Goodbye, Charles Lindbergh*
Brown, Don. *Ruth Law thrills a nation*
Joseph, Lynn. *Fly, Bessie, fly*
Krementz, Jill. *Jamie goes on an airplane*
Lindbergh, Reeve. *A view from the air*
Morgan, Allen. *Matthew and the midnight pilot*
Schomp, Virginia. *If you were a . . . pilot*
Seymour, Peter S. *Pilots*
Young, Miriam Burt. *If I flew a plane*

Careers – archaeologists

Addy, Sharon Hart. *Right here on this spot*
Brighton, Catherine. *The fossil girl*
Cole, Joanna. *The magic school bus shows and tells*
Duke, Kate. *Archaeologists dig for clues*

Careers – architects

Clinton, Susan. *I can be an architect*
Cooper, Elisha. *Building*
Demi. *The artist and the architect*
Hudson, Wade. *Jamal's busy day*
Hunter, Ryan Ann. *Into the sky*

Careers – artists *see also* Activities – painting; Careers – painters

Adams, Adrienne. *The great Valentine's Day balloon race*
Angelo, Nancy Carolyn Harrison. *Camembert*
Anholt, Laurence. *Camille and the sunflowers*
Baker, Alan. *Benjamin's portrait*
Baynton, Martin. *Fifty gets the picture*
Carrick, Donald. *Morgan and the artist*
Christelow, Eileen. *What do authors do?*
Collins, Pat Lowery. *I am an artist*
Deeter, Catherine. *Seymour Bleu*
Demi. *The artist and the architect*
Dunrea, Olivier. *The painter who loved chickens*
Edwards, Michelle. *A baker's portrait*
Eve and Smithy
Ekoomiak, Normee. *Arctic memories*
Everett, Gwen. *Li'l Sis and Uncle Willie*
Florian, Douglas. *A painter*
Galli, Letizia. *Mona Lisa*
Gardner, Jane Mylum. *Henry Moore*
Gibbons, Gail. *The art box*
Goffstein, M. B. (Marilyn Brooke). *An artist*
Green, Donna. *My little artist*

Guarnieri, Paolo. *A boy named Giotto*
Havill, Juanita. *Sato and the elephants*
Heller, Nicholas. *The giant*
Hest, Amy. *Nana's birthday party*
Isom, Joan Shaddox. *The first starry night*
Johnson, Angela. *Daddy calls me man*
Kleven, Elisa. *The lion and the little red bird*
Laden, Nina. *When Pigasso met Mootisse*
Lager, Claude. *A tale of two rats*
Lakin, Pat (Patricia). *Subway sonata*
Leaf, Margaret. *Eyes of the dragon*
Lehan, Daniel. *This is not a book about dodos*
Le Tord, Bijou. *A bird or two*
Levine, Arthur A. *The boy who drew cats*
Lionni, Leo. *Matthew's dream*
Littlesugar, Amy. *Jonkonnu*
Josiah True and the art maker
Marie in fourth position
Locker, Thomas. *The man who paints nature*
Miranda's smile
The young artist
McClintock, Barbara. *The fantastic drawings of Danielle*
McPhail, David M. *Drawing lessons from a bear*
Mayhew, James. *Katie and the Mona Lisa*
Katie meets the Impressionists
Maynard, Bill. *Incredible Ned*
Miller, Warren. *Pablo paints a picture*
Moss, Marissa. *Regina's big mistake*
Nicholson, Nicholas B. A. *Little girl in a red dress with cat and dog*
Nickens, Bessie. *Walking the log*
Parillo, Tony. *Michelangelo's surprise*
Payne, Joan Balfour. *The stable that stayed*
Pinkwater, Daniel Manus. *The bear's picture*
Porte, Barbara Ann. *Chickens! Chickens!*
Ross, Tom. *Eggbert, the slightly cracked egg*
Sharon, Mary Bruce. *Scenes from childhood*
Sloan, Carolyn. *Carter is a painter's cat*
Stevenson, James. *Fun, no fun*
I meant to tell you
Thomas, Abigail. *Pearl paints*
Turnbull, Ann. *The sand horse*
Velthuijs, Max. *Crocodile's masterpiece*
The painter and the bird
Ventura, Piero. *The painter's trick*
Waddell, Martin. *Alice the artist*
Walsh, Jill Paton. *Pepi and the secret names*
Weisgard, Leonard. *Mr. Peaceable paints*
Willard, Nancy. *Pish posh, said Hieronymous Bosch*
Winter, Jeanette. *Cowboy Charlie*
Winter, Jonah. *Diego*
Wolkstein, Diane. *Little Mouse's painting*
Wooding, Sharon L. *The painter's cat*
Yacowitz, Caryn. *The jade stone*

Careers – astronauts

Agee, Jon. *Dmitri the astronaut*
Anderson, Joan. *Richie's rocket*
Barton, Byron. *I want to be an astronaut*
Behrens, June. *I can be an astronaut*
Branley, Franklyn M. (Mansfield). *Floating in space*
Brown, Don. *One giant leap*
Catalanotto, Peter. *Dad and me*
Eco, Umberto. *The three astronauts*
Greene, Carol. *Astronauts work in space*

Careers – astronomers

Crew, Gary. *Bright star*
Hopkinson, Deborah. *Maria's comet*
Pinkney, Andrea Davis. *Dear Benjamin Banneker*

Careers – authors

Manuel, Lynn. *Lucy Maud and the Cavendish cat*
Myers, Walter Dean. *Harlem*
Walsh, Ellen Stoll. *Jack's tale*

Careers – bakers

Allard, Harry. *The cactus flower bakery*
Barkan, Joanne. *Whiskerville bake shop*
Bunting, Eve (Anne Evelyn). *Barney the Beard*
Caple, Kathy. *Inspector Aardvark and the perfect cake*
Carle, Eric. *Walter the baker*
Craig, M. Jean. *The man whose name was not Thomas*
De Paola, Tomie (Thomas Anthony). *Tony's bread*
Edwards, Michelle. *A baker's portrait*
Forest, Heather. *The baker's dozen*
Green, Melinda. *Bembelman's bakery*
Greeson, Janet. *The stingy baker*
Hartman, Bob. *Who brought the bread?*
Hayward, Linda. *Baker, baker, cookie maker*
    The biggest cookie in the world
Heath, Amy. *Sofie's role*
Helldorfer, M. C. (Mary Claire). *The darling boys*
Kessler, Leonard P. *Soup for the king*
Langford, Sondra Gordon. *Mishka and Plishka*
Levitin, Sonia. *Boom town*
Lillegard, Dee. *I can be a baker*
Mayer, Marianna. *Marcel the pastry chef*
Pinkwater, Daniel Manus. *The Frankenbagel monster*
Rylant, Cynthia. *The cookie-store cat*
Schwartz, Ellen. *Mr. Belinsky's bagels*
Shepard, Aaron. *The baker's dozen*
Stewart, Sarah. *The gardener*
Sundvall, Viveca. *Mimi and the biscuit factory*
Tzannes, Robin. *Sanji and the baker*
Westcott, Nadine Bernard. *Peanut butter and jelly*
Worthington, Phoebe. *Teddy bear baker*
Young, Miriam Burt. *The sugar mouse cake*
Ziegler, Sandra. *A visit to the bakery*

Careers – barbers

Appell, Clara. *Now I have a daddy haircut*
Auerbach, Marjorie. *King Lavra and the barber*
Barry, Robert E. *Next please*
Freeman, Don. *Mop Top*
Kunhardt, Dorothy. *Billy the barber*
Mahiri, Jabari. *The day they stole the letter J*
Mitchell, Margaree King. *Uncle Jed's barbershop*
Peet, Bill (William Bartlett). *Hubert's hair-raising adventures*
Portlock, Rob. *Someone's trying to cut off my head*
Rockwell, Anne F. *My barber*

Careers – beggars

Scott, Sally. *The three wonderful beggars*

Careers – boat builders

Hunt, Jonathan. *Leif's saga*
Rand, Gloria. *Salty dog*

Careers – bus drivers

Brown, Marc Tolon. *Arthur lost and found*
Denslow, Sharon Phillips. *Bus riders*
Flanagan, Alice K. *Riding the school bus with Mrs. Kramer*
Harrison, Troon. *Lavender Moon*
Lakin, Pat (Patricia). *Up a tree*
Pulver, Robin. *Axle Annie*
Young, Miriam Burt. *If I drove a bus*

Careers – butchers

Kobayashi, Robert. *Maria Mazaretti loves spaghetti*
Yorinks, Arthur. *Louis the fish*

Careers – cab drivers *see* Careers – taxi drivers

Careers – carpenters

Baker, Keith. *The magic fan*
Denslow, Sharon Phillips. *At Taylor's place*
Florian, Douglas. *A carpenter*
Greene, Carla. *I want to be a carpenter*
Hest, Amy. *The ring and the window seat*
Lillegard, Dee. *I can be a carpenter*
Lucado, Max. *Jacob's gift*
Pickthall, Marjorie L. C. (Marjorie Lowry Christie). *The worker in sandalwood*
Prøysen, Alf. *Christmas eve at Santa's*

Careers – chefs, cooks

Florian, Douglas. *A chef*
Guthrie, Donna. *This little pig stayed home*
Harrison, Troon. *Lavender Moon*
Kidd, Richard. *Monsieur Thermidor*
Loomis, Christine. *In the diner*
Medearis, Angela Shelf. *The ghost of Sifty-Sifty Sam*
Moss, Marissa. *Mel's diner*
Myers, Edward. *Forri the baker*
Pillar, Marjorie. *Pizza man*
Poskanzer, Susan Cornell. *What's it like to be a chef?*
Tomchek, Ann Heinrichs. *I can be a chef*
Wellington, Monica. *Mr. Cookie Baker*

Careers – clockmakers

Ardizzone, Edward. *Johnny the clockmaker*
Henwood, Simon. *The clock shop*

Careers – coaches

Flanagan, Alice K. *Coach John and his soccer team*

Careers – composers

Brighton, Catherine. *Mozart*
Dineen, Jacqueline. *Frédéric Chopin*

Careers – construction workers

Hennessy, B. G. (Barbara G.). *Road builders*
Johnson, Angela. *Those building men*
Rex, Michael. *Who builds?*
    Who digs?
Wallace, Karen. *Big machines*

Careers – custodians, janitors

Lakin, Pat (Patricia). *Trash and treasure*

Careers – dancers

Isadora, Rachel. *Lili on stage*
Komaiko, Leah. *Aunt Elaine does the dance from Spain*
Pinkney, Andrea Davis. *Alvin Ailey*

Careers – dentists

Ambrus, Victor G. *What's the time, Dracula?*
Barnett, Naomi. *I know a dentist*
Berenstain, Stan. *The Berenstain bears visit the dentist*
Curious George goes to the dentist
Duvoisin, Roger Antoine. *Crocus*
Gomi, Taro. *The crocodile and the dentist*
Hallinan, P. K. (Patrick K.). *My dentist, my friend*
Krementz, Jill. *Taryn goes to the dentist*
Kuklin, Susan. *When I see my dentist*
Lapp, Carolyn. *The dentists' tools*
Linn, Margot. *A trip to the dentist*
Luttrell, Ida. *Milo's toothache*
Mitra, Annie. *Tusk! Tusk!*
Richter, Alice Numeroff. *You can't put braces on spaces*
Rockwell, Harlow. *My dentist*
Steig, William. *Doctor De Soto goes to Africa*
Watson, Jane Werner. *My friend the dentist*
Wolf, Bernard. *Michael and the dentist*
Zalben, Jane Breskin. *Buster gets braces*

Careers – detectives

Allen, Laura Jean. *Rollo and Tweedy and the case of the missing cheese*
Rollo and Tweedy and the ghost of Dougal Castle
Where is Freddy?
Berenstain, Stan. *The bear detectives*
Bunting, Eve (Anne Evelyn). *Jane Martin, dog detective*
Christelow, Eileen. *Gertrude, the bulldog detective*
Cox, Paul. *The case of the botched book*
The great eucalyptus mystery
The riddle of the floating island
Cushman, Doug. *The ABC mystery*
The mystery of King Karfu
The mystery of the monkey's maze
Harrison, David Lee. *Detective Bob and the great ape escape*
Kitamura, Satoshi. *Sheep in wolves' clothing*
Kraus, Robert. *The detective of London*
Latimer, Jim. *The fox under first base*
Lawrence, James. *Binky Brothers and the fearless four*
Binky Brothers, detectives
O'Malley, Kevin. *Who killed Cock Robin?*
Ostheeren, Ingrid. *Jonathan Mouse, detective*
Panek, Dennis. *Detective Whoo*
Sharmat, Marjorie Weinman. *Nate the Great*
Nate the Great and the lost list
Nate the Great and the phony clue
Nate the Great goes undercover
Stortz, Diane M. *Barnaby Mouse, detective, and the mystery of the big book*
Supraner, Robyn. *Sam Sunday and the mystery at the Ocean Beach Hotel*
Thomson, Ruth. *Peabody all at sea*
Peabody's first case
Tryon, Leslie. *Albert's Halloween*

Careers – doctors

Arnold, Caroline. *Who keeps us healthy?*
Baggette, Susan K. *Jonathan goes to the doctor*
Berenstain, Stan. *The Berenstain bears go to the doctor*
Bertrand, Lynne. *One day, two dragons*
Breckler, Rosemary K. *Sweet dried apples*
Breinburg, Petronella. *Doctor Shawn*
Charlip, Remy. *"Mother, mother I feel sick"*
Chislett, Gail. *Melinda's no's cold*
Cobb, Vicki. *How the doctor knows you're fine*
Corey, Dorothy. *A shot for baby bear*
Davison, Martine. *Robby visits the doctor*
DeSantis, Kenny. *A doctor's tools*
Fine, Anne. *Poor Monty*
Freeman, Don. *Corduroy's busy street and Corduroy goes to the doctor*
Gilbert, Helen Earle. *Dr. Trotter and his big gold watch*
Goodsell, Jane. *Katie's magic glasses*
Greene, Carla. *Doctors and nurses*
Hallinan, P. K. (Patrick K.). *My doctor, my friend*
Hanklin, Rebecca. *I can be a doctor*
Kraus, Robert. *Boris bad enough*
Dr. Mouse, Bungle Jungle doctor
Kroll, Steven. *Doctor on an elephant*
Kuklin, Susan. *When I see my doctor*
Lerner, Marguerite Rush. *Doctors' tools*
Linn, Margot. *A trip to the doctor*
Marcus, Susan. *Casey visits the doctor*
Oxenbury, Helen. *The checkup*
Robison, Deborah. *Your turn, doctor*
Rockwell, Harlow. *My doctor*
Rogers, Fred. *Going to the doctor*
Roop, Peter. *Stick out your tongue!*
Rylant, Cynthia. *Silver packages*
Stein, Sara Bonnett. *A hospital story*
Viorst, Judith. *The tenth good thing about Barney*
Wahl, Jan. *Doctor Rabbit's foundling*
Watson, Jane Werner. *My friend the doctor*
Wolde, Gunilla. *Betsy and the doctor*

Careers – electricians

Cole, Joanna. *The magic school bus and the electric field trip*
Lillegard, Dee. *I can be an electrician*

Careers – engineers

Moss, Marissa. *True heart*

Careers – entertainers

Ahlberg, Allan. *Mr. and Mrs. Hay the horse*

Careers – explorers

Conrad, Pam. *Call me Ahnighito*
DeRubertis, Barbara. *Columbus Day*
Edwards, Pamela Duncan. *Livingstone Mouse*
Hunt, Jonathan. *Leif's saga*
Jendresen, Erik. *The first story ever told*
Kroll, Steven. *Lewis and Clark*
Yorinks, Arthur. *The Miami giant*

Careers – farmers

Ackerman, Karen. *Bingleman's midway*
Aliki. *Milk from cow to carton*
Allen, Pamela. *Belinda*
Ambrus, Victor G. *Never laugh at bears*
Anderson, Janet S. *Sunflower Sal*
Asch, Frank. *Barnyard lullaby*
Aylesworth, Jim. *My son John*
Birchman, David F. *Jigsaw Jackson*
Booth, David. *The dust bowl*
Brown, Craig McFarland. *City sounds*
    Patchwork farmer
Buehner, Caralyn. *Fanny's dream*
Carney, Margaret (Margaret Rose). *At Grandpa's sugar bush*
Chorao, Kay. *Little farm by the sea*
Christelow, Eileen. *The great pig escape*
Cowley, Joy. *The rusty, trusty tractor*
Crebbin, June. *Cows in the kitchen*
Cronin, Doreen. *Click, clack, moo*
Demarest, Chris L. *Farmer Nat*
Demuth, Patricia Brennan. *Ornery morning*
Dunrea, Olivier. *The trow-wife's treasure*
Ehrlich, Amy. *Parents in the pigpen, pigs in the tub*
A farmer boy birthday
The farmer in the dell. *The farmer in the dell*, ill. by John O'Brien
    The farmer in the dell, ill. by Kathy Parkinson
    The farmer in the dell, ill. by Mary Maki Rae
    The farmer in the dell, ill. by Diane Stanley
    The farmer in the dell, ill. by Alexandra Wallner
Flanagan, Alice K. *A visit to the Gravesens' farm*
Friedrich, Elizabeth. *Leah's pony*
Hall, Donald. *The milkman's boy*
Hamm, Diane Johnston. *Rock-a-bye farm*
Hazen, Barbara Shook. *Turkey in the straw*
Henderson, Kathy. *I can be a farmer*
Henley, Claire. *Farm day*
Hutchins, H. J. (Hazel J.). *One duck*
Johnson, Angela. *Casey Jones*
Johnson, Paul Brett. *Farmers' market*
Kaufman, Jeff. *Milk rock*
Ketteman, Helen. *I remember papa*
Kightley, Rosalinda. *The farmer*
Kunhardt, Edith. *I'm going to be a farmer*
Laird, Elizabeth. *The day the ducks went skating*
    The day Veronica was nosy
Lasky, Kathryn. *The emperor's old clothes*
Love, Ann. *Farming*
Ludy, Mark. *The farmer*
Lunn, Janet Louise Swoboda. *Come to the fair*
Maccarone, Grace. *Oink! moo! how do you do?*
Most, Bernard. *Cock-a-doodle-moo!*
Nordqvist, Sven. *The fox hunt*
Old MacDonald had a farm. *E I E I O*
    Old MacDonald, ill. by Rosemary Wells
    Old MacDonald had a farm, ill. by Holly Berry
    Old MacDonald had a farm, ill. by Lorinda Bryan Cauley
    Old MacDonald had a farm, ill. by Mel Crawford
    Old MacDonald had a farm, ill. by Tracey English
    Old MacDonald had a farm, ill. by David Frankland
    Old MacDonald had a farm, ill. by Abner Graboff
    Old MacDonald had a farm, ill. by Nancy Hellen
    Old MacDonald had a farm, ill. by Carol Jones
    Old MacDonald had a farm, ill. by Tracey Campbell Pearson
    Old MacDonald had a farm, ill. by Robert M. Quackenbush
    Old MacDonald had a farm, ill. by Glen Rounds
    Old MacDonald had a farm, ill. by Jessica Souhami
    Old MacDonald had a farm, ill. by William Stobbs
    Old MacDonald had a farm, ill. by Prue Theobalds
Peterson, Cris. *Extra cheese, please!*
Poskanzer, Susan Cornell. *Dairy farmer*
Riecken, Nancy. *Today is the day*
Sandburg, Carl (Charles August). *The Huckabuck family and how they raised popcorn in Nebraska and quit and came back*
Scott, C. Anne (Cynthia Anne). *Old Jake's skirts*
Sloat, Teri. *The thing that bothered Farmer Brown*
Steig, William. *Wizzil*
Sugar snow
Tafuri, Nancy. *This is the farmer*
Trottier, Maxine. *Prairie willow*
Van Leeuwen, Jean. *Nothing here but trees*
Waddell, Martin. *Farmer Duck*
    The pig in the pond
Ward, Nick. *Farmer George and the fieldmice*
    Farmer George and the lost chick
Yee, Wong Herbert. *Fireman Small to the rescue*

Careers – firefighters

Averill, Esther. *The fire cat*
Barbaresi, Nina. *Firemouse*
Barkan, Joanne. *Whiskerville firehouse*
Barr, Jene. *Fire snorkel number 7*
Baumann, Kurt. *Piro and the fire brigade*
Bester, Roger. *Fireman Jim*
Boucher, Jerry. *Fire truck nuts and bolts*
Bourgeois, Paulette. *Fire fighters*
Bridwell, Norman. *Clifford's good deeds*
Brown, Margaret Wise. *Five little firemen*
    The little fireman
Bundt, Nancy. *The fire station book*
Bunting, Eve (Anne Evelyn). *On Call Back Mountain*
Bushey, Jerry. *Building a fire truck*
Chalmers, Mary. *Throw a kiss, Harry*
Curious George at the fire station
DeLage, Ida. *ABC fire dogs*
Dubowski, Cathy East. *Fire engine to the rescue*
Elliott, Dan. *A visit to the Sesame Street firehouse*
Fast rolling fire trucks
Firehouse, ill. by Zokeisha
Fisher, Leonard Everett. *Pumpers, boilers, hooks and ladders*
Flanagan, Alice K. *Ms. Murphy fights fires*
Fowler, Richard. *Mr. Little's noisy fire engine*
Gibbons, Gail. *Fire! Fire!*
Gramatky, Hardie. *Hercules*
Greydanus, Rose. *Big red fire engine*
Hammar, Asa. *Fit for pigs*
Hanklin, Rebecca. *I can be a fire fighter*
Hansen, Jeff. *Being a fire fighter isn't just squirtin' water*
Hill, Mary Lou. *My dad's a smokejumper*
Homme, Bob. *The friendly giant's book of fire engines*
Keeping, Charles. *Willie's fire-engine*
Killingback, Julia. *Busy Bears at the fire station*
Kuklin, Susan. *Lighting fires*
Kunhardt, Edith. *I'm going to be a fire fighter*
Lenski, Lois. *The little fire engine*
Leonard, Marcia. *Jeffrey Lee, future fireman*
Lewison, Wendy Cheyette. *A trip to the firehouse*

Liebman, Daniel. *I want to be a firefighter*
Marston, Hope Irvin. *Fire trucks*
Martin, Ann M. *Fire truck to the rescue*
Martin, Bill (William Ivan). *Fire! Fire! said Mrs. McGuire*
Mayer, Mercer. *Fireman critter*
Mitton, Tony. *Flashing fire engines*
Morgan, Allen. *Matthew and the midnight firemen*
Munsch, Robert N. *The fire station*
Rex, Michael. *My fire engine*
Rey, H. A. (Hans Augusto). *Curious George*
    The original Curious George
Robinson, Nancy K. *Firefighters!*
Rockwell, Anne F. *Fire engines*
Royston, Angela. *Fire fighters*
Santoro, Scott. *Isaac the Ice Cream Truck*
Sis, Peter. *Fire truck*
Spiegel, Doris. *Danny and Company 92*
Spier, Peter. *Firehouse*
Steel, Danielle. *Max's daddy goes to the hospital*
Weiss, Harvey. *The sooner hound*
Wilson-Max, Ken. *Big red fire truck*
Winkleman, Katherine K. *Firehouse*
Yee, Wong Herbert. *Fireman Small*
    Fireman Small, fire down below
    Fireman Small to the rescue
Zaffo, George J. *Big book of real fire engines*

Careers – fishermen

Adams, Jeanie. *Going for oysters*
Aldridge, Josephine Haskell. *Fisherman's luck*
Beim, Lorraine. *Lucky Pierre*
Brown, Marcia. *Henry fisherman*
Brown, Margaret Wise. *The little fisherman*
Bunting, Eve (Anne Evelyn). *Magic and the night river*
Dunbar, Joyce. *Indigo and the whale*
Edwards, Roberta. *Five silly fishermen*
Flora, James. *Fishing with dad*
Florian, Douglas. *A fisher*
Galchutt, David. *There was magic inside*
Garland, Sherry. *My father's boat*
Garne, S. T. *By a blazing blue sea*
Gibbons, Gail. *Surrounded by sea*
Gramatky, Hardie. *Nikos and the sea god*
Guiberson, Brenda Z. *Lobster boat*
Le Tord, Bijou. *Joseph and Nellie*
Lewin, Ted. *Nilo and the tortoise*
Love, Ann. *Fishing*
Matsutani, Miyoko. *The fisherman under the sea*
Miles, Miska. *No, no, Rosina*
Mills, Patricia. *On an island in the bay*
Mitchell, Barbara. *Waterman's child*
Moxley, Susan. *Abdul's treasure*
Nakawatari, Harutaka. *The sea and I*
Napoli, Guillier. *Adventure at Mont-Saint-Michel*
Pallotta, Jerry. *Going lobstering*
Parker, Dorothy D. *Liam's catch*
Rettich, Margret. *The voyage of the jolly boat*
San Souci, Robert D. *Nicholas Pipe*
Tomlinson, Theresa. *Little stowaway*
Weil, Lisl. *Gertie and Gus*
Williams, Laura E. *Torch fishing with the sun*
Yolen, Jane. *Greyling*

Careers – forest rangers *see* Careers – park rangers

Careers – fortune tellers

Alexander, Lloyd. *Fortune tellers*
Jeschke, Susan. *Firerose*
Shepard, Aaron. *Forty fortunes*
Weiss, Ellen. *Clara the fortune-telling chicken*

Careers – garbage collectors *see* Careers – sanitation workers

Careers – geologists

Cole, Joanna. *The magic school bus inside the earth*
Sipiera, Paul P. *I can be a geologist*

Careers – handymen

Mazer, Anne. *The Fixits*
Rockwell, Anne F. *Handy Hank will fix it*

Careers – hatters

Chetwin, Grace. *Box and Cox*

Careers – housekeepers

McKissack, Patricia C. *Ma Dear's aprons*
Widman, Christine. *Housekeeper of the wind*

Careers – illustrators

Locker, Thomas. *The man who paints nature*
Myers, Walter Dean. *Harlem*

Careers – inventors

Denslow, Sharon Phillips. *Radio boy*
Himmelman, John. *The Clover County carrot contest*
    The super camper caper
Lustig, Michael. *Willy Whyner, cloud designer*

Careers – janitors *see* Careers – custodians, janitors

Careers – journalists

Leedy, Loreen. *The Furry News*

Careers – judges

Flanagan, Alice K. *A day in court with Mrs. Trinh*
Mirkovic, Irene. *The greedy shopkeeper*
Zemach, Harve. *The judge*

Careers – lawyers

Flanagan, Alice K. *A day in court with Mrs. Trinh*

Careers – librarians

Baggette, Susan K. *Jonathan goes to the library*
Baker, Donna. *I want to be a librarian*
Brillhart, Julie. *Story hour - starring Megan!*
Greene, Carol. *I can be a librarian*
Lakin, Pat (Patricia). *Information, please*
Mann, Pamela. *The frog princess?*
Mora, Pat. *Tomás and the library lady*
Pinkwater, Daniel Manus. *Aunt Lulu*
Porte, Barbara Ann. *Harry in trouble*

Williams, Suzanne. *Library Lil*

Careers – lifeguards

Borden, Louise. *Albie the lifeguard*
Pinkwater, Daniel Manus. *At the Hotel Larry*

Careers – lumberjacks

Emberley, Barbara. *The story of Paul Bunyan*
Gleeson, Brian. *Paul Bunyan*
Hines, Gary. *The day of the high climber*
Kellogg, Steven (Stephen). *Paul Bunyan*
Lasky, Kathryn. *Marven of the Great North Woods*

Careers – magicians

Graham, Bob. *Benny*
Grejniec, Michael. *Who is my neighbor?*
Hodges, Margaret. *Comus*
Howe, James. *Rabbit-Cadabra!*
My first Raggedy Ann, Raggedy Ann and Andy and the nice police officer

Careers – mail carriers *see* Careers – postal workers

Careers – mechanics

Aldag, Kurt. *Some things never change*
Broekel, Ray. *I can be an auto mechanic*
Dupasquier, Philippe. *A busy day at the garage*
Florian, Douglas. *An auto mechanic*
Kirk, Daniel. *Lucky's twenty-four hour garage*
Radford, Derek. *Harry at the garage*

Careers – migrant workers

Altman, Linda Jacobs. *Amelia's road*
Covault, Ruth M. *Pablo and Pimienta*
Dorros, Arthur. *Radio Man/Don Radio*
Hanson, Regina. *The tangerine tree*
Mora, Pat. *Tomás and the library lady*
Thomas, Jane Resh. *Lights on the river*
Williams, Sherley Anne. *Working cotton*

Careers – military

Ambrus, Victor G. *Brave soldier Janosch*
Aragon, Jane Chelsea. *The major and the mousehole mice*
Brown, Marcia. *Stone soup*
Bunting, Eve (Anne Evelyn). *The wall*
Chin, Charlie. *China's bravest girl*
Conrad, Pam. *The lost sailor*
Emberley, Barbara. *Drummer Hoff*
Hoff, Syd. *Captain Cat*
Jewell, Nancy. *Sailor song*
Kimmel, Eric A. *Billy Lazroe and the King of the Sea*
Langstaff, John M. *Soldier, soldier, won't you marry me?*
Lee, Jeanne M. *The song of Mu Lan*
Little, Mimi Otey. *Yoshiko and the foreigner*
McGowen, Tom (Thomas). *The only glupmaker in the U.S. Navy*
McKinley, Robin. *My father is in the Navy*
Mahy, Margaret. *Sailor Jack and the twenty orphans*
Van Rynbach, Iris. *The soup stone*

Careers – miners

Bartoletti, Susan Campbell. *Silver at night*
Brown, Margaret Wise. *Two little miners*
Eversole, Robyn Harbert. *The gift stone*
Harris, Marian. *Tuesday in Arizona*
Kay, Verla. *Gold fever*
Levitin, Sonia. *Boom town*
Lyon, George Ella. *Mama is a miner*
Nixon, Joan Lowery. *Fat chance, Claude*

Careers – models

Greene, Carol. *I can be a model*
Littlesugar, Amy. *Marie in fourth position*

Careers – museum workers

L'Hommedieu, Arthur John. *Working at a museum*

Careers – musicians

Arrhenius, Peter. *The Penguin Quartet*
Birchman, David Francis. *A green horn blowing*
Brighton, Catherine. *Mozart*
Chocolate, Deborah M. Newton. *The piano man*
England, Linda. *The old cotton blues*
3 kids dreamin'
Gillmor, Don. *The fabulous song*
Harranth, Wolf. *The flute concert*
Hoff, Syd. *Arturo's baton*
Isherwood, Shirley. *The band over the hill*
Komaiko, Leah. *Broadway Banjo Bill*
Krementz, Jill. *A very young musician*
Leonard, Marcia. *Big Ben*
Linscott, Jody. *Once upon A to Z*
London, Jonathan. *Hip cat*
McKee, David. *The sad story of Veronica who played the violin*
Martin, Bill (William Ivan). *Maestro plays*
Pinkney, Andrea Davis. *Duke Ellington*
Pinkwater, Daniel Manus. *Bongo Larry*
Poole, Valerie. *Obadiah Coffee and the music contest*
Raschka, Christopher. *Charlie Parker played be bop*
Mysterious Thelonious
Ray, Mary Lyn. *Pianna*
Shepard, Aaron. *The sea king's daughter*
Ungerer, Tomi. *Tortoni Tremelo the cursed musician*
Weller, Frances Ward. *The angel of Mill Street*

Careers – nuns

Routh, Jonathan. *The Nuns go to Africa*

Careers – nurses

Arnold, Caroline. *Who keeps us healthy?*
Behrens, June. *I can be a nurse*
Davison, Martine. *Kevin and the school nurse*
Greene, Carla. *Doctors and nurses*
Karim, Roberta. *This is a hospital, not a zoo!*
Kraus, Robert. *Rebecca Hatpin*
Lakin, Pat (Patricia). *The mystery illness*
Stein, Sara Bonnett. *A hospital story*
Whitney, Alma Marshak. *Just awful*
Woolf, Virginia. *Nurse Lugton's curtain*

Careers – opera singers

Fleming, Candace. *Westward ho, Carlotta!*

Careers – organists

Ketcham, Sallie. *Bach's big adventure*

Careers – painters *see also* Activities – painting; Careers – artists

Flanagan, Alice K. *The Wilsons, a house-painting team*

Careers – paleontologists

Atkins, Jeannine. *Mary Anning and the sea dragon*
Day, Marie. *Dragon in the rocks*
Hawcock, David. *Dinosaur hunt*

Careers – park rangers

Bunting, Eve (Anne Evelyn). *On Call Back Mountain*
Butterworth, Nick. *The rescue party*
    The secret path
Christian, Peggy. *Chocolate, a glacier grizzly*
Greene, Carol. *I can be a forest ranger*
Hill, Mary Lou. *My dad's a park ranger*
Muller, Gerda. *Around the oak*

Careers – peddlers

Crossley-Holland, Kevin. *The pedlar of Swaffham*
DeGross, Monalisa. *Granddaddy's street songs*
DeLage, Ida. *Good morning, lady*
Haley, Gail E. *Dream peddler*
Jacobs, Joseph. *The crock of gold*
Johnson, Angela. *The Rolling Store*
Lewis, J. Patrick. *The moonbow of Mr. B. Bones*
London, Sara. *Firehouse Max*
McDonald, Megan. *The potato man*
Miller, William. *Jenny and the peddler*
Rockwell, Anne F. *A bear, a bobcat and three ghosts*
Shefelman, Janice Jordan. *A peddler's dream*
Slobodkina, Esphyr. *Caps for sale*
    Pezzo the peddler and the circus elephant
    Pezzo the peddler and the thirteen silly thieves
Suba, Susanne. *The monkeys and the pedlar*
Waller, Barrett. *New feet for old*

Careers – photographers

Johnson, Dinah. *All around town*
Martin, Jacqueline Briggs. *Snowflake Bentley*

Careers – physicians *see* Careers – doctors

Careers – plasterers

Carle, Eric. *My apron*

Careers – plumbers

Adinolfi, JoAnn. *Tina's diner*
Ahlberg, Allan. *Mrs. Plug the plumber*
Duvall, Jill. *Who keeps the water clean? Ms. Schindler!*
Morgan, Allen. *Matthew and the midnight flood*

Careers – police officers

Adelson, Leone. *Who blew that whistle?*
Ahlberg, Allan. *Cops and robbers*
Baker, Donna. *I want to be a police officer*

Bare, Colleen Stanley. *Sammy, dog detective*
Bourgeois, Paulette. *Police officers*
Brown, David. *Someone always needs a policeman*
Chapin, Cynthia. *Squad car 55*
Chwast, Seymour. *Traffic jam*
Erdoes, Richard. *Policemen around the world*
Flanagan, Alice K. *Officer Brown keeps neighborhoods safe*
Goodall, John S. *Paddy's new hat*
Guilfoile, Elizabeth. *Have you seen my brother?*
Keats, Ezra Jack. *My dog is lost!*
Kunhardt, Edith. *I'm going to be a police officer*
Lakin, Pat (Patricia). *Aware and alert*
Lattin, Anne. *Peter's policeman*
Lenski, Lois. *Policeman Small*
Liebman, Daniel. *I want to be a police officer*
McCloskey, Robert. *Make way for ducklings*
Mayer, Mercer. *Policeman critter*
My first Raggedy Ann, Raggedy Ann and Andy and the nice police officer
Rathmann, Peggy. *Officer Buckle and Gloria*
Schlein, Miriam. *The amazing Mr. Pelgrew*
Vreeken, Elizabeth. *The boy who would not say his name*
Yee, Wong Herbert. *The Officers' Ball*

Careers – postal workers

Ahlberg, Janet. *The jolly Christmas postman*
    The jolly pocket postman
    The jolly postman
Barkan, Joanne. *Whiskerville post office*
Beim, Jerrold. *Country mailman*
Boelts, Maribeth. *Grace and Joe*
Bourgeois, Paulette. *Postal workers*
Bradby, Marie. *The longest wait*
Brandt, Betty. *Special delivery*
Buchheimer, Naomi. *Let's go to a post office*
Craven, Carolyn. *What the mailman brought*
Drummond, Violet H. *The flying postman*
Flanagan, Alice K. *Here comes Mr. Eventoff with the mail!*
Gibbons, Gail. *The post office book*
Glass, Andrew. *The sweetwater run*
Haley, Gail E. *The post office cat*
Hedderwick, Mairi. *Katie Morag delivers the mail*
Henkes, Kevin. *Good-bye, Curtis*
Henri, Adrian. *The postman's palace*
Holabird, Katharine. *Angelina's Christmas*
Kightley, Rosalinda. *The postman*
Koscielniak, Bruce. *Euclid Bunny delivers the mail*
Lakin, Pat (Patricia). *Red letter day*
Lillegard, Dee. *Tortoise brings the mail*
Marshak, S. (Samuil). *Hail to mail*
Maury, Inez. *My mother the mail carrier*
Morgan, Allen. *Matthew and the midnight ball game*
Pryor, Bonnie. *Mr. Munday and the space creatures*
Rylant, Cynthia. *Mr. Griggs' work*
Scarry, Richard. *Richard Scarry's Postman Pig and his busy neighbors*
Siracusa, Catherine. *No mail for Mitchell*
Skurzynski, Gloria. *Here comes the mail*
Spinelli, Eileen. *Somebody loves you, Mr. Hatch*
Tunnell, Michael O. *Mailing May*
Watts, Bernadette. *Harvey Hare, postman extraordinaire*
    Harvey Hare's Christmas

Careers – preachers

Gillerlain, Gayle. *Reverend Thomas's false teeth*
McKissack, Patricia C. *Booker T. Washington*

Careers – printers

Chetwin, Grace. *Box and Cox*
Edwards, Michelle. *Dora's book*
Fisher, Leonard Everett. *Gutenberg*
Krensky, Stephen. *Breaking into print*
Monsell, Mary Elise. *Crackle Creek*

Careers – puppeteers

Poskanzer, Susan Cornell. *Puppeteer*

Careers – race car drivers

Wilkinson, Sylvia. *I can be a race car driver*

Careers – railroad engineers

Lenski, Lois. *The little train*

Careers – ranchers

Henderson, Kathy. *I can be a rancher*

Careers – rangers *see* Careers – park rangers

Careers – sailors *see* Careers – military; Sailors

Careers – salesmen

Palatini, Margie. *Ding dong ding dong*

Careers – sanitation workers

Bourgeois, Paulette. *Garbage collectors*
Glaser, Linda. *Stop that garbage truck!*
Hartmann, Wendy. *All the magic in the world*
Kirk, Daniel. *Trash trucks!*
Maass, Robert. *Garbage*
Showers, Paul. *Where does the garbage go?*
Steig, William. *Tiffky Doofky*
Zimmerman, Andrea Griffing. *Trashy town*
Zion, Gene. *Dear garbage man*

Careers – school principals

Calmenson, Stephanie. *The principal's new clothes*
Cocca-Leffler, Maryann. *Mr. Tanen's ties*

Careers – scientists

Accorsi, William. *Rachel Carson*
Lehn, Barbara. *What is a scientist?*
Martin, Jacqueline Briggs. *Snowflake Bentley*

Careers – seamstresses

Chevance, Audrey. *Tutu*
Olds, Helen Diehl. *Miss Hattie and the monkey*

Careers – shepherds

Ada, Alma Flor. *Jordi's star*
Aichinger, Helga. *The shepherd*

Ben-´Ezer, Ehud. *Hosni the dreamer*
Calhoun, Mary. *A shepherd's gift*
Eversole, Robyn Harbert. *Red berry wool*
Gantschev, Ivan. *The moon lake*
Garaway, Margaret Kahn. *Ashkii and his grandfather*
Guarnieri, Paolo. *A boy named Giotto*
Lewis, Kim. *The shepherd boy*
Mills, Claudia. *One small lost sheep*
Safran, Sheri. *The musical cherub*
Wellington, Monica. *The sheep follow*

Careers – sheriffs

Yorinks, Arthur. *Whitefish Will rides again*

Careers – shoemakers

Aiken, Joan. *The shoemaker's boy*
Gilbert, Helen Earle. *Mr. Plum and the little green tree*
Grimm, Jacob. *The elves and the shoemaker*, ill. by Doug Cushman
  The elves and the shoemaker, ill. by Paul Galdone
  The elves and the shoemaker, ill. by Margaret Walty
  The elves and the shoemaker, ill. by Bernadette Watts
  The shoemaker and the elves, ill. by Adrienne Adams
  The shoemaker and the elves, ill. by Cynthia and William Birrer
  The shoemaker and the elves, ill. by Ilse Plume
Hodges, Margaret. *The hero of Bremen*
Lieberman, Syd. *The wise shoemaker of Studena*
Lowell, Susan. *The bootmaker and the elves*
Oppenheim, Joanne. *Left and right*
Prose, Francine. *You never know*
Ross, Tony. *The greedy little cobbler*
San Souci, Robert D. *The red heels*
Sheldon, Aure. *Of cobblers and kings*

Careers – sign painters

Roth, Roger. *The sign painter's dream*

Careers – singers

Littlesugar, Amy. *Shake Rag*
McKissack, Patricia C. *Paul Robeson*

Careers – soldiers *see* Careers – military

Careers – storekeepers

Asch, Frank. *George's store*
Carling, Amelia Lau. *Mama and Papa have a store*
Fleming, Candace. *The hatmaker's sign*
Heo, Yumi. *Father's rubber shoes*
Kimmelman, Leslie. *Frannie's fruits*
Melmed, Laura Krauss. *The Marvelous Market on Mermaid*
Pearson, Tracey Campbell. *The storekeeper*
Shefelman, Janice Jordan. *A peddler's dream*
Shelby, Anne. *We keep a store*

Careers – tailors

Ackerman, Karen. *Just like Max*
Ambrus, Victor G. *The three poor tailors*
Armstrong, Jennifer. *Pockets*

Calmenson, Stephanie. *The principal's new clothes*
Galdone, Paul. *The monster and the tailor*
Grimm, Jacob. *The brave little tailor*, ill. by Mark Corcoran
   The brave little tailor, ill. by Daniel San Souci
   The brave little tailor, ill. by Svend Otto S
   The brave little tailor, ill. by Eve Tharlet
   The brave little tailor, ill. by James Warhola
   Seven at one blow
   The valiant little tailor
Hest, Amy. *The purple coat*
Hilton, Nette. *Dirty Dave*
Potter, Beatrix. *The tailor of Gloucester*
Sanfield, Steve. *Bit by bit*
Schotter, Roni. *Dreamland*
West, Colin. *I brought my love a tabby cat*
Yorinks, Arthur. *Oh, brother*

Careers – taxi drivers

Moore, Lilian. *Papa Albert*
Ross, Jessica. *Ms. Klondike*
Svend Otto S (Svend Otto Sorensen). *Taxi dog*

Careers – teachers

Allard, Harry. *Miss Nelson is back*
   Miss Nelson is missing!
Amper, Thomas. *Booker T. Washington*
Arnold, Caroline. *Where do you go to school?*
Barkan, Joanne. *Whiskerville school*
Beckman, Beatrice. *I can be a teacher*
Bognomo, Joel Eboueme. *Madoulina*
Brillhart, Julie. *Anna's goodbye apron*
Bunting, Eve (Anne Evelyn). *Our teacher's having a baby*
Calmenson, Stephanie. *The teeny tiny teacher*
Cole, Joanna. *The magic school bus in the time of the dinosaurs*
   The magic school bus inside a beehive
   The magic school bus lost in the solar system
   The magic school bus on the ocean floor
Cummings, W. T. (Walter Thies). *Miss Esta Maude's secret*
Daniel, Kira. *Teacher*
Denslow, Sharon Phillips. *On the trail with Miss Pace*
Feder, Paula Kurzband. *Where does the teacher live?*
Glennon, Karen M. *Miss Eva and the red balloon*
Greene, Carol. *Teachers help us learn*
Hallinan, P. K. (Patrick K.). *My teacher's my friend*
Havill, Juanita. *Jamaica and the substitute teacher*
Henkes, Kevin. *Lilly's purple plastic purse*
Houston, Gloria. *My Great-Aunt Arizona*
James, Simon. *Dear Mr. Blueberry*
Johnson, Jean. *Teachers A to Z*
Kraus, Robert. *Good morning, Miss Gator*
Krensky, Stephen. *My teacher's secret life*
Lorbiecki, Marybeth. *Sister Anne's hands*
McKissack, Patricia C. *Booker T. Washington*
Munsch, Robert N. *Thomas' snowsuit*
Myers, Bernice. *It happens to everyone*
Paraskevas, Betty. *Gracie Graves and the kids from room 402*
Park, Barbara. *Junie B. Jones and some sneaky peeky spying*
Polacco, Patricia. *Thank you, Mr. Falker*
Powers, Mary E. *Our teacher's in a wheelchair*
Priceman, Marjorie. *Emeline at the circus*
Pulver, Robin. *Mrs. Toggle and the dinosaur*

   Mrs. Toggle's beautiful blue shoe
   Mrs. Toggle's zipper
Schomp, Virginia. *If you were a . . . teacher*
Tabor, Nancy (Maria Grande). *Bottles break*
Weiss, Leatie. *My teacher sleeps in school*

Careers – telephone operators

Allen, Jeffrey. *Mary Alice, operator number 9*
   Mary Alice returns

Careers – toy makers

Gallaz, Christophe. *Threadbear*
Hoffmann, E. T. A. *The nutcracker*, ill. by Francesca Crespi
   The nutcracker, ill. by Carolyn Ewing
   The nutcracker, ill. by Rachel Isadora
   The nutcracker, ill. by Joanna Isles
   The nutcracker, ill. by Maurice Sendak
   The nutcracker, ill. by Lisbeth Zwerger
McMullan, Kate (Hall). *Nutcracker Noel*
Thurber, James. *The great Quillow*
Waddell, Martin. *The toymaker*

Careers – train engineers *see* Careers – railroad engineers

Careers – truck drivers

Behrens, June. *I can be a truck driver*
Cartlidge, Michelle. *Teddy trucks*
Cowley, Joy. *Gracias, the Thanksgiving turkey*
Day, Alexandra. *Frank and Ernest on the road*
Horenstein, Henry. *Sam goes trucking*
Mitchell, Joyce Slayton. *Tractor-trailer trucker*
Royston, Angela. *Truck trouble*
Sturges, Philemon. *I love trucks!*
Young, Miriam Burt. *If I drove a truck*

Careers – veterinarians

Bellville, Rod. *Large animal veterinarians*
Coffey, Maria. *A seal in the family*
Dodd, Lynley. *Hairy Maclary's rumpus at the vet*
Gibbons, Gail. *Say woof!*
Herriot, James. *Moses the kitten*
   Only one woof
Hewett, Joan. *Fly away free*
Kuklin, Susan. *Taking my dog to the vet*
Kunhardt, Edith. *I'm going to be a vet*
Leonard, Marcia. *The pet vet*
Lumley, Katheryn Wentzel. *I can be an animal doctor*
Martin, C. L. G. *Down Dairy Farm Road*
Polhamus, Jean Burt. *Doctor Dinosaur*

Careers – waiters, waitresses

Ahlberg, Allan. *Mrs. Wobble the waitress*
Krementz, Jill. *Benjy goes to a restaurant*
Loomis, Christine. *In the diner*
Mooser, Stephen. *Funnyman's first case*
Moss, Marissa. *Mel's diner*
Peters, Sharon. *Happy Jack*

Careers – waitresses *see* Careers – waiters, waitresses

Careers – welders

Lillegard, Dee. *I can be a welder*

Careers – whalers

Drummond, Allan. *Moby Dick*

Careers – window cleaners

Dahl, Roald. *The giraffe and the pelly and me*
Rey, H. A. (Hans Augusto). *Curious George takes a job*

Careers – woodcarvers

Rosen, Michael J. (1954-). *Elijah's angel*
Steven, Kenneth C. *The bearer of gifts*
Wojciechowski, Susan. *The Christmas miracle of Jonathan Toomey*

Careers – writers

Broekel, Ray. *I can be an author*
Brown, Margaret Wise. *The days before now*
Christelow, Eileen. *What do authors do?*
Edwards, Michelle. *Dora's book*
Goffstein, M. B. (Marilyn Brooke). *A writer*
Harness, Cheryl. *Mark Twain and the queens of the Mississippi*
Hurwitz, Johanna. *A dream come true*
Johnson, Jane. *My dear Noel*
Lester, Helen. *Author*
London, Jonathan. *Tell me a story*
Lyon, George Ella. *A sign*
Muntean, Michaela. *Kermit and Robin's scary story*
Rylant, Cynthia. *Best wishes*
Schotter, Roni. *Nothing ever happens on 90th Street*
Stevenson, James. *Fun, no fun*
  I meant to tell you
Wallner, Alexandra. *Beatrix Potter*

Careers – zoo keepers

Knight, Bertram T. *Working at a zoo*
Löfgren, Ulf. *Alvin the zookeeper*
Rathmann, Peggy. *Good night, Gorilla*

Carelessness *see* Behavior – carelessness

Caribbean Islands *see* Foreign lands – Caribbean Islands

Caribou *see* Animals – reindeer

Carnivals *see* Fairs

Carousels *see* Merry-go-rounds

Carpenters *see* Careers – carpenters

Carrier *see* Indians of North America – Carrier

Cars *see* Automobiles

Castles

Allen, Laura Jean. *Rollo and Tweedy and the ghost of Dougal Castle*
Crebbin, June. *Into the castle*
Duquennoy, Jacques. *The ghosts in the cellar*
Dürr, Ursula. *The secret of Trembleton Hall*
Gabler, Mirko. *Brakus, Krakus . . . Or the incredible adventure of Mr. Skola's Tourist Club*
Krensky, Stephen. *We just moved!*
Leonard, Marcia. *King Lionheart's castle*
Love, Ann. *Ice cream at the castle*
Oberman, Sheldon. *The white stone in the castle wall*
Yee, Brenda Shannon. *Sand castle*

Caterpillars *see* Insects – butterflies, caterpillars

Cats *see* Animals – cats

Cave drawings *see* Petroglyphs

Cavemen

Baylor, Byrd. *One small blue bead*
Hoff, Syd. *Stanley*
Seyton, Marion. *The hole in the hill*
Slobodkin, Louis. *Dinny and Danny*
Wood, Audrey. *The Tickleoctopus*

Caves

Baynes, Pauline. *How dog began*
Brett, Jan. *The first dog*
Day, Marie. *Quennu and the cave bear*
DeLage, Ida. *The old witch and the snores*
Tettelbaum, Michael. *The cave of the lost Fraggle*
Ungerer, Tomi. *The Mellops go spelunking*

Central America *see* Foreign lands – Central America

Cerebral palsy *see* Handicaps – cerebral palsy

Chairs *see* Furniture – chairs

Chameleons *see* Reptiles – chameleons

Chanukah *see* Holidays – Hanukkah

Character traits

Buehner, Caralyn. *I did it, I'm sorry*
Burdett, Lois. *Twelfth night*
Johnson, Crockett. *The emperor's gifts*
Seignobosc, Françoise. *Jeanne-Marie in gay Paris*
Wahl, Jan. *Mrs. Owl and Mr. Pig*
Walker, Alice. *Finding the green stone*
Wilson-Kelly, Becky. *Mother Grumpy's dog biscuits*

Character traits – ambition

Balet, Jan B. *Joanjo*
Barton, Byron. *I want to be an astronaut*
Chottin, Ariane. *Beaver gets lost*
Claude-Lafontaine, Pascale. *Monsieur Bussy, the celebrated hamster*

Dunrea, Olivier. *The painter who loved chickens*
Graham, Al. *Timothy Turtle*
Gramatky, Hardie. *Little Toot*
Greaves, Margaret. *Henry's wild morning*
Herman, R. A. (Ronnie Ann). *Pal the pony*
Horwitz, Elinor Lander. *Sometimes it happens*
Kumin, Maxine W. *Speedy digs downside up*
Ringi, Kjell (Arne Sorensen). *My father and I*
Root, Phyllis. *Sam, who was swallowed by a shark*
Seignobosc, Françoise. *What do you want to be?*
Shecter, Ben. *Hester the jester*
Shefelman, Janice Jordan. *A peddler's dream*
Turska, Krystyna. *The magician of Cracow*
Uchida, Yoshiko. *Sumi's prize*

Character traits – appearance

Andersen, H. C. (Hans Christian). *The ugly duck-ling*, ill. by Adrienne Adams
  The ugly duckling, ill. by Lorinda Bryan Cauley
  The ugly duckling, ill. by Troy Howell
  The ugly duckling, ill. by Tadasu Izawa and Shigemi Hijikata
  The ugly duckling, ill. by Monika Laimgruber
  The ugly duckling, ill. by Johannes Larsen
  The ugly duckling, ill. by Thomas Locker
  The ugly duckling, ill. by Alan Marks
  The ugly duckling, ill. by Josef Palecek
  The ugly duckling, ill. by Jerry Pinkney
  The ugly duckling, ill. by Maria Ruis
  The ugly duckling, ill. by Daniel San Souci
  The ugly duckling, ill. by Robert Van Nutt
  The ugly duckling, ill. by Bernadette Watts
  The ugly little duck, ill. by Peggy Perry Anderson
Asch, Frank. *I can blink*
Balestrino, Philip. *Fat and skinny*
Beim, Jerrold. *Freckle face*
Bonsall, Crosby Newell. *Listen, listen!*
Boyle, Vere. *Beauty and the beast*
Butterworth, Nick. *Making faces*
Carter, Anne. *Beauty and the beast*
Caseley, Judith. *Molly Pink goes hiking*
Charles, Donald. *Shaggy dog's Halloween*
  Ugly bug
Chevalier, Christa. *Spence isn't Spence anymore*
Cohen, Burton. *Nelson makes a face*
Collins, Judith Graham. *Josh's scary dad*
Crowley, Arthur. *The ugly book*
Dellinger, Annetta. *You are special to Jesus*
De Paola, Tomie (Thomas Anthony). *Big Anthony and the magic ring*
Eco, Umberto. *The three astronauts*
Edwards, Lisa. *Disney's Beauty and the beast, a book of manners*
Elborn, Andrew. *Big Al*
  Bird Adalbert
Fatio, Louise. *The happy lion and the bear*
Freeman, Don. *Dandelion*
Ginsburg, Mirra. *The Chinese mirror*
Girion, Barbara. *The boy with the special face*
Goble, Paul. *Star boy*
Greenfield, Eloise. *Grandpa's face*
Hale, Irina. *Brown bear in a brown chair*
Heine, Helme. *The most wonderful egg in the world*
Hillert, Margaret. *The funny baby*
Hutton, Warwick. *Beauty and the beast*
Iké, Jane Hori. *A Japanese fairy tale*
Joly, Fanny. *Mr. Fine, porcupine*
Kasza, Keiko. *The pigs' picnic*

Keller, Irene. *The Thingumajig book of manners*
Lieberman, Syd. *The wise shoemaker of Studena*
Lindenbaum, Pija. *Boodil, my dog*
McDermott, Gerald. *The magic tree*
Maestro, Betsy. *On the town*
Mayer, Marianna. *Beauty and the beast*
Mayer, Mercer. *How the trollusk got his hat*
Moore, Sheila. *Samson Svenson's baby*
Munsch, Robert N. *The paper bag princess*
  Stephanie's ponytail
Myers, Amy. *I know a monster*
Nesbit, Edith. *Beauty and the beast*
Ness, Evaline. *The girl and the goatherd*
Numeroff, Laura Joffe. *Amy for short*
  Why a disguise?
Ormerod, Jan. *Just like me*
  Our Ollie
  Silly goose
Ormondroyd, Edward. *Theodore*
Otto, Carolyn. *What color is camouflage?*
Palatini, Margie. *Piggie pie*
Paraskevas, Betty. *The tangerine bear*
Park, Ruth. *When the wind changed*
Pfister, Marcus. *The rainbow fish*
  Rainbow fish to the rescue!
Primavera, Elise. *Basil and Maggie*
Quinsey, Mary Beth. *Why does that man have such a big nose?*
Ring, Elizabeth. *Tiger lilies and other beastly plants*
Salus, Naomi Panush. *My daddy's mustache*
Schaffer, Libor. *Arthur sets sail*
Scott, Natalie (Anderson). *Firebrand, push your hair out of your eyes*
Small, David. *Imogene's antlers*
Stren, Patti. *Mountain Rose*
Thomson, Peggy. *The king has horse's ears*
Willis, Jeanne. *What did I look like when I was a baby?*
Wright, Freire. *Beauty and the beast*
Yep, Laurence. *The city of dragons*

Character traits – assertiveness

Dunbar, Joyce. *A cake for Barney*
Ingoglia, Gina. *The art class*
Lindgren, Astrid. *Pippi Longstocking's after-Christmas party*
Martchenko, Michael. *Bird feeder banquet*
Moss, Marissa. *After-school monster*
Winthrop, Elizabeth. *I'm the Boss!*

Character traits – being different

Aggs, Patrice. *The visitor*
Alborough, Jez. *Cuddly Dudley*
Allinson, Beverley. *Effie*
Andersen, H. C. (Hans Christian). *The ugly duck-ling*, ill. by Adrienne Adams
  The ugly duckling, ill. by Lorinda Bryan Cauley
  The ugly duckling, ill. by Troy Howell
  The ugly duckling, ill. by Tadasu Izawa and Shigemi Hijikata
  The ugly duckling, ill. by Monika Laimgruber
  The ugly duckling, ill. by Johannes Larsen
  The ugly duckling, ill. by Thomas Locker
  The ugly duckling, ill. by Alan Marks
  The ugly duckling, ill. by Josef Palecek
  The ugly duckling, ill. by Jerry Pinkney
  The ugly duckling, ill. by Maria Ruis
  The ugly duckling, ill. by Daniel San Souci

The ugly duckling, ill. by Robert Van Nutt
The ugly duckling, ill. by Bernadette Watts
The ugly little duck, ill. by Peggy Perry Anderson
Arnold, Tedd. Green Wilma
Aulaire, Ingri Mortenson d'. Nils
Baumann, Hans. Mischa and his brothers
Beim, Jerrold. Freckle face
Blos, Joan W. Old Henry
Blue, Rose. I am here
Brandenberg, Franz. Otto is different
Brightman, Alan. Like me
Burningham, John. Borka
Cannon, Janell. Stellaluna
   Stellaluna: a pop-up book and mobile
Caple, Kathy. The biggest nose
Carle, Eric. The mixed-up chameleon
Carrick, Carol. Two very little sisters
Chapman, Elizabeth. Suzy
Cibula, Matt S. The contrary kid
Clément, Claude. The hungry duckling
Cohen, Miriam. It's George!
Coombs, Patricia. The lost playground
Corbalis, Judy. Porcellus, the flying pig
Counsel, June. But Martin!
Crossley-Holland, Kevin. The green children
De Veaux, Alexis. An enchanted hair tale
Dinan, Carolyn. Say cheese!
Drescher, Henrik. The strange appearance of Howard
   Cranebill, Jr.
Dubanevich, Arlene. Pigs at Christmas
Duvoisin, Roger Antoine. Our Veronica goes to Petu-
   nia's farm
   Veronica
Emberley, Ed (Edward Randolph). Rosebud
Escudie, René. Paul and Sebastian
Fern, Eugene. Pepito's story
Fleming, Denise. Mama cat has three kittens
Frieden, Sarajo. The care and feeding of fish
Garcia, Carolyn. Moonboy
Hayes, Sarah. Mary Mary
Heine, Helme. Superhare
Hennessy, B. G. (Barbara G.). Meet Winslow whale
Hillert, Margaret. The funny baby
Hoff, Syd. Mrs. Brice's mice
Imai, Miko. Lilly's secret
Jeram, Anita. Daisy Dare
Karlin, Nurit. The blue frog
Keller, Holly. Horace
Krasilovsky, Phyllis. The very tall little girl
Kuklin, Susan. Thinking big
Leech, Bryan Jeffery. John Jeremy Colton
Leedy, Loreen. Pingo the plaid panda
Lerner, Marguerite Rush. Lefty, the story of left-hand-
   edness
Levine, Rhoda. Harrison loved his umbrella
Lionni, Leo. Cornelius
McGovern, Ann. Mr. Skinner's skinny house
Machado, Ana Maria. Nina Bonita
McKee, David. Elmer
McKelvey, David. Bobby the mostly silky
Modarressi, Mitra. The beastly visits
Mora, Pat. The rainbow tulip
Moser, Madeline. Ever heard of an aardwolf?
Murphy, Pat. Pigasus
Myers, Christopher A. Wings
Nones, Eric Jon. Angela's wings
Nordlicht, Lillian. I love to laugh
Ostrow, Vivian. My brother is from outer space
Paek, Min. Aekyung's dream

Passen, Lisa. Fat, fat Rose Marie
Payne, Sherry Neuwirth. A contest
Peet, Bill (William Bartlett). The spooky tail of Pre-
   witt Peacock
Polacco, Patricia. I can hear the sun
Polisar, Barry Louis. The trouble with Ben
Quinsey, Mary Beth. Why does that man have such a
   big nose?
Rankin, Joan. You're somebody special, Walliwigs!
Reesink, Marijke. The princess who always ran away
Reidy, Hannah. Crazy creature contrasts
Rey, Margret (Margret Elisabeth Waldstein). Spotty
Riddell, Chris. Bird's new shoes
Rubinetti, Donald. Cappy the lonely camel
Sansone, Adele. The little green goose
Schertle, Alice. Jeremy Bean's St. Patrick's Day
Schotter, Roni. Captain Snap and the children of
   Vinegar Lane
Sharmat, Marjorie Weinman. Helga high-up
Shles, Larry. Moths and mothers, feathers and fathers
Shub, Elizabeth. Dragon Franz
Simon, Francesca. The Topsy-Turvies
Simon, Norma. Why am I different?
Simon, Sidney B. The armadillo who had no shell
Slyder, Ingrid. The Fabulous Flying Fandinis
Stapler, Sarah. Cordellia, dance!
Thurber, James. The great Quillow
Voake, Charlotte. Mrs. Goose's baby
Wadhams, Margaret. Anna
Wallace, Barbara Brooks. Argyle
Walsh, Ellen Stoll. For Pete's sake
Weedn, Flavia. The enchanted tree
Wells, Rosemary. Abdul
Whitcomb, Mary E. Odd Velvet
Whitmore, Adam. Max in America
   Max in Australia
   Max in India
   Max leaves home
Wilkon, Piotr. Rosie the cool cat
Willis, Jeanne. The long blue blazer
Wood, Audrey. Weird parents
Yep, Laurence. The city of dragons

Character traits – bravery

Aitken, Amy. Ruby, the red knight
Alborough, Jez. There's something at the mail slot
Aliki. George and the cherry tree
Andersen, H. C. (Hans Christian). The snow queen,
   ill. by Angela Barrett
   The snow queen, ill. by Toma Bogdanovic
   The snow queen, ill. by June Atkin Corwin
   The snow queen, ill. by Sally Holmes
   The snow queen, ill. by Susan Jeffers
   The snow queen, ill. by Errol Le Cain
   The snow queen, ill. by Bernadette Watts
   The snow queen, ill. by Arieh Zeldich
Anglund, Joan Walsh. The brave cowboy
Ardizzone, Edward. Little Tim and the brave sea cap-
   tain
   Paul, the hero of the fire
   Peter the wanderer
   Tim and Charlotte
   Tim to the rescue
Aulaire, Ingri Mortenson d'. Wings for Per
Bailey, Linda. When Addie was scared
Baillie, Allan. Rebel!
Baldner, Gaby. Joba and the wild boar
Bannon, Laura. Hat for a hero

Barr, Cathrine. *Little Ben*
Barrows, Marjorie Wescott. *Fraidy cat*
Baumann, Kurt. *Piro and the fire brigade*
Bawden, Nina. *William Tell*
Beim, Jerrold. *Eric on the desert*
Benchley, Nathaniel. *The deep dives of Stanley Whale*
Benjamin, Anne. *Young Pocahontas*
Blegvad, Lenore. *Anna Banana and me*
Bornstein, Ruth Lercher. *Jim*
Brook, Judy. *Tim mouse goes down the stream*
Brown, Margaret Wise. *Streamlined pig*
Burgert, Hans-Joachim. *Samulo and the giant*
Cameron, Ann. *Harry (the monster)*
Carleton, Barbee Oliver. *Benny and the bear*
Carlson, Nancy L. *Arnie and the skateboard gang*
    Harriet and the roller coaster
Chaffin, Lillie D. *We be warm till springtime comes*
Chapouton, Anne-Marie. *Billy the brave*
Charlton, Elizabeth. *Jeremy and the ghost*
Chocolate, Deborah M. Newton. *Imani in the belly*
Church, Kristine. *My brother John*
Coles, Robert. *The story of Ruby Bridges*
Conford, Ellen. *Eugene the brave*
Coombs, Patricia. *Molly Mullett*
Coville, Bruce. *The foolish giant*
Craft, Ruth. *Carrie Hepple's garden*
De Beer, Hans. *Little polar bear and the brave little hare*
De La Mare, Walter (Walter John). *Molly Whuppie*
De Posadas Mane, Carmen. *Mister North Wind*
Derby, Sally. *King Kenrick's splinter*
Douglas, Richardo Keens. *The nutmeg princess*
Dreifus, Miriam W. *Brave Betsy*
Driscoll, Laura. *The bravest cat!*
Duncan, Jane. *Brave Janet Reachfar*
Dyke, John. *Pigwig*
Ehlert, Lois. *Cuckoo: a Mexican folktale = Cucú: un cuento folklórico mexicano*
Erickson, Karen. *I'm brave!*
Fatio, Louise. *The red bantam*
Fern, Eugene. *The most frightened hero*
Fuchshuber, Annegert. *Giant story – Mouse tale*
Furchgott, Terry. *Phoebe and the hot water bottles*
Gackenbach, Dick. *Beauty, brave and beautiful*
Gantschev, Ivan. *The Christmas train*
Ginsburg, Mirra. *The strongest one of all*
Goodall, John S. *Paddy to the rescue*
Grant, Joan. *The monster that grew small*
    Grasshopper to the rescue
Greaves, Margaret. *Once there were no pandas*
Grimm, Jacob. *The brave little tailor*, ill. by Mark Corcoran
    The brave little tailor, ill. by Daniel San Souci
    The brave little tailor, ill. by Svend Otto S
    The brave little tailor, ill. by Eve Tharlet
    The brave little tailor, ill. by James Warhola
    Seven at one blow
    The valiant little tailor
Haley, Gail E. *Jack and the fire dragon*
Harris, Leon A. *The great diamond robbery*
Harshman, Marc. *A little excitement*
Hayes, Sarah. *This is the bear and the scary night*
Hazen, Barbara Shook. *Fang*
    The new dog
Hearne, Betsy Gould. *Seven brave women*
Heide, Florence Parry. *Timothy Twinge*
Helldorfer, M. C. (Mary Claire). *The mapmaker's daughter*
Henkes, Kevin. *Sheila Rae, the brave*

Herman, Gail. *Fievel's big showdown*
Heyer, Carol. *Robin Hood*
Hiser, Berniece T. *The adventure of Charlie and his wheat-straw hat*
Hoban, Lillian. *No, no, Sammy Crow*
Holl, Adelaide. *Sir Kevin of Devon*
Hooks, William H. *Peach boy*
Hort, Lenny. *The boy who held back the sea*
Horvath, Betty F. *Jasper and the hero business*
Howard, Elizabeth Fitzgerald. *Papa tells Chita a story*
Hughes, Monica. *Little Fingerling*
Hulpach, Vladimir. *Ahaiyute and Cloud Eater*
Hürlimann, Bettina. *Barry*
Jackson, Shelley. *The old woman and the wave*
Jakes, John. *Susanna of the Alamo*
James, J. Alison. *The drums of Noto Hanto*
Jaques, Faith. *Tilly's rescue*
Jeram, Anita. *Daisy Dare*
Keller, Beverly. *Pimm's place*
Keller, Holly. *Brave Horace*
Kerins, Tony (Anthony). *The brave ones*
Kimmel, Eric A. *The four gallant sisters*
Kurtz, Jane. *Miro in the kingdom of the sun*
Lagercrantz, Rose. *Brave little Pete of Geranium Street*
Lee, Jeanne M. *The song of Mu Lan*
Le Guin, Ursula K. *A ride on the red mare's back*
Lemaître, Pascal. *Emily the giraffe*
Leonard, Alain. *Barnaby and the big gorilla*
Lewis, Robin Baird. *Friska, the sheep that was too small*
Lexau, Joan M. *It all began with a drip, drip, drip*
Little, Jean. *Jess was the brave one*
Little, Lessie Jones. *I can do it by myself*
Littlewood, Valerie. *The season clock*
Low, Joseph. *Benny rabbit and the owl*
    Boo to a goose
Lunge-Larsen, Lise. *The legend of the lady slipper*
Maitland, Barbara. *The bear who didn't like honey*
Mallat, Kathy. *Brave bear*
Manushkin, Fran. *Be brave, baby rabbit*
Marshak, S. (Samuil). *The tale of a hero nobody knows*
Martin, Bill (William Ivan). *Knots on a counting rope*
Martin, Rafe. *The monkey bridge*
Matsutani, Miyoko. *The witch's magic cloth*
May, Kara. *Big brave brother Ben*
Mayer, Marianna. *The unicorn and the lake*
Mayer, Mercer. *Liverwurst is missing*
    Liza Lou and the Yeller Belly Swamp
Milne, A. A. (Alan Alexander). *Winnie-the-Pooh*
Mitchell, Margaree King. *Granddaddy's gift*
Moss, Marissa. *After-school monster*
Namioka, Lensey. *The loyal cat*
Nash, Ogden. *The adventures of Isabel*, ill. by Walter Lorraine
    The adventures of Isabel, ill. by James Marshall
    Custard the dragon
    Custard the dragon and the wicked knight, ill. by Lynn Munsinger
    Custard the dragon and the wicked knight, ill. by Linell Nash
Nishikawa, Osamu. *Alexander and the blue ghost*
Olson, Arielle North. *The lighthouse keeper's daughter*
Oppenheim, Shulamith Levey. *The lily cupboard*
Palecek, Libuse. *Brave as a tiger*
Peet, Bill (William Bartlett). *Cowardly Clyde*
Polushkin, Maria. *The little hen and the giant*
Pryor, Bonnie. *The porcupine mouse*
Raglus, Jeff. *Schnorky the wave puncher*

Rappaport, Doreen. *The long-haired girl*
Roth, Susan L. *Brave Martha and the dragon*
San Souci, Robert D. *The enchanted tapestry*
    The samurai's daughter
Scarry, Richard. *Richard Scarry's Peasant Pig and the terrible dragon*
Scheffler, Ursel. *Be brave, little lion!*
Schertle, Alice. *The gorilla in the hall*
Schumacher, Claire. *Brave Lily*
Sewell, Helen Moore. *Jimmy and Jemima*
Shire, Ellen. *The mystery at number seven, Rue Petite*
Shute, Linda. *Momotaro, the peach boy*
Small, Terry. *The legend of William Tell*
Stanek, Muriel. *All alone after school*
Steig, William. *Brave Irene*
Stevenson, Drew. *The ballad of Penelope Lou . . . and me*
Taylor, Mark. *Henry explores the jungle*
    Henry explores the mountains
    Henry the explorer
Titus, Eve. *Anatole and the cat*
Uchida, Yoshiko. *The magic purse*
Va, Leong. *A letter to the king*
Van Woerkom, Dorothy. *Becky and the bear*
Wells, H. G. (Herbert George). *The adventures of Tommy*
Wetterer, Margaret. *Kate Shelley and the midnight express*
Wilkon, Piotr. *The brave little kittens*
Wolkstein, Diane. *The banza*
Yolen, Jane. *Beneath the ghost moon*

Character traits – cleanliness

Adelborg, Ottilia. *Clean Peter and the children of Grubbylea*
Ahlberg, Allan. *Mrs. Lather's laundry*
Allen, Jonathan. *Mucky moose*
Bonning, Tony. *Another fine mess*
Bowling, David Louis. *Dirty Dingy Daryl*
Bucknall, Caroline. *One bear in the picture*
Burch, Robert. *The jolly witch*
Carlstrom, Nancy White. *Jesse Bear's yum-yum crumble*
Cobb, Vicki. *Keeping clean*
Cole, Babette. *Dr. Dog*
Conrad, Pam. *This mess*
Cummings, Pat. *Clean your room, Harvey Moon!*
De Paola, Tomie (Thomas Anthony). *Marianna May and Nursey*
Dickinson, Mary. *Alex's bed*
Eagle, Ellen. *Gypsy's cleaning day*
Edwards, Frank B. *Mortimer Mooner stopped taking a bath*
Ernst, Lisa Campbell. *Duke, the Dairy Delight dog*
Flot, Jeannette B. *Princess Kalina and the hedgehog*
Gantos, Jack (John, Jr.). *Swampy alligator*
Groves-Raines, Antony. *The tidy hen*
Hamsa, Bobbie. *Dirty Larry*
Hare, Lorraine. *Who needs her?*
Haseley, Dennis. *The soap bandit*
Hickman, Martha Whitmore. *Eeps creeps, it's my room!*
Howells, Mildred. *The woman who lived in Holland*
Hurd, Edith Thacher. *Stop, stop*
Hutchins, Pat. *Where's the baby?*
Jackson, Ellen B. *The bear in the bathtub*
Krasilovsky, Phyllis. *The man who didn't wash his dishes*

Kraus, Robert. *Buggy Bear cleans up*
Krensky, Stephen. *What a mess!*
Kroll, Steven. *The pigrates clean up*
Landström, Olof. *Boo and Baa on a cleaning spree*
Lattimore, Deborah Nourse. *Cinderhazel*
Lindbergh, Anne. *Tidy lady*
Loomis, Christine. *The cleanup surprise*
McKay, Hilary. *Where's bear?*
McKissack, Patricia C. *Ada, la desordenada*
    Messy Bessey
    Messy Bessey and the birthday overnight
    Messy Bessey's holidays
McQueen, Lucinda. *Tidy pig*
Madden, Don. *The Wartville wizard*
Mahy, Margaret. *Keeping house*
Miller, Edward. *The curse of Claudia*
Moon, Nicola. *Alligator tails and crocodile cakes*
Morris, Ann. *Eleanora Mousie makes a mess*
Munsch, Robert N. *Mud puddle*
Nerlove, Miriam. *I meant to clean my room today*
Peters, Sharon. *Messy Mark*
Polushkin, Maria. *Bubba and Babba*
Potter, Beatrix. *The tale of Mrs. Tittlemouse*
Rockwell, Anne F. *Nice and clean*
Root, Phyllis. *Mrs. Potter's pig*
Rounds, Glen. *Washday on Noah's ark*
Schwartz, Mary. *Spiffen*
Serfozo, Mary. *Dirty Kurt*
Sharmat, Marjorie Weinman. *Mooch the messy*
Sharmat, Mitchell. *The seven sloppy days of Phineas Pig*
Stanton, Elizabeth. *The very messy room*
Teague, Mark. *Pigsty*
Wabbes, Marie. *Rose is muddy*
Wells, Rosemary. *Fritz and the mess fairy*
    Max cleans up
Wilhelm, Hans. *Oh, what a mess*
Willis, Jeanne. *The tale of Georgie Grub*
Wilson, Sarah. *The day that Henry cleaned his room*
Ziefert, Harriet. *A clean house for Mole and Mouse*
    Hurry up, Jessie!

Character traits – cleverness

Ahlberg, Janet. *It was a dark and stormy night*
Alberts, Nancy Markham. *No toys on Sunday*
Alderson, Sue Ann. *Ida and the wool smugglers*
Alexander, Sue. *Peacocks are very special*
Aliki. *The eggs*
Andersen, H. C. (Hans Christian). *The swineherd*, ill. by Erik Blegvad
    The swineherd, ill. by Dorothée Duntze
    The swineherd, ill. by Deborah Hahn
    The swineherd, ill. by Lisbeth Zwerger
Anderson, Paul S. *Red fox and the hungry tiger*
Ardizzone, Edward. *Peter the wanderer*
Arnold, Katya. *Baba Yaga and the little girl*
Asbjørnsen, P. C. (Peter Christen). *Billy goats Gruff*, ill. by Wendy Edelson
    Billy goats Gruff, ill. by Susan Hellard
    The three billy goats Gruff, ill. by Tim Arnold
    The three billy goats Gruff, ill. by Robert Bender
    The three billy goats Gruff, ill. by Marcia Brown
    The three billy goats Gruff, ill. by Stephen Carpenter
    Three billy goats Gruff, ill. by Tom Dunnington
    The three billy goats Gruff, ill. by Paul Galdone
    The three billy goats Gruff, ill. by David Jorgensen
    The three billy goats Gruff, ill. by Dennis Kendrick

The three billygoats Gruff, ill. by Eric Kincaid
The three billy goats Gruff, ill. by Jonathan Langley
The three billy goats Gruff, ill. by Loretta Lustig
The three billy goats Gruff, ill. by Thomas Newbury
The three billy goats Gruff, ill. by Lilian Obligado
The three billy goats Gruff, ill. by Ed Parker
The three billy goats Gruff, ill. by Heidi Petach
The three billy goats Gruff, ill. by Laura Rader
The three billy goats Gruff, ill. by Glen Rounds
The three billy goats Gruff, ill. by Janet Stevens
The three billy goats Gruff, ill. by William Stobbs
The three billy goats Gruff, ill. by Svend Otto S
The truth about three billy goats Gruff
Asch, Frank. *Ziggy Piggy and the three little pigs*
Baker, Betty. *And me, coyote!*
    Partners
Bang, Betsy. *The old woman and the red pumpkin*
    The old woman and the rice thief
Bang, Molly. *Wiley and the hairy man*
Bannerman, Helen. *The story of Little Babaji*
    The story of little black Sambo
Barbosa, Rogério Andrade. *African animal tales*
Barry, David. *The Rajah's rice*
Bason, Lillian. *Those foolish Molboes!*
Bell, Anthea. *The wise queen*
Bemelmans, Ludwig. *Welcome home!*
Berson, Harold. *How the devil gets his due*
    Joseph and the snake
    Why the jackal won't speak to the hedgehog
Bishop, Claire Huchet. *The five Chinese brothers*
Blundell, Tony. *Beware of boys*
Bodnar, Judit Z. *A wagonload of fish*
Boegehold, Betty. *Pawpaw's run*
Brett, Jan. *Fritz and the beautiful horses*
    The trouble with trolls
Brown, Marcia. *The bun*
    Stone soup
Brown, Margaret Wise. *Don't frighten the lion*
Buchanan, Heather S. *George Mouse's first summer*
Burningham, John. *Harquin*
    The shopping basket
Byfield, Barbara Ninde. *The haunted churchbell*
Calhoun, Mary. *Cross-country cat*
    Jack and the whoopee wind
Cameron, John. *If mice could fly*
Caseley, Judith. *Ada potato*
Castle, Caroline. *Herbert Binns and the flying tricycle*
Cauley, Lorinda Bryan. *The trouble with Tyrannosaurus Rex*
Christelow, Eileen. *Jerome the babysitter*
Climo, Shirley. *King of the birds*
Coatsworth, Elizabeth. *Pika and the roses*
Cohen, Caron Lee. *Renata, Whizbrain and the ghost*
Cole, Joanna. *Doctor Change*
Compton, Kenn. *Jack the giant chaser*
Costa, Nicoletta. *The clever dog*
Crompton, Anne Eliot. *The lifting stone*
Damjan, Mischa. *The wolf and the kid*
Daniels, Guy. *The Tsar's riddles*
Dee, Ruby. *Two ways to count to ten*
DeFelice, Cynthia C. *Clever crow*
    Three perfect peaches
De La Mare, Walter (Walter John). *Molly Whuppie*
Demi. *One grain of rice*
    Under the shade of the mulberry tree
De Regniers, Beatrice Schenk. *Catch a little fox*
Dickens, Frank. *Boffo*
Dines, Glen. *Gilly and the wicharoo*
Dodd, Lynley. *Hairy Maclary's bone*

Domanska, Janina. *The best of the bargain*
    King Krakus and the dragon
    Why so much noise?
Dos Santos, Joyce Audy. *The diviner*
Elkin, Benjamin. *Gillespie and the guards*
    Lucky and the giant
Erickson, Russell E. *Warton and the traders*
Ernst, Lisa Campbell. *The prize pig surprise*
Forest, Heather. *Stone soup*
Frankel, Bernice. *Half-As-Big and the tiger*
Frascino, Edward. *My cousin the king*
French, Vivian. *Red Hen and Sly Fox*
Freschet, Berniece. *Elephant and friends*
Galdone, Paul. *The monkey and the crocodile*
    What's in fox's sack?
Ginsburg, Mirra. *The fisherman's son*
Goldman, Dara. *There's no such thing!*
Gorbachev, Valeri. *The Fool of the world and the flying ship*
Greeson, Janet. *An American army of two*
Grimm, Jacob. *The four clever brothers*
Harrison, David Lee. *Little boy soup*
Hayes, Sarah. *Nine ducks nine*
Hazen, Barbara Shook. *The Fat Cats, Cousin Scraggs and the monster mice*
Helldorfer, M. C. (Mary Claire). *The darling boys*
    Jack, Skinny Bones, and the golden pancakes
Hillert, Margaret. *The three goats*
Hirsh, Marilyn. *The Rabbi and the twenty-nine witches*
Hogrogian, Nonny. *Rooster brother*
Hooks, William H. *The Gruff brothers*
    Three rounds with rabbit
Huck, Charlotte S. *Princess Furball*
Hughes, Monica. *Little Fingerling*
Hutton, Warwick. *The nose tree*
Jackson, Ellen B. *The impossible riddle*
Jaffe, Rona. *Last of the wizards*
Jameson, Cynthia. *The house of five bears*
Kennedy, Richard. *The contests at Cowlick*
Kimmel, Eric A. *Count Silvernose*
Kipling, Rudyard. *Rikki-tikki-tavi*
Kraus, Robert. *Big Squeak, Little Squeak*
Laroche, Michel. *The snow rose*
Leverich, Kathleen. *The hungry fox and the foxy duck*
Lieberman, Syd. *The wise shoemaker of Studena*
The little red hen. The cock, the mouse and the little red hen, ill. by Lorinda Bryan Cauley
Lobel, Anita. *The straw maid*
Lobel, Arnold. *How the rooster saved the day*
    Mouse soup
Logue, Christopher. *The magic circus*
Lorenz, Lee. *The feathered ogre*
Lowell, Susan. *The three little javelinas*
McClenathan, Louise. *My mother sends her wisdom*
McCormack, John E. *Rabbit tales*
McCurdy, Michael. *The devils who learned to be good*
McNaughton, Colin. *Oops!*
Mahy, Margaret. *The seven Chinese brothers*
Mantinband, Gerda. *Three clever mice*
Martin, Charles E. *Dunkel takes a walk*
Mathers, Petra. *Lottie's new beach towel*
Metaxas, Eric. *The fool and the flying ship*
    Puss in boots
Mogensen, Jan. *The tiger's breakfast*
Myers, Edward. *Forri the baker*
Obrist, Jürg. *The miser who wanted the sun*
Olaleye, Isaac. *Bitter bananas*
Parish, Peggy. *Zed and the monsters*
Parry, Marian. *King of the fish*

Paterson, A. B. (Andrew Barton). *The man from Ironbark*
Patron, Susan. *Burgoo stew*
Paul, Anthony. *The tiger who lost his stripes*
Perrault, Charles. *Puss in boots*, ill. by Marcia Brown
  Puss in boots, ill. by Lorinda Bryan Cauley
  Puss in boots, ill. by Jean Claverie
  Puss in boots, ill. by Andrea Da Rif
  Puss in boots, ill. by Stasys Eidrigevicius
  Puss in boots, ill. by Hans Fischer
  Puss in boots, ill. by Paul Galdone
  Puss in boots, retold and ill. by John S. Goodall
  Puss in boots, retold and ill. by Gail E. Haley
  Puss in boots, ill. by Giuliano Lunelli
  Puss in boots, ill. by Fred Marcellino [pub. by Farrar, 1990]
  Puss in boots, ill. by Fred Marcellino [pub. by Farrar, 1998]
  Puss in boots, ill. by Julia Noonan
  Puss in boots, ill. by Tony Ross
  Puss in boots, ill. by William Stobbs
  Puss in boots, ill. by Yan Thomas
  Puss in boots, ill. by Alain Vaës
  Puss in boots, ill. by Barry Wilkinson
Peterson, Julienne. *Caterina, the clever farm girl*
Pittman, Helena Clare. *A grain of rice*
Potter, Beatrix. *The sly old cat*
  The tale of the Flopsy Bunnies
Prokofiev, Sergei Sergeievitch. *Peter and the wolf*, ill. by Reg Cartwright
  Peter and the wolf, ill. by Warren Chappell
  Peter and the wolf, ill. by Barbara Cooney
  Peter and the wolf, ill. by Julia Gukova
  Peter and the wolf, ill. by Frans Haacken
  Peter and the wolf, ill. by Alan Howard
  Peter and the wolf, ill. by Charles Mikolaycak
  Peter and the wolf, ill. by Jörg Müller
  Peter and the wolf, ill. by Josef Palecek
  Peter and the wolf, ill. by Kozo Shimizu
  Peter and the wolf, retold and ill. by Vladimir Vagin
  Peter and the wolf, ill. by Erna Voigt
Ransome, Arthur. *The fool of the world and the flying ship*
Reneaux, J. J. *Why Alligator hates Dog*
Rockwell, Anne F. *Big boss*
  The bump in the night
  The stolen necklace
Ross, Tony. *Stone soup*
San Souci, Robert D. *Callie Ann and Mistah Bear*
Schatell, Brian. *Sam's no dummy, Farmer Goff*
Schatz, Letta. *The extraordinary tug-of-war*
Shannon, George. *Laughing all the way*
  Lizard's home
Sheldon, Aure. *Of cobblers and kings*
Siddiqui, Ashraf. *Bhombal Dass, the uncle of lion*
Sierra, Judy. *Wiley and the Hairy Man*
Simon, Sidney B. *Henry, the uncatchable mouse*
Singh, Jacquelin. *Fat Gopal*
Small, David. *Paper John*
Steig, William. *Doctor De Soto*
Stevens, Janet. *Tops and bottoms*
Stewig, John Warren. *Clever Gretchen*
  Stone soup
Storr, Catherine (Cole). *Clever Polly and the stupid wolf*
Threadgall, Colin. *Proud rooster and the fox*
The three little pigs. *The original three little pigs retold*, ill. by Jonathan Smith

The story of the three little pigs, ill. by L. Leslie Brooke
The story of the three little pigs, ill. by William Stobbs
Three little pigs [Facsimile ed]
The three little pigs, ill. by Val Biro
The three little pigs, ill. by Gavin Bishop
The three little pigs, ill. by Erik Blegvad
The three little pigs, ill. by Caroline Bucknall
The three little pigs, ill. by Stephen Cartwright
The three little pigs, ill. by Lorinda Bryan Cauley
The three little pigs, ill. by Jean Claverie
The three little pigs, ill. by Doug Cushman
The three little pigs, ill. by William Pène Du Bois
The three little pigs, ill. by Paul Galdone
The three little pigs, ill. by Madelaine Gill
The three little pigs, ill. by Steven Kellogg
The three little pigs, ill. by David McPhail
The three little pigs, ill. by James Marshall
The three little pigs, ill. by Paul Meisel
The three little pigs, ill. by Rodney Peppé
The three little pigs, ill. by Edda Reinl
The three little pigs, ill. by John Wallner
The three little pigs, ill. by Irma Wilde
The three little pigs, ill. by Margot Zemach
The three little pigs and the big bad wolf
The three little pigs and the fox
The three pigs, ill. by Tony Ross
Who's at the door?
Thurber, James. *The great Quillow*
Troughton, Joanna. *Mouse-Deer's market*
Van Rynbach, Iris. *The soup stone*
Van Woerkom, Dorothy. *The rat, the ox and the zodiac*
Wahl, Jan. *Little Johnny Buttermilk*
Walker, Barbara K. (Barbara Kerlin). *Teeny-Tiny and the witch-woman*
Walsh, Ellen Stoll. *Jack's tale*
Ward, Helen. *The king of the birds*
Westwood, Jennifer. *Going to Squintum's*
Wetterer, Margaret. *Patrick and the fairy thief*
Wild, Robin. *Little Pig and the big bad wolf*
Williams, Jay. *School for sillies*
Winthrop, Elizabeth. *The little humpbacked horse*
Wolkstein, Diane. *The cool ride in the sky*
Wood, Audrey. *Heckedy Peg*
Young, Ed (Edward). *Little Plum*
  The terrible Nung Gwama
Zakhoder, Boris Vladimirovich. *The good stepmother*
Zemach, Harve. *Nail soup*

Character traits – clumsiness

Kroll, Steven. *Oh, Tucker!*
McNaughton, Colin. *Preston's goal!*
Naylor, Phyllis Reynolds. *"I can't take you anywhere!"*

Character traits – completing things

Flack, Marjorie. *Angus and the cat*
Ness, Evaline. *Do you have the time, Lydia?*
Petrides, Heidrun. *Hans and Peter*

Character traits – compromising

Hogrogian, Nonny. *Carrot cake*
Wildsmith, Brian. *The owl and the woodpecker*

Character traits – conceit

Bellows, Cathy. *The royal raccoon*
Brenner, Barbara A. *Mr. Tall and Mr. Small*
Flack, Marjorie. *Angus and the ducks*
Goble, Paul. *Iktomi and the boulder*
   Iktomi and the buffalo skull
Grimm, Jacob. *King Grisly-Beard*
Martin, Ann M. *Rachel Parker, kindergarten show-off*
Modarressi, Mitra. *The dream pillow*
Peet, Bill (William Bartlett). *Ella*
Sharmat, Marjorie Weinman. *I'm terrific*
Williams, Barbara. *So what if I'm a sore loser?*

Character traits – confidence

Alexander, Martha G. *My outrageous friend Charlie*
Barrett, Joyce Durham. *Willie's not the hugging kind*
Callan, Elizabeth Koda. *Good luck pony*
Caseley, Judith. *Harry and Willy and Carrothead*
Chottin, Ariane. *Little Kangaroo finds his way*
Hoff, Syd. *Stanley*
Lasky, Kathryn. *The solo*
Pocock, Rita. *Annabelle and the big slide*
Seed, Jenny. *Ntombi's song*
Waddell, Martin. *Good job, Little Bear!*
Wagner, Karen. *Bravo, Mildred and Ed!*
Wilhelm, Hans. *A cool kid - like me!*

Character traits – courage *see* Character traits – bravery

Character traits – cruelty to animals *see* Character traits – kindness to animals

Character traits – curiosity

Adamson, Gareth. *Old man up a tree*
Alden, Laura. *When?*
Allen, Jeffrey. *Nosey Mrs. Rat*
Ames, Mildred. *The wonderful box*
Bang, Molly. *Dawn*
Bird, E. J. *How do bears sleep?*
Bograd, Larry. *Egon*
Broome, Errol. *The smallest koala*
Campbell, Rod. *Buster's afternoon*
   Buster's morning
Chottin, Ariane. *The curious little dolphin*
Clark, Roberta. *Why?*
Climo, Shirley. *The adventure of Walter*
Cooper, Patrick. *Never trust a squirrel*
Cornette. *Purple coyote*
Curious George and the dump truck
Curious George and the pizza
Curious George at the fire station
Curious George goes hiking
Curious George goes sledding
Curious George goes to the aquarium
Curious George goes to the circus
Curious George visits the zoo
Demarest, Chris L. *Clemens' kingdom*
Domanska, Janina. *Spring is*
Fisher, Aileen Lucia. *Anybody home?*
Flack, Marjorie. *Angus and the cat*
   Angus and the ducks
Gackenbach, Dick. *The pig who saw everything*
Gottlieb, Dale. *Seeing Eye Willie*
Kanao, Keiko. *Kitten up a tree*

Kipling, Rudyard. *The elephant's child*, ill. by Louise Brierley
   The elephant's child, ill. by Lorinda Bryan Cauley
   The elephant's child, ill. by Tim Raglin
   The elephant's child, ill. by John A. Rowe
McBratney, Sam. *The dark at the top of the stairs*
MacGregor, Marilyn. *Baby takes a trip*
Meeks, Esther K. *The curious cow*
Moncure, Jane Belk. *Where?*
Morgan-Vanroyen, Mary. *Curious Rosie*
Napoli, Guillier. *Adventure at Mont-Saint-Michel*
Parker, Steve. *I wonder why tunnels are round*
Pinkwater, Daniel Manus. *Devil in the drain*
Ravilious, Robin. *The runaway chick*
Reece, Colleen L. *What?*
Rey, H. A. (Hans Augusto). *Curious George*
   Curious George gets a medal
   Curious George learns the alphabet
   Curious George rides a bike
   Curious George takes a job
   The original Curious George
Rey, Margret (Margret Elisabeth Waldstein). *Curious George flies a kite*
   Curious George goes to the hospital
Rylant, Cynthia. *Miss Maggie*
Sandberg, Inger. *Dusty wants to borrow everything*
Schoenherr, John. *Rebel*
Waber, Bernard. *Lorenzo*
Weil, Lisl. *Pandora's box*
Yolen, Jane. *Eeny, meeny, miney mole*

Character traits – flattery

Æsop. *Three Æsop fox fables*
Chaucer, Geoffrey. *Chanticleer and the fox*

Character traits – foolishness

Aardema, Verna. *Sebgugugu the glutton*
Alexander, Lloyd. *The house Gobbaleen*
Bason, Lillian. *Those foolish Molboes!*
Bradman, Tony. *Not like this, like that*
Brenner, Barbara A. *Rosa and Marco and the three wishes*
Butterworth, Nick. *The house on the rock*
Carlson, Nancy L. *Arnie and the skateboard gang*
Gackenbach, Dick. *Harvey, the foolish pig*
Gammell, Stephen. *The story of Mr. and Mrs. Vinegar*
Ginsburg, Mirra. *The king who tried to fry an egg on his head*
Gordon, Ruth. *Feathers*
Grimm, Jacob. *Hans in luck*, ill. by Paul Galdone
   Hans in luck, ill. by Felix Hoffmann
   Jack in luck
   Lucky Hans
Jacobs, Joseph. *The three sillies*, ill. by Kathryn Hewitt
   The three sillies, ill. by Steven Kellogg
Johnson, Evelyne. *The cow in the kitchen*
Keenen, George. *The preposterous week*
Lazy Jack. *Lazy Jack*, ill. by Barry Wilkinson
Maitland, Antony. *Idle Jack*
Mike, Jan M. *Juan Bobo and the horse of seven colors*
Miller, William. *The knee-high man*
Morgan, Michaela. *Helpful Betty to the rescue*
Phillips, Louis. *The brothers Wrong and Wrong Again*
San Souci, Robert D. *Six foolish fishermen*
Schwartz, Amy. *Yossel Zissel and the wisdom of Chelm*

Scruton, Clive. *Circus cow*
Van Nutt, Julia. *Pignapped!*
Zemach, Margot. *The three wishes*

Character traits – fortune *see* Character traits – luck

Character traits – freedom

Andersen, H. C. (Hans Christian). *The emperor and the nightingale*, ill. by Meilo So
The emperor and the nightingale, ill. by James Watling
The emperor's nightingale, ill. from the Disney arcives
The emperor's nightingale, ill. by Georges Lemoine
The nightingale, ill. by Harold Berson
The nightingale, ill. by Nancy Ekholm Burkert
The nightingale, ill. by Alison Claire Darke
The nightingale, ill. by Demi
The nightingale, ill. by Beni Montresor
The nightingale, ill. by Josef Palecek
The nightingale, ill. by Regolo Ricci
The nightingale, ill. by Christopher Santoro
The nightingale, ill. by Lisbeth Zwerger
Babbitt, Natalie. *Nellie, a cat on her own*
Bayar, Steven. *Rachel and Mischa*
Baylor, Byrd. *Hawk, I'm your brother*
Benjamin, Anne. *Young Harriet Tubman*
Blaustein, Muriel. *Baby Mabu and Auntie Moose*
Bradford, Ann. *The mystery of the missing raccoon*
Buehner, Caralyn. *The escape of Marvin the ape*
Bunting, Eve (Anne Evelyn). *How many days to America?*
Crew, Gary. *Bright star*
De Beer, Hans. *Little polar bear finds a friend*
Dennis, Wesley. *Tumble, the story of a mustang*
Fatio, Louise. *Hector and Christina*
Fujita, Tamao. *The boy and the bird*
Hawkinson, John. *Where the wild apples grow*
McKenna, Virginia. *Back to the blue*
McPhail, David M. *A wolf story*
Maugham, W. Somerset (William Somerset). *Princess September and the nightingale*
Meade, Holly. *John Willy and Freddy McGee*
Oram, Hiawyn. *Princess Chamomile gets her way*
Park, Frances. *My freedom trip*
Polacco, Patricia. *The butterfly*
Rascal. *Oregon's journey*
Riddle, Tohby. *The great escape from City Zoo*
Sanders, Scott R. (Scott Russell). *A place called Freedom*
Shulevitz, Uri. *What is a wise bird like you doing in a silly tale like this*
Siegelson, Kim L. *In the time of the drums*
Steiner, Jörg. *Rabbit Island*
Stern, Mark. *It's a dog's life*
Sundgaard, Arnold. *The lamb and the butterfly*
Wright, Courtni Crump. *Journey to freedom*

Character traits – generosity

Ainsworth, Ruth. *The mysterious Baba and her magic caravan*
Aliki. *The story of Johnny Appleseed*
Anglund, Joan Walsh. *Christmas is a time of giving*
Bawden, Nina. *St. Francis of Assisi*
Behrens, June. *Christmas-magic wagon*
Bohanon, Paul. *Golden Kate*

Brown, Palmer. *Something for Christmas*
Chalmers, Mary. *A hat for Amy Jean*
Chinn, Karen. *Sam and the lucky money*
Christian, Mary Blount. *The devil take you, Barnabas Beane!*
Chute, Beatrice Joy. *Journey to Christmas*
Cohen, Barbara. *Even higher*
Cohen, Miriam. *Liar, liar, pants on fire!*
Davis, Aubrey. *Bone button borscht*
Emberley, Michael. *The present*
Erickson, Russell E. *Warton and the traders*
Evans, Richard Paul. *The Christmas candle*
Farjeon, Eleanor. *Mrs. Malone*
Fearnley, Jan. *Little Robin's Christmas*
Fine, Edith Hope. *Under the lemon moon*
Fontane, Theodor. *Nick Ribbeck of Ribbeck of Havelland*
Sir Ribbeck of Ribbeck of Havelland
Fox, Mem. *With love, at Christmas*
French, Vivian. *Why the sea is salt*
Grimm, Jacob. *The falling stars*
One gift deserves another
Hänel, Wolfram. *The gold at the end of the rainbow*
Hayes, Geoffrey. *Christmas in Puttyville*
Henry, O. *The gift of the Magi*
Hoban, Russell. *Emmet Otter's jug-band Christmas*
The mole family's Christmas
Hodges, Margaret. *Saint Patrick and the peddler*
Houston, John A. *The bright yellow rope*
Hughes, Shirley. *Giving*
Hush little baby. *Hush little baby*, ill. by Aliki
Hush little baby, ill. by Shari Halpern
Hush little baby, ill. by Jeanette Winter
Hush little baby, ill. by Margot Zemach
Janice. *Little Bear's Christmas*
Johnson, Crockett. *The emperor's gifts*
Kasza, Keiko. *The wolf's chicken stew*
Kunnas, Mauri. *Twelve gifts for Santa Claus*
Kvasnosky, Laura McGee. *Zelda and Ivy one Christmas*
Lattimore, Deborah Nourse. *The dragon's robe*
Lexau, Joan M. *A house so big*
Lindman, Maj. *Snipp, Snapp, Snurr and the red shoes*
Lionni, Leo. *Tico and the golden wings*
Lussert, Anneliese. *The Christmas visitor*
McBratney, Sam. *Just one!*
McClenathan, Louise. *The Easter pig*
McCourt, Lisa. *Chicken soup for little souls: The best night out with Dad*
Macdonald, Maryann. *Rosie and the poor rabbits*
Marton, Jirina. *Flowers for mom*
Munsch, Robert N. *Ribbon rescue*
Muntean, Michaela. *Mokey and the festival of the bells*
Ness, Evaline. *Josefina February*
Patron, Susan. *Five bad boys, Billy Que, and the dustdobbin*
Pilkey, Dav. *Dragon's merry Christmas*
Rockwell, Anne F. *Gogo's pay day*
Rodanas, Kristina. *The story of Wali Dâd*
Ross, Christine. *Lily and the present*
Roth, Roger. *The sign painter's dream*
Rylant, Cynthia. *Silver packages*
Sandman, Rochel. *Perfect porridge*
Schotter, Roni. *Captain Snap and the children of Vinegar Lane*
Shecter, Ben. *If I had a ship*
Shepard, Aaron. *The baker's dozen*
Silverstein, Shel. *The giving tree*
Testa, Fulvio. *Wolf's favor*

Timmermans, Felix. *A gift from Saint Nicholas*
Tolstoy, Aleksey Nikolayevich. *Shoemaker Martin*
Wallner, Alexandra. *An Alcott family Christmas*
Wang, Rosalind C. *The fourth question*
　The treasure chest
Ward, Sally G. *What goes around comes around*
Yep, Laurence. *The junior thunder lord*

Character traits – helpfulness

Adelson, Leone. *Who blew that whistle?*
Adshead, Gladys L. *Brownies - hush!*
　Brownies - they're moving
Æsop. *Androcles and the lion*, ill. by Janusz Grabianski
　Androcles and the lion, ill. by Dennis Nolan
　Androcles and the lion, ill. by Robert Rayevsky
　Androcles and the lion, ill. by Janet Stevens
　The ant and the dove
　The lion and the mouse, ill. by Carol Jones
　The lion and the mouse, ill. by Lisa McCue
　The lion and the mouse, ill. by Gerald Rose
　The lion and the mouse, ill. by Bernadette Watts
　The lion and the mouse, ill. by Ed Young
Aliki. *The two of them*
Aller, Susan B. *Emma and the night dogs*
Ancona, George. *Helping out*
Asch, Frank. *Baby Bird's first nest*
Aylesworth, Jim. *Mr. McGill goes to town*
Baillie, Marilyn. *Side by side*
Baker, Betty. *Partners*
Bakken, Harold. *The special string*
Beard, Darleen Bailey. *Twister*
Beim, Jerrold. *Country mailman*
Best, Cari. *Top banana*
Biro, Val. *Gumdrop and the birthday surprise*
　Gumdrop beats the clock
Borovsky, Paul. *Nico*
Bridwell, Norman. *Clifford's good deeds*
Bright, Robert. *Georgie and the baby birds*
　Georgie and the ball of yarn
　Georgie and the little dog
　Georgie and the runaway balloon
Brown, Myra Berry. *Company's coming for dinner*
Buchanan, Heather S. *Emily Mouse saves the day*
Bunting, Eve (Anne Evelyn). *December*
Burningham, John. *Harvey Slumfenburger's Christmas present*
Butterworth, Nick. *The two sons*
Calhoun, Mary. *Blue-ribbon Henry*
　Euphonia and the flood
　Jack the wise and the Cornish cuckoos
Calmenson, Stephanie. *The little witch sisters*
Carey, Valerie Scho. *Harriet and William and the terrible creature*
Chevalier, Christa. *Spence is small*
Clements, Andrew. *Santa's secret helper*
Clifton, Lucille. *My friend Jacob*
Cole, William. *Aunt Bella's umbrella*
Collier, Ethel. *Who goes there in my garden?*
Collington, Peter. *A small miracle*
Cooper, Susan. *Danny and the Kings*
Curle, Jock J. *The four good friends*
Cuyler, Margery. *Fat Santa*
Daly, Niki. *Thank you Henrietta*
Davis, Alice Vaught. *Timothy Turtle*
Day, Alexandra. *Frank and Ernest*
　Helping the animals
　Helping the flowers and trees

　Helping the night
　Helping the sun
Day, Shirley. *Waldo's back yard*
DeLage, Ida. *What does a witch need?*
Devlin, Wende. *Cranberry autumn*
　Cranberry Christmas
Dowling, Paul. *You can do it, Rabbit*
Du Bois, William Pène. *Bear circus*
Edwards, Michelle. *Eve and Smithy*
Erickson, Karen. *I like to help*
Ets, Marie Hall. *Elephant in a well*
Galdone, Paul. *Androcles and the lion*
Gibbons, Gail. *Emergency!*
Graham, Al. *Timothy Turtle*
Graham, Margaret Bloy. *Benjy and his friend Fifi*
Gray, Genevieve. *Send Wendell*
Green, Norma B. *The hole in the dike*
Greene, Laura. *Help*
Grimm, Jacob. *The elves and the shoemaker*, ill. by Doug Cushman
　The elves and the shoemaker, ill. by Paul Galdone
　The elves and the shoemaker, ill. by Margaret Walty
　The elves and the shoemaker, ill. by Bernadette Watts
　Mother Holly
　The shoemaker and the elves, ill. by Adrienne Adams
　The shoemaker and the elves, ill. by Cynthia and William Birrer
　The shoemaker and the elves, ill. by Ilse Plume
Hague, Kathleen. *The legend of the Veery bird*
Haley, Gail E. *Birdsong*
Han, Oki S. *Kongi and Potgi*
Hassett, John. *Cat up a tree*
Hayes, Sarah. *This is the bear and the bad little girl*
Herold, Ann Bixby. *The helping day*
Hill, Elizabeth Starr. *Evan's corner*
Hol, Coby. *Tippy Bear hunts for honey*
Holmes, Efner Tudor. *Amy's goose*
Houston, John A. *The bright yellow rope*
Hürlimann, Bettina. *Barry*
Janovitz, Marilyn. *Can I help?*
Jensen, Patricia. *Little Donkey learns to help*
　Little Squirrel's special nest
Joyce, William. *Bently and egg*
　The Leaf Men and the brave good bugs
Kishida, Eriko. *The lion and the bird's nest*
Kraus, Robert. *Herman the helper*
　Rebecca Hatpin
La Fontaine, Jean de. *The lion and the rat*
Landa, Norbert. *Rabbit and chicken find a box*
Lewis, Eils Moorhouse. *The snug little house*
Lindman, Maj. *Flicka, Ricka, Dicka and the new dotted dress*
　Snipp, Snapp, Snurr and the red shoes
Lively, Penelope. *One, two, three, jump!*
Lloyd, Errol. *Nini at carnival*
Lowell, Susan. *The bootmaker and the elves*
Ludy, Mark. *The farmer*
McConnachie, Brian. *Flying boy*
McKissack, Patricia C. *Messy Bessey and the birthday overnight*
McMullan, Kate (Hall). *No no Jo*
McPhail, David M. *Santa's book of names*
Marcus, Susan. *The missing button adventure*
Marshall, James. *What's the matter with Carruthers?*
Mayer, Mercer. *Just for you*
Mayne, William. *The blue book of Hob stories*
　The green book of Hob stories

The red book of Hob stories
The yellow book of Hob stories
Michael, Emory H. *Androcles and the lion*
Miller, M. L. *The enormous snore*
Monsell, Mary Elise. *Crackle Creek*
Morgan, Michaela. *Helpful Betty solves a mystery*
  Helpful Betty to the rescue
Nakano, Hirotaka. *Elephant blue*
Ness, Evaline. *Pavo and the princess*
Okimoto, Jean Davies. *A place for Grace*
Oxenbury, Helen. *Mother's helper*
Paraskevas, Betty. *Maggie and the Ferocious Beast, the big carrot*
Parker, Nancy Winslow. *Cooper, the McNallys' big black dog*
Partridge, Jenny. *Peterkin Pollensnuff*
Paul, Sherry. *2-B and the rock 'n roll band*
Peet, Bill (William Bartlett). *The ant and the elephant*
  Cyrus the unsinkable sea serpent
Porte, Barbara Ann. *Harry in trouble*
Potter, Beatrix. *The tailor of Gloucester*
Quackenbush, Robert M. *Chuck lends a paw*
Rayner, Mary. *The rain cloud*
Rockwell, Anne F. *Big bad goat*
  The bump in the night
  Can I help?
  Handy Hank will fix it
Rosa-Casanova, Sylvia. *Mama Provi and the pot of rice*
Rylant, Cynthia. *Mr. Putter and Tabby walk the dog*
Schwartz, Roslyn. *The mole sisters and the piece of moss*
Schweiger-Dmi'el, Itzhak. *Hanna's Sabbath dress*
Seuss, Dr. *Horton hatches the egg*
Simon, Norma. *What do I do?*
Slawski, Wolfgang. *Captain Jonathan sails the sea*
Slobodkin, Louis. *Dinny and Danny*
Snow, Pegeen. *Mrs. Periwinkle's groceries*
Soto, Gary. *The old man and his door*
Stevenson, James. *Will you please feed our cat?*
Suhl, Yuri. *The Purim goat*
Thomas, Shelley Moore. *Somewhere today*
Udry, Janice May. *Is Susan here?*, ill. by Peter Edwards
  Is Susan here?, ill. by Karen Gundersheimer
Venino, Suzanne. *Animals helping people*
Waber, Bernard. *Lyle, Lyle Crocodile*
Waddell, Martin. *Farmer Duck*
  Good job, Little Bear!
Weller, Frances Ward. *Madaket Millie*
Williams, Barbara. *Someday, said Mitchell*
Wittmann, Patricia. *Go ask Giorgio!*
Wolde, Gunilla. *Betsy's fixing day*
Zemach, Margot. *To Hilda for helping*

Character traits – honesty

Aardema, Verna. *Pedro and the padre*
Alexander, Lloyd. *The truthful harp*
Aliki. *Diogenes*
Ardizzone, Edward. *Peter the wanderer*
Bunting, Eve (Anne Evelyn). *A day's work*
Demi. *Chen Ping and his magic axe*
  The empty pot
Gallant, Kathryn. *The flute player of Beppu*
Gikow, Louise. *Jim Henson's Muppets in Rowlf's big test*
Goldsmith, Howard. *Little lost dog*
Gretz, Susanna. *Rabbit rambles on*
Hathorn, Libby (Elizabeth). *Freya's fantastic surprise*

Havill, Juanita. *Jamaica's find*
Heyer, Carol. *Robin Hood*
Himmelman, John. *Honest Tulio*
Keller, Holly. *That's mine, Horace*
Langton, Jane. *The hedgehog boy*
McLenighan, Valjean. *I know you cheated*
Matsuno, Masako. *A pair of red clogs*
  Taro and the Tofu
Mayer, Mercer. *How the trollusk got his hat*
Moss, Marissa. *Who was it?*
O'Connor, Jane. *Nina, Nina, star ballerina*
Schroeder, Alan. *The stone lion*
Torre, Betty L. *The luminous pearl*
Turkle, Brinton. *The adventures of Obadiah*
Wilson, Julia. *Becky*

Character traits – incentive *see* Character traits – ambition

Character traits – individuality

Abolafia, Yossi. *My three uncles*
Alderson, Sue Ann. *Bonnie McSmithers is at it again!*
Aliki. *Jack and Jake*
Allamand, Pascale. *The animals who changed their colors*
Anglund, Joan Walsh. *Look out the window*
Anholt, Catherine. *Kids*
  What I like
Baker, Jeannie. *Millicent*
Bates, Ivan. *All by myself*
Beim, Jerrold. *Country train*
  Freckle face
Berliner, Franz. *Wildebeest*
Boland, Janice. *Annabel*
Bowen, Keith. *Katy's gift*
Bradman, Tony. *Michael*
Bright, Robert. *Which is Willy?*
Brimner, Larry Dane. *Nana's hog*
Burke-Weiner, Kimberly. *The maybe garden*
Carey, Mary. *The owl who loved sunshine*
Carey, Valerie Scho. *Tsugele's broom*
Carlson, Nancy L. *I like me*
Caseley, Judith. *Cousins*
Charlip, Remy. *Hooray for me!*
Cibula, Matt S. *What's up with you, Taquandra Fu?*
Conford, Ellen. *Impossible, possum*
Cowan, Catherine. *My life with the wave*
Delaney, Ned. *One dragon to another*
Dellinger, Annetta. *You are special to Jesus*
Delton, Judy. *I'm telling you now*
De Paola, Tomie (Thomas Anthony). *Oliver Button is a sissy*
Dobkin, Bonnie. *Everybody says*
Duvoisin, Roger Antoine. *Jasmine*
Eduar, Gilles. *Jooka saves the day*
Fatio, Louise. *Hector penguin*
Fuchshuber, Annegert. *Two peas in a pod*
Gerrard, Roy. *Mik's mammoth*
Gramatky, Hardie. *Little Toot through the Golden Gate*
Grejniec, Michael. *What do you like?*
Guy, Rosa. *Billy the Great*
Hallinan, P. K. (Patrick K.). *A rainbow of friends*
Hendry, Diana. *Back soon!*
Hines, Anna Grossnickle. *What Joe saw*
Horvath, Betty F. *Will the real Tommy Wilson please stand up?*

Jaynes, Ruth M. *What is a birthday child?*
Jeffery, Graham. *Thomas the tortoise*
Jeram, Anita. *Contrary Mary*
Katz, Karen. *The colors of us*
Keens-Douglas, Richardo. *The Miss Meow pageant*
Keller, Holly. *Harry and Tuck*
King, Stephen Michael. *Henry and Amy (right-way-round and upside down)*
Knowles, Sheena. *Edward the emu*
Kraus, Robert. *Owliver*
Kuskin, Karla. *I am me*
    Which horse is William?
Lachner, Dorothea. *Meredith, the witch who wasn't*
Lampert, Emily. *A little touch of monster*
Latimer, Jim. *Snail and Buffalo*
Leaf, Munro. *The story of Ferdinand the bull*
Leonard, Marcia. *Best friends*
Lester, Alison. *Celeste sails to Spain*
    Clive eats alligators
    Tessa snaps snakes
Lester, Helen. *Tacky the penguin*
    Three cheers for Tacky
Levine, Rhoda. *Harrison loved his umbrella*
Lewison, Wendy Cheyette. *Shy Vi*
Lidz, Jane. *Zak, the one-of-a-kind dog*
Lionni, Leo. *A color of his own*
    Pezzettino
    Tico and the golden wings
Littledale, Freya. *The magic plum tree*
Lopshire, Robert. *I want to be somebody new!*
Lystad, Mary H. *That new boy*
McConnachie, Brian. *Flying boy*
McCormack, John E. *Rabbit tales*
MacGregor, Marilyn. *On top*
Manning, Mick. *My body, your body*
Manushkin, Fran. *Shirleybird*
Martin, Bill (William Ivan). *Chicken Chuck*
Mayer, Marianna. *The prince and the pauper*
Mills, Lauren A. *Tatterhood and the hobgoblins*
Mitchell, Lori. *Different just like me*
Modesitt, Jeanne. *Mama, if you had a wish*
Morris, Ann. *Families*
Moss, Marissa. *But not Kate*
Newman, Lesléa. *Belinda's bouquet*
Ogburn, Jacqueline K. *The Masked Maverick*
Olsen, Alfa-Betty. *Gabby the shrew*
Oram, Hiawyn. *Ned and the Joybaloo*
Parr, Todd. *The okay book*
Peet, Bill (William Bartlett). *Buford the little bighorn*
    The spooky tail of Prewitt Peacock
Percy, Graham. *24 strange little animals in a haunted house*
Pinkwater, Daniel Manus. *The big orange splot*
Rand, Gloria. *Salty dog*
Rankin, Joan. *You're somebody special, Walliwigs!*
Redies, Rainer. *The cats' party*
Rockwell, Anne F. *Show and tell day*
Rogers, Fred. *If we were all the same*
Ross, Tom. *Eggbert, the slightly cracked egg*
Rotner, Shelley. *Faces*
Rubel, Nicole. *Sam and Violet are twins*
    Sam and Violet go camping
Ruck-Pauquèt, Gina. *Mumble bear*
Schami, Rafik. *Albert and Lila*
    The crow who stood on his beak
Schotter, Roni. *Dreamland*
Sendak, Maurice. *Pierre*
Seuling, Barbara. *The triplets*
Seuss, Dr. *I can draw it myself*

Shannon, David. *A bad case of stripes*
Sharmat, Marjorie Weinman. *What are we going to do about Andrew?*
Sharmat, Mitchell. *Sherman is a slowpoke*
Silverstein, Shel. *The missing piece*
Simon, Norma. *All kinds of children*
    I know what I like
    Why am I different?
Simont, Marc. *The goose that almost got cooked*
Singer, Marilyn. *The dog who insisted he wasn't*
    The one and only me
    Pickle plan
Slobodkin, Louis. *Millions and millions and millions*
Tafuri, Nancy. *Have you seen my duckling?*
Thomas, Joyce Carol. *Cherish me*
Thomson, Pat. *Beware of the aunts!*
Tusa, Tricia. *Camilla's new hairdo*
Tyrrell, Anne. *Mary Ann always can*
Viorst, Judith. *Try it again, Sam*
Waber, Bernard. *"You look ridiculous," said the rhinoceros to the hippopotamus*
Walsh, Ellen Stoll. *For Pete's sake*
Waxman, Stephanie. *What is a girl? What is a boy?*
Wells, Rosemary. *Shy Charles*
Weninger, Brigitte. *Why are you fighting, Davy?*
Whitney, Dorothy B. *Creatures of an exceptional kind*

Character traits – kindness

Aliki. *The story of William Penn*
Bang, Molly. *The paper crane*
Barber, Antonia. *Satchelmouse and the doll's house*
Barbour, Karen. *Mr. Bow Tie*
Barrett, Mary Brigid. *The man of the house at Huffington Row*
Baumann, Kurt. *The prince and the lute*
Bishop, Adela. *The Easter wolf*
Brown, Margaret Wise. *Dr. Squash the doll doctor*
Butterworth, Nick. *Amanda's butterfly*
Calhoun, Mary. *The thieving dwarfs*
Caswell, Helen Rayburn. *Parable of the good Samaritan*
Cazet, Denys. *A fish in his pocket*
Chmielarz, Sharon. *Down at Angel's*
Cole, Brock. *The king at the door*
Cole, Joanna. *A gift from Saint Francis*
Compton, Joanne. *Ashpet*
Coville, Bruce. *The foolish giant*
    Sarah and the dragon
Curry, Jane Louise. *The Christmas knight*
Davis, Maggie S. *Grandma's secret letter*
DeArmond, Dale. *The seal oil lamp*
Elzbieta. *Dikou and the baby star*
    Dikou the little troon who walks at night
Fatio, Louise. *The happy lion's rabbits*
Fleischman, Sid. *The scarebird*
Fyleman, Rose. *A fairy went a-marketing*
Gannett, Ruth Stiles. *Katie and the sad noise*
Gerstein, Mordicai. *The wild boy*
Goodsell, Jane. *Toby's toe*
Grimm, Jacob. *The golden goose*, ill. by Dorothée Duntze
    The golden goose, ill. by Isadore Seltzer
    The golden goose, ill. by Martin Ursell
Hasler, Eveline. *Martin is our friend*
Hastings, Selina. *The singing ringing tree*
Heyward, Du Bose. *The country bunny and the little gold shoes*
Karlin, Nurit. *The tooth witch*

Kent, Jack. *Clotilda*
Kraus, Robert. *The first robin*
Lamstein, Sarah Marwil. *I like your buttons!*
LaRochelle, David. *A Christmas guest*
Lee, Jeanne M. *Ba-Nam*
Lipkind, William. *The magic feather duster*
McCourt, Lisa. *Chicken soup for little souls: The Goodness Gorillas*
  Chicken soup for little souls: The never-forgotten doll
MacDonald, Margaret Read. *Slop!*
Martin, Nora. *The stone dancers*
Mayer, Marianna. *The little jewel box*
Meddaugh, Susan. *Beast*
Mizumura, Kazue. *If I built a village*
Munsch, Robert N. *David's father*
Nesbit, Edith. *The last of the dragons*
Newton, Patricia Montgomery. *The five sparrows*
Noble, Trinka Hakes. *Hansy's mermaid*
Ormondroyd, Edward. *Theodore*
Paterson, Katherine. *Celia and the sweet, sweet water*
Peterson, Hans. *Erik and the Christmas horse*
Postgate, Oliver. *Noggin the king*
Richard, Françoise. *On Cat Mountain*
Rider, Joanne. *First grade valentines*
Rohmer, Harriet. *Atariba and Niguayona*
San Souci, Robert D. *The talking eggs*
Schaefer, Carole Lexa. *Under the midsummer sky*
Schnur, Steven. *The tie man's miracle*
Schotter, Roni. *Captain Snap and the children of Vinegar Lane*
Schroeder, Alan. *The stone lion*
Seuss, Dr. *Horton hears a Who!*
Shibano, Tamizo. *The old man who made the trees bloom*
Silverman, Erica. *Gittel's hands*
Simmons, Steven J. *Alice and Greta*
Singer, Marilyn. *The maiden on the moor*
Small, David. *Eulalie and the hopping head*
Steig, William. *Wizzil*
Steptoe, John. *Mufaro's beautiful daughters*
Stevens, Carla. *Stories from a snowy meadow*
Stock, Catherine. *Secret Valentine*
Stroud, Bettye. *Down home at Miss Dessa's*
Tolstoy, Aleksey Nikolayevich. *Shoemaker Martin*
Torre, Betty L. *The luminous pearl*
Ungerer, Tomi. *Zeralda's ogre*
Vigna, Judith. *Anyhow, I'm glad I tried*
Warren, Cathy. *Saturday belongs to Sara*
Weedn, Flavia. *The giant's garden*
Wells, H. G. (Herbert George). *The adventures of Tommy*
Wilde, Oscar. *Fairy tales of Oscar Wilde*
  The selfish giant, ill. by S. Saelig Gallagher
  The selfish giant, ill. by Dom Mansell
  The selfish giant, ill. by Fabian Negrin
  The selfish giant, ill. by Lisbeth Zwerger
Wittman, Sally. *The boy who hated Valentine's Day*
Yep, Laurence. *The junior thunder lord*
Zolotow, Charlotte (Shapiro). *I know a lady*

Character traits – kindness to animals

Aardema, Verna. *Koi and the kola nuts*
Æsop. *Androcles and the lion*, ill. by Janusz Grabianski
  Androcles and the lion, ill. by Dennis Nolan
  Androcles and the lion, ill. by Robert Rayevsky
  Androcles and the lion, ill. by Janet Stevens
Albert, Richard E. *Alejandro's gift*

Allred, Mary. *Grandmother Poppy and the funny-looking bird*
Anderson, C. W. (Clarence Williams). *Lonesome little colt*
  The rumble seat pony
Aragon, Jane Chelsea. *Winter harvest*
Armstrong, Jennifer. *King crow*
Baker, Jeannie. *Home in the sky*
Barnhart, Peter. *The wounded duck*
Baumann, Hans. *Chip has many brothers*
Beatty, Hetty Burlingame. *Moorland pony*
Bergman, Donna. *City fox*
Berson, Harold. *Joseph and the snake*
Bianchi, John. *The lab rats of Doctor Eclair*
Birrer, Cynthia. *The lady and the unicorn*
Bodkin, Odds. *The crane wife*
Bolliger, Max. *The magic bird*
Boon, Emilie. *It's spring, Peterkin*
Brenner, Barbara A. *Two orphan cubs*
Brighton, Catherine. *Hope's gift*
Brock, Emma Lillian. *The birds' Christmas tree*
Brown, Katherine. *The Small One*
Brown, Ruth. *The grizzly revenge*
Brunhoff, Laurent de. *Babar's little girl*
Brutschy, Jennifer. *The winter fox*
Bryan, Ashley. *Sh-ko and his eight wicked brothers*
Buchanan, Heather S. *Emily Mouse's first adventure*
Bunting, Eve (Anne Evelyn). *Night tree*
Burch, Robert. *The hunting trip*
Butterworth, Nick. *One blowy night*
  One snowy night
Cannon, Annie. *The bat in the boot*
Carey, Mary. *The owl who loved sunshine*
Carter, Anne. *Bella's secret garden*
Chase, Jan Brinckerhoff. *The golden song*
Clark, Elizabeth. *Father Christmas and the donkey*
Clewes, Dorothy. *The wild wood*
Coffey, Maria. *A seal in the family*
Collicott, Sharleen. *Toestomper and the caterpillars*
Cowcher, Helen. *Tigress*
Cowley, Joy. *The video shop sparrow*
Curle, Jock J. *The four good friends*
Daugherty, James Henry. *Andy and the lion*
De Beer, Hans. *Little polar bear and the husky pup*
De Marolles, Chantal. *The lonely wolf*
Devlin, Wende. *Cranberry summer*
Dobson, Clive. *Fred's TV*
Dragonwagon, Crescent. *Bat in the dining room*
Drew, Patricia. *Spotter Puff*
Dunn, Judy. *The little lamb*
Duvoisin, Roger Antoine. *The happy hunter*
Easterling, Bill. *Prize in the snow*
Elbling, Peter. *Aria*
Falk, Barbara Bustetter. *Grusha*
Fowler, Susi Gregg. *Circle of thanks*
Freeman, Don. *The seal and the slick*
Galdone, Paul. *Androcles and the lion*
Gantschev, Ivan. *Otto the bear*
Georgiady, Nicholas P. *Gertie the duck*
Geraghty, Paul. *The hunter*
Gilbert, Suzie. *Hawk Hill*
Gleeson, Brian. *Koi and the kola nuts*
Goffstein, M. B. (Marilyn Brooke). *Natural history*
  The good-hearted youngest brother
Graham, Bob. *Pete and Roland*
  Queenie, one of the family
Grant, Joan. *The monster that grew small*
Haas, Jessie. *Mowing*
Hader, Berta Hoerner. *Mister Billy's gun*

Harriott, Ted. *Coming home*
Harrison, David Lee. *Little turtle's big adventure*
Hendry, Diana. *Dog Donovan*
Herriot, James. *Christmas Day kitten*
Hewett, Joan. *Rosalie*
Himmelman, John. *Ibis*
Hirsh, Marilyn. *Deborah the dybbuk*
Hodges, Margaret. *The golden deer*
    St. Jerome and the lion
Hol, Coby. *Niki's little donkey*
Holmes, Efner Tudor. *Amy's goose*
    Carrie's gift
Hoose, Philip M. *Hey little ant*
Houk, Randy. *Rico's hawk*
Hutchins, H. J. (Hazel J.). *The catfish palace*
    One duck
Ichikawa, Satomi. *Nora's duck*
Ikeda, Daisaku. *Kanta and the deer*
    The snow country prince
Ishii, Momoko. *The tongue-cut sparrow*
Jeffery, Graham. *Thomas the tortoise*
Joosse, Barbara M. *Nugget and Darling*
Keats, Ezra Jack. *Jennie's hat*
Keller, Holly. *Island baby*
Keo, Ena. *The crane wife*
Kimmel, Eric A. *The birds' gift*
Kroll, Steven. *Queen of the May*
Kroll, Virginia L. *Sweet Magnolia*
Kumin, Maxine W. *Mittens in May*
Laird, Elizabeth. *The day the ducks went skating*
Lathrop, Dorothy Pulis. *Who goes there?*
Lears, Laurie. *Waiting for Mr. Goose*
Levitin, Sonia. *All the cats in the world*
Lewis, Paul Owen. *Frog girl*
Lipkind, William. *The boy and the forest*
London, Jonathan. *Jackrabbit*
McClure, Gillian. *Selkie*
McDonnell, Flora. *I love animals*
McFarlane, Sheryl. *Eagle dreams*
McMillan, Bruce. *Nights of the pufflings*
McNally, Darcie. *In a cabin in a wood*
McNulty, Faith. *The lady and the spider*
    Mouse and Tim
McPhail, David M. *The bear's toothache*
    A wolf story
Mamin-Sibiryak, D. N. *Grey Neck*
Martchenko, Michael. *Bird feeder banquet*
Martin, Jacqueline Briggs. *Washing the willow tree loon*
Meddaugh, Susan. *Tree of birds*
Michael, Emory H. *Androcles and the lion*
Miklowitz, Gloria D. *Save that raccoon!*
Miller, Edna. *Mousekin's frosty friend*
Mogensen, Jan. *Teddy's Christmas gift*
Moore, Inga. *Rose and the nightingale*
Moore, Sheila. *Samson Svenson's baby*
Nakatani, Chiyoko. *Fumio and the dolphins*
Newberry, Clare Turlay. *Percy, Polly and Pete*
Novak, Matt. *Mr. Floop's lunch*
Numeroff, Laura Joffe. *If you give a moose a muffin*
    If you give a mouse a cookie
    If you give a pig a pancake
Orstadius, Brita. *The dolphin journey*
Pedersen, Judy. *The tiny patient*
Peet, Bill (William Bartlett). *Huge Harold*
Pinkwater, Daniel Manus. *Rainy morning*
Rossiter, Nan Parson. *The way home*
Roy, Ronald. *A thousand pails of water*
Rylant, Cynthia. *The bookshop dog*

Sandburg, Helga. *Anna and the baby buzzard*
Sayre, April Pulley. *Turtle, turtle, watch out!*
Schlein, Miriam. *Deer in the snow*
Sheldon, Dyan. *The whales' song*
Strand, Keith. *Grandfather's Christmas tree*
Strete, Craig Kee. *The lost boy and the monster*
Thomas, Frances. *The Bear and Mr. Bear*
Thomas, Jane Resh. *Scaredy dog*
Turkle, Brinton. *Thy friend, Obadiah*
Turska, Krystyna. *The woodcutter's duck*
Tyler, Linda Wagner. *After Christmas tree*
Van West, Patricia E. *The crab man*
Varley, Dimitry. *The whirly bird*
Velthuijs, Max. *Little Man to the rescue*
Wallace, Ian. *The sparrow's song*
Ward, Lynd. *The biggest bear*
Waterton, Betty. *A salmon for Simon*
Wersba, Barbara. *Do tigers ever bite kings?*
Whitney, Alma Marshak. *Leave Herbert alone*
Wildsmith, Brian. *Hunter and his dog*
Wondriska, William. *The stop*
Yagawa, Sumiko. *The crane wife*

Character traits – laziness

Armstrong, Jennifer. *Pierre's dream*
Aylesworth, Jim. *Hush up!*
Baker, Betty. *Partners*
Bolognese, Elaine. *The sleepy watchdog*
Bowen, Vernon. *The lazy beaver*
Bright, Robert. *Gregory, the noisiest and strongest boy in Grangers Grove*
Coleman, Michael. *Lazy Ozzie*
De Paola, Tomie (Thomas Anthony). *Jamie O'Rourke and the big potato*
    Jamie O'Rourke and the pooka
Du Bois, William Pène. *Lazy Tommy pumpkinhead*
Geraghty, Paul. *Slobcat*
Grimm, Jacob. *Mother Holly*
Holding, James. *The lazy little Zulu*
Koscielniak, Bruce. *Bear and Bunny grow tomatoes*
Krasilovsky, Phyllis. *The man who didn't wash his dishes*
    The man who tried to save time
    The man who was too lazy to fix things
Lazy Jack. *Lazy Jack*, ill. by Bert Dodson
    Lazy Jack, ill. by Tony Ross
    Lazy Jack, ill. by Kurt Werth
    Lazy Jack, ill. by Barry Wilkinson
The little red hen. *The cock, the mouse and the little red hen*
    The little red hen, ill. by Byron Barton
    The little red hen, ill. by Emily Bolam
    The little red hen, ill. by Janina Domanska
    The little red hen, ill. by Paul Galdone
    The little red hen, ill. by Dennis Hockerman
    Little red hen, ill. by Norman Messenger
    The little red hen, ill. by Mel Pekarsky
    The little red hen, ill. by William Stobbs
    The little red hen, ill. by Margot Zemach
    The Little Red Hen makes a pizza
Lobel, Arnold. *A treeful of pigs*
Lorenz, Lee. *Big Gus and Little Gus*
Martin, Antoinette Truglio. *Famous seaweed soup*
Mathews, Louise. *The great take-away*
Melmed, Laura Krauss. *Prince Nautilus*
Metaxas, Eric. *The monkey people*
Mwenye Hadithi. *Lazy lion*
Namioka, Lensey. *The laziest boy in the world*

Nobisso, Josephine. *For the sake of a cake*
Oppenheim, Joanne. *"Not now!" said the cow*
Pack, Robert. *How to catch a crocodile*
Papas, William. *Taresh the tea planter*
Root, Phyllis. *Aunt Nancy and Cousin Lazybones*
San Souci, Robert D. *The hired hand*
Schmidt, Eric von. *The young man who wouldn't hoe corn*
Sharmat, Marjorie Weinman. *Burton and Dudley*
Snyder, Dianne. *The boy of the three-year nap*
Taylor, Sydney. *Mr. Barney's beard*
Wells, Ruth. *The farmer and the poor god*
Wildsmith, Brian. *The lazy bear*
Wolf, Gita. *The very hungry lion*

Character traits – littleness *see* Character traits – smallness

Character traits – loyalty

Aliki. *The two of them*
Ardizzone, Edward. *Tim to the rescue*
Boyle, Vere. *Beauty and the beast*
Bridwell, Norman. *Clifford goes to Hollywood*
Calhoun, Mary. *The witch who lost her shadow*
Carter, Anne. *Beauty and the beast*
Collodi, Carlo. *The adventures of Pinocchio*
   Pinocchio
Cooney, Barbara. *Little brother and little sister*
Crompton, Anne Eliot. *The winter wife*
Cullen, Lynn. *The mightiest heart*
Edwards, Lisa. *Disney's Beauty and the beast, a book of manners*
Gregory, Nan. *How Smudge came*
Grimm, Jacob. *Little brother and little sister*
Hautzig, Deborah. *Beauty and the beast*
Haywood, Carolyn. *How the reindeer saved Santa*
Hurd, Edith Thacher. *Under the lemon tree*
Hutton, Warwick. *Beauty and the beast*
Ichikawa, Satomi. *Fickle Barbara*
Lasker, Joe. *He's my brother*
McCrea, James. *The king's procession*
McLerran, Alice. *The mountain that loved a bird*
Mayer, Marianna. *Beauty and the beast*
Montenegro, Laura Nyman. *Sweet Tooth*
Nesbit, Edith. *Beauty and the beast*
Parsons, Virginia. *Pinocchio and Gepetto*
Pollock, Penny. *The turkey girl*
Potter, Beatrix. *The tale of the faithful dove*
Stanovich, Betty Jo. *Hedgehog adventures*
Va, Leong. *A letter to the king*
Waite, Michael P. *Jojofu*
Whittier, John Greenleaf. *Barbara Frietchie*
Wright, Freire. *Beauty and the beast*

Character traits – luck

Aldridge, Josephine Haskell. *Fisherman's luck*
Alexander, Lloyd. *The house Gobbaleen*
Aliki. *Three gold pieces*
Beim, Lorraine. *Lucky Pierre*
Benjamin, A. H. *It could have been worse*
Bond, Michael. *Paddington's lucky day*
Breckler, Rosemary K. *Hoang breaks the lucky teapot*
Brown, Margaret Wise. *Wheel on the chimney*
Butler, Dorothy. *Another happy tale*
   A happy tale
Callan, Elizabeth Koda. *Good luck pony*
Cazet, Denys. *Lucky me*

Chausse, Sylvie. *The egg and I*
Cocca-Leffler, Maryann. *Ice-cold birthday*
Conrad, Pam. *The lost sailor*
Delton, Judy. *I never win!*
   It happened on Thursday
Dillon, Jana. *Lucky O'Leprechaun*
Elkin, Benjamin. *Lucky and the giant*
Gackenbach, Dick. *Harvey, the foolish pig*
Geraghty, Paul. *Look out, Patrick!*
Grimm, Jacob. *Hans in luck*, ill. by Paul Galdone
   Hans in luck, ill. by Felix Hoffmann
   Lucky Hans
Hann, Jacquie. *Up day, down day*
Hearn, Diane Dawson. *Bad luck Boswell*
Henwood, Simon. *A piece of luck*
Hodges, Margaret. *Saint Patrick and the peddler*
Holland, Janice. *You never can tell*
Ivanov, Anatoly. *Ol' Jake's lucky day*
Lecher, Doris. *Angelita's magic yarn*
Long, Jan Freeman. *The bee and the dream*
Mayer, Marianna. *The little jewel box*
Moeri, Louise. *The unicorn and the plow*
Russell, Betty. *Big store, funny door*
Seuss, Dr. *Did I ever tell you how lucky you are?*
Stafford, Kay. *Ling Tang and the lucky cricket*
Stanley, Diane. *The good-luck pencil*
Underhill, Liz. *The lucky coin*
Velthuijs, Max. *Little Man's lucky day*
Walsh, Jill Paton. *Lost and found*
Ziefert, Harriet. *Good luck, bad luck*

Character traits – meanness

Bellows, Cathy. *Four fat rats*
Bottner, Barbara. *Mean Maxine*
Brown, Marc Tolon. *D. W., go to your room!*
Burningham, John. *Borka*
Carey, Valerie Scho. *The devil and mother Crump*
Carlson, Nancy L. *How to lose all your friends*
Carr, Jan. *Dark day, light night*
Carrick, Carol. *Old Mother Witch*
Clayton, Elaine. *Pup in school*
Coville, Bruce. *Sarah's unicorn*
David, Lawrence. *The good little girl*
Edwards, Richard. *The forest child*
Euvremer, Teryl. *Triple whammy*
Freeman, Don. *Tilly Witch*
Gantos, Jack (John, Jr.). *Rotten Ralph's rotten Christmas*
   Rotten Ralph's show and tell
   Rotten Ralph's trick or treat
   Worse than Rotten Ralph
Glazer, Lee. *Cookie Becker casts a spell*
Goble, Paul. *The lost children*
Goodsell, Jane. *Toby's toe*
Himmelman, John. *Amanda and the witch switch*
Hoban, Russell. *Big John Turkle*
   The little Brute family
Jones, Rebecca C. *The biggest, meanest, ugliest dog in the whole wide world*
Kidd, Bruce. *Hockey showdown*
Kismaric, Carole. *The rumor of Pavel and Paali*
Kraus, Robert. *The Christmas cookie sprinkle snitcher*
McCrea, James. *The magic tree*
McCully, Emily Arnold. *Little Kit, or, The Industrious Flea Circus girl*
Mahy, Margaret. *The boy with two shadows*
Manushkin, Fran. *Hocus and Pocus at the circus*
Nickl, Peter. *Ra ta ta tam*

Patz, Nancy. *Gina Farina and the Prince of Mintz*
Prelutsky, Jack. *The mean old mean hyena*
Price, Michelle. *Mean Melissa*
San Souci, Robert D. *Sootface*
Seuss, Dr. *How the Grinch stole Christmas*
Shibano, Tamizo. *The old man who made the trees bloom*
Silverman, Erica. *Gittel's hands*
Simmons, Steven J. *Alice and Greta*
Snyder, Anne. *The old man and the mule*
Steptoe, John. *Mufaro's beautiful daughters*
Stevenson, James. *Fried feathers for Thanksgiving*
  Happy Valentine's Day, Emma!
  The worst person's Christmas
Udry, Janice May. *The mean mouse and other mean stories*
Wooldridge, Connie Nordhielm. *Wicked Jack*
Zimelman, Nathan. *Mean Murgatroyd and the ten cats*
Zion, Gene. *The meanest squirrel I ever met*

Character traits – optimism

Alexander, Sue. *Marc the Magnificent*
Aliki. *The twelve months*
Anglund, Joan Walsh. *Rainbow love*
Atwood, Margaret. *Anna's pet*
Ayer, Jacqueline. *The paper-flower tree*
Brisson, Pat. *Wanda's roses*
Butterworth, Nick. *One blowy night*
Carey, Valerie Scho. *Maggie Mab and the bogey beast*
Delton, Judy. *My mother lost her job today*
Dionetti, Michelle V. *Coal mine peaches*
Gregory, Valiska. *Sunny side up*
  Terribly wonderful
Hall, Malcolm. *The friends of Charlie Ant Bear*
Hoff, Syd. *Oliver*
Krauss, Ruth. *The carrot seed*
Lindgren, Astrid. *Of course Polly can do almost everything*
Lionni, Leo. *Theodore and the talking mushroom*
Martin, Jacqueline Briggs. *Good times on Grandfather Mountain*
Peet, Bill (William Bartlett). *The Whingdingdilly*
Piatti, Celestino. *The happy owls*
Rice, Inez. *A long long time*
Saltzman, David. *The jester has lost his jingle*
Schwartz, Roslyn. *The mole sisters and the piece of moss*
Seuss, Dr. *Would you rather be a bullfrog?*
Tapio, Pat Decker. *The lady who saw the good side of everything*
Wiesner, William. *Happy-Go-Lucky*
Zakhoder, Boris Vladimirovich. *Rosachok*

Character traits – orderliness

Dale, Penny. *Bet you can't*
Dubowski, Cathy East. *Megan's messy room*
Duncan, Alice Faye. *Miss Viola and Uncle Ed Lee*
Grohmann, Susan. *The dust under Mrs. Merriweather's bed*
Leonard, Marcia. *I like mess*
Lillie, Patricia. *Everything has a place*
MacDonald, Alan. *Beware of the bears!*
McKenzie, Ellen Kindt. *The perfectly orderly house*
McKissack, Patricia C. *Messy Bessey*
Miller, Margaret. *Where does it go?*
O'Malley, Kevin. *Bud*
Peguero, Leone. *Lionel and Amelia*

Perkins, Lynne Rae. *Clouds for dinner*
Piers, Helen. *Who's in my bed?*
Prigger, Mary Skillings. *Aunt Minnie McGranahan*
Root, Phyllis. *Mrs. Potter's pig*
Sutherland, Colleen. *Jason goes to show-and-tell*
Teague, Mark. *Pigsty*

Character traits – ostracism *see* Character traits – being different

Character traits – patience

Appelt, Kathi. *Watermelon day*
Barbosa, Rogério Andrade. *African animal tales*
Barton, Byron. *Hester*
Butler, Stephen. *The mouse and the apple*
Clark, Gus. *How many days to my birthday?*
Cyrus, Kurt. *Slow train to Oxmox*
Erickson, Karen. *Waiting my turn*
Gerstein, Mordicai. *The wild boy*
Grindley, Sally. *Why is the sky blue?*
Grunwald, Lisa. *Now, soon, later*
Hellen, Nancy. *Bus stop*
Jensen, Patricia. *Be patient, Little Chick*
Ketteman, Helen. *Not yet, Yvette*
Kibbey, Marsha. *My grammy*
Koski, Mary. *Impatient Pamela calls 9-1-1*
Kulling, Monica. *Waiting for Amos*
Laurin, Anne. *Little things*
Ludy, Mark. *The farmer*
Mollel, Tololwa M. (Tololwa Marti). *Subira subira*
Morgan-Vanroyen, Mary. *Patient Rosie*
Poydar, Nancy. *Mailbox magic*
Steiner, Charlotte. *What's the hurry, Harry?*
Walters, Catherine. *When will it be spring?*
Weiss, Nicki. *Waiting*
Wells, Rosemary. *Max's breakfast*

Character traits – perseverance

Abisch, Roz. *Sweet Betsy from Pike*
Æsop. *The miller, his son and their donkey*, ill. by Roger Antoine Duvoisin
  The miller, his son and their donkey, ill. by Eugen Sopko
Alexander, Martha G. *Move over, Twerp*
  We never get to do anything
Aliki. *A weed is a flower*
Ambrus, Victor G. *The little cockerel*
  Mishka
Barber, Barbara E. *Allie's basketball dream*
Baumgardner, Mary Alice. *Alexandra, keeper of dreams*
Bethell, Jean. *Hooray for Henry*
Blades, Ann. *Mary of mile 18*
Boynton, Sandra. *If at first . . .*
Brennan, Joseph Killorin. *Gobo and the river*
Calhoun, Mary. *Old man Whickutt's donkey*
Carle, Eric. *The very clumsy click beetle*
Choldenko, Gennifer. *Moonstruck*
Conford, Ellen. *Just the thing for Geraldine*
Day, Shirley. *Ruthie's big tree*
Erickson, Karen. *I'll try*
Gray, Genevieve. *How far, Felipe?*
Hoff, Syd. *Slugger Sal's slump*
Jensen, Virginia Allen. *Sara and the door*
Kahl, Virginia. *Maxie*
Keats, Ezra Jack. *John Henry*
Kent, Jack. *Mrs. Mooley*

Lester, Julius. *John Henry*
Lindgren, Astrid. *Of course Polly can do almost everything*
Ludy, Mark. *The farmer*
Mitchell, Margaree King. *Uncle Jed's barbershop*
Pinkney, J. Brian. *Jojo's flying side kick*
Piper, Watty. *The little engine that could*
Riordan, James. *The three magic gifts*
Shearer, Marilyn J. *The crown of fools*
Shine, Deborah. *The little engine that could pudgy word book*
Skorpen, Liesel Moak. *All the Lassies*
Steig, William. *Brave Irene*
Thomas, Jane Resh. *Scaredy dog*
Thomas, Kathy. *The angel's quest*
Ungerer, Tomi. *The Mellops go spelunking*
Watanabe, Shigeo. *I can build a house!*
   I can ride it!
   Where's my daddy?
Waterton, Betty. *Orff, 27 dragons (and a snarkel)*
Weedn, Flavia. *The elephant prince*
Weller, Frances Ward. *Madaket Millie*

Character traits – persistence

Adler, David A. *A picture book of Helen Keller*
Birdseye, Tom. *Airmail to the moon*
Brown, Ruth. *The ghost of Greyfriar's Bobby*
Brutschy, Jennifer. *Celeste and Crabapple Sam*
Bulla, Clyde Robert. *The stubborn old woman*
Day, Marie. *Dragon in the rocks*
Glass, Andrew. *Charles T. McBiddle*
Hodges, Margaret. *Hidden in sand*
Lattimore, Deborah Nourse. *The sailor who captured the sea*
Lexau, Joan M. *Go away, dog*, ill. by Crosby Newell Bonsall
   Go away, dog, ill. by Paul Meisel
McCully, Emily Arnold. *The ballot box battle*
   Mouse practice
Marsh, Jeri. *Hurrah for Alexander*
Patz, Nancy. *Gina Farina and the Prince of Mintz*
Rigby, Rodney. *Hello, this is your penguin speaking*
Ross, Tony. *I want a cat*
Siomades, Lorianne. *The itsy bitsy spider*
Trapani, Iza. *The itsy bitsy spider*
Ward, Sally G. *Molly and Grandpa*
West, Colin. *"Pardon?" said the giraffe*

Character traits – practicality

Aylesworth, Jim. *Mother Halverson's new cat*
Evans, Katherine. *The man, the boy and the donkey*
Gág, Wanda. *Millions of cats*
Gretz, Susanna. *Roger loses his marbles!*
La Fontaine, Jean de. *The miller, the boy and the donkey*, adapt. and ill. by Brian Wildsmith
Modell, Frank. *One zillion valentines*
Oppenheim, Joanne. *Donkey's tale*
Schlein, Miriam. *The pile of junk*

Character traits – pride

Andersen, H. C. (Hans Christian). *The emperor's new clothes*, ill. by Angela Barrett
   The emperor's new clothes, ill. by Erik Blegvad
   The emperor's new clothes, ill. by Virginia Lee Burton
   The emperor's new clothes, ill. by Robert Byrd
   The emperor's new clothes, ill. by Jack and Irene Delano
   The emperor's new clothes, ill. by Hélène Desputeaux
   The emperor's new clothes, ill. by Birte Dietz
   The emperor's new clothes, ill. by Dorothée Duntze
   The emperor's new clothes, ill. by Pamela Baldwin Ford
   The emperor's new clothes, ill. by Jack Kent
   The emperor's new clothes, ill. by Monika Laimgruber
   The emperor's new clothes, ill. by Anne F. Rockwell
   The emperor's new clothes, ill. by Janet Stevens
   The emperor's new clothes, ill. by Robert Van Nutt
   The emperor's new clothes, ill. by Nadine Bernard Westcott
   The red shoes
Armstrong, Jennifer. *Chin Yu Min and the ginger cat*
Atkins, Jeannine. *Get set! Swim!*
Bemelmans, Ludwig. *Rosebud*
Birch, David. *The king's chessboard*
Burningham, John. *Humbert, Mister Firkin and the Lord Mayor of London*
Calhoun, Mary. *The runaway brownie*
Calmenson, Stephanie. *The principal's new clothes*
Clifton, Lucille. *All us come cross the water*
Conrad, Pam. *The rooster's gift*
Crary, Elizabeth. *I'm proud*
DeLuise, Dom. *King Bob's new clothes*
Dionetti, Michelle V. *Thalia Brown and the blue bug*
Duvoisin, Roger Antoine. *Crocus*
   Petunia
Edwards, Dorothy. *A wet Monday*
Ehrhardt, Reinhold. *Kikeri*
Friskey, Margaret (Margaret Richards). *Indian Two Feet rides alone*
Gackenbach, Dick. *The dog and the deep dark woods*
Goode, Diane. *The dinosaur's new clothes*
Grifalconi, Ann. *Osa's pride*
Hamberger, John. *The peacock who lost his tail*
Hürlimann, Ruth. *The proud white cat*
Keats, Ezra Jack. *John Henry*
Lester, Julius. *John Henry*
McKissack, Patricia C. *The king's new clothes*
McLenighan, Valjean. *What you see is what you get*
McMullan, Kate (Hall). *Noel the first*
Perlman, Janet. *The Emperor Penguin's new clothes*
Pomerantz, Charlotte. *The ballad of the long-tailed rat*
Rogasky, Barbara. *The water of life*
Ross, Anna. *I did it!*
Rylant, Cynthia. *Mr. Griggs' work*
Schwartz, Amy. *Annabelle Swift, kindergartner*
Sharmat, Marjorie Weinman. *I'm terrific*
Tettelbaum, Michael. *The cave of the lost Fraggle*
Whitney, Alex. *Once a bright red tiger*
Wilde, Oscar. *The Star Child*
Winthrop, Elizabeth. *Tough Eddie*
Yolen, Jane. *King Long Shanks*
Zimnik, Reiner. *The proud circus horse*

Character traits – questioning

Adler, David A. *A little at a time*
Alden, Laura. *When?*
Alexander, Martha G. *Where does the sky end, Grandpa?*
Allard, Harry. *May I stay?*
Anholt, Catherine. *All about you*

Baynton, Martin. *Why do you love me?*
Bird, E. J. *How do bears sleep?*
Brown, Margaret Wise. *Wait till the moon is full*
Camp, Lindsay. *Why?*
Carlstrom, Nancy White. *Goodbye geese*
Clark, Gus. *How many days to my birthday?*
Clark, Roberta. *Why?*
De Veaux, Alexis. *Na-ni*
Dunbar, Joyce. *Why is the sky up?*
Gorbachev, Valeri. *Where is the apple pie?*
Haswell, Peter. *Pog*
Hazen, Barbara Shook. *Santa clues*
Hines, Anna Grossnickle. *Even if I spill my milk?*
Hopkins, Lee Bennett. *Animals from Mother Goose*
    People from Mother Goose
    Questions
Hulbert, Jay. *Armando asked "Why?"*
Jacobs, Leland B. (Leland Blair). *Is somewhere always far away?*, ill. by John E. Johnson
    Is somewhere always far away?, ill. by Jeff Kaufman
Keven, Elisa. *Ernest*
Krauze, Andrzej. *What's so special about today?*
Lindbergh, Reeve. *What is the sun?*
Lionni, Leo. *Tico and the golden wings*
McKaughan, Larry. *Why are your fingers cold?*
Mahood, Kenneth. *Why are there more questions than answers, Grandad?*
Miller, M. L. *Dizzy from fools*
Miller, Margaret. *Can you guess?*
Moncure, Jane Belk. *Where?*
Reece, Colleen L. *What?*
Ripley, Catherine. *Why do stars twinkle?*
    Why is soap so slippery?
Schertle, Alice. *That's what I thought*
Simont, Marc. *How come elephants?*
Slater, Teddy. *The cow that could tap dance*
Stover, Jo Ann. *Why? Because*
Thaler, Mike. *Owley*
Tucker, Kathy. *Do cowboys ride bikes?*
Vance, Eleanor Graham. *Jonathan*
Williams, Barbara. *If he's my brother*
Wormell, Mary. *Why not?*
Young, Ruth. *Who says moo?*
Ziefert, Harriet. *Sarah's questions*

Character traits – responsibility

Gregory, Valiska. *When stories fell like shooting stars*
Haas, Jessie. *Busybody Brandy*
Oberman, Sheldon. *King Solomon, Sheba, and the hoopoe bird*
Schachner, Judith Byron. *The Grannyman*

Character traits – selfishness

Andersen, H. C. (Hans Christian). *The swineherd*, ill. by Erik Blegvad
    The swineherd, ill. by Dorothée Duntze
    The swineherd, ill. by Deborah Hahn
    The swineherd, ill. by Lisbeth Zwerger
Angelo, Valenti. *The acorn tree*
Baba, Noboru. *Eleven cats and a pig*
    Eleven cats and albatrosses
    Eleven cats in a bag
    Eleven hungry cats
Bahous, Sally. *Sitti and the cats*
Barrett, John M. *Oscar the selfish octopus*
Bascom, Joe. *Malcolm Softpaws*
Berquist, Grace. *The boy who couldn't roar*

Berry, Joy Wilt. *Being selfish*
Bryant, Bernice. *Follow the leader*
Carlson, Nancy L. *How to lose all your friends*
Chang, Margaret Scrogin. *The beggar's magic*
Christian, Mary Blount. *The devil take you, Barnabas Beane!*
Coombs, Patricia. *Mouse Café*
Demi. *One grain of rice*
Douglas, Richardo Keens. *The nutmeg princess*
Egan, Tim. *Chestnut Cove*
Elkin, Benjamin. *Lucky and the giant*
Gantos, Jack (John, Jr.). *Back to school for Rotten Ralph*
Garrett, Jennifer. *The queen who stole the sky*
Henkes, Kevin. *A weekend with Wendell*
Hooks, William H. *The rainbow ribbon*
Kahl, Virginia. *The perfect pancake*
Kraus, Robert. *Rebecca Hatpin*
Lattimore, Deborah Nourse. *The dragon's robe*
Lester, Helen. *Me first*
    Princess Penelope's parrot
Lewin, Betsy. *Chubbo's pool*
Lipkind, William. *Even Steven*
    Finders keepers
Martin, Jane Read. *Now everybody really hates me*
Mollel, Tololwa M. (Tololwa Marti). *The princess who lost her hair*
Peet, Bill (William Bartlett). *The ant and the elephant*
Rankin, Joan. *The little cat and the greedy old woman*
Reader, Dennis. *I want one!*
Reesink, Marijke. *The golden treasure*
Remkiewicz, Frank. *Greedyanna*
Rosen, Michael (1946-). *This is our house*
Sanfield, Steve. *Just rewards, or, Who is that man in the moon and what's he doing up there anyway?*
Schroeder, Alan. *The stone lion*
Warburton, Nick. *Mr. Tite's belongings*
Ward, Helen. *The moonrat and the white turtle*
Weedn, Flavia. *The giant's garden*
Wilde, Oscar. *Fairy tales of Oscar Wilde*
    The selfish giant, ill. by S. Saelig Gallagher
    The selfish giant, ill. by Dom Mansell
    The selfish giant, ill. by Fabian Negrin
    The selfish giant, ill. by Lisbeth Zwerger
    The Star Child
Winthrop, Elizabeth. *The Best Friends Club*
Yep, Laurence. *Tiger woman*

Character traits – shyness

Blaustein, Muriel. *Jim chimp's story*
Brice, Tony. *The bashful goldfish*
Cooney, Nancy Evans. *Chatter-box Jamie*
Devlin, Wende. *Cranberry Valentine*
Dines, Glen. *A tiger in the cherry tree*
Glaser, Linda. *Stop that garbage truck!*
Goble, Paul. *Love flute*
Goffstein, M. B. (Marilyn Brooke). *Neighbors*
Hamilton, Morse. *How do you do, Mr. Birdsteps?*
Hogrogian, Nonny. *Carrot cake*
Hutchins, Pat. *Titch and Daisy*
Keats, Ezra Jack. *Louie*
Keller, Beverly. *Fiona's bee*
Krasilovsky, Phyllis. *The shy little girl*
Lester, Helen. *The shy people's picnic*
Levine, Arthur A. *Sheep dreams*
Lewison, Wendy Cheyette. *Shy Vi*

Lexau, Joan M. *Benjie*
McCourt, Lisa. *The new kid and the cookie thief*
McCully, Emily Arnold. *Speak up, Blanche!*
Mathers, Petra. *Sophie and Lou*
Metcalf, Paula. *Norma No Friends*
Moore, Inga. *A big day for Little Jack*
Richardson, Jean. *Clara's dancing feet*
Rosenberry, Vera. *Vera's first day of school*
Schaefer, Charles E. *Cat's got your tongue?*
Smith, Wendy. *Say hello, Tilly*
Udry, Janice May. *What Mary Jo shared*
Wold, Jo Anne. *Tell them my name is Amanda*
Yashima, Taro. *Crow boy*
   The youngest one
Zalben, Jane Breskin. *Miss Violet's shining day*
Zolotow, Charlotte (Shapiro). *A tiger called Thomas*, ill. by Catherine Stock
   A tiger called Thomas, ill. by Kurt Werth

Character traits – smallness

Andersen, H. C. (Hans Christian). *Thumbelina*, ill. by Adrienne Adams
   Thumbelina, ill. by Wayne Anderson
   Thumbelina, ill. by Emma Chichester
   Thumbelina, ill. by Alison Claire Darke
   Thumbelina, ill. by Demi
   Thumbelina, ill. by Arlene Graston
   Thumbelina, ill. by Susan Jeffers
   Thumbelina, ill. by Kaarina Kaila
   Thumbelina, ill. by Christine Willis Nigognossian
   Thumbelina, ill. by Gustaf Tenggren
   Thumbelina, ill. by Lisbeth Zwerger, tr. by Richard and Clara Winston
   Thumbeline, ill. by Lisbeth Zwerger; tr. by Anthea Bell
Bang, Betsy. *The cucumber stem*
Beim, Jerrold. *The smallest boy in the class*
Benjamin, A. H. *A duck so small*
Bromhall, Winifred. *Bridget's growing day*
Burgess, Gelett. *The little father*
Chevalier, Christa. *Spence is small*
Cooper, Susan. *The silver cow*
Cuneo, Mary Louise. *Inside a sandcastle and other secrets*
Curry, Jane Louise. *Little, little sister*
De Paola, Tomie (Thomas Anthony). *Andy (that's my name)*
Gay, Michel. *Little helicopter*
Glass, Andrew. *Chickpea and the talking cow*
Hoff, Syd. *The littlest leaguer*
Horvath, Betty F. *Hooray for Jasper*
Johnston, Johanna. *Sugarplum*
Kraus, Robert. *The littlest rabbit*
Kumin, Maxine W. *Sebastian and the dragon*
Kuskin, Karla. *Herbert hated being small*
Lindgren, Barbro. *Shorty takes off*
Lipkind, William. *The little tiny rooster*
Lurie, Morris. *The story of Imelda, who was small*
Meddaugh, Susan. *Too short Fred*
Miles, Miska. *No, no, Rosina*
Moore, Inga. *Oh, little Jack*
Orgel, Doris. *On the sand dune*
Prøysen, Alf. *Mrs. Pepperpot and the moose*
Rigby, Shirley Lincoln. *Smaller than most*
Schlein, Miriam. *Billy, the littlest one*
Stanley, John. *It's nice to be little*
Tresselt, Alvin R. *Smallest elephant in the world*

Williams, Barbara. *Someday, said Mitchell*
Yolen, Jane. *The emperor and the kite*
Young, Ed (Edward). *Little Plum*

Character traits – stubbornness

Beatty, Hetty Burlingame. *Droopy*
Bulla, Clyde Robert. *The stubborn old woman*
Coplans, Peta. *Spaghetti for Suzy*
Garrett, Jennifer. *The queen who stole the sky*
Keller, Holly. *Merry Christmas, Geraldine*
Leaf, Margaret. *Eyes of the dragon*
Minarik, Else Holmelund. *The little girl and the dragon*
O'Brien, Anne Sibley. *I'm not tired*
Plourde, Lynn. *Pigs in the mud in the middle of the rud*
Steig, William. *Spinky sulks*
Tarbescu, Edith. *The boy who stuck out his tongue*
Tusa, Tricia. *Miranda*
Viorst, Judith. *Alexander, who's not (Do you hear me? I mean it!) going to move*

Character traits – vanity

Andersen, H. C. (Hans Christian). *The emperor's new clothes*, ill. by Angela Barrett
   The emperor's new clothes, ill. by Erik Blegvad
   The emperor's new clothes, ill. by Virginia Lee Burton
   The emperor's new clothes, ill. by Robert Byrd
   The emperor's new clothes, ill. by Jack and Irene Delano
   The emperor's new clothes, ill. by Hélène Desputeaux
   The emperor's new clothes, ill. by Birte Dietz
   The emperor's new clothes, ill. by Dorothée Duntze
   The emperor's new clothes, ill. by Pamela Baldwin Ford
   The emperor's new clothes, ill. by Jack Kent
   The emperor's new clothes, ill. by Monika Laimgruber
   The emperor's new clothes, ill. by Anne F. Rockwell
   The emperor's new clothes, ill. by Janet Stevens
   The emperor's new clothes, ill. by Robert Van Nutt
   The emperor's new clothes, ill. by Nadine Bernard Westcott
   It's perfectly true!
Armstrong, Jennifer. *Chin Yu Min and the ginger cat*
Brown, Marcia. *Once a mouse . . .*
Brown, Margaret Wise. *The duck*
Browne, Anthony. *The big baby*
Calmenson, Stephanie. *The principal's new clothes*
DeLuise, Dom. *King Bob's new clothes*
Elborn, Andrew. *Bird Adalbert*
Fleming, Candace. *Madame LaGrande and her so high, to the sky, uproarious pompadour*
Frascino, Edward. *My cousin the king*
Goode, Diane. *The dinosaur's new clothes*
Hausman, Gerald. *Coyote walks on two legs*
Kajpust, Melissa. *The peacock's pride*
Kepes, Juliet. *The story of a bragging duck*
McCormack, John E. *Rabbit tales*
MacDonald, Margaret Read. *The girl who wore too much*
McKissack, Patricia C. *The king's new clothes*
Marshall, James. *George and Martha, tons of fun*
Peppé, Rodney. *The color catalog*
Perlman, Janet. *The Emperor Penguin's new clothes*

Sharmat, Marjorie Weinman. *Sasha the silly*
Shields, Carol Diggory. *I am really a princess*
Wall, Lina Mao. *Judge Rabbit and the tree spirit*
Winter, Paula. *Sir Andrew*
Yolen, Jane. *King Long Shanks*
　　Pegasus, the flying horse

Character traits – willfulness

Albert, Shirley. *Doll party*
Alexander, Sue. *Nadia the willful*
Boyd, Lizi. *Half wild and half child*
Cox, David. *Bossyboots*
Grimm, Jacob. *The princess and the frog*
Lattimore, Deborah Nourse. *The prince and the
　　golden ax*
Lester, Helen. *Pookins gets her way*
Quin-Harkin, Janet. *Benjamin's balloon*
Vesey, A. *The princess and the frog*

Cheerleading

Carlson, Nancy L. *Louanne Pig in making the team*
Lester, Helen. *Three cheers for Tacky*

Cheetahs *see* Animals – cheetahs

Chefs *see* Careers – chefs, cooks

Cherokee Indians *see* Indians of North
　　America – Cherokee

Cherubs *see* Angels

Cheyenne (Sioux) Indians *see* Indians of
　　North America – Cheyenne (Sioux)

Chickasaw Indians *see* Indians of North
　　America – Chickasaw

Chicken pox *see* Illness – chicken pox

Chickens *see* Birds – chickens

Child abuse

Caines, Jeannette. *Chilly stomach*
Kleven, Sandy. *The right touch*
Spelman, Cornelia. *Your body belongs to you*
Trottier, Maxine. *A safe place*

Children as authors

Baskin, Leonard. *Hosie's alphabet*
　　Hosie's aviary
Burdett, Lois. *Hamlet for kids*
　　Macbeth for kids
　　A midsummer night's dream for kids
　　Romeo and Juliet for kids
　　The tempest for kids
　　Twelfth night
　　Children's prayers from around the world
Haidle, Elizabeth. *Elmer the grump*
Harper, Isabelle. *My dog Rosie*
Jay, Betsy. *Swimming lessons*
Kershen, L. Michael (Lloyd Michael). *Why buffalo
　　roam*

Komaiko, Leah. *A million moms and mine*
Krauss, Ruth. *Somebody else's nut tree, and other tales
　　from children*
Kroll, Steven. *Patches*
Lady Eden's School. *Just how stories*
MacKeen, Leslie Ann. *Who can fix it?*
　　Night time
O'Reilly, Edward. *Brown pelican at the pond*
　　The palm of my heart
Phumla. *Nomi and the magic fish*
St. Pierre, Wendy. *Henry finds a home*
Salter, Heidi. *Taddy McFinley and the great grey
　　grimly*
Waldman, Sarah. *Light*
Wiener, Lori. *Be a friend*

Children as illustrators

Arnold, Lynda. *My Mommy has AIDS*
Burdett, Lois. *Hamlet for kids*
　　Macbeth for kids
　　A midsummer night's dream for kids
　　Romeo and Juliet for kids
　　The tempest for kids
　　Twelfth night
De Paola, Tomie (Thomas Anthony). *Criss-cross
　　applesauce*
Feldman, Eve B. *Birthdays!*
Giuliano, Katie. *All the way to God*
Haidle, Elizabeth. *Elmer the grump*
Hughes, Langston. *The sweet and sour animal book*
Kamish, Daniel. *The night scary beasties popped out of
　　my head*
Komaiko, Leah. *A million moms and mine*
Kroll, Steven. *Patches*
MacKeen, Leslie Ann. *Who can fix it?*
　　Night time
Salter, Heidi. *Taddy McFinley and the great grey
　　grimly*
Tusa, Tricia. *Bunnies in my head*
Wiener, Lori. *Be a friend*

Chile *see* Foreign lands – Chile

Chimpanzees *see* Animals – chimpanzees

China *see* Foreign lands – China

Chinese Americans *see* Ethnic groups in the
　　U.S. – Asian Americans; Ethnic groups in
　　the U.S. – Chinese Americans

Chinese New Year *see* Holidays – Chinese
　　New Year

Chinook Indians *see* Indians of North Ameri-
　　ca – Chinook

Chipmunks *see* Animals – chipmunks

Chippewa *see* Indians of North America –
　　Chippewa

Chol Indians *see* Indians of North America –
　　Chol

Christmas *see* Holidays – Christmas

Chumash Indians *see* Indians of North America – Chumash

Cinco de Mayo *see* Holidays – Cinco de Mayo

Circular tales

Ada, Alma Flor. *The gold coin*
Arnold, Tedd. *Ollie forgot*
Bonners, Susan. *Just in passing*
Bonning, Tony. *Another fine mess*
Carle, Eric. *Draw me a star*
Coco, Eugene Bradley. *The wishing well*
Dodds, Dayle Ann. *Wheel away!*
Fanelli, Sara. *Button*
Gorbachev, Valeri. *Where is the apple pie?*
Greeley, Valerie. *Where's my share?*
Hoban, Russell. *The marzipan pig*
Jackson, Ellen B. *Brown cow, green grass, yellow mellow sun*
Janovitz, Marilyn. *Look out, bird!*
Johnston, Tony. *Big red apple*
   The last snow of winter
Kalan, Robert. *Stop, thief!*
Leemis, Ralph. *Mister Momboo's hat*
Lichtveld, Noni. *I lost my arrow in a kankan tree*
McAllister, Angela. *Matepo*
MacDonald, Elizabeth. *The very windy day*
McGuire, Richard. *What goes around comes around*
Numeroff, Laura Joffe. *If you give a moose a muffin*
   If you give a mouse a cookie
   If you give a pig a pancake
Rogers, Paul (Patrick). *Don't blame me!*
Root, Phyllis. *The old red rocking chair*
Rosenberg, Liz. *Window, mirror, moon*
Runcie, Jill. *Cock-a-doodle-doo*
Schories, Pat. *Mouse around*
Stevens, Harry. *Fat mouse*
Ueno, Noriko. *Elephant buttons*
Van Laan, Nancy. *The big fat worm*
   This is the hat
Vyner, Sue. *The stolen egg*
Whybrow, Ian. *Quacky quack-quack!*
Wolf, Sallie. *Peter's trucks*
Wolff, Ferida. *The woodcutter's coat*
Ziefert, Harriet. *A polar bear can swim*
Zolotow, Charlotte (Shapiro). *Wake up and goodnight*

Circus

Adler, David A. *You think it's fun to be a clown!*
Ahlberg, Allan. *Mr. and Mrs. Hay the horse*
Aitken, Amy. *Wanda's circus*
Allen, Jeffrey. *Bonzini! the tattooed man*
Ambrus, Victor G. *Mishka*
Amoit, Pierre. *Bijou, the little bear*
Anno, Mitsumasa. *Dr. Anno's magical midnight circus*
Armstrong, Jennifer. *Pierre's dream*
Austin, Margot. *Barney's adventure*
Bach, Alice. *Millicent the magnificent*
Balet, Jan B. *Five Rollatinis*
Banigan, Sharon Stearns. *Circus magic*
Barnes-Murphy, Rowan. *Numbers*
Barr, Cathrine. *Sammy seal ov the sircus*
Barton, Byron. *Harry is a scaredy-cat*

Blance, Ellen. *Monster goes to the circus*
Blumberg, Rhoda. *Jumbo*
Blume, Karin. *Circus*
Bond, Michael. *Paddington at the circus*
Bonfils, Bolette. *Peter joins the circus*
Booth, Eugene. *At the circus*
Bourguignon, Laurence. *A friend for Tiger*
Bowden, Joan Chase. *Boo and the flying flews*
Brown, Marc Tolon. *Arthur's chicken pox*
   Lenny and Lola
Brunhoff, Laurent de. *Babar's little circus star*
Burningham, John. *Cannonball Simp*
Cameron, Polly. *The cat who thought he was a tiger*
Carrick, Carol. *Two very little sisters*
Cassidy, Dianne. *Circus animals*
   Circus people
Chardiet, Bernice. *C is for circus*
Chorao, Kay. *Number one number fun*
Chwast, Seymour. *The twelve circus rings*
Collington, Peter. *The midnight circus*
Come to the circus
Coontz, Otto. *A real class clown*
Cooper, Melrose. *Pets!*
Coxe, Molly. *Louella and the yellow balloon*
Curious George goes to the circus
Damjan, Mischa. *The clown said no*
Darling, Kathy (Mary Kathleen). *Bug circus*
Day, Alexandra. *Paddy's pay-day*
Dayton, Laura. *LeRoy's birthday circus*
Dedieu, Thierry. *Baby clown*
De Paola, Tomie (Thomas Anthony). *Jingle, the Christmas clown*
De Regniers, Beatrice Schenk. *Circus*
Dreamer, Sue. *Circus ABC*
   Circus 1, 2, 3
Drescher, Henrik. *Klutz*
Dubanevich, Arlene. *The piggest show on earth*
Du Bois, William Pène. *Bear circus*
Ehlert, Lois. *Circus*
Ehrlich, Amy. *Lucy's winter tale*
Elks, Wendy. *Charles B. Wombat and the very strange thing*
Emberley, Rebecca. *My mother's secret life*
Ernst, Lisa Campbell. *Ginger jumps*
Ets, Marie Hall. *Mister Penny's circus*
Everton, Macduff. *El circo magico modelo*
Falk, Barbara Bustetter. *Grusha*
Falwell, Cathryn. *Clowning around*
Fazzi, Maura. *The circus of mystery*
Flack, Marjorie. *Wait for William*
Fox, Charles Philip. *Come to the circus*
Freeman, Don. *Bearymore*
Garbutt, Bernard. *Roger, the rosin back*
Garland, Michael. *Circus girl*
Gascoigne, Bamber. *Why the rope went tight*
Gay, Michel. *Night ride*
Goennel, Heidi. *The circus*
Goodall, John S. *The adventures of Paddy Pork*
Gramatky, Hardie. *Homer and the circus train*
Greaves, Margaret. *Little Bear and the Papagini circus*
Hale, Irina. *Donkey's dreadful day*
Harris, Steven Michael. *This is my trunk*
Herrmann, Frank. *The giant Alexander and the circus*
Hill, Eric. *Spot goes to the circus*
Hoff, Syd. *Barkley*
   Henrietta, circus star
   Oliver
Hol, Coby. *Henrietta saves the show*
Holl, Adelaide. *Mrs. McGarrity's peppermint sweater*

Hopkins, Lee Bennett. *Circus! Circus!*
The house that Jack built. *The house that Jack built,* ill. by Janet Stevens
Johnson, Crockett. *Harold's circus*
Johnson, Jane. *Bertie on the beach*
Johnson, Neil. *Big-top circus*
Karn, George. *Circus big and small*
　　Circus colors
Kastner, Jill. *Barnyard big top*
Lacome, Julie. *Funny business*
Lent, Blair. *Pistachio*
Lipkind, William. *Circus rucus*
Lisowski, Gabriel. *Roncalli's magnificent circus*
Logue, Christopher. *The magic circus*
London, Jonathan. *Little Red Monkey*
Lopshire, Robert. *New tricks I can do!*
　　Put me in the zoo
McCourt, Lisa. *Chicken soup for little souls: The best night out with Dad*
McCully, Emily Arnold. *Little Kit, or, The Industrious Flea Circus girl*
MacDonald, Suse. *Elephants on board*
Maestro, Betsy. *Busy day*
　　Harriet goes to the circus
Maley, Anne. *Have you seen my mother?*
Marokvia, Merelle. *A French school for Paul*
Martin, Bill (William Ivan). *Chicken Chuck*
Mayer, Mercer. *Liverwurst is missing*
Miranda, Anne. *The elephant at the Waldorf*
Modell, Frank. *Seen any cats?*
Montenegro, Laura Nyman. *Sweet Tooth*
Munari, Bruno. *The circus in the mist*
Murphy, Stuart J. *Circus shapes*
Myers, Bernice. *Herman and the bears and the giants*
Ness, Evaline. *Fierce*
Nightingale, Sandy. *Pink pigs aplenty*
O'Kelley, Mattie Lou. *Circus!*
Ostheeren, Ingrid. *Jonathan Mouse at the circus*
Panek, Dennis. *Detective Whoo*
Paré, Roger. *Circus days*
Peet, Bill (William Bartlett). *Chester the worldly pig*
　　Ella
　　Randy's dandy lions
Pellowski, Michael. *Clara joins the circus*
Peppé, Rodney. *Circus numbers*
　　Little circus
　　Thumbprint circus
Petersham, Maud. *The circus baby*
Pinkwater, Daniel Manus. *Rainy morning*
Piumini, Roberto. *The saint and the circus*
Prater, John. *The greatest show on earth*
Prelutsky, Jack. *Circus*
Price, Mathew. *Do you see what I see?*
　　Dumbo
Priceman, Marjorie. *Emeline at the circus*
Quackenbush, Robert M. *The man on the flying trapeze*
Rascal. *Oregon's journey*
Rey, H. A. (Hans Augusto). *Curious George rides a bike*
　　See the circus
Rounds, Glen. *The day the circus came to Lone Tree*
Saville, Lynn. *Horses in the circus ring*
Scheffrin-Falk, Gladys. *Another celebrated dancing bear*
Schulz, Charles M. *Life is a circus, Charlie Brown*
Seignobosc, Françoise. *Small-Trot*
Seligson, Susan. *The amazing Amos and the greatest couch on earth*

Seuss, Dr. *If I ran the circus*
Slobodkina, Esphyr. *Pezzo the peddler and the circus elephant*
Slocum, Rosalie. *Breakfast with the clowns*
Slyder, Ingrid. *The Fabulous Flying Fandinis*
Spier, Peter. *Peter Spier's circus!*
Taylor, Mark. *Henry explores the jungle*
Teague, Mark. *Baby tamer*
Tester, Sylvia Root. *Parade!*
Tresselt, Alvin R. *Smallest elephant in the world*
Varga, Judy. *Circus cannonball*
　　Miss Lollipop's lion
Vincent, Gabrielle. *Ernest and Celestine at the circus*
Wahl, Jan. *Sylvester Bear overslept*
　　The toy circus
Wallace, Ian. *Morgan the magnificent*
Weil, Lisl. *Let's go to the circus*
Westman, Barbara. *Dancing dogs*
Wildsmith, Brian. *Brian Wildsmith's circus*
Winn, Chris. *Archie's acrobats*
Wiseman, Bernard. *Morris and Boris at the circus*
Yaccarino, Dan. *Deep in the jungle*
Zimnik, Reiner. *The bear on the motorcycle*
　　The proud circus horse

City

Adinolfi, JoAnn. *Tina's diner*
Adoff, Arnold. *Street music*
　　Where wild Willie?
Æsop. *The country mouse and the city mouse*
　　The town mouse and the country mouse, ill. by Lorinda Bryan Cauley
　　The town mouse and the country mouse, ill. by Helen Craig
　　The town mouse and the country mouse, ill. by Paul Galdone
　　The town mouse and the country mouse, ill. by Tom Garcia
　　The town mouse and the country mouse, ill. by Janet Stevens
　　The town mouse and the country mouse, ill. by Bernadette Watts
　　Town mouse, country mouse, ill. by Jan Brett
　　Town mouse, country mouse, ill. by Carol Jones
Allamand, Pascale. *The pop rooster*
Asch, Frank. *City sandwich*
　　Dear brother
Asch, George. *Linda*
Baker, Jeannie. *Home in the sky*
　　Millicent
Bank Street College of Education. *Around the city*
　　Green light, go
　　In the city
　　My city
　　Uptown, downtown
Barracca, Debra. *Maxi, the hero*
　　A taxi dog Christmas
Barracca, Sal. *The adventures of taxi dog*
Barrett, Judi. *Old MacDonald had an apartment house*
Bartone, Elisa. *Peppe the lamplighter*
Bash, Barbara. *Urban roosts*
Baum, Susan. *City shapes*
Baylor, Byrd. *The best town in the world*
Bemelmans, Ludwig. *Sunshine*
Bergere, Thea. *Paris in the rain with Jean and Jacqueline*
Bergman, Donna. *City fox*
Bible. Old Testament. Psalms. *Psalm twenty-three*

Binzen, Bill. *Carmen*
Blance, Ellen. *Monster comes to the city*
Blegvad, Lenore. *Once upon a time and Grandma*
Blue, Rose. *How many blocks is the world?*
Bowden, Joan Chase. *Emilio's summer day*
Bozzo, Maxine Zohn. *Toby in the country, Toby in the city*
Bright, Robert. *Georgie to the rescue*
Brock, Emma Lillian. *Nobody's mouse*
Brown, Craig McFarland. *City sounds*
Brown, Jane Clark. *Whonk, and whonk again*
Brown, Marcia. *The little carousel*
Brown, Margaret Wise. *Three little animals*
Brown, Tricia. *The city by the bay*
Buehner, Caralyn. *The escape of Marvin the ape*
Bunting, Eve (Anne Evelyn). *Secret place*
   Smoky night
Burstein, Fred. *The dancer*
Burton, Virginia Lee. *Katy and the big snow*
   The little house
   Maybelle, the cable car
Busch, Phyllis S. *City lots*
Calmenson, Stephanie. *Hotter than a hot dog!*
Cannon, Janell. *Trupp*
Carrick, Carol. *Left behind*
Casey, Patricia. *Beep! Beep! Oink! Oink! animals in the city*
Chalmers, Mary. *Kevin*
Chapouton, Anne-Marie. *Ben finds a friend*
Christian, Mary Blount. *Christmas reflections*
Chwast, Seymour. *Tall city, wide country*
   Traffic jam
City, ill. by Roser Capdevila
Cleveland-Peck, Patricia. *City cat, country cat*
Clifton, Lucille. *The boy who didn't believe in spring*
   Everett Anderson's Christmas coming
Coats, Laura Jane. *City cat*
Cohen, Miriam. *Down in the subway*
Colman, Hila. *Peter's brownstone house*
Come out to play
Corcos, Lucille. *The city book*
Craft, Ruth. *The day of the rainbow*
Craig, Helen. *Susie and Alfred in a busy day in town*
Crews, Donald. *Parade*
Crews, Nina. *One hot summer day*
Crowell, Maryalicia. *A horse in the house*
Daly, Niki. *Not so fast Songololo*
Decker, Dorothy W. *Stripe visits New York*
Demarest, Chris L. *Bus*
De Paola, Paula. *Rosie and the yellow ribbon*
De Veaux, Alexis. *Na-ni*
DiSalvo-Ryan, DyAnne. *City green*
Donnelly, Liza. *Dinosaur beach*
   Dinosaur garden
   Dinosaurs' Halloween
Dorros, Arthur. *Abuela*
Dunrea, Olivier. *The painter who loved chickens*
Duvoisin, Roger Antoine. *Lonely Veronica*
   Veronica
Ellis, Anne Leo. *Dabble Duck*
Emberley, Michael. *Ruby*
Emberley, Rebecca. *City sounds*
   Three cool kids
Enderle, Judith (Ann) Ross. *Upstairs*
   Where are you, little Zack?
Fife, Dale. *Adam's ABC*
Finsand, Mary Jane. *The town that moved*
Florian, Douglas. *The city*
   City street

Fraser, Kathleen. *Adam's world, San Francisco*
Freeman, Don. *Fly high, fly low*
   The guard mouse
French, Fiona. *Snow White in New York*
Garland, Sarah. *Polly's puffin*
Geisert, Bonnie. *Prairie town*
Gibbons, Gail. *Up goes the skyscraper!*
Giff, Patricia Reilly. *I love Saturday*
Goodall, John S. *The story of a main street*
   The story of an English village
Gramatky, Hardie. *Little Toot through the Golden Gate*
Greenberg, Melanie Hope. *My father's luncheonette*
Greenfield, Eloise. *Night on Neighborhood Street*
Grifalconi, Ann. *City rhythms*
Griffith, Helen V. *Grandaddy's stars*
Grimes, Nikki. *C is for city*
   Danitra Brown leaves town
   Meet Danitra Brown
Grossbart, Francine. *A big city*
Guilfoile, Elizabeth. *Have you seen my brother?*
Guthrie, Donna. *A rose for Abby*
Harvey, Brett. *Immigrant girl*
Hawkesworth, Jenny. *The lonely skyscraper*
Hayward, Linda. *The city worm and the country worm*
Hazelaar, Cor. *Dogs everywhere*
Helldorfer, M. C. (Mary Claire). *Silver Rain Brown*
Henderson, Kathy. *In the middle of the night*
   A year in the city
Henwood, Simon. *The hidden jungle*
Heo, Yumi. *One afternoon*
   One Sunday morning
Hest, Amy. *Nana's birthday party*
   Ruby's storm
   Weekend girl
Himler, Ronald. *The girl on the yellow giraffe*
Hoban, Tana. *Is it red? Is it yellow? Is it blue?*
Holl, Adelaide. *A mouse story*
Hopkins, Lee Bennett. *I think I saw a snail*
   A song in stone
Hubbell, Patricia. *Sidewalk trip*
Hughes, Shirley. *The big concrete lorry*
Hurd, Thacher. *Zoom City*
Ingle, Annie. *The big city book*
Isadora, Rachel. *City seen from A to Z*
   Listen to the city
Ivory, Lesley Anne. *A day in London*
   A day in New York
Jam, Teddy. *Night cars*
Jenkins, Priscilla Belz. *Falcons nest on skyscrapers*
Johnson, Dinah. *Sunday week*
Johnson, Stephen T. *Alphabet city*
Johnston, Tony. *How many miles to Jacksonville?*
Jonas, Ann. *Round trip*
Jones, Rebecca C. *Matthew and Tilly*
Joosse, Barbara M. *The morning chair*
Jordan, June. *Kimako's story*
Kahn, Joan. *Hi, Jock, run around the block*
Kanome, Kayoko. *Little Mop lost*
Karlins, Mark. *Music over Manhattan*
Kaufman, Curt. *Hotel boy*
Keats, Ezra Jack. *Apt. 3*
   Goggles
   Hi, cat!
Keeping, Charles. *Alfie finds the other side of the world*
   Through the window
Kesselman, Wendy Ann. *Angelita*
Kightley, Rosalinda. *The postman*

Konigsburg, E. L. (Elaine Lobl). *Amy Elizabeth explores Bloomingdale's*
Koralek, Jenny. *Cat and Kit*
Kovalski, Maryann. *Jingle bells*
Krementz, Jill. *A visit to Washington, D.C.*
Kroll, Steven. *Mary McLean and the St. Patrick's Day parade*
Kroll, Virginia L. *Faraway drums*
Krudop, Walter Lyon. *Something is growing*
Kuskin, Karla. *City noise*
 Jerusalem, shining still
Lakin, Pat (Patricia). *Subway sonata*
Lasky, Kathryn. *I have an aunt on Marlborough Street*
Lenski, Lois. *Policeman Small*
 Sing a song of people
Lent, Blair. *Bayberry Bluff*
 Molasses flood
Lerman, Rory S. *Charlie's checklist*
Levine, Arthur A. *Pearl Moscowitz's last stand*
Levinson, Riki. *Our home is the sea*
Lewin, Hugh. *Jafta - the town*
Lewin, Ted. *Amazon boy*
Lewis, Stephen. *Zoo city*
Lexau, Joan M. *Benjie on his own*
 Come here, cat
 Me day
Little, Jean. *Gruntle Piggle takes off*
London, Jonathan. *Hip cat*
Loomis, Christine. *Rush hour*
Lorenz, Lee. *A weekend in the city*
Lotz, Karen E. *Can't sit still*
Low, Alice. *David's windows*
McCloskey, Kevin. *Mrs. Fitz's flamingos*
McCloskey, Robert. *Make way for ducklings*
McGinley, Phyllis. *All around the town*
McKissack, Patricia C. *Country mouse and city mouse*
Maestro, Betsy. *Big city port*
 Delivery van
 Taxi
Maestro, Giulio. *The remarkable plant in apartment 4*
Maizlish, Lisa. *The ring*
Manushkin, Fran. *Let's go riding in our strollers*
Martin, Jacqueline Briggs. *The green truck garden giveaway*
Mathers, Petra. *Maria Theresa*
Mayer, Mercer. *Little Monster's neighborhood*
Mennen, Ingrid. *Somewhere in Africa*
Merriam, Eve. *Bam, bam, bam*
 Fighting words
 On my street
Miles, Miska. *No, no, Rosina*
 Rolling the cheese
Milich, Melissa. *Miz Fannie Mae's fine new Easter hat*
Mizumura, Kazue. *If I built a village*
Moak, Allan. *A big city ABC*
Moore, Elaine. *Good morning, city*
Moreton, Daniel. *La Cucaracha Martina*
Morris, Jill. *The boy who painted the sun*
Muller, Gerda. *The garden in the city*
Munro, Roxie. *Christmastime in New York City*
 The inside-outside book of London
 The inside-outside book of New York City
 The inside-outside book of Paris
 The inside-outside book of Washington, D.C.
Myers, Christopher A. *Sparrows*
Myers, Walter Dean. *Harlem*
Nichols, Cathy. *Tuxedo Sam*
Nims, Bonnie Larkin. *Where is the bear in the city?*
Numeroff, Laura Joffe. *What daddies do best*

O'Donnell, Peter. *Oscar*
O'Kelley, Mattie Lou. *Moving to town*
Olds, Elizabeth. *Little Una*
Olsen, Ib Spang. *Cat alley*
O'Shell, Marcia. *Alphabet Annie announces an all-American album*
Otto, Carolyn. *Ducks, ducks, ducks*
Our house
Peet, Bill (William Bartlett). *Fly, Homer, fly*
Perera, Lydia. *Frisky*
Poydar, Nancy. *Cool Ali*
Proimos, James. *The loudness of Sam*
Provensen, Alice. *Punch in New York*
 Shaker Lane
 Town and country
Pryor, Bonnie. *The dream jar*
Quackenbush, Robert M. *City trucks*
Raskin, Ellen. *Franklin Stein*
 Nothing ever happens on my block
Ressner, Phil. *Dudley Pippin*
Rice, Eve. *City night*
Ringgold, Faith. *Tar Beach*
Roach, Marilynne K. *Two Roman mice*
Rockwell, Anne F. *Come to town*
 Hugo at the window
Rogers, Paul (Patrick). *Tumbledown*
Rosario, Idalia. *Idalia's project ABC*
Rosenblum, Richard. *The old synagogue*
Roth, Harold. *Let's look all around the town*
Rotner, Shelley. *Citybook*
Rowe, Jeanne A. *City workers*
Rush, Ken. *Friday's journey*
Russo, Marisabina. *Mama talks too much*
Ryder, Joanne. *The night flight*
Sara. *Across town*
Sauer, Julia Lina. *Mike's house*
Scarry, Richard. *Richard Scarry's Postman Pig and his busy neighbors*
Schick, Eleanor. *City green*
 City in the winter
 One summer night
 Peter and Mr. Brandon
Schotter, Roni. *Nothing ever happens on 90th Street*
Schwartz, Amy. *A teeny, tiny baby*
Scott, Ann Herbert. *Let's catch a monster*
Shannon, George. *Beanboy*
Shecter, Ben. *Emily, girl witch of New York*
Shulevitz, Uri. *One Monday morning*
 Snow
Silverman, Erica. *Mrs. Peachtree and the Eighth Avenue cat*
 On Grandma's roof
Simon, Norma. *What do I do?*
Smalls-Hector, Irene. *Irene and the big, fine nickel*
 Jonathan and his mommy
Smucker, Anna Egan. *No star nights*
Sonneborn, Ruth A. *Friday night is papa night*
 I love Gram
 Lollipop's party
Sopko, Eugen. *Townsfolk and countryfolk*
Soto, Gary. *Chato's kitchen*
Stadler, John. *The cats of Mrs. Calamari*
Stanley, Diane. *A country tale*
Steel, Barry. *Greek cities*
Steptoe, John. *Uptown*
Stevenson, James. *Grandpa's great city tour*
Summers, Kate. *Milly and Tilly*
Tamar, Erika. *The garden of happiness*
Taylor, Harriet Peck. *Two days in May*

Thomas, Ianthe. *Walk home tired, Billy Jenkins*
Thornhill, Jan. *Wild in the city*
Torres, Daniel. *Tom*
Tresselt, Alvin R. *It's time now!*
    Wake up, city!
Trimby, Elisa. *Mr. Plum's paradise*
Van Laan, Nancy. *People, people, everywhere*
Vasiliu, Mircea. *What's happening?*
Wallace, Karen. *City pig*
Wallace-Brodeur, Ruth. *Home by five*
Walters, Marguerite. *The city-country ABC*
Weitzman, Jacqueline Preiss. *You can't take a bal-
    loon into the Metropolitan Museum*
    You can't take a balloon into the National Gallery
Wellington, Monica. *Night city*
Wilde, Oscar. *The happy prince*
Wilder, Laura Ingalls. *Going to town*
Williams, Jay. *The city witch and the country witch*
Williams, Sherley Anne. *Girls together*
Williamson, Mel. *Walk on!*
Wold, Jo Anne. *Well! Why didn't you say so?*
Wyeth, Sharon Dennis. *Something beautiful*
Yashima, Taro. *Umbrella*
Yezback, Steven A. *Pumpkinseeds*
Zarin, Cynthia. *Rose and Sebastian*
Zimmerman, Andrea Griffing. *Trashy town*
Zion, Gene. *Dear garbage man*
    Hide and seek day
Zolotow, Charlotte (Shapiro). *One step, two . . .*
    The park book

Clallam Indians *see* Indians of North Ameri-
    ca – Clallam

Cleanliness *see* Character traits – cleanliness

Cleverness *see* Character traits – cleverness

Clockmakers *see* Careers – clockmakers

Clocks, watches

Aiken, Conrad Potter. *Tom, Sue and the clock*
Ambrus, Victor G. *What's the time, Dracula?*
Anderson, Lena. *Tick-tock*
Ardizzone, Edward. *Johnny the clockmaker*
Axelrod, Amy. *Pigs on a blanket*
Aylesworth, Jim. *The completed hickory dickory dock*
Bassett, Lisa. *A clock for Beany*
Berg, Jean Horton. *The noisy clock shop*
Bloom, Becky. *Mr. Cuckoo*
Bragdon, Lillian J. *Tell me the time, please*
Bram, Elizabeth. *Woodruff and the clocks*
Briggs, Raymond. *The snowman tell-the-time book*
Brown, Kathryn. *Muledred*
Browne, Eileen. *Tick-tock*
Cohen, Carol L. *Wake up, groundhog!*
Colman, Hila. *Watch that watch*
Dunbar, James. *Tick-tock*
Duquennoy, Jacques. *Operation ghost*
Gibbons, Gail. *Clocks and how they go*
Gilbert, Helen Earle. *Dr. Trotter and his big gold
    watch*
Gordon, Sharon. *Tick tock clock*
Gould, Deborah. *Brendan's best-timed birthday*
Harper, Dan. *Telling time with Big Mama Cat*
Henwood, Simon. *The clock shop*
Hutchins, Pat. *Clocks and more clocks*

Johns, Linda. *Sarah's secret plan*
Jones, Carol. *What's the time, Mr. Wolf?*
Katz, Bobbi. *Tick-tock, let's read the clock*
Kramsky, Jerry. *The cranky sun*
Llewellyn, Claire. *My first book of time*
Lloyd, David. *The stopwatch*
McGinley, Phyllis. *Wonderful time*
McKee, David. *The school bus comes at eight o'clock*
McMillan, Bruce. *Time to . . .*
Maestro, Betsy. *Around the clock with Harriet*
Mother Goose. *Hickory dickory dock*, ill. by Doug
    Cushman
    Hickory, dickory, dock, ill. by Suzanne Duranceau
    Hickory dickory dock, ill. by Marilyn Janovitz
    Hickory, dickory, dock, ill. by Moira Kemp
    The real Mother Goose clock book
Mueller, Virginia. *Monster goes to school*
Myers, Bernice. *The gold watch*
Pienkowski, Jan. *Time*
Richards, Kitty. *It's about time, Max!*
Slobodkin, Louis. *The late cuckoo*
Stanley, Diane. *Siegfried*
Steinmetz, Leon. *Clocks in the woods*
Thomas, Patricia. *The one and only, super-duper,
    golly-whopper, jim-dandy, really-handy clock-tock-
    stopper*
Thompson, Carol. *Time*
Verdet, Andre. *All about time*

Clothing

Alborough, Jez. *Clothesline*
Alda, Arlene. *Matthew and his dad*
Allen, Jonathan. *Purple sock, pink sock*
Allen, Robert. *Ten little babies count*
    Ten little babies dress
Andersen, H. C. (Hans Christian). *The emperor's
    new clothes*, ill. by Angela Barrett
    The emperor's new clothes, ill. by Erik Blegvad
    The emperor's new clothes, ill. by Virginia Lee Bur-
    ton
    The emperor's new clothes, ill. by Robert Byrd
    The emperor's new clothes, ill. by Jack and Irene
    Delano
    The emperor's new clothes, ill. by Hélène Des-
    puteaux
    The emperor's new clothes, ill. by Birte Dietz
    The emperor's new clothes, ill. by Dorothée Duntze
    The emperor's new clothes, ill. by Pamela Baldwin
    Ford
    The emperor's new clothes, ill. by Jack Kent
    The emperor's new clothes, ill. by Monika Laimgru-
    ber
    The emperor's new clothes, ill. by Anne F. Rockwell
    The emperor's new clothes, ill. by Janet Stevens
    The emperor's new clothes, ill. by Robert Van Nutt
    The emperor's new clothes, ill. by Nadine Bernard
    Westcott
Anglund, Joan Walsh. *The Emily book*
Apple, Margot. *Blanket*
Armstrong, Jennifer. *Pockets*
Arnold, Tedd. *Huggly gets dressed*
Asch, Frank. *Yellow, yellow*
Azaad, Meyer (Mahmud). *Half for you*
Babbitt, Lorraine. *Pink like the geranium*
Bailey, Debbie. *Clothes*
Barrett, Judi. *Animals should definitely not wear cloth-
    ing*
    Peter's pocket

Slobodkina, Esphyr. *Pezzo the peddler and the circus elephant*
    Pezzo the peddler and the thirteen silly thieves
Smith, Donald. *Who's wearing my bow tie?*
Spohn, Kate. *Clementine's winter wardrobe*
Stinson, Kathy. *The dressed up book*
Stoeke, Janet Morgan. *A hat for Minerva Louise*
Sutherland, Colleen. *Jason goes to show-and-tell*
Sutton, Jane. *What should a hippo wear?*
Szekeres, Cyndy. *The mouse that Jack built*
Thayer, Jane. *Gus was a gorgeous ghost*
Topek, Susan Remick. *A costume for Noah*
Townsend, Kenneth. *Felix, the bald-headed lion*
Tucker, Sian. *My clothes*
Tusa, Tricia. *Maebelle's suitcase*
Tyrrell, Anne. *Elizabeth Jane gets dressed*
Vulliamy, Clara. *Blue hat, red coat*
Watanabe, Shigeo. *How do I put it on?*
Weiss, Nicki. *The world turns round and round*
Wells, Rosemary. *Max's dragon shirt*
    Max's new suit
West, Colin. *I brought my love a tabby cat*
Wright, Jill. *The old woman and the Willy Nilly Man*
Yeoman, John. *Old Mother Hubbard's dog dresses up*
Yolen, Jane. *King Long Shanks*
Yorinks, Arthur. *Christmas in July*
Ziefert, Harriet. *Bear gets dressed*
    Clara Ann Cookie
    Let's get dressed!
Zion, Gene. *No roses for Harry*

Clothing – aprons

Brillhart, Julie. *Anna's goodbye apron*
Carle, Eric. *My apron*
McKissack, Patricia C. *Ma Dear's aprons*
Payne, Emmy. *Katy no-pocket*

Clothing – boots

Emerson, Scott. *The magic boots*
Havill, Juanita. *Jamaica and Brianna*
Lewison, Wendy Cheyette. *So many boots*
London, Jonathan. *Puddles*
Lowell, Susan. *The bootmaker and the elves*
MacKinnon, Debbie. *Billy's boots*
Morck, Irene. *Tyler's new boots*
Roche, Harriet. *Pete's puddles*

Clothing – coats

Bible. Old Testament. Joseph. *Joseph and his brothers*
De Paola, Tomie (Thomas Anthony). *Charlie needs a cloak*
Fagan, Cary. *Gogol's coat*
Garelick, May. *Just my size*
Hest, Amy. *The purple coat*
Kassirer, Sue. *Joseph and his coat of many colors*
Lacome, Julie. *Ruthie's big old coat*
Parton, Dolly. *Coat of many colors*
Pulver, Robin. *Mrs. Toggle's zipper*
Taback, Simms. *Joseph had a little overcoat*
Tafuri, Nancy. *One wet jacket*
Watson, Pauline. *The walking coat*
Williams, Marcia. *Joseph and his magnificent coat of many colors*
Wolff, Ferida. *The woodcutter's coat*
Woodruff, Elvira. *The memory coat*

Ziefert, Harriet. *A new coat for Anna*
Zinnemann-Hope, Pam. *Find your coat, Ned*

Clothing – costumes

Cousins, Lucy. *Maisy dresses up*
De Groat, Diane. *Trick or treat, smell my feet*
DeLage, Ida. *The old witch goes to the ball*
Ford, Miela. *My day in the garden*
Gauch, Patricia Lee. *Tanya and the magic wardrobe*
Geddes, Anne. *Shapes*
Gretz, Susanna. *Frog, duck, and rabbit*
Hasler, Eveline. *The giantess*
Kessler, Leonard P. *That's not Santa!*
London, Jonathan. *Froggy's Halloween*
McDonald, Megan. *Ant and Honey Bee*
Rockwell, Anne F. *Halloween day*
Saltzberg, Barney. *Soccer mom from outer space*
Wojciechowski, Susan. *The best Halloween of all*

Clothing – dresses

Daly, Niki. *Jamela's dress*
Dörrie, Doris. *Lottie's princess dress*
Jocelyn, Marthe. *Hannah and the seven dresses*
Munsch, Robert N. *Ribbon rescue*
Schweiger-Dmi'el, Itzhak. *Hanna's Sabbath dress*
Spalding, Andrea. *Sarah May and the new red dress*

Clothing – gloves, mittens

Bannon, Laura. *Red mittens*
Kay, Helen. *One mitten Lewis*
Kellogg, Steven (Stephen). *The mystery of the missing red mitten*
Kumin, Maxine W. *Mittens in May*
Rogers, Jean. *Runaway mittens*
Siomades, Lorianne. *Three little kittens*

Clothing – hats

Bailey, Debbie. *Hats*
Bancroft, Catherine. *Felix's hat*
Bannon, Laura. *Hat for a hero*
Barrett, Judi. *The wind thief*
Barrows, Marjorie Wescott. *The funny hat*
Blos, Joan W. *Martin's hats*
Bowden, Joan Chase. *A hat for the queen*
Boyd, Lizi. *Princess, cowboy, pirate, elf*
Carlson, Laurie M. *Boss of the plains*
Carrick, Malcolm. *The extraordinary hatmaker*
Chalmers, Mary. *A hat for Amy Jean*
Christelow, Eileen. *Olive and the magic hat*
Cousins, Lucy. *Portly's hat*
Demi. *Little bitty bunny*
Fisher, Leonard Everett. *A head full of hats*
Geringer, Laura. *A three hat day*
Gill, Madelaine. *The spring hat*
Grifalconi, Ann. *Tiny's hat*
Hindley, Judy. *Uncle Harold and the green hat*
Hiser, Berniece T. *The adventure of Charlie and his wheat-straw hat*
Holland, Isabelle. *Kevin's hat*
Howard, Elizabeth Fitzgerald. *Aunt Flossie's hats (and crab cakes later)*
Hürlimann, Ruth. *The mouse with the daisy hat*
Iwamura, Kazuo. *Tan Tan's hat*
Jaynes, Ruth M. *Benny's four hats*
Johnson, B. J. *A hat like that*

Johnston, Tony. *The witch's hat*
Kahn, Rosemary. *Grandma's hat*
Karon, Jan. *Miss Fannie's hat*
Keats, Ezra Jack. *Jennie's hat*
Keller, Holly. *Rosata*
Krisher, Trudy. *Kathy's hats*
Kroll, Steven. *Princess Abigail and the wonderful hat*
Landström, Olof. *Will's new cap*
Lattimore, Deborah Nourse. *The lady with the ship on her head*
Lear, Edward. *Of pelicans and pussycats*
  The quangle wangle's hat, ill. by Emma Crosby
  The quangle wangle's hat, ill. by Helen Oxenbury
  The quangle wangle's hat, ill. by Janet Stevens
  Two laughable lyrics
Leemis, Ralph. *Mister Momboo's hat*
Lexau, Joan M. *Who took the farmer's hat?*
Lowell, Susan. *Little Red Cowboy Hat*
Mayer, Mercer. *Two moral tales*
Milich, Melissa. *Miz Fannie Mae's fine new Easter hat*
Miller, Margaret. *What's on my head?*
  Whose hat?
Moore, Inga. *Fifty red night-caps*
Morris, Ann. *Hats, hats, hats*
Morris, Neil. *Where's my hat?*
Murphey, Sara. *The animal hat shop*
Parr, Letitia. *A man and his hat*
Pearson, Tracey Campbell. *The purple hat*
Reed, Lynn Rowe. *Pedro, his perro, and the alphabet sombrero*
Roche, Hannah. *Sandra's sun hat*
Roy, Ronald. *Whose hat is that?*
Ryder, Eileen. *Winston's new cap*
Scheller, Melanie. *My grandfather's hat*
Slobodkina, Esphyr. *Caps for sale*
Smath, Jerry. *A hat so simple*
Smith, Donald. *Who's wearing my baseball cap?*
Thayer, Jane. *The horse with the Easter bonnet*
Ungerer, Tomi. *The hat*
Van der Meer, Ron. *Funny hats*
Van Laan, Nancy. *This is the hat*
Walbrecker, Dirk. *Benny's hat*
Ward, Nanda Weedon. *The black sombrero*
Weedn, Flavia. *The magic cap*
Weiss, Harvey. *My closet full of hats*
Weninger, Brigitte. *The elf's hat*
Westerberg, Christine. *The cap that mother made*
Williams, Karen Lynn. *Tap-tap*
Wittmann, Patricia. *Go ask Giorgio!*
Ziefert, Harriet. *Hats off for the Fourth of July!*

Clothing – neckties

Cocca-Leffler, Maryann. *Mr. Tanen's ties*

Clothing – pajamas

De Paola, Tomie (Thomas Anthony). *Kit and Kat*
Jackson, Isaac. *Somebody's new pajamas*

Clothing – pants

Gerstein, Mordicai. *Stop those pants!*
Hissey, Jane. *Little Bear's trousers*
Kraus, Robert. *The king's trousers*
Raschka, Christopher. *Moosey Moose*
Rice, Eve. *Peter's pockets*
Uttley, Alison. *Sam Pig and the wind*

Clothing – shirts

Anderson, Leone Castell. *The wonderful shrinking shirt*
Gould, Deborah. *Aaron's shirt*
Rudolph, Marguerita. *How a shirt grew in the field*, ill. by Erika Weihs
  How a shirt grew in the field, ill. by Yaroslava

Clothing – shoes

Andersen, H. C. (Hans Christian). *The red shoes*
Bailey, Debbie. *Shoes*
Balzola, Asun. *Munia and the red shoes*
Banks, Kate (Katherine A.). *Peter and the talking shoes*
Berridge, Celia. *Hannah's new boots*
Blos, Joan W. *Hello, shoes!*
Bourgeois, Paulette. *Big Sarah's little boots*
Brenner, Barbara A. *Somebody's slippers, somebody's shoes*
Browne, Anthony. *Willy the wizard*
Calmenson, Stephanie. *One red shoe (the other's blue!)*
Cote, Nancy. *Flip-flops*
Cottle, Joan. *Emily's shoes*
Denton, Kady MacDonald. *Christmas boot*
Dixon, Ann. *The blueberry shoe*
Dornbusch, Erica. *Finding Kate's shoes*
Gay, Michel. *Little shoe*
Geeslin, Campbell. *How Nanita learned to make flan*
Hampshire, Susan. *Rosie's ballet slippers*
Harper, Jessica. *I forgot my shoes*
Heo, Yumi. *Father's rubber shoes*
Hughes, Shirley. *Two shoes, new shoes*
Hurwitz, Johanna. *New shoes for Silvia*
Johnson, Angela. *Shoes like Miss Alice's*
Komaiko, Leah. *Shoeshine Shirley*
Lawston, Lisa. *A pair of red sneakers*
LeRoy, Gen. *Billy's shoes*
Lunge-Larsen, Lise. *The legend of the lady slipper*
McKee, David. *King Rollo and the new shoes*
Matsuno, Masako. *A pair of red clogs*
Miller, Margaret. *Whose shoe?*
Morris, Ann. *Shoes, shoes, shoes*
Myers, Bernice. *The flying shoes*
Neidigh, Sherry. *Creatures at my feet*
Paul, Ann Whitford. *Hello toes! Hello feet!*
Pulver, Robin. *Mrs. Toggle's beautiful blue shoe*
Rice, Eve. *New blue shoes*
Riddell, Chris. *Bird's new shoes*
Rollings, Susan. *New shoes, red shoes*
Roy, Ronald. *Whose shoes are these?*
Smith, Donald. *Who's wearing my sneakers?*
Tafuri, Nancy. *Two new sneakers*
Uff, Caroline. *Hello, Lulu*
Vigna, Judith. *Boot weather*
Weiss, Leatie. *Funny feet!*
Wells, Ruth. *The farmer and the poor god*
Winthrop, Elizabeth. *Shoes*

Clothing – socks

Baird, Anne. *Baby socks*
Balian, Lorna. *The socksnatchers*
Daly, Niki. *Joseph's other red sock*
Glaser, Linda. *Keep your socks on, Albert!*
Mathews, Judith. *An egg and seven socks*
Murphy, Stuart J. *A pair of socks*

Selden, George. *Sparrow socks*

Clothing – sweaters

Diller, Harriett. *The faraway drawer*
Lunn, Janet Louise Swoboda. *Amos's sweater*

Clouds *see* Weather – clouds

Clowns, jesters

Adler, David A. *You think it's fun to be a clown!*
Allen, Jeffrey. *Bonzini! the tattooed man*
Amoit, Pierre. *Bijou, the little bear*
Anno, Mitsumasa. *Dr. Anno's magical midnight circus*
Austin, Margot. *Barney's adventure*
Barr, Cathrine. *Sammy seal ov the sircus*
Bradford, Ann. *The mystery of the midget clown*
Burningham, John. *Cannonball Simp*
Cole, Joanna. *The Clown-Arounds*
  The Clown-Arounds go on vacation
  The Clown-Arounds have a party
  Get well, Clown-Arounds!
  Sweet dreams, Clown-Arounds!
Coontz, Otto. *A real class clown*
Daly, Niki. *Bravo, Zan Angelo!*
Damjan, Mischa. *The clown said no*
Dedieu, Thierry. *Baby clown*
De Paola, Tomie (Thomas Anthony). *Jingle, the Christmas clown*
  Sing, Pierrot, sing
Douglass, Barbara. *The chocolate chip cookie contest*
Drescher, Henrik. *Klutz*
Faulkner, Nancy. *Small clown*
Fazzi, Maura. *The circus of mystery*
Freeman, Don. *Forever laughter*
Garland, Michael. *Circus girl*
Harris, Steven Michael. *This is my trunk*
Krahn, Fernando. *A funny friend from heaven*
Lacome, Julie. *Funny business*
Lent, Blair. *Pistachio*
Lobel, Anita. *Pierrot's ABC garden*
Long, Kathy. *Hallelujah the clown*
Lynn, Sara. *Colors*
McGuire, Richard. *What's wrong with this book?*
Marceau, Marcel. *The story of Bip*
Mendoza, George. *The Marcel Marceau counting book*
Miller, M. L. *Dizzy from fools*
Olds, Elizabeth. *Plop plop ploppie*
Pellowski, Michael. *Clara joins the circus*
Petersham, Maud. *The circus baby*
Politi, Leo. *Lito and the clown*
Prater, John. *The greatest show on earth*
Quackenbush, Robert M. *The man on the flying trapeze*
Rascal. *Oregon's journey*
Richardson, Jean. *Tall inside*
Rockwell, Anne F. *Gogo's pay day*
Saltzman, David. *The jester has lost his jingle*
Schreiber, Georges. *Bambino goes home*
  Bambino the clown
Shecter, Ben. *Hester the jester*
Slocum, Rosalie. *Breakfast with the clowns*
Sobol, Harriet Langsam. *Clowns*
Thurber, James. *Many moons*, ill. by Marc Simont
  Many moons, ill. by Louis Slobodkin

Clubs, gangs

Alexander, Sue. *Seymour the prince*
Berenstain, Stan. *The Berenstain bears no girls allowed*
Bourgeois, Paulette. *Franklin's secret club*
Bradford, Ann. *The mystery at Misty Falls*
  The mystery in the secret club house
  The mystery of the blind writer
  The mystery of the midget clown
  The mystery of the missing dogs
  The mystery of the square footsteps
  The mystery of the tree house
Christian, Mary Blount. *The green thumb thief*
Collicott, Sharleen. *Toestomper and the caterpillars*
Crowley, Michael. *New kid on Spurwick Ave.*
  Shack and back
Hoffman, Mary. *Henry's baby*
Howe, James. *Horace and Morris but mostly Dolores*
Jackson, Ellen B. *Monsters in my mailbox*
Johnson-Petrov, Arden. *The Lost Tooth Club*
Kotzwinkle, William. *The day the gang got rich*
Leedy, Loreen. *The monster money book*
McCourt, Lisa. *Chicken soup for little souls: The Goodness Gorillas*
Stanley, Diane. *The conversation club*
Thaler, Mike. *Pack 109*
Winthrop, Elizabeth. *The Best Friends Club*

Clumsiness *see* Character traits – clumsiness

Coaches *see* Careers – coaches

Coats *see* Clothing – coats

Cockatoos *see* Birds – cockatoos

Cockroaches *see* Insects – cockroaches

Codes *see* Secret codes

Cold *see* Concepts – cold and heat; Illness – cold (disease); Weather – cold

Cold and heat *see* Concepts – cold and heat

Cold (disease) *see* Illness – cold (disease)

Collecting things *see* Behavior – collecting things

Colombia *see* Foreign lands – Colombia

Color *see* Concepts – color

Columbus Day *see* Holidays – Columbus Day

Comanche Indians *see* Indians of North America – Comanche

Communication

Allington, Richard L. *Talking Words*
Ancona, George. *Handtalk zoo*
Arnold, Caroline. *How do we communicate?*

Bohdal, Susi. *Tom cat*
Borchers, Elisabeth. *Dear Sarah*
Brown, Margaret Wise. *The big fur secret*
Buchheimer, Naomi. *Let's go to a post office*
Charlip, Remy. *Handtalk*
Chukovskii, Kornei Ivanovich. *The telephone*
Clifford, Eth. *A bear before breakfast*
Coleman, Evelyn. *The glass bottle tree*
Dewey, Jennifer Owings. *Stories on stone*
Dorros, Arthur. *Radio Man/Don Radio*
Elbling, Peter. *Aria*
Emberley, Ed (Edward Randolph). *Green says go*
Engdahl, Sylvia. *Our world is earth*
Ets, Marie Hall. *Talking without words*
Fisher, Leonard Everett. *Gutenberg*
Gibbons, Gail. *The post office book*
　Puff - flash - bang!
Goor, Ron. *Signs*
Hirschi, Ron. *A time for singing*
Hoban, Tana. *I read signs*
　I read symbols
Hughes, Shirley. *Chatting*
Joslin, Sesyle. *Dear dragon*
Klove, Lars. *I see a sign*
Lachner, Dorothea. *Andrew's angry words*
Leedy, Loreen. *The Furry News*
LoMonaco, Palmyra. *Night letters*
Potter, Beatrix. *Yours affectionately, Peter Rabbit*
Seuss, Dr. *Gerald McBoing Boing*
Showers, Paul. *How you talk*
Stanley, Diane. *The conversation club*
Telephones
Tolkien, J. R. R. (John Ronald Reuel). *The Father Christmas letters*
Van Woerkom, Dorothy. *Hidden messages*
Walton, Rick. *My two hands, my two feet*
Wheeler, Cindy. *More simple signs*
　Simple signs

Communities, neighborhoods

Ahlberg, Allan. *Mr. Buzz the beeman*
Ancona, George. *Barrio*
Appelt, Kathi. *A red wagon year*
Arnold, Caroline. *What is a community?*
　Where do you go to school?
　Who works here?
Arnold, Tedd. *The simple people*
Baggette, Susan K. *Jonathan goes to the grocery store*
　Jonathan goes to the library
Bailey, Debbie. *The playground*
Barber, Barbara E. *Saturday at the new you*
Bartone, Elisa. *American, too*
Berridge, Celia. *On my street*
Blakeley, Peggy. *Two little ducks*
Bourgeois, Paulette. *Fire fighters*
　Garbage collectors
　Police officers
　Postal workers
Brisson, Pat. *Wanda's roses*
Brown, Marc Tolon. *Arthur's neighborhood*
Bunting, Eve (Anne Evelyn). *Smoky night*
Crowley, Michael. *New kid on Spurwick Ave.*
Denslow, Sharon Phillips. *Hazel's circle*
DiSalvo-Ryan, DyAnne. *City green*
Dooley, Norah. *Everybody bakes bread*
Dowling, Paul. *Where are you going, Jimmy?*
Duke, Kate. *If you walk down this road*
Dupasquier, Philippe. *A busy day at the garage*

Edwards, Michelle. *Chicken Man*
Flanagan, Alice K. *Coach John and his soccer team*
　Here comes Mr. Eventoff with the mail!
　Ms. Murphy fights fires
　Officer Brown keeps neighborhoods safe
　Riding the school bus with Mrs. Kramer
　A visit to the Gravesens' farm
Freeman, Don. *Corduroy's busy street and Corduroy goes to the doctor*
Gackenbach, Dick. *Claude has a picnic*
Gauch, Patricia Lee. *Christina Katerina and Fats and the Great Neighborhood War*
Geisert, Bonnie. *Prairie town*
Gray, Libba Moore. *Miss Tizzy*
Greenfield, Eloise. *Night on Neighborhood Street*
Grejniec, Michael. *Look*
　Who is my neighbor?
Groner, Judyth Saypol. *My very own Jewish community*
Hartmann, Wendy. *All the magic in the world*
Haskins, Francine. *I remember "121"*
Helldorfer, M. C. (Mary Claire). *Silver Rain Brown*
Henkes, Kevin. *Good-bye, Curtis*
　Once around the block
Henwood, Simon. *The troubled village*
Heo, Yumi. *One afternoon*
Hest, Amy. *How to get famous in Brooklyn*
Hubbell, Patricia. *Sidewalk trip*
Hughes, Shirley. *Chatting*
Isadora, Rachel. *Over the green hills*
Jennings, Linda M. *Franklin's neighborhood*
Komaiko, Leah. *My perfect neighborhood*
Krensky, Stephen. *My teacher's secret life*
Lakin, Pat (Patricia). *Aware and alert*
　Information, please
　Red letter day
Leedy, Loreen. *The Furry News*
Lewison, Wendy Cheyette. *A trip to the firehouse*
Liebman, Daniel. *I want to be a firefighter*
　I want to be a police officer
Loomis, Christine. *At the laundromat*
　At the mall
Low, William. *Chinatown*
Martin, Jacqueline Briggs. *The green truck garden giveaway*
Medearis, Angela Shelf. *Rum-a-tum-tum*
Merriam, Eve. *On my street*
Miller, Margaret. *On my street*
Modarressi, Mitra. *Yard sale*
Modesitt, Jeanne. *Vegetable soup*
Nolan, Lucy A. *The Lizard Man of Crabtree County*
Novak, Matt. *The Robobots*
Pedersen, Judy. *When night time comes near*
Pinkney, J. Brian. *The adventures of sparrowboy*
Pittman, Helena Clare. *The angel tree*
Ratz de Tagyos, Paul. *A coney tale*
Robinson, Aminah Brenda Lynn. *A street called home*
Rogers, Fred. *Moving*
Rosen, Michael (1946-). *A Thanksgiving wish*
Russo, Marisabina. *Mama talks too much*
Scheffler, Ursel. *Stop your crowing, Kasimir!*
Smalls-Hector, Irene. *Irene and the big, fine nickel*
　Jonathan and his mommy
Smith, Barry. *Cumberland Road*
Spinelli, Eileen. *Somebody loves you, Mr. Hatch*
Swope, Sam. *The Araboolies of Liberty Street*
Tamar, Erika. *The garden of happiness*
Taulbert, Clifton L. *Little Cliff and the porch people*

Ward, Sally G. *What goes around comes around*
Wyeth, Sharon Dennis. *Something beautiful*
Yeoman, John. *Our village*
Yoaker, Harry. *The view*
Yolen, Jane. *Raising Yoder's barn*
Zarin, Cynthia. *Rose and Sebastian*

Competition *see* Sibling rivalry

Completing things *see* Character traits – completing things

Composers *see* Careers – composers

Compromising *see* Character traits – compromising

Computers

Baker, Eugene H. *I want to be a computer operator*
Brown, Marc Tolon. *Arthur's computer disaster*
Carrick, Carol. *Patrick's dinosaurs on the Internet*
D'Ignazio, Fred. *Katie and the computer*
Greene, Carol. *A computer went a-courting*
Lyon, David. *The brave little computer*
Matthias, Catherine. *I can be a computer operator*
Modell, Frank. *Skeeter and the computer*
Ross, Dave (David). *Space Monster Gorp and the runaway computer*
Skulavik, Mary Alys. *Bert*
Steadman, Ralph. *The little red computer*

Conceit *see* Character traits – conceit

Concepts

Ahlberg, Allan. *Big bad pig*
   Fee fi fo fum
   Happy worm
   Help!
Albert, Burton. *Mine, yours, ours*
Allen, Judy. *What is a wall, after all?*
Anholt, Catherine. *One, two, three, count with me*
Anno, Mitsumasa. *Anno's math games*
   Anno's math games II
   Anno's math games III
Arvetis, Chris. *Why is it dark?*
Balestrino, Philip. *Hot as an ice cube*
Bauman, A. F. *Guess where you're going, guess what you'll do*
Beisner, Monika. *Topsy turvy*
Berenstain, Stan. *Inside outside upside down*
Berkley, Ethel S. *Ups and down*
Blackstone, Stella. *Baby high, baby low*
Blos, Joan W. *Hello, shoes!*
Bodger, Joan. *Belinda's ball*
Booth, Eugene. *At the circus*
   At the fair
   In the air
   In the garden
   In the jungle
   Under the ocean
Borten, Helen. *Do you see what I see?*
Brown, Marcia. *Touch will tell*
   Walk with your eyes
Browne, Philippa-Alys. *A gaggle of geese*
Browner, Richard. *Look again!*
Bruna, Dick. *Dick Bruna's picture word book*

Bulloch, Ivan. *Patterns*
Burningham, John. *First steps*
Carle, Eric. *My very first book of motion*
Charosh, Mannis. *Number ideas through pictures*
Chase, Catherine. *Hot and cold*
Corey, Dorothy. *You go away*
Cousins, Lucy. *Katy Cat and Beaky Boo*
Crews, Donald. *Light*
   We read
Cushman, Doug. *Nasty Kyle the crocodile*
Dantzer-Rosenthal, Marya. *Some things are different, some things are the same*
Davis, Lee. *The lifesize animal opposites book*
Duke, Kate. *Guinea pigs far and near*
   What bounces?
Emberley, Ed (Edward Randolph). *Ed Emberley's amazing look through book*
Fisher, Leonard Everett. *Boxes! Boxes!*
Freudberg, Judy. *Some, more, most*
Froman, Robert. *Angles are easy as pie*
   A game of functions
Garland, Sarah. *All gone!*
Gillham, Bill. *Where does it go?*
Gomi, Taro. *Guess what?*
Green, Mary McBurney. *Is it hard? Is it easy?*
Greene, Laura. *Change*
Greenway, Shirley. *Two's company . . .*
Griest, Virginia. *In between*
Hartman, Gail. *For sand castles or seashells*
   For strawberry jam or fireflies
Hayward, Linda. *Wet foot, dry foot, low foot, high foot*
Heide, Florence Parry. *The bigness contest*
Heller, Nicholas. *Ten old pails*
Hennessy, B. G. (Barbara G.). *A, B, C, D, tummy, toes, hands, knee*
Hoban, Tana. *All about where*
   Black on white
   Dots, spots, speckles, and stripes
   Is it rough? Is it smooth? Is it shiny?
   Look! Look! Look!
   More, fewer, less
   Over, under and through
   Take another look
   White on black
Hughes, Shirley. *Lucy and Tom's 1, 2, 3*
Jenkins, Steve. *Biggest, strongest, fastest*
Jensen, Virginia Allen. *What's that?*
Johnson, Ryerson. *Upstairs and downstairs*
Johnson, Stephen T. *Alphabet city*
Jonas, Ann. *Reflections*
Klove, Lars. *I see a sign*
Kulman, Andrew. *Red light stop, green light go*
Kuskin, Karla. *All sizes of noises*
Lember, Barbara Hirsch. *A book of fruit*
Leonard, Marcia. *Spots*
Lewis, Zoe. *Disney's Beauty and the beast teacup mix-up*
Lopshire, Robert. *The biggest, smallest, fastest, tallest things you've ever heard of*
McMillan, Bruce. *Becca backward, Becca forward*
   Dry or wet?
   One, two, one pair!
   Sense suspense
Maestro, Betsy. *Temperature and you*
   Where is my friend?
Magnus, Erica. *Around me*
Marzollo, Jean. *I love you*
Matthias, Catherine. *Arriba y abajo*
Matthiesen, Thomas. *Things to see*

Mayer, Mercer. *Mine!*
Mazer, Anne. *The yellow button*
Murphy, Stuart J. *The greatest gymnast of all*
  Missing mittens
Once I was . . .
Pelletier, David. *The graphic alphabet*
Peppé, Rodney. *Odd one out*
  Rodney Peppé's puzzle book
Pluckrose, Henry Arthur. *Beginnings and endings*
Pragoff, Fiona. *Let's find Teddy*
  Odd one out
Rahn, Joan Elma. *Holes*
Rockwell, Anne F. *What we like*
Ruben, Patricia. *True or false?*
Scarry, Richard. *Richard Scarry's best first book ever!*
Schwartz, David M. *If you hopped like a frog*
Sesame Street. *The Sesame Street book of people and
  things*
Seuss, Dr. *Gerald McBoing Boing*
Shannon, George. *Tomorrow's alphabet*
Sis, Peter. *Beach ball*
Supraner, Robyn. *Giggly-wiggly, snickety-snick*
Swinburne, Stephen R. *What's a pair? What's a
  dozen?*
Tompert, Ann. *Just a little bit*
Wallner, John C. *Look and find*
Webb, Angela. *Talkabout light*
  Talkabout reflections
  Talkabout sound
Wood, A. J. *Look! The ultimate spot-the-difference book*
Yektai, Niki. *Bears in pairs*
Zaslavsky, Claudia. *Zero! Is it something? Is it noth-
  ing?*
Ziefert, Harriet. *My getting-ready-for-school book*
  Rabbit and Hare divide an apple

Concepts – cold and heat

McAllister, Angela. *The ice palace*

Concepts – color

Abisch, Roz. *Open your eyes*
Adoff, Arnold. *Greens*
Allamand, Pascale. *The animals who changed their
  colors*
Allen, Jonathan. *Purple sock, pink sock*
Allen, Robert. *Ten little babies play*
Allington, Richard L. *Colors*
Anholt, Catherine. *Tom's rainbow walk*
Arnold, Tedd. *Colors*
Asch, Frank. *Yellow, yellow*
Baby's first book of colors
Baker, Alan. *Benjamin's portrait*
  White Rabbit's color book
Barasch, Lynne. *A winter walk*
Bassède, Francine. *George paints his house*
Berger, Judith. *Butterflies and rainbows*
Bond, Michael. *Paddington's colors*
Boyd, Lizi. *Black dog red house*
Bradman, Tony. *The bad babies' book of colors*
Brenner, Barbara A. *The color wizard*
Briggs, Raymond. *The snowman, a lift-the-flap board
  book*
Bright, Robert. *I like red*
Brophy, Nannette. *The color of my fur*
Brown, Margaret Wise. *Afro-bets*
  Red light, green light
Bruna, Dick. *My shirt is white*

Brunhoff, Laurent de. *Babar's book of color*
Burningham, John. *First steps*
  John Burningham's colors
Burton, Katherine. *One gray mouse*
Campbell, Ann. *Let's find out about color*
Can you see the red balloon?
Carle, Eric. *Hello, red fox*
  The mixed-up chameleon
  My very first book of colors
Carroll, Kathleen Sullivan. *One red rooster*
Charles, N. N. *What am I? Looking through shapes at
  apples and grapes*
Charlip, Remy. *Harlequin and the gift of many colors*
Chermayeff, Ivan. *Tomato and other colors*
Chocolate, Deborah M. Newton. *Kente colors*
Clifford, Eth. *Red is never a mouse*
Cousins, Lucy. *Maisy's colors*
Deeter, Catherine. *Seymour Bleu*
De Paola, Paula. *Rosie and the yellow ribbon*
Dines, Glen. *Pitadoe, the color maker*
Dodds, Dayle Ann. *The color box*
Dunbar, Joyce. *Indigo and the whale*
Dunham, Meredith. *Colors*
Duvoisin, Roger Antoine. *The house of four seasons*
  See what I am
Ehlert, Lois. *Color farm*
  Color zoo
  Fish eyes
Emberley, Ed (Edward Randolph). *Green says go*
Ernst, Lisa Campbell. *A colorful adventure of the bee
  who left home one Monday morning and what he
  found along the way*
Falwell, Cathryn. *Nicky's walk*
Feeney, Stephanie. *Hawaii is a rainbow*
Field, Susan. *The sun, the moon, and the silver baboon*
Fisher, Leonard Everett. *Boxes! Boxes!*
Fleming, Denise. *Lunch*
Flora. *Feathers like a rainbow*
Fosberg, John. *Ice cream colors*
Fowler, Allan. *Hard-to-see animals*
Freeman, Don. *The chalk box story*
  A rainbow of my own
French, Vivian. *Oh no, Anna!*
Garland, Sarah. *Seeing red*
Garne, S. T. *By a blazing blue sea*
Giffard, Hannah. *Red bus*
Gillham, Bill. *Let's look for colors*
Ginsburg, Mirra. *Three kittens*
Godwin, Laura. *Little white dog*
Goennel, Heidi. *Colors*
Goffstein, M. B. (Marilyn Brooke). *Artists' helpers
  enjoy the evening*
Gold-Vukson, Marji. *The colors of my Jewish Year*
Graff, Nancy Price. *In the hush of the evening*
Graham, Amanda. *Picasso, the green tree frog*
Graham, Bob. *The red woolen blanket*
Greeley, Valerie. *White is the moon*
Greenway, Shirley. *Color me bright*
Groening, Maggie. *Maggie Simpson's book of colors
  and shapes*
Gundersheimer, Karen. *Colors to know*
Haring, Keith. *Big*
Haskins, Ilma. *Color seems*
Heller, Ruth. *Color, color, color, color*
Hest, Amy. *The purple coat*
Hill, Eric. *Spot looks at colors*
  *Spot's big book of colors, shapes and numbers; El libro
  grande de Spot*
  Spot's big book of colours, shapes, and numbers

Wood, Jakki. *Moo moo, brown cow*
Yates, Irene. *All about color*
Yee, Patrick. *Rosie Rabbit's colors*
Youldon, Gillian. *Colors*
Young, James. *A million chameleons*
Youngs, Betty. *Pink pigs in mud*
Zacharias, Thomas. *But where is the green parrot?*
Ziefert, Harriet. *No more! Piggety Pig*
Zolotow, Charlotte (Shapiro). *Mr. Rabbit and the lovely present*

Concepts – counting *see* Counting, numbers

Concepts – distance

Axelrod, Amy. *Pigs on the move*
Giuliano, Katie. *All the way to God*
Rosen, Sidney. *How far is a star?*
Tresselt, Alvin R. *How far is far?*

Concepts – in and out

Banchek, Linda. *Snake in, snake out*
Daughtry, Duanne. *What's inside?*
Duerrstein, Richard. *In . . . out*
Matthias, Catherine. *Sal y entra*
Ueno, Noriko. *Elephant buttons*

Concepts – left and right

Chase, Catherine. *Feet*
McMillan, Bruce. *Beach ball - left, right*
Oppenheim, Joanne. *Left and right*
Rehm, Karl. *Left or right?*
Stanek, Muriel. *Left, right, left, right!*

Concepts – measurement

Adler, David A. *3D, 2D, 1D*
Allington, Richard L. *Measuring*
Axelrod, Amy. *Pigs on the move*
Branley, Franklyn M. (Mansfield). *How little and how much*
Dunbar, James. *Tick-tock*
Enderle, Judith (Ann) Ross. *What would Mama do?*
Ganeri, Anita. *The longest and tallest*
Hightower, Susan. *Twelve snails to one lizard*
Lionni, Leo. *Inch by inch*
Myller, Rolf. *How big is a foot?*
Thompson, Brenda. *The winds that blow*

Concepts – opposites

Ahlberg, Allan. *Big bad pig*
　Fee fi fo fum
　Happy worm
Allen, Jeffrey. *Up the steps, down the slide*
Allington, Richard L. *Opposites*
Anglund, Joan Walsh. *Emily and Adam book of opposites*
Anholt, Catherine. *Good days, bad days*
Arnold, Tedd. *Opposites*
Asch, Frank. *Short train, long train*
Banchek, Linda. *Snake in, snake out*
Barrett, Judi. *I'm too small, you're too big*
Blackstone, Stella. *Baby high, baby low*
Blake, Quentin. *Simpkin*
Bond, Michael. *Paddington's opposites*
Boynton, Sandra. *Opposites*

Burningham, John. *First steps*
Butterworth, Nick. *Nice or nasty*
Crews, Nina. *A high, low, near, far, loud, quiet story*
Crowther, Robert. *The most amazing hide-and-seek opposites book*
Demi. *Demi's opposites*
Dijs, Carla. *Big and small*
Fujita, Miho. *The little choo-choo*
Giffard, Hannah. *Fast car*
Gillham, Bill. *Let's look for opposites*
　What's the difference?
Grejniec, Michael. *Good morning, good night*
Harris, Pamela. *Hot, cold, shy, bold*
Hill, Eric. *Spot looks at opposites*
Hillman, Priscilla. *The Merry-Mouse book of opposites*
Hoban, Tana. *Exactly the opposite*
　Push-pull, empty-full
Hughes, Shirley. *Bathwater's hot*
Inkpen, Mick. *Kipper's book of opposites*
Karn, George. *Circus big and small*
Kightley, Rosalinda. *Opposites*
King, Stephen Michael. *Henry and Amy (right-way-round and upside down)*
Koch, Michelle. *By the sea*
Lankford, Mary D. *Is it dark? Is it light?*
Leonard, Marcia. *The kitten twins*
　The opposite of stop is go
Lippman, Peter. *Peter Lippman's opposites*
Maccarone, Grace. *Pumpkin faces*
McKissack, Patricia C. *Big bug book of opposites*
McLenighan, Valjean. *Stop-go, fast-slow*
McMillan, Bruce. *Becca backward, Becca forward*
　Here a chick, there a chick
McNaughton, Colin. *At home*
　At playschool
　At the park
　At the party
　At the stores
Maestro, Betsy. *Traffic*
Matthias, Catherine. *Over-under*
Mendoza, George. *The Sesame Street book of opposites with Zero Mostel*
Milios, Rita. *Yo soy = I am*
Miller, Margaret. *Big and little*
　Playtime
Minters, Frances. *Too big, too small, just right*
Murphy, Chuck. *Black cat, white cat*
Oliver, Stephen. *Opposites*
Pragoff, Fiona. *Opposites*
Provensen, Alice. *Karen's opposites*
Serfozo, Mary. *What's what?*
Shirotani, Hideo. *Opposites*
Spier, Peter. *Fast-slow, high-low*
Stevenson, James. *Fun, no fun*
Stickland, Paul. *Dinosaur roar!*
Swinburne, Stephen R. *What's opposite?*
Tullet, Hervé. *Night / day*
Wagner, Karen. *A friend like Ed*
Watson, Carol. *Opposites*
Wilbur, Richard. *Runaway opposites*
Wildsmith, Brian. *What the moon saw*
Yee, Patrick. *Rosie Rabbit's opposites*
Young, Ruth. *Daisy's taxi*
Ziefert, Harriet. *Let's go! Piggety Pig*

Concepts – perspective

Adler, David A. *3D, 2D, 1D*
Cohen, Caron Lee. *Pigeon, pigeon*

Where's the fly?
Davies, Kay. *My balloon*
  My mirror
Gore, Sheila. *My shadow*
Hutchins, Pat. *Shrinking mouse*
Mainwaring, Jane. *My feather*
Rotner, Shelley. *Close, closer, closest*
Titherington, Jeanne. *Big world, small world*
Wakefield, Joyce. *From where you are*
Yolen, Jane. *All those secrets of the world*

Concepts – self *see* Self-concept

Concepts – shape

Adler, David A. *3D, 2D, 1D*
Allen, Robert. *Round and square*
Allington, Richard L. *Shapes*
Anderson, Janet S. *Sunflower Sal*
Anno, Mitsumasa. *Anno's faces*
Atwood, Ann. *The little circle*
Axelrod, Amy. *Pigs on the ball*
Baker, Alan. *Brown Rabbit's shape book*
Barner, Bob. *Space race*
Baum, Susan. *City shapes*
Berenstain, Stan. *Old hat, new hat*
Bishop, Roma. *Shapes*
Blackstone, Stella. *Bear in a square*
Brown, Marcia. *Listen to a shape*
Brown, Margaret Wise. *Afro-bets*
  The little fireman
Budney, Blossom. *A kiss is round*
Bulloch, Ivan. *Patterns*
Carle, Eric. *Little cloud*
  Little cloud, a board book
  My very first book of shapes
Charles, N. N. *What am I? Looking through shapes at apples and grapes*
Charosh, Mannis. *The ellipse*
Coxe, Molly. *6 sticks*
Craig, M. Jean. *Boxes*
Crews, Donald. *Ten black dots*
De Mejo, Oscar. *La Bella Magellona and the little cavalier*
Dodds, Dayle Ann. *The shape of things*
Dotlich, Rebecca Kai. *What is round?*
  What is square?
Dunbar, Fiona. *You'll never guess!*
Dunham, Meredith. *Shapes*
Ehlert, Lois. *Color farm*
  Color zoo
Engel, Diana. *Circle song*
Esbensen, Barbara Juster. *Echoes for the eye*
Falwell, Cathryn. *Clowning around*
  Shape space
Feldman, Judy. *Shapes in nature*
Fisher, Leonard Everett. *Look around!*
Fosberg, John. *Cookie shapes*
Fowler, Allan. *What do you see in a cloud?*
Friskey, Margaret (Margaret Richards). *Three sides and the round one*
Gardner, Beau. *Guess what?*
  What is it?
Geddes, Anne. *Shapes*
Gerstein, Mordicai. *The gigantic baby*
Gillham, Bill. *Let's look for shapes*
Godwin, Laura. *Little white dog*
Goldblatt, Eli. *Leo loves round*
Gomi, Taro. *The big book of boxes*

Groening, Maggie. *Maggie Simpson's book of colors and shapes*
Gundersheimer, Karen. *Shapes to show*
Hatcher, Charles. *What shape is it?*
Hefter, Richard. *The strawberry book of shapes*
Heinst, Marie. *My first number book*
Henkes, Kevin. *The biggest boy*
  Circle dogs
Hill, Eric. *Spot looks at shapes*
  Spot's big book of colors, shapes and numbers; El libro grande de Spot
  Spot's big book of colours, shapes, and numbers
Hindley, Judy. *Ten bright eyes*
  The wheeling and whirling-around book
Hoban, Tana. *Circles, triangles, and squares*
  Dots, spots, speckles, and stripes
  Is it red? Is it yellow? Is it blue?
  Round and round and round
  Shapes and things
  Shapes, shapes, shapes
  So many circles, so many squares
  Spirals, curves, fanshapes and lines
Hughes, Peter. *The emperor's oblong pancake*
Hughes, Shirley. *All shapes and sizes*
Jensen, Virginia Allen. *Catching*
Joyce, William. *Rolie Polie Olie*
Kightley, Rosalinda. *Shapes*
Kimmel, Eric A. *Ten suns*
Lacome, Julie. *Funny business*
Lionni, Leo. *Pezzettino*
Lopshire, Robert. *New tricks I can do!*
MacDonald, Suse. *Sea shapes*
MacKinnon, Debbie. *Eye spy shapes*
  What shape?
McMillan, Bruce. *Fire engine shapes*
Maisner, Heather. *Planet monster*
Mayer, Marianna. *The Brambleberrys animal book of big and small shapes*
Murphy, Stuart J. *Captain Invincible and the space shapes*
  Circus shapes
Newth, Philip. *Roly goes exploring*
Oliver, Stephen. *My first look at shapes*
Parker, Steve. *I wonder why tunnels are round*
Pienkowski, Jan. *Shapes*
Pilegard, Virginia Walton. *The warlord's puzzle*
Pluckrose, Henry Arthur. *Shape*
Podendorf, Illa. *Shapes, sides, curves and corners*
Poydar, Nancy. *Cool Ali*
Pragoff, Fiona. *Shapes*
Priddy, Roger. *Baby's book of nature*
Radunsky, Eugenia. *Square, triangle, round, skinny*
Reiss, John J. *Shapes*
Reit, Seymour. *Round things everywhere*
Roberts, Cliff. *The dot*
  Start with a dot
Rogers, Paul (Patrick). *The shapes game*
Salazar, Violet. *Squares are not bad*
Santoro, Christopher. *Book of shapes*
Schlein, Miriam. *Shapes*
Serfozo, Mary. *There's a square*
Sesame Street. *The Sesame Street book of shapes*
Seuss, Dr. *The shape of me and other stuff*
Shapes
Shapiro, Arnold L. *Circle*
  Square
  Triangles
Shaw, Charles Green. *It looked like spilt milk*
Silverman, Maida. *Mouse's shape book*

Silverstein, Shel. *The missing piece*
Smith, Mavis. *Circles*
Smith-Moore, J. J. *Sally Small*
Stoddard, Sandol. *Curl up small*
Tafuri, Nancy. *The brass ring*
Testa, Fulvio. *If you look around*
Thong, Roseanne. *Round is a mooncake*
Turner, Gwenda. *Shapes*
Van Fleet, Matthew. *Fuzzy yellow ducklings*
  Spotted yellow frogs
Wallwork, Amanda. *Find the fish that looks like this*
Watson, Carol. *Shapes*
Wells, Tony. *Allsorts*
Wildsmith, Brian. *Animal shapes*
  Brian Wildsmith 1 2 3
Wilson, April. *April Wilson's magpie magic*
Yates, Irene. *All about pattern*
  All about shape
Yee, Patrick. *Rosie Rabbit's shapes*
Youldon, Gillian. *Shapes*
Zimmermann, H. Werner (Heinz Werner).
  Alphonse knows . . . a circle is not a Valentine
Zwetchkenbaum, G. *The Peanuts shape circus puzzle
  book*

Concepts – size

Alborough, Jez. *Watch out! Big Bro's coming!*
Alexander, Martha G. *Blackboard Bear*
Allen, Jonathan. *Big owl, little towel*
Allington, Richard L. *Shapes*
Anderson, Janet S. *Sunflower Sal*
Anno, Mitsumasa. *The king's flower*
Aulaire, Ingri Mortenson d'. *Too big*
Balian, Lorna. *Where in the world is Henry?*
Barrett, Judi. *I hate to take a bath*
Benson, Patrick. *Little penguin*
Berenstain, Stan. *Old hat, new hat*
Black, Irma (Simonton). *Big puppy and little puppy*
Blackstone, Stella. *Bear in a square*
Blue, Rose. *How many blocks is the world?*
Bowman, Peter. *I wish I were big*
Brown, Marcia. *Once a mouse . . .*
Brown, Margaret Wise. *Big dog, little dog*
  Bumble bugs and elephants
  The little fireman
Bulette, Sara. *The splendid belt of Mr. Big*
Cantieni, Benita. *Little Elephant and Big Mouse*
Chalmers, Audrey. *Hector and Mr. Murfit*
Cole, Babette. *The trouble with grandad*
Cole, Joanna. *Big Goof and Little Goof*
Cooke, Trish. *When I grow bigger*
Craig, M. Jean. *Boxes*
Croswell, Volney. *How to hide a hippopotamus*
Cuneo, Mary Louise. *What can a giant do?*
Cuyler, Margery. *The biggest, best snowman*
Damjan, Mischa. *The big squirrel and the little rhinoc-
  eros*
De Mejo, Oscar. *La Bella Magellona and the little cav-
  alier*
Donohue, Dorothy. *Big and little on the farm*
Du Quette, Keith. *Hotel Animal*
Facklam, Margery. *The big bug book*
Finzel, Julia. *Large as life*
French, Fiona. *Little Inchkin*
French, Vivian. *Molly in the middle*
Gackenbach, Dick. *Tiny for a day*
Gerstein, Mordicai. *The gigantic baby*
Gliori, Debi. *When I'm big*

Gray, Nigel. *Pigs can't fly*
Green-Armytage, Stephen. *Dudley, the little terrier
  that could*
Greenway, Shirley. *How big am I?*
Grindley, Sally. *Too big bear*
Haring, Keith. *Big*
Hellings, Colette. *Too little, too big*
Henkes, Kevin. *The biggest boy*
Herman, R. A. (Ronnie Ann). *Pal the pony*
Hindley, Judy. *Little and big*
Hoban, Tana. *Big ones, little ones*
  Is it larger? Is it smaller?
  Is it red? Is it yellow? Is it blue?
  Spirals, curves, fanshapes and lines
Hughes, Shirley. *All shapes and sizes*
Hutchins, Pat. *Shrinking mouse*
  Titch
Ipcar, Dahlov. *The biggest fish in the sea*
  The land of flowers
Iwamura, Kazuo. *Ton and Pon*
Jenkins, Steve. *Big and little*
Jensen, Patricia. *Be patient, Little Chick*
Jonell, Lynne. *Mommy go away!*
Joyce, William. *George shrinks*
Kalan, Robert. *Blue sea*
Karlin, Nurit. *Little big mouse*
Keller, Holly. *Jacob's tree*
Kimmel, Eric A. *Ten suns*
Kirk, Daniel. *Bigger*
Kraus, Robert. *The little giant*
Krauss, Ruth. *Big and little*
  A bouquet of littles
Kuskin, Karla. *Herbert hated being small*
Lipkind, William. *Chaga*
Little, Jean. *Revenge of the small Small*
Long, Earlene. *Gone fishing*
MacKinnon, Debbie. *What shape?*
  What size?
McPhail, David M. *A bug, a bear, and a boy*
Mangan, Anne. *Browny, the smallest bear of all*
Masurel, Claire. *Too big!*
Mayer, Marianna. *The Brambleberrys animal book of
  big and small shapes*
Meister, Cari. *Tiny goes to the library*
  Tiny's bath
  When Tiny was tiny
Miller, Margaret. *Big and little*
  Now I'm big
Mitchell, Adrian. *Twice my size*
Moers, Hermann. *Little Ben*
Mogensen, Jan. *The Land of the Big*
Most, Bernard. *How big were the dinosaurs?*
Nakabayashi, Ei. *The rainy day puddle*
Nathan, Cheryl. *The long and short of it*
Nickle, John. *The ant bully*
O'Brien, Patrick. *Gigantic!*
Oliver, Stephen. *My first look at sizes*
Packard, Edward. *Big numbers*
Palazzo-Craig, Janet. *Little Danny Dinosaur*
Patron, Susan. *Five bad boys, Billy Que, and the dust-
  dobbin*
Peet, Bill (William Bartlett). *Huge Harold*
Pienkowski, Jan. *Sizes*
Pluckrose, Henry Arthur. *Big and little*
Poydar, Nancy. *Cool Ali*
Pragoff, Fiona. *Shapes*
Prøysen, Alf. *Mrs. Pepperpot and the moose*
Rotner, Shelley. *Close, closer, closest*
Schwartz, David M. *How much is a million?*

Shapp, Martha. *Let's find out what's big and what's small*
Sizes
Smith, Mavis. *Circles*
Smith-Moore, J. J. *Sally Small*
Stickland, Paul. *Machines as big as monsters*
Stoddard, Sandol. *Curl up small*
Tafuri, Nancy. *The brass ring*
Tangvald, Christine Harder. *The Rinky Dinky Donkey*
Ueno, Noriko. *Elephant buttons*
Van Emst, Charlotte. *Little Rabbit's big day*
Wallwork, Amanda. *Find the fish that looks like this*
Watson, Carol. *Sizes*
Wells, Tony. *Puzzle doubles*
Wilson, April. *April Wilson's magpie magic*
Youldon, Gillian. *Sizes*

Concepts – speed

Schlein, Miriam. *Fast is not a ladybug*
Spier, Peter. *Fast-slow, high-low*

Concepts – up and down

Berkley, Ethel S. *Ups and down*
Hoban, Tana. *Look up, look down*
Johnson, Crockett. *Upside down*
Knight, Hilary. *Sylvia the sloth*
Matthias, Catherine. *Sal y entra*
Seuss, Dr. *A great day for up*
Slobodkin, Louis. *Up high and down low*
Zion, Gene. *All falling down*

Concepts – weight

Enderle, Judith (Ann) Ross. *What would Mama do?*
Fischer, Vera Kistiakowsky. *One way is down*
MacDonald, George. *The light princess*, ill. by Katie Thamer Treherne
Pluckrose, Henry Arthur. *Weight*
Schlein, Miriam. *Heavy is a hippopotamus*

Condors *see* Birds – condors

Confidence *see* Character traits – confidence

Conservation *see* Ecology

Construction workers *see* Careers – construction workers

Contests

Bond, Michael. *Paddington Bear and the Busy Bee Carnival*
Cole, Joanna. *The Clown-Arounds*
Dalmais, Anne-Marie. *And may the best animal win!*
Dunbar, Joyce. *Eggday*
Gray, Nigel. *The dog show*
Himmelman, John. *The Clover County carrot contest*
Lattimore, Deborah Nourse. *The lady with the ship on her head*
Loredo, Elizabeth. *Boogie Bones*
Marshall, James. *The Cut-Ups carry on*
Mathers, Petra. *A cake for Herbie*
Most, Bernard. *The very boastful kangaroo*
Neugebauer, Charise. *The real winner*

Olaleye, Isaac. *In the Rainfield*
Park, Frances. *The royal bee*
Root, Phyllis. *Rosie's fiddle*
Saltzberg, Barney. *Phoebe and the spelling bee*
Samuels, Barbara. *Aloha, Dolores*
White, Linda Arms. *Comes a wind*

Cooking *see* Activities – cooking

Cooks *see* Careers – bakers; Careers – chefs, cooks

Coquelle *see* Indians of North America – Coquelle

Cora *see* Indians of North America – Cora

Coral Islands *see* Foreign lands – South Sea Islands

Cormorants *see* Birds – cormorants

Costa Rica *see* Foreign lands – Costa Rica

Costumes *see* Clothing – costumes

Couches, sofas *see* Furniture – couches, sofas

Cougars *see* Animals – cougars

Counting, numbers

Adams, Pam. *This old man*
Adler, David A. *Base five*
Ahlberg, Allan. *Fee fi fo fum*
Alda, Arlene. *Arlene Alda's 1 2 3*
Alexander, Anne (Anna Barbara Cooke). *My daddy and I*
Allbright, Viv. *Ten go hopping*
Allen, Jonathan. *One with a bun*
Allen, Robert. *Numbers*
    Ten little babies count
    Ten little babies dress
    Ten little babies eat
    Ten little babies play
Allington, Richard L. *Numbers*
Ambler, C. Gifford (Christopher Gifford). *Ten little foxhounds*
Ambrus, Victor G. *Count, Dracula*
Anholt, Catherine. *One, two, three, count with me*
Animal 123's
Anno, Mitsumasa. *Anno's counting book*
    Anno's counting house
    Anno's hat tricks
    Anno's magic seeds
    Anno's math games
    Anno's math games II
    Anno's math games III
Appelt, Kathi. *Bats on parade*
Archambault, John. *Counting sheep*
Arnold, Tedd. *Bisnipian blast-off*
    Five ugly monsters
Arnosky, Jim. *Mouse numbers and letters*
Asch, Frank. *Little Devil's 123*
Ashton, Elizabeth Allen. *An old-fashioned one two three book*

Astley, Judy. *When one cat woke up*
Axelrod, Amy. *Pigs in the pantry*
  Pigs on the ball
Aylesworth, Jim. *The completed hickory dickory dock*
  One crow
Baker, Alan. *Gray Rabbit's one, two, three*
  Little Rabbit's first number book
Baker, Bonnie Jeanne. *A pear by itself*
Baker, Jeannie. *One hungry spider*
Ballart, Elisabet. *Let's count*
Bang, Molly. *Ten, nine, eight*
Barner, Bob. *Space race*
  Too many dinosaurs
Barnes-Murphy, Rowan. *Numbers*
Barry, David. *The Rajah's rice*
Bassède, Francine. *George's store at the shore*
Baum, Arline. *One bright Monday morning*
Bawden, Juliet. *One year old*
Bayley, Nicola. *One old Oxford ox*
Beck, Ian. *Five little ducks*
Becker, John Leonard. *Seven little rabbits*
Bennett, David. *One cow moo moo*
Berenstain, Stan. *Bears on wheels*
  The Berenstain bears' counting book
Bertrand, Lynne. *Dragon naps*
  One day, two dragons
Bishop, Claire Huchet. *Twenty-two bears*
Bishop, Roma. *Easter counting*
  Numbers
Blackstone, Stella. *Bear in a square*
Blake, Quentin. *Cockatoos*
Blegvad, Lenore. *One is for the sun*
Blumenthal, Nancy. *Count-a-saurus*
Bohdal, Susi. *1,2,3, what do you see?*
Bond, Felicia. *Tumble bumble*
Bond, Michael. *Paddington's 1 2 3*
Boon, Emilie. *1 2 3 how many animals can you see?*
Bourke, Linda. *Eye count*
Bowden, Miriam. *The adventure of Paz in the land of numbers*
Boynton, Sandra. *Hippos go berserk*
  One, two, three!
Bradman, Tony. *The bad babies' counting book*
  Not like this, like that
Breeze, Lynn. *Baby's food*
Brenner, Barbara A. *The snow parade*
Bridgman, Elizabeth. *All the little bunnies*
Bridwell, Norman. *Clifford counts bubbles*
Briggs, Raymond. *The snowman, a lift-the-flap board book*
Bright, Robert. *My red umbrella*
Brooks, Alan. *Frogs jump*
Brown, Marc Tolon. *Count to ten*
Brown, Rick. *Who built the ark?*
Bruna, Dick. *I can count*
  I can count more
  I know more about numbers
  Poppy Pig goes to market
Brunhoff, Laurent de. *Babar's counting book*
Bucknall, Caroline. *One bear all alone*
Burningham, John. *Count up*
  First steps
  Five down
  John Burningham's 1 2 3
  Just cats
  Pigs plus
  Read one
  Ride off
Burton, Katherine. *One gray mouse*

Butler, John. *While you were sleeping*
Calmenson, Stephanie. *Come to my party*
  Dinner at the Panda Palace
  One little monkey
  Ten furry monsters
Carle, Eric. *My very first book of numbers*
  1, 2, 3 to the zoo
  The rooster who set out to see the world
  Rooster's off to see the world
Carlstrom, Nancy White. *Graham cracker animals 1-2-3*
  Let's count it out, Jesse Bear
Carroll, Kathleen Sullivan. *One red rooster*
Cave, Kathryn. *Out for the count*
Challoner, Jack. *The science book of numbers*
Chandra, Deborah. *Miss Mabel's table*
Charles, Faustin. *A Caribbean counting book*
Charlip, Remy. *Thirteen*
Charosh, Mannis. *Number ideas through pictures*
Chester, Jonathan. *Splash!*
Chichester Clark, Emma. *Little Miss Muffet's count-along surprise*
Chorao, Kay. *Number one number fun*
Chouinard, Roger. *One magic box*
Christelow, Eileen. *Five little monkeys jumping on the bed*
  Five little monkeys sitting in a tree
Chwast, Seymour. *Still another number book*
  The twelve circus rings
Clarke, Gus. *Ten green monsters*
Clements, Andrew. *Mother Earth's counting book*
Cleveland, David. *The April rabbits*
Coats, Laura Jane. *Ten little animals*
Coats, Lucy. *One hungry baby*
Cole, Joanna. *Animal sleepyheads*
Coleman, Michael. *One, two, three, oops!*
Conover, Chris. *Six little ducks*
Coplans, Peta. *Cat and dog*
Corbett, Grahame. *What number now?*
Count in the dark with Glo Worm
Count me in
Counting rhymes
Cousins, Lucy. *Count with Maisy*
Cowley, Stewart. *Down Ladybug Lane*
  Five little kittens
  Hide-and-seek puppies
  In dragonfly forest
  In songbird jungle
  Little chick
  Little lost rabbit
  The naughty ducklings
  On Butterfly Farm
Coxe, Molly. *6 sticks*
Cretan, Gladys Yessayan. *Ten brothers with camels*
Crews, Donald. *Bicycle race*
  Ten black dots
Crowther, Robert. *Hide and seek counting book*
  My pop-up surprise 1 2 3
Daily, Don. *The twelve days of Christmas cats*
Dale, Penny. *Ten out of bed*
Dalmais, Anne-Marie. *In my garden*
Dayton, Laura. *LeRoy's birthday circus*
DeCaprio, Annie. *One, two*
Demi. *Demi's count the animals 1-2-3*
  One grain of rice
De Regniers, Beatrice Schenk. *So many cats!*
Dijs, Carla. *How many?*
Dodd, Lynley. *The nickle nackle tree*
Dodds, Dayle Ann. *The Great Divide*

Dodds, Siobhan. *Elizabeth Hen*
Doolittle, Eileen. *World of wonders*
Dreamer, Sue. *Circus 1, 2, 3*
Duerrstein, Richard. *One Mickey Mouse*
Dunham, Meredith. *Numbers: how do you say it?*
Dunrea, Olivier. *Deep down underground*
Duvoisin, Roger Antoine. *Two lonely ducks*
Edwards, Pamela Duncan. *Warthogs in the kitchen*
Edwards, Richard. *Ten tall oaktrees*
Edwards, Roberta. *Five silly fishermen*
Ehlert, Lois. *Fish eyes*
Eichenberg, Fritz. *Dancing in the moon*
Elkin, Benjamin. *Six foolish fishermen*
Enderle, Judith (Ann) Ross. *Six creepy sheep*
   Six sandy sheep
   Six snowy sheep
   Where are you, little Zack?
Ernst, Lisa Campbell. *Up to ten and down again*
Evans, Lezlie. *Can you count ten toes?*
Everett, Percival L. *The one that got away*
Falwell, Cathryn. *Christmas for 10*
   Feast for ten
   Nicky, 1-2-3
Fancher, Lou. *The quest for the One Big Thing*
Farber, Norma. *Up the down elevator*
Feelings, Muriel. *Menjo means one*
Fisher, Leonard Everett. *Boxes! Boxes!*
Flather, Lisa. *Ten silly dogs*
Fleming, Denise. *Count!*
Florian, Douglas. *A summer day*
Foreman, Michael. *Dad! I can't sleep*
Fowler, Richard. *Happy birthday, Mouse!*
Freeman, Lydia. *Corduroy's day*
French, Vivian. *One ballerina two*
Freschet, Berniece. *The ants go marching*
   Where's Henrietta's hen?
Friedman, Aileen. *The king's commissioners*
Friskey, Margaret (Margaret Richards). *Chicken Little, count-to-ten*
   Seven diving ducks
Fuchshuber, Annegert. *Two peas in a pod*
Fujikawa, Gyo. *Ten little babies*
Gantz, David. *Captain Swifty counts to 50*
Gardner, Beau. *Can you imagine . . . ?*
Geisert, Arthur. *Pigs from 1 to 10*
George, Kristine O'Connell. *The great frog race and other poems*
Gerstein, Mordicai. *Guess what?*
   Roll over!
Giganti, Paul. *Each orange had eight slices*
   How many snails?
Gikow, Louise. *Count with me*
Gill, Shelley. *The big buck adventure*
Gillham, Bill. *Let's look for numbers*
Ginsburg, Mirra. *Kitten from one to ten*
Goennel, Heidi. *Odds and evens*
Gregor, Arthur S. *1, 2, 3, 4, 5*
Gretz, Susanna. *Teddy bears ABC*
   Teddy bears 1 - 10
Grimm, Jacob. *Mrs. Fox's wedding*
Groening, Maggie. *Maggie Simpson's counting book*
Grossman, Bill. *My little sister ate one hare*
Grossman, Virginia. *Ten little rabbits*
Gryspeerdt, Rebecca. *Counting friends*
Guettier, Bénédicte. *The father who had ten children*
Gundersheimer, Karen. *1, 2, 3, play with me*
Guy, Ginger Foglesong. *Fiesta!*
Hague, Kathleen. *Numbears*
   Ten little bears

Halpern, Shari. *Moving from one to ten*
Hamm, Diane Johnston. *How many feet in the bed?*
Hamsa, Bobbie. *Polly wants a cracker*
Harada, Joyce. *It's the 0-1-2-3 book*
Haring, Keith. *10*
Harshman, Marc. *Only one*
Hartmann, Wendy. *One sun rises*
Haskins, Jim (James). *Count your way through Africa*
   Count your way through Brazil
   Count your way through Canada
   Count your way through China
   Count your way through France
   Count your way through Germany
   Count your way through Greece
   Count your way through India
   Count your way through Ireland
   Count your way through Israel
   Count your way through Italy
   Count your way through Japan
   Count your way through Korea
   Count your way through Mexico
   Count your way through Russia
   Count your way through the Arab world
Hassett, John. *Cat up a tree*
Hawkins, Colin. *Take away monsters*
Hay, Dean. *Now I can count*
Hayward, Linda. *Did I ever tell you how high you can count?*
   I can add upside down!
   I can count to ten and back again
   Oh, the things you can count from 1-10
Heinst, Marie. *My first number book*
Henderson, Kathy. *Counting farm*
Henley, Claire. *Joe's pool*
Hennessy, B. G. (Barbara G.). *One little, two little, three little pilgrims*
Hill, Eric. *Spot counts from 1 to 10*
   Spot's big book of colors, shapes and numbers; El libro grande de Spot
   Spot's big book of colours, shapes, and numbers
   Spot's favorite numbers
   Spot's first 1, 2, 3 frieze
Hillman, Priscilla. *The Merry-Mouse counting and colors book*
Hindley, Judy. *How many twos?*
   One by one
   Ten bright eyes
Hoban, Russell. *Ten what?*
Hoban, Tana. *Count and see*
   Let's count
   More, fewer, less
   1, 2, 3
   26 letters and 99 cents
Holder, Heidi. *Crows*
Holland, Cheri. *Maccabee jamboree*
Holmes, Stephen. *Hidden numbers*
Hooks, William H. *A dozen dizzy dogs*
   Read-a-rebus
Hooper, Meredith. *Seven eggs*
Howard, Katherine. *I can count to 100 . . . can you?*
Howe, Caroline Walton. *Counting penguins*
Hubbard, Patricia. *Trick or treat countdown*
Hubbard, Woodleigh Marx. *2 is for dancing*
Huck, Charlotte S. *A creepy countdown*
Hudson, Cheryl Willis. *Let's count, baby*
Hughes, Shirley. *Lucy and Tom's 1, 2, 3*
   When we went to the park
Hulme, Joy N. *Sea squares*
   Sea sums

Sharratt, Nick. *Rocket countdown*
Sheppard, Jeff. *The right number of elephants*
Shostak, Myra. *Rainbow candles*
Silverman, Erica. *The Halloween house*
Simmons, Al. *Counting feathers*
Sis, Peter. *Fire truck*
  Going up!
  Waving
Sitomer, Mindel. *How did numbers begin?*
Smith, Donald. *Farm numbers*
Smith, Maggie. *Dear Daisy, get well soon*
Smith, Maggie (Margaret C.). *Counting our way to Maine*
Staake, Bob. *My little 1 2 3 book*
Stanek, Muriel. *One, two, three for fun*
Steiner, Charlotte. *Five little finger playmates*
Stickland, Paul. *Ten terrible dinosaurs*
Stobbs, Joanna. *One sun, two eyes, and a million stars*
Stobbs, William. *This little piggy*
Sturges, Philemon. *Ten flashing fireflies*
Sugita, Yutaka. *Good night 1, 2, 3*
Sullivan, Charles. *Numbers at play*
Swinburne, Stephen R. *Water for one, water for everyone*
  What's a pair? What's a dozen?
Szekeres, Cyndy. *Cyndy Szekeres' counting book, 1 to 10*
  Cyndy Szekeres' learn to count, funny bunnies
  I can count 100 bunnies, and so can you!
Tafuri, Nancy. *Counting to Christmas*
  Who's counting?
Testa, Fulvio. *If you take a pencil*
Thompson, Susan L. *One more thing, dad*
Thornhill, Jan. *The wildlife 1-2-3*
The Timbertoes 1 2 3 counting book
Toft, Kim Michelle. *One less fish*
Trinca, Rod. *One woolly wombat*
Tudor, Tasha. *1 is one*
Turner, Gwenda. *Over on the farm*
Turner, Priscilla. *Among the odds and evens*
VanderKlipp, Michael A. *Joy to the world!*
Van der Meer, Ron. *Funny hats*
Van Fleet, Matthew. *One yellow lion*
Van Laan, Nancy. *Mama rocks, Papa sings*
  A tree for me
Voce, Louise. *Over in the meadow*
Wadsworth, Ginger. *One tiger growls*
Wadsworth, Olive A. *Over in the meadow*
Walker, Jane. *Ten little penguins*
Wallner, John C. *Look and find*
Walsh, Ellen Stoll. *Mouse count*
Walton, Rick. *How many, how many, how many*
  One more bunny
  So many bunnies
Ward, Jennifer. *Somewhere in the ocean*
Warren, Cathy. *The ten-alarm camp-out*
Watson, Nancy Dingman. *What is one?*
Weihs, Erika. *Count the cats*
Weiss, Monica. *Mmmm . . . cookies!*
Wells, Rosemary. *Emily's first 100 days of school*
  Max's toys
Weston, Martha. *Bea's four bears*
Wild, Robin. *The bears' counting book*
Wildsmith, Brian. *Brian Wildsmith 1 2 3*
Williams, Garth. *The chicken book*
Williams, Jenny (Jennifer). *One, two, buckle my shoe*
  Playtime 1 2 3
Williams, Sue. *Let's go visiting*
Wilson, Barbara Ker. *ABC et = and 123*

Wojtowycz, David. *Animal antics from 1 to 10*
Wolfe, Art. *1, 2, 3 moose*
Wolff, Ferida. *On Halloween night*
Wood, Jakki. *Moo moo, brown cow*
  One bear with bees in his hair
Wyllie, Stephen. *Snappity snap*
Yee, Patrick. *Rosie Rabbit's numbers*
Yektai, Niki. *Bears at the beach*
Yolen, Jane. *An invitation to the butterfly ball*
  Old Dame Counterpane
  Street rhymes around the world
Yoshi. *One, two, three*
Youldon, Gillian. *Counting*
  Numbers
Youngs, Betty Ferrell. *One panda*
Zabar, Abbie. *Fifty-five friends*
Zaslavsky, Claudia. *Count on your fingers African style*
  Zero! Is it something? Is it nothing?
Ziefert, Harriet. *A dozen dogs*
  Math riddles
  Mother Goose math
  Rabbit and Hare divide an apple
  Two little witches
Zimmermann, H. Werner (Heinz Werner). *Alphonse knows . . . zero is not enough*
Ziner, Feenie. *Counting carnival*
Zirbes, Laura. *How many bears?*
Zolotow, Charlotte (Shapiro). *One step, two . . .*

Countries, foreign *see* Foreign lands

Country

Æsop. *The country mouse and the city mouse*
  The town mouse and the country mouse, ill. by Lorinda Bryan Cauley
  The town mouse and the country mouse, ill. by Helen Craig
  The town mouse and the country mouse, ill. by Paul Galdone
  The town mouse and the country mouse, ill. by Tom Garcia
  The town mouse and the country mouse, ill. by Janet Stevens
  The town mouse and the country mouse, ill. by Bernadette Watts
  Town mouse, country mouse, ill. by Jan Brett
  Town mouse, country mouse, ill. by Carol Jones
Anderson, Janet S. *Sunflower Sal*
Asch, Frank. *Country pie*
  Dear brother
Atwood, Margaret. *Anna's pet*
Aylesworth, Jim. *Wake up, little children*
Barklem, Jill. *The big book of Brambly Hedge*
Barton, Pat. *A week is a long time*
Birdseye, Tom. *A regular flood of mishap*
  She'll be comin' round the mountain
Borden, Louise. *The watching game*
Bozzo, Maxine Zohn. *Toby in the country, Toby in the city*
Bröger, Achim. *Francie's paper puppy*
Brown, Margaret Wise. *The country noisy book*
Browne, Caroline. *Mrs. Christie's farmhouse*
Burns, Maurice. *Go ducks, go!*
Burton, Virginia Lee. *The little house*
Carlstrom, Nancy White. *The snow speaks*
Caudill, Rebecca. *Contrary Jenkins*
Chorao, Kay. *Ida and Betty and the secret eggs*
Christian, Mary Blount. *Christmas reflections*

Chwast, Seymour. *Tall city, wide country*
Cleveland-Peck, Patricia. *City cat, country cat*
Cole, Sheila. *When the rain stops*
Cooper, Elisha. *Country fair*
Cousins, Lucy. *Country animals*
Crowther, Robert. *Who lives in the country?*
Dale, Ruth Bluestone. *Benjamin . . . and Sylvester also*
Day, Alexandra. *Paddy's pay-day*
DeFelice, Cynthia C. *When Grampa kissed his elbow*
Dickinson, Mary. *Alex's outing*
Florian, Douglas. *A year in the country*
Geisert, Bonnie. *Prairie town*
Gibbons, Faye. *Mountain wedding*
Gibbons, Gail. *County fair*
Goffstein, M. B. (Marilyn Brooke). *Our prairie home*
Griffith, Helen V. *Grandaddy's place*
Grimes, Nikki. *Danitra Brown leaves town*
Harshman, Marc. *A little excitement*
Hawkesworth, Jenny. *The lonely skyscraper*
Hayward, Linda. *The city worm and the country worm*
Hendershot, Judith. *Up the tracks to Grandma's*
Hirschi, Ron. *Harvest song*
Hodeir, André. *Warwick's 3 bottles*
Holl, Adelaide. *A mouse story*
Jam, Teddy. *The year of fire*
Johnson, Angela. *Down the winding road*
Kingman, Lee. *Peter's long walk*
Kiser, SuAnn. *The hog call to end all!*
Kraus, Robert. *Robert Kraus' Babytown express*
Kuskin, Karla. *City dog*
Levinson, Riki. *Country dawn to dusk*
Lewin, Ted. *Fair!*
Lewis, Kim. *One summer day*
Loomis, Christine. *Cowboy bunnies*
Lorenz, Lee. *A weekend in the city*
    A weekend in the country
Lunn, Janet Louise Swoboda. *Come to the fair*
McKissack, Patricia C. *Country mouse and city mouse*
MacLachlan, Patricia. *All the places to love*
    What you know first
McPartland, Suzy. *Zoom, car, zoom*
McPhail, David M. *Ed and me*
Maestro, Betsy. *Delivery van*
Martin, Bill (William Ivan). *Barn dance!*
Merriam, Eve. *Fighting words*
Miller, William. *Jenny and the peddler*
Mollel, Tololwa M. (Tololwa Marti). *Ananse's feast*
Moore, Elaine. *Grandma's house*
    Grandma's promise
Moore, Inga. *Little dog lost*
    The truffle hunter
Nikola-Lisa, W. *Night is coming*
    Storm
    Till year's good end
Nolan, Lucy A. *The Lizard Man of Crabtree County*
Payne, Joan Balfour. *The stable that stayed*
Pedersen, Judy. *Out in the country*
Pender, Lydia. *Barnaby and the horses*
Polacco, Patricia. *Meteor!*
Provensen, Alice. *Town and country*
Roach, Marilynne K. *Two Roman mice*
Rockwell, Anne F. *Willy can count*
Roe, Eileen. *Staying with Grandma*
Rylant, Cynthia. *Appalachia*
    Night in the country
    Scarecrow
Scheffler, Ursel. *Stop your crowing, Kasimir!*
Schertle, Alice. *Down the road*

Sopko, Eugen. *Townsfolk and countryfolk*
Stanley, Diane. *A country tale*
Stevens, Kathleen. *Aunt Skilly and the stranger*
Summers, Kate. *Milly and Tilly*
Tucker, Kathy. *Do cowboys ride bikes?*
Van Allsburg, Chris. *The stranger*
Walters, Marguerite. *The city-country ABC*
    The weekend
Williams, David. *Walking to the creek*
Williams, Jay. *The city witch and the country witch*
Wyeth, Sharon Dennis. *Always my dad*
Yolen, Jane. *Letting Swift River go*

Courage *see* Character traits – bravery

Cousins *see* Family life – cousins

Cowboys

Anderson, C. W. (Clarence Williams). *Blaze and the Indian cave*
    Blaze and the lost quarry
    Blaze and the mountain lion
    Blaze and Thunderbolt
    Blaze finds forgotten roads
    Blaze finds the trail
Anglund, Joan Walsh. *The brave cowboy*
    Cowboy and his friend
    The cowboy's Christmas
    Cowboy's secret life
Antle, Nancy. *Sam's Wild West Show*
Appelt, Kathi. *Cowboy dreams*
Aulaire, Ingri Mortenson d'. *Nils*
Beatty, Hetty Burlingame. *Bucking horse*
Birney, Betty G. *Tyrannosaurus Tex*
Bishop, Ann. *Wild Bill Hiccup's riddle book*
Bright, Robert. *Georgie goes west*
Brimner, Larry Dane. *Cowboy up!*
Carter, Anne. *Tall in the saddle*
Chandler, Edna Walker. *Cattle drive*
    Cowboy Andy
    Pony rider
    Secret tunnel
Cohen, Caron Lee. *Bronco dogs*
Demarest, Chris L. *The cowboy ABC*
Denslow, Sharon Phillips. *On the trail with Miss Pace*
Dewey, Ariane. *Pecos Bill*
Doughtie, Charles. *High Henry . . . the cowboy who was too tall to ride a horse*
Enderle, Judith (Ann) Ross. *Nell Nugget and the cow caper*
Everett, Percival L. *The one that got away*
Fain, James W. *Rodeos*
Felton, Harold W. *Pecos Bill and the mustang*
Fitzhugh, Louise. *Bang, bang, you're dead*
Gardella, Tricia. *Just like my dad*
Garland, Sherry. *Goodnight, cowboy*
Gerrard, Roy. *Rosie and the rustlers*
Gibbons, Gail. *Yippee-yay!*
Grossman, Bill. *Cowboy Ed*
Hancock, Sibyl. *Old Blue*
Heap, Sue. *Cowboy Baby*
Herzig, Alison Cragin. *Bronco busters*
Hill, Eric. *Spot goes to a party*
Hillert, Margaret. *The little cowboy and the big cowboy*
Hooker, Ruth. *Matthew the cowboy*
Johnson, Neil. *Jack Creek cowboy*
Johnston, Tony. *The cowboy and the black-eyed pea*

Sparky and Eddie, wild, wild rodeo!
Karas, G. Brian. *Home on the bayou*
Kellogg, Steven (Stephen). *Pecos Bill*
Kennedy, Richard. *The contests at Cowlick*
Ketteman, Helen. *Bubba the cowboy prince*
Kimmel, Eric A. *Four dollars and fifty cents*
    Grizz!
Kinerk, Robert. *Slim and Miss Prim*
Krasilovsky, Phyllis. *The girl who was a cowboy*
Lenski, Lois. *Cowboy Small*
Lester, Julius. *Black cowboy, wild horses*
Liebman, Daniel. *I want to be a cowboy*
Loomis, Christine. *Cowboy bunnies*
Lowell, Susan. *The bootmaker and the elves*
McAllister, Angela. *The clever cowboy*
Mayer, Mercer. *Cowboy critter*
Medearis, Angela Shelf. *The zebra-riding cowboy*
Miller, Robert H. (Robert Henry). *The story of Nat*
    Love
Moon, Dolly M. *My very first book of cowboy songs*
Mora, Jo. *Budgee Budgee Cottontail*
Morck, Irene. *Tyler's new boots*
Pinkney, Andrea Davis. *Bill Pickett, rodeo ridin' cowboy*
Quackenbush, Robert M. *Pete Pack Rat*
Rounds, Glen. *Cowboys*
Sanfield, Steve. *The great turtle drive*
Scott, Ann Herbert. *Big Cowboy Western*
    One good horse
    Someday rider
Sewall, Marcia. *Ridin' that strawberry roan*
Stadler, John. *The ballad of Wilbur and the moose*
Stutson, Caroline. *Cowpokes*
Sullivan, Silky. *Grandpa was a cowboy*
Tucker, Kathy. *Do cowboys ride bikes?*
Ulmer, Wendy K. *A campfire for cowboy Billy*
Ward, Nanda Weedon. *The black sombrero*
Watson, Esther (Pearl). *The adventures of Jules and*
    Gertie
Winter, Jeanette. *Cowboy Charlie*
Wood, Nancy C. *Little wrangler*

Cows *see* Animals – bulls, cows

Coyotes *see* Animals – coyotes

Crabs *see* Crustaceans

Cradles *see* Furniture – cradles

Crafts *see* Activities – making things

Cranes (birds) *see* Birds – cranes

Creation

Alexander, Cecil Frances. *All things bright and beautiful*
Aronow, Sara. *Seven days of creation*
Baker, Betty. *And me, coyote!*
Bernstein, Margery. *Earth namer*
Bible. Old Testament. Genesis. *Genesis*
    The story of the creation
Bierhorst, John. *The woman who fell from the sky*
Blake, William. *The tyger*
Bratton, Heidi. *Imagine*
Cassidy, Sheila. *The creation*

Caswell, Helen Rayburn. *God must like to laugh*
Cooner, Donna D. (Donna Danell). *The world God made*
Crespo, George. *How the sea began*
Davidson, Alice J. *The story of creation*
Davol, Marguerite W. *Batwings and the curtain of night*
Dwyer, Mindy. *Coyote in love*
Field, Edward. *Magic words*
Fisher, Leonard Everett. *The seven days of creation*
Foreman, Juli. *Great beginnings*
Frank, Penny. *In the beginning*
French, Fiona. *Lord of the animals*
Gates, Frieda. *Owl eyes*
Goble, Paul. *The great race of the birds and animals*
    I sing for the animals
    Remaking the earth
Goffe, Toni. *The story of creation*
Greene, Carol. *God's good creation*
Grimes, Nikki. *At break of day*
Haley, Gail E. *Two bad boys*
Harper, Piers. *How the world was saved and other Native American tales*
Hartman, Bob. *The morning of the world*
Helldorfer, M. C. (Mary Claire). *Clap clap!*
Hickman, Martha Whitmore. *And God created squash*
Jackson, Ellen B. *The precious gift*
Jaffe, Nina. *The golden flower*
Jendresen, Erik. *The first story ever told*
Johnson, James Weldon. *The Creation*
Keams, Geri. *Snail girl brings water*
Kimmel, Eric A. *The rooster's antlers*
Lattimore, Deborah Nourse. *Why there is no arguing in heaven*
Lester, Julius. *What a truly cool world*
Le Tord, Bijou. *The deep blue sea*
Levin, Miriam Ramsfelder. *In the beginning*
Lindbergh, Reeve. *The circle of days*
McDermott, Beverly Brodsky. *The dreamtime*
MacDonald, Amy. *The spider who created the world*
McFall, Gardner. *Naming the animals*
Maddern, Eric. *The fire children*
Matthews, Caitlin. *The blessing seed*
Neitzel, Shirley. *From the land of the white birch*
Oliviero, Jamie. *The day Sun was stolen*
Oppenheim, Shulamith Levey. *And the earth trembled*
    Iblis
Ortiz, Simon. *The people shall continue*
Pohrt, Tom. *Coyote goes walking*
Poole, Amy Lowry. *How the rooster got his crown*
Quattlebaum, Mary. *In the beginning*
Reed, Allison. *Genesis*
Rich, Scharlotte. *Who made the wild woods?*
Riordan, James. *The coming of Night*
Rodanas, Kristina. *Follow the stars*
Rohmer, Harriet. *How we came to the fifth world*
Rose, Anne K. *Spider in the sky*
Rosen, Michael J. (1954-). *The dog who walked with God*
Sage, James. *Coyote makes man*
Sattgast, L. J. *Look what God made*
Simms, Laura. *The bone man*
Slate, Joseph. *Story time for Little Porcupine*
Sneve, Virginia Driving Hawk. *The Cherokees*
    The Nez Perce
Strauss, Susan. *When woman became the sea*
Swartz, Nancy Sohn. *In our image*

Troughton, Joanna. *Who will be the sun?*
Van Laan, Nancy. *Rainbow crow*
Waldman, Sarah. *Light*
Williams, Sheron. *And in the beginning . . .*
Wood, Audrey. *The rainbow bridge*
Wood, Douglas. *Making the world*
Yolen, Jane. *Old Dame Counterpane*
Zeman, Ludmila. *The first red maple leaf*
Zhang, Song Nan. *The five heavenly emperors and other Chinese myths from the creation*
Ziefert, Harriet. *First He made the sun*

Creatures *see* Monsters; Mythical creatures

Cree Indians *see* Indians of North America – Cree

Creek Indians *see* Indians of North America – Creek

Creeks *see* Rivers

Crickets *see* Insects – crickets

Crime

Ada, Alma Flor. *The gold coin*
Adamson, Gareth. *Old man up a tree*
Ahlberg, Allan. *Cops and robbers*
Ahlberg, Janet. *Burglar Bill*
  It was a dark and stormy night
Alderson, Sue Ann. *Ida and the wool smugglers*
Allard, Harry. *It's so nice to have a wolf around the house*
Anderson, C. W. (Clarence Williams). *Blaze and the gypsies*
Antle, Nancy. *Sam's Wild West Show*
Auch, Mary Jane. *Eggs mark the spot*
Barracca, Debra. *Maxi, the hero*
Berson, Harold. *The thief who hugged a moonbeam*
Biro, Val. *Gumdrop finds a friend*
  Gumdrop in double trouble
Blake, Quentin. *Snuff*
Bradford, Ann. *The mystery in the secret club house*
  The mystery of the blind writer
  The mystery of the tree house
Brandenberg, Franz. *A robber! A robber!*
Bright, Robert. *Georgie and the robbers*
Brunhoff, Laurent de. *Babar's mystery*
  The rescue of Babar
Burdett, Lois. *Hamlet for kids*
  Macbeth for kids
Calders, Pere. *Brush*
Carlson, Nancy L. *Arnie and the stolen markers*
Cass, Joan E. *The cat thief*
Christelow, Eileen. *The robbery at the diamond dog diner*
Christian, Mary Blount. *The doggone mystery*
Cohen, Caron Lee. *Bronco dogs*
Cohn, Janice I. *"Why did it happen?"*
Coltman, Paul. *Tinker Jim*
Cox, David. *Bossyboots*
Cressey, James. *Max the mouse*
  Pet parrot
Dahl, Roald. *The giraffe and the pelly and me*
Daly, Niki. *Vim, the rag mouse*
Dixon, Chuck. *Batman*

Dodd, Lynley. *Slinky Malinki*
Dumas, Philippe. *Laura and the bandits*
Duvoisin, Roger Antoine. *Petunia and the song*
Egan, Tim. *The blunder of the Rogues*
Euvremer, Teryl. *The thieves of Peck's pocket*
Foreman, Michael. *Look! Look!*
French, Fiona. *Snow White in New York*
Gage, Wilson. *Down in the boondocks*
Gerrard, Roy. *Jocasta Carr, movie star*
  Rosie and the rustlers
Goodall, John S. *Paddy to the rescue*
Grimm, Jacob. *The Bremen town band*
  The Bremen town musicians, ill. by Donna Diamond
  The Bremen town musicians, ill. by Janina Domanska
  The Bremen town musicians, ill. by Paul Galdone
  Bremen town musicians, ill. by Josef Palecek
  The Bremen town musicians, ill. by Ilse Plume
  The Bremen town musicians, ill. by Bernadette Watts
Harris, Leon A. *The great diamond robbery*
  The great picture robbery
Haseley, Dennis. *The thieves' market*
Heller, George. *Hiroshi's wonderful kite*
Heymans, Margriet. *Pippin and Robber Grumblecroak's big baby*
Hickman, Martha Whitmore. *When Andy's father went to prison*
High, Linda Oatman. *A Christmas Star*
Hilton, Nette. *Dirty Dave*
Hogrogian, Nonny. *The contest*
  Rooster brother
Jacobs, Joseph. *Hereafterthis*
Janice. *Mr. and Mrs. Button's wonderful watchdogs*
Johnson, Paul Brett. *Frank Fister's hidden talent*
Kimmel, Eric A. *Four dollars and fifty cents*
Kinerk, Robert. *Slim and Miss Prim*
Kirn, Ann. *I spy*
Krahn, Fernando. *Mr. Top*
Kraus, Robert. *The detective of London*
Kroll, Steven. *Looking for Daniela*
  Woof, woof!
Lakin, Pat (Patricia). *Aware and alert*
Levitin, Sonia. *Nobody stole the pie*
Lewis, J. Patrick. *The night of the goat children*
Lobel, Anita. *The straw maid*
Lobel, Arnold. *How the rooster saved the day*
McCully, Emily Arnold. *An outlaw Thanksgiving*
McKean, Thomas. *Hooray for Grandma Jo!*
McKee, David. *123456789 Benn*
McPhail, David M. *Moony B. Finch, fastest draw in the West*
  Stanley: Henry Bear's friend
Mahy, Margaret. *Beaten by a balloon*
Marzollo, Jean. *Jed and the space bandits*
Mathews, Louise. *The great take-away*
Mayer, Mercer. *Liverwurst is missing*
Mead, Alice. *Billy and Emma*
Miles, Miska. *The raccoon and Mrs. McGinnis*
Moore, John. *Granny Stickleback*
Mooser, Stephen. *Funnyman and the penny dodo*
Moss, P. Buckley (Pat Buckley). *Reuben and the quilt*
Myller, Rolf. *A very noisy day*
Noyes, Alfred. *The highwayman*
Ogburn, Jacqueline K. *Scarlett Angelina Wolverton-Manning*
O'Malley, Kevin. *Who killed Cock Robin?*

Oram, Hiawyn. *Princess Chamomile gets her way*
Parish, Peggy. *The cats' burglar*
　Granny and the desperadoes
Partch, Virgil Franklin. *The Christmas cookie sprinkle snitcher*
Politi, Leo. *Emmet*
Propp, James. *Tuscanini*
Pryor, Bonnie. *Mr. Munday and the rustlers*
Reidel, Marlene. *Jacob and the robbers*
Rose, Gerald. *The tiger-skin rug*
Rosenbloom, Joseph. *Deputy Dan and the bank robbers*
Ruby-Spears Enterprises. *The puppy's new adventures*
Scarry, Richard. *Richard Scarry's great big mystery book*
Seabrooke, Brenda. *The best burglar alarm*
Shire, Ellen. *The mystery at number seven, Rue Petite*
Skolsky, Mindy Warshaw. *Hannah and the whistling tea kettle*
Slobodkina, Esphyr. *Pezzo the peddler and the thirteen silly thieves*
Solotareff, Grégoire. *Don't call me little bunny*
Stevens, Kathleen. *Aunt Skilly and the stranger*
Thomson, Ruth. *Peabody all at sea*
　Peabody's first case
Titus, Eve. *Anatole and the thirty thieves*
Tompert, Ann. *The hungry black bag*
Ungerer, Tomi. *The three robbers*
Van Nutt, Julia. *The monster in the shadows*
Wahl, Jan. *The adventures of Underwater Dog*
Watson, Nancy Dingman. *The birthday goat*
Wolff, Ferida. *The woodcutter's coat*
Wright, Betty Ren. *Pet detectives!*
Yee, Wong Herbert. *The Officers' Ball*

Criminals *see* Crime; Prisons

Crippled *see* Handicaps – physical handicaps

Crocodiles *see* Reptiles – alligators, crocodiles

Crow Indians *see* Indians of North America – Crow

Crows *see* Birds – crows

Cruelty to animals *see* Character traits – kindness to animals

Crustaceans

Carle, Eric. *A house for Hermit Crab*
Carrick, Carol. *The blue lobster*
Childress, Mark. *Joshua and the big bad blue crabs*
Coldrey, Jennifer. *The world of crabs*
Griffith, Helen V. *Emily and the enchanted frog*
Guiberson, Brenda Z. *Lobster boat*
Hartman, Bob. *Lobster for lunch*
Heller, Ruth. *How to hide an octopus*
Heyduck-Huth, Hilde. *The starfish*
Horio, Seishi. *The monkey and the crab*
James, Simon. *Sally and the limpet*
Kalan, Robert. *Moving day*
Kidd, Richard. *Monsieur Thermidor*
Kipling, Rudyard. *The crab that played with the sea*
Knutson, Barbara. *Why the crab has no head*

Krudop, Walter Lyon. *Blue claws*
Maccarone, Grace. *The classroom pet*
McDonald, Megan. *Is this a house for Hermit Crab?*
Manson, Christopher. *The crab prince*
Mogensen, Jan. *Teddy in the undersea kingdom*
Peet, Bill (William Bartlett). *Kermit the hermit*
Pratt, Kristin Joy. *A swim through the sea*
Royston, Angela. *Sea animals*
Spooner, Michael. *Old Meshikee and the little crabs*
Tafuri, Nancy. *Follow me!*
Van West, Patricia E. *The crab man*
West, Colin. *"Only joking!" laughed the lobster*
Yamaguchi, Tohr. *Two crabs and the moonlight*

Crying *see* Emotions

Cuckoos *see* Birds – cuckoos

Cumulative tales

Aardema, Verna. *Bringing the rain to Kapiti Plain*
　The riddle of the drum
Ada, Alma Flor. *El Arbol de Navidad : The Christmas tree*
　The gold coin
　The rooster who went to his uncle's wedding
Adoff, Arnold. *The cabbages are chasing the rabbits*
Alda, Arlene. *Pig, horse, or cow, don't wake me now*
Alexander, Lloyd. *Fortune tellers*
Alger, Leclaire Gowans. *Always room for one more*
Aliki. *June 7!*
Allbright, Viv. *Ten go hopping*
Arnold, Katya. *Knock, knock, teremok!*
Arnold, Tedd. *No more water in the tub!*
Asbjørnsen, P. C. (Peter Christen). *Billy goats Gruff*, ill. by Wendy Edelson
　Billy goats Gruff, ill. by Susan Hellard
　The three billy goats Gruff, ill. by Robert Bender
　The three billy goats Gruff, ill. by Marcia Brown
　Three billy goats Gruff, ill. by Tom Dunnington
　The three billy goats Gruff, ill. by Paul Galdone
　The three billy goats Gruff, ill. by David Jorgensen
　The three billy goats Gruff, ill. by Dennis Kendrick
　The three billygoats Gruff, ill. by Eric Kincaid
　The three billy goats Gruff, ill. by Jonathan Langley
　The three billy goats Gruff, ill. by Loretta Lustig
　The three billy goats Gruff, ill. by Lilian Obligado
　The three billy goats Gruff, ill. by Ed Parker
　The three billy goats Gruff, ill. by Heidi Petach
　The three billy goats Gruff, ill. by Laura Rader
　The three billy goats Gruff, ill. by Glen Rounds
　The three billy goats Gruff, ill. by Janet Stevens
　The three billy goats Gruff, ill. by William Stobbs
　The three billy goats Gruff, ill. by Svend Otto S
　The truth about three billy goats Gruff
Aylesworth, Jim. *Mr. McGill goes to town*
Baehr, Patricia. *Mouse in the house*
Baker, Alan. *Black and White Rabbit's ABC*
Baker, Betty. *Rat is dead and ant is sad*
Banks, Kate (Katherine A.). *Peter and the talking shoes*
Baron, Alan. *Little Pig's bouncy ball*
　Red Fox dances
Barton, Byron. *Buzz, buzz, buzz*
Bennett, David. *One cow moo moo*
Berson, Harold. *The boy, the baker, the miller and more*
Birdseye, Tom. *Soap! Soap! Don't forget the soap!*

Ormerod, Jan. *Ms. MacDonald has a class*
Oxenbury, Helen. *It's my birthday*
Pace, David. *Shouting Sharon*
Pack, Robert. *Then what did you do?*
Parkinson, Kathy. *The enormous turnip*
Patron, Susan. *Dark cloud strong breeze*
Peet, Bill (William Bartlett). *The ant and the elephant*
Petie, Haris. *The seed the squirrel dropped*
Piers, Helen. *Is there room on the bus?*
   Who's in my bed?
Polacco, Patricia. *In Enzo's splendid gardens*
Polette, Nancy. *The little old woman and the hungry cat*
Prelutsky, Jack. *The terrible tiger*
Preston, Edna Mitchell. *One dark night*
Quackenbush, Robert M. *No mouse for me*
Raskin, Ellen. *Ghost in a four-room apartment*
Reider, Katja. *Snail started it!*
Reiser, Lynn. *Christmas counting*
Riddell, Chris. *Bird's new shoes*
Robart, Rose. *The cake that Mack ate*
Rockwell, Anne F. *Honk honk!*
   Poor Goose
   Root-a-toot-toot
Roddie, Shen. *Animal stew*
Rose, Anne K. *The talking turnip*
Rydell, Katy. *Wind says good night*
Sanfield, Steve. *Bit by bit*
Sawyer, Ruth. *Journey cake, ho!*
Schaefer, Lola M. *This is the sunflower*
Scieszka, Jon. *The book that Jack wrote*
Scott, William R. *This is the milk that Jack drank*
Seeger, Pete. *The foolish frog*
Segal, Lore. *All the way home*
Seuss, Dr. *Green eggs and ham*
Seymour, Dorothy Z. *The tent*
Shannon, George. *Beanboy*
   Oh, I love!
Sierra, Judy. *The house that Drac built*
Silverman, Erica. *On the morn of Mayfest*
Silverstein, Shel. *A giraffe and a half*
Simms, Laura. *The squeaky door*
Skorpen, Liesel Moak. *All the Lassies*
   We were tired of living in a house
Sloat, Teri. *There was an old lady who swallowed a trout*
Snow, Pegeen. *Mrs. Periwinkle's groceries*
Steger, Hans-Ulrich. *Traveling to Tripiti*
Stevens, Jan Romero. *Twelve lizards leaping*
Stockdale, Susan. *Some sleep standing up*
Stoddard, Sandol. *Bedtime mouse*
Stojic, Manya. *Rain*
Stone, Rosetta. *Because a little bug went ka-choo!*
Stutson, Caroline. *By the light of the Halloween moon*
Suhl, Yuri. *Simon Boom gives a wedding*
Sutherland, Colleen. *Jason goes to show-and-tell*
Sutton, Eve. *My cat likes to hide in boxes*
Sweet, Melissa. *Fiddle-i-fee*
Szekeres, Cyndy. *The mouse that Jack built*
Tafuri, Nancy. *This is the farmer*
Tanaka, Beatrice. *The chase*
Thomas, Shelley Moore. *Putting the world to sleep*
Tolstoy, Aleksey Nikolayevich. *The gigantic turnip*, ill. by Niamh Sharkey
   The great big enormous turnip, ill. by Helen Oxenbury
Tompert, Ann. *Just a little bit*
Tresselt, Alvin R. *Rain drop splash*

Trosclair. *Cajun night before Christmas*
Troughton, Joanna. *The quail's egg*
The twelve days of Christmas.. English folk song.
   Brian Wildsmith's The twelve days of Christmas
   Jack Kent's twelve days of Christmas
   The twelve days of Christmas, ill. by Jan Brett
   The twelve days of Christmas, ill. by Ilonka Karasz
   The twelve days of Christmas, ill. by Ilse Plume
   The twelve days of Christmas, ill. by Erika Schneider
   The twelve days of Christmas, ill. by Vladimir Vagin
   The twelve days of Christmas, ill. by Sophie Windham
Tworkov, Jack. *The camel who took a walk*
Vagin, Vladimir Vasil'evich. *The enormous carrot*
Van Laan, Nancy. *Mama rocks, Papa sings*
   Possum come a-knocking
Varga, Judy. *The monster behind Black Rock*
Waddell, Martin. *The pig in the pond*
Wahl, Jan. *Follow me cried Bee*
Wallner, John C. *Old MacDonald had a farm*
Weninger, Brigitte. *The elf's hat*
West, Colin. *Go tell it to the toucan*
   Have you seen the crocodile?
   The king of Kennelwick castle
   The king's toothache
   One day in the jungle
Wiesner, William. *Happy-Go-Lucky*
Wildsmith, Brian. *Goat's trail*
Williams, Linda. *The little old lady who was not afraid of anything*
Wolkstein, Diane. *The magic wings*
Wood, Audrey. *The napping house*
   Silly Sally
Wood, Jakki. *Fiddle-i-fee*
Yee, Brenda Shannon. *Sand castle*
Yee, Wong Herbert. *Eek! There's a mouse in the house*
Yolen, Jane. *Jane Yolen's Old MacDonald songbook*
Zabar, Abbie. *Fifty-five friends*
Ziefert, Harriet. *I swapped my dog*
   The turnip
   When I first came to this land
Ziner, Feenie. *Counting carnival*
Zolotow, Charlotte (Shapiro). *The quarreling book*

Curiosity *see* Character traits – curiosity

Currency *see* Money

Custodians *see* Careers – custodians, janitors

Cycles *see* Motorcycles; Sports – bicycling

Czechoslovakia *see* Foreign lands – Czechoslovakia

Czechoslovakian Americans *see* Ethnic groups in the U.S. – Czechoslovakian Americans

Dakota (Sioux) Indians *see* Indians of North America – Dakota (Sioux)

Damselflies *see* Insects – damselflies

Dancers *see* Careers – dancers

Dancing *see* Activities – dancing; Ballet

Daniel *see* Religion – Daniel

Dark *see* Night

Darkness – fear *see* Emotions – fear

Daughters *see* Family life – daughters

David and Goliath *see* Religion – David

Dawn *see* Morning

Day

George, Jean Craighead. *Morning, noon, and night*

Day of the Dead *see* Holidays – Day of the Dead

Days of the week, months of the year

Alberts, Nancy Markham. *No toys on Sunday*
Anglund, Joan Walsh. *A child's year*
   How many days has Baby to play?
Anholt, Catherine. *One, two, three, count with me*
Appelt, Kathi. *A red wagon year*
Arnold, Tedd. *Mother Goose's words of wit and wisdom*
Baden, Robert. *And Sunday makes seven*
Borchers, Elisabeth. *There comes a time*
Butterworth, Nick. *Jasper's beanstalk*
Carle, Eric. *Today is Monday*
   The very hungry caterpillar
Carlstrom, Nancy White. *How do you say it today, Jesse Bear?*
Charles, Donald. *Calico Cat's year*
   A child's calendar
Clark, Gus. *How many days to my birthday?*
Clifton, Lucille. *Some of the days of Everett Anderson*
Cocca-Leffler, Maryann. *Wednesday is spaghetti day*
Coleridge, Sara. *January brings the snow*
Damjan, Mischa. *December's travels*
Day, Nancy Raines. *A kitten's year*
De Regniers, Beatrice Schenk. *Little Sister and the Month Brothers*
Dragonwagon, Crescent. *Alligators and others all year long!*
Gág, Flavia. *Chubby's first year*
Gerstein, Mordicai. *The story of May*

Giff, Patricia Reilly. *I love Saturday*
Ginsburg, Mirra. *The old man and his birds*
Hague, Kathleen. *Calendarbears*
Halsey, Megan. *Jump for joy*
Harmer, Juliet. *Prayers for children*
Henderson, Kathy. *A year in the city*
Hillman, Priscilla. *A Merry-Mouse book of months*
Hooper, Meredith. *Seven eggs*
Howell, Lynn. *Winifred's new bed*
Johnson, Dinah. *Sunday week*
Keenen, George. *The preposterous week*
Lasker, Joe. *Lentil soup*
Lesser, Carolyn. *What a wonderful day to be a cow*
Lewis, J. Patrick. *July is a mad mosquito*
Lewis, Robin Baird. *Hello, Mr. Scarecrow*
Lillie, Patricia. *When this box is full*
Llewellyn, Claire. *My first book of time*
Lobel, Anita. *One lighthouse, one moon*
Lord, Beman. *The days of the week*
MacDonald, Elizabeth. *My aunt and the animals*
Maestro, Betsy. *Through the year with Harriet*
Manning, Linda. *Dinosaur days*
Martin, Bill (William Ivan). *The turning of the year*
Min, Laura. *Mrs. Sato's hens*
Molnar, Dorothy E. *Who will pick me up when I fall?*
Nikola-Lisa, W. *Till year's good end*
Otten, Charlotte F. *January rides the wind*
Owen, Annie. *From snowflakes to sandcastles*
Peters, Lisa Westberg. *October smiled back*
Plotz, Helen. *A week of lullabies*
Prater, John. *On Friday something funny happened*
Provensen, Alice. *The year at Maple Hill Farm*
Rylant, Cynthia. *Bless us all*
   Give me grace
Scarry, Richard. *Richard Scarry's best first book ever!*
Sendak, Maurice. *Chicken soup with rice*
Sharratt, Nick. *Monday run-day*
Shiefman, Vicky. *Sunday potatoes, Monday potatoes*
Shields, Carol Diggory. *Day by day a week goes round*
   Month by month a year goes round
Shulevitz, Uri. *One Monday morning*
Singer, Marilyn. *Turtle in July*
Smith, Maggie. *Dear Daisy, get well soon*
Smith, William Jay. *The sun is up*
Tafuri, Nancy. *All year long*
   Snowy flowy blowy
Thomas, Joyce Carol. *Gingerbread days*
Tudor, Tasha. *Around the year*
Tyrrell, Anne. *Elizabeth Jane gets dressed*
Verdet, Andre. *All about time*
Vojtech, Anna. *Marushka and the Month Brothers*
Ward, Cindy. *Cookie's week*
Wolff, Ashley. *A year of beasts*
   A year of birds
Wood, Audrey. *Heckedy Peg*
Yolen, Jane. *No bath tonight*
Young, Ed (Edward). *Seven blind mice*
Zimmermann, H. Werner (Heinz Werner). *Alphonse knows . . . twelve months make a year*

Deafness *see* Anatomy – ears; Handicaps – deafness; Senses – hearing

Death

Adoff, Arnold. *The return of Rex and Ethel*
Aliki. *Mummies made in Egypt*
Anaya, Rudolfo A. *Farolitos for Abuelo*

Anders, Rebecca. *A look at death*
Andersen, H. C. (Hans Christian). *It's perfectly true!*
   The little match girl, ill. by Rachel Isadora
   The little match girl, ill. by Blair Lent
   The little match girl, ill. by Jerry Pinkney
Anderson, Leone Castell. *It's O.K. to cry*
Arnold, Caroline. *What we do when someone dies*
Baker, Betty. *Rat is dead and ant is sad*
Barker, Peggy. *What happened when grandma died*
Barnhart, Peter. *The wounded duck*
Barron, T. A. *Where is Grandpa?*
Bartoli, Jennifer. *Nonna*
Beim, Jerrold. *With dad alone*
Bernstein, Joanne E. *When people die*
Breckler, Rosemary K. *Sweet dried apples*
Breebaart, Joeri. *When I die, will I get better?*
Brown, Laurie Krasny. *When dinosaurs die*
Brown, Margaret Wise. *The dead bird*
Bunting, Eve (Anne Evelyn). *The big red barn*
   The day before Christmas
   The happy funeral
   On Call Back Mountain
   Rudi's pond
Burningham, John. *Grandpa*
Carlstrom, Nancy White. *Blow me a kiss, Miss Lilly*
Carrick, Carol. *The accident*
Carson, Jo. *You hold me and I'll hold you*
Caseley, Judith. *When Grandpa came to stay*
Cazet, Denys. *A fish in his pocket*
Cazzola, Gus. *The bells of Santa Lucia*
Clifton, Lucille. *Everett Anderson's goodbye*
Cock Robin. *The courtship, merry marriage, and feast of Cock Robin and Jenny Wren*
   Who killed Cock Robin?, ill. by William Stobbs
Coerr, Eleanor. *Sadako*
Cohen, Miriam. *Jim's dog Muffins*
Cohn, Janice I. *I had a friend named Peter*
   Molly's rosebush
Cooney, Barbara. *Island boy*
Coutant, Helen. *First snow*
Coville, Bruce. *My grandfather's house*
Dabcovich, Lydia. *Mrs. Huggins and her hen Hannah*
DeArmond, Dale. *The seal oil lamp*
De Paola, Tomie (Thomas Anthony). *Nana upstairs and Nana downstairs*
DiSalvo-Ryan, DyAnne. *A dog like Jack*
Ehrlich, Amy. *Maggie and Silky and Joe*
Engel, Diana. *Eleanor, Arthur, and Claire*
Fassler, Joan. *My grandpa died today*
Fowler, Susi Gregg. *Beautiful*
Fox, Louisa. *Every Monday in the mailbox*
Fox, Mem. *Sophie*
   With love, at Christmas
Garland, Michael. *Angel cat*
Gerstein, Mordicai. *The mountains of Tibet*
   The shadow of a flying bird
Goble, Paul. *Beyond the ridge*
Gould, Deborah. *Grandpa's slide show*
Greenlee, Sharon. *When someone dies*
Gregory, Valiska. *Through the mickle woods*
Griffith, Helen V. *Dream meadow*
Grimm, Wilhelm. *Dear Mili*
Hallinan, P. K. (Patrick K.). *Three freckles past a hair*
Harranth, Wolf. *My old grandad*
Harriott, Ted. *Coming home*
Harshman, Marc. *Uncle James*
Haseley, Dennis. *Ghost catcher*
Hastings, Selina. *The man who wanted to live forever*

Hazen, Barbara Shook. *Why did Grandpa die?*
Hesse, Karen. *Poppy's chair*
Heymans, Annemie. *The princess in the kitchen garden*
Hickcox, Ruth. *Great-Grandmother's treasure*
Hines, Anna Grossnickle. *Remember the butterflies*
Hoffmann, E. T. A. *The strange child*
Hogan, Bernice. *My grandmother died but I won't forget her*
Hoopes, Lyn Littlefield. *Nana*
Horio, Seishi. *The monkey and the crab*
Howard, Ellen. *Murphy and Kate*
Hurd, Edith Thacher. *The black dog who went into the woods*
Hutton, Warwick. *Theseus and the Minotaur*
Jewell, Nancy. *Time for Uncle Joe*
Joosse, Barbara M. *Better with two*
Joslin, Mary. *The goodbye boat*
Jukes, Mavis. *I'll see you in my dreams*
Kaldhol, Marit. *Goodbye Rune*
Kantrowitz, Mildred. *When Violet died*
Keats, Ezra Jack. *Maggie and the pirate*
Keller, Holly. *Goodbye, Max*
Kooharian, David. *Sammy's story*
Kroll, Virginia L. *Fireflies, peach pies, and lullabies*
   Helen the fish
Kübler-Ross, Elisabeth. *Remember the secret*
Lanton, Sandy. *Daddy's chair*
Leavy, Una. *Good-bye, Papa*
Le Tord, Bijou. *My Grandma Leonie*
Levete, Sarah. *When people die*
Limb, Sue. *Come back, Grandma*
London, Jonathan. *Gray fox*
   Liplap's wish
Luenn, Nancy. *A gift for Abuelita*
Lyon, George Ella. *Ada's pal*
McFarlane, Sheryl. *Waiting for the whales*
Madenski, Melissa. *Some of the pieces*
Maguire, Gregory. *Lucas Fishbone*
Maple, Marilyn J. *On the wings of a butterfly*
Mattingley, Christobel. *The angel with a mouth-organ*
Meeker, Clare Hodgson. *A tale of two rice birds*
Mendoza, George. *The hunter I might have been*
Mills, Joyce C. *Gentle Willow*
Morehead, Debby. *A special place for Charlee*
Newman, Lesléa. *Too far away to touch*
Nobisso, Josephine. *Grandpa loved*
Nodar, Carmen Santiago. *Abuelita's paradise*
Old, Wendie C. *Stacy had a little sister*
Oliviero, Jamie. *Som See and the magic elephant*
Peavy, Linda. *Allison's grandfather*
Pollack, Eileen. *Whisper whisper Jesse, whisper whisper Josh*
Porte, Barbara Ann. *Harry's mom*
Rappaport, Doreen. *Journey of Meng*
   The new king
Rogers, Fred. *When a pet dies*
Rosen, Michael (1946-). *A Thanksgiving wish*
Rosen, Michael J. (1954-). *Bonesy and Isabel*
Rosenberg, Liz. *The carousel*
Roth, Susan L. *Another Christmas*
Russo, Marisabina. *Grandpa Abe*
Rylant, Cynthia. *Dog Heaven*
Sanford, Doris. *David has AIDS*
Scheller, Melanie. *My grandfather's hat*
Schick, Eleanor. *Mama*
Schneider, Antonie. *Good-bye, Vivi!*
Simmonds, Posy. *Fred*
Simon, Norma. *The saddest time*

Smith-Ayala, Emilie. *Marisol and the yellow messenger*
Spohn, David. *Nate's treasure*
Stein, Sara Bonnett. *About dying*
Stevens, Carla. *Stories from a snowy meadow*
Stevens, Margaret (Dean). *When grandpa died*
Stiles, Norman. *I'll miss you, Mr. Hooper*
Stilz, Carol Curtis. *Kirsty's kite*
Taha, Karen T. *A gift for Tia Rose*
Tejima, Keizaburo. *Swan sky*
Thomas, Jane Resh. *Saying good-bye to grandma*
Townsend, Maryann. *Pop's secret*
Trottier, Maxine. *Prairie willow*
Van den Berg, Marinus. *The three birds*
Varley, Susan. *Badger's parting gifts*
Velthuijs, Max. *Frog and the birdsong*
Vigna, Judith. *Saying goodbye to daddy*
Viorst, Judith. *The tenth good thing about Barney*
Wahl, Jan. *Tiger watch*
Wahl, Mats. *Grandfather's laika*
Walker, Alice. *To hell with dying*
Wallace, Ian. *The sparrow's song*
Wallace-Brodeur, Ruth. *Goodbye, Mitch*
Weitzman, Elizabeth. *Let's talk about when a parent dies*
Wells, Rosemary. *The language of doves*
Whelan, Gloria. *Bringing the farmhouse home*
White Deer of Autumn. *The great change*
Wild, Margaret. *Old Pig*
  Toby
  The very best of friends
Wilhelm, Hans. *I'll always love you*
Williams, Laura E. *The long silk strand*
Wittbold, Maureen. *Mending Peter's heart*
Wood, Douglas. *Grandad's prayers of the earth*
Wright, Betty Ren. *The cat next door*
Zalben, Jane Breskin. *Pearl's marigolds for grandpa*
Zolotow, Charlotte (Shapiro). *My grandson Lew*
  The old dog

Deer *see* Animals – deer

Delaware Indians *see* Indians of North America – Delaware

Demons *see* Devil; Monsters

Denmark *see* Foreign lands – Denmark

Dentists *see* Careers – dentists

Department stores *see* Stores

Desert

Albert, Richard E. *Alejandro's gift*
Apperley, Dawn. *In the sand*
Arnold, Caroline. *A walk in the desert*
Asch, Frank. *Cactus poems*
Bash, Barbara. *Desert giant*
Baylor, Byrd. *The desert is theirs*
  Desert voices
  I'm in charge of celebrations
  We walk in sandy places
Beim, Jerrold. *Eric on the desert*
Buchanan, Ken. *It rained on the desert today*
  This house is made of mud
Busch, Phyllis S. *Cactus in the desert*

Catchpole, Clive. *Deserts*
Caudill, Rebecca. *Wind, sand and sky*
Chinery, Michael. *Desert animals*
Clark, Ann Nolan. *Tia Maria's garden*
Córdova, Amy. *Abuelita's heart*
Cretan, Gladys Yessayan. *Ten brothers with camels*
Darling, Kathy (Mary Kathleen). *Desert babies*
Dunphy, Madeleine. *Here is the southwestern desert*
Geis, Jacqueline. *Where the buffalo roam*
Guiberson, Brenda Z. *Cactus hotel*
Haarhoff, Dorian. *Desert December*
Holmes, Anita. *The 100-year-old cactus*
Irbinskas, Heather. *How Jackrabbit got his very long ears*
John, Naomi. *Roadrunner*
Johnson, Paul Brett. *Lost*
Johnston, Tony. *Desert song*
Keats, Ezra Jack. *Clementina's cactus*
Kessler, Cristina. *One night*
Levy, Elizabeth. *Cleo and the coyote*
London, Jonathan. *Ali, child of the desert*
Lowell, Susan. *The tortoise and the jackrabbit*
McDonald, Megan. *The bone keeper*
McKee, David. *The day the tide went out and out and out*
McLerran, Alice. *Roxaboxen*
  The year of the ranch
Marsh, T. J. *Way out in the desert*
Mora, Pat. *Delicious hullabaloo = Pachanga deliciosa*
  The desert is my mother = El desierto es mi madre
  Listen to the desert = Oye al desierto
  This big sky
Moreillon, Judi. *Sing down the rain*
Nunes, Susan Miho. *Coyote dreams*
Pearce, Q. L. *In the desert*
Pohrt, Tom. *Having a wonderful time*
Reynolds, Jan. *Sahara*
Roberts, Bethany. *Camel caravan*
Siebert, Diane. *Mojave*
Silverman, Erica. *Fixing the crack of dawn*
Ungerer, Tomi. *Orlando, the brave vulture*
Upper, Jonathan. *Spin's really wild Africa tour*
Wondriska, William. *The stop*
Yolen, Jane. *Welcome to the sea of sand*
Young, Ed (Edward). *Donkey trouble*

Detective stories *see* Problem solving

Detectives *see* Careers – detectives

Devil

Alger, Leclaire Gowans. *Kellyburn Braes*
Asch, Frank. *Little Devil's ABC*
  Little Devil's 123
Berson, Harold. *How the devil gets his due*
Carey, Valerie Scho. *The devil and mother Crump*
Coombs, Patricia. *The magic pot*
Elwell, Peter. *The king of the pipers*
Galdone, Joanna. *Amber day*
Grimm, Jacob. *The bearskinner*
  The devil with the green hairs
Helldorfer, M. C. (Mary Claire). *Jack, Skinny Bones, and the golden pancakes*
Joyce, James. *The cat and the devil*
Kimmel, Eric A. *Grizz!*
McCurdy, Michael. *The devils who learned to be good*
Magnus, Erica. *The boy and the devil*

Olson, Arielle North. *Noah's cats and the devil's fire*
Oppenheim, Shulamith Levey. *Iblis*
Pinkwater, Daniel Manus. *Devil in the drain*
Root, Phyllis. *Rosie's fiddle*
Scribner, Charles. *The devil's bridge*
Shute, Linda. *Momotaro, the peach boy*
Stalder, Valerie. *Even the devil is afraid of a shrew*
Stewig, John Warren. *Clever Gretchen*
Turska, Krystyna. *The magician of Cracow*
Wooldridge, Connie Nordhielm. *Wicked Jack*
Zemach, Harve. *Duffy and the devil*

Diabetes *see* Illness – diabetes

Dictionaries

Ahlberg, Allan. *Me and my friend*
Bruna, Dick. *Dick Bruna's picture word book*
Bunting, Jane. *The children's visual dictionary*
    My first word book
Burnstein, Chaya M. *The Jewish kids' Hebrew-English wordbook*
Cartlidge, Michelle. *Michelle Cartlidge's book of words*
A child's picture English-Hebrew dictionary
Daly, Kathleen N. *The Macmillan picture wordbook*
Day, Alexandra. *Frank and Ernest play ball*
Dodds, Siobhan. *Words and pictures*
Floyd, Lucy. *Agatha's alphabet, with her very own dictionary*
Halsey, William D. *The magic world of words*
Howard, Katherine. *My first picture dictionary*
Kelley, True. *Hammers and mops, pencils and pots*
Krensky, Stephen. *My first dictionary*
MacBean, Dilla Wittemore. *Picture book dictionary*
McIntire, Alta. *Follett beginning to read picture dictionary*
Parke, Margaret B. *Young reader's color-picture dictionary*
Rand McNally picturebook dictionary
Scarry, Richard. *Richard Scarry's biggest word book ever!*
    Richard Scarry's storybook dictionary
Schulz, Charles M. *The Charlie Brown dictionary*
Seuss, Dr. *The cat in the hat dictionary*
Wilkes, Angela. *My first word book*
Williams, Sam. *The baby's word book*

Diggers *see* Machines

Digging *see* Activities – digging

Diners *see* Restaurants

Dinosaurs

Ahlberg, Allan. *Dinosaur dreams*
Aliki. *Digging up dinosaurs*
    Dinosaur bones
    Dinosaurs are different
    Fossils tell of long ago
    My visit to the dinosaurs
Atkins, Jeannine. *Mary Anning and the sea dragon*
Barber, Antonia. *Satchelmouse and the dinosaurs*
Barner, Bob. *Too many dinosaurs*
Barton, Byron. *Bones, bones, dinosaur bones*
    Dinosaurs, dinosaurs
Berenstain, Stan. *After the dinosaurs*
    The day of the dinosaur

Berger, Melvin. *Why did the dinosaurs disappear?*
Binnamin, Vivian. *The case of the snoring stegosaurus*
Birchman, David Francis. *Brother Billy Bronto's bygone blues band*
Birney, Betty G. *Tyrannosaurus Tex*
Bishop, Roma. *My first pop-up book of dinosaurs*
Blackwood, Mary. *Derek the knitting dinosaur*
Blumenthal, Nancy. *Count-a-saurus*
Bourgeois, Paulette. *Franklin's class trip*
Boynton, Sandra. *Dinosaur's binkit*
    Oh my oh my oh dinosaurs!
Bradman, Tony. *Dilly speaks up*
Brasch, Kate. *Prehistoric monsters*
Brenner, Barbara A. *Dinosaurium*
Brighton, Catherine. *The fossil girl*
Brillhart, Julie. *The dino expert*
Brown, Laurie Krasny. *Dinosaurs alive and well*
    Dinosaurs divorce
    Dinosaurs to the rescue
    Dinosaurs travel
    How to be a friend
    Rex and Lilly school time
    When dinosaurs die
Brown, Marc Tolon. *Dinosaurs, beware!*
Camp, Lindsay. *Dinosaurs at the supermarket*
Carrick, Carol. *Big old bones*
    The crocodiles still wait
    Patrick's dinosaurs
    Patrick's dinosaurs on the Internet
    What happened to Patrick's dinosaurs?
Cauley, Lorinda Bryan. *The trouble with Tyrannosaurus Rex*
Charlton, Elizabeth. *Terrible tyrannosaurus*
Chausse, Sylvie. *The egg and I*
Cohen, Daniel. *Dinosaurs*
Cole, Joanna. *The magic school bus in the time of the dinosaurs*
Craig, M. Jean. *Dinosaurs and more dinosaurs*
Cremins, Robert. *Pop up baby brontosaurus*
    Pop up baby coelophysis
    Pop up baby pteranodon
    Pop up baby stegosaurus
    Pop up baby triceratops
    Pop up baby tyrannosaurus rex
Curious George and the dinosaur
Cutts, David. *More about dinosaurs*
Cuyler, Margery. *Baby Dot*
Daly, Kathleen N. *Dinosaurs*
Damjan, Mischa. *How do Dinosaurs say goodnight?*
Demi. *Find Demi's dinosaurs*
De Paola, Tomie (Thomas Anthony). *Little Grunt and the big egg*
Dinosaurs and monsters
Donnelly, Liza. *Dinosaur beach*
    Dinosaur garden
    Dinosaurs' Halloween
Eastman, David. *The story of dinosaurs*
Edwards, Pamela Duncan. *Dinorella*
Emberley, Michael. *More dinosaurs!*
Faulkner, Keith. *Amble has a dream*
    David dreaming of dinosaurs
    Munch looks for lunch
    Rumble frightens himself
    Swoop flies too high
Fleischman, Paul. *Time train*
Gay, Tenner Ottley. *Dinosaurs and their relatives in action*
Gibbons, Gail. *Dinosaurs*
Goode, Diane. *The dinosaur's new clothes*

Disbelief *see* Behavior – disbelief

Disguises

Hale, Irina. *Boxman*
Heller, Ruth. *How to hide a crocodile and other reptiles*
  How to hide a gray treefrog and other amphibians
  How to hide a parakeet and other birds
  How to hide a whip-poor-will and other birds
Kraus, Robert. *Strudwick, a sheep in wolf's clothing*
Lewis, J. Patrick. *The night of the goat children*
McNaughton, Colin. *Boo!*
Riddle, Tohby. *The great escape from City Zoo*
The three little pigs. *Who's at the door?*
Tildes, Phyllis Limbacher. *Animals in camouflage*

Dissatisfaction *see* Behavior – dissatisfaction

Distance *see* Concepts – distance

Divali *see* Holidays – Divali

Diving *see* Sports – skin diving

Divorce

Ackerman, Karen. *In the park with dad*
Ballard, Robin. *Gracie*
Baum, Louis. *One more time*
Berger, Terry. *How does it feel when your parents get divorced?*
Best, Cari. *Taxi! Taxi!*
Bienenfeld, Florence. *My mom and dad are getting a divorce*
Binch, Caroline. *Since Dad left*
Boegehold, Betty. *Daddy doesn't live here anymore*
Brown, Laurie Krasny. *Dinosaurs divorce*
Caines, Jeannette. *Daddy*
Christiansen, C. B. *My mother's house, my father's house*
Cole, Babette. *The un-wedding*
Cole, Julia. *My parents' divorce*
Dragonwagon, Crescent. *Always, always*
Girard, Linda Walvoord. *At Daddy's on Saturdays*
Goff, Beth. *Where's daddy?*
Hazen, Barbara Shook. *Two homes to live in*
Hickman, Martha Whitmore. *Robert lives with his grandparents*
Lansky, Vicki. *It's not your fault, KoKo Bear*
Lexau, Joan M. *Me day*
Lisker, Sonia O. *Two special cards*
Mayle, Peter. *Divorce can happen to the nicest people*
  Why are we getting a divorce?
Newman, Lesléa. *Saturday is Pattyday*
Noble, June. *Two homes for Lynn*
Norris, Lori P. (Peters). *D is for divorce*
Paris, Lena. *Mom is single*
Perry, Patricia. *Mommy and daddy are divorced*
Peterson, Jeanne Whitehouse. *That is that*
Pursell, Margaret Sanford. *A look at divorce*
Rodell, Susanna. *Dear Fred*
Rogers, Fred. *Divorce*
Rogers, Helen Spelman. *Morris and his brave lion*
Roy, Ronald. *Breakfast with my father*
Rush, Ken. *Friday's journey*
Schindel, John. *Dear Daddy*
Schuchman, Joan. *Two places to sleep*
Simon, Norma. *The daddy days*

Spelman, Cornelia. *Mama and Daddy Bear's divorce*
Steel, Danielle. *Martha's new daddy*
Stein, Sara Bonnett. *On divorce*
Stinson, Kathy. *Mom and dad don't live together any more*
Tangvald, Christine Harder. *Mom and dad don't live together anymore*
Thomas, Pat (1959-). *My family's changing*
Vigna, Judith. *Daddy's new baby*
  Grandma without me
  She's not my real mother
Watson, Jane Werner. *Sometimes a family has to split up*
Weninger, Brigitte. *Good-bye, daddy!*
Willhoite, Michael. *Daddy's roommate*
Winthrop, Elizabeth. *As the crow flies*

Doctors *see* Careers – doctors

Dodos *see* Birds – dodos

Dogs *see* Animals – dogs

Dolls *see* Toys – dolls

Dolphins *see* Animals – dolphins

Donkeys *see* Animals – donkeys

Dormice *see* Animals – dormice

Doves *see* Birds – doves

Down and up *see* Concepts – up and down

Down syndrome *see* Handicaps – Down syndrome

Dragonflies *see* Insects – dragonflies

Dragons

Agell, Charlotte. *The sailor's book*
Alexander, Sue. *World famous Muriel and the scary dragon*
Anderson, Wayne. *Dragon*
Aruego, José. *The king and his friends*
Asch, Frank. *Milk and cookies*
Atkins, Jeannine. *Mary Anning and the sea dragon*
Baumgart, Klaus. *Anna and the little green dragon*
  The little green dragon steps out
Bertrand, Lynne. *Dragon naps*
  One day, two dragons
Biro, Val. *Tobias and the dragon*
Boswell, Stephen. *King Gorboduc's fabulous zoo*
Bradfield, Roger (Jolly Roger). *A good night for dragons*
Buckaway, C. M. *Alfred, the dragon who lost his flame*
Burnside, Julian. *Matilda and the dragon*
Carle, Eric. *Dragons dragons and other creatures that never were*
Chalmers, Mary. *George Appleton*
Cherry, Lynne. *The dragon and the unicorn*
Christelow, Eileen. *Henry and the dragon*
Christian, Mary Blount. *The bookstore mouse*
Company González, Mercé. *Killian and the dragons*

Conover, Chris. *Sam Panda and Thunder Dragon*
Cooper, Susan. *Matthew's dragon*
Coville, Bruce. *Sarah and the dragon*
Craig, M. Jean. *The dragon in the clock box*
Cressey, James. *The dragon and George*
Cretien, Paul D. *Sir Henry and the dragon*
Davis, Reda. *Martin's dinosaur*
Day, Marie. *Dragon in the rocks*
DeLage, Ida. *The old witch and the dragon*
Delaney, Ned. *One dragon to another*
Demi. *Demi's dragons and fantastic creatures*
    Dragon kites and dragonflies
    The dragon's tale and other animal fables of the Chinese zodiac
De Paola, Tomie (Thomas Anthony). *The knight and the dragon*
Dewey, Ariane. *Dorin and the dragon*
Domanska, Janina. *King Krakus and the dragon*
Dragon poems
Eduar, Gilles. *Jooka saves the day*
Emberley, Ed (Edward Randolph). *Klippity klop*
Enderle, Judith (Ann) Ross. *The good-for-something dragon*
Falwell, Cathryn. *Dragon tooth*
Fassler, Joan. *The man of the house*
Gág, Wanda. *The funny thing*
Galchutt, David. *There was magic inside*
Garrison, Christian. *The dream eater*
Goode, Diane. *I hear a noise*
Grimm, Jacob. *The four clever brothers*
Haley, Gail E. *Jack and the fire dragon*
Hillert, Margaret. *Happy birthday, dear dragon*
    Merry Christmas, dear dragon
Hillman, Elizabeth. *Min-Yo and the moon dragon*
Hoban, Russell. *Ace Dragon Ltd.*
Hodges, Margaret. *Saint George and the dragon*
Holabird, Katharine. *Alexander and the dragon*
Howe, James. *There's a dragon in my sleeping bag*
Janosch. *Just one apple*
Jeschke, Susan. *Firerose*
Jones, Maurice. *I'm going on a dragon hunt*
Joslin, Sesyle. *Dear dragon*
Kent, Jack. *The once-upon-a-time dragon*
    There's no such thing as a dragon
Kimmel, Eric A. *The four gallant sisters*
    The rooster's antlers
Kimmel, Margaret Mary. *Magic in the mist*
Krahn, Fernando. *The secret in the dungeon*
Kumin, Maxine W. *Sebastian and the dragon*
Lattimore, Deborah Nourse. *The dragon's robe*
Lawson, Julie. *The dragon's pearl*
Leaf, Margaret. *Eyes of the dragon*
Leedy, Loreen. *A dragon Christmas*
    The dragon Halloween party
    The dragon Thanksgiving feast
    A number of dragons
Lifton, Betty Jean. *Joji and the dragon*
Lindgren, Astrid. *The dragon with red eyes*
Lobel, Arnold. *Prince Bertram the bad*
Long, Claudia. *Albert's story*
McCaughrean, Geraldine. *Saint George and the dragon*
McCrea, James. *The story of Olaf*
McMullen, Eunice. *Dragon for breakfast*
Mahood, Kenneth. *The laughing dragon*
Mahy, Margaret. *The dragon of an ordinary family*
    A lion in the meadow
Manushkin, Fran. *Moon dragon*
Martin, C. L. G. *The dragon nanny*

Mathews, Judith. *An egg and seven socks*
Mayer, Mercer. *Whinnie the lovesick dragon*
Minarik, Else Holmelund. *The little girl and the dragon*
Mogensen, Jan. *Teddy and the Chinese dragon*
Munsch, Robert N. *The paper bag princess*
Murphy, Shirley Rousseau. *Valentine for a dragon*
Myers, Walter Dean. *The dragon takes a wife*
Nash, Ogden. *Custard the dragon*
    Custard the dragon and the wicked knight, ill. by Lynn Munsinger
    Custard the dragon and the wicked knight, ill. by Linell Nash
Nesbit, Edith. *The last of the dragons*
Noble, Kate. *The dragon of Navy Pier*
Nolan, Dennis. *The castle builder*
Nolen, Jerdine. *Raising dragons*
Nunes, Susan Miho. *The last dragon*
Oksner, Robert M. *The incompetent wizard*
Pattison, Darcy. *The river dragon*
Pavey, Peter. *One dragon's dream*
Peet, Bill (William Bartlett). *How Droofus the dragon lost his head*
Pendziwol, Jean. *No dragons for tea*
Phillips, Louis. *The brothers Wrong and Wrong Again*
Pilkey, Dav. *Dragon's fat cat*
    Dragon's merry Christmas
    A friend for Dragon
Price, Roger. *The last little dragon*
Reddix, Valerie. *Dragon kite of the autumn moon*
Robinson, Fay. *Where did all the dragons go?*
Rosen, Winifred. *Dragons hate to be discreet*
Roth, Susan L. *Brave Martha and the dragon*
Scarry, Richard. *Richard Scarry's Peasant Pig and the terrible dragon*
Schotter, Richard. *There's a dragon about*
Scullard, Sue. *Miss Fanshawe and the great dragon adventure*
Sherman, Nancy. *Gwendolyn the miracle hen*
Shub, Elizabeth. *Dragon Franz*
Slote, Elizabeth. *Nelly's garden*
Stern, Peter. *Max the dragon*
Stern, Simon. *Vasily and the dragon*
Stock, Catherine. *Emma's dragon hunt*
Sutcliff, Rosemary. *The minstrel and the dragon pup*
Thayer, Jane. *The popcorn dragon*, ill. by Jay Hyde Barnum
    The popcorn dragon, ill. by Lisa McCue
Thomas, Shelley Moore. *Good night, Good Knight*
Torre, Betty L. *The luminous pearl*
Trevelyan, Kathy. *Don't be surprised!*
Trez, Denise. *The little knight's dragon*
Uttley, Alison. *Sam Pig and the dragon*
Van Woerkom, Dorothy. *Alexandra the rock-eater*
Vaughan, Marcia Kapok. *The dancing dragon*
Waterton, Betty. *Orff, 27 dragons (and a snarkel)*
Wiesner, David. *Free fall*
    The loathsome dragon
Williams, Arlene. *Dragon soup*
Williams, Jay. *Everyone knows what a dragon looks like*
Willis, Val. *The secret in the matchbox*
Wilson, Sarah. *Beware the dragons!*
Yep, Laurence. *Dragon prince*
Zirkel, Lynn. *The shell dragon*

Drawing *see* Activities – drawing

Drawing games *see* Games

Dreams

Adlerman, Dan. *Africa calling*
Adoff, Arnold. *Flamboyan*
Ahlberg, Allan. *Dinosaur dreams*
Aichinger, Helga. *The shepherd*
Alborough, Jez. *Ice cream bear*
Alexander, Martha G. *Bobo's dream*
   You're a genius, Blackboard Bear
Allison, Diane Worfolk. *In window eight, the moon is late*
Anrooy, Frans van. *The sea horse*
Appelt, Kathi. *Cowboy dreams*
Armstrong, Jennifer. *Pierre's dream*
Arnold, Tedd. *Green Wilma*
   No jumping on the bed!
Asch, Frank. *Milk and cookies*
   Moonbear's dream
Axworthy, Anni. *Ben's Wednesday*
Aylesworth, Jim. *The bad dream*
   Tonight's the night
Balet, Jan B. *Joanjo*
Balzola, Asun. *Munia and the orange crocodile*
Bancroft, Catherine. *Felix's hat*
Banks, Kate (Katherine A.). *And if the moon could talk*
Barasch, Lynne. *Old friends*
Baumgart, Klaus. *The little green dragon steps out*
Berenstain, Stan. *The Berenstain bears and the bad dream*
Berger, Barbara Helen. *The donkey's dream*
Bider, Djemma. *A drop of honey*
Bohdal, Susi. *The magic honey jar*
Bond, Felicia. *Wake up, Vladimir*
Boyd, Lizi. *Sweet dreams, Willy*
Brown, M. K. (Mary K.). *Let's go swimming with Mr. Sillypants*
Brown, Margaret Wise. *Dream book*
   The little farmer
Brown, Ruth. *Mad summer night's dream*
Browne, Anthony. *Willy the dreamer*
Bruna, Dick. *Miffy's dream*
Buckley, Helen Elizabeth. *Someday with my father*
Burdett, Lois. *A midsummer night's dream for kids*
Burningham, John. *Hey! Get off our train*
Burnside, Julian. *Matilda and the dragon*
Callen, Larry. *Dashiel and the night*
Carlson, Nancy L. *It's going to be perfect*
Carpenter, Mary-Chapin. *Dreamland*
Carroll, Lewis. *The nursery "Alice"*
Casler, Leigh. *The boy who dreamed of an acorn*
Cazet, Denys. *Daydreams*
Chesworth, Michael. *Rainy day dream*
Chorao, Kay. *Lemon moon*
Chwast, Seymour. *Still another children's book*
Cole, Babette. *The slimy book*
Collington, Peter. *Little pickle*
   The midnight circus
Cooper, Susan. *Matthew's dragon*
Cousins, Lucy. *Maisy's bedtime*
Craig, M. Jean. *What did you dream?*
Crew, Gary. *Bright star*
Crossley-Holland, Kevin. *Sleeping Nanna*
Crowley, Arthur. *The wagon man*
Cuyler, Margery. *Fat Santa*
Dahl, Roald. *Dirty beasts*
Daugherty, Charles Michael. *Wisher*
Davis, Katie (Katie I.). *I hate to go to bed!*
Davis, Maggie S. *A garden of whales*

Davol, Marguerite W. *Batwings and the curtain of night*
Dennis, Wesley. *Flip*
DeSaix, Frank. *The girl who danced with dolphins*
Dewey, Ariane. *Dorin and the dragon*
Doherty, Berlie. *The midnight man*
Donaldson, Lois. *Karl's wooden horse*
Dragonwagon, Crescent. *Half a moon and one whole star*
Drescher, Henrik. *Simon's book*
Dunbar, Joyce. *The sand children*
   Tell me something happy before I go to sleep
Duncan, Lois. *Horses of dreamland*
Dürr, Ursula. *The secret of Trembleton Hall*
Duvoisin, Roger Antoine. *The missing milkman*
Eduar, Gilles. *Dream journey*
Elzbieta. *Dikou and the mysterious moon sheep*
Emberley, Rebecca. *My mother's secret life*
Erskine, Jim. *Bedtime story*
Esbensen, Barbara Juster. *The dream mouse*
Farber, Norma. *I swim an ocean in my sleep*
Faulkner, Keith. *Amble has a dream*
Fazio, Brenda Lena. *Grandfather's story*
Field, Rachel Lyman. *A road might lead to anywhere*
Foreman, Michael. *Jack's fantastic voyage*
   Land of dreams
Francis, Anna B. *Pleasant dreams*
Francis, Frank. *The magic wallpaper*
Galouchko, Annouchka. *Shô and the demons of the deep*
Gantos, Jack (John, Jr.). *Greedy Greeny*
Garrison, Christian. *The dream eater*
Gay, Marie-Louise. *Moonbeam on a cat's ear*
Giff, Patricia Reilly. *Next year I'll be special*
Gile, John. *Oh, how I wished I could read!*
Ginsburg, Mirra. *Across the stream*
   Four brave sailors
Goldsmith, Howard. *Sleepy little owl*
Goodhart, Pippa. *Row, row, row your boat*
Goodman, Joan Elizabeth. *Bernard's nap*
Gorbachev, Valeri. *Nicky and the big, bad wolves*
Gould, Deborah. *Grandpa's slide show*
Greenfield, Eloise. *Africa dream*
Greenwood, Ann. *A pack of dreams*
Griffith, Helen V. *Pluck's dreams*
Hague, Kathleen. *Out of the nursery, into the night*
Hale, Irina. *Donkey's dreadful day*
Haley, Gail E. *Dream peddler*
Harrison, Troon. *The dream collector*
Hayes, Geoffrey. *The secret inside*
Hazelaar, Cor. *Zoo dreams*
Heckman, Philip. *Waking upside down*
Heine, Helme. *The marvelous journey through the night*
Heller, Nicholas. *Mathilda the dream bear*
   Peas
Henri, Adrian. *The postman's palace*
Hill, Susan. *Go away, bad dreams!*
Hodgetts, Blake Christopher. *Dream of the dinosaurs*
Hurd, Edith Thacher. *Little dog, dreaming*
Ipcar, Dahlov. *Black and white*
Isadora, Rachel. *Caribbean dream*
Jacobs, Joseph. *The crock of gold*
James, Betsy. *The dream stair*
Jendresen, Erik. *The first story ever told*
Jennings, Michael. *The bears who came to breakfix*
Johnson, Jane. *Bertie on the beach*
Jonas, Ann. *The quilt*

Weisgard, Leonard. *Who dreams of cheese?*
Wende, Philip. *Bird boy*
Wersba, Barbara. *Amanda dreaming*
Wiesner, David. *Free fall*
Wild, Margaret. *Going home*
Wildsmith, Brian. *Carousel*
Willard, Nancy. *The mountains of quilt*
  Night story
Wood, Audrey. *Sweet dream pie*
Yaccarino, Dan. *Good night, Mr. Night*
Yolen, Jane. *Moon ball*
Yorinks, Arthur. *Hey, Al*
Young, Ed (Edward). *Night visitors*
Zemach, Kaethe. *The funny dream*
Ziefert, Harriet. *Moonride*
Zolotow, Charlotte (Shapiro). *I have a horse of my own*
  Someday
  Wake up and goodnight
  Who is Ben?

Dressers *see* Furniture – dressers

Dresses *see* Clothing – dresses

Driving *see* Activities – driving

Droughts *see* Weather – droughts

Drug addiction *see* Illness – drug addiction

Ducks *see* Birds – ducks

Dutch Americans *see* Ethnic groups in the U.S. – Dutch Americans

Dwarfs, midgets

Bruna, Dick. *Dick Bruna's Snow-White and the seven dwarfs*
  Dick Bruna's Tom Thumb
Calhoun, Mary. *The thieving dwarfs*
French, Fiona. *Snow White in New York*
Grimm, Jacob. *Rose Red and the bear prince*
  Snow White, ill. by Trina Schart Hyman
  Snow White, ill. by Bernadette Watts
  Snow White and Rose Red, ill. by Adrienne Adams
  Snow White and Rose Red, ill. by John Wallner
  Snow White and Rose Red, ill. by Bernadette Watts
  Snow White and the seven dwarfs, ill. by Wanda Gág
  Snow White and the seven dwarves, ill. by Chihiro Iwasaki
Jennings, Michael. *Robin Goodfellow and the giant dwarf*
Lobel, Anita. *The dwarf giant*
Rascal. *Oregon's journey*
Sikundar, Sylvia. *Forest singer*
Walt Disney Productions. *Walt Disney's Snow White and the seven dwarfs*

Dwellings *see* Buildings; Homes, houses

Dying *see* Death

Eagles *see* Birds – eagles

Ears *see* Anatomy – ears; Handicaps – deafness; Senses – hearing

Earth

Anno, Mitsumasa. *Anno's sundial*
Asch, Frank. *The earth and I*
Asimov, Isaac. *The best new thing*
Benson, Laura Lee. *This is our earth*
Bernstein, Margery. *Earth namer*
Branley, Franklyn M. (Mansfield). *Earthquakes*
  What makes day and night
Burningham, John. *Whaddayamean*
Carson, Jo. *The great shaking*
Clements, Andrew. *Mother Earth's counting book*
Cole, Joanna. *The magic school bus inside the earth*
Dayton, Mona. *Earth and sky*
DeMunn, Michael. *The earth is good*
Engdahl, Sylvia. *Our world is earth*
Johnston, Tony. *We love the dirt*
Lauber, Patricia. *How we learned the earth is round*
  You're aboard spaceship Earth
Leutscher, Alfred. *Earth*
Lewis, Claudia Louise. *When I go to the moon*
Luenn, Nancy. *Mother earth*
Milgrim, David. *Here in space*
Reiser, Lynn. *Earthdance*
Rucki, Ani. *When the Earth wakes*
Schmid, Eleonore. *The living earth*
Simon, Seymour. *Beneath your feet*
Siomades, Lorianne. *A place to bloom*
Staub, Leslie. *Bless this house*
Wyler, Rose. *The starry sky*
Zoehfeld, Kathleen Weidner. *How mountains are made*

Earthquakes

Carson, Jo. *The great shaking*
Enderle, Judith (Ann) Ross. *Francis, the earthquake dog*
Givon, Hannah Gelman. *We shake in a quake*

East Indian Americans *see* Ethnic groups in the U.S. – East Indian Americans

Easter *see* Holidays – Easter

Eating *see* Food

Ecology

Accorsi, William. *Rachel Carson*
Aldridge, Josephine Haskell. *A possible tree*
Aliki. *My visit to the zoo*
Allen, Judy. *Seal*
  Whale

Fly, Homer, fly
   The gnats of knotty pine
   The wump world
Radley, Gail. *The spinner's gift*
Rand, Gloria. *Prince William*
Ray, Mary Lyn. *Pumpkins*
Reed-Jones, Carol. *The tree in the ancient forest*
Roach, Marilynne K. *Dune fox*
Sadler, Marilyn. *Elizabeth, Larry, and Ed*
Sanders, Scott R. (Scott Russell). *Crawdad Creek*
Santore, Charles. *William the Curious*
Schmid, Eleonore. *The living earth*
Selzer, Meyer. *Here comes the recycling truck!*
Seuss, Dr. *The Lorax*
Short, Mayo. *Andy and the wild ducks*
Showers, Paul. *Where does the garbage go?*
Siomades, Lorianne. *A place to bloom*
Snape, Juliet. *Frog odyssey*
Staub, Leslie. *Bless this house*
Stone, A. Harris. *The last free bird*
Swamp, Jake. *Giving thanks*
Tate, Suzanne. *Crabby's water wish*
Thornhill, Jan. *A tree in a forest*
   Wild in the city
Torgersen, Don Arthur. *The troll who lived in the lake*
Tresselt, Alvin R. *The beaver pond*
   The dead tree
   The gift of the tree
Van Laan, Nancy. *Round and round again*
Wahl, Jan. *Once when the world was green*
Wegen, Ron. *Where can the animals go?*
Wildsmith, Brian. *Professor Noah's spaceship*
Williams, Terry Tempest. *Between cattails*
Wood, Douglas. *Old Turtle*
Yardley, Thompson. *Buy now, pay later*
Yolen, Jane. *Welcome to the sea of sand*

Ecuador *see* Foreign lands – Ecuador

Education *see* School

Eggs

Andersen, H. C. (Hans Christian). *The woman with the eggs*
Asch, Frank. *MacGooses's grocery*
Auch, Mary Jane. *The Easter egg farm*
   Eggs mark the spot
Back, Christine. *Chicken and egg*
Barber, Antonia. *Gemma and the baby chick*
Bourke, Linda. *Ethel's exceptional egg*
Brown, Margaret Wise. *The golden egg book*
Burton, Robert. *The egg*
Campbell, Rod. *Oh dear!*
Casey, Patricia. *Quack quack*
Chausse, Sylvie. *The egg and I*
Chorao, Kay. *Ida and Betty and the secret eggs*
Claret, Maria. *The chocolate rabbit*
Coontz, Otto. *The quiet house*
Demi. *Little chick chick*
Dodds, Siobhan. *Elizabeth Hen*
Dunbar, Joyce. *Eggday*
Dunrea, Olivier. *The trow-wife's treasure*
Eastman, P. D. (Philip D.). *Flap your wings*
Eggs
Ernst, Lisa Campbell. *Zinnia and Dot*
Goffin, Josse. *Yes*

Gordon, Sharon. *Easter Bunny's lost egg*
Halperin, Wendy Anderson. *When chickens grow teeth*
Hariton, Anca. *Egg story*
Hartmann, Wendy. *The dinosaurs are back and it's all your fault, Edward!*
Heller, Ruth. *Chickens aren't the only ones*
Hill, Eric. *Spot's first Easter*
Hoban, Lillian. *The case of the two masked robbers*
Hooks, William H. *Mr. Dinosaur*
Hooper, Meredith. *Seven eggs*
Imai, Miko. *Little Lumpty*
Isami, Ikuyo. *The fox's egg*
Jenkins, Priscilla Belz. *A nest full of eggs*
Joyce, William. *Bently and egg*
Kay, Helen. *An egg is for wishing*
Kellogg, Steven (Stephen). *A penguin pup for Pinkerton*
Kent, Jack. *The egg book*
Kimmel, Eric A. *The birds' gift*
Knüppel, Helga. *Christabel Crocodile's birthday egg*
Krauss, Ruth. *The happy egg*
Kumin, Maxine W. *Eggs of things*
Kwitz, Mary DeBall. *Little chick's story*
Landa, Norbert. *Rabbit and chicken count eggs*
   Rabbit and chicken play with colors
Lasell, Fen. *Fly away goose*
Lauber, Patricia. *What's hatching out of that egg?*
Leedy, Loreen. *Tracks in the sand*
Legg, Gerald. *From egg to chicken*
Levitin, Sonia. *A single speckled egg*
Lionni, Leo. *An extraordinary egg*
Lloyd, Megan. *Chicken tricks*
London, Jonathan. *Condor's egg*
Long, Earlene. *Johnny's egg*
Lorenz, Lee. *Dinah's egg*
McCrea, Lilian. *Mother hen*
MacDonald, Elizabeth. *Mr. MacGregor's breakfast egg*
McGovern, Ann. *Eggs on your nose*
Mathews, Louise. *Cluck one*
Merrick, Patrick. *Easter bunnies*
Milgrom, Harry. *Egg-ventures*
Milhous, Katherine. *The egg tree*
Min, Laura. *Mrs. Sato's hens*
Mother Goose. *Humpty Dumpty*, ill. by Moira Kemp
Myers, Bernice. *The millionth egg*
Nethery, Mary. *Mary Veronica's egg*
Nicoll, Helen. *Meg's eggs*
Nolen, Jerdine. *Raising dragons*
O'Neill, Mary. *Big red hen*
Peet, Bill (William Bartlett). *The pinkish, purplish, bluish egg*
Polacco, Patricia. *Chicken Sunday*
   Just plain Fancy
   Rechenka's eggs
Potter, Beatrix. *The tale of Jemima Puddle-Duck*
Powell, Jillian. *Eggs*
Pursell, Margaret Sanford. *Jessie the chicken*
   Sprig the tree frog
Rockwell, Anne F. *The gollywhopper egg*
   The wonderful eggs of Furicchia
Roddie, Shen. *Hatch, egg, hatch!*
Ross, Tom. *Eggbert, the slightly cracked egg*
San Souci, Robert D. *The talking eggs*
Scamell, Ragnhild. *Solo plus one*
Scarry, Richard. *Egg in the hole*
Schertle, Alice. *Down the road*
Schick, Eleanor. *A surprise in the forest*
Schubert, Ingrid. *Bear's eggs*

Selsam, Millicent E. *Egg to chick*
Seuss, Dr. *Horton hatches the egg*
Simmons, Jane. *Daisy and the egg*
Smith, Mavis. *A snake mistake*
Standon, Anna. *Little duck lost*
Stevenson, James. *The great big especially beautiful Easter egg*
Sundgaard, Arnold. *Jethro's difficult dinosaur*
Sutcliff, Rosemary. *The minstrel and the dragon pup*
Sykes, Julie. *Dora's eggs*
Taylor, Shirley. *The cross in the egg*
Tildes, Phyllis Limbacher. *The magic babushka*
Tresselt, Alvin R. *The world in the candy egg*
Troughton, Joanna. *The quail's egg*
Vyner, Sue. *The stolen egg*
Waber, Bernard. *How to go about laying an egg*
Wahl, Jan. *The five in the forest*
Wilhelm, Hans. *More bunny trouble*
Wilkes, Larry. *The king's egg dance*
Wormell, Mary. *Hilda Hen's search*
Wright, Dare. *Edith and the duckling*
Ziefert, Harriet. *Happy Easter, Grandma!*

Egrets *see* Birds – egrets

Egypt *see* Foreign lands – Egypt

Egyptian language *see* Hieroglyphics

El Salvador *see* Foreign lands – El Salvador

Elderly *see* Old age

Electricians *see* Careers – electricians

Elephant seals *see* Animals – elephant seals

Elephants *see* Animals – elephants

Elevators, escalators

Barner, Bob. *Elevator escalator book*
Farber, Norma. *Up the down elevator*
Murphy, Stuart J. *Elevator magic*
Reasoner, Charles. *The big busy building*
Sis, Peter. *Going up!*

Elk *see* Animals – elk

Elves *see* Mythical creatures – elves

Embarrassment *see* Emotions – embarrassment

Emergencies *see* Hospitals

Emotions

Aliki. *Feelings*
Allington, Richard L. *Feelings*
Ancona, George. *I feel*
Andersen, H. C. (Hans Christian). *The snow queen*, ill. by Bernadette Watts
Andersen, Karen Born. *What's the matter, Sylvie, can't you ride?*
Anholt, Catherine. *What I like*

What makes me happy?
Bach, Alice. *The day after Christmas*
Berger, Terry. *How does it feel when your parents get divorced?*
I have feelings
I have feelings too
Bienenfeld, Florence. *My mom and dad are getting a divorce*
Binch, Caroline. *Since Dad left*
Bogacki, Tomasz. *I hate you! I like you!*
Borten, Helen. *Do you move as I do?*
Brenner, Barbara A. *Faces, faces, faces*
Brown, Laurie Krasny. *When dinosaurs die*
Brown, Tricia. *Someone special, just like you*
Brownridge, William Roy. *The moccasin goalie*
Bunting, Eve (Anne Evelyn). *I don't want to go to camp*
Sunshine home
Train to somewhere
Burdett, Lois. *The tempest for kids*
Burningham, John. *The baby*
Butterworth, Nick. *Making faces*
Cadnum, Michael. *The lost and found house*
Calhoun, Mary. *The witch who lost her shadow*
Campbell, Ann. *Dora's box*
Castle, Sue. *Face talk, hand talk, body talk*
Christiansen, C. B. *My mother's house, my father's house*
Clark, Sue. *Feelings*
Clifford, Eth. *Your face is a picture*
Cole, William. *Frances face-maker*
Conta, Marcia Maher. *Feelings between brothers and sisters*
Feelings between friends
Feelings between kids and grownups
Feelings between kids and parents
Crary, Elizabeth. *I'm frustrated*
Cunningham, Julia. *A mouse called Junction*
Curtis, Gavin. *Grandma's baseball*
Curtis, Jamie Lee. *Today I feel silly and other moods that make my day*
Dragonwagon, Crescent. *Rainy day together*
Duerrstein, Richard. *Mickey is happy*
Eisenstein, Marilyn. *Periwinkle isn't Paris*
Emberley, Ed (Edward Randolph). *Glad monster, sad monster*
England, Linda. *The old cotton blues*
English, Karen. *Neeny coming, Neeny going*
Galdone, Paul. *The teeny-tiny woman*
Gallaz, Christophe. *Threadbear*
Grifalconi, Ann. *Kinda blue*
Grimes, Nikki. *Something on my mind*
Gugler, Laurel Dee. *Facing the day*
Hann, Jacquie. *Crybaby*
Harley, Bill. *Nothing happened*
Harshman, Marc. *Moving days*
Hausman, Bonnie. *A to Z, do you ever feel like me?*
Hazen, Barbara Shook. *Good-bye/Hello*
Happy, sad, silly, mad
Two homes to live in
Heiligman, Deborah. *Mike Swan, sink or swim*
Helena, Ann. *The lie*
Hines, Anna Grossnickle. *Even if I spill my milk?*
Hoban, Russell. *La corona and the tin frog*
The marzipan pig
The stone doll of Sister Brute
Hobbie, Holly. *Toot and Puddle, you are my sunshine*
Hopkins, Lee Bennett. *I loved Rose Ann*

Horvath, Betty F. *Will the real Tommy Wilson please stand up?*
Hubbard, Woodleigh Marx. *C is for curious*
Hulme, Joy N. *Eerie feary feeling*
Inkpen, Mick. *Wibbly Pig is upset*
Isadora, Rachel. *At the crossroads*
Jenkins, Jessica. *Thinking about colors*
Johnson, Angela. *The leaving morning*
Johnson, Julie. *How do I feel about my stepfamily*
Johnston, Marianne. *Dealing with bullying*
Kaiser Johnson, Lee. *If I ran the family*
Karas, Jacqueline. *The doll house*
Keller, Holly. *Lizzie's invitation*
Kherdian, David. *Right now*
Kiser, Kevin. *Buzzy Widget*
Knight, Joan. *Opal in the closet*
Knox-Wagner, Elaine. *My grandpa retired today*
Krauss, Ruth. *The bundle book*
　You're just what I need
Lalli, Judy. *Feelings alphabet*
Laskin, Pamela L. *Wish upon a star*
Levete, Sarah. *Looking after myself*
Lewin, Hugh. *Jafta*
　Jafta - the homecoming
　Jafta - the journey
　Jafta - the town
Maccarone, Grace. *The lunch box surprise*
McCrea, James. *The magic tree*
McGovern, Ann. *Feeling mad, feeling sad, feeling bad, feeling glad*
MacLachlan, Patricia. *What you know first*
McLerran, Alice. *Hugs*
Mayer, Mercer. *Mine!*
Mayers, Patrick. *Just one more block*
Millen, C. M. *The low-down laundry line blues*
Miller, Kathryn Ann. *Did my first mother love me?*
Millward, David Wynn. *Jenny and Bob*
Mitchell, Cynthia. *Playtime*
Modesitt, Jeanne. *Sometimes I feel like a mouse*
　The story of Z
Munsch, Robert N. *Aaron's hair*
Murphy, Mary. *I feel happy, and sad, and angry, and glad*
Musgrave, Susan. *Dreams are more real than bathtubs*
Nave, Yolanda. *Goosebumps and butterflies*
Ness, Evaline. *Pavo and the princess*
Nicholls, Judith. *Someone I like*
O'Donnell, Elizabeth Lee. *Maggie doesn't want to move*
Parr, Todd. *Things that make you feel good, things that make you feel bad*
Peacock, Carol Antoinette. *Mommy far, Mommy near*
Proimos, James. *The loudness of Sam*
Pursell, Margaret Sanford. *A look at divorce*
Ransom, Candice F. *When the whippoorwill calls*
Raschka, Christopher. *Ring! Yo?*
　Yo! Yes?
Rogers, Fred. *Adoption*
　Making friends
　Moving
Ross, Dave (David). *A book of hugs*
　A book of kisses
　More hugs!
Say, Allen. *Allison*
Selway, Martina. *Don't forget to write*
Senisi, Ellen B. *Hurray for pre-K!*
Sesame Street. *The Sesame Street book of people and things*

Sharratt, Nick. *I look like this*
Simon, Norma. *How do I feel?*
　I am not a crybaby!
Smith, Wendy. *Twice mice*
Spelman, Cornelia. *Mama and Daddy Bear's divorce*
Stanton, Elizabeth. *Sometimes I like to cry*
Stevenson, James. *Fun, no fun*
Strauss, Gwen. *Trail of stones*
Sussman, Susan. *Hippo thunder*
Taberski, Sharon. *Morning, noon, and night*
Thomas, Jane Resh. *Lights on the river*
Tobias, Tobi. *Moving day*
Tresselt, Alvin R. *What did you leave behind?*
Turner, Ethel. *Walking to school*
Vigna, Judith. *Saying goodbye to daddy*
Waber, Bernard. *Ira says goodbye*
Walsh, Ellen Stoll. *Two too much*
Weninger, Brigitte. *Good-bye, daddy!*
Weston, Martha. *Bad baby brother*
Wild, Margaret. *Toby*
Wittels, Harriet. *Things I hate!*
Wolde, Gunilla. *This is Betsy*
Yudell, Lynn Deena. *Make a face*

Emotions – anger

Alexander, Martha G. *And my mean old mother will be sorry, Blackboard Bear*
Aliki. *We are best friends*
Andrews, F. Emerson (Frank Emerson). *Nobody comes to dinner*
Andrews, Jan. *The auction*
Aseltine, Lorraine. *I'm deaf and it's okay*
Bang, Molly. *When Sophie gets angry – really, really angry . . .*
Berridge, Celia. *Hannah's temper*
Boegehold, Betty. *Daddy doesn't live here anymore*
Bunting, Eve (Anne Evelyn). *Smoky night*
Carr, Jan. *Dark day, light night*
Cohn, Janice I. *"Why did it happen?"*
Cooper, Susan. *Jethro and the jumbie*
Couture, Susan Arkin. *Melanie Jane*
Craft, Ruth. *The day of the rainbow*
Crary, Elizabeth. *I'm mad*
　When you're mad and you know it
Cummings, Pat. *Carousel*
Du Bois, William Pène. *Bear party*
Duncan, Riana. *When Emily woke up angry*
Enright, Elizabeth. *Zeee*
Erickson, Karen. *I was so mad*
Everitt, Betsy. *Mean soup*
French, Vivian. *Tiger and the temper tantrum*
Hapgood, Miranda. *Martha's mad day*
Harshman, Marc. *The storm*
Hautzig, Deborah. *Why are you so mean to me?*
Henkes, Kevin. *Lilly's purple plastic purse*
Hoban, Lillian. *Arthur's great big Valentine*
Ikeda, Daisaku. *The princess and the moon*
Johnston, Marianne. *Dealing with anger*
Joosse, Barbara M. *Dinah's mad, bad wishes*
Lachner, Dorothea. *Andrew's angry words*
　Danny, the angry lion
Langreuter, Jutta. *Little Bear and the big fight*
Lasky, Kathryn. *The tantrum*
Leonard, Marcia. *Angry*
Lester, Helen. *Princess Penelope's parrot*
Lewis, Kim. *Friends*
Lillie, Patricia. *Floppy teddy bear*
McBratney, Sam. *I'll always be your friend*

I'm sorry
Mahy, Margaret. *Beaten by a balloon*
Oram, Hiawyn. *Angry Arthur*
Parkison, Jami. *Amazing Mallika*
Rankin, Joan. *The little cat and the greedy old woman*
Shannon, David. *The amazing Christmas extravaganza*
Sharmat, Marjorie Weinman. *Attila the angry*
   I'm not Oscar's friend any more
   Rollo and Juliet . . . forever!
Shields, Carol Diggory. *I wish my brother was a dog*
Simon, Norma. *I was so mad!*
Small, David. *Paper John*
Spelman, Cornelia. *When I feel angry*
Stein, Stephanie. *Lucy's feet*
Sykes, Julie. *Little Tiger's big surprise*
Tulloch, Richard. *Danny in the toybox*
Watson, Jane Werner. *Sometimes I get angry*
Widman, Christine. *Housekeeper of the wind*
Wilhelm, Hans. *Let's be friends again!*
Yorinks, Arthur. *Harry and Lulu*
Zolotow, Charlotte (Shapiro). *The quarreling book*

Emotions – embarrassment

Alexander, Martha G. *Sabrina*
Aylesworth, Jim. *Shenandoah Noah*
Boyd, Selma. *The how: making the best of a mistake*
Brown, Marc Tolon. *Arthur's underwear*
Bulla, Clyde Robert. *Daniel's duck*
Bunting, Eve (Anne Evelyn). *A picnic in October*
Carlson, Nancy L. *Loudmouth George and the big race*
Caseley, Judith. *Molly Pink*
Cazet, Denys. *Great-Uncle Felix*
Cooney, Nancy Evans. *Donald says thumbs down*
Corrigan, Kathy. *Emily Umily*
Davis, Gibbs. *Katy's first haircut*
Freeman, Don. *Quiet! There's a canary in the library*
Hirsh, Marilyn. *The pink suit*
Hoff, Syd. *A walk past Ellen's house*
Lexau, Joan M. *I should have stayed in bed*
Raschka, Christopher. *The blushful hippopotamus*
Shalev, Meir. *My father always embarrasses me*
Stanek, Muriel. *Left, right, left, right!*
Townsend, Kenneth. *Felix, the bald-headed lion*
Udry, Janice May. *How I faded away*
Wood, Audrey. *Weird parents*

Emotions – envy, jealousy

Abisch, Roz. *Mai-Ling and the mirror*
Alexander, Martha G. *Nobody asked me if I wanted a baby sister*
   When the new baby comes, I'm moving out
Armstrong, Jennifer. *King crow*
Asch, Frank. *Bear's bargain*
Aylesworth, Jim. *Mary's mirror*
Bach, Alice. *Millicent the magnificent*
Baker, Charlotte. *Little brother*
Beim, Jerrold. *Country mailman*
Best, Cari. *Top banana*
Brown, Ruth. *I don't like it!*
Bruna, Dick. *Dick Bruna's Snow-White and the seven dwarfs*
Buck, Pearl S. (Pearl Sydenstricker). *The Chinese story teller*
Bullock, Kathleen. *A surprise for Mitzi Mouse*
Bunting, Eve (Anne Evelyn). *Monkey in the middle*

Burningham, John. *Humbert, Mister Firkin and the Lord Mayor of London*
Caines, Jeannette. *I need a lunch box*
Calhoun, Mary. *High-wire Henry*
Carlson, Nancy L. *Poor Carl*
Castle, Caroline. *Herbert Binns and the flying tricycle*
Chottin, Ariane. *A home for Little Turtle*
   Little Goat's new horns
Chwast, Seymour. *Bushy bride*
Cole, Babette. *Hurray for Ethelyn*
Cole, Joanna. *The new baby at your house*
Conford, Ellen. *Why can't I be William?*
Cooper, Helen (Helen F.). *Little monster did it!*
Corey, Dorothy. *Will it ever be my birthday?*
Cottringer, Anne. *Ella and the naughty lion*
Cretan, Gladys Yessayan. *Lobo and Brewster*
Croft, Priscilla. *Dealing with jealousy*
Cutler, Jane. *Darcy and Gran don't like babies*
DeLage, Ida. *A bunny ride*
Demi. *The artist and the architect*
Doherty, Berlie. *Paddiwak and cozy*, ill. by Alison Bartlett
   Paddiwak and cozy, ill. by Teresa O'Brien
Drescher, Joan E. *My mother's getting married*
Eriksson, Eva. *Jealousy*
Ernst, Lisa Campbell. *Miss Penny and Mr. Grubbs*
Ferguson, Alane. *That new pet!*
Fonteyn, Margot, Dame. *Coppélia*
Gantos, Jack (John, Jr.). *Back to school for Rotten Ralph*
   Rotten Ralph's rotten Christmas
Ganz, Yaffa. *The story of Mimmy and Simmy*
Gill, Joan. *Hush, Jon!*
Graham, Margaret Bloy. *Benjy and the barking bird*
Graham, Richard. *Jack and the monster*
Greenfield, Eloise. *She come bringing me that little baby girl*
Gretz, Susanna. *Frog in the middle*
Grimm, Jacob. *Snow White*, ill. by Trina Schart Hyman
   Snow White, ill. by Bernadette Watts
   Snow White and the seven dwarves, ill. by Chihiro Iwasaki
Hathorn, Libby (Elizabeth). *Freya's fantastic surprise*
Hautzig, Deborah. *Grover's bad dream*
Havill, Juanita. *Jamaica and Brianna*
Hazen, Barbara Shook. *Why couldn't I be an only kid like you, Wigger?*
Hedderwick, Mairi. *Katie Morag and the tiresome Ted*
Hest, Amy. *You're the boss, Baby Duck*
Hoban, Russell. *A baby sister for Frances*
   A birthday for Frances
Hoffman, Rosekrans. *Sister Sweet Ella*
Howe, James. *I wish I were a butterfly*
Jenkin-Pearce, Susie. *Bad Boris and the new kitten*
Joosse, Barbara M. *Nugget and Darling*
Joseph, Lynn. *Jump up time*
Keller, Holly. *Geraldine's baby brother*
Kellogg, Steven (Stephen). *Best friends*
Kimmel, Eric A. *Rimonah of the Flashing Sword*
Levete, Sarah. *Being jealous*
Levine, Abby. *Sometimes I wish I were Mindy*
Lindgren, Astrid. *I want a brother or sister*
Lionni, Leo. *Alexander and the wind-up mouse*
McAllister, Angela. *The battle of Sir Cob and Sir Filbert*
Macdonald, Maryann. *The pink party*
McGeorge, Constance W. *Boomer's big surprise*
McLenighan, Valjean. *You can go jump*

McMullan, Kate (Hall). *Nutcracker Noel*
Manushkin, Fran. *Little rabbit's baby brother*
Mario, Heidi Stetson. *I'd rather have an iguana*
Martin, Ann M. *Rachel Parker, kindergarten show-off*
Mathers, Petra. *Lottie's new friend*
Mayer, Mercer. *One frog too many*
Mayne, William. *Pandora*
Miller, Warren. *The goings on at Little Wishful*
Mills, Claudia. *A visit to Amy-Claire*
Mills, Lauren A. *The goblin baby*
Moodie, Fiona. *Nabulela*
Ormondroyd, Edward. *Theodore's rival*
Peet, Bill (William Bartlett). *The luckiest one of all*
Pushkin, Aleksandr Sergeevich. *The tale of Tsar Saltan*
Roop, Peter. *The buffalo jump*
Schick, Eleanor. *Peggy's new brother*
Shyer, Marlene Fanta. *Stepdog*
Skorpen, Liesel Moak. *His mother's dog*
Smalls-Hector, Irene. *Because you're lucky*
Stanley, Diane. *Siegfried*
Stephens, Helen. *What about me?*
Sykes, Julie. *Little Tiger's big surprise*
Velthuijs, Max. *Little Man to the rescue*
Vigna, Judith. *Couldn't we have a turtle instead?*
Voake, Charlotte. *Ginger*
Waber, Bernard. *Lyle and the birthday party*
Wahl, Jan. *Mabel ran away with the toys*
Walt Disney Productions. *Walt Disney's Snow White and the seven dwarfs*
Watson, Jane Werner. *Sometimes I'm jealous*
Winter, Susan. *A baby just like me*
Yep, Laurence. *Dragon prince*
Zemach, Margot. *To Hilda for helping*
Ziefert, Harriet. *Getting ready for new baby*
Zolotow, Charlotte (Shapiro). *It's not fair*

Emotions – fear

Aaron, Jane. *When I'm afraid*
Akass, Susan. *Number nine duckling*
Alborough, Jez. *It's the bear*
  Watch out! Big Bro's coming!
Alcantara, Ricardo. *Dog and cat*
Alderson, Sue Ann. *Wherever bears be*
Alexander, Anne (Anna Barbara Cooke). *Noise in the night*
Alexander, Martha G. *I'll protect you from the jungle beasts*
  Maybe a monster
Alexander, Sally Hobart. *Sarah's surprise*
Alexander, Sue. *Witch, Goblin and sometimes Ghost*
Anrooy, Frans van. *The sea horse*
Apple, Margot. *Brave Martha*
Aseltine, Lorraine. *I'm deaf and it's okay*
Auch, Mary Jane. *Monster brother*
Aylesworth, Jim. *Siren in the night*
  Teddy bear tears
  Two terrible frights
Babbitt, Natalie. *The something*
Bailey, Linda. *When Addie was scared*
Bannon, Laura. *Little people of the night*
  The scary thing
Barton, Byron. *Harry is a scaredy-cat*
Baumgart, Klaus. *Don't be afraid, Tommy*
Benedek, Elissa P. *The secret worry*
Berenstain, Stan. *The Berenstain bears get stage fright*
  The Berenstain bears learn about strangers
Bergström, Gunilla. *Who's scaring Alfie Atkins?*

Berry, Christine. *Mama went walking*
Blegvad, Lenore. *Anna Banana and me*
Bonsall, Crosby Newell. *Who's afraid of the dark?*
Bourgeois, Paulette. *Franklin and the thunderstorm*
  Franklin in the dark
Bradbury, Ray. *Switch on the night*, ill. by Leo and Diane Dillion
  Switch on the night, ill. by Madeleine Gekiere
Brown, Margaret Wise. *Night and day*
Buck, Nola. *The basement stairs*
Bunting, Eve (Anne Evelyn). *Ghost's hour, spook's hour*
  Terrible things
Byfield, Barbara Ninde. *The haunted churchbell*
Caines, Jeannette. *Chilly stomach*
Callan, Elizabeth Koda. *Good luck pony*
Calmenson, Stephanie. *The kindergarten book*
  No stage fright for me!
Cameron, Ann. *Harry (the monster)*
Carlson, Nancy L. *Harriet's recital*
  Witch lady
Carrick, Carol. *Dark and full of secrets*
Cazet, Denys. *Mud baths for everyone*
Chorao, Kay. *Lester's overnight*
Church, Kristine. *My brother John*
Clifton, Lucille. *Amifika*
  Good, says Jerome
Cohen, Miriam. *Jim meets the thing*
  The real-skin rubber monster mask
Coles, Alison. *Michael and the sea*
  Michael in the dark
  Michael's first day
Company González, Mercé. *Killian and the dragons*
Compton, Kenn. *Granny Greenteeth and the noise in the night*
Conford, Ellen. *Eugene the brave*
Cooney, Nancy Evans. *Go away monsters, lickety split!*
Cooper, Helen (Helen F.). *The bear under the stairs*
Corey, Dorothy. *You go away*
Credle, Ellis. *Big fraid, little fraid*
Crowe, Robert L. *Clyde monster*
Cunningham, Julia. *A mouse called Junction*
Devlin, Wende. *Aunt Agatha, there's a lion under the couch!*
Dickens, Lucy. *Go fish*
Dinardo, Jeffrey. *Timothy and the night noises*
Dodd, Lynley. *Hairy Maclary from Donaldson's dairy*
Dragonwagon, Crescent. *Will it be okay?*
Emberley, Ed (Edward Randolph). *Go away, big green monster!*
Erickson, Karen. *It's dark – but I'm not scared*
Erlbruch, Wolf. *Leonard*
Farber, Werner. *Night lion*
Figueredo, D. H. *When this world was new*
Flood, Bo. *I'll go to school if . . .*
Foreman, Michael. *Surprise! Surprise!*
Freschet, Berniece. *Furlie Cat*
Frost, Robert. *The runaway*
Gackenbach, Dick. *Harry and the terrible whatzit*
Gantos, Jack (John, Jr.). *Back to school for Rotten Ralph*
Gay, Zhenya. *Who's afraid?*
Gifford, Kathie Lee. *Giff the scaredy bear*
Gikow, Louise. *Boober Fraggle's ghosts*
Girard, Linda Walvoord. *Jeremy's first haircut*
Glaser, Linda. *Keep your socks on, Albert!*
Gliori, Debi. *A lion at bedtime*
Goode, Diane. *I hear a noise*
Goodenow, Earle. *The owl who hated the dark*

Raschka, Christopher. *Can't sleep*
Ratnett, Michael. *Marmaduke and the scary story*
Reed, Jonathan. *Do armadillos come in houses?*
Reeves, Mona Rabun. *The spooky eerie night noise*
Robison, Deborah. *No elephants allowed*
Roddie, Shen. *Help, Mama, help!*
Rodgers, Frank. *Who's afraid of the ghost train?*
Rosenberry, Vera. *Vera's first day of school*
Ross, Pat. *Your first airplane trip*
Ross, Tony. *Happy blanket*
   I'm coming to get you!
Sabraw, John. *I wouldn't be scared*
Sanromán, Susana. *Señora Reganona*
Schaefer, Charles E. *Cat's got your tongue?*
Scheffler, Ursel. *Be brave, little lion!*
Schertle, Alice. *The gorilla in the hall*
Scruton, Clive. *Scaredy cat*
Seuss, Dr. *The Sneetches, and other stories*
Shortall, Leonard W. *Tony's first dive*
Simms, Laura. *The squeaky door*
Slepian, Jan. *Emily just in time*
Smith, Janice Lee. *The monster in the third dresser drawer and other stories about Adam Joshua*
Smith, Maggie (Margaret C.). *There's a witch under the stairs*
Steel, Danielle. *Max and the baby sitter*
Stevenson, Drew. *The ballad of Penelope Lou . . . and me*
Stevenson, Harvey. *Big scary wolf*
Stevenson, James. *What's under my bed?*
Stock, Catherine. *Halloween monster*
Strand, Mark. *The night book*
Stubbs, Joanna. *With cat's eyes you'll never be scared of the dark*
Szilagyi, Mary. *Thunderstorm*
Taylor, Anelise. *Lights on, lights off*
Tompert, Ann. *The Tzar's bird*
   Will you come back for me?
Townson, Hazel. *Terrible Tuesday*
Trez, Denise. *The royal hiccups*
Tsutsui, Yoriko. *Anna in charge*
Udry, Janice May. *Alfred*
Vigna, Judith. *Nobody wants a nuclear war*
Viorst, Judith. *My mama says there aren't any zombies, ghosts, vampires, creatures, demons, monsters, fiends, goblins, or things*
Vogel, Ilse-Margret. *The don't be scared book*
Waddell, Martin. *Can't you sleep, Little Bear?*
   Let's go home, Little Bear
   Owl babies
   Owl babies, a board book
   The park in the dark
Waldron, Jan L. *John Pig's Halloween*
Wallace, Ian. *Chin Chiang and the dragon's dance*
Walsh, Ellen Stoll. *Pip's magic*
Watson, Jane Werner. *Sometimes I'm afraid*
Weston, Martha. *Tuck in the pool*
Wharton, Thomas. *Hildegard sings*
Whishaw, Iona. *Henry and the cow problem*
Widerberg, Siv. *The boy and the dog*
Williams, Gweneira Maureen. *Timid Timothy, the kitten who learned to be brave*
Williams, Linda. *The little old lady who was not afraid of anything*
Willis, Jeanne. *The monster bed*
   The monster storm
Winters, Kay. *The teeny tiny ghost*
   Whooo's haunting the teeny tiny ghost?
Winthrop, Elizabeth. *Potbellied possums*

Winton, Tim. *The deep*
Wolf, Bernard. *Michael and the dentist*
Wondriska, William. *The stop*
Zarin, Cynthia. *Rose and Sebastian*
Zolotow, Charlotte (Shapiro). *The storm book*

Emotions – grief

Adoff, Arnold. *The return of Rex and Ethel*
Arnold, Caroline. *What we do when someone dies*
Baker, Betty. *Rat is dead and ant is sad*
Barker, Peggy. *What happened when grandma died*
Barron, T. A. *Where is Grandpa?*
Bartoli, Jennifer. *Nonna*
Bernstein, Joanne E. *When people die*
Brown, Margaret Wise. *The dead bird*
Bunting, Eve (Anne Evelyn). *Rudi's pond*
Burningham, John. *Grandpa*
Carlstrom, Nancy White. *Blow me a kiss, Miss Lilly*
Carrick, Carol. *The accident*
Carson, Jo. *You hold me and I'll hold you*
Caseley, Judith. *When Grandpa came to stay*
Clifton, Lucille. *Everett Anderson's goodbye*
Cohen, Miriam. *Jim's dog Muffins*
Cohn, Janice I. *I had a friend named Peter*
   Molly's rosebush
Cooney, Barbara. *Island boy*
Coutant, Helen. *First snow*
Coville, Bruce. *My grandfather's house*
Dabcovich, Lydia. *Mrs. Huggins and her hen Hannah*
De Paola, Tomie (Thomas Anthony). *Nana upstairs and Nana downstairs*
DiSalvo-Ryan, DyAnne. *A dog like Jack*
Fassler, Joan. *My grandpa died today*
Fox, Louisa. *Every Monday in the mailbox*
Gould, Deborah. *Grandpa's slide show*
Greenlee, Sharon. *When someone dies*
Grifalconi, Ann. *Tiny's hat*
Hallinan, P. K. (Patrick K.). *Three freckles past a hair*
Harranth, Wolf. *My old grandad*
Harriott, Ted. *Coming home*
Hazen, Barbara Shook. *Why did Grandpa die?*
Hesse, Karen. *Poppy's chair*
Heymans, Annemie. *The princess in the kitchen garden*
Hines, Anna Grossnickle. *Remember the butterflies*
Hoffmann, E. T. A. *The strange child*
Hogan, Bernice. *My grandmother died but I won't forget her*
Hoopes, Lyn Littlefield. *Nana*
Howard, Ellen. *Murphy and Kate*
Jewell, Nancy. *Time for Uncle Joe*
Joslin, Mary. *The goodbye boat*
Kadono, Eiko. *Grandpa's soup*
Kaldhol, Marit. *Goodbye Rune*
Kantrowitz, Mildred. *When Violet died*
Keller, Holly. *Goodbye, Max*
Lanton, Sandy. *Daddy's chair*
Leavy, Una. *Good-bye, Papa*
Le Tord, Bijou. *My Grandma Leonie*
Levete, Sarah. *When people die*
Limb, Sue. *Come back, Grandma*
London, Jonathan. *Liplap's wish*
Lyon, George Ella. *Ada's pal*
Madenski, Melissa. *Some of the pieces*
Maguire, Gregory. *Lucas Fishbone*
Maple, Marilyn J. *On the wings of a butterfly*

Martin, Jacqueline Briggs. *Grandmother Bryant's pocket*
Mendoza, George. *The hunter I might have been*
Morehead, Debby. *A special place for Charlee*
Newman, Lesléa. *Too far away to touch*
Nobisso, Josephine. *Grandpa loved*
Nodar, Carmen Santiago. *Abuelita's paradise*
Old, Wendie C. *Stacy had a little sister*
Oliviero, Jamie. *Som See and the magic elephant*
Peavy, Linda. *Allison's grandfather*
Pollack, Eileen. *Whisper whisper Jesse, whisper whisper Josh*
Porte, Barbara Ann. *Harry's mom*
Rappaport, Doreen. *The new king*
Rogers, Fred. *When a pet dies*
Rosen, Michael J. (1954-). *Bonesy and Isabel*
Rosenberg, Liz. *The carousel*
Roth, Susan L. *Another Christmas*
Russo, Marisabina. *Grandpa Abe*
Sanford, Doris. *David has AIDS*
Scheller, Melanie. *My grandfather's hat*
Schick, Eleanor. *Mama*
Simmonds, Posy. *Fred*
Simon, Norma. *The saddest time*
Smith-Ayala, Emilie. *Marisol and the yellow messenger*
Stein, Sara Bonnett. *About dying*
Stevens, Margaret (Dean). *When grandpa died*
Stiles, Norman. *I'll miss you, Mr. Hooper*
Stilz, Carol Curtis. *Kirsty's kite*
Thomas, Jane Resh. *Saying good-bye to grandma*
Townsend, Maryann. *Pop's secret*
Trottier, Maxine. *Prairie willow*
Ulmer, Wendy K. *A campfire for cowboy Billy*
Van den Berg, Marinus. *The three birds*
Vigna, Judith. *Saying goodbye to daddy*
Viorst, Judith. *The tenth good thing about Barney*
Wahl, Mats. *Grandfather's laika*
Wallace-Brodeur, Ruth. *Goodbye, Mitch*
Weitzman, Elizabeth. *Let's talk about when a parent dies*
Wilhelm, Hans. *I'll always love you*
Wittbold, Maureen. *Mending Peter's heart*
Wood, Douglas. *Grandad's prayers of the earth*
Wright, Betty Ren. *The cat next door*
Zalben, Jane Breskin. *Pearl's marigolds for grandpa*
Zolotow, Charlotte (Shapiro). *My grandson Lew*
The old dog

Emotions – happiness

Asch, George. *Linda*
Carlson, Nancy L. *Life is fun*
Czernecki, Stefan. *Pancho's piñata*
Dodd, Lynley. *Schnitzel von Krumm's basketwork*
Low, Joseph. *The Christmas grump*
McCrea, James. *The magic tree*
McCully, Emily Arnold. *Crossing the new bridge*
Miller, Edward. *The curse of Claudia*
Miryam. *The happy man and his dump truck*
Paschkis, Julie. *So happy/So sad*
Piatti, Celestino. *The happy owls*
Rice, Eve. *What Sadie sang*
Steig, William. *Spinky sulks*
Tapio, Pat Decker. *The lady who saw the good side of everything*
Tobias, Tobi. *Jane wishing*
Tripp, Paul. *The strawman who smiled by mistake*
Weedn, Flavia. *The ragged peddler*
Williams, Barbara. *Someday, said Mitchell*

Wondriska, William. *Mr. Brown and Mr. Gray*
Yabuki, Seiji. *I love the morning*

Emotions – hate

Udry, Janice May. *Let's be enemies*
Zolotow, Charlotte (Shapiro). *The hating book*

Emotions – jealousy *see* Emotions – envy, jealousy

Emotions – loneliness

Aardema, Verna. *The lonely lioness and the ostrich chicks*
Alborough, Jez. *My friend bear*
Alexander, Sue. *Dear Phoebe*
Aliki. *We are best friends*
Allan, Nicholas. *The bird*
Allard, Harry. *Crash helmet*
Ardizzone, Edward. *Lucy Brown and Mr. Grimes*
Ballard, Robin. *My father is far away*
Battles, Edith. *One to teeter-totter*
Blegvad, Lenore. *Mr. Jensen and cat*
Bolliger, Max. *The lonely prince*
Brett, Jan. *Annie and the wild animals*
Bröger, Achim. *Francie's paper puppy*
Brown, Marcia. *The little carousel*
Buck, Pearl S. (Pearl Sydenstricker). *The little fox in the middle*
Buckley, Helen Elizabeth. *Moonlight kite*
Buntain, Ruth Jaeger. *The birthday story*
Bunting, Eve (Anne Evelyn). *The big cheese*
Burningham, John. *Aldo*
Chenault, Nell. *Parsifal the Poddley*
Chess, Victoria. *Poor Esmé*
Clewes, Dorothy. *Happiest day*
Coatsworth, Elizabeth. *Lonely Maria*
Conaway, Judith. *I'll get even*
Conger, Marion. *The chipmunk that went to church*
Coontz, Otto. *The quiet house*
Craven, Carolyn. *What the mailman brought*
Cummings, W. T. (Walter Thies). *The kid*
Delton, Judy. *Lee Henry's best friend*
My grandma's in a nursing home
Drawson, Blair. *Flying Dimitri*
Duvoisin, Roger Antoine. *Periwinkle*
Ellis, Anne Leo. *Dabble Duck*
Fatio, Louise. *The happy lion roars*
Fujikawa, Gyo. *Shags finds a kitten*
Funazaki, Yasuko. *Baby owl*
Gág, Wanda. *Nothing at all*
Gliori, Debi. *The snowchild*
Godard, Alex. *Idora*
Goffstein, M. B. (Marilyn Brooke). *Neighbors*
Golembe, Carla. *Annabelle's big move*
Harranth, Wolf. *My old grandad*
Hobbs, Will. *Howling Hill*
Hofsepian, Sylvia A. *Why not?*
Hughes, Shirley. *Abel's moon*
Moving Molly
Jackson, Ellen B. *Boris the boring boar*
Kadono, Eiko. *Grandpa's soup*
Keats, Ezra Jack. *The trip*
Kesselman, Wendy Ann. *Angelita*
Emma
Khalsa, Dayal Kaur. *How pizza came to Queens*
Knaff, Jean Christian. *Manhattan*
Lachner, Dorothea. *Look out, Cinder!*

Levete, Sarah. *Making friends*
Levin, Miriam Ramsfelder. *In the beginning*
Lewin, Ted. *Nilo and the tortoise*
Lukesová, Milena. *The little girl and the rain*
Lund, Jillian. *Two cool coyotes*
Luttrell, Ida. *Lonesome Lester*
McClure, Gillian. *What's the time, Rory Wolf?*
McCormick, Wendy. *Daddy, will you miss me?*
McGovern, Ann. *Mr. Skinner's skinny house*
   Nicholas Bentley Stoningpot III
McNeer, May Yonge. *My friend Mac*
Munthe, Adam John. *I believe in unicorns*
Murphy, Shirley Rousseau. *Valentine for a dragon*
Nomura, Takaaki. *Grandpa's town*
Norton, Natalie. *A little old man*
Novak, Matt. *Gertie and Gumbo*
Olsen, Ib Spang. *The grown-up trap*
Park, W. B. *The costume party*
Pearson, Tracey Campbell. *The howling dog*
Pfister, Marcus. *The rainbow fish*
Pilkey, Dav. *A friend for Dragon*
Ring, Elizabeth. *Some stuff*
Rylant, Cynthia. *Mr. Putter and Tabby pour the tea*
Sanfield, Steve. *The girl who wanted a song*
Sarton, May. *Punch's secret*
Scamell, Ragnhild. *Who likes Wolfie?*
Seignobosc, Françoise. *The story of Colette*
Siekkinen, Raija. *Mister King*
Skurzynski, Gloria. *Martin by himself*
Slate, Joseph. *Lonely Lula cat*
Smith, Wendy. *The lonely, only mouse*
Sonneborn, Ruth A. *Lollipop's party*
Spang, Günter. *Clelia and the little mermaid*
Spinelli, Eileen. *Somebody loves you, Mr. Hatch*
Spurr, Elizabeth. *The long, long letter*
Stage, Mads. *The lonely squirrel*
Stanek, Muriel. *All alone after school*
Stevenson, James. *Mr. Hacker*
Stren, Patti. *Hug me*
Sugita, Yutaka. *Helena the unhappy hippopotamus*
Surany, Anico. *Kati and Kormos*
Timlock, Jason. *Basil, the loneliest boy*
Titherington, Jeanne. *A place for Ben*
Waber, Bernard. *Gina*
Waddell, Martin. *The hidden house*
   Sam Vole and his brothers
Wagener, Gerda. *Leo the lion*
Wallner, Alexandra. *Beatrix Potter*
Walter, Mildred Pitts. *My mama needs me*
Wright, Dare. *The lonely doll*
Yashima, Taro. *Crow boy*
Zindel, Paul. *I love my mother*
Zolotow, Charlotte (Shapiro). *The bunny who found Easter*
   Janey
   Three funny friends
   A tiger called Thomas, ill. by Catherine Stock
   A tiger called Thomas, ill. by Kurt Werth

Emotions – love

Adoff, Arnold. *Love letters*
Agostinelli, Maria Enrica. *On wings of love*
Alexander, Sue. *Dear Phoebe*
   Nadia the willful
Andersen, H. C. (Hans Christian). *The snow queen*, ill. by Angela Barrett
   The snow queen, ill. by Toma Bogdanovic
   The snow queen, ill. by June Atkin Corwin
   The snow queen, ill. by Sally Holmes
   The snow queen, ill. by Susan Jeffers
   The snow queen, ill. by Errol Le Cain
   The snow queen, ill. by Arieh Zeldich
Anglund, Joan Walsh. *Christmas is love*
   Love is a baby
   Love is a special way of feeling
Babbitt, Natalie. *Bub, or, The very best thing*
Baker, Keith. *The dove's letter*
Barrett, Joyce Durham. *Willie's not the hugging kind*
Bartoletti, Susan Campbell. *Silver at night*
Baynton, Martin. *Why do you love me?*
Berger, Barbara Helen. *The jewel heart*
Bergström, Gunilla. *You have a girlfriend, Alfie Atkins?*
Bianco, Margery Williams. *The velveteen rabbit*, ill. by Allen Atkinson
   The velveteen rabbit, ill. by Michael Green
   The velveteen rabbit, ill. by Michael Hague
   The velveteen rabbit, ill. by David Jorgensen
   The velveteen rabbit, ill. by William Nicholson
   The velveteen rabbit, ill. by Ilse Plume
   The velveteen rabbit, ill. by S. D. Schindler
   The velveteen rabbit, ill. by Tien
Billam, Rosemary. *Fuzzy rabbit*
Birdseye, Tom. *A song of stars*
Boegehold, Betty. *Pawpaw's run*
Boyle, Vere. *Beauty and the beast*
Brown, Palmer. *Something for Christmas*
Buckley, Helen Elizabeth. *Grandmother and I*
Burdett, Lois. *Romeo and Juliet for kids*
Carmichael, Clay. *Used-up Bear*
Carter, Anne. *Beauty and the beast*
Caseley, Judith. *Dear Annie*
Clifton, Lucille. *Everett Anderson's goodbye*
Cole, Babette. *Cupid*
Davenier, Christine. *Leon and Albertine*
De Mejo, Oscar. *La Bella Magellona and the little cavalier*
De Paola, Tomie (Thomas Anthony). *Helga's dowry*
Dragonwagon, Crescent. *Wind Rose*
Drummond, Allan. *The willow pattern story*
Dyke, John. *Pigwig*
Edwards, Lisa. *Disney's Beauty and the beast, a book of manners*
Eisenberg, Phyllis Rose. *You're my Nikki*
Elzbieta. *Jon-Jon and Annette*
Fatio, Louise. *The happy lion's treasure*
Flack, Marjorie. *Ask Mr. Bear*
Flanders, Michael. *The hippopotamus song*
Fowler, Susi Gregg. *Beautiful*
Fox, Mem. *Koala Lou*
   Sophie
Freedman, Florence B. *Brothers*
Freeman, Don. *Corduroy*
Gerstein, Mordicai. *Prince Sparrow*
Girard, Linda Walvoord. *At Daddy's on Saturdays*
Giuliano, Katie. *All the way to God*
Glass, Andrew. *Chickpea and the talking cow*
Gliori, Debi. *No matter what*
Goble, Paul. *Love flute*
Graham, Georgia. *The strongest man this side of Cremona*
Greene, Carol. *The golden locket*
Haseley, Dennis. *Ghost catcher*
Hautzig, Deborah. *Beauty and the beast*
Havill, Juanita. *I love you more*
Hazen, Barbara Shook. *Even if I did something awful*
Heine, Helme. *The boxer and the princess*

Hest, Amy. *The go-between*
Hill, Eric. *Puppy love*
Hines, Anna Grossnickle. *When we married Gary*
Hodges, Margaret. *The kitchen knight*
Hoopes, Lyn Littlefield. *When I was little*
Huss, Sally. *I love you with all my hearts*
Hutton, Warwick. *Beauty and the beast*
Jacobs, Joseph. *Tattercoats*
Jaffe, Nina. *The way meat loves salt*
Jenkins, Jordan. *Learning about love*
Jewell, Nancy. *The snuggle bunny*
Johnson, Dolores. *Grandma's hands*
Joosse, Barbara M. *Mama, do you love me?*
Kasza, Keiko. *A mother for Choco*
Kern, Noris. *I love you with all my heart*
Kinerk, Robert. *Slim and Miss Prim*
King-Smith, Dick. *Puppy love*
Kirk, David. *Little Miss Spider*
Kocí, Marta. *Sarah's bear*
Kohlenberg, Sherry. *Sammy's mommy has cancer*
Kraus, Robert. *Buggy Bear cleans up*
Krauss, Ruth. *Big and little*
Lagerlöf, Selma. *The changeling*
Laird, Elizabeth. *A book of promises*
Lasky, Kathryn. *I have four names for my grandfather*
Lawrence, Michael (Michael C.). *Baby loves*
Levitin, Sonia. *The man who kept his heart in a bucket*
Lexau, Joan M. *A house so big*
Lindbergh, Reeve. *Grandfather's lovesong*
London, Jonathan. *Froggy's first kiss*
   A koala for Katie
   What do you love?
McBratney, Sam. *Guess how much I love you*
McCloskey, Kevin. *Mrs. Fitz's flamingos*
McCourt, Lisa. *I love you, Stinky Face*
Macken, JoAnn Early. *Cats on Judy*
McNaughton, Colin. *Oomph!*
McPhail, David M. *Sisters*
Mangas, Brian. *A nice surprise for Father Rabbit*
Manna, Anthony L. *Mr. Semolina-Semolinus*
Marshall, Edward. *Fox in love*
Martin, Bill (William Ivan). *Knots on a counting rope*
Marzollo, Jean. *I love you*
Mayer, Marianna. *Beauty and the beast*
Mayer, Mercer. *Just for you*
   Whinnie the lovesick dragon
Mayne, William. *The patchwork cat*
Meeker, Clare Hodgson. *A tale of two rice birds*
Miles, Betty. *Around and around . . . love*
Mizumura, Kazue. *If I were a cricket . . .*
Moore, Elaine. *Grammy, do you love me?*
Morgan-Vanroyen, Mary. *Guess who I love?*
Morris, Ann. *Loving*
Munsch, Robert N. *Love you forever*
Naylor, Phyllis Reynolds. *The baby, the bed, and the rose*
Nesbit, Edith. *Beauty and the beast*
Newton, Laura P. *Me and my aunts*
Nobisso, Josephine. *Grandpa loved*
Norac, Carl. *I love you so much*
Noyes, Alfred. *The highwayman*
Oppenheim, Shulamith Levey. *I love you, Bunny Rabbit*
Otsuka, Yuzo. *Suho and the white horse*
Paterson, Diane. *Wretched Rachel*
Pochocki, Ethel. *Rosebud and red flannel*
Porter-Gaylord, Laurel. *I love my daddy because . . .*
   I love my mommy because . . .
Price, Leontyne. *Aïda*

Rankin, Joan. *You're somebody special, Walliwigs!*
Reinl, Edda. *The little snake*
Reiser, Lynn. *The surprise family*
Rohmer, Harriet. *Mother scorpion country*
Rowand, Phyllis. *Every day in the year*
Samuels, Barbara. *Faye and Dolores*
San Souci, Robert D. *Nicholas Pipe*
Scott, Ann Herbert. *On mother's lap*
Shecter, Ben. *If I had a ship*
Shipton, Jonathan. *Busy! Busy! Busy!*
Silverman, Maida. *The magic well*
Steig, William. *Tiffky Doofky*
Stuve-Bodeen, Stephanie. *Elizabeti's doll*
Summers, Kate. *Milly's wedding*
Tafuri, Nancy. *I love you, little one*
Tedesco, Donna. *Do you know how much I love you?*
Thompson, Richard. *Foo*
Tudor, Tasha. *Miss Kiss and the nasty beast*
Vaës, Alain. *The porcelain pepper pot*
Velthuijs, Max. *Frog in love*
Waddell, Martin. *The toymaker*
   Who do you love?
Wade, Barrie. *Little monster*
Wahl, Jan. *Old Hippo's Easter egg*
Ward, Heather Patricia. *I promise I'll find you*
Watson, Clyde. *Love's a sweet*
Watson, Wendy. *A Valentine for you*
Wilson, Sarah. *Love and kisses*
Woychuk, Denis. *The other side of the wall*
Wright, Freire. *Beauty and the beast*
Yezerski, Thomas. *Together in Pinecone Patch*
Yorinks, Arthur. *Harry and Lulu*
Zalben, Jane Breskin. *A perfect nose for Ralph*
Ziefert, Harriet. *With love from Grandma*
Zindel, Paul. *I love my mother*
Zola, Meguido. *Only the best*
Zolotow, Charlotte (Shapiro). *Do you know what I'll do?*
   May I visit?
   A rose, a bridge, and a wild black horse
   Say it!
   The sky was blue
   Some things go together

Emotions – sadness

Alexander, Sue. *Nadia the willful*
Allen, Frances Charlotte. *Little hippo*
Andrews, Jan. *The auction*
Baker, Betty. *Rat is dead and ant is sad*
Cole, Joanna. *The Clown-Arounds have a party*
Delton, Judy. *I'll never love anything ever again*
De Veaux, Alexis. *Na-ni*
Hanson, Regina. *The tangerine tree*
Havill, Juanita. *Jamaica's blue marker*
Johnson, Angela. *The aunt in our house*
Lindgren, Astrid. *My nightingale is singing*
Low, Joseph. *The Christmas grump*
McLerran, Alice. *The mountain that loved a bird*
Paschkis, Julie. *So happy/So sad*
Sharmat, Marjorie Weinman. *I don't care*
Singer, Marilyn. *In the palace of the Ocean King*
Sugita, Yutaka. *Helena the unhappy hippopotamus*
Wolff, Ashley. *The bells of London*

Emotions – unhappiness *see* Emotions – happiness; Emotions – sadness

Emperors *see* Royalty – emperors

Emus *see* Birds – emus

Endangered animals *see* Animals – endangered animals

Engineered books *see* Format, unusual – toy and movable books

Engineers *see* Careers – engineers

England *see* Foreign lands – England

Entertainers *see* Careers – entertainers

Entertainment *see* Theater

Envy *see* Emotions – envy, jealousy

Escalators *see* Elevators, escalators

Eskimos

Andrews, Jan. *Very last first time*
Beim, Lorraine. *The little igloo*
Bernhard, Emery. *How Snowshoe Hare rescued the sun*
Bushey, Jeanne. *A sled dog for Moshi*
Carlstrom, Nancy White. *Northern lullaby*
Conway, Diana Cohen. *Northern lights*
Dabcovich, Lydia. *The polar bear son*
Damjan, Mischa. *Atuk*
DeArmond, Dale. *The seal oil lamp*
Ekoomiak, Normee. *Arctic memories*
George, Jean Craighead. *Arctic son*
    Snow bear
Gerber, Carole. *Arctic dreams*
Harlow, Joan Hiatt. *Shadow bear*
Heinz, Brian J. *Nanuk, lord of the ice*
Hopkins, Marjorie. *Three visitors*
Houston, James. *Kiviok's magic journey*
Jessell, Tim. *Amorak*
Joosse, Barbara M. *Mama, do you love me?*
Kroll, Virginia L. *The seasons and someone*
Loverseed, Amanda. *Tikkatoo's journey*
Luenn, Nancy. *Nessa's fish*
    Nessa's story
McDonald, Megan. *Tundra mouse*
Machetanz, Sara. *A puppy named Gia*
Magdanz, James S. *Go home, river*
Martin, Rafe. *The eagle's gift*
Morrow, Suzanne Stark. *Inatuck's friend*
Munsch, Robert N. *A promise is a promise*
Nicolai, Margaret. *Kitaq goes ice fishing*
Parish, Peggy. *Ootah's lucky day*
San Souci, Robert D. *Song of Sedna*
Scott, Ann Herbert. *On mother's lap*
Steiner, Barbara (Annette). *The whale brother*
Villoldo, Alberto. *Skeleton woman*

Estonia *see* Foreign lands – Estonia

Ethiopia *see* Foreign lands – Ethiopia

Ethnic groups in the U.S.

Appelt, Kathi. *Bayou lullaby*
Bailey, Debbie. *Grandma*
    Grandpa
Banish, Roslyn. *A forever family*
Barrett, Joyce Durham. *Willie's not the hugging kind*
Belpré, Pura. *Santiago*
Bettinger, Craig. *Follow me, everybody*
Blue, Rose. *I am here*
Brenner, Barbara A. *Faces, faces, faces*
Bunting, Eve (Anne Evelyn). *Smoky night*
Caseley, Judith. *Apple pie and onions*
Clifford, Eth. *Your face is a picture*
Cohen, Miriam. *Will I have a friend?*
Córdova, Amy. *Abuelita's heart*
Cox, Judy. *Now we can have a wedding!*
Crume, Marion W. *Listen!*
Cummings, Pat. *Petey Moroni's Camp Runamok diary*
Davol, Marguerite W. *Black, white, just right*
Dickens, Lucy. *Dancing class*
Dooley, Norah. *Everybody bakes bread*
    Everybody cooks rice
Dorros, Arthur. *Abuela*
Feldman, Eve B. *Animals don't wear pajamas*
Fisher, Iris L. *Katie-Bo*
Greene, Roberta. *Two and me makes three*
Heinst, Marie. *My first number book*
Hoffman, Phyllis. *Meatball*
Hogan, Paula Z. *The hospital scares me*
Hughes, Shirley. *The big concrete lorry*
James, Betsy. *The dream stair*
Jaynes, Ruth M. *Benny's four hats*
    Friends! friends! friends!
    Tell me please! What's that?
    That's what it is!
    What is a birthday child?
Jenkins, Jessica. *Thinking about colors*
Johnson, Angela. *The aunt in our house*
Kaiser Johnson, Lee. *If I ran the family*
Katz, Karen. *The colors of us*
Keats, Ezra Jack. *My dog is lost!*
Kesselman, Wendy Ann. *Angelita*
Klein, Leonore. *Just like you*
Kroll, Virginia L. *New friends, true friends, stuck-like-glue friends*
Kuklin, Susan. *How my family lives in America*
Lansdown, Brenda. *Galumph*
Levy, Janice. *Totally uncool*
Lippman, Sidney. *A you're adorable*
MacKinnon, Debbie. *My first ABC*
Maestro, Betsy. *Coming to America*
May, Julian. *Why people are different colors*
Medearis, Angela Shelf. *The zebra-riding cowboy*
Merriam, Eve. *Boys and girls, girls and boys*
Merrill, Jean. *How many kids are hiding on my block?*
Moss, Marissa. *After-school monster*
Nikola-Lisa, W. *America: my land, your land, our land*
    Bein' with you this way
Paek, Min. *Aekyung's dream*
Pellegrini, Nina. *Families are different*
Prager, Annabelle. *The baseball birthday party*
Reit, Seymour. *Round things everywhere*
Rosa-Casanova, Sylvia. *Mama Provi and the pot of rice*
Rosenberg, Maxine B. *Being adopted*
Rotner, Shelley. *Lots of moms*
Sage, James. *The little band*
Schaefer, Carole Lexa. *Snow pumpkin*
Shelby, Anne. *Potluck*

Simon, Norma. *I am not a crybaby!*
  What do I say?
Sobol, Harriet Langsam. *We don't look like our mom
  and dad*
Stanek, Muriel. *One, two, three for fun*
Udry, Janice May. *What Mary Jo shared*
Valentine, Johnny. *One dad, two dads, brown dad,
  blue dads*
Watson, Mary. *The butterfly seeds*
Weiss, Nicki. *The world turns round and round*
Williams, Vera B. *"More more more," said the baby*
Wing, Natasha. *Jalapeño bagels*
Wong, Janet S. *This next New Year*
Zarin, Cynthia. *What do you see when you shut your
  eyes?*

Ethnic groups in the U.S. – Acadians

Trosclair. *Cajun night before Christmas*

Ethnic groups in the U.S. – African Americans

Ackerman, Karen. *By the dawn's early light*
Adler, David A. *A picture book of Martin Luther King,
  Jr.*
Adoff, Arnold. *Big sister tells me that I'm black*
  I am the running girl
  In for winter, out for spring
  Where wild Willie?
Alexander, Martha G. *Bobo's dream*
  The story grandmother told
Aliki. *A weed is a flower*
All the pretty little horses
Allison, Diane Worfolk. *This is the key to the kingdom*
Altman, Susan. *Followers of the north star*
Amper, Thomas. *Booker T. Washington*
Ashley Bryan's abc of African American poetry
Bang, Molly. *Ten, nine, eight*
  Wiley and the hairy man
Barber, Barbara E. *Allie's basketball dream*
  Saturday at the new you
Barner, Bob. *Dem bones*
Barnwell, Ysaye M. *No mirrors in my Nana's house*
Beim, Jerrold. *The swimming hole*
Beim, Lorraine. *Two is a team*
Benjamin, Anne. *Young Harriet Tubman*
Bible. New Testament. *The Lord's prayer*, ill. by Tim
  Ladwig
Bible. Old Testament. Psalms. *Psalm twenty-three*
Blackstone, Stella. *Bear on a bike*
Blue, Rose. *Black, black, beautiful black*
  How many blocks is the world?
Bogart, Jo Ellen. *Daniel's dog*
Bowen, Keith. *Katy's gift*
Bradby, Marie. *More than anything else*
Breinburg, Petronella. *Doctor Shawn*
  Shawn goes to school
  Shawn's red bike
Bryan, Ashley. *All night, all day*
  I'm going to sing
Bunting, Eve (Anne Evelyn). *The blue and the gray*
Burch, Robert. *Joey's cat*
Burden-Patmon, Denise. *Carnival*
  Imani's gift at Kwanzaa
Caines, Jeannette. *Abby*
  Daddy
  Just us women
Calhoun, Mary. *Big Sixteen*

Calloway, Northern J. *Northern J. Calloway presents
  Super-vroomer!*
Carlstrom, Nancy White. *Wild wild sunflower child
  Anna*
Chapman, Cheryl. *Snow on snow on snow*
Children go where I send thee
Chocolate, Deborah M. Newton. *Kwanzaa*
  The piano man
Clifton, Lucille. *All us come cross the water*
  Amifika
  The boy who didn't believe in spring
  Don't you remember?
  Everett Anderson's Christmas coming
  Everett Anderson's friend
  Everett Anderson's goodbye
  Everett Anderson's nine months long
  Everett Anderson's 1-2-3
  Everett Anderson's year
  Good, says Jerome
  My brother fine with me
  My friend Jacob
  Some of the days of Everett Anderson
  Three wishes, ill. by Stephanie Douglas
  Three wishes, ill. by Michael Hays
Coleman, Evelyn. *The glass bottle tree*
  To be a drum
  White socks only
Coles, Robert. *The story of Ruby Bridges*
Cooke, Trish. *Mr. Pam Pam and the Hullabazoo*
Cooper, Floyd. *Coming home*
Cooper, Melrose. *Gettin' through Thursday*
Cowley, Joy. *Singing down the rain*
Crews, Donald. *Shortcut*
Crews, Nina. *One hot summer day*
  You are here
Cummings, Pat. *Carousel*
  Clean your room, Harvey Moon!
  Jimmy Lee did it
  My aunt came back
Curtis, Gavin. *The bat boy and his violin*
  Grandma's baseball
Dale, Penny. *Bet you can't*
DeFelice, Cynthia C. *Willy's silly grandma*
DeGross, Monalisa. *Granddaddy's street songs*
Derby, Sally. *My steps*
De Veaux, Alexis. *An enchanted hair tale*
Dionetti, Michelle V. *Thalia Brown and the blue bug*
Dobkin, Bonnie. *Everybody says*
Dragonwagon, Crescent. *Home place*
Duncan, Alice Faye. *Miss Viola and Uncle Ed Lee*
Dupré, Rick. *Agassu*
  The wishing chair
Edwards, Pamela Duncan. *Barefoot*
Engel, Diana. *Circle song*
  Fishing
England, Linda. *The old cotton blues*
English, Karen. *Big wind coming!*
  Just right stew
  Neeny coming, Neeny going
Evans, Mari. *Singing black*
Everett, Gwen. *Li'l Sis and Uncle Willie*
Falwell, Cathryn. *Christmas for 10*
  Feast for ten
Fassler, Joan. *Don't worry dear*
Faulkner, William J. *Brer Tiger and the big wind*
Fife, Dale. *Adam's ABC*
Flournoy, Valerie. *The best time of day*
  The patchwork quilt
Ford, Juwanda G. *K is for Kwanzaa*

Fraser, Kathleen. *Adam's world, San Francisco*
Freeman, Don. *Corduroy*
  A pocket for Corduroy
Gambill, Henrietta D. *Self-control*
George, Jean Craighead. *The wentletrap trap*
Gilchrist, Jan Spivey. *Indigo and moonlight gold*
Gill, Joan. *Hush, Jon!*
Giovanni, Nikki. *The genie in the jar*
  Spin a soft black song
  The sun is so quiet
Glaser, Linda. *Stop that garbage truck!*
Gray, Genevieve. *Send Wendell*
Gray, Libba Moore. *Miss Tizzy*
Gray, Nigel. *I'll take you to Mrs. Cole!*
Greenberg, Polly. *Oh, Lord, I wish I was a buzzard*
Greene, Carol. *Katherine Dunham*
Greenfield, Eloise. *Angels*
  Big friend, little friend
  Daddy and I
  Daydreamers
  Easter parade
  First pink light
  I make music
  Kia Tanisha
  Lisa's daddy and daughter day
  Me and Nessie
  My doll, Keshia
  Nathaniel talking
  Night on Neighborhood Street
  On my horse
  She come bringing me that little baby girl
  Sweet baby coming
  Water, water
  William and the good old days
Greenfield, Monica. *The baby*
  Waiting for Christmas
Grifalconi, Ann. *City rhythms*
  Electric Yancy
  Kinda blue
  Tiny's hat
Grimes, Nikki. *Baby's bedtime*
  Come Sunday
  Danitra Brown leaves town
  From a child's heart
  It's raining laughter
  Meet Danitra Brown
  Wild, wild hair
Guthrie, Donna. *A rose for Abby*
Guy, Rosa. *Billy the Great*
Hamilton, Virginia. *Drylongso*
Haseley, Dennis. *Crosby*
Haskins, Francine. *I remember "121"*
Hathorn, Libby (Elizabeth). *Sky sash so blue*
Havill, Juanita. *Jamaica and Brianna*
  Jamaica Tag-Along
  Jamaica's blue marker
  Jamaica's find
Hayes, Sarah. *Eat up, Gemma*
  Happy Christmas, Gemma
Hayward, Linda. *Hello, house!*
Heath, Amy. *Sofie's role*
Helldorfer, M. C. (Mary Claire). *Silver Rain Brown*
Hesse, Karen. *Come on, rain*
Hest, Amy. *Jamaica Louise James*
Hill, Elizabeth Starr. *Evan's corner*
Hoffman, Mary. *Amazing Grace*
  An angel just like me
  Grace and family
Hoffman, Phyllis. *Steffie and me*

Hogan, Paula Z. *The hospital scares me*
Holman, Sandy Lynne. *Grandpa, is everything black bad?*
Hooks, Bell. *Happy to be nappy*
Hooks, William H. *Where's Lulu?*
Hopkins, Lee Bennett. *I think I saw a snail*
Hort, Lenny. *How many stars in the sky*
Horvath, Betty F. *Hooray for Jasper*
  Jasper and the hero business
  Jasper makes music
Howard, Elizabeth Fitzgerald. *Aunt Flossie's hats (and crab cakes later)*
  Chita's Christmas tree
  Mac and Marie and the train toss surprise
  Papa tells Chita a story
  What's in Aunt Mary's room?
  When will Sarah come?
Hru, Dakari. *Joshua's Masai mask*
Hudson, Cheryl Willis. *Animal sounds for baby*
  Bright eyes, brown skin
  Good morning baby
  Good night baby
  Let's count, baby
Hudson, Wade. *Afro-bets kids I'm gonna be*
  I love my family
  Pass it on
Hughes, Langston. *Carol of the brown king*
Hulbert, Jay. *Armando asked "Why?"*
Hutchins, Pat. *My best friend*
Igus, Toyomi. *Two Mrs. Gibsons*
  When I was little
In daddy's arms I am tall
Isadora, Rachel. *Ben's trumpet*
  Bring on that beat
Jackson, Bobby L. *Little Red Ronnika*
Jackson, Isaac. *Somebody's new pajamas*
Jaquith, Priscilla. *Bo Rabbit smart for true*
Jensen, Virginia Allen. *Sara and the door*
Johnson, Angela. *Casey Jones*
  Daddy calls me man
  Do like Kyla
  Down the winding road
  The girl who wore snakes
  Joshua by the sea
  Joshua's night whispers
  Julius
  The leaving morning
  Mama bird, baby birds
  One of three
  Rain feet
  The Rolling Store
  Shoes like Miss Alice's
  The wedding
  When I am old with you
  When mules flew on Magnolia Street
Johnson, Dinah. *All around town*
  Sunday week
Johnson, Dolores. *The best bug to be*
  Grandma's hands
  My mom is my show-and-tell
  Now let me fly
  Papa's stories
  Seminole diary
  What kind of baby-sitter is this?
  What will mommy do when I'm at school?
  Your dad was just like you
Johnson, James Weldon. *The Creation*
  Lift ev'ry voice and sing
Johnson, Janet P. *How Mr. Dog got tame*

Keelboat Annie
Johnston, Tony. *The wagon*
Jonas, Ann. *Splash!*
Jones, Joy. *Tambourine moon*
Jones, Rebecca C. *Matthew and Tilly*
Joseph, Lynn. *Fly, Bessie, fly*
Kaufman, Curt. *Hotel boy*
Keats, Ezra Jack. *Apt. 3*
  Dreams
  Goggles
  Hi, cat!
  John Henry
  A letter to Amy
  Louie
  Pet show!
  Peter's chair
  Skates
  The snowy day
  The snowy day(a board book)
  The trip
  Whistle for Willie
Kessler, Brad. *Brer Rabbit and Boss Lion*
Ketteman, Helen. *Not yet, Yvette*
Kirn, Ann. *Beeswax catches a thief*
Koplow, Lesley. *Tanya and the tobo man = Tanya y el*
  hombre tobo
Kroll, Virginia L. *Africa brothers and sisters*
  Can you dance, Dalila?
  Faraway drums
  Masai and I
  Sweet Magnolia
  Wood-hoopoe Willie
Lansdown, Brenda. *Galumph*
Lauture, Denizé. *Father and son*
Leonard, Marcia. *Get the ball, Slim*
  My camp-out
  My pal Al
Lester, Julius. *Black cowboy, wild horses*
  John Henry
  The knee-high man and other tales
  What a truly cool world
Lexau, Joan M. *Benjie*
  Benjie on his own
  I should have stayed in bed
  Me day
  The rooftop mystery
Liddell, Janice. *Imani and the Flying Africans*
Lillie, Patricia. *Jake and Rosie*
Lindbergh, Reeve. *Nobody owns the sky*
Lipkind, William. *Four-leaf clover*
Little, Lessie Jones. *Children of long ago*
Little, Mimi Otey. *Yoshiko and the foreigner*
Littlesugar, Amy. *Jonkonnu*
  Shake Rag
  Tree of hope
Livingston, Myra Cohn. *Keep on singing*
Lorbiecki, Marybeth. *Sister Anne's hands*
Lotz, Karen E. *Can't sit still*
MacDonald, Margaret Read. *Pickin' peas*
McGill, Alice. *Molly Bannaky*
McGovern, Ann. *Black is beautiful*
McKissack, Patricia C. *Ada, la desordenada*
  Booker T. Washington
  Flossie and the fox
  Ma Dear's aprons
  Messy Bessey
  Messy Bessey's closet
  Messy Bessey's holidays
  Mirandy and brother wind

Paul Robeson
Mandel, Peter. *Say hey*
Martin, Ann M. *Rachel Parker, kindergarten show-off*
Mayer, Mercer. *Liza Lou and the Yeller Belly Swamp*
Medearis, Angela Shelf. *The adventures of Sugar and*
  Junior
  Annie's gifts
  Dancing with the Indians
  The freedom riddle
  The ghost of Sifty-Sifty Sam
  Kyle's first Kwanzaa
  Our people
  Picking peas for a penny
  Poppa's new pants
  Rum-a-tum-tum
  Tailypo
Merriam, Eve. *Epaminondas*
Miles, Calvin. *Calvin's Christmas wish*
Milich, Melissa. *Can't scare me!*
  Miz Fannie Mae's fine new Easter hat
Miller, Thomas Patton. *Can a coal scuttle fly?*
Miller, William. *The bus ride*
  The conjure woman
  Frederick Douglass
  A house by the river
  Jenny and the peddler
  The knee-high man
  Night golf
  The piano
  Richard Wright and the library card
Milstein, Linda Breiner. *Coconut mon*
Mitchell, Margaree King. *Granddaddy's gift*
  Susie Mae
  Uncle Jed's barbershop
Mitchell, Rhonda. *The talking cloth*
Monjo, F. N. *The drinking gourd*
Moore, Dessie. *Getting dressed*
  Good morning
  Good night
  Let's pretend
Moss, Marissa. *Mel's diner*
Moss, Thylias. *I want to be*
Myers, Christopher A. *Sparrows*
Myers, Walter Dean. *Brown angels*
  Glorious angels
  Harlem
  Young Martin's promise
Nickens, Bessie. *Walking the log*
Nikola-Lisa, W. *Bein' with you this way*
  Hallelujah!
Nolan, Madeena Spray. *My daddy don't go to work*
Nolen, Jerdine. *Big Jabe*
Oppenheim, Shulamith Levey. *Fireflies for Nathan*
The palm of my heart
Patrick, Denise Lewis. *No diapers for baby!*
Perkins, Charles. *Swinging on a rainbow*
Peterson, Jeanne Whitehouse. *My mama sings*
Pinkney, Andrea Davis. *Alvin Ailey*
  Bill Pickett, rodeo ridin' cowboy
  Dear Benjamin Banneker
  Duke Ellington
Pinkney, Gloria Jean. *Back home*
  The Sunday outing
Pinkney, J. Brian. *The adventures of sparrowboy*
Polacco, Patricia. *Chicken Sunday*
  I can hear the sun
  Mrs. Katz and Tush
Poydar, Nancy. *Busy Bea*
Price, Hope Lynne. *These hands*

Raschka, Christopher. *Charlie Parker played be bop*
  Mysterious Thelonious
  Yo! Yes?
Riggio, Anita. *Secret signs*
Ringgold, Faith. *Bonjour, Lonnie*
  Dinner at Aunt Connie's house
  My dream of Martin Luther King
  Tar Beach
Robinson, Aminah Brenda Lynn. *A street called
  home*
Rochelle, Belinda. *Jewels*
Rodriguez, Anita. *Jamal and the angel*
Rosales, Melodye Benson. *Double Dutch and the
  voodoo shoes*
  Leola and the honeybears
  'Twas the night b'fore Christmas
Rosen, Michael J. (1954-). *Elijah's angel*
Sadu, Itah. *Christopher changes his name*
Saint James, Synthia. *The gifts of Kwanzaa*
  Sunday
Samton, Sheila White. *Amazing Aunt Agatha*
Samuels, Vyanne. *Carry go bring come*
Sanders, Scott R. (Scott Russell). *A place called Free-
  dom*
San Souci, Robert D. *The boy and the ghost*
  Callie Ann and Mistah Bear
  The hired hand
  The secret of the stones
  Sukey and the mermaid
Schertle, Alice. *Down the road*
Schrier, Jeffrey. *On the wings of eagles*
Schroeder, Alan. *Ragtime Tumpie*
Scott, Ann Herbert. *Big Cowboy Western*
  Let's catch a monster
  Sam
Scruggs, Afi. *Jump rope magic*
Serfozo, Mary. *What's what?*
Shange, Ntozake. *Whitewash*
Sharmat, Marjorie Weinman. *I don't care*
Shelby, Anne. *We keep a store*
Showers, Paul. *Look at your eyes*
  Your skin and mine
Siegelson, Kim L. *In the time of the drums*
Sierra, Judy. *Wiley and the Hairy Man*
Singer, Marilyn. *In the palace of the Ocean King*
Smalls-Hector, Irene. *Because you're lucky*
  Beginning school
  Irene and the big, fine nickel
  Irene Jennie and the Christmas masquerade
  Jenny Reen and the Jack Muh Lantern
  Jonathan and his mommy
  Kevin and his dad
  Louise's gift
Smith, Edward Biko. *A lullaby for Daddy*
Stephens, Helen. *What about me?*
Steptoe, John. *Birthday*
  Creativity
  My special best words
  Stevie
  Uptown
Stolz, Mary Slattery. *Storm in the night*
Straight, Susan. *Bear E. Bear*
Strom, Maria Diaz. *Rainbow Joe and me*
Stroud, Bettye. *Down home at Miss Dessa's*
Swanson-Natsues, Lyn. *Days of adventure*
Tarpley, Natasha. *I love my hair!*
Taulbert, Clifton L. *Little Cliff and the porch people*
Taylor, Ann. *Baby dance*
Taylor, Sydney. *The dog who came to dinner*

Teague, Mark. *Baby tamer*
Temple, Charles A. *Train*
Thomas, Ianthe. *Lordy, Aunt Hattie*
  Walk home tired, Billy Jenkins
Thomas, Jane Resh. *Celebration!*
Thomas, Joyce Carol. *Brown honey in broomwheat tea*
  Cherish me
  Gingerbread days
  You are my perfect baby
Thomas, Naturi. *Uh-oh! It's Mama's birthday!*
Turner, Ann Warren. *Nettie's trip south*
Udry, Janice May. *Mary Ann's mud day*
  Mary Jo's grandmother
  What Mary Jo shared
  What Mary Jo wanted
Wahl, Jan. *The singing geese*
Walker, Alice. *Finding the green stone*
  To hell with dying
Walsh, Ellen Stoll. *Two too much*
Walter, Mildred Pitts. *My mama needs me*
Washington, Donna L. *The story of Kwanzaa*
Watts, Jeri Hanel. *Keepers*
Weatherford, Carole Boston. *Juneteenth jamboree*
Williams, Sherley Anne. *Girls together*
  Working cotton
Williams, Vera B. *Cherries and cherry pits*
Williams-Garcia, Rita. *Catching the wild waiyuuzee*
Williamson, Mel. *Walk on!*
Williamson, Stan. *The no-bark dog*
Wilson, Beth P. *Jenny*
Wilson, Julia. *Becky*
Winter, Jeanette. *Follow the drinking gourd*
Woodson, Jacqueline. *We had a picnic this Sunday
  past*
Woodtor, Dee. *Big meeting*
Wright, Courtni Crump. *Journey to freedom*
  Jumping the broom
  Wagon train
Wyeth, Sharon Dennis. *Always my dad*
  Something beautiful
Yezback, Steven A. *Pumpkinseeds*
Yolen, Jane. *Miz Berlin walks*
Young, Ruth. *Golden Bear*
Zemach, Margot. *Jake and Honeybunch go to heaven*
Ziner, Feenie. *Counting carnival*
Zolotow, Charlotte (Shapiro). *Do you know what I'll
  do?*
  The old dog

Ethnic groups in the U.S. – Amish

Ammon, Richard. *An Amish wedding*
Good, Merle. *Amos and Susie*
  Reuben and the fire
Good, Phyllis Pellman. *Plain Pig's ABCs*
Gregory, Valiska. *Babysitting for Benjamin*
Mitchell, Barbara. *Down Buttermilk Lane*
Moss, P. Buckley (Pat Buckley). *Reuben and the
  quilt*
Smucker, Barbara Claasen. *Selina and the bear paw
  quilt*
Turkle, Brinton. *The adventures of Obadiah*
  Obadiah the Bold
  Rachel and Obadiah
  Thy friend, Obadiah
Wood, Douglas. *Northwoods cradle song*
Yolen, Jane. *Raising Yoder's barn*

Ethnic groups in the U.S. – Arab Americans

Nye, Naomi Shihab. *Sitti's secrets*

Ethnic groups in the U.S. – Asian Americans

Gabel, Susan L. *Where the sun kisses the sea*
Havill, Juanita. *Jamaica and Brianna*
Min, Laura. *Mrs. Sato's hens*
Molarsky, Osmond. *A sky full of kites*
Swanson-Natsues, Lyn. *Days of adventure*

Ethnic groups in the U.S. – Black Americans *see* Ethnic groups in the U.S. – African Americans

Ethnic groups in the U.S. – Cambodian Americans

Chiemruom, Sothea. *Dara's Cambodian New Year*

Ethnic groups in the U.S. – Chinese Americans

Behrens, June. *Soo Ling finds a way*
Bunting, Eve (Anne Evelyn). *The happy funeral*
Chin, Steven A. *Dragon Parade*
Chinn, Karen. *Sam and the lucky money*
Coerr, Eleanor. *Chang's paper pony*
D'Antonio, Nancy. *Our baby from China*
Hoyt-Goldsmith, Diane. *Celebrating Chinese New Year*
Lee, Milly. *Nim and the war effort*
Levine, Ellen. *I hate English!*
Lin, Grace. *The ugly vegetables*
Look, Lenore. *Love as strong as ginger*
Low, William. *Chinatown*
McCunn, Ruthanne L. *Pie-Biter*
Molnar-Fenton, Stephan. *An Mei's strange and wondrous journey*
Nunes, Susan Miho. *The last dragon*
Peacock, Carol Antoinette. *Mommy far, Mommy near*
Politi, Leo. *Moy Moy*
Pomeranc, Marion Hess. *The American Wei*
Sing, Rachel. *Chinese New Year's dragon*
Thong, Roseanne. *Round is a mooncake*
Trottier, Maxine. *The tiny kite of Eddie Wing*
Vaughan, Marcia Kapok. *The dancing dragon*
Wallace, Ian. *Chin Chiang and the dragon's dance*
Waters, Kate. *Lion dancer*
Ye, Ting-xing. *Share the sky*
Yee, Paul. *Roses sing on new snow*
Yee, Wong Herbert. *A drop of rain*

Ethnic groups in the U.S. – Czechoslovakian Americans

Nelson, Nan Ferring. *My day with Anka*

Ethnic groups in the U.S. – Dutch Americans

Joosse, Barbara M. *The morning chair*

Ethnic groups in the U.S. – East Indian Americans

Gilmore, Rachna. *Lights for Gita*

Ethnic groups in the U.S. – French Americans

McCully, Emily Arnold. *Mirette and Bellini cross Niagara Falls*

Ethnic groups in the U.S. – German Americans

Nivola, Claire A. *Elisabeth*

Ethnic groups in the U.S. – Greek Americans

Bunting, Eve (Anne Evelyn). *I have an olive tree*

Ethnic groups in the U.S. – Hispanic Americans

Aliki. *Tabby*
Ancona, George. *Barrio*
Carlson, Lori Marie. *Hurray for Three Kings' Day*
Carlstrom, Nancy White. *Barney is best*
Cisneros, Sandra. *Hairs = Pelitos*
Figueredo, D. H. *When this world was new*
Hayes, Joe. *A spoon for every bite*
Hughes, Monica. *A handful of seeds*
Lomas Garza, Carmen. *In my family*
Medearis, Angela Shelf. *The adventures of Sugar and Junior*
Miller, Elizabeth I. *Just like home = Como en mi tierra*
Shea, Pegi Deitz. *New moon*
Slate, Joseph. *The secret stars*
Weiss, Nicki. *On a hot, hot day*

Ethnic groups in the U.S. – Hmong Americans

Shea, Pegi Deitz. *The whispering cloth*

Ethnic groups in the U.S. – Irish Americans

Kroll, Steven. *Mary McLean and the St. Patrick's Day parade*
Weller, Frances Ward. *The angel of Mill Street*
Yezerski, Thomas. *Together in Pinecone Patch*

Ethnic groups in the U.S. – Italian Americans

Bartoletti, Susan Campbell. *Silver at night*
Bartone, Elisa. *American, too*
    Peppe the lamplighter
Bunting, Eve (Anne Evelyn). *A picnic in October*
Dionetti, Michelle V. *Coal mine peaches*

Ethnic groups in the U.S. – Japanese Americans

Bunting, Eve (Anne Evelyn). *So far from the sea*
Copeland, Helen. *Meet Miki Takino*
Hawkinson, Lucy (Ozone). *Dance, dance, Amy-Chan!*
Igus, Toyomi. *Two Mrs. Gibsons*

Johnston, Tony. *Fishing Sunday*
Kroll, Virginia L. *Pink paper swans*
McCoy, Karen Kawamoto. *Bon Odori dancer*
Mochizuki, Ken. *Baseball saved us*
 Heroes
Sakai, Kimiko. *Sachiko means happiness*
Say, Allen. *Grandfather's journey*
Trottier, Maxine. *Flags*
Uchida, Yoshiko. *The bracelet*
Yashima, Mitsu. *Momo's kitten*
Yashima, Taro. *Umbrella*
 The youngest one

Ethnic groups in the U.S. – Korean Americans

Choi, Sook Nyul. *Halmoni and the picnic*
 Yunmi and Halmoni's trip
Ginsburg, Mirra. *We adopted you, Benjamin Koo*
Heo, Yumi. *Father's rubber shoes*
Paek, Min. *Aekyung's dream*
Pak, Soyung. *Dear Juno*
Pellegrini, Nina. *Families are different*

Ethnic groups in the U.S. – Lebanese Americans

Shefelman, Janice Jordan. *A peddler's dream*

Ethnic groups in the U.S. – Lithuanian Americans

Moss, Marissa. *In America*

Ethnic groups in the U.S. – Mexican Americans

Anaya, Rudolfo A. *Farolitos for Abuelo*
Behrens, June. *Fiesta!*
Bertrand, Diane Gonzales. *Family / familia*
Bolognese, Don. *A new day*
Brown, Tricia. *Hello, amigos!*
Bunting, Eve (Anne Evelyn). *A day's work*
 Going home
Calhoun, Mary. *Tonio's cat*
Cazet, Denys. *Born in the gravy*
Covault, Ruth M. *Pablo and Pimienta*
Cuyler, Margery. *From here to there*
Dorros, Arthur. *Radio Man/Don Radio*
Ets, Marie Hall. *Bad boy, good boy*
 Gilberto and the wind
 Nine days to Christmas
Felt, Sue. *Rosa-too-little*
Fife, Dale. *Rosa's special garden*
Fraser, James Howard. *Los Posadas*
Havill, Juanita. *Treasure nap*
Jaynes, Ruth M. *Melinda's Christmas stocking*
 Tell me please! What's that?
 That's what it is!
 What is a birthday child?
Johnston, Tony. *Uncle rain cloud*
Levy, Janice. *Abuelito eats with his fingers*
Lopez, Loretta. *The birthday swap*
Luenn, Nancy. *A gift for Abuelita*
Molnar, Joe. *Graciela*
Mora, Pat. *A birthday basket for Tía*
 Confetti
 Pablo's tree
 The rainbow tulip

Tomás and the library lady
Ormsby, Virginia H. *Twenty-one children plus ten*
Politi, Leo. *Juanita*
 Pedro, the angel of Olvera Street
 Song of the swallows
Roe, Eileen. *Con mi hermano = With my brother*
Serfozo, Mary. *Welcome Roberto! Bienvenido, Roberto!*
Soto, Gary. *The old man and his door*
 Snapshots from the wedding
 Too many tamales
Taha, Karen T. *A gift for Tia Rose*
Thomas, Jane Resh. *Lights on the river*

Ethnic groups in the U.S. – Pakistani Americans

English, Karen. *Nadia's hands*

Ethnic groups in the U.S. – Polish Americans

Leighton, Maxinne Rhea. *An Ellis Island Christmas*
Levinson, Riki. *Soon, Annala*
Yezerski, Thomas. *Together in Pinecone Patch*

Ethnic groups in the U.S. – Puerto Rican Americans

Atkins, Jeannine. *Get set! Swim!*
Belpré, Pura. *Santiago*
Blue, Rose. *I am here*
Bowden, Joan Chase. *Emilio's summer day*
Cowley, Joy. *Gracias, the Thanksgiving turkey*
Keats, Ezra Jack. *My dog is lost!*
Kesselman, Wendy Ann. *Angelita*
Simon, Norma. *What do I do?*
 What do I say?
Sonneborn, Ruth A. *Friday night is papa night*
 Lollipop's party
 Seven in a bed
Steptoe, John. *Creativity*

Ethnic groups in the U.S. – Russian Americans

Cohen, Barbara. *Make a wish, Molly*
Cohen, Miriam. *Mimmy and Sophie*
Levitin, Sonia. *A piece of home*
Pryor, Bonnie. *The dream jar*
Rosenberg, Liz. *Grandmother and the runaway*
 shadow
Rosenblum, Richard. *Journey to the golden land*
Tarbescu, Edith. *Annushka's voyage*
Woodruff, Elvira. *The memory coat*

Ethnic groups in the U.S. – Shakers

Ray, Mary Lyn. *Shaker boy*

Ethnic groups in the U.S. – Vietnamese Americans

Breckler, Rosemary K. *Hoang breaks the lucky teapot*
Garland, Sherry. *The lotus seed*
 My father's boat
McKay, Lawrence. *Journey home*
Surat, Michele Maria. *Angel child, dragon child*
Trottier, Maxine. *The walking stick*

Etiquette

Ackley, Edith Flack. *Please
    Thank you*
Alden, Laura. *Saying I'm sorry*
Aliki. *Manners*
Anastasio, Dina. *Pass the peas, please*
Anderson, Peggy Perry. *Out to lunch*
Austin, Virginia. *Say please*
Behrens, June. *The manners book*
Berenstain, Stan. *The Berenstain bears forget their
    manners*
Betz, Betty. *Manners for moppets*
Brown, Marc Tolon. *Perfect pigs*
Brown, Myra Berry. *Company's coming for dinner*
Buehner, Caralyn. *It's a spoon, not a shovel*
Carlson, Nancy L. *How to lose all your friends*
Chapman, Cheryl. *Pass the fritters, critters*
Charles, Donald. *Shaggy dog's birthday*
Cho, Shinta. *The gas we pass*
Cole, Babette. *The bad good manners book*
Cole, Joanna. *Monster manners*
Cuneo, Diane. *Mary Louise loses her manners*
Demuth, Patricia Brennan. *Max, the bad-talking par-
    rot*
Duvoisin, Roger Antoine. *Periwinkle*
Edwards, Lisa. *Disney's Beauty and the beast, a book of
    manners*
Gardner, Martin. *Never make fun of a turtle, my son*
Gordon, Margaret. *Wilberforce goes to a party*
Hartman, Bob. *Aunt Mabel's table*
Hawkins, Colin. *Max and the magic word*
Himmelman, John. *A guest is a guest*
Hoban, Russell. *Dinner at Alberta's
    The little Brute family*
Ichikawa, Satomi. *Nora's surprise*
Jefferds, Vincent. *Disney's elegant book of manners*
Joslin, Sesyle. *Dear dragon
    What do you do, dear?
    What do you say, dear?*
Kandoian, Ellen. *Is anybody up?*
Keenan, Martha. *The mannerly adventures of Little
    Mouse*
Keller, Irene. *The Thingumajig book of manners*
Keller, John G. *Krispin's fair*
Leaf, Munro. *A flock of watchbirds
    How to behave and why
    Manners can be fun*
Lewison, Wendy Cheyette. *Say thank you, Theodore*
Lexau, Joan M. *Cathy is company*
Miller, Virginia. *On your potty!*
Munsch, Robert N. *Good families don't*
Myller, Lois. *No! No!*
Parish, Peggy. *Mind your manners*
Parr, Todd. *Do's and don'ts*
Patterson, Geoffrey. *The naughty boy and the straw-
    berry horse*
Paxton, Tom. *Engelbert the elephant*
Petersham, Maud. *The circus baby*
Polhamus, Jean Burt. *Dinosaur do's and don'ts*
Polisar, Barry Louis. *Don't do that!*
Potter, Beatrix. *The sly old cat*
Quackenbush, Robert M. *I don't want to go, I don't
    know how to act*
Rix, Jamie. *The last chocolate cookie*
Ross, Anna. *Say the magic word, please*
Scarry, Richard. *Richard Scarry's please and thank
    you book*
Seignobosc, Françoise. *The thank-you book*

Sherman, Ivan. *I do not like it when my friend comes to
    visit*
Slobodkin, Louis. *Thank you - you're welcome*
Smaridge, Norah. *You know better than that*
Smith, Barry. *A child's guide to bad behavior*
Stover, Jo Ann. *If everybody did*
Super, Gretchen. *Family traditions*
Turner, Priscilla. *Among the odds and evens*
Weiss, Ellen. *Telephone time*
Yee, Wong Herbert. *Big black bear*

Europe *see* Foreign lands – Europe

Evening *see* Twilight

Exercise *see* Health and fitness – exercise

Experiments *see* Science

Explorers *see* Careers – explorers

Eye glasses *see* Glasses

Eyes *see* Anatomy – eyes; Handicaps – blind-
    ness; Senses – seeing

Fables *see* Folk and fairy tales

Faces *see* Anatomy – faces

Fairies

Allingham, William. *The fairies*
Alper, Ann Fitzerald. *Harry McNairy, Tooth Fairy*
Anderson, Lonzo. *Two hundred rabbits*
Asch, Frank. *The flower faerie*
Barber, Antonia. *Catkin*
Barker, Cicely Mary. *Berry flower fairies
    Blossom flower fairies
    Flower fairies of the garden
    Flower fairies of the seasons
    Flower fairies of the spring
    Flower fairies of the summer
    Flower fairies of the trees
    Flower fairies postcard book
    Spring flower fairies
    Summer flower fairies*
Bate, Lucy. *Little rabbit's loose tooth*
Beim, Lorraine. *Sasha and the samovar*
Bennett, Rowena. *Songs from around a toadstool table*
Boujon, Claude. *The fairy with the long nose*
Briggs, Raymond. *The man*
Brown, Marc Tolon. *Arthur tricks the tooth fairy*
Butterworth, Nick. *Amanda's butterfly*
Carrick, Carol. *Norman fools the tooth fairy*
Cartlidge, Michelle. *Fairy letters*
Chardiet, Bernice. *Martin and the tooth fairy*
Christiana, David. *A Tooth Fairy's tale
    White nineteens*

Collington, Peter. *On Christmas eve*
   The tooth fairy
Coombs, Patricia. *Lisa and the grompet*
DeLage, Ida. *Weeny witch*
Elves, fairies and gnomes
Enright, Elizabeth. *Zeee*
Erlbruch, Wolf. *Leonard*
Fairy poems for the very young
Forest, Heather. *The woman who flummoxed the*
   fairies
Fyleman, Rose. *A fairy went a-marketing*
Gardner, Mercedes. *Scooter and the magic star*
Griffith, Helen V. *Nata*
Gunther, Louise. *A tooth for the tooth fairy*
Heller, Nicholas. *The tooth tree*
Hoffmann, E. T. A. *The nutcracker*, ill. by Rachel
   Isadora
   The nutcracker, ill. by Maurice Sendak
Hollyn, Lynn. *Lynn Hollyn's Christmas toyland*
Hooks, William H. *The mystery of the missing tooth*
Jeschke, Susan. *Mia, Grandma and the genie*
Karlin, Nurit. *The tooth witch*
Kaye, Marilyn. *The real tooth fairy*
Keith, Adrienne. *Fairies from A to Z*
Kennedy, Kim. *Mr. Bumble*
Kent, Jack. *Clotilda*
Kimmel, Eric A. *Asher and the capmakers*
Kroll, Steven. *Loose tooth*
Lagerlöf, Selma. *The changeling*
Lester, Helen. *The wizard, the fairy and the magic*
   chicken
Lowell, Susan. *Cindy Ellen*
McClintock, Barbara. *Molly and the magic wishbone*
MacDonald, George. *Little Daylight*
MacDonald, Margaret Read. *Slop!*
MacDonald, Maryann. *Rosie's baby tooth*
Mahy, Margaret. *Pillycock's shop*
Manson, Beverlie. *The fairies' alphabet book*
Mayne, William. *The green book of Hob stories*
   The red book of Hob stories
   The yellow book of Hob stories
Metaxas, Eric. *The boy and the whale*
Mills, Lauren A. *Fairy wings*
Morris, Ann. *The Cinderella rebus book*
Munsch, Robert N. *Andrew's loose tooth*
Myers, Bernice. *Sidney Rella and the glass sneaker*
Myers, Walter Dean. *The dragon takes a wife*
Nesbit, Edith. *Melisande*
Newbolt, Henry John, Sir. *Rilloby-rill*
Nightingale, Sandy. *Cider apples*
Paxton, Tom. *The story of the Tooth Fairy*
Pomeranc, Marion Hess. *The American Wei*
Prelutsky, Jack. *Monday's troll*
Ross, Tony. *A fairy tale*
San José, Christine. *Sleeping Beauty*
Sierra, Judy. *The gift of the crocodile*
Silverman, Maida. *The magic well*
Smee, Nicola. *The Tusk Fairy*
Taylor, Jane. *Twinkle, twinkle, little star*
Turnbull, Ann. *The tapestry cats*
Waddell, Martin. *The tough princess*
Wallace, Daisy. *Fairy poems*
Wells, Rosemary. *Fritz and the mess fairy*
Weninger, Brigitte. *The elf's hat*
Wetterer, Margaret. *Patrick and the fairy thief*
Wilder, Laura Ingalls. *Laura Ingalls Wilder's fairy*
   poems
Yolen, Jane. *Child of faerie, child of earth*

Fairs

Ackerman, Karen. *Bingleman's midway*
Amery, H. *Going to the fair*
Ancona, George. *Pablo remembers*
Aylesworth, Jim. *Mr. McGill goes to town*
Baker, Jill. *Basil of Bywater Hollow*
Ballard, Robin. *Carnival*
Barker, Melvern J. *Country fair*
Baynton, Martin. *Fifty and the great race*
Bond, Michael. *Paddington at the fair*
   Paddington Bear and the Busy Bee Carnival
Booth, Eugene. *At the fair*
Bourke, Linda. *Ethel's exceptional egg*
Brunhoff, Laurent de. *Babar's fair will be opened*
   next Sunday
Bunting, Eve (Anne Evelyn). *Market day*
   The pumpkin fair
Burden-Patmon, Denise. *Carnival*
Calhoun, Mary. *Blue-ribbon Henry*
Calmenson, Stephanie. *Get well, gators!*
Carrick, Carol. *The highest balloon on the common*
Castaneda, Omar S. *Abuela's weave*
Chiefari, Janet. *Kids are baby goats*
Cooper, Elisha. *Country fair*
Crews, Donald. *Night at the fair*
Crowther, Robert. *All the fun of the fair*
Daly, Niki. *Bravo, Zan Angelo!*
Delaney, A. *Pearl's first prize plant*
Delton, Judy. *Penny wise, fun foolish*
Devlin, Wende. *Old Witch and the polka-dot ribbon*
Dorros, Arthur. *Tonight is carnaval*
Ernst, Lisa Campbell. *Miss Penny and Mr. Grubbs*
Ets, Marie Hall. *Mr. Penny's race horse*
Gauch, Patricia Lee. *On to Widecombe Fair*
Gibbons, Gail. *County fair*
Gikow, Louise. *Jim Henson's Muppets in What's fair is*
   fair
Greenstein, Elaine. *Mrs. Rose's garden*
Guy, Ginger Foglesong. *Fiesta!*
Harshman, Marc. *Only one*
Hedderwick, Mairi. *Katie Morag and the two grand-*
   mothers
Helldorfer, M. C. (Mary Claire). *Carnival*
Herriot, James. *Bonny's big day*
Hill, Eric. *Spot at the fair*
Hoff, Syd. *Henrietta goes to the fair*
Holabird, Katharine. *Angelina at the fair*
Jacobson, Jennifer Richard. *A net of stars*
Joseph, Lynn. *Jump up time*
Kalman, Bobbie. *Celebrating the powwow*
Kiser, SuAnn. *The hog call to end all!*
Kroll, Steven. *Queen of the May*
Lasky, Kathryn. *Science fair bunnies*
Leech, Jay. *Bright Fawn and me*
Lewin, Ted. *Fair!*
Livingston, Myra Cohn. *Festivals*
Lunn, Janet Louise Swoboda. *Come to the fair*
McFarlane, Sheryl. *Going to the fair*
Miles, Miska. *Jump frog jump*
Mitchell, Barbara. *Red Bird*
Moore, Elaine. *Grandma's smile*
Mott, Evelyn Clarke. *Dancing rainbows*
Muntean, Michaela. *The very bumpy bus ride*
Murphy, Stuart J. *The penny pot*
Nikola-Lisa, W. *Wheels go round*
O'Malley, Kevin. *Roller coaster*
Sathre, Vivian. *Carnival time*
Schatell, Brian. *Farmer Goff and his turkey Sam*

Seignobosc, Françoise. *Jeanne-Marie at the fair*
Singer, Marilyn. *Will you take me to town on strawberry day?*
Speed, Toby. *Brave potatoes*
Stevens, Janet. *Animal fair*
Stevenson, James. *All aboard!*
Stoeke, Janet Morgan. *Minerva Louise at the fair*
Talley, Carol. *Clarissa*
Tudor, Tasha. *Corgiville fair*
Van Nutt, Julia. *Pumpkins from the sky?*
Watson, Clyde. *Applebet*
    Tom Fox and the apple pie
Watson, Nancy Dingman. *The birthday goat*
    Widdecombe Fair
Wildsmith, Brian. *Carousel*
Yacowitz, Caryn. *Pumpkin fiesta*
Ziefert, Harriet. *Pumpkin Pie*

Fairy tales *see* Folk and fairy tales

Falcons *see* Birds – falcons

Fall *see* Seasons – fall

Families *see* Family life

Family life

Aaron, Jane. *When I'm afraid*
Abercrombie, Barbara. *Charlie Anderson*
Ackerman, Karen. *I know a place*
    In the park with dad
    Just like Max
    The sleeping porch
Adams, Jeanie. *Going for oysters*
Adler, David A. *Hiding from the Nazis*
Adoff, Arnold. *Big sister tells me that I'm black*
    Black is brown is tan
    In for winter, out for spring
    Ma nDa La
    Make a circle, keep us in
Agell, Charlotte. *Mud makes me dance in the spring*
Ahlberg, Allan. *Master Salt the sailor's son*
    Miss Brick, the builder's baby
    Mr. and Mrs. Hay the horse
    Mr. Biff the boxer
    Mr. Buzz the beeman
    Mockingbird
    Mrs. Lather's laundry
    Mrs. Plug the plumber
    Mrs. Wobble the waitress
Ahlberg, Janet. *The baby's catalogue*
    Bye-bye, baby
    Peek-a-boo!
Aitken, Amy. *Wanda's circus*
Alcott, Louisa May. *An old-fashioned Thanksgiving*
Aldis, Dorothy (Keeley). *Hiding*
Alexander, Martha G. *Even that moose won't listen to me*
    I'll be the horse if you'll play with me
    Marty McGee's space lab, no girls allowed
Alexander, Sue. *Dear Phoebe*
    Nadia the willful
Aliki. *Christmas tree memories*
    Jack and Jake
    June 7!
    Keep your mouth closed, dear

    Marianthe's story one: painted words; Marianthe's story two: spoken memories
    Those summers
    Welcome, little baby
Allard, Harry. *The Stupids have a ball*
    The Stupids step out
    The Stupids take off
Allen, Laura Jean. *Ottie and the star*
Allen, Thomas B. (Thomas Burt). *On grandaddy's farm*
Altman, Linda Jacobs. *Amelia's road*
Anderson, C. W. (Clarence Williams). *Billy and Blaze*
Anderson, Douglas. *Let's draw a story*
Anderson, Laurie Halse. *Turkey pox*
Anderson, Lonzo. *The day the hurricane happened*
Anderson, Peggy Perry. *Out to lunch*
Anholt, Catherine. *Catherine and Laurence Anholt's big book of families*
    Good days, bad days
    When I was a baby
Appelt, Kathi. *Someone's come to our house*
    Watermelon day
Arbeit, Eleanor Werner. *Mrs. Cat hides something*
Arcellana, Francisco. *The mats*
Arkin, Alan. *Tony's hard work day*
Armitage, Ronda. *The bossing of Josie*
    Don't forget, Matilda
    One moonlit night
Arnold, Marsha Diane. *The chicken salad club*
Arthur, Catherine. *My sister's silent world*
Asbjørnsen, P. C. (Peter Christen). *The man who kept house*
Asch, Frank. *Dear brother*
    Good night, Baby Bear
    Goodbye house
Asher, Sandy. *Princess Bee and the royal good-night story*
Aulaire, Ingri Mortenson d'. *Children of the northlights*
    Nils
Auzary-Luton, Sylvie. *1, 2, 3, music!*
Axelrod, Amy. *Pigs on the ball*
    Pigs will be pigs
Ayer, Jacqueline. *A wish for little sister*
Aylesworth, Jim. *The bad dream*
    Siren in the night
Babbitt, Lorraine. *Pink like the geranium*
Babbitt, Natalie. *Bub, or, The very best thing*
Bach, Alice. *Millicent the magnificent*
    The smartest bear and his brother Oliver
Bailey, Debbie. *My family*
    The playground
Baird, Anne. *Kiss, kiss*
Baisch, Cris. *When the lights went out*
Baker, Betty. *Sonny-Boy Sim*
Baker, Sanna Anderson. *Mississippi going north*
Balet, Jan B. *The fence*
    Five Rollatinis
Ballard, Robin. *Good-bye, house*
    Gracie
    Granny and me
    When we get home
Balzola, Asun. *Munia and the day things went wrong*
Banish, Roslyn. *A forever family*
Banks, Kate (Katherine A.). *Alphabet soup*
Bannerman, Helen. *The story of Little Babaji*
    The story of little black Sambo
Barasch, Lynne. *Old friends*

Barbato, Juli. *From bed to bus*
Barbour, Karen. *Little Nino's pizzeria*
   Mr. Bow Tie
Barrett, Joyce Durham. *Willie's not the hugging kind*
Barrett, Mary Brigid. *Day care days*
Bartoli, Jennifer. *Nonna*
Bascom, Joe. *Malcolm's job*
Bassett, Jeni. *The chicks' trick*
Bates, Artie Ann. *Ragsale*
Battles, Edith. *One to teeter-totter*
Bawden, Nina. *Princess Alice*
Baylor, Byrd. *The table where rich people sit*
Beard, Darleen Bailey. *Twister*
Beatty, Hetty Burlingame. *Moorland pony*
Beckman, Kaj. *Lisa cannot sleep*
Beim, Jerrold. *Jay's big job*
Beim, Lorraine. *Lucky Pierre*
Bemelmans, Ludwig. *Quito express*
   Sunshine
Benjamin, Alan. *A change of plans*
Bennett, Olivia. *A Turkish afternoon*
Benson, Ellen. *Philip's little sister*
Benton, Robert. *Little brother, no more*
Berenstain, Michael. *The dwarks*
Berenstain, Stan. *The Berenstain bears and the truth*
   The Berenstain bears and too much TV
   The Berenstain bears' Christmas tree
   The Berenstain bears forget their manners
   The Berenstain bears in the dark
   The Berenstain bears learn about strangers
   The Berenstain bears' moving day
Berger, Terry. *How does it feel when your parents get divorced?*
Bernhard, Durga. *What's Maggie up to?*
Bernheim, Marc. *In Africa*
Berridge, Celia. *At my house*
Bertrand, Diane Gonzales. *Family / familia*
Bianchi, John. *Swine snafu*
Bible, Charles. *Jennifer's new chair*
Binch, Caroline. *Since Dad left*
Birdseye, Tom. *A regular flood of mishap*
Bishop, Claire Huchet. *The five Chinese brothers*
Bittner, Wolfgang. *Wake up, Grizzly!*
Blades, Ann. *Back to the cabin*
Blaine, Marge (Margery Kay). *The terrible thing that happened at our house*
Blake, Claire. *The paper chain*
Blake, Jon. *Wriggly Pig*
Blake, Quentin. *Clown*
Blaustein, Muriel. *Bedtime, Zachary!*
Bloom, Suzanne. *A family for Jamie*
Blue, Rose. *How many blocks is the world?*
Blume, Judy. *The one in the middle is a green kangaroo*
   The Pain and The Great One
Boegehold, Betty. *Daddy doesn't live here anymore*
   You are much too small
Bogart, Jo Ellen. *Jeremiah learns to read*
Bograd, Larry. *Felix in the attic*
Boholm-Olsson, Eva. *Tuan*
Bolliger, Max. *The fireflies*
   The golden apple
Bolognese, Don. *A new day*
Bond, Felicia. *Poinsettia and her family*
Bond, Michael. *Paddington Bear*, ill. by John Lobban
   Paddington's garden
Bond, Rebecca. *Just like a baby*
Bonsall, Crosby Newell. *The day I had to play with my sister*

Boon, Emilie. *Belinda's balloon*
Booth, David. *The dust bowl*
Bornstein, Ruth Lercher. *Of course a goat*
Bos, Burny. *Meet the Molesons*
   Ollie the elephant
Bourgeois, Paulette. *Big Sarah's little boots*
Bowden, Joan Chase. *The bouncy baby bunny*
Bowen, Keith. *Katy's gift*
Bradman, Tony. *A bad week for the three bears*
   A goodnight kind of feeling
   That's not a fish
   Through my window
   Wait and see
Brady, Susan. *Find my blanket*
Brandenberg, Franz. *Everyone ready?*
   A fun weekend
   What's wrong with a van?
Brann, Esther. *A book for baby*
Breckler, Rosemary K. *Hoang breaks the lucky teapot*
Breeze, Lynn. *This little baby's bedtime*
Brennan, Jan. *Born two-gether*
Brenner, Barbara A. *The prince and the pink blanket*
Bresnick-Perry, Roslyn. *Leaving for America*
Brett, Jan. *Armadillo rodeo*
Bright, Robert. *Georgie*
Brimner, Larry Dane. *Elliot Fry's good-bye*
Brisson, Pat. *Your best friend, Kate*
Brock, Emma Lillian. *Mr. Wren's house*
   A pet for Barbie
Bromhall, Winifred. *Middle Matilda*
Brooks, Robert B. *So that's how I was born*
Brothers, Aileen. *Sad Mrs. Sam Sack*
Brothers and sisters are like that!
Brown, Jeff. *Flat Stanley*
Brown, Laurie Krasny. *What's the big secret?*
   When dinosaurs die
Brown, Marc Tolon. *Arthur's chicken pox*
   Arthur's family vacation
   D. W., the picky eater
   D. W.'s lost blankie
Brown, Margaret Wise. *The little scarecrow boy*
   On Christmas eve, ill. by Nancy Edwards Calder
   On Christmas eve, ill. by Beni Montresor
Brown, Myra Berry. *Pip camps out*
Brown, Tricia. *Hello, amigos!*
Browne, Anthony. *Changes*
   Zoo
Bruna, Dick. *Miffy*
   Miffy's birthday
Brutschy, Jennifer. *The winter fox*
Buchanan, Heather S. *Emily Mouse saves the day*
Buck, Pearl S. (Pearl Sydenstricker). *The little fox in the middle*
Buckley, Helen Elizabeth. *Where did Josie go?*
Bunin, Catherine. *Is that your sister?*
Bunting, Eve (Anne Evelyn). *The big red barn*
   Ghost's hour, spook's hour
   Going home
   I have an olive tree
   My backpack
   Night tree
   A picnic in October
   The wall
   The Wednesday surprise
Burch, Robert. *The hunting trip*
   Joey's cat
Burden-Patmon, Denise. *Imani's gift at Kwanzaa*
Burdett, Lois. *Romeo and Juliet for kids*
Burningham, John. *Avocado baby*

David, Lawrence. *The good little girl*
Davis, Jennifer. *Before you were born*
Davis, Katie (Katie I.). *I hate to go to bed!*
Davis, Maggie S. *Something magic*
Davol, Marguerite W. *Black, white, just right*
Day, Alexandra. *The Christmas we moved to the barn*
De Angeli, Marguerite. *Yonie Wondernose*
Deedy, Carmen Agra. *The secret of Old Zeb*
Deetlefs, Rene. *Tabu and the dancing elephants*
Delton, Judy. *Brimhall comes to stay*
　　It happened on Thursday
Denim, Sue. *The Dumb Bunnies*
　　The Dumb Bunnies' Easter
　　The Dumb Bunnies go to the zoo
　　Make way for Dumb Bunnies
Denison, Carol. *A part-time dog for Nick*
Dennis, Lynne. *Raymond Rabbit's early morning*
Denton, Kady MacDonald. *The picnic*
De Paola, Tomie (Thomas Anthony). *The art lesson*
　　The family Christmas tree book
　　Katie, Kit and cousin Tom
　　Too many Hopkins
De Regniers, Beatrice Schenk. *The giant story*
　　A little house of your own
DeSaix, Deborah Durland. *In the back seat*
Dickens, Lucy. *At the beach*
　　Our day
　　Outside
　　Playtime
Dixon, Ann. *The blueberry shoe*
Dodds, Dayle Ann. *Sing, Sophie!*
Doherty, Berlie. *Snowy*
Dooley, Norah. *Everybody cooks rice*
Douglass, Ann. *Baby science*
Dowling, Paul. *Meg and Jack are moving*
Dragonwagon, Crescent. *Diana, maybe*
　　Home place
　　Rainy day together
　　The sun begun
Drescher, Henrik. *Klutz*
　　The strange appearance of Howard Cranebill, Jr.
Drescher, Joan E. *The birth-order blues*
　　I'm in charge!
　　The marvelous mess
　　Your family, my family
Duke, Kate. *Bedtime*
　　Clean-up day
　　If you walk down this road
　　The playground
　　What bounces?
Dunbar, Joyce. *When I was young*
　　Why is the sky up?
Dupasquier, Philippe. *I can't sleep*
Edwards, Frank B. *Mortimer Mooner stopped taking a bath*
Edwards, Michelle. *Alef-bet*
Ehlert, Lois. *Hands*
Ehrlich, Amy. *Bunnies at Christmastime*
　　Bunnies on their own
　　Zeek Silver Moon
Elzbieta. *Brave Babette and sly Tom*
　　Dikou and the mysterious moon sheep
Emberley, Michael. *Welcome back, Sun*
Emerman, Ellen. *Just right*
Engel, Diana. *Gino Badino*
　　Josephina hates her name
English, Karen. *Just right stew*
　　Nadia's hands
Escudie, René. *Paul and Sebastian*

Estes, Kristyn Rehling. *Manuela's gift*
Ets, Marie Hall. *Bad boy, good boy*
Factor, Jane. *Summer*
Falwell, Cathryn. *Feast for ten*
　　We have a baby
Farber, Norma. *The boy who longed for a lift*
Fassler, Joan. *One little girl*
Faulkner, Keith. *The monster in my bathroom*
　　The monster in my toybox
Feiffer, Jules. *I lost my bear*
Felt, Sue. *Rosa-too-little*
Fenton, Edward. *Fierce John*
Fiday, Beverly. *Time to go*
Figley, Marty Rhodes. *Noah's wife*
Figueredo, D. H. *When this world was new*
Fisher, Aileen Lucia. *In one door and out the other*
Flack, Marjorie. *Wait for William*
Flanagan, Alice K. *A visit to the Gravesens' farm*
Fleisher, Robbin. *Quilts in the attic*
Florian, Douglas. *A summer day*
　　A winter day
Flournoy, Valerie. *The best time of day*
Fontenot, Mary Alice. *Tah-Tye*
Ford, Christine. *Snow!*
Foreman, Michael. *The angel and the wild animal*
Foster, Karen Sharp. *Good night my little chicks = Buenas noches mis pollitos*
Fowler, Susi Gregg. *Fog*
Fox, Charles Philip. *Mr. Stripes the gopher*
Fox, Mem. *A bedtime story*
　　Time for bed
Fraser, Kathleen. *Adam's world, San Francisco*
French, Vivian. *A song for little toad*
　　Tiger and the temper tantrum
Freudberg, Judy. *Susan and Gordon adopt a baby*
Friedman, Ina R. *How my parents learned to eat*
Gackenbach, Dick. *Where are Momma, Poppa, and Sister June?*
Galbraith, Kathryn Osebold. *Katie did!*
Galdone, Paul. *Obedient Jack*
Ganly, Helen. *Jyoti's journey*
Garland, Michael. *Circus girl*
　　My cousin Katie
Garland, Sarah. *Going shopping*
　　Having a picnic
Gauch, Patricia Lee. *Christina Katerina and the time she quit the family*
Gay, Marie-Louise. *Rainy day magic*
Gelsanliter, Wendy. *Dancin' in the kitchen*
Giffard, Hannah. *Red Fox on the move*
Gill, Joan. *Hush, Jon!*
Gillmor, Don. *The fabulous song*
Ginsburg, Mirra. *We adopted you, Benjamin Koo*
Girard, Linda Walvoord. *Adoption is for always*
　　At Daddy's on Saturdays
Glass, Andrew. *Chickpea and the talking cow*
Gliori, Debi. *Mr. Bear's new baby*
　　New big house
　　No matter what
　　The princess and the pirate king
Gobhai, Mehlli. *Usha, the mouse-maiden*
Goffstein, M. B. (Marilyn Brooke). *Family scrapbook*
　　Our prairie home
　　Our snowman
Goldman, Susan. *Cousins are special*
Good, Merle. *Reuben and the fire*
Goodman, Joan Elizabeth. *Bernard's bath*
Goudey, Alice E. *The day we saw the sun come up*
Gould, Deborah. *Camping in the Temple of the Sun*

Melmed, Laura Krauss. *Little Oh*
Merriam, Eve. *The Christmas box*
Merrill, Jean. *Emily Emerson's moon*
Miles, Calvin. *Calvin's Christmas wish*
Milgram, Mary. *Brothers are all the same*
Miller, Edna. *Mousekin's family*
Miller, J. P. (John Parr). *Good night, Little Rabbit*
Miller, Kathryn Ann. *Did my first mother love me?*
Miller, M. L. *Those Bottles!*
Miller, Margaret. *At my house*
   Family time
   I can help
   I love colors
   I'm grown up!
   In my room
   My first words: me and my clothes
   Time to eat
Mills, Claudia. *A visit to Amy-Claire*
Millward, David Wynn. *Jenny and Bob*
Milord, Sue. *Maggie and the goodbye gift*
Mintzberg, Yvette. *Sally, where are you?*
Miranda, Anne. *Baby talk*
Mitchell, Barbara. *Red Bird*
   Waterman's child
Modarressi, Mitra. *The parent thief*
Moers, Hermann. *Hugo's baby brother*
Molnar, Dorothy E. *Who will pick me up when I fall?*
Monjo, F. N. *Rudi and the distelfink*
Moore, Inga. *Oh, little Jack*
Moore, Lilian. *Papa Albert*
Moorman, Margaret. *Light the lights!*
Morgan-Vanroyen, Mary. *Guess who I love?*
Morimoto, Junko. *The inch boy*
Morozumi, Atsuko. *Helping daddy*
Morris, Ann. *The baby book*
   Families
   Loving
Morrow, Barbara. *Edward's portrait*
Moses, Will. *Silent night*
Mosley, Francis. *The dinosaur eggs*
Moss, Marissa. *Mel's diner*
Motyka, Sally Mitchell. *An ordinary day*
Munsch, Robert N. *Good families don't*
   I have to go!
   Mmm, cookies!
Murphy, Jill. *All in one piece*
   Five minutes' peace
   The last noo-noo
   A quiet night in
Murphy, Stuart J. *The best vacation ever*
Myller, Lois. *No! No!*
Namioka, Lensey. *The laziest boy in the world*
Nayer, Judy. *The happy little engine*
Nelson, Vaunda Micheaux. *Always Gramma*
Nerlove, Miriam. *Easter*
Ness, Evaline. *Exactly alike*
Neville, Emily Cheney. *The bridge*
Neville, Mary. *The Christmas tree ride*
Newton, Jill. *Don't sit there!*
Nicholls, Judith. *Someone I like*
Nicholson, Nicholas B. A. *Little girl in a red dress*
   with cat and dog
Nikola-Lisa, W. *One, two, three Thanksgiving!*
Nilsson, Ulf. *Little sister rabbit*
Nivola, Claire A. *Elisabeth*
Nixon, Joan Lowery. *You bet your britches, Claude*
Noble, June. *Two homes for Lynn*
Nolan, Madeena Spray. *My daddy don't go to work*
Nolen, Jerdine. *In my momma's kitchen*

Nones, Eric Jon. *Wendell*
Norac, Carl. *I love you so much*
Novak, Matt. *Mouse TV*
O'Brien, John (1953-). *Poof!*
O'Donnell, Elizabeth Lee. *Maggie doesn't want to move*
O'Kelley, Mattie Lou. *Circus!*
Olsen, Ib Spang. *The grown-up trap*
Oppenheim, Joanne. *Rooter remembers*
Oram, Hiawyn. *Reckless Ruby*
Ormerod, Jan. *Moonlight*
   Who's whose?
Osofsky, Audrey. *Dreamcatcher*
Ostheeren, Ingrid. *The blue monster*
Ovenell-Carter, Julie. *Adam's daycare*
Overend, Jenni. *Welcome with love*
Oxenbury, Helen. *Beach day*
   Family
   Our dog
Paraskevas, Betty. *The tangerine bear*
Paterson, Diane. *Wretched Rachel*
Peacock, Carol Antoinette. *Mommy far, Mommy near*
Pearce, Philippa. *Emily's own elephant*
Pearson, Susan. *Saturday, I ran away*
Pedersen, Judy. *Out in the country*
Pellegrini, Nina. *Families are different*
Pellowski, Anne. *Stairstep farm*
Perkins, Lynne Rae. *Clouds for dinner*
   Home lovely
Pilkey, Dav. *The Hallo-wiener*
Pinkney, Gloria Jean. *Back home*
   The Sunday outing
Pinkney, J. Brian. *Jojo's flying side kick*
Pinkwater, Daniel Manus. *Wempires*
Politi, Leo. *Little Leo*
Pomerantz, Charlotte. *The mango tooth*
   Posy
Porte, Barbara Ann. *Harry's mom*
Portnoy, Mindy Avra. *Mommy never went to Hebrew school*
Poulin, Stéphane. *My mother's loves*
   Travels for two
Powell, Consie. *Old dog Cora and the Christmas tree*
Powell, E. Sandy. *A chance to grow*
Prater, John. *Along came Tom*
   The greatest show on earth
Price, Mathew. *Peekaboo!*
Pringle, Laurence P. *Everybody has a bellybutton*
   Octopus hug
Provensen, Alice. *An owl and three pussycats*
Prøysen, Alf. *Christmas eve at Santa's*
Prusski, Jeffrey. *Bring back the deer*
Pryor, Bonnie. *The dream jar*
Pulver, Robin. *Alicia's tutu*
Purdy, Carol. *Iva Dunnit and the big wind*
   Least of all
Quackenbush, Robert M. *Funny bunnies on the run*
   Henry's world tour
   I don't want to go, I don't know how to act
   Mouse feathers
Quindlen, Anna. *The tree that came to stay*
Raffi. *One light, one sun*
Rand, Gloria. *Baby in a basket*
   The cabin key
Ransom, Candice F. *When the whippoorwill calls*
Raphael, Elaine. *Turnabout*
Raskin, Ellen. *Ghost in a four-room apartment*
Raven, Margot. *Angels in the dust*

Family life – aunts, uncles

Fowler, Susi Gregg. *Beautiful*
Froissart, Bénédicte. *Uncle Henry's dinner guests*
Gantos, Jack (John, Jr.). *Aunt Bernice*
Gauch, Patricia Lee. *Uncle Magic*
Go tell Aunt Rhody. *Go tell Aunt Rhody*, ill. by Aliki
    Go tell Aunt Rhody, ill. by Robert M. Quacken-
    bush
Gray, Libba Moore. *When Uncle took the fiddle*
Green, Phyllis. *Uncle Roland, the perfect guest*
Greenblat, Rodney Alan. *Aunt Ippy's museum of
    junk*
    Uncle Wizzmo's new used car
Gregory, Valiska. *The oatmeal cookie giant*
Gretz, Susanna. *Rabbit food*
Grifalconi, Ann. *Kinda blue*
Guthrie, Donna. *One hundred and two steps*
Hallinan, P. K. (Patrick K.). *We're very good friends,
    my aunt and I*
Harshman, Marc. *Uncle James*
Hartman, Bob. *Aunt Mabel's table*
    The one and only Delgado Cheese
Helldorfer, M. C. (Mary Claire). *Sailing to the sea*
Hermes, Patricia. *When snow lay soft on the mountain*
Hesse, Karen. *Lavender*
Hest, Amy. *Fancy Aunt Jess*
Hindley, Judy. *Uncle Harold and the green hat*
Hines, Anna Grossnickle. *Mean old Uncle Jack*
Hoff, Syd. *My Aunt Rosie*
Honeycutt, Natalie. *Whistle home*
Houston, Gloria. *But no candy*
    My Great-Aunt Arizona
Howard, Elizabeth Fitzgerald. *Aunt Flossie's hats
    (and crab cakes later)*
    What's in Aunt Mary's room?
Jewell, Nancy. *Time for Uncle Joe*
Johnson, Angela. *The aunt in our house*
    The girl who wore snakes
Johnston, Tony. *Uncle rain cloud*
Jones, Rebecca C. *Great Aunt Martha*
Jukes, Mavis. *I'll see you in my dreams*
Ketteman, Helen. *Aunt Hilarity's bustle*
Kimmelman, Leslie. *Sound the shofar!*
Komaiko, Leah. *Great Aunt Ida and her Great Dane,
    Doc*
Lakin, Pat (Patricia). *The palace of stars*
Lasky, Kathryn. *I have an aunt on Marlborough Street*
Levoy, Myron. *The Hanukkah of Great-Uncle Otto*
Lewis, Robin Baird. *Aunt Armadillo*
Lewison, Wendy Cheyette. *I am a flower girl*
Lobel, Arnold. *Uncle Elephant*
Lööf, Jan. *Uncle Louie's fantastic sea voyage*
MacDonald, Elizabeth. *My aunt and the animals*
Mahy, Margaret. *The horrendous hullabaloo*
Martin, Jacqueline Briggs. *Bizzy Bones and Uncle
    Ezra*
Merriam, Eve. *Epaminondas*
Mitchell, Margaree King. *Uncle Jed's barbershop*
Mitchell, Rhonda. *The talking cloth*
Mogensen, Jan. *The Land of the Big*
Mora, Pat. *A birthday basket for Tía*
Moss, Marissa. *In America*
Muntean, Michaela. *Bicycle Bear rides again*
    Kermit and Robin's scary story
Naylor, Phyllis Reynolds. *"I can't take you anywhere!"*
Newman, Lesléa. *Too far away to touch*
Newton, Laura P. *Me and my aunts*
Nielsen, Laura F. *Jeremy's muffler*
Nunes, Susan Miho. *The last dragon*
Oliviero, Jamie. *Som See and the magic elephant*

Parker, Nancy Winslow. *Love from Aunt Betty*
    Love from Uncle Clyde
Paterson, Diane. *Smile for auntie*
Pearson, Susan. *Karin's Christmas walk*
Perkins, Lynne Rae. *Clouds for dinner*
Pinkwater, Daniel Manus. *Aunt Lulu*
Pollack, Eileen. *Whisper whisper Jesse, whisper whisper
    Josh*
Porte, Barbara Ann. *When Aunt Lucy rode a mule
    and other stories*
Potok, Chaim. *The sky of now*
Prigger, Mary Skillings. *Aunt Minnie McGranahan*
Proimos, James. *The loudness of Sam*
Rubel, Nicole. *Uncle Henry and Aunt Henrietta's hon-
    eymoon*
Schwartz, Amy. *Her Majesty, Aunt Essie*
Selway, Martina. *Don't forget to write*
Sharratt, Nick. *Snazzy aunties*
Spurr, Elizabeth. *The long, long letter*
Stevenson, James. *Worse than the worst*
Stewart, Sarah. *The gardener*
Sullivan, Silky. *Grandpa was a cowboy*
Thomas, Ianthe. *Lordy, Aunt Hattie*
Thomson, Pat. *Beware of the aunts!*
Thorne, Jenny. *My uncle*
Tripp, Wallace. *My Uncle Podger*
Vigna, Judith. *My two uncles*
Weller, Frances Ward. *The closet gorilla*
Whitcher, Susan. *Something for everyone*
Willey, Margaret. *Thanksgiving with me*
Woodtor, Dee. *Big meeting*
Wyse, Lois. *Two guppies, a turtle and Aunt Edna*

Family life – brothers see also Family life;
    Family life – brothers and sisters; Sibling
    rivalry
Afanas'ev, Aleksandr N. *Salt*
Amoss, Berthe. *Tom in the middle*
Arnold, Tedd. *The twin princes*
Asch, Frank. *Dear brother*
Auch, Mary Jane. *Monster brother*
Ayers, Rebecca Hickox. *Per and the Dala horse*
Baumann, Hans. *Mischa and his brothers*
Bible. Old Testament. Joseph. *Joseph and his
    brothers*
Blades, Ann. *Summer*
    Winter
Bradman, Tony. *Billy and the baby*
Breebaart, Joeri. *When I die, will I get better?*
Buckley, Helen Elizabeth. *"Take care of things,"
    Edward said*
Butterworth, Nick. *The two sons*
Byars, Betsy Cromer. *Ant plays bear*
    My brother, Ant
Caseley, Judith. *Sophie and Sammy's library sleepover*
Clarke, Gus. *Along came Eric*
Cole, Babette. *Babette Cole's brother*
Cole, Joanna. *I'm a big brother*
Collins, Pat Lowery. *Don't tease the guppies*
Croll, Carolyn. *The three brothers*
Cummings, Pat. *Jimmy Lee did it*
Dale, Penny. *Big Brother, Little Brother*
Degen, Bruce. *Teddy bear towers*
Donaldson, Joan. *The real pretend*
Edwards, Becky. *My brother Sammy*
Edwards, Pamela Duncan. *Four famished foxes and
    Fosdyke*
Falwell, Cathryn. *Nicky and Alex*

Freedman, Florence B. *Brothers*
Grimm, Jacob. *One gift deserves another*
Hanson, Joan. *I don't like Timmy*
Harber, Frances. *The brothers' promise*
Harley, Bill. *Nothing happened*
Hartmann, Wendy. *The dinosaurs are back and it's all your fault, Edward!*
Havill, Juanita. *Magic fort*
Hiatt, Fred. *Baby talk*
Himmelman, John. *J.J. versus the babysitter*
Hoban, Russell. *Best friends for Frances*
    Harvey's hideout
Hoffman, Mary. *Henry's baby*
Hooker, Ruth. *Sara loves her big brother*
Hooks, William H. *Mr. Baseball*
    Mr. Dinosaur
    Mr. Monster
Howe, James. *There's a dragon in my sleeping bag*
Jacobs, Kate. *A sister's wish*
Jaffe, Nina. *Older brother, younger brother*
Johnston, Tony. *The iguana brothers, a perfect day*
    Slither McCreep and his brother, Joe
Jonell, Lynne. *It's my birthday, too!*
Joosse, Barbara M. *I love you the purplest*
Keller, Holly. *Harry and Tuck*
Kleven, Elisa. *A monster in the house*
Kovacs, Deborah. *Moonlight on the river*
Kraus, Robert. *Little Louie the baby bloomer*
Kroll, Virginia L. *Helen the fish*
Lakin, Pat (Patricia). *Just like me*
Levine, Arthur A. *All the lights in the night*
London, Jonathan. *Moshi moshi*
Maccarone, Grace. *Sharing time troubles*
Mackinnon, Debbie. *Tom's train*
Nixon, Joan Lowery. *When I am eight*
Oppenheim, Joanne. *Left and right*
Packard, Mary. *When I am big*
Pryor, Bonnie. *Louie and Dan are friends*
Robins, Joan. *My brother, Will*
Roche, P. K. (Patrick K.). *Webster and Arnold go camping*
Roe, Eileen. *Con mi hermano = With my brother*
Rumford, James. *The Island-below-the-star*
Russo, Marisabina. *The big brown box*
San Souci, Robert D. *The enchanted tapestry*
Schertle, Alice. *Witch Hazel*
Schnitter, Jane. *William is my brother*
Shields, Carol Diggory. *I wish my brother was a dog*
Silverman, Erica. *Follow the leader*
Spohn, David. *Starry night*
Steig, William. *The toy brother*
Stevenson, James. *That's exactly the way it wasn't*
Stuve-Bodeen, Stephanie. *Mama Elizabeti*
Titherington, Jeanne. *A place for Ben*
Vulliamy, Clara. *Ellen and Penguin and the new baby*
Waddell, Martin. *Sam Vole and his brothers*
White, Linda Arms. *Comes a wind*
Wilhelm, Hans. *More bunny trouble*
Woodruff, Elvira. *Mrs. McCloskey's monkeys*
Yorinks, Arthur. *Oh, brother*
    Ugh

Family life – brothers and sisters

Adoff, Arnold. *Today we are brother and sister*
Alborough, Jez. *Cuddly Dudley*
    Watch out! Big Bro's coming!
Alexander, Martha G. *Good night, Lily*
    Lily and Willy
    Where's Willy?
    Willy's boot
Anglund, Joan Walsh. *Baby brother*
Armitage, Ronda. *Harry hates shopping!*
Barrett, Mary Brigid. *The man of the house at Huffington Row*
Bartone, Elisa. *Peppe the lamplighter*
Beck, Ian. *Emily and the golden acorn*
Berenstain, Stan. *The Berenstain bears no girls allowed*
Blake, Quentin. *Simpkin*
Bogart, Jo Ellen. *Daniel's dog*
Brenner, Barbara A. *Rosa and Marco and the three wishes*
Brown, Laurie Krasny. *Rex and Lilly school time*
Brown, Marc Tolon. *Arthur tricks the tooth fairy*
    Arthur's first sleepover
    D. W. rides again!
    D. W. thinks big, a board book
    Glasses for D. W.
Browne, Anthony. *The tunnel*
Buck, Nola. *Hey, little baby!*
Burningham, John. *The baby*
Caple, Kathy. *The coolest place in town*
    The wimp
Carlstrom, Nancy White. *Wishing at dawn in summer*
Carter, Alden R. *Big brother Dustin*
Chall, Marsha Wilson. *Mattie*
Church, Kristine. *My brother John*
Collins, Pat Lowery. *Waiting for baby Joe*
Craig, Helen. *Susie and Alfred in a busy day in town*
Crews, Nina. *A high, low, near, far, loud, quiet story*
Dale, Penny. *Bet you can't*
Daly, Niki. *Monsters are like that*
De Groat, Diane. *Trick or treat, smell my feet*
Denchfield, Nick. *Desmond the dog*
    Desmond the dog, a wag-the-tail pop-up book
De Paola, Tomie (Thomas Anthony). *The bubble factory*
Dilley, Becki. *Sixty fingers, sixty toes*
Driscoll, Debbie. *Baby comes home*
Dubois, Claude K. *Looking for Ginny*
Dunbar, Joyce. *Tell me something happy before I go to sleep*
Eaton, Deborah. *The rainy day grump*
Farmer, Patti. *What's he doing now?*
Fleming, Denise. *Mama cat has three kittens*
Franklin, Jonathan. *Don't wake the baby*
French, Vivian. *A Christmas star called Hannah*
    Molly in the middle
    Tiger and the new baby
Gerstein, Mordicai. *The gigantic baby*
Givens, Terryl. *Dragon scales and willow leaves*
Gliori, Debi. *My little brother*
Goode, Diane. *Mama's perfect present*
Green, Jen. *Our new baby*
Grimm, Jacob. *The six swans*, ill. by Daniel San Souci
Hains, Harriet. *My baby brother*
Hallinan, P. K. (Patrick K.). *Today is Easter!*
Havill, Juanita. *Jamaica Tag-Along*
Helldorfer, M. C. (Mary Claire). *The darling boys*
Hendrickson, Karen. *Baby and I can play*
Herrick, Amy. *Kimbo's marble*
Hest, Amy. *You're the boss, Baby Duck*
Heymans, Annemie. *The princess in the kitchen garden*
Hiatt, Fred. *If I were queen of the world*

Hines, Anna Grossnickle. *Big help*
Hoban, Lillian. *Arthur's back to school day*
   No, no, Sammy Crow
Hoberman, Mary Ann. *And to think that we thought*
   that we'd never be friends
Hodges, Margaret. *Comus*
Hoffman, Rosekrans. *Sister Sweet Ella*
Holcomb, Nan. *Patrick and Emma Lou*
Hooks, William H. *The legend of the Christmas rose*
   Rough, tough, Rowdy
Horowitz, Ruth. *Mommy's lap*
Howard, Elizabeth Fitzgerald. *Mac and Marie and*
   the train toss surprise
   When will Sarah come?
Hughes, Shirley. *Alfie's ABC*
   Rhymes for Annie Rose
Hutchins, Pat. *Silly Billy!*
Impey, Rose. *Joe's café*
   Jumble Joan
Johnson, Angela. *Do like Kyla*
   When mules flew on Magnolia Street
Joyce, William. *Santa calls*
Keller, Holly. *Geraldine and Mrs. Duffy*
   Maxine in the middle
   What Alvin wanted
Kinsey-Warnock, Natalie. *The summer of Stanley*
Komaiko, Leah. *Where can Daniel be?*
Kudler, David. *The Seven Gods of Luck*
Kurtz, Jane. *Fire on the mountain*
Lasky, Kathryn. *Starring Lucille*
Lawlor, Laurie. *The biggest pest on Eighth Avenue*
Lears, Laurie. *Ian's walk*
Le Guin, Ursula K. *A ride on the red mare's back*
Leonard, Marcia. *Get the ball, Slim*
Lester, Alison. *The journey home*
Lester, Helen. *Help! I'm stuck!*
Leuck, Laura. *My baby brother has ten tiny toes*
Levine, Arthur A. *The boardwalk princess*
Lewison, Wendy Cheyette. *My baby brother*
   Our new baby
   Say thank you, Theodore
Little, Jean. *Revenge of the small Small*
Livingston, Myra Cohn. *Poems for brothers, poems for*
   sisters
McAllister, Angela. *The clever cowboy*
   The snow angel
McClintock, Barbara. *Molly and the magic wishbone*
Macdonald, Maryann. *Ben at the beach*
Magorian, Michelle. *Who's going to take care of me?*
Manushkin, Fran. *Be brave, baby rabbit*
Mario, Heidi Stetson. *I'd rather have an iguana*
May, Kara. *Big brave brother Ben*
Mazer, Anne. *The Fixits*
Meddaugh, Susan. *Cinderella's rat*
Mills, Claudia. *Phoebe's parade*
Mills, Lauren A. *The goblin baby*
Moon, Nicola. *Something special*
Munsch, Robert N. *Alligator baby*
Murdocca, Sal (Salvatore). *Baby wants the moon*
Naylor, Phyllis Reynolds. *The baby, the bed, and the*
   rose
Novak, Matt. *The Pillow War*
Offen, Hilda. *Good girl, Gracie Growler!*
Palatini, Margie. *Good as Goldie*
Pelham, David. *Sam's pizza*
   Sam's sandwich
Pitcher, Caroline. *The snow whale*
Polacco, Patricia. *My rotten redheaded older brother*
Prigger, Mary Skillings. *Aunt Minnie McGranahan*

Pulver, Robin. *Way to go, Alex!*
Radunsky, Eugenia. *Yucka Drucka Droni*
Raschka, Christopher. *The blushful hippopotamus*
Reader, Dennis. *Butterfingers*
Rockwell, Lizzy. *Hello baby!*
Roddie, Shen. *Toes are to tickle*
Rodell, Susanna. *Dear Fred*
Rogers, Jacqueline. *Tiptoe into kindergarten*
Rosenberg, Maxine B. *Brothers and sisters*
Russo, Marisabina. *Hannah's baby sister*
Sanders, Scott R. (Scott Russell). *Crawdad Creek*
Scheffler, Ursel. *Taking care of Sister Bear*
Shea, Pegi Deitz. *New moon*
Simmons, Jane. *Daisy and the egg*
Skorpen, Liesel Moak. *We were tired of living in a*
   house
Stimson, Joan. *Big Panda, Little Panda*
Stuve-Bodeen, Stephanie. *We'll paint the octopus red*
Super, Gretchen. *Sisters and brothers*
Topek, Susan Remick. *A costume for Noah*
Waddell, Martin. *When the teddy bears came*
Walsh, Ellen Stoll. *Two too much*
Warner, Sunny. *The magic sewing machine*
Wells, Rosemary. *Bunny cakes*
   Bunny money
   Goodnight Max
   Max and Ruby's Midas
   Max cleans up
   Max's dragon shirt
Wiesner, David. *Hurricane*
Wild, Margaret. *Toby*
Wilkowski, Susan. *Baby's Bris*
Williams, Susan. *Poppy's first year*
Winthrop, Elizabeth. *Bear and Roly-Poly*
Wishinsky, Frieda. *Oonga boonga*, ill. by Suçie
   Stevenson
   Oonga boonga, ill. by Carol Thompson
Woodruff, Elvira. *Tubtime*
Zalben, Jane Breskin. *Buster gets braces*

Family life – cousins

Carlstrom, Nancy White. *Guess who's coming, Jesse*
   Bear
Caseley, Judith. *Cousins*
Chausse, Sylvie. *The egg and I*
Chorao, Kay. *Annie and cousin Precious*
Craig, Helen. *Charlie and Tyler at the seashore*
English, Karen. *Neeny coming, Neeny going*
French, Vivian. *Spider watching*
Greenfield, Eloise. *Easter parade*
Hautzig, Deborah. *Little Witch's bad dream*
Hesse, Karen. *Lavender*
Hest, Amy. *Nana's birthday party*
Holabird, Katharine. *Angelina's Christmas*
Impey, Rose. *Scare yourself to sleep*
Levitin, Sonia. *A piece of home*
Luttrell, Ida. *Be nice to Marilyn*
Northway, Jennifer. *Get lost, Laura!*
   Lucy's day trip
Rodriguez, Bobbie. *Sarah's sleepover*
Root, Phyllis. *Aunt Nancy and Cousin Lazybones*
Smalls-Hector, Irene. *Because you're lucky*
Thomassie, Tynia. *Cajun through and through*
Wagner, Jenny. *Amy's monster*

Family life – daughters

Balgassi, Haemi. *Peacebound trains*

Family life – fathers

Hudson, Wade. *Jamal's busy day*
Hughes, Shirley. *Abel's moon*
Impey, Rose. *My mom and our dad*
In daddy's arms I am tall
Jaffe, Nina. *The way meat loves salt*
Jam, Teddy. *Night cars*
Janovitz, Marilyn. *Can I help?*
Is it time?
Jensen, Patricia. *Be careful, Little Antelope*
Johnson, Angela. *Casey Jones*
Joshua's night whispers
Johnson, Dolores. *Papa's stories*
Your dad was just like you
Jolin, Dominique. *It's not fair!*
Joosse, Barbara M. *Lewis and papa*
Kauffman, Lois. *What's that noise?*
Kessler, Leonard P. *Are we lost, daddy?*
Ketteman, Helen. *I remember papa*
Not yet, Yvette
Kidd, Nina. *June Mountain secret*
Kilroy, Sally. *Market day*
Kinsey-Warnock, Natalie. *When spring comes*
Komaiko, Leah. *Just my dad and me*
Kraus, Robert. *Daddy Long Ears*
Kroll, Steven. *Happy Father's Day*
Kroll, Virginia L. *Africa brothers and sisters*
Lakin, Pat (Patricia). *Dad and me in the morning*
Hurricane!
Lanton, Sandy. *Daddy's chair*
Lauture, Denizé. *Father and son*
Leblanc, Anne. *Benjamin in the snow*
Lenski, Lois. *Papa Small*
Leonard, Marcia. *The tin can man*
Levy, Janice. *Totally uncool*
Lewin, Hugh. *Jafta - the homecoming*
Jafta's father
Lexau, Joan M. *Every day a dragon*
Me day
Lindbergh, Reeve. *If I'd known then what I know now*
Lindenbaum, Pija. *Else-Marie and her seven little daddies*
Lindsay, Jeanne Warren. *Do I have a daddy?*
Little, Mimi Otey. *Daddy has a pair of striped shorts*
Livingston, Myra Cohn. *Poems for fathers*
Locker, Thomas. *Miranda's smile*
London, Jonathan. *At the edge of the forest*
Loon Lake
Old salt, young salt
Long, Earlene. *Gone fishing*
Lubell, Winifred. *Here comes daddy*
McAfee, Annalena. *The visitors who came to stay*
McAllister, Angela. *The ice palace*
McBratney, Sam. *Guess how much I love you*
McCormick, Wendy. *Daddy, will you miss me?*
McCourt, Lisa. *Chicken soup for little souls: The best night out with Dad*
McCully, Emily Arnold. *Popcorn at the palace*
McDonald, Megan. *Bedbugs*
McGinnis, Lila Sprague. *If Daddy only knew me*
McKay, Lawrence. *Caravan*
McKee, David. *Prince Peter and the teddy bear*
McKinley, Robin. *My father is in the Navy*
McMullan, Kate (Hall). *Papa's song*
McPhail, David M. *Ed and me*
Henry Bear's park
The party
McQuade, Jacqueline. *At preschool with Teddy Bear*
Madenski, Melissa. *Some of the pieces*

Mahy, Margaret. *Down the dragon's tongue*
Mangas, Brian. *A nice surprise for Father Rabbit*
Manushkin, Fran. *Peeping and sleeping*
Martin, David. *Piggy and Dad*
Marzollo, Jean. *Amy goes fishing*
Close your eyes
Papa, papa
Mayer, Mercer. *Just me and my dad*
Shibumi and the kitemaker
Medearis, Angela Shelf. *Our people*
Meredith, Carol. *Jamie Anderson wouldn't . . .*
Milich, Melissa. *Miz Fannie Mae's fine new Easter hat*
Minarik, Else Holmelund. *Father Bear comes home*
Monjo, F. N. *The one bad thing about father*
Morgan, Allen. *Nicole's boat*
Morris, Ann. *The daddy book*
Munsch, Robert N. *Get me another one!*
Something good
Where is Gah-Ning?
Myers, Bernice. *The gold watch*
Newton-John, Olivia. *A pig tale*
Nolan, Madeena Spray. *My daddy don't go to work*
Novak, Matt. *Gertie and Gumbo*
Numeroff, Laura Joffe. *What daddies do best*
O'Donnell, Elizabeth Lee. *Sing me a window*
Oppenheim, Shulamith Levey. *Yanni rubbish*
Ormerod, Jan. *Dad's back*
Messy baby
Reading
Sleeping
Paradis, Susan. *My Daddy*
Paris, Lena. *Mom is single*
Parker, Kristy. *My dad the magnificent*
Patron, Susan. *Dark cloud strong breeze*
Paxton, Tom. *The marvelous toy*
Pettigrew, Eileen. *Night-time*
Pfister, Marcus. *Penguin Pete and Little Tim*
Pingry, Patricia. *Joseph's story*
Pitcher, Caroline. *The time of the lion*
Pittman, Helena Clare. *Uncle Phil's diner*
Polacco, Patricia. *My ol' man*
Some birthday!
Porte, Barbara Ann. *Harry's dog*
Harry's mom
Porter-Gaylord, Laurel. *I love my daddy because . . .*
Posey, Lee. *Night rabbits*
Puner, Helen Walker. *Daddys, what they do all day*
Quinlan, Patricia. *My dad takes care of me*
Rabe, Berniece. *Where's Chimpy?*
Radlauer, Ruth Shaw. *Molly at the library*
Rappaport, Doreen. *The new king*
Ray, Mary Lyn. *Basket moon*
Regan, Dian Curtis. *Daddies*
Repchuk, Caroline. *The forgotten garden*
Rice, Eve. *Swim!*
Riecken, Nancy. *Today is the day*
Ringi, Kjell (Arne Sorensen). *My father and I*
Roberts, Bethany. *Waiting-for-Papa stories*
Rockwell, Anne F. *Ducklings and pollywogs*
Root, Phyllis. *Contrary bear*
Rush, Ken. *Friday's journey*
Ryder, Joanne. *My father's hands*
Sachar, Louis. *Monkey soup*
Sandberg, Inger. *Come on out, Daddy!*
San Souci, Robert D. *The samurai's daughter*
Schindel, John. *Dear Daddy*
Schwartz, Amy. *Bea and Mr. Jones*
Shalev, Meir. *My father always embarrasses me*
Shannon, George. *Dancing the breeze*

Sharp, N. L. *Today I'm going fishing with my dad*
Shepard, Steve. *Elvis Hornbill, international business bird*
Shipton, Jonathan. *How to be a happy hippo*
Simmonds, Posy. *Lulu and the flying babies*
Simon, Norma. *The daddy days*
　I wish I had my father
Singer, Marilyn. *In the palace of the Ocean King*
Slate, Joseph. *Story time for Little Porcupine*
Slater, Teddy. *Jan and Dan and the super dads*
Smalls-Hector, Irene. *Kevin and his dad*
Smee, Nicola. *Finish the story, dad*
Smith-Ayala, Emilie. *Marisol and the yellow messenger*
Sonneborn, Ruth A. *Friday night is papa night*
Spinelli, Eileen. *Night shift daddy*
Spohn, David. *Starry night*
　Winter wood
Stafford, Kim Robert. *We got here together*
Stanley, Sanna. *Monkey Sunday*
Stecher, Miriam B. *Daddy and Ben together*
Steel, Danielle. *Max's daddy goes to the hospital*
Steig, William. *Pete's a pizza*
Steiner, Charlotte. *Daddy comes home*
Steptoe, John. *Daddy is a monster . . . sometimes*
Stevens, Bryna. *Handel and the famous sword swallower of Halle*
Stevenson, James. *I meant to tell you*
　Sam the Zamboni man
Stevenson, Suçie. *Jessica the blue streak*
Stewart, Robert S. *The daddy book*
Stock, Catherine. *Christmas time*
Tarbescu, Edith. *Annushka's voyage*
Taylor, Ann. *Baby dance*
Thomas, Ianthe. *Willie blows a mean horn*
Thompson, Richard. *I have to see this*
Townson, Hazel. *What on earth . . . ?*
Trottier, Maxine. *A safe place*
Tyler, Linda Wagner. *When daddy comes home*
Udry, Janice May. *What Mary Jo shared*
Valentine, Johnny. *One dad, two dads, brown dad, blue dads*
Van Woerkom, Dorothy. *Something to crow about*
Vigna, Judith. *Daddy's new baby*
　I wish my daddy didn't drink so much
　Saying goodbye to daddy
Waboose, Jan Bourdeau. *Morning on the lake*
Waddell, Martin. *Can't you sleep, Little Bear?*
　Let's go home, Little Bear
　The toymaker
Wadsworth, Ginger. *Tomorrow is Daddy's birthday*
Wahl, Jan. *Once when the world was green*
Walters, Virginia. *Are we there yet, Daddy?*
Watanabe, Shigeo. *Daddy, play with me!*
　I can take a bath!
　Let's go swimming
　Where's my daddy?
Watson, Pauline. *Days with Daddy*
Welch, Willy. *Dancing with Daddy*
Wells, Rosemary. *The island light*
Weninger, Brigitte. *Good-bye, daddy!*
Willhoite, Michael. *Daddy's roommate*
Winthrop, Elizabeth. *As the crow flies*
Wolf, Jake. *Daddy, could I have an elephant?*
Wood, Douglas. *What dads can't do*
Wood, Jakki. *Dads are such fun*
Worley, Daryl. *Billy and the attic adventure*
Wyeth, Sharon Dennis. *Always my dad*
Yolen, Jane. *All those secrets of the world*
　The emperor and the kite
　Owl moon
Young, Ed (Edward). *Mouse match*
Zagwÿn, Deborah Turney. *Papa's latkes*
Ziefert, Harriet. *When daddy had the chicken pox*
Zimelman, Nathan. *Treed by a pride of irate lions*
Zola, Meguido. *Only the best*
Zolotow, Charlotte (Shapiro). *The summer night*

Family life – grandfathers

Ackerman, Karen. *Song and dance man*
Adams, Ken. *When I was your age*
Adler, David A. *A little at a time*
Alexander, Martha G. *Where does the sky end, Grandpa?*
Aliki. *The two of them*
Anaya, Rudolfo A. *Farolitos for Abuelo*
Anderson, Lena. *Stina*
　Stina's visit
Andrews, Jan. *The auction*
Arkin, Alan. *One present from Flekman's*
Auzary-Luton, Sylvie. *1, 2, 3, music!*
Bahr, Mary. *The memory box*
Bailey, Debbie. *Grandpa*
Balmer, Helen. *Jungle adventure*
Barrett, Judi. *Cloudy with a chance of meatballs*
Barron, T. A. *Where is Grandpa?*
Behrens, June. *Soo Ling finds a way*
Blades, Ann. *A boy of Taché*
Blos, Joan W. *The grandpa days*
　Hello, shoes!
Bond, Ruskin. *Cherry tree*
Borack, Barbara. *Grandpa*
Brady, Kimberley Smith. *Keeper for the sea*
Brooks, Ron. *Timothy and Gramps*
Brown, Kathryn. *Muledred*
Buckley, Helen Elizabeth. *Grandfather and I*
Bunting, Eve (Anne Evelyn). *Butterfly house*
　The day before Christmas
　A day's work
　The happy funeral
　Magic and the night river
　So far from the sea
Burningham, John. *Grandpa*
Butterworth, Nick. *My grandpa is amazing*
Carlson, Melody. *What Nick and Holly found in grandpa's attic*
Carlstrom, Nancy White. *Grandpappy*
Carrick, Carol. *Melanie*
Caseley, Judith. *Dear Annie*
　When Grandpa came to stay
Castle, Caroline. *Grandpa Baxter and the photographs*
Cazet, Denys. *Christmas moon*
　December 24th
Christian, Mary Blount. *Grandfathers, God's gift to children*
Clement, Rod. *Grandpa's teeth*
Coatsworth, Elizabeth. *Lonely Maria*
Cole, Babette. *The trouble with grandad*
Conrad, Pam. *The Tub grandfather*
Coville, Bruce. *My grandfather's house*
Cowley, Joy. *The rusty, trusty tractor*
Daly, Niki. *Papa Lucky's shadow*
Darling, Benjamin. *Valerie and the silver pear*
DeFelice, Cynthia C. *When Grampa kissed his elbow*
DeGross, Monalisa. *Granddaddy's street songs*
De Paola, Tomie (Thomas Anthony). *The bubble factory*
　Kit and Kat

Noll, Sally. *Lucky morning*
Nomura, Takaaki. *Grandpa's town*
Oberman, Sheldon. *The always prayer shawl*
  By the Hanukkah light
Ogburn, Jacqueline K. *The jukebox man*
O'Malley, Kevin. *Bud*
Onyefulu, Ifeoma. *Grandfather's work*
Oram, Hiawyn. *A boy wants a dinosaur*
Otto, Carolyn. *That sky, that rain*
Paraskevas, Betty. *Monster Beach*
Paterson, Diane. *Hey, cowboy!*
Paul, Ann Whitford. *Everything to spend the night . . .*
  from A to Z
Pearson, Susan. *Happy birthday, Grampie*
Peavy, Linda. *Allison's grandfather*
Pfister, Marcus. *The happy hedgehog*
Pomerantz, Charlotte. *Buffy and Albert*
  The outside dog
  Timothy Tall Feather
Pope, Geraldine. *The empty creel*
Proimos, James. *Joe's wish*
Raczek, Linda Theresa. *The night the grandfathers*
  danced
Radin, Ruth Yaffe. *High in the mountains*
Rael, Elsa. *When Zaydeh danced on Eldridge Street*
Reddix, Valerie. *Dragon kite of the autumn moon*
Rice, Eve. *Aren't you coming too?*
Rigby, Shirley Lincoln. *Smaller than most*
Rodgers, Frank. *Who's afraid of the ghost train?*
Roth, Susan L. *We'll ride elephants through Brooklyn*
Rumford, James. *The cloudmakers*
Russo, Marisabina. *Grandpa Abe*
Salter, Heidi. *Taddy McFinley and the great grey*
  grimly
Sandberg, Inger. *Dusty wants to help*
Sathre, Vivian. *On Grandpa's farm*
Savageau, Cheryl. *Muskrat will be swimming*
Say, Allen. *Grandfather's journey*
Scheller, Melanie. *My grandfather's hat*
Schlein, Miriam. *Go with the sun*
Schwartz, David M. *Sugargrandpa*
Selway, Martina. *Don't forget to write*
Shields, Carol Diggory. *Lucky pennies and hot choco-*
  late
Shulevitz, Uri. *Dawn*
Stevens, Margaret (Dean). *When grandpa died*
Stevenson, Harvey. *Grandpa's house*
Stevenson, James. *Brr!*
  "Could be worse!"
  Grandpa's great city tour
  Grandpa's too-good garden
  The great big especially beautiful Easter egg
  No friends
  That dreadful day
  That terrible Halloween night
  That's exactly the way it wasn't
  There's nothing to do!
  We can't sleep
  What's under my bed?
  Will you please feed our cat?
  Worse than Willy!
Stiles, Martha Bennett. *Island magic*
Stilz, Carol Curtis. *Kirsty's kite*
Stock, Catherine. *Emma's dragon hunt*
  Thanksgiving treat
Stolz, Mary Slattery. *Storm in the night*
Sullivan, Silky. *Grandpa was a cowboy*
Titherington, Jeanne. *Where are you going, Emma?*
Tompert, Ann. *Grandfather Tang's story*

Townsend, Maryann. *Pop's secret*
Ulmer, Wendy K. *A campfire for cowboy Billy*
Valgardson, W. D. *Winter rescue*
Van Leeuwen, Jean. *The tickle stories*
Vigna, Judith. *My two uncles*
Wahl, Jan. *The fishermen*
Wahl, Mats. *Grandfather's laika*
Wallace, Ian. *Chin Chiang and the dragon's dance*
Wallace, Nancy Elizabeth. *Snow*
Walsh, Jill Paton. *Lost and found*
Ward, Sally G. *Molly and Grandpa*
  Punky goes fishing
Wardlaw, Lee. *Bow-wow birthday*
Webb, Denise. *The same sun was in the sky*
Wells, Rosemary. *The language of doves*
White Deer of Autumn. *The great change*
Williams, Laura E. *Torch fishing with the sun*
Wood, Douglas. *Grandad's prayers of the earth*
Woodruff, Elvira. *Can you guess where we're going?*
Ye, Ting-xing. *Share the sky*
Zalben, Jane Breskin. *Pearl plants a tree*
  Pearl's marigolds for grandpa
Ziefert, Harriet. *Happy birthday, Grandpa!*
Zolotow, Charlotte (Shapiro). *My grandson Lew*

Family life – grandmothers

Ackerman, Karen. *By the dawn's early light*
Addy, Sharon Hart. *A visit with great-grandma*
Alcott, Louisa May. *An old-fashioned Thanksgiving*
Alda, Arlene. *Hurry Granny Annie*
Alexander, Martha G. *The story grandmother told*
Allen, Linda. *Mr. Simkin's grandma*
Allred, Mary. *Grandmother Poppy and the children's*
  tea party
  Grandmother Poppy and the funny-looking bird
Ambrus, Victor G. *Grandma, Felix, and Mustapha*
  Biscuit
Anderson, Laurie Halse. *Turkey pox*
Anholt, Catherine. *Tom's rainbow walk*
Anholt, Laurence. *Summerhouse*
Bailey, Debbie. *Grandma*
Bailey, Linda. *When Addie was scared*
Baker, Jeannie. *Grandmother*
Balgassi, Haemi. *Peacebound trains*
Balian, Lorna. *Humbug rabbit*
Ballard, Robin. *Granny and me*
Barker, Peggy. *What happened when grandma died*
Barnwell, Ysaye M. *No mirrors in my Nana's house*
Bartoli, Jennifer. *Nonna*
Base, Graeme. *My grandma lived in Gooligulch*
Bauer, Marion Dane. *When I go camping with*
  Grandma
Bea, Holly. *Where does God live?*
Belton, Sandra. *May'naise sandwiches and sunshine*
  tea
Berenstain, Stan. *The Berenstain bears and the week at*
  grandma's
Berridge, Celia. *Grandmother's tales*
Best, Cari. *Three cheers for Catherine the Great!*
Bible, Charles. *Jennifer's new chair*
Blegvad, Lenore. *Once upon a time and Grandma*
Boon, Debbie. *My gran*
Borden, Louise. *The watching game*
Bottner, Barbara. *Nana Hannah's piano*
Bowles, Brad. *Grandma's band*
Brandenberg, Franz. *A secret for grandmother's birth-*
  day
Brimner, Larry Dane. *Nana's hog*

Bryan, Ashley. *Turtle knows your name*
Buckley, Helen Elizabeth. *Grandmother and I*
Bunting, Eve (Anne Evelyn). *Sunshine home*
 The Wednesday surprise
Butterworth, Nick. *My grandma is wonderful*
Caines, Jeannette. *Window wishing*
Calmenson, Stephanie. *Hotter than a hot dog!*
 Zip, whiz, zoom!
Carlson, Nancy L. *A visit to grandma's*
Carlstrom, Nancy White. *The moon came too*
Carrick, Carol. *Valentine*
Caseley, Judith. *Apple pie and onions*
Castaneda, Omar S. *Abuela's weave*
Cazzola, Gus. *The bells of Santa Lucia*
Cech, John. *My grandmother's journey*
Chanin, Michael. *Chief's blanket*
Choi, Sook Nyul. *Halmoni and the picnic*
 Yunmi and Halmoni's trip
Chorao, Kay. *Lemon moon*
Christian, Mary Blount. *Grandmothers, God's gift to children*
Cole, Babette. *The trouble with Gran*
Coleman, Evelyn. *The glass bottle tree*
Corbalis, Judy. *The cuckoo bird*
Cornish, Sam. *Grandmother's pictures*
Coutant, Helen. *First snow*
Cowley, Joy. *Big moon tortilla*
Cutler, Jane. *Darcy and Gran don't like babies*
Daly, Niki. *Not so fast Songololo*
DeJong, David Cornel. *Looking for Alexander*
Delton, Judy. *My grandma's in a nursing home*
Denton, Kady MacDonald. *Granny is a darling*
De Paola, Tomie (Thomas Anthony). *The baby sister*
 Haircuts for the Woolseys
 Nana upstairs and Nana downstairs
Devlin, Wende. *Cranberry autumn*
Dexter, Alison. *Grandma*
Dodd, Anne Westcott. *The story of the sea glass*
Dorros, Arthur. *Abuela*
Drucker, Malka. *Grandma's latkes*
Dupré, Rick. *The wishing chair*
Easwaran, Eknath. *The monkey and the mango*
Ehrlich, Amy. *Bunnies and their grandma*
Eisenberg, Phyllis Rose. *A mitzvah is something special*
Erdrich, Louise. *Grandmother's pigeon*
Ernst, Lisa Campbell. *Little Red Riding Hood*
Farmer, Nancy. *Runnery granary*
Fellows, Rebecca Nevers. *A lei for Tutu*
Fernandes, Kim. *Visiting granny*
Finfer, Celentha. *Grandmother dear*
Flournoy, Valerie. *The patchwork quilt*
Gackenbach, Dick. *With love from Gran*
Garland, Sherry. *The lotus seed*
George, Jean Craighead. *Dear Katie, the volcano is a girl*
 Dear Rebecca, winter is here
Goffstein, M. B. (Marilyn Brooke). *Fish for supper*
Goldman, Susan. *Grandma is somebody special*
Gomi, Taro. *Coco can't wait!*
Goodman, Louise. *Ida's doll*
Gordon, Shirley. *Grandma zoo*
Gorog, Judith. *Zilla Sasparilla and the mud baby*
Green, Donna. *My little artist*
Greenfield, Eloise. *William and the good old days*
Grifalconi, Ann. *Osa's pride*
Grindley, Sally. *A flag for Grandma*
Guback, Georgia. *Luka's quilt*

Halak, Glenn. *A grandmother's story*
Hamm, Diane Johnston. *Grandma drives a motor bed*
Hautzig, Deborah. *Big Bird at the beach*
 Get well, Granny Bird
Hawxhurst, Joan C. *Bubbe and Gram, my two grandmothers*
Hayashi, Akiko. *Aki and the fox*
Hayes, Sarah. *Happy Christmas, Gemma*
Hayward, Linda. *Sunny Day Bunny*
Hedderwick, Mairi. *Katie Morag and the big boy cousins*
 Katie Morag and the two grandmothers
 Katie Morag delivers the mail
Helldorfer, M. C. (Mary Claire). *Harmonica night*
Heller, Nicholas. *This little piggy*
Hendershot, Judith. *Up the tracks to Grandma's*
Hennessy, B. G. (Barbara G.). *When you were just a little girl*
Henriod, Lorraine. *Grandma's wheelchair*
Hershey, Kathleen. *Cotton mill town*
Hest, Amy. *The go-between*
 Jamaica Louise James
 The midnight eaters
 Nana's birthday party
Hines, Anna Grossnickle. *Come to the meadow*
 Gramma's walk
 Grandma gets grumpy
Hippely, Hilary Horder. *A song for Lena*
Hirschi, Ron. *Harvest song*
Hiser, Berniece T. *The adventure of Charlie and his wheat-straw hat*
Hogan, Bernice. *My grandmother died but I won't forget her*
Hol, Coby. *Niki's little donkey*
Hoopes, Lyn Littlefield. *Nana*
Howard, Elizabeth Fitzgerald. *When will Sarah come?*
Howard, Ellen. *The log cabin quilt*
Howard, Kim. *In wintertime*
Ichikawa, Satomi. *Nora's stars*
Igus, Toyomi. *Two Mrs. Gibsons*
Isadora, Rachel. *Over the green hills*
Jackson, Bobby L. *Little Red Ronnika*
James, Betsy. *The dream stair*
Jarrell, Mary. *The knee baby*
Jeschke, Susan. *Mia, Grandma and the genie*
Jessup, Harley. *Grandma summer*
Johnson, Dolores. *Grandma's hands*
Johnston, Tony. *Goblin walk*
Jones, Diana Wynne. *Yes, dear*
Kahn, Rosemary. *Grandma's hat*
Karkowsky, Nancy. *Grandma's soup*
Kay, Helen. *A stocking for a kitten*
Keller, Holly. *The best present*
Ketner, Mary Grace. *Ganzy remembers*
Ketteman, Helen. *Grandma's cat*
Khalsa, Dayal Kaur. *Tales of a gambling grandma*
Kibbey, Marsha. *My grammy*
Kimmelman, Leslie. *Me and Nana*
Kojima, Naomi. *The flying grandmother*
Konigsburg, E. L. (Elaine Lobl). *Amy Elizabeth explores Bloomingdale's*
Koralek, Jenny. *The boy and the cloth of dreams*
 Night ride to Nanna's
Kovalski, Maryann. *Take me out to the ball game*
 The wheels on the bus
Kraus, Robert. *Rebecca Hatpin*
Kroll, Steven. *Annie's four grannies*
 If I could be my grandmother

Kroll, Virginia L. *Sweet Magnolia*
Kunhardt, Edith. *Danny's mystery Valentine*
Kuskin, Karla. *Paul*
Lakin, Pat (Patricia). *Jet black pickup truck*
Laminack, Lester L. *Trevor's wiggly-wobbly tooth*
Lasky, Kathryn. *My island grandma*, ill. by Emily
    Arnold McCully
   My island grandma, ill. by Amy Schwartz
Leedahl, Shelley A. (Shelley Ann). *The bone talker*
Lenski, Lois. *Debbie and her grandma*
Lester, Alison. *Isabella's bed*
Le Tord, Bijou. *My Grandma Leonie*
Levine, Evan. *Not the piano, Mrs. Medley!*
Levinson, Riki. *I go with my family to Grandma's*
   Watch the stars come out
Lexau, Joan M. *Benjie*
   Benjie on his own
Limb, Sue. *Come back, Grandma*
Lindbergh, Reeve. *The hippie grandmother*
Linden, Ann Marie. *One smiling grandma*
Lindgren, Astrid. *The ghost of Skinny Jack*
Little, Jean. *Bats about baseball*
Lloyd, David. *Duck*
   Grandma and the pirate
   The stopwatch
London, Jonathan. *Liplap's wish*
   The sugaring-off party
Look, Lenore. *Love as strong as ginger*
Low, Alice. *David's windows*
Low, William. *Chinatown*
Lowell, Susan. *Little Red Cowboy Hat*
Luenn, Nancy. *A gift for Abuelita*
   Nessa's fish
   Nessa's story
Lum, Kate. *What! cried Granny*
McCain, Becky R. (Becky Ray). *Grandmother's*
   dreamcatcher
McCully, Emily Arnold. *The grandma mix-up*
McKean, Thomas. *Hooray for Grandma Jo!*
McQueen, John Troy. *A world full of monsters*
Maguire, Gregory. *Lucas Fishbone*
Mahy, Margaret. *A busy day for a good grandmother*
Manuel, Lynn. *The night the moon blew kisses*
Martin, C. L. G. *Three brave women*
Mason, Ann Maree. *The weird things in Nanna's*
   house
Mathews, Judith. *Nathaniel Willy, scared silly*
Melmed, Laura Krauss. *The Marvelous Market on*
   Mermaid
Milstein, Linda Breiner. *Grandma's jewelry box*
   Miami-Nanny stories
Mitchell, Lori. *Different just like me*
Moore, Elaine. *Grammy, do you love me?*
   Grandma's garden
   Grandma's house
   Grandma's promise
   Grandma's smile
Morris, Ann. *The grandma book*
Morris, Winifred. *Just listen*
Mower, Nancy. *I visit my Tūtū and Grandma*
Neasi, Barbara J. *Listen to me*
Nelson, Vaunda Micheaux. *Always Gramma*
Nethery, Mary. *Hannah and Jack*
Newman, Lesléa. *Matzo ball moon*
   Remember that
Nightingale, Sandy. *Cider apples*
Nobisso, Josephine. *Grandma's scrapbook*
Nodar, Carmen Santiago. *Abuelita's paradise*
Noll, Sally. *I have a loose tooth*

Nye, Naomi Shihab. *Benito's dream bottle*
   Sitti's secrets
O'Callahan, Jay. *Orange cheeks*
   Tulips
Ogburn, Jacqueline K. *The magic nesting doll*
Olson, Arielle North. *Hurry home, Grandma!*
Oppenheim, Shulamith Levey. *Waiting for Noah*
Orbach, Ruth. *Please send a panda*
Pak, Soyung. *Dear Juno*
Palmisciano, Diane. *Garden partners*
Parish, Peggy. *Granny and the desperadoes*
   Granny and the Indians
   Granny, the baby and the big gray thing
Passen, Lisa. *Grammy and Sammy*
Peters, Lisa Westberg. *Purple delicious blackberry jam*
Peterson, Jeanne Whitehouse. *Sometimes I dream*
   horses
Polacco, Patricia. *Babushka's Mother Goose*
   Chicken Sunday
   Thunder cake
Poskanzer, Susan Cornell. *Puppeteer*
Powers, Daniel. *Jiro's pearl*
Poydar, Nancy. *Busy Bea*
Pulver, Robin. *Alicia's tutu*
Reiser, Lynn. *Cherry pies and lullabies*
Roberts, Sarah. *I want to go home!*
Robertson, Joanne. *Sea witches*
Rockwell, Anne F. *When I go visiting*
Roe, Eileen. *Staying with Grandma*
Rogers, Paul (Patrick). *From me to you*
Root, Phyllis. *Gretchen's grandma*
Rosenberg, Liz. *Grandmother and the runaway*
   shadow
Roth, Susan L. *Another Christmas*
   Patchwork tales
Rothenberg, Joan. *Inside-out grandma*
Sakai, Kimiko. *Sachiko means happiness*
Sasso, Sandy Eisenberg. *For heaven's sake*
Satterfield, Barbara. *The story dance*
Scheffler, Ursel. *A walk in the rain*
Schertle, Alice. *Maisie*
Schneider, Antonie. *Good-bye, Vivi!*
Schwartz, Amy. *Oma and Bobo*
Scott, Ann Herbert. *Grandmother's chair*
Seymour, Tres. *Too quiet for these old bones*
Shea, Pegi Deitz. *The whispering cloth*
Shecter, Ben. *Grandma remembers*
Shelby, Anne. *Homeplace*
Sheldon, Dyan. *The whales' song*
Silverman, Erica. *On Grandma's roof*
Slate, Joseph. *The secret stars*
Slepian, Jan. *Emily just in time*
Smee, Nicola. *The Tusk Fairy*
Smith, Barry. *Grandma Rabbitty's visit*
Smith, Maggie (Margaret C.). *My grandma's chair*
Smucker, Barbara Claasen. *Selina and the bear paw*
   quilt
Sonneborn, Ruth A. *I love Gram*
Spalding, Andrea. *Sarah May and the new red dress*
Stanovich, Betty Jo. *Big boy, little boy*
Steiner, Charlotte. *Kiki and Muffy*
Stilz, Carol Curtis. *Grandma Buffalo, May, and me*
Storr, Catherine (Cole). *Hugo and his grandma*
Stroud, Virginia A. *A walk to the Great Mystery*
Tan, Amy. *The moon lady*
Theroux, Phyllis. *Serefina under the circumstances*
Thomas, Jane Resh. *Saying good-bye to grandma*
Thompson, Mary. *Gran's bees*
Torres, Leyla. *Liliana's grandmothers*

Saturday sancocho
Udry, Janice May. *Mary Jo's grandmother*
Vigna, Judith. *Everyone goes as a pumpkin*
Grandma without me
Waddell, Martin. *Amy said*
Wahl, Jan. *"I remember," cried Grandma Pinky*
Walsh, Jill Paton. *When Grandma came*
When I was little like you
Ward, Sally G. *Charlie and Grandma*
What goes around comes around
Waterton, Betty. *Pettranella*
Watkins, Sherrin. *White Bead Ceremony*
Watts, Jeri Hanel. *Keepers*
Weitzman, Jacqueline Preiss. *You can't take a balloon into the Metropolitan Museum*
You can't take a balloon into the National Gallery
Wells, Rosemary. *Bunny cakes*
Bunny money
Whelan, Gloria. *Bringing the farmhouse home*
Whitlock, Susan Love. *Donovan scares the monsters*
Wild, Margaret. *Big cat dreaming*
Old Pig
Our granny
Remember me
Wilhelm, Hans. *A cool kid - like me!*
Willard, Nancy. *The mountains of quilt*
Williams, Barbara. *Kevin's grandma*
Williams, Laura E. *The long silk strand*
Williams, Sophy. *Nana's garden*
Williams, Vera B. *Music, music for everyone*
Wilson, Beth P. *Jenny*
Wolf, Janet. *The best present is me*
Wood, Audrey. *The napping house*
The napping house wakes up
Wood, Joyce. *Grandmother Lucy goes on a picnic*
Grandmother Lucy in her garden
Wright, Betty Ren. *The cat next door*
Wyse, Lois. *How to take your grandmother to the museum*
Yolen, Jane. *No bath tonight*
Zagwÿn, Deborah Turney. *The winter gift*
Zelinsky, Paul O. *The wheels on the bus*
Ziefert, Harriet. *Little Red Riding Hood*
With love from Grandma
Zolotow, Charlotte (Shapiro). *William's doll*

Family life – grandparents

Allen, Linda. *Mr. Simkin's grandma*
Baggette, Susan K. *Jonathan goes to the grocery store*
Jonathan goes to the library
Barrett, Judi. *Pickles to Pittsburgh*
Bat-Ami, Miriam. *Sea, salt, and air*
Bate, Lucy. *How Georgina drove the car very carefully from Boston to New York*
Bonners, Susan. *The wooden doll*
Bosak, Susan V. *Something to remember me by*
Bunting, Eve (Anne Evelyn). *Winter's coming*
Caseley, Judith. *Grandpa's garden lunch*
Cazet, Denys. *Big shoe, little shoe*
Saturday
Child, Lydia Maria. *Over the river and through the wood*
Chocolate, Deborah M. Newton. *The piano man*
Copeland, Helen. *Meet Miki Takino*
Curtis, Gavin. *Grandma's baseball*
Dalmais, Anne-Marie. *Henry the hedgehog*
DeFelice, Cynthia C. *Willy's silly grandma*

De Paola, Tomie (Thomas Anthony). *Pajamas for Kit*
Dunbar, Joyce. *When I was young*
Eisenberg, Phyllis Rose. *A mitzvah is something special*
Engel, Diana. *Eleanor, Arthur, and Claire*
Eversole, Robyn Harbert. *The gift stone*
Farber, Norma. *How does it feel to be old?*
Feldman, Barbara. *Stephen's frog*
Flory, Jane. *The unexpected grandchildren*
French, Vivian. *Oliver's vegetables*
Gantschev, Ivan. *The train to Grandma's*
Gould, Deborah. *Grandpa's slide show*
Greve, Andreas. *Christopher's dream car*
Haas, Irene. *A summertime song*
Haas, Jessie. *No foal yet*
Sugaring
Hamm, Diane Johnston. *Grandma drives a motor bed*
Hawes, Judy. *Fireflies in the night*
Haywood, Carolyn. *Hello, star*
Heller, Linda. *The castle on Hester Street*
Hesse, Karen. *Poppy's chair*
Hest, Amy. *Gabby growing up*
Weekend girl
Hickman, Martha Whitmore. *Robert lives with his grandparents*
Hill, Eric. *Spot visits his grandparents*
Hooker, Ruth. *At Grandma and Grandpa's house*
Hooper, Meredith. *A cow, a bee, a cookie, and me*
Hurd, Edith Thacher. *I dance in my red pajamas*
James, Betsy. *Flashlight*
Joosse, Barbara M. *Jam day*
Joseph, Daniel M. *All dressed up and nowhere to go*
Kilroy, Sally. *Grandpa's garden*
Kitamura, Satoshi. *Captain Toby*
Kroll, Steven. *Toot! Toot!*
Kunhardt, Edith. *Pat the puppy*
Lakin, Pat (Patricia). *Grandparents*
Laminack, Lester L. *The sunsets of Miss Olivia Wiggins*
Lebentritt, Julia. *The Kooken*
Lemieux, Margo. *The fiddle ribbon*
Levinson, Riki. *Grandpa's hotel*
Lohans, Alison. *Sundog rescue*
McAllister, Angela. *The wind garden*
Maccarone, Grace. *Baby visits grandma and grandpa*
Maris, Ron. *Is anyone home?*
Martin, Jacqueline Briggs. *Grandmother Bryant's pocket*
Minarik, Else Holmelund. *Little Bear's visit*
Mollel, Tololwa M. (Tololwa Marti). *Kele's secret*
Morgan, Michaela. *Visitors for Edward*
Moss, Marissa. *The ugly menorah*
Newman, Shirlee. *Tell me, grandma; tell me, grandpa*
Oechsli, Helen. *Fly away!*
Oppenheim, Shulamith Levey. *Fireflies for Nathan*
Oxenbury, Helen. *Grandma and Grandpa*
Palacios, Argentina. *A Christmas surprise for Chabelita*
Polacco, Patricia. *My rotten redheaded older brother*
Porte, Barbara Ann. *Harry's mom*
Raynor, Dorka. *Grandparents around the world*
Rice, Eve. *At Grammy's house*
Rockwell, Anne F. *When I go visiting*
Rosen, Michael (1946-). *A Thanksgiving wish*
Rosen, Winifred. *Henrietta and the gong from Hong Kong*
Rosenberg, Liz. *The silence in the mountains*
Saint James, Synthia. *Sunday*

Sandberg, Inger. *Dusty wants to borrow everything*
Scheffler, Ursel. *A walk in the rain*
Schneider, Antonie. *The birthday bear*
Skofield, James. *Snow country*
Skolsky, Mindy Warshaw. *Hannah and the whistling tea kettle*
Stevenson, James. *Higher on the door*
    July
Tsubakiyama, Margaret (Holloway). *Mei-Mei loves the morning*
Tunnell, Michael O. *Mailing May*
Van Haeringen, Annemarie. *The cats' tale*
Van Leeuwen, Jean. *Touch the sky summer*
Waboose, Jan Bourdeau. *Firedancers*
Waddell, Martin. *Grandma's Bill*
Wardlaw, Lee. *The tales of Grandpa Cat*
Watanabe, Shigeo. *It's my birthday*
Watson, Mary. *The butterfly seeds*
Woodtor, Dee. *Big meeting*
Wyeth, Sharon Dennis. *Always my dad*
Yolen, Jane. *Off we go!*
Ziefert, Harriet. *Chocolate mud cake*

Family life – great-grandparents

Arnold, Marsha Diane. *The chicken salad club*
Bornstein, Ruth Lercher. *A beautiful seashell*
Budd, Lillian. *The people on Long Ago Street*
Cross, Verda. *Great-grandma tells of threshing day*
Diller, Harriett. *The faraway drawer*
Greenburg, Dan. *Great-Grandpa's in the litter box*
Guthrie, Donna. *The secret admirer*
Herter, Jonina. *Eighty-eight kisses*
Hickcox, Ruth. *Great-Grandmother's treasure*
Hooks, William H. *The mighty Santa Fe*
Ketner, Mary Grace. *Ganzy remembers*
Knotts, Howard. *Great-grandfather, the baby and me*
MacLachlan, Patricia. *Three names*
Matthews, Wendy. *The gift of a traveler*
Reiser, Lynn. *Cherry pies and lullabies*
Rochelle, Belinda. *Jewels*
Russo, Marisabina. *A visit to Oma*
Waddell, Martin. *My great grandpa*
Whittington, Mary K. *Carmina, come dance!*

Family life – mothers

Ackerman, Karen. *By the dawn's early light*
    When mama retires
Albert, Shirley. *Doll party*
Alborough, Jez. *It's the bear*
Alda, Arlene. *Sonya's mommy works*
Alexander, Sue. *One more time, Mama*
All the pretty little horses
Anderson, Laurie Halse. *No time for Mother's Day*
Anderson, Lena. *Bunny box*
Arnold, Lynda. *My Mommy has AIDS*
Asch, Frank. *Bread and honey*
Bailey, Debbie. *My mom*
Baker, Alan. *Where's mouse?*
Baker, Gayle. *Special delivery*
Balgassi, Haemi. *Peacebound trains*
Balian, Lorna. *Mother's Mother's Day*
Banks, Kate (Katherine A.). *Spider, spider*
Barber, Antonia. *Gemma and the baby chick*
Barber, Barbara E. *Saturday at the new you*
Bauer, Caroline Feller. *My mom travels a lot*
Baum, Louis. *After dark*
Benjamin, Amanda. *Two's company*

Berry, Christine. *Mama went walking*
Blaine, Marge (Margery Kay). *The terrible thing that happened at our house*
Blake, Claire. *The paper chain*
Breeze, Lynn. *This little baby goes out*
    This little baby's morning
Bridges, Margaret Park. *Will you take care of me?*
Brillhart, Julie. *Story hour - starring Megan!*
Browne, Anthony. *Piggybook*
Bunting, Eve (Anne Evelyn). *The day before Christmas*
    Flower garden
    I don't want to go to camp
    Someday a tree
Burke-Weiner, Kimberly. *The maybe garden*
Butterworth, Nick. *My mom is excellent*
Cain, Sheridan. *Why so sad, Brown Rabbit?*
Cannon, Janell. *Stellaluna*
    Stellaluna: a pop-up book and mobile
Carle, Eric. *Does a kangaroo have a mother, too?*
Carrick, Carol. *Valentine*
Carter, Dorothy (Dorothy A.). *Wilhe'mina Miles after the stork night*
Carton, Lonnie Caming. *Mommies*
Caseley, Judith. *Mama, coming and going*
Charlip, Remy. *Sleepytime rhyme*
Chichester Clark, Emma. *More!*
Christelow, Eileen. *Don't wake up Mama!*
Cole, Babette. *Mum*
    The trouble with mom
Cowan, Catherine. *My friend the piano*
Cowen-Fletcher, Jane. *Mama zooms*
Coyne, Rachel. *Daughter, have I told you?*
Dale, Elizabeth. *How long?*
Daly, Niki. *Ben's gingerbread man*
    Teddy's ear
Damjan, Mischa. *How do Dinosaurs say goodnight?*
Delton, Judy. *The best mom in the world*
    My mom made me go to camp
    My mom made me go to school
    My Mom made me take piano lessons
    My mother lost her job today
Demarest, Chris L. *Honk!*
Dijs, Carla. *Mommy, would you love me if . . . ?*
Dionetti, Michelle V. *The day Eli went looking for bear*
Dodds, Siobhan. *Ting-a-ling!*
Dornbusch, Erica. *Finding Kate's shoes*
Dörrie, Doris. *Lottie's princess dress*
Doyle, Charlotte Lackner. *Where's Bunny's mommy?*
Dragonwagon, Crescent. *Will it be okay?*
Drescher, Joan E. *My mother's getting married*
Dubowski, Cathy East. *Megan's messy room*
Eastman, P. D. (Philip D.). *Are you my mother?*
Eccles, Jane. *Maxwell's birthday*
Edwards, Richard. *Copy me, Copycub*
Eisenberg, Phyllis Rose. *You're my Nikki*
Emberley, Rebecca. *My mother's secret life*
English, Jennifer. *My mommy's special*
Evans, Lezlie. *If I were the wind*
Falwell, Cathryn. *Nicky's walk*
    P.J. & Puppy
Farber, Norma. *All those mothers at the manger*
    Without wings, mother, how can I fly?
Fassler, Joan. *The man of the house*
Feldman, Barbara. *Going, going*
Fine, Anne. *Poor Monty*
Fisher, Aileen Lucia. *Do bears have mothers too?*
    My mother and I

Yezerski, Thomas. *Queen of the world*
Yim, Natasha. *Otto's rainy day*
Yolen, Jane. *Nocturne*
Ziefert, Harriet. *Clara Ann Cookie*
   Mommies are for counting stars
   Sarah's questions
   Surprise!
   Where's mommy's truck?
Zindel, Paul. *I love my mother*
Zinnemann-Hope, Pam. *Time for bed, Ned*
Zolotow, Charlotte (Shapiro). *I like to be little*
   Mr. Rabbit and the lovely present
   Say it!
   The seashore book
   This quiet lady

Family life – new sibling

Alexander, Martha G. *Nobody asked me if I wanted a baby sister*
   When the new baby comes, I'm moving out
Allen, Robert. *Ten little babies count*
Andry, Andrew C. *Hi, new baby*
Anholt, Catherine. *Aren't you lucky!*
   Here come the babies
Arnstein, Helene S. *Billy and our new baby*
Auch, Mary Jane. *Monster brother*
Baker, Charlotte. *Little brother*
Banish, Roslyn. *Let me tell you about my baby*
Birdseye, Tom. *Waiting for baby*
Bogart, Jo Ellen. *Daniel's dog*
Boyd, Lizi. *Sam is my half brother*
Bradman, Tony. *Billy and the baby*
Brown, Marc Tolon. *Arthur's baby*
Byars, Betsy Cromer. *Go and hush the baby*
Carlstrom, Nancy White. *Kiss your sister, Rose Marie*
Caseley, Judith. *Mama, coming and going*
   Silly baby
Chess, Victoria. *Poor Esmé*
Clarke, Gus. *Along came Eric*
Clifton, Lucille. *Everett Anderson's nine months long*
Cole, Joanna. *The new baby at your house*
Collins, Pat Lowery. *Waiting for baby Joe*
Corey, Dorothy. *Will there be a lap for me?*
Cottringer, Anne. *Ella and the naughty lion*
Cutler, Jane. *Darcy and Gran don't like babies*
De Paola, Tomie (Thomas Anthony). *The baby sister*
Driscoll, Debbie. *Baby comes home*
Fisher, Iris L. *Katie-Bo*
Foreman, Michael. *Ben's baby*
Franklin, Jonathan. *Don't wake the baby*
Galbraith, Kathryn Osebold. *Waiting for Jennifer*
Garland, Sarah. *Billy and Belle*
Gewing, Lisa. *Mama, daddy, baby and me*
Gliori, Debi. *New big sister*
Graham, Richard. *Jack and the monster*
Greenfield, Eloise. *She come bringing me that little baby girl*
   Sweet baby coming
Haarhoff, Dorian. *Desert December*
Hains, Harriet. *My baby brother*
Hamilton-Merritt, Jane. *Our new baby*
Hanson, Joan. *I don't like Timmy*
Harper, Anita. *It's not fair!*
Hathorn, Libby (Elizabeth). *Freya's fantastic surprise*
Hedderwick, Mairi. *Katie Morag and the tiresome Ted*
Helmering, Doris Wild. *We're going to have a baby*
Hobson, Laura Z. *"I'm going to have a baby!"*

Hoffman, Rosekrans. *Sister Sweet Ella*
Holabird, Katharine. *Angelina's baby sister*
Holland, Viki. *We are having a baby*
Hooker, Ruth. *Sara loves her big brother*
Horowitz, Ruth. *Mommy's lap*
Hughes, Shirley. *Angel Mae*
Hutchins, Pat. *Our baby is best*
Keats, Ezra Jack. *Peter's chair*
Keller, Holly. *Geraldine's baby brother*
Knight, Joan. *Opal in the closet*
Krasilovsky, Phyllis. *The very little boy*
   The very little girl
Lakin, Pat (Patricia). *Don't touch my room*
Lasky, Kathryn. *A baby for Max*
Levi, Dorothy Hoffman. *A very special sister*
Levinson, Riki. *Me baby!*
Lewison, Wendy Cheyette. *Our new baby*
Lindgren, Astrid. *I want a brother or sister*
Malecki, Maryann. *Mom and dad and I are having a baby!*
Manushkin, Fran. *Little rabbit's baby brother*
Mario, Heidi Stetson. *I'd rather have an iguana*
Mills, Lauren A. *The goblin baby*
Munsch, Robert N. *Alligator baby*
Murdocca, Sal (Salvatore). *Baby wants the moon*
Old, Wendie C. *Stacy had a little sister*
Polushkin, Maria. *Baby brother blues*
Reader, Dennis. *Butterfingers*
Rheingrover, Jean Sasso. *Veronica's first year*
Robins, Joan. *My brother, Will*
Rockwell, Lizzy. *Hello baby!*
Rogers, Fred. *The new baby*
Rosenberg, Maxine B. *Mommy's in the hospital having a baby*
Ross, Christine. *Lily and the present*
Russo, Marisabina. *Hannah's baby sister*
Schick, Eleanor. *Peggy's new brother*
Schindel, John. *Frog face, my little sister and me*
Schlein, Miriam. *Laurie's new brother*
Shields, Carol Diggory. *I wish my brother was a dog*
Simmons, Jane. *Daisy and the egg*
Smith, Peter. *Jenny's baby brother*
Steel, Danielle. *Max's new baby*
Stevenson, James. *Worse than Willy!*
Stimson, Joan. *Big Panda, Little Panda*
Stuve-Bodeen, Stephanie. *Mama Elizabeti*
Sykes, Julie. *Little Tiger's big surprise*
Thomas, Iolette. *Janine and the new baby*
Thomas, Joyce Carol. *You are my perfect baby*
Titherington, Jeanne. *A place for Ben*
Topek, Susan Remick. *A costume for Noah*
Vigna, Judith. *Couldn't we have a turtle instead?*
Vulliamy, Clara. *Ellen and Penguin and the new baby*
Waddell, Martin. *Rosie's babies*
   When the teddy bears came
Wahl, Jan. *Mabel ran away with the toys*
Walters, Catherine. *Are you there, Baby Bear?*
Watts, Bernadette. *David's waiting day*
Weninger, Brigitte. *Will you mind the baby, Davy?*
West, Keith. *Little Pig's special day*
Weston, Martha. *Bad baby brother*
Whybrow, Ian. *A baby for Grace*
Wild, Margaret. *Rosie and Tortoise*
Winter, Susan. *A baby just like me*
Young, Ruth. *The new baby*
Zagwÿn, Deborah Turney. *Turtle spring*
Ziefert, Harriet. *Getting ready for new baby*
   Talk, baby!
   Waiting for baby

Family life – only child

Bertrand, Cécile. *Mr. and Mrs. Smith have only one child, but what a child!*
Conford, Ellen. *Why can't I be William?*
Dragonwagon, Crescent. *Rainy day together*
Hallinan, P. K. (Patrick K.). *I'm glad to be me*
  Just being alone
Hamberger, John. *Hazel was an only pet*
Hazen, Barbara Shook. *Tight times*
  Why couldn't I be an only kid like you, Wigger?
Iwasaki, Chihiro. *Staying home alone on a rainy day*
Schick, Eleanor. *City in the winter*
Sharmat, Marjorie Weinman. *I want mama*
Shyer, Marlene Fanta. *Here I am, an only child*
Skorpen, Liesel Moak. *All the Lassies*
Smith, Wendy. *The lonely, only mouse*

Family life – parents

Hest, Amy. *Gabby growing up*

Family life – sisters *see also* Family life; Family life – brothers and sisters; Sibling rivalry

Ackerman, Karen. *Moveable Mabeline*
Adoff, Arnold. *Hard to be six*
Adorjan, Carol Madden. *I can! Can you?*
Alexander, Martha G. *Nobody asked me if I wanted a baby sister*
Anholt, Catherine. *Aren't you lucky!*
Bang, Molly. *When Sophie gets angry – really, really angry . . .*
Blades, Ann. *Summer*
  Winter
Brown, Marc Tolon. *Arthur meets the president*
  D. W., go to your room!
Brown, Ruth. *Cry baby*
Bullock, Kathleen. *A surprise for Mitzi Mouse*
Bunting, Eve (Anne Evelyn). *Twinnies*
Calmenson, Stephanie. *The little witch sisters*
Carlstrom, Nancy White. *Kiss your sister, Rose Marie*
Caseley, Judith. *My sister Celia*
Cohen, Miriam. *Mimmy and Sophie*
Cole, Joanna. *I'm a big sister*
Curry, Jane Louise. *Little, little sister*
Dahlbäck-Lutteman, Helena. *My sister Lotta and me*
Dale, Penny. *All about Alice*
Delaney, Molly. *My sister*
De Paola, Tomie (Thomas Anthony). *The baby sister*
Edelman, Elaine. *I love my baby sister (most of the time)*
Eversole, Robyn Harbert. *The magic house*
Galbraith, Kathryn Osebold. *Roommates*
  Waiting for Jennifer
Garland, Sarah. *Billy and Belle*
Gauch, Patricia Lee. *Christina Katerina and the great bear train*
Glaser, Linda. *Keep your socks on, Albert!*
Goodman, Louise. *Ida's doll*
Greeson, Janet. *An American army of two*
Hamilton, Morse. *Little sister for sale*
Hanrahan, Barbara. *My sisters love my clothes*
Harper, Isabelle. *Our new puppy*
Henkes, Kevin. *Sheila Rae, the brave*
Herman, Gail. *Flower girl*
Hines, Anna Grossnickle. *Jackie's lunch box*
Hoban, Russell. *Best friends for Frances*

Harvey's hideout
Hodges, Margaret. *Up the chimney*
Holabird, Katharine. *Angelina's baby sister*
Howard, Elizabeth Fitzgerald. *The train to Lulu's*
  What's in Aunt Mary's room?
Hru, Dakari. *The magic moonberry jump ropes*
Hutchins, Pat. *Our baby is best*
Johnson, Angela. *One of three*
  The wedding
Joseph, Lynn. *Jump up time*
Kalman, Maira. *Hey Willy, see the pyramids!*
Kroll, Virginia L. *Faraway drums*
  My sister, then and now
Kvasnosky, Laura McGee. *Zelda and Ivy*
  Zelda and Ivy and the boy next door
  Zelda and Ivy one Christmas
Lattimore, Deborah Nourse. *Punga the goddess of ugly*
Leech, Jay. *Bright Fawn and me*
Lerner, Harriet Goldhor. *What's so terrible about swallowing an apple seed?*
Levi, Dorothy Hoffman. *A very special sister*
Lillie, Patricia. *Floppy teddy bear*
Little, Jean. *Jess was the brave one*
McGinnis, Lila Sprague. *If Daddy only knew me*
Martin, Jacqueline Briggs. *The finest horse in town*
Martin, Rafe. *The rough-face girl*
Mathews, Judith. *An egg and seven socks*
Millen, C. M. *The low-down laundry line blues*
Mills, Claudia. *A visit to Amy-Claire*
Noll, Sally. *That bothered Kate*
Northway, Jennifer. *Get lost, Laura!*
Numeroff, Laura Joffe. *The Chicken sisters*
O'Connor, Jane. *Kate skates*
Old, Wendie C. *Stacy had a little sister*
Oram, Hiawyn. *The second princess*
Porazinska, Janina. *The enchanted book*
Porte, Barbara Ann. *When Aunt Lucy rode a mule and other stories*
Prall, Jo. *My sister's special*
Price, Mathew. *Have you seen my sister?*
Pryor, Bonnie. *Amanda and April*
  Merry Christmas, Amanda and April
Rheingrover, Jean Sasso. *Veronica's first year*
Rosenberg, Liz. *The carousel*
Rothenberg, Joan. *Matzah ball soup*
Sage, Chris. *That's mine, that's yours*
Samuels, Barbara. *Aloha, Dolores*
  Duncan and Dolores
  What's so great about Cindy Snappleby?
San Souci, Robert D. *Sootface*
Schindel, John. *Frog face, my little sister and me*
Schwartz, Roslyn. *The mole sisters and the piece of moss*
  The mole sisters and the rainy day
Stevenson, Suçie. *Christmas eve*
Stroud, Bettye. *Down home at Miss Dessa's*
Tarbescu, Edith. *Annushka's voyage*
Weiss, Nicki. *A family story*
  Princess Pearl
Whybrow, Ian. *A baby for Grace*
Wilder, Laura Ingalls. *Going to town*
Wilhelm, Hans. *Let's be friends again!*
  More bunny trouble
Winter, Susan. *A baby just like me*
Yep, Laurence. *Dragon prince*
Yezerski, Thomas. *Queen of the world*

Family life – sons

Ambrus, Victor G. *Son of Dracula*
Chichester Clark, Emma. *More!*
Hartman, Bob. *Who wrecked the roof?*
Joosse, Barbara M. *Lewis and papa*
Lakin, Pat (Patricia). *Dad and me in the morning*
Lauture, Denizé. *Father and son*
London, Jonathan. *At the edge of the forest*
    Loon Lake
McKay, Lawrence. *Caravan*
Newman, Lesléa. *Saturday is Pattyday*

Family life – step families

Arnold, Katya. *Baba Yaga and the little girl*
Ballard, Robin. *When I am a sister*
Benjamin, Amanda. *Two's company*
Best, Cari. *Getting used to Harry*
Boyd, Lizi. *The not-so-wicked stepmother*
    Sam is my half brother
Brodzinsky, Anne Braff. *The mulberry bird*
Bunting, Eve (Anne Evelyn). *Train to somewhere*
Chwast, Seymour. *Bushy bride*
Coburn, Jewell Reinhart. *Angkat*
    Jouanah
Day, Nancy Raines. *The lion's whiskers*
French, Fiona. *Snow White in New York*
Gibbons, Faye. *Mountain wedding*
Grimm, Jacob. *Cinderella*, ill. by Nonny Hogrogian
    Cinderella, ill. by Svend Otto S
    Little brother and little sister
Han, Oki S. *Kongi and Potgi*
Helmering, Doris Wild. *I have two families*
Hickox, Rebecca. *The golden sandal*
Hines, Anna Grossnickle. *When we married Gary*
Howard, Ellen. *The big seed*
Johnson, Julie. *How do I feel about my stepfamily*
Knight, Hilary. *Hilary Knight's Cinderella*
Kroll, Steven. *Annie's four grannies*
    Queen of the May
Leach, Norman. *My wicked stepmother*
Lewis, Naomi. *The stepsister*
Lowell, Susan. *Cindy Ellen*
McCaughrean, Geraldine. *Grandma Chickenlegs*
McKissack, Patricia C. *Cinderella*
Perrault, Charles. *Cinderella*, ill. by Sheilah Beckett
    Cinderella, ill. by Marcia Brown
    Cinderella, ill. by Paul Galdone
    Cinderella, ill. by Diane Goode
    Cinderella, ill. by Susan Jeffers
    Cinderella, ill. by Loek Koopmans
    Cinderella, ill. by Emanuele Luzzati
    Cinderella, ill. by James Marshall
    Cinderella, ill. by Phil Smith
Seuling, Barbara. *What kind of family is this?*
Sierra, Judy. *The gift of the crocodile*
Steel, Danielle. *Martha's new daddy*
Vojtech, Anna. *Marushka and the Month Brothers*
Zakhoder, Boris Vladimirovich. *The good stepmother*

Family life – stepchildren *see* Divorce; Family life – step families

Family life – stepparents *see* Divorce; Family life – step families

Farmers *see* Careers – farmers

Farms

Adams, Pam. *This old man*
Addy, Sharon Hart. *Right here on this spot*
Akass, Susan. *Number nine duckling*
Alborough, Jez. *The grass is always greener*
Allen, Pamela. *Fancy that!*
Allen, Thomas B. (Thomas Burt). *On grandaddy's farm*
Amery, H. *The farm picture book*
Andrews, Jan. *The auction*
Anholt, Catherine. *Chaos at Cold Custard Farm*
Arnosky, Jim. *Raccoons and ripe corn*
At the farm
Auch, Mary Jane. *The nutquacker*
Augarde, Steve (Stephen). *Pig*
Aulaire, Ingri Mortenson d'. *Wings for Per*
Ayers, Rebecca Hickox. *Per and the Dala horse*
Aylesworth, Jim. *My son John*
    One crow
Azarian, Mary. *A farmer's alphabet*
Bailey, Linda. *When Addie was scared*
Baker, Betty. *Partners*
Balian, Lorna. *A garden for a groundhog*
Balzano, Jeanne. *The wee moose*
Barber, Antonia. *Gemma and the baby chick*
Barr, Cathrine. *A horse for Sherry*
Barrett, Judi. *Old MacDonald had an apartment house*
Baruch, Dorothy. *Kappa's tug-of-war with the big brown horse*
Bax, Martin. *Edmond went far away*
Baynton, Martin. *Fifty and the fox*
    Fifty and the great race
    Fifty gets the picture
    Fifty saves his friend
Berends, Polly Berrien. *I heard said the bird*
Berkowitz, Linda. *Alfonse, where are you?*
Birchman, David F. *Jigsaw Jackson*
Biro, Val. *Gumdrop and the farmyard caper*
Blades, Ann. *Mary of mile 18*
    Summer
Blanchard, Arlene. *The naughty lamb*
Blocksma, Mary. *Where's that duck?*
Bloom, Suzanne. *We keep a pig in the parlor*
Bohanon, Paul. *Golden Kate*
Bonino, Louise. *The cozy little farm*
Borton, Lady. *Fat chance!*
Boynton, Sandra. *Barnyard dance!*
Brand, Millen. *This little pig named Curly*
Brandenberg, Franz. *Cock-a-doodle-doo*
Braun, Trudi. *My goose Betsy*
Bright, Robert. *Georgie*
Brook, Judy. *Tim mouse visits the farm*
Brown, Craig McFarland. *My barn*
    Patchwork farmer
Brown, Ken (Ken James). *Mucky Pup*
    Mucky Pup's Christmas
Brown, Margaret Wise. *Big red barn*, ill. by Felicia Bond
    Big red barn, ill. by Rosella Hartman
    The little farmer
    The summer noisy book
Brown, Ruth. *The big sneeze*
Browne, Caroline. *Mrs. Christie's farmhouse*
Bruna, Dick. *Farmer John*
    Little bird tweet
Budbill, David. *Christmas tree farm*
Buehner, Caralyn. *Fanny's dream*
Bulla, Clyde Robert. *Dandelion Hill*

Bunting, Eve (Anne Evelyn). *Goose dinner*
   Winter's coming
Burton, Marilee Robin. *Aaron awoke*
Butler, Dorothy. *Another happy tale*
Campbell, Rod. *Oh dear!*
Carlson, Natalie Savage. *Time for the white egret*
Carlstrom, Nancy White. *Rise and shine!*
Carrick, Carol. *In the moonlight, waiting*
Carrick, Donald. *The deer in the pasture*
   Harold and the giant knight
   Milk
Cartwright, Ann. *Norah's ark*
Casey, Patricia. *Cluck cluck*
Caudill, Rebecca. *A pocketful of cricket*
Cazet, Denys. *Nothing at all*
Chandra, Deborah. *A is for Amos*
Chaucer, Geoffrey. *Chanticleer and the fox*
Child, Lydia Maria. *Over the river and through the
   wood*
Chorao, Kay. *Little farm by the sea*
Cimarusti, Marie Torres. *Peek-a-moo*
Cleary, Beverly. *The hullabaloo ABC*, ill. by Ted
   Rand
   The hullabaloo ABC, ill. by Earl Thollander
Clewes, Dorothy. *Hide and seek*
Climo, Lindee. *Chester's barn*
Collier, Ethel. *I know a farm*
Cook, Bernadine. *Looking for Susie*
Coulter, Hope Norman. *Uncle Chuck's truck*
Cousins, Lucy. *Farm animals*
   Hen on the farm
   Maisy at the farm
Coxe, Molly. *Whose footprints?*
Croll, Carolyn. *The three brothers*
Cronin, Doreen. *Click, clack, moo*
Cross, Verda. *Great-grandma tells of threshing day*
Crowther, Robert. *Who lives on the farm?*
Curry, Jane Louise. *Little, little sister*
Dalgliesh, Alice. *The little wooden farmer*
Daniel, Doris Temple. *Pauline and the peacock*
Davis, Aubrey. *The enormous potato*
Day, Betsy. *Stefan and Olga*
De Angeli, Marguerite. *Yonie Wondernose*
Delaney, Ned. *Cosmic chickens*
Demarest, Chris L. *Farmer Nat*
Demuth, Patricia Brennan. *Ornery morning*
Dennis, Wesley. *Flip*
   Flip and the cows
Denslow, Sharon Phillips. *At Taylor's place*
De Paola, Tomie (Thomas Anthony). *Country farm*
De Regniers, Beatrice Schenk. *Going for a walk*
Dewey, Ariane. *Febold Feboldson*
DeWitt, Jamie. *Jamie's turn*
DiFiori, Lawrence. *The farm*
Dodds, Siobhan. *Elizabeth Hen*
Domanska, Janina. *The turnip*
Donohue, Dorothy. *Big and little on the farm*
Dorros, Arthur. *Radio Man/Don Radio*
   Tonight is carnaval
Dragonwagon, Crescent. *Jemima remembers*
Dreier, Ted. *Moozie's kind adventure*
Duncan, Jane. *Janet Reachfar and Chickabird*
Dunn, Judy. *The animals of Buttercup Farm*
   The little lamb
Dunrea, Olivier. *Eddy B, pigboy*
   The painter who loved chickens
Duvoisin, Roger Antoine. *The crocodile in the tree*
   Crocus
   Jasmine

Our Veronica goes to Petunia's farm
Petunia
Petunia and the song
Petunia, beware!
Petunia, I love you
Petunia, the silly goose
Petunia's treasure
Two lonely ducks
Veronica
Veronica and the birthday present
Edwards, Pamela Duncan. *The grumpy morning*
Ehrlich, Amy. *Maggie and Silky and Joe*
   Parents in the pigpen, pigs in the tub
English, Karen. *Big wind coming!*
Eriksson, Ake. *Joel, Jasper, and Julia*
Ets, Marie Hall. *Mister Penny*
   Mr. Penny's race horse
Euvremer, Teryl. *Sun's up*
Farm animals [Macmillan, 1991]
Farm house
The farmer in the dell. The farmer in the dell, ill. by
   John O'Brien
   The farmer in the dell, ill. by Kathy Parkinson
   The farmer in the dell, ill. by Mary Maki Rae
   The farmer in the dell, ill. by Diane Stanley
   The farmer in the dell, ill. by Alexandra Wallner
Fatio, Louise. *The red bantam*
Feldman, Barbara. *Stephen's frog*
Fiday, Beverly. *Time to go*
Flanagan, Alice K. *A visit to the Gravesens' farm*
Fleischman, Paul. *The animal hedge*
Fleischman, Sid. *The scarebird*
Fleming, Denise. *Barnyard banter*
Flora, James. *Grandpa's farm*
Florian, Douglas. *A year in the country*
Fox, Mem. *Hattie and the fox*
Frascino, Edward. *Nanny Noony and the dust queen*
   Nanny Noony and the magic spell
Freedman, Russell. *Farm babies*
Freschet, Berniece. *Where's Henrietta's hen?*
Gackenbach, Dick. *Crackle, Gluck and the sleeping
   toad*
   The pig who saw everything
Galdone, Paul. *Cat goes fiddle-i-fee*
Gammell, Stephen. *Once upon MacDonald's farm*
Garland, Michael. *My cousin Katie*
Gibbons, Gail. *Farming*
   The milk makers
Gibson, Betty. *The story of Little Quack*
Glass, Andrew. *Chickpea and the talking cow*
Glasscock, Sarah. *My prairie summer*
Good, Phyllis Pellman. *Plain Pig's ABCs*
Goodall, John S. *The story of a farm*
Goode, Diane. *The little book of farm friends*
Graham, Georgia. *The strongest man this side of Cre-
   mona*
Gray, Libba Moore. *Is there room on the feather bed?*
Greeley, Valerie. *Farm animals*
Green, Mary McBurney. *Everybody has a house and
   everybody eats*
Greenberg, Polly. *Oh, Lord, I wish I was a buzzard*
Greene, Rhonda Gowler. *Barnyard song*
Grifalconi, Ann. *Kinda blue*
Gunthrop, Karen. *Rina at the farm*
Haas, Jessie. *Busybody Brandy*
   Mowing
   No foal yet
Hader, Berta Hoerner. *Cock-a-doodle doo*
Hale, Kathleen. *Orlando buys a farm*

Hale, Sarah Josepha Buell. *Mary had a little lamb*
Hall, Donald. *Lucy's summer*
   The ox-cart man
Hamilton, Virginia. *Drylongso*
Hamm, Diane Johnston. *Rock-a-bye farm*
Hansen, Carla. *Barnaby Bear visits the farm*
Harold, Jerdine Nolen. *Harvey Potter's balloon farm*
Harranth, Wolf. *My old grandad*
Harshman, Marc. *A little excitement*
   The storm
   Uncle James
Harvey, Brett. *My prairie year*
Haseley, Dennis. *The old banjo*
Hawes, Judy. *Fireflies in the night*
Haywood, Carolyn. *Hello, star*
Hazen, Barbara Shook. *Turkey in the straw*
Hellen, Nancy. *Circle farm*
   A visit to the farm
Helweg, Hans. *Farm animals*
Henderson, Kathy. *Counting farm*
   I can be a farmer
Henley, Claire. *Farm day*
Herriot, James. *Blossom comes home*
   Bonny's big day
Hess, Paul. *Farmyard animals*
Hill, Eric. *Spot goes to the farm*
   Spot on the farm
Himmelman, John. *A guest is a guest*
Hines, Anna Grossnickle. *I'll tell you what they say*
Hirschi, Ron. *Harvest song*
Hoban, Julia. *Quick chick*
Hol, Coby. *A visit to the farm*
Hopkins, Lee Bennett. *On the farm*
Houk, Randy. *Rico's hawk*
Hudson, Wade. *I love my family*
Hurd, Edith Thacher. *Under the lemon tree*
Hurd, Thacher. *Blackberry ramble*
   Tomato soup
Hutchins, H. J. (Hazel J.). *One duck*
Hutchins, Pat. *Rosie's walk*
   Rosie's walk, a board book
Ipcar, Dahlov. *Bright barnyard*
   Brown cow farm
   Hard scrabble harvest
   One horse farm
   Ten big farms
Isenbart, Hans-Heinrich. *Baby animals on the farm*
Israel, Marion Louise. *The tractor on the farm*
Jackson, Ellen B. *Brown cow, green grass, yellow mellow sun*
Jacobs, Joseph. *Hereafterthis*
James, Shirley Kerby. *Going to a horse farm*
Jennings, Linda M. *Tom's tail*
Jensen, Patricia. *Kitty's special job*
Johnson, Angela. *Casey Jones*
Johnson, Dolores. *Grandma's hands*
Johnson, Paul Brett. *The cow who wouldn't come down*
   Farmers' market
Johnston, Tony. *Farmer Mack measures his pig*
   Once in the country
   The promise
   We love the dirt
Jones, Carol. *This old man*
Jordan, Sandra. *Christmas tree farm*
   Down on Casey's farm
Karim, Roberta. *Mandy Sue Day*
Kastner, Jill. *Barnyard big top*
Kaufman, Jeff. *Milk rock*

Kent, Jack. *Little Peep*
Kessler, Ethel. *Are there hippos on the farm?*
Ketteman, Helen. *Heat wave*
   The year of no more corn
Kightley, Rosalinda. *The farmer*
King-Smith, Dick. *Cuckoobush farm*
   Farmer Bungle forgets
Kinsey-Warnock, Natalie. *The summer of Stanley*
   When spring comes
Kiser, SuAnn. *The catspring somersault flying one-handed flip-flop*
   The hog call to end all!
Koch, Dorothy Clarke. *When the cows got out*
Komaiko, Leah. *On Sally Perry's farm*
Koontz, Robin Michal. *This old man*
Koralek, Jenny. *Cat and Kit*
   The friendly fox
Kovalski, Maryann. *Queen Nadine*
Kunhardt, Edith. *I'm going to be a farmer*
   Which pig would you choose?
Kwitz, Mary DeBall. *Little chick's breakfast*
Lacome, Julie. *On the farm*
Laird, Elizabeth. *The day Patch stood guard*
   The day Sidney ran off
   The day the ducks went skating
   The day Veronica was nosy
Lapp, Eleanor. *The mice came in early this year*
Lasson, Robert. *Orange Oliver*
Lemieux, Margo. *The fiddle ribbon*
Lenski, Lois. *The little farm*
Lerman, Rory S. *Charlie's checklist*
Lesser, Carolyn. *What a wonderful day to be a cow*
Lester, Alison. *My farm*
Levitin, Sonia. *A single speckled egg*
Lewis, Kim. *Emma's lamb*
   First snow
   Friends
   Just like Floss
   Little Baa
   Little calf
   Little lamb
   Little puppy
Lewison, Wendy Cheyette. *Going to sleep on the farm*
   The rooster who lost his crow
Lexau, Joan M. *Who took the farmer's hat?*
Lillie, Patricia. *When the rooster crowed*
Lilly, Kenneth. *Animals on the farm*
Lindbergh, Reeve. *Benjamin's barn*
   The day the goose got loose
   Midnight farm
Lindgren, Astrid. *The dragon with red eyes*
   The tomten
Lindman, Maj. *Flicka, Ricka, Dicka and the big red hen*
   Snipp, Snapp, Snurr and the buttered bread
Ling, Mary. *Calf*
   Foal
   Pig
Lionni, Leo. *Six crows*
Little, Jean. *Gruntle Piggle takes off*
The little red hen. *The cock, the mouse and the little red hen*
   The little red hen, ill. by Byron Barton
   The little red hen, ill. by Emily Bolam
   The little red hen, ill. by Janina Domanska
   The little red hen, ill. by Paul Galdone
   The little red hen, ill. by Dennis Hockerman
   Little red hen, ill. by Norman Messenger
   The little red hen, ill. by Mel Pekarsky

Raven, Margot. *Angels in the dust*
Reddix, Valerie. *Millie and the mudhole*
Reynolds, Marilynn. *The new land*
    The prairie fire
Rider, Alex. *A la ferme = At the farm*
Riecken, Nancy. *Today is the day*
Robart, Rose. *The cake that Mack ate*
Robinson, W. W. (William Wilcox). *On the farm*
Rockwell, Anne F. *The gollywhopper egg*
Rogers, Paul (Patrick). *Quacky Duck*
Rojankovsky, Feodor. *Animals on the farm*
    The great big animal book
Root, Phyllis. *One windy Wednesday*
    What Baby wants
Rosen, Michael J. (1954-). *Bonesy and Isabel*
Rossiter, Nan Parson. *The way home*
Roth, Harold. *Let's look all around the farm*
Royston, Angela. *Cow*
    The goat
    The hen
    The pig
    The pony
    The sheep
Runcie, Jill. *Cock-a-doodle-doo*
Russell, Sandra Joanne. *A farmer's dozen*
Rylant, Cynthia. *Scarecrow*
Sandburg, Carl (Charles August). *The Huckabuck family and how they raised popcorn in Nebraska and quit and came back*
Sathre, Vivian. *On Grandpa's farm*
Scheidl, Gerda Marie. *Pickle and Patch*
Schertle, Alice. *Maisie*
Schlein, Miriam. *Something for now, something for later*
Schmid, Eleonore. *Farm animals*
Schmidt, Eric von. *The young man who wouldn't hoe corn*
Schnur, Steven. *Spring thaw*
Schoenherr, John. *The barn*
Schulz, Charles M. *Snoopy's facts and fun book about farms*
Scott, C. Anne (Cynthia Anne). *Old Jake's skirts*
Seabrooke, Brenda. *The swan's gift*
Seignobosc, Françoise. *The big rain*
Selsam, Millicent E. *Keep looking!*
    More potatoes!
Selway, Martina. *Don't forget to write*
Sewell, Helen Moore. *Blue barns*
Sherman, Nancy. *Gwendolyn and the weathercock*
Short, Mayo. *Andy and the wild ducks*
Simon, Carly. *Midnight farm*
Simont, Marc. *The goose that almost got cooked*
Skofield, James. *Snow country*
Sloat, Teri. *Farmer Brown goes round and round*
    Farmer Brown shears his sheep
Slobodkina, Esphyr. *The wonderful feast*
Smith, Donald. *Farm numbers*
Smith, Mavis. *A snake mistake*
Sneed, Brad. *Lucky Russell*
Snow, Alan. *Cluck!*
    Oink!
    Quack!
    Woof!
Staines, Bill. *All God's critters got a place in the choir*
Steers, Billy. *Tractor Mac*
Stevenson, James. *"Could be worse!"*
Stoeke, Janet Morgan. *Hide and seek*
Stott, Dorothy. *Little Duck's bicycle ride*
Strete, Craig Kee. *How the Indians bought the farm*

Stutson, Caroline. *Prairie primer A to Z*
Sweet, Melissa. *Fiddle-i-fee*
Sykes, Julie. *Dora's eggs*
    This and that
Tafuri, Nancy. *Early morning in the barn*
    This is the farmer
    Who's counting?
Talley, Carol. *Clarissa*
Tennyson, Alfred, Baron. *The brook*
Thiele, Colin. *Farmer Schulz's ducks*
Thomas, Jane Resh. *Lights on the river*
Thompson, Mary. *Gran's bees*
Threadgall, Colin. *Proud rooster and the fox*
Tiller, Ruth. *Cats vanish slowly*
Tolstoy, Aleksey Nikolayevich. *The gigantic turnip*, ill. by Niamh Sharkey
    The great big enormous turnip, ill. by Helen Oxenbury
Tompert, Ann. *The hungry black bag*
Torgersen, Don Arthur. *The girl who tricked the troll*
Tresselt, Alvin R. *Sun up*, ill. by author
    Sun up, ill. by Henri Sorensen
    Wake up, farm!, ill. by author
    Wake up, farm!, ill. by Carolyn Ewing
Tripp, Paul. *The strawman who smiled by mistake*
Turner, Ann Warren. *Dakota dugout*
    Dust for dinner
Turner, Gwenda. *Over on the farm*
Twinem, Neecy. *Changing colors*
Udry, Janice May. *Emily's autumn*
Vaës, Alain. *The porcelain pepper pot*
Vagin, Vladimir Vasil'evich. *The enormous carrot*
Van Horn, Grace. *Little red rooster*
Van Leeuwen, Jean. *The strange adventures of Blue Dog*
Verboven, Agnes. *Ducks like to swim*
Waddell, Martin. *Farmer Duck*
Wallace, Nancy Elizabeth. *Apples, apples, apples*
Wallner, John C. *Old MacDonald had a farm*
Ward, Nick. *Farmer George and the fieldmice*
    Farmer George and the lost chick
Watson, Nancy Dingman. *What does A begin with?*
    What is one?
Weidt, Maryann N. *Daddy played music for the cows*
Wellington, Monica. *The sheep follow*
Westcott, Nadine Bernard. *Skip to my Lou*
    There's a hole in the bucket
Wheeler, Cindy. *Rose*
Wiesner, William. *Happy-Go-Lucky*
Wild, Margaret. *The very best of friends*
Willis, Val. *Silly little chick*
Wolff, Ashley. *A year of beasts*
Wood, Jakki. *Moo moo, brown cow*
Wormell, Mary. *Hilda Hen's happy birthday*
    Hilda Hen's search
    Why not?
Worthington, Phoebe. *Teddy bear farmer*
Wright, Dare. *Look at a calf*
    Look at a colt
Yolen, Jane. *The giant's farm*
    Jane Yolen's Old MacDonald songbook
    Raising Yoder's barn
Zalben, Jane Breskin. *Basil and Hillary*
Ziefert, Harriet. *I swapped my dog*
    Nicky's Christmas surprise
    Nicky's friends
    Oh, what a noisy farm!
    On our way to the barn
    Pumpkin Pie

The turnip
Zwetchkenbaum, G. *The Snoopy farm puzzle book*

Fathers *see* Family life – fathers

Father's Day *see* Holidays – Father's Day

Fear *see* Emotions – fear

Feeling *see* Senses – touching

Feelings *see* Emotions

Feet *see* Anatomy – feet

Ferrets *see* Animals – ferrets

Fidgeting *see* Behavior – fidgeting

Fighting *see* Behavior – fighting, arguing

Fiji *see* Foreign lands – Fiji

Fingers *see* Anatomy – hands

Finishing things *see* Character traits – completing things

Finland *see* Foreign lands – Finland

Fire

Anderson, C. W. (Clarence Williams). *Blaze and the forest fire*
Augarde, Steve (Stephen). *Pig*
Baker, Eugene H. *Fire*
Barr, Jene. *Fire snorkel number 7*
Baumann, Kurt. *Piro and the fire brigade*
Beatty, Hetty Burlingame. *Little Owl Indian*
Belloc, Hilaire. *Matilda who told lies and was burned to death*
Bernstein, Margery. *Coyote goes hunting for fire*
Bester, Roger. *Fireman Jim*
Bible, Charles. *Jennifer's new chair*
Blathwayt, Benedict. *Tangle and the firesticks*
Bond, Ruskin. *Flames in the forest*
Brenner, Barbara A. *Mr. Tall and Mr. Small*
Brown, Margaret Wise. *The little fireman*
Bruna, Dick. *Snuffy and the fire*
Charles, Donald. *Chancay and the secret of fire*
De Regniers, Beatrice Schenk. *Willy O'Dwyer jumped in the fire*
Driscoll, Laura. *The bravest cat!*
Du Bois, William Pène. *Otto and the magic potatoes*
Dubowski, Cathy East. *Fire engine to the rescue*
Ehlert, Lois. *Cuckoo: a Mexican folktale = Cucú: un cuento folklórico mexicano*
Elliott, Dan. *A visit to the Sesame Street firehouse*
Fire
Firehouse, ill. by Zokeisha
Foreman, Michael. *Panda and the bushfire*
Fraser, Mary Ann. *Forest fire!*
Good, Merle. *Reuben and the fire*
Gramatky, Hardie. *Hercules*
Greene, Graham. *The little fire engine*
Haines, Gail Kay. *Fire*

Hammar, Asa. *Fit for pigs*
Harshman, Marc. *A little excitement*
Jam, Teddy. *The year of fire*
Kirn, Ann. *The tale of a crocodile*
Kraus, Robert. *Freddy, the fire engine*
Kuklin, Susan. *Lighting fires*
Lawrence, John. *Pope Leo's elephant*
Leech, Bryan Jeffery. *John Jeremy Colton*
Lemaître, Pascal. *Emily the giraffe*
Liebman, Daniel. *I want to be a firefighter*
London, Jonathan. *Fire race*
Mahood, Kenneth. *The laughing dragon*
Martin, Bill (William Ivan). *Fire! Fire! said Mrs. McGuire*
Martin, Jacqueline Briggs. *Grandmother Bryant's pocket*
Mike, Jan M. *Opossum and the great firemaker*
Miklowitz, Gloria D. *Save that raccoon!*
Miles, Miska. *The fox and the fire*
Moskin, Marietta D. *Lysbet and the fire kittens*
Newton, James R. *A forest is reborn*
Pendziwol, Jean. *No dragons for tea*
Polacco, Patricia. *Tikvah means hope*
Quackenbush, Robert M. *There'll be a hot time in the old town tonight*
Rex, Michael. *My fire engine*
Reynolds, Marilynn. *The prairie fire*
Roth, Susan L. *Fire came to the earth people*
Spiegel, Doris. *Danny and Company 92*
Taylor, Mark. *Henry explores the mountains*
Thompson, Colin (Colin Edward). *Unknown*
Troughton, Joanna. *How rabbit stole the fire*
Ungerer, Tomi. *The Mellops strike oil*
Van Laan, Nancy. *Rainbow crow*
Wilson-Max, Ken. *Big red fire truck*
Yee, Wong Herbert. *Fireman Small*
  Fireman Small, fire down below
  Fireman Small to the rescue
Ziefert, Harriet. *Lewis the fire fighter*

Fire engines *see* Careers – firefighters; Trucks

Firefighters *see* Careers – firefighters

Fireflies *see* Insects – fireflies

Fires

Garland, Michael. *Angel cat*
Royston, Angela. *Fire fighters*

Fish

Adams, Georgie. *Fish fish fish*
Aliki. *The long lost coelacanth and other living fossils*
  My visit to the aquarium
Arnosky, Jim. *Crinkleroot's 25 fish every child should know*
Aruego, José. *Pilyo the piranha*
Asch, Frank. *Moonbear's pet*
Balet, Jan B. *Joanjo*
Beisert, Heide Helene. *Poor fish*
Borovsky, Paul. *The fish that wasn't*
Brenner, Barbara A. *Rosa and Marco and the three wishes*
Brice, Tony. *The bashful goldfish*
Broekel, Ray. *Dangerous fish*
Brown, Margaret Wise. *The little fisherman*

Bruna, Dick. *The fish*
Burstein, Fred. *Whispering in the park*
Bush, John. *The fish who could wish*
Cain, Sheridan. *Look out for the big bad fish!*
Calder, S. J. *If you were a fish*
Carlstrom, Nancy White. *Fish and flamingo*
Coatsworth, Elizabeth. *Under the green willow*
Cole, Joanna. *A fish hatches*
Cook, Bernadine. *The little fish that got away*
Cooper, Elizabeth K. *The fish from Japan*
Curious George goes to the aquarium
Damjan, Mischa. *The little sea horse*
Darby, Gene. *What is a fish?*
Demi. *Find Demi's sea creatures*
Eastman, David. *What is a fish?*
Ehlert, Lois. *Fish eyes*
Elborn, Andrew. *Big Al*
Frieden, Sarajo. *The care and feeding of fish*
Gliori, Debi. *Willie Bear and the Wish Fish*
Gomi, Taro. *Where's the fish?*
Hall, Bill. *Fish tale*
Hawes, Judy. *Shrimps*
Henley, Claire. *In the ocean*
Himmelman, John. *Ellen and the goldfish*
Hirschi, Ron. *Ocean*
Hogan, Paula Z. *The salmon*
Hutchins, H. J. (Hazel J.). *The catfish palace*
Ipcar, Dahlov. *The biggest fish in the sea*
Jonas, Ann. *Splash!*
Kalan, Robert. *Blue sea*
Kelly, Irene. *Ebbie and Flo*
Kite, L. Patricia. *Down in the sea. The jellyfish*
Komaiko, Leah. *Just my dad and me*
Kroll, Virginia L. *A carp for Kimiko*
    Helen the fish
Lewis, J. Patrick. *At the wish of the fish*
Lionni, Leo. *Fish is fish*
    Swimmy
Love, Ann. *Fishing*
Lubach, Peter. *Harry and the singing fish*
MacGill-Callahan, Sheila. *Finn MacCool and the talking fish*
McMullan, Kate (Hall). *Fishy riddles*
Maddern, Eric. *Curious clownfish*
Mallory, Kenneth. *Families of the deep blue sea*
Mendoza, George. *The gillygoofang*
Metaxas, Eric. *Princess Scargo and the birthday pumpkin*
Mudd-Ruth, Maria. *The ultimate ocean book*
Muzik, Katharine. *At home in the coral reef*
Nayer, Judy. *Sea creatures*
Newton, Jill. *Cat-fish*
O'Malley, Kevin. *Carl caught a flying fish*
Pallotta, Jerry. *The dory story*
Parnall, Peter. *The great fish*
Parry, Marian. *King of the fish*
Paulsen, Gary. *Canoe days*
Pfeffer, Wendy. *What's it like to be a fish?*
Pfister, Marcus. *The rainbow fish*
    Rainbow fish and the big blue whale
    Rainbow fish to the rescue!
Pratt, Kristin Joy. *A swim through the sea*
Raschka, Christopher. *Arlene sardine*
Royston, Angela. *Sea animals*
Schatell, Brian. *Midge and Fred*
Schlein, Miriam. *That's not Goldie!*
Schumacher, Claire. *Alto and Tango*
Seuss, Dr. *McElligot's pool*
    One fish, two fish, red fish, blue fish

Shaw, Evelyn S. *Fish out of school*
Sloat, Teri. *There was an old lady who swallowed a trout*
Stevenson, James. *Which one is Whitney?*
Toft, Kim Michelle. *One less fish*
Turnage, Sheila. *Trout the magnificent*
Valens, Evans G. *Wingfin and Topple*
Van Laan, Nancy. *Little Fish lost*
Waber, Bernard. *Lorenzo*
Waechter, Friedrich Karl. *Three is company*
Walton, Rick. *Something's fishy!*
Weeks, Sarah. *Splish splash*
Wezel, Peter. *The good bird*
Wilcox, Cathy. *Enzo the Wonderfish*
Wildsmith, Brian. *Fishes*
Wong, Herbert H. *My goldfish*
Wood, John Norris. *Oceans*
Wyse, Lois. *Two guppies, a turtle and Aunt Edna*
Yerxa, Leo. *A fish tale, or, The little one that got away*
Yorinks, Arthur. *Louis the fish*
Zimelman, Nathan. *The great adventure of Wo Ti*

Fish – sharks

Cole, Joanna. *Hungry, hungry sharks*
Gay, Tenner Ottley. *Sharks in action*
Gibbons, Gail. *Sharks*
Laird, Donivee Martin. *The three little Hawaiian pigs and the magic shark*
Mahy, Margaret. *The great white man-eating shark*
Mellor, Corinne. *Clark the toothless shark*
Pfister, Marcus. *Rainbow fish to the rescue!*
Selsam, Millicent E. *A first look at sharks*
West, Colin. *"Only joking!" laughed the lobster*
Zoehfeld, Kathleen Weidner. *Great white shark, ruler of the sea*

Fishermen *see* Careers – fishermen

Fishing *see* Sports – fishing

Fitness *see* Health and fitness

Flamingos *see* Birds – flamingos

Flattery *see* Character traits – flattery

Fleas *see* Insects – fleas

Flies *see* Insects – flies

Floods *see* Weather – floods

Flowers

Aksakov, Sergei. *The scarlet flower*
Allison, Diane Worfolk. *This is the key to the kingdom*
Andersen, H. C. (Hans Christian). *Little Ida's flowers*
Anderson, Janet S. *Sunflower Sal*
Anno, Mitsumasa. *The king's flower*
Baker, Jeffrey J. W. *Patterns of nature*
Barker, Cicely Mary. *Berry flower fairies*
    Blossom flower fairies
    Flower fairies of the garden
    Flower fairies of the seasons
    Flower fairies of the spring

Flower fairies of the summer
Flower fairies of the trees
Flower fairies postcard book
Spring flower fairies
Summer flower fairies
Best, Cari. *Top banana*
Brisson, Pat. *Wanda's roses*
Bruce, Lisa. *Fran's flower*
Bunting, Eve (Anne Evelyn). *Flower garden*
   Sunflower house
Campbell, Rod. *Buster's afternoon*
Chapman, Carol. *Barney Bipple's magic dandelions*
Cooney, Barbara. *Miss Rumphius*
Cousins, Lucy. *Flower in the garden*
Day, Alexandra. *Helping the flowers and trees*
DeLage, Ida. *Frannie's flower*
Delaney, A. *The gunnywolf*
Denver, John. *The children and the flowers*
De Paola, Tomie (Thomas Anthony). *The legend of the bluebonnet*
   The legend of the Indian paintbrush
Ehlert, Lois. *Planting a rainbow*
Ellentuck, Shan. *A sunflower as big as the sun*
Fellows, Rebecca Nevers. *A lei for Tutu*
Fisher, Aileen Lucia. *And a sunflower grew*
   Petals yellow and petals red
Ford, Miela. *Sunflower*
Givens, Janet Eaton. *Something wonderful happened*
Greene, Ellin. *Ling-li and the phoenix fairy*
Harper, Wilhelmina. *The gunniwolf*
Hearn, Diane Dawson. *Anna in the garden*
Heilbroner, Joan. *Robert the rose horse*
Heller, Ruth. *The reason for a flower*
Heyduck-Huth, Hilde. *The strawflower*
Hidaka, Masako. *Girl from the snow country*
Himmelman, John. *A dandelion's life*
Hines, Anna Grossnickle. *Miss Emma's wild garden*
Hoban, Julia. *Amy loves the sun*
Ichikawa, Satomi. *Nora's roses*
   Suzanne and Nicholas in the garden
Ipcar, Dahlov. *The land of flowers*
King, Elizabeth. *Backyard sunflower*
Kirkpatrick, Rena K. *Look at flowers*
Lagerlöf, Selma. *The legend of the Christmas rose*
Legg, Gerald. *From seed to sunflower*
Lerner, Carol. *Flowers of a woodland spring*
Lillegard, Dee. *The day the daisies danced*
Lin, Grace. *The ugly vegetables*
Lobel, Anita. *Alison's zinnia*
Lobel, Arnold. *The rose in my garden*
Lucht, Irmgard. *The red poppy*
Lunge-Larsen, Lise. *The legend of the lady slipper*
McMillan, Bruce. *Counting wildflowers*
Maris, Ron. *In my garden*
Marshall, Janet Perry. *A honey of a day*
Marton, Jirina. *Flowers for mom*
Marzollo, Jean. *I'm a seed*
Medearis, Angela Shelf. *Seeds grow*
Merriam, Eve. *Ten rosy roses*
Mockford, Caroline. *What's this?*
Montresor, Beni. *The witches of Venice*
Newman, Lesléa. *Belinda's bouquet*
O'Callahan, Jay. *Tulips*
Olson, Arielle North. *The lighthouse keeper's daughter*
Posada, Mia. *Dandelions, stars in the grass*
Preller, James. *Cardinal and sunflower*
Rockwell, Anne F. *Bumblebee, bumblebee, do you know me?*
   My spring robin

Samson, Suzanne M. *Fairy dusters and blazing stars*
Schaefer, Lola M. *This is the sunflower*
Selsam, Millicent E. *A first look at flowers*
Shannon, George. *Dancing the breeze*
Slobodkina, Esphyr. *Pinky and the petunias*
Slote, Elizabeth. *Nelly's garden*
Spalding, Andrea. *Me and Mr. Mah*
Steig, William. *Rotten island*
Stern, Maggie. *The missing sunflowers*
Sugita, Yutaka. *The flower family*
Tamar, Erika. *The garden of happiness*
Turner, Ann Warren. *Red flower goes West*
Umezawa, Rui. *Aiko's flowers*
Waber, Bernard. *A lion named Shirley Williamson*
Wallace, Nancy Elizabeth. *Paperwhite*
Williams, Barbara. *Hello, dandelions!*
Wilson-Max, Ken. *Max loves sunflowers*

Flowers – roses

Hooks, William H. *The legend of the Christmas rose*

Flying *see* Activities – flying

Fog *see* Weather – fog

Fold out books *see* Format, unusual – toy and movable books

Folk and fairy tales

Aardema, Verna. *Anansi does the impossible!*
   Anansi finds a fool
   Bimwili and the Zimwi
   Borreguita and the coyote
   Bringing the rain to Kapiti Plain
   Half-a-ball-of-kenki
   Jackal's flying lesson
   Ji-nongo-nongo means riddles
   Koi and the kola nuts
   The lonely lioness and the ostrich chicks
   Misoso
   Oh, Kojo! How could you!
   Pedro and the padre
   Princess Gorilla and a new kind of water
   The riddle of the drum
   Sebgugugu the glutton
   Traveling to Tondo
   The vingananee and the tree toad
   Who's in Rabbit's house?
   Why mosquitoes buzz in people's ears
Abisch, Roz. *The clever turtle*
   Mai-Ling and the mirror
   Sweet Betsy from Pike
Ada, Alma Flor. *Dear Peter Rabbit*
   The malachite palace
   The rooster who went to his uncle's wedding
Adshead, Gladys L. *Brownies - hush!*
Æsop. *Æsop*
   Æsop's fables, ill. by Gisela Dürr
   Æsop's fables, ill. by Michael Hague
   Æsop's fables, ill. by Heidi Holder
   Æsop's fables, ill. by Claire Littlejohn
   Æsop's fables, ill. by Jerry Pinkney
   Æsop's fables, ill. by Nick Price
   Æsop's fables, ill. by Lisbeth Zwerger
   Androcles and the lion, ill. by Janusz Grabianski
   Androcles and the lion, ill. by Dennis Nolan

Androcles and the lion, ill. by Robert Rayevsky
Androcles and the lion, ill. by Janet Stevens
Animal fables from Æsop
The ant and the dove
The best of Æsop's fables
The children's Æsop
The country mouse and the city mouse
The fables of Æsop
The hare and the frogs
The hare and the tortoise, ill. by Paul Galdone
The hare and the tortoise, ill. by Carol Jones
The hare and the tortoise, ill. by Gerald Rose
The hare and the tortoise, ill. by Helen Ward
The hare and the tortoise, ill. by Peter Weevers
The lion and the mouse, ill. by Carol Jones
The lion and the mouse, ill. by Lisa McCue
The lion and the mouse, ill. by Gerald Rose
The lion and the mouse, ill. by Bernadette Watts
The lion and the mouse, ill. by Ed Young
The lion and the mouse and other Æsop fables
The miller, his son and their donkey, ill. by Roger
 Antoine Duvoisin
The miller, his son and their donkey, ill. by Eugen
 Sopko
Once in a wood
The raven and the fox
Seven fables from Æsop
Tales from Æsop
Three Æsop fox fables
The tortoise and the hare
The town mouse and the country mouse, ill. by
 Lorinda Bryan Cauley
The town mouse and the country mouse, ill. by
 Helen Craig
The town mouse and the country mouse, ill. by Paul
 Galdone
The town mouse and the country mouse, ill. by Tom
 Garcia
The town mouse and the country mouse, ill. by Janet
 Stevens
The town mouse and the country mouse, ill. by
 Bernadette Watts
Town mouse, country mouse, ill. by Jan Brett
Town mouse, country mouse, ill. by Carol Jones
Wolf! Wolf!
Afanas'ev, Aleksandr N. *Russian folk tales*
 Salt
Ahlberg, Allan. *The Cinderella show*
Aiken, Joan. *The shoemaker's boy*
Aleichem, Sholem. *Hanukah money*
Alexander, Ellen. *Llama and the great flood*
Alexander, Lloyd. *The king's fountain*
 The truthful harp
Alger, Leclaire Gowans. *All in the morning early*
 Always room for one more
Aliki. *Diogenes*
 The eggs
 George and the cherry tree
 The story of Johnny Appleseed
 Three gold pieces
 The twelve months
The all-amazing ha ha book
Allard, Harry. *May I stay?*
Allen, Jonathan. *Wake up, Sleeping Beauty*
Allen, Linda. *The giant who had no heart*
 The mouse bride
Ambrus, Victor G. *The little cockerel*
 Never laugh at bears
 The seven skinny goats

The Sultan's bath
The three poor tailors
Anaya, Rudolfo A. *Maya's children*
Andersen, H. C. (Hans Christian). *The emperor and
 the nightingale,* ill. by Meilo So
The emperor and the nightingale, ill. by James
 Watling
The emperor's new clothes, ill. by Angela Barrett
The emperor's new clothes, ill. by Erik Blegvad
The emperor's new clothes, ill. by Virginia Lee Bur-
 ton
The emperor's new clothes, ill. by Robert Byrd
The emperor's new clothes, ill. by Jack and Irene
 Delano
The emperor's new clothes, ill. by Hélène Des-
 puteaux
The emperor's new clothes, ill. by Birte Dietz
The emperor's new clothes, ill. by Dorothée Duntze
The emperor's new clothes, ill. by Pamela Baldwin
 Ford
The emperor's new clothes, ill. by Jack Kent
The emperor's new clothes, ill. by Monika Laimgru-
 ber
The emperor's new clothes, ill. by Anne F. Rockwell
The emperor's new clothes, ill. by Janet Stevens
The emperor's new clothes, ill. by Robert Van Nutt
The emperor's new clothes, ill. by Nadine Bernard
 Westcott
The emperor's nightingale, ill. from the Disney
 arcives
The emperor's nightingale, ill. by Georges Lemoine
The fir tree, ill. by Stephanie Britt
The fir tree, ill. by Nancy Elkholm Burkert
The fir tree, ill. by Diane Goode
The fir tree, ill. by Rita Marshall
The fir tree, ill. by Bernadette Watts
It's perfectly true!
Little Ida's flowers
The little match girl, ill. by Rachel Isadora
The little match girl, ill. by Blair Lent
The little match girl, ill. by Jerry Pinkney
The little mermaid, ill. by Edward Frascino
The little mermaid, ill. by Michael Hague
The little mermaid, ill. by Rachel Isadora
The little mermaid, ill. by Chihiro Iwasaki
The little mermaid, ill. by Dorothy Pulis Lathrop
The little mermaid, ill. by Darcy May
The little mermaid, ill. by Josef Palecek
The little mermaid, ill. by Daniel San Souci
The little mermaid, ill. by Katie Thamer Treherne
The nightingale, ill. by Harold Berson
The nightingale, ill. by Nancy Ekholm Burkert
The nightingale, ill. by Alison Claire Darke
The nightingale, ill. by Demi
The nightingale, ill. by Beni Montresor
The nightingale, ill. by Josef Palecek
The nightingale, ill. by Regolo Ricci
The nightingale, ill. by Christopher Santoro
The nightingale, ill. by Lisbeth Zwerger
The old man is always right
The princess and the pea, ill. by Emily Bolam
The princess and the pea, ill. by Dorothée Duntze
The princess and the pea, ill. by Dick Gackenbach
The princess and the pea, ill. by Paul Galdone
The princess and the pea, ill. by Camille Semelet
The princess and the pea, ill. by Janet Stevens
The princess and the pea, ill. by Suçie Stevenson
The princess and the pea, ill. by Eve Tharlet
The snow queen, ill. by Angela Barrett

Barrie, J. M. (James M.). *Peter Pan*
Barry, David. *The Rajah's rice*
Bartels, Alice L. *The beast*
Bartos-Hoppner, Barbara. *The pied piper of Hamelin*
Baruch, Dorothy. *Kappa's tug-of-war with the big brown horse*
Basile, Giambattista. *Petrosinella*
Bason, Lillian. *Those foolish Molboes!*
Bateman, Teresa. *Leprechaun gold*
Bateson-Hill, Margaret. *Lao Lao of Dragon Mountain*
Baumann, Hans. *Chip has many brothers*
  The hare's race
Baumann, Kurt. *The prince and the lute*
Bawden, Nina. *William Tell*
Baylor, Byrd. *The desert is theirs*
  A God on every mountain top
  Moon song
  The way to start a day
Bazilian, Barbara. *Princess Lily*
Bechstein, Ludwig. *The rabbit catcher and other fairy tales*
The bedtime book
Beeler, Selby B. *Throw your tooth on the roof*
Behan, Brendan. *The king of Ireland's son*
Bell, Anthea. *Swan Lake*
  The wise queen
Belling the cat and other stories
Belpré, Pura. *Dance of the animals*
  Pérez and Martina
Belting, Natalia Maree. *The sun is a golden earring*
Bemelmans, Ludwig. *Rosebud*
Ben-'Ezer, Ehud. *Hosni the dreamer*
Bennett, Jill. *Teeny tiny*
Berenstain, Michael. *The troll book*
Berenzy, Alix. *A frog prince*
  Rapunzel
Beresford, Elisabeth. *Jack and the magic stove*
Berg, Leila. *Folk tales for reading and telling*
Bergen, Lara Rice. *Washington Irving's Rip Van Winkle*
Berger, Barbara Helen. *Grandfather Twilight*
Bernhard, Emery. *The girl who wanted to hunt*
  How Snowshoe Hare rescued the sun
  Spotted Eagle and Black Crow
  The tree that rains
Bernhard, Josephine Butkowska. *Lullaby*
  Nine cry-baby dolls
Bernstein, Margery. *Coyote goes hunting for fire*
  Earth namer
  The first morning
  How the sun made a promise and kept it
Bernstein, Robin. *Terrible, terrible!*
Berry, James. *Don't leave an elephant to go and chase a bird*
  First palm trees
Berson, Harold. *Balarin's goat*
  Barrels to the moon
  The boy, the baker, the miller and more
  Charles and Claudine
  How the devil gets his due
  Joseph and the snake
  Kassim's shoes
  Larbi and Leila
  Raminagrobis and the mice
  Why the jackal won't speak to the hedgehog
Bess, Clayton. *The truth about the moon*
Bianco, Margery Williams. *The velveteen rabbit*, ill. by Allen Atkinson

The velveteen rabbit, ill. by Michael Green
The velveteen rabbit, ill. by Michael Hague
The velveteen rabbit, ill. by David Jorgensen
The velveteen rabbit, ill. by William Nicholson
The velveteen rabbit, ill. by Ilse Plume
The velveteen rabbit, ill. by S. D. Schindler
The velveteen rabbit, ill. by Tien
Bible, Charles. *Hamdaani*
Bider, Djemma. *The buried treasure*
  A drop of honey
Bierhorst, John. *Doctor Coyote*
  The ring in the prairie
Billy Boy (folk-song). *Billy Boy*
Birdseye, Tom. *Soap! Soap! Don't forget the soap!*
  A song of stars
Biro, Val. *The pied piper of Hamelin*
  Tobias and the dragon
Birrer, Cynthia. *The lady and the unicorn*
  Song to Demeter
Bishop, Claire Huchet. *The five Chinese brothers*
Bishop, Gavin. *Maui and the sun*
Black, Algernon D. *The woman of the wood*
Blackmore, Vivien. *Why corn is golden*
Blake, Quentin. *The story of the dancing frog*
Bodkin, Odds. *The crane wife*
Bodnar, Judit Z. *A wagonload of fish*
Bolliger, Max. *The fireflies*
Bouhuys, Mies. *The lady of Stavoren*
Boutwell, Edna. *Red rooster*
Bowden, Joan Chase. *Strong John*
Boyle, Vere. *Beauty and the beast*
Brand, Oscar. *When I first came to this land*
Brennan, Patricia D. *Hitchety hatchety up I go!*
Brentano, Clemens. *Schoolmaster Whackwell's wonderful sons*
Brett, Jan. *Fritz and the beautiful horses*
  The mitten
Briggs, Raymond. *Jim and the beanstalk*
Bro, Marguerite (Harmon). *The animal friends of Peng-u*
Brodmann, Aliana. *Such a noise!*
Brown, Marcia. *The blue jackal*
  The bun
  Once a mouse . . .
  Stone soup
Browne, Vee. *Monster birds*
Browning, Robert. *The pied piper of Hamelin*, ill. by Patricia and Robin DeWitt
  The pied piper of Hamelin, ill. by Kate Greenaway
  The pied piper of Hamelin, ill. by Anatoly Ivanov
  The pied piper of Hamelin, ill. by Errol Le Cain
  The pied piper of Hamelin, ill. by Drahos Zak
Bruchac, Joseph. *The circle of thanks*
  The first strawberries
  Gluskabe and the four wishes
  The great ball game
  Thirteen moons on turtle's back
Bruna, Dick. *Dick Bruna's Cinderella*
  Dick Bruna's Little Red Riding Hood
  Dick Bruna's Snow-White and the seven dwarfs
  Dick Bruna's Tom Thumb
Brusca, María Cristina. *The cook and the king*
  When jaguars ate the moon
Bryan, Ashley. *Beat the story-drum, pum-pum*
  The cat's purr
  The dancing granny
  Lion and the ostrich chicks
  Sh-ko and his eight wicked brothers
  The story of lightning and thunder

Dalton, Anne. *Prince Starr*

Daly, Niki. *Why the sun and moon live in the sky*

Daniels, Guy. *The Tsar's riddles*

Dasent, George W. *East o' the sun, west o' the moon*

Daugherty, Sonia (Medvedeva). *Vanka's donkey*

Davis, Aubrey. *Bone button borscht*
  The enormous potato
  Sody salleratus

Davis, Douglas F. *The lion's tail*

Davol, Marguerite W. *Batwings and the curtain of night*

Day, David. *The swan children*

Day, Nancy Raines. *The lion's whiskers*

Dayrell, Elphinstone. *Why the sun and the moon live in the sky*

DeArmond, Dale. *The seal oil lamp*

DeChristopher, Marlowe. *Greencoat and the swanboy*

Dee, Ruby. *Tower to heaven*
  Two ways to count to ten

Deetlefs, Rene. *Tabu and the dancing elephants*

DeFelice, Cynthia C. *Three perfect peaches*

De Gerez, Toni. *Louhi, witch of North Farm*

Del Negro, Janice. *Lucy Dove*

DeLuise, Dom. *King Bob's new clothes*

De Mejo, Oscar. *La Bella Magellona and the little cavalier*

Demi. *The artist and the architect*
  Chen Ping and his magic axe
  A Chinese zoo
  Demi's reflective fables
  The dragon's tale and other animal fables of the Chinese zodiac
  The empty pot
  The greatest treasure
  The hallowed horse
  The magic boat
  The magic tapestry
  One grain of rice
  The stonecutter
  Under the shade of the mulberry tree

De Montaño, Martha Kreipe. *Coyote in love with a star*

De Paola, Tomie (Thomas Anthony). *Big Anthony, his story*
  Favorite nursery tales
  Fin M'Coul
  Jamie O'Rourke and the big potato
  The legend of Old Befana
  The legend of the bluebonnet
  The legend of the Indian paintbrush
  The legend of the persian carpet
  Little Grunt and the big egg
  The mysterious giant of Barletta
  The Prince of the Dolomites
  Strega Nona meets her match
  Tony's bread

De Regniers, Beatrice Schenk. *Everyone is good for something*
  Little Sister and the Month Brothers
  Red Riding Hood

DeSpain, Pleasant. *The dancing turtle*

Dewan, Ted. *The sorcerer's apprentice*

Dewey, Ariane. *The fish Peri*
  Laffite, the pirate
  The thunder god's son

Diakité, Baba Wagué. *The hunterman and the crocodiles*

Dick Whittington and his cat. *Dick Whittington*, ill. by Edward Ardizzone

Dick Whittington, ill. by Antony Maitland

Dick Whittington and his cat, ill. by Marcia Brown

Dick Whittington and his cat, ill. by Kurt Werth

Diller, Harriett. *The waiting day*

Dinardo, Jeffrey. *The wolf who cried boy*

Dixon, Ann. *How raven brought light to people*

Dobbs, Rose. *More once-upon-a-time stories*
  Once-upon-a-time story book

Domanska, Janina. *The best of the bargain*
  Busy Monday morning
  King Krakus and the dragon
  Look, there is a turtle flying
  Marek, the little fool
  Palmiero and the ogre
  A scythe, a rooster and a cat
  The tortoise and the tree
  The turnip
  Why so much noise?

Dos Santos, Joyce Audy. *The diviner*
  Henri and the Loup-Garou

Doucet, Sharon Arms. *Why Lapin's ears are long and other stories of the Louisiana bayou*

Drummond, Allan. *The willow pattern story*

Du Bois, William Pène. *The hare and the tortoise and the tortoise and the hare*

Duff, Maggie (Margaret K.). *Dancing turtle*
  The princess and the pumpkin
  Rum pum pum

Dukas, P. (Paul Abraham). *The sorcerer's apprentice*

Duncan, Lois. *The magic of Spider Woman*

Dupré, Judith. *The mouse bride*

Dupré, Rick. *Agassu*

Durell, Ann. *The Diane Goode book of American folk tales and songs*

Dwyer, Mindy. *Coyote in love*

Easwaran, Eknath. *The monkey and the mango*

Edens, Cooper. *A present for Rose*

Edwards, Lisa. *Disney's Beauty and the beast, a book of manners*

Edwards, Pamela Duncan. *Dinorella*

Edwards, Roberta. *Five silly fishermen*

Ehlert, Lois. *Cuckoo: a Mexican folktale = Cucú: un cuento folklórico mexicano*
  Mole's hill
  Moon rope

Ehrlich, Amy. *Pome and Peel*

Elkin, Benjamin. *The king's wish and other stories*
  Six foolish fishermen
  Such is the way of the world
  The wisest man in the world

Elwell, Peter. *The king of the pipers*

Elzbieta. *Dikou and the Snivelly Snoak*

Emberley, Barbara. *One wide river to cross*

Emberley, Rebecca. *Three cool kids*

Ernst, Lisa Campbell. *Little Red Riding Hood*

Esbensen, Barbara Juster. *The great buffalo race*
  Ladder to the sky
  The star maiden

Esterl, Arnica. *The fine round cake*

Evans, Katherine. *The boy who cried wolf*
  A bundle of sticks
  The maid and her pail of milk
  The man, the boy and the donkey

Farley, Carol J. *Mr. Pak buys a story*

Farris, Pamela J. *Young Mouse and Elephant*

Faulkner, William J. *Brer Tiger and the big wind*

Fiddle-i-fee, ill. by Diane Stanley

Field, Edward. *Magic words*

The firebird, ill. by Reg Cartwright

The legend of the cranberry
Ling-li and the phoenix fairy
Greene, Jacqueline Dembar. *What his father did*
Greeson, Janet. *The stingy baker*
Gregg, Andy. *Great Rabbit and the long-tailed Wildcat*
Gregorowski, Christopher. *Fly, eagle, fly!*
Gregory, Valiska. *Through the mickle woods*
Grieg, E. H. (Edvard Hagerup). *E. H. Grieg's Peer Gynt*
Grifalconi, Ann. *The village of round and square houses*
Grimm, Jacob. *The bear and the kingbird*
   The bearskinner
   The brave little tailor, ill. by Mark Corcoran
   The brave little tailor, ill. by Daniel San Souci
   The brave little tailor, ill. by Svend Otto S
   The brave little tailor, ill. by Eve Tharlet
   The brave little tailor, ill. by James Warhola
   The Bremen town band
   The Bremen town musicians, ill. by Donna Diamond
   The Bremen town musicians, ill. by Janina Domanska
   The Bremen town musicians, ill. by Paul Galdone
   The Bremen town musicians, ill. by David Johnson
   Bremen town musicians, ill. by Josef Palecek
   The Bremen town musicians, ill. by Ilse Plume
   The Bremen town musicians, ill. by Janet Stevens
   The Bremen town musicians, ill. by Bernadette Watts
   Cinderella, ill. by Nonny Hogrogian
   Cinderella, ill. by Svend Otto S
   Clever Kate
   The devil with the green hairs
   The donkey prince
   The earth gnome
   The elves and the shoemaker, ill. by Doug Cushman
   The elves and the shoemaker, ill. by Paul Galdone
   The elves and the shoemaker, ill. by Margaret Walty
   The elves and the shoemaker, ill. by Bernadette Watts
   The falling stars
   The fisherman and his wife, ill. by Eleanor Hubbard
   The fisherman and his wife, ill. by Monika Laimgruber
   The fisherman and his wife, ill. by Alan Marks
   The fisherman and his wife, ill. by Laurinda Spear
   The fisherman and his wife, ill. by Margot Tomes
   The fisherman and his wife, ill. by Margot Zemach
   Fitcher's bird
   The four clever brothers
   The frog prince, ill. by Paul Galdone
   The frog prince, ill. by Binette Schroeder
   The glass mountain, ill. by Louisa Bauer
   The glass mountain, ill. by Nonny Hogrogian
   Godfather Cat and Mousie
   The golden bird, ill. by Isabelle Brent
   The golden bird, ill. by Sandro Nardini
   The golden goose, ill. by Dorothée Duntze
   The golden goose, ill. by Isadore Seltzer
   The golden goose, ill. by Martin Ursell
   The goose girl, ill. by Sabine Bruntjen
   The goose girl, ill. by Robert Sauber
   Hans in luck, ill. by Paul Galdone
   Hans in luck, ill. by Felix Hoffmann
   Hansel and Gretel, ill. by Adrienne Adams
   Hansel and Gretel, ill. by Anthony Browne
   Hansel and Gretel, ill. by Susan Jeffers

Hansel and Gretel, ill. by Winslow P. Pels
Hansel and Gretel, ill. by Jane Ray
Hansel and Gretel, ill. by Conxita Rodriguez
Hansel and Gretel, ill. by Christopher Santoro
Hansel and Gretel, ill. by John Wallner
Hansel and Gretel, ill. by Paul O. Zelinsky
Hansel and Gretel, ill. by Lisbeth Zwerger
The horse, the fox, and the lion
Iron Hans
Iron John, ill. by Trina Schart Hyman
Iron John, ill. by Winslow Pels
Jack in luck
Jorinda and Joringel, ill. by Adrienne Adams
Jorinda and Joringel, ill. by Jutta Ash
Jorinda and Joringel, ill. by Margot Tomes
King Grisly-Beard
Little brother and little sister
Little red cap
Little Red Riding Hood, ill. by Frank E. Aloise
Little Red Riding Hood, ill. by Gwen Connelly
Little Red Riding Hood, ill. by Paul Galdone
Little Red Riding Hood, ill. by John S. Goodall
Little Red Riding Hood, ill. by Trina Schart Hyman
Little Red Riding Hood, ill. by Mireille Levert
Little Red Riding Hood, ill. by Jean-François Martin
Little Red Riding Hood, ill. by David M. McPhail
Little Red Riding Hood, ill. by Bernadette Watts
Lucky Hans
Mother Holly
Mrs. Fox's wedding
The musicians of Bremen, ill. by John Segal
The musicians of Bremen, ill. by Svend Otto S
The musicians of Bremen, ill. by Martin Ursell
Nanny goat and the seven little kids
The princess and the frog
Rapunzel, ill. by Jutta Ash
Rapunzel, ill. by Sheilah Beckett
Rapunzel, ill. by Bert Dodson
Rapunzel, ill. by Maja Dusíkova
Rapunzel, ill. by Michael Hague
Rapunzel, ill. by Trina Schart Hyman
Rapunzel, ill. by Kris Waldherr
Rapunzel, ill. by Bernadette Watts
Rapunzel, ill. by Paul O. Zelinsky
Rose Red and the bear prince
Rumpelstiltskin, ill. by Jacqueline Ayer
Rumpelstiltskin, ill. by Donna Diamond
Rumpelstiltskin, ill. by Paul Galdone
Rumpelstiltskin, ill. by Jonathan Langley
Rumpelstiltskin, ill. by Gennady Spirin
Rumpelstiltskin, ill. by John Wallner
Rumpelstiltskin, ill. by Bernadette Watts
Rumpelstiltskin, ill. by Paul O. Zelinsky
Seven at one blow
The seven ravens, ill. by Felix Hoffmann
The seven ravens, ill. by Lisbeth Zwerger
The shoemaker and the elves, ill. by Adrienne Adams
The shoemaker and the elves, ill. by Cynthia and William Birrer
The shoemaker and the elves, ill. by Ilse Plume
The six servants
The six swans, ill. by Dorothée Duntze
The six swans, ill. by Daniel San Souci
The six swans, ill. by Margot Tomes
The sleeping beauty, ill. by Warwick Hutton
The sleeping beauty, ill. by Trina Schart Hyman

Rooster brother
Holland, Janice. *You never can tell*
Hong, Lily Toy. *How the ox star fell from heaven*
Hooks, William H. *Feed me!*
　The Gruff brothers
　Moss gown
　Peach boy
　Snowbear Whittington, an Appalachian Beauty and the Beast
Hort, Lenny. *The boy who held back the sea*
Houston, James. *Kiviok's magic journey*
How the cock wrecked the manor
Howland, Naomi. *Latkes, latkes, good to eat*
Huck, Charlotte S. *Princess Furball*
Hughes, Monica. *Little Fingerling*
Hulpach, Vladimir. *Ahaiyute and Cloud Eater*
Hunt, Angela Elwell. *The tale of three trees*
Hunt, Jonathan. *Leif's saga*
Hunter, C. W. *The green gourd*
Hürlimann, Ruth. *The proud white cat*
Hush little baby. *Hush little baby*, ill. by Jeanette Winter
Hutton, Warwick. *Beauty and the beast*
　The nose tree
　Perseus
　The Trojan horse
Ichikawa, Satomi. *A child's book of seasons*
Sun through small leaves
Iké, Jane Hori. *A Japanese fairy tale*
Ikeda, Daisaku. *The snow country prince*
Illyés, Gyula. *Matt the gooseherd*
Irbinskas, Heather. *How Jackrabbit got his very long ears*
Irving, Washington. *Rip Van Winkle*, ill. by John Howe
　Rip Van Winkle, ill. by Thomas Locker
　Rip Van Winkle, ill. by Peter Wingham
Isele, Elizabeth. *The frog princess*
Ishii, Momoko. *The tongue-cut sparrow*
Ivanov, Anatoly. *Ol' Jake's lucky day*
I've been working on the railroad
Jack and the beanstalk. *The history of Mother Twaddle and the marvelous achievements of her son Jack*
　Jack and the beanstalk, ill. by Val Biro
　Jack and the beanstalk, ill. by Lorinda Bryan Cauley
　Jack and the beanstalk, ill. by Lydia Halverson
　Jack and the beanstalk, ill. by Julek Heller
　Jack and the beanstalk, ill. by John Howe
　Jack and the beanstalk, ill. by Steven Kellogg
　Jack and the beanstalk, ill. by Ed Parker
　Jack and the beanstalk, ill. by Tony Ross
　Jack and the beanstalk, ill. by by Niamh Sharkey
　Jack and the beanstalk, ill. by Gennady Spirin
　Jack and the beanstalk, ill. by William Stobbs
　Jack and the beanstalk, ill. by James Warhola
　Jack and the beanstalk, ill. by Anne Wilsdorf
　Jack and the beanstalk / Juan y los frijoles magicos
　Jack the giant killer, ill. by Anne Wilsdorf
　Jack the giantkiller, ill. by Tony Ross
Jackson, Alison. *I know an old lady who swallowed a pie*
Jackson, Bobby L. *Little Red Ronnika*
Jackson, Ellen B. *Cinder Edna*
Jacobs, Joseph. *The crock of gold*
　Hereafterthis
　Hudden and Dudden and Donald O'Neary
　Johnny-cake, ill. by Emma Lillian Brock
　Johnny-cake, ill. by William Stobbs

Master of all masters
Old Mother Wiggle-Waggle
Tattercoats
The three sillies, ill. by Paul Galdone
The three sillies, ill. by Kathryn Hewitt
The three sillies, ill. by Steven Kellogg
Jacobs, Shannon K. *The boy who loved morning*
Jaffe, Nina. *The golden flower*
　In the month of Kislev
　Older brother, younger brother
　The way meat loves salt
Jagendorf, Moritz A. *Kwi-na the eagle*
Jameson, Cynthia. *The house of five bears*
A January fog will freeze a hog
Jaquith, Priscilla. *Bo Rabbit smart for true*
Jenkins, Steve. *Duck's breath and mouse pie*
Jennings, Linda M. *Coppelia*
　The sleeping beauty
Jessell, Tim. *Amorak*
Johnson, Crockett. *Harold's fairy tale*
Johnson, Janet P. *How Mr. Dog got tame*
　Keelboat Annie
Johnston, Tony. *Alice Nizzy Nazzy, the Witch of Santa Fe*
　The badger and the magic fan
　Bigfoot Cinderrrrella
　The cowboy and the black-eyed pea
　The tale of Rabbit and Coyote
Jones, Jennifer Berry. *Heetunka's harvest*
Kajpust, Melissa. *The peacock's pride*
Keams, Geri. *Snail girl brings water*
Keats, Ezra Jack. *John Henry*
Kellogg, Steven (Stephen). *Chicken Little*
　I was born about 10,000 years ago
　Johnny Appleseed
Kent, Jack. *Jack Kent's happy-ever-after book*
　Jack Kent's hokus pokus bedtime book
Keo, Ena. *The crane wife*
Kessler, Brad. *Brer Rabbit and Boss Lion*
Ketteman, Helen. *Bubba the cowboy prince*
Kherdian, David. *The golden bracelet*
Kimmel, Eric A. *Anansi and the magic stick*
　Anansi and the moss-covered rock
　Anansi and the talking melon
　Anansi goes fishing
　Asher and the capmakers
　Baba Yaga
　Bearhead
　Bernal and Florinda
　Billy Lazroe and the King of the Sea
　The birds' gift
　Boots and his brothers
　The Chanukkah tree
　Count Silvernose
　Easy work!
　The four gallant sisters
　The greatest of all
　Grizz!
　The magic dreidels
　One Eye, Two Eyes, Three Eyes
　Onions and garlic
　Rimonah of the Flashing Sword
　The runaway tortilla
　Sirko and the wolf
　Squash it!
　The tale of Ali Baba and the forty thieves
　The three princes
　Three sacks of truth
　The two mountains

Luenn, Nancy. *The dragon kite*
  Miser on the mountain
Lunge-Larsen, Lise. *The legend of the lady slipper*
MacBeth, George. *Jonah and the Lord*
McCaughrean, Geraldine. *Grandma Chickenlegs*
  Saint George and the dragon
  Unicorns! Unicorns!
McClure, Gillian. *Selkie*
McCurdy, Michael. *The devils who learned to be good*
McDermott, Beverly Brodsky. *The crystal apple*
  The dreamtime
  The Golem
McDermott, Gerald. *Anansi the spider*
  Arrow to the sun
  Coyote
  Daniel O'Rourke
  Daughter of earth
  The fox and the stork
  Musicians of the sun
  Raven
  The stonecutter
  Tim O'Toole and the wee folk
  The voyage of Osiris
MacDonald, Amy. *Please, Malese!*
MacDonald, George. *The light princess*, ill. by Maurice Sendak
  The light princess, ill. by Katie Thamer Treherne
  Little Daylight
MacDonald, Margaret Read. *The girl who wore too much*
  The old woman who lived in a vinegar bottle
  Pickin' peas
  Slop!
MacDonald, Suse. *Once upon another*
McFarland, John. *The exploding frog and other fables from Æsop*
MacGill-Callahan, Sheila. *And still the turtle watched*
  The children of Lir
  Finn MacCool and the talking fish
  The last snake in Ireland
  The seal prince
  To capture the wind
  When Solomon was king
McGuire-Turcotte, Casey A. *How Honu the turtle got his shell*
McHale, Ethel Kharasch. *Son of thunder*
McKee, David. *The man who was going to mind the house*
McKissack, Patricia C. *Cinderella*
  A million fish . . . more or less
  Mirandy and brother wind
McLenighan, Valjean. *Turtle and rabbit*
  What you see is what you get
  You are what you are
  You can go jump
McNaughton, Colin. *Guess who's just moved in next door?*
Maddern, Eric. *The fire children*
Maestro, Giulio. *The tortoise's tug of war*
Magnus, Erica. *The boy and the devil*
  Old Lars
Mahy, Margaret. *The seven Chinese brothers*
Maitland, Antony. *Idle Jack*
Malkovych, Ivan. *The cat and the rooster*
Malotki, Ekkehart. *The magic hummingbird*
Mamin-Sibiryak, D. N. *Grey Neck*
Mann, Pamela. *The frog princess?*
Manna, Anthony L. *Mr. Semolina-Semolinus*
Manson, Christopher. *The crab prince*

  A gift for the king
  The tree in the wood
Mantinband, Gerda. *Blabbermouths*
Mark, Jan. *The Midas touch*
  The tale of Tobias
Marshall, James. *Hansel and Gretel*
  Red Riding Hood
Marston, Elsa. *The fox maiden*
Martin, Bill (William Ivan). *Sounds of laughter*
Martin, Claire. *Boots and the glass mountain*, ill. by Gennady Spirin
  The race of the golden apples
Martin, Francesca. *Clever Tortoise*
  The honey hunters
Martin, Rafe. *The eagle's gift*
  Foolish rabbit's big mistake
  The hungry tigress
  The rough-face girl
Mason, Jane B. *The flying horse*
Mathews, Judith. *Nathaniel Willy, scared silly*
Matsuno, Masako. *Taro and the bamboo shoot*
Matsutani, Miyoko. *The fisherman under the sea*
  The witch's magic cloth
Maugham, W. Somerset (William Somerset). *Princess September and the nightingale*
Mayer, Marianna. *Baba Yaga and Vasilisa the Brave*
  Beauty and the beast
  The black horse
  The little jewel box
  My first book of nursery tales
  Pegasus
  Perseus
  The spirit of the blue light
Mayer, Mercer. *The pied piper of Hamelin*
Mead, Katherine. *How spiders got eight legs*
Medearis, Angela Shelf. *The freedom riddle*
  Seven spools of thread
  The singing man
  Tailypo
  Too much talk
Medicine Crow, Joseph. *Brave Wolf and the Thunderbird*
Melmed, Laura Krauss. *Moishe's miracle*
  Prince Nautilus
  The rainbabies
Mendelson, S. T. *Stupid Emilien*
Merriam, Eve. *Epaminondas*
Metaxas, Eric. *The boy and the whale*
  The fool and the flying ship
  The gardener's apprentice
  The monkey people
  Puss in boots
  The white cat
Michael, Emory H. *Androcles and the lion*
Midge, Tiffany. *Buffalo*
Mike, Jan M. *The bird maiden*
  Clever Karlis
  Gift of the Nile
  Juan Bobo and the horse of seven colors
  Opossum and the great firemaker
Milhous, Katherine. *The turnip*
Miller, Edna. *Mousekin's fables*
Miller, Moira. *The moon dragon*
Miller, William. *The knee-high man*
Mills, Lauren A. *Fairy wings*
  Tatterhood and the hobgoblins
Milne, A. A. (Alan Alexander). *Prince Rabbit*
Minters, Frances. *Cinder-Elly*
  Sleepless Beauty

Mirkovic, Irene. *The greedy shopkeeper*
Mobley, Jane. *The star husband*
Moeri, Louise. *Star Mother's youngest child*
Mollel, Tololwa M. (Tololwa Marti). *Ananse's feast*
   Big boy
   Dume's roar
   The flying tortoise
   The king and the tortoise
   Kitoto the mighty
   Orphan boy
   The princess who lost her hair
   Shadow dance
   Song bird
   Subira subira
Moncure, Jane Belk. *The talking tabby cat*
Moon, Dolly M. *My very first book of cowboy songs*
Moore, Inga. *The sorcerer's apprentice*
Mora, Pat. *The night the moon fell*
   The race of toad and deer
Morel, Eve. *Fairy tales*
   Fairy tales and fables
Moreton, Daniel. *La Cucaracha Martina*
Morimoto, Junko. *The inch boy*
   Mouse's marriage
   The two bullies
Morley, Carol. *A spider and a pig*
Moroney, Lynn. *The boy who loved bears*
   Elinda who danced in the sky
   Moontellers
Morris, Ann. *The Cinderella rebus book*
   The Little Red Riding Hood rebus book
Morris, Winifred. *The future of Yen-Tzu*
   The magic leaf
Mosel, Arlene. *Tikki Tikki Tembo*
Moser, Barry. *Tucker Pfeffercorn*
Mother Goose. *The golden goose book*, ill. by L. Leslie Brooke
   London Bridge is falling down, ill. by Ed Emberley
   London Bridge is falling down, ill. by Peter Spier
Moxley, Susan. *Abdul's treasure*
Muller, Robin. *The lucky old woman*
   Mollie Whuppie and the giant
   The sorcerer's apprentice
Munsch, Robert N. *A promise is a promise*
Murphy, Shirley Rousseau. *Wind child*
Mwalimu. *Awful aardvark*
Mwenye Hadithi. *Greedy zebra*
Myers, Walter Dean. *The dragon takes a wife*
   The golden serpent
Namioka, Lensey. *The loyal cat*
Neale, J. M. (John Mason). *Good King Wenceslas*
Neitzel, Shirley. *From the land of the white birch*
Nesbit, Edith. *Beauty and the beast*
   The last of the dragons
   Melisande
Ness, Evaline. *The girl and the goatherd*
Newton, Patricia Montgomery. *The five sparrows*
   The stonecutter
Nikly, Michelle. *The princess on the nut*
Nikola-Lisa, W. *The dancin' fox*
Nister, Ernest. *Little tales from long ago*
Nixon, Joan Lowery. *Bigfoot makes a movie*
Nones, Eric Jon. *Canary prince*
Norman, Howard A. *Who-Paddled-Backward-With-Trout*
Nunes, Susan Miho. *Tiddalick the frog*
O'Connor, Jane. *The teeny tiny woman*
Odoyevsky, Vladimir. *Old Father Frost*
Ogburn, Jacqueline K. *The magic nesting doll*

O Huigin, Sean. *King of the birds*
Olaleye, Isaac. *In the Rainfield*
The old woman and her pig. *The old woman and her pig*, ill. by Paul Galdone
   The old woman and her pig, ill. by Giyora Karmi
   The old woman and her pig, ill. by Rosanne Litzinger
   The troublesome pig
The old-fashioned children's storybook
Oliviero, Jamie. *The day Sun was stolen*
   The fish skin
Olson, Arielle North. *Noah's cats and the devil's fire*
Onyefulu, Obi. *Chinye*
Oppenheim, Joanne. *The Christmas witch*
   Donkey's tale
Oram, Hiawyn. *Baba Yaga and the wise doll*
   Skittlewonder and the wizard
Orgel, Doris. *Button soup*
Osborne, Mary Pope. *Kate and the beanstalk*
Osofsky, Audrey. *Dreamcatcher*
Oughton, Jerrie. *How the stars fell into the sky*
   The magic weaver of rugs
Over in the meadow, ill. by Ezra Jack Keats
P'an, Ts'ai-ying. *Monkey creates havoc in heaven*
Pancheri, Jan. *The twelve poodle princess*
A paper of pins
Parkinson, Kathy. *The enormous turnip*
Parnall, Peter. *The great fish*
Parry, Marian. *King of the fish*
Parsons, Virginia. *Pinocchio and Gepetto*
   Pinocchio and the money tree
   Pinocchio goes on the stage
   Pinocchio plays truant
Paterson, Katherine. *The tale of the Mandarin ducks*
Patron, Susan. *Burgoo stew*
Pattison, Darcy. *The river dragon*
Paxton, Tom. *Belling the cat and other Æsop fables*
   The story of Santa Claus
   The story of the Tooth Fairy
Pearson, Kit. *The singing basket*
The peasant's pea patch
Peck, Jan. *The giant carrot*
Pellowski, Anne. *The nine crying dolls*
Penney, Ian. *Ian Penney's book of fairy tales*
Perlman, Janet. *The Emperor Penguin's new clothes*
Perrault, Charles. *Cinderella*, ill. by Sheilah Beckett
   Cinderella, ill. by Marcia Brown
   Cinderella, ill. by Paul Galdone
   Cinderella, ill. by Diane Goode
   Cinderella, ill. by Susan Jeffers
   Cinderella, ill. by Loek Koopmans
   Cinderella, ill. by Emanuele Luzzati
   Cinderella, ill. by James Marshall
   Cinderella, ill. by Phil Smith
   Puss in boots, ill. by Marcia Brown
   Puss in boots, ill. by Lorinda Bryan Cauley
   Puss in boots, ill. by Jean Claverie
   Puss in boots, ill. by Andrea Da Rif
   Puss in boots, ill. by Stasys Eidrigevicius
   Puss in boots, ill. by Hans Fischer
   Puss in boots, ill. by Paul Galdone
   Puss in boots, retold and ill. by John S. Goodall
   Puss in boots, retold and ill. by Gail E. Haley
   Puss in boots, ill. by Giuliano Lunelli
   Puss in boots, ill. by Fred Marcellino [pub. by Farrar, 1990]
   Puss in boots, ill. by Fred Marcellino [pub. by Farrar, 1998]
   Puss in boots, ill. by Julia Noonan

Puss in boots, ill. by Tony Ross
Puss in boots, ill. by William Stobbs
Puss in boots, ill. by Yan Thomas
Puss in boots, ill. by Alain Vaës
Puss in boots, ill. by Barry Wilkinson
The sleeping beauty, ill. by David Walker
Petach, Heidi. *Goldilocks and the three hares*
Peters, Andrew. *Salt is sweeter than gold*
Peterson, Julienne. *Caterina, the clever farm girl*
Pevear, Richard. *Mister Cat-and-a-Half*
  Our king has horns!
Phillips, Mildred. *The sign in Mendel's window*
Philpot, Graham. *Fabulous fairy tale follies*
Phumla. *Nomi and the magic fish*
Pilegard, Virginia Walton. *The warlord's puzzle*
Pitcher, Caroline. *Mariana and the merchild*
Pitre, Felix. *Paco and the witch*
Pittman, Helena Clare. *The gift of the willows*
  A grain of rice
Plante, Patricia. *The turtle and the two ducks*
Plume, Ilse. *The story of Befana*
Podwal, Mark H. *Golem*
Pohrt, Tom. *Coyote goes walking*
Polacco, Patricia. *Babushka's Mother Goose*
  Luba and the wren
  Rechenka's eggs
Pollock, Penny. *The turkey girl*
Polushkin, Maria. *Bubba and Babba*
  The little hen and the giant
Poole, Amy Lowry. *How the rooster got his crown*
Porazinska, Janina. *The enchanted book*
Powers, Daniel. *Jiro's pearl*
Prather, Ray. *The ostrich girl*
Presencer, Alain. *Roaring lion tales*
Preussler, Otfried. *The tale of the unicorn*
The prince who knew his fate
Prokofiev, Sergei Sergeievitch. *Peter and the wolf,* ill.
  by Reg Cartwright
  Peter and the wolf, ill. by Warren Chappell
  Peter and the wolf, ill. by Barbara Cooney
  Peter and the wolf, ill. by Julia Gukova
  Peter and the wolf, ill. by Frans Haacken
  Peter and the wolf, ill. by Alan Howard
  Peter and the wolf, ill. by Charles Mikolaycak
  Peter and the wolf, ill. by Jörg Müller
  Peter and the wolf, ill. by Josef Palecek
  Peter and the wolf, ill. by Kozo Shimizu
  Peter and the wolf, retold and ill. by Vladimir
    Vagin
  Peter and the wolf, ill. by Erna Voigt
Prose, Francine. *The angel's mistake*
  Dybbuk
  You never know
Pushkin, Aleksandr Sergeevich. *The tale of Tsar
  Saltan*
Pyle, Howard. *The Swan Maiden*
Quackenbush, Robert M. *Clementine*
  She'll be comin' 'round the mountain
  Skip to my Lou
  There'll be a hot time in the old town tonight
Quigley, Lillian Fox. *The blind men and the elephant*
Ransome, Arthur. *The fool of the world and the flying
  ship*
Raphael, Elaine. *Turnabout*
Rappaport, Doreen. *Journey of Meng*
  The long-haired girl
  The new king
Rattigan, Jama Kim. *The woman in the moon*
Rayevsky, Inna. *The talking tree*

Reesink, Marijke. *The golden treasure*
  The princess who always ran away
Reit, Seymour. *Rebus bears*
Renberg, Dalia Hardof. *King Solomon and the bee*
Richard, Françoise. *On Cat Mountain*
Richardson, Jean. *The sleeping beauty*
Riggio, Anita. *Beware the Brindlebeast*
Riordan, James. *The coming of Night*
  The Snowmaiden
  The three magic gifts
Robbins, Ruth. *Baboushka and the three kings*
  How the first rainbow was made
Robertson, Joanne. *Sea witches*
Robins, Arthur. *The teeny tiny woman*
Robinson, Adjai. *Femi and old grandaddie*
Robinson, Fay. *Where did all the dragons go?*
Rockwell, Anne F. *The acorn tree and other folktales*
  Bafana
  The boy who wouldn't obey
  The old woman and her pig and 10 other stories
  Poor Goose
  Romulus and Remus
  The three bears and 15 other stories
  Thump thump thump!
  The wolf who had a wonderful dream
  The wonderful eggs of Furicchia
Rodanas, Kristina. *The dragonfly's tale*
  Follow the stars
Rogasky, Barbara. *The water of life*
Rogers, Margaret. *Green is beautiful*
Rohmer, Harriet. *How we came to the fifth world*
  The invisible hunters
  Mother scorpion country
Ronay, Jadja. *Ginger*
Root, Phyllis. *Aunt Nancy and Old Man Trouble*
  Grandmother Winter
  Soup for supper
Rosales, Melodye Benson. *Leola and the honeybears*
Rose, Anne K. *Akimba and the magic cow*
  Pot full of luck
  Spider in the sky
  The talking turnip
  The triumphs of Fuzzy Fogtop
Rosen, Michael (1946-). *Crow and Hawk*
  How the animals got their colors
Ross, Gayle. *How Turtle's back was cracked*
  The legend of the Windigo
Ross, Tony. *The boy who cried wolf*
  The enchanted pig
  Hansel and Gretel
  The pied piper of Hamelin
  Stone soup
Roth, Susan L. *Brave Martha and the dragon*
  Fire came to the earth people
  Kanahena
  The story of light
Rothenberg, Joan. *Inside-out grandma*
Roughsey, Dick. *The giant devil-dingo*
Rounds, Glen. *The boll weevil*
  Casey Jones
  Sweet Betsy from Pike
Rumford, James. *The cloudmakers*
Sage, James. *Coyote makes man*
Sahagun, Bernardino de. *Spirit child*
San José, Christine. *Sleeping Beauty*
Sanderson, Ruth. *The enchanted wood*
  Papa Gatto
Sanfield, Steve. *Bit by bit*

Goldilocks and the three bears, ill. by Lorinda Bryan Cauley
Goldilocks and the three bears, ill. by Jane Dyer
Goldilocks and the three bears, ill. by Lynn Bywaters Ferris
Goldilocks and the three bears, ill. by Madelaine Gill Linden
Goldilocks and the three bears, ill. by David McPhail
Goldilocks and the three bears, ill. by James Marshall
Goldilocks and the three bears, ill. by Laura Rader
Goldilocks and the three bears, ill. by Tony Ross
Goldilocks and the three bears, ill. by Janet Stevens
Goldilocks and the three bears, ill. by Bernadette Watts
Goldilocks and the three bears, ill. by Bari Weissman
The story of the three bears, ill. by L. Leslie Brooke
The story of the three bears, ill. by William Stobbs
The three bears, ill. by Byron Barton
The three bears, ill. by Paul Galdone
The three bears, ill. by Feodor Rojankovsky
The three bears, ill. by Robin Spowart
The three little pigs. *The original three little pigs retold*, ill. by Jonathan Smith
The story of the three little pigs, ill. by L. Leslie Brooke
The story of the three little pigs, ill. by William Stobbs
Three little pigs [Facsimile ed]
The three little pigs, ill. by Val Biro
The three little pigs, ill. by Gavin Bishop
The three little pigs, ill. by Caroline Bucknall
The three little pigs, ill. by Stephen Cartwright
The three little pigs, ill. by Lorinda Bryan Cauley
The three little pigs, ill. by Jean Claverie
The three little pigs, ill. by Doug Cushman
The three little pigs, ill. by William Pène Du Bois
The three little pigs, ill. by Paul Galdone
The three little pigs, ill. by Madelaine Gill
The three little pigs, ill. by Steven Kellogg
The three little pigs, ill. by David McPhail
The three little pigs, ill. by James Marshall
The three little pigs, ill. by Paul Meisel
The three little pigs, ill. by Rodney Peppé
The three little pigs, ill. by Edda Reinl
The three little pigs, ill. by John Wallner
The three little pigs, ill. by Irma Wilde
The three little pigs, ill. by Margot Zemach
The three little pigs and the big bad wolf
The three little pigs and the fox
The three pigs, ill. by Tony Ross
Who's at the door?
Tildes, Phyllis Limbacher. *The magic babushka*
Tolhurst, Marilyn. *Somebody and the three Blairs*
Tolstoy, Aleksey Nikolayevich. *The gigantic turnip*, ill. by Niamh Sharkey
The great big enormous turnip, ill. by Helen Oxenbury
Tom Thumb. *Grimm Tom Thumb*
Tom Thumb, ill. by L. Leslie Brooke
Tom Thumb, ill. by Dennis Hockerman
Tom Thumb, ill. by Felix Hoffmann
Tom Thumb, ill. by Lidia Postma
Tom Thumb, ill. by Richard Jesse Watson
Tom Thumb, ill. by William Wiesner
Tom Tit Tot. *Tom Tit Tot*
Tompert, Ann. *The jade horse, the cricket, and the peach stone*
Saint Nicholas

Torre, Betty L. *The luminous pearl*
Towle, Faith M. *The magic cooking pot*
Toye, William. *Fire stealer*
  How summer came to Canada
  The loon's necklace
  The mountain goats of Temlaham
Tresselt, Alvin R. *The mitten*
Tripp, Wallace. *The tale of a pig*
Troughton, Joanna. *How rabbit stole the fire*
  How the birds changed their feathers
  Make-believe tales
  The quail's egg
  Tortoise's dream
  What made Tiddalik laugh
  Who will be the sun?
Tseng, Grace. *White tiger, blue serpent*
Tsultim, Yeshe. *The mouse king*
Tune, Suelyn Ching. *How Maui slowed the sun*
Turkle, Brinton. *Deep in the forest*
Turska, Krystyna. *The magician of Cracow*
  The woodcutter's duck
Uchida, Yoshiko. *The magic purse*
  The two foolish cats
  The wise old woman
Va, Leong. *A letter to the king*
Vagin, Vladimir Vasil'evich. *The enormous carrot*
Valentine, Johnny. *The duke who outlawed jelly beans and other stories*
Van Laan, Nancy. *The legend of El Dorado*
  The magic bean tree
  Rainbow crow
  Shingebiss
  So say the little monkeys
Van Rynbach, Iris. *The soup stone*
Van Woerkom, Dorothy. *Alexandra the rock-eater*
  The queen who couldn't bake gingerbread
  The rat, the ox and the zodiac
  Sea frog, city frog
Varga, Judy. *The mare's egg*
Vernon, Adele. *The riddle*
Vesey, A. *The princess and the frog*
Villoldo, Alberto. *Skeleton woman*
Vojtech, Anna. *Marushka and the Month Brothers*
Volkmer, Jane Anne. *Song of Chirimia*
Vozar, David. *Yo, hungry wolf!*
Waddell, Martin. *The tough princess*
Wahl, Jan. *Little Eight John*
  Little Johnny Buttermilk
Waite, Michael P. *Jojofu*
Walker, Barbara K. (Barbara Kerlin). *New patches for old*
Wall, Lina Mao. *Judge Rabbit and the tree spirit*
Wallis, Diz. *Battle of the beasts*
Walsh, Ellen Stoll. *Jack's tale*
Walsh, Grahame L. *Didane the koala*
  The goori goori bird
Walsh, Jill Paton. *Pepi and the secret names*
Walt Disney Productions. *Walt Disney's Snow White and the seven dwarfs*
Walter, Mildred Pitts. *Ty's one-man band*
Wang, Rosalind C. *The fourth question*
  The treasure chest
Ward, Helen. *The golden pear*
Watkins, Hope (Brister). *The cunning fox and other tales*
Watts, Bernadette. *St. Francis and the proud crow*
Weedn, Flavia. *The elephant prince*
  The enchanted tree
  The giant's garden

The magic cap
The moon maiden
The ragged peddler
The star gift
Weil, Lisl. *Pandora's box*
Weiss, Harvey. *The sooner hound*
Weiss, Nicki. *If you're happy and you know it*
Wells, Rosemary. *The little lame prince*
Wells, Ruth. *The farmer and the poor god*
Westcott, Nadine Bernard. *Skip to my Lou*
Westerberg, Christine. *The cap that mother made*
Westwood, Jennifer. *Going to Squintum's*
White, Carolyn. *Whuppity Stoorie*
Whitethorne, Baje. *Sunpainters*
Widdecombe Fair
Wiesner, David. *The loathsome dragon*
Wilde, Oscar. *Fairy tales of Oscar Wilde*
    The happy prince
    The selfish giant, ill. by S. Saelig Gallagher
    The selfish giant, ill. by Dom Mansell
    The selfish giant, ill. by Fabian Negrin
    The selfish giant, ill. by Lisbeth Zwerger
    The Star Child
Wildsmith, Brian. *The true cross*
Willard, Nancy. *Shadow story*
Williams, Arlene. *Dragon soup*
Williams, Jay. *The practical princess*
    The surprising things Maui did
Williams, Julie Stewart. *And the birds appeared*
Williams, Laura E. *The long silk strand*
    Torch fishing with the sun
Williams, Sheron. *And in the beginning . . .*
Wilson, Barbara Ker. *The turtle and the island*
Wilson, Sarah. *Beware the dragons!*
Winter, Jeanette. *The girl and the moon man*
Winthrop, Elizabeth. *The little humpbacked horse*
    Vasilissa the beautiful
Wisniewski, David. *Elfwyn's saga*
    Golem
    Sundiata
    The warrior and the wise man
Wolf, Ann. *The rabbit and the turtle*
Wolf, Gita. *The very hungry lion*
Wolff, Ferida. *The emperor's garden*
Wolfson, Margaret. *Turtle songs*
Wolkstein, Diane. *The banza*
    Bouki dances the Kokioko
    The cool ride in the sky
    The legend of Sleepy Hollow
    The magic wings
    Oom razoom; or, Go I know not where, Bring back I know not what
    White wave
Wood, Audrey. *Heckedy Peg*
    The rainbow bridge
Wood, Douglas. *Rabbit and the moon*
Woodworth, Viki. *Fairy tale jokes*
Wooldridge, Connie Nordhielm. *Wicked Jack*
Wright, Freire. *Beauty and the beast*
Wright, Jill. *The old woman and the Willy Nilly Man*
Wright, Sue (Sue M.). *The Christmas path*
Xiong, Blia. *Nine-in-one Grr! Grr!*
Yacowitz, Caryn. *The jade stone*
Yagawa, Sumiko. *The crane wife*
Yashima, Taro. *Seashore story*
Ye, Ting-xing. *Three monks, no water*
Yeoman, John. *The wild washerwomen*
Yep, Laurence. *Dragon prince*
    The junior thunder lord

The Khan's daughter
The shell woman and the king
Tiger woman
Yolen, Jane. *Child of faerie, child of earth*
    The girl in the golden bower
    Greyling
    King Long Shanks
    Little Mouse and Elephant
    Pegasus, the flying horse
    Sky dogs
    The three bears rhyme book
Young, Ed (Edward). *Cat and Rat*
    Donkey trouble
    High on a hill
    Little Plum
    Lon Po Po
    The lost horse
    Night visitors
    The rooster's horns
    The terrible Nung Gwama
Zelinsky, Paul O. *The maid and the mouse and the odd-shaped house*
Zemach, Harve. *Duffy and the devil*
    Nail soup
Zemach, Kaethe. *The beautiful rat*
Zemach, Margot. *It could always be worse*
    Jake and Honeybunch go to heaven
    The little tiny woman
    The three wishes
Zeman, Ludmila. *Sinbad*
Zhang, Song Nan. *The five heavenly emperors and other Chinese myths from the creation*
Ziefert, Harriet. *Cow in the house*
    Little Red Riding Hood
    The turnip
    When I first came to this land
Zijlstra, Tjerk. *Benny and his geese*
Zola, Meguido. *The dream of promise*

Food

Adler, David A. *Bunny rabbit rebus*
Ahlberg, Janet. *Yum yum*
Alborough, Jez. *Ice cream bear*
    It's the bear
Alcott, Louisa May. *An old-fashioned Thanksgiving*
Alderson, Sue Ann. *Wherever bears be*
Aliki. *Milk from cow to carton*
Allamand, Pascale. *Cocoa beans and daisies*
Allard, Harry. *The cactus flower bakery*
Allen, Laura Jean. *Rollo and Tweedy and the case of the missing cheese*
Allen, Robert. *Ten little babies eat*
Ambrus, Victor G. *Country wedding*
Andersen, H. C. (Hans Christian). *The nightingale,* ill. by Christopher Santoro
Andrews, Jan. *Very last first time*
Appelt, Kathi. *Watermelon day*
Armitage, Ronda. *Ice creams for Rosie*
    The lighthouse keeper's lunch
Arnold, Caroline. *Mealtime for zoo animals*
Arnosky, Jim. *Raccoons and ripe corn*
Aronin, Ben. *The secret of the Sabbath fish*
Asch, Frank. *Good lemonade*
    Moonbear
    Popcorn
Axelrod, Amy. *Pigs in the pantry*
    Pigs will be pigs

Azarian, Mary. *The tale of John Barleycorn or, From barley to beer*
Bach, Alice. *The smartest bear and his brother Oliver*
Balan, Bruce. *Pie in the sky*
Banks, Kate (Katherine A.). *Alphabet soup*
Barasch, Lynne. *Rodney's inside story*
Barbato, Juli. *Mom's night out*
Barbour, Karen. *Little Nino's pizzeria*
Barklem, Jill. *The secret staircase*
Barrett, Judi. *An apple a day*
  Cloudy with a chance of meatballs
  Pickles to Pittsburgh
Basso, Bill. *The top of the pizzas*
Baugh, Dolores M. *Supermarket*
Beil, Karen Magnuson. *A cake all for me!*
Benchley, Nathaniel. *Walter the homing pigeon*
Benedictus, Roger. *Fifty million sausages*
Benjamin, Alan. *Ribtickle Town*
Berenstain, Stan. *The Berenstain bears and too much junk food*
Berson, Harold. *Pop! goes the turnip*
  The rats who lived in the delicatessen
Beskow, Elsa Maartman. *Peter in Blueberry Land*
  Peter's adventures in Blueberry Land
Bethell, Jean. *Hooray for Henry*
Biro, Val. *Gumdrop and the great sausage caper*
Black, Irma (Simonton). *Is this my dinner?*
Bolliger, Max. *The giants' feast*
  The golden apple
Bond, Michael. *Paddington and the knickerbocker rainbow*
Boutell, Clarence Burley. *The fat baron*
Brandenberg, Franz. *Fresh cider and apple pie*
Breeze, Lynn. *Baby's food*
Brierley, Louise. *King Lion and his cooks*
Bright, Robert. *Gregory, the noisiest and strongest boy in Grangers Grove*
Brimner, Larry Dane. *Country Bear's good neighbor*
Broome, Errol. *The smallest koala*
Brown, Judith Gwyn. *Max and the truffle pig*
Brown, Marc Tolon. *D. W., the picky eater*
  Pickle things
Brown, Marcia. *Stone soup*
Bruna, Dick. *The fish*
Budd, Lillian. *The pie wagon*
Buehner, Caralyn. *A job for Wittilda*
Burch, Robert. *The hunting trip*
Burningham, John. *Avocado baby*
  The cupboard
  Where's Julius?
Burt, Olive (Woolley). *Let's find out about bread*
Burton, Jane. *Animals eating*
Calhoun, Mary. *Audubon cat*
  The hungry leprechaun
Calmenson, Stephanie. *Dinner at the Panda Palace*
  Kinderkittens, who took the cookie from the cookie jar?
Carle, Eric. *My very first book of food*
  Pancakes, pancakes
  Today is Monday
  Walter the baker
Carlstrom, Nancy White. *Moose in the garden*
Carney, Margaret (Margaret Rose). *At Grandpa's sugar bush*
Carrick, Donald. *Milk*
Caseley, Judith. *Grandpa's garden lunch*
Cauley, Lorinda Bryan. *Pease porridge hot*
Cazet, Denys. *Lucky me*
Chadwick, Tim. *Cabbage moon*

Chalmers, Audrey. *Hundreds and hundreds of pancakes*
Chichester Clark, Emma. *Lunch with Aunt Augusta*
Childress, Mark. *Joshua and the big bad blue crabs*
Christelow, Eileen. *Don't wake up Mama!*
Clément, Claude. *The hungry duckling*
Coatsworth, Elizabeth. *Under the green willow*
Cocca-Leffler, Maryann. *Wednesday is spaghetti day*
Cohen, Peter Zachary. *Olson's meat pies*
Coltman, Paul. *Tinker Jim*
Conrad, Pam. *Molly and the strawberry day*
Coontz, Otto. *Starring Rosa*
Coplans, Peta. *Spaghetti for Suzy*
Cousins, Lucy. *Maisy makes gingerbread*
Cowley, Joy. *Big moon tortilla*
Cox, Judy. *Now we can have a wedding!*
  Rabbit pirates
  The West Texas chili monster
Croll, Carolyn. *Too many babas*
Crook, Connie Brummel. *Maple moon*
Curious George and the pizza
Curious George goes to a chocolate factory
Curious George goes to an ice cream shop
Cushman, Doug. *Possum stew*
Czernecki, Stefan. *The sleeping bread*
Daly, Niki. *Ben's gingerbread man*
Darling, Abigail. *Teddy bears' picnic cookbook*
Davies, Kay. *My apple*
Davis, Aubrey. *Bone button borscht*
  The enormous potato
  Sody salleratus
Davis, Maggie S. *The rinky-dink café*
Davison, Martine. *Kevin and the school nurse*
Degen, Bruce. *Jamberry*
Delton, Judy. *Rabbit finds a way*
Demarest, Chris L. *No peas for Nellie*
De Paola, Tomie (Thomas Anthony). *Pancakes for breakfast*
  The popcorn book
  Tony's bread
De Regniers, Beatrice Schenk. *Sam and the impossible thing*
Desimini, Lisa. *Moon soup*
Devlin, Wende. *Old Witch and the polka-dot ribbon*
Dixon, Ann. *The blueberry shoe*
Dodd, Lynley. *The apple tree*
Dooley, Norah. *Everybody bakes bread*
  Everybody cooks rice
Downey, Lynn. *Sing, Henrietta! Sing!*
Doyle, Malachy. *Jody's beans*
Dragonwagon, Crescent. *This is the bread I baked for Ned*
Drescher, Henrik. *The boy who ate around*
Drucker, Malka. *Grandma's latkes*
Dubowski, Cathy East. *Picky Nicky*
Du Quette, Keith. *Ripping day for a picnic*
Durant, Alan. *Snake supper*
Edwards, Frank B. *Is the spaghetti ready?*
Edwards, Pamela Duncan. *Four famished foxes and Fosdyke*
Egan, Tim. *Chestnut Cove*
Ehlert, Lois. *Eating the alphabet*
  Growing vegetable soup
Engel, Diana. *Gino Badino*
English, Karen. *Just right stew*
Esterl, Arnica. *The fine round cake*
Evans, Katie. *Hunky Dory ate it*
Everitt, Betsy. *Mean soup*
Facklam, Margery. *I eat dinner*

Kraus, Robert. *Big Squeak, Little Squeak*
  The Christmas cookie sprinkle snitcher
  Klunky Monkey, new kid in class
Krensky, Stephen. *The pizza book*
Krings, Antoon. *Oliver's strawberry patch*
Kroll, Steven. *The Hokey-Pokey man*
Kroll, Virginia L. *Lunching and munching*
Krudwig, Vickie Leigh. *Cucumber soup*
Kwitz, Mary DeBall. *Little chick's breakfast*
Landström, Olof. *Boo and Baa in windy weather*
Lapp, Eleanor. *The blueberry bears*
Lasker, Joe. *Lentil soup*
Lass, Bonnie. *Who took the cookies from the cookie jar?*
Lauber, Patricia. *Who eats what?*
Lear, Edward. *The new vestments*
Leavitt, Melvin. *Grena and the magic pomegranate*
Leblanc, Anne. *Shopping with Benjamin*
Lebrun, Claude. *Little Brown Bear does not want to eat*
Lee, Hector Viveros. *I had a hippopotamus*
Leedy, Loreen. *The dragon Thanksgiving feast*
  The edible pyramid
Lember, Barbara Hirsch. *A book of fruit*
Lemerise, Bruce. *Sheldon's lunch*
Lent, Blair. *Molasses flood*
Leonard, Marcia. *Alphabet bandits*
  Food is fun!
  Rainboots for breakfast
Levine, Abby. *Too much mush!*
Levitin, Sonia. *Nobody stole the pie*
Lewin, Betsy. *Animal snackers*
Lillegard, Dee. *The wild bunch*
Lin, Grace. *The ugly vegetables*
Lindsey, Treska. *When Batistine made bread*
Lobel, Anita. *The pancake*
London, Jonathan. *Candystore man*
  Crunch munch
  Shawn and Keeper and the birthday party
  The sugaring-off party
Losi, Carol A. *The 512 ants on Sullivan Street*
Love, Ann. *Ice cream at the castle*
Lurie, Morris. *The story of Imelda, who was small*
Lynn, Sara. *Food*
Lyon, David. *The crumbly coast*
Lyon, George Ella. *The outside inn*
Maccarone, Grace. *The lunch box surprise*
  Pizza party
McCloskey, Robert. *Blueberries for Sal*
McCully, Emily Arnold. *Popcorn at the palace*
MacDonald, Elizabeth. *Mr. MacGregor's breakfast egg*
Macdonald, Maryann. *Hedgehog bakes a cake*
McGovern, Ann. *Eggs on your nose*
MacGregor, Marilyn. *Helen the hungry bear*
McGuire, Richard. *The orange book*
Machotka, Hana. *Pasta factory*
McKee, David. *King Rollo and the bread*
MacKinnon, Debbie. *Cathy's cake*
  Find my cake!
McPhail, David M. *Pigs aplenty, pigs galore!*
Maestro, Betsy. *How do apples grow?*
Mahy, Margaret. *Boom Baby boom, boom*
  A busy day for a good grandmother
  Jam
  Simply delicious!
Manushkin, Fran. *The matzah that Papa brought home*
  Moon dragon
Marcellino, Fred. *I, crocodile*
Marshall, James. *Miss Dog's Christmas*

  Yummers!
  Yummers too
Marshall, Janet Perry. *Banana moon*
Martchenko, Michael. *Bird feeder banquet*
Martin, Antoinette Truglio. *Famous seaweed soup*
Martin, Bill (William Ivan). *Rock it, sock it, number line*
Mayer, Mercer. *Frog goes to dinner*
Meddaugh, Susan. *Martha blah blah*
Medearis, Angela Shelf. *Eat, babies, eat!*
Meijer, Marie. *The bake-a-cake book*
Miller, Edna. *Mousekin's frosty friend*
Miller, Margaret. *Time to eat*
Miller, Virginia. *Eat your dinner!*
Mitgutsch, Ali. *From lemon to lemonade*
Modesitt, Jeanne. *Lunch with Milly*
  Vegetable soup
Moffatt, Judith. *Who stole the cookies?*
Moncure, Jane Belk. *A tasting party*
Morris, Ann. *Bread, bread, bread*
Mott, Evelyn Clarke. *Dancing rainbows*
Munsch, Robert N. *Mmm, cookies!*
Munsterberg, Peggy. *Beastly banquet*
Murphey, Sara. *The roly poly cookie*
Murphy, Jill. *A piece of cake*
Murphy, Stuart J. *A fair bear share*
  Just enough carrots
Myers, Christopher A. *Turnip soup*
Myers, Edward. *Forri the baker*
Myers, Walter Dean. *How Mr. Monkey saw the whole world*
Naylor, Phyllis Reynolds. *Sweet strawberries*
Neitzel, Shirley. *We're making breakfast for mother*
Newman, Lesléa. *Matzo ball moon*
Nilsén, Anna. *Where is Percy's dinner?*
Nordqvist, Sven. *Pancake pie*
Norman, Philip Ross. *The carrot war*
Offen, Hilda. *Elephant pie*
O'Keefe, Susan Heyboer. *One hungry monster*
Okrend, Elise. *Blintzes for Blitzen*
Olaleye, Isaac. *Bitter bananas*
Orbach, Ruth. *Apple pigs*
Orgel, Doris. *Button soup*
Owen, Annie. *Hungry panda*
Oxenbury, Helen. *Eating out*
  It's my birthday
Palatini, Margie. *Zak's lunch*
Paraskevas, Betty. *The ferocious beast with the polka-dot hide*
Paterson, Diane. *Eat*
Patron, Susan. *Burgoo stew*
Patz, Nancy. *No thumpin' no bumpin' no rumpus tonight!*
Peck, Jan. *The giant carrot*
Pelham, David. *Sam's pizza*
  Sam's sandwich
Peters, Lisa Westberg. *Purple delicious blackberry jam*
Peterson, Cris. *Extra cheese, please!*
Petie, Haris. *The seed the squirrel dropped*
Pienkowski, Jan. *Food*
Pillar, Marjorie. *Pizza man*
Pinkwater, Daniel Manus. *The phantom of the lunch wagon*
  Rainy morning
Pittman, Helena Clare. *Still-life stew*
  Uncle Phil's diner
Polacco, Patricia. *In Enzo's splendid gardens*
Pomeranc, Marion Hess. *The can-do Thanksgiving*
Pomeroy, Diana. *One potato*

Porter, Sue. *One potato*
Portnoy, Mindy Avra. *Matzah ball*
Powell, Jillian. *Eggs*
Powell, Polly. *Just dessert*
Priceman, Marjorie. *How to make an apple pie and see the world*
Rabe, Berniece. *The first Christmas candy cane*
Radlauer, Ruth Shaw. *Breakfast by Molly*
Raschka, Christopher. *Arlene sardine*
Rayner, Mary. *Mrs. Pig's bulk buy*
Retan, Walter. *The steam shovel that wouldn't eat dirt*
Rice, Eve. *Sam who never forgets*
Riley, Linnea Asplind. *Mouse mess*
Ringgold, Faith. *Dinner at Aunt Connie's house*
Rix, Jamie. *The last chocolate cookie*
Robart, Rose. *The cake that Mack ate*
Rockwell, Anne F. *Apples and pumpkins*
　　The Mother Goose cookie-candy book
　　The wolf who had a wonderful dream
Rockwell, Harlow. *My kitchen*
Roffey, Maureen. *Mealtime*
Rogers, Paul (Patrick). *Somebody's awake*
Rogow, Zak. *Oranges*
Root, Phyllis. *The hungry monster*
　　Soup for supper
　　Turnover Tuesday
Rosa-Casanova, Sylvia. *Mama Provi and the pot of rice*
Rothenberg, Joan. *Matzah ball soup*
Rotner, Shelley. *Hold the anchovies!*
Rowe, John A. *Baby Crow*
Rylant, Cynthia. *Mr. Putter and Tabby bake the cake*
　　Mr. Putter and Tabby pick the pears
Saltzberg, Barney. *The Flying Garbanzos*
Sandman, Rochel. *Perfect porridge*
Scarry, Richard. *Pie rats ahoy!*
Schaefer, Jackie Jasina. *Miranda's day to dance*
Schneider, Christine M. *Picky Mrs. Pickle*
Schotter, Roni. *That extraordinary pig of Paris*
Schwalje, Marjory. *Mr. Angelo*
Schwartz, Ellen. *Mr. Belinsky's bagels*
Seabrooke, Brenda. *The swan's gift*
Senisi, Ellen B. *For my family, Love, Allie*
Seuss, Dr. *Green eggs and ham*
　　Scrambled eggs super!
Sharmat, Marjorie Weinman. *Nate the Great*
　　Nate the Great and the lost list
　　Nate the Great and the phony clue
　　Nate the Great goes undercover
Sharmat, Mitchell. *Gregory, the terrible eater*
Sharratt, Nick. *Ketchup on your cornflakes?*
Shaw, Nancy (Nancy E.). *Sheep out to eat*
Shecter, Ben. *The big stew*
Shelby, Anne. *Potluck*
Shiefman, Vicky. *Sunday potatoes, Monday potatoes*
Shirotani, Hideo. *Let's eat = Vamos a comer*
Shott, Steve (Stephen). *Mealtime*
Slepian, Jan. *The hungry thing returns*
Slobodkina, Esphyr. *The wonderful feast*
Slocum, Rosalie. *Breakfast with the clowns*
Sobol, Harriet Langsam. *A book of vegetables*
Sondheimer, Ilse. *The magic of Pomme*
Soto, Gary. *Chato's kitchen*
　　The old man and his door
　　Too many tamales
Speed, Toby. *Hattie baked a wedding cake*
Spier, Peter. *Food market*
Spohn, Kate. *Introducing Fanny*
Springer, Sally. *Let's make latkes*

Spurr, Elizabeth. *The biggest birthday cake in the world*
Stadler, John. *Animal café*
Stamaty, Mark Alan. *Minnie Maloney and Macaroni*
Steig, William. *Pete's a pizza*
Stevens, Janet. *Cook-a-doodle-doo!*
Stevenson, Jocelyn. *Red and the pumpkins*
Stewig, John Warren. *Stone soup*
Stock, Catherine. *Alexander's midnight snack*
Szekeres, Cyndy. *Suppertime for Frieda Fuzzypaws*
Taulbert, Clifton L. *Little Cliff and the porch people*
Taylor, Judy. *Dudley and the strawberry shake*
　　Dudley in a jam
Testa, Fulvio. *The land where the ice cream grows*
Thayer, Jane. *The popcorn dragon*, ill. by Jay Hyde Barnum
　　The popcorn dragon, ill. by Lisa McCue
Thompson, Vivian Laubach. *The horse that liked sandwiches*
Torres, Leyla. *Saturday sancocho*
Towle, Faith M. *The magic cooking pot*
Tunnell, Michael O. *Halloween pie*
Tusa, Tricia. *Sisters*
Uchida, Yoshiko. *The two foolish cats*
Van Rynbach, Iris. *The soup stone*
Van Woerkom, Dorothy. *Alexandra the rock-eater*
Vevers, Gwynne. *Animals that store food*
Vulliamy, Clara. *Yum yum*
Wabbes, Marie. *Rose is hungry*
Waddell, Martin. *Yum, yum, yummy*
Wallace, Karen. *Scarlette Beane*
Wallner, Alexandra. *Munch*
Ward, Sally G. *Molly and Grandpa*
Wasmuth, Eleanor. *The picnic basket*
Watanabe, Shigeo. *What a good lunch!*
Watson, Clyde. *Tom Fox and the apple pie*
　　Valentine foxes
Watson, Nancy Dingman. *Sugar on snow*
Weeks, Sarah. *Noodles*
Weir, Bob. *Panther dream*
Weiss, Monica. *Mmmm . . . cookies!*
Wellington, Monica. *Mr. Cookie Baker*
Wells, Rosemary. *Max and Ruby's Midas*
　　Yoko
Westcott, Nadine Bernard. *Peanut butter and jelly*
White, Linda Arms. *Too many pumpkins*
Wikler, Madeline. *My first seder*
Willard, Nancy. *The marzipan moon*
Williams, Arlene. *Dragon soup*
Williams, Gweneira Maureen. *Timid Timothy, the kitten who learned to be brave*
Wilson, Sarah. *Muskrat, muskrat, eat your peas!*
Wilson-Kelly, Becky. *Mother Grumpy's dog biscuits*
Windham, Sophie. *Noah's ark*
Wing, Natasha. *Jalapeño bagels*
Winthrop, Elizabeth. *Potbellied possums*
Wisniewski, David. *Tough cookie*
Wood, Audrey. *Heckedy Peg*
Wood, Leslie. *A dog called Mischief*
Wyllie, Stephen. *Dinner with fox*
Wynot, Jillian. *The Mother's Day sandwich*
Yee, Patrick. *Let's go*
Yee, Wong Herbert. *Hamburger Heaven*
Young, Miriam Burt. *The sugar mouse cake*
Zagwÿn, Deborah Turney. *Apple batter*
　　Papa's latkes
Zamorano, Ana. *Let's eat!*
Ziefert, Harriet. *Breakfast time!*
　　Rabbit and Hare divide an apple

Surprise!
Zweifel, Frances W. *The Make-Something Club*

Foolishness *see* Character traits – foolishness

Football *see* Sports – football

Foreign lands

Ada, Alma Flor. *The rooster who went to his uncle's wedding*
Aleichem, Sholem. *Hanukah money*
Aliki. *Marianthe's story one: painted words; Marianthe's story two: spoken memories*
Allen, Thomas B. (Thomas Burt). *Where children live*
Anglund, Joan Walsh. *Love one another*
Anno, Mitsumasa. *All in a day*
Baylor, Byrd. *The way to start a day*
Benjamin, Floella. *Skip across the ocean*
Berg, Leila. *Folk tales for reading and telling*
Borchers, Elisabeth. *Dear Sarah*
Brann, Esther. *'Round the world*
Bridgman, Elizabeth. *How to travel with grownups*
Bryson, Bernarda. *The twenty miracles of Saint Nicolas*
Climo, Shirley. *Stolen thunder*
Coburn, Jewell Reinhart. *Jouanah*
Darling, Kathy (Mary Kathleen). *Rain forest babies*
De Regniers, Beatrice Schenk. *Little Sister and the Month Brothers*
Domanska, Janina. *Marek, the little fool*
Dorros, Arthur. *This is my house*
Douglas, Michael. *Round, round world*
Feldman, Eve B. *Birthdays!*
Gerrard, Roy. *Jocasta Carr, movie star*
    Sir Francis Drake
Goffstein, M. B. (Marilyn Brooke). *Across the sea*
Gray, Nigel. *A country far away*
Handford, Martin. *Where's Waldo?*
Hess, Paul. *Rainforest animals*
Knight, Margy Burns. *Talking walls*
Listen to the storyteller
Low, Robert. *Peoples of the rain forest*
McDonald, Megan. *My house has stars*
Mitchell, Cynthia. *Here a little child I stand*
Morris, Ann. *Houses and homes*
    Loving
    On the go
    Play
    Work
Orstadius, Brita. *The dolphin journey*
Quackenbush, Robert M. *Henry's world tour*
Raffi. *Like me and you*
Rehnman, Mats. *The clay flute*
Robb, Brian. *My grandmother's djinn*
Schulz, Charles M. *Bon voyage, Charlie Brown (and don't come back!!)*
Scott, Sally. *The magic horse*
Sheldon, Dyan. *Love, your bear, Pete*
Shohet, Marti. *Market days*
Singer, Marilyn. *Nine o'clock lullaby*
Sis, Peter. *Madlenka*
Soto, Gary. *The old man and his door*
Svend Otto S (Svend Otto Sorensen). *The giant fish and other stories*
Van Laan, Nancy. *Sleep, sleep, sleep*

Van Woerkom, Dorothy. *Alexandra the rock-eater*
Yolen, Jane. *Street rhymes around the world*

Foreign lands – Afghanistan

Khan, Rukhsana. *The roses in my carpets*
McKay, Lawrence. *Caravan*

Foreign lands – Africa

Aardema, Verna. *Anansi does the impossible!*
    Bimwili and the Zimwi
    Bringing the rain to Kapiti Plain
    Half-a-ball-of-kenki
    Jackal's flying lesson
    Ji-nongo-nongo means riddles
    The lonely lioness and the ostrich chicks
    Misoso
    Oh, Kojo! How could you!
    Princess Gorilla and a new kind of water
    Rabbit makes a monkey of lion
    Sebgugugu the glutton
    The vingananee and the tree toad
    What's so funny, Ketu?
    Who's in Rabbit's house?
    Why mosquitoes buzz in people's ears
Abisch, Roz. *The clever turtle*
Adamson, Joy. *Elsa*
    Elsa and her cubs
    Pippa the cheetah and her cubs
Adoff, Arnold. *Ma nDa La*
Alexander, Lloyd. *Fortune tellers*
Allen, Judy. *Elephant*
Appelt, Kathi. *Elephants aloft*
Arkin, Alan. *Black and white*
Arnott, Kathleen. *Spiders, crabs and creepy crawlers*
Aruego, José. *We hide, you seek*
Barbosa, Rogério Andrade. *African animal tales*
Bare, Colleen Stanley. *Who comes to the water hole?*
Bateman, Robert. *Safari*
Bemelmans, Ludwig. *Rosebud*
Bernard, Robin. *Juma and the honey-guild*
Bernheim, Marc. *In Africa*
    A week in Aya's world
Bernstein, Margery. *The first morning*
Berson, Harold. *Kassim's shoes*
    Why the jackal won't speak to the hedgehog
Bess, Clayton. *The truth about the moon*
Bible, Charles. *Hamdaani*
Bishop, Roma. *On a safari*
Bond, Jean Carey. *A is for Africa*
Borden, Beatrice Brown. *Wild animals of Africa*
Bozylinsky, Hannah Heritage. *Lala Salama*
Bryan, Ashley. *Beat the story-drum, pum-pum*
    Lion and the ostrich chicks
    The story of lightning and thunder
Butler, Andrea. *Mr. Sun and Mr. Sea*
Carrick, Malcolm. *I can squash elephants!*
Cendrars, Blaise. *Shadow*
Ching. *The baboon's umbrella*
Chocolate, Deborah M. Newton. *Imani in the belly*
    Kente colors
Cole, Babette. *Nungu and the elephant*
    Nungu and the hippopotamus
Coleman, Evelyn. *To be a drum*
Daly, Niki. *Not so fast Songololo*
Davis, Douglas F. *The lion's tail*
Davol, Marguerite W. *How snake got his hiss*

Dayrell, Elphinstone. *Why the sun and the moon live in the sky*

Dee, Ruby. *Two ways to count to ten*

De Paola, Tomie (Thomas Anthony). *Bill and Pete*

Diakité, Baba Wagué. *The hunterman and the crocodiles*

Domanska, Janina. *The tortoise and the tree*

Du Bois, William Pène. *Otto in Africa*

Dupré, Rick. *Agassu*

Economakis, Olga. *Oasis of the stars*

Elkin, Benjamin. *Such is the way of the world*

Farris, Pamela J. *Young Mouse and Elephant*

Fatio, Louise. *The happy lion in Africa*

Feelings, Muriel. *Jambo means hello*
Menjo means one

Fournier, Catharine. *The coconut thieves*

Franklin, Kristine L. *The old, old man and the very little boy*

French, Fiona. *King of another country*

Geraghty, Paul. *The hunter*

Gershator, Phillis. *Zzzng! zzzng! zzzng!*

Graham, Lorenz B. *Song of the boat*

Greenfield, Eloise. *Africa dream*

Gregorowski, Christopher. *Fly, eagle, fly!*

Grifalconi, Ann. *Darkness and the butterfly*
Flyaway girl
Osa's pride
The village of round and square houses

Grimsdell, Jeremy. *Kalinzu*

Guthrie, Donna. *Nobiah's well*

Guy, Rosa. *Mother crocodile*

Haley, Gail E. *A story, a story*

Hanna, Jack. *Jungle Jack Hanna's safari adventure*

Hartmann, Wendy. *One sun rises*

Haskins, Jim (James). *Count your way through Africa*

Heatwole, Marsha. *Jambo, watoto!*

Hess, Paul. *Safari animals*

Hetfield, Jamie. *The Yoruba of West Africa*

Hill, Susan. *Simba's A-Z*

Holding, James. *The lazy little Zulu*

Ichikawa, Satomi. *The first bear in Africa!*

Isadora, Rachel. *A South African night*

Jackson, Bobby L. *Makimba's animal world*

Kennaway, Adrienne. *Bushbaby*
Little elephant's walk

Kessler, Cristina. *One night*

Kimmel, Eric A. *Anansi and the magic stick*
Anansi and the talking melon
Anansi goes fishing

Kipling, Rudyard. *The elephant's child*, ill. by Louise Brierley
The elephant's child, ill. by Lorinda Bryan Cauley
The elephant's child, ill. by Tim Raglin
The elephant's child, ill. by John A. Rowe
How the camel got his hump, ill. by Quentin Blake
How the camel got his hump, ill. by Tim Raglin

Kirn, Ann. *The tale of a crocodile*

Kitchen, Bert. *Tenrec's twigs*

Knutson, Barbara. *Why the crab has no head*

Kroll, Virginia L. *Africa brothers and sisters*
Faraway drums
Jaha and Jamil went down the hill
Masai and I

Laskowski, Jerzy. *Master of the royal cats*

Lester, Julius. *Shining*

Lewin, Hugh. *An elephant came to swim*
Jafta
Jafta and the wedding
Jafta - the journey
Jafta - the town
Jafta's father
Jafta's mother

Lexau, Joan M. *Crocodile and hen*

McCormick, Wendy. *Daddy, will you miss me?*

McDermott, Gerald. *Anansi the spider*
Zomo the rabbit

MacDonald, Suse. *Nanta's lion*

McKissack, Patricia C. *Who is coming?*

Maddern, Eric. *The fire children*

Mantegazza, Giovanna. *The hippopotamus*

Manushkin, Fran. *My Christmas safari*

Martin, Francesca. *The honey hunters*

Melmed, Laura Krauss. *Jumbo's lullaby*

Mitchell, Rhonda. *The talking cloth*

Moers, Hermann. *Evie to the rescue!*

Mollel, Tololwa M. (Tololwa Marti). *Dume's roar*
Kitoto the mighty
The princess who lost her hair
To dinner, for dinner

Morozumi, Atsuko. *My friend gorilla*

Morrison, Taylor. *Cheetah*

Musgrove, Margaret. *Ashanti to Zulu*

Mwalimu. *Awful aardvark*

Mwenye Hadithi. *Greedy zebra*
Hot hippo

Noble, Kate. *Bubble gum*
Oh look, it's a nosserus

Olaleye, Isaac. *Bitter bananas*
Lake of the Big Snake

Onyefulu, Obi. *Chinye*
Over in the Grasslands

Padt, Maartje. *Shanti*

Pearce, Q. L. *In the African grasslands*

Phumla. *Nomi and the magic fish*

Pitcher, Caroline. *The time of the lion*

Pohrt, Tom. *Having a wonderful time*

Prather, Ray. *The ostrich girl*

Purcell, John Wallace. *African animals*

Radcliffe, Theresa. *Bashi, elephant baby*

Riordan, James. *The coming of Night*

Robinson, Adjai. *Femi and old grandaddie*

Rose, Anne K. *Akimba and the magic cow*
Pot full of luck

Roth, Susan L. *Fire came to the earth people*

Routh, Jonathan. *The Nuns go to Africa*

Ryden, Hope. *Wild animals of Africa ABC*

Sackett, Elisabeth. *Danger on the African grassland*

Sayre, April Pulley. *If you should hear a honey guide*

Schatz, Letta. *The extraordinary tug-of-war*

Scheffler, Ursel. *Be brave, little lion!*

Schrier, Jeffrey. *On the wings of eagles*

Shepard, Steve. *Elvis Hornbill, international business bird*

Sikundar, Sylvia. *Forest singer*

Souhami, Jessica. *The leopard's drum*

Stanley, Sanna. *Monkey Sunday*

Steig, William. *Doctor De Soto goes to Africa*

Steptoe, John. *Mufaro's beautiful daughters*

Stojic, Manya. *Rain*

Swann, Brian. *The house with no door*

Swinburne, Stephen R. *Water for one, water for everyone*

Troughton, Joanna. *Tortoise's dream*

Tulloch, Shirley. *Who made me?*

Unobagha, Uzoamaka Chinyelu. *Off to the sweet shores of Africa and other talking drum rhymes*

Upper, Jonathan. *Spin's really wild Africa tour*

Van Laan, Nancy. *Little Fish lost*

Walter, Mildred Pitts. *Brother to the wind*
Ward, Leila. *I am eyes, ni macho*
Weir, Bob. *Panther dream*
Williams, Karen Lynn. *Galimoto*
　　When Africa was home
Williams, Sheron. *And in the beginning . . .*
Yoshida, Toshi. *Elephant crossing*
　　Rhinoceros mother
　　Young lions
Zaslavsky, Claudia. *Count on your fingers African style*
Zimelman, Nathan. *Treed by a pride of irate lions*

Foreign lands – Amazon

Darling, Kathy (Mary Kathleen). *Amazon A B C*
Gilliland, Judith Heide. *River*

Foreign lands – Antarctic

Benson, Patrick. *Little penguin*
Chester, Jonathan. *Splash!*
Faulkner, Keith. *The puzzled penguin*
Geraghty, Paul. *Solo*
Gibbons, Gail. *Penguins!*
Hooper, Meredith. *Tom's rabbit*
Inkpen, Mick. *Penguin small*
Seibold, J. Otto. *Penguin dreams*
Wood, Audrey. *Little Penguin's tale*
Yee, Patrick. *Baby penguin*

Foreign lands – Arabia

Alexander, Sue. *Nadia the willful*
Arabian Nights. *The first book of tales of ancient Araby*
Haskins, Jim (James). *Count your way through the Arab world*
Kimmel, Eric A. *The three princes*
Zeman, Ludmila. *Sinbad*

Foreign lands – Arctic

Carlstrom, Nancy White. *Swim the silver sea, Joshie Otter*
Dabcovich, Lydia. *The polar bear son*
Damjan, Mischa. *Atuk*
Darling, Kathy (Mary Kathleen). *Arctic babies*
De Beer, Hans. *Little polar bear and the brave little hare*
　　Little polar bear finds a friend
Dunphy, Madeleine. *Here is the Arctic winter*
Foa, Maryclare. *Songs are thoughts*
Ford, Miela. *Mom and me*
George, Jean Craighead. *Arctic son*
　　Snow bear
Gerber, Carole. *Arctic dreams*
Griese, Arnold A. *Anna's Athabaskan summer*
Grigg, Carol. *The singing snow bear*
Grindley, Sally. *Polar Star*
Hayles, Karen. *What is stuck*
Heinz, Brian J. *Nanuk, lord of the ice*
Hess, Paul. *Polar animals*
Inkpen, Mick. *Penguin small*
Kroll, Virginia L. *The seasons and someone*
London, Jonathan. *Ice Bear and Little Fox*
Low, Robert. *Peoples of the Arctic*
Luenn, Nancy. *Nessa's story*
Newton, Jill. *Polar bear scare*
Pinczes, Elinor J. *Arctic fives arrive*
Raffi. *Baby beluga*

Reynolds, Jan. *Far north*
Ryder, Joanne. *White bear, ice bear*
Sabuda, Robert James. *The Blizzard's robe*
Sackett, Elisabeth. *Danger on the Arctic ice*
Taylor, Harriet Peck. *Ulaq and the northern lights*
Trottier, Maxine. *Dreamstones*
Wild, Margaret. *Thank you, Santa*
Yolen, Jane. *Welcome to the icehouse*

Foreign lands – Argentina

Van Laan, Nancy. *The magic bean tree*

Foreign lands – Armenia

Bider, Djemma. *A drop of honey*
Hogrogian, Nonny. *The contest*
Kherdian, David. *The golden bracelet*
San Souci, Robert D. *A weave of words*

Foreign lands – Asia

Chin-Lee, Cynthia. *A is for Asia*

Foreign lands – Australia

Adams, Jeanie. *Going for oysters*
The all-amazing ha ha book
Argent, Kerry. *Animal capers*
　　Wombat and Bandicoot
Arnold, Caroline. *A walk on the Great Barrier Reef*
Baker, Jeannie. *The story of rosy dock*
　　Where the forest meets the sea
　　Window
Base, Graeme. *My grandma lived in Gooligulch*
Bassett, Lisa. *Koala Christmas*
Bodsworth, Nan. *A nice walk in the jungle*
Cox, David. *Bossyboots*
　　Tin Lizzie and Little Nell
Crew, Gary. *Bright star*
Czernecki, Stefan. *The singing snake*
Dumbleton, Mike. *Dial-a-croc*
Eversole, Robyn Harbert. *The gift stone*
Factor, Jane. *Summer*
Foreman, Michael. *Panda and the bunyips*
　　Panda and the bushfire
Fox, Mem. *Because of the bloomers*
　　Possum magic
Gelman, Rita Golden. *A koala grows up*
Harrison, Troon. *Don't dig so deep, Nicholas!*
Hathorn, Libby (Elizabeth). *The tram to Bondi beach*
Henry, Lenny. *Charlie, queen of the desert*
Hilton, Nette. *Dirty Dave*
Jacka, Martin. *Waiting for Billy*
Katz, Avner. *The little pickpocket*
Kipling, Rudyard. *The sing-song of old man kangaroo*
Lester, Alison. *Ernie dances to the didgeridoo*
　　My farm
　　Rosie sips spiders
McDermott, Beverly Brodsky. *The dreamtime*
Morpurgo, Michael. *Wombat goes walkabout*
Niland, Kilmeny. *A bellbird in a flame tree*
Nunes, Susan Miho. *Tiddalick the frog*
Paterson, A. B. (Andrew Barton). *Mulga Bill's bicycle*
　　Waltzing Matilda
Pershall, Mary K. *Hello, Barney!*
Pittaway, Margaret. *The rainforest children*
Powzyk, Joyce Ann. *Tasmania*

Reynolds, Jan. *Down under*
Rodda, Emily. *Yay!*
Roth, Susan L. *The biggest frog in Australia*
Roughsey, Dick. *The giant devil-dingo*
Thiele, Colin. *Farmer Schulz's ducks*
Trinca, Rod. *One woolly wombat*
Troughton, Joanna. *What made Tiddalik laugh*
Turner, Ethel. *Walking to school*
Vaughan, Marcia Kapok. *Wombat stew*
Wagner, Jenny. *The bunyip of Berkeley's Creek*
Walsh, Grahame L. *Didane the koala*
    The goori goori bird
Whitmore, Adam. *Max in Australia*
Wild, Margaret. *Thank you, Santa*

Foreign lands – Austria

Kahl, Virginia. *Away went Wolfgang*
Tompert, Ann. *A carol for Christmas*
Wenning, Elisabeth. *The Christmas mouse*

Foreign lands – Bali

Cox, David. *Ayu and the perfect moon*

Foreign lands – Bavaria *see* Foreign lands – Austria; Foreign lands – Germany

Foreign lands – Belize

London, Jonathan. *The village basket weaver*

Foreign lands – Borneo

Climo, Shirley. *The match between the winds*
Cushman, Doug. *The mystery of the monkey's maze*

Foreign lands – Botswana

Lewin, Betsy. *Chubbo's pool*

Foreign lands – Brazil

Cherry, Lynne. *The great kapok tree*
DeSpain, Pleasant. *The dancing turtle*
Lewin, Ted. *Amazon boy*
    When the rivers go home
Machado, Ana Maria. *Nina Bonita*
Van Laan, Nancy. *So say the little monkeys*

Foreign lands – Burma

Baillie, Allan. *Rebel!*
Froese, Deborah L. *The wise washerman*
Troughton, Joanna. *Make-believe tales*

Foreign lands – Cambodia

Coburn, Jewell Reinhart. *Angkat*
Ho, Minfong. *Brother Rabbit*
    The two brothers
Lee, Jeanne M. *Silent lotus*
Wall, Lina Mao. *Judge Rabbit and the tree spirit*

Foreign lands – Cameroon

Alexander, Lloyd. *Fortune tellers*
Bognomo, Joel Eboueme. *Madoulina*

Mollel, Tololwa M. (Tololwa Marti). *The king and the tortoise*
Njeng, Pierre Yves. *Vacation in the village*

Foreign lands – Canada

Andrews, Jan. *Very last first time*
Bannatyne-Cugnet, Jo. *A prairie alphabet*
Blades, Ann. *A boy of Taché*
    Mary of mile 18
Booth, David. *The dust bowl*
Bouchard, Dave. *Prairie born*
Brebeuf, Jean de, Saint. *The Huron carol*
Butler, Geoff. *The hangashore*
Carney, Margaret (Margaret Rose). *At Grandpa's sugar bush*
Carrier, Roch. *The longest home run*
Cleaver, Elizabeth. *The enchanted caribou*
Climo, Lindee. *Chester's barn*
Crook, Connie Brummel. *Maple moon*
Dos Santos, Joyce Audy. *The diviner*
    Henri and the Loup-Garou
Garay, Luis. *The long road*
Harrison, Ted. *O Canada*
Haskins, Jim (James). *Count your way through Canada*
Holling, Holling C. (Holling Clancy). *Paddle-to-the-sea*
Jam, Teddy. *The year of fire*
Jessell, Tim. *Amorak*
Kinsey-Warnock, Natalie. *The fiddler of the Northern Lights*
    Wilderness cat
Little old lady who swallowed a fly. *I know an old lady*, ill. by Abner Graboff
    I know an old lady who swallowed a fly, ill. by William Stobbs
    There was an old lady who swallowed a fly, ill. by Pam Adams
London, Jonathan. *The sugaring-off party*
Moak, Allan. *A big city ABC*
Munsch, Robert N. *From far away*
    Get me another one!
    Good families don't
    Love you forever
    Mud puddle
    Murmel, Murmel, Murmel
    A promise is a promise
    Thomas' snowsuit
    Wait and see
    Where is Gah-Ning?
Nichol, Barbara. *Biscuits in the cupboard*
Norman, Howard A. *The owl-scatterer*
    Who-Paddled-Backward-With-Trout
Oberman, Sheldon. *The white stone in the castle wall*
Pearson, Kit. *The singing basket*
Pickthall, Marjorie L. C. (Marjorie Lowry Christie). *The worker in sandalwood*
Poulin, Stéphane. *Can you catch Josephine?*
    Have you seen Josephine?
Smith-Ayala, Emilie. *Marisol and the yellow messenger*
Smucker, Barbara Claasen. *Selina and the bear paw quilt*
Speare, Jean. *A candle for Christmas*
Thornhill, Jan. *A tree in a forest*
Toye, William. *How summer came to Canada*
    The loon's necklace
    The mountain goats of Temlaham
Trottier, Maxine. *Prairie willow*

Valgardson, W. D. *Winter rescue*
Van Camp, Richard. *What's the most beautiful thing you know about horses?*
Ward, Lynd. *The biggest bear*
 Nic of the woods
Waterton, Betty. *Pettranella*
Woolaver, Lance. *Christmas with the rural mail*
Zagwÿn, Deborah Turney. *The pumpkin blanket*
Zeman, Ludmila. *The first red maple leaf*

Foreign lands – Caribbean Islands

Agard, John. *No hickory no dickory no dock*
Anderson, Lonzo. *The day the hurricane happened*
 Izzard
Appelbaum, Diana Karter. *Cocoa ice*
Berry, James. *First palm trees*
Bryan, Ashley. *Sing to the sun*
Buffett, Jimmy. *The jolly mon*
Carlstrom, Nancy White. *Baby-O*
Charles, Faustin. *A Caribbean counting book*
Cohen, Miriam. *Down in the subway*
Comissiong, Lynette. *Mind me good now!*
Cooper, Susan. *Jethro and the jumbie*
Dobrin, Arnold Jack. *Josephine's 'magination*
Douglas, Richardo Keens. *The nutmeg princess*
Garne, S. T. *By a blazing blue sea*
George, Jean Craighead. *The wentletrap trap*
Gershator, David. *Palampam Day*
Gershator, Phillis. *Sweet, sweet fig banana*
Gottlieb, Dale. *Where Jamaica go?*
Greenfield, Eloise. *Under the Sunday tree*
Hallworth, Grace. *Down by the river*
Huth, Holly Young. *Darkfright*
Isadora, Rachel. *Caribbean dream*
Jekyll, Walter. *I have a news*
Lessac, Frané. *Caribbean canvas*
 My little island
Linden, Ann Marie. *One smiling grandma*
McMillan, Bruce. *Sense suspense*
Milstein, Linda Breiner. *Coconut mon*
Moreton, Daniel. *La Cucaracha Martina*
Ness, Evaline. *Josefina February*
Rahaman, Vashanti. *O Christmas tree*
San Souci, Robert D. *Cendrillon*
 The faithful friend
 The house in the sky

Foreign lands – Central America

Ada, Alma Flor. *The gold coin*
Anaya, Rudolfo A. *Maya's children*
Tortillas and lullabies = Tortillas y cancioncitas
Wisniewski, David. *Rain player*

Foreign lands – Chile

Pitcher, Caroline. *Mariana and the merchild*

Foreign lands – China

Abisch, Roz. *Mai-Ling and the mirror*
Allen, Judy. *Panda*
 Tiger
Andersen, H. C. (Hans Christian). *The emperor and the nightingale*, ill. by Meilo So
 The emperor and the nightingale, ill. by James Watling

The emperor's nightingale, ill. from the Disney arcives
The emperor's nightingale, ill. by Georges Lemoine
The nightingale, ill. by Harold Berson
The nightingale, ill. by Nancy Ekholm Burkert
The nightingale, ill. by Alison Claire Darke
The nightingale, ill. by Demi
The nightingale, ill. by Beni Montresor
The nightingale, ill. by Josef Palecek
The nightingale, ill. by Regolo Ricci
The nightingale, ill. by Christopher Santoro
The nightingale, ill. by Lisbeth Zwerger
Armstrong, Jennifer. *Chin Yu Min and the ginger cat*
Bateson-Hill, Margaret. *Lao Lao of Dragon Mountain*
Behrens, June. *Soo Ling finds a way*
Birdseye, Tom. *A song of stars*
Bishop, Claire Huchet. *The five Chinese brothers*
Bright, Robert. *The travels of Ching*
Bro, Marguerite (Harmon). *The animal friends of Peng-u*
Buck, Pearl S. (Pearl Sydenstricker). *The Chinese story teller*
Chang, Margaret Scrogin. *The beggar's magic*
 The cricket warrior
Cheng, Hou-Tien. *The Chinese New Year*
Chiang, Wei. *The legend of Mu Lan = La heroina Hua Mulan*
Chin, Charlie. *China's bravest girl*
Czernecki, Stefan. *The cricket's cage*
D'Antonio, Nancy. *Our baby from China*
Dawson, Zöe. *China*
Demi. *The adventures of Marco Polo*
 The artist and the architect
 Chen Ping and his magic axe
 A Chinese zoo
 Demi's reflective fables
 Dragon kites and dragonflies
 The dragon's tale and other animal fables of the Chinese zodiac
 The empty pot
 The greatest treasure
 Liang and the magic paintbrush
 The magic boat
 The magic tapestry
 The stonecutter
 Under the shade of the mulberry tree
Diller, Harriett. *The waiting day*
Drummond, Allan. *The willow pattern story*
Fairclough, Chris. *Take a trip to China*
Flack, Marjorie. *The story about Ping*
Foley, Bernice Williams. *A walk among clouds*
Fribourg, Marjorie G. *Ching-Ting and the ducks*
Granfield, Linda. *The legend of the panda*
Greene, Ellin. *Ling-li and the phoenix fairy*
Handforth, Thomas. *Mei Li*
Haskins, Jim (James). *Count your way through China*
Heyer, Marilee. *The weaving of a dream*
Hillman, Elizabeth. *Min-Yo and the moon dragon*
Ho, Minfong. *Maples in the mist*
Hodges, Margaret. *The voice of the great bell*
Holland, Janice. *You never can tell*
Hong, Lily Toy. *How the ox star fell from heaven*
Jensen, Helen Zane. *When Panda came to our house*
Lattimore, Deborah Nourse. *The dragon's robe*
Lawson, Julie. *The dragon's pearl*
Leaf, Margaret. *Eyes of the dragon*
Lee, Jeanne M. *Legend of the Li River*
 The legend of the milky way

The song of Mu Lan
Levinson, Riki. *Our home is the sea*
Littlefield, William. *The whiskers of Ho Ho*
Lobel, Arnold. *Ming Lo moves the mountain*
Louie, Ai-Ling. *Yeh Shen*
Mahy, Margaret. *The seven Chinese brothers*
Miles, Miska. *The pointed brush . . .*
Miller, Moira. *The moon dragon*
Morimoto, Junko. *The two bullies*
Morris, Winifred. *The future of Yen-Tzu*
   The magic leaf
Mosel, Arlene. *Tikki Tikki Tembo*
Namioka, Lensey. *The laziest boy in the world*
P'an, Ts'ai-ying. *Monkey creates havoc in heaven*
Pattison, Darcy. *The river dragon*
Perkins, Al. *Tubby and the lantern*
Pilegard, Virginia Walton. *The warlord's puzzle*
Pittman, Helena Clare. *A grain of rice*
Poole, Amy Lowry. *How the rooster got his crown*
Rappaport, Doreen. *Journey of Meng*
   The long-haired girl
Rumford, James. *The cloudmakers*
Sanfield, Steve. *Just rewards, or, Who is that man in the moon and what's he doing up there anyway?*
San Souci, Robert D. *The enchanted tapestry*
Shi, Zhang Xiu. *Monkey and the white bone demon*
Skipper, Mervyn. *The fooling of King Alexander*
Slobodkin, Louis. *Moon Blossom and the golden penny*
Stafford, Kay. *Ling Tang and the lucky cricket*
Stone, Jon. *Big Bird in China*
Tan, Amy. *The Chinese Siamese cat*
   The moon lady
Tompert, Ann. *Grandfather Tang's story*
   The jade horse, the cricket, and the peach stone
Torre, Betty L. *The luminous pearl*
Tseng, Grace. *White tiger, blue serpent*
Tsubakiyama, Margaret (Holloway). *Mei-Mei loves the morning*
Va, Leong. *A letter to the king*
Van Woerkom, Dorothy. *The rat, the ox and the zodiac*
Wang, Rosalind C. *The fourth question*
   The treasure chest
Whitfield, Susan. *The animals of the Chinese zodiac*
Wiese, Kurt. *Fish in the air*
Williams, Jay. *Everyone knows what a dragon looks like*
Wolff, Ferida. *The emperor's garden*
Wolkstein, Diane. *The magic wings*
   White wave
Yacowitz, Caryn. *The jade stone*
Ye, Ting-xing. *Share the sky*
   Three monks, no water
Yen, Clara. *Why rat comes first*
Yep, Laurence. *Dragon prince*
   The junior thunder lord
   The man who tricked a ghost
   The shell woman and the king
   Tiger woman
Yolen, Jane. *The emperor and the kite*
   The seeing stick
Young, Ed (Edward). *Cat and Rat*
   High on a hill
   Little Plum
   Lon Po Po
   The lost horse
   Monkey King
   Mouse match
   Night visitors

The rooster's horns
   The terrible Nung Gwama
Young, Evelyn. *The tale of Tai Wu and Lu and Li*
Zhang, Song Nan. *The ballad of Mulan*
   The five heavenly emperors and other Chinese myths from the creation
Zimelman, Nathan. *The great adventure of Wo Ti*

Foreign lands – Colombia

Metaxas, Eric. *The monkey people*
Torres, Leyla. *Saturday sancocho*

Foreign lands – Congo (Democratic Republic)

Aardema, Verna. *Traveling to Tondo*

Foreign lands – Costa Rica

Baden, Robert. *And Sunday makes seven*
Franklin, Kristine L. *When the monkeys came back*
Keister, Douglas. *Fernando's gift = El regalo de Fernando*
Strauss, Susan. *When woman became the sea*

Foreign lands – Czechoslovakia

Bolliger, Max. *The fireflies*
Cohen, Barbara. *Here come the Purim players!*, ill. by Shoshana Mekibel
Ginsburg, Mirra. *How the sun was brought back to the sky*
Marshak, S. (Samuil). *The Month-Brothers*
Peters, Andrew. *Salt is sweeter than gold*
Vojtech, Anna. *Marushka and the Month Brothers*
Wisniewski, David. *Golem*

Foreign lands – Denmark

Andersen, H. C. (Hans Christian). *The snow queen*, ill. by Toma Bogdanovic
Bason, Lillian. *Those foolish Molboes!*
Blegvad, Lenore. *Mr. Jensen and cat*
Bodecker, N. M. (Nils Mogens). *"It's raining," said John Twaining*
Brande, Marlie. *Sleepy Nicholas*
Burdett, Lois. *Hamlet for kids*
A Christmas book
Conover, Chris. *The wizard's daughter*
Coombs, Patricia. *The magic pot*
Haviland, Virginia. *The talking pot*
Kent, Jack. *Hoddy doddy*
Lobel, Anita. *King Rooster, Queen Hen*

Foreign lands – Ecuador

Bemelmans, Ludwig. *Quito express*

Foreign lands – Egypt

Adinolfi, JoAnn. *The Egyptian polar bear*
Aliki. *Mummies made in Egypt*
Angeletti, Roberta. *Nefertari, princess of Egypt*
Bible. Old Testament. Joseph. *Joseph and his brothers*
Clements, Andrew. *Temple cat*, ill. by Kate Kiesler
   Temple cat, ill. by Alan Marks
Climo, Shirley. *The Egyptian Cinderella*

Cushman, Doug. *The mystery of King Karfu*
Daly, Niki. *Mary Malloy and the baby who wouldn't sleep*
De Paola, Tomie (Thomas Anthony). *Bill and Pete go down the Nile*
Gerrard, Roy. *Croco'nile*
Goodenow, Earle. *The last camel*
Grant, Joan. *The monster that grew small*
Hayward, Linda. *Baby Moses*
Heide, Florence Parry. *The day of Ahmed's secret*
Hutton, Warwick. *Moses in the bulrushes*
Ife, Elaine. *Moses in the bulrushes*
Kimmel, Eric A. *Rimonah of the Flashing Sword*
Laskowski, Jerzy. *Master of the royal cats*
Lewin, Betsy. *What's the matter, Habibi?*
McDermott, Gerald. *The voyage of Osiris*
McMullan, Kate (Hall). *Mummy riddles*
Marcellino, Fred. *I, crocodile*
Mayers, Florence Cassen. *Egyptian art from the Brooklyn Museum*
Mike, Jan M. *Gift of the Nile*
Oppenheim, Shulamith Levey. *The hundredth name*
Price, Leontyne. *Aïda*
The prince who knew his fate
Sabuda, Robert James. *The mummy's tomb*
Tutankhamen's gift
Stolz, Mary Slattery. *Zekmet, the stone carver*
Walsh, Jill Paton. *Pepi and the secret names*
Wynne-Jones, Tim. *Zoom upstream*

Foreign lands – El Salvador

Argueta, Manlio. *The magic dogs of the volcanoes*

Foreign lands – England

Ahlberg, Allan. *Cops and robbers*
Ambler, C. Gifford (Christopher Gifford). *Ten little foxhounds*
Anno, Mitsumasa. *Anno's Britain*
Ardizzone, Edward. *Lucy Brown and Mr. Grimes*
Armitage, Ronda. *Don't forget, Matilda*
Atkins, Jeannine. *Mary Anning and the sea dragon*
Azarian, Mary. *The tale of John Barleycorn or, From barley to beer*
Barber, Antonia. *The mousehole cat*
Beatty, Hetty Burlingame. *Moorland pony*
Belting, Natalia Maree. *Christmas folk*
Summer's coming in
Bemelmans, Ludwig. *Madeline in London*
Bennett, Jill. *Teeny tiny*
Bennett, Olivia. *A Turkish afternoon*
Bentley, Anne. *The Groggs' day out*
The Groggs have a wonderful summer
Blathwayt, Benedict. *The runaway train*
Bond, Michael. *Paddington and the knickerbocker rainbow*
Paddington at the circus
Paddington at the fair
Paddington at the palace
Paddington at the seaside
Paddington at the tower
Paddington at the zoo
Paddington Bear, ill. by John Lobban
Paddington cleans up
Paddington's art exhibit
Paddington's garden
Paddington's lucky day
Brighton, Catherine. *The fossil girl*

Brown, Ruth. *A dark, dark tale*
Burningham, John. *Borka*
Calhoun, Mary. *The pixy and the lazy housewife*
The witch's pig
Carrick, Donald. *Harold and the great stag*
Christian, Mary Blount. *April fool*
Clayton, Elaine. *The yeoman's daring daughter and the princes in the tower*
Cole, Brock. *The king at the door*
Coltman, Paul. *Tinker Jim*
Conger, Lesley. *Tops and bottoms*
Cooper, Susan. *The silver cow*
Cressey, James. *The dragon and George*
Crompton, Margaret. *The house where Jack lives*
Crossley-Holland, Kevin. *The green children*
Davidson, Amanda. *Teddy at the seashore*
Davis, Reda. *Martin's dinosaur*
Dick Whittington and his cat. *Dick Whittington*, ill. by Edward Ardizzone
Dick Whittington, ill. by Antony Maitland
Dick Whittington and his cat, ill. by Marcia Brown
Dick Whittington and his cat, ill. by Kurt Werth
Dines, Glen. *Gilly and the wicharoo*
Dominguez, Angel. *Diary of a Victorian mouse*
Drummond, Violet H. *The flying postman*
Emecheta, Buchi. *Nowhere to play*
Esterl, Arnica. *The fine round cake*
Fairclough, Chris. *Take a trip to England*
Freeman, Don. *The guard mouse*
Will's quill
Freschet, Berniece. *Bernard of Scotland Yard*
A frog he would a-wooing go (folk-song). *Mr. Frog went a-courting*
Ganly, Helen. *Jyoti's journey*
Garland, Sarah. *Seeing red*
Gauch, Patricia Lee. *On to Widecombe Fair*
Gerrard, Jean. *Matilda Jane*
Goodall, John S. *An Edwardian Christmas*
An Edwardian summer
Great days of a country house
The story of a castle
The story of a farm
The story of an English village
Gramatky, Hardie. *Little Toot on the Thames*
Greaves, Margaret. *Kate Crackernuts*
Mother Cuspen
The witch cat
The witch's servant
Haley, Gail E. *Dream peddler*
The post office cat
Herrmann, Frank. *The giant Alexander*
The giant Alexander and the circus
The Hippopotamus's birthday and other poems about animals and birds
Hodges, Margaret. *Molly Limbo*
Saint George and the dragon
Up the chimney
Hughes, Shirley. *Bathwater's hot*
Lucy and Tom's A.B.C.
Lucy and Tom's Christmas
Noisy
Out and about
The snow lady
When we went to the park
Ivory, Lesley Anne. *A day in London*
Jacobs, Joseph. *The crock of gold*
Tattercoats
James, Simon. *Leon and Bob*

Keeping, Charles. *Alfie finds the other side of the world*
    Through the window
Laird, Elizabeth. *The day Patch stood guard*
    The day Sidney ran off
Lawrence, John. *The giant of Grabbist*
Lerman, Rory S. *Charlie's checklist*
Lewis, J. Patrick. *The Christmas of the reddle moon*
Lewis, Kim. *The last train*
Little old lady who swallowed a fly. *Fancy that!*
    I know an old lady, ill. by G. Brian Karas
    I know an old lady, ill. by Steve McInturff
    I know an old lady who swallowed a fly, ill. by Glen Rounds
    I know an old lady who swallowed a fly, ill. by Nadine Bernard Westcott
    There was an old lady, ill. by Nick Bantock
    There was an old lady who swallowed a fly, ill. by Colin Hawkins
Lodge, Bernard. *Door to door*
McCully, Emily Arnold. *Popcorn at the palace*
MacDonald, Margaret Read. *The old woman who lived in a vinegar bottle*
Menter, Ian. *Carnival*
Mother Goose. *London Bridge is falling down*, ill. by Ed Emberley
    London Bridge is falling down, ill. by Peter Spier
Muller, Robin. *Mollie Whuppie and the giant*
Munro, Roxie. *The inside-outside book of London*
Newcome, Zita. *Rosie goes shopping*
Nikola-Lisa, W. *Till year's good end*
Northway, Jennifer. *Lucy's day trip*
Oakley, Graham. *The church cat abroad*
    The church mice and the moon
    The church mice at bay
    The church mice spread their wings
    The church mouse
Oldfield, Pamela. *Melanie Brown climbs a tree*
Oxenbury, Helen. *The queen and Rosie Randall*
Penney, Ian. *Ian Penney's ABC*
Petty, Kate. *On a plane*
Riggio, Anita. *Beware the Brindlebeast*
Robins, Arthur. *The teeny tiny woman*
Rogers, Paul (Patrick). *Don't blame me!*
Ross, Diana. *The story of the little red engine*
San Souci, Robert D. *The Hobyahs*
Service, Pamela F. *The wizard of wind and rock*
Seuling, Barbara. *The teeny tiny woman*
Sewall, Marcia. *The Green Mist*
    The little wee tyke
Shannon, Mark. *Gawain and the Green Knight*
Shulman, Milton. *Prep, the little pigeon of Trafalgar Square*
Smith, Barry. *Minnie and Ginger*
Solomon, Joan. *A present for Mum*
Southey, Robert. *The cataract of Lodore*
Storr, Catherine (Cole). *Robin Hood*
Tennyson, Alfred, Baron. *The brook*
Thompson, Harwood. *The witch's cat*
Unwin, Pippa. *Tomcat takes a walk*
Wahl, Jan. *Little Johnny Buttermilk*
    Widdecombe Fair
Willard, Barbara. *To London! To London!*
Wolff, Ashley. *The bells of London*
Wood, Joyce. *Grandmother Lucy in her garden*
Worthington, Phoebe. *Teddy bear baker*
    Teddy bear coalman
Zemach, Harve. *Duffy and the devil*

Foreign lands – Estonia

Moroney, Lynn. *Elinda who danced in the sky*

Foreign lands – Ethiopia

Day, Nancy Raines. *The lion's whiskers*
Kurtz, Jane. *Fire on the mountain*
    Only a pigeon
Schrier, Jeffrey. *On the wings of eagles*
Schur, Maxine Rose. *Day of delight*

Foreign lands – Europe

Bornstein, Ruth Lercher. *The dancing man*
Dunrea, Olivier. *The trow-wife's treasure*
Jaffe, Nina. *The way meat loves salt*
Sopko, Eugen. *Townsfolk and countryfolk*

Foreign lands – Fiji

Wolfson, Margaret. *Turtle songs*

Foreign lands – Finland

Allen, Linda. *The mouse bride*
De Gerez, Toni. *Louhi, witch of North Farm*

Foreign lands – France

Aliki. *The king's day*
Allen, Laura Jean. *Rollo and Tweedy and the case of the missing cheese*
Angelo, Nancy Carolyn Harrison. *Camembert*
Baker, Leslie A. *Paris cat*
Bemelmans, Ludwig. *Madeline*
    Madeline [pop-up book]
    Madeline and the bad hat
    Madeline and the gypsies
    Madeline's Christmas
    Madeline's rescue
Bergere, Thea. *Paris in the rain with Jean and Jacqueline*
Berson, Harold. *Barrels to the moon*
    Charles and Claudine
    How the devil gets his due
    Joseph and the snake
Bingham, Mindy. *Minou*
Bishop, Claire Huchet. *The truffle pig*
Brighton, Catherine. *My Napoleon*
Bring a torch, Jeannette, Isabella
Brown, Judith Gwyn. *Max and the truffle pig*
Brunhoff, Jean de. *The story of Babar, the little elephant*
Charlip, Remy. *Harlequin and the gift of many colors*
Collier, Mary Jo. *The king's giraffe*
Cox, Judy. *Rabbit pirates*
Daudet, Alphonse. *The brave little goat of Monsieur Séguin*
Dauphin, Francine Legrand. *A French A. B. C.*
DeFelice, Cynthia C. *Three perfect peaches*
De Paola, Tomie (Thomas Anthony). *Bonjour, Mister Satie*
Diska, Pat. *Andy says . . . Bonjour!*
Dumas, Philippe. *Caesar, cock of the village*
    Laura loses her head
    The story of Edward
Eisenstein, Marilyn. *Periwinkle isn't Paris*
Elzbieta. *Dikou and the Snivelly Snoak*

Fatio, Louise. *The happy lion*
   The happy lion and the bear
   The happy lion in Africa
   The happy lion roars
   The happy lion's quest
   The happy lion's rabbits
   The happy lion's treasure
   The three happy lions
Fender, Kay. *Odette!*
Fleming, Candace. *Madame LaGrande and her so high, to the sky, uproarious pompadour*
Froment, Eugène. *The story of a round loaf*
Gamgee, John. *Journey through France*
Goffstein, M. B. (Marilyn Brooke). *Artists' helpers enjoy the evening*
Goode, Diane. *Mama's perfect present*
   Where's our mama?
Harris, Leon A. *The great picture robbery*
Haseley, Dennis. *Horses with wings*
Haskins, Jim (James). *Count your way through France*
Hautzig, Esther (Rudomin). *At home*
   In the park
Hoestlandt, Jo. *Star of fear, star of hope*
Ichikawa, Satomi. *Suzanne and Nicholas at the market*
   Suzanne and Nicholas in the garden
Ingman, Bruce. *A night on the tiles*
Joslin, Sesyle. *Baby elephant's trunk*
Kimmel, Eric A. *Three sacks of truth*
Kirby, David K. *Cows are going to Paris*
Klein, Leonore. *Henri's walk to Paris*
Knight, Joan. *Bon appetit, Bertie!*
Le Tord, Bijou. *A bird or two*
Lubell, Winifred. *Rosalie, the bird market turtle*
McCully, Emily Arnold. *Mirette on the high wire*
Manson, Christopher. *Here begins the tale of the marvellous blue mouse*
Marcellino, Fred. *I, crocodile*
Marokvia, Merelle. *A French school for Paul*
Meddaugh, Susan. *Maude and Claude go abroad*
Mendoza, George. *Henri Mouse, the juggler*
Milton, Nancy. *The giraffe that walked to Paris*
Moore, Inga. *The truffle hunter*
Moore, Lilian. *Papa Albert*
Morris, Ann. *The Cinderella rebus book*
   Hello Peter = Bonjour, Rémy
Munro, Roxie. *The inside-outside book of Paris*
Napoli, Guillier. *Adventure at Mont-Saint-Michel*
O'Callahan, Jay. *Tulips*
Orgel, Doris. *Button soup*
Patron, Susan. *Burgoo stew*
Perrault, Charles. *Puss in boots*, ill. by Julia Noonan
Polacco, Patricia. *The butterfly*
Poole, Josephine. *Joan of Arc*
Raffi. *Wheels on the bus*
Rider, Alex. *A la ferme = At the farm*
   Chez nous = At our house
Ringgold, Faith. *Bonjour, Lonnie*
Rockwell, Anne F. *Poor Goose*
   The wolf who had a wonderful dream
Schiller, Barbara. *The white rat's tale*
Schotter, Roni. *That extraordinary pig of Paris*
Scribner, Charles. *The devil's bridge*
Seignobosc, Françoise. *The big rain*
   Biquette, the white goat
   Chouchou
   Jeanne-Marie at the fair
   Jeanne-Marie counts her sheep
   Jeanne-Marie in gay Paris
   Minou

   Noël for Jeanne-Marie
   Springtime for Jeanne-Marie
Shannon, Mark. *The acrobat and the angel*
Shecter, Ben. *Partouche plants a seed*
Slobodkin, Louis. *Colette and the princess*
Titus, Eve. *Anatole*
   Anatole and the cat
   Anatole and the piano
   Anatole and the Pied Piper
   Anatole and the poodle
   Anatole and the robot
   Anatole and the thirty thieves
   Anatole and the toyshop
   Anatole over Paris
Ungerer, Tomi. *Adelaide*
   The beast of Monsieur Racine
Weelen, Guy. *The little red train*
Yorinks, Arthur. *Harry and Lulu*

Foreign lands – French Guiana

Ryder, Joanne. *Jaguar in the rain forest*

Foreign lands – Galapagos Islands

Lewin, Ted. *Nilo and the tortoise*

Foreign lands – Galilee

Stewart, Dana. *Friends from Galilee*

Foreign lands – Gambia

Hoffman, Mary. *Grace and family*

Foreign lands – Germany

Allard, Harry. *May I stay?*
Attenberger, Walburga. *The little man in winter*
   Who knows the little man?
Babbitt, Natalie. *Ouch!*
Bartos-Hoppner, Barbara. *The pied piper of Hamelin*
Bechstein, Ludwig. *The rabbit catcher and other fairy tales*
Biro, Val. *The pied piper of Hamelin*
Browning, Robert. *The pied piper of Hamelin*, ill. by Patricia and Robin DeWitt
   The pied piper of Hamelin, ill. by Kate Greenaway
   The pied piper of Hamelin, ill. by Anatoly Ivanov
   The pied piper of Hamelin, ill. by Errol Le Cain
   The pied piper of Hamelin, ill. by Drahos Zak
Calhoun, Mary. *The thieving dwarfs*
Coombs, Patricia. *Tilabel*
Cooney, Barbara. *Little brother and little sister*
Croll, Carolyn. *The three brothers*
Delaney, A. *The gunnywolf*
Fairclough, Chris. *Take a trip to West Germany*
Grimm, Jacob. *The elves and the shoemaker*, ill. by Doug Cushman
   The elves and the shoemaker, ill. by Paul Galdone
   The elves and the shoemaker, ill. by Margaret Walty
   The elves and the shoemaker, ill. by Bernadette Watts
   Iron Hans
   Iron John, ill. by Trina Schart Hyman
   Iron John, ill. by Winslow Pels
   Seven at one blow
   The shoemaker and the elves, ill. by Adrienne Adams

The shoemaker and the elves, ill. by Cynthia and
  William Birrer
The shoemaker and the elves, ill. by Ilse Plume
Harper, Wilhelmina. *The gunniwolf*
Haskins, Jim (James). *Count your way through Germany*
Hodges, Margaret. *The hero of Bremen*
Hürlimann, Ruth. *The proud white cat*
Kahl, Virginia. *Droopsi*
  Maxie
Kimmel, Eric A. *The four gallant sisters*
Kinter, Judith. *King of magic, man of glass*
Latimer, Jim. *The Irish piper*
Mayer, Marianna. *The spirit of the blue light*
Mayer, Mercer. *The pied piper of Hamelin*
Morgenstern, Elizabeth. *The little gardeners*
Root, Phyllis. *Grandmother Winter*
Ross, Tony. *The pied piper of Hamelin*
Spang, Günter. *Clelia and the little mermaid*
Van Woerkom, Dorothy. *The queen who couldn't
  bake gingerbread*

Foreign lands – Ghana

Appiah, Sonia. *Amoko and Efua Bear*
Berry, James. *Don't leave an elephant to go and chase
  a bird*
Dee, Ruby. *Tower to heaven*
Lake, Mary Dixon. *The royal drum*
Medearis, Angela Shelf. *Seven spools of thread*
  Too much talk
Mollel, Tololwa M. (Tololwa Marti). *Ananse's feast*

Foreign lands – Gilbert Islands *see* Foreign
  lands – South Sea Islands

Foreign lands – Greece

Aliki. *Diogenes*
  The eggs
  Three gold pieces
  The twelve months
Allen, Judy. *Seal*
Anderson, Lonzo. *Arion and the dolphins*
Birrer, Cynthia. *Song to Demeter*
Brown, Marcia. *Tamarindo!*
Bunting, Eve (Anne Evelyn). *I have an olive tree*
Delton, Judy. *My Uncle Nikos*
Haskins, Jim (James). *Count your way through Greece*
Hol, Coby. *Niki's little donkey*
Hutton, Warwick. *Persephone*
  Theseus and the Minotaur
  The Trojan horse
Manna, Anthony L. *Mr. Semolina-Semolinus*
Mason, Jane B. *The flying horse*
Mayer, Marianna. *Pegasus*
  Perseus
Oppenheim, Shulamith Levey. *Yanni rubbish*
Steel, Barry. *Greek cities*
Stewig, John Warren. *King Midas*
Walker, Barbara K. (Barbara Kerlin). *Pigs and
  pirates*

Foreign lands – Greenland

Conrad, Pam. *Call me Ahnighito*
Hertz, Ole. *Tobias catches trout*
  Tobias goes ice fishing
  Tobias goes seal hunting

Tobias has a birthday

Foreign lands – Guatemala

Carling, Amelia Lau. *Mama and Papa have a store*
Castaneda, Omar S. *Abuela's weave*
Czernecki, Stefan. *The sleeping bread*
Mora, Pat. *The race of toad and deer*

Foreign lands – Guyana

Agard, John. *Dig away two-hole Tim*

Foreign lands – Haiti

Lauture, Denizé. *Running the road to ABC*
MacDonald, Amy. *Please, Malese!*
Van Laan, Nancy. *Mama rocks, Papa sings*
Williams, Karen Lynn. *Painted dreams*
  Tap-tap
Wolkstein, Diane. *Bouki dances the Kokioko*

Foreign lands – Himalayas

Fleming, Candace. *When Agnes caws*

Foreign lands – Holland

Anholt, Laurence. *Camille and the sunflowers*
Bouhuys, Mies. *The lady of Stavoren*
Bromhall, Winifred. *Johanna arrives*
Chasek, Judith. *Have you seen Wilhelmina Krumpf?*
Fairclough, Chris. *Take a trip to Holland*
Green, Norma B. *The hole in the dike*
Howells, Mildred. *The woman who lived in Holland*
Krasilovsky, Phyllis. *The cow who fell in the canal*
Oppenheim, Shulamith Levey. *The lily cupboard*
Reesink, Marijke. *The golden treasure*
Schubert, Ingrid. *The magic bubble trip*
Van Stockum, Hilda. *A day on skates*

Foreign lands – Hungary

Ambrus, Victor G. *Brave soldier Janosch*
  The three poor tailors
Bodnar, Judit Z. *A wagonload of fish*
Brown, Margaret Wise. *Wheel on the chimney*
Ginsburg, Mirra. *Two greedy bears*
  The good-hearted youngest brother
Hippely, Hilary Horder. *A song for Lena*
Illyés, Gyula. *Matt the gooseherd*
Kimmel, Eric A. *The valiant red rooster*
Lieberman, Syd. *The wise shoemaker of Studena*
Surany, Anico. *Kati and Kormos*
Varga, Judy. *Janko's wish*

Foreign lands – Iceland

McMillan, Bruce. *Gletta the foal*
  Nights of the pufflings
Wisniewski, David. *Elfwyn's saga*

Foreign lands – India

Alan, Sandy. *The plaid peacock*
Ambrus, Victor G. *The Sultan's bath*
Appelt, Kathi. *Elephants aloft*
Backstein, Karen. *The blind men and the elephant*
Bang, Betsy. *The cucumber stem*
  The old woman and the red pumpkin

The old woman and the rice thief
Tuntuni the tailor bird
Bannerman, Helen. *Sambo and the twins*
The story of Little Babaji
The story of little black Sambo
Barry, David. *The Rajah's rice*
Bond, Ruskin. *Cherry tree*
Flames in the forest
Bonnici, Peter. *The festival*
Brown, Marcia. *The blue jackal*
Once a mouse . . .
Bush, Barbara. *In the heart of the village*
Cassedy, Sylvia. *Moon-uncle, moon-uncle*
Cathon, Laura E. *Tot Botot and his little flute*
Chase, Catherine. *The nightingale and the fool*
Demi. *The hallowed horse*
Domanska, Janina. *Why so much noise?*
Duff, Maggie (Margaret K.). *Rum pum pum*
Easwaran, Eknath. *The monkey and the mango*
Galdone, Paul. *The monkey and the crocodile*
Ganly, Helen. *Jyoti's journey*
Gleeson, Brian. *The tiger and the Brahmin*
Gobhai, Mehlli. *Lakshmi, the water buffalo who wouldn't*
Usha, the mouse-maiden
Haskins, Jim (James). *Count your way through India*
Hirsh, Marilyn. *Leela and the watermelon*
Hodges, Margaret. *The golden deer*
Hidden in sand
Kajpust, Melissa. *The peacock's pride*
Kamal, Aleph. *The bird who was an elephant*
Kipling, Rudyard. *The miracle of the mountain*
Rikki-tikki-tavi
Kroll, Steven. *Doctor on an elephant*
Lexau, Joan M. *It all began with a drip, drip, drip*
Martin, Rafe. *The monkey bridge*
Myers, Walter Dean. *The golden serpent*
Newton, Patricia Montgomery. *The stonecutter*
Papas, William. *Taresh the tea planter*
Parkison, Jami. *Amazing Mallika*
Quigley, Lillian Fox. *The blind men and the elephant*
Rockwell, Anne F. *The stolen necklace*
Rodanas, Kristina. *The story of Wali Dâd*
Shank, Ned. *The sanyasin's first day*
Shepard, Aaron. *The gifts of Wali Dad*
Siberell, Anne. *A journey to paradise*
Singh, Jacquelin. *Fat Gopal*
Slobodkin, Louis. *The polka-dot goat*
Souhami, Jessica. *No dinner!*
Rama and the demon king
Towle, Faith M. *The magic cooking pot*
Trez, Denise. *Maila and the flying carpet*
Villarejo, Mary. *The tiger hunt*
Wahl, Jan. *Tiger watch*
Ward, Nanda Weedon. *The elephant that ga-lumped*
Whitmore, Adam. *Max in India*
Wolf, Gita. *The very hungry lion*
Young, Ed (Edward). *Seven blind mice*

Foreign lands – Indonesia

Sierra, Judy. *The gift of the crocodile*

Foreign lands – Iran

Hofmeyr, Dianne. *The stone*
Shepard, Aaron. *Forty fortunes*

Foreign lands – Iraq

Hickox, Rebecca. *The golden sandal*

Foreign lands – Ireland

Balian, Lorna. *Leprechauns never lie*
Behan, Brendan. *The king of Ireland's son*
Blazek, Sarah Kirwan. *An Irish Hallowe'en*
Bromhall, Winifred. *Bridget's growing day*
Bunting, Eve (Anne Evelyn). *Clancy's coat*
Market day
Calhoun, Mary. *The hungry leprechaun*
Climo, Shirley. *The Irish Cinderlad*
Cooper, Susan. *The Selkie girl*
Cormack, M. Grant. *Animal tales from Ireland*
Day, David. *The swan children*
De Paola, Tomie (Thomas Anthony). *Fin M'Coul*
Jamie O'Rourke and the big potato
Jamie O'Rourke and the pooka
Patrick
Gerber, Carole. *Hush! a Gaelic lullaby*
Gleeson, Brian. *Finn McCoul*
Graham, Steve. *Dear old Donegal*
Greene, Ellin. *Billy Beg and his bull*
Hänel, Wolfram. *The gold at the end of the rainbow*
Haskins, Jim (James). *Count your way through Ireland*
Haugaard, Erik Christian. *Prince Boghole*
Hodges, Margaret. *Saint Patrick and the peddler*
Jacobs, Joseph. *Hudden and Dudden and Donald O'Neary*
Kennedy, Richard. *The leprechaun's story*
Lattimore, Deborah Nourse. *The sailor who captured the sea*
McCully, Emily Arnold. *The pirate queen*
McDermott, Gerald. *Daniel O'Rourke*
MacGill-Callahan, Sheila. *The children of Lir*
Finn MacCool and the talking fish
The last snake in Ireland
To capture the wind
O'Donnell, Elizabeth Lee. *Patrick's day*
Parker, Dorothy D. *Liam's catch*
San Souci, Robert D. *Brave Margaret*
Stuart, Chad. *The Ballymara flood*
Taylor, Alice. *A child's treasury of Irish rhymes*
What do you feed your donkey on?
Zimelman, Nathan. *To sing a song as big as Ireland*

Foreign lands – Israel

Adler, David A. *A picture book of Israel*
Bible. Old Testament. David. *David and Goliath*
Brin, Ruth F. *David and Goliath*
The story of Esther
Carlstrom, Nancy White. *I am Christmas*
De Regniers, Beatrice Schenk. *David and Goliath*, ill. by Scott Cameron
David and Goliath, ill. by Richard M. Powers
Edwards, Michelle. *Chicken Man*
Elkin, Benjamin. *The wisest man in the world*
Fairclough, Chris. *Take a trip to Israel*
Haskins, Jim (James). *Count your way through Israel*
Karmi, Giora. *And Shira imagined*
Kuskin, Karla. *Jerusalem, shining still*
Metaxas, Eric. *David and Goliath*
Segal, Sheila. *Joshua's dream*

Foreign lands – Italy

Æsop. *Androcles and the lion*, ill. by Janusz Grabianski
  Androcles and the lion, ill. by Dennis Nolan
  Androcles and the lion, ill. by Robert Rayevsky
  Androcles and the lion, ill. by Janet Stevens
Anno, Mitsumasa. *Anno's Italy*
Atene, Ann (Anna). *The golden guitar*
Basile, Giambattista. *Petrosinella*
Bettina (Bettina Ehrlich). *Pantaloni*
Brighton, Catherine. *Five secrets in a box*
Brown, Marcia. *Felice*
Cauley, Lorinda Bryan. *The goose and the golden coins*
Cazzola, Gus. *The bells of Santa Lucia*
Cecil, Laura. *The frog princess*
Chafetz, Henry. *The legend of Befana*
Chapman, Jean. *Moon-Eyes*
Daly, Niki. *Bravo, Zan Angelo!*
De Paola, Tomie (Thomas Anthony). *Big Anthony, his story*
  The clown of God
  Jingle, the Christmas clown
  The legend of Old Befana
  Merry Christmas, Strega Nona
  The mysterious giant of Barletta
  The Prince of the Dolomites
  Tony's bread
Ehrlich, Amy. *Pome and Peel*
Fairclough, Chris. *Take a trip to Italy*
Fleming, Candace. *Gabriella's song*
Gál, László. *The parrot*
Galdone, Paul. *Androcles and the lion*
Gerrard, Roy. *The Roman twins*
Giannini, Enzo. *Little Parsley*
Guarnieri, Paolo. *A boy named Giotto*
Guy, Suzanne. *The music box*
Haskins, Jim (James). *Count your way through Italy*
Kimmel, Eric A. *Count Silvernose*
Kroll, Steven. *Looking for Daniela*
Lager, Claude. *A tale of two rats*
McCully, Emily Arnold. *The orphan singer*
Manson, Christopher. *The crab prince*
Michael, Emory H. *Androcles and the lion*
Morpurgo, Michael. *Jo-Jo the melon donkey*
Nones, Eric Jon. *Canary prince*
Parillo, Tony. *Michelangelo's surprise*
Peterson, Julienne. *Caterina, the clever farm girl*
Plume, Ilse. *The story of Befana*
Politi, Leo. *Little Leo*
Rayevsky, Inna. *The talking tree*
Rockwell, Anne F. *Romulus and Remus*
  The wonderful eggs of Furicchia
Sanderson, Ruth. *Papa Gatto*
Seibold, J. Otto. *Mr. Lunch borrows a canoe*
Seidler, Rosalie. *Grumpus and the Venetian cat*
Titus, Eve. *Anatole in Italy*
Ungerer, Tomi. *The hat*
Yorinks, Arthur. *The Miami giant*

Foreign lands – Jamaica

Carter, Donna Renee. *Music in the family*
Gleeson, Brian. *Anansi*
Hanson, Regina. *The tangerine tree*
Hausman, Gerald. *Doctor Bird*
Temple, Frances. *Tiger soup*
Van West, Patricia E. *The crab man*

Foreign lands – Japan

Baker, Keith. *The magic fan*
Bang, Molly. *Dawn*
Bartoli, Jennifer. *Snow on bear's nose*
Baruch, Dorothy. *Kappa's tug-of-war with the big brown horse*
Battles, Edith. *What does the rooster say, Yoshio?*
Bodkin, Odds. *The crane wife*
Bryan, Ashley. *Sh-ko and his eight wicked brothers*
Bunting, Eve (Anne Evelyn). *Magic and the night river*
Cassedy, Sylvia. *Red dragonfly on my shoulder*
Charles, Veronika Martenova. *The crane girl*
Cocagnac, A. M. (Augustin Maurice). *The three trees of the Samurai*
Coerr, Eleanor. *Sadako*
Cook, Joel. *The rat's daughter*
Damjan, Mischa. *The little prince and the tiger cat*
Dawson, Zöe. *Japan*
DeForest, Charlotte B. *The prancing pony*
Demi. *The leaky umbrella*
Dines, Glen. *A tiger in the cherry tree*
Don't tell the scarecrow
Edens, Cooper. *A present for Rose*
Fazio, Brenda Lena. *Grandfather's story*
Fifield, Flora. *Pictures for the palace*
French, Fiona. *Little Inchkin*
Fujita, Tamao. *The boy and the bird*
Gackenbach, Dick. *The perfect mouse*
Galouchko, Annouchka. *Shô and the demons of the deep*
Garrison, Christian. *The dream eater*
Hamanaka, Sheila. *Screen of frogs*
Hamilton, Morse. *Belching Hill*
Hanson, Regina. *The face at the window*
Haskins, Jim (James). *Count your way through Japan*
Heller, George. *Hiroshi's wonderful kite*
Hidaka, Masako. *Girl from the snow country*
Hodges, Margaret. *The wave*
Honda, Tetsuya. *Wild horse winter*
Hooks, William H. *Peach boy*
Hughes, Monica. *Little Fingerling*
Iké, Jane Hori. *A Japanese fairy tale*
Ikeda, Daisaku. *The cherry tree*
  Kanta and the deer
  The snow country prince
Ishii, Momoko. *The tongue-cut sparrow*
James, J. Alison. *The drums of Noto Hanto*
Johnson, Ryerson. *Kenji and the magic geese*
Johnston, Tony. *The badger and the magic fan*
Kalman, Maira. *Sayonara, Mrs. Kackleman*
Keo, Ena. *The crane wife*
Kimmel, Eric A. *The greatest of all*
Kroll, Virginia L. *A carp for Kimiko*
Kudler, David. *The Seven Gods of Luck*
Langston, Laura. *The fox's kettle*
Laurin, Anne. *Perfect crane*
Levine, Arthur A. *The boy who drew cats*
Lifton, Betty Jean. *Joji and the Amanojaku*
  Joji and the dragon
  The many lives of Chio and Goro
  The rice-cake rabbit
Little, Mimi Otey. *Yoshiko and the foreigner*
Lobel, Anita. *The dwarf giant*
London, Jonathan. *Moshi moshi*
Long, Jan Freeman. *The bee and the dream*
Luenn, Nancy. *The dragon kite*
McDermott, Gerald. *The stonecutter*

Mado, Michio. *The magic pocket*
Marston, Elsa. *The fox maiden*
Matsuno, Masako. *A pair of red clogs*
   Taro and the bamboo shoot
   Taro and the Tofu
Matsutani, Miyoko. *The fisherman under the sea*
   How the withered trees blossomed
   The witch's magic cloth
Mayer, Mercer. *Shibumi and the kitemaker*
Melmed, Laura Krauss. *The first song ever sung*
Merrill, Jean. *The girl who loved caterpillars*
Morimoto, Junko. *The two bullies*
Mosel, Arlene. *The funny little woman*
Nakatani, Chiyoko. *Fumio and the dolphins*
Namioka, Lensey. *The loyal cat*
Newton, Patricia Montgomery. *The five sparrows*
Nomura, Takaaki. *Grandpa's town*
Paterson, Katherine. *The tale of the Mandarin ducks*
Pittman, Helena Clare. *The gift of the willows*
Powers, Daniel. *Jiro's pearl*
Richard, Françoise. *On Cat Mountain*
Roy, Ronald. *A thousand pails of water*
San Souci, Robert D. *The samurai's daughter*
   The snow wife
Say, Allen. *The bicycle man*
   Grandfather's journey
   Once under the cherry blossom tree
   Tree of cranes
Shannon, George. *Spring*
Shute, Linda. *Momotaro, the peach boy*
Sierra, Judy. *Tasty baby belly buttons*
Slobodkin, Louis. *Yasu and the strangers*
Takeshita, Fumiko. *The park bench*
Tejima, Keizaburo. *Ho-limlim*
Uchida, Yoshiko. *The magic purse*
   Sumi's prize
   Sumi's special happening
   The wise old woman
Van Woerkom, Dorothy. *Sea frog, city frog*
Waite, Michael P. *Jojofu*
Weedn, Flavia. *The moon maiden*
Wells, Ruth. *The farmer and the poor god*
Williams, Laura E. *The long silk strand*
Wisniewski, David. *The warrior and the wise man*
Yagawa, Sumiko. *The crane wife*
Yashima, Mitsu. *Plenty to watch*
Yashima, Taro. *Crow boy*
   The village tree

Foreign lands – Kenya

Anderson, Laurie Halse. *Ndito runs*
McLean, Virginia O. *Kenya, jambo!*
Mollel, Tololwa M. (Tololwa Marti). *Orphan boy*
   A promise to the sun
   Rhinos for lunch and elephants for supper
Wilson-Max, Ken. *Faraha means happy*

Foreign lands – Korea

Balgassi, Haemi. *Peacebound trains*
Choi, Sook Nyul. *Yunmi and Halmoni's trip*
Choi, Yangsook. *The sun girl and the moon boy*
Climo, Shirley. *The Korean Cinderella*
Farley, Carol J. *Mr. Pak buys a story*
Fregosi, Claudia. *The pumpkin sparrow*
Ginsburg, Mirra. *The Chinese mirror*
Gukova, Julia. *Mole's daughter*
Han, Oki S. *Kongi and Potgi*

   Sir Whong and the golden pig
Haskins, Jim (James). *Count your way through Korea*
Heo, Yumi. *The green frogs*
Jaffe, Nina. *Older brother, younger brother*
Kwon, Holly H. *The moles and the mireuk*
Park, Frances. *The royal bee*
Parry, Marian. *King of the fish*
San Souci, Daniel. *In the moonlight mist*

Foreign lands – Korea (North)

Park, Frances. *My freedom trip*

Foreign lands – Kurdistan

Gerstein, Mordicai. *The shadow of a flying bird*

Foreign lands – Laos

Xiong, Blia. *Nine-in-one Grr! Grr!*

Foreign lands – Lapland

Aulaire, Ingri Mortenson d'. *Children of the north-lights*
Borg, Inga. *Plupp builds a house*
Lindman, Maj. *Snipp, Snapp, Snurr and the red shoes*
McHale, Ethel Kharasch. *Son of thunder*
Reynolds, Jan. *Far north*
Stalder, Valerie. *Even the devil is afraid of a shrew*

Foreign lands – Latin America

Garay, Luis. *Pedrito's day*
Hurwitz, Johanna. *New shoes for Silvia*
Robbins, Sandra. *The firefly star*
Torres, Leyla. *Liliana's grandmothers*

Foreign lands – Latvia

Langton, Jane. *The hedgehog boy*
Mike, Jan M. *Clever Karlis*

Foreign lands – Lebanon

Heide, Florence Parry. *Sami and the time of the troubles*
Munsch, Robert N. *From far away*

Foreign lands – Liberia

Aardema, Verna. *Koi and the kola nuts*
   The vingananee and the tree toad
Gleeson, Brian. *Koi and the kola nuts*

Foreign lands – Madagascar

Rappaport, Doreen. *The new king*

Foreign lands – Malaysia

Kaye, Geraldine. *The sea monkey*

Foreign lands – Mali

Wisniewski, David. *Sundiata*

Foreign lands – Martinique

San Souci, Robert D. *The faithful friend*

Foreign lands – Mexico

Aardema, Verna. *Borreguita and the coyote*
  Pedro and the padre
  The riddle of the drum
Alarcón, Francisco X. *From the bellybutton of the moon and other summer poems / poems = Del ombligo de la luna y otros poemas de verano / poemas*
Anaya, Rudolfo A. *Maya's children*
Ancona, George. *Pablo remembers*
Balet, Jan B. *The fence*
Bannon, Laura. *Hat for a hero*
  Manuela's birthday
Bernhard, Emery. *The tree that rains*
Blackmore, Vivien. *Why corn is golden*
Bunting, Eve (Anne Evelyn). *Going home*
Climo, Shirley. *The little red ant and the great big crumb*
Crane, Alan. *Pepita bonita*
Czernecki, Stefan. *The hummingbird's gift*
  Pancho's piñata
De Gerez, Toni. *My song is a piece of jade*
De Paola, Tomie (Thomas Anthony). *The Lady of Guadalupe*
Dupré, Judith. *The mouse bride*
Ehlert, Lois. *Cuckoo: a Mexican folktale = Cucú: un cuento folklórico mexicano*
Estes, Kristyn Rehling. *Manuela's gift*
Ets, Marie Hall. *Nine days to Christmas*
Everton, Macduff. *El circo magico modelo*
Fine, Edith Hope. *Under the lemon moon*
Fraser, James Howard. *Los Posadas*
Geeslin, Campbell. *How Nanita learned to make flan*
Gollub, Matthew. *The twenty-five Mixtec cats*
Grifalconi, Ann. *The bravest flute*
  The toy trumpet
Grossman, Patricia. *Saturday market*
Guy, Ginger Foglesong. *Fiesta!*
Hader, Berta Hoerner. *The story of Pancho and the bull with the crooked tail*
Haskins, Jim (James). *Count your way through Mexico*
Johnston, Tony. *Day of the Dead*
  The iguana brothers, a perfect day
  Isabel's house of butterflies
  Lorenzo the naughty parrot
  My Mexico = México mío
  The old lady and the birds
  The tale of Rabbit and Coyote
Kent, Jack. *The Christmas piñata*
Kimmel, Eric A. *The two mountains*
  The witch's face
Kroll, Virginia L. *Butterfly boy*
Krull, Kathleen. *Maria Molina and the Days of the Dead*
Krupp, Robin Rector. *Let's go traveling in Mexico*
Lewis, Thomas P. *Hill of fire*
McDermott, Gerald. *Musicians of the sun*
Madrigal, Antonio Hernandez. *Erandi's braids*
Martin, Bill (William Ivan). *My days are made of butterflies*
Mike, Jan M. *Opossum and the great firemaker*
Miles, Miska. *Friend of Miguel*
Mora, Pat. *The gift of the poinsettia = El regalo de la flor de nochebuena*
  The night the moon fell
Morrow, Elizabeth Cutter. *The painted pig*
Politi, Leo. *Lito and the clown*
  Rosa
Riecken, Nancy. *Today is the day*
Rohmer, Harriet. *How we came to the fifth world*
Sahagun, Bernardino de. *Spirit child*
Sanromán, Susana. *Señora Regañona*
Swope, Sam. *Gotta go! Gotta go!*
Tompert, Ann. *The silver whistle*
Ungerer, Tomi. *Orlando, the brave vulture*
Van Laan, Nancy. *La boda*
Volkmer, Jane Anne. *Song of Chirimia*
Wisniewski, David. *Rain player*
Yacowitz, Caryn. *Pumpkin fiesta*

Foreign lands – Middle East

Figley, Marty Rhodes. *The story of Zacchaeus*
Kimmel, Eric A. *The tale of Ali Baba and the forty thieves*
Matze, Claire Sidhom. *The stars in my Geddoh's sky*
Weedn, Flavia. *The ragged peddler*

Foreign lands – Mongolia

Yep, Laurence. *The Khan's daughter*

Foreign lands – Morocco

Czernecki, Stefan. *Zorah's magic carpet*
Lewin, Ted. *The storytellers*
London, Jonathan. *Ali, child of the desert*

Foreign lands – Namibia

Aardema, Verna. *Jackal's flying lesson*
Haarhoff, Dorian. *Desert December*

Foreign lands – Nepal

Reynolds, Jan. *Himalaya*

Foreign lands – Netherlands *see* Foreign lands – Holland

Foreign lands – New Guinea

Anderson, Robin. *Sinabouda Lily*
Wilson, Barbara Ker. *The turtle and the island*

Foreign lands – New Zealand

Bishop, Gavin. *Maui and the sun*
Lattimore, Deborah Nourse. *Punga the goddess of ugly*
Turner, Gwenda. *Over on the farm*

Foreign lands – Nicaragua

Rohmer, Harriet. *The invisible hunters*
  Mother scorpion country

Foreign lands – Nigeria

Daly, Niki. *Why the sun and moon live in the sky*
Gerson, Mary-Joan. *Why the sky is far away*
Medearis, Angela Shelf. *The singing man*
Mollel, Tololwa M. (Tololwa Marti). *The flying tortoise*
Olaleye, Isaac. *Bikes for rent!*
  Bitter bananas

The distant talking drum
In the Rainfield
Onyefulu, Ifeoma. *Grandfather's work*
Ogbo

Foreign lands – Norway

Allard, Harry. *May I stay?*
Allen, Linda. *The giant who had no heart*
Asbjørnsen, P. C. (Peter Christen). *The man who
kept house*
Aulaire, Ingri Mortenson d'. *East of the sun and west
of the moon*
Ola
The terrible troll-bird
Chwast, Seymour. *Bushy bride*
Dasent, George W. *East o' the sun, west o' the moon*
Emberley, Michael. *Welcome back, Sun*
French, Vivian. *Why the sea is salt*
Grieg, E. H. (Edvard Hagerup). *E. H. Grieg's Peer
Gynt*
Hague, Kathleen. *East of the sun and west of the moon*
The man who kept house
Howard, Kim. *In wintertime*
Kimmel, Eric A. *Boots and his brothers*
Easy work!
Magnus, Erica. *The boy and the devil*
Old Lars
Martin, Claire. *Boots and the glass mountain*, ill. by
Gennady Spirin
Mills, Lauren A. *Tatterhood and the hobgoblins*
Reynolds, Jan. *Far north*
The squire's bride
Wiesner, William. *Happy-Go-Lucky*
Turnabout

Foreign lands – Pakistan

Shepard, Aaron. *The gifts of Wali Dad*
Siddiqui, Ashraf. *Bhombal Dass, the uncle of lion*

Foreign lands – Palestine

Bahous, Sally. *Sitti and the cats*
Nye, Naomi Shihab. *Sitti's secrets*
Stewart, Dana. *Friends from Galilee*

Foreign lands – Panama

Janosch. *The trip to Panama*
Palacios, Argentina. *A Christmas surprise for Chabelita*

Foreign lands – Persia

Chaikin, Miriam. *Esther*
De Paola, Tomie (Thomas Anthony). *The legend of
the persian carpet*
Foley, Bernice Williams. *The gazelle and the hunter*
Manson, Christopher. *A gift for the king*

Foreign lands – Peru

Alexander, Ellen. *Chaska and the golden doll*
Llama and the great flood
Ayers, Rebecca Hickox. *Zorro and Quwi*
Charles, Donald. *Chancay and the secret of fire*
Dewey, Ariane. *The thunder god's son*
Dorros, Arthur. *Tonight is carnaval*

Ehlert, Lois. *Moon rope*
Loverseed, Amanda. *The thunder king*

Foreign lands – Philippines

Allen, Judy. *Eagle*
Arcellana, Francisco. *The mats*
Aruego, José. *A crocodile's tale*
Look what I can do
Rockabye crocodile
Charlot, Martin. *Felisa and the magic tikling bird*
San Souci, Robert D. *Pedro and the monkey*

Foreign lands – Poland

Adler, David A. *The children of Chelm*
Bernhard, Josephine Butkowska. *Lullaby*
Nine cry-baby dolls
Carey, Valerie Scho. *Tsugele's broom*
Clement, Gary. *Just stay put*
Din dan don, it's Christmas
Domanska, Janina. *The best of the bargain*
Busy Monday morning
King Krakus and the dragon
Look, there is a turtle flying
Gordon, Ruth. *Feathers*
Nerlove, Miriam. *Flowers on the wall*
Pellowski, Anne. *The nine crying dolls*
Porazinska, Janina. *The enchanted book*
Turska, Krystyna. *The magician of Cracow*
The woodcutter's duck

Foreign lands – Portugal

Balet, Jan B. *The gift*
Joanjo

Foreign lands – Puerto Rico

Belpré, Pura. *Dance of the animals*
Pérez and Martina
Crespo, George. *How the sea began*
Ichikawa, Satomi. *Isabela's ribbons*
Jaffe, Nina. *The golden flower*
London, Jonathan. *Hurricane!*
Martel, Cruz. *Yagua days*
Mike, Jan M. *Juan Bobo and the horse of seven colors*
Nodar, Carmen Santiago. *Abuelita's paradise*
Pitre, Felix. *Paco and the witch*
Pomerantz, Charlotte. *The outside dog*
Rohmer, Harriet. *Atariba and Niguayona*
Roth, Susan L. *Another Christmas*
Wallner, Alexandra. *Sergio and the hurricane*

Foreign lands – Romania

Matthews, Wendy. *The gift of a traveler*
Metaxas, Eric. *The gardener's apprentice*
Olson, Arielle North. *Noah's cats and the devil's fire*

Foreign lands – Russia

Afanas'ev, Aleksandr N. *Russian folk tales*
Salt
Aksakov, Sergei. *The scarlet flower*
Arnold, Katya. *Baba Yaga and the little girl*
Knock, knock, teremok!
Ayres, Becky Hickox. *Matreshka*
Beim, Lorraine. *Sasha and the samovar*

Foreign lands – Rwanda

Foreign lands – Sahara Desert

Foreign lands – Scandinavia

Foreign lands – Scotland

Kellyburn Braes
Blegvad, Erik. *Burnie's hill*
Brown, Ruth. *The ghost of Greyfriar's Bobby*
Burdett, Lois. *Macbeth for kids*
Calhoun, Mary. *The runaway brownie*
Cate, Rikki. *A cat's tale*
Cooper, Susan. *The Selkie girl*
    Tam Lin
Del Negro, Janice. *Lucy Dove*
Duncan, Jane. *Janet Reachfar and Chickabird*
Fern, Eugene. *The most frightened hero*
Forest, Heather. *The woman who flummoxed the fairies*
A frog he would a-wooing go (folk-song). *The frog went a-courting*, adapt. and ill. by Dominic Catalano
Gramatky, Hardie. *Little Toot and the Loch Ness monster*
Hedderwick, Mairi. *Katie Morag and the big boy cousins*
    Katie Morag and the tiresome Ted
    Katie Morag and the two grandmothers
    Katie Morag delivers the mail
Jeffers, Susan. *Wild Robin*
Leaf, Munro. *Wee Gillis*
Lewis, Naomi. *Puffin*
MacGill-Callahan, Sheila. *The seal prince*
Manning, Mick. *A ruined house*
Robertson, Joanne. *Sea witches*
Sewall, Marcia. *The wee, wee mannie and the big, big coo*
White, Carolyn. *Whuppity Stoorie*
Yolen, Jane. *Greyling*

Foreign lands – Serbia

Mike, Jan M. *The bird maiden*

Foreign lands – Siam *see* Foreign lands – Thailand

Foreign lands – Siberia

Bernhard, Emery. *The girl who wanted to hunt*
    How Snowshoe Hare rescued the sun

Foreign lands – South Africa

Angelou, Maya. *My painted house, my friendly chicken, and me*
Daly, Niki. *The boy on the beach*
    Jamela's dress
    Not so fast Songololo
Deetlefs, Rene. *Tabu and the dancing elephants*
Haarhoff, Dorian. *Desert December*
Isadora, Rachel. *At the crossroads*
    Over the green hills
    A South African night
Kahn, Rosemary. *Grandma's hat*
Lewin, Hugh. *Jafta - the homecoming*
Mennen, Ingrid. *Somewhere in Africa*
Moodie, Fiona. *Nabulela*
Schermbrucker, Reviva. *Charlie's house*
Seed, Jenny. *Ntombi's song*
Wilson-Max, Ken. *Halala means welcome*

Foreign lands – South America

Alexander, Ellen. *Chaska and the golden doll*

Aruego, José. *Pilyo the piranha*
Brusca, María Cristina. *The cook and the king*
    When jaguars ate the moon
Cowcher, Helen. *Rain forest*
Fischetto, Laura. *The jungle is my home*
Flora. *Feathers like a rainbow*
Frasconi, Antonio. *The snow and the sun = la nieve y el sol*
Gramatky, Hardie. *Bolivar*
Jordan, Martin. *Amazon alphabet*
    Jungle days, jungle nights
Maestro, Giulio. *The tortoise's tug of war*
Maiorano, Robert. *Francisco*
Reynolds, Jan. *Amazon*
Rockwell, Anne F. *The good llama*
Schaefer, Jackie Jasina. *Miranda's day to dance*
Smith-Ayala, Emilie. *Marisol and the yellow messenger*
Surany, Anico. *Ride the cold wind*
Thomson, Ruth. *The Rainforest Indians*
Troughton, Joanna. *How the birds changed their feathers*
Van Laan, Nancy. *The legend of El Dorado*

Foreign lands – South Sea Islands

Mordvinoff, Nicolas. *Coral Island*

Foreign lands – Soviet Union

Malkovych, Ivan. *The cat and the rooster*
Polacco, Patricia. *Luba and the wren*

Foreign lands – Spain

Duff, Maggie (Margaret K.). *The princess and the pumpkin*
García Lorca, Federico. *The Lieutenant Colonel and the gypsy*
Hautzig, Esther (Rudomin). *At home*
    In the park
Kimmel, Eric A. *Bernal and Florinda*
    Squash it!
Leaf, Munro. *The story of Ferdinand the bull*
Oleson, Claire. *For Pipita, an orange tree*
Sierra, Judy. *The beautiful butterfly*
Vernon, Adele. *The riddle*
Zamorano, Ana. *Let's eat!*

Foreign lands – Sri Lanka

Troughton, Joanna. *The quail's egg*

Foreign lands – Sudan

Aardema, Verna. *What's so funny, Ketu?*

Foreign lands – Suriname

Lichtveld, Noni. *I lost my arrow in a kankan tree*

Foreign lands – Sweden

Ayers, Rebecca Hickox. *Per and the Dala horse*
Beskow, Elsa Maartman. *Children of the forest*
    Pelle's new suit
    Peter in Blueberry Land
    Peter's adventures in Blueberry Land
Hooks, William H. *The legend of the Christmas rose*
Langton, Jane. *The queen's necklace*

Lindgren, Astrid. *A calf for Christmas*
   Christmas in noisy village
   Christmas in the stable
   Do you know Pippi Longstocking?
   Lotta's Christmas surprise
   Pippi Longstocking's after-Christmas party
   The tomten
   The tomten and the fox
Lindman, Maj. *Flicka, Ricka, Dicka and a little dog*
   Flicka, Ricka, Dicka and the new dotted dress
   Flicka, Ricka, Dicka bake a cake
   Sailboat time
   Snipp, Snapp, Snurr and the buttered bread
   Snipp, Snapp, Snurr and the magic horse
   Snipp, Snapp, Snurr and the reindeer
   Snipp, Snapp, Snurr and the seven dogs
   Snipp, Snapp, Snurr and the yellow sled
Peterson, Hans. *Erik and the Christmas horse*
Schaefer, Carole Lexa. *Under the midsummer sky*
Schwartz, David M. *Sugargrandpa*
Sundvall, Viveca. *Mimi and the biscuit factory*
Weedn, Flavia. *The magic cap*
Westerberg, Christine. *The cap that mother made*
Zemach, Harve. *Nail soup*

Foreign lands – Switzerland

Allamand, Pascale. *Cocoa beans and daisies*
Baumann, Kurt. *Piro and the fire brigade*
Bawden, Nina. *William Tell*
Carigiet, Alois. *The pear tree, the birch tree and the barberry bush*
Chönz, Selina. *A bell for Ursli*
   Florina and the wild bird
   The snowstorm
Fisher, Leonard Everett. *William Tell*
Freeman, Don. *Ski pup*
Ostheeren, Ingrid. *The new dog*
Stone, Marti. *The singing fir tree*

Foreign lands – Taiwan

Reddix, Valerie. *Dragon kite of the autumn moon*

Foreign lands – Tanzania

Grimes, Nikki. *Is it far to Zanzibar?*
Martin, Francesca. *Clever Tortoise*
Mollel, Tololwa M. (Tololwa Marti). *Big boy*
   Kele's secret
   My rows and piles of coins
   Shadow dance
   Song bird
   Subira subira
Stuve-Bodeen, Stephanie. *Elizabeti's doll*
   Mama Elizabeti

Foreign lands – Thailand

Ayer, Jacqueline. *Nu Dang and his kite*
   The paper-flower tree
   A wish for little sister
Ho, Minfong. *Hush!*
Krudop, Walter Lyon. *The man who caught fish*
MacDonald, Margaret Read. *The girl who wore too much*
Maugham, W. Somerset (William Somerset). *Princess September and the nightingale*
Northrup, Mili. *The watch cat*

Oliviero, Jamie. *Som See and the magic elephant*
Shea, Pegi Deitz. *The whispering cloth*

Foreign lands – Tibet

Schroeder, Alan. *The stone lion*
Tsultim, Yeshe. *The mouse king*

Foreign lands – Trinidad

Joseph, Lynn. *Coconut kind of day*
   An island Christmas
   Jasmine's parlour day
   Jump up time

Foreign lands – Turkey

Bennett, Olivia. *A Turkish afternoon*
Dewey, Ariane. *The fish Peri*
Walker, Barbara K. (Barbara Kerlin). *Teeny-Tiny and the witch-woman*
Yolen, Jane. *Little Mouse and Elephant*

Foreign lands – Tyrol

Bemelmans, Ludwig. *Hansi*
Sawyer, Ruth. *The remarkable Christmas of the cobbler's sons*

Foreign lands – Ukraine

Brett, Jan. *The mitten*
Gorbachev, Valeri. *The Fool of the world and the flying ship*
Hale, Irina. *The naughty crow*
Kay, Helen. *An egg is for wishing*
Kimmel, Eric A. *The birds' gift*
   One Eye, Two Eyes, Three Eyes
   Sirko and the wolf
Lisowski, Gabriel. *How Tevye became a milkman*
Malkovych, Ivan. *The cat and the rooster*
Ransome, Arthur. *The fool of the world and the flying ship*
Rudolph, Marguerita. *How a shirt grew in the field*, ill. by Erika Weihs
   How a shirt grew in the field, ill. by Yaroslava
Tresselt, Alvin R. *The mitten*

Foreign lands – Uzbekistan

Sandman, Rochel. *Perfect porridge*

Foreign lands – Vatican City

Lawrence, John. *Pope Leo's elephant*

Foreign lands – Venezuela

Barbot, Daniel. *A bicycle for Rosaura*
Cowcher, Helen. *Jaguar*

Foreign lands – Vietnam

Boholm-Olsson, Eva. *Tuan*
Breckler, Rosemary K. *Sweet dried apples*
Garland, Sherry. *The lotus seed*
   Why ducks sleep on one leg
Keller, Holly. *Grandfather's dream*
Lee, Jeanne M. *Ba-Nam*
McKay, Lawrence. *Journey home*

Shepard, Aaron. *The crystal heart*
Trân-Khánh-Tuyê. *The little weaver of Thái-Yên Village*

Foreign lands – Wales

Cullen, Lynn. *The mightiest heart*
MacDonald, Margaret Read. *Slop!*

Foreign lands – West Indies

Burgie, Irving. *Caribbean carnival*
Rahaman, Vashanti. *O Christmas tree*

Foreign lands – Zaire

Aardema, Verna. *Traveling to Tondo*
Knutson, Barbara. *Why the crab has no head*

Foreign lands – Zanzibar

Aardema, Verna. *Bimwili and the Zimwi*
Grimes, Nikki. *Is it far to Zanzibar?*

Foreign languages

ABCDEFGHIJKLMNOPQRSTUVWXYZ in English and Spanish
Ada, Alma Flor. *El Arbol de Navidad : The Christmas tree*
 Gathering the sun
Alarcón, Francisco X. *From the bellybutton of the moon and other summer poems / poems = Del ombligo de la luna y otros poemas de verano / poemas*
Alger, Leclaire Gowans. *Kellyburn Braes*
Anglund, Joan Walsh. *Love one another*
Baden, Robert. *And Sunday makes seven*
Baldner, Gaby. *Joba and the wild boar*
Bateson-Hill, Margaret. *Lao Lao of Dragon Mountain*
Bernard, Robin. *Juma and the honey-guild*
Bertrand, Diane Gonzales. *Family / familia*
Blue, Rose. *I am here*
Borlenghi, Patricia. *From albatross to zoo*
Bowden, Miriam. *The adventure of Paz in the land of numbers*
Bozylinsky, Hannah Heritage. *Lala Salama*
Breckler, Rosemary K. *Hoang breaks the lucky teapot*
Brown, Ruth. *Alphabet times four*
Chiang, Wei. *The legend of Mu Lan = La heroina Hua Mulan*
A child's picture English-Hebrew dictionary
Cisneros, Sandra. *Hairs = Pelitos*
Conrad, Pam. *Animal lingo*
Córdova, Amy. *Abuelita's heart*
Covault, Ruth M. *Pablo and Pimienta*
Dabcovich, Lydia. *The keys to my kingdom*
Dauphin, Francine Legrand. *A French A. B. C.*
De Gerez, Toni. *My song is a piece of jade*
Delacre, Lulu. *Arroz con leche*
 Las Navidades
De Zutter, Hank. *Who says a dog goes bow-wow?*
Diska, Pat. *Andy says . . . Bonjour!*
Dorros, Arthur. *Abuela*
Du Bois, William Pène. *The hare and the tortoise and the tortoise and the hare*
Duerrstein, Richard. *In . . . out*
 One Mickey Mouse

Dunham, Meredith. *Colors*
 Numbers: how do you say it?
 Picnic
 Shapes
Edwards, Michelle. *Alef-bet*
Ehlert, Lois. *Cuckoo: a Mexican folktale = Cucú: un cuento folklórico mexicano*
 Moon rope
Elya, Susan Middleton. *Say hola to Spanish*
Evans, Lezlie. *Can you count ten toes?*
Everton, Macduff. *El circo magico modelo*
Faulkner, Keith. *My first one hundred words in French and English*
Feder, Jane. *Table, chair, bear*
Feelings, Muriel. *Jambo means hello*
 Menjo means one
Foster, Karen Sharp. *Good night my little chicks = Buenas noches mis pollitos*
Frasconi, Antonio. *See again, say again*
 See and say
 The snow and the sun = la nieve y el sol
Geraty, Virginia Mixson. *Gullah night before Christmas*
Gerber, Carole. *Hush! a Gaelic lullaby*
Gershator, David. *Palampam Day*
Gunning, Monica. *The two Georges*
Guy, Ginger Foglesong. *Fiesta!*
Hammond, Anna. *This home we have made*
Haring, Keith. *10*
Haskins, Jim (James). *Count your way through Africa*
 Count your way through Brazil
 Count your way through France
 Count your way through Germany
 Count your way through Greece
 Count your way through India
 Count your way through Israel
 Count your way through Italy
 Count your way through Korea
 Count your way through Mexico
Hautzig, Esther (Rudomin). *At home*
 In the park
Hill, Eric. *Spot's big book of colors, shapes and numbers; El libro grande de Spot*
 Spot's big book of words; El libro grande de las palabras de Spot
The house that Jack built. *The house that Jack built, ill. by Antonio Frasconi*
Jack and the beanstalk. *Jack and the beanstalk / Juan y los frijoles magicos*
Jaynes, Ruth M. *Tell me please! What's that?*
Johnson, Diana F. *Princesa and Friskie*
Johnston, Tony. *My Mexico = México mío*
 The old lady and the birds
Joslin, Sesyle. *Baby elephant goes to China*
 Baby elephant's trunk
 Señor Baby Elephant, the pirate
Kahn, Michèle. *My everyday Spanish word book*
Keats, Ezra Jack. *My dog is lost!*
Keister, Douglas. *Fernando's gift = El regalo de Fernando*
Koplow, Lesley. *Tanya and the tobo man = Tanya y el hombre tobo*
Leventhal, Debra. *What is your language?*
Lomas Garza, Carmen. *In my family*
Luenn, Nancy. *A gift for Abuelita*
McKissack, Patricia C. *Ada, la desordenada*
Macsolis. *Baile de luna*
Mado, Michio. *The magic pocket*
Matsutani, Miyoko. *How the withered trees blossomed*

Matthias, Catherine. *Arriba y abajo*
   Demasidados globos
   Sal y entra
Maury, Inez. *My mother the mail carrier*
Milios, Rita. *Yo soy = I am*
Miller, Elizabeth I. *Just like home = Como en mi tierra*
Moore, Lilian. *Papa Albert*
Mora, Pat. *Confetti*
   Delicious hullabaloo = Pachanga deliciosa
   The desert is my mother = El desierto es mi madre
   The gift of the poinsettia = El regalo de la flor de nochebuena
   Listen to the desert = Oye al desierto
   The race of toad and deer
   Uno, dos, tres = One, two, three
Moreton, Daniel. *La Cucaracha Martina*
Morris, Ann. *Hello Peter = Bonjour, Rémy*
Mother Goose. *Mother Goose in French*
   Mother Goose in Spanish
   Rimes de la Mere Oie
Nomura, Takaaki. *Grandpa's town*
Nye, Naomi Shihab. *Sitti's secrets*
On the little hearth
Pak, Soyung. *Dear Juno*
Pomerantz, Charlotte. *If I had a Paka*
   The tamarindo puppy and other poems
Rattigan, Jama Kim. *The woman in the moon*
Reasoner, Charles. *Who pretends?*
Reed, Lynn Rowe. *Pedro, his perro, and the alphabet sombrero*
Ricklen, Neil. *My clothes = Mi ropa*
   My colors = Mis colores
   My family = Mi familia
   My numbers = Mi numeros
Rider, Alex. *A la ferme = At the farm*
   Chez nous = At our house
Roe, Eileen. *Con mi hermano = With my brother*
Rosario, Idalia. *Idalia's project ABC*
Rothman, Joel. *This can lick a lollipop*
Schaffer, Marion. *I love my cat!*
Schotter, Roni. *That extraordinary pig of Paris*
Serfozo, Mary. *Welcome Roberto! Bienvenido, Roberto!*
Shirotani, Hideo. *Let's eat = Vamos a comer*
   Let's take a walk = Vamos a caminar
   What color? = Qué color?
Simon, Norma. *What do I say?*
Soto, Gary. *Chato's kitchen*
   Too many tamales
Standon, Anna. *Three little cats*
Steiner, Charlotte. *A friend is "Amie"*
Stevens, Cat. *Teaser and the firecat*
Takeshita, Fumiko. *The park bench*
Tortillas and lullabies = Tortillas y cancioncitas
Va, Leong. *A letter to the king*
Vagin, Vladimir Vasil'evich. *Here comes the cat!*
Van Laan, Nancy. *La boda*
   Sleep, sleep, sleep
Volkmer, Jane Anne. *Song of Chirimia*
Wiese, Kurt. *You can write Chinese*
Wilson, Barbara Ker. *ABC et = and 123*
Wilson-Max, Ken. *Faraha means happy*
   Halala means welcome
Winter, Jonah. *Diego*
Yolen, Jane. *Street rhymes around the world*
Zola, Meguido. *The dream of promise*

Forest rangers *see* Careers – park rangers

Forest, woods

Ada, Alma Flor. *The unicorn of the west*
Adler, David A. *Redwoods are the tallest trees in the world*
Ahlberg, Janet. *Jeremiah in the dark wood*
Alborough, Jez. *Where's my teddy?*
Allen, Gertrude E. *Everyday animals*
Anglund, Joan Walsh. *Nibble nibble mousekin*
Anholt, Laurence. *The forgotten forest*
Armer, Laura Adams. *The forest pool*
Arneson, D. J. *Secret places*
Arnold, Caroline. *The terrible Hodag*
   A walk in the woods
Arnosky, Jim. *Crinkleroot's guide to knowing the trees*
Baker, Jeannie. *Where the forest meets the sea*
Baumann, Hans. *Mischa and his brothers*
Berenstain, Stan. *The Berenstain bears and the ghost of the forest*
Beskow, Elsa Maartman. *Children of the forest*
Blake, Robert J. *The perfect spot*
Bond, Ruskin. *Flames in the forest*
Bowen, Betsy. *Antler, bear, canoe*
   Tracks in the wild
Bradman, Tony. *Look out, he's behind you*
Buff, Mary (Marsh). *Dash and Dart*
   Forest folk
Carrick, Carol. *A clearing in the forest*
Carrick, Donald. *Harold and the great stag*
Carrier, Lark. *A tree's tale*
Cartlidge, Michelle. *Bear in the forest*
Chall, Marsha Wilson. *Up north at the cabin*
Cherry, Lynne. *Archie, follow me*
Christiana, David. *White nineteens*
Cooper, Ann (Ann C.). *In the forest*
Cowcher, Helen. *Rain forest*
Cristini, Ermanno. *In the woods*
Darling, Kathy (Mary Kathleen). *Rain forest babies*
Davidson, Jill A. *And that's what happened to little Lucy*
Day, David. *King of the woods*
Dunphy, Madeleine. *Here is the tropical rain forest*
Edwards, Richard. *The forest child*
Ets, Marie Hall. *Another day*
   In the forest
Franklin, Kristine L. *When the monkeys came back*
Fraser, Mary Ann. *Forest fire!*
Frost, Robert. *Stopping by woods on a snowy evening*
Gaffney, Michael. *Secret forests*
George, Lindsay Barrett. *In the woods*
George, William T. *Christmas at Long Pond*
Geraghty, Paul. *The great green forest*
Gibbons, Gail. *Nature's green umbrella*
Gilliland, Judith Heide. *River*
Grahame, Kenneth. *The wind in the willows*
Greenaway, Shirley. *Forests*
Greene, Carol. *I can be a forest ranger*
Gregory, Valiska. *Through the mickle woods*
Grimm, Jacob. *Hansel and Gretel*, ill. by Adrienne Adams
   Hansel and Gretel, ill. by Anthony Browne
   Hansel and Gretel, ill. by Susan Jeffers
   Hansel and Gretel, ill. by Winslow P. Pels
   Hansel and Gretel, ill. by Jane Ray
   Hansel and Gretel, ill. by Conxita Rodriguez
   Hansel and Gretel, ill. by Christopher Santoro
   Hansel and Gretel, ill. by John Wallner
   Hansel and Gretel, ill. by Paul O. Zelinsky
   Hansel and Gretel, ill. by Lisbeth Zwerger

Grindley, Sally. *Little Sibu*
Grupper, Jonathan. *Destination, rain forest*
Hague, Kathleen. *The legend of the Veery bird*
Haseley, Dennis. *My father doesn't know about the woods and me*
Helldorfer, M. C. (Mary Claire). *Night of the white stag*
Hess, Paul. *Rainforest animals*
Hill, Eric. *Spot's walk in the woods*
Hill, Mary Lou. *My dad's a smokejumper*
Himmelman, John. *A wood frog's life*
Hines, Gary. *The day of the high climber*
Hirschi, Ron. *Faces in the forest*
  Forest
  Who lives in . . . Alligator Swamp?
  Who lives in . . . the forest?
Hodges, Margaret. *Buried moon*
  Comus
Holder, Heidi. *Carmine the crow*
Holmes, Efner Tudor. *Deer in the hollow*
Hyman, Trina Schart. *The enchanted forest*
Iwamura, Kazuo. *The fourteen forest mice and the harvest moon watch*
  The fourteen forest mice and the spring meadow picnic
  The fourteen forest mice and the summer laundry day
  The fourteen forest mice and the winter sledding day
Jam, Teddy. *The year of fire*
Jaspersohn, William. *Timber!*
Johnston, Tony. *Bigfoot Cinderrrrella*
Jones, Chuck. *William the backwards skunk*
Keister, Douglas. *Fernando's gift = El regalo de Fernando*
Kerins, Tony (Anthony). *The brave ones*
Krupinski, Loretta. *Into the woods*
Lasky, Kathryn. *Marven of the Great North Woods*
Latimer, Jim. *Going the moose way home*
Leister, Mary. *The silent concert*
Lerner, Carol. *Flowers of a woodland spring*
Le Tord, Bijou. *The river and the rain*
Lipkind, William. *The boy and the forest*
Low, Robert. *Peoples of the rain forest*
Luenn, Nancy. *Song for the ancient forest*
Lukesová, Milena. *Julian in the autumn woods*
Lyon, George Ella. *Counting on the woods*
McConnachie, Brian. *Lily of the forest*
McCourt, Lisa. *The rainforest counts!*
Mantegazza, Giovanna. *Look inside a rainforest*
Maris, Ron. *Hold tight, bear!*
Marshall, Edward. *Troll country*
Marshall, James. *Hansel and Gretel*
Martin, Bill (William Ivan). *A beasty story*
Miklowitz, Gloria D. *Save that raccoon!*
Miles, Miska. *The fox and the fire*
  Sylvester Jones and the voice in the forest
Miller, Edna. *Mousekin's ABC*
  Mousekin's close call
  Mousekin's lost woodland
  Mousekin's Thanksgiving
Moore, Inga. *Fifty red night-caps*
Mora, Emma. *Animals of the forest*
  Gideon, the little bear cub
Muller, Gerda. *Around the oak*
Nail, James T. *Whose tracks are these?*
Newton, James R. *A forest is reborn*
  Forest log
O'Donnell, Peter. *Moonlit journey*
Olaleye, Isaac. *Lake of the Big Snake*
Osborne, Mary Pope. *Molly and the prince*
Owen, Roy. *My night forest*

Parnall, Peter. *The rock*
Pascoe, Gwen. *Deep in a rainforest*
Paul, Anthony. *The tiger who lost his stripes*
Pearson, Tracey Campbell. *The purple hat*
Peet, Bill (William Bartlett). *Big bad Bruce*
Peters, Lisa Westberg. *Meg and dad discover treasure in the air*
Peyo. *The Smurfs and their woodland friends*
Porter, Sue. *Little Wolf and the giant*
Prather, Ray. *The ostrich girl*
Prusski, Jeffrey. *Bring back the deer*
Reed-Jones, Carol. *The tree in the ancient forest*
Rich, Scharlotte. *Who made the wild woods?*
Ross, Tony. *Hansel and Gretel*
Ryder, Joanne. *Jaguar in the rain forest*
Schaefer, Carole Lexa. *Down in the woods at sleepytime*
Scheidl, Gerda Marie. *Can we help you, Saint Nicholas?*
Schick, Eleanor. *A surprise in the forest*
Seligson, Susan. *Amos camps out*
Seymour, Peter S. *What's in the prehistoric forest?*
Sikundar, Sylvia. *Forest singer*
Simple gifts
Slobodkin, Louis. *Melvin, the moose child*
Spohn, David. *Winter wood*
Storr, Catherine (Cole). *Robin Hood*
Tejima, Keizaburo. *Fox's dream*
  Woodpecker forest
Thomson, Ruth. *The Rainforest Indians*
Thornhill, Jan. *A tree in a forest*
Tresselt, Alvin R. *The gift of the tree*
Upton, Pat. *Who lives in the woods?*
Waddell, Martin. *Let's go home, Little Bear*
Wahl, Jan. *The five in the forest*
Wallace, Karen. *Bears in the forest*
Ward, Lynd. *Nic of the woods*
Weir, Bob. *Panther dream*
Wells, Rosemary. *Moss pillows*
Wilds, Kazumi Inose. *Hajime in the North Woods*
Wood, Douglas. *Northwoods cradle song*
Woodman, Allen. *The bear who came to stay*
Yolen, Jane. *All in the woodland early*
  Owl moon
Zalben, Jane Breskin. *Norton's nighttime*
Ziefert, Harriet. *On our way to the forest*

Forgetfulness *see* Behavior – forgetfulness

Format, unusual

Adams, Pam. *This old man*
Ahlberg, Janet. *The jolly Christmas postman*
Aliki. *Marianthe's story one: painted words; Marianthe's story two: spoken memories*
Amery, H. *The zoo picture book*
Andersen, H. C. (Hans Christian). *The emperor's new clothes*, ill. by Robert Van Nutt
Anno, Mitsumasa. *Anno's faces*
  Anno's peekaboo
Axworthy, Anni. *Guess what I am*
  Guess what I'll be
Barker, Cicely Mary. *Berry flower fairies*
  Blossom flower fairies
  Spring flower fairies
  Summer flower fairies
Barrows, Marjorie Wescott. *Fraidy cat*
  The funny hat
Blake, William. *The tyger*

Boyd, Lizi. *Mouse in a house*
Bratton, John. *The teddy bears' picnic*, ill. by Renate Kozikowski
Brown, Margaret Wise. *The little fur family*
Brown, Rick. *Who built the ark?*
Burlson, Joe. *Space colony*
Burton, Jane. *ABC*
  Chick
Cahill, Chris. *Spider magic*
  Turtle magic
Cameron, Alice. *The cat sat on the mat*
Campbell, Rod. *Henry's busy day*
  Misty's mischief
Carle, Eric. *My very first book of colors*
  My very first book of growth
  My very first book of homes
  My very first book of motion
  My very first book of numbers
  My very first book of shapes
  My very first book of touch
  My very first book of words
  The very hungry caterpillar
  The very quiet cricket
Carrier, Lark. *There was a hill . . .*
Cars and trucks and other vehicles
Carter, Noelle. *I'm a little mouse*
Chwast, Seymour. *Tall city, wide country*
Count in the dark with Glo Worm
Cousins, Lucy. *Flower in the garden*
  Hen on the farm
  Kite in the park
  Teddy in the house
De Paola, Tomie (Thomas Anthony). *Country farm*
Dodds, Dayle Ann. *Wheel away!*
Dryden, Emma. *Good morning - good night*
Durant, Alan. *Snake supper*
Dürr, Ursula. *The secret of Trembleton Hall*
Ehlert, Lois. *Color farm*
  Color zoo
Elias, Joyce. *Whose toes are those?*
Emberley, Ed (Edward Randolph). *Ed Emberley's amazing look through book*
Ernst, Lisa Campbell. *The rescue of Aunt Pansy*
Falwell, Cathryn. *Nicky and Alex*
  Nicky and grandpa
  Nicky loves daddy
  Nicky, 1-2-3
  Nicky's walk
  Where's Nicky?
Fort, Patrick. *Redbird*
Fowler, Richard. *Happy birthday, Mouse!*
Gantschev, Ivan. *The train to Grandma's*
  Where is Mr. Mole?
Ghigna, Charles. *Good cats/Bad cats*
  Good dogs/Bad dogs
Golden tales from long ago
Gomi, Taro. *Hi, butterfly!*
Goodall, John S. *The adventures of Paddy Pork*
  The ballooning adventures of Paddy Pork
  Creepy castle
  An Edwardian Christmas
  An Edwardian summer
  Jacko
  The midnight adventures of Kelly, Dot and Esmeralda
  Naughty Nancy
  Naughty Nancy goes to school
  Paddy goes traveling
  Paddy Pork
  Paddy Pork's holiday

Paddy under water
Paddy's evening out
Paddy's new hat
Shrewbettina's birthday
The story of a castle
The story of a farm
The story of a main street
The story of an English village
The surprise picnic
Gorey, Edward (St. John). *The tunnel calamity*
Grimm, Jacob. *Little Red Riding Hood*, ill. by John S. Goodall
Grindley, Sally. *Shhh!*
Hague, Michael. *Michael Hague's world of unicorns*
Hannant, Judith Stuller. *Doorknob collection of nursery rhymes*
Hauptmann, Tatjana. *A day in the life of Petronella Pig*
Hayden, Lea. *Sunny day - rainy day*
Hedderwick, Mairi. *P. D. Pebbles' summer or winter book*
Hellard, Susan. *This little piggy*
Hellen, Nancy. *Bus stop*
Hill, Eric. *Spot's first 1, 2, 3 frieze*
Hoban, Tana. *Look! Look! Look!*
  26 letters and 99 cents
Hooper, Meredith. *Seven eggs*
Howell, Lynn. *Winifred's new bed*
Hyman, Trina Schart. *The enchanted forest*
Imershein, Betsy. *Finding red, finding yellow*
Inkpen, Mick. *The blue balloon*
  Threadbear
Jenkins, Martin. *Wings, stings, and wriggly things*
Jensen, Virginia Allen. *Catching*
  Red thread riddles
Jonas, Ann. *Reflections*
  The thirteenth clue
Jones, Carol. *This old man*
Kent, Lorna. *No, no, Charlie Rascal!*
Ladybug, ladybug, and other nursery rhymes
Lenski, Lois. *Sing a song of people*
Lewis, Stephen. *Zoo city*
Lewison, Wendy Cheyette. *Where is Sammy's smile?*
Little old lady who swallowed a fly. There was an old lady who swallowed a fly, ill. by Simms Taback
Lodge, Bernard. *Door to door*
  Rhyming Nell
MacDonald, Suse. *Nanta's lion*
  Once upon another
Mackinnon, Debbie. *Eye spy colors*
  Eye spy shapes
McNaughton, Colin. *Guess who's just moved in next door?*
Magnus, Erica. *Around me*
Mari, Iela. *Eat and be eaten*
Marshall, James. *Hey, diddle, daddle*
Martin, Jerome. *Carrot/parrot*
  Mitten/kitten
Meijer, Marie. *The bake-a-cake book*
Miranda, Anne. *Baby walk*
Moffatt, Judith. *Christmas lights*
  Halloween frights
  Trick-or-treat faces
Monfried, Lucia. *Baby's world*
Mother Goose. *Hickory dickory dock and other nursery rhymes*, ill. by Carol Jones
Munari, Bruno. *The circus in the mist*
Newell, Peter. *Topsys and turvys*
Newth, Philip. *Roly goes exploring*

Nilsén, Anna. *Drive your car*
  Drive your tractor
  Let's all hang and dangle
Old MacDonald had a farm. *Old MacDonald had a*
  farm, ill. by Carol Jones
Ormerod, Jan. *Come back, kittens*
  Come back, puppies
Pacovská, Kveta. *One, five, many*
Padt, Maartje. *Shanti*
Page, Robin. *The alphabet sticker book*
Paschkis, Julie. *So happy/So sad*
Potter, Beatrix. *Where's Peter Rabbit?*
Potter, Tony. *See how it works: cars*
  See how it works: earth movers
  See how it works: planes
  See how it works: trucks
Price, Mathew. *Do you see what I see?*
  Have you seen my sister?
Radunsky, Eugenia. *Square, triangle, round, skinny*
Rey, H. A. (Hans Augusto). *Anybody at home?*
  How do you get there?
  See the circus
  Where's my baby?
Roddie, Shen. *Animal stew*
Roffey, Maureen. *Family scramble*
  Here, kitty kitty!
  Look, there's my hat!
  Quick, catch Dan!
Ross, Tony. *Happy blanket*
Roth, Carol. *Ten dirty pigs / Ten clean pigs*
Royston, Angela. *Shells*
  Small animals
Russell, Naomi. *The tree*
Scarry, Richard. *Egg in the hole*
  Pig Will and Pig Won't
  Richard Scarry's biggest word book ever!
Scruton, Clive. *Mary's pets*
Scullard, Sue. *Miss Fanshawe and the great dragon*
  adventure
Sharratt, Nick. *I look like this*
  Look what I found!
Steer, Dougald. *Just one more story*
Steiner, Charlotte. *The climbing book*
Tafuri, Nancy. *What the sun sees / What the moon sees*
Tarrant, Graham. *Rabbits*
The three bears. *Goldilocks and the three bears*, ill. by
  Madelaine Gill Linden
Tison, Annette. *The adventures of the three colors*
  Animal hide-and-seek
  Animals in color magic
  Inside and outside
The twelve days of Christmas.. English folk song.
  The twelve days of Christmas, ill. by Erika
  Schneider
Vaughan, Marcia Kapok. *The dancing dragon*
Waber, Bernard. *The snake*
Wahl, Jan. *Dracula's cat and Frankenstein's dog*
Walters, Marguerite. *The city-country ABC*
Wattenberg, Jane. *Mrs. Mustard's baby faces*
Watts, Barrie. *Rabbit*
Wildsmith, Brian. *Give a dog a bone*
  Goat's trail
  Pelican
Wilson-Max, Ken. *Wake up; Sleep tight*
Windham, Sophie. *Noah's ark*
Wood, John Norris. *Jungles*
  Oceans
Wyllie, Stephen. *Ghost train*
  The great race

  White Rabbit builds a dream house
Youldon, Gillian. *Counting*
  Shapes
  Sizes
Young, Ed (Edward). *Mouse match*
Ziefert, Harriet. *Where's the cat?*
  Where's the dog?
  Where's the guinea pig?
  Where's the turtle?
Zolotow, Charlotte (Shapiro). *Wake up and good-
  night*

Format, unusual – board books

Alexander, Martha G. *Good night, Lily*
  Lily and Willy
  Where's Willy?
  Willy's boot
Allen, Jonathan. *Big owl, little towel*
  One with a bun
  Purple sock, pink sock
Allen, Robert. *Ten little babies count*
  Ten little babies dress
  Ten little babies eat
  Ten little babies play
Anderson, Lena. *Bunny bath*
  Bunny box
  Bunny fun
  Bunny party
  Bunny story
  Bunny surprise
Anglund, Joan Walsh. *Christmas is here*
Arnold, Tedd. *Actions*
  Colors
  My first drawing book
  Opposites
  Sounds
Aronin, Ben. *The secret of the Sabbath fish*
Asch, Frank. *Moonbear's books*
  Moonbear's canoe
At the farm
Baby's first book of colors
Baby's words
Baggette, Susan K. *Jonathan goes to the doctor*
  Jonathan goes to the grocery store
Bailey, Debbie. *Clothes*
  Grandma
  Grandpa
  Hats
  My dad
  My family
  My mom
  The playground
  Shoes
  Toys
Bailey, Jill. *Eyes*
  Feet
  Mouths
  Noses
Baird, Anne. *Baby socks*
  Kiss, kiss
  Little tree
  No sheep
Bambi
Barkan, Joanne. *Boxcar*
  Caboose
  Locomotive
  Passenger car
  Whiskerville bake shop

Whiskerville firehouse
Whiskerville post office
Whiskerville school
Bedtime
Bible. Old Testament. Daniel. *Daniel in the lions' den,* ill. by Jim Cummins
Bible. Old Testament. Jonah. *Jonah and the great fish,* ill. by Jim Cummins
Bible. Old Testament. Joseph. *Joseph and his brothers*
Bishop, Roma. *Animals*
  Numbers
  Shapes
  Toys
Blades, Ann. *Fall*
  Spring
  Summer
  Winter
Blegvad, Lenore. *This is me*
Blume, Karin. *Circus*
  My new friends
Bohdal, Susi. *Bobby the bear*
  Harry the hare
Boon, Émilie. *It's spring, Peterkin*
  Peterkin's very own garden
Bos, Claire. *Maurice the hippo*
  Webster's wardrobe
Bowman, Peter. *Goodnight, teddy bear*
Boyd, Lizi. *Baby play*
  Bunny hop
Boynton, Sandra. *Barnyard dance!*
  Birthday monsters!
  But not the hippopotamus
  Dinosaur's binkit
  Doggies
  The going to bed book
  Horns to toes and in between
  Moo, baa, lalala
  Oh my oh my oh dinosaurs!
  One, two, three!
  Opposites
Bratton, Heidi. *Imagine*
  Yes, I can!
Breeze, Lynn. *Baby's animals*
  Baby's clothes
  Baby's food
  Baby's toys
  This little baby goes out
  This little baby's bedtime
  This little baby's morning
Brett, Jan. *The mitten*
Brown, Marc Tolon. *Arthur goes to school*
  Arthur's new puppy (board book)
  Count to ten
  D. W. thinks big, a board book
  Marc Brown's Boat book
Brown, Margaret Wise. *Bumble bee*
Buck, Nola. *How a baby grows*
Burningham, John. *Count up*
  The dog
  Five down
  Just cats
  Pigs plus
  Read one
  Ride off
Burton, Jane. *Kitten*
  Puppy
Busy baby
Butterworth, Nick. *When there's work to do*

When we go shopping
When we play together
Cabrera, Jane. *Panda Big and Panda Small*
Cahill, Chris. *Bear magic*
  Bunny magic
  Spider magic
  Turtle magic
Calmenson, Stephanie. *Meet Penny*
  Meet Timmy
Campbell, Rod. *Look inside! All kinds of places*
  Look inside! Land, sea, air
Carle, Eric. *From head to toe*
  Little cloud, a board book
Carlstrom, Nancy White. *Jesse Bear's tra-la tub*
  Jesse Bear's tum-tum tickle
  Jesse Bear's wiggle-jiggle jump-up
  Jesse Bear's yum-yum crumble
Cars and trucks
Cartlidge, Michelle. *Baby mice at home*
  Bear in the forest
  Bears on the go
  Bunny's birthday
  Doggy days
  Duck in the pond
  Elephant in the jungle
  Mouse in the house
Cassidy, Dianne. *Circus animals*
  Circus people
The caterpillar who turned into a butterfly
Cherry, Lynne. *Grizzly bear*
  Orangutan
  Seal
  Snow leopard
Children's Television Workshop. *Muppets in my neighborhood*
Chorao, Kay. *Peekaboo! Was it you?*
  Rock, rock, my baby
City, ill. by Roser Capdevila
Clark, Sue. *Bodies*
  Clothes
  Faces
  Feelings
Cock Robin. *Who killed Cock Robin?,* ill. by William Stobbs
Come to the circus
Corbett, Grahame. *Guess who?*
  What number now?
  Who is hiding?
  Who is inside?
  Who is next?
Cosgrove, Stephen (Edward). *Sleepy time bunny*
Costa, Nicoletta. *The birthday party, a board book*
  Dressing up
  A friend comes to play
  The missing cat
Cousins, Lucy. *Count with Maisy*
  Country animals
  Farm animals
  Garden animals
  Humpty Dumpty and other nursery rhymes
  Jack and Jill
  Little Miss Muffet
  Pet animals
  Wee Willie Winkie and other nursery rhymes
Cowley, Stewart. *Down Ladybug Lane*
  Five little kittens
  Hide-and-seek puppies
  In dragonfly forest
  In songbird jungle

Little bunny
Little chick
Little lost rabbit
The naughty ducklings
On Butterfly Farm
"Tweet, tweet, tweet"
What's that sound?
Crary, Elizabeth. When you're mad and you know it
Crozat, François. I am a little cat
I am a little caterpillar
I am a little dog
Curti, Anna. Seasons
Daly, Kathleen N. Jesus our friend
Davidson, Amanda. Teddy goes outside
Day, Alexandra. Helping the animals
Helping the flowers and trees
Helping the night
Helping the sun
Demarest, Chris L. Bus
Plane
Train
Demi. Cuddly chick
Demi's Christmas surprise
Downy duckling
Fleecy bunny
Fleecy lamb
Fuzzy wuzzy puppy
Little baby lamb
Little bitty bunny
Little chick chick
Little lucky ducky
So soft kitty
De Paola, Tomie (Thomas Anthony). Get dressed, Santa!
Katie and Kit at the beach
Katie, Kit and cousin Tom
Katie's good idea
My first Chanukah
Pajamas for Kit
Dickens, Lucy. At the beach
Our day
Outside
Playtime
DiFiori, Lawrence. Baby animals
The farm
If I had a little car
My first book
My toys
Domestic animals
Douzou, Olivier. Wolf's lunch
Dreamer, Sue. Circus ABC
Circus 1, 2, 3
Dubov, Christine Salac. Aleksandra, where are your toes?
Aleksandra, where is your nose?
Ding dong! and other sounds
Knock! and other sounds
Oink! and other sounds
Duerrstein, Richard. Mickey is happy
Duke, Kate. Bedtime
Clean-up day
The playground
What bounces?
Dunn, Phoebe. Baby's animal friends
Busy, busy toddlers
I'm a baby!
Edwards, Roberta. Anna Bear's first winter
Eisenberg, Ann. I can celebrate
Emberley, Ed (Edward Randolph). Animals

Cars, boats, and planes
Home
Sounds
Farjeon, Eleanor. Cats
Farm animals, photos sel. by Debby Slier
Farm house
Fast rolling fire trucks
Fast rolling work trucks
Fechner, Amrei. I am a little dog
I am a little elephant
I am a little lion
Firehouse, ill. by Zokeisha
Fitzsimons, Cecilia. My first birds
My first butterflies
Five little pumpkins
Fosberg, John. Cookie shapes
Ice cream colors
Fowler, Richard. Cat's story
Freeman, Don. Corduroy's busy street and Corduroy goes to the doctor
Corduroy's party
Freeman, Lydia. Corduroy's day
Fujikawa, Gyo. Let's grow a garden
Millie's secret
My favorite thing
See what I can be!
Surprise! Surprise!
Fujita, Miho. The little choo-choo
Gelbard, Jane. My bye-bye bottle book
My dressing book
My eating book
My sharing book
Gellman, Ellie. It's Chanukah!
It's Rosh Hashanah!
Shai's Shabbat walk
Giffard, Hannah. Fast car
Hens say cluck
Red bus
Striped zebra
Gikow, Louise. Bye-bye, pacifier
I am Kermit
Gliori, Debi. Mr. Bear says peek-a-boo
Gold-Vukson, Marji. The colors of my Jewish Year
Gomboli, Mario. Look inside a house
Look inside a ship
Gomi, Taro. Guess what?
Guess who?
Gorbaty, Norman. Get up and go, little dinosaur!
Grahame, Kenneth. Duck song
Greeley, Valerie. Animals
Farm animals
Field animals
Pets
Zoo animals
Greenfield, Eloise. Big friend, little friend
Daddy and I
I make music
My doll, Keshia
Sweet baby coming
Greenfield, Monica. The baby
Greenway, Shirley. Color me bright
Here's ears
Legs and all
A tale of tails
Gretz, Susanna. Hide-and-seek
I'm not sleepy
Ready for bed
Too dark!
Grimes, Nikki. Baby's bedtime

Groner, Judyth Saypol. *Where is the Afikomen?*
Gundersheimer, Karen. *Find cat, wear hat*
Haddon, Mark. *At home*
    At playgroup
    In the garden
    On vacation
Haldane, Suzanne. *Teddies and machines*
    Teddies and trucks
Hands, Hargrave. *Bunny sees*
    Duckling sees
    Little lamb sees
Hannant, Judith Stuller. *Doorknob collection of nursery rhymes*
    The doorknob collection of pets and pals
    Three little kittens
Haring, Keith. *Big*
    10
Hathon, Elizabeth. *We go to school*
    We go to the zoo
Haus, Felice. *Beep! Beep! I'm a jeep*
Hawkins, Colin. *Hey diddle diddle*
Hayes, Geoffrey. *Patrick and his grandpa*
Hayward, Linda. *Sunny Day Bunny*
Hello, baby
Henley, Claire. *Dinnertime*
    I'm a baby, too!
    Playtime
    Quack, quack
Hill, Eric. *Puppy love*
    Spot at home
    Spot at the fair
    Spot counts from 1 to 10
    Spot goes to the circus
    Spot goes to the farm
    Spot in the garden
    Spot looks at colors
    Spot looks at opposites
    Spot looks at shapes
    Spot looks at weather
    Spot on the farm
    Spot visits his grandparents
    Spot's favorite baby animals
    Spot's favorite colors
    Spot's favorite numbers
    Spot's favorite words
    Spot's first words
    Spot's magical Christmas
    Spot's toy box
Hines, Anna Grossnickle. *What can you do in the rain?*
    What can you do in the snow?
    What can you do in the sun?
    What can you do in the wind?
Hissey, Jane. *Little bear's bedtime*
    Little Bear's day
    Old bear, a board book
Hoban, Lillian. *Big Little Otter*
Hoban, Tana. *1, 2, 3*
    Panda, panda
    Red, blue, yellow shoe
    What is it?
    What is that?
    White on black
    Who are they?
Holabird, Katharine. *Angelina dances*
Hopkins, Margaret. *Sleepytime for baby mouse*
Hubbell, Patricia. *Pots and pans*
    Wrapping paper romp
Hudson, Cheryl Willis. *Animal sounds for baby*

Good morning baby
Good night baby
Let's count, baby
Hughes, Shirley. *Being together*
    Playing
Hutchins, Pat. *Rosie's walk, a board book*
Inkpen, Mick. *Wibbly Pig can make a tent*
    Wibbly Pig is upset
    Wibbly Pig likes bananas
    Wibbly Pig makes pictures
    Wibbly Pig opens his presents
Intrater, Roberta Grobel. *Peek-a-boo!*
    Smile!
Jaramillo, Raquel. *Ride, baby, ride!*
Johnson, Angela. *Joshua by the sea*
    Joshua's night whispers
    Mama bird, baby birds
    Rain feet
Johnson, John Emil. *My first book of things*
Josephs, Rhoda. *The baby bubble book*
Joyce, William. *Baseball Bob*
    Life with Bob
    Rolie Polie Olie, how many howdys?
Kahn, Katherine Janus. *The shofar calls to us*
Kangas, Juli. *Fluffy Bunny's friend*
    Ginger Kitten's surprise
    Hello, Honey Bear
Karn, George. *Circus big and small*
    Circus colors
Keats, Ezra Jack. *One red sun*
    The snowy day (a board book)
Keeshan, Robert. *Itty Bitty Kitty*
    Itty Bitty Kitty makes a big splash
Kelley, True. *Hammers and mops, pencils and pots*
Kemp, Moira. *I'm a little teapot*
    Knock at the door
    Round and round the garden
Kessler, Ethel. *Are there hippos on the farm?*
    Are there seals in the sandbox?
    Is there a gorilla in the band?
    Is there a horse in your house?
    Is there a penguin at your party?
    Is there an elephant in your kitchen?
Kilroy, Sally. *Animal noises*
    Babies' bodies
    Babies' homes
    Babies' outings
    Babies' zoo
    Baby colors
    Busy babies
    Noisy homes
Koelling, Caryl. *Animal mix and match*
    Mad monsters mix and match
    Silly stories mix and match
Koenner, Alfred. *Be quite quiet beside the lake*
    High flies the ball
Kraus, Robert. *Animal families*
    Freddy, the fire engine
    Mouse work
    Robert Kraus' a sunny day in Babytown
    Robert Kraus' Babytown express
    Robert Kraus' meet the babies
    Robert Kraus' welcome to Babytown
    Tony, the tow truck
Krauss, Ruth. *I can fly*
Krementz, Jill. *Benjy goes to a restaurant*
    Jack goes to the beach
    Jamie goes on an airplane
    Katharine goes to nursery school

Lily goes to the playground
Taryn goes to the dentist
Kress, Camille. *Tot Shabbat*
Kvasnosky, Laura McGee. *One, two, three, play with me!*
    Pink, red, blue, what are you?
Lacome, Julie. *Seashore*
Laden, Nina. *Peek-a-who?*
Landa, Norbert. *Rabbit and chicken count eggs*
    Rabbit and chicken find a box
    Rabbit and chicken play with colors
Lawrence, Michael (Michael C.). *Baby loves*
Leblanc, Anne. *Benjamin in the snow*
    Benjamin takes care of Mommy
    Benjamin's busy day
    Shopping with Benjamin
Leonard, Marcia. *Bye-bye, Baby-boo*
    What's that, Baby-boo?
    Where's Baby-boo?
Lewis, Shari. *Baby Lamb Chop loves animals*
    Baby Lamb Chop loves numbers
    Baby Lamb Chop loves nursery school
    Baby Lamb Chop loves the beach
    Baby Lamb Chop loves words
Lewison, Wendy Cheyette. *Baby has a boo-boo*
    Happy Thanksgiving!
    Nighty-night
Lilly, Kenneth. *Animal builders*
    Animal climbers
    Animal jumpers
    Animal runners
    Animal swimmers
    Animals at the zoo
    Animals in the country
    Animals in the jungle
    Animals of the ocean
    Animals on the farm
Lionni, Leo. *Colors to talk about*
    Letters to talk about
    Numbers to talk about
    What?
    When?
    Where?
    Who?
    Words to talk about
A little ABC book
A little book of colors
A little book of numbers
Losordo, Stephen. *Cow moo me*
Lundell, Margo. *Teddy bear's birthday*
Lynn, Sara. *Big animals*
    Clothes
    Farm animals
    Food
    Garden animals
    Home
    Jungle friends
    Small animals
    Toys
    Wheels
Maccarone, Grace. *Baby visits grandma and grandpa*
    Baby's toys
McCue, Lisa. *Corduroy's party*
    Corduroy's toys
    The little chick
MacDonald, Amy. *Let's do it*
    Let's go
    Let's make a noise
    Let's play

Let's pretend
Let's try
McKee, David. *Elmer's colors*
    Elmer's day
    Elmer's friends
    Elmer's weather
McNaught, Harry. *Baby animals*
McNaughton, Colin. *At home*
    At playschool
    At the park
    At the party
    At the stores
    Autumn
    Spring
    Summer
    Winter
McQuade, Jacqueline. *At preschool with Teddy Bear*
    At the petting zoo with Teddy Bear
Maestro, Betsy. *Harriet at home*
    Harriet at play
    Harriet at school
    Harriet at work
Mantegazza, Giovanna. *The cat*
    The hippopotamus
    Look how a baby grows
Maris, Ron. *Ducks quack*
    Frogs jump
Marzollo, Jean. *Do you know new?*
    I spy little animals
    I spy little book
    I spy little wheels
    Mama, Mama
    Papa, papa
Mayer, Mercer. *Astronaut critter*
    Cowboy critter
    Fireman critter
    Policeman critter
Medearis, Angela Shelf. *Bye-bye, babies!*
    Eat, babies, eat!
Melmed, Laura Krauss. *I love you as much . . .*
Merriam, Eve. *The hole story*
Miller, J. P. (John Parr). *Good night, Little Rabbit*
Miller, Margaret. *At my house*
    At the shore
    Baby faces
    Every day
    Family time
    Guess who?
    Happy days
    Here we go!
    I can help
    I can make it!
    I love colors
    I'm grown up!
    In my room
    Let's play!
    Let's pretend!
    Me and my bear
    My best friends
    My birthday
    My first words: me and my clothes
    On my street
    Playtime
    Time to eat
    Water play
    What's on my head?
    Wheels go 'round
Moore, Dessie. *Getting dressed*
    Good morning

Good night
Let's pretend
Morgan-Vanroyen, Mary. *Guess who I love?*
   The Pudgy merry Christmas book
Morozumi, Atsuko. *Helping daddy*
   In the park
   Playing
   Time for bed
Most, Bernard. *Moo-ha!*
   Oink-ha!
Mother Goose. *ABC rhymes*
   Baa, baa, black sheep, ill. by Moira Kemp
   Baa baa black sheep, ill. by Sue Porter
   Baa baa black sheep, ill. by Ferelith Eccles
      Williams
   Baby's first Mother Goose
   Hey diddle, diddle, ill. by Moira Kemp
   Hey diddle diddle, ill. by Nita Sowter
   Hey diddle diddle, ill. by Eleanor Wasmuth
   Hickory, dickory, dock, ill. by Moira Kemp
   Humpty Dumpty, ill. by Colin and Jacqui Hawkins
   Humpty Dumpty and other rhymes, ill. by Rosemary
      Wells
   Jack and Jill
   Kate Greenaway's Mother Goose
   Kitten rhymes
   Little Boy Blue
   Little Boy Blue and other rhymes
   Mother Goose house
   My first real Mother Goose board book, ill. by
      Blanche Fisher Wright
   The old woman in a shoe
   Pat-a-cake, pat-a-cake, ill. by Moira Kemp
   Pussy cat, pussy cat
   Pussycat, pussycat and other rhymes
   The real Mother Goose board book, ill. by Diane
      Muldrow
   Sing a song of sixpence, ill. by Margaret Chamber-
      lain
   Sing a song of sixpence, ill. by Ferelith Eccles
      Williams
   This little pig, ill. by Eleanor Wasmuth
   This little pig went to market, ill. by Ferelith Eccles
      Williams
   This little piggy
   The three little kittens, ill. by Dorothy Stott
   Wee Willie Winkie and other rhymes
Mott, Evelyn Clarke. *Cool cat*
   Hot dog
Mouse house
Murphy, Chuck. *Colors*
My body
My first book of baby animals
Nayer, Judy. *Bath*
   Jungle life
   Night animals
   Reptiles
   Sea creatures
Nickl, Peter. *Ra ta ta tam*
O'Brien, Anne Sibley. *Come play with us*
   I want that!
   I'm not tired
   Where's my truck?
Our house
Owen, Annie. *Goodnight bear!*
   Hungry panda
   Playtime duck
   Wake up Frog!
Oxenbury, Helen. *All fall down*

Beach day
Clap hands
Dressing
Family
Friends
I can
I hear
I see
I touch
Playing
Say goodnight
729 curious creatures
729 merry mix-ups
729 puzzle people
The shopping trip
Tickle, tickle
Parish, Peggy. *I can - can you?*
Paterson, Bettina. *In my house*
   In my yard
   My clothes
   My toys
Patrick, Denise Lewis. *No diapers for baby!*
Pearson, Susan. *Baby and the bear*
   When baby went to bed
Peppé, Rodney. *Little circus*
   Little dolls
   Little games
   Little numbers
   Little wheels
Pfister, Marcus. *Where is my friend?*
Pfloog, Jan. *Kittens*
   Puppies
Phillips, Joan. *Peek-a-boo! I see you!*
Pienkowski, Jan. *Faces*
   Food
Pragoff, Fiona. *Odd one out*
   Opposites
   Shapes
The pudgy book of babies
The pudgy book of farm animals
The pudgy book of here we go
The pudgy book of make-believe
The pudgy book of Mother Goose
The pudgy book of toys
The pudgy bunny book
The pudgy fingers counting book
The pudgy pals
The pudgy pat-a-cake book
The pudgy peek-a-boo book
The pudgy rock-a-bye book
Puppies and kittens
Reasoner, Charles. *The big busy building*
Reidy, Hannah. *Crazy creature contrasts*
Ricklen, Neil. *My clothes = Mi ropa*
   My colors = Mis colores
   My family = Mi familia
   My numbers = Mi numeros
Roosevelt, Michelle Chopin. *Zoo animals*
Roth, Harold. *Autumn days*
   A checkup
   Nursery school
   Winter days
Royston, Angela. *Cars*
Sage, Chris. *Happy baby*
   Sleepy baby
Scarry, Richard. *My first word book*
   Richard Scarry's busy houses
   Richard Scarry's Lowly Worm word book
Schanzer, Rosalyn. *In the synagogue*

Schindel, John. *Busy penguins*
Schmid, Eleonore. *Farm animals*
Schroeder, Binette. *Tuffa and her friends*
    Tuffa and the bone
    Tuffa and the ducks
    Tuffa and the picnic
    Tuffa and the snow
Sesame Street. *Ernie and Bert can . . . can you?*
Shea, Pegi Deitz. *I see me!*
Shine, Deborah. *The little engine that could pudgy word book*
Shirotani, Hideo. *Let's eat = Vamos a comer*
    Let's play
    Let's take a walk = Vamos a caminar
    What color? = Qué color?
Shostak, Myra. *Rainbow candles*
Shott, Steve (Stephen). *Bathtime*
    Look at me
    Mealtime
    Playtime
Sieveking, Anthea. *Mary had a little lamb and other animal rhymes*
    Polly put the kettle on and other play rhymes
    Rub-a-dub-dub and other splashy rhymes
    Twinkle, twinkle, little star and other bedtime rhymes
Silverman, Maida. *Bunny's ABC*
    Ladybug's color book
    Mouse's shape book
Simmons, Jane. *Daisy says Coo!*
    Daisy's day out
    Daisy's favorite things
Smith, Donald. *Who's wearing my baseball cap?*
    Who's wearing my bow tie?
    Who's wearing my sneakers?
    Who's wearing my sunglasses?
Snow, Alan. *Cluck!*
    Oink!
    Quack!
    Woof!
Spanner, Helmut. *I am a little cat*
Spier, Peter. *Bill's service station*
    Firehouse
    Food market
    Little cats
    Little dogs
    Little ducks
    Little rabbits
    My school
    The pet store
    The toy shop
Spohn, Kate. *Piglet's bath*
Springer, Sally. *Let's make latkes*
Staake, Bob. *My little ABC book*
    My little 1 2 3 book
Stephens, Helen. *I'm too busy*
Stevens, Harry. *Fat mouse*
    Parrot told snake
Stoeke, Janet Morgan. *Hide and seek*
Struppi
Suben, Eric. *Pigeon takes a trip*
Szekeres, Cyndy. *Cyndy Szekeres' learn to count, funny bunnies*
    Good night, Sammy
    Hide-and-seek duck
    Nothing-to-do puppy
    Suppertime for Frieda Fuzzypaws
Tabler, Judith. *The new puppy*
Tafuri, Nancy. *In a red house*
    My friends

    One wet jacket
    Two new sneakers
    Where we sleep
Taylor, Ann. *Baby dance*
Taylor, Kim. *Frog*
The three bears. *Goldilocks and the three bears*, ill. by Jane Dyer
The three little pigs. *The three little pigs*, ill. by Val Biro
Tildes, Phyllis Limbacher. *Baby animals black and white*
Titherington, Jeanne. *Baby's boat, a board book*
Topek, Susan Remick. *Shalom, Shabbat*
Tucker, Sian. *At home*
    Going out
    My clothes
    My toys
Twinem, Neecy. *In the air*
VanderKlipp, Michael A. *Joy to the world!*
A visit to a pond
Vulliamy, Clara. *Bang and shout*
    Blue hat, red coat
    Boo baby boo!
    Good night, baby
    Wide awake
    Yum yum
Waddell, Martin. *Owl babies, a board book*
Watson, Carol. *Rabbit*
Watts, Barrie. *Duck*
Weiss, Nicki. *Where does the brown bear go? A board book*
Wellington, Monica. *Baby at home*
    Baby in a buggy
    Baby in a car
    Bunny's first snowflake
    Bunny's rainbow day
Wells, Rosemary. *Bingo*
    Hooray for Max
    The itsy-bitsy spider
    Max's bath
    Max's bedtime
    Max's birthday
    Max's breakfast
    Max's first word
    Max's new suit
    Max's ride
    Max's toys
    What do babies do?
    What do toddlers do?
Wijngaard, Juan. *Bear*
    Cat
    Dog
    Duck
Wikler, Madeline. *Let's build a Sukkah*
    My first seder
    The Purim parade
Willis, Val. *The mystery in the bottle*
Winn, Chris. *Helping*
    Holiday
    My day
    Playing
Yee, Patrick. *Baby bear*
    Baby lion
    Baby monkey
    Baby penguin
    Let's go
    Let's make friends
    Let's play
    Rosie Rabbit's colors

Rosie Rabbit's numbers
Rosie Rabbit's opposites
Rosie Rabbit's shapes
Yee, Paul. *Let's eat*
You can name 100 trucks!
Young animals in the zoo
Young domestic animals
Ziefert, Harriet. *Baby Ben's bow-wow book*
Baby Ben's busy book
Baby Ben's go-go book
Baby Ben's noisy book
My getting-ready-for-school book
Nicky's friends
No, no, Nicky!
On our way to the barn
On our way to the forest
On our way to the water
On our way to the zoo
Where's the cat?
Where's the dog?
Where's the guinea pig?
Where's the turtle?
Zoo animals, (Imported Pubs., 1983)

Format, unusual – toy and movable books

Æsop. *Æsop's fables*, ill. by Gisela Dürr
Æsop's fables, ill. by Claire Littlejohn
The children's Æsop
The hare and the tortoise, ill. by Carol Jones
Ahlberg, Janet. *The bear nobody wanted*
The jolly pocket postman
The jolly postman
Peek-a-boo!
Playmates
Yum yum
Alborough, Jez. *Can you jump like a kangaroo?*
Can you peck like a hen?
Clothesline
Hide and seek
Alexander, Martha G. *3 magic flip books*
Anno, Mitsumasa. *Anno's magical ABC*
Anno's masks
Anno's sundial
Apperley, Dawn. *In the jungle*
In the sand
Argent, Kerry. *Happy birthday wombat!*
Arnold, Tedd. *Bisnipian blast-off*
My first drawing book
Artell, Mike. *Legs*
Asbjørnsen, P. C. (Peter Christen). *The three billy goats Gruff*, ill. by Thomas Newbury
The three billy goats Gruff, ill. by Laura Rader
Asch, Frank. *I can blink*
I can roar
Short train, long train
Baker, Alan. *Where's mouse?*
Baker, Keith. *Cat tricks*
Balmer, Helen. *Jungle adventure*
Bantock, Nick. *Runners, sliders, bouncers, climbers*
Barnes-Murphy, Rowan. *Numbers*
Bees
Belloc, Hilaire. *The bad child's pop-up book of beasts*
Bemelmans, Ludwig. *Madeline [pop-up book]*
Benjamin, Alan. *1000 monsters*
Berger, Melvin. *Early humans*
Prehistoric mammals
Bishop, Roma. *Animals*
Christmas songs

Easter counting
Easter egg hunt
Holiday cheer
My first pop-up book of dinosaurs
My first pop-up book of prehistoric animals
Numbers
On a safari
Santa pays a visit
Shapes
Toys
Bonfils, Bolette. *Peter joins the circus*
Bowman, Peter. *The Christmas songbook*
Boyd, Lizi. *Baby play*
Bunny hop
Boynton, Sandra. *Dinosaur's binkit*
Bradman, Tony. *Look out, he's behind you*
See you later, alligator
Breverton, David. *Here comes bulldozer*
Here comes fire truck
Here comes the dump truck
Here comes the tow truck
Briggs, Raymond. *The snowman, a lift-the-flap board book*
The snowman tell-the-time book
Brooks, Bruce. *Each a piece*
Brown, Marc Tolon. *Arthur goes to school*
Arthur's neighborhood
Can you jump like a frog?
Monster's lunchbox
One, two buckle my shoe
Teddy bear, teddy bear
Two little monkeys
What do you call a dumb bunny? and other rabbit riddles, games, jokes and cartoons
Brown, Ruth. *If at first you do not see*
Browne, Gerard. *The aircraft lift-the-flap book*
Bruna, Dick. *My toys*
Buck, Nola. *The basement stairs*
Christmas in the manger
Gotcha!
Halloween parade
The littlest witch
Burns, Kate. *How does your garden grow?*
In the snow
Butler, Andrea. *Mr. Sun and Mr. Sea*
Butterworth, Nick. *All together now!*
Making faces
The rescue party
When it's time for bed
Campbell, Rod. *Buster gets dressed*
Buster keeps warm
Buster's afternoon
Buster's morning
Dear zoo
Funwheels with moving parts!
It's mine
My pop-up garden friends
Oh dear!
Playwheels with moving parts!
Cannon, Janell. *Stellaluna: a pop-up book and mobile*
Capucilli, Alyssa Satin. *Peekaboo bunny*
Carle, Eric. *My very first book of food*
My very first book of heads and tails
My very first book of sounds
My very first book of tools
Papa, please get the moon for me
The secret birthday message
The very lonely firefly
Watch out! A giant!

Carlstrom, Nancy White. *Ten Christmas sheep*
  What would you do if you lived at the zoo?
Carter, David A. *How many bugs in a box?*
Carter, Noelle. *My house*
  My pet
  Where's my squishy ball?
Cartlidge, Michelle. *Fairy letters*
  Mouse birthday
  Mouse Christmas
  Mouse letters
  Mouse theater
  Mouse time
  Mouse's scrapbook
Cassidy, Dianne. *Circus animals*
  Circus people
Charles, N. N. *What am I? Looking through shapes at apples and grapes*
Chen, Tony. *Animals showing off*
Chwast, Seymour. *Mr. Merlin and the turtle*
  Traffic jam
Cimarusti, Marie Torres. *Peek-a-moo*
Clarke, Gus. *Ten green monsters*
Cole, Babette. *Babette Cole's beastly birthday book*
  Babette Cole's brother
  Babette Cole's ponies
  Dad
  Don't go out tonight
  Mum
Cole, Henry. *I took a walk*
Cousins, Lucy. *Happy birthday, Maisy*
  Katy Cat and Beaky Boo
  Maisy at the farm
  Maisy goes swimming
  Maisy goes to bed
  Maisy goes to school
  Maisy goes to the playground
  Maisy's ABC
  Maisy's pop-up playhouse
  What can Pinky hear?
  What can Pinky see?
  What can rabbit hear?
  What can rabbit see?
Cowley, Stewart. *Five little kittens*
  From my window
  Hide-and-seek puppies
  Little lost rabbit
  The naughty ducklings
Cremins, Robert. *My animal ABC*
  My animal Mother Goose
  Pop up baby brontosaurus
  Pop up baby coelophysis
  Pop up baby pteranodon
  Pop up baby stegosaurus
  Pop up baby triceratops
  Pop up baby tyrannosaurus rex
Crespi, Francesca. *Make a joyful noise*
  Santa Claus is coming!
  Silent night
Crowther, Robert. *All the fun of the fair*
  Animal rap!
  Animal snap!
  Dump trucks and diggers
  Hide and seek counting book
  The most amazing hide-and-seek alphabet book
  The most amazing hide-and-seek opposites book
  My pop-up surprise ABC
  My pop-up surprise 1 2 3
  Pop goes the weasel!
  Who lives in the country?

Who lives in the garden?
Who lives on the farm?
Curtis, Jamie Lee. *Today I feel silly and other moods that make my day*
Davis, Jennifer. *Before you were born*
Day, Alexandra. *Carl pops up*
DeBoer, Jesslyn. *Follow the star*
  Getting ready for Christmas
Dedieu, Thierry. *Baby clown*
Demarest, Chris L. *Fall*
  Farmer Nat
  Honk!
  Spring
  Summer
  Winter
Demi. *Cuddly chick*
  Demi's dragons and fantastic creatures
  Downy duckling
  Fuzzy wuzzy puppy
  Little bitty bunny
  Little chick chick
  The peek-a-boo ABC
  So soft kitty
  Three little elephants
  Where is Willie Worm?
Denchfield, Nick. *Desmond the dog, a wag-the-tail pop-up book*
Dijs, Carla. *Are you my daddy?*
  Are you my mommy?
  Big and small
  How many?
  Mommy, would you love me if . . . ?
  Pretend you're a hippo
Dodds, Dayle Ann. *The color box*
Dowling, Paul. *Jimmy's snowy book*
  The night journey
Drescher, Henrik. *Pat the beastie*
Easter babies
Edwards, Richard. *Fly with the birds*
Ehlert, Lois. *Hands*
Elson, Raymond. *Clothes*
  Pets
  Toys
Emberley, Ed (Edward Randolph). *Glad monster, sad monster*
  Go away, big green monster!
Facklam, Margery. *But not like mine*
  So can I
Faulkner, Keith. *Amble has a dream*
  Bertie's big blue binoculars
  Butterfly
  David dreaming of dinosaurs
  Frog
  The long-nosed pig
  Munch looks for lunch
  My first one hundred words in French and English
  My pets
  The puzzled penguin
  Rumble frightens himself
  Sam at the seaside
  Sam helps out
  Swoop flies too high
  This is me
  The wide-mouthed frog
Ferguson, Don. *Winnie the Pooh's A to Zzzz*
Fowler, Richard. *Honeybee's busy day*
  Ladybug on the move
  Little Chick's big adventure
  Mr. Little's noisy car

Mr. Little's noisy fire engine
Mr. Little's noisy truck
Pop-up trucks
French, Vivian. *Oh no, Anna!*
Fuchshuber, Annegert. *Giant story – Mouse tale*
Ganeri, Anita. *Animal hideaways*
Gantschev, Ivan. *Where the moon lives*
Gardner, Beau. *What is it?*
 Whooo's a fright on Halloween night?
Garrett, Ann. *What's for lunch?*
Gauch, Patricia Lee. *Tanya steps out*
Gay, Tenner Ottley. *Dinosaurs and their relatives in action*
 Sharks in action
Gerrard, Roy. *A pocket full of posies*
Gerstein, Mordicai. *Guess what?*
 William, where are you?
The gingerbread boy. *Gingerbread baby*, ill. by Jan Brett
Gliori, Debi. *Mr. Bear says, "Are you there, Baby Bear?"*
Goffin, Josse. *Oh!*
Gomi, Taro. *Santa through the window*
Gorbaty, Norman. *Tow truck*
Gordon, Lynn. *The witch's revenge*
Grimm, Jacob. *Sleeping Beauty*, ill. by John Wallner
Grindley, Sally. *Too big bear*
Hague, Michael. *The perfect present*
Hanna, Jack. *The petting zoo*
Hansen, Biruta Akerbergs. *Parading with piglets*
Harper, Dan. *Telling time with Big Mama Cat*
Hathon, Elizabeth. *We go to school*
 We go to the zoo
Hawcock, David. *Ant*
 Bee
 Beetle
 Brontosaurus
 Dinosaur hunt
 Fly
 Spider
 Stegosaurus
 Triceratops
 Tyrannosaurus
 Wasp
 Whose coat?
 Whose home?
 Whose nose?
Hawkins, Colin. *Come for a ride on the ghost train*
 The elephant
 Incy wincy spider
 Jen the hen
 Mig the pig
 Round the garden
 Take away monsters
 This little pig
 Tog the dog
 What time is it, Mr. Wolf?
Hellard, Susan. *Time to get up*
Hellen, Nancy. *Circle farm*
 Circle zoo
 A visit to the farm
 A visit to the zoo
Henderson, Kathy. *Don't interrupt!*
Hennessy, B. G. (Barbara G.). *Corduroy's birthday*
 Corduroy's Christmas
 Corduroy's Easter
 Corduroy's Halloween
Hergé. *Explorers on the moon*
Hide-and-seek bunnies

Hill, Eric. *Spot and friends dress up*
 Spot and friends play
 Spot bakes a cake
 Spot goes on holiday
 Spot goes to a party
 Spot goes to school
 Spot goes to the beach
 Spot goes to the park
 Spot sleeps over
 Spot's baby sister
 Spot's birthday party
 Spot's first Christmas
 Spot's first Easter
 Spot's first walk
 Spot's walk in the woods
 Where's Spot?
Hillman, Priscilla. *A Merry-Mouse book of months*
Hindley, Judy. *The big red bus*
 Ten bright eyes
Hissey, Jane. *Old Bear, a pop-up book*
Hoban, Tana. *Just look*
 Look book
Holmes, Stephen. *Hidden numbers*
The house that Jack built. *The house that Jack built*, ill. by Seymour Chwast
 The house that Jack built, ill. by Nadine Bernard Westcott
Howe, James. *Bunnicula escapes!*
Hulme, Joy N. *Eerie feary feeling*
Hurd, Thacher. *A night in the swamp*
Inkpen, Mick. *Anything cuddly will do!*
 Crocodile!
 Kipper's bathtime
 Kipper's bedtime
 Kipper's playtime
 Kipper's snacktime
 Lullabyhullaballoo!
 Penguin small
 This troll, that troll
 The very good dinosaur
 Where, oh where, is Kipper's bear?
Isaacs, Gwynne L. *Baby face*
It feels like Christmas!. *It feels like Christmas!*
Ives, Penny. *The golden angel*
 On Christmas eve
 The snow angel
Johnson, B. J. *A hat like that*
 My blanket Burt
Jolley, Mike. *Grunter, a pig with an attitude!*
Jonas, Ann. *Where can it be?*
Jones, Carol. *What's the time, Mr. Wolf?*
Kemp, Moira. *Lift-the-flap chick*
 Lift-the-flap kitten
 Lift-the-flap mouse
 Lift-the-flap puppy
Kopper, Lisa. *Ten little babies*
Kraus, Robert. *See the Christmas lights*
 See the moon
Kunhardt, Edith. *Pat the cat*
 Pat the puppy
Kurokawa, Mitsuhiro. *Dinosaur valley*
Lacome, Julie. *Funny business*
 Garden
 Hocus pocus
Lagerlöf, Selma. *The changeling*
Laidlaw, Ken. *The amazing I spy ABC*
Lattimore, Deborah Nourse. *I wonder what's under there?*
Leonard, Marcia. *The best snowman ever*

Leslie, Amanda. *Are chickens stripy?*
  Do crocodiles moo?
  Flappy, waggy, wiggly
  Let's look inside the red car
  Let's look inside the yellow truck
  Play kitten play
  Play puppy play
Lewison, Wendy Cheyette. *Bye-bye, baby*
  My baby brother
  My favorite doll
  My new puppy
  Ten little ballerinas
  Uh oh, baby
  Where's baby?
  Where's my teddy?
Lippman, Peter. *Peter Lippman's numbers*
  Peter Lippman's opposites
Lishak, Anthony. *Row your boat*
Little old lady who swallowed a fly. *Fancy that!*
  I know an old lady, ill. by Steve McInturff
  There was an old lady, ill. by Nick Bantock
  There was an old lady who swallowed a fly, ill. by
    Pam Adams
  There was an old lady who swallowed a fly, ill. by
    Colin Hawkins
Llewellyn, Claire. *My first book of time*
Lobel, Arnold. *The frog and toad pop-up book*
Longfellow, Layne. *Imaginary menagerie*
Lundell, Margo. *The furry bedtime book*
Maccarone, Grace. *Pumpkin faces*
McGowan, Alan. *Sailing ships*
McGuire, Richard. *What's wrong with this book?*
McKee, David. *I can too!*
MacKinnon, Debbie. *Billy's boots*
  Cathy's cake
  Daniel's duck
  Find monkey!
  Find my boots!
  Find my cake!
  Ken's kitten
  Let's play: I can do it!
  Meg's monkey
  My day: I can do it!
  My kitty!
  Pippa's puppy
  Sarah's shovel
  Tom's train
McMullan, Kate (Hall). *Hearty har har*
  No no Jo
  Trick or eeek!
McNaughton, Colin. *Shh! (Don't tell Mr. Wolf!)*
  Who's that banging on the ceiling?
McPartland, Suzy. *Good morning, sun*
  Sleepy-time moon
  Toy-shop surprise
  Zoom, car, zoom
Maisner, Heather. *Find Mouse in the house*
  Find Mouse in the yard
Mantegazza, Giovanna. *Look how a baby grows*
  Look inside a car
  Look inside a farm
  Look inside a rainforest
Maris, Ron. *Bernard's boring day*
  Is anyone home?
Marshall, James. *Hey, diddle, diddle*
Marshall, Janet Perry. *Banana moon*
Marshall, Ray. *Pop-up numbers #1*
  Pop-up numbers #2
  Pop-up numbers #3

Pop-up numbers #4
  The train
Martin, Bill (William Ivan). *Chicka chicka sticka
    sticka*
Martin, Sarah Catherine. *Old Mother Hubbard*
Mason, Lura. *A book of boxes*
Meeuwissen, Tony. *Remarkable animals*
Meggendorfer, Lothar. *The genius of Lothar Meggen-
    dorfer*
Melcher, Mary. *Mommy, who does God love?*
Mellor, Corinne. *Bruce the balding moose*
  Clark the toothless shark
Merriam, Eve. *What in the world?*
Meryl, Debra. *Baby's peek-a-boo album*
Milne, A. A. (Alan Alexander). *House at Pooh corner*
    [a pop-up book]
  Pooh and some bees
  Pooh goes visiting
  Winnie-the-Pooh
Milstein, Linda Breiner. *Grandma's jewelry box*
Miranda, Anne. *Baby talk*
  Baby-sit
Monfried, Lucia. *Dishes all done*
Moon, Nicola. *At the beginning of a pig*
Moore, Karen Ann. *The baby king*
Moseley, Keith. *Dinosaurs*
Most, Bernard. *Peek-a-moo!*
Mother Goose. *Humpty Dumpty*, ill. by Moira Kemp
  Little Miss Muffet
  1, 2 buckle my shoe
  Sing a song of sixpence, ill. by Ray Marshall and
    Korky Paul
  This little pig went to market, ill. by Denise Fleming
Mudd-Ruth, Maria. *The beetle*
  The ultimate ocean book
Mullins, Patricia. *Dinosaur encore*
Munari, Bruno. *The elephant's wish*
  Jimmy has lost his cap
  Tic, Tac and Toc
  Who's there? Open the door
Murphy, Chuck. *Black cat, white cat*
  Chuck Murphy's alphabet magic
Nappa, Mike. *Do you see the star?*
Nayer, Judy. *Funny bunnies*
  Mice are nice
  Pig in a wig
  Tricky puppies
Nilsén, Anna. *Where are Percy's friends?*
  Where is Percy's dinner?
Oakley, Graham. *Graham Oakley's magical changes*
Old MacDonald had a farm. *Old MacDonald had a
    farm*, ill. by Jessica Souhami
Olyff, Clotilde. *1,2,3. One, two, three*
Ormerod, Jan. *Ben goes swimming*
  Emily dances
  Rock-a-baby
Pearson, Tracey Campbell. *A apple pie*
Pelham, David. *A is for animals*
  Crawlies creep
  Sam's pizza
  Sam's sandwich
  Worms wiggle
Pfister, Marcus. *Milo and the magical stones*
Philpot, Lorna. *Amazing Anthony Ant*
Pienkowski, Jan. *Good night, a pop-up lullaby*
Piers, Helen. *Who's in my bed?*
Porter, Sue. *Parsnip*
  Parsnip and the pink blanket
  Parsnip and the runaway tractor

Potter, Beatrix. *The two bad mice*
Presencer, Alain. *Roaring lion tales*
Price, Mathew. *Patch and the rabbits*
　Peekaboo!
Priestley, Alice. *Someone is reading this book*
Prokofiev, Sergei Sergeievitch. *Peter and the wolf*, ill.
　by Barbara Cooney
Reasoner, Charles. *The big busy building*
　Who drives this?
　Who pretends?
Rex, Michael. *Who builds?*
　Who digs?
Richards, Kitty. *Merry Christmas, Rugrats!*
Richardson, John. *Ten bears in a bed*
　Where's Jack?
Robinson, Aminah Brenda Lynn. *A street called*
　home
Roddie, Shen. *Hatch, egg, hatch!*
　Help, Mama, help!
Roffey, Maureen. *Home sweet home*
Rose, Emma. *Ballet magic*
Ross, Tony. *This old man*
Roth, Harold. *Let's look all around the farm*
　Let's look all around the house
　Let's look all around the town
　Let's look for surprises all around
Rowe, Jeannette. *Whose ears?*
　Whose feet?
　Whose nose?
Ruby-Spears Enterprises. *The puppy's new adventures*
Ruschak, Lynette. *The counting zoo*
Sabuda, Robert. *ABC Disney*
Sabuda, Robert James. *The Christmas alphabet*
　The movable Mother Goose
　The mummy's tomb
Safran, Sheri. *The musical cherub*
　The painted cherub
Saunders, Dave. *Ten times better*
Savage, Stephen. *Making tracks*
Scarry, Huck. *Looking into the Middle Ages*
Scarry, Richard. *Richard Scarry's mix or match story-*
　book
Schlein, Miriam. *Sleep safe, little whale*
Scuderi, Lucia. *To fly*
See the dinosaurs
Selberg, Ingrid. *Nature's hidden world*
Seymour, Peter S. *Animals in disguise*
　How the weather works
　Insects
　Pilots
　The pop-up book of big trucks
　What lives in the sea?
　What's in the deep blue sea?
　What's in the prehistoric forest?
Shapiro, Arnold L. *Circle*
　Square
　Triangles
Sharratt, Nick. *Ketchup on your cornflakes?*
　Rocket countdown
Shields, Carol Diggory. *Colors*
Shopping
Sibbick, John. *Creatures of long ago*
Sis, Peter. *Fire truck*
　Trucks, trucks, trucks
Skwarek, Skip. *The horrors of Howling Hall*
　Mystery of Maggoty Mill
Smallman, Clare. *Outside in*
Smith, Mavis. *Fred, is that you?*
Spiegelman, Art. *I'm a dog!*

Stapler, Sarah. *Trilby's trumpet*
Stickland, Paul. *Dinosaur stomp!*
　Truck jam
The Superman mix or match storybook
Thomas's big railway pop-up book
The three little pigs. The three little pigs, ill. by John
　Wallner
　Who's at the door?
Tilden, Ruth. *Freddie works out*
　Sophie's dance class
Trevelyan, Kathy. *Don't be surprised!*
Tucker, Sian. *A is for astronaut*
Tullet, Hervé. *Night / day*
Underhill, Liz. *The lucky coin*
Van der Meer, Ron. *Funny hats*
　Pigs at home
Van Fleet, Matthew. *Fuzzy yellow ducklings*
　One yellow lion
　Spotted yellow frogs
Varekamp, Marjolein. *Little Sam takes a bath*
Verdet, Andre. *All about time*
Walker, Jane. *Ten little penguins*
Wallner, John C. *Look and find*
　Old MacDonald had a farm
Watson, Claire. *Big creatures from the past*
Watson, Wendy. *The bunnies' Christmas eve*
Weeks, Sarah. *Noodles*
Wells, Rosemary. *Goodnight Max*
Whales
Wilson-Max, Ken. *Big blue engine*
　Big red fire truck
　Little red plane
　Max loves sunflowers
Wood, Audrey. *The napping house wakes up*
Wood, David. *Silly spider!*
Wyllie, Stephen. *Dinner with fox*
　Snappity snap
Yee, Patrick. *Bedtime for Rosie Rabbit*
　Little Buddy meets Bobo
Yoshi. *Who's hiding here?*
Youldon, Gillian. *Colors*
　Numbers
Zager, Karen. *Bubbles*
Zelinsky, Paul O. *The wheels on the bus*
Ziefert, Harriet. *Animals of the Bible*
　Bear all year
　Bear gets dressed
　Bear goes shopping
　Bear's busy morning
　Daddies are for catching fireflies
　Dancing
　Mommies are for counting stars
　People of the Bible
　Talk, baby!
　Where's daddy's car?
　Where's mommy's truck?

Fortune *see* Character traits – luck

Fortune tellers *see* Careers – fortune tellers

Fourth of July *see* Holidays – Fourth of July

Foxes *see* Animals – foxes

France *see* Foreign lands – France

Freedom *see* Character traits – freedom

French Americans *see* Ethnic groups in the U.S. – French Americans

French Guiana *see* Foreign lands – French Guiana

Friendship

Ada, Alma Flor. *Jordi's star*
   The unicorn of the west
Adinolfi, JoAnn. *The Egyptian polar bear*
Æsop. *The ant and the dove*
Alborough, Jez. *My friend bear*
Alcantara, Ricardo. *Dog and cat*
Aldridge, Josephine Haskell. *The best of friends*
Alexander, Martha G. *My outrageous friend Charlie*
Alexander, Sue. *Ellsworth and Millicent*
   Small plays for you and a friend
   What's wrong now, Millicent?
   Witch, Goblin and sometimes Ghost
Aliki. *Best friends together again*
   Feelings
   Overnight at Mary Bloom's
   We are best friends
Allard, Harry. *The cactus flower bakery*
Allen, Pamela. *My cat Maisie*
Allinson, Beverley. *Effie*
Anderson, Lena. *Stina's visit*
Anderson, Leone Castell. *My friend next door*
Anderson, Paul S. *Red fox and the hungry tiger*
Anglund, Joan Walsh. *Cowboy and his friend*
   A friend is someone who likes you
Anholt, Catherine. *Snow fairy and the spaceman*
Anholt, Laurence. *Camille and the sunflowers*
Ardizzone, Edward. *Tim and Lucy go to sea*
Argent, Kerry. *Wombat and Bandicoot*
Arnold, Caroline. *My friend from outer space*
Artis, Vicki Kimmel. *Pajama walking*
Aruego, José. *The king and his friends*
Asare, Meshack. *Cat . . . in search of a friend*
Asch, Frank. *Moonbear's friend*
   Moonbear's pet
   Oats and wild apples
Auch, Mary Jane. *Bird dogs can't fly*
Aylesworth, Jim. *McGraw's Emporium*
   Mr. McGill goes to town
Baker, Alan. *Benjamin and the box*
Baker, Barbara. *Digby and Kate*
   Digby and Kate again
Baker, Betty. *Partners*
Balian, Lorna. *Wilbur's space machine*
Ballard, Robin. *Carnival*
Barasch, Lynne. *Old friends*
Barbour, Karen. *Nancy*
Barrett, Joyce Durham. *Willie's not the hugging kind*
Bassett, Lisa. *Beany wakes up for Christmas*
Bastin, Marjolein. *My name is Vera*
   Vera and her friends
Batchelor, Louise. *Whoops!*
Battles, Edith. *One to teeter-totter*
Baylor, Byrd. *Guess who my favorite person is*
Baynton, Martin. *Fifty saves his friend*
Bedard, Michael. *Sitting ducks*
Begaye, Lisa Shook. *Building a bridge*
Beim, Jerrold. *The swimming hole*
Beim, Lorraine. *Two is a team*

Bell, Norman. *Linda's airmail letter*
Belton, Sandra. *May'naise sandwiches and sunshine tea*
Bender, Robert. *A little witch magic*
Berends, Polly Berrien. *Ladybug and dog and the night walk*
Berenstain, Stan. *The Berenstain bears and the trouble with friends*
   The Berenstain bears' moving day
Berger, Barbara Helen. *When the sun rose*
Berger, Terry. *Friends*
Bergman, Donna. *City fox*
Bergstrom, Corinne. *Losing your best friend*
Bianchi, John. *Swine snafu*
Binzen, Bill. *Carmen*
Birdseye, Tom. *She'll be comin' round the mountain*
Blake, Quentin. *Clown*
Blance, Ellen. *Monster looks for a friend*
Blaustein, Muriel. *Make friends, Zachary!*
Bliss, Corinne Demas. *That dog Melly!*
Bluthenthal, Diana Cain. *Matilda the moocher*
Boelts, Maribeth. *Grace and Joe*
   Little Bunny's cool tool set
Bohdal, Susi. *Bobby the bear*
Bolliger, Max. *The lonely prince*
Bond, Felicia. *Four Valentines in a rainstorm*
Bonsall, Crosby Newell. *It's mine! A greedy book*
Bornstein, Ruth Lercher. *The seedling child*
Borton, Lady. *Junk pile!*
Bos, Burny. *Prince Valentino*
Bottner, Barbara. *Horrible Hannah*
   Mean Maxine
Bourgeois, Paulette. *Franklin's new friend*
   Franklin's secret club
Bourguignon, Laurence. *A friend for Tiger*
Bowen, Keith. *Katy's gift*
Boyd, Lizi. *Black dog red house*
Boyd, Selma. *The how: making the best of a mistake*
Boynton, Sandra. *Chloë and Maude*
Bradbury, Ray. *Switch on the night*, ill. by Leo and Diane Dillion
   Switch on the night, ill. by Madeleine Gekiere
Breinburg, Petronella. *Shawn goes to school*
Brenner, Barbara A. *Lion and Lamb*
Brewster, Patience. *Two bushy badgers*
Briggs, Raymond. *The snowman*
Bright, Robert. *Me and the bears*
Brimner, Larry Dane. *Aggie and Will*
   Dinosaurs dance
   Max and Felix
Brophy, Nannette. *The color of my fur*
Brown, Laurie Krasny. *How to be a friend*
Brown, Marc Tolon. *Arthur's birthday*
   The cloud over Clarence
   The true Francine
Brown, Myra Berry. *Best friends*
   First night away from home
Browne, Anthony. *Willy and Hugh*
Browne, Eileen. *Where's that bus?*
Bruna, Dick. *A story to tell*
Brutschy, Jennifer. *Celeste and Crabapple Sam*
Bryan, Dorothy. *Friendly little Jonathan*
Buck, Pearl S. (Pearl Sydenstricker). *The little fox in the middle*
Buntain, Ruth Jaeger. *The birthday story*
Bunting, Eve (Anne Evelyn). *The blue and the gray*
   Clancy's coat
   Monkey in the middle
   On Call Back Mountain

Lindgren, Astrid. *Do you know Pippi Longstocking?*
Lindgren, Barbro. *A worm's tale*
Lionni, Leo. *Alexander and the wind-up mouse*
  An extraordinary egg
  Fish is fish
  Little blue and little yellow
  Mr. McMouse
  Nicholas, where have you been?
Lipkind, William. *The two reds*
Lipniacka, Ewa. *To bed . . . or else!*
Lobato, Arcadio. *The greatest treasure*
Lobel, Arnold. *Days with Frog and Toad*
  Frog and Toad all year
  Frog and Toad are friends
  Frog and Toad together
London, Jonathan. *Shawn and Keeper: show-and-tell*
  What Newt could do for Turtle
Loomis, Christine. *In the diner*
Lund, Doris Herold. *You ought to see Herbert's house*
Lund, Jillian. *Two cool coyotes*
Luttrell, Ida. *Ottie Slockett*
Lyon, George Ella. *A day at damp camp*
  Together
Lystad, Mary H. *That new boy*
McBratney, Sam. *I'm sorry*
McClure, Gillian. *What's the time, Rory Wolf?*
McCormack, John E. *Rabbit tales*
  Rabbit travels
McCourt, Lisa. *Della Splatnuk birthday girl*
  The new kid and the cookie thief
MacDonald, Amy. *Little Beaver and the echo*
Macdonald, Maryann. *The pink party*
McDonald, Megan. *Lucky star*
  The night Iguana left home
MacGregor, Ellen. *Mr. Pingle and Mr. Buttonhouse*
McKay, Louise. *Marny's ride with the wind*
McKee, David. *Elmer and Wilbur*
  Elmer in the snow
  Elmer's friends
McKissack, Patricia C. *Messy Bessey and the birthday overnight*
MacLachlan, Patricia. *Moon, stars, frogs and friends*
McPhail, David M. *Big Pig and Little Pig*
  A bug, a bear, and a boy
  A girl, a goat, and a goose
Maestro, Giulio. *Leopard is sick*
Mahy, Margaret. *Making friends*
Majewski, Joe. *A friend for Oscar Mouse*
Mallett, Anne. *Here comes Tagalong*
Malone, Nola Langner. *A home*
Mandry, Kathy. *The cat and the mouse and the mouse and the cat*
Manson, Christopher. *Two travelers*
Marshall, Edward. *Fox all week*
  Three by the sea
Marshall, James. *The Cut-Ups cut loose*
  George and Martha
  George and Martha back in town
  George and Martha encore
  George and Martha one fine day
  George and Martha rise and shine
  George and Martha 'round and 'round
  The guest
  Speedboat
  What's the matter with Carruthers?
  Willis
Martin, Ann M. *Rachel Parker, kindergarten show-off*
Martin, David. *Lizzie and her friend*

Martin, Jacqueline Briggs. *Bizzy Bones and Moose-mouse*
  Bizzy Bones and the lost quilt
Mathers, Petra. *Lottie's new friend*
Mayer, Mercer. *A boy, a dog, a frog and a friend*
  A boy, a dog and a frog
  Frog, where are you?
Mead, Alice. *Billy and Emma*
Medearis, Angela Shelf. *The adventures of Sugar and Junior*
  Best friends in the snow
  We eat dinner in the bathtub
Mellor, Corinne. *Bruce the balding moose*
Merriam, Eve. *Boys and girls, girls and boys*
Metcalf, Paula. *Norma No Friends*
Miles, Betty. *Having a friend*
Miles, Sally. *Alfi and the dark*
Millais, Raoul. *Elijah and Pin-Pin*
Miller, Edna. *Mousekin finds a friend*
Mills, Lauren A. *The rag coat*
Min, Willemien. *Peter's patchwork dream*
Minarik, Else Holmelund. *Little Bear's friend*
Modarressi, Mitra. *The beastly visits*
  The dream pillow
Moers, Hermann. *Katie and the big, brave bear*
Monsell, Mary Elise. *Armadillo*
Monson, A. M. *Wanted . . . best friend*
Montenegro, Laura Nyman. *Sweet Tooth*
Moon, Nicola. *Alligator tails and crocodile cakes*
Moore, Inga. *Little dog lost*
Morozumi, Atsuko. *My friend gorilla*
Morris, Ann. *Eleanora Mousie's gray day*
Morrow, Suzanne Stark. *Inatuck's friend*
Mostacchi, Massimo. *A dog's best friend*
Munsch, Robert N. *Millicent and the wind*
  Murmel, Murmel, Murmel
  Wait and see
Murphy, Jill. *All for one*
Murphy, Stuart J. *Betcha!*
  Give me half!
Narahashi, Keiko. *Two girls can!*
Naylor, Phyllis Reynolds. *King of the playground*
Nelson, Brenda. *Mud for sale*
Nelson, Nan Ferring. *My day with Anka*
Neuhaus, David. *His finest hour*
Neville, Mary. *The Christmas tree ride*
Newberry, Clare Turlay. *Marshmallow*
Newsome, Jill. *Shadow*
Nicholls, Judith. *Someone I like*
Nikly, Michelle. *The emperor's plum tree*
Nikola-Lisa, W. *Bein' with you this way*
Nilsén, Anna. *Where are Percy's friends?*
Njeng, Pierre Yves. *Vacation in the village*
Nolen, Jerdine. *Raising dragons*
Nomura, Takaaki. *Grandpa's town*
Nones, Eric Jon. *Caleb's friend*
Novak, Matt. *Claude and Sun*
  Jazzbo and Googy
Numeroff, Laura Joffe. *Amy for short*
Oakley, Graham. *The church mice and the ring*
O'Callahan, Jay. *Herman and Marguerite*
O'Donnell, Peter. *Pinkie goes south*
Oppenheim, Shulamith Levey. *The lily cupboard*
Oram, Hiawyn. *Badger's bad mood*
  Badger's bring something party
  Mine!
Oxenbury, Helen. *First day of school*
  Friends
  Tom and Pippo and the dog

Wilfred the rat
The worst person in the world
The worst person in the world at Crab Beach
Stewart, Paul. *A little bit of winter*
Stone, Phoebe. *Go away, Shelley Boo!*
Strauss, Gwen. *The night shimmy*
Strete, Craig Kee. *Big thunder magic*
Strom, Maria Diaz. *Rainbow Joe and me*
Sugita, Yutaka. *Helena the unhappy hippopotamus*
Supraner, Robyn. *Sam Sunday and the mystery at the Ocean Beach Hotel*
Tafuri, Nancy. *My friends*
  Will you be my friend?
Taha, Karen T. *A gift for Tia Rose*
Talbott, Hudson. *Going Hollywood! A dinosaur's dream*
Taulbert, Clifton L. *Little Cliff and the porch people*
Taylor, Mark. *Old Blue, you good dog you*
Tether, Graham. *Skunk and possum*
Thaler, Mike. *It's me, hippo!*
  Moonkey
Tharlet, Eve. *Little pig, big trouble*
Thayer, Jane. *Gus was a friendly ghost*
  The popcorn dragon, ill. by Jay Hyde Barnum
  The popcorn dragon, ill. by Lisa McCue
Thompson, Richard. *Effie's bath*
  Jenny's neighbours
Tibo, Gilles. *Simon and the snowflakes*
Torres, Daniel. *Tom*
Trimble, Patti. *What day is it?*
Tripp, Paul. *The strawman who smiled by mistake*
Trivas, Irene. *Annie . . . Anya*
Tsutsui, Yoriko. *Anna's secret friend*
Tudor, Bethany. *Samuel's tree house*
Uchida, Yoshiko. *The bracelet*
Udry, Janice May. *Let's be enemies*
Uff, Caroline. *Hello, Lulu*
Van Woerkom, Dorothy. *Harry and Shelburt*
Varley, Susan. *Badger's parting gifts*
Velthuijs, Max. *Frog is a hero*
  Frog is frightened
Venable, Alan. *The checker players*
VerDorn, Bethea. *Day breaks*
Vigna, Judith. *The hiding house*
Vincent, Gabrielle. *Breakfast time, Ernest and Celestine*
  Ernest and Celestine's patchwork quilt
  Merry Christmas, Ernest and Celestine
Viorst, Judith. *Rosie and Michael*
Waber, Bernard. *Gina*
  Ira says goodbye
  Ira sleeps over
  Lovable Lyle
  Nobody is perfick
Waddell, Martin. *We love them*
Wade, Anne. *A promise is for keeping*
Waechter, Friedrich Karl. *Three is company*
Wagner, Karen. *Bravo, Mildred and Ed!*
  A friend like Ed
Walker, Alice. *To hell with dying*
Wallace, Nancy Elizabeth. *Paperwhite*
Ward, Helen. *The golden pear*
Warren, Cathy. *Fred's first day*
Wayne-von-Königslöw, Andrea. *Bing and Chutney*
Weedn, Flavia. *The little snow bear*
Weil, Lisl. *Gillie and the flattering fox*
Weiss, Ellen. *Mokey's birthday present*
Weiss, Nicki. *Battle day at Camp Delmont*
  A family story

Maude and Sally
Weninger, Brigitte. *Why are you fighting, Davy?*
Whitcher, Susan. *Something for everyone*
White, Linda Arms. *Too many pumpkins*
Wiesner, William. *Tops*
Wild, Margaret. *Mr. Nick's knitting*
  The very best of friends
Wildsmith, Brian. *The lazy bear*
Wilhelm, Hans. *Let's be friends again!*
  A new home, a new friend
Williams, Barbara. *Kevin's grandma*
Williams, Karen Lynn. *When Africa was home*
Williams, Sherley Anne. *Girls together*
Winthrop, Elizabeth. *The Best Friends Club*
  Katharine's doll
  Lizzie and Harold
  Sloppy kisses
Wittbold, Maureen. *Mending Peter's heart*
Wittman, Sally. *The boy who hated Valentine's Day*
  Pelly and Peak
  Plenty of Pelly and Peak
  A special trade
  The wonderful Mrs. Trumbly
Wojciechowski, Susan. *The Christmas miracle of Jonathan Toomey*
Wolcott, Patty. *Double-decker, double-decker, double-decker bus*
Wolde, Gunilla. *Betsy and Peter are different*
Wolkstein, Diane. *Little Mouse's painting*
  Step by step
Wood, Audrey. *Jubal's wish*
Wormell, Christopher. *Blue Rabbit and friends*
Yashima, Taro. *The youngest one*
Yee, Patrick. *Let's make friends*
Yee, Paul. *The boy in the attic*
Yeoman, John. *Mouse trouble*
You and me
Young, Ruth. *Golden Bear*
Zabar, Abbie. *Fifty-five friends*
Zalben, Jane Breskin. *Beni's first Chanukah*
  Oliver and Alison's week
Zarin, Cynthia. *Rose and Sebastian*
Zelinsky, Paul O. *The lion and the stoat*
Ziefert, Harriet. *Mike and Tony*
  Nicky's friends
Zion, Gene. *The meanest squirrel I ever met*
Zolotow, Charlotte (Shapiro). *The hating book*
  Hold my hand
  Janey
  My friend John
  The new friend
  Three funny friends
  Timothy too!
  The unfriendly book
  The white marble

Frogs and toads

Æsop. *The hare and the frogs*
Alexander, Martha G. *No ducks in our bathtub*
Anderson, Peggy Perry. *Out to lunch*
  Time for bed, the babysitter said
  To the tub
Arnold, Tedd. *Green Wilma*
Asch, Frank. *Baby Bird's first nest*
  Moonbear's pet
Back, Christine. *Tadpole and frog*
Bancroft, Catherine. *Felix's hat*
Berenzy, Alix. *A frog prince*

Noll, Sally. *Off and counting*
Nunes, Susan Miho. *Tiddalick the frog*
Ogburn, Jacqueline K. *The reptile ball*
Owen, Annie. *Wake up Frog!*
Parker, Nancy Winslow. *Working frog*
Partridge, Jenny. *Hopfellow*
Pavey, Peter. *I'm Taggarty Toad*
Pendery, Rosemary. *A home for Hopper*
Pfeffer, Wendy. *From tadpole to frog*
Pfister, Marcus. *Hopper hunts for spring*
Policoff, Stephen Phillip. *Cesar's amazing journey*
Popov, Nikolai. *Why?*
Potter, Beatrix. *The tale of Mr. Jeremy Fisher*, ill. by author
    The tale of Mr. Jeremy Fisher, ill. by David Jorgensen
Priceman, Marjorie. *Friend or frog*
Pursell, Margaret Sanford. *Sprig the tree frog*
Rockwell, Anne F. *Big boss*
    Toad
Roth, Susan L. *The biggest frog in Australia*
Samton, Sheila White. *Frogs in clogs*
Samuels, Barbara. *What's so great about Cindy Snappleby?*
Santore, Charles. *William the Curious*
Saul, Carol P. *Peter's song*
Schertle, Alice. *Advice for a frog and other poems*
    Little Frog's song
Schubert, Ingrid. *The magic bubble trip*
Schumacher, Claire. *Brave Lily*
Scieszka, Jon. *The frog prince, continued*
Seeger, Pete. *The foolish frog*
Seuss, Dr. *Would you rather be a bullfrog?*
Shannon, George. *April showers*
    Frog legs
Simms, Laura. *Moon and Otter and Frog*
Small, David. *Eulalie and the hopping head*
Smith, Jim. *The frog band and Durrington Dormouse*
    The frog band and the onion seller
    The frog band and the owlnapper
Snape, Juliet. *Frog odyssey*
Solotareff, Grégoire. *The ogre and the frog king*
Steig, William. *Gorky rises*
Steptoe, John. *The story of jumping mouse*
Stevenson, James. *Monty*
Stratemeyer, Clara Georgeanna. *Frog fun*
    Tuggy
Talley, Linda. *Jackson's plan*
Taylor, Kim. *Frog*
Thayer, Mike. *In the middle of the puddle*
Tilden, Ruth. *Freddie works out*
Tresselt, Alvin R. *Frog in the well*
Troughton, Joanna. *What made Tiddalik laugh*
Turska, Krystyna. *The woodcutter's duck*
Van Woerkom, Dorothy. *Sea frog, city frog*
Velthuijs, Max. *Frog and the birdsong*
    Frog in love
    Frog is a hero
    Frog is frightened
    Little Man to the rescue
Vesey, A. *The princess and the frog*
Wahl, Jan. *Doctor Rabbit's foundling*
Walsh, Ellen Stoll. *Jack's tale*
Walt Disney Productions. *Walt Disney's The adventures of Mr. Toad*
Weiss, Monica. *Mmmm . . . cookies!*
West, Colin. *"Pardon?" said the giraffe*
Wiesner, David. *Tuesday*
Wood, Audrey. *Jubal's wish*

Wynne-Jones, Tim. *The hour of the frog*
Yeoman, John. *The bear's water picnic*
Yolen, Jane. *King Long Shanks*
Zakhoder, Boris Vladimirovich. *Rosachok*

Frontier life *see* U.S. history – frontier and pioneer life

Furniture

Devlin, Wende. *Aunt Agatha, there's a lion under the couch!*
Hutchins, H. J. (Hazel J.). *Leanna builds a genie trap*
Lillegard, Dee. *Wake up house!*
Thompson, Carol. *Piggy goes to bed*

Furniture – beds

Allen, Linda. *Mrs. Simkin's bed*
Arnold, Tedd. *No jumping on the bed!*
Buckingham, Simon. *Alec and his flying bed*
Camp, Lindsay. *The biggest bed in the world*
Deedy, Carmen Agra. *Agatha's feather bed*
Dickinson, Mary. *Alex's bed*
Dillon, Barbara. *The beast in the bed*
Freedman, Sally. *Devin's new bed*
Greenberg, Dan. *The bed who ran away from home*
Grindley, Sally. *Wake up, dad!*
Grossblatt, Ruby M. *Who's that sleeping on my sofabed?*
Hamm, Diane Johnston. *Grandma drives a motor bed*
Hawkins, Mark. *A lion under her bed*
Hines, Anna Grossnickle. *My own big bed*
Howe, James. *There's a monster under my bed*
Howell, Lynn. *Winifred's new bed*
Klein, Suzanne. *An elephant in my bed*
Knutson, Kimberley. *Bed bouncers*
Lewis, J. Patrick. *Isabella Abnormella and the very, very finicky Queen of Trouble*
Lum, Kate. *What! cried Granny*
Parker, Nancy Winslow. *The crocodile under Louis Finneberg's bed*
Pulver, Robin. *Alicia's tutu*
Rosen, Michael (1946-). *Under the bed*
Schubert, Ingrid. *There's a crocodile under my bed!*
Stevenson, James. *What's under my bed?*
Storm, Theodor. *Little Hobbin*
Swain, Ruth Freeman. *Bedtime!*
Thaler, Mike. *There's a hippopotamus under my bed*
Willis, Jeanne. *The monster bed*
Winthrop, Elizabeth. *Bunk beds*

Furniture – chairs

Bible, Charles. *Jennifer's new chair*
Cappetta, Cynthia. *Chairs, chairs, chairs!*
Graham, Thomas. *Mr. Bear's chair*
Hale, Irina. *Brown bear in a brown chair*
Jackson, Jean. *Mrs. Piccolo's easy chair*
Joosse, Barbara M. *The morning chair*
Keats, Ezra Jack. *Peter's chair*
Kessler, Ethel. *Do baby bears sit in chairs?*
Lanteigne, Helen. *The seven chairs*
Lanton, Sandy. *Daddy's chair*
Nordqvist, Sven. *Porker finds a chair*
Root, Phyllis. *The old red rocking chair*
Schweitzer, Iris. *Hilda's restful chair*
Scott, Ann Herbert. *Grandmother's chair*
Smith, Maggie (Margaret C.). *My grandma's chair*

Tennyson, Noel. *The lady's chair and the ottoman*
Williams, Vera B. *A chair for my mother*
Zander, Hans. *My blue chair*

Furniture – couches, sofas

Grossblatt, Ruby M. *Who's that sleeping on my sofabed?*
Newton, Jill. *Don't sit there!*
Seligson, Susan. *The amazing Amos and the greatest couch on earth*
    Amos ahoy
    Amos camps out
    Amos

Furniture – cradles

Bond, Rebecca. *Just like a baby*

Furniture – dressers

Montenegro, Laura Nyman. *One stuck drawer*

Furniture – tables

Grimm, Jacob. *The table, the donkey and the stick*
    The wishing table
Heller, Linda. *Lily at the table*

Galapagos Islands *see* Foreign lands – Galapagos Islands

Galilee *see* Foreign lands – Galilee

Gambia *see* Foreign lands – Gambia

Games

Agostinelli, Maria Enrica. *I know something you don't know*
Ahlberg, Janet. *Each peach pear plum*
    Peek-a-boo!
Alexander, Martha G. *We never get to do anything*
    Where's Willy?
Allen, Jeffrey. *The secret life of Mr. Weird*
Allington, Richard L. *Letters*
Anderson, Douglas. *Let's draw a story*
Anglund, Joan Walsh. *The brave cowboy*
    Cowboy's secret life
Anno, Mitsumasa. *Anno's animals*
    Anno's Britain
    Anno's counting house
    Anno's flea market
    Anno's Italy
    Anno's journey
    Anno's magical ABC
    Anno's U.S.A.
    Topsy turvies
    Topsy turvies
    Upside-downers
Appelbaum, Neil. *Is there a hole in your head?*

Aruego, José. *Look what I can do*
    We hide, you seek
Asch, Frank. *Goodnight horsey*
Baillie, Allan. *Drac and the gremlin*
Baker, Keith. *Hide and snake*
Ball, Duncan. *Jeremy's tail*
Battles, Edith. *One to teeter-totter*
Bauman, A. F. *Guess where you're going, guess what you'll do*
Baylor, Byrd. *Guess who my favorite person is*
Beach, Stewart. *Good morning, sun's up!*
Behrens, June. *Can you walk the plank?*
Berkowitz, Linda. *Alfonse, where are you?*
The big Peter Rabbit book
Blacker, Terence. *Herbie Hamster, where are you?*
Blake, Quentin. *Cockatoos*
Blanchard, Arlene. *The naughty lamb*
Blizzard, Gladys S. *Come look with me*
Bonsall, Crosby Newell. *The day I had to play with my sister*
Booth, Eugene. *At the circus*
    At the fair
    In the air
    In the garden
    In the jungle
    Under the ocean
Brinckloe, Julie. *Playing marbles*
Brown, Marc Tolon. *Finger rhymes*
    Hand rhymes
    One, two buckle my shoe
    Play rhymes
    What do you call a dumb bunny? and other rabbit riddles, games, jokes and cartoons
Brown, Margaret Wise. *The indoor noisy book*
Buck, Nola. *Santa's short suit shrunk and other Christmas tongue twisters*
Buckley, Helen Elizabeth. *Where did Josie go?*
Byars, Betsy Cromer. *Go and hush the baby*
Capucilli, Alyssa Satin. *Peekaboo bunny*
Carroll, Ruth. *Where's the bunny?*
Cauley, Lorinda Bryan. *Clap your hands*
Charlip, Remy. *Arm in arm*
    Where is everybody?
Chorao, Kay. *Peekaboo! Was it you?*
Civardi, Anne. *Things people do*
Clark, Harry. *The first story of the whale*
Cohen, Peter Zachary. *Authorized autumn charts of the Upper Red Canoe River country*
Cole, Joanna. *Pin the tail on the donkey and other party games*
Cowley, Stewart. *Hide-and-seek puppies*
Craig, M. Jean. *Boxes*
Delacre, Lulu. *Arroz con leche*
Delaney, Ned. *One dragon to another*
Delton, Judy. *I never win!*
Demi. *Demi's opposites*
De Paola, Tomie (Thomas Anthony). *Andy (that's my name)*
    Things to make and do for Valentine's Day
De Regniers, Beatrice Schenk. *What can you do with a shoe?*
Dubanevich, Arlene. *Pigs in hiding*
Duffy, Dee Dee (Deborah). *Barnyard tracks*
Dunbar, Fiona. *You'll never guess!*
Elting, Mary. *Q is for duck*
Emberley, Ed (Edward Randolph). *Ed Emberley's crazy mixed-up face game*
    Klippity klop
Falwell, Cathryn. *Where's Nicky?*

The farmer in the dell. *The farmer in the dell*, ill. by John O'Brien
  The farmer in the dell, ill. by Kathy Parkinson
  The farmer in the dell, ill. by Mary Maki Rae
  The farmer in the dell, ill. by Diane Stanley
  The farmer in the dell, ill. by Alexandra Wallner
Finzel, Julia. *Large as life*
Fisher, Leonard Everett. *Look around!*
Fleisher, Robbin. *Quilts in the attic*
Fowler, Allan. *What do you see in a cloud?*
Fox, Dorothea Warren. *Follow me the leader*
French, Fiona. *Hunt the thimble*
Gardner, Beau. *Guess what?*
  What is it?
Gillham, Bill. *Can you see it?*
  What can you do?
  What's the difference?
  Where does it go?
Gliori, Debi. *Mr. Bear says peek-a-boo*
Go tell Aunt Rhody. *Go tell Aunt Rhody*, ill. by Aliki
  Go tell Aunt Rhody, ill. by Robert M. Quackenbush
Gomi, Taro. *Guess who?*
  Who ate it?
  Who hid it?
Gretz, Susanna. *Hide-and-seek*
  I'm not sleepy
Grindley, Sally. *Knock, knock! Who's there?*
  Silly Goose and Dizzy Duck play hide-and-seek
Hague, Michael. *Teddy bear, teddy bear*
Hahn, Hannelore. *Take a giant step*
Handford, Martin. *Find Waldo now*
  The great Waldo search
  Where's Waldo?
  Where's Waldo? In Hollywood
  Where's Waldo now?
  Where's Waldo? The fantastic journey
  Where's Waldo? The wonder book
Hann, Jacquie. *Follow the leader*
Hawkins, Colin. *Incy wincy spider*
  Round the garden
  This little pig
Hayes, Sarah. *Clap your hands*
Haynes, Max. *Sparky's rainbow repair*
  Ticklemonster and me
Heinst, Marie. *My first number book*
Henrietta. *A mouse in the house*
Hillert, Margaret. *Play ball*
Hines, Anna Grossnickle. *What can you do in the wind?*
Hissey, Jane. *Little Bear lost*
Hoban, Russell. *How Tom beat Captain Najork and his hired sportsmen*
Hoff, Syd. *The littlest leaguer*
Hoguet, Susan Ramsay. *I unpacked my grandmother's trunk*
Holmes, Stephen. *Hidden numbers*
Houghton, Eric. *The crooked apple tree*
Hurd, Edith Thacher. *Last one home is a green pig*
Hutchins, Pat. *What game shall we play?*
  Which witch is which?
Intrater, Roberta Grobel. *Peek-a-boo!*
Johnson, Elizabeth. *All in free but Janey*
Jonas, Ann. *The trek*
Kahn, Joan. *Seesaw*
Keeshan, Robert. *She loves me, she loves me not*
Kemp, Moira. *Knock at the door*
Khalsa, Dayal Kaur. *Tales of a gambling grandma*
Knight, Joan. *Tickle-toe rhymes*

Koch, Dorothy Clarke. *I play at the beach*
Krauss, Ruth. *The bundle book*
  Mama, I wish I was snow. Child, you'd be very cold
  You're just what I need
Kroll, Steven. *The tyrannosaurus game*
Kunhardt, Edith. *Where's Peter?*
Landa, Norbert. *Rabbit and chicken play hide and seek*
Leonard, Marcia. *Peek-a-boo, baby!*
  Where's Baby-boo?
Leslie, Amanda. *Hidden toys*
  Play kitten play
  Play puppy play
Let's count and count out
Lewis, J. Patrick. *The bookworm's feast*
Lexau, Joan M. *Every day a dragon*
  I hate red rover
Lipkind, William. *Sleepyhead*
Livermore, Elaine. *Find the cat*
  Lost and found
  One to ten, count again
  Three little kittens lost their mittens
Lopshire, Robert. *How to make snop snappers and other fine things*
McCarthy, Bobette. *Happy hiding hippos*
MacDonald, Amy. *Let's do it*
McGee, Shelagh. *I'm a little teapot*
Machotka, Hana. *Breathtaking noses*
  What neat feet!
MacKinnon, Debbie. *My kitty!*
McToots, Rudi. *The kid's book of games for cars, trains and planes*
Maestro, Giulio. *The tortoise's tug of war*
Maisner, Heather. *Find Mouse in the yard*
Major, Beverly. *Playing sardines*
Marshall, Janet Perry. *My camera*
Martin, David. *Lizzie and her dolly*
Merrill, Jean. *How many kids are hiding on my block?*
Meryl, Debra. *Baby's peek-a-boo album*
Miles, Miska. *Rolling the cheese*
Miller, Margaret. *Whose shoe?*
Milne, A. A. (Alan Alexander). *Pooh's quiz book*
Mitchell, Cynthia. *Halloweena Hecatee*
Monson, A. M. *Wanted . . . best friend*
Montgomerie, Norah. *This little pig went to market*
Moon, Nicola. *Alligator tails and crocodile cakes*
Morris, Neil. *Find the canary*
  Hide and seek
  Search for Sam
  Where's my hat?
Most, Bernard. *Peek-a-moo!*
  There's an ape behind the drape
Mother Goose. *London Bridge is falling down*, ill. by Ed Emberley
  London Bridge is falling down, ill. by Peter Spier
  Mother Goose in hieroglyphics
  Pat-a-cake, pat-a-cake, ill. by Moira Kemp
  This little pig went to market, ill. by Ferelith Eccles Williams
  The three little kittens, ill. by Lorinda Bryan Cauley
  The three little kittens, ill. by Shelley Thornton
Munari, Bruno. *The birthday present*
Murphy, Stuart J. *Monster musical chairs*
Myers, Amy. *I know a monster*
Nail, James T. *Whose tracks are these?*
Nayer, Judy. *Games*
Nelson, Esther L. *Holiday singing and dancing games*
Nims, Bonnie Larkin. *Where is the bear at school?*
Offen, Hilda. *The sheep made a leap*

Oppenheim, Joanne. *The eency weency spider*
Oram, Hiawyn. *Skittlewonder and the wizard*
Ormerod, Jan. *To baby with love*
Oxenbury, Helen. *All fall down*
 The queen and Rosie Randall
Packard, Mary. *Where is Jake?*
Patterson, Elizabeth Burman. *Whose eyes are these?*
Patterson, Pat. *Hickory dickory duck*
Peppé, Rodney. *Little games*
 Odd one out
 Rodney Peppé's puzzle book
Philpot, Graham. *Fabulous fairy tale follies*
Pragoff, Fiona. *Let's find Teddy*
 Odd one out
The pudgy pat-a-cake book
The pudgy peek-a-boo book
Ra, Carol F. *Trot, trot to Boston*
Raebeck, Lois. *Who am I?*
Ray, Karen. *Sleep song*
Ripley, Catherine. *Two dozen dinosaurs*
Rockwell, Norman. *Norman Rockwell's counting book*
Rodda, Emily. *Power and glory*
Roddie, Shen. *Toes are to tickle*
Rodriguez, Bobbie. *Sarah's sleepover*
Rosales, Melodye Benson. *Double Dutch and the
 voodoo shoes*
Rosen, Michael (1946-). *We're going on a bear hunt*
Russo, Marisabina. *The big brown box*
 The line up book
 Where is Ben?
Sandberg, Inger. *Little Anna saved*
Scruggs, Afi. *Jump rope magic*
Scruton, Clive. *Mary's pets*
Selsam, Millicent E. *Is this a baby dinosaur?*
Seymour, Tres. *We played marbles*
Sharratt, Nick. *I look like this*
Shaw, Charles Green. *The blue guess book*
 The guess book
 It looked like spilt milk
Siewert, Margaret. *Bear hunt*
Sivulich, Sandra Stroner. *I'm going on a bear hunt*
Steig, William. *The bad speller*
 Pete's a pizza
Steiner, Charlotte. *Five little finger playmates*
 Red Ridinghood's little lamb
Stine, Jovial Bob. *Pork and beans*
Stoeke, Janet Morgan. *Hide and seek*
Sykes, Julie. *Robbie Rabbit and the little ones*
Taylor, Mark. *Old Blue, you good dog you*
Thwaite, Ann. *The day with the Duke*
Tison, Annette. *Animal hide-and-seek*
Trapani, Iza. *What am I?*
Ueno, Noriko. *Elephant buttons*
Ungerer, Tomi. *One, two, where's my shoe?*
 Snail, where are you?
Van Allsburg, Chris. *Jumanji*
Venable, Alan. *The checker players*
Viorst, Judith. *The Alphabet from Z to A*
Vulliamy, Clara. *Bang and shout*
 Boo baby boo!
Walsh, Melanie. *Hide and sleep*
Weil, Lisl. *Owl and other scrambles*
Wells, Tony. *Allsorts*
 Puzzle doubles
Westcott, Nadine Bernard. *The lady with the alliga-
 tor purse*
Wildsmith, Brian. *Animal games*
 Brian Wildsmith's puzzles
Williams, Jenny (Jennifer). *Ring around a rosy*

Wilner, Isabel. *The baby's game book*
Wisniewski, David. *Rain player*
Withers, Carl. *The tale of a black cat*
 The wild ducks and the goose
Wittington, Mary K. *Troll games*
Wood, A. J. *Look! The ultimate spot-the-difference book*
Wood, David. *Piggies*
Yektai, Niki. *What's missing?*
Yolen, Jane. *The lap-time song and play book*
 Street rhymes around the world
Yudell, Lynn Deena. *Make a face*
Zacharias, Thomas. *But where is the green parrot?*
Ziefert, Harriet. *Bear all year*
 Bear gets dressed
 Bear goes shopping
 Bear's busy morning
Zion, Gene. *Hide and seek day*
 Jeffie's party

Gangs *see* Clubs, gangs

Garage sales, rummage sales

Devlin, Wende. *Cranberry autumn*
Rockwell, Anne F. *Our garage sale*
Stevenson, James. *Yard sale*

Garbage collectors *see* Careers – sanitation workers

Gardens, gardening

Aliki. *Corn is maize*
 The story of Johnny Appleseed
Anno, Mitsumasa. *Anno's magic seeds*
Balian, Lorna. *A garden for a groundhog*
Barker, Cicely Mary. *Flower fairies of the garden*
Barrett, Judi. *Old MacDonald had an apartment house*
Berson, Harold. *Pop! goes the turnip*
Bishop, Gavin. *Mrs. McGinty and the bizarre plant*
Bond, Michael. *Paddington's garden*
Boon, Emilie. *Peterkin's very own garden*
Boyd, Lizi. *Lulu Crow's garden*
Boyle, Constance. *Little Owl and the weed*
Brisson, Pat. *Wanda's roses*
Brown, Marc Tolon. *Your first garden book*
Browne, Caroline. *Mrs. Christie's farmhouse*
Bruce, Lisa. *Fran's flower*
Bryan, Ashley. *The dancing granny*
Buchanan, Heather S. *Emily Mouse's garden*
Bunting, Eve (Anne Evelyn). *A day's work*
 Flower garden
 Sunflower house
Burke-Weiner, Kimberly. *The maybe garden*
Burns, Kate. *How does your garden grow?*
Butterworth, Nick. *The secret path*
Campbell, Rod. *My pop-up garden friends*
Carlstrom, Nancy White. *Moose in the garden*
Caseley, Judith. *Grandpa's garden lunch*
Cavagnaro, David. *The pumpkin people*
Coats, Laura Jane. *Alphabet garden*
Cole, Babette. *The trouble with grandad*
Cole, Henry. *Jack's garden*
Collier, Ethel. *Who goes there in my garden?*
Cowley, Stewart. *From my window*
Craft, Ruth. *Carrie Hepple's garden*
Cristini, Ermanno. *In my garden*
Crowther, Robert. *Who lives in the garden?*

Cuneo, Mary Louise. *How to grow a picket fence*
Cutler, Jane. *Mr. Carey's garden*
Davidson, Amanda. *Teddy in the garden*
Davis, Maggie S. *A garden of whales*
Delaney, A. *Pearl's first prize plant*
Demi. *The empty pot*
De Paola, Tomie (Thomas Anthony). *Four stories for four seasons*
  Too many Hopkins
Dietl, Ulla. *The plant-and-grow project book*
DiSalvo-Ryan, DyAnne. *City green*
Domanska, Janina. *The best of the bargain*
Donnelly, Liza. *Dinosaur garden*
Douglas, Richardo Keens. *The nutmeg princess*
Downey, Lynn. *Sing, Henrietta! Sing!*
Doyle, Malachy. *Jody's beans*
Dyjak, Elisabeth. *Bertha's garden*
Edwards, Michelle. *Eve and Smithy*
Ehlert, Lois. *Growing vegetable soup*
  Planting a rainbow
Ernst, Lisa Campbell. *Hamilton's art show*
  Miss Penny and Mr. Grubbs
Ezra, Mark. *The sleepy dormouse*
Farjeon, Eleanor. *Mr. Garden*
Fatio, Louise. *Marc and Pixie and the walls in Mrs. Jones's garden*
Fife, Dale. *Rosa's special garden*
Firmin, Peter. *Chicken stew*
Fisher, Aileen Lucia. *Mysteries in the garden*
Florian, Douglas. *Vegetable garden*
Fontaine, Jan. *The spaghetti tree*
Ford, Miela. *Sunflower*
Fowler, Susi Gregg. *Beautiful*
French, Vivian. *Oliver's vegetables*
Fujikawa, Gyo. *Let's grow a garden*
Gage, Wilson. *Anna's garden songs*
  Mrs. Gaddy and the fast-growing vine
Gans, Roma. *Hummingbirds in the garden*
Gershator, Phillis. *Sweet, sweet fig banana*
Gerstein, Mordicai. *Daisy's garden*
Glaser, Linda. *Compost!*
  Spectacular spiders
Godkin, Celia. *What about ladybugs?*
Goldin, Augusta. *Where does your garden grow?*
Greenstein, Elaine. *Mrs. Rose's garden*
Griffith, Helen V. *Georgia music*
Haddon, Mark. *In the garden*
Hader, Berta Hoerner. *Mister Billy's gun*
Hall, Fergus. *Groundsel*
Hall, Zoe. *The surprise garden*
Hawkins, Colin. *Round the garden*
Hearn, Diane Dawson. *Anna in the garden*
Higgs, Liz Curtis. *The parable of the lily*
Hill, Eric. *Spot in the garden*
Himmelman, John. *Amanda and the magic garden*
  The Clover County carrot contest
Hines, Anna Grossnickle. *Miss Emma's wild garden*
Howard, Ellen. *The big seed*
Hughes, Monica. *A handful of seeds*
Hurd, Thacher. *The pea patch jig*
Huriet, Genevieve. *Dandelion's vanishing vegetable garden*
Ichikawa, Satomi. *Suzanne and Nicholas in the garden*
Ipcar, Dahlov. *The land of flowers*
Jacobs, Laurie A. *So much in common*
Janovitz, Marilyn. *Can I help?*
Jenkin-Pearce, Susie. *The enchanted garden*
Johnston, Tony. *The old lady and the birds*

Jordan, Helene J. (Helene Jamieson). *How a seed grows*
Joslin, Mary. *The tale of the heaven tree*
Joyce, William. *The Leaf Men and the brave good bugs*
Keeping, Charles. *Joseph's yard*
Kemp, Anthea. *Mr. Percy's magic greenhouse*
Kemp, Moira. *Round and round the garden*
Kilroy, Sally. *Grandpa's garden*
King, Elizabeth. *Backyard sunflower*
  Pumpkin patch
Komaiko, Leah. *On Sally Perry's farm*
Koscielniak, Bruce. *Bear and Bunny grow tomatoes*
Krauss, Ruth. *The carrot seed*
Krementz, Jill. *A very young gardener*
Krings, Antoon. *Oliver's strawberry patch*
Krudop, Walter Lyon. *Something is growing*
Lacome, Julie. *Garden*
Legg, Gerald. *From seed to sunflower*
Leonard, Marcia. *Gregory and Mr. Grump*
Le Tord, Bijou. *Rabbit seeds*
  Sing a new song
Levenson, George. *Pumpkin circle*
Lin, Grace. *The ugly vegetables*
Lobel, Anita. *Pierrot's ABC garden*
Lobel, Arnold. *The rose in my garden*
Lord, John Vernon. *Mr. Mead and his garden*
Lynn, Sara. *Garden animals*
Maass, Robert. *Garden*
McAllister, Angela. *The wind garden*
MacDonald, Margaret Read. *Pickin' peas*
Maguire, Gregory. *Lucas Fishbone*
Mahy, Margaret. *The pumpkin man and the crafty creeper*
Mallett, David. *Inch by inch*
Marino, Dorothy. *Buzzy Bear in the garden*
Maris, Ron. *In my garden*
Marston, Elsa. *A griffin in the garden*
Martin, Jacqueline Briggs. *Button, bucket, sky*
  The green truck garden giveaway
Medearis, Angela Shelf. *The friendship garden*
Miles, Miska. *Rabbit garden*
Mockford, Caroline. *What's this?*
Molk, Laurel. *Good job, Oliver!*
Moore, Elaine. *Grandma's garden*
Moore, Inga. *The vegetable thieves*
Morgenstern, Elizabeth. *The little gardeners*
Muller, Gerda. *The garden in the city*
Muntean, Michaela. *Alligator's garden*
Musicant, Elke. *The night vegetable eater*
Nordqvist, Sven. *Festus and Mercury: ruckus in the garden*
O'Callahan, Jay. *Tulips*
Oechsli, Helen. *In my garden*
O'Malley, Kevin. *Bud*
Oxenbury, Helen. *Tom and Pippo in the garden*
Palmisciano, Diane. *Garden partners*
Paraskevas, Betty. *Maggie and the Ferocious Beast, the big carrot*
Perkins, Lynne Rae. *Home lovely*
Pike, Norman. *The peach tree*
Pittman, Helena Clare. *Still-life stew*
Primavera, Elise. *Plantpet*
Ray, Mary Lyn. *Pumpkins*
Repchuk, Caroline. *The forgotten garden*
Rockwell, Anne F. *How my garden grew*
Rockwell, Harlow. *The compost heap*
Russo, Marisabina. *Waiting for Hannah*
Ryder, Joanne. *Dancers in the garden*
  First grade ladybugs

My father's hands
Rylant, Cynthia. *This year's garden*
Schumaker, Ward. *In my garden*
Seabrook, Elizabeth. *Cabbages and kings*
Sharpe, Sara. *Gardener George goes to town*
Shecter, Ben. *Partouche plants a seed*
Slote, Elizabeth. *Nelly's garden*
Smith, Maggie (Margaret C.). *This is your garden*
Sobol, Harriet Langsam. *A book of vegetables*
Spalding, Andrea. *Me and Mr. Mah*
Spurr, Elizabeth. *The gumdrop tree*
Stevens, Janet. *Tops and bottoms*
Stevenson, James. *Grandpa's too-good garden*
Stewart, Sarah. *The gardener*
Tamar, Erika. *The garden of happiness*
Taylor, Judy. *Sophie and Jack help out*
Titherington, Jeanne. *Pumpkin pumpkin*
Trimby, Elisa. *Mr. Plum's paradise*
Trottier, Maxine. *Flags*
Van Haeringen, Annemarie. *The cats' tale*
Wabbes, Marie. *Little Rabbit's garden*
Wallace, Karen. *Scarlette Beane*
Wallace, Nancy Elizabeth. *Paperwhite*
Watts, Barrie. *Tomato*
Watts, Bernadette. *Tattercoats*
Weedn, Flavia. *The giant's garden*
Weeks, Sarah. *Mrs. McNosh and the great big squash*
Wells, Rosemary. *First tomato*
Westcott, Nadine Bernard. *The giant vegetable garden*
Wilde, Oscar. *Fairy tales of Oscar Wilde*
  The selfish giant, ill. by S. Saelig Gallagher
  The selfish giant, ill. by Dom Mansell
  The selfish giant, ill. by Fabian Negrin
  The selfish giant, ill. by Lisbeth Zwerger
Williams, Sophy. *Nana's garden*
Wilner, Isabel. *A garden alphabet*
Wolf, Janet. *The rosy fat magenta radish*
Wolff, Ferida. *The emperor's garden*
Yacowitz, Caryn. *Pumpkin fiesta*
Zagwÿn, Deborah Turney. *The pumpkin blanket*
Zalben, Jane Breskin. *Pearl plants a tree*

Geese *see* Birds – geese

Gender roles

Alexander, Martha G. *Marty McGee's space lab, no girls allowed*
Blackwood, Mary. *Derek the knitting dinosaur*
Ernst, Lisa Campbell. *Sam Johnson and the blue ribbon quilt*
Fine, Anne. *Poor Monty*
Gág, Wanda. *Gone is gone*
Gibbons, Faye. *Mama and me and the Model-T*
Hilton, Nette. *The long red scarf*
Hines, Anna Grossnickle. *Daddy makes the best spaghetti*
Ives, Penny. *Mrs. Santa Claus*
Lane, Megan Halsey. *Something to crow about*
Le Guin, Ursula K. *Fish soup*
Lyon, George Ella. *Mama is a miner*
Richardson, Jean. *Thomas's sitter*
Winthrop, Elizabeth. *Tough Eddie*

Genealogy

Dunbar, Joyce. *When I was young*

Generosity *see* Character traits – generosity

Geography

Cuyler, Margery. *From here to there*
Schuett, Stacey. *Somewhere in the world right now*

Geologists *see* Careers – geologists

Gerbils *see* Animals – gerbils

German Americans *see* Ethnic groups in the U.S. – German Americans

Germany *see* Foreign lands – Germany

Ghana *see* Foreign lands – Ghana

Ghosts

Ahlberg, Janet. *Funnybones*
Alexander, Sue. *More Witch, Goblin, and Ghost stories*
  Witch, Goblin and Ghost are back
  Witch, Goblin, and Ghost in the haunted woods
  Witch, Goblin and sometimes Ghost
Allard, Harry. *Bumps in the night*
Allen, Laura Jean. *Rollo and Tweedy and the ghost of Dougal Castle*
Bennett, Jill. *Teeny tiny*
Berenstain, Stan. *The Berenstain bears and the ghost of the forest*
Bergström, Gunilla. *Who's scaring Alfie Atkins?*
Birchman, David Francis. *Brother Billy Bronto's bygone blues band*
Biro, Val. *Gumdrop finds a ghost*
Bright, Robert. *Georgie*
  Georgie and the baby birds
  Georgie and the ball of yarn
  Georgie and the buried treasure
  Georgie and the little dog
  Georgie and the magician
  Georgie and the noisy ghost
  Georgie and the robbers
  Georgie and the runaway balloon
  Georgie goes west
  Georgie to the rescue
  Georgie's Christmas carol
  Georgie's Halloween
Brown, Marc Tolon. *Spooky riddles*
Brown, Ruth. *One stormy night*
Brunhoff, Laurent de. *Babar and the ghost*
  Babar and the ghost
Buck, Nola. *Gotcha!*
Bunting, Eve (Anne Evelyn). *In the haunted house*
Calmenson, Stephanie. *The teeny tiny teacher*
Capucilli, Alyssa Satin. *Inside a house that is haunted*
Charlton, Elizabeth. *Jeremy and the ghost*
Cohen, Caron Lee. *Bronco dogs*
  Renata, Whizbrain and the ghost
Cutts, David. *I can read about creatures of the night*
Cuyler, Margery. *Sir William and the pumpkin monster*
DeFelice, Cynthia C. *Willy's silly grandma*
DeLage, Ida. *The old witch and the ghost parade*
Du Bois, William Pène. *Elisabeth, the cow ghost*
Duquennoy, Jacques. *The ghosts in the cellar*
  Operation ghost
Dürr, Ursula. *The secret of Trembleton Hall*

Faulkner, Keith. *Hector Specter*
Flora, James. *Grandpa's ghost stories*
French, Vivian. *Little Ghost*
Friedrich, Priscilla. *The marshmallow ghosts*
Gabler, Mirko. *Brakus, Krakus . . . Or the incredible adventure of Mr. Skola's Tourist Club*
Gage, Wilson. *Mrs. Gaddy and the ghost*
Galdone, Joanna. *The tailypo*
Galdone, Paul. *King of the cats*
   The monster and the tailor
   The teeny-tiny woman
Gikow, Louise. *Boober Fraggle's ghosts*
Hancock, Sibyl. *Esteban and the ghost*
Harness, Cheryl. *Midnight in the cemetery*
Haseley, Dennis. *Ghost catcher*
Hawkins, Colin. *Come for a ride on the ghost train*
Hayes, Geoffrey. *The mystery of the pirate ghost*
Herman, Emily. *Hubknuckles*
Herman, Gail. *The haunted house*
Hirsh, Marilyn. *Deborah the dybbuk*
Hodges, Margaret. *Molly Limbo*
   Saint Patrick and the peddler
Johnston, Tony. *Four scary stories*
   The ghost of Nicholas Greebe
Khdir, Kate. *Little ghost*
Kraus, Robert. *Mummy knows best*
Kroll, Steven. *Amanda and the giggling ghost*
   Branigan's cat and the Halloween ghost
Kunnas, Mauri. *One spooky night and other scary stories*
Lewis, J. Patrick. *The house of Boo*
Lexau, Joan M. *Millicent's ghost*
Lindgren, Astrid. *The ghost of Skinny Jack*
McMillan, Bruce. *Ghost doll*
McMullan, Kate (Hall). *Creepy riddles*
Maitland, Barbara. *The bookstore ghost*
Martin, Bill (William Ivan). *Old devil wind*
Martín Larrañaga, Ana. *Woo!*
Medearis, Angela Shelf. *The ghost of Sifty-Sifty Sam*
Michelson, Richard. *Did you say ghosts?*
Milich, Melissa. *Can't scare me!*
Mooser, Stephen. *The ghost with the Halloween hiccups*
Nishikawa, Osamu. *Alexander and the blue ghost*
Nixon, Joan Lowery. *The Thanksgiving mystery*
O'Connor, Jane. *The teeny tiny woman*
Olson, Helen Kronberg. *The strange thing that happened to Oliver Wendell Iscovitch*
Ostheeren, Ingrid. *Martin and the Pumpkin Ghost*
Pinkwater, Daniel Manus. *The phantom of the lunch wagon*
Polisar, Barry Louis. *The haunted house party*
Raskin, Ellen. *Ghost in a four-room apartment*
Robins, Arthur. *The teeny tiny woman*
Rockwell, Anne F. *A bear, a bobcat and three ghosts*
Rodgers, Frank. *Who's afraid of the ghost train?*
Rubel, Nicole. *The ghost family meets its match*
Sandberg, Inger. *Little ghost Godfry*
San Souci, Robert D. *The boy and the ghost*
Seuling, Barbara. *The teeny tiny woman*
Sharmat, Marjorie Weinman. *Two ghosts on a bench*
Sherrow, Victoria. *There goes the ghost*
Silverman, Erica. *The Halloween house*
Skwarek, Skip. *The horrors of Howling Hall*
   Mystery of Maggoty Mill
Standiford, Natalie. *The headless horseman*
Thayer, Jane. *Gus and the baby ghost*
   Gus loved his happy home
   Gus was a friendly ghost
   Gus was a gorgeous ghost
   Gus was a real dumb ghost
   What's a ghost going to do?
Wallace, Daisy. *Ghost poems*
Wick, Walter. *I spy spooky night*
Williams, Sophy. *Nana's garden*
Winters, Kay. *The teeny tiny ghost*
   Whooo's haunting the teeny tiny ghost?
Wolkstein, Diane. *The legend of Sleepy Hollow*
Wyllie, Stephen. *Ghost train*
Yee, Paul. *The boy in the attic*
Yep, Laurence. *The man who tricked a ghost*
Zemach, Margot. *The little tiny woman*
Ziefert, Harriet. *Who can boo the loudest?*

Giants

Allen, Linda. *The giant who had no heart*
Auer, Martin. *Now, now Markus*
Balian, Lorna. *A sweetheart for Valentine*
Benjamin, Alan. *Ribtickle Town*
Bible. Old Testament. David. *David and Goliath*
   David and the giant
Biro, Val. *Miranda's umbrella*
Bodwell, Gaile. *The long day of the giants*
Bolliger, Max. *The giants' feast*
   The magic bird
Bradfield, Roger (Jolly Roger). *Giants come in different sizes*
Briggs, Raymond. *Jim and the beanstalk*
Brin, Ruth F. *David and Goliath*
Carle, Eric. *Watch out! A giant!*
Christiana, David. *A Tooth Fairy's tale*
Cole, Brock. *The giant's toe*
Compton, Kenn. *Jack the giant chaser*
Coville, Bruce. *The foolish giant*
Cuneo, Mary Louise. *What can a giant do?*
Cunliffe, John. *Sara's giant and the upside down house*
Cushman, Doug. *Giants*
De La Mare, Walter (Walter John). *Molly Whuppie*
De Paola, Tomie (Thomas Anthony). *Fin M'Coul*
   The mysterious giant of Barletta
De Regniers, Beatrice Schenk. *David and Goliath*, ill. by Scott Cameron
   David and Goliath, ill. by Richard M. Powers
   The giant story
Desimini, Lisa. *Sun and moon*
Du Bois, William Pène. *Giant Otto*
   Otto and the magic potatoes
   Otto at sea
   Otto in Africa
   Otto in Texas
Dunbar, Joyce. *The sand children*
Elkin, Benjamin. *Lucky and the giant*
Farley, Jacqui. *Giant hiccups*
Fisher, Leonard Everett. *David and Goliath*
Foreman, Michael. *The two giants*
Fritz, Jean. *The good giants and the bad Pukwudgies*
Fuchshuber, Annegert. *Giant story – Mouse tale*
Gleeson, Brian. *Finn McCoul*
Greene, Ellin. *The pumpkin giant*
Gregory, Valiska. *Kate's giants*
Grimm, Jacob. *The brave little tailor*, ill. by Mark Corcoran
   The brave little tailor, ill. by Daniel San Souci
   The brave little tailor, ill. by Svend Otto S
   The brave little tailor, ill. by Eve Tharlet
   The brave little tailor, ill. by James Warhola

The glass mountain, ill. by Nonny Hogrogian
Seven at one blow
The valiant little tailor
Grindley, Sally. *Shhh!*
Haley, Gail E. *Jack and the bean tree*
Harris, Jim. *Jack and the giant*
Hasler, Eveline. *The giantess*
Hawkes, Kevin. *His Royal Buckliness*
Hayes, Sarah. *Mary Mary*
Heller, Nicholas. *The giant*
Herrmann, Frank. *The giant Alexander*
    The giant Alexander and the circus
Hillert, Margaret. *The magic beans*
Homme, Bob. *The friendly giant's birthday*
    The friendly giant's book of fire engines
Jack and the beanstalk. *The history of Mother Twaddle and the marvelous achievements of her son Jack*
Jack and the beanstalk, ill. by Val Biro
Jack and the beanstalk, ill. by Lorinda Bryan Cauley
Jack and the beanstalk, ill. by Lydia Halverson
Jack and the beanstalk, ill. by Julek Heller
Jack and the beanstalk, ill. by John Howe
Jack and the beanstalk, ill. by Steven Kellogg
Jack and the beanstalk, ill. by Ed Parker
Jack and the beanstalk, ill. by Tony Ross
Jack and the beanstalk, ill. by by Niamh Sharkey
Jack and the beanstalk, ill. by Gennady Spirin
Jack and the beanstalk, ill. by William Stobbs
Jack and the beanstalk, ill. by James Warhola
Jack and the beanstalk, ill. by Anne Wilsdorf
Jack and the beanstalk / Juan y los frijoles magicos
Jack the giant killer, ill. by Anne Wilsdorf
Jack the giantkiller, ill. by Tony Ross
Jennings, Michael. *Robin Goodfellow and the giant dwarf*
Johnson, Odette. *One prickly porcupine*
Kahl, Virginia. *Giants, indeed!*
Kasza, Keiko. *The mightiest*
Kraus, Robert. *The little giant*
Kreye, Walter. *The giant from the little island*
Kroll, Steven. *Big Jeremy*
Lawrence, John. *The giant of Grabbist*
Lobel, Anita. *The dwarf giant*
Lobel, Arnold. *Giant John*
Löfgren, Ulf. *The boy who ate more than the giant and other Swedish folktales*
McNeill, Janet. *The giant's birthday*
Minarik, Else Holmelund. *The little giant girl and the elf boys*
Mollel, Tololwa M. (Tololwa Marti). *Big boy*
Muller, Robin. *Mollie Whuppie and the giant*
Munsch, Robert N. *David's father*
Nash, Ogden. *The adventures of Isabel*, ill. by Walter Lorraine
    The adventures of Isabel, ill. by James Marshall
O Huigin, Sean. *King of the birds*
Osborne, Mary Pope. *Kate and the beanstalk*
Podwal, Mark H. *Golem*
Polushkin, Maria. *The little hen and the giant*
Pomerantz, Charlotte. *Mangaboom*
Porter, Sue. *Little Wolf and the giant*
Priestley, Alice. *Someone is reading this book*
Roddie, Shen. *Animal stew*
Root, Phyllis. *Soup for supper*
San Souci, Robert D. *Brave Margaret*
Schami, Rafik. *Fatima and the dream thief*
Selway, Martina. *Greedyguts*
Sherman, Ivan. *I am a giant*

Still, James. *Jack and the wonder beans*
Thurber, James. *The great Quillow*
Tompert, Ann. *Charlotte and Charles*
Ungerer, Tomi. *Zeralda's ogre*
Van Haeringen, Annemarie. *The cats' tale*
Wallace, Daisy. *Giant poems*
Ward, Nick. *Giant*
Weedn, Flavia. *The giant's garden*
Wiesner, William. *Tops*
Wilde, Oscar. *Fairy tales of Oscar Wilde*
    The selfish giant, ill. by S. Saelig Gallagher
    The selfish giant, ill. by Dom Mansell
    The selfish giant, ill. by Fabian Negrin
    The selfish giant, ill. by Lisbeth Zwerger
Yep, Laurence. *The city of dragons*
Yolen, Jane. *The giant's farm*
    The giants go camping
Yorinks, Arthur. *The Miami giant*

Gifts

Albert, Richard E. *Alejandro's gift*
Anderson, Laurie Halse. *No time for Mother's Day*
Balet, Jan B. *The gift*
Best, Cari. *Three cheers for Catherine the Great!*
Bohdal, Susi. *1,2,3, what do you see?*
Bourgeois, Paulette. *Franklin's Christmas gift*
Brighton, Catherine. *Hope's gift*
Brown, Marc Tolon. *Arthur's Christmas*
Burden-Patmon, Denise. *Imani's gift at Kwanzaa*
Byars, Betsy Cromer. *The lace snail*
Calhoun, Mary. *A shepherd's gift*
Charlip, Remy. *Harlequin and the gift of many colors*
Conrad, Pam. *The rooster's gift*
Czernecki, Stefan. *The hummingbird's gift*
De Groat, Diane. *Happy Birthday to you, you belong in a zoo*
Delton, Judy. *No time for Christmas*
    The perfect Christmas gift
Dubowski, Cathy East. *Cave boy*
Estes, Kristyn Rehling. *Manuela's gift*
Fern, Eugene. *Birthday presents*
Gerstein, Mordicai. *Guess what?*
Gliori, Debi. *A present for Big Pig*
    What can I give him?
Goble, Paul. *The gift of the sacred dog*
Gomi, Taro. *Santa through the window*
Grimm, Jacob. *One gift deserves another*
Grosz, Peter. *The special gifts*
Hague, Michael. *The perfect present*
Helldorfer, M. C. (Mary Claire). *Daniel's gift*
Henry, O. *The gift of the Magi*
Higgs, Liz Curtis. *The parable of the lily*
High, Linda Oatman. *A Christmas Star*
Hobbie, Holly. *Toot and Puddle, a present for Toot*
Holmes, Efner Tudor. *Carrie's gift*
Hoopes, Lyn Littlefield. *Half a button*
Hubbell, Patricia. *Wrapping paper romp*
Hughes, Shirley. *Alfie and the birthday surprise*
Hutchins, Pat. *It's my birthday!*
Inkpen, Mick. *Wibbly Pig opens his presents*
Jackson, Ellen B. *The precious gift*
Johnson, Crockett. *The emperor's gifts*
Keister, Douglas. *Fernando's gift = El regalo de Fernando*
Keller, Holly. *A bear for Christmas*
Keselman, Gabriela. *The gift*
Krahn, Fernando. *How Santa Claus had a long and difficult journey delivering his presents*

Kunnas, Mauri. *Twelve gifts for Santa Claus*
Lubin, Leonard B. *Christmas gift-bringers*
McCourt, Lisa. *Chicken soup for little souls: The never-forgotten doll*
McCully, Emily Arnold. *The Christmas gift*
McKee, David. *Prince Peter and the teddy bear*
Manson, Christopher. *A gift for the king*
Mathers, Petra. *Lottie's new beach towel*
Medearis, Angela Shelf. *Annie's gifts*
Milord, Sue. *Maggie and the goodbye gift*
Mogensen, Jan. *Teddy's Christmas gift*
Mora, Pat. *A birthday basket for Tia*
   The gift of the poinsettia = El regalo de la flor de nochebuena
Naylor, Phyllis Reynolds. *Keeping a Christmas secret*
Neugebauer, Charise. *Santa's gift*
Politi, Leo. *The nicest gift*
Pomerantz, Charlotte. *You're not my best friend anymore*
Prater, John. *The gift*
Quattrocki, Carolyn. *The little drummer boy*
Radley, Gail. *The spinner's gift*
Riordan, James. *The three magic gifts*
Rylant, Cynthia. *Birthday presents*
Sabuda, Robert James. *Tutankhamen's gift*
Saint James, Synthia. *The gifts of Kwanzaa*
Seabrooke, Brenda. *The swan's gift*
Shepard, Aaron. *The gifts of Wali Dad*
Skolsky, Mindy Warshaw. *Hannah and the whistling tea kettle*
Smalls-Hector, Irene. *Louise's gift*
Steven, Kenneth C. *The bearer of gifts*
Stewart, Paul. *The birthday presents*
Taha, Karen T. *A gift for Tia Rose*
Thomas, Naturi. *Uh-oh! It's Mama's birthday!*
Thury, Frederick. *The last straw*
Timmermans, Felix. *A gift from Saint Nicholas*
Varley, Susan. *Badger's parting gifts*
Wallace, John. *Tiny Rabbit goes to a birthday party*
Watts, Bernadette. *Harvey Hare, postman extraordinaire*
Weedn, Flavia. *The star gift*
Wells, Rosemary. *Morris's disappearing bag*
Williams, Vera B. *Something special for me*

Gilbert Islands *see* Foreign lands – South Sea Islands

Giraffes *see* Animals – giraffes

Glasses

Brown, Marc Tolon. *Arthur's eyes*
   Glasses for D. W.
Cousins, Lucy. *What can rabbit see?*
Delaney, Ned. *Two strikes, four eyes*
Geoghegan, Adrienne. *Dogs don't wear glasses*
Giff, Patricia Reilly. *Watch out, Ronald Morgan!*
Goodsell, Jane. *Katie's magic glasses*
Hest, Amy. *Baby Duck and the bad eyeglasses*
Keller, Holly. *Cromwell's glasses*
Kessler, Leonard P. *Mr. Pine's mixed-up signs*
Lasson, Robert. *Orange Oliver*
MacDonald, Maryann. *Little Hippo gets glasses*
McKean, Thomas. *Hooray for Grandma Jo!*
Marshall, James. *Willis*
Motomora, Mitchell. *Specs*
Paul, Korky. *Winnie flies again*

Rascal. *Socrates*
Raskin, Ellen. *Spectacles*
Smith, Donald. *Who's wearing my sunglasses?*
Smith, Lane. *Glasses . . . who needs 'em?*
Stadler, John. *The cats of Mrs. Calamari*
Thayer, Jane. *Mr. Turtle's magic glasses*
Tusa, Tricia. *Libby's new glasses*

Gloves *see* Clothing – gloves, mittens

Gnats *see* Insects – gnats

Gnomes *see* Mythical creatures – gnomes

Goats *see* Animals – goats

Goblins *see* Mythical creatures – goblins

Golf *see* Sports – golf

Gorillas *see* Animals – gorillas

Gossip *see* Behavior – gossip

Grammar *see* Language

Grandfathers *see* Family life – grandfathers; Family life – grandparents

Grandmothers *see* Family life – grandmothers; Family life – grandparents

Grandparents *see* Family life – grandfathers; Family life – grandmothers; Family life – grandparents

Grasshoppers *see* Insects – grasshoppers

Great-grandparents *see* Family life – great-grandparents

Great Plains Indians *see* Indians of North America – Great Plains

Greece *see* Foreign lands – Greece

Greed *see* Behavior – greed

Greek Americans *see* Ethnic groups in the U.S. – Greek Americans

Greenland *see* Foreign lands – Greenland

Grief *see* Emotions – grief

Griffins *see* Mythical creatures – griffins

Grocery stores *see* Shopping; Stores

Groundhog Day *see* Holidays – Groundhog Day

Groundhogs *see* Animals – groundhogs

Growing up *see* Behavior – growing up

Guatemala *see* Foreign lands – Guatemala

Guinea fowl *see* Birds – guinea fowl

Guinea pigs *see* Animals – guinea pigs

Guns *see* Weapons

Guy Fawkes Day *see* Holidays – Guy Fawkes Day

Guyana *see* Foreign lands – Guyana

Gymnastics *see* Sports – gymnastics

Gypsies

Anderson, C. W. (Clarence Williams). *Blaze and the gypsies*
Bemelmans, Ludwig. *Madeline and the gypsies*
García Lorca, Federico. *The Lieutenant Colonel and the gypsy*
Kellogg, Steven (Stephen). *The mystery of the magic green ball*
Mahy, Margaret. *Mrs. Discombobulous*
Oram, Hiawyn. *Skittlewonder and the wizard*
Patterson, Geoffrey. *The lion and the gypsy*
Tompert, Ann. *Savina, the gypsy dancer*

Habits *see* Thumb sucking

Haida Indians *see* Indians of North America – Haida

Hair

Abisch, Roz. *The Pumpkin Heads*
Appell, Clara. *Now I have a daddy haircut*
B-52's (Musical group). *Wig!*
Bright, Robert. *I like red*
Cisneros, Sandra. *Hairs = Pelitos*
Cole, Babette. *The hairy book*
Davis, Gibbs. *Katy's first haircut*
De Veaux, Alexis. *An enchanted hair tale*
Duncan, Lois. *The longest hair in the world*
Fleming, Candace. *Madame LaGrande and her so high, to the sky, uproarious pompadour*
Freeman, Don. *Mop Top*
Girard, Linda Walvoord. *Jeremy's first haircut*
Goldin, Augusta. *Straight hair, curly hair*
Grimes, Nikki. *Wild, wild hair*
Grimm, Jacob. *Rapunzel*, ill. by Jutta Ash
 Rapunzel, ill. by Sheilah Beckett
 Rapunzel, ill. by Bert Dodson

Rapunzel, ill. by Maja Dusíkova
Rapunzel, ill. by Michael Hague
Rapunzel, ill. by Trina Schart Hyman
Rapunzel, ill. by Kris Waldherr
Rapunzel, ill. by Bernadette Watts
Rapunzel, ill. by Paul O. Zelinsky
Hair
Hest, Amy. *Gabby growing up*
Hooks, Bell. *Happy to be nappy*
Johnson, Lindsay Lee. *Hurricane Henrietta*
Joly, Fanny. *Mr. Fine, porcupine*
Krisher, Trudy. *Kathy's hats*
Kunhardt, Dorothy. *Billy the barber*
Landström, Olof. *Will gets a haircut*
MacDonald, Allan. *The pig in a wig*
Madrigal, Antonio Hernandez. *Erandi's braids*
Marton, Jirina. *I'll do it myself*
Milstein, Linda Breiner. *Amanda's perfect hair*
Mollel, Tololwa M. (Tololwa Marti). *The princess who lost her hair*
Munsch, Robert N. *Aaron's hair*
 Stephanie's ponytail
Nesbit, Edith. *Melisande*
Palatini, Margie. *Bedhead*
 Moosetache
Parr, Todd. *This is my hair*
Portlock, Rob. *Someone's trying to cut off my head*
Quin-Harkin, Janet. *Helpful Hattie*
Robins, Joan. *Addie's bad day*
Rockwell, Anne F. *My barber*
Sandeman, Anna. *Skin, teeth, and hair*
Scott, Natalie (Anderson). *Firebrand, push your hair out of your eyes*
Tarpley, Natasha. *I love my hair!*
Tether, Graham. *The hair book*
Townsend, Kenneth. *Felix, the bald-headed lion*
Tusa, Tricia. *Camilla's new hairdo*
Wilhelm, Hans. *Don't cut my hair*
Williams-Garcia, Rita. *Catching the wild waiyuuzee*

Haiti *see* Foreign lands – Haiti

Halloween *see* Holidays – Halloween

Hamsters *see* Animals – hamsters

Handicaps

Adler, David A. *A picture book of Helen Keller*
Arnold, Katrin. *Anna joins in*
Borton, Lady. *Junk pile!*
Bradford, Ann. *The mystery of the missing dogs*
Briscoe, Jill. *The innkeeper's daughter*
Brown, Tricia. *Someone special, just like you*
Brownridge, William Roy. *The moccasin goalie*
Cairo, Shelley. *Our brother has Down's syndrome*
Carter, Alden R. *Seeing things my way*
Charlot, Martin. *Felisa and the magic tikling bird*
Clifton, Lucille. *My friend Jacob*
Corrigan, Kathy. *Emily Umily*
Dwight, Laura. *We can do it!*
English, Jennifer. *My mommy's special*
Fanshawe, Elizabeth. *Rachel*
Fassler, Joan. *Howie helps himself*
Foreman, Michael. *Seal surfer*
Hamm, Diane Johnston. *Grandma drives a motor bed*
Hasler, Eveline. *Martin is our friend*
Henriod, Lorraine. *Grandma's wheelchair*

Hoffman, Alice. *Fireflies*
Kaufman, Curt. *Rajesh*
Kuklin, Susan. *Thinking big*
Larsen, Hanne. *Don't forget Tom*
Lasker, Joe. *He's my brother*
Lears, Laurie. *Waiting for Mr. Goose*
Lester, Helen. *Author*
    Hooway for Wodney Wat
Lester, Julius. *Shining*
Marron, Carol A. *No trouble for Grandpa*
Naylor, Phyllis Reynolds. *Jennifer Jean, the Cross-Eyed Queen*
Polacco, Patricia. *Thank you, Mr. Falker*
Powers, Mary E. *Our teacher's in a wheelchair*
Prall, Jo. *My sister's special*
Pulver, Robin. *Way to go, Alex!*
Rabe, Berniece. *The balancing girl*
    Where's Chimpy?
Rogers, Fred. *Extraordinary friends*
Rosenberg, Maxine B. *My friend Leslie*
Schatell, Brian. *The McGoonys have a party*
Senisi, Ellen B. *Just kids*
Small, David. *Ruby Mae has something to say*
Smith, Lucia B. *A special kind of sister*
Stein, Sara Bonnett. *About handicaps*
Wahl, Jan. *Button eye's orange*
White, Paul. *Janet at school*
Whitney, Dorothy B. *Creatures of an exceptional kind*
Wisniewski, David. *Sundiata*
Wolf, Bernard. *Don't feel sorry for Paul*

Handicaps – ADD

Rotner, Shelley. *The A.D.D. book for kids*

Handicaps – autism

Amenta, Charles A. (Charles Anthony). *Russell is extra special*
Edwards, Becky. *My brother Sammy*
Lears, Laurie. *Ian's walk*

Handicaps – blindness

Armstrong, Jennifer. *King crow*
Backstein, Karen. *The blind men and the elephant*
Balian, Lorna. *Elephant?*
Bradford, Ann. *The mystery of the blind writer*
Brighton, Catherine. *My hands, my world*
Carrick, Carol. *Melanie*
Chapman, Elizabeth. *Suzy*
Cohen, Miriam. *See you tomorrow*
Condra, Estelle. *See the ocean*
DeArmond, Dale. *The seal oil lamp*
Goldin, Barbara Diamond. *Cakes and miracles*
Herman, Bill. *Jenny's magic wand*
Jensen, Virginia Allen. *Catching*
    Red thread riddles
    What's that?
Johnson, Donna Kay. *Brighteyes*
Karim, Roberta. *Mandy Sue Day*
Keats, Ezra Jack. *Apt. 3*
Kroll, Virginia L. *Naomi knows it's springtime*
Litchfield, Ada B. *A cane in her hand*
McMahon, Patricia. *Listen for the bus*
Martin, Bill (William Ivan). *Knots on a counting rope*
Moon, Nicola. *Lucy's picture*
Newth, Philip. *Roly goes exploring*
Quigley, Lillian Fox. *The blind men and the elephant*

Rau, Dana Meachen. *The secret code*
Reuter, Margaret. *My mother is blind*
Rodriguez, Bobbie. *Sarah's sleepover*
Sargent, Susan. *My favorite place*
Saxe, John Godfrey. *The blind men and the elephant*
Strom, Maria Diaz. *Rainbow Joe and me*
Wheeler, Cindy. *More simple signs*
Wisniewski, David. *Elfwyn's saga*
Yolen, Jane. *The seeing stick*
Young, Ed (Edward). *Seven blind mice*

Handicaps – cerebral palsy

Moran, George. *Imagine me on a sit-ski!*
Payne, Sherry Neuwirth. *A contest*

Handicaps – deafness

Ancona, George. *Handtalk zoo*
Arthur, Catherine. *My sister's silent world*
Aseltine, Lorraine. *I'm deaf and it's okay*
Baker, Pamela J. *My first book of sign*
Bove, Linda. *Sign language ABC with Linda Bove*
Chaplin, Susan Gibbons. *I can sign my ABCs*
Charlip, Remy. *Handtalk*
    Handtalk birthday
Gage, Wilson. *Down in the boondocks*
Greenberg, Judith E. *What is the sign for friend?*
Hesse, Karen. *Lester's dog*
Lee, Jeanne M. *Silent lotus*
Levi, Dorothy Hoffman. *A very special sister*
Litchfield, Ada B. *A button in her ear*
Millman, Isaac. *Moses goes to a concert*
Moore, Clement C. *The night before Christmas in signed English*
Mother Goose. *Nursery rhymes from Mother Goose in signed English*
Okimoto, Jean Davies. *A place for Grace*
Pace, Elizabeth. *Chris gets ear tubes*
Rankin, Laura. *The handmade counting book*
Wahl, Jan. *Jamie's tiger*
Wheeler, Cindy. *Simple signs*
Wolf, Bernard. *Anna's silent world*

Handicaps – Down syndrome

Butler, Geoff. *The hangashore*
Carter, Alden R. *Big brother Dustin*
Fleming, Virginia M. *Be good to Eddie Lee*
Gregory, Nan. *How Smudge came*
Rheingrover, Jean Sasso. *Veronica's first year*
Stuve-Bodeen, Stephanie. *We'll paint the octopus red*

Handicaps – mental handicaps

Brightman, Alan. *Like me*
Fassler, Joan. *One little girl*

Handicaps – physical handicaps

Baggette, Susan K. *Jonathan goes to the grocery store*
Carlson, Nancy L. *Arnie and the new kid*
Caseley, Judith. *Harry and Willy and Carrothead*
Cowen-Fletcher, Jane. *Mama zooms*
Damrell, Liz. *With the wind*
Edwards, Michelle. *Alef-bet*
Harshman, Marc. *The storm*
Hines, Anna Grossnickle. *Gramma's walk*
Hodges, Margaret. *The hero of Bremen*

Holcomb, Nan. *Patrick and Emma Lou*
Kirk, Daniel. *Breakfast at the Liberty Diner*
Lakin, Pat (Patricia). *Dad and me in the morning*
Lasker, Joe. *Nick joins in*
Lee, Jeanne M. *Silent lotus*
Moran, George. *Imagine me on a sit-ski!*
Osofsky, Audrey. *My buddy*
Waddell, Martin. *My great grandpa*
Wells, Rosemary. *The little lame prince*

Hands *see* Anatomy – hands

Handymen *see* Careers – handymen

Hanukkah *see* Holidays – Hanukkah

Happiness *see* Emotions – happiness

Hares *see* Animals – rabbits

Hate *see* Emotions – hate

Hats *see* Clothing – hats

Hatters *see* Careers – hatters

Hawaii

Coste, Marion. *Honu*
Fellows, Rebecca Nevers. *A lei for Tutu*
Funai, Mamoru. *Moke and Poki in the rain forest*
George, Jean Craighead. *Dear Katie, the volcano is a girl*
Guback, Georgia. *Luka's quilt*
Laird, Donivee Martin. *The three little Hawaiian pigs and the magic shark*
Lewis, Richard. *In the night, still dark*
McGuire-Turcotte, Casey A. *How Honu the turtle got his shell*
Mower, Nancy. *I visit my Tūtū and Grandma*
Rand, Gloria. *Aloha, Salty!*
Rattigan, Jama Kim. *The woman in the moon*
Rumford, James. *The Island-below-the-star*
Samuels, Barbara. *Aloha, Dolores*
Tune, Suelyn Ching. *How Maui slowed the sun*
Williams, Jay. *The surprising things Maui did*
Williams, Julie Stewart. *And the birds appeared*
Williams, Laura E. *Torch fishing with the sun*

Hawks *see* Birds – hawks

Heads *see* Anatomy – heads

Health and fitness

Arnold, Caroline. *Who keeps us healthy?*
Berger, Melvin. *Ouch! a book about cuts, scratches and scrapes*
  Why I cough, sneeze, shiver, hiccup and yawn
Borten, Helen. *Do you move as I do?*
Brown, Laurie Krasny. *Dinosaurs alive and well*
Burnstein, John. *Slim Goodbody*
Cobb, Vicki. *How the doctor knows you're fine*
Cole, Babette. *Dr. Dog*
Egielski, Richard. *Buz*
Fassler, David. *What's a virus, anyway?*

Glyman, Caroline A. *Learning your ABC's of nutrition*
Gross, Ruth Belov. *A book about your skeleton*
Kuklin, Susan. *When I see my dentist*
Leaf, Munro. *Health can be fun*
Leedy, Loreen. *The edible pyramid*
Levete, Sarah. *Looking after myself*
Loewen, Nancy. *School safety*
Marcus, Susan. *Casey visits the doctor*
Marshall, Lyn. *Yoga for your children*
Moncure, Jane Belk. *Happy healthkins*
  The healthkin food train
  Healthkins help
Morgan, Allen. *Matthew and the midnight hospital*
Newman, Lesléa. *Belinda's bouquet*
Onyefulu, Ifeoma. *Grandfather's work*
Oxenbury, Helen. *The checkup*
Radlauer, Ruth Shaw. *Of course, you're a horse!*
Rockwell, Harlow. *My doctor*
Roth, Harold. *A checkup*
Seuss, Dr. *The tooth book*
Sharmat, Marjorie Weinman. *Lucretia the unbearable*
Showers, Paul. *Sleep is for everyone*
Slangerup, Erik Jon. *Dirt Boy*
Spelman, Cornelia. *Your body belongs to you*
Tilden, Ruth. *Freddie works out*
Watson, Jane Werner. *My friend the dentist*
  My friend the doctor
Yagya, Genichiro. *All about scabs*
Zamorano, Ana. *Let's eat!*

Health and fitness – exercise

Charles, Donald. *Calico Cat's exercise book*
Isenberg, Barbara. *Albert the running bear's exercise book*
Moncure, Jane Belk. *Healthkins exercise!*
Newcome, Zita. *Animal fun*
  Toddlerobics
Tsubakiyama, Margaret (Holloway). *Mei-Mei loves the morning*

Hearing *see* Handicaps – deafness; Senses – hearing

Heat *see* Concepts – cold and heat

Heavy equipment *see* Machines

Hedgehogs *see* Animals – hedgehogs

Helicopters

Anderson, Joan. *Harry's helicopter*
Cartwright, Ann. *The winter hedgehog*
Drummond, Violet H. *The flying postman*
Duchess of York. *Budgie at Bendick's Point*
  Budgie the little helicopter
Gay, Michel. *Little helicopter*
Ingoglia, Gina. *The big book of real airplanes*
Taylor, Mark. *Henry explores the mountains*
Zaffo, George J. *The book of real airplanes*

Helpfulness *see* Character traits – helpfulness

Hens *see* Birds – chickens

Herons *see* Birds – herons

Hibernation

Arnosky, Jim. *Every autumn comes the bear*
Barrett, John M. *The bear who slept through Christmas*
Bartoli, Jennifer. *Snow on bear's nose*
Bassett, Lisa. *Beany wakes up for Christmas*
Bird, E. J. *How do bears sleep?*
Cohen, Carol L. *Wake up, groundhog!*
De Beer, Hans. *Bernard Bear's amazing adventure*
DeLage, Ida. *The old witch and the snores*
De Paola, Tomie (Thomas Anthony). *Four stories for four seasons*
Evans, Eva Knox. *Sleepy time*
Fisher, Aileen Lucia. *Where does everyone go?*
Fleming, Denise. *Time to sleep*
Freeman, Don. *Bearymore*
Gammell, Stephen. *Wake up, bear . . . It's Christmas!*
Grindley, Sally. *What will I do without you?*
Hobbs, Will. *Beardream*
Janice. *Little Bear's Christmas*
Kepes, Juliet. *Frogs, merry*
Kesselman, Wendy Ann. *Time for Jody*
Krauss, Ruth. *The happy day*
Lawson, Julie. *Bear on the train*
London, Jonathan. *Froggy gets dressed*
Ludwig, Warren. *Good morning, Granny Rose*
McClure, Gillian. *Prickly pig*
Marshall, James. *What's the matter with Carruthers?*
Miller, Edna. *Mousekin's golden house*
Moret, Brigitte Frey. *The bear's Christmas*
Patz, Nancy. *Sarah Bear and Sweet Sidney*
Piers, Helen. *Grasshopper and butterfly*
Rascal. *Orson*
Stewart, Paul. *A little bit of winter*
Stott, Rowena. *The hedgehog feast*
Walters, Catherine. *When will it be spring?*
Ward, Andrew. *Baby bear and the long sleep*
Watson, Wendy. *Has winter come?*
Yulya. *Bears are sleeping*
Zagwÿn, Deborah Turney. *Turtle spring*

Hiccups

Black, Charles C. *The royal nap*
Farley, Jacqui. *Giant hiccups*
Kelley, True. *Buggly Bear's hiccup cure*
McKee, David. *Zebra's hiccups*

Hiding *see* Behavior – hiding

Hiding things *see* Behavior – hiding things

Hieroglyphics

Mother Goose. *Mother Goose in hieroglyphics*
The prince who knew his fate
Walsh, Jill Paton. *Pepi and the secret names*

Hiking *see* Sports – hiking

Himalayas *see* Foreign lands – Himalayas

Hinduism *see* Religion – Hinduism

Hippopotamuses *see* Animals – Hippopotamuses

Hispanic Americans *see* Ethnic groups in the U.S. – Hispanic Americans

Hmong Americans *see* Ethnic groups in the U.S. – Hmong Americans

Hobby horses *see* Toys – rocking horses

Hockey *see* Sports – hockey

Hogs *see* Animals – pigs

Hohokam Indians *see* Indians of North America – Hohokam

Holidays

Adler, David A. *The children's book of Jewish holidays*
  A picture book of Jewish holidays
Alexander, Sue. *Small plays for special days*
Belting, Natalia Maree. *Summer's coming in*
Bonnici, Peter. *The festival*
Carle, Eric. *Hello, red fox*
Carlson, Lori Marie. *Hurray for Three Kings' Day*
Cazet, Denys. *December 24th*
Chaikin, Miriam. *Esther*
Cohen, Barbara. *Even higher*
Conger, Marion. *The little golden holiday book*
Cooney, Barbara. *The story of Christmas*
Crespi, Francesca. *Little Bear and the oompah-pah*
Drucker, Malka. *A Jewish holiday ABC*
Eisenberg, Ann. *I can celebrate*
Fisher, Aileen Lucia. *Arbor day*
  Skip around the year
Forrester, Victoria. *Oddward*
Gellman, Ellie. *Shai's Shabbat walk*
Groner, Judyth Saypol. *Where is the Afikomen?*
Hest, Amy. *Gabby growing up*
Hopkins, Lee Bennett. *Ring out, wild bells*
Kress, Camille. *Tot Shabbat*
Kroll, Virginia L. *A carp for Kimiko*
Kumin, Maxine W. *Follow the fall*
Livingston, Myra Cohn. *Celebrations*
Mason, Lura. *A book of boxes*
Menter, Ian. *Carnival*
Meyer, Elizabeth C. *The blue china pitcher*
Morris, Ann. *Light the candle! Bang the drum!*
Most, Bernard. *Happy holidaysaurus!*
Noll, Sally. *Surprise!*
Pennington, Daniel. *Itse selu*
Robbins, Sandra. *The firefly star*
Roop, Peter. *Let's celebrate!*
Ross, Tony. *Hugo and the bureau of holidays*
Schaefer, Carole Lexa. *Under the midsummer sky*
Shulevitz, Uri. *The magician*
Silverman, Maida. *My first book of Jewish holidays*
Stanley, Sanna. *Monkey Sunday*
Tunnell, Michael O. *Halloween pie*
Wikler, Madeline. *Let's build a Sukkah*
Winn, Chris. *Holiday*
Worth, Valerie. *At Christmastime*
Yolen, Jane. *The three bears holiday rhyme book*
Zolotow, Charlotte (Shapiro). *Over and over*

Holidays – April Fools' Day

Brown, Marc Tolon. *Arthur's April fool*
Christian, Mary Blount. *April fool*
Krahn, Fernando. *April fools*
Kroll, Steven. *It's April Fools' Day!*
Modell, Frank. *Look out, it's April Fools' Day*
Rockwell, Norman. *Norman Rockwell's counting book*
Wegen, Ron. *Billy Gorilla*

Holidays – Chanukah *see* Holidays – Hanukkah

Holidays – Chinese New Year

Cheng, Hou-Tien. *The Chinese New Year*
Chin, Steven A. *Dragon Parade*
Chinn, Karen. *Sam and the lucky money*
Handforth, Thomas. *Mei Li*
Hoyt-Goldsmith, Diane. *Celebrating Chinese New Year*
Low, William. *Chinatown*
Politi, Leo. *Moy Moy*
Sing, Rachel. *Chinese New Year's dragon*
Vaughan, Marcia Kapok. *The dancing dragon*
Wallace, Ian. *Chin Chiang and the dragon's dance*
Waters, Kate. *Lion dancer*
Wong, Janet S. *This next New Year*
Young, Evelyn. *The tale of Tai*

Holidays – Christmas

Abisch, Roz. *'Twas in the moon of wintertime*
Ada, Alma Flor. *El Arbol de Navidad : The Christmas tree*
Adams, Adrienne. *The Christmas party*
Adams, Georgie. *The first Christmas*
Adshead, Gladys L. *Brownies - it's Christmas*
Ahlberg, Allan. *Cops and robbers*
Ahlberg, Janet. *The jolly Christmas postman*
Aichinger, Helga. *The shepherd*
Aldridge, Josephine Haskell. *A possible tree*
Aliki. *Christmas tree memories*
Allan, Nicholas. *Jesus' Christmas party*
Ambrus, Victor G. *Santa Claus takes off*
Ammon, Richard. *An Amish Christmas*
Amoss, Berthe. *What did you lose, Santa?*
Anaya, Rudolfo A. *Farolitos for Abuelo*
Andersen, H. C. (Hans Christian). *The fir tree*, ill. by Stephanie Britt
The fir tree, ill. by Nancy Elkholm Burkert
The fir tree, ill. by Diane Goode
The fir tree, ill. by Rita Marshall
The fir tree, ill. by Bernadette Watts
Anglund, Joan Walsh. *Christmas is a time of giving*
Christmas is here
Christmas is love
The cowboy's Christmas
Teddy bear tales
Aoki, Hisako. *Santa's favorite story*
Ardizzone, Aingelda. *The night ride*
Armour, Richard Willard. *The year Santa went modern*
Arnold, Katya. *The adventures of Snowwoman*
Arnold, Mary. *The fussy angel*
Ashley, Jill. *Riddles about Christmas*
Auch, Mary Jane. *The nutquacker*
Axelrod, Amy. *Pigs on the move*
Bach, Alice. *The day after Christmas*

Bach, Othello. *Hector McSnector and the mail-order Christmas witch*
Baird, Anne. *The Christmas lamb*
Baker, Laura Nelson. *The friendly beasts*
O children of the wind and pines
Balet, Jan B. *The gift*
Balian, Lorna. *Bah! Humbug?*
Barracca, Debra. *A taxi dog Christmas*
Barrett, John M. *The bear who slept through Christmas*
Barrett, Mary Brigid. *The man of the house at Huffington Row*
Barry, Robert E. *Mr. Willowby's Christmas tree*
Bassett, Lisa. *Beany wakes up for Christmas*
Koala Christmas
Baumgart, Klaus. *Laura's Christmas star*
Becker, Bonny. *The Christmas crocodile*
Behrens, June. *Christmas-magic wagon*
Belting, Natalia Maree. *Christmas folk*
Bemelmans, Ludwig. *Hansi*
Madeline's Christmas
Berenstain, Stan. *The Berenstain bears' Christmas tree*
The Berenstain bears meet Santa Bear
Berger, Barbara Helen. *The donkey's dream*
Bernardoni, Robert. *Christmas all over*
Berry, James. *Celebration song*
Bible. New Testament. Gospels. *Christmas*
The first Christmas, ill. by Barbara Neustadt
The Nativity
The story of Christmas, ill. by Jane Ray
Bishop, Adela. *The Christmas polar bear*
Bishop, Roma. *Christmas songs*
Holiday cheer
Santa pays a visit
Blough, Glenn O. *Christmas trees and how they grow*
Bolognese, Don. *A new day*
Bond, Felicia. *Christmas in the chicken coop*
Bond, Michael. *Paddington Bear and the Christmas surprise*
Bourgeois, Paulette. *Franklin's Christmas gift*
Bowman, Peter. *The Christmas songbook*
Breathed, Berkeley. *A wish for wings that work*
Brebeuf, Jean de, Saint. *The Huron carol*
Brett, Jan. *Christmas trolls*
The wild Christmas reindeer
Briggs, Raymond. *Father Christmas*
Father Christmas goes on holiday
Bright, Robert. *Georgie's Christmas carol*
Bright star shining
Bring a torch, Jeannette, Isabella
Briscoe, Jill. *The innkeeper's daughter*
Brock, Emma Lillian. *The birds' Christmas tree*
Bröger, Achim. *The Santa Clauses*
Brown, Abbie Farwell. *The Christmas angel*
Brown, Ken (Ken James). *Mucky Pup's Christmas*
Brown, Marc Tolon. *Arthur's Christmas*
Brown, Margaret Wise. *Christmas in the barn*
The little fir tree
On Christmas eve, ill. by Nancy Edwards Calder
On Christmas eve, ill. by Beni Montresor
A pussycat's Christmas, ill. by Anne Mortimer
Pussycat's Christmas, ill. by Helen Stone
The steamroller
Brown, Palmer. *Something for Christmas*
Bruna, Dick. *Christmas*
The Christmas book
Brunhoff, Jean de. *Babar and Father Christmas*
Bryson, Bernarda. *The twenty miracles of Saint Nicolas*
Buck, Nola. *Christmas in the manger*

Forward, Toby. *Ben's Christmas carol*
Fox, Mem. *With love, at Christmas*
    Wombat divine
Fraser, James Howard. *Los Posadas*
Freeman, Jean Todd. *Cynthia and the unicorn*
French, Vivian. *Christmas kitten*
    A Christmas star called Hannah
The friendly beasts, ill. by Sarah Chamberlain
The friendly beasts and a partridge in a pear tree, ill. by
    Virginia Pearsons
Funakoshi, Canna. *One Christmas*
Gackenbach, Dick. *Claude the dog*
Gaffington, Urslan Judith. *Silver berries and Christ-*
    mas magic
Gambill, Henrietta D. *Little Christmas animals*
Gammell, Stephen. *Wake up, bear . . . It's Christmas!*
Ganeri, Anita. *The story of Christmas*
Gannett, Ruth Stiles. *Katie and the sad noise*
Gantos, Jack (John, Jr.). *Rotten Ralph's rotten Christ-*
    mas
Gantschev, Ivan. *The Christmas teddy bear*
    The Christmas train
Gardam, Catharine. *The animals' Christmas*
Garland, Michael. *The mouse before Christmas*
Gay, Michel. *The Christmas wolf*
George, William T. *Christmas at Long Pond*
Geraty, Virginia Mixson. *Gullah night before Christ-*
    mas
Gikow, Louise. *Baby Kermit's Christmas*
    Sprocket's Christmas tale
Ginolfi, Arthur. *The tiny star*
Gleeson, Brian. *The Savior is born*
Gliori, Debi. *What can I give him?*
Goffin, Josse. *The Christmas story*
    Silent Christmas
Gomi, Taro. *Santa through the window*
Goodall, John S. *An Edwardian Christmas*
Gordon, Sharon. *Christmas surprise*
Grahame, Kenneth. *The wind in the willows*
Granfield, Linda. *Silent night*
Greenfield, Monica. *Waiting for Christmas*
Haarhoff, Dorian. *Desert December*
Hague, Michael. *Deck the halls*
    The perfect present
Hale, Linda. *The glorious Christmas soup party*
Hall, Donald. *Lucy's Christmas*
Harness, Cheryl. *Papa's Christmas gift*
Hartman, Bob. *The birthday of a king*
    A night the stars danced for joy
Harvey, Brett. *My prairie Christmas*
Hautzig, Deborah. *The Christmas story*
Hawxhurst, Joan C. *Bubbe and Gram, my two grand-*
    mothers
Hayes, Geoffrey. *Christmas in Puttyville*
Hayes, Sarah. *Away in a manger*
    A bad start for Santa
    Happy Christmas, Gemma
Hayward, Linda. *The runaway Christmas toy*
Haywood, Carolyn. *A Christmas fantasy*
    How the reindeer saved Santa
    Santa Claus forever!
Hazen, Barbara Shook. *Santa clues*
Heath, Amy. *Sofie's role*
Heck, Elisabeth. *The black sheep*
Helldorfer, M. C. (Mary Claire). *Daniel's gift*
    Night of the white stag
Heller, Nicholas. *The monster in the cave*
Hennessy, B. G. (Barbara G.). *Corduroy's Christmas*
    The first night

Henry, O. *The gift of the Magi*
Herriot, James. *Christmas Day kitten*
High, Linda Oatman. *A Christmas Star*
Hill, Eric. *Spot's first Christmas*
    Spot's magical Christmas
Hill, Susan. *Can it be true?*
    King of kings
Hillert, Margaret. *Merry Christmas, dear dragon*
Hillman, Priscilla. *A Merry-Mouse Christmas A B C*
Hines, Anna Grossnickle. *The secret keeper*
Hines, Gary. *A Christmas tree in the White House*
Hoban, Lillian. *Arthur's Christmas cookies*
    It's really Christmas
Hoban, Russell. *Emmet Otter's jug-band Christmas*
    The mole family's Christmas
Hobbie, Holly. *Toot and Puddle, I'll be home for*
    Christmas
Hodges, Margaret. *Silent night*
Hoff, Syd. *Merry Christmas, Henrietta!*
    Santa's moose
    Where's Prancer?
Hoffman, Mary. *An angel just like me*
    Three wise women
Hoffmann, E. T. A. *The nutcracker*, ill. by Francesca
    Crespi
    The nutcracker, ill. by Carolyn Ewing
    The nutcracker, ill. by Rachel Isadora
    The nutcracker, ill. by Joanna Isles
    The nutcracker, ill. by Maurice Sendak
    The nutcracker, ill. by Lisbeth Zwerger
    The nutcracker ballet, ill. by Vladimir Vasil'evich
    Vagin
Hoffmann, Felix. *The story of Christmas*
Hogrogian, Nonny. *The first Christmas*
Hol, Coby. *Tippy Bear's Christmas*
Holabird, Katharine. *Angelina's Christmas*
    Christmas with Angelina
Holder, Mig. *The fourth wise man*
Hollyn, Lynn. *Lynn Hollyn's Christmas toyland*
Holm, Mayling Mack. *A forest Christmas*
Holmes, Efner Tudor. *The Christmas cat*
    Deer in the hollow
Hooks, William H. *The legend of the Christmas rose*
    The mighty Santa Fe
Hooper, Meredith. *Tom's rabbit*
Houston, Gloria. *The year of the perfect Christmas tree*
Howard, Elizabeth Fitzgerald. *Chita's Christmas tree*
Huffaker, Alice. *That first Christmas day*
Hughes, Langston. *Carol of the brown king*
Hughes, Shirley. *Angel Mae*
    Lucy and Tom's Christmas
Hurd, Edith Thacher. *Christmas eve*
Hurd, Thacher. *Santa Mouse and the ratdeer*
Hutchins, Pat. *King Henry's palace*
    The silver Christmas tree
Inkpen, Mick. *Kipper's Christmas Eve*
Ipcar, Dahlov. *My wonderful Christmas tree*
It feels like Christmas!. *It feels like Christmas!*
Ives, Penny. *Mrs. Santa Claus*
    On Christmas eve
Janice. *Little Bear's Christmas*
Janovitz, Marilyn. *What could be keeping Santa?*
Jaques, Faith. *Tilly's rescue*
Jaynes, Ruth M. *Melinda's Christmas stocking*
Johnson, Crockett. *Harold at the North Pole*
Johnson, Russell. *Trouble at Christmas*
Johnston, Tony. *Lorenzo the naughty parrot*
    Mole and Troll trim the tree
Jones, Jessie Mae Orton. *A little child*

Jordan, Sandra. *Christmas tree farm*
Joseph, Daniel M. *All dressed up and nowhere to go*
Joseph, Lynn. *An island Christmas*
Joslin, Sesyle. *Baby elephant and the secret wishes*
Jüchen, Aurel von. *The Holy Night*
Kahl, Virginia. *Plum pudding for Christmas*
Kajpust, Melissa. *A dozen silk diapers*
Keats, Ezra Jack. *The little drummer boy*
Keller, Holly. *A bear for Christmas*
  Merry Christmas, Geraldine
Kellogg, Steven (Stephen). *The Christmas witch*
Kennedy, Jimmy. *The teddy bears' Christmas*
Kennedy, X. J. *The beasts of Bethlehem*
Kent, Jack. *The Christmas piñata*
Kerr, Judith. *Mog's Christmas*
Kessler, Leonard P. *That's not Santa!*
Kimpton, Diana. *The bear Santa Claus forgot*
King, B. A. *The very best Christmas tree*
Knight, Hilary. *Angels and berries and candy canes*
Knotts, Howard. *The lost Christmas*
Knowlton, Laurie Lazzaro. *The Nativity*
Koralek, Jenny. *The cobweb curtain*
Koscielniak, Bruce. *Hector and Prudence - all aboard!*
Kovalski, Maryann. *Jingle bells*
Krahn, Fernando. *The biggest Christmas tree on earth*
Kraus, Robert. *The Christmas cookie sprinkle snitcher*
  See the Christmas lights
  The tree that stayed up until next Christmas
  Wise Old Owl's Christmas adventure
Krensky, Stephen. *How Santa got his job*
  How Santa lost his job
Kroll, Steven. *Santa's crash-bang Christmas*
Kroll, Virginia L. *The Christmas cow*
Kunhardt, Edith. *Danny's Christmas star*
Kunnas, Mauri. *Santa Claus and his elves*
  Twelve gifts for Santa Claus
Kvasnosky, Laura McGee. *Zelda and Ivy one Christmas*
Lachner, Dorothea. *The gift from Saint Nicholas*
Lagerlöf, Selma. *The legend of the Christmas rose*
Landa, Norbert. *Little Bear's Christmas*
Langstaff, John M. *On Christmas day in the morning*
LaRochelle, David. *A Christmas guest*
Lathrop, Dorothy Pulis. *An angel in the woods*
Laurence, Margaret. *The Christmas birthday story*
Leedy, Loreen. *A dragon Christmas*
Leighton, Maxinne Rhea. *An Ellis Island Christmas*
Leonard, Marcia. *The best snowman ever*
Lewis, J. Patrick. *The Christmas of the reddle moon*
  Long was the winter road they traveled
Linch, Elizabeth Johanna. *Samson*
Lindgren, Astrid. *A calf for Christmas*
  Christmas in noisy village
  Christmas in the stable
  Lotta's Christmas surprise
  Of course Polly can do almost everything
  Pippi Longstocking's after-Christmas party
Lines, Kathleen. *Once in royal David's city*
Lipkind, William. *The Christmas bunny*
London, Jonathan. *Froggy's first Christmas*
Low, Joseph. *The Christmas grump*
Lubin, Leonard B. *Christmas gift-bringers*
Lucado, Max. *Alabaster's song*
Lussert, Anneliese. *The Christmas visitor*
McAllister, Angela. *The Christmas wish*
Maccarone, Grace. *A child was born*
McCaughrean, Geraldine. *The story of the Nativity*
McCully, Emily Arnold. *The Christmas gift*
McCutcheon, Marc. *Grandfather's Christmas camp*

McDermott, Gerald. *The light of the world*
MacDonald, Alan. *The not-so-wise man*
McGinley, Phyllis. *How Mrs. Santa Claus saved Christmas*
McKissack, Patricia C. *Messy Bessey's holidays*
McPhail, David M. *Henry Bear's Christmas*
  Mistletoe
  Santa's book of names
McQuade, Jacqueline. *Christmas with Teddy Bear*
Mahy, Margaret. *The Christmas tree tangle*
Maloney, Peter. *Redbird at Rockefeller Center*
Mamchur, Carolyn Marie. *The popcorn tree*
Manushkin, Fran. *My Christmas safari*
  The perfect Christmas picture
Mariana. *The journey of Bangwell Putt*
Marshall, James. *Merry Christmas, space case*
  Miss Dog's Christmas
Martin, Judith. *The tree angel*
Marzollo, Jean. *Christmas cats*
  I spy little Christmas
Masurel, Claire. *Christmas is coming*
Matthews, Wendy. *The gift of a traveler*
Mattingley, Christobel. *The angel with a mouth-organ*
Maxfield, Christine. *Christmas in Water Village*
May, Robert Lewis. *Rudolph the red-nosed reindeer*
Mayper, Monica. *Come and see*
Medearis, Angela Shelf. *Poppa's itchy Christmas*
Merriam, Eve. *The Christmas box*
Metaxas, Eric. *The boy and the whale*
  Uncle Mugsy and the terrible twins of Christmas
Miles, Calvin. *Calvin's Christmas wish*
Miller, Edna. *Mousekin's Christmas eve*
Moeri, Louise. *Star Mother's youngest child*
Moffatt, Judith. *Christmas lights*
Mogensen, Jan. *Teddy's Christmas gift*
Mohr, Joseph. *Silent night*
Monsell, Helen Albee. *Paddy's Christmas*
Moore, Clement C. *The night before Christmas*, ill. by Jan Brett
  The night before Christmas, ill. by Tomie de Paola
  The night before Christmas, comp. by Cooper Edens and Harold Darling; ill. by various nineteenth- and twentieth-century artists
  The night before Christmas, ill. by Michael Foreman
  The night before Christmas, ill. by Gyo Fujikawa
  The night before Christmas, ill. by Scott Gustafson
  The night before Christmas, ill. by Cheryl Harness
  The night before Christmas, ill. by Loretta Krupinski
  The night before Christmas, ill. by Anita Lobel
  The night before Christmas, ill. by James Marshall
  The night before Christmas, ill. by Jacqueline Rogers
  The night before Christmas, ill. by Robin Spowart
  The night before Christmas, ill. by Gustaf Tenggren
  The night before Christmas, ill. by Tasha Tudor
  The night before Christmas, ill. by Wendy Watson
  The night before Christmas, ill. by Jody Wheeler
  The night before Christmas in signed English
  The teddy bears' night before Christmas
  A visit from St. Nicholas
Moore, Karen Ann. *The baby king*
Moorman, Margaret. *Light the lights!*
Mora, Jo. *Budgee Budgee Cottontail*
Mora, Pat. *The gift of the poinsettia = El regalo de la flor de nochebuena*
Moret, Brigitte Frey. *The bear's Christmas*

Morgan-Vanroyen, Mary. *The Pudgy merry Christmas book*
Moses, Will. *Silent night*
Munro, Roxie. *Christmastime in New York City*
Murdocca, Sal (Salvatore). *Christmas bear*
Nayer, Judy. *Little bear's first Christmas*
Naylor, Phyllis Reynolds. *Keeping a Christmas secret*
    Old Sadie and the Christmas bear
Neale, J. M. (John Mason). *Good King Wenceslas*
Nerlove, Miriam. *Christmas*
Neugebauer, Charise. *Santa's gift*
Neville, Mary. *The Christmas tree ride*
Newland, Mary Reed. *Good King Wenceslas*
Nikola-Lisa, W. *Hallelujah!*
Niland, Kilmeny. *A bellbird in a flame tree*
Nixon, Joan Lowery. *That's the spirit, Claude*
Noble, Trinka Hakes. *Apple tree Christmas*
Novak, Matt. *The last Christmas present*
Numeroff, Laura Joffe. *If you take a mouse to the movies*
Nussbaumer, Mares. *Away in a manger*
O Christmas tree
Oakley, Graham. *The church mice at Christmas*
O'Brien, John (1953-). *Mother Hubbard's Christmas*
O'Connor, Francine M. *The ABC's of Christmas*
Okrend, Elise. *Blintzes for Blitzen*
Olson, Arielle North. *Hurry home, Grandma!*
Oppenheim, Joanne. *The Christmas witch*
Ostheeren, Ingrid. *I'm the real Santa Claus!*
Paraskevas, Betty. *A very Kroll Christmas*
Parker, Nancy Winslow. *The Christmas camel*
Partch, Virgil Franklin. *The Christmas cookie sprinkle snitcher*
Paxton, Tom. *The story of Santa Claus*
Pearson, Susan. *Karin's Christmas walk*
Peet, Bill (William Bartlett). *Countdown to Christmas*
Peterson, Hans. *Erik and the Christmas horse*
Pfister, Marcus. *The Christmas star*
    Wake up, Santa Claus!
Phifer, Martha Nelson. *The colors of Christmas*
Pickthall, Marjorie L. C. (Marjorie Lowry Christie). *The worker in sandalwood*
Pierpont, James. *Jingle bells*
Pilkey, Dav. *Dragon's merry Christmas*
Pingry, Patricia. *Joseph's story*
Pinkwater, Daniel Manus. *Wolf Christmas*
Pittman, Helena Clare. *The angel tree*
Plume, Ilse. *The story of Befana*
Polacco, Patricia. *Welcome Comfort*
Politi, Leo. *The nicest gift*
    Pedro, the angel of Olvera Street
    Rosa
Powell, Consie. *Old dog Cora and the Christmas tree*
Prøysen, Alf. *Christmas eve at Santa's*
Pryor, Bonnie. *Merry Christmas, Amanda and April*
Quattrocki, Carolyn. *The little drummer boy*
Quindlen, Anna. *The tree that came to stay*
Rabe, Berniece. *The first Christmas candy cane*
Rahaman, Vashanti. *O Christmas tree*
Ransom, Candice F. *The Christmas dolls*
Reiser, Lynn. *Christmas counting*
Richards, Kitty. *Merry Christmas, Rugrats!*
Richardson, Jean. *Stephen's feast*
Richardson, John. *Where's Jack?*
Robbins, Ruth. *Baboushka and the three kings*
Roberts, Bethany. *Waiting-for-Christmas stories*
Rockwell, Anne F. *Bafana*

Rosales, Melodye Benson. *'Twas the night b'fore Christmas*
Rosen, Michael J. (1954-). *Elijah's angel*
Roth, Susan L. *Another Christmas*
Rowand, Phyllis. *Every day in the year*
Rylant, Cynthia. *Mr. Putter and Tabby bake the cake*
    Silver packages
Sabuda, Robert James. *The Christmas alphabet*
Sahagun, Bernardino de. *Spirit child*
Sawyer, Ruth. *The Christmas Anna angel*
    The remarkable Christmas of the cobbler's sons
Say, Allen. *Tree of cranes*
Scarry, Richard. *Richard Scarry's best Christmas book ever!*
Scheidl, Gerda Marie. *Can we help you, Saint Nicholas?*
Schenk, Esther M. *Christmas time*
Schrecker, Judie. *Santa's new reindeer*
Schumacher, Claire. *Nutty's Christmas*
Schweninger, Ann. *Christmas secrets*
Seignobosc, Françoise. *Noël for Jeanne-Marie*
Selden, George. *The mice, the monks and the Christmas tree*
Seuss, Dr. *How the Grinch stole Christmas*
Shannon, David. *The amazing Christmas extravaganza*
Sharmat, Marjorie Weinman. *I'm Santa Claus and I'm famous*
A small treasury of Christmas poems and prayers
Smalls-Hector, Irene. *Irene Jennie and the Christmas masquerade*
Soto, Gary. *Too many tamales*
Speare, Jean. *A candle for Christmas*
Spier, Peter. *Peter Spier's Christmas!*
Spinelli, Eileen. *Coming through the blizzard*
Steiner, Charlotte. *The climbing book*
Stephenson, Dorothy. *The night it rained toys*
Stern, Elsie-Jean. *Wee Robin's Christmas song*
Steven, Kenneth C. *The bearer of gifts*
Stevens, Jan Romero. *Twelve lizards leaping*
Stevenson, James. *The worst person's Christmas*
Stevenson, Suçie. *Christmas eve*
Stock, Catherine. *Christmas time*
    Sampson the Christmas cat
Stone, Phoebe. *What night do the angels wander?*
Strand, Keith. *Grandfather's Christmas tree*
Sykes, Julie. *Hurry, Santa!*
Tafuri, Nancy. *Counting to Christmas*
Tangvald, Christine Harder. *The best thing about Christmas*
    Hey, Mr. Angel!
Tazewell, Charles. *The littlest angel*
Teasdale, Sara. *Christmas carol*
Thayer, Jane. *The puppy who wanted a boy*, ill. by Seymour Fleishman
    The puppy who wanted a boy, ill. by Lisa McCue
Thompson, Lauren. *Mouse's first Christmas*
Thury, Frederick. *The last straw*
Timmermans, Felix. *A gift from Saint Nicholas*
Tippett, James Sterling. *Counting the days*
Tolkien, J. R. R. (John Ronald Reuel). *The Father Christmas letters*
Tompert, Ann. *A carol for Christmas*
    The silver whistle
Tornqvist, Rita. *The Christmas carp*
Trent, Robbie. *The first Christmas*
Trivas, Irene. *Emma's Christmas*
Trosclair. *Cajun night before Christmas*
Tryon, Leslie. *Albert's Christmas*

Tudor, Tasha. *The doll's Christmas*
  Snow before Christmas
Türk, Hanne. *Merry Christmas Max*
Turner, Ann Warren. *The Christmas house*
Tutt, Kay Cunningham. *And now we call him Santa Claus*
The twelve days of Christmas.. English folk song.
  Brian Wildsmith's The twelve days of Christmas
  Jack Kent's twelve days of Christmas
  The twelve days of Christmas, ill. by Jan Brett
  The twelve days of Christmas, ill. by Ilonka Karasz
  The twelve days of Christmas, ill. by Ilse Plume
  The twelve days of Christmas, ill. by Erika Schneider
  The twelve days of Christmas, ill. by Vladimir Vagin
  The twelve days of Christmas, ill. by Sophie Windham
Tyler, Linda Wagner. *After Christmas tree*
Ungerer, Tomi. *Christmas eve at the Mellops*
Uttley, Alison. *The Christmas box*
Vainio, Pirkko. *The Christmas angel*
Valgardson, W. D. *Winter rescue*
Van Allsburg, Chris. *The polar express*
Vesey, A. *Merry Christmas, Thomas!*
Vincent, Gabrielle. *Merry Christmas, Ernest and Celestine*
Waber, Bernard. *Lyle at Christmas*
Waddell, Martin. *Mimi's Christmas*
Wahl, Jan. *The Muffletumps' Christmas party*
Waldron, Jan L. *Angel Pig and the hidden Christmas*
Wallner, Alexandra. *An Alcott family Christmas*
Watson, Clyde. *How Brown Mouse kept Christmas*
Watson, Wendy. *The bunnies' Christmas eve*
Watts, Bernadette. *The Christmas bird*
  Harvey Hare's Christmas
We wish you a merry Christmas
Weil, Lisl. *Santa Claus around the world*
Weller, Frances Ward. *The angel of Mill Street*
Wells, Joel. *The manger mouse*
Wells, Rosemary. *McDuff's new friend*
  Max's Christmas
  Morris's disappearing bag
Weninger, Brigitte. *A Letter to Santa Claus*
  Lumina
  Merry Christmas, Davy!
Wenning, Elisabeth. *The Christmas mouse*
Westman, Barbara. *The day before Christmas*
  What a morning!
Wheeler, Cindy. *Marmalade's Christmas present*
Wick, Walter. *I spy Christmas*
Wijngaard, Juan. *The Nativity*
Wild, Margaret. *Thank you, Santa*
Wildsmith, Brian. *A Christmas story*
Wilhelm, Hans. *Schnitzel's first Christmas*
Wilkon, Józef. *Lullaby for a newborn king*
Williams, Marcia. *The first Christmas*
Wilson, Robina Beckles. *Merry Christmas!*
Winter, Jeanette. *The Christmas tree ship*
Winthrop, Elizabeth. *Bear's Christmas surprise*
  A child is born
Wiseman, Bernard. *Christmas with Morris and Borris*
Wojciechowski, Susan. *The Christmas miracle of Jonathan Toomey*
Wood, Audrey. *The Christmas adventure of Space Elf Sam*
Wooding, Sharon L. *Arthur's Christmas wish*
Woolaver, Lance. *Christmas with the rural mail*
Worth, Valerie. *At Christmastime*
Wright, Cliff. *Santa's ark*

Wright, Sue (Sue M.). *The Christmas path*
Yeomans, Thomas. *For every child a star*
Yorinks, Arthur. *Christmas in July*
Zagwÿn, Deborah Turney. *The winter gift*
Zakhoder, Boris Vladimirovich. *How a piglet crashed the Christmas party*
Ziefert, Harriet. *Nicky's Christmas surprise*
Zimelman, Nathan. *The star of Melvin*
Zolotow, Charlotte (Shapiro). *The beautiful Christmas tree*

Holidays – Cinco de Mayo

Behrens, June. *Fiesta!*

Holidays – Columbus Day

Showers, Paul. *Columbus Day*

Holidays – Day of the Dead

Ancona, George. *Pablo remembers*
Czernecki, Stefan. *The hummingbird's gift*
Johnston, Tony. *Day of the Dead*
Krull, Kathleen. *Maria Molina and the Days of the Dead*
Luenn, Nancy. *A gift for Abuelita*

Holidays – Divali

Gilmore, Rachna. *Lights for Gita*

Holidays – Easter

Adams, Adrienne. *The Easter egg artists*
Armour, Richard Willard. *The adventures of Egbert the Easter egg*
Auch, Mary Jane. *The Easter egg farm*
Balian, Lorna. *Humbug rabbit*
Barrett, John M. *The Easter bear*
Bishop, Adela. *The Easter wolf*
Bishop, Roma. *Easter counting*
  Easter egg hunt
Brown, Margaret Wise. *The golden egg book*
  The runaway bunny
Carrick, Carol. *A rabbit for Easter*
Chalmers, Mary. *Easter parade*
Claret, Maria. *The chocolate rabbit*
Compton, Joanne. *Little Rabbit's Easter surprise*
Cross, Genevieve. *My bunny book*
Darling, Kathy (Mary Kathleen). *The Easter bunny's secret*
Delacre, Lulu. *Peter Cottontail's Easter book*
DeLage, Ida. *ABC Easter bunny*
Demi. *Demi's basket of books*
  Little bitty bunny
  Little chick chick
Denim, Sue. *The Dumb Bunnies' Easter*
Devlin, Wende. *Cranberry Easter*
Dunn, Judy. *The little rabbit*
Duvoisin, Roger Antoine. *Easter treat*
Easter babies
Fisher, Aileen Lucia. *The story of Easter*
Friedrich, Priscilla. *The Easter bunny that overslept*
Gibbons, Gail. *Easter*
Gordon, Sharon. *Easter Bunny's lost egg*
Green, Adam. *The funny bunny factory*
Greenfield, Eloise. *Easter parade*
Griest, Lisa. *Lost at the White House*

Hallinan, P. K. (Patrick K.). *The small town children's Easter*
  Today is Easter!
Hawxhurst, Joan C. *Bubbe and Gram, my two grandmothers*
Hennessy, B. G. (Barbara G.). *Corduroy's Easter*
Heyward, Du Bose. *The country bunny and the little gold shoes*
Higgs, Liz Curtis. *The parable of the lily*
Hill, Eric. *Spot's first Easter*
Hoban, Lillian. *Silly Tilly and the Easter bunny*
Hopkins, Lee Bennett. *Easter buds are springing*
Houselander, Caryll. *Petook*
Kay, Helen. *An egg is for wishing*
Kimmel, Eric A. *The birds' gift*
Kraus, Robert. *Daddy Long Ears*
  How Spider saved Easter
Kroll, Steven. *The big bunny and the Easter eggs*
  The big bunny and the magic show
Kunhardt, Edith. *Danny and the Easter egg*
Lachner, Dorothea. *Smoky's special Easter present*
Landa, Norbert. *Rabbit and chicken play with colors*
Littlefield, William. *The whiskers of Ho Ho*
McClenathan, Louise. *The Easter pig*
Maril, Lee. *Mr. Bunny paints the eggs*
Merrick, Patrick. *Easter bunnies*
Milhous, Katherine. *The egg tree*
Milich, Melissa. *Miz Fannie Mae's fine new Easter hat*
Miller, Edna. *Mousekin's Easter basket*
Modesitt, Jeanne. *Little Bunny's Easter surprise*
Nerlove, Miriam. *Easter*
Ostheeren, Ingrid. *Coriander's Easter adventure*
Pienkowski, Jan. *Easter*
Polacco, Patricia. *Chicken Sunday*
A small treasury of Easter poems and prayers
Stock, Catherine. *Easter surprise*
Taylor, Shirley. *The cross in the egg*
Thayer, Jane. *The horse with the Easter bonnet*
Tildes, Phyllis Limbacher. *The magic babushka*
Tresselt, Alvin R. *The world in the candy egg*
Tudor, Tasha. *A tale for Easter*
Wahl, Jan. *The five in the forest*
Watson, Wendy. *Happy Easter day!*
Weil, Lisl. *The candy egg bunny*
Wells, Rosemary. *Max's chocolate chicken*
Wiese, Kurt. *Happy Easter*
Wildsmith, Brian. *The Easter story*
Wilhelm, Hans. *More bunny trouble*
Winthrop, Elizabeth. *He is risen*
Wolf, Winfried. *The Easter bunny*
Young, Miriam Burt. *Miss Suzy's Easter surprise*
Ziefert, Harriet. *Happy Easter, Grandma!*
Zolotow, Charlotte (Shapiro). *The bunny who found Easter*
  Mr. Rabbit and the lovely present

Holidays – Father's Day

Bunting, Eve (Anne Evelyn). *A perfect Father's Day*
Butterworth, Nick. *My dad is awesome*
Kroll, Steven. *Happy Father's Day*
Livingston, Myra Cohn. *Poems for fathers*
Sharmat, Marjorie Weinman. *Hooray for Father's Day!*
Simon, Norma. *I wish I had my father*

Holidays – Fourth of July

Devlin, Wende. *Cranberry summer*

Hines, Anna Grossnickle. *Mean old Uncle Jack*
Houck, Eric L. *Rabbit surprise*
Joosse, Barbara M. *Fourth of July*
Keller, Holly. *Henry's Fourth of July*
Lasky, Kathryn. *Fourth of July bear*
Paraskevas, Betty. *On the day the tall ships sailed*
Shortall, Leonard W. *One way*
Thomas, Jane Resh. *Celebration!*
Watson, Wendy. *Hurray for the Fourth of July*
Ziefert, Harriet. *Hats off for the Fourth of July!*
Zion, Gene. *The summer snowman*

Holidays – Groundhog Day

Balian, Lorna. *A garden for a groundhog*
Bartalos, Michael. *Shadowville*
Cohen, Carol L. *Wake up, groundhog!*
Delton, Judy. *Groundhog's Day at the doctor*
Farber, Norma. *Return of the shadows*
Glass, Marvin. *What happened today, Freddy Groundhog?*
Hamberger, John. *This is the day*
Johnson, Crockett. *Will spring be early or will spring be late?*
Kesselman, Wendy Ann. *Time for Jody*
Koscielniak, Bruce. *Geoffrey Groundhog predicts the weather*
Kroll, Steven. *It's Groundhog Day!*
Levine, Abby. *Gretchen Groundhog, it's your day!*
Lewin, Betsy. *Groundhog day*
Palazzo, Tony (Anthony D.). *Waldo the woodchuck*
Tompert, Ann. *Nothing sticks like a shadow*

Holidays – Guy Fawkes Day

Buchanan, Heather S. *George and Matilda Mouse and the moon rocket*

Holidays – Halloween

Adams, Adrienne. *A Halloween happening*
  A woggle of witches
Alexander, Sue. *Who goes out on Halloween?*
Anderson, Lonzo. *The Halloween party*
Asch, Frank. *Popcorn*
Balian, Lorna. *Humbug witch*
Battles, Edith. *The terrible trick or treat*
Beim, Jerrold. *Sir Halloween*
Benarde, Anita. *The pumpkin smasher*
Bender, Robert. *A little witch magic*
Berenstain, Stan. *The Berenstain bears trick or treat*
Blazek, Sarah Kirwan. *An Irish Hallowe'en*
Bond, Felicia. *The Halloween performance*
  The Halloween play
Borten, Helen. *Halloween*
Bradford, Ann. *The mystery of the live ghosts*
Bridwell, Norman. *Clifford's Halloween*
Bright, Robert. *Georgie's Halloween*
Brown, Marc Tolon. *Arthur's Halloween*
Buck, Nola. *Creepy crawly critters and other Halloween tongue twisters*
  Gotcha!
  Halloween parade
  The littlest witch
Bunting, Eve (Anne Evelyn). *In the haunted house*
  Scary, scary Halloween
Calhoun, Mary. *The witch of Hissing Hill*
  Wobble the witch cat
Carlson, Natalie Savage. *Spooky and the ghost cat*

Spooky and the wizard's bats
Spooky night
Carlstrom, Nancy White. *What a scare, Jesse Bear!*
    Who said boo?
Carrick, Carol. *Old Mother Witch*
Caseley, Judith. *Witch mama*
Cassedy, Sylvia. *The best cat suit of all*
Cavagnaro, David. *The pumpkin people*
Cecil, Mirabel. *Lottie's cats*
Charles, Donald. *Shaggy dog's Halloween*
Charlton, Elizabeth. *Jeremy and the ghost*
Christelow, Eileen. *Jerome and the Witchcraft kids*
Cohen, Miriam. *The real-skin rubber monster mask*
Cooper, Paulette. *Let's find out about Halloween*
Corey, Dorothy. *Will it ever be my birthday?*
Cummings, E. E. (Edward Estlin). *Hist whist*
Cuyler, Margery. *Sir William and the pumpkin monster*
Davis, Maggie S. *Rickety witch*
Degen, Bruce. *Aunt Possum and the pumpkin man*
De Groat, Diane. *Trick or treat, smell my feet*
DeLage, Ida. *ABC Halloween witch*
    The old witch and her magic basket
    The old witch goes to the ball
    The old witch's party
Devlin, Wende. *Cranberry Halloween*
    Old Witch rescues Halloween
Dillon, Jana. *Jeb Scarecrow's pumpkin patch*
Donnelly, Liza. *Dinosaurs' Halloween*
Embry, Margaret. *The blue-nosed witch*
Enderle, Judith (Ann) Ross. *Six creepy sheep*
Feczko, Kathy. *Halloween party*
Five little pumpkins
Foster, Doris Van Liew. *Tell me, Mr. Owl*
Freeman, Don. *Space witch*
    Tilly Witch
Friedrich, Priscilla. *The marshmallow ghosts*
Friskey, Margaret (Margaret Richards). *The perky little pumpkin*
Gantos, Jack (John, Jr.). *Rotten Ralph's Halloween howl*
    Rotten Ralph's trick or treat
Gardner, Beau. *Whooo's a fright on Halloween night?*
Gibbons, Gail. *Halloween*
Gordon, Lynn. *The witch's revenge*
Greene, Carol. *The thirteen days of Halloween*
Greene, Ellin. *The pumpkin giant*
Guthrie, Donna. *The witch who lives down the hall*
Hall, Zoe. *It's pumpkin time!*
Hallinan, P. K. (Patrick K.). *Today is Halloween*
Heinz, Brian J. *The monsters' test*
Hellsing, Lennart. *The wonderful pumpkin*
Hennessy, B. G. (Barbara G.). *Corduroy's Halloween*
Herman, Emily. *Hubknuckles*
Hines, Anna Grossnickle. *When the goblins came knocking*
Hoff, Syd. *Henrietta's Halloween*
Hopkins, Lee Bennett. *Ragged shadows*
Howe, James. *Scared silly*
Hubbard, Patricia. *Trick or treat countdown*
Hubbell, Patricia. *Wrapping paper romp*
Huck, Charlotte S. *A creepy countdown*
Hurd, Edith Thacher. *The so-so cat*
Hutchins, Pat. *Which witch is which?*
Johnston, Tony. *Soup bone*
    The vanishing pumpkin
Keats, Ezra Jack. *The trip*
Kellogg, Steven (Stephen). *The mystery of the flying orange pumpkin*

Khdir, Kate. *Little ghost*
King, Elizabeth. *Pumpkin patch*
Kraus, Robert. *How Spider saved Halloween*
    Jack O'Lantern's scary Halloween
Kroll, Steven. *Branigan's cat and the Halloween ghost*
    The candy witch
Kunhardt, Edith. *Trick or treat, Danny!*
Kunnas, Mauri. *One spooky night and other scary stories*
Kutner, Merrily. *Z is for zombie*
Leedy, Loreen. *The dragon Halloween party*
    2 x 2 = boo!
Leiner, Katherine. *Halloween*
Levine, Abby. *This is the pumpkin*
Lewis, J. Patrick. *The house of Boo*
London, Jonathan. *Froggy's Halloween*
Low, Alice. *The witch who was afraid of witches*
    Witch's holiday
Maccarone, Grace. *Pumpkin faces*
McMullan, Kate (Hall). *Trick or eeek!*
Maestro, Giulio. *Halloween howls*
Manushkin, Fran. *Be brave, baby rabbit*
    Hocus and Pocus at the circus
Marshall, Edward. *Space case*
Martin, Bill (William Ivan). *The magic pumpkin*
    Old devil wind
Massey, Jeanne. *The littlest witch*
Meddaugh, Susan. *The witches' supermarket*
Merriam, Eve. *Halloween ABC*
Miller, Edna. *Mousekin's golden house*
Moffatt, Judith. *Halloween frights*
    The pumpkin man
    Trick-or-treat faces
Mooser, Stephen. *The ghost with the Halloween hiccups*
Mueller, Virginia. *A Halloween mask for Monster*
Nerlove, Miriam. *Halloween*
Nicoll, Helen. *Meg and Mog*
Nikola-Lisa, W. *Shake dem Halloween bones*
Nolan, Dennis. *Witch Bazooza*
Novak, Matt. *No zombies allowed*
Numeroff, Laura Joffe. *Emily's bunch*
O'Malley, Kevin. *Welcome*
Ott, John. *Peter Pumpkin*
Palatini, Margie. *Piggie pie*
Paul, Sherry. *2-B and the space visitor*
Peters, Sharon. *Trick or treat Halloween*
Pilkey, Dav. *The Hallo-wiener*
Polacco, Patricia. *Picnic at Mudsock Meadow*
Polisar, Barry Louis. *The haunted house party*
Prager, Annabelle. *The spooky Halloween party*
Preston, Edna Mitchell. *One dark night*
Racioppo, Larry. *Halloween*
Reeves, Howard W. *There was an old witch*
Riggio, Anita. *Beware the Brindlebeast*
Rockwell, Anne F. *Apples and pumpkins*
    A bear, a bobcat and three ghosts
    Halloween day
    Pumpkin day, pumpkin night
Rose, David S. *It hardly seems like Halloween*
Ross, Eileen. *The Halloween showdown*
St. George, Judith. *The Halloween pumpkin smasher*
San Souci, Robert D. *The legend of Sleepy Hollow*
Schertle, Alice. *Bill and the google-eyed goblins*
    Hob Goblin and the skeleton
Schweninger, Ann. *Halloween surprises*
Scott, Ann Herbert. *Let's catch a monster*
Shaw, Nancy (Nancy E.). *Sheep trick or treat*
Shaw, Richard. *The kitten in the pumpkin patch*

Shute, Linda. *Halloween party*
Sierra, Judy. *The house that Drac built*
Silverman, Erica. *The Halloween house*
Slobodkin, Louis. *Trick or treat*
Smalls-Hector, Irene. *Jenny Reen and the Jack Muh Lantern*
Standiford, Natalie. *The headless horseman*
Stevenson, James. *That terrible Halloween night*
Stock, Catherine. *Halloween monster*
Stutson, Caroline. *By the light of the Halloween moon*
Teague, Mark. *One Halloween night*
Thayer, Jane. *Gus was a gorgeous ghost*
Thompson, Lauren. *Mouse's first Halloween*
Titherington, Jeanne. *Pumpkin pumpkin*
Tryon, Leslie. *Albert's Halloween*
Van Rynbach, Iris. *Five little pumpkins*
Vigna, Judith. *Everyone goes as a pumpkin*
Von Hippel, Ursula. *The craziest Halloween*
Wahl, Jan. *Pleasant Fieldmouse's Halloween party*
Waldron, Jan L. *John Pig's Halloween*
Watson, Jane Werner. *Which is the witch?*
Watson, Wendy. *Boo! It's Halloween*
Wegen, Ron. *The Halloween costume party*
Weller, Frances Ward. *The closet gorilla*
West, Kipling. *A rattle of bones*
Wick, Walter. *I spy spooky night*
Winters, Kay. *The teeny tiny ghost*
    Whooo's haunting the teeny tiny ghost?
Wojciechowski, Susan. *The best Halloween of all*
Wolff, Ferida. *On Halloween night*
Wolkstein, Diane. *The legend of Sleepy Hollow*
Yolen, Jane. *Beneath the ghost moon*
    Child of faerie, child of earth
Ziefert, Harriet. *Two little witches*
Zimmer, Dirk. *The trick-or-treat trap*
Zolotow, Charlotte (Shapiro). *A tiger called Thomas, ill. by Catherine Stock*
    A tiger called Thomas, ill. by Kurt Werth

Holidays – Hanukkah

Adler, David A. *A picture book of Hanukkah*
    A picture book of Jewish holidays
Aleichem, Sholem. *Hanukah money*
Behrens, June. *Hanukkah*
Chaikin, Miriam. *Hanukkah*
Chanover, Hyman. *Happy Hanukah everybody*
Conway, Diana Cohen. *Northern lights*
Coopersmith, Jerome. *A Chanukah fable for Christmas*
De Paola, Tomie (Thomas Anthony). *My first Chanukah*
Drucker, Malka. *Grandma's latkes*
Fisher, Aileen Lucia. *My first Hanukkah book*
Fishman, Cathy Goldberg. *On Hanukkah*
Gellman, Ellie. *It's Chanukah!*
Glaser, Linda. *The borrowed Hanukkah latkes*
Goffstein, M. B. (Marilyn Brooke). *Laughing latkes*
Goldin, Barbara Diamond. *Just enough is plenty*
Groner, Judyth Saypol. *All about Hanukkah*
Hawxhurst, Joan C. *Bubbe and Gram, my two grandmothers*
Hirsh, Marilyn. *I love Hanukkah*
    Potato pancakes all around
Holland, Cheri. *Maccabee jamboree*
Howland, Naomi. *Latkes, latkes, good to eat*
Jaffe, Nina. *In the month of Kislev*
Kimmel, Eric A. *Asher and the capmakers*
    The Chanukkah guest

    The Chanukkah tree
    Hershel and the Hanukkah goblins
    The magic dreidels
    One winter night
    Ten suns
Kimmelman, Leslie. *Hanukkah lights, Hanukkah nights*
    The runaway latkes
Koralek, Jenny. *Hanukkah*
Kuskin, Karla. *A great miracle happened there*
Levine, Arthur A. *All the lights in the night*
Levoy, Myron. *The Hanukkah of Great-Uncle Otto*
McKissack, Patricia C. *Messy Bessey's holidays*
Manushkin, Fran. *Hooray for Hanukkah!*
    Latkes and applesauce
Melmed, Laura Krauss. *Moishe's miracle*
Modesitt, Jeanne. *It's Hanukkah!*
    Songs of Chanukah
Moorman, Margaret. *Light the lights!*
Moss, Marissa. *The ugly menorah*
Nayer, Judy. *The eight nights of Hanukka*
Nerlove, Miriam. *Hanukkah*
Oberman, Sheldon. *By the Hanukkah light*
Okrend, Elise. *Blintzes for Blitzen*
Podwal, Mark H. *The menorah story*
Poskanzer, Susan Cornell. *Riddles about Hannukah*
Rosen, Michael J. (1954-). *Elijah's angel*
Rothenberg, Joan. *Inside-out grandma*
Schnur, Steven. *The tie man's miracle*
Schotter, Roni. *Hanukkah!*
Sherman, Eileen Bluestone. *The odd potato*
Shostak, Myra. *Rainbow candles*
Simon, Norma. *The story of Hanukkah*
Stillerman, Marci. *Nine spoons*
Zagwÿn, Deborah Turney. *Papa's latkes*
Zalben, Jane Breskin. *Beni's first Chanukah*
    Pearl's eight days of Chanukah

Holidays – Independence Day *see* Holidays – Fourth of July

Holidays – Juneteenth

Weatherford, Carole Boston. *Juneteenth jamboree*

Holidays – Kwanzaa

Burden-Patmon, Denise. *Imani's gift at Kwanzaa*
Chocolate, Deborah M. Newton. *Kente colors*
    Kwanzaa
Ford, Juwanda G. *K is for Kwanzaa*
Kroll, Virginia L. *Wood-hoopoe Willie*
McKissack, Patricia C. *Messy Bessey's holidays*
Medearis, Angela Shelf. *Kyle's first Kwanzaa*
    Seven spools of thread
Saint James, Synthia. *The gifts of Kwanzaa*
Washington, Donna L. *The story of Kwanzaa*

Holidays – Mardi Gras *see* Mardi Gras

Holidays – May Day

Mora, Pat. *The rainbow tulip*
Silverman, Erica. *On the morn of Mayfest*

Holidays – Memorial Day

Scott, Geoffrey. *Memorial Day*

Holidays – Mother's Day

Anderson, Laurie Halse. *No time for Mother's Day*
Balian, Lorna. *Mother's Mother's Day*
Bunting, Eve (Anne Evelyn). *The Mother's Day mice*
Howe, James. *The case of the missing mother*
Kroll, Steven. *Happy Mother's Day*
Livingston, Myra Cohn. *Poems for mothers*
Morgan, Allen. *Matthew and the midnight money van*
Sharmat, Marjorie Weinman. *Hooray for Mother's Day!*
Tripp, Valerie. *Happy, happy Mother's Day*
Wynot, Jillian. *The Mother's Day sandwich*

Holidays – New Year's

Andersen, H. C. (Hans Christian). *The little match girl*, ill. by Rachel Isadora
   The little match girl, ill. by Blair Lent
   The little match girl, ill. by Jerry Pinkney
Chiemruom, Sothea. *Dara's Cambodian New Year*
Grifalconi, Ann. *The bravest flute*
Holabird, Katharine. *Angelina ice skates*
Janice. *Little Bear's New Year's party*
Kudler, David. *The Seven Gods of Luck*
Modell, Frank. *Goodbye old year, hello new year*
Ziefert, Harriet. *First Night*

Holidays – Passover

Adler, David A. *A picture book of Jewish holidays*
   A picture book of Passover
Auerbach, Julie Jaslow. *Everything's changing - It's pesach!*
Behrens, June. *Passover*
Feder, Harriet K. *Not yet, Elijah!*
Fishman, Cathy Goldberg. *On Passover*
Hawxhurst, Joan C. *Bubbe and Gram, my two grandmothers*
Hirsh, Marilyn. *I love Passover*
   One little goat
Kimmelman, Leslie. *Hooray! it's Passover!*
Manushkin, Fran. *The matzah that Papa brought home*
   Miriam's cup
Newman, Lesléa. *Matzo ball moon*
Portnoy, Mindy Avra. *Matzah ball*
Rosen, Anne. *A family Passover*
Rothenberg, Joan. *Matzah ball soup*
Rouss, Sylvia A. *Sammy Spider's first Passover*
Schotter, Roni. *Passover magic*
Schwartz, Lynne Sharon. *The four questions*
Silverman, Erica. *Gittel's hands*
Simon, Norma. *The story of Passover*
Swartz, Leslie. *A first Passover*
Wikler, Madeline. *My first seder*
Wohl, Lauren L. *Matzoh mouse*
Zalben, Jane Breskin. *Happy Passover, Rosie*
Zusman, Evelyn. *The Passover parrot*

Holidays – Purim

Cohen, Barbara. *Here come the Purim players!*, ill. by Beverly Brodsky McDermott
   Here come the Purim players!, ill. by Shoshana Mekibel
Gerstein, Mordicai. *Queen Esther the morning star*
Nerlove, Miriam. *Purim*
Schotter, Roni. *Purim play*

Suhl, Yuri. *The Purim goat*
Topek, Susan Remick. *A costume for Noah*
Wikler, Madeline. *The Purim parade*

Holidays – Ramadan

Ghazi, Suhaib Hamid. *Ramadan*

Holidays – Rosh Hashanah

Fishman, Cathy Goldberg. *On Rosh Hashanah and Yom Kippur*
Gellman, Ellie. *It's Rosh Hashanah!*
Goldin, Barbara Diamond. *World's birthday*
Kahn, Katherine Janus. *The shofar calls to us*
Kimmelman, Leslie. *Sound the shofar!*

Holidays – St. Patrick's Day

Bunting, Eve (Anne Evelyn). *St. Patrick's Day in the morning*
Calhoun, Mary. *The hungry leprechaun*
Dillon, Jana. *Lucky O'Leprechaun*
Janice. *Little Bear marches in the St. Patrick's Day parade*
Kroll, Steven. *Mary McLean and the St. Patrick's Day parade*
O'Donnell, Elizabeth Lee. *Patrick's day*
Schertle, Alice. *Jeremy Bean's St. Patrick's Day*
Zimelman, Nathan. *To sing a song as big as Ireland*

Holidays – Sukkot

Groner, Judyth Saypol. *All about Sukkot*
Lepon, Shoshana. *Hillel builds a house*
Polacco, Patricia. *Tikvah means hope*
Zalben, Jane Breskin. *Leo and Blossom's Sukkah*

Holidays – Thanksgiving

Alcott, Louisa May. *An old-fashioned Thanksgiving*
Anderson, Laurie Halse. *Turkey pox*
Balian, Lorna. *Sometimes it's turkey*
Behrens, June. *The feast of Thanksgiving*
Berenstain, Stan. *The Berenstain bears and the prize pumpkin*
Borden, Louise. *Thanksgiving is . . .*
Brown, Marc Tolon. *Arthur's Thanksgiving*
Bunting, Eve (Anne Evelyn). *How many days to America?*
   A turkey for Thanksgiving
Carlson, Nancy L. *A visit to grandma's*
Child, Lydia Maria. *Over the river and through the wood*
Cowley, Joy. *Gracias, the Thanksgiving turkey*
Dalgliesh, Alice. *The Thanksgiving story*
De Paola, Tomie (Thomas Anthony). *My first Thanksgiving*
Devlin, Wende. *Cranberry Thanksgiving*
Dragonwagon, Crescent. *Alligator arrived with apples*
George, Jean Craighead. *The first Thanksgiving*
Gibbons, Gail. *Thanksgiving Day*
Hopkins, Lee Bennett. *Merrily comes our harvest in*
Ipcar, Dahlov. *Hard scrabble harvest*
Jackson, Alison. *I know an old lady who swallowed a pie*
Janice. *Little Bear's Thanksgiving*
Koller, Jackie French. *Nickommoh!*
Kraus, Robert. *How Spider saved Turkey*

Kroll, Steven. *Oh, what a Thanksgiving!*
  One tough turkey
  The squirrels' Thanksgiving
Leedy, Loreen. *The dragon Thanksgiving feast*
Levine, Abby. *This is the turkey*
Lowitz, Sadyebeth. *The pilgrims' party*
McCully, Emily Arnold. *An outlaw Thanksgiving*
Marzollo, Jean. *Thanksgiving cats*
Melmed, Laura Krauss. *1-2-3 Thanksgiving*
Miller, Edna. *Mousekin's Thanksgiving*
Nerlove, Miriam. *Thanksgiving*
Nikola-Lisa, W. *One, two, three Thanksgiving!*
Nixon, Joan Lowery. *The Thanksgiving mystery*
Ott, John. *Peter Pumpkin*
Paraskevas, Betty. *A very Kroll Christmas*
Pilkey, Dav. *'Twas the night before Thanksgiving*
Pomeranc, Marion Hess. *The can-do Thanksgiving*
Quackenbush, Robert M. *Sheriff Sally Gopher and the Thanksgiving caper*
Rockwell, Anne F. *Thanksgiving Day*
Rosen, Michael (1946-). *A Thanksgiving wish*
Spinelli, Eileen. *Thanksgiving at Tappletons'*
Stock, Catherine. *Thanksgiving treat*
Tresselt, Alvin R. *Autumn harvest*
Watson, Wendy. *Thanksgiving at our house*
Willey, Margaret. *Thanksgiving with me*
Williams, Barbara. *Chester Chipmunk's Thanksgiving*
Zion, Gene. *The meanest squirrel I ever met*

Holidays – Valentine's Day

Adams, Adrienne. *The great Valentine's Day balloon race*
Balian, Lorna. *A sweetheart for Valentine*
Blos, Joan W. *One very best Valentine's Day*
Bond, Felicia. *Four Valentines in a rainstorm*
Brown, Marc Tolon. *Arthur's Valentine*
Buckley, Kate. *Love notes*
Bulla, Clyde Robert. *The story of Valentine's Day*
  Valentine cat
Bunting, Eve (Anne Evelyn). *The Valentine bears*
Carlson, Nancy L. *Louanne Pig in the mysterious valentine*
Carrick, Carol. *Valentine*
Cohen, Miriam. *Bee my Valentine!*
De Groat, Diane. *Roses are pink, your feet really stink*
De Paola, Tomie (Thomas Anthony). *Things to make and do for Valentine's Day*
Devlin, Wende. *Cranberry Valentine*
Gantos, Jack (John, Jr.). *Rotten Ralph's rotten romance*
Geringer, Laura. *Yours 'til the ice cracks*
Gibbons, Gail. *Valentine's Day*
Greene, Carol. *A computer went a-courting*
Gregory, Valiska. *A valentine for Norman Noggs*
Greydanus, Rose. *Someone's baby-sitting*
Guilfoile, Elizabeth. *Valentine's Day*
Guthrie, Donna. *The secret admirer*
Hallinan, P. K. (Patrick K.). *Today is Valentine's Day!*
Hoban, Lillian. *Arthur's great big Valentine*
  Silly Tilly's Valentine
Hurd, Thacher. *Little Mouse's big Valentine*
Keeshan, Robert. *She loves me, she loves me not*
Kelley, True. *A valentine for Fuzzboom*
Krahn, Fernando. *Little love story*
Kraus, Robert. *How Spider saved Valentine's Day*
Kroll, Steven. *Will you be my valentine?*
Kunhardt, Edith. *Danny's mystery Valentine*

Livingston, Myra Cohn. *Valentine poems*
London, Jonathan. *Froggy's first kiss*
McMullan, Kate (Hall). *Hearty har har*
Marzollo, Jean. *Valentine cats*
Maurer-Mathison, Diane V. *Make your own spectacular Valentines*
Modell, Frank. *One zillion valentines*
Murphy, Shirley Rousseau. *Valentine for a dragon*
Nerlove, Miriam. *Valentine's Day*
Nixon, Joan Lowery. *The Valentine mystery*
Rider, Joanne. *First grade valentines*
Roberts, Bethany. *Valentine mice!*
Sabuda, Robert James. *St. Valentine*
Schweninger, Ann. *The hunt for rabbit's galosh*
  Valentine friends
Shannon, George. *Heart to heart*
Sharmat, Marjorie Weinman. *The best Valentine in the world*
Spinelli, Eileen. *Somebody loves you, Mr. Hatch*
Stevenson, James. *Happy Valentine's Day, Emma!*
  A village full of valentines
Stock, Catherine. *Secret Valentine*
Watson, Clyde. *Valentine foxes*
Watson, Wendy. *A Valentine for you*
Wittman, Sally. *The boy who hated Valentine's Day*
Zimmermann, H. Werner (Heinz Werner).
  Alphonse knows . . . a circle is not a Valentine

Holidays – Washington's Birthday

Bulla, Clyde Robert. *Washington's birthday*

Holidays – Yom Kippur

Cohen, Barbara. *First fast*
Fishman, Cathy Goldberg. *On Rosh Hashanah and Yom Kippur*
Kimmelman, Leslie. *Sound the shofar!*
Singer, Marilyn. *Minnie's Yom Kippur birthday*
Weilerstein, Sadie Rose. *K'tonton's Yom Kippur kitten*

Holland *see* Foreign lands – Holland

Holocaust

Adler, David A. *Hiding from the Nazis*
Hoestlandt, Jo. *Star of fear, star of hope*
Lakin, Pat (Patricia). *Don't forget*
Nerlove, Miriam. *Flowers on the wall*
Oberman, Sheldon. *By the Hanukkah light*
Oppenheim, Shulamith Levey. *The lily cupboard*
Schnur, Steven. *The tie man's miracle*
Stillerman, Marci. *Nine spoons*

Homeless

Andersen, H. C. (Hans Christian). *The little match girl*, ill. by Rachel Isadora
  The little match girl, ill. by Blair Lent
  The little match girl, ill. by Jerry Pinkney
Barbour, Karen. *Mr. Bow Tie*
Bunting, Eve (Anne Evelyn). *December*
  Fly away home
Cannon, Janell. *Trupp*
Chinn, Karen. *Sam and the lucky money*
Clément, Claude. *The man who lit the stars*
Coltman, Paul. *Tinker Jim*
Davis, Aubrey. *Bone button borscht*

Gerstein, Mordicai. *The wild boy*
Gottlieb, Dale. *Seeing Eye Willie*
Guthrie, Donna. *A rose for Abby*
Hammond, Anna. *This home we have made*
Hughes, Monica. *A handful of seeds*
Khan, Rukhsana. *The roses in my carpets*
Komaiko, Leah. *Lenora O'Grady*
Martin, Ann M. *Leo the Magnificat*
Myers, Christopher A. *Sparrows*
Polacco, Patricia. *I can hear the sun*
Powell, E. Sandy. *A chance to grow*
Rascal. *Socrates*
Rosen, Michael J. (1954-). *Home*
Vainio, Pirkko. *The Christmas angel*
Weninger, Brigitte. *Lumina*

Homes, houses

Ackerman, Karen. *I know a place*
   The sleeping porch
   This old house
Adler, David A. *The house on the roof*
Alger, Leclaire Gowans. *Always room for one more*
Altman, Linda Jacobs. *Amelia's road*
Angelou, Maya. *My painted house, my friendly chicken, and me*
Aragon, Jane Chelsea. *The major and the mousehole mice*
Arkin, Alan. *Tony's hard work day*
Arnold, Katya. *Knock, knock, teremok!*
Ayars, James Sterling. *Caboose on the roof*
Ballard, Robin. *Good-bye, house*
Bannon, Laura. *The best house in the world*
Barton, Byron. *Building a house*
Bassède, Francine. *George paints his house*
Becker, Edna. *Nine hundred buckets of paint*
Bemelmans, Ludwig. *Sunshine*
Berridge, Celia. *At my house*
Binzen, Bill. *Alfred goes house hunting*
Blegvad, Lenore. *The parrot in the garret and other rhymes about dwellings*
Blos, Joan W. *Old Henry*
Boland, Janice. *Annabel again*
Borg, Inga. *Plupp builds a house*
Bour, Danièle. *The house from morning to night*
Boyd, Lizi. *Mouse in a house*
Brown, Marc Tolon. *There's no place like home*
Brown, Marcia. *The neighbors*
Brown, Margaret Wise. *House of a hundred windows*
   The wonderful house
Buchanan, Ken. *This house is made of mud*
Bunting, Eve (Anne Evelyn). *In the haunted house*
Burton, Virginia Lee. *The little house*
Butterworth, Nick. *The house on the rock*
Calhoun, Mary. *Mrs. Dog's own house*
Calmenson, Stephanie. *Where will the animals stay?*
Campbell, Rod. *Buster's morning*
Carle, Eric. *My very first book of homes*
Carter, Katharine. *Houses*
Carter, Noelle. *My house*
Carter, Penny. *A new house for the Morrisons*
Cartlidge, Michelle. *A house for Lily Mouse*
   Mouse in the house
Chase, Catherine. *The mouse in my house*
Chorao, Kay. *Cathedral mouse*
Christensen, Gardell Dano. *Mrs. Mouse needs a house*
Clymer, Eleanor Lowenton. *The tiny little house*
Colby, C. B. (Carroll Burleigh). *Who lives there?*

Colman, Hila. *Peter's brownstone house*
Cousins, Lucy. *Maisy's pop-up playhouse*
Crompton, Margaret. *The house where Jack lives*
Curry, Nancy. *The littlest house*
Cutler, Ivor. *The animal house*
Dale, Penny. *Daisy Rabbit's tree house*
Dalmais, Anne-Marie. *Petey the puppy*
Dauer, Rosamond. *Bullfrog builds a house*
De Regniers, Beatrice Schenk. *A little house of your own*
Desimini, Lisa. *My house*
Dorros, Arthur. *This is my house*
Dragonwagon, Crescent. *Home place*
Du Quette, Keith. *The house book*
Durant, Alan. *Mouse party*
Emberley, Ed (Edward Randolph). *Home*
Emerman, Ellen. *Just right*
Enderle, Judith (Ann) Ross. *Upstairs*
Erickson, Phoebe. *Just follow me*
Farm house
Feder, Paula Kurzband. *Where does the teacher live?*
Firehouse, ill. by Zokeisha
Fisher, Aileen Lucia. *Best little house*
   The house of a mouse
Flanagan, Alice K. *The Wilsons, a house-painting team*
Flint, Russ. *Let's build a house*
Flory, Jane. *The bear on the doorstep*
Gedin, Birgitta. *The little house from the sea*
Gerstein, Mordicai. *The room*
Gibbons, Gail. *How a house is built*
Gliori, Debi. *New big house*
Goffstein, M. B. (Marilyn Brooke). *A house, a home*
Gomboli, Mario. *Look inside a house*
Goodall, John S. *Great days of a country house*
Graham, Bob. *Spirit of Hope*
Grahame, Kenneth. *The wind in the willows*
Green, Mary McBurney. *Everybody has a house and everybody eats*
Greenway, Shirley. *Animal homes: burrows*
Greydanus, Rose. *Tree house fun*
Grosz, Peter. *The special gifts*
Hammar, Asa. *Fit for pigs*
Harper, Anita. *How we live*
Harrison, David Lee. *When cows come home*
Hawcock, David. *Whose home?*
Hayward, Linda. *Hello, house!*
Herman, Gail. *The haunted house*
Hoberman, Mary Ann. *A house is a house for me*
Hodges, Margaret. *Molly Limbo*
Hoff, Syd. *Stanley*
Högner, Franz. *From blueprint to house*
Holl, Adelaide. *Small Bear builds a playhouse*
Houses
Hughes, Shirley. *Alfie gets in first*
   The big concrete lorry
   Sally's secret
Hunter, Norman. *Professor Branestawn's building bust-up*
Ichikawa, Satomi. *Nora's castle*
Jaques, Faith. *Tilly's house*
Jaynes, Ruth M. *The biggest house*
Joerns, Consuelo. *The lost and found house*
Katz, Avner. *Tortoise solves a problem*
Kaune, Merriman B. *My own little house*
Kay, Verla. *Covered wagons, bumpy trails*
Kessler, Ethel. *Is there an elephant in your kitchen?*
Kilroy, Sally. *Babies' homes*
Kirk, Barbara. *Grandpa, me and our house in the tree*

Kitchen, Bert. *And so they build*
Koller, Jackie French. *Mole and Shrew*
Krauss, Ruth. *A very special house*
Kroll, Steven. *Pigs in the house*
Kwitz, Mary DeBall. *Rabbits' search for a little house*
Lepon, Shoshana. *Hillel builds a house*
Le Tord, Bijou. *Good wood bear*
Lewis, Eils Moorhouse. *The snug little house*
Liersch, Anne. *A house is not a home*
Lillegard, Dee. *Wake up house!*
Lindbergh, Reeve. *If I'd known then what I know now*
Lippman, Peter. *The Know-It-Alls help out*
Lynn, Sara. *Home*
Lyon, George Ella. *One lucky girl*
McCarty, Peter. *Little bunny on the move*
McDonald, Megan. *My house has stars*
McGough, Roger. *Until I met Dudley*
McGovern, Ann. *Mr. Skinner's skinny house*
McNaughton, Colin. *Who's that banging on the ceiling?*
McPhail, David M. *Lorenzo*
Maestro, Betsy. *Harriet at home*
Malone, Nola Langner. *A home*
Manning, Mick. *A ruined house*
Maris, Ron. *Better move on, frog!*
Marzollo, Jean. *Home sweet home*
Mason, Ann Maree. *The weird things in Nanna's house*
Mathis, Melissa Bay. *Animal house*
Mayer, Mercer. *Little Monster at home*
Maynard, Joyce. *New house*
Meddaugh, Susan. *The best place*
Medearis, Angela Shelf. *The ghost of Sifty-Sifty Sam*
We eat dinner in the bathtub
Mendoza, George. *Need a house? Call Ms. Mouse*
Merriam, Eve. *The birthday door*
Miles, Betty. *A house for everyone*
Miller, Elizabeth I. *Just like home = Como en mi tierra*
Miller, William. *A house by the river*
Milne, A. A. (Alan Alexander). *House at Pooh corner [a pop-up book]*
Minarik, Else Holmelund. *Percy and the five houses*
Miranda, Anne. *Does a mouse have a house?*
Mizumura, Kazue. *If I built a village*
Morris, Ann. *Houses and homes*
Mother Goose. *Mother Goose house*
Mouse house
Mozelle, Shirley. *The pig is in the pantry, the cat is on the shelf*
Muntean, Michaela. *The house that bear built*
Murphy, Shirley Rousseau. *Tattie's river journey*
Neitzel, Shirley. *The house I'll build for the wrens*
Nolan, Dennis. *Witch Bazooza*
Nolen, Jerdine. *In my momma's kitchen*
Novak, Matt. *Elmer Blunt's open house*
Oakley, Graham. *The church mice and the ring*
Okimoto, Jean Davies. *No dear, not here*
Our house
Pape, D. L. (Donna Lugg). *Doghouse for sale*
Pedersen, Judy. *Out in the country*
Peppé, Rodney. *The mice who lived in a shoe*
Pfanner, Louise. *Louise builds a house*
Pienkowski, Jan. *Homes*
Pilkey, Dav. *The Silly Gooses build a house*
Pinkwater, Daniel Manus. *The big orange splot*
Rainy morning
Polisar, Barry Louis. *The haunted house party*
Posey, Lee. *Night rabbits*

Pryor, Bonnie. *The beaver boys*
Quackenbush, Robert M. *Batbaby finds a home*
Radford, Derek. *Harry builds a house*
Rey, H. A. (Hans Augusto). *Anybody at home?*
Rockwell, Anne F. *Nice and clean*
Roffey, Maureen. *Home sweet home*
Rosen, Michael (1946-). *This is our house*
Roth, Harold. *Let's look all around the house*
Rounds, Glen. *Sod houses on the Great Plains*
Rusling, Albert. *The mouse and Mrs. Proudfoot*
Ryan, Pam Muñoz. *Armadillos sleep in dugouts*
Ryder, Joanne. *A house by the sea*
Rylant, Cynthia. *The bird house*
Bunny bungalow
San Souci, Robert D. *The boy and the ghost*
The house in the sky
Sattler, Helen Roney. *No place for a goat*
Scarry, Richard. *Is this the house of Mistress Mouse?*
Richard Scarry's busy houses
Schaaf, Peter. *An apartment house close up*
Scharer, Niko. *Emily's house*
Schermbrucker, Reviva. *Charlie's house*
Schertle, Alice. *In my treehouse*
Schlein, Miriam. *My house*
Schulz, Charles M. *Snoopy's facts and fun book about houses*
Seuss, Dr. *Come over to my house*
In a people house
Shannon, George. *Lizard's home*
Shapp, Martha. *Let's find out about houses*
Sharr, Christine. *Homes*
Shecter, Ben. *Emily, girl witch of New York*
Shefelman, Janice Jordan. *Victoria House*
Shelby, Anne. *The someday house*
Sherrow, Victoria. *There goes the ghost*
Sierra, Judy. *The house that Drac built*
Silsbe, Brenda. *Just one more color*
Silverman, Erica. *On Grandma's roof*
Skorpen, Liesel Moak. *We were tired of living in a house*
Stern, Simon. *Mrs. Vinegar*
Strathdee, Jean. *The house that grew*
Swinburne, Stephen R. *Swallows in the birdhouse*
Tallarico, Tony. *At home*
Testa, Fulvio. *The ideal home*
Thayer, Jane. *What's a ghost going to do?*
Tison, Annette. *Inside and outside*
Tudor, Bethany. *Samuel's tree house*
Turner, Ann Warren. *The Christmas house*
Vainio, Pirkko. *The dream house*
Van Allsburg, Chris. *Two bad ants*
Velthuijs, Max. *Little Man finds a home*
Vevers, Gwynne. *Animal homes*
Vizurraga, Susan. *Our old house*
Waddell, Martin. *The hidden house*
Mimi and the dream house
Waite, Judy. *Mouse, look out!*
Wallace, John. *Building a house with Mr. Bumble*
Ward, Nick. *Farmer George and the fieldmice*
Watanabe, Shigeo. *I can build a house!*
Weeks, Sarah. *Drip, drop*
Mrs. McNosh and the great big squash
Wellington, Monica. *Baby at home*
Wildsmith, Brian. *Animal homes*
Winch, Madeleine. *Come by chance*
Worley, Daryl. *Billy and the attic adventure*
Wormell, Christopher. *Blue Rabbit and friends*
Wyllie, Stephen. *White Rabbit builds a dream house*
Yee, Wong Herbert. *Eek! There's a mouse in the house*

Mrs. Brown went to town
Yoaker, Harry. *The view*
Zelinsky, Paul O. *The maid and the mouse and the odd-shaped house*
Ziefert, Harriet. *Cow in the house*
A new house for Mole and Mouse

Homosexuality

Newman, Lesléa. *Heather has two mommies*
Saturday is Pattyday
Vigna, Judith. *My two uncles*
Willhoite, Michael. *Daddy's roommate*

Honesty *see* Character traits – honesty

Honey bees *see* Insects – bees

Hope

Ikeda, Daisaku. *The cherry tree*

Hopi Indians *see* Indians of North America – Hopi

Hornbills *see* Birds – hornbills

Hornets *see* Insects – hornets

Horses *see* Animals – horses, ponies

Horses, rocking *see* Toys – rocking horses

Hospitals

Baker, Gayle. *Special delivery*
Bemelmans, Ludwig. *Madeline*
Madeline [pop-up book]
Blance, Ellen. *Monster goes to the hospital*
Bruna, Dick. *Miffy in the hospital*
Bucknall, Caroline. *One bear in the hospital*
Carlstrom, Nancy White. *Barney is best*
Ciliotta, Claire. *"Why am I going to the hospital?"*
Collier, James Lincoln. *Danny goes to the hospital*
Davison, Martine. *Maggie and the emergency room*
Rita goes to the hospital
Dooley, Virginia. *Tubes in my ears*
Elliott, Ingrid Glatz. *Hospital roadmap*
Goodall, Jane. *Dr. White*
Hautzig, Deborah. *A visit to the Sesame Street hospital*
Hill, Eric. *Spot visits the hospital*
Hogan, Paula Z. *The hospital scares me*
Karim, Roberta. *This is a hospital, not a zoo!*
Keller, Holly. *The best present*
Ketner, Mary Grace. *Ganzy remembers*
Marino, Barbara Pavis. *Eric needs stitches*
Martin, Charles E. *Island rescue*
Morgan, Allen. *Matthew and the midnight hospital*
Moses, Amy. *At the hospital*
Pace, Elizabeth. *Chris gets ear tubes*
Pirner, Connie White. *Even little kids get diabetes*
Pope, Billy N. *Your world*
Rey, Margret (Margret Elisabeth Waldstein). *Curious George goes to the hospital*
Rockwell, Anne F. *The emergency room*
Rogers, Fred. *Going to the hospital*

Rosenberg, Maxine B. *Mommy's in the hospital having a baby*
Shay, Arthur. *What happens when you go to the hospital*
Sobol, Harriet Langsam. *Jeff's hospital book*
Sonneborn, Ruth A. *I love Gram*
Steel, Danielle. *Max's daddy goes to the hospital*
Stein, Sara Bonnett. *A hospital story*
Stone, Bernard. *Emergency mouse*
Tamburine, Jean. *I think I will go to the hospital*
Watts, Marjorie-Ann. *Crocodile medicine*
Crocodile plaster
Weber, Alfons. *Elizabeth gets well*
Wild, Margaret. *Going home*
Mr. Nick's knitting
Wolde, Gunilla. *Betsy and the doctor*

Hotels

Brewster, Patience. *Rabbit Inn*
Du Quette, Keith. *Hotel Animal*
Keeshan, Robert. *Itty Bitty Kitty makes a big splash*
Knight, Joan. *Bon appetit, Bertie!*
Levinson, Riki. *Grandpa's hotel*
Mahy, Margaret. *Rooms for rent*
Naylor, Phyllis Reynolds. *Ducks disappearing*
Parkin, Rex. *The red carpet*
Pinkwater, Daniel Manus. *At the Hotel Larry*
Schneider, Howie. *No dogs allowed*
Simmie, Lois. *Mister got to go/No cats allowed*
Stevenson, James. *The Sea View Hotel*
Supraner, Robyn. *Sam Sunday and the mystery at the Ocean Beach Hotel*
Vaughan, Marcia Kapok. *The Sea-Breeze Hotel*
Waber, Bernard. *Do you see a mouse?*
Wojtowycz, David. *Animal antics from 1 to 10*
Yee, Wong Herbert. *Fireman Small, fire down below*

Housekeepers *see* Careers – housekeepers

Houses *see* Homes, houses

Huichol Indians *see* Indians of North America – Huichol

Humming birds *see* Birds – humming birds

Humor

Aardema, Verna. *Oh, Kojo! How could you!*
What's so funny, Ketu?
Who's in Rabbit's house?
Accorsi, William. *Short short short stories*
Adams, Richard (Richard Newbold). *The tyger voyage*
Adamson, Gareth. *Old man up a tree*
Adinolfi, JoAnn. *The Egyptian polar bear*
Adler, David A. *The children of Chelm*
Æsop. *The miller, his son and their donkey*, ill. by Roger Antoine Duvoisin
Ahlberg, Allan. *The ghost train*
Mystery tour
Ahlberg, Janet. *The little worm book*
Alexander, Martha G. *Move over, Twerp*
My outrageous friend Charlie
Alexander, Sue. *World famous Muriel*
Aliki. *Digging up dinosaurs*
The eggs

The all-amazing ha ha book

Allamand, Pascale. *The animals who changed their colors*

Allard, Harry. *Miss Nelson has a field day*
Miss Nelson is back
Miss Nelson is missing!
The Stupids die
The Stupids have a ball
The Stupids step out
The Stupids take off
There's a party at Mona's tonight

Allen, Jonathan. *A bad case of animal nonsense*

Allen, Linda. *Mr. Simkin's grandma*
Mrs. Simkin's bed

Allen, Marjorie N. *One, two, three – ah-choo!*

Allen, Pamela. *Mr. Archimedes' bath*
Mr. McGee

Ambrus, Victor G. *Grandma, Felix, and Mustapha Biscuit*

Andersen, H. C. (Hans Christian). *The emperor's new clothes*, ill. by Erik Blegvad
The emperor's new clothes, ill. by Virginia Lee Burton
The emperor's new clothes, ill. by Robert Byrd
The emperor's new clothes, ill. by Jack and Irene Delano
The emperor's new clothes, ill. by Hélène Desputeaux
The emperor's new clothes, ill. by Birte Dietz
The emperor's new clothes, ill. by Dorothée Duntze
The emperor's new clothes, ill. by Pamela Baldwin Ford
The emperor's new clothes, ill. by Jack Kent
The emperor's new clothes, ill. by Monika Laimgruber
The emperor's new clothes, ill. by Anne F. Rockwell
The emperor's new clothes, ill. by Janet Stevens
The emperor's new clothes, ill. by Nadine Bernard Westcott
The old man is always right

Anderson, Leone Castell. *The wonderful shrinking shirt*

Armour, Richard Willard. *Animals on the ceiling*

Arnosky, Jim. *Outdoors on foot*

Asch, Frank. *Sand cake*
Turtle tale

Auch, Mary Jane. *Bantam of the opera*

Aulaire, Ingri Mortenson d'. *Don't count your chicks*

Ayars, James Sterling. *Caboose on the roof*

Aylesworth, Jim. *Hush up!*
Shenandoah Noah

Baker, Alan. *Benjamin and the box*
Benjamin bounces back
Benjamin's balloon
Benjamin's book
Benjamin's dreadful dream
Benjamin's portrait

Baker, Betty. *Sonny-Boy Sim*
Three fools and a horse
Worthington Botts and the steam machine

Bakken, Harold. *The special string*

Balian, Lorna. *Leprechauns never lie*

Barr, Cathrine. *Hound dog's bone*

Barrett, John M. *The bear who slept through Christmas*

Behn, Harry. *What a beautiful noise*

Beisner, Monika. *Monika Beisner's book of riddles*

Belloc, Hilaire. *The bad child's book of beasts*
The bad child's book of beasts, and more beasts for worse children

Bemelmans, Ludwig. *Rosebud*
Sunshine

Benchley, Nathaniel. *Walter the homing pigeon*

Benedictus, Roger. *Fifty million sausages*

Benjamin, Alan. *1000 monsters*

Bennett, Jill. *Roger was a razor fish and other poems*

Benton, Robert. *Don't ever wish for a 7-foot bear*

Bishop, Ann. *Chicken riddle*
The Ella Fannie elephant riddle book
Hey riddle riddle
Merry-go-riddle
Noah riddle?
Oh, riddlesticks!
The riddle ages
Riddle-iculous rid-alphabet book
Wild Bill Hiccup's riddle book

Bishop, Claire Huchet. *The man who lost his head*

Blake, Quentin. *Mister Magnolia*
Mrs. Armitage on wheels
Quentin Blake's nursery rhyme book

Bodecker, N. M. (Nils Mogens). *"It's raining," said John Twaining*
"Let's marry" said the cherry, and other nonsense poems
Snowman Sniffles and other verse

Bohman, Nils Axel Erik. *Jim, Jock and Jumbo*

Borten, Helen. *Do you go where I go?*

Bossom, Naomi. *A scale full of fish and other turnabouts*

Boynton, Sandra. *If at first . . .*

Bradfield, Roger (Jolly Roger). *The flying hockey stick*

Brecht, Bertolt. *Uncle Eddie's moustache*

Brenner, Barbara A. *A dog I know*

Bridwell, Norman. *The witch grows up*

Briggs, Raymond. *Jim and the beanstalk*

Brock, Emma Lillian. *Mr. Wren's house*
Nobody's mouse
Skipping Island

Brodmann, Aliana. *Such a noise!*

Bröger, Achim. *Little Harry*
The Santa Clauses

Brothers, Aileen. *Sad Mrs. Sam Sack*

Brown, Jeff. *Flat Stanley*

Brown, Marc Tolon. *Spooky riddles*
What do you call a dumb bunny? and other rabbit riddles, games, jokes and cartoons

Brown, Margaret Wise. *Once upon a time in pigpen and three other stories*

Brown, Ruth. *The big sneeze*

Browne, Caroline. *Mrs. Christie's farmhouse*

Bruna, Dick. *Kitten Nell*

Brunhoff, Laurent de. *Serafina the giraffe*

Bryant, Sara Cone. *Epaminondas and his auntie*

Buchanan, Joan. *It's a good thing*

Buehner, Caralyn. *It's a spoon, not a shovel*

Bunting, Eve (Anne Evelyn). *The big cheese*

Burningham, John. *The shopping basket*

Burroway, Janet. *The truck on the track*

Burton, Marilee Robin. *The elephant's nest*

Byfield, Barbara Ninde. *The haunted churchbell*

Calhoun, Mary. *The nine lives of Homer C. Cat*
Old man Whickutt's donkey
The traveling ball of string

Cameron, Polly. *A child's book of nonsense*

Carrick, Donald. *Harold and the giant knight*
Harold and the great stag

Carroll, Lewis. *Jabberwocky*, ill. by Graeme Base
Jabberwocky, ill. from Disney archives

Jennifer and Josephine
Jethro and Joel were a troll
Kermit the hermit
Merle the high flying squirrel
Randy's dandy lions
Phillips, Louis. *The upside down riddle book*
Pilkey, Dav. *The Silly Gooses*
  The Silly Gooses build a house
Pinkney, J. Brian. *The adventures of sparrowboy*
Pinkwater, Daniel Manus. *At the Hotel Larry*
  Bongo Larry
  Young Larry
Plourde, Lynn. *Pigs in the mud in the middle of the rud*
Polacco, Patricia. *In Enzo's splendid gardens*
Postgate, Oliver. *Noggin and the whale*
  Noggin the king
Potter, Beatrix. *The tale of Tom Kitten*
Prather, Ray. *Double dog dare*
Prelutsky, Jack. *The baby uggs are hatching*
  The queen of Eene
  The Random House book of poetry for children
  The snopp on the sidewalk and other poems
Preston, Edna Mitchell. *Horrible Hepzibah*
  Pop Corn and Ma Goodness
Pulver, Robin. *Mrs. Toggle's zipper*
Puner, Helen Walker. *The sitter who didn't sit*
Quackenbush, Robert M. *Funny bunnies*
  Pete Pack Rat
Ragz, M. M. *Lost little angel*
Raskin, Ellen. *Franklin Stein*
  Nothing ever happens on my block
Rayner, Shoo. *My first picture joke book*
Reid, Alastair. *Supposing*
Rey, H. A. (Hans Augusto). *Cecily G and the nine monkeys*
  Curious George
  Curious George gets a medal
  Curious George rides a bike
  Curious George takes a job
  Elizabite
  Elizabite, adventures of a carnivorous plant
  The original Curious George
  Tit for tat
Rey, Margret (Margret Elisabeth Waldstein). *Billy's picture*
  Curious George flies a kite
  Curious George goes to the hospital
Riddell, Chris. *Mr. Underbed*
Rix, Jamie. *The last chocolate cookie*
Rosen, Michael (1946-). *Smelly jelly smelly fish*
  You can't catch me!
Rossner, Judith. *What kind of feet does a bear have?*
Rounds, Glen. *The day the circus came to Lone Tree*
Roy, Ronald. *Three ducks went wandering*
Rubel, Nicole. *It came from the swamp*
Rusling, Albert. *The mouse and Mrs. Proudfoot*
Saddler, Allen. *The Archery contest*
  The king gets fit
Sage, Michael. *Dippy dos and don'ts*
  If you talked to a boar
Saltzberg, Barney. *Cromwell*
Samuels, Barbara. *Duncan and Dolores*
Sandburg, Carl (Charles August). *The Huckabuck family and how they raised popcorn in Nebraska and quit and came back*
Sazer, Nina. *What do you think I saw?*
Schatell, Brian. *Midge and Fred*
Scheer, Julian. *Rain makes applesauce*

Schmidt, Eric von. *The young man who wouldn't hoe corn*
Schwalje, Marjory. *Mr. Angelo*
Schwartz, Alvin. *All of our noses are here and other stories*
Seligson, Susan. *The amazing Amos and the greatest couch on earth*
  Amos
Sendak, Maurice. *Pierre*
Seuss, Dr. *And to think that I saw it on Mulberry Street*
  Bartholomew and the Oobleck
  The cat in the hat
  The cat in the hat comes back!
  The cat in the hat dictionary
  The cat's quizzer
  Did I ever tell you how lucky you are?
  Dr. Seuss's ABC
  Dr. Seuss's sleep book
  The foot book
  Fox in socks
  Gerald McBoing Boing
  A great day for up
  Green eggs and ham
  Happy birthday to you!
  Hooper Humperdink . . . ? Not him!
  Hop on Pop
  Horton hatches the egg
  Horton hears a Who!
  How the Grinch stole Christmas
  I am not going to get up today!
  I can lick 30 tigers today and other stories
  I can read with my eyes shut
  I can write!
  I had trouble getting to Solla Sollew
  If I ran the circus
  If I ran the zoo
  In a people house
  The king's stilts
  The Lorax
  McElligot's pool
  Marvin K. Mooney, will you please go now!
  Mr. Brown can moo! Can you?
  Oh say can you say?
  Oh, the thinks you can think!
  On beyond zebra
  One fish, two fish, red fish, blue fish
  Please try to remember the first of Octember!
  Scrambled eggs super!
  The shape of me and other stuff
  The Sneetches, and other stories
  There's a wocket in my pocket
  Thidwick, the big-hearted moose
  Wacky Wednesday
Shannon, George. *Beanboy*
Showalter, Jean B. *The donkey ride*
Silverstein, Shel. *A giraffe and a half*
Singer, Marilyn. *The dog who insisted he wasn't*
  Solomon sneezes
Sloat, Teri. *There was an old lady who swallowed a trout*
Slobodkina, Esphyr. *Caps for sale*
  Pezzo the peddler and the circus elephant
  Pezzo the peddler and the thirteen silly thieves
Smith, Jim. *The frog band and the onion seller*
  The frog band and the owlnapper
Smith, Robert Paul. *Jack Mack*
Smith, William Jay. *Puptents and pebbles*
Speed, Toby. *Watervoices*
Spier, Peter. *Bored - nothing to do!*

Oh, were they ever happy!
Spilka, Arnold. *A lion I can do without*
    A rumbudgin of nonsense
Spinelli, Eileen. *Thanksgiving at Tappletons'*
Stamaty, Mark Alan. *Minnie Maloney and Macaroni*
Steig, William. *Farmer Palmer's wagon ride*
Stevenson, James. *Don't make me laugh*
    Happy Valentine's Day, Emma!
    The worst person in the world at Crab Beach
Stone, Rosetta. *Because a little bug went ka-choo!*
Stroyer, Poul. *It's a deal*
Suba, Susanne. *The monkeys and the pedlar*
Suhl, Yuri. *Simon Boom gives a wedding*
Sundgaard, Arnold. *Jethro's difficult dinosaur*
Tapio, Pat Decker. *The lady who saw the good side of*
    everything
Thaler, Mike. *Pack 109*
    The yellow brick toad
Thomas, Patricia. *"Stand back," said the elephant,*
    "I'm going to sneeze!"
Tobias, Tobi. *Jane wishing*
Tomkins, Jasper. *The catalog*
Tripp, Wallace. *My Uncle Podger*
Tulloch, Richard. *Stories from our house*
The twelve days of Christmas.. English folk song.
    Jack Kent's twelve days of Christmas
Ueno, Noriko. *Elephant buttons*
Ulrich, George. *The spook matinee*
Ungerer, Tomi. *The beast of Monsieur Racine*
    Crictor
    Emile
Van der Meer, Ron. *Oh Lord!*
Van Laan, Nancy. *Little baby Bobby*
Van Woerkom, Dorothy. *Donkey Ysabel*
    The queen who couldn't bake gingerbread
Vaughan, Marcia Kapok. *The lemonade stand*
Viorst, Judith. *Sunday morning*
Waber, Bernard. *How to go about laying an egg*
    Nobody is perfick
Wahl, Jan. *Cabbage moon*
Watanabe, Shigeo. *What a good lunch!*
Watson, Clyde. *Hickory stick rag*
Watson, Esther (Pearl). *The adventures of Jules and*
    Gertie
Weatherill, Stephen. *The very first Lucy Goose book*
Weeks, Sarah. *Happy birthday, Frankie*
    Mrs. McNosh hangs up her wash
Westcott, Nadine Bernard. *The lady with the alliga-*
    tor purse
Wiese, Kurt. *Fish in the air*
Wiesner, William. *Happy-Go-Lucky*
    Turnabout
Willard, Nancy. *Simple pictures are best*
Williams, Barbara. *Jeremy isn't hungry*
Williams, Jay. *School for sillies*
Wiseman, Bernard. *Tails are not for painting*
Wisniewski, David. *Tough cookie*
Wolkstein, Diane. *The legend of Sleepy Hollow*
Wood, Audrey. *King Bidgood's in the bathtub*
Wright, Jill. *The old woman and the Willy Nilly Man*
Yorinks, Arthur. *Company's coming*
Zemach, Harve. *The tricks of Master Dabble*
Zemach, Margot. *It could always be worse*
Ziefert, Harriet. *Math riddles*
Zimmerman, Andrea Griffing. *Yetta, the trickster*

Hungary *see* Foreign lands – Hungary

Hungry

Milne, A. A. (Alan Alexander). *Pooh's quiz book*

Hunting *see* Sports – hunting

Huron Indians *see* Indians of North America
   – Huron

Hurricanes *see* Weather – hurricanes

Hurrying *see* Behavior – hurrying

Hyenas *see* Animals – hyenas

Hygiene

Cole, Babette. *Dr. Dog*
Langreuter, Jutta. *Little Bear brushes his teeth*
Yagya, Genichiro. *All about scabs*

Ibis *see* Birds – ibis

Ice skating *see* Sports – ice skating

Iceland *see* Foreign lands – Iceland

Identity *see* Self-concept

Iguanas *see* Reptiles – iguanas

Illness

Anholt, Catherine. *Truffles is sick*
Arnold, Katrin. *Anna joins in*
Aylesworth, Jim. *McGraw's Emporium*
Baggette, Susan K. *Jonathan goes to the doctor*
Bains, Rae. *Hiccups, hiccups*
Barrett, Judi. *An apple a day*
Bartels, Alice L. *The grandmother doll*
Bemelmans, Ludwig. *Madeline's Christmas*
Berger, Melvin. *Germs make me sick!*
    Ouch! a book about cuts, scratches and scrapes
    Why I cough, sneeze, shiver, hiccup and yawn
Bertrand, Lynne. *One day, two dragons*
Biro, Val. *Gumdrop catches a cold*
Borton, Lady. *Fat chance!*
Bradman, Tony. *Through my window*
Brandenberg, Franz. *I wish I was sick, too!*
Brown, Margaret Wise. *When the wind blew*
Bruna, Dick. *Miffy in the hospital*
Buckley, Helen Elizabeth. *Someday with my father*
Bucknall, Caroline. *One bear in the hospital*
Calmenson, Stephanie. *Get well, gators!*
    Rosie, a visiting dog's story
Carrick, Carol. *Old Mother Witch*
Carter, Alden R. *Seeing things my way*
Cassedy, Sylvia. *The best cat suit of all*
Chalmers, Mary. *Come to the doctor, Harry*

Schick, Eleanor. *Mama*
Seignobosc, Françoise. *Biquette, the white goat*
Shannon, Mark. *The acrobat and the angel*
Sharmat, Marjorie Weinman. *I want mama*
Shay, Arthur. *What happens when you go to the hospital*
Simon, Charnan. *The good bad day*
Siracusa, Catherine. *No mail for Mitchell*
Sonneborn, Ruth A. *I love Gram*
Sonnenschein, Harriet. *Harold's runaway nose*
Steel, Danielle. *Max's daddy goes to the hospital*
Stein, Sara Bonnett. *A hospital story*
Stephenson, Dorothy. *How to scare a lion*
Stroud, Bettye. *Down home at Miss Dessa's*
Thurber, James. *Many moons*, ill. by Marc Simont
 Many moons, ill. by Louis Slobodkin
Tobias, Tobi. *A day off*
Trez, Denise. *The royal hiccups*
Tyler, Linda Wagner. *The sick-in-bed birthday book*
Udry, Janice May. *Mary Jo's grandmother*
Vigna, Judith. *I wish my daddy didn't drink so much*
Waddell, Martin. *The toymaker*
Wadhams, Margaret. *Anna*
Wahl, Jan. *Jamie's tiger*
Watson, Wendy. *Tales for a winter's eve*
Watts, Marjorie-Ann. *Crocodile medicine*
 Crocodile plaster
Weber, Alfons. *Elizabeth gets well*
Wells, Rosemary. *The island light*
West, Colin. *The king's toothache*
Whitney, Alma Marshak. *Just awful*
Wickstrom, Sylvie (Sylvie Kantrovitz). *Mothers can't get sick*
Wild, Margaret. *Mr. Nick's knitting*
Wildsmith, Brian. *Carousel*
Williams, Barbara. *Albert's toothache*
Williams, Vera B. *Music, music for everyone*
Wolde, Gunilla. *Betsy and the chicken pox*
 Betsy and the doctor
Ziefert, Harriet. *When daddy had the chicken pox*

Illness – AIDS

Arnold, Lynda. *My Mommy has AIDS*
Newman, Lesléa. *Too far away to touch*
Pollack, Eileen. *Whisper whisper Jesse, whisper whisper Josh*
Wiener, Lori. *Be a friend*

Illness – alcoholism

Carrick, Carol. *Banana beer*
Langsen, Richard C. *When someone in the family drinks too much*
Oppenheim, Joanne. *No way, Slippery Slick!*
Tabor, Nancy (Maria Grande). *Bottles break*

Illness – allergies

Harrison, Troon. *Aaron's awful allergies*

Illness – Alzheimer's

Bahr, Mary. *The memory box*
Guthrie, Donna. *Grandpa doesn't know it's me*
Karkowsky, Nancy. *Grandma's soup*
Kroll, Virginia L. *Fireflies, peach pies, and lullabies*
Nelson, Vaunda Micheaux. *Always Gramma*
Sakai, Kimiko. *Sachiko means happiness*

Weitzman, Elizabeth. *Let's talk about when someone you love has Alzheimer's disease*

Illness – asthma

Carter, Alden R. *I'm tougher than asthma!*
London, Jonathan. *The lion who had asthma*

Illness – cancer

Blake, Claire. *The paper chain*
Kohlenberg, Sherry. *Sammy's mommy has cancer*
Krisher, Trudy. *Kathy's hats*
Maple, Marilyn J. *On the wings of a butterfly*
Tusa, Tricia. *Bunnies in my head*
Van den Berg, Marinus. *The three birds*

Illness – chicken pox

Anderson, Laurie Halse. *Turkey pox*
Brown, Marc Tolon. *Arthur's chicken pox*
Fine, Anne. *Poor Monty*
Kelley, True. *I've got chicken pox*
Maccarone, Grace. *Itchy, itchy chicken pox*
Rosa-Casanova, Sylvia. *Mama Provi and the pot of rice*
Rosenberry, Vera. *When Vera was sick*
Smith, Maggie. *Dear Daisy, get well soon*

Illness – cold (disease)

Maccarone, Grace. *I have a cold*

Illness – diabetes

Pirner, Connie White. *Even little kids get diabetes*

Illness – drug addiction

Oppenheim, Joanne. *No way, Slippery Slick!*

Illness – measles

Cole, Babette. *Don't go out tonight*
Duquennoy, Jacques. *Operation ghost*

Illness – mental illness

Houk, Randy. *Rico's hawk*

Illness – mumps

Lerner, Marguerite Rush. *Dear little mumps child*
Ostrovsky, Vivian. *Mumps!*
Showers, Paul. *No measles, no mumps for me*

Illness – muscular dystrophy

Osofsky, Audrey. *My buddy*

Illness – tonsillectomy

Carlstrom, Nancy White. *Barney is best*
Davison, Martine. *Rita goes to the hospital*

Illusions, optical *see* Optical illusions

Illustrators *see* Careers – illustrators

Illustrators, children *see* Children as illustrators

Imaginary friends *see* Imagination – imaginary friends

Imagination

Abisch, Roz. *Open your eyes*
Adam, Barbara. *The big, big box*
Adler, David A. *I know I'm a witch*
Agee, Jon. *Ellsworth*
  The incredible painting of Felix Clousseau
Agell, Charlotte. *Mud makes me dance in the spring*
Aiken, Joan. *Arabel and Mortimer*
Aitken, Amy. *Kate and Mona in the jungle*
  Ruby!
  Ruby, the red knight
Alexander, Martha G. *Bobo's dream*
  Marty McGee's space lab, no girls allowed
Allan, Nicholas. *The thing that ate Aunt Julia*
Allen, Jeffrey. *The secret life of Mr. Weird*
Allen, Pamela. *I wish I had a pirate suit*
  A lion in the night
Anastasio, Dina. *Baby Piggy and giant bubble*
Andersen, H. C. (Hans Christian). *The emperor's new clothes*, ill. by Angela Barrett
  The emperor's new clothes, ill. by Erik Blegvad
  The emperor's new clothes, ill. by Virginia Lee Burton
  The emperor's new clothes, ill. by Robert Byrd
  The emperor's new clothes, ill. by Jack and Irene Delano
  The emperor's new clothes, ill. by Hélène Desputeaux
  The emperor's new clothes, ill. by Birte Dietz
  The emperor's new clothes, ill. by Dorothée Duntze
  The emperor's new clothes, ill. by Pamela Baldwin Ford
  The emperor's new clothes, ill. by Jack Kent
  The emperor's new clothes, ill. by Monika Laimgruber
  The emperor's new clothes, ill. by Anne F. Rockwell
  The emperor's new clothes, ill. by Janet Stevens
  The emperor's new clothes, ill. by Robert Van Nutt
  The emperor's new clothes, ill. by Nadine Bernard Westcott
Anderson, C. W. (Clarence Williams). *Linda and the Indians*
Anderson, Joan. *Harry's helicopter*
  Sally's submarine
Anderson, Lonzo. *The haganinny*
Anderson, Wayne. *Dragon*
Angeletti, Roberta. *Nefertari, princess of Egypt*
Anglund, Joan Walsh. *Cowboy's secret life*
Anholt, Laurence. *Summerhouse*
Anno, Mitsumasa. *Anno's alphabet*
  Anno's animals
  Anno's Britain
  Anno's counting book
  Anno's counting house
  Anno's flea market
  Anno's Italy
  Anno's journey
  Anno's magical ABC
  Anno's U.S.A.
  Dr. Anno's magical midnight circus
  The king's flower

  Topsy turvies
  Topsy turvies
  Upside-downers
Armour, Richard Willard. *Animals on the ceiling*
Armstrong, Jennifer. *Pockets*
Arnold, Caroline. *My friend from outer space*
Arnold, Tedd. *No jumping on the bed!*
  No more water in the tub!
Asch, Frank. *City sandwich*
  Goodnight horsey
  Rebecka
Ayal, Ora. *The adventures of Chester the chest*
  Ugbu
Bach, Othello. *Lilly, Willy and the mail-order witch*
Baillie, Allan. *Drac and the gremlin*
Baker, Alan. *Benjamin bounces back*
Baker, Betty. *My sister says*
Baker, Keith. *The magic fan*
Balet, Jan B. *Ned and Ed and the lion*
Bang, Molly. *The grey lady and the strawberry snatcher*
Banks, Kate (Katherine A.). *Alphabet soup*
  Spider, spider
Bannon, Laura. *The best house in the world*
Barber, Antonia. *Satchelmouse and the dinosaurs*
Barrett, Judi. *Cloudy with a chance of meatballs*
  I hate to go to bed
Barry, Katharina. *A bug to hug*
Bartels, Alice L. *The grandmother doll*
Barthelme, Donald. *The slightly irregular fire engine*
Bate, Lucy. *How Georgina drove the car very carefully from Boston to New York*
Baumann, Kurt. *The paper airplane*
Bayley, Nicola. *Crab cat*
  Elephant cat
  Parrot cat
  Polar bear cat
  Spider cat
Beck, Ian. *Emily and the golden acorn*
Beech, Caroline. *Peas again for lunch*
Behrens, June. *Can you walk the plank?*
Beifuss, John. *Armadillo Ray*
Beim, Jerrold. *The taming of Toby*
Benedictus, Roger. *Fifty million sausages*
Benjamin, Alan. *Ribtickle Town*
Bennett, Rowena. *The day is dancing and other poems*
  Songs from around a toadstool table
Berenstain, Stan. *The Berenstain bears in the dark*
Bergman, Donna. *Timmy Green's blue lake*
Berry, Christine. *Mama went walking*
Berson, Harold. *I'm bored, Ma!*
Bertrand, Cécile. *Let's pretend!*
Bishop, Gavin. *Little Rabbit and the sea*
Bittner, Wolfgang. *Wake up, Grizzly!*
Blakeley, Peggy. *What shall I be tomorrow?*
Blathwayt, Benedict. *Tangle and the firesticks*
Blaustein, Muriel. *Jim chimp's story*
Blegvad, Lenore. *Anna Banana and me*
  Rainy day Kate
Blocksma, Mary. *The pup went up*
Blos, Joan W. *Martin's hats*
Blundell, Tony. *Joe on Sunday*
Bodsworth, Nan. *Monkey business*
Boegehold, Betty. *Hurray for Pippa!*
  In the castle of cats
Boon, Emilie. *Peterkin meets a star*
  Peterkin's wet walk
Bottner, Barbara. *Mean Maxine*
  Myra
  There was nobody there

Félix, Monique. *The further adventures of the little mouse trapped in a book*
  The story of a little mouse trapped in a book
Fenner, Carol. *Tigers in the cellar*
Fenton, Edward. *Fierce John*
Fleischman, Paul. *Rondo in C*
Fontaine, Jan. *The spaghetti tree*
Ford, Miela. *My day in the garden*
Fowler, Allan. *What do you see in a cloud?*
Francis, Frank. *The magic wallpaper*
Franklin, Jonathan. *Don't wake the baby*
Freeman, Don. *The paper party*
  Quiet! There's a canary in the library
Fujikawa, Gyo. *See what I can be!*
Furtado, Jo. *Sorry, Miss Folio!*
Gackenbach, Dick. *Harry and the terrible whatzit*
  Mag the magnificent
  Supposes
Gage, Wilson. *Mrs. Gaddy and the ghost*
Galbraith, Kathryn Osebold. *Spots are special*
Gay, Marie-Louise. *Rainy day magic*
Gillham, Bill. *What can you do?*
Givens, Terryl. *Dragon scales and willow leaves*
Glass, Andrew. *My brother tries to make me laugh*
Glassman, Peter. *The wizard next door*
Gliori, Debi. *When I'm big*
Godwin, Laura. *Little white dog*
Goennel, Heidi. *I pretend*
  If I were a penguin . . .
Goode, Diane. *The dinosaur's new clothes*
Gottlieb, Dale. *Seeing Eye Willie*
Greenblat, Rodney Alan. *Thunder Bunny*
Greenburg, Dan. *Great-Grandpa's in the litter box*
  Through the medicine cabinet
Greenfield, Eloise. *On my horse*
Greenstein, Elaine. *Emily and the crows*
Grejniec, Michael. *When I open my eyes*
Greve, Andreas. *Christopher's dream car*
Greydanus, Rose. *Let's pretend*
Grifalconi, Ann. *Electric Yancy*
Guy, Ginger Foglesong. *Black crow, black crow*
Gwynne, Fred. *A chocolate moose for dinner*
  A little pigeon toad
Haas, Irene. *A summertime song*
Haggerty, Mary Elizabeth. *A crack in the wall*
Hamanaka, Sheila. *I look like a girl*
Hamsa, Bobbie. *Your pet bear*
  Your pet beaver
  Your pet camel
  Your pet elephant
  Your pet giraffe
  Your pet kangaroo
  Your pet penguin
  Your pet sea lion
Handford, Martin. *Where's Waldo? The fantastic journey*
Hanlon, Emily. *What if a lion eats me and I fall into a hippopotamus' mud hole?*
Harrison, Troon. *The dream collector*
Hartmann, Wendy. *All the magic in the world*
Haseley, Dennis. *My father doesn't know about the woods and me*
  The thieves' market
Haus, Felice. *Beep! Beep! I'm a jeep*
Heckman, Philip. *Waking upside down*
Heller, Nicholas. *An adventure at sea*
  The front hall carpet
  A troll story
  Up the wall

Hennessy, B. G. (Barbara G.). *The dinosaur who lived in my backyard*
Henry, Lenny. *Charlie and the big chill*
  Charlie, queen of the desert
Hiatt, Fred. *If I were queen of the world*
Hill, Susan. *Beware, beware*
Hillert, Margaret. *What is it?*
Himler, Ronald. *The girl on the yellow giraffe*
Himmelman, John. *Lights out!*
Hindley, Judy. *Maybe it's a pirate*
  Uncle Harold and the green hat
Hines, Anna Grossnickle. *Bethany for real*
  Gramma's walk
Hoban, Russell. *The flight of Bembel Rudzuk*
  Goodnight
  The great gum drop robbery
  Monsters
  The rain door
Hoffmann, E. T. A. *The nutcracker*, ill. by Francesca Crespi
  The nutcracker, ill. by Carolyn Ewing
  The nutcracker, ill. by Rachel Isadora
  The nutcracker, ill. by Joanna Isles
  The nutcracker, ill. by Maurice Sendak
  The nutcracker, ill. by Lisbeth Zwerger
  The nutcracker ballet, ill. by Vladimir Vasil'evich Vagin
Holabird, Katharine. *Alexander and the magic boat*
Holl, Adelaide. *Most-of-the-time Maxie*
Holleyman, Sonia. *Mona the vampire*
Holman, Felice. *Victoria's castle*
Hood, Thomas. *Before I go to sleep*
Hooker, Ruth. *Matthew the cowboy*
Horwitz, Elinor Lander. *Sometimes it happens*
Howard, Jane R. *When I'm sleepy*
Hughes, Shirley. *Abel's moon*
  Up and up
Hurd, Edith Thacher. *The white horse*
Hutchins, H. J. (Hazel J.). *Nicholas at the library*
Ichikawa, Satomi. *Isabela's ribbons*
Imagine that! poems of never-was
Inkpen, Mick. *The blue balloon*
  If I had a pig
  If I had a sheep
  Lullabyhullaballoo!
  One bear at bedtime
Isadora, Rachel. *The pirates of Bedford Street*
Ivanov, Anatoly. *Ol' Jake's lucky day*
James, Simon. *Dear Mr. Blueberry*
Janosch. *Hey Presto! You're a bear!*
Jenkin-Pearce, Susie. *The enchanted garden*
Jeschke, Susan. *Tamar and the tiger*
Jewell, Nancy. *Try and catch me*
Johnson, B. J. *A hat like that*
Johnson, Crockett. *The blue ribbon puppies*
  Ellen's lion
  Harold and the purple crayon
  Harold at the North Pole
  Harold's ABC
  Harold's circus
  Harold's fairy tale
  Harold's trip to the sky
  A picture for Harold's room
Johnson, Elizabeth. *All in free but Janey*
Johnson, Jane. *Sybil and the blue rabbit*
Johnston, Deborah. *Mathew Michael's beastly day*
Jonas, Ann. *The trek*
Jonell, Lynne. *Mommy go away!*
Jones, Diana Wynne. *Yes, dear*

Moser, Erwin. *The crow in the snow and other bedtime stories*
Most, Bernard. *If the dinosaurs came back*
Murphy, Jill. *What next, baby bear!*
Narahashi, Keiko. *Is that Josie?*
Neitzel, Shirley. *I'm taking a trip on my train*
Nerlove, Miriam. *I meant to clean my room today*
    If all the world were paper
Nesbit, Edith. *Cockatoucan*
Ness, Evaline. *Sam, Bangs, and moonshine*
Newcome, Zita. *Rosie goes exploring*
Newton, Laura P. *William the vehicle king*
Nightingale, Sandy. *I'm a little monster*
Nixon, Joan Lowery. *When I am eight*
Nolan, Dennis. *The castle builder*
Norman, Philip Ross. *A mammoth imagination*
Numeroff, Laura Joffe. *Chimps don't wear glasses*
Nunes, Susan Miho. *Coyote dreams*
Nygren, Tord. *The red thread*
Oakley, Graham. *Graham Oakley's magical changes*
Olofsdotter, Marie. *Frej the fearless*
Olsen, Ib Spang. *The grown-up trap*
O'Malley, Kevin. *The box*
Oram, Hiawyn. *In the attic*
Ormerod, Jan. *Ben goes swimming*
    The saucepan game
Ottley, Matt. *What Faust saw*
Oxenbury, Helen. *729 curious creatures*
    729 merry mix-ups
    729 puzzle people
Pack, Robert. *How to catch a crocodile*
Palatini, Margie. *Zak's lunch*
Pallotta, Jerry. *The dory story*
Paterson, Diane. *The bathtub ocean*
Pavey, Peter. *I'm Taggarty Toad*
Peppé, Rodney. *The kettleship pirates*
Perkins, Charles. *Swinging on a rainbow*
Perlman, Janet. *The Emperor Penguin's new clothes*
Perry, Sarah. *If . . .*
Peters, Lisa Westberg. *Cold little duck, duck, duck*
Pfanner, Louise. *Louise builds a house*
Pinkwater, Daniel Manus. *I was a second grade werewolf*
    Tooth-gnasher superflash
    Wempires
Pirani, Felix. *Abigail at the beach*
Pittman, Helena Clare. *Once when I was scared*
Polacco, Patricia. *Appelemando's dreams*
    My ol' man
Pomerantz, Charlotte. *Timothy Tall Feather*
Ponti, Claude. *Adele's album*
Portlock, Rob. *Someone's trying to cut off my head*
Postma, Lidia. *The stolen mirror*
Powell, Polly. *Just dessert*
Prater, John. *Once upon a picnic*
    Once upon a time
Prelutsky, Jack. *The baby uggs are hatching*
    Ride a purple pelican
    The snopp on the sidewalk and other poems
Price, Mathew. *Have you seen my sister?*
Price-Thomas, Brian. *The magic ark*
Pringle, Laurence P. *Jesse builds a road*
The pudgy book of make-believe
Radlauer, Ruth Shaw. *Of course, you're a horse!*
Radley, Gail. *The night Stella hid the stars*
Raschka, Christopher. *Elizabeth imagined an iceberg*
Raskin, Ellen. *Franklin Stein*
    Spectacles
Ratnett, Michael. *Jenny's bear*

Reasoner, Charles. *Who pretends?*
Reavin, Sam. *Hurray for Captain Jane!*
Reid, Alastair. *Supposing*
Reiser, Lynn. *Any kind of dog*
    Best friends think alike
Renberg, Dalia Hardof. *Hello, clouds!*
Ressner, Phil. *Dudley Pippin*
Rex, Michael. *My fire engine*
Rice, Inez. *A long long time*
    The March wind
Riches, Judith. *Giraffes have more fun*
Riddle, Tohby. *Careful with that ball, Eugene!*
Rinder, Lenore. *A big mistake*
Ringgold, Faith. *Bonjour, Lonnie*
Ringi, Kjell (Arne Sorensen). *My father and I*
Roberts, Thom. *Pirates in the park*
Rodgers, Frank. *Who's afraid of the ghost train?*
Root, Phyllis. *Moon tiger*
Rosen, Michael J. (1954-). *With a dog like that, a kid like me . . .*
Rosen, Winifred. *Dragons hate to be discreet*
Rosenberg, Liz. *The carousel*
Rosner, Ruth. *Arabba gah zee, Marissa and Me!*
Rush, Ken. *Friday's journey*
Russ, Lavinia. *Alec's sand castle*
Russo, Marisabina. *The big brown box*
    Why do grownups have all the fun?
Ryder, Joanne. *Bears out there*
    Tyrannosaurus time
Sabraw, John. *I wouldn't be scared*
Salter, Heidi. *Taddy McFinley and the great grey grimly*
Samton, Sheila White. *Jenny's journey*
Sato, Satoru. *I wish I had a big, big tree*
Schoberle, Ceile. *Beyond the Milky Way*
Schotter, Roni. *Captain Bob sets sail*
    Dreamland
Schreier, Joshua. *Luigi's all-night parking lot*
Schrier, Jeffrey. *On the wings of eagles*
Scott, Ann Herbert. *Big Cowboy Western*
Seligson, Susan. *The amazing Amos and the greatest couch on earth*
    Amos ahoy
    Amos
Sendak, Maurice. *In the night kitchen*
    The sign on Rosie's door
    Where the wild things are
Seuss, Dr. *And to think that I saw it on Mulberry Street*
    McElligot's pool
    Oh say can you say?
    Oh, the thinks you can think!
Sharmat, Marjorie Weinman. *My mother never listens to me*
Shaw, Charles Green. *It looked like spilt milk*
Shecter, Ben. *Conrad's castle*
    If I had a ship
Shelby, Anne. *The someday house*
Sheldon, Dyan. *Unicorn dreams*
Sherman, Ivan. *I am a giant*
Shields, Carol Diggory. *I am really a princess*
Shimin, Symeon. *I wish there were two of me*
Shipton, Jonathan. *What if?*
Shulevitz, Uri. *One Monday morning*
Sicotte, Virginia. *A riot of quiet*
Siepmann, Jane. *The lion on Scott Street*
Simmonds, Posy. *Lulu and the flying babies*
Sis, Peter. *Dinosaur!*
    Madlenka
    Ship ahoy!

Skorpen, Liesel Moak. *If I had a lion*
Sleator, William. *That's silly*
Slobodkin, Louis. *Clear the track for Michael's magic train*
  Magic Michael
Smith, Jim. *Nimbus the explorer*
Smith, Maggie (Margaret C.). *My grandma's chair*
  There's a witch under the stairs
Stanley, Diane. *Birdsong lullaby*
Steig, William. *Pete's a pizza*
Steiner, Charlotte. *Look what Tracy found*
Stemp, Robin. *Guy and the flowering plum tree*
Stevens, Cat. *Teaser and the firecat*
Stevenson, James. *Worse than Willy!*
Stevenson, Jocelyn. *Red and the pumpkins*
Stevenson, Robert Louis. *Block city*
Stinson, Kathy. *The dressed up book*
  Those green things
Stoddard, Sandol. *Curl up small*
  The thinking book
Stone, Kazuko G. *Goodnight Twinklegator*
Stone, Phoebe. *Go away, Shelley Boo!*
Stuve-Bodeen, Stephanie. *Elizabeti's doll*
Sundgaard, Arnold. *Meet Jack Appleknocker*
Supraner, Robyn. *Would you rather be a tiger?*
Sutherland, Harry A. *Dad's car wash*
Swanson-Natsues, Lyn. *Days of adventure*
Sweeney, Jacqueline. *Katie and the night noises*
Tafuri, Nancy. *Junglewalk*
Tamar, Erika. *Donnatalee*
Taniuchi, Kota. *Trolley*
Teague, Mark. *The lost and found*
Testa, Fulvio. *The land where the ice cream grows*
Thayer, Jane. *Andy and the wild worm*
Theroux, Phyllis. *Serefina under the circumstances*
Thomas, Frances. *What if?*
Thomas, Ianthe. *Walk home tired, Billy Jenkins*
Thompson, Richard. *Effie's bath*
  Gurgle, bubble, splash
  Jenny's neighbours
  Jesse on the night train
  Sky full of babies
Tompert, Ann. *Little Fox goes to the end of the world*
Townson, Hazel. *Terrible Tuesday*
  What on earth . . . ?
Trottier, Maxine. *The tiny kite of Eddie Wing*
Turkle, Brinton. *The sky dog*
Turner, Ann Warren. *Let's be animals*
Tusa, Tricia. *Bunnies in my head*
  Camilla's new hairdo
Udry, Janice May. *Is Susan here?*, ill. by Peter Edwards
  Is Susan here?, ill. by Karen Gundersheimer
Ulmer, Wendy K. *A campfire for cowboy Billy*
Updike, David. *An autumn tale*
Utton, Peter. *Jennifer's room*
Valfre, Edward. *Backseat buckaroo*
  Vacationers from outer space
Van Allsburg, Chris. *Bad day at Riverbend*
  The garden of Abdul Gasazi
  Jumanji
  The mysteries of Harris Burdick
  The polar express
Van Caster, Nancy. *An alligator lives in Benjamin's house*
Velthuijs, Max. *Crocodile's masterpiece*
  The painter and the bird
Vigna, Judith. *Boot weather*
Viorst, Judith. *The good-bye book*

My mama says there aren't any zombies, ghosts, vampires, creatures, demons, monsters, fiends, goblins, or things
Vogel, Ilse-Margret. *The don't be scared book*
Vreeken, Elizabeth. *The boy who would not say his name*
Wahl, Jan. *I met a dinosaur*
  My cat Ginger
Wahl, Robert. *Pyxx*
Wallace, Karen. *Imagine you are a tiger*
Wallner, Alexandra. *Beatrix Potter*
Walsh, Jill Paton. *Connie came to play*
Walsh, Joanna. *What if?*
Warner, Sunny. *Madison finds a line*
Watson, Clyde. *Midnight moon*
Wayland, April Halprin. *To Rabbittown*
Wells, Rosemary. *Good night, Fred*
  A lion for Lewis
Westell, Kerry. *Amanda's book*
Whatley, Bruce. *Captain Pajamas*
Whitcher, Susan. *The key to the cupboard*
Whittington, Mary K. *Carmina, come dance!*
Whybrow, Ian. *Sammy and the dinosaurs*
Wick, Walter. *I spy fantasy*
Wiesner, David. *Hurricane*
Willard, Nancy. *The tale I told Sasha*
  A visit to William Blake's inn
Williams, Vera B. *Cherries and cherry pits*
Williams-Garcia, Rita. *Catching the wild waiyuuzee*
Winthrop, Elizabeth. *Bunk beds*
  A very noisy girl
Wood, Audrey. *The flying dragon room*
Woodruff, Elvira. *Tubtime*
Woolf, Virginia. *Nurse Lugton's curtain*
Yardley, Joanna. *The red ball*
Yolen, Jane. *King Long Shanks*
Yorinks, Arthur. *Harry and Lulu*
  Hey, Al
  Louis the fish
Young, Miriam Burt. *Jellybeans for breakfast*
Young, Ruth. *Golden Bear*
  A trip to Mars
Zarin, Cynthia. *What do you see when you shut your eyes?*
Ziefert, Harriet. *Lewis the fire fighter*
Zimelman, Nathan. *Once when I was five*
Zolotow, Charlotte (Shapiro). *The seashore book*
  When I have a son

Imagination – imaginary friends

Alexander, Martha G. *And my mean old mother will be sorry, Blackboard Bear*
  Blackboard Bear
  I sure am glad to see you, Blackboard Bear
  I'll protect you from the jungle beasts
  We're in big trouble, Blackboard Bear
  You're a genius, Blackboard Bear
Andrews, F. Emerson (Frank Emerson). *Nobody comes to dinner*
Anglund, Joan Walsh. *Cowboy and his friend*
  The cowboy's Christmas
Berger, Barbara Helen. *When the sun rose*
Bogart, Jo Ellen. *Daniel's dog*
Bornstein, Ruth Lercher. *The seedling child*
Bram, Elizabeth. *There is someone standing on my head*
Brewster, Patience. *Nobody*
Brighton, Catherine. *My hands, my world*

Burningham, John. *Aldo*
Cottringer, Anne. *Ella and the naughty lion*
Cummings, Pat. *Jimmy Lee did it*
Cuneo, Mary Louise. *What can a giant do?*
Dauer, Rosamond. *My friend, Jasper Jones*
Dillon, Barbara. *The beast in the bed*
Dinan, Carolyn. *The lunch box monster*
Geringer, Laura. *Look out, look out, it's coming!*
Greenfield, Eloise. *Me and Nessie*
Guthrie, Donna. *Mrs. Gigglebelly is coming for tea*
Hazen, Barbara Shook. *The gorilla did it!*
   Gorilla wants to be the baby
Henkes, Kevin. *Jessica*
Hiller, Catherine. *Argentaybee and the boonie*
Hoff, Syd. *The horse in Harry's room*
Howe, James. *There's a dragon in my sleeping bag*
James, Simon. *Leon and Bob*
Jeschke, Susan. *Angela and Bear*
   The devil did it
Joosse, Barbara M. *The thinking place*
Khalsa, Dayal Kaur. *The snow cat*
Kherdian, David. *By myself*
Kornblatt, Marc. *Eli and the Dimplemeyers*
Krahn, Fernando. *The creepy thing*
Krensky, Stephen. *The lion upstairs*
Langner, Nola. *By the light of the silvery moon*
Marx, Patricia (Patricia A.). *Meet my staff*
Moers, Hermann. *Katie and the big, brave bear*
Morris, Terry Nell. *Good night, dear monster!*
Noble, June. *Two homes for Lynn*
Oram, Hiawyn. *Ned and the Joybaloo*
Patz, Nancy. *No thumpin' no bumpin' no rumpus tonight!*
Pinkwater, Daniel Manus. *Pickle creature*
Ross, Tony. *Hugo and Oddsock*
Rovetch, Lissa. *Trigwater did it*
St. George, Judith. *The Halloween pumpkin smasher*
Steiner, Charlotte. *Lulu*
Strauss, Gwen. *The night shimmy*
Thaler, Mike. *My puppy*
Thayer, Jane. *Andy and his fine friends*
Vries, Anke de. *My elephant can do almost anything*
Watts, Marjorie-Ann. *Zebra goes to school*
Zemke, Deborah. *The shadow of Matilda Hunt*
Zolotow, Charlotte (Shapiro). *Three funny friends*

Imitation *see* Behavior – imitation

Immigrants

Carling, Amelia Lau. *Mama and Papa have a store*
Cohen, Miriam. *Mimmy and Sophie*
Figueredo, D. H. *When this world was new*
Garay, Luis. *The long road*
Hearne, Betsy Gould. *Seven brave women*
Joosse, Barbara M. *The morning chair*
Levinson, Riki. *Soon, Annala*
McCully, Emily Arnold. *Mirette and Bellini cross Niagara Falls*
McGill, Alice. *Molly Bannaky*
Miller, Elizabeth I. *Just like home = Como en mi tierra*
Nivola, Claire A. *Elisabeth*
Oberman, Sheldon. *The always prayer shawl*
Park, Frances. *My freedom trip*
Polacco, Patricia. *The keeping quilt*
Pomeranc, Marion Hess. *The American Wei*
Pryor, Bonnie. *The dream jar*
Reynolds, Marilynn. *The new land*
Rosenberg, Liz. *The silence in the mountains*

Sandman, Rochel. *Perfect porridge*
Tarbescu, Edith. *Annushka's voyage*
Trottier, Maxine. *The walking stick*
Yezerski, Thomas. *Together in Pinecone Patch*
Ziefert, Harriet. *When I first came to this land*

Immigration

Woodruff, Elvira. *The memory coat*

Imps *see* Mythical creatures – imps

In and out *see* Concepts – in and out

Incas *see* Indians of South America – Incas

Incentive *see* Character traits – ambition

Independence Day *see* Holidays – Fourth of July

India *see* Foreign lands – India

Indians, American *see* Indians of Central America; Indians of North America; Indians of South America

Indians of Central America – Black Carib

London, Jonathan. *The village basket weaver*

Indians of Central America – Maya

Dupré, Judith. *The mouse bride*
Ehlert, Lois. *Cuckoo: a Mexican folktale = Cucú: un cuento folklórico mexicano*
Grifalconi, Ann. *The bravest flute*
Lattimore, Deborah Nourse. *Why there is no arguing in heaven*
Mora, Pat. *The night the moon fell*
Rockwell, Anne F. *The boy who wouldn't obey*
Volkmer, Jane Anne. *Song of Chirimia*
Wahl, Jan. *Once when the world was green*
Wisniewski, David. *Rain player*

Indians of North America

Aliki. *Corn is maize*
Anderson, C. W. (Clarence Williams). *Linda and the Indians*
Anderson, Leone Castell. *Surprise at Muddy Creek*
Baker, Betty. *And me, coyote!*
Baker, Laura Nelson. *O children of the wind and pines*
Baker, Olaf. *Where the buffaloes begin*
Bandes, Hanna. *Sleepy river*
Baylor, Byrd. *A God on every mountain top*
   Hawk, I'm your brother
   Moon song
   When clay sings
Beatty, Hetty Burlingame. *Little Owl Indian*
Behrens, June. *Powwow*
Belting, Natalia Maree. *Verity Mullens and the Indian*
Benjamin, Anne. *Young Pocahontas*
Blake, Robert J. *Yudonsi*
Boegehold, Betty. *A horse called Starfire*

Bornstein, Ruth Lercher. *Indian bunny*
Brock, Emma Lillian. *One little Indian boy*
Brownridge, William Roy. *The moccasin goalie*
Bruchac, Joseph. *The circle of thanks*
   Many nations
   Thirteen moons on turtle's back
Ehrlich, Amy. *Zeek Silver Moon*
Flöethe, Louise Lee. *The Indian and his pueblo*
Friskey, Margaret (Margaret Richards). *Indian Two*
   Feet and his eagle feather
   Indian Two Feet and his horse
   Indian Two Feet and the wolf cubs
   Indian Two Feet rides alone
Goble, Paul. *Buffalo woman*
   The girl who loved wild horses
Gorsline, Marie. *North American Indians*
Grossman, Virginia. *Ten little rabbits*
Hader, Berta Hoerner. *The mighty hunter*
Harper, Piers. *How the world was saved and other*
   Native American tales
Hausman, Gerald. *How Chipmunk got tiny feet*
   Turtle Island ABC
Hayes, Joe. *A spoon for every bite*
Jacobs, Shannon K. *The boy who loved morning*
Jagendorf, Moritz A. *Kwi-na the eagle*
Jones, Hettie. *The trees stand shining*
Kalman, Bobbie. *Celebrating the powwow*
Krensky, Stephen. *Children of the wind and water*
Kroll, Virginia L. *The seasons and someone*
Locker, Thomas. *The land of gray wolf*
London, Jonathan. *Fireflies, fireflies, light my way*
Luenn, Nancy. *Nessa's fish*
McDermott, Gerald. *Raven*
McLerran, Alice. *The ghost dance*
Mariana. *Doki, the lonely papoose*
Martin, Bill (William Ivan). *Brave little Indian*
   Knots on a counting rope
Midge, Tiffany. *Buffalo*
Moon, Grace Purdie. *One little Indian*
Native Americans
Ortiz, Simon. *The people shall continue*
Parish, Peggy. *Good hunting, Blue Sky*
   Good hunting, Little Indian
   Granny and the Indians
   Granny, the baby and the big gray thing
   Little Indian
   Snapping turtle's all wrong day
Parnall, Peter. *The great fish*
Pomerantz, Charlotte. *Timothy Tall Feather*
Prusski, Jeffrey. *Bring back the deer*
Robbins, Ruth. *How the first rainbow was made*
Rose, Anne K. *Spider in the sky*
Siberell, Anne. *Whale in the sky*
Smith, Cynthia Leitich. *Jingle dancer*
Speare, Jean. *A candle for Christmas*
Stan-Padilla, Viento. *Dream Feather*
Strete, Craig Kee. *How the Indians bought the farm*
Taylor, Harriet Peck. *Coyote and the laughing butter-*
   flies
Toye, William. *The loon's necklace*
Troughton, Joanna. *How rabbit stole the fire*
Van Camp, Richard. *What's the most beautiful thing*
   you know about horses?
Wheeler, M. J. (Mary Jane). *First came the Indians*
White Deer of Autumn. *The great change*
Wondriska, William. *The stop*
Wood, Douglas. *Northwoods cradle song*
Zeman, Ludmila. *The first red maple leaf*

Indians of North America – Abnaki

Bruchac, Joseph. *Gluskabe and the four wishes*
Crompton, Anne Eliot. *The winter wife*

Indians of North America – Aleuts

Villoldo, Alberto. *Skeleton woman*

Indians of North America – Algonquian

Gregg, Andy. *Great Rabbit and the long-tailed Wildcat*
Martin, Rafe. *The rough-face girl*
Ross, Gayle. *The legend of the Windigo*
Toye, William. *Fire stealer*

Indians of North America – Anasazi

James, Betsy. *The mud family*

Indians of North America – Apache

Baker, Betty. *Three fools and a horse*
Lacapa, Michael. *Antelope Woman*

Indians of North America – Athabascan

Griese, Arnold A. *Anna's Athabaskan summer*

Indians of North America – Aztec

Bierhorst, John. *Doctor Coyote*
Kimmel, Eric A. *The two mountains*
McDermott, Gerald. *Musicians of the sun*

Indians of North America – Blackfoot

Goble, Paul. *The lost children*
Roop, Peter. *The buffalo jump*
San Souci, Robert D. *The legend of Scarface*
Yolen, Jane. *Sky dogs*

Indians of North America – Bungee

Bernstein, Margery. *How the sun made a promise and*
   kept it

Indians of North America – Carrier

Blades, Ann. *A boy of Taché*

Indians of North America – Cherokee

Bruchac, Joseph. *The first strawberries*
Haley, Gail E. *Two bad boys*
Pennington, Daniel. *Itse selu*
Ross, Gayle. *How Turtle's back was cracked*
Roth, Susan L. *Kanahena*
   The story of light
Sneve, Virginia Driving Hawk. *The Cherokees*
Stroud, Virginia A. *A walk to the Great Mystery*

Indians of North America – Cheyenne (Sioux)

Bunting, Eve (Anne Evelyn). *Cheyenne again*
Goble, Paul. *Death of the iron horse*
   The great race of the birds and animals
   Her seven brothers
Leech, Jay. *Bright Fawn and me*

Indians of North America – Kato

Rosen, Michael J. (1954-). *The dog who walked with God*

Indians of North America – Kutenai

Tanaka, Beatrice. *The chase*
Troughton, Joanna. *Who will be the sun?*

Indians of North America – Lakota (Sioux)

Bateson-Hill, Margaret. *Shota and the star quilt*
Bernhard, Emery. *Spotted Eagle and Black Crow*
Goble, Paul. *Adopted by the eagles*
    The legend of the White Buffalo Woman
    The return of the buffaloes

Indians of North America – Lenape

Van Laan, Nancy. *Rainbow crow*

Indians of North America – Maidu

Bernstein, Margery. *Earth namer*

Indians of North America – Micmac

Toye, William. *How summer came to Canada*

Indians of North America – Missisauga

Crook, Connie Brummel. *Maple moon*

Indians of North America – Miwok

French, Fiona. *Lord of the animals*
San Souci, Robert D. *Two bear cubs*

Indians of North America – Modoc

Simms, Laura. *The bone man*
    Moon and Otter and Frog

Indians of North America – Mohawk

Gates, Frieda. *Owl eyes*
Swamp, Jake. *Giving thanks*

Indians of North America – Muskogee

Bruchac, Joseph. *The great ball game*

Indians of North America – Nanticoke

Mitchell, Barbara. *Red Bird*

Indians of North America – Narragansett

Koller, Jackie French. *Nickommoh!*

Indians of North America – Navajo

Begaye, Lisa Shook. *Building a bridge*
Blood, Charles L. *The goat in the rug*
Browne, Vee. *Monster birds*
Chanin, Michael. *Chief's blanket*
Duncan, Lois. *The magic of Spider Woman*
Garaway, Margaret Kahn. *Ashkii and his grandfather*
Hausman, Gerald. *Coyote walks on two legs*

Eagle boy
Jackson, Ellen B. *The precious gift*
Keams, Geri. *Snail girl brings water*
Nez, Redwing T. *Forbidden talent*
Oughton, Jerrie. *How the stars fell into the sky*
    The magic weaver of rugs
Perrine, Mary. *Salt boy*
Schick, Eleanor. *My Navajo sister*
Tapahonso, Luci. *Navajo ABC*
Whitethorne, Baje. *Sunpainters*

Indians of North America – Nez Perce

Krupinski, Loretta. *Best friends*
Sneve, Virginia Driving Hawk. *The Nez Perce*

Indians of North America – Nishnawbe

Yerxa, Leo. *Last leaf first snowflake to fall*

Indians of North America – Nisqually

Luenn, Nancy. *Miser on the mountain*

Indians of North America – Nobscusset

Metaxas, Eric. *Princess Scargo and the birthday pumpkin*

Indians of North America – Ojibwa

Bernstein, Margery. *How the sun made a promise and kept it*
Esbensen, Barbara Juster. *Ladder to the sky*
    The star maiden
Larry, Charles. *Peboan and Seegwun*
Lunge-Larsen, Lise. *The legend of the lady slipper*
Neitzel, Shirley. *From the land of the white birch*
Osofsky, Audrey. *Dreamcatcher*
Rodanas, Kristina. *Follow the stars*
San Souci, Robert D. *Sootface*
Spooner, Michael. *Old Meshikee and the little crabs*
Van Laan, Nancy. *Shingebiss*
Waboose, Jan Bourdeau. *Firedancers*
    Morning on the lake

Indians of North America – Paiute

Hodges, Margaret. *The fire bringer*

Indians of North America – Papago

Baylor, Byrd. *The desert is theirs*
Clark, Ann Nolan. *The little Indian basket maker*

Indians of North America – Pawnee

Cohen, Caron Lee. *The mud pony*
Moroney, Lynn. *The boy who loved bears*

Indians of North America – Penobscot

Day, Michael E. *Berry Ripe Moon*

Indians of North America – Pima

Moreillon, Judi. *Sing down the rain*

Indians of North America – Potawatomi

De Montaño, Martha Kreipe. *Coyote in love with a star*

Indians of North America – Powhaton

Accorsi, William. *My name is Pocahontas*
Aulaire, Ingri Mortenson d'. *Pocahontas*

Indians of North America – Pueblo

Baker, Betty. *Rat is dead and ant is sad*
Carey, Valerie Scho. *Quail song*
Clark, Ann Nolan. *The little Indian pottery maker*
Dewey, Jennifer Owings. *Stories on stone*
Hausman, Gerald. *The story of Blue Elk*
Lyon, George Ella. *Dreamplace*
McDermott, Gerald. *Arrow to the sun*
Rosen, Michael (1946-). *Crow and Hawk*
Strete, Craig Kee. *Big thunder magic*

Indians of North America – Seminole

Johnson, Dolores. *Seminole diary*
Medearis, Angela Shelf. *Dancing with the Indians*

Indians of North America – Seneca

Ehlert, Lois. *Mole's hill*
Esbensen, Barbara Juster. *The great buffalo race*
Savageau, Cheryl. *Muskrat will be swimming*

Indians of North America – Shawnee

Bierhorst, John. *The ring in the prairie*
Watkins, Sherrin. *White Bead Ceremony*

Indians of North America – Shoshone

Gleiter, Jan. *Sacagawea*
Stevens, Janet. *Old bag of bones*

Indians of North America – Siksika

Goble, Paul. *The lost children*
  Star boy
San Souci, Robert D. *The legend of Scarface*
Yolen, Jane. *Sky dogs*

Indians of North America – Sioux

Sheldon, Dyan. *Under the moon*

Indians of North America – Southwest

McDermott, Gerald. *Coyote*
Strete, Craig Kee. *The lost boy and the monster*

Indians of North America – Taino

Crespo, George. *How the sea began*
Jaffe, Nina. *The golden flower*

Indians of North America – Tarascan

Czernecki, Stefan. *The hummingbird's gift*

Indians of North America – Tewa

Clark, Ann Nolan. *In my mother's house*

Indians of North America – Tlingit

Dixon, Ann. *How raven brought light to people*
Lewis, Paul Owen. *Frog girl*
Sleator, William. *The angry moon*

Indians of North America – Tohono O'Odham

Cowley, Joy. *Big moon tortilla*

Indians of North America – Tsimshian

Toye, William. *The mountain goats of Temlaham*

Indians of North America – Twa

Mott, Evelyn Clarke. *Dancing rainbows*

Indians of North America – Ute

Hobbs, Will. *Beardream*
Raczek, Linda Theresa. *The night the grandfathers danced*

Indians of North America – Wampanoag

Fritz, Jean. *The good giants and the bad Pukwudgies*
Hennessy, B. G. (Barbara G.). *One little, two little, three little pilgrims*

Indians of North America – Windigos

Ross, Gayle. *The legend of the Windigo*

Indians of North America – Yana

Bernstein, Margery. *Coyote goes hunting for fire*

Indians of North America – Yupik

McDonald, Megan. *Tundra mouse*

Indians of North America – Zapotec

Grossman, Patricia. *Saturday market*
Johnston, Tony. *The tale of Rabbit and Coyote*
Van Laan, Nancy. *La boda*

Indians of North America – Zuni

Hulpach, Vladimir. *Ahaiyute and Cloud Eater*
Pollock, Penny. *The turkey girl*
Rodanas, Kristina. *The dragonfly's tale*

Indians of South America

Alexander, Ellen. *Chaska and the golden doll*
Flora. *Feathers like a rainbow*
Metaxas, Eric. *The monkey people*
Reynolds, Jan. *Amazon*
Van Laan, Nancy. *The legend of El Dorado*

Indians of South America – Incas

Jendresen, Erik. *The first story ever told*

Kurtz, Jane. *Miro in the kingdom of the sun*

Indians of South America – Quechua

Van Laan, Nancy. *The magic bean tree*

Indians of South America – Yanomamo

Thomson, Ruth. *The Rainforest Indians*

Indifference *see* Behavior – indifference

Individuality *see* Character traits – individuality

Indonesia *see* Foreign lands – Indonesia

Indonesian Archipelago *see* Foreign lands – South Sea Islands

Insects

Adelson, Leone. *Please pass the grass*
Aldis, Dorothy (Keeley). *Quick as a wink*
Asch, Frank. *Insects from outer space*
Barrett, Judi. *Snake is totally tail*
Belpré, Pura. *Pérez and Martina*
Bernstein, Joanne E. *Creepy crawly critter riddles*
Boegehold, Betty. *Bear underground*
Bond, Felicia. *Tumble bumble*
Brouillette, Jeanne S. *Moths*
Buck, Nola. *Creepy crawly critters and other Halloween tongue twisters*
Bugs
Carter, David A. *How many bugs in a box?*
Charles, Donald. *Ugly bug*
Colby, C. B. (Carroll Burleigh). *Who lives there?*
Cole, Joanna. *Find the hidden insect*
Conklin, Gladys. *I caught a lizard*
    We like bugs
    When insects are babies
Cristini, Ermanno. *In the pond*
Darling, Kathy (Mary Kathleen). *Bug circus*
Dubowski, Cathy East. *Snug Bug*
    Snug Bug's play day
Dussling, Jennifer. *Bugs! bugs! bugs!*
Edwards, Pamela Duncan. *The wacky wedding*
Egielski, Richard. *Buz*
    Jazper
Facklam, Margery. *The big bug book*
Farber, Norma. *Never say ugh to a bug*
Fisher, Aileen Lucia. *When it comes to bugs*
Florian, Douglas. *Insectlopedia*
Gackenbach, Dick. *Little bug*
Gaffney, Michael. *Secret forests*
George, Jean Craighead. *All upon a stone*
Geraghty, Paul. *Over the steamy swamp*
Goudey, Alice E. *Red legs*
Greenberg, David (David T.). *Bugs!*
Griffen, Elizabeth. *A dog's book of bugs*
Heller, Ruth. *How to hide a butterfly*
Hepworth, Catherine. *Bug off!*
Hines, Anna Grossnickle. *Miss Emma's wild garden*
Hopkins, Lee Bennett. *Flit, flutter, fly!*
Ipcar, Dahlov. *Bug city*
Jaynes, Ruth M. *That's what it is!*
Jenkins, Martin. *Wings, stings, and wriggly things*
Johnston, Tony. *Sparky and Eddie, trouble with bugs*

Joyce, William. *The Leaf Men and the brave good bugs*
Katz, Bobbi. *The creepy crawly book*
Kaufmann, John. *Flying giants of long ago*
Kirk, David. *Little Miss Spider at Sunny Patch School*
    Miss Spider's ABC
    Miss Spider's new car
Kraus, Robert. *How Spider saved Halloween*
    How Spider saved Valentine's Day
Krudwig, Vickie Leigh. *Cucumber soup*
Lavies, Bianca. *Tree trunk traffic*
Lewis, J. Patrick. *The little buggers*
Lewison, Wendy Cheyette. *So many boots*
Lifton, Betty Jean. *Tell me a real adoption story*
Lionni, Leo. *Inch by inch*
Llewellyn, Claire. *Some bugs glow in the dark*
Lobel, Arnold. *Grasshopper on the road*
McDonald, Megan. *Bedbugs*
    Insects are my life
McKissack, Patricia C. *Big bug book of counting*
    Big bug book of opposites
    Big bug book of places to go
    Big bug book of the alphabet
McPhail, David M. *A bug, a bear, and a boy*
    A bug, a bear, and a boy go to school
Martin, Bill (William Ivan). *The little squeegy bug*
Maxner, Joyce. *Lady Bugatti*
Milne, A. A. (Alan Alexander). *Pooh and some bees*
Miranda, Anne. *Does a mouse have a house?*
Mitchell, Adrian. *Twice my size*
Mogensen, Jan. *The Land of the Big*
Morgan-Vanroyen, Mary. *Benjamin's bugs*
Murphy, Stuart J. *The best bug parade*
    Bug dance
Nathan, Cheryl. *Bugs and beasties ABC*
O'Neil, Amanda. *I wonder why spiders spin webs*
Oppenheim, Joanne. *Have you seen bugs?*
Parker, Nancy Winslow. *Bugs*
Paulsen, Gary. *Canoe days*
Penner, Lucille Recht. *Monster bugs*
Petie, Haris. *Billions of bugs*
Peyo. *The Smurfs and their woodland friends*
Pinczes, Elinor J. *A remainder of one*
Pratt, Kristin Joy. *A fly in the sky*
Rockwell, Anne F. *Bumblebee, bumblebee, do you know me?*
Roop, Peter. *Going buggy!*
Rounds, Glen. *The boll weevil*
Ryder, Joanne. *My father's hands*
Sabuda, Robert James. *The movable Mother Goose*
Samton, Sheila White. *Frogs in clogs*
Sardegna, Jill. *The roly-poly spider*
Selsam, Millicent E. *Where do they go? Insects in winter*
Seymour, Peter S. *Insects*
Soya, Kiyoshi. *A house of leaves*
Stone, Rosetta. *Because a little bug went ka-choo!*
Sturges, Philemon. *What's that sound, Woolly Bear?*
Tison, Annette. *Animal hide-and-seek*
Van Woerkom, Dorothy. *Hidden messages*
Warner, Sunny. *Madison finds a line*

Insects – ants

Æsop. *The ant and the dove*
Allinson, Beverley. *Effie*
Andreae, Giles. *Rumble in the jungle*
Byars, Betsy Cromer. *My brother, Ant*
Calder, S. J. *If you were an ant*
Cameron, Polly. *"I can't," said the ant*

Ciardi, John. *John J. Plenty and Fiddler Dan*
Clay, Pat. *Ants*
Climo, Shirley. *The little red ant and the great big crumb*
Dorros, Arthur. *Ant cities*
Edwards, Pamela Duncan. *The wacky wedding*
Fancher, Lou. *The quest for the One Big Thing*
Fichter, George S. *Bees, wasps, and ants*
Freschet, Berniece. *The ants go marching*
Hawcock, David. *Ant*
Hepworth, Catherine. *ANTics! an alphabetical anthology*
Hoose, Philip M. *Hey little ant*
Lass, Bonnie. *Who took the cookies from the cookie jar?*
Losi, Carol A. *The 512 ants on Sullivan Street*
McDonald, Megan. *Ant and Honey Bee*
Nickle, John. *The ant bully*
Peet, Bill (William Bartlett). *The ant and the elephant*
Philpot, Lorna. *Amazing Anthony Ant*
Pluckrose, Henry Arthur. *Ants*
Trimble, Patti. *Lost!*
　What day is it?
Van Allsburg, Chris. *Two bad ants*
Wolkstein, Diane. *Step by step*
Young, Ed (Edward). *Night visitors*

Insects – bees

Ahlberg, Allan. *Mr. Buzz the beeman*
Baran, Tancy. *Bees*
Barton, Byron. *Buzz, buzz, buzz*
Bees
Brown, Margaret Wise. *Bumble bee*
　The whispering rabbit
Cole, Joanna. *The magic school bus inside a beehive*
Crewe, Sabrina. *The bee*
Ernst, Lisa Campbell. *A colorful adventure of the bee who left home one Monday morning and what he found along the way*
Fichter, George S. *Bees, wasps, and ants*
Fowler, Richard. *Honeybee's busy day*
Galdone, Joanna. *Honeybee's party*
Gibbons, Faye. *Mountain wedding*
Hawcock, David. *Bee*
Hawes, Judy. *Watch honeybees with me*
High, Linda Oatman. *Beekeepers*
Hogan, Paula Z. *The honeybee*
Keller, Beverly. *Fiona's bee*
Kennedy, Kim. *Mr. Bumble*
Lobel, Arnold. *The rose in my garden*
Long, Jan Freeman. *The bee and the dream*
McDonald, Megan. *Ant and Honey Bee*
Pizer, Abigail. *Nosey Gilbert*
Pluckrose, Henry Arthur. *Bees and wasps*
Polacco, Patricia. *In Enzo's splendid gardens*
Renberg, Dalia Hardof. *King Solomon and the bee*
Rockwell, Anne F. *Big bad goat*
　Bumblebee, bumblebee, do you know me?
Sayre, April Pulley. *If you should hear a honey guide*
Thompson, Mary. *Gran's bees*
Wahl, Jan. *Follow me cried Bee*
Wallace, John. *Building a house with Mr. Bumble*
Wong, Janet S. *Buzz*

Insects – beetles

Carle, Eric. *The very clumsy click beetle*
Clay, Pat. *Beetles*
Conklin, Gladys. *I like beetles*
Hawcock, David. *Beetle*
Hoban, Russell. *Jim Frog*
Inkpen, Mick. *Billy's beetle*
Mudd-Ruth, Maria. *The beetle*

Insects – butterflies, caterpillars

Aardema, Verna. *Who's in Rabbit's house?*
Abisch, Roz. *Let's find out about butterflies*
Arnosky, Jim. *Crinkleroot's guide to knowing butterflies and moths*
Brown, Ruth. *If at first you do not see*
Bunting, Eve (Anne Evelyn). *Butterfly house*
Carle, Eric. *The very hungry caterpillar*
Carrick, Malcolm. *I can squash elephants!*
The caterpillar who turned into a butterfly
Collicott, Sharleen. *Toestomper and the caterpillars*
Conklin, Gladys. *I like butterflies*
　I like caterpillars
Crozat, François. *I am a little caterpillar*
Cutts, David. *Look . . . a butterfly*
Darby, Gene. *What is a butterfly?*
Delaney, A. *The butterfly*
Delaney, Ned. *One dragon to another*
DeLuise, Dom. *Charlie the caterpillar*
Denslow, Sharon Phillips. *Woollybear good-bye*
Ernst, Lisa Campbell. *Bubba and Trixie*
Faulkner, Keith. *Butterfly*
Fitzsimons, Cecilia. *My first butterflies*
Fleming, Denise. *In the tall, tall grass*
French, Vivian. *Caterpillar, caterpillar*
Garelick, May. *Where does the butterfly go when it rains?*, ill. by Leonard Weisgard
　Where does the butterfly go when it rains?, ill. by Nicholas Wilton
Gibbons, Gail. *Monarch butterfly*
Glaser, Linda. *Wonderful worms*
Gomi, Taro. *Hi, butterfly!*
Grifalconi, Ann. *Darkness and the butterfly*
Hariton, Anca. *Butterfly story*
Heiligman, Deborah. *From caterpillar to butterfly*
Heller, Ruth. *How to hide a butterfly*
Hines, Anna Grossnickle. *Remember the butterflies*
Hogan, Paula Z. *The butterfly*
Inkpen, Mick. *Butterfly*
Johnston, Tony. *Isabel's house of butterflies*
Kent, Jack. *The caterpillar and the polliwog*
Kroll, Virginia L. *Butterfly boy*
Legg, Gerald. *From caterpillar to butterfly*
Lewis, Naomi. *The butterfly collector*
Ling, Mary. *Butterfly*
McBratney, Sam. *The caterpillow fight*
McClung, Robert. *Sphinx*
Maple, Marilyn J. *On the wings of a butterfly*
Marzollo, Jean. *I'm a caterpillar*
May, Kara. *Creepy crawly caterpillar*
Merrill, Jean. *The girl who loved caterpillars*
Murphy, Mary. *Caterpillar's wish*
O'Callahan, Jay. *Herman and Marguerite*
O'Hagan, Caroline. *It's easy to have a caterpillar visit you*
Pallandt, Nicholas van . *The butterfly night of Old Brown Bear*
Piers, Helen. *Grasshopper and butterfly*
Pluckrose, Henry Arthur. *Butterflies and moths*
Polacco, Patricia. *The butterfly*
Roscoe, William. *The butterfly's ball and the grasshopper's feast*

Hooks, William H. *The monster from the sea*
Hoopes, Lyn Littlefield. *Mommy, daddy, me*
Horse, Harry. *A friend for Little Bear*
Ichikawa, Satomi. *Isabela's ribbons*
Ikeda, Daisaku. *Over the deep blue sea*
Isadora, Rachel. *Caribbean dream*
Jauck, Andrea. *Assateague*
Jekyll, Walter. *I have a news*
Johnston, Tony. *Pages of music*
Joseph, Lynn. *Coconut kind of day*
　Jasmine's parlour day
Keller, Holly. *Island baby*
Kellogg, Steven (Stephen). *The island of the skog*
Kessler, Leonard P. *The pirates' adventure on Spooky Island*
King, Deborah. *Sirius and Saba*
Kinsey-Warnock, Natalie. *The wild horses of Sweetbriar*
Krahn, Fernando. *The great ape*
Lasky, Kathryn. *My island grandma*, ill. by Emily Arnold McCully
　My island grandma, ill. by Amy Schwartz
Lent, Blair. *Bayberry Bluff*
Lessac, Frané. *My little island*
Lewin, Betsy. *Booby hatch*
Lewin, Ted. *Nilo and the tortoise*
Lewis, J. Patrick. *The la-di-da hare*
McCloskey, Robert. *Time of wonder*
McClure, Gillian. *Selkie*
McGovern, Ann. *Nicholas Bentley Stoningpot III*
McPhail, David M. *Great cat*
Martin, Charles E. *For rent*
　Island rescue
　Island winter
Millhouse, Nicholas. *Blue-footed booby*
Mills, Patricia. *On an island in the bay*
Monfried, Lucia. *The Daddies Boat*
Mordvinoff, Nicolas. *Coral Island*
Morley, Carol. *A spider and a pig*
Olson, Arielle North. *The lighthouse keeper's daughter*
Poulin, Stéphane. *Travels for two*
Raglus, Jeff. *Schnorky the wave puncher*
Rahaman, Vashanti. *O Christmas tree*
Rockwell, Anne F. *Ferryboat ride!*
　On our vacation
Rohmann, Eric. *The cinder-eyed cats*
Round, Graham. *Hangdog*
Rumford, James. *The Island-below-the-star*
Simon, Carly. *Midnight farm*
Smith, Roger. *The empty island*
Steig, William. *Abel's Island*
　Rotten island
Stiles, Martha Bennett. *Island magic*
Stock, Catherine. *An island summer*
Thaxter, Celia. *Celia's island journal*
Wallis, Lisa. *Island child*
Wallner, Alexandra. *Sergio and the hurricane*
Wilson, Barbara Ker. *The turtle and the island*

Israel *see* Foreign lands – Israel

Italian Americans *see* Ethnic groups in the U.S. – Italian Americans

Italy *see* Foreign lands – Italy

Jackals *see* Animals – jackals

Jackets *see* Clothing – coats

Jaguars *see* Animals – jaguars

Jails *see* Prisons

Jamaica *see* Foreign lands – Jamaica

Janitors *see* Careers – custodians, janitors

Japan *see* Foreign lands – Japan

Japanese Americans *see* Ethnic groups in the U.S. – Asian Americans; Ethnic groups in the U.S. – Japanese Americans

Jealousy *see* Emotions – envy, jealousy

Jesters *see* Clowns, jesters

Jewelry

Langton, Jane. *The queen's necklace*

Jewish culture

Adler, David A. *The children of Chelm*
　The children's book of Jewish holidays
　Hiding from the Nazis
　The house on the roof
　The number on my grandfather's arm
　A picture book of Hanukkah
　A picture book of Israel
　A picture book of Jewish holidays
　A picture book of Passover
Aleichem, Sholem. *Hanukah money*
Aronin, Ben. *The secret of the Sabbath fish*
Auerbach, Julie Jaslow. *Everything's changing - It's pesach!*
Bayar, Steven. *Rachel and Mischa*
Behrens, June. *Hanukkah*
　Passover
Bernstein, Robin. *Terrible, terrible!*
Bogot, Howard. *I'm growing*
Bresnick-Perry, Roslyn. *Leaving for America*
Brodmann, Aliana. *Such a noise!*
Buckley, Ray. *God's love is like . . .*
Burnstein, Chaya M. *The Jewish kids' Hebrew-English wordbook*
Burstein, Chaya M. *Joseph and Anna's time capsule*
Caseley, Judith. *When Grandpa came to stay*
Chaikin, Miriam. *Esther*
　Exodus
　Hanukkah
Chanover, Hyman. *Happy Hanukah everybody*
Chapman, Carol. *The tale of Meshka the Kvetch*

A child's picture English-Hebrew dictionary
Clement, Gary. *Just stay put*
Cohen, Barbara. *Even higher*
  First fast
  Gooseberries to oranges
  Here come the Purim players!, ill. by Beverly Brodsky McDermott
  Here come the Purim players!, ill. by Shoshana Mekibel
  Make a wish, Molly
Cole, Joanna. *It's too noisy*
Conway, Diana Cohen. *Northern lights*
Coopersmith, Jerome. *A Chanukah fable for Christmas*
Davis, Aubrey. *Bone button borscht*
De Paola, Tomie (Thomas Anthony). *My first Chanukah*
Drucker, Malka. *Grandma's latkes*
  A Jewish holiday ABC
Edwards, Michelle. *Alef-bet*
  A baker's portrait
Ehrlich, Amy. *The story of Hannukah*
Eisenberg, Ann. *I can celebrate*
Eisenberg, Phyllis Rose. *A mitzvah is something special*
Emerman, Ellen. *Just right*
Fass, David E. *The shofar that lost its voice*
Fassler, Joan. *My grandpa died today*
Feder, Harriet K. *Not yet, Elijah!*
  What can you do with a bagel?
Fisher, Aileen Lucia. *My first Hanukkah book*
Fishman, Cathy Goldberg. *On Hanukkah*
  On Passover
  On Rosh Hashanah and Yom Kippur
Freedman, Florence B. *Brothers*
Ganz, Yaffa. *The story of Mimmy and Simmy*
Gellman, Ellie. *It's Chanukah!*
  It's Rosh Hashanah!
  Shai's Shabbat walk
Gershator, Phillis. *Honi and his magic circle*
Gerstein, Mordicai. *Queen Esther the morning star*
  The shadow of a flying bird
Glaser, Linda. *The borrowed Hanukkah latkes*
Goffstein, M. B. (Marilyn Brooke). *Laughing latkes*
Goldin, Barbara Diamond. *Cakes and miracles*
  Just enough is plenty
  World's birthday
Gold-Vukson, Marji. *The colors of my Jewish Year*
Gordon, Ruth. *Feathers*
Greene, Jacqueline Dembar. *Butchers and bakers, rabbis and kings*
  What his father did
Groner, Judyth Saypol. *All about Hanukkah*
  All about Sukkot
  My very own Jewish community
  Thank you, God!
  Where is the Afikomen?
Gross, Michael. *The fable of the fig tree*
Grossblatt, Ruby M. *Who's that sleeping on my sofabed?*
Harber, Frances. *The brothers' promise*
Harvey, Brett. *Immigrant girl*
Hawxhurst, Joan C. *Bubbe and Gram, my two grandmothers*
Hest, Amy. *Fancy Aunt Jess*
Hirsh, Marilyn. *Captain Jiri and Rabbi Jacob*
  Could anything be worse?
  I love Hanukkah
  I love Passover

Joseph who loved the Sabbath
  One little goat
  The pink suit
  Potato pancakes all around
  The Rabbi and the twenty-nine witches
  Where is Yonkela?
Hoestlandt, Jo. *Star of fear, star of hope*
Holland, Cheri. *Maccabee jamboree*
Howland, Naomi. *Latkes, latkes, good to eat*
Hutton, Warwick. *Moses in the bulrushes*
Ife, Elaine. *Moses in the bulrushes*
Jaffe, Nina. *In the month of Kislev*
  The way meat loves salt
Kahn, Katherine Janus. *The shofar calls to us*
Karkowsky, Nancy. *Grandma's soup*
Karlinsky, Ruth Schild. *My first book of Mitzvos*
Kessler, Brad. *Moses in Egypt*
Kimmel, Eric A. *Asher and the capmakers*
  The Chanukkah guest
  The Chanukkah tree
  Hershel and the Hanukkah goblins
  The magic dreidels
  One winter night
  Onions and garlic
  Ten suns
Kimmelman, Leslie. *Hanukkah lights, Hanukkah nights*
  Hooray! it's Passover!
  The runaway latkes
  Sound the shofar!
Koralek, Jenny. *Hanukkah*
Kress, Camille. *Tot Shabbat*
Kuskin, Karla. *A great miracle happened there*
Lakin, Pat (Patricia). *Don't forget*
Lamstein, Sarah Marwil. *Annie's Shabbat*
Lepon, Shoshana. *Hillel builds a house*
Levine, Arthur A. *All the lights in the night*
Levinson, Riki. *Soon, Annala*
Levoy, Myron. *The Hanukkah of Great-Uncle Otto*
Levy, Sara G. *Mother Goose rhymes for Jewish children*
Lieberman, Syd. *The wise shoemaker of Studena*
Lisowski, Gabriel. *How Tevye became a milkman*
London, Jonathan. *Into this night we are rising*
McDermott, Beverly Brodsky. *The Golem*
MacGill-Callahan, Sheila. *When Solomon was king*
Manushkin, Fran. *Hooray for Hanukkah!*
  Latkes and applesauce
  The matzah that Papa brought home
  Miriam's cup
  Starlight and candles
Margalit, Avishai. *The Hebrew alphabet book*
Melmed, Laura Krauss. *Moishe's miracle*
Metaxas, Eric. *David and Goliath*
Miller, William. *Jenny and the peddler*
Milstein, Linda Breiner. *Miami-Nanny stories*
Modesitt, Jeanne. *It's Hanukkah!*
  Songs of Chanukah
Moss, Marissa. *In America*
  The ugly menorah
Nayer, Judy. *The eight nights of Hanukka*
Nerlove, Miriam. *Flowers on the wall*
  Hanukkah
  Passover
  Purim
  Shabbat
  The Ten Commandments for Jewish children
Newman, Lesléa. *Matzo ball moon*
Nivola, Claire A. *Elisabeth*
Oberman, Sheldon. *The always prayer shawl*

King Solomon, Sheba, and the hoopoe bird
Sound of the shofar
On the little hearth
Oppenheim, Shulamith Levey. *The lily cupboard*
Orgel, Doris. *The flower of Sheba*
Patterson, José. *Mazal-Tov*
Phillips, Mildred. *The sign in Mendel's window*
Podwal, Mark H. *Golem*
  The menorah story
Polacco, Patricia. *The keeping quilt*
  Mrs. Katz and Tush
  Tikvah means hope
Portnoy, Mindy Avra. *Ima on the Bima*
  Matzah ball
  Mommy never went to Hebrew school
Prose, Francine. *The angel's mistake*
  Dybbuk
  You never know
Rael, Elsa. *When Zaydeh danced on Eldridge Street*
Renberg, Dalia Hardof. *King Solomon and the bee*
Rosen, Anne. *A family Passover*
Rosen, Michael J. (1954-). *Elijah's angel*
Rosenberg, Liz. *Grandmother and the runaway shadow*
Rosenblum, Richard. *Journey to the golden land*
  The old synagogue
Ross, Lillian Hammer. *Buba Leah and her paper children*
  The little old man and his dreams
Rothenberg, Joan. *Inside-out grandma*
  Matzah ball soup
Rouss, Sylvia A. *Sammy Spider's first Passover*
  Sammy Spider's first Shabbat
Sanfield, Steve. *Bit by bit*
Schanzer, Rosalyn. *In the synagogue*
Schnur, Steven. *The tie man's miracle*
Schotter, Roni. *Hanukkah!*
  Passover magic
  Purim play
Schrier, Jeffrey. *On the wings of eagles*
Schur, Maxine Rose. *Day of delight*
Schwartz, Amy. *Mrs. Moskowitz and the Sabbath candlesticks*
  Yossel Zissel and the wisdom of Chelm
Schwartz, Lynne Sharon. *The four questions*
Schweiger-Dmi'el, Itzhak. *Hanna's Sabbath dress*
Segal, Lore. *Tell me a Mitzi*
  Tell me a Trudy
Segal, Sheila. *Joshua's dream*
Sherman, Eileen Bluestone. *The odd potato*
Shostak, Myra. *Rainbow candles*
Silverman, Erica. *Gittel's hands*
Silverman, Maida. *My first book of Jewish holidays*
Simon, Norma. *The story of Hanukkah*
  The story of Passover
Singer, Marilyn. *Minnie's Yom Kippur birthday*
Springer, Sally. *Let's make latkes*
Stillerman, Marci. *Nine spoons*
Suhl, Yuri. *Simon Boom gives a wedding*
Swartz, Leslie. *A first Passover*
Tarbescu, Edith. *Annushka's voyage*
  The boy who stuck out his tongue
Topek, Susan Remick. *A costume for Noah*
  Shalom, Shabbat
Weedn, Flavia. *The ragged peddler*
Weilerstein, Sadie Rose. *The best of K'tonton*
  K'tonton's Yom Kippur kitten
Wikler, Madeline. *Let's build a Sukkah*
  My first seder

The Purim parade
Wilkowski, Susan. *Baby's Bris*
Wisniewski, David. *Golem*
Wohl, Lauren L. *Matzoh mouse*
Woodruff, Elvira. *The memory coat*
Yorinks, Arthur. *The Miami giant*
Zagwÿn, Deborah Turney. *Papa's latkes*
Zalben, Jane Breskin. *Beni's first Chanukah*
  Beni's first wedding
  Happy Passover, Rosie
  Leo and Blossom's Sukkah
  Pearl's eight days of Chanukah
Zemach, Margot. *It could always be worse*
Zola, Meguido. *The dream of promise*
Zusman, Evelyn. *The Passover parrot*

Jewish culture – Passover

Shulevitz, Uri. *The magician*

Jobs *see* Careers

Jokes *see* Riddles

Jonah *see* Religion – Jonah

Journalists *see* Careers – journalists

Judges *see* Careers – judges

Jumping *see* Activities – jumping

Jumping rope *see* Sports – jumping rope

Juneteenth *see* Holidays – Juneteenth

Jungle

Aardema, Verna. *Rabbit makes a monkey of lion*
Adlerman, Dan. *Africa calling*
Aitken, Amy. *Kate and Mona in the jungle*
Allen, Judy. *Eagle*
Andreae, Giles. *Rumble in the jungle*
Apperley, Dawn. *In the jungle*
Balmer, Helen. *Jungle adventure*
Bare, Colleen Stanley. *Who comes to the water hole?*
Bodsworth, Nan. *A nice walk in the jungle*
Booth, Eugene. *In the jungle*
Bush, John. *The giraffe who got in a knot*
Calmenson, Stephanie. *One little monkey*
Cannon, Janell. *Verdi*
Cartlidge, Michelle. *Elephant in the jungle*
Catchpole, Clive. *Jungles*
Cherry, Lynne. *The great kapok tree*
Chichester Clark, Emma. *Lunch with Aunt Augusta*
Cole, Babette. *Tarzanna!*
Corddry, Thomas I. *Kibby's big feat*
Dale, Penny. *The elephant tree*
Demi. *Three little elephants*
Dijs, Carla. *Pretend you're a hippo*
Drescher, Henrik. *The yellow umbrella*
Elbling, Peter. *Aria*
Emberley, Rebecca. *Jungle sounds*
Engel, Diana. *The shelf-paper jungle*
Fischetto, Laura. *The jungle is my home*
Geraghty, Paul. *Stop that noise!*
Greenaway, Shirley. *Jungles*

Harter, Debbie. *Walking through the jungle*
Hellen, Nancy. *Animals of the jungle*
Henley, Claire. *Jungle day*
Hennessy, B. G. (Barbara G.). *Eeney, Meeney, Miney, Mo*
Hindley, Judy. *Into the jungle*
Isadora, Rachel. *A South African night*
Jordan, Martin. *Amazon alphabet*
   Jungle days, jungle nights
Kemp, Anthea. *Mr. Percy's magic greenhouse*
Kitchen, Bert. *Tenrec's twigs*
Lacome, Julie. *Walking through the jungle*
Lilly, Kenneth. *Animals in the jungle*
London, Jonathan. *Little Red Monkey*
Loomis, Christine. *The Hippo Hop*
Lynn, Sara. *Jungle friends*
McAllister, Angela. *Matepo*
MacDonald, Suse. *Nanta's lion*
McPhail, David M. *Edward in the jungle*
Mahy, Margaret. *17 kings and 42 elephants*
   Simply delicious!
Morgan, Michaela. *Helpful Betty solves a mystery*
   Helpful Betty to the rescue
Most, Bernard. *Hippopotamus hunt*
Mwenye Hadithi. *Tricky tortoise*
Nayer, Judy. *Jungle life*
O'Donnell, Peter. *Oscar*
Royston, Angela. *Jungle animals*
Sage, Angie. *Monkeys in the jungle*
Smith, Jim. *Nimbus the explorer*
Steig, William. *The Zabajaba Jungle*
Tafuri, Nancy. *Junglewalk*
Upper, Jonathan. *Spin's really wild Africa tour*
Van Allsburg, Chris. *Jumanji*
West, Colin. *One day in the jungle*
Willis, Jeanne. *The boy who lost his bellybutton*
Wood, John Norris. *Jungles*
Wundrow, Deanna. *Jungle drum*

Kangaroos *see* Animals – kangaroos

Karate *see* Sports – karate

Karok Indians *see* Indians of North America – Karok

Kato *see* Indians of North America – Kato

Kelpies *see* Mythical creatures – kelpies

Kenya *see* Foreign lands – Kenya

Khans *see* Royalty – khans

Kindness *see* Character traits – kindness

Kindness to animals *see* Character traits – kindness to animals

Kings *see* Royalty – kings

Kissing

McLerran, Alice. *Kisses*

Kites

Ayer, Jacqueline. *Nu Dang and his kite*
Brown, Marcia. *The little carousel*
Buckley, Helen Elizabeth. *Moonlight kite*
Cooper, Elizabeth K. *The fish from Japan*
Cousins, Lucy. *Kite in the park*
French, Vivian. *Little Tiger finds a friend*
Galouchko, Annouchka. *Shô and the demons of the deep*
Gerstein, Mordicai. *The mountains of Tibet*
Haseley, Dennis. *Crosby*
   Kite flier
Heller, George. *Hiroshi's wonderful kite*
How Raggedy Ann got her candy heart
Kroll, Virginia L. *A carp for Kimiko*
Lies, Brian. *Hamlet and the enormous Chinese dragon kite*
Lobato, Arcadio. *Paper bird*
Luenn, Nancy. *The dragon kite*
MacDonald, Elizabeth. *Mike's kite*
MacDonald, Maryann. *Rabbit's birthday kite*
Mayer, Mercer. *Shibumi and the kitemaker*
Miller, Moira. *The moon dragon*
Molarsky, Osmond. *A sky full of kites*
Packard, Mary. *The kite*
Peet, Bill (William Bartlett). *Merle the high flying squirrel*
Reddix, Valerie. *Dragon kite of the autumn moon*
Rey, Margret (Margret Elisabeth Waldstein). *Curious George flies a kite*
Roche, Hannah. *Corey's kite*
Romanelli, Serena. *Little Bobo saves the day*
Ruthstrom, Dorotha. *The big kite contest*
Stadler, John. *One seal*
Stilz, Carol Curtis. *Kirsty's kite*
Strauss, Gwen. *The night shimmy*
Thayer, Jane. *Gus loved his happy home*
Titus, Eve. *Anatole over Paris*
Trottier, Maxine. *The tiny kite of Eddie Wing*
Uchida, Yoshiko. *Sumi's prize*
Vaughan, Marcia Kapok. *The Sea-Breeze Hotel*
Wiese, Kurt. *Fish in the air*
Ye, Ting-xing. *Share the sky*
Yolen, Jane. *The emperor and the kite*

Knights

Blake, Quentin. *Snuff*
Boutell, Clarence Burley. *The fat baron*
Bradfield, Roger (Jolly Roger). *A good night for dragons*
Carrick, Donald. *Harold and the giant knight*
Cressey, James. *The dragon and George*
Cretien, Paul D. *Sir Henry and the dragon*
Curry, Jane Louise. *The Christmas knight*
De Paola, Tomie (Thomas Anthony). *The knight and the dragon*
Emberley, Ed (Edward Randolph). *Klippity klop*
Fradon, Dana. *Sir Dana - a knight*
Gerrard, Roy. *Sir Cedric*
   Sir Cedric rides again
Gibbons, Gail. *Knights in shining armor*

Goodall, John S. *Creepy castle*
Haley, Gail E. *The green man*
Hazen, Barbara Shook. *The knight who was afraid of the dark*
  The knight who was afraid to fight
Hodges, Margaret. *The hero of Bremen*
  The kitchen knight
Holl, Adelaide. *Sir Kevin of Devon*
Ipcar, Dahlov. *Sir Addlepate and the unicorn*
Krensky, Stephen. *A good knight's sleep*
Lasker, Joe. *A tournament of knights*
Löfgren, Ulf. *Alvin the Knight*
McCrea, James. *The story of Olaf*
Mayer, Mercer. *Terrible troll*
Myers, Walter Dean. *The dragon takes a wife*
Nash, Ogden. *Custard the dragon and the wicked knight*, ill. by Lynn Munsinger
  Custard the dragon and the wicked knight, ill. by Linell Nash
Nolan, Dennis. *The castle builder*
Peet, Bill (William Bartlett). *Cowardly Clyde*
  How Droofus the dragon lost his head
Scarry, Huck. *Looking into the Middle Ages*
Shannon, Mark. *Gawain and the Green Knight*
Thomas, Shelley Moore. *Good night, Good Knight*
Trez, Denise. *The little knight's dragon*
Tucker, Kathy. *Do knights take naps?*

Knitting *see* Activities – knitting

Koala bears *see* Animals – koalas

Komodo dragons *see* Reptiles – Komodo dragons

Korea *see* Foreign lands – Korea

Korea (North) *see* Foreign lands – Korea (North)

Korean Americans *see* Ethnic groups in the U.S. – Asian Americans; Ethnic groups in the U.S. – Korean Americans

Kurdistan *see* Foreign lands – Kurdistan

Kutenai Indians *see* Indians of North America – Kutenai

Kwanzaa *see* Holidays – Kwanzaa

Lady birds *see* Insects – ladybugs

Ladybugs *see* Insects – ladybugs

Lakes, ponds

Capucilli, Alyssa Satin. *Good morning, pond*

Cartlidge, Michelle. *Duck in the pond*
Fleming, Denise. *In the small, small pond*
Gantschev, Ivan. *The moon lake*
George, Lindsay Barrett. *Around the pond*
Lasky, Kathryn. *Pond year*
London, Jonathan. *Loon Lake*
Mills, Judith Christine. *The stonehook schooner*
Rockwell, Anne F. *Ducklings and pollywogs*
Rosen, Michael J. (1954-). *All eyes on the pond*
Schoenherr, John. *Rebel*
Seymour, Tres. *The gulls of the Edmund Fitzgerald*
Taylor, Harriet Peck. *Coyote and the laughing butterflies*
Valgardson, W. D. *Winter rescue*
Van Leeuwen, Jean. *Touch the sky summer*
Waddell, Martin. *The pig in the pond*

Lakota (Sioux) Indians *see* Indians of North America – Lakota (Sioux)

Lambs *see* Animals – sheep

Language

Ahlberg, Allan. *Big bad pig*
  Fee fi fo fum
  Happy worm
  Help!
Aliki. *Communication*
  Hello! Good-bye!
The all-amazing ha ha book
Allington, Richard L. *Letters*
  Talking
  Words
Ancona, George. *Handtalk zoo*
Anglund, Joan Walsh. *The Adam book*
  Emily and Adam book of opposites
  The Emily book
Anholt, Catherine. *All about you*
  First words and pictures
Antoine, Héloïse. *Curious kids go to preschool*
Asch, Frank. *Short train, long train*
Baby's words
Baer, Edith. *Words are like faces*
Baker, Pamela J. *My first book of sign*
Barrett, Judi. *The things that are most in the world*
Barton, Byron. *Tools*
Battles, Edith. *What does the rooster say, Yoshio?*
Bender, Robert. *The A to Z beastly jamboree*
Benjamin, Alan. *Rat-a-tat, pitter pat*
Berson, Harold. *A moose is not a mouse*
Bond, Michael. *Paddington and the knickerbocker rainbow*
Bossom, Naomi. *A scale full of fish and other turnabouts*
Bourke, Linda. *Eye count*
Bove, Linda. *Sign language ABC with Linda Bove*
Brown, Marc Tolon. *Arthur's really helpful word book*
Bruce, Lisa. *Oliver's alphabets*
Buck, Nola. *Creepy crawly critters and other Halloween tongue twisters*
  Oh, cats!
  Santa's short suit shrunk and other Christmas tongue twisters
  Sid and Sam
Bunting, Eve (Anne Evelyn). *Say it fast*
Bunting, Jane. *The children's visual dictionary*
  My first ABC

My first word book
Burnstein, Chaya M. *The Jewish kids' Hebrew-English wordbook*
Carle, Eric. *My very first book of words*
Carlson, Nancy L. *ABC, I like me!*
Cartlidge, Michelle. *Michelle Cartlidge's book of words*
Chaplin, Susan Gibbons. *I can sign my ABCs*
Chapman, Cheryl. *Snow on snow on snow*
Charlip, Remy. *Handtalk*
    Handtalk birthday
Chislett, Gail. *Melinda's no's cold*
Clements, Andrew. *Double trouble in Walla Walla*
Clifford, Eth. *A bear before breakfast*
Cohen, Caron Lee. *Three yellow dogs*
Cole, Babette. *Tarzanna!*
Day, Alexandra. *Frank and Ernest*
    Frank and Ernest on the road
    Frank and Ernest play ball
DeRubertis, Barbara. *Janey Crane*
    Joey Goat
    Suzy Mule
    Tiny Tiger
    Zeely Zebra
Dodds, Dayle Ann. *Do bunnies talk?*
Dunham, Meredith. *Colors*
    Numbers: how do you say it?
    Picnic
    Shapes
Edwards, Richard. *Fly with the birds*
Ellentuck, Shan. *Did you see what I said?*
Everett, Percival L. *The one that got away*
Falwell, Cathryn. *Clowning around*
    Word wizard
Folsom, Marcia. *Easy as pie*
Gibbons, Gail. *Weather words and what they mean*
Gifaldi, David. *The boy who spoke colors*
Gomi, Taro. *Seeing, saying, doing, playing*
Goodspeed, Peter. *Hugh and Fitzhugh*
Gordon, Jeffie Ross. *Six sleepy sheep*
Greenberg, Judith E. *What is the sign for friend?*
Grover, Max. *The accidental zucchini*
Gwynne, Fred. *A chocolate moose for dinner*
    A little pigeon toad
Hartman, Gail. *For strawberry jam or fireflies*
Hawkins, Colin. *Tog the dog*
Hayward, Linda. *Wet foot, dry foot, low foot, high foot*
Heller, Ruth. *A cache of jewels and other collective nouns*
    Fantastic! wow! and unreal!
    Kites sail high
    Many luscious lollipops
    Merry-go-round
    Mine, all mine
Hepworth, Catherine. *Bug off!*
Hiatt, Fred. *Baby talk*
Hill, Eric. *Spot's big book of words; El libro grande de las palabras de Spot*
    Spot's favorite words
    Spot's first words
Hill, Susan. *Simba's A-Z*
Hirschi, Ron. *Seya's song*
Hoban, Tana. *All about where*
    More than one
Hooper, Patricia. *A bundle of beasts*
Horenstein, Henry. *Arf! beg! catch!*
Hunt, Bernice Kohn. *Your ant is a which*
Inkpen, Mick. *Kipper's book of opposites*
Jackson, Bobby L. *Makimba's animal world*
Johnston, Tony. *Uncle rain cloud*

Jonas, Ann. *Watch William walk*
Karlin, Nurit. *I see, you saw*
King-Smith, Dick. *Dick King-Smith's Alphabeasts*
Koch, Michelle. *By the sea*
    Just one more
Kopper, Lisa. *I'm a baby, you're a baby*
Kraus, Robert. *Ella the bad speller*
Krauss, Ruth. *A hole is to dig*
Krupp, Robin Rector. *Get set to wreck!*
Lachner, Dorothea. *Andrew's angry words*
Lacome, Julie. *My first book of words*
Leaf, Munro. *Grammar can be fun*
Leedy, Loreen. *There's a frog in my throat*
Leeton, Will C. *The Tower of Babel*
Lenssen, Ann. *A rainbow balloon*
Levine, Ellen. *I hate English!*
Levinson, Riki. *Soon, Annala*
Lewin, Betsy. *Wiley learns to spell*
Lewis, Shari. *Baby Lamb Chop loves words*
Lionni, Leo. *Words to talk about*
Little, Jean. *Bats about baseball*
MacCarthy, Patricia. *Herds of words*
McMillan, Bruce. *One sun*
    Play day
    Super, super, superwords
McNaught, Harry. *Words to grow on*
Maestro, Betsy. *All aboard overnight*
    Camping out
    Delivery van
    On the go
    Taxi
Magee, Doug. *Let's fly from A to Z*
Marks, Alan. *Nowhere to be found*
Martin, Bill (William Ivan). *Words*
Martin, Jerome. *Carrot/parrot*
    Mitten/kitten
Maynard, Bill. *Quiet, Wyatt!*
Miller, Margaret. *Every day*
    I'm grown up!
    My birthday
    On my street
    Playtime
    Where's Jenna?
Millman, Isaac. *Moses goes to a concert*
Moncure, Jane Belk. *Word Bird's fall words*
    Word Bird's spring words
    Word Bird's summer words
    Word Bird's winter words
Monfried, Lucia. *Baby's world*
Most, Bernard. *Hippopotamus hunt*
    Pets in trumpets and other word-play riddles
    There's an ape behind the drape
Nayer, Judy. *Mice are nice*
    Pig in a wig
O'Brien, John (1953-). *Sam and Spot*
100 words about transportation
100 words about working
Owen, Annie. *From snowflakes to sandcastles*
Pluckrose, Henry Arthur. *Join it!*
Preiss, Byron. *The first crazy word book*
Rand, Ann. *Sparkle and spin*
Rankin, Laura. *The handmade counting book*
Richardson, Jack E. *Six in a mix*
Riddell, Edwina. *One hundred first words*
Rockwell, Anne F. *What we like*
Root, Phyllis. *Gretchen's grandma*
Rose, Gerald. *The bird garden*
Sage, Michael. *If you talked to a boar*
Salt, Jane. *See and say picture word book*

Sattler, Helen Roney. *Train whistles*
Scarry, Richard. *Richard Scarry's biggest word book ever!*
Serfozo, Mary. *What's what?*
Sesame Street. *Sesame Street sign language fun*
  Sesame Street word book
Sherman, Ivan. *Walking talking words*
Showers, Paul. *How you talk*
Small, David. *Ruby Mae has something to say*
Snell, Nigel. *A bird in hand . . .*
Snow, Alan. *My first dictionary*
Steig, William. *The bad speller*
Steptoe, John. *My special best words*
Tapahonso, Luci. *Navajo ABC*
Tester, Sylvia Root. *Never monkey with a monkey*
  What did you say?
Tobias, Tobi. *A world of words*
Trân-Khánh-Tuyê. *The little weaver of Thái-Yên Village*
Tullet, Hervé. *Night / day*
Viorst, Judith. *The Alphabet from Z to A*
Wall, Lina Mao. *Judge Rabbit and the tree spirit*
Wells, Rosemary. *Max's first word*
  Max's ride
West, Kipling. *A rattle of bones*
Wheeler, Cindy. *More simple signs*
  Simple signs
Wiesner, William. *The Tower of Babel*
Wildsmith, Brian. *What the moon saw*
Wilkes, Angela. *My first word book*
Wood, Audrey. *Elbert's bad word*

Language, foreign *see* Foreign languages

Languages

Moore, Clement C. *The night before Christmas in signed English*

Laos *see* Foreign lands – Laos

Lapland *see* Foreign lands – Lapland

Larks *see* Birds – larks

Latin America *see* Foreign lands – Latin America

Latvia *see* Foreign lands – Latvia

Laundry

Ahlberg, Allan. *Mrs. Lather's laundry*
Behrens, June. *Soo Ling finds a way*
Freeman, Don. *A pocket for Corduroy*
Iwamura, Kazuo. *The fourteen forest mice and the summer laundry day*
Ormondroyd, Edward. *Theodore*
Straight, Susan. *Bear E. Bear*
Weeks, Sarah. *Mrs. McNosh hangs up her wash*

Law *see* Careers – judges; Careers – lawyers; Careers – police officers; Crime; Prisons

Lawyers *see* Careers – lawyers

Laziness *see* Character traits – laziness

Lebanese Americans *see* Ethnic groups in the U.S. – Lebanese Americans

Lebanon *see* Foreign lands – Lebanon

Left and right *see* Concepts – left and right

Left-handedness

Lerner, Marguerite Rush. *Lefty, the story of left-handedness*

Legends *see* Folk and fairy tales

Legs *see* Anatomy – legs

Lemmings *see* Animals – lemmings

Lemurs *see* Animals – lemurs

Lenape *see* Indians of North America – Lenape

Leopards *see* Animals – leopards

Leprechauns *see* Mythical creatures – leprechauns

Letters, cards

Ada, Alma Flor. *Dear Peter Rabbit*
Adoff, Arnold. *Love letters*
Asch, Frank. *Dear brother*
Baker, Keith. *The dove's letter*
Bell, Norman. *Linda's airmail letter*
Brandt, Betty. *Special delivery*
Brisson, Pat. *Kate on the coast*
  Your best friend, Kate
Cartlidge, Michelle. *Fairy letters*
  Mouse letters
Caseley, Judith. *Dear Annie*
Dunbar, Joyce. *The secret friend*
Fox, Louisa. *Every Monday in the mailbox*
Harrison, Joanna. *Dear bear*
Hobbie, Holly. *Toot and Puddle*
Holub, Joan. *Pen pals*
James, Simon. *Dear Mr. Blueberry*
Johnson, Jane. *My dear Noel*
Keats, Ezra Jack. *A letter to Amy*
Leedy, Loreen. *Messages in the mailbox*
Lester, Alison. *Ernie dances to the didgeridoo*
Lillegard, Dee. *Tortoise brings the mail*
Pak, Soyung. *Dear Juno*
Poydar, Nancy. *Mailbox magic*
Raffi. *Like me and you*
Rodell, Susanna. *Dear Fred*
Ross, Lillian Hammer. *Buba Leah and her paper children*
Schindel, John. *Dear Daddy*
Schumacher, Claire. *Tommy the winner*
Selway, Martina. *Don't forget to write*
Seuss, Dr. *On beyond zebra*
Siracusa, Catherine. *No mail for Mitchell*
Skurzynski, Gloria. *Here comes the mail*
Spurr, Elizabeth. *The long, long letter*
Stewart, Sarah. *The gardener*

Weninger, Brigitte. *A Letter to Santa Claus*
Wild, Margaret. *Thank you, Santa*

Liberia *see* Foreign lands – Liberia

Librarians *see* Careers – librarians

Libraries

Alexander, Martha G. *How my library grew by Dinah*
Alexander, Sue. *World famous Muriel and the magic mystery*
Aliki. *How a book is made*
Baggette, Susan K. *Jonathan goes to the library*
Baker, Donna. *I want to be a librarian*
Bartlett, Susan. *Libraries*
Bauer, Caroline Feller. *Too many books!*
Baugh, Dolores M. *Let's take a trip*
Brillhart, Julie. *Story hour - starring Megan!*
Brimner, Larry Dane. *Aggie and Will*
Caseley, Judith. *The noisemakers*
   Sophie and Sammy's library sleepover
Charles, Donald. *Calico Cat meets bookworm*
Daly, Maureen. *Patrick visits the library*
Daugherty, James Henry. *Andy and the lion*
Demarest, Chris L. *Clemens' kingdom*
De Paola, Tomie (Thomas Anthony). *The knight and the dragon*
Ernst, Lisa Campbell. *Stella Louella's runaway book*
Felt, Sue. *Rosa-too-little*
Freeman, Don. *Quiet! There's a canary in the library*
Furtado, Jo. *Sorry, Miss Folio!*
Gay, Zhenya. *Look!*
Gibbons, Gail. *Check it out!*
Hautzig, Deborah. *A visit to the Sesame Street library*
Hest, Amy. *The babies are coming!*
Houghton, Eric. *Walter's magic wand*
Huff, Barbara A. *Once inside the library*
Hulbert, Jay. *Armando asked "Why?"*
Hutchins, H. J. (Hazel J.). *Nicholas at the library*
Jaspersohn, William. *My hometown library*
Kimmel, Eric A. *I took my frog to the library*
Krensky, Stephen. *Breaking into print*
Levinson, Nancy Smiler. *Clara and the bookwagon*
Lewis, Robin Baird. *Aunt Armadillo*
Little, Mary E. *ABC for the library*
   Ricardo and the puppets
Loomis, Christine. *At the library*
Meister, Cari. *Tiny goes to the library*
Miller, William. *Richard Wright and the library card*
Mora, Pat. *Tomás and the library lady*
Munro, Roxie. *The inside-outside book of libraries*
Polacco, Patricia. *Aunt Chip and the great Triple Creek dam affair*
Radlauer, Ruth Shaw. *Molly at the library*
Rahaman, Vashanti. *Read for me, Mama*
Rockwell, Anne F. *I like the library*
Sadler, Marilyn. *Alistair in outer space*
Sauer, Julia Lina. *Mike's house*
Stewart, Sarah. *The library*
Tudor, Tasha. *Mildred and the mummy*
Weil, Lisl. *Let's go to the library*
Woodruff, Elvira. *Can you guess where we're going?*

Lice *see* Insects – lice

Lifeguards *see* Careers – lifeguards

Lighthouses

Armitage, Ronda. *The lighthouse keeper's catastrophe*
   The lighthouse keeper's lunch
   The lighthouse keeper's rescue
Barker, Melvern J. *Little island star*
Brett, Jan. *Comet's nine lives*
Hoff, Syd. *The lighthouse children*
Hopkinson, Deborah. *Birdie's lighthouse*
Lobel, Anita. *One lighthouse, one moon*
Metaxas, Eric. *The boy and the whale*
Olson, Arielle North. *The lighthouse keeper's daughter*
Perrow, Angeli. *Captain's castaway*
Rowinski, Kate. *Cats in the dark*
Strahl, Rudi. *Sandman in the lighthouse*
Swift, Hildegarde Hoyt. *The little red lighthouse and the great gray bridge*
Thaxter, Celia. *Celia's island journal*
Vaughan, Marcia Kapok. *Abbie against the storm*
Wells, Rosemary. *The island light*

Lightning bugs *see* Insects – fireflies

Lights

Baisch, Cris. *When the lights went out*
Berger, Melvin. *Switch on, switch off*
Crews, Donald. *Light*
Graham, Joan Bransfield. *Flicker flash*
Schnur, Steven. *Night lights*
Swinburne, Stephen R. *Guess whose shadow?*
Weninger, Brigitte. *Lumina*
Wright, Sue (Sue M.). *The Christmas path*

Lions *see* Animals – lions

Lithuanian Americans *see* Ethnic groups in the U.S. – Lithuanian Americans

Little people

Barber, Antonia. *Catkin*
Berg, Jean Horton. *The wee little man*
Beskow, Elsa Maartman. *Peter in Blueberry Land*
   Peter's adventures in Blueberry Land
Brennan, Patricia D. *Hitchety hatchety up I go!*
Carrick, Carol. *Two very little sisters*
French, Fiona. *Little Inchkin*
Hughes, Monica. *Little Fingerling*
Krauss, Ruth. *Everything under a mushroom*
Mogensen, Jan. *The forty-six little men*
Morimoto, Junko. *The inch boy*
Tom Thumb. *Grimm Tom Thumb*
   Tom Thumb, ill. by L. Leslie Brooke
   Tom Thumb, ill. by Dennis Hockerman
   Tom Thumb, ill. by Felix Hoffmann
   Tom Thumb, ill. by Lidia Postma
   Tom Thumb, ill. by Richard Jesse Watson
   Tom Thumb, ill. by William Wiesner

Littleness *see* Character traits – smallness

Lizards *see* Reptiles – lizards

Llamas *see* Animals – llamas

Lobsters *see* Crustaceans

Loneliness *see* Emotions – loneliness

Loons *see* Birds – loons

Losing things *see* Behavior – losing things

Lost *see* Behavior – lost

Love *see* Emotions – love

Loyalty *see* Character traits – loyalty

Luck *see* Character traits – luck

Lullabies

Ahlberg, Allan. *Mockingbird*
All the pretty little horses
Appelt, Kathi. *Bayou lullaby*
Aragon, Jane Chelsea. *Lullaby*
Asch, Frank. *Barnyard lullaby*
Bang, Molly. *Ten, nine, eight*
Benjamin, Floella. *Skip across the ocean*
Bernhard, Josephine Butkowska. *Lullaby*
Bozylinsky, Hannah Heritage. *Lala Salama*
Calmenson, Stephanie. *All aboard the goodnight train*
Carlstrom, Nancy White. *Northern lullaby*
Carpenter, Mary-Chapin. *Dreamland*
Chorao, Kay. *Rock, rock, my baby*
Conrad, Pam. *Animal lullabies*
Duncan, Lois. *Songs from dreamland*
Engvick, William. *Lullabies and night songs*
Fox, Mem. *Sleepy bears*
French, Vivian. *A song for little toad*
Gerber, Carole. *Hush! a Gaelic lullaby*
Gilbert, Yvonne. *Baby's book of lullabies and cradle songs*
Ginsburg, Mirra. *Asleep, asleep*
Highwater, Jamake. *Moonsong lullaby*
Hindley, Judy. *The sleepy book*
Ho, Minfong. *Hush!*
Hopkins, Lee Bennett. *And God bless me*
Hush little baby. *Hush little baby*, ill. by Aliki
Hush little baby, ill. by Shari Halpern
Hush little baby, ill. by Jeanette Winter
Hush little baby, ill. by Margot Zemach
Khan, Rukhsana. *Bedtime ba-a-a-lk*
Kherdian, David. *Lullaby for Emily*
Kirk, Daniel. *Hush, little alien*
Lambert, Paulette Livers. *Evening*
Lansky, Bruce. *Sweet dreams*
London, Jonathan. *Fireflies, fireflies, light my way*
Lullaby and goodnight
McMullan, Kate (Hall). *If you were my bunny*
Marzollo, Jean. *Close your eyes*
Meigs, Mildred Plew. *Moon song*
Melmed, Laura Krauss. *Jumbo's lullaby*
Merriam, Eve. *Goodnight to Annie*, ill. by Carol Schwartz
Messenger, Jannat. *Lullabies and baby songs*
Miranda, Anne. *Night songs*
Morgenstern, Christian. *Lullabies, lyrics and gallows songs*
Nichol, B. P. *Once*
Nye, Naomi Shihab. *Lullaby raft*
Ogburn, Jacqueline K. *Noise lullaby*

Pfister, Marcus. *I see the moon*
Pienkowski, Jan. *Good night, a pop-up lullaby*
Plotz, Helen. *A week of lullabies*
Pomerantz, Charlotte. *All asleep*
Root, Phyllis. *What Baby wants*
Schlein, Miriam. *Sleep safe, little whale*
Slate, Joseph. *The star rocker*
Sleep, baby, sleep
Smith, Edward Biko. *A lullaby for Daddy*
Stanley, Diane. *Birdsong lullaby*
Staub, Leslie. *Bless this house*
Swados, Elizabeth. *Lullaby*
Taylor, Livingston. *Pajamas*
Titherington, Jeanne. *Baby's boat*
Baby's boat, a board book
Van Laan, Nancy. *Sleep, sleep, sleep*
When winter comes
Van Vorst, M. L. *A Norse lullaby*
Walty, Margaret. *Rock-a-bye baby*
Watson, Clyde. *Fisherman lullabies*
Whiteside, Karen. *Lullaby of the wind*
Wilkon, Józef. *Lullaby for a newborn king*
Wood, Douglas. *Northwoods cradle song*
Yolen, Jane. *Dragon night and other lullabies*
The lullaby songbook

Lumberjacks *see* Careers – lumberjacks

Lying *see* Behavior – lying

Lynx *see* Animals – lynx

Macaws *see* Birds – macaws

Machines

Adkins, Jan. *Heavy equipment*
Baker, Betty. *Worthington Botts and the steam machine*
Balterman, Lee. *Girders and cranes*
Barton, Byron. *Machines at work*
Bate, Norman. *Vulcan*
Who built the bridge?
Who built the highway?
Baugh, Dolores M. *Let's take a trip*
Benedictus, Roger. *Fifty million sausages*
Bennett, Jill. *Machine poems*
Biro, Val. *Gumdrop and the steamroller*
Bradfield, Roger (Jolly Roger). *The flying hockey stick*
Breverton, David. *Here comes bulldozer*
Brown, Margaret Wise. *The diggers*
The steamroller
Burton, Virginia Lee. *Katy and the big snow*
Mike Mulligan and his steam shovel
Calhoun, Mary. *Jack and the whoopee wind*
Climo, Lindee. *Clyde*
Cowcher, Helen. *Rain forest*
Cox, David. *Tin Lizzie and Little Nell*
Crowther, Robert. *Dump trucks and diggers*
Du Bois, William Pène. *Lazy Tommy pumpkinhead*

Fleishman, Seymour. *Too hot in Potzburg*
Fleming, Candace. *Professor Fergus Fahrenheit and his wonderful weather machine*
Gackenbach, Dick. *Dog for a day*
Geringer, Laura. *Molly's new washing machine*
Goor, Ron. *In the driver's seat*
Haldane, Suzanne. *Teddies and machines*
  Teddies and trucks
Hennessy, B. G. (Barbara G.). *Road builders*
Henstra, Friso. *Wait and see*
Hill, Eric. *Spot goes to the farm*
Hoban, Tana. *Construction zone*
  Dig, drill, dump, fill
Holl, Adelaide. *The ABC of cars, trucks and machines*
Hopkins, Lee Bennett. *Click, rumble, roar*
Hunter, Norman. *Professor Branestawm's building bust-up*
Hutchings, Tony. *Things that go word book*
Ipcar, Dahlov. *One horse farm*
Jacobs, Daniel. *What does it do?*
Löfgren, Ulf. *The traffic stopper that became a grandmother visitor*
Love, Ann. *Farming*
Lustig, Michael. *Willy Whyner, cloud designer*
MacDonald, Suse. *Elephants on board*
McGough, Roger. *Until I met Dudley*
Machotka, Hana. *Pasta factory*
Merriam, Eve. *Bam, bam, bam*
Munsch, Robert N. *Jonathan cleaned up - then he heard a sound*
Neville, Emily Cheney. *The bridge*
Nikola-Lisa, W. *One hole in the road*
Olney, Ross R. *Construction giants*
  Farm giants
Parker, Steve. *I wonder why tunnels are round*
Pluckrose, Henry Arthur. *On the farm*
  On the move
Potter, Tony. *See how it works: earth movers*
Pringle, Laurence P. *Jesse builds a road*
Radford, Derek. *Building machines and what they do*
  Cargo machines and what they do
Retan, Walter. *The snowplow that tried to go south*
  The steam shovel that wouldn't eat dirt
Rockwell, Anne F. *Big wheels*
  Machines
Royston, Angela. *Big machines*
  Diggers and dump trucks
  Monster road builders
Sadler, Marilyn. *Alistair's time machine*
Small, David. *Ruby Mae has something to say*
Smucker, Anna Egan. *No star nights*
Stevenson, James. *Sam the Zamboni man*
Stickland, Paul. *Machines as big as monsters*
Wallace, Karen. *Big machines*
Ward, Nick. *Farmer George and the fieldmice*
Wolde, Gunilla. *Betsy and the vacuum cleaner*
Yagelski, Robert. *The day the lifting bridge stuck*
Zaffo, George J. *The giant nursery book of things that work*

Madagascar *see* Foreign lands – Madagascar

Magic

Alexander, Martha G. *My outrageous friend Charlie*
  3 magic flip books
Alexander, Sue. *Marc the Magnificent*
  World famous Muriel and the magic mystery
Aliki. *The wish workers*

Andersen, H. C. (Hans Christian). *The tinderbox,* ill. by Warwick Hutton
  The tinderbox, ill. by Barry Moser
  The wild swans, ill. by Angela Barrett
  The wild swans, ill. by Susan Jeffers
Anderson, Lonzo. *Two hundred rabbits*
Anderson, Robin. *Sinabouda Lily*
Anno, Mitsumasa. *Anno's hat tricks*
Arabian Nights. *The flying carpet*
  The tale of Aladdin and the wonderful lamp
Argueta, Manlio. *The magic dogs of the volcanoes*
Armitage, Ronda. *The bossing of Josie*
Atwell, Debby. *Humphrey Thud*
Ayers, Rebecca Hickox. *Per and the Dala horse*
Aylesworth, Jim. *The full belly bowl*
Ayres, Becky Hickox. *Victoria flies high*
Babbitt, Samuel F. *The forty-ninth magician*
Bach, Othello. *Hector McSnector and the mail-order Christmas witch*
  Lilly, Willy and the mail-order witch
Balian, Lorna. *Humbug potion*
Ballard, Robin. *Cat and Alex and the magic flying carpet*
Banigan, Sharon Stearns. *Circus magic*
Barber, Antonia. *The enchanter's daughter*
  Satchelmouse and the dinosaurs
Baumann, Hans. *Chip has many brothers*
Baumgart, Klaus. *Laura's Christmas star*
Behrens, June. *Christmas-magic wagon*
Beisner, Monika. *Secret spells and curious charms*
Bell, Anthea. *Swan Lake*
Bemelmans, Ludwig. *Madeline's Christmas*
Bentley, Nancy. *I've got your nose!*
Berenstain, Stan. *The Berenstain bears and the sitter*
Berson, Harold. *Charles and Claudine*
  The thief who hugged a moonbeam
Beskow, Elsa Maartman. *Peter in Blueberry Land*
  Peter's adventures in Blueberry Land
Bianco, Margery Williams. *The velveteen rabbit,* ill. by Allen Atkinson
  The velveteen rabbit, ill. by Michael Green
  The velveteen rabbit, ill. by Michael Hague
  The velveteen rabbit, ill. by David Jorgensen
  The velveteen rabbit, ill. by William Nicholson
  The velveteen rabbit, ill. by Ilse Plume
  The velveteen rabbit, ill. by S. D. Schindler
  The velveteen rabbit, ill. by Tien
Birrer, Cynthia. *The lady and the unicorn*
Blance, Ellen. *Monster and the magic umbrella*
Boujon, Claude. *The fairy with the long nose*
Bowden, Joan Chase. *Who took the top hat trick?*
Boyle, Vere. *Beauty and the beast*
Brenner, Barbara A. *The flying patchwork quilt*
Bridwell, Norman. *The witch grows up*
Bright, Robert. *Georgie and the magician*
Brown, Marcia. *Once a mouse . . .*
Browne, Anthony. *Through the magic mirror*
Bruna, Dick. *Dick Bruna's Snow-White and the seven dwarfs*
Brunhoff, Laurent de. *Babar the magician*
Buckaway, C. M. *Alfred, the dragon who lost his flame*
Buckley, Paul. *Amy Belligera and the fireflies*
Buffett, Jimmy. *Trouble dolls*
Bunting, Eve (Anne Evelyn). *The man who could call down owls*
Burdett, Lois. *The tempest for kids*
Calmenson, Stephanie. *The little witch sisters*
Carlson, Natalie Savage. *Spooky and the ghost cat*
  Spooky and the witch's goat

Marionettes *see* Puppets

Markets *see* Stores

Marriage, interracial

Adoff, Arnold. *Black is brown is tan*
Davol, Marguerite W. *Black, white, just right*
Igus, Toyomi. *Two Mrs. Gibsons*
McGill, Alice. *Molly Bannaky*
Northway, Jennifer. *Lucy's day trip*
Senisi, Ellen B. *For my family, Love, Allie*

Marriages *see* Weddings

Martinique *see* Foreign lands – Martinique

Masks

Anno, Mitsumasa. *Anno's masks*
Cohen, Miriam. *The real-skin rubber monster mask*
Emberley, Ed (Edward Randolph). *Glad monster, sad monster*
Hoban, Lillian. *The case of the two masked robbers*
Hru, Dakari. *Joshua's Masai mask*
Masks and puppets
Mueller, Virginia. *A Halloween mask for Monster*

Math *see* Counting, numbers

Maya Indians *see* Indians of Central America – Maya

Mazes

Madgwick, Wendy. *Animaze!*

Meanness *see* Character traits – meanness

Measles *see* Illness – measles

Measurement *see* Concepts – measurement

Mechanical men *see* Robots

Mechanics *see* Careers – mechanics

Memorial Day *see* Holidays – Memorial Day

Memories, memory

Aliki. *Christmas tree memories*
Bahr, Mary. *The memory box*
Clifton, Lucille. *Don't you remember?*
Dragonwagon, Crescent. *Jemima remembers*
Ekoomiak, Normee. *Arctic memories*
Foreman, Michael. *Cat in the manger*
Griffith, Helen V. *Alex remembers*
Grindley, Sally. *A flag for Grandma*
Guthrie, Donna. *One hundred and two steps*
Harper, Jessica. *I forgot my shoes*
Haskins, Francine. *I remember "121"*
Hazelton, Elizabeth Baldwin. *Sammy, the crow who remembered*
Hickcox, Ruth. *Great-Grandmother's treasure*
Hines, Anna Grossnickle. *Remember the butterflies*

When the goblins came knocking
Hines, Gary. *A ride in the crummy*
Hoban, Lillian. *Silly Tilly's Valentine*
Hoopes, Lyn Littlefield. *Half a button*
Johnson, Angela. *The Rolling Store*
Ketner, Mary Grace. *Ganzy remembers*
Kramlich, Carolyn Walz. *Mary's treasure box*
Kroll, Virginia L. *Fireflies, peach pies, and lullabies*
Kübler-Ross, Elisabeth. *Remember the secret*
Laminack, Lester L. *The sunsets of Miss Olivia Wiggins*
Laser, Michael. *The rain*
Leedahl, Shelley A. (Shelley Ann). *The bone talker*
Lyon, George Ella. *A sign*
Marshak, S. (Samuil). *The absentminded fellow*
Martin, Bill (William Ivan). *Sounds I remember*
Martin, Jacqueline Briggs. *The finest horse in town*
Newman, Lesléa. *Remember that*
Nobisso, Josephine. *Grandma's scrapbook*
Oppenheim, Joanne. *Rooter remembers*
Priceman, Marjorie. *My nine lives / by Clio*
Raven, Margot. *Angels in the dust*
Repchuk, Caroline. *The forgotten garden*
Rochelle, Belinda. *Jewels*
Rowe, John A. *Smudge*
Satterfield, Barbara. *The story dance*
Schaefer, Carole Lexa. *The copper tin cup*
Schick, Eleanor. *Mama*
Scott, Geoffrey. *Memorial Day*
Seuss, Dr. *Please try to remember the first of Octember!*
Shecter, Ben. *Grandma remembers*
Spalding, Andrea. *Me and Mr. Mah*
Sarah May and the new red dress
Tompert, Ann. *Little Otter remembers and other stories*
Vizurraga, Susan. *Our old house*
Wahl, Jan. *"I remember," cried Grandma Pinky*
Walsh, Jill Paton. *When I was little like you*
Watson, Mary. *The butterfly seeds*
Weinberg, Lawrence. *The Forgetful Bears meet Mr. Memory*
Wild, Margaret. *Remember me*
Woodruff, Elvira. *The memory coat*
Zagwÿn, Deborah Turney. *The winter gift*
Zalben, Jane Breskin. *Pearl's marigolds for grandpa*

Menehunes *see* Mythical creatures – menehunes

Mental handicaps *see* Handicaps – mental handicaps

Mental illness *see* Illness – mental illness

Mermaids *see* Mythical creatures – mermaids, mermen

Mermen *see* Mythical creatures – mermaids, mermen

Merry-go-rounds

Ardizzone, Edward. *Paul, the hero of the fire*
Bowdish, Lynea. *The carousel ride*
Brown, Marcia. *The little carousel*
Charles, R. H. (Robert Henry). *The roundabout turn*
Chorao, Kay. *Carousel round and round*

Clements, Andrew. *Workshop*
Crews, Donald. *Carousel*
Cummings, Pat. *Carousel*
Greaves, Margaret. *The star horse*
Leigh, Oretta. *The merry-go-round*
Martin, Bill (William Ivan). *Up and down on the merry-go-round*
Murphy, Stuart J. *Animals on board*
Noble, Kate. *The dragon of Navy Pier*
Perera, Lydia. *Frisky*
Rosenberg, Liz. *The carousel*
Schneider, Elisa. *The merry-go-round dog*
Thomas, Art. *Merry-go-rounds*
Wildsmith, Brian. *Carousel*

Messy *see* Behavior – messy

Metamorphosis

Abisch, Roz. *Let's find out about butterflies*
Bunting, Eve (Anne Evelyn). *Butterfly house*
Carle, Eric. *The very hungry caterpillar*
The caterpillar who turned into a butterfly
Crozat, François. *I am a little caterpillar*
Cutts, David. *Look . . . a butterfly*
Darby, Gene. *What is a butterfly?*
Delaney, Ned. *One dragon to another*
DeLuise, Dom. *Charlie the caterpillar*
Ernst, Lisa Campbell. *Bubba and Trixie*
French, Vivian. *Caterpillar, caterpillar*
Gibbons, Gail. *Monarch butterfly*
Glaser, Linda. *Wonderful worms*
Hariton, Anca. *Butterfly story*
Heiligman, Deborah. *From caterpillar to butterfly*
Hogan, Paula Z. *The butterfly*
Kent, Jack. *The caterpillar and the polliwog*
Legg, Gerald. *From caterpillar to butterfly*
McClung, Robert. *Sphinx*
Maple, Marilyn J. *On the wings of a butterfly*
Marzollo, Jean. *I'm a caterpillar*
May, Kara. *Creepy crawly caterpillar*
Murphy, Mary. *Caterpillar's wish*
O'Hagan, Caroline. *It's easy to have a caterpillar visit you*
Ryder, Joanne. *Where butterflies grow*
Selsam, Millicent E. *A first look at caterpillars*
Sturges, Philemon. *What's that sound, Woolly Bear?*
Thompson, Susan L. *Diary of a monarch butterfly*
Watts, Barrie. *Butterfly and caterpillar*
Wong, Herbert H. *Our caterpillars*

Mexican Americans *see* Ethnic groups in the U.S. – Hispanic Americans; Ethnic groups in the U.S. – Mexican Americans

Mexico *see* Foreign lands – Mexico

Mice *see* Animals – mice

Micmac Indians *see* Indians of North America – Micmac

Middle Ages

Aiken, Joan. *The shoemaker's boy*
Althea. *Castle life*
Arnold, Tedd. *Ollie forgot*
Azarian, Mary. *The tale of John Barleycorn or, From barley to beer*
Babbitt, Natalie. *Bub, or, The very best thing*
Bahous, Sally. *Sitti and the cats*
Biro, Val. *The pied piper of Hamelin*
Bishop, Ann. *The riddle ages*
Black, Charles C. *The royal nap*
Carrick, Donald. *Harold and the great stag*
Cecil, Laura. *The frog princess*
Cohen, Barbara. *Here come the Purim players!*, ill. by Beverly Brodsky McDermott
Coombs, Patricia. *The magician and McTree*
Cressey, James. *The dragon and George*
Curry, Jane Louise. *The Christmas knight*
Dick Whittington and his cat. *Dick Whittington*, ill. by Edward Ardizzone
  Dick Whittington, ill. by Antony Maitland
  Dick Whittington and his cat, ill. by Marcia Brown
  Dick Whittington and his cat, ill. by Kurt Werth
Fradon, Dana. *Sir Dana - a knight*
Gerrard, Roy. *Sir Cedric*
  Sir Cedric rides again
Gibbons, Gail. *Knights in shining armor*
Hazen, Barbara Shook. *The knight who was afraid of the dark*
  The knight who was afraid to fight
Herford, Oliver. *The most timid in the land*
Hodges, Margaret. *The kitchen knight*
  Saint George and the dragon
Kahl, Virginia. *The Baron's booty*
  The Duchess bakes a cake
Krensky, Stephen. *We just moved!*
Löfgren, Ulf. *Alvin the Knight*
McAllister, Angela. *The battle of Sir Cob and Sir Filbert*
Manson, Christopher. *Here begins the tale of the marvellous blue mouse*
Mayer, Mercer. *Whinnie the lovesick dragon*
Phillips, Louis. *The brothers Wrong and Wrong Again*
Richardson, Jean. *Stephen's feast*
Saltzman, David. *The jester has lost his jingle*
Scarry, Huck. *Looking into the Middle Ages*
Scarry, Richard. *Richard Scarry's Peasant Pig and the terrible dragon*
Shannon, Mark. *The acrobat and the angel*
  Gawain and the Green Knight
Singer, Marilyn. *The maiden on the moor*
Steig, William. *The toy brother*
Storr, Catherine (Cole). *Robin Hood*
Tompert, Ann. *Charlotte and Charles*
Tucker, Kathy. *Do knights take naps?*
Woychuk, Denis. *The other side of the wall*
Yep, Laurence. *The man who tricked a ghost*

Middle East *see* Foreign lands – Middle East

Migrant workers *see* Careers – migrant workers

Migration

Manning, Mick. *Honk! honk!*
Sayre, April Pulley. *Home at last*
  Turtle, turtle, watch out!
  Swan flyway
Swope, Sam. *Gotta go! Gotta go!*

Military *see* Careers – military

Mimes *see* Clowns, jesters

Miners *see* Careers – miners

Minks *see* Animals – minks

Minorities *see* Ethnic groups in the U.S.

Mirages *see* Optical illusions

Mirrors

Day, Alexandra. *Mirror*

Misbehavior *see* Behavior – misbehavior

Missions

Politi, Leo. *Song of the swallows*

Missisauga *see* Indians of North America – Missisauga

Mist *see* Weather – fog

Mistakes *see* Behavior – mistakes

Misunderstanding *see* Behavior – misunderstanding

Mittens *see* Clothing – gloves, mittens

Miwok Indians *see* Indians of North America – Miwok

Mockingbirds *see* Birds – mockingbirds

Models *see* Careers – models

Modoc Indians *see* Indians of North America – Modoc

Mohawk Indians *see* Indians of North America – Mohawk

Moles *see* Animals – moles

Money

Arnold, Caroline. *What will we buy?*
Axelrod, Amy. *Pigs will be pigs*
Baylor, Byrd. *The table where rich people sit*
Berenstain, Stan. *The Berenstain bears' trouble with money*
Brenner, Barbara A. *The five pennies*
Brooks, Ben. *Lemonade parade*
Brown, Marc Tolon. *Arthur's TV trouble*
Brown, Marcia. *The little carousel*
Caple, Kathy. *The purse*
Chardiet, Bernice. *Martin and the tooth fairy*
Cole, Joanna. *Don't tell the whole world*
Day, Alexandra. *Paddy's pay-day*
Gill, Shelley. *The big buck adventure*
Hoban, Lillian. *Arthur's funny money*
Inkpen, Mick. *The great pet sale*

Kent, Jack. *Piggy Bank Gonzalez*
Kimmel, Eric A. *Four dollars and fifty cents*
Langford, Sondra Gordon. *Mishka and Plishka*
Leedy, Loreen. *The monster money book*
Love, Ann. *Ice cream at the castle*
McMillan, Bruce. *Jelly beans for sale*
Maestro, Betsy. *Dollars and cents for Harriet*
Mantinband, Gerda. *Blabbermouths*
Mollel, Tololwa M. (Tololwa Marti). *My rows and piles of coins*
Murphy, Stuart J. *The penny pot*
A paper of pins
Rockwell, Anne F. *Gogo's pay day*
Rose, Anne K. *As right as right can be*
Slobodkin, Louis. *Moon Blossom and the golden penny*
Smalls-Hector, Irene. *Irene and the big, fine nickel*
Stewart, Sarah. *The money tree*
Turkle, Brinton. *Rachel and Obadiah*
Underhill, Liz. *The lucky coin*
Vaughan, Marcia Kapok. *The lemonade stand*
Vincent, Gabrielle. *Bravo, Ernest and Celestine!*
Viorst, Judith. *Alexander, who used to be rich last Sunday*
Wells, Rosemary. *Bunny money*
Wondriska, William. *Mr. Brown and Mr. Gray*
Yardley, Thompson. *Buy now, pay later*
Zimelman, Nathan. *How the second grade got $8,205.50 to visit the Statue of Liberty*

Mongolia *see* Foreign lands – Mongolia

Mongooses *see* Animals – mongooses

Monitor lizards *see* Reptiles – monitor lizards

Monkeys *see* Animals – monkeys

Monsters

Ahlberg, Allan. *The ghost train*
Me and my friend
Alexander, Lloyd. *The house Gobbaleen*
Alexander, Martha G. *Maybe a monster*
Alexander, Sue. *Who goes out on Halloween?*
Allen, Martha Dickson. *Real life monsters*
Ambrus, Victor G. *Count, Dracula*
Son of Dracula
What's the time, Dracula?
Apple, Margot. *Brave Martha*
Arnold, Caroline. *The terrible Hodag*
Arnold, Tedd. *Five ugly monsters*
Huggly gets dressed
Huggly takes a bath
Auch, Mary Jane. *Monster brother*
Axworthy, Anni. *Ben's Wednesday*
Babbitt, Natalie. *The something*
Baggette, Susan K. *Jonathan goes to the library*
Bang, Molly. *Wiley and the hairy man*
Barden, Rosalind. *TV monster*
Bartels, Alice L. *The beast*
Basso, Bill. *The top of the pizzas*
Benjamin, Alan. *1000 monsters*
Bennett, Jill. *Spooky poems*
Bergström, Gunilla. *Is that a monster, Alfie Atkins?*
Berlan, Kathryn Hook. *Andrew's amazing monsters*
Bird, Malcolm. *The school in Murky Wood*
Blake, Quentin. *Zagazoo*

Hutton, Warwick. *Theseus and the Minotaur*
Impey, Rose. *The ankle grabber*
  The flat man
  Scare yourself to sleep
Jackson, Ellen B. *Monsters in my mailbox*
Jackson, Jean. *Big lips and hairy arms*
  Thorndike and Nelson
Johnson, Jane. *Today I thought I'd run away*
Johnston, Tony. *Four scary stories*
Kahl, Virginia. *Giants, indeed!*
  How do you hide a monster?
Kamish, Daniel. *The night scary beasties popped out of my head*
Kasza, Keiko. *Grandpa Toad's last secret*
Kellogg, Steven (Stephen). *The island of the skog*
  The mysterious tadpole
Kimura, Yasuko. *Fergus and the sea monster*
Kleven, Elisa. *A monster in the house*
Koelling, Caryl. *Mad monsters mix and match*
Koller, Jackie French. *No such thing*
Krahn, Fernando. *The mystery of the giant footprints*
Kraus, Robert. *The phantom of Creepy Hollow*
Kunnas, Mauri. *One spooky night and other scary stories*
LaRose, Linda. *Jessica takes charge*
Laslett, Stephanie. *The monster party*
Leedy, Loreen. *The monster money book*
Lerner, Sharon. *Follow the monsters!*
Leuck, Laura. *My monster mama loves me so*
Lewin, Betsy. *Wiley learns to spell*
Lifton, Betty Jean. *Goodnight orange monster*
Logue, Christopher. *The magic circus*
Lottridge, Celia B. (Celia Barker). *Something might be hiding*
McDonald, Megan. *Bedbugs*
McKee, David. *The monster and the teddy bear*
  Two monsters
McMullan, Kate (Hall). *Creepy riddles*
McPhail, David M. *The Glerp*
McQueen, John Troy. *A world full of monsters*
Maisner, Heather. *Save Brave Ted*
Marshall, Edward. *Four on the shore*
Marshall, James. *Three up a tree*
Martin, Bill (William Ivan). *A beasty story*
Mason, Jane B. *The flying horse*
Mayer, Marianna. *Pegasus*
Mayer, Mercer. *Little Monster at home*
  Little Monster at school
  Little Monster at work
  Little Monster's alphabet book
  Little Monster's bedtime book
  Little Monster's counting book
  Little Monster's neighborhood
  Liza Lou and the Yeller Belly Swamp
  Mrs. Beggs and the wizard
  Terrible troll
  There's a nightmare in my closet
Meddaugh, Susan. *Beast*
Medearis, Angela Shelf. *Tailypo*
Medicine Crow, Joseph. *Brave Wolf and the Thunderbird*
Memling, Carl. *What's in the dark?*
Michelson, Richard. *Did you say ghosts?*
Miller, Edward. *The curse of Claudia*
Mills, Lauren A. *The dog prince*
Minsberg, David. *The book monster*
Miranda, Anne. *Monster math*
Modarressi, Mitra. *The beastly visits*
Moffatt, Judith. *Trick-or-treat faces*

Mollel, Tololwa M. (Tololwa Marti). *Song bird*
Monster poems
Monster soup and other spooky poems
Moodie, Fiona. *Nabulela*
Moore, Lilian. *See my lovely poison ivy, and other verses about witches, ghosts and things*
Mooser, Stephen. *Funnyman meets the monster from outer space*
Morris, Ann. *Eleanora Mousie in the dark*
Morris, Terry Nell. *Good night, dear monster!*
Mosel, Arlene. *The funny little woman*
Moss, Marissa. *After-school monster*
Most, Bernard. *Boo!*
Mueller, Virginia. *A Halloween mask for Monster*
  Monster and the baby
  Monster can't sleep
  Monster goes to school
  Monster's birthday hiccups
  A playhouse for Monster
Murphy, Jill. *All for one*
  The last noo-noo
Murphy, Shirley Rousseau. *Valentine for a dragon*
Myers, Amy. *I know a monster*
Namm, Diane. *Monsters!*
Newsham, Wendy. *The monster hunt*
Nightingale, Sandy. *I'm a little monster*
Niland, Deborah. *ABC of monsters*
Nixon, Joan Lowery. *Bigfoot makes a movie*
Nolan, Lucy A. *The Lizard Man of Crabtree County*
Numeroff, Laura Joffe. *Monster munchies*
O'Keefe, Susan Heyboer. *One hungry monster*
Olofsdotter, Marie. *Sofia and the Heartmender*
O'Malley, Kevin. *Velcome*
Packard, Mary. *We are monsters*
Paige, Rob. *Some of my best friends are monsters*
Paraskevas, Betty. *Cecil Bunions and the midnight train*
  Maggie and the Ferocious Beast, the big carrot
  Maggie and the Ferocious Beast, the big scare
  Monster Beach
Parish, Peggy. *No more monsters for me!*
  Zed and the monsters
Park, Barbara. *Pssst! It's me . . . the Bogeyman*
Parker, Nancy Winslow. *Love from Aunt Betty*
Peet, Bill (William Bartlett). *Cyrus the unsinkable sea serpent*
Pinkney, J. Brian. *Cosmo and the robot*
Pinkwater, Daniel Manus. *The Frankenbagel monster*
  I was a second grade werewolf
Polacco, Patricia. *Some birthday!*
Polisar, Barry Louis. *The haunted house party*
Prelutsky, Jack. *The baby uggs are hatching*
Riddell, Chris. *Mr. Underbed*
  The wish factory
Riggio, Anita. *Beware the Brindlebeast*
Rix, Jamie. *The last chocolate cookie*
Robison, Nancy. *Ten tall soldiers*
Rockwell, Anne F. *The one-eyed giant and other monsters from the Greek Myths*
  Thump thump thump!
Root, Phyllis. *The hungry monster*
Ross, Dave (David). *Gorp and the space pirates*
  Space monster
  Space Monster Gorp and the runaway computer
Ross, Gayle. *The legend of the Windigo*
Ross, H. L. *Not counting monsters*
Ross, Tony. *I'm coming to get you!*
  Towser and the terrible thing
Sabraw, John. *I wouldn't be scared*

Salter, Heidi. *Taddy McFinley and the great grey grimly*
Samton, Sheila White. *Ten tiny monsters*
San Souci, Robert D. *The Hobyahs*
  Pedro and the monkey
Schroder, William. *Pea soup and serpents*
Seeger, Pete. *Abiyoyo*
Selsam, Millicent E. *Sea monsters of long ago*
Sendak, Maurice. *Seven little monsters*
  Where the wild things are
Seymour, Peter S. *What's at the beach?*
Shannon, Margaret. *Gullible's troubles*
Shannon, Mark. *Gawain and the Green Knight*
Sharmat, Marjorie Weinman. *The pizza monster*
  Scarlet Monster lives here
Sierra, Judy. *The house that Drac built*
  Wiley and the Hairy Man
Silverman, Erica. *The Halloween house*
Simms, Laura. *The bone man*
Sis, Peter. *Ship ahoy!*
Skwarek, Skip. *Mystery of Maggoty Mill*
Smith, Janice Lee. *The monster in the third dresser drawer and other stories about Adam Joshua*
Snow, Alan. *The monster book of ABC sounds*
Solotareff, Grégoire. *The ogre and the frog king*
Steig, William. *Rotten island*
Steptoe, John. *Daddy is a monster . . . sometimes*
Stern, Peter. *Max the dragon*
Stevens, Kathleen. *The beast in the bathtub*
Stevenson, James. *"Could be worse!"*
Strete, Craig Kee. *The lost boy and the monster*
Taylor, Judy. *Dudley and the monster*
Thomas, Frances. *What if?*
Tunnell, Michael O. *Halloween pie*
Turkle, Brinton. *Do not open*
Ungerer, Tomi. *The beast of Monsieur Racine*
  Zeralda's ogre
Van Nutt, Julia. *The monster in the shadows*
Viorst, Judith. *My mama says there aren't any zombies, ghosts, vampires, creatures, demons, monsters, fiends, goblins, or things*
Wagner, Jenny. *Amy's monster*
  The bunyip of Berkeley's Creek
Wahl, Jan. *Dracula's cat*
  Dracula's cat and Frankenstein's dog
  Frankenstein's dog
Waldron, Jan L. *John Pig's Halloween*
Watson, Pauline. *Wriggles, the little wishing pig*
Weeks, Sarah. *Happy birthday, Frankie*
Whitlock, Susan Love. *Donovan scares the monsters*
Willis, Jeanne. *The monster bed*
  The monster storm
Willoughby, Elaine Macmann. *Boris and the monsters*
Winthrop, Elizabeth. *Maggie and the monster*
Yep, Laurence. *The Khan's daughter*
Young, Ed (Edward). *The terrible Nung Gwama*
Zemach, Harve. *The judge*

Monsters – vampires

Gralley, Jean. *Hogula, dread pig of night*
Holleyman, Sonia. *Mona the vampire*

Months of the year *see* Days of the week, months of the year

Moon

Agee, Jon. *Dmitri the astronaut*
Alexander, Martha G. *Maggie's moon*
Asch, Frank. *Happy birthday, moon!*
  Moonbear
  Mooncake
  Moondance
  Moongame
Asimov, Isaac. *The moon*
Babcock, Chris. *No moon, no milk!*
Bacon, Ethel. *To see the moon*
Balet, Jan B. *Amos and the moon*
Balzola, Asun. *Munia and the moon*
Banks, Kate (Katherine A.). *And if the moon could talk*
Baum, Louis. *I want to see the moon*
Baylor, Byrd. *Moon song*
Beifuss, John. *Armadillo Ray*
Berenstain, Stan. *The Berenstain bears on the moon*
Berger, Barbara Helen. *Grandfather Twilight*
  A lot of otters
Bess, Clayton. *The truth about the moon*
Branley, Franklyn M. (Mansfield). *The moon seems to change*
  What the moon is like
Brown, Margaret Wise. *Goodnight moon*
  The sleepy men
  Wait till the moon is full
Buchanan, Heather S. *George and Matilda Mouse and the moon rocket*
Bunting, Eve (Anne Evelyn). *Moonstick*
Carle, Eric. *Papa, please get the moon for me*
Carlstrom, Nancy White. *Who gets the sun out of bed?*
Cazet, Denys. *Christmas moon*
Chadwick, Tim. *Cabbage moon*
Choldenko, Gennifer. *Moonstruck*
Coats, Laura Jane. *Marcella and the moon*
Come out to play
Crews, Nina. *I'll catch the moon*
Daly, Niki. *Mary Malloy and the baby who wouldn't sleep*
  Why the sun and moon live in the sky
Dayrell, Elphinstone. *Why the sun and the moon live in the sky*
De Gerez, Toni. *Louhi, witch of North Farm*
Demarest, Chris L. *The lunatic adventure of Kitman and Willy*
De Paola, Tomie (Thomas Anthony). *The Prince of the Dolomites*
  The unicorn and the moon
De Regniers, Beatrice Schenk. *Willy O'Dwyer jumped in the fire*
Desimini, Lisa. *Moon soup*
  Sun and moon
Doherty, Berlie. *The midnight man*
Duncan, Lois. *Birthday moon*
Ehlert, Lois. *Moon rope*
Fowler, Allan. *So that's how the moon changes shape!*
Fowler, Susi Gregg. *I'll see you when the moon is full*
Freeman, Mae Blacker. *The sun, the moon and the stars*
  You will go to the moon
Fuchs, Erich. *Journey to the moon*
Gantschev, Ivan. *Good morning, good night*
  The moon lake
  Where the moon lives
Garcia, Carolyn. *Moonboy*

Garelick, May. *Look at the moon*, ill. by Barbara Garrison
    Look at the moon, ill. by Leonard Weisgard
Gay, Marie-Louise. *Moonbeam on a cat's ear*
Gregory, Valiska. *When stories fell like shooting stars*
Griffith, Helen V. *Alex remembers*
Haddon, Mark. *The Sea of Tranquillity*
Heckman, Philip. *The moon is following me*
Hergé. *Explorers on the moon*
Hillert, Margaret. *Up, up and away*
Hillman, Elizabeth. *Min-Yo and the moon dragon*
Hines, Anna Grossnickle. *Moon's wish*
Hodges, Margaret. *Buried moon*
Hughes, Shirley. *Abel's moon*
Hunter, Anne. *Possum's harvest moon*
Ikeda, Daisaku. *The princess and the moon*
Iwamura, Kazuo. *The fourteen forest mice and the harvest moon watch*
Janosch. *Joshua and the magic fiddle*
Jones, Joy. *Tambourine moon*
King, Christopher L. *The boy who ate the moon*
Kirk, Daniel. *Moondogs*
Kraus, Robert. *See the moon*
Kurt, Kemal. *The five fingers and the moon*
Lankford, Mary D. *Is it dark? Is it light?*
Lester, Robin. *Wuzzy takes off*
Levitin, Sonia. *Who owns the moon?*
Lewis, Claudia Louise. *When I go to the moon*
Lewis, J. Patrick. *The moonbow of Mr. B. Bones*
Lewison, Wendy Cheyette. *Nighty-night*
Lifton, Betty Jean. *The rice-cake rabbit*
Lindbergh, Reeve. *What is the sun?*
Little, Mimi Otey. *Blue moon soup spoon*
Lussert, Anneliese. *The farmer and the moon*
McDermott, Gerald. *Anansi the spider*
    Papagayo, the mischief maker
McPartland, Suzy. *Sleepy-time moon*
Macsolis. *Baile de luna*
Manuel, Lynn. *The night the moon blew kisses*
Manushkin, Fran. *Moon dragon*
Marton, Jirina. *Midnight visit at Molly's house*
Matura, Mustapha. *Moon jump*
Merrill, Jean. *Emily Emerson's moon*
Mitra, Annie. *Penguin moon*
Moché, Dinah L. *The astronauts*
Mora, Pat. *The night the moon fell*
Moroney, Lynn. *Moontellers*
Mother Goose. *Hey diddle, diddle*, ill. by Moira Kemp
Nicoll, Helen. *Meg on the moon*
Oakley, Graham. *The church mice and the moon*
Olsen, Ib Spang. *The boy in the moon*
Oppenheim, Shulamith Levey. *What is the full moon full of?*
Oram, Hiawyn. *Mole's moon*
Oxenbury, Helen. *Tom and Pippo see the moon*
Pfister, Marcus. *I see the moon*
Pierson, Judith Patterson. *The always moon*
Powell, Roxanne Dyer. *Cat, mouse and moon*
Preston, Edna Mitchell. *Squawk to the moon, little goose*
Raschka, Christopher. *Can't sleep*
Rattigan, Jama Kim. *The woman in the moon*
Rosen, Sidney. *Where does the moon go?*
Rosenberg, Liz. *Window, mirror, moon*
Rowe, John A. *Rabbit moon*
Salter, Mary Jo. *The moon comes home*
Sanfield, Steve. *Just rewards, or, Who is that man in the moon and what's he doing up there anyway?*

Schaefer, Carole Lexa. *Sometimes moon*
Scheidl, Gerda Marie. *The moon man*
Schertle, Alice. *Witch Hazel*
Schmid, Eleonore. *The squirrel and the moon*
Schweninger, Ann. *The man in the moon as he sails the sky and other moon verse*
Shea, Pegi Deitz. *New moon*
Simms, Laura. *Moon and Otter and Frog*
Skofield, James. *Crow moon, worm moon*
Sleator, William. *The angry moon*
Speed, Toby. *Two cool cows*
Stevens, Cat. *Teaser and the firecat*
Stevenson, Robert Louis. *The moon*
Storm, Theodor. *Little Hobbin*
Tafuri, Nancy. *What the sun sees / What the moon sees*
Tan, Amy. *The moon lady*
Thaler, Mike. *Moonkey*
Thurber, James. *Many moons*, ill. by Marc Simont
    Many moons, ill. by Louis Slobodkin
Turner, Charles. *The turtle and the moon*
Turska, Krystyna. *The magician of Cracow*
Udry, Janice May. *The moon jumpers*
Ungerer, Tomi. *Moon man*
Vail, Rachel. *Over the moon*
Vaughn, Jenny. *On the moon*
VerDorn, Bethea. *Moon glows*
Wahl, Jan. *Cabbage moon*
Ward, Helen. *The moonrat and the white turtle*
Watson, Clyde. *Midnight moon*
Weedn, Flavia. *The moon maiden*
Wildsmith, Brian. *What the moon saw*
Willard, Nancy. *The nightgown of the sullen moon*
Winter, Jeanette. *The girl and the moon man*
Wood, Audrey. *Moonflute*
Wood, Douglas. *Rabbit and the moon*
Wynne-Jones, Tim. *Builder of the moon*
Yaccarino, Dan. *Zoom! Zoom! Zoom! I'm off to the moon!*
Yamaguchi, Tohr. *Two crabs and the moonlight*
Young, James. *Everyone loves the moon*
Ziefert, Harriet. *Moonride*
    Who can boo the loudest?
Ziegler, Ursina. *Squaps the moonling*
Zolotow, Charlotte (Shapiro). *The moon was the best*

Moose *see* Animals – moose

Mopeds *see* Motorcycles

Morning

Alda, Arlene. *Pig, horse, or cow, don't wake me now*
Anglund, Joan Walsh. *Morning is a little child*
Aylesworth, Jim. *Wake up, little children*
Barbato, Juli. *From bed to bus*
Beach, Stewart. *Good morning, sun's up!*
Brown, Margaret Wise. *A child's good morning book*
    The quiet noisy book
Caldwell, Mary. *Morning, rabbit, morning*
Capucilli, Alyssa Satin. *Good morning, pond*
Carlstrom, Nancy White. *Who gets the sun out of bed?*
Chall, Marsha Wilson. *Rupa raises the sun*
Chase, Edith Newlin. *Secret dawn*
Chorao, Kay. *The baby's good morning book*
Christiansen, C. B. *Mara in the morning*
Conrad, Pam. *The rooster's gift*
Craig, M. Jean. *Spring is like the morning*
    What did you dream?

Dale, Penny. *Wake up, Mr. B.!*
Dennis, Lynne. *Raymond Rabbit's early morning*
Dennis, Wesley. *Flip and the morning*
Dragonwagon, Crescent. *Katie in the morning*
Dryden, Emma. *Good morning - good night*
Farjeon, Eleanor. *Morning has broken*
Funakoshi, Canna. *One morning*
Grindley, Sally. *Wake up, dad!*
Harrison, David Lee. *Wake up, sun!*
Hellard, Susan. *Time to get up*
Henkes, Kevin. *Shhhh*
Hill, Eric. *Good morning, baby bear*
Himler, Ronald. *Wake up, Jeremiah*
Hudson, Cheryl Willis. *Good morning baby*
Jacobs, Shannon K. *The boy who loved morning*
Johnston, Deborah. *Mathew Michael's beastly day*
Kandoian, Ellen. *Under the sun*
Lakin, Pat (Patricia). *Dad and me in the morning*
Lapp, Eleanor. *In the morning mist*
McNulty, Faith. *When a boy wakes up in the morning*
McPartland, Suzy. *Good morning, sun*
Mann, Peggy. *King Laurence, the alarm clock*
Meeker, Clare Hodgson. *Who wakes rooster?*
Moore, Dessie. *Good morning*
Moore, Elaine. *Good morning, city*
Most, Bernard. *Cock-a-doodle-moo!*
Mueller, Virginia. *In the morning*
Murphy, Stuart J. *Get up and go!*
Ormerod, Jan. *Sunshine*
Oxenbury, Helen. *Good night, good morning*
Pilkey, Dav. *The paperboy*
Pittman, Helena Clare. *Sunrise*
Polushkin, Maria. *Morning*
Raffi. *Rise and shine*
Ray, Deborah Kogan. *Fog drift morning*
Rogers, Paul (Patrick). *Somebody's awake*
Shulevitz, Uri. *Dawn*
Silverman, Erica. *Fixing the crack of dawn*
Tafuri, Nancy. *Early morning in the barn*
Tresselt, Alvin R. *Wake up, city!*
    Wake up, farm!, ill. by author
    Wake up, farm!, ill. by Carolyn Ewing
Tworkov, Jack. *The camel who took a walk*
VerDorn, Bethea. *Day breaks*
Westcott, Nadine Bernard. *Getting up*
Whitman, Candace. *Now it is morning*
Yabuki, Seiji. *I love the morning*
Ziefert, Harriet. *Good morning, sun!*
    Say good night!
Zolotow, Charlotte (Shapiro). *Something is going to happen*
    Wake up and goodnight

Morocco *see* Foreign lands – Morocco

Moses *see* Religion – Moses

Mosquitoes *see* Insects – mosquitoes

Mother Goose *see* Nursery rhymes

Mothers *see* Family life – mothers

Mother's Day *see* Holidays – Mother's Day

Moths *see* Insects – moths

Motorcycles

Cave, Ron. *Motorcycles*
Cleary, Beverly. *Lucky Chuck*
Dickens, Frank. *Boffo*
McPhail, David M. *Captain Toad and the motorbike*
Zimnik, Reiner. *The bear on the motorcycle*

Mountain climbing *see* Sports – mountain climbing

Mountain lions *see* Animals – cougars

Mountains

Arnold, Caroline. *A walk up the mountain*
Hirschi, Ron. *Mountain*
Kimmel, Eric A. *The two mountains*
Lasky, Kathryn. *The Gates of the Wind*
Lawson, Julie. *Midnight in the mountains*
Luenn, Nancy. *Miser on the mountain*
Ray, Mary Lyn. *Basket moon*
Swanson, June. *Summit up*
Wells, Rosemary. *The bear went over the mountain*
Zoehfeld, Kathleen Weidner. *How mountains are made*

Mouths *see* Anatomy – mouths

Moving

Ackerman, Karen. *The sleeping porch*
Adshead, Gladys L. *Brownies - they're moving*
Aliki. *Best friends together again*
    We are best friends
Asch, Frank. *Goodbye house*
Ballard, Robin. *Good-bye, house*
Barbour, Karen. *Nancy*
Becker, Edna. *Nine hundred buckets of paint*
Berenstain, Stan. *The Berenstain bears' moving day*
Berg, Jean Horton. *The O'Learys and friends*
Bond, Felicia. *Poinsettia and her family*
Bottner, Barbara. *Horrible Hannah*
Bresnick-Perry, Roslyn. *Leaving for America*
Cadnum, Michael. *The lost and found house*
Carlstrom, Nancy White. *I'm not moving, mama!*
Carter, Anne. *Molly in danger*
Carter, Penny. *A new house for the Morrisons*
Cartlidge, Michelle. *A house for Lily Mouse*
Cassedy, Sylvia. *The best cat suit of all*
Clifton, Lucille. *Good, says Jerome*
Clymer, Eleanor Lowenton. *A yard for John*
Cohen, Barbara. *Gooseberries to oranges*
Davies, Sally. *When William went away*
Day, Alexandra. *The Christmas we moved to the barn*
DeLage, Ida. *The old witch finds a new house*
Delton, Judy. *Lee Henry's best friend*
Denslow, Sharon Phillips. *Woollybear good-bye*
Disher, Garry. *Switch cat*
Dowling, Paul. *Meg and Jack are moving*
    Meg and Jack's new friends
Dugan, Barbara. *Leaving home with a pickle jar*
Engel, Diana. *Fishing*
Felt, Sue. *Hello-goodbye*
Fiday, Beverly. *Time to go*
Figueredo, D. H. *When this world was new*
Finsand, Mary Jane. *The town that moved*
Fisher, Aileen Lucia. *Best little house*

Giffard, Hannah. *Red Fox on the move*
Gilmore, Rachna. *Lights for Gita*
Graham, Bob. *First there was Frances*
    Spirit of Hope
Gretz, Susanna. *Teddy bears' moving day*
Halpern, Shari. *Moving from one to ten*
Harper, Jo. *Prairie dog pioneers*
Harshman, Marc. *Moving days*
Havill, Juanita. *Jamaica's blue marker*
Hazen, Barbara Shook. *Good-bye/Hello*
Hendry, Diana. *Not anywhere house*
Hest, Amy. *Best-ever good-bye party*
Hickman, Martha Whitmore. *My friend William*
    moved away
Hilton, Nette. *Andrew Jessup*
Hoff, Syd. *Who will be my friends?*
Hughes, Shirley. *Moving Molly*
Ilsley, Velma. *M is for moving*
Isadora, Rachel. *The Potters' kitchen*
James, Betsy. *Mary Ann*
Jennings, Michael. *The bears who came to breakfix*
Johnson, Angela. *The leaving morning*
Johnston, Tony. *The quilt story*
Jones, Penelope. *I'm not moving!*
Kalan, Robert. *Moving day*
Karas, G. Brian. *Home on the bayou*
Keats, Ezra Jack. *The trip*
Keyworth, C. L. *New day*
Kinsey-Warnock, Natalie. *Wilderness cat*
Koller, Jackie French. *Mole and Shrew*
Komaiko, Leah. *Annie Bananie*
Krensky, Stephen. *We just moved!*
Leighton, Maxinne Rhea. *An Ellis Island Christmas*
Lexau, Joan M. *The rooftop mystery*
Lobel, Arnold. *Ming Lo moves the mountain*
Lottridge, Celia B. (Celia Barker). *Something might*
    be hiding
Lystad, Mary H. *That new boy*
McCarthy, Bobette. *See you later, alligator*
McGeorge, Constance W. *Boomer's big day*
MacLachlan, Patricia. *What you know first*
McLerran, Alice. *I want to go home*
McNaughton, Colin. *Guess who's just moved in next*
    door?
Malone, Nola Langner. *A home*
Marshak, S. (Samuil). *In the van*
Maschler, Fay. *T. G. and Moonie move out of town*
Milord, Sue. *Maggie and the goodbye gift*
Moore, Inga. *Little dog lost*
Morris, Jill. *The boy who painted the sun*
Morrow, Barbara. *Help for Mr. Peale*
Munsch, Robert N. *From far away*
Newsome, Jill. *Shadow*
Obrist, Jürg. *Fluffy*
O'Donnell, Elizabeth Lee. *Maggie doesn't want to*
    move
O'Kelley, Mattie Lou. *Moving to town*
Patz, Nancy. *To Annabella Pelican from Thomas Hip-*
    popotamus
Pedersen, Judy. *Out in the country*
Provensen, Alice. *Shaker Lane*
Pryor, Bonnie. *The beaver boys*
Pulver, Robin. *Homer and the house next door*
Rabe, Berniece. *A smooth move*
Ransom, Candice F. *When the whippoorwill calls*
Rodell, Susanna. *Dear Fred*
Rogers, Fred. *Moving*
Ross, Lillian Hammer. *Buba Leah and her paper chil-*
    dren

Schlein, Miriam. *My house*
Schulman, Janet. *The big hello*
Sharmat, Marjorie Weinman. *Gila monsters meet you*
    at the airport
    Mitchell is moving
    Scarlet Monster lives here
Shecter, Ben. *Grandma remembers*
Shefelman, Janice Jordan. *Victoria House*
Sherrow, Victoria. *There goes the ghost*
Singer, Marilyn. *Archer Armadillo's secret room*
Snape, Juliet. *Frog odyssey*
Steel, Danielle. *Martha's new school*
Stevenson, James. *No friends*
Strathdee, Jean. *The house that grew*
Teague, Mark. *The trouble with the Johnsons*
Tobias, Tobi. *Moving day*
Tsutsui, Yoriko. *Anna's secret friend*
Turner, Ann Warren. *Dust for dinner*
    Stars for Sarah
Van Leeuwen, Jean. *Going west*
Viorst, Judith. *Alexander, who's not (Do you hear me?*
    I mean it!) going to move
Waber, Bernard. *Gina*
    Ira says goodbye
Watson, Jane Werner. *Sometimes a family has to move*
Watson, Wendy. *Moving*
Whitcher, Susan. *Something for everyone*
Wilhelm, Hans. *A new home, a new friend*
Woodruff, Elvira. *The wing shop*
Zagwÿn, Deborah Turney. *The winter gift*
Ziefert, Harriet. *A new house for Mole and Mouse*
Zolotow, Charlotte (Shapiro). *Janey*

Mules *see* Animals – mules

Multi-ethnic *see* Ethnic groups in the U.S.

Multiple birth children *see* Multiple births –
    sextuplets; Multiple births – triplets; Mul-
    tiple births – twins

Multiple births – sextuplets

Dilley, Becki. *Sixty fingers, sixty toes*

Multiple births – triplets

Abolafia, Yossi. *My three uncles*
Brunhoff, Jean de. *Babar and his children*
Lacoe, Addie. *Just not the same*
Lindman, Maj. *Flicka, Ricka, Dicka and a little dog*
    Flicka, Ricka, Dicka and the big red hen
    Flicka, Ricka, Dicka and the new dotted dress
    Flicka, Ricka, Dicka and the three kittens
    Flicka, Ricka, Dicka bake a cake
    Snipp, Snapp, Snurr and the buttered bread
    Snipp, Snapp, Snurr and the magic horse
    Snipp, Snapp, Snurr and the red shoes
    Snipp, Snapp, Snurr and the reindeer
    Snipp, Snapp, Snurr and the seven dogs
    Snipp, Snapp, Snurr and the yellow sled
Pirani, Felix. *Triplets*
Seuling, Barbara. *The triplets*

Multiple births – twins

Aliki. *Jack and Jake*
Anholt, Catherine. *Twins, two by two*

Balet, Jan B. *Ned and Ed and the lion*
Bos, Burny. *Meet the Molesons*
Brennan, Jan. *Born two-gether*
Brown, Marc Tolon. *Arthur babysits*
Browne, Vee. *Monster birds*
Bruna, Dick. *Lisa and Lynn*
   Tilly and Tess
Bunting, Eve (Anne Evelyn). *Twinnies*
Cleary, Beverly. *The growing-up feet*
   The real hole
   Two dog biscuits
Dalmais, Anne-Marie. *Molly and Mimi the mouse twins*
Denslow, Sharon Phillips. *On the trail with Miss Pace*
De Paola, Tomie (Thomas Anthony). *The bubble factory*
Doro, Ann. *Twin pickle*
Fuchshuber, Annegert. *Two peas in a pod*
Gabler, Mirko. *The alphabet soup*
Gerrard, Roy. *The Roman twins*
Givens, Terryl. *Dragon scales and willow leaves*
Gliori, Debi. *New big sister*
Gordon, Jeffie Ross. *Two badd babies*
Greenberg, Dan. *The bed who ran away from home*
Himmelman, John. *J.J. versus the babysitter*
Hoban, Lillian. *Here come raccoons*
Hutchins, Pat. *Which witch is which?*
Impey, Rose. *My mom and our dad*
Keller, Holly. *Harry and Tuck*
King-Smith, Dick. *Cuckoobush farm*
Kismaric, Carole. *The rumor of Pavel and Paali*
Lattimore, Deborah Nourse. *Punga the goddess of ugly*
Lawrence, James. *Binky Brothers and the fearless four*
   Binky Brothers, detectives
Leonard, Marcia. *Get the ball, Slim*
   The kitten twins
   Spots
Levi, Dorothy Hoffman. *A very special sister*
McDermott, Gerald. *The magic tree*
Mackinnon, Debbie. *Tom's train*
McKissack, Patricia C. *Who is who?*
Mahy, Margaret. *Down the dragon's tongue*
Metaxas, Eric. *Uncle Mugsy and the terrible twins of Christmas*
Moore, Lilian. *Little Raccoon and no trouble at all*
Neasi, Barbara J. *Just like me*
Obrist, Jürg. *Bear business*
Perkins, Al. *Don and Donna go to bat*
Rockwell, Anne F. *Romulus and Remus*
Rubel, Nicole. *Sam and Violet are twins*
   Sam and Violet go camping
Saint James, Synthia. *Sunday*
Simon, Carly. *Midnight farm*
Simon, Norma. *How do I feel?*
Steel, Danielle. *Max's new baby*
Stewart, Elizabeth Laing. *The lion twins*
Thompson, Vivian Laubach. *Camp-in-the-yard*
Wagner, Jenny. *Amy's monster*
Wagner, Karen. *Chocolate chip cookies*
Walters, Catherine. *Are you there, Baby Bear?*
Wisniewski, David. *The warrior and the wise man*
Yeoman, John. *The young performing horse*
Yorinks, Arthur. *Oh, brother*

Mummies

Allard, Harry. *Crash helmet*

Mumps *see* Illness – mumps

Muppets *see* Puppets

Muscular dystrophy *see* Illness – muscular dystrophy

Museum workers *see* Careers – museum workers

Museums

Alexander, Liza. *A visit to the Sesame Street Museum*
Aliki. *My visit to the dinosaurs*
Berenstain, Stan. *The Berenstain bears and the missing dinosaur bone*
Binnamin, Vivian. *The case of the snoring stegosaurus*
Blance, Ellen. *Monster goes to the museum*
Boehm, Arlene P. *Jack in search of Art*
Bourgeois, Paulette. *Franklin's class trip*
Brenner, Barbara A. *Dinosaurium*
Brown, Laurie Krasny. *Visiting the art museum*
Bunting, Eve (Anne Evelyn). *Night of the gargoyles*
Butterworth, Nick. *The school trip*
Carmack, Lisa Jobe. *Philippe in Monet's garden*
The Christmas story
Clayton, Elaine. *Ella's trip to the museum*
Clement, Rod. *Frank's great museum adventure*
Cohen, Miriam. *Lost in the museum*
De Paola, Tomie (Thomas Anthony). *Bill and Pete go down the Nile*
Everett, Gwen. *Li'l Sis and Uncle Willie*
Faulkner, Keith. *David dreaming of dinosaurs*
Floca, Brian. *The frightful story of Harry Walfish*
Fradon, Dana. *Sir Dana - a knight*
Freeman, Don. *Norman the doorman*
Gramatky, Hardie. *Hercules*
Hayward, Linda. *Ernie and Bert's summer project*
Hurd, Thacher. *Art dog*
J. Paul Getty Museum. *A is for artist*
Kellogg, Steven (Stephen). *Prehistoric Pinkerton*
Krementz, Jill. *A visit to Washington, D.C.*
L'Hommedieu, Arthur John. *Working at a museum*
Lionni, Leo. *Matthew's dream*
Löfgren, Ulf. *Alvin the Knight*
Mayers, Florence Cassen. *Egyptian art from the Brooklyn Museum*
   The Museum of Fine Arts, Boston
   The Museum of Modern Art, New York
   The National Air and Space Museum
Mayhew, James. *Katie and the dinosaurs*
   Katie and the Mona Lisa
   Katie meets the Impressionists
Morrow, Barbara. *Help for Mr. Peale*
Munro, Roxie. *The inside-outside book of Washington, D.C.*
Papajani, Janet. *Museums*
Rohmann, Eric. *Time flies*
Simmonds, Posy. *Lulu and the flying babies*
Stevenson, James. *The most amazing dinosaur*
Thayer, Jane. *Gus and the baby ghost*
Van Nutt, Julia. *Pignapped!*
Vincent, Gabrielle. *Where are you, Ernest and Celestine?*
Wahl, Jan. *The field mouse and the dinosaur named Sue*
   I met a dinosaur
Weil, Lisl. *Let's go to the museum*

Weitzman, Jacqueline Preiss. *You can't take a balloon into the Metropolitan Museum*
  You can't take a balloon into the National Gallery
Wellington, Monica. *Squeaking of art, the mice go to the museum*
Wyse, Lois. *How to take your grandmother to the museum*
Zadrzynska, Ewa. *The Peaceable Kingdom*

Music

Abisch, Roz. *Sweet Betsy from Pike*
  'Twas in the moon of wintertime
Alexander, Cecil Frances. *All things bright and beautiful*
Alexander, Lloyd. *The truthful harp*
Alger, Leclaire Gowans. *Always room for one more*
  Kellyburn Braes
Ambrus, Victor G. *Mishka*
  The seven skinny goats
Appelt, Kathi. *Bats on parade*
Arkin, Alan. *Black and white*
Asch, Frank. *Barnyard lullaby*
Ash, Jutta. *Wedding birds*
Atene, Ann (Anna). *The golden guitar*
Auzary-Luton, Sylvie. *1, 2, 3, music!*
Azarian, Mary. *The tale of John Barleycorn or, From barley to beer*
Bach, Othello. *Lilly, Willy and the mail-order witch*
Baer, Gene. *Thump thump rat-a-tat-tat*
Baker, Laura Nelson. *The friendly beasts*
  O children of the wind and pines
Bascom, Joe. *Malcolm's job*
Behn, Harry. *What a beautiful noise*
Berger, Barbara Helen. *The jewel heart*
Bianco, Margery Williams. *The hurdy-gurdy man*
Birchman, David Francis. *Brother Billy Bronto's bygone blues band*
  A green horn blowing
Birdseye, Tom. *She'll be comin' round the mountain*
Bishop, Roma. *Christmas songs*
Black, Charles C. *The royal nap*
Boesel, Ann Sterling. *Sing and sing again*
  Singing with Peter and Patsy
Bolliger, Max. *The most beautiful song*
Bottner, Barbara. *Nana Hannah's piano*
  Zoo song
Botwin, Esther. *A treasury of songs for little children*
Bowles, Brad. *Grandma's band*
Bowman, Peter. *The Christmas songbook*
Boynton, Sandra. *Good night, good night*
Bratton, John. *The teddy bears' picnic*, ill. by Renate Kozikowski
Brebeuf, Jean de, Saint. *The Huron carol*
Brett, Jan. *Berlioz the bear*
Bring a torch, Jeannette, Isabella
Brott, Ardyth. *Jeremy's decision*
Brown, Marc Tolon. *Play rhymes*
Brown, Margaret Wise. *The little brass band*
Bruna, Dick. *The orchestra*
Bryan, Ashley. *All night, all day*
Buffett, Jimmy. *The jolly mon*
Bunting, Eve (Anne Evelyn). *The traveling men of Ballycoo*
Burden-Patmon, Denise. *Carnival*
Burgie, Irving. *Caribbean carnival*
Burningham, John. *Jangle twang*
  Trubloff
Carle, Eric. *I see a song*

Carryl, Charles E. (Charles Edward). *A capital ship*
Carter, Donna Renee. *Music in the family*
Caseley, Judith. *Ada potato*
Cathon, Laura E. *Tot Botot and his little flute*
Causley, Charles. *Early in the morning*
Cech, John. *Django*
Chalk, Gary. *Yankee Doodle*
Chanover, Hyman. *Happy Hanukah everybody*
Children go where I send thee
Chocolate, Deborah M. Newton. *The piano man*
Clément, Claude. *The voice of the wood*
Coco, Eugene Bradley. *The fiddler's son*
Colette, Sidonie Gabrielle. *The boy and the magic*
Conover, Chris. *Six little ducks*
Count me in
Cowan, Catherine. *My friend the piano*
Craver, Mike. *Beaver ball at the bug club*
Crespi, Francesca. *Little Bear and the oompah-pah*
  Make a joyful noise
Cummings, W. T. (Walter Thies). *The kid*
Curtis, Gavin. *The bat boy and his violin*
Dallas-Smith, Peter. *Trumpets in Grumpetland*
Dalton, Alene. *My new picture book of songs*
Davies, Kay. *My drum*
Davol, Marguerite W. *The heart of the wood*
Day, Betsy. *Stefan and Olga*
Delacre, Lulu. *Arroz con leche*
  Las Navidades
Delton, Judy. *My Mom made me take piano lessons*
Diller, Harriett. *Big band sound*
Dillon, Eilis. *The cats' opera*
Dineen, Jacqueline. *Frédéric Chopin*
Domanska, Janina. *Busy Monday morning*
Donovan, Mary Lee. *Won't you come and play with me?*
Dunbar, Joyce. *Indigo and the whale*
Duncan, Lois. *Songs from dreamland*
Durell, Ann. *The Diane Goode book of American folk tales and songs*
Emerson, Sally. *The Kingfisher nursery rhyme songbook*
England, Linda. *3 kids dreamin'*
Engvick, William. *Lullabies and night songs*
Fair, David. *The fabulous four skunks*
The farmer in the dell. The farmer in the dell, ill. by John O'Brien
  The farmer in the dell, ill. by Kathy Parkinson
  The farmer in the dell, ill. by Mary Maki Rae
  The farmer in the dell, ill. by Diane Stanley
  The farmer in the dell, ill. by Alexandra Wallner
Flack, Marjorie. *The restless robin*
Flanders, Michael. *The hippopotamus song*
Fleischman, Paul. *Rondo in C*
Fleming, Candace. *Gabriella's song*
Fowler, Susi Gregg. *Fog*
Freeman, Lydia. *Pet of the Met*
The friendly beasts, ill. by Sarah Chamberlain
The friendly beasts and a partridge in a pear tree, ill. by Virginia Pearsons
A frog he would a-wooing go (folk-song). *The frog went a-courting*, adapt. and ill. by Dominic Catalano
  Froggie went a-courting, ill. by Chris Conover
  Mr. Frog went a-courting
  Wendy Watson's frog went a-courting
Gilbert, Yvonne. *Baby's book of lullabies and cradle songs*
Go tell Aunt Rhody. Go tell Aunt Rhody, ill. by Robert M. Quackenbush

McMillan, Bruce. *The alphabet symphony*
McNally, Darcie. *In a cabin in a wood*
McPhail, David M. *Mole music*
Maiorano, Robert. *A little interlude*
Mallett, David. *Inch by inch*
Manushkin, Fran. *My Christmas safari*
Maril, Lee. *Mr. Bunny paints the eggs*
Maxner, Joyce. *Nicholas Cricket*
Mayer, Mercer. *The queen always wanted to dance*
Medearis, Angela Shelf. *The singing man*
    The zebra-riding cowboy
Micucci, Charles. *A little night music*
Miller, William. *The piano*
Millman, Isaac. *Moses goes to a concert*
Mills, Alan. *The hungry goat*
Modesitt, Jeanne. *Songs of Chanukah*
Morley, Carol. *Farmyard song*
Moss, Lloyd. *Our marching band*
    Zin! zin! zin! A violin
Mother Goose. *Hey diddle diddle*, ill. by Marilyn
    Janovitz
    The Mother Goose songbook
    Mother Goose's rhymes and melodies
    Pat-a-cake, ill. by Marilyn Janovitz
    Sing hey diddle diddle
    Thirty old-time nursery songs
Myers, Walter Dean. *The blues of Flats Brown*
Neale, J. M. (John Mason). *Good King Wenceslas*
Nelson, Esther L. *The funny songbook*
    Holiday singing and dancing games
    The silly songbook
Newbolt, Henry John, Sir. *Rilloby-rill*
Newland, Mary Reed. *Good King Wenceslas*
Nichol, B. P. *Once*
Niland, Kilmeny. *A bellbird in a flame tree*
Novak, Matt. *Gertie and Gumbo*
Nussbaumer, Mares. *Away in a manger*
Nygaard, Elizabeth. *Snake alley band*
Oates, Eddie Hershel. *Making music*
Ogburn, Jacqueline K. *The jukebox man*
Old MacDonald had a farm. *E I E I O*
    Old MacDonald had a farm, ill. by Holly Berry
    Old MacDonald had a farm, ill. by Lorinda Bryan
    Cauley
    Old MacDonald had a farm, ill. by Mel Crawford
    Old MacDonald had a farm, ill. by Tracey English
    Old MacDonald had a farm, ill. by David Frank-
    land
    Old MacDonald had a farm, ill. by Abner Graboff
    Old MacDonald had a farm, ill. by Nancy Hellen
    Old MacDonald had a farm, ill. by Carol Jones
    Old MacDonald had a farm, ill. by Tracey Camp-
    bell Pearson
    Old MacDonald had a farm, ill. by Robert M.
    Quackenbush
    Old MacDonald had a farm, ill. by Glen Rounds
    Old MacDonald had a farm, ill. by William Stobbs
    Old MacDonald had a farm, ill. by Prue Theobalds
On the little hearth
Paker, Josephine. *I wonder why flutes have holes*
Paraskevas, Betty. *Junior Kroll and Company*
    On the day the tall ships sailed
Patterson, Geoffrey. *The lion and the gypsy*
Paxton, Tom. *Going to the zoo*
Peek, Merle. *The balancing act*
Perrault, Charles. *Cinderella*, ill. by Emanuele Luz-
    zati
Peterson, Jeanne Whitehouse. *My mama sings*
Pierpont, James. *Jingle bells*

Pillar, Marjorie. *Join the band!*
Pinkney, Andrea Davis. *Duke Ellington*
Pinkwater, Daniel Manus. *Doodle flute*
Poole, Valerie. *Obadiah Coffee and the music contest*
Poston, Elizabeth. *Baby's song book*
Poulin, Stéphane. *Benjamin and the pillow saga*
Price, Leontyne. *Aïda*
Prokofiev, Sergei Sergeievitch. *Peter and the wolf*, ill.
    by Warren Chappell
    Peter and the wolf, ill. by Barbara Cooney
    Peter and the wolf, ill. by Julia Gukova
    Peter and the wolf, ill. by Frans Haacken
    Peter and the wolf, ill. by Alan Howard
    Peter and the wolf, ill. by Charles Mikolaycak
    Peter and the wolf, ill. by Jörg Müller
    Peter and the wolf, ill. by Josef Palecek
    Peter and the wolf, ill. by Kozo Shimizu
    Peter and the wolf, retold and ill. by Vladimir
    Vagin
    Peter and the wolf, ill. by Erna Voigt
Purdy, Carol. *Mrs. Merriwether's musical cat*
Quackenbush, Robert M. *Clementine*
    The man on the flying trapeze
    Pop! goes the weasel and Yankee Doodle
    She'll be comin' 'round the mountain
    Skip to my Lou
    There'll be a hot time in the old town tonight
Quattrocki, Carolyn. *The little drummer boy*
Raffi. *Baby beluga*
    Down by the bay
    Everything grows
    Like me and you
    One light, one sun
    Rise and shine
    Shake my sillies out
    Wheels on the bus
Raposo, Joe. *The Sesame Street song book*
Raschka, Christopher. *Charlie Parker played be bop*
Ray, Mary Lyn. *Pianna*
    Shaker boy
Rayner, Mary. *One by one*
    Ten pink piglets
Rehnman, Mats. *The clay flute*
Rey, H. A. (Hans Augusto). *Humpty Dumpty and
    other Mother Goose songs*
Richardson, Jean. *Stephen's feast*
Robbins, Ruth. *Baboushka and the three kings*
Rodgers, Richard. *A real nice clambake*
Root, Phyllis. *Rosie's fiddle*
    Soup for supper
Ross, Tony. *This old man*
Rounds, Glen. *The boll weevil*
    Casey Jones
    The strawberry roan
    Sweet Betsy from Pike
Safran, Sheri. *The musical cherub*
Sage, James. *The little band*
Schaaf, Peter. *The violin close up*
Schackburg, Richard. *Yankee Doodle*
Schick, Eleanor. *One summer night*
    A piano for Julie
Scholey, Arthur. *Baboushka*
Scott, Lesbia. *I sing a song of the saints of God*
Seeger, Pete. *The foolish frog*
Sendak, Maurice. *Maurice Sendak's Really Rosie*
Simple gifts
Singer, Marilyn. *Will you take me to town on straw-
    berry day?*
Slavin, Bill. *The cat came back*

Slobodkin, Louis. *Wide-awake owl*
Smith, Edward Biko. *A lullaby for Daddy*
Spier, Peter. *The Erie Canal*
Stadler, John. *Hector, the accordion-nosed dog*
Staines, Bill. *All God's critters got a place in the choir*
Stapler, Sarah. *Trilby's trumpet*
Stecher, Miriam B. *Max, the music-maker*
Steig, William. *Roland, the minstrel pig*
  Zeke Pippin
Stern, Elsie-Jean. *Wee Robin's Christmas song*
Stevens, Bryna. *Handel and the famous sword swal-
  lower of Halle*
Stevens, Jan Romero. *Twelve lizards leaping*
Stevenson, James. *Clams can't sing*
Strom, Maria Diaz. *Rainbow Joe and me*
Sweet, Melissa. *Fiddle-i-fee*
Takao, Yuko. *A winter concert*
Taylor, Mark. *The bold fisherman*
  Old Blue, you good dog you
Thomas, Ianthe. *Willie blows a mean horn*
Titus, Eve. *Anatole and the piano*
  Anatole and the Pied Piper
Trapani, Iza. *The itsy bitsy spider*
  Mary had a little lamb
Tudor, Tasha. *Junior's tune*
Tusa, Tricia. *Miranda*
The twelve days of Christmas. English folk song.
  Brian Wildsmith's The twelve days of Christmas
  Jack Kent's twelve days of Christmas
  The twelve days of Christmas, ill. by Jan Brett
  The twelve days of Christmas, ill. by Ilonka Karasz
  The twelve days of Christmas, ill. by Ilse Plume
  The twelve days of Christmas, ill. by Erika Schnei-
    der
  The twelve days of Christmas, ill. by Vladimir Vagin
  The twelve days of Christmas, ill. by Sophie Wind-
    ham
Ungerer, Tomi. *Tortoni Tremelo the cursed musician*
Uttley, Alison. *Sam Pig and the hurdy-gurdy man*
Vainio, Pirkko. *The Christmas angel*
Vaughan, Marcia Kapok. *Wombat stew*
Vincent, Gabrielle. *Bravo, Ernest and Celestine!*
Waddell, Martin. *The happy hedgehog band*
Wallace, Nancy Elizabeth. *Apples, apples, apples*
Wallner, John C. *Old MacDonald had a farm*
Walter, Mildred Pitts. *Ty's one-man band*
Walty, Margaret. *Rock-a-bye baby*
Warner, Sunny. *Madison finds a line*
Watson, Clyde. *Father Fox's feast of songs*
  Fisherman lullabies
Weeks, Sarah. *Crocodile smile*
Weidt, Maryann N. *Daddy played music for the cows*
Weil, Lisl. *The magic of music*
Weiss, Nicki. *If you're happy and you know it*
Wells, Rosemary. *Bingo*
Wenning, Elisabeth. *The Christmas mouse*
Westcott, Nadine Bernard. *Skip to my Lou*
  There's a hole in the bucket
What a morning!
Wheeler, Opal. *Sing in praise*
  Sing Mother Goose
Whippo, Walt. *Little white duck*
Whittington, Mary K. *Carmina, come dance!*
Widdecombe Fair
Wilder, Laura Ingalls. *My little house songbook*
Williams, Vera B. *Music, music for everyone*
Winter, Jeanette. *The girl and the moon man*
Wolkstein, Diane. *The banza*
Wood, Jakki. *Fiddle-i-fee*

Yeoman, John. *Old Mother Hubbard's dog learns to
  play*
Yolen, Jane. *Jane Yolen's Old MacDonald songbook*
  The lap-time song and play book
  The lullaby songbook
Yulya. *Bears are sleeping*
Zalben, Jane Breskin. *Miss Violet's shining day*
Zelinsky, Paul O. *The wheels on the bus*
Zemach, Harve. *Mommy, buy me a China doll*
Ziefert, Harriet. *Animal music*
Zimelman, Nathan. *To sing a song as big as Ireland*

Musical instruments *see* Music

Musicians *see* Careers – musicians

Muskogee Indians *see* Indians of North
  America – Muskogee

Muskrats *see* Animals – muskrats

Mystery stories

Alexander, Sue. *World famous Muriel*
  World famous Muriel and the magic mystery
Allen, Laura Jean. *Rollo and Tweedy and the case of
  the missing cheese*
  Rollo and Tweedy and the ghost of Dougal Castle
  Where is Freddy?
Amoore, Susannah. *Motley the cat*
Balian, Lorna. *The socksnatchers*
Berenstain, Stan. *The bear detectives*
  The Berenstain bears and the messy room
  The Berenstain bears and the missing dinosaur bone
  The Berenstain bears and the missing honey
Binnamin, Vivian. *The case of the anteater's missing
  lunch*
  The case of the planetarium puzzle
  The case of the snoring stegosaurus
Bradford, Ann. *The mystery at Misty Falls*
  The mystery in the secret club house
  The mystery of the blind writer
  The mystery of the live ghosts
  The mystery of the midget clown
  The mystery of the missing dogs
  The mystery of the missing raccoon
  The mystery of the square footsteps
  The mystery of the tree house
Bunting, Eve (Anne Evelyn). *Jane Martin, dog detec-
  tive*
Christelow, Eileen. *Gertrude, the bulldog detective*
Christian, Mary Blount. *The doggone mystery*
Clement, Rod. *Grandpa's teeth*
Cox, Paul. *The case of the botched book*
  The great eucalyptus mystery
  The riddle of the floating island
Cushman, Doug. *The ABC mystery*
  The mystery of King Karfu
  The mystery of the monkey's maze
Darling, Kathy (Mary Kathleen). *The mystery in
  Santa's toyshop*
Davoll, Barbara. *Dusty Mole, private eye*
Fowler, Richard. *Inspector Smart gets the message!*
Freschet, Berniece. *Bernard of Scotland Yard*
Gibbons, Gail. *The missing maple syrup sap mystery*
Hare, Norma Q. *Mystery at mouse house*
Harrison, David Lee. *Detective Bob and the great ape
  escape*

Hayes, Geoffrey. *The mystery of the pirate ghost*
Hayward, Linda. *The case of the missing Duckie*
Hoban, Julia. *Buzby to the rescue*
Hoban, Lillian. *The case of the two masked robbers*
Holl, Adelaide. *Small Bear solves a mystery*
Hurd, Thacher. *Art dog*
  Mystery on the docks
Isherwood, Shirley. *Something for James*
Jonas, Ann. *The thirteenth clue*
Kellogg, Steven (Stephen). *The mystery of the flying orange pumpkin*
  The mystery of the magic green ball
  The mystery of the missing red mitten
  The mystery of the stolen blue paint
Kitamura, Satoshi. *Sheep in wolves' clothing*
Krahn, Fernando. *Arthur's adventure in the abandoned house*
  The mystery of the giant footprints
Kraus, Robert. *The detective of London*
  Mummy knows best
Laden, Nina. *Private I. Guana, the case of the missing chameleon*
Lass, Bonnie. *Who took the cookies from the cookie jar?*
Lawrence, James. *Binky Brothers and the fearless four*
  Binky Brothers, detectives
Lewis, Thomas P. *Call for Mr. Sniff*
  Mr. Sniff and the motel mystery
Lexau, Joan M. *The dog food caper*
  The rooftop mystery
McDonald, Megan. *The great pumpkin switch*
McKee, David. *123456789 Benn*
Mason, Jane B. *The shadow stealer*
Miller, Edna. *Mousekin's mystery*
Mooser, Stephen. *Funnyman and the penny dodo*
  Funnyman's first case
Morgan, Michaela. *Helpful Betty solves a mystery*
Musicant, Elke. *The night vegetable eater*
Nixon, Joan Lowery. *The Thanksgiving mystery*
  The Valentine mystery
O'Malley, Kevin. *Who killed Cock Robin?*
Ostheeren, Ingrid. *Jonathan Mouse, detective*
Panek, Dennis. *Detective Whoo*
Pape, D. L. (Donna Lugg). *Snoino mystery*
Park, Barbara. *Junie B. Jones and some sneaky peeky spying*
Sharmat, Marjorie Weinman. *Nate the Great*
  Nate the Great and the fishy prize
  Nate the Great and the lost list
  Nate the Great and the phony clue
  Nate the Great goes undercover
Shire, Ellen. *The mystery at number seven, Rue Petite*
Stern, Maggie. *The missing sunflowers*
Stortz, Diane M. *Barnaby Mouse, detective, and the mystery of the big book*
Supraner, Robyn. *Sam Sunday and the mystery at the Ocean Beach Hotel*
Taylor, Mark. *The case of the missing kittens*
Thomson, Ruth. *Peabody all at sea*
  Peabody's first case
Tryon, Leslie. *Albert's Halloween*
Van Nutt, Julia. *The mystery of Mineral Gorge*
Wick, Walter. *I spy treasure hunt*

Mythical creatures

Aardema, Verna. *Anansi finds a fool*
Ahlberg, Janet. *Jeremiah in the dark wood*
Arabian Nights. *The tale of Aladdin and the wonderful lamp*

Arnold, Tedd. *Bisnipian blast-off*
Aruego, José. *The king and his friends*
Berenstain, Michael. *The dwarks*
Bryan, Ashley. *The dancing granny*
Bunting, Eve (Anne Evelyn). *Night of the gargoyles*
Campbell, Ann. *Dora's box*
Cannon, Janell. *Trupp*
Carle, Eric. *Dragons dragons and other creatures that never were*
Carroll, Lewis. *Jabberwocky*, ill. by Graeme Base
  Jabberwocky, ill. from Disney archives
  Jabberwocky, ill. by Jane Breskin Zalben
Chenault, Nell. *Parsifal the Poddley*
Climo, Shirley. *Stolen thunder*
Cole, Babette. *Cupid*
Cooper, Susan. *Jethro and the jumbie*
Coville, Bruce. *Sarah and the dragon*
Dallas-Smith, Peter. *Trumpets in Grumpetland*
Darling, Kathy (Mary Kathleen). *Pecos Bill finds a horse*
Decker, Dorothy W. *Stripe and the merbear*
De Paola, Tomie (Thomas Anthony). *The Prince of the Dolomites*
Dunrea, Olivier. *Ravena*
Elzbieta. *Dikou the little troon who walks at night*
Fish, Helen Dean. *When the root children wake up*, published by Lippincott, 1930
  When the root children wake up, published by Green Tiger Pr., 1988
Fisher, Leonard Everett. *Cyclops*
  Theseus and the minotaur
Foreman, Michael. *Panda and the bunyips*
  Panda and the bushfire
George, Jean Craighead. *Dear Katie, the volcano is a girl*
Gilleo, Alma. *Learning about monsters*
Goble, Paul. *Iktomi and the coyote*
Gramatky, Hardie. *Nikos and the sea god*
Hodges, Margaret. *Comus*
Hutton, Warwick. *Persephone*
  Perseus
  Theseus and the Minotaur
Johnston, Tony. *Bigfoot Cinderrrrella*
Keeshan, Robert. *She loves me, she loves me not*
Kimmel, Eric A. *Billy Lazroe and the King of the Sea*
Krupp, Robin Rector. *Let's go traveling in Mexico*
Kurt, Kemal. *The five fingers and the moon*
McDonald, Megan. *The bone keeper*
McLenighan, Valjean. *You can go jump*
Mayer, Mercer. *Terrible troll*
Mayne, William. *The blue book of Hob stories*
  The green book of Hob stories
  The red book of Hob stories
  The yellow book of Hob stories
Medicine Crow, Joseph. *Brave Wolf and the Thunderbird*
Moore, Christopher J. *Ishtar and Tammuz*
Nones, Eric Jon. *Wendell*
Oram, Hiawyn. *Jenna and the troublemaker*
Osborne, Mary Pope. *Molly and the prince*
Peet, Bill (William Bartlett). *Cyrus the unsinkable sea serpent*
  No such things
  The pinkish, purplish, bluish egg
Plourde, Lynn. *Wild child*
  Winter waits
Robb, Brian. *My grandmother's djinn*
Rockwell, Anne F. *Buster and the bogeyman*

The one-eyed giant and other monsters from the Greek Myths
Sabuda, Robert James. *The Blizzard's robe*
Schroder, William. *Pea soup and serpents*
Shepard, Aaron. *The sea king's daughter*
Small, David. *Paper John*
Steiner, Charlotte. *Red Ridinghood's little lamb*
Takamado no Miya Hisako. *Katie and the dream-eater*
Vojtech, Anna. *Marushka and the Month Brothers*
Wagner, Jenny. *The bunyip of Berkeley's Creek*
Willis, Val. *The mystery in the bottle*
Wisniewski, David. *Golem*
Wood, Audrey. *The Bunyans*
   The Tickleoctopus
Yolen, Jane. *Greyling*
   Pegasus, the flying horse
   Wings
Zeman, Ludmila. *The first red maple leaf*
Zimelman, Nathan. *To sing a song as big as Ireland*

Mythical creatures – aliens *see* Aliens

Mythical creatures – elves

Adshead, Gladys L. *Brownies - hush!*
   Brownies - it's Christmas
   Brownies - they're moving
Bergen, Lara Rice. *Washington Irving's Rip Van Winkle*
Bernardoni, Robert. *Christmas all over*
Bulette, Sara. *The elf in the singing tree*
Calhoun, Mary. *The runaway brownie*
Cole, Joanna. *Mixed-up magic*
Compton, Kenn. *Happy Christmas to all!*
Cooper, Susan. *Tam Lin*
Cox, Palmer. *Another Brownie book*
   The Brownies
Davis, Maggie S. *Grandma's secret letter*
Dubowski, Cathy East. *The Christmas Santa almost missed*
Dürr, Ursula. *The secret of Trembleton Hall*
Elves, fairies and gnomes
Grimm, Jacob. *The elves and the shoemaker*, ill. by Doug Cushman
   The elves and the shoemaker, ill. by Paul Galdone
   The elves and the shoemaker, ill. by Margaret Walty
   The elves and the shoemaker, ill. by Bernadette Watts
   The shoemaker and the elves, ill. by Adrienne Adams
   The shoemaker and the elves, ill. by Cynthia and William Birrer
   The shoemaker and the elves, ill. by Ilse Plume
Haidle, Elizabeth. *Elmer the grump*
Irving, Washington. *Rip Van Winkle*, ill. by John Howe
   Rip Van Winkle, ill. by Thomas Locker
   Rip Van Winkle, ill. by Peter Wingham
Joyce, William. *The Leaf Men and the brave good bugs*
Krensky, Stephen. *How Santa lost his job*
Kunnas, Mauri. *Santa Claus and his elves*
   Twelve gifts for Santa Claus
Lowell, Susan. *The bootmaker and the elves*
May, Robert Lewis. *Rudolph the red-nosed reindeer*
Minarik, Else Holmelund. *The little giant girl and the elf boys*
Norby, Lisa. *The Herself the elf storybook*
Novak, Matt. *The last Christmas present*

Smith, Mary. *Long ago elf*
Yolen, Jane. *Elfabet*

Mythical creatures – gnomes

Elves, fairies and gnomes
Farmer, Nancy. *Runnery granary*
Grimm, Jacob. *The earth gnome*
Lester, Helen. *Pookins gets her way*
Maris, Ron. *Bernard's boring day*
Smith, Mary. *Long ago elf*

Mythical creatures – goblins

Alexander, Lloyd. *The house Gobbaleen*
Alexander, Sue. *More Witch, Goblin, and Ghost stories*
   Who goes out on Halloween?
   Witch, Goblin and Ghost are back
   Witch, Goblin, and Ghost in the haunted woods
   Witch, Goblin and sometimes Ghost
Bang, Molly. *The goblins giggle and other stories*
Blazek, Sarah Kirwan. *An Irish Hallowe'en*
Bunting, Eve (Anne Evelyn). *Scary, scary Halloween*
Calhoun, Mary. *The goblin under the stairs*
De Paola, Tomie (Thomas Anthony). *Jamie O'Rourke and the pooka*
Haley, Gail E. *Go away, stay away*
Heller, Nicholas. *Goblins in green*
Impey, Rose. *The flat man*
Johnston, Tony. *Four scary stories*
   Goblin walk
Kimmel, Eric A. *Hershel and the Hanukkah goblins*
Lifton, Betty Jean. *Joji and the Amanojaku*
Mills, Lauren A. *Tatterhood and the hobgoblins*
Schertle, Alice. *Bill and the google-eyed goblins*
Sendak, Maurice. *Outside over there*
Tobias, Tobi. *Chasing the goblins away*

Mythical creatures – griffins

Marston, Elsa. *A griffin in the garden*

Mythical creatures – imps

Baruch, Dorothy. *Kappa's tug-of-war with the big brown horse*

Mythical creatures – kelpies

Duncan, Jane. *Janet Reachfar and the kelpie*

Mythical creatures – leprechauns

Balian, Lorna. *Leprechauns never lie*
Bateman, Teresa. *Leprechaun gold*
Calhoun, Mary. *The hungry leprechaun*
De Paola, Tomie (Thomas Anthony). *Jamie O'Rourke and the big potato*
Dillon, Jana. *Lucky O'Leprechaun*
Hänel, Wolfram. *The gold at the end of the rainbow*
Kennedy, Richard. *The leprechaun's story*
Shub, Elizabeth. *Seeing is believing*
Shute, Linda. *Clever Tom and the leprechaun*

Mythical creatures – menehunes

Funai, Mamoru. *Moke and Poki in the rain forest*

Mythical creatures – mermaids, mermen

Andersen, H. C. (Hans Christian). *The little mermaid*, ill. by Edward Frascino
  The little mermaid, ill. by Michael Hague
  The little mermaid, ill. by Rachel Isadora
  The little mermaid, ill. by Chihiro Iwasaki
  The little mermaid, ill. by Dorothy Pulis Lathrop
  The little mermaid, ill. by Darcy May
  The little mermaid, ill. by Josef Palecek
  The little mermaid, ill. by Daniel San Souci
  The little mermaid, ill. by Katie Thamer Treherne
Binnamin, Vivian. *The case of the mysterious mermaid*
Haley, Gail E. *Sea tale*
Noble, Trinka Hakes. *Hansy's mermaid*
Nones, Eric Jon. *Caleb's friend*
Pitcher, Caroline. *Mariana and the merchild*
San Souci, Robert D. *Nicholas Pipe*
  Sukey and the mermaid
Spang, Günter. *Clelia and the little mermaid*
Tamar, Erika. *Donnatalee*

Mythical creatures – ogres

Domanska, Janina. *Palmiero and the ogre*
Hamilton, Morse. *Belching Hill*
Heller, Nicholas. *Ogres! ogres! ogres!*
Lorenz, Lee. *The feathered ogre*
Sierra, Judy. *Tasty baby belly buttons*
Solotareff, Grégoire. *Never trust an ogre*
  The ogre and the frog king
Ungerer, Tomi. *Zeralda's ogre*
Willard, Nancy. *Shadow story*

Mythical creatures – Pegasus

Mason, Jane B. *The flying horse*
Mayer, Marianna. *Pegasus*
Yolen, Jane. *Pegasus, the flying horse*

Mythical creatures – phoenix

Greene, Ellin. *Ling-li and the phoenix fairy*
Todaro, John. *Phillip the flower-eating phoenix*

Mythical creatures – pixies

Barrie, J. M. (James M.). *Peter Pan*
Calhoun, Mary. *The pixy and the lazy housewife*

Mythical creatures – pooka spirit

McDermott, Gerald. *Daniel O'Rourke*

Mythical creatures – sandman

Christiana, David. *A Tooth Fairy's tale*
Laimgruber, Monika. *Susannah and the Sandman*
Shepperson, Rob. *The sandman*
Strahl, Rudi. *Sandman in the lighthouse*
Twining, Edith. *Sandman*

Mythical creatures – selkies

Cooper, Susan. *The Selkie girl*
McClure, Gillian. *Selkie*
MacGill-Callahan, Sheila. *The seal prince*

Mythical creatures – trolls

Aardema, Verna. *Bimwili and the Zimwi*
Asbjørnsen, P. C. (Peter Christen). *Billy goats Gruff*, ill. by Wendy Edelson
  Billy goats Gruff, ill. by Susan Hellard
  The three billy goats Gruff, ill. by Tim Arnold
  The three billy goats Gruff, ill. by Robert Bender
  The three billy goats Gruff, ill. by Marcia Brown
  The three billy goats Gruff, ill. by Stephen Carpenter
  Three billy goats Gruff, ill. by Tom Dunnington
  The three billy goats Gruff, ill. by Paul Galdone
  The three billy goats Gruff, ill. by David Jorgensen
  The three billy goats Gruff, ill. by Dennis Kendrick
  The three billygoats Gruff, ill. by Eric Kincaid
  The three billy goats Gruff, ill. by Jonathan Langley
  The three billy goats Gruff, ill. by Loretta Lustig
  The three billy goats Gruff, ill. by Thomas Newbury
  The three billy goats Gruff, ill. by Lilian Obligado
  The three billy goats Gruff, ill. by Ed Parker
  The three billy goats Gruff, ill. by Heidi Petach
  The three billy goats Gruff, ill. by Laura Rader
  The three billy goats Gruff, ill. by Glen Rounds
  The three billy goats Gruff, ill. by Janet Stevens
  The three billy goats Gruff, ill. by William Stobbs
  The three billy goats Gruff, ill. by Svend Otto S
  The truth about three billy goats Gruff
Aulaire, Ingri Mortenson d'. *The terrible troll-bird*
Ayers, Rebecca Hickox. *Per and the Dala horse*
Berenstain, Michael. *The troll book*
Brett, Jan. *Christmas trolls*
  The trouble with trolls
Carrick, Carol. *Melanie*
De Paola, Tomie (Thomas Anthony). *The cat on the Dovrefell*
  Helga's dowry
Dunrea, Olivier. *The trow-wife's treasure*
Grimm, Jacob. *The glass mountain*, ill. by Louisa Bauer
Havill, Juanita. *Kentucky troll*
Hawkes, Kevin. *Then the troll heard the squeak*
Heller, Nicholas. *A troll story*
Herrick, Amy. *Kimbo's marble*
Hillert, Margaret. *The three goats*
Hooks, William H. *The Gruff brothers*
Inkpen, Mick. *This troll, that troll*
Johnston, Tony. *Mole and Troll trim the tree*
Lagerlöf, Selma. *The changeling*
Leedy, Loreen. *The potato party and other troll tales*
Le Guin, Ursula K. *A ride on the red mare's back*
Lindgren, Astrid. *The tomten*
  The tomten and the fox
Lobel, Anita. *The troll music*
McMullan, Kate (Hall). *Hey, Pipsqueak!*
Marshall, Edward. *Troll country*
Martin, Claire. *Boots and the glass mountain*, ill. by Gennady Spirin
Mayer, Mercer. *Terrible troll*
Mills, Lauren A. *Fairy wings*
Peet, Bill (William Bartlett). *Jethro and Joel were a troll*
Prelutsky, Jack. *Monday's troll*
Schertle, Alice. *Hob Goblin and the skeleton*
Svendsen, Carol. *Hulda*
Torgersen, Don Arthur. *The girl who tricked the troll*
  The troll who lived in the lake

Tudor, Tasha. *Corgiville fair*
Wahl, Jan. *Peter and the troll baby*
Walsh, Ellen Stoll. *Jack's tale*
Wittington, Mary K. *Troll games*
Wolff, Patricia Rae. *The toll-bridge troll*

Mythical creatures – unicorns

Ada, Alma Flor. *The unicorn of the west*
Birrer, Cynthia. *The lady and the unicorn*
Cherry, Lynne. *The dragon and the unicorn*
Coville, Bruce. *Sarah's unicorn*
De Paola, Tomie (Thomas Anthony). *The unicorn and the moon*
Freeman, Jean Todd. *Cynthia and the unicorn*
Greaves, Margaret. *The naming*
Hague, Michael. *Michael Hague's world of unicorns*
Ipcar, Dahlov. *Sir Addlepate and the unicorn*
McCaughrean, Geraldine. *Unicorns! Unicorns!*
Mayer, Marianna. *The unicorn alphabet*
The unicorn and the lake
Mitchell, Adrian. *Nobody rides the unicorn*
Moeri, Louise. *The unicorn and the plow*
Munthe, Adam John. *I believe in unicorns*
Preussler, Otfried. *The tale of the unicorn*
Sheldon, Dyan. *Unicorn dreams*

Mythical creatures – werewolves

Ogburn, Jacqueline K. *Scarlett Angelina Wolverton-Manning*

Nagging *see* Behavior – nagging

Name calling *see* Behavior – name calling

Names

Ackerman, Karen. *Flannery Row*
Alexander, Martha G. *Sabrina*
Bayer, Jane. *A my name is Alice*
Beim, Jerrold. *The smallest boy in the class*
Benton, Robert. *Little brother, no more*
Browner, Richard. *Everyone has a name*
Bryan, Ashley. *Turtle knows your name*
Capucilli, Alyssa Satin. *Hello, Biscuit!*
Carter, Alden R. *Big brother Dustin*
Cross, Diana Harding. *Some birds have funny names*
Some plants have funny names
Davis, Gibbs. *The other Emily*
De Paola, Tomie (Thomas Anthony). *Andy (that's my name)*
Tom
Dragonwagon, Crescent. *Wind Rose*
Engel, Diana. *Josephina hates her name*
Goffstein, M. B. (Marilyn Brooke). *School of names*
Greaves, Margaret. *The naming*
Henkes, Kevin. *Chrysanthemum*
Hinton, S. E. *Big David, Little David*
Hoban, Julia. *Quick chick*
Hogan, Inez. *About Nono, the baby elephant*

Inkpen, Mick. *Nothing*
Jacobs, Shannon K. *The boy who loved morning*
Johnson, Janice (Janice Kay). *Rosamund*
Kraus, Robert. *Squirmy's big secret*
Kroll, Virginia L. *The seasons and someone*
Lester, Helen. *A porcupine named Fluffy*
Lester, Robin. *Roy Foy's special name*
Low, Joseph. *Adam's book of odd creatures*
Lyne, Alice. *A, my name is . . .*
McFall, Gardner. *Naming the animals*
McKee, David. *Two can toucan*
MacLachlan, Patricia. *Three names*
Martin, Mary Jane. *From Anne to Zach*
Mosel, Arlene. *Tikki Tikki Tembo*
Moser, Barry. *Tucker Pfeffercorn*
Most, Bernard. *Catbirds and dogfish*
A dinosaur named after me
Munsch, Robert N. *From far away*
Norac, Carl. *Hello, sweetie pie*
Norman, Howard A. *Who-Paddled-Backward-With-Trout*
Oppenheim, Shulamith Levey. *The hundredth name*
Parish, Peggy. *Little Indian*
Peterson, Scott K. *What's your name?*
Pitre, Felix. *Paco and the witch*
Pringle, Laurence P. *Naming the cat*
Raskin, Ellen. *A & The*
Rice, Eve. *Ebbie*
Ryan, Pam Muñoz. *A pinky is a baby mouse, and other baby animal names*
Sadu, Itah. *Christopher changes his name*
Sanders, Marilyn. *What's your name?*
Sasso, Sandy Eisenberg. *In God's name*
Tom Tit Tot. *Tom Tit Tot*
Vreeken, Elizabeth. *The boy who would not say his name*
Waber, Bernard. *But names will never hurt me*
A lion named Shirley Williamson
Walsh, Jill Paton. *Pepi and the secret names*
Watkins, Sherrin. *White Bead Ceremony*
White, Carolyn. *Whuppity Stoorie*
Wilkowski, Susan. *Baby's Bris*
Williams, Jay. *I wish I had another name*
Williams, Suzanne. *Mommy doesn't know my name*
Wilson, Sarah. *Good zap, little grog*
Wold, Jo Anne. *Tell them my name is Amanda*
Wolf, Janet. *Adelaide to Zeke*

Namibia *see* Foreign lands – Namibia

Nanticoke Indians *see* Indians of North America – Nanticoke

Napping *see* Sleep

Narragansett *see* Indians of North America – Narragansett

Native Americans *see* Eskimos; Indians of Central America; Indians of North America; Indians of South America

Nativity *see* Religion – Nativity

Nature

Alarcón, Francisco X. *From the bellybutton of the moon and other summer poems / poems = Del ombligo de la luna y otros poemas de verano / poemas*

Alexander, Cecil Frances. *All things bright and beautiful*

Alexander, Martha G. *Where does the sky end, Grandpa?*

Alexander, Sue. *One more time, Mama*

Allen, Marjorie N. *Changes*

Aragon, Jane Chelsea. *Salt hands*

Arnosky, Jim. *Come out, muskrats*
   Crinkleroot's guide to knowing animal habitats
   Crinkleroot's guide to knowing the trees
   Crinkleroot's guide to walking in wild places
   Crinkleroot's 25 birds every child should know
   Crinkleroot's 25 fish every child should know
   Crinkleroot's 25 mammals every child should know
   Crinkleroot's visit to Crinkle Cove
   I see animals hiding

Asch, Frank. *The earth and I*
   Water

Ayres, Pam. *When dad cuts down the chestnut tree*
   When dad fills in the garden pond

Bailey, Jill. *The life cycle of a spider*

Baker, Alan. *Two tiny mice*

Baker, Sanna Anderson. *Mississippi going north*

Banks, Merry. *Animals of the night*

Bare, Colleen Stanley. *Never grab a deer by the ear*

Bash, Barbara. *Urban roosts*

Baskwill, Jane. *Somewhere*

Bastin, Marjolein. *Vera's special hobbies*

Baylor, Byrd. *I'm in charge of celebrations*
   The other way to listen
   The table where rich people sit

Bendick, Jeanne. *All around you*

Bennett, Rowena. *Songs from around a toadstool table*

Benson, Laura Lee. *This is our earth*

Berenstain, Stan. *The Berenstain bears and the wild, wild honey*

Berger, Melvin. *Look out for turtles!*

Bernhard, Durga. *Alphabeasts*

Bernhard, Emery. *Dragonfly*
   Eagles
   Ladybug
   The way of the willow branch

Blake, Robert J. *The perfect spot*

Bliss, Corinne Demas. *Matthew's meadow*

Blyler, Allison. *Finding foxes*

Bornstein, Ruth Lercher. *Rabbit's good news*

Bowen, Betsy. *Antler, bear, canoe*
   Tracks in the wild

Boyle, Doe. *Summer coat, winter coat*

Brenner, Barbara A. *Two orphan cubs*

Brownell, Barbara. *Spin's really wild U.S.A. tour*

Bruchac, Joseph. *The circle of thanks*

Bryan, Ashley. *Sing to the sun*

Bunting, Eve (Anne Evelyn). *Moonstick*
   Secret place

Burke, Katie. *Lightning bug thunder*

Burton, Jane. *Animals at home*
   Animals at night
   Animals at rest
   Animals at work
   Animals eating
   Animals fighting
   Animals keeping clean
   Animals keeping cool
   Animals keeping safe
   Animals keeping warm
   Animals learning
   Animals talking

Bush, Barbara. *In the heart of the village*

Campbell, Rod. *Buster's afternoon*

Capucilli, Alyssa Satin. *Good morning, pond*

Carlstrom, Nancy White. *Northern lullaby*

Carter, Anne. *Molly in danger*
   Scurry's treasure

Chall, Marsha Wilson. *Up north at the cabin*

Cherry, Lynne. *A river ran wild*

Chester, Jonathan. *Splash!*

Clay, Pat. *Ants*

Cole, Babette. *Supermoo!*

Cole, Henry. *I took a walk*

Cooner, Donna D. (Donna Danell). *The world God made*

Cooper, Ann (Ann C.). *In the forest*

Cousins, Lucy. *Za-Za's baby brother*

Cousteau Society. *Albatross*
   Dolphins
   Manatees
   Otters
   Penguins
   Seals
   Turtles
   Whales

Crewe, Sabrina. *The bear*
   The bee

Davies, Kay. *My apple*

DeMunn, Michael. *The earth is good*

Diviny, Sean. *Snow inside the house*

Drawson, Blair. *Mary Margaret's tree*

Dunbar, Joyce. *Why is the sky up?*

Eaton, Deborah. *The rainy day grump*

Esbensen, Barbara Juster. *Dance with me*
   Echoes for the eye

Facklam, Margery. *Only a star*

Farjeon, Eleanor. *Between the earth and sun*

Feldman, Judy. *The alphabet in nature*
   Shapes in nature

Fife, Dale. *Empty lot*

Fisher, Aileen Lucia. *Like nothing at all*

Flatt, Lizann. *My first nature treasury*

Fleming, Denise. *In the tall, tall grass*
   Where once there was a wood

Fleming, Virginia M. *Be good to Eddie Lee*

Florian, Douglas. *Nature walk*

Ford, Miela. *Sunflower*

Gackenbach, Dick. *Mighty tree*

Ganeri, Anita. *The hunt for food*

Gans, Roma. *How do birds find their way?*

George, Jean Craighead. *Dear Rebecca, winter is here*
   Everglades

George, Kristine O'Connell. *The great frog race and other poems*

George, Lindsay Barrett. *Around the pond*
   In the woods

George, William T. *Beaver at Long Pond*
   Box turtle at Long Pond
   Christmas at Long Pond

Geraghty, Paul. *Over the steamy swamp*

Giovanni, Nikki. *The sun is so quiet*

Glaser, Linda. *Compost!*
   Wonderful worms

Goble, Paul. *I sing for the animals*

Godkin, Celia. *What about ladybugs?*

Graham, Bob. *The wild*
Greeley, Valerie. *White is the moon*
Greenaway, Shirley. *Forests*
  Jungles
Greene, Carol. *I can be a forest ranger*
Greenway, Shirley. *Can you see me?*
  Color me bright
  Here's ears
  How do I move?
  Legs and all
  A tale of tails
  Where do I live?
  Whose baby am I?
Griffith, Helen V. *Georgia music*
Grupper, Jonathan. *Destination, rain forest*
Guiberson, Brenda Z. *Into the sea*
  Spoonbill swamp
Hall, Zoe. *The apple pie tree*
Hallinan, P. K. (Patrick K.). *For the love of our earth*
Hands, Hargrave. *Bunny sees*
Hathorn, Libby (Elizabeth). *The wonder thing*
Heinz, Brian J. *The wolves*
Hershey, Kathleen. *Cotton mill town*
Himmelman, John. *A wood frog's life*
Hines, Anna Grossnickle. *Gramma's walk*
Hirschi, Ron. *Loon lake*
  Summer
Hoban, Tana. *Look book*
Hoopes, Lyn Littlefield. *Mommy, daddy, me*
  My own home
Howell, Will C. *I call it sky*
Hurd, Edith Thacher. *Look for a bird*
Iverson, Diane. *Discover the seasons*
Jackson, Ellen B. *The book of slime*
  Brown cow, green grass, yellow mellow sun
Jackson, Shelley. *The old woman and the wave*
Jackson, Woody. *Counting cows*
James, Simon. *The wild woods*
Jenkins, Martin. *Chameleons are cool*
Johnston, Tony. *Once in the country*
Jordan, Helene J. (Helene Jamieson). *How a seed grows*
Kherdian, David. *By myself*
Kinsey-Warnock, Natalie. *On a starry night*
Kitchen, Bert. *When hunger calls*
Koch, Michelle. *Hoot, howl, hiss*
Krull, Kathleen. *It's my earth too*
Krupinski, Loretta. *Into the woods*
Lamm, C. Drew. *Screech Owl at Midnight Hollow*
Lasky, Kathryn. *Pond year*
Lavies, Bianca. *Lily pad pond*
  Tree trunk traffic
Leach, Michael. *Rabbits*
Lewin, Betsy. *Booby hatch*
Lewis, J. Patrick. *July is a mad mosquito*
Lewis, Naomi. *Swan*
Lindbergh, Reeve. *North country spring*
  A view from the air
Ling, Mary. *Fox*
Lionni, Leo. *A busy year*
Llewellyn, Claire. *Some bugs glow in the dark*
Locker, Thomas. *The land of gray wolf*
  The man who paints nature
LoMonaco, Palmyra. *Night letters*
London, Jonathan. *Dream weaver*
  Gray fox
  Honey Paw and Lightfoot
  I see the moon and the moon sees me
  Phantom of the prairie

  Red wolf country
Loomis, Christine. *Across America, I love you*
Loomis, Jennifer A. *A duck in a tree*
Lucht, Irmgard. *The red poppy*
Luenn, Nancy. *Squish!*
Lyon, George Ella. *Counting on the woods*
  The outside inn
Maestro, Betsy. *Why do leaves change color?*
Manning, Mick. *A ruined house*
Maris, Ron. *Better move on, frog!*
Martin, Jacqueline Briggs. *Snowflake Bentley*
Marzollo, Jean. *Home sweet home*
Merriam, Eve. *Low song*
Merrill, Jean. *The girl who loved caterpillars*
Michels, Tilde. *Rabbit spring*
  What a beautiful day!
Miller, Debbie S. *A caribou journey*
Miller, Edna. *Patches finds a new home*
  Scamper
Moore, Lilian. *Adam Mouse's book of poems*
Myers, Walter Dean. *The story of the three kingdoms*
Norman, Charles. *The hornbean tree and other poems*
Olaleye, Isaac. *In the Rainfield*
Oliver, Stephen. *Nature*
Pallotta, Jerry. *The dory story*
Pandell, Karen. *I love you sun, I love you moon*
Patterson, Elizabeth Burman. *Whose eyes are these?*
Paul, Korky. *Winnie in winter*
Peddle, Daniel. *Snow day*
Peters, Lisa Westberg. *Meg and dad discover treasure in the air*
  The sun, the wind and the rain
  This way home
  Water's way
Pets
Pfeffer, Wendy. *From tadpole to frog*
Pfister, Marcus. *Hopper's treetop adventure*
Powell, Consie. *A bold carnivore*
Powzyk, Joyce Ann. *Tasmania*
Poydar, Nancy. *Snip, snip . . . snow!*
Preller, James. *Cardinal and sunflower*
Priddy, Roger. *Baby's book of nature*
Radin, Ruth Yaffe. *High in the mountains*
Rand, Gloria. *The cabin key*
Ring, Elizabeth. *Lucky mouse*
Rosen, Michael J. (1954-). *All eyes on the pond*
Rosman, Steven M. *Deena the damselfly*
Royston, Angela. *Small animals*
Rucki, Ani. *When the Earth wakes*
Russell, Naomi. *The stream*
  The tree
Ryder, Joanne. *Catching the wind*
  Chipmunk song
  Dancers in the garden
  Hello, tree!
  Lizard in the sun
  Mockingbird morning
  Step into the night
  Under your feet
  Where butterflies grow
  White bear, ice bear
  Winter whale
Sarton, May. *A walk through the woods*
Schaefer, Lola M. *This is the sunflower*
Schnur, Steven. *Spring thaw*
Schoenherr, John. *Bear*
Schulz, Charles M. *Snoopy's facts and fun book about nature*
Schweninger, Ann. *Summertime*

Selsam, Millicent E. *How to be a nature detective*
Seymour, Peter S. *What's at the beach?*
Shulevitz, Uri. *Snow*
Siddals, Mary McKenna. *I'll play with you*
Siebert, Diane. *Sierra*
Simmons, Jane. *Come along, Daisy!*
Simon, Seymour. *Icebergs and glaciers*
Singer, Marilyn. *Turtle in July*
Skofield, James. *Crow moon, worm moon*
Sohi, Morteza E. *Look what I did with a leaf!*
The song of the Three Holy Children
Speed, Toby. *Watervoices*
Stafford, Kim Robert. *We got here together*
Stiles, Martha Bennett. *Island magic*
Stone, Phoebe. *When the Wind Bears go dancing*
Stroud, Virginia A. *A walk to the Great Mystery*
Swamp, Jake. *Giving thanks*
Sweetland, Nancy. *God's quiet things*
Tafuri, Nancy. *What the sun sees / What the moon sees*
Taylor, Kim. *Too fast to see*
   Too small to see
Tejima, Keizaburo. *Owl lake*
   Woodpecker forest
Thornhill, Jan. *Wildlife ABC*
   The wildlife 1-2-3
Tucker, Sian. *Going out*
Waboose, Jan Bourdeau. *Morning on the lake*
Wahl, Jan. *My cat Ginger*
Wallace, Karen. *Bears in the forest*
   Scarlette Beane
Walsh, Melanie. *Do donkeys dance?*
Walters, Catherine. *When will it be spring?*
Ward, Leila. *I am eyes, ni macho*
Watts, Barrie. *Apple tree*
Weiss, George (George David). *What a wonderful world*
Wells, Rosemary. *Forest of dreams*
Wildsmith, Brian. *Seasons*
Williams, David. *Walking to the creek*
Willington, Monica. *Seasons of swans*
Wilson, Ron. *Mice*
Winters, Kay. *Tiger trail*
   Wolf watch
Winton, Tim. *The deep*
Wood, Audrey. *The Bunyans*
Wood, Douglas. *Grandad's prayers of the earth*
   Making the world
Wood, Jakki. *Across the big blue sea*
Wood, Jenny. *The animal kingdom*
Wyler, Rose. *Puddles and ponds*
Yerxa, Leo. *Last leaf first snowflake to fall*
Yolen, Jane. *Welcome to the icehouse*
Yoshida, Toshi. *Rhinoceros mother*
Ziefert, Harriet. *Sarah's questions*
Zolotow, Charlotte (Shapiro). *Say it!*
   The song
   When the wind stops
Zoo animals, (Macmillan, 1991)
Zweifel, Frances W. *Animal baby-sitters*

Naughty *see* Behavior – misbehavior

Navajo Indians *see* Indians of North America – Navajo

Neckties *see* Clothing – neckties

Needing someone *see* Behavior – needing someone

Neighborhoods *see* Communities, neighborhoods

Nepal *see* Foreign lands – Nepal

Netherlands *see* Foreign lands – Holland

New Guinea *see* Foreign lands – New Guinea

New Year's *see* Holidays – New Year's

New Zealand *see* Foreign lands – New Zealand

Nez Perce Indians *see* Indians of North America – Nez Perce

Nicaragua *see* Foreign lands – Nicaragua

Nigeria *see* Foreign lands – Nigeria

Night

Ackerman, Karen. *The banshee*
Adoff, Arnold. *Make a circle, keep us in*
Ahlberg, Allan. *Mystery tour*
Ahlberg, Janet. *Funnybones*
Alexander, Anne (Anna Barbara Cooke). *Noise in the night*
Alexander, Martha G. *Maggie's moon*
   We're in big trouble, Blackboard Bear
   You're a genius, Blackboard Bear
Aliki. *Overnight at Mary Bloom's*
Anrooy, Frans van. *The sea horse*
Appelt, Kathi. *Bayou lullaby*
   Cowboy dreams
Apple, Margot. *Brave Martha*
Aragon, Jane Chelsea. *Salt hands*
   Winter harvest
Ardizzone, Aingelda. *The night ride*
Armitage, Ronda. *One moonlit night*
Arnold, Tedd. *Huggly gets dressed*
   Huggly takes a bath
Arnosky, Jim. *All night near the water*
   Raccoons and ripe corn
Artis, Vicki Kimmel. *Pajama walking*
Asch, Frank. *Moonbear*
Axworthy, Anni. *Ben's Wednesday*
Aylesworth, Jim. *The good-night kiss*
   Through the night
   Tonight's the night
   Two terrible frights
Babbitt, Natalie. *The something*
Balzola, Asun. *Munia and the moon*
Bandes, Hanna. *Sleepy river*
Banks, Kate (Katherine A.). *And if the moon could talk*
Banks, Merry. *Animals of the night*
Bannon, Laura. *Little people of the night*
Bartels, Alice L. *The beast*
Baumgart, Klaus. *The little green dragon steps out*
Bennett, Rainey. *After the sun goes down*

Hort, Lenny. *How many stars in the sky*
Horwitz, Elinor Lander. *When the sky is like lace*
Howe, James. *There's a monster under my bed*
Hudson, Cheryl Willis. *Good night baby*
Hurd, Thacher. *A night in the swamp*
 The quiet evening
Huth, Holly Young. *Darkfright*
Impey, Rose. *The ankle grabber*
 The flat man
 Scare yourself to sleep
Ingman, Bruce. *A night on the tiles*
Ipcar, Dahlov. *The cat at night*
 "The song of the day birds" and "The song of the night birds"
Isadora, Rachel. *A South African night*
Jacobson, Jennifer Richard. *A net of stars*
Jam, Teddy. *Night cars*
James, Betsy. *Flashlight*
Johnson, Angela. *Joshua's night whispers*
Johnston, Tony. *The Chizzywink and the Alamagoozlum*
 Desert song
 Little Rabbit goes to sleep
Jones, Joy. *Tambourine moon*
Kamish, Daniel. *The night scary beasties popped out of my head*
Kandoian, Ellen. *Under the sun*
Kauffman, Lois. *What's that noise?*
Keats, Ezra Jack. *Dreams*
Kessler, Cristina. *One night*
Kinsey-Warnock, Natalie. *On a starry night*
Koenig, Marion. *The wonderful world of night*
Koralek, Jenny. *The boy and the cloth of dreams*
Kovacs, Deborah. *Moonlight on the river*
Kraus, Robert. *Good night little one*
 Good night Richard Rabbit
 See the moon
Krensky, Stephen. *Fraidy Cats*
Kunnas, Mauri. *The nighttime book*
Landalf, Helen. *The secret night world of cats*
LaRose, Linda. *Jessica takes charge*
Larrick, Nancy. *When the dark comes dancing*
Leaf, Munro. *Boo, who used to be scared of the dark*
Lesser, Carolyn. *The goodnight circle*
Lesynski, Loris. *Night school*
Lewison, Wendy Cheyette. *Nighty-night*
Lexau, Joan M. *Millicent's ghost*
Lifton, Betty Jean. *Goodnight orange monster*
Lindbergh, Reeve. *Midnight farm*
Lindgren, Barbro. *The wild baby gets a puppy*
Lionni, Leo. *When?*
Lipniacka, Ewa. *To bed . . . or else!*
Lively, Penelope. *Good night, sleep tight*
Lloyd, Errol. *Nandy's bedtime*
LoMonaco, Palmyra. *Night letters*
London, Jonathan. *Fireflies, fireflies, light my way*
 Into this night we are rising
 Let the lynx come in
 The owl who became the moon
Lucht, Irmgard. *In this night*
Lyon, David. *The biggest truck*
McDonald, Megan. *My house has stars*
 Whoo-oo is it?
McPartland, Suzy. *Sleepy-time moon*
McPhail, David M. *Adam's smile*
 The dream child
McQueen, John Troy. *A world full of monsters*
Maitland, Barbara. *The bear who didn't like honey*
Manushkin, Fran. *Peeping and sleeping*

Martin, Bill (William Ivan). *Barn dance!*
Marton, Jirina. *Midnight visit at Molly's house*
Matus, Greta. *Where are you, Jason?*
Mayer, Mercer. *There's something in my attic*
 You're the scaredy cat
Memling, Carl. *What's in the dark?*
Michelson, Richard. *Did you say ghosts?*
Micucci, Charles. *A little night music*
Miles, Sally. *Alfi and the dark*
Miranda, Anne. *Night songs*
Modesitt, Jeanne. *The night call*
Montgomery, Michael. *'Night, America*
 The moon's the north wind's cooky
Moore, Dessie. *Good night*
Mora, Pat. *Delicious hullabaloo = Pachanga deliciosa*
Morgan-Vanroyen, Mary. *Night ride*
Morris, Ann. *Cuddle up*
 Eleanora Mousie in the dark
 Kiss time
 Night counting
 Sleepy, sleepy
Murphy, Jill. *What next, baby bear!*
Murphy, Jim. *Backyard bear*
Murray, Marjorie Dennis. *The stars are waiting*
Mwalimu. *Awful aardvark*
Nayer, Judy. *Night animals*
Newman, Lesléa. *Cats, cats, cats*
Nichol, B. P. *Once*
Night time
Nikola-Lisa, W. *Night is coming*
Nobisso, Josephine. *Shh! the whale is smiling*
Nye, Naomi Shihab. *Lullaby raft*
O'Donnell, Peter. *Moonlit journey*
Olofsdotter, Marie. *Sofia and the Heartmender*
Oppenheim, Shulamith Levey. *What is the full moon full of?*
Ormerod, Jan. *Midnight pillow fight*
Osborne, Mary Pope. *Moonhorse*, ill. by David McPhail
 Moonhorse, ill. by S. M. Saelig
Ottley, Matt. *What Faust saw*
Owen, Annie. *Goodnight bear!*
Paraskevas, Betty. *Cecil Bunions and the midnight train*
Pearson, Tracey Campbell. *The howling dog*
Pedersen, Judy. *When night time comes near*
Percy, Graham. *24 strange little animals in a haunted house*
Peters, Sharon. *Animals at night*
Pettigrew, Eileen. *Night-time*
Pfister, Marcus. *I see the moon*
Pierson, Judith Patterson. *The always moon*
Pilkey, Dav. *The Moonglow Roll-O-Rama*
Pittman, Helena Clare. *Once when I was scared*
Pizer, Abigail. *Harry's night out*
A Pocketful of stars
Posey, Lee. *Night rabbits*
Powell, Polly. *Just dessert*
Powell, Roxanne Dyer. *Cat, mouse and moon*
Prater, John. *On top of the world*
Preston, Edna Mitchell. *Monkey in the jungle*
Raschka, Christopher. *Can't sleep*
Rathmann, Peggy. *Good night, Gorilla*
Ray, Deborah Kogan. *Stargazing sky*
Reeves, Mona Rabun. *The spooky eerie night noise*
Reidel, Marlene. *Jacob and the robbers*
Rice, Eve. *City night*
 Goodnight, goodnight
Riddell, Chris. *Mr. Underbed*

Riley, Linnea Asplind. *Mouse mess*
Riordan, James. *The coming of Night*
Ripley, Catherine. *Why do stars twinkle?*
Rockwell, Anne F. *The night we slept outside*
Rodriguez, Bobbie. *Sarah's sleepover*
Rohmann, Eric. *The cinder-eyed cats*
Rosenberg, Liz. *Adelaide and the night train*
  Window, mirror, moon
Roth, Susan L. *Night-time numbers*
Rowand, Phyllis. *It is night*
Rowinski, Kate. *Cats in the dark*
Royston, Angela. *Night-time animals*
Rukeyser, Muriel. *More night*
Ryan, Cheli Durán. *Hildilid's night*
Rydell, Katy. *Wind says good night*
Ryder, Joanne. *The night flight*
  The snail's spell
  Step into the night
Rylant, Cynthia. *Night in the country*
Salter, Mary Jo. *The moon comes home*
Sanromán, Susana. *Señora Regañona*
Schlein, Miriam. *Here comes night*
Schneider, Nina. *While Susie sleeps*
Schnur, Steven. *Night lights*
Schotter, Roni. *Bunny's night out*
Selsam, Millicent E. *Night animals*
Shipton, Jonathan. *In the night*
Simmons, Jane. *Daisy's favorite things*
Sloat, Teri. *The thing that bothered Farmer Brown*
Spinelli, Eileen. *Night shift daddy*
Spohn, David. *Starry night*
Stanley, Diane. *Birdsong lullaby*
Stepto, Michele. *Snuggle Piggy and the magic blanket*
Stevens, Cat. *Teaser and the firecat*
Stevenson, Robert Louis. *The moon*
Stolz, Mary Slattery. *Storm in the night*
Stone, Kazuko G. *Goodnight Twinklegator*
Strand, Mark. *The night book*
Stubbs, Joanna. *With cat's eyes you'll never be scared of
  the dark*
Sturges, Philemon. *Ten flashing fireflies*
Tafuri, Nancy. *Do not disturb*
  What the sun sees / What the moon sees
Takamado no Miya Hisako. *Katie and the dream-
  eater*
Taylor, Anelise. *Lights on, lights off*
Tejima, Keizaburo. *Owl lake*
Thomas, Shelley Moore. *Putting the world to sleep*
Thompson, Richard. *I have to see this*
  Jesse on the night train
Thornhill, Jan. *Wild in the city*
Tobias, Tobi. *Chasing the goblins away*
Tyers, Jenny. *When it is night and when it is day*
Updike, David. *An autumn tale*
Van Allsburg, Chris. *The polar express*
VerDorn, Bethea. *Moon glows*
Vevers, Gwynne. *Animals of the dark*
Waboose, Jan Bourdeau. *Firedancers*
Waddell, Martin. *The big big sea*
  Can't you sleep, Little Bear?
  Owl babies
  Owl babies, a board book
  The park in the dark
Wahl, Jan. *My cat Ginger*
  The sleepytime book
Wallace, Daisy. *Ghost poems*
Walsh, Ellen Stoll. *Pip's magic*
Walter, Mildred Pitts. *Darkness*
Weir, Alison. *Peter, good night*

Weiss, Nicki. *Where does the brown bear go?*
  Where does the brown bear go? A board book
Wellington, Monica. *Night city*
  Night rabbits
Westcott, Nadine Bernard. *Going to bed*
Weston, Martha. *Space guys!*
Whatley, Bruce. *Captain Pajamas*
Whitman, Candace. *The night is like an animal*
Wiesner, David. *Tuesday*
Willard, Nancy. *Night story*
  The nightgown of the sullen moon
  The well-mannered balloon
Williams, Laura E. *Torch fishing with the sun*
Winthrop, Elizabeth. *Potbellied possums*
Wittington, Mary K. *Troll games*
Wolff, Ashley. *Only the cat saw*
Wood, Audrey. *Moonflute*
Wood, Douglas. *Northwoods cradle song*
Wouters, Anne. *This book is for us*
Wynne-Jones, Tim. *The hour of the frog*
Yaccarino, Dan. *Good night, Mr. Night*
Yeomans, Thomas. *For every child a star*
Yolen, Jane. *Nocturne*
  Owl moon
Zalben, Jane Breskin. *Norton's nighttime*
Ziefert, Harriet. *Hurry up, Jessie!*
  Moonride
  Say good night!
Zolotow, Charlotte (Shapiro). *I have a horse of my
  own*
  Wake up and goodnight
  When the wind stops
  The white marble
  Who is Ben?

Nightingales *see* Birds – nightingales

Nightmares *see* Bedtime; Monsters; Mythical
  creatures – goblins; Night; Sleep

Nishnawbe Indians *see* Indians of North
  America – Nishnawbe

Nisqually *see* Indians of North America –
  Nisqually

No text *see* Wordless

Noah *see* Religion – Noah

Nobscusset *see* Indians of North America –
  Nobscusset

Noise, sounds

Ahlberg, Allan. *Crash, bang, wallop!*
Alda, Arlene. *Pig, horse, or cow, don't wake me now*
Alexander, Anne (Anna Barbara Cooke). *Noise in
  the night*
Alexander, Martha G. *Pigs say oink*
Allard, Harry. *Bumps in the night*
Allen, Pamela. *Bertie and the bear*
Arnold, Caroline. *Noisytime for zoo animals*
Arnold, Katya. *Meow!*
Arnold, Tedd. *Sounds*
Asch, Frank. *Barnyard lullaby*
  I can roar

Aylesworth, Jim. *Country crossing*
  Hush up!
  Siren in the night
Bassett, Preston R. *Raindrop stories*
Behn, Harry. *What a beautiful noise*
Benjamin, Alan. *Rat-a-tat, pitter pat*
Bennett, David. *One cow moo moo*
Bennett, Jill. *Noisy poems*
Berenstain, Stan. *Bears in the night*
Berg, Jean Horton. *The noisy clock shop*
  The wee little man
Bilezikian, Gary. *While I slept*
Blanchard, Arlene. *Sounds my feet make*
Blocksma, Mary. *Did you hear that?*
Bond, Felicia. *Poinsettia and the firefighters*
Borten, Helen. *Do you hear what I hear?*
Boynton, Sandra. *Moo, baa, lalala*
Brandenberg, Franz. *Cock-a-doodle-doo*
  A robber! A robber!
Branley, Franklyn M. (Mansfield). *High sounds, low*
  sounds
Breeze, Lynn. *Baby's animals*
  Baby's clothes
Bright, Robert. *Georgie and the noisy ghost*
  Gregory, the noisiest and strongest boy in Grangers
  Grove
Brodmann, Aliana. *Such a noise!*
Brown, Craig McFarland. *City sounds*
Brown, Jane Clark. *Whonk, and whonk again*
Brown, Margaret Wise. *The country noisy book*
  Five little firemen
  The indoor noisy book
  Noisy book
  The quiet noisy book
  The seashore noisy book
  SHHhhh . . . . Bang
  The summer noisy book
  The winter noisy book
Burningham, John. *Cluck baa*
  Jangle twang
  Skip trip
  Slam bang
  Sniff shout
  Wobble pop
Burton, Jane. *Animals talking*
Cabrera, Jane. *Rory and the lion*
Capucilli, Alyssa Satin. *Inside a barn in the country*
Carle, Eric. *My very first book of sounds*
  The very quiet cricket
Caseley, Judith. *The noisemakers*
Casey, Patricia. *Beep! Beep! Oink! Oink! animals in*
  the city
  Cluck cluck
Causley, Charles. *"Quack!" said the billy-goat*
Cazet, Denys. *Dancing*
  Nothing at all
Christiansen, C. B. *Mara in the morning*
Chukovskii, Kornei Ivanovich. *Good morning, chick*
Cleary, Beverly. *The hullabaloo ABC*, ill. by Ted
  Rand
  The hullabaloo ABC, ill. by Earl Thollander
Coffelt, Nancy. *The dog who cried woof*
Cole, Joanna. *It's too noisy*
Compton, Kenn. *Granny Greenteeth and the noise in*
  the night
Conrad, Pam. *Animal lingo*
Cousins, Lucy. *What can Pinky hear?*
  What can rabbit hear?
Cowley, Stewart. *"Tweet, tweet, tweet"*

  What's that sound?
Crowe, Robert L. *Tyler Toad and the thunder*
Crowther, Robert. *Animal rap!*
DeLage, Ida. *The old witch and the snores*
Demarest, Chris L. *Farmer Nat*
  Honk!
DeRubertis, Barbara. *Janey Crane*
  Joey Goat
  Suzy Mule
  Tiny Tiger
  Zeely Zebra
De Zutter, Hank. *Who says a dog goes bow-wow?*
Diller, Harriett. *Big band sound*
Dinardo, Jeffrey. *Timothy and the night noises*
Dodds, Dayle Ann. *Do bunnies talk?*
Domanska, Janina. *Why so much noise?*
Dubov, Christine Salac. *Ding dong! and other sounds*
  Knock! and other sounds
  Oink! and other sounds
Durant, Alan. *Snake supper*
Duvoisin, Roger Antoine. *Petunia and the song*
Emberley, Ed (Edward Randolph). *Sounds*
Emberley, Rebecca. *City sounds*
  Jungle sounds
Evans, Mel. *The tiniest sound*
Farber, Norma. *There once was a woman who married*
  a man
Feiffer, Jules. *Bark, George*
Fleming, Candace. *When Agnes caws*
Fleming, Denise. *Barnyard banter*
Forrester, Victoria. *The magnificent moo*
Fowler, Richard. *Mr. Little's noisy car*
  Mr. Little's noisy fire engine
  Mr. Little's noisy truck
Fox, Mem. *Night noises*
Fujita, Miho. *The little choo-choo*
Gaeddert, LouAnn Bigge. *Noisy Nancy Norris*
Galdone, Paul. *Cat goes fiddle-i-fee*
Gannett, Ruth Stiles. *Katie and the sad noise*
Garelick, May. *Sounds of a summer night*
Geisert, Arthur. *Oink*
Geraghty, Paul. *The great green forest*
  Stop that noise!
Giffard, Hannah. *Hens say cluck*
Graff, Nancy Price. *In the hush of the evening*
Graham, John. *A crowd of cows*
Grambling, Lois G. *Night sounds*
Greene, Rhonda Gowler. *Barnyard song*
Grossman, Bill. *The banging book*
Gundersheimer, Karen. *Find cat, wear hat*
  Splish splash bang crash!
Hancock, Joy Elizabeth. *The loudest little lion*
Harrison, David Lee. *The animals' song*
Harshman, Marc. *All the way to morning*
Henley, Claire. *Quack, quack*
Heo, Yumi. *One afternoon*
  One Sunday morning
Hersom, Kathleen. *The copycat*
Hindley, Judy. *Soft and noisy*
Hirschi, Ron. *A time for singing*
Ho, Minfong. *Hush!*
Horvath, Betty F. *The cheerful quiet*
Howard, Elizabeth Fitzgerald. *When will Sarah*
  come?
Hubbell, Patricia. *Pots and pans*
Hudson, Cheryl Willis. *Animal sounds for baby*
Hughes, Shirley. *Noisy*
Hutchins, H. J. (Hazel J.). *Katie's babbling brother*
Hutchins, Pat. *Good night owl*

Daisy's day out
  Go to sleep, Daisy
Simms, Laura. *The squeaky door*
Simon, Francesca. *But what does the hippopotamus say?*
Skaar, Grace Marion. *What do the animals say?*
Skolsky, Mindy Warshaw. *Hannah and the whistling tea kettle*
Sloat, Teri. *Farmer Brown goes round and round*
  The thing that bothered Farmer Brown
Slobodkin, Louis. *Colette and the princess*
Smith, Barry. *Grandma Rabbitty's visit*
Snow, Alan. *Cluck!*
  The monster book of ABC sounds
  Oink!
  Quack!
  Woof!
Spence, Robert, III. *Clickety clack*
Spier, Peter. *Crash! bang! boom!*
  Gobble, growl, grunt
Spooner, Michael. *Old Meshikee and the little crabs*
Stafford, William. *The animal that drank up sound*
Stanley, Diane. *The conversation club*
Stapler, Sarah. *Trilby's trumpet*
Steiner, Charlotte. *Listen to my seashell*
Stevenson, Harvey. *Big scary wolf*
Stevenson, James. *Clams can't sing*
Strand, Mark. *The planet of lost things*
Sturges, Philemon. *What's that sound, Woolly Bear?*
Sweeney, Jacqueline. *Katie and the night noises*
Tafuri, Nancy. *Do not disturb*
Thayer, Jane. *Quiet on account of dinosaur*
Thomas, Patricia. *The one and only, super-duper, golly-whopper, jim-dandy, really-handy clock-tock-stopper*
Titus, Eve. *The kitten who couldn't purr*
Tresselt, Alvin R. *Wake up, farm!*, ill. by author
  Wake up, farm!, ill. by Carolyn Ewing
Tyers, Jenny. *When it is night and when it is day*
Velthuijs, Max. *Frog is frightened*
Verboven, Agnes. *Ducks like to swim*
Voake, Charlotte. *Tom's cat*
Waber, Bernard. *The mouse that snored*
Waddell, Martin. *Let's go home, Little Bear*
  Squeak-a-lot
Wadsworth, Ginger. *One tiger growls*
Walsh, Melanie. *Do monkeys tweet?*
Walter, Virginia. *"Hi, pizza man!"*
Walton, Rick. *Little dogs say "Rough!"*
Watson, John. *We're the noisy dinosaurs!*
Webb, Angela. *Talkabout sound*
West, Colin. *One day in the jungle*
West, Judy. *Have you got my purr?*
Wheeler, Cindy. *Marmalade's nap*
Whybrow, Ian. *Quacky quack-quack!*
Wildsmith, Brian. *Goat's trail*
Winthrop, Elizabeth. *A very noisy girl*
Wong, Janet S. *Buzz*
Wood, Jakki. *Fiddle-i-fee*
Wundrow, Deanna. *Jungle drum*
Wynne-Jones, Tim. *The hour of the frog*
Young, Ruth. *Who says moo?*
Zalben, Jane Breskin. *Norton's nighttime*
Zarin, Cynthia. *Rose and Sebastian*
Ziefert, Harriet. *Cow in the house*
  Listen! Piggety Pig
  Oh, what a noisy farm!
  On our way to the barn
  On our way to the forest

On our way to the water
  On our way to the zoo
Zolotow, Charlotte (Shapiro). *The poodle who barked at the wind*
  The quiet mother and the noisy little boy

North Pole *see* Foreign lands – Arctic

Norway *see* Foreign lands – Norway

Noses *see* Anatomy – noses; Senses – smelling

Numbers *see* Counting, numbers

Nuns *see* Careers – nuns

Nursery rhymes

Agard, John. *No hickory no dickory no dock*
Ahlberg, Janet. *The jolly Christmas postman*
Allison, Diane Worfolk. *This is the key to the kingdom*
Anholt, Catherine. *Come back, Jack!*
Arnold, Tedd. *Actions*
  Colors
  Mother Goose's words of wit and wisdom
  Opposites
  Sounds
Aylesworth, Jim. *The cat and the fiddle and more*
  The completed hickory dickory dock
  My son John
B. B. Blacksheep and Company
Barchilon, Jacques. *The authentic Mother Goose fairy tales and nursery rhymes*
Bartlett, Robert Merrill. *Jack Horner and song of six-pence*
Baum, L. Frank (Lyman Frank). *Mother Goose in prose*
Bayley, Nicola. *Nicola Bayley's book of nursery rhymes*
Benjamin, Floella. *Skip across the ocean*
Blake, Pamela. *Peep-show*
Blake, Quentin. *Quentin Blake's nursery rhyme book*
Blegvad, Erik. *Burnie's hill*
Blegvad, Lenore. *Hark! Hark! The dogs do bark, and other poems about dogs*
  Mittens for kittens and other rhymes about cats
  This little pig-a-wig and other rhymes about pigs
Bodecker, N. M. (Nils Mogens). *"It's raining," said John Twaining*
Bowman, Peter. *Goodnight, teddy bear*
Briggs, Raymond. *Fee fi fo fum*
  Ring-a-ring o' roses
  The white land
Brooke, L. Leslie (Leonard Leslie). *Oranges and lemons*
  Ring o'roses
Brown, Marc Tolon. *Can you jump like a frog?*
  Finger rhymes
  Hand rhymes
  One, two buckle my shoe
  Play rhymes
  Two little monkeys
Brown, Marcia. *Peter Piper's alphabet*
Brown, Ruth. *Ladybug, ladybug*
Butterworth, Nick. *Nick Butterworth's book of nursery rhymes*
Cakes and custard
Caldecott, Randolph. *Panjandrum picture book*
  The Queen of Hearts

London, Jonathan. *I see the moon and the moon sees me*
Lord, Beman. *The days of the week*
McGee, Shelagh. *I'm a little teapot*
Manson, Christopher. *A farmyard song*
Marshak, S. (Samuel). *The merry starlings*
Marshall, James. *Hey, diddle, diddle*
Martin, Bill (William Ivan). *Fire! Fire! said Mrs. McGuire*
 Sounds I remember
Martin, Sarah Catherine. *The comic adventures of Old Mother Hubbard and her dog*
 Old Mother Hubbard
 Old Mother Hubbard and her dog, ill. by Lisa Amoroso
 Old Mother Hubbard and her dog, ill. by Paul Galdone
 Old Mother Hubbard and her dog, ill. by Evaline Ness
 Old Mother Hubbard and her wonderful dog
Marzollo, Jean. *The rebus treasury*
Mendoza, George. *Silly sheep and other sheepish rhymes*
Miranda, Anne. *To market, to market*
Montgomerie, Norah. *This little pig went to market*
Morley, Carol. *Farmyard song*
Most, Bernard. *Four and twenty dinosaurs*
Mother Goose. *A child's book of old nursery rhymes*
 ABC rhymes
 The annotated Mother Goose
 As I was going up and down
 Baa baa, black sheep, ill. by Marilyn Janovitz
 Baa, baa, black sheep, ill. by Moira Kemp
 Baa baa black sheep, ill. by Sue Porter
 Baa baa black sheep, ill. by Ferelith Eccles Williams
 Baby's first Mother Goose
 The baby's lap book
 Beatrix Potter's nursery rhyme book
 Blessed Mother Goose
 Brian Wildsmith's Mother Goose
 Carolyn Wells' edition of Mother Goose
 Cats by Mother Goose
 The Charles Addams Mother Goose
 The Chinese Mother Goose rhymes
 The city and country Mother Goose
 Frank Baber's Mother Goose
 The gay Mother Goose
 The glorious Mother Goose
 Grafa' Grig had a pig
 Gray goose and gander and other Mother Goose rhymes
 Gregory Griggs and other nursery rhyme people
 Hey diddle diddle, ill. by Marilyn Janovitz
 Hey diddle, diddle, ill. by Moira Kemp
 Hey diddle diddle, ill. by Marc Mongeau
 Hey diddle diddle, ill. by Nita Sowter
 Hey diddle diddle, ill. by Eleanor Wasmuth
 Hey diddle diddle, and Baby bunting, ill. by Randolph Caldecott
 Hey diddle diddle picture book, ill. by Randolph Caldecott
 Hickory dickory dock, ill. by Marilyn Janovitz
 Hickory, dickory, dock, ill. by Moira Kemp
 Hickory dickory dock and other nursery rhymes, ill. by Carol Jones
 Humpty Dumpty, ill. by Colin and Jacqui Hawkins
 Humpty Dumpty, ill. by Moira Kemp
 Humpty Dumpty and other first rhymes

 Humpty Dumpty and other rhymes, ill. by Rosemary Wells
 Hurrah, we're outward bound!
 Hush-a-bye baby
 Ian Penney's book of nursery rhymes
 In a pumpkin shell
 Jack and Jill
 Jack Kent's merry Mother Goose
 James Marshall's Mother Goose
 Kate Greenaway's Mother Goose
 Kitten rhymes
 The Larousse book of nursery rhymes
 Lavender's blue
 Little Boy Blue
 Little Boy Blue and other rhymes
 Little Miss Muffet
 The little Mother Goose
 London Bridge is falling down, ill. by Ed Emberley
 London Bridge is falling down, ill. by Peter Spier
 Michael Foreman's Mother Goose
 Mother Goose, ill. by Scott Cook
 Mother Goose, ill. by Roger Antoine Duvoisin
 Mother Goose, ill. by Miss Elliott
 Mother Goose, ill. by C. B. Falls
 Mother Goose, ill. by Gyo Fujikawa
 Mother Goose, ill. by Vernon Grant
 Mother Goose, ill. by Kate Greenaway
 Mother Goose, ill. by Michael Hague
 Mother Goose, ill. by Violet La Mont
 Mother Goose, ill. by Arthur Rackham
 Mother Goose, ill. by Frederick Richardson, 1915
 Mother Goose, ill. by Frederick Richardson, 1976
 Mother Goose, ill. by Gustaf Tenggren
 Mother Goose, ill. by Tasha Tudor
 Mother Goose and nursery rhymes, ill. by Philip Reed
 A Mother Goose book, ill. by Joan Walsh Anglund
 The Mother Goose book, ill. by Alice and Martin Provensen
 The Mother Goose book, ill. by Sonia Roetter
 Mother Goose house
 Mother Goose in French
 Mother Goose in hieroglyphics
 Mother Goose in Spanish
 Mother Goose melodies
 Mother Goose nursery rhymes, ill. by Arthur Rackham, 1969
 Mother Goose nursery rhymes, ill. by Arthur Rackham, 1975
 Mother Goose rhymes, ill. by Eulalie M. Banks and Lois Lenski
 The Mother Goose songbook
 The Mother Goose treasury
 Mother Goose's melodies
 Mother Goose's melody
 Mother Goose's nursery rhymes
 Mother Goose's rhymes and melodies
 My first real Mother Goose board book, ill. by Blanche Fisher Wright
 Nursery rhyme book
 Nursery rhymes, ill. by Douglas W. Gorsline
 Nursery rhymes, ill. by Eloise Wilkin
 Nursery rhymes from Mother Goose in signed English
 The old woman in a shoe
 One I love, two I love, and other loving Mother Goose rhymes
 One misty moisty morning
 1, 2 buckle my shoe
 The only true Mother Goose melodies

Over the moon
Pat-a-cake, ill. by Marilyn Janovitz
Pat-a-cake, pat-a-cake, ill. by Moira Kemp
The piper's son, ill. by Emily Newton Barto
A pocket full of posies
Pussy cat, pussy cat
Pussycat, pussycat and other rhymes
The rainbow Mother Goose
The real Mother Goose
The real Mother Goose board book, ill. by Diane
  Muldrow
The real Mother Goose clock book
Richard Scarry's best Mother Goose ever
Richard Scarry's favorite Mother Goose rhymes
Rimes de la Mere Oie
Ring o' roses
The Sesame Street players present Mother Goose
Sing a song of Mother Goose
Sing a song of sixpence, ill. by Randolph Calde-
  cott; Barron's, 1988
Sing a song of sixpence, ill. by Randolph Calde-
  cott; Hart, 1977
Sing a song of sixpence, ill. by Margaret Chamber-
  lain
Sing a song of sixpence, ill. by Leonard Lubin
Sing a song of sixpence, ill. by Ray Marshall and
  Korky Paul
Sing a song of sixpence, ill. by Ferelith Eccles
  Williams
Sing hey diddle diddle
Songs for Mother Goose
The tall Mother Goose
Thirty old-time nursery songs
This little pig, ill. by Leonard Lubin
This little pig, ill. by Eleanor Wasmuth
This little pig went to market, ill. by L. Leslie
  Brooke
This little pig went to market, ill. by Denise Fleming
This little pig went to market, ill. by Ferelith Eccles
  Williams
This little piggy
The three jovial huntsmen, ill. by Susan Jeffers
The three little kittens, ill. by Lorinda Bryan Cauley
The three little kittens, ill. by Paul Galdone
The three little kittens, ill. by Dorothy Stott
The three little kittens, ill. by Shelley Thornton
To market! To market!, ill. by Emma Lillian Brock
To market! To market!, ill. by Peter Spier
Tom, Tom the piper's son
Twenty nursery rhymes
Vernon Grant's Mother Goose
Wee Willie Winkie and other rhymes
Wendy Watson's Mother Goose
Willy Pogany's Mother Goose
*The moving adventures of Old Dame Trot and her comi-
  cal cat*
My first nursery rhymes
My first songs
Namm, Diane. *Favorite nursery rhymes*
Nayer, Judy. *Rhymes*
Nichols, Grace. *Asana and the animals*
Nursery rhymes, ill. by Gertrude Elliott
One, two, buckle my shoe, ill. by Rowan Barnes-Mur-
  phy
One, two, buckle my shoe, ill. by Gail E. Haley
One, two, skip a few!
Ormerod, Jan. *To baby with love*
Over in the meadow, ill. by Paul Galdone

Palazzo, Tony (Anthony D.). *Animals 'round the
  mulberry bush*
Paparone, Pamela. *Five little ducks*
Patterson, Pat. *Hickory dickory duck*
Patz, Nancy. *Moses supposes his toeses are roses and 7
  other silly old rhymes*
Pearson, Tracey Campbell. *A apple pie*
  Sing a song of sixpence
Peppé, Rodney. *Cat and mouse*
  Hey riddle diddle
Percy, Graham. *Elephants never forget*
Petersham, Maud. *The rooster crows*
Polacco, Patricia. *Babushka's Mother Goose*
Potter, Beatrix. *Appley Dapply's nursery rhymes*
  Cecily Parsley's nursery rhymes
The pudgy book of Mother Goose
Rey, H. A. (Hans Augusto). *Humpty Dumpty and
  other Mother Goose songs*
Robbins, Ruth. *The harlequin and Mother Goose*
Rosenberg, Liz. *Mama Goose*
Sabuda, Robert James. *The movable Mother Goose*
Scarry, Richard. *Richard Scarry's animal nursery tales*
Scieszka, Jon. *The book that Jack wrote*
Sendak, Maurice. *Hector Protector, and As I went over
  the water*
Sieveking, Anthea. *Mary had a little lamb and other
  animal rhymes*
  Polly put the kettle on and other play rhymes
  Rub-a-dub-dub and other splashy rhymes
  Twinkle, twinkle, little star and other bedtime rhymes
Simple Simon. *The adventures of Simple Simon*
  The history of Simple Simon
  Simple Simon
Siomades, Lorianne. *The itsy bitsy spider*
  Three little kittens
Stobbs, William. *This little piggy*
Tarrant, Margaret. *The Margaret Tarrant nursery
  rhyme book*
Taylor, Alice. *A child's treasury of Irish rhymes*
Taylor, Jane. *Twinkle, twinkle, little star*
Thomson, Pat. *Rhymes around the day*
Trapani, Iza. *The itsy bitsy spider*
  Mary had a little lamb
Tucker, Nicholas. *Mother Goose abroad*
Vail, Rachel. *Over the moon*
Voce, Louise. *Over in the meadow*
Wadsworth, Olive A. *Over in the meadow*
Walton, Rick. *How many, how many, how many*
Watson, Wendy. *Thanksgiving at our house*
Weil, Lisl. *Mother Goose picture riddles*
What do you feed your donkey on?
Wheeler, Opal. *Sing Mother Goose*
Williams, Garth. *The chicken book*
Williams, Jenny (Jennifer). *Here's a ball for baby*
  One, two, buckle my shoe
  Ride a cockhorse
  Ring around a rosy
Williams, Sarah. *Ride a cock-horse*
Yolen, Jane. *The lap-time song and play book*
  Street rhymes around the world
Ziefert, Harriet. *Mother Goose math*

Nursery school *see* School

Nurses *see* Careers – nurses

Oceans *see* Sea and seashore

Octopuses

Barrett, John M. *Oscar the selfish octopus*
Brandenberg, Franz. *Otto is different*
Carrick, Carol. *Octopus*
Drdek, Richard E. *Horace the friendly octopus*
Heller, Ruth. *How to hide an octopus*
Kite, L. Patricia. *Down in the sea. The octopus*
Kraus, Robert. *Herman the helper*
Lauber, Patricia. *An octopus is amazing*
Most, Bernard. *My very own octopus*
Shaw, Evelyn S. *Octopus*
Spohn, Kate. *Ruth's bake shop*
Ungerer, Tomi. *Emile*
Waber, Bernard. *I was all thumbs*
Yaccarino, Dan. *An octopus followed me home*

Odors *see* Senses – smelling

Ogres *see* Mythical creatures – ogres

Oil

Berger, Melvin. *Oil spill!*
Freeman, Don. *The seal and the slick*
Rand, Gloria. *Prince William*
Ungerer, Tomi. *The Mellops strike oil*

Ojibwa Indians *see* Indians of North America
– Ojibwa

Old age

Ackerman, Karen. *Just like Max*
    Walking with Clara Belle
Allard, Harry. *It's so nice to have a wolf around the
    house*
Anderson, Lena. *Stina's visit*
Ardizzone, Edward. *Lucy Brown and Mr. Grimes*
Armitage, Ronda. *The lighthouse keeper's rescue*
Arnold, Marsha Diane. *The chicken salad club*
Barasch, Lynne. *Old friends*
Bergman, Donna. *City fox*
Bogart, Jo Ellen. *Jeremiah learns to read*
Bosak, Susan V. *Something to remember me by*
Briggs, Raymond. *Jim and the beanstalk*
Bunting, Eve (Anne Evelyn). *The big cheese*
    Sunshine home
Calmenson, Stephanie. *Rosie, a visiting dog's story*
Carlstrom, Nancy White. *Blow me a kiss, Miss Lilly*
Coats, Laura Jane. *Mr. Jordan in the park*
Collington, Peter. *A small miracle*
Delton, Judy. *My grandma's in a nursing home*
Dugan, Barbara. *Loop the loop*
Duncan, Alice Faye. *Miss Viola and Uncle Ed Lee*
Edelman, Elaine. *Boom-de-boom*
Farber, Norma. *How does it feel to be old?*

Fassler, Joan. *My grandpa died today*
Fender, Kay. *Odette!*
Fink, Dale Borman. *Mr. Silver and Mrs. Gold*
Fox, Louisa. *Every Monday in the mailbox*
Fox, Mem. *Wilfrid Gordon McDonald Partridge*
Franklin, Kristine L. *The gift*
    The old, old man and the very little boy
Gammell, Stephen. *Git along, old Scudder*
Glaser, Linda. *The borrowed Hanukkah latkes*
Goffstein, M. B. (Marilyn Brooke). *Fish for supper*
Graham, Bob. *Rose meets Mr. Wintergarten*
Greene, Carol. *The old ladies who liked cats*
Gregory, Valiska. *The oatmeal cookie giant*
Griffith, Helen V. *Dream meadow*
    Georgia music
    How many candles?
Grimm, Jacob. *The Bremen town band*
    The Bremen town musicians, ill. by Donna Dia-
    mond
    The Bremen town musicians, ill. by Janina Doman-
    ska
    The Bremen town musicians, ill. by Paul Galdone
    The Bremen town musicians, ill. by David Johnson
    Bremen town musicians, ill. by Josef Palecek
    The Bremen town musicians, ill. by Ilse Plume
    The Bremen town musicians, ill. by Janet Stevens
    The Bremen town musicians, ill. by Bernadette
    Watts
    The horse, the fox, and the lion
    The musicians of Bremen, ill. by John Segal
    The musicians of Bremen, ill. by Svend Otto S
    The musicians of Bremen, ill. by Martin Ursell
    The traveling musicians of Bremen
Grosz, Peter. *The special gifts*
Guthrie, Donna. *Grandpa doesn't know it's me*
    The secret admirer
Hamm, Diane Johnston. *Grandma drives a motor bed*
Hazen, Barbara Shook. *Digby*
    Why did Grandpa die?
Herriot, James. *Blossom comes home*
Hest, Amy. *The midnight eaters*
Hewett, Joan. *Rosalie*
Hickcox, Ruth. *Great-Grandmother's treasure*
Hill, Susan. *King of kings*
Hindley, Judy. *The little train*
Hoff, Syd. *Barkley*
Holder, Heidi. *Carmine the crow*
Hughes, Shirley. *The snow lady*
Johnson, Angela. *When I am old with you*
Johnston, Tony. *Grandpa's song*
Jones, Rebecca C. *Great Aunt Martha*
Joyce, William. *The Leaf Men and the brave good bugs*
Jung, Minna. *William's ninth life*
Kahl, Virginia. *Maxie*
Karkowsky, Nancy. *Grandma's soup*
Keeping, Charles. *Molly o' the moors*
Ketner, Mary Grace. *Ganzy remembers*
Kibbey, Marsha. *My grammy*
Klein, Leonore. *Old, older, oldest*
Knox-Wagner, Elaine. *My grandpa retired today*
Krasilovsky, Phyllis. *The woman who saved things*
Kroll, Virginia L. *Fireflies, peach pies, and lullabies*
Kunhardt, Dorothy. *Billy the barber*
Kvasnosky, Laura McGee. *Zelda and Ivy one Christ-
    mas*
Lakin, Pat (Patricia). *Grandparents*
Laminack, Lester L. *The sunsets of Miss Olivia Wig-
    gins*
Lasky, Kathryn. *Sea swan*

Leedahl, Shelley A. (Shelley Ann). *The bone talker*
Leonard, Marcia. *Gregory and Mr. Grump*
Lewis, J. Patrick. *The tsar and the amazing cow*
Littledale, Freya. *The snow child*
Miller, William. *The piano*
Nelson, Vaunda Micheaux. *Always Gramma*
Newman, Lesléa. *Remember that*
Nordqvist, Sven. *Festus and Mercury wishing to go fishing*
Peet, Bill (William Bartlett). *Smokey*
Peters, Lisa Westberg. *Good morning, river!*
Pomerantz, Charlotte. *Buffy and Albert*
Powell, Consie. *Old dog Cora and the Christmas tree*
Proimos, James. *Joe's wish*
Rawlins, Donna. *Digging to China*
Ross, Lillian Hammer. *The little old man and his dreams*
Rylant, Cynthia. *Mr. Putter and Tabby bake the cake*
    Mr. Putter and Tabby pick the pears
    Mr. Putter and Tabby pour the tea
    Mr. Putter and Tabby walk the dog
Sakai, Kimiko. *Sachiko means happiness*
Schachner, Judith Byron. *The Grannyman*
Schwartz, David M. *Sugargrandpa*
Seligson, Susan. *Amos*
Skorpen, Liesel Moak. *Old Arthur*
Slobodkina, Esphyr. *Billy, the condominium cat*
Smith, Barry. *Minnie and Ginger*
Snow, Pegeen. *Mrs. Periwinkle's groceries*
Sonneborn, Ruth A. *I love Gram*
Spalding, Andrea. *Me and Mr. Mah*
    Sarah May and the new red dress
Stevens, Janet. *Old bag of bones*
Stroud, Bettye. *Down home at Miss Dessa's*
Sullivan, Silky. *Grandpa was a cowboy*
Taber, Anthony. *Cats' eyes*
Taylor, Mark. *Old Blue, you good dog you*
Tejima, Keizaburo. *Ho-limlim*
Tusa, Tricia. *Maebelle's suitcase*
Uchida, Yoshiko. *Sumi's special happening*
    The wise old woman
Waggoner, Karen. *The lemonade babysitter*
Wahl, Jan. *"I remember," cried Grandma Pinky*
Watts, Jeri Hanel. *Keepers*
Wild, Margaret. *Old Pig*
    Remember me
Wittman, Sally. *A special trade*
Yolen, Jane. *Miz Berlin walks*
Zolotow, Charlotte (Shapiro). *I know a lady*

Olympics *see* Sports – Olympics

Only child *see* Family life – only child

Opera singers *see* Careers – opera singers

Opossums *see* Animals – possums

Opposites *see* Concepts – opposites

Optical illusions

Anno, Mitsumasa. *Anno's alphabet*
    Anno's counting book
    Anno's counting house
    Anno's flea market
    Anno's Italy
    Anno's journey
    Anno's magical ABC
    Dr. Anno's magical midnight circus
    Topsy turvies
    Topsy turvies
    Upside-downers
Baum, Arline. *Opt*
Doty, Roy. *Eye fooled you*
Gardner, Beau. *The look again . . . and again, and again, and again book*
    The turn about, think about, look about book
Noll, Sally. *Watch where you go*

Optimism *see* Character traits – optimism

Orangutans *see* Animals – orangutans

Orderliness *see* Character traits – orderliness

Organists *see* Careers – organists

Orphans

Ardizzone, Edward. *Lucy Brown and Mr. Grimes*
The babes in the woods. *The old ballad of the babes in the woods*
Bemelmans, Ludwig. *Madeline*
    Madeline [pop-up book]
    Madeline and the bad hat
    Madeline and the gypsies
    Madeline in London
    Madeline's Christmas
    Madeline's rescue
Bulla, Clyde Robert. *Poor boy, rich boy*
Bunting, Eve (Anne Evelyn). *Train to somewhere*
Burton, Jane. *Fancy the fox*
Calhoun, Mary. *A shepherd's gift*
Gabel, Susan L. *Where the sun kisses the sea*
Gibson, Kari Smalley. *Mooki's secret*
Goble, Paul. *The lost children*
Jeram, Anita. *All together now*
Lyon, David. *The crumbly coast*
McCully, Emily Arnold. *Little Kit, or, The Industrious Flea Circus girl*
    The orphan singer
McKay, Lawrence. *Journey home*
Mahy, Margaret. *Sailor Jack and the twenty orphans*
Martin, Jacqueline Briggs. *The water gift and the pig of the pig*
Mollel, Tololwa M. (Tololwa Marti). *Orphan boy*
Moore, Inga. *The vegetable thieves*
Polacco, Patricia. *Welcome Comfort*
Prigger, Mary Skillings. *Aunt Minnie McGranahan*
Rylant, Cynthia. *The bird house*
Sanfield, Steve. *The girl who wanted a song*
San Souci, Robert D. *The secret of the stones*
Sullivan, Silky. *Grandpa was a cowboy*
Thomas, Kathy. *The angel's quest*
Ungerer, Tomi. *The three robbers*
Warner, Sunny. *The magic sewing machine*
Weedn, Flavia. *The star gift*
Weninger, Brigitte. *Lumina*
Willard, Nancy. *Shadow story*
Yolen, Jane. *The girl in the golden bower*
Yorinks, Arthur. *Oh, brother*

Ostracism *see* Character traits – being different

Ostriches *see* Birds – ostriches

Otters *see* Animals – otters

Outer space *see* Space and spaceships

Owls *see* Birds – owls

Oxen *see* Animals – oxen

Pack rats *see* Animals – pack rats

Painters *see* Activities – painting; Careers – artists

Painting *see* Activities – painting

Paiute Indians *see* Indians of North America – Paiute

Pajamas *see* Clothing – pajamas

Pakistan *see* Foreign lands – Pakistan

Paleontologists *see* Careers – paleontologists

Palestine *see* Foreign lands – Palestine

Panama *see* Foreign lands – Panama

Pandas *see* Animals – pandas

Panthers *see* Animals – leopards

Pants *see* Clothing – pants

Papago Indians *see* Indians of North America – Papago

Paper

Bateson-Hill, Margaret. *Lao Lao of Dragon Mountain*
Curtis, Neil. *How paper is made*
Engel, Diana. *The shelf-paper jungle*
Gibbons, Gail. *Deadline!*
   Paper, paper everywhere
Huff, Vivian. *Let's make paper dolls*
Jaspersohn, William. *Timber!*
Kleven, Elisa. *The paper princess*
Kroll, Virginia L. *Pink paper swans*
Lobato, Arcadio. *Paper bird*
Lohf, Sabine. *Things I can make with paper*
Melmed, Laura Krauss. *Little Oh*
Mitgutsch, Ali. *From wood to paper*
Monsell, Mary Elise. *Crackle Creek*
Rumford, James. *The cloudmakers*

Small, David. *Paper John*
Tagore, Rabindranath. *Paper boats*
Testa, Fulvio. *The paper airplane*

Parades

Anderson, C. W. (Clarence Williams). *The rumble seat pony*
Baer, Gene. *Thump thump rat-a-tat-tat*
Ballard, Robin. *Carnival*
Brenner, Barbara A. *The snow parade*
Butler, Dorothy. *Higgledy, piggledy, hobbledy hoy*
Chalmers, Mary. *Easter parade*
Chwast, Seymour. *Alphabet parade*
Crews, Donald. *Parade*
Derby, Sally. *King Kenrick's splinter*
Emberley, Ed (Edward Randolph). *The parade book*
Ets, Marie Hall. *Another day*
   In the forest
Feczko, Kathy. *Umbrella parade*
Flack, Marjorie. *Wait for William*
Greenfield, Eloise. *Easter parade*
Gretz, Susanna. *Frog, duck, and rabbit*
Hayes, Ann. *Meet the Marching Smithereens*
Janice. *Little Bear marches in the St. Patrick's Day parade*
Joosse, Barbara M. *Fourth of July*
Kraus, Robert. *Springfellow's parade*
Kroll, Steven. *The goat parade*
   Mary McLean and the St. Patrick's Day parade
Lasky, Kathryn. *Fourth of July bear*
Leonard, Marcia. *The tin can man*
Mahy, Margaret. *When the king rides by*
Mills, Claudia. *Phoebe's parade*
Mora, Pat. *The rainbow tulip*
O'Donnell, Elizabeth Lee. *Patrick's day*
Richter, Mischa. *Eric and Matilda*
Roth, Susan L. *We'll ride elephants through Brooklyn*
Silverman, Erica. *On the morn of Mayfest*
Slobodkina, Esphyr. *Pezzo the peddler and the circus elephant*
Spier, Peter. *Crash! bang! boom!*
Ziefert, Harriet. *First Night*
Ziner, Feenie. *Counting carnival*

Parakeets *see* Birds – parakeets, parrots

Park rangers *see* Careers – park rangers

Parks

Ackerman, Karen. *In the park with dad*
Bauer, Helen. *Good times at the park*
Browne, Anthony. *Voices in the park*
Burstein, Fred. *Whispering in the park*
Coats, Laura Jane. *Mr. Jordan in the park*
Cousins, Lucy. *Kite in the park*
Curious George and the dump truck
Ernst, Lisa Campbell. *Squirrel Park*
Fife, Dale. *The little park*
Hautzig, Esther (Rudomin). *In the park*
Heo, Yumi. *One Sunday morning*
Hill, Eric. *The park*
   Spot goes to the park
Hill, Mary Lou. *My dad's a park ranger*
Hughes, Shirley. *When we went to the park*
Kessler, Ethel. *Are there seals in the sandbox?*
McNaughton, Colin. *At the park*

McPhail, David M. *Henry Bear's park*
Mahy, Margaret. *Down the dragon's tongue*
Matje, Martin. *Celeste*
Merriam, Eve. *Where's that cat?*
Morozumi, Atsuko. *In the park*
O'Donnell, Peter. *Carnegie's excuse*
Roberts, Thom. *Pirates in the park*
Rockwell, Anne F. *Hugo at the park*
Rodda, Emily. *Yay!*
Takeshita, Fumiko. *The park bench*
Van der Beek, Deborah. *Superbabe!*
Waddell, Martin. *The park in the dark*
Zolotow, Charlotte (Shapiro). *The park book*

Parrots *see* Birds – parakeets, parrots

Participation

Agostinelli, Maria Enrica. *I know something you don't know*
Barrett, Judi. *What's left?*
Bauman, A. F. *Guess where you're going, guess what you'll do*
Bendick, Jeanne. *Why can't I?*
Berry, Holly. *Busy Lizzie*
Bester, Roger. *Guess what?*
Black, Irma (Simonton). *Is this my dinner?*
Blake, Quentin. *All join in*
Booth, Eugene. *At the circus*
   At the fair
   In the air
   In the garden
   In the jungle
   Under the ocean
Brown, Marc Tolon. *Finger rhymes*
Brown, Margaret Wise. *The country noisy book*
   The indoor noisy book
   Noisy book
   The quiet noisy book
   The seashore noisy book
   The summer noisy book
   The winter noisy book
Cameron, Polly. *"I can't," said the ant*
Carroll, Ruth. *Where's the bunny?*
Charlip, Remy. *Fortunately*
Cole, William. *Frances face-maker*
Corbett, Grahame. *Guess who?*
   What number now?
   Who is hiding?
   Who is inside?
   Who is next?
Craig, M. Jean. *Boxes*
Crume, Marion W. *Let me see you try*
   Listen!
   What do you say?
De Regniers, Beatrice Schenk. *It does not say meow!*
Elting, Mary. *Q is for duck*
Emberley, Ed (Edward Randolph). *Ed Emberley's amazing look through book*
   Klippity klop
Ets, Marie Hall. *Just me*
   Talking without words
Fowler, Allan. *What do you see in a cloud?*
French, Fiona. *Hunt the thimble*
Garten, Jan. *The alphabet tale*
Heilbroner, Joan. *This is the house where Jack lives*
Hewett, Anita. *The tale of the turnip*
Hoban, Tana. *Look again*
   Where is it?

The house that Jack built. *The house that Jack built,* ill. by Seymour Chwast
   The house that Jack built, ill. by Nadine Bernard Westcott
Hutchins, Pat. *Good night owl*
Ipcar, Dahlov. *Lost and found*
Jaynes, Ruth M. *Benny's four hats*
Johnson, Ryerson. *Let's walk up the wall*
Kepes, Juliet. *Run little monkeys, run, run, run*
Kunhardt, Edith. *Which one would you choose?*
   Which pig would you choose?
Kuskin, Karla. *Roar and more*
Leonard, Marcia. *King Lionheart's castle*
Löfgren, Ulf. *One-two-three*
MacGregor, Ellen. *Theodor Turtle*
Martin, Bill (William Ivan). *Brave little Indian*
Montgomerie, Norah. *This little pig went to market*
Ogle, Lucille. *I hear*
Paterson, Diane. *If I were a toad*
Rosen, Michael (1946-). *We're going on a bear hunt*
Seignobosc, Françoise. *The things I like*
Seuss, Dr. *Mr. Brown can moo! Can you?*
   Wacky Wednesday
Shaw, Charles Green. *It looked like spilt milk*
Siewert, Margaret. *Bear hunt*
Simon, Norma. *What do I say?*
Sivulich, Sandra Stroner. *I'm going on a bear hunt*
Skaar, Grace Marion. *What do the animals say?*
Skorpen, Liesel Moak. *All the Lassies*
Slobodkina, Esphyr. *Caps for sale*
   Pezzo the peddler and the circus elephant
   Pezzo the peddler and the thirteen silly thieves
Spier, Peter. *Crash! bang! boom!*
   Gobble, growl, grunt
Steiner, Charlotte. *Five little finger playmates*
Sutton, Eve. *My cat likes to hide in boxes*
Ueno, Noriko. *Elephant buttons*
Watanabe, Shigeo. *How do I put it on?*
Weil, Lisl. *Owl and other scrambles*
Yudell, Lynn Deena. *Make a face*

Parties

Adams, Adrienne. *The Christmas party*
   A Halloween happening
Albert, Shirley. *Doll party*
Allard, Harry. *The Stupids have a ball*
   There's a party at Mona's tonight
Allred, Mary. *Grandmother Poppy and the children's tea party*
Anderson, Lena. *Bunny party*
Anderson, Lonzo. *The Halloween party*
Anholt, Catherine. *Snow fairy and the spaceman*
Asch, Frank. *Insects from outer space*
   Popcorn
Barbour, Karen. *Nancy*
Berenstain, Stan. *The Berenstain bears and the slumber party*
Berlan, Kathryn Hook. *Andrew's amazing monsters*
Bible, Charles. *Jennifer's new chair*
Blance, Ellen. *Monster has a party*
Bowden, Joan Chase. *The bear's surprise party*
Brandenberg, Franz. *The hit of the party*
Briggs, Raymond. *The party*
Brimner, Larry Dane. *Country Bear's surprise*
Brooke, L. Leslie (Leonard Leslie). *Johnny Crow's party*
Brown, Marc Tolon. *Arthur's birthday*
Brown, Myra Berry. *Company's coming for dinner*

Calder, Lyn. *Walt Disney's Alice's tea party*
Carlstrom, Nancy White. *Happy birthday, Jesse Bear!*
Cartlidge, Michelle. *Bunny's birthday*
Caseley, Judith. *Slumber party!*
Chalmers, Mary. *Six dogs, twenty-three cats, forty-five mice, and one hundred sixteen spiders*
Chichester Clark, Emma. *Little Miss Muffet's count-along surprise*
Childress, Mark. *Joshua and Bigtooth*
Claverie, Jean. *The party*
Cocca-Leffler, Maryann. *Ice-cold birthday*
Cohen, Barbara. *Make a wish, Molly*
Cohen, Miriam. *Tough Jim*
Cole, Joanna. *Pin the tail on the donkey and other party games*
Conrad, Pam. *Doll Face has a party!*
Corey, Dorothy. *Will it ever be my birthday?*
Costa, Nicoletta. *The birthday party, a board book*
  Molly and Tom, the birthday party
Cousins, Lucy. *Maisy dresses up*
Craver, Mike. *Beaver ball at the bug club*
Crothers, Samuel McChord. *Miss Muffet's Christmas party*
Davis, Katie (Katie I.). *I hate to go to bed!*
Day, Alexandra. *Carl's masquerade*
De Groat, Diane. *Happy Birthday to you, you belong in a zoo*
DeLage, Ida. *The old witch's party*
  The squirrel's tree party
Delessert, Etienne. *The endless party*
Dewey, Ariane. *The tea squall*
Dowling, Paul. *Happy birthday, Owl*
Du Bois, William Pène. *Bear party*
Dubowski, Cathy East. *A cake for Jake*
Durant, Alan. *Mouse party*
Ehrlich, Amy. *Bunnies at Christmastime*
Enderle, Judith (Ann) Ross. *Six creepy sheep*
Ets, Marie Hall. *The cow's party*
  Nine days to Christmas
Feczko, Kathy. *Halloween party*
Fowler, Richard. *Happy birthday, Mouse!*
Freedman, Sally. *Monster birthday party*
Freeman, Don. *Corduroy's party*
  Dandelion
  The paper party
Gackenbach, Dick. *Annie and the mud monster*
Galdone, Joanna. *Honeybee's party*
Gantos, Jack (John, Jr.). *Rotten Ralph's rotten romance*
Gay, Michel. *Bibi's birthday surprise*
Goennel, Heidi. *It's my birthday*
Gordon, Margaret. *Wilberforce goes to a party*
Gould, Deborah. *Brendan's best-timed birthday*
Goyder, Alice. *Party in Catland*
Guthrie, Donna. *Mrs. Gigglebelly is coming for tea*
Harshman, Terry Webb. *Porcupine's pajama party*
Hautzig, Deborah. *Grover's bad dream*
Heller, Nicholas. *The monster in the cave*
Hennessy, B. G. (Barbara G.). *Corduroy's birthday*
Herman, Gail. *There is a town*
Hill, Eric. *Spot goes to a party*
Hiskey, Iris. *Cassandra who?*
Hissey, Jane. *Ruff*
Hoff, Syd. *Henrietta's Halloween*
Hol, Coby. *Tippy Bear goes to a party*
Hughes, Shirley. *Alfie and the birthday surprise*
  Alfie gives a hand
Hunter, Anne. *Possum's harvest moon*
Hutchins, Pat. *The surprise party*

  Titch and Daisy
  Which witch is which?
Hynard, Julia. *Percival's party*
Ichikawa, Satomi. *Nora's castle*
  Nora's surprise
Inkpen, Mick. *Kipper's birthday*
Jahn-Clough, Lisa. *1 2 3 yippie*
Janice. *Little Bear's New Year's party*
  Little Bear's pancake party
Jeram, Anita. *Birthday happy, Contrary Mary*
Johnston, Tony. *Lorenzo the naughty parrot*
Jonas, Ann. *The thirteenth clue*
Jonell, Lynne. *It's my birthday, too!*
Jones, Penelope. *I didn't want to be nice*
Jungman, Ann. *When the people are away*
Keats, Ezra Jack. *A letter to Amy*
Keller, Holly. *Brave Horace*
  Henry's happy birthday
Kennedy, Jimmy. *The teddy bears' Christmas*
Kessler, Ethel. *Is there a penguin at your party?*
Ketteman, Helen. *Bubba the cowboy prince*
Kirk, David. *Miss Spider's tea party*
Koller, Jackie French. *Mole and Shrew step out*
Koontz, Robin Michal. *Chicago and the cat, the family reunion*
Kunhardt, Edith. *Danny's birthday*
Landström, Olof. *Boo and Baa in a party mood*
Laslett, Stephanie. *The monster party*
Lazard, Naomi. *What Amanda saw*
Leedy, Loreen. *The dragon Halloween party*
Lenski, Lois. *A surprise for Davy*
Lifton, Betty Jean. *Tell me a real adoption story*
Lillegard, Dee. *The Big Bug Ball*
Lillie, Patricia. *One very, very quiet afternoon*
Lindgren, Astrid. *Pippi Longstocking's after-Christmas party*
Lipkind, William. *The Christmas bunny*
Lobe, Mira. *Christoph wants a party*
Lodge, Bernard. *Mouldylocks*
London, Jonathan. *Shawn and Keeper and the birthday party*
Loomis, Christine. *The Hippo Hop*
Lopez, Loretta. *The birthday swap*
McAllister, Angela. *Snail's birthday problem*
McCourt, Lisa. *Della Splatnuk birthday girl*
McDonald, Megan. *Ant and Honey Bee*
MacKay, Jed. *The big secret*
MacKinnon, Debbie. *Cathy's cake*
  Find my cake!
McMullan, Kate (Hall). *Hey, Pipsqueak!*
McNaughton, Colin. *At the party*
McPhail, David M. *The party*
Martin, Bill (William Ivan). *Rock it, sock it, number line*
Maxner, Joyce. *Lady Bugatti*
Meyer, Elizabeth C. *The blue china pitcher*
Millais, Raoul. *Elijah and Pin-Pin*
Miller, Margaret. *My birthday*
Miranda, Anne. *Monster math*
Modell, Frank. *Ice cream soup*
Moore, Inga. *A big day for Little Jack*
Mora, Pat. *Delicious hullabaloo = Pachanga deliciosa*
Mother Goose. *Hickory, dickory, dock*, ill. by Suzanne Duranceau
Mueller, Virginia. *Monster's birthday hiccups*
Munsch, Robert N. *Moira's birthday*
Murphy, Stuart J. *Too many kangaroo things to do!*
Nikola-Lisa, W. *Shake dem Halloween bones*
Novak, Matt. *No zombies allowed*

Ogburn, Jacqueline K. *The reptile ball*
Oram, Hiawyn. *Badger's bring something party*
Oxenbury, Helen. *The queen and Rosie Randall*
Park, W. B. *The costume party*
Paterson, Bettina. *Bun's birthday*
Paxton, Tom. *Engelbert the elephant*
Polacco, Patricia. *Some birthday!*
Polisar, Barry Louis. *The haunted house party*
Pomerantz, Charlotte. *The birthday letters*
Potter, Beatrix. *The sly old cat*
Prager, Annabelle. *The baseball birthday party*
   The spooky Halloween party
   The surprise party
Pryor, Bonnie. *Amanda and April*
Quackenbush, Robert M. *Funny bunnies on the run*
Quin-Harkin, Janet. *Helpful Hattie*
Redies, Rainer. *The cats' party*
Reid, Barbara. *The party*
Rollings, Susan. *New shoes, red shoes*
Samuels, Barbara. *Happy birthday, Dolores*
Schertle, Alice. *Jeremy Bean's St. Patrick's Day*
Schindel, John. *Who are you?*
Schweninger, Ann. *Birthday wishes*
Selkowe, Valrie M. *Spring green*
Shute, Linda. *Halloween party*
Soto, Gary. *Chato and the party animals*
   The old man and his door
Springer, Margaret. *A royal ball*
Spurr, Elizabeth. *The biggest birthday cake in the world*
Stapler, Sarah. *Spruce the moose cuts loose*
Stock, Catherine. *The birthday present*
Stott, Rowena. *The hedgehog feast*
Tafuri, Nancy. *The barn party*
Trimble, Patti. *What day is it?*
Tryon, Leslie. *Albert's birthday*
Tudor, Tasha. *The doll's Christmas*
Vincent, Gabrielle. *Merry Christmas, Ernest and Celestine*
Waldron, Jan L. *John Pig's Halloween*
Wallace, John. *Tiny Rabbit goes to a birthday party*
Wallace, Nancy Elizabeth. *Tell-a-bunny*
Wardlaw, Lee. *Bow-wow birthday*
Wegen, Ron. *The Halloween costume party*
Weninger, Brigitte. *Happy birthday, Davy*
West, Colin. *Go tell it to the toucan*
Wilson, Sarah. *Uncle Albert's flying birthday*
Wiseman, Bernard. *Morris has a birthday party!*
Worth, Bonnie. *Peter Cottontail's surprise*
Yolen, Jane. *Piggins*
Zimmer, Dirk. *The trick-or-treat trap*
Zion, Gene. *Jeffie's party*

Passover *see* Holidays – Passover

Patience *see* Character traits – patience

Pawnee Indians *see* Indians of North America – Pawnee

Peacocks, peahens *see* Birds – peacocks, peahens

Peddlers *see* Careers – peddlers

Pegasus *see* Mythical creatures – Pegasus

Pelicans *see* Birds – pelicans

Pen pals

Calmenson, Stephanie. *Wanted*
Caple, Kathy. *Harry's smile*
Holub, Joan. *Pen pals*

Penguins *see* Birds – penguins

Penobscot Indians *see* Indians of North America – Penobscot

Perseverance *see* Character traits – perseverance

Persia *see* Foreign lands – Persia

Persistence *see* Character traits – persistence

Perspective *see* Concepts – perspective

Peru *see* Foreign lands – Peru

Petroglyphs

Webb, Denise. *The same sun was in the sky*

Petroleum *see* Oil

Pets

Abercrombie, Barbara. *Charlie Anderson*
Adoff, Arnold. *The return of Rex and Ethel*
Ahlberg, Allan. *The pet shop*
Aiken, Joan. *Arabel and Mortimer*
Alexander, Martha G. *No ducks in our bathtub*
Allard, Harry. *It's so nice to have a wolf around the house*
Allen, Jonathan. *My cat*
   My dog
Allen, Marjorie N. *One, two, three – ah-choo!*
Allen, Pamela. *My cat Maisie*
Ambrus, Victor G. *Count, Dracula*
Anholt, Laurence. *The new puppy*
Ardizzone, Edward. *Diana and her rhinoceros*
Asch, Frank. *The last puppy*
Atwood, Margaret. *Anna's pet*
Baehr, Patricia. *Mouse in the house*
Baldner, Gaby. *Joba and the wild boar*
Balian, Lorna. *Amelia's nine lives*
Barasch, Marc Ian. *No plain pets!*
Bare, Colleen Stanley. *Guinea pigs don't read books*
   To love a cat
   To love a dog
Barton, Byron. *Jack and Fred*
Barwin, Gary. *The racing worm brothers*
Bastin, Marjolein. *A little dog for Vera*
Baylor, Byrd. *Amigo*
Beatty, Hetty Burlingame. *Moorland pony*
Belpré, Pura. *Santiago*
Benchley, Peter. *Jonathan visits the White House*
Berenstain, Stan. *The Berenstain bears' trouble with pets*
Bishop, Claire Huchet. *The truffle pig*
Blackwood, Gladys Rourke. *Whistle for Cindy*
Blance, Ellen. *Monster buys a pet*

Blegvad, Lenore. *The great hamster hunt*
Bliss, Corinne Demas. *That dog Melly!*
Boegehold, Betty. *Pawpaw's run*
Borovsky, Paul. *The fish that wasn't*
Breeze, Lynn. *Baby's animals*
    Baby's clothes
Brenner, Barbara A. *The five pennies*
Brett, Jan. *Annie and the wild animals*
    The first dog
Brice, Tony. *The bashful goldfish*
Brock, Emma Lillian. *A pet for Barbie*
Bröger, Achim. *Bruno takes a trip*
    Francie's paper puppy
Brothers, Aileen. *Jiffy, Miss Boo and Mr. Roo*
Brown, Marc Tolon. *Arthur's new puppy*
    Arthur's new puppy (board book)
    Arthur's pet business
    Arthur's TV trouble
Brown, Margaret Wise. *The days before now*
Brown, Ruth. *Our puppy's vacation*
Brunhoff, Laurent de. *Babar and the Wully-Wully*
Brutschy, Jennifer. *Celeste and Crabapple Sam*
Bryant, Donna. *My rabbit Roberta*
Burningham, John. *The rabbit*
Burns, Theresa. *You're not my cat*
Burton, Jane. *Ginger the kitten*
    Gipper the guinea pig
    Hoppy the toad
    Jack the puppy
Bushey, Jeanne. *A sled dog for Moshi*
Calder, S. J. *If you were a cat*
Calders, Pere. *Brush*
Calhoun, Mary. *High-wire Henry*
    Tonio's cat
Calmenson, Stephanie. *Shaggy, waggy dogs (and others)*
Capucilli, Alyssa Satin. *Bathtime for Biscuit*
    Happy birthday, Biscuit!
Carlson, Natalie Savage. *Spooky night*
Carlstrom, Nancy White. *Who gets the sun out of bed?*
Carr, Jan. *The nature of the beast*
Carrick, Carol. *The accident*
    A clearing in the forest
    The foundling
    Lost in the storm
Carroll, Ruth. *Pet tale*
Carter, Noelle. *My pet*
Caseley, Judith. *Mr. Green Peas*
Casey, Patricia. *My cat Jack*
Chalmers, Mary. *Six dogs, twenty-three cats, forty-five mice, and one hundred sixteen spiders*
Chapouton, Anne-Marie. *Ben finds a friend*
Chase, Jan Brinckerhoff. *The golden song*
Chenery, Janet. *Pickles and Jake*
Child, Lauren. *I want a pet*
Childress, Mark. *Joshua and Bigtooth*
Chittum, Ida. *The cat's pajamas*
Christian, Mary Blount. *Devin and Goliath*
Chwast, Seymour. *Mr. Merlin and the turtle*
Cleveland-Peck, Patricia. *City cat, country cat*
Coerr, Eleanor. *The Josefina story quilt*
Coffelt, Nancy. *Good night, Sigmund*
Coffey, Maria. *A cat in a kayak*
Cohen, Miriam. *Jim's dog Muffins*
Cole, Babette. *Princess Smartypants*
Cole, Joanna. *Big Goof and Little Goof*
Collington, Peter. *My darling kitten*
Collins, Pat Lowery. *Tumble, tumble, tumbleweed*
Cooney, Nancy Evans. *Go away monsters, lickety split!*

Cooper, Elizabeth K. *The fish from Japan*
Cooper, Melrose. *Pets!*
Copeland, Eric. *Milton, my father's dog*
Corrin, Ruth. *Mister cat*
Cousins, Lucy. *Pet animals*
Cowley, Stewart. *What's that sound?*
Crane, Donn. *Flippy and Skippy*
Crawford, Ron. *Pet?*
Crowell, Maryalicia. *A horse in the house*
Cummings, Betty Sue. *Turtle*
Cuyler, Margery. *Freckles and Jane*
Dale, Penny. *Wake up, Mr. B.!*
Daly, Kathleen N. *Strawberry Shortcake and pets on parade*
Daly, Niki. *Just like Archie*
Darling, Kathy (Mary Kathleen). *ABC cats*
    ABC dogs
Davenier, Christine. *Leon and Albertine*
Davies, Andrew. *Poonam's pets*
Day, Betsy. *Stefan and Olga*
De Hamel, Joan. *Hemi's pet*
Delton, Judy. *I'll never love anything ever again*
    A pet for Duck and Bear
Dennard, Deborah. *Do cats have nine lives?*
De Paola, Tomie (Thomas Anthony). *Little Grunt and the big egg*
DiSalvo-Ryan, DyAnne. *A dog like Jack*
Dubois, Claude K. *Looking for Ginny*
Dubowski, Cathy East. *A cake for Jake*
Dunn, Judy. *The little goat*
    The little puppy
    The little rabbit
Elson, Raymond. *Pets*
Enell, Trinka. *Roll over, Rosie*
Ernst, Lisa Campbell. *Walter's tail*
Evans, Mark. *Guinea pigs*
    Kitten
    Puppy
    Rabbit
Falwell, Cathryn. *P.J. & Puppy*
Faulkner, Keith. *My pets*
Feldman, Barbara. *Stephen's frog*
Ferguson, Alane. *That new pet!*
Foster, Sally. *A pup grows up*
Fujita, Tamao. *The boy and the bird*
Furchgott, Terry. *Phoebe and the hot water bottles*
Gackenbach, Dick. *Mother Rabbit's son Tom*
Gantos, Jack (John, Jr.). *The perfect pal*
Garland, Michael. *Angel cat*
Garland, Sarah. *Billy and Belle*
Geoghegan, Adrienne. *Dogs don't wear glasses*
    There's a wardrobe in my monster!
George, Lindsay Barrett. *William and Boomer*
Gerson, Corinne. *Good dog, bad dog*
Ghigna, Charles. *Mice are nice*
Gibson, Betty. *The story of Little Quack*
Giff, Patricia Reilly. *Good luck, Ronald Morgan*
Goennel, Heidi. *My dog*
Graham, Bob. *The wild*
Grambling, Lois G. *Can I have a Stegosaurus, Mom? Can I? Please!?*
Greeley, Valerie. *Pets*
Gregoire, Caroline. *Uglypuss*
Gregory, Nan. *How Smudge came*
Greydanus, Rose. *Let's get a pet*
Griessman, Annette. *Jenny's prayer*
Griffith, Helen V. *Mine will, said John*
Gwynne, Fred. *Easy to see why*
Hafner, Marylin. *A year with Molly and Emmett*

Primavera, Elise. *Plantpet*
Pringle, Laurence P. *Naming the cat*
Provensen, Alice. *An owl and three pussycats*
Pursell, Margaret Sanford. *Polly the guinea pig*
   Shelley the sea gull
Quackenbush, Robert M. *No mouse for me*
Rathmann, Peggy. *10 minutes till bedtime*
Rayner, Mary. *Marathon and Steve*
Reiser, Lynn. *Any kind of dog*
Remkiewicz, Frank. *The last time I saw Harris*
Ridlon, Marcia. *Kittens and more kittens*
Rockwell, Anne F. *I love my pets*
Roffey, Maureen. *Here, kitty kitty!*
   Quick, catch Dan!
Rogers, Fred. *When a pet dies*
Rosen, Michael J. (1954-). *Bonesy and Isabel*
Rosen, Winifred. *Henrietta and the day of the iguana*
Ross, George Maxim. *When Lucy went away*
Ross, Tony. *I want a cat*
Rotner, Shelley. *Pick a pet*
Sandberg, Inger. *Nicholas' favorite pet*
Schaffer, Marion. *I love my cat!*
Schick, Alice. *Just this once*
Schlein, Miriam. *That's not Goldie!*
Schmeltz, Susan Alton. *Pets I wouldn't pick*
Schwartz, Henry. *Albert goes Hollywood*
   How I captured a dinosaur
Scruton, Clive. *Mary's pets*
Seabrooke, Brenda. *The best burglar alarm*
Seeber, Dorothea P. *A pup just for me . . . A boy just*
   for me
Seignobosc, Françoise. *The story of Colette*
Sendak, Maurice. *Some swell pup*
Seymour, Tres. *I love my buzzard*
Sharmat, Marjorie Weinman. *I'm the best*
   Nate the Great and the fishy prize
Sierra, Judy. *There's a zoo in room 22*
Simon, Norma. *Cats do, dogs don't*
   Mama cat's year
   Oh, that cat!
Skorpen, Liesel Moak. *All the Lassies*
Smath, Jerry. *But no elephants*
Smith, Lane. *The big pets*
Smyth, Gwenda. *A pet for Mrs. Arbuckle*
Sneed, Brad. *Lucky Russell*
Snow, Pegeen. *A pet for Pat*
Spier, Peter. *The pet store*
Spooner, J. B. *The story of the little Black Dog*
Springer, Margaret. *A royal ball*
Steiner, Charlotte. *Polka Dot*
Stevenson, James. *Mr. Hacker*
   Will you please feed our cat?
Stevenson, Suçie. *Jessica the blue streak*
Stoddard, Sandol. *My very own special particular pri-*
   vate and personal cat
   Turtle time
Szilagyi, Mary. *Thunderstorm*
Tabler, Judith. *The new puppy*
Tallon, Robert. *Latouse my moose*
Thaler, Mike. *My puppy*
Thomas, Jane Resh. *Scaredy dog*
Tidd, Louise Vitellaro. *The best pet yet*
Trapani, Iza. *How much is that doggie in the window?*
   Row, row, row your boat
Tusa, Tricia. *Chicken*
Udry, Janice May. *"Oh no, cat!"*
   What Mary Jo wanted
Uff, Caroline. *Hello, Lulu*
Vaës, Alain. *The wild hamster*

Varga, Judy. *Miss Lollipop's lion*
Vaughan, Marcia Kapok. *Whistling Dixie*
Viorst, Judith. *The tenth good thing about Barney*
Vreeken, Elizabeth. *Henry*
Vries, Anke de. *My elephant can do almost anything*
Wahl, Jan. *Dracula's cat and Frankenstein's dog*
   My cat Ginger
Wahl, Mats. *Grandfather's laika*
Wallace-Brodeur, Ruth. *Goodbye, Mitch*
Ward, Lynd. *The biggest bear*
Wayland, April Halprin. *To Rabbittown*
Weird pet poems
Wells, Rosemary. *Lucy comes to stay*
Whatley, Bruce. *That magnetic dog*
Wilcox, Cathy. *Enzo the Wonderfish*
Wilhelm, Hans. *I'll always love you*
Williams, Sue. *Let's go visiting*
Wirth, Beverly. *Margie and me*
Wisbeski, Dorothy Gross. *Pícaro, a pet otter*
Wittbold, Maureen. *Mending Peter's heart*
Wolf, Jake. *Daddy, could I have an elephant?*
Wolski, Slawomir. *Tiger cat*
Wong, Herbert H. *My goldfish*
Wright, Dare. *The lonely doll learns a lesson*
Yaccarino, Dan. *An octopus followed me home*
Zimelman, Nathan. *Positively no pets allowed*
Zinnemann-Hope, Pam. *Find your coat, Ned*
Zolotow, Charlotte (Shapiro). *The old dog*
   The poodle who barked at the wind
Zweifel, Frances W. *Bony*

Pharaohs *see* Royalty – pharaohs

Philippines *see* Foreign lands – Philippines

Phoenix *see* Mythical creatures – phoenix

Photographers *see* Careers – photographers

Photography *see* Activities – photographing

Physical handicaps *see* Handicaps – physical
handicaps

Physicians *see* Careers – doctors

Piano

Miller, William. *The piano*

Picnics *see* Activities – picnicking

Picture puzzles

Anno, Mitsumasa. *Anno's alphabet*
   Anno's animals
   Anno's counting book
   Anno's counting house
   Anno's flea market
   Anno's Italy
   Anno's journey
   Anno's magical ABC
   Dr. Anno's magical midnight circus
Blyler, Allison. *Finding foxes*
Day, Shirley. *Waldo's back yard*
Grimm, Jacob. *The elves and the shoemaker*, ill. by
   Doug Cushman

Handford, Martin. *Find Waldo now*
　The great Waldo search
　Where's Waldo?
Horenstein, Henry. *A is for – ?*
King, Dave. *Counting book*
Laidlaw, Ken. *The amazing I spy ABC*
MacDonald, Suse. *Look whooo's counting*
　Peck, slither and slide
McGuire, Richard. *What's wrong with this book?*
McMillan, Bruce. *Mouse views*
Maisner, Heather. *Save Brave Ted*
Marsh, T. J. *Way out in the desert*
Marzollo, Jean. *I spy little animals*
　I spy little book
　I spy little Christmas
　I spy little letters
　I spy little numbers
　I spy little wheels
　I spy, mystery
Nims, Bonnie Larkin. *Where is the bear at school?*
O'Malley, Kevin. *Who killed Cock Robin?*
Palazzo, Tony (Anthony D.). *Waldo the woodchuck*
Rogers, Paul Patrick. *What can you see?*
Schwartz, David M. *If you hopped like a frog*
Steiner, Joan (Joan Catherine). *Look-alikes*
　Look-alikes, Jr.
The three little pigs. *The three little pigs*, ill. by Doug
　Cushman
Tildes, Phyllis Limbacher. *Animals in camouflage*
Toft, Kim Michelle. *Neptune's nursery*
　One less fish
Turner, Ann Warren. *Angel hide and seek*
Twinem, Neecy. *In the air*
Wallner, John C. *Look and find*
Wallwork, Amanda. *Find the fish that looks like this*
Weitzman, Jacqueline Preiss. *You can't take a bal-
　loon into the National Gallery*
Wick, Walter. *I spy Christmas*
　I spy extreme challenger
　I spy fantasy
　I spy gold challenger!
　I spy school days
　I spy spooky night
　I spy super challenger!
　I spy treasure hunt

Pigeons *see* Birds – pigeons

Pigs *see* Animals – pigs

Pilgrims

Behrens, June. *The feast of Thanksgiving*
Bunting, Eve (Anne Evelyn). *How many days to
　America?*
Dalgliesh, Alice. *The Thanksgiving story*
DeLage, Ida. *Pilgrim children on the Mayflower*
George, Jean Craighead. *The first Thanksgiving*
Gibbons, Gail. *Thanksgiving Day*
Harness, Cheryl. *Three young pilgrims*
Hennessy, B. G. (Barbara G.). *One little, two little,
　three little pilgrims*
Kroll, Steven. *One tough turkey*
Lowitz, Sadyebeth. *The pilgrims' party*
Szekeres, Cyndy. *Long ago*
Van Leeuwen, Jean. *Across the wide dark sea*

Pilots *see* Careers – airplane pilots

Pima *see* Indians of North America – Pima

Pioneer life *see* U.S. history – frontier and
　pioneer life

Pirates

Ahlberg, Allan. *Skeleton crew*
Ahlberg, Janet. *It was a dark and stormy night*
Allen, Pamela. *I wish I had a pirate suit*
Baum, Louis. *JuJu and the pirate*
Burningham, John. *Come away from the water, Shirley*
Carryl, Charles E. (Charles Edward). *A capital ship*
　The walloping window-blind, ill. by Jim LaMarche
　The walloping window blind
Cole, Babette. *The trouble with Uncle*
Collington, Peter. *The angel and the soldier boy*
DeLage, Ida. *ABC pirate adventure*
Devlin, Harry. *The walloping window blind*
Dewey, Ariane. *Laffite, the pirate*
Dyke, John. *Pigwig and the pirates*
Farber, Erica. *Ooey gooey*
Faulkner, Matt. *The amazing voyage of Jackie Grace*
Fox, Mem. *Tough Boris*
Ginsburg, Mirra. *Four brave sailors*
Gliori, Debi. *The princess and the pirate king*
Graham, Mary Stuart (Campbell). *The pirates'
　bridge*
Haseley, Dennis. *The pirate who tried to capture the
　moon*
Hayes, Geoffrey. *The mystery of the pirate ghost*
Hutchins, Pat. *One-eyed Jake*
Impey, Rose. *Who's a bright girl?*
Isadora, Rachel. *The pirates of Bedford Street*
Joslin, Sesyle. *Señor Baby Elephant, the pirate*
Keats, Ezra Jack. *Maggie and the pirate*
Kessler, Leonard P. *The pirates' adventure on Spooky
　Island*
Kimmel, Eric A. *Robin Hook, pirate hunter!*
Kroll, Steven. *Are you pirates?*
　The pigrates clean up
Leonard, Marcia. *Violet and the pirates*
Lichtenheld, Tom. *Everything I know about pirates*
Lloyd, David. *Grandma and the pirate*
Löfgren, Ulf. *Alvin the pirate*
McAllister, Angela. *The babies of Cockle Bay*
McCully, Emily Arnold. *The pirate queen*
McFarland, Lyn Rossiter. *The pirate's parrot*
MacGill-Callahan, Sheila. *To capture the wind*
McNaughton, Colin. *Captain Abdul's pirate school*
　Jolly Roger and the pirates of Captain Abdul
McPhail, David M. *Edward and the pirates*
Mahy, Margaret. *The horrendous hullabaloo*
　The man whose mother was a pirate
　Sailor Jack and the twenty orphans
Marston, Elsa. *Cynthia and the runaway gazebo*
Morgan, Allen. *Matthew and the midnight pirates*
*My first Raggedy Ann, Raggedy Ann and Andy and the
　camel with the wrinkled knees*
Nash, Ogden. *Custard the dragon*
Peppé, Rodney. *The kettleship pirates*
Perkins, Al. *Tubby and the lantern*
Roberts, Thom. *Pirates in the park*
Ross, Dave (David). *Gorp and the space pirates*
Ross, Tony. *Treasure of Cozy Cove*
Scarry, Richard. *Pie rats ahoy!*
Schotter, Roni. *Captain Bob sets sail*
Sharratt, Nick. *Mrs. Pirate*

Thompson, Brenda. *Pirates*
Tucker, Kathy. *Do pirates take baths?*
Walker, Barbara K. (Barbara Kerlin). *Pigs and pirates*
Ward, Helen. *The moonrat and the white turtle*
Weiss, Ellen. *The pirates of Tarnoonga*
Wick, Walter. *I spy treasure hunt*
Woychuk, Denis. *Pirates*
Young, James. *Penelope and the pirates*

Pixies *see* Mythical creatures – pixies

Planes *see* Airplanes, airports

Planets

Branley, Franklyn M. (Mansfield). *The planets in our solar system*
Cecil, Laura. *Noah and the space ark*
Gibbons, Gail. *The planets*
Glyman, Caroline A. *What's above the sky?*
Pinkney, J. Brian. *Cosmo and the robot*
Wethered, Peggy. *Touchdown Mars!*

Plants

Adelson, Leone. *Please pass the grass*
Aliki. *Corn is maize*
  My visit to the aquarium
Appelt, Kathi. *Watermelon day*
Arnold, Caroline. *A walk by the seashore*
  A walk in the desert
  A walk in the woods
  A walk on the Great Barrier Reef
  A walk up the mountain
Ayer, Jacqueline. *The paper-flower tree*
Back, Christine. *Bean and plant*
Baker, Jeannie. *The story of rosy dock*
Baker, Jeffrey J. W. *Patterns of nature*
Bash, Barbara. *Desert giant*
Berenstain, Stan. *The Berenstain bears and the prize pumpkin*
Berson, Harold. *Pop! goes the turnip*
Bishop, Gavin. *Mrs. McGinty and the bizarre plant*
Blackmore, Vivien. *Why corn is golden*
Brown, Marc Tolon. *Your first garden book*
Brownell, Barbara. *Spin's really wild U.S.A. tour*
Bruce, Lisa. *Fran's flower*
Bryant-Mole, Karen. *Moving*
Bulla, Clyde Robert. *A tree is a plant*
Busch, Phyllis S. *Cactus in the desert*
  Lions in the grass
Butterworth, Nick. *Jasper's beanstalk*
Carle, Eric. *The tiny seed*
Chapman, Carol. *Barney Bipple's magic dandelions*
Christian, Mary Blount. *The green thumb thief*
Cohn, Janice I. *Molly's rosebush*
Cole, Henry. *Jack's garden*
Cole, Joanna. *Evolution*
  Plants in winter
Craig, M. Jean. *Spring is like the morning*
Credle, Ellis. *Down, down the mountain*
Cristini, Ermanno. *In the pond*
Cross, Diana Harding. *Some plants have funny names*
Cross, Genevieve. *A trip to the yard*
Darby, Gene. *What is a plant?*
Davis, Aubrey. *The enormous potato*
Delaney, A. *Pearl's first prize plant*

Dietl, Ulla. *The plant-and-grow project book*
Dobson, David. *Can we save them?*
Domanska, Janina. *The turnip*
Dunphy, Madeleine. *Here is the tropical rain forest*
Ellentuck, Shan. *A sunflower as big as the sun*
Euvremer, Teryl. *The thieves of Peck's pocket*
Fisher, Aileen Lucia. *And a sunflower grew*
  As the leaves fall down
  Mysteries in the garden
  Now that spring is here
  Plant magic
  Prize performance
  Seeds on the go
  Swords and daggers
  We went looking
Five little pumpkins
Fleming, Denise. *Where once there was a wood*
Ford, Miela. *Sunflower*
Fowler, Allan. *Corn . . . on and off the cob*
Gage, Wilson. *Anna's garden songs*
  Anna's summer songs
Geis, Jacqueline. *Where the buffalo roam*
Gibbons, Gail. *From seed to plant*
  Nature's green umbrella
Ginsburg, Mirra. *Mushroom in the rain*
The green grass grows all around
Greenberg, Polly. *Oh, Lord, I wish I was a buzzard*
Guiberson, Brenda Z. *Cactus hotel*
Hall, Zoe. *It's pumpkin time!*
Harris, Jim. *Jack and the giant*
Heller, Ruth. *Plants that never ever bloom*
Henderson, Douglas. *Dinosaur tree*
Hewett, Anita. *The tale of the turnip*
Hillert, Margaret. *The magic beans*
Himmelman, John. *A dandelion's life*
Hines, Anna Grossnickle. *Miss Emma's wild garden*
Hogan, Paula Z. *The dandelion*
Holmes, Anita. *The 100-year-old cactus*
Hutchins, Pat. *Titch*
Ipcar, Dahlov. *Hard scrabble harvest*
Jack and the beanstalk. *The history of Mother Twaddle and the marvelous achievements of her son Jack*
  Jack and the beanstalk, ill. by Val Biro
  Jack and the beanstalk, ill. by Lorinda Bryan Cauley
  Jack and the beanstalk, ill. by Lydia Halverson
  Jack and the beanstalk, ill. by Julek Heller
  Jack and the beanstalk, ill. by John Howe
  Jack and the beanstalk, ill. by Steven Kellogg
  Jack and the beanstalk, ill. by Ed Parker
  Jack and the beanstalk, ill. by Tony Ross
  Jack and the beanstalk, ill. by by Niamh Sharkey
  Jack and the beanstalk, ill. by Gennady Spirin
  Jack and the beanstalk, ill. by William Stobbs
  Jack and the beanstalk, ill. by James Warhola
  Jack and the beanstalk, ill. by Anne Wilsdorf
  Jack and the beanstalk / Juan y los frijoles magicos
  Jack the giant killer, ill. by Anne Wilsdorf
  Jack the giantkiller, ill. by Tony Ross
Jenkins, Martin. *Fly traps!*
Johnson, Janice (Janice Kay). *Rosamund*
Johnston, Tony. *Big red apple*
Jordan, Helene J. (Helene Jamieson). *Seeds of wind and water*
Keats, Ezra Jack. *Clementina's cactus*
Kepes, Juliet. *The seed that peacock planted*
Ketteman, Helen. *The year of no more corn*
Kirkpatrick, Rena K. *Leaves*
  Seeds and weeds

Kite, L. Patricia. *Dandelion adventures*
Krauss, Ruth. *The carrot seed*
Krings, Antoon. *Oliver's strawberry patch*
Kuchalla, Susan. *All about seeds*
Lember, Barbara Hirsch. *A book of fruit*
Le Tord, Bijou. *Picking and weaving*
Lewis, Naomi. *Leaves*
Little, Lessie Jones. *I can do it by myself*
The little red hen. *The cock, the mouse and the little red hen*
   The little red hen, ill. by Byron Barton
   The little red hen, ill. by Emily Bolam
   The little red hen, ill. by Janina Domanska
   The little red hen, ill. by Paul Galdone
   Little red hen, ill. by Norman Messenger
   The little red hen, ill. by Mel Pekarsky
   The little red hen, ill. by William Stobbs
   The little red hen, ill. by Margot Zemach
Littledale, Freya. *The magic plum tree*
Maass, Robert. *Garden*
Maccarone, Grace. *Pumpkin faces*
McDonald, Megan. *The great pumpkin switch*
Maestro, Giulio. *The remarkable plant in apartment 4*
Mahy, Margaret. *The pumpkin man and the crafty creeper*
Martin, Bill (William Ivan). *Rock it, sock it, number line*
Marzollo, Jean. *I'm a seed*
   Sun song
Medearis, Angela Shelf. *Seeds grow*
Milhous, Katherine. *The turnip*
Miller, Judith Ransom. *Nabob and the geranium*
Moreillon, Judi. *Sing down the rain*
Nash, Ogden. *The animal garden*
Newcome, Zita. *Rosie goes exploring*
Oleson, Claire. *For Pipita, an orange tree*
Osborne, Mary Pope. *Kate and the beanstalk*
Petie, Haris. *The seed the squirrel dropped*
Posada, Mia. *Dandelions, stars in the grass*
Pouyanne, Rési. *What I see hidden by the pond*
Primavera, Elise. *Plantpet*
Pulver, Robin. *Nobody's mother is in second grade*
Ray, Mary Lyn. *Pumpkins*
Reiser, Lynn. *Earthdance*
Relf, Patricia. *The magic school bus plants seeds*
Rey, H. A. (Hans Augusto). *Elizabite*
   Elizabite, adventures of a carnivorous plant
Rich, Scharlotte. *Who made the wild woods?*
Ring, Elizabeth. *Tiger lilies and other beastly plants*
Ringi, Kjell (Arne Sorensen). *The sun and the cloud*
Robbins, Ken. *Autumn leaves*
Rockwell, Anne F. *One bean*
   Pumpkin day, pumpkin night
Rockwell, Harlow. *The compost heap*
Rudolph, Marguerita. *How a shirt grew in the field*, ill. by Erika Weihs
   How a shirt grew in the field, ill. by Yaroslava
Schaefer, Lola M. *This is the sunflower*
Schertle, Alice. *Witch Hazel*
Seabrook, Elizabeth. *Cabbages and kings*
Selberg, Ingrid. *Nature's hidden world*
Selsam, Millicent E. *A first look at the world of plants*
   More potatoes!
   Seeds and more seeds
Shecter, Ben. *Partouche plants a seed*
Shields, Carol Diggory. *Martian rock*
Simon, Carly. *Midnight farm*
Speed, Toby. *Brave potatoes*
Stern, Maggie. *The missing sunflowers*

Sugita, Yutaka. *The flower family*
Tolstoy, Aleksey Nikolayevich. *The gigantic turnip*, ill. by Niamh Sharkey
   The great big enormous turnip, ill. by Helen Oxenbury
Trottier, Maxine. *Flags*
Vagin, Vladimir Vasil'evich. *The enormous carrot*
Van Rynbach, Iris. *Five little pumpkins*
Wallace, Karen. *Scarlette Beane*
Wallace, Nancy Elizabeth. *Paperwhite*
Watts, Barrie. *Dandelion*
   Mushrooms
   Tomato
Weeks, Sarah. *Mrs. McNosh and the great big squash*
Wexler, Jerome (LeRoy). *Flowers, fruits, seeds*
   Wonderful pussy willows
Williams, Barbara. *Hello, dandelions!*
Wilson-Max, Ken. *Max loves sunflowers*
Wondriska, William. *The tomato patch*
Wong, Herbert H. *My plant*
Yacowitz, Caryn. *Pumpkin fiesta*
Yolen, Jane. *Welcome to the sea of sand*
Ziefert, Harriet. *The turnip*
Zion, Gene. *The plant sitter*
Zoehfeld, Kathleen Weidner. *What's alive?*
Zolotow, Charlotte (Shapiro). *In my garden*

Plasterers *see* Careers – plasterers

Playing *see* Activities – playing

Plays *see* Theater

Plovers *see* Birds – plovers

Plumbers *see* Careers – plumbers

Poems

Asch, Frank. *Cactus poems*

Poetry

Abrons, Mary. *For Alice a palace*
Absolutely angels
Ada, Alma Flor. *Gathering the sun*
Adams, Richard (Richard Newbold). *The tyger voyage*
Adelborg, Ottilia. *Clean Peter and the children of Grubbylea*
Adelson, Leone. *Please pass the grass*
Adoff, Arnold. *Big sister tells me that I'm black*
   Birds
   The cabbages are chasing the rabbits
   I am the running girl
   In for winter, out for spring
   Love letters
   Make a circle, keep us in
   OUTside INside Poems
   Street music
   Today we are brother and sister
   Tornado!
   Touch the poem
   Where wild Willie?
Alarcón, Francisco X. *From the bellybutton of the moon and other summer poems / poems = Del ombligo de la luna y otros poemas de verano / poemas*

Aldis, Dorothy (Keeley). *All together*
  Before things happen
  Hello day
  Hiding
  Quick as a wink
Alexander, Anne (Anna Barbara Cooke). *ABC of*
  cars and trucks
  My daddy and I
Alger, Leclaire Gowans. *All in the morning early*
  Kellyburn Braes
All year round
Allen, Jonathan. *A bad case of animal nonsense*
Allingham, William. *The fairies*
Alphabestiary
Altman, Susan. *Followers of the north star*
Andre, Evelyn M. *Places I like to be*
Andreae, Giles. *Rumble in the jungle*
Angelou, Maya. *My painted house, my friendly chicken,*
  and me
Anglund, Joan Walsh. *Christmas is love*
  Love is a baby
  Morning is a little child
  Poems of childhood
Anholt, Catherine. *Here come the babies*
Archambault, John. *The birth of a whale*
Armour, Richard Willard. *Have you ever wished you*
  were something else?
Asch, Frank. *City sandwich*
  Country pie
Ashley Bryan's abc of African American poetry
Ashley, Jill. *Riddles about Christmas*
Aylesworth, Jim. *The cat and the fiddle and more*
Azarian, Mary. *The tale of John Barleycorn or, From*
  barley to beer
The babes in the woods. The old ballad of the babes
  in the woods
Bagert, Brod. *Chicken socks and other contagious*
  poems
  The gooch machine
Barker, Cicely Mary. *Berry flower fairies*
  Blossom flower fairies
  Flower fairies of the garden
  Flower fairies of the seasons
  Flower fairies of the spring
  Flower fairies of the summer
  Flower fairies of the trees
  Flower fairies postcard book
  Spring flower fairies
  Summer flower fairies
Barry, Katharina. *A is for anything*
  A bug to hug
Barry, Robert E. *Animals around the world*
Barto, Emily Newton. *Chubby bear*
Baruch, Dorothy. *I would like to be a pony and other*
  wishes
Baylor, Byrd. *The other way to listen*
Behn, Harry. *Crickets and bullfrogs and whispers of*
  thunder
  Trees
Belloc, Hilaire. *The bad child's book of beasts, and*
  more beasts for worse children
  The bad child's pop-up book of beasts
  Matilda who told lies and was burned to death
  More beasts for worse children
Belting, Natalia Maree. *Christmas folk*
  Summer's coming in
Benét, William Rose. *Timothy's angels*
Benjamin, Alan. *A nickel buys a rhyme*
Bennett, Jill. *Animal fair*

  A cup of starshine
  Days are where we live and other poems
  Machine poems
  Noisy poems
  People poems
  Roger was a razor fish and other poems
  Spooky poems
Bennett, Rainey. *The secret hiding place*
Bennett, Rowena. *The day is dancing and other poems*
  Songs from around a toadstool table
Berry, James. *Celebration song*
Billy Boy (folk-song). *Billy Boy*
Blake, Quentin. *All join in*
Blake, William. *The tyger*
Blegvad, Lenore. *The parrot in the garret and other*
  rhymes about dwellings
Blos, Joan W. *A seed, a flower, a minute, an hour*
Bodecker, N. M. (Nils Mogens). *Hurry, hurry, Mary*
  dear!
  "Let's marry" said the cherry, and other nonsense
  poems
  Snowman Sniffles and other verse
Borchers, Elisabeth. *There comes a time*
Bornstein, Ruth Lercher. *That's how it is when we*
  draw
Bouchard, Dave. *Prairie born*
Bouton, Josephine. *Favorite poems for the children's*
  hour
Bowman, Peter. *Goodnight, teddy bear*
A boy went out to gather pears
Brecht, Bertolt. *Uncle Eddie's moustache*
Bright star shining
Brooks, Gwendolyn. *Bronzeville boys and girls*
Brown, Beatrice Curtis. *Jonathan Bing*, ill. by Judith
  Gwyn Brown
  Jonathan Bing, ill. by Pelagie Doane
Brown, Margaret Wise. *Bumble bee*
  The diggers
  Four fur feet
  Little Donkey close your eyes
  Nibble nibble
  Under the sun and the moon and other poems
  Where have you been?
  The wonderful story book
Brown, Myra Berry. *Best friends*
Browner, Richard. *Everyone has a name*
Browning, Robert. *The pied piper of Hamelin*, ill. by
  Patricia and Robin DeWitt
  The pied piper of Hamelin, ill. by Kate Greenaway
  The pied piper of Hamelin, ill. by Anatoly Ivanov
  The pied piper of Hamelin, ill. by Errol Le Cain
  The pied piper of Hamelin, ill. by Drahos Zak
Bruce, Sheilah B. *The radish day jubilee*
Bruchac, Joseph. *The circle of thanks*
  Thirteen moons on turtle's back
Bruna, Dick. *The fish*
Bryan, Ashley. *Sing to the sun*
Buchanan, Ken. *It rained on the desert today*
Buckley, Kate. *Love notes*
Budney, Blossom. *A kiss is round*
Buell, Ellen Lewis. *Read me a poem*
Burdekin, Harold. *A child's grace*
Burgess, Gelett. *The little father*
Burgunder, Rose. *From summer to summer*
Cahill, Chris. *Bear magic*
  Bunny magic
Calmenson, Stephanie. *Never take a pig to lunch and*
  other funny poems about animals
Cameron, Polly. *A child's book of nonsense*

On a summer day
Spring is here
Susie Mariar
Lessac, Frané. *Caribbean canvas*
Lesser, Carolyn. *What a wonderful day to be a cow*
Let's count and count out
Levens, George. *Kippy the koala*
Lewin, Betsy. *Animal snackers*
  Cat count
Lewis, J. Patrick. *The bookworm's feast*
  Doodle dandies
  The Fat-Cats at sea
  A hippopotamusn't
  July is a mad mosquito
  The la-di-da hare
  The little buggers
  Long was the winter road they traveled
  Riddle-icious
  Two-legged, four-legged, no-legged rhymes
Lewis, Richard. *In a spring garden*
  In the night, still dark
Lexau, Joan M. *More beautiful than flowers*
Liatsos, Sandra Olson. *Bicycle riding and other poems*
Lillegard, Dee. *Hello school!*
  Wake up house!
  The wild bunch
Lindbergh, Reeve. *Grandfather's lovesong*
Little, Lessie Jones. *Children of long ago*
Livingston, Myra Cohn. *Abraham Lincoln*
  B is for baby
  Birthday poems
  Cat poems
  Celebrations
  Dog poems
  Festivals
  Keep on singing
  Poems for brothers, poems for sisters
  Poems for fathers
  Poems for mothers
Lobel, Arnold. *Whiskers and rhymes*
London, Jonathan. *Fall rap*
Longfellow, Henry Wadsworth. *Hiawatha*
  Hiawatha's childhood
  Paul Revere's ride, ill. by Paul Galdone
  Paul Revere's ride, ill. by Nancy Winslow Parker
Lord, Beman. *The days of the week*
Low, Joseph. *Adam's book of odd creatures*
Lullaby and goodnight
Lüton, Mildred. *Little chicks' mothers and all the others*
Lyon, George Ella. *Book*
  Counting on the woods
  Dreamplace
  A sign
  Together
McClintock, Marshall. *What have I got?*
McCord, David. *Every time I climb a tree*
  The star in the pail
McCurdy, Michael. *The sailor's alphabet*
McGovern, Ann. *Feeling mad, feeling sad, feeling bad, feeling glad*
McMillan, Bruce. *One sun*
  Play day
Mado, Michio. *The animals*
  The magic pocket
Maestro, Betsy. *Fat polka-dot cat and other haiku*
Margolis, Richard J. *Secrets of a small brother*
Marks, Marcia Bliss. *Swing me, swing tree*
Marshak, S. (Samuil). *Hail to mail*

In the van
The merry starlings
The tale of a hero nobody knows
Marshall, James. *Pocketful of nonsense*
Martin, Bill (William Ivan). *Sounds around the clock*
  Sounds of home
  Sounds of laughter
  Sounds of numbers
Marzollo, Jean. *I love you*
  The teddy bear book
Massie, Diane Redfield. *Cockle stew and other rhymes*
  Tiny pin
Mathers, Petra. *A cake for Herbie*
Mayer, Mercer. *Little Monster's bedtime book*
Medina, Nina. *Have you ever noticed that rabbits don't sing?*
Melmed, Laura Krauss. *The first song ever sung*
  1-2-3 Thanksgiving
Mendoza, George. *The hunter I might have been*
  The scribbler
Merriam, Eve. *Bam, bam, bam*
  The birthday cow
  Blackberry ink
  Halloween ABC
  Higgle wiggle
  The hole story
  A poem for a pickle
Messenger, Jannat. *Lullabies and baby songs*
Michelson, Richard. *Animals that ought to be*
Miles, Betty. *Around and around . . . love*
Mitchell, Cynthia. *Halloweena Hecatee*
  Here a little child I stand
  Playtime
  Under the cherry tree
Mizumura, Kazue. *If I were a cricket . . .*
Monster poems
Monster soup and other spooky poems
Moon, Pat. *This is the earth*
The moon's the north wind's cooky
Moore, Clement C. *The night before Christmas*, ill. by Jan Brett
  The night before Christmas, ill. by Tomie de Paola
  The night before Christmas, comp. by Cooper Edens and Harold Darling; ill. by various nineteenth- and twentieth-century artists
  The night before Christmas, ill. by Michael Foreman
  The night before Christmas, ill. by Gyo Fujikawa
  The night before Christmas, ill. by Scott Gustafson
  The night before Christmas, ill. by Cheryl Harness
  The night before Christmas, ill. by Loretta Krupinski
  The night before Christmas, ill. by Anita Lobel
  The night before Christmas, ill. by James Marshall
  The night before Christmas, ill. by Jacqueline Rogers
  The night before Christmas, ill. by Robin Spowart
  The night before Christmas, ill. by Gustaf Tenggren
  The night before Christmas, ill. by Tasha Tudor
  The night before Christmas, ill. by Wendy Watson
  The night before Christmas, ill. by Jody Wheeler
  The night before Christmas in signed English
  The teddy bears' night before Christmas
  A visit from St. Nicholas
Moore, Lilian. *Adam Mouse's book of poems*
  I feel the same way
  I never did that before
  I'm small and other verses

Wolman, Bernice. *Taking turns*
Wood, Douglas. *Northwoods cradle song*
Woolaver, Lance. *Christmas with the rural mail*
  From Ben Loman to the sea
Worth, Valerie. *At Christmastime*
Wright, Josephine Lord. *Cotton Cat and Martha Mouse*
Yeoman, John. *Our village*
Yerxa, Leo. *Last leaf first snowflake to fall*
Yolen, Jane. *Bird watch*
  Child of faerie, child of earth
  How beastly!
  Nocturne
  Ring of earth
  Snow, snow
  The three bears holiday rhyme book
  The three bears rhyme book
  Welcome to the sea of sand
You and me
Ziner, Feenie. *Counting carnival*
Zolotow, Charlotte (Shapiro). *River winding*
  Some things go together

Poland *see* Foreign lands – Poland

Polar bears *see* Animals – polar bears

Police officers *see* Careers – police officers

Polish Americans *see* Ethnic groups in the U.S. – Polish Americans

Poltergeists *see* Ghosts

Ponds *see* Lakes, ponds

Ponies *see* Animals – horses, ponies

Pooka spirit *see* Mythical creatures – pooka spirit

Poor *see* Homeless; Poverty

Pop-up books *see* Format, unusual – toy and movable books

Porcupines *see* Animals – porcupines

Porpoises *see* Animals – dolphins

Portugal *see* Foreign lands – Portugal

Possums *see* Animals – possums

Post office

Ahlberg, Janet. *The jolly Christmas postman*
  The jolly pocket postman
  The jolly postman
Barkan, Joanne. *Whiskerville post office*
Beim, Jerrold. *Country mailman*
Bell, Norman. *Linda's airmail letter*
Brandt, Betty. *Special delivery*
Buchheimer, Naomi. *Let's go to a post office*
Gibbons, Gail. *The post office book*

Haley, Gail E. *The post office cat*
Hedderwick, Mairi. *Katie Morag delivers the mail*
Henri, Adrian. *The postman's palace*
Kightley, Rosalinda. *The postman*
Koscielniak, Bruce. *Euclid Bunny delivers the mail*
Landström, Olof. *Will goes to the post office*
Marshak, S. (Samuil). *Hail to mail*
Maury, Inez. *My mother the mail carrier*
Rylant, Cynthia. *Mr. Griggs' work*
Scarry, Richard. *Richard Scarry's Postman Pig and his busy neighbors*
Scott, Ann Herbert. *Hi!*
Skurzynski, Gloria. *Here comes the mail*

Postal workers *see* Careers – postal workers

Potawatomi *see* Indians of North America – Potawatomi

Potty training *see* Toilet training

Poverty

Alexander, Lloyd. *The king's fountain*
Ambrus, Victor G. *The three poor tailors*
Andersen, H. C. (Hans Christian). *The little match girl*, ill. by Rachel Isadora
  The little match girl, ill. by Blair Lent
  The little match girl, ill. by Jerry Pinkney
Balet, Jan B. *The fence*
Bates, Artie Ann. *Ragsale*
Belton, Sandra. *May'naise sandwiches and sunshine tea*
Bettina (Bettina Ehrlich). *Pantaloni*
Brand, Oscar. *When I first came to this land*
Carey, Valerie Scho. *Maggie Mab and the bogey beast*
Coltman, Paul. *Tinker Jim*
Cooper, Susan. *Danny and the Kings*
Czernecki, Stefan. *The sleeping bread*
De Paola, Tomie (Thomas Anthony). *Helga's dowry*
De Veaux, Alexis. *Na-ni*
Diller, Harriett. *The waiting day*
Friedman, Elizabeth. *Leah's pony*
Garay, Luis. *Pedrito's day*
Goodman, Louise. *Ida's doll*
Greene, Jacqueline Dembar. *What his father did*
Haggerty, Mary Elizabeth. *A crack in the wall*
Harshman, Marc. *Uncle James*
Hazen, Barbara Shook. *Tight times*
Hoban, Lillian. *Stick-in-the-mud turtle*
Keeping, Charles. *Joseph's yard*
Kudler, David. *The Seven Gods of Luck*
Levine, Abby. *Too much mush!*
Lindgren, Astrid. *My nightingale is singing*
Littlesugar, Amy. *Tree of hope*
McCrea, James. *The king's procession*
Maiorano, Robert. *Francisco*
Mills, Lauren A. *The rag coat*
Namioka, Lensey. *The loyal cat*
Nickens, Bessie. *Walking the log*
Nolan, Madeena Spray. *My daddy don't go to work*
Park, Frances. *The royal bee*
Parton, Dolly. *Coat of many colors*
Powell, E. Sandy. *A chance to grow*
Provensen, Alice. *Shaker Lane*
Rose, Anne K. *How does a czar eat potatoes?*
Sawyer, Ruth. *Journey cake, ho!*
Schermbrucker, Reviva. *Charlie's house*

Seabrooke, Brenda. *The swan's gift*
Shiefman, Vicky. *Sunday potatoes, Monday potatoes*
Sonneborn, Ruth A. *Friday night is papa night*
   Seven in a bed
Steptoe, John. *Uptown*
Thomas, Jane Resh. *Lights on the river*
Turner, Ann Warren. *Dust for dinner*
Vainio, Pirkko. *The Christmas angel*
Wells, Ruth. *The farmer and the poor god*
Wilde, Oscar. *The happy prince*
Ziefert, Harriet. *When I first came to this land*

Power failures

Baisch, Cris. *When the lights went out*
Cölle, Gisela. *The star tree*
Freeman, Don. *The night the lights went out*
Grejniec, Michael. *Who is my neighbor?*
Leavy, Una. *Harry's stormy night*
Quackenbush, Robert M. *Funny bunnies on the run*
Rockwell, Anne F. *Blackout*
Rodriguez, Bobbie. *Sarah's sleepover*

Powhaton Indians *see* Indians of North America – Powhaton

Practicality *see* Character traits – practicality

Prairie dogs *see* Animals – prairie dogs

Prairie wolves *see* Animals – coyotes

Praying mantis *see* Insects – praying mantis

Preachers *see* Careers – preachers

Prehistoric man *see* Cavemen

Prejudice

Ada, Alma Flor. *The malachite palace*
Anders, Rebecca. *A look at prejudice and understanding*
Brophy, Nannette. *The color of my fur*
Carlson, Nancy L. *Loudmouth George and the new neighbors*
Coleman, Evelyn. *White socks only*
Coles, Robert. *The story of Ruby Bridges*
Egan, Tim. *Metropolitan cow*
Escudie, René. *Paul and Sebastian*
Glen, Maggie. *Ruby*
Ikeda, Daisaku. *Over the deep blue sea*
Le Guin, Ursula K. *Fish soup*
Littlesugar, Amy. *Jonkonnu*
Lorbiecki, Marybeth. *Sister Anne's hands*
McCourt, Lisa. *Della Splatnuk birthday girl*
Miller, M. L. *Those Bottles!*
Miller, William. *The bus ride*
   Night golf
Mitchell, Margaree King. *Susie Mae*
Mostacchi, Massimo. *The beast and the boy*
Rosen, Michael (1946-). *This is our house*
Rubinetti, Donald. *Cappy the lonely camel*
Schami, Rafik. *Albert and Lila*
Shange, Ntozake. *Whitewash*
Ungerer, Tomi. *Flix*

Valentine, Johnny. *One dad, two dads, brown dad, blue dads*
Van Allsburg, Chris. *The widow's broom*
Wells, Rosemary. *Yoko*
Yezerski, Thomas. *Together in Pinecone Patch*

Pride *see* Character traits – pride

Princes *see* Royalty – princes

Princesses *see* Royalty – princesses

Printers *see* Careers – printers

Prisons

Butterworth, Oliver. *A visit to the big house*
DuPasquier, Philippe. *The great escape*
Hickman, Martha Whitmore. *When Andy's father went to prison*
McKee, David. *123456789 Benn*
Solotareff, Grégoire. *Don't call me little bunny*

Problem solving

Adler, David A. *The children of Chelm*
Alexander, Martha G. *I'll protect you from the jungle beasts*
   Move over, Twerp
   Out! Out! Out!
   We never get to do anything
   We're in big trouble, Blackboard Bear
Allington, Richard L. *Thinking*
Ames, Mildred. *The wonderful box*
Armitage, Ronda. *Ice creams for Rosie*
   The lighthouse keeper's catastrophe
   The lighthouse keeper's lunch
Arnosky, Jim. *Mud time and more*
Ashley, Bernard. *Dinner ladies don't count*
Bakken, Harold. *The special string*
Balet, Jan B. *The fence*
Barklem, Jill. *The secret staircase*
Barrett, Judi. *What's left?*
Barry, Katharina. *A bug to hug*
Beim, Lorraine. *Two is a team*
Benarde, Anita. *The pumpkin smasher*
Berg, Jean Horton. *The O'Learys and friends*
Bester, Roger. *Guess what?*
Blaine, Marge (Margery Kay). *The terrible thing that happened at our house*
Booth, Eugene. *At the circus*
   At the fair
   In the air
   In the garden
   In the jungle
   Under the ocean
Brillhart, Julie. *Story hour - starring Megan!*
Brodmann, Aliana. *Such a noise!*
Bröger, Achim. *Little Harry*
Brown, Jeff. *Flat Stanley*
Brown, Margaret Wise. *They all saw it*
Browne, Anthony. *Bear hunt*
Buchanan, Heather S. *George and Matilda Mouse and the floating school*
   George Mouse's first summer
Bulette, Sara. *The splendid belt of Mr. Big*
Burton, Marilee Robin. *Tail toes eyes ears nose*
Butterworth, Nick. *Jingle bells*

The secret path
Calhoun, Mary. *Audubon cat*
Carlson, Nancy L. *Harriet and the garden*
Carrick, Carol. *Ben and the porcupine*
Chaffin, Lillie D. *Tommy's big problem*
Chapman, Carol. *Herbie's troubles*
Christensen, Gardell Dano. *Mrs. Mouse needs a house*
Cleary, Beverly. *The real hole*
Clymer, Ted. *The horse and the bad morning*
Cole, Babette. *Princess Smartypants*
Cole, Joanna. *It's too noisy*
Cooney, Nancy Evans. *The blanket that had to go*
   Donald says thumbs down
Cooper, Jacqueline. *Angus and the Mona Lisa*
Corbalis, Judy. *The cuckoo bird*
Cressey, James. *Fourteen rats and a rat-catcher*
Cummings, Pat. *Jimmy Lee did it*
Davis, Aubrey. *The enormous potato*
Deedy, Carmen Agra. *Agatha's feather bed*
Demarest, Chris L. *Kitman and Willy at sea*
De Paola, Tomie (Thomas Anthony). *Charlie needs a cloak*
Dewey, Ariane. *The fish Peri*
Dickinson, Mary. *Alex's bed*
Domanska, Janina. *The turnip*
Economakis, Olga. *Oasis of the stars*
Elkin, Benjamin. *Such is the way of the world*
Emberley, Ed (Edward Randolph). *Rosebud*
Farber, Norma. *How the left-behind beasts built Ararat*
Fassler, Joan. *Boy with a problem*
Feder, Paula Kurzband. *Where does the teacher live?*
George, Lindsay Barrett. *In the woods*
Gerstein, Mordicai. *Stop those pants!*
Gordon, Margaret. *The supermarket mice*
Greene, Carol. *The golden locket*
Hancock, Sibyl. *Freaky Francie*
Harber, Frances. *My king has donkey ears*
Heitler, Susan M. (Susan McCrensky). *David decides, no more thumb-sucking*
Henwood, Simon. *The troubled village*
Hines, Anna Grossnickle. *Maybe a band-aid will help*
Hoban, Lillian. *Arthur's funny money*
Horvath, Betty F. *The cheerful quiet*
Houston, John A. *The bright yellow rope*
   A mouse in my house
Hughes, Shirley. *An evening at Alfie's*
Hulse, Gillian. *Morris, where are you?*
Ives, Penny. *Mrs. Santa Claus*
Jonas, Ann. *Holes and peeks*
Keats, Ezra Jack. *Goggles*
   Whistle for Willie
Keenen, George. *The preposterous week*
Klimowicz, Barbara. *The strawberry thumb*
Kroll, Steven. *Looking for Daniela*
Lebentritt, Julia. *The Kooken*
Leonard, Marcia. *Birthday in a bathtub*
   Little owl leaves the nest
Levitin, Sonia. *Who owns the moon?*
Lexau, Joan M. *Benjie*
   Benjie on his own
Lobel, Arnold. *On the day Peter Stuyvesant sailed into town*
London, Sara. *Firehouse Max*
Low, Joseph. *What if . . . ?*
Lyon, David. *The brave little computer*
McCloskey, Robert. *Lentil*
Maestro, Betsy. *The guessing game*
Maiorano, Robert. *Francisco*

Manson, Christopher. *Here begins the tale of the marvellous blue mouse*
Marie, Geraldine. *The magic box*
Maris, Ron. *Hold tight, bear!*
Marshall, James. *Four little troubles*
Marshall, Margaret. *Mike*
Martinez, Ruth. *Mrs. McDockerty's knitting*
Mayer, Mercer. *What do you do with a kangaroo?*
Merriam, Eve. *The birthday door*
Milhous, Katherine. *The turnip*
Munsch, Robert N. *Jonathan cleaned up - then he heard a sound*
Murphy, Stuart J. *The best vacation ever*
Myers, Walter Dean. *The golden serpent*
Myrick, Jean Lockwood. *Ninety-nine pockets*
Ness, Evaline. *Do you have the time, Lydia?*
Oakley, Graham. *The church mice in action*
Obrist, Jürg. *They do things right in Albern*
Olaleye, Isaac. *Bitter bananas*
Partridge, Jenny. *Hopfellow*
   Mr. Squint
   Peterkin Pollensnuff
Payne, Emmy. *Katy no-pocket*
Rice, Eve. *Peter's pockets*
Robb, Brian. *My grandmother's djinn*
Robison, Deborah. *Bye-bye, old buddy*
   No elephants allowed
Schermer, Judith. *Mouse in house*
Schurr, Cathleen. *The long and the short of it*
Segal, Lore. *The story of old Mrs. Brubeck and how she looked for trouble and where she found him*
Seuss, Dr. *Did I ever tell you how lucky you are?*
   Hunches in bunches
Sharmat, Marjorie Weinman. *The pizza monster*
Singh, Jacquelin. *Fat Gopal*
Smith, Donald. *Who's wearing my baseball cap?*
   Who's wearing my bow tie?
   Who's wearing my sneakers?
   Who's wearing my sunglasses?
Smith, Jim. *The frog band and the onion seller*
Sondheimer, Ilse. *The magic of Pomme*
Steel, Danielle. *Max and the baby sitter*
Stevenson, James. *Quick! Turn the page!*
Talbot, John. *Pins and needles*
Thayer, Jane. *What's a ghost going to do?*
Thomas, Patricia. *"There are rocks in my socks!" said the ox to the fox*
Thompson, Vivian Laubach. *Camp-in-the-yard*
Titus, Eve. *Anatole and the cat*
   Anatole and the Pied Piper
   Anatole and the poodle
   Anatole and the robot
   Anatole and the thirty thieves
   Anatole and the toyshop
   Anatole in Italy
Tolstoy, Aleksey Nikolayevich. *The gigantic turnip*, ill. by Niamh Sharkey
   The great big enormous turnip, ill. by Helen Oxenbury
Türk, Hanne. *Max versus the cube*
   A surprise for Max
Tusa, Tricia. *Camilla's new hairdo*
Twinem, Neecy. *Changing colors*
   High in the trees
Uhlberg, Myron. *Mad Dog McGraw*
Vagin, Vladimir Vasil'evich. *The enormous carrot*
Van Horn, William. *Twitchtoe, the beastfinder*
Wilhelm, Hans. *I lost my tooth!*
Williams, Karen Lynn. *Painted dreams*

Winthrop, Elizabeth. *Maggie and the monster*
Wiseman, Bernard. *Doctor Duck and Nurse Swan*
Wold, Jo Anne. *Tell them my name is Amanda*
Wynne-Jones, Tim. *Builder of the moon*
Wyse, Lois. *Two guppies, a turtle and Aunt Edna*
Yagelski, Robert. *The day the lifting bridge stuck*
Yektai, Niki. *What's missing?*
Yolen, Jane. *Piggins*
Yorinks, Arthur. *Bravo, Minski*
Zemach, Margot. *It could always be worse*
Ziefert, Harriet. *The turnip*

Progress

Barton, Byron. *Wheels*
Burton, Virginia Lee. *The little house*
Duvoisin, Roger Antoine. *Lonely Veronica*
Fife, Dale. *Empty lot*
   The little park
Goodall, John S. *The story of an English village*
Greene, Graham. *The little fire engine*
Harrison, David Lee. *Little turtle's big adventure*
Heine, Helme. *Prince Bear*
Hoban, Russell. *Arthur's new power*
Ipcar, Dahlov. *One horse farm*
MacGill-Callahan, Sheila. *And still the turtle watched*
Murschetz, Luis. *Mister Mole*
Peet, Bill (William Bartlett). *Countdown to Christmas*
   Farewell to Shady Glade
   The wump world
Ray, Mary Lyn. *Pumpkins*
Shecter, Ben. *Emily, girl witch of New York*
Steiner, Jörg. *The bear who wanted to be a bear*
Tusa, Tricia. *Sherman and Pearl*

Proverbs

Kneen, Maggie. *"Too many cooks . . ."*
Swann, Brian. *A basket full of white eggs*

Pueblo Indians *see* Indians of North America – Pueblo

Puerto Rican Americans *see* Ethnic groups in the U.S. – Hispanic Americans; Ethnic groups in the U.S. – Puerto Rican Americans

Puerto Rico *see* Foreign lands – Puerto Rico

Puffins *see* Birds – puffins

Pumas *see* Animals – cougars

Punchball *see* Sports – punchball

Puppeteers *see* Careers – Puppeteers

Puppets

Anastasio, Dina. *Baby Piggy and giant bubble*
Atene, Ann (Anna). *The golden guitar*
Blau, Judith. *Bunny Mitten's book*
Brandenberg, Franz. *Aunt Nina's visit*
Brennan, Joseph Killorin. *Gobo and the river*
Bruce, Sheilah B. *The radish day jubilee*

Cahill, Chris. *Bear magic*
   Bunny magic
   Spider magic
   Turtle magic
Calmenson, Stephanie. *ABC*
Chernoff, Goldie Taub. *Puppet party*
Children's Television Workshop. *Muppets in my neighborhood*
Cleaver, Elizabeth. *The enchanted caribou*
Collodi, Carlo. *The adventures of Pinocchio*
   Pinocchio
Eaton, Su. *Punch and Judy in the rain*
Elliott, Dan. *Ernie's little lie*
   A visit to the Sesame Street firehouse
Freeman, Don. *The paper party*
Freudberg, Judy. *Susan and Gordon adopt a baby*
Gikow, Louise. *Baby Kermit's Christmas*
   Boober Fraggle's ghosts
   Bye-bye, pacifier
   Count with me
   Follow that Fraggle!
   For every child, a better world
   I am Kermit
   Jim Henson's Muppets in Rowlf's big test
   Jim Henson's Muppets in What's fair is fair
   Sprocket's Christmas tale
Gilmour, H. B. *Why Wembley Fraggle couldn't sleep*
Greaves, Margaret. *Petrushka*
Hautzig, Deborah. *Big Bird at the beach*
   Ernie and Bert's new kitten
   Grover's bad dream
   It's not fair!
   A visit to the Sesame Street hospital
   A visit to the Sesame Street library
Hayward, Linda. *Baker, baker, cookie maker*
   The biggest cookie in the world
   The case of the missing Duckie
   A day in the life of Oscar the Grouch
   Elmo goes to day camp
   Ernie and Bert's summer project
   Grover's summer vacation
   I can count to ten and back again
Heymans, Margriet. *Pippin and Robber Grumblecroak's big baby*
Howe, James. *The case of the missing mother*
Kates, Bobbi Jane. *We're different, we're the same*
Keats, Ezra Jack. *Louie*
Klimowicz, Barbara. *The strawberry thumb*
Lerner, Sharon. *Big Bird's copycat day*
   Follow the monsters!
Lewis, Shari. *Baby Lamb Chop loves animals*
   Baby Lamb Chop loves numbers
   Baby Lamb Chop loves nursery school
   Baby Lamb Chop loves the beach
   Baby Lamb Chop loves words
Little, Mary E. *Ricardo and the puppets*
Masks and puppets
Moss, Jeffrey. *The Sesame Street ABC storybook*
   The songs of Sesame Street in poems and pictures
Mother Goose. *The Sesame Street players present Mother Goose*
Muntean, Michaela. *Kermit and Robin's scary story*
   Mokey and the festival of the bells
   Muppet babies through the year
The Muppet Show book
One rubber duckie
Parsons, Virginia. *Pinocchio and Gepetto*
   Pinocchio and the money tree
   Pinocchio goes on the stage

Pinocchio plays truant
Peters, Sharon. *Puppet show*
Poskanzer, Susan Cornell. *Puppeteer*
Provensen, Alice. *Punch in New York*
Roberts, Sarah. *Bert and the missing mop mix-up*
   Ernie's big mess
   I want to go home!
Ross, Anna. *I did it!*
   I have to go
   Naptime
   Say the magic word, please
Ryder, Joanne. *Hello, first grade*
Sesame Street. *Ernie and Bert can . . . can you?*
   Sesame Street sign language fun
   Sesame Street word book
Steiner, Charlotte. *Pete's puppets*
Stevenson, Jocelyn. *Jim Henson's Muppets at sea*
   Red and the pumpkins
Stiles, Norman. *I'll miss you, Mr. Hooper*
Stone, Jon. *Big Bird in China*
Tettelbaum, Michael. *The cave of the lost Fraggle*
The Timbertoes 1 2 3 counting book
The Timbertoes ABC alphabet book
Tornborg, Pat. *The Sesame Street cookbook*
Weiss, Ellen. *Mokey's birthday present*
   Pigs in space
   You are the star of a Muppet adventure
Weiss, George (George David). *What a wonderful world*
Young, Ed (Edward). *The rooster's horns*

Purim *see* Holidays – Purim

Puzzles *see also* Picture puzzles; Rebuses; Riddles
Birchman, David F. *Jigsaw Jackson*
Bourke, Linda. *Eye count*
Demi. *Find Demi's baby animals*
   Find Demi's dinosaurs
   Find Demi's sea creatures
Geisert, Arthur. *Pigs from 1 to 10*
Kneen, Maggie. *When you're not looking*
Owen, Annie. *From snowflakes to sandcastles*
Waber, Bernard. *Do you see a mouse?*

Quail *see* Birds – quail

Quechua *see* Indians of South America – Quechua

Queens *see* Royalty – queens

Questioning *see* Character traits – questioning

Quicksand *see* Sand

Quilts

Bateson-Hill, Margaret. *Shota and the star quilt*
Brenner, Barbara A. *The flying patchwork quilt*
Chorao, Kay. *Kate's quilt*
Coerr, Eleanor. *The Josefina story quilt*
Cole, Barbara Hancock. *Texas star*
Ernst, Lisa Campbell. *Sam Johnson and the blue ribbon quilt*
Fleisher, Robbin. *Quilts in the attic*
Flournoy, Valerie. *The patchwork quilt*
Guback, Georgia. *Luka's quilt*
Hermes, Patricia. *When snow lay soft on the mountain*
Hesse, Karen. *Lavender*
Howard, Ellen. *The log cabin quilt*
Ipcar, Dahlov. *The calico jungle*
Johnston, Tony. *The quilt story*
Jonas, Ann. *The quilt*
Koralek, Jenny. *The boy and the cloth of dreams*
Kuskin, Karla. *Patchwork island*
Leedahl, Shelley A. (Shelley Ann). *The bone talker*
Martin, Jacqueline Briggs. *Bizzy Bones and the lost quilt*
Min, Willemien. *Peter's patchwork dream*
Moss, P. Buckley (Pat Buckley). *Reuben and the quilt*
Paul, Ann Whitford. *Eight hands round*
Polacco, Patricia. *The keeping quilt*
Radley, Gail. *The spinner's gift*
Ransom, Candice F. *The promise quilt*
Ringgold, Faith. *Tar Beach*
Smucker, Barbara Claasen. *Selina and the bear paw quilt*
Steiner, Charlotte. *The sleepy quilt*
Stevens, Kathleen. *Aunt Skilly and the stranger*
Torres, Leyla. *Liliana's grandmothers*
Vincent, Gabrielle. *Ernest and Celestine's patchwork quilt*
Whelan, Gloria. *Bringing the farmhouse home*
Whittington, Mary K. *The patchwork lady*
Willard, Nancy. *The mountains of quilt*
Yolen, Jane. *Old Dame Counterpane*
Zagwÿn, Deborah Turney. *The pumpkin blanket*
Ziefert, Harriet. *Before I was born*

Rabbits *see* Animals – rabbits

Raccoons *see* Animals – raccoons

Race car drivers *see* Careers – race car drivers

Racing *see* Sports – racing

Radio

Dorros, Arthur. *Radio Man/Don Radio*

Railroad engineers *see* Careers – railroad engineers

Railroads *see* Trains

Rain *see* Weather – rain

Rainbows *see* Weather – rainbows

Rajahs *see* Royalty – rajahs

Ramadan *see* Holidays – Ramadan

Ranchers *see* Careers – ranchers

Rangers *see* Careers – park rangers

Rats *see* Animals – rats

Ravens *see* Birds – ravens

Reading *see* Activities – reading

Rebuses

Adler, David A. *Bunny rabbit rebus*
Asbjørnsen, P. C. (Peter Christen). *The three billy goats Gruff*, ill. by Heidi Petach
Banks, Kate (Katherine A.). *The bird, the monkey, and the snake in the jungle*
Capucilli, Alyssa Satin. *Inside a barn in the country*
  Inside a house that is haunted
Cole, Joanna. *Monster and Muffin*
Coletta, Irene. *From A to Z*
Dodds, Siobhan. *Words and pictures*
Doolittle, Eileen. *The ark in the attic*
Downie, Jill. *Alphabet puzzle*
Dubowski, Cathy East. *Picky Nicky*
Grimm, Jacob. *Sleeping Beauty*, ill. by John Wallner
Hayward, Linda. *D is for doll*
Herman, Gail. *Otto the cat*
Heuck, Sigrid. *Pony and Bear are friends*
  Who stole the apples?
Hill, Eric. *Spot's walk in the woods*
Hooks, William H. *The Gruff brothers*
  Read-a-rebus
The house that Jack built. *The house that Jack built*, ill. by Jeanette Winter
Lewison, Wendy Cheyette. *Don't wake the baby!*
Marzollo, Jean. *I love you*
  The rebus treasury
Morris, Ann. *The Cinderella rebus book*
  The Little Red Riding Hood rebus book
Mother Goose. *Mother Goose in hieroglyphics*
Neitzel, Shirley. *The bag I'm taking to Grandma's*
  The dress I'll wear to the party
  The house I'll build for the wrens
  I'm not feeling well today
  I'm taking a trip on my train
  We're making breakfast for mother
O'Connor, Jane. *Benny's big bubble*
Partch, Virgil Franklin. *The Christmas cookie sprinkle snitcher*
Pizer, Abigail. *It's a perfect day*
Reit, Seymour. *Rebus bears*
The three bears. *Goldilocks and the three bears*, ill. by Madelaine Gill Linden
The three little pigs. *The three little pigs*, ill. by Madelaine Gill
Weil, Lisl. *Mother Goose picture riddles*

Wyllie, Stephen. *The great race*

Reindeer *see* Animals – reindeer

Religion

Adler, David A. *A picture book of Hanukkah*
  A picture book of Israel
Æsop. *Androcles and the lion*, ill. by Janusz Grabianski
  Androcles and the lion, ill. by Janet Stevens
Aichinger, Helga. *The shepherd*
Aleichem, Sholem. *Hanukah money*
Alexander, Cecil Frances. *All things bright and beautiful*
Aliki. *Mummies made in Egypt*
Ammon, Richard. *An Amish Christmas*
Anderson, Debby. *Let's talk about Heaven*
Angeletti, Roberta. *Nefertari, princess of Egypt*
Anglund, Joan Walsh. *A book of good tidings from the Bible*
Aoki, Hisako. *Santa's favorite story*
Araten, Harry. *Two by two*
Aronow, Sara. *Seven days of creation*
Baker, Betty. *And me, coyote!*
Baker, Sanna Anderson. *Who's a friend of the water-spurting whale*
Balet, Jan B. *The gift*
Barker, Peggy. *What happened when grandma died*
Bawden, Nina. *St. Francis of Assisi*
Bayar, Steven. *Rachel and Mischa*
Baylor, Byrd. *The way to start a day*
Baynes, Pauline. *Let there be light*
  Thanks be to God
Bea, Holly. *Where does God live?*
Behrens, June. *Hanukkah*
  Passover
Berger, Barbara Helen. *The donkey's dream*
Bernhard, Emery. *The tree that rains*
Bible. *Best-loved Bible verses for children*
Bible. New Testament. *The Lord's prayer*, Catholic version, ill. by Ingri and Edgar Parin d'Aulaire
  The Lord's prayer, Protestant version, ill. by Ingri and Edgar Parin d'Aulaire
  The Lord's prayer, ill. by George Kraus
  The Lord's prayer, ill. by Tim Ladwig
Bible. Old Testament. Daniel. *Daniel in the lions' den*, ill. by Jim Cummins
  Daniel in the lions' den, ill. by Diana Mayo
  Shadrach, Meshack, and Abednego
Bible. Old Testament. Genesis. *Genesis*
  The story of the creation
Bible. Old Testament. Jonah. *Jonah and the great fish*, ill. by Jim Cummins
Bible. Old Testament. Joseph. *Joseph and his brothers*
Bible. Old Testament. Psalms. *The Lord is my shepherd*, ill. by George Kraus
  The Lord is my shepherd, ill. by Tasha Tudor
  Psalm twenty-three
  The twenty-third Psalm
Bratton, Heidi. *Imagine*
  Yes, I can!
Brin, Ruth F. *The story of Esther*
Briscoe, D. Stuart. *Where is God?*
Briscoe, Jill. *The innkeeper's daughter*
Brown, Katherine. *The Small One*

Brown, Margaret Wise. *On Christmas eve*, ill. by
 Nancy Edwards Calder
 On Christmas eve, ill. by Beni Montresor
Bruna, Dick. *Christmas*
Bryan, Ashley. *All night, all day*
Buckley, Helen Elizabeth. *Moonlight kite*
Buckley, Ray. *God's love is like . . .*
Burdekin, Harold. *A child's grace*
Burningham, John. *Whaddayamean*
Butterworth, Nick. *The house on the rock*
 The lost sheep
 The precious pearl
 The two sons
Carlson, Lori Marie. *Hurray for Three Kings' Day*
Carlstrom, Nancy White. *Does God know how to tie
 shoes?*
Caswell, Helen Rayburn. *God must like to laugh*
 Parable of the good Samaritan
Chaikin, Miriam. *Exodus*
Chanover, Hyman. *Happy Hanukah everybody*
Chapman, Jean. *Moon-Eyes*
Chase, Catherine. *The miracles at Cana*
Children go where I send thee
Children's prayers from around the world
A child's book of prayers
Christian, Mary Blount. *Anna and the strangers*
 Grandfathers, God's gift to children
 Grandmothers, God's gift to children
Coatsworth, Elizabeth. *Song of the camels*
Cohen, Barbara. *The binding of Isaac*
 The donkey's story
 First fast
 Here come the Purim players!, ill. by Shoshana Mek-
 ibel
Cole, Joanna. *A gift from Saint Francis*
Cooner, Donna D. (Donna Danell). *The world God
 made*
Cooney, Barbara. *A little prayer*
Daly, Kathleen N. *Jesus our friend*
Davidson, Alice J. *The story of creation*
Dellinger, Annetta. *You are special to Jesus*
De Paola, Tomie (Thomas Anthony). *Christopher*
 The clown of God
 The Lady of Guadalupe
 The legend of Old Befana
 My first Chanukah
 The night of Las Posadas
 The parables of Jesus
 Patrick
Din dan don, it's Christmas
Douglas, Robert W. *John Paul II*
Downes, Belinda. *Every little angel's handbook*
Drucker, Malka. *Grandma's latkes*
 A Jewish holiday ABC
Easwaran, Eknath. *The monkey and the mango*
Ehrlich, Amy. *The story of Hannukkah*
Eisenberg, Ann. *Bible heroes I can be*
 I can celebrate
Farber, Norma. *How the hibernators came to Bethle-
 hem*
 When it snowed that night
Fass, David E. *The shofar that lost its voice*
Feder, Harriet K. *Not yet, Elijah!*
Field, Rachel Lyman. *Prayer for a child*
Figley, Marty Rhodes. *The story of Zacchaeus*
First graces
First prayers, ill. by Anna Maria Magagna
First prayers, ill. by Tasha Tudor
Fisher, Aileen Lucia. *The story of Easter*

Fisher, Leonard Everett. *The seven days of creation*
Fishman, Cathy Goldberg. *On Hanukkah*
 On Passover
 On Rosh Hashanah and Yom Kippur
Fitch, Florence Mary. *A book about God*
Foreman, Juli. *Great beginnings*
Foreman, Michael. *Cat in the manger*
Forrester, Victoria. *Poor Gabriella*
Frank, Penny. *In the beginning*
Fraser, James Howard. *Los Posadas*
The friendly beasts, ill. by Sarah Chamberlain
The friendly beasts and a partridge in a pear tree, ill. by
 Virginia Pearsons
Galdone, Paul. *The first seven days*
Gauch, Patricia Lee. *The little friar who flew*
Geisert, Arthur. *After the flood*
Gerstein, Mordicai. *Queen Esther the morning star*
Ghazi, Suhaib Hamid. *Ramadan*
Giuliano, Katie. *All the way to God*
Gleeson, Brian. *The Savior is born*
Goddard, Carrie Lou. *Isn't it a wonder!*
Goldin, Barbara Diamond. *Cakes and miracles*
Gold-Vukson, Marji. *The colors of my Jewish Year*
Good, Merle. *Amos and Susie*
Graham, Lorenz B. *David he no fear*
 Hongry catch the foolish boy
 A road down in the sea
Gramatky, Hardie. *Nikos and the sea god*
Greene, Carol. *God's good creation*
Griessman, Annette. *Jenny's prayer*
Grimes, Nikki. *At break of day*
 Come Sunday
 From a child's heart
Groner, Judyth Saypol. *All about Hanukkah*
 All about Sukkot
 Thank you, God!
Haas, Dorothy. *My first communion*
Hallinan, P. K. (Patrick K.). *The small town chil-
 dren's Easter*
Hamil, Thomas Arthur. *Brother Alonzo*
Harber, Frances. *The brothers' promise*
Harmer, Juliet. *Prayers for children*
Hartman, Bob. *The birthday of a king*
 The morning of the world
 A night the stars danced for joy
 Who brought the bread?
 Who wrecked the roof?
Hawxhurst, Joan C. *Bubbe and Gram, my two grand-
 mothers*
Heck, Elisabeth. *The black sheep*
Heine, Helme. *One day in paradise*
Helldorfer, M. C. (Mary Claire). *Clap clap!*
Hennessy, B. G. (Barbara G.). *The first night*
Higgs, Liz Curtis. *Go away, dark night*
Hillman, Priscilla. *The Merry-Mouse book of prayers
 and graces*
Hirsh, Marilyn. *I love Passover*
 Joseph who loved the Sabbath
 Potato pancakes all around
Hodges, Margaret. *The golden deer*
 Saint Christopher
 St. Jerome and the lion
Holland, Cheri. *Maccabee jamboree*
Hopkins, Lee Bennett. *All God's children*
 And God bless me
Houselander, Caryll. *Petook*
Hughes, Shirley. *Lucy and Tom's Christmas*
Hunt, Angela Elwell. *The tale of three trees*
Hutton, Warwick. *Adam and Eve*

Persephone
Theseus and the Minotaur
Ife, Elaine. *The childhood of Jesus*
Stories Jesus told
Johnson, Dinah. *Sunday week*
Johnson, James Weldon. *The Creation*
Jones, Jessie Mae Orton. *A little child*
Small rain
Jüchen, Aurel von. *The Holy Night*
Kahn, Katherine Janus. *The shofar calls to us*
Kajpust, Melissa. *A dozen silk diapers*
Karlinsky, Ruth Schild. *My first book of Mitzvos*
Karon, Jan. *Miss Fannie's hat*
Kassirer, Sue. *Joseph and his coat of many colors*
Keats, Ezra Jack. *God is in the mountain*
The little drummer boy
Kennedy, X. J. *The beasts of Bethlehem*
Kimmel, Eric A. *The Chanukkah guest*
The Chanukkah tree
Hershel and the Hanukkah goblins
One winter night
Ten suns
Kimmelman, Leslie. *Hanukkah lights, Hanukkah
nights*
Hooray! it's Passover!
The runaway latkes
Sound the shofar!
Kipling, Rudyard. *The miracle of the mountain*
Knapp, John, II. *A pillar of pepper and other Bible
nursery rhymes*
Koralek, Jenny. *Hanukkah*
Krull, Kathleen. *Songs of praise*
Kuskin, Karla. *A great miracle happened there*
Jerusalem, shining still
Lamstein, Sarah Marwil. *Annie's Shabbat*
Lattimore, Deborah Nourse. *The sailor who captured
the sea*
Lee, Jeanne M. *I once was a monkey*
Leeton, Will C. *The Tower of Babel*
Lepon, Shoshana. *Hillel builds a house*
Lester, Julius. *What a truly cool world*
Le Tord, Bijou. *The deep blue sea*
God's little seeds
The river and the rain
Sing a new song
Levine, Arthur A. *All the lights in the night*
The boy who drew cats
Lexau, Joan M. *More beautiful than flowers*
Lindbergh, Reeve. *The circle of days*
Lines, Kathleen. *Once in royal David's city*
Little book of prayers
London, Jonathan. *Into this night we are rising*
Long, Kathy. *Hallelujah the clown*
Maccarone, Grace. *A child's good night prayer*
McDermott, Gerald. *The voyage of Osiris*
McDonough, Yona Zeldis. *Eve and her sisters*
McKissack, Patricia C. *My Bible ABC book*
McLerran, Alice. *The ghost dance*
Manushkin, Fran. *Hooray for Hanukkah!*
Latkes and applesauce
The matzah that Papa brought home
Miriam's cup
Starlight and candles
Mark, Jan. *The tale of Tobias*
Marshall, Lyn. *Yoga for your children*
Martin, Ann M. *Leo the Magnificat*
Martin, Bill (William Ivan). *Adam, Adam, what do
you see?*
Matthews, Caitlin. *The blessing seed*

Mayer, Marianna. *Perseus*
Melcher, Mary. *Mommy, who does God love?*
Metaxas, Eric. *Bible ABC*
David and Goliath
Michael, Emory H. *Androcles and the lion*
Mitchell, Cynthia. *Here a little child I stand*
Miyoshi, Sekiya. *Singing David*
Modesitt, Jeanne. *It's Hanukkah!*
Songs of Chanukah
Moorman, Margaret. *Light the lights!*
Moss, Marissa. *The ugly menorah*
Murphy, Elspeth Campbell. *Do you see me God?*
Namioka, Lensey. *The loyal cat*
Nayer, Judy. *The eight nights of Hanukka*
Nerlove, Miriam. *Easter*
Hanukkah
Passover
Purim
Shabbat
The Ten Commandments for Jewish children
Newman, Lesléa. *Matzo ball moon*
Nomura, Noriko S. *I am Shinto*
Oberman, Sheldon. *King Solomon, Sheba, and the
hoopoe bird*
Sound of the shofar
O'Keefe, Susan Heyboer. *Angel prayer*
Good night, God bless
Oppenheim, Shulamith Levey. *The hundredth name*
Iblis
Orgel, Doris. *The flower of Sheba*
Otto, Carolyn. *Pioneer church*
Parton, Dolly. *Coat of many colors*
Pienkowski, Jan. *Easter*
Podwal, Mark H. *The menorah story*
Polacco, Patricia. *Chicken Sunday*
Poole, Josephine. *Joan of Arc*
Price, Christine. *One is God*
Quattlebaum, Mary. *In the beginning*
Quintero-Spongberg, Emily. *Hannibal and the king*
Rael, Elsa. *When Zaydeh danced on Eldridge Street*
Ragz, M. M. *Lost little angel*
Ray, Mary Lyn. *Shaker boy*
Reed, Allison. *Genesis*
Renberg, Dalia Hardof. *King Solomon and the bee*
Rich, Scharlotte. *Who made the wild woods?*
Rosenblum, Richard. *The old synagogue*
Rothenberg, Joan. *Inside-out grandma*
Rouss, Sylvia A. *Sammy Spider's first Passover*
Sammy Spider's first Shabbat
Rylant, Cynthia. *Bless us all*
Give me grace
Sabuda, Robert James. *St. Valentine*
Sasso, Sandy Eisenberg. *For heaven's sake*
God's paintbrush
In God's name
Sattgast, L. J. *Look what God made*
Schanzer, Rosalyn. *In the synagogue*
Scholey, Arthur. *Baboushka*
Schotter, Roni. *Hanukkah!*
Passover magic
Purim play
Schrier, Jeffrey. *On the wings of eagles*
Schur, Maxine Rose. *Day of delight*
Schwartz, Amy. *Mrs. Moskowitz and the Sabbath can-
dlesticks*
Schwartz, Lynne Sharon. *The four questions*
Schweiger-Dmi'el, Itzhak. *Hanna's Sabbath dress*
Scott, Lesbia. *I sing a song of the saints of God*
Seignobosc, Françoise. *The thank-you book*

Shulevitz, Uri. *The magician*
Silverman, Erica. *Gittel's hands*
Silverman, Maida. *My first book of Jewish holidays*
Simon, Norma. *The story of Hanukkah*
   The story of Passover
Singer, Marilyn. *Minnie's Yom Kippur birthday*
Slate, Joseph. *Who is coming to our house?*
A small treasury of Easter poems and prayers
The song of the Three Holy Children
Springer, Sally. *Let's make latkes*
Stan-Padilla, Viento. *Dream Feather*
Stevens, Jan Romero. *Twelve lizards leaping*
Stillerman, Marci. *Nine spoons*
Stortz, Diane M. *Barnaby Mouse, detective, and the mystery of the big book*
Swamp, Jake. *Giving thanks*
Swartz, Nancy Sohn. *In our image*
Tarbescu, Edith. *Annushka's voyage*
Taylor, Mark. *"Lamb," said the lion, "I am here."*
Taylor, Shirley. *The cross in the egg*
Thomas, Kathy. *The angel's quest*
Thorne, Jenny. *Adam and Eve*
   The walls of Jericho
Titherington, Jeanne. *A child's prayer*
Tolstoy, Aleksey Nikolayevich. *Shoemaker Martin*
Tompert, Ann. *Saint Nicholas*
Topek, Susan Remick. *Shalom, Shabbat*
Trist, Glenda. *A child's book of prayers*
Trottier, Maxine. *The walking stick*
Tudor, Tasha. *More prayers*
Tulloch, Shirley. *Who made me?*
Turner, Ann Warren. *Angel hide and seek*
   Shaker hearts
Van der Meer, Ron. *Oh Lord!*
Van Leeuwen, Jean. *Across the wide dark sea*
Vasiliu, Mircea. *Everything is somewhere*
Volkmer, Jane Anne. *Song of Chirimia*
Waldman, Sarah. *Light*
Weilerstein, Sadie Rose. *K'tonton's Yom Kippur kitten*
What a morning!
Wheeler, Opal. *Sing in praise*
Wiesner, William. *The Tower of Babel*
Wildsmith, Brian. *The Easter story*
   Joseph
   The true cross
Wilkon, Józef. *Lullaby for a newborn king*
Wilkowski, Susan. *Baby's Bris*
Williams, Marcia. *Joseph and his magnificent coat of many colors*
Winthrop, Elizabeth. *He is risen*
Wohl, Lauren L. *Matzoh mouse*
Wojciechowski, Susan. *The Christmas miracle of Jonathan Toomey*
Wood, Douglas. *Old Turtle*
Woodtor, Dee. *Big meeting*
Yenne, Bill. *Joshua and the battle of Jericho*
Zagwyn, Deborah Turney. *Papa's latkes*
Zalben, Jane Breskin. *Happy Passover, Rosie*
   Leo and Blossom's Sukkah
   Pearl's eight days of Chanukah
Ziefert, Harriet. *Animals of the Bible*
   First He made the sun
   People of the Bible

Religion – Daniel

Bible. Old Testament. Daniel. *Daniel in the lions' den*, ill. by Leon Baxter

Religion – David

Bible. Old Testament. David. *David and Goliath*
   David and the giant
Brin, Ruth F. *David and Goliath*
De Regniers, Beatrice Schenk. *David and Goliath*, ill. by Scott Cameron
   David and Goliath, ill. by Richard M. Powers
Fisher, Leonard Everett. *David and Goliath*

Religion – Hinduism

Gilmore, Rachna. *Lights for Gita*

Religion – Islam

Oppenheim, Shulamith Levey. *And the earth trembled*

Religion – Jonah

Baumann, Kurt. *The story of Jonah*
Bible. Old Testament. Jonah. *The Book of Jonah*
   Jonah, ill. by Kurt Mitchell
   Jonah and the great fish, ill. by Leon Baxter
Bulla, Clyde Robert. *Jonah and the great fish*
Gerstein, Mordicai. *Jonah and the two great fish*
Haiz, Danah. *Jonah's journey*
Hutton, Warwick. *Jonah and the great fish*
MacBeth, George. *Jonah and the Lord*
McDermott, Beverly Brodsky. *Jonah*
Patterson, Geoffrey. *Jonah and the whale*
Thorne, Jenny. *Jonah and the whale*
Williams, Marcia. *Jonah and the whale*

Religion – Moses

Gerstein, Mordicai. *The shadow of a flying bird*
Hayward, Linda. *Baby Moses*
Hodges, Margaret. *Moses*
Hutton, Warwick. *Moses in the bulrushes*
Ife, Elaine. *Moses in the bulrushes*
Kessler, Brad. *Moses in Egypt*
Paterson, Katherine. *The angel and the donkey*

Religion – Nativity

Adams, Georgie. *The first Christmas*
Allan, Nicholas. *Jesus' Christmas party*
Arnold, Mary. *The fussy angel*
Berry, James. *Celebration song*
Bible. New Testament. Gospels. *Christmas*
   The first Christmas, ill. by Barbara Neustadt
   The Nativity
   The story of Christmas, ill. by Jane Ray
Bolognese, Don. *A new day*
Buck, Nola. *Christmas in the manger*
Butterfield, Moira. *The Christmas story*
Butterworth, Nick. *The Nativity play*
Calhoun, Mary. *A shepherd's gift*
Cardillo-Young, Donatella. *The yellow coat*
Carlson, Melody. *King of the stable*
   What Nick and Holly found in grandpa's attic
Carlstrom, Nancy White. *I am Christmas*
Chalmers, Mary. *A Christmas story*
Chorao, Kay. *The Christmas story*
Christmas in the stable, ill. by Beverly K. Duncan
The Christmas story
Clements, Andrew. *Bright Christmas*

Cooney, Barbara. *The story of Christmas*
Crawford, Sheryl Ann. *The baby who changed the world*
Daffis-Felicelli, Christine. *The little star of Bethlehem*
DeBoer, Jesslyn. *Getting ready for Christmas*
De Paola, Tomie (Thomas Anthony). *The Christmas pageant*
  The story of the three wise kings
DeVajay, Szabolcs. *The animals' gift*
Farber, Norma. *All those mothers at the manger*
Fleetwood, Jenni. *While shepherds watched*
Foote, Dan. *The cobbler, the princess, and the newborn King*
Gambill, Henrietta D. *Little Christmas animals*
Ganeri, Anita. *The story of Christmas*
Ginolfi, Arthur. *The tiny star*
Gliori, Debi. *What can I give him?*
Goffin, Josse. *The Christmas story*
  Silent Christmas
Graham, Lorenz B. *Every man heart lay down*
Hautzig, Deborah. *The Christmas story*
Hayes, Sarah. *Away in a manger*
Helldorfer, M. C. (Mary Claire). *Daniel's gift*
Hoffman, Mary. *Three wise women*
Hoffmann, Felix. *The story of Christmas*
Hofmeyr, Dianne. *The stone*
Hogrogian, Nonny. *The first Christmas*
Holcomb, Nan. *Leah's night of wonder*
Holder, Mig. *The fourth wise man*
Hooks, William H. *The legend of the Christmas rose*
Huffaker, Alice. *That first Christmas day*
Hughes, Langston. *Carol of the brown king*
Jewell, Nancy. *Christmas lullaby*
Knowlton, Laurie Lazzaro. *The Nativity*
Kramlich, Carolyn Walz. *Mary's treasure box*
Kroll, Virginia L. *The Christmas cow*
Laurence, Margaret. *The Christmas birthday story*
Lewis, J. Patrick. *Long was the winter road they traveled*
Lindgren, Astrid. *Christmas in the stable*
Lucado, Max. *Jacob's gift*
Lussert, Anneliese. *The Christmas visitor*
Maccarone, Grace. *A child was born*
McCaughrean, Geraldine. *The story of the nativity*
McDermott, Gerald. *The light of the world*
MacDonald, Alan. *The not-so-wise man*
Mackall, Dandi Daley. *Off to Bethlehem!*
Mayper, Monica. *Come and see*
Mills, Claudia. *One small lost sheep*
Moore, Karen Ann. *The baby king*
Moret, Brigitte Frey. *The bear's Christmas*
Nappa, Mike. *Do you see the star?*
Nikola-Lisa, W. *Hallelujah!*
Nussbaumer, Mares. *Away in a manger*
O'Connor, Francine M. *The ABC's of Christmas*
Oppenheim, Joanne. *The Christmas witch*
Pfister, Marcus. *The Christmas star*
Phifer, Martha Nelson. *The colors of Christmas*
Pingry, Patricia. *Joseph's story*
Quattrocki, Carolyn. *The little drummer boy*
Rabe, Berniece. *The first Christmas candy cane*
Safran, Sheri. *The musical cherub*
Sahagun, Bernardino de. *Spirit child*
A small treasury of Christmas poems and prayers
Summers, Susan. *The fourth wise man*
Tangvald, Christine Harder. *The best thing about Christmas*
  Hey, Mr. Angel!
  The Rinky Dinky Donkey

They followed a bright star
Thury, Frederick. *The last straw*
Trent, Robbie. *The first Christmas*
VanderKlipp, Michael A. *Joy to the world!*
Watts, Bernadette. *The Christmas bird*
Wells, Joel. *The manger mouse*
Wijngaard, Juan. *The Nativity*
Wildsmith, Brian. *A Christmas story*
Williams, Marcia. *The first Christmas*
Winthrop, Elizabeth. *A child is born*
Wright, Sue (Sue M.). *The Christmas path*

Religion – Noah

Alberts, Nancy Markham. *No toys on Sunday*
Allan, Jonathan. *Two by two by two*
Allan, Nicholas. *The bird*
Bible. Old Testament. Noah. *Noah and the ark*, ill. by Pauline Baynes
  Noah and the ark, ill. by Jim Cummins
Bolliger, Max. *Noah and the rainbow*
Brent, Isabelle. *Noah's ark*
Brown, Rick. *Who built the ark?*
Chase, Catherine. *Noah's ark*
Cousins, Lucy. *Noah's ark*
Delessert, Etienne. *The endless party*
De Paola, Tomie (Thomas Anthony). *Noah and the ark*
Duvoisin, Roger Antoine. *A for the ark*
Elborn, Andrew. *Noah and the ark and the animals*
Emberley, Barbara. *One wide river to cross*
Farber, Norma. *How the left-behind beasts built Ararat*
  Where's Gomer?
Figley, Marty Rhodes. *Noah's wife*
Fischetto, Laura. *Inside Noah's ark*
French, Fiona. *Rise and shine*
Fussenegger, Gertrud. *Noah's ark*
Gauch, Patricia Lee. *Noah*
Geisert, Arthur. *The ark*
Gerstein, Mordicai. *Noah and the great flood*
Goffstein, M. B. (Marilyn Brooke). *My Noah's ark*
Goodhart, Pippa. *Noah makes a boat*
Graham, Lorenz B. *God wash the world and start again*
Greenfield, Karen R. *Sister Yessa's story*
Haley, Gail E. *Noah's ark*
Haubensak-Tellenbach, Margrit. *The story of Noah's ark*
Hayward, Linda. *Noah's ark*
Henrioud, Charles. *Mr. Noah and the animals*
Hewitt, Kathryn. *Two by two*
Hogrogian, Nonny. *Noah's ark*
Hutton, Warwick. *Noah and the great flood*
Ife, Elaine. *Noah and the ark*
Janisch, Heinz. *Noah's ark*
Jonas, Ann. *Aardvarks, disembark!*
Kuskin, Karla. *The animals and the ark*
Lenski, Lois. *Mr. and Mrs. Noah*
Le Tord, Bijou. *Noah's trees*
Lewis, J. Patrick. *The boat of many rooms*
Ludwig, Warren. *Old Noah's elephants*
MacBeth, George. *Noah's journey*
McCaughrean, Geraldine. *The story of Noah and the ark*
  Unicorns! Unicorns!
McKié, Roy. *Noah's ark*
Martin, Charles E. *Noah's ark*
Mee, Charles L. *Noah*
Olson, Arielle North. *Noah's cats and the devil's fire*

Palazzo, Tony (Anthony D.). *Noah's ark*
Rose, Gerald. *Trouble in the ark*
Rounds, Glen. *Washday on Noah's ark*
Santore, Charles. *A stowaway on Noah's Ark*
Sasso, Sandy Eisenberg. *A prayer for the earth*
Singer, Isaac Bashevis. *Why Noah chose the dove*
Smith, Elmer Boyd. *The story of Noah's ark*
Smith, Roger. *How the animals saved the ark and put two and two together*
Spier, Peter. *Noah's ark*
Thorne, Jenny. *Noah's ark*
Turnbull, Ann. *Too tired*
Walton, Rick. *Noah's square dance*
Webb, Clifford. *The story of Noah*
Wiesner, William. *Noah's ark*
Windham, Sophie. *Noah's ark*

Remembering

Ackerman, Karen. *Walking with Clara Belle*

Repetitive stories *see* Cumulative tales

Reptiles

Barrett, Judi. *Snake is totally tail*
Colby, C. B. (Carroll Burleigh). *Who went there?*
Cortesi, Wendy W. *Explore a spooky swamp*
Cristini, Ermanno. *In the pond*
Harris, Susan. *Reptiles*
Heller, Ruth. *How to hide a crocodile and other reptiles*
Kuchalla, Susan. *What is a reptile?*
Nayer, Judy. *Reptiles*
Ogburn, Jacqueline K. *The reptile ball*
Pluckrose, Henry Arthur. *Reptiles*
Vyner, Sue. *The stolen egg*

Reptiles – alligators, crocodiles

Aliki. *Keep your mouth closed, dear*
  Use your head, dear
Aruego, José. *A crocodile's tale*
  Rockabye crocodile
Balzola, Asun. *Munia and the orange crocodile*
Bare, Colleen Stanley. *Never kiss an alligator*
Becker, Bonny. *The Christmas crocodile*
Bedard, Michael. *Sitting ducks*
Bradman, Tony. *See you later, alligator*
Brown, Ruth. *Crazy Charlie*
Calmenson, Stephanie. *Get well, gators!*
Campbell, M. Rudolph. *The talking crocodile*
Carrick, Carol. *The crocodiles still wait*
  Norman fools the tooth fairy
Cazet, Denys. *The duck with squeaky feet*
Childress, Mark. *Joshua and Bigtooth*
Christelow, Eileen. *Five little monkeys sitting in a tree*
  Jerome and the Witchcraft kids
  Jerome camps out
  Jerome the babysitter
Cushman, Doug. *Nasty Kyle the crocodile*
Dahl, Roald. *The enormous crocodile*
Daly, Niki. *Mary Malloy and the baby who wouldn't sleep*
De Groat, Diane. *Alligator's toothache*
De Paola, Tomie (Thomas Anthony). *Bill and Pete*
  Bill and Pete go down the Nile
  Bill and Pete to the rescue
Dorros, Arthur. *Alligator shoes*
Dragonwagon, Crescent. *Alligator arrived with apples*

Dumbleton, Mike. *Dial-a-croc*
Duvoisin, Roger Antoine. *The crocodile in the tree*
  Crocus
Eastman, P. D. (Philip D.). *Flap your wings*
Eduar, Gilles. *Jooka saves the day*
Engel, Diana. *Josephina hates her name*
Galdone, Paul. *The monkey and the crocodile*
Gantos, Jack (John, Jr.). *Swampy alligator*
Garrett, Ann. *Keeper of the swamp*
Gerrard, Roy. *Croco'nile*
Gomi, Taro. *The crocodile and the dentist*
Gross, Ruth Belov. *Alligators and other crocodilians*
Guiberson, Brenda Z. *Spoonbill swamp*
Guy, Rosa. *Mother crocodile*
Hartelius, Margaret A. *The chicken's child*
Heller, Ruth. *How to hide a crocodile and other reptiles*
Hill, Eric. *Spot's baby sister*
Hirschi, Ron. *Who lives in . . . Alligator Swamp?*
Hoban, Russell. *Arthur's new power*
  Dinner at Alberta's
Hodeir, André. *Warwick's 3 bottles*
Holland, Isabelle. *Kevin's hat*
Hurd, Thacher. *Mama don't allow*
Inkpen, Mick. *Crocodile!*
Jaquith, Priscilla. *Bo Rabbit smart for true*
Keeshan, Robert. *Alligator in the basement*
Keven, Elisa. *Ernest*
Kinnell, Galway. *How the alligator missed breakfast*
Kipling, Rudyard. *The elephant's child*, ill. by John A. Rowe
Kirn, Ann. *The tale of a crocodile*
Knüppel, Helga. *The adventures of Christabel Crocodile*
  Christabel Crocodile's birthday egg
Kraus, Robert. *Good morning, Miss Gator*
Kunhardt, Edith. *Danny and the Easter egg*
  Danny's birthday
  Danny's Christmas star
  Danny's mystery Valentine
  Trick or treat, Danny!
Lexau, Joan M. *Crocodile and hen*
Lionni, Leo. *Cornelius*
  An extraordinary egg
McCarthy, Bobette. *See you later, alligator*
McPhail, David M. *Alligators are awful (and they have terrible manners, too)*
Marcellino, Fred. *I, crocodile*
Markle, Sandra. *Outside and inside alligators*
Mayer, Marianna. *Alley oop!*
Mayer, Mercer. *There's an alligator under my bed*
Minarik, Else Holmelund. *No fighting, no biting!*
Mollel, Tololwa M. (Tololwa Marti). *Shadow dance*
Moon, Nicola. *Alligator tails and crocodile cakes*
Muntean, Michaela. *Alligator's garden*
Nobisso, Josephine. *For the sake of a cake*
Novak, Matt. *Gertie and Gumbo*
Offen, Hilda. *Elephant pie*
Pack, Robert. *How to catch a crocodile*
Parker, Nancy Winslow. *The crocodile under Louis Finneberg's bed*
Peterson, Esther Allen. *Frederick's alligator*
Pickett, Carla. *Calvin Crocodile and the terrible noise*
Reneaux, J. J. *Why Alligator hates Dog*
Rice, James. *Gaston goes to Texas*
Rubel, Nicole. *It came from the swamp*
Sadler, Marilyn. *Elizabeth, Larry, and Ed*
Schubert, Ingrid. *There's a crocodile under my bed!*
Sendak, Maurice. *Alligators all around*
Shaw, Evelyn S. *Alligator*

Oppenheim, Joanne. *Mrs. Peloki's snake*
Parsons, Alexandra. *Amazing snakes*
Patton, Don. *Pythons*
Pilkey, Dav. *A friend for Dragon*
Prather, Ray. *The ostrich girl*
Reinl, Edda. *The little snake*
Shannon, George. *Lizard's home*
Smith, Mavis. *A snake mistake*
Strete, Craig Kee. *The lost boy and the monster*
Tseng, Grace. *White tiger, blue serpent*
Ungerer, Tomi. *Crictor*
Waber, Bernard. *The snake*
Walsh, Ellen Stoll. *Mouse count*
Wildsmith, Brian. *Python's party*

Reptiles – turtles, tortoises

Abisch, Roz. *The clever turtle*
Æsop. *The hare and the tortoise*, ill. by Paul Galdone
    The hare and the tortoise, ill. by Carol Jones
    The hare and the tortoise, ill. by Gerald Rose
    The hare and the tortoise, ill. by Helen Ward
    The hare and the tortoise, ill. by Peter Weevers
    The tortoise and the hare
Asch, Frank. *Turtle tale*
Augarde, Steve (Stephen). *Barnaby Shrew, Black Dan and . . . the mighty wedgwood*
    Barnaby Shrew goes to sea
Baumann, Hans. *The hare's race*
Berger, Melvin. *Look out for turtles!*
Bourgeois, Paulette. *Franklin and the thunderstorm*
    Franklin in the dark
    Franklin rides a bike
    Franklin's Christmas gift
    Franklin's class trip
    Franklin's new friend
    Franklin's secret club
Bryan, Ashley. *Turtle knows your name*
Buckley, Richard. *The foolish tortoise*
Cahill, Chris. *Turtle magic*
Chottin, Ariane. *A home for Little Turtle*
Christian, Mary Blount. *Devin and Goliath*
Chwast, Seymour. *Mr. Merlin and the turtle*
Collins, Pat Lowery. *Tomorrow, up and away!*
Coste, Marion. *Honu*
Cousteau Society. *Turtles*
Creighton, Jill. *One day there was nothing to do*
Cromie, William J. *Steven and the green turtle*
Cummings, Betty Sue. *Turtle*
Darby, Gene. *What is a turtle?*
Davis, Alice Vaught. *Timothy Turtle*
DeSpain, Pleasant. *The dancing turtle*
Dodd, Lynley. *The smallest turtle*
Domanska, Janina. *Look, there is a turtle flying*
    The tortoise and the tree
Du Bois, William Pène. *The hare and the tortoise and the tortoise and the hare*
Elks, Wendy. *Charles B. Wombat and the very strange thing*
Emberley, Ed (Edward Randolph). *Rosebud*
Florian, Douglas. *Turtle day*
Freeman, Don. *The turtle and the dove*
Freschet, Berniece. *Turtle pond*
George, William T. *Box turtle at Long Pond*
Goldsmith, Howard. *Toto the timid turtle*
Graham, Al. *Timothy Turtle*
Guiberson, Brenda Z. *Into the sea*
Harris, Dorothy Joan. *Four seasons for Toby*
Harrison, David Lee. *Little turtle's big adventure*

Hoban, Lillian. *Stick-in-the-mud turtle*
    Turtle spring
Horn, Peter. *When I grow up –*
Jeffery, Graham. *Thomas the tortoise*
Jennings, Linda M. *Franklin's neighborhood*
Joyce, William. *Bently and egg*
Katz, Avner. *Tortoise solves a problem*
Kimmel, Eric A. *Anansi goes fishing*
Kraus, Robert. *Wise Old Owl's canoe trip adventure*
Kulling, Monica. *Waiting for Amos*
La Fontaine, Jean de. *The hare and the tortoise*
Leedy, Loreen. *Tracks in the sand*
Lesikin, Joan. *Down the road*
Lillegard, Dee. *Tortoise brings the mail*
London, Jonathan. *What Newt could do for Turtle*
Lowell, Susan. *The tortoise and the jackrabbit*
Lubell, Winifred. *Rosalie, the bird market turtle*
MacGill-Callahan, Sheila. *And still the turtle watched*
MacGregor, Ellen. *Theodor Turtle*
McGuire-Turcotte, Casey A. *How Honu the turtle got his shell*
McLenighan, Valjean. *Turtle and rabbit*
Maestro, Giulio. *The tortoise's tug of war*
Maris, Ron. *I wish I could fly*
Marshall, James. *Yummers too*
Martin, Francesca. *Clever Tortoise*
Matsutani, Miyoko. *The fisherman under the sea*
Métral, Yvette. *The turtle*
Mollel, Tololwa M. (Tololwa Marti). *Ananse's feast*
    The flying tortoise
    The king and the tortoise
Murdocca, Sal (Salvatore). *Tuttle's shell*
O'Donnell, Elizabeth Lee. *I can't get my turtle to move*
Palazzo-Craig, Janet. *Turtles*
Parry, Marian. *King of the fish*
Patton, Don. *Sea turtles*
Ross, Gayle. *How Turtle's back was cracked*
St. Pierre, Wendy. *Henry finds a home*
Sanfield, Steve. *The great turtle drive*
Sayre, April Pulley. *Turtle, turtle, watch out!*
Shearer, Marilyn J. *The crown of fools*
Spooner, Michael. *Old Meshikee and the little crabs*
Stoddard, Sandol. *Turtle time*
Thayer, Jane. *Mr. Turtle's magic glasses*
Thayer, Mike. *In the middle of the puddle*
Troughton, Joanna. *Tortoise's dream*
Turner, Charles. *The turtle and the moon*
Van Woerkom, Dorothy. *Harry and Shelburt*
Vozar, David. *M. C. Turtle and the hip hop hare*
Ward, Helen. *The moonrat and the white turtle*
Wiese, Kurt. *The cunning turtle*
Williams, Barbara. *Albert's toothache*
Wilson, Barbara Ker. *The turtle and the island*
Wolf, Ann. *The rabbit and the turtle*
Wolfson, Margaret. *Turtle songs*
Wyse, Lois. *Two guppies, a turtle and Aunt Edna*
Yashima, Taro. *Seashore story*
Zagwÿn, Deborah Turney. *Turtle spring*
Ziefert, Harriet. *Where's the turtle?*

Responsibility *see* Character traits – responsibility

Rest *see* Sleep

Restaurants

Adinolfi, JoAnn. *Tina's diner*
Anderson, Peggy Perry. *Out to lunch*
Christelow, Eileen. *The robbery at the diamond dog diner*
Coombs, Patricia. *Mouse Café*
Davis, Maggie S. *The rinky-dink café*
Egan, Tim. *Friday night at Hodges' café*
Herman, Gail. *Pizza cats*
Impey, Rose. *Joe's café*
Kirk, Daniel. *Breakfast at the Liberty Diner*
Krementz, Jill. *Benjy goes to a restaurant*
Loomis, Christine. *In the diner*
Moss, Marissa. *Mel's diner*
Pearson, Tracey Campbell. *Where does Joe go?*
Pittman, Helena Clare. *Uncle Phil's diner*
Polacco, Patricia. *In Enzo's splendid gardens*
Stadler, John. *Animal café*
Yee, Wong Herbert. *Hamburger Heaven*

Rhinoceros *see* Animals – rhinoceros

Rhyming text

Aardema, Verna. *Bringing the rain to Kapiti Plain*
The riddle of the drum
Ackerman, Karen. *The banshee*
Flannery Row
This old house
Ada, Alma Flor. *El Arbol de Navidad : The Christmas tree*
Adler, David A. *You think it's fun to be a clown!*
Adoff, Arnold. *Black is brown is tan*
Greens
Adorjan, Carol Madden. *I can! Can you?*
Æsop. *Androcles and the lion*, ill. by Robert Rayevsky
Once in a wood
Agard, John. *No hickory no dickory no dock*
Agell, Charlotte. *To the island*
Ahlberg, Allan. *Cops and robbers*
Monkey do!
Ahlberg, Janet. *Each peach pear plum*
The jolly Christmas postman
The jolly pocket postman
The jolly postman
Peek-a-boo!
Aiken, Conrad Potter. *Tom, Sue and the clock*
Alborough, Jez. *Bare bear*
Duck in the truck
Esther's trunk
Ice cream bear
It's the bear
There's something at the mail slot
Where's my teddy?
Alda, Arlene. *Pig, horse, or cow, don't wake me now*
Sheep, sheep, sheep, help me fall asleep
Alderson, Sue Ann. *Bonnie McSmithers is at it again!*
Alexander, Anne (Anna Barbara Cooke). *I want to whistle*
Alexander, Sue. *Who goes out on Halloween?*
All year round
Allard, Harry. *The hummingbirds' day*
Allen, Jeffrey. *Up the steps, down the slide*
Allen, Jonathan. *Big owl, little towel*
One with a bun
Purple sock, pink sock
Allen, Judy. *What is a wall, after all?*
Allen, Marjorie N. *Changes*

Allen, Pamela. *Mr. McGee*
Who sank the boat?
Allen, Robert. *Ten little babies eat*
Allison, Diane Worfolk. *In window eight, the moon is late*
Ambler, C. Gifford (Christopher Gifford). *Ten little foxhounds*
Anastasio, Dina. *Baby Piggy and giant bubble*
Pass the peas, please
Anderson, Lena. *Tick-tock*
Anderson, Peggy Perry. *Out to lunch*
Andreae, Giles. *Love is a handful of honey*
Anglund, Joan Walsh. *A child's year*
Christmas is here
How many days has Baby to play?
Anholt, Catherine. *Bear and baby*
Kids
One, two, three, count with me
Toddlers
What I like
What makes me happy?
Appelt, Kathi. *Bats on parade*
Cowboy dreams
A red wagon year
Someone's come to our house
Aragon, Jane Chelsea. *Salt hands*
Winter harvest
Archambault, John. *A beautiful feast for a big king cat*
Counting sheep
Armour, Richard Willard. *The adventures of Egbert the Easter egg*
Animals on the ceiling
Sea full of whales
The year Santa went modern
Arnold, Katya. *Knock, knock, teremok!*
Arnold, Tedd. *Five ugly monsters*
Green Wilma
Ollie forgot
Parts
Aronow, Sara. *Seven days of creation*
Asch, Frank. *The alphabet zoo*
Baby in the box
Ashton, Elizabeth Allen. *An old-fashioned ABC book*
An old-fashioned one two three book
Attenberger, Walburga. *The little man in winter*
Who knows the little man?
Atwood, Ann. *The little circle*
Auerbach, Julie Jaslow. *Everything's changing - It's pesach!*
Aylesworth, Jim. *The folks in the valley*
Mary's mirror
Mr. McGill goes to town
My sister's rusty bike
Old Black Fly
One crow
Wake up, little children
Ayres, Pam. *Guess what?*
Guess who?
When dad cuts down the chestnut tree
When dad fills in the garden pond
Babson, Jane F. *Babson's bestiary*
Bach, Othello. *Lilly, Willy and the mail-order witch*
Baer, Edith. *This is the way we go to school*
Words are like faces
Baker, Keith. *Cat tricks*
Hide and snake
Who is the beast?

Baker, Sanna Anderson. *Who's a friend of the water-spurting whale*
Ballart, Elisabet. *Let's count*
Bang, Molly. *Ten, nine, eight*
Banigan, Sharon Stearns. *Circus magic*
Barasch, Marc Ian. *No plain pets!*
Barracca, Debra. *Maxi, the hero*
   Maxi, the star
   A taxi dog Christmas
Barracca, Sal. *The adventures of taxi dog*
Barrett, Judi. *Pickles have pimples*
Barrett, Mary Brigid. *Day care days*
Barry, Robert E. *Mr. Willowby's Christmas tree*
Bartalos, Michael. *Shadowville*
Base, Graeme. *My grandma lived in Gooligulch*
Baskin, Leonard. *Hosie's zoo*
Baskwill, Jane. *Somewhere*
Bauer, Steven. *The strange and wonderful tale of Robert McDoodle*
Baylor, Byrd. *Amigo*
   The desert is theirs
   Desert voices
   Everybody needs a rock
   One small blue bead
Beck, Ian. *Five little ducks*
Becker, Bonny. *Tickly prickly*
Beil, Karen Magnuson. *A cake all for me!*
Beisner, Monika. *Catch that cat!*
   Topsy turvy
Bemelmans, Ludwig. *Madeline*
   Madeline and the bad hat
   Madeline and the gypsies
   Madeline in London
   Madeline's Christmas
   Madeline's rescue
   Welcome home!
Benjamin, Alan. *A change of plans*
   Rat-a-tat, pitter pat
   Ribtickle Town
Berends, Polly Berrien. *I heard said the bird*
Berenstain, Stan. *The bear detectives*
   The Berenstain bears and the missing dinosaur bone
   The Berenstain bears and the spooky old tree
   The Berenstain bears' Christmas tree
   He bear, she bear
Berg, Jean Horton. *The wee little man*
Berger, Judith. *Butterflies and rainbows*
Bernardoni, Robert. *Christmas all over*
Berridge, Celia. *Hannah's temper*
Beskow, Elsa Maartman. *Children of the forest*
   Peter in Blueberry Land
   Peter's adventures in Blueberry Land
Betz, Betty. *Manners for moppets*
Birchman, David Francis. *Brother Billy Bronto's bygone blues band*
Birchmore, Daniel A. *Pilly, Polly, and Wee*
Bird, E. J. *How do bears sleep?*
Black, Irma (Simonton). *Is this my dinner?*
Blackstone, Stella. *Baby high, baby low*
Blackwood, Mary. *Derek the knitting dinosaur*
Blake, Quentin. *Mister Magnolia*
   Quentin Blake's ABC
   Simpkin
Blazek, Sarah Kirwan. *An Irish Hallowe'en*
Blegvad, Lenore. *One is for the sun*
   This is me
Blocksma, Mary. *Where's that duck?*
Bloom, Suzanne. *We keep a pig in the parlor*
Blos, Joan W. *Old Henry*

Blumenthal, Nancy. *Count-a-saurus*
Blyler, Allison. *Finding foxes*
Bodwell, Gaile. *The long day of the giants*
Boegehold, Betty. *The fight*
   Pawpaw's run
Boesky, Amy. *Planet Was*
Bond, Felicia. *Tumble bumble*
Boon, Debbie. *My gran*
Bornstein, Ruth Lercher. *The seedling child*
Borten, Helen. *Do you go where I go?*
   Do you hear what I hear?
   Do you know what I know?
Bos, Claire. *Maurice the hippo*
   Webster's wardrobe
Bottner, Barbara. *There was nobody there*
Bowie, C. W. *Busy toes*
Boyd, Lizi. *Lulu Crow's garden*
   Mouse in a house
Boynton, Sandra. *Birthday monsters!*
   But not the hippopotamus
   Dinosaur's binkit
   The going to bed book
   Good night, good night
   Hippos go berserk
   Moo, baa, lalala
   Oh my oh my oh dinosaurs!
   One, two, three!
Bradman, Tony. *The bad babies' book of colors*
   The bad babies' counting book
   A bad week for the three bears
   This little baby
Braun, Kathy. *Kangaroo and kangaroo*
Breeze, Lynn. *Baby's animals*
   Baby's clothes
   Baby's food
   Baby's toys
   This little baby goes out
   This little baby's bedtime
   This little baby's morning
Brenner, Barbara A. *The color wizard*
Brent, Isabelle. *Cameo cats*
Bridgman, Elizabeth. *All the little bunnies*
Bright, Robert. *My hopping bunny*
Brillhart, Julie. *When daddy came to school*
   When Daddy took us camping
Brimner, Larry Dane. *Cowboy up!*
   Nana's hog
   What good is a tree?
Brink, Carol Ryrie. *Goody O'Grumpity*
Brooke, L. Leslie (Leonard Leslie). *Johnny Crow's garden*
   Johnny Crow's new garden
Brooks, Bruce. *Each a piece*
Brouillard, Anne. *The bathtub prima donna*
Brown, Judith Gwyn. *Alphabet dreams*
Brown, Marc Tolon. *Monster's lunchbox*
   Pickle things
   The silly tail book
   Teddy bear, teddy bear
   There's no place like home
   Wings on things
   Witches four
Brown, Margaret Wise. *Another important book*
   Big red barn, ill. by Felicia Bond
   Big red barn, ill. by Rosella Hartman
   The diggers
   Sleepy ABC
   Two little trains
   Whistle for the train

Brown, Ruth. *Mad summer night's dream*
 Toad
Browne, Philippa-Alys. *A gaggle of geese*
Bruna, Dick. *Christmas*
 The happy apple
 Kitten Nell
 Little bird tweet
 The orchestra
 Poppy Pig goes to market
 Tilly and Tess
Bryan, Ashley. *Beat the story-drum, pum-pum*
 The cat's purr
Buck, Nola. *Christmas in the manger*
 Gotcha!
 Halloween parade
 How a baby grows
 The littlest witch
 Oh, cats!
Buckley, Helen Elizabeth. *Josie and the snow*
 Josie's Buttercup
 Where did Josie go?
Buckley, Richard. *The foolish tortoise*
 The greedy python
Bucknall, Caroline. *One bear all alone*
 One bear in the hospital
 One bear in the picture
Buff, Mary (Marsh). *Hurry, Skurry and Flurry*
Bullard, Lisa. *Not enough beds!*
Buller, Jon. *Toad on the road*
Bullock, Kathleen. *It chanced to rain*
Bunting, Eve (Anne Evelyn). *Butterfly house*
 Flower garden
 Happy birthday, dear duck
 My backpack
 The pumpkin fair
 Red fox running
 Scary, scary Halloween
 Sunflower house
Burdett, Lois. *Hamlet for kids*
 A midsummer night's dream for kids
 Romeo and Juliet for kids
 The tempest for kids
Burleigh, Robert. *It's funny where Ben's train takes him*
Burnside, Julian. *Matilda and the dragon*
Burnstein, John. *Slim Goodbody*
Burroway, Janet. *The truck on the track*
Burton, Katherine. *One gray mouse*
Bush, John. *The cross-with-us rhinoceros*
 The fish who could wish
 The giraffe who got in a knot
Butler, Dorothy. *Higgledy, piggledy, hobbledy hoy*
Butterworth, Nick. *All together now!*
Bynum, Janie. *Altoona Baboona*
Cabrera, Jane. *Panda Big and Panda Small*
Caffey, Donna. *Yikes-lice!*
Calmenson, Stephanie. *Dinner at the Panda Palace*
 Engine, engine, number nine
 It begins with an A
 One little monkey
 Roller skates!
 Shaggy, waggy dogs (and others)
 Ten furry monsters
 Where will the animals stay?
Cameron, John. *If mice could fly*
Cappetta, Cynthia. *Chairs, chairs, chairs!*
Capucilli, Alyssa Satin. *Inside a barn in the country*
 Inside a house that is haunted
 Peekaboo bunny

Carlson, Nancy L. *Take time to relax*
Carlstrom, Nancy White. *Better not get wet, Jesse Bear*
 Goodbye geese
 Guess who's coming, Jesse Bear
 Happy birthday, Jesse Bear!
 How do you say it today, Jesse Bear?
 It's about time, Jesse Bear
 Jesse Bear's tra-la tub
 Jesse Bear's tum-tum tickle
 Jesse Bear's wiggle-jiggle jump-up
 Jesse Bear's yum-yum crumble
 Kiss your sister, Rose Marie
 Let's count it out, Jesse Bear
 The moon came too
 No nap for Benjamin Badger
 Northern lullaby
 Rise and shine!
 Ten Christmas sheep
 What a scare, Jesse Bear!
 What would you do if you lived at the zoo?
 Wild wild sunflower child Anna
Carmack, Lisa Jobe. *Philippe in Monet's garden*
Carroll, Kathleen Sullivan. *One red rooster*
Carter, Noelle. *My house*
 My pet
Cassidy, Dianne. *Circus animals*
 Circus people
Caswell, Helen Rayburn. *God must like to laugh*
Cate, Rikki. *A cat's tale*
Cauley, Lorinda Bryan. *Treasure hunt*
Causley, Charles. *"Quack!" said the billy-goat*
Cave, Kathryn. *Out for the count*
Cazet, Denys. *Nothing at all*
Chandra, Deborah. *A is for Amos*
 Miss Mabel's table
Chapman, Cheryl. *Pass the fritters, critters*
Chardiet, Bernice. *C is for circus*
Charles, Donald. *Calico Cat at school*
 Calico Cat at the zoo
 Calico Cat meets bookworm
 Calico Cat's exercise book
 Calico Cat's year
 Time to rhyme with Calico Cat
Charles, Faustin. *A Caribbean counting book*
Charlip, Remy. *Sleepytime rhyme*
Cherry, Lynne. *The armadillo from Amarillo*
 Who's sick today?
Chesworth, Michael. *Archibald Frisby*
Chönz, Selina. *A bell for Ursli*
 Florina and the wild bird
 The snowstorm
Chorao, Kay. *Carousel round and round*
 Knock at the door and other baby action rhymes
 Number one number fun
 Peekaboo! Was it you?
Christelow, Eileen. *Five little monkeys sitting in a tree*
Chukovskii, Kornei Ivanovich. *The telephone*
Cibula, Matt S. *The contrary kid*
 Slumgullion, the executive pig
Civardi, Anne. *The wacky book of witches*
Clarke, Gus. *Ten green monsters*
Cleary, Beverly. *The hullabaloo ABC*, ill. by Ted Rand
 The hullabaloo ABC, ill. by Earl Thollander
Clifton, Lucille. *Everett Anderson's friend*
 Everett Anderson's goodbye
 Everett Anderson's nine months long
 Everett Anderson's 1-2-3
 Everett Anderson's year

Coats, Laura Jane. *Ten little animals*
Coats, Lucy. *One hungry baby*
Coatsworth, Elizabeth. *The children come running*
   The giant golden book of cat stories
Cobb, Annie. *Wheels!*
Cohen, Caron Lee. *Whiffle Squeek*
Cohen, Nora. *From apple to zipper*
Cole, Babette. *Babette Cole's beastly birthday book*
   Babette Cole's brother
   Babette Cole's ponies
   The bad good manners book
   Dad
   The hairy book
   Mum
   Silly book
   The slimy book
   The smelly book
Cole, Joanna. *Animal sleepyheads*
   Fun on wheels, ill. by Whitney Darrow
   Fun on wheels, ill. by Don Gauthier
Cole, William. *Frances face-maker*
   Have I got dogs!
   That pest Jonathan
   What's good for a four-year-old?
   What's good for a six-year-old?
   What's good for a three-year-old?
Coleman, Michael. *One, two, three, oops!*
Coletta, Irene. *From A to Z*
Coltman, Paul. *Tinker Jim*
Conover, Chris. *Six little ducks*
Cooner, Donna D. (Donna Danell). *The world God made*
Cooney, Barbara. *A garland of games and other diversions*
Cooper, Melrose. *I got a family*
   Pets!
Copp, James (Andrew James). *Martha Matilda O'Toole*
Count in the dark with Glo Worm
Count me in
Couture, Susan Arkin. *The biggest horse I ever did see*
   The block book
Cowen-Fletcher, Jane. *Baby angels*
Cowley, Stewart. *Five little kittens*
   Hide-and-seek puppies
   Little bunny
   Little chick
   Little lost rabbit
   The naughty ducklings
   "Tweet, tweet, tweet"
Craft, Ruth. *The winter bear*
Crebbin, June. *Cows in the kitchen*
   Into the castle
Crowley, Arthur. *Bonzo Beaver*
   The wagon man
Cuetara, Mittie. *The crazy crawler crane and other very short truck stories*
   Terrible Teresa and other very short stories
Cummings, Pat. *Clean your room, Harvey Moon!*
   Jimmy Lee did it
   My aunt came back
Cummings, Phil. *Goodness gracious!*
Cuneo, Mary Louise. *What can a giant do?*
Curtis, Jamie Lee. *Today I feel silly and other moods that make my day*
Curtiss, A. B. *In the company of bears*
Cushman, Doug. *The ABC mystery*
   Once upon a pig
Daly, Niki. *The boy on the beach*

Davis, Lee. *The lifesize animal opposites book*
Davis, Maggie S. *The rinky-dink café*
Davol, Marguerite W. *The heart of the wood*
Dayton, Laura. *LeRoy's birthday circus*
DeFelice, Cynthia C. *Clever crow*
Degen, Bruce. *Jamberry*
   Sailaway home
   Teddy bear towers
Delaunay, Sonia. *Sonia Delaunay's alphabet*
Demarest, Chris L. *Bus*
   Fall
   Farmer Nat
   Plane
   Ship
   Spring
   Summer
   Train
   Winter
Demi. *Demi's count the animals 1-2-3*
   Demi's dragons and fantastic creatures
Demuth, Patricia Brennan. *Busy at day care head to toe*
   Max, the bad-talking parrot
De Paola, Tomie (Thomas Anthony). *Get dressed, Santa!*
   Songs of the fog maiden
De Regniers, Beatrice Schenk. *May I bring a friend?*
   Red Riding Hood
   Sam and the impossible thing
   So many cats!
   Something special
   Was it a good trade?
DeRubertis, Barbara. *Janey Crane*
   Joey Goat
   Suzy Mule
   Tiny Tiger
   Zeely Zebra
Dijs, Carla. *Pretend you're a hippo*
Dionne, Wanda. *Little Thumb*
Disher, Garry. *Switch cat*
Diviny, Sean. *Snow inside the house*
Dodd, Lynley. *A dragon in a wagon*
   Find me a tiger
   Hairy Maclary from Donaldson's dairy
   Hairy Maclary, Scattercat
   Hairy Maclary, sit
   Hairy Maclary's bone
   Hairy Maclary's caterwaul caper
   Hairy Maclary's rumpus at the vet
   Hairy Maclary's showbusiness
   The nickle nackle tree
   Schnitzel von Krumm forget-me-not
   Schnitzel von Krumm's basketwork
   Slinky Malinki
   Slinky Malinki catflaps
   Slinky Malinki, open the door
Dodds, Dayle Ann. *Do bunnies talk?*
   The Great Divide
   Sing, Sophie!
   Wheel away!
Dodge, Mary Mapes. *Mary Anne*
Domanska, Janina. *What do you see?*
Donaldson, Julia. *The gruffalo*
Doolittle, Eileen. *World of wonders*
Doro, Ann. *Twin pickle*
Dotlich, Rebecca Kai. *What is round?*
   What is square?
Doyle, Charlotte Lackner. *You can't catch me*
Dragonwagon, Crescent. *Annie flies the birthday bike*

Bat in the dining room
Half a moon and one whole star
The itch book
Jemima remembers
The sun begun
This is the bread I baked for Ned
Drake, John. *The beginning of the river*
Drury, Tim. *When I'm big*
Dubanevich, Arlene. *Tom's tail*
Dubowski, Cathy East. *Snug Bug*
Snug Bug's play day
Duke, Kate. *Seven froggies went to school*
Dunbar, Joyce. *Baby bird*
Duncan, Lois. *Birthday moon*
Dunphy, Madeleine. *Here is the Arctic winter*
Du Quette, Keith. *The house book*
Eberstadt, Isabel (Nash). *What is for my birthday?*
Edelman, Elaine. *Boom-de-boom*
Eduar, Gilles. *Dream journey*
Edwards, Pamela Duncan. *Ed and Fred Flea*
The grumpy morning
Warthogs in the kitchen
Edwards, Richard. *Fly with the birds*
Ten tall oaktrees
Edwards, Roland. *Tigers*
Ehlert, Lois. *Feathers for lunch*
Fish eyes
Nuts to you!
Top cat
Eichenberg, Fritz. *Dancing in the moon*
Elborn, Andrew. *Bird Adalbert*
Elkin, Benjamin. *The king who could not sleep*
Engel, Diana. *Circle song*
Esbensen, Barbara Juster. *Jumping day*
Ladder to the sky
The star maiden
Euvremer, Teryl. *After dark*
Evans, Katie. *Hunky Dory ate it*
Evans, Lezlie. *Can you count ten toes?*
If I were the wind
Evans, Nate. *The mixed-up zoo of professor Yahoo*
Factor, Jane. *Summer*
Falwell, Cathryn. *Christmas for 10*
Feast for ten
Shape space
Farber, Erica. *Ooey gooey*
Farber, Norma. *All those mothers at the manger*
The boy who longed for a lift
I swim an ocean in my sleep
Without wings, mother, how can I fly?
Farjeon, Eleanor. *Mrs. Malone*
Faulkner, Keith. *David dreaming of dinosaurs*
The snake's mistake
Feder, Harriet K. *Not yet, Elijah!*
Fehlner, Paul. *Dog and cat*
Ferguson, Don. *Winnie the Pooh's A to Zzzz*
Field, Rachel Lyman. *A road might lead to anywhere*
Fisher, Aileen Lucia. *And a sunflower grew*
Anybody home?
Going barefoot
Now that spring is here
Petals yellow and petals red
Plant magic
Prize performance
Seeds on the go
Sing, little mouse
Swords and daggers
Fisher, Leonard Everett. *Boxes! Boxes!*
Five little pumpkins

Flather, Lisa. *Ten silly dogs*
Fleischman, Paul. *Rondo in C*
Fleming, Denise. *Barnyard banter*
In the small, small pond
Florian, Douglas. *A potter*
Vegetable garden
A winter day
Foord, Jo. *The book of babies*
Fowler, Richard. *Cat's story*
Fox, Mem. *Boo to a goose*
Shoes from grandpa
Sleepy bears
Time for bed
Zoo-looking
Fox, Perla. *The Wooodles*
Freeman, Don. *The day is waiting*
Mop Top
Frith, Michael K. *I'll teach my dog 100 words*
Fujikawa, Gyo. *Ten little babies*
Gág, Wanda. *ABC bunny*
Gage, Wilson. *Down in the boondocks*
Galdone, Joanna. *Gertrude, the goose who forgot*
Gardner, Beau. *Whooo's a fright on Halloween night?*
Garelick, May. *Look at the moon*, ill. by Barbara Garrison
Look at the moon, ill. by Leonard Weisgard
Where does the butterfly go when it rains?, ill. by Leonard Weisgard
Where does the butterfly go when it rains?, ill. by Nicholas Wilton
Garland, Michael. *The mouse before Christmas*
Garne, S. T. *By a blazing blue sea*
Garrett, Ann. *What's for lunch?*
Gay, Marie-Louise. *Moonbeam on a cat's ear*
Rainy day magic
Gelbard, Jane. *My bye-bye bottle book*
My dressing book
My eating book
My sharing book
Gelman, Rita Golden. *Hey, kid*
Gelsanliter, Wendy. *Dancin' in the kitchen*
Geringer, Laura. *The cow is mooing anyhow*
Gerrard, Roy. *Croco'nile*
The Favershams
Jocasta Carr, movie star
Mik's mammoth
The Roman twins
Rosie and the rustlers
Sir Cedric
Sir Cedric rides again
Gershator, Phillis. *When it starts to snow*
Gerstein, Mordicai. *Daisy's garden*
Gewing, Lisa. *Mama, daddy, baby and me*
Ghigna, Charles. *Mice are nice*
Gilchrist, Theo E. *Halfway up the mountain*
Gile, John. *Oh, how I wished I could read!*
The gingerbread boy. *The gingerbread boy*, ill. by Paul Galdone
Whiff, sniff, nibble and chew
Ginsburg, Mirra. *Four brave sailors*
Kitten from one to ten
The sun's asleep behind the hill
Gliori, Debi. *Mr. Bear says, "Are you there, Baby Bear?"*
No matter what
What can I give him?
Godwin, Laura. *Little white dog*
Goldblatt, Eli. *Leo loves round*
Golding, Kim. *Alphababies*

Gomi, Taro. *Toot!*
Good, Merle. *Amos and Susie*
Goode, Molly. *Mama loves*
Goodspeed, Peter. *A rhinoceros wakes me up in the morning*
Gordon, Jeffie Ross. *Two badd babies*
Gottlieb, Dale. *Where Jamaica go?*
Graham, Lorenz B. *Song of the boat*
Grahame, Kenneth. *Duck song*
Graves, Keith. *Frank was a monster who wanted to dance*
Gray, Libba Moore. *Is there room on the feather bed?*
  Small green snake
Gray, Nigel. *Fly*
  The grocer's daughter
Greaves, Margaret. *The mice of Nibbling Village*
Greeley, Valerie. *The acorn's story*
  White is the moon
Greenberg, Dan. *The bed who ran away from home*
Greenberg, David (David T.). *Bugs!*
  Slugs
Greene, Carol. *The world's biggest birthday cake*
Greene, Rhonda Gowler. *Barnyard song*
Greenfield, Eloise. *Kia Tanisha*
  On my horse
  Water, water
Greenwood, Ann. *A pack of dreams*
Grimes, Nikki. *Baby's bedtime*
  C is for city
  Wild, wild hair
Grimm, Jacob. *The traveling musicians of Bremen*
Grossman, Bill. *The banging book*
  The bear whose bones were Jezebel Jones
  Cowboy Ed
  Donna O'Neeshuck was chased by some cows
  The guy who was five minutes late
  My little sister ate one hare
  Tommy at the grocery store
Grossman, Virginia. *Ten little rabbits*
Gryspeerdt, Rebecca. *Counting friends*
Guarino, Deborah. *Is your mama a llama?*
Gugler, Laurel Dee. *Facing the day*
Gundersheimer, Karen. *Find cat, wear hat*
  Happy winter
  Splish splash bang crash!
Haas, Irene. *The Maggie B*
Hague, Kathleen. *Alphabears*
  Calendarbears
  Out of the nursery, into the night
  Ten little bears
Hallinan, P. K. (Patrick K.). *I know I belong*
  I know who I am
  Just open a book
  Let's learn all we can!
  Let's play as a team
  My dentist, my friend
  My doctor, my friend
  A rainbow of friends
  The small town children's Easter
  That's what a friend is
  Today is Easter!
  Today is Halloween
  Today is Valentine's Day!
  We're very good friends, my aunt and I
  When I grow up
Hamanaka, Sheila. *I look like a girl*
Hamsa, Bobbie. *Fast-draw Freddie*
  Polly wants a cracker
Harder, Dan (Dan Wymbs). *Colliding with Chris*

Hardy, Tad. *Lost cat*
Harness, Cheryl. *Midnight in the cemetery*
Harper, Jessica. *I forgot my shoes*
Harris, Pamela. *Hot, cold, shy, bold*
Harrison, David Lee. *The animals' song*
  The case of Og, the missing frog
  When cows come home
Harrison, Sarah. *In granny's garden*
Hathorn, Libby (Elizabeth). *Sky sash so blue*
Hawkes, Kevin. *His Royal Buckliness*
  Then the troll heard the squeak
Hawkins, Colin. *Boo! Who?*
  Jen the hen
  Mig the pig
  Snap! Snap!
  Take away monsters
  Tog the dog
Hayes, Sarah. *The grumpalump*
  Nine ducks nine
  This is the bear
  This is the bear and the picnic lunch
  This is the bear and the scary night
Hayward, Linda. *Baker, baker, cookie maker*
  D is for doll
Hazen, Barbara Shook. *Good-bye/Hello*
  Santa clues
  Where do bears sleep?, ill. by Mary Morgan-Van-royen
  Where do bears sleep?, ill. by Ian E. Staunton
  World, world, what can I do?
Heide, Florence Parry. *Timothy Twinge*
Heiligman, Deborah. *Into the night*
Heine, Helme. *Mollywoop*
Heinz, Brian J. *The monsters' test*
Hellard, Susan. *Time to get up*
Heller, Ruth. *A cache of jewels and other collective nouns*
  Color, color, color, color
  Fantastic! wow! and unreal!
  How to hide a butterfly
  How to hide a crocodile and other reptiles
  How to hide a gray treefrog and other amphibians
  How to hide a parakeet and other birds
  How to hide a polar bear
  How to hide a whip-poor-will and other birds
  How to hide an octopus
  Kites sail high
  Many luscious lollipops
  Merry-go-round
  Mine, all mine
  The reason for a flower
Henderson, Kathy. *Bounce, bounce, bounce*
  Bumpety bump
  Don't interrupt!
Henkes, Kevin. *Oh!*
Hennessy, B. G. (Barbara G.). *A, B, C, D, tummy, toes, hands, knee*
  Eeney, Meeney, Miney, Mo
  Jake baked the cake
  The missing tarts
  School days
  Sleep tight
  When you were just a little girl
Henrietta. *A mouse in the house*
Hersom, Kathleen. *The copycat*
  Hide-and-seek bunnies
Highwater, Jamake. *Moonsong lullaby*
Hill, Susan. *Beware, beware*
  Can it be true?

Simba's A-Z
Hillert, Margaret. *What is it?*
Hillman, Priscilla. *A Merry-Mouse book of months*
   The Merry-Mouse book of prayers and graces
Hindley, Judy. *The big red bus*
   Eyes, nose, fingers and toes
   Little and big
   One by one
   Uncle Harold and the green hat
Hines, Anna Grossnickle. *The greatest picnic in the world*
   It's just me, Emily
   When the goblins came knocking
Hippely, Hilary Horder. *Adventure on Klickitat Island*
Hiskey, Iris. *I like a snack on an iceberg*
Hissey, Jane. *Little bear's bedtime*
   Little Bear's day
Hoban, Tana. *One little kitten*
   Where is it?
Hoberman, Mary Ann. *And to think that we thought that we'd never be friends*
   A house is a house for me
   I like old clothes
   One of each
Hoffman, Phyllis. *We play*
Hofstrand, Mary. *Albion pig*
   By the sea
Holl, Adelaide. *Mrs. McGarrity's peppermint sweater*
   Sir Kevin of Devon
Holsonback, Anita. *Monkey see, monkey do*
Hood, Susan. *The new kid*
Hood, Thomas. *Before I go to sleep*
Hooks, William H. *A dozen dizzy dogs*
   How do you make a bubble?
   Read-a-rebus
Hoopes, Lyn Littlefield. *Mommy, daddy, me*
Houk, Randy. *Chessie, the travelin' man*
   Rico's hawk
   Ruffle, Coo and Hoo Doo
Houston, John A. *The bright yellow rope*
Howells, Mildred. *The woman who lived in Holland*
Hubbard, Patricia. *My crayons talk*
   Trick or treat countdown
Hubbell, Patricia. *Pots and pans*
   Sidewalk trip
   Wrapping paper romp
Huck, Charlotte S. *A creepy countdown*
Hudson, Cheryl Willis. *Animal sounds for baby*
   Good morning baby
   Good night baby
   Let's count, baby
Huffaker, Alice. *That first Christmas day*
Hughes, Shirley. *All shapes and sizes*
   Bathwater's hot
   Colors
   Noisy
   Out and about
   Rhymes for Annie Rose
   Two shoes, new shoes
   When we went to the park
Hulme, Joy N. *Bubble trouble*
   Sea squares
   Sea sums
Hunt, Jonathan. *One is a mouse*
Hurd, Edith Thacher. *Caboose*
   Come and have fun
Huss, Sally. *I love you with all my hearts*
Hutchins, Pat. *The tale of Thomas Mead*

Which witch is which?
   The wind blew
Inkpen, Mick. *Anything cuddly will do!*
   Crocodile!
   This troll, that troll
   The very good dinosaur
   Where, oh where, is Kipper's bear?
Intrater, Roberta Grobel. *Two eyes, a nose, and a mouth*
Inwald, Robin. *Cap it off with a smile*
Ipcar, Dahlov. *Black and white*
   The cat came back
   Hard scrabble harvest
   My wonderful Christmas tree
Isaacs, Gwynne L. *Baby face*
Isadora, Rachel. *Bring on that beat*
Jabar, Cynthia. *Bored blue? Think what you can do!*
Jack and the beanstalk. *The history of Mother Twaddle and the marvelous achievements of her son Jack*
   Jack and the beanstalk, ill. by Anne Wilsdorf
   Jack the giant killer, ill. by Anne Wilsdorf
Jackson, Alison. *I know an old lady who swallowed a pie*
Jacobs, Kate. *A sister's wish*
Jakob, Donna. *My bike*
Jam, Teddy. *Night cars*
Janosch. *Tonight at nine*
Janovitz, Marilyn. *Bowl patrol!*
   Can I help?
   Is it time?
   What could be keeping Santa?
Jefferds, Vincent. *Disney's elegant book of manners*
Jenkin-Pearce, Susie. *The seashell song*
Jensen, Patricia. *The mess*
Jewell, Nancy. *ABC cat*
   Christmas lullaby
   Five little kittens
Johnson, Angela. *Mama bird, baby birds*
Johnson, B. J. *A hat like that*
   My blanket Burt
Johnston, Tony. *Little bear sleeping*
Jones, Bill T. *Dance*
Jorgensen, Gail. *Crocodile Beat*
Joyce, Susan. *ABC animal riddles*
   Alphabet riddles
Joyce, William. *Rolie Polie Olie*
Kahl, Virginia. *The Baron's booty*
   The Duchess bakes a cake
   How do you hide a monster?
   The perfect pancake
   Plum pudding for Christmas
Kahn, Joan. *Hi, Jock, run around the block*
Kaiser Johnson, Lee. *If I ran the family*
Kalan, Robert. *Moving day*
Kamen, Gloria. *"Paddle," said the swan*
Karlin, Nurit. *The fat cat sat on the mat*
   Ten little bunnies
Kates, Bobbi Jane. *We're different, we're the same*
Kavanaugh, James J. *The crooked angel*
Kay, Verla. *Covered wagons, bumpy trails*
   Gold fever
   Iron horses
Keillor, Garrison. *Cat, you better come home*
   The old man who loved cheese
Keith, Adrienne. *Fairies from A to Z*
Keller, Holly. *What I see*
Kemp, Moira. *I'm a little teapot*
   Knock at the door
   Round and round the garden

Kesselman, Wendy Ann. *Sand in my shoes*
Kessler, Ethel. *Do baby bears sit in chairs?*
Ketteman, Helen. *Grandma's cat*
Kharms, Daniil. *The story of a boy named Will, who
    went sledding down the hill*
Kinerk, Robert. *Slim and Miss Prim*
King, Christopher L. *The vegetables go to bed*
King, Larry L. *Because of Lozo Brown*
Kingman, Lee. *Catch the baby!*
Kirk, Daniel. *Moondogs*
    Trash trucks!
Kirk, David. *Little Miss Spider*
    Little Miss Spider at Sunny Patch School
    Miss Spider's ABC
    Miss Spider's new car
    Miss Spider's tea party
Kitchen, Bert. *Pig in a barrow*
Klimowicz, Barbara. *The strawberry thumb*
Knutson, Kimberley. *Bed bouncers*
    Jungle jamboree
    Muddigush
Kolar, Bob. *Stomp, stomp!*
Koller, Jackie French. *Bouncing on the bed*
    Fish fry tonight
    One monkey too many
Komaiko, Leah. *Annie Bananie*
    Aunt Elaine does the dance from Spain
    Broadway Banjo Bill
    Earl's too cool for me
    Fritzi Fox flew in from Florida
    Great Aunt Ida and her Great Dane, Doc
    I like the music
    Just my dad and me
    Lenora O'Grady
    My perfect neighborhood
    Shoeshine Shirley
Kopper, Lisa. *Ten little babies*
Kraus, Robert. *The Christmas cookie sprinkle snitcher*
    Ladybug, ladybug!
    Mouse work
    Whose mouse are you?
Krauss, Ruth. *Everything under a mushroom*
    I can fly
Krensky, Stephen. *Fraidy Cats*
    My loose tooth
Kroll, Steven. *Annie's four grannies*
    The pigrates clean up
    Pigs in the house
Kroll, Virginia L. *Girl, you're amazing!*
    Lunching and munching
    Motherlove
    New friends, true friends, stuck-like-glue friends
Kudrna, C. Imbior. *To bathe a boa*
Kumin, Maxine W. *Follow the fall*
    Sebastian and the dragon
    Speedy digs downside up
Kuskin, Karla. *A boy had a mother who bought him a
        hat*
    City dog
    Herbert hated being small
    In the flaky frosty morning
    James and the rain
    Roar and more
Kutner, Merrily. *Z is for zombie*
Kwitz, Mary DeBall. *When it rains*
Lacome, Julie. *I'm a jolly farmer*
Laden, Nina. *Peek-a-who?*
Lagercrantz, Rose. *Brave little Pete of Geranium Street*
Lakin, Pat (Patricia). *Jet black pickup truck*

Larios, Julie Hofstrand. *On the stairs*
LaRochelle, David. *A Christmas guest*
Lass, Bonnie. *Who took the cookies from the cookie jar?*
Lawrence, John. *Rabbit and pork*
Lawston, Lisa. *A pair of red sneakers*
Leavy, Una. *Harry's stormy night*
Leech, Bryan Jeffery. *John Jeremy Colton*
Leedy, Loreen. *A dragon Christmas*
    The dragon Halloween party
    The dragon Thanksgiving feast
    A number of dragons
Leemis, Ralph. *Mister Momboo's hat*
Leichman, Seymour. *Shaggy dogs and spotty dogs
        and shaggy and spotty dogs*
    The wicked wizard and the wicked witch
Leigh, Oretta. *The merry-go-round*
Lenski, Lois. *Sing a song of people*
Leonard, Marcia. *Best friends*
    Big Ben
    Birthday in a bathtub
    Dan and Dan
    Dress-up
    Hop, skip, run
    I like mess
    My camp-out
    My pal Al
    No new pants!
    The pet vet
    Spots
    The tin can man
Lerner, Marguerite Rush. *Dear little mumps child*
Lerner, Sharon. *Follow the monsters!*
Lester, Alison. *Magic beach*
    Yikes!
Leuck, Laura. *My baby brother has ten tiny toes*
    My monster mama loves me so
Levenson, George. *Pumpkin circle*
Levine, Abby. *This is the pumpkin*
    This is the turkey
    You push, I ride
Levine, Arthur A. *Bono and Nonno*
Lewis, J. Patrick. *The boat of many rooms*
    The house of Boo
    *Isabella Abnormella and the very, very finicky Queen
        of Trouble*
    Riddle-lightful
Lewis, Kevin. *Chugga-chugga choo-choo*
Lewis, Naomi. *The butterfly collector*
    Once upon a rainbow
Lewison, Wendy Cheyette. *"Buzz," said the bee*
    Going to sleep on the farm
    Happy Thanksgiving!
    Hello, snow!
    Mud
    Nighty-night
    So many boots
    Ten little ballerinas
Lifton, Betty Jean. *Tell me a real adoption story*
Lillegard, Dee. *The Big Bug Ball*
    The day the daisies danced
Lindbergh, Reeve. *The awful aardvarks go to school*
    The awful Aardvarks shop for school
    Benjamin's barn
    The hippie grandmother
    If I'd known then what I know now
    Johnny Appleseed
    Nobody owns the sky
    North country spring
    There's a cow in the road!

A view from the air
Linden, Madelaine Gill. Under the blanket
Lindgren, Barbro. The wild baby
  The wild baby gets a puppy
Lipkind, William. Sleepyhead
Little, Mimi Otey. Blue moon soup spoon
Little old lady who swallowed a fly. I know an old
  lady, ill. by G. Brian Karas
  There was an old lady who swallowed a fly, ill. by
    Simms Taback
Livingston, Myra Cohn. Higgledy-Piggledy
Lloyd, Megan. Chicken tricks
Lobe, Mira. Valerie and the good-night swing
Lobel, Arnold. Martha, the movie mouse
  On Market Street
  On the day Peter Stuyvesant sailed into town
  The rose in my garden
Lodge, Bernard. Cloud Cuckoo Land (and other odd
    spots)
  Rhyming Nell
London, Jonathan. Candystore man
  Fireflies, fireflies, light my way
  I see the moon and the moon sees me
  Little Red Monkey
  Park beat
  What do you love?
  Who bop
Longfellow, Layne. Imaginary menagerie
Loomans, Diane. The lovables in the kingdom of self-
    esteem
Loomis, Christine. Astro Bunnies
  At the laundromat
  At the library
  The cleanup surprise
  Cowboy bunnies
  The Hippo Hop
  One cow coughs
  Rush hour
Lopshire, Robert. I want to be somebody new!
  New tricks I can do!
  Put me in the zoo
Lorbiecki, Marybeth. Sister Anne's hands
Lord, John Vernon. Mr. Mead and his garden
Losordo, Stephen. Cow moo me
Lotz, Karen E. Snowsong whistling
Low, Alice. Witch's holiday
Lund, Doris Herold. The paint-box sea
Lundell, Margo. The furry bedtime book
Lunn, Carolyn. A buzz is part of a bee
Lyne, Alice. A, my name is . . .
Lyon, George Ella. A day at damp camp
  Mama is a miner
  The outside inn
McAfee, Annalena. Kirsty knows best
McAllister, Angela. Sleepy Ella
MacBeth, George. Noah's journey
McBratney, Sam. The caterpillow fight
Maccarone, Grace. Cars! Cars! Cars!
  A child was born
  The class trip
  The classroom pet
  I have a cold
  I shop with my daddy
  Itchy, itchy chicken pox
  Oink! moo! how do you do?
  Pizza party
  Sharing time troubles
McCarthy, Bobette. Dreaming
  See you later, alligator

Ten little hippos
McCurdy, Michael. The old man and the fiddle
MacDonald, Amy. Cousin Ruth's tooth
  Rachel Fister's blister
MacDonald, Elizabeth. Miss Poppy and the honey
  cake
McDonald, Megan. Bedbugs
MacDonald, Suse. Elephants on board
McGinley, Phyllis. All around the town
  How Mrs. Santa Claus saved Christmas
  Lucy McLockett
  Wonderful time
McGough, Roger. Counting by numbers
McGovern, Ann. Eggs on your nose
McGuire, Richard. What's wrong with this book?
Mackall, Dandi Daley. Off to Bethlehem!
McKié, Roy. Snow
McKissack, Patricia C. Messy Bessey and the birthday
    overnight
  Messy Bessey's closet
  Messy Bessey's holidays
McLean, Janet. Dog tales
MacLeod, Elizabeth. I heard a little baa
McLerran, Alice. Hugs
  Kisses
McMillan, Bruce. Puffins climb, penguins rhyme
McNaughton, Colin. If dinosaurs were cats and dogs
McPartland, Suzy. Good morning, sun
  Sleepy-time moon
  Toy-shop surprise
  Zoom, car, zoom
McPhail, David M. Big brown bear
  Pigs ahoy
  Pigs aplenty, pigs galore!
  Those can-do pigs
Maestro, Marco. Geese find the missing piece
Maguire, Gregory. Lucas Fishbone
Mahy, Margaret. The Christmas tree tangle
  17 kings and 42 elephants
  A summery Saturday morning
  When the king rides by
Maloney, Peter. The magic hockey stick
  Redbird at Rockefeller Center
Mandel, Peter. Say hey
Manning, Linda. Animal hours
Manushkin, Fran. Let's go riding in our strollers
Marcin, Marietta. A zoo in her bed
Mark, Jan. Fun with Mrs. Thumb
Marsh, T. J. Way out in the desert
Marshak, S. (Samuil). The absentminded fellow
  The Month-Brothers
  The pup grew up!
Marshall, James. Hey, diddle, daddle
Marshall, Janet Perry. Ohmygosh, my pocket
Martin, Bill (William Ivan). Adam, Adam, what do
    you see?
  Barn dance!
  Brown bear, brown bear, what do you see?
  Chicka chicka boom boom
  Chicka chicka sticka sticka
  The happy hippopotami
  Here are my hands
  Listen to the rain
  Maestro plays
  The magic pumpkin
  Polar bear, polar bear, what do you hear?
  The turning of the year
  The wizard
Martin, David. Lizzie and her dolly

Valentine's Day
Newberry, Clare Turlay. *The kittens' ABC*
Newcome, Zita. *Animal fun*
    Toddlerobics
Newman, Lesléa. *Cats, cats, cats*
Newton-John, Olivia. *A pig tale*
Nichols, Grace. *Asana and the animals*
Nightingale, Sandy. *A giraffe on the moon*
Nikola-Lisa, W. *No babies asleep*
    Shake dem Halloween bones
    Tangletalk
    Wheels go round
Nims, Bonnie Larkin. *Where is the bear?*
    Where is the bear at school?
    Where is the bear in the city?
Nobisso, Josephine. *For the sake of a cake*
    Hot-cha-cha!
Nolan, Dennis. *Wizard McBean and his flying*
    machine
Noll, Sally. *Off and counting*
Novak, Matt. *The Pillow War*
Numeroff, Laura Joffe. *Chimps don't wear glasses*
    Monster munchies
O'Book, Irene. *Maybe my baby*
O'Brien, John (1953-). *Mother Hubbard's Christmas*
O'Connor, Francine M. *The ABC's of Christmas*
O'Donnell, Elizabeth Lee. *Winter visitors*
Offen, Hilda. *As quiet as a mouse*
    A fox got my socks
    The sheep made a leap
O'Keefe, Susan Heyboer. *Angel prayer*
    Good night, God bless
Olsen, Ib Spang. *The grown-up trap*
O'Malley, Kevin. *Carl caught a flying fish*
    Who killed Cock Robin?
Once I was . . .
One, two, skip a few!
O'Neill, Mary. *Big red hen*
Oppenheim, Joanne. *Do you like cats?*
    Donkey's tale
    Have you seen bugs?
    The story book prince
    You can't catch me!
Orbach, Ruth. *Apple pigs*
Orgel, Doris. *Two crows counting*
Ormerod, Jan. *Rock-a-baby*
Osborne, Valerie. *One big yo to go*
Over in the meadow, ill. by Ezra Jack Keats
Owens, Mary Beth. *A caribou alphabet*
Oxenbury, Helen. *Pig tale*
Packard, Mary. *Bubble trouble*
    The kite
    We are monsters
Pacovská, Kveta. *One, five, many*
Paraskevas, Betty. *Cecil Bunions and the midnight*
    train
    The ferocious beast with the polka-dot hide
Parr, Letitia. *A man and his hat*
Partch, Virgil Franklin. *The Christmas cookie sprinkle*
    snitcher
Paschkis, Julie. *Play all day*
Patron, Susan. *Dark cloud strong breeze*
Patterson, Elizabeth Burman. *Whose eyes are these?*
Paul, Ann Whitford. *Everything to spend the night . . .*
    from A to Z
Paulsen, Gary. *Worksong*
Pavey, Peter. *One dragon's dream*
Paxton, Tom. *The marvelous toy*
Pearson, Tracey Campbell. *Where does Joe go?*

Peck, Robert Newton. *Hamilton*
Peek, Merle. *The balancing act*
Peet, Bill (William Bartlett). *Ella*
    Hubert's hair-raising adventures
    Huge Harold
    The kweeks of Kookatumdee
    The luckiest one of all
    No such things
    The pinkish, purplish, bluish egg
    Randy's dandy lions
    Smokey
    Zella, Zack, and Zodiac
Pelham, David. *Sam's pizza*
    Sam's sandwich
Pendziwol, Jean. *No dragons for tea*
Perkins, Al. *The ear book*
    Hand, hand, fingers, thumb
    The nose book
Perkins, Charles. *Swinging on a rainbow*
Peters, Lisa Westberg. *October smiled back*
Petie, Haris. *Billions of bugs*
    The seed the squirrel dropped
Peyo. *What do smurfs do all day?*
Phifer, Martha Nelson. *The colors of Christmas*
Phillips, Joan. *Peek-a-boo! I see you!*
Phillips, Louis. *The upside down riddle book*
Pike, Carol. *The nutty queen*
Pilkey, Dav. *The Moonglow Roll-O-Rama*
    'Twas the night before Thanksgiving
Pinczes, Elinor J. *Arctic fives arrive*
    A remainder of one
Pittman, Helena Clare. *Sunrise*
Plourde, Lynn. *Wild child*
    Winter waits
Plummer, David. *Counting kittens*
Polisar, Barry Louis. *The haunted house party*
Pomerantz, Charlotte. *The ballad of the long-tailed*
    rat
    Flap your wings and try
    Here comes Henny
    How many trucks can a tow truck tow?
    The piggy in the puddle
Poskanzer, Susan Cornell. *Riddles about Hannukah*
Prater, John. *"No!" said Joe*
    Once upon a picnic
    Once upon a time
Prelutsky, Jack. *The mean old mean hyena*
    The terrible tiger
Preston, Edna Mitchell. *Pop Corn and Ma Goodness*
Price, Hope Lynne. *These hands*
Provensen, Alice. *Karen's opposites*
Puner, Helen Walker. *Daddys, what they do all day*
    The sitter who didn't sit
Puppies and kittens
Raphael, Elaine. *Turnabout*
Raskin, Ellen. *Ghost in a four-room apartment*
    Who, said Sue, said whoo?
Ray, Karen. *Sleep song*
Reddix, Valerie. *Millie and the mudhole*
Reeves, Howard W. *There was an old witch*
Reeves, Mona Rabun. *I had a cat*
    The spooky eerie night noise
Regan, Dian Curtis. *Daddies*
Reid, Barbara. *The party*
Reid, Rob. *Wave goodbye*
Rey, H. A. (Hans Augusto). *Elizabite*
    Elizabite, adventures of a carnivorous plant
    Feed the animals
    See the circus

Shortall, Leonard W. *One way*
Shulevitz, Uri. *Rain rain rivers*
Shute, Linda. *Halloween party*
Siddals, Mary McKenna. *Millions of snowflakes*
   Tell me a season
Siebert, Diane. *Plane song*
   Train song
   Truck song
Sierra, Judy. *The house that Drac built*
   There's a zoo in room 22
Silverman, Erica. *Follow the leader*
   The Halloween house
   On the morn of Mayfest
Silverstein, Shel. *A giraffe and a half*
   The giving tree
Simmons, Jane. *Daisy's favorite things*
Simon, Charnan. *Mud!*
Simon, Francesca. *But what does the hippopotamus say?*
   Calling all toddlers
Simon, Mina Lewiton. *Is anyone here?*
Singer, Marilyn. *Solomon sneezes*
Singh, Jacquelin. *Fat Gopal*
Siomades, Lorianne. *Kangaroo and cricket*
   A place to bloom
Skwarek, Skip. *The horrors of Howling Hall*
Slate, Joseph. *Who is coming to our house?*
Slepian, Jan. *The hungry thing returns*
Sloat, Teri. *Farmer Brown goes round and round*
   Farmer Brown shears his sheep
   Patty's pumpkin patch
   There was an old lady who swallowed a trout
   The thing that bothered Farmer Brown
Slobodkin, Louis. *Clear the track for Michael's magic train*
   Friendly animals
   Millions and millions and millions
   One is good, but two are better
   The seaweed hat
   Up high and down low
Small, David. *George Washington's cows*
Smalls-Hector, Irene. *Kevin and his dad*
Smath, Jerry. *A hat so simple*
Smith, Mavis. *Fred, is that you?*
Smith-Moore, J. J. *Sally Small*
Snow, Alan. *The monster book of ABC sounds*
Snow, Pegeen. *A pet for Pat*
Speed, Toby. *Two cool cows*
Spence, Robert, III. *Clickety clack*
Spier, Peter. *Noah's ark*
Spilka, Arnold. *A lion I can do without*
   Little birds don't cry
Spinelli, Eileen. *When Mama comes home tonight*
Stadler, John. *Cat is back at bat*
Steiner, Joan (Joan Catherine). *Look-alikes*
   Look-alikes, Jr.
Stevenson, Drew. *The ballad of Penelope Lou . . . and me*
Stewart, Sarah. *The library*
Stickland, Paul. *Dinosaur roar!*
   Dinosaur stomp!
   Ten terrible dinosaurs
Stobbs, William. *This little piggy*
Stoddard, Sandol. *Bedtime for bear*
   Bedtime mouse
   My very own special particular private and personal cat
   Turtle time
Stone, Phoebe. *What night do the angels wander?*

Stone, Rosetta. *Because a little bug went ka-choo!*
Stover, Jo Ann. *If everybody did*
Stuart, Chad. *The Ballymara flood*
Sturges, Philemon. *I love trucks!*
   Ten flashing fireflies
Stutson, Caroline. *By the light of the Halloween moon*
   Cowpokes
   Prairie primer A to Z
Suen, Anastasia. *Delivery*
   Window music
Sullivan, Charles. *Numbers at play*
Sundgaard, Arnold. *Jethro's difficult dinosaur*
Supraner, Robyn. *Would you rather be a tiger?*
Sutton, Eve. *My cat likes to hide in boxes*
Svendsen, Carol. *Hulda*
Sweeney, Jacqueline. *Katie and the night noises*
Sweetland, Nancy. *God's quiet things*
Szekeres, Cyndy. *Cyndy Szekeres' learn to count, funny bunnies*
Tafuri, Nancy. *Snowy flowy blowy*
Tangvald, Christine Harder. *Hey, Mr. Angel!*
Taylor, Scott. *Dinosaur James*
Temple, Charles A. *Train*
Tether, Graham. *The hair book*
Thomas, Patricia. *The one and only, super-duper, golly-whopper, jim-dandy, really-handy clock-tock-stopper*
   "Stand back," said the elephant, "I'm going to sneeze!"
   "There are rocks in my socks!" said the ox to the fox
Thomas, Shelley Moore. *Putting the world to sleep*
Thompson, Carol. *Baby days*
Thomson, Ruth. *My bear: I can . . . can you?*
   My bear: I like . . . do you?
The three little pigs. *The three little pigs*, ill. by Erik Blegvad
   The three little pigs, ill. by Caroline Bucknall
   The three little pigs, ill. by William Pène Du Bois
   The three little pigs and the big bad wolf
Tippett, James Sterling. *Counting the days*
Toft, Kim Michelle. *Neptune's nursery*
   One less fish
Trapani, Iza. *Row, row, row your boat*
   What am I?
Trent, Robbie. *The first Christmas*
Tresselt, Alvin R. *Follow the wind*
Tripp, Valerie. *Happy, happy Mother's Day*
   Sillyhen's big surprise
Tryon, Leslie. *Albert's Christmas*
   Albert's play
Tucker, Kathy. *Do cowboys ride bikes?*
   Do knights take naps?
   Do pirates take baths?
Turner, Ann Warren. *Angel hide and seek*
   Shaker hearts
Turner, Gwenda. *Over on the farm*
Tyrrell, Anne. *Elizabeth Jane gets dressed*
   Mary Ann always can
Van der Beek, Deborah. *Superbabe!*
VanderKlipp, Michael A. *Joy to the world!*
Van Laan, Nancy. *Little baby Bobby*
   Little Fish lost
   Mama rocks, Papa sings
   A mouse in my house
   People, people, everywhere
   Possum come a-knocking
   Round and round again
   So say the little monkeys
   This is the hat

Riddles

Aardema, Verna. *Ji-nongo-nongo means riddles*
Adler, David A. *The carsick zebra and other riddles*
Anno, Mitsumasa. *Anno's math games*
   Anno's math games II
   Anno's math games III
Ashley, Jill. *Riddles about Christmas*
Barber, Antonia. *Catkin*
Beisner, Monika. *Catch that cat!*
   Monika Beisner's book of riddles
Bell, Anthea. *The wise queen*
Bernstein, Joanne E. *Creepy crawly critter riddles*
   What was the wicked witch's real name?
The big Peter Rabbit book
Bishop, Ann. *Chicken riddle*
   The Ella Fannie elephant riddle book
   Hey riddle riddle
   Merry-go-riddle
   Noah riddle?
   Oh, riddlesticks!
   The riddle ages
   Riddle-iculous rid-alphabet book
   Wild Bill Hiccup's riddle book
Brown, Marc Tolon. *Spooky riddles*
   What do you call a dumb bunny? and other rabbit
     riddles, games, jokes and cartoons
Burns, Diane L. *Elephants never forget!*
Burton, Marilee Robin. *Tail toes eyes ears nose*
Calmenson, Stephanie. *It begins with an A*
   What am I?
Cerf, Bennett Alfred. *Bennett Cerf's book of animal*
   riddles
   Bennett Cerf's book of laughs
   Bennett Cerf's book of riddles
   More riddles
Charles, N. N. *What am I? Looking through shapes at*
   apples and grapes
Cole, Joanna. *The Clown-Arounds go on vacation*
   Get well, Clown-Arounds!
   Why did the chicken cross the road?
Crowley, Arthur. *The wagon man*
Daniels, Guy. *The Tsar's riddles*
Degen, Bruce. *The little witch and the riddle*
Delaney, M. C. (Michael Clark). *The marigold monster*
De Regniers, Beatrice Schenk. *It does not say meow!*
Demi. *Where is it?*
Doolittle, Eileen. *The ark in the attic*
Downie, Jill. *Alphabet puzzle*
Duncan, Riana. *A nutcracker in a tree*
Elias, Joyce. *Whose toes are those?*
Elkin, Benjamin. *The wisest man in the world*
Emberley, Ed (Edward Randolph). *Ed Emberley's*
   amazing look through book
Fleischman, Sid. *Kate's secret riddle*
Fletcher, Elizabeth. *What am I?*
Gackenbach, Dick. *Supposes*
Goundaud, Karen Jo. *A very mice joke book*
Gregorich, Barbara. *My friend goes left*
Grimm, Jacob. *Rumpelstiltskin*, ill. by Jacqueline
   Ayer
   Rumpelstiltskin, ill. by Donna Diamond
   Rumpelstiltskin, ill. by Paul Galdone
   Rumpelstiltskin, ill. by Jonathan Langley
   Rumpelstiltskin, ill. by Gennady Spirin
   Rumpelstiltskin, ill. by John Wallner
   Rumpelstiltskin, ill. by Bernadette Watts
   Rumpelstiltskin, ill. by Paul O. Zelinsky

Hall, Malcolm. *CariCATures*
Hample, Stoo. *Stoo Hample's silly joke book*
   Yet another big fat funny silly book
Hathorn, Libby (Elizabeth). *The wonder thing*
Hoffman, Mary. *Clever Katya*
Hopkins, Lee Bennett. *How do you make an elephant*
   float?
Jackson, Ellen B. *The impossible riddle*
Jensen, Virginia Allen. *Red thread riddles*
Joyce, Susan. *ABC animal riddles*
   Alphabet riddles
Karim, Roberta. *Kindle me a riddle*
Keller, Charles. *School daze*
Koontz, Robin Michal. *I see something you don't see*
Lewis, J. Patrick. *Riddle-icious*
   Riddle-lightful
Lewis, Naomi. *The butterfly collector*
Low, Joseph. *Five men under one umbrella*
   A mad wet hen and other riddles
Lyfick, Warren. *Animal tales*
   The little book of fowl jokes
McKié, Roy. *The riddle book*
McMullan, Kate (Hall). *Batty riddles*
   Bunny riddles
   Chickie riddles
   Creepy riddles
   Dinosaur riddles
   Fishy riddles
   Hearty har har
   Kitty riddles
   Mummy riddles
   Puppy riddles
   Sheepish riddles
   Snakey riddles
   Spacey riddles
   Trick or eeek!
Maestro, Giulio. *Halloween howls*
   A raft of riddles
   Riddle romp
Maestro, Marco. *Geese find the missing piece*
   What do you hear when cows sing?
Marzollo, Jean. *I spy, mystery*
Medearis, Angela Shelf. *The freedom riddle*
Modell, Frank. *Look out, it's April Fools' Day*
Moncure, Jane Belk. *Riddle me a riddle*
Mooser, Stephen. *Funnyman's first case*
Most, Bernard. *Pets in trumpets and other word-play*
   riddles
   Zoodles
Nims, Bonnie Larkin. *Just beyond reach and other rid-*
   dle poems
Peppé, Rodney. *Hey riddle diddle*
Peterson, Scott K. *What's your name?*
Phillips, Louis. *The upside down riddle book*
Poskanzer, Susan Cornell. *Riddles about Hannukah*
Potter, Beatrix. *The tale of Squirrel Nutkin*
Romanoli, Robert. *What's so funny?!!*
Roop, Peter. *Going buggy!*
   Let's celebrate!
   Stick out your tongue!
Rosenbloom, Joseph. *The funniest joke book ever!*
Selberg, Ingrid. *Nature's hidden world*
Seuss, Dr. *The cat's quizzer*
Shields, Carol Diggory. *Colors*
Sloat, Teri. *Rib-ticklers*
Speed, Toby. *Watervoices*
Swann, Brian. *A basket full of white eggs*
   The house with no door
Swanson, June. *Summit up*

Thaler, Mike. *The yellow brick toad*
Türk, Hanne. *Max versus the cube*
Wakefield, Joyce. *Ask a silly question*
Walton, Rick. *Dumb clucks!*
  How many, how many, how many
  Something's fishy!
Wick, Walter. *I spy Christmas*
  I spy extreme challenger
  I spy fantasy
  I spy gold challenger!
  I spy school days
  I spy spooky night
  I spy super challenger!
  I spy treasure hunt
Wolff, Patricia Rae. *The toll-bridge troll*
Woodworth, Viki. *Fairy tale jokes*
Young, Ed (Edward). *High on a hill*
Young, Ruth. *Who says moo?*
Ziefert, Harriet. *Math riddles*
Zwetchkenbaum, G. *The Peanuts shape circus puzzle book*
  The Peanuts sleepy time puzzle book
  The Snoopy farm puzzle book
  Snoopy safari puzzle book

Right and left *see* Concepts – left and right

Riots

Bunting, Eve (Anne Evelyn). *Smoky night*

Rivers

Atwell, Debby. *River*
Baker, Sanna Anderson. *Mississippi going north*
Bandes, Hanna. *Sleepy river*
Brennan, Joseph Killorin. *Gobo and the river*
Brook, Judy. *Tim mouse goes down the stream*
Burke, Timothy. *Tugboats in action*
Bush, Timothy. *Three at sea*
Bushey, Jerry. *The barge book*
Carlstrom, Nancy White. *Raven and river*
Carrick, Carol. *The brook*
Cherry, Lynne. *A river ran wild*
Craighead, Charles. *The eagle and the river*
Cunningham, David. *A crow's journey*
Dabcovich, Lydia. *Follow the river*
Day, Alexandra. *River parade*
Drake, John. *The beginning of the river*
Flack, Marjorie. *The boats on the river*
George, Jean Craighead. *Everglades*
Gerrard, Roy. *Croco'nile*
Gilliland, Judith Heide. *River*
Gorog, Judith. *Zilla Sasparilla and the mud baby*
Grahame, Kenneth. *The wind in the willows*
Gramatky, Hardie. *Little Toot on the Mississippi*
Grasshopper to the rescue
Greene, Carol. *Reading about the river otter*
  Sunflower Island
Grifalconi, Ann. *Flyaway girl*
Halpern, Shari. *My river*
Harness, Cheryl. *Mark Twain and the queens of the Mississippi*
Holling, Holling C. (Holling Clancy). *Paddle-to-the-sea*
Keeping, Charles. *Alfie finds the other side of the world*
Kellogg, Steven (Stephen). *Mike Fink*
Kovacs, Deborah. *Moonlight on the river*

Kurtz, Jane. *River friendly, river wild*
Lewin, Ted. *Amazon boy*
Lillegard, Dee. *The hee-haw river*
Locker, Thomas. *Where the river begins*
London, Jonathan. *White water*
MacDonald, Elizabeth. *Dilly-Dally and the nine secrets*
Magdanz, James S. *Go home, river*
Michl, Reinhard. *A day on the river*
Murphy, Shirley Rousseau. *Tattie's river journey*
Mwenye Hadithi. *Hot hippo*
Oakley, Graham. *The church mice adrift*
Peters, Lisa Westberg. *Good morning, river!*
Reynolds, Jan. *Amazon*
Russell, Naomi. *The stream*
Sanders, Scott R. (Scott Russell). *Crawdad Creek*
Schmid, Eleonore. *The water's journey*
Tennyson, Alfred, Baron. *The brook*

Roads

Bate, Norman. *Who built the highway?*
Field, Rachel Lyman. *A road might lead to anywhere*
Goodall, John S. *The story of a main street*
Hennessy, B. G. (Barbara G.). *Road builders*
Hindley, Judy. *The big red bus*
Johnston, Tony. *Amber on the mountain*
Kehoe, Michael. *Road closed*
Kroninger, Stephen. *If I crossed the road*
Lyon, George Ella. *Who came down that road?*
Nikola-Lisa, W. *One hole in the road*
Plourde, Lynn. *Pigs in the mud in the middle of the rud*
Pringle, Laurence P. *Jesse builds a road*
Roennfeldt, Robert. *A day on the avenue*
Royston, Angela. *Monster road builders*
Tusa, Tricia. *Sherman and Pearl*

Robbers *see* Crime

Robins *see* Birds – robins

Robots

Barner, Bob. *Space race*
Bradford, Ann. *The mystery of the square footsteps*
Bunting, Eve (Anne Evelyn). *The robot birthday*
Bush, Timothy. *Benjamin McFadden and the robot babysitter*
Cole, Babette. *The trouble with dad*
Dewan, Ted. *The sorcerer's apprentice*
Dupasquier, Philippe. *A robot named chip*
Greene, Carol. *Robots*
Hoban, Lillian. *The laziest robot in zone one*
Joyce, William. *Rolie Polie Olie*
  Rolie Polie Olie, how many howdys?
  Snowie Rolie
Kiser, Kevin. *Buzzy Widget*
Krahn, Fernando. *Robot-bot-bot*
Kroll, Steven. *Otto*
Lauber, Patricia. *Get ready for robots!*
Loomis, Christine. *The cleanup surprise*
Marshall, Edward. *Space case*
Marzollo, Jean. *Jed and the space bandits*
  Jed's junior space patrol
Novak, Matt. *The Robobots*
Paul, Sherry. *2-B and the rock 'n roll band*
  2-B and the space visitor

Pinkney, J. Brian. *Cosmo and the robot*
Titus, Eve. *Anatole and the robot*
Yaccarino, Dan. *If I had a robot*

Rock climbing *see* Sports – rock climbing

Rockets *see* Space and space ships

Rocking chairs *see* Furniture – chairs

Rocking horses *see* Toys – rocking horses

Rocks

Baylor, Byrd. *Everybody needs a rock*
Chetwin, Grace. *Mr. Meredith and the truly remarkable stone*
Christian, Peggy. *If you find a rock*
Cole, Joanna. *The magic school bus inside the earth*
Gans, Roma. *Let's go rock collecting*
    Rock collecting
Goble, Paul. *Iktomi and the boulder*
Harshman, Marc. *Rocks in my pocket*
Kaufman, Jeff. *Milk rock*
Kehoe, Michael. *The rock quarry book*
Lee, Jeanne M. *Legend of the Li River*
Lionni, Leo. *On my beach there are many pebbles*
McKee, David. *The hill and the rock*
Marston, Elsa. *A griffin in the garden*
Mills, Judith Christine. *The stonehook schooner*
Parnall, Peter. *The rock*
Peters, Lisa Westberg. *Meg and dad discover treasure in the air*
Polacco, Patricia. *My ol' man*
Selsam, Millicent E. *A first look at rocks*
Stuve-Bodeen, Stephanie. *Elizabeti's doll*
Trimble, Marcia. *Malinda Martha and her stepping stones*
Walker, Alice. *Finding the green stone*
Weller, Frances Ward. *Matthew Wheelock's wall*

Rodeos

Gibbons, Gail. *Yippee-yay!*

Roller skating *see* Sports – roller skating

Romania *see* Foreign lands – Romania

Roosters *see* Birds – chickens

Rosh Hashanah *see* Holidays – Rosh Hashanah

Royalty

Aardema, Verna. *The riddle of the drum*
Abrons, Mary. *For Alice a palace*
Adinolfi, JoAnn. *The Egyptian polar bear*
Aitken, Amy. *Ruby, the red knight*
Allen, Pamela. *Bertie and the bear*
    A lion in the night
Andersen, H. C. (Hans Christian). *The swineherd*, ill. by Dorothée Duntze
Anderson, Lonzo. *Two hundred rabbits*
Asher, Sandy. *Princess Bee and the royal good-night story*

Babbitt, Natalie. *Bub, or, The very best thing*
Babbitt, Samuel F. *The forty-ninth magician*
Bang, Betsy. *Tuntuni the tailor bird*
Bang, Molly. *Tye May and the magic brush*
Baring, Maurice. *The blue rose*
Barry, David. *The Rajah's rice*
Basile, Giambattista. *Petrosinella*
Berenzy, Alix. *A frog prince*
Beresford, Elisabeth. *Jack and the magic stove*
Berson, Harold. *The thief who hugged a moonbeam*
Bohdal, Susi. *The magic honey jar*
Bolliger, Max. *The most beautiful song*
Bond, Michael. *Paddington at the palace*
Bowden, Joan Chase. *A new home for Snow Ball*
Brierley, Louise. *King Lion and his cooks*
Browne, Caroline. *Mrs. Christie's farmhouse*
Burningham, John. *Time to get out of the bath, Shirley*
Carle, Eric. *Walter the baker*
Chapman, Gaynor. *The luck child*
Climo, Shirley. *The Egyptian Cinderella*
    King of the birds
Company González, Mercé. *Killian and the dragons*
Coombs, Patricia. *Tilabel*
Cooney, Barbara. *Little brother and little sister*
Cretien, Paul D. *Sir Henry and the dragon*
Day, David. *The swan children*
De La Mare, Walter (Walter John). *Molly Whuppie*
De Regniers, Beatrice Schenk. *May I bring a friend?*
Dewey, Ariane. *Dorin and the dragon*
Domanska, Janina. *Look, there is a turtle flying*
Dos Santos, Joyce Audy. *The diviner*
Duke, Kate. *Aunt Isabel tells a good one*
Elkin, Benjamin. *Gillespie and the guards*
    The wisest man in the world
Espenscheid, Gertrude E. *The oh ball*
Fisher, Leonard Everett. *Theseus and the minotaur*
Fleischman, Sid. *Longbeard the wizard*
Foreman, Michael. *War and peas*
Freeman, Don. *Forever laughter*
Galdone, Paul. *The amazing pig*
    The monster and the tailor
Gay, Michel. *Bibi's birthday surprise*
Gianni, Peg. *Alex, the amazing juggler*
Gill, Janet. *Basket Weaver and Catches Many Mice*
Glass, Andrew. *Chickpea and the talking cow*
The golden goose, ill. by William Stobbs
Grimm, Jacob. *The earth gnome*
    The goose girl, ill. by Sabine Bruntjen
    The goose girl, ill. by Robert Sauber
    King Grisly-Beard
    Rumpelstiltskin, ill. by Jacqueline Ayer
    Rumpelstiltskin, ill. by Donna Diamond
    Rumpelstiltskin, ill. by Paul Galdone
    Rumpelstiltskin, ill. by Jonathan Langley
    Rumpelstiltskin, ill. by Gennady Spirin
    Rumpelstiltskin, ill. by John Wallner
    Rumpelstiltskin, ill. by Bernadette Watts
    Rumpelstiltskin, ill. by Paul O. Zelinsky
Hayes, Sarah. *Bad egg*
Heine, Helme. *The most wonderful egg in the world*
Helldorfer, M. C. (Mary Claire). *Cabbage Rose*
Hilton, Nette. *Prince Lachlan*
Hoffmann, E. T. A. *The nutcracker*, ill. by Francesca Crespi
    The nutcracker, ill. by Carolyn Ewing
    The nutcracker, ill. by Joanna Isles
    The nutcracker, ill. by Lisbeth Zwerger
    The nutcracker ballet, ill. by Vladimir Vasil'evich Vagin

Kahl, Virginia. *The Baron's booty*
  The Duchess bakes a cake
  Plum pudding for Christmas
Kennedy, Richard. *The lost kingdom of Karnica*
Kimmel, Eric A. *The four gallant sisters*
Kroll, Steven. *Fat magic*
Kurtz, Jane. *Miro in the kingdom of the sun*
Langner, Nola. *By the light of the silvery moon*
Langton, Jane. *The hedgehog boy*
  The queen's necklace
Lasker, David. *The boy who loved music*
Laskowski, Jerzy. *Master of the royal cats*
Lee, Jeanne M. *Toad is the uncle of heaven*
Littledale, Freya. *The magic plum tree*
Lobel, Anita. *Sven's bridge*
Locker, Thomas. *The young artist*
Lorenz, Lee. *The feathered ogre*
McCrea, James. *The magic tree*
McDermott, Gerald. *The voyage of Osiris*
McLenighan, Valjean. *What you see is what you get*
  You are what you are
McNaughton, Colin. *The rat race*
Mahood, Kenneth. *The laughing dragon*
Martin, Bill (William Ivan). *Rock it, sock it, number line*
Matsutani, Miyoko. *The fisherman under the sea*
Mayer, Marianna. *Baba Yaga and Vasilisa the Brave*
  The black horse
  The spirit of the blue light
Miller, M. L. *Dizzy from fools*
Montresor, Beni. *The witches of Venice*
Mother Goose. *The golden goose book*, ill. by L. Leslie Brooke
  Sing a song of sixpence, ill. by Leonard Lubin
Moxley, Susan. *Abdul's treasure*
Muller, Robin. *The sorcerer's apprentice*
Myers, Walter Dean. *The golden serpent*
Myller, Rolf. *Rolling round*
Nesbit, Edith. *The last of the dragons*
Nishikawa, Osamu. *Alexander and the blue ghost*
Oram, Hiawyn. *Skittlewonder and the wizard*
Orgel, Doris. *The flower of Sheba*
Pittman, Helena Clare. *A grain of rice*
Price, Leontyne. *Aïda*
Pushkin, Aleksandr Sergeevich. *The tale of Tsar Saltan*
Radley, Gail. *The spinner's gift*
Rappaport, Doreen. *The new king*
Richter, Mischa. *To bed, to bed!*
Rogasky, Barbara. *The water of life*
Rose, Anne K. *How does a czar eat potatoes?*
Rose, Gerald. *The bird garden*
Ross, Tony. *Towser and the terrible thing*
Saddler, Allen. *The Archery contest*
San Souci, Robert D. *The white cat*
Schiller, Barbara. *The white rat's tale*
Scholey, Arthur. *Baboushka*
Schwartz, Amy. *Her Majesty, Aunt Essie*
Scott, Sally. *The magic horse*
Seuss, Dr. *Bartholomew and the Oobleck*
Shulevitz, Uri. *One Monday morning*
Steig, William. *Roland, the minstrel pig*
Stephenson, Dorothy. *The night it rained toys*
Thomas, Shelley Moore. *Good night, Good Knight*
Tompert, Ann. *The Tzar's bird*
Torre, Betty L. *The luminous pearl*
Trez, Denise. *Maila and the flying carpet*
  The royal hiccups
Vernon, Adele. *The riddle*

Wahl, Jan. *Cabbage moon*
Wiesner, David. *The loathsome dragon*
Williams, Jay. *School for sillies*
Winthrop, Elizabeth. *Vasilissa the beautiful*
Wisniewski, David. *The warrior and the wise man*
Yen, Clara. *Why rat comes first*
Yolen, Jane. *The seeing stick*
Young, Miriam Burt. *The sugar mouse cake*
Zemach, Harve. *The tricks of Master Dabble*

Royalty – emperors

Andersen, H. C. (Hans Christian). *The emperor's new clothes*, ill. by Angela Barrett
  The emperor's new clothes, ill. by Erik Blegvad
  The emperor's new clothes, ill. by Virginia Lee Burton
  The emperor's new clothes, ill. by Robert Byrd
  The emperor's new clothes, ill. by Jack and Irene Delano
  The emperor's new clothes, ill. by Hélène Desputeaux
  The emperor's new clothes, ill. by Birte Dietz
  The emperor's new clothes, ill. by Dorothée Duntze
  The emperor's new clothes, ill. by Pamela Baldwin Ford
  The emperor's new clothes, ill. by Jack Kent
  The emperor's new clothes, ill. by Monika Laimgruber
  The emperor's new clothes, ill. by Anne F. Rockwell
  The emperor's new clothes, ill. by Janet Stevens
  The emperor's new clothes, ill. by Robert Van Nutt
  The emperor's new clothes, ill. by Nadine Bernard Westcott
  The emperor's nightingale, ill. from the Disney arcives
  The emperor's nightingale, ill. by Georges Lemoine
  The nightingale, ill. by Harold Berson
  The nightingale, ill. by Nancy Ekholm Burkert
  The nightingale, ill. by Demi
  The nightingale, ill. by Beni Montresor
  The nightingale, ill. by Regolo Ricci
  The nightingale, ill. by Christopher Santoro
  The nightingale, ill. by Lisbeth Zwerger
Asch, Frank. *The flower faerie*
Brighton, Catherine. *My Napoleon*
Chang, Margaret Scrogin. *The cricket warrior*
Demi. *The empty pot*
Goode, Diane. *The dinosaur's new clothes*
Hughes, Peter. *The emperor's oblong pancake*
Johnson, Crockett. *The emperor's gifts*
Lasky, Kathryn. *The emperor's old clothes*
Manson, Christopher. *Here begins the tale of the marvellous blue mouse*
Marcellino, Fred. *I, crocodile*
Mayer, Mercer. *Shibumi and the kitemaker*
Morris, Winifred. *The future of Yen-Tzu*
Nikly, Michelle. *The emperor's plum tree*
Perlman, Janet. *The Emperor Penguin's new clothes*
Shulevitz, Uri. *What is a wise bird like you doing in a silly tale like this*
Tompert, Ann. *The jade horse, the cricket, and the peach stone*
Wolff, Ferida. *The emperor's garden*
Yacowitz, Caryn. *The jade stone*
Yolen, Jane. *The emperor and the kite*

Young, Ed (Edward). *Cat and Rat*

Royalty – khans

Yep, Laurence. *The Khan's daughter*

Royalty – kings

Alexander, Lloyd. *The king's fountain*
Alexander, Sue. *World famous Muriel and the scary dragon*
Aliki. *The king's day*
Anno, Mitsumasa. *The king's flower*
Armstrong, Jennifer. *Little Salt Lick and the Sun King*
Arnold, Tedd. *The twin princes*
Aroner, Miriam. *The kingdom of singing birds*
Aruego, José. *The king and his friends*
Auerbach, Marjorie. *King Lavra and the barber*
Balet, Jan B. *The king and the broom maker*
Birch, David. *The king's chessboard*
Black, Charles C. *The royal nap*
Borchers, Elisabeth. *There comes a time*
Boswell, Stephen. *King Gorboduc's fabulous zoo*
Brown, Ruth. *The grizzly revenge*
Brunhoff, Jean de. *Babar the king*
   Babar the king, facsimile ed
Brunhoff, Laurent de. *Babar's visit to Bird Island*
Brusca, María Cristina. *The cook and the king*
Buffett, Jimmy. *The jolly mon*
Bunting, Eve (Anne Evelyn). *Demetrius and the golden goblet*
Burdett, Lois. *Macbeth for kids*
Chwast, Seymour. *Bushy bride*
Cole, Babette. *King Change-A-Lot*
Cole, Brock. *The king at the door*
Collier, Mary Jo. *The king's giraffe*
Crabtree, Judith. *The sparrow's story at the king's command*
Cunliffe, John. *The king's birthday cake*
Curry, Jane Louise. *The Christmas knight*
Cushman, Doug. *The mystery of King Karfu*
Day, David. *King of the woods*
Degen, Bruce. *Teddy bear towers*
DeLuise, Dom. *King Bob's new clothes*
De Paola, Tomie (Thomas Anthony). *The legend of the persian carpet*
Derby, Sally. *King Kenrick's splinter*
Domanska, Janina. *King Krakus and the dragon*
Elkin, Benjamin. *The king who could not sleep*
   The king's wish and other stories
Fern, Eugene. *The king who was too busy*
French, Fiona. *King of another country*
Friedman, Aileen. *The king's commissioners*
Froese, Deborah L. *The wise washerman*
Gackenbach, Dick. *Harvey, the foolish pig*
   King Wacky
Gifaldi, David. *The boy who spoke colors*
Ginsburg, Mirra. *The king who tried to fry an egg on his head*
Gregory, Valiska. *Through the mickle woods*
Grimm, Jacob. *The golden bird*, ill. by Isabelle Brent
   The golden bird, ill. by Sandro Nardini
   Iron Hans
   Iron John, ill. by Trina Schart Hyman
   Iron John, ill. by Winslow Pels
Harber, Frances. *My king has donkey ears*
Harness, Cheryl. *The queen with bees in her hair*
Haywood, Carolyn. *The king's monster*

Heine, Helme. *King Bounce the 1st*
Hewitt, Kathryn. *King Midas and the golden touch*
Hughes, Peter. *The king who loved candy*
Hutchins, Pat. *King Henry's palace*
Jackson, Ellen B. *The impossible riddle*
Karlin, Nurit. *A train for the king*
Kessler, Leonard P. *Soup for the king*
Kherdian, David. *The golden bracelet*
Kimmel, Eric A. *Squash it!*
   Three sacks of truth
Kraus, Robert. *The king's trousers*
Krudop, Walter Lyon. *The man who caught fish*
Lang, Andrew. *The flying ship*
Leonard, Marcia. *King Lionheart's castle*
Love, Ann. *Ice cream at the castle*
   The prince who wrote a letter
Luttrell, Ida. *The star counters*
McCrea, James. *The king's procession*
MacDonald, Alan. *The not-so-wise man*
MacGill-Callahan, Sheila. *The children of Lir*
   When Solomon was king
McKee, David. *King Rollo and the birthday*
   King Rollo and the bread
   King Rollo and the new shoes
McKissack, Patricia C. *King Midas and his gold*
   The king's new clothes
McMullen, Eunice. *Dragon for breakfast*
Mahy, Margaret. *17 kings and 42 elephants*
   When the king rides by
Manson, Christopher. *A gift for the king*
Mark, Jan. *The Midas touch*
Martin, C. L. G. *The dragon nanny*
Martin, Rafe. *The monkey bridge*
Mayer, Marianna. *Marcel the pastry chef*
   The prince and the pauper
Medearis, Angela Shelf. *Too much talk*
Metaxas, Eric. *David and Goliath*
   Puss in boots
Miller, M. L. *The enormous snore*
Milton, Nancy. *The giraffe that walked to Paris*
Mitchell, Adrian. *Nobody rides the unicorn*
Mollel, Tololwa M. (Tololwa Marti). *Dume's roar*
   The king and the tortoise
Muller, Robin. *The magic paintbrush*
Myller, Rolf. *How big is a foot?*
Noble, Trinka Hakes. *The king's tea*
Noyes, Alfred. *The highwayman*
Oberman, Sheldon. *King Solomon, Sheba, and the hoopoe bird*
Paterson, Katherine. *The angel and the donkey*
Peet, Bill (William Bartlett). *How Droofus the dragon lost his head*
Perkins, Al. *King Midas and the golden touch*
Perrault, Charles. *Puss in boots*, ill. by Marcia Brown
   Puss in boots, ill. by Lorinda Bryan Cauley
   Puss in boots, ill. by Jean Claverie
   Puss in boots, ill. by Andrea Da Rif
   Puss in boots, ill. by Stasys Eidrigevicius
   Puss in boots, ill. by Hans Fischer
   Puss in boots, ill. by Paul Galdone
   Puss in boots, retold and ill. by John S. Goodall
   Puss in boots, retold and ill. by Gail E. Haley
   Puss in boots, ill. by Giuliano Lunelli
   Puss in boots, ill. by Fred Marcellino [pub. by Farrar, 1990]
   Puss in boots, ill. by Fred Marcellino [pub. by Farrar, 1998]
   Puss in boots, ill. by Julia Noonan
   Puss in boots, ill. by Tony Ross

Puss in boots, ill. by William Stobbs
Puss in boots, ill. by Yan Thomas
Puss in boots, ill. by Alain Vaës
Puss in boots, ill. by Barry Wilkinson
Peters, Andrew. *Salt is sweeter than gold*
Peterson, Julienne. *Caterina, the clever farm girl*
Pevear, Richard. *Our king has horns!*
Pfister, Marcus. *How Leo learned to be king*
Postgate, Oliver. *Noggin and the whale*
   Noggin the king
Reit, Seymour. *The king who learned to smile*
Robison, Nancy. *Ten tall soldiers*
Saddler, Allen. *The king gets fit*
San Souci, Robert D. *A weave of words*
Santore, Charles. *William the Curious*
Sawyer, Ruth. *The remarkable Christmas of the cobbler's sons*
Seuss, Dr. *The king's stilts*
Sexton, Gwain. *There once was a king*
Siekkinen, Raija. *Mister King*
Sierra, Judy. *The beautiful butterfly*
Skipper, Mervyn. *The fooling of King Alexander*
Slate, Joseph. *The secret stars*
Souhami, Jessica. *Rama and the demon king*
Steptoe, John. *Mufaro's beautiful daughters*
Stewig, John Warren. *King Midas*
Storr, Catherine (Cole). *King Midas*
Thomson, Peggy. *The king has horse's ears*
Va, Leong. *A letter to the king*
Van Laan, Nancy. *The legend of El Dorado*
Ward, Helen. *The king of the birds*
Wersba, Barbara. *Do tigers ever bite kings?*
West, Colin. *The king of Kennelwick castle*
   The king's toothache
Wilde, Oscar. *The happy prince*
Wilkes, Larry. *The king's egg dance*
Wisniewski, David. *Sundiata*
Wolkstein, Diane. *Bouki dances the Kokioko*
Wood, Audrey. *King Bidgood's in the bathtub*
Yep, Laurence. *The shell woman and the king*
Yolen, Jane. *King Long Shanks*

Royalty – pharaohs

Mike, Jan M. *Gift of the Nile*
Sabuda, Robert James. *Tutankhamen's gift*

Royalty – princes

Allen, Jonathan. *Wake up, Sleeping Beauty*
Arnold, Tedd. *The twin princes*
Aulaire, Ingri Mortenson d'. *East of the sun and west of the moon*
Baum, Arline. *Opt*
Baumann, Kurt. *The prince and the lute*
Behan, Brendan. *The king of Ireland's son*
Berenzy, Alix. *Rapunzel*
Birrer, Cynthia. *The lady and the unicorn*
Boesky, Amy. *Planet Was*
Brenner, Barbara A. *The prince and the pink blanket*
Bruna, Dick. *Dick Bruna's Cinderella*
Burdett, Lois. *Hamlet for kids*
Canfield, Jane White. *The frog prince*
Cecil, Laura. *The frog princess*
Clayton, Elaine. *The yeoman's daring daughter and the princes in the tower*
Coburn, Jewell Reinhart. *Angkat*
   Jouanah
Cole, Babette. *King Change-A-Lot*

Prince Cinders
Damjan, Mischa. *The little prince and the tiger cat*
Dasent, George W. *East o' the sun, west o' the moon*
The firebird, ill. by Reg Cartwright
The firebird, ill. by Francesca Crespi
The firebird, ill. by Demi
The firebird, adapt. and ill. by Rachel Isadora
The firebird, ill. by Moira Kemp
The firebird, ill. by Kris Waldherr
The firebird, ill. by Boris Zvorykin
Gál, László. *The parrot*
Gray, Nigel. *The frog prince*
Greene, Ellin. *Billy Beg and his bull*
Grimm, Jacob. *Cinderella*, ill. by Nonny Hogrogian
   Cinderella, ill. by Svend Otto S
   The donkey prince
   The frog prince, ill. by Paul Galdone
   The frog prince, ill. by Binette Schroeder
   The golden bird, ill. by Isabelle Brent
   The golden bird, ill. by Sandro Nardini
   Iron Hans
   Iron John, ill. by Trina Schart Hyman
   Iron John, ill. by Winslow Pels
   Rapunzel, ill. by Jutta Ash
   Rapunzel, ill. by Sheilah Beckett
   Rapunzel, ill. by Bert Dodson
   Rapunzel, ill. by Maja Dusíkova
   Rapunzel, ill. by Michael Hague
   Rapunzel, ill. by Trina Schart Hyman
   Rapunzel, ill. by Kris Waldherr
   Rapunzel, ill. by Bernadette Watts
   Rapunzel, ill. by Paul O. Zelinsky
   Rose Red and the bear prince
Hague, Kathleen. *East of the sun and west of the moon*
Han, Oki S. *Kongi and Potgi*
Hastings, Selina. *The singing ringing tree*
Haugaard, Erik Christian. *Prince Boghole*
Heine, Helme. *Prince Bear*
Helldorfer, M. C. (Mary Claire). *The mapmaker's daughter*
Hilton, Nette. *Prince Lachlan*
Ikeda, Daisaku. *The snow country prince*
Jackson, Ellen B. *Cinder Edna*
Jacobs, Joseph. *Tattercoats*
Johnson, Crockett. *The frowning prince*
Kimmel, Eric A. *One Eye, Two Eyes, Three Eyes*
   The three princes
Knight, Hilary. *Hilary Knight's Cinderella*
Kvasnosky, Laura McGee. *What shall I dream?*
Lattimore, Deborah Nourse. *Cinderhazel*
   The prince and the golden ax
Lester, Helen. *Princess Penelope's parrot*
Lobel, Arnold. *Prince Bertram the bad*
Love, Ann. *Ice cream at the castle*
MacDonald, George. *Little Daylight*
McKee, David. *Prince Peter and the teddy bear*
McKissack, Patricia C. *Cinderella*
Mann, Pamela. *The frog princess?*
Manson, Christopher. *The crab prince*
Metaxas, Eric. *The white cat*
Mike, Jan M. *The bird maiden*
Mills, Lauren A. *The dog prince*
   Fairy wings
Milne, A. A. (Alan Alexander). *Prince Rabbit*
Minters, Frances. *Cinder-Elly*
Morris, Ann. *The Cinderella rebus book*
Murphy, Shirley Rousseau. *Wind child*
Nones, Eric Jon. *Canary prince*

Oppenheim, Joanne. *The story book prince*
Osborne, Mary Pope. *Molly and the prince*
Patz, Nancy. *Gina Farina and the Prince of Mintz*
Perrault, Charles. *Cinderella*, ill. by Sheilah Beckett
   Cinderella, ill. by Marcia Brown
   Cinderella, ill. by Paul Galdone
   Cinderella, ill. by Diane Goode
   Cinderella, ill. by Susan Jeffers
   Cinderella, ill. by Loek Koopmans
   Cinderella, ill. by Emanuele Luzzati
   Cinderella, ill. by James Marshall
   Cinderella, ill. by Phil Smith
Priestley, Alice. *Someone is reading this book*
The prince who knew his fate
Pyle, Howard. *The Swan Maiden*
Rogers, Paul (Patrick). *Tumbledown*
Sanderson, Ruth. *The enchanted wood*
   Papa Gatto
Scieszka, Jon. *The frog prince, continued*
Sherman, Josepha. *Vassilisa the wise*
Souhami, Jessica. *Rama and the demon king*
Springer, Margaret. *A royal ball*
Wells, Rosemary. *The little lame prince*
Yolen, Jane. *Wings*

Royalty – princesses

Ada, Alma Flor. *The malachite palace*
Afanas'ev, Aleksandr N. *Salt*
Allen, Jonathan. *Wake up, Sleeping Beauty*
Allen, Linda. *The mouse bride*
Andersen, H. C. (Hans Christian). *The princess and the pea*, ill. by Emily Bolam
   The princess and the pea, ill. by Dorothée Duntze
   The princess and the pea, ill. by Dick Gackenbach
   The princess and the pea, ill. by Paul Galdone
   The princess and the pea, ill. by Camille Semelet
   The princess and the pea, ill. by Janet Stevens
   The princess and the pea, ill. by Suçie Stevenson
   The princess and the pea, ill. by Eve Tharlet
Angeletti, Roberta. *Nefertari, princess of Egypt*
Bawden, Nina. *Princess Alice*
Bazilian, Barbara. *Princess Lily*
Cecil, Laura. *The frog princess*
Cole, Babette. *Princess Smartypants*
Cooper, Susan. *Tam Lin*
Costa, Nicoletta. *The mischievous princess*
DeChristopher, Marlowe. *Greencoat and the swanboy*
DeFelice, Cynthia C. *Three perfect peaches*
Flot, Jeannette B. *Princess Kalina and the hedgehog*
French, Vivian. *The thistle princess*
Gál, László. *The parrot*
Gekiere, Madeleine. *The frilly lily and the princess*
Gliori, Debi. *The princess and the pirate king*
Gray, Nigel. *The frog prince*
Greaves, Margaret. *Kate Crackernuts*
   Sarah's lion
Greene, Ellin. *Billy Beg and his bull*
Grimm, Jacob. *The frog prince*, ill. by Paul Galdone
   The frog prince, ill. by Binette Schroeder
   The golden goose, ill. by Dorothée Duntze
   The golden goose, ill. by Isadore Seltzer
   The golden goose, ill. by Martin Ursell
   The princess and the frog
   The six servants
   The twelve dancing princesses, ill. by Kinuko Y. Craft
   The twelve dancing princesses, ill. by Anne Dalton

The twelve dancing princesses, ill. by Dennis Hockerman
The twelve dancing princesses, ill. by Errol Le Cain
The twelve dancing princesses, ill. by Gerald McDermott
The twelve dancing princesses, ill. by Jane Ray
The twelve dancing princesses, ill. by Uri Shulevitz
The twelve dancing princesses, ill. by Suçie Stevenson
Gwynne, Fred. *Pondlarker*
Hastings, Selina. *The singing ringing tree*
Haugaard, Erik Christian. *Princess Horrid*
Heine, Helme. *The boxer and the princess*
   Prince Bear
Hooks, William H. *The monster from the sea*
Huck, Charlotte S. *Princess Furball*
Inkpen, Mick. *Lullabyhullaballoo!*
Isele, Elizabeth. *The frog princess*
Kimmel, Eric A. *Rimonah of the Flashing Sword*
   The three princes
Kleven, Elisa. *The paper princess*
Kroll, Steven. *Princess Abigail and the wonderful hat*
Lang, Andrew. *The flying ship*
Laroche, Michel. *The snow rose*
Lester, Helen. *Princess Penelope's parrot*
Lewis, J. Patrick. *The frog princess*
   The night of the goat children
Lewison, Wendy Cheyette. *The princess and the potty*
Lobel, Anita. *A birthday for the princess*
Love, Ann. *The prince who wrote a letter*
MacDonald, George. *The light princess*, ill. by Katie Thamer Treherne
   Little Daylight
Martin, Claire. *Boots and the glass mountain*, ill. by Gennady Spirin
   The race of the golden apples
Marzollo, Jean. *Welcome to the Shanna show*
Maugham, W. Somerset (William Somerset). *Princess September and the nightingale*
Mayer, Mercer. *Shibumi and the kitemaker*
Meeker, Clare Hodgson. *A tale of two rice birds*
Metaxas, Eric. *Princess Scargo and the birthday pumpkin*
Mike, Jan M. *The bird maiden*
   Clever Karlis
   Juan Bobo and the horse of seven colors
Miller, M. L. *Dizzy from fools*
Mills, Lauren A. *Tatterhood and the hobgoblins*
Mollel, Tololwa M. (Tololwa Marti). *The princess who lost her hair*
Nesbit, Edith. *Melisande*
Ness, Evaline. *Pavo and the princess*
Nikly, Michelle. *The princess on the nut*
Nones, Eric Jon. *Canary prince*
Oram, Hiawyn. *Princess Chamomile gets her way*
   The second princess
Pancheri, Jan. *The twelve poodle princess*
Peters, Andrew. *Salt is sweeter than gold*
Reesink, Marijke. *The princess who always ran away*
Scieszka, Jon. *The frog prince, continued*
Shearer, Marilyn J. *The Nubian princess*
Shields, Carol Diggory. *I am really a princess*
Slobodkin, Louis. *Colette and the princess*
Springer, Margaret. *A royal ball*
Thurber, James. *Many moons*, ill. by Marc Simont
   Many moons, ill. by Louis Slobodkin
Turnbull, Ann. *The tapestry cats*
Vesey, A. *The princess and the frog*
Waddell, Martin. *The tough princess*

Walsh, Ellen Stoll. *Jack's tale*
Williams, Jay. *The practical princess*
Wolfson, Margaret. *Turtle songs*
Zakhoder, Boris Vladimirovich. *The good stepmother*

Royalty – queens

Bell, Anthea. *The wise queen*
Bowden, Joan Chase. *A hat for the queen*
Brown, Ruth. *The grizzly revenge*
Burdett, Lois. *Macbeth for kids*
Evans, Nate. *The mixed-up zoo of professor Yahoo*
Garrett, Jennifer. *The queen who stole the sky*
Greaves, Margaret. *Kate Crackernuts*
Grimm, Jacob. *The six servants*
Harness, Cheryl. *The queen with bees in her hair*
Hennessy, B. G. (Barbara G.). *The missing tarts*
Hiatt, Fred. *If I were queen of the world*
Lewis, J. Patrick. *Isabella Abnormella and the very, very finicky Queen of Trouble*
Lobato, Arcadio. *The greatest treasure*
Mahy, Margaret. *The queen's goat*
Mayer, Mercer. *The queen always wanted to dance*
Myers, Bernice. *The flying shoes*
Oxenbury, Helen. *The queen and Rosie Randall*
Paxton, Tom. *Engelbert the elephant*
Pike, Carol. *The nutty queen*
San Souci, Robert D. *A weave of words*
Sharratt, Nick. *The green queen*
Silverman, Maida. *The magic well*
Turnbull, Ann. *The tapestry cats*
Van Woerkom, Dorothy. *The queen who couldn't bake gingerbread*
Wild, Margaret. *The queen's holiday*

Royalty – rajahs

Demi. *One grain of rice*

Royalty – sultans

Ambrus, Victor G. *The Sultan's bath*
Kimmel, Eric A. *The valiant red rooster*

Royalty – tsars

Gorbachev, Valeri. *The Fool of the world and the flying ship*
Hoffman, Mary. *Clever Katya*
Lottridge, Celia B. (Celia Barker). *Music for the Tsar of the Sea*
Metaxas, Eric. *The fool and the flying ship*
Ogburn, Jacqueline K. *The magic nesting doll*
Ransome, Arthur. *The fool of the world and the flying ship*
Winthrop, Elizabeth. *The little humpbacked horse*

Rummage sales *see* Garage sales, rummage sales

Running *see* Activities – Running

Running away *see* Behavior – running away

Russia *see* Foreign lands – Russia

Russian Americans *see* Ethnic groups in the U.S. – Russian Americans

Rwanda *see* Foreign lands – Rwanda

Sadness *see* Emotions – sadness

Safety

Arnold, Caroline. *Who keeps us safe?*
Bahr, Amy C. *It's ok to say no*
   Sometimes it's ok to tell secrets
   What should you do when . . . ?
   Your body is your own
Baker, Eugene H. *Bicycles*
   Fire
   Home
   Outdoors
   School
   Water
Berenstain, Stan. *The Berenstain bears learn about strangers*
Brown, Marc Tolon. *Dinosaurs, beware!*
Brown, Margaret Wise. *Red light, green light*
Chlad, Dorothy. *Bicycles are fun to ride*
   Matches, lighters, and firecrackers are not toys
   Poisons make you sick
Cleary, Beverly. *Lucky Chuck*
Emecheta, Buchi. *Nowhere to play*
Girard, Linda Walvoord. *My body is private*
   Who is a stranger, and what should I do?
Hoban, Lillian. *Arthur's back to school day*
Joyce, Irma. *Never talk to strangers*
Lakin, Pat (Patricia). *Aware and alert*
Leaf, Munro. *Safety can be fun*
Levete, Sarah. *Looking after myself*
Lindgren, Barbro. *Sam's lamp*
Loewen, Nancy. *Bicycle safety*
   Emergencies
   School safety
   Traffic safety
McKissack, Patricia C. *Who is coming?*
McLeod, Emilie Warren. *The bear's bicycle*
Maestro, Betsy. *Bike trip*
Mattern, Joanne. *Safety at school*
   Safety in public places
   Safety in the water
Meyer, Linda D. *Safety zone*
Moss, Elaine. *Polar*
Myller, Lois. *No! No!*
Pendziwol, Jean. *No dragons for tea*
Petty, Kate. *Being careful with strangers*
Pfister, Marcus. *Hang on, Hopper!*
Rand, Gloria. *Willie takes a hike*
Rex, Michael. *My fire engine*
Royston, Angela. *Fire fighters*
Russell, Pamela. *Do you have a secret?*
Schulson, Rachel Ellenberg. *Guns . . . what you should know*
Shortall, Leonard W. *One way*
Smaridge, Norah. *Watch out!*
Spelman, Cornelia. *Your body belongs to you*
Trottier, Maxine. *A safe place*
Viorst, Judith. *Try it again, Sam*

Vogel, Carole Garbuny. *The dangers of strangers*
Yamashita, Haruo. *Mice at the beach*
Ziefert, Harriet. *No, no, Nicky!*

Sahara Desert *see* Foreign lands – Sahara Desert

Sailing *see* Sports – sailing

Sailors

Agell, Charlotte. *The sailor's book*
Ahlberg, Allan. *Master Salt the sailor's son*
Anderson, Lena. *Stina's visit*
Bruna, Dick. *The sailor*
Calhoun, Mary. *Henry the sailor cat*
Conrad, Pam. *The lost sailor*
Crews, Donald. *Sail away*
Denton, Terry. *Home is the sailor*
Friedman, Ina R. *How my parents learned to eat*
Ginsburg, Mirra. *Four brave sailors*
Helldorfer, M. C. (Mary Claire). *Sailing to the sea*
Hest, Amy. *A sort-of sailor*
Jewell, Nancy. *Sailor song*
Kimmel, Eric A. *Billy Lazroe and the King of the Sea*
Lattimore, Deborah Nourse. *The sailor who captured the sea*
Locker, Thomas. *Sailing with the wind*
Maass, Robert. *Tugboats*
McCurdy, Michael. *The sailor's alphabet*
McKinley, Robin. *My father is in the Navy*
Mahy, Margaret. *Sailor Jack and the twenty orphans*
Metaxas, Eric. *Stormalong, the legendary sea captain*
Mills, Judith Christine. *The stonehook schooner*
O'Neill, Alexis. *Loud Emily*
Slawski, Wolfgang. *Captain Jonathan sails the sea*
Stevenson, Drew. *The ballad of Penelope Lou . . . and me*
Van Allsburg, Chris. *The wreck of the Zephyr*
Waddell, Martin. *Sailor Bear*
Waters, Tony. *Sailor's bride*
Whittle, Emily. *Sailor cats*
Winter, Jeanette. *Follow the drinking gourd*
Zeman, Ludmila. *Sinbad*

Saint Patrick's Day *see* Holidays – St. Patrick's Day

St. Patrick's Day *see* Holidays – St. Patrick's Day

Salamanders *see* Reptiles – salamanders

Salesmen *see* Careers – salesmen

Sand

Apperley, Dawn. *In the sand*
Bason, Lillian. *Castles and mirrors and cities of sand*
Garland, Sherry. *Summer sands*
Inkpen, Mick. *Sandcastle*
Jones, Rebecca C. *Down at the bottom of the deep dark sea*
Krementz, Jill. *Jack goes to the beach*
Lloyd, David. *Grandma and the pirate*
Macdonald, Maryann. *Ben at the beach*
Nolan, Dennis. *The castle builder*

Ormondroyd, Edward. *Johnny Castleseed*
Roach, Marilynne K. *Dune fox*
Robbins, Ken. *Beach days*
Turnbull, Ann. *The sand horse*
Vasiliu, Mircea. *A day at the beach*
Watanabe, Shigeo. *I'm the king of the castle!*
Webb, Angela. *Talkabout sand*
Yee, Brenda Shannon. *Sand castle*

Sandcastles *see* Sand

Sandman *see* Mythical creatures – sandman

Sandpipers *see* Birds – sandpipers

Sandstorms *see* Weather – sandstorms

Sanitation workers *see* Careers – sanitation workers

Santa Claus

Ambrus, Victor G. *Santa Claus takes off*
Amoss, Berthe. *What did you lose, Santa?*
Aoki, Hisako. *Santa's favorite story*
Ardizzone, Aingelda. *The night ride*
Armour, Richard Willard. *The year Santa went modern*
Arnold, Katya. *The adventures of Snowwoman*
Bernardoni, Robert. *Christmas all over*
Bishop, Roma. *Santa pays a visit*
Brett, Jan. *The wild Christmas reindeer*
Briggs, Raymond. *Father Christmas*
  Father Christmas goes on holiday
Bröger, Achim. *The Santa Clauses*
Brown, Marc Tolon. *Arthur's Christmas*
Burningham, John. *Harvey Slumfenburger's Christmas present*
Catalanotto, Peter. *Christmas always . . .*
Chalmers, Mary. *Merry Christmas, Harry*
Clark, Elizabeth. *Father Christmas and the donkey*
Clements, Andrew. *Santa's secret helper*
Collington, Peter. *On Christmas eve*
Compton, Kenn. *Happy Christmas to all!*
Conrad, Pam. *The Tub People's Christmas*
Crespi, Francesca. *Santa Claus is coming!*
Cuyler, Margery. *Fat Santa*
Darling, Kathy (Mary Kathleen). *The mystery in Santa's toyshop*
DeLage, Ida. *ABC Santa Claus*
Delamare, David. *The Christmas secret*
Denton, Kady MacDonald. *Christmas boot*
De Paola, Tomie (Thomas Anthony). *Get dressed, Santa!*
Drescher, Henrik. *Looking for Santa Claus*
Dubowski, Cathy East. *The Christmas Santa almost missed*
Duvoisin, Roger Antoine. *The Christmas whale*
  One thousand Christmas beards
Edens, Cooper. *Nicholi*
Ehrlich, Amy. *Bunnies at Christmastime*
Ephron, Delia. *Santa and Alex*
Fearnley, Jan. *Little Robin's Christmas*
Foreman, Michael. *The perfect present*
French, Vivian. *Christmas kitten*
Gaffington, Urslan Judith. *Silver berries and Christmas magic*
Gammell, Stephen. *Wake up, bear . . . It's Christmas!*

Gomi, Taro. *Santa through the window*
Hayes, Sarah. *A bad start for Santa*
Hayward, Linda. *The runaway Christmas toy*
Haywood, Carolyn. *A Christmas fantasy*
　How the reindeer saved Santa
　Santa Claus forever!
Hazen, Barbara Shook. *Santa clues*
　The story of Santa Claus
Hill, Eric. *Spot's magical Christmas*
Hoff, Syd. *Santa's moose*
　Where's Prancer?
Hurd, Thacher. *Santa Mouse and the ratdeer*
Ives, Penny. *Mrs. Santa Claus*
Janovitz, Marilyn. *What could be keeping Santa?*
Johnson, Crockett. *Harold at the North Pole*
Johnson, Russell. *Trouble at Christmas*
Joyce, William. *Santa calls*
Kessler, Leonard P. *That's not Santa!*
Kimpton, Diana. *The bear Santa Claus forgot*
Knight, Hilary. *Angels and berries and candy canes*
Krahn, Fernando. *How Santa Claus had a long and difficult journey delivering his presents*
Krensky, Stephen. *How Santa got his job*
　How Santa lost his job
Kroll, Steven. *Santa's crash-bang Christmas*
Kunnas, Mauri. *Santa Claus and his elves*
　Twelve gifts for Santa Claus
Landa, Norbert. *Little Bear's Christmas*
Lewis, J. Patrick. *The Christmas of the reddle moon*
Lubin, Leonard B. *Christmas gift-bringers*
McGinley, Phyllis. *How Mrs. Santa Claus saved Christmas*
McPhail, David M. *Mistletoe*
　Santa's book of names
Maloney, Peter. *Redbird at Rockefeller Center*
May, Robert Lewis. *Rudolph the red-nosed reindeer*
Maynard, Bill. *Santa's time off*
Miles, Calvin. *Calvin's Christmas wish*
Mogensen, Jan. *Teddy's Christmas gift*
Moore, Clement C. *The night before Christmas*, ill. by Jan Brett
　The night before Christmas, ill. by Tomie de Paola
　The night before Christmas, comp. by Cooper Edens and Harold Darling; ill. by various nineteenth- and twentieth-century artists
　The night before Christmas, ill. by Michael Foreman
　The night before Christmas, ill. by Gyo Fujikawa
　The night before Christmas, ill. by Scott Gustafson
　The night before Christmas, ill. by Cheryl Harness
　The night before Christmas, ill. by Loretta Krupinski
　The night before Christmas, ill. by Anita Lobel
　The night before Christmas, ill. by James Marshall
　The night before Christmas, ill. by Jacqueline Rogers
　The night before Christmas, ill. by Robin Spowart
　The night before Christmas, ill. by Gustaf Tenggren
　The night before Christmas, ill. by Tasha Tudor
　The night before Christmas, ill. by Wendy Watson
　The night before Christmas, ill. by Jody Wheeler
　The night before Christmas in signed English
　The teddy bears' night before Christmas
　A visit from St. Nicholas
Murdocca, Sal (Salvatore). *Christmas bear*
Neugebauer, Charise. *Santa's gift*
Nixon, Joan Lowery. *That's the spirit, Claude*
Novak, Matt. *The last Christmas present*
Ostheeren, Ingrid. *I'm the real Santa Claus!*

Paxton, Tom. *The story of Santa Claus*
Pearson, Tracey Campbell. *Where does Joe go?*
Peet, Bill (William Bartlett). *Countdown to Christmas*
Pfister, Marcus. *Wake up, Santa Claus!*
Polacco, Patricia. *Welcome Comfort*
Prøysen, Alf. *Christmas eve at Santa's*
Rosales, Melodye Benson. *'Twas the night b'fore Christmas*
Schrecker, Judie. *Santa's new reindeer*
Sharmat, Marjorie Weinman. *I'm Santa Claus and I'm famous*
Steven, Kenneth C. *The bearer of gifts*
Sykes, Julie. *Hurry, Santa!*
Tompert, Ann. *Saint Nicholas*
Trosclair. *Cajun night before Christmas*
Tryon, Leslie. *Albert's Christmas*
Tutt, Kay Cunningham. *And now we call him Santa Claus*
Van Allsburg, Chris. *The polar express*
Weil, Lisl. *Santa Claus around the world*
Wells, Rosemary. *McDuff's new friend*
　Max's Christmas
Weninger, Brigitte. *A Letter to Santa Claus*
Wilhelm, Hans. *Schnitzel's first Christmas*
Wood, Audrey. *The Christmas adventure of Space Elf Sam*
Wright, Cliff. *Santa's ark*
Yorinks, Arthur. *Christmas in July*

Saving things *see* Behavior – saving things

Scandinavia *see* Foreign lands – Scandinavia

Scarecrows

Bolliger, Max. *The wooden man*
Brown, Margaret Wise. *The little scarecrow boy*
Cazet, Denys. *Nothing at all*
Dillon, Jana. *Jeb Scarecrow's pumpkin patch*
Farber, Norma. *There goes feathertop!*
Fleischman, Sid. *The scarebird*
Gordon, Sharon. *Sam the scarecrow*
Hart, Jeanne McGahey. *Scareboy*
Lewis, Robin Baird. *Hello, Mr. Scarecrow*
Lifton, Betty Jean. *Joji and the Amanojaku*
　Joji and the dragon
　Joji and the fog
Maris, Ron. *Ducks quack*
Martin, Bill (William Ivan). *Barn dance!*
Miller, Edna. *Pebbles, a pack rat*
Oana, Kay D. *Robbie and the raggedy scarecrow*
Rylant, Cynthia. *Scarecrow*
San Souci, Robert D. *Feathertop*
Schaefer, Carole Lexa. *Under the midsummer sky*
Schertle, Alice. *Witch Hazel*
Tripp, Paul. *The strawman who smiled by mistake*
Watts, Bernadette. *Tattercoats*
Williams, Linda. *The little old lady who was not afraid of anything*

School

Adelson, Leone. *All ready for school*
Ahlberg, Allan. *The Cinderella show*
　Me and my friend
Alexander, Martha G. *Move over, Twerp*

Aliki. *Marianthe's story one: painted words; Marianthe's story two: spoken memories*
Allard, Harry. *Miss Nelson has a field day*
  Miss Nelson is back
  Miss Nelson is missing!
Ambrus, Victor G. *Son of Dracula*
Amper, Thomas. *Booker T. Washington*
Ancona, George. *Ricardo's day*
Annett, Cora. *The dog who thought he was a boy*
Antoine, Héloïse. *Curious kids go to preschool*
Arkin, Alan. *Black and white*
Arnold, Caroline. *Where do you go to school?*
Arnold, Katrin. *Anna joins in*
Arnold, Tedd. *Green Wilma*
Aseltine, Lorraine. *First grade can wait*
Ashley, Bernard. *Dinner ladies don't count*
Aulaire, Ingri Mortenson d'. *Children of the northlights*
  Nils
Babbitt, Lorraine. *Pink like the geranium*
Baehr, Patricia. *School isn't fair*
Baer, Edith. *This is the way we go to school*
Baird, Anne. *The guppies of Hilly Dale House*
Baker, Eugene H. *School*
Ballart, Elisabet. *Let's count*
Bare, Colleen Stanley. *Critter, the class cat*
Barkan, Joanne. *Whiskerville school*
Barrett, Mary Brigid. *Day care days*
Behrens, June. *Who am I?*
Beim, Jerrold. *The taming of Toby*
Bemelmans, Ludwig. *Madeline*
Berenstain, Stan. *The Berenstain bears' trouble at school*
Berquist, Grace. *Speckles goes to school*
Binnamin, Vivian. *The case of the anteater's missing lunch*
  The case of the mysterious mermaid
Bird, Malcolm. *The school in Murky Wood*
Biro, Val. *Gumdrop goes to school*
Blance, Ellen. *Monster at school*
  Monster goes to school
Blaustein, Muriel. *Jim chimp's story*
Blue, Rose. *How many blocks is the world?*
Bluthenthal, Diana Cain. *Matilda the moocher*
Boegehold, Betty. *The fight*
Boelts, Maribeth. *Little Bunny's cool tool set*
  Summer's end
Bogart, Jo Ellen. *Jeremiah learns to read*
Bognomo, Joel Eboueme. *Madoulina*
Bond, Felicia. *The Halloween performance*
  The Halloween play
Boon, Emilie. *1 2 3 how many animals can you see?*
Bourgeois, Paulette. *Franklin's class trip*
  Too many chickens
Boyd, Selma. *I met a polar bear*
Bradman, Tony. *It came from outer space*
  Michael
Brandenberg, Franz. *No school today!*
Brillhart, Julie. *Anna's goodbye apron*
  When daddy came to school
Brooks, Ron. *Timothy and Gramps*
Brown, Kathryn. *Muledred*
Brown, Laurie Krasny. *Rex and Lilly school time*
Brown, Marc Tolon. *Arthur and the true Francine*
  Arthur goes to school
  Arthur's teacher trouble
  Arthur's underwear
  Arthur's Valentine
  The true Francine

Brown, Ruth. *The shy little angel*
Brown, Tricia. *Hello, amigos!*
Bruna, Dick. *The school*
Buchanan, Heather S. *George and Matilda Mouse and the floating school*
Buchheimer, Naomi. *Let's go to a school*
Buckley, Kate. *Love notes*
Budney, Blossom. *N is for nursery school*
Bunting, Eve (Anne Evelyn). *Cheyenne again*
  Our teacher's having a baby
Burningham, John. *John Patrick Norman McHennessy - the boy who was always late*
  The school
Butler, Dorothy. *My brown bear Barney*
Butterworth, Nick. *Field day*
  The Nativity play
  The school trip
Calmenson, Stephanie. *The after school book*
  The kindergarten book
  Kinderkittens, show-and-tell
  Kinderkittens, who took the cookie from the cookie jar?
  The principal's new clothes
  The teeny tiny teacher
Caple, Kathy. *The biggest nose*
Carlson, Nancy L. *Arnie and the new kid*
  Louanne Pig in making the team
  Sit still!
Carrick, Carol. *Left behind*
  Patrick's dinosaurs on the Internet
Caseley, Judith. *Ada potato*
  Mickey's class play
  Mr. Green Peas
  Molly Pink
Caudill, Rebecca. *A pocketful of cricket*
Cazet, Denys. *Are there any questions?*
  Daydreams
  A fish in his pocket
  Frosted glass
Cecil, Ivon. *Kirby Kelvin and the not laughing lessons*
Chapouton, Anne-Marie. *Sebastian is always late*
Chardiet, Bernice. *Martin and the tooth fairy*
Charles, Donald. *Calico Cat at school*
Charmatz, Bill. *The Troy St. bus*
Cibula, Matt S. *What's up with you, Taquandra Fu?*
Clayton, Elaine. *Pup in school*
Clement, Rod. *Just another ordinary day*
Clements, Andrew. *Double trouble in Walla Walla*
Clewes, Dorothy. *Happiest day*
Clifton, Lucille. *All us come cross the water*
Cocca-Leffler, Maryann. *Missing: one stuffed rabbit*
  Mr. Tanen's ties
Cohen, Miriam. *Bee my Valentine!*
  Best friends
  Don't eat too much turkey!
  First grade takes a test
  It's George!
  Jim meets the thing
  Liar, liar, pants on fire!
  Lost in the museum
  The new teacher
  No good in art
  The real-skin rubber monster mask
  See you in second grade!
  See you tomorrow
  So what?
  Starring first grade
  Tough Jim
  When will I read?
Coker, Gylbert. *Naptime*

Panek, Dennis. *Ba ba sheep wouldn't go to sleep*
Paraskevas, Betty. *Gracie Graves and the kids from room 402*
Parish, Peggy. *Jumper goes to school*
Park, Barbara. *Junie B. Jones and some sneaky peeky spying*
Park, Frances. *The royal bee*
Payne, Sherry Neuwirth. *A contest*
Pearson, Susan. *Everybody knows that!*
Phillips, Tamara. *Day care ABC*
Pillar, Marjorie. *Join the band!*
Polacco, Patricia. *Thank you, Mr. Falker*
  Welcome Comfort
Polisar, Barry Louis. *The trouble with Ben*
Pomeranc, Marion Hess. *The can-do Thanksgiving*
Porte, Barbara Ann. *Harry's mom*
Poulin, Stéphane. *Can you catch Josephine?*
Powers, Mary E. *Our teacher's in a wheelchair*
Poydar, Nancy. *Busy Bea*
  Snip, snip . . . snow!
Price, Michelle. *Mean Melissa*
Priceman, Marjorie. *Emeline at the circus*
Pulver, Robin. *Axle Annie*
  Mrs. Toggle and the dinosaur
  Mrs. Toggle's beautiful blue shoe
  Mrs. Toggle's zipper
  Nobody's mother is in second grade
Rabe, Berniece. *The balancing girl*
Rathmann, Peggy. *Officer Buckle and Gloria*
  Ruby the copycat
Rayner, Mary. *Crocodarling*
Reiser, Lynn. *Earthdance*
Rider, Joanne. *First grade valentines*
Rockwell, Anne F. *Career day*
  Halloween day
  Show and tell day
  Thanksgiving Day
  When Hugo went to school
Rockwell, Harlow. *My nursery school*
Rogers, Fred. *Going to day care*
Rogers, Jacqueline. *Tiptoe into kindergarten*
Rosenberg, Maxine B. *My friend Leslie*
Ross, Pat. *Molly and the slow teeth*
Roth, Harold. *Nursery school*
Rowe, Jeanne A. *A trip through a school*
Rubel, Nicole. *Goldie's nap*
Ryder, Eileen. *Winklet goes to school*
Ryder, Joanne. *First grade ladybugs*
  Hello, first grade
Sadler, Marilyn. *Alistair's time machine*
Saltzberg, Barney. *Phoebe and the spelling bee*
Schertle, Alice. *Jeremy Bean's St. Patrick's Day*
Schick, Eleanor. *The little school at Cottonwood Corners*
Schomp, Virginia. *If you were a . . . teacher*
Selsam, Millicent E. *More potatoes!*
Senisi, Ellen B. *Hurray for pre-K!*
  Just kids
  Kindergarten kids
Shannon, David. *David goes to school*
Sheldon, Dyan. *Unicorn dreams*
Shields, Carol Diggory. *Lunch money and other poems about school*
Shipton, Jonathan. *No biting, horrible crocodile!*
Sierra, Judy. *There's a zoo in room 22*
Simms, Laura. *Rotten teeth*
Simon, Charnan. *Show-and-tell Sam*
Simon, Francesca. *Spider school*
Simon, Norma. *I'm busy, too*

What do I do?
What do I say?
Singer, Marilyn. *All we needed to say*
Smath, Jerry. *Elephant goes to school*
Solomon, Chuck. *Moving up from kindergarten to first grade*
Spier, Peter. *My school*
Spurr, Elizabeth. *Mrs. Minetta's car pool*
Stanley, Diane. *The good-luck pencil*
Staunton, Ted. *Taking care of Crumley*
Steptoe, John. *Creativity*
  Jeffrey Bear cleans up his act
Stevens, Carla. *Pig and the blue flag*
Stoeke, Janet Morgan. *Minerva Louise at school*
Sundvall, Viveca. *Mimi and the biscuit factory*
Surat, Michele Maria. *Angel child, dragon child*
Sutherland, Colleen. *Jason goes to show-and-tell*
Teague, Mark. *The Lost and found*
  The secret shortcut
Thayer, Jane. *Gus was a real dumb ghost*
Tidd, Louise Vitellaro. *I'll do it later*
Topek, Susan Remick. *A costume for Noah*
Tryon, Leslie. *Albert's alphabet*
Turner, Gwenda. *Playbook*
Tyler, Linda Wagner. *Waiting for mom*
Udry, Janice May. *What Mary Jo shared*
Valens, Amy. *Jesse's day care*
Vigna, Judith. *Anyhow, I'm glad I tried*
Watson, Clyde. *Hickory stick rag*
Weiss, Leatie. *My teacher sleeps in school*
Welch, Willy. *Grumpy Bunnies*
Wells, Rosemary. *First tomato*
  Yoko
Whitcomb, Mary E. *Odd Velvet*
White, Florence Meiman. *How to lose your lunch money*
White, Paul. *Janet at school*
Whitney, Alma Marshak. *Just awful*
Wick, Walter. *I spy school days*
Wiesner, David. *Sector 7*
Williams, Barbara. *Donna Jean's disaster*
Willis, Jeanne. *The long blue blazer*
Willis, Val. *The mystery in the bottle*
  The secret in the matchbox
Wing, Natasha. *Jalapeño bagels*
Winthrop, Elizabeth. *Tough Eddie*
Wiseman, Bernard. *Tails are not for painting*
Wittman, Sally. *The boy who hated Valentine's Day*
  The wonderful Mrs. Trumbly
Wolff, Patricia Rae. *The toll-bridge troll*
Woodruff, Elvira. *Show and tell*
Yashima, Taro. *Crow boy*
Zimelman, Nathan. *How the second grade got $8,205.50 to visit the Statue of Liberty*

School – first day

Ahlberg, Janet. *Starting school*
Alexander, Martha G. *Sabrina*
Anholt, Laurence. *Billy and the big new school*
Begaye, Lisa Shook. *Building a bridge*
Berenstain, Stan. *The Berenstain bears go to school*
Blue, Rose. *I am here*
Boelts, Maribeth. *Little Bunny's preschool countdown*
Bram, Elizabeth. *I don't want to go to school*
Brandenberg, Franz. *Six new students*
Breinburg, Petronella. *Shawn goes to school*
Bruna, Dick. *Miffy goes to school*
Calmenson, Stephanie. *The kindergarten book*

Carlson, Nancy L. *Look out kindergarten, here I come!*
Cazet, Denys. *Born in the gravy*
   Never spit on your shoes
Charlton, Nancy Lee. *Derek's dog days*
Chorao, Kay. *Molly's lies*
Clarke, Gus. *Eddie and Teddy*
Cohen, Miriam. *Will I have a friend?*
Coles, Alison. *Michael's first day*
Cooney, Nancy Evans. *The blanket that had to go*
Coontz, Otto. *A real class clown*
Delton, Judy. *My mom made me go to school*
   The new girl at school
Flood, Bo. *I'll go to school if . . .*
Gantos, Jack (John, Jr.). *Back to school for Rotten Ralph*
Goodall, John S. *Naughty Nancy goes to school*
Hains, Harriet. *My new school*
Hamilton-Merritt, Jane. *My first days of school*
Hautzig, Deborah. *Little Witch goes to school*
Henkes, Kevin. *Jessica*
Hest, Amy. *Off to school, Baby Duck*
Hill, Eric. *Spot goes to school*
Hillman, Priscilla. *The Merry-Mouse schoolhouse*
Howe, James. *When you go to kindergarten*
Jenkin-Pearce, Susie. *Bad Boris goes to school*
Johnston, Tony. *Sparky and Eddie, the first day of school*
Kantrowitz, Mildred. *Willy Bear*
Keller, Holly. *Harry and Tuck*
Kirk, David. *Little Miss Spider at Sunny Patch School*
Krementz, Jill. *Katharine goes to nursery school*
Langreuter, Jutta. *Little Bear goes to kindergarten*
Lasker, Joe. *Nick joins in*
Lasky, Kathryn. *Lunch bunnies*
Leonard, Marcia. *Hannah the hamster hunter*
Lester, Mike. *A is for salad*
London, Jonathan. *Froggy goes to school*
MacDonald, Maryann. *Little Hippo starts school*
McMahon, Patricia. *Listen for the bus*
McQuade, Jacqueline. *At preschool with Teddy Bear*
Meredith, Carol. *Jamie Anderson wouldn't . . .*
Musgrave, Susan. *Dreams are more real than bathtubs*
Novak, Matt. *Jazzbo goes to school*
Oxenbury, Helen. *First day of school*
Poydar, Nancy. *First day, hooray!*
Quackenbush, Robert M. *First grade jitters*
Riddell, Edwina. *My first day at preschool*
Rosenberry, Vera. *Vera's first day of school*
Schaefer, Charles E. *Cat's got your tongue?*
Schwartz, Amy. *Annabelle Swift, kindergartner*
Schweninger, Ann. *Off to school!*
Sellers, Ronnie. *My first day at school*
Sharmat, Mitchell. *Sherman is a slowpoke*
Slate, Joseph. *Miss Bindergarten gets ready for kindergarten*
Smalls-Hector, Irene. *Beginning school*
Steel, Danielle. *Martha's new school*
Stein, Sara Bonnett. *A child goes to school*
Stevenson, James. *That dreadful day*
Tompert, Ann. *Will you come back for me?*
Turner, Ethel. *Walking to school*
Warren, Cathy. *Fred's first day*
Watts, Marjorie-Ann. *Zebra goes to school*
Weiss, Nicki. *Barney is big*
Wells, Rosemary. *Emily's first 100 days of school*
   Timothy goes to school
Wild, Margaret. *Tom goes to kindergarten*
Wolde, Gunilla. *Betsy's first day at nursery school*
Wolf, Bernard. *Adam Smith goes to school*

School principals *see* Careers – school principals

Science

Abisch, Roz. *Let's find out about butterflies*
Adler, David A. *Redwoods are the tallest trees in the world*
Aliki. *Corn is maize*
   Digging up dinosaurs
   Dinosaurs are different
   Fossils tell of long ago
   The long lost coelacanth and other living fossils
   My feet
   My hands
   My visit to the dinosaurs
   A weed is a flower
   Wild and woolly mammoths
Allen, Gertrude E. *Everyday animals*
Allen, Martha Dickson. *Real life monsters*
Allen, Pamela. *Mr. Archimedes' bath*
   Who sank the boat?
Allington, Richard L. *Science*
   Talking
Anderson, Lucia Z. *The smallest life around us*
Andry, Andrew C. *How babies are made*
Annixter, Jane. *Brown rats, black rats*
Applebaum, Stan. *Going my way?*
Appleby, Leonard G. *Snakes*
Ariane. *Small Cloud*
Arnold, Caroline. *The biggest living thing*
   Five nests
   Sun fun
Arnosky, Jim. *All about deer*
   Crinkleroot's guide to knowing butterflies and moths
Aruego, José. *Symbiosis*
Arvetis, Chris. *Why does it fly?*
   Why is it dark?
Asimov, Isaac. *The best new thing*
   The moon
Back, Christine. *Bean and plant*
   Chicken and egg
   Spider's web
   Tadpole and frog
Bailey, Jill. *The life cycle of a spider*
Baker, Gayle. *Special delivery*
Baker, Jeannie. *One hungry spider*
Baker, Jeffrey J. W. *Patterns of nature*
Balestrino, Philip. *Hot as an ice cube*
   The skeleton inside you
Balian, Lorna. *Where in the world is Henry?*
Bancroft, Henrietta. *Animals in winter*
Baran, Tancy. *Bees*
Barner, Bob. *Elephant facts*
Barrett, Norman S. *Spiders*
Bartlett, Margaret Farrington. *The clean brook*
   Down the mountain
   Where the brook begins
Bason, Lillian. *Castles and mirrors and cities of sand*
   Spiders
Batherman, Muriel. *Animals live here*
Baylor, Byrd. *If you are a hunter of fossils*
Behrens, June. *Whales of the world*
   Whalewatch!
Bendick, Jeanne. *All around you*
   What made you you?
   Why can't I?
Berenstain, Stan. *The Berenstain bears' science fair*
Berger, Melvin. *Early humans*

Davies, Kay. *My apple*
  My balloon
  My drum
  My mirror
DeLuise, Dom. *Charlie the caterpillar*
Dietl, Ulla. *The plant-and-grow project book*
Dobson, David. *Can we save them?*
Dodd, Lynley. *The smallest turtle*
Dorros, Arthur. *Ant cities*
  Follow the water from brook to ocean
Eastman, David. *What is a fish?*
Eastman, Patricia. *Sometimes things change*
Engdahl, Sylvia. *Our world is earth*
Engelbrektson, Sune. *Gravity at work and play*
  The sun is a star
Fischer, Vera Kistiakowsky. *One way is down*
Fischer-Nagel, Heiderose. *A kitten is born*
  A puppy is born
Fisher, Aileen Lucia. *And a sunflower grew*
  As the leaves fall down
  Like nothing at all
  Mysteries in the garden
  Now that spring is here
  Petals yellow and petals red
  Plant magic
  Prize performance
  Seeds on the go
  Swords and daggers
Florian, Douglas. *A bird can fly*
Flower, Phyllis. *Barn owl*
Fowler, Allan. *Cubs and colts and calves and kittens*
  So that's how the moon changes shape!
  Spiders are not insects
  What do you see in a cloud?
Freedman, Russell. *Hanging on*
  Tooth and claw
  When winter comes
Freeman, Mae Blacker. *The sun, the moon and the stars*
Freschet, Berniece. *Bear mouse*
  The little woodcock
  Moose baby
  Wood duck baby
Friskey, Margaret (Margaret Richards). *Birds we know*
Frith, Michael K. *Some of us walk, some fly, some swim*
Gans, Roma. *Rock collecting*
  When birds change their feathers
Gelman, Rita Golden. *A koala grows up*
George, Jean Craighead. *All upon a stone*
Gibbons, Gail. *From seed to plant*
  Monarch butterfly
  Prehistoric animals
  Sharks
  Soaring with the wind
  Sun up, sun down
Girard, Linda Walvoord. *You were born on your very first birthday*
Glaser, Linda. *Wonderful worms*
Goldin, Augusta. *Ducks don't get wet*
  Salt
  The shape of water
  Spider silk
  Straight hair, curly hair
  Where does your garden grow?
Gore, Sheila. *My shadow*
Graeber, Jean B. *Bantie and her chicks*
Granowsky, Alvin. *The dinosaurs' last days*
  Meat-eating dinosaurs

Gross, Ruth Belov. *Alligators and other crocodilians*
Grosvenor, Donna. *Pandas*
Haines, Gail Kay. *Fire*
Hamberger, John. *The day the sun disappeared*
Hariton, Anca. *Butterfly story*
Harris, Louise Dyer. *Flash, the life of a firefly*
Harris, Susan. *Creatures that look alike*
  Reptiles
Hawes, Judy. *Fireflies in the night*
  Ladybug, ladybug, fly away home
  Shrimps
  Spring peepers
  Watch honeybees with me
  Why frogs are wet
Hawkinson, Lucy (Ozone). *Birds in the sky*
Heiligman, Deborah. *From caterpillar to butterfly*
Heller, Ruth. *Chickens aren't the only ones*
Hirschi, Ron. *What is a bird?*
  Where do birds live?
  Who lives in . . . Alligator Swamp?
Hirst, Robin. *My place in space*
Hoffman, Mary. *Animals in the wild: elephant*
  Animals in the wild: monkey
  Animals in the wild: panda
  Animals in the wild: tiger
Hogan, Paula Z. *The black swan*
  The butterfly
  The dandelion
  The frog
  The honeybee
  The oak tree
  The penguin
  The salmon
Holmes, Anita. *The 100-year-old cactus*
  House mouse
Howell, Ruth. *Splash and flow*
Hurd, Edith Thacher. *Look for a bird*
  The mother kangaroo
  Sandpipers
  Starfish
Isenbart, Hans-Heinrich. *A duckling is born*
Jackson, Jacqueline. *Chicken ten thousand*
Jenkins, Priscilla Belz. *A nest full of eggs*
Johnston, Johanna. *Penguin's way*
  Whale's way
Johnston, Tony. *Sparky and Eddie, trouble with bugs*
  Sparky and Eddie, trouble with rats
Jolliffe, Anne. *From pots to plastics*
  Water, wind and wheels
Jones, Brian. *Space*
Jordan, Helene J. (Helene Jamieson). *How a seed grows*
Justice, Jennifer. *The tiger*
Kaizuki, Kiyonori. *A calf is born*
Kalas, Sybille. *The beaver family book*
Kane, Henry B. *Wings, legs, or fins*
Kaufmann, John. *Birds are flying*
  Flying giants of long ago
Kelly, Irene. *Ebbie and Flo*
Kirkpatrick, Rena K. *Leaves*
  Look at flowers
  Magnets
  Pond life
  Rainbow colors
  Seeds and weeds
  Trees
  Weather
Knight, David C. *Dinosaur days*
Komori, Atsushi. *Animal mothers*

Krupinski, Loretta. *Into the woods*
Krupp, E. C. *The comet and you*
Kuchalla, Susan. *All about seeds*
Kumin, Maxine W. *Eggs of things*
Landshoff, Ursula. *Cats are good company*
Lane, Margaret. *The frog*
   The squirrel
Lasky, Kathryn. *Science fair bunnies*
Lauber, Patricia. *Be a friend to trees*
   How we learned the earth is round
   Snakes are hunters
   What's hatching out of that egg?
   Who eats what?
Leach, Michael. *Rabbits*
Legg, Gerald. *From egg to chicken*
   From seed to sunflower
Lehn, Barbara. *What is a scientist?*
Leutscher, Alfred. *Earth*
   Water
Lewis, Naomi. *Swan*
Lilly, Kenneth. *Animal builders*
   Animal climbers
   Animal jumpers
   Animal runners
   Animal swimmers
Lloyd, David. *Air*
Locker, Thomas. *Sky tree*
Mabey, Richard. *Oak and company*
McCauley, Jane R. *Baby birds and how they grow*
McClung, Robert. *How animals hide*
   Sphinx
McKeever, Katherine. *A family for Minerva*
McMillan, Bruce. *Counting wildflowers*
McNulty, Faith. *Woodchuck*
Madgwick, Wendy. *Up in the air*
   Water play
Maestro, Betsy. *How do apples grow?*
   Why do leaves change color?
Mainwaring, Jane. *My feather*
Marzollo, Jean. *I'm a caterpillar*
May, Charles Paul. *High-noon rocket*
Merrill, Jean. *The girl who loved caterpillars*
Meshover, Leonard. *The guinea pigs that went to
   school*
   The monkey that went to school
Meyers, Susan. *The truth about gorillas*
Michels, Tilde. *At the frog pond*
Milgrom, Harry. *Egg-ventures*
Miller, Edna. *Jumping bean*
Miller, Judith Ransom. *Nabob and the geranium*
Millhouse, Nicholas. *Blue-footed booby*
Mitgutsch, Ali. *From gold to money*
   From graphite to pencil
   From sea to salt
   From swamp to coal
Moché, Dinah L. *The astronauts*
Moseley, Keith. *Dinosaurs*
Most, Bernard. *Where to look for a dinosaur*
Newton, James R. *A forest is reborn*
   Forest log
Oleson, Jens. *Snail*
Oxford Scientific Films. *Grey squirrel*
   The spider's web
Palazzo-Craig, Janet. *Our friend the sun*
   Turtles
Parish, Peggy. *Dinosaur time*
Parker, Nancy Winslow. *Bugs*
Parsons, Alexandra. *Amazing birds*
   Amazing mammals

Amazing snakes
Amazing spiders
Pascoe, Gwen. *Deep in a rainforest*
Patterson, Elizabeth Burman. *Whose eyes are these?*
Penner, Lucille Recht. *Dinosaur babies*
   Monster bugs
Penrose, Gordon. *More science surprises from Dr. Zed*
Peters, Lisa Westberg. *The sun, the wind and the rain*
   Water's way
Pfeffer, Wendy. *From tadpole to frog*
Pluckrose, Henry Arthur. *Ants*
   Bears
   Bees and wasps
   Butterflies and moths
   Elephants
   Floating and sinking
   Horses
   Hot and cold
   Reptiles
   Whales
Polacco, Patricia. *Meteor!*
Posada, Mia. *Dandelions, stars in the grass*
Pouyanne, Rési. *What I see hidden by the pond*
Powzyk, Joyce Ann. *Tasmania*
Pursell, Margaret Sanford. *A look at birth*
   Polly the guinea pig
   Shelley the sea gull
   Sprig the tree frog
Rabinowitz, Sandy. *What's happening to Daisy?*
Relf, Patricia. *The magic school bus plants seeds*
Richards, Jane. *A horse grows up*
Rockwell, Anne F. *One bean*
Russell, Solveig Paulson. *What good is a tail?*
Ryder, Joanne. *Fireflies*
   Rainbow wings
   Snail in the woods
   The spiders dance
   Where butterflies grow
Sadler, Marilyn. *Alistair's time machine*
Samson, Suzanne M. *Fairy dusters and blazing stars*
Sandeman, Anna. *Skin, teeth, and hair*
Schilling, Betty. *Two kittens are born*
Schlein, Miriam. *Lucky porcupine!*
   What's wrong with being a skunk?
Schmid, Eleonore. *The water's journey*
Schneider, Herman. *Follow the sunset*
Schoberle, Ceile. *Beyond the Milky Way*
Schulz, Charles M. *Snoopy's facts and fun book about
   nature*
Schwartz, David M. *If you hopped like a frog*
Selberg, Ingrid. *Nature's hidden world*
Selsam, Millicent E. *All kinds of babies*
   Egg to chick
   A first look at bird nests
   A first look at caterpillars
   A first look at cats
   A first look at flowers
   *A first look at kangaroos, koalas and other animals
      with pouches*
   A first look at monkeys
   A first look at owls, eagles and other hunters of the sky
   A first look at rocks
   A first look at seashells
   A first look at sharks
   A first look at spiders
   A first look at the world of plants
   A first look at whales
   How kittens grow
   How puppies grow

Is this a baby dinosaur?
More potatoes!
Seeds and more seeds
Where do they go? Insects in winter
Seymour, Peter S. *How the weather works*
What's in the deep blue sea?
What's in the prehistoric forest?
Shapp, Martha. *Let's find out about babies*
Shaw, Evelyn S. *Alligator*
Fish out of school
Nest of wood ducks
Octopus
Sea otters
Sheehan, Angela. *The beaver*
The duck
The otter
The penguin
Sheffield, Margaret. *Before you were born*
Where do babies come from?
Showers, Paul. *Before you were a baby*
A drop of blood
Ears are for hearing
Look at your eyes
No measles, no mumps for me
Sleep is for everyone
Where does the garbage go?
You can't make a move without your muscles
Silverman, Maida. *Dinosaur babies*
Simon, Seymour. *Beneath your feet*
Icebergs and glaciers
Stecher, Miriam B. *Max, the music-maker*
Steig, William. *The toy brother*
Stein, Sara Bonnett. *Cat*
Mouse
Strange, Florence. *Rock-a-bye whale*
Sugita, Yutaka. *The flower family*
Thompson, Susan L. *Diary of a monarch butterfly*
Toft, Kim Michelle. *Neptune's nursery*
Townsend, Anita. *The kangaroo*
Tresselt, Alvin R. *How far is far?*
Rain drop splash
Van Woerkom, Dorothy. *Hidden messages*
Vasiliu, Mircea. *A day at the beach*
Vyner, Sue. *The stolen egg*
Wandelmaier, Roy. *Stars*
Watts, Barrie. *Apple tree*
Bird's nest
Butterfly and caterpillar
Dandelion
Hamster
Ladybug
Mushrooms
Rabbit
Tomato
Webb, Angela. *Talkabout air*
Talkabout light
Talkabout reflections
Talkabout sand
Talkabout soil
Talkabout sound
Talkabout water
Wexler, Jerome (LeRoy). *Flowers, fruits, seeds*
Wonderful pussy willows
Williams, Gweneira Maureen. *Timid Timothy, the kitten who learned to be brave*
Wilson, Ron. *Mice*
Wilson-Max, Ken. *Max loves sunflowers*
Wong, Herbert H. *My goldfish*
My ladybug

My plant
Our caterpillars
Our earthworms
Our tree
Wyler, Rose. *Puddles and ponds*
Raindrops and rainbows
The starry sky
Yabuuchi, Masayuki. *Animals sleeping*
Yolen, Jane. *Welcome to the icehouse*
Zallinger, Peter. *Dinosaurs*
Ziefert, Harriet. *Getting ready for new baby*
Zoehfeld, Kathleen Weidner. *How mountains are made*
What lives in a shell?
What's alive?
Zoll, Max Alfred. *A flamingo is born*

Scientists *see* Careers – scientists

Scotland *see* Foreign lands – Scotland

Scuba diving *see* Sports – skin diving

Sea and seashore

Agell, Charlotte. *The sailor's book*
Albert, Burton. *Where does the trail lead?*
Alexander, Sally Hobart. *Sarah's surprise*
Aliki. *Those summers*
Allen, Laura Jean. *Ottie and the star*
Allen, Pamela. *Hidden treasure*
Amoss, Berthe. *Old Hannibal and the hurricane*
Anderson, Lena. *Stina*
Andrews, Jan. *Very last first time*
Anrooy, Frans van. *The sea horse*
Apperley, Dawn. *In the sand*
Ardizzone, Edward. *Little Tim and the brave sea captain*
Peter the wanderer
Ship's cook Ginger
Tim all alone
Tim and Charlotte
Tim and Ginger
Tim and Lucy go to sea
Tim in danger
Tim to the rescue
Tim's friend Towser
Tim's last voyage
Arnold, Caroline. *A walk by the seashore*
A walk on the Great Barrier Reef
Asch, Frank. *Sand cake*
Starbaby
Axelrod, Amy. *Pigs on a blanket*
Bang, Molly. *Yellow ball*
Barber, Antonia. *The mousehole cat*
Bare, Colleen Stanley. *Elephants on the beach*
Barklem, Jill. *Sea story*
Bat-Ami, Miriam. *Sea, salt, and air*
Bate, Norman. *What a wonderful machine is a submarine*
Baum, Susan. *The beach*
Bennett, Rainey. *The secret hiding place*
Bentley, Anne. *The Groggs have a wonderful summer*
Berger, Melvin. *Oil spill!*
Bernhard, Emery. *The way of the willow branch*
Biro, Val. *Gumdrop floats away*
Bishop, Gavin. *Little Rabbit and the sea*
Blake, Quentin. *Mrs. Armitage and the big wave*

Blake, Robert J. *Spray*
Blance, Ellen. *Monster goes to the beach*
Blathwayt, Benedict. *The runaway train*
Bond, Michael. *Paddington at the seaside*
Bonsall, Crosby Newell. *Mine's the best*
Booth, Eugene. *Under the ocean*
Bornstein, Ruth Lercher. *A beautiful seashell*
Boyle, Doe. *Otter on his own*
Brady, Kimberley Smith. *Keeper for the sea*
Bright, Robert. *Georgie and the noisy ghost*
Brown, Marc Tolon. *D. W. all wet*
Brown, Margaret Wise. *The seashore noisy book*
Bruna, Dick. *Miffy at the beach*
    Miffy at the seaside
Brutschy, Jennifer. *Celeste and Crabapple Sam*
Buchanan, Heather S. *Emily Mouse's beach house*
    George Mouse's covered wagon
Bundey, Nikki. *In the water*
Bunting, Eve (Anne Evelyn). *Demetrius and the golden goblet*
Burdett, Lois. *Twelfth night*
Burningham, John. *Come away from the water, Shirley*
Bush, Timothy. *Three at sea*
Butler, Andrea. *Mr. Sun and Mr. Sea*
Calhoun, Mary. *Henry the sailor cat*
Calmenson, Stephanie. *Hotter than a hot dog!*
Carle, Eric. *A house for Hermit Crab*
Carlstrom, Nancy White. *Swim the silver sea, Joshie Otter*
Carmichael, Clay. *Bear at the beach*
Carrick, Carol. *Beach bird*
Carter, Debby L. *Clipper*
Cohen, Caron Lee. *Whiffle Squeek*
Cohen, Miriam. *See you in second grade!*
Cole, Babette. *The trouble with Uncle*
Cole, Joanna. *The magic school bus on the ocean floor*
Cole, Sheila. *When the tide is low*
Coles, Alison. *Michael and the sea*
Collicott, Sharleen. *Seeing stars*
Condra, Estelle. *See the ocean*
Conrad, Pam. *The lost sailor*
Cooney, Barbara. *Hattie and the wild waves*
Coplans, Peta. *Cat and dog*
Corney, Estelle. *Pa's top hat*
Cote, Nancy. *Flip-flops*
Cousins, Lucy. *Za-Za's baby brother*
Cousteau Society. *Albatross*
    Dolphins
    Manatees
    Otters
    Penguins
    Seals
    Turtles
    Whales
Cowan, Catherine. *My life with the wave*
Craig, Helen. *Charlie and Tyler at the seashore*
Crane, Alan. *Pepita bonita*
Daly, Niki. *The boy on the beach*
    Why the sun and moon live in the sky
Damjan, Mischa. *The little sea horse*
Darling, Kathy (Mary Kathleen). *Seashore babies*
Davidson, Amanda. *Teddy at the seashore*
Davies, Nicola. *Big blue whale*
Decker, Dorothy W. *Stripe and the merbear*
Demarest, Chris L. *My blue boat*
    Summer
Denton, Terry. *Home is the sailor*
De Paola, Tomie (Thomas Anthony). *Katie and Kit at the beach*

DeRubertis, Barbara. *Columbus Day*
DeSaix, Frank. *The girl who danced with dolphins*
Dexter, Alison. *Grandma*
Dickens, Lucy. *At the beach*
Dodd, Anne Westcott. *The story of the sea glass*
Dodd, Lynley. *The smallest turtle*
Domanska, Janina. *If all the seas were one sea*
Donnelly, Liza. *Dinosaur beach*
Dos Santos, Joyce Audy. *Sand dollar, sand dollar*
Doubilet, Anne. *Under the sea from A to Z*
Drummond, Allan. *Moby Dick*
Dunbar, Joyce. *The sand children*
Dunphy, Madeleine. *Here is the coral reef*
Dupasquier, Philippe. *Dear Daddy . . .*
    Jack at sea
Dyke, John. *Pigwig and the pirates*
Ehrlich, H. M. *Louie's goose*
Enderle, Judith (Ann) Ross. *Six sandy sheep*
Esbensen, Barbara Juster. *Sponges are skeletons*
Farber, Norma. *I swim an ocean in my sleep*
Faulkner, Keith. *Sam at the seaside*
Field, Eugene. *Wynken, Blynken and Nod*, ill. by Barbara Cooney
    Wynken, Blynken and Nod, ill. by Susan Jeffers
    Wynken, Blynken and Nod, ill. by Holly Johnson
    Wynken, Blynken and Nod, ill. by Johanna Westerman
Florian, Douglas. *Beach day*
    In the swim
Foreman, Michael. *Jack's fantastic voyage*
    One world
    Seal surfer
Fowler, Allan. *The biggest animal ever*
    Friendly dolphins
Francia, Silvia. *Roberta's vacation*
Frasier, Debra. *Out of the ocean*
Freeman, Don. *Come again, pelican*
French, Vivian. *Whale journey*
    Why the sea is salt
Garelick, May. *Down to the beach*
Garland, Sherry. *Summer sands*
Gay, Michel. *Little auto*
Gebert, Warren. *The old ball and the sea*
Gedin, Birgitta. *The little house from the sea*
George, Jean Craighead. *The wentletrap trap*
Gerrard, Jean. *Matilda Jane*
Gerrard, Roy. *Sir Francis Drake*
Ginsburg, Mirra. *Four brave sailors*
Goodall, John S. *Paddy under water*
Gordon, Sharon. *Dolphins and porpoises*
Goudey, Alice E. *Houses from the sea*
Graham, Bob. *Greetings from Sandy Beach*
Greenberg, Melanie Hope. *At the beach*
Gretz, Susanna. *Teddy bears at the seaside*
Grindley, Sally. *A flag for Grandma*
    Peter's place
Guiberson, Brenda Z. *Into the sea*
    Lobster boat
Haas, Irene. *The Maggie B*
Halak, Glenn. *A grandmother's story*
Haley, Gail E. *Sea tale*
Hallinan, P. K. (Patrick K.). *Three freckles past a hair*
Hänel, Wolfram. *Mia the beach cat*
Hanze. *Yann and the whale*
Harrison, Troon. *Don't dig so deep, Nicholas!*
Hautzig, Deborah. *Big Bird at the beach*
Hayles, Karen. *What is stuck*
Helldorfer, M. C. (Mary Claire). *Harmonica night*
Hellen, Nancy. *Creatures of the ocean*

Pryor, Bonnie. *Lottie's dream*
Quinlan, Patricia. *Emma's sea journey*
Rand, Gloria. *Aloha, Salty!*
  Salty sails north
Ray, Deborah Kogan. *Fog drift morning*
Reiser, Lynn. *Little clam*
Richardson, Judith Benét. *The way home*
Robbins, Ken. *Beach days*
Roberts, Sarah. *I want to go home!*
Rockwell, Anne F. *At the beach*
  Ferryboat ride!
  The storm
Rodgers, Richard. *A real nice clambake*
Roffey, Maureen. *I spy on vacation*
Root, Phyllis. *Sam, who was swallowed by a shark*
Round, Graham. *Hangdog*
Rowinski, Kate. *L. L. Bear's island adventure*
Royston, Angela. *Sea animals*
  Shells
Russ, Lavinia. *Alec's sand castle*
Russo, Susan. *The ice cream ocean and other delectable poems of the sea*
Ryder, Joanne. *Beach party*
  A house by the sea
  A wet and sandy day
Rylant, Cynthia. *The whales*
Samton, Sheila White. *Beside the bay*
San Souci, Robert D. *Brave Margaret*
  Nicholas Pipe
Schlein, Miriam. *The sun, the wind, the sea and the rain*
Schulz, Charles M. *Snoopy's facts and fun book about seashores*
Schumacher, Claire. *Alto and Tango*
Schweninger, Ann. *Summertime*
The Sea World alphabet book
Seaside poems
Selby, Jennifer. *Beach bunny*
Selsam, Millicent E. *A first look at seashells*
  Sea monsters of long ago
Seymour, Peter S. *What lives in the sea?*
  What's at the beach?
  What's in the deep blue sea?
Sharratt, Nick. *Look what I found!*
  Mrs. Pirate
Shaw, Alison. *Until I saw the sea*
Shaw, Evelyn S. *Fish out of school*
  Octopus
Shea, Pegi Deitz. *Bungalow fungalow*
Shepard, Aaron. *The sea king's daughter*
Simmons, Jane. *Ebb and Flo and the greedy gulls*
Simon, Mina Lewiton. *Is anyone here?*
Sis, Peter. *Beach ball*
  An ocean world
  Ship ahoy!
Slawski, Wolfgang. *Captain Jonathan sails the sea*
Slobodkin, Louis. *The seaweed hat*
Smith, Raymond Kenneth. *The long dive*
Smith, Theresa Kalab. *The fog is secret*
Spooner, J. B. *The story of the little Black Dog*
Stadler, John. *One seal*
Stafford, Kim Robert. *We got here together*
Steiner, Barbara (Annette). *The whale brother*
Steiner, Charlotte. *Listen to my seashell*
Stevenson, James. *Clams can't sing*
  July
  Which one is Whitney?
Stevenson, Jocelyn. *Jim Henson's Muppets at sea*
Stevenson, Robert Louis. *Block city*

Stock, Catherine. *Sophie's bucket*
Strahl, Rudi. *Sandman in the lighthouse*
Straker, Joan Ann. *Animals that live in the sea*
Strauss, Susan. *When woman became the sea*
Tamar, Erika. *Donnatalee*
Tate, Suzanne. *Crabby's water wish*
Taylor, Mark. *The bold fisherman*
Thaxter, Celia. *Celia's island journal*
Thompson, Brenda. *The winds that blow*
Thompson, Richard. *Gurgle, bubble, splash*
Titherington, Jeanne. *Baby's boat*
  Baby's boat, a board book
Tobias, Tobi. *At the beach*
Toft, Kim Michelle. *Neptune's nursery*
Tokuda, Wendy. *Humphrey the lost whale*
Tomlinson, Theresa. *Little stowaway*
Tresselt, Alvin R. *Hide and seek fog*
  I saw the sea come in
Trimble, Marcia. *Malinda Martha and her stepping stones*
Tucker, Kathy. *Do pirates take baths?*
Turbak, Gary. *Ocean animals in danger*
Turkle, Brinton. *Do not open*
  Obadiah the Bold
  The sky dog
Turnbull, Ann. *The sand horse*
Ungerer, Tomi. *The Mellops go diving for treasure*
Vasiliu, Mircea. *A day at the beach*
Vaughan, Marcia Kapok. *Abbie against the storm*
Vernon, Tannis. *Little Pig and the blue-green sea*
Vinson, Pauline. *Willie goes to the seashore*
Vullo, Vera. *About things you find at the beach*
Waber, Bernard. *I was all thumbs*
Waddell, Martin. *The big big sea*
  Sailor Bear
Wahl, Jan. *The adventures of Underwater Dog*
Ward, Jennifer. *Somewhere in the ocean*
Waters, Tony. *Sailor's bride*
Watson, Nancy Dingman. *When is tomorrow?*
The weekend
Wegen, Ron. *Sand castle*
Weiss, Nicki. *Sun sand sea sail*
Weller, Frances Ward. *Madaket Millie*
  Riptide
Whittle, Emily. *Sailor cats*
Wild, Margaret. *The queen's holiday*
Willard, Nancy. *The voyage of the Ludgate Hill*
Windham, Sophie. *Down in the marvelous deep*
Winton, Tim. *The deep*
Wolfson, Margaret. *Turtle songs*
Wood, Jakki. *Across the big blue sea*
Wood, John Norris. *Oceans*
Woolaver, Lance. *From Ben Loman to the sea*
Yamashita, Haruo. *Mice at the beach*
Yashima, Taro. *Seashore story*
Yee, Brenda Shannon. *Sand castle*
Yektai, Niki. *Bears at the beach*
Young, Ruth. *Daisy's taxi*
Zeman, Ludmila. *Sinbad*
Ziefert, Harriet. *A dozen dogs*
  Good night, Jessie!
  Keeping daddy awake on the way home from the beach
Zoehfeld, Kathleen Weidner. *Great white shark, ruler of the sea*
  What lives in a shell?
Zolotow, Charlotte (Shapiro). *The seashore book*

Sea lions *see* Animals – sea lions

Sea serpents *see* Monsters; Mythical creatures

Seagulls *see* Birds – seagulls

Seahorses *see* Crustaceans

Seals *see* Animals – seals

Seamstresses *see* Careers – seamstresses

Seashore *see* Sea and seashore

Seasons

Adoff, Arnold. *In for winter, out for spring*
All year round
Anholt, Catherine. *Sun, snow, stars, sky*
Anno, Mitsumasa. *Anno's counting book*
Appelt, Kathi. *A red wagon year*
Arnosky, Jim. *Outdoors on foot*
Barker, Cicely Mary. *Flower fairies of the seasons*
Bartels, Alice L. *The beast*
Beskow, Elsa Maartman. *Children of the forest*
Birnbaum, Abe. *Green eyes*
Blegvad, Erik. *Burnie's hill*
Blocksma, Mary. *Apple tree! Apple tree!*
Borden, Louise. *Caps, hats, socks and mittens*
    The watching game
Bowen, Betsy. *Antler, bear, canoe*
Boyle, Doe. *Summer coat, winter coat*
Branley, Franklyn M. (Mansfield). *Sunshine makes the seasons*
Brown, Margaret Wise. *The little island*
Browne, Anthony. *Voices in the park*
Bruchac, Joseph. *Thirteen moons on turtle's back*
Bunting, Eve (Anne Evelyn). *Moonstick*
Burningham, John. *Seasons*
Calmenson, Stephanie. *My book of the seasons*
Carle, Eric. *The tiny seed*
Carlstrom, Nancy White. *How does the wind walk?*
    Midnight dance of the snowshoe hare
Carrick, Carol. *The old barn*
Charles, Donald. *Calico Cat's year*
Chorao, Kay. *Little farm by the sea*
Clifton, Lucille. *Everett Anderson's year*
Cole, Joanna. *Big Goof and Little Goof*
Coleridge, Sara. *January brings the snow*
Curti, Anna. *Seasons*
De Paola, Tomie (Thomas Anthony). *Four stories for four seasons*
Derby, Sally. *My steps*
Desimini, Lisa. *My house*
Domanska, Janina. *Spring is*
Don't tell the scarecrow
Dow, Katharine. *My time of year*
Dragonwagon, Crescent. *Jemima remembers*
Drawson, Blair. *Mary Margaret's tree*
DuPasquier, Philippe. *Our house on the hill*
Duvoisin, Roger Antoine. *The house of four seasons*
Edens, Cooper. *A present for Rose*
Edwards, Richard. *Copy me, Copycub*
Ehlert, Lois. *Red leaf, yellow leaf*
Farjeon, Eleanor. *Around the seasons*
Fisher, Aileen Lucia. *As the leaves fall down*
    Going barefoot
    Like nothing at all
Fleming, Denise. *In the small, small pond*
Florian, Douglas. *A year in the country*

Foster, Doris Van Liew. *A pocketful of seasons*
Fowler, Susi Gregg. *When summer ends*
Fox, Charles Philip. *Mr. Stripes the gopher*
Gackenbach, Dick. *Ida Fanfanny*
Geisert, Bonnie. *Prairie town*
George, Jean Craighead. *Dear Rebecca, winter is here*
    Look to the north
George, Kristine O'Connell. *Old Elm speaks*
Gerstein, Mordicai. *Daisy's garden*
    The story of May
Gibbons, Gail. *Farming*
    The reasons for seasons
    The seasons of Arnold's apple tree
Ginsburg, Mirra. *The old man and his birds*
Goennel, Heidi. *Seasons*
Gomi, Taro. *Spring is here*
Good, Merle. *Amos and Susie*
Gray, Libba Moore. *My mama had a dancing heart*
Greydanus, Rose. *Changing seasons*
Grohmann, Susan. *The dust under Mrs. Merri-weather's bed*
Haley, Gail E. *Go away, stay away*
    The green man
Hall, Donald. *The ox-cart man*
Hall, Fergus. *Groundsel*
Hall, Zoe. *The apple pie tree*
Harris, Dorothy Joan. *Four seasons for Toby*
Hawkes, Kevin. *His Royal Buckliness*
Helldorfer, M. C. (Mary Claire). *Gather up, gather in*
Henderson, Kathy. *A year in the city*
Heyduck-Huth, Hilde. *The strawflower*
Hirschi, Ron. *Seya's song*
Hopkins, Lee Bennett. *Ring out, wild bells*
Horton, Barbara Savadge. *What comes in spring?*
Howell, Ruth. *Everything changes*
Howell, Will C. *I call it sky*
Hunter, Anne. *Possum's harvest moon*
Hurd, Edith Thacher. *The day the sun danced*
Hutton, Warwick. *Persephone*
Ichikawa, Satomi. *A child's book of seasons*
Iverson, Diane. *Discover the seasons*
Jacobs, Leland B. (Leland Blair). *Just around the corner*
Jauck, Andrea. *Assateague*
Johnston, Tony. *Once in the country*
    Yonder
Jordan, Sandra. *Christmas tree farm*
Kandoian, Ellen. *Molly's seasons*
Kelley, Marty. *Fall is not easy*
King-Smith, Dick. *Cuckoobush farm*
Kroll, Virginia L. *The seasons and someone*
Krull, Kathleen. *Songs of praise*
Krupp, Robin Rector. *Let's go traveling in Mexico*
Kwitz, Mary DeBall. *Mouse at home*
Leonard, Marcia. *Bear's busy year*
Lesser, Carolyn. *Great crystal bear*
    What a wonderful day to be a cow
Lewis, J. Patrick. *July is a mad mosquito*
Lewis, Naomi. *Leaves*
Lionni, Leo. *A busy year*
    Mouse days
    When?
Littlewood, Valerie. *The season clock*
Llewellyn, Claire. *My first book of time*
Lobel, Arnold. *Frog and Toad all year*
Locker, Thomas. *Sky tree*
London, Jonathan. *Park beat*
    What Newt could do for Turtle

Lotz, Karen E. *Can't sit still*
McDermott, Gerald. *Daughter of earth*
MacKinnon, Debbie. *The seasons*
Maestro, Betsy. *Through the year with Harriet*
Mangin, Marie-France. *Suzette and Nicholas and the seasons clock*
Manushkin, Fran. *The best toy of all*
Marshak, S. (Samuil). *The Month-Brothers*
Martin, Bill (William Ivan). *The turning of the year*
Miller, Edna. *Mousekin's fables*
Miller, Jane. *Seasons on the farm*
Miller, Moira. *The search for spring*
Moore, Christopher J. *Ishtar and Tammuz*
Mora, Emma. *Gideon, the little bear cub*
Muller, Gerda. *Around the oak*
  Circle of seasons
Muntean, Michaela. *Muppet babies through the year*
Murphy, Mary. *Here comes spring, and summer and fall and winter*
Nightingale, Sandy. *The witch's spell*
Oliver, Stephen. *Seasons*
Oppenheim, Joanne. *Have you seen trees?*, ill. by Irwin Rosenhouse
  Have you seen trees?, ill. by Jean and Mou-sien Tseng
Owen, Roy. *The ibis and the egret*
Pearson, Susan. *My favorite time of year*
Peters, Lisa Westberg. *Good morning, river!*
Pizer, Abigail. *Charlie the puppy*
  Hattie the goat
  Penelope pig
  Percy the duck
Provensen, Alice. *A book of seasons*
  The year at Maple Hill Farm
Roach, Marilynne K. *Dune fox*
Rockwell, Anne F. *Ducklings and pollywogs*
  First comes spring
Rosenberry, Vera. *Run, jump, whiz, splash*
Rucki, Ani. *When the Earth wakes*
Ryder, Joanne. *Under your feet*
Schulz, Charles M. *Snoopy's facts and fun book about seasons*
Shields, Carol Diggory. *Month by month a year goes round*
Siddals, Mary McKenna. *Tell me a season*
Silverman, Erica. *Warm in winter*
Simon, Norma. *Mama cat's year*
Smith, William Jay. *The sun is up*
Spohn, David. *Nate's treasure*
Stewart, Sarah. *The money tree*
Tafuri, Nancy. *Snowy flowy blowy*
Tresselt, Alvin R. *It's time now!*
  Johnny Maple-Leaf
Tudor, Tasha. *Around the year*
Udry, Janice May. *A tree is nice*
Verdet, Andre. *All about time*
Watts, Bernadette. *Tattercoats*
Weiss, Nicki. *On a hot, hot day*
Welber, Robert. *Song of the seasons*
Wellington, Anne. *Apple pie*
Wells, Rosemary. *Night sounds, morning colors*
Wildsmith, Brian. *Seasons*
Wolff, Ashley. *A year of birds*
Wood, Joyce. *Grandmother Lucy in her garden*
Yolen, Jane. *Ring of earth*
  Welcome to the icehouse
Zagwÿn, Deborah Turney. *Turtle spring*
Zeman, Ludmila. *The first red maple leaf*
Ziefert, Harriet. *Bear all year*

Zimmermann, H. Werner (Heinz Werner). *Alphonse knows . . . twelve months make a year*
Zolotow, Charlotte (Shapiro). *In my garden*
  The song

Seasons – fall

Adelson, Leone. *All ready for school*
Allington, Richard L. *Autumn*
Arnosky, Jim. *Every autumn comes the bear*
Barklem, Jill. *Autumn story*
  The high hills
Blades, Ann. *Fall*
Bliss, Corinne Demas. *Matthew's meadow*
Bunting, Eve (Anne Evelyn). *The pumpkin fair*
Cavagnaro, David. *The pumpkin people*
Cohen, Peter Zachary. *Authorized autumn charts of the Upper Red Canoe River country*
Demarest, Chris L. *Fall*
Denslow, Sharon Phillips. *At Taylor's place*
Dutton, Sandra. *The cinnamon hen's autumn day*
Fregosi, Claudia. *The happy horse*
Freschet, Berniece. *Owl in the garden*
George, Lindsay Barrett. *In the woods*
Griffith, Helen V. *Alex remembers*
Hirschi, Ron. *Fall*
Hoban, Julia. *Amy loves the wind*
Hopkins, Lee Bennett. *Merrily comes our harvest in*
Iwamura, Kazuo. *The fourteen forest mice and the harvest moon watch*
Knutson, Kimberley. *Ska-tat!*
Koller, Jackie French. *Nickommoh!*
Kumin, Maxine W. *Follow the fall*
Lapp, Eleanor. *The mice came in early this year*
Lenski, Lois. *Now it's fall*
London, Jonathan. *Fall rap*
Lotz, Karen E. *Snowsong whistling*
Maass, Robert. *When autumn comes*
McNaughton, Colin. *Autumn*
Maestro, Betsy. *Why do leaves change color?*
Moncure, Jane Belk. *Word Bird's fall words*
Moore, Elaine. *Grandma's smile*
Ott, John. *Peter Pumpkin*
Plourde, Lynn. *Wild child*
Potter, Beatrix. *The tale of Squirrel Nutkin*
Potter, Tessa. *Digger, the story of a mole in the fall*
Robbins, Ken. *Autumn leaves*
Roth, Harold. *Autumn days*
Schnur, Steven. *Autumn*
Schweninger, Ann. *Autumn days*
Spetter, Jung-Hee. *Lily and Trooper's fall*
Taylor, Mark. *Henry explores the mountains*
Tejima, Keizaburo. *The bears' autumn*
Tresselt, Alvin R. *Autumn harvest*
  Johnny Maple-Leaf
Udry, Janice May. *Emily's autumn*
Updike, David. *An autumn tale*
Van Allsburg, Chris. *The stranger*
Wheeler, Cindy. *Marmalade's yellow leaf*
Yerxa, Leo. *Last leaf first snowflake to fall*
Zolotow, Charlotte (Shapiro). *Say it!*

Seasons – spring

Agell, Charlotte. *Mud makes me dance in the spring*
Alexander, Sue. *There's more . . . much more*
Allington, Richard L. *Spring*
Anglund, Joan Walsh. *Spring is a new beginning*
Barker, Cicely Mary. *Flower fairies of the spring*

Barklem, Jill. *Spring story*
Barrett, John M. *The Easter bear*
Baum, Arline. *One bright Monday morning*
Beer, Kathleen Costello. *What happens in the spring*
Belting, Natalia Maree. *Summer's coming in*
Blades, Ann. *Spring*
Boon, Emilie. *It's spring, Peterkin*
Bornstein, Ruth Lercher. *Rabbit's good news*
Brown, Craig McFarland. *In the spring*
Carlstrom, Nancy White. *Raven and river*
Chönz, Selina. *A bell for Ursli*
Clifton, Lucille. *The boy who didn't believe in spring*
Cohen, Carol L. *Wake up, groundhog!*
Craig, M. Jean. *Spring is like the morning*
Cummings, E. E. (Edward Estlin). *In just-spring*
Dabcovich, Lydia. *Sleepy bear*
Delton, Judy. *Three friends find spring*
Demarest, Chris L. *Spring*
Demi. *Demi's basket of books*
    Little baby lamb
De Posadas Mane, Carmen. *Mister North Wind*
Dewey, Ariane. *The tea squall*
Dodd, Lynley. *Wake up, bear*
Dragonwagon, Crescent. *Strawberry dress escape*
Emberley, Michael. *Welcome back, Sun*
Fish, Helen Dean. *When the root children wake up*,
    published by Lippincott, 1930
    When the root children wake up, published by
    Green Tiger Pr., 1988
Fisher, Aileen Lucia. *My mother and I*
    Now that spring is here
    The story of Easter
Forrester, Victoria. *The touch said hello*
Harness, Cheryl. *The queen with bees in her hair*
Hest, Amy. *Ruby's storm*
Hirschi, Ron. *Spring*
Hoban, Lillian. *The sugar snow spring*
    Turtle spring
Hopkins, Lee Bennett. *Easter buds are springing*
Hunter, Anne. *Possum and the peeper*
Hurd, Edith Thacher. *The day the sun danced*
Hurd, Thacher. *Blackberry ramble*
Ichikawa, Satomi. *Sun through small leaves*
Iwamura, Kazuo. *The fourteen forest mice and the
    spring meadow picnic*
Janice. *Little Bear's pancake party*
Johnson, Crockett. *Time for spring*
    Will spring be early or will spring be late?
Kesselman, Wendy Ann. *Time for Jody*
Kinsey-Warnock, Natalie. *When spring comes*
Kite, L. Patricia. *Dandelion adventures*
Koscielniak, Bruce. *Geoffrey Groundhog predicts the
    weather*
Kraus, Robert. *The first robin*
    Springfellow's parade
Krauss, Ruth. *The happy day*
Kroll, Steven. *I love spring!*
Kroll, Virginia L. *Naomi knows it's springtime*
Larry, Charles. *Peboan and Seegwun*
Lenski, Lois. *Spring is here*
Lerner, Carol. *Flowers of a woodland spring*
Levens, George. *Kippy the koala*
Lindbergh, Reeve. *North country spring*
Lucht, Irmgard. *In this night*
Maass, Robert. *When spring comes*
McNaughton, Colin. *Spring*
Martin, Charles E. *Island rescue*
Miller, Edna. *Mousekin's Easter basket*
Minarik, Else Holmelund. *It's spring!*

Moncure, Jane Belk. *Word Bird's spring words*
Moore, Elaine. *Grandma's garden*
Morgan-Vanroyen, Mary. *Night ride*
Nordqvist, Sven. *Festus and Mercury: ruckus in the
    garden*
Oppenheim, Joanne. *Could it be?*
Patz, Nancy. *Sarah Bear and Sweet Sidney*
Peters, Lisa Westberg. *Cold little duck, duck, duck*
Pfister, Marcus. *Hopper*
    Hopper hunts for spring
Ray, Mary Lyn. *Mud*
Richardson, Judith Benét. *Old winter*
Rockwell, Anne F. *My spring robin*
Schlein, Miriam. *Little Red Nose*
Schnur, Steven. *Spring thaw*
Seignobosc, Françoise. *Springtime for Jeanne-Marie*
Selkowe, Valrie M. *Spring green*
Sewall, Marcia. *The Green Mist*
Shannon, George. *Spring*
Silverman, Erica. *On the morn of Mayfest*
Skofield, James. *Crow moon, worm moon*
Spetter, Jung-Hee. *Lily and Trooper's spring*
Stafford, William. *The animal that drank up sound*
Taylor, Harriet Peck. *Two days in May*
Taylor, Judy. *Dudley and the monster*
Taylor, Mark. *Henry the castaway*
Tresselt, Alvin R. *Hi, Mister Robin*
Wallace, Nancy Elizabeth. *Paperwhite*
Walters, Catherine. *When will it be spring?*
Warren, Cathy. *Springtime bears*
Waterton, Betty. *Pettranella*
Weedn, Flavia. *The giant's garden*
Wells, Rosemary. *Forest of dreams*
    Max's chocolate chicken
Whittington, Mary K. *Winter's child*
Wilde, Oscar. *Fairy tales of Oscar Wilde*
    The selfish giant, ill. by S. Saelig Gallagher
    The selfish giant, ill. by Dom Mansell
    The selfish giant, ill. by Fabian Negrin
    The selfish giant, ill. by Lisbeth Zwerger
Wolkstein, Diane. *The magic wings*
Wood, Joyce. *Grandmother Lucy in her garden*
Woolaver, Lance. *From Ben Loman to the sea*
Worth, Bonnie. *Peter Cottontail's surprise*
Zimmermann, H. Werner (Heinz Werner).
    Alphonse knows . . . the colour of spring
Zion, Gene. *Really spring*

Seasons – summer

Ackerman, Karen. *In the park with dad*
Adelson, Leone. *All ready for summer*
Alarcón, Francisco X. *From the bellybutton of the
    moon and other summer poems / poems = Del
    ombligo de la luna y otros poemas de verano / poe-
    mas*
Aliki. *Those summers*
Allington, Richard L. *Summer*
Appelt, Kathi. *Watermelon day*
Barker, Cicely Mary. *Flower fairies of the summer*
Barklem, Jill. *Summer story*
Bat-Ami, Miriam. *Sea, salt, and air*
Beim, Jerrold. *The swimming hole*
Belting, Natalia Maree. *Summer's coming in*
Bentley, Anne. *The Groggs have a wonderful summer*
Berenstain, Stan. *The Berenstain bears go to camp*
Blades, Ann. *Back to the cabin*
    Summer
Boelts, Maribeth. *Little Bunny's preschool countdown*

Seasons – winter

Foreman, Michael. *Panda's puzzle, and his voyage of discovery*
Fox, Mem. *The straight line wonder*
Fujikawa, Gyo. *See what I can be!*
Gauch, Patricia Lee. *Presenting Tanya, the Ugly Duckling*
Gibson, Kari Smalley. *Mooki's secret*
Gifford, Kathie Lee. *Moochie's surprise*
Girard, Linda Walvoord. *My body is private*
Glen, Maggie. *Ruby to the rescue*
Goldin, Barbara Diamond. *Cakes and miracles*
Gordon, Gaelyn. *Duckat*
Green-Armytage, Stephen. *Dudley, the little terrier that could*
Greenburg, Dan. *Through the medicine cabinet*
Gregorowski, Christopher. *Fly, eagle, fly!*
Gregory, Valiska. *A valentine for Norman Noggs*
Gwynne, Fred. *Pondlarker*
Hallinan, P. K. (Patrick K.). *I know I belong*
　I know who I am
　I'm glad to be me
　Where's Michael?
Harsh, Fred. *Alfie*
Hartman, Bob. *The one and only Delgado Cheese*
Hasler, Eveline. *The giantess*
Heide, Florence Parry. *The bigness contest*
Hellings, Colette. *Too little, too big*
Hest, Amy. *You're the boss, Baby Duck*
Hines, Anna Grossnickle. *All by myself*
Hoban, Russell. *A near thing for Captain Najork*
Hoffman, Mary. *Amazing Grace*
Holman, Sandy Lynne. *Grandpa, is everything black bad?*
Howard, Arthur. *Cosmo zooms*
Inkpen, Mick. *Nothing*
Irbinskas, Heather. *How Jackrabbit got his very long ears*
Jennings, Linda M. *Tom's tail*
Johnston, Deborah. *Mathew Michael's beastly day*
Joly, Fanny. *Mr. Fine, porcupine*
Kaiser Johnson, Lee. *If I ran the family*
Karlin, Nurit. *Little big mouse*
　A train for the king
Keats, Ezra Jack. *Peter's chair*
　Whistle for Willie
Keller, Holly. *Horace*
King-Smith, Dick. *The spotty pig*
Kirk, Daniel. *Bigger*
Krauss, Ruth. *The carrot seed*
Kroll, Virginia L. *The Christmas cow*
Kuskin, Karla. *What did you bring me?*
Lane, Megan Halsey. *Something to crow about*
Leaf, Munro. *Noodle*
Lionni, Leo. *Mr. McMouse*
　Pezzettino
Lipkind, William. *The little tiny rooster*
Lipson, Beth Weiner. *Benjamin's perfect solution*
Loomans, Diane. *The lovables in the kingdom of self-esteem*
McAllister, Angela. *The enchanted flute*
MacDonald, Allan. *The pig in a wig*
McKee, David. *Elmer and the kangaroo*
Mangan, Anne. *Browny, the smallest bear of all*
Martín Larrañaga, Ana. *The big wide-mouthed frog*
Medearis, Angela Shelf. *Annie's gifts*
Milios, Rita. *Yo soy = I am*
Mills, Joyce C. *Little Tree*
Minarik, Else Holmelund. *Am I beautiful?*
Monks, Lydia. *The cat barked?*

Moss, Marissa. *But not Kate*
　Regina's big mistake
Murphy, Jill. *A piece of cake*
O'Donnell, Elizabeth Lee. *Patrick's day*
Oram, Hiawyn. *Just Dog*
Palmer, Mary Babcock. *No-sort-of-animal*
Parr, Todd. *The okay book*
Pearson, Susan. *Lenore's big break*
Peet, Bill (William Bartlett). *Pamela Camel*
Polisar, Barry Louis. *The trouble with Ben*
Prater, John. *The greatest show on earth*
Purdy, Carol. *Least of all*
Raschka, Christopher. *Arlene sardine*
Richardson, Jean. *Tall inside*
Robertson, Janet. *Oscar's spots*
Roe, Eileen. *All I am*
Sadler, Marilyn. *It's not easy being a bunny*
Savageau, Cheryl. *Muskrat will be swimming*
Scamell, Ragnhild. *Who likes Wolfie?*
Schneider, Christine M. *Picky Mrs. Pickle*
Schroeder, Binette. *Laura*
Seuss, Dr. *Oh, the places you'll go!*
Sharmat, Marjorie Weinman. *I'm terrific*
　Taking care of Melvin
　The 329th friend
Shields, Carol Diggory. *I am really a princess*
Shipton, Jonathan. *What if?*
Shott, Steve (Stephen). *Look at me*
Simon, Norma. *All kinds of children*
　Why am I different?
Skulavik, Mary Alys. *Bert*
Slobodkin, Louis. *Magic Michael*
Smalls-Hector, Irene. *Louise's gift*
Stadler, John. *Ready, set, go!*
Steers, Billy. *Tractor Mac*
Stren, Patti. *Mountain Rose*
Supraner, Robyn. *Would you rather be a tiger?*
Talbott, Hudson. *Going Hollywood! A dinosaur's dream*
Talley, Carol. *Clarissa*
Titherington, Jeanne. *Big world, small world*
Tobias, Tobi. *Jane wishing*
Turnage, Sheila. *Trout the magnificent*
Tusa, Tricia. *Chicken*
　Libby's new glasses
Udry, Janice May. *How I faded away*
Waber, Bernard. *"You look ridiculous," said the rhinoceros to the hippopotamus*
Wagner, Karen. *Silly Fred*
Weedn, Flavia. *The enchanted tree*
Williams, Barbara. *Donna Jean's disaster*
Wold, Jo Anne. *Tell them my name is Amanda*
Wondriska, William. *Puff*
Yolen, Jane. *Little Mouse and Elephant*
Zola, Meguido. *The dream of promise*

Self-esteem *see* Self-concept

Self-image *see* Self-concept

Self-reliance *see* Character traits – confidence

Selfishness *see* Character traits – selfishness

Selkies *see* Mythical creatures – selkies

Seminole Indians *see* Indians of North America – Seminole

Seneca Indians *see* Indians of North America – Seneca

Senses

Calmenson, Stephanie. *My book of the seasons*
Cole, Joanna. *You can't smell a flower with your ear*
Crossley-Holland, Kevin. *Sleeping Nanna*
Falwell, Cathryn. *Nicky loves daddy*
It feels like Christmas!. *It feels like Christmas!*
Kasperson, James. *Little brother moose*
Lears, Laurie. *Ian's walk*
McMillan, Bruce. *Sense suspense*
Miller, Margaret. *My five senses*
Murphy, Mary. *You smell and taste and feel and see and hear*
Seuss, Dr. *Gerald McBoing Boing*
Topek, Susan Remick. *Shalom, Shabbat*
Wells, Rosemary. *Night sounds, morning colors*
Zarin, Cynthia. *What do you see when you shut your eyes?*

Senses – hearing

Aliki. *My five senses*
Allington, Richard L. *Hearing*
Ancona, George. *Handtalk zoo*
Arthur, Catherine. *My sister's silent world*
Aseltine, Lorraine. *I'm deaf and it's okay*
Baker, Pamela J. *My first book of sign*
Borten, Helen. *Do you hear what I hear?*
   Do you know what I know?
Bove, Linda. *Sign language ABC with Linda Bove*
Brenner, Barbara A. *Faces, faces, faces*
Chaplin, Susan Gibbons. *I can sign my ABCs*
Charlip, Remy. *Handtalk*
   Handtalk birthday
Cousins, Lucy. *What can Pinky hear?*
   What can rabbit hear?
Fowler, Allan. *Hearing things*
Greenberg, Judith E. *What is the sign for friend?*
Hindley, Judy. *Soft and noisy*
Isadora, Rachel. *I hear*
Jaynes, Ruth M. *Melinda's Christmas stocking*
Lionni, Leo. *What?*
Litchfield, Ada B. *A button in her ear*
Locker, Thomas. *Anna and the bagpiper*
Moncure, Jane Belk. *Sounds all around*
Morris, Winifred. *Just listen*
Ogle, Lucille. *I hear*
Oxenbury, Helen. *I hear*
Pace, Elizabeth. *Chris gets ear tubes*
Perkins, Al. *The ear book*
Pluckrose, Henry Arthur. *Hearing*
   Things we hear
Rauzon, Mark J. *Eyes and ears*
Shirotani, Hideo. *Sounds*
Showers, Paul. *Ears are for hearing*
   The listening walk
Soto, Gary. *The old man and his door*
Wahl, Jan. *Jamie's tiger*
Wolf, Bernard. *Anna's silent world*
Wright, Lillian. *Hearing*

Senses – seeing

Aliki. *My five senses*
Allington, Richard L. *Looking*
Backstein, Karen. *The blind men and the elephant*
Balian, Lorna. *Elephant?*
Borten, Helen. *Do you know what I know?*
   Do you see what I see?
Bram, Elizabeth. *One day I closed my eyes and the world disappeared*
Brenner, Barbara A. *Faces, faces, faces*
Brighton, Catherine. *My hands, my world*
Brown, Marc Tolon. *Arthur's eyes*
Brown, Marcia. *Walk with your eyes*
Chapman, Elizabeth. *Suzy*
Cohen, Miriam. *See you tomorrow*
Cousins, Lucy. *What can Pinky see?*
   What can rabbit see?
DeArmond, Dale. *The seal oil lamp*
Faulkner, Keith. *Bertie's big blue binoculars*
Fowler, Allan. *Seeing things*
Geoghegan, Adrienne. *Dogs don't wear glasses*
Giff, Patricia Reilly. *Watch out, Ronald Morgan!*
Goodsell, Jane. *Katie's magic glasses*
Hay, Dean. *I see a lot of things*
Herman, Bill. *Jenny's magic wand*
Hoban, Tana. *Look again*
Isadora, Rachel. *I see*
Jaynes, Ruth M. *Melinda's Christmas stocking*
Jensen, Virginia Allen. *Catching*
   Red thread riddles
   What's that?
Johnson, Donna Kay. *Brighteyes*
Keats, Ezra Jack. *Apt. 3*
Keller, Holly. *Cromwell's glasses*
   What I see
Kelley, True. *Look again at funny animals*
Kessler, Leonard P. *Mr. Pine's mixed-up signs*
Lasson, Robert. *Orange Oliver*
Lionni, Leo. *What?*
Litchfield, Ada B. *A cane in her hand*
MacDonald, Maryann. *Little Hippo gets glasses*
Martin, Bill (William Ivan). *Knots on a counting rope*
Matthiesen, Thomas. *Things to see*
Moncure, Jane Belk. *The look book*
Newth, Philip. *Roly goes exploring*
Ogle, Lucille. *I spy*
Oxenbury, Helen. *I see*
Pluckrose, Henry Arthur. *Seeing*
   Things we see
Quigley, Lillian Fox. *The blind men and the elephant*
Raskin, Ellen. *Spectacles*
Rauzon, Mark J. *Eyes and ears*
Reuter, Margaret. *My mother is blind*
Sargent, Susan. *My favorite place*
Saxe, John Godfrey. *The blind men and the elephant*
Shecter, Ben. *The stocking child*
Showers, Paul. *Look at your eyes*
Smith, Lane. *Glasses . . . who needs 'em?*
Thayer, Jane. *Mr. Turtle's magic glasses*
Thomson, Ruth. *Eyes*
Tusa, Tricia. *Libby's new glasses*
Wright, Lillian. *Seeing*
Yolen, Jane. *The seeing stick*
Young, Ed (Edward). *Seven blind mice*

Senses – smelling

Aliki. *My five senses*

Allen, Jonathan. *Mucky moose*
Allington, Richard L. *Smelling*
Borten, Helen. *Do you know what I know?*
Brenner, Barbara A. *Faces, faces, faces*
Cole, Babette. *The smelly book*
Doughtie, Charles. *Gabriel Wrinkles, the bloodhound who couldn't smell*
Fair, David. *The fabulous four skunks*
Fowler, Allan. *Smelling things*
Gackenbach, Dick. *Barker's crime*
Jaynes, Ruth M. *Melinda's Christmas stocking*
Keillor, Garrison. *The old man who loved cheese*
Knutson, Kimberley. *Ska-tat!*
Lionni, Leo. *What?*
Moncure, Jane Belk. *What your nose knows!*
Nikly, Michelle. *The perfume of memory*
Perkins, Al. *The nose book*
Pluckrose, Henry Arthur. *Smelling*
Rose, Gerald. *Scruff*
Saunders, Susan. *A sniff in time*
Wright, Lillian. *Smelling and tasting*

Senses – tasting

Aliki. *My five senses*
Allington, Richard L. *Tasting*
Borten, Helen. *Do you know what I know?*
Brenner, Barbara A. *Faces, faces, faces*
Fowler, Allan. *Tasting things*
Jaynes, Ruth M. *Melinda's Christmas stocking*
Lionni, Leo. *What?*
Moncure, Jane Belk. *A tasting party*
Pluckrose, Henry Arthur. *Tasting*
Wright, Lillian. *Smelling and tasting*

Senses – touching

Adoff, Arnold. *Touch the poem*
Aliki. *My five senses*
Allington, Richard L. *Touching*
Becker, Bonny. *Tickly prickly*
Borten, Helen. *Do you know what I know?*
Brenner, Barbara A. *Faces, faces, faces*
Brown, Marcia. *Touch will tell*
Carle, Eric. *My very first book of touch*
Fowler, Allan. *Feeling things*
Gibson, Myra Tomback. *What is your favorite thing to touch?*
Isadora, Rachel. *I touch*
Jaynes, Ruth M. *Melinda's Christmas stocking*
Lionni, Leo. *What?*
Moncure, Jane Belk. *The touch book*
Oliver, Stephen. *Touch*
Otto, Carolyn. *I can tell by touching*
Oxenbury, Helen. *I touch*
Pluckrose, Henry Arthur. *Things we touch*
   Touching
Wright, Lillian. *Touching*
Yates, Irene. *All about touch*

Serbia *see* Foreign lands – Serbia

Sewing *see* Activities – sewing

Sex instruction

Brown, Laurie Krasny. *What's the big secret?*

Sex roles

Impey, Rose. *Who's a bright girl?*
Kroll, Virginia L. *A carp for Kimiko*
   Girl, you're amazing!
Lattimore, Deborah Nourse. *Frida Maria*
Moss, Marissa. *True heart*
Numeroff, Laura Joffe. *What daddies do best*
   What mommies do best
Pearson, Susan. *Everybody knows that!*
San Souci, Robert D. *Brave Margaret*
   A weave of words
Sierra, Judy. *Tasty baby belly buttons*
Yaroshevskaya, Kim. *Little Kim's doll*
Zhang, Song Nan. *The ballad of Mulan*

Sextuplets *see* Multiple births – sextuplets

Shadows

Anno, Mitsumasa. *Anno's sundial*
   In shadowland
Asch, Frank. *Bear shadow*
Bartalos, Michael. *Shadowville*
Berger, Barbara Helen. *The jewel heart*
Bond, Felicia. *Wake up, Vladimir*
Bulla, Clyde Robert. *What makes a shadow?*
Calmenson, Stephanie. *Kinderkittens, show-and-tell*
Cendrars, Blaise. *Shadow*
Christelow, Eileen. *Henry and the dragon*
De Regniers, Beatrice Schenk. *The shadow book*
Dodd, Anne Westcott. *Footprints and shadows*
Dorros, Arthur. *Me and my shadow*
Farber, Norma. *Return of the shadows*
Gackenbach, Dick. *Barker's crime*
   Mr. Wink and his shadow, Ned
Goor, Ron. *Shadows*
Gore, Sheila. *My shadow*
Haseley, Dennis. *Ghost catcher*
Hoban, Tana. *Shadows and reflections*
Kent, Jack. *The biggest shadow in the zoo*
Lewin, Betsy. *Groundhog day*
McHargue, Georgess. *Private zoo*
Mahy, Margaret. *The boy with two shadows*
Marol, Jean-Claude. *Vagabul and his shadow*
Michaels, William. *Clare and her shadow*
Narahashi, Keiko. *I have a friend*
Olofsdotter, Marie. *Sofia and the Heartmender*
Robison, Nancy. *Ten tall soldiers*
Rosenberg, Liz. *Grandmother and the runaway shadow*
Severn, Jeffrey. *George and his giant shadow*
Simon, Seymour. *Shadow magic*
Swinburne, Stephen R. *Guess whose shadow?*
Tompert, Ann. *Nothing sticks like a shadow*
Van Nutt, Julia. *The monster in the shadows*
Walter, Mildred Pitts. *Darkness*
Willard, Nancy. *Shadow story*
Winter, Susan. *My shadow*
Zemke, Deborah. *The shadow of Matilda Hunt*

Shakers *see* Ethnic groups in the U.S. – Shakers

Shakespeare

Freeman, Don. *Will's quill*

Shape *see* Concepts – shape

Shaped books *see* Format, unusual

Sharing *see* Behavior – sharing

Sharks *see* Fish – sharks

Shawnee Indians *see* Indians of North America – Shawnee

Sheep *see* Animals – sheep

Shells *see* Sea and seashore

Shepherds *see* Careers – shepherds

Sheriffs *see* Careers – sheriffs

Ships *see* Boats, ships

Shirts *see* Clothing – shirts

Shoemakers *see* Careers – shoemakers

Shoes *see* Clothing – shoes

Shopping

Allard, Harry. *I will not go to market today*
Anholt, Catherine. *Truffles in trouble*
Ardizzone, Edward. *The little girl and the tiny doll*
Armitage, Ronda. *Harry hates shopping!*
Arnold, Caroline. *What will we buy?*
Baggette, Susan K. *Jonathan goes to the grocery store*
Bates, Artie Ann. *Ragsale*
Baugh, Dolores M. *Supermarket*
Bertrand, Cécile. *Let's pretend!*
Birdseye, Tom. *Soap! Soap! Don't forget the soap!*
Black, Irma (Simonton). *The little old man who could not read*
Bond, Michael. *Paddington's lucky day*
Bradman, Tony. *Dilly speaks up*
   Wait and see
Brenner, Barbara A. *Somebody's slippers, somebody's shoes*
Bunting, Eve (Anne Evelyn). *Market day*
Burningham, John. *The shopping basket*
Butterworth, Nick. *Just like Jasper*
   When we go shopping
Calmenson, Stephanie. *The birthday hat*
Cass, Joan E. *The cats go to market*
Chase, Catherine. *Baby mouse goes shopping*
Chorao, Kay. *Molly's Moe*
Claverie, Jean. *Shopping*
Daly, Niki. *Mama, papa and baby Joe*
   Not so fast Songololo
Day, Alexandra. *Carl goes shopping*
Edwards, Linda Strauss. *The downtown day*
Enderle, Judith (Ann) Ross. *What would Mama do?*
Faulkner, Keith. *Sam helps out*
Fyleman, Rose. *A fairy went a-marketing*
Garland, Sarah. *Going shopping*
Gershator, Phillis. *Sweet, sweet fig banana*

Gill, Shelley. *The big buck adventure*
Gretz, Susanna. *Teddy bears go shopping*
Greydanus, Rose. *Susie goes shopping*
Grossman, Bill. *Tommy at the grocery store*
Grossman, Patricia. *Saturday market*
Guzzo, Sandra E. *Fox and Heggie*
Hamm, Diane Johnston. *Laney's lost momma*
Hastings, Evelyn Beilhart. *The department store*
Hines, Anna Grossnickle. *Don't worry, I'll find you*
Hutchins, Pat. *Don't forget the bacon!*
Ichikawa, Satomi. *Suzanne and Nicholas at the market*
Kilroy, Sally. *Market day*
Leblanc, Anne. *Shopping with Benjamin*
Leonard, Marcia. *No new pants!*
   Shopping for snowflakes
Lindbergh, Reeve. *The awful Aardvarks shop for school*
Lobel, Arnold. *On Market Street*
London, Jonathan. *Ali, child of the desert*
Loomis, Christine. *At the mall*
Maccarone, Grace. *I shop with my daddy*
McPhail, David M. *The cereal box*
Martin, David. *Five little piggies*
Maschler, Fay. *T. G. and Moonie go shopping*
Mother Goose. *To market! To market!*, ill. by Emma Lillian Brock
Munsch, Robert N. *Something good*
   Where is Gah-Ning?
Murphy, Stuart J. *Just enough carrots*
Nethery, Mary. *Orange cat goes to market*
Newcome, Zita. *Rosie goes shopping*
Oliver, Stephen. *Shopping*
Oxenbury, Helen. *The shopping trip*
   Tom and Pippo go shopping
Patz, Nancy. *Pumpernickel tickle and mean green cheese*
Potter, Beatrix. *The tale of Little Pig Robinson*
Prater, John. *"No!" said Joe*
Rice, Eve. *New blue shoes*
Rockwell, Anne F. *The supermarket*
Ross, Christine. *Lily and the present*
Rubel, Nicole. *Goldie*
Russell, Betty. *Big store, funny door*
Russo, Marisabina. *Mama talks too much*
Shaw, Nancy (Nancy E.). *Sheep in a shop*
Shohet, Marti. *Market days*
Shopping
Smith, Barry. *Tom and Annie go shopping*
Solomon, Joan. *A present for Mum*
Spier, Peter. *Food market*
Winn, Chris. *My day*
Yardley, Thompson. *Buy now, pay later*
Ziefert, Harriet. *Bear goes shopping*
Zinnemann-Hope, Pam. *Let's go shopping, Ned*

Shops *see* Stores

Shoshone Indians *see* Indians of North America – Shoshone

Shows *see* Theater

Shrews *see* Animals – shrews

Shrimp *see* Crustaceans

Shyness *see* Character traits – shyness

Siam *see* Foreign lands – Thailand

Siberia *see* Foreign lands – Siberia

Sibling rivalry

Adoff, Arnold. *Hard to be six*
Aitken, Amy. *Wanda's circus*
Alexander, Martha G. *I'll be the horse if you'll play with me*
   Marty McGee's space lab, no girls allowed
   Nobody asked me if I wanted a baby sister
   When the new baby comes, I'm moving out
Allen, Pamela. *Hidden treasure*
Amoss, Berthe. *It's not your birthday*
   Tom in the middle
Anholt, Catherine. *Aren't you lucky!*
Armitage, Ronda. *The bossing of Josie*
Arnstein, Helene S. *Billy and our new baby*
Bach, Alice. *The smartest bear and his brother Oliver*
Baker, Betty. *My sister says*
Baker, Charlotte. *Little brother*
Bassett, Lisa. *Koala Christmas*
Beecroft, John. *What? Another cat!*
Benson, Ellen. *Philip's little sister*
Berenstain, Stan. *The Berenstain bears and the double dare*
   The Berenstain bears get in a fight
Bernhard, Emery. *Spotted Eagle and Black Crow*
Bider, Djemma. *A drop of honey*
Blume, Judy. *The Pain and The Great One*
Bond, Felicia. *Poinsettia and her family*
Bottner, Barbara. *Big boss! Little boss!*
   Jungle day
Boyd, Lizi. *Sam is my half brother*
Bradman, Tony. *Dilly speaks up*
Brothers and sisters are like that!
Brown, Marc Tolon. *D. W. all wet*
Bruna, Dick. *Dick Bruna's Cinderella*
Buchanan, Heather S. *Emily Mouse's garden*
Bulla, Clyde Robert. *Keep running, Allen!*
Bullock, Kathleen. *A surprise for Mitzi Mouse*
Byrne, David. *Stay up late*
Caines, Jeannette. *Abby*
Carlson, Nancy L. *Harriet and Walt*
   Louanne Pig in the perfect family
Carlstrom, Nancy White. *Kiss your sister, Rose Marie*
Caseley, Judith. *Silly baby*
Castiglia, Julie. *Jill the pill*
Chalmers, Audrey. *Fancy be good*
Chenery, Janet. *Wolfie*
Chorao, Kay. *George told Kate*
Clarke, Gus. *Along came Eric*
Cleary, Beverly. *Janet's thingamajigs*
Clifton, Lucille. *My brother fine with me*
Climo, Shirley. *The Egyptian Cinderella*
Coburn, Jewell Reinhart. *Angkat*
   Jouanah
Cole, Joanna. *The new baby at your house*
Conaway, Judith. *I'll get even*
Conta, Marcia Maher. *Feelings between brothers and sisters*
Cooke, Trish. *When I grow bigger*
Cooper, Helen (Helen F.). *Little monster did it!*
Corey, Dorothy. *Will there be a lap for me?*
Cottringer, Anne. *Ella and the naughty lion*

Cousins, Lucy. *Za-Za's baby brother*
Croft, Priscilla. *Dealing with jealousy*
Crowley, Arthur. *Bonzo Beaver*
Cutler, Jane. *Darcy and Gran don't like babies*
Daly, Niki. *Look at me!*
De Hamel, Joan. *Hemi's pet*
Delaney, Molly. *My sister*
De Lynam, Alicia Garcia. *It's mine!*
Dragonwagon, Crescent. *I hate my brother Harry*
   I hate my sister Maggie
Drescher, Joan E. *The birth-order blues*
   The marvelous mess
Dubanevich, Arlene. *Pig William*
Dubois, Claude K. *He's my jumbo!*
Duncan, Lois. *Giving away Suzanne*
Edelman, Elaine. *I love my baby sister (most of the time)*
Ehrlich, Amy. *Bunnies at Christmastime*
   Bunnies on their own
Engel, Diana. *Josephina, the great collector*
Etherington, Frank. *The spaghetti word race*
Fair, Sylvia. *The bedspread*
Fife, Dale. *Rosa's special garden*
Fisher, Iris L. *Katie-Bo*
Franklin, Jonathan. *Don't wake the baby*
Galbraith, Kathryn Osebold. *Katie did!*
   Roommates
Gauch, Patricia Lee. *Christina Katerina and the time she quit the family*
Gewing, Lisa. *Mama, daddy, baby and me*
Gili, Phillida. *Fanny and Charles*
Ginsburg, Mirra. *Two greedy bears*
Graham, Richard. *Jack and the monster*
Greene, Carol. *Hinny Winny Bunco*
Greenfield, Eloise. *She come bringing me that little baby girl*
Grimm, Jacob. *Cinderella*, ill. by Nonny Hogrogian
   Cinderella, ill. by Svend Otto S
Hamilton, Morse. *Big sisters are bad witches*
   Little sister for sale
   My name is Emily
Harper, Anita. *It's not fair!*
Hazen, Barbara Shook. *If it weren't for Benjamin (I'd always get to lick the icing spoon)*
   Why couldn't I be an only kid like you, Wigger?
Heckman, Philip. *Waking upside down*
Hedderwick, Mairi. *Katie Morag and the tiresome Ted*
Heide, Florence Parry. *Oh, grow up!*
Heller, Nicholas. *An adventure at sea*
Helmering, Doris Wild. *We're going to have a baby*
Henkes, Kevin. *Julius, the baby of the world*
Henriod, Lorraine. *Grandma's wheelchair*
Hines, Anna Grossnickle. *They really like me!*
Hoban, Lillian. *Arthur's pen pal*
Hoban, Russell. *A baby sister for Frances*
   The battle of Zormla
   The great gum drop robbery
   Some snow said hello
   They came from Aargh!
Holabird, Katharine. *Angelina's baby sister*
Hooker, Ruth. *Sara loves her big brother*
Hoopes, Lyn Littlefield. *When I was little*
Hutchins, H. J. (Hazel J.). *Katie's babbling brother*
Hutchins, Pat. *The very worst monster*
Jacobs, Kate. *A sister's wish*
Johnston, Tony. *I'm gonna tell mama I want an iguana*
   Slither McCreep and his brother, Joe
Jonell, Lynne. *It's my birthday, too!*

Max's bedtime
Max's breakfast
Max's chocolate chicken
Peabody
Stanley and Rhoda
Williams, Barbara. *Donna Jean's disaster*
Winter, Susan. *A baby just like me*
Winthrop, Elizabeth. *I think he likes me*
   That's mine
Wolde, Gunilla. *Betsy and the chicken pox*
Wolff, Ashley. *Stella and Roy go camping*
Yep, Laurence. *Dragon prince*
Yezerski, Thomas. *Queen of the world*
Yorinks, Arthur. *Ugh*
Young, Ruth. *The new baby*
Zalben, Jane Breskin. *Buster gets braces*
Ziefert, Harriet. *Getting ready for new baby*
Zolotow, Charlotte (Shapiro). *If it weren't for you*
   Timothy too!

Siblings *see* Family life – brothers; Family life – brothers and sisters; Family life – sisters

Sickness *see* Health and fitness; Illness

Sight *see* Anatomy – eyes; Glasses; Handicaps – blindness; Senses – seeing

Sign painters *see* Careers – sign painters

Siksika Indians *see* Indians of North America – Siksika

Singers *see* Careers – singers

Singing *see* Activities – singing

Sioux Indians *see* Indians of North America – Cheyenne (Sioux); Indians of North America – Dakota (Sioux); Indians of North America – Lakota (Sioux); Indians of North America – Sioux

Sisters *see* Family life; Family life – brothers and sisters; Family life – sisters; Sibling rivalry

Size *see* Concepts – size

Skateboarding *see* Sports – skateboarding

Skating *see* Sports – ice skating; Sports – hockey; Sports – roller skating

Skeletons *see* Anatomy – skeletons

Skiing *see* Sports – skiing

Skin *see* Anatomy – skin

Skin diving *see* Sports – skin diving

Skunks *see* Animals – skunks

Sky

Asch, Frank. *Starbaby*
Belting, Natalia Maree. *The sun is a golden earring*
Birdseye, Tom. *A song of stars*
Branley, Franklyn M. (Mansfield). *Comets*
   The sky is full of stars
Carle, Eric. *Little cloud*
   Little cloud, a board book
Dalton, Anne. *Prince Starr*
Dayrell, Elphinstone. *Why the sun and the moon live in the sky*
Dayton, Mona. *Earth and sky*
Dee, Ruby. *Tower to heaven*
Dewey, Ariane. *The sky*
Gerson, Mary-Joan. *Why the sky is far away*
Glyman, Caroline A. *What's above the sky?*
Hines, Anna Grossnickle. *Sky all around*
Hopkinson, Deborah. *Maria's comet*
Ichikawa, Satomi. *Nora's stars*
Jacobson, Jennifer Richard. *A net of stars*
Moroney, Lynn. *Elinda who danced in the sky*
Osborne, Mary Pope. *Moonhorse*, ill. by David McPhail
   Moonhorse, ill. by S. M. Saelig
Otto, Carolyn. *That sky, that rain*
Oughton, Jerrie. *How the stars fell into the sky*
Rosen, Sidney. *Where's the big dipper?*
Schoberle, Ceile. *Beyond the Milky Way*
Shaw, Charles Green. *It looked like spilt milk*
Spier, Peter. *Dreams*
Standiford, Natalie. *Dollhouse mouse*
Stone, Kazuko G. *Goodnight Twinklegator*
Taylor, Jane. *Twinkle, twinkle, little star*
Wyler, Rose. *The starry sky*

Slavery

Benjamin, Anne. *Young Harriet Tubman*
Bible. Old Testament. Joseph. *Joseph and his brothers*
Coleman, Evelyn. *To be a drum*
Dupré, Rick. *Agassu*
Edwards, Pamela Duncan. *Barefoot*
Gerrard, Roy. *The Roman twins*
Hathorn, Libby (Elizabeth). *Sky sash so blue*
Hopkinson, Deborah. *Sweet Clara and the freedom quilt*
Johnson, Dolores. *Now let me fly*
   Seminole diary
Johnson, James Weldon. *Lift ev'ry voice and sing*
Johnston, Tony. *The wagon*
McGill, Alice. *Molly Bannaky*
Medearis, Angela Shelf. *The freedom riddle*
Miller, Robert H. (Robert Henry). *The story of Nat Love*
Miller, William. *Frederick Douglass*
Monjo, F. N. *The drinking gourd*
Nolen, Jerdine. *Big Jabe*
Pinkney, Andrea Davis. *Dear Benjamin Banneker*
Riggio, Anita. *Secret signs*
Rochelle, Belinda. *Jewels*
Sanders, Scott R. (Scott Russell). *A place called Freedom*
Siegelson, Kim L. *In the time of the drums*
Smalls-Hector, Irene. *Irene Jennie and the Christmas masquerade*
   Jenny Reen and the Jack Muh Lantern
Uchida, Yoshiko. *The bracelet*

Weatherford, Carole Boston. *Juneteenth jamboree*
Winter, Jeanette. *Follow the drinking gourd*
Wright, Courtni Crump. *Journey to freedom*
  Jumping the broom

Sledding *see* Sports – sledding

Sleep

Alexander, Martha G. *I'll protect you from the jungle beasts*
Andersen, H. C. (Hans Christian). *The princess and the pea*, ill. by Emily Bolam
  The princess and the pea, ill. by Dorothée Duntze
  The princess and the pea, ill. by Dick Gackenbach
  The princess and the pea, ill. by Paul Galdone
  The princess and the pea, ill. by Camille Semelet
  The princess and the pea, ill. by Janet Stevens
  The princess and the pea, ill. by Suçie Stevenson
  The princess and the pea, ill. by Eve Tharlet
Arnold, Caroline. *Sleepytime for zoo animals*
Arnold, Tedd. *Five ugly monsters*
Asch, Frank. *Good night, Baby Bear*
Asher, Sandy. *Princess Bee and the royal good-night story*
Aylesworth, Jim. *The bad dream*
  Tonight's the night
Bach, Alice. *The smartest bear and his brother Oliver*
Bauer, Marion Dane. *Sleep, little one, sleep*
Baum, Louis. *I want to see the moon*
Beckman, Kaj. *Lisa cannot sleep*
Bergen, Lara Rice. *Washington Irving's Rip Van Winkle*
Bertrand, Lynne. *Dragon naps*
Bilezikian, Gary. *While I slept*
Black, Charles C. *The royal nap*
Bottner, Barbara. *There was nobody there*
Brande, Marlie. *Sleepy Nicholas*
Bright, Robert. *Me and the bears*
Brown, Margaret Wise. *A child's good night book*
  Sleepy ABC
  The sleepy little lion
  The sleepy men
Brown, Myra Berry. *First night away from home*
Bunting, Eve (Anne Evelyn). *No nap*
Burstein, Fred. *Rebecca's nap*
Burton, Jane. *Animals at rest*
Butler, John. *While you were sleeping*
Calhoun, Mary. *While I sleep*
Camp, Lindsay. *The biggest bed in the world*
Carlstrom, Nancy White. *No nap for Benjamin Badger*
Carpenter, Mary-Chapin. *Dreamland*
Caseley, Judith. *Slumber party!*
  Sophie and Sammy's library sleepover
Cazet, Denys. *I'm not sleepy*
  Mother night
Chalmers, Mary. *Take a nap, Harry*
Chislett, Gail. *Whump*
Chorao, Kay. *Lester's overnight*
Ciardi, John. *Scrappy, the pup*
Clise, Michele Durkson. *Ophelia's bedtime book*
Coker, Gylbert. *Naptime*
Collington, Peter. *Little pickle*
Crossley-Holland, Kevin. *Sleeping Nanna*
Dale, Penny. *Ten out of bed*
Daly, Niki. *Mary Malloy and the baby who wouldn't sleep*

De Paola, Tomie (Thomas Anthony). *Fight the night*
  When everyone was fast asleep
Dodd, Lynley. *Wake up, bear*
Dowling, Paul. *Are you sleepy, Puff?*
Dupasquier, Philippe. *I can't sleep*
Edwards, Patricia Kier. *Chester and Uncle Willoughby*
Edwards, Roberta. *Anna Bear's first winter*
Elkin, Benjamin. *The king who could not sleep*
Esbensen, Barbara Juster. *The dream mouse*
Evans, Eva Knox. *Sleepy time*
Facklam, Margery. *I go to sleep*
Farber, Werner. *Night lion*
Feldman, Eve B. *Animals don't wear pajamas*
Field, Eugene. *Wynken, Blynken and Nod*, ill. by Barbara Cooney
  Wynken, Blynken and Nod, ill. by Susan Jeffers
  Wynken, Blynken and Nod, ill. by Holly Johnson
  Wynken, Blynken and Nod, ill. by Johanna Westerman
Foreman, Michael. *Dad! I can't sleep*
Fox, Mem. *Night noises*
  Sleepy bears
Gerber, Carole. *Arctic dreams*
Gilmour, H. B. *Why Wembley Fraggle couldn't sleep*
Goodman, Joan Elizabeth. *Bernard's nap*
Grambling, Lois G. *Night sounds*
Grejniec, Michael. *Albert's nap*
Gretz, Susanna. *I'm not sleepy*
Hamm, Diane Johnston. *Rock-a-bye farm*
Harshman, Marc. *All the way to morning*
Harshman, Terry Webb. *Porcupine's pajama party*
Haseley, Dennis. *The cave of snores*
Hazelaar, Cor. *Zoo dreams*
Hazen, Barbara Shook. *Where do bears sleep?*, ill. by Mary Morgan-Vanroyen
  Where do bears sleep?, ill. by Ian E. Staunton
Heine, Helme. *King Bounce the 1st*
  The marvelous journey through the night
Henkes, Kevin. *Shhhh*
Hennessy, B. G. (Barbara G.). *Sleep tight*
Hindley, Judy. *The sleepy book*
Hirschi, Ron. *A time for sleeping*
Hopkins, Lee Bennett. *Still as a star*
Howard, Jane R. *When I'm sleepy*
Hutchins, Pat. *Good night owl*
Inkpen, Mick. *Kipper*
Irving, Washington. *Rip Van Winkle*, ill. by John Howe
  Rip Van Winkle, ill. by Thomas Locker
  Rip Van Winkle, ill. by Peter Wingham
James, Betsy. *The dream stair*
Janovitz, Marilyn. *Is it time?*
Jeffers, Susan. *All the pretty horses*
Jensen, Patricia. *Go to sleep, little groundhog*
Johnston, Tony. *The Chizzywink and the Alamagoozlum*
  Little Rabbit goes to sleep
Kajikawa, Kimiko. *Sweet dreams*
Kamish, Daniel. *The night scary beasties popped out of my head*
Kantrowitz, Mildred. *Willy Bear*
Karlin, Nurit. *The dream factory*
Katz, Avner. *The little pickpocket*
Keats, Ezra Jack. *Dreams*
Kemp, Moira. *Lift-the-flap kitten*
Khalsa, Dayal Kaur. *Sleepers*
Khan, Rukhsana. *Bedtime ba-a-a-lk*
Koralek, Jenny. *The boy and the cloth of dreams*

Kotzwinkle, William. *The nap master*
Krahn, Fernando. *Sleep tight, Alex Pumpernickel*
Kraus, Robert. *Good night little one*
    Good night Richard Rabbit
    Milton the early riser
    See the moon
Laimgruber, Monika. *Susannah and the Sandman*
Lewis, J. Patrick. *Isabella Abnormella and the very,
    very finicky Queen of Trouble*
Lewison, Wendy Cheyette. *Going to sleep on the farm*
Lively, Penelope. *Good night, sleep tight*
Lucas, Barbara (Barbara M.). *Sleeping over*
McCarthy, Bobette. *Dreaming*
McCauley, Jane R. *The way animals sleep*
McMullan, Kate (Hall). *Good night, Stella*
    The noisy giant's tea party
    Papa's song
McPartland, Suzy. *Sleepy-time moon*
McPhail, David M. *The dream child*
Mallat, Kathy. *Seven stars, more!*
Marino, Dorothy. *Edward and the boxes*
Martin, Jacqueline Briggs. *Grandmother Bryant's
    pocket*
Massie, Diane Redfield. *The baby beebee bird*
Merriam, Eve. *Goodnight to Annie*, ill. by Carol
    Schwartz
Miller, M. L. *The enormous snore*
Moore, Julia. *While you sleep*
Most, Bernard. *Z-Z-Zoink!*
Mueller, Virginia. *Monster can't sleep*
Munsch, Robert N. *Get out of bed!*
Murphy, Jill. *Peace at last*
Mwalimu. *Awful aardvark*
Nichol, B. P. *Once*
Nobisso, Josephine. *The yawn*
Novak, Matt. *The Pillow War*
    While the shepherd slept
O'Brien, Mary. *Counting sheep to sleep*
Oppenheim, Joanne. *The story book prince*
Ormerod, Jan. *Moonlight*
    Sleeping
Owen, Roy. *My night forest*
Oxenbury, Helen. *Say goodnight*
Panek, Dennis. *Ba ba sheep wouldn't go to sleep*
Pfister, Marcus. *The sleepy owl*
Plath, Sylvia. *The bed book*
Polushkin, Maria. *Mother, Mother, I want another*
Preston, Edna Mitchell. *Monkey in the jungle*
Reidel, Marlene. *Jacob and the robbers*
Reiser, Lynn. *Night thunder and the Queen of the Wild
    Horses*
Richardson, Judith Benét. *Old winter*
Riddell, Chris. *The wish factory*
Riggio, Anita. *Wake up, William!*
Rosenberg, Liz. *Adelaide and the night train*
Ross, Anna. *Naptime*
Roth, Carol. *Little Bunny's sleepless night*
Rowand, Phyllis. *It is night*
Rubel, Nicole. *Goldie's nap*
Sage, Chris. *Sleepy baby*
Sage, James. *To sleep*
Saleh, Harold J. *Even tiny ants must sleep*
Schneider, Nina. *While Susie sleeps*
Seuss, Dr. *Dr. Seuss's sleep book*
    I am not going to get up today!
Shepperson, Rob. *The sandman*
Showers, Paul. *Sleep is for everyone*
Simmons, Jane. *Go to sleep, Daisy*
Simon, Norma. *Where does my cat sleep?*

Sloat, Teri. *The thing that bothered Farmer Brown*
Slobodkin, Louis. *Wide-awake owl*
Sonneborn, Ruth A. *Seven in a bed*
Spinelli, Eileen. *Where is the night train going?*
Stanley, Diane. *Birdsong lullaby*
Steel, Danielle. *Freddie's first night away*
Stevenson, James. *We can't sleep*
Stockdale, Susan. *Some sleep standing up*
Sugita, Yutaka. *Good night 1, 2, 3*
Swain, Ruth Freeman. *Bedtime!*
Szekeres, Cyndy. *Good night, Sammy*
Tafuri, Nancy. *Where we sleep*
Takamado no Miya Hisako. *Katie and the dream-
    eater*
Tobias, Tobi. *Chasing the goblins away*
Trez, Denise. *Good night, Veronica*
Tucker, Kathy. *Do knights take naps?*
Twining, Edith. *Sandman*
Van Laan, Nancy. *Sleep, sleep, sleep*
Van Vorst, M. L. *A Norse lullaby*
Vulliamy, Clara. *Good night, baby*
Waber, Bernard. *Ira sleeps over*
Waddell, Martin. *Can't you sleep, Little Bear?*
Wahl, Jan. *The sleepytime book*
    Sylvester Bear overslept
    The toy circus
Walton, Rick. *So many bunnies*
Weir, Alison. *Peter, good night*
Weisgard, Leonard. *Who dreams of cheese?*
Weiss, Nicki. *Where does the brown bear go?*
    Where does the brown bear go? A board book
Wersba, Barbara. *Amanda dreaming*
Whatley, Bruce. *Captain Pajamas*
Wheeler, Cindy. *Marmalade's nap*
Whiteside, Karen. *Lullaby of the wind*
Wolcott, Patty. *Eeeeeek!*
Wood, Audrey. *Moonflute*
    The napping house
    The napping house wakes up
Woolf, Virginia. *Nurse Lugton's curtain*
Yabuuchi, Masayuki. *Animals sleeping*
Yolen, Jane. *Dragon night and other lullabies*
Yulya. *Bears are sleeping*
Zagone, Theresa. *No nap for me*
Ziefert, Harriet. *Cow in the house*
    Good night everyone!
    I want to sleep in your bed!
    Say good night!
    Sleepy dog
Zolotow, Charlotte (Shapiro). *The sleepy book*, ill. by
    Vladimir Bobri
    The sleepy book, ill. by Ilse Plume
Zwetchkenbaum, G. *The Peanuts sleepy time puzzle
    book*

Sleepovers

Berenstain, Stan. *The Berenstain bears and the slum-
    ber party*
Brown, Marc Tolon. *Arthur's first sleepover*
Caseley, Judith. *Slumber party!*
Dale, Penny. *Daisy Rabbit's tree house*
Harshman, Terry Webb. *Porcupine's pajama party*
Hill, Eric. *Spot sleeps over*
Jackson, Isaac. *Somebody's new pajamas*
Lipniacka, Ewa. *To bed . . . or else!*
Lucas, Barbara (Barbara M.). *Sleeping over*
McKissack, Patricia C. *Messy Bessey and the birthday
    overnight*

Murphy, Stuart J. *Rabbit's pajama party*
Rodriguez, Bobbie. *Sarah's sleepover*
Steel, Danielle. *Freddie's first night away*
Waber, Bernard. *Bearsie Bear and the surprise sleepover party*

Sleight-of-hand *see* Magic

Sloths *see* Animals – sloths

Slugs *see* Animals – slugs

Smallness *see* Character traits – smallness

Smelling *see* Anatomy – noses; Senses – smelling

Snails *see* Animals – snails

Snakes *see* Reptiles – snakes

Snow *see* Weather – blizzards; Weather – snow

Snow plows *see* Machines

Snowmen

Arnold, Katya. *The adventures of Snowwoman*
Bauer, Caroline Feller. *Midnight snowman*
Briggs, Raymond. *Building the snowman*
   Dressing up
   The party
   The snowman
   The snowman, a lift-the-flap board book
   The snowman storybook
   The snowman tell-the-time book
   Walking in the air
Carlson, Nancy L. *Snowden*
Chorao, Kay. *Kate's snowman*
Cuyler, Margery. *The biggest, best snowman*
Ehlert, Lois. *Snowballs*
Erskine, Jim. *The snowman*
Goffstein, M. B. (Marilyn Brooke). *Our snowman*
Gordon, Sharon. *Friendly snowman*
Hoban, Julia. *Amy loves the snow*
Hol, Coby. *Lisa and the snowman*
Holl, Adelaide. *The runaway giant*
Hughes, Shirley. *The snow lady*
Inkpen, Mick. *Penguin small*
Janosch. *Dear snowman*
Johnson, Crockett. *Time for spring*
Joos, Françoise. *The golden snowflake*
Joyce, William. *Snowie Rolie*
Kellogg, Steven (Stephen). *The mystery of the missing red mitten*
Komoda, Beverly. *The winter day*
Kuskin, Karla. *In the flaky frosty morning*
Leonard, Marcia. *The best snowman ever*
Lobe, Mira. *The snowman who went for a walk*
Loretan, Sylvia. *Bob the snowman*
Mack, Gail. *Yesterday's snowman*
McKee, David. *Snow woman*
Miller, Edna. *Mousekin's frosty friend*
Morgan, Allen. *Sadie and the snowman*
Parillo, Tony. *Michelangelo's surprise*
Peddle, Daniel. *Snow day*

Schaefer, Carole Lexa. *Snow pumpkin*
Weedn, Flavia. *The little snow bear*
Whybrow, Ian. *Harry and the snow king*
Yee, Patrick. *Winter rabbit*
Zion, Gene. *The summer snowman*

Soccer *see* Sports – soccer

Society Islands *see* Foreign lands – South Sea Islands

Socks *see* Clothing – socks

Sofas *see* Furniture – couches, sofas

Soldiers *see* Careers – military

Soldiers, toy *see* Toys – soldiers

Solitude *see* Behavior – solitude

Songs

Abisch, Roz. *Sweet Betsy from Pike*
Adams, Pam. *This old man*
Alexander, Cecil Frances. *All things bright and beautiful*
Alger, Leclaire Gowans. *All in the morning early*
   Kellyburn Braes
Arkin, Alan. *Black and white*
Ash, Jutta. *Wedding birds*
B-52's (Musical group). *Wig!*
Bangs, Edward. *Yankee Doodle*
Barner, Bob. *Dem bones*
Billy Boy (folk-song). *Billy Boy*
Birdseye, Tom. *She'll be comin' round the mountain*
Boesel, Ann Sterling. *Sing and sing again*
   Singing with Peter and Patsy
Botwin, Esther. *A treasury of songs for little children*
Bowman, Peter. *The Christmas songbook*
Boynton, Sandra. *Good night, good night*
Brand, Oscar. *When I first came to this land*
Bratton, John. *The teddy bears' picnic*, ill. by Renate Kozikowski
Briggs, Raymond. *The white land*
Bring a torch, Jeannette, Isabella
Brown, Marc Tolon. *Play rhymes*
Bryan, Ashley. *All night, all day*
   I'm going to sing
   Lion and the ostrich chicks
Buffett, Jimmy. *The jolly mon*
Burgie, Irving. *Caribbean carnival*
Byrne, David. *Stay up late*
Carle, Eric. *Today is Monday*
Carpenter, Mary-Chapin. *Halley came to Jackson*
Carryl, Charles E. (Charles Edward). *A capital ship*
Caseley, Judith. *Molly Pink*
Cazet, Denys. *Dancing*
Chalk, Gary. *Yankee Doodle*
Child, Lydia Maria. *Over the river and through the wood*
Christmas carols
Cohen, Miriam. *Down in the subway*
Conover, Chris. *Six little ducks*
Cooner, Donna D. (Donna Danell). *I know an old Texan who swallowed a fly*
Count me in

Craver, Mike. *Beaver ball at the bug club*
Cutler, Ivor. *Doris*
Daily, Don. *The twelve days of Christmas cats*
Dalton, Alene. *My new picture book of songs*
Delacre, Lulu. *Arroz con leche*
    Las Navidades
Delaney, A. *The gunnywolf*
Delessert, Etienne. *A long long song*
Denslow, W. W. *Denslow's picture book treasury*
Denver, John. *The children and the flowers*
De Regniers, Beatrice Schenk. *Was it a good trade?*
Devlin, Harry. *The walloping window blind*
Din dan don, it's Christmas
Domanska, Janina. *Busy Monday morning*
Donovan, Mary Lee. *Won't you come and play with me?*
Duncan, Lois. *Songs from dreamland*
Durell, Ann. *The Diane Goode book of American folk tales and songs*
Duvoisin, Roger Antoine. *Petunia and the song*
Emberley, Barbara. *One wide river to cross*
    Simon's song
Emerson, Sally. *The Kingfisher nursery rhyme songbook*
Farjeon, Eleanor. *Morning has broken*
The farmer in the dell. *The farmer in the dell*, ill. by John O'Brien
    The farmer in the dell, ill. by Kathy Parkinson
    The farmer in the dell, ill. by Mary Maki Rae
    The farmer in the dell, ill. by Diane Stanley
    The farmer in the dell, ill. by Alexandra Wallner
Fern, Eugene. *Birthday presents*
Flanders, Michael. *The hippopotamus song*
Fleming, Candace. *Gabriella's song*
The fox went out on a chilly night
French, Fiona. *Rise and shine*
The friendly beasts and a partridge in a pear tree, ill. by Virginia Pearsons
A frog he would a-wooing go (folk-song). *Frog went a-courtin'*, ill. by Feodor Rojankovsky
    The frog went a-courting, adapt. and ill. by Dominic Catalano
    Froggie went a courting, ill. by Marjorie Priceman
    Froggie went a-courting, ill. by Chris Conover
    Mr. Frog went a-courting
    Wendy Watson's frog went a-courting
Gilbert, Yvonne. *Baby's book of lullabies and cradle songs*
Go tell Aunt Rhody. *Go tell Aunt Rhody*, ill. by Aliki
    Go tell Aunt Rhody, ill. by Robert M. Quackenbush
Goode, Diane. *Diane Goode's book of silly stories & songs*
Goodhart, Pippa. *Row, row, row your boat*
Graham, Steve. *Dear old Donegal*
Granfield, Linda. *Silent night*
The green grass grows all around
Greene, Carol. *A computer went a-courting*
    Hinny Winny Bunco
    The thirteen days of Halloween
Guthrie, Woody. *This land is your land*
    Woody's 20 grow big songs
Hale, Sarah Josepha Buell. *Mary had a little lamb*
Hallworth, Grace. *Down by the river*
Halpern, Shari. *What shall we do when we all go out?*
Harris, Leon A. *The great diamond robbery*
Harrison, David Lee. *The animals' song*
Hirsh, Marilyn. *One little goat*
Hoban, Brom. *Skunk Lane*

Hoban, Lillian. *Harry's song*
Hobzek, Mildred. *We came a-marching . . . 1, 2, 3*
Hodges, Margaret. *Silent night*
Hogrogian, Nonny. *The cat who loved to sing*
Homme, Bob. *The friendly giant's birthday*
Hoose, Philip M. *Hey little ant*
Hot cross buns, and other old street cries
Houston, John A. *The bright yellow rope*
    A mouse in my house
    A room full of animals
Ipcar, Dahlov. *The cat came back*
    "The song of the day birds" and "The song of the night birds"
I've been working on the railroad
Ivimey, John William. *The complete story of the three blind mice*, ill. by Paul Galdone
    The complete version of ye three blind mice, ill. by Walton Corbould
    Three blind mice, ill. by Lorinda Bryan Cauley
    Three blind mice, ill. by Victoria Chess
Johnson, James Weldon. *Lift ev'ry voice and sing*
Johnston, Mary Anne. *Sing me a song*
Johnston, Tony. *Grandpa's song*
Jonas, Ann. *Bird talk*
Jones, Carol. *This old man*
Kapp, Paul. *Cock-a-doodle-doo! Cock-a-doodle-dandy!*
Keats, Ezra Jack. *The little drummer boy*
Kellogg, Steven (Stephen). *A-hunting we will go!*
    Give the dog a bone
    I was born about 10,000 years ago
    Yankee Doodle
Kemp, Moira. *I'm a little teapot*
Kennedy, Jimmy. *The teddy bears' picnic*, ill. by Michael Hague
Key, Francis Scott. *The Star-Spangled Banner*, ill. by Paul Galdone
    The Star-Spangled Banner, ill. by Peter Spier
Kimmel, Eric A. *Why worry?*
King, Bob. *Sitting on the farm*
Koontz, Robin Michal. *This old man*
Kovalski, Maryann. *Jingle bells*
    Take me out to the ball game
    The wheels on the bus
Kroll, Steven. *By the dawn's early light*
Krull, Kathleen. *Songs of praise*
Kuskin, Karla. *Paul*
Lambert, Paulette Livers. *Evening*
Langstaff, John M. *Oh, a-hunting we will go*
    Ol' Dan Tucker
    On Christmas day in the morning
    Over in the meadow
    Soldier, soldier, won't you marry me?
    The swapping boy
    The two magicians
Lansky, Bruce. *Sweet dreams*
Lear, Edward. *The pelican chorus*, ill. by Harold Berson
    The pelican chorus and the quangle wangle's hat, ill. by Kevin W. Maddison
Lenski, Lois. *At our house*
    Davy and his dog
    Davy goes places
    Debbie and her grandma
    A dog came to school
    I like winter
    I went for a walk
    The life I live
Lester, Alison. *Isabella's bed*
Leventhal, Debra. *What is your language?*

Lippman, Sidney. *A you're adorable*
Lishak, Anthony. *Row your boat*
Little old lady who swallowed a fly. *Fancy that!*
  Golly Gump swallowed a fly
  I know an old lady, ill. by Abner Graboff
  I know an old lady, ill. by G. Brian Karas
  I know an old lady, ill. by Steve McInturff
  I know an old lady, ill. by Albert Miller
  I know an old lady who swallowed a fly, ill. by Glen
    Rounds
  I know an old lady who swallowed a fly, ill. by
    William Stobbs
  I know an old lady who swallowed a fly, ill. by
    Nadine Bernard Westcott
  There was an old lady, ill. by Nick Bantock
  There was an old lady who swallowed a fly, ill. by
    Pam Adams
  There was an old lady who swallowed a fly, ill. by
    Colin Hawkins
  There was an old lady who swallowed a fly, ill. by
    Simms Taback
  There was an old woman, ill. by Steven Kellogg
Lord, Beman. *The days of the week*
Lubach, Peter. *Harry and the singing fish*
Lullaby and goodnight
McCarthy, Bobette. *Buffalo girls*
McCutcheon, John. *Happy adoption day!*
McGee, Shelagh. *I'm a little teapot*
Mack, Stanley (Stan). *Ten bears in my bed*
McLerran, Alice. *Dreamsong*
McNally, Darcie. *In a cabin in a wood*
Mallett, David. *Inch by inch*
Manson, Christopher. *A farmyard song*
  The tree in the wood
Maril, Lee. *Mr. Bunny paints the eggs*
Medearis, Angela Shelf. *The zebra-riding cowboy*
Melmed, Laura Krauss. *The first song ever sung*
Mills, Alan. *The hungry goat*
Modesitt, Jeanne. *Songs of Chanukah*
Mohr, Joseph. *Silent night*
Moon, Dolly M. *My very first book of cowboy songs*
Morgenstern, Christian. *Lullabies, lyrics and gallows
  songs*
Morley, Carol. *Farmyard song*
Moses, Will. *Silent night*
Moss, Jeffrey. *The songs of Sesame Street in poems and
  pictures*
Moss, Marissa. *Knick knack paddywack*
Most, Bernard. *Row, row, row your goat*
Mother Goose. *London Bridge is falling down*, ill. by
  Ed Emberley
  London Bridge is falling down, ill. by Peter Spier
  The Mother Goose songbook
  Mother Goose's melodies
  Thirty old-time nursery songs
Munsch, Robert N. *Mortimer*
My first songs
Neale, J. M. (John Mason). *Good King Wenceslas*
Nelson, Esther L. *The funny songbook*
  Holiday singing and dancing games
  The silly songbook
Newbolt, Henry John, Sir. *Rilloby-rill*
Newland, Mary Reed. *Good King Wenceslas*
Niland, Kilmeny. *A bellbird in a flame tree*
Norworth, Jack. *Take me out to the ballgame*
O Christmas tree
Old MacDonald had a farm. *E I E I O*
  Old MacDonald, ill. by Rosemary Wells
  Old MacDonald had a farm, ill. by Holly Berry

Old MacDonald had a farm, ill. by Lorinda Bryan
  Cauley
Old MacDonald had a farm, ill. by Mel Crawford
Old MacDonald had a farm, ill. by Tracey English
Old MacDonald had a farm, ill. by David Frank-
  land
Old MacDonald had a farm, ill. by Abner Graboff
Old MacDonald had a farm, ill. by Nancy Hellen
Old MacDonald had a farm, ill. by Carol Jones
Old MacDonald had a farm, ill. by Tracey Camp-
  bell Pearson
Old MacDonald had a farm, ill. by Robert M.
  Quackenbush
Old MacDonald had a farm, ill. by Glen Rounds
Old MacDonald had a farm, ill. by Jessica Souhami
Old MacDonald had a farm, ill. by William Stobbs
Old MacDonald had a farm, ill. by Prue Theobalds
On the little hearth
Oppenheim, Joanne. *The eency weency spider*
Ormerod, Jan. *Ms. MacDonald has a class*
Over in the meadow, ill. by Ezra Jack Keats
A paper of pins
Parton, Dolly. *Coat of many colors*
Paterson, A. B. (Andrew Barton). *Waltzing Matilda*
Paxton, Tom. *Going to the zoo*
  The marvelous toy
Peek, Merle. *The balancing act*
  *Mary wore her red dress and Henry wore his green
    sneakers*
Pfister, Marcus. *I see the moon*
Philpot, Lorna. *Amazing Anthony Ant*
Pierpont, James. *Jingle bells*
Poston, Elizabeth. *Baby's song book*
Preston, Edna Mitchell. *Pop Corn and Ma Goodness*
Price, Christine. *One is God*
Quackenbush, Robert M. *Clementine*
  The man on the flying trapeze
  Pop! goes the weasel and Yankee Doodle
  She'll be comin' 'round the mountain
  Skip to my Lou
  There'll be a hot time in the old town tonight
Raebeck, Lois. *Who am I?*
Raffi. *Baby beluga*
  Down by the bay
  Everything grows
  Like me and you
  One light, one sun
  Rise and shine
  Shake my sillies out
  Wheels on the bus
Raposo, Joe. *The Sesame Street song book*
Ray, Mary Lyn. *Shaker boy*
Rayner, Mary. *One by one*
  Ten pink piglets
Rey, H. A. (Hans Augusto). *Humpty Dumpty and
  other Mother Goose songs*
Richardson, Jean. *Stephen's feast*
Robbins, Ruth. *Baboushka and the three kings*
Rodgers, Richard. *A real nice clambake*
Roll over!, ill. by Merle Peek
Root, Phyllis. *Soup for supper*
Ross, Tony. *This old man*
Rounds, Glen. *The boll weevil*
  Casey Jones
  The strawberry roan
  Sweet Betsy from Pike
Sanfield, Steve. *The girl who wanted a song*
Schackburg, Richard. *Yankee Doodle*
Scott, Lesbia. *I sing a song of the saints of God*

Seeger, Pete. *The foolish frog*
Sewall, Marcia. *Animal song*
Shannon, George. *Lizard's song*
   Oh, I love!
Simon, Paul. *At the zoo*
Simple gifts
Singer, Marilyn. *The maiden on the moor*
   Will you take me to town on strawberry day?
Slavin, Bill. *The cat came back*
Slobodkin, Louis. *Wide-awake owl*
The song of the Three Holy Children
Spier, Peter. *The Erie Canal*
Staines, Bill. *All God's critters got a place in the choir*
Stern, Elsie-Jean. *Wee Robin's Christmas song*
Stevens, Jan Romero. *Twelve lizards leaping*
Stobbs, William. *There's a hole in my bucket*
Sweet, Melissa. *Fiddle-i-fee*
Taylor, Jane. *Twinkle, twinkle, little star*
Taylor, Mark. *The bold fisherman*
   Old Blue, you good dog you
Tompert, Ann. *A carol for Christmas*
Trapani, Iza. *How much is that doggie in the window?*
   The itsy bitsy spider
   Mary had a little lamb
Trivas, Irene. *Emma's Christmas*
The twelve days of Christmas.. English folk song.
   Brian Wildsmith's The twelve days of Christmas
   Jack Kent's twelve days of Christmas
   The twelve days of Christmas, ill. by Jan Brett
   The twelve days of Christmas, ill. by Ilonka Karasz
   The twelve days of Christmas, ill. by Ilse Plume
   The twelve days of Christmas, ill. by Erika Schnei-
   der
   The twelve days of Christmas, ill. by Vladimir Vagin
   The twelve days of Christmas, ill. by Sophie Wind-
   ham
Vaughan, Marcia Kapok. *Wombat stew*
Wallace, Nancy Elizabeth. *Apples, apples, apples*
Wallner, John C. *Old MacDonald had a farm*
We wish you a merry Christmas
Weeks, Sarah. *Crocodile smile*
Weiss, George (George David). *What a wonderful
   world*
Weiss, Nicki. *If you're happy and you know it*
Welch, Willy. *Playing right field*
Wells, Rosemary. *The bear went over the mountain*
   Bingo
   The itsy-bitsy spider
Wenning, Elisabeth. *The Christmas mouse*
Westcott, Nadine Bernard. *Skip to my Lou*
   There's a hole in the bucket
What a morning!
Wheeler, Opal. *Sing in praise*
   Sing Mother Goose
Whippo, Walt. *Little white duck*
Widdecombe Fair
Wilder, Laura Ingalls. *My little house songbook*
Wolff, Ashley. *The bells of London*
Yolen, Jane. *Jane Yolen's Old MacDonald songbook*
   The lap-time song and play book
Yulya. *Bears are sleeping*
Zelinsky, Paul O. *The wheels on the bus*
Zemach, Harve. *Mommy, buy me a China doll*
Ziefert, Harriet. *When I first came to this land*
Zolotow, Charlotte (Shapiro). *The song*

Sons *see* Family life – sons

Sorcerers *see* Wizards

Sounds *see* Noise, sounds

South Africa *see* Foreign lands – South Africa

South America *see* Foreign lands – South
America

South Pole *see* Foreign lands – Antarctic

South Sea Islands *see* Foreign lands – South
Sea Islands

Southwest Indians *see* Indians of North
America – Southwest

Soviet Union *see* Foreign lands – Russia; Foreign lands – Soviet Union

Space and space ships

Agee, Jon. *Dmitri the astronaut*
Alexander, Martha G. *Marty McGee's space lab, no
   girls allowed*
   You're a genius, Blackboard Bear
Anderson, Joan. *Richie's rocket*
Asimov, Isaac. *The best new thing*
Barden, Rosalind. *TV monster*
Barner, Bob. *Space race*
Barton, Byron. *I want to be an astronaut*
Behrens, June. *I can be an astronaut*
Berenstain, Stan. *The Berenstain bears on the moon*
Blocksma, Mary. *Easy-to-make spaceships that really fly*
Bradman, Tony. *It came from outer space*
   Michael
Branley, Franklyn M. (Mansfield). *Floating in space*
   Is there life in outer space?
   Journey into a black hole
   The planets in our solar system
Brewster, Patience. *Ellsworth and the cats from Mars*
Brunhoff, Laurent de. *Babar visits another planet*
Carey, Valerie Scho. *Harriet and William and the ter-
   rible creature*
Carrick, Carol. *Patrick's dinosaurs on the Internet*
Catalanotto, Peter. *Dad and me*
Cecil, Laura. *Noah and the space ark*
Coffelt, Nancy. *Dogs in space*
Cole, Babette. *The trouble with Gran*
Cole, Joanna. *The magic school bus lost in the solar sys-
   tem*
Collicott, Sharleen. *Seeing stars*
Counsel, June. *But Martin!*
Cox, Judy. *The West Texas chili monster*
Delaney, Ned. *Cosmic chickens*
Demarest, Chris L. *The lunatic adventure of Kitman
   and Willy*
Eco, Umberto. *The three astronauts*
Freeman, Don. *Space witch*
Freeman, Mae Blacker. *You will go to the moon*
Fuchs, Erich. *Journey to the moon*
Glass, Andrew. *My brother tries to make me laugh*
Graham, Ian. *The best book of spaceships*
Greene, Carol. *Astronauts work in space*
Greydanus, Rose. *Trouble in space*
Haddon, Mark. *The Sea of Tranquillity*
Hergé. *Explorers on the moon*

Hillert, Margaret. *Up, up and away*
Hirst, Robin. *My place in space*
Hopkins, Lee Bennett. *Blast off!*
Johnson, Crockett. *Harold's trip to the sky*
Jones, Brian. *Space*
Keats, Ezra Jack. *Regards to the man in the moon*
Kirk, Daniel. *Moondogs*
Kroll, Steven. *The magic rocket*
Kuskin, Karla. *A space story*
Lauber, Patricia. *You're aboard spaceship Earth*
Leedy, Loreen. *Blast off to Earth!*
    How humans make friends
    Postcards from Pluto
Loomis, Christine. *Astro Bunnies*
Lorenz, Lee. *Hugo and the spacedog*
MacDonald, Suse. *Space spinners*
McMullan, Kate (Hall). *Spacey riddles*
McNaughton, Colin. *Here come the aliens!*
McPhail, David M. *Tinker and Tom and the Star Baby*
Maisner, Heather. *Planet monster*
Marshall, Edward. *Space case*
Marshall, James. *Merry Christmas, space case*
Marzollo, Jean. *Jed and the space bandits*
    Jed's junior space patrol
May, Charles Paul. *High-noon rocket*
Mayer, Mercer. *Astronaut critter*
Mayers, Florence Cassen. *The National Air and Space Museum*
Moché, Dinah L. *The astronauts*
Mooser, Stephen. *Funnyman meets the monster from outer space*
Moss, Marissa. *Knick knack paddywack*
Murphy, Jill. *What next, baby bear!*
Osborne, Mary Pope. *Moonhorse*, ill. by S. M. Saelig
Ostrow, Vivian. *My brother is from outer space*
Ottley, Matt. *What Faust saw*
Oxenbury, Helen. *Tom and Pippo see the moon*
Paul, Sherry. *2-B and the space visitor*
Peet, Bill (William Bartlett). *The wump world*
Pinkney, J. Brian. *Cosmo and the robot*
Pinkwater, Daniel Manus. *Guys from space*
    Wallpaper from space
Podendorf, Illa. *Space*
Pryor, Bonnie. *Mr. Munday and the space creatures*
Rey, H. A. (Hans Augusto). *Curious George gets a medal*
Robison, Nancy. *UFO kidnap*
Rockwell, Anne F. *Space vehicles*
Root, Phyllis. *The hungry monster*
Rosen, Michael (1946-). *Mission Ziffoid*
Rosen, Sidney. *How far is a star?*
    Where does the moon go?
Ross, Dave (David). *Gorp and the space pirates*
    Space monster
    Space Monster Gorp and the runaway computer
Ross, Tony. *I'm coming to get you!*
Sadler, Marilyn. *Alistair in outer space*
    Alistair's time machine
Schoberle, Ceile. *Beyond the Milky Way*
Sharratt, Nick. *Rocket countdown*
Shields, Carol Diggory. *Martian rock*
Sis, Peter. *Starry messenger*
Snow, Alan. *The truth about cats*
Steadman, Ralph. *The little red computer*
Thompson, Richard. *Sky full of babies*
Ungerer, Tomi. *Moon man*
Vaughn, Jenny. *On the moon*
Weiss, Ellen. *Pigs in space*
Weston, Martha. *Space guys!*

Wethered, Peggy. *Touchdown Mars!*
Wildsmith, Brian. *Professor Noah's spaceship*
Willis, Jeanne. *Earth mobiles as explained by Professor Xargle*
    Earth tigerlets as explained by Professor Xargle
    Earthlets as explained by Professor Xargle
    The long blue blazer
Wood, Audrey. *The Christmas adventure of Space Elf Sam*
Wynne-Jones, Tim. *Builder of the moon*
Yaccarino, Dan. *Zoom! Zoom! Zoom! I'm off to the moon!*
Yolen, Jane. *Moon ball*
Yorinks, Arthur. *Company's coming*
Young, Ruth. *A trip to Mars*
Zaffo, George J. *The giant book of things in space*
Ziegler, Ursina. *Squaps the moonling*

Spain *see* Foreign lands – Spain

Sparrows *see* Birds – sparrows

Special Olympics *see* Sports – Special Olympics

Spectacles *see* Glasses

Speech *see* Language

Speed *see* Concepts – speed

Spelunking *see* Caves

Spiders

Aardema, Verna. *Anansi does the impossible!*
    Anansi finds a fool
    The vingananee and the tree toad
Adelson, Leone. *Please pass the grass*
Back, Christine. *Spider's web*
Bailey, Jill. *The life cycle of a spider*
Baker, Jeannie. *One hungry spider*
Banks, Kate (Katherine A.). *Spider, spider*
Barrett, Norman S. *Spiders*
Bason, Lillian. *Spiders*
Berman, Ruth. *Spinning spiders*
Berry, James. *First palm trees*
Brandenberg, Franz. *Fresh cider and apple pie*
Bryan, Ashley. *The dancing granny*
Cahill, Chris. *Spider magic*
Carle, Eric. *The very busy spider*
Chenery, Janet. *Wolfie*
Climo, Shirley. *The cobweb Christmas*
Conklin, Gladys. *I caught a lizard*
Crothers, Samuel McChord. *Miss Muffet's Christmas party*
Fisher, Aileen Lucia. *When it comes to bugs*
Fowler, Allan. *Spiders are not insects*
French, Vivian. *Spider watching*
Freschet, Berniece. *The web in the grass*
Galdone, Joanna. *Honeybee's party*
George, Jean Craighead. *All upon a stone*
Gibbons, Gail. *Spiders*
Glaser, Linda. *Spectacular spiders*
Gleeson, Brian. *Anansi*
Goldin, Augusta. *Spider silk*
Graham, Margaret Bloy. *Be nice to spiders*

Hawcock, David. *Spider*
Hawes, Judy. *My daddy longlegs*
Hawkins, Colin. *Incy wincy spider*
Joosse, Barbara M. *Spiders in the fruit cellar*
Kajpust, Melissa. *A dozen silk diapers*
Kimmel, Eric A. *Anansi and the magic stick*
   Anansi and the moss-covered rock
   Anansi and the talking melon
   Anansi goes fishing
Kirk, David. *Little Miss Spider*
   Little Miss Spider at Sunny Patch School
   Miss Spider's ABC
   Miss Spider's new car
   Miss Spider's tea party
Koralek, Jenny. *The cobweb curtain*
Kraus, Robert. *Dance, Spider, dance!*
   How Spider saved Easter
   How Spider saved Halloween
   How Spider saved Turkey
   How Spider saved Valentine's Day
   The trouble with spider
Lake, Mary Dixon. *The royal drum*
Lasky, Kathryn. *Show and tell bunnies*
Lewis, J. Patrick. *The little buggers*
Llewellyn, Claire. *Some bugs glow in the dark*
   Spiders have fangs
London, Jonathan. *Dream weaver*
McDermott, Gerald. *Anansi the spider*
MacDonald, Amy. *The spider who created the world*
MacDonald, Suse. *Space spinners*
McNulty, Faith. *The lady and the spider*
Mead, Katherine. *How spiders got eight legs*
Mollel, Tololwa M. (Tololwa Marti). *Ananse's feast*
Morley, Carol. *A spider and a pig*
O'Neil, Amanda. *I wonder why spiders spin webs*
Oppenheim, Joanne. *The eency weency spider*
   Have you seen bugs?
Oxford Scientific Films. *The spider's web*
Parsons, Alexandra. *Amazing spiders*
Penner, Lucille Recht. *Monster bugs*
Policoff, Stephen Phillip. *Cesar's amazing journey*
Rose, Anne K. *Spider in the sky*
Rouss, Sylvia A. *Sammy Spider's first Passover*
   Sammy Spider's first Shabbat
Ryder, Joanne. *The spiders dance*
Sardegna, Jill. *The roly-poly spider*
Selsam, Millicent E. *A first look at spiders*
Simon, Francesca. *Spider school*
Siomades, Lorianne. *The itsy bitsy spider*
Temple, Frances. *Tiger soup*
Trapani, Iza. *The itsy bitsy spider*
Wagner, Jenny. *Aranea*
Wells, Rosemary. *The itsy-bitsy spider*
Wood, David. *Silly spider!*
Yolen, Jane. *Spider Jane*

Split page books *see* Format, unusual

Sponges *see* Animals – sponges

Spooks *see* Ghosts; Mythical creatures – goblins

Spoonbills *see* Birds – spoonbills

Sports

Axelrod, Amy. *Pigs on the ball*

Berenstain, Stan. *The Berenstain bears go out for the team*
Blaustein, Muriel. *Play ball, Zachary!*
Bundey, Nikki. *In the park*
   In the snow
   In the water
Bush, Timothy. *Three at sea*
Butterworth, Nick. *Field day*
Carlson, Nancy L. *Bunnies and their sports*
Carr, Jan. *Frozen noses*
Carrick, Carol. *The climb*
Caseley, Judith. *Molly Pink goes hiking*
Cole, Babette. *Three cheers for Errol!*
Cole, Joanna. *Riding Silver Star*
Dadey, Debbie. *Shooting star: Annie Oakley, the legend*
Hoberman, Mary Ann. *Mr. and Mrs. Muddle*
Johnston, Tony. *Sparky and Eddie, wild, wild rodeo!*
Liatsos, Sandra Olson. *Bicycle riding and other poems*
London, Jonathan. *White water*
Martin, Bill (William Ivan). *White Dynamite and Curly Kidd*
Millen, C. M. *The low-down laundry line blues*
Miller, Margaret. *Here we go!*
   Water play
Ormerod, Jan. *Bend and stretch*
Peterson, Esther Allen. *Penelope gets wheels*
Rayner, Mary. *Marathon and Steve*
Riddle, Tohby. *Careful with that ball, Eugene!*
Rotenberg, Lisa. *Rodeo pup*
Saddler, Allen. *The Archery contest*
Tinkelman, Murray. *Cowgirl*
Yeoman, John. *Old Mother Hubbard's dog takes up sport*

Sports – archery

Fisher, Leonard Everett. *William Tell*

Sports – baseball

Blackstone, Margaret. *This is baseball*
Bottner, Barbara. *Nana Hannah's piano*
Burleigh, Robert. *Home run*
Carrier, Roch. *The longest home run*
Christian, Mary Blount. *The sand lot*
Cohen, Ron. *My dad's baseball*
Cooper, Elisha. *Ballpark*
Curtis, Gavin. *The bat boy and his violin*
Day, Alexandra. *Frank and Ernest play ball*
Delaney, Ned. *Two strikes, four eyes*
Downing, Joan. *Baseball is our game*
Eaton, Deborah. *The rainy day grump*
Giff, Patricia Reilly. *Ronald Morgan goes to bat*
Gordon, Sharon. *Play ball, Kate!*
Greene, Carol. *I can be a baseball player*
Herman, Gail. *Double-header*
Hillert, Margaret. *Play ball*
Hoff, Syd. *The littlest leaguer*
   Slugger Sal's slump
Hooks, William H. *Mr. Baseball*
Isadora, Rachel. *Max*
Joyce, William. *Baseball Bob*
Ketteman, Helen. *I remember papa*
Kovalski, Maryann. *Take me out to the ball game*
Latimer, Jim. *The fox under first base*
Lexau, Joan M. *I'll tell on you*
Little, Jean. *Bats about baseball*

McConnachie, Brian. *Elmer and the chickens vs. the big league*
McCully, Emily Arnold. *Mouse practice*
Mandel, Peter. *Say hey*
Mochizuki, Ken. *Baseball saved us*
Morgan, Allen. *Matthew and the midnight ball game*
Motomora, Mitchell. *Specs*
Norworth, Jack. *Take me out to the ballgame*
Paxton, Tom. *The jungle baseball game*
Perkins, Al. *Don and Donna go to bat*
Portnoy, Mindy Avra. *Matzah ball*
Prager, Annabelle. *The baseball birthday party*
Rubin, Jeff. *Baseball brothers*
Sachs, Marilyn. *Fleet-footed Florence*
Matt's mitt
Schulman, Janet. *Camp Kee Wee's secret weapon*
Stadler, John. *Hooray for snail!*
Thayer, Ernest Lawrence. *Casey at the bat*, ill. by Christopher Bing
Casey at the bat, ill. by Gerald Fitzgerald
Casey at the bat, ill. by Patricia Polacco
Waber, Bernard. *Gina*
Welch, Willy. *Playing right field*
Yolen, Jane. *Moon ball*
Zagwÿn, Deborah Turney. *Apple batter*

Sports – basketball

Barber, Barbara E. *Allie's basketball dream*
Henderson, Kathy. *I can be a basketball player*
Martin, Bill (William Ivan). *Swish!*
Porte, Barbara Ann. *Harry's visit*

Sports – bicycling

Andersen, Karen Born. *What's the matter, Sylvie, can't you ride?*
Aylesworth, Jim. *My sister's rusty bike*
Baker, Eugene H. *Bicycles*
Bang, Molly. *Delphine*
Barbot, Daniel. *A bicycle for Rosaura*
Baugh, Dolores M. *Bikes*
Bentley, Anne. *The Groggs' day out*
Blackstone, Stella. *Bear on a bike*
Blake, Quentin. *Mrs. Armitage on wheels*
Blance, Ellen. *Monster, Lady Monster and the bike ride*
Bourgeois, Paulette. *Franklin rides a bike*
Breinburg, Petronella. *Shawn's red bike*
Brown, Marc Tolon. *D. W. rides again!*
Bruna, Dick. *Miffy's bicycle*
Bundey, Nikki. *On a bike*
Bunting, Eve (Anne Evelyn). *Summer wheels*
Cabban, Vanessa. *Bertie and Small and the fast bike ride*
Chlad, Dorothy. *Bicycles are fun to ride*
Crews, Donald. *Bicycle race*
Crowley, Michael. *Shack and back*
De Paola, Tomie (Thomas Anthony). *Kit and Kat*
Dowling, Paul. *You can do it, Rabbit*
Dragonwagon, Crescent. *Annie flies the birthday bike*
Glass, Andrew. *Charles T. McBiddle*
Harder, Dan (Dan Wymbs). *Colliding with Chris*
Heine, Helme. *Friends*
Holabird, Katharine. *Angelina's birthday surprise*
Hughes, Shirley. *Wheels*
Jakob, Donna. *My bike*
Johnston, Tony. *Three little bikers*
Krings, Antoon. *Oliver's bicycle*
Liebler, John. *Frog counts to ten*

Loewen, Nancy. *Bicycle safety*
London, Jonathan. *Let's go, Froggy!*
McLeod, Emilie Warren. *The bear's bicycle*
Maestro, Betsy. *Bike trip*
Mason, Jane B. *Hello, two-wheeler!*
Mollel, Tololwa M. (Tololwa Marti). *My rows and piles of coins*
Morgan-Vanroyen, Mary. *Night ride*
Muntean, Michaela. *Bicycle bear*
Bicycle Bear rides again
Myers, Bernice. *Herman and the bears and the giants*
Olaleye, Isaac. *Bikes for rent!*
Paterson, A. B. (Andrew Barton). *Mulga Bill's bicycle*
Rey, H. A. (Hans Augusto). *Curious George rides a bike*
Rockwell, Anne F. *Bikes*
Say, Allen. *The bicycle man*
Schwartz, David M. *Sugargrandpa*
Stott, Dorothy. *Little Duck's bicycle ride*
Strub, Susanne. *Lulu on her bike*
Sueyoshi, Akiko. *Ladybird on a bicycle*
Thomas, Jane Resh. *Wheels*
Yorinks, Arthur. *Ugh*

Sports – bowling

Egan, Tim. *The blunder of the Rogues*

Sports – boxing

Ahlberg, Allan. *Mr. Biff the boxer*

Sports – camping *see* Camps, camping

Sports – fishing

Aldridge, Josephine Haskell. *Fisherman's luck*
A penny and a periwinkle
Alexander, Sally Hobart. *Maggie's whopper*
Anderson, Lena. *Bunny fun*
Bettina (Bettina Ehrlich). *Pantaloni*
Bodnar, Judit Z. *Tale of a tail*
A wagonload of fish
Bradman, Tony. *That's not a fish*
Brady, Kimberley Smith. *Keeper for the sea*
Carlstrom, Nancy White. *Wishing at dawn in summer*
Cech, John. *The southernmost cat*
Cook, Bernadine. *The little fish that got away*
Delacre, Lulu. *Nathan's fishing trip*
Delton, Judy. *Duck goes fishing*
Demarest, Chris L. *Orville's odyssey*
Elkin, Benjamin. *Six foolish fishermen*
Engel, Diana. *Fishing*
Franklin, Kristine L. *The gift*
George, William T. *Fishing at Long Pond*
Gibbons, Gail. *Surrounded by sea*
Goffstein, M. B. (Marilyn Brooke). *Fish for supper*
Gray, Catherine. *Tammy and the gigantic fish*
Griffith, Helen V. *Grandaddy's place*
Hall, Bill. *Fish tale*
Hann, Jacquie. *Up day, down day*
Hanze. *Yann and the whale*
Hertz, Ole. *Tobias catches trout*
Tobias goes ice fishing
Hest, Amy. *Rosie's fishing trip*
Igus, Toyomi. *When I was little*
Ipcar, Dahlov. *The biggest fish in the sea*

Johnston, Tony. *Fishing Sunday*
Joosse, Barbara M. *I love you the purplest*
Kidd, Nina. *June Mountain secret*
Koller, Jackie French. *Fish fry tonight*
Kovacs, Deborah. *Moonlight on the river*
Krudop, Walter Lyon. *Blue claws*
    The man who caught fish
Lapp, Eleanor. *In the morning mist*
London, Jonathan. *Old salt, young salt*
Long, Earlene. *Gone fishing*
Luenn, Nancy. *Nessa's fish*
McKissack, Patricia C. *A million fish . . . more or less*
Maris, Ron. *Bernard's boring day*
Marzollo, Jean. *Amy goes fishing*
Mayer, Mercer. *A boy, a dog, a frog and a friend*
    A boy, a dog and a frog
Miles, Miska. *No, no, Rosina*
Moore, Elaine. *Deep river*
Munsch, Robert N. *Get me another one!*
Ness, Evaline. *Sam, Bangs, and moonshine*
Nicolai, Margaret. *Kitaq goes ice fishing*
Noll, Sally. *Lucky morning*
Nordqvist, Sven. *Festus and Mercury wishing to go
    fishing*
Parker, Dorothy D. *Liam's catch*
Pope, Geraldine. *The empty creel*
Potter, Beatrix. *The tale of Mr. Jeremy Fisher*, ill. by
    author
    The tale of Mr. Jeremy Fisher, ill. by David Jor-
    gensen
Rey, Margret (Margret Elisabeth Waldstein). *Curi-
    ous George flies a kite*
Roth, Roger. *Fishing for Methuselah*
San Souci, Robert D. *Six foolish fishermen*
Say, Allen. *A river dream*
Sharp, N. L. *Today I'm going fishing with my dad*
Stevenson, Robert Louis. *The moon*
Surany, Anico. *Ride the cold wind*
Taylor, Mark. *The bold fisherman*
Thorne, Jenny. *My uncle*
Valgardson, W. D. *Winter rescue*
Wahl, Jan. *The fishermen*
Waldron, Kathleen Cook. *Loon Lake fishing derby*
Ward, Sally G. *Punky goes fishing*
Waterton, Betty. *A salmon for Simon*
Watson, Nancy Dingman. *Tommy's mommy's fish*, ill.
    by Aldren Auld Watson
    Tommy's mommy's fish, ill. by Thomas Aldren
    Dingman Watson
Wildsmith, Brian. *Pelican*
Wilson, Bob. *Stanley Bagshaw and the twenty-two ton
    whale*
Yerxa, Leo. *A fish tale, or, The little one that got away*

Sports – football

Carlson, Nancy L. *Louanne Pig in making the team*
Gifford, Kathie Lee. *Giff's big game*
Kuskin, Karla. *The Dallas Titans get ready for bed*
Myers, Bernice. *Sidney Rella and the glass sneaker*
Stadler, John. *Snail saves the day*

Sports – golf

Miller, William. *Night golf*

Sports – gymnastics

Brown, Marc Tolon. *D. W. flips!*

Kuklin, Susan. *Going to my gymnastics class*
Newcome, Zita. *Toddlerobics*
Stevens, Carla. *Pig and the blue flag*
Wood, Tim. *Gymnastics*

Sports – hiking

Curious George goes hiking
Johnson, D. B. (Donald B.). *Henry hikes to Fitchburg*
Lester, Helen. *Lin's backpack*
London, Jonathan. *The waterfall*
Rand, Gloria. *Willie takes a hike*
Shaw, Nancy (Nancy E.). *Sheep take a hike*

Sports – hockey

Brownridge, William Roy. *The moccasin goalie*
Kidd, Bruce. *Hockey showdown*
Maloney, Peter. *The magic hockey stick*
Stevenson, James. *Sam the Zamboni man*

Sports – hunting

Allen, Judy. *Tiger*
Backovsky, Jan. *Trouble in Paradise*
Baker, Betty. *Sonny-Boy Sim*
Bemelmans, Ludwig. *Parsley*
Bernhard, Emery. *The girl who wanted to hunt*
Browne, Anthony. *Bear hunt*
Burch, Robert. *The hunting trip*
Burningham, John. *Harquin*
Calhoun, Mary. *Houn' dog*
Carrick, Donald. *The deer in the pasture*
    Harold and the great stag
Cowcher, Helen. *Jaguar*
De Paola, Tomie (Thomas Anthony). *The hunter
    and the animals*
De Regniers, Beatrice Schenk. *Catch a little fox*
Dionetti, Michelle V. *The day Eli went looking for
    bear*
Drummond, Allan. *Moby Dick*
Duvoisin, Roger Antoine. *The happy hunter*
Gage, Wilson. *Cully Cully and the bear*
Geraghty, Paul. *The hunter*
Hader, Berta Hoerner. *The mighty hunter*
Heinz, Brian J. *Nanuk, lord of the ice*
Hertz, Ole. *Tobias goes seal hunting*
Hoban, Russell. *The dancing tigers*
Hodges, Margaret. *The golden deer*
Jones, Maurice. *I'm going on a dragon hunt*
Kahl, Virginia. *How do you hide a monster?*
Kamen, Gloria. *The ringdoves*
Kastner, Jill. *Snake hunt*
Kellogg, Steven (Stephen). *Tallyho, Pinkerton!*
Kilroy, Sally. *The baron's hunting party*
Krause, Ute. *Nora and the great bear*
Kroll, Steven. *One tough turkey*
Lacapa, Michael. *Antelope Woman*
Langstaff, John M. *Oh, a-hunting we will go*
Livermore, Elaine. *Looking for Henry*
MacDonald, Suse. *Nanta's lion*
Mari, Iela. *Eat and be eaten*
Mendoza, George. *The hunter I might have been*
Michels, Tilde. *Who's that knocking at my door?*
Parish, Peggy. *Good hunting, Blue Sky*
    Ootah's lucky day
Peet, Bill (William Bartlett). *Buford the little bighorn*
    The gnats of knotty pine
Prusski, Jeffrey. *Bring back the deer*

Rohmer, Harriet. *The invisible hunters*
Roop, Peter. *The buffalo jump*
Rosen, Michael (1946-). *We're going on a bear hunt*
Steiner, Charlotte. *Pete and Peter*
Turnbull, Ann. *Rob goes a-hunting*
Wahl, Jan. *Tiger watch*
Wildsmith, Brian. *Hunter and his dog*
Withers, Carl. *The wild ducks and the goose*
Wolcott, Patty. *Eeeeeek!*

Sports – ice skating

Blackstone, Margaret. *This is figure skating*
Carlson, Nancy L. *Snowden*
DiVito, Anna. *Elephants on ice*
Hoban, Lillian. *Mr. Pig and Sonny too*
Holabird, Katharine. *Angelina ice skates*
Isadora, Rachel. *Sophie skates*
Khalsa, Dayal Kaur. *The snow cat*
Lindman, Maj. *Snipp, Snapp, Snurr and the yellow sled*
Medearis, Angela Shelf. *Poppa's itchy Christmas*
Morris, Ann. *Little skaters*
O'Connor, Jane. *Kate skates*
Radin, Ruth Yaffe. *A winter place*
Stadler, John. *Ready, set, go!*
Stevenson, James. *Sam the Zamboni man*
Van Stockum, Hilda. *A day on skates*
Wallace-Brodeur, Ruth. *Home by five*
Weiss, Nicki. *Dog boy cap skate*

Sports – jumping rope

Brown, Marc Tolon. *Teddy bear, teddy bear*
Hru, Dakari. *The magic moonberry jump ropes*

Sports – karate

Morris, Ann. *Karate boy*

Sports – mountain climbing

George, Jean Craighead. *To climb a waterfall*
Haswell, Peter. *Pog climbs Mount Everest*

Sports – Olympics

Hennessy, B. G. (Barbara G.). *Olympics!*
Mariotti, Mario. *Hand games*
Schulz, Charles M. *You're the greatest, Charlie Brown*

Sports – punchball

Best, Cari. *Last licks*

Sports – racing

Aarle, Thomas Van. *Don't put your cart before the horse race*
Adams, Adrienne. *The great Valentine's Day balloon race*
Æsop. *The hare and the tortoise*, ill. by Paul Galdone
   The hare and the tortoise, ill. by Carol Jones
   The hare and the tortoise, ill. by Gerald Rose
   The hare and the tortoise, ill. by Helen Ward
   The hare and the tortoise, ill. by Peter Weevers
   The tortoise and the hare
Alborough, Jez. *Running Bear*
Anderson, Laurie Halse. *Ndito runs*

Ashforth, Camilla. *Calamity*
Bacon, Ethel. *To see the moon*
Baumann, Hans. *The hare's race*
Baynton, Martin. *Fifty and the great race*
Benchley, Nathaniel. *Walter the homing pigeon*
Berenstain, Stan. *The Berenstain bears and the big road race*
Biro, Val. *Gumdrop on the Brighton run*
   Gumdrop races a train
Blake, Robert J. *Akiak*
Calloway, Northern J. *Northern J. Calloway presents Super-vroomer!*
Crews, Donald. *Bicycle race*
Crowley, Michael. *Shack and back*
Dickens, Frank. *Boffo*
Dodds, Dayle Ann. *The Great Divide*
Hall, Derek. *Tiger runs*
Heine, Helme. *Three little friends: the racing cart*
Hurd, Edith Thacher. *Last one home is a green pig*
Isenberg, Barbara. *The adventures of Albert, the running bear*
   Albert the running bear gets the jitters
Kessler, Leonard P. *The big mile race*
Kurtz, Jane. *Only a pigeon*
La Fontaine, Jean de. *The hare and the tortoise*
Leedy, Loreen. *The race*
Lowell, Susan. *The tortoise and the jackrabbit*
McLenighan, Valjean. *Turtle and rabbit*
McNaughton, Colin. *The rat race*
McPhail, David M. *The great race*
Marshall, Edward. *Fox on wheels*
Miranda, Anne. *Vroom, chugga, vroom-vroom*
Moore, John. *Granny Stickleback*
Mora, Pat. *The race of toad and deer*
Neuhaus, David. *His finest hour*
Otsuka, Yuzo. *Suho and the white horse*
Reimold, Mary Gallagher. *My mom is a runner*
Schwartz, David M. *Sugargrandpa*
Seibert, Patricia. *Mush!*
Shearer, Marilyn J. *The crown of fools*
Van Woerkom, Dorothy. *Harry and Shelburt*
Vozar, David. *M. C. Turtle and the hip hop hare*
Wilkinson, Sylvia. *I can be a race car driver*
Wood, Tim. *Motor racing*
   Motorcycling
Wyllie, Stephen. *The great race*

Sports – rock climbing

London, Jonathan. *The waterfall*

Sports – roller skating

Calmenson, Stephanie. *Roller skates!*
Crary, Elizabeth. *I'm frustrated*
Gifford, Kathie Lee. *Giff the scaredy bear*
Johnson, Mildred D. *Wait, skates!*
Kemp, Moira. *Round and round the garden*
Pilkey, Dav. *The Moonglow Roll-O-Rama*
Wahl, Jan. *Rabbits on roller skates!*

Sports – sailing

Agell, Charlotte. *To the island*
Ahlberg, Allan. *Skeleton crew*
Crews, Donald. *Sail away*
Greydanus, Rose. *Climb aboard*
Marshall, Janet Perry. *Banana moon*
Whittle, Emily. *Sailor cats*

Sports – skateboarding

Carlson, Nancy L. *Arnie and the skateboard gang*
Havill, Juanita. *Embarcadero upset*
Howard, Arthur. *Cosmo zooms*
Mammano, Julie. *Rhinos who skateboard*

Sports – skiing

Calhoun, Mary. *Cross-country cat*
Freeman, Don. *Ski pup*
Hutchins, H. J. (Hazel J.). *Ben's snow song*
Krementz, Jill. *A very young skier*
Lindman, Maj. *Snipp, Snapp, Snurr and the red shoes*
Marol, Jean-Claude. *Vagabul goes skiing*
Moran, George. *Imagine me on a sit-ski!*
Peet, Bill (William Bartlett). *Buford the little bighorn*
Simon, Francesca. *Camels don't ski*

Sports – skin diving

Carrick, Carol. *Dark and full of secrets*
Ungerer, Tomi. *The Mellops go diving for treasure*

Sports – sledding

Bacon, Ethel. *To see the moon*
Curious George goes sledding
Iwamura, Kazuo. *The fourteen forest mice and the winter sledding day*
Kharms, Daniil. *The story of a boy named Will, who went sledding down the hill*
Seibert, Patricia. *Mush!*
Winthrop, Elizabeth. *Sledding*

Sports – soccer

Browne, Anthony. *Willy the wizard*
Brownridge, William Roy. *The final game*
Catalanotto, Peter. *Dylan's day out*
Flanagan, Alice K. *Coach John and his soccer team*
Lakin, Pat (Patricia). *A good sport*
London, Jonathan. *Froggy plays soccer*
McNaughton, Colin. *Preston's goal!*
Saltzberg, Barney. *Soccer mom from outer space*

Sports – Special Olympics

Pulver, Robin. *Way to go, Alex!*

Sports – surfing

Blake, Quentin. *Mrs. Armitage and the big wave*
Bundey, Nikki. *In the water*
Ormondroyd, Edward. *Broderick*
Raglus, Jeff. *Schnorky the wave puncher*

Sports – swimming

Alexander, Martha G. *We never get to do anything*
Anderson, Lena. *Bunny fun*
Atkins, Jeannine. *Get set! Swim!*
Beatty, Hetty Burlingame. *Droopy*
Beim, Jerrold. *The swimming hole*
Berridge, Celia. *Going swimming*
Borden, Louise. *Albie the lifeguard*
Brown, M. K. (Mary K.). *Let's go swimming with Mr. Sillypants*
Bundey, Nikki. *In the water*
Cohn, Norma. *Brother and sister*

Coles, Alison. *Michael and the sea*
Cousins, Lucy. *Maisy goes swimming*
    Maisy's pool
Day, Alexandra. *River parade*
George, Lindsay Barrett. *William and Boomer*
Ginsburg, Mirra. *The chick and the duckling*
Hall, Derek. *Otter swims*
Heiligman, Deborah. *Mike Swan, sink or swim*
Henley, Claire. *Joe's pool*
Herman, Gail. *The littlest duckling*
Jay, Betsy. *Swimming lessons*
Keeshan, Robert. *Itty Bitty Kitty makes a big splash*
Khalsa, Dayal Kaur. *The snow cat*
Krings, Antoon. *Oliver's pool*
Lasky, Kathryn. *Sea swan*
London, Jonathan. *Froggy learns to swim*
Mattern, Joanne. *Safety in the water*
Moore, Inga. *Aktil's big swim*
Ormerod, Jan. *Ben goes swimming*
Pfister, Marcus. *Hang on, Hopper!*
Rice, Eve. *Swim!*
Riley, Linda Capus. *Elephants swim*
Schwartz, Roslyn. *The mole sisters and the rainy day*
Shortall, Leonard W. *Tony's first dive*
Stevens, Carla. *Hooray for pig!*
Stott, Dorothy. *Too much*
Strub, Susanne. *Lulu goes swimming*
Umansky, Kay. *You can swim, Jim*
Van Leeuwen, Jean. *Too hot for ice cream*
Waddell, Martin. *The pig in the pond*
Watanabe, Shigeo. *Let's go swimming*
Weston, Martha. *Tuck in the pool*
Winton, Tim. *The deep*

Sports – T-ball

Bunting, Eve (Anne Evelyn). *Trouble on the T-ball team*
Gemme, Leila Boyle. *T-ball is our game*

Sports – Tae Kwon Do

Pinkney, J. Brian. *Jojo's flying side kick*

Sports – wrestling

Morgan, Allen. *Matthew and the midnight wrestlers*
Novak, Matt. *Gertie and Gumbo*
Ogburn, Jacqueline K. *The Masked Maverick*
Stren, Patti. *Mountain Rose*

Sportsmanship

Gifford, Kathie Lee. *Giff's big game*

Spring *see* Seasons – spring

Squirrels *see* Animals – squirrels

Stage *see* Theater

Stars

Ada, Alma Flor. *Jordi's star*
Allen, Laura Jean. *Ottie and the star*
Asch, Frank. *Starbaby*
Baumgart, Klaus. *Laura's Christmas star*
Birdseye, Tom. *A song of stars*
Boon, Emilie. *Peterkin meets a star*

Branley, Franklyn M. (Mansfield). *Journey into a black hole*
 The sky is full of stars
Carpenter, Mary-Chapin. *Halley came to Jackson*
Clément, Claude. *The man who lit the stars*
Coatsworth, Elizabeth. *Good night*
Cölle, Gisela. *The star tree*
Daffis-Felicelli, Christine. *The little star of Bethlehem*
Davis, Karen. *Star light, star bright*
DeBoer, Jesslyn. *Follow the star*
De Montaño, Martha Kreipe. *Coyote in love with a star*
Doherty, Berlie. *The midnight man*
Dussling, Jennifer. *Stars*
Elzbieta. *Dikou and the baby star*
Facklam, Margery. *Only a star*
Field, Susan. *The sun, the moon, and the silver baboon*
Freeman, Mae Blacker. *The sun, the moon and the stars*
Gibbons, Gail. *Stargazers*
Ginolfi, Arthur. *The tiny star*
Glyman, Caroline A. *What's above the sky?*
Goble, Paul. *The lost children*
Hillman, Elizabeth. *Min-Yo and the moon dragon*
Hines, Anna Grossnickle. *Sky all around*
Hoffman, Mary. *Three wise women*
Hort, Lenny. *How many stars in the sky*
Ichikawa, Satomi. *Nora's stars*
Kuskin, Karla. *A space story*
Lee, Jeanne M. *The legend of the milky way*
London, Jonathan. *Liplap's wish*
Luttrell, Ida. *The star counters*
McDonald, Megan. *My house has stars*
Mallat, Kathy. *Seven stars, more!*
Mitton, Jacqueline. *Zoo in the sky*
Mobley, Jane. *The star husband*
Modesitt, Jeanne. *The night call*
Nappa, Mike. *Do you see the star?*
Newman, Lesléa. *Too far away to touch*
Oughton, Jerrie. *How the stars fell into the sky*
Pfister, Marcus. *The Christmas star*
Radley, Gail. *The night Stella hid the stars*
Ray, Deborah Kogan. *Stargazing sky*
Robbins, Sandra. *The firefly star*
Rosen, Sidney. *How far is a star?*
 Where's the big dipper?
Sis, Peter. *Starry messenger*
Slate, Joseph. *The secret stars*
 The star rocker
Stone, Kazuko G. *Goodnight Twinklegator*
Taylor, Jane. *Twinkle, twinkle, little star*
 They followed a bright star
Tibo, Gilles. *Simon and the snowflakes*
Wandelmaier, Roy. *Stars*
Weedn, Flavia. *The star gift*
Widman, Christine. *The star grazers*
Winter, Jeanette. *Follow the drinking gourd*
Wyler, Rose. *The starry sky*
Yeomans, Thomas. *For every child a star*
Zimelman, Nathan. *The star of Melvin*

Stealing *see* Behavior – stealing; Crime

Steam shovels *see* Machines

Steamrollers *see* Machines

Step families *see* Divorce; Family life – step families

Stepchildren *see* Divorce; Family life – step families

Stepparents *see* Divorce; Family life – step families

Stones *see* Rocks

Storekeepers *see* Careers – storekeepers

Stores

Alexander, Liza. *Ernie gets lost*
Anholt, Catherine. *Truffles in trouble*
Arkin, Alan. *One present from Flekman's*
Baggette, Susan K. *Jonathan goes to the grocery store*
Baugh, Dolores M. *Let's go Supermarket*
Bograd, Larry. *Lost in the store*
Bond, Michael. *Paddington Bear and the Christmas surprise*
Carling, Amelia Lau. *Mama and Papa have a store*
Carlstrom, Nancy White. *Baby-O*
Christian, Mary Blount. *The bookstore mouse*
Cooper, Letice Ulpha. *The bear who was too big*
Cowley, Joy. *The video shop sparrow*
Cowley, Stewart. *What's that sound?*
Day, Alexandra. *Carl goes shopping*
DeLage, Ida. *ABC pigs go to market*
Field, Rachel Lyman. *General store*, ill. by Giles Laroche
 General store, ill. by Nancy Winslow Parker
Fleming, Candace. *The hatmaker's sign*
Freeman, Don. *Corduroy*
Gibbons, Gail. *Department store*
Gordon, Margaret. *The supermarket mice*
Graham, Amanda. *Who wants Arthur?*
Grossman, Bill. *Tommy at the grocery store*
Hale, Kathleen. *Orlando, the frisky housewife*
Hamm, Diane Johnston. *Laney's lost momma*
Harris, Leon A. *The great diamond robbery*
Haseley, Dennis. *The thieves' market*
Hastings, Evelyn Beilhart. *The department store*
Hoff, Syd. *Merry Christmas, Henrietta!*
Houston, Gloria. *But no candy*
Jackson, Jean. *Mrs. Piccolo's easy chair*
Johnson, Angela. *The Rolling Store*
Johnson, Paul Brett. *Farmers' market*
Lewin, Ted. *Market!*
Lippman, Peter. *The Know-It-Alls mind the store*
Lobel, Arnold. *On Market Street*
London, Jonathan. *Candystore man*
Loomis, Christine. *At the mall*
McNaughton, Colin. *At the stores*
McPartland, Suzy. *Toy-shop surprise*
Maitland, Barbara. *The bookstore ghost*
Maschler, Fay. *T. G. and Moonie go shopping*
Meddaugh, Susan. *The witches' supermarket*
Melmed, Laura Krauss. *The Marvelous Market on Mermaid*
Miller, Alice P. *The little store on the corner*
Miranda, Anne. *To market, to market*
Modarressi, Mitra. *Yard sale*
Munsch, Robert N. *Something good*

Murphy, Stuart J. *Just enough carrots*
Naylor, Phyllis Reynolds. *Sweet strawberries*
Oliver, Stephen. *Shopping*
Paraskevas, Betty. *The tangerine bear*
Pearson, Tracey Campbell. *The storekeeper*
Potter, Beatrix. *Ginger and Pickles*
Rockwell, Anne F. *The supermarket*
Rubel, Nicole. *Goldie*
Sawyer, Jean. *Our village shop*
Scarry, Richard. *Richard Scarry's great big mystery
    book*
Shelby, Anne. *We keep a store*
Skolsky, Mindy Warshaw. *Hannah and the whistling
    tea kettle*
Solomon, Joan. *A present for Mum*
Spier, Peter. *Food market*
    The pet store
    The toy shop
Steiner, Jörg. *The bear who wanted to be a bear*
Wells, Rosemary. *Max's dragon shirt*
Williams, Barbara. *I know a salesperson*
Williams, Karen Lynn. *Tap-tap*
Young, Ed (Edward). *Donkey trouble*

Stories in rhyme *see* Rhyming text

Storks *see* Birds – storks

Storms *see* Weather – storms

Storytelling *see* Activities – storytelling

Strangers *see* Behavior – talking to strangers

Streams *see* Rivers

Streets *see* Roads

String

Bakken, Harold. *The special string*
Calhoun, Mary. *The traveling ball of string*
Hindley, Judy. *A piece of string is a wonderful thing*

Stubbornness *see* Character traits – stubbornness

Sukkot *see* Holidays – Sukkot

Sullivan Islands *see* Foreign lands – South
Sea Islands

Sultans *see* Royalty – sultans

Summer *see* Seasons – summer

Sun

Alda, Arlene. *Hurry Granny Annie*
Anno, Mitsumasa. *Anno's sundial*
    In shadowland
Arnold, Caroline. *Sun fun*
Baylor, Byrd. *The way to start a day*
Bernstein, Margery. *How the sun made a promise and
    kept it*
Bishop, Gavin. *Maui and the sun*

Branley, Franklyn M. (Mansfield). *Eclipse*
    The planets in our solar system
    The sun, our nearest star
    Sunshine makes the seasons
Butler, Andrea. *Mr. Sun and Mr. Sea*
Carlstrom, Nancy White. *Who gets the sun out of bed?*
Chall, Marsha Wilson. *Rupa raises the sun*
Daly, Niki. *Why the sun and moon live in the sky*
Day, Alexandra. *Helping the sun*
Dayrell, Elphinstone. *Why the sun and the moon live
    in the sky*
De Gerez, Toni. *Louhi, witch of North Farm*
Derby, Sally. *The mouse who owned the sun*
De Regniers, Beatrice Schenk. *Who likes the sun?*
Desimini, Lisa. *Sun and moon*
Elkin, Benjamin. *Why the sun was late*
Emberley, Michael. *Welcome back, Sun*
Engelbrektson, Sune. *The sun is a star*
Euvremer, Teryl. *Sun's up*
Field, Susan. *The sun, the moon, and the silver baboon*
Freeman, Mae Blacker. *The sun, the moon and the
    stars*
Gantschev, Ivan. *Good morning, good night*
Gerstein, Mordicai. *The sun's day*
Gibbons, Gail. *Sun up, sun down*
Ginsburg, Mirra. *How the sun was brought back to the
    sky*
    Where does the sun go at night?
Goudey, Alice E. *The day we saw the sun come up*
Greene, Carol. *Shine, sun!*
Gregory, Valiska. *When stories fell like shooting stars*
Hamberger, John. *The day the sun disappeared*
Harrison, David Lee. *Wake up, sun!*
Hendra, Sue. *Oliver's wood*
Henley, Claire. *Sunny day*
Hines, Anna Grossnickle. *What can you do in the
    sun?*
Hurd, Edith Thacher. *The day the sun danced*
Ivory, Lesley Anne. *Cats in the sun*
Kandoian, Ellen. *Under the sun*
Kinney, Jean. *What does the sun do?*
Kramsky, Jerry. *The cranky sun*
La Fontaine, Jean de. *The north wind and the sun*
Lindbergh, Reeve. *What is the sun?*
London, Jonathan. *Like butter on pancakes*
McDermott, Gerald. *Musicians of the sun*
McPartland, Suzy. *Good morning, sun*
Markoe, Merrill. *The day my dogs became guys*
Marzollo, Jean. *Sun song*
Meeker, Clare Hodgson. *Who wakes rooster?*
Mollel, Tololwa M. (Tololwa Marti). *A promise to the
    sun*
Novak, Matt. *Claude and Sun*
Obrist, Jürg. *The miser who wanted the sun*
Oliviero, Jamie. *The fish skin*
Ormerod, Jan. *Sunshine*
Palazzo-Craig, Janet. *Our friend the sun*
Peet, Bill (William Bartlett). *Cock-a-doodle Dudley*
Polacco, Patricia. *I can hear the sun*
Ringi, Kjell (Arne Sorensen). *The sun and the cloud*
Roche, Hannah. *Sandra's sun hat*
Roth, Susan L. *The story of light*
Schlein, Miriam. *The sun looks down*
    The sun, the wind, the sea and the rain
Schneider, Herman. *Follow the sunset*
Shulevitz, Uri. *Dawn*
Slate, Joseph. *Story time for Little Porcupine*
Storm, Theodor. *Little Hobbin*
Tafuri, Nancy. *What the sun sees / What the moon sees*

Best, Cari. *Taxi! Taxi!*
Maestro, Betsy. *Taxi*
Mitchell, Lucy Sprague. *The taxi that hurried*
Moore, Lilian. *Papa Albert*
Nordqvist, Sven. *Porker's taxi*
Ross, Jessica. *Ms. Klondike*

Teachers *see* Careers – teachers

Teasing *see* Behavior – bullying

Teddy bears *see* Toys – bears

Teeth

Alper, Ann Fitzerald. *Harry McNairy, Tooth Fairy*
Balzola, Asun. *Munia and the orange crocodile*
Barnett, Naomi. *I know a dentist*
Bate, Lucy. *Little rabbit's loose tooth*
Beeler, Selby B. *Throw your tooth on the roof*
Berridge, Celia. *Hannah's temper*
Birdseye, Tom. *Airmail to the moon*
Brown, Marc Tolon. *Arthur's tooth*
Brown, Ruth. *Crazy Charlie*
Bunting, Eve (Anne Evelyn). *Trouble on the T-ball team*
Carrick, Carol. *Norman fools the tooth fairy*
Carson, Jo. *Pulling my leg*
Catalanotto, Peter. *Christmas always . . .*
Chardiet, Bernice. *Martin and the tooth fairy*
Clement, Rod. *Grandpa's teeth*
Cole, Joanna. *The missing tooth*
Collington, Peter. *The tooth fairy*
Cooney, Nancy Evans. *The wobbly tooth*
Curious George goes to the dentist
De Groat, Diane. *Alligator's toothache*
Dinan, Carolyn. *Say cheese!*
Duvoisin, Roger Antoine. *Crocus*
Eriksson, Eva. *The tooth trip*
Falwell, Cathryn. *Dragon tooth*
Farber, Erica. *Ooey gooey*
Gillerlain, Gayle. *Reverend Thomas's false teeth*
Gomi, Taro. *The crocodile and the dentist*
Gunther, Louise. *A tooth for the tooth fairy*
Hallinan, P. K. (Patrick K.). *My dentist, my friend*
Heller, Nicholas. *The tooth tree*
Hooks, William H. *The mystery of the missing tooth*
Jenkin-Pearce, Susie. *Boris's big ache*
Johnson-Petrov, Arden. *The Lost Tooth Club*
Kaye, Marilyn. *The real tooth fairy*
Krensky, Stephen. *My loose tooth*
Kroll, Steven. *Loose tooth*
Laminack, Lester L. *Trevor's wiggly-wobbly tooth*
Luttrell, Ida. *Milo's toothache*
Maccarone, Grace. *My tooth is about to fall out*
McCloskey, Robert. *One morning in Maine*
MacDonald, Amy. *Cousin Ruth's tooth*
MacDonald, Maryann. *Rosie's baby tooth*
McGinley, Phyllis. *Lucy McLockett*
McPhail, David M. *The bear's toothache*
Mellor, Corinne. *Clark the toothless shark*
Mitra, Annie. *Tusk! Tusk!*
Munsch, Robert N. *Andrew's loose tooth*
Nerlove, Miriam. *Just one tooth*
Noll, Sally. *I have a loose tooth*
Paxton, Tom. *The story of the Tooth Fairy*
Pomerantz, Charlotte. *The mango tooth*
Quin-Harkin, Janet. *Helpful Hattie*

Richter, Alice Numeroff. *You can't put braces on spaces*
Ricketts, Michael. *Teeth*
Rockwell, Harlow. *My dentist*
Ross, Pat. *Molly and the slow teeth*
Sandeman, Anna. *Skin, teeth, and hair*
Scamell, Ragnhild. *Who likes Wolfie?*
Seuss, Dr. *The tooth book*
Silverman, Martin. *My tooth is loose*
Simms, Laura. *Rotten teeth*
Sis, Peter. *Madlenka*
Sundvall, Viveca. *Mimi and the biscuit factory*
West, Colin. *The king's toothache*
Wilhelm, Hans. *I lost my tooth!*
Williams, Barbara. *Albert's toothache*
Wolf, Bernard. *Michael and the dentist*
Zalben, Jane Breskin. *Buster gets braces*

Telephone

Allen, Jeffrey. *Mary Alice, operator number 9*
Mary Alice returns
Chukovskii, Kornei Ivanovich. *Telephone*
Dodds, Siobhan. *Ting-a-ling!*
Jackson, Jean. *Big lips and hairy arms*
King, Bob. *Sitting on the farm*
Koski, Mary. *Impatient Pamela calls 9-1-1*
Raschka, Christopher. *Ring! Yo?*
Telephones
Weiss, Ellen. *Telephone time*
Wyse, Lois. *Two guppies, a turtle and Aunt Edna*

Telephone operators *see* Careers – telephone operators

Television

Barden, Rosalind. *TV monster*
Barracca, Debra. *Maxi, the star*
Berenstain, Stan. *The Berenstain bears and too much TV*
Brown, Marc Tolon. *The bionic bunny show*
Davis, Gary. *Working at a TV station*
Dobson, Clive. *Fred's TV*
Heilbroner, Joan. *Tom the TV cat*
Krauss, Ronnie. *Take a look, it's in a book*
McCully, Emily Arnold. *Zaza's big break*
McPhail, David M. *Fix-it*
Novak, Matt. *Mouse TV*
Polacco, Patricia. *Aunt Chip and the great Triple Creek dam affair*
Rodda, Emily. *Power and glory*

Telling stories *see* Activities – storytelling

Telling time *see* Clocks, watches; Time

Temper tantrums *see* Emotions – anger

Textless *see* Wordless

Thailand *see* Foreign lands – Thailand

Thanksgiving *see* Holidays – Thanksgiving

Theater

Ahlberg, Allan. *The Cinderella show*
Alexander, Sue. *Seymour the prince*
  Small plays for special days
  Small plays for you and a friend
Behrens, June. *Christmas-magic wagon*
  The feast of Thanksgiving
Berenstain, Stan. *The Berenstain bears get stage fright*
Bond, Felicia. *The Halloween play*
Boyd, Lizi. *Princess, cowboy, pirate, elf*
Brighton, Catherine. *Hope's gift*
Brown, Marc Tolon. *Arthur's Thanksgiving*
Brown, Ruth. *The shy little angel*
Butterworth, Nick. *The Nativity play*
Calmenson, Stephanie. *No stage fright for me!*
Caple, Kathy. *Starring Hillary*
Carlson, Nancy L. *The talent show*
Cartlidge, Michelle. *Mouse theater*
Caseley, Judith. *Mickey's class play*
Cazet, Denys. *The duck with squeaky feet*
Cohen, Miriam. *Starring first grade*
Curious George goes to a movie
Daly, Kathleen N. *Strawberry Shortcake and pets on parade*
Daly, Niki. *Bravo, Zan Angelo!*
De Paola, Tomie (Thomas Anthony). *The Christmas pageant*
  The night of Las Posadas
  Sing, Pierrot, sing
De Regniers, Beatrice Schenk. *Picture book theater*
Ernst, Lisa Campbell. *When Bluebell sang*
Ets, Marie Hall. *Another day*
Ford, Miela. *My day in the garden*
Fox, Mem. *Wombat divine*
Freeman, Don. *Hattie the backstage bat*
  Will's quill
Freeman, Lydia. *Pet of the Met*
French, Vivian. *A Christmas star called Hannah*
A frog he would a-wooing go (folk-song). *The frog went a-courting*, adapt. and ill. by Dominic Catalano
Frye, Dean. *Days of sunshine, days of rain*
Gallwey, Kay. *Dancing Daisy*
Gauch, Patricia Lee. *Tanya and the magic wardrobe*
Giff, Patricia Reilly. *The almost awful play*
Goffstein, M. B. (Marilyn Brooke). *An actor*
Goodall, John S. *Paddy's evening out*
Grimm, Jacob. *King Grisly-Beard*
Hartman, Bob. *The one and only Delgado Cheese*
Hodges, Margaret. *Comus*
Hoffman, Mary. *Amazing Grace*
Hoffmann, E. T. A. *The nutcracker*, ill. by Maurice Sendak
Holabird, Katharine. *Angelina ice skates*
  Angelina on stage
Hughes, Shirley. *Angel Mae*
Isadora, Rachel. *Jesse and Abe*
  Lili on stage
  Opening night
Isherwood, Shirley. *Flora the frog*
Johnson, Dolores. *The best bug to be*
Komaiko, Leah. *Aunt Elaine does the dance from Spain*
Krauss, Ronnie. *Take a look, it's in a book*
Krementz, Jill. *A very young actress*
Lakin, Pat (Patricia). *The palace of stars*
Lawlor, Laurie. *The biggest pest on Eighth Avenue*
Layton, Aviva. *The squeakers*

Leedy, Loreen. *The bunny play*
Levine, Arthur A. *Sheep dreams*
Lewison, Wendy Cheyette. *Shy Vi*
Littlesugar, Amy. *Tree of hope*
Lobel, Arnold. *Martha, the movie mouse*
Lubach, Peter. *Harry and the singing fish*
McClintock, Barbara. *The battle of Luke and Long-nose*
McCully, Emily Arnold. *The evil spell*
  My real family
  Speak up, Blanche!
  Zaza's big break
Maiorano, Robert. *Backstage*
Marshall, James. *Swine lake*
Martin, Judith. *The tree angel*
Novak, Matt. *While the shepherd slept*
Oppenheim, Joanne. *Mrs. Peloki's class play*
Patz, Nancy. *Gina Farina and the Prince of Mintz*
Pearson, Susan. *Lenore's big break*
Philpot, Graham. *Fabulous fairy tale follies*
Rockwell, Anne F. *Thanksgiving Day*
Rose, Mitchell. *Norman*
Sage, James. *The boy and the dove*
Schotter, Roni. *Purim play*
Schwartz, Henry. *Albert goes Hollywood*
Sendak, Maurice. *Maurice Sendak's Really Rosie*
Steiner, Charlotte. *Kiki is an actress*
Tangvald, Christine Harder. *Hey, Mr. Angel!*
Tryon, Leslie. *Albert's play*
Vail, Rachel. *Over the moon*
Wharton, Thomas. *Hildegard sings*
Whippo, Walt. *Little white duck*
Yeoman, John. *The young performing horse*

Thumb sucking

Cooney, Nancy Evans. *Donald says thumbs down*
Dionne, Wanda. *Little Thumb*
Ernst, Kathryn F. *Danny and his thumb*
Heitler, Susan M. (Susan McCrensky). *David decides, no more thumb-sucking*
Inkpen, Mick. *Arnold*
Klimowicz, Barbara. *The strawberry thumb*
Sonnenschein, Harriet. *Harold's hideaway thumb*
Tobias, Tobi. *The quitting deal*
Tufts, Mary L. *The wee kitten who sucked her thumb*

Thunder *see* Weather – storms; Weather – thunder

Tibet *see* Foreign lands – Tibet

Tigers *see* Animals – tigers

Time

Aiken, Conrad Potter. *Tom, Sue and the clock*
Aldag, Kurt. *Some things never change*
Allen, Jeffrey. *Mary Alice, operator number 9*
Allington, Richard L. *Time*
Ambrus, Victor G. *What's the time, Dracula?*
Ancona, George. *Handtalk zoo*
Anderson, Lena. *Tick-tock*
Anno, Mitsumasa. *Anno's sundial*
Axelrod, Amy. *Pigs on a blanket*
Aylesworth, Jim. *The completed hickory dickory dock*
Bloom, Becky. *Mr. Cuckoo*
Bodwell, Gaile. *The long day of the giants*

Bragdon, Lillian J. *Tell me the time, please*
Carle, Eric. *The grouchy ladybug*
Cartlidge, Michelle. *Mouse time*
Colman, Hila. *Watch that watch*
Dale, Elizabeth. *How long?*
Dunbar, James. *Tick-tock*
Fleischman, Paul. *Time train*
Gerstein, Mordicai. *The sun's day*
Gibbons, Gail. *Clocks and how they go*
Gordon, Sharon. *Tick tock clock*
Grunwald, Lisa. *Now, soon, later*
Handford, Martin. *Find Waldo now*
    Where's Waldo now?
Harper, Dan. *Telling time with Big Mama Cat*
Hawkins, Colin. *What time is it, Mr. Wolf?*
Hay, Dean. *Now I can count*
Henderson, Douglas. *Dinosaur tree*
Henwood, Simon. *The clock shop*
Hoff, Syd. *Henrietta, the early bird*
Hopkins, Lee Bennett. *It's about time*
Hutchins, Pat. *Clocks and more clocks*
Jakob, Donna. *My bike*
Jones, Carol. *What's the time, Mr. Wolf?*
Katz, Bobbi. *Tick-tock, let's read the clock*
Killingback, Julia. *What time is it, Mrs. Bear?*
Krasilovsky, Phyllis. *The man who tried to save time*
Krensky, Stephen. *The big time bears*
Littlewood, Valerie. *The season clock*
Llewellyn, Claire. *My first book of time*
Lyon, George Ella. *Father Time and the day boxes*
McGinley, Phyllis. *Wonderful time*
McGuire, Richard. *Night becomes day*
McKee, David. *The school bus comes at eight o'clock*
McMillan, Bruce. *Time to . . .*
Maestro, Betsy. *Around the clock with Harriet*
Manning, Linda. *Animal hours*
May, Charles Paul. *High-noon rocket*
Merriam, Eve. *Train leaves the station*
Mother Goose. *The real Mother Goose clock book*
Mueller, Virginia. *Monster goes to school*
Murphy, Stuart J. *Get up and go!*
Ness, Evaline. *Do you have the time, Lydia?*
Nobens, C. A. *Montgomery's time zone*
Pienkowski, Jan. *Time*
Plourde, Lynn. *Winter waits*
Pluckrose, Henry Arthur. *Time*
Richards, Kitty. *It's about time, Max!*
Rockwell, Anne F. *Bear Child's book of hours*
Rohmann, Eric. *Time flies*
Sadler, Marilyn. *Alistair's time machine*
Schlein, Miriam. *It's about time*
Schuett, Stacey. *Somewhere in the world right now*
Seignobosc, Françoise. *What time is it, Jeanne-Marie?*
Sharratt, Nick. *The time it took Tom*
Singer, Marilyn. *Nine o'clock lullaby*
Skutina, Vladimir. *Nobody has time for me*
Slobodkin, Louis. *The late cuckoo*
Steinmetz, Leon. *Clocks in the woods*
Thompson, Carol. *Time*
Turner, Gwenda. *Once upon a time*
Verdet, Andre. *All about time*
Watson, Nancy Dingman. *When is tomorrow?*
Wilson-Max, Ken. *Wake up; Sleep tight*
Ziner, Feenie. *The true book of time*
Zolotow, Charlotte (Shapiro). *Over and over*

Tin soldiers *see* Toys – soldiers

Tlingit Indians *see* Indians of North America
    – Tlingit

Toads *see* Frogs and toads

Toes *see* Anatomy – toes

Toilet training

Allison, Alida. *The toddler's potty book*
Caseley, Judith. *Annie's potty*
Civardi, Anne. *Potty time*
Cole, Joanna. *Your new potty*
Falwell, Cathryn. *P.J. & Puppy*
Lewison, Wendy Cheyette. *The princess and the potty*
Lindgren, Barbro. *Sam's potty*
Miller, Virginia. *On your potty!*
Patrick, Denise Lewis. *No diapers for baby!*
Reichmeier, Betty. *Potty time!*
Rogers, Fred. *Going to the potty*
Ross, Tony. *I want my potty*
Young, Ruth. *My potty chair*

Tongue twisters

Bodecker, N. M. (Nils Mogens). *Snowman Sniffles
    and other verse*
Brown, Marcia. *Peter Piper's alphabet*
Buck, Nola. *Creepy crawly critters and other Halloween
    tongue twisters*
    *Santa's short suit shrunk and other Christmas tongue
    twisters*
Bunting, Eve (Anne Evelyn). *Say it fast*
Gordon, Jeffie Ross. *Six sleepy sheep*
Johnson, Odette. *One prickly porcupine*
Keller, Charles. *Tongue twisters*
Mahy, Margaret. *Simply delicious!*
Monster poems
Obligado, Lilian. *Faint frogs feeling feverish and other
    terrifically tantalizing tongue twisters*
Patz, Nancy. *Pumpernickel tickle and mean green cheese*
Pomerantz, Charlotte. *The piggy in the puddle*
Radunsky, Eugenia. *Yucka Drucka Droni*
Smith, Robert Paul. *Jack Mack*

Tonsillectomy *see* Illness – tonsillectomy

Tools

Barton, Byron. *Tools*
Beim, Jerrold. *Tim and the tool chest*
Boelts, Maribeth. *Little Bunny's cool tool set*
Carle, Eric. *My very first book of tools*
Clements, Andrew. *Workshop*
DeSantis, Kenny. *A doctor's tools*
Gibbons, Gail. *The art box*
    Tool book
Kelley, True. *Hammers and mops, pencils and pots*
Kesselman, Judi R. *I can use tools*
Lerner, Marguerite Rush. *Doctors' tools*
Miller, Margaret. *Who uses this?*
Morris, Ann. *Tools*
Neitzel, Shirley. *The house I'll build for the wrens*
Pluckrose, Henry Arthur. *Things we cut*
Rockwell, Anne F. *The toolbox*
Wallace, John. *Building a house with Mr. Bumble*
Zaffo, George J. *The giant nursery book of things that
    work*

Tortoises *see* Reptiles – turtles, tortoises

Toucans *see* Birds – toucans

Touching *see* Senses – touching

Towns *see* City

Toy and movable books *see* Format, unusual – toy and movable books

Toy makers *see* Careers – toy makers

Toys

Abolafia, Yossi. *Yanosh's Island*
Adlerman, Dan. *Africa calling*
Alexander, Martha G. *Good night, Lily*
   Lily and Willy
   The story grandmother told
   Where's Willy?
   Willy's boot
Anderson, Lena. *Bunny box*
Ardizzone, Aingelda. *The night ride*
Arkin, Alan. *One present from Flekman's*
Asch, Frank. *Baby in the box*
Ashforth, Camilla. *Calamity*
   Horatio's bed
   Monkey tricks
Atwell, Debby. *Humphrey Thud*
Ayer, Jacqueline. *Nu Dang and his kite*
Ayers, Rebecca Hickox. *Per and the Dala horse*
Bailey, Debbie. *Toys*
Bambi
Bang, Molly. *One fall day*
Beck, Andrea. *Elliot bakes a cake*
Beckman, Kaj. *Lisa cannot sleep*
Bianco, Margery Williams. *The velveteen rabbit*, ill. by Allen Atkinson
   The velveteen rabbit, ill. by Michael Green
   The velveteen rabbit, ill. by Michael Hague
   The velveteen rabbit, ill. by David Jorgensen
   The velveteen rabbit, ill. by William Nicholson
   The velveteen rabbit, ill. by Ilse Plume
   The velveteen rabbit, ill. by S. D. Schindler
   The velveteen rabbit, ill. by Tien
Billam, Rosemary. *Fuzzy rabbit*
Binzen, Bill. *Alfred goes house hunting*
Bishop, Roma. *Toys*
Blake, Quentin. *Clown*
Boegehold, Betty. *Hurray for Pippa!*
Bohdal, Susi. *Harry the hare*
Bornstein, Ruth Lercher. *Annabelle*
Bowman, Peter. *I wish I were big*
Brandenberg, Franz. *Aunt Nina and her nephews and nieces*
Breese, Gillian. *The amazing adventures of Teddy Tum Tum*
Breeze, Lynn. *Baby's toys*
Brown, Ruth. *I don't like it!*
Browne, Anthony. *Gorilla*
Bruna, Dick. *My toys*
Bryant, Dean. *See the bear*
Buchanan, Heather S. *George and Matilda Mouse and the floating school*
Bunting, Eve (Anne Evelyn). *Ducky*
Burdick, Margaret. *Bobby Otter and the blue boat*

Burns, Maurice. *Go ducks, go!*
Butterworth, Nick. *All together now!*
   Just like Jasper
   When it's time for bed
   When there's work to do
   When we go shopping
   When we play together
Cabban, Vanessa. *Bertie and Small and the brave sea journey*
   Bertie and Small and the fast bike ride
Campbell, Rod. *Buster's morning*
Carlstrom, Nancy White. *Barney is best*
Cartlidge, Michelle. *Good night, Teddy*
Chichester Clark, Emma. *I love you, Blue Kangaroo!*
Chorao, Kay. *Carousel round and round*
   Kate's car
   Molly's Moe
Cocca-Leffler, Maryann. *Missing: one stuffed rabbit*
Collington, Peter. *The midnight circus*
Conrad, Pam. *Doll Face has a party!*
   The Tub grandfather
   The Tub People
   The Tub People's Christmas
Coombs, Patricia. *The lost playground*
Corbett, Grahame. *Guess who?*
   Who is hiding?
   Who is inside?
   Who is next?
Couture, Susan Arkin. *The block book*
Craig, M. Jean. *Boxes*
Dale, Penny. *Ten out of bed*
   Ten play hide-and-seek
Daly, Niki. *Vim, the rag mouse*
Davenport, Zoë. *Toys*
Dedieu, Thierry. *The little Christmas soldier*
De Lynam, Alicia Garcia. *It's mine!*
Demarest, Chris L. *My blue boat*
   My little red car
Demi. *The magic boat*
DiFiori, Lawrence. *My toys*
Dobrin, Arnold Jack. *Josephine's 'magination*
Dodds, Siobhan. *Grandpa Bud*
   Ting-a-ling!
Dowling, Paul. *Meg and Jack's new friends*
Drescher, Henrik. *Look-alikes*
Drummond, Violet H. *Phewtus the squirrel*
Dugan, Barbara. *Loop the loop*
Dunbar, Joyce. *Lollopy*
Ehrlich, H. M. *Louie's goose*
Elson, Raymond. *Toys*
Ernst, Lisa Campbell. *The letters are lost!*
   The rescue of Aunt Pansy
Farber, Werner. *Night lion*
Faulkner, Keith. *The monster in my toybox*
Feiffer, Jules. *I lost my bear*
Field, Eugene. *The gingham dog and the calico cat*, ill. by Janet Street
   The gingham dog and the calico cat, ill. by Johanna Westerman
Fox, Mem. *A bedtime story*
Francis, Anna B. *Pleasant dreams*
Frankel, Ben. *Tertius and Pliny*
Freeman, Don. *Corduroy's party*
Gackenbach, Dick. *Poppy the panda*
Galbraith, Kathryn Osebold. *Laura Charlotte*
Garay, Luis. *Pedrito's day*
Gay, Michel. *Bibi's birthday surprise*
Gerstein, Mordicai. *Bedtime, everybody!*
Ginsburg, Mirra. *Four brave sailors*

Gomi, Taro. *Guess who?*
Goodhart, Pippa. *Row, row, row your boat*
Greenfield, Eloise. *Kia Tanisha drives her car*
Greenleaf, Ann. *No room for Sarah*
Grifalconi, Ann. *The toy trumpet*
Grimes, Nikki. *Someone's baby-sitting*
　　Someone's fighting
Gundersheimer, Karen. *Shapes to show*
Hale, Irina. *Chocolate mouse and sugar pig*
　　The lost toys
Haus, Felice. *Beep! Beep! I'm a jeep*
Hayashi, Akiko. *Aki and the fox*
Hayes, Sarah. *This is the bear and the bad little girl*
Hayward, Linda. *The runaway Christmas toy*
Heap, Sue. *Cowboy Baby*
Henderson, Kathy. *The little boat*
Herman, Gail. *There is a town*
Hill, Eric. *Spot's toy box*
Hillert, Margaret. *The birthday car*
Hillman, Priscilla. *The Merry-Mouse book of toys*
Hippely, Hilary Horder. *Adventure on Klickitat Island*
Hissey, Jane. *Hoot*
　　Jolly snow
　　Jolly Tall
　　Little Bear lost
　　Old Bear
　　Old bear, a board book
　　Old Bear, a pop-up book
　　Ruff
Hoban, Russell. *La corona and the tin frog*
Hollyn, Lynn. *Lynn Hollyn's Christmas toyland*
Hooks, William H. *Mr. Monster*
Hoopes, Lyn Littlefield. *Wing-a-ding*
Howell, Lynn. *Winifred's new bed*
Hughes, Richard. *Gertrude's child*
Hughes, Shirley. *David and dog*
　　Dogger
Hutchins, Pat. *Tidy Titch*
Ichikawa, Satomi. *Nora's castle*
　　Nora's stars
Inkpen, Mick. *Kipper's bathtime*
　　Kipper's snowy day
　　Kipper's toybox
　　Nothing
　　Thing
Isherwood, Shirley. *Something for James*
Ivory, Lesley Anne. *The birthday cat*
Jahn-Clough, Lisa. *My friend and I*
Johnson, Crockett. *The blue ribbon puppies*
　　Ellen's lion
Johnson, Jane. *Sybil and the blue rabbit*
Jonas, Ann. *Now we can go*
Jones, Harold. *There and back again*
Joyce, William. *The Leaf Men and the brave good bugs*
Kahn, Joan. *Seesaw*
Kent, Jack. *Piggy Bank Gonzalez*
Kerins, Tony (Anthony). *The brave ones*
　　Tat Rabbit's treasure
Kerr, Judith. *Mog and bunny*
Kraus, Robert. *The tree that stayed up until next Christmas*
Kroll, Steven. *The magic rocket*
Leonard, Alain. *Barnaby and the big gorilla*
Leonard, Marcia. *My pal Al*
Leslie, Amanda. *Hidden toys*
Lewis, Kim. *My friend Harry*
Linden, Madelaine Gill. *Under the blanket*
Lindgren, Barbro. *Sam's car*
　　Sam's wagon
　　The wild baby goes to sea
Lionni, Leo. *Alexander and the wind-up mouse*
Lively, Penelope. *Good night, sleep tight*
Low, Joseph. *Don't drag your feet . . .*
Lynn, Sara. *Toys*
Lyon, David. *The runaway duck*
Maccarone, Grace. *Baby's toys*
McClintock, Barbara. *The battle of Luke and Long-nose*
McCue, Lisa. *Corduroy's toys*
McCully, Emily Arnold. *The Christmas gift*
MacDonald, Amy. *Let's play*
McDonnell, Flora. *I love boats*
Mackinnon, Debbie. *Daniel's duck*
　　Find monkey!
　　Sarah's shovel
　　What am I?
McPartland, Suzy. *Toy-shop surprise*
McPhail, David M. *Mistletoe*
　　The party
　　The puddle
Maisner, Heather. *Save Brave Ted*
Manushkin, Fran. *The best toy of all*
Marcin, Marietta. *A zoo in her bed*
Maris, Ron. *Are you there, bear?*
Mark, Jan. *Fun with Mrs. Thumb*
Marshall, James. *The Cut-Ups*
Marzollo, Jean. *I spy little wheels*
Masurel, Claire. *Christmas is coming*
　　Too big!
Mathews, Judith. *Tuti, Blue Horse, and the Nipnope Man*
Meggendorfer, Lothar. *The genius of Lothar Meggendorfer*
Miller, Margaret. *Where does it go?*
Miller, Moira. *The proverbial mouse*
Modesitt, Jeanne. *The night call*
Mogensen, Jan. *Teddy runs away*
　　Teddy's birthday bugle
Moore, Clement C. *The teddy bears' night before Christmas*
Moss, Marissa. *Want to play?*
Murrow, Liza Ketchum. *Good-bye, Sammy*
My first Raggedy Ann, Raggedy Ann and Andy and the camel with the wrinkled knees
Nayer, Judy. *Toys*
Newton, Laura P. *William the vehicle king*
Noll, Sally. *Off and counting*
Oliver, Stephen. *Things that go*
O'Malley, Kevin. *Leo Cockroach . . . toy tester*
Oppenheim, Shulamith Levey. *I love you, Bunny Rabbit*
Ormerod, Jan. *Messy baby*
Oxenbury, Helen. *Pippo gets lost*
　　Playing
　　Tom and Pippo and the dog
　　Tom and Pippo go shopping
　　Tom and Pippo in the garden
　　Tom and Pippo on the beach
　　Tom and Pippo see the moon
　　Tom and Pippo's day
Paterson, Bettina. *My toys*
Paxton, Tom. *The marvelous toy*
Peppé, Rodney. *Little circus*
　　Little dolls
　　Little games
　　Little numbers
　　Little wheels

Toys – balloons

Toys – balls

Toys – bears

Anglund, Joan Walsh. *How many days has Baby to play?*
  Teddy bear tales
Anholt, Catherine. *Bear and baby*
Appiah, Sonia. *Amoko and Efua Bear*
Ardizzone, Aingelda. *The night ride*
Arnold, Tedd. *My first drawing book*
Asch, Frank. *In the eye of the teddy*
Ashforth, Camilla. *Horatio's bed*
  Monkey tricks
Atwell, Debby. *Humphrey Thud*
Aylesworth, Jim. *Teddy bear tears*
Bansemer, Roger. *Rachael's splendifilous adventure*
Barker, Inga-Lil. *Why teddy bears are brown*
Behrens, June. *The manners book*
Bohdal, Susi. *Bobby the bear*
Bowman, Peter. *Goodnight, teddy bear*
Boyle, Constance. *The story of little owl*
Breese, Gillian. *The amazing adventures of Teddy Tum Tum*
Brown, Myra Berry. *First night away from home*
Buchholz, Quint. *Sleep well, little bear*
Bucknall, Caroline. *One bear all alone*
  One bear in the hospital
  One bear in the picture
Butler, Dorothy. *My brown bear Barney*
  My brown bear Barney in trouble
Carmichael, Clay. *Used-up Bear*
Cartlidge, Michelle. *Good night, Teddy*
  Teddy's cat
  Teddy's Christmas
  Teddy's friends
Castle, Caroline. *Grandpa Baxter and the photographs*
Clarke, Gus. *Eddie and Teddy*
Clise, Michele Durkson. *Ophelia's bedtime book*
Cooper, Letice Ulpha. *The bear who was too big*
Cousins, Lucy. *Maisy's bedtime*
Craft, Ruth. *The winter bear*
Daly, Niki. *Teddy's ear*
Darling, Abigail. *Teddy bears' picnic cookbook*
Davidson, Amanda. *Teddy at the seashore*
  Teddy goes outside
  Teddy in the garden
  Teddy's birthday
  Teddy's first Christmas
Davis, Douglas F. *There's an elephant in the garage*
Decker, Dorothy W. *Stripe and the merbear*
  Stripe visits New York
Degen, Bruce. *Teddy bear towers*
Douglass, Barbara. *Good as new*
Feiffer, Jules. *I lost my bear*
Ferguson, Don. *Winnie the Pooh's A to Zzzz*
Flora, James. *Sherwood walks home*
Freeman, Don. *Beady Bear*
  Corduroy
  Corduroy's busy street and Corduroy goes to the doctor
  Corduroy's party
  A pocket for Corduroy
Freeman, Lydia. *Corduroy's day*
Galbraith, Richard. *Reuben runs away*
Gallaz, Christophe. *Threadbear*
Gantschev, Ivan. *The Christmas teddy bear*
Gauch, Patricia Lee. *Bravo, Tanya*
  Christina Katerina and the great bear train
  Dance, Tanya
Glen, Maggie. *Ruby*
Greene, Carol. *Margarete Steiff, toy maker*
Gretz, Susanna. *Hide-and-seek*
  I'm not sleepy

Teddy bears ABC
Teddy bears at the seaside
Teddy bears cure a cold
Teddy bears go shopping
Teddy bears' moving day
Teddy bears 1 - 10
Teddy bears stay indoors
Teddy bears take the train
Teddybears cookbook
Too dark!
Greydanus, Rose. *Trouble in space*
Grindley, Sally. *Knock, knock! Who's there?*
  Too big bear
Hague, Kathleen. *Alphabears*
  Bear hugs
  Numbears
  Out of the nursery, into the night
Hague, Michael. *Teddy bear, teddy bear*
Haldane, Suzanne. *Teddies and machines*
  Teddies and trucks
Hale, Irina. *Brown bear in a brown chair*
  How I found a friend
Harrison, Joanna. *Dear bear*
Hawkins, Colin. *Dip, dip, dip*
  One finger, one thumb
  Oops-a-Daisy
  Where's bear?
Hayes, Geoffrey. *Bear by himself*
Hayes, Sarah. *This is the bear*
  This is the bear and the picnic lunch
  This is the bear and the scary night
Henderson, Kathy. *Disney's Pooh's grand adventure: the search for Christopher Robin*
Hennessy, B. G. (Barbara G.). *Corduroy's birthday*
  Corduroy's Christmas
  Corduroy's Easter
  Corduroy's Halloween
Herman, Gail. *Teddy bear for sale*
Hines, Anna Grossnickle. *I'll tell you what they say*
Hissey, Jane. *Jolly snow*
  Jolly Tall
  Little Bear lost
  Little bear's bedtime
  Little Bear's day
  Little Bear's trousers
  Old Bear
  Old bear, a board book
  Old Bear, a pop-up book
Horse, Harry. *A friend for Little Bear*
Howe, Caroline Walton. *Teddy Bear's bird and beast band*
Hutchins, H. J. (Hazel J.). *It's raining, Yancy and Bear*
Ichikawa, Satomi. *Fickle Barbara*
  The first bear in Africa!
Ingpen, Robert. *The idle bear*
Inkpen, Mick. *One bear at bedtime*
  Threadbear
  Where, oh where, is Kipper's bear?
Joerns, Consuelo. *The forgotten bear*
Kantrowitz, Mildred. *Willy Bear*
Keller, Holly. *A bear for Christmas*
Kelley, True. *Day-care teddy bear*
Kemp, Moira. *Round and round the garden*
Kennedy, Jimmy. *The teddy bears' Christmas*
  The teddy bears' picnic, ill. by Alexandra Day
  The teddy bears' picnic, ill. by Michael Hague
  The teddy bears' picnic, ill. by Prue Theobalds

Kimpton, Diana. *The bear Santa Claus forgot*
Kocí, Marta. *Sarah's bear*
Lawson, Carol. *Teddy bear, teddy bear*
Leblanc, Anne. *Benjamin finds a friend*
   Shopping with Benjamin
Lester, Robin. *Wuzzy takes off*
Le-Tan, Pierre. *Visit to the North Pole*
Lewis, Kim. *First snow*
Lewis, Naomi. *Once upon a rainbow*
Lewison, Wendy Cheyette. *Where's my teddy?*
Lillie, Patricia. *Floppy teddy bear*
Lindgren, Barbro. *Sam's teddy bear*
Lindsay, Elizabeth. *A letter for Maria*
Little, Jean. *Jess was the brave one*
Lundell, Margo. *Teddy bear's birthday*
McCue, Lisa. *Corduroy's party*
   Corduroy's toys
MacDonald, Maryann. *Sam's worries*
McFarland, Lyn Rossiter. *The pirate's parrot*
McKay, Hilary. *Where's bear?*
McKee, David. *Elmer and the lost teddy*
   The monster and the teddy bear
   Prince Peter and the teddy bear
MacLeod, Elizabeth. *I heard a little baa*
McLeod, Emilie Warren. *The bear's bicycle*
McPhail, David M. *The dream child*
   First flight
McQuade, Jacqueline. *At preschool with Teddy Bear*
   At the petting zoo with Teddy Bear
   Christmas with Teddy Bear
   Good times with Teddy Bear
Magnus, Erica. *My secret place*
Maisner, Heather. *Save Brave Ted*
Maitland, Barbara. *My bear and me*
Mansell, Dom. *My old teddy*
Marcus, Susan. *The missing button adventure*
Maris, Ron. *Are you there, bear?*
Marzollo, Jean. *Jed's junior space patrol*
   The teddy bear book
Matje, Martin. *Celeste*
Milne, A. A. (Alan Alexander). *House at Pooh corner*
   [a pop-up book]
   Pooh and some bees
   Pooh goes visiting
   Pooh's alphabet book
   Pooh's counting book
   Pooh's quiz book
   Winnie-the-Pooh
Mogensen, Jan. *Lost and found Teddy*
   Teddy and the Chinese dragon
   Teddy in the undersea kingdom
   Teddy runs away
   Teddy's birthday bugle
   Teddy's Christmas gift
   When Teddy woke early
Moore, Clement C. *The teddy bears' night before*
   Christmas
Moss, Elaine. *Polar*
Naylor, Phyllis Reynolds. *The picnic*
Nims, Bonnie Larkin. *Where is the bear?*
   Where is the bear at school?
Novak, Matt. *Jazzbo and Googy*
O'Donnell, Elizabeth Lee. *Sing me a window*
O'Donnell, Peter. *Moonlit journey*
O'Malley, Kevin. *The box*
Ormondroyd, Edward. *Theodore*
   Theodore's rival
Paraskevas, Betty. *The tangerine bear*
Pearson, Susan. *Baby and the bear*

Phillips, Joan. *Lucky bear*
Pike, Carol. *The nutty queen*
Prince, Pamela. *The secret world of teddy bears*
Rascal. *Orson*
Ratnett, Michael. *Jenny's bear*
Richardson, Jean. *The bear who went to the ballet*
Romanek, Enid Warner. *Teddy*
Root, Phyllis. *Contrary bear*
Schroeder, Binette. *Laura*
Sheldon, Dyan. *Love, your bear, Pete*
Siewert, Margaret. *Bear hunt*
Skorpen, Liesel Moak. *Charles*
Steger, Hans-Ulrich. *Traveling to Tripiti*
Straight, Susan. *Bear E. Bear*
Sutherland, Colleen. *Jason goes to show-and-tell*
Thomson, Ruth. *My bear: I can . . . can you?*
   My bear: I like . . . do you?
Tobias, Tobi. *Moving day*
Van Laan, Nancy. *Little baby Bobby*
Waber, Bernard. *Ira sleeps over*
Waddell, Martin. *Night night Cuddly Bear*
   Sailor Bear
   Small Bear lost
   When the teddy bears came
Wahl, Jan. *Humphrey's bear*
Weninger, Brigitte. *Good-bye, daddy!*
Weston, Martha. *Bea's four sisters*
Wilhelm, Hans. *A cool kid - like me!*
Worthington, Phoebe. *Teddy bear baker*
   Teddy bear coalman
   Teddy bear farmer
Wright, Dare. *The doll and the kitten*
   Edith and Midnight
   Edith and Mr. Bear
   Edith and the duckling
   The lonely doll
   The lonely doll learns a lesson
Yektai, Niki. *Hi bears, bye bears*
Young, Ruth. *Golden Bear*
Zalben, Jane Breskin. *A perfect nose for Ralph*
Ziefert, Harriet. *Clara Ann Cookie go to bed!*

Toys – blocks

Hutchins, Pat. *Changes, changes*
Mayers, Patrick. *Just one more block*
Winthrop, Elizabeth. *That's mine*
Wynne-Jones, Tim. *Builder of the moon*

Toys – dolls

Ackerman, Karen. *Moveable Mabeline*
Ainsworth, Ruth. *The mysterious Baba and her magic*
   caravan
Albert, Shirley. *Doll party*
Alberts, Nancy Markham. *No toys on Sunday*
Ardizzone, Aingelda. *The night ride*
Ardizzone, Edward. *The little girl and the tiny doll*
Ayer, Jacqueline. *Little Silk*
Ayres, Becky Hickox. *Matreshka*
Bannon, Laura. *Manuela's birthday*
Barber, Antonia. *Satchelmouse and the doll's house*
Bartels, Alice L. *The grandmother doll*
Beck, Andrea. *Elliot's emergency*
Bernhard, Josephine Butkowska. *Nine cry-baby dolls*
Blegvad, Lenore. *Rainy day Kate*
Bonners, Susan. *The wooden doll*
Bright, Robert. *The travels of Ching*
Brown, Margaret Wise. *Dr. Squash the doll doctor*

Brown, Ruth. *I don't like it!*
Buffett, Jimmy. *Trouble dolls*
Conrad, Pam. *Doll Face has a party!*
Dahlbäck-Lutteman, Helena. *My sister Lotta and me*
Dalmais, Anne-Marie. *Betsy the bunny*
Demas, Corinne. *The littlest matryoshka*
Dodge, Mary Mapes. *Mary Anne*
Dreifus, Miriam W. *Brave Betsy*
English, Karen. *Big wind coming!*
Fonteyn, Margot, Dame. *Coppélia*
Francis, Frank. *Natasha's new doll*
Garelick, May. *Just my size*
Goffstein, M. B. (Marilyn Brooke). *Me and my captain*
  Our prairie home
Goodman, Louise. *Ida's doll*
Greenfield, Eloise. *My doll, Keshia*
Hammerschlag, Carl A. *The go away doll*
Hermes, Patricia. *When snow lay soft on the mountain*
Hines, Anna Grossnickle. *Don't worry, I'll find you*
  Keep your old hat
  Maybe a band-aid will help
  Moompa, Toby, and Bomp
Hoban, Russell. *The stone doll of Sister Brute*
How Raggedy Ann got her candy heart
Huff, Vivian. *Let's make paper dolls*
James, Betsy. *The mud family*
Jaques, Faith. *Tilly's house*
  Tilly's rescue
Jennings, Linda M. *Coppelia*
Johnston, Johanna. *Sugarplum*
Karas, Jacqueline. *The doll house*
Keller, Holly. *Geraldine's blanket*
Kroll, Steven. *The hand-me-down doll*
Krupinski, Loretta. *Best friends*
Kuklin, Susan. *From head to toe*
Kunhardt, Dorothy. *Kitty's new doll*
Lamm, C. Drew. *Anniranni and Mollymishi, the wild-haired doll*
Lasky, Kathryn. *Sophie and Rose*
Lenski, Lois. *Debbie and her dolls*
  Let's play house
Lewison, Wendy Cheyette. *My favorite doll*
Lexau, Joan M. *The rooftop mystery*
McGinley, Phyllis. *The most wonderful doll in the world*
McGuire, Richard. *What goes around comes around*
McKissack, Patricia C. *Nettie Jo's friends*
McMillan, Bruce. *Ghost doll*
Mariana. *The journey of Bangwell Putt*
Maris, Ron. *Hold tight, bear!*
Mark, Jan. *Fun with Mrs. Thumb*
Martin, David. *Lizzie and her dolly*
Mayer, Marianna. *Baba Yaga and Vasilisa the Brave*
My first Raggedy Ann, Raggedy Ann and Andy and the camel with the wrinkled knees
My first Raggedy Ann, Raggedy Ann and Andy and the nice police officer
My first Raggedy Ann, Raggedy Ann's wishing pebble
Nivola, Claire A. *Elisabeth*
Ogburn, Jacqueline K. *The magic nesting doll*
Oram, Hiawyn. *Baba Yaga and the wise doll*
Ormerod, Jan. *Making friends*
  Miss Mouse takes off
Pellowski, Anne. *The nine crying dolls*
Pincus, Harriet. *Minna and Pippin*
Polacco, Patricia. *Babushka's doll*
Politi, Leo. *Rosa*
Pomerantz, Charlotte. *The chalk doll*

Pryor, Ainslie. *The baby blue cat and the smiley worm doll*
  The baby blue cat and the whole batch of cookies
Ransom, Candice F. *The Christmas dolls*
Rosenberg, Liz. *The scrap doll*
Sandburg, Carl (Charles August). *The wedding procession of the rag doll and the broom handle and who was in it*
Schulman, Janet. *The big hello*
  The great big dummy
Shecter, Ben. *The stocking child*
Skorpen, Liesel Moak. *Elizabeth*
Smith, Maggie (Margaret C.). *Noly Poly Rabbit Tail and me*
Steig, William. *Yellow and pink*
Stuve-Bodeen, Stephanie. *Elizabeti's doll*
Tudor, Tasha. *The doll's Christmas*
Turner, Ann Warren. *Secrets from the dollhouse*
Udry, Janice May. *Emily's autumn*
  Thump and Plunk, ill. by Geoffrey Hayes
  Thump and Plunk, ill. by Ann Schweninger
Waddell, Martin. *The hidden house*
  The toymaker
Wahl, Jan. *The Muffletumps*
  The Muffletumps' Christmas party
  The Muffletumps' Halloween scare
Wells, Rosemary. *Peabody*
Wilson, Julia. *Becky*
Winthrop, Elizabeth. *Katharine's doll*
  Vasilissa the beautiful
Wiseman, Bernard. *Oscar is a mama*
Wright, Dare. *The doll and the kitten*
  Edith and Midnight
  Edith and Mr. Bear
  Edith and the duckling
  The lonely doll
  The lonely doll learns a lesson
Yaroshevskaya, Kim. *Little Kim's doll*
Zemach, Harve. *Mommy, buy me a China doll*
Zolotow, Charlotte (Shapiro). *William's doll*

Toys – hobby horses *see* Toys – rocking horses

Toys – pandas *see* Toys – bears

Toys – rocking horses

Chandra, Deborah. *A is for Amos*
Donaldson, Lois. *Karl's wooden horse*
Lindman, Maj. *Snipp, Snapp, Snurr and the magic horse*
Roberts, Thom. *Pirates in the park*
Robertson, Lilian. *Runaway rocking horse*

Toys – soldiers

Andersen, H. C. (Hans Christian). *The steadfast tin soldier*, ill. by Thomas di Grazia
  The steadfast tin soldier, ill. by Paul Galdone
  The steadfast tin soldier, ill. by Rachel Isadora
  The steadfast tin soldier, ill. by David Jorgensen
  The steadfast tin soldier, ill. by Monika Laimgruber
  The steadfast tin soldier, ill. by P. J. Lynch
  The steadfast tin soldier, ill. by Fred Marcellino
  The steadfast tin soldier, ill. by Alain Vaës
Brown, Margaret Wise. *Dr. Squash the doll doctor*

Collington, Peter. *The angel and the soldier boy*
Nicholson, William, Sir. *Clever Bill*
Sowden, Henry. *The grand old Duke of York*

Toys – teddy bears *see* Toys – bears

Toys – tin soldiers *see* Toys – soldiers

Toys – trains

Fujita, Miho. *The little choo-choo*
Heller, Nicholas. *Peas*
Hindley, Judy. *The little train*
Hooks, William H. *The mighty Santa Fe*
Kroll, Steven. *Toot! Toot!*
Lewis, Kevin. *Chugga-chugga choo-choo*
McPhail, David M. *The train*
Merriam, Eve. *Train leaves the station*

Tractors

Baynton, Martin. *Fifty and the fox*
  Fifty and the great race
  Fifty gets the picture
  Fifty saves his friend
Cowley, Joy. *The rusty, trusty tractor*
Israel, Marion Louise. *The tractor on the farm*
Laird, Elizabeth. *The day Patch stood guard*
  The day Sidney ran off
  The day the ducks went skating
  The day Veronica was nosy
Lewis, Kim. *One summer day*
Nilsén, Anna. *Drive your tractor*
Porter, Sue. *Parsnip and the runaway tractor*
Rickard, Graham. *Let's look at tractors*
Steers, Billy. *Tractor Mac*
Young, Miriam Burt. *If I drove a tractor*

Trading *see* Activities – trading

Traffic, traffic signs

Arnold, Tedd. *The signmaker's assistant*
Bank Street College of Education. *Green light, go*
Baugh, Dolores M. *Bikes*
Brown, Margaret Wise. *Red light, green light*
Chwast, Seymour. *Traffic jam*
Krahn, Fernando. *Mr. Top*
Kulman, Andrew. *Red light stop, green light go*
Loewen, Nancy. *Traffic safety*
Maestro, Betsy. *Traffic*
Mendoza, George. *Traffic jam*
Mitchell, Lucy Sprague. *The taxi that hurried*
Shortall, Leonard W. *One way*
Thayer, Jane. *Andy and the runaway horse*
Yagelski, Robert. *The day the lifting bridge stuck*

Train engineers *see* Careers – railroad engineers

Trains

Ahlberg, Allan. *The ghost train*
Ammon, Richard. *Trains at work*
Ardizzone, Edward. *Nicholas and the fast-moving diesel*
Ayars, James Sterling. *Caboose on the roof*
Aylesworth, Jim. *Country crossing*

Ayres, Pam. *Piggo has a train ride*
Balgassi, Haemi. *Peacebound trains*
Barkan, Joanne. *Boxcar*
  Caboose
  Locomotive
  Passenger car
Barton, Byron. *Trains*
Beim, Jerrold. *Country train*
Bemelmans, Ludwig. *Quito express*
Big book of trains
Biro, Val. *Gumdrop races a train*
Blathwayt, Benedict. *The runaway train*
Bontemps, Arna Wendell. *The fast sooner hound*
Brandenberg, Franz. *Everyone ready?*
Broekel, Ray. *Trains*
Bröger, Achim. *Bruno takes a trip*
Brown, Margaret Wise. *The train to Timbuctoo*
  Two little trains
  Whistle for the train
Bunce, William. *Freight trains*
Bunting, Eve (Anne Evelyn). *Train to somewhere*
Burleigh, Robert. *It's funny where Ben's train takes him*
Burningham, John. *Hey! Get off our train*
Burton, Virginia Lee. *Choo choo*
Calmenson, Stephanie. *Engine, engine, number nine*
Cohen, Miriam. *Down in the subway*
Collicutt, Paul. *This train*
Corney, Estelle. *Pa's top hat*
Crews, Donald. *Freight train*
  Shortcut
Cushman, Jerome. *Marvella's hobby*
Cyrus, Kurt. *Slow train to Oxmox*
Demarest, Chris L. *Train*
Ehrlich, Amy. *The everyday train*
Emmett, Fredrick Rowland. *New world for Nellie*
Fleischman, Paul. *Time train*
Gantschev, Ivan. *The Christmas train*
  The train to Grandma's
Gibbons, Gail. *Trains*
Goble, Paul. *Death of the iron horse*
Gramatky, Hardie. *Homer and the circus train*
Greene, Graham. *The little train*
Gretz, Susanna. *Teddy bears take the train*
Hathorn, Libby (Elizabeth). *The tram to Bondi beach*
Hawkins, Colin. *Come for a ride on the ghost train*
Hayashi, Akiko. *Aki and the fox*
Hayward, Linda. *The runaway Christmas toy*
Hines, Gary. *A ride in the crummy*
Howard, Elizabeth Fitzgerald. *Mac and Marie and the train toss surprise*
Hurd, Edith Thacher. *Caboose*
  Engine, engine no. 9
Hurd, Thacher. *Hobo dog*
I've been working on the railroad
Johnson, Angela. *Casey Jones*
Johnston, Tony. *How many miles to Jacksonville?*
Kay, Verla. *Iron horses*
Kirby, David K. *Cows are going to Paris*
Kirk, Daniel. *Breakfast at the Liberty Diner*
Koscielniak, Bruce. *Hector and Prudence - all aboard!*
Kroll, Steven. *Toot! Toot!*
Lakin, Pat (Patricia). *Subway sonata*
Lawson, Julie. *Bear on the train*
  Emma and the silk train
Le Guin, Ursula K. *Tom Mouse*
Lenski, Lois. *The little train*
Lewis, Kim. *The last train*
London, Jonathan. *The owl who became the moon*

Loomis, Christine. *We're going on a trip*
Lyon, George Ella. *A regular rolling Noah*
McAllister, Angela. *Jessie's journey*
Macaulay, David. *Black and white*
McCully, Emily Arnold. *An outlaw Thanksgiving*
Mackinnon, Debbie. *Tom's train*
McPhail, David M. *Moony B. Finch, fastest draw in the West*
   The train
Maestro, Betsy. *All aboard overnight*
Magee, Doug. *All aboard ABC*
Marshak, S. (Samuil). *The pup grew up!*
Marshall, Ray. *The train*
Martin, Bill (William Ivan). *Smoky Poky*
Martin, C. L. G. *The blueberry train*
Meeks, Esther K. *One is the engine*, ill. by Ernie King
   One is the engine, ill. by Joe Rogers
Mogensen, Jan. *Lost and found Teddy*
Moss, Marissa. *True heart*
Mott, Evelyn Clarke. *Steam train ride*
Munsch, Robert N. *Jonathan cleaned up - then he heard a sound*
Murphy, Mary. *My puffer train*
Neitzel, Shirley. *I'm taking a trip on my train*
Nickl, Peter. *Ra ta ta tam*
Paraskevas, Betty. *Cecil Bunions and the midnight train*
Peet, Bill (William Bartlett). *The caboose who got loose*
   Smokey
Pierce, Jack. *The freight train book*
Pinkney, Gloria Jean. *The Sunday outing*
Piper, Watty. *The little engine that could*
Quattlebaum, Mary. *Underground train*
Richards, Jon. *Trains*
Rockwell, Anne F. *Trains*
Rodgers, Frank. *Who's afraid of the ghost train?*
Rosenberg, Liz. *Adelaide and the night train*
Ross, Diana. *The story of the little red engine*
Rounds, Glen. *Casey Jones*
Rush, Ken. *Friday's journey*
Rylant, Cynthia. *Silver packages*
Sasaki, Isao. *Snow*
Sattler, Helen Roney. *Train whistles*
Scarry, Huck. *Huck Scarry's steam train journey*
Shine, Deborah. *The little engine that could pudgy word book*
Siebert, Diane. *Train song*
Slobodkin, Louis. *Clear the track for Michael's magic train*
Spence, Robert, III. *Clickety clack*
Stevenson, James. *All aboard!*
Stinson, Kathy. *Teddy Rabbit*
Suen, Anastasia. *Window music*
Temple, Charles A. *Train*
Thayer, Jane. *I like trains*
Thomas's big railway pop-up book
Thompson, Richard. *Jesse on the night train*
Trains
Tunnell, Michael O. *Mailing May*
Van Allsburg, Chris. *The polar express*
Voake, Charlotte. *Here comes the train*
Weelen, Guy. *The little red train*
Wells, Rosemary. *Don't spill it again, James*
Wetterer, Margaret. *Kate Shelley and the midnight express*
Wilson-Max, Ken. *Big blue engine*
Wondriska, William. *Puff*
Wyllie, Stephen. *Ghost train*

Young, Miriam Burt. *If I drove a train*
Ziefert, Harriet. *Train song*

Trains, toy *see* Toys – trains

Transportation

Ardizzone, Edward. *Nicholas and the fast-moving diesel*
Arnold, Caroline. *How do we travel?*
Baer, Edith. *This is the way we go to school*
Bagwell, Richard. *This is an airport*
Barkan, Joanne. *Boxcar*
   Caboose
   Locomotive
   Passenger car
Barner, Bob. *Elevator escalator book*
Barton, Byron. *Airport*
Baugh, Dolores M. *Trucks and cars to ride*
Billout, Guy. *By camel or by car*
Broekel, Ray. *Trains*
   Trucks
Burton, Virginia Lee. *Maybelle, the cable car*
Calmenson, Stephanie. *Zip, whiz, zoom!*
Campbell, Rod. *Look inside! Land, sea, air*
Cars and trucks
Cars and trucks and other vehicles
Cave, Ron. *Airplanes*
   Automobiles
   Motorcycles
Cleary, Beverly. *Lucky Chuck*
Collicutt, Paul. *This train*
Crews, Donald. *School bus*
   Truck
Dalmais, Anne-Marie. *The Elephant's airplane and other machines*
Demarest, Chris L. *Lindbergh*
   My little red car
Emberley, Ed (Edward Randolph). *Cars, boats, and planes*
Gay, Michel. *Little truck*
Gibbons, Gail. *New road!*
Gomi, Taro. *Bus stop*
Gramatky, Hardie. *Sparky*
Haas, Jessie. *Getting ready to drive a horse and cart*
Hellen, Nancy. *Bus stop*
Hoberman, Mary Ann. *How do I go?*
Ingoglia, Gina. *The big book of real airplanes*
Kimmel, Eric A. *Charlie drives the stage*
Koren, Edward. *Behind the wheel*
Lawson, Julie. *Emma and the silk train*
Lenski, Lois. *Davy goes places*
   Lois Lenski's big book of Mr. Small
Levinson, Riki. *I go with my family to Grandma's*
Lishak, Anthony. *Row your boat*
Loomis, Christine. *Rush hour*
Maass, Robert. *Tugboats*
McAllister, Angela. *Jessie's journey*
MacDonald, Suse. *Elephants on board*
McNaught, Harry. *The truck book*
McNaughton, Colin. *Walk rabbit walk*
Mahy, Margaret. *A busy day for a good grandmother*
Mantegazza, Giovanna. *Look inside a car*
   Look inside an airplane
Marston, Hope Irvin. *Big rigs*
Martin, C. L. G. *The blueberry train*
Miranda, Anne. *Vroom, chugga, vroom-vroom*
Morris, Ann. *On the go*
Munari, Bruno. *The birthday present*

Nikola-Lisa, W. *Wheels go round*
Old MacDonald had a farm. *Old MacDonald had a farm*, ill. by Jessica Souhami
Oliver, Stephen. *Things that go*
Olschewski, Alfred. *The wheel rolls over*
100 words about transportation
Oppenheim, Joanne. *Have you seen roads?*
Pluckrose, Henry Arthur. *On the move*
Quattlebaum, Mary. *Underground train*
Reasoner, Charles. *Who drives this?*
Rey, H. A. (Hans Augusto). *How do you get there?*
Richards, Jon. *Jetliners*
Trains
Rockwell, Anne F. *Ferryboat ride!*
Planes
Things that go
Trains
Rotner, Shelley. *Boats afloat*
Rylant, Cynthia. *Silver packages*
Scarry, Richard. *Richard Scarry's hop aboard! Here we go!*
Schomp, Virginia. *If you were a . . . pilot*
Seibold, J. Otto. *Mr. Lunch takes a plane ride*
Simon, Seymour. *Seymour Simon's book of trucks*
Stevenson, James. *No need for Monty*
Stickland, Paul. *Truck jam*
Suen, Anastasia. *Delivery*
Temple, Charles A. *Train*
Thayer, Jane. *I like trains*
Trucks
Tunnell, Michael O. *Mailing May*
Willis, Jeanne. *Earth mobiles as explained by Professor Xargle*
Yee, Paul. *Let's eat*
Young, Miriam Burt. *If I drove a bus*
If I drove a car
If I drove a train
If I drove a truck
If I flew a plane
Zaffo, George J. *The book of real airplanes*
The giant nursery book of things that go
The giant nursery book of things that work

Traveling *see* Activities – traveling

Trees

Ada, Alma Flor. *El Arbol de Navidad : The Christmas tree*
Adler, David A. *Redwoods are the tallest trees in the world*
Adoff, Arnold. *Flamboyan*
Aldridge, Josephine Haskell. *A possible tree*
Aliki. *Christmas tree memories*
The story of Johnny Appleseed
Altman, Linda Jacobs. *Amelia's road*
Andersen, H. C. (Hans Christian). *The fir tree*, ill. by Stephanie Britt
The fir tree, ill. by Nancy Elkholm Burkert
The fir tree, ill. by Diane Goode
The fir tree, ill. by Rita Marshall
The fir tree, ill. by Bernadette Watts
Angelo, Valenti. *The acorn tree*
Arnold, Caroline. *The biggest living thing*
Arnosky, Jim. *Crinkleroot's guide to knowing the trees*
Ayres, Pam. *When dad cuts down the chestnut tree*
Baird, Anne. *Little tree*
Baker, Jeffrey J. W. *Patterns of nature*
Barker, Cicely Mary. *Flower fairies of the seasons*

Flower fairies of the trees
Barry, Robert E. *Mr. Willowby's Christmas tree*
Bason, Lillian. *Pick a raincoat, pick a whistle*
Baumgart, Klaus. *Laura's Christmas star*
Beck, Ian. *Emily and the golden acorn*
Behn, Harry. *Trees*
Bemelmans, Ludwig. *Parsley*
Berenstain, Stan. *The Berenstain bears and the spooky old tree*
The Berenstain bears' Christmas tree
Bernhard, Emery. *The tree that rains*
The way of the willow branch
Blocksma, Mary. *Apple tree! Apple tree!*
Blough, Glenn O. *Christmas trees and how they grow*
Bond, Felicia. *Christmas in the chicken coop*
Bond, Ruskin. *Cherry tree*
Brenner, Barbara A. *The tremendous tree book*
Brimner, Larry Dane. *What good is a tree?*
Brown, Margaret Wise. *The little fir tree*
Budbill, David. *Christmas tree farm*
Bulla, Clyde Robert. *A tree is a plant*
Bunting, Eve (Anne Evelyn). *I have an olive tree*
Night tree
Someday a tree
Burns, Diane L. *Arbor Day*
Busch, Phyllis S. *Once there was a tree*
Bush, Barbara. *In the heart of the village*
Butcher, Julia. *The sheep and the rowan tree*
Carigiet, Alois. *The pear tree, the birch tree and the barberry bush*
Carney, Margaret (Margaret Rose). *At Grandpa's sugar bush*
Carrier, Lark. *A Christmas promise*
A tree's tale
Casler, Leigh. *The boy who dreamed of an acorn*
Chalmers, Mary. *A Christmas story*
Chase, Edith Newlin. *Secret dawn*
Cherry, Lynne. *The great kapok tree*
Cleary, Beverly. *The real hole*
Clément, Claude. *The voice of the wood*
Coats, Laura Jane. *The oak tree*
Cole, Joanna. *Plants in winter*
Coleman, Evelyn. *The glass bottle tree*
Conrad, Pam. *The Tub People's Christmas*
Cooper, Susan. *Danny and the Kings*
Cummings, E. E. (Edward Estlin). *Little tree*, ill. by Deborah Kogan Ray
Little tree, ill. by Mary C. Smith
Cushman, Doug. *Mouse and Mole and the Christmas walk*
Dale, Penny. *Daisy Rabbit's tree house*
The elephant tree
Day, Alexandra. *Helping the flowers and trees*
Day, Shirley. *Ruthie's big tree*
DeLage, Ida. *The squirrel's tree party*
De Paola, Tomie (Thomas Anthony). *The family Christmas tree book*
Dodd, Lynley. *The apple tree*
Hairy Maclary's caterwaul caper
Drawson, Blair. *Mary Margaret's tree*
Edwards, Richard. *Ten tall oaktrees*
Ehlert, Lois. *Red leaf, yellow leaf*
Ernst, Lisa Campbell. *Squirrel Park*
Fenner, Carol. *Christmas tree on the mountain*
Fisher, Aileen Lucia. *Arbor day*
As the leaves fall down
Fleischman, Paul. *The birthday tree*
Franklin, Kristine L. *When the monkeys came back*
Gackenbach, Dick. *Mighty tree*

George, Kristine O'Connell. *Old Elm speaks*
George, William T. *Christmas at Long Pond*
Gibbons, Gail. *The missing maple syrup sap mystery*
    The seasons of Arnold's apple tree
Gilbert, Helen Earle. *Mr. Plum and the little green tree*
Gordon, Sharon. *Trees*
Gove, Doris. *My mother talks to trees*
Greeley, Valerie. *The acorn's story*
Greydanus, Rose. *Tree house fun*
Haas, Jessie. *Sugaring*
Hall, Derek. *Panda climbs*
Hall, Zoe. *The apple pie tree*
Havill, Juanita. *Magic fort*
Hawkinson, John. *The old stump*
Heller, Nicholas. *The tooth tree*
Henderson, Douglas. *Dinosaur tree*
Henwood, Simon. *The hidden jungle*
High, Linda Oatman. *A Christmas Star*
Himmelman, John. *The great leaf blast-off*
    The talking tree
Hindley, Judy. *The tree*
Hines, Gary. *A Christmas tree in the White House*
    The day of the high climber
Hogan, Paula Z. *The oak tree*
Hoopes, Lyn Littlefield. *Wing-a-ding*
Houghton, Eric. *The crooked apple tree*
Houston, Gloria. *The year of the perfect Christmas tree*
Hunt, Angela Elwell. *The tale of three trees*
Hutchins, Pat. *The silver Christmas tree*
Ikeda, Daisaku. *The cherry tree*
Jaspersohn, William. *Timber!*
Johnston, Tony. *Big red apple*
    Isabel's house of butterflies
    Mole and Troll trim the tree
Jordan, Sandra. *Christmas tree farm*
Joslin, Mary. *The tale of the heaven tree*
Karpin, Florence Baker. *Tree spirits*
Keister, Douglas. *Fernando's gift = El regalo de Fernando*
Kelley, Marty. *Fall is not easy*
Kellogg, Steven (Stephen). *Johnny Appleseed*
King, B. A. *The very best Christmas tree*
Kirk, Barbara. *Grandpa, me and our house in the tree*
Kirkpatrick, Rena K. *Trees*
Krahn, Fernando. *The biggest Christmas tree on earth*
Kraus, Robert. *The tree that stayed up until next Christmas*
Lakin, Pat (Patricia). *Oh, brother!*
Lauber, Patricia. *Be a friend to trees*
Lavies, Bianca. *Lily pad pond*
    Tree trunk traffic
Le Tord, Bijou. *Noah's trees*
Levine, Arthur A. *Pearl Moscowitz's last stand*
Lewis, Naomi. *Leaves*
Lindbergh, Reeve. *Johnny Appleseed*
Lindgren, Astrid. *Lotta's Christmas surprise*
    Of course Polly can do almost everything
Lionni, Leo. *A busy year*
Lloyd, David. *Hello, goodbye*
Locker, Thomas. *Sky tree*
Löfgren, Ulf. *The wonderful tree*
London, Jonathan. *The sugaring-off party*
Lyon, George Ella. *A B Cedar*
Mabey, Richard. *Oak and company*
McCord, David. *Every time I climb a tree*
McPhail, David M. *Henry Bear's Christmas*
Maestro, Betsy. *How do apples grow?*
    Why do leaves change color?

Mahy, Margaret. *The Christmas tree tangle*
Maloney, Peter. *Redbird at Rockefeller Center*
Mamchur, Carolyn Marie. *The popcorn tree*
Manson, Christopher. *The tree in the wood*
Margolis, Richard J. *Big bear, spare that tree*
Marshall, James. *Three up a tree*
Martin, Bill (William Ivan). *Chicka chicka boom boom*
    Chicka chicka sticka sticka
Martin, Jacqueline Briggs. *Button, bucket, sky*
Mathis, Melissa Bay. *Animal house*
Maynard, Joyce. *New house*
Miles, Miska. *Apricot ABC*
Mills, Joyce C. *Gentle Willow*
    Little Tree
Muller, Gerda. *Around the oak*
Munsch, Robert N. *Up, up, down!*
Myers, Bernice. *Charlie's birthday present*
Neville, Mary. *The Christmas tree ride*
Newton, James R. *Forest log*
Nightingale, Sandy. *Cider apples*
Nikly, Michelle. *The emperor's plum tree*
Noble, Trinka Hakes. *Apple tree Christmas*
O Christmas tree
Oana, Kay D. *Robbie and the raggedy scarecrow*
Oppenheim, Joanne. *Have you seen trees?*, ill. by Irwin Rosenhouse
    Have you seen trees?, ill. by Jean and Mou-sien Tseng
Orbach, Ruth. *Apple pigs*
Peet, Bill (William Bartlett). *Merle the high flying squirrel*
Petie, Haris. *The seed the squirrel dropped*
Pfister, Marcus. *Hopper's treetop adventure*
Pike, Norman. *The peach tree*
Pittman, Helena Clare. *The angel tree*
Pomerantz, Charlotte. *Mangaboom*
Powell, Consie. *Old dog Cora and the Christmas tree*
Pyle, Howard. *The Swan Maiden*
Quindlen, Anna. *The tree that came to stay*
Rayevsky, Inna. *The talking tree*
Reed-Jones, Carol. *The tree in the ancient forest*
Reiser, Lynn. *Christmas counting*
Robbins, Ken. *Autumn leaves*
Rogow, Zak. *Oranges*
Russell, Naomi. *The tree*
Ryder, Joanne. *Hello, tree!*
Sato, Satoru. *I wish I had a big, big tree*
Schertle, Alice. *In my treehouse*
Schmid, Eleonore. *The squirrel and the moon*
Spurr, Elizabeth. *The gumdrop tree*
Stemp, Robin. *Guy and the flowering plum tree*
Stewart, Sarah. *The money tree*
Stone, Marti. *The singing fir tree*
Thelen, Gerda. *The toy maker*
Thornhill, Jan. *A tree in a forest*
Tresselt, Alvin R. *The dead tree*
    The gift of the tree
    Johnny Maple-Leaf
Trottier, Maxine. *Prairie willow*
Tudor, Bethany. *Samuel's tree house*
Udry, Janice May. *A tree is nice*
Van Laan, Nancy. *A tree for me*
Van Leeuwen, Jean. *Nothing here but trees*
Vieira, Linda. *The ever-living tree*
Watts, Barrie. *Apple tree*
Weedn, Flavia. *The enchanted tree*
Welch, Willy. *Dancing with Daddy*
Winter, Jeanette. *The Christmas tree ship*
Wong, Herbert H. *Our tree*

Yashima, Taro. *The village tree*
Young, Ed (Edward). *Up a tree*
Zalben, Jane Breskin. *Pearl plants a tree*
Zolotow, Charlotte (Shapiro). *The beautiful Christmas tree*

Trickery *see* Behavior – trickery

Tricks *see* Magic

Trinidad *see* Foreign lands – Trinidad

Trolleys *see* Cable cars, trolleys

Trolls *see* Mythical creatures – trolls

Truck drivers *see* Careers – truck drivers

Trucks

Adkins, Jan. *Heavy equipment*
Alborough, Jez. *Duck in the truck*
Alexander, Anne (Anna Barbara Cooke). *ABC of cars and trucks*
Barr, Jene. *Fire snorkel number 7*
Barton, Byron. *Trucks*
Baugh, Dolores M. *Trucks and cars to ride*
Boucher, Jerry. *Fire truck nuts and bolts*
Breverton, David. *Here comes bulldozer*
    Here comes fire truck
    Here comes the dump truck
    Here comes the tow truck
Broekel, Ray. *Trucks*
Burroway, Janet. *The truck on the track*
Bushey, Jerry. *Building a fire truck*
Campbell, Rod. *Playwheels with moving parts!*
Cars and trucks
Cars and trucks and other vehicles
Cartlidge, Michelle. *Teddy trucks*
Coulter, Hope Norman. *Uncle Chuck's truck*
Crews, Donald. *Truck*
Crowther, Robert. *Dump trucks and diggers*
Cuetara, Mittie. *The crazy crawler crane and other very short truck stories*
Curious George and the dump truck
Curious George and the dump truck
Day, Alexandra. *Frank and Ernest on the road*
Diller, Harriett. *Grandaddy's highway*
Dubowski, Cathy East. *Dumpy the dump truck*
    Fire engine to the rescue
Fast rolling fire trucks
Fast rolling work trucks
Fisher, Leonard Everett. *Pumpers, boilers, hooks and ladders*
Floca, Brian. *Five trucks*
Fowler, Richard. *Mr. Little's noisy fire engine*
    Mr. Little's noisy truck
    Pop-up trucks
Gay, Michel. *Little truck*
Gibbons, Gail. *Emergency!*
    Trucks
Giffard, Hannah. *Fast car*
Gorbaty, Norman. *Tow truck*
Gramatky, Hardie. *Hercules*
Gray, Libba Moore. *The little black truck*
Greydanus, Rose. *Big red fire engine*
Herman, Gail. *Make way for trucks*

Holl, Adelaide. *The ABC of cars, trucks and machines*
Homme, Bob. *The friendly giant's book of fire engines*
Horenstein, Henry. *Sam goes trucking*
Johnston, Tony. *The bull and the fire truck*
Kirk, Daniel. *Trash trucks!*
Kraus, Robert. *Freddy, the fire engine*
    Tony, the tow truck
Kuklin, Susan. *Lighting fires*
Lakin, Pat (Patricia). *Jet black pickup truck*
Leslie, Amanda. *Let's look inside the yellow truck*
Lyon, David. *The biggest truck*
MacDonald, Suse. *Elephants on board*
McNaught, Harry. *The truck book*
McPhail, David M. *Ed and me*
Magee, Doug. *Trucks you can count on*
Marston, Hope Irvin. *Big rigs*
    Fire trucks
Martin, Ann M. *Fire truck to the rescue*
Miranda, Anne. *Beep! beep!*
Miryam. *The happy man and his dump truck*
Mitchell, Joyce Slayton. *Tractor-trailer trucker*
Mitton, Tony. *Flashing fire engines*
Morgan, Allen. *Matthew and the midnight tow truck*
Newton, Laura P. *William the vehicle king*
Peppé, Rodney. *Little wheels*
Petrie, Catherine. *Joshua James likes trucks*
Pomerantz, Charlotte. *How many trucks can a tow truck tow?*
Potter, Tony. *See how it works: trucks*
Quackenbush, Robert M. *City trucks*
Reasoner, Charles. *Who drives this?*
Relf, Patricia. *Tonka big book of trucks*
Rex, Michael. *My fire engine*
Robbins, Ken. *Trucks of every sort*
Rockwell, Anne F. *Fire engines*
    Trucks
Royston, Angela. *Big machines*
    Diggers and dump trucks
    Truck trouble
Santoro, Scott. *Isaac the Ice Cream Truck*
Scarry, Richard. *The great big car and truck book*
Schulz, Charles M. *Snoopy's facts and fun book about trucks*
Seiden, Art. *Trucks*
Selzer, Meyer. *Here comes the recycling truck!*
Seymour, Peter S. *The pop-up book of big trucks*
Siebert, Diane. *Truck song*
Simon, Seymour. *Seymour Simon's book of trucks*
Sis, Peter. *Fire truck*
    Trucks, trucks, trucks
Stickland, Paul. *Truck jam*
Sturges, Philemon. *I love trucks!*
Trucks
Wallace, Karen. *Big machines*
Williams, Karen Lynn. *Tap-tap*
Winkleman, Katherine K. *Firehouse*
Wolf, Sallie. *Peter's trucks*
Wolfe, Robert L. *The truck book*
You can name 100 trucks!
Young, Miriam Burt. *If I drove a truck*
Zaffo, George J. *The giant nursery book of things that go*
Ziefert, Harriet. *Where's mommy's truck?*

Tsars *see* Royalty – tsars

Tsimshian Indians *see* Indians of North America – Tsimshian

Tsunamis

Hodges, Margaret. *The wave*

Turkey *see* Foreign lands – Turkey

Turkeys *see* Birds – turkeys

Turtles *see* Reptiles – turtles, tortoises

TV *see* Television

Twa *see* Indians of North America – Twa

Twilight

Berger, Barbara Helen. *Grandfather Twilight*
Fletcher, Ralph J. *Twilight comes twice*
Major, Beverly. *Playing sardines*
Udry, Janice May. *The moon jumpers*

Tyrol *see* Foreign lands – Tyrol

U.S. history

Abisch, Roz. *The Pumpkin Heads*
Accorsi, William. *My name is Pocahontas*
Ackerman, Karen. *The tin heart*
Addy, Sharon Hart. *Right here on this spot*
Adler, David A. *A picture book of Abraham Lincoln*
  A picture book of Benjamin Franklin
  A picture book of Eleanor Roosevelt
  A picture book of George Washington
  A picture book of John F. Kennedy
  A picture book of Martin Luther King, Jr.
  A picture book of Thomas Jefferson
Aliki. *George and the cherry tree*
  The many lives of Benjamin Franklin
  The story of William Penn
  A weed is a flower
Altman, Susan. *Followers of the north star*
Andersen, H. C. (Hans Christian). *The tinderbox*,
  ill. by Barry Moser
Appelbaum, Diana Karter. *Cocoa ice*
Aulaire, Ingri Mortenson d'. *Abraham Lincoln*
  Pocahontas
Balgassi, Haemi. *Peacebound trains*
Bangs, Edward. *Yankee Doodle*
Barner, Bob. *Which way to the Revolution?*
Benchley, Peter. *Jonathan visits the White House*
Benjamin, Anne. *Young Pocahontas*
Bethell, Jean. *Three cheers for Mother Jones!*
Blumberg, Rhoda. *Bloomers!*
Borden, Louise. *Goodbye, Charles Lindbergh*
  A. Lincoln and me
Brink, Carol Ryrie. *Goody O'Grumpity*
Brownell, Barbara. *Spin's really wild U.S.A. tour*
Bulla, Clyde Robert. *Washington's birthday*
Bunting, Eve (Anne Evelyn). *The blue and the gray*
  Train to somewhere

Calhoun, Mary. *Flood!*
Carlson, Laurie M. *Boss of the plains*
Carrier, Lark. *A tree's tale*
Chalk, Gary. *Yankee Doodle*
Chenault, Nell. *Parsifal the Poddley*
Cherry, Lynne. *A river ran wild*
Chial, Debra. *M is for Minnesota*
Coleman, Evelyn. *To be a drum*
  White socks only
Cooney, Barbara. *Eleanor*
Dadey, Debbie. *Shooting star: Annie Oakley, the legend*
  Will Rogers: larger than life
Dalgliesh, Alice. *The Thanksgiving story*
DeLage, Ida. *Pilgrim children on the Mayflower*
Demarest, Chris L. *Lindbergh*
De Paola, Tomie (Thomas Anthony). *An early American Christmas*
  My first Thanksgiving
DeRubertis, Barbara. *Columbus Day*
Dewey, Ariane. *Laffite, the pirate*
Dupré, Rick. *The wishing chair*
Edwards, Pamela Duncan. *Barefoot*
Everett, Gwen. *Li'l Sis and Uncle Willie*
Fischetto, Laura. *All pigs on deck*
Fisher, Leonard Everett. *Stars and stripes*
Fleming, Candace. *A big cheese for the White House*
  The hatmaker's sign
Friedrich, Elizabeth. *Leah's pony*
George, Jean Craighead. *The first Thanksgiving*
Gerrard, Roy. *Wagons west!*
Giblin, James Cross. *George Washington*
Gleiter, Jan. *Paul Revere*
  Sacagawea
Gorsline, Marie. *North American Indians*
Greenfield, Eloise. *Easter parade*
Greeson, Janet. *An American army of two*
Griest, Lisa. *Lost at the White House*
Haley, Gail E. *Jack Jouett's ride*
Hall, Donald. *Lucy's Christmas*
  Lucy's summer
Harness, Cheryl. *Mark Twain and the queens of the Mississippi*
  Three young pilgrims
Haskins, Jim (James). *The Statue of Liberty*
Hearne, Betsy Gould. *Seven brave women*
Hines, Gary. *A Christmas tree in the White House*
Hiser, Berniece T. *The adventure of Charlie and his wheat-straw hat*
Holbrook, Stewart. *America's Ethan Allen*
Houston, Gloria. *But no candy*
Johnson, D. B. (Donald B.). *Henry hikes to Fitchburg*
Johnson, Dinah. *All around town*
Johnson, Dolores. *Now let me fly*
  Seminole diary
Johnston, Tony. *The wagon*
Jones, Rebecca C. *The biggest (and best) flag that ever flew*
Kay, Verla. *Covered wagons, bumpy trails*
  Iron horses
Keller, Laurie. *The scrambled states of America*
Kellogg, Steven (Stephen). *Johnny Appleseed*
  Mike Fink
  Yankee Doodle
Key, Francis Scott. *The Star-Spangled Banner*, ill. by Paul Galdone
  The Star-Spangled Banner, ill. by Peter Spier
Kirk, Daniel. *Breakfast at the Liberty Diner*
Kroll, Steven. *By the dawn's early light*

Lewis and Clark
Oh, what a Thanksgiving!
Krupinski, Loretta. *Best friends*
Kurtz, Jane. *River friendly, river wild*
Lee, Milly. *Nim and the war effort*
Lent, Blair. *Molasses flood*
Levinson, Riki. *Watch the stars come out*
Lindbergh, Reeve. *Johnny Appleseed*
Littlesugar, Amy. *Tree of hope*
Livingston, Myra Cohn. *Abraham Lincoln*
Keep on singing
Lobel, Arnold. *On the day Peter Stuyvesant sailed into town*
Longfellow, Henry Wadsworth. *Paul Revere's ride*, ill. by Paul Galdone
Paul Revere's ride, ill. by Nancy Winslow Parker
Loomis, Christine. *Across America, I love you*
Love, Ann. *Fishing*
Lowitz, Sadyebeth. *The pilgrims' party*
Lowrey, Janette Sebring. *Six silver spoons*
Lyon, George Ella. *Cecil's story*
McCully, Emily Arnold. *The ballot box battle*
An outlaw Thanksgiving
McGill, Alice. *Molly Bannaky*
McKissack, Patricia C. *Booker T. Washington*
Paul Robeson
McPhail, David M. *Farm boy's year*
Maestro, Betsy. *The story of the Statue of Liberty*
Magdanz, James S. *Go home, river*
Martin, Jacqueline Briggs. *Snowflake Bentley*
Maxfield, Christine. *Christmas in Water Village*
Medearis, Angela Shelf. *The freedom riddle*
Picking peas for a penny
Melmed, Laura Krauss. *1-2-3 Thanksgiving*
Miller, William. *The bus ride*
Frederick Douglass
Mills, Judith Christine. *The stonehook schooner*
Mitchell, Barbara. *Waterman's child*
Mitchell, Margaree King. *Granddaddy's gift*
Mochizuki, Ken. *Baseball saved us*
Heroes
Monjo, F. N. *The drinking gourd*
The one bad thing about father
Poor Richard in France
Morrow, Barbara. *Edward's portrait*
Moskin, Marietta D. *Lysbet and the fire kittens*
Myers, Walter Dean. *Young Martin's promise*
Nicholson, Nicholas B. A. *Little girl in a red dress with cat and dog*
Nickens, Bessie. *Walking the log*
Nikola-Lisa, W. *America: my land, your land, our land*
Ortiz, Simon. *The people shall continue*
Otto, Carolyn. *Pioneer church*
Paraskevas, Betty. *On the day the tall ships sailed*
Petersham, Maud. *An American ABC*
Pinkney, Andrea Davis. *Dear Benjamin Banneker*
Precek, Katharine Wilson. *Penny in the road*
Pryor, Bonnie. *The house on Maple Street*
Quackenbush, Robert M. *Clementine*
Pop! goes the weasel and Yankee Doodle
There'll be a hot time in the old town tonight
Rand, Gloria. *Baby in a basket*
Ransom, Candice F. *The promise quilt*
Raven, Margot. *Angels in the dust*
Ray, Mary Lyn. *Pianna*
Shaker boy
Riggio, Anita. *Secret signs*
Ringgold, Faith. *Dinner at Aunt Connie's house*
My dream of Martin Luther King

Robinson, Aminah Brenda Lynn. *A street called home*
Rochelle, Belinda. *Jewels*
Ryan, Pam Muñoz. *Amelia and Eleanor go for a ride*
The flag we love
St. George, Judith. *So you want to be president?*
Schackburg, Richard. *Yankee Doodle*
Schulz, Walter A. *Will and Orv*
Seymour, Tres. *We played marbles*
Showers, Paul. *Columbus Day*
Siebert, Diane. *Heartland*
Small, David. *George Washington's cows*
Smalls-Hector, Irene. *Jenny Reen and the Jack Muh Lantern*
Smith, Barry. *The first voyage of Christopher Columbus*
Smucker, Barbara Claasen. *Selina and the bear paw quilt*
Sneve, Virginia Driving Hawk. *The Cherokees*
The Nez Perce
Spier, Peter. *The Erie Canal*
The legend of New Amsterdam
We the people
Stewart, Sarah. *The gardener*
Stier, Catherine. *If I were president*
Szekeres, Cyndy. *Long ago*
Trottier, Maxine. *Flags*
Tunnell, Michael O. *Mailing May*
Turkle, Brinton. *The adventures of Obadiah*
Obadiah the Bold
Thy friend, Obadiah
Turner, Ann Warren. *Dust for dinner*
Shaker hearts
Uchida, Yoshiko. *The bracelet*
Uhlberg, Myron. *Flying over Brooklyn*
Van Leeuwen, Jean. *Across the wide dark sea*
Vaughan, Marcia Kapok. *Abbie against the storm*
Vaughn, Jenny. *On the moon*
Vieira, Linda. *The ever-living tree*
Wallner, Alexandra. *Betsy Ross*
The first air voyage in the United States
Washington, Donna L. *The story of Kwanzaa*
Weatherford, Carole Boston. *Juneteenth jamboree*
Weller, Frances Ward. *Madaket Millie*
Wetterer, Margaret. *Kate Shelley and the midnight express*
Whittier, John Greenleaf. *Barbara Frietchie*
Winter, Jeanette. *The Christmas tree ship*
Follow the drinking gourd
Wright, Courtni Crump. *Journey to freedom*
Jumping the broom
Yolen, Jane. *Letting Swift River go*

U.S. history – frontier and pioneer life

Abisch, Roz. *Sweet Betsy from Pike*
Ackerman, Karen. *Araminta's paint box*
Aliki. *The story of Johnny Appleseed*
Anderson, Leone Castell. *Surprise at Muddy Creek*
Belting, Natalia Maree. *Verity Mullens and the Indian*
Bishop, Ann. *Wild Bill Hiccup's riddle book*
Brandt, Betty. *Special delivery*
Chandler, Edna Walker. *Cattle drive*
Pony rider
Secret tunnel
Cohen, Caron Lee. *Bronco dogs*
Dewey, Ariane. *Pecos Bill*
Doughtie, Charles. *High Henry . . . the cowboy who was too tall to ride a horse*

Enderle, Judith (Ann) Ross. *Nell Nugget and the cow caper*
Everett, Percival L. *The one that got away*
A farmer boy birthday
Felton, Harold W. *Pecos Bill and the mustang*
Fleming, Candace. *Westward ho, Carlotta!*
Gerrard, Roy. *Rosie and the rustlers*
Wagons west!
Gibbons, Gail. *Yippee-yay!*
Glass, Andrew. *The sweetwater run*
Glasscock, Sarah. *My prairie summer*
Gleeson, Brian. *Paul Bunyan*
Grossman, Bill. *Cowboy Ed*
Hancock, Sibyl. *Old Blue*
Harper, Jo. *Jalapeno Hal*
Prairie dog pioneers
Harvey, Brett. *Cassie's journey*
My prairie year
Hooker, Ruth. *Matthew the cowboy*
Howard, Ellen. *The log cabin quilt*
Isaacs, Anne. *Swamp Angel*
Jakes, John. *Susanna of the Alamo*
Johnston, Tony. *The cowboy and the black-eyed pea*
Joosse, Barbara M. *Lewis and papa*
Karim, Roberta. *Kindle me a riddle*
Kay, Verla. *Gold fever*
Kellogg, Steven (Stephen). *Paul Bunyan*
Pecos Bill
Sally Ann Thunder Ann Whirlwind Crockett
Kennedy, Richard. *The contests at Cowlick*
Ketteman, Helen. *Shoeshine Whittaker*
Kimmel, Eric A. *Charlie drives the stage*
Four dollars and fifty cents
Kinsey-Warnock, Natalie. *The bear that heard crying*
Kramer, Sydelle. *Wagon train*
Kunstler, James Howard. *Annie Oakley*
Lawson, Robert. *They were strong and good*
Levitin, Sonia. *Nine for California*
Taking charge
Lowell, Susan. *The bootmaker and the elves*
Cindy Ellen
Dusty Locks and the three bears
Lyndon, Kerry Raines. *A birthday for Blue*
MacLachlan, Patricia. *What you know first*
McLerran, Alice. *The year of the ranch*
Medearis, Angela Shelf. *The zebra-riding cowboy*
Miller, Robert H. (Robert Henry). *The story of Nat Love*
Nixon, Joan Lowery. *If you say so, Claude*
That's the spirit, Claude
You bet your britches, Claude
Pryor, Bonnie. *Lottie's dream*
Quackenbush, Robert M. *Pete Pack Rat*
Reynolds, Marilynn. *The new land*
The prairie fire
Rounds, Glen. *Cowboys*
Sod houses on the Great Plains
Sanders, Scott R. (Scott Russell). *A place called Freedom*
Warm as wool
Scott, Ann Herbert. *Big Cowboy Western*
Sewall, Marcia. *Ridin' that strawberry roan*
Sorensen, Henri. *New Hope*
Stadler, John. *The ballad of Wilbur and the moose*
Stilz, Carol Curtis. *Grandma Buffalo, May, and me*
Strand, Keith. *Grandfather's Christmas tree*
Stutson, Caroline. *Prairie primer A to Z*
Sugar snow

Turner, Ann Warren. *Dakota dugout*
Red flower goes West
Van Leeuwen, Jean. *Going west*
Nothing here but trees
Van Woerkom, Dorothy. *Becky and the bear*
Walton, Rick. *Dance, pioneer, dance!*
Whiteley, Opal Stanley. *Only Opal*
Wilder, Laura Ingalls. *Going to town*
My little house songbook
Winter, Jeanette. *Cowboy Charlie*
Wittmann, Patricia. *Buffalo Thunder*
Wood, Audrey. *The Bunyans*
Wright, Courtni Crump. *Wagon train*
Yorinks, Arthur. *Whitefish Will rides again*

Ukraine *see* Foreign lands – Ukraine

Umbrellas

Biro, Val. *Miranda's umbrella*
Blance, Ellen. *Monster and the magic umbrella*
Bright, Robert. *My red umbrella*
Chesworth, Michael. *Rainy day dream*
Ching. *The baboon's umbrella*
Chorao, Kay. *Maudie's umbrella*
Cole, William. *Aunt Bella's umbrella*
Demi. *The leaky umbrella*
Drescher, Henrik. *The yellow umbrella*
Feczko, Kathy. *Umbrella parade*
Levine, Rhoda. *Harrison loved his umbrella*
Lipkind, William. *Professor Bull's umbrella*
Pinkwater, Daniel Manus. *Roger's umbrella*
Smath, Jerry. *Mr. Digby's bad day*
Yashima, Taro. *Umbrella*

Uncles *see* Family life – aunts, uncles

Unhappiness *see* Emotions – happiness; Emotions – sadness

UNICEF

Coatsworth, Elizabeth. *The children come running*

Unicorns *see* Mythical creatures – unicorns

Unnoticed *see* Behavior – unnoticed, unseen

Unseen *see* Behavior – unnoticed, unseen

Unusual format *see* Format, unusual

Up and down *see* Concepts – up and down

Ute Indians *see* Indians of North America – Ute

Uzbekistan *see* Foreign lands – Uzbekistan

Vacationing *see* Activities – vacationing

Vacuum cleaners *see* Machines

Valentine's Day *see* Holidays – Valentine's Day

Values

Mahy, Margaret. *Pillycock's shop*
Schlein, Miriam. *The pile of junk*

Vampires *see* Monsters

Vanity *see* Character traits – vanity

Vatican City *see* Foreign lands – Vatican City

Venezuela *see* Foreign lands – Venezuela

Veterinarians *see* Careers – veterinarians

Vietnam *see* Foreign lands – Vietnam

Vietnamese Americans *see* Ethnic groups in the U.S. – Asian Americans; Ethnic groups in the U.S. – Vietnamese Americans

Violence, nonviolence

Charters, Janet. *The general*
Cohn, Janice I. *"Why did it happen?"*
Duvoisin, Roger Antoine. *The happy hunter*
Fitzhugh, Louise. *Bang, bang, you're dead*
Foreman, Michael. *Moose*
Hader, Berta Hoerner. *Mister Billy's gun*
Leaf, Munro. *The story of Ferdinand the bull*
Lobel, Anita. *Potatoes, potatoes*
Peet, Bill (William Bartlett). *The pinkish, purplish, bluish egg*
Sharmat, Marjorie Weinman. *Walter the wolf*
Wiesner, William. *Tops*
Wondriska, William. *The tomato patch*

Volcanoes

Branley, Franklyn M. (Mansfield). *Volcanoes*
George, Jean Craighead. *Dear Katie, the volcano is a girl*
Grifalconi, Ann. *The village of round and square houses*
Kimmel, Eric A. *The two mountains*
Lewis, Paul Owen. *Frog girl*
Lewis, Thomas P. *Hill of fire*

Vultures *see* Birds – vultures

Waiters *see* Careers – waiters, waitresses

Waitresses *see* Careers – waiters, waitresses

Wales *see* Foreign lands – Wales

Walking *see* Activities – walking

Walruses *see* Animals – walruses

Wampanoag Indians *see* Indians of North America – Wampanoag

War

Ackerman, Karen. *The tin heart*
    When mama retires
Adler, David A. *The number on my grandfather's arm*
Ambrus, Victor G. *Brave soldier Janosch*
Armstrong, Jennifer. *King crow*
Aulaire, Ingri Mortenson d'. *Wings for Per*
Baillie, Allan. *Rebel!*
Balgassi, Haemi. *Peacebound trains*
Baumann, Kurt. *The prince and the lute*
Breckler, Rosemary K. *Sweet dried apples*
Briggs, Raymond. *The tin-pot foreign general and the old iron woman*
Brunhoff, Laurent de. *Babar's battle*
Bunting, Eve (Anne Evelyn). *The blue and the gray*
    So far from the sea
    The wall
Chiang, Wei. *The legend of Mu Lan = La heroina Hua Mulan*
Coerr, Eleanor. *Sadako*
De Paola, Tomie (Thomas Anthony). *The mysterious giant of Barletta*
Dupasquier, Philippe. *Jack at sea*
Eco, Umberto. *The bomb and the general*
Elzbieta. *Jon-Jon and Annette*
Fitzhugh, Louise. *Bang, bang, you're dead*
Foreman, Michael. *War and peas*
Fox, Mem. *Feathers and fools*
Garland, Sherry. *The lotus seed*
Gauch, Patricia Lee. *Once upon a Dinkelsbühl*
Gleiter, Jan. *Paul Revere*
Goble, Paul. *Death of the iron horse*
Gold, Julie. *From a distance*
Greenfield, Eloise. *Easter parade*
Greeson, Janet. *An American army of two*
Grimm, Wilhelm. *Dear Mili*
Haseley, Dennis. *Horses with wings*
Hearne, Betsy Gould. *Seven brave women*
Heide, Florence Parry. *Sami and the time of the troubles*
Hest, Amy. *The ring and the window seat*
Hodges, Margaret. *The hero of Bremen*
Hoestlandt, Jo. *Star of fear, star of hope*
Holbrook, Stewart. *America's Ethan Allen*

Houston, Gloria. *But no candy*

Howard, Elizabeth Fitzgerald. *Papa tells Chita a story*

Hughes, Peter. *The king who loved candy*

Hutton, Warwick. *The Trojan horse*

Ikeda, Daisaku. *The cherry tree*

James, J. Alison. *The drums of Noto Hanto*

Jones, Rebecca C. *The biggest (and best) flag that ever flew*

Khan, Rukhsana. *The roses in my carpets*

Lee, Milly. *Nim and the war effort*

Lyon, George Ella. *Cecil's story*

McAllister, Angela. *The battle of Sir Cob and Sir Filbert*

McKee, David. *Tusk tusk*

Mattingley, Christobel. *The angel with a mouth-organ*

Miller, Edward. *Frederick Ferdinand Fox*

Mochizuki, Ken. *Baseball saved us Heroes*

Morimoto, Junko. *My Hiroshima*

Munsch, Robert N. *From far away*

Myers, Edward. *Forri the baker*

Nerlove, Miriam. *Flowers on the wall*

Nivola, Claire A. *Elisabeth*

Norman, Philip Ross. *The carrot war*

Oberman, Sheldon. *By the Hanukkah light*

Oppenheim, Shulamith Levey. *The lily cupboard*

Phillips, Louis. *The brothers Wrong and Wrong Again*

Polacco, Patricia. *The butterfly*

Poole, Josephine. *Joan of Arc*

Popov, Nikolai. *Why?*

Rupprecht, Siegfried P. *The tale of the vanishing rainbow*

Sandman, Rochel. *Perfect porridge*

Seuss, Dr. *The butter battle book*

Seymour, Tres. *We played marbles*

Shea, Pegi Deitz. *The whispering cloth*

Smucker, Barbara Claasen. *Selina and the bear paw quilt*

Stillerman, Marci. *Nine spoons*

Stone, Bernard. *The charge of the mouse brigade*

Trottier, Maxine. *Flags*

Vigna, Judith. *Nobody wants a nuclear war*

Wells, Rosemary. *The language of doves*

Whittier, John Greenleaf. *Barbara Frietchie*

Wild, Margaret. *Let the celebrations begin!*

Yenne, Bill. *Joshua and the battle of Jericho*

Yolen, Jane. *All those secrets of the world*

Zhang, Song Nan. *The ballad of Mulan*

Ziefert, Harriet. *A new coat for Anna*

Warthogs *see* Animals – warthogs

Washing machines *see* Machines

Washington's Birthday *see* Holidays – Washington's Birthday

Wasps *see* Insects – wasps

Watches *see* Clocks, watches

Water

Asch, Frank. *Water*

Atwell, Debby. *River*

Cole, Joanna. *The magic school bus at the waterworks*

Cunningham, David. *A crow's journey*

Dorros, Arthur. *Follow the water from brook to ocean*

Duvall, Jill. *Who keeps the water clean? Ms. Schindler!*

George, Jean Craighead. *To climb a waterfall*

Greenfield, Eloise. *Water, water*

Grindley, Sally. *Peter's place*

Guthrie, Donna. *Nobiah's well*

Hathorn, Libby (Elizabeth). *The wonder thing*

Jackson, Ellen B. *The precious gift*

Jackson, Shelley. *The old woman and the wave*

Jolliffe, Anne. *Water, wind and wheels*

Keams, Geri. *Snail girl brings water*

Koch, Michelle. *World water watch*

Leutscher, Alfred. *Water*

McDonnell, Flora. *Splash!*

Madgwick, Wendy. *Water play*

Martin, David. *Lizzie and her friend*

Mattern, Joanne. *Safety in the water*

Miller, Margaret. *Water play*

Paterson, Katherine. *Celia and the sweet, sweet water*

Peters, Lisa Westberg. *Water's way*

Pitcher, Caroline. *The snow whale*

Pollock, Penny. *Water is wet*

Rauzon, Mark J. *Water, water everywhere*

Riley, Linda Capus. *Elephants swim*

Russell, Naomi. *The stream*

Schmid, Eleonore. *The water's journey*

Sheppard, Jeff. *Splash, splash*

Southey, Robert. *The cataract of Lodore*

Speed, Toby. *Watervoices*

Stafford, Kim Robert. *We got here together*

Verboven, Agnes. *Ducks like to swim*

Wyler, Rose. *Puddles and ponds*

Yolen, Jane. *Letting Swift River go*

Water buffaloes *see* Animals – water buffaloes

Weapons

Bolliger, Max. *The wooden man*

Duvoisin, Roger Antoine. *The happy hunter*

Emberley, Barbara. *Drummer Hoff*

Fitzhugh, Louise. *Bang, bang, you're dead*

Hader, Berta Hoerner. *Mister Billy's gun*

Schulson, Rachel Ellenberg. *Guns . . . what you should know*

Wondriska, William. *The tomato patch*

Weasels *see* Animals – weasels

Weather

Allington, Richard L. *Autumn*
Spring
Summer
Winter

Anholt, Catherine. *Sun, snow, stars, sky*

Ardizzone, Edward. *Tim to the rescue*

Asch, Frank. *Country pie*

Barrett, Judi. *Cloudy with a chance of meatballs*
Pickles to Pittsburgh

Baum, Arline. *One bright Monday morning*

Bell, Norman. *Linda's airmail letter*

Berger, Melvin. *How's the weather?*

Bolliger, Max. *The wooden man*

Branley, Franklyn M. (Mansfield). *Down comes the rain*
Rain and hail

Brenner, Barbara A. *The snow parade*
Brown, Margaret Wise. *The little island*
Burgert, Hans-Joachim. *Samulo and the giant*
Calmenson, Stephanie. *Hotter than a hot dog!*
Davidson, Amanda. *Teddy goes outside*
Dewey, Ariane. *Febold Feboldson*
DeWitt, Lyndia. *What will the weather be?*
Dunphy, Madeleine. *Here is the tropical rain forest*
Fisher, Aileen Lucia. *I like weather*
Fowler, Allan. *What's the weather today?*
Frye, Dean. *Days of sunshine, days of rain*
Gackenbach, Dick. *Ida Fanfanny*
Gibbons, Gail. *Weather words and what they mean*
Ginsburg, Mirra. *Four brave sailors*
Gliori, Debi. *Willie Bear and the Wish Fish*
Gould, Deborah. *Camping in the Temple of the Sun*
Greenberg, Barbara. *The bravest babysitter*
Grohmann, Susan. *The dust under Mrs. Merri-
    weather's bed*
Havill, Juanita. *Treasure nap*
Hayden, Lea. *Sunny day - rainy day*
Hayward, Linda. *Sunny Day Bunny*
Hill, Eric. *Spot looks at weather*
Hines, Anna Grossnickle. *What can you do in the
    sun?*
Howell, Will C. *I call it sky*
Inkpen, Mick. *Kipper's book of weather*
A January fog will freeze a hog
Jaynes, Ruth M. *Benny's four hats*
Ketteman, Helen. *Heat wave*
Kirkpatrick, Rena K. *Weather*
Koscielniak, Bruce. *Geoffrey Groundhog predicts the
    weather*
Lewin, Betsy. *Hip, hippo, hooray!*
Lotz, Karen E. *Can't sit still*
McCloskey, Robert. *Time of wonder*
McKee, David. *Elmer's weather*
Maestro, Betsy. *Temperature and you*
Through the year with Harriet
Marshak, S. (Samuil). *The Month-Brothers*
Mollel, Tololwa M. (Tololwa Marti). *A promise to the
    sun*
Moore, Elaine. *Grandma's garden*
Palazzo-Craig, Janet. *What makes the weather*
Peters, Lisa Westberg. *The sun, the wind and the rain*
Water's way
Pienkowski, Jan. *Weather*
Roche, Hannah. *Sandra's sun hat*
Rockwell, Anne F. *Blackout*
Rogers, Paul (Patrick). *What will the weather be like
    today?*
Schlein, Miriam. *The sun, the wind, the sea and the
    rain*
Schweninger, Ann. *Summertime*
Seymour, Peter S. *How the weather works*
Sherrow, Victoria. *Wilbur waits*
Stevenson, James. *Heat wave at Mud Flat*
Tresselt, Alvin R. *Sun up*, ill. by author
Sun up, ill. by Henri Sorensen
Vance, Eleanor Graham. *Jonathan*
Van Leeuwen, Jean. *Too hot for ice cream*
Vigna, Judith. *Boot weather*
Watts, Bernadette. *Tattercoats*
Zolotow, Charlotte (Shapiro). *The storm book*

Weather – blizzards

Hobbie, Holly. *Toot and Puddle, I'll be home for
    Christmas*

Spinelli, Eileen. *Coming through the blizzard*

Weather – clouds

Ariane. *Small Cloud*
Burningham, John. *Cloudland*
Carle, Eric. *Little cloud*
Little cloud, a board book
Cummings, Pat. *C.L.O.U.D.S.*
De Paola, Tomie (Thomas Anthony). *The cloud
    book*
Fowler, Allan. *What do you see in a cloud?*
Greenblat, Rodney Alan. *Thunder Bunny*
Greene, Carol. *Hi, clouds*
Locker, Thomas. *Cloud dance*
Lustig, Michael. *Willy Whyner, cloud designer*
McFall, Gardner. *Jonathan's cloud*
Manushkin, Fran. *Swinging and swinging*
Marol, Jean-Claude. *Vagabul in the clouds*
Oliviero, Jamie. *The fish skin*
Ray, Deborah Kogan. *The cloud*
Rayner, Mary. *The rain cloud*
Renberg, Dalia Hardof. *Hello, clouds!*
Ringi, Kjell (Arne Sorensen). *The sun and the cloud*
Shaw, Charles Green. *It looked like spilt milk*
Spier, Peter. *Dreams*
Turkle, Brinton. *The sky dog*
Wandelmaier, Roy. *Clouds*
Wegen, Ron. *Sky dragon*
Wiesner, David. *Sector 7*
Williams, Leslie. *A bear in the air*

Weather – cold

Baker, Susan. *First look at keeping warm*
Faulkner, Keith. *The puzzled penguin*
Hoban, Lillian. *The sugar snow spring*

Weather – droughts

Aardema, Verna. *Bringing the rain to Kapiti Plain*
Booth, David. *The dust bowl*
Burke, Katie. *Lightning bug thunder*
Cowley, Joy. *Singing down the rain*
Czernecki, Stefan. *The hummingbird's gift*
Fleming, Candace. *Professor Fergus Fahrenheit and
    his wonderful weather machine*
Frascino, Edward. *Nanny Noony and the dust queen*
Friedrich, Elizabeth. *Leah's pony*
Guthrie, Donna. *Nobiah's well*
Hamilton, Virginia. *Drylongso*
Harper, Jo. *Jalapeno Hal*
James, Betsy. *The mud family*
Malotki, Ekkehart. *The magic hummingbird*
Metaxas, Eric. *Princess Scargo and the birthday pump-
    kin*
Oliviero, Jamie. *The fish skin*
Rappaport, Doreen. *The long-haired girl*
Yep, Laurence. *The junior thunder lord*

Weather – floods

Alexander, Ellen. *Llama and the great flood*
Bernhard, Emery. *The tree that rains*
Bible. Old Testament. Noah. *Noah and the ark*, ill.
    by Pauline Baynes
Noah and the ark, ill. by Jim Cummins
Bolliger, Max. *Noah and the rainbow*
Brent, Isabelle. *Noah's ark*

Brown, Rick. *Who built the ark?*
Calhoun, Mary. *Flood!*
Carson, Jo. *The great shaking*
Cartwright, Ann. *Norah's ark*
Cech, John. *Django*
Chase, Catherine. *Noah's ark*
Cousins, Lucy. *Noah's ark*
Delessert, Etienne. *The endless party*
De Paola, Tomie (Thomas Anthony). *Noah and the ark*
Duvoisin, Roger Antoine. *A for the ark*
Elborn, Andrew. *Noah and the ark and the animals*
Emberley, Barbara. *One wide river to cross*
Farber, Norma. *How the left-behind beasts built Ararat Where's Gomer?*
Figley, Marty Rhodes. *Noah's wife*
Fischetto, Laura. *Inside Noah's ark*
French, Fiona. *Rise and shine*
Fussenegger, Gertrud. *Noah's ark*
Gauch, Patricia Lee. *Noah*
Geisert, Arthur. *The ark*
Gerstein, Mordicai. *Noah and the great flood*
Goble, Paul. *Remaking the earth*
Goffstein, M. B. (Marilyn Brooke). *My Noah's ark*
Goodhart, Pippa. *Noah makes a boat*
Graham, Lorenz B. *God wash the world and start again*
Haley, Gail E. *Noah's ark*
Haubensak-Tellenbach, Margrit. *The story of Noah's ark*
Hayward, Linda. *Noah's ark*
Hendrick, Mary Jean. *If anything ever goes wrong at the zoo*
Henrioud, Charles. *Mr. Noah and the animals*
Hewitt, Kathryn. *Two by two*
Hogrogian, Nonny. *Noah's ark*
Hutton, Warwick. *Noah and the great flood*
Ife, Elaine. *Noah and the ark*
Ipcar, Dahlov. *A flood of creatures*
James, Betsy. *The mud family*
Janisch, Heinz. *Noah's ark*
Jonas, Ann. *Aardvarks, disembark!*
Ketteman, Helen. *The year of no more corn*
Kishida, Eriko. *The hippo boat*
Kurtz, Jane. *River friendly, river wild*
Kuskin, Karla. *The animals and the ark*
Lenski, Lois. *Mr. and Mrs. Noah*
Le Tord, Bijou. *Noah's trees*
Lewis, J. Patrick. *The boat of many rooms*
Ludwig, Warren. *Old Noah's elephants*
Lyon, George Ella. *Come a tide*
MacBeth, George. *Noah's journey*
McCaughrean, Geraldine. *The story of Noah and the ark*
McKié, Roy. *Noah's ark*
Martin, Charles E. *Noah's ark*
Mee, Charles L. *Noah*
Miller, M. L. *Those Bottles!*
Morgan, Allen. *Matthew and the midnight flood*
Morpurgo, Michael. *Jo-Jo the melon donkey*
Olson, Arielle North. *Noah's cats and the devil's fire*
Palazzo, Tony (Anthony D.). *Noah's ark*
Rose, Gerald. *Trouble in the ark*
Rosen, Michael J. (1954-). *The dog who walked with God*
Rounds, Glen. *Washday on Noah's ark*
Sasso, Sandy Eisenberg. *A prayer for the earth*
Singer, Isaac Bashevis. *Why Noah chose the dove*
Smith, Elmer Boyd. *The story of Noah's ark*

Smith, Roger. *How the animals saved the ark and put two and two together*
Spier, Peter. *Noah's ark*
Stuart, Chad. *The Ballymara flood*
Tapio, Pat Decker. *The lady who saw the good side of everything*
Thorne, Jenny. *Noah's ark*
Turnbull, Ann. *Too tired*
Velthuijs, Max. *Frog is a hero*
Walton, Rick. *Noah's square dance*
Webb, Clifford. *The story of Noah*
Wiesner, William. *Noah's ark*
Windham, Sophie. *Noah's ark*

Weather – fog

Bacheller, Irving. *Lost in the fog*
Fowler, Susi Gregg. *Fog*
Fry, Christopher. *The boat that mooed*
Keeping, Charles. *Alfie finds the other side of the world*
Lifton, Betty Jean. *Joji and the fog*
May, Robert Lewis. *Rudolph the red-nosed reindeer*
Morse, Samuel French. *Sea sums*
Munari, Bruno. *The circus in the mist*
Pearson, Susan. *Silver morning*
Ryder, Joanne. *Fog in the meadow*
Schroder, William. *Pea soup and serpents*
Smith, Theresa Kalab. *The fog is secret*
Tresselt, Alvin R. *Hide and seek fog*

Weather – hurricanes

Cole, Joanna. *The magic school bus inside a hurricane*
Egan, Tim. *Distant Feathers*
Lakin, Pat (Patricia). *Hurricane!*
London, Jonathan. *Hurricane!*
Wallner, Alexandra. *Sergio and the hurricane*

Weather – mist *see* Weather – fog

Weather – rain

Aardema, Verna. *Bringing the rain to Kapiti Plain*
Ariane. *Small Cloud*
Arnosky, Jim. *Rabbits and raindrops*
Baker, Jill. *Basil of Bywater Hollow*
Bassett, Preston R. *Raindrop stories*
Bergere, Thea. *Paris in the rain with Jean and Jacqueline*
Bible. Old Testament. Noah. *Noah and the ark*, ill. by Pauline Baynes
  Noah and the ark, ill. by Jim Cummins
Blegvad, Lenore. *Rainy day Kate*
Bolliger, Max. *Noah and the rainbow*
Bonnici, Peter. *The first rains*
Boon, Emilie. *Peterkin's wet walk*
Bourgeois, Paulette. *Big Sarah's little boots*
Branley, Franklyn M. (Mansfield). *Down comes the rain*
  Rain and hail
Brent, Isabelle. *Noah's ark*
Bright, Robert. *My red umbrella*
Brouillard, Anne. *The bathtub prima donna*
Brown, Rick. *Who built the ark?*
Buchanan, Ken. *It rained on the desert today*
Bullock, Kathleen. *It chanced to rain*
Burningham, John. *Mr. Gumpy's motor car*
Calhoun, Mary. *Euphonia and the flood*

Carle, Eric. *Little cloud*
   Little cloud, a board book
Carlson, Nancy L. *What if it never stops raining?*
Carlstrom, Nancy White. *What does the rain play?*
Carrick, Carol. *Sleep out*
   The washout
Cartwright, Ann. *Norah's ark*
Cazet, Denys. *You make the angels cry*
Charlip, Remy. *Where is everybody?*
Chase, Catherine. *Noah's ark*
Claverie, Jean. *The picnic*
Cole, Sheila. *When the rain stops*
Cole, William. *Aunt Bella's umbrella*
Conover, Chris. *Sam Panda and Thunder Dragon*
Cousins, Lucy. *Noah's ark*
Cowley, Joy. *Singing down the rain*
Crary, Elizabeth. *I'm mad*
Crews, Nina. *You are here*
Delessert, Etienne. *The endless party*
De Paola, Tomie (Thomas Anthony). *Katie and Kit at the beach*
   Noah and the ark
Dragonwagon, Crescent. *Rainy day together*
Drury, Tim. *When I'm big*
Dubanevich, Arlene. *Pig William*
Duvoisin, Roger Antoine. *A for the ark*
Eaton, Deborah. *The rainy day grump*
Edwards, Dorothy. *A wet Monday*
Elborn, Andrew. *Noah and the ark and the animals*
Emberley, Barbara. *One wide river to cross*
Evans, Lezlie. *Rain song*
Farber, Norma. *How the left-behind beasts built Ararat*
   Where's Gomer?
Ferro, Beatriz. *Caught in the rain*
Figley, Marty Rhodes. *Noah's wife*
Fischetto, Laura. *Inside Noah's ark*
Fleming, Candace. *Professor Fergus Fahrenheit and his wonderful weather machine*
Ford, Miela. *My day in the garden*
Freeman, Don. *Dandelion*
French, Fiona. *Rise and shine*
Fussenegger, Gertrud. *Noah's ark*
Garelick, May. *Where does the butterfly go when it rains?*, ill. by Leonard Weisgard
   Where does the butterfly go when it rains?, ill. by Nicholas Wilton
Gauch, Patricia Lee. *Noah*
Gay, Marie-Louise. *Rainy day magic*
Geisert, Arthur. *The ark*
Gerstein, Mordicai. *Noah and the great flood*
Ginsburg, Mirra. *Mushroom in the rain*
Goffstein, M. B. (Marilyn Brooke). *My Noah's ark*
Goodhart, Pippa. *Noah makes a boat*
Goudey, Alice E. *The good rain*
Graham, Lorenz B. *God wash the world and start again*
Greene, Carol. *Rain! Rain!*
Greenfield, Karen R. *Sister Yessa's story*
Haley, Gail E. *Noah's ark*
Harper, Jo. *Jalapeno Hal*
Haubensak-Tellenbach, Margrit. *The story of Noah's ark*
Hayden, Lea. *Sunny day - rainy day*
Hayward, Linda. *Noah's ark*
Helldorfer, M. C. (Mary Claire). *Silver Rain Brown*
Henrioud, Charles. *Mr. Noah and the animals*
Hershenhorn, Esther. *There goes Lowell's party!*
Hesse, Karen. *Come on, rain*
Hest, Amy. *In the rain with Baby Duck*

Hewitt, Kathryn. *Two by two*
Hines, Anna Grossnickle. *The greatest picnic in the world*
   Taste the raindrops
   What can you do in the rain?
Hoban, Julia. *Amy loves the rain*
Hoban, Russell. *The rain door*
Hogrogian, Nonny. *Noah's ark*
Holl, Adelaide. *The rain puddle*
Hurd, Edith Thacher. *Johnny Lion's rubber boots*
Hutchins, H. J. (Hazel J.). *It's raining, Yancy and Bear*
Hutton, Warwick. *Noah and the great flood*
Ife, Elaine. *Noah and the ark*
Inkpen, Mick. *Splosh!*
Iwasaki, Chihiro. *Staying home alone on a rainy day*
James, Betsy. *The mud family*
Janisch, Heinz. *Noah's ark*
Johnson, Angela. *Rain feet*
Jonas, Ann. *Aardvarks, disembark!*
Kalan, Robert. *Rain*
Keats, Ezra Jack. *A letter to Amy*
Keith, Eros. *Nancy's backyard*
Keller, Holly. *Will it rain?*
Kennedy, Kim. *Napoleon*
Kishida, Eriko. *The hippo boat*
Knutson, Kimberley. *Jungle jamboree*
   Muddigush
Krings, Antoon. *Oliver's bicycle*
Kroll, Steven. *Doctor on an elephant*
Kuskin, Karla. *The animals and the ark*
   James and the rain
Kwitz, Mary DeBall. *When it rains*
Laser, Michael. *The rain*
Lee, Jeanne M. *Toad is the uncle of heaven*
Lenski, Lois. *Mr. and Mrs. Noah*
Le Tord, Bijou. *Noah's trees*
Lewis, J. Patrick. *The boat of many rooms*
Lewison, Wendy Cheyette. *So many boots*
Lindbergh, Reeve. *What is the sun?*
Lloyd, David. *Hello, goodbye*
London, Jonathan. *Puddles*
Ludwig, Warren. *Old Noah's elephants*
Lukesová, Milena. *The little girl and the rain*
MacBeth, George. *Noah's journey*
McCaughrean, Geraldine. *The story of Noah and the ark*
McKié, Roy. *Noah's ark*
McPhail, David M. *The puddle*
Marino, Dorothy. *Good-bye thunderstorm*
Martin, Bill (William Ivan). *Listen to the rain*
Martin, Charles E. *Noah's ark*
Medearis, Angela Shelf. *We play on a rainy day*
Mee, Charles L. *Noah*
Munsch, Robert N. *Mud puddle*
Murphy, Shirley Rousseau. *Tattie's river journey*
Nakabayashi, Ei. *The rainy day puddle*
Olaleye, Isaac. *In the Rainfield*
Oliviero, Jamie. *The fish skin*
Olson, Arielle North. *Noah's cats and the devil's fire*
Otto, Carolyn. *That sky, that rain*
Palazzo, Tony (Anthony D.). *Noah's ark*
Patron, Susan. *Dark cloud strong breeze*
Pinkwater, Daniel Manus. *Rainy morning*
Plourde, Lynn. *Pigs in the mud in the middle of the rud*
Potter, Tessa. *Digger, the story of a mole in the fall*
Prelutsky, Jack. *Rainy rainy Saturday*
Preston, Edna Mitchell. *Pop Corn and Ma Goodness*

Radley, Gail. *Rainy day rhymes*
Raskin, Ellen. *And it rained*
Rayner, Mary. *One by one*
Ricketts, Michael. *Rain*
Robbins, Ruth. *How the first rainbow was made*
Roche, Harriet. *Pete's puddles*
Rose, Gerald. *Trouble in the ark*
Rounds, Glen. *Washday on Noah's ark*
Ryder, Joanne. *A wet and sandy day*
Sasso, Sandy Eisenberg. *A prayer for the earth*
Scheer, Julian. *Rain makes applesauce*
Scheffler, Ursel. *A walk in the rain*
Schlein, Miriam. *The sun, the wind, the sea and the rain*
Schwartz, Roslyn. *The mole sisters and the rainy day*
Seignobosc, Françoise. *The big rain*
Serfozo, Mary. *Rain talk*
Shannon, David. *The rain came down*
Shannon, George. *April showers*
Sherman, Nancy. *Gwendolyn and the weathercock*
Shulevitz, Uri. *Rain rain rivers*
Simmie, Lois. *Mister got to go/No cats allowed*
Simms, Laura. *The bone man*
Simon, Norma. *The wet world*, ill. by Jane Miller
    The wet world, ill. by Alexi Natchev
Singer, Isaac Bashevis. *Why Noah chose the dove*
Skofield, James. *All wet! All wet!*
Smath, Jerry. *Mr. Digby's bad day*
Smith, Elmer Boyd. *The story of Noah's ark*
Smith, Roger. *How the animals saved the ark and put two and two together*
Soya, Kiyoshi. *A house of leaves*
Spetter, Jung-Hee. *Lily and Trooper's winter*
Spier, Peter. *Noah's ark*
    Peter Spier's rain
Stanley, Sanna. *The rains are coming*
Stevenson, James. *Heat wave at Mud Flat*
Stojic, Manya. *Rain*
Sykes, Julie. *Smudge*
Tapio, Pat Decker. *The lady who saw the good side of everything*
Taylor, Mark. *Henry the castaway*
Thayer, Mike. *In the middle of the puddle*
Thorne, Jenny. *Noah's ark*
Tresselt, Alvin R. *Rain drop splash*
Türk, Hanne. *Rainy day Max*
Turnbull, Ann. *Too tired*
Velthuijs, Max. *Little Man finds a home*
Verboven, Agnes. *Ducks like to swim*
Vincent, Gabrielle. *Ernest and Celestine's picnic*
Wagner, Jenny. *Aranea*
Wahl, Jan. *Follow me cried Bee*
Walton, Rick. *Noah's square dance*
Wandelmaier, Roy. *Clouds*
Webb, Clifford. *The story of Noah*
Weeks, Sarah. *Drip, drop*
Wellington, Monica. *Bunny's rainbow day*
Wells, Rosemary. *Don't spill it again, James*
Wiesner, William. *Noah's ark*
Windham, Sophie. *Noah's ark*
Wyler, Rose. *Raindrops and rainbows*
Yashima, Taro. *Umbrella*
Yee, Wong Herbert. *A drop of rain*
Yep, Laurence. *The junior thunder lord*
Yim, Natasha. *Otto's rainy day*
Zinnemann-Hope, Pam. *Find your coat, Ned*
Zolotow, Charlotte (Shapiro). *The quarreling book*
    The storm book

Weather – rainbows

Anglund, Joan Walsh. *Rainbow love*
Asch, Frank. *Skyfire*
Bible. Old Testament. Noah. *Noah and the ark*, ill. by Pauline Baynes
Bolliger, Max. *Noah and the rainbow*
Brent, Isabelle. *Noah's ark*
Chase, Catherine. *Noah's ark*
Cousins, Lucy. *Noah's ark*
Craft, Ruth. *The day of the rainbow*
De Paola, Tomie (Thomas Anthony). *Noah and the ark*
Elborn, Andrew. *Noah and the ark and the animals*
Fischetto, Laura. *Inside Noah's ark*
Freeman, Don. *A rainbow of my own*
Fussenegger, Gertrud. *Noah's ark*
Gauch, Patricia Lee. *Noah*
Geisert, Arthur. *After the flood*
Goodhart, Pippa. *Noah makes a boat*
Haley, Gail E. *Noah's ark*
Haubensak-Tellenbach, Margrit. *The story of Noah's ark*
Haynes, Max. *Sparky's rainbow repair*
Henrioud, Charles. *Mr. Noah and the animals*
Hewitt, Kathryn. *Two by two*
Hines, Anna Grossnickle. *What can you do in the sun?*
Hogrogian, Nonny. *Noah's ark*
Hooper, Patricia. *How the sky's housekeeper wore her scarves*
Hutton, Warwick. *Noah and the great flood*
Ife, Elaine. *Noah and the ark*
Janisch, Heinz. *Noah's ark*
Kirkpatrick, Rena K. *Rainbow colors*
Kunhardt, Edith. *Red day, green day*
Kwitz, Mary DeBall. *When it rains*
Ludwig, Warren. *Old Noah's elephants*
MacBeth, George. *Noah's journey*
McCaughrean, Geraldine. *The story of Noah and the ark*
McKié, Roy. *Noah's ark*
Marino, Dorothy. *Buzzy Bear and the rainbow*
Martin, Charles E. *Noah's ark*
Mee, Charles L. *Noah*
Palazzo, Tony (Anthony D.). *Noah's ark*
Robbins, Ruth. *How the first rainbow was made*
Rupprecht, Siegfried P. *The tale of the vanishing rainbow*
Shannon, David. *The rain came down*
Singer, Isaac Bashevis. *Why Noah chose the dove*
Smith, Elmer Boyd. *The story of Noah's ark*
Thorne, Jenny. *Noah's ark*
Walsh, Melanie. *Ned's rainbow*
Webb, Clifford. *The story of Noah*
Wellington, Monica. *Bunny's rainbow day*
Weston, Martha. *Peony's rainbow*
Williams, Leslie. *A bear in the air*
Wyler, Rose. *Raindrops and rainbows*
Zolotow, Charlotte (Shapiro). *The storm book*

Weather – sandstorms

London, Jonathan. *Ali, child of the desert*

Weather – snow

Alborough, Jez. *Ice cream bear*
Bahr, Robert. *Blizzard at the zoo*

Barklem, Jill. *Winter story*
Bartoli, Jennifer. *Snow on bear's nose*
Bauer, Caroline Feller. *Midnight snowman*
Blades, Ann. *Winter*
Bogacki, Tomasz. *Cat and mouse in the snow*
Bradby, Marie. *The longest wait*
Branley, Franklyn M. (Mansfield). *Snow is falling*
Briggs, Raymond. *The snowman tell-the-time book*
Brown, Margaret Wise. *The winter noisy book*
Bruna, Dick. *Another story to tell*
   Miffy in the snow
Buckley, Helen Elizabeth. *Josie and the snow*
Bundey, Nikki. *In the snow*
Burningham, John. *The snow*
   Trubloff
Burns, Kate. *In the snow*
Burton, Virginia Lee. *Katy and the big snow*
Bushey, Jeanne. *A sled dog for Moshi*
Butterworth, Nick. *One snowy night*
Carlson, Nancy L. *Take time to relax*
Carlstrom, Nancy White. *The snow speaks*
Cech, John. *First snow, magic snow*
Chapman, Cheryl. *Snow on snow on snow*
Chönz, Selina. *The snowstorm*
Claverie, Jean. *Working*
Cocca-Leffler, Maryann. *Ice-cold birthday*
Crews, Nina. *Snowball*
Croll, Carolyn. *The little snowgirl*
Cunningham, David. *A crow's journey*
Curious George in the snow
Cuyler, Margery. *The biggest, best snowman*
Delaney, A. *Monster tracks?*
Delton, Judy. *Brimhall turns detective*
   A walk on a snowy night
Diviny, Sean. *Snow inside the house*
Dorian, Marguerite. *When the snow is blue*
Dowling, Paul. *Jimmy's snowy book*
Duncan, Jane. *Brave Janet Reachfar*
Enderle, Judith (Ann) Ross. *Six snowy sheep*
Fain, Moira. *Snow day*
Figueredo, D. H. *When this world was new*
Ford, Christine. *Snow!*
Frost, Robert. *The runaway*
Funakoshi, Canna. *One evening*
Galbraith, Kathryn Osebold. *Look! Snow!*
Gammell, Stephen. *Is that you, winter?*
Gantschev, Ivan. *The Christmas teddy bear*
George, Jean Craighead. *Snow bear*
Gershator, Phillis. *When it starts to snow*
Gipson, Morrell. *Whose tracks are these?*
Gliori, Debi. *The snow lambs*
   The snowchild
Greene, Carol. *Snow Joe*
Gunther, Louise. *Anna's snow day*
Hader, Berta Hoerner. *The big snow*
Harshman, Marc. *Snow company*
Henderson, Kathy. *Disney's Bambi: the winter trail*
Henkes, Kevin. *Oh!*
Hidaka, Masako. *Girl from the snow country*
Himmelman, John. *The day-off machine*
Hines, Anna Grossnickle. *What can you do in the snow?*
Hissey, Jane. *Jolly snow*
Hoban, Julia. *Amy loves the snow*
Hoban, Lillian. *Silly Tilly's Valentine*
   The sugar snow spring
Hoban, Russell. *Some snow said hello*
Hobbie, Holly. *Toot and Puddle, I'll be home for Christmas*

Hoff, Syd. *When will it snow?*
Honda, Tetsuya. *Wild horse winter*
Hughes, Shirley. *The snow lady*
Hutchins, H. J. (Hazel J.). *Ben's snow song*
   Norman's snowball
Inkpen, Mick. *Kipper's snowy day*
Ives, Penny. *The snow angel*
Iwasaki, Chihiro. *The birthday wish*
Janosch. *Dear snowman*
Johnston, Tony. *The last snow of winter*
Joos, Françoise. *The golden snowflake*
Joosse, Barbara M. *Snow day!*
Joyce, William. *Snowie Rolie*
Keats, Ezra Jack. *The snowy day*
   The snowy day (a board book)
Keller, Holly. *Geraldine's big snow*
Keown, Elizabeth. *Emily's snowball*
Kharms, Daniil. *The story of a boy named Will, who went sledding down the hill*
Kovalski, Maryann. *Jingle bells*
Krauss, Ruth. *The happy day*
Kuskin, Karla. *In the flaky frosty morning*
Lachner, Dorothea. *The gift from Saint Nicholas*
Lakin, Pat (Patricia). *Snow day!*
Landa, Norbert. *Little Bear's Christmas*
Landström, Olof. *Boo and Baa in windy weather*
Leblanc, Anne. *Benjamin in the snow*
Lewis, Kim. *First snow*
Lewison, Wendy Cheyette. *Hello, snow!*
London, Jonathan. *Froggy gets dressed*
Loretan, Sylvia. *Bob the snowman*
Lucas, Barbara (Barbara M.). *Snowed in*
Ludwig, Warren. *Good morning, Granny Rose*
McAllister, Angela. *The snow angel*
McCully, Emily Arnold. *First snow*
   An outlaw Thanksgiving
McCutcheon, Marc. *Grandfather's Christmas camp*
McGuirk, Leslie. *Tucker flips!*
McKee, David. *Elmer in the snow*
McKié, Roy. *Snow*
McPhail, David M. *Snow lion*
Manuel, Lynn. *The night the moon blew kisses*
Martin, Jacqueline Briggs. *Snowflake Bentley*
Marzollo, Jean. *Snow angel*
Mayper, Monica. *Oh snow*
Medearis, Angela Shelf. *Best friends in the snow*
   Here comes the snow
Munsch, Robert N. *Thomas' snowsuit*
Norman, Philip Ross. *A mammoth imagination*
Parillo, Tony. *Michelangelo's surprise*
Parnall, Peter. *Alfalfa Hill*
Peddle, Daniel. *Snow day*
Pfister, Marcus. *Penguin Pete and Little Tim*
Pitcher, Caroline. *The snow whale*
Poydar, Nancy. *Snip, snip . . . snow!*
Pulver, Robin. *Axle Annie*
Raphael, Elaine. *Donkey, it's snowing*
Retan, Walter. *The snowplow that tried to go south*
Rockwell, Anne F. *The first snowfall*
Root, Phyllis. *Grandmother Winter*
Rosen, Michael J. (1954-). *Avalanche*
Sanfield, Steve. *Snow*
Sasaki, Isao. *Snow*
Sauer, Julia Lina. *Mike's house*
Saunders, Dave. *Snowtime*
Schaefer, Carole Lexa. *Snow pumpkin*
Schick, Eleanor. *City in the winter*
Schlein, Miriam. *Deer in the snow*
Schmid, Eleonore. *The water's journey*

Schroeder, Binette. *Tuffa and the snow*
Shulevitz, Uri. *Snow*
Siddals, Mary McKenna. *Millions of snowflakes*
Simmonds, Posy. *Lulu and the flying babies*
Skofield, James. *Snow country*
Spetter, Jung-Hee. *Lily and Trooper's winter*
Steig, William. *Brave Irene*
Tibo, Gilles. *Simon and the snowflakes*
Todd, Kathleen. *Snow*
Tresselt, Alvin R. *White snow, bright snow*
Tudor, Tasha. *Snow before Christmas*
Udry, Janice May. *Mary Jo's grandmother*
Uhlberg, Myron. *Flying over Brooklyn*
Updike, David. *A winter's journey*
Wabbes, Marie. *It's snowing, Little Rabbit*
Wallace, Nancy Elizabeth. *Snow*
Watanabe, Shigeo. *Ice cream is falling!*
Watson, Nancy Dingman. *Sugar on snow*
Weller, Frances Ward. *The angel of Mill Street*
Wellington, Monica. *Bunny's first snowflake*
Wheeler, Cindy. *Marmalade's snowy day*
Whybrow, Ian. *Harry and the snow king*
Yerxa, Leo. *Last leaf first snowflake to fall*
Yolen, Jane. *Snow, snow*
Zion, Gene. *The summer snowman*
Zolotow, Charlotte (Shapiro). *Hold my hand*
    Something is going to happen

Weather – storms

Adoff, Arnold. *Make a circle, keep us in*
    Tornado!
Aldridge, Josephine Haskell. *Fisherman's luck*
Amoss, Berthe. *Old Hannibal and the hurricane*
Anderson, Lena. *Stina*
Anderson, Lonzo. *The day the hurricane happened*
Arvetis, Chris. *Why does it thunder and lightning?*
Bahr, Robert. *Blizzard at the zoo*
Barber, Antonia. *The mousehole cat*
Beard, Darleen Bailey. *Twister*
Bourgeois, Paulette. *Franklin and the thunderstorm*
Bradby, Marie. *The longest wait*
Branley, Franklyn M. (Mansfield). *Hurricane watch*
    Tornado alert
Brown, Ruth. *One stormy night*
Bryan, Ashley. *The story of lightning and thunder*
Buchanan, Ken. *It rained on the desert today*
Burdett, Lois. *The tempest for kids*
Burstein, Fred. *Anna's rain*
Bushey, Jeanne. *A sled dog for Moshi*
Butterworth, Nick. *One blowy night*
Carrick, Carol. *Lost in the storm*
Chesworth, Michael. *Rainy day dream*
Chönz, Selina. *The snowstorm*
Cocca-Leffler, Maryann. *Ice-cold birthday*
Crews, Donald. *Sail away*
Delamare, David. *The Christmas secret*
Delton, Judy. *A walk on a snowy night*
Dennis, Morgan. *The sea dog*
Dodds, Dayle Ann. *Sing, Sophie!*
Duncan, Jane. *Brave Janet Reachfar*
English, Karen. *Big wind coming!*
Faulkner, Matt. *The amazing voyage of Jackie Grace*
Foreman, Michael. *Jack's fantastic voyage*
Gantschev, Ivan. *The Christmas teddy bear*
Gedin, Birgitta. *The little house from the sea*
Gliori, Debi. *The snow lambs*
Graham, Georgia. *The strongest man this side of Cre-
    mona*

Gray, Libba Moore. *Is there room on the feather bed?*
Greenfield, Karen R. *Sister Yessa's story*
Harshman, Marc. *Snow company*
    The storm
Harvey, Brett. *My prairie Christmas*
Henderson, Kathy. *The storm*
Henley, Claire. *Stormy day*
Hershenhorn, Esther. *There goes Lowell's party!*
Hest, Amy. *Ruby's storm*
Hines, Anna Grossnickle. *Rumble thumble boom!*
Hippely, Hilary Horder. *Adventure on Klickitat
    Island*
Hobbie, Holly. *Toot and Puddle, I'll be home for
    Christmas*
    Toot and Puddle, you are my sunshine
Hopkinson, Deborah. *Birdie's lighthouse*
Keats, Ezra Jack. *Clementina's cactus*
Keller, Holly. *Will it rain?*
Kitamura, Satoshi. *Captain Toby*
Kovacs, Deborah. *Moonlight on the river*
Landström, Olof. *Boo and Baa in windy weather*
Leavy, Una. *Harry's stormy night*
Lee, Jeanne M. *Ba-Nam*
Lewis, Paul Owen. *Storm boy*
McBratney, Sam. *Just you and me*
Marino, Dorothy. *Good-bye thunderstorm*
Martin, David. *Little Chicken Chicken*
Miller, William. *A house by the river*
Morley, Carol. *A spider and a pig*
Nikola-Lisa, W. *Storm*
Noble, Trinka Hakes. *Apple tree Christmas*
Olson, Arielle North. *The lighthouse keeper's daughter*
Polacco, Patricia. *Thunder cake*
Quackenbush, Robert M. *Batbaby*
Raglus, Jeff. *Schnorky the wave puncher*
Rand, Gloria. *Aloha, Salty!*
Rettich, Margret. *The voyage of the jolly boat*
Rockwell, Anne F. *The storm*
Rowinski, Kate. *L. L. Bear's island adventure*
Simmie, Lois. *Mister got to go/No cats allowed*
Steig, William. *Brave Irene*
Stolz, Mary Slattery. *Storm in the night*
Stone, Phoebe. *When the Wind Bears go dancing*
Szilagyi, Mary. *Thunderstorm*
Tafuri, Nancy. *Will you be my friend?*
Taylor, Judy. *Sophie and Jack help out*
Trapani, Iza. *Row, row, row your boat*
Vainio, Pirkko. *The dream house*
Van Allsburg, Chris. *The wreck of the Zephyr*
Van Nutt, Julia. *Pumpkins from the sky?*
Wellington, Monica. *Bunny's rainbow day*
    Night rabbits
Wiesner, David. *Hurricane*
Willard, Nancy. *The voyage of the Ludgate Hill*
Willis, Jeanne. *The monster storm*
Wilson, Sarah. *Beware the dragons!*
Wondriska, William. *The stop*
Yolen, Jane. *Before the storm*
Young, Ed (Edward). *The lost horse*

Weather – thunder

Arvetis, Chris. *Why does it thunder and lightning?*
Bourgeois, Paulette. *Franklin and the thunderstorm*
Branley, Franklyn M. (Mansfield). *Flash, crash,
    rumble, and roll*
Bryan, Ashley. *The story of lightning and thunder*
Burke, Katie. *Lightning bug thunder*
Climo, Shirley. *Stolen thunder*

Crowe, Robert L. *Tyler Toad and the thunder*
Henley, Claire. *Stormy day*
Hines, Anna Grossnickle. *Rumble thumble boom!*
Hobbie, Holly. *Toot and Puddle, you are my sunshine*
Marino, Dorothy. *Good-bye thunderstorm*
Martin, David. *Little Chicken Chicken*
Nikola-Lisa, W. *Storm*
Novak, Matt. *Rolling*
Polacco, Patricia. *Thunder cake*
Reiser, Lynn. *Night thunder and the Queen of the Wild Horses*
Sussman, Susan. *Hippo thunder*
Szilagyi, Mary. *Thunderstorm*

Weather – tornadoes

Beard, Darleen Bailey. *Twister*
Lyon, George Ella. *One lucky girl*
Sloat, Teri. *Farmer Brown goes round and round*

Weather – wind

Ardizzone, Edward. *Tim's last voyage*
Barrett, Judi. *The wind thief*
Birchmore, Daniel A. *The white curtain*
Boegehold, Betty. *What the wind told*
Brown, Margaret Wise. *When the wind blew*
Burgess, Thornton. *Old Mother West Wind*
Butterworth, Nick. *One blowy night*
Calhoun, Mary. *Jack and the whoopee wind*
Carlstrom, Nancy White. *How does the wind walk?*
Cartwright, Ann. *The winter hedgehog*
Climo, Shirley. *The match between the winds*
De Posadas Mane, Carmen. *Mister North Wind*
Dorros, Arthur. *Feel the wind*
Ets, Marie Hall. *Gilberto and the wind*
Garrison, Christian. *Little pieces of the west wind*
Greene, Carol. *Please, wind?*
Hamilton, Virginia. *Drylongso*
Henderson, Kathy. *The storm*
Hines, Anna Grossnickle. *What can you do in the wind?*
Hoban, Julia. *Amy loves the wind*
Hutchins, Pat. *The wind blew*
Karas, G. Brian. *The windy day*
Keats, Ezra Jack. *A letter to Amy*
Ketteman, Helen. *The year of no more corn*
La Fontaine, Jean de. *The north wind and the sun*
Lasky, Kathryn. *The Gates of the Wind*
Leemis, Ralph. *Mister Momboo's hat*
Lexau, Joan M. *Who took the farmer's hat?*
Lindbergh, Reeve. *What is the sun?*
Lipson, Michael. *How the wind plays*
Littledale, Freya. *Peter and the north wind*
Lobel, Arnold. *The turnaround wind*
McAllister, Angela. *The wind garden*
MacDonald, Elizabeth. *The very windy day*
McKay, Louise. *Marny's ride with the wind*
McKee, David. *Elmer and the wind*
    Elmer takes off
McPhail, David M. *The day the dog said, "Cock-a-doodle doo!"*
Martin, Bill (William Ivan). *Old devil wind*
Munsch, Robert N. *Millicent and the wind*
Murphy, Shirley Rousseau. *Wind child*
Olaleye, Isaac. *In the Rainfield*
Patron, Susan. *Dark cloud strong breeze*
Purdy, Carol. *Iva Dunnit and the big wind*
Rice, Inez. *The March wind*

Roche, Hannah. *Corey's kite*
Root, Phyllis. *One windy Wednesday*
Saltzberg, Barney. *It must have been the wind*
Schick, Eleanor. *City in the winter*
Schlein, Miriam. *The sun, the wind, the sea and the rain*
Stone, Phoebe. *When the Wind Bears go dancing*
Thompson, Brenda. *The winds that blow*
Tresselt, Alvin R. *Follow the wind*
    The wind and Peter
Ungerer, Tomi. *The hat*
Uttley, Alison. *Sam Pig and the wind*
Vaughan, Marcia Kapok. *The Sea-Breeze Hotel*
White, Linda Arms. *Comes a wind*
Whiteside, Karen. *Lullaby of the wind*
Widman, Christine. *Housekeeper of the wind*
Wilhelm, Hans. *It's too windy!*
Yolen, Jane. *The girl who loved the wind*
Zolotow, Charlotte (Shapiro). *When the wind stops*

Weaving *see* Activities – weaving

Weddings

Ambrus, Victor G. *Country wedding*
Ammon, Richard. *An Amish wedding*
Ash, Jutta. *Wedding birds*
Balian, Lorna. *A sweetheart for Valentine*
Barklem, Jill. *Summer story*
Beck, Martine. *The wedding of Brown Bear and White Bear*
Benjamin, Amanda. *Two's company*
Brown, Marc Tolon. *D. W. thinks big, a board book*
Caseley, Judith. *My sister Celia*
Claret, Maria. *Melissa Mouse*
Cock Robin. *The courtship, merry marriage, and feast of Cock Robin and Jenny Wren*
Coombs, Patricia. *Mouse Café*
Cox, Judy. *Now we can have a wedding!*
De Paola, Tomie (Thomas Anthony). *Helga's dowry*
Drescher, Joan E. *My mother's getting married*
Edwards, Pamela Duncan. *The wacky wedding*
English, Karen. *Nadia's hands*
Euvremer, Teryl. *Triple whammy*
A frog he would a-wooing go (folk-song). *The frog went a-courting*, adapt. and ill. by Dominic Catalano
    Froggie went a courting, ill. by Marjorie Priceman
    Froggie went a-courting, ill. by Chris Conover
    Mr. Frog went a-courting
    Wendy Watson's frog went a-courting
Ganly, Helen. *Jyoti's journey*
Gantos, Jack (John, Jr.). *Wedding bells for Rotten Ralph*
Gibbons, Faye. *Mountain wedding*
Goodall, John S. *Naughty Nancy*
Greene, Ellin. *Ling-li and the phoenix fairy*
Gregory, Valiska. *Babysitting for Benjamin*
Grimm, Jacob. *The goose girl*, ill. by Sabine Bruntjen
    The goose girl, ill. by Robert Sauber
    Mrs. Fox's wedding
    Rumpelstiltskin, ill. by Jacqueline Ayer
    Rumpelstiltskin, ill. by Donna Diamond
    Rumpelstiltskin, ill. by Paul Galdone
    Rumpelstiltskin, ill. by Jonathan Langley
    Rumpelstiltskin, ill. by Gennady Spirin
    Rumpelstiltskin, ill. by John Wallner
    Rumpelstiltskin, ill. by Bernadette Watts
    Rumpelstiltskin, ill. by Paul O. Zelinsky

Snow White and Rose Red, ill. by Adrienne Adams
Snow White and Rose Red, ill. by John Wallner
Snow White and Rose Red, ill. by Bernadette Watts
Gross, Ruth Belov. *The girl who wouldn't get married*
Heine, Helme. *The pigs' wedding*
Hennessy, B. G. (Barbara G.). *Jake baked the cake*
Herman, Gail. *Flower girl*
Hest, Amy. *Fancy Aunt Jess*
    The go-between
Hoban, Lillian. *Mr. Pig and Sonny too*
Hogrogian, Nonny. *Carrot cake*
Hürlimann, Ruth. *The mouse with the daisy hat*
Jaffe, Nina. *The way meat loves salt*
Johnson, Angela. *The wedding*
Johnston, Tony. *The cowboy and the black-eyed pea*
Karlins, Mark. *Music over Manhattan*
Kimmel, Eric A. *The greatest of all*
Kroll, Steven. *The pigrates clean up*
Langton, Jane. *The hedgehog boy*
Lewin, Hugh. *Jafta and the wedding*
Lewison, Wendy Cheyette. *I am a flower girl*
Lillegard, Dee. *The day the daisies danced*
Little, Mimi Otey. *Yoshiko and the foreigner*
Marshall, Janet Perry. *A honey of a day*
Mathers, Petra. *Dodo gets married*
Mayer, Marianna. *Marcel the pastry chef*
Morris, Ann. *Weddings*
Munsch, Robert N. *Ribbon rescue*
Naylor, Phyllis Reynolds. *"I can't take you anywhere!"*
Patterson, José. *Mazal-Tov*
Pilkey, Dav. *The Silly Gooses*
Prose, Francine. *Dybbuk*
Quin-Harkin, Janet. *Peter Penny's dance*
Ross, Lillian Hammer. *The little old man and his dreams*
Rylant, Cynthia. *The bookshop dog*
Samuels, Vyanne. *Carry go bring come*
Sandburg, Carl (Charles August). *The wedding procession of the rag doll and the broom handle and who was in it*
Seguin-Fontes, Marthe. *A wedding book*
Simmonds, Posy. *The chocolate wedding*
Smith, Barry. *Minnie and Ginger*
Soto, Gary. *Snapshots from the wedding*
Speed, Toby. *Hattie baked a wedding cake*
    The squire's bride
Stadler, John. *The cats of Mrs. Calamari*
Suhl, Yuri. *Simon Boom gives a wedding*
Summers, Kate. *Milly's wedding*
Trivas, Irene. *Emma's Christmas*
Van Laan, Nancy. *La boda*
Varga, Judy. *Janko's wish*
West, Colin. *I brought my love a tabby cat*
Williams, Barbara. *Whatever happened to Beverly Bigler's birthday?*
Williams, Garth. *The rabbits' wedding*
Wittman, Sally. *The wonderful Mrs. Trumbly*
Wright, Courtni Crump. *Jumping the broom*
Yep, Laurence. *The Khan's daughter*
Yezerski, Thomas. *Together in Pinecone Patch*
Young, Ed (Edward). *Mouse match*
Young, James. *Everyone loves the moon*
Zalben, Jane Breskin. *Beni's first wedding*

Weekdays *see* Days of the week, months of the year

Weight *see* Concepts – weight

Welders *see* Careers – welders

Werewolves *see* Mythical creatures – werewolves

West *see* U.S. history

West Indies *see* Foreign lands – West Indies

Whalers *see* Careers – whalers

Whales *see* Animals – whales

Wheels

Barton, Byron. *Wheels*
Berenstain, Stan. *Bears on wheels*
Cobb, Annie. *Wheels!*
Cole, Joanna. *Fun on wheels*, ill. by Whitney Darrow
    Fun on wheels, ill. by Don Gauthier
Dubowski, Cathy East. *Cave boy*
Hindley, Judy. *The wheeling and whirling-around book*
Lynn, Sara. *Wheels*
Miller, Margaret. *Wheels go 'round*
Myller, Rolf. *Rolling round*
Nikola-Lisa, W. *Wheels go round*
Olschewski, Alfred. *The wheel rolls over*
Rotner, Shelley. *Wheels around*
Snoopy on wheels

Whistling *see* Activities – whistling

Wildebeests *see* Animals – wildebeests

Willfulness *see* Character traits – willfulness

Wind *see* Weather – wind

Windigos Indians *see* Indians of North America – Windigos

Windmills

Yeoman, John. *Mouse trouble*

Window cleaners *see* Careers – window cleaners

Wings

Myers, Christopher A. *Wings*

Winter *see* Seasons – winter

Wishing *see* Behavior – wishing

Witches

Adams, Adrienne. *A Halloween happening*
    A woggle of witches
Adler, David A. *I know I'm a witch*
Alexander, Sue. *More Witch, Goblin, and Ghost stories*
    Who goes out on Halloween?
    Witch, Goblin and Ghost are back
    Witch, Goblin, and Ghost in the haunted woods
    Witch, Goblin and sometimes Ghost

Andersen, H. C. (Hans Christian). *The tinderbox*, ill. by Warwick Hutton
The tinderbox, ill. by Barry Moser
Anderson, Robin. *Sinabouda Lily*
Anglund, Joan Walsh. *Nibble nibble mousekin*
Armitage, Ronda. *The bossing of Josie*
Arnold, Katya. *Baba Yaga and the little girl*
Aulaire, Ingri Mortenson d'. *East of the sun and west of the moon*
Ayres, Becky Hickox. *Matreshka*
Bach, Othello. *Hector McSnector and the mail-order Christmas witch*
Lilly, Willy and the mail-order witch
Baden, Robert. *And Sunday makes seven*
Balian, Lorna. *Humbug potion*
Humbug witch
Basile, Giambattista. *Petrosinella*
Benarde, Anita. *The pumpkin smasher*
Bender, Robert. *A little witch magic*
Bentley, Nancy. *I've got your nose!*
Berenzy, Alix. *Rapunzel*
Berridge, Celia. *Grandmother's tales*
Berson, Harold. *Charles and Claudine*
Biro, Val. *Miranda's umbrella*
Bridwell, Norman. *The witch grows up*
The witch next door
Brown, Marc Tolon. *Spooky riddles*
Witches four
Bruna, Dick. *Dick Bruna's Snow-White and the seven dwarfs*
Buck, Nola. *The littlest witch*
Buckley, Paul. *Amy Belligera and the fireflies*
Buehner, Caralyn. *A job for Wittilda*
Burch, Robert. *The jolly witch*
Calhoun, Mary. *The witch of Hissing Hill*
The witch who lost her shadow
The witch's pig
Wobble the witch cat
Calmenson, Stephanie. *The little witch sisters*
Campbell, Ann. *Dora's box*
Carlson, Nancy L. *Witch lady*
Carlson, Natalie Savage. *Spooky and the bad luck raven*
Spooky and the witch's goat
Spooky and the wizard's bats
Spooky night
Christelow, Eileen. *Glenda Feathers casts a spell*
Christian, Mary Blount. *Scarabee, the witch's cat*
Civardi, Anne. *The wacky book of witches*
Cole, Babette. *Don't go out tonight*
The trouble with mom
Cole, Joanna. *Bony-legs*
Comissiong, Lynette. *Mind me good now!*
Coombs, Patricia. *Dorrie and the haunted schoolhouse*
Cooney, Barbara. *Little brother and little sister*
Coville, Bruce. *Sarah and the dragon*
Sarah's unicorn
Cretien, Paul D. *Sir Henry and the dragon*
Dasent, George W. *East o' the sun, west o' the moon*
Davis, Maggie S. *Rickety witch*
Degen, Bruce. *The little witch and the riddle*
De Gerez, Toni. *Louhi, witch of North Farm*
DeLage, Ida. *ABC Halloween witch*
Beware! Beware! A witch won't share
The old witch and her magic basket
The old witch and the crows
The old witch and the dragon
The old witch and the ghost parade
The old witch and the snores

The old witch and the wizard
The old witch finds a new house
The old witch gets a surprise
The old witch goes to the ball
The old witch's party
Weeny witch
What does a witch need?
The witchy broom
De Paola, Tomie (Thomas Anthony). *Big Anthony, his story*
Merry Christmas, Strega Nona
Strega Nona
Strega Nona meets her match
Strega Nona takes a vacation
Strega Nona's magic lessons
De Regniers, Beatrice Schenk. *Willy O'Dwyer jumped in the fire*
Devlin, Wende. *Old Black Witch!*
Old Witch and the polka-dot ribbon
Old Witch rescues Halloween
Edmund and the White Witch
Embry, Margaret. *The blue-nosed witch*
Euvremer, Teryl. *Triple whammy*
Flora, James. *Grandpa's ghost stories*
Fox, Mem. *Guess what?*
Francis, Frank. *Natasha's new doll*
Frascino, Edward. *Nanny Noony and the dust queen*
Nanny Noony and the magic spell
Freeman, Don. *Space witch*
Tilly Witch
Gabler, Mirko. *The alphabet soup*
Giannini, Enzo. *Little Parsley*
Ginsburg, Mirra. *Pampalche of the silver teeth*
Glassman, Peter. *My working mom*
Gordon, Lynn. *The witch's revenge*
Gordon, Sharon. *Three little witches*
Greaves, Margaret. *Kate Crackernuts*
Mother Cuspen
The witch cat
The witch's servant
Greene, Carol. *The thirteen days of Halloween*
Greeson, Janet. *The stingy baker*
Grimm, Jacob. *Hansel and Gretel*, ill. by Adrienne Adams
Hansel and Gretel, ill. by Anthony Browne
Hansel and Gretel, ill. by Susan Jeffers
Hansel and Gretel, ill. by Winslow P. Pels
Hansel and Gretel, ill. by Jane Ray
Hansel and Gretel, ill. by Conxita Rodriguez
Hansel and Gretel, ill. by Christopher Santoro
Hansel and Gretel, ill. by John Wallner
Hansel and Gretel, ill. by Paul O. Zelinsky
Hansel and Gretel, ill. by Lisbeth Zwerger
Jorinda and Joringel, ill. by Adrienne Adams
Jorinda and Joringel, ill. by Jutta Ash
Jorinda and Joringel, ill. by Margot Tomes
Rapunzel, ill. by Jutta Ash
Rapunzel, ill. by Sheilah Beckett
Rapunzel, ill. by Bert Dodson
Rapunzel, ill. by Maja Dusíkova
Rapunzel, ill. by Michael Hague
Rapunzel, ill. by Trina Schart Hyman
Rapunzel, ill. by Kris Waldherr
Rapunzel, ill. by Bernadette Watts
Rapunzel, ill. by Paul O. Zelinsky
Snow White, ill. by Trina Schart Hyman
Snow White, ill. by Bernadette Watts
Snow White and the seven dwarves, ill. by Chihiro Iwasaki

Guthrie, Donna. *The witch has an itch*
   The witch who lives down the hall
Hamilton, Morse. *Big sisters are bad witches*
Harrison, David Lee. *Little boy soup*
Haugaard, Erik Christian. *Princess Horrid*
Hautzig, Deborah. *Little Witch goes to school*
   Little Witch's bad dream
Hayes, Geoffrey. *Elroy and the witch's child*
Hearn, Diane Dawson. *Bad luck Boswell*
Heinz, Brian J. *The monsters' test*
Helldorfer, M. C. (Mary Claire). *The mapmaker's daughter*
Himmelman, John. *Amanda and the magic garden*
   Amanda and the witch switch
Hirsh, Marilyn. *The Rabbi and the twenty-nine witches*
Hodges, Margaret. *Up the chimney*
Hooks, William H. *Snowbear Whittington, an Appalachian Beauty and the Beast*
Howe, James. *Scared silly*
Hurd, Edith Thacher. *The so-so cat*
Hutton, Warwick. *The nose tree*
Isele, Elizabeth. *The frog princess*
Jackson, Ellen B. *The wacky witch war*
Jeschke, Susan. *Rima and Zeppo*
Johnson, Paul Brett. *A perfect pork stew*
Johnston, Tony. *Alice Nizzy Nazzy, the Witch of Santa Fe*
   The vanishing pumpkin
   The witch's hat
Karlin, Nurit. *The fat cat sat on the mat*
   The tooth witch
Keith, Eros. *Bedita's bad day*
Kellogg, Steven (Stephen). *The Christmas witch*
Kimmel, Eric A. *Baba Yaga*
   Bearhead
   One Eye, Two Eyes, Three Eyes
   The witch's face
Kroll, Steven. *The candy witch*
Kuskin, Karla. *What did you bring me?*
Lachner, Dorothea. *Meredith, the witch who wasn't*
   Meredith's mixed-up magic
Langstaff, John M. *The two magicians*
Laslett, Stephanie. *The monster party*
Lattimore, Deborah Nourse. *Cinderhazel*
Leedy, Loreen. *2 x 2 = boo!*
Leichman, Seymour. *The wicked wizard and the wicked witch*
Lester, Helen. *Me first*
Levine, Arthur A. *The boardwalk princess*
Lewis, J. Patrick. *The frog princess*
Lexau, Joan M. *The dog food caper*
Little old lady who swallowed a fly. *I know an old lady*, ill. by G. Brian Karas
Lobato, Arcadio. *The greatest treasure*
Lobel, Arnold. *Prince Bertram the bad*
Lodge, Bernard. *Mouldylocks*
   Rhyming Nell
Low, Alice. *The witch who was afraid of witches*
   Witch's holiday
Lucy steps through the wardrobe
McAllister, Angela. *Nesta, the little witch*
McCaughrean, Geraldine. *Grandma Chickenlegs*
MacDonald, George. *The light princess*, ill. by Katie Thamer Treherne
MacLachlan, Patricia. *Moon, stars, frogs and friends*
McLenighan, Valjean. *You can go jump*
McMullan, Kate (Hall). *Creepy riddles*
Mahy, Margaret. *The boy who was followed home*
   The boy with two shadows

Manson, Christopher. *The crab prince*
Manushkin, Fran. *Hocus and Pocus at the circus*
Marshall, James. *Hansel and Gretel*
Massey, Jeanne. *The littlest witch*
Matsutani, Miyoko. *The witch's magic cloth*
Mayer, Marianna. *Baba Yaga and Vasilisa the Brave*
Meddaugh, Susan. *The witches' supermarket*
Mike, Jan M. *The bird maiden*
Minters, Frances. *Sleepless Beauty*
Montresor, Beni. *The witches of Venice*
Moore, Lilian. *See my lovely poison ivy, and other verses about witches, ghosts and things*
Morley, Carol. *Dots and spots*
Nash, Ogden. *The adventures of Isabel*, ill. by Walter Lorraine
   The adventures of Isabel, ill. by James Marshall
Nicoll, Helen. *Meg and Mog*
   Meg at sea
   Meg on the moon
   Meg's eggs
   Mog's box
Nightingale, Sandy. *Cat's knees and bee's whiskers*
   The witch's spell
Nolan, Dennis. *Witch Bazooza*
Novak, Matt. *No zombies allowed*
O'Brien, John (1953-). *Poof!*
Oppenheim, Joanne. *The Christmas witch*
Oram, Hiawyn. *Baba Yaga and the wise doll*
   Skittlewonder and the wizard
Palatini, Margie. *Piggie pie*
   Zoom Broom
Paul, Korky. *Winnie flies again*
   Winnie in winter
Peet, Bill (William Bartlett). *Big bad Bruce*
   The Whingdingdilly
Pitre, Felix. *Paco and the witch*
Prather, Ray. *The ostrich girl*
Prelutsky, Jack. *Monday's troll*
Reeves, Howard W. *There was an old witch*
Rehnman, Mats. *The clay flute*
Robertson, Joanne. *Sea witches*
Rosner, Ruth. *Nattie witch*
Ross, Eileen. *The Halloween showdown*
Ross, Tony. *The enchanted pig*
   Hansel and Gretel
San Souci, Robert D. *Feathertop*
   The red heels
Schubert, Ingrid. *Little big feet*
Scieszka, Jon. *The frog prince, continued*
Serraillier, Ian. *Suppose you met a witch*
Shaw, Richard. *The kitten in the pumpkin patch*
Shecter, Ben. *The big stew*
   Emily, girl witch of New York
Shute, Linda. *Halloween party*
Silverman, Erica. *The Halloween house*
Simmons, Steven J. *Alice and Greta*
   Alice and Greta's color magic
   Greta's revenge
Slate, Joseph. *The mean, clean, giant canoe machine*
Smith, Maggie (Margaret C.). *There's a witch under the stairs*
Springstubb, Tricia. *The magic guinea pig*
Steig, William. *Caleb and Kate*
   Wizzil
Stevenson, James. *Emma*
   Fried feathers for Thanksgiving
   Happy Valentine's Day, Emma!
   Yuck!
Thompson, Harwood. *The witch's cat*

Tunnell, Michael O. *Halloween pie*
Utton, Peter. *The witch's hand*
Van Allsburg, Chris. *The widow's broom*
Wahl, Jan. *Little Johnny Buttermilk*
Walker, Barbara K. (Barbara Kerlin). *Teeny-Tiny and the witch-woman*
Walt Disney Productions. *Walt Disney's Snow White and the seven dwarfs*
Watson, Jane Werner. *Which is the witch?*
Weil, Lisl. *The candy egg bunny*
Whitcher, Susan. *The key to the cupboard*
White, Carolyn. *Whuppity Stoorie*
Williams, Jay. *The city witch and the country witch*
Winthrop, Elizabeth. *Vasilissa the beautiful*
Witch poems
Wolff, Ferida. *On Halloween night*
Wood, Audrey. *Heckedy Peg*
Yolen, Jane. *The girl in the golden bower*
Ziefert, Harriet. *Two little witches*
Zimmer, Dirk. *The trick-or-treat trap*

Wizards

Barber, Antonia. *The enchanter's daughter*
Bazilian, Barbara. *Princess Lily*
Bradfield, Roger (Jolly Roger). *Giants come in different sizes*
Brenner, Barbara A. *The color wizard*
Carlson, Natalie Savage. *Spooky and the wizard's bats*
Conover, Chris. *The wizard's daughter*
DeLage, Ida. *The old witch and the wizard*
De Regniers, Beatrice Schenk. *Picture book theater*
Dewan, Ted. *The sorcerer's apprentice*
Dines, Glen. *Pitadoe, the color maker*
Fleischman, Sid. *Longbeard the wizard*
Glassman, Peter. *The wizard next door*
Grimm, Jacob. *The donkey prince*
Haseley, Dennis. *The cave of snores*
Kherdian, David. *The golden bracelet*
Kimmel, Margaret Mary. *Magic in the mist*
Leichman, Seymour. *The wicked wizard and the wicked witch*
Lester, Helen. *The wizard, the fairy and the magic chicken*
Lobel, Arnold. *The great blueness and other predicaments*
McCrea, James. *The story of Olaf*
Madden, Don. *The Wartville wizard*
Martin, Bill (William Ivan). *The wizard*
Mayer, Mercer. *Mrs. Beggs and the wizard*
Nolan, Dennis. *Wizard McBean and his flying machine*
O'Brien, John (1953-). *Poof!*
Oksner, Robert M. *The incompetent wizard*
Oram, Hiawyn. *Skittlewonder and the wizard*
Saunders, Susan. *A sniff in time*
Scott, Sally. *The magic horse*
Service, Pamela F. *The wizard of wind and rock*
Smith, Janice Lee. *Wizard and Wart in trouble*
Snyder, Zilpha Keatley. *The changing maze*
Walsh, Ellen Stoll. *Mouse magic*
Whitcher, Susan. *The key to the cupboard*
Zijlstra, Tjerk. *Benny and his geese*
Zimmermann, H. Werner (Heinz Werner).
   Alphonse knows . . . a circle is not a Valentine
   Alphonse knows . . . the colour of spring
   Alphonse knows . . . twelve months make a year
   Alphonse knows . . . zero is not enough

Wolves *see* Animals – wolves

Wombats *see* Animals – wombats

Woodcarvers *see* Careers – woodcarvers

Woodchucks *see* Animals – groundhogs

Wood-hoopoe *see* Birds – wood-hoopoe

Woodpeckers *see* Birds – woodpeckers

Woods *see* Forest, woods

Word games *see* Language

Wordless

Alexander, Martha G. *Bobo's dream*
   Out! Out! Out!
   3 magic flip books
Aliki. *Tabby*
Andersen, H. C. (Hans Christian). *The ugly duckling*, ill. by Maria Ruis
Anderson, Lena. *Bunny bath*
   Bunny box
   Bunny fun
   Bunny party
   Bunny story
   Bunny surprise
Anno, Mitsumasa. *Anno's animals*
   Anno's Britain
   Anno's counting book
   Anno's counting house
   Anno's flea market
   Anno's Italy
   Anno's journey
   Anno's peekaboo
   Anno's U.S.A.
   Dr. Anno's magical midnight circus
   Topsy turvies
   Topsy turvies
Arnosky, Jim. *Mouse numbers and letters*
   Mouse writing
   Mud time and more
Asch, Frank. *In the eye of the teddy*
Asch, George. *Linda*
Baker, Jeannie. *Window*
Bakken, Harold. *The special string*
   Bambi
Banchek, Linda. *Snake in, snake out*
Bang, Molly. *The grey lady and the strawberry snatcher*
Barton, Byron. *Where's Al?*
Baum, Willi. *Birds of a feather*
Blades, Ann. *Fall*
   Spring
   Summer
   Winter
Blake, Quentin. *Clown*
Bonners, Susan. *Just in passing*
Briggs, Raymond. *Building the snowman*
   Dressing up
   Father Christmas
   Father Christmas goes on holiday
   The party
   The snowman
   Walking in the air

Brown, Craig McFarland. *Patchwork farmer*
Bruna, Dick. *Another story to tell*
   A story to tell
Bullock, Kathleen. *Rabbits are coming*
Bunting, Eve (Anne Evelyn). *We need a bigger zoo!*
Burlson, Joe. *Space colony*
Burton, Marilee Robin. *The elephant's nest*
Butterworth, Nick. *Amanda's butterfly*
Campbell, Rod. *Look inside! All kinds of places*
   Look inside! Land, sea, air
Carle, Eric. *Do you want to be my friend?*
   I see a song
Carroll, Ruth. *What Whiskers did*
   Where's the bunny?
Charlot, Martin. *Sunnyside up*
Chesworth, Michael. *Rainy day dream*
Chwast, Seymour. *Alphabet parade*
   Still another alphabet book
City, ill. by Roser Capdevila
Collington, Peter. *The angel and the soldier boy*
   Little pickle
   The midnight circus
   On Christmas eve
   A small miracle
   The tooth fairy
Cousins, Lucy. *Flower in the garden*
   Hen on the farm
   Kite in the park
   Teddy in the house
Crews, Donald. *Truck*
Cristini, Ermanno. *In my garden*
   In the woods
Daughtry, Duanne. *What's inside?*
Day, Alexandra. *Carl goes shopping*
   Carl pops up
   Carl's afternoon in the park
   Carl's Christmas
   Carl's masquerade
   Follow Carl!
   Good dog, Carl
Degen, Bruce. *Aunt Possum and the pumpkin man*
De Groat, Diane. *Alligator's toothache*
Demarest, Chris L. *Orville's odyssey*
Demi. *Follow the line*
De Paola, Tomie (Thomas Anthony). *Country farm*
   Flicks
   The hunter and the animals
   Pancakes for breakfast
   Sing, Pierrot, sing
Domestic animals
Dornbusch, Erica. *Finding Kate's shoes*
Drescher, Henrik. *The yellow umbrella*
Dubois, Claude K. *He's my jumbo!*
   Looking for Ginny
DuPasquier, Philippe. *The great escape*
   I can't sleep
   Our house on the hill
Emberley, Ed (Edward Randolph). *Ed Emberley's*
   big green drawing book
Euvremer, Teryl. *Sun's up*
Feldman, Barbara. *Stephen's frog*
Feldman, Judy. *The alphabet in nature*
   Shapes in nature
Félix, Monique. *The further adventures of the little*
   mouse trapped in a book
   The story of a little mouse trapped in a book
Florian, Douglas. *The city*
Freeman, Don. *Forever laughter*
Fromm, Lilo. *Muffel and Plums*

Fuchs, Erich. *Journey to the moon*
Fujikawa, Gyo. *Millie's secret*
   My favorite thing
Gill, Madelaine. *The spring hat*
Goffin, Josse. *Oh!*
   Silent Christmas
Goodall, John S. *The adventures of Paddy Pork*
   The ballooning adventures of Paddy Pork
   Creepy castle
   An Edwardian Christmas
   An Edwardian summer
   Jacko
   The midnight adventures of Kelly, Dot and Esmeralda
   Naughty Nancy
   Naughty Nancy goes to school
   Paddy goes traveling
   Paddy Pork
   Paddy Pork's holiday
   Paddy to the rescue
   Paddy under water
   Paddy's evening out
   Paddy's new hat
   Shrewbettina's birthday
   The story of a castle
   The story of a farm
   The story of a main street
   The story of an English village
   The surprise picnic
Gorey, Edward (St. John). *The tunnel calamity*
Greeley, Valerie. *Farm animals*
   Field animals
   Pets
   Zoo animals
Grimm, Jacob. *Hansel and Gretel*, ill. by Conxita
   Rodriguez
   Little Red Riding Hood, ill. by John S. Goodall
   Sleeping Beauty, ill. by Fina Rifa
Hamberger, John. *The lazy dog*
Hartelius, Margaret A. *The chicken's child*
Hauptmann, Tatjana. *A day in the life of Petronella*
   Pig
Heller, Linda. *Lily at the table*
Herriot, James. *Christmas Day kitten*
Hill, Eric. *At home*
   The park
   Up there
Hoban, Tana. *Big ones, little ones*
   Black on white
   Circles, triangles, and squares
   Colors everywhere
   Dig, drill, dump, fill
   Exactly the opposite
   Is it larger? Is it smaller?
   Is it red? Is it yellow? Is it blue?
   Is it rough? Is it smooth? Is it shiny?
   Just look
   Look again
   Look book
   Look! Look! Look!
   More, fewer, less
   1, 2, 3
   Shadows and reflections
   Shapes and things
   Shapes, shapes, shapes
   So many circles, so many squares
   Spirals, curves, fanshapes and lines
   Take another look
   What is it?
   What is that?

Raking leaves with Max
The rope skips Max
Snapshot Max
A surprise for Max
Turkle, Brinton. *Deep in the forest*
Ueno, Noriko. *Elephant buttons*
Ungerer, Tomi. *One, two, where's my shoe?*
　　Snail, where are you?
Vincent, Gabrielle. *Breakfast time, Ernest and Celestine*
　　Ernest and Celestine's patchwork quilt
A visit to a pond
Ward, Lynd. *The silver pony*
Wegen, Ron. *The balloon trip*
Weitzman, Jacqueline Preiss. *You can't take a balloon into the Metropolitan Museum*
　　You can't take a balloon into the National Gallery
Wezel, Peter. *The good bird*
　　The naughty bird
Wiesner, David. *Free fall*
　　Sector 7
Wilson, April. *April Wilson's magpie magic*
Winter, Paula. *The bear and the fly*
　　Sir Andrew
Wood, A. J. *Look! The ultimate spot-the-difference book*
Wouters, Anne. *This book is for us*
　　This book is too small
Young animals in the zoo
Young domestic animals
Young, Ed (Edward). *Up a tree*
Zager, Karen. *Bubbles*
Zoo animals, (Imported Pubs., 1983)

Words *see* Language

Working *see* Activities – working; Careers

World

Anno, Mitsumasa. *All in a day*
Bendick, Jeanne. *All around you*
Branley, Franklyn M. (Mansfield). *The planets in our solar system*
Brann, Esther. *'Round the world*
Brown, Margaret Wise. *Four fur feet*
Delessert, Etienne. *How the mouse was hit on the head by a stone and so discovered the world*
Derby, Sally. *The mouse who owned the sun*
Domanska, Janina. *What do you see?*
Douglas, Michael. *Round, round world*
Ekker, Ernest A. *What is beyond the hill?*
Gikow, Louise. *For every child, a better world*
Goffstein, M. B. (Marilyn Brooke). *School of names*
Johnson, Crockett. *Upside down*
Lakin, Pat (Patricia). *Family*
　　Grandparents
Nesbit, Edith. *The ice dragon*
Peet, Bill (William Bartlett). *Chester the worldly pig*
Quin-Harkin, Janet. *Peter Penny's dance*
Schlein, Miriam. *Herman McGregor's world*
Schneider, Herman. *Follow the sunset*
Schuett, Stacey. *Somewhere in the world right now*
Snow, Alan. *My first atlas*
Spier, Peter. *People*
Weiss, Nicki. *The world turns round and round*
Wood, Douglas. *Making the world*

Worms *see* Animals – worms

Worrying *see* Behavior – worrying

Wrecking machines *see* Machines

Wrens *see* Birds – wrens

Wrestling *see* Sports – wrestling

Writers *see* Careers – writers

Writing *see* Activities – writing

Writing letters *see* Letters, cards

Yaks *see* Animals – yaks

Yana Indians *see* Indians of North America – Yana

Yanomamo Indians *see* Indians of South America – Yanomamo

Yom Kippur *see* Holidays – Yom Kippur

Yupik *see* Indians of North America – Yupik

Zaire *see* Foreign lands – Zaire

Zanzibar *see* Foreign lands – Zanzibar

Zapotec Indians *see* Indians of North America – Zapotec

Zebras *see* Animals – zebras

Zodiac

Demi. *The dragon's tale and other animal fables of the Chinese zodiac*
Fisher, Leonard Everett. *Star signs*
Kimmel, Eric A. *The rooster's antlers*
Van Woerkom, Dorothy. *The rat, the ox and the zodiac*
Yen, Clara. *Why rat comes first*
Young, Ed (Edward). *Cat and Rat*

Zookeepers *see* Careers – zoo keepers

Zoos

Ahlberg, Allan. *Monkey do!*
Aitken, Amy. *Kate and Mona in the jungle*
Aliki. *My visit to the zoo*
Allamand, Pascale. *The camel who left the zoo*
Allen, Robert. *The zoo book*
Amery, H. *At the zoo*
  The zoo picture book
Ancona, George. *Handtalk zoo*
Argent, Kerry. *Animal capers*
Arnold, Caroline. *Mealtime for zoo animals*
  Mother and baby zoo animals
  Noisytime for zoo animals
  Playtime for zoo animals
  Sleepytime for zoo animals
  Splashtime for zoo animals
Arthur, Catherine. *My sister's silent world*
Ashabranner, Brent. *I'm in the zoo, too*
Bahr, Robert. *Blizzard at the zoo*
Barry, Robert E. *Next please*
Barton, Byron. *Zoo animals*
Baskin, Leonard. *Hosie's zoo*
Bauer, Helen. *Good times at the park*
Belloc, Hilaire. *Jim, who ran away from his nurse, and was eaten by a lion*
Biro, Val. *Gumdrop at the zoo*
Bishop, Bonnie. *Ralph rides away*
Blance, Ellen. *Monster goes to the zoo*
Blue, Rose. *Black, black, beautiful black*
Blumberg, Rhoda. *Jumbo*
Bodsworth, Nan. *Monkey business*
Bolliger, Max. *Sandy at the children's zoo*
Bond, Michael. *Paddington at the zoo*
Boswell, Stephen. *King Gorboduc's fabulous zoo*
Bottner, Barbara. *Zoo song*
Brennan, John. *Zoo day*
Bridges, William. *Lion Island*
Bright, Robert. *Me and the bears*
Brown, Margaret Wise. *The big fur secret*
  Don't frighten the lion
Browne, Anthony. *Zoo*
Bruna, Dick. *Miffy at the zoo*
Buehner, Caralyn. *The escape of Marvin the ape*
Bunting, Eve (Anne Evelyn). *We need a bigger zoo!*
Calmenson, Stephanie. *Where will the animals stay?*
Campbell, Rod. *Dear zoo*
Canning, Kate. *A painted tale*
Carle, Eric. *1, 2, 3 to the zoo*
Carlstrom, Nancy White. *What would you do if you lived at the zoo?*
Carrick, Carol. *Patrick's dinosaurs*
Chalmers, Audrey. *Hundreds and hundreds of pancakes*
Charles, Donald. *Calico Cat at the zoo*
Chichester Clark, Emma. *The story of Horrible Hilda and Henry*
Cohen, Caron Lee. *Pigeon, pigeon*
Colonius, Lillian. *At the zoo*
Curious George visits the zoo
Cutler, Ivor. *The animal house*
Cuyler, Margery. *That's good! that's bad!*
DeLage, Ida. *ABC triplets at the zoo*
Denim, Sue. *The Dumb Bunnies go to the zoo*
Drescher, Henrik. *The yellow umbrella*
Evans, Nate. *The mixed-up zoo of professor Yahoo*
Fatio, Louise. *The happy lion*
  The happy lion and the bear
  The happy lion in Africa

The happy lion roars
The happy lion's rabbits
The happy lion's treasure
Hector and Christina
The three happy lions
Fay, Hermann. *My zoo*
Flora, James. *Leopold, the see-through crumbpicker*
Florian, Douglas. *At the zoo*
Ford, Miela. *Watch us play*
Fox, Mem. *Zoo-looking*
Gibbons, Gail. *Zoo*
Gordon, Shirley. *Grandma zoo*
Graham, Margaret Bloy. *Be nice to spiders*
Greeley, Valerie. *Zoo animals*
Greydanus, Rose. *Animals at the zoo*
Groening, Maggie. *Maggie Simpson's book of animals*
Grossman, Bill. *The bear whose bones were Jezebel Jones*
Grosvenor, Donna. *Zoo babies*
Hader, Berta Hoerner. *Lost in the zoo*
Hanlon, Emily. *What if a lion eats me and I fall into a hippopotamus' mud hole?*
Hanna, Jack. *The petting zoo*
Harrison, David Lee. *Detective Bob and the great ape escape*
Hathon, Elizabeth. *We go to the zoo*
Hazelaar, Cor. *Zoo dreams*
Hellen, Nancy. *Circle zoo*
  A visit to the zoo
Hendrick, Mary Jean. *If anything ever goes wrong at the zoo*
Henley, Claire. *At the zoo*
Hewett, Joan. *Tiger, tiger, growing up*
Hoban, Tana. *A children's zoo*
Hoff, Syd. *Sammy the seal*
Hopkins, Lee Bennett. *To the zoo*
Howe, James. *The day the teacher went bananas*
Irvine, Georgeanne. *Bo the orangutan*
  Elmer the elephant
  Georgie the giraffe
  Lindi the leopard
  The nursery babies
  Sasha the cheetah
  Sydney the koala
  Tully the tree kangaroo
Isenberg, Barbara. *The adventures of Albert, the running bear*
Jeram, Anita. *Bill's belly button*
Johnson, Louise. *Malunda*
Kilroy, Sally. *Babies' zoo*
Kishida, Eriko. *The hippo boat*
Knight, Bertram T. *Working at a zoo*
Knight, Hilary. *Where's Wallace?*
Knowles, Sheena. *Edward the emu*
Lewis, Stephen. *Zoo city*
Lilly, Kenneth. *Animals at the zoo*
Lippman, Peter. *New at the zoo*
Lisker, Sonia O. *Lost*
Lobel, Arnold. *A holiday for Mister Muster*
  A zoo for Mister Muster
Löfgren, Ulf. *Alvin the zookeeper*
London, Jonathan. *A koala for Katie*
Lööf, Jan. *Uncle Louie's fantastic sea voyage*
Maccarone, Grace. *The class trip*
McCarthy, Ruth. *Katie and the smallest bear*
McGovern, Ann. *Zoo, where are you?*
Machotka, Hana. *What do you do at a petting zoo?*
McKean, Thomas. *Hooray for Grandma Jo!*
McQuade, Jacqueline. *At the petting zoo with Teddy Bear*

Marshall, Janet Perry. *My camera*
Martin, Bill (William Ivan). *Polar bear, polar bear, what do you hear?*
Matthias, Catherine. *Too many balloons*
Mead, Alice. *Billy and Emma*
Meeks, Esther K. *Something new at the zoo*
Miklowitz, Gloria D. *The zoo that moved*
Morozumi, Atsuko. *My friend gorilla*
Moses, Amy. *At the zoo*
Munari, Bruno. *Bruno Munari's zoo*
Munsch, Robert N. *Alligator baby*
Noble, Kate. *The blue elephant*
Ormerod, Jan. *When we went to the zoo*
Oxenbury, Helen. *Monkey see, monkey do*
Panek, Dennis. *Catastrophe Cat at the zoo*
Parker, Nancy Winslow. *Working frog*
Paxton, Tom. *Going to the zoo*
Pienkowski, Jan. *Zoo*
Policoff, Stephen Phillip. *Cesar's amazing journey*
Propp, James. *Tuscanini*
Rathmann, Peggy. *Good night, Gorilla*
Ray, Deborah Kogan. *Sunday morning we went to the zoo*
Reitveld, Jane Klatt. *Monkey island*
Rey, H. A. (Hans Augusto). *Curious George takes a job*
  Feed the animals

Rice, Eve. *Sam who never forgets*
Riddle, Tohby. *The great escape from City Zoo*
Roffey, Maureen. *I spy at the zoo*
Rojankovsky, Feodor. *Animals in the zoo*
Roosevelt, Michelle Chopin. *Zoo animals*
Ross, Christine. *Lily and the bears*
Rowan, James P. *I can be a zoo keeper*
San Diego Zoological Society. *Families*
  A visit to the zoo
Schneider, Antonie. *Luke the Lionhearted*
Schumacher, Claire. *King of the zoo*
Seuss, Dr. *If I ran the zoo*
Simon, Paul. *At the zoo*
Snyder, Dick. *One day at the zoo*
  Talk to me tiger
Tensen, Ruth M. *Come to the zoo!*
Tester, Sylvia Root. *A visit to the zoo*
Unwin, Pippa. *The great zoo hunt!*
Waber, Bernard. *A lion named Shirley Williamson*
Woodruff, Elvira. *Mrs. McCloskey's monkeys*
Ylla. *Look who's talking*
Young, Miriam Burt. *Please don't feed Horace*
Ziefert, Harriet. *On our way to the zoo*

Zuni Indians *see* Indians of North America – Zuni

Bibliographic Guide

Arranged alphabetically by author's name in boldface (or by title, if author is unknown), each entry includes title, illustrator, publisher, publication date, and subjects. Joint authors and their titles appear as short entries, with the main author name (in parentheses after the title) citing where the complete entry will be found. Where only an author and title are given, complete information is listed under the title as the main entry. ISBNs are included for titles that have been added since the second edition.

A is for alphabet by Cathy, Marly and Wendy; ill. by George Suyeoka. Scott, 1968. Subj: ABC books.

Aardema, Verna. *Anansi does the impossible! an Ashanti tale* ill. by Lisa Desimini. Atheneum, 1997. ISBN 0-689-81092-X Subj: Folk and fairy tales. Foreign lands – Africa. Spiders.

Anansi finds a fool: an Ashanti tale ill. by Bryna Waldman. Dial, 1992. ISBN 0-8037-1165-4 Subj: Behavior – trickery. Folk and fairy tales. Mythical creatures. Spiders.

Bimwili and the Zimwi ill. by Susan Meddaugh. Dial, 1985. ISBN 0-8037-0213-2 Subj: Folk and fairy tales. Foreign lands – Africa. Foreign lands – Zanzibar. Mythical creatures – trolls.

Borreguita and the coyote ill. by Petra Mathers. Knopf, 1991. ISBN 0-679-90921-4 Subj: Animals – coyotes. Animals – sheep. Behavior – trickery. Folk and fairy tales. Foreign lands – Mexico.

Bringing the rain to Kapiti Plain: a Nandi tale ill. by Beatriz A. Vidal. Dial, 1981. ISBN 0-8037-0807-6 Subj: Cumulative tales. Folk and fairy tales. Foreign lands – Africa. Rhyming text. Weather – droughts. Weather – rain.

Half-a-ball-of-kenki: an Ashanti tale retold by Verna Aardema; ill. by Diane Stanley Zuromskis. Warne, 1979. ISBN 0-7232-6158-X Subj: Animals – leopards. Folk and fairy tales. Foreign lands – Africa. Insects – flies.

Jackal's flying lesson: a Khoikhoi tale ill. by Dale Gottlieb. Knopf, 1995. ISBN 0-679-95813-4 Subj: Activities – flying. Animals – jackals. Behavior – trickery. Birds. Folk and fairy tales. Foreign lands – Africa. Foreign lands – Namibia.

Ji-nongo-nongo means riddles ill. by Jerry Pinkney. Four Winds, 1978. ISBN 0-590-07474-1 Subj: Folk and fairy tales. Foreign lands – Africa. Riddles.

Koi and the kola nuts: a tale from Liberia ill. by Joe Cepeda. Atheneum, 1999. ISBN 0-689-81760-6 Subj: Character traits – kindness to animals. Folk and fairy tales. Foreign lands – Liberia.

The lonely lioness and the ostrich chicks: a Masai tale ill. by Yumi Heo. Owen, 1992. ISBN 0-679-96934-9 Subj: Animals – lions. Animals – mongooses. Behavior – needing someone. Birds – ostriches. Emotions – loneliness. Folk and fairy tales. Foreign lands – Africa.

Misoso ill. by Reynold Ruffins. Knopf, 1994. ISBN 0-679-93430-8 Subj: Folk and fairy tales. Foreign lands – Africa.

Oh, Kojo! How could you! an Ashanti tale ill. by Marc Brown. Dial, 1984. ISBN 0-8037-0007-5 Subj: Folk and fairy tales. Foreign lands – Africa. Humor.

Pedro and the padre ill. by Friso Henstra. Dial, 1991. ISBN 0-8037-0523-9 Subj: Character traits – honesty. Folk and fairy tales. Foreign lands – Mexico.

Princess Gorilla and a new kind of water ill. by Victoria Chess. Dial, 1988. ISBN 0-8037-0413-5 Subj: Animals. Animals – gorillas. Folk and fairy tales. Foreign lands – Africa.

Rabbit makes a monkey of lion ill. by Jerry Pinkney. Dial, 1988. ISBN 0-8037-0298-1 Subj: Animals. Behavior – trickery. Foreign lands – Africa. Jungle.

The riddle of the drum: a tale from Tizapan, Mexico ill. by Tony Chen. Four Winds, 1978. ISBN 0-590-07489-X Subj: Cumulative tales. Folk and fairy tales. Foreign lands – Mexico. Rhyming text. Royalty.

Sebgugugu the glutton: a Bantu tale from Rwanda ill. by Nancy L. Clouse. Eerdmans, 1993. ISBN 0-8028-5073-1 Subj: Behavior – greed. Character traits – foolishness. Folk and fairy tales. Foreign lands – Africa. Foreign lands – Rwanda.

Traveling to Tondo: a tale of the Nkundo of Zaire ill. by Will Hillenbrand. Knopf, 1991. ISBN 0-679-90081-0 Subj: Activities – traveling. Animals. Folk and fairy tales. Foreign lands – Congo (Democratic Republic). Foreign lands – Zaire.

The vingananee and the tree toad: a Liberian tale ill. by Ellen Weiss. Warne, 1983. ISBN 0-7232-6217-9 Subj: Animals. Folk and fairy tales. Foreign lands – Africa. Foreign lands – Liberia. Spiders.

What's so funny, Ketu? a Nuer tale ill. by Marc Brown. Dial, 1982. ISBN 0-8037-9370-7 Subj: Animals. Behavior – secrets. Foreign lands – Africa. Foreign lands – Sudan. Humor. Reptiles – snakes.

Who's in Rabbit's house? ill. by Leo and Diane Dillon. Dial, 1977. ISBN 0-8037-9551-3 Subj: Animals. Folk and fairy tales. Foreign lands – Africa. Humor. Insects – butterflies, caterpillars.

Why mosquitoes buzz in people's ears: a West African tale ill. by Leo and Diane Dillon. Dial, 1975. ISBN 0-8037-6087-6 Subj: Animals. Caldecott award books. Folk and fairy tales. Foreign lands – Africa. Insects – mosquitoes.

Aarle, Thomas Van. *Don't put your cart before the horse race* ill. by Bob Barner. Houghton Mifflin, 1980. ISBN 0-395-29095-3 Subj: Animals – horses, ponies. Sports – racing.

Aaron, Jane. *When I'm afraid* ill. by author. St. Martin's, 1998. ISBN 0-307-44057-5 Subj: Emotions – fear. Family life.

Abbot, Sara. *see* Zolotow, Charlotte (Shapiro)

ABCDEFGHIJKLMNOPQRSTUVWXYZ in English and Spanish ill. by Robert Tallon. Lion, 1981. ISBN 0-874-60359-5 Subj: ABC books. Foreign languages.

Abel, Laurie. *Bisnipian blast-off: an action counting book* (Arnold, Tedd)

Abel, Ray. *The new sitter* (Abel, Ruth)

Abel, Ruth. *The new sitter* by Ruth and Ray Abel; ill. by Ray Abel. Oxford Univ. Pr., 1950. Subj: Activities – babysitting.

Abercrombie, Barbara. *Charlie Anderson* ill. by Mark Graham. Macmillan, 1990. ISBN 0-689-50486-1 Subj: Animals – cats. Family life. Pets.

Michael and the cats ill. by Mark Graham. Margaret K. McElderry, 1993. ISBN 0-689-50543-4 Subj: Animals – cats. Family life – aunts, uncles.

Abisch, Roslyn Kroop. *see* Abisch, Roz

Abisch, Roz. *The clever turtle* ill. by Boche Kaplan. Prentice-Hall, 1969. Subj: Animals. Folk and fairy tales. Foreign lands – Africa. Reptiles – turtles, tortoises.

Let's find out about butterflies ill. by Boche Kaplan. Watts, 1972. ISBN 0-531-00077-X Subj: Insects – butterflies, caterpillars. Metamorphosis. Science.

Mai-Ling and the mirror: a Chinese folktale ill. by Boche Kaplan. Prentice-Hall, 1969. Subj: Emo-

tions – envy, jealousy. Folk and fairy tales. Foreign lands – China.

Open your eyes ill. by Boche Kaplan. Parents, 1964. Subj: Concepts – color. Imagination.

The Pumpkin Heads ill. by Boche Kaplan. Prentice-Hall, 1968. Based on an anecdote from general history of Connecticut, by Reverend Samuel Peters. Subj: Hair. U.S. history.

Sweet Betsy from Pike by Roz Abisch and Boche Kaplan; ill. by Boche Kaplan. McCall, 1970. ISBN 0-8415-2006-2 Subj: Character traits – perseverance. Folk and fairy tales. Music. Songs. U.S. history – frontier and pioneer life.

'Twas in the moon of wintertime: the first American Christmas carol adapt. by Roz Abisch; ill. by Boche Kaplan. Prentice-Hall, 1969. ISBN 0-1393-3358-4 Subj: Holidays – Christmas. Indians of North America – Huron. Music.

Abolafia, Yossi. *A fish for Mrs. Gardenia* ill. by author. Greenwillow, 1988. ISBN 0-688-07468-5 Subj: Activities – cooking. Behavior – losing things.

Fox tale ill. by author. Greenwillow, 1991. ISBN 0-688-09542-9 Subj: Animals. Animals – foxes. Behavior – trickery.

My three uncles ill. by author. Greenwillow, 1984. ISBN 0-688-04025-X Subj: Character traits – individuality. Family life – aunts, uncles. Multiple births – triplets.

Yanosh's Island ill. by author. Greenwillow, 1987. ISBN 0-688-06817-0 Subj: Activities – flying. Behavior – seeking better things. Islands. Toys.

Abrons, Mary. *For Alice a palace* ill. by Gertrude Barrer-Russell. W. R. Scott, 1966. Subj: ABC books. Birthdays. Poetry. Royalty.

Absolutely angels: *poems for children and other believers* sel. by Mary Lou Carney; ill. by Viqui Maggio. Wordsong, 1998. ISBN 1-56397-708-7 Subj: Angels. Poetry.

Accorsi, William. *My name is Pocahontas* ill. by author. Holiday, 1992. ISBN 0-8234-0932-5 Subj: Indians of North America – Powhatan. U.S. history.

Rachel Carson ill. by author. Holiday, 1993. ISBN 0-8234-0994-5 Subj: Careers – scientists. Ecology.

Short short short stories ill. by author. Greenwillow, 1991. ISBN 0-688-10181-X Subj: Activities. Humor.

Ackerman, Diane. *Monk seal hideaway* photos by Bill Curtsinger. Crown, 1995. ISBN 0-517-59674-1 Subj: Animals – endangered animals. Animals – seals. Islands.

Ackerman, Karen. *Araminta's paint box* ill. by Betsy Lewin. Macmillan, 1990. ISBN 0-689-31462-0 Subj: Behavior – losing things. U.S. history – frontier and pioneer life.

The banshee ill. by David Ray. Putnam, 1990. ISBN 0-399-21924-2 Subj: Night. Rhyming text.

Bingleman's midway ill. by Barry Moser. Boyds Mills, 1995. ISBN 1-563-97366-9 Subj: Behavior – running away. Careers – farmers. Fairs.

By the dawn's early light ill. by Catherine Stock. Atheneum, 1994. ISBN 0-689-31788-3 Subj: Activities – working. Ethnic groups in the U.S. – African Americans. Family life – grandmothers. Family life – mothers.

Flannery Row ill. by Karen Ann Weinhaus. Little, 1986. ISBN 0-87113-054-8 Subj: ABC books. Names. Rhyming text.

I know a place ill. by Deborah Kogan Ray. Houghton Mifflin, 1992. ISBN 0-395-53932-3 Subj: Family life. Homes, houses.

In the park with dad: a story for kids whose parents don't live together ill. by Linda Crockett-Blassingame. St. Paul Books & Media, 1996. ISBN 0-8198-3669-9 Subj: Divorce. Family life. Family life – fathers. Parks. Seasons – summer.

Just like Max ill. by George Schmidt. Knopf, 1990. ISBN 0-394-90176-2 Subj: Careers – tailors. Family life. Old age.

Moveable Mabeline ill. by Linda Allen. Putnam, 1990. ISBN 0-399-21580-8 Subj: Family life – sisters. Toys – dolls.

The sleeping porch ill. by Elizabeth Sayles. Morrow, 1995. ISBN 0-688-12823-8 Subj: Family life. Homes, houses. Moving.

Song and dance man ill. by Stephen Gammell. Knopf, 1988. ISBN 0-394-99330-6 Subj: Activities – dancing. Caldecott award books. Family life – grandfathers.

This old house ill. by Sylvie Wickstrom. Atheneum, 1992. ISBN 0-689-31741-7 Subj: Animals. Homes, houses. Rhyming text.

The tin heart ill. by Michael Hays. Macmillan, 1990. ISBN 0-689-31461-2 Subj: U.S. history. War.

Walking with Clara Belle ill. by Debbie Mason. St. Paul Books & Media, 1993. ISBN 0-8198-8243-7 Subj: Activities – walking. Old age. Remembering.

When mama retires ill. by Alexa Grace. Knopf, 1992. ISBN 0-679-90289-9 Subj: Activities – working. Family life – mothers. War.

Ackley, Edith Flack. *Please* ill. by Telka Ackley. Stokes, 1941. Subj: Etiquette.

Thank you ill. by Telka Ackley. Stokes, 1942. Subj: Etiquette.

Ada, Alma Flor. *El Arbol de Navidad: The Christmas tree* ill. by Terry Ybáñez. Hyperion, 1997. ISBN 0-7868-0151-4 Subj: Cumulative tales. Foreign languages. Holidays – Christmas. Rhyming text. Trees.

Dear Peter Rabbit ill. by Leslie Tryon. Atheneum, 1994. ISBN 0-689-31850-2 Subj: Animals. Folk and fairy tales. Letters, cards.

Gathering the sun: an alphabet in Spanish and English ill. by Simon Silva. Lothrop, 1997. ISBN 0-688-13904-3 Subj: ABC books. Foreign languages. Poetry.

The gold coin ill. by Neil Waldman. Macmillan, 1991. ISBN 0-689-31633-X Subj: Behavior – stealing. Circular tales. Crime. Cumulative tales. Foreign lands – Central America.

Jordi's star ill. by Susan Gaber. Atheneum, 1994. ISBN 0-399-22832-2 Subj: Animals – goats. Careers – shepherds. Friendship. Stars.

The malachite palace ill. by Leonid Gore. Atheneum, 1998. ISBN 0-689-31972-X Subj: Birds. Folk and fairy tales. Prejudice. Royalty – princesses.

The rooster who went to his uncle's wedding ill. by Kathleen Kuchera. Atheneum, 1993. ISBN 0-399-22412-2 Subj: Birds – chickens. Cumulative tales. Folk and fairy tales. Foreign lands.

The unicorn of the west ill. by Abigail Pizer. Atheneum, 1994. ISBN 0-689-31778-6 Subj: Animals. Forest, woods. Friendship. Mythical creatures – unicorns.

Adam, Barbara. *The big, big box* ill. by author. Doubleday, 1960. Subj: Activities – playing. Animals – cats. Imagination.

Adams, Adrienne. *The Christmas party* ill. by author. Scribners, 1978. ISBN 0684159309 Subj: Animals – rabbits. Holidays – Christmas. Parties.

The Easter egg artists ill. by author. Scribners, 1976. ISBN 0-684-14652-5 Subj: Activities – painting. Activities – vacationing. Animals – rabbits. Holidays – Easter.

The great Valentine's Day balloon race ill. by author. Scribners, 1980. ISBN 0-684-16640-2 Subj: Activities – ballooning. Animals – rabbits. Careers – artists. Holidays – Valentine's Day. Sports – racing.

A Halloween happening ill. by author. Scribners, 1981. ISBN 0-684-17166-X Subj: Holidays – Halloween. Parties. Witches.

Two hundred rabbits (Anderson, Lonzo)

A woggle of witches ill. by author. Scribners, 1971. ISBN 0-684-12506-4 Subj: Holidays – Halloween. Witches.

Adams, Georgie. *The first Christmas* ill. by Anna C. Leplar. Broadman & Holman, 1997. ISBN 0-8054-0175-X Subj: Holidays – Christmas. Religion – Nativity.

Fish fish fish ill. by Brigitte Willgoss. Dial, 1993. ISBN 0-8037-1208-1 Subj: Fish.

Adams, Jeanie. *Going for oysters* ill. by author. Albert Whitman, 1994. ISBN 0-8075-2978-8 Subj: Careers – fishermen. Family life. Foreign lands – Australia.

Adams, Ken. *When I was your age* ill. by Bal Biro. Barron's, 1991. ISBN 0-8120-6249-3 Subj: Family life – grandfathers. Tall tales.

Adams, Lisa K. *Dealing with teasing* ill. with photos. Rosen, 1997. ISBN 0-8239-5070-0 Subj: Behavior – misbehavior.

Adams, Pam. *There was an old lady who swallowed a fly* (Little old lady who swallowed a fly)

This old man ill. by author. Child's Play, 1990. ISBN 0-85953-026-4 Subj: Counting, numbers. Farms. Format, unusual. Songs.

Adams, Richard (Richard Newbold). *The tyger voyage* ill. by Nicola Bayley. Knopf, 1976. ISBN 0-394-40796-2 Subj: Animals – tigers. Humor. Poetry.

Adamson, Deb. *Monkey see, monkey do: an animal exercise book for you!* (Holsonback, Anita)

Adamson, Gareth. *Old man up a tree* ill. by author. Abelard-Schuman, 1963. Subj: Character traits – curiosity. Crime. Humor.

Adamson, Joy. *Elsa: the true story of a lioness* photos by author. Pantheon, 1961. Subj: Animals – lions. Foreign lands – Africa.

Elsa and her cubs photos by author. Harcourt, 1965. Subj: Animals – lions. Foreign lands – Africa.

Pippa the cheetah and her cubs photos by author. Harcourt, 1971. ISBN 0-15-262125-3 Subj: Animals – cheetahs. Foreign lands – Africa.

Addy, Sharon Hart. *Right here on this spot* ill. by John Clapp. Houghton Mifflin, 1999. ISBN 0-395-73091-0 Subj: Careers – archaeologists. Farms. U.S. history.

A visit with great-grandma ill. by author. Albert Whitman, 1988. ISBN 0-8075-8497-5 Subj: Family life – grandmothers.

Adedjouma, Davida. *The palm of my heart: poetry by African American children* (The palm of my heart)

Adelberg, Doris. *see* Orgel, Doris

Adelborg, Ottilia. *Clean Peter and the children of Grubbylea* trans. by Ada Wallas; ill. by author. Platt, 1968. Subj: Character traits – cleanliness. Poetry.

Adelson, Leone. *All ready for school* ill. by Kathleen Elgin. McKay, 1957. Subj: School. Seasons – fall.

All ready for summer ill. by Kathleen Elgin. McKay, 1955. Subj: Seasons – summer.

All ready for winter ill. by Kathleen Elgin. McKay, 1952. Subj: Seasons – winter.

Please pass the grass ill. by Roger Antoine Duvoisin. McKay, 1960. Subj: Insects. Plants. Poetry. Spiders.

Who blew that whistle? ill. by Oscar Fabrès. W. R. Scott, 1946. Subj: Careers – police officers. Character traits – helpfulness.

Adinolfi, JoAnn. *The Egyptian polar bear* ill. by author. Houghton Mifflin, 1994. ISBN 0-395-68074-3 Subj: Animals – polar bears. Foreign lands – Egypt. Friendship. Humor. Royalty.

Tina's diner ill. by author. Simon & Schuster, 1997. ISBN 0-689-80634-5 Subj: Activities – cooking. Careers – plumbers. City. Restaurants.

Adkins, Jan. *Heavy equipment* ill. by author. Scribners, 1980. ISBN 0-684-16641-0 Subj: Machines. Trucks.

Adler, David A. *Base five* ill. by Larry Ross. Crowell, 1975. ISBN 0-690-00669-1 Subj: Counting, numbers.

Bunny rabbit rebus ill. by Madelaine Gill Linden. Crowell, 1983. ISBN 0-690-04197-7 Subj: Animals – rabbits. Food. Rebuses.

The carsick zebra and other riddles ill. by Tomie de Paola. Holiday, 1983. ISBN 0-8234-0479-X Subj: Animals. Riddles.

The children of Chelm ill. by Arthur Friedman. Bonim Books, 1980. ISBN 0-88482-773-9 Subj: Foreign lands – Poland. Humor. Jewish culture. Problem solving.

The children's book of Jewish holidays ill. by David Sears. Mesorah, 1987. ISBN 0-89906-810-3 Subj: Holidays. Jewish culture.

Hiding from the Nazis ill. by Karen Ritz. Holiday, 1997. ISBN 0-8234-1288-1 Subj: Behavior – hiding. Family life. Holocaust. Jewish culture.

The house on the roof: a Sukkot story ill. by Marilyn Hirsh. Bonim Books, 1976. ISBN 0-8848-2905-7 Subj: Homes, houses. Jewish culture.

I know I'm a witch ill. by Suçie Stevenson. Holt, 1988. ISBN 0-8050-0427-0 Subj: Imagination. Witches.

A little at a time ill. by author. Random House, 1976. ISBN 0-394-92533-5 Subj: Character traits – questioning. Family life – grandfathers.

The number on my grandfather's arm ill. by Rose Eichenbaum. UAHC Pr., 1987. ISBN 0-8074-0328-8 Subj: Jewish culture. War.

A picture book of Abraham Lincoln ill. by John and Alexandra Wallner. Holiday, 1989. ISBN 0-8234-0731-4 Subj: U.S. history.

A picture book of Amelia Earhart ill. by Jeff Fisher. Holiday, 1998. ISBN 0-8234-1315-2 Subj: Careers – airplane pilots.

A picture book of Benjamin Franklin ill. by John and Alexandra Wallner. Holiday, 1990. ISBN 0-8234-0792-6 Subj: U.S. history.

A picture book of Eleanor Roosevelt ill. by Robert Casilla. Holiday, 1991. ISBN 0-8234-0856-6 Subj: U.S. history.

A picture book of George Washington ill. by John and Alexandra Wallner. Holiday, 1989. ISBN 0-8234-0732-2 Subj: U.S. history.

A picture book of Hanukkah ill. by Linda Heller. Holiday, 1982. ISBN 0-8234-0458-7 Subj: Holidays – Hanukkah. Jewish culture. Religion.

A picture book of Helen Keller ill. by John and Alexandra Wallner. Holiday, 1990. ISBN 0-8234-0818-3 Subj: Character traits – persistence. Handicaps.

A picture book of Israel ill. with photos. Holiday, 1984. ISBN 0-8234-0513-3 Subj: Foreign lands – Israel. Jewish culture. Religion.

A picture book of Jewish holidays ill. by Linda Heller. Holiday, 1981. ISBN 0-8234-0396-3 Subj: Holidays. Holidays – Hanukkah. Holidays – Passover. Jewish culture.

A picture book of John F. Kennedy ill. by Robert Casilla. Holiday, 1991. ISBN 0-8234-0884-1 Subj: U.S. history.

A picture book of Martin Luther King, Jr. ill. by Robert Casilla. Holiday, 1989. ISBN 0-8234-0770-5 Subj: Ethnic groups in the U.S. – African Americans. U.S. history.

A picture book of Passover ill. by Linda Heller. Holiday, 1982. ISBN 0-8234-0439-0 Subj: Holidays – Passover. Jewish culture.

A picture book of Thomas Jefferson ill. by John and Alexandra Wallner. Holiday, 1990. ISBN 0-8234-0791-8 Subj: U.S. history.

Redwoods are the tallest trees in the world ill. by Kazue Mizumura. Crowell, 1978. ISBN 0-690-01368-X Subj: Forest, woods. Science. Trees.

3D, 2D, 1D ill. by Harvey Weiss. Crowell, 1975. ISBN 0-690-00543-1 Subj: Concepts – measurement. Concepts – perspective. Concepts – shape.

You think it's fun to be a clown! ill. by Ray Cruz. Doubleday, 1980. ISBN 0-385-14460-1 Subj: Circus. Clowns, jesters. Rhyming text.

Adler, Irene. *see* Storr, Catherine (Cole)

Adlerman, Dan. *Africa calling: nighttime falling* ill. by Kimberly Adlerman. Whispering Coyote, 1996. ISBN 1-879085-98-4 Subj: Animals. Dreams. Jungle. Toys.

Adoff, Arnold. *Big sister tells me that I'm black* ill. by Lorenzo Lynch. Holt, 1976. ISBN 0-03-014546-5 Subj: Ethnic groups in the U.S. – African Americans. Family life. Poetry.

Birds ill. by Troy Howell. Lippincott, 1982. ISBN 0-397-31974-6 Subj: Birds. Poetry.

Black is brown is tan ill. by Emily Arnold McCully. HarperCollins, 1973. ISBN 0-06-020084-7 Subj: Family life. Marriage, interracial. Rhyming text.

The cabbages are chasing the rabbits ill. by Janet Stevens. Harcourt, 1985. ISBN 0-15-213875-7 Subj: Cumulative tales. Poetry.

Flamboyan ill. by Karen Barbour. Harcourt, 1988. ISBN 0-15-228404-4 Subj: Activities – flying. Dreams. Islands. Trees.

Greens ill. by Betsy Lewin. Lothrop, 1988. ISBN 0-688-04277-5 Subj: Concepts – color. Rhyming text.

Hard to be six ill. by Cheryl Hanna. Lothrop, 1990. ISBN 0-688-09579-8 Subj: Family life – sisters. Sibling rivalry.

I am the running girl ill. by Ronald Himler. Harper, 1979. ISBN 0-06-020095-2 Subj: Activities – running. Ethnic groups in the U.S. – African Americans. Poetry.

In for winter, out for spring ill. by Jerry Pinkney. Harcourt, 1991. ISBN 0-15-238637-8 Subj: Ethnic groups in the U.S. – African Americans. Family life. Poetry. Seasons.

Love letters ill. by Lisa Desimini. Blue Sky, 1997. ISBN 0-590-48478-8 Subj: Emotions – love. Letters, cards. Poetry.

Ma nDa La ill. by Emily Arnold McCully. HarperCollins, 1971. ISBN 0-06-020085-5 Subj: Family life. Foreign lands – Africa.

Make a circle, keep us in: poems for a good day ill. by Ronald Himler. Delacorte, 1975. ISBN 0-440-05909-7 Subj: Family life. Night. Poetry. Weather – storms.

OUTside INside Poems ill. by John Steptoe. Lothrop, 1981. ISBN 0-688-51942-3 Subj: Poetry.

The return of Rex and Ethel ill. by Catherine Deeter. Harcourt, 1996. ISBN 0-15266-367-3 Subj: Animals – dogs. Death. Emotions – grief. Pets.

Street music: city poems ill. by Karen Barbour. HarperCollins, 1994. ISBN 0-06-021523-2 Subj: City. Poetry.

Today we are brother and sister ill. by Glo Coalson. Lothrop, 1981. ISBN 0-688-51973-3 Subj: Family life – brothers and sisters. Poetry.

Tornado! poems ill. by Ronald Himler. Delacorte, 1977. ISBN 0-440-08965-4 Subj: Poetry. Weather – storms.

Touch the poem ill. by Bill Creevy. Scholastic, 1996. ISBN 0-590-47970-9 Subj: Poetry. Senses – touching.

Where wild Willie? ill. by Emily Arnold McCully. HarperCollins, 1978. ISBN 0-06-020093-6 Subj: Behavior – running away. City. Ethnic groups in the U.S. – African Americans. Poetry.

Adorjan, Carol Madden. *I can! Can you?* ill. by Miriam Nerlove. Rev. ed. Albert Whitman, 1990. Orignal title: Someone I know. ISBN 0-8075-3491-9 Subj: Activities – playing. Family life – sisters. Rhyming text.

Adshead, Gladys L. *Brownies - hush!* ill. by Elizabeth Orton Jones. Oxford Univ. Pr., 1938. Subj: Character traits – helpfulness. Folk and fairy tales. Mythical creatures – elves.

Brownies - it's Christmas ill. by Velma Ilsley. Oxford Univ. Pr., 1955. Subj: Holidays – Christmas. Mythical creatures – elves.

Brownies - they're moving ill. by Richard Lebenson. Walck, 1970. ISBN 0-8098-1163-4 Subj: Character traits – helpfulness. Moving. Mythical creatures – elves.

Æsop. *Æsop* sel. and ill. by Gaynor Chapman. Atheneum, 1972. ISBN 0-689-30024-7 Subj: Folk and fairy tales.

Æsop's fables retold by Werner Thuswaldner; trans. by Anthea Bell; ill. by Giselda Dürr. North-South, 1994. ISBN 1-55858-340-8 Subj: Folk and fairy tales. Format, unusual – toy and movable books.

Æsop's fables sel. and ill. by Michael Hague. Holt, 1985. ISBN 0-03-002038-7 Subj: Folk and fairy tales.

Æsop's fables sel. and ill. by Heidi Holder. Viking, 1981. ISBN 0-670-10643-7 Subj: Folk and fairy tales.

Æsop's fables: a pull-the-tab-pop-up-book ill. by Claire Littlejohn. Dial, 1988. ISBN 0-8037-0487-9 Subj: Folk and fairy tales. Format, unusual – toy and movable books.

Æsop's fables ill. by Jerry Pinkney. SeaStar, 2000. ISBN 1-587-17003-5 Subj: Folk and fairy tales.

Æsop's fables retold by Carol Watson; ill. by Nick Price. Usborne, 1982. ISBN 0-86020-667-X Subj: Folk and fairy tales.

Æsop's fables ill. by Lisbeth Zwerger. Picture Book Studio, 1991. ISBN 0-88708-108-8 Subj: Folk and fairy tales.

Androcles and the lion ill. by Janusz Grabianski. Watts, 1970. ISBN 0-531-01856-3 Subj: Animals – lions. Character traits – helpfulness. Character traits – kindness to animals. Folk and fairy tales. Foreign lands – Italy. Religion.

Androcles and the lion retold and ill. by Dennis Nolan. Harcourt, 1997. ISBN 0-15-203355-6 Subj: Animals – lions. Character traits – helpfulness. Character traits – kindness to animals. Folk and fairy tales. Foreign lands – Italy.

Androcles and the lion: and other Æsop fables adapt. by Tom Paxton; ill. by Robert Rayevsky. Morrow, 1991. ISBN 0-688-09683-2 Subj: Animals – lions. Character traits – helpfulness. Character traits – kindness to animals. Folk and fairy tales. Foreign lands – Italy. Rhyming text.

Androcles and the lion adapt. and ill. by Janet Stevens. Holiday, 1989. ISBN 0-8234-0768-3 Subj: Animals – lions. Character traits – helpfulness. Character traits – kindness to animals. Folk and fairy tales. Foreign lands – Italy. Religion.

Animal fables from Æsop adapt. and ill. by Barbara McClintock. Godine, 2000. ISBN 1-56792-144-2 Subj: Animals. Folk and fairy tales.

Anno's Æsop: a book of fables by Æsop and Mr. Fox (Anno, Mitsumasa)

The ant and the dove retold by Mary Lewis Wang; ill. by Ching. Childrens Pr., 1989. ISBN 0-516-02367-5 Subj: Birds – doves. Character traits – helpfulness. Folk and fairy tales. Friendship. Insects – ants.

Belling the cat and other Æsop fables (Paxton, Tom)

The best of Æsop's fables retold by Margaret Clark; ill. by Charlotte Voake. Little, 1990. ISBN 0-316-14499-1 Subj: Folk and fairy tales.

The children's Æsop retold by Stephanie Calmenson; ill. by Robert Byrd. Doubleday, 1988. ISBN 1-56397-041-4 Subj: Folk and fairy tales. Format, unusual – toy and movable books.

The country mouse and the city mouse ill. by Laura Lydecker. Knopf, 1987. ISBN 0-394-99027-7 Subj: Animals – mice. City. Country. Folk and fairy tales.

The dancin' fox (Nikola-Lisa, W.)

Doctor Coyote: a Native American Æsop's fables (Bierhorst, John)

The donkey ride (Showalter, Jean B.)

The fables of Æsop ed. by Ruth Spriggs; ill. by Frank Baber. Rand McNally, 1975. ISBN 0-528-82070-2 Subj: Folk and fairy tales.

Feed me! an Æsop fable (Hooks, William H.)

The hare and the frogs adapt. and ill. by William Stobbs. Merrimack, 1979. ISBN 0-370-30098-X Subj: Animals – rabbits. Folk and fairy tales. Frogs and toads.

The hare and the tortoise ill. by Paul Galdone. Whittlesey House, 1962. Subj: Animals – rabbits. Folk and fairy tales. Reptiles – turtles, tortoises. Sports – racing.

The hare and the tortoise retold and ill. by Carol Jones. Houghton Mifflin, 1996. ISBN 0-395-81368-9 Subj: Animals – rabbits. Folk and fairy tales. Format, unusual – toy and movable books. Reptiles – turtles, tortoises. Sports – racing.

The hare and the tortoise adapt. and ill. by Gerald Rose. Macmillan, 1988. ISBN 0-689-71197-2 Subj: Animals – rabbits. Folk and fairy tales. Reptiles – turtles, tortoises. Sports – racing.

The hare and the tortoise retold and ill. by Helen Ward. Millbrook, 1999. ISBN 0-7613-1318-4 Subj: Animals – rabbits. Folk and fairy tales. Reptiles – turtles, tortoises. Sports – racing.

The hare and the tortoise adapt. by Caroline Castle; ill. by Peter Weevers. Dial, 1985. ISBN 0-8037-0138-1 Subj: Animals – rabbits. Folk and fairy tales. Reptiles – turtles, tortoises. Sports – racing.

The lion and the mouse adapt. and ill. by Carol Jones. Random House, 1998. ISBN 0-395-86956-0 Subj: Animals – lions. Animals – mice. Character traits – helpfulness. Folk and fairy tales.

The lion and the mouse told by Gail Herman; ill. by Lisa McCue. Random House, 1998. ISBN 0-679-98674-X Subj: Animals – lions. Animals – mice. Character traits – helpfulness. Folk and fairy tales.

The lion and the mouse adapt. and ill. by Gerald Rose. Macmillan, 1988. ISBN 0-689-71196-4 Subj: Animals – lions. Animals – mice. Character traits – helpfulness. Folk and fairy tales.

The lion and the mouse retold and ill. by Bernadette Watts. North-South, 2000. ISBN 0-7358-1221-7 Subj: Animals – lions. Animals – mice. Character traits – helpfulness. Folk and fairy tales.

The lion and the mouse: an Æsop fable ill. by Ed Young. Doubleday, 1980. ISBN 0-385-15463-1 Subj: Animals – lions. Animals – mice. Character traits – helpfulness. Folk and fairy tales.

The lion and the mouse and other Æsop fables retold by Doris Orgel; ill. by Bert Kitchen. DK, 2000. ISBN 0-7894-2665-X Subj: Animals. Folk and fairy tales.

The miller, his son and their donkey ill. by Roger Antoine Duvoisin. McGraw-Hill, 1962. Subj: Animals – donkeys. Character traits – perseverance. Folk and fairy tales. Humor.

The miller, his son and their donkey ill. by Eugen Sopko. Holt, 1985. ISBN 0-8050-0475-0 Subj: Animals – donkeys. Character traits – perseverance. Folk and fairy tales.

Milly and Tilly: the story of a town mouse and a country mouse (Summers, Kate)

Once in a wood: ten tales from Æsop adapt. and ill. by Eve Rice. Greenwillow, 1980. ISBN 0-688-84191-0 Subj: Folk and fairy tales. Rhyming text.

The raven and the fox adapt. and ill. by Gerald Rose. Macmillan, 1988. ISBN 0-689-71194-8 Subj: Animals – foxes. Birds – ravens. Folk and fairy tales.

Seven fables from Æsop retold and ill. by R. W. Alley. Dodd, 1986. ISBN 0-396-08820-1 Subj: Animals. Folk and fairy tales.

Tales from Æsop retold and ill. by Harold Jones. Watts, 1982. ISBN 0-531-04074-7 Subj: Folk and fairy tales.

Three Æsop fox fables ill. by Paul Galdone. Seabury Pr., 1971. ISBN 0-395-28810-X Subj: Animals – foxes. Behavior – trickery. Character traits – flattery. Folk and fairy tales.

The tortoise and the hare: an Æsop fable adapt. and ill. by Janet Stevens. Holiday, 1984. ISBN 0-8234-0510-9 Subj: Animals – rabbits. Folk and fairy tales. Reptiles – turtles, tortoises. Sports – racing.

The town mouse and the country mouse ill. by Lorinda Bryan Cauley. Putnam, 1984. ISBN 0-399-21123-3 Subj: Animals – mice. City. Country. Folk and fairy tales.

The town mouse and the country mouse retold and ill. by Helen Craig. Candlewick, 1992. ISBN 1-56402-102-5 Subj: Animals – mice. City. Country. Folk and fairy tales.

The town mouse and the country mouse ill. by Paul Galdone. McGraw-Hill, 1971. ISBN 0-07-022694-6 Subj: Animals – mice. City. Country. Folk and fairy tales.

The town mouse and the country mouse ill. by Tom Garcia. Troll, 1979. ISBN 0-89375-109-X Subj: Animals – mice. City. Country. Folk and fairy tales.

The town mouse and the country mouse adapt. and ill. by Janet Stevens. Holiday, 1987. ISBN 0-8234-0633-4 Subj: Animals – mice. City. Country. Folk and fairy tales.

The town mouse and the country mouse: an Æsop fable retold and ill. by Bernadette Watts. North-South, 1998. ISBN 1-55858-988-0 Subj: Animals – mice. City. Country. Folk and fairy tales.

Town mouse, country mouse retold and ill. by Jan Brett. Putnam, 1994. ISBN 0-399-22622-2 Subj: Animals – cats. Animals – mice. Birds – owls. City. Country. Folk and fairy tales.

Town mouse, country mouse retold and ill. by Carol Jones. Houghton Mifflin, 1995. ISBN 0-395-71129-0 Subj: Animals – mice. City. Country. Folk and fairy tales.

Twelve tales from Æsop (Carle, Eric)

Wolf! Wolf! adapt. and ill. by Gerald Rose. Macmillan, 1988. ISBN 0-689-71195-6 Subj: Behavior – lying. Behavior – trickery. Folk and fairy tales.

Afanas'ev, Aleksandr N. *Russian folk tales* trans. by Robert Chandler; ill. by Ivan I. Bilibin. Random House, 1980. ISBN 0-87773-195-0 Subj: Folk and fairy tales. Foreign lands – Russia.

Salt: from a Russian folktale adapt. by Jane Langton; trans. by Alice Plume; ill. by Ilse Plume. Walt Disney, 1992. ISBN 1-56282-179-2 Subj: Behavior – greed. Family life – brothers. Folk and fairy tales. Foreign lands – Russia. Royalty – princesses.

Agard, John. *Dig away two-hole Tim* ill. by Jennifer Northway. Bodley Head, 1982. ISBN 0-370-30421-7 Subj: Activities – digging. Behavior – misbehavior. Foreign lands – Guyana.

No hickory no dickory no dock: Caribbean nursery rhymes by John Agard and Grace Nichols; ill. by Cynthia Jabar. Candlewick, 1995. ISBN 1-56402-156-4 Subj: Foreign lands – Caribbean Islands. Nursery rhymes. Rhyming text.

Agee, Joel. *The crow in the snow and other bedtime stories* (Moser, Erwin)

Agee, Jon. *Dmitri the astronaut* ill. by author. HarperCollins, 1996. ISBN 0-06-205075-3 Subj: Animals. Careers – astronauts. Moon. Space and space ships.

Ellsworth ill. by author. Pantheon, 1983. ISBN 0-394-95995-7 Subj: Activities – playing. Animals – dogs. Imagination.

The incredible painting of Felix Clousseau ill. by author. Farrar, 1988. ISBN 0-374-33633-4 Subj: Activities – painting. Art. Imagination.

Agell, Charlotte. *Mud makes me dance in the spring* ill. by author. Tilbury House, 1994. ISBN 0-88448-112-3 Subj: Family life. Imagination. Seasons – spring.

The sailor's book ill. by author. Firefly, 1991. ISBN 0-920668-90-9 Subj: Boats, ships. Dragons. Sailors. Sea and seashore.

To the island ill. by author. DK, 1998. ISBN 0-7894-2505-X Subj: Animals. Islands. Rhyming text. Sports – sailing.

Aggs, Patrice. *The visitor* ill. by author. Orchard, 1999. ISBN 0-531-33059-1 Subj: Animals – cats. Animals – giraffes. Character traits – being different.

Agostinelli, Maria Enrica. *I know something you don't know* ill. by author. Watts, 1970. Translation of Ich weiss etwas, was du nicht weisst. ISBN 0-531-01920-9 Subj: Games. Participation.

On wings of love: the United Nations declaration of the rights of the child ill. by author. Collins-World, 1979. ISBN 0-529-05529-5 Subj: Birds – doves. Emotions – love.

Ahlberg, Allan. *The baby's catalogue* (Ahlberg, Janet)

The bear nobody wanted (Ahlberg, Janet)

Big bad pig by Allan Ahlberg and Colin McNaughton; ill. by Colin McNaughton. Random House, 1985. ISBN 0-394-87194-4 Subj: Animals. Concepts. Concepts – opposites. Language.

The black cat ill. by André Amstutz. Greenwillow, 1990. ISBN 0-688-09904-1 Subj: Anatomy – skeletons. Animals – cats.

Burglar Bill (Ahlberg, Janet)

Bye-bye, baby: a sad story with a happy ending (Ahlberg, Janet)

The Cinderella show by Allan and Janet Ahlberg; ill. by authors. Viking, 1987. ISBN 0-670-81037-1 Subj: Folk and fairy tales. School. Theater.

Cops and robbers ill. by Janet Ahlberg. Greenwillow, 1979. ISBN 0-688-84178-3 Subj: Careers – police officers. Crime. Foreign lands – England. Holidays – Christmas. Rhyming text.

Crash, bang, wallop! ill. by Colin McNaughton. Random House, 1986. ISBN 0-394-87198-7 Subj: Noise, sounds.

Dinosaur dreams ill. by André Amstutz. Greenwillow, 1991. ISBN 0-688-09956-4 Subj: Anatomy – skeletons. Dinosaurs. Dreams.

Each peach pear plum: an "I spy" story (Ahlberg, Janet)

Fee fi fo fum by Allan Ahlberg and Colin McNaughton; ill. by Colin McNaughton. Random House, 1985. ISBN 0-394-97193-0 Subj: Concepts. Concepts – opposites. Counting, numbers. Language.

Funnybones (Ahlberg, Janet)

The ghost train ill. by André Amstutz. Greenwillow, 1992. ISBN 0-688-11435-0 Subj: Anatomy – skeletons. Humor. Monsters. Trains.

Happy worm by Allan Ahlberg and Colin McNaughton; ill. by Colin McNaughton. Random House, 1985. ISBN 0-394-97196-5 Subj: Concepts. Concepts – opposites. Language.

Help! by Allan Ahlberg and Colin McNaughton; ill. by Colin McNaughton. Random House, 1985. ISBN 0-394-97190-6 Subj: Concepts. Language.

It was a dark and stormy night (Ahlberg, Janet)

Jeremiah in the dark wood (Ahlberg, Janet)

The jolly Christmas postman (Ahlberg, Janet)

The jolly pocket postman (Ahlberg, Janet)

The jolly postman (Ahlberg, Janet)

The little worm book (Ahlberg, Janet)

Master Salt the sailor's son ill. by André Amstutz. Golden Pr., 1982, c1980. ISBN 0-307-61708-4 Subj: Behavior – hiding. Family life. Islands. Sailors.

Me and my friend ill. by Colin McNaughton. Random House, 1986. ISBN 0-394-87199-5 Subj: Activities. Activities – playing. Dictionaries. Monsters. School.

Miss Brick, the builder's baby ill. by Colin McNaughton. Golden Pr., 1982. ISBN 0-307-61702-5 Subj: Activities – making things. Babies. Family life.

Mr. and Mrs. Hay the horse ill. by Colin McNaughton. Golden Pr., 1982. ISBN 0-307-61704-1 Subj: Careers – entertainers. Circus. Family life.

Mr. Biff the boxer ill. by Janet Ahlberg. Western, 1982. ISBN 0-307-61701-7 Subj: Family life. Sports – boxing.

Mr. Buzz the beeman ill. by Faith Jaques. Golden Pr., 1982. ISBN 0-307-61703-3 Subj: Communities, neighborhoods. Family life. Insects – bees.

Mockingbird ill. by Paul Howard. Candlewick, 1998. ISBN 0-7636-0439-9 Subj: Babies. Family life. Lullabies.

Monkey do! ill. by André Amstutz. Candlewick, 1998. ISBN 0-7636-0466-6 Subj: Animals – monkeys. Behavior – misbehavior. Behavior – running away. Rhyming text. Zoos.

Mrs. Lather's laundry ill. by André Amstutz. Golden Pr., 1982. ISBN 0-307-61705-X Subj: Character traits – cleanliness. Family life. Laundry.

Mrs. Plug the plumber ill. by Joe Wright. Golden Pr., 1982. ISBN 0-307-61706-8 Subj: Careers – plumbers. Family life.

Mrs. Wobble the waitress ill. by Janet Ahlberg. Golden Books, 1982. ISBN 0-307-61707-6 Subj: Activities – working. Careers – waiters, waitresses. Family life.

Mystery tour ill. by André Amstutz. Greenwillow, 1991. ISBN 0-688-09958-0 Subj: Anatomy – skeletons. Behavior – losing things. Humor. Night.

Peek-a-boo! (Ahlberg, Janet)

The pet shop ill. by André Amstutz. Greenwillow, 1990. ISBN 0-688-09906-8 Subj: Anatomy – skeletons. Pets.

Playmates (Ahlberg, Janet)

Skeleton crew ill. by André Amstutz. Greenwillow, 1992. ISBN 0-688-11436-9 Subj: Activities – vacationing. Anatomy – skeletons. Boats, ships. Pirates. Sports – sailing.

Starting school (Ahlberg, Janet)

Yum yum (Ahlberg, Janet)

Ahlberg, Janet. *The baby's catalogue* by Janet and Allan Ahlberg; ill. by authors. Little, 1983. ISBN 0-316-02037-0 Subj: Babies. Family life.

The bear nobody wanted by Janet and Allan Ahlberg; ill. by authors. Viking, 1992. ISBN 0-670-83982-5 Subj: Format, unusual – toy and movable books. Self-concept.

Burglar Bill by Janet and Allan Ahlberg; ill. by authors. Greenwillow, 1977. ISBN 0-688-84078-7 Subj: Crime.

Bye-bye, baby: a sad story with a happy ending by Janet and Allan Ahlberg; ill. by Janet Ahlberg. Little, 1989. ISBN 0-316-02034-6 Subj: Babies. Behavior – needing someone. Family life.

The Cinderella show (Ahlberg, Allan)

Each peach pear plum: an "I spy" story by Janet and Allan Ahlberg; ill. by authors. Viking, 1978. ISBN 0-670-28705-9 Subj: Games. Rhyming text.

Funnybones by Janet and Allan Ahlberg; ill. by authors. Greenwillow, 1981. ISBN 0-688-84238-0 Subj: Activities – playing. Anatomy – skeletons. Ghosts. Night.

It was a dark and stormy night by Janet and Allan Ahlberg; ill. by Janet Ahlberg. Viking, 1993. ISBN 0-670-84620-1 Subj: Activities – storytelling. Character traits – cleverness. Crime. Pirates.

Jeremiah in the dark wood by Janet and Allan Ahlberg; ill. by Janet Ahlberg. Viking, 1987. ISBN 0-670-40637-6 Subj: Behavior – stealing. Forest, woods. Mythical creatures.

The jolly Christmas postman by Janet and Allan Ahlberg; ill. by authors. Little, 1991. ISBN 0-316-02033-8 Subj: Careers – postal workers. Format, unusual. Holidays – Christmas. Nursery rhymes. Post office. Rhyming text.

The jolly pocket postman by Janet and Allan Ahlberg; ill. by authors. Little, 1995. ISBN 0-316-60202-7 Subj: Careers – postal workers. Format, unusual – toy and movable books. Post office. Rhyming text.

The jolly postman by Janet and Allan Ahlberg; ill. by authors. Little, 1986. ISBN 0-316-02036-2 Subj: Careers – postal workers. Format, unusual – toy and movable books. Post office. Rhyming text.

The little worm book by Janet and Allan Ahlberg; ill. by authors. Viking, 1980. ISBN 0-670-43438-8 Subj: Animals – worms. Humor.

Peek-a-boo! by Janet and Allan Ahlberg; ill. by authors. Viking, 1981. ISBN 0-670-54598-8 Subj: Babies. Family life. Format, unusual – toy and movable books. Games. Rhyming text.

Playmates by Janet and Allan Ahlberg; ill. by authors. Viking, 1985. ISBN 0-670-55988-1 Subj: Activities – playing. Format, unusual – toy and movable books.

Starting school by Janet and Allan Ahlberg; ill. by authors. Viking, 1988. ISBN 0-670-82175-6 Subj: School – first day.

Yum yum by Janet and Allan Ahlberg; ill. by authors. Viking, 1985. ISBN 0-670-79620-4 Subj: Food. Format, unusual – toy and movable books.

Aichinger, Helga. *The shepherd* ill. by author. Crowell, 1967. Subj: Angels. Careers – shepherds. Dreams. Holidays – Christmas. Religion.

Aiello, Susan. *A hat like that* (Johnson, B. J.)

My blanket Burt (Johnson, B. J.)

Aiken, Conrad Potter. *Tom, Sue and the clock* ill. by Julie Maas. Macmillan, 1966. Subj: Clocks, watches. Rhyming text. Time.

Aiken, Joan. *Arabel and Mortimer* ill. by Quentin Blake. Doubleday, 1981. ISBN 0-385-15643-X Subj: Birds – ravens. Imagination. Pets.

The shoemaker's boy ill. by Victor G. Ambrus. Simon & Schuster, 1994. ISBN 0-671-86647-8 Subj: Careers – shoemakers. Folk and fairy tales. Middle Ages.

Ainsworth, Ruth. *The mysterious Baba and her magic caravan* ill. by Joan Hickson. André Deutsch, 1980. ISBN 0-233-97200-5 Subj: Character traits – generosity. Toys – dolls.

Aitken, Amy. *Kate and Mona in the jungle* ill. by author. Bradbury, 1981. ISBN 0-878-88167-0 Subj: Animals. Imagination. Jungle. Zoos.

Ruby! ill. by author. Bradbury, 1979. ISBN 0-878-88144-1 Subj: Careers. Imagination.

Ruby, the red knight ill. by author. Bradbury, 1983. ISBN 0-02-700340-X Subj: Character traits – bravery. Imagination. Royalty.

Wanda's circus ill. by author. Bradbury, 1985. ISBN 0-02-700370-1 Subj: Animals. Circus. Family life. Sibling rivalry.

Akass, Susan. *Number nine duckling* ill. by Alex Ayliffe. Boyds Mills, 1993. ISBN 1-56397-224-7 Subj: Activities – jumping. Animals. Birds – ducks. Emotions – fear. Farms.

Akers, Floyd. *see* Baum, L. Frank (Lyman Frank)

Aksakov, Sergei. *The scarlet flower* trans. by Isadora Levin; ill. by Boris Diodorov. Harcourt, 1989. ISBN 0-15-270487-6 Subj: Activities – traveling. Family life – fathers. Flowers. Foreign lands – Russia.

Alan, Sandy. *The plaid peacock* ill. by Kelly Oechsli. Pantheon, 1965. Subj: Birds – peacocks, peahens. Foreign lands – India.

Alarcón, Francisco X. *From the bellybutton of the moon and other summer poems / poems = Del ombligo de la luna y otros poemas de verano / poemas* ill. by Maya Christina Gonzalez. Childrens Pr., 1998. ISBN 0-89239-153-7 Subj: Foreign lands – Mexico. Foreign languages. Nature. Poetry. Seasons – summer.

Alavedra, Joan. *They followed a bright star* (They followed a bright star)

Albert, Burton. *Mine, yours, ours* ill. by Lois Axeman. Albert Whitman, 1977. ISBN 0-807-55148-1 Subj: Behavior – sharing. Concepts.

Where does the trail lead? ill. by J. Brian Pinkney. Simon & Schuster, 1991. ISBN 0-671-73409-1 Subj: Islands. Sea and seashore.

Albert, Richard E. *Alejandro's gift* ill. by Sylvia Long. Chronicle, 1994. ISBN 0-8118-0436-4 Subj: Animals. Character traits – kindness to animals. Desert. Gifts.

Albert, Shirley. *Doll party* ill. by Amy Flynn. Grosset, 1994. ISBN 0-448-40183-5 Subj: Animals – mice. Character traits – willfulness. Family life – mothers. Parties. Toys – dolls.

Alberts, Nancy Markham. *No toys on Sunday* ill. by Erin McGonigle Brammer. Morehouse, 1998. ISBN 0-8192-1740-9 Subj: Activities – playing. Character traits – cleverness. Days of the week, months of the year. Religion – Noah. Toys – dolls.

Alborough, Jez. *Bare bear* ill. by author. Knopf, 1984. ISBN 0-394-96808-5 Subj: Activities – bathing. Animals – polar bears. Rhyming text.

Beaky ill. by author. Houghton Mifflin, 1990. ISBN 0-395-53348-1 Subj: Animals. Birds. Self-concept.

Can you jump like a kangaroo? ill. by author. Candlewick, 1996. ISBN 1-56402-880-1 Subj: Activities. Animals. Format, unusual – toy and movable books.

Can you peck like a hen? ill. by author. Candlewick, 1996. ISBN 1-56402-881-X Subj: Animals. Format, unusual – toy and movable books.

Clothesline ill. by author. Candlewick, 1993. ISBN 1-56402-243-9 Subj: Animals. Clothing. Format, unusual – toy and movable books.

Cuddly Dudley ill. by author. Candlewick, 1993. ISBN 1-56402-095-9 Subj: Behavior – solitude. Birds – penguins. Character traits – being different. Family life – brothers and sisters.

Duck in the truck ill. by author. HarperCollins, 2000. ISBN 0-06-028685-7 Subj: Animals. Birds – ducks. Rhyming text. Trucks.

Esther's trunk ill. by author. Warner, 1988. ISBN 1-55782-007-4 Subj: Animals – elephants. Rhyming text.

The grass is always greener ill. by author. Dial, 1987. ISBN 0-8037-0468-2 Subj: Animals – sheep. Behavior – seeking better things. Farms.

Hide and seek ill. by author. Candlewick, 1994. ISBN 1-56402-369-9 Subj: Activities – playing. Animals. Behavior – hiding. Format, unusual – toy and movable books.

Ice cream bear ill. by author. Candlewick, 1997. ISBN 0-7636-0293-0 Subj: Animals – bears. Dreams. Food. Rhyming text. Weather – snow.

It's the bear ill. by author. Candlewick, 1994. ISBN 1-56402-486-5 Subj: Activities – picnicking. Animals – bears. Behavior – stealing. Emotions – fear. Family life – mothers. Food. Rhyming text.

My friend bear ill. by author. Candlewick, 1998. ISBN 0-7636-0583-2 Subj: Animals – bears. Emotions – loneliness. Friendship. Toys – bears.

Running Bear ill. by author. Knopf, 1985. ISBN 0-394-97963-X Subj: Animals – polar bears. Behavior – bad day. Sports – racing.

There's something at the mail slot ill. by author. Candlewick, 1995. ISBN 1-56402-523-3 Subj: Animals. Character traits – bravery. Rhyming text.

Watch out! Big Bro's coming! ill. by author. Candlewick, 1997. ISBN 0-7636-0130-6 Subj: Animals. Animals – mice. Concepts – size. Emotions – fear. Family life – brothers and sisters.

Where's my teddy? ill. by author. Candlewick, 1992. ISBN 1-56402-048-7 Subj: Animals – bears. Forest, woods. Rhyming text. Toys – bears.

Alcantara, Ricardo. *Dog and cat* ill. by Gusti; trans. by Elizabeth Uhlig. Millbrook, 1999. ISBN 0-7613-1420-2 Subj: Animals – cats. Animals – dogs. Emotions – fear. Friendship.

Alcott, Louisa May. *An old-fashioned Thanksgiving* ill. by Jody Wheeler. Ideals, 1993. ISBN 0-8249-8630-X Subj: Family life. Family life – grandmothers. Food. Holidays – Thanksgiving.

Alda, Arlene. *Arlene Alda's ABC* photos by author. Tricycle, 1993. ISBN 1-883672-01-5 Subj: ABC books.

Arlene Alda's 1 2 3: what do you see? photos by author. Tricycle, 1998. ISBN 1-883672-71-6 Subj: Counting, numbers.

Hurry Granny Annie ill. by Aldridge, Eve. Tricycle, 1999. ISBN 1-883672-72-4 Subj: Behavior – hurrying. Family life – grandmothers. Sun.

Matthew and his dad photos by author. Simon & Schuster, 1983. ISBN 0-671-45158-8 Subj: Clothing. Family life – fathers.

Pig, horse, or cow, don't wake me now photos by author. Doubleday, 1994. ISBN 0-385-32032-9 Subj: Animals. Cumulative tales. Morning. Noise, sounds. Rhyming text.

Sheep, sheep, sheep, help me fall asleep photos by author. Delacorte, 1992. ISBN 0-385-30791-8 Subj: Animals. Animals – sheep. Bedtime. Rhyming text.

Sonya's mommy works photos by author. Messner, 1982. ISBN 0-671-46167-2 Subj: Activities – working. Family life – mothers.

Aldag, Kurt. *Some things never change* ill. by Ken Rush. Macmillan, 1992. ISBN 0-02-700205-5 Subj: Automobiles. Careers – mechanics. Time.

Alden, Jack. *see* Barrows, Marjorie Wescott

Alden, Laura. *Saying I'm sorry* ill. by Dan Siculan. Child's World, 1983. ISBN 0-89565-247-1 Subj: Etiquette.

When? ill. by Lois Axeman. Childrens Pr., 1983. ISBN 0-516-06592-0 Subj: Character traits – curiosity. Character traits – questioning.

Alderson, Brian W. *Cakes and custard: children's rhymes* (Cakes and custard)

The Helen Oxenbury nursery rhyme book (The Helen Oxenbury nursery rhyme book)

Alderson, Sue Ann. *Bonnie McSmithers is at it again!* ill. by Fiona Garrick. Tree Frog Pr., 1980. ISBN 0-88967-028-5 Subj: Activities. Character traits – individuality. Rhyming text.

Ida and the wool smugglers ill. by Ann Blades. Macmillan, 1987. ISBN 0-689-50440-3 Subj: Character traits – cleverness. Crime. Islands.

Wherever bears be: a story for two voices ill. by Arden Johnson. Tricycle, 1999. ISBN 1-883672-77-5 Subj: Animals – bears. Emotions – fear. Food.

Aldis, Dorothy (Keeley). *All together: a child's treasury of verse* ill. by Helen D. Jameson, Marjorie Flack, and Margaret Freeman. Putnam, 1952. ISBN 0-399-20006-1 Subj: Poetry.

Before things happen ill. by Margaret Freeman. Putnam, 1939. Subj: Poetry.

Hello day ill. by Susan Elson. Putnam, 1959. Subj: Poetry.

Hiding ill. by Heather Collins. Viking, 1994. ISBN 0-670-85410-7 Subj: Behavior – hiding. Family life. Poetry. Toys – bears.

Quick as a wink ill. by Peggy Westphal. Putnam, 1960. Subj: Insects. Poetry.

Aldridge, Josephine Haskell. *The best of friends* ill. by Betty Peterson. Parnassus, 1963. Subj: Animals. Friendship.

Fisherman's luck ill. by Ruth Robbins. Parnassus, 1966. Subj: Careers – fishermen. Character traits – luck. Sports – fishing. Weather – storms.

A penny and a periwinkle ill. by Ruth Robbins. Parnassus, 1961. Subj: Sports – fishing.

A possible tree ill. by Daniel San Souci. Macmillan, 1993. ISBN 0-02-700407-4 Subj: Animals. Ecology. Holidays – Christmas. Trees.

Aleichem, Sholem. *Hanukah money* ill. by Uri Shulevitz. Greenwillow, 1978. ISBN 0-688-84120-1 Subj: Folk and fairy tales. Foreign lands. Holidays – Hanukkah. Jewish culture. Religion.

Alemany, Norah E. *My mother the mail carrier: Mi mama la cartera* (Maury, Inez)

Alexander, Anne (Anna Barbara Cooke). *ABC of cars and trucks* ill. by Ninon. Doubleday, 1956. Subj: ABC books. Automobiles. Poetry. Trucks.

Boats and ships from A to Z ill. by Will Huntington. Rand McNally, 1961. Subj: Boats, ships.

I want to whistle ill. by Abner Graboff. Abelard-Schuman, 1958. Subj: Activities – whistling. Rhyming text.

My daddy and I ill. by Cyril Satorsky. Abelard-Schuman, 1961. Subj: Counting, numbers. Family life – fathers. Poetry.

Noise in the night ill. by Abner Graboff. Rand McNally, 1960. Subj: Emotions – fear. Night. Noise, sounds.

Alexander, Cecil Frances. *All things bright and beautiful: a hymn* ill. by Leo Politi. Scribners, 1962. Subj: Creation. Music. Nature. Religion. Songs.

Alexander, Ellen. *Chaska and the golden doll* ill. by author. Arcade, 1994. ISBN 1-55970-241-9 Subj: Foreign lands – Peru. Foreign lands – South America. Indians of South America.

Llama and the great flood ill. by author. HarperCollins, 1989. ISBN 0-690-04729-0 Subj: Animals – llamas. Folk and fairy tales. Foreign lands – Peru. Weather – floods.

Alexander, Liza. *Ernie gets lost* ill. by Tom Cooke. Childrens Pr., 1985. ISBN 0-307-62115-4 Subj: Behavior – lost. Stores.

A visit to the Sesame Street Museum ill. by Joe Mathieu. Random House, 1987. ISBN 0-394-98715-2 Subj: Museums.

Alexander, Lloyd. *Fortune tellers* ill. by Trina Schart Hyman. Dutton, 1992. ISBN 0-525-44849-7 Subj: Careers – fortune tellers. Cumulative tales. Foreign lands – Africa. Foreign lands – Cameroon.

The house Gobbaleen ill. by Diane Goode. Dutton, 1995. ISBN 0-525-45289-3 Subj: Animals – cats. Behavior – trickery. Character traits – foolishness. Character traits – luck. Monsters. Mythical creatures – goblins.

The king's fountain ill. by Ezra Jack Keats. Dutton, 1971. ISBN 0-525-33240-5 Subj: Folk and fairy tales. Poverty. Royalty – kings.

The truthful harp ill. by Evaline Ness. Holt, 1967. Subj: Character traits – honesty. Folk and fairy tales. Music.

Alexander, Martha G. *And my mean old mother will be sorry, Blackboard Bear* ill. by author. Candlewick, 2000. ISBN 0-7636-0668-5 Subj: Animals – bears. Behavior – running away. Emotions – anger. Imagination – imaginary friends.

Blackboard Bear ill. by author. 2nd ed. Candlewick, 1999. ISBN 0-7636-0667-7 Subj: Activities – playing. Animals – bears. Concepts – size. Imagination – imaginary friends.

Bobo's dream ill. by author. Dial, 1970. Subj: Animals – dogs. Dreams. Ethnic groups in the U.S. – African Americans. Imagination. Wordless.

Even that moose won't listen to me ill. by author. Dial, 1988. ISBN 0-8037-0188-8 Subj: Animals – moose. Behavior – disbelief. Family life.

Good night, Lily ill. by author. Candlewick, 1993. ISBN 1-56402-164-5 Subj: Activities – playing. Bedtime. Family life – brothers and sisters. Format, unusual – board books. Toys.

How my library grew by Dinah ill. by author. H. W. Wilson, 1982. ISBN 0-8242-0670-3 Subj: Libraries.

I sure am glad to see you, Blackboard Bear ill. by author. Dial, 1976. ISBN 0-8037-4003-4 Subj: Animals – bears. Behavior – bullying. Imagination – imaginary friends.

I'll be the horse if you'll play with me ill. by author. Dial, 1975. ISBN 0-8037-5511-2 Subj: Activities – playing. Behavior – fighting, arguing. Family life. Sibling rivalry.

I'll protect you from the jungle beasts ill. by author. Dial, 1973. ISBN 0-8037-4309-2 Subj: Emotions – fear. Imagination – imaginary friends. Problem solving. Sleep. Toys – bears.

Lily and Willy ill. by author. Candlewick, 1993. ISBN 1-56402-163-7 Subj: Activities – playing. Family life – brothers and sisters. Format, unusual – board books. Toys.

Maggie's moon ill. by author. Dial, 1982. ISBN 0-8037-5721-2 Subj: Animals – dogs. Moon. Night.

Marty McGee's space lab, no girls allowed ill. by author. Dial, 1981. ISBN 0-8037-5156-7 Subj: Family life. Gender roles. Imagination. Sibling rivalry. Space and space ships.

Maybe a monster ill. by author. Dial, 1968. ISBN 0-8037-5508-2 Subj: Emotions – fear. Monsters.

Move over, Twerp ill. by author. Dial, 1981. ISBN 0-8037-6140-6 Subj: Behavior – bullying. Character traits – perseverance. Humor. Problem solving. School.

My outrageous friend Charlie ill. by author. Dial, 1989. ISBN 0-8037-0588-3 Subj: Character traits – confidence. Friendship. Humor. Magic.

No ducks in our bathtub ill. by author. Dial, 1973. ISBN 0-8037-6217-8 Subj: Frogs and toads. Pets.

Nobody asked me if I wanted a baby sister ill. by author. Dial, 1971. ISBN 0-8037-6402-2 Subj: Babies. Emotions – envy, jealousy. Family life – new sibling. Family life – sisters. Sibling rivalry.

Out! Out! Out! ill. by author. Dial, 1968. ISBN 0-685-01457-6 Subj: Birds. Problem solving. Wordless.

Pigs say oink: a first book of sounds ill. by author. Random House, [1981] c1978. ISBN 0-394-93838-0 Subj: Animals. Noise, sounds.

Sabrina ill. by author. Dial, 1971. ISBN 0-8037-7547-4 Subj: Emotions – embarrassment. Names. School – first day.

The story grandmother told ill. by author. Dial, 1969. Subj: Ethnic groups in the U.S. – African Americans. Family life – grandmothers. Toys.

3 magic flip books: The magic hat; The magic box; The magic picture ill. by author. Dial, 1984. ISBN 0-8037-0051-2 Subj: Format, unusual – toy and movable books. Magic. Wordless.

We never get to do anything ill. by author. Dial, 1970. ISBN 0-8037-9416-9 Subj: Behavior – boredom. Character traits – perseverance. Games. Problem solving. Sports – swimming.

We're in big trouble, Blackboard Bear ill. by author. Dial, 1980. ISBN 0-8037-9742-7 Subj: Animals – bears. Behavior – misbehavior. Imagination – imaginary friends. Night. Problem solving.

When the new baby comes, I'm moving out ill. by author. Dial, 1979. ISBN 0-8037-9558-0 Subj: Animals – babies. Emotions – envy, jealousy. Family life – new sibling. Sibling rivalry.

Where does the sky end, Grandpa? ill. by author. Harcourt, 1992. ISBN 0-15-295603-4 Subj: Activities – walking. Character traits – questioning. Family life – grandfathers. Nature.

Where's Willy? ill. by author. Candlewick, 1993. ISBN 1-56402-161-0 Subj: Activities – playing. Family life – brothers and sisters. Format, unusual – board books. Games. Toys.

Willy's boot ill. by author. Candlewick, 1993. ISBN 1-56402-162-9 Subj: Activities – playing. Family life – brothers and sisters. Format, unusual – board books. Toys.

You're a genius, Blackboard Bear ill. by author. Candlewick, 1995. ISBN 1-56402-238-2 Subj: Animals – bears. Dreams. Imagination – imaginary friends. Night. Space and space ships.

Alexander, Sally Hobart. *Maggie's whopper* ill. by Deborah Kogan Ray. Macmillan, 1992. ISBN 0-02-700201-2 Subj: Animals – bears. Family life – aunts, uncles. Sports – fishing.

Sarah's surprise ill. by Jill Kastner. Macmillan, 1990. ISBN 0-02-700391-4 Subj: Emotions – fear. Sea and seashore.

Alexander, Sue. *Dear Phoebe* ill. by Eileen Christelow. Little, 1984. ISBN 0-316-03123-1 Subj: Animals – dormice. Behavior – growing up. Emotions – loneliness. Emotions – love. Family life.

Ellsworth and Millicent ill. by David Scott Meier. Picture Book Studio, 1992. ISBN 0-88708-247-5

Subj: Animals – hippopotamuses. Behavior – dissatisfaction. Friendship.

Marc the Magnificent ill. by Tomie de Paola. Pantheon, 1978. ISBN 0-394-93728-7 Subj: Character traits – optimism. Magic.

More Witch, Goblin, and Ghost stories ill. by Jeanette Winter. Pantheon, 1978. ISBN 0-394-93933-6 Subj: Ghosts. Mythical creatures – goblins. Witches.

Nadia the willful ill. by Lloyd Bloom. Pantheon, 1983. ISBN 0-394-95265-0 Subj: Character traits – willfulness. Emotions – love. Emotions – sadness. Family life. Foreign lands – Arabia.

One more time, Mama ill. by David Soman. Cavendish, 1999. ISBN 0-7614-5051-3 Subj: Birth. Family life – mothers. Nature.

Peacocks are very special ill. by Victoria Chess. Doubleday, 1976. ISBN 0-385-02169-0 Subj: Animals – jackals. Birds – peacocks, peahens. Character traits – cleverness.

Seymour the prince ill. by Lillian Hoban. Pantheon, 1979. ISBN 0-394-94141-1 Subj: Clubs, gangs. Theater.

Small plays for special days ill. by Tom Huffman. Seabury Pr., 1977. ISBN 0-8164-3184-1 Subj: Holidays. Theater.

Small plays for you and a friend ill. by Olivia Cole. Houghton Mifflin, 1974. ISBN 0-8164-3125-6 Subj: Friendship. Theater.

There's more . . . much more ill. by Patience Brewster. Harcourt, 1987. ISBN 0-15-200605-2 Subj: Animals – squirrels. Seasons – spring.

What's wrong now, Millicent? ill. by David Scott Meier. Simon & Schuster, 1996. ISBN 0-689-80680-9 Subj: Animals – hippopotamuses. Behavior – dissatisfaction. Friendship.

Who goes out on Halloween? ill. by G. Brian Karas. Bantam, 1990. ISBN 0-553-05891-6 Subj: Holidays – Halloween. Monsters. Mythical creatures – goblins. Rhyming text. Witches.

Witch, Goblin and Ghost are back ill. by Jeanette Winter. Pantheon, 1985. ISBN 0-394-96296-6 Subj: Ghosts. Mythical creatures – goblins. Witches.

Witch, Goblin, and Ghost in the haunted woods ill. by Jeanette Winter. Pantheon, 1981. ISBN 0-394-94443-7 Subj: Ghosts. Mythical creatures – goblins. Witches.

Witch, Goblin and sometimes Ghost ill. by Jeanette Winter. Pantheon, 1976. ISBN 0-394-93216-1 Subj: Behavior – forgetfulness. Emotions – fear. Friendship. Ghosts. Mythical creatures – goblins. Witches.

World famous Muriel ill. by Chris L. Demarest. Little, 1984. ISBN 0-316-03131-3 Subj: Birthdays. Humor. Mystery stories.

World famous Muriel and the magic mystery ill. by Marla Frazee. HarperCollins, 1990. ISBN 0-690-04789-4 Subj: Libraries. Magic. Mystery stories.

World famous Muriel and the scary dragon ill. by Chris L. Demarest. Little, 1985. ISBN 0-316-03134-8 Subj: Dragons. Royalty – kings.

Alger, Leclaire Gowans. *All in the morning early* ill. by Evaline Ness. Holt, 1963. Subj: Caldecott award honor books. Folk and fairy tales. Foreign lands – Scotland. Poetry. Songs.

Always room for one more ill. by Nonny Hogrogian. Holt, 1965. Children's story based on the Scottish ballad of the same title. ISBN 0-8050-0331-2 Subj: Caldecott award books. Cumulative tales. Folk and fairy tales. Foreign lands – Scotland. Homes, houses. Music.

Kellyburn Braes ill. by Evaline Ness. Harcourt, 1968. Subj: Devil. Foreign lands – Scotland. Foreign languages. Music. Poetry. Songs.

Aliki. *At Mary Bloom's* ill. by author. Greenwillow, 1976. ISBN 0-688-84048-8 Subj: Animals – babies. Animals – mice.

Best friends together again ill. by author. Greenwillow, 1995. ISBN 0-688-13754-7 Subj: Friendship. Moving.

Christmas tree memories ill. by author. HarperCollins, 1991. ISBN 0-06-020008-1 Subj: Family life. Holidays – Christmas. Memories, memory. Trees.

Communication ill. by author. Greenwillow, 1993. ISBN 0-688-11248-X Subj: Activities – writing. Language.

Corn is maize: the gift of the Indians ill. by author. Crowell, 1976. ISBN 0-690-00976-3 Subj: Gardens, gardening. Indians of North America. Plants. Science.

Digging up dinosaurs ill. by author. Rev. ed. Crowell, 1988. ISBN 0-690-04716-9 Subj: Activities – digging. Dinosaurs. Humor. Science.

Dinosaur bones ill. by author. HarperCollins, 1988. ISBN 0-690-04550-6 Subj: Dinosaurs.

Dinosaurs are different ill. by author. Crowell, 1985. ISBN 0-690-04458-5 Subj: Dinosaurs. Science.

Diogenes: the story of the Greek philosopher ill. by author. Prentice-Hall, 1969. Subj: Character traits – honesty. Folk and fairy tales. Foreign lands – Greece.

The eggs: a Greek folk tale ill. by adapt. Pantheon, 1969. ISBN 0-06-443385-4 Subj: Behavior – greed. Character traits – cleverness. Folk and fairy tales. Foreign lands – Greece. Humor.

Feelings ill. by author. Greenwillow, 1984. ISBN 0-688-03832-8 Subj: Emotions. Friendship.

Fossils tell of long ago ill. by author. Rev. ed. Crowell, 1990. ISBN 0-690-31379-9 Subj: Dinosaurs. Science.

George and the cherry tree ill. by author. Dial, 1964. Subj: Character traits – bravery. Folk and fairy tales. U.S. history.

Hello! Good-bye! ill. by author. Greenwillow, 1996. ISBN 0-688-14334-2 Subj: Language.

How a book is made ill. by author. HarperCollins, 1986. ISBN 0-690-04498-4 Subj: Activities – reading. Libraries.

I'm growing! ill. by author. HarperCollins, 1992. ISBN 0-06-020245-9 Subj: Behavior – growing up.

Jack and Jake ill. by author. Greenwillow, 1986. ISBN 0-688-06100-1 Subj: Behavior – mistakes. Character traits – individuality. Family life. Multiple births – twins.

June 7! ill. by author. Macmillan, 1972. Subj: Birthdays. Cumulative tales. Family life.

Keep your mouth closed, dear ill. by author. Dial, 1966. ISBN 0-8037-4418-8 Subj: Behavior – carelessness. Family life. Reptiles – alligators, crocodiles.

The king's day ill. by author. HarperCollins, 1989. ISBN 0-690-04590-5 Subj: Foreign lands – France. Royalty – kings.

The long lost coelacanth and other living fossils ill. by author. Crowell, 1973. ISBN 0-690-50478-0 Subj: Fish. Science.

Manners ill. by author. Greenwillow, 1990. ISBN 0-688-09199-7 Subj: Etiquette.

The many lives of Benjamin Franklin ill. by author. Simon & Schuster, 1988. ISBN 0-671-66119-1 Subj: U.S. history.

Marianthe's story one: painted words; Marianthe's story two: spoken memories ill. by author. Greenwillow, 1998. ISBN 0-688-15662-2 Subj: Family life. Foreign lands. Format, unusual. School.

Milk from cow to carton ill. by author. HarperCollins, 1992. ISBN 0-06-020435-4 Subj: Animals – bulls, cows. Careers – farmers. Food.

Mummies made in Egypt ill. by author. Crowell, 1979. ISBN 0-690-03859-3 Subj: Death. Foreign lands – Egypt. Religion.

My feet ill. by author. HarperCollins, 1990. ISBN 0-690-04815-7 Subj: Anatomy – feet. Science.

My five senses ill. by author. Rev. ed. HarperCollins, 1989. ISBN 0-690-04794-0 Subj: Senses – hearing. Senses – seeing. Senses – smelling. Senses – tasting. Senses – touching.

My hands ill. by author. Rev. ed. Harper, 1992. ISBN 0-06-445096-1 Subj: Anatomy – hands. Science.

My visit to the aquarium ill. by author. HarperCollins, 1993. ISBN 0-06-021459-7 Subj: Animals. Aquariums. Fish. Plants.

My visit to the dinosaurs ill. by author. Rev. ed. Crowell, 1985. ISBN 0-690-04423-2 Subj: Dinosaurs. Museums. Science.

My visit to the zoo ill. by author. HarperCollins, 1997. ISBN 0-06-024943-9 Subj: Animals. Animals – endangered animals. Birds. Ecology. Zoos.

Overnight at Mary Bloom's ill. by author. Greenwillow, 1987. ISBN 0-688-06765-4 Subj: Activities. Activities – playing. Friendship. Night.

The story of Johnny Appleseed ill. by author. Simon & Schuster, 1988. Reprint. Originally published: Englewood Cliffs, N.J.: Prentice-Hall, c1963. ISBN 0-671-66298-8 Subj: Character traits – generosity. Folk and fairy tales. Gardens, gardening. Trees. U.S. history – frontier and pioneer life.

The story of William Penn ill. by author. Simon & Schuster, 1994. ISBN 0-671-88558-8 Subj: Character traits – kindness. U.S. history.

Tabby ill. by author. HarperCollins, 1995. ISBN 0-06-024916-1 Subj: Animals – cats. Ethnic groups in the U.S. – Hispanic Americans. Wordless.

Those summers ill. by author. HarperCollins, 1996. ISBN 0-06-024938-2 Subj: Family life. Sea and seashore. Seasons – summer.

Three gold pieces: a Greek folk tale ill. by author. Pantheon, 1967. ISBN 0-394-91737-5 Subj: Character traits – luck. Folk and fairy tales. Foreign lands – Greece.

The twelve months: a Greek folktale ill. by adapt. Greenwillow, 1978. ISBN 0-688-84164-3 Subj: Behavior – dissatisfaction. Character traits – optimism. Folk and fairy tales. Foreign lands – Greece.

The two of them ill. by author. Greenwillow, 1979. ISBN 0-688-84225-9 Subj: Character traits – helpfulness. Character traits – loyalty. Family life – grandfathers.

Use your head, dear ill. by author. Greenwillow, 1983. ISBN 0-688-01812-2 Subj: Behavior – forgetfulness. Birthdays. Reptiles – alligators, crocodiles.

We are best friends ill. by author. Greenwillow, 1982. ISBN 0-688-00823-2 Subj: Emotions – anger. Emotions – loneliness. Friendship. Moving.

A weed is a flower: the life of George Washington Carver ill. by author. Simon & Schuster, 1988. ISBN 0-671-66118-3 Subj: Character traits – perseverance. Ethnic groups in the U.S. – African Americans. Science. U.S. history.

Welcome, little baby ill. by author. Greenwillow, 1987. ISBN 0-688-06811-1 Subj: Babies. Family life.

Wild and woolly mammoths ill. by author. HarperCollins, 1996. ISBN 0-06-026277-X Subj: Animals. Science.

The wish workers ill. by author. Dial, 1962. Subj: Behavior – dissatisfaction. Behavior – wishing. Birds. Magic.

The all-amazing ha ha book ill. by Max Dann. Oxford Univ. Pr., 1987. ISBN 0-19-554581-8 Subj: Folk and fairy tales. Foreign lands – Australia. Humor. Language.

All the pretty little horses ill. by Linda Saport. Clarion, 1999. ISBN 0-395-93097-9 Subj: Animals – horses, ponies. Ethnic groups in the U.S. –

African Americans. Family life – mothers. Lullabies.

All year round: *a book to benefit children in need* by Lisa Desimini . . . [et al.]; ill. by Lisa Desimini. Scholastic, 1997. Written and illustrated in conjunction with the Robin Hood Foundation to benefit a Women in Need (WIN) shelter for homeless women and children in New York. ISBN 0-590-36097-3 Subj: Poetry. Rhyming text. Seasons.

Allamand, Pascale. *The animals who changed their colors* ill. by Elizabeth Watson Taylor. Morrow, 1979. ISBN 0-688-51900-8 Subj: Animals. Behavior – imitation. Character traits – individuality. Concepts – color. Humor.

The camel who left the zoo ill. by author; English version by Michael Bullock. Scribners, 1976. ISBN 0-684-14824-2 Subj: Animals. Behavior – running away. Zoos.

Cocoa beans and daisies: how Swiss chocolate is made photos by author. Warne, 1978. ISBN 0-7232-6156-3 Subj: Food. Foreign lands – Switzerland.

The little goat in the mountains trans. by Michael Bullock; ill. by author. Warne, 1978. ISBN 0-7232-6149-0 Subj: Animals – goats.

The pop rooster ill. by author; English version by Michael Bullock. Scribners, 1975. ISBN 0-224-01113-8 Subj: Activities – singing. Birds – chickens. City.

Allan, Jonathan. *Two by two by two* ill. by author. Dial, 1995. ISBN 0-8037-1838-1 Subj: Animals. Behavior – sharing. Boats, ships. Religion – Noah.

Allan, Nicholas. *The bird* ill. by author. Doubleday, 1998. ISBN 0-385-32573-8 Subj: Behavior – sharing. Birds – pigeons. Emotions – loneliness. Islands. Religion – Noah.

Jesus' Christmas party ill. by author. Random House, 1991. ISBN 0-679-82688-2 Subj: Holidays – Christmas. Religion – Nativity.

The thing that ate Aunt Julia ill. by author. Dial, 1991. ISBN 0-8037-0872-6 Subj: Family life – aunts, uncles. Imagination.

Allard, Harry. *Bumps in the night* ill. by James Marshall. Doubleday, 1979. ISBN 0-385-12943-2 Subj: Animals. Ghosts. Noise, sounds.

The cactus flower bakery ill. by Ned Delaney. HarperCollins, 1991. ISBN 0-06-020047-2 Subj: Animals – armadillos. Careers – bakers. Food. Friendship. Reptiles – snakes.

Crash helmet ill. by Jean-Claude Suarès. Prentice-Hall, 1977. ISBN 0-13-188961-3 Subj: Birds – vultures. Emotions – loneliness. Mummies.

The hummingbirds' day ill. by Betsy Lewin. Houghton Mifflin, 1991. ISBN 0-395-55029-7 Subj: Birds – humming birds. Rhyming text.

I will not go to market today ill. by James Marshall. Dial, 1979. ISBN 0-8037-4020-4 Subj: Birds – chickens. Shopping.

It's so nice to have a wolf around the house ill. by James Marshall. Doubleday, 1977. ISBN 0-385-11301-3 Subj: Crime. Old age. Pets.

May I stay? ill. by F. A. Fitzgerald. Prentice-Hall, 1977. ISBN 0-13-566323-7 Subj: Character traits – questioning. Folk and fairy tales. Foreign lands – Germany. Foreign lands – Norway.

Miss Nelson has a field day ill. by James Marshall. Houghton Mifflin, 1985. ISBN 0-395-36690-9 Subj: Behavior – secrets. Humor. School.

Miss Nelson is back by Harry Allard and James Marshall; ill. by James Marshall. Houghton Mifflin, 1982. ISBN 0-395-32956-6 Subj: Behavior – misbehavior. Careers – teachers. Humor. School.

Miss Nelson is missing! by Harry Allard and James Marshall; ill. by James Marshall. Houghton Mifflin, 1977. ISBN 0-395-25296-2 Subj: Behavior – misbehavior. Careers – teachers. Humor. School.

The Stupids die ill. by James Marshall. Houghton Mifflin, 1981. ISBN 0-395-30347-8 Subj: Behavior – misunderstanding. Humor.

The Stupids have a ball by Harry Allard and James Marshall; ill. by James Marshall. Houghton Mifflin, 1978. ISBN 0-395-26497-9 Subj: Family life. Humor. Parties.

The Stupids step out ill. by James Marshall. Houghton Mifflin, 1974. ISBN 0-395-18513-0 Subj: Activities. Family life. Humor.

The Stupids take off by Harry Allard and James Marshall; ill. by James Marshall. Houghton Mifflin, 1989. ISBN 0-395-50068-0 Subj: Activities – flying. Family life. Humor.

There's a party at Mona's tonight ill. by James Marshall. Doubleday, 1981. ISBN 0-385-15186-1 Subj: Animals – pigs. Behavior – trickery. Humor. Parties.

Three is company (Waechter, Friedrich Karl)

Allbright, Viv. *Ten go hopping* ill. by author. Faber, 1985. ISBN 0-571-13473-4 Subj: Counting, numbers. Cumulative tales.

Allen, Alex B. *see* Heide, Florence Parry

Allen, Allyn. *see* Eberle, Irmengarde

Allen, Frances Charlotte. *Little hippo* ill. by Laura Jean Allen. Putnam, 1971. Subj: Animals – hippopotamuses. Emotions – sadness.

Allen, Gertrude E. *Everyday animals* ill. by author. Houghton Mifflin, 1961. Subj: Animals. Forest, woods. Science.

Allen, Jeffrey. *Bonzini! the tattooed man* ill. by James Marshall. Little, 1976. ISBN 0-316-03427-4 Subj: Circus. Clowns, jesters.

Mary Alice, operator number 9 ill. by James Marshall. Little, 1975. ISBN 0-316-03425-8 Subj: Activities – working. Animals. Birds – ducks. Careers – telephone operators. Telephone. Time.

Mary Alice returns ill. by James Marshall. Little, 1986. ISBN 0-316-03429-0 Subj: Birds – ducks. Careers – telephone operators. Telephone.

Nosey Mrs. Rat ill. by James Marshall. Viking, 1985. ISBN 0-670-80880-6 Subj: Animals. Behavior – gossip. Character traits – curiosity.

The secret life of Mr. Weird ill. by Ned Delaney. Little, 1982. ISBN 0-316-03428-2 Subj: Animals – dogs. Behavior – dissatisfaction. Behavior – seeking better things. Games. Imagination.

Up the steps, down the slide ill. by author. Tambourine, 1992. ISBN 0-688-11784-8 Subj: Animals – cats. Concepts – opposites. Rhyming text.

Allen, Jonathan. *A bad case of animal nonsense* ill. by author. Godine, 1997. ISBN 1-567-92083-7 Subj: Animals. Humor. Poetry.

Big owl, little towel ill. by author. Tambourine, 1992. ISBN 0-688-11783-X Subj: Concepts – size. Format, unusual – board books. Rhyming text.

Mucky moose ill. by author. Macmillan, 1991. ISBN 0-02-700251-9 Subj: Animals – moose. Animals – wolves. Character traits – cleanliness. Senses – smelling.

My cat ill. by author. Dial, 1986. ISBN 0-8037-0292-2 Subj: Animals – cats. Pets.

My dog ill. by author. Gareth Stevens, 1989. ISBN 0-8368-0095-8 Subj: Animals – dogs. Pets.

One with a bun ill. by author. Tambourine, 1992. ISBN 0-688-11781-3 Subj: Counting, numbers. Format, unusual – board books. Rhyming text.

Purple sock, pink sock ill. by author. Tambourine, 1992. ISBN 0-688-11782-1 Subj: Animals – cats. Clothing. Concepts – color. Format, unusual – board books. Rhyming text.

Wake up, Sleeping Beauty ill. by author. Dial, 1997. ISBN 0-8037-2212-5 Subj: Folk and fairy tales. Royalty – princes. Royalty – princesses.

Who's at the door? (The three little pigs)

Allen, Judy. *Eagle* ill. by Tudor Humphries. Candlewick, 1994. ISBN 1-56402-143-2 Subj: Animals – endangered animals. Birds – eagles. Foreign lands – Philippines. Jungle.

Elephant ill. by Tudor Humphries. Candlewick, 1993. ISBN 1-56402-069-X Subj: Animals – elephants. Animals – endangered animals. Foreign lands – Africa.

Panda ill. by Tudor Humphries. Candlewick, 1993. ISBN 1-56402-142-4 Subj: Animals – endangered animals. Animals – pandas. Foreign lands – China.

Seal ill. by Tudor Humphries. Candlewick, 1994. ISBN 1-56402-145-9 Subj: Animals – endangered animals. Animals – seals. Ecology. Foreign lands – Greece.

Tiger ill. by Tudor Humphries. Candlewick, 1992. ISBN 1-56402-083-5 Subj: Animals – endangered animals. Animals – tigers. Foreign lands – China. Sports – hunting.

Whale ill. by Tudor Humphries. Candlewick, 1993. ISBN 1-56402-160-2 Subj: Animals – endangered animals. Animals – whales. Ecology.

What is a wall, after all? ill. by Alan Baron. Candlewick, 1995. ISBN 1-56402-248-8 Subj: Concepts. Rhyming text.

Allen, Laura Jean. *Ottie and the star* ill. by author. HarperCollins, 1979. ISBN 0-06-020108-8 Subj: Animals – otters. Family life. Sea and seashore. Stars.

Rollo and Tweedy and the case of the missing cheese ill. by author. HarperCollins, 1983. ISBN 0-06-020097-9 Subj: Animals – mice. Careers – detectives. Food. Foreign lands – France. Mystery stories.

Rollo and Tweedy and the ghost of Dougal Castle ill. by author. HarperCollins, 1992. ISBN 0-06-020107-X Subj: Careers – detectives. Castles. Ghosts. Mystery stories.

Where is Freddy? ill. by author. HarperCollins, 1986. ISBN 0-06-020099-5 Subj: Activities – flying. Behavior – lost. Careers – detectives. Mystery stories.

Allen, Linda. *The giant who had no heart* ill. by author. Philomel, 1988. ISBN 0-399-21446-1 Subj: Folk and fairy tales. Foreign lands – Norway. Giants.

Mr. Simkin's grandma ill. by Loretta Lustig. Morrow, 1979. ISBN 0-688-32191-7 Subj: Family life – grandmothers. Family life – grandparents. Humor.

The mouse bride ill. by author. Putnam, 1992. ISBN 0-399-22136-0 Subj: Animals – mice. Folk and fairy tales. Foreign lands – Finland. Royalty – princesses.

Mrs. Simkin's bed ill. by Loretta Lustig. Morrow, 1980. ISBN 0-688-32233-6 Subj: Animals. Furniture – beds. Humor.

Allen, Marjorie N. *Changes* by Marjorie N. Allen and Shelley Rotner; photos by Shelley Rotner. Macmillan, 1991. ISBN 0-02-700252-7 Subj: Nature. Rhyming text.

One, two, three – ah-choo! ill. by Dick Gackenbach. Coward, 1980. ISBN 0-698-30718-6 Subj: Animals. Humor. Pets.

Allen, Martha Dickson. *Real life monsters* ill. by author. Prentice-Hall, 1979. ISBN 0-13-766568-7 Subj: Animals. Monsters. Science.

Allen, Pamela. *Belinda* ill. by author. Viking, 1992. ISBN 0-670-84372-5 Subj: Animals – bulls, cows. Careers – farmers.

Bertie and the bear ill. by author. Coward, 1984. ISBN 0-698-20600-2 Subj: Activities – dancing. Animals – bears. Animals – dogs. Noise, sounds. Royalty.

Fancy that! ill. by author. Orchard, 1988. ISBN 0-531-08363-2 Subj: Birds – chickens. Farms.

Hidden treasure ill. by author. Putnam, 1987. Orig. published as Herbert and Harry. ISBN 0-399-21427-5 Subj: Behavior – greed. Behavior – hiding things. Sea and seashore. Sibling rivalry.

I wish I had a pirate suit ill. by author. Viking, 1990. ISBN 0-670-82475-5 Subj: Activities – playing. Behavior – wishing. Imagination. Pirates.

A lion in the night ill. by author. Putnam, 1986. ISBN 0-399-21203-5 Subj: Animals – lions. Babies. Behavior – wishing. Imagination. Royalty.

Mr. Archimedes' bath ill. by author. Lothrop, 1980. ISBN 0-688-51919-9 Subj: Activities – bathing. Animals. Humor. Science.

Mr. McGee ill. by author. Nelson, 1987. ISBN 0-17-006908-7 Subj: Humor. Rhyming text.

My cat Maisie ill. by author. Viking, 1991. ISBN 0-670-83251-0 Subj: Animals – cats. Friendship. Pets.

Who sank the boat? ill. by author. Coward, 1983. ISBN 0-698-20576-6 Subj: Animals. Boats, ships. Rhyming text. Science.

Allen, Robert. *Numbers: a first counting book* photos by Mottke Weissman. Platt, 1968. Subj: Counting, numbers.

Round and square ill. by Philippe Thomas. Platt, 1965. Subj: Concepts – shape.

Ten little babies count by Janet Martin [pseud.]; photos by Michael Watson. St. Martin's, 1986. ISBN 0-312-79112-7 Subj: Babies. Clothing. Counting, numbers. Family life – new sibling. Format, unusual – board books.

Ten little babies dress by Janet Martin [pseud.]; photos by Michael Watson. St. Martin's, 1986. ISBN 0-312-79113-5 Subj: Babies. Clothing. Counting, numbers. Format, unusual – board books.

Ten little babies eat by Janet Martin [pseud.]; photos by Michael Watson. St. Martin's, 1986. ISBN 0-312-79114-3 Subj: Anatomy. Babies. Counting, numbers. Food. Format, unusual – board books. Rhyming text.

Ten little babies play: a book of colors by Janet Martin [pseud.]; photos by Michael Watson. St. Martin's, 1986. ISBN 0-312-79115-1 Subj: Activities – playing. Babies. Concepts – color. Counting, numbers. Format, unusual – board books.

The zoo book: a child's world of animals photos by Peter Sahula. Platt, 1968. Subj: Animals. Zoos.

Allen, Thomas B. (Thomas Burt). *On grandaddy's farm* ill. by author. Knopf, 1989. ISBN 0-394-99613-5 Subj: Family life. Farms.

Where children live ill. by author. Prentice-Hall, 1980. ISBN 0-13-957126-4 Subj: Foreign lands.

Allende, Ricardo. *Princesa and Friskie* (Johnson, Diana F.)

Aller, Susan B. *Emma and the night dogs* ill. by Marni Backer. Albert Whitman, 1997. ISBN 0-8075-1993-6 Subj: Animals – dogs. Behavior – lost. Character traits – helpfulness.

Alley, R. W. (Robert W.). *Seven fables from Æsop* (Æsop)

Alleyne, Ellen. *see* Rossetti, Christina Georgina

Allingham, William. *The fairies* ill. by Michael Hague. Holt, 1989. ISBN 0-8050-1003-3 Subj: Fairies. Poetry.

Allington, Richard L. *Autumn* by Richard L. Allington and Kathleen Krull; ill. by Bruce Bond. Raintree, 1985. ISBN 0-8172-1343-0 Subj: Seasons – fall. Weather.

Colors ill. by Noel Spangler. Raintree, 1985. ISBN 0-8172-1280-9 Subj: Concepts – color.

Feelings by Richard L. Allington and Kathleen Cowles; ill. by Brian Cody. Raintree, 1985. ISBN 0-8172-1295-7 Subj: Activities. Emotions.

Hearing by Richard L. Allington and Kathleen Cowles; ill. by Wayne Dober. Raintree, 1985. ISBN 0-8172-1291-4 Subj: Activities. Senses – hearing.

Letters ill. by Tom Garcia. Raintree, 1985. ISBN 0-8172-1384-8 Subj: ABC books. Games. Language.

Looking by Richard L. Allington and Kathleen Cowles; ill. by Bill Bober. Raintree, 1981. ISBN 0-8172-1290-6 Subj: Activities. Senses – seeing.

Measuring by Richard L. Allington and Kathleen Krull; ill. by Noel Spangler. Raintree, 1985. ISBN 0-8172-1389-9 Subj: Concepts – measurement.

Numbers ill. by Tom Garcia. Raintree, 1985. ISBN 0-8172-1278-7 Subj: Counting, numbers.

Opposites ill. by Eulala Conner. Raintree, 1985. ISBN 0-8172-1279-5 Subj: Concepts – opposites.

Reading by Richard L. Allington and Kathleen Krull; ill. by Joel Naprstek. Raintree, 1985. ISBN 0-8172-1322-8 Subj: Activities – reading.

Science by Richard L. Allington and Kathleen Krull; ill. by James Teason. Raintree, 1985. ISBN 0-8172-1387-2 Subj: Science.

Shapes ill. by Lois Ehlert. Raintree, 1985. ISBN 0-8172-1277-9 Subj: Concepts – shape. Concepts – size.

Smelling by Richard L. Allington and Kathleen Cowles; ill. by Rick Thrun. Raintree, 1981. ISBN 0-8172-1293-0 Subj: Activities. Senses – smelling.

Spring by Richard L. Allington and Kathleen Krull; ill. by Lynn Uhde. Raintree, 1981. ISBN 0-8172-1342-2 Subj: Seasons – spring. Weather.

Summer by Richard L. Allington and Kathleen Krull; ill. by Dennis Hockerman. Raintree, 1985. ISBN 0-8172-1341-4 Subj: Seasons – summer. Weather.

Talking by Richard L. Allington and Kathleen Krull; ill. by Rick Thrun. Raintree, 1985. ISBN 0-8172-2492-0 Subj: Communication. Language. Science.

Tasting by Richard L. Allington and Kathleen Cowles; ill. by Noel Spangler. Raintree, 1985. ISBN 0-8172-1292-2 Subj: Activities. Senses – tasting.

Thinking by Richard L. Allington and Kathleen Krull; ill. by Tom Garcia. Raintree, 1985. ISBN 0-8172-1319-8 Subj: Problem solving.

Time by Richard L. Allington and Kathleen Krull; ill. by Yoshi Miyake. Raintree, 1985. ISBN 0-8172-1388-0 Subj: Time.

Touching by Richard L. Allington and Kathleen Cowles; ill. by Yoshi Miyake. Raintree, 1985. ISBN 0-8172-1294-9 Subj: Activities. Senses – touching.

Winter by Richard L. Allington and Kathleen Krull; ill. by John Wallner. Raintree, 1985. ISBN 0-8172-1340-6 Subj: Seasons – winter. Weather.

Words by Richard L. Allington and Kathleen Krull; ill. by Ray Cruz. Raintree, 1982. ISBN 0-8172-1385-6 Subj: Communication. Language.

Writing by Richard L. Allington and Kathleen Krull; ill. by Yoshi Miyake. Raintree, 1985. ISBN 0-8175-1321-X Subj: Activities – writing.

Allinson, Beverley. *Effie* ill. by Barbara Reid. Scholastic, 1991. ISBN 0-590-44045-4 Subj: Animals – elephants. Character traits – being different. Friendship. Insects – ants.

Allison, Alida. *The toddler's potty book* by Alida Allison and Paula Sapphire. Price Stern Sloan, 1981, 1979. ISBN 0-8431-0673-5 Subj: Behavior – growing up. Toilet training.

Allison, Diane Worfolk. *In window eight, the moon is late* ill. by author. Little, 1988. ISBN 0-316-03435-5 Subj: Bedtime. Dreams. Rhyming text.

This is the key to the kingdom ill. by reteller. Little, 1992. ISBN 0-316-03432-0 Subj: Ethnic groups in the U.S. – African Americans. Flowers. Nursery rhymes.

Allred, Mary. *Grandmother Poppy and the children's tea party* ill. by Paul Behrens. Broadman & Holman, 1984. ISBN 0-8054-4292-8 Subj: Family life – grandmothers. Parties.

Grandmother Poppy and the funny-looking bird ill. by Paul Behrens. Broadman & Holman, 1981. ISBN 0-8054-4269-3 Subj: Birds. Character traits – kindness to animals. Family life – grandmothers.

Alper, Ann Fitzerald. *Harry McNairy, Tooth Fairy* ill. by Bridget Starr Taylor. Albert Whitman, 1998. ISBN 0-8075-3166-9 Subj: Fairies. Teeth.

Alphabestiary: animal poems from A to Z sel. by Jane Yolen; ill. by Allen Eitzen. Boyds Mills, 1995. ISBN 1-56397-222-0 Subj: Animals. Poetry.

Alphaus, N. Y. *see* Rubin, Cynthia Elyce

Althea. *Castle life* ill. by Maureen Galvani. Merrimack, 1980. Subj: Middle Ages.

Jeremy Mouse and cat ill. by author. Merrimack, 1980. ISBN 0-8659-2562-3 Subj: Animals – cats. Animals – mice. Behavior – trickery.

Altman, Linda Jacobs. *Amelia's road* ill. by Enrique O. Sánchez. Lee & Low, 1993. ISBN 1-880000-04-0 Subj: Activities – working. Behavior – seeking better things. Careers – migrant workers. Family life. Homes, houses. Trees.

Altman, Susan. *Followers of the north star: rhymes about African American heroes, heroines, and historical times* by Susan Altman and Susan Lechner; ill. by Byron Wooden. Childrens Pr., 1993. ISBN 0-516-05151-2 Subj: Ethnic groups in the U.S. – African Americans. Poetry. U.S. history.

Ambler, C. Gifford (Christopher Gifford). *Ten little foxhounds.* Childrens Pr., 1968. Subj: Animals – dogs. Counting, numbers. Foreign lands – England. Rhyming text.

Ambrus, Gyozo Laszlo. *see* Ambrus, Victor G.

Ambrus, Victor G. *Brave soldier Janosch* ill. by author. Harcourt, 1967. Subj: Careers – military. Foreign lands – Hungary. War.

Count, Dracula ill. by author. Crown, 1992. ISBN 0-517-58969-9 Subj: Counting, numbers. Monsters. Pets.

Country wedding ill. by author. Addison-Wesley, 1975. ISBN 0-20-100197-7 Subj: Animals – foxes. Animals – wolves. Food. Weddings.

Grandma, Felix, and Mustapha Biscuit ill. by author. Morrow, 1982. ISBN 0-688-01287-6 Subj: Animals – cats. Animals – hamsters. Family life – grandmothers. Humor.

The little cockerel ill. by author. Harcourt, 1968. Subj: Birds – chickens. Character traits – perseverance. Folk and fairy tales.

Mishka ill. by author. Warne, 1978. ISBN 0-7232-6150-4 Subj: Animals – elephants. Character traits – perseverance. Circus. Music.

Never laugh at bears: a Transylvanian folk tale ill. by author. Peter Bedrick, 1992. ISBN 0-8722-6465-3 Subj: Animals – bears. Careers – farmers. Folk and fairy tales.

Santa Claus takes off ill. by Glenys Ambrus. Oxford Univ. Pr., 1991. ISBN 0-19-279878-2 Subj: Holidays – Christmas. Santa Claus.

The seven skinny goats ill. by author. Harcourt, 1969. Subj: Activities – dancing. Animals – goats. Folk and fairy tales. Music.

Son of Dracula ill. by author. Oxford Univ. Pr., 1990. ISBN 0-19-279813-8 Subj: Family life – sons. Monsters. School.

The Sultan's bath ill. by author. Oxford Univ. Pr., 1971. ISBN 0-1927-9677-1 Subj: Activities – bathing. Folk and fairy tales. Foreign lands – India. Royalty – sultans.

The three poor tailors ill. by author. Harcourt, 1966. Subj: Activities – whistling. Animals – goats. Careers – tailors. Folk and fairy tales. Foreign lands – Hungary. Poverty.

What's the time, Dracula? ill. by author. Crown, 1992. ISBN 0-517-58970-2 Subj: Careers – dentists. Clocks, watches. Monsters. Time.

Amenta, Charles A. (Charles Anthony). *Russell is extra special: a book about autism for children* written and ill. by Charles A. Amenta III. Magination Pr., 1992. ISBN 0-94535-443-6 Subj: Handicaps – autism.

Amery, H. *At the zoo* ill. by author. Educational Development, 1984. ISBN 0-86020-854-0 Subj: Animals. Zoos.

The farm picture book ill. by author. Educational Development, 1988. ISBN 0-7460-0128-2 Subj: Animals. Farms.

Going to the fair ill. by author. Educational Development, 1987. ISBN 0-88110-262-8 Subj: Fairs.

Goldilocks and the three bears (The three bears)

The three little pigs (The three little pigs)

The zoo picture book ill. by author. Educational Development, 1988. ISBN 0-7460-0127-4 Subj: Animals. Format, unusual. Zoos.

Ames, Mildred. *The wonderful box* ill. by Richard Cuffari. Dutton, 1978. ISBN 0-525-43200-0 Subj: Character traits – curiosity. Problem solving.

Ames, Noel. *see* Barrows, Marjorie Wescott

Ames, Rose. *see* Wyler, Rose

Ammon, Richard. *An Amish Christmas* ill. by Pamela Patrick. Atheneum, 1996. ISBN 0-689-80377-X Subj: Holidays – Christmas. Religion.

An Amish wedding ill. by Pamela Patrick. Atheneum, 1998. ISBN 0-689-81677-4 Subj: Ethnic groups in the U.S. – Amish. Weddings.

Trains at work photos by Darrell Peterson and Richard Ammon. Atheneum, 1993. ISBN 0-689-31740-9 Subj: Trains.

Amoit, Pierre. *Bijou, the little bear.* Coward, 1950. Subj: Animals – bears. Circus. Clowns, jesters.

Amoore, Susannah. *Motley the cat* ill. by Mary Fedden. Viking, 1997. ISBN 0-670-87730-1 Subj: Animals – cats. Mystery stories.

Amoss, Berthe. *It's not your birthday* ill. by author. HarperCollins, 1966. Subj: Birthdays. Sibling rivalry.

Old Hannibal and the hurricane ill. by author. Walt Disney, 1991. ISBN 1-56282-098-2 Subj: Boats, ships. Sea and seashore. Weather – storms.

Tom in the middle ill. by author. HarperCollins, 1988. ISBN 0-06-020064-2 Subj: Family life – brothers. Sibling rivalry.

What did you lose, Santa? ill. by author. Harper-Collins, 1987. ISBN 0-694-00197-X Subj: Behavior – losing things. Holidays – Christmas. Santa Claus.

Amper, Thomas. *Booker T. Washington* ill. by Jeni Reeves. Carolrhoda, 1998. ISBN 1-57505-094-3 Subj: Careers – teachers. Ethnic groups in the U.S. – African Americans. School.

Anastasio, Dina. *Baby Piggy and giant bubble* ill. by Tom Cooke. Muppet Pr., 1986. ISBN 0-8713-5096-3 Subj: Bubbles. Imagination. Puppets. Rhyming text.

Pass the peas, please: a book of manners ill. by Katy Keck Arnsteen. Warner, 1988. ISBN 1-55782-021-X Subj: Etiquette. Rhyming text.

Anaya, Rudolfo A. *Farolitos for Abuelo* ill. by Edward Gonzales. Hyperion, 1998. ISBN 0-7868-2186-8 Subj: Death. Ethnic groups in the U.S. – Mexican Americans. Family life – grandfathers. Holidays – Christmas.

Maya's children: the story of La Llorona ill. by Maria Baca. Hyperion, 1997. ISBN 0-7868-2124-8 Subj: Folk and fairy tales. Foreign lands – Central America. Foreign lands – Mexico.

Anchondo, Mary. *How we came to the fifth world: a creation story from Ancient Mexico* (Rohmer, Harriet)

Ancona, George. *Barrio: José's neighborhood* ill. by author. Harcourt, 1998. ISBN 0-15-201049-1 Subj: Communities, neighborhoods. Ethnic groups in the U.S. – Hispanic Americans.

Dancing is ill. by author. Dutton, 1981. ISBN 0-525-28490-7 Subj: Activities – dancing.

Handtalk: an ABC of finger spelling and sign language (Charlip, Remy)

Handtalk zoo by George and Mary Beth Ancona; photos by George Ancona. Macmillan, 1989. ISBN 0-02-700801-0 Subj: Animals. Communication. Handicaps – deafness. Language. Senses – hearing. Time. Zoos.

Helping out photos by author. Clarion, 1985. ISBN 0-89919-278-5 Subj: Character traits – helpfulness.

I feel: a picture book of emotions ill. by author. Dutton, 1977. ISBN 0-525-32525-5 Subj: Emotions.

It's a baby! ill. by author. Dutton, 1979. ISBN 0-525-32598-0 Subj: Babies.

Let's dance! ill. by author. Morrow, 1998. ISBN 0-688-16212-6 Subj: Activities – dancing.

Pablo remembers: the fiesta of the Day of the Dead ill. by author. Lothrop, 1993. ISBN 0-688-11250-1 Subj: Fairs. Foreign lands – Mexico. Holidays – Day of the Dead.

Ricardo's day photos by author. Scholastic, 1995. ISBN 0-590-29257-9 Subj: School.

Ancona, Mary Beth. *Handtalk: an ABC of finger spelling and sign language* (Charlip, Remy)

Handtalk zoo (Ancona, George)

Anders, Rebecca. *A look at death* photos by Maria S. Forrai; foreword by Robert C. Slater. Lerner, 1978. ISBN 0-822-51308-0 Subj: Death.

A look at prejudice and understanding ill. by Maria S. Forrai. Lerner, 1976. ISBN 0-8225-1306-4 Subj: Prejudice.

Andersen, H. C. (Hans Christian). *The dinosaur's new clothes* (Goode, Diane)

The emperor and the nightingale retold and ill. by Meilo So. Bradbury, 1992. ISBN 0-02-786045-0 Subj: Birds – nightingales. Character traits – freedom. Folk and fairy tales. Foreign lands – China.

The emperor and the nightingale ill. by James Watling. Troll, 1979. ISBN 0-89375-112-X Subj: Birds – nightingales. Character traits – freedom. Folk and fairy tales. Foreign lands – China.

The emperor's new clothes ill. by Angela Barrett. Candlewick, 1997. ISBN 0-7636-0119-5 Subj: Character traits – pride. Character traits – vanity. Clothing. Folk and fairy tales. Imagination. Royalty – emperors.

The emperor's new clothes ill. by Erik Blegvad. Harcourt, 1959. Translation of Kejserens nye klæder by Erik Blegvad. Subj: Character traits – pride. Character traits – vanity. Clothing. Folk and fairy tales. Humor. Imagination. Royalty – emperors.

The emperor's new clothes ill. by Virginia Lee Burton. Houghton Mifflin, 1949. Translation of Kejserens nye klæder. Subj: Character traits – pride. Character traits – vanity. Clothing. Folk and fairy tales. Humor. Imagination. Royalty – emperors.

The emperor's new clothes retold by Riki Levinson; ill. by Robert Byrd. Dutton, 1991. ISBN 0-525-44611-7 Subj: Animals. Character traits – pride. Character traits – vanity. Clothing. Folk and fairy tales. Humor. Imagination. Royalty – emperors.

The emperor's new clothes adapt. by Jean Van Leeuwen; ill. by Jack and Irene Delano. Random House, 1971. Translation of Kejserens nye klæder. Text adapted from Hans Christian Andersen and other sources by Jean Van Leeuwen. ISBN 0-394-82105-4 Subj: Character traits – pride. Character traits – vanity. Clothing. Folk and fairy tales. Humor. Imagination. Royalty – emperors.

The emperor's new clothes ill. by Hélène Desputeaux. Gallery Books, 1984. ISBN 0-8317-2736-5 Subj: Character traits – pride. Character traits – vanity. Clothing. Folk and fairy tales. Humor. Imagination. Royalty – emperors.

The emperor's new clothes ill. by Birte Dietz; trans. by M. R. James; adapt. by Jean Van Leeuwen. Van Nostrand, 1972. Translation of Kejserens nye klæder. Subj: Character traits – pride. Character traits – vanity. Clothing. Folk and fairy tales. Humor. Imagination. Royalty – emperors.

The emperor's new clothes adapt. by Anthea Bell; ill. by Dorothée Duntze. Holt, 1986. ISBN 0-8050-0010-0 Subj: Character traits – pride. Character traits – vanity. Clothing. Folk and fairy tales. Humor. Imagination. Royalty – emperors.

The emperor's new clothes ill. by Dorothée Duntze. North-South, 1997. ISBN 1-55858-689-X Subj: Character traits – pride. Character traits – vanity. Clothing. Folk and fairy tales. Imagination. Royalty – emperors.

The emperor's new clothes ill. by Pamela Baldwin Ford. Troll, 1979. Translation of Kejserens nye klæder. ISBN 0-8937-5132-4 Subj: Character traits – pride. Character traits – vanity. Clothing. Folk and fairy tales. Humor. Imagination. Royalty – emperors.

The emperor's new clothes a new English version by Ruth Belov Gross; ill. by Jack Kent. Four Winds, 1977. Adapt. of Kejserens nye klæder by Ruth Belov Gross. ISBN 0-590-07502-0 Subj: Character traits – pride. Character traits – vanity. Clothing. Folk and fairy tales. Humor. Imagination. Royalty – emperors.

The emperor's new clothes ill. by Monika Laimgruber. Addison-Wesley, 1973. Translation of Kejserens nye klæder. Subj: Character traits – pride. Character traits – vanity. Clothing. Folk and fairy tales. Humor. Imagination. Royalty – emperors.

The emperor's new clothes ill. by Anne F. Rockwell. Crowell, 1982. Translation of Kejserens nye klæder by H. W. Dulcken. ISBN 0-690-04149-7 Subj: Character traits – pride. Character traits – vanity. Clothing. Folk and fairy tales. Humor. Imagination. Royalty – emperors.

The emperor's new clothes adapt. and ill. by Janet Stevens. Holiday, 1985. ISBN 0-8234-0566-4 Subj: Character traits – pride. Character traits – vanity. Clothing. Folk and fairy tales. Humor. Imagination. Royalty – emperors.

The emperor's new clothes adapt. by Eric Metaxas; ill. by Robert Van Nutt. Minibook ed. Simon & Schuster, 1995. ISBN 0-689-80058-4 Subj: Character traits – pride. Character traits – vanity. Clothing. Folk and fairy tales. Format, unusual. Imagination. Royalty – emperors.

The emperor's new clothes ill. by Nadine Bernard Westcott. Little, 1984. Subj: Character traits – pride. Character traits – vanity. Clothing. Folk and fairy tales. Humor. Imagination. Royalty – emperors.

The emperor's nightingale retold by Teddy Slater; ill. from the Disney archives. Walt Disney, 1992. ISBN 1-56282-134-2 Subj: Birds – nightingales. Character traits – freedom. Folk and fairy tales. Foreign lands – China. Royalty – emperors.

The emperor's nightingale trans. by Erik Haugaard; ill. by Georges Lemoine. Schocken, 1981. ISBN 0-8052-3780-1 Subj: Birds – nightingales. Character traits – freedom. Folk and fairy tales. Foreign lands – China. Royalty – emperors.

The fir tree ill. by Stephanie Britt. HarperCollins, 1988. ISBN 0-60-020078-2 Subj: Folk and fairy tales. Holidays – Christmas. Trees.

The fir tree trans. by H. W. Dulcken; ill. by Nancy Ekholm Burkert. HarperCollins, 1970. Tr. of Grantræet. ISBN 0-8249-8389-0 Subj: Folk and fairy tales. Holidays – Christmas. Trees.

The fir tree adapt. and ill. by Diane Goode. Random House, 1988. ISBN 0-394-81941-1 Subj: Folk and fairy tales. Holidays – Christmas. Trees.

The fir tree adapt. by Marcel Imsand; ill. by Rita Marshall. Creative Ed., 1983. ISBN 0-87191-949-4 Subj: Folk and fairy tales. Holidays – Christmas. Trees.

The fir tree adapt. and ill. by Bernadette Watts. North-South, 1990. ISBN 1-55858-093-X Subj: Folk and fairy tales. Holidays – Christmas. Trees.

It's perfectly true! adapt. and ill. by Janet Stevens. Holiday, 1987. ISBN 0-8234-0672-5 Subj: Behavior – gossip. Character traits – vanity. Death. Folk and fairy tales.

Little Ida's flowers ill. by Linda Allen. Putnam, 1990. ISBN 0-399-21571-9 Subj: Flowers. Folk and fairy tales.

The little match girl ill. by Rachel Isadora. Putnam, 1987. Translation of Den lille pige med svovlstikkeren. ISBN 0-399-21336-8 Subj: Death. Folk and fairy tales. Holidays – New Year's. Homeless. Poverty.

The little match girl ill. by Blair Lent. Houghton Mifflin, 1968. Translation of Den lille pige med svovlstikkerne. ISBN 1-56397-470-3 Subj: Death. Folk and fairy tales. Holidays – New Year's. Homeless. Poverty.

The little match girl ill. by Jerry Pinkney. Fogelman, 1999. ISBN 0-8037-2314-8 Subj: Death. Folk and fairy tales. Holidays – New Year's. Homeless. Poverty.

The little mermaid trans. by Eva Le Gallienne; ill. by Edward Frascino. HarperCollins, 1971. ISBN 0-06-023783-X Subj: Folk and fairy tales. Mythical creatures – mermaids, mermen.

The little mermaid ill. by Michael Hague. Holt, 1993. ISBN 0-8050-1010-6 Subj: Folk and fairy tales. Mythical creatures – mermaids, mermen.

The little mermaid retold and ill. by Rachel Isadora. Putnam, 1998. ISBN 0-399-22813-6 Subj: Folk and fairy tales. Mythical creatures – mermaids, mermen.

The little mermaid adapt. by Anthea Bell; ill. by Chihiro Iwasaki. Alphabet Pr., 1984. Adapt. of Den lille havfrue. ISBN 0-907234-59-3 Subj: Folk and fairy tales. Mythical creatures – mermaids, mermen.

The little mermaid ill. by Dorothy Pulis Lathrop. Macmillan, 1939. Subj: Folk and fairy tales. Mythical creatures – mermaids, mermen.

The little mermaid retold by Deborah Hautzig; ill. by Darcy May. Random House, 1991. ISBN 0-679-92241-5 Subj: Folk and fairy tales. Mythical creatures – mermaids, mermen.

The little mermaid ill. by Josef Palecek. Faber, 1981. Translation of Den lille havfrue by M. R. James. ISBN 0-571-11847-X Subj: Folk and fairy tales. Mythical creatures – mermaids, mermen.

The little mermaid adapt. by Freya Littledale; ill. by Daniel San Souci. Scholastic, 1986. ISBN 0-590-33590-1 Subj: Folk and fairy tales. Mythical creatures – mermaids, mermen.

The little mermaid retold and ill. by Katie Thamer Treherne. Harcourt, 1989. ISBN 0-15-246320-8 Subj: Folk and fairy tales. Mythical creatures – mermaids, mermen.

The nightingale ill. by Harold Berson. Lippincott, 1962. Subj: Birds – nightingales. Character traits – freedom. Folk and fairy tales. Foreign lands – China. Royalty – emperors.

The nightingale trans. by Eva Le Gallienne; ill. by Nancy Ekholm Burkert. HarperCollins, 1965. Subj: Birds – nightingales. Character traits – freedom. Folk and fairy tales. Foreign lands – China. Royalty – emperors.

The nightingale ill. by Alison Claire Darke. Doubleday, 1989. ISBN 0-385-26082-2 Subj: Birds – nightingales. Character traits – freedom. Folk and fairy tales. Foreign lands – China.

The nightingale adapt. by Anna Bier; ill. by Demi. Harcourt, 1985. Adapt. of Nattergalen. ISBN 0-15-257427-1 Subj: Birds – nightingales. Character traits – freedom. Folk and fairy tales. Foreign lands – China. Royalty – emperors.

The nightingale adapt. by Alan Benjamin; ill. by Beni Montresor. Crown, 1985. Adapt. of Nattergalen. ISBN 0-517-55211-6 Subj: Birds – nightingales. Character traits – freedom. Folk and fairy tales. Foreign lands – China. Royalty – emperors.

The nightingale trans. by Naomi Lewis; ill. by Josef Palecek. North-South, 1990. ISBN 1-55858-090-5 Subj: Birds – nightingales. Character traits – freedom. Folk and fairy tales. Foreign lands – China.

The nightingale retold by Michael Bedard; ill. by Regolo Ricci. Houghton Mifflin, 1992. ISBN 0-395-60735-3 Subj: Birds – nightingales. Character traits – freedom. Folk and fairy tales. Foreign lands – China. Royalty – emperors.

The nightingale retold by Dom DeLuise; ill. by Christopher Santoro. Simon & Schuster, 1998. ISBN 0-689-81749-5 Subj: Activities – cooking. Birds – nightingales. Character traits – freedom.

Folk and fairy tales. Food. Foreign lands – China. Royalty – emperors.

The nightingale ill. by Lisbeth Zwerger; trans. from Danish by Anthea Bell. North-South, 1999. Adapt. of Nattergalen. ISBN 0-7358-1118-0 Subj: Birds – nightingales. Character traits – freedom. Folk and fairy tales. Foreign lands – China. Royalty – emperors.

The old man is always right ill. by Feodor Rojankovsky. HarperCollins, 1940. Subj: Activities – trading. Folk and fairy tales. Humor.

The princess and the pea retold by Harriet Ziefert; ill. by Emily Bolam. Viking, 1996. ISBN 0-670-86054-9 Subj: Folk and fairy tales. Royalty – princesses. Sleep.

The princess and the pea ill. by Dorothée Duntze. Holt, 1985. ISBN 0-8050-0170-0 Subj: Folk and fairy tales. Royalty – princesses. Sleep.

The princess and the pea ill. by Dick Gackenbach. Macmillan, 1983. ISBN 0-02-735800-3 Subj: Folk and fairy tales. Royalty – princesses. Sleep.

The princess and the pea ill. by Paul Galdone. Seabury Pr., 1978. Translation of Den prindsessen paa aerten. ISBN 0-8164-3202-3 Subj: Folk and fairy tales. Royalty – princesses. Sleep.

The princess and the pea ill. by Camille Semelet. Abbeville, 1999. ISBN 0-7892-0515-7 Subj: Folk and fairy tales. Royalty – princesses. Sleep.

The princess and the pea adapt. and ill. by Janet Stevens. Holiday, 1982. ISBN 0-8234-0442-0 Subj: Folk and fairy tales. Royalty – princesses. Sleep.

The princess and the pea retold and ill. by Suçie Stevenson. Doubleday, 1992. ISBN 0-385-41376-9 Subj: Folk and fairy tales. Royalty – princesses. Sleep.

The princess and the pea trans. by Anthea Bell; ill. by Eve Tharlet. Picture Book Studio, 1987. ISBN 0-88708-052-9 Subj: Folk and fairy tales. Royalty – princesses. Sleep.

The red shoes trans. from Danish by Anthea Bell; ill. by Chihiro Iwasaki. Alphabet Pr., 1983. ISBN 0-907234-26-7 Subj: Activities – dancing. Angels. Character traits – pride. Clothing – shoes.

The snow queen trans. by Naomi Lewis; ill. by Angela Barrett. Candlewick, 1993. ISBN 1-56402-215-3 Subj: Character traits – bravery. Emotions – love. Folk and fairy tales.

The snow queen ill. by Toma Bogdanovic. Scroll Pr., n.d. An adapt. of Sneedronningen by Naomi Lewis. Subj: Character traits – bravery. Emotions – love. Folk and fairy tales. Foreign lands – Denmark.

The snow queen ill. by June Atkin Corwin. Atheneum, 1968. ISBN 0-689-30018-2 Subj: Character traits – bravery. Emotions – love. Folk and fairy tales.

The snow queen sel. and ed. by Neil Philip; ill. by Sally Holmes. Lothrop, 1989. ISBN 0-688-09048-6 Subj: Character traits – bravery. Emotions – love. Folk and fairy tales.

The snow queen adapt. by Amy Ehrlich; ill. by Susan Jeffers. Dial, 1982. ISBN 0-8037-8029-X Subj: Character traits – bravery. Emotions – love. Folk and fairy tales.

The snow queen adapt. by Naomi Lewis; ill. by Errol Le Cain. Viking, 1979. ISBN 0-670-65378-0 Subj: Character traits – bravery. Emotions – love. Folk and fairy tales.

The snow queen: a fairy tale adapt. by Anthea Bell; ill. by Bernadette Watts. Holt, 1987. First pub. in Sweden under the title Die Schneekönigin. ISBN 0-8050-0485-8 Subj: Character traits – bravery. Emotions. Folk and fairy tales.

The snow queen trans. by Eva Le Gallienne; ill. by Arieh Zeldich. HarperCollins, 1985. ISBN 0-06-023695-7 Subj: Character traits – bravery. Emotions – love. Folk and fairy tales.

The snow queen and other stories from Hans Andersen ill. by Edmund Dulac. Doubleday, 1976. ISBN 0-385-11678-0 Subj: Folk and fairy tales.

The steadfast tin soldier ill. by Thomas di Grazia. Prentice-Hall, 1981. ISBN 0-13-846295-X Subj: Folk and fairy tales. Toys – soldiers.

The steadfast tin soldier ill. by Paul Galdone. Houghton Mifflin, 1979. Translation of Den standhaftige tinsoldat. ISBN 0-395-28964-5 Subj: Folk and fairy tales. Toys – soldiers.

The steadfast tin soldier retold and ill. by Rachel Isadora. Putnam, 1996. ISBN 0-399-22676-1 Subj: Folk and fairy tales. Toys – soldiers.

The steadfast tin soldier adapt. by Joel Tuber; ill. by David Jorgensen. Knopf, 1986. ISBN 0-394-88402-7 Subj: Folk and fairy tales. Toys – soldiers.

The steadfast tin soldier ill. by Monika Laimgruber. Atheneum, 1971. Translation of Den standhaftige tinsoldat. Subj: Folk and fairy tales. Toys – soldiers.

The steadfast tin soldier trans. from Danish by Naomi Lewis; ill. by P. J. Lynch. Harcourt, 1992. ISBN 0-15-200599-4 Subj: Folk and fairy tales. Toys – soldiers.

The steadfast tin soldier retold by Tor Seidler; ill. by Fred Marcellino. HarperCollins, 1992. ISBN 0-06-205001-X Subj: Folk and fairy tales. Toys – soldiers.

The steadfast tin soldier ill. by Alain Vaës. Little, 1983. Translation of Den standhaftige tinsoldat. ISBN 0-316-03949-7 Subj: Folk and fairy tales. Toys – soldiers.

The swineherd ill. by Erik Blegvad. Harcourt, 1958. Translation of Den svinedrengen by Erik Blegvad. Subj: Character traits – cleverness. Character traits – selfishness. Folk and fairy tales.

The swineherd ill. by Dorothée Duntze. Holt, 1987. Translation of Den svinedrengen by Naomi Lewis. ISBN 0-8050-0232-4 Subj: Character traits –

cleverness. Character traits – selfishness. Folk and fairy tales. Royalty.

The swineherd adapt. and ill. by Deborah Hahn. Lothrop, 1991. ISBN 0-688-10053-8 Subj: Character traits – cleverness. Character traits – selfishness. Folk and fairy tales.

The swineherd trans. from Danish by Anthea Bell; ill. by Lisbeth Zwerger. Morrow, 1982. Tr. of Den svinedrengen. ISBN 0-688-00930-1 Subj: Character traits – cleverness. Character traits – selfishness. Folk and fairy tales.

Thumbelina trans. by R. P. Keigwin; ill. by Adrienne Adams. Scribners, 1961. Tr. of Tommelise. Subj: Character traits – smallness. Folk and fairy tales.

Thumbelina retold by James Riordan; ill. by Wayne Anderson. Putnam, 1991. ISBN 0-399-21756-8 Subj: Character traits – smallness. Folk and fairy tales.

Thumbelina retold by Jane Falloon; ill. by Emma Chichester Clark. Margaret K. McElderry, 1996. ISBN 0-689-81181-0 Subj: Character traits – smallness. Folk and fairy tales.

Thumbelina ill. by Alison Claire Darke. Doubleday, 1991. ISBN 0-385-41404-8 Subj: Character traits – smallness. Folk and fairy tales.

Thumbelina ill. by Demi. Putnam, 1987. ISBN 0-396-09241-1 Subj: Character traits – smallness. Folk and fairy tales.

Thumbelina trans. by Erik Haugaard; ill. by Arlene Graston. Delacorte, 1997. ISBN 0-385-32251-8 Subj: Character traits – smallness. Folk and fairy tales.

Thumbelina ill. by Susan Jeffers; retold by Amy Ehrlich. Dial, 1979. Translation of Tommelise. ISBN 0-8037-8815-0 Subj: Character traits – smallness. Folk and fairy tales.

Thumbelina retold by Deborah Hautzig; ill. by Kaarina Kaila. Knopf, 1990. ISBN 0-679-90667-3 Subj: Character traits – smallness. Folk and fairy tales.

Thumbelina ill. by Christine Willis Nigognossian. Troll, 1979. Translation of Tommelise. ISBN 0-89375-141-3 Subj: Character traits – smallness. Folk and fairy tales.

Thumbelina ill. by Gustaf Tenggren. Simon & Schuster, 1953. Translation of Tommelise. Subj: Character traits – smallness. Folk and fairy tales.

Thumbelina trans. by Richard and Clara Winston; ill. by Lisbeth Zwerger. Morrow, 1980. Tr. of Tommelise. ISBN 0-688-32235-2 Subj: Character traits – smallness. Folk and fairy tales.

Thumbeline trans. by Anthea Bell; ill. by Lisbeth Zwerger. Picture Book Studio, 1985. ISBN 0-88708-006-5 Subj: Character traits – smallness. Folk and fairy tales.

The tinderbox ill. by Warwick Hutton. Macmillan, 1988. ISBN 0-689-50458-6 Subj: Folk and fairy tales. Magic. Witches.

The tinderbox ill. by Barry Moser. Little, 1990. ISBN 0-316-03938-1 Subj: Folk and fairy tales. Magic. U.S. history. Witches.

The ugly duckling ill. by Adrienne Adams. Scribners, 1965. Translation of Den grimme ælling by R. P. Keigwin. Subj: Birds – ducks. Birds – swans. Character traits – appearance. Character traits – being different. Folk and fairy tales.

The ugly duckling ill. by Lorinda Bryan Cauley. Harcourt, 1979. ISBN 0-15-292435-3 Subj: Birds – ducks. Birds – swans. Character traits – appearance. Character traits – being different. Folk and fairy tales.

The ugly duckling retold and ill. by Troy Howell. Putnam, 1990. ISBN 0-399-22158-1 Subj: Birds – ducks. Birds – swans. Character traits – appearance. Character traits – being different. Folk and fairy tales.

The ugly duckling trans. by Phyllis Palecek; ill. by Tadasu Izawa and Shigemi Hijikata. Grosset, 1971. Tr. of Den grimme ælling. ISBN 0-4480-4235-5 Subj: Birds – ducks. Birds – swans. Character traits – appearance. Character traits – being different. Folk and fairy tales.

The ugly duckling trans. by Anne Stewart; ill. by Monika Laimgruber. Greenwillow, 1985. ISBN 0-688-04951-6 Subj: Birds – ducks. Birds – swans. Character traits – appearance. Character traits – being different. Folk and fairy tales.

The ugly duckling trans. by R. P. Keigwin; ill. by Johannes Larsen. Ward, 1956. Tr. of Den grimme ælling. Subj: Birds – ducks. Birds – swans. Character traits – appearance. Character traits – being different. Folk and fairy tales.

The ugly duckling adapt. by Marianna Mayer; ill. by Thomas Locker. Macmillan, 1987. ISBN 0-02-765130-4 Subj: Birds – ducks. Birds – swans. Character traits – appearance. Character traits – being different. Folk and fairy tales.

The ugly duckling trans. by Anthea Bell; ill. by Alan Marks. Picture Book Studio, 1990. ISBN 0-88708-116-9 Subj: Birds – ducks. Birds – swans. Character traits – appearance. Character traits – being different. Folk and fairy tales.

The ugly duckling adapt. by Phyllis Hoffman; ill. by Josef Palecek. Abelard-Schuman, 1972. ISBN 0-200-71739-1 Subj: Birds – ducks. Birds – swans. Character traits – appearance. Character traits – being different. Folk and fairy tales.

The ugly duckling adapt. and ill. by Jerry Pinkney. Morrow, 1999. ISBN 0-688-15933-8 Subj: Birds – ducks. Birds – swans. Caldecott award honor books. Character traits – appearance. Character traits – being different. Folk and fairy tales.

The ugly duckling retold by M. Eulalia Valeri; trans. from Spanish by Leland Northam; ill. by Maria Ruis. Silver Burdett, 1985. ISBN 0-382-09071-3 Subj: Birds – ducks. Birds – swans. Character traits – appearance. Character traits – being different. Folk and fairy tales. Wordless.

The ugly duckling adapt. by Lilian Moore; ill. by Daniel San Souci. Scholastic, 1987. ISBN 0-590-40957-3 Subj: Birds – ducks. Birds – swans. Character traits – appearance. Character traits – being different. Folk and fairy tales.

The ugly duckling adapt. by Joel Tuber and Clara Stites; ill. by Robert Van Nutt. Knopf, 1986. ISBN 0-394-88403-5 Subj: Birds – ducks. Birds – swans. Character traits – appearance. Character traits – being different. Folk and fairy tales.

The ugly duckling retold and ill. by Bernadette Watts. North-South, 2000. Subj: Birds – ducks. Birds – swans. Character traits – appearance. Character traits – being different. Folk and fairy tales.

The ugly little duck adapt. by Patricia C. and Fredrick McKissack; ill. by Peggy Perry Anderson. Childrens Pr., 1986. Prepared under the direction of Robert Hillerick. ISBN 0-516-03982-2 Subj: Birds – ducks. Birds – swans. Character traits – appearance. Character traits – being different. Folk and fairy tales.

The wild swans trans. from Danish by Naomi Lewis; ill. by Angela Barrett. HarperCollins, 1984. ISBN 0-911745-36-X Subj: Birds – swans. Folk and fairy tales. Magic.

The wild swans retold by Amy Ehrlich; ill. by Susan Jeffers. Dial, 1981. ISBN 0-8037-9391-X Subj: Birds – swans. Folk and fairy tales. Magic.

The woman with the eggs adapt. by Jan Wahl; ill. by Ray Cruz. Crown, 1974. An adaptation of a poem by H. C. Andersen pub. in Den danske bondeven, 1836. ISBN 0-517-51587-3 Subj: Behavior – greed. Eggs. Folk and fairy tales.

Andersen, Karen Born. *An alphabet in five acts* ill. by Flint Born. Dial, 1993. ISBN 0-8037-1441-6 Subj: ABC books.

What's the matter, Sylvie, can't you ride? ill. by author. Dial, 1981. ISBN 0-8037-9621-8 Subj: Emotions. Sports – bicycling.

Anderson, Adrienne Adams. *see* Adams, Adrienne

Anderson, C. W. (Clarence Williams). *Billy and Blaze* ill. by author. Aladdin, 1992. ISBN 0-689-71608-7 Subj: Animals – horses, ponies. Birthdays. Family life.

Blaze and the forest fire ill. by author. Macmillan, 1938. ISBN 0-02-702080-0 Subj: Animals – horses, ponies. Fire.

Blaze and the gray spotted pony ill. by author. Macmillan, 1968. ISBN 0-02-701150-X Subj: Animals – horses, ponies.

Blaze and the gypsies ill. by author. Macmillan, 1937. Subj: Animals – horses, ponies. Crime. Gypsies.

Blaze and the Indian cave ill. by author. Macmillan, 1964. ISBN 0-02-702470-9 Subj: Animals – horses, ponies. Cowboys.

Blaze and the lost quarry ill. by author. Macmillan, 1966. ISBN 0-606-05758-7 Subj: Animals – horses, ponies. Cowboys.

Blaze and the mountain lion ill. by author. Macmillan, 1959. Subj: Animals – cougars. Animals – horses, ponies. Cowboys.

Blaze and Thunderbolt ill. by author. Macmillan, 1955. ISBN 0-689-71712-1 Subj: Animals – horses, ponies. Cowboys.

Blaze finds forgotten roads ill. by author. Macmillan, 1970. ISBN 0-02-701340-5 Subj: Animals – horses, ponies. Behavior – lost. Cowboys.

Blaze finds the trail ill. by author. Macmillan, 1950. ISBN 0-02-041450-1 Subj: Animals – horses, ponies. Behavior – lost. Cowboys.

Blaze shows the way ill. by author. Macmillan, 1969. ISBN 0-606-05759-5 Subj: Animals – horses, ponies.

The crooked colt ill. by author. Macmillan, 1954. Subj: Animals – horses, ponies.

Linda and the Indians ill. by author. Macmillan, 1952. Subj: Animals – horses, ponies. Imagination. Indians of North America.

Lonesome little colt ill. by author. Macmillan, 1961. ISBN 0-02-041490-0 Subj: Animals – horses, ponies. Character traits – kindness to animals.

A pony for Linda ill. by author. Macmillan, 1951. Subj: Animals – horses, ponies.

A pony for three ill. by author. Macmillan, 1958. Subj: Animals – horses, ponies.

The rumble seat pony ill. by author. Macmillan, 1971. Subj: Animals – horses, ponies. Character traits – kindness to animals. Parades.

Anderson, Debby. *Let's talk about Heaven* ill. by author. Chariot Books, 1991. ISBN 1-55513-531-5 Subj: Religion.

Anderson, Douglas. *Let's draw a story* ill. by author. Sterling, 1959. Subj: Animals – cats. Animals – dogs. Art. Family life. Games.

Anderson, James. *A letter to the king* (Va, Leong)

Anderson, Janet S. *Sunflower Sal* ill. by Elizabeth Johns. Albert Whitman, 1997. ISBN 0-8075-7662-X Subj: Careers – farmers. Concepts – shape. Concepts – size. Country. Flowers.

Anderson, Joan. *Harry's helicopter* ill. by George Ancona. Morrow, 1990. ISBN 0-688-09187-3 Subj: Activities – flying. Helicopters. Imagination.

Richie's rocket photos by George Ancona. Morrow, 1993. ISBN 0-688-11305-2 Subj: Careers – astronauts. Space and space ships.

Sally's submarine photos by George Ancona. Morrow, 1995. ISBN 0-688-12691-X Subj: Boats, ships. Family life – fathers. Imagination.

Anderson, John L. *see* Anderson, Lonzo

Anderson, Laurie Halse. *Ndito runs* ill. by Anita Van der Merwe. Holt, 1996. ISBN 0-8050-3265-7 Subj: Animals. Foreign lands – Kenya. Sports – racing.

No time for Mother's Day ill. by Dorothy Donohue. Albert Whitman, 1999. ISBN 0-8075-4955-X Subj: Family life – mothers. Gifts. Holidays – Mother's Day.

Turkey pox ill. by Dorothy Donohue. Albert Whitman, 1996. ISBN 0-8075-8127-5 Subj: Family life. Family life – grandmothers. Holidays – Thanksgiving. Illness – chicken pox.

Anderson, Lena. *Bunny bath* ill. by author. Farrar, 1991. ISBN 91-29-59652-1 Subj: Activities – bathing. Animals – rabbits. Format, unusual – board books. Wordless.

Bunny box ill. by author. Farrar, 1991. ISBN 91-29-59858-3 Subj: Animals – rabbits. Bedtime. Family life – mothers. Format, unusual – board books. Toys. Wordless.

Bunny fun ill. by author. Farrar, 1991. ISBN 91-29-59860-5 Subj: Animals – rabbits. Format, unusual – board books. Sports – fishing. Sports – swimming. Wordless.

Bunny party ill. by author. Farrar, 1991. ISBN 91-29-59134-1 Subj: Animals – rabbits. Format, unusual – board books. Parties. Wordless.

Bunny story ill. by author. Farrar, 1991. ISBN 91-29-59132-5 Subj: Animals. Animals – rabbits. Bedtime. Format, unusual – board books. Wordless.

Bunny surprise ill. by author. Farrar, 1991. ISBN 91-29-59654-8 Subj: Animals – rabbits. Format, unusual – board books. Wordless.

Stina ill. by author. Greenwillow, 1989. ISBN 0-688-08881-3 Subj: Family life – grandfathers. Sea and seashore. Weather – storms.

Stina's visit ill. by author. Greenwillow, 1991. ISBN 0-688-09666-2 Subj: Birthdays. Family life – grandfathers. Friendship. Old age. Sailors.

Tick-tock ill. by author. Doubleday, 1998. ISBN 0-385-32554-1 Subj: Animals. Clocks, watches. Family life – aunts, uncles. Rhyming text. Time.

Anderson, Leone Castell. *It's O.K. to cry* ill. by Richard Wahl. Child's World, 1979. ISBN 0-8956-5094-0 Subj: Death. Family life – aunts, uncles.

My friend next door ill. by Pat Karch. Dandelion, 1983. ISBN 0-8969-3212-5 Subj: Friendship.

Surprise at Muddy Creek ill. by Helen Endres. Dandelion, 1984. ISBN 0-8969-3222-2 Subj: Indians of North America. U.S. history – frontier and pioneer life.

The wonderful shrinking shirt ill. by Irene Trivas. Albert Whitman, 1983. ISBN 0-8075-9171-8 Subj: Clothing – shirts. Humor.

Anderson, Lonzo. *Arion and the dolphins* ill. by Adrienne Adams. Scribners, 1978. Based on an ancient Greek legend. ISBN 0-684-15128-6 Subj: Animals – dolphins. Boats, ships. Folk and fairy tales. Foreign lands – Greece.

The day the hurricane happened ill. by Ann Grifalconi. Scribners, 1974. ISBN 0-684-13495-0 Subj: Family life. Foreign lands – Caribbean Islands. Weather – storms.

The haganinny ill. by Susan Harris Andersen. Ginn, 1973. ISBN 0-663-25493-0 Subj: Imagination.

The Halloween party ill. by Adrienne Adams. Scribners, 1974. ISBN 0-684-14002-0 Subj: Holidays – Halloween. Parties.

Izzard ill. by Adrienne Adams. Scribners, 1973. ISBN 0-684-13247-8 Subj: Foreign lands – Caribbean Islands. Reptiles – lizards.

Mr. Biddle and the birds ill. by Adrienne Adams. Scribners, 1971. ISBN 0-684-12315-0 Subj: Activities – flying. Birds.

Two hundred rabbits by Lonzo Anderson and Adrienne Adams; ill. by Adrienne Adams. Viking, 1968. Subj: Animals – rabbits. Fairies. Magic. Royalty.

Anderson, Lucia Z. *The smallest life around us* ill. by Leigh Grant. Crown, 1978. ISBN 0-517-53227-1 Subj: Science.

Anderson, Neil. *see* Beim, Jerrold

Anderson, Paul S. *Red fox and the hungry tiger* ill. by Robert Kraus. Addison-Wesley, 1962. Subj: Animals – foxes. Animals – tigers. Character traits – cleverness. Friendship.

Anderson, Peggy Perry. *Out to lunch* ill. by author. Houghton Mifflin, 1998. ISBN 0-395-89826-9 Subj: Behavior – misbehavior. Etiquette. Family life. Frogs and toads. Restaurants. Rhyming text.

Time for bed, the babysitter said ill. by author. Houghton Mifflin, 1987. ISBN 0-395-41851-8 Subj: Activities – babysitting. Bedtime. Frogs and toads.

To the tub ill. by author. Houghton Mifflin, 1996. ISBN 0-395-77614-7 Subj: Activities – bathing. Family life – fathers. Frogs and toads.

Anderson, Robin. *Sinabouda Lily: a folk tale from Papua New Guinea* ill. by Jennifer Allen. Oxford Univ. Pr., 1979. ISBN 0-19-554201-0 Subj: Activities – swinging. Folk and fairy tales. Foreign lands – New Guinea. Magic. Witches.

Anderson, Scoular. *MacPelican's American adventure* ill. by author. Candlewick, 1998. ISBN 0-7636-0443-7 Subj: Activities – traveling. Behavior – lost.

Anderson, Wayne. *Dragon* ill. by author. Simon & Schuster, 1992. ISBN 0-671-78397-1 Subj: Dragons. Imagination. Self-concept.

Andre, Evelyn M. *Places I like to be* photos by author. Abingdon, 1980. ISBN 0-687-31540-9 Subj: Activities. Poetry.

Andreae, Giles. *Love is a handful of honey* ill. by Vanessa Cabban. Little Tiger, 1999. ISBN 1-888444-58-4 Subj: Animals – bears. Rhyming text.

Rumble in the jungle ill. by David Wojtowycz. Little Tiger, 1997. ISBN 1-888444-08-8 Subj: Animals. Insects – ants. Jungle. Poetry.

Andreasen, Dan. *Rose Red and the bear prince* (Grimm, Jacob)

Andrews, F. Emerson (Frank Emerson). *Nobody comes to dinner* ill. by Lydia Dabcovich. Little, 1977. ISBN 0-316-04221-8 Subj: Behavior – bad day. Emotions – anger. Imagination – imaginary friends.

Andrews, Jan. *The auction* ill. by Karen Reczuch. Macmillan, 1991. ISBN 0-02-705535-3 Subj: Emotions – anger. Emotions – sadness. Family life – grandfathers. Farms.

Very last first time ill. by Ian Wallace. Atheneum, 1986. ISBN 0-689-50388-1 Subj: Eskimos. Food. Foreign lands – Canada. Sea and seashore.

Andrews, Wayne. *Snow White and Rose Red* (Grimm, Jacob)

Andry, Andrew C. *Hi, new baby: a book to help your child learn about the new baby* by Andrew C. Andry and Suzanne C. Kratka; ill. by Thomas di Grazia. Simon & Schuster, 1979, c1968. ISBN 0-671-65132-3 Subj: Babies. Birth. Family life – new sibling.

How babies are made by Andrew C. Andry and Steven Schepp; ill. by Blake Hampton. Rev. ed. Time-Life, 1979. ISBN 0-316-04227-7 Subj: Babies. Birth. Science.

Andújar, Gloria. *Cuckoo: a Mexican folktale = Cucú: un cuento folklórico mexicano* (Ehlert, Lois)

Angeletti, Roberta. *Nefertari, princess of Egypt* ill. by author. Oxford Univ. Pr., 1998. ISBN 0-19-521507-9 Subj: Foreign lands – Egypt. Imagination. Religion. Royalty – princesses.

Angeli, Marguerite De. *see* De Angeli, Marguerite

Angelis, Nancy de. *see* Angelo, Nancy Carolyn Harrison

Angelo, Nancy Carolyn Harrison. *Camembert* ill. by author. Houghton Mifflin, 1958. Subj: Animals – mice. Art. Careers – artists. Foreign lands – France.

Angelo, Valenti. *The acorn tree* ill. by author. Viking, 1958. Subj: Animals – chipmunks. Animals – squirrels. Birds – bluejays. Character traits – selfishness. Trees.

The candy basket ill. by author. Viking, 1960. Subj: Animals – mice. Behavior – greed.

Angelou, Maya. *My painted house, my friendly chicken, and me* photos by Margaret Courtney-Clarke. Potter/Crown, 1994. ISBN 0-517-59667-9 Subj: Art. Foreign lands – South Africa. Homes, houses. Poetry.

Anglund, Joan Walsh. *A is for always: an ABC book* ill. by author. Harcourt, 1968. ISBN 0-15-200670-2 Subj: ABC books.

The Adam book ill. by author. Random House, 1979. ISBN 0-394-94227-2 Subj: Language.

Baby brother ill. by author. Random House, 1985. ISBN 0-394-96837-9 Subj: Babies. Family life – brothers and sisters.

A book of good tidings from the Bible ill. by author. Harcourt, 1965. Subj: Religion.

The brave cowboy ill. by author. Harcourt, 1959. ISBN 0-15-614050-0 Subj: Character traits – bravery. Cowboys. Games.

A child's year ill. by author. Golden Books, 1992. ISBN 0-307-00141-5 Subj: Days of the week, months of the year. Rhyming text.

Christmas is a time of giving ill. by author. Harcourt, 1961. ISBN 0-15-217863-5 Subj: Character traits – generosity. Holidays – Christmas.

Christmas is here ill. by author. Random House, 1986. ISBN 0-694-88404-3 Subj: Format, unusual – board books. Holidays – Christmas. Rhyming text.

Christmas is love ill. by author. Harcourt, 1988. ISBN 0-15-200425-4 Subj: Emotions – love. Holidays – Christmas. Poetry.

Cowboy and his friend ill. by author. Harcourt, 1961. ISBN 0-15-220369-9 Subj: Animals – bears. Cowboys. Friendship. Imagination – imaginary friends.

The cowboy's Christmas ill. by author. Atheneum, 1972. ISBN 0-689-30301-7 Subj: Animals – bears. Cowboys. Holidays – Christmas. Imagination – imaginary friends.

Cowboy's secret life ill. by author. Harcourt, 1963. ISBN 0-15-223565-9 Subj: Cowboys. Games. Imagination.

Emily and Adam book of opposites ill. by author. Random House, 1979. ISBN 0-394-94230-2 Subj: Concepts – opposites. Language.

The Emily book ill. by author. Random House, 1979. ISBN 0-394-94237-X Subj: Clothing. Language.

A friend is someone who likes you ill. by author. Harcourt, 1958. ISBN 0-15-229678-6 Subj: Friendship.

How many days has Baby to play? ill. by author. Harcourt, 1988. ISBN 0-15-200460-2 Subj: Babies. Days of the week, months of the year. Rhyming text. Toys – bears.

Look out the window ill. by author. Random House, 1978. Subj: Character traits – individuality.

Love is a baby ill. by author. Harcourt, 1992. ISBN 0-15-200517-X Subj: Babies. Emotions – love. Poetry.

Love is a special way of feeling ill. by author. Harcourt, 1960. ISBN 0-15-249724-2 Subj: Emotions – love.

Love one another ill. by author. Determined Prod., 1981. ISBN 0-915696-45-2 Subj: Foreign lands. Foreign languages.

Morning is a little child: poems ill. by author. Harcourt, 1969. ISBN 0-15-255652-4 Subj: Morning. Poetry.

Nibble nibble mousekin: a tale of Hansel and Gretel ill. by author. Harcourt, 1962. ISBN 0-15-257400-X Subj: Folk and fairy tales. Forest, woods. Witches.

Poems of childhood ill. by author. Harcourt, 1996. ISBN 0-15-262961-0 Subj: Poetry.

Rainbow love ill. by author. Determined Prod., 1982. ISBN 0-915696-51-7 Subj: Character traits – optimism. Weather – rainbows.

Spring is a new beginning ill. by author. Harcourt, 1963. ISBN 0-15-278161-7 Subj: Seasons – spring.

Teddy bear tales ill. by author. Random House, 1985. ISBN 0-394-97171-X Subj: Holidays – Christmas. Toys – bears.

Anholt, Catherine. *All about you* by Catherine and Laurence Anholt; ill. by authors. Viking, 1992. ISBN 0-670-84488-8 Subj: Character traits – questioning. Language.

Aren't you lucky! ill. by author. Little, 1991. ISBN 0-316-04264-1 Subj: Babies. Family life – new sibling. Family life – sisters. Sibling rivalry.

Bear and baby written and ill. by Catherine and Laurence Anholt. Candlewick, 1993. ISBN 1-56402-235-8 Subj: Rhyming text. Toys – bears.

Catherine and Laurence Anholt's big book of families by Catherine and Laurence Anholt; ill. by authors. Candlewick, 1998. ISBN 0-7636-0323-6 Subj: Family life.

Chaos at Cold Custard Farm ill. by author. Oxford Univ. Pr., 1988. ISBN 0-19-520645-2 Subj: Animals. Farms.

Come back, Jack! written and ill. by Catherine and Laurence Anholt. Candlewick, 1994. ISBN 1-56402-313-3 Subj: Activities – reading. Behavior – boredom. Nursery rhymes.

First words and pictures by Catherine and Laurence Anholt; ill. by authors. Candlewick, 1996. ISBN 0-763-60041-5 Subj: Language.

Good days, bad days ill. by author. Putnam, 1991. ISBN 0-399-22283-9 Subj: Concepts – opposites. Family life.

Here come the babies written and ill. by Catherine and Laurence Anholt. Candlewick, 1995. ISBN 1-56402-209-9 Subj: Babies. Family life – new sibling. Poetry.

Kids written and ill. by Catherine and Laurence Anholt. Candlewick, 1992. ISBN 1-56402-097-5 Subj: Character traits – individuality. Rhyming text.

A kiss like this by Catherine and Laurence Anholt; ill. by authors. Barron's, 1997. ISBN 0-7641-5068-5 Subj: Animals. Animals – lions.

One, two, three, count with me written and ill. by Catherine and Laurence Anholt. Viking, 1994. ISBN 0-670-85261-9 Subj: Anatomy. Concepts. Counting, numbers. Days of the week, months of the year. Rhyming text.

Snow fairy and the spaceman ill. by author. Delacorte, 1991. ISBN 0-385-30422-6 Subj: Birthdays. Friendship. Parties.

Sun, snow, stars, sky by Catherine and Laurence Anholt; ill. by authors. Viking, 1995. ISBN 0-670-86196-0 Subj: Seasons. Weather.

Toddlers written and ill. by Catherine and Laurence Anholt. Candlewick, 1993. ISBN 1-56402-242-0 Subj: Babies. Rhyming text.

Tom's rainbow walk ill. by author. Little, 1990. ISBN 0-316-04261-7 Subj: Activities – knitting. Concepts – color. Family life – grandmothers.

Truffles in trouble ill. by author. Little, 1987. ISBN 0-316-04260-9 Subj: Animals – pigs. Shopping. Stores.

Truffles is sick ill. by author. Little, 1987. ISBN 0-316-04259-5 Subj: Animals – pigs. Illness.

Twins, two by two by Catherine and Laurence Anholt; ill. by authors. Candlewick, 1992. ISBN 1-56402-041-X Subj: Animals. Bedtime. Multiple births – twins.

What I like by Catherine and Laurence Anholt; ill. by Catherine Anholt. Putnam, 1991. ISBN 0-399-21863-7 Subj: Character traits – individuality. Emotions. Rhyming text.

What makes me happy? written and ill. by Catherine and Laurence Anholt. Candlewick, 1995. ISBN 1-56402-482-2 Subj: Babies. Emotions. Rhyming text.

When I was a baby ill. by author. Little, 1989. ISBN 0-316-04262-5 Subj: Babies. Behavior – growing up. Family life.

Anholt, Laurence. *All about you* (Anholt, Catherine)

Bear and baby (Anholt, Catherine)

Billy and the big new school ill. by Catherine Anholt. Albert Whitman, 1999. ISBN 0-8075-0743-1 Subj: Behavior – growing up. Birds. School – first day.

Camille and the sunflowers: a story about Vincent Van Gogh ill. by author. Barron's, 1994. ISBN 0-8120-6409-7 Subj: Art. Careers – artists. Foreign lands – Holland. Friendship.

Catherine and Laurence Anholt's big book of families (Anholt, Catherine)

Come back, Jack! (Anholt, Catherine)

First words and pictures (Anholt, Catherine)

The forgotten forest ill. by author. Sierra Club, 1992. ISBN 0-87156-569-2 Subj: Ecology. Forest, woods.

Here come the babies (Anholt, Catherine)

Kids (Anholt, Catherine)

A kiss like this (Anholt, Catherine)

The new puppy ill. by Catherine Anholt. Artists & Writers Guild, 1995. ISBN 0-307-17516-2 Subj: Animals – dogs. Pets.

One, two, three, count with me (Anholt, Catherine)

Summerhouse ill. by Lynne Russell. DK, 1999. ISBN 0-7894-4377-5 Subj: Family life – grandmothers. Imagination. Seasons – winter.

Sun, snow, stars, sky (Anholt, Catherine)

Toddlers (Anholt, Catherine)

Twins, two by two (Anholt, Catherine)

What I like (Anholt, Catherine)

What makes me happy? (Anholt, Catherine)

Animal 123's ill. with photos. Cedco, 1998. World Wildlife Fund: Saving life on earth. ISBN 0-7683-2033-X Subj: Animals. Counting, numbers.

Annett, Cora. *The dog who thought he was a boy* ill. by Walter Lorraine. Houghton Mifflin, 1965. ISBN 0-395-18471-1 Subj: Animals – dogs. Birthdays. School.

When the porcupine moved in ill. by Peter Parnall. Watts, 1971. ISBN 0-531-01987-X Subj: Animals – porcupines. Animals – rabbits. Behavior – trickery.

Annixter, Jane. *Brown rats, black rats* by Jane and Paul Annixter; ill. by Gilbert Riswold. Prentice-Hall, 1977. ISBN 0-13-084400-4 Subj: Animals – rats. Science.

Annixter, Paul. *Brown rats, black rats* (Annixter, Jane)

Anno, Masaichiro. *Anno's magical ABC: an anamorphic alphabet* (Anno, Mitsumasa)

Anno, Mitsumasa. *All in a day* by Mitsumasa Anno and others; ill. by Mitsumasa Anno. Putnam, 1986. ISBN 0-399-21311-2 Subj: Activities. Foreign lands. World.

Anno's Æsop: a book of fables by Æsop and Mr. Fox adapt. and ill. by author. Watts, 1989. ISBN 0-531-08374-8 Subj: Animals – foxes. Folk and fairy tales.

Anno's alphabet: an adventure in imagination ill. by author. Crowell, 1975. ISBN 0-690-00546-5 Subj: ABC books. Imagination. Optical illusions. Picture puzzles.

Anno's animals ill. by author. Collins-World, 1979. ISBN 0-529-05546-5 Subj: Animals. Games. Imagination. Picture puzzles. Wordless.

Anno's Britain ill. by author. Philomel, 1982. ISBN 0-399-20861-5 Subj: Foreign lands – England. Games. Imagination. Wordless.

Anno's counting book ill. by author. Crowell, 1975. ISBN 0-690-01288-8 Subj: Counting, numbers. Imagination. Optical illusions. Picture puzzles. Seasons. Wordless.

Anno's counting house ill. by author. Philomel, 1982. Translation of 10-nin no yukai na hikkoshi. ISBN 0-399-20896-8 Subj: Counting, numbers. Games. Imagination. Optical illusions. Picture puzzles. Wordless.

Anno's faces ill. by author. Putnam, 1989. ISBN 0-399-21711-8 Subj: Anatomy – faces. Concepts – shape. Format, unusual.

Anno's flea market ill. by author. Philomel, 1984. Translation of Nomi no ichi. ISBN 0-399-21033-8 Subj: Games. Imagination. Optical illusions. Picture puzzles. Wordless.

Anno's hat tricks ill. by author. Putnam, 1985. ISBN 0-399-21212-4 Subj: Counting, numbers. Magic.

Anno's Italy ill. by author. Collins-World, 1980. Japanese ed. entitled My journey II, a translation of Tabi no ehon, II. ISBN 0-529-05560-0 Subj: Foreign lands – Italy. Games. Imagination. Optical illusions. Picture puzzles. Wordless.

Anno's journey ill. by author. Putnam, 1981. Pub. in 1977 under title: My journey, a translation of Tabi no ehon. ISBN 0-529-05419-1 Subj: Games. Imagination. Optical illusions. Picture puzzles. Wordless.

Anno's magic seeds ill. by author. Philomel, 1995. ISBN 0-399-22538-2 Subj: Counting, numbers. Gardens, gardening. Seeds.

Anno's magical ABC: an anamorphic alphabet by Mitsumasa and Masaichiro Anno; ill. by authors. Putnam, 1981. ISBN 0-399-20788-0 Subj: ABC books. Format, unusual – toy and movable books. Games. Imagination. Optical illusions. Picture puzzles.

Anno's masks ill. by author. Philomel, 1990. ISBN 0-399-21860-2 Subj: Animals. Format, unusual – toy and movable books. Masks.

Anno's math games ill. by author. Philomel, 1987. ISBN 0-399-21151-9 Subj: Concepts. Counting, numbers. Riddles.

Anno's math games II ill. by author. Putnam, 1989. ISBN 0-399-21615-4 Subj: Concepts. Counting, numbers. Riddles.

Anno's math games III ill. by author. Putnam, 1991. ISBN 0-399-22274-X Subj: Concepts. Counting, numbers. Riddles.

Anno's peekaboo ill. by author. Putnam, 1988. ISBN 0-399-21520-4 Subj: Format, unusual. Wordless.

Anno's sundial ill. by author. Philomel, 1987. ISBN 0-399-21374-0 Subj: Earth. Format, unusual – toy and movable books. Shadows. Sun. Time.

Anno's U.S.A. ill. by author. Philomel, 1983. Translation of Tabi no ehon, IV. ISBN 0-399-20974-3 Subj: Games. Imagination. Wordless.

Dr. Anno's magical midnight circus ill. by author. Weatherhill, 1972. ISBN 0-8348-2011-0 Subj: Circus. Clowns, jesters. Imagination. Optical illusions. Picture puzzles. Wordless.

In shadowland ill. by author. Watts, 1988. ISBN 0-531-08341-1 Subj: Folk and fairy tales. Shadows. Sun.

The king's flower ill. by author. Collins-World, 1979. ISBN 0-529-05459-0 Subj: Concepts – size. Flowers. Imagination. Royalty – kings.

Topsy turvies: more pictures to stretch the imagination ill. by author. Putnam, 1989. ISBN 0-399-21557-3 Subj: Games. Imagination. Optical illusions. Wordless.

Topsy turvies: pictures to stretch the imagination ill. by author. Weatherhill, 1970. Subj: Games. Imagination. Optical illusions. Wordless.

Upside-downers: more pictures to stretch the imagination adapt. into English by Meredith Weatherby and Susan Trumbull; ill. by author. Weatherhill, 1971. ISBN 0-8348-2005-6 Subj: Games. Imagination. Optical illusions.

Anrooy, Frans van. *The sea horse* ill. by Jaap Tol. Harcourt, 1968, c1967. Originally pub. in Holland under the title of Het Zeepaardje. Subj: Dreams. Emotions – fear. Night. Sea and seashore.

Antle, Nancy. *Sam's Wild West Show* ill. by Simms Taback. Dial, 1995. ISBN 0-8037-1533-1 Subj: Cowboys. Crime.

Antoine, Héloïse. *Curious kids go to preschool* ill. by Ingrid Godon. Peachtree, 1996. ISBN 1-56145-129-0 Subj: Language. School.

Aoki, Hisako. *Santa's favorite story* by Hisako Aoki and Ivan Gantschev; ill. by authors. Neugebauer, 1982. ISBN 0-90-723416-X Subj: Animals. Holidays – Christmas. Religion. Santa Claus.

Appelbaum, Diana Karter. *Cocoa ice* ill. by Holly Meade. Orchard, 1997. ISBN 0-531-33040-0 Subj: Foreign lands – Caribbean Islands. U.S. history.

Appelbaum, Neil. *Is there a hole in your head?* ill. by author. Ivan Obolensky, 1963. ISBN 0-8392-3012-5 Subj: Animals – whales. Games.

Appell, Clara. *Now I have a daddy haircut* by Clara and Morey Appell; photos by authors. Dodd, 1960. Subj: Behavior – growing up. Careers – barbers. Hair. Self-concept.

Appell, Morey. *Now I have a daddy haircut* (Appell, Clara)

Appelt, Kathi. *Bats on parade* ill. by Melissa Sweet. Morrow, 1999. ISBN 0-688-15666-5 Subj: Animals – bats. Counting, numbers. Music. Rhyming text.

Bayou lullaby ill. by Neil Waldman. Morrow, 1995. ISBN 0-688-12856-4 Subj: Bedtime. Ethnic groups in the U.S. Lullabies. Night.

Cowboy dreams ill. by Barry Root. HarperCollins, 1999. ISBN 0-06-027764-5 Subj: Bedtime. Cowboys. Dreams. Night. Rhyming text.

Elephants aloft ill. by Keith Baker. Harcourt, 1993. ISBN 0-15-225384-X Subj: Activities – ballooning. Animals – elephants. Foreign lands – Africa. Foreign lands – India.

A red wagon year ill. by Laura McGee Kvasnosky. Harcourt, 1996. ISBN 0-15-277991-4 Subj: Communities, neighborhoods. Days of the week, months of the year. Rhyming text. Seasons.

Someone's come to our house ill. by Nancy Carpenter. Eerdmans, 1999. ISBN 0-8028-5144-4 Subj: Babies. Family life. Rhyming text.

Watermelon day ill. by Dale Gottlieb. Holt, 1996. ISBN 0-8050-2304-6 Subj: Character traits – patience. Family life. Food. Plants. Seasons – summer.

Apperley, Dawn. *How does your garden grow?* (Burns, Kate)

In the jungle by Dawn Apperley and Kate Burns; ill. by Dawn Apperley. Little, 1996. ISBN 0-316-11821-4 Subj: Animals. Behavior – hiding. Format, unusual – toy and movable books. Jungle.

In the sand ill. by Kate Burns. Little, 1996. ISBN 0-316-11822-2 Subj: Desert. Format, unusual – toy and movable books. Sand. Sea and seashore.

Appiah, Sonia. *Amoko and Efua Bear* ill. by Carol Easmon. Macmillan, 1989. ISBN 0-02-705591-4 Subj: Foreign lands – Ghana. Toys – bears.

Apple, Margot. *Blanket* ill. by author. Houghton Mifflin, 1990. ISBN 0-395-51522-X Subj: Animals. Bedtime. Clothing.

Brave Martha ill. by author. Houghton Mifflin, 1999. ISBN 0-395-59422-7 Subj: Animals – cats. Bedtime. Emotions – fear. Monsters. Night.

Applebaum, Stan. *Going my way?* by Stan Applebaum and Victoria Cox; ill. by Leonard W. Shortall. Harcourt, 1976. ISBN 0-15-231125-4 Subj: Animals. Science.

Appleby, Leonard G. *Snakes* photos by author. A & C Black, 1983. ISBN 0-7136-2350-0 Subj: Reptiles – snakes. Science.

Arabian Nights. *The first book of tales of ancient Araby* comp. by Charles Mozley. Watts, 1960. Subj: Folk and fairy tales. Foreign lands – Arabia.

The flying carpet ill. by Marcia Brown. Scribners, 1956. Subj: Activities – flying. Folk and fairy tales. Magic.

The magic horse (Scott, Sally)

The tale of Aladdin and the wonderful lamp: a story from the Arabian Nights adapt. by Eric A. Kimmel; ill. by Ju-Hong Chen. Holiday, 1992. ISBN 0-8234-0938-4 Subj: Folk and fairy tales. Magic. Mythical creatures.

The tale of Ali Baba and the forty thieves: a story from the Arabian nights (Kimmel, Eric A.)

Aragon, Jane Chelsea. *Lullaby* ill. by Kandy Radzinski. Chronicle, 1989. ISBN 0-87701-576-7 Subj: Lullabies.

The major and the mousehole mice ill. by John O'Brien. Simon & Schuster, 1990. ISBN 0-671-68853-7 Subj: Animals – mice. Careers – military. Homes, houses.

Salt hands ill. by Ted Rand. Dutton, 1989. ISBN 0-525-44489-0 Subj: Animals – deer. Nature. Night. Rhyming text.

Winter harvest ill. by Leslie A. Baker. Little, 1989. ISBN 0-316-04937-9 Subj: Animals – deer. Character traits – kindness to animals. Night. Rhyming text. Seasons – winter.

Araten, Harry. *Two by two* ill. by author. Kar-Ben Copies, 1991. ISBN 0-929371-53-4 Subj: Religion.

Arbeit, Eleanor Werner. *Mrs. Cat hides something* ill. by author. Gibbs Smith, 1985. ISBN 0-87905-205-8 Subj: Animals – babies. Animals – cats. Family life.

Arcellana, Francisco. *The mats* ill. by Hermès Alègrè. Kane/Miller, 1999. ISBN 0-916291-86-3 Subj: Family life. Foreign lands – Philippines.

Archambault, John. *A beautiful feast for a big king cat* by John Archambault and Bill Martin, Jr.; ill. by Bruce Degen. HarperCollins, 1994. ISBN 0-06-022904-7 Subj: Animals – cats. Animals – mice. Behavior – misbehavior. Rhyming text.

The birth of a whale ill. by Janet Skiles. Silver Burdett, 1996. ISBN 0-382-39566-2 Subj: Animals – whales. Birth. Poetry.

Chicka chicka boom boom (Martin, Bill [William Ivan])

Chicka chicka sticka sticka: an ABC sticker book (Martin, Bill [William Ivan])

Counting kittens (Plummer, David)

Counting sheep ill. by John Rombola. Holt, 1989. ISBN 0-8050-1135-8 Subj: Animals. Bedtime. Counting, numbers. Rhyming text.

Here are my hands (Martin, Bill [William Ivan])

Knots on a counting rope (Martin, Bill [William Ivan])

Listen to the rain (Martin, Bill [William Ivan])

The magic pumpkin (Martin, Bill [William Ivan])

Up and down on the merry-go-round (Martin, Bill [William Ivan])

White Dynamite and Curly Kidd (Martin, Bill [William Ivan])

Words (Martin, Bill [William Ivan])

Archbold, Rick. *Safari* (Bateman, Robert)

Ardizzone, Aingelda. *The night ride* ill. by Edward Ardizzone. Windmill, 1975. ISBN 0-5256-1535-0 Subj: Holidays – Christmas. Night. Santa Claus. Toys. Toys – bears. Toys – dolls.

Ardizzone, Edward. *Diana and her rhinoceros* ill. by author. Oxford Univ. Pr., [1979] c1964. Reprint of the ed. published by Bodley Head, London. ISBN 0-19-520172-8 Subj: Animals – rhinoceros. Pets.

Johnny the clockmaker ill. by author. Walck, 1960. Subj: Careers – clockmakers. Clocks, watches.

The little girl and the tiny doll ill. by author. Delacorte, 1967. Subj: Behavior – losing things. Shopping. Toys – dolls.

Little Tim and the brave sea captain ill. by author. Walck, 1955. Subj: Boats, ships. Character traits – bravery. Sea and seashore.

Lucy Brown and Mr. Grimes ill. by author. Walck, 1970. A new version of a story published in 1937. ISBN 0-8098-1179-0 Subj: Emotions – loneliness. Foreign lands – England. Old age. Orphans.

Nicholas and the fast-moving diesel ill. by author. Eyre & Spottiswoode, 1980. ISBN 0-19-520230-9 Subj: Trains. Transportation.

Paul, the hero of the fire ill. by author. Walck, 1963. A new version of a story published in 1949. Subj: Activities – working. Behavior – growing up. Character traits – bravery. Merry-go-rounds.

Peter the wanderer ill. by author. Walck, 1963. Subj: Character traits – bravery. Character traits – cleverness. Character traits – honesty. Sea and seashore.

Ship's cook Ginger ill. by author. Macmillan, 1978, c1977. First published in London by Bodley Head, 1977. ISBN 0-02-705680-5 Subj: Boats, ships. Sea and seashore.

Tim all alone ill. by author. Oxford Univ. Pr., 1957. ISBN 0-19-272125-9 Subj: Boats, ships. Sea and seashore.

Tim and Charlotte ill. by author. Oxford Univ. Pr., 1979. ISBN 0-19-279562-7 Subj: Boats, ships. Character traits – bravery. Sea and seashore.

Tim and Ginger ill. by author. Walck, 1965. ISBN 0-19-272113-5 Subj: Boats, ships. Sea and seashore.

Tim and Lucy go to sea ill. by author. Walck, 1958. Subj: Boats, ships. Friendship. Sea and seashore.

Tim in danger ill. by author. Walck, 1953. ISBN 0-19-272106-2 Subj: Boats, ships. Sea and seashore.

Tim to the rescue ill. by author. Walck, 1949. Subj: Boats, ships. Character traits – bravery. Character traits – loyalty. Sea and seashore. Weather.

Tim's friend Towser ill. by author. Walck, 1962. ISBN 0-19-272112-7 Subj: Animals – dogs. Boats, ships. Sea and seashore.

Tim's last voyage ill. by author. Walck, 1972. ISBN 0-8098-1200-2 Subj: Boats, ships. Sea and seashore. Weather – wind.

Argent, Kerry. *Animal capers* ill. by author. Dial, 1990. ISBN 0-8037-0752-5 Subj: ABC books. Animals. Foreign lands – Australia. Zoos.

Happy birthday wombat! ill. by author. Little, 1991. ISBN 0-316-05097-0 Subj: Animals – wombats. Birthdays. Format, unusual – toy and movable books.

One woolly wombat (Trinca, Rod)

Wombat and Bandicoot: best friends ill. by author. Little, 1990. ISBN 0-316-05096-2 Subj: Animals – bandicoots. Animals – wombats. Foreign lands – Australia. Friendship.

Argueta, Manlio. *The magic dogs of the volcanoes* trans. from Spanish by Stacey Ross; ill. by Elly Simmons. Childrens Book Pr., 1990. ISBN 0-89239-064-6 Subj: Animals – dogs. Foreign lands – El Salvador. Magic.

Ariane. *Animal stories* ill. by Feodor Rojankovsky. Western, 1944. Subj: Animals.

Small Cloud ill. by Annie Gusman. Dutton, 1984. ISBN 0-525-44085-2 Subj: Folk and fairy tales. Science. Weather – clouds. Weather – rain.

Arkin, Alan. *Black and white* music by Earl Robinson; ill. by author. Golden Pr., 1966. Subj: Foreign lands – Africa. Music. School. Songs.

One present from Flekman's ill. by Richard Egielski. HarperCollins, 1999. ISBN 0-06-024531-X Subj: Family life – grandfathers. Stores. Toys.

Tony's hard work day ill. by James Stevenson. HarperCollins, 1972. ISBN 0-06-020138-X Subj: Activities – working. Family life. Homes, houses.

Armalyte, Olimpija. *How the cock wrecked the manor* (How the cock wrecked the manor)

Armer, Laura Adams. *The forest pool* ill. by author. Longman, 1938. Subj: Caldecott award honor books. Forest, woods.

Armitage, David. *Harry hates shopping!* (Armitage, Ronda)

Ice creams for Rosie (Armitage, Ronda)

The lighthouse keeper's catastrophe (Armitage, Ronda)

My brother Sammy (Edwards, Becky)

One moonlit night (Armitage, Ronda)

Armitage, Marcia. *Lupatelli's favorite nursery tales* ill. by Anthony Lupatelli. Grosset, 1977. ISBN 0-488-13065-3 Subj: Folk and fairy tales.

Armitage, Ronda. *The bossing of Josie* ill. by David Armitage. Elsevier-Dutton, 1980. ISBN 0-233-97231-5 Subj: Birthdays. Family life. Magic. Sibling rivalry. Witches.

Don't forget, Matilda ill. by David Armitage. Elsevier-Dutton, 1979. ISBN 0-233-97075-4 Subj: Family life. Foreign lands – England.

Harry hates shopping! by Ronda and David Armitage; ill. by David Armitage. Scholastic, 1992. ISBN 0-590-45886-8 Subj: Animals – koalas. Behavior. Family life – brothers and sisters. Shopping.

Ice creams for Rosie by Ronda and David Armitage; ill. by David Armitage. Elsevier-Dutton, 1981. ISBN 0-233-97361-3 Subj: Food. Islands. Problem solving.

The lighthouse keeper's catastrophe by Ronda and David Armitage; ill. by David Armitage. Dutton, 1986. ISBN 0-233-97891-7 Subj: Animals – cats. Behavior – losing things. Lighthouses. Problem solving.

The lighthouse keeper's lunch ill. by David Armitage. Elsevier-Dutton, 1979. ISBN 0-233-96869-7 Subj: Birds – seagulls. Food. Lighthouses. Problem solving.

The lighthouse keeper's rescue ill. by David Armitage. Dutton, 1989. ISBN 0-233-98428-3 Subj: Animals – whales. Lighthouses. Old age.

One moonlit night by Ronda and David Armitage; ill. by David Armitage. Dutton, 1983. ISBN 0-233-97540-3 Subj: Camps, camping. Family life. Night.

Armour, Richard Willard. *The adventures of Egbert the Easter egg* ill. by Paul Galdone. McGraw-Hill, 1965. Subj: Holidays – Easter. Rhyming text.

Animals on the ceiling ill. by Paul Galdone. McGraw-Hill, 1966. Subj: Animals. Humor. Imagination. Rhyming text.

Have you ever wished you were something else? ill. by Scott Gustafson. Childrens Pr., 1983. ISBN 0-516-03475-8 Subj: Animals. Poetry.

Sea full of whales ill. by Paul Galdone. McGraw-Hill, 1974. ISBN 0-07-002280-1 Subj: Animals – whales. Rhyming text.

The year Santa went modern ill. by Paul Galdone. McGraw-Hill, 1964. Subj: Holidays – Christmas. Rhyming text. Santa Claus.

Armstrong, Jennifer. *Chin Yu Min and the ginger cat* ill. by Mary GrandPré. Crown, 1993. ISBN 0-517-58657-6 Subj: Animals – cats. Character traits – pride. Character traits – vanity. Foreign lands – China.

King crow ill. by Eric Rohmann. Crown, 1995. ISBN 0-517-59635-0 Subj: Birds – crows. Character traits – kindness to animals. Emotions – envy, jealousy. Handicaps – blindness. War.

Little Salt Lick and the Sun King ill. by Jon Goodell. Crown, 1994. ISBN 0-517-59621-0 Subj: Activities – cooking. Animals – dogs. Royalty – kings.

Pierre's dream ill. by Susan Gaber. Dial, 1999. ISBN 0-8037-2460-8 Subj: Character traits – laziness. Circus. Dreams.

Pockets ill. by Mary GrandPré. Crown, 1998. ISBN 0-517-70927-9 Subj: Activities – sewing. Careers – tailors. Clothing. Imagination.

Arneson, D. J. *Secret places* ill. by Peter Arnold. Holt, 1971. ISBN 0-0308-6225-6 Subj: Ecology. Forest, woods.

Arnold, Caroline. *The biggest living thing* ill. by author. Carolrhoda, 1983. ISBN 0-87614-245-5 Subj: Science. Trees.

Everybody has a birthday ill. by Anthony Accardo. Watts, 1987. ISBN 0-531-10094-4 Subj: Birthdays.

Five nests ill. by Ruth Sanderson. Dutton, 1980. Includes index. ISBN 0-525-29760-X Subj: Animals. Birds. Science.

How do we communicate? photos by Ginger Giles. Watts, 1983. ISBN 0-531-04505-6 Subj: Communication.

How do we have fun? photos by Ginger Giles. Watts, 1983. ISBN 0-531-04506-4 Subj: Activities. Activities – playing.

How do we travel? photos by Ginger Giles. Watts, 1983. ISBN 0-531-04507-2 Subj: Activities – traveling. Transportation.

Mealtime for zoo animals photos by Richard Hewett. Carolrhoda, 1999. ISBN 1-57505-389-6 Subj: Animals. Food. Zoos.

Mother and baby zoo animals photos by Richard Hewett. Carolrhoda, 1999. ISBN 1-57505-285-7 Subj: Animals. Animals – babies. Zoos.

My friend from outer space ill. by Carol Nicklaus. Watts, 1981. ISBN 0-531-04192-1 Subj: Friendship. Imagination.

Noisytime for zoo animals photos by Richard Hewett. Carolrhoda, 1999. ISBN 1-57505-289-X Subj: Animals. Noise, sounds. Zoos.

Playtime for zoo animals photos by Richard Hewett. Carolrhoda, 1999. ISBN 1-57505-287-3 Subj: Activities – playing. Animals. Zoos.

Sleepytime for zoo animals photos by Richard Hewett. Carolrhoda, 1999. ISBN 1-57505-290-3 Subj: Animals. Sleep. Zoos.

Splashtime for zoo animals photos by Richard Hewett. Carolrhoda, 1999. ISBN 1-57505-288-1 Subj: Activities – playing. Animals. Zoos.

Sun fun ill. by author. Watts, 1981. ISBN 0-531-04312-6 Subj: Science. Sun.

The terrible Hodag ill. by Lambert Davis. Harcourt, 1989. ISBN 0-15-284750-2 Subj: Behavior – greed. Folk and fairy tales. Forest, woods. Monsters.

A walk by the seashore ill. by Freya Tanz. Silver Burdett, 1990. ISBN 0-671-68662-3 Subj: Animals. Ecology. Plants. Sea and seashore.

A walk in the desert ill. by Freya Tanz. Silver Burdett, 1990. ISBN 0-671-68664-X Subj: Animals. Desert. Ecology. Plants.

A walk in the woods ill. by Freya Tanz. Silver Burdett, 1990. ISBN 0-671-68665-8 Subj: Animals. Ecology. Forest, woods. Plants.

A walk on the Great Barrier Reef ill. with photos by Arthur Arnold and Marty Snyderman. Silver Burdett, 1988. ISBN 0-87614-285-4 Subj: Animals. Ecology. Foreign lands – Australia. Plants. Sea and seashore.

A walk up the mountain ill. by Freya Tanz. Silver Burdett, 1990. ISBN 0-671-68663-1 Subj: Animals. Ecology. Mountains. Plants.

What is a community? ill. by Carole Bertole. Watts, 1982. ISBN 0-531-04444-0 Subj: Careers. Communities, neighborhoods.

What we do when someone dies ill. by Helen K. Davie. Watts, 1987. ISBN 0-531-10095-2 Subj: Death. Emotions – grief.

What will we buy? photos by Ginger Giles. Watts, 1983. ISBN 0-531-04508-0 Subj: Money. Shopping.

Where do you go to school? ill. by Carole Bertole. Watts, 1982. Includes index. ISBN 0-531-04442-4 Subj: Careers – teachers. Communities, neighborhoods. School.

Who keeps us healthy? ill. by Carole Bertole. Watts, 1982. ISBN 0-531-04440-8 Subj: Careers – doctors. Careers – nurses. Health and fitness.

Who keeps us safe? photos by Carole Bertole. Watts, 1983. ISBN 0-531-04441-6 Subj: Careers. Safety.

Who works here? ill. by Carole Bertole. Watts, 1982. ISBN 0-531-04443-2 Subj: Careers. Communities, neighborhoods.

Arnold, Katrin. *Anna joins in* ill. by Renate Seelig. Abingdon, 1983. ISBN 0-687-01530-8 Subj: Handicaps. Illness. School.

Arnold, Katya. *The adventures of Snowwoman* retold and ill. by Katya Arnold. Holiday, 1998. Based on a story by V. Suteev. ISBN 0-8234-1390-X Subj: Animals. Holidays – Christmas. Santa Claus. Snowmen.

Baba Yaga and the little girl ill. by reteller. North-South, 1994. ISBN 1-55858-288-6 Subj: Character traits – cleverness. Family life – step families. Folk and fairy tales. Foreign lands – Russia. Witches.

Knock, knock, teremok! ill. by adapt. North-South, 1994. ISBN 1-55858-330-0 Subj: Cumulative tales. Folk and fairy tales. Foreign lands – Russia. Homes, houses. Rhyming text.

Meow! retold and ill. by Katya Arnold. Holiday, 1998. Based on a story by V. Suteev. ISBN 0-8234-

1361-6 Subj: Animals. Animals – cats. Animals – dogs. Noise, sounds.

Arnold, Lynda. *My Mommy has AIDS* ill. by Ellen M. Monahan and students of Rosemont School of the Holy Child. Dream Pub., 1998. ISBN 1-892073-01-3 Subj: Children as illustrators. Family life – mothers. Illness – AIDS.

Arnold, Marsha Diane. *The chicken salad club* ill. by Julie Downing. Dial, 1998. ISBN 0-8037-1916-7 Subj: Family life. Family life – great-grandparents. Old age.

Arnold, Mary. *The fussy angel* ill. by Patsy Nealon. Bethlehem Books, 1995. ISBN 1-883937-10-8 Subj: Angels. Holidays – Christmas. Religion – Nativity.

Arnold, Tedd. *Actions* ill. by author. Little Simon, 1985. ISBN 0-671-55492-1 Subj: Format, unusual – board books. Nursery rhymes.

Bisnipian blast-off: an action counting book ill. by Tedd Arnold; written by Laurie Abel; designed and paper engineered by Vincent Morales. Discovery Toys, 1990. ISBN 0-9399-7927-6 Subj: Counting, numbers. Format, unusual – toy and movable books. Mythical creatures.

Colors ill. by author. Little Simon, 1985. ISBN 0-671-55493-X Subj: Concepts – color. Format, unusual – board books. Nursery rhymes.

Five ugly monsters ill. by author. Scholastic, 1995. ISBN 0-590-22226-0 Subj: Counting, numbers. Monsters. Rhyming text. Sleep.

Green Wilma ill. by author. Dial, 1993. ISBN 0-8037-1314-2 Subj: Character traits – being different. Dreams. Frogs and toads. Rhyming text. School.

Huggly gets dressed ill. by author. Scholastic, 1997. ISBN 0-590-11759-9 Subj: Clothing. Monsters. Night.

Huggly takes a bath ill. by author. Scholastic, 1998. ISBN 0-590-91820-6 Subj: Behavior – misbehavior. Monsters. Night.

Mother Goose's words of wit and wisdom: a book of months ill. by author. Dial, 1990. ISBN 0-8037-0826-2 Subj: Behavior. Days of the week, months of the year. Nursery rhymes.

My first drawing book ill. by author. Workman, 1986. ISBN 0-89480-350-6 Subj: Format, unusual – board books. Format, unusual – toy and movable books. Toys – bears.

No jumping on the bed! ill. by author. Dial, 1987. ISBN 0-8037-0039-3 Subj: Bedtime. Behavior – misbehavior. Dreams. Furniture – beds. Imagination.

No more water in the tub! ill. by author. Dial, 1995. ISBN 0-8037-1583-8 Subj: Activities – bathing. Cumulative tales. Imagination.

Ollie forgot ill. by author. Dial, 1988. ISBN 0-8037-0488-7 Subj: Behavior – forgetfulness. Circular tales. Middle Ages. Rhyming text.

Opposites ill. by author. Little Simon, 1985. ISBN 0-671-55494-8 Subj: Concepts – opposites. Format, unusual – board books. Nursery rhymes.

Parts ill. by author. Dial, 1997. ISBN 0-8037-2041-6 Subj: Anatomy. Rhyming text.

The signmaker's assistant ill. by author. Dial, 1992. ISBN 0-8037-1011-9 Subj: Behavior – misbehavior. Traffic, traffic signs.

The simple people ill. by Andrew Shachat. Dial, 1992. ISBN 0-8037-1013-5 Subj: Activities – making things. Communities, neighborhoods.

Sounds ill. by author. Little Simon, 1985. ISBN 0-671-77826-9 Subj: Animals. Format, unusual – board books. Noise, sounds. Nursery rhymes.

The twin princes ill. by author. Dial, 1998. ISBN 0-8037-1418-1 Subj: Family life – brothers. Royalty – kings. Royalty – princes.

Arnold, Tim. *The three billy goats Gruff* (Asbjørnsen, P. C. [Peter Christen])

Arnosky, Jim. *All about deer* ill. by author. Scholastic, 1996. ISBN 0-590-46792-1 Subj: Animals – deer. Science.

All about turkeys ill. by author. Scholastic, 1998. ISBN 0-590-48147-9 Subj: Birds – turkeys.

All night near the water ill. by author. Putnam, 1994. ISBN 0-399-22629-X Subj: Birds – ducks. Night.

Come out, muskrats ill. by author. Lothrop, 1989. ISBN 0-688-05458-7 Subj: Animals – muskrats. Nature.

Crinkleroot's guide to knowing animal habitats ill. by author. Simon & Schuster, 1997. ISBN 0-689-80583-7 Subj: Animals. Nature.

Crinkleroot's guide to knowing butterflies and moths ill. by author. Simon & Schuster, 1996. ISBN 0-689-80587-X Subj: Insects – butterflies, caterpillars. Insects – moths. Science.

Crinkleroot's guide to knowing the trees ill. by author. Macmillan, 1992. ISBN 0-02-705855-7 Subj: Forest, woods. Nature. Trees.

Crinkleroot's guide to walking in wild places ill. by author. Bradbury, 1990. ISBN 0-02-705842-5 Subj: Activities – walking. Nature.

Crinkleroot's 25 birds every child should know ill. by author. Bradbury, 1993. ISBN 0-02-705859-X Subj: Birds. Nature.

Crinkleroot's 25 fish every child should know ill. by author. Bradbury, 1993. ISBN 0-02-705844-1 Subj: Fish. Nature.

Crinkleroot's 25 mammals every child should know ill. by author. Bradbury, 1994. ISBN 0-02-705845-X Subj: Animals. Nature.

Crinkleroot's visit to Crinkle Cove ill. by author. Simon & Schuster, 1998. ISBN 0-689-81602-2 Subj: Ecology. Nature. Reptiles – snakes.

Deer at the brook ill. by author. Lothrop, 1986. ISBN 0-688-04100-0 Subj: Animals – deer.

Every autumn comes the bear ill. by author. Putnam, 1993. ISBN 0-399-22508-0 Subj: Animals. Animals – bears. Hibernation. Seasons – fall. Seasons – winter.

I see animals hiding ill. by author. Scholastic, 1995. ISBN 0-590-48143-6 Subj: Animals. Behavior – hiding. Nature.

Mouse numbers and letters ill. by author. Harcourt, 1982. ISBN 0-15-256022-X Subj: ABC books. Animals – mice. Counting, numbers. Wordless.

Mouse writing ill. by author. Harcourt, 1983. ISBN 0-15-256028-9 Subj: ABC books. Activities – writing. Animals – mice. Birds. Wordless.

Mud time and more: Nathaniel stories ill. by author. Addison-Wesley, 1979. ISBN 0-20-100173-X Subj: Problem solving. Wordless.

Outdoors on foot ill. by author. Coward, 1978. ISBN 0-698-30684-8 Subj: Activities – walking. Humor. Seasons.

Rabbits and raindrops ill. by author. Putnam, 1997. ISBN 0-399-22635-4 Subj: Animals – rabbits. Weather – rain.

Raccoons and ripe corn ill. by author. Lothrop, 1987. ISBN 0-688-05456-0 Subj: Animals – raccoons. Farms. Food. Night.

Watching foxes ill. by author. Lothrop, 1985. ISBN 0-688-04260-0 Subj: Activities – playing. Animals – foxes.

Arnott, Kathleen. *Spiders, crabs and creepy crawlers: two African folktales* ill. by Bette Davis. Garrard, 1978. ISBN 0-8116-4412-X Subj: Folk and fairy tales. Foreign lands – Africa.

Arnsteen, Katy Keck. *Mrs. Gigglebelly is coming for tea* (Guthrie, Donna)

Arnstein, Helene S. *Billy and our new baby* ill. by M. Jane Smyth. Human Sciences Pr., 1973. ISBN 0-8770-5093-7 Subj: Babies. Family life – new sibling. Sibling rivalry.

Aroner, Miriam. *The kingdom of singing birds* ill. by Shelly O. Haas. Kar-Ben Copies, 1993. ISBN 0-929371-43-7 Subj: Activities – singing. Birds. Folk and fairy tales. Royalty – kings.

Aronin, Ben. *The secret of the Sabbath fish* ill. by Shay Rieger. Jewish Publication Society, 1979. ISBN 0-8276-0110-7 Subj: Folk and fairy tales. Food. Format, unusual – board books. Jewish culture.

Aronow, Sara. *Seven days of creation* ill. by Lynne Cassouto. Sepher-Hermon Pr., 1985. ISBN 0-87203-119-5 Subj: Creation. Religion. Rhyming text.

Arquette, Lois S. *see* Duncan, Lois

Arrhenius, Peter. *The Penguin Quartet* ill. by Ingela Peterson. Carolrhoda, 1998. ISBN 1-57505-252-0 Subj: Birds – penguins. Careers – musicians.

Artell, Mike. *Legs: a who's-under-the-flap book* ill. by author. Little Simon, 1996. ISBN 0-689-80621-3 Subj: Anatomy. Animals. Format, unusual – toy and movable books.

Arthur, Catherine. *My sister's silent world* ill. by Nathan Talbot. Childrens Pr., 1979. ISBN 0-516-02022-6 Subj: Birthdays. Family life. Handicaps – deafness. Senses – hearing. Zoos.

Arthur, Malcolm. *Puss in boots* (Perrault, Charles)

Artis, Vicki Kimmel. *Pajama walking* ill. by Emily Arnold McCully. Houghton Mifflin, 1981. ISBN 0-395-30343-5 Subj: Activities – playing. Friendship. Night.

Artzybasheff, Boris. *Seven Simeons* ill. by author. Viking, 1937. Subj: Caldecott award honor books.

Aruego, Ariane. *see* Dewey, Ariane

Aruego, José. *A crocodile's tale: a Philippine folk story* by José Aruego and Ariane Dewey; ill. by authors. Scribners, 1972. ISBN 0-684-12806-3 Subj: Folk and fairy tales. Foreign lands – Philippines. Reptiles – alligators, crocodiles.

The king and his friends ill. by author. Scribners, 1969. Subj: Dragons. Friendship. Mythical creatures. Royalty – kings.

Look what I can do ill. by author. Aladdin, 1988, c1971. ISBN 0-689-71205-7 Subj: Animals. Behavior – imitation. Folk and fairy tales. Foreign lands – Philippines. Games.

Pilyo the piranha ill. by author. Macmillan, 1971. Subj: Fish. Foreign lands – South America.

Rockabye crocodile: a folktale from the Philippines by José Aruego and Ariane Dewey; ill. by authors. Mulberry, 1993. ISBN 0-688-06739-5 Subj: Animals – pigs. Folk and fairy tales. Foreign lands – Philippines. Reptiles – alligators, crocodiles.

Symbiosis: a book of unusual friendships ill. by author. Scribners, 1970. Subj: Science.

We hide, you seek by José Aruego and Ariane Dewey; ill. by authors. Greenwillow, 1979. ISBN 0-688-84201-1 Subj: Animals. Behavior – hiding. Foreign lands – Africa. Games.

Arundel, Anne. *see* Arundel, Jocelyn

Arundel, Jocelyn. *Shoes for Punch* ill. by Wesley Dennis. McGraw-Hill, 1964. Subj: Animals – horses, ponies.

Arvetis, Chris. *Why does it fly?* by Chris Arvetis and Carole Palmer; ill. by James Buckley. Rand McNally, 1984. ISBN 0-528-82074-5 Subj: Activities – flying. Animals. Science.

Why does it thunder and lightning? by Chris Arvetis and Carole Palmer; ill. by James Buckley. Macmillan, 1985. ISBN 0-528-82671-9 Subj: Weather – storms. Weather – thunder.

Why is it dark? by Chris Arvetis and Carole Palmer; ill. by James Buckley. Rand McNally, 1984. ISBN 0-528-82075-3 Subj: Animals. Concepts. Science.

Asare, Meshack. *Cat . . . in search of a friend* ill. by author. Kane/Miller, 1986. ISBN 0-916291-07-3 Subj: Animals – cats. Behavior – needing someone. Friendship.

Asbjørnsen, P. C. (Peter Christen). *Billy goats Gruff* retold by Stephen Cosgrove; ill. by Wendy Edelson. Ideals Children's Books, 1988. ISBN 0-8249-8271-1 Subj: Animals – goats. Character traits – cleverness. Cumulative tales. Folk and fairy tales. Mythical creatures – trolls.

Billy goats Gruff retold and ill. by Susan Hellard. Putnam, 1986. ISBN 0-399-21291-4 Subj: Animals – goats. Character traits – cleverness. Cumulative tales. Folk and fairy tales. Mythical creatures – trolls.

The man who kept house by P. C. Asbjørnsen and J. E. Moe; ill. by Svend Otto S. Macmillan, 1992. ISBN 0-689-50560-4 Subj: Animals. Family life. Folk and fairy tales. Foreign lands – Norway.

The squire's bride: a Norwegian folk tale (The squire's bride)

The three billy goats Gruff adapt. and ill. by Tim Arnold. Margaret K. McElderry, 1993. ISBN 0-689-50575-2 Subj: Animals – goats. Character traits – cleverness. Folk and fairy tales. Mythical creatures – trolls.

The three billy goats Gruff adapt. and ill. by Robert Bender. Holt, 1993. ISBN 0-8050-2529-4 Subj: Animals – goats. Character traits – cleverness. Cumulative tales. Folk and fairy tales. Mythical creatures – trolls.

The three billy goats Gruff ill. by Marcia Brown. Harcourt, 1957. Subj: Animals – goats. Character traits – cleverness. Cumulative tales. Folk and fairy tales. Mythical creatures – trolls.

The three billy goats Gruff retold and ill. by Stephen Carpenter. HarperCollins, 1998. ISBN 0-694-01033-2 Subj: Animals – goats. Character traits – cleverness. Folk and fairy tales. Mythical creatures – trolls.

Three billy goats Gruff adapt. by Patricia C. and Fredrick McKissack; ill. by Tom Dunnington. Childrens Pr., 1987. ISBN 0-516-02366-7 Subj: Animals – goats. Character traits – cleverness. Cumulative tales. Folk and fairy tales. Mythical creatures – trolls.

The three billy goats Gruff ill. by Paul Galdone. Seabury Pr., 1973. Translation of De tre bukkene Bruse. ISBN 0-8164-3080-2 Subj: Animals – goats. Character traits – cleverness. Cumulative tales. Folk and fairy tales. Mythical creatures – trolls.

The three billy goats Gruff retold by Tom Roberts; ill. by David Jorgensen. Simon & Schuster, 1995. ISBN 0-689-80060-6 Subj: Animals – goats. Character traits – cleverness. Cumulative tales. Folk and fairy tales. Mythical creatures – trolls.

The three billy goats Gruff retold and ill. by Dennis Kendrick. Random House, 1979. ISBN 0-394-62044-5 Subj: Animals – goats. Character traits – cleverness. Cumulative tales. Folk and fairy tales. Mythical creatures – trolls.

The three billygoats Gruff adapted by Lucy Kincaid; ill. by Eric Kincaid. Rourke, 1983. ISBN 0-8659-2184-9 Subj: Animals – goats. Character traits – cleverness. Cumulative tales. Folk and fairy tales. Mythical creatures – trolls.

The three billy goats Gruff retold and ill. by Jonathan Langley. HarperCollins, 1998. ISBN 0-06-021474-0 Subj: Animals – goats. Character traits – cleverness. Cumulative tales. Folk and fairy tales. Mythical creatures – trolls.

The three billy goats Gruff retold by Jennifer Greenway; ill. by Loretta Lustig. Andrews & McMeel, 1991. Adapt. of Peter Christen Asbjørnsen's Tre bukkene Bruse. ISBN 0-8362-4913-5 Subj: Animals – goats. Character traits – cleverness. Cumulative tales. Folk and fairy tales. Mythical creatures – trolls.

The three billy goats Gruff retold by Alvin Granowsky; ill. by Thomas Newbury. Steck-Vaughn, 1996. ISBN 0-8114-7128-4 Subj: Animals – goats. Character traits – cleverness. Folk and fairy tales. Format, unusual – toy and movable books. Mythical creatures – trolls.

The three billy goats Gruff retold by Ellen Rudin; ill. by Lilian Obligado. Golden Pr., 1982. ISBN 0-307-68117-3 Subj: Animals – goats. Character traits – cleverness. Cumulative tales. Folk and fairy tales. Mythical creatures – trolls.

The three billy goats Gruff ill. by Ed Parker. Troll, 1979. ISBN 0-89375-121-9 Subj: Animals – goats. Character traits – cleverness. Cumulative tales. Folk and fairy tales. Mythical creatures – trolls.

The three billy goats Gruff retold by Lisa Meltzer; ill. by Heidi Petach. Checkerboard, 1989. ISBN 0-02-898242-8 Subj: Animals – goats. Character traits – cleverness. Cumulative tales. Folk and fairy tales. Mythical creatures – trolls. Rebuses.

The three billy goats Gruff retold by Harriet Ziefert; ill. by Laura Rader. Tambourine, 1994. ISBN 0-688-13259-6 Subj: Animals – goats. Character traits – cleverness. Cumulative tales. Folk and fairy tales. Format, unusual – toy and movable books. Mythical creatures – trolls.

The three billy goats Gruff retold and ill. by Glenn Rounds. Holiday, 1993. ISBN 0-8234-1015-3 Subj: Animals – goats. Character traits – cleverness. Cumulative tales. Folk and fairy tales. Mythical creatures – trolls.

The three billy goats Gruff adapt. and ill. by Janet Stevens. Harcourt, 1987. ISBN 0-15-286396-6 Subj: Animals – goats. Character traits – cleverness.

Cumulative tales. Folk and fairy tales. Mythical creatures – trolls.

The three billy goats Gruff ill. by William Stobbs. McGraw-Hill, 1967. Subj: Animals – goats. Character traits – cleverness. Cumulative tales. Folk and fairy tales. Mythical creatures – trolls.

The three billy goats Gruff adapt. and ill. by Svend Otto S. D. C. Heath, 1989. ISBN 0-669-13287-X Subj: Animals – goats. Character traits – cleverness. Cumulative tales. Folk and fairy tales. Mythical creatures – trolls.

The truth about three billy goats Gruff as told to Steven Otfinoski; pictures by Rowan Barnes-Murphy. WhistleStop, 1994. ISBN 0-8167-3013-X Subj: Animals – goats. Character traits – cleverness. Cumulative tales. Folk and fairy tales. Mythical creatures – trolls.

Asch, Frank. *The alphabet zoo* ill. by Lee Lee Brazeal. Scott Foresman, 1989. ISBN 0-673-74984-3 Subj: ABC books. Activities. Rhyming text.

Baby Bird's first nest ill. by author. Harcourt, 1999. ISBN 0-15-201726-7 Subj: Birds. Birds – babies. Character traits – helpfulness. Frogs and toads.

Baby in the box ill. by author. Holiday, 1989. ISBN 0-8234-0725-X Subj: Babies. Rhyming text. Toys.

Barnyard lullaby ill. by author. Simon & Schuster, 1998. ISBN 0-689-81363-5 Subj: Animals. Careers – farmers. Lullabies. Music. Noise, sounds.

Bear shadow ill. by author. Prentice-Hall, 1985. ISBN 0-13-071580-8 Subj: Animals – bears. Shadows.

Bear's bargain ill. by author. Prentice-Hall, 1985. ISBN 0-13-071606-5 Subj: Animals – bears. Birds. Emotions – envy, jealousy.

Bread and honey ill. by author. Parents, 1981. Adapt. from the author's Monkey face. ISBN 0-8193-1078-6 Subj: Activities – painting. Animals. Animals – bears. Family life – mothers.

Cactus poems photos by Ted Levin. Harcourt, 1998. ISBN 0-15-200676-1 Subj: Desert. Ecology. Poems.

City sandwich ill. by author. Greenwillow, 1978. ISBN 0-688-84156-2 Subj: City. Imagination. Poetry.

Country pie ill. by author. Greenwillow, 1979. ISBN 0-688-84188-0 Subj: Country. Poetry. Weather.

Dear brother by Frank Asch and Vladimir Vagin; ill. by authors. Scholastic, 1992. ISBN 0-590-43107-2 Subj: Activities – reading. Animals – mice. City. Country. Family life. Family life – brothers. Letters, cards.

The earth and I ill. by author. Gulliver, 1994. ISBN 0-15-200443-2 Subj: Earth. Nature.

The flower faerie by Frank Asch and Vladimir Vagin; ill. by Frank Asch. Scholastic, 1993. ISBN 0-590-45493-5 Subj: Fairies. Folk and fairy tales. Royalty – emperors.

George's store ill. by author. Parents, 1983. ISBN 0-8368-0877-0 Subj: Birds – parakeets, parrots. Careers – storekeepers.

Gia and the one hundred dollars worth of bubblegum based on a story by Cresent Giasullo; ill. by author with a little help from Russell Alan Bush and Linda and Pat Galle. McGraw-Hill, 1974. ISBN 0-07-002418-9 Subj: Activities.

Good lemonade ill. by author. Watts, 1976. ISBN 0-531-01093-7 Subj: Activities – working. Food.

Good night, Baby Bear ill. by author. Harcourt, 1998. ISBN 0-15-200836-5 Subj: Animals – bears. Bedtime. Family life. Seasons – winter. Sleep.

Goodbye house ill. by author. Prentice-Hall, 1986. ISBN 0-13-360272-9 Subj: Animals – bears. Family life. Moving.

Goodnight horsey ill. by author. Prentice-Hall, 1981. ISBN 0-13-360461-6 Subj: Animals – horses, ponies. Bedtime. Family life – fathers. Games. Imagination.

Happy birthday, moon! ill. by author. Prentice-Hall, 1982. ISBN 0-13-383687-8 Subj: Animals – bears. Birthdays. Moon.

Here comes the cat! (Vagin, Vladimir Vasil'evich)

I can blink ill. by author. Crown, 1986. ISBN 0-517-56119-0 Subj: Animals. Character traits – appearance. Format, unusual – toy and movable books.

I can roar ill. by author. Crown, 1986. ISBN 1-55074-382-1 Subj: Animals. Format, unusual – toy and movable books. Noise, sounds.

In the eye of the teddy ill. by author. Harper, 1973. ISBN 0-06-020152-5 Subj: Toys – bears. Wordless.

Insects from outer space by Frank Asch and Vladimir Vagin; ill. by Vladimir Vagin. Scholastic, 1994. ISBN 0-590-45489-7 Subj: Insects. Parties.

Just like daddy ill. by author. Prentice-Hall, 1981. ISBN 0-1351-4042-0 Subj: Animals – bears. Behavior – imitation. Family life – fathers.

The last puppy ill. by author. Prentice-Hall, 1980. ISBN 0-1352-4058-1 Subj: Animals – dogs. Pets.

Little Devil's ABC ill. by author. Scribners, 1979. ISBN 0-684-16096-X Subj: ABC books. Devil.

Little Devil's 123 ill. by author. Scribners, 1979. ISBN 0-684-16294-6 Subj: Counting, numbers. Devil.

MacGooses's grocery ill. by James Marshall. Dial, 1978. ISBN 0-8037-5231-8 Subj: Birds – geese. Eggs.

Milk and cookies ill. by author. Parents, 1992. ISBN 0-8368-0878-9 Subj: Animals – bears. Bedtime. Dragons. Dreams.

Monkey face ill. by author. Parents, 1977. ISBN 0-819-30863-3 Subj: Activities – drawing. Animals. Behavior – dissatisfaction.

Moonbear ill. by author. Little Simon, 1993. ISBN 0-671-86743-1 Subj: Animals – bears. Birds. Food. Moon. Night.

Moonbear's books ill. by author. Little Simon, 1993. ISBN 0-671-86744-X Subj: Activities – reading. Animals – bears. Format, unusual – board books.

Moonbear's canoe ill. by author. Little Simon, 1993. ISBN 0-671-86745-8 Subj: Animals – bears. Canoes and canoeing. Format, unusual – board books.

Moonbear's dream ill. by author. Simon & Schuster, 1999. ISBN 0-689-82244-8 Subj: Animals. Animals – bears. Behavior – misbehavior. Birds. Dreams.

Moonbear's friend ill. by author. Little Simon, 1993. ISBN 0-671-86746-6 Subj: Animals – bears. Friendship.

Moonbear's pet ill. by author. Simon & Schuster, 1997. ISBN 0-689-80794-5 Subj: Animals – bears. Birds. Fish. Friendship. Frogs and toads.

Mooncake ill. by author. Prentice-Hall, 1983. ISBN 0-1360-1013-X Subj: Animals – bears. Birds. Moon. Seasons – winter.

Moondance ill. by author. Scholastic, 1993. ISBN 0-590-45487-0 Subj: Activities – dancing. Animals – bears. Moon.

Moongame ill. by author. Prentice-Hall, 1984. ISBN 0-13-600503-9 Subj: Activities – dancing. Animals – bears. Behavior – hiding. Moon.

Oats and wild apples ill. by author. Holiday, 1988. ISBN 0-8234-0677-6 Subj: Animals – bulls, cows. Animals – deer. Friendship.

Popcorn ill. by author. Parents, 1979. ISBN 0-819-31002-6 Subj: Animals – bears. Food. Holidays – Halloween. Parties.

Rebecka ill. by author. HarperCollins, 1972. ISBN 0-06-020149-5 Subj: Activities – playing. Animals – dogs. Imagination.

Sand cake ill. by author. Parents, 1979. ISBN 0-8193-0986-9 Subj: Activities – picnicking. Animals – bears. Humor. Sea and seashore.

Short train, long train ill. by author. Scholastic, 1992. ISBN 0-590-44493-X Subj: Concepts – opposites. Format, unusual – toy and movable books. Language.

Skyfire ill. by author. Simon & Schuster, 1988. ISBN 0-671-66692-4 Subj: Animals – bears. Weather – rainbows.

Starbaby ill. by author. Scribners, 1980. ISBN 0-684-16490-6 Subj: Babies. Sea and seashore. Sky. Stars.

Turtle tale ill. by author. Dial, 1978. ISBN 0-8037-8783-9 Subj: Humor. Reptiles – turtles, tortoises.

Water ill. by author. Harcourt, 1995. ISBN 0-15-200189-1 Subj: Nature. Water.

Yellow, yellow ill. by Mark Alan Stamaty. McGraw-Hill, 1971. Subj: Clothing. Concepts – color.

Ziggy Piggy and the three little pigs ill. by author. Kids Can Pr., 1998. ISBN 1-55074-515-8 Subj: Animals – pigs. Animals – wolves. Character traits – cleverness. Folk and fairy tales.

Asch, George. *Linda* ill. by author. McGraw-Hill, 1969. Subj: City. Emotions – happiness. Wordless.

Aseltine, Lorraine. *First grade can wait* ill. by Virginia Wright-Frierson. Albert Whitman, 1988. ISBN 0-8075-2451-4 Subj: Behavior – growing up. School.

I'm deaf and it's okay by Lorraine Aseltine, Evelyn Mueller and Nancy Tait; ill. by Helen Cogancherry. Albert Whitman, 1986. ISBN 0-8075-3472-2 Subj: Emotions – anger. Emotions – fear. Handicaps – deafness. Senses – hearing.

Ash, Jutta. *Rapunzel* (Grimm, Jacob)

Wedding birds ill. by author. Little, 1987. ISBN 0-87113-122-6 Subj: Birds. Music. Songs. Weddings.

Ashabranner, Brent. *I'm in the zoo, too* ill. by Janet Stevens. Dutton, 1989. ISBN 0-525-65002-4 Subj: Animals. Animals – squirrels. Zoos.

Asher, Sandy. *Princess Bee and the royal good-night story* ill. by Cat Bowman Smith. Albert Whitman, 1989. ISBN 0-8075-6624-1 Subj: Bedtime. Behavior – needing someone. Family life. Royalty. Sleep.

Ashey, Bella. *see* Breinburg, Petronella

Ashforth, Camilla. *Calamity* ill. by author. Candlewick, 1993. ISBN 1-56402-252-8 Subj: Animals. Sports – racing. Toys.

Horatio's bed ill. by author. Candlewick, 1992. ISBN 1-56402-057-6 Subj: Bedtime. Toys. Toys – bears.

Monkey tricks ill. by author. Candlewick, 1992. ISBN 1-56402-170-X Subj: Behavior – misbehavior. Toys. Toys – bears.

Ashley, Bernard. *Dinner ladies don't count* ill. by Janet Duchesne. Watts, 1981. ISBN 0-531-04281-2 Subj: Behavior – misbehavior. Birthdays. Problem solving. School.

Ashley Bryan's abc of African American poetry ill. by Ashley Bryan. Atheneum, 1997. ISBN 0-689-81209-4 Subj: ABC books. Ethnic groups in the U.S. – African Americans. Poetry.

Ashley, Jill. *Riddles about Christmas* photos by Rob Gray. Silver Pr., 1990. ISBN 0-671-70552-0 Subj: Holidays – Christmas. Poetry. Riddles.

Ashton, Elizabeth Allen. *An old-fashioned ABC book* ill. by Jessie Willcox Smith. Viking, 1990. ISBN 0-670-83048-8 Subj: ABC books. Rhyming text.

An old-fashioned one two three book ill. by Jessie Willcox Smith. Viking, 1991. ISBN 0-670-83499-8 Subj: Counting, numbers. Rhyming text.

Asimov, Isaac. *Animals of the Bible* ill. by Howard Berelson. Doubleday, 1978. ISBN 0-385-07215-5 Subj: Animals.

The best new thing ill. by Symeon Shimin. Collins-World, 1971. Subj: Earth. Science. Space and space ships.

The moon ill. by Alex Ebel. Follett, 1967. Subj: Moon. Science.

Askar, Saoussan. *From far away* (Munsch, Robert N.)

Astley, Judy. *When one cat woke up* ill. by author. Dial, 1990. ISBN 0-8037-0782-7 Subj: Animals – cats. Counting, numbers.

At the farm ill. by Roser Capdevila. Firefly, 1985. ISBN 0-920303-08-0 Subj: Farms. Format, unusual – board books.

Ata, Te. *Baby Rattlesnake* adapt. by Lynn Moroney; ill. by Veg Reisberg. Childrens Book Pr., 1989. ISBN 0-89239-049-2 Subj: Folk and fairy tales. Indians of North America – Chickasaw.

Atene, Ann (Anna). *The golden guitar* ill. by author. Little, 1967. Subj: Foreign lands – Italy. Music. Puppets.

Atkins, Jeannine. *Get set! Swim!* ill. by Hector Viveros Lee. Lee & Low, 1998. ISBN 1-880000-66-0 Subj: Character traits – pride. Ethnic groups in the U.S. – Puerto Rican Americans. Sports – swimming.

Mary Anning and the sea dragon ill. by Michael Dooling. Farrar, 1999. ISBN 0-374-34840-5 Subj: Careers – paleontologists. Dinosaurs. Dragons. Foreign lands – England.

Attenberger, Walburga. *The little man in winter* ill. by author. Random House, 1972. Translation of Het mannetje in de winter. ISBN 0-394-92428-2 Subj: Foreign lands – Germany. Rhyming text. Seasons – winter.

Who knows the little man? ill. by author. Random House, 1972. Translation of Wie kent dat kleine mannetje? ISBN 0-394-92427-4 Subj: Foreign lands – Germany. Rhyming text.

Attenborough, Elizabeth. *Walk rabbit walk* (McNaughton, Colin)

Atwell, Debby. *Barn* ill. by author. Houghton Mifflin, 1996. ISBN 0-395-78568-5 Subj: Barns.

Humphrey Thud ill. by author. Candlewick, 1995. ISBN 1-56402-538-1 Subj: Animals. Magic. Toys. Toys – bears.

River ill. by author. Houghton Mifflin, 1999. ISBN 0-395-93546-6 Subj: Ecology. Rivers. Water.

Atwood, Ann. *The little circle* ill. by author. Scribners, 1967. Subj: Concepts – shape. Rhyming text.

Atwood, Margaret. *Anna's pet* by Margaret Atwood and Joyce Barkhouse; ill. by Ann Blades. Lori-

mer, 1980. ISBN 0-88862-249-X Subj: Animals. Character traits – optimism. Country. Pets.

Auch, Mary Jane. *Bantam of the opera* ill. by author. Holiday, 1997. ISBN 0-8234-1312-8 Subj: Activities – singing. Birds – chickens. Humor.

Bird dogs can't fly ill. by author. Holiday, 1993. ISBN 0-8234-1050-1 Subj: Animals – dogs. Birds – geese. Friendship. Seasons – winter.

The Easter egg farm ill. by author. Holiday, 1992. ISBN 0-8234-0917-1 Subj: Birds – chickens. Eggs. Holidays – Easter.

Eggs mark the spot ill. by author. Holiday, 1996. ISBN 0-8234-1242-3 Subj: Art. Birds – chickens. Crime. Eggs.

Hen lake ill. by author. Holiday, 1995. ISBN 0-8234-1188-5 Subj: Activities – dancing. Ballet. Birds – chickens. Birds – peacocks, peahens.

Monster brother ill. by author. Holiday, 1994. ISBN 0-8234-1095-1 Subj: Babies. Bedtime. Emotions – fear. Family life – brothers. Family life – new sibling. Monsters.

The nutquacker ill. by author. Holiday, 1999. ISBN 0-8234-1524-4 Subj: Animals. Birds – ducks. Farms. Holidays – Christmas.

Peeping Beauty ill. by author. Holiday, 1993. ISBN 0-8234-1001-3 Subj: Activities – dancing. Animals – foxes. Ballet. Birds – chickens.

Auer, Martin. *Now, now Markus* by Martin Auer and Simone Klages; ill. by authors. Greenwillow, 1989. ISBN 0-688-08975-5 Subj: Behavior – misbehavior. Birds – swans. Giants.

Auerbach, Julie Jaslow. *Everything's changing - It's pesach!* ill. by Chari Radin. Kar-Ben Copies, 1986. ISBN 0-930494-53-9 Subj: Holidays – Passover. Jewish culture. Rhyming text.

Auerbach, Marjorie. *King Lavra and the barber* ill. by author. Knopf, 1964. Subj: Behavior – secrets. Careers – barbers. Folk and fairy tales. Royalty – kings.

Augarde, Steve (Stephen). *Barnaby Shrew, Black Dan and . . . the mighty wedgwood* ill. by author. Elsevier-Dutton, 1980. ISBN 0-233-97104-1 Subj: Animals – mice. Animals – rats. Animals – shrews. Behavior – boasting. Birds – parakeets, parrots. Reptiles – turtles, tortoises.

Barnaby Shrew goes to sea ill. by author. Elsevier-Dutton, 1979. ISBN 0-233-96957-8 Subj: Animals – rats. Animals – shrews. Boats, ships. Reptiles – turtles, tortoises.

Humpty Dumpty (Mother Goose)

Pig ill. by author. Bradbury, 1977. ISBN 0-87888-099-2 Subj: Animals – pigs. Farms. Fire.

Aulaire, Edgar Parin d'. *Abraham Lincoln* (Aulaire, Ingri Mortenson d')

Animals everywhere (Aulaire, Ingri Mortenson d')

Children of the northlights (Aulaire, Ingri Mortenson d')

Don't count your chicks (Aulaire, Ingri Mortenson d')

East of the sun and west of the moon (Aulaire, Ingri Mortenson d')

Foxie, the singing dog (Aulaire, Ingri Mortenson d')

Nils (Aulaire, Ingri Mortenson d')

Ola (Aulaire, Ingri Mortenson d')

Pocahontas (Aulaire, Ingri Mortenson d')

The terrible troll-bird (Aulaire, Ingri Mortenson d')

Too big (Aulaire, Ingri Mortenson d')

The two cars (Aulaire, Ingri Mortenson d')

Wings for Per (Aulaire, Ingri Mortenson d')

Aulaire, Ingri Mortenson d'. *Abraham Lincoln* by Ingri and Edgar Parin d'Aulaire; ill. by authors. Rev. ed. Doubleday, 1957. ISBN 0-385-07674-6 Subj: Caldecott award books. U.S. history.

Animals everywhere by Ingri and Edgar Parin d'Aulaire; ill. by authors. Doubleday, 1940. Subj: Animals.

Children of the northlights by Ingri and Edgar Parin d'Aulaire; ill. by authors. Viking, 1962. Subj: Activities – bathing. Activities – playing. Animals. Family life. Folk and fairy tales. Foreign lands – Lapland. School. Seasons – winter.

Don't count your chicks by Ingri and Edgar Parin d'Aulaire; ill. by authors. Doubleday, 1943. ISBN 0-440-40771-0 Subj: Behavior – greed. Birds – chickens. Folk and fairy tales. Humor.

East of the sun and west of the moon ed. by Ingri and Edgar Parin d'Aulaire; ill. by eds. Viking, 1938. ISBN 0-670-28748-2 Subj: Animals – polar bears. Folk and fairy tales. Foreign lands – Norway. Royalty – princes. Witches.

Foxie, the singing dog by Ingri and Edgar Parin d'Aulaire; ill. by authors. Doubleday, 1949. Subj: Animals – cats. Animals – dogs. Birds – chickens.

Nils by Ingri and Edgar Parin d'Aulaire; ill. by authors. Doubleday, 1948. Subj: Character traits – being different. Cowboys. Family life. School.

Ola by Ingri and Edgar Parin d'Aulaire; ill. by authors. Doubleday, 1932. Subj: Foreign lands – Norway.

Pocahontas by Ingri and Edgar Parin d'Aulaire; ill. by authors. Doubleday, [1985] c1946. ISBN 0-385-07454-9 Subj: Indians of North America – Powhaton. Pilgrims. U.S. history.

The terrible troll-bird by Ingri and Edgar Parin d'Aulaire; ill. by authors. Doubleday, 1976. ISBN 0-385-03475-X Subj: Foreign lands – Norway. Mythical creatures – trolls.

Too big by Ingri and Edgar Parin d'Aulaire; ill. by authors. Doubleday, 1945. Subj: Behavior – growing up. Concepts – size.

The two cars by Ingri and Edgar Parin d'Aulaire; ill. by authors. Doubleday, 1955. Subj: Automobiles.

Wings for Per by Ingri and Edgar Parin d'Aulaire; ill. by authors. Doubleday, 1944. Subj: Activities – flying. Character traits – bravery. Farms. War.

Auld, Mary. *Daniel in the lions' den* (Bible. Old Testament. Daniel)

Austin, Margot. *Barney's adventure* ill. by author. Dutton, 1941. Subj: Circus. Clowns, jesters.

A friend for Growl Bear ill. by David McPhail. HarperCollins, 1999. ISBN 0-06-027802-1 Subj: Animals. Animals – bears. Behavior – needing someone.

Austin, Virginia. *Say please* ill. by author. Candlewick, 1995. ISBN 1-56402-496-2 Subj: Activities – reading. Animals. Etiquette.

Auzary-Luton, Sylvie. *1, 2, 3, music!* ill. by author. Orchard, 1999. ISBN 0-531-30188-5 Subj: Family life. Family life – grandfathers. Music.

Averill, Esther. *The fire cat* ill. by author. HarperCollins, 1960. ISBN 0-06-020196-7 Subj: Animals – cats. Careers – firefighters.

Axelrod, Amy. *Pigs in the pantry: fun with math and cooking* ill. by Sharon McGinley-Nally. Simon & Schuster, 1997. ISBN 0-689-80665-5 Subj: Activities – cooking. Animals – pigs. Counting, numbers. Food.

Pigs on a blanket ill. by Sharon McGinley-Nally. Simon & Schuster, 1996. ISBN 0-689-80505-5 Subj: Animals – pigs. Behavior – tardiness. Clocks, watches. Sea and seashore. Time.

Pigs on the ball: fun with math and sports ill. by Sharon McGinley-Nally. Simon & Schuster, 1998. ISBN 0-689-81565-4 Subj: Animals – pigs. Concepts – shape. Counting, numbers. Family life. Sports.

Pigs on the move: fun with math and travel ill. by Sharon McGinley-Nally. Simon & Schuster, 1999. ISBN 0-689-81070-9 Subj: Activities – traveling. Animals – pigs. Concepts – distance. Concepts – measurement. Holidays – Christmas.

Pigs will be pigs ill. by Sharon McGinley-Nally. Four Winds, 1994. ISBN 0-02-765415-X Subj: Animals – pigs. Family life. Food. Money.

Axworthy, Anni. *Along came Toto* ill. by author. Candlewick, 1993. ISBN 1-56402-172-6 Subj: Animals – cats. Animals – dogs. Behavior – needing someone.

Ben's Wednesday ill. by author. David & Charles, 1986. ISBN 0-340-33289-1 Subj: Dreams. Monsters. Night.

Guess what I am ill. by author. Candlewick, 1998. ISBN 0-7636-0625-1 Subj: Animals. Format, unusual.

Guess what I'll be ill. by author. Candlewick, 1998. ISBN 0-7636-0626-X Subj: Animals. Format, unusual.

Ayal, Ora. *The adventures of Chester the chest* by Ora Ayal and Naomi Löw Nakao; ill. by Ora Ayal. HarperCollins, 1982. ISBN 0-06-020306-4 Subj: Activities – flying. Behavior – boredom. Imagination.

Ugbu trans. by Naomi Löw Nakao; ill. by author. HarperCollins, 1979. ISBN 0-06-020308-0 Subj: Activities – playing. Imagination.

Ayars, James Sterling. *Caboose on the roof* ill. by Bob Hodgell. Abelard-Schuman, 1956. Subj: Homes, houses. Humor. Trains.

Contrary Jenkins (Caudill, Rebecca)

Aye, Nila. *When I'm big* (Drury, Tim)

Ayer, Jacqueline. *Little Silk* ill. by author. Harcourt, 1970. ISBN 0-15-247450-1 Subj: Behavior – lost. Toys – dolls.

Nu Dang and his kite ill. by author. Harcourt, 1959. Subj: Behavior – losing things. Foreign lands – Thailand. Kites. Toys.

The paper-flower tree: a tale from Thailand ill. by author. Harcourt, 1962. Subj: Character traits – optimism. Foreign lands – Thailand. Plants.

A wish for little sister ill. by author. Harcourt, 1962. Subj: Behavior – wishing. Birds. Birthdays. Family life. Foreign lands – Thailand.

Ayers, Rebecca Hickox. *Per and the Dala horse* ill. by Yvonne Gilbert. Doubleday, 1993. ISBN 0-385-32075-2 Subj: Animals – horses, ponies. Family life – brothers. Farms. Folk and fairy tales. Foreign lands – Sweden. Magic. Mythical creatures – trolls. Toys.

Zorro and Quwi: tales of a trickster pig ill. by Kim Howard. Doubleday, 1997. ISBN 0-385-32122-8 Subj: Animals – foxes. Animals – guinea pigs. Folk and fairy tales. Foreign lands – Peru.

Aylesworth, Jim. *The bad dream* ill. by Judith Friedman. Albert Whitman, 1985. ISBN 0-8075-0506-4 Subj: Animals – dogs. Dreams. Family life. Sleep.

The cat and the fiddle and more ill. by Richard Hull. Atheneum, 1992. ISBN 0-689-31715-8 Subj: Nursery rhymes. Poetry.

The completed hickory dickory dock ill. by Eileen Christelow. Macmillan, 1990. ISBN 0-689-31606-2 Subj: Animals – mice. Clocks, watches. Counting, numbers. Nursery rhymes. Time.

Country crossing ill. by Ted Rand. Macmillan, 1991. ISBN 0-689-31580-5 Subj: Noise, sounds. Trains.

The folks in the valley ill. by Stefano Vitale. Harper-Collins, 1992. ISBN 0-06-021929-7 Subj: ABC books. Rhyming text.

The full belly bowl ill. by Wendy Halperin. Atheneum, 1998. ISBN 0-689-81033-4 Subj: Folk and fairy tales. Magic.

The gingerbread man (The gingerbread boy)

The good-night kiss ill. by Walter Lyon Krudop. Atheneum, 1993. ISBN 0-689-31515-5 Subj: Animals. Bedtime. Night.

Hanna's hog ill. by Glen Rounds. Atheneum, 1988. ISBN 0-689-31367-5 Subj: Animals – pigs. Behavior – stealing. Behavior – trickery.

Hush up! ill. by Glen Rounds. Holt, 1980. ISBN 0-03-054841-1 Subj: Character traits – laziness. Humor. Noise, sounds.

McGraw's Emporium ill. by Mavis Smith. Holt, 1995. ISBN 0-8050-3192-8 Subj: Animals – cats. Friendship. Illness.

Mary's mirror ill. by Richard Egielski. Holt, 1982. ISBN 0-03-060392-7 Subj: Behavior – greed. Emotions – envy, jealousy. Rhyming text.

Mr. McGill goes to town ill. by Thomas Graham. Holt, 1989. ISBN 0-8050-0772-5 Subj: Character traits – helpfulness. Cumulative tales. Fairs. Friendship. Rhyming text.

Mother Halverson's new cat ill. by Toni Goffe. Macmillan, 1989. ISBN 0-689-31465-5 Subj: Animals – cats. Character traits – practicality.

My sister's rusty bike ill. by Richard Hull. Atheneum, 1996. ISBN 0-689-31798-0 Subj: Activities – traveling. Rhyming text. Sports – bicycling. Tall tales.

My son John woodcuts by David Frampton. Holt, 1994. ISBN 0-8050-1725-9 Subj: Careers – farmers. Farms. Nursery rhymes.

Old Black Fly ill. by Stephen Gammell. Holt, 1992. ISBN 0-8050-1401-2 Subj: ABC books. Insects – flies. Rhyming text.

One crow: a counting rhyme ill. by Ruth Young. HarperCollins, 1988. ISBN 0-397-32175-9 Subj: Animals. Counting, numbers. Farms. Rhyming text.

Shenandoah Noah ill. by Glen Rounds. Holt, 1985. ISBN 0-03-003749-2 Subj: Activities – working. Emotions – embarrassment. Humor.

Siren in the night ill. by Tom Centola. Albert Whitman, 1983. ISBN 0-8075-7374-4 Subj: Activities – walking. Emotions – fear. Family life. Noise, sounds.

Teddy bear tears ill. by Jo Ellen McAllister-Stammen. Atheneum, 1997. ISBN 0-689-31776-X Subj: Bedtime. Emotions – fear. Toys – bears.

Through the night ill. by Pamela Patrick. Simon & Schuster, 1998. ISBN 0-689-80642-6 Subj: Activities – driving. Family life – fathers. Night.

Tonight's the night ill. by John Wallner. Albert Whitman, 1981. ISBN 0-8075-8020-1 Subj: Bedtime. Dreams. Night. Sleep.

Two terrible frights ill. by Eileen Christelow. Atheneum, 1987. ISBN 0-689-31327-6 Subj: Animals – mice. Emotions – fear. Night.

Wake up, little children: a rise-and-shine rhyme ill. by Walter Lyon Krudop. Atheneum, 1996. ISBN 0-689-31857-X Subj: Activities. Country. Morning. Rhyming text.

Ayres, Becky Hickox. *Matreshka* ill. by Alexi Natchev. Doubleday, 1992. ISBN 0-385-30657-1 Subj: Folk and fairy tales. Foreign lands – Russia. Toys – dolls. Witches.

Victoria flies high ill. by Robin Michal Koontz. Dutton, 1990. ISBN 0-525-65014-8 Subj: Activities – flying. Animals – pigs. Magic.

Ayres, Pam. *Guess what?* ill. by Julie Lacome. Knopf, 1988. ISBN 0-394-99287-3 Subj: Rhyming text.

Guess who? ill. by Julie Lacome. Knopf, 1988. ISBN 0-394-99288-1 Subj: Rhyming text.

Piggo and the nosebag ill. by Andy Ellis. Parkwest, 1991. ISBN 0-563-20922-4 Subj: Animals – pigs.

Piggo has a train ride ill. by Andy Ellis. Parkwest, 1992. ISBN 0-563-20921-6 Subj: Animals – pigs. Trains.

When dad cuts down the chestnut tree ill. by Percy Graham. Knopf, 1988. ISBN 0-394-90435-4 Subj: Family life – fathers. Nature. Rhyming text. Trees.

When dad fills in the garden pond ill. by Percy Graham. Knopf, 1988. ISBN 0-394-90441-4 Subj: Activities – digging. Family life – fathers. Nature. Rhyming text.

Azaad, Meyer (Mahmud). *Half for you* ill. by Nahid Haqiqat. Carolrhoda, 1971. ISBN 0-87614-016-9 Subj: Behavior – sharing. Birds. Careers. Clothing.

Azarian, Mary. *A farmer's alphabet* ill. by author. Godine, 1981. ISBN 0-87923-394-X Subj: ABC books. Activities. Farms.

The tale of John Barleycorn or, From barley to beer: a traditional English ballad ill. by author. Godine, 1983. ISBN 0-87923-446-6 Subj: Folk and fairy tales. Food. Foreign lands – England. Middle Ages. Music. Poetry.

B. B. Blacksheep and Company: *a collection of favorite nursery rhymes* ill. by Nick Butterworth.

Grosset, 1982. ISBN 0-448-16577-5 Subj: Animals. Nursery rhymes.

B-52's (Musical group). *Wig!* ill. by Laura Levine. Hyperion, 1995. ISBN 0-7868-2064-0 Subj: Hair. Songs.

Baba, Noboru. *Eleven cats and a pig* ill. by author. Carolrhoda, 1988. ISBN 0-87614-338-9 Subj: Animals – cats. Behavior – misbehavior. Character traits – selfishness.

Eleven cats and albatrosses ill. by author. Carolrhoda, 1988. ISBN 0-87614-335-4 Subj: Animals – cats. Behavior – misbehavior. Character traits – selfishness.

Eleven cats in a bag ill. by author. Carolrhoda, 1988. ISBN 0-87614-336-2 Subj: Animals – cats. Behavior – misbehavior. Character traits – selfishness.

Eleven hungry cats ill. by author. Carolrhoda, 1988. ISBN 0-87614-337-0 Subj: Animals – cats. Behavior – misbehavior. Character traits – selfishness.

Babbitt, Lorraine. *Pink like the geranium* ill. by author. Childrens Pr., 1973. ISBN 0-516-08841-6 Subj: Behavior. Clothing. Family life. School.

Babbitt, Natalie. *Bub, or, The very best thing* ill. by author. HarperCollins, 1994. ISBN 0-06-205045-1 Subj: Emotions – love. Family life. Middle Ages. Royalty.

Nellie, a cat on her own ill. by author. Farrar, 1989. ISBN 0-374-35506-1 Subj: Activities – dancing. Animals – cats. Character traits – freedom.

Ouch! a tale from Grimm retold by Natalie Babbitt; ill. by Fred Marcellino. HarperCollins, 1998. ISBN 0-06-205067-2 Subj: Folk and fairy tales. Foreign lands – Germany.

The something ill. by author. Farrar, 1970. ISBN 0-374-37137-7 Subj: Emotions – fear. Monsters. Night.

Babbitt, Samuel F. *The forty-ninth magician* ill. by Natalie Babbitt. Pantheon, 1966. Subj: Magic. Royalty.

Babcock, Chris. *No moon, no milk!* ill. by Mark Teague. Crown, 1993. ISBN 0-517-58780-7 Subj: Animals – bulls, cows. Moon.

The babes in the woods. *The old ballad of the babes in the woods* ed. by Kathleen Lines; ill. by Edward Ardizzone. Walck, 1972. Derived from a Chapbook ed. published in 1640. ISBN 0-8098-1197-9 Subj: Folk and fairy tales. Orphans. Poetry.

Babson, Jane F. *Babson's bestiary* ill. by author. Winstead Pr., 1991. ISBN 0-940787-02-4 Subj: ABC books. Animals. Rhyming text.

Baby's first book of colors ill. by Nina Barbaresi. Platt, 1986. ISBN 0-448-10827-5 Subj: Animals – rabbits. Concepts – color. Format, unusual – board books.

Baby's words photos sel. by Debby Slier. Macmillan, 1988. ISBN 0-02-688751-7 Subj: Babies. Format, unusual – board books. Language.

Bach, Alice. *The day after Christmas* ill. by Mary Chalmers. HarperCollins, 1975. ISBN 0-06-020314-5 Subj: Emotions. Holidays – Christmas.

Millicent the magnificent ill. by Steven Kellogg. HarperCollins, 1978. ISBN 0-06-020312-9 Subj: Animals – bears. Circus. Emotions – envy, jealousy. Family life.

The smartest bear and his brother Oliver ill. by Steven Kellogg. HarperCollins, 1975. ISBN 0-06-020335-8 Subj: Animals – bears. Family life. Food. Sibling rivalry. Sleep.

Warren Weasel's worse than measles ill. by Hilary Knight. HarperCollins, 1980. ISBN 0-06-020327-7 Subj: Animals – bears. Animals – weasels. Self-concept.

Bach, Othello. *Hector McSnector and the mail-order Christmas witch* ill. by Timothy Hildebrandt. Caedmon, 1984. ISBN 0-89845-342-9 Subj: Holidays – Christmas. Magic. Witches.

Lilly, Willy and the mail-order witch ill. by Timothy Hildebrandt. Caedmon, 1983. ISBN 0-89845-048-9 Subj: Activities – working. Imagination. Magic. Music. Rhyming text. Witches.

Bacheller, Irving. *Lost in the fog* adapt. and ill. by Loretta Krupinski. Little, 1990. ISBN 0-316-07462-4 Subj: Behavior – lost. Birds – geese. Weather – fog.

Back, Christine. *Bean and plant* photos by Barrie Watts. Silver Burdett, 1986. ISBN 0-382-09286-4 Subj: Plants. Science. Seeds.

Chicken and egg photos by Bo Jarner. Silver Burdett, 1986. ISBN 0-382-09284-8 Subj: Birds – chickens. Eggs. Science.

Spider's web photos by Barrie Watts. Silver Burdett, 1986. ISBN 0-382-09288-8 Subj: Science. Spiders.

Tadpole and frog photos by Barrie Watts. Silver Burdett, 1986. ISBN 0-382-09285-6 Subj: Frogs and toads. Science.

Backhouse, Joy. *The voyage of the jolly boat* (Rettich, Margret)

Backovsky, Jan. *Trouble in Paradise* ill. by author. Tambourine, 1992. ISBN 0-688-11858-5 Subj: Animals. Islands. Sports – hunting.

Backstein, Karen. *The blind men and the elephant* ill. by Annie Mitra. Scholastic, 1992. ISBN 0-590-45813-2 Subj: Animals – elephants. Folk and fairy tales. Foreign lands – India. Handicaps – blindness. Senses – seeing.

Bacon, Ethel. *To see the moon* ill. by David Ray. BridgeWater, 1996. ISBN 0-8167-3822-X Subj: Animals – dogs. Moon. Sports – racing. Sports – sledding.

Bacon, Joan Chase. *see* Bowden, Joan Chase

Baden, Robert. *And Sunday makes seven* ill. by Michelle Edwards. Albert Whitman, 1990. ISBN 0-8075-0356-8 Subj: Days of the week, months of the year. Folk and fairy tales. Foreign lands – Costa Rica. Foreign languages. Witches.

Baehr, Patricia. *Mouse in the house* ill. by Laura Lydecker. Holiday, 1994. ISBN 0-8234-1102-8 Subj: Animals – mice. Cumulative tales. Pets.

School isn't fair ill. by R. W. Alley. Macmillan, 1992. ISBN 0-689-71544-7 Subj: School.

Baer, Edith. *This is the way we go to school* ill. by Steve Björkman. Scholastic, 1990. ISBN 0-590-43161-7 Subj: Rhyming text. School. Transportation.

The wonder of hands photos by Tana Hoban. Macmillan, 1992. ISBN 0-02-708138-9 Subj: Anatomy – hands.

Words are like faces ill. by Karen Gundersheimer. Pantheon, 1980. ISBN 0-394-94028-8 Subj: Language. Rhyming text.

Baer, Gene. *Thump thump rat-a-tat-tat* ill. by Lois Ehlert. HarperCollins, 1989. ISBN 0-06-020362-5 Subj: Music. Parades.

Bagert, Brod. *Chicken socks and other contagious poems* ill. by Tim Ellis. Boyds Mills, 1993. ISBN 1-56397-292-1 Subj: Poetry.

The gooch machine: a collection of humorous poems to perform ill. by Tim Ellis. Boyds Mills, 1997. ISBN 1-56397-294-8 Subj: Poetry.

Baggette, Susan K. *Jonathan goes to the doctor* photos by William J. Moriarty. Brookfield, 1998. ISBN 0-9660172-1-8 Subj: Careers – doctors. Format, unusual – board books. Illness.

Jonathan goes to the grocery store photos by William J. Moriarty. Brookfield, 1998. ISBN 0-9660172-2-6 Subj: Communities, neighborhoods. Family life – grandparents. Format, unusual – board books. Handicaps – physical handicaps. Shopping. Stores.

Jonathan goes to the library photos by William J. Moriarty. Brookfield, 1998. ISBN 0-9660172-3-4 Subj: Activities – reading. Careers – librarians. Communities, neighborhoods. Family life – grandparents. Libraries. Monsters.

Bagwell, Elizabeth. *This is an airport* (Bagwell, Richard)

Bagwell, Richard. *This is an airport* by Richard and Elizabeth Bagwell; photos by Lee Balterman. Follett, 1967. Subj: Airplanes, airports. Transportation.

Bahous, Sally. *Sitti and the cats* ill. by Nancy Malick. Bookmakers Guild, 1993. ISBN 1-879373-61-0 Subj: Animals – cats. Character traits – selfishness. Folk and fairy tales. Foreign lands – Palestine. Middle Ages.

Bahr, Amy C. *It's ok to say no: a book for parents and children to read together* ill. by Frederick Bennett Green. Grosset, 1986. ISBN 0-448-15328-9 Subj: Behavior – talking to strangers. Safety. Self-concept.

Sometimes it's ok to tell secrets: a book for parents and children to read together ill. by Frederick Bennett Green. Grosset, 1986. ISBN 0-448-15325-4 Subj: Behavior – secrets. Safety. Self-concept.

What should you do when . . . ? a book for parents and children to read together ill. by Frederick Bennett Green. Grosset, 1986. ISBN 0-448-15327-0 Subj: Safety. Self-concept.

Your body is your own: a book for parents and children to read together ill. by Frederick Bennett Green. Grosset, 1986. ISBN 0-448-15326-2 Subj: Safety. Self-concept.

Bahr, Mary. *The memory box* ill. by David Cunningham. Albert Whitman, 1992. ISBN 0-8075-5052-3 Subj: Family life – grandfathers. Illness – Alzheimer's. Memories, memory.

Bahr, Robert. *Blizzard at the zoo* ill. by Consuelo Joerns. Lothrop, 1982. ISBN 0-688-00424-5 Subj: Animals. Weather – snow. Weather – storms. Zoos.

Bailey, Debbie. *Clothes* photos by Susan Huszar. Firefly, 1991. ISBN 1-55037-167-3 Subj: Clothing. Format, unusual – board books.

Grandma photos by Susan Huszar. Firefly, 1994. ISBN 1-55037-966-6 Subj: Ethnic groups in the U.S. Family life – grandmothers. Format, unusual – board books.

Grandpa photos by Susan Huszar. Firefly, 1994. ISBN 1-55037-967-4 Subj: Ethnic groups in the U.S. Family life – grandfathers. Format, unusual – board books.

Hats photos by Susan Huszar. Firefly, 1991. ISBN 1-55037-159-2 Subj: Clothing – hats. Format, unusual – board books.

My dad photos by Susan Huszar. Firefly, 1991. ISBN 1-55037-164-9 Subj: Family life – fathers. Format, unusual – board books.

My family photos by Susan Huszar. Annick, 1998. ISBN 1-55037-510-5 Subj: Family life. Format, unusual – board books.

My mom photos by Susan Huszar. Firefly, 1991. ISBN 1-55037-163-0 Subj: Family life – mothers. Format, unusual – board books.

The playground photos by Susan Huszar. Annick, 1998. ISBN 1-55037-511-3 Subj: Activities – playing. Communities, neighborhoods. Family life. Format, unusual – board books.

Shoes photos by Susan Huszar. Firefly, 1991. ISBN 1-55037-161-4 Subj: Clothing – shoes. Format, unusual – board books.

Toys photos by Susan Huszar. Firefly, 1991. ISBN 1-55037-165-7 Subj: Format, unusual – board books. Toys.

Bailey, Donna. *Camels* ill. with photos. Steck-Vaughn, 1991. ISBN 0-8114-2644-0 Subj: Animals – camels.

Dolphins ill. with photos. Steck-Vaughn, 1991. ISBN 0-8114-2647-5 Subj: Animals – dolphins.

Giraffes ill. with photos. Steck-Vaughn, 1991. ISBN 0-8114-2646-7 Subj: Animals – giraffes.

Bailey, Jill. *Eyes* photos by Jim Bailey. Putnam, 1984. ISBN 0-399-21026-1 Subj: Anatomy – eyes. Animals. Birds. Format, unusual – board books.

Feet photos by Jim Bailey. Putnam, 1984. ISBN 0-399-21029-6 Subj: Anatomy – feet. Animals. Birds. Format, unusual – board books.

The life cycle of a spider ill. by Jackie Harland. Bookwright, 1989. ISBN 0-531-18288-6 Subj: Nature. Science. Spiders.

Mouths photos by Jim Bailey. Putnam, 1984. ISBN 0-399-21028-8 Subj: Anatomy – mouths. Animals. Birds. Format, unusual – board books.

Noses photos by Jim Bailey. Putnam, 1984. ISBN 0-399-21027-X Subj: Anatomy – noses. Animals. Format, unusual – board books.

Bailey, Linda. *Gordon Loggins and the three bears* ill. by Tracy Walker. Kids Can Pr., 1997. ISBN 1-55074-362-7 Subj: Animals – bears. Folk and fairy tales.

When Addie was scared ill. by Wendy Bailey. Kids Can Pr., 1999. ISBN 1-55074-431-3 Subj: Character traits – bravery. Emotions – fear. Family life – grandmothers. Farms.

Bailey, Philip H. *What shall we do when we all go out?* (Halpern, Shari)

Baillie, Allan. *Drac and the gremlin* ill. by Jane Tanner. Dial, 1989. ISBN 0-8037-0628-6 Subj: Activities – playing. Games. Imagination.

Rebel! ill. by Di Wu. Ticknor & Fields, 1994. ISBN 0-395-63250-4 Subj: Character traits – bravery. Foreign lands – Burma. War.

Baillie, Marilyn. *More science surprises from Dr. Zed* (Penrose, Gordon)

Side by side: animals who help each other ill. by Romi Caron. Firefly, 1997. ISBN 1-895688-56-6 Subj: Animals. Character traits – helpfulness.

Bains, Rae. *Hiccups, hiccups* ill. by Otto Coontz. Troll, 1981. ISBN 0-89375-537-0 Subj: Illness.

Baird, Anne. *Baby socks* ill. by author. Morrow, 1984. ISBN 0-688-02436-X Subj: Babies. Clothing – socks. Format, unusual – board books.

The Christmas lamb ill. by author. Morrow, 1989. ISBN 0-688-07775-7 Subj: Animals – sheep. Holidays – Christmas.

The guppies of Hilly Dale House ill. by Mary Morgan. Simon & Schuster, 1991. ISBN 0-671-69201-1 Subj: Activities. School.

Kiss, kiss ill. by author. Morrow, 1984. ISBN 0-688-02493-9 Subj: Babies. Family life. Format, unusual – board books.

Little tree ill. by author. Morrow, 1984. ISBN 0-688-02421-9 Subj: Format, unusual – board books. Trees.

No sheep ill. by author. Morrow, 1984. ISBN 0-688-02377-0 Subj: Bedtime. Format, unusual – board books.

Baisch, Cris. *When the lights went out* ill. by Ulises Wensell. Putnam, 1987. ISBN 0-399-21415-1 Subj: Family life. Lights. Power failures.

Baker, Alan. *Benjamin and the box* ill. by author. Lippincott, 1978. ISBN 0-397-31774-3 Subj: Animals – hamsters. Friendship. Humor.

Benjamin bounces back ill. by author. Lippincott, 1978. ISBN 0-397-31809-X Subj: Animals – hamsters. Humor. Imagination.

Benjamin's balloon ill. by author. Lothrop, 1990. ISBN 0-688-09744-8 Subj: Animals – hamsters. Humor. Toys – balloons.

Benjamin's book ill. by author. Lothrop, 1983. ISBN 0-688-01697-9 Subj: Animals – hamsters. Behavior – misbehavior. Humor.

Benjamin's dreadful dream ill. by author. Lippincott, 1980. ISBN 0-397-31903-7 Subj: Animals – hamsters. Behavior – misbehavior. Humor.

Benjamin's portrait ill. by author. Lothrop, 1987. ISBN 0-688-06878-2 Subj: Activities – painting. Animals – hamsters. Behavior – bad day. Careers – artists. Concepts – color. Humor.

Black and White Rabbit's ABC ill. by author. Kingfisher, 1994. ISBN 1-85697-851-2 Subj: ABC books. Activities – painting. Animals – rabbits. Cumulative tales.

Brown Rabbit's shape book ill. by author. Kingfisher, 1994. ISBN 1-85697-950-4 Subj: Animals – rabbits. Concepts – shape. Toys – balloons.

Gray Rabbit's one, two, three ill. by author. Kingfisher, 1994. ISBN 1-85697-952-0 Subj: Animals. Animals – rabbits. Counting, numbers.

Little Rabbit's first number book ill. by author. Kingfisher, 1998. ISBN 0-7534-5167-0 Subj: Animals – rabbits. Counting, numbers.

Two tiny mice ill. by author. Dial, 1991. ISBN 0-8037-0973-0 Subj: Animals. Animals – mice. Nature.

Where's mouse? ill. by author. Kingfisher, 1992. ISBN 1-85697-821-4 Subj: Animals. Animals – mice. Behavior – losing things. Family life – mothers. Format, unusual – toy and movable books.

White Rabbit's color book ill. by author. Kingfisher, 1994. ISBN 1-85697-953-9 Subj: Activities – painting. Animals – rabbits. Concepts – color.

Baker, Barbara. *Digby and Kate* ill. by Marsha Winborn. Dutton, 1988. ISBN 0-525-44370-3 Subj: Animals – cats. Animals – dogs. Friendship.

Digby and Kate again ill. by Marsha Winborn. Dutton, 1989. ISBN 0-525-44477-7 Subj: Animals – cats. Animals – dogs. Friendship.

Baker, Betty. *And me, coyote!* ill. by Maria Horvath. Macmillan, 1982. ISBN 0-02-708280-6 Subj: Animals – coyotes. Character traits – cleverness. Creation. Folk and fairy tales. Indians of North America. Religion.

My sister says ill. by Tricia Taggart. Macmillan, 1984. ISBN 0-02-708160-5 Subj: Behavior – wishing. Boats, ships. Family life – fathers. Imagination. Sibling rivalry.

Partners ill. by Emily Arnold McCully. Greenwillow, 1978. ISBN 0688841511 Subj: Animals – badgers. Animals – coyotes. Character traits – cleverness. Character traits – helpfulness. Character traits – laziness. Farms. Friendship.

Rat is dead and ant is sad: based on a Pueblo Indian tale ill. by Mamoru Funai. HarperCollins, 1981. ISBN 0-06-020347-1 Subj: Cumulative tales. Death. Emotions – grief. Emotions – sadness. Folk and fairy tales. Indians of North America – Pueblo.

Sonny-Boy Sim ill. by Susanne Suba. Rand McNally, 1948. Subj: Animals. Family life. Humor. Sports – hunting.

Three fools and a horse ill. by Glen Rounds. Macmillan, 1975. ISBN 0-02-708250-4 Subj: Animals – horses, ponies. Humor. Indians of North America – Apache.

Worthington Botts and the steam machine ill. by Sal Murdocca. Macmillan, 1981. ISBN 0-02-708190-7 Subj: Activities – reading. Humor. Machines.

Baker, Bonnie Jeanne. *A pear by itself* ill. by author. Childrens Pr., 1982. ISBN 0-516-02032-3 Subj: Counting, numbers.

Baker, Charlotte. *Little brother* ill. by author. McKay, 1959. Subj: Animals – dogs. Babies. Emotions – envy, jealousy. Family life – new sibling. Sibling rivalry.

Baker, Donna. *I want to be a librarian* ill. by Richard Wahl. Childrens Pr., 1978. ISBN 0-516-01715-2 Subj: Careers – librarians. Libraries.

I want to be a pilot ill. by Richard Wahl. Childrens Pr., 1978. ISBN 0-516-01720-9 Subj: Airplanes, airports. Careers – airplane pilots.

I want to be a police officer ill. by Richard Wahl. Childrens Pr., 1978. ISBN 0-516-01721-7 Subj: Careers – police officers.

Baker, Eugene H. *Bicycles* ill. by Tom Dunnington. Creative Ed., 1980. ISBN 0-87191-738-6 Subj: Animals. Safety. Sports – bicycling.

Fire ill. by Tom Dunnington. Creative Ed., 1980. ISBN 0-87191-735-1 Subj: Animals. Fire. Safety.

Home ill. by Tom Dunnington. Creative Ed., 1980. ISBN 0-87191-739-4 Subj: Animals. Safety.

I want to be a computer operator ill. by Tom Dunnington. Childrens Pr., 1973. ISBN 0-516-01741-1 Subj: Careers. Computers.

Outdoors ill. by Tom Dunnington. Creative Ed., 1980. ISBN 0-87191-736-X Subj: Animals. Safety.

School ill. by Tom Dunnington. Creative Ed., 1980. ISBN 0-87191-737-8 Subj: Animals. Safety. School.

Water ill. by Tom Dunnington. Creative Ed., 1980. ISBN 0-87191-740-8 Subj: Animals. Safety.

Baker, Gayle. *Special delivery: a book for kids about cesarean and vaginal birth* ill. by Debra Hillyer. Chas. Franklin Pr., 1981. ISBN 0-9603516-2-0 Subj: Babies. Birth. Family life – mothers. Hospitals. Science.

Baker, Jeannie. *Grandmother* ill. by author. Elsevier-Dutton, 1979. ISBN 0-233-96975-6 Subj: Art. Family life – grandmothers.

Home in the sky ill. by author. Greenwillow, 1984. ISBN 0-688-03842-5 Subj: Animals – dogs. Birds – pigeons. Character traits – kindness to animals. City.

Millicent ill. by author. Elsevier-Dutton, 1980. ISBN 0-233-97201-3 Subj: Birds – pigeons. Character traits – individuality. City.

One hungry spider ill. by author. Elsevier-Dutton, 1983. ISBN 0-233-97429-6 Subj: Counting, numbers. Science. Spiders.

The story of rosy dock ill. by author. Greenwillow, 1995. ISBN 0-688-11493-8 Subj: Ecology. Foreign lands – Australia. Plants.

Where the forest meets the sea ill. by author. Greenwillow, 1988. ISBN 0-688-06364-0 Subj: Ecology. Foreign lands – Australia. Forest, woods.

Window ill. by author. Greenwillow, 1991. ISBN 0-688-08918-6 Subj: Ecology. Foreign lands – Australia. Wordless.

Baker, Jeffrey J. W. *Patterns of nature* photos by Jaroslav Salek. Doubleday, 1967. Subj: Animals. Birds. Flowers. Plants. Science. Trees.

Baker, Jill. *Basil of Bywater Hollow* ill. by Lynn Bywaters Ferris. Holt, 1987. ISBN 0-8050-0268-5 Subj: Animals – bears. Fairs. Weather – rain.

Baker, Karen Lee. *Seneca* ill. by author. Greenwillow, 1997. ISBN 0-688-14030-0 Subj: Animals – horses, ponies.

Baker, Keith. *Cat tricks* ill. by author. Harcourt, 1997. ISBN 0-15-292857-X Subj: Animals – cats. Format, unusual – toy and movable books. Rhyming text.

The dove's letter ill. by author. Harcourt, 1988. ISBN 0-15-224133-7 Subj: Birds – doves. Emotions – love. Letters, cards.

Hide and snake ill. by author. Harcourt, 1991. ISBN 0-15-233986-8 Subj: Games. Reptiles – snakes. Rhyming text.

The magic fan ill. by author. Harcourt, 1989. ISBN 0-15-250750-7 Subj: Careers – carpenters. Foreign lands – Japan. Imagination.

Who is the beast? ill. by author. Harcourt, 1990. ISBN 0-15-296057-0 Subj: Animals – tigers. Rhyming text.

Baker, Laura Nelson. *The friendly beasts* ill. by Nicolas Sidjakov. Parnassus, 1958. Adapt. from an old English Christmas carol of the same title. Subj: Animals. Holidays – Christmas. Music.

O children of the wind and pines ill. by Inez Storer. Lippincott, 1967. Subj: Holidays – Christmas. Indians of North America. Music.

Baker, Leslie A. *The antique store cat* ill. by author. Little, 1992. ISBN 0-316-07837-9 Subj: Animals – cats. Behavior – running away.

Paris cat ill. by author. Little, 1999. ISBN 0-316-07309-1 Subj: Animals – cats. Behavior – losing things. Behavior – lost. Foreign lands – France.

The third-story cat ill. by author. Little, 1987. ISBN 0-316-07832-8 Subj: Animals – cats. Behavior – running away.

Baker, Margaret. *A puppy called Spinach* by Margaret and Mary Baker; ill. by Mary Baker. Dodd, 1939. Subj: Animals – dogs. Behavior – misbehavior.

Baker, Mary. *A puppy called Spinach* (Baker, Margaret)

Baker, Olaf. *Where the buffaloes begin* ill. by Stephen Gammell. Warne, 1981. ISBN 0-670-82760-6 Subj: Animals – buffaloes. Caldecott award honor books. Folk and fairy tales. Indians of North America.

Baker, Pamela J. *My first book of sign* ill. by Patricia Bellan Gillen. Gallaudet Univ. Pr., 1986. ISBN 0-930323-20-3 Subj: Handicaps – deafness. Language. Senses – hearing.

Baker, Sanna Anderson. *Mississippi going north* ill. by Bill Farnsworth. Albert Whitman, 1996. ISBN 0-8075-5164-3 Subj: Canoes and canoeing. Family life. Nature. Rivers.

Who's a friend of the water-spurting whale handlettered and ill. by Tomie de Paola. David C. Cook, 1987. ISBN 0-89191-587-7 Subj: Religion. Rhyming text.

Baker, Susan. *First look at keeping warm* ill. by author. Gareth Stevens, 1991. ISBN 0-8368-0704-9 Subj: Weather – cold.

Baker, Taftt. *The hokey pokey* (La Prise, Larry)

Bakken, Harold. *The special string* ill. by Mischa Richter. Prentice-Hall, 1981. ISBN 0-13-826370-1

Subj: Character traits – helpfulness. Humor. Problem solving. String. Wordless.

Balan, Bruce. *Pie in the sky* ill. by Clare Skilbeck. Viking, 1993. ISBN 0-670-85150-7 Subj: Birthdays. Food.

Baldner, Gaby. *Joba and the wild boar: Joba und das wildschwein* ill. by Gerhard Oberländer. Hastings House, 1961. Text in English and German. Subj: Animals – pigs. Character traits – bravery. Foreign languages. Pets.

Balestrino, Philip. *Fat and skinny* ill. by Pam Makie. Crowell, 1975. ISBN 0-690-00665-9 Subj: Character traits – appearance.

Hot as an ice cube ill. by Tomie de Paola. Crowell, 1971. ISBN 0-690-40415-8 Subj: Concepts. Science.

The skeleton inside you ill. by True Kelley. Rev. ed. HarperCollins, 1989. ISBN 0-690-04733-9 Subj: Anatomy – skeletons. Science.

Balet, Jan B. *Amos and the moon* ill. by author. Oxford Univ. Pr., 1948. Subj: Moon.

The fence: a Mexican tale ill. by author. Delacorte, 1969. Translation of Der Zaun. ISBN 0-356-02847-X Subj: Family life. Folk and fairy tales. Foreign lands – Mexico. Poverty. Problem solving.

Five Rollatinis ill. by author. Lippincott, 1959. Subj: Animals – horses, ponies. Circus. Family life.

The gift: a Portuguese Christmas tale ill. by author. Delacorte, 1967. Subj: Foreign lands – Portugal. Gifts. Holidays – Christmas. Religion.

Joanjo: a Portuguese tale ill. by author. Delacorte, 1967. Subj: Character traits – ambition. Dreams. Fish. Foreign lands – Portugal.

The king and the broom maker ill. by author. Delacorte, 1968. Translation of König und der Besenbinder. Subj: Behavior – dissatisfaction. Royalty – kings.

Ned and Ed and the lion ill. by author. Oxford Univ. Pr., 1949. Subj: Animals – lions. Imagination. Multiple births – twins.

Balgassi, Haemi. *Peacebound trains* ill. by Chris K. Soentpiet. Houghton Mifflin, 1996. ISBN 0-395-72093-1 Subj: Family life – daughters. Family life – grandmothers. Family life – mothers. Foreign lands – Korea. Trains. U.S. history. War.

Balian, Lorna. *Amelia's nine lives* ill. by author. Abingdon, 1986. ISBN 0-687-01250-3 Subj: Animals – cats. Behavior – lost. Pets.

Bah! Humbug? ill. by author. Abingdon, 1977. ISBN 0-687-02345-9 Subj: Holidays – Christmas.

Elephant? ill. by adapt. Abingdon, 1964. Adapt. [by Lorna Balian] from a poem by John Godfrey Saxe. Subj: Animals – elephants. Handicaps – blindness. Senses – seeing.

A garden for a groundhog ill. by author. Abingdon, 1985. ISBN 0-687-14009-9 Subj: Animals – groundhogs. Farms. Gardens, gardening. Holidays – Groundhog Day.

Humbug potion: an A B Cipher ill. by author. Abingdon, 1984. ISBN 0-687-18021-X Subj: ABC books. Magic. Secret codes. Witches.

Humbug rabbit ill. by author. Abingdon, 1974. ISBN 0-687-18046-5 Subj: Animals – rabbits. Family life – grandmothers. Holidays – Easter.

Humbug witch ill. by author. Abingdon, 1965. ISBN 1-881772-24-1 Subj: Holidays – Halloween. Witches.

Leprechauns never lie ill. by author. Abingdon, 1980. ISBN 0-687-21371-1 Subj: Animals – cats. Folk and fairy tales. Foreign lands – Ireland. Humor. Mythical creatures – leprechauns.

Mother's Mother's Day ill. by author. Abingdon, 1982. ISBN 0-685-57645-0 Subj: Animals – mice. Family life – mothers. Holidays – Mother's Day.

The socksnatchers ill. by author. Abingdon, 1988. ISBN 0-687-39047-8 Subj: Clothing – socks. Mystery stories.

Sometimes it's turkey ill. by author. Abingdon, 1973. ISBN 0-687-39074-5 Subj: Birds – turkeys. Holidays – Thanksgiving.

A sweetheart for Valentine ill. by author. Abingdon, 1987. ISBN 0-687-40771-0 Subj: Giants. Holidays – Valentine's Day. Weddings.

Where in the world is Henry? ill. by author. Bradbury, 1972. ISBN 1-881772-27-6 Subj: Concepts – size. Science.

Wilbur's space machine ill. by author. Holiday, 1990. ISBN 0-8234-0836-1 Subj: Activities – flying. Ecology. Friendship.

Ball, Duncan. *Jeremy's tail* ill. by Donna Rawlins. Orchard, 1991. ISBN 0-531-08551-1 Subj: Activities – traveling. Games.

Ballard, Robin. *Carnival* ill. by author. Greenwillow, 1995. ISBN 0-688-13237-5 Subj: Fairs. Friendship. Parades.

Cat and Alex and the magic flying carpet ill. by author. HarperCollins, 1991. ISBN 0-06-020390-0 Subj: Animals – cats. Magic.

Good-bye, house ill. by author. Greenwillow, 1994. ISBN 0-688-12526-3 Subj: Family life. Homes, houses. Moving.

Gracie ill. by author. Greenwillow, 1993. ISBN 0-688-11807-0 Subj: Divorce. Family life.

Granny and me ill. by author. Greenwillow, 1992. ISBN 0-688-10549-1 Subj: Family life. Family life – grandmothers.

My father is far away ill. by author. Greenwillow, 1992. ISBN 0-688-10954-3 Subj: Emotions – loneliness. Family life – fathers.

When I am a sister ill. by author. Greenwillow, 1998. ISBN 0-688-15398-4 Subj: Babies. Family life – fathers. Family life – step families.

When we get home ill. by author. Greenwillow, 1999. ISBN 0-688-16168-5 Subj: Activities – traveling. Bedtime. Family life.

Ballart, Elisabet. *Let's count* ill. by Roser Capdevila. Thomasson-Grant, 1992. ISBN 1-56566-011-0 Subj: Animals. Animals – sheep. Counting, numbers. Rhyming text. School.

Balmer, Helen. *Jungle adventure* ill. by author. Simon & Schuster, 1993. ISBN 0-671-86768-7 Subj: Animals. Family life – grandfathers. Format, unusual – toy and movable books. Jungle.

Balog, James. *James Balog's animals A to Z* ill. by author. Chronicle, 1996. ISBN 0-8118-1339-8 Subj: ABC books. Animals. Animals – endangered animals.

Balterman, Lee. *Girders and cranes* photos by author. Albert Whitman, 1990. ISBN 0-8075-2923-0 Subj: Activities – making things. Buildings. Machines.

Balzano, Jeanne. *The wee moose* ill. by Enrico Arno. Parents, 1964. Subj: Animals – mice. Farms.

Balzola, Asun. *Munia and the day things went wrong* ill. by author. Cambridge Univ. Pr., 1988. ISBN 0-521-35643-1 Subj: Behavior – bad day. Family life.

Munia and the moon ill. by author. Cambridge Univ. Pr., 1989. ISBN 0-521-37143-0 Subj: Moon. Night.

Munia and the orange crocodile ill. by author. Cambridge Univ. Pr., 1988. ISBN 0-521-35642-3 Subj: Dreams. Reptiles – alligators, crocodiles. Teeth.

Munia and the red shoes ill. by author. Cambridge Univ. Pr., 1989. ISBN 0-521-37142-2 Subj: Behavior – growing up. Clothing – shoes.

Bambi ill. by Christa Stephan. Imported Pubs., 1983. ISBN 0-8285-2584-6 Subj: Format, unusual – board books. Toys. Wordless.

Banbery, Fred. *Paddington at the circus* (Bond, Michael)

Banchek, Linda. *Snake in, snake out* ill. by Elaine Arnold. Crowell, 1978. ISBN 0-690-03853-4 Subj: Birds – parakeets, parrots. Concepts – in and out. Concepts – opposites. Reptiles – snakes. Wordless.

Bancroft, Catherine. *Felix's hat* by Catherine Bancroft and Hannah Coale Gruenberg; ill. by Hannah Coal Gruenberg. Four Winds, 1993. ISBN 0-02-708325-X Subj: Clothing – hats. Dreams. Frogs and toads.

Bancroft, Henrietta. *Animals in winter* by Henrietta Bancroft and Richard G. Van Gelder; ill. by Helen K. Davie. HarperCollins, 1997. ISBN 0-06-445165-8 Subj: Animals. Birds. Science. Seasons – winter.

Bancroft, Laura. *see* Baum, L. Frank (Lyman Frank)

Bandes, Hanna. *Sleepy river* ill. by Jeanette Winter. Putnam/Philomel, 1993. ISBN 0-399-22349-5 Subj: Animals. Indians of North America. Night. Rivers.

Bang, Betsy. *The cucumber stem* ill. by Tony Chen. Greenwillow, 1980. Adapt. from a Bengali folk tale. ISBN 0-688-84213-5 Subj: Character traits – smallness. Foreign lands – India. Tall tales.

The old woman and the red pumpkin ill. by Molly Bang. Macmillan, 1975. Adapt. and tr. from a Bengali folk tale by Betsy Bang. ISBN 0-02-708360-8 Subj: Animals. Character traits – cleverness. Folk and fairy tales. Foreign lands – India.

The old woman and the rice thief ill. by Molly Bang. Greenwillow, 1978. Adapt. and tr. from a Bengali folk tale by Betsy Bang. ISBN 0-688-84098-1 Subj: Animals. Character traits – cleverness. Folk and fairy tales. Foreign lands – India.

Tuntuni the tailor bird ill. by Molly Bang. Greenwillow, 1978. Adapt. and tr. from a Bengali folk tale by Betsy Bang. ISBN 0-688-84167-8 Subj: Birds. Folk and fairy tales. Foreign lands – India. Royalty.

Bang, Molly. *Dawn* ill. by author. Morrow, 1983. An adaptation of the Japanese folk tale: Tsuru Nyōbō. Also known as The Crane Wife. ISBN 0-688-02404-1 Subj: Activities – weaving. Behavior – secrets. Birds – cranes. Character traits – curiosity. Folk and fairy tales. Foreign lands – Japan.

Delphine ill. by author. Morrow, 1988. ISBN 0-688-05637-7 Subj: Animals. Sports – bicycling.

The goblins giggle and other stories ill. by author. Peter Smith, 1988. ISBN 0-8446-6360-3 Subj: Mythical creatures – goblins.

Goose ill. by author. Blue Sky, 1996. ISBN 0-590-89005-0 Subj: Activities – flying. Animals – groundhogs. Birds – geese.

The grey lady and the strawberry snatcher ill. by author. Four Winds, 1980. ISBN 0-590-07547-0 Subj: Caldecott award honor books. Imagination. Wordless.

One fall day ill. by author. Greenwillow, 1994. ISBN 0-688-07016-7 Subj: Activities – playing. Bedtime. Toys.

The paper crane ill. by author. Greenwillow, 1985. ISBN 0-688-04109-4 Subj: Birds – cranes. Character traits – kindness. Folk and fairy tales.

Ten, nine, eight ill. by author. Greenwillow, 1983. ISBN 0-688-00907-7 Subj: Bedtime. Caldecott award honor books. Counting, numbers. Ethnic groups in the U.S. – African Americans. Lullabies. Rhyming text.

Tye May and the magic brush ill. by author. Greenwillow, 1981. ISBN 0-688-84290-9 Subj: Activities – painting. Royalty.

When Sophie gets angry – really, really angry . . . ill. by author. Blue Sky, 1999. ISBN 0-590-18979-4 Subj: Caldecott award honor books. Emotions – anger. Family life – sisters.

Wiley and the hairy man ill. by adapt. Macmillan, 1976. ISBN 0-02-708370-5 Subj: Bedtime. Character traits – cleverness. Ethnic groups in the U.S. – African Americans. Folk and fairy tales. Monsters.

Yellow ball ill. by author. Morrow, 1991. ISBN 0-688-06315-2 Subj: Activities – playing. Sea and seashore. Toys – balls.

Bangs, Edward. *Yankee Doodle* ill. by Steven Kellogg. Parents, 1976. ISBN 0-819-30834-X Subj: Songs. U.S. history.

Banigan, Sharon Stearns. *Circus magic* ill. by Katharina Maillard. Dutton, 1958. Subj: Circus. Magic. Rhyming text.

Banish, Roslyn. *A forever family* ill. by author with Jennifer Jordan-Wong. HarperCollins, 1992. ISBN 0-06-021674-3 Subj: Adoption. Ethnic groups in the U.S. Family life.

Let me tell you about my baby photos by author. HarperCollins, 1988. Previously published as: I want to tell you about my baby, HarperCollins 1982. ISBN 0-06-020383-8 Subj: Babies. Birth. Family life – new sibling.

Bank Street College of Education. *Around the city* ill. by Aurelius Battaglia and others. Rev. ed. Macmillan, 1972. Subj: City.

Green light, go ill. by Jack Endewelt and others. Rev. ed. Macmillan, 1972. Subj: City. Traffic, traffic signs.

In the city ill. by Dan Dickas. Rev. ed. Macmillan, 1972. ISBN 0-02-258930-9 Subj: City.

My city ill. by Ron Becker and others. Macmillan, 1965. Subj: City.

People read ill. by Dan Dickas. Rev. ed. Macmillan, 1972. ISBN 0-02-258940-6 Subj: Activities – reading. Careers.

Uptown, downtown ill. by Ron Becker and others. Macmillan, 1965. Subj: City.

Banks, Kate (Katherine A.). *Alphabet soup* ill. by Peter Sis. Knopf, 1988. ISBN 0-394-99151-6 Subj: Family life. Food. Imagination.

And if the moon could talk ill. by Georg Hallensleben. Farrar, 1998. ISBN 0-374-30299-5 Subj: Bedtime. Dreams. Moon. Night.

Baboon ill. by Georg Hallensleben. Farrar, 1997. ISBN 0-374-30474-2 Subj: Animals – baboons.

The bird, the monkey, and the snake in the jungle ill. by Tomek Bogacki. Farrar, 1999. ISBN 0-374-

30729-6 Subj: Animals – monkeys. Behavior – sharing. Birds. Rebuses. Reptiles – snakes.

Peter and the talking shoes ill. by Marc Rosenthal. Knopf, 1994. ISBN 0-394-92723-0 Subj: Behavior – losing things. Clothing – shoes. Cumulative tales.

Spider, spider ill. by Georg Hallensleben. Farrar, 1996. ISBN 0-374-37151-2 Subj: Family life – mothers. Imagination. Spiders.

Banks, Merry. *Animals of the night* ill. by Ronald Himler. Macmillan, 1990. ISBN 0-684-19093-1 Subj: Animals. Nature. Night.

Bannatyne-Cugnet, Jo. *A prairie alphabet* ill. by Yvette Moore. Tundra, 1992. ISBN 0-88776-282-1 Subj: ABC books. Foreign lands – Canada.

Bannerman, Helen. *Sambo and the twins* ill. by author. Stokes, 1936. Subj: Folk and fairy tales. Foreign lands – India.

The story of Little Babaji ill. by Fred Marcellino. HarperCollins, 1996. ISBN 0-06-205065-6 Subj: Animals – tigers. Character traits – cleverness. Family life. Foreign lands – India.

The story of little black Sambo ill. by author. Lippincott, 1943. First published in the U.S. by Stokes in 1900. Subj: Animals – tigers. Character traits – cleverness. Family life. Foreign lands – India.

The story of the teasing monkey ill. by author. Lippincott, 1907. Subj: Animals – lions. Animals – monkeys.

Bannon, Laura. *The best house in the world* ill. by author. Houghton Mifflin, 1952. Subj: Animals. Homes, houses. Imagination.

Hat for a hero: a Tarasean boy of Mexico ill. by author. Albert Whitman, 1954. Subj: Character traits – bravery. Clothing – hats. Foreign lands – Mexico.

Little people of the night ill. by author. Houghton Mifflin, 1963. Subj: Animals. Emotions – fear. Night.

Manuela's birthday ill. by author. Albert Whitman, 1972. Orig. pub. in 1939. ISBN 0-8075-4973-8 Subj: Birthdays. Foreign lands – Mexico. Toys – dolls.

Red mittens ill. by author. Houghton Mifflin, 1946. ISBN 0-395-19863-1 Subj: Animals. Behavior – losing things. Clothing – gloves, mittens.

The scary thing ill. by author. Houghton Mifflin, 1956. Subj: Animals. Emotions – fear.

Bansemer, Roger. *Rachael's splendifilous adventure* by Roger Bansemer and Daryl May; ill. by Roger Bansemer. Windswept House, 1991. ISBN 0-932433-83-9 Subj: Activities – ballooning. Activities – traveling. Toys – bears.

Bantock, Nick. *Runners, sliders, bouncers, climbers* by Nick Bantock and Stacie Strong; designed by Nick Bantock and Doug Bergstreser; paper engineering by Rodger Smith; ill. by Nick Bantock.

Hyperion, 1992. ISBN 1-56282-219-5 Subj: Activities. Animals. Format, unusual – toy and movable books.

There was an old lady (Little old lady who swallowed a fly)

Baran, Tancy. *Bees* ill. by author. Grosset, 1971. Subj: Insects – bees. Science.

Barasch, Lynne. *Old friends* ill. by author. Farrar, 1998. ISBN 0-374-35611-4 Subj: Animals – dogs. Dreams. Family life. Friendship. Old age.

Rodney's inside story ill. by author. Watts, 1992. ISBN 0-531-08593-7 Subj: Activities – reading. Animals – rabbits. Bedtime. Food.

A winter walk ill. by author. Ticknor & Fields, 1993. ISBN 0-395-65937-X Subj: Concepts – color. Seasons – winter.

Barasch, Marc Ian. *No plain pets!* ill. by Henrik Drescher. HarperCollins, 1991. ISBN 0-06-022473-8 Subj: Animals. Pets. Rhyming text.

Barbaresi, Nina. *Firemouse* ill. by author. Crown, 1987. ISBN 0-517-56337-1 Subj: Animals – cats. Animals – mice. Careers – firefighters.

Barbato, Juli. *From bed to bus* ill. by Brian Schatell. Macmillan, 1985. ISBN 0-02-708380-2 Subj: Family life. Morning.

Mom's night out ill. by Brian Schatell. Macmillan, 1985. ISBN 0-02-708480-9 Subj: Family life – fathers. Food.

Barber, Antonia. *Catkin* ill. P. J. Lynch. Candlewick, 1994. ISBN 1-56402-485-7 Subj: Animals – cats. Fairies. Little people. Riddles.

The enchanter's daughter ill. by Errol Le Cain. Farrar, 1988. ISBN 0-374-32170-1 Subj: Birds. Magic. Wizards.

Gemma and the baby chick ill. by Karin Littlewood. Scholastic, 1993. ISBN 0-590-45479-X Subj: Birds – chickens. Eggs. Family life – mothers. Farms.

The mousehole cat ill. by Nicola Bayley. Macmillan, 1990. ISBN 0-02-708331-4 Subj: Animals – cats. Foreign lands – England. Sea and seashore. Weather – storms.

Satchelmouse and the dinosaurs ill. by Claudio Muñoz. Barron's, 1988. ISBN 0-8120-5872-0 Subj: Dinosaurs. Imagination. Magic.

Satchelmouse and the doll's house ill. by Claudio Muñoz. Barron's, 1988. ISBN 0-8120-5873-9 Subj: Character traits – kindness. Toys – dolls.

Barber, Barbara E. *Allie's basketball dream* ill. by Darryl Ligasan. Lee & Low, 1996. ISBN 1-880000-38-5 Subj: Character traits – perseverance. Ethnic groups in the U.S. – African Americans. Sports – basketball.

Saturday at the new you ill. by Anna Rich. Lee & Low, 1994. ISBN 1-880000-06-7 Subj: Activities – working. Beauty shops. Careers. Communities, neighborhoods. Ethnic groups in the U.S. – African Americans. Family life – mothers.

Barbosa, Rogério Andrade. *African animal tales* adapt. by Feliz Guthrie; ill. by Cica Fittipaldi. Volcano Pr., 1993. ISBN 0-912078-96-0 Subj: Animals. Character traits – cleverness. Character traits – patience. Folk and fairy tales. Foreign lands – Africa.

Barbot, Daniel. *A bicycle for Rosaura* ill. by Morella Fuenmayor. Kane/Miller, 1991. ISBN 0-916291-34-0 Subj: Animals. Birds – chickens. Birthdays. Foreign lands – Venezuela. Sports – bicycling.

Barbour, Karen. *Little Nino's pizzeria* ill. by author. Harcourt, 1987. ISBN 0-15-247650-4 Subj: Family life. Food.

Mr. Bow Tie ill. by author. Harcourt, 1991. ISBN 0-15-256165-X Subj: Character traits – kindness. Family life. Homeless.

Nancy ill. by author. Harcourt, 1989. ISBN 0-15-256675-9 Subj: Friendship. Moving. Parties.

Barchilon, Jacques. *The authentic Mother Goose fairy tales and nursery rhymes* ed. by Jacques Barchilon and Henry Pettit. Alan Swallow, 1960. Subj: Nursery rhymes.

Barclay, William. *The cobweb curtain: a Christmas story* (Koralek, Jenny)

Barden, Rosalind. *TV monster* ill. by author. Crown, 1989. ISBN 0-517-56934-5 Subj: Monsters. Space and space ships. Television.

Bare, Colleen Stanley. *Busy, busy squirrels* photos by author. Dutton, 1991. ISBN 0-525-65063-6 Subj: Animals – squirrels.

Critter, the class cat photos by author. Putnam, 1989. ISBN 0-399-21710-X Subj: Animals – cats. School.

Elephants on the beach photos by author. Dutton, 1990. ISBN 0-525-65018-0 Subj: Animals – elephant seals. Sea and seashore.

Guinea pigs don't read books photos by author. Dodd, 1985. ISBN 0-396-08538-5 Subj: Animals – guinea pigs. Pets.

Never grab a deer by the ear photos by author. Cobblehill, 1993. ISBN 0-525-65112-8 Subj: Animals – deer. Nature.

Never kiss an alligator photos by author. Dutton, 1989. ISBN 0-525-65003-2 Subj: Reptiles – alligators, crocodiles.

Sammy, dog detective photos by author. Dutton, 1998. ISBN 0-525-65253-1 Subj: Animals – dogs. Careers – police officers.

To love a cat photos by author. Dodd, 1986. ISBN 0-396-08834-1 Subj: Animals – cats. Pets.

To love a dog photos by author. Dodd, 1987. ISBN 0-396-09057-5 Subj: Animals – dogs. Pets.

Tree squirrels photos by author. Dodd, 1983. ISBN 0-396-08208-4 Subj: Animals – squirrels.

Who comes to the water hole? photos by author. Dutton, 1991. ISBN 0-525-65073-3 Subj: Animals. Foreign lands – Africa. Jungle.

Baring, Maurice. *The blue rose* ill. by Anne Dalton. Heinemann, 1987. ISBN 0-7182-2100-1 Subj: Folk and fairy tales. Royalty.

Baring-Gould, Ceil. *The annotated Mother Goose: nursery rhymes old and new* (Mother Goose)

Baring-Gould, William S. *The annotated Mother Goose: nursery rhymes old and new* (Mother Goose)

Barish, Wendy. *Trains* (Trains)

Barkan, Joanne. *Boxcar* ill. by Richard Walz. Macmillan, 1992. ISBN 0-689-71573-0 Subj: Format, unusual – board books. Trains. Transportation.

Caboose ill. by Richard Walz. Macmillan, 1992. ISBN 0-689-71574-9 Subj: Format, unusual – board books. Trains. Transportation.

Locomotive ill. by Richard Walz. Macmillan, 1992. ISBN 0-689-71576-5 Subj: Format, unusual – board books. Trains. Transportation.

Passenger car ill. by Richard Walz. Macmillan, 1992. ISBN 0-689-71575-7 Subj: Format, unusual – board books. Trains. Transportation.

Whiskerville bake shop ill. by Karen Lee Schmidt. Putnam, 1990. ISBN 0-448-19467-8 Subj: Animals – mice. Buildings. Careers – bakers. Format, unusual – board books.

Whiskerville firehouse ill. by Karen Lee Schmidt. Putnam, 1990. ISBN 0-448-19468-6 Subj: Animals – mice. Buildings. Careers – firefighters. Format, unusual – board books.

Whiskerville post office ill. by Karen Lee Schmidt. Putnam, 1990. ISBN 0-448-19466-X Subj: Animals – mice. Buildings. Careers – postal workers. Format, unusual – board books. Post office.

Whiskerville school ill. by Karen Lee Schmidt. Putnam, 1990. ISBN 0-448-19465-1 Subj: Animals – mice. Buildings. Careers – teachers. Format, unusual – board books. School.

Barker, Carol. *Achilles and Diana* (Bates, H. E. [Herbert Ernest])

Achilles the donkey (Bates, H. E. [Herbert Ernest])

Barker, Cicely Mary. *Berry flower fairies* ill. by author. Putnam, 1981. Vol. [2] of a set of 4 v. issued in a case with title: Flower fairies miniature library. ISBN 0-399-20823-2 Subj: Fairies. Flowers. Format, unusual. Poetry.

Blossom flower fairies ill. by author. Putnam, 1981. Vol. [1] of a set of 4 v. issued in a case with title: Flower fairies miniature library. ISBN 0-399-20823-2 Subj: Fairies. Flowers. Format, unusual. Poetry.

Flower fairies of the garden ill. by author. Viking, 1991. ISBN 0-7232-3758-1 Subj: Fairies. Flowers. Gardens, gardening. Poetry.

Flower fairies of the seasons ill. by author. HarperCollins, 1984. First published in 1923. ISBN 0-911745-48-3 Subj: Fairies. Flowers. Poetry. Seasons. Trees.

Flower fairies of the spring ill. by author. Warne, 1991. ISBN 0-7232-4433-2 Subj: Fairies. Flowers. Poetry. Seasons – spring.

Flower fairies of the summer ill. by author. Warne, 1991. ISBN 0-7232-3754-9 Subj: Fairies. Flowers. Poetry. Seasons – summer.

Flower fairies of the trees ill. by author. Viking, 1991. ISBN 0-872-26022-4 Subj: Fairies. Flowers. Poetry. Trees.

Flower fairies postcard book ill. by author. Warne, 1991. ISBN 0-7232-3710-7 Subj: Fairies. Flowers. Poetry.

Spring flower fairies ill. by author. Putnam, 1981. Vol. [3] of a set of 4 v. issued in a case with title: Flower fairies miniature library. ISBN 0-399-20823-2 Subj: Fairies. Flowers. Format, unusual. Poetry.

Summer flower fairies ill. by author. Putnam, 1981. Vol. [4] of a set of 4 v. issued in a case with title: Flower fairies miniature library. ISBN 0-399-20823-2 Subj: Fairies. Flowers. Format, unusual. Poetry.

Barker, George. *Why teddy bears are brown* (Barker, Inga-Lil)

Barker, Inga-Lil. *Why teddy bears are brown* by Inga-Lil and George Barker; ill. by authors. Crowell, 1946. Subj: Behavior – greed. Toys – bears.

Barker, Melvern J. *Country fair.* Oxford Univ. Pr., 1955. Subj: Animals – bulls, cows. Fairs.

Little island star. Oxford Univ. Pr., 1954. Subj: Lighthouses.

Barker, Peggy. *What happened when grandma died* ill. by Patricia Mattozzi. Concordia, 1984. ISBN 0-570-04090-6 Subj: Death. Emotions – grief. Family life – grandmothers. Religion.

Barkhouse, Joyce. *Anna's pet* (Atwood, Margaret)

Barklem, Jill. *Autumn story* ill. by author. Atheneum, 1999. ISBN 0-689-83054-8 Subj: Animals – mice. Behavior – lost. Seasons – fall.

The big book of Brambly Hedge ill. by author. Putnam, 1981. ISBN 0-399-20833-X Subj: Animals – mice. Country.

The high hills ill. by author. Atheneum, 1999. ISBN 0-689-83091-2 Subj: Activities – traveling. Animals – mice. Seasons – fall.

Sea story ill. by author. Putnam, 1991. ISBN 0-399-21844-0 Subj: Sea and seashore.

The secret staircase ill. by author. Putnam, 1983. ISBN 0-689-83090-4 Subj: Animals – mice. Behavior – secrets. Food. Problem solving. Seasons – winter.

Spring story ill. by author. Putnam, 1980. Subj: Animals – mice. Birthdays. Seasons – spring.

Summer story ill. by author. Putnam, 1980. ISBN 0-399-61157-6 Subj: Animals – mice. Seasons – summer. Weddings.

Winter story ill. by author. Putnam, 1980. ISBN 0-689-83057-2 Subj: Animals – mice. Seasons – winter. Weather – snow.

Barnard, A. M. *see* Alcott, Louisa May

Barner, Bob. *Dem bones* ill. by author. Chronicle, 1996. ISBN 0-8118-0827-0 Subj: Anatomy. Ethnic groups in the U.S. – African Americans. Songs.

Elephant facts ill. by author. Dutton, 1979. ISBN 0-525-29200-4 Subj: Animals – elephants. Science.

Elevator escalator book ill. by author. Doubleday, 1990. ISBN 0-385-26667-7 Subj: Animals – dogs. Elevators, escalators. Transportation.

Space race ill. by author. Bantam, 1995. ISBN 0-553-37567-9 Subj: Concepts – shape. Counting, numbers. Robots. Space and space ships.

Too many dinosaurs ill. by author. Bantam, 1995. ISBN 0-553-37566-0 Subj: Counting, numbers. Dinosaurs.

Which way to the Revolution? ill. by author. Holiday, 1998. ISBN 0-8234-1352-7 Subj: Animals – mice. Maps. U.S. history.

Barnes-Murphy, Rowan. *Numbers* ill. by author. Ideals, 1992. ISBN 0-8249-8531-1 Subj: Animals – cats. Animals – mice. Circus. Counting, numbers. Format, unusual – toy and movable books.

One, two, buckle my shoe: a book of counting rhymes (One, two, buckle my shoe)

Barnett, Naomi. *I know a dentist* ill. by Linda Boehm. Putnam, 1977. ISBN 0-399-61097-9 Subj: Careers – dentists. Teeth.

Barnhart, Peter. *The wounded duck* ill. by Adrienne Adams. Scribners, 1979. ISBN 0-684-16255-5 Subj: Birds – ducks. Character traits – kindness to animals. Death. Seasons – winter.

Barnwell, Ysaye M. *No mirrors in my Nana's house* ill. by Synthia Saint James. Harcourt, 1999. ISBN 0-15-201825-5 Subj: Ethnic groups in the U.S. – African Americans. Family life – grandmothers. Self-concept.

Baron, Alan. *Little Pig's bouncy ball* ill. by author. Candlewick, 1996. ISBN 1-56402-805-4 Subj: Activities – playing. Animals. Animals – dogs. Animals – pigs. Behavior – misunderstanding. Cumulative tales. Toys – balls.

Red Fox dances ill. by author. Candlewick, 1996. ISBN 1-56402-803-8 Subj: Activities – dancing. Animals. Animals – foxes. Behavior – trickery. Cumulative tales.

Barr, Cathrine. *A horse for Sherry* ill. by author. Walck, 1963. Subj: Animals – horses, ponies. Farms.

Hound dog's bone ill. by author. Walck, 1961. Subj: Animals – dogs. Animals – foxes. Behavior – stealing. Humor.

Little Ben ill. by author. Walck, 1960. Subj: Animals – beavers. Character traits – bravery.

Sammy seal ov the sircus ill. by author. [1st initial teaching alphabet ed.]. Walck, 1955, 1964. Subj: Animals – seals. Circus. Clowns, jesters.

Barr, Jene. *Fire snorkel number 7* ill. by Joe Rogers. Albert Whitman, 1965. Subj: Careers – firefighters. Fire. Trucks.

Barracca, Debra. *The adventures of taxi dog* (Barracca, Sal)

Maxi, the hero by Debra and Sal Barracca; ill. by Mark Buehner. Dial, 1991. ISBN 0-8037-0940-4 Subj: Animals – dogs. City. Crime. Rhyming text.

Maxi, the star by Debra and Sal Barracca; ill. by Alan Ayers. Dial, 1993. ISBN 0-8037-1349-5 Subj: Activities – traveling. Animals – dogs. Rhyming text. Television.

A taxi dog Christmas by Debra and Sal Barracca; ill. by Alan Ayers. Dial, 1994. ISBN 0-8037-1368-1 Subj: Animals – dogs. City. Holidays – Christmas. Rhyming text. Taxis.

Barracca, Sal. *The adventures of taxi dog* by Sal and Debra Barracca; ill. by Mark Buehner. Dial, 1990. ISBN 0-8037-0672-3 Subj: Animals – dogs. City. Rhyming text. Taxis.

Maxi, the hero (Barracca, Debra)

Maxi, the star (Barracca, Debra)

A taxi dog Christmas (Barracca, Debra)

Barrett, John M. *The bear who slept through Christmas* ill. by Rick Reinert Productions. Ideals, 1980. ISBN 0-8249-7175-2 Subj: Animals – bears. Hibernation. Holidays – Christmas. Humor.

The Easter bear ill. by Rick Reinert Productions. Childrens Pr., 1981. ISBN 0-516-09190-5 Subj: Animals – bears. Animals – rabbits. Holidays – Easter. Seasons – spring.

Oscar the selfish octopus ill. by Joe Servello. Human Sciences Pr., 1978. ISBN 0-87705-355-9 Subj: Character traits – selfishness. Octopuses.

Barrett, Joyce Durham. *Willie's not the hugging kind* ill. by Pat Cummings. HarperCollins, 1989. ISBN 0-06-020417-6 Subj: Character traits – confidence. Emotions – love. Ethnic groups in the U.S. Family life. Friendship.

Barrett, Judi. *Animals should definitely not act like people* ill. by Ron Barrett. Atheneum, 1980. ISBN 0-689-30768-3 Subj: Animals. Behavior – imitation.

Animals should definitely not wear clothing ill. by Ron Barrett. Atheneum, 1970. ISBN 0-689-20592-9 Subj: Animals. Behavior – imitation. Clothing.

An apple a day ill. by Tim Lewis. Atheneum, 1973. ISBN 0-689-30105-7 Subj: Food. Illness.

Benjamin's 365 birthdays ill. by Ron Barrett. Atheneum, 1974. ISBN 0-689-30130-8 Subj: Birthdays.

Cloudy with a chance of meatballs ill. by Ron Barrett. Atheneum, 1978. ISBN 0-689-30647-4 Subj: Family life – grandfathers. Food. Imagination. Weather.

I hate to go to bed ill. by Ray Cruz. Four Winds, 1977. ISBN 0-590-07472-5 Subj: Bedtime. Imagination.

I hate to take a bath ill. by Charles B. Slackman. Atheneum, 1981. ISBN 0-590-07429-6 Subj: Behavior – growing up. Concepts – size.

I'm too small, you're too big ill. by David S. Rose. Atheneum, 1981. ISBN 0-689-30800-0 Subj: Behavior – growing up. Concepts – opposites. Family life – fathers.

Old MacDonald had an apartment house ill. by Ron Barrett. Atheneum, 1969. ISBN 0-689-81757-6 Subj: City. Farms. Gardens, gardening.

Peter's pocket ill. by Julia Noonan. Atheneum, 1974. ISBN 0-689-30403-X Subj: Clothing.

Pickles have pimples ill. by Lonni Sue Johnson. Atheneum, 1986. ISBN 0-689-31187-7 Subj: Rhyming text.

Pickles to Pittsburgh: the sequel to Cloudy with a chance of meatballs written and colored by Judi Barrett; drawn by Ron Barrett. Atheneum, 1997. ISBN 0-689-80104-1 Subj: Family life – grandparents. Food. Weather.

Snake is totally tail ill. by L. S. Johnson. Atheneum, 1983. ISBN 0-689-30979-1 Subj: Animals. Insects. Reptiles.

The things that are most in the world ill. by John Nickle. Atheneum, 1998. ISBN 0-689-81333-3 Subj: Language.

What's left? ill. by author. Atheneum, 1983. ISBN 0-689-30874-4 Subj: Participation. Problem solving.

The wind thief Ill. by Diane Dawson Hearn. Atheneum, 1977. ISBN 0-689-30564-8 Subj: Clothing – hats. Weather – wind.

Barrett, Lawrence Louis. *Twinkle, the baby colt* ill. by author. Knopf, 1945. Subj: Animals – horses, ponies. Behavior – running away.

Barrett, Mary Brigid. *Day care days* ill. by Patti Beling Murphy. Little, 1999. ISBN 0-316-08456-5 Subj: Family life. Rhyming text. School.

The man of the house at Huffington Row: a Christmas story ill. by author. Harcourt, 1998. ISBN 0-15-201580-9 Subj: Character traits – kindness. Family life – brothers and sisters. Holidays – Christmas.

Barrett, Norman S. *Spiders* ill. by author. Watts, 1989. ISBN 0-531-10702-7 Subj: Science. Spiders.

Barrie, J. M. (James M.). *Peter Pan* ill. by Diane Goode. Random House, 1983. ISBN 0-394-95717-2 Subj: Folk and fairy tales. Mythical creatures – pixies.

Barron, T. A. *Where is Grandpa?* ill. by Chris K. Soentpiet. Philomel, 2000. ISBN 0-399-23037-8 Subj: Death. Emotions – grief. Family life – grandfathers.

Barrows, Marjorie Wescott. *Fraidy cat* ill. by Barbara Maynard. Rand McNally, 1942. Subj: Animals – cats. Character traits – bravery. Format, unusual.

The funny hat ill. by Norv Mink. Rand McNally, 1943. Subj: Behavior – losing things. Clothing – hats. Format, unusual.

Muggins' big balloon ill. by Anne Sellers Leaf. Rand McNally, 1967. ISBN 0-8382-0557-7 Subj: Animals – mice. Toys – balloons.

Muggins Mouse ill. by Anne Sellers Leaf. Rand McNally, 1965, c1964. Subj: Animals – mice.

Muggins takes off ill. by Anne Sellers Leaf. Rand McNally, 1964. ISBN 0-8382-0559-3 Subj: Animals – mice.

The Rand McNally book of favorite Muggins Mouse stories ill. by Anne Sellers Leaf. Rand McNally, 1965. Subj: Animals – mice.

Timothy Tiger ill. by Keith Ward. Rand McNally, 1943. Subj: Animals – tigers.

Barry, David. *The Rajah's rice* ill. by Donna Perrone. Scientific American, 1994. ISBN 0-7167-6568-3 Subj: Animals – elephants. Character traits – cleverness. Counting, numbers. Folk and fairy tales. Foreign lands – India. Royalty.

Barry, Katharina. *A is for anything* ill. by author. Harcourt, 1961. Subj: ABC books. Poetry.

A bug to hug ill. by author. Harcourt, 1964. Subj: Imagination. Poetry. Problem solving.

Barry, Robert E. *Animals around the world* ill. by author. McGraw-Hill, 1967. Subj: ABC books. Animals. Poetry.

Mr. Willowby's Christmas tree ill. by Paul Galdone. McGraw-Hill, 1963. ISBN 0-89966-935-2 Subj: Holidays – Christmas. Rhyming text. Trees.

Next please ill. by author. Houghton Mifflin, 1961. Subj: Careers – barbers. Zoos.

Bartalos, Michael. *Shadowville* ill. by author. Viking, 1995. ISBN 0-67086-161-8 Subj: Holidays – Groundhog Day. Rhyming text. Shadows.

Bartels, Alice L. *The beast* ill. by Gilles Tibo. Firefly, 1990. ISBN 1-55037-101-0 Subj: Folk and fairy tales. Monsters. Night. Seasons.

The grandmother doll ill. by Duſan Petricic. Firefly, 2001. ISBN 1-55037-667-5 Subj: Activities – making things. Illness. Imagination. Toys – dolls.

Barth, Dominic. *George paints his house* (Bassède, Francine)

Barthelme, Donald. *The slightly irregular fire engine: or, The hithering thithering djinn* ill. by author. Farrar, 1971. Collage ill. made from nineteenth-century engravings. ISBN 0-374-37038-9 Subj: Imagination.

Bartlett, Margaret Farrington. *The clean brook* ill. by Aldren Auld Watson. McGraw-Hill, 1960. ISBN 0-690-19556-7 Subj: Science.

Down the mountain: a book about the ever-changing soil ill. by Rhys Caparn. Addison-Wesley, 1963. Subj: Science.

Raindrop stories (Bassett, Preston R.)

Where the brook begins ill. by Aldren Auld Watson. Crowell, 1961. Subj: Science.

Bartlett, Robert Merrill. *Jack Horner and song of sixpence* ill. by Emily Newton Barto. Longman, 1943. Subj: Nursery rhymes.

Bartlett, Susan. *Libraries* ill. by Gioia Fiammenghi. Holt, 1964. Subj: Libraries.

Barto, Emily Newton. *Chubby bear* ill. by author. Longman, 1941. Subj: Animals – bears. Poetry.

Bartoletti, Susan Campbell. *Silver at night* ill. by David Ray. Crown, 1994. ISBN 0-517-59427-7 Subj: Activities – working. Careers – miners. Emotions – love. Ethnic groups in the U.S. – Italian Americans.

Bartoli, Jennifer. *In a meadow, two hares hide* ill. by Takeo Ishida; ed. by Kathy Pacini. Albert Whitman, 1978. Subj: Animals – rabbits. Seasons – winter.

Nonna ill. by Joan E. Drescher. Harvey House, 1975. ISBN 0-8178-5212-3 Subj: Death. Emotions – grief. Family life. Family life – grandmothers.

Snow on bear's nose: a story of a Japanese moon bear cub ed. by Caroline Rubin; ill. by Takeo Ishida. Albert Whitman, 1972. ISBN 0-8075-7520-8 Subj: Animals – bears. Behavior – lost. Foreign lands – Japan. Hibernation. Seasons – winter. Weather – snow.

Barton, Byron. *Airplanes* ill. by author. Crowell, 1986. ISBN 0-690-04532-8 Subj: Airplanes, airports.

Airport ill. by author. Crowell, 1982. ISBN 0-690-04169-1 Subj: Airplanes, airports. Careers – airplane pilots. Transportation.

Boats ill. by author. Crowell, 1986. ISBN 0-690-04563-0 Subj: Boats, ships.

Bones, bones, dinosaur bones ill. by author. Harper-Collins, 1990. ISBN 0-690-04827-0 Subj: Dinosaurs.

Building a house ill. by author. Greenwillow, 1981. ISBN 0-688-84291-7 Subj: Homes, houses.

Buzz, buzz, buzz ill. by author. Macmillan, 1973. ISBN 0-02-708450-7 Subj: Cumulative tales. Insects – bees.

Dinosaurs, dinosaurs ill. by author. HarperCollins, 1989. ISBN 0-690-04768-1 Subj: Dinosaurs.

Harry is a scaredy-cat ill. by author. Macmillan, 1974. ISBN 0-02-708440-X Subj: Circus. Emotions – fear.

Hester ill. by author. Greenwillow, 1975. ISBN 0-688-84009-4 Subj: Character traits – patience.

I want to be an astronaut ill. by author. Crowell, 1988. ISBN 0-690-04744-4 Subj: Careers – astronauts. Character traits – ambition. Space and space ships.

Jack and Fred ill. by author. Macmillan, 1974. ISBN 0-02-708400-0 Subj: Animals – dogs. Animals – rabbits. Pets.

The little red hen (The little red hen)

Machines at work ill. by author. HarperCollins, 1987. ISBN 0-690-04573-5 Subj: Activities – working. Machines.

The three bears (The three bears)

Tools ill. by author. HarperFestival, 1995. ISBN 0-694-00623-8 Subj: Language. Tools.

Trains ill. by author. Crowell, 1986. ISBN 0-690-04534-4 Subj: Trains.

Trucks ill. by author. Crowell, 1986. ISBN 0-690-04530-1 Subj: Trucks.

The wee little woman ill. by author. HarperCollins, 1995. ISBN 0-06-023388-5 Subj: Animals – cats. Behavior – running away. Behavior – stealing.

Wheels ill. by author. Crowell, 1979. ISBN 0-690-03952-2 Subj: Progress. Wheels.

Where's Al? ill. by author. Seabury Pr., 1972. Subj: Animals – dogs. Behavior – lost. Wordless.

Zoo animals ill. by author. HarperFestival, 1995. ISBN 0-694-00620-3 Subj: Animals. Zoos.

Barton, Julia. *Are you asleep, rabbit?* (Campbell, Alison)

Barton, Pat. *A week is a long time* ill. by Jutta Ash. Academy Chicago, 1980. ISBN 0-200-72464-9 Subj: Clothing. Country.

Bartone, Elisa. *American, too* ill. by Ted Lewin. Lothrop, 1996. ISBN 0-688-13279-0 Subj: Communities, neighborhoods. Ethnic groups in the U.S. – Italian Americans.

Peppe the lamplighter ill. by Ted Lewin. Lothrop, 1993. ISBN 0-688-10269-7 Subj: Caldecott award honor books. City. Ethnic groups in the U.S. – Italian Americans. Family life – brothers and sisters. Family life – fathers.

Bartos-Hoppner, Barbara. *The pied piper of Hamelin* trans. by Anthea Bell; ill. by Annegert Fuchshuber. Lippincott, 1987. Adapt. of the poem The pied piper of Hamelin by Robert Browning. ISBN 0-397-32240-2 Subj: Animals – rats. Behavior – trickery. Folk and fairy tales. Foreign lands – Germany.

Baruch, Dorothy. *I would like to be a pony and other wishes* ill. by Mary Chalmers. HarperCollins, 1959. Subj: Behavior – wishing. Poetry.

Kappa's tug-of-war with the big brown horse: the story of a Japanese water imp ill. by Sanryo Sakai. Tuttle, 1962. Subj: Animals. Farms. Folk and fairy tales. Foreign lands – Japan. Mythical creatures – imps.

Barwin, Gary. *The racing worm brothers* ill. by Kitty Macaulay. Annick, 1998. ISBN 1-55037-541-5 Subj: Animals – worms. Pets.

Bascom, Joe. *Malcolm Softpaws* ill. by author. Lippincott, 1958. Subj: Animals – cats. Behavior – greed. Character traits – selfishness.

Malcolm's job ill. by author. Lippincott, 1959. Subj: Animals – cats. Family life. Music.

Base, Graeme. *Animalia* ill. by author. Abrams, 1987. ISBN 0-8109-1868-4 Subj: ABC books. Animals.

My grandma lived in Gooligulch ill. by author. Australian Book Source, 1988, 1983. ISBN 0-944176-01-1 Subj: Animals. Family life – grandmothers. Foreign lands – Australia. Rhyming text.

Bash, Barbara. *Desert giant: the world of the Saguaro cactus* ill. by author. Little, 1988. ISBN 0-316-08301-1 Subj: Desert. Plants.

Urban roosts ill. by author. Little, 1990. ISBN 0-316-08306-2 Subj: Birds. City. Nature.

Bashevis, Isaac. *see* Singer, Isaac Bashevis

Basile, Giambattista. *Petrosinella: a Neapolitan Rapunzel* adapt. by John Edward Taylor; ill. by Diane Stanley. Warne, 1981. ISBN 0-7232-6196-2 Subj: Folk and fairy tales. Foreign lands – Italy. Royalty. Witches.

Baskin, Leonard. *Hosie's alphabet* ill. by author; words by Hosea, Tobias and Lisa Baskin. Viking, 1972. ISBN 0-670-37958-1 Subj: ABC books. Caldecott award honor books. Children as authors.

Hosie's aviary ill. by author; words mostly by Tobias Baskin and others. Viking, 1979. ISBN 0-670-37965-4 Subj: Birds. Children as authors.

Hosie's zoo ill. by author; words by Tobias Baskin and others. Viking, 1981. ISBN 0-670-37968-9 Subj: Animals. Rhyming text. Zoos.

Baskin, Tobias. *Hosie's aviary* (Baskin, Leonard)

Hosie's zoo (Baskin, Leonard)

Baskwill, Jane. *Somewhere* ill. by Trish Hill. Mondo, 1996. ISBN 1-57255-132-1 Subj: Nature. Rhyming text.

Bason, Lillian. *Castles and mirrors and cities of sand* ill. by Allan Eitzen. Lothrop, 1968. Subj: Animals. Sand. Science.

Pick a raincoat, pick a whistle ill. by Allan Eitzen. Lothrop, 1966. Subj: Activities – whistling. Trees.

Spiders ill. with photos. National Geographic, 1974. ISBN 0-870-44156-6 Subj: Science. Spiders.

Those foolish Molboes! ill. by Margot Tomes. Coward, 1977. ISBN 0-698-30642-2 Subj: Behavior – hiding things. Character traits – cleverness. Character traits – foolishness. Folk and fairy tales. Foreign lands – Denmark.

Bassède, Francine. *George paints his house* ill. by author; trans. by Dominic Barth. Orchard, 1999. ISBN 0-531-33150-4 Subj: Activities – painting. Animals – cats. Birds – ducks. Concepts – color. Homes, houses.

George's store at the shore ill. by author. Orchard, 1998. ISBN 0-531-33083-4 Subj: Counting, numbers.

Bassett, Jeni. *The chicks' trick* ill. by author. Cobblehill, 1995. ISBN 0-525-65152-7 Subj: Behavior – fighting, arguing. Birds – chickens. Family life.

Bassett, Lisa. *Beany and Scamp* ill. by Jeni Bassett. Dodd, 1987. ISBN 0-396-08822-8 Subj: Animals – bears. Animals – squirrels. Behavior – losing things. Behavior – lost. Seasons – winter.

Beany wakes up for Christmas ill. by Jeni Bassett. Putnam, 1988. ISBN 0-399-21668-5 Subj: Animals – bears. Animals – squirrels. Friendship. Hibernation. Holidays – Christmas.

A clock for Beany ill. by Jeni Bassett. Dodd, 1985. ISBN 0-396-08484-2 Subj: Animals. Animals – bears. Birthdays. Clocks, watches.

Koala Christmas ill. by Jeni Bassett. Dutton, 1991. ISBN 0-525-65065-2 Subj: Animals – koalas. Foreign lands – Australia. Holidays – Christmas. Sibling rivalry.

Bassett, Preston R. *Raindrop stories* by Preston R. Bassett and Margaret Farrington Bartlett; ill. by Jim Arnosky. Four Winds, 1981. ISBN 0-590-07628-0 Subj: Noise, sounds. Weather – rain.

Basso, Bill. *The top of the pizzas* ill. by author. Dodd, 1977. ISBN 0-396-07463-4 Subj: Activities – working. Food. Monsters.

Bastin, Marjolein. *A little dog for Vera* ill. by author. Stewart, Tabori & Chang, 1991. ISBN 0-55670-208-6 Subj: Animals – dogs. Animals – mice. Pets.

My name is Vera ill. by author. Barron's, 1985. ISBN 0-8120-5690-6 Subj: Animals – mice. Friendship.

Vera and her friends ill. by author. Barron's, 1985. ISBN 0-8120-5689-2 Subj: Animals – mice. Friendship.

Vera dresses up ill. by author. Barron's, 1985. ISBN 0-8120-5691-4 Subj: Animals – mice. Clothing.

Vera in the kitchen ill. by author. Barron's, 1988. ISBN 0-8120-6087-3 Subj: Activities – cooking. Animals – mice.

Vera the mouse ill. by author. Barron's, 1986. ISBN 0-8120-7391-6 Subj: Animals – mice.

Vera's special hobbies ill. by author. Barron's, 1985. ISBN 0-8120-5692-2 Subj: Animals – mice. Nature.

Bat-Ami, Miriam. *Sea, salt, and air* ill. by Mary O'Keefe Young. Simon & Schuster, 1993. ISBN 0-02-708495-7 Subj: Behavior – growing up. Family life – grandparents. Sea and seashore. Seasons – summer.

Batchelor, Louise. *Whoops!* ill. by author. Zero to Ten, 1998. ISBN 1-8408-9024-X Subj: Activities – playing. Friendship.

Bate, Lucy. *How Georgina drove the car very carefully from Boston to New York* ill. by Tamar Taylor. Crown, 1989. ISBN 0-517-57142-0 Subj: Activities – traveling. Family life – grandparents. Imagination.

Little rabbit's loose tooth ill. by Diane de Groat. Crown, 1975. ISBN 0-517-52240-3 Subj: Animals – rabbits. Fairies. Teeth.

Bate, Norman. *Vulcan* ill. by author. Scribners, 1960. Subj: Machines.

What a wonderful machine is a submarine ill. by author. Scribners, 1961. Subj: Boats, ships. Sea and seashore.

Who built the bridge? ill. by author. Crown, 1975. ISBN 0-684-13449-7 Subj: Machines.

Who built the highway? ill. by author. Scribners, 1953. Subj: Machines. Roads.

Bateman, Robert. *Safari* by Robert Bateman and Rick Archbold; ill. by authors. Little, 1998. ISBN 0-316-08265-1 Subj: Animals. Foreign lands – Africa.

Bateman, Teresa. *Leprechaun gold* ill. by Rosanne Litzinger. Holiday, 1998. ISBN 0-8234-1344-6 Subj: Folk and fairy tales. Mythical creatures – leprechauns.

Bates, Artie Ann. *Ragsale* ill. by Jeff Chapman-Crane. Houghton Mifflin, 1995. ISBN 0-395-70030-2 Subj: Family life. Poverty. Shopping.

Bates, H. E. (Herbert Ernest). *Achilles and Diana* by H. E. Bates and Carol Barker; ill. by Carol Barker. Dobson, 1963. Subj: Animals – donkeys.

Achilles the donkey by H. E. Bates and Carol Barker; ill. by Carol Barker. Watts, 1963. Subj: Animals – donkeys. Behavior – running away.

Bates, Ivan. *All by myself* ill. by author. Harper-Collins, 2000. ISBN 0-06-028585-0 Subj: Animals. Animals – elephants. Character traits – individuality.

Bateson-Hill, Margaret. *Lao Lao of Dragon Mountain* ill. by Francesca Pelizzoli; Chinese text by Manyee Wan; paper cuts by Shaliu Qu. Zero to Ten, 1996. ISBN 1-899883-64-9 Subj: Folk and fairy tales. Foreign lands – China. Foreign languages. Paper.

Shota and the star quilt ill. by Christine Fowler; Lakota text by Philomine Lakota. Zero to Ten, 1998. ISBN 1-8408-9021-5 Subj: Indians of North America – Lakota (Sioux). Quilts.

Batherman, Muriel. *Animals live here* ill. by author. Greenwillow, 1979. ISBN 0-688-84206-2 Subj: Animals. Science.

Some things you should know about my dog ill. by author. Prentice-Hall, 1976. ISBN 0-13-822544-3 Subj: Animals – dogs.

Battles, Edith. *One to teeter-totter* ill. by Rosalind Fry. Albert Whitman, 1973. ISBN 0-8075-6103-7 Subj: Emotions – loneliness. Family life. Friendship. Games.

The terrible terrier ill. by Tom Funk. Addison-Wesley, 1972. ISBN 0-20-109366-9 Subj: Animals – dogs. Behavior – greed.

The terrible trick or treat ill. by Tom Funk. Addison-Wesley, 1970. Subj: Behavior – greed. Holidays – Halloween.

What does the rooster say, Yoshio? ill. by Toni Hormann. Albert Whitman, 1978. ISBN 0-8075-3628-8 Subj: Animals. Foreign lands – Japan. Language.

Bauer, Caroline Feller. *Midnight snowman* ill. by Catherine Stock. Atheneum, 1987. ISBN 0-689-31294-6 Subj: Seasons – winter. Snowmen. Weather – snow.

My mom travels a lot ill. by Nancy Winslow Parker. Warne, 1981. ISBN 0-7232-6203-9 Subj: Careers. Family life – mothers.

Too many books! ill. by Diane Paterson. Viking, 1986. ISBN 0-670-81130-0 Subj: Activities – reading. Behavior – collecting things. Libraries.

Bauer, Helen. *Good times at the park* photos by Hubert A. Lowman. Melmont, 1954. Subj: Activities – playing. Birthdays. Parks. Zoos.

Bauer, Marion Dane. *If you were born a kitten* ill. by JoEllen McAllister Stammen. Simon & Schuster, 1997. ISBN 0-689-80111-4 Subj: Animals. Animals – babies.

Sleep, little one, sleep ill. by author. Simon & Schuster, 1999. ISBN 0-689-82250-2 Subj: Animals. Bedtime. Family life – fathers. Sleep.

When I go camping with Grandma ill. by Allen Garns. BridgeWater, 1995. ISBN 0-8167-3448-8 Subj: Camps, camping. Family life – grandmothers.

Bauer, Steven. *The strange and wonderful tale of Robert McDoodle* ill. by Brad Sneed. Simon & Schuster, 1999. ISBN 0-689-80619-1 Subj: Animals – dogs. Behavior – dissatisfaction. Behavior – running away. Birthdays. Rhyming text.

Baugh, Dolores M. *Bikes* by Dolores M. Baugh and Marjorie P. Pulsifer; ill. by Eve Hoffmann. Rev. ed. Chandler, 1965. Subj: Sports – bicycling. Traffic, traffic signs.

Let's go by Dolores M. Baugh and Marjorie P. Pulsifer; ill. by Eve Hoffmann. Noble, 1970. Subj: Stores.

Let's see the animals by Dolores M. Baugh and Marjorie P. Pulsifer; ill. by Eve Hoffmann. Chandler, 1965. Subj: Animals.

Let's take a trip by Dolores M. Baugh and Marjorie P. Pulsifer; ill. by Richard Szumski and others. Chandler, 1965. Subj: Libraries. Machines.

Slides by Dolores M. Baugh and Marjorie P. Pulsifer; ill. by Eve Hoffmann. Noble, 1970. Subj: Activities – playing.

Supermarket by Dolores M. Baugh and Marjorie P. Pulsifer; ill. by Eve Hoffmann. Noble, 1970. Subj: Food. Shopping. Stores.

Swings by Dolores M. Baugh and Marjorie P. Pulsifer; ill. by Eve Hoffmann. Noble, 1970. Subj: Activities – playing. Activities – swinging.

Trucks and cars to ride by Dolores M. Baugh and Marjorie P. Pulsifer; ill. by Eve Hoffmann. Noble, 1970. Subj: Automobiles. Transportation. Trucks.

Baum, Arline. *One bright Monday morning* by Arline and Joseph Baum; ill. by Joseph Baum. Random House, 1973, c1962. ISBN 0-394-82650-7 Subj: Counting, numbers. Seasons – spring. Weather.

Opt: an illusionary tale by Arline and Joseph Baum; ill. by authors. Viking, 1987. ISBN 0-670-80870-9 Subj: Birthdays. Optical illusions. Royalty – princes.

Baum, Joseph. *One bright Monday morning* (Baum, Arline)

Opt: an illusionary tale (Baum, Arline)

Baum, L. Frank (Lyman Frank). *Mother Goose in prose* ill. by Maxfield Parrish. Bounty Books, 1986, c1901. ISBN 0-685-16878-6 Subj: Nursery rhymes.

Baum, Louis. *After dark* ill. by Susan Varley. Overlook Pr., 1990. ISBN 0-87951-382-9 Subj: Family life – mothers.

I want to see the moon ill. by Niki Daly. Overlook Pr., 1989. ISBN 0-87951-367-5 Subj: Bedtime. Moon. Sleep.

Juju and the pirate ill. by Philippe Matter. HarperCollins, 1984. ISBN 0-911745-14-9 Subj: Activities – traveling. Birds – parakeets, parrots. Pirates.

One more time ill. by Paddy Bouma. Morrow, 1986. ISBN 0-688-06587-2 Subj: Divorce. Family life – fathers.

Baum, Susan. *The beach* ill. by author. HarperCollins, 1991. ISBN 0-06-107416-0 Subj: Sea and seashore.

City shapes ill. by author. HarperCollins, 1991. ISBN 0-06-107417-9 Subj: City. Concepts – shape.

Baum, Willi. *Birds of a feather* ill. by author. Addison-Wesley, 1969. Subj: Birds. Wordless.

Bauman, A. F. *Guess where you're going, guess what you'll do* ill. by True Kelley. Houghton Mifflin, 1989. ISBN 0-395-50211-X Subj: Concepts. Games. Participation.

Bauman, Amy. *I know an old lady* (Little old lady who swallowed a fly)

Baumann, Hans. *Chip has many brothers* ill. by Eric Carle. Philomel, 1985. ISBN 0-399-21283-3 Subj: Animals. Character traits – kindness to animals. Folk and fairy tales. Magic.

The hare's race ill. by Antoni Boratynski; trans. from German by Elizabeth D. Crawford. Morrow, 1976. ISBN 0-688-32067-8 Subj: Animals – rabbits. Folk and fairy tales. Reptiles – turtles, tortoises. Sports – racing.

Mischa and his brothers trans. from German by Peter F. Neumeyer; ill. by Reinhard Michl. Green Tiger Pr., 1985. ISBN 0-88138-051-2 Subj: Character traits – being different. Family life – brothers. Forest, woods.

Baumann, Kurt. *The paper airplane* ill. by Fulvio Testa. Little, 1982. ISBN 0-316-08389-5 Subj: Airplanes, airports. Imagination.

Piro and the fire brigade ill. by Jiri Bernard. Faber, 1981. Translation of: Piro und die Feuerwehr. ISBN 0-571-11843-7 Subj: Animals – dogs. Careers – firefighters. Character traits – bravery. Fire. Foreign lands – Switzerland.

The prince and the lute ill. by Jean Claverie. North-South, 1986. First pub. in Switzerland under the title Der Prinz und die Laute. ISBN 0-03-008018-5 Subj: Character traits – kindness. Folk and fairy tales. Royalty – princes. War.

Puss in boots (Perrault, Charles)

The story of Jonah trans. from German by Jock J. Curle; ill. by Allison Reed. Holt, 1987. ISBN 0-8050-0233-2 Subj: Animals – whales. Behavior – misbehavior. Religion – Jonah.

Baumgardner, Mary Alice. *Alexandra, keeper of dreams* ill. by author. Rocky River, 1993. ISBN 0-944576-08-7 Subj: Activities – dancing. Ballet. Birds – ducks. Character traits – perseverance.

Baumgart, Klaus. *Anna and the little green dragon* ill. by author. Walt Disney, 1992. ISBN 1-56282-167-9 Subj: Behavior – misbehavior. Dragons.

Don't be afraid, Tommy ill. by author. Little Tiger, 1998. ISBN 1-888444-32-0 Subj: Animals – dogs. Behavior – growing up. Emotions – fear.

Laura's Christmas star ill. by author. Little Tiger, 1999. ISBN 1-888444-59-2 Subj: Holidays – Christmas. Magic. Stars. Trees.

The little green dragon steps out ill. by author. Hyperion, 1992. ISBN 1-56282-255-1 Subj: Activities – reading. Dragons. Dreams. Night.

Bawden, Juliet. *One year old* photos by Helen Pask. Holt, 1990. ISBN 0-8050-1257-5 Subj: Counting, numbers.

Bawden, Nina. *Princess Alice* ill. by Phillida Gili. Dutton, 1986. ISBN 0-233-97746-5 Subj: Adoption. Family life. Royalty – princesses.

St. Francis of Assisi ill. by Pascale Allamand. Lothrop, 1983. ISBN 0-688-01653-7 Subj: Character traits – generosity. Religion.

William Tell ill. by Pascale Allamand. Lothrop, 1981. ISBN 0-688-51985-7 Subj: Character traits – bravery. Folk and fairy tales. Foreign lands – Switzerland.

Bax, Martin. *Edmond went far away* ill. by Michael Foreman. Harcourt, 1989. ISBN 0-15-225105-7 Subj: Activities – walking. Animals. Farms.

Bayar, Ilene. *Rachel and Mischa* (Bayar, Steven)

Bayar, Steven. *Rachel and Mischa* by Steven and Ilene Bayar; ill. by Marlene Lobell Ruthen; photos by Joanne Strauss. Kar-Ben Copies, 1988. ISBN 0-930-49477-6 Subj: Character traits – freedom. Jewish culture. Religion.

Bayer, Jane. *A my name is Alice* ill. by Steven Kellogg. Dial, 1984. ISBN 0-8037-0124-1 Subj: ABC books. Animals. Names.

Bayley, Nicola. *Crab cat* ill. by author. Knopf, 1984. ISBN 0-394-86499-0 Subj: Animals – cats. Imagination.

Elephant cat ill. by author. Knopf, 1984. ISBN 0-394-86497-2 Subj: Animals – cats. Imagination.

Nicola Bayley's book of nursery rhymes ill. by author. Knopf, 1975. ISBN 0-394-83561-1 Subj: Nursery rhymes.

One old Oxford ox ill. by author. Atheneum, 1977. ISBN 0-689-30608-3 Subj: Animals. Counting, numbers.

Parrot cat ill. by author. Knopf, 1984. ISBN 0-394-86496-4 Subj: Animals – cats. Imagination.

Polar bear cat ill. by author. Knopf, 1984. ISBN 0-394-86501-4 Subj: Animals – cats. Imagination.

Spider cat ill. by author. Knopf, 1984. ISBN 0-394-86500-6 Subj: Animals – cats. Imagination.

Baylor, Byrd. *Amigo* ill. by Garth Williams. Macmillan, 1963. ISBN 0-606-03982-1 Subj: Animals – prairie dogs. Pets. Rhyming text.

The best town in the world ill. by Ronald Himler. Scribners, 1983. ISBN 0-684-18035-9 Subj: City.

Coyote cry ill. by Symeon Shimin. Lothrop, 1972. Subj: Animals – coyotes. Animals – dogs.

The desert is theirs ill. by Peter Parnall. Scribners, 1975. ISBN 0-684-14266-X Subj: Caldecott award honor books. Desert. Ecology. Folk and fairy tales. Indians of North America – Papago. Rhyming text.

Desert voices ill. by Peter Parnall. Scribners, 1981. ISBN 0-684-16712-3 Subj: Animals. Desert. Rhyming text.

Everybody needs a rock ill. by Peter Parnall. Scribners, 1974. ISBN 0-684-13899-9 Subj: Rhyming text. Rocks.

A God on every mountain top: stories of southwest Indian sacred mountains ill. by Carol Brown. Scribners, 1981. ISBN 0-684-16758-1 Subj: Folk and fairy tales. Indians of North America.

Guess who my favorite person is ill. by Robert Andrew Parker. Scribners, 1977. ISBN 0-684-15197-9 Subj: Friendship. Games.

Hawk, I'm your brother ill. by Peter Parnall. Scribners, 1976. ISBN 0-684-14571-5 Subj: Birds – hawks. Caldecott award honor books. Character traits – freedom. Indians of North America.

If you are a hunter of fossils ill. by Peter Parnall. Macmillan, 1980. ISBN 0-684-16419-1 Subj: Science.

I'm in charge of celebrations ill. by Peter Parnall. Scribners, 1986. ISBN 0-684-18579-2 Subj: Desert. Nature.

Moon song ill. by Ronald Himler. Scribners, 1982. ISBN 0-684-17463-4 Subj: Animals – coyotes. Folk and fairy tales. Indians of North America. Moon.

One small blue bead ill. by Ronald Himler. Scribners, 1992. ISBN 0-684-19334-5 Subj: Cavemen. Rhyming text.

The other way to listen ill. by Peter Parnall. Scribners, 1978. ISBN 0-684-16017-X Subj: Nature. Poetry.

The table where rich people sit ill. by Peter Parnall. Scribners, 1994. ISBN 0-684-19653-0 Subj: Family life. Money. Nature.

The way to start a day ill. by Peter Parnall. Aladdin, 1986, c1978. ISBN 0-684-15651-2 Subj: Caldecott award honor books. Folk and fairy tales. Foreign lands. Religion. Sun.

We walk in sandy places ill. by Marilyn Schweitzer. Scribners, 1976. ISBN 0-684-14526-X Subj: Animals. Desert.

When clay sings ill. by Tom Bahti. Scribners, 1972. ISBN 0-684-12807-1 Subj: Art. Caldecott award honor books. Indians of North America.

Your own best secret place ill. by Peter Parnall. Scribners, 1979. ISBN 0-684-16111-7 Subj: Behavior – hiding things. Behavior – secrets.

Baynes, Pauline. *How dog began* ill. by author. Holt, 1987. ISBN 0-8050-0011-9 Subj: Animals – dogs. Animals – wolves. Caves.

Let there be light ill. by author. Macmillan, 1991. ISBN 0-02-708542-2 Subj: Religion.

Noah and the ark (Bible. Old Testament. Noah)

Thanks be to God ill. by author. Macmillan, 1990. ISBN 0-02-708541-4 Subj: Religion.

Baynton, Martin. *Fifty and the fox* ill. by author. Crown, 1986. ISBN 0-517-56069-0 Subj: Animals – foxes. Farms. Tractors.

Fifty and the great race ill. by author. Crown, 1987. ISBN 0-517-56354-1 Subj: Fairs. Farms. Sports – racing. Tractors.

Fifty gets the picture ill. by author. Crown, 1987. ISBN 0-517-56355-X Subj: Activities – digging. Careers – artists. Farms. Tractors.

Fifty saves his friend ill. by author. Crown, 1986. ISBN 0-517-56022-4 Subj: Animals – rats. Farms. Friendship. Tractors.

Why do you love me? ill. by author. Greenwillow, 1990. ISBN 0-688-09157-1 Subj: Character traits – questioning. Emotions – love. Family life – fathers.

Bazilian, Barbara. *Princess Lily* by Barbara Bazilian and Judith Fine; ill. by Barbara Bazilian. Whispering Coyote, 1998. ISBN 1-58089-006-7 Subj: Folk and fairy tales. Royalty – princesses. Wizards.

Bea, Holly. *Where does God live?* ill. by Kim Howard. Starseed Pr., 1997. ISBN 0-915811-73-1 Subj: Family life – grandmothers. Religion.

Beach, Stewart. *Good morning, sun's up!* ill. by Yutaka Sugita. Scroll Pr., 1970. German ed. has title: Guten Morgen, liebe Sonne! Subj: Animals. Games. Morning.

Beard, Darleen Bailey. *Twister* ill. by Nancy Carpenter. Farrar, 1999. ISBN 0-374-37977-7 Subj: Character traits – helpfulness. Family life. Weather – storms. Weather – tornadoes.

Beatty, Hetty Burlingame. *Bucking horse* ill. by author. Houghton Mifflin, 1957. Subj: Animals – horses, ponies. Cowboys.

Droopy ill. by author. Houghton Mifflin, 1954. Subj: Animals – mules. Character traits – stubbornness. Sports – swimming.

Little Owl Indian ill. by author. Houghton Mifflin, 1951. Subj: Animals – horses, ponies. Fire. Indians of North America.

Moorland pony ill. by author. Houghton Mifflin, 1961. Subj: Activities – traveling. Animals – horses, ponies. Character traits – kindness to animals. Family life. Foreign lands – England. Pets.

Bechstein, Ludwig. *The rabbit catcher and other fairy tales* tr. and intro. by Randall Jarrell; ill. by Ugo Fontana. Macmillan, 1962. Subj: Folk and fairy tales. Foreign lands – Germany.

Beck, Andrea. *Elliot bakes a cake* ill. by author. Kids Can Pr., 1999. ISBN 1-55074-443-7 Subj: Activities – cooking. Animals. Birthdays. Toys.

Elliot's emergency ill. by author. Kids Can Pr., 1998. ISBN 1-55074-441-0 Subj: Toys – dolls.

Beck, Ian. *Emily and the golden acorn* ill. by author. Simon & Schuster, 1992. ISBN 0-671-75979-5 Subj: Boats, ships. Family life – brothers and sisters. Imagination. Trees.

Five little ducks ill. by author. Holt, 1993. ISBN 0-8050-2525-1 Subj: Animals – foxes. Birds – ducks. Counting, numbers. Rhyming text.

Beck, Martine. *Rescue of Brown Bear and White Bear* ill. by Marie H. Henry. Little, 1991. ISBN 0-316-08654-1 Subj: Animals – bears.

The wedding of Brown Bear and White Bear trans. from French by Aliyah Morgenstern; ill. by Marie H. Henry. Little, 1990. ISBN 0-316-08652-5 Subj: Animals – bears. Weddings.

Becker, Bonny. *The Christmas crocodile* ill. by David Small. Simon & Schuster, 1997. ISBN 0-689-81503-4 Subj: Behavior – mistakes. Holidays – Christmas. Reptiles – alligators, crocodiles.

Tickly prickly ill. by Shari Halpern. HarperFestival, 1999. ISBN 0-694-01239-4 Subj: Animals. Rhyming text. Senses – touching.

Becker, Edna. *Nine hundred buckets of paint* ill. by Margaret Bradfield. Abingdon, 1945. Subj: Activities – painting. Homes, houses. Moving.

Becker, John Leonard. *Seven little rabbits* ill. by Barbara Cooney. Walker, 1973. ISBN 0-8027-6130-5 Subj: Animals – rabbits. Counting, numbers.

Becker, May Lamberton. *The rainbow Mother Goose* (Mother Goose)

Beckett, Hilary. *The rooster's horns: a Chinese puppet play to make and perform* (Young, Ed [Edward])

Beckman, Beatrice. *I can be a teacher* ill. with photos. Childrens Pr., 1985. ISBN 0-516-01843-4 Subj: Careers – teachers.

Beckman, Kaj. *Lisa cannot sleep* ill. by Per Beckman. Watts, 1970. ISBN 0-531-01931-4 Subj: Bedtime. Family life. Sleep. Toys.

Bedard, Michael. *The nightingale* (Andersen, H. C. [Hans Christian])

Sitting ducks ill. by author. Putnam, 1998. ISBN 0-399-22847-0 Subj: Birds – ducks. Friendship. Reptiles – alligators, crocodiles.

Bedford, A. N. (Annie North). *see* Watson, Jane Werner

Bedtime ed. by Mary Lee Donovan. Candlewick, 1999. ISBN 0-7636-0932-3 Subj: Bedtime. Format, unusual – board books.

The bedtime book: *a collection of fairy tales* ill. by Daniel San Souci. Messner, 1985. ISBN 0-671-60505-4 Subj: Folk and fairy tales.

Beech, Caroline. *Peas again for lunch* ill. by Gina Calleja. Annick, 1981. Subj: Behavior – misbehavior. Imagination.

Beecroft, John. *What? Another cat!* ill. by Kurt Wiese. Dodd, 1960. Subj: Animals – cats. Sibling rivalry.

Beeler, Selby B. *Throw your tooth on the roof: tooth traditions from around the world* ill. by G. Brian Karas. Houghton Mifflin, 1998. ISBN 0-395-89108-6 Subj: Folk and fairy tales. Teeth.

Beer, Kathleen Costello. *What happens in the spring* ill. with photos. National Geographic, 1977. ISBN 0-8704-4242-2 Subj: Seasons – spring.

Bees created by Gallimard Jeunesse, Ute Fuhr and Raoul Sautai; ill. by Ute Fuhr and Raoul Sautai. Scholastic, 1997. ISBN 0-590-93780-4 Subj: Format, unusual – toy and movable books. Insects – bees.

Begaye, Lisa Shook. *Building a bridge* ill. by Libba Tracy. Northland, 1993. ISBN 0-87358-557-7 Subj: Friendship. Indians of North America – Navajo. School – first day.

Behan, Brendan. *The king of Ireland's son* ill. by P. J. Lynch. Orchard, 1997. ISBN 0-531-09549-5 Subj: Folk and fairy tales. Foreign lands – Ireland. Royalty – princes.

Behn, Harry. *Crickets and bullfrogs and whispers of thunder* sel. by Lee Bennett Hopkins; ill. by author. Harcourt, 1984. ISBN 0-15-220885-2 Subj: Poetry.

Trees ill. by James R. Endicott. Holt, 1992. ISBN 0-8050-1926-X Subj: Poetry. Trees.

What a beautiful noise ill. by Harold Berson. Collins-World, 1970. Subj: Humor. Music. Noise, sounds.

Behrens, June. *Can you walk the plank?* ill. by Michele and Tom Grimm. Childrens Pr., 1976. ISBN 0-516-03673-4 Subj: Activities. Games. Imagination.

Christmas-magic wagon ill. by Marjorie Burgeson. Childrens Pr., 1975. ISBN 0-516-08880-7 Subj: Character traits – generosity. Holidays – Christmas. Magic. Theater.

The feast of Thanksgiving ill. by Anne Siberell. Childrens Pr., 1974. ISBN 0-516-08725-8 Subj: Holidays – Thanksgiving. Pilgrims. Theater.

Fiesta! ill. by Scott Taylor. Childrens Pr., 1978. ISBN 0-516-08815-7 Subj: Ethnic groups in the U.S. – Mexican Americans. Holidays – Cinco de Mayo.

Hanukkah ill. by Terry Behrens. Childrens Pr., 1983. ISBN 0-516-02386-1 Subj: Holidays – Hanukkah. Jewish culture. Religion.

I can be a nurse ill. with photos. Childrens Pr., 1986. ISBN 0-516-01893-0 Subj: Careers – nurses.

I can be a pilot ill. with photos. Childrens Pr., 1985. ISBN 0-516-01888-4 Subj: Careers – airplane pilots.

I can be a truck driver ill. with photos. Childrens Pr., 1985. ISBN 0-516-01848-5 Subj: Careers – truck drivers.

I can be an astronaut ill. with photos. Childrens Pr., 1984. ISBN 0-516-01837-X Subj: Careers – astronauts. Space and space ships.

The manners book: what's right, Ned? ill. by Michele and Tom Grimm. Childrens Pr., 1980. ISBN 0-516-08750-9 Subj: Etiquette. Toys – bears.

Passover photos by Terry Behrens. Childrens Pr., 1987. ISBN 0-516-02389-6 Subj: Holidays – Passover. Jewish culture. Religion.

Powwow photos comp. by Terry Behrens. Childrens Pr., 1983. ISBN 0-516-02387-X Subj: Indians of North America.

Soo Ling finds a way ill. by Taro Yashima. Childrens Pr., 1965. Subj: Ethnic groups in the U.S. – Chinese Americans. Family life – grandfathers. Foreign lands – China. Laundry.

Whales of the world. Childrens Pr., 1987. ISBN 0-516-08877-7 Subj: Animals – dolphins. Animals – whales. Science.

Whalewatch! ill. by John Olguin. Childrens Pr., 1978. Photographs collected by John Olguin. ISBN 0-516-08873-4 Subj: Animals – whales. Science.

Who am I? photos by Ray Ambraziunas. Elk Grove Pr., 1968. Subj: School. Self-concept.

Beifuss, John. *Armadillo Ray* ill. by Peggy Turley. Chronicle, 1995. ISBN 0-8118-2277-X Subj: Animals. Animals – armadillos. Birds – owls. Imagination. Moon.

Beil, Karen Magnuson. *A cake all for me!* ill. by Paul Meisel. Holiday, 1998. ISBN 0-8234-1368-3 Subj: Activities – cooking. Animals. Animals – pigs. Food. Rhyming text.

Beim, Jerrold. *Country mailman* ill. by Leonard W. Shortall. Morrow, 1958. Subj: Careers – postal workers. Character traits – helpfulness. Emotions – envy, jealousy. Post office.

Country train ill. by Leonard W. Shortall. Morrow, 1950. Subj: Character traits – individuality. Trains.

Eric on the desert ill. by Louis Darling. Morrow, 1953. Subj: Animals. Character traits – bravery. Desert.

Freckle face ill. by Barbara Cooney. Crowell, 1957. Subj: Character traits – appearance. Character traits – being different. Character traits – individuality.

Jay's big job ill. by Tracy Sugarman. Morrow, 1957. Subj: Activities – painting. Activities – working. Family life.

The little igloo (Beim, Lorraine)

Lucky Pierre (Beim, Lorraine)

Sasha and the samovar (Beim, Lorraine)

Sir Halloween ill. by Tracy Sugarman. Morrow, 1959. Subj: Holidays – Halloween.

The smallest boy in the class ill. by Meg Wohlberg. Morrow, 1949. ISBN 0-688-31442-2 Subj: Behavior – sharing. Character traits – smallness. Names.

The swimming hole ill. by Louis Darling. Morrow, 1950. Subj: Behavior. Ethnic groups in the U.S. – African Americans. Friendship. Seasons – summer. Sports – swimming.

The taming of Toby ill. by Tracy Sugarman. Morrow, 1953. Subj: Behavior – misbehavior. Imagination. School.

Tim and the tool chest ill. by Tracy Sugarman. Morrow, 1951. Subj: Tools.

Two is a team (Beim, Lorraine)

With dad alone ill. by Don Sibley. Harcourt, 1954. Subj: Death. Family life – fathers.

Beim, Lorraine. *The little igloo* by Lorraine and Jerrold Beim; ill. by Howard Simon. Harcourt, 1941. Subj: Animals – dogs. Eskimos.

Lucky Pierre by Lorraine and Jerrold Beim; ill. by Howard Simon. Harcourt, 1940. Subj: Behavior – collecting things. Careers – fishermen. Character traits – luck. Family life.

Sasha and the samovar by Lorraine and Jerrold Beim; ill. by Rafaello Busoni. Harcourt, 1944. Subj: Fairies. Foreign lands – Russia.

Two is a team by Lorraine and Jerrold Beim; ill. by Ernest Crichlow. Harcourt, 1945. Subj: Behavior – fighting, arguing. Ethnic groups in the U.S. – African Americans. Friendship. Problem solving.

Beisert, Heide Helene. *Poor fish* trans. from German by Marion Koenig; ill. by author. HarperCollins, 1982. ISBN 0-571-12514-X Subj: Birds. Ecology. Fish.

Beisner, Monika. *Catch that cat!* ill. by author. Farrar, 1990. ISBN 0-374-31226-5 Subj: Animals – cats. Rhyming text. Riddles.

Monika Beisner's book of riddles ill. by author. Farrar, 1983. ISBN 0-374-30866-7 Subj: Humor. Riddles.

Secret spells and curious charms ill. by author. Farrar, 1986. ISBN 0-374-36692-6 Subj: Behavior – secrets. Magic.

Topsy turvy: the world of upside down ill. by author. Farrar, 1987. ISBN 0-374-37679-4 Subj: Concepts. Rhyming text.

Bell, Anthea. *Æsop's fables* (Æsop)

Albert and Lila (Schami, Rafik)

Billy the brave (Chapouton, Anne-Marie)

The brave little tailor (Grimm, Jacob)

The Bremen town musicians (Grimm, Jacob)

The Christmas angel (Vainio, Pirkko)

Cinderella (Perrault, Charles)

The clown said no (Damjan, Mischa)

The crow who stood on his beak (Schami, Rafik)

The emperor's new clothes (Andersen, H. C. [Hans Christian])

The fake flamingos (Damjan, Mischa)

The farmer and the moon (Lussert, Anneliese)

Fatima and the dream thief (Schami, Rafik)

The fisherman and his wife (Grimm, Jacob)

The five fingers and the moon (Kurt, Kemal)

Frog in love (Velthuijs, Max)

The gold at the end of the rainbow (Hänel, Wolfram)

The golden goose (Grimm, Jacob)

Goodbye little bird (Damjan, Mischa)

The goose girl (Grimm, Jacob)

Grimm Tom Thumb (Tom Thumb)

Jack in luck (Grimm, Jacob)

Little brother and little sister (Grimm, Jacob)

Little Hobbin (Storm, Theodor)

The little mermaid (Andersen, H. C. [Hans Christian])

Lullabies, lyrics and gallows songs (Morgenstern, Christian)

Lumina: a story for the dark time of the year (Weninger, Brigitte)

The magic honey jar (Bohdal, Susi)

Mumble bear (Ruck-Pauquèt, Gina)

Nick Ribbeck of Ribbeck of Havelland (Fontane, Theodor)

The nightingale (Andersen, H. C. [Hans Christian])

Noah's ark (Fussenegger, Gertrud)

The nutcracker (Hoffmann, E. T. A.)

Peter and the wolf (Prokofiev, Sergei Sergeievitch)

The pied piper of Hamelin (Bartos-Hoppner, Barbara)

The princess and the pea (Andersen, H. C. [Hans Christian])

The proud white cat (Hürlimann, Ruth)

Puss in boots (Perrault, Charles)

The red shoes (Andersen, H. C. [Hans Christian])

Rumpelstiltskin (Grimm, Jacob)

Sandman in the lighthouse (Strahl, Rudi)

The six servants (Grimm, Jacob)

The six swans (Grimm, Jacob)

The sleeping beauty (Grimm, Jacob)

The snow queen: a fairy tale (Andersen, H. C. [Hans Christian])

Snow White and the seven dwarves (Grimm, Jacob)

The strange child (Hoffmann, E. T. A.)

Swan Lake: a traditional folktale ill. by Chihiro Iwasaki. Picture Book Studio, 1986. Adapt. of Tchaikovsky's Lebedinoe ozero. ISBN 0-88708-028-6 Subj: Activities – dancing. Ballet. Birds – swans. Folk and fairy tales. Magic.

The swineherd (Andersen, H. C. [Hans Christian])

Thumbeline (Andersen, H. C. [Hans Christian])

The trip to Panama (Janosch)

The ugly duckling (Andersen, H. C. [Hans Christian])

The wise queen ill. by Chihiro Iwasaki. Picture Book Studio, 1986. ISBN 0-88708-014-6 Subj: Character traits – cleverness. Folk and fairy tales. Riddles. Royalty – queens.

The wishing table (Grimm, Jacob)

Bell, Janet. *see* Clymer, Eleanor Lowenton

Bell, Norman. *Linda's airmail letter* ill. by Patricia Villemain. Follett, 1964. Subj: Birthdays. Friendship. Letters, cards. Post office. Weather.

Bellamy, David. *How green are you?* ill. by Penny Dann. Crown, 1991. ISBN 0-517-58447-6 Subj: Animals – whales. Ecology.

The roadside ill. by Jill Dow. Crown, 1988. ISBN 0-517-56976-0 Subj: Ecology.

The rock pool ill. by Jill Dow. Crown, 1988. ISBN 0-517-56977-9 Subj: Ecology.

Beller, Janet. *A-B-C-ing: an action alphabet* ill. with photos. Crown, 1984. ISBN 0-517-55208-6 Subj: ABC books. Activities.

Belling the cat and other stories retold by Leland B. Jacobs; ill. by Harold Berson. Golden Pr., 1960. Subj: Animals. Folk and fairy tales.

Belloc, Hilaire. *The bad child's book of beasts* ill. by Basil T. Blackwood [B.A.T.]. Knopf, 1965. Origi-

nally published in 1896. Subj: Animals. Behavior. Humor.

The bad child's book of beasts, and more beasts for worse children ill. by Harold Berson. Grosset, 1966. Subj: Animals. Humor. Poetry.

The bad child's pop-up book of beasts ill. by Wallace Tripp. Putnam, 1987. ISBN 0-399-21431-3 Subj: Animals. Format, unusual – toy and movable books. Poetry.

Jim, who ran away from his nurse, and was eaten by a lion ill. by Victoria Chess. Little, 1987. ISBN 0-316-13815-0 Subj: Animals – lions. Behavior – misbehavior. Behavior – running away. Zoos.

Matilda who told lies and was burned to death ill. by Steven Kellogg. Dial, 1970. Subj: Behavior – lying. Behavior – misbehavior. Fire. Poetry.

More beasts for worse children ill. by Basil T. Blackwood [B.A.T.]. Knopf, 1966. Subj: Animals. Poetry.

Bellows, Cathy. *Four fat rats* ill. by author. Macmillan, 1987. ISBN 0-02-708830-8 Subj: Animals – rats. Behavior – greed. Character traits – meanness.

The Grizzly sisters ill. by author. Macmillan, 1991. ISBN 0-02-709032-9 Subj: Animals – bears. Behavior – misbehavior.

The royal raccoon ill. by author. Macmillan, 1989. ISBN 0-02-709031-0 Subj: Animals – raccoons. Character traits – conceit.

Bellville, Cheryl Walsh. *Large animal veterinarians* (Bellville, Rod)

Bellville, Rod. *Large animal veterinarians* by Rod and Cheryl Walsh Bellville; photos by authors. Carolrhoda, 1983. ISBN 0-87614-211-0 Subj: Animals. Careers – veterinarians.

Belpré, Pura. *Dance of the animals: a Puerto Rican folk tale* ill. by Paul Galdone. Warne, 1972. ISBN 0-7232-6039-7 Subj: Animals. Folk and fairy tales. Foreign lands – Puerto Rico.

Pérez and Martina: a Portorican folk tale ill. by Carlos Sanchez. Rev. ed. Warne, 1961. Originally pub. in 1960. ISBN 0-7232-6017-6 Subj: Animals – mice. Folk and fairy tales. Foreign lands – Puerto Rico. Insects.

Santiago ill. by Symeon Shimin. Warne, 1969. Subj: Birds – chickens. Ethnic groups in the U.S. Ethnic groups in the U.S. – Puerto Rican Americans. Pets.

Belting, Natalia Maree. *Christmas folk* ill. by Barbara Cooney. Holt, 1969. ISBN 0-03-072375-2 Subj: Foreign lands – England. Holidays – Christmas. Poetry.

Summer's coming in ill. by Adrienne Adams. Holt, 1970. ISBN 0-03-084250-6 Subj: Foreign lands – England. Holidays. Poetry. Seasons – spring. Seasons – summer.

The sun is a golden earring ill. by Bernarda Bryson. Holt, 1962. Subj: Caldecott award honor books. Folk and fairy tales. Sky.

Verity Mullens and the Indian ill. by Leonard Everett Fisher. Holt, 1960. Subj: Animals – dogs. Behavior – lost. Indians of North America. U.S. history – frontier and pioneer life.

Belton, Sandra. *May'naise sandwiches and sunshine tea* ill. by Gail Gordon Carter. Four Winds, 1994. ISBN 0-02-709035-3 Subj: Family life – grandmothers. Friendship. Poverty.

Bemelmans, Ludwig. *Hansi* ill. by author. Viking, 1934. Subj: Activities – vacationing. Foreign lands – Tyrol. Holidays – Christmas.

Madeline ill. by author. Viking, 1939. Subj: Caldecott award honor books. Foreign lands – France. Hospitals. Orphans. Rhyming text. School.

Madeline [pop-up book] ill. by author. Viking, 1987. ISBN 0-670-81667-1 Subj: Foreign lands – France. Format, unusual – toy and movable books. Hospitals. Orphans.

Madeline and the bad hat ill. by author. Viking, 1956. Subj: Behavior – animals, dislike of. Behavior – misbehavior. Foreign lands – France. Orphans. Rhyming text.

Madeline and the gypsies ill. by author. Viking, 1959. ISBN 0-670-44682-3 Subj: Behavior – lost. Foreign lands – France. Gypsies. Orphans. Rhyming text.

Madeline in London ill. by author. Viking, 1978, c1961. ISBN 0-14-050199-1 Subj: Animals – horses, ponies. Birthdays. Foreign lands – England. Orphans. Rhyming text.

Madeline's Christmas ill. by author. Viking, 1985. ISBN 0-670-80666-8 Subj: Foreign lands – France. Holidays – Christmas. Illness. Magic. Orphans. Rhyming text.

Madeline's rescue ill. by author. Viking, 1978, c1953. ISBN 0-14-050207-6 Subj: Animals – dogs. Caldecott award books. Foreign lands – France. Orphans. Rhyming text.

Parsley ill. by author. HarperCollins, 1955. ISBN 0-06-020455-9 Subj: Animals – deer. Sports – hunting. Trees.

Quito express ill. by author. Viking, 1938. Subj: Activities – traveling. Family life. Foreign lands – Ecuador. Trains.

Rosebud ill. by author. Random House, 1993, c1942. ISBN 0-679-94913-5 Subj: Animals. Character traits – pride. Folk and fairy tales. Foreign lands – Africa. Humor.

Sunshine ill. by author. Simon & Schuster, 1950. Subj: City. Family life. Homes, houses. Humor.

Welcome home! ill. by author. HarperCollins, 1970. Based on a poem by Beverley Bogert. Subj: Animals – foxes. Character traits – cleverness. Rhyming text.

Benarde, Anita. *The pumpkin smasher* ill. by author. Walker, 1972. ISBN 0-8027-6109-7 Subj: Holidays – Halloween. Problem solving. Witches.

Benchley, Nathaniel. *The deep dives of Stanley Whale* ill. by Mischa Richter. HarperCollins, 1973. ISBN 0-06-020464-8 Subj: Animals – whales. Character traits – bravery.

The flying lessons of Gerald Pelican ill. by Mamoru Funai. HarperCollins, 1970. ISBN 0-06-020482-6 Subj: Activities – flying. Birds – pelicans.

Walter the homing pigeon ill. by Whitney Darrow, Jr. HarperCollins, 1981. ISBN 0-06-020508-3 Subj: Birds – pigeons. Food. Humor. Sports – racing.

Benchley, Peter. *Jonathan visits the White House* ill. by Richard Bergere. McGraw-Hill, 1964. Subj: Animals – dogs. Birthdays. Pets. U.S. history.

Bender, Robert. *The A to Z beastly jamboree* ill. by author. Lodestar, 1996. ISBN 0-525-67520-5 Subj: ABC books. Activities. Animals. Language.

A little witch magic ill. by author. Holt, 1992. ISBN 0-8050-2126-4 Subj: Friendship. Holidays – Halloween. Witches.

The three billy goats Gruff (Asbjørnsen, P. C. [Peter Christen])

Bendick, Jeanne. *All around you: a first look at the world* foreword by Glenn O. Blough; ill. by author. McGraw-Hill, 1951. ISBN 0-07-004464-3 Subj: Nature. Science. World.

What made you you? ill. by author. McGraw-Hill, 1971. ISBN 0-07-004502-X Subj: Babies. Science.

Why can't I? ill. by author. McGraw-Hill, 1969. ISBN 0-07-004491-0 Subj: Animals. Behavior – imitation. Participation. Science.

Benedek, Elissa P. *The secret worry* ill. by Patricia Rosamilia. Human Sciences Pr., 1984. ISBN 0-89885-133-5 Subj: Behavior – worrying. Emotions – fear.

Benedictus, Roger. *Fifty million sausages* ill. by Kenneth Mahood. Elsevier-Dutton, 1979. ISBN 0-233-96692-7 Subj: Food. Humor. Imagination. Machines.

Beneduce, Ann Keay. *Jack and the beanstalk* (Jack and the beanstalk)

Benét, William Rose. *Mother Goose: a comprehensive collection of the rhymes* (Mother Goose)

Timothy's angels ill. by Constantin Alajalov. Crowell, 1947. Subj: Activities – playing. Angels. Poetry.

Ben-'Ezer, Ehud. *Hosni the dreamer: an Arabian tale* ill. by Uri Shulevitz. Farrar, 1997. ISBN 0-374-33340-8 Subj: Careers – shepherds. Folk and fairy tales.

Beni, Ruth. *Sir Baldergog the great* ill. by author. Dutton, 1985. ISBN 0-233-97628-0 Subj: Activities. Behavior – lost. Islands.

Benjamin, A. H. *A duck so small* ill. by Elisabeth Holstien. Little Tiger, 1998. ISBN 1-888444-30-4 Subj: Birds – ducks. Character traits – smallness. Self-concept.

It could have been worse ill. by Tim Warnes. Little Tiger, 1998. ISBN 1-888444-26-6 Subj: Animals – mice. Character traits – luck.

Benjamin, Alan. *Busy bunnies* ill. by Christopher Santoro. Simon & Schuster, 1988. ISBN 0-671-64807-1 Subj: Activities. Animals – rabbits.

A change of plans ill. by Steven Kellogg. Four Winds, 1982. ISBN 0-590-07730-9 Subj: Activities – picnicking. Boats, ships. Family life. Rhyming text.

A nickel buys a rhyme ill. by Karen Lee Schmidt. Morrow, 1993. ISBN 0-688-06699-2 Subj: Poetry.

The nightingale (Andersen, H. C. [Hans Christian])

1000 monsters ill. by Sal Murdocca. Four Winds, 1979. ISBN 0-590-07636-1 Subj: Format, unusual – toy and movable books. Humor. Monsters.

Rat-a-tat, pitter pat ill. by Margaret Miller. Harper-Collins, 1987. ISBN 0-690-04611-1 Subj: Language. Noise, sounds. Rhyming text.

Ribtickle Town ill. by Ann Schweninger. Four Winds, 1983. ISBN 0-590-07880-3 Subj: Behavior – lost. Food. Giants. Imagination. Rhyming text.

Benjamin, Amanda. *Two's company* ill. by author. Viking, 1995. ISBN 0-670-84876-X Subj: Family life – mothers. Family life – step families. Weddings.

Benjamin, Anne. *Young Harriet Tubman: freedom fighter* ill. by Ellen Beier. Troll, 1992. ISBN 0-8167-2538-1 Subj: Character traits – freedom. Ethnic groups in the U.S. – African Americans. Slavery.

Young Pocahontas: Indian princess ill. by Christine Powers. Troll, 1997. ISBN 0-8167-2534-9 Subj: Character traits – bravery. Indians of North America. U.S. history.

Benjamin, Floella. *Skip across the ocean: nursery rhymes from around the world* ill. by Sheila Moxley. Orchard, 1995. ISBN 0-531-09455-3 Subj: Foreign lands. Lullabies. Nursery rhymes.

Bennett, David. *One cow moo moo* ill. by Andy Cooke. Holt, 1990. ISBN 0-8050-1416-0 Subj: Animals. Counting, numbers. Cumulative tales. Noise, sounds.

Bennett, Jill. *Animal fair* ill. by Susie Jenkin-Pearce. Viking, 1990. ISBN 0-670-82691-X Subj: Animals. Poetry.

A cup of starshine ill. by Graham Percy. Harcourt, 1992. ISBN 0-15-220982-4 Subj: Poetry.

Days are where we live and other poems ill. by Maureen Roffey. Lothrop, 1982. ISBN 0-688-00852-6 Subj: Activities. Poetry.

Machine poems by Jill Bennett and Nick Sharratt; ill. by Nick Sharratt. Oxford Univ. Pr., 1991. ISBN 0-19-276094-7 Subj: Machines. Poetry.

Noisy poems ill. by Nick Sharratt. Oxford Univ. Pr., 1990. ISBN 0-19-276063-7 Subj: Noise, sounds. Poetry.

People poems ill. by Nick Sharratt. Oxford Univ. Pr., 1991. ISBN 0-19-276086-6 Subj: Poetry.

Roger was a razor fish and other poems ill. by Maureen Roffey. Lothrop, 1981. ISBN 0-688-51986-5 Subj: Humor. Poetry.

Seaside poems (Seaside poems)

Spooky poems coll. by Jill Bennett; ill. by Mary Rees. Little, 1989. ISBN 0-316-08987-7 Subj: Monsters. Poetry.

Teeny tiny ill. by Tomie de Paola. Putnam, 1986. ISBN 0-399-21293-0 Subj: Folk and fairy tales. Foreign lands – England. Ghosts.

Tiny Tim: verses for children (Oxenbury, Helen)

Bennett, Olivia. *A Turkish afternoon* photos by Christopher Cormack. David & Charles, 1984. Subj: Family life. Foreign lands – England. Foreign lands – Turkey.

Bennett, Rainey. *After the sun goes down* ill. by author. Collins-World, 1961. Subj: Birds – owls. Night.

The secret hiding place ill. by author. Collins-World, 1960. Subj: Animals – hippopotamuses. Behavior – solitude. Poetry. Sea and seashore.

Bennett, Rowena. *The day is dancing and other poems* ill. by Rainey Bennett. Follett, 1968. Subj: Imagination. Poetry.

Songs from around a toadstool table ill. by Betty Fraser. Follett, 1967. Subj: Fairies. Imagination. Nature. Poetry.

Benson, Ellen. *Philip's little sister* ill. by Rachael Davis. Childrens Pr., 1979. ISBN 0-516-02023-4 Subj: Family life. Sibling rivalry.

Benson, Kathleen. *Count your way through Brazil* (Haskins, Jim [James])

Benson, Laura Lee. *This is our earth* ill. by John Carrozza. Charlesbridge, 1994. ISBN 0-88106-445-9 Subj: Earth. Ecology. Nature.

Benson, Patrick. *Little penguin* ill. by author. Putnam, 1991. ISBN 0-399-21757-6 Subj: Birds – penguins. Concepts – size. Foreign lands – Antarctic.

Bentley, Anne. *The Groggs' day out* ill. by Roy Bentley. Elsevier-Dutton, 1981. ISBN 0-233-97348-6 Subj: Foreign lands – England. Sports – bicycling.

The Groggs have a wonderful summer by Anne and Roy Bentley; ill. by Roy Bentley. Elsevier-Dutton, 1980. ISBN 0-233-97199-8 Subj: Foreign lands – England. Sea and seashore. Seasons – summer.

Bentley, Nancy. *I've got your nose!* ill. by Don Madden. Doubleday, 1991. ISBN 0-385-41296-7 Subj: Anatomy – noses. Behavior – dissatisfaction. Behavior – wishing. Magic. Self-concept. Witches.

Bentley, Roy. *The Groggs have a wonderful summer* (Bentley, Anne)

Benton, Robert. *Don't ever wish for a 7-foot bear* ill. by Sally Benton. Knopf, 1972. ISBN 0-394-92399-5 Subj: Animals – bears. Behavior – wishing. Humor.

Little brother, no more ill. by author. Knopf, 1960. Subj: Family life. Names.

Berends, Polly Berrien. *I heard said the bird* ill. by Brad Sneed. Dial, 1995. ISBN 0-14-056426-8 Subj: Animals. Babies. Birds. Farms. Rhyming text.

Ladybug and dog and the night walk ill. by Cyndy Szekeres. Random House, 1980. ISBN 0-394-93398-2 Subj: Animals – dogs. Friendship. Insects – fireflies. Insects – ladybugs. Night.

Berenstain, Jan. *After the dinosaurs* (Berenstain, Stan)

The bear detectives: the case of the missing pumpkin (Berenstain, Stan)

Bears in the night (Berenstain, Stan)

Bears on wheels (Berenstain, Stan)

The Berenstain bears and mama's new job (Berenstain, Stan)

The Berenstain bears and the bad dream (Berenstain, Stan)

The Berenstain bears and the bad habit (Berenstain, Stan)

The Berenstain bears and the big road race (Berenstain, Stan)

The Berenstain bears and the double dare (Berenstain, Stan)

The Berenstain bears and the ghost of the forest (Berenstain, Stan)

The Berenstain bears and the messy room (Berenstain, Stan)

The Berenstain bears and the missing dinosaur bone (Berenstain, Stan)

The Berenstain bears and the missing honey (Berenstain, Stan)

The Berenstain bears and the prize pumpkin (Berenstain, Stan)

The Berenstain bears and the sitter (Berenstain, Stan)

The Berenstain bears and the slumber party (Berenstain, Stan)

The Berenstain bears and the spooky old tree (Berenstain, Stan)

The Berenstain bears and the trouble with friends (Berenstain, Stan)

The Berenstain bears and the truth (Berenstain, Stan)

The Berenstain bears and the week at grandma's (Berenstain, Stan)

The Berenstain bears and the wild, wild honey (Berenstain, Stan)

The Berenstain bears and too much birthday (Berenstain, Stan)

The Berenstain bears and too much junk food (Berenstain, Stan)

The Berenstain bears and too much TV (Berenstain, Stan)

The Berenstain bears and too much vacation (Berenstain, Stan)

The Berenstain bears blaze a trail (Berenstain, Stan)

The Berenstain bears' Christmas tree (Berenstain, Stan)

The Berenstain bears' counting book (Berenstain, Stan)

The Berenstain bears don't pollute anymore (Berenstain, Stan)

The Berenstain bears forget their manners (Berenstain, Stan)

The Berenstain bears get in a fight (Berenstain, Stan)

The Berenstain bears get stage fright (Berenstain, Stan)

The Berenstain bears get the gimmies (Berenstain, Stan)

The Berenstain bears go out for the team (Berenstain, Stan)

The Berenstain bears go to camp (Berenstain, Stan)

The Berenstain bears go to school (Berenstain, Stan)

The Berenstain bears go to the doctor (Berenstain, Stan)

The Berenstain bears in the dark (Berenstain, Stan)

The Berenstain bears learn about strangers (Berenstain, Stan)

The Berenstain bears meet Santa Bear (Berenstain, Stan)

The Berenstain bears' moving day (Berenstain, Stan)

The Berenstain bears no girls allowed (Berenstain, Stan)

The Berenstain bears on the moon (Berenstain, Stan)

The Berenstain bears ready, set, go! (Berenstain, Stan)

The Berenstain bears' science fair (Berenstain, Stan)

The Berenstain bears trick or treat (Berenstain, Stan)

The Berenstain bears' trouble at school (Berenstain, Stan)

The Berenstain bears' trouble with money (Berenstain, Stan)

The Berenstain bears' trouble with pets (Berenstain, Stan)

The Berenstain bears visit the dentist (Berenstain, Stan)

The Berenstains' B book (Berenstain, Stan)

The day of the dinosaur (Berenstain, Stan)

He bear, she bear (Berenstain, Stan)

Inside outside upside down (Berenstain, Stan)

Old hat, new hat (Berenstain, Stan)

Berenstain, Michael. *The dwarks: book 1* ill. by author. Bantam, 1983. ISBN 0-553-15341-2 Subj: Family life. Mythical creatures.

Peat Moss and Ivy and the birthday present ill. by author. Random House, 1986. ISBN 0-394-97605-3 Subj: Animals – chipmunks. Birthdays.

Peat Moss and Ivy's backyard adventure ill. by author. Random House, 1986. ISBN 0-394-97604-5 Subj: Animals – chipmunks.

The ship book ill. by author. McKay, 1978. ISBN 0-679-20449-0 Subj: Boats, ships.

The troll book ill. by author. Random House, 1980. ISBN 0-394-94295-7 Subj: Folk and fairy tales. Mythical creatures – trolls.

Berenstain, Stan. *After the dinosaurs* by Stan and Jan Berenstain; ill. by authors. Random House, 1988. ISBN 0-394-90518-0 Subj: Animals – bears. Dinosaurs.

The bear detectives: the case of the missing pumpkin by Stan and Jan Berenstain; ill. by authors. Random House, 1975. ISBN 0-394-93127-0 Subj: Animals – bears. Careers – detectives. Mystery stories. Rhyming text.

Bears in the night by Stan and Jan Berenstain; ill. by authors. Random House, 1971. ISBN 0-394-92286-7 Subj: Animals – bears. Bedtime. Night. Noise, sounds.

Bears on wheels by Stan and Jan Berenstain; ill. by authors. Random House, 1969. ISBN 0-394-90967-4 Subj: Animals – bears. Counting, numbers. Wheels.

The Berenstain bears and mama's new job by Stan and Jan Berenstain; ill. by authors. Random House, 1984. ISBN 0-394-96881-6 Subj: Animals – bears. Careers.

The Berenstain bears and the bad dream by Stan and Jan Berenstain; ill. by authors. Random House, 1988. ISBN 0-394-97341-0 Subj: Animals – bears. Dreams.

The Berenstain bears and the bad habit by Stan and Jan Berenstain; ill. by authors. Random House, 1987. ISBN 0-394-97340-2 Subj: Animals – bears.

The Berenstain bears and the big road race by Stan and Jan Berenstain; ill. by authors. Random House, 1987. ISBN 0-394-99134-6 Subj: Animals – bears. Sports – racing.

The Berenstain bears and the double dare by Stan and Jan Berenstain; ill. by authors. Random House, 1988. ISBN 0-394-99748-4 Subj: Animals – bears. Sibling rivalry.

The Berenstain bears and the ghost of the forest by Stan and Jan Berenstain; ill. by authors. Random House, 1988. ISBN 0-394-90565-2 Subj: Animals – bears. Forest, woods. Ghosts.

The Berenstain bears and the messy room by Stan and Jan Berenstain; ill. by authors. Random House, 1983. ISBN 0-394-95639-7 Subj: Animals – bears. Mystery stories.

The Berenstain bears and the missing dinosaur bone by Stan and Jan Berenstain; ill. by authors. Random House, 1980. ISBN 0-394-94447-X Subj: Animals – bears. Museums. Mystery stories. Rhyming text.

The Berenstain bears and the missing honey by Stan and Jan Berenstain; ill. by authors. Random House, 1987. ISBN 0-394-99133-8 Subj: Animals – bears. Mystery stories.

The Berenstain bears and the prize pumpkin by Stan and Jan Berenstain; ill. by authors. Random House, 1990. ISBN 0-679-90847-1 Subj: Animals – bears. Holidays – Thanksgiving. Plants.

The Berenstain bears and the sitter by Stan and Jan Berenstain; ill. by authors. Random House, 1981. ISBN 0-394-94837-8 Subj: Activities – babysitting. Animals – bears. Magic.

The Berenstain bears and the slumber party by Stan and Jan Berenstain; ill. by authors. McKay, 1990. ISBN 0-679-90419-0 Subj: Animals – bears. Bedtime. Parties. Sleepovers.

The Berenstain bears and the spooky old tree by Stan and Jan Berenstain; ill. by authors. Random House, 1978. ISBN 0-394-93910-7 Subj: Animals – bears. Rhyming text. Trees.

The Berenstain bears and the trouble with friends by Stan and Jan Berenstain; ill. by authors. Random House, 1987. ISBN 0-394-97339-9 Subj: Animals – bears. Friendship.

The Berenstain bears and the truth by Stan and Jan Berenstain; ill. by authors. Random House, 1983. ISBN 0-394-95640-0 Subj: Animals – bears. Behavior – lying. Behavior – misbehavior. Family life.

The Berenstain bears and the week at grandma's by Stan and Jan Berenstain; ill. by authors. Random House, 1986. ISBN 0-394-97335-6 Subj: Animals – bears. Family life – grandmothers.

The Berenstain bears and the wild, wild honey by Stan and Jan Berenstain; ill. by authors. Random House, 1983. ISBN 0-394-85924-3 Subj: Animals – bears. Nature.

The Berenstain bears and too much birthday by Stan and Jan Berenstain; ill. by authors. Random

House, 1986. ISBN 0-394-97332-1 Subj: Animals – bears. Birthdays.

The Berenstain bears and too much junk food by Stan and Jan Berenstain; ill. by authors. Random House, 1985. ISBN 0-394-97217-1 Subj: Animals – bears. Food.

The Berenstain bears and too much TV by Stan and Jan Berenstain; ill. by authors. Random House, 1984. ISBN 0-394-96570-1 Subj: Animals – bears. Family life. Television.

The Berenstain bears and too much vacation by Stan and Jan Berenstain; ill. by authors. Random House, 1989. ISBN 0-394-93014-2 Subj: Activities – vacationing. Animals – bears.

The Berenstain bears blaze a trail by Stan and Jan Berenstain; ill. by authors. Random House, 1987. ISBN 0-394-99132-X Subj: Animals – bears.

The Berenstain bears' Christmas tree by Stan and Jan Berenstain; ill. by authors. Random House, 1980. ISBN 0-394-94566-2 Subj: Animals – bears. Family life. Holidays – Christmas. Rhyming text. Trees.

The Berenstain bears' counting book by Stan and Jan Berenstain; ill. by authors. Random House, 1976. ISBN 0-394-83246-9 Subj: Animals – bears. Counting, numbers.

The Berenstain bears don't pollute anymore by Stan and Jan Berenstain; ill. by authors. Random House, 1991. ISBN 0-679-92351-9 Subj: Animals – bears. Ecology.

The Berenstain bears forget their manners by Stan and Jan Berenstain; ill. by authors. Random House, 1985. ISBN 0-394-97333-X Subj: Animals – bears. Etiquette. Family life.

The Berenstain bears get in a fight by Stan and Jan Berenstain; ill. by authors. Random House, 1982. ISBN 0-394-95132-8 Subj: Animals – bears. Behavior – bad day. Sibling rivalry.

The Berenstain bears get stage fright by Stan and Jan Berenstain; ill. by authors. Random House, 1986. ISBN 0-394-97337-2 Subj: Animals – bears. Emotions – fear. Theater.

The Berenstain bears get the gimmies by Stan and Jan Berenstain; ill. by authors. Random House, 1988. ISBN 0-394-90566-0 Subj: Animals – bears. Behavior – greed.

The Berenstain bears go out for the team by Stan and Jan Berenstain; ill. by authors. Random House, 1987. ISBN 0-394-97338-0 Subj: Animals – bears. Sports.

The Berenstain bears go to camp by Stan and Jan Berenstain; ill. by authors. Random House, 1982. ISBN 0-394-95131-X Subj: Animals – bears. Camps, camping. Seasons – summer.

The Berenstain bears go to school by Stan and Jan Berenstain; ill. by authors. Random House, 1978. ISBN 0-394-93736-8 Subj: Animals – bears. School – first day.

The Berenstain bears go to the doctor by Stan and Jan Berenstain; ill. by authors. Random House, 1981.

ISBN 0-394-94835-1 Subj: Animals – bears. Careers – doctors.

The Berenstain bears in the dark by Stan and Jan Berenstain; ill. by authors. Random House, 1982. Subj: Animals – bears. Family life. Imagination. Night.

The Berenstain bears learn about strangers by Stan and Jan Berenstain; ill. by authors. Random House, 1985. ISBN 0-394-87334-3 Subj: Animals – bears. Behavior – talking to strangers. Emotions – fear. Family life. Safety.

The Berenstain bears meet Santa Bear by Stan and Jan Berenstain; ill. by authors. Random House, 1988. ISBN 0-394-89797-8 Subj: Animals – bears. Holidays – Christmas.

The Berenstain bears' moving day by Stan and Jan Berenstain; ill. by authors. Random House, 1981. Subj: Animals – bears. Family life. Friendship. Moving.

The Berenstain bears no girls allowed by Stan and Jan Berenstain; ill. by authors. Random House, 1986. ISBN 0-394-97331-3 Subj: Animals – bears. Clubs, gangs. Family life – brothers and sisters.

The Berenstain bears on the moon by Stan and Jan Berenstain; ill. by authors. Random House, 1985. ISBN 0-394-97180-9 Subj: Animals – bears. Animals – dogs. Moon. Space and space ships.

The Berenstain bears ready, set, go! by Stan and Jan Berenstain; ill. by authors. Random House, 1988. ISBN 0-394-90564-4 Subj: Animals – bears.

The Berenstain bears' science fair by Stan and Jan Berenstain; ill. by authors. Random House, 1977. Subj: Animals – bears. Science.

The Berenstain bears trick or treat by Stan and Jan Berenstain; ill. by authors. Random House, 1989. ISBN 0-679-90091-8 Subj: Animals – bears. Holidays – Halloween.

The Berenstain bears' trouble at school by Stan and Jan Berenstain; ill. by authors. Random House, 1987. ISBN 0-394-97336-4 Subj: Animals – bears. Behavior. School.

The Berenstain bears' trouble with money by Stan and Jan Berenstain; ill. by authors. Random House, 1983. Subj: Animals – bears. Money.

The Berenstain bears' trouble with pets by Stan and Jan Berenstain; ill. by authors. Random House, 1990. ISBN 0-679-90848-X Subj: Animals – bears. Pets.

The Berenstain bears visit the dentist by Stan and Jan Berenstain; ill. by authors. Random House, 1981. Subj: Animals – bears. Careers – dentists.

The Berenstains' B book by Stan and Jan Berenstain; ill. by authors. Random House, 1971. Subj: ABC books. Animals – bears.

The day of the dinosaur by Stan and Jan Berenstain; ill. by Michael Berenstain. Random House, 1987. ISBN 0-394-99130-3 Subj: Dinosaurs.

He bear, she bear by Stan and Jan Berenstain; ill. by authors. Random House, 1974. Subj: Animals – bears. Rhyming text.

Inside outside upside down by Stan and Jan Berenstain; ill. by authors. Random House, 1968. Subj: Animals – bears. Concepts.

Old hat, new hat by Stan and Jan Berenstain; ill. by authors. Random House, 1970. Subj: Animals – bears. Concepts – shape. Concepts – size.

Berenzy, Alix. *A frog prince* ill. by author. Holt, 1989. ISBN 0-8050-0426-2 Subj: Folk and fairy tales. Frogs and toads. Royalty.

Rapunzel retold and ill. by Alix Berenzy. Holt, 1995. ISBN 0-8050-1283-4 Subj: Folk and fairy tales. Royalty – princes. Witches.

Beresford, Elisabeth. *Jack and the magic stove* ill. by Rita van Bilsen. Hutchinson, 1984. Subj: Behavior – wishing. Folk and fairy tales. Royalty.

Snuffle to the rescue ill. by Gunvor Edwards. Penguin, 1975. Subj: Animals – dogs.

Berg, Charles Ramírez. *The gift of the poinsettia = El regalo de la flor de nochebuena* (Mora, Pat)

Berg, Jean Horton. *The little red hen* (The little red hen)

The noisy clock shop ill. by Art Seiden. Grosset, 1950. Subj: Clocks, watches. Noise, sounds.

The O'Learys and friends ill. by Mary Stevens. Follett, 1961. Subj: Animals – cats. Behavior – misunderstanding. Moving. Problem solving.

The wee little man ill. by Charles Geer. Follett, 1963. Subj: Animals – cats. Little people. Night. Noise, sounds. Rhyming text.

Berg, Leila. *Folk tales for reading and telling* ill. by George Him. Collins-World, 1966. Subj: Folk and fairy tales. Foreign lands.

Bergen, Lara Rice. *Washington Irving's Rip Van Winkle* ill. by Donald Cook. Grosset, 1997. ISBN 0-448-41733-2 Subj: Behavior – lost. Folk and fairy tales. Mythical creatures – elves. Sleep.

Berger, Barbara Helen. *The donkey's dream* ill. by author. Philomel, 1986. ISBN 0-399-21233-7 Subj: Animals – donkeys. Dreams. Holidays – Christmas. Religion.

Grandfather Twilight ill. by author. Putnam, 1986. ISBN 0-399-20996-4 Subj: Folk and fairy tales. Moon. Twilight.

The jewel heart ill. by author. Philomel, 1994. ISBN 0-399-22681-8 Subj: Activities – dancing. Ballet. Emotions – love. Music. Shadows.

A lot of otters ill. by author. Philomel, 1997. ISBN 0-399-22910-8 Subj: Animals – otters. Behavior – lost. Moon.

When the sun rose ill. by author. Philomel, 1986. ISBN 0-399-21360-0 Subj: Friendship. Imagination – imaginary friends.

Berger, Gilda. *How do airplanes fly?* (Berger, Melvin)

How's the weather? (Berger, Melvin)

Why did the dinosaurs disappear? the great dinosaur mystery (Berger, Melvin)

Berger, Judith. *Butterflies and rainbows* by Judith Berger and Terry Landau; ill. by Carmen Lowhar. Bande House, 1982. Subj: Concepts – color. Rhyming text.

Berger, Melvin. *Early humans: a pop-up book* ill. by Michael Welply. Putnam, 1988. ISBN 0-399-21476-3 Subj: Format, unusual – toy and movable books. Science.

Germs make me sick! ill. by Marylin Hafner. Crowell, 1985. ISBN 0-690-04429-1 Subj: Illness. Science.

How do airplanes fly? by Melvin and Gilda Berger; ill. by Paul Babb. Ideals, 1996. ISBN 1-57102-058-6 Subj: Activities – flying. Airplanes, airports. Science.

How's the weather? by Melvin and Gilda Berger; ill. by John Emil Cymerman. Ideals, 1996. ISBN 0-8249-8641-5 Subj: Science. Weather.

Look out for turtles! ill. by Megan Lloyd. HarperCollins, 1992. ISBN 0-06-022540-8 Subj: Nature. Reptiles – turtles, tortoises. Science.

Oil spill! ill. by Paul Mirocha. HarperCollins, 1994. ISBN 0-06-022912-8 Subj: Ecology. Oil. Science. Sea and seashore.

Ouch! a book about cuts, scratches and scrapes ill. by Pat Stewart. Dutton, 1991. ISBN 0-525-67323-7 Subj: Health and fitness. Illness.

Prehistoric mammals devised and designed by Keith Moseley; ill. by Robert Cremins. Putnam, 1986. ISBN 0-399-21312-0 Subj: Animals. Format, unusual – toy and movable books.

Switch on, switch off ill. by Carolyn Croll. HarperCollins, 1992. ISBN 0-690-04786-X Subj: Lights. Science.

Why did the dinosaurs disappear? the great dinosaur mystery by Melvin and Gilda Berger; ill. by Susan Harrison. Ideals, 1995. ISBN 1-57102-033-0 Subj: Dinosaurs.

Why I cough, sneeze, shiver, hiccup and yawn ill. by Holly Keller. Crowell, 1983. Subj: Health and fitness. Illness.

Berger, Terry. *Ben's ABC day* photos by Alice Kandell. Lothrop, 1982. Subj: ABC books.

Friends photos by Alice Kandell. Messner, 1981. Subj: Friendship.

How does it feel when your parents get divorced? photos by Miriam Shapiro. Messner, 1977. Subj: Divorce. Emotions. Family life.

I have feelings ill. by Howard Spivak. Behavioral, 1971. Subj: Emotions. Self-concept.

I have feelings too photos by Michael E. Ach. Human Sciences Pr., 1979. Subj: Emotions.

The turtles' picnic and other nonsense stories ill. by Erkki Alanen. Crown, 1977. Subj: Activities – picnicking. Animals.

Bergere, Thea. *Paris in the rain with Jean and Jacqueline* ill. by Richard Bergere. McGraw-Hill, 1963. Subj: City. Foreign lands – France. Weather – rain.

Bergman, David. *The turtle and the two ducks: animal fables* (Plante, Patricia)

Bergman, Donna. *City fox* ill. by Peter E. Hanson. Atheneum, 1992. ISBN 0-689-31687-9 Subj: Animals – foxes. Character traits – kindness to animals. City. Friendship. Old age.

Timmy Green's blue lake ill. by Ib Ohlsson. Tambourine, 1992. ISBN 0-688-10748-6 Subj: Activities – playing. Ecology. Imagination.

Bergstreser, Doug. *Runners, sliders, bouncers, climbers* (Bantock, Nick)

Bergstrom, Corinne. *Losing your best friend* ill. by Patricia Rosamilia. Human Sciences Pr., 1980. Subj: Friendship.

Bergström, Gunilla. *Is that a monster, Alfie Atkins?* ill. by Robert Swindells. Farrar, 1989. ISBN 9-12-959136-8 Subj: Animals – rabbits. Monsters.

Who's scaring Alfie Atkins? trans. by Joan Sandin; ill. by author. Farrar, 1987. ISBN 91-29-58318-7 Subj: Emotions – fear. Family life – fathers. Ghosts.

You have a girlfriend, Alfie Atkins? ill. by Joan Sandin. Farrar, 1988. ISBN 9-12-959062-0 Subj: Emotions – love.

Beris, Sandra. *The cat's surprise* (Seguin-Fontes, Marthe)

A wedding book (Seguin-Fontes, Marthe)

Berkley, Ethel S. *Ups and down: a first book of space* ill. by Kathleen Elgin. Addison-Wesley, 1951. Subj: Concepts. Concepts – up and down.

Berkowitz, Linda. *Alfonse, where are you?* ill. by author. Crown, 1996. ISBN 0-517-70046-8 Subj: Activities – playing. Animals. Birds – chickens. Birds – geese. Farms. Games.

Berlan, Kathryn Hook. *Andrew's amazing monsters* ill. by Maxie Chambliss. Atheneum, 1993. ISBN 0-689-31739-5 Subj: Activities – drawing. Monsters. Night. Parties.

Berliner, Franz. *Miserable Marabou* ill. by Irene Hedlund. Gareth Stevens, 1989. ISBN 0-8368-0094-X Subj: Birds. Birds – storks. Self-concept.

Wildebeest ill. by Lilian Brogger. Ideals, 1991. ISBN 0-8249-8488-9 Subj: Animals – wildebeests. Behavior – sharing. Character traits – individuality.

Berman, Linda. *The goodbye painting* ill. by Mark Hannon. Human Sciences Pr., 1983. Subj: Activities – babysitting.

Berman, Ruth. *Buzzing rattlesnakes* photos by David T. Roberts and David M. Schleser. Lerner, 1998. ISBN 0-8225-3603-X Subj: Reptiles – snakes.

Climbing tree frogs photos by John Netherton. Lerner, 1998. ISBN 0-8225-3605-6 Subj: Frogs and toads.

Fishing bears photos by Lynn M. Stone. Lerner, 1998. ISBN 0-8225-3601-3 Subj: Animals – bears.

Spinning spiders photos by David T. Roberts and David M. Schleser. Lerner, 1998. ISBN 0-8225-3604-8 Subj: Spiders.

Squeaking bats ill. with photos. Lerner, 1998. ISBN 0-8225-3602-1 Subj: Animals – bats.

Watchful wolves photos by William Muñoz. Lerner, 1998. ISBN 0-8225-3600-5 Subj: Animals – wolves.

Bernadette. *see* Watts, Bernadette

Bernard, Robin. *Juma and the honey-guild* ill. by Nneka Bennett. Silver Burdett, 1996. ISBN 0-382-39162-4 Subj: Behavior – sharing. Birds. Family life – fathers. Foreign lands – Africa. Foreign languages.

Bernardoni, Robert. *Christmas all over* ill. by Ruth Hunter McAnespy. Pelican, 1996. ISBN 1-56554-205-3 Subj: Holidays – Christmas. Mythical creatures – elves. Rhyming text. Santa Claus.

Bernhard, Durga. *Alphabeasts: a hide and seek alphabet book* ill. by author. Holiday, 1993. ISBN 0-8234-0993-7 Subj: ABC books. Animals. Behavior – hiding. Nature.

What's Maggie up to? ill. by author. Holiday, 1992. ISBN 0-8234-0969-4 Subj: Animals – cats. Birds. Family life.

Bernhard, Emery. *Dragonfly* ill. by Durga Bernhard. Holiday, 1993. ISBN 0-8234-1033-1 Subj: Insects – dragonflies. Nature. Science.

Eagles: lions of the sky ill. by Durga Bernhard. Holiday, 1994. ISBN 0-8234-1105-2 Subj: Birds – eagles. Nature. Science.

The girl who wanted to hunt ill. by Durga Bernhard. Holiday, 1994. ISBN 0-8234-1125-7 Subj: Birds – owls. Folk and fairy tales. Foreign lands – Russia. Foreign lands – Siberia. Sports – hunting.

How Snowshoe Hare rescued the sun: a tale from the Arctic ill. by Durga Bernhard. Holiday, 1993. ISBN 0-8234-1043-9 Subj: Animals. Eskimos. Folk and fairy tales. Foreign lands – Russia. Foreign lands – Siberia.

Ladybug ill. by Durga Bernhard. Holiday, 1992. ISBN 0-8234-0986-4 Subj: Insects – ladybugs. Nature. Science.

Reindeer ill. by Durga Bernhard. Holiday, 1994. ISBN 0-8234-1097-8 Subj: Animals – reindeer. Science.

Salamanders ill. by Durga Bernhard. Holiday, 1995. ISBN 0-8234-1148-6 Subj: Reptiles – salamanders. Science.

Spotted Eagle and Black Crow: a Lakota legend ill. by Durga Bernhard. Holiday, 1993. ISBN 0-8234-1007-2 Subj: Birds – eagles. Folk and fairy tales. Indians of North America – Lakota (Sioux). Sibling rivalry.

The tree that rains: the flood myth of the Huichol Indians of Mexico ill. by Durga Bernhard. Holiday, 1994. ISBN 0-8234-1108-7 Subj: Folk and fairy tales. Foreign lands – Mexico. Indians of North America – Huichol. Religion. Trees. Weather – floods.

The way of the willow branch ill. by Durga Bernhard. Harcourt, 1996. ISBN 0-15-200844-6 Subj: Nature. Sea and seashore. Trees.

Bernhard, Josephine Butkowska. *Lullaby: why the pussy-cat washes himself so often; a folk-tale adapted from the Polish* ill. by Irena Lorentowicz. Roy Pub., 1944. Subj: Animals – cats. Folk and fairy tales. Foreign lands – Poland. Lullabies.

Nine cry-baby dolls ill. by Irena Lorentowicz. Roy Pub., 1945. Subj: Folk and fairy tales. Foreign lands – Poland. Toys – dolls.

Bernheim, Evelyne. *In Africa* (Bernheim, Marc)

A week in Aya's world: the Ivory Coast (Bernheim, Marc)

Bernheim, Marc. *In Africa* by Marc and Evelyne Bernheim; photos by authors. Atheneum, 1973. ISBN 0-689-30315-7 Subj: Family life. Foreign lands – Africa.

A week in Aya's world: the Ivory Coast by Marc and Evelyne Bernheim; photos by authors. Macmillan, 1970. Subj: Foreign lands – Africa.

Bernstein, Alan. *Regal the golden eagle* (Klinting, Lars)

Bernstein, Joanne E. *Creepy crawly critter riddles* by Joanne E. Bernstein and Paul Cohen; ill. by Rosekrans Hoffman. Albert Whitman, 1986. ISBN 0-8075-1345-8 Subj: Animals. Insects. Riddles.

What was the wicked witch's real name? and other character riddles by Joanne E. Bernstein and Paul Cohen; ill. by Ann Iosa. Albert Whitman, 1986. ISBN 0-8075-8854-7 Subj: Riddles.

When people die by Joanne E. Bernstein and Steven V. Gullo; photos by Rosmarie Hausherr. Dutton, 1977. ISBN 0-525-42545-4 Subj: Death. Emotions – grief.

Bernstein, Margery. *Coyote goes hunting for fire: a California Indian myth* by Margery Bernstein and Janet Kobrin; ill. by Ed Heffernan. Scribners, 1974. ISBN 0-684-13768-2 Subj: Animals. Animals – coyotes. Fire. Folk and fairy tales. Indians of North America – Yana.

Earth namer: a California Indian myth by Margery Bernstein and Janet Kobrin; ill. by Ed Heffernan. Scribners, 1974. ISBN 0-684-13769-0 Subj: Creation. Earth. Folk and fairy tales. Indians of North America – Maidu.

The first morning: an African myth by Margery Bernstein and Janet Kobrin; ill. by Enid Warner Romanek. Scribners, 1976. ISBN 0-684-14533-2 Subj: Animals. Folk and fairy tales. Foreign lands – Africa.

How the sun made a promise and kept it: a Canadian Indian myth retold by Margery Bernstein and Janet Kobrin; ill. by Ed Heffernan. Scribners, 1974. ISBN 0-684-13770-4 Subj: Animals – beavers. Folk and fairy tales. Indians of North America – Bungee. Indians of North America – Ojibwa. Sun.

Bernstein, Robin. *Terrible, terrible!* ill. by Shauna Mooney Kawaski. Kar-Ben Copies, 1998. ISBN 1-58013-016-X Subj: Folk and fairy tales. Jewish culture.

Berquist, Grace. *The boy who couldn't roar* ill. by Ruth Van Sciver. Abingdon, 1960. Subj: Behavior – bullying. Character traits – selfishness.

Speckles goes to school ill. by Kathleen Elgin. Abingdon, 1952. Subj: Birds – chickens. School.

Berridge, Celia. *At my house* ill. by author. Random House, 1987. ISBN 0-394-99166-4 Subj: Family life. Homes, houses.

Going swimming ill. by author. Random House, 1987. ISBN 0-394-99165-6 Subj: Sports – swimming.

Grandmother's tales ill. by author. Elsevier-Dutton, 1981. ISBN 0-233-97357-5 Subj: Bedtime. Family life – grandmothers. Witches.

Hannah's new boots ill. by author. Scholastic, 1993. ISBN 0-590-45888-4 Subj: Clothing – shoes.

Hannah's temper ill. by author. Scholastic, 1992. ISBN 0-590-45887-6 Subj: Behavior – misbehavior. Emotions – anger. Rhyming text. Teeth.

On my street ill. by author. Random House, 1987. ISBN 0-394-88163-X Subj: Communities, neighborhoods.

Berry, Christine. *Mama went walking* ill. by María Cristina Brusca. Holt, 1990. ISBN 0-8050-1261-3 Subj: Activities – walking. Emotions – fear. Family life – mothers. Imagination.

Berry, Holly. *Busy Lizzie* ill. by author. North-South, 1994. ISBN 1-55858-324-6 Subj: Activities – playing. Bedtime. Participation.

Berry, James. *Celebration song* ill. by Louise Brierley. Simon & Schuster, 1994. ISBN 0-671-89446-3 Subj: Birth. Holidays – Christmas. Poetry. Religion – Nativity.

Don't leave an elephant to go and chase a bird ill. by Ann Grifalconi. Simon & Schuster, 1996. ISBN 0-689-80464-4 Subj: Animals – elephants. Behavior – trickery. Folk and fairy tales. Foreign lands – Ghana.

First palm trees: an Anancy Spiderman story ill. by Greg Couch. Simon & Schuster, 1997. ISBN 0-689-81060-1 Subj: Folk and fairy tales. Foreign lands – Caribbean Islands. Spiders.

Berry, Joy Wilt. *Being destructive* ill. by John Costanza. Rev. ed. Childrens Pr., 1984. ISBN 0-516-02681-X Subj: Behavior – misbehavior.

Being selfish ill. by John Costanza. Rev. ed. Childrens Pr., 1984. ISBN 0-516-02682-8 Subj: Behavior – misbehavior. Character traits – selfishness.

Disobeying ill. by John Costanza. Rev. ed. Childrens Pr., 1984. ISBN 0-516-02683-6 Subj: Behavior – misbehavior.

Fighting ill. by John Costanza. Rev. ed. Childrens Pr., 1984. ISBN 0-516-02684-4 Subj: Behavior – fighting, arguing. Behavior – misbehavior.

Throwing tantrums ill. by John Costanza. Rev. ed. Childrens Pr., 1984. ISBN 0-516-02685-2 Subj: Behavior – misbehavior.

Whining ill. by John Costanza. Rev. ed. Childrens Pr., 1984. ISBN 0-516-02686-0 Subj: Behavior – misbehavior.

Berson, Harold. *Balarin's goat* ill. by author. Crown, 1972. ISBN 0-517-50105-8 Subj: Animals – goats. Folk and fairy tales.

Barrels to the moon ill. by author. Coward, 1982. ISBN 0-698-20551-0 Subj: Folk and fairy tales. Foreign lands – France.

The boy, the baker, the miller and more ill. by author. Crown, 1974. The story is based on a French folk tale called Un Morceau de pain. ISBN 0-517-50326-3 Subj: Cumulative tales. Folk and fairy tales.

Charles and Claudine ill. by adapt. Macmillan, 1980. ISBN 0-02-709230-5 Subj: Folk and fairy tales. Foreign lands – France. Frogs and toads. Magic. Witches.

Henry Possum ill. by author. Crown, 1973. ISBN 0-517-50297-6 Subj: Animals – foxes. Animals – possums. Behavior – lost.

How the devil gets his due ill. by adapt. Crown, 1972. Subj: Character traits – cleverness. Devil. Folk and fairy tales. Foreign lands – France.

I'm bored, Ma! Ill. by author. Crown, 1976. ISBN 0-517-52508-9 Subj: Animals. Behavior – boredom. Imagination.

Joseph and the snake ill. by author. Macmillan, 1979. ISBN 0-02-709200-3 Subj: Animals – foxes.

Character traits – cleverness. Character traits – kindness to animals. Folk and fairy tales. Foreign lands – France. Reptiles – snakes.

Kassim's shoes ill. by adapt. Crown, 1977. ISBN 0-517-53063-5 Subj: Behavior – misunderstanding. Folk and fairy tales. Foreign lands – Africa.

Larbi and Leila: a tale of two mice ill. by author. Seabury Pr., 1974. ISBN 0-8164-3113-2 Subj: Behavior – greed. Folk and fairy tales.

A moose is not a mouse ill. by author. Crown, 1975. ISBN 0-517-51869-4 Subj: Animals – mice. Language.

Pop! goes the turnip ill. by author. Grosset, 1966. Subj: Animals – rabbits. Food. Gardens, gardening. Plants.

Raminagrobis and the mice ill. by author. Seabury Pr., 1966. Subj: Animals – cats. Animals – mice. Folk and fairy tales.

The rats who lived in the delicatessen ill. by author. Crown, 1976. ISBN 0-517-52604-2 Subj: Animals – rats. Behavior – greed. Food.

The thief who hugged a moonbeam ill. by author. Seabury Pr., 1972. ISBN 0-395-28767-7 Subj: Behavior – gossip. Crime. Magic. Royalty.

Truffles for lunch ill. by author. Macmillan, 1980. ISBN 0-02-709800-1 Subj: Animals – pigs. Behavior – wishing.

Why the jackal won't speak to the hedgehog: a Tunisian folk tale ill. by adapt. Seabury Pr., 1970. Subj: Animals. Animals – hedgehogs. Character traits – cleverness. Folk and fairy tales. Foreign lands – Africa.

Bertrand, Cécile. *Let's pretend!* ill. by author. Lothrop, 1993. ISBN 0-688-12378-3 Subj: Animals – dogs. Imagination. Shopping.

Mr. and Mrs. Smith have only one child, but what a child! ill. and trans. from French by author. Lothrop, 1992. ISBN 0-688-11330-3 Subj: Behavior. Family life – only child. Self-concept.

Bertrand, Diane Gonzales. *Family / familia* ill. by Pauline Rodriguez Howard; Spanish trans. by Julia Mercedes Castilla. Piñata Books, 1999. ISBN 1-55885-269-7 Subj: Ethnic groups in the U.S. – Mexican Americans. Family life. Foreign languages.

Bertrand, Lynne. *Dragon naps* ill. by Janet Street. Viking, 1996. ISBN 0-670-85403-4 Subj: Bedtime. Counting, numbers. Dragons. Sleep.

One day, two dragons ill. by Janet Street. Potter/Crown, 1992. ISBN 0-517-58413-1 Subj: Careers – doctors. Counting, numbers. Dragons. Illness.

Beskow, Elsa Maartman. *Children of the forest* adapt. from the Swedish by William Jay Smith; ill. by author. Delacorte, 1969. ISBN 0-86315-049-7 Subj: Foreign lands – Sweden. Forest, woods. Rhyming text. Seasons.

Pelle's new suit based on the original by Elsa Beskow; edited by Nova Nestrick; ill. by Bruno Frost. Platt, 1962. ISBN 0-06-020496-6 Subj: Animals – sheep. Clothing. Foreign lands – Sweden.

Peter in Blueberry Land ill. by author. Merrimack, 1984. A new ed. of a 100-year-old picture book. ISBN 0-510-00129-7 Subj: Birthdays. Food. Foreign lands – Sweden. Little people. Magic. Rhyming text.

Peter's adventures in Blueberry Land adapt. by Sheila La Farge; ill. by author. Delacorte, 1975. Pub. in Sweden in 1901. ISBN 0-440-04435-9 Subj: Birthdays. Food. Foreign lands – Sweden. Little people. Magic. Rhyming text.

Bess, Clayton. *The truth about the moon* ill. by Rosekrans Hoffman. Houghton Mifflin, 1983. ISBN 0-395-34551-0 Subj: Folk and fairy tales. Foreign lands – Africa. Moon.

Best, Cari. *Getting used to Harry* ill. by Diane Palmisciano. Orchard, 1996. ISBN 0-531-08794-8 Subj: Family life – step families.

Last licks: a Spaldeen story ill. by Diane Palmisciano. DK, 1999. ISBN 0-7894-2513-0 Subj: Activities – playing. Sports – punchball.

Montezuma's revenge ill. by Diane Palmisciano. Orchard, 1999. ISBN 0-531-33198-9 Subj: Activities – vacationing. Animals – dogs. Behavior – dissatisfaction.

Taxi! Taxi! ill. by Dale Gottlieb. Little, 1994. ISBN 0-316-09259-2 Subj: Activities – playing. Divorce. Family life – fathers. Taxis.

Three cheers for Catherine the Great! ill. by Giselle Potter. DK, 1999. ISBN 0-7894-2622-6 Subj: Birthdays. Family life – grandmothers. Gifts.

Top banana ill. by Erika Oller. Orchard, 1997. ISBN 0-531-33009-5 Subj: Birds – parakeets, parrots. Character traits – helpfulness. Emotions – envy, jealousy. Flowers.

Bester, Roger. *Fireman Jim* photos by author. Crown, 1981. ISBN 0-517-54290-0 Subj: Careers – firefighters. Fire.

Guess what? photos by author. Crown, 1980. ISBN 0-517-54104-1 Subj: Animals. Participation. Problem solving.

Bethell, Jean. *Bathtime.* Holt, 1979. ISBN 0-03-044636-8 Subj: Activities – bathing. Animals.

Hooray for Henry ill. by Sergio Leone. Grosset, 1966. Subj: Character traits – perseverance. Food.

Playmates photos by author. Holt, 1981. ISBN 0-03-053821-1 Subj: Activities – playing. Animals.

Three cheers for Mother Jones! ill. by Kathleen Garry-McCord. Holt, 1980. ISBN 0-03-054831-4 Subj: Activities – working. U.S. history.

Bettina (Bettina Ehrlich). *Cocolo comes to America* ill. by author. HarperCollins, 1949. Subj: Animals – donkeys.

Cocolo's home ill. by author. HarperCollins, 1950. Subj: Animals – donkeys.

Of uncles and aunts ill. by author. Norton, 1964. Subj: Family life – aunts, uncles.

Pantaloni ill. by author. HarperCollins, 1957. Subj: Animals – dogs. Foreign lands – Italy. Poverty. Sports – fishing.

Piccolo ill. by author. HarperCollins, 1954. Subj: Animals – donkeys.

Bettinger, Craig. *Follow me, everybody* ill. by Edward S. Hollander. Doubleday, 1968. Subj: Ethnic groups in the U.S.

Betz, Betty. *Manners for moppets* ill. by author. Grosset, 1962. Subj: Etiquette. Rhyming text.

Bianchi, John. *The lab rats of Doctor Eclair* ill. by author. Firefly, 1997. ISBN 0-921285-49-3 Subj: Animals – rats. Character traits – kindness to animals.

Swine snafu ill. by author. Firefly, 1988. ISBN 0-921285-14-0 Subj: Animals – pigs. Family life. Friendship.

Bianco, Margery Williams. *The hurdy-gurdy man* ill. by Robert Lawson. Gregg, 1979, c1933. Subj: Activities – dancing. Music.

The velveteen rabbit: or, How toys became real ill. by Allen Atkinson. Knopf, 1983. ISBN 0-394-53221-X Subj: Animals – rabbits. Emotions – love. Folk and fairy tales. Magic. Toys.

The velveteen rabbit: or, How toys became real ill. by Michael Green. Running Pr., 1984. ISBN 0-89741-291-8 Subj: Animals – rabbits. Emotions – love. Folk and fairy tales. Magic. Toys.

The velveteen rabbit: or, How toys became real ill. by Michael Hague. Holt, 1983. ISBN 0-03-063517-9 Subj: Animals – rabbits. Emotions – love. Folk and fairy tales. Magic. Toys.

The velveteen rabbit ill. by David Jorgensen. Knopf, 1985. ISBN 0-394-87711-X Subj: Animals – rabbits. Emotions – love. Folk and fairy tales. Magic. Toys.

The velveteen rabbit: or, How toys became real ill. by William Nicholson. Doubleday, 1991. ISBN 0-385-07748-3 Subj: Animals – rabbits. Emotions – love. Folk and fairy tales. Magic. Toys.

The velveteen rabbit: or, How toys became real ill. by Ilse Plume. Godine, 1983. ISBN 0-87923-444-X Subj: Animals – rabbits. Emotions – love. Folk and fairy tales. Magic. Toys.

The velveteen rabbit: or, How toys became real ed. by David Eastman; ill. by S. D. Schindler. Troll, 1987. ISBN 0-8167-1061-9 Subj: Animals – rabbits. Emotions – love. Folk and fairy tales. Magic. Toys.

The velveteen rabbit: or, How toys became real ill. by Tien. Simon & Schuster, 1983. ISBN 0-671-46784-8 Subj: Animals – rabbits. Emotions – love. Folk and fairy tales. Magic. Toys.

Bibb, Eric. *The dolphin journey* (Orstadius, Brita)

Bible. *Best-loved Bible verses for children* ill. by Anna Maria Magagna. Grosset, 1983. ISBN 0-448-46626-0 Subj: Religion.

Bible, Charles. *Hamdaani: a traditional tale from Zanzibar* ill. by adapt. Holt, 1977. ISBN 0-03-020846-7 Subj: Animals. Folk and fairy tales. Foreign lands – Africa.

Jennifer's new chair ill. by author. Holt, 1978. ISBN 0-03-022801-8 Subj: Birthdays. Family life. Family life – grandmothers. Fire. Furniture – chairs. Parties.

Bible. New Testament. *The Lord's prayer* ill. by Ingri and Edgar Parin d'Aulaire. Catholic version. Doubleday, 1934. Subj: Religion.

The Lord's prayer ill. by Ingri and Edgar Parin d'Aulaire. Protestant version. Doubleday, 1934. Subj: Religion.

The Lord's prayer ill. by George Kraus. Dutton, 1970. ISBN 0-6716-6524-3 Subj: Religion.

The Lord's prayer ill. by Tim Ladwig. Eerdmans, 1999. ISBN 0-8028-5180-0 Subj: Ethnic groups in the U.S. – African Americans. Religion.

Bible. New Testament. Gospels. *Christmas: the King James Version* ill. by Jan Pienkowski. Knopf, 1984. ISBN 0-394-86923-0 Subj: Holidays – Christmas. Religion – Nativity.

The first Christmas: from the Gospels according to Saint Luke and Saint Matthew ill. by Barbara Neustadt. Crowell, 1960. Subj: Holidays – Christmas. Religion – Nativity.

The Nativity ill. by Julie Vivas. Harcourt, 1988. Text consists of excerpts from the authorized King James version of the Bible. ISBN 0-15-200535-8 Subj: Holidays – Christmas. Religion – Nativity.

The story of Christmas: words from the Gospels of Matthew and Luke ill. by Jane Ray. Dutton, 1991. ISBN 0-525-44768-7 Subj: Holidays – Christmas. Religion – Nativity.

Bible. Old Testament. Daniel. *Daniel in the lions' den* adapt. by Belinda Hollyer; ill. by Leon Baxter. Silver Burdett, 1984. ISBN 0-382-06790-8 Subj: Animals – lions. Religion – Daniel.

Daniel in the lions' den text by Kathleen N. Daly; ill. by Jim Cummins. Rand McNally, 1984. ISBN 0-528-82492-9 Subj: Animals – lions. Format, unusual – board books. Religion.

Daniel in the lions' den retold by Mary Auld; ill. by Diana Mayo. Simon & Schuster, 1999. ISBN 0-531-14514-X Subj: Animals – lions. Religion.

Shadrach, Meshack, and Abednego ill. by Paul Galdone. McGraw-Hill, 1965. Subj: Religion.

Bible. Old Testament. David. *David and Goliath* adapt. by Belinda Hollyer; ill. by Leon Baxter. Silver Burdett, 1984. ISBN 0-382-06791-6 Subj: Foreign lands – Israel. Giants. Religion – David.

David and the giant text by Emily Little; ill. by Hans Wilhelm. Random House, 1987. ISBN 0-394-98867-1 Subj: Behavior – bullying. Giants. Religion – David.

Bible. Old Testament. Genesis. *Genesis* ill. by Ed Young. Laura Geringer, 1997. ISBN 0-06-025356-8 Subj: Creation. Religion.

The story of the creation ill. by Jane Ray. Dutton, 1993. ISBN 0-525-44946-9 Subj: Creation. Religion.

Bible. Old Testament. Jonah. *The Book of Jonah* adapt. and ill. by Peter Spier. Doubleday, 1985. ISBN 0-385-19335-1 Subj: Animals – whales. Religion – Jonah.

Jonah: the complete text of Jonah from the Holy Bible, New International version ill. by Kurt Mitchell. Crossway, 1981. ISBN 0-89107-224-1 Subj: Animals – cats. Animals – mice. Animals – whales. Religion – Jonah.

Jonah and the great fish adapt. by Belinda Hollyer; ill. by Leon Baxter. Silver Burdett, 1984. ISBN 0-382-06792-4 Subj: Animals – whales. Religion – Jonah.

Jonah and the great fish text by Kathleen N. Daly; ill. by Jim Cummins. Rand McNally, 1984. ISBN 0-528-82495-3 Subj: Animals – whales. Format, unusual – board books. Religion.

Bible. Old Testament. Joseph. *Joseph and his brothers* text by Kathleen N. Daly; ill. by Jim Cummins. Rand McNally, 1984. ISBN 0-528-82493-7 Subj: Clothing – coats. Family life – brothers. Foreign lands – Egypt. Format, unusual – board books. Religion. Slavery.

Bible. Old Testament. Noah. *Noah and the ark* adapt. and ill. by Pauline Baynes. Holt, 1988. ISBN 0-8050-0886-1 Subj: Animals. Boats, ships. Religion – Noah. Weather – floods. Weather – rain. Weather – rainbows.

Noah and the ark text by Kathleen N. Daly; ill. by Jim Cummins. Rand McNally, 1984. ISBN 0-528-82490-2 Subj: Animals. Boats, ships. Religion – Noah. Weather – floods. Weather – rain.

Bible. Old Testament. Psalms. *The Lord is my shepherd* ill. by George Kraus. Dutton, 1971. ISBN 0-87807-015-X Subj: Religion.

The Lord is my shepherd: the twenty-third Psalm ill. by Tasha Tudor. Putnam, 1980. ISBN 0-399-20756-2 Subj: Religion.

Psalm twenty-three ill. by Tim Ladwig. African American Family Pr., 1993. ISBN 1-56977-025-5

Subj: City. Ethnic groups in the U.S. – African Americans. Religion.

The twenty-third Psalm: from the King James Bible ill. by Michael Hague. Holt, 1997. ISBN 0-8050-3820-5 Subj: Religion.

Bider, Djemma. *The buried treasure* ill. by Debby L. Carter. Dodd, 1982. ISBN 0-396-07991-1 Subj: Folk and fairy tales. Foreign lands – Russia.

A drop of honey ill. by Armen Kojoyian. Simon & Schuster, 1989. ISBN 0-671-66265-1 Subj: Dreams. Folk and fairy tales. Foreign lands – Armenia. Sibling rivalry.

Bienenfeld, Florence. *My mom and dad are getting a divorce* ill. by Art Scott. EMC, 1980. ISBN 0-88436-753-3 Subj: Divorce. Emotions.

Bier, Anna. *The nightingale* (Andersen, H. C. [Hans Christian])

Bierhorst, John. *Doctor Coyote: a Native American Æsop's fables* ill. by Wendy Watson. Macmillan, 1987. ISBN 0-02-709780-3 Subj: Animals. Animals – coyotes. Folk and fairy tales. Indians of North America – Aztec.

The ring in the prairie: a Shawnee legend trans. by John Bierhorst; ill. by Leo and Diane Dillon. Dial, 1970. ISBN 0-8037-7455-9 Subj: Folk and fairy tales. Indians of North America – Shawnee.

Spirit child: a story of the Nativity (Sahagun, Bernardino de)

The woman who fell from the sky: the Iroquois story of creation ill. by Robert Andrew Parker. Morrow, 1993. ISBN 0-688-10681-1 Subj: Creation. Indians of North America – Iroquois.

Big book of trains: *National Railway Museum, York, England* ill. with photos. DK, 1998. ISBN 0-7894-3436-9 Subj: Trains.

The big Peter Rabbit book: *things to do, games to play, stories, presents to make* ill. by Beatrix Potter. Warne, 1986. ISBN 0-7232-3409-4 Subj: Activities – making things. Animals. Games. Riddles.

Bileck, Marvin. *Rain makes applesauce* (Scheer, Julian)

Bilezikian, Gary. *While I slept* ill. by author. Orchard, 1990. ISBN 0-531-08475-2 Subj: Night. Noise, sounds. Sleep.

Billam, Rosemary. *Fuzzy rabbit* ill. by Vanessa Julian-Ottie. Random House, 1984. ISBN 0-394-96346-6 Subj: Behavior – needing someone. Birthdays. Emotions – love. Toys.

Billington, Elizabeth T. *The Randolph Caldecott treasury* (Caldecott, Randolph)

Billout, Guy. *By camel or by car: a look at transportation* ill. by author. Prentice-Hall, 1979. ISBN 0-13-109603-6 Subj: Activities – traveling. Transportation.

Billy Boy (folk-song). *Billy Boy* verses sel. by Richard Chase; ill. by Glen Rounds. Childrens Pr., 1966. Subj: Folk and fairy tales. Poetry. Songs.

Binch, Caroline. *Since Dad left* ill. by author. Millbrook, 1998. ISBN 0-7613-0357-X Subj: Divorce. Emotions. Family life.

Bingham, Mindy. *Minou* ill. by Itoko Maeno. Advocacy Pr., 1987. ISBN 0-911655-36-0 Subj: Animals – cats. Behavior – needing someone. Foreign lands – France.

My way Sally by Mindy Bingham and Penelope Colville Paine; ill. by Itoko Maeno. Advocacy Pr., 1988. ISBN 0-911655-27-1 Subj: Animals – dogs. Animals – foxes. Behavior – trickery.

Binnamin, Vivian. *The case of the anteater's missing lunch* ill. by Jeffrey S. Nelsen. Silver Pr., 1990. ISBN 0-671-68816-2 Subj: Activities – picnicking. Animals – anteaters. Mystery stories. School.

The case of the mysterious mermaid ill. by Jeffrey S. Nelsen. Silver Pr., 1990. ISBN 0-671-68817-0 Subj: Aquariums. Mythical creatures – mermaids, mermen. School.

The case of the planetarium puzzle ill. by Jeffrey S. Nelsen. Silver Pr., 1990. ISBN 0-671-68819-7 Subj: Mystery stories.

The case of the snoring stegosaurus ill. by Jeffrey S. Nelsen. Silver Pr., 1990. ISBN 0-671-68818-9 Subj: Dinosaurs. Museums. Mystery stories.

Binzen, Bill. *Alfred goes house hunting* ill. by author. Doubleday, 1974. ISBN 0-385-08223-1 Subj: Animals. Homes, houses. Toys.

Carmen photos by author. Coward, 1970. ISBN 0-698-30034-3 Subj: City. Friendship.

Birch, David. *The king's chessboard* ill. by Devis Grebu. Dial, 1988. ISBN 0-8037-0367-8 Subj: Character traits – pride. Royalty – kings.

Birchman, David F. *Jigsaw Jackson* ill. by Daniel San Souci. Lothrop, 1996. ISBN 0-688-11633-7 Subj: Behavior – misbehavior. Careers – farmers. Farms. Puzzles.

Birchman, David Francis. *Brother Billy Bronto's bygone blues band* ill. by John O'Brien. Lothrop, 1992. ISBN 0-688-10424-X Subj: Dinosaurs. Ghosts. Music. Rhyming text.

A green horn blowing ill. by Thomas B. Allen. Lothrop, 1997. ISBN 0-688-12389-9 Subj: Careers – musicians. Music.

Birchmore, Daniel A. *Harry, the happy snake of Happy Hollow* ill. by Gail E. Lucas. Cucumber Island, 1996. ISBN 1-887813-06-3 Subj: Reptiles – snakes.

Pilly, Polly, and Wee ill. by Gail E. Lucas. Cucumber Island, 1996. ISBN 1-887813-15-2 Subj: Animals. Rhyming text.

The white curtain ill. by Gail E. Lucas. Cucumber Island, 1996. ISBN 1-887813-09-8 Subj: Weather – wind.

Bird, E. J. *How do bears sleep?* ill. by author. Carolrhoda, 1989. ISBN 0-87614-384-2 Subj: Animals – bears. Character traits – curiosity. Character traits – questioning. Hibernation. Rhyming text.

Bird, Malcolm. *The school in Murky Wood* ill. by author. Chronicle, 1993. ISBN 0-8118-0544-1 Subj: Monsters. Night. School.

Birdseye, Debbie Holsclaw. *She'll be comin' round the mountain* (Birdseye, Tom)

Birdseye, Tom. *Airmail to the moon* ill. by Stephen Gammell. Holiday, 1988. ISBN 0-8234-0683-0 Subj: Behavior – losing things. Character traits – persistence. Teeth.

A regular flood of mishap ill. by Megan Lloyd. Holiday, 1994. ISBN 0-8234-1070-6 Subj: Behavior – bad day. Country. Family life.

She'll be comin' round the mountain by Tom Birdseye and Debbie Holsclaw Birdseye; ill. by Andrew Glass. Holiday, 1994. ISBN 0-8234-1032-3 Subj: Activities – singing. Country. Friendship. Music. Songs.

Soap! Soap! Don't forget the soap! an Appalachian folktale ill. by Andrew Glass. Holiday, 1993. ISBN 0-8234-1005-6 Subj: Behavior – forgetfulness. Cumulative tales. Folk and fairy tales. Shopping.

A song of stars ill. by Ju-Hong Chen. Holiday, 1990. ISBN 0-8234-0790-X Subj: Emotions – love. Folk and fairy tales. Foreign lands – China. Sky. Stars.

Waiting for baby ill. by Loreen Leedy. Holiday, 1991. ISBN 0-8234-0892-2 Subj: Babies. Family life – new sibling.

Birnbaum, Abe. *Green eyes* ill. by author. Golden Books, 2001. ISBN 0-307-20203-8 Subj: Animals – cats. Caldecott award honor books. Seasons.

Birney, Betty G. *Tyrannosaurus Tex* ill. by John O'Brien. Houghton Mifflin, 1994. ISBN 0-395-67648-7 Subj: Cowboys. Dinosaurs.

Biro, B. S. *see* Biro, Val

Biro, Val. *Gumdrop and the birthday surprise* ill. by author. Gareth Stevens, 1986. ISBN 1-55532-010-4 Subj: Automobiles. Character traits – helpfulness.

Gumdrop and the farmyard caper ill. by author. Gareth Stevens, 1985. ISBN 0-918831-11-3 Subj: Animals. Automobiles. Farms.

Gumdrop and the great sausage caper ill. by author. Gareth Stevens, 1985. ISBN 0-918831-13-X Subj: Animals. Automobiles. Food.

Gumdrop and the secret switches ill. by author. Children's Book Co., 1982. ISBN 0-685-42941-5 Subj: Animals – dogs. Automobiles.

Gumdrop and the steamroller ill. by author. Gareth Stevens, 1986. ISBN 1-55532-013-9 Subj: Accidents. Automobiles. Machines.

Gumdrop at the zoo ill. by author. Gareth Stevens, 1985. ISBN 0-918831-10-5 Subj: Automobiles. Zoos.

Gumdrop beats the clock ill. by author. Gareth Stevens, 1986. First published as Gumdrop in a hurry in the United Kingdom by Hodder & Stoughton Children's Books. ISBN 1-55532-011-2 Subj: Automobiles. Behavior – hurrying. Character traits – helpfulness.

Gumdrop catches a cold ill. by author. Gareth Stevens, 1985. ISBN 0-918831-14-8 Subj: Automobiles. Illness.

Gumdrop finds a friend ill. by author. Children's Book Co., 1982. ISBN 0-685-42940-7 Subj: Automobiles. Crime.

Gumdrop finds a ghost ill. by author. Children's Book Co., 1982. ISBN 0-685-11061-3 Subj: Automobiles. Ghosts.

Gumdrop floats away ill. by author. Gareth Stevens, 1985. ISBN 0-918831-09-1 Subj: Automobiles. Sea and seashore.

Gumdrop gets a lift ill. by author. Gareth Stevens, 1986. ISBN 1-55532-009-0 Subj: Automobiles. Behavior – carelessness. Behavior – needing someone.

Gumdrop gets his wings ill. by author. Children's Book Co., 1982. ISBN 0-685-42939-3 Subj: Automobiles.

Gumdrop goes to school ill. by author. Gareth Stevens, 1986. ISBN 1-55532-008-2 Subj: Automobiles. Behavior – misbehavior. School.

Gumdrop has a birthday ill. by author. Children's Book Co., 1982. ISBN 0-89813-055-7 Subj: Automobiles. Birthdays.

Gumdrop in double trouble ill. by author. Children's Book Co., 1982. ISBN 0-898130-54-9 Subj: Automobiles. Crime.

Gumdrop is the best ill. by author. Gareth Stevens, 1985. ISBN 0-918831-12-1 Subj: Automobiles.

Gumdrop on the Brighton run ill. by author. Hodder & Stoughton, 1976. ISBN 0-34020-213-0 Subj: Automobiles. Sports – racing.

Gumdrop races a train ill. by author. Gareth Stevens, 1986. ISBN 1-55532-012-0 Subj: Automobiles. Sports – racing. Trains.

Gumdrop, the adventures of a vintage car ill. by author. Follett, 1967, c1966. Subj: Automobiles.

Jack and the beanstalk (Jack and the beanstalk)

Miranda's umbrella ill. by author. Peter Bedrick, 1990. ISBN 0-87226-429-7 Subj: Giants. Umbrellas. Witches.

The pied piper of Hamelin ill. by reteller. Silver Burdett, 1985. ISBN 0-382-09014-4 Subj: Animals –

rats. Behavior – trickery. Folk and fairy tales. Foreign lands – Germany. Middle Ages.

The three little pigs (The three little pigs)

Tobias and the dragon: a Hungarian folk tale ill. by author. Bedrick/Blackie, 1989. ISBN 0-8722-6427-0 Subj: Dragons. Folk and fairy tales.

The wind in the willows: home sweet home (Grahame, Kenneth)

The wind in the willows: the open road (Grahame, Kenneth)

The wind in the willows: the river bank (Grahame, Kenneth)

The wind in the willows: the wild wood (Grahame, Kenneth)

Birrer, Cynthia. *The lady and the unicorn* by Cynthia and William Birrer; ill. by authors. Lothrop, 1987. ISBN 0-688-04038-1 Subj: Character traits – kindness to animals. Folk and fairy tales. Magic. Mythical creatures – unicorns. Royalty – princes.

Song to Demeter by Cynthia and William Birrer; ill. by authors. Lothrop, 1987. ISBN 0-688-04041-1 Subj: Folk and fairy tales. Foreign lands – Greece.

Birrer, William. *The lady and the unicorn* (Birrer, Cynthia)

Song to Demeter (Birrer, Cynthia)

Bischhoff-Miersch, Andrea. *Do you know the difference?* by Andrea and Michael Bischhoff-Miersch; ill. by Christine Faltermayr. North-South, 1995. Translated by Rosemary Lanning. ISBN 1-55858-372-6 Subj: Animals.

Bischhoff-Miersch, Michael. *Do you know the difference?* (Bischhoff-Miersch, Andrea)

Bishop, Adela. *The Christmas polar bear* ill. by Carole Czapla. DOT Garnet, 1991. ISBN 0-9625620-2-5 Subj: Animals – polar bears. Holidays – Christmas.

The Easter wolf ill. by Carole Czapla. Garnet, 1988. ISBN 0-9625620-1-7 Subj: Animals – rabbits. Animals – wolves. Birds – chickens. Character traits – kindness. Holidays – Easter.

Bishop, Ann. *Chicken riddle* ill. by Jerry Warshaw. Albert Whitman, 1972. ISBN 0-8075-1170-4 Subj: Birds – chickens. Humor. Riddles.

The Ella Fannie elephant riddle book ill. by Jerry Warshaw. Albert Whitman, 1974. ISBN 0-8075-1966-9 Subj: Animals – elephants. Humor. Riddles.

Hey riddle riddle ill. by Jerry Warshaw. Albert Whitman, 1968. ISBN 0-8075-3257-6 Subj: Humor. Riddles.

Merry-go-riddle ill. by Jerry Warshaw. Albert Whitman, 1973. ISBN 0-8075-5072-8 Subj: Humor. Riddles.

Noah riddle? ill. by Jerry Warshaw. Albert Whitman, 1970. ISBN 0-8075-5702-1 Subj: Humor. Riddles.

Oh, riddlesticks! ill. by Jerry Warshaw. Albert Whitman, 1976. ISBN 0-8075-5916-4 Subj: Humor. Riddles.

The riddle ages ill. by Jerry Warshaw. Albert Whitman, 1977. ISBN 0-8075-6965-8 Subj: Humor. Middle Ages. Riddles.

Riddle-iculous rid-alphabet book ill. by Jerry Warshaw. Albert Whitman, 1971. ISBN 0-8075-6970-4 Subj: ABC books. Humor. Riddles.

Wild Bill Hiccup's riddle book ed. by Caroline Rubin; ill. by Jerry Warshaw. Albert Whitman, 1969. ISBN 0-8075-9097-5 Subj: Cowboys. Humor. Riddles. U.S. history – frontier and pioneer life.

Bishop, Bonnie. *No one noticed Ralph* ill. by Jack Kent. Doubleday, 1979. ISBN 0-385-12159-8 Subj: Behavior – unnoticed, unseen. Birds – parakeets, parrots.

Ralph rides away ill. by Jack Kent. Doubleday, 1979. ISBN 0-385-14214-5 Subj: Activities – picnicking. Birds – parakeets, parrots. Zoos.

Bishop, Claire Huchet. *The five Chinese brothers* by Claire Huchet Bishop and Kurt Wiese; ill. by Kurt Wiese. Coward, 1938. ISBN 0-698-20044-6 Subj: Character traits – cleverness. Family life. Folk and fairy tales. Foreign lands – China.

The man who lost his head ill. by Robert McCloskey. Viking, 1942. ISBN 0-670-45349-8 Subj: Anatomy – heads. Humor.

The truffle pig ill. by Kurt Wiese. Coward, 1971. Subj: Animals – pigs. Foreign lands – France. Pets.

Twenty-two bears ill. by Kurt Wiese. Viking, 1964. Subj: Animals – bears. Counting, numbers. Cumulative tales.

Bishop, Gavin. *Chicken Licken* (Chicken Little)

Little Rabbit and the sea ill. by author. North-South, 1997. ISBN 1-55858-810-8 Subj: Animals – rabbits. Imagination. Sea and seashore.

Maui and the sun: a Maori tale ill. by author. North-South, 1996. ISBN 1-55858-578-8 Subj: Behavior – trickery. Folk and fairy tales. Foreign lands – New Zealand. Sun.

Mrs. McGinty and the bizarre plant ill. by author. Oxford Univ. Pr., 1983. ISBN 0-19-558074-5 Subj: Gardens, gardening. Plants.

The three little pigs (The three little pigs)

Bishop, Roma. *Animals* ill. by author. Simon & Schuster, 1991. ISBN 0-671-74833-5 Subj: Animals. Format, unusual – board books. Format, unusual – toy and movable books.

Christmas songs ill. by author; paper engineering by Ruth Mawdsley; designed and conceived by Graham Brown. Little Simon, 1994. ISBN 0-671-

89516-8 Subj: Format, unusual – toy and movable books. Holidays – Christmas. Music.

Easter counting ill. by author; paper engineering by Ruth Mawdsley. Little Simon, 1996. ISBN 0-689-80612-4 Subj: Counting, numbers. Format, unusual – toy and movable books. Holidays – Easter.

Easter egg hunt ill. by author; paper engineering by Ruth Mawdsley. Little Simon, 1996. ISBN 0-689-80613-2 Subj: Format, unusual – toy and movable books. Holidays – Easter.

Holiday cheer ill. by author; paper engineering by Ruth Mawdsley; designed and conceived by Graham Brown. Simon & Schuster, 1994. ISBN 0-671-89518-4 Subj: Format, unusual – toy and movable books. Holidays – Christmas.

My first pop-up book of dinosaurs ill. by author; conceived and designed by Graham Brown and Ruth Mawdsley; paper engineering by Ruth Mawdsley; written by Sarah Fabiny. Simon & Schuster, 1993. ISBN 0-671-86723-7 Subj: Dinosaurs. Format, unusual – toy and movable books.

My first pop-up book of prehistoric animals ill. by author; conceived and designed by Graham Brown and Ruth Mawdsley; paper engineering by Ruth Mawdsley; written by Sarah Hewetson. Little Simon, 1994. ISBN 0-671-89556-7 Subj: Animals. Format, unusual – toy and movable books.

Numbers ill. by author. Simon & Schuster, 1991. ISBN 0-671-74832-7 Subj: Counting, numbers. Format, unusual – board books. Format, unusual – toy and movable books.

On a safari ill. by author. Little Simon, 1993. ISBN 0-671-88309-7 Subj: Animals. Foreign lands – Africa. Format, unusual – toy and movable books.

Santa pays a visit ill. by author; paper engineering by Ruth Mawdsley; designed and conceived by Graham Brown. Simon & Schuster, 1994. ISBN 0-671-89519-2 Subj: Format, unusual – toy and movable books. Holidays – Christmas. Santa Claus.

Shapes ill. by author. Simon & Schuster, 1991. ISBN 0-671-74830-0 Subj: Concepts – shape. Format, unusual – board books. Format, unusual – toy and movable books.

Toys ill. by author. Simon & Schuster, 1991. ISBN 0-671-74831-9 Subj: Format, unusual – board books. Format, unusual – toy and movable books. Toys.

Bishop, Rudine Sims. *Wonders: the best children's poems of Effie Lee Newsome* (Newsome, Effie Lee)

Bittner, Wolfgang. *Wake up, Grizzly!* ill. by Gustavo Rosemffet; trans. by J. Alison James. North-South, 1996. ISBN 1-55858-519-2 Subj: Animals – bears. Family life. Family life – fathers. Imagination.

Bix, Cynthia Overbeck. *Water, water everywhere* (Rauzon, Mark J.)

Black, Algernon D. *The woman of the wood: a tale from old Russia* ill. by Evaline Ness. Holt, 1973. ISBN 0-03-007436-3 Subj: Folk and fairy tales. Foreign lands – Russia.

Black, Charles C. *The royal nap* ill. by James Stevenson. Viking, 1995. ISBN 0-670-85863-3 Subj: Animals. Hiccups. Middle Ages. Music. Royalty – kings. Sleep.

Black, Floyd. *Alphabet cat* ill. by Carol Nicklaus. Elsevier-Dutton, 1979. ISBN 0-525-69009-3 Subj: ABC books. Animals – cats. Animals – rats.

Black, Irma (Simonton). *Big puppy and little puppy* ill. by Theresa Sherman. Holiday, 1960. Subj: Animals – dogs. Concepts – size.

Is this my dinner? ill. by Rosalind Fry. Albert Whitman, 1972. ISBN 0-8075-3665-2 Subj: Food. Participation. Rhyming text.

The little old man who could not read ill. by Seymour Fleishman. Albert Whitman, 1968. ISBN 0-8075-4621-6 Subj: Activities – reading. Shopping.

The taxi that hurried (Mitchell, Lucy Sprague)

Blacker, Terence. *Herbie Hamster, where are you?* ill. by Pippa Unwin. Random House, 1990. ISBN 0-679-80838-8 Subj: Animals – hamsters. Behavior – hiding. Games.

Blackmore, Vivien. *Why corn is golden: stories about plants* ill. by Susana Martínez-Ostos. Little, 1984. ISBN 0-316-54820-0 Subj: Folk and fairy tales. Foreign lands – Mexico. Plants.

Blackstone, Margaret. *This is baseball* ill. by John O'Brien. Holt, 1993. ISBN 0-8050-2390-9 Subj: Sports – baseball.

This is figure skating ill. by John O'Brien. Holt, 1998. ISBN 0-8050-3706-3 Subj: Sports – ice skating.

Blackstone, Stella. *Baby high, baby low* ill. by Denise [Fraifield] and Fernando [Azevedo]. Holiday, 1998. ISBN 0-8234-1345-4 Subj: Babies. Concepts. Concepts – opposites. Rhyming text.

Bear in a square ill. by Debbie Harter. Barefoot, 1998. ISBN 1-84148-120-3 Subj: Animals – bears. Concepts – shape. Concepts – size. Counting, numbers.

Bear on a bike ill. by Debbie Harter. Barefoot, 1999. ISBN 1-84148-121-1 Subj: Animals – bears. Ethnic groups in the U.S. – African Americans. Sports – bicycling.

Blackwood, Gladys Rourke. *Whistle for Cindy* ill. by author. Albert Whitman, 1952. Subj: Activities – whistling. Animals – dogs. Pets.

Blackwood, Mary. *Derek the knitting dinosaur* ill. by Kerry Argent. Carolrhoda, 1990. ISBN 0-87614-400-8 Subj: Activities – knitting. Dinosaurs. Gender roles. Rhyming text.

Blades, Ann. *Back to the cabin* ill. by author. Orca, 1997. ISBN 1-55143-049-5 Subj: Activities – vacationing. Family life. Seasons – summer.

A boy of Taché ill. by author. Tundra, 1995. ISBN 0-8877-6350-2 Subj: Family life – grandfathers. Foreign lands – Canada. Indians of North America – Carrier.

Fall ill. by author. Lothrop, 1990. ISBN 0-688-09232-2 Subj: Format, unusual – board books. Seasons – fall. Wordless.

Mary of mile 18 ill. by author. Tundra, 1971. ISBN 0-88776-015-5 Subj: Animals – wolves. Character traits – perseverance. Farms. Foreign lands – Canada.

Spring ill. by author. Lothrop, 1990. ISBN 0-688-09230-6 Subj: Format, unusual – board books. Seasons – spring. Wordless.

Summer ill. by author. Lothrop, 1989. ISBN 0-888-99091-X Subj: Family life – brothers. Family life – sisters. Farms. Format, unusual – board books. Seasons – summer. Wordless.

Winter ill. by author. Lothrop, 1990. ISBN 0-888-99093-6 Subj: Family life – brothers. Family life – sisters. Format, unusual – board books. Seasons – winter. Weather – snow. Wordless.

Blaine, Marge (Margery Kay). *The terrible thing that happened at our house* ill. by John Wallner. Parents, 1975. ISBN 0-819-30782-3 Subj: Family life. Family life – mothers. Problem solving.

Blake, Claire. *The paper chain* by Claire Blake, Eliza Blanchard, Kathy Parkinson; ill. by Kathy Parkinson. Health Pr., 1998. ISBN 0-929173-28-7 Subj: Family life. Family life – mothers. Illness – cancer.

Blake, Jon. *Wriggly Pig* ill. by Susie Jenkin-Pearce. Morrow, 1992. ISBN 0-688-11296-X Subj: Animals – pigs. Behavior. Family life.

You're a hero, Daley B.! ill. by Axel Scheffler. Candlewick, 1994. ISBN 1-56402-367-2 Subj: Animals – rabbits. Animals – weasels.

Blake, Olive. *see* Supraner, Robyn

Blake, Pamela. *Peep-show: a little book of rhymes* ill. by author. Macmillan, 1973. Subj: Nursery rhymes.

Blake, Quentin. *All join in* ill. by author. Little, 1991. ISBN 0-316-09934-1 Subj: Participation. Poetry.

Clown ill. by author. Holt, 1996. ISBN 0-8050-4399-3 Subj: Family life. Friendship. Toys. Wordless.

Cockatoos ill. by author. Little, 1992. ISBN 0-316-09951-1 Subj: Behavior – hiding. Birds – cockatoos. Counting, numbers. Games.

Mister Magnolia ill. by author. Jonathan Cape, 1980. ISBN 0-224-10612-1 Subj: Humor. Rhyming text.

Mrs. Armitage and the big wave ill. by author. Harcourt, 1997. ISBN 0-15-201642-2 Subj: Animals – dogs. Sea and seashore. Sports – surfing.

Mrs. Armitage on wheels ill. by author. Knopf, 1988. ISBN 0-394-99498-1 Subj: Humor. Sports – bicycling.

Quentin Blake's ABC ill. by author. Knopf, 1989. ISBN 0-394-94149-7 Subj: ABC books. Rhyming text.

Quentin Blake's nursery rhyme book ill. by author. HarperCollins, 1984. ISBN 0-06-020532-6 Subj: Humor. Nursery rhymes.

Simpkin ill. by author. Viking, 1994. ISBN 0-670-85371-2 Subj: Concepts – opposites. Family life – brothers and sisters. Rhyming text.

Snuff ill. by author. Lippincott, 1973. ISBN 0-397-31469-8 Subj: Crime. Knights.

The story of the dancing frog ill. by author. Knopf, 1985. ISBN 0-394-97033-0 Subj: Folk and fairy tales.

Zagazoo ill. by author. Orchard, 1998. ISBN 0-531-30178-8 Subj: Animals. Animals – babies. Behavior – imitation. Monsters.

Blake, Robert J. *Akiak: a tale from the Iditarod* ill. by author. Philomel, 1997. ISBN 0-399-22798-9 Subj: Alaska. Animals – dogs. Sports – racing.

The perfect spot ill. by author. Putnam, 1992. ISBN 0-399-22132-8 Subj: Family life – fathers. Forest, woods. Nature.

Spray ill. by author. Philomel, 1996. ISBN 0-399-22770-9 Subj: Boats, ships. Islands. Sea and seashore.

Yudonsi: a tale from the canyons ill. by author. Philomel, 1999. ISBN 0-399-23320-2 Subj: Behavior – misbehavior. Indians of North America.

Blake, William. *The tyger* ill. by Neil Waldman. Harcourt, 1993. ISBN 0-15-292375-6 Subj: Animals – tigers. Creation. Format, unusual. Poetry.

Blakeley, Peggy. *Two little ducks* ill. by Kenzo Kobayashi. Alphabet Pr., 1984. ISBN 0-9072-3407-0 Subj: Communities, neighborhoods.

What shall I be tomorrow? ill. by Helga Aichinger. Alphabet Pr., 1984. ISBN 0-907234-51-8 Subj: Behavior – imitation. Imagination.

Blance, Ellen. *Lady Monster has a plan* by Ellen Blance and Ann Cook; ill. by Quentin Blake. Bowmar, 1977. ISBN 0-8372-2135-8 Subj: Monsters.

Lady Monster helps out by Ellen Blance and Ann Cook; ill. by Quentin Blake. Bowmar, 1977. ISBN 0-8372-2126-9 Subj: Monsters.

Monster and the magic umbrella by Ellen Blance and Ann Cook; ill. by Quentin Blake. Bowmar, 1973. ISBN 0-8372-0835-1 Subj: Magic. Monsters. Umbrellas.

Monster and the mural by Ellen Blance and Ann Cook; ill. by Quentin Blake. Bowmar, 1977. ISBN 0-8372-2124-2 Subj: Monsters.

Monster and the surprise cookie by Ellen Blance and Ann Cook; ill. by Quentin Blake. Bowmar, 1977. ISBN 0-8372-2131-5 Subj: Monsters.

Monster at school by Ellen Blance and Ann Cook; ill. by Quentin Blake. Bowmar, 1973. ISBN 0-8372-0834-3 Subj: Monsters. School.

Monster buys a pet by Ellen Blance and Ann Cook; ill. by Quentin Blake. Bowmar, 1977. ISBN 0-8372-2134-X Subj: Monsters. Pets.

Monster cleans his house by Ellen Blance and Ann Cook; ill. by Quentin Blake. Bowmar, 1973. ISBN 0-8372-0828-9 Subj: Monsters.

Monster comes to the city by Ellen Blance and Ann Cook; ill. by Quentin Blake. Bowmar, 1973. ISBN 0-8372-0826-2 Subj: City. Monsters.

Monster gets a job by Ellen Blance and Ann Cook; ill. by Quentin Blake. Bowmar, 1977. ISBN 0-8372-2130-7 Subj: Activities – working. Monsters.

Monster goes around the town by Ellen Blance and Ann Cook; ill. by Quentin Blake. Bowmar, 1977. ISBN 0-8372-2132-3 Subj: Monsters.

Monster goes to school by Ellen Blance and Ann Cook; ill. by Quentin Blake. Bowmar, 1973. ISBN 0-8372-0834-3 Subj: Monsters. School.

Monster goes to the beach by Ellen Blance and Ann Cook; ill. by Quentin Blake. Bowmar, 1977. ISBN 0-8372-2129-3 Subj: Monsters. Sea and seashore.

Monster goes to the circus by Ellen Blance and Ann Cook; ill. by Quentin Blake. Bowmar, 1977. ISBN 0-8372-2127-7 Subj: Circus. Monsters.

Monster goes to the hospital by Ellen Blance and Ann Cook; ill. by Quentin Blake. Bowmar, 1977. ISBN 0-8372-2128-5 Subj: Hospitals. Monsters.

Monster goes to the museum by Ellen Blance and Ann Cook; ill. by Quentin Blake. Bowmar, 1973. ISBN 0-8372-0832-7 Subj: Monsters. Museums.

Monster goes to the zoo by Ellen Blance and Ann Cook; ill. by Quentin Blake. Bowmar, 1973. ISBN 0-8372-0837-8 Subj: Monsters. Zoos.

Monster has a party by Ellen Blance and Ann Cook; ill. by Quentin Blake. Bowmar, 1973. ISBN 0-8372-0836-X Subj: Monsters. Parties.

Monster, Lady Monster and the bike ride by Ellen Blance and Ann Cook; ill. by Quentin Blake. Bowmar, 1977. ISBN 0-8372-2125-0 Subj: Monsters. Sports – bicycling.

Monster looks for a friend by Ellen Blance and Ann Cook; ill. by Quentin Blake. Bowmar, 1973. ISBN 0-8372-0829-7 Subj: Friendship. Monsters.

Monster looks for a house by Ellen Blance and Ann Cook; ill. by Quentin Blake. Bowmar, 1973. ISBN 0-8372-0827-0 Subj: Monsters.

Monster meets Lady Monster by Ellen Blance and Ann Cook; ill. by Quentin Blake. Bowmar, 1973. ISBN 0-8372-0831-9 Subj: Monsters.

Monster on the bus by Ellen Blance and Ann Cook; ill. by Quentin Blake. Bowmar, 1973. ISBN 0-8372-0830-0 Subj: Buses. Monsters.

Blanchard, Arlene. *The naughty lamb* ill. by Tony Wells. Dial, 1989. ISBN 0-8037-0605-7 Subj: Animals – sheep. Behavior – hiding. Farms. Games.

Sounds my feet make ill. by Vanessa Julian-Ottie. Random House, 1989. ISBN 0-394-89648-3 Subj: Anatomy – feet. Noise, sounds.

Blanchard, Eliza. *The paper chain* (Blake, Claire)

Bland, Fabian. *see* Nesbit, Edith

Blathwayt, Benedict. *Bear's adventure* ill. by author. Knopf, 1988. ISBN 0-394-90568-7 Subj: Animals – bears.

The runaway train ill. by author. Trafalgar Square, 1996. ISBN 1-85681-077-1 Subj: Foreign lands – England. Sea and seashore. Trains.

Tangle and the firesticks ill. by author. Knopf, 1997. ISBN 0-394-98827-2 Subj: Fire. Imagination.

Tangle and the silver bird ill. by author. Knopf, 1989. ISBN 0-394-92780-X Subj: Activities – flying. Animals.

Blau, Judith. *Bunny Mitten's book* ill. by author. Random House, 1991. ISBN 0-679-81315-2 Subj: Animals – rabbits. Puppets.

Blaustein, Muriel. *Baby Mabu and Auntie Moose* ill. by author. Four Winds, 1983. ISBN 0-590-07874-7 Subj: Activities – babysitting. Behavior – misbehavior. Character traits – freedom. Family life – aunts, uncles.

Bedtime, Zachary! ill. by author. HarperCollins, 1987. ISBN 0-06-020537-7 Subj: Animals – tigers. Bedtime. Behavior – misbehavior. Family life.

Jim chimp's story ill. by author. Simon & Schuster, 1992. ISBN 0-671-74779-7 Subj: Animals – chimpanzees. Character traits – shyness. Imagination. School.

Make friends, Zachary! ill. by author. HarperCollins, 1990. ISBN 0-06-020546-6 Subj: Animals – tigers. Camps, camping. Friendship.

Play ball, Zachary! ill. by author. HarperCollins, 1988. ISBN 0-06-020544-X Subj: Family life – fathers. Sports.

Blazek, Sarah Kirwan. *An Irish Hallowe'en* ill. by James Rice. Pelican, 1999. ISBN 1-56554-413-7 Subj: Foreign lands – Ireland. Holidays – Halloween. Mythical creatures – goblins. Rhyming text.

Blech, Dietlind. *Hello Irina* ill. by author; trans. by Yaak Karsunke. Holt, 1971. Tr. of Allo Irina. ISBN 0-582-16422-2 Subj: Activities – traveling. Animals – horses, ponies.

Blegvad, Erik. *Burnie's hill: a traditional rhyme* ill. by author. Atheneum, 1977. ISBN 0-689-50070-X Subj: Cumulative tales. Foreign lands – Scotland. Nursery rhymes. Seasons.

The emperor's new clothes (Andersen, H. C. [Hans Christian])

One is for the sun (Blegvad, Lenore)

The swineherd (Andersen, H. C. [Hans Christian])

Blegvad, Lenore. *Anna Banana and me* ill. by Erik Blegvad. Atheneum, 1985. ISBN 0-689-50274-5 Subj: Character traits – bravery. Emotions – fear. Imagination.

The great hamster hunt ill. by Erik Blegvad. Harcourt, 1969. ISBN 0-15-232500-X Subj: Animals – hamsters. Pets.

Hark! Hark! The dogs do bark, and other poems about dogs ill. by Erik Blegvad. Atheneum, 1975. ISBN 0-689-50035-1 Subj: Animals – dogs. Nursery rhymes.

Mr. Jensen and cat ill. by Erik Blegvad. Harcourt, 1965. ISBN 0-15-256214-1 Subj: Animals – cats. Emotions – loneliness. Foreign lands – Denmark.

Mittens for kittens and other rhymes about cats ill. by Erik Blegvad. Atheneum, 1974. ISBN 0-689-50003-3 Subj: Animals – cats. Nursery rhymes.

Once upon a time and Grandma ill. by author. Margaret K. McElderry, 1993. ISBN 0-689-50548-5 Subj: City. Family life – grandmothers.

One is for the sun by Lenore and Erik Blegvad; ill. by Erik Blegvad. Harcourt, 1968. Subj: Counting, numbers. Rhyming text.

The parrot in the garret and other rhymes about dwellings ill. by Erik Blegvad. Atheneum, 1982. ISBN 0-689-50217-6 Subj: Birds – parakeets, parrots. Homes, houses. Poetry.

Rainy day Kate ill. by Erik Blegvad. Macmillan, 1988. ISBN 0-689-50442-X Subj: Activities – playing. Imagination. Toys – dolls. Weather – rain.

This is me ill. by Erik Blegvad. Random House, 1986. ISBN 0-394-87816-7 Subj: Anatomy. Format, unusual – board books. Rhyming text. Self-concept.

This little pig-a-wig and other rhymes about pigs ill. by Erik Blegvad. Atheneum, 1978. ISBN 0-689-50110-2 Subj: Animals – pigs. Nursery rhymes.

Bliss, Austin. *That dog Melly!* (Bliss, Corinne Demas)

Bliss, Corinne Demas. *Matthew's meadow* ill. by Ted Lewin. Harcourt, 1992. ISBN 0-15-200759-8 Subj: Birds – hawks. Nature. Seasons – fall.

That dog Melly! by Corinne Demas Bliss with Austin Bliss; photos by Corinne Demas Bliss and Jim Judkis. Hastings House, 1981. ISBN 0-8038-7217-8 Subj: Animals – dogs. Friendship. Pets.

Blizzard, Gladys S. *Come look with me: enjoying art with children.* Thomasson-Grant, 1991. ISBN 0-934738-76-9 Subj: Art.

Come look with me: world of play ill. by author. Thomasson-Grant, 1993. ISBN 1-56566-031-5 Subj: Activities – playing. Art. Games.

Blocksma, Dewey. *Easy-to-make spaceships that really fly* (Blocksma, Mary)

Blocksma, Mary. *Apple tree! Apple tree!* ill. by Sandra Cox Kalthoff. Childrens Pr., 1983. ISBN 0-516-01584-2 Subj: Seasons. Trees.

The best dressed bear ill. by Sandra Cox Kalthoff. Childrens Pr., 1984. ISBN 0-516-01585-0 Subj: Activities – dancing. Animals – bears. Clothing.

Did you hear that? ill. by Sandra Cox Kalthoff. Childrens Pr., 1983. ISBN 0-516-01581-8 Subj: Bedtime. Night. Noise, sounds.

Easy-to-make spaceships that really fly by Mary and Dewey Blocksma; ill. by Marisabina Russo. Prentice-Hall, 1983. ISBN 0-13-223180-8 Subj: Activities – making things. Space and space ships.

Grandma Dragon's birthday ill. by Sandra Cox Kalthoff. Childrens Pr., 1983. ISBN 0-516-01582-6 Subj: Birthdays.

The pup went up ill. by Sandra Cox Kalthoff. Childrens Pr., 1983. ISBN 0-516-01583-4 Subj: Animals – dogs. Imagination.

Rub-a-dub-dub: what's in the tub? ill. by Sandra Cox Kalthoff. Childrens Pr., 1984. ISBN 0-516-01586-9 Subj: Activities – bathing. Animals – dogs.

Where's that duck? ill. by Sandra Cox Kalthoff. Childrens Pr., 1985. ISBN 0-516-01587-7 Subj: Birds – ducks. Farms. Rhyming text.

Blood, Charles L. *The goat in the rug* by Charles L. Blood and Martin A. Link; ill. by Nancy Winslow Parker. Parents, 1976. ISBN 0-819-30828-5 Subj: Activities – weaving. Animals – goats. Indians of North America – Navajo.

Bloom, Becky. *Mr. Cuckoo* ill. by author. Mondo, 1998. ISBN 1-57255-626-9 Subj: Animals. Birds – cuckoos. Clocks, watches. Time.

Wolf ill. by author. Orchard, 1999. ISBN 0-531-33155-5 Subj: Activities – reading. Animals. Animals – wolves.

Bloom, Suzanne. *A family for Jamie* ill. by author. Crown, 1991. ISBN 0-517-57493-4 Subj: Adoption. Family life.

We keep a pig in the parlor ill. by author. Potter/Crown, 1988. ISBN 0-517-56829-2 Subj: Animals – pigs. Farms. Rhyming text.

Bloome, Enid. *The air we breathe!* ill. with photos. Doubleday, 1972. Subj: Ecology.

The water we drink! ill. with photos. Doubleday, 1971. ISBN 0-385-00392-7 Subj: Ecology.

Blos, Joan W. *The days before now: an autobiographical note* (Brown, Margaret Wise)

The grandpa days ill. by Emily Arnold McCully. Simon & Schuster, 1989. ISBN 0-671-64640-0 Subj: Activities – making things. Family life – grandfathers.

Hello, shoes! ill. by Ann Boyajian. Simon & Schuster, 1999. ISBN 0-689-81441-0 Subj: Behavior – losing things. Clothing – shoes. Concepts. Family life – grandfathers.

Martin's hats ill. by Marc Simont. Morrow, 1984. ISBN 0-688-02033-X Subj: Clothing – hats. Imagination.

Old Henry ill. by Stephen Gammell. Morrow, 1987. ISBN 0-688-06400-0 Subj: Behavior – indifference. Character traits – being different. Homes, houses. Rhyming text.

One very best Valentine's Day ill. by Emanuel Schongut. Little Simon, 1989. ISBN 0-671-64639-7 Subj: Holidays – Valentine's Day.

A seed, a flower, a minute, an hour ill. by Hans Poppel. Simon & Schuster, 1992. ISBN 0-671-73214-5 Subj: Poetry.

Blough, Glenn O. *Christmas trees and how they grow* ill. by Jeanne Bendick. McGraw-Hill, 1961. Subj: Holidays – Christmas. Trees.

Who lives in this meadow? ill. by Jeanne Bendick. McGraw-Hill, 1961. Subj: Animals.

Blue, Rose. *Black, black, beautiful black* ill. by Emmett Wigglesworth. Watts, 1969. Subj: Ethnic groups in the U.S. – African Americans. Zoos.

How many blocks is the world? ill. by Harold James. Watts, 1970. ISBN 0-531-01836-9 Subj: City. Concepts – size. Ethnic groups in the U.S. – African Americans. Family life. School.

I am here: Yo estoy aqui ill. by Moneta Barnett. Watts, 1971. ISBN 0-531-01943-8 Subj: Character traits – being different. Ethnic groups in the U.S. Ethnic groups in the U.S. – Puerto Rican Americans. Foreign languages. School – first day.

Blumberg, Rhoda. *Bloomers!* ill. by Mary Morgan-Vanroyen. Bradbury, 1993. ISBN 0-02-711684-0 Subj: Clothing. U.S. history.

Jumbo ill. by Jonathan Hunt. Macmillan, 1992. ISBN 0-02-711683-2 Subj: Animals – elephants. Circus. Zoos.

Blume, Judy. *The one in the middle is a green kangaroo* ill. by Irene Trivas. Macmillan, 1991. ISBN 0-02-711055-9 Subj: Family life. Self-concept.

The Pain and The Great One ill. by Irene Trivas. Bradbury, 1984. Orig. pub. in Free to be . . . you and me, McGraw-Hill, 1974. ISBN 0-02-711100-8 Subj: Family life. Sibling rivalry.

Blume, Karin. *Circus* written and ill. by Karin Blume and Brigitte Blume. Abbeville, 1996. ISBN 0-7892-0179-8 Subj: Circus. Format, unusual – board books.

My new friends written and ill. by Karin Blume and Brigitte Blume. Abbeville, 1996. ISBN 0-7892-0180-1 Subj: Anatomy – hands. Format, unusual – board books.

Blumenthal, Nancy. *Count-a-saurus* ill. by Robert Jay Kaufman. Macmillan, 1989. ISBN 0-02-749391-1 Subj: Counting, numbers. Dinosaurs. Rhyming text.

Blundell, Tony. *Beware of boys* ill. by author. Greenwillow, 1992. ISBN 0-688-10925-X Subj: Activities – cooking. Animals – wolves. Character traits – cleverness.

Joe on Sunday ill. by author. Dial, 1987. ISBN 0-8037-0446-1 Subj: Behavior. Imagination.

Bluthenthal, Diana Cain. *Matilda the moocher* ill. by author. Orchard, 1997. ISBN 0-531-33003-6 Subj: Behavior. Friendship. School.

Blutig, Eduard. *see* Gorey, Edward (St. John)

Blyler, Allison. *Finding foxes* ill. by Robert J. Blake. Putnam, 1991. ISBN 0-399-22264-2 Subj: Animals – foxes. Nature. Picture puzzles. Rhyming text.

Blyth, Alan. *Cinderella: the story of Rossini's opera* (Perrault, Charles)

Bodecker, N. M. (Nils Mogens). *Good night little one* (Kraus, Robert)

Good night Richard Rabbit (Kraus, Robert)

Hurry, hurry, Mary dear! ill. by Erik Blegvad. Margaret K. McElderry, 1998. ISBN 0-689-81770-3 Subj: Poetry. Seasons – winter.

"It's raining," said John Twaining: Danish nursery rhymes ill. by author. Atheneum, 1973. ISBN 0-689-30316-5 Subj: Foreign lands – Denmark. Humor. Nursery rhymes.

"Let's marry" said the cherry, and other nonsense poems ill. by author. Atheneum, 1974. ISBN 0-689-50004-1 Subj: Humor. Poetry.

Snowman Sniffles and other verse ill. by author. Atheneum, 1983. ISBN 0-689-50263-X Subj: Humor. Poetry. Tongue twisters.

Bodger, Joan. *Belinda's ball* ill. by Mark Thurman. Atheneum, 1981. ISBN 0-689-30836-1 Subj: Concepts.

Bodkin, Odds. *The crane wife* ill. by Gennady Spirin. Harcourt, 1998. ISBN 0-15-201407-1 Subj: Activities – weaving. Birds – cranes. Character traits – kindness to animals. Folk and fairy tales. Foreign lands – Japan.

Bodnar, Judit Z. *Tale of a tail* ill. by John Sandford. Lothrop, 1998. ISBN 0688121756 Subj: Animals – bears. Animals – foxes. Sports – fishing.

A wagonload of fish tr. and adapt. by Judit Z. Bodnar; ill. by Alexi Natchev. Lothrop, 1996. ISBN 0-688-12173-X Subj: Animals – foxes. Character traits – cleverness. Folk and fairy tales. Foreign lands – Hungary. Sports – fishing.

Bodsworth, Nan. *Monkey business* ill. by author. Dial, 1987. ISBN 0-8037-0393-7 Subj: Animals. Behavior – wishing. Imagination. Zoos.

A nice walk in the jungle ill. by author. Viking, 1990. ISBN 0-670-82476-3 Subj: Activities – walking. Foreign lands – Australia. Jungle. Reptiles – snakes.

Bodwell, Gaile. *The long day of the giants* ill. by Leon Steinmetz. McGraw-Hill, 1975. Subj: Giants. Rhyming text. Time.

Boegehold, Betty. *Bear underground* ill. by Jim Arnosky. Doubleday, 1980. ISBN 0-385-15063-6 Subj: Animals – bears. Insects. Science.

Daddy doesn't live here anymore: a book about divorce ill. by Deborah Borgo. Childrens Pr., 1985. ISBN 0-307-62480-3 Subj: Divorce. Emotions – anger. Family life.

The fight ill. by Robin Oz. Bantam, 1991. ISBN 0-553-07086-X Subj: Behavior – fighting, arguing. Rhyming text. School.

A horse called Starfire ill. by Neil Waldman. Gareth Stevens, 1998. ISBN 0-8368-1763-X Subj: Animals – horses, ponies. Indians of North America.

Hurray for Pippa! ill. by Cyndy Szekeres. Knopf, 1980. ISBN 0-394-94067-9 Subj: Behavior – talking to strangers. Imagination. Toys.

In the castle of cats ill. by Jan Brett. Dutton, 1981. ISBN 0-525-32541-7 Subj: Animals – cats. Imagination.

Pawpaw's run ill. by Christine Price. Dutton, 1968. Subj: Animals – cats. Behavior – lost. Character traits – cleverness. Emotions – love. Pets. Rhyming text.

Pippa Mouse ill. by Cyndy Szekeres. Knopf, 1973. ISBN 0-394-92671-4 Subj: Animals – mice.

Pippa pops out! ill. by Cyndy Szekeres. Knopf, 1979. ISBN 0-394-94057-1 Subj: Animals – mice.

The rainbow ribbon (Hooks, William H.)

Read-a-rebus (Hooks, William H.)

Small Deer's magic tricks ill. by Jacqueline Chwast. Coward, 1977. ISBN 0-698-30659-7 Subj: Animals – deer. Behavior – trickery.

Three to get ready ill. by Mary Chalmers. HarperCollins, 1965. ISBN 0-06-020551-2 Subj: Animals – cats. Behavior.

What the wind told ill. by Emanuel Schongut. Parents' Magazine, 1974. ISBN 0-8193-0757-2 Subj: Weather – wind.

You are much too small ill. by Valérie Michaut. Bantam, 1990. ISBN 0-553-05895-9 Subj: Animals – pigs. Family life.

Boehm, Arlene P. *Jack in search of Art* ill. by author. Roberts Rinehart, 1998. ISBN 1-57098-244-9 Subj: Animals – bears. Art. Behavior – mistakes. Museums.

Boelts, Maribeth. *Grace and Joe* ill. by Martine Gourbault. Albert Whitman, 1994. ISBN 0-8075-3019-0 Subj: Careers – postal workers. Friendship.

Little Bunny's cool tool set ill. by Kathy Parkinson. Albert Whitman, 1997. ISBN 0-8075-4584-8 Subj: Animals – rabbits. Behavior – sharing. Friendship. School. Tools.

Little Bunny's pacifier plan ill. by Kathy Parkinson. Albert Whitman, 1999. ISBN 0-8075-4581-3 Subj: Animals – rabbits. Behavior – growing up.

Little Bunny's preschool countdown ill. by Kathy Parkinson. Albert Whitman, 1996. ISBN 0-8075-4582-1 Subj: Animals – rabbits. Behavior – worrying. School – first day. Seasons – summer.

Summer's end ill. by Ellen Kandoian. Houghton Mifflin, 1995. ISBN 0-395-70559-2 Subj: School. Seasons – summer.

Boesel, Ann Sterling. *Sing and sing again* ill. by Louise Costello. Oxford Univ. Pr., 1938. Subj: Music. Songs.

Singing with Peter and Patsy ill. by Pelagie Doane. Oxford Univ. Pr., 1944. Subj: Music. Songs.

Boesky, Amy. *Planet Was* ill. by Nadine Bernard Westcott. Little, 1990. ISBN 0-316-10084-6 Subj: Rhyming text. Royalty – princes.

Bofill, Francesc. *Jack and the beanstalk / Juan y los frijoles magicos* (Jack and the beanstalk)

Bogacki, Tomasz. *Cat and mouse in the night* ill. by author. Farrar, 1998. ISBN 0-374-31190-0 Subj: Animals – cats. Animals – mice. Night.

Cat and mouse in the snow ill. by author. Farrar, 1999. ISBN 0-374-31192-7 Subj: Activities – playing. Animals – cats. Animals – mice. Weather – snow.

I hate you! I like you! ill. by author. Farrar, 1997. ISBN 0-374-33544-3 Subj: Animals. Emotions.

Bogart, Jo Ellen. *Daniel's dog* ill. by Janet Wilson. Scholastic, 1990. ISBN 0-590-43402-0 Subj: Babies. Ethnic groups in the U.S. – African Americans. Family life – brothers and sisters. Family life – new sibling. Imagination – imaginary friends.

Jeremiah learns to read ill. by Laura Fernandez and Rick Jacobson. Orchard, 1999. ISBN 0-531-33190-3 Subj: Activities – reading. Family life. Old age. School.

Boggiss, Lisa. *Maisy at the farm* (Cousins, Lucy)

Bognomo, Joel Eboueme. *Madoulina* ill. by author. Boyds Mills, 1999. ISBN 1-56397-769-9 Subj: Careers – teachers. Foreign lands – Cameroon. School.

Bogot, Howard. *I'm growing* by Howard Bogot and Daniel B. Syme; ill. by Janet Compere. UAHC Pr., 1982. ISBN 0-8074-0167-6 Subj: Behavior – growing up. Jewish culture.

Bograd, Larry. *Egon* ill. by Dirk Zimmer. Macmillan, 1980. ISBN 0-02-710970-4 Subj: Animals. Character traits – curiosity.

Felix in the attic ill. by Dirk Zimmer. Harvey House, 1978. ISBN 0-8178-5917-9 Subj: Family life.

Lost in the store ill. by Victoria Chess. Macmillan, 1981. ISBN 0-02-710980-1 Subj: Behavior – lost. Stores.

Bohanon, Paul. *Golden Kate* ill. by Gertrude Howe. Oxford Univ. Pr., 1943. Subj: Character traits – generosity. Farms.

Bohdal, Susi. *Bobby the bear* ill. by author. Holt, 1986. ISBN 0-03-008028-2 Subj: Format, unusual – board books. Friendship. Toys – bears.

Harry the hare ill. by author. Holt, 1986. ISBN 0-03-008029-0 Subj: Format, unusual – board books. Toys.

The magic honey jar trans. by Anthea Bell; ill. by author. North-South, 1987. ISBN 0-8050-0491-2 Subj: Behavior – greed. Dreams. Royalty.

1,2,3, what do you see? an animal counting book ill. by author. North-South, 1997. ISBN 1-55858-647-4 Subj: Animals. Counting, numbers. Gifts.

Tom cat ill. by author. Doubleday, 1977. ISBN 0-385-13612-9 Subj: Animals. Animals – cats. Communication.

Bohman, Nils Axel Erik. *Jim, Jock and Jumbo* ill. by Einar Norelius. Dutton, 1946. Subj: Animals – elephants. Animals – hippopotamuses. Animals – lions. Humor.

Boholm-Olsson, Eva. *Tuan* trans. by Dianne Jonasson; ill. by Pham van Don. Farrar, 1988. ISBN 91-29-58766-2 Subj: Family life. Foreign lands – Vietnam.

Bois, Ivy Du. *see* DuBois, Ivy

Bois, William Pène Du. *see* Du Bois, William Pène

Boland, Janice. *Annabel* ill. by Megan Halsey. Dial, 1993. ISBN 0-8037-1255-3 Subj: Animals – pigs. Character traits – individuality.

Annabel again ill. by Megan Halsey. Dial, 1995. ISBN 0-8037-1757-1 Subj: Animals – pigs. Homes, houses.

A dog named Sam ill. by G. Brian Karas. Dial, 1996. ISBN 0-8037-1531-5 Subj: Animals – dogs. Behavior – misbehavior.

Bolliger, Max. *The fireflies* tr. and adapt. by Roseanna Hoover; ill. by Jiri Trnka. Atheneum, 1970. Based on a Czechoslovakian story: Broučci, by Jan Karafiát, first published in 1875; translated by Roseanna Hoover. Subj: Family life. Folk and fairy tales. Foreign lands – Czechoslovakia. Insects – fireflies. Night.

The giants' feast ill. by Monica Laimgruber. Addison-Wesley, 1976. Translation of Das Reisenfest; English version by Barbara Willard. ISBN 0-241-89255-4 Subj: Food. Giants.

The golden apple ill. by Celestino Piatti; trans. by Roseanna Hoover. Atheneum, 1970. Subj: Behavior – greed. Family life. Food.

The lonely prince ill. by Jürg Obrist. Atheneum, 1982. ISBN 0-689-50215-X Subj: Emotions – loneliness. Friendship.

The magic bird ill. by Jan Lenica. David & Charles, 1988. ISBN 0-86264-146-2 Subj: Behavior – growing up. Character traits – kindness to animals. Giants.

The most beautiful song ill. by Jindra Capek. Little, 1981. ISBN 0-316-10117-6 Subj: Music. Royalty.

Noah and the rainbow: an ancient story trans. by Clyde Robert Bulla; ill. by Helga Aichinger. Crowell, 1972. ISBN 0-698-58449-0 Subj: Animals. Boats, ships. Religion – Noah. Weather – floods. Weather – rain. Weather – rainbows.

The rabbit with the sky blue ears ill. by Jürg Obrist. David & Charles, 1989. ISBN 0-86241-204-8 Subj: Anatomy – ears. Animals – rabbits. Self-concept.

Sandy at the children's zoo trans. from German by Elisabeth Gemming; ill. by Klaus Brunner. Crowell, 1967. ISBN 0-690-71956-6 Subj: Behavior – lost. Zoos.

The wooden man ill. by Fred Bauer. Seabury Pr., 1974. Translation of Der Mann aus Holz. ISBN 0-816-43129-9 Subj: Scarecrows. Weapons. Weather.

Bolognese, Don. *Donkey and Carlo* (Raphael, Elaine)

Donkey, it's snowing (Raphael, Elaine)

A new day ill. by author. Delacorte, 1970. Subj: Activities – traveling. Babies. Ethnic groups in the U.S. – Mexican Americans. Family life. Holidays – Christmas. Religion – Nativity.

The sleepy watchdog (Bolognese, Elaine)

Turnabout (Raphael, Elaine)

Bolognese, Elaine. *The sleepy watchdog* by Elaine and Don Bolognese; ill. by Don Bolognese. Lothrop, 1964. Subj: Animals – dogs. Character traits – laziness.

Bolton, Evelyn. *see* Bunting, Eve (Anne Evelyn)

Bond, Felicia. *Christmas in the chicken coop* ill. by author. Crowell, 1983. ISBN 0-690-04333-3 Subj: Birds – chickens. Holidays – Christmas. Trees.

Four Valentines in a rainstorm ill. by author. Crowell, 1983. ISBN 0-690-04307-4 Subj: Friendship. Holidays – Valentine's Day.

The Halloween performance ill. by author. Crowell, 1983. ISBN 0-690-04309-0 Subj: Animals – mice. Holidays – Halloween. School.

The Halloween play ill. by author. HarperCollins, 1999. ISBN 0-06-028684-9 Subj: Animals – mice. Holidays – Halloween. School. Theater.

Mary Betty Lizzie McNutt's birthday ill. by author. Crowell, 1983. ISBN 0-690-04256-6 Subj: Animals – pigs. Birthdays.

Poinsettia and her family ill. by author. Harper-Collins, 1981. ISBN 0-690-04145-4 Subj: Animals – pigs. Behavior. Family life. Moving. Sibling rivalry.

Poinsettia and the firefighters ill. by author. Crowell, 1984. ISBN 0-690-04400-3 Subj: Animals – pigs. Bedtime. Night. Noise, sounds.

Tumble bumble ill. by author. Front Street, 1996. ISBN 1-886910-15-4 Subj: Animals. Counting, numbers. Insects. Rhyming text.

Wake up, Vladimir ill. by author. Crowell, 1987. ISBN 0-690-04453-4 Subj: Animals – groundhogs. Behavior – running away. Dreams. Shadows.

Bond, Jean Carey. *A is for Africa* ill. by author. Watts, 1969. Subj: ABC books. Foreign lands – Africa.

Bond, Michael. *Paddington and the knickerbocker rainbow* ill. by David McKee. Putnam, 1985. ISBN 0-399-21202-7 Subj: Animals – bears. Food. Foreign lands – England. Language.

Paddington at the circus by Michael Bond and Fred Banbery; ill. by Fred Banbery. Random House, 1973. ISBN 0-394-92918-7 Subj: Animals – bears. Circus. Foreign lands – England.

Paddington at the fair ill. by David McKee. Putnam, 1986. ISBN 0-399-21271-X Subj: Animals – bears. Fairs. Foreign lands – England.

Paddington at the palace ill. by David McKee. Putnam, 1986. ISBN 0-399-21340-6 Subj: Animals – bears. Foreign lands – England. Royalty.

Paddington at the seaside ill. by Fred Banbery. Random House, 1975. ISBN 0-394-93801-1 Subj: Activities – vacationing. Animals – bears. Foreign lands – England. Sea and seashore.

Paddington at the tower ill. by Fred Banbery. Random House, 1975. ISBN 0-394-93802-X Subj: Animals – bears. Foreign lands – England.

Paddington at the zoo ill. by David McKee. Putnam, 1985. ISBN 0-399-21201-9 Subj: Animals – bears. Behavior – losing things. Foreign lands – England. Zoos.

Paddington Bear ill. by R. W. Alley. HarperCollins, 1998. ISBN 0-06-027854-4 Subj: Animals – bears.

Paddington Bear ill. by John Lobban. Harper-Collins, 1992. ISBN 0-694-00394-8 Subj: Animals – bears. Family life. Foreign lands – England.

Paddington Bear and the Busy Bee Carnival ill. by R. W. Alley. HarperCollins, 1998. ISBN 0-06-027765-3 Subj: Animals – bears. Contests. Fairs.

Paddington Bear and the Christmas surprise ill. by R. W. Alley. HarperCollins, 1997. ISBN 0-694-00897-4 Subj: Animals – bears. Careers. Holidays – Christmas. Stores.

Paddington cleans up ill. by David McKee. Putnam, 1986. ISBN 0-399-21339-2 Subj: Activities – working. Animals – bears. Foreign lands – England.

Paddington's ABC ill. by John Lobban. Viking, 1991. ISBN 0-670-84104-8 Subj: ABC books. Animals – bears.

Paddington's art exhibit ill. by David McKee. Putnam, 1986. ISBN 0-399-21270-1 Subj: Activities – painting. Animals – bears. Art. Foreign lands – England.

Paddington's colors ill. by John Lobban. Viking, 1991. ISBN 0-670-84102-1 Subj: Animals – bears. Concepts – color.

Paddington's garden ill. by Fred Banbery. Random House, 1973. ISBN 0-394-92643-9 Subj: Animals – bears. Family life. Foreign lands – England. Gardens, gardening.

Paddington's lucky day ill. by Fred Banbery. Random House, 1974, c1973. ISBN 0-394-92919-5 Subj: Animals – bears. Character traits – luck. Foreign lands – England. Shopping.

Paddington's 1 2 3 ill. by John Lobban. Viking, 1991. ISBN 0-670-84103-X Subj: Animals – bears. Counting, numbers.

Paddington's opposites ill. by John Lobban. Viking, 1991. ISBN 0-670-84105-6 Subj: Animals – bears. Concepts – opposites.

Bond, Rebecca. *Just like a baby* ill. by author. Little, 1999. ISBN 0-316-10416-7 Subj: Babies. Cumulative tales. Family life. Furniture – cradles.

Bond, Ruskin. *Cherry tree* ill. by Allan Eitzen. Boyds Mills, 1991. ISBN 1-878093-21-5 Subj: Family life – grandfathers. Foreign lands – India. Trees.

Flames in the forest ill. by Valerie Littlewood. Watts, 1981. ISBN 0-531-04282-0 Subj: Fire. Foreign lands – India. Forest, woods.

Bonfils, Bolette. *Peter joins the circus* ill. by Jan Mogensen. Crocodile Books, 1994. ISBN 1-56656-154-X Subj: Animals. Animals – rabbits. Circus. Format, unusual – toy and movable books.

Bonino, Louise. *The cozy little farm* ill. by Angelia Straeter. Random House, 1946. Subj: Animals. Farms.

Bonne, Rose. *I know an old lady* (Little old lady who swallowed a fly)

I know an old lady who swallowed a fly (Little old lady who swallowed a fly)

Bonners, Susan. *Hunter in the snow: the lynx* ill. by author. Little, 1994. ISBN 0-316-10201-6 Subj: Animals – lynx. Science.

Just in passing ill. by author. Lothrop, 1989. ISBN 0-688-07712-9 Subj: Circular tales. Wordless.

Why does the cat do that? ill. by author. Holt, 1998. ISBN 0-8050-4377-2 Subj: Animals – cats. Behavior.

The wooden doll ill. by author. Lothrop, 1991. ISBN 0-688-08282-3 Subj: Family life – grandparents. Toys – dolls.

Bonnici, Peter. *The festival* ill. by Lisa Kopper. Carolrhoda, 1985. ISBN 0-87614-229-3 Subj: Behavior – growing up. Foreign lands – India. Holidays.

The first rains ill. by Lisa Kopper. Carolrhoda, 1985. ISBN 0-87614-228-5 Subj: Weather – rain.

Bonning, Tony. *Another fine mess* ill. by Sally Hobson. Little Tiger, 1998. ISBN 1-888444-43-6 Subj: Animals. Animals – foxes. Character traits – cleanliness. Circular tales.

Bonsall, Crosby Newell. *The amazing the incredible super dog* ill. by author. HarperCollins, 1986. ISBN 0-06-020591-1 Subj: Animals – cats. Animals – dogs. Behavior – boasting.

And I mean it, Stanley ill. by author. HarperCollins, 1974. ISBN 0-06-020568-7 Subj: Activities – playing. Animals – dogs.

The day I had to play with my sister ill. by author. HarperCollins, 1972. ISBN 0-06-020576-8 Subj: Family life. Games.

I'll show you cats (Ylla)

It's mine! A greedy book ill. by author. HarperCollins, 1964. ISBN 0-06-020586-5 Subj: Behavior – greed. Friendship.

Listen, listen! by Crosby Newell Bonsall and Ylla; photos by Ylla. HarperCollins, 1961. Subj: Animals – cats. Animals – dogs. Character traits – appearance.

Look who's talking (Ylla)

Mine's the best ill. by author. HarperCollins, 1973. ISBN 0-06-020578-4 Subj: Behavior – boasting. Sea and seashore. Toys – balloons.

Polar bear brothers (Ylla)

Who's afraid of the dark? ill. by author. HarperCollins, 1980. ISBN 0-06-020598-9 Subj: Animals – dogs. Emotions – fear. Night.

Bontemps, Arna Wendell. *The fast sooner hound* by Arna Wendell Bontemps and Jack Conroy; ill. by Virginia Lee Burton. Houghton Mifflin, 1942. ISBN 0-395-18657-9 Subj: Animals – dogs. Trains.

Boojum. *see* Barrows, Marjorie Wescott

Bookman, Charlotte. *see* Zolotow, Charlotte (Shapiro)

Boon, Debbie. *My gran* ill. by author. Millbrook, 1998. ISBN 0-7613-0312-X Subj: Family life – grandmothers. Rhyming text.

Boon, Emilie. *Belinda's balloon* ill. by author. Knopf, 1985. ISBN 0-394-97342-9 Subj: Animals – bears. Family life. Toys – balloons.

It's spring, Peterkin ill. by author. Random House, 1986. ISBN 0-394-87997-X Subj: Character traits – kindness to animals. Format, unusual – board books. Seasons – spring.

1 2 3 how many animals can you see? ill. by author. Random House, 1987. ISBN 0-531-08301-2 Subj: Animals. Counting, numbers. School.

Peterkin meets a star ill. by author. Random House, 1984. ISBN 0-394-96284-2 Subj: Imagination. Stars.

Peterkin's very own garden ill. by author. Random House, 1987. ISBN 0-394-88666-6 Subj: Animals. Format, unusual – board books. Gardens, gardening.

Peterkin's wet walk ill. by author. Random House, 1984. ISBN 0-394-96285-0 Subj: Animals. Imagination. Weather – rain.

Booth, David. *The dust bowl* ill. by author. Kids Can Pr., 1997. ISBN 1-55074-295-7 Subj: Careers – farmers. Family life. Foreign lands – Canada. Weather – droughts.

Booth, Eugene. *At the circus* ill. by Derek Collard. Raintree, 1977. ISBN 0-8393-0112-X Subj: Circus. Concepts. Games. Participation. Problem solving.

At the fair ill. by Derek Collard. Raintree, 1977. ISBN 0-8393-0114-6 Subj: Concepts. Fairs. Games. Participation. Problem solving.

In the air ill. by Derek Collard. Raintree, 1977. ISBN 0-8393-0105-7 Subj: Concepts. Games. Participation. Problem solving.

In the garden ill. by Derek Collard. Raintree, 1977. ISBN 0-8393-0115-4 Subj: Concepts. Games. Participation. Problem solving.

In the jungle ill. by Derek Collard. Raintree, 1977. ISBN 0-8393-0104-9 Subj: Concepts. Games. Jungle. Participation. Problem solving.

Under the ocean ill. by Derek Collard. Raintree, 1977. ISBN 0-8393-0108-1 Subj: Concepts. Games. Participation. Problem solving. Sea and seashore.

Borack, Barbara. *Grandpa* ill. by Ben Shecter. HarperCollins, 1967. Subj: Family life – grandfathers.

Borchers, Elisabeth. *Dear Sarah* tr. and adapt. from German by Elizabeth Shub; ill. by Wilhelm Schlote. Greenwillow, 1980. ISBN 0-688-84277-1 Subj: Activities – traveling. Communication. Foreign lands.

There comes a time trans. by Babette Deutsch; ill. by Dietlind Blech. Doubleday, 1969. Subj: Days of the week, months of the year. Poetry. Royalty – kings.

Borden, Beatrice Brown. *Wild animals of Africa* photos by author. Random House, 1982. ISBN 0-394-95306-1 Subj: Animals. Birds. Foreign lands – Africa.

Borden, Louise. *A. Lincoln and me* ill. by Ted Lewin. Scholastic, 2000. ISBN 0-590-45714-4 Subj: Birthdays. Self-concept. U.S. history.

Albie the lifeguard ill. by Elizabeth Sayles. Scholastic, 1993. ISBN 0-590-44585-5 Subj: Behavior – growing up. Careers – lifeguards. Sports – swimming.

Caps, hats, socks and mittens ill. by Lillian Hoban. Scholastic, 1989. ISBN 0-590-41257-4 Subj: Clothing. Seasons.

Goodbye, Charles Lindbergh: based on a true story ill. by Thomas B. Allen. Margaret K. McElderry, 1998. ISBN 0-689-81536-0 Subj: Activities – flying. Careers – airplane pilots. U.S. history.

Thanksgiving is . . . ill. by Steve Björkman. Scholastic, 1997. ISBN 0-590-33128-0 Subj: Holidays – Thanksgiving.

The watching game ill. by Teri Weidner. Scholastic, 1991. ISBN 0-590-43600-7 Subj: Country. Family life – grandmothers. Seasons.

Borg, Inga. *Plupp builds a house* ill. by author. Warne, 1961. Subj: Animals. Foreign lands – Lapland. Homes, houses.

Borlenghi, Patricia. *From albatross to zoo* ill. by Piers Harper. Scholastic, 1992. ISBN 0-590-45483-8 Subj: ABC books. Animals. Foreign languages.

Bornstein, Ruth Lercher. *Annabelle* ill. by author. Crowell, 1978. ISBN 0-690-03810-0 Subj: Behavior – lost. Toys.

A beautiful seashell ill. by author. HarperCollins, 1990. ISBN 0-06-020595-4 Subj: Family life – great-grandparents. Sea and seashore.

The dancing man ill. by author. Seabury Pr., 1978. ISBN 0-8164-3214-7 Subj: Activities – dancing. Foreign lands – Europe.

I'll draw a meadow ill. by author. HarperCollins, 1979. ISBN 0-06-020613-6 Subj: Activities – vacationing. Animals – dogs.

Indian bunny ill. by author. Childrens Pr., 1973. ISBN 0-516-08723-1 Subj: Animals – rabbits. Indians of North America.

Jim ill. by author. Seabury Pr., 1978. ISBN 0-8164-3204-X Subj: Animals – dogs. Behavior – lost. Character traits – bravery.

Of course a goat ill. by author. HarperCollins, 1980. ISBN 0-06-020609-8 Subj: Animals – goats. Family life.

Rabbit's good news ill. by author. Clarion, 1995. ISBN 0-395-68700-4 Subj: Animals – rabbits. Nature. Seasons – spring.

The seedling child ill. by author. Harcourt, 1987. ISBN 0-15-272459-1 Subj: Friendship. Imagination – imaginary friends. Rhyming text.

That's how it is when we draw ill. by author. Clarion, 1997. ISBN 0-395-82509-1 Subj: Activities – drawing. Art. Poetry.

Borovsky, Paul. *The fish that wasn't* ill. by author. Hyperion, 1994. ISBN 1-56282-582-8 Subj: Animals – whales. Birthdays. Fish. Pets.

Nico ill. by author. Hyperion, 1993. ISBN 0-517-58855-2 Subj: Animals – monkeys. Behavior – greed. Character traits – helpfulness.

Borten, Helen. *Do you go where I go?* ill. by author. Abelard-Schuman, 1972. Subj: Humor. Rhyming text.

Do you hear what I hear? ill. by author. Abelard-Schuman, 1960. Subj: Noise, sounds. Rhyming text. Senses – hearing.

Do you know what I know? ill. by author. Abelard-Schuman, 1970. ISBN 0-20-071695-6 Subj: Rhyming text. Senses – hearing. Senses – seeing. Senses – smelling. Senses – tasting. Senses – touching.

Do you move as I do? ill. by author. Abelard-Schuman, 1963. Subj: Emotions. Health and fitness.

Do you see what I see? ill. by author. Abelard-Schuman, 1959. Subj: Art. Concepts. Senses – seeing.

Halloween ill. by author. Crowell, 1965. ISBN 0-690-36314-1 Subj: Holidays – Halloween.

A picture has a special look ill. by author. Abelard-Schuman, 1961. Subj: Art.

Borton, Lady. *Fat chance!* ill. by Deborah Kogan Ray. Putnam, 1993. ISBN 0-399-21963-3 Subj: Animals – cats. Farms. Illness.

Junk pile! ill. by Kimberly Bulcken Root. Philomel, 1997. ISBN 0-399-22728-8 Subj: Friendship. Handicaps.

Bos, Burny. *Meet the Molesons* ill. by Hans de Beer; trans. by J. Alison James. North-South, 1994. ISBN 1-55858-258-4 Subj: Animals – moles. Family life. Multiple births – twins.

Ollie the elephant ill. by Hans de Beer. North-South, 1989. ISBN 1-55858-012-3 Subj: Animals – elephants. Behavior – wishing. Family life.

Prince Valentino ill. by Hans de Beer. North-South, 1990. ISBN 1-55858-089-1 Subj: Birds – storks. Friendship. Frogs and toads.

Bos, Claire. *Maurice the hippo* by Claire and Maarten Bos; ill. by authors. Orchard, 1998. ISBN 0-531-30098-6 Subj: Animals – hippopotamuses. Format, unusual – board books. Rhyming text.

Webster's wardrobe by Claire and Maarten Bos; ill. by authors. Orchard, 1998. ISBN 0-531-30097-8 Subj: Animals – seals. Clothing. Format, unusual – board books. Rhyming text.

Bos, Maarten. *Maurice the hippo* (Bos, Claire)

Webster's wardrobe (Bos, Claire)

Bosak, Susan V. *Something to remember me by* ill. by author. Communication Project, 1999. ISBN 1-896232-01-9 Subj: Family life – grandparents. Old age.

Bossom, Naomi. *A scale full of fish and other turnabouts* ill. by author. Greenwillow, 1979. ISBN 0-688-84203-8 Subj: Humor. Language.

Boston. Children's Hospital Medical Center. *Curious George goes to the hospital* (Rey, Margret [Margret Elisabeth Waldstein])

Boswell, Stephen. *King Gorboduc's fabulous zoo* ill. by Beverley Gooding. Dutton, 1986. ISBN 0-525-44267-7 Subj: Dragons. Royalty – kings. Zoos.

Botel, Morton. *Sad Mrs. Sam Sack* (Brothers, Aileen)

Bothwell, Jean. *Paddy and Sam* ill. by Margaret Ayer. Abelard-Schuman, 1952. Subj: Behavior – lost. Birds – ducks.

Bottner, Barbara. *Big boss! Little boss!* ill. by author. Pantheon, 1978. ISBN 0-394-93939-5 Subj: Behavior – losing things. Sibling rivalry.

Bootsie Barker bites ill. by Peggy Rathmann. Putnam, 1992. ISBN 0-399-22125-5 Subj: Activities – playing. Behavior – bullying.

Horrible Hannah ill. by Joan E. Drescher. Crown, 1980. ISBN 0-517-53973-X Subj: Animals – dogs. Friendship. Moving.

Jungle day: or, How I learned to love my nosey little brother ill. by author. Delacorte, 1978. ISBN 0-440-04384-0 Subj: Sibling rivalry.

Mean Maxine ill. by author. Pantheon, 1980. ISBN 0-394-94219-1 Subj: Character traits – meanness. Friendship. Imagination.

Messy ill. by author. Delacorte, 1979. ISBN 0-440-05493-1 Subj: Activities – dancing. Behavior – carelessness.

Myra ill. by author. Macmillan, 1979. ISBN 0-02-711740-5 Subj: Activities – dancing. Imagination.

Nana Hannah's piano ill. by Diana Cain Bluthenthal. Putnam, 1996. ISBN 0-399-22656-7 Subj: Family life – grandmothers. Music. Sports – baseball.

There was nobody there ill. by author. Macmillan, 1978. ISBN 0-02-711000-1 Subj: Bedtime. Imagination. Rhyming text. Sleep.

Zoo song ill. by Lynn Munsinger. Scholastic, 1987. ISBN 0-590-41005-9 Subj: Animals. Music. Zoos.

Botwin, Esther. *A treasury of songs for little children* ill. by Evelyn Urbanowich. Hart, 1954. Subj: Music. Songs.

Bouchard, Dave. *Prairie born* ill. by Peter Shostak. Orca, 1997. ISBN 1-55143-092-4 Subj: Foreign lands – Canada. Poetry.

Boucher, Jerry. *Fire truck nuts and bolts* photos by author. Carolrhoda, 1993. ISBN 0-87614-783-X Subj: Activities – making things. Careers – firefighters. Trucks.

Bouhuys, Mies. *The lady of Stavoren: a story from Holland* ill. by Francien Van Westering. Penguin, 1979. ISBN 0-14-030802-4 Subj: Folk and fairy tales. Foreign lands – Holland.

Boujon, Claude. *The fairy with the long nose* ill. by author. Macmillan, 1987. ISBN 0-689-50424-1 Subj: Anatomy – noses. Fairies. Magic.

Boulton, Jane. *Only Opal: the diary of a young girl* (Whiteley, Opal Stanley)

Bour, Danièle. *The house from morning to night* ill. by author. Kane, 1985. ISBN 0-916291-01-4 Subj: Homes, houses.

Bourgeois, Paulette. *Big Sarah's little boots* ill. by Brenda Clark. Scholastic, 1987. ISBN 0-590-42622-2 Subj: Behavior – growing up. Clothing – shoes. Family life. Weather – rain.

Fire fighters ill. by Kim LaFave. Kids Can Pr., 1998. ISBN 1-55074-438-0 Subj: Careers – firefighters. Communities, neighborhoods.

Franklin and the thunderstorm ill. by Brenda Clark. Scholastic, 1998. ISBN 0-590-02635-6 Subj: Animals. Emotions – fear. Reptiles – turtles, tortoises. Weather – storms. Weather – thunder.

Franklin in the dark ill. by Brenda Clark. Kids Can Pr., 1986. ISBN 0-919964-93-1 Subj: Emotions – fear. Night. Reptiles – turtles, tortoises.

Franklin rides a bike ill. by Brenda Clark. Kids Can Pr., 1997. ISBN 1-55074-414-3 Subj: Animals. Reptiles – turtles, tortoises. Sports – bicycling.

Franklin's Christmas gift ill. by Brenda Clark. Kids Can Pr., 1998. ISBN 1-55074-466-6 Subj: Gifts. Holidays – Christmas. Reptiles – turtles, tortoises.

Franklin's class trip by Paulette Bourgeois and Sharon Jennings; ill. by Brenda Clark. Kids Can Pr., 1999. ISBN 1-55074-470-4 Subj: Animals. Dinosaurs. Museums. Reptiles – turtles, tortoises. School.

Franklin's new friend ill. by Brenda Clark. Scholastic, 1997. ISBN 0-590-02592-9 Subj: Animals – moose. Friendship. Reptiles – turtles, tortoises.

Franklin's secret club ill. by Brenda Clark. Kids Can Pr., 1998. ISBN 0-59013-000-5 Subj: Animals. Clubs, gangs. Friendship. Reptiles – turtles, tortoises.

Garbage collectors ill. by Kim LaFave. Kids Can Pr., 1998. ISBN 1-55074-440-2 Subj: Careers – sanitation workers. Communities, neighborhoods.

Police officers ill. by Kim LaFave. Kids Can Pr., 1999. ISBN 1-55074-502-6 Subj: Careers – police officers. Communities, neighborhoods.

Postal workers ill. by Kim LaFave. Kids Can Pr., 1998. ISBN 1-55074-504-2 Subj: Birthdays. Careers – postal workers. Communities, neighborhoods.

Too many chickens ill. by Bill Slavin. Little, 1991. ISBN 0-316-10358-6 Subj: Animals. Birds – chickens. School.

Bourguignon, Laurence. *A friend for Tiger* ill. by Laurence Henno. BridgeWater, 1994. ISBN 0-8167-3907-2 Subj: Animals – rabbits. Animals – tigers. Circus. Friendship.

Bourke, Linda. *Ethel's exceptional egg* ill. by author. Harvey House, 1977. ISBN 0-817-85622-6 Subj: Birds – chickens. Eggs. Fairs.

Eye count: a book of counting puzzles ill. by author. Chronicle, 1995. ISBN 0-8118-0732-0 Subj: ABC books. Counting, numbers. Language. Puzzles.

Boutell, Clarence Burley. *The fat baron* ill. by Frank Lieberman. Houghton Mifflin, 1946. Subj: Food. Imagination. Knights.

Bouton, Josephine. *Favorite poems for the children's hour* ill. by Bonnie and Bill Rutherford; foreword by Carolyn Sherwin Bailey. Platt, 1967. Subj: Poetry.

Boutwell, Edna. *Red rooster* ill. by Bernard Garbutt. Atheneum, 1950. Subj: Birds – chickens. Cumulative tales. Folk and fairy tales.

Bove, Linda. *Sign language ABC with Linda Bove* ill. by Tom Cooke. Random House, 1985. ISBN 0-394-97516-2 Subj: ABC books. Handicaps – deafness. Language. Senses – hearing.

Bowden, Joan Chase. *The bear's surprise party* ill. by Jerry Scott. Golden Pr., 1975. ISBN 0-307-60809-3 Subj: Animals – bears. Parties.

Boo and the flying flews ill. by Don Leake. Western, 1974. Subj: Animals – dogs. Circus.

The bouncy baby bunny ill. by Patience Brewster. Golden Books, 1999. ISBN 0-307-10217-3 Subj: Animals – rabbits. Family life.

Bouncy baby bunny finds his bed ill. by Christine Westerberg. Western, 1977. ISBN 0-307-60029-7 Subj: Animals – rabbits. Bedtime.

Emilio's summer day ill. by Ben Shecter. HarperCollins, 1966. Subj: City. Ethnic groups in the U.S. – Puerto Rican Americans. Seasons – summer.

The Ginghams and the backward picnic ill. by Joane Koenig. Western, 1979. ISBN 0-307-60148-X Subj: Activities – picnicking.

A hat for the queen ill. by Olindo Giacomini. Golden Pr., 1974. Subj: Clothing – hats. Royalty – queens.

Little grey rabbit ill. by Lorinda Bryan Cauley. Western, 1979. ISBN 0-307-68651-5 Subj: Animals – rabbits.

A new home for Snow Ball ill. by Jan Pyk. Western, 1979. ISBN 0-307-60800-X Subj: Animals – horses, ponies. Royalty.

Strong John ill. by Sal Murdocca. Macmillan, 1980. ISBN 0-02-711790-1 Subj: Behavior – trickery. Folk and fairy tales.

Who took the top hat trick? ill. by Jim Cummins. Golden Pr., 1974. Subj: Behavior – losing things. Magic.

Bowden, Miriam. *The adventure of Paz in the land of numbers* ill. by Anna-Maria Crum. Humanics, 1992. ISBN 0-89334-450-9 Subj: Animals. Animals – koalas. Counting, numbers. Foreign languages.

Bowdish, Lynea. *The carousel ride* ill. by Patrick Girouard. Childrens Pr., 1998. ISBN 0-516-20967-1 Subj: Imagination. Merry-go-rounds.

Bowen, Betsy. *Antler, bear, canoe* ill. by author. Little, 1991. ISBN 0-316-10376-4 Subj: ABC books. Forest, woods. Nature. Seasons.

Tracks in the wild ill. by author. Houghton Mifflin, 1998. ISBN 0-316-10377-2 Subj: Animals. Forest, woods. Nature.

Bowen, Keith. *Katy's gift* ill. by author; words by Dan Gutman. Courage Books, 1998. ISBN 0-7624-0169-9 Subj: Character traits – individuality. Ethnic groups in the U.S. – African Americans. Family life. Friendship.

Bowen, Vernon. *The lazy beaver* ill. by Jim Davis. McKay, 1948. Subj: Animals – beavers. Character traits – laziness.

Bowers, Kathleen Rice. *At this very minute* ill. by Linda Shute. Little, 1983. ISBN 0-316-10400-0 Subj: Bedtime. Imagination.

Bowie, C. W. *Busy toes* ill. by Fred Willingham. Whispering Coyote, 1998. ISBN 1-879085-72-0 Subj: Activities. Anatomy – toes. Rhyming text.

Bowles, Brad. *Grandma's band* ill. by Anthony Chan. Stemmer House, 1989. ISBN 0-88045-112-2 Subj: Family life – grandmothers. Music.

Bowling, David Louis. *Dirty Dingy Daryl* ill. by Patricia Hendy Bowling. Inka Dinka Ink, 1981. ISBN 0-939700-00-X Subj: Character traits – cleanliness.

Bowman, Peter. *The Christmas songbook* ill. by author. Putnam, 1990. ISBN 0-399-21918-8 Subj: Format, unusual – toy and movable books. Holidays – Christmas. Music. Songs.

Goodnight, teddy bear ill. by author. Kingfisher, 1995. ISBN 1-85697-552-5 Subj: Bedtime. Format, unusual – board books. Night. Nursery rhymes. Poetry. Toys – bears.

I wish I were big ill. by author. Hutchinson, 1997. ISBN 0-09-176588-9 Subj: Animals. Behavior – wishing. Concepts – size. Self-concept. Toys.

Boxer, Devorah. *26 ways to be somebody else* ill. by author. Pantheon, 1960. Subj: ABC books. Careers.

A boy went out to gather pears: *an old verse* ill. by Felix Hoffmann. Harcourt, 1966. Subj: Cumulative tales. Poetry.

Boyd, Lizi. *Baby play* ill. by author. Workman, 1992. ISBN 1-56305-310-1 Subj: Animals – cats. Babies. Format, unusual – board books. Format, unusual – toy and movable books.

Baby's journal ill. by author. Chronicle, 1995. ISBN 0-8118-0780-0 Subj: Babies.

Bailey the big bully ill. by author. Viking, 1989. ISBN 0-670-82719-3 Subj: Behavior – bullying.

Black dog red house ill. by author. Little, 1993. ISBN 0-316-10443-4 Subj: Animals – dogs. Concepts – color. Friendship.

Bunny hop ill. by author. Workman, 1992. ISBN 1-56305-308-X Subj: Animals – rabbits. Format, unusual – board books. Format, unusual – toy and movable books.

Half wild and half child ill. by author. Viking, 1988. ISBN 0-670-82072-5 Subj: Behavior – misbehavior. Character traits – willfulness.

Lulu Crow's garden ill. by author. Little, 1998. ISBN 0-316-10419-1 Subj: Animals. Birds – crows. Gardens, gardening. Rhyming text.

Mouse in a house ill. by author. Little, 1993. ISBN 0-316-10444-2 Subj: Animals – mice. Format, unusual. Homes, houses. Rhyming text.

The not-so-wicked stepmother ill. by author. Viking, 1987. ISBN 0-670-81589-6 Subj: Activities. Behavior – misunderstanding. Birds – ducks. Family life – step families.

Princess, cowboy, pirate, elf ill. by author. Hyperion, 1995. ISBN 0-7868-1059-9 Subj: Clothing – hats. Imagination. Theater.

Sam is my half brother ill. by author. Viking, 1990. ISBN 0-670-83046-1 Subj: Babies. Family life – new sibling. Family life – step families. Sibling rivalry.

Sweet dreams, Willy ill. by author. Viking, 1992. ISBN 0-670-84382-2 Subj: Bedtime. Dreams. Imagination. Night.

Willy and the cardboard boxes ill. by author. Viking, 1991. ISBN 0-670-83636-2 Subj: Activities – playing. Imagination.

Boyd, Pauline. *The how: making the best of a mistake* (Boyd, Selma)

I met a polar bear (Boyd, Selma)

Boyd, Selma. *The how: making the best of a mistake* by Selma and Pauline Boyd; ill. by Peggy Luks. Human Sciences Pr., 1981. ISBN 0-87705-076-3 Subj: Behavior – mistakes. Emotions – embarrassment. Friendship.

I met a polar bear by Selma and Pauline Boyd; ill. by Patience Brewster. Lothrop, 1983. ISBN 0-688-01885-8 Subj: Animals. Behavior – tardiness. Imagination. School.

Boyle, Constance. *Little Owl and the weed* ill. by author. Barron's, 1985. ISBN 0-8120-5639-6 Subj: Birds. Gardens, gardening.

The story of Little Owl ill. by author. Barron's, 1985. ISBN 0-8120-5638-8 Subj: Behavior – losing things. Birds – owls. Toys – bears.

Boyle, Doe. *Gray wolf pup* ill. by Jeff Domm. Soundprints Pr., 1993. ISBN 1-56899-010-3 Subj: Alaska. Animals – wolves.

Otter on his own ill. by Lisa Bonforte. Soundprints Pr., 1995. ISBN 1-56899-129-0 Subj: Animals – otters. Sea and seashore.

Summer coat, winter coat: the story of a snowshoe hare ill. by Allen Davis. Soundprints Pr., 1993. ISBN 1-56899-015-4 Subj: Animals – rabbits. Nature. Seasons.

Boyle, Vere. *Beauty and the beast* ill. by author. Barron's, 1988. ISBN 0-8120-5902-6 Subj: Character traits – appearance. Character traits – loyalty. Emotions – love. Folk and fairy tales. Magic.

Boynton, Sandra. *A is for angry* ill. by author. Workman, 1983. ISBN 0-89480-453-7 Subj: ABC books. Animals.

Barnyard dance! ill. by author. Workman, 1993. ISBN 1-56305-442-6 Subj: Activities – dancing. Animals. Farms. Format, unusual – board books.

Birthday monsters! ill. by author. Workman, 1993. ISBN 1-56305-443-4 Subj: Birthdays. Format, unusual – board books. Monsters. Rhyming text.

But not the hippopotamus ill. by author. Simon & Schuster, 1982. ISBN 0-671-44904-4 Subj: Animals – hippopotamuses. Format, unusual – board books. Rhyming text.

Chloë and Maude ill. by author. Little, 1985. ISBN 0-316-10492-2 Subj: Animals – cats. Friendship.

Dinosaur's binkit ill. by author. Little Simon, 1998. ISBN 0-689-82203-0 Subj: Bedtime. Dinosaurs. Format, unusual – board books. Format, unusual – toy and movable books. Rhyming text.

Doggies ill. by author. Simon & Schuster, 1984. ISBN 0-671-49318-3 Subj: Animals – dogs. Format, unusual – board books.

The going to bed book ill. by author. Simon & Schuster, 1982. ISBN 0-671-44902-8 Subj: Animals. Bedtime. Format, unusual – board books. Rhyming text.

Good night, good night ill. by author. Random House, 1985. ISBN 0-394-97285-6 Subj: Animals. Bedtime. Music. Rhyming text. Songs.

Hester in the wild ill. by author. HarperCollins, 1979. ISBN 0-06-020654-3 Subj: Animals – hippopotamuses. Animals – pigs. Camps, camping.

Hippos go berserk ill. by author. Little, 1979. ISBN 0-316-16488-4 Subj: Animals – hippopotamuses. Counting, numbers. Rhyming text.

Horns to toes and in between ill. by author. Simon & Schuster, 1984. ISBN 0-671-49319-1 Subj: Anatomy. Format, unusual – board books.

If at first . . . ill. by author. Little, 1980. ISBN 0-316-10487-6 Subj: Animals – elephants. Animals – mice. Character traits – perseverance. Humor.

Moo, baa, lalala ill. by author. Simon & Schuster, 1982. ISBN 0-671-44901-X Subj: Animals. Format, unusual – board books. Noise, sounds. Rhyming text.

Oh my oh my oh dinosaurs! ill. by author. Workman, 1993. ISBN 1-56305-441-8 Subj: Dinosaurs. Format, unusual – board books. Rhyming text.

One, two, three! ill. by author. Workman, 1993. ISBN 1-56305-444-2 Subj: Counting, numbers. Format, unusual – board books. Rhyming text.

Opposites ill. by author. Simon & Schuster, 1982. ISBN 0-671-44903-6 Subj: Concepts – opposites. Format, unusual – board books.

Bozylinsky, Hannah Heritage. *Lala Salama* ill. by author. Putnam, 1993. ISBN 0-399-22022-4 Subj: Animals. Bedtime. Foreign lands – Africa. Foreign languages. Lullabies.

Bozzo, Maxine Zohn. *Toby in the country, Toby in the city* ill. by Frank Modell. Greenwillow, 1982. ISBN 0-688-00917-4 Subj: City. Country.

Bradbury, Ray. *Switch on the night* ill. by Leo and Diane Dillon. Knopf, 1993. ISBN 0-394-90486-4 Subj: Emotions – fear. Friendship. Night.

Switch on the night ill. by Madeleine Gekiere. Pantheon, 1955. Subj: Emotions – fear. Friendship. Night.

Bradby, Marie. *The longest wait* ill. by Peter Catalanotto. Orchard, 1998. ISBN 0-531-08721-2 Subj: Careers – postal workers. Weather – snow. Weather – storms.

More than anything else ill. by Chris K. Soentpiet. Orchard, 1995. ISBN 0-531-08764-6 Subj: Activities – reading. Behavior – seeking better things. Ethnic groups in the U.S. – African Americans.

Bradfield, Roger (Jolly Roger). *The flying hockey stick* ill. by author. Rand McNally, 1966. Subj: Activities – flying. Humor. Machines.

Giants come in different sizes ill. by author. Rand McNally, 1966. Subj: Giants. Wizards.

A good night for dragons ill. by author. Addison-Wesley, 1967. ISBN 0-201-09201-8 Subj: Dragons. Knights.

Bradford, Ann. *The mystery at Misty Falls* by Ann Bradford and Kal Gezi; ill. by Mina Gow McLean. Childrens Pr., 1980. ISBN 0-516-06491-6 Subj: Animals – raccoons. Clubs, gangs. Mystery stories.

The mystery in the secret club house by Ann Bradford and Kal Gezi; ill. by Mina Gow McLean. Childrens Pr., 1978. ISBN 0-89565-027-4 Subj: Clubs, gangs. Crime. Mystery stories.

The mystery of the blind writer by Ann Bradford and Kal Gezi; ill. by Mina Gow McLean. Childrens Pr., 1980. ISBN 0-516-06493-2 Subj: Animals – dogs. Clubs, gangs. Crime. Handicaps – blindness. Mystery stories.

The mystery of the live ghosts by Ann Bradford and Kal Gezi; ill. by Mina Gow McLean. Childrens Pr., 1978. ISBN 0-89565-026-6 Subj: Holidays – Halloween. Mystery stories.

The mystery of the midget clown by Ann Bradford and Kal Gezi; ill. by Mina Gow McLean. Childrens Pr., 1980. ISBN 0-516-06495-9 Subj: Clowns, jesters. Clubs, gangs. Mystery stories.

The mystery of the missing dogs by Ann Bradford and Kal Gezi; ill. by Mina Gow McLean. Childrens Pr., 1980. ISBN 0-516-06492-4 Subj: Animals – dogs. Clubs, gangs. Handicaps. Mystery stories.

The mystery of the missing raccoon by Ann Bradford and Kal Gezi; ill. by Mina Gow McLean. Childrens Pr., 1978. ISBN 0-89565-025-8 Subj: Animals – raccoons. Character traits – freedom. Mystery stories.

The mystery of the square footsteps by Ann Bradford and Kal Gezi; ill. by Mina Gow McLean. Childrens Pr., 1980. ISBN 0-516-06496-7 Subj: Clubs, gangs. Mystery stories. Robots.

The mystery of the tree house by Ann Bradford and Kal Gezi; ill. by Mina Gow McLean. Childrens Pr., 1980. ISBN 0-516-06494-0 Subj: Birds – parakeets, parrots. Clubs, gangs. Crime. Mystery stories.

Bradman, Tony. *The bad babies' book of colors* ill. by Deborah Van der Beek. Knopf, 1987. ISBN 0-394-99046-3 Subj: Behavior – misbehavior. Birthdays. Concepts – color. Rhyming text.

The bad babies' counting book ill. by Deborah Van der Beek. Knopf, 1986. ISBN 0-394-98352-1 Subj: Behavior – misbehavior. Counting, numbers. Rhyming text.

A bad week for the three bears ill. by Jenny Williams. Random House, 1993. ISBN 0-679-83379-X Subj: Animals – bears. Behavior – misbehavior. Family life. Rhyming text.

Billy and the baby ill. by Jan Lewis. Barron's, 1992. ISBN 0-8120-6328-7 Subj: Babies. Family life – brothers. Family life – new sibling.

Dilly speaks up ill. by Susan Hellard. Viking, 1991. ISBN 0-670-83680-X Subj: Dinosaurs. Shopping. Sibling rivalry.

A goodnight kind of feeling ill. by Clive Scruton. Holiday, 1998. ISBN 0-8234-1351-9 Subj: Animals – cats. Family life.

It came from outer space ill. by Carol Wright. Dial, 1992. ISBN 0-8037-1098-4 Subj: School. Space and space ships.

Look out, he's behind you ill. by Margaret Chamberlain. Putnam, 1988. ISBN 0-399-21485-2 Subj: Animals – wolves. Behavior – talking to strangers. Forest, woods. Format, unusual – toy and movable books.

Michael ill. by Tony Ross. Macmillan, 1991. ISBN 0-02-711850-9 Subj: Behavior – misbehavior. Character traits – individuality. School. Space and space ships.

Not like this, like that ill. by Joanna Burroughes. Oxford Univ. Pr., 1988. ISBN 0-19-520712-2 Subj: Character traits – foolishness. Counting, numbers. Family life – fathers.

See you later, alligator ill. by Colin Hawkins. Dial, 1986. ISBN 0-8037-0267-1 Subj: Animals. Format, unusual – toy and movable books. Reptiles – alligators, crocodiles.

That's not a fish ill. by Susie Jenkin-Pearce. Trafalgar Square, 1993. ISBN 0-460-88121-3 Subj: Family life. Sports – fishing.

This little baby ill. by Jenny Williams. Putnam, 1990. ISBN 0-399-22202-2 Subj: Babies. Rhyming text.

Through my window ill. by Eileen Browne. Silver Burdett, 1986. ISBN 0-382-09258-9 Subj: Family life. Illness.

Wait and see ill. by Eileen Browne. Oxford Univ. Pr., 1988. ISBN 0-19-520644-4 Subj: Family life. Shopping.

Brady, Irene. *Wild mouse* ill. by author. Scribners, 1976. ISBN 0-684-14664-9 Subj: Animals – mice. Science.

Brady, Kimberley Smith. *Keeper for the sea* ill. by Peter M. Fiore. Simon & Schuster, 1995. ISBN 0-689-80472-5 Subj: Family life – grandfathers. Sea and seashore. Sports – fishing.

Brady, Susan. *Find my blanket* ill. by author. HarperCollins, 1988. ISBN 0-397-32248-8 Subj: Animals – mice. Behavior – hiding things. Family life.

Bragdon, Lillian J. *Tell me the time, please* ill. by Frank and Margaret Phares. Lippincott, 1937. Subj: Clocks, watches. Time.

Bram, Elizabeth. *I don't want to go to school* ill. by author. Greenwillow, 1977. ISBN 0-688-84095-7 Subj: School – first day.

One day I closed my eyes and the world disappeared ill. by author. Dial, 1978. ISBN 0-8037-6613-0 Subj: Senses – seeing.

Saturday morning lasts forever ill. by author. Dial, 1978. ISBN 0-8037-7628-4 Subj: Activities – playing.

There is someone standing on my head ill. by author. Dial, 1979. ISBN 0-8037-8649-2 Subj: Imagination – imaginary friends.

Woodruff and the clocks ill. by author. Dial, 1980. ISBN 0-8037-9633-1 Subj: Behavior – collecting things. Clocks, watches.

Branagh, Kenneth. *Hamlet for kids* (Burdett, Lois)

Brand, Millen. *This little pig named Curly* ill. by John Hamberger. Crown, 1968. Subj: Animals – pigs. Farms.

Brand, Oscar. *When I first came to this land* ill. by Doris Burn. Putnam, 1974. ISBN 0-399-60906-7 Subj: Cumulative tales. Folk and fairy tales. Poverty. Songs.

Brande, Marlie. *Sleepy Nicholas* adapt. by Noel Streatfield; ill. by author. Follett, 1970. ISBN 0-695-40071-3 Subj: Foreign lands – Denmark. Sleep.

Brandenberg, Alexa. *I am me!* ill. by author. Harcourt, 1996. ISBN 0-15-200974-4 Subj: Careers. Self-concept.

Brandenberg, Aliki. *see* Aliki

Brandenberg, Franz. *Aunt Nina and her nephews and nieces* ill. by Aliki. Greenwillow, 1983. ISBN 0-688-01870-X Subj: Animals. Animals – babies. Animals – cats. Birthdays. Family life – aunts, uncles. Toys.

Aunt Nina, good night ill. by Aliki. Greenwillow, 1989. ISBN 0-688-07464-2 Subj: Bedtime. Family life – aunts, uncles.

Aunt Nina's visit ill. by Aliki. Greenwillow, 1984. ISBN 0-688-01766-5 Subj: Animals – cats. Family life – aunts, uncles. Puppets.

Cock-a-doodle-doo ill. by Aliki. Greenwillow, 1986. ISBN 0-688-06104-4 Subj: Animals. Farms. Noise, sounds.

Everyone ready? ill. by Aliki. Greenwillow, 1979. ISBN 0-688-84198-8 Subj: Activities – traveling. Animals – mice. Family life. Trains.

Fresh cider and apple pie ill. by Aliki. Macmillan, 1973. ISBN 0-02-711910-6 Subj: Food. Insects – flies. Spiders.

A fun weekend ill. by Alexa Brandenberg. Greenwillow, 1991. ISBN 0-688-09721-9 Subj: Activities – vacationing. Animals – bears. Family life.

The hit of the party ill. by Aliki. Greenwillow, 1985. ISBN 0-688-04241-4 Subj: Animals – hamsters. Parties.

I wish I was sick, too! ill. by Aliki. Greenwillow, 1976. ISBN 0-688-84047-7 Subj: Behavior – wishing. Illness.

No school today! ill. by Aliki. Macmillan, 1975. ISBN 0-02-711930-0 Subj: Animals – cats. Behavior – mistakes. School.

Otto is different ill. by James Stevenson. Greenwillow, 1985. ISBN 0-688-04254-6 Subj: Activities. Character traits – being different. Octopuses.

A robber! A robber! ill. by Aliki. Greenwillow, 1975. ISBN 0-688-84027-2 Subj: Animals – cats. Crime. Night. Noise, sounds.

A secret for grandmother's birthday ill. by Aliki. Greenwillow, 1975. ISBN 0-688-84012-4 Subj: Behavior – secrets. Birthdays. Family life – grandmothers.

Six new students ill. by Aliki. Greenwillow, 1978. ISBN 0-688-84124-4 Subj: Animals – mice. School – first day.

What's wrong with a van? ill. by Aliki. Greenwillow, 1987. ISBN 0-688-06775-1 Subj: Animals – cats. Automobiles. Behavior – seeking better things. Family life.

Brandt, Betty. *Special delivery* ill. by Kathy Haubrich. Carolrhoda, 1988. ISBN 0-87614-312-5 Subj: Careers – postal workers. Letters, cards. Post office. U.S. history – frontier and pioneer life.

Branley, Franklyn M. (Mansfield). *Air is all around you* ill. by Holly Keller. Rev. ed. Crowell, 1986. ISBN 0-690-04503-4 Subj: Science.

Comets ill. by Giulio Maestro. Crowell, 1984. Subj: Science. Sky.

Down comes the rain ill. by James Graham Hale. HarperCollins, 1997. ISBN 0-06-025338-X Subj: Science. Weather. Weather – rain.

Earthquakes ill. by Richard Rosenblum. HarperCollins, 1990. ISBN 0-690-04663-4 Subj: Earth. Science.

Eclipse: darkness in daytime ill. by Donald Crews. Rev. ed. HarperCollins, 1988. ISBN 0-690-04619-7 Subj: Science. Sun.

Flash, crash, rumble, and roll ill. by Barbara and Ed Emberley. Rev. ed. Crowell, 1985. ISBN 0-690-04425-9 Subj: Science. Weather – thunder.

Floating and sinking ill. by Robert Galster. Crowell, 1967. ISBN 0-690-30918-X Subj: Science.

Floating in space ill. by True Kelley. HarperCollins, 1998. ISBN 0-06-025433-5 Subj: Careers – astronauts. Science. Space and space ships.

Gravity is a mystery ill. by Don Madden. Rev. ed. Crowell, 1986. ISBN 0-690-04527-1 Subj: Science.

High sounds, low sounds ill. by Paul Galdone. Crowell, 1967. ISBN 0-690-38018-6 Subj: Noise, sounds. Science.

How little and how much: a book about scales ill. by Byron Barton. Crowell, 1976. ISBN 0-690-01058-3 Subj: Concepts – measurement.

Hurricane watch ill. by Giulio Maestro. Crowell, 1985. ISBN 0-690-04471-2 Subj: Science. Weather – storms.

Is there life in outer space? ill. by Don Madden. Crowell, 1984. ISBN 0-690-04375-9 Subj: Science. Space and space ships.

Journey into a black hole ill. by Marc Simont. Crowell, 1986. ISBN 0-690-04544-1 Subj: Science. Space and space ships. Stars.

Light and darkness ill. by Stacey Schuett. Rev. ed. HarperCollins, 1998. ISBN 0-06-027295-3 Subj: Science.

The moon seems to change ill. by Barbara and Ed Emberley. Crowell, 1987. ISBN 0-690-04585-9 Subj: Moon. Science.

North, south, east and west ill. by Robert Galster. Crowell, 1966. ISBN 0-690-58609-4 Subj: Science.

The planets in our solar system ill. by Don Madden. Crowell, 1981. ISBN 0-690-04026-1 Subj: Planets. Science. Space and space ships. Sun. World.

Rain and hail ill. by Harriett Barton. Rev. ed. Crowell, 1983. ISBN 0-690-04353-8 Subj: Science. Weather. Weather – rain.

The sky is full of stars ill. by Felicia Bond. Crowell, 1981. ISBN 0-690-04123-3 Subj: Science. Sky. Stars.

Snow is falling ill. by Holly Keller. Rev. ed. Crowell, 1986. ISBN 0-690-04548-4 Subj: Science. Weather – snow.

The sun, our nearest star ill. by Helen Borten. Crowell, 1961. ISBN 0-690-79483-5 Subj: Science. Sun.

Sunshine makes the seasons ill. by Giulio Maestro. Rev. ed. Crowell, 1985. ISBN 0-690-04482-8 Subj: Science. Seasons. Sun.

Tornado alert ill. by Giulio Maestro. Crowell, 1988. ISBN 0-690-04688-X Subj: Science. Weather – storms.

Volcanoes ill. by Marc Simont. Crowell, 1985. ISBN 0-690-04431-3 Subj: Science. Volcanoes.

What makes a magnet? ill. by True Kelley. HarperCollins, 1996. ISBN 0-06-026442-X Subj: Science.

What makes day and night ill. by Arthur Dorros. Rev. ed. Crowell, 1986. ISBN 0-690-04524-7 Subj: Earth. Science.

What the moon is like ill. by True Kelley. Rev. ed. Crowell, 1986. ISBN 0-690-04512-3 Subj: Moon. Science.

Brann, Esther. *A book for baby* ill. by author. Macmillan, 1945. Subj: Activities. Babies. Family life.

'Round the world ill. by author. Macmillan, 1935. Subj: Activities – traveling. Foreign lands. World.

Brannen, Ann. *E. H. Grieg's Peer Gynt* (Grieg, E. H. [Edvard Hagerup])

The sorcerer's apprentice (Dukas, P. [Paul Abraham])

Brasch, Kate. *Prehistoric monsters* photos by Jean-Philippe Varin. Merrimack, 1985. ISBN 0-88162-098-X Subj: Animals. Dinosaurs. Science.

Bratton, Heidi. *Imagine: a story about the beginning* ill. by author. Paulist Pr., 1997. ISBN 0-8091-6642-9 Subj: Creation. Format, unusual – board books. Religion.

Yes, I can! ill. by author. Paulist Pr., 1997. ISBN 0-8091-6639-9 Subj: Format, unusual – board books. Religion.

Bratton, John. *The teddy bears' picnic* ill. by Renate Kozikowski. Macmillan, 1990. ISBN 0-690-04703-7 Subj: Activities – picnicking. Format, unusual. Music. Songs.

Braun, Kathy. *Kangaroo and kangaroo* ill. by Jim McMullan. Doubleday, 1965. Subj: Animals – kangaroos. Behavior – collecting things. Rhyming text.

Braun, Trudi. *My goose Betsy* ill. by John Bendall-Brunello. Candlewick, 1998. ISBN 0-7636-0449-6 Subj: Birds – geese. Farms.

Breathed, Berkeley. *A wish for wings that work* ill. by author. Little, 1991. ISBN 0-316-10758-1 Subj: Activities – flying. Behavior – wishing. Birds – penguins. Holidays – Christmas.

Brebeuf, Jean de, Saint. *The Huron carol* ill. by Frances Tyrrell. Dutton, 1992. ISBN 0-525-44909-4 Subj: Foreign lands – Canada. Holidays – Christmas. Indians of North America – Huron. Music.

Brecht, Bertolt. *Uncle Eddie's moustache* ill. by Ursula Kirchberg; trans. by Muriel Rukeyser. Pantheon, 1974. Tr. of Onkel Ede hat einen Schnurrbart. ISBN 0-394-92819-9 Subj: Family life – aunts, uncles. Humor. Poetry.

Breckler, Rosemary K. *Hoang breaks the lucky teapot* ill. by Adrian Frankel. Houghton Mifflin, 1992. ISBN 0-395-57031-X Subj: Character traits – luck. Ethnic groups in the U.S. – Vietnamese Americans. Family life. Foreign languages.

Sweet dried apples: a Vietnamese wartime childhood ill. by Deborah Kogan Ray. Houghton Mifflin, 1996. ISBN 0-395-73570-X Subj: Careers – doctors. Death. Foreign lands – Vietnam. War.

Breda, Tjalmar. *see* DeJong, David Cornel

Breebaart, Joeri. *When I die, will I get better?* by Joeri and Piet Breebaart; ill. by Piet Breebaart. Peter Bedrick, 1993. ISBN 0-87226-375-4 Subj: Animals. Death. Family life – brothers.

Breebaart, Piet. *When I die, will I get better?* (Breebaart, Joeri)

Breese, Gillian. *The amazing adventures of Teddy Tum Tum* by Gillian Breese and Tony Langham;

ill. by Patrick Lowry. Arcade, 1992. ISBN 1-55970-185-4 Subj: Toys. Toys – bears.

Breeze, Lynn. *Baby's animals* ill. by author. Barron's, 1994. ISBN 0-812-06411-9 Subj: Animals. Babies. Format, unusual – board books. Noise, sounds. Pets. Rhyming text.

Baby's clothes ill. by author. Barron's, 1994. ISBN 0-812-06410-0 Subj: Babies. Clothing. Format, unusual – board books. Noise, sounds. Pets. Rhyming text.

Baby's food ill. by author. Barron's, 1994. ISBN 0-812-06413-5 Subj: Babies. Counting, numbers. Food. Format, unusual – board books. Rhyming text.

Baby's toys ill. by author. Barron's, 1994. ISBN 0-812-06412-7 Subj: Babies. Format, unusual – board books. Rhyming text. Toys.

This little baby goes out by Lynn Breeze and Ann Morris; ill. by Lynn Breeze. Little, 1993. ISBN 0-316-10854-5 Subj: Babies. Family life – mothers. Format, unusual – board books. Rhyming text.

This little baby's bedtime by Lynn Breeze and Ann Morris; ill. by Lynn Breeze. Little, 1993. ISBN 0-316-58419-3 Subj: Babies. Bedtime. Family life. Format, unusual – board books. Rhyming text.

This little baby's morning by Lynn Breeze and Ann Morris; ill. by Lynn Breeze. Barron's, 1993. ISBN 0-316-10855-3 Subj: Activities – playing. Babies. Family life – mothers. Format, unusual – board books. Rhyming text.

Breinburg, Petronella. *Doctor Shawn* ill. by Errol Lloyd. Crowell, 1975. ISBN 0-690-00722-1 Subj: Activities – playing. Careers – doctors. Ethnic groups in the U.S. – African Americans.

Shawn goes to school ill. by Errol Lloyd. Crowell, 1973. ISBN 0-690-00277-7 Subj: Ethnic groups in the U.S. – African Americans. Friendship. School – first day.

Shawn's red bike ill. by Errol Lloyd. Crowell, 1976. ISBN 0-690-01115-6 Subj: Ethnic groups in the U.S. – African Americans. Sports – bicycling.

Brennan, Jan. *Born two-gether* photos by Leo Brennan. J & L Books, 1984. ISBN 0-9613536-1-9 Subj: Family life. Multiple births – twins.

Brennan, John. *Zoo day* by John Brennan and Leonie Keaney; ill. with photos. Carolrhoda, 1989. ISBN 0-87614-358-3 Subj: Animals. Zoos.

Brennan, Joseph Killorin. *Gobo and the river* ill. by Diane Dawson Hearn. Holt, 1985. ISBN 0-03-004552-5 Subj: Character traits – perseverance. Puppets. Rivers.

Brennan, Patricia D. *Hitchety hatchety up I go!* ill. by Robert Rayevsky. Macmillan, 1985. ISBN 0-02-712300-6 Subj: Behavior – stealing. Folk and fairy tales. Little people.

Brenner, Anita. *I want to fly* ill. by Lucienne Bloch. Addison-Wesley, 1943. Subj: Airplanes, airports. Imagination.

Brenner, Barbara A. *The color wizard* ill. by Leo and Diane Dillon. Bantam, 1989. ISBN 0-553-05825-8 Subj: Concepts – color. Rhyming text. Wizards.

Dinosaurium ill. by Donna Bragenitz. Bantam, 1993. ISBN 0-553-07614-0 Subj: Dinosaurs. Imagination. Museums.

A dog I know ill. by Fred Brenner. HarperCollins, 1983. ISBN 0-06-020685-3 Subj: Animals – dogs. Humor.

Faces, faces, faces photos by George Ancona. Dutton, 1970. ISBN 0-525-29518-6 Subj: Anatomy – faces. Emotions. Ethnic groups in the U.S. Senses – hearing. Senses – seeing. Senses – smelling. Senses – tasting. Senses – touching.

The five pennies ill. by Erik Blegvad. Knopf, 1964. Subj: Money. Pets.

The flying patchwork quilt ill. by Fred Brenner. Addison-Wesley, 1965. Subj: Activities – flying. Magic. Quilts.

Good news ill. by Kate Duke. Bantam, 1991. ISBN 0-553-07091-6 Subj: Behavior – gossip. Birds – geese. Cumulative tales.

How do you make a bubble? (Hooks, William H.)

Lion and Lamb by Barbara A. Brenner and William H. Hooks; ill. by Bruce Degen. Gareth Stevens, 1998, c1990. ISBN 0-553-05829-0 Subj: Animals – lions. Animals – sheep. Friendship.

Mr. Tall and Mr. Small ill. by Tomi Ungerer. Addison-Wesley, 1966. ISBN 0-8050-2757-2 Subj: Animals – giraffes. Animals – mice. Character traits – conceit. Fire.

No way, Slippery Slick! a child's first book about drugs (Oppenheim, Joanne)

Ostrich feathers ill. by Vera B. Williams and Evelyn Armstrong. Parents, 1979. ISBN 0-8193-0922-2 Subj: Animals. Behavior – greed.

The prince and the pink blanket ill. by Nola Langner. Four Winds, 1980. ISBN 0-590-07614-0 Subj: Family life. Royalty – princes.

Rosa and Marco and the three wishes ill. by Megan Halsey. Bradbury, 1992. ISBN 0-02-712315-4 Subj: Behavior – wishing. Character traits – foolishness. Family life – brothers and sisters. Fish.

The snow parade ill. by Mary Tara O'Keefe. Crown, 1984. ISBN 0-571-55210-8 Subj: Counting, numbers. Parades. Weather.

Somebody's slippers, somebody's shoes ill. by Leslie Jacobs. Addison-Wesley, 1957. Subj: Clothing – shoes. Shopping.

The tremendous tree book by Barbara Brenner and May Garelick; ill. by Fred Brenner. Caroline House, 1992, c1979. ISBN 1-8780-9356-8 Subj: Science. Trees.

Two orphan cubs by Barbara Brenner and May Garelick; ill. by Erika Kors. Walker, 1989. ISBN 0-8027-6869-5 Subj: Animals – bears. Character traits – kindness to animals. Nature.

Where's that cat? ill. by Carol Schwartz. Scholastic, 1995. ISBN 0-590-45216-9 Subj: Animals – cats. Science.

Brent, Isabelle. *Cameo cats* ill. by sel. Little, 1992. ISBN 0-316-10836-7 Subj: Animals – cats. Art. Rhyming text.

Noah's ark ill. by author. Little, 1992. ISBN 0-316-10837-5 Subj: Animals. Boats, ships. Religion – Noah. Weather – floods. Weather – rain. Weather – rainbows.

Brentano, Clemens. *Schoolmaster Whackwell's wonderful sons* ill. by Maurice Sendak. Random House, 1962. Subj: Behavior – growing up. Careers. Folk and fairy tales.

Bresnick-Perry, Roslyn. *Leaving for America* ill. by Mira Reisberg. Childrens Pr., 1992. ISBN 0-89239-105-7 Subj: Family life. Foreign lands – Russia. Jewish culture. Moving.

Brett, Jan. *Annie and the wild animals* ill. by author. Houghton Mifflin, 1985. ISBN 0-395-37800-1 Subj: Animals. Animals – cats. Emotions – loneliness. Pets.

Armadillo rodeo ill. by author. Putnam, 1995. ISBN 0-399-22803-9 Subj: Animals. Animals – armadillos. Behavior – mistakes. Family life.

Berlioz the bear ill. by author. Putnam, 1991. ISBN 0-399-22248-0 Subj: Animals. Animals – bears. Cumulative tales. Music.

Christmas trolls ill. by author. Putnam, 1993. ISBN 0-399-22507-2 Subj: Animals – hedgehogs. Behavior – sharing. Behavior – stealing. Holidays – Christmas. Mythical creatures – trolls.

Comet's nine lives ill. by author. Putnam, 1996. ISBN 0-399-22931-0 Subj: Animals – cats. Animals – dogs. Behavior – carelessness. Lighthouses.

The first dog ill. by author. Harcourt, 1988. ISBN 0-15-227650-5 Subj: Animals – dogs. Animals – wolves. Art. Caves. Pets.

Fritz and the beautiful horses ill. by author. Houghton Mifflin, 1981. ISBN 0-395-30850-X Subj: Animals – horses, ponies. Behavior – wishing. Character traits – cleverness. Folk and fairy tales.

Gingerbread baby (The gingerbread boy)

Goldilocks and the three bears (The three bears)

The hat ill. by author. Putnam, 1997. ISBN 0-399-23101-3 Subj: Animals. Animals – hedgehogs. Clothing.

The mitten ill. by author. Putnam, 1990. ISBN 0-399-23109-9 Subj: Behavior – losing things. Folk and fairy tales. Foreign lands – Ukraine. Format, unusual – board books.

Town mouse, country mouse (Æsop)

The trouble with trolls ill. by author. Putnam, 1992. ISBN 0-399-22336-3 Subj: Animals – dogs. Character traits – cleverness. Clothing. Mythical creatures – trolls.

The wild Christmas reindeer ill. by author. Putnam, 1990. ISBN 0-399-22192-1 Subj: Animals – reindeer. Holidays – Christmas. Santa Claus.

Breverton, David. *Here comes bulldozer* ill. by Brian Bartle. Grosset, 1992. ISBN 0-448-40590-1 Subj: Format, unusual – toy and movable books. Machines. Trucks.

Here comes fire truck ill. by Brian Bartle. Grosset, 1992. ISBN 0-448-40592-X Subj: Format, unusual – toy and movable books. Trucks.

Here comes the dump truck ill. by Brian Bartle. Grosset, 1992. ISBN 0-448-40591-1 Subj: Format, unusual – toy and movable books. Trucks.

Here comes the tow truck ill. by Brian Bartle. Grosset, 1992. ISBN 0-448-40593-8 Subj: Format, unusual – toy and movable books. Trucks.

Brewster, Patience. *Ellsworth and the cats from Mars* ill. by author. Houghton Mifflin, 1981. ISBN 0-395-29612-9 Subj: Animals – cats. Behavior – lost. Space and space ships.

Nobody ill. by author. Houghton Mifflin, 1982. ISBN 0-89919-110-X Subj: Behavior – dissatisfaction. Imagination – imaginary friends.

Rabbit Inn ill. by author. Little, 1991. ISBN 0-316-10747-6 Subj: Animals – rabbits. Hotels.

Two bushy badgers ill. by author. Little, 1995. ISBN 0-316-10862-6 Subj: Animals – badgers. Friendship.

Brice, Tony. *Baby animals* ill. by author. Rand McNally, 1945. Subj: Animals. Babies.

The bashful goldfish ill. by author. Rand McNally, 1942. Subj: Character traits – shyness. Fish. Pets.

Bridges, Margaret Park. *If I were your father* ill. by Kady MacDonald. Morrow, 1999. ISBN 0-688-15193-0 Subj: Family life – fathers. Imagination.

Will you take care of me? ill. by Melissa Sweet. Morrow, 1998. ISBN 0-688-15195-7 Subj: Animals – kangaroos. Family life – mothers.

Bridges, William. *Lion Island* photos by Emmy Haas and Sam Dunton. Morrow, 1965. ISBN 0-688-31519-4 Subj: Animals – lions. Zoos.

Ookie, the walrus who likes people photos by Emmy Haas and Sam Dunton. Morrow, 1962. Subj: Animals – walruses.

Bridgman, Elizabeth. *All the little bunnies: a counting book* ill. by author. Atheneum, 1977. ISBN 0-689-50068-7 Subj: Counting, numbers. Rhyming text.

How to travel with grownups ill. by Eleanor Hazard. Crowell, 1980. ISBN 0-690-04010-5 Subj: Activities – traveling. Foreign lands.

Nanny bear's cruise ill. by author. HarperCollins, 1981. ISBN 0-06-020689-6 Subj: Activities – traveling. Animals – bears. Boats, ships.

A new dog next door ill. by author. HarperCollins, 1978. ISBN 0-06-020673-X Subj: Animals – dogs.

Bridle, Martin. *Punch and Judy in the rain* (Eaton, Su)

Bridwell, Norman. *Clifford counts bubbles* ill. by author. Scholastic, 1992. ISBN 0-590-45872-8 Subj: Animals – dogs. Bubbles. Counting, numbers.

Clifford goes to Hollywood ill. by author. Scholastic, 1981. ISBN 0-606-03090-5 Subj: Animals – dogs. Character traits – loyalty.

Clifford's ABC ill. by author. Scholastic, 1984. ISBN 0-590-48694-2 Subj: ABC books. Animals – dogs.

Clifford's good deeds ill. by author. Four Winds, 1975. ISBN 0-590-07439-3 Subj: Animals – dogs. Automobiles. Behavior – mistakes. Careers – firefighters. Character traits – helpfulness.

Clifford's Halloween ill. by author. Four Winds, 1967. ISBN 0-590-66159-0 Subj: Animals – dogs. Holidays – Halloween.

The witch grows up ill. by author. Scholastic, 1980. ISBN 0-590-30045-8 Subj: Humor. Magic. Witches.

The witch next door ill. by author. Four Winds, 1966. ISBN 0-590-40433-4 Subj: Witches.

Brierley, Louise. *King Lion and his cooks* ill. by author. Holt, 1982. ISBN 0-03-061218-7 Subj: Animals. Food. Royalty.

Briggs, Raymond. *The bear* ill. by author. Random House, 1994. ISBN 0-679-96944-6 Subj: Animals – polar bears. Imagination. Seasons – winter.

Building the snowman ill. by author. Little, 1985. ISBN 0-316-10813-8 Subj: Snowmen. Wordless.

Dressing up ill. by author. Little, 1985. ISBN 0-316-10814-6 Subj: Clothing. Snowmen. Wordless.

Father Christmas ill. by author. Random House, 1997. ISBN 0-679-88776-8 Subj: Holidays – Christmas. Santa Claus. Wordless.

Father Christmas goes on holiday ill. by author. Coward, 1975. ISBN 0-14-050187-8 Subj: Activities – vacationing. Holidays – Christmas. Santa Claus. Wordless.

Fee fi fo fum ill. by author. Coward, 1964. Subj: Nursery rhymes.

Jim and the beanstalk ill. by author. Coward, 1970. ISBN 0-698-11577-5 Subj: Folk and fairy tales. Giants. Humor. Old age.

The man ill. by author. Random House, 1995. ISBN 0-679-87643-X Subj: Fairies.

The party ill. by author. Little, 1985. ISBN 0-316-10816-2 Subj: Parties. Snowmen. Wordless.

Ring-a-ring o' roses ill. by author. Coward, 1962. Subj: Nursery rhymes.

The snowman ill. by author. Random House, 1978. ISBN 0-394-93973-5 Subj: Friendship. Snowmen. Wordless.

The snowman, a lift-the-flap board book ill. by author. Random House, 1998. ISBN 0-679-88896-9 Subj: Concepts – color. Counting, numbers. Format, unusual – toy and movable books. Snowmen.

The snowman storybook ill. by author. Random House, 1997. ISBN 0-679-98343-0 Subj: Snowmen.

The snowman tell-the-time book ill. by author. H. Hamilton, 1991. ISBN 0-241-13112-X Subj: Clocks, watches. Format, unusual – toy and movable books. Snowmen. Weather – snow.

The tin-pot foreign general and the old iron woman ill. by author. H. Hamilton, 1984. ISBN 0-241-11362-8 Subj: War.

Walking in the air ill. by author. Little, 1985. ISBN 0-316-10815-4 Subj: Imagination. Snowmen. Wordless.

The white land: a picture book of traditional rhymes and verses comp. and ill. by Raymond Briggs. Coward, 1963. Subj: Nursery rhymes. Songs.

Bright, Robert. *Georgie* ill. by author. Doubleday, 1944. ISBN 0-385-07307-0 Subj: Family life. Farms. Ghosts.

Georgie and the baby birds ill. by author. Doubleday, 1983. ISBN 0-385-17246-X Subj: Birds. Character traits – helpfulness. Ghosts.

Georgie and the ball of yarn ill. by author. Doubleday, 1983. ISBN 0-385-17244-3 Subj: Character traits – helpfulness. Ghosts.

Georgie and the buried treasure ill. by author. Doubleday, 1979. ISBN 0-385-14626-4 Subj: Ghosts.

Georgie and the little dog ill. by author. Doubleday, 1983. ISBN 0-385-17247-8 Subj: Animals – dogs. Character traits – helpfulness. Ghosts.

Georgie and the magician ill. by author. Doubleday, 1966. ISBN 0-385-01021-4 Subj: Ghosts. Magic.

Georgie and the noisy ghost ill. by author. Doubleday, 1971. ISBN 0-590-20614-1 Subj: Activities – vacationing. Ghosts. Noise, sounds. Sea and seashore.

Georgie and the robbers ill. by author. Doubleday, 1963. ISBN 0-389-01470-8 Subj: Crime. Ghosts.

Georgie and the runaway balloon ill. by author. Doubleday, 1983. ISBN 0-385-17245-1 Subj: Animals – mice. Character traits – helpfulness. Ghosts. Toys – balloons.

Georgie goes west ill. by author. Doubleday, 1973. ISBN 0-385-05277-4 Subj: Cowboys. Ghosts.

Georgie to the rescue ill. by author. Doubleday, 1956. Subj: Birds – owls. City. Ghosts.

Georgie's Christmas carol ill. by author. Doubleday, 1975. ISBN 0-385-02410-X Subj: Ghosts. Holidays – Christmas.

Georgie's Halloween ill. by author. Doubleday, 1958. Subj: Ghosts. Holidays – Halloween.

Gregory, the noisiest and strongest boy in Grangers Grove ill. by author. Doubleday, 1969. Subj: Character traits – laziness. Food. Noise, sounds.

I like red ill. by author. Doubleday, 1955. Subj: Concepts – color. Hair.

Me and the bears ill. by author. Doubleday, 1951. Subj: Animals – bears. Behavior – wishing. Friendship. Sleep. Zoos.

Miss Pattie ill. by author. Doubleday, 1954. Subj: Animals – cats.

My hopping bunny ill. by author. Doubleday, 1971. Subj: Activities – jumping. Animals – rabbits. Rhyming text.

My red umbrella ill. by author. Morrow, 1959. ISBN 0-688-31619-0 Subj: Counting, numbers. Umbrellas. Weather – rain.

The travels of Ching ill. by author. Addison-Wesley, 1943. Subj: Foreign lands – China. Toys – dolls.

Which is Willy? ill. by author. Doubleday, 1962. Subj: Birds – penguins. Character traits – individuality.

Bright star shining: *poems for Christmas* sel. by Michael Harrison and Christopher Stuart-Clark. Eerdmans, 1998. ISBN 0-8028-5177-0 Subj: Holidays – Christmas. Poetry.

Brightman, Alan. *Like me* ill. by author. Little, 1976. ISBN 0-316-10808-1 Subj: Character traits – being different. Handicaps – mental handicaps.

Brighton, Catherine. *Five secrets in a box* ill. by author. Dutton, 1987. ISBN 0-525-44318-5 Subj: Behavior – secrets. Foreign lands – Italy. Science.

The fossil girl: Mary Anning's dinosaur discovery ill. by author. Millbrook, 1999. ISBN 0-7613-1468-7 Subj: Careers – archaeologists. Dinosaurs. Foreign lands – England. Science.

Hope's gift ill. by author. Doubleday, 1988. ISBN 0-385-24598-X Subj: Character traits – kindness to animals. Gifts. Theater.

Mozart ill. by author. Doubleday, 1990. ISBN 0-385-41538-9 Subj: Careers – composers. Careers – musicians.

My hands, my world ill. by author. Macmillan, 1984. ISBN 0-02-712900-4 Subj: Handicaps – blindness. Imagination – imaginary friends. Senses – seeing.

My Napoleon ill. by author. Millbrook, 1997. ISBN 0-7613-0106-2 Subj: Foreign lands – France. Royalty – emperors.

Nijinsky ill. by author. Doubleday, 1989. ISBN 0-385-24926-8 Subj: Activities – dancing. Ballet. Foreign lands – Russia.

Brillhart, Julie. *Anna's goodbye apron* ill. by author. Albert Whitman, 1990. ISBN 0-8075-0375-4 Subj: Careers – teachers. Clothing – aprons. School.

The dino expert ill. by author. Albert Whitman, 1993. ISBN 0-8075-1597-3 Subj: Birds. Dinosaurs.

Story hour - starring Megan! ill. by author. Albert Whitman, 1992. ISBN 0-8075-7628-X Subj: Activities – reading. Careers – librarians. Family life – mothers. Libraries. Problem solving.

When daddy came to school ill. by author. Albert Whitman, 1995. ISBN 0-8075-8878-4 Subj: Birthdays. Family life – fathers. Rhyming text. School.

When Daddy took us camping ill. by author. Albert Whitman, 1997. ISBN 0-8075-8879-2 Subj: Camps, camping. Family life – fathers. Rhyming text.

Brimner, Larry Dane. *Aggie and Will* ill. by Rebecca McKillip Thornburgh. Childrens Pr., 1998. ISBN 0-516-20754-7 Subj: Activities – reading. Friendship. Libraries.

Country Bear's good neighbor ill. by Ruth Tietjen Councell. Watts, 1988. ISBN 0-531-08308-X Subj: Animals – bears. Food.

Country Bear's surprise ill. by Ruth Tietjen Councell. Orchard, 1991. ISBN 0-531-08411-6 Subj: Animals – bears. Birthdays. Parties.

Cowboy up! ill. by Susan Miller. Childrens Pr., 1999. ISBN 0-516-21199-4 Subj: Animals – horses, ponies. Cowboys. Rhyming text.

Dinosaurs dance ill. by Patrick Girouard. Childrens Pr., 1998. ISBN 0-516-20752-0 Subj: Animals. Animals – dogs. Friendship.

Elliot Fry's good-bye ill. by Eugenie Fernandes. Boyds Mills, 1994. ISBN 1-56397-113-5 Subj: Behavior – running away. Family life.

If dogs had wings ill. by Chris L. Demarest. Boyds Mills, 1996. ISBN 1-56397-146-1 Subj: Activities – flying. Animals – dogs.

Max and Felix ill. by Les Gray. Boyds Mills, 1993. ISBN 1-56397-010-4 Subj: Activities – photographing. Friendship. Frogs and toads.

Nana's hog ill. by Susan Miller. Childrens Pr., 1998. ISBN 0-516-20755-5 Subj: Animals – pigs. Character traits – individuality. Family life – grandmothers. Rhyming text.

What good is a tree? ill. by Leo Landry. Childrens Pr., 1998. ISBN 0-516-20953-1 Subj: Rhyming text. Trees.

Brin, Ruth F. *David and Goliath* ill. by H. Hechtkopf. Lerner, 1977. ISBN 0-8225-0365-4 Subj: Foreign lands – Israel. Giants. Religion – David.

The story of Esther ill. by H. Hechtkopf. Lerner, 1976. ISBN 0-8225-0364-6 Subj: Foreign lands – Israel. Religion.

Brinckloe, Julie. *Fireflies!* ill. by author. Macmillan, 1985. ISBN 0-02-713310-9 Subj: Behavior – growing up. Insects – fireflies.

Gordon's house ill. by author. Doubleday, 1976. ISBN 0-385-06905-7 Subj: Animals – bears.

Playing marbles ill. by author. Morrow, 1988. ISBN 0-688-07144-9 Subj: Activities – playing. Games.

Bring a torch, Jeannette, Isabella ill. by Adrienne Adams. Scribners, 1963. A provincial carol attributed to Nicholas Saboly, seventeenth century. Subj: Foreign lands – France. Holidays – Christmas. Music. Songs.

Brink, Carol Ryrie. *Goody O'Grumpity* ill. by Ashley Wolff. North-South, 1994. ISBN 1-55858-328-9 Subj: Activities – cooking. Rhyming text. U.S. history.

Brion, David. *Space vehicles* (Rockwell, Anne F.)

Briscoe, D. Stuart. *Where is God?* ill. by Sally Marinin. Baker Book House, 1993. ISBN 0-8010-1038-1 Subj: Religion.

Briscoe, Jill. *The innkeeper's daughter* ill. by Dennis Hockerman. Childrens Pr., 1984. ISBN 0-516-09484-X Subj: Handicaps. Holidays – Christmas. Religion.

Brisson, Pat. *Kate on the coast* ill. by Rick Brown. Bradbury, 1992. ISBN 0-02-714341-4 Subj: Activities – traveling. Activities – vacationing. Letters, cards.

Magic carpet ill. by Amy Schwartz. Macmillan, 1991. ISBN 0-02-714340-6 Subj: Activities – traveling. Family life – aunts, uncles. Imagination.

Wanda's roses ill. by Maryann Cocca-Leffler. Boyds Mills, 1994. ISBN 1-56397-136-4 Subj: Behavior – disbelief. Character traits – optimism. Communities, neighborhoods. Flowers. Gardens, gardening.

Your best friend, Kate ill. by Rick Brown. Bradbury, 1989. ISBN 0-02-714350-3 Subj: Activities – traveling. Activities – vacationing. Family life. Letters, cards.

Bro, Marguerite (Harmon). *The animal friends of Peng-u* ill. by Seong Moy. Doubleday, 1965. Subj: Animals. Folk and fairy tales. Foreign lands – China.

Brock, Emma Lillian. *The birds' Christmas tree* ill. by author. Knopf, 1946. Subj: Birds. Character traits – kindness to animals. Holidays – Christmas.

Mr. Wren's house ill. by author. Knopf, 1944. Subj: Birds – wrens. Family life. Humor.

Nobody's mouse ill. by author. Knopf, 1938. Subj: Animals. City. Humor.

One little Indian boy ill. by author. Hale, 1932. Subj: Indians of North America.

A pet for Barbie ill. by author. Knopf, 1947. Subj: Family life. Pets.

Pig with a front porch ill. by author. Knopf, 1937. Subj: Animals – pigs. Behavior – dissatisfaction.

A present for Auntie ill. by author. Knopf, 1939. Subj: Family life – aunts, uncles.

Skipping Island ill. by author. Knopf, 1958. Subj: Humor. Islands.

Surprise balloon ill. by author. Knopf, 1949. Subj: Activities – flying. Animals. Toys – balloons.

Brocket, Ray. *Even the devil is afraid of a shrew: a folktale of Lapland* (Stalder, Valerie)

Brodmann, Aliana. *Such a noise!* trans. from German by Aliana Brodmann and David Fillingham; ill. by Hans Poppel. Kane/Miller, 1989. Translation of: Ein Wunderlicher Rat. ISBN 0-916291-25-1 Subj: Folk and fairy tales. Humor. Jewish culture. Noise, sounds. Problem solving.

Brodsky, Beverly. *see* McDermott, Beverly Brodsky

Brodzinsky, Anne Braff. *The mulberry bird* ill. by Diana L. Stanley. Rev. ed. Perspectives Pr., 1996. ISBN 0-944934-15-3 Subj: Adoption. Birds. Family life – step families.

Broekel, Ray. *Dangerous fish* ill. with photos. Childrens Pr., 1982. ISBN 0-516-01635-0 Subj: Fish.

I can be an author ill. by author. Childrens Pr., 1986. ISBN 0-516-01891-4 Subj: Careers – writers.

I can be an auto mechanic. Childrens Pr., 1985. ISBN 0-516-01885-X Subj: Automobiles. Careers – mechanics.

The painter and the bird (Velthuijs, Max)

Trains ill. with photos. Childrens Pr., 1981. ISBN 0-516-01652-0 Subj: Trains. Transportation.

Trucks ill. with photos. Childrens Pr., 1983. ISBN 0-516-01688-1 Subj: Transportation. Trucks.

Brogan, Peggy. *Sounds around the clock* (Martin, Bill [William Ivan])

Sounds I remember (Martin, Bill [William Ivan])

Sounds of home (Martin, Bill [William Ivan])

Sounds of laughter (Martin, Bill [William Ivan])

Sounds of numbers (Martin, Bill [William Ivan])

Bröger, Achim. *Bruno takes a trip* trans. from German by Caroline Gueritz; ill. by Gisela Kalow. Morrow, 1978. ISBN 0-688-32138-0 Subj: Activities – traveling. Pets. Trains.

Francie's paper puppy ill. by Michele Sambin. Alphabet Pr., 1984. Translation of: Wollen wir Freunde sein? ISBN 0-907234-56-9 Subj: Animals – dogs. Art. Country. Emotions – loneliness. Imagination. Pets.

Little Harry trans. from German by Elizabeth D. Crawford; ill. by Judy Morgan. Morrow, 1979. ISBN 0-688-32185-2 Subj: Humor. Imagination. Problem solving.

The Santa Clauses ill. by Ute Krause. Dial, 1986. ISBN 0-8037-0266-3 Subj: Holidays – Christmas. Humor. Santa Claus.

Bromhall, Winifred. *Bridget's growing day* ill. by author. Knopf, 1957. Subj: Behavior – growing up. Character traits – smallness. Foreign lands – Ireland.

Johanna arrives ill. by author. Knopf, 1941. Subj: Activities – traveling. Foreign lands – Holland.

Mary Ann's first picture ill. by author. Knopf, 1947. Subj: Activities – painting. Art. Birthdays.

Middle Matilda ill. by author. Knopf, 1962. Subj: Behavior – losing things. Clothing. Family life.

Brook, Judy. *Hector and Harriet the night hamsters: two adventures* ill. by author. Dutton, 1985. ISBN 0-233-97625-6 Subj: Animals – hamsters.

Tim mouse goes down the stream ill. by author. Lothrop, 1975. ISBN 0-688-51698-X Subj: Animals – hedgehogs. Animals – mice. Character traits – bravery. Rivers.

Tim mouse visits the farm ill. by author. Lothrop, 1977. ISBN 0-688-51796-X Subj: Animals – hedgehogs. Animals – mice. Farms.

Brooke, L. Leslie (Leonard Leslie). *The golden goose book* (Mother Goose)

Johnny Crow's garden ill. by author. Warne, 1903. ISBN 0-7232-3429-9 Subj: Animals. Rhyming text.

Johnny Crow's new garden ill. by author. Warne, 1935. ISBN 0-7232-0568-X Subj: Animals. Rhyming text.

Johnny Crow's party ill. by author. Warne, 1907. ISBN 0-7232-0566-3 Subj: Animals. Parties.

Oranges and lemons ill. by author. Warne, 1913. Subj: Nursery rhymes.

Ring o'roses ill. by author. Houghton Mifflin, 1992. ISBN 0-395-61304-3 Subj: Nursery rhymes.

This little pig went to market (Mother Goose)

Brooks, Alan. *Frogs jump* ill. by Steven Kellogg. Scholastic, 1996. ISBN 0-590-45528-1 Subj: Animals. Counting, numbers.

Brooks, Andrea. *The guinea pigs' adventure* ill. by author. Little, 1980. ISBN 0-316-10961-4 Subj: Animals – guinea pigs.

Brooks, Ben. *Lemonade parade* ill. by Bill Slavin. Albert Whitman, 1992. ISBN 0-8075-4432-9 Subj: Activities – working. Family life – fathers. Money.

Brooks, Bruce. *Each a piece* ill. by Elena Pavlov. HarperCollins, 1998. ISBN 0-06-023595-0 Subj: Format, unusual – toy and movable books. Rhyming text.

Brooks, Gregory. *Monroe's island* ill. by author. Bradbury, 1979. ISBN 0-87888-140-9 Subj: Imagination.

Brooks, Gwendolyn. *Bronzeville boys and girls* ill. by Ronni Solbert. HarperCollins, 1956. ISBN 0-06-020651-9 Subj: Poetry.

Brooks, Robert B. *So that's how I was born* ill. by Susan Perl. Simon & Schuster, 1983. ISBN 0-671-44501-4 Subj: Babies. Birth. Family life. Science.

Brooks, Ron. *Timothy and Gramps* ill. by author. Bradbury, 1978. ISBN 0-8788-8139-5 Subj: Family life – grandfathers. School.

Broome, Errol. *The smallest koala* ill. by Gwen Mason. Australian Book Source, 1988. ISBN 0-949447-65-X Subj: Animals – koalas. Character traits – curiosity. Food.

Brophy, Nannette. *The color of my fur* ill. by author. Winston-Derek, 1992. ISBN 1-55523-456-9 Subj: Animals – rabbits. Concepts – color. Friendship. Prejudice.

Brothers, Aileen. *Jiffy, Miss Boo and Mr. Roo* ill. by Audean Johnson. Follett, 1966. Subj: Birds – chickens. Pets.

Sad Mrs. Sam Sack by Aileen Brothers and Morton Botel; ill. by Muriel and Jim Collins. Follett, 1963. Subj: Behavior – dissatisfaction. Family life. Humor.

Brothers and sisters are like that! Sel. by the Child Study Association of America; ill. by Michael Hampshire. Crowell, 1971. ISBN 0-690-16042-9 Subj: Family life. Sibling rivalry.

Brott, Ardyth. *Jeremy's decision* ill. by Michael Martchenko. Kane/Miller, 1990. ISBN 0-916291-31-6 Subj: Careers. Music.

Brouillard, Anne. *The bathtub prima donna* ill. by author. Abrams, 1999. ISBN 0-8109-4093-0 Subj: Activities – bathing. Activities – singing. Rhyming text. Weather – rain.

Brouillette, Jeanne S. *Moths* ill. by Bill Barss. Follett, 1966. Subj: Insects. Science.

Brown, Abbie Farwell. *The Christmas angel* ill. by Reginald Birch. Houghton Mifflin, 1910. Subj: Angels. Holidays – Christmas.

Brown, Andrew. *Armored animals* ill. by author. Crabtree, 1997. ISBN 0-8650-5558-0 Subj: Animals.

Baby animals ill. by author. Crabtree, 1997. ISBN 0-8650-5559-9 Subj: Animals – babies.

Dangerous animals ill. by author. Crabtree, 1997. ISBN 0-8650-5560-2 Subj: Animals.

Brown, Beatrice Curtis. *Jonathan Bing* ill. by Judith Gwyn Brown. Lothrop, 1968. Subj: Poetry.

Jonathan Bing ill. by Pelagie Doane. Oxford Univ. Pr., 1937. Subj: Poetry.

Brown, Craig McFarland. *City sounds* ill. by author. Greenwillow, 1992. ISBN 0-688-10029-5 Subj: Careers – farmers. City. Noise, sounds.

In the spring ill. by author. Greenwillow, 1994. ISBN 0-688-10984-5 Subj: Animals – babies. Babies. Birth. Seasons – spring.

My barn ill. by author. Greenwillow, 1991. ISBN 0-688-08786-8 Subj: Animals. Barns. Farms.

Patchwork farmer ill. by author. Greenwillow, 1989. ISBN 0-688-07736-6 Subj: Activities – sewing. Careers – farmers. Clothing. Farms. Wordless.

Brown, Daphne Faunce. *see* Faunce-Brown, Daphne

Brown, David. *Someone always needs a policeman* ill. by author. Simon & Schuster, 1972. ISBN 0-671-65168-4 Subj: Careers – police officers.

Brown, Don. *Alice Ramsey's grand adventure* ill. by author. Houghton Mifflin, 1997. ISBN 0-395-70127-9 Subj: Activities – traveling. Automobiles.

One giant leap: the story of Neil Armstrong ill. by author. Houghton Mifflin, 1998. ISBN 0-395-88401-2 Subj: Careers – astronauts.

Ruth Law thrills a nation ill. by author. Ticknor & Fields, 1993. ISBN 0-395-66404-7 Subj: Airplanes, airports. Careers – airplane pilots.

Brown, Elinor. *The little story book* ill. by author. Oxford Univ. Pr., 1940. Subj: Activities.

Brown, Graham. *Christmas songs* (Bishop, Roma)

Holiday cheer (Bishop, Roma)

My first pop-up book of dinosaurs (Bishop, Roma)

My first pop-up book of prehistoric animals (Bishop, Roma)

Santa pays a visit (Bishop, Roma)

Brown, Jane Clark. *Whonk, and whonk again* ill. by author. Houghton Mifflin, 1989. ISBN 0-395-49211-4 Subj: Behavior – lost. Boats, ships. City. Noise, sounds.

Brown, Jeff. *Flat Stanley* ill. by Tomi Ungerer. HarperCollins, 1961. ISBN 0-06-020681-0 Subj: Family life. Humor. Problem solving.

Brown, Judith Gwyn. *Alphabet dreams* ill. by author. Prentice-Hall, 1976. ISBN 0-13-022806-0 Subj: ABC books. Rhyming text.

The happy voyage ill. by author. Macmillan, 1965. Subj: Boats, ships.

Max and the truffle pig ill. by author. Abingdon, 1963. Subj: Animals – pigs. Behavior – lost. Food. Foreign lands – France.

Brown, Katherine. *The Small One: a good Samaritan* ill. by author. Disney Pr., 1998. ISBN 0-7868-0481-5 Subj: Animals – donkeys. Character traits – kindness to animals. Religion.

Brown, Kathryn. *Muledred* ill. by author. Harcourt, 1990. ISBN 0-15-256265-6 Subj: Animals – mules. Clocks, watches. Family life – grandfathers. School.

Brown, Ken (Ken James). *Mucky Pup* ill. by author. Dutton, 1997. ISBN 0-525-45886-7 Subj: Animals. Animals – dogs. Farms.

Mucky Pup's Christmas ill. by author. Dutton, 1999. ISBN 0-525-46141-8 Subj: Animals – dogs. Animals – pigs. Behavior – misbehavior. Farms. Holidays – Christmas.

Nellie's knot ill. by author. Four Winds, 1993. ISBN 0-02-714930-7 Subj: Animals – elephants. Behavior – forgetfulness.

Brown, Laurie Krasny. *The bionic bunny show* (Brown, Marc Tolon)

Dinosaurs alive and well by Laurie Krasny Brown and Marc Tolon Brown; ill. by authors. Little, 1990. ISBN 0-316-10998-3 Subj: Dinosaurs. Health and fitness.

Dinosaurs divorce by Laurene Krasny Brown and Marc Brown; ill. by Marc Brown. Atlantic Monthly, 1986. ISBN 0-8711-3089-0 Subj: Dinosaurs. Divorce.

Dinosaurs to the rescue by Laurie Krasny Brown and Marc Tolon Brown; ill. by Marc Tolon Brown. Little, 1992. ISBN 0-316-11087-6 Subj: Dinosaurs. Ecology.

Dinosaurs travel by Laurie Krasny Brown and Marc Brown; ill. by Marc Brown. Little, 1988. ISBN 0-316-11076-0 Subj: Activities – traveling. Dinosaurs.

How to be a friend: a guide to making friends and keeping them by Laurie Krasny Brown and Marc Brown; ill. by Marc Brown. Little, 1998. ISBN 0-316-10913-4 Subj: Dinosaurs. Friendship.

Rex and Lilly school time by Laurie Krasny Brown and Marc Brown; ill. by Marc Brown. Little, 1997. ISBN 0-316-10920-7 Subj: Dinosaurs. Family life – brothers and sisters. School.

Visiting the art museum by Laurene Krasny Brown and Marc Brown; ill. by authors. Dutton, 1986. ISBN 0-525-44233-2 Subj: Art. Museums.

What's the big secret? talking about sex with girls and boys by Laurie Krasny Brown and Marc Brown; ill. by Marc Brown. Little, 1997. ISBN 0-316-10915-0 Subj: Anatomy. Family life. Sex instruction.

When dinosaurs die: a guide to understanding death by Laurie Krasny Brown and Marc Tolon Brown; ill. by Marc Tolon Brown. Little, 1996. ISBN 0-316-10917-7 Subj: Death. Dinosaurs. Emotions. Family life.

Brown, M. K. (Mary K.). *Let's go swimming with Mr. Sillypants* ill. by author. Crown, 1986. ISBN 0-517-56185-9 Subj: Dreams. Sports – swimming.

Brown, Marc Tolon. *Arthur and the true Francine* ill. by author. Little, 1996. ISBN 0-316-11136-8 Subj: Animals. Behavior – lying. School.

Arthur babysits ill. by author. Little, 1992. ISBN 0-316-11293-3 Subj: Activities – babysitting. Animals – aardvarks. Multiple births – twins.

Arthur goes to camp ill. by author. Little, 1982. ISBN 0-316-11218-6 Subj: Animals. Camps, camping.

Arthur goes to school ill. by author. Random House, 1995. ISBN 0-679-86734-1 Subj: Animals – aardvarks. Format, unusual – board books. Format, unusual – toy and movable books. School.

Arthur lost and found ill. by author. Little, 1998. ISBN 0-316-10912-6 Subj: Animals – aardvarks. Behavior – lost. Buses. Careers – bus drivers.

Arthur meets the president ill. by author. Little, 1991. ISBN 0-316-11265-8 Subj: Activities – traveling. Animals – aardvarks. Family life – sisters.

Arthur tricks the tooth fairy ill. by author. Random House, 1997. ISBN 0-679-98464-X Subj: Animals – aardvarks. Behavior – trickery. Fairies. Family life – brothers and sisters.

Arthur writes a story ill. by author. Little, 1996. ISBN 0-316-10916-9 Subj: Activities – writing. Animals – aardvarks.

Arthur's April fool ill. by author. Little, 1983. ISBN 0-316-11196-1 Subj: Animals. Holidays – April Fools' Day.

Arthur's baby ill. by author. Little, 1987. ISBN 0-316-11123-6 Subj: Animals – aardvarks. Babies. Family life – new sibling.

Arthur's birthday ill. by author. Little, 1989. ISBN 0-316-11073-6 Subj: Animals – aardvarks. Birthdays. Friendship. Parties.

Arthur's chicken pox ill. by author. Little, 1994. ISBN 0-316-11384-0 Subj: Animals – aardvarks. Circus. Family life. Illness – chicken pox.

Arthur's Christmas ill. by author. Little, 1984. ISBN 0-316-11180-5 Subj: Animals. Gifts. Holidays – Christmas. Santa Claus.

Arthur's computer disaster ill. by author. Little, 1997. ISBN 0-316-11016-7 Subj: Animals – aardvarks. Behavior – misbehavior. Computers.

Arthur's eyes ill. by author. Little, 1979. ISBN 0-316-11063-9 Subj: Animals. Glasses. Senses – seeing.

Arthur's family vacation ill. by author. Little, 1993. ISBN 0-316-11312-3 Subj: Activities – vacationing. Animals – aardvarks. Family life.

Arthur's first sleepover ill. by author. Little, 1994. ISBN 0-316-11445-6 Subj: Animals – aardvarks. Behavior – misbehavior. Camps, camping. Family life – brothers and sisters. Monsters. Sleepovers.

Arthur's Halloween ill. by author. Little, 1982. ISBN 0-316-11116-3 Subj: Animals. Holidays – Halloween.

Arthur's neighborhood ill. by author. Random House, 1996. ISBN 0-679-86737-6 Subj: Animals – aardvarks. Communities, neighborhoods. Format, unusual – toy and movable books.

Arthur's new puppy ill. by author. Little, 1993. ISBN 0-316-11355-7 Subj: Animals – aardvarks. Animals – dogs. Pets.

Arthur's new puppy (board book) ill. by author. 1st board book ed. Little, 1997. ISBN 0-316-11133-3 Subj: Animals – aardvarks. Animals – dogs. Format, unusual – board books. Pets.

Arthur's nose ill. by author. Little, 1976. ISBN 0-316-11193-7 Subj: Anatomy – noses. Animals – aardvarks.

Arthur's pet business ill. by author. Little, 1990. ISBN 0-316-11262-3 Subj: Animals – aardvarks. Animals – dogs. Pets.

Arthur's really helpful word book ill. by author. Random House, 1997. ISBN 0-679-98735-5 Subj: Activities – reading. Animals – aardvarks. Language.

Arthur's teacher trouble ill. by author. Little, 1986. ISBN 0-87113-091-2 Subj: Animals. School.

Arthur's Thanksgiving ill. by author. Little, 1983. ISBN 0-316-11060-4 Subj: Animals. Holidays – Thanksgiving. Theater.

Arthur's tooth ill. by author. Little, 1985. ISBN 0-87113-006-8 Subj: Animals. Teeth.

Arthur's TV trouble ill. by author. Little, 1995. ISBN 0-316-10919-3 Subj: Animals – aardvarks. Money. Pets.

Arthur's underwear ill. by author. Little, 1999. ISBN 0-316-11012-4 Subj: Animals. Animals – aardvarks. Behavior – worrying. Clothing. Emotions – embarrassment. School.

Arthur's Valentine ill. by author. Little, 1980. ISBN 0-316-11062-0 Subj: Animals. Holidays – Valentine's Day. School.

The bionic bunny show by Marc Brown and Laurene Krasny Brown; ill. by Marc Brown. Little, 1984. ISBN 0-316-11120-1 Subj: Animals. Animals – rabbits. Television.

Can you jump like a frog? ill. by author. Dutton, 1989. ISBN 0-525-44463-7 Subj: Format, unusual – toy and movable books. Frogs and toads. Nursery rhymes.

The cloud over Clarence ill. by author. Dutton, 1979. ISBN 0-525-28013-8 Subj: Animals – cats. Behavior – carelessness. Friendship.

Count to ten ill. by author. Western, 1982. ISBN 0-307-10627-6 Subj: Counting, numbers. Format, unusual – board books.

D. W. all wet ill. by author. Little, 1988. ISBN 0-316-11077-9 Subj: Animals – anteaters. Sea and seashore. Sibling rivalry.

D. W. flips! ill. by author. Little, 1987. ISBN 0-316-11239-9 Subj: Animals – anteaters. Sports – gymnastics.

D. W., go to your room! ill. by author. Little, 1999. ISBN 0-316-10905-3 Subj: Animals – aardvarks. Character traits – meanness. Family life – sisters.

D. W. rides again! ill. by author. Little, 1998. ISBN 0-316-11128-7 Subj: Animals – aardvarks. Family life – brothers and sisters. Sports – bicycling.

D. W., the picky eater ill. by author. Little, 1995. ISBN 0-316-10957-6 Subj: Animals – aardvarks. Family life. Food.

D. W. thinks big, a board book ill. by author. Little, 1998. ISBN 0-316-11112-0 Subj: Accidents. Animals – aardvarks. Family life – brothers and sisters. Format, unusual – board books. Weddings.

D. W.'s lost blankie ill. by author. Little, 1998. ISBN 0-316-10914-2 Subj: Animals – aardvarks. Behavior – losing things. Family life.

Dinosaurs alive and well (Brown, Laurie Krasny)

Dinosaurs, beware! a safety guide by Marc Brown and Stephen Krensky; ill. by authors. Little, 1982. ISBN 0-316-11228-3 Subj: Dinosaurs. Safety.

Dinosaurs divorce (Brown, Laurie Krasny)

Dinosaurs to the rescue (Brown, Laurie Krasny)

Dinosaurs travel (Brown, Laurie Krasny)

Finger rhymes ill. by author. Dutton, 1980. ISBN 0-525-29732-4 Subj: Games. Nursery rhymes. Participation.

Glasses for D. W. ill. by author. Random House, 1995. ISBN 0-679-98043-1 Subj: Animals – aardvarks. Family life – brothers and sisters. Glasses.

Hand rhymes ill. by sel. Dutton, 1985. ISBN 0-525-44201-4 Subj: Games. Nursery rhymes.

How to be a friend: a guide to making friends and keeping them (Brown, Laurie Krasny)

Lenny and Lola ill. by author. Dutton, 1978. ISBN 0-525-33465-3 Subj: Circus.

Marc Brown's Boat book ill. by author. Golden Pr., 1982. ISBN 0-307-12262-X Subj: Animals – aardvarks. Boats, ships. Format, unusual – board books.

Marc Brown's full house ill. by author. Addison-Wesley, 1977. ISBN 0-201-00341-4 Subj: Monsters.

Monster's lunchbox ill. by author. Little, 1995. ISBN 0-316-11313-1 Subj: Format, unusual – toy and movable books. Monsters. Rhyming text.

Moose and goose ill. by author. Dutton, 1978. ISBN 0-525-35175-2 Subj: Animals – moose. Birds – geese.

One, two buckle my shoe ill. by author. Dutton, 1989. ISBN 0-525-44462-9 Subj: Animals – rabbits. Format, unusual – toy and movable books. Games. Nursery rhymes.

Perfect pigs: an introduction to manners by Marc Brown and Stephen Krensky; ill. by authors. Little, 1983. ISBN 0-316-11079-5 Subj: Animals – pigs. Etiquette.

Pickle things ill. by author. Parents, 1980. ISBN 0-8193-1028-X Subj: Food. Rhyming text.

Play rhymes ill. by author. Dutton, 1987. ISBN 0-525-44336-3 Subj: Games. Music. Nursery rhymes. Songs.

Rex and Lilly school time (Brown, Laurie Krasny)

The silly tail book ill. by author. Parents, 1983. ISBN 0-8193-1109-X Subj: Animals. Rhyming text.

Spooky riddles ill. by author. Random House, 1983. ISBN 0-394-96093-9 Subj: Ghosts. Humor. Monsters. Riddles. Witches.

Teddy bear, teddy bear ill. by author. Dutton, 1989. ISBN 0-525-44531-5 Subj: Format, unusual – toy and movable books. Rhyming text. Sports – jumping rope.

There's no place like home ill. by author. Parents, 1984. ISBN 0-8193-1125-1 Subj: Homes, houses. Rhyming text.

The true Francine ill. by author. Little, 1987. ISBN 0-316-11212-7 Subj: Animals – aardvarks. Behavior. Friendship. School.

Two little monkeys ill. by author. Dutton, 1989. ISBN 0-525-44533-1 Subj: Format, unusual – toy and movable books. Nursery rhymes.

Visiting the art museum (Brown, Laurie Krasny)

What do you call a dumb bunny? and other rabbit riddles, games, jokes and cartoons ill. by author. Little, 1983. ISBN 0-316-11117-1 Subj: Animals – rabbits. Format, unusual – toy and movable books. Games. Humor. Riddles.

What's the big secret? talking about sex with girls and boys (Brown, Laurie Krasny)

When dinosaurs die: a guide to understanding death (Brown, Laurie Krasny)

Wings on things ill. by author. Random House, 1982. ISBN 0-394-95130-1 Subj: Activities – flying. Rhyming text.

Witches four ill. by author. Parents, 1993. ISBN 0-8368-0893-2 Subj: Rhyming text. Witches.

Your first garden book ill. by author. Little, 1981. ISBN 0-316-11217-8 Subj: Gardens, gardening. Plants.

Brown, Marcia. *All butterflies: an ABC* ill. by author. Scribners, 1974. ISBN 0-684-13771-2 Subj: ABC books.

The blue jackal ill. by author. Scribners, 1977. ISBN 0-684-14905-2 Subj: Animals. Behavior – trickery. Folk and fairy tales. Foreign lands – India.

The bun: a tale from Russia ill. by author. Harcourt, 1972. ISBN 0-152-13450-6 Subj: Animals. Behavior – greed. Character traits – cleverness. Cumulative tales. Folk and fairy tales.

Dick Whittington and his cat (Dick Whittington and his cat)

Felice ill. by author. Scribners, 1958. Subj: Animals – cats. Foreign lands – Italy.

Henry fisherman ill. by author. Scribners, 1949. Subj: Caldecott award honor books. Careers – fishermen.

How, hippo! ill. by author. Scribners, 1969. Subj: Animals – hippopotamuses.

Listen to a shape photos by author. Watts, 1979. ISBN 0-531-02930-1 Subj: Concepts – shape.

The little carousel ill. by author. Scribners, 1946. Subj: City. Emotions – loneliness. Kites. Merry-go-rounds. Money.

The neighbors ill. by author. Scribners, 1967. Text adapted from Afanas'yev. Subj: Animals – foxes. Animals – rabbits. Cumulative tales. Foreign lands – Russia. Homes, houses.

Once a mouse . . . adapt. and ill. by author. Scribners, 1961. An adaption of Hitopadeśa, a tale from ancient India. ISBN 0-684-12662-1 Subj: Animals. Caldecott award books. Character traits – vanity. Concepts – size. Folk and fairy tales. Foreign lands – India. Magic.

Peter Piper's alphabet ill. by author. Scribners, 1959. Subj: ABC books. Nursery rhymes. Tongue twisters.

Shadow (Cendrars, Blaise)

Skipper John's cook ill. by author. Scribners, 1951. Subj: Activities – cooking. Boats, ships. Caldecott award honor books.

Stone soup ill. by author. Scribners, 1947. ISBN 0-684-92296-7 Subj: Caldecott award honor books. Careers – military. Character traits – cleverness. Folk and fairy tales. Food. Foreign lands – Russia.

Tamarindo! ill. by author. Scribners, 1960. Subj: Animals – donkeys. Behavior – lost. Foreign lands – Greece.

Touch will tell photos by author. Watts, 1979. ISBN 0-531-02931-X Subj: Concepts. Senses – touching.

Walk with your eyes photos by author. Watts, 1979. ISBN 0-531-02925-5 Subj: Concepts. Senses – seeing.

Brown, Margaret Wise. *Afro-bets: book of colors* ill. by Culverson Blair. Just Us Books, 1991. ISBN 0-940975-29-7 Subj: Concepts – color.

Afro-bets: book of shapes ill. by Culverson Blair. Just Us Books, 1991. ISBN 0-940975-28-9 Subj: Concepts – shape.

Another important book ill. by Christopher Raschka. HarperCollins, 1999. ISBN 0-06-026283-4 Subj: Behavior – growing up. Rhyming text.

Baby animals ill. by Mary Cameron. Random House, 1941. Subj: Animals.

Baby animals ill. by Susan Jeffers. Rev. ed. Random House, 1989. ISBN 0-394-92040-6 Subj: Animals.

Big dog, little dog ill. by Leonard Weisgard. Doubleday, 1943. Subj: Animals – dogs. Concepts – size.

The big fur secret ill. by Robert De Veyrac. HarperCollins, 1944. Subj: Animals. Communication. Zoos.

Big red barn ill. by Felicia Bond. HarperCollins, 1989. ISBN 0-06-020749-3 Subj: Animals. Barns. Farms. Rhyming text.

Big red barn ill. by Rosella Hartman. Addison-Wesley, 1956. ISBN 0-201-09114-1 Subj: Animals. Barns. Farms. Rhyming text.

Bumble bee ill. by Victoria Raymond. Harper-Collins, 1999. ISBN 0-694-01749-3 Subj: Format, unusual – board books. Insects – bees. Poetry.

Bumble bugs and elephants ill. by Clement Hurd. W. R. Scott, 1938. Subj: Concepts – size.

A child's good morning book ill. by Jean Charlot. HarperCollins, 1995. Previously published as: A child's good morning. 1952. ISBN 0-06-024539-5 Subj: Animals. Morning.

A child's good night book ill. by Jean Charlot. Addison-Wesley, 1950. ISBN 0-06-020752-3 Subj: Bedtime. Caldecott award honor books. Night. Sleep.

Christmas in the barn ill. by Barbara Cooney. Crowell, 1952. ISBN 0-690-19272-X Subj: Holidays – Christmas.

The country noisy book ill. by Leonard Weisgard. HarperCollins, 1994. ISBN 0-06-020811-2 Subj: Animals – dogs. Country. Noise, sounds. Participation.

The days before now: an autobiographical note adapt. by Joan W. Blos; ill. by Thomas B. Allen. Simon & Schuster, 1994. ISBN 0-671-79628-3 Subj: Animals. Careers – writers. Pets.

The dead bird ill. by Remy Charlip. W. R. Scott, 1958. ISBN 0-06-020758-2 Subj: Death. Emotions – grief.

The diggers ill. by Daniel Kirk. Hyperion, 1995. ISBN 0-7868-2001-2 Subj: Activities – digging. Animals. Machines. Poetry. Rhyming text.

Dr. Squash the doll doctor ill. by J. P. Miller. Simon & Schuster, 1952. Subj: Character traits – kindness. Toys – dolls. Toys – soldiers.

Don't frighten the lion ill. by H. A. Rey. Harper-Collins, 1942. ISBN 0-06-443262-9 Subj: Animals. Animals – dogs. Character traits – cleverness. Zoos.

Dream book ill. by Richard Flöethe. Random House, 1950. ISBN 1-56282-211-X Subj: Dreams.

The duck photos by Ylla. HarperCollins, 1953. Subj: Animals. Birds – ducks. Character traits – vanity.

Five little firemen by Margaret Wise Brown and Edith Thacher Hurd; ill. by Tibor Gergely. Simon & Schuster, 1948. Subj: Careers – firefighters. Noise, sounds.

Four fur feet ill. by Remy Charlip. W. R. Scott, 1961. ISBN 0-7868-2000-4 Subj: Activities – walking. Poetry. World.

Fox eyes ill. by Garth Williams. Pantheon, 1977, 1951. ISBN 0-394-93116-5 Subj: Animals. Animals – foxes.

The golden birthday book ill. by Leonard Weisgard. Western, 1989. ISBN 0-307-12096-1 Subj: Animals. Birthdays.

The golden egg book ill. by Leonard Weisgard. Simon & Schuster, 1947. ISBN 0-685-05367-9 Subj: Animals – rabbits. Birds – ducks. Eggs. Holidays – Easter.

Goodnight moon ill. by Clement Hurd. Harper-Collins, 1934. ISBN 0-590-73302-8 Subj: Animals – rabbits. Bedtime. Moon.

House of a hundred windows Cat and architecture by Robert de Veyrac; ill. by Henri Rousseau and others. HarperCollins, 1945. Subj: Animals – cats. Homes, houses.

The indoor noisy book ill. by Leonard Weisgard. HarperCollins, 1942. ISBN 0-06-020821-X Subj: Animals – dogs. Games. Noise, sounds. Participation.

The little brass band ill. by Clement Hurd. Harper-Collins, 1948. Subj: Cumulative tales. Music.

Little chicken ill. by Leonard Weisgard. Harper-Collins, 1943. ISBN 0-06-020740-X Subj: Animals – rabbits. Birds – chickens.

Little Donkey close your eyes ill. by Ashley Wolff. HarperCollins, 1995. ISBN 0-06-024483-6 Subj: Animals – donkeys. Bedtime. Night. Poetry.

The little farmer ill. by Esphyr Slobodkina. Addison-Wesley, 1948. Subj: Dreams. Farms.

The little fir tree ill. by Barbara Cooney. Crowell, 1954. ISBN 0-06-028190-1 Subj: Holidays – Christmas. Trees.

The little fireman ill. by Esphyr Slobodkina. HarperCollins, 1993. ISBN 0-06-021476-7 Subj: Careers – firefighters. Concepts – shape. Concepts – size. Fire.

The little fisherman ill. by Dahlov Ipcar. Addison-Wesley, 1945. Subj: Careers – fishermen. Fish.

The little fur family ill. by Garth Williams. Harper-Collins, 1946. ISBN 0-06-020746-9 Subj: Activities. Animals. Format, unusual.

The little island ill. by Leonard Weisgard. Double-day, 1946. Subj: Caldecott award books. Islands. Seasons. Weather.

Little lost lamb ill. by Leonard Weisgard. Double-day, 1945. ISBN 0-7868-2322-4 Subj: Animals – sheep. Behavior – lost. Caldecott award honor books.

The little scarecrow boy ill. by David Diaz. Harper-Collins, 1998. ISBN 0-06-026290-7 Subj: Family life. Scarecrows.

Nibble nibble ill. by Leonard Weisgard. Addison-Wesley, 1959. ISBN 0-201-09291-3 Subj: Poetry.

Night and day ill. by Leonard Weisgard. Harper-Collins, 1942. Subj: Animals – cats. Emotions – fear. Night.

Noisy book ill. by Leonard Weisgard. Harper-Collins, 1939. ISBN 0-06-020831-7 Subj: Noise, sounds. Participation.

On Christmas eve ill. by Nancy Edwards Calder. HarperCollins, 1996. ISBN 0-06-023649-3 Subj: Family life. Holidays – Christmas. Night. Religion.

On Christmas eve ill. by Beni Montresor. Harper, 1985, c1961. ISBN 0-201-09297-2 Subj: Family life. Holidays – Christmas. Night. Religion.

Once upon a time in pigpen and three other stories ill. by Ann Strugnell. Addison-Wesley, 1980. ISBN 0-201-00343-0 Subj: Animals. Humor.

A pussycat's Christmas ill. by Anne Mortimer. HarperCollins, 1994. ISBN 0-06-023533-0 Subj: Animals – cats. Holidays – Christmas.

Pussycat's Christmas ill. by Helen Stone. Harper-Collins, 1949. ISBN 0-690-65993-8 Subj: Animals – cats. Holidays – Christmas.

The quiet noisy book ill. by Leonard Weisgard. HarperCollins, 1950. ISBN 0-06-021220-9 Subj: Animals – dogs. Morning. Noise, sounds. Participation.

Red light, green light ill. by Leonard Weisgard. Scholastic, 1992. ISBN 0-590-44558-8 Subj: Concepts – color. Safety. Traffic, traffic signs.

The runaway bunny ill. by Clement Hurd. Harper, 1972, c1942. ISBN 0-06-020766-3 Subj: Animals – rabbits. Behavior – running away. Holidays – Easter.

The seashore noisy book ill. by Leonard Weisgard. HarperCollins, 1993, c1941. ISBN 0-06-020841-4 Subj: Animals – dogs. Noise, sounds. Participation. Sea and seashore.

SHHhhh . . . . Bang: a whispering book ill. by Robert De Veyrac. HarperCollins, 1943. Subj: Noise, sounds.

Sleepy ABC ill. by Esphyr Slobodkina. Harper-Collins, 1994. ISBN 0-06-024285-X Subj: ABC books. Bedtime. Rhyming text. Sleep.

The sleepy little lion ill. by Ylla. HarperCollins, 1947. ISBN 0-06-020771-X Subj: Animals – lions. Sleep.

The sleepy men ill. by Robert Rayevsky. Hyperion, 1996. ISBN 0-7868-0154-9 Subj: Bedtime. Moon. Sleep.

Sneakers ill. by Jean Charlot. Addison-Wesley, 1979, 1955. Reissue of 1955 ed. published by W. R. Scott under title Seven stories about a cat named Sneakers. ISBN 0-2010-0625-1 Subj: Animals – cats. Behavior – misbehavior.

The steamroller: a fantasy ill. by Evaline Ness. Walker, 1974. Published in 1938 in the author's collection, The fish with the deep sea smile. ISBN

0-8027-6192-5 Subj: Holidays – Christmas. Machines.

Streamlined pig ill. by Kurt Wiese. HarperCollins, 1938. Subj: Activities – flying. Airplanes, airports. Animals. Character traits – bravery.

The summer noisy book ill. by Leonard Weisgard. HarperCollins, 1993, c1951. ISBN 0-06-020856-2 Subj: Animals – dogs. Farms. Noise, sounds. Participation. Seasons – summer.

They all saw it photos by Ylla. HarperCollins, 1944. Subj: Animals. Problem solving.

Three little animals ill. by Garth Williams. Harper-Collins, 1956. Subj: Activities – traveling. Animals. Behavior – lost. City.

The train to Timbuctoo ill. by Art Seiden. Golden Books, 1999. ISBN 0-307-10215-7 Subj: Trains.

Two little miners ill. by Edith Thacher Hurd. Simon & Schuster, 1949. Subj: Careers – miners.

Two little trains ill. by Jean Charlot. Addison-Wesley, 1949. ISBN 0-201-09381-2 Subj: Rhyming text. Trains.

Under the sun and the moon and other poems ill. by Tom Leonard. Hyperion, 1993. ISBN 1-56282-355-8 Subj: Poetry.

Wait till the moon is full ill. by Garth Williams. HarperCollins, 1948. ISBN 0-06-020801-5 Subj: Animals. Animals – raccoons. Character traits – questioning. Moon. Night.

Wheel on the chimney by Margaret Wise Brown and Tibor Gergely; ill. by Tibor Gergely. Lippincott, 1954. ISBN 0-397-30296-7 Subj: Birds – storks. Caldecott award honor books. Character traits – luck. Foreign lands – Hungary.

When the wind blew ill. by Geoffrey Hayes. Harper-Collins, 1977, 1937. ISBN 0-06-020868-6 Subj: Animals – cats. Illness. Weather – wind.

Where have you been? ill. by Barbara Cooney. Reissue of Crowell, 1952 ed. Hastings House, 1981. ISBN 0-8038-8018-9 Subj: Animals. Poetry.

The whispering rabbit ill. by Cyndy Szekeres. Western, 1992. ISBN 0-307-00138-5 Subj: Animals – rabbits. Insects – bees.

Whistle for the train ill. by Leonard Weisgard. Doubleday, 1956. Subj: Rhyming text. Trains.

The winter noisy book ill. by Charles Green Shaw. HarperCollins, 1994. ISBN 0-06-020866-X Subj: Animals – dogs. Noise, sounds. Participation. Seasons – winter. Weather – snow.

The wonderful house ill. by J. P. Miller. Simon & Schuster, 1950. ISBN 0-307-20313-1 Subj: Homes, houses.

The wonderful story book ill. by J. P. Miller. Simon & Schuster, 1948. Subj: Poetry.

Young kangaroo ill. by Symeon Shimin. Addison-Wesley, 1955. ISBN 1-56282-410-4 Subj: Animals – kangaroos.

Brown, Myra Berry. *Benjy's blanket* ill. by Dorothy Marino. Watts, 1962. Subj: Animals – cats. Behavior – growing up.

Best friends ill. by Don Freeman. Golden Gate, 1967. Subj: Friendship. Poetry.

Company's coming for dinner ill. by Dorothy Marino. Watts, 1960. Subj: Character traits – helpfulness. Etiquette. Parties.

First night away from home ill. by Dorothy Marino. Watts, 1960. Subj: Activities – playing. Friendship. Sleep. Toys – bears.

Pip camps out ill. by Phyllis Graham. Golden Gate, 1966. Subj: Camps, camping. Family life. Night.

Brown, Palmer. *Something for Christmas* ill. by author. HarperCollins, 1958. Subj: Animals – mice. Character traits – generosity. Emotions – love. Holidays – Christmas.

Brown, Richard Eric. *One hundred words about animals* ill. by author. Harcourt, 1987. ISBN 0-15-200550-1 Subj: Animals.

Brown, Rick. *Who built the ark?* ill. by author. Viking, 1994. ISBN 0-670-85160-4 Subj: Animals. Boats, ships. Counting, numbers. Format, unusual. Religion – Noah. Weather – floods. Weather – rain.

Brown, Ruth. *Alphabet times four* ill. by author. Dutton, 1991. ISBN 0-525-44831-4 Subj: ABC books. Foreign languages.

The big sneeze ill. by author. Lothrop, 1985. ISBN 0-688-04666-5 Subj: Farms. Humor.

Copycat ill. by author. Dutton, 1994. ISBN 0-525-45326-1 Subj: Animals. Animals – cats. Behavior.

Crazy Charlie ill. by author. Rourke, 1982. ISBN 0-86592-124-5 Subj: Reptiles – alligators, crocodiles. Self-concept. Teeth.

Cry baby ill. by author. Dutton, 1997. ISBN 0-525-45902-2 Subj: Family life – sisters.

A dark, dark tale ill. by author. Dial, 1981. ISBN 0-8037-1673-7 Subj: Cumulative tales. Foreign lands – England.

The ghost of Greyfriar's Bobby ill. by author. Dutton, 1996. ISBN 0-525-45581-7 Subj: Animals – dogs. Character traits – persistence. Foreign lands – Scotland.

The grizzly revenge ill. by author. Andersen, 1983. ISBN 0-8626-4024-5 Subj: Animals. Character traits – kindness to animals. Royalty – kings. Royalty – queens.

I don't like it! ill. by author. Dutton, 1990. ISBN 0-525-44559-5 Subj: Animals – dogs. Emotions – envy, jealousy. Toys. Toys – dolls.

If at first you do not see ill. by author. Holt, 1983. ISBN 0-03-063521-7 Subj: Format, unusual – toy and movable books. Insects – butterflies, caterpillars.

Ladybug, ladybug ill. by author. Dutton, 1988. ISBN 0-525-44423-8 Subj: Insects – ladybugs. Nursery rhymes.

Mad summer night's dream ill. by author. Dutton, 1999. ISBN 0-525-46010-1 Subj: Dreams. Rhyming text.

One stormy night ill. by author. Dutton, 1993. ISBN 0-525-45091-2 Subj: Animals. Ghosts. Night. Weather – storms.

Our cat Flossie ill. by author. Dutton, 1986. ISBN 0-525-44256-1 Subj: Activities. Animals – cats.

Our puppy's vacation ill. by author. Dutton, 1987. ISBN 0-525-44326-6 Subj: Activities – playing. Activities – vacationing. Animals – dogs. Pets.

The picnic ill. by author. Dutton, 1992. ISBN 0-525-45012-2 Subj: Activities – picnicking. Animals.

The shy little angel ill. by author. Dutton, 1998. ISBN 0-525-46079-9 Subj: Angels. School. Theater.

Toad ill. by author. Dutton, 1997. ISBN 0-525-45757-7 Subj: Frogs and toads. Rhyming text.

The world that Jack built ill. by author. Dutton, 1991. ISBN 0-525-44635-4 Subj: Cumulative tales. Ecology.

Brown, Tricia. *The city by the bay: a magical journey around San Francisco* by Tricia Brown and the Junior League of San Francisco; ill. by Elisa Kleven. Chronicle, 1993. ISBN 0-811-80233-7 Subj: Activities – traveling. City.

Hello, amigos! photos by Fran Ortiz. Holt, 1986. ISBN 0-8050-0090-9 Subj: Birthdays. Ethnic groups in the U.S. – Mexican Americans. Family life. School.

Someone special, just like you photos by Fran Ortiz. Holt, 1984. ISBN 0-03-069706-9 Subj: Emotions. Handicaps.

Browne, Anthony. *Bear goes to town* ill. by author. Doubleday, 1989. ISBN 0-385-26524-7 Subj: Animals. Animals – bears. Art. Imagination.

Bear hunt ill. by author. Atheneum, 1980. ISBN 0-689-30733-0 Subj: Animals – bears. Art. Problem solving. Sports – hunting.

The big baby ill. by author. Knopf, 1994. ISBN 0-679-84737-5 Subj: Babies. Character traits – vanity. Family life – fathers.

Changes ill. by author. Julia MacRae Books, 1991. ISBN 0-679-91029-8 Subj: Babies. Family life. Imagination.

Gorilla ill. by author. Knopf, 1985, 1983. ISBN 0-394-97525-1 Subj: Animals – gorillas. Birthdays. Family life – fathers. Imagination. Toys.

I like books ill. by author. Knopf, 1989. ISBN 0-394-84186-7 Subj: Activities – reading. Animals – chimpanzees.

The little bear book ill. by author. Doubleday, 1989. ISBN 0-385-26006-7 Subj: Animals. Animals – bears. Art. Imagination.

Look what I've got! ill. by author. Watts, 1980. ISBN 0-394-99860-X Subj: Behavior – boasting. Imagination.

Piggybook ill. by author. Knopf, 1986. ISBN 0-394-98416-1 Subj: Animals – pigs. Family life – mothers.

Things I like ill. by author. Knopf, 1989. ISBN 0-394-94192-6 Subj: Activities – playing. Animals – chimpanzees.

Through the magic mirror ill. by author. Greenwillow, 1992. ISBN 0-688-10725-7 Subj: Imagination. Magic.

The tunnel ill. by author. Knopf, 1989. ISBN 0-3949-4582-4 Subj: Family life – brothers and sisters.

Voices in the park ill. by author. DK, 1998. ISBN 0-7894-2522-X Subj: Animals – dogs. Animals – gorillas. Parks. Seasons.

Willy and Hugh ill. by author. Knopf, 1991. ISBN 0-679-91446-3 Subj: Animals – chimpanzees. Animals – gorillas. Friendship.

Willy the champ ill. by author. Knopf, 1986. ISBN 0-394-97907-9 Subj: Animals – chimpanzees. Animals – gorillas. Behavior – bullying.

Willy the dreamer ill. by author. Candlewick, 1998. ISBN 0-7636-0378-3 Subj: Animals – chimpanzees. Dreams.

Willy the wimp ill. by author. Knopf, 1985. ISBN 0-394-97061-6 Subj: Animals – chimpanzees. Animals – gorillas. Self-concept.

Willy the wizard ill. by author. Knopf, 1995. ISBN 0-679-97644-2 Subj: Animals – chimpanzees. Clothing – shoes. Sports – soccer.

Zoo ill. by author. Knopf, 1992. ISBN 0-679-93946-6 Subj: Animals. Family life. Zoos.

Browne, Caroline. *Mrs. Christie's farmhouse* ill. by author. Doubleday, 1977. ISBN 0-385-13275-1 Subj: Country. Farms. Gardens, gardening. Humor. Royalty.

Browne, Eileen. *No problem* ill. by David Parkins. Candlewick, 1993. ISBN 1-56402-200-5 Subj: Activities – reading. Airplanes, airports. Animals. Birthdays.

Tick-tock ill. by David Parkins. Candlewick, 1994. ISBN 1-56402-300-1 Subj: Animals – squirrels. Behavior – misbehavior. Clocks, watches.

Where's that bus? ill. by author. Simon & Schuster, 1991. ISBN 0-671-73810-0 Subj: Activities – picnicking. Animals – moles. Animals – rabbits. Animals – squirrels. Buses. Friendship.

Browne, Gerard. *The aircraft lift-the-flap book* ill. by author. Lodestar, 1992. ISBN 0-525-67351-2 Subj: Airplanes, airports. Format, unusual – toy and movable books.

Browne, Philippa-Alys. *A gaggle of geese: the collective names of the animal kingdom* ill. by author. Atheneum, 1996. ISBN 0-689-80761-9 Subj: Animals. Birds. Concepts. Rhyming text.

Browne, Vee. *Monster birds: a Navajo folktale* ill. by Baje Whitethorne. Northland, 1993. ISBN 0-87359-558-5 Subj: Birds. Folk and fairy tales. Indians of North America – Navajo. Monsters. Multiple births – twins.

Brownell, Barbara. *Spin's really wild U.S.A. tour* ill. by Barbara Gibson. National Geographic, 1996. ISBN 0-7922-3422-7 Subj: Animals. Nature. Plants. U.S. history.

Browner, Richard. *Everyone has a name* ill. by Emma Landau. Walck, 1961. Subj: Animals. Names. Poetry.

Look again! ill. by Emma Landau. Atheneum, 1962. Subj: Concepts.

Browning, Robert. *The pied piper of Hamelin* (Bartos-Hoppner, Barbara)

The pied piper of Hamelin (Mayer, Mercer)

The pied piper of Hamelin adapt. by Sharon Chmielarz; ill. by Patricia and Robin DeWitt. Stemmer House, 1990. ISBN 0-88045-115-7 Subj: Animals – rats. Behavior – trickery. Folk and fairy tales. Foreign lands – Germany. Poetry.

The pied piper of Hamelin ill. by Kate Greenaway. Warne, [1910]. ISBN 0-688-03810-7 Subj: Animals – rats. Behavior – trickery. Folk and fairy tales. Foreign lands – Germany. Poetry.

The pied piper of Hamelin ill. by Anatoly Ivanov. Lothrop, 1986. ISBN 0-688-03810-1 Subj: Animals – rats. Behavior – trickery. Folk and fairy tales. Foreign lands – Germany. Poetry.

The pied piper of Hamelin adapt. by Sara and Stephen Corrin; ill. by Errol Le Cain. Harcourt, 1989. ISBN 0-15-261596-2 Subj: Animals – rats. Behavior – trickery. Folk and fairy tales. Foreign lands – Germany. Poetry.

The pied piper of Hamelin retold by Robert Holden; ill. by Drahos Zak. Houghton Mifflin, 1997. ISBN 0-395-89918-4 Subj: Animals – rats. Behavior – trickery. Folk and fairy tales. Foreign lands – Germany. Poetry.

Brownridge, William Roy. *The final game: the further adventures of the moccasin goalie* ill. by author. Orca, 1997. ISBN 1-55143-100-9 Subj: Behavior – sharing. Sports – soccer.

The moccasin goalie ill. by author. Orca, 1996. ISBN 1-55143-042-8 Subj: Emotions. Handicaps. Indians of North America. Sports – hockey.

Bruandet, Jerome. *Baby clown* (Dedieu, Thierry)

Bruce, Lisa. *Fran's flower* ill. by Rosalind Beardshaw. HarperCollins, 2000. ISBN 0-06-028621-0 Subj: Flowers. Gardens, gardening. Plants.

Oliver's alphabets ill. by Debi Gliori. Bradbury, 1993. ISBN 0-02-735996-4 Subj: ABC books. Language.

Bruce, Sheilah B. *The radish day jubilee* ill. by Lawrence DiFiori. Holt, 1983. ISBN 0-03-068678-4 Subj: Imagination. Poetry. Puppets.

Bruchac, Joseph. *A boy called Slow: the true story of Sitting Bull* ill. by Rocco Baviera. Philomel, 1994. ISBN 0-399-22692-3 Subj: Behavior – growing up. Indians of North America – Dakota (Sioux).

The circle of thanks: native American poems and songs of Thanksgiving ill. by Murv Jacob. BridgeWater, 1996. ISBN 0-8167-4012-7 Subj: Folk and fairy tales. Indians of North America. Nature. Poetry.

The first strawberries: a Cherokee story ill. by Anna Vojtech. Dial, 1993. ISBN 0-8037-1332-0 Subj: Folk and fairy tales. Indians of North America – Cherokee.

Gluskabe and the four wishes ill. by Christine Nyburg Shrader. Cobblehill, 1995. ISBN 0-525-65164-0 Subj: Behavior – wishing. Folk and fairy tales. Indians of North America – Abnaki.

The great ball game: a Muskogee story ill. by Susan L. Roth. Dial, 1994. ISBN 0-8037-1540-4 Subj: Animals. Behavior – fighting, arguing. Birds. Folk and fairy tales. Indians of North America – Creek. Indians of North America – Muskogee.

Many nations: an alphabet of Native America ill. by Robert F. Goetzl. BridgeWater, 1997. ISBN 0-8167-4389-4 Subj: ABC books. Indians of North America.

Thirteen moons on turtle's back by Joseph Bruchac and Jonathan London; ill. by Thomas Locker. Putnam, 1992. ISBN 0-399-22141-7 Subj: Folk and fairy tales. Indians of North America. Poetry. Seasons.

Bruna, Dick. *Another story to tell* ill. by author. Methuen, 1978. ISBN 0-458-92680-9 Subj: Weather – snow. Wordless.

B is for bear: an A-B-C ill. by author. Methuen, 1971. ISBN 0-416-93100-6 Subj: ABC books.

Christmas ill. by author; tr. and English verse by Eve Merriam. Doubleday, 1969. Tr. of Kerstmis. Subj: Holidays – Christmas. Religion. Rhyming text.

The Christmas book ill. by author. Methuen, 1964. Subj: Holidays – Christmas.

Dick Bruna's Cinderella ill. by author. Follett, 1966. Subj: Folk and fairy tales. Royalty – princes. Sibling rivalry.

Dick Bruna's Little Red Riding Hood by Jacob and Wilhelm Grimm; ill. by Dick Bruna. Follett, 1966. Subj: Animals – wolves. Behavior – talking to strangers. Folk and fairy tales.

Dick Bruna's picture word book ill. by author. Random House, 1989. ISBN 0-517-05662-3 Subj: Concepts. Dictionaries.

Dick Bruna's Snow-White and the seven dwarfs ill. by author. Follett, 1966. Subj: Dwarfs, midgets. Emotions – envy, jealousy. Folk and fairy tales. Magic. Witches.

Dick Bruna's Tom Thumb ill. by author. Follett, 1966. Subj: Dwarfs, midgets. Folk and fairy tales.

Farmer John ill. by author. Price Stern Sloan, 1984. ISBN 0-8431-1526-2 Subj: Farms.

The fish ill. by author. Follett, 1963. English verse tr. from the Dutch by Sandra Greifenstein. ISBN 0-416-30341-2 Subj: Fish. Food. Poetry.

The happy apple by Dick Bruna and and Judith Klugmann; ill. by Dick Bruna. Hart, 1959. Subj: Activities – flying. Behavior – wishing. Rhyming text.

I can count ill. by author. Two Continents, 1975. ISBN 0-8467-0082-4 Subj: Counting, numbers.

I can count more ill. by author. Two Continents, 1976. ISBN 0-8467-0168-5 Subj: Counting, numbers.

I can dress myself ill. by author. Methuen, 1977. ISBN 0-458-93270-1 Subj: Behavior – growing up. Clothing.

I can read ill. by author. Two Continents, 1975. ISBN 0-8467-0086-7 Subj: Activities – reading.

I can read difficult words ill. by author. Methuen, 1978. ISBN 0-458-92690-6 Subj: Activities – reading.

I can read more ill. by author. Two Continents, 1976. ISBN 0-8431-1539-4 Subj: Activities – reading.

I know more about numbers ill. by author. Methuen, 1981. ISBN 0-416-20870-3 Subj: Counting, numbers.

Kitten Nell ill. by author. Follett, 1963. Subj: Animals – cats. Humor. Rhyming text.

Lisa and Lynn ill. by author. Two Continents, 1975. ISBN 0-8431-1537-8 Subj: Multiple births – twins.

The little bird ill. by author. Two Continents, 1975. ISBN 0-8431-1541-6 Subj: Birds.

Little bird tweet ill. by author. Follett, 1963. Subj: Birds. Farms. Rhyming text.

Miffy ill. by author. Follett, 1970. Translation of Nijntje. ISBN 0-695-80117-1 Subj: Animals – rabbits. Family life.

Miffy at the beach ill. by author. Methuen, 1980. ISBN 0-416-30151-7 Subj: Animals – rabbits. Sea and seashore.

Miffy at the playground ill. by author. Methuen, 1980. ISBN 0-416-30161-4 Subj: Activities – playing. Animals – rabbits.

Miffy at the seaside ill. by author. Follett, 1970. Translation of Nijntje aan zee. ISBN 0-695-80118-X Subj: Animals – rabbits. Sea and seashore.

Miffy at the zoo ill. by author. Follett, 1970. Translation of Nijntje in de dierentuin. ISBN 0-695-80121-X Subj: Animals – rabbits. Zoos.

Miffy goes flying ill. by author. Two Continents, 1976. New York. ISBN 0-8431-1535-1 Subj: Activities – flying. Animals – rabbits.

Miffy goes to school ill. by author. Price Stern Sloan, 1984. ISBN 0-8431-1530-0 Subj: Animals – rabbits. School – first day.

Miffy in the hospital ill. by author. Methuen, 1978. ISBN 0-458-92700-7 Subj: Animals – rabbits. Hospitals. Illness.

Miffy in the snow ill. by author. Follett, 1970. Translation of Nijntje in de sneeuw. ISBN 0-695-80119-8 Subj: Animals – rabbits. Seasons – winter. Weather – snow.

Miffy's bicycle ill. by author. Price Stern Sloan, 1984. ISBN 0-8431-1527-0 Subj: Animals – rabbits. Sports – bicycling.

Miffy's birthday ill. by author. Two Continents, 1976. ISBN 0-8431-1545-9 Subj: Animals – rabbits. Birthdays. Family life.

Miffy's dream ill. by author. Methuen, 1980. ISBN 0-416-88650-7 Subj: Activities – playing. Animals – rabbits. Dreams.

My shirt is white ill. by author. Two Continents, 1975. ISBN 0-416-30291-2 Subj: Clothing. Concepts – color.

My toys ill. by author. Methuen, 1980. ISBN 0-416-30761-2 Subj: Format, unusual – toy and movable books. Toys.

The orchestra ill. by author. Price Stern Sloan, 1984. ISBN 0-8431-1529-7 Subj: Music. Rhyming text.

Poppy Pig goes to market ill. by author. Methuen, 1981. ISBN 0-416-20890-8 Subj: Animals – pigs. Counting, numbers. Rhyming text.

The sailor ill. by author. Methuen, 1980. ISBN 0-416-30171-1 Subj: Activities – traveling. Boats, ships. Sailors.

The school ill. by author. Methuen, 1980. ISBN 0-416-30181-9 Subj: School.

Snuffy ill. by author. Two Continents, 1975. ISBN 0-8431-1548-3 Subj: Animals – dogs. Behavior – lost.

Snuffy and the fire ill. by author. Two Continents, 1975. ISBN 0-8431-1549-1 Subj: Animals – dogs. Fire.

A story to tell ill. by author. Two Continents, 1975. ISBN 0-8431-1576-9 Subj: Friendship. Wordless.

Tilly and Tess ill. by author. Follett, 1963. Subj: Birthdays. Multiple births – twins. Rhyming text.

Brunhoff, Jean de. *Babar and Father Christmas* trans. by Merle Haas; ill. by author. Random House, 1940. Translation of Babar et le Père Nöel. ISBN 0-394-89265-8 Subj: Animals – elephants. Holidays – Christmas.

Babar and his children trans. by Merle Haas; ill. by author. Random House, 1938. ISBN 0-394-90577-6 Subj: Animals – elephants. Multiple births – triplets.

Babar and Zephir trans. from French by Merle Haas; ill. by author. Reprint of 1937 ed. Random House, 1942. Subj: Animals – elephants. Animals – monkeys.

Babar the king trans. by Merle Haas; ill. by author. Random House, 1935. ISBN 0-394-90580-6 Subj: Animals – elephants. Royalty – kings.

Babar the king trans. by Merle Haas; ill. by author. Facsimile ed. Random House, 1986. ISBN 0-394-88245-8 Subj: Animals – elephants. Royalty – kings.

The story of Babar, the little elephant trans. by Merle Haas; ill. by author. Random House, 1984, c1933. ISBN 0-394-86823-4 Subj: Animals – elephants. Behavior – running away. Foreign lands – France.

The travels of Babar trans. by Merle Haas; ill. by author. Random House, 1934, 1961. ISBN 0-394-90576-8 Subj: Activities – traveling. Animals – elephants.

Brunhoff, Laurent de. *Babar and the ghost* ill. by author. Random House, 1981. ISBN 0-394-94660-X Subj: Animals – elephants. Ghosts.

Babar and the ghost ill. by author. Easy-to-read ed. Random House, 1986. ISBN 0-394-97908-7 Subj: Animals – elephants. Ghosts.

Babar and the Wully-Wully ill. by author. Random House, 1975. ISBN 0-394-93077-0 Subj: Animals – elephants. Pets.

Babar comes to America trans. by M. Jean Craig; ill. by author. Random House, 1965. Translation of Babar en Amérique. Subj: Animals – elephants.

Babar learns to cook ill. by author. Random House, 1979. ISBN 0-394-94108-X Subj: Activities – cooking. Animals – elephants.

Babar the magician ill. by author. Random House, 1980. ISBN 0-394-84360-6 Subj: Animals – elephants. Animals – monkeys. Magic.

Babar visits another planet trans. by Merle Haas; ill. by author. Random House, 1972. Translation of Babar sur la planète molle. ISBN 0-394-92429-0 Subj: Animals – elephants. Space and space ships.

Babar's ABC ill. by author. Random House, 1983. ISBN 0-394-95920-5 Subj: ABC books. Animals – elephants.

Babar's battle ill. by author. Random House, 1992. ISBN 0-679-91068-9 Subj: Animals – elephants. Animals – rhinoceros. War.

Babar's birthday surprise ill. by author. Random House, 1970. Translation of Anniversaire de Babar. ISBN 0-394-90591-1 Subj: Animals – elephants. Birthdays.

Babar's book of color ill. by author. Random House, 1984. ISBN 0-394-86896-X Subj: Animals – elephants. Concepts – color.

Babar's castle trans. by Merle Haas; ill. by author. Random House, 1962. ISBN 0-394-90586-5 Subj: Animals – elephants.

Babar's counting book ill. by author. Random House, 1986. ISBN 0-394-97517-0 Subj: Animals. Animals – elephants. Counting, numbers.

Babar's cousin, that rascal Arthur trans. by Merle Haas; ill. by author. Random House, 1948. Translation of Babar et ce coquin d'Arthur. A continuation of the Babar stories of Jean de Brunhoff. ISBN 0-394-90581-4 Subj: Activities – vacationing. Animals – elephants. Behavior – misbehavior.

Babar's fair will be opened next Sunday trans. by Merle Haas; ill. by author. Random House, 1954. Translation of La fête de Célesteville. ISBN 0-394-90584-9 Subj: Animals – elephants. Fairs.

Babar's little circus star ill. by author. Random House, 1988. ISBN 0-394-98959-7 Subj: Animals. Animals – elephants. Circus.

Babar's little girl ill. by author. Random House, 1987. ISBN 0-394-98689-X Subj: Animals – elephants. Behavior – carelessness. Behavior – lost. Character traits – kindness to animals.

Babar's mystery ill. by author. Random House, 1978. ISBN 0-394-93920-4 Subj: Activities – vacationing. Animals – elephants. Crime.

Babar's picnic ill. by author. Random House, 1991. ISBN 0-679-81245-8 Subj: Activities – picnicking. Animals – elephants.

Babar's visit to Bird Island ill. by author. Random House, 1952. Subj: Animals – elephants. Birds. Islands. Royalty – kings.

The rescue of Babar ill. by author. Random House, 1993. ISBN 0-679-93897-4 Subj: Animals. Animals – elephants. Crime.

Serafina the giraffe ill. by author. Collins-World, 1961. Subj: Animals – giraffes. Birthdays. Humor.

Brusca, María Cristina. *The cook and the king* by María Cristina Brusca and Toña Wilson; ill. by María Cristina Brusca. Holt, 1993. ISBN 0-8050-2355-0 Subj: Folk and fairy tales. Foreign lands – South America. Royalty – kings.

When jaguars ate the moon: and other stories about animals and plants of the Americas by María Cristina Brusca and Toña Wilson; ill. by María Cristina Brusca. Holt, 1995. ISBN 0-8050-2797-1 Subj: ABC books. Animals. Animals – jaguars. Folk and fairy tales. Foreign lands – South America.

Brustlein, Janice Tworkov. *see* Janice

Brutschy, Jennifer. *Celeste and Crabapple Sam* ill. by Eileen Christelow. Lodestar, 1994. ISBN 0-525-67416-0 Subj: Animals. Behavior – hiding. Character traits – persistence. Friendship. Pets. Sea and seashore.

Just one more story ill. by Cat Bowman Smith. Orchard, 2001. ISBN 0-531-33296-9 Subj: Activities – storytelling. Activities – traveling. Family life – fathers.

The winter fox ill. by Allen Garns. Knopf, 1993. ISBN 0-679-91524-9 Subj: Animals – foxes. Animals – rabbits. Character traits – kindness to animals. Family life. Seasons – winter.

Bryan, Ashley. *All night, all day: a child's first book of African-American spirituals* ill. by sel. Macmillan, 1991. ISBN 0-689-31662-3 Subj: Ethnic groups in the U.S. – African Americans. Music. Religion. Songs.

Beat the story-drum, pum-pum ill. by adapt. Atheneum, 1980. ISBN 0-689-30769-1 Subj: Cumulative tales. Folk and fairy tales. Foreign lands – Africa. Rhyming text.

The cat's purr ill. by author. Atheneum, 1985. ISBN 0-689-31086-2 Subj: Animals – cats. Animals – rats. Folk and fairy tales. Rhyming text.

The dancing granny retold and ill. by Ashley Bryan. Aladdin, 1987. ISBN 0-689-71149-2 Subj: Folk and fairy tales. Gardens, gardening. Mythical creatures. Spiders.

I'm going to sing: Black American spirituals, Vol. II ill. by author. Atheneum, 1982. ISBN 0-689-30915-5 Subj: Ethnic groups in the U.S. – African Americans. Songs.

Lion and the ostrich chicks: and other African tales ill. by author. Atheneum, 1986. ISBN 0-689-31311-X Subj: Folk and fairy tales. Foreign lands – Africa. Songs.

Sh-ko and his eight wicked brothers ill. by Fumio Yoshimura. Atheneum, 1988. ISBN 0-689-31446-9 Subj: Character traits – kindness to animals. Folk and fairy tales. Foreign lands – Japan.

Sing to the sun ill. by author. HarperCollins, 1992. ISBN 0-06-020833-3 Subj: Foreign lands – Caribbean Islands. Nature. Poetry.

The story of lightning and thunder ill. by author. Atheneum, 1993. ISBN 0-689-31836-7 Subj: Folk and fairy tales. Foreign lands – Africa. Weather – storms. Weather – thunder.

Turtle knows your name ill. by author. Macmillan, 1989. ISBN 0-689-31578-3 Subj: Family life – grandmothers. Folk and fairy tales. Names. Reptiles – turtles, tortoises.

Bryan, Dorothy. *Friendly little Jonathan* by Dorothy and Marguerite Bryan; ill. by Marguerite Bryan. Dodd, 1939. Subj: Animals – dogs. Friendship.

Just Tammie! by Dorothy and Marguerite Bryan; ill. by Marguerite Bryan. Dodd, 1951. Subj: Animals – dogs.

Bryan, Marguerite. *Friendly little Jonathan* (Bryan, Dorothy)

Just Tammie! (Bryan, Dorothy)

Bryant, Bernice. *Follow the leader* ill. by author. Houghton Mifflin, 1950. Subj: Behavior – bullying. Behavior – growing up. Character traits – selfishness.

Bryant, Dean. *Here am I* ill. by author. Rand McNally, 1947. Subj: Activities.

See the bear ill. by author. Rand McNally, 1947. Subj: Toys.

Bryant, Donna. *My rabbit Roberta* ill. by Jakki Wood. Barron's, 1991. ISBN 0-8120-6210-8 Subj: Animals – rabbits. Pets.

Bryant, Michael. *The story of Nat Love* (Miller, Robert H. [Robert Henry])

Bryant, Sara Cone. *Epaminondas* (Merriam, Eve)

Epaminondas and his auntie ill. by Inez Hogan. Houghton Mifflin, 1938. Subj: Behavior – misunderstanding. Family life – aunts, uncles. Folk and fairy tales. Humor.

Bryant-Mole, Karen. *Moving* ill. by author. Heinemann Interactive, 1998. ISBN 1-57572-630-0 Subj: Animals. Plants. Science.

Bryson, Bernarda. *The twenty miracles of Saint Nicolas* ill. by author. Atlantic Monthly, 1960. Subj: Folk and fairy tales. Foreign lands. Holidays – Christmas.

Buchanan, Debby. *It rained on the desert today* (Buchanan, Ken)

Buchanan, Heather S. *Emily Mouse saves the day* ill. by author. Dial, 1985. ISBN 0-8037-0175-6 Subj: Animals – mice. Character traits – helpfulness. Family life.

Emily Mouse's beach house ill. by author. Dial, 1987. ISBN 0-8037-0263-9 Subj: Animals – mice. Sea and seashore.

Emily Mouse's first adventure ill. by author. Dial, 1985. ISBN 0-8037-0174-8 Subj: Animals – mice. Character traits – kindness to animals.

Emily Mouse's garden ill. by author. Dial, 1987. ISBN 0-8037-0261-2 Subj: Animals – mice. Gardens, gardening. Sibling rivalry.

George and Matilda Mouse and the floating school ill. by author. Simon & Schuster, 1990. ISBN 0-671-70613-6 Subj: Animals – mice. Problem solving. School. Toys.

George and Matilda Mouse and the moon rocket ill. by author. Simon & Schuster, 1992. ISBN 0-671-75864-0 Subj: Animals – mice. Holidays – Guy Fawkes Day. Moon.

George Mouse learns to fly ill. by author. Dial, 1985. ISBN 0-8037-0172-1 Subj: Activities – flying. Airplanes, airports. Animals – mice.

George Mouse's covered wagon ill. by author. Dial, 1987. ISBN 0-8037-0258-2 Subj: Activities – traveling. Activities – vacationing. Animals – mice. Sea and seashore.

George Mouse's first summer ill. by author. Dial, 1985. ISBN 0-8037-0173-X Subj: Animals – mice. Character traits – cleverness. Problem solving. Seasons – summer.

George Mouse's riverboat band ill. by author. Dial, 1987. ISBN 0-8037-0260-4 Subj: Animals – mice. Boats, ships.

Buchanan, Joan. *It's a good thing* ill. by Barbara Di Lella. Firefly, 1984. ISBN 0-920236-72-3 Subj: Activities – walking. Behavior – carelessness. Humor.

Buchanan, Ken. *It rained on the desert today* by Ken and Debby Buchanan; ill. by Libba Tracey. Northland, 1994. ISBN 0-87358-575-5 Subj: Desert. Poetry. Weather – rain. Weather – storms.

This house is made of mud ill. by Libba Tracy. Northland, 1991. ISBN 0-87358-518-6 Subj: Desert. Homes, houses.

Buchheimer, Naomi. *Let's go to a post office* ill. by Ruth Van Sciver. Putnam, 1957. Subj: Careers – postal workers. Communication. Post office.

Let's go to a school ill. by Ruth Van Sciver. Putnam, 1957. Subj: School.

Buchholz, Quint. *Sleep well, little bear* trans. from German by Peter F. Neumeyer; by ill. by author. Farrar, 1994. ISBN 0-374-37026-5 Subj: Bedtime. Night. Toys – bears.

Buck, Frank. *Jungle animals* by Frank Buck; text by Ferrin Fraser; ill. by Roger Vernam. Random House, 1945. Subj: Animals.

Buck, Nola. *The basement stairs* ill. by Jonathan Lambert. HarperCollins, 1993. ISBN 0-694-00649-1 Subj: Emotions – fear. Format, unusual – toy and movable books.

Christmas in the manger ill. by Felicia Bond. HarperFestival, 1994. ISBN 0-694-00605-X Subj: Format, unusual – toy and movable books. Holidays – Christmas. Religion – Nativity. Rhyming text.

Creepy crawly critters and other Halloween tongue twisters ill. by Sue Truesdell. HarperCollins, 1995. ISBN 0-06-024809-2 Subj: Animals. Holidays – Halloween. Insects. Language. Tongue twisters.

Gotcha! ill. by Jonathan Lambert. HarperCollins, 1994. ISBN 0-694-00648-3 Subj: Format, unusual – toy and movable books. Ghosts. Holidays – Halloween. Rhyming text.

Halloween parade ill. by Jonathan Lambert. HarperCollins, 1994. ISBN 0-694-00646-7 Subj: Format, unusual – toy and movable books. Holidays – Halloween. Rhyming text.

Hey, little baby! ill. by R. W. Alley. HarperFestival, 1999. ISBN 0-694-01200-9 Subj: Babies. Behavior – growing up. Family life – brothers and sisters.

How a baby grows ill. by Pamela Paparone. HarperFestival, 1998. ISBN 0-694-00873-7 Subj:

Babies. Format, unusual – board books. Rhyming text.

The littlest witch ill. by Jonathan Lambert. HarperCollins, 1994. ISBN 0-694-00647-5 Subj: Format, unusual – toy and movable books. Holidays – Halloween. Rhyming text. Witches.

Oh, cats! ill. by Nadine Bernard Westcott. HarperCollins, 1997. ISBN 0-06-025374-6 Subj: Activities – playing. Animals – cats. Language. Rhyming text.

Santa's short suit shrunk and other Christmas tongue twisters ill. by Sue Truesdell. HarperCollins, 1997. ISBN 0-06-026663-5 Subj: Games. Holidays – Christmas. Language. Tongue twisters.

Sid and Sam ill. by G. Brian Karas. HarperCollins, 1996. ISBN 0-06-025372-X Subj: Activities – playing. Activities – singing. Language.

Buck, Pearl S. (Pearl Sydenstricker). *The Chinese story teller* ill. by Regina Shekerjian. John Day, 1971. Subj: Animals – cats. Animals – dogs. Emotions – envy, jealousy. Folk and fairy tales. Foreign lands – China.

The little fox in the middle ill. by Robert Jones. Collier, 1966. Subj: Animals – foxes. Emotions – loneliness. Family life. Friendship.

Buckaway, C. M. *Alfred, the dragon who lost his flame* ill. by Sarie Jenkins. Firefly, 1982. Subj: Dragons. Imagination. Magic.

Buckingham, Simon. *Alec and his flying bed* ill. by author. Lothrop, 1991. ISBN 0-688-10556-4 Subj: Activities – flying. Furniture – beds. Imagination.

Buckley, Helen Elizabeth. *Grandfather and I* ill. by Paul Galdone. Lothrop, 1959. ISBN 0-688-12534-4 Subj: Activities – walking. Family life – grandfathers.

Grandmother and I ill. by Paul Galdone. Lothrop, 1961. ISBN 0-688-12532-8 Subj: Emotions – love. Family life – grandmothers.

Josie and the snow ill. by Evaline Ness. Lothrop, 1964. Subj: Rhyming text. Seasons – winter. Weather – snow.

Josie's Buttercup ill. by Evaline Ness. Lothrop, 1967. Subj: Animals – dogs. Rhyming text.

The leftover bridge ill. by Oki S. Han. Lothrop, 1999. ISBN 0-688-13485-8 Subj: Bridges.

Moonlight kite ill. by Elise Primavera. Lothrop, 1997. ISBN 0-688-10932-2 Subj: Behavior – sharing. Emotions – loneliness. Kites. Religion.

Someday with my father ill. by Ellen Eagle. HarperCollins, 1985. ISBN 0-06-020877-5 Subj: Dreams. Family life – fathers. Illness.

"Take care of things," Edward said ill. by Katherine Coville. Lothrop, 1991. ISBN 0-688-07732-3 Subj: Activities – playing. Family life – brothers.

Where did Josie go? ill. by Jan Ormerod. Lothrop, 1999. ISBN 0-688-16507-9 Subj: Family life. Games. Rhyming text.

Buckley, Kate. *Love notes* ill. by author. Albert Whitman, 1988. ISBN 0-8075-4780-8 Subj: Behavior – growing up. Holidays – Valentine's Day. Poetry. School.

Buckley, Paul. *Amy Belligera and the fireflies* ill. by Kate Buckley. Albert Whitman, 1987. ISBN 0-8075-0324-X Subj: Insects – fireflies. Magic. Night. Witches.

Buckley, Ray. *God's love is like . . .* ill. by author. Abingdon, 1998. ISBN 0-687-05626-8 Subj: Jewish culture. Religion.

Buckley, Richard. *The foolish tortoise* ill. by Eric Carle. Picture Book Studio, 1985. ISBN 0-88708-002-2 Subj: Behavior – seeking better things. Folk and fairy tales. Reptiles – turtles, tortoises. Rhyming text.

The greedy python ill. by Eric Carle. Picture Book Studio, 1985. ISBN 0-88708-001-4 Subj: Behavior – greed. Folk and fairy tales. Reptiles – snakes. Rhyming text.

Buckmaster, Henrietta. *Lucy and Loki* ill. by Barbara Cooney. Scribners, 1958. Subj: Animals – cats. Animals – dogs. Behavior – imitation.

Bucknall, Caroline. *One bear all alone* ill. by author. Dial, 1986. ISBN 0-8037-0238-8 Subj: Counting, numbers. Rhyming text. Toys – bears.

One bear in the hospital ill. by author. Dial, 1991. ISBN 0-8037-0847-5 Subj: Hospitals. Illness. Rhyming text. Toys – bears.

One bear in the picture ill. by author. Dial, 1988. ISBN 0-8037-0463-1 Subj: Character traits – cleanliness. Rhyming text. Toys – bears.

The three little pigs (The three little pigs)

Budbill, David. *Christmas tree farm* ill. by Donald Carrick. Macmillan, 1974. ISBN 0-02-715330-4 Subj: Farms. Holidays – Christmas. Science. Trees.

Budd, Lillian. *The people on Long Ago Street* ill. by Marilyn Miller. Rand McNally, 1964. Subj: Family life – great-grandparents. Imagination.

The pie wagon ill. by Marilyn Miller. Lothrop, 1960. Subj: ABC books. Food.

Budney, Blossom. *After dark* ill. by Tony Chen. Lothrop, 1975. ISBN 068851703X Subj: Night.

A kiss is round ill. by Vladimir Bobri. Lothrop, 1954. ISBN 0-688-51177-5 Subj: Concepts – shape. Poetry.

N is for nursery school ill. by Vladimir Bobri. Lothrop, 1956. Subj: ABC books. School.

Buehner, Caralyn. *The escape of Marvin the ape* by Caralyn and Mark Buehner; ill. by Mark Buehner. Dial, 1992. ISBN 0-8037-1124-7 Subj: Animals – gorillas. Character traits – freedom. City. Zoos.

Fanny's dream ill. by Mark Buehner. Dial, 1996. ISBN 0-8037-1497-1 Subj: Behavior – wishing. Careers – farmers. Farms. Folk and fairy tales.

I did it, I'm sorry ill. by Mark Buehner. Dial, 1998. ISBN 0-8037-2011-4 Subj: Animals. Behavior. Character traits.

It's a spoon, not a shovel ill. by Mark Buehner. Dial, 1998. ISBN 0-8037-1495-5 Subj: Etiquette. Humor.

A job for Wittilda by Caralyn and Mark Buehner; ill. by Mark Buehner. Dial, 1993. ISBN 0-8037-1150-6 Subj: Activities – working. Food. Witches.

Buehner, Mark. *The escape of Marvin the ape* (Buehner, Caralyn)

A job for Wittilda (Buehner, Caralyn)

Buell, Ellen Lewis. *Read me a poem: children's favorite poetry* ill. by Anna Maria Magagna. Grosset, 1965. Subj: Poetry.

Buff, Conrad. *Dash and Dart* (Buff, Mary [Marsh])

Forest folk (Buff, Mary [Marsh])

Hurry, Skurry and Flurry (Buff, Mary [Marsh])

Buff, Mary (Marsh). *Dash and Dart* by Mary and Conrad Buff; ill. by authors. Viking, 1942. Subj: Animals – deer. Caldecott award honor books. Forest, woods.

Forest folk by Mary and Conrad Buff; ill. by authors. Viking, 1962. Subj: Animals. Animals – deer. Forest, woods.

Hurry, Skurry and Flurry by Mary and Conrad Buff; ill. by authors. Viking, 1954. Subj: Animals – squirrels. Rhyming text.

Buffett, Jimmy. *The jolly mon* by Jimmy and Savannah Jane Buffett; ill. by Lambert Davis. Harcourt, 1988. ISBN 0-15-240530-5 Subj: Activities – traveling. Foreign lands – Caribbean Islands. Music. Royalty – kings. Songs.

Trouble dolls by Jimmy and Savannah Jane Buffet; ill. by Lambert Davis. Harcourt, 1991. ISBN 0-15-290790-4 Subj: Behavior – lost. Magic. Toys – dolls.

Buffett, Savannah Jane. *The jolly mon* (Buffett, Jimmy)

Trouble dolls (Buffett, Jimmy)

Bugs ill. with photos. Cedco, 1998. ISBN 0-7683-2032-1 Subj: Insects.

Bulette, Sara. *The elf in the singing tree* ill. by Tom Dunnington. Follett, 1964. Reading consultant: Morton Botel. Subj: Imagination. Mythical creatures – elves.

The splendid belt of Mr. Big ill. by Lou Myers. Follett, 1964. Reading consultant: Morton Botel. Subj: Animals – monkeys. Clothing. Concepts – size. Problem solving.

Bulla, Clyde Robert. *Dandelion Hill* ill. by Bruce Degen. Dutton, 1982. ISBN 0-525-45101-3 Subj: Animals – bulls, cows. Behavior – growing up. Farms.

Daniel's duck ill. by Joan Sandin. HarperCollins, 1979. ISBN 0-06-020909-7 Subj: Activities. Art. Emotions – embarrassment.

Jonah and the great fish ill. by Helga Aichinger. Crowell, 1970. Subj: Animals – whales. Religion – Jonah.

Keep running, Allen! ill. by Satomi Ichikawa. Crowell, 1978. ISBN 0690013752 Subj: Behavior – solitude. Sibling rivalry.

Noah and the rainbow: an ancient story (Bolliger, Max)

Poor boy, rich boy ill. by Marcia Sewall. HarperCollins, 1982. ISBN 0-06-020897-X Subj: Orphans.

The story of Valentine's Day ill. by Susan Estelle Kwas. HarperCollins, 1999. ISBN 0-06-027884-6 Subj: Holidays – Valentine's Day.

The stubborn old woman ill. by Anne F. Rockwell. Crowell, 1980. ISBN 0-690-03946-8 Subj: Behavior – needing someone. Character traits – persistence. Character traits – stubbornness.

A tree is a plant ill. by Lois Lignell. Crowell, 1960. Subj: Plants. Trees.

Valentine cat ill. by Leonard Weisgard. Crowell, 1959. ISBN 0-690-85730-6 Subj: Animals – cats. Holidays – Valentine's Day.

Washington's birthday ill. by Don Bolognese. Crowell, 1967. ISBN 0-690-86796-4 Subj: Holidays – Washington's Birthday. U.S. history.

What makes a shadow? ill. by June Otani. HarperCollins, 1994. ISBN 0-06-022915-2 Subj: Shadows.

Bullard, Lisa. *Not enough beds! a Christmas alphabet book* ill. by Joni Oeltjenbruns. Carolrhoda, 1999. ISBN 1-57505-356-X Subj: ABC books. Bedtime. Holidays – Christmas. Rhyming text.

Buller, Jon. *Toad on the road* by Jon Buller and Susan Schade; ill. by authors. Random House, 1992. ISBN 0-679-92689-5 Subj: Animals. Automobiles. Frogs and toads. Rhyming text.

Bulloch, Ivan. *Patterns* consultants, Wendy and David Clemson; ill. with photos. World Book, 1997. ISBN 0-7166-4903-9 Subj: Concepts. Concepts – shape.

Bullock, Kathleen. *It chanced to rain* ill. by author. Simon & Schuster, 1992. ISBN 0-671-66005-5 Subj: Activities – walking. Animals. Rhyming text. Weather – rain.

Rabbits are coming ill. by author. Simon & Schuster, 1991. ISBN 0-671-72963-2 Subj: Animals – rabbits. Toys – balloons. Wordless.

A surprise for Mitzi Mouse ill. by author. Simon & Schuster, 1989. ISBN 0-671-67331-9 Subj: Animals

– mice. Emotions – envy, jealousy. Family life – sisters. Sibling rivalry.

Bullock, Michael. *The camel who left the zoo* (Allamand, Pascale)

The pop rooster (Allamand, Pascale)

Bunce, William. *Freight trains* ill. by Lemuel B. Line. Putnam, 1954. Subj: Trains.

Bundey, Nikki. *In the park* ill. by Virginia Gray. Carolrhoda, 1998. ISBN 1-57505-277-6 Subj: Activities. Science. Sports.

In the snow ill. by Virginia Gray. Carolrhoda, 1998. ISBN 1-57505-086-2 Subj: Activities. Science. Seasons – winter. Sports. Weather – snow.

In the water ill. by Virginia Gray. Carolrhoda, 1998. ISBN 1-57505-085-4 Subj: Activities. Science. Sea and seashore. Sports. Sports – surfing. Sports – swimming.

On a bike ill. by Virginia Gray. Carolrhoda, 1998. ISBN 1-57505-278-4 Subj: Science. Sports – bicycling.

Bundt, Nancy. *The fire station book* text by Jeff Linzer; photos by Nancy Bundt. Carolrhoda, 1981. ISBN 0-87614-126-2 Subj: Careers – firefighters.

Bunin, Catherine. *Is that your sister? a true story of adoption* by Catherine Bunin and Sherry Bunin; ill. with photos. Pantheon, 1976. ISBN 0-394-93230-7 Subj: Adoption. Family life.

Bunin, Sherry. *Is that your sister? a true story of adoption* (Bunin, Catherine)

Buntain, Ruth Jaeger. *The birthday story* ill. by Eloise Wilkin. Holiday, 1953. Subj: Birthdays. Emotions – loneliness. Friendship.

Bunting, Eve (Anne Evelyn). *Barney the Beard* ill. by Imero Gobbato. Parents, 1975. ISBN 0-8193-0729-7 Subj: Activities – cooking. Careers – bakers.

The big cheese ill. by Sal Murdocca. Macmillan, 1977. ISBN 0-02-715370-3 Subj: Cumulative tales. Emotions – loneliness. Humor. Old age.

The big red barn ill. by Howard Knotts. Harcourt, 1979. ISBN 0-15-207145-8 Subj: Death. Family life.

The blue and the gray ill. by Ned Bittinger. Scholastic, 1996. ISBN 0-590-60197-0 Subj: Ethnic groups in the U.S. – African Americans. Friendship. U.S. history. War.

Box, fox, ox, and the peacock ill. by Leslie H. Morrill. Ginn, 1974. ISBN 0-663-25470-1 Subj: Animals – foxes. Animals – oxen. Behavior – fighting, arguing. Birds – peacocks, peahens.

Butterfly house ill. by Greg Shed. Scholastic, 1999. ISBN 0-590-84884-4 Subj: Family life – grandfathers. Insects – butterflies, caterpillars. Metamorphosis. Rhyming text.

Cheyenne again ill. by Irving Toddy. Clarion, 1995. ISBN 0-395-70364-6 Subj: Indians of North America – Cheyenne (Sioux). Indians of North America – Great Plains. School.

Clancy's coat ill. by Lorinda Bryan Cauley. Warne, 1984. ISBN 0-7232-6252-7 Subj: Foreign lands – Ireland. Friendship.

The day before Christmas ill. by Beth Peck. Clarion, 1992. ISBN 0-89919-866-X Subj: Activities – dancing. Death. Family life – grandfathers. Family life – mothers. Holidays – Christmas.

A day's work ill. by Ronald Himler. Clarion, 1994. ISBN 0-395-67321-6 Subj: Activities – working. Character traits – honesty. Ethnic groups in the U.S. – Mexican Americans. Family life – grandfathers. Gardens, gardening.

December ill. by David Diaz. Harcourt, 1997. ISBN 0-15-201434-9 Subj: Character traits – helpfulness. Holidays – Christmas. Homeless.

Demetrius and the golden goblet ill. by Michael Hague. Harcourt, 1980. ISBN 0-15-223186-2 Subj: Royalty – kings. Sea and seashore.

Ducky ill. by David Wisniewski. Clarion, 1997. ISBN 0-395-75185-3 Subj: Activities – traveling. Toys.

Flower garden ill. by Kathryn Hewitt. Harcourt, 1994. ISBN 0-15-228776-0 Subj: Birthdays. Family life – mothers. Flowers. Gardens, gardening. Rhyming text.

Fly away home ill. by Ronald Himler. Houghton Mifflin, 1991. ISBN 0-395-55962-6 Subj: Airplanes, airports. Family life – fathers. Homeless.

Ghost's hour, spook's hour ill. by author. Clarion, 1987. ISBN 0-89919-484-2 Subj: Animals – dogs. Emotions – fear. Family life. Night.

Going home ill. by David Diaz. HarperCollins, 1996. ISBN 0-06-026296-6 Subj: Ethnic groups in the U.S. – Mexican Americans. Family life. Foreign lands – Mexico. Holidays – Christmas.

Goose dinner ill. by Howard Knotts. Harcourt, 1981. ISBN 0-05-232224-8 Subj: Birds – geese. Farms.

Happy birthday, dear duck ill. by Jan Brett. Clarion, 1988. ISBN 0-89919-541-5 Subj: Animals. Birds – ducks. Birthdays. Rhyming text.

The happy funeral ill. by Vo-Dinh Mai. HarperCollins, 1982. ISBN 0-06-020894-5 Subj: Death. Ethnic groups in the U.S. – Chinese Americans. Family life – grandfathers.

How many days to America? a Thanksgiving story ill. by Beth Peck. Clarion, 1988. ISBN 0-89919-521-0 Subj: Character traits – freedom. Holidays – Thanksgiving. Pilgrims.

I don't want to go to camp ill. by Maryann Cocca-Leffler. Boyds Mills, 1996. ISBN 1-56397-393-6 Subj: Camps, camping. Emotions. Family life – mothers.

I have an olive tree ill. by Karen Barbour. HarperCollins, 1999. ISBN 0-06-027574-X Subj: Ethnic groups in the U.S. – Greek Americans. Family life. Foreign lands – Greece. Trees.

In the haunted house ill. by Susan Meddaugh. Houghton Mifflin, 1990. ISBN 0-395-51589-0 Subj: Ghosts. Holidays – Halloween. Homes, houses.

Jane Martin, dog detective ill. by Amy Schwartz. Harcourt, 1984. ISBN 0-15-239586-5 Subj: Animals – dogs. Behavior – lost. Careers – detectives. Mystery stories.

Magic and the night river ill. by Allen Say. HarperCollins, 1978. ISBN 0-06-020913-5 Subj: Birds – cormorants. Careers – fishermen. Family life – grandfathers. Foreign lands – Japan.

The man who could call down owls ill. by Charles Mikolaycak. Macmillan, 1984. ISBN 0-02-715380-0 Subj: Behavior – greed. Birds – owls. Magic.

Market day ill. by Holly Berry. HarperCollins, 1996. ISBN 0-06-025368-1 Subj: Fairs. Foreign lands – Ireland. Shopping.

Monkey in the middle ill. by Lynn Munsinger. Harcourt, 1984. ISBN 0-15-255316-9 Subj: Animals – monkeys. Emotions – envy, jealousy. Friendship.

Moonstick: the seasons of the Sioux ill. by John Sandford. HarperCollins, 1997. ISBN 0-06-024805-X Subj: Indians of North America – Dakota (Sioux). Moon. Nature. Seasons.

The Mother's Day mice ill. by Jan Brett. Clarion, 1986. ISBN 0-89919-387-0 Subj: Animals – mice. Holidays – Mother's Day.

My backpack ill. by Maryann Cocca-Leffler. Boyds Mills, 1997. ISBN 1-56397-433-9 Subj: Behavior. Family life. Rhyming text.

Night of the gargoyles ill. by David Wiesner. Clarion, 1994. ISBN 0-395-66553-1 Subj: Buildings. Monsters. Museums. Mythical creatures.

Night tree ill. by Ted Rand. Harcourt, 1991. ISBN 0-15-257425-5 Subj: Animals. Character traits – kindness to animals. Family life. Holidays – Christmas. Trees.

No nap ill. by Susan Meddaugh. Houghton Mifflin, 1989. ISBN 0-89919-813-9 Subj: Bedtime. Sleep.

On Call Back Mountain ill. by Barry Moser. Blue Sky, 1997. ISBN 0-590-25929-6 Subj: Animals – wolves. Careers – firefighters. Careers – park rangers. Death. Friendship.

Our teacher's having a baby ill. by Diane de Groat. Clarion, 1992. ISBN 0-395-60470-2 Subj: Babies. Careers – teachers. School.

A perfect Father's Day ill. by Susan Meddaugh. Houghton Mifflin, 1991. ISBN 0-395-52590-X Subj: Family life – fathers. Holidays – Father's Day.

A picnic in October ill. by Nancy Carpenter. Harcourt, 1999. ISBN 0-15-201656-2 Subj: Activities – traveling. Emotions – embarrassment. Ethnic groups in the U.S. – Italian Americans. Family life.

The pumpkin fair ill. by Eileen Christelow. Clarion, 1997. ISBN 0-395-70060-4 Subj: Fairs. Rhyming text. Seasons – fall.

Red fox running ill. by Wendell Minor. Clarion, 1993. ISBN 0-395-58919-3 Subj: Animals – foxes. Rhyming text. Seasons – winter.

The robot birthday ill. by Marie DeJohn. Dutton, 1980. ISBN 0-525-38542-8 Subj: Birthdays. Robots.

Rudi's pond ill. by Ronald Himler. Clarion, 1999. ISBN 0-395-89067-5 Subj: Death. Emotions – grief. Friendship.

St. Patrick's Day in the morning ill. by Jan Brett. Houghton Mifflin, 1980. ISBN 0-395-29098-8 Subj: Holidays – St. Patrick's Day.

Say it fast ill. by True Kelley. Ginn, 1974. ISBN 0-663-25467-1 Subj: Language. Tongue twisters.

Scary, scary Halloween ill. by Jan Brett. Houghton Mifflin, 1986. ISBN 0-89919-414-1 Subj: Holidays – Halloween. Monsters. Mythical creatures – goblins. Rhyming text.

Secret place ill. by Ted Rand. Clarion, 1996. ISBN 0-395-64367-8 Subj: City. Nature.

Smoky night ill. by David Diaz. Harcourt, 1994. ISBN 0-15-269954-6 Subj: Caldecott award books. City. Communities, neighborhoods. Emotions – anger. Ethnic groups in the U.S. Riots.

So far from the sea ill. by Chris Soentpiet. Clarion, 1998. ISBN 0-395-72095-8 Subj: Ethnic groups in the U.S. – Japanese Americans. Family life – grandfathers. War.

Someday a tree ill. by Ronald Himler. Clarion, 1993. ISBN 0-395-61309-4 Subj: Activities – picnicking. Ecology. Family life – mothers. Trees.

Summer wheels ill. by Thomas B. Allen. Harcourt, 1992. ISBN 0-15-207000-1 Subj: Friendship. Sports – bicycling.

Sunflower house ill. by Kathryn Hewitt. Harcourt, 1996. ISBN 0-15-200483-1 Subj: Flowers. Gardens, gardening. Rhyming text. Seasons – summer.

Sunshine home ill. by Diane de Groat. Clarion, 1994. ISBN 0-395-63309-5 Subj: Emotions. Family life – grandmothers. Old age.

Terrible things ill. by Stephen Gammell. HarperCollins, 1980. ISBN 0-06-020904-6 Subj: Animals. Emotions – fear.

Train to somewhere ill. by Ronald Himler. Clarion, 1996. ISBN 0-395-71325-0 Subj: Emotions. Family life – step families. Orphans. Trains. U.S. history.

The traveling men of Ballycoo ill. by Kaethe Zemach. Harcourt, 1983. ISBN 0-15-289792-5 Subj: Activities – traveling. Music.

Trouble on the T-ball team ill. by Irene Trivas. Clarion, 1997. ISBN 0-395-66060-2 Subj: Sports – T-ball. Teeth.

A turkey for Thanksgiving ill. by Diane de Groat. Ticknor & Fields, 1991. ISBN 0-89919-793-0 Subj:

Animals – moose. Birds – turkeys. Holidays – Thanksgiving.

Twinnies ill. by Nancy Carpenter. Harcourt, 1997. ISBN 0-15-291592-3 Subj: Babies. Family life – sisters. Multiple births – twins.

The Valentine bears ill. by Jan Brett. Seabury Pr., 1983. ISBN 0-89919-138-X Subj: Animals – bears. Holidays – Valentine's Day.

The wall ill. by Ronald Himler. Clarion, 1990. ISBN 0-395-51588-2 Subj: Careers – military. Family life. War.

We need a bigger zoo! ill. by Bob Barner. Ginn, 1974. ISBN 0-663-25446-9 Subj: Animals. Wordless. Zoos.

The Wednesday surprise ill. by Donald Garrick. Ticknor & Fields, 1989. ISBN 0-89919-721-3 Subj: Activities – reading. Birthdays. Family life. Family life – grandmothers.

Winter's coming ill. by Howard Knotts. Harcourt, 1977. ISBN 0-15-298036-9 Subj: Family life – grandparents. Farms. Seasons – winter.

Bunting, Jane. *The children's visual dictionary* ill. by David Hopkins. DK, 1995. ISBN 1-56458-881-5 Subj: Dictionaries. Language.

My first ABC ill. by author. DK, 1993. ISBN 1-56458-403-8 Subj: ABC books. Language.

My first word book ill. by author. DK, 1996. ISBN 0-7894-0463-X Subj: Activities. Dictionaries. Language.

Burch, Robert. *The hunting trip* ill. by Susanne Suba. Scribners, 1971. ISBN 0-684-12495-5 Subj: Character traits – kindness to animals. Family life. Food. Sports – hunting.

Joey's cat ill. by Don Freeman. Viking, 1969. ISBN 0-670-40789-5 Subj: Animals – cats. Animals – possums. Ethnic groups in the U.S. – African Americans. Family life.

The jolly witch ill. by Leigh Grant. Dutton, 1975. ISBN 0-525-32797-5 Subj: Character traits – cleanliness. Witches.

Burchard, Peter. *The Carol Moran* ill. by author. Macmillan, 1958. Subj: Boats, ships.

Burdekin, Harold. *A child's grace* by Harold Burdekin and Ernest Claxton; the grace by Mrs. E. Rutter Leatham; photos by Harold Burdekin. Dutton, 1938. Subj: Activities. Poetry. Religion.

Burden-Patmon, Denise. *Carnival* by Denise Burden-Patmon with Kathryn D. Jones; ill. by Reynold Ruffins. Modern Curriculum, 1992. ISBN 0-8136-2275-1 Subj: Ethnic groups in the U.S. – African Americans. Fairs. Music.

Imani's gift at Kwanzaa ill. by Floyd Cooper. Modern Curriculum, 1992. ISBN 0-8136-2244-1 Subj: Ethnic groups in the U.S. – African Americans. Family life. Gifts. Holidays – Kwanzaa.

Burdett, Lois. *Hamlet for kids* intro. by Kenneth Branagh; written and ill. by children. Firefly, 2000. ISBN 1-55209-522-3 Subj: Children as authors. Children as illustrators. Crime. Foreign lands – Denmark. Rhyming text. Royalty – princes.

Macbeth for kids written and ill. by children. Black Moss, 1996. ISBN 0-8875-3287-X Subj: Behavior – fighting, arguing. Children as authors. Children as illustrators. Crime. Foreign lands – Scotland. Royalty – kings. Royalty – queens.

A midsummer night's dream for kids written and ill. by children. Firefly, 1997. ISBN 1-55209-130-9 Subj: Children as authors. Children as illustrators. Dreams. Rhyming text.

Romeo and Juliet for kids written and ill. by children. Firefly, 1998. ISBN 1-55209-244-5 Subj: Behavior – fighting, arguing. Children as authors. Children as illustrators. Emotions – love. Family life. Rhyming text.

The tempest for kids written and ill. by children. Firefly, 1999. ISBN 1-55209-355-7 Subj: Children as authors. Children as illustrators. Emotions. Islands. Magic. Rhyming text. Weather – storms.

Twelfth night written and ill. by children. Firefly, 1997. ISBN 0-8875-3233-0 Subj: Behavior – mistakes. Behavior – trickery. Boats, ships. Character traits. Children as authors. Children as illustrators. Sea and seashore.

Burdick, Margaret. *Bobby Otter and the blue boat* ill. by author. Little, 1987. ISBN 0-316-11616-5 Subj: Activities – trading. Animals. Animals – otters. Toys.

Sara Raccoon and the secret place ill. by author. Little, 1992. ISBN 0-316-11617-3 Subj: Animals. Animals – raccoons. Behavior – solitude. Friendship.

Burgert, Hans-Joachim. *Samulo and the giant* ill. by author. Holt, 1970. ISBN 0-03081-493-6 Subj: Character traits – bravery. Weather.

Burgess, Anthony. *The land where the ice cream grows* (Testa, Fulvio)

Burgess, Gelett. *The little father* ill. by Richard Egielski. Farrar, 1985. ISBN 0-374-34596-1 Subj: Character traits – smallness. Family life – fathers. Poetry.

Burgess, Thornton. *Old Mother West Wind* ill. by Michael Hague. Holt, 1990. ISBN 0-8050-1005-X Subj: Animals. Weather – wind.

Burgie, Irving. *Caribbean carnival: songs of the West Indies* ill. by Frané Lessac; afterword by Rosa Guy. Tambourine, 1992. ISBN 0-688-10780-X Subj: Foreign lands – West Indies. Music. Songs.

Burgunder, Rose. *From summer to summer* ill. by author. Viking, 1965. Subj: Poetry. Seasons – summer.

Burke, Katie. *Lightning bug thunder* ill. by Sheila McGraw. Firefly, 1998. ISBN 1-55209-271-2 Subj:

Imagination. Insects – fireflies. Nature. Weather – droughts. Weather – thunder.

Burke, Timothy. *Tugboats in action* photos by author. Albert Whitman, 1993. ISBN 0-8075-8112-7 Subj: Activities – working. Boats, ships. Rivers.

Burke-Weiner, Kimberly. *The maybe garden* ill. by Fredrika Spillman. Beyond Words, 1992. ISBN 0-941831-56-6 Subj: Character traits – individuality. Family life – mothers. Gardens, gardening. Imagination.

Burland, Brian. *St. Nicholas and the tub* ill. by Joseph Low. Holiday, 1964. Subj: Folk and fairy tales. Holidays – Christmas.

Burleigh, Robert. *Home run: the story of Babe Ruth* ill. by Mike Wimmer. Silver Whistle, 1998. ISBN 0-15-200970-1 Subj: Sports – baseball.

It's funny where Ben's train takes him ill. by Joanna Yardley. Orchard, 1999. ISBN 0-531-33106-7 Subj: Bedtime. Imagination. Rhyming text. Trains.

Burlingham, Mary. *The climbing book* (Steiner, Charlotte)

Burlson, Joe. *Space colony* ill. by author. Putnam, 1984. ISBN 0-399-21058-X Subj: Format, unusual. Wordless.

Burn, Doris. *The summerfolk* ill. by author. Coward, 1968. Subj: Seasons – summer.

Burningham, Helen Oxenbury. *see* Oxenbury, Helen

Burningham, John. *Aldo* ill. by author. Crown, 1992. ISBN 0-517-58699-1 Subj: Emotions – loneliness. Friendship. Imagination – imaginary friends.

Avocado baby ill. by author. Crowell, 1982. ISBN 0-690-04244-2 Subj: Babies. Family life. Food.

The baby ill. by author. Candlewick, 1994. ISBN 1-56402-334-6 Subj: Babies. Emotions. Family life – brothers and sisters.

The blanket ill. by author. Crowell, 1976, 1975. ISBN 0-690-01270-5 Subj: Behavior – losing things. Night.

Borka: the adventures of a goose with no feathers ill. by author. Random House, 1963. ISBN 0-394-90727-2 Subj: Birds – geese. Character traits – being different. Character traits – meanness. Foreign lands – England.

Cannonball Simp ill. by author. Bobbs-Merrill, 1966. ISBN 1-56402-338-9 Subj: Animals – dogs. Circus. Clowns, jesters.

Cloudland ill. by author. Crown, 1996. ISBN 0-051-70929-5 Subj: Imagination. Weather – clouds.

Cluck baa ill. by author. Viking, 1985. ISBN 0-670-22580-0 Subj: Animals. Noise, sounds.

Come away from the water, Shirley ill. by author. Crowell, 1977. ISBN 0-690-01361-2 Subj: Imagination. Pirates. Sea and seashore.

Count up: learning sets ill. by author. Viking, 1983. ISBN 0-670-24410-4 Subj: Counting, numbers. Format, unusual – board books.

Courtney ill. by author. Crown, 1994. ISBN 0-517-59884-1 Subj: Animals – dogs. Family life.

The cupboard ill. by author. Crowell, 1977. ISBN 0-224-01134-0 Subj: Food.

The dog ill. by author. Crowell, 1975. ISBN 0-690-01272-1 Subj: Animals – dogs. Format, unusual – board books.

First steps: letters, numbers, colors, opposites ill. by author. Candlewick, 1994. ISBN 1-56402-205-6 Subj: ABC books. Concepts. Concepts – color. Concepts – opposites. Counting, numbers.

Five down: numbers as signs ill. by author. Viking, 1983. ISBN 0-670-31698-9 Subj: Counting, numbers. Format, unusual – board books.

The friend ill. by author. Crowell, 1975. ISBN 0-690-01274-8 Subj: Friendship.

Grandpa ill. by author. Crown, 1985. ISBN 0-517-55643-X Subj: Death. Emotions – grief. Family life – grandfathers.

Harquin: the fox who went down to the valley ill. by author. Bobbs-Merrill, 1968. Subj: Animals – foxes. Character traits – cleverness. Sports – hunting.

Harvey Slumfenburger's Christmas present ill. by author. Candlewick, 1993. ISBN 1-56402-246-3 Subj: Character traits – helpfulness. Holidays – Christmas. Santa Claus.

Hey! Get off our train ill. by author. Crown, 1990. ISBN 0-517-57643-0 Subj: Animals. Dreams. Trains.

Humbert, Mister Firkin and the Lord Mayor of London ill. by author. Bobbs-Merrill, 1967. ISBN 0-517-57312-1 Subj: Animals – horses, ponies. Character traits – pride. Emotions – envy, jealousy.

Jangle twang ill. by author. Viking, 1985. ISBN 0-670-40570-5 Subj: Music. Noise, sounds.

John Burningham's ABC ill. by author. Crown, 1993. ISBN 0-517-59504-4 Subj: ABC books.

John Burningham's colors ill. by author. Crown, 1986. ISBN 0-517-55961-7 Subj: Concepts – color.

John Burningham's 1 2 3 ill. by author. Crown, 1985. ISBN 0-517-55962-5 Subj: Counting, numbers.

John Patrick Norman McHennessy - the boy who was always late ill. by author. Crown, 1987. ISBN 0-517-56805-5 Subj: Behavior – tardiness. Imagination. School.

Just cats: learning groups ill. by author. Viking, 1983. ISBN 0-670-41094-2 Subj: Counting, numbers. Format, unusual – board books.

Mr. Gumpy's motor car ill. by author. Macmillan, 1975, 1973. ISBN 0-02-716200-1 Subj: Automobiles. Weather – rain.

Mr. Gumpy's outing ill. by author. Macmillan, 1971. ISBN 0-03-086613-8 Subj: Animals. Behavior – fighting, arguing. Boats, ships. Cumulative tales.

Pigs plus: learning addition ill. by author. Viking, 1983. ISBN 0-670-55508-8 Subj: Counting, numbers. Format, unusual – board books.

The rabbit ill. by author. Crowell, 1975. ISBN 0-690-00907-0 Subj: Animals – rabbits. Pets.

Read one: numbers as words ill. by author. Viking, 1983. ISBN 0-670-58986-1 Subj: Counting, numbers. Format, unusual – board books.

Ride off: learning subtraction ill. by author. Viking, 1983. ISBN 0-670-59798-8 Subj: Counting, numbers. Format, unusual – board books.

The school ill. by author. Crowell, 1975. Activities. ISBN 0-690-00903-8 Subj: School.

Seasons ill. by author. Bobbs-Merrill, 1970. Subj: Seasons.

The shopping basket ill. by author. Candlewick, 1996. ISBN 1-56402-688-4 Subj: Animals. Character traits – cleverness. Humor. Shopping.

Skip trip ill. by author. Viking, 1984. ISBN 0-670-65016-1 Subj: Activities. Noise, sounds.

Slam bang ill. by author. Viking, 1985. ISBN 0-670-65076-5 Subj: Automobiles. Noise, sounds.

Sniff shout ill. by author. Viking, 1984. ISBN 0-670-65349-7 Subj: Activities. Noise, sounds.

The snow ill. by author. Crowell, 1975. ISBN 0-690-00905-4 Subj: Family life. Weather – snow.

Time to get out of the bath, Shirley ill. by author. Crowell, 1978. ISBN 0-690-01379-5 Subj: Activities – bathing. Imagination. Royalty.

Trubloff: the mouse who wanted to play the balalaika ill. by author. Random House, 1965. ISBN 0-394-97316-X Subj: Animals – mice. Music. Weather – snow.

Whaddayamean ill. by author. Crown, 1999. ISBN 0-517-80067-5 Subj: Earth. Ecology. Religion.

Where's Julius? ill. by author. Crown, 1986. ISBN 0-517-56511-0 Subj: Activities – playing. Family life. Food. Imagination.

Wobble pop ill. by author. Viking, 1984. Subj: Activities. Noise, sounds.

Would you rather . . . ill. by author. Crowell, 1978. ISBN 0-690-03918-2 Subj: Imagination.

Burns, Diane L. *Arbor Day* ill. by Kathy Rogers. Carolrhoda, 1988. ISBN 0-87614-346-X Subj: Trees.

Elephants never forget! ill. by Joan Hanson. Lerner, 1987. ISBN 0-8225-0992-X Subj: Animals – elephants. Riddles.

Burns, Kate. *How does your garden grow?* by Kate Burns and Dawn Apperley. Levinson Books, 1997. ISBN 1-899607-51-X Subj: Format, unusual – toy and movable books. Gardens, gardening.

In the jungle (Apperley, Dawn)

In the snow ill. by author. Little, 1996. ISBN 0-316-11820-6 Subj: Animals. Behavior – hiding. Format, unusual – toy and movable books. Weather – snow.

Burns, Marilyn. *Amanda Bean's amazing dream* (Neuschwander, Cindy)

The 512 ants on Sullivan Street (Losi, Carol A.)

Burns, Maurice. *Go ducks, go!* ill. by Ron Brooks. Scholastic, 1988. ISBN 0-590-41167-5 Subj: Activities – playing. Country. Family life. Toys.

Burns, Theresa. *You're not my cat* ill. by author. HarperCollins, 1989. ISBN 0-397-32341-7 Subj: Animals – cats. Pets.

Burnside, Julian. *Matilda and the dragon* ill. by Bettina Guthridge. Allen & Unwin, 1993. ISBN 1-86373-127-X Subj: Dragons. Dreams. Night. Rhyming text.

Burnstein, Chaya M. *The Jewish kids' Hebrew-English wordbook* ill. by author. Jewish Publication Society, 1993. ISBN 0-8276-0381-9 Subj: ABC books. Dictionaries. Jewish culture. Language.

Burnstein, John. *Slim Goodbody: what can go wrong and how to be strong* ill. with photos and drawings. McGraw-Hill, 1978. ISBN 0-07-009242-7 Subj: Health and fitness. Rhyming text.

Burroway, Janet. *The truck on the track* ill. by John Vernon Lord. Bobbs-Merrill, 1970. ISBN 0-224-61807-5 Subj: Humor. Rhyming text. Trucks.

Bursik, Rose. *Amelia's fantastic flight* ill. by author. Holt, 1992. ISBN 0-8050-1872-7 Subj: Activities – traveling. Airplanes, airports. Imagination.

Burstein, Chaya M. *Joseph and Anna's time capsule* ill. by Nancy Edwards Calder. Simon & Schuster, 1984. ISBN 0-671-50712-5 Subj: Jewish culture.

Burstein, Fred. *Anna's rain* ill. by Harvey Stevenson. Orchard, 1990. ISBN 0-531-08427-2 Subj: Birds. Family life – fathers. Weather – storms.

The dancer ill. by Joan Auclair. Bradbury, 1993. ISBN 0-02-715625-7 Subj: Activities – dancing. Ballet. City. Family life – fathers.

Rebecca's nap ill. by Helen Cogancherry. Bradbury, 1988. ISBN 0-02-715620-6 Subj: Family life. Sleep.

Whispering in the park ill. by Helen Cogancherry. Macmillan, 1992. ISBN 0-02-715621-4 Subj: Activities – playing. Fish. Parks.

Burt, Olive (Woolley). *Let's find out about bread* ill. by Mimi Korach. Watts, 1966. Subj: Food. Science.

Burton, Jane. *ABC* photos by author. Snapshot, 1994. ISBN 1-56458-533-6 Subj: ABC books. Format, unusual.

Animals at home ill. with photos. Newington, 1991. ISBN 1-878137-12-3 Subj: Animals. Nature.

Animals at night ill. with photos. Newington, 1991. ISBN 1-878137-13-1 Subj: Animals. Nature. Night.

Animals at rest ill. with photos. Newington, 1991. ISBN 1-878137-14-X Subj: Animals. Nature. Sleep.

Animals at work ill. with photos. Newington, 1991. ISBN 1-878137-15-8 Subj: Animals. Nature.

Animals eating ill. with photos. Newington, 1991. ISBN 1-878137-00-X Subj: Animals. Food. Nature.

Animals fighting ill. with photos. Newington, 1991. ISBN 1-878137-03-4 Subj: Animals. Behavior – fighting, arguing. Nature.

Animals keeping clean ill. with photos. Random House, 1989. ISBN 0-394-92261-1 Subj: Animals. Nature.

Animals keeping cool ill. with photos. Random House, 1989. ISBN 0-394-92260-3 Subj: Animals. Nature.

Animals keeping safe ill. with photos. Random House, 1989. ISBN 0-394-92263-8 Subj: Animals. Nature.

Animals keeping warm ill. with photos. Random House, 1989. ISBN 0-394-92262-X Subj: Animals. Nature.

Animals learning ill. with photos. Newington, 1991. ISBN 1-878137-01-8 Subj: Animals. Nature.

Animals talking ill. with photos. Newington, 1991. ISBN 1-878137-02-6 Subj: Animals. Nature. Noise, sounds.

Buffy the barn owl photos by Jane Burton and Kim Taylor. Gareth Stevens, 1989. ISBN 0-8368-0202-0 Subj: Birds – owls.

Caper the kid photos by author. Gareth Stevens, 1989. ISBN 0-8368-0203-9 Subj: Animals – babies. Animals – goats. Behavior – growing up.

Chester the chick photos by Jane Burton and Kim Taylor. Gareth Stevens, 1989. ISBN 0-8368-0204-7 Subj: Birds – chickens.

Chick [written and ed. by Angela Royston] ill. by Rowan Clifford; photos by author. Dutton, 1992. ISBN 0-525-67355-5 Subj: Birds – chickens. Birth. Format, unusual. Science.

Dabble the duckling photos by Jane Burton and Kim Taylor. Gareth Stevens, 1989. ISBN 0-8368-0205-5 Subj: Birds – ducks.

Dazy the guinea pig photos by Jane Burton and Kim Taylor. Gareth Stevens, 1989. ISBN 0-8368-0206-3 Subj: Animals – guinea pigs.

Dizzie the pony photos by author. Gareth Stevens, 1989. ISBN 0-8368-0207-1 Subj: Animals – babies. Animals – horses, ponies. Behavior – growing up.

Fancy the fox photos by author. Random House, 1988. ISBN 0-394-99963-0 Subj: Animals – babies. Animals – foxes. Behavior – growing up. Orphans.

Freckles the rabbit photos by Jane Burton and Kim Taylor. Gareth Stevens, 1989. ISBN 0-8368-0208-X Subj: Animals – rabbits.

Ginger the kitten photos by Jane Burton and Kim Taylor. Gareth Stevens, 1989. ISBN 0-8368-0213-6 Subj: Animals – babies. Animals – cats. Behavior – growing up. Pets.

Gipper the guinea pig photos by author. Random House, 1988. ISBN 0-394-99961-4 Subj: Animals – babies. Animals – guinea pigs. Behavior – growing up. Pets.

Hoppy the toad photos by author. Random House, 1989. ISBN 0-394-92270-0 Subj: Animals – babies. Behavior – growing up. Frogs and toads. Pets.

Jack the puppy photos by author. Random House, 1988. ISBN 0-394-99641-0 Subj: Animals – babies. Animals – dogs. Behavior – growing up. Pets.

Kitten [written and ed. by Angela Royston] photos by author. Dutton, 1991. ISBN 0-525-67343-1 Subj: Animals – cats. Birth. Format, unusual – board books.

Pacer, the pony photos by author. Random House, 1989. ISBN 0-394-92271-9 Subj: Animals – babies. Animals – horses, ponies. Behavior – growing up.

Puppy [written and ed. by Angela Royston] photos by author. Dutton, 1991. ISBN 0-525-67342-3 Subj: Animals – dogs. Birth. Format, unusual – board books.

Rabbit (Watson, Carol)

Snowy, the barn owl photos by author. Random House, 1989. ISBN 0-394-92268-9 Subj: Behavior – growing up. Birds – owls.

Surfer the seal photos by author. Random House, 1989. ISBN 0-394-92269-7 Subj: Animals – babies. Animals – seals. Behavior – growing up.

Taddy the toad photos by author. Gareth Stevens, 1989. ISBN 0-8368-0211-X Subj: Behavior – growing up. Frogs and toads.

Trill the fox cub photos by Jane Burton and Kim Taylor. Gareth Stevens, 1989. ISBN 0-8368-0212-8 Subj: Animals – foxes.

Burton, Katherine. *One gray mouse* by Katherine Burton and Kim Fernandes; ill. by Kim Fernandes. Kids Can Pr., 1997. ISBN 1-55074-225-6 Subj: Animals. Animals – mice. Concepts – color. Counting, numbers. Rhyming text.

Burton, Marilee Robin. *Aaron awoke: an alphabet story* ill. by author. HarperCollins, 1982. ISBN 0-06-020892-9 Subj: ABC books. Farms.

The elephant's nest ill. by author. HarperCollins, 1979. ISBN 0-06-020906-2 Subj: Animals. Humor. Wordless.

Oliver's birthday ill. by author. HarperCollins, 1986. ISBN 0-06-020880-5 Subj: Birds – ostriches. Birthdays.

Tail toes eyes ears nose ill. by author. HarperCollins, 1988. ISBN 0-06-020874-0 Subj: Animals. Problem solving. Riddles.

Burton, Robert. *The egg* photos by Jan Burton and Kim Taylor. DK, 1994. ISBN 1-56458-460-7 Subj: Birds. Eggs.

Burton, Virginia Lee. *Choo choo: the story of a little engine who ran away* ill. by author. Houghton Mifflin, 1937. ISBN 0-395-17684-0 Subj: Behavior – running away. Trains.

Katy and the big snow ill. by author. Houghton Mifflin, 1943. ISBN 0-606-03726-8 Subj: City. Cumulative tales. Machines. Seasons – winter. Weather – snow.

The little house ill. by author. Houghton Mifflin, 1939. ISBN 0-606-01531-0 Subj: Caldecott award books. City. Country. Ecology. Homes, houses. Progress.

Maybelle, the cable car ill. by author. Houghton Mifflin, 1939. ISBN 0-395-24905-8 Subj: Cable cars, trolleys. City. Transportation.

Mike Mulligan and his steam shovel ill. by author. Houghton Mifflin, 1967. ISBN 0-395-16961-5 Subj: Activities – working. Machines.

Busch, Phyllis S. *Cactus in the desert* ill. by Harriett Barton. Crowell, 1979. ISBN 0-690-01336-1 Subj: Desert. Plants. Science.

City lots: living things in vacant spots photos by Arline Strong. Collins-World, 1970. Subj: City. Science.

Lions in the grass: the story of the dandelion, a green plant photos by Arline Strong. Collins-World, 1968. Subj: Plants. Science.

Once there was a tree: the story of the tree, a changing home for plants and animals photos by Arline Strong. Collins-World, 1968. Subj: Science. Trees.

Puddles and ponds: living things in watery places photos by Arline Strong. Collins-World, 1969. Subj: Ecology. Science.

Bush, Barbara. *In the heart of the village: the world of the Indian Banyan tree* photos by author. Sierra Club, 1996. ISBN 0-87156-575-7 Subj: Foreign lands – India. Nature. Trees.

Bush, John. *The cross-with-us rhinoceros* ill. by Paul Geraghty. Dutton, 1988. ISBN 0-525-44411-4 Subj: Animals – rhinoceros. Behavior – misunderstanding. Rhyming text.

The fish who could wish ill. by Korky Paul. Kane/Miller, 1991. ISBN 0-916291-35-9 Subj: Behavior – wishing. Fish. Rhyming text.

The giraffe who got in a knot by John Bush and Paul Geraghty; ill. by Paul Geraghty. Price Stern Sloan, 1987. ISBN 0-8431-1993-4 Subj: Animals. Animals – giraffes. Jungle. Rhyming text.

Bush, Timothy. *Benjamin McFadden and the robot babysitter* ill. by author. Crown, 1998. ISBN 0-517-79985-5 Subj: Activities – babysitting. Behavior – wishing. Robots.

James in the house of Aunt Prudence ill. by author. Crown, 1993. ISBN 0-517-58882-X Subj: Family life – aunts, uncles. Imagination.

Three at sea ill. by author. Crown, 1994. ISBN 0-517-59300-9 Subj: Animals. Rivers. Sea and seashore. Sports.

Bushey, Jeanne. *A sled dog for Moshi* ill. by Germaine Arnaktauyok. Hyperion, 1994. ISBN 1-56282-632-8 Subj: Animals – dogs. Eskimos. Indians of North America – Inuit. Pets. Weather – snow. Weather – storms.

Bushey, Jerry. *The barge book* photos by author. Carolrhoda, 1984. ISBN 0-87614-205-6 Subj: Activities – trading. Boats, ships. Rivers.

Building a fire truck photos by author. Carolrhoda, 1981. ISBN 0-87614-170-X Subj: Careers – firefighters. Trucks.

Busy baby photos sel. by Debby Slier. Macmillan, 1988. ISBN 0-02-688753-3 Subj: Babies. Format, unusual – board books.

Butcher, Julia. *The sheep and the rowan tree* ill. by author. Holt, 1984. ISBN 0-03-071602-0 Subj: Behavior – wishing. Trees.

Butler, Andrea. *Mr. Sun and Mr. Sea* ill. by Lily Toy Hong. Scott Foresman, 1994. ISBN 0-673-36198-5 Subj: Folk and fairy tales. Foreign lands – Africa. Format, unusual – toy and movable books. Sea and seashore. Sun.

Butler, Dorothy. *Another happy tale* ill. by John Hurford. Interlink, 1991. ISBN 0-940793-88-1 Subj: Character traits – luck. Family life. Farms.

A happy tale ill. by John Hurford. Interlink, 1990. ISBN 0-940793-61-X Subj: Activities – traveling. Airplanes, airports. Character traits – luck.

Higgledy, piggledy, hobbledy hoy ill. by Lyn Kriegerd. Greenwillow, 1991. ISBN 0-688-08661-6 Subj: Activities – picnicking. Animals. Parades. Rhyming text.

My brown bear Barney ill. by Elizabeth Fuller. Greenwillow, 1989. ISBN 0-688-08568-7 Subj: Activities – traveling. School. Toys – bears.

My brown bear Barney in trouble ill. by Elizabeth Fuller. Greenwillow, 1993. ISBN 0-688-10522-X Subj: Friendship. Toys – bears.

Butler, Geoff. *The hangashore* ill. by author. Tundra, 1998. ISBN 0-8877-6444-4 Subj: Behavior. Foreign lands – Canada. Handicaps – Down syndrome.

Butler, John. *While you were sleeping* ill. by author. Peachtree, 1999. ISBN 1-56145-211-4 Subj: Animals. Bedtime. Counting, numbers. Night. Sleep.

Butler, Stephen. *Henny Penny* (Chicken Little)

The mouse and the apple ill. by author. Tambourine, 1994. ISBN 0-688-12811-4 Subj: Animals. Animals – mice. Character traits – patience.

Butterfield, Moira. *Brown, fierce, and furry* ill. by Wayne Ford. Raintree, 1997. ISBN 0-8172-4586-3 Subj: Animals – bears.

The Christmas story ill. with soft sculptures by Christine Potter; designs and concept by Rachael O'Neill. Gold Key Book, 1994. ISBN 0-307-16176-5 Subj: Holidays – Christmas. Religion – Nativity.

Fast, strong, and striped ill. by Wayne Ford. Raintree, 1997. ISBN 0-8172-4583-9 Subj: Animals – tigers.

Butterfield-Campbell, Jill. *The queen and Rosie Randall* (Oxenbury, Helen)

Butterworth, Nick. *All together now!* ill. by author. Little, 1995. ISBN 0-316-11932-6 Subj: Activities – picnicking. Format, unusual – toy and movable books. Rhyming text. Toys.

Amanda's butterfly ill. by author. Delacorte, 1991. ISBN 0-385-30434-X Subj: Character traits – kindness. Fairies. Wordless.

Busy people ill. by author. Candlewick, 1992. ISBN 1-56402-056-8 Subj: Careers.

Field day by Nick Butterworth and Mick Inkpen; ill. by Mick Inkpen. Delacorte, 1991. ISBN 0-385-30328-9 Subj: School. Sports.

The house on the rock by Nick Butterworth and Mick Inkpen; ill. by Mick Inkpen. Multnomah, 1986. ISBN 0-8807-0146-3 Subj: Character traits – foolishness. Homes, houses. Religion.

Jasper's beanstalk by Nick Butterworth and Mick Inkpen; ill. by Mick Inkpen. Bradbury, 1993. ISBN 0-02-716231-1 Subj: Animals – cats. Behavior – dissatisfaction. Days of the week, months of the year. Plants.

Jingle bells ill. by author. Orchard, 1998. ISBN 0-531-30124-9 Subj: Animals – cats. Animals – mice. Holidays – Christmas. Problem solving.

Just like Jasper ill. by Mick Inkpen. Little, 1989. ISBN 0-316-11917-2 Subj: Animals – cats. Shopping. Toys.

The lost sheep ill. by Mick Inkpen. Multnomah, 1986. ISBN 0-88-070147-1 Subj: Animals – sheep. Behavior – lost. Religion.

Making faces ill. by author. Candlewick, 1993. ISBN 1-56402-212-9 Subj: Anatomy – faces. Character traits – appearance. Emotions. Format, unusual – toy and movable books.

My dad is awesome ill. by author. Candlewick, 1992. ISBN 1-56402-033-9 Subj: Behavior – boasting. Family life – fathers. Holidays – Father's Day.

My grandma is wonderful ill. by author. Candlewick, 1991. ISBN 1-56402-100-9 Subj: Family life – grandmothers.

My grandpa is amazing ill. by author. Candlewick, 1992. ISBN 1-56402-099-1 Subj: Behavior – boasting. Family life – grandfathers.

My mom is excellent ill. by author. Candlewick, 1994. ISBN 1-56402-289-7 Subj: Family life – mothers.

The Nativity play by Nick Butterworth and Mick Inkpen; ill. by authors. Little, 1985. ISBN 0-316-11903-2 Subj: Holidays – Christmas. Religion – Nativity. School. Theater.

Nice or nasty by Nick Butterworth and Mick Inkpen; ill. by authors. Little, 1987. ISBN 0-316-11915-6 Subj: Concepts – opposites.

Nick Butterworth's book of nursery rhymes ill. by sel. Viking, 1991. ISBN 0-670-83551-X Subj: Nursery rhymes.

One blowy night ill. by author. Little, 1992. ISBN 0-316-11919-9 Subj: Animals. Character traits – kindness to animals. Character traits – optimism. Weather – storms. Weather – wind.

One snowy night ill. by author. Little, 1990. ISBN 0-316-11918-0 Subj: Animals. Character traits – kindness to animals. Night. Weather – snow.

The precious pearl ill. by Mick Inkpen. Multnomah, 1986. ISBN 0-88-070145-5 Subj: Religion.

The rescue party ill. by author. Little, 1993. ISBN 0-316-11923-7 Subj: Activities – picnicking. Animals. Careers – park rangers. Format, unusual – toy and movable books.

The school trip by Nick Butterworth and Mick Inkpen; ill. by Mick Inkpen. Delacorte, 1990. ISBN 0-385-30243-6 Subj: Museums. School.

The secret path ill. by author. Little, 1994. ISBN 0-316-11914-8 Subj: Animals. Careers – park rangers. Gardens, gardening. Problem solving.

The two sons ill. by Mick Inkpen. Multnomah, 1986. ISBN 0-88-070148-X Subj: Character traits – helpfulness. Family life – brothers. Family life – fathers. Religion.

When it's time for bed ill. by author. Little, 1994. ISBN 0-316-11902-4 Subj: Bedtime. Format, unusual – toy and movable books. Toys.

When there's work to do ill. by author. Little, 1994. ISBN 0-316-11906-7 Subj: Activities – working. Format, unusual – board books. Toys.

When we go shopping ill. by author. Little, 1994. ISBN 0-316-11900-8 Subj: Format, unusual – board books. Shopping. Toys.

When we play together ill. by author. Little, 1994. ISBN 0-316-11901-6 Subj: Activities – playing. Format, unusual – board books. Toys.

Butterworth, Oliver. *A visit to the big house* ill. by Susan Avishai. Houghton Mifflin, 1993. ISBN 0-395-52805-4 Subj: Family life – fathers. Prisons.

Buxbaum, Susan Kovacs. *Splash! all about baths* by Susan Kovacs Buxbaum and Rita Golden Gelman; ill. by Maryann Cocca-Leffler. Little, 1987. ISBN 0-316-30726-2 Subj: Activities – bathing.

Byars, Betsy Cromer. *Ant plays bear* ill. by Marc Simont. Viking, 1997. ISBN 0-670-86776-4 Subj: Family life – brothers. Friendship.

Go and hush the baby ill. by Emily Arnold McCully. Puffin, 1982, 1971. ISBN 0-14-050396-X Subj: Babies. Family life – new sibling. Games.

The groober ill. by author. Harper, 1967. Subj: Animals. Behavior – dissatisfaction.

The lace snail ill. by author. Viking, 1975. ISBN 0-670-41614-2 Subj: Animals. Animals – snails. Gifts.

My brother, Ant ill. by Marc Simont. Viking, 1996. ISBN 0-670-86664-4 Subj: Family life – brothers. Insects – ants.

Byers, Rinda M. *Mycca's baby* ill. by David Tamura. Orchard, 1990. ISBN 0-531-08428-0 Subj: Babies. Family life.

Byfield, Barbara Ninde. *The haunted churchbell* ill. by author. Doubleday, 1971. Subj: Character traits – cleverness. Emotions – fear. Humor.

Bynum, Janie. *Altoona Baboona* ill. by author. Harcourt, 1999. ISBN 0-15-201860-3 Subj: Activities – ballooning. Animals. Islands. Rhyming text.

Byrd, Robert. *Marcella was bored* ill. by author. Dutton, 1985. ISBN 0-525-44156-5 Subj: Animals – cats. Behavior – running away. Family life.

Byrne, David. *Stay up late* ill. by Maira Kalman. Viking, 1987. ISBN 0-670-81895-X Subj: Babies. Family life. Sibling rivalry. Songs.

Cabban, Vanessa. *Bertie and Small and the brave sea journey* ill. by author. Candlewick, 1999. ISBN 0-7636-0878-5 Subj: Activities – traveling. Imagination. Toys.

Bertie and Small and the fast bike ride ill. by author. Candlewick, 1999. ISBN 0-7636-0879-3 Subj: Activities – playing. Sports – bicycling. Toys.

Cabrera, Jane. *Panda Big and Panda Small* ill. by author. DK, 1998. ISBN 0-7894-3485-7 Subj: Animals – pandas. Format, unusual – board books. Friendship. Rhyming text.

Rory and the lion ill. by author. DK, 1999. ISBN 0-7894-4843-2 Subj: Animals – lions. Noise, sounds.

Cadnum, Michael. *The lost and found house* ill. by Steve Johnson and Lou Fancher. Viking, 1997. ISBN 0-670-84884-0 Subj: Emotions. Family life. Moving.

Caen, Herb. *The cable car and the dragon* ill. by Barbara Ninde Byfield. Chronicle, 1972. ISBN 0-87701-390-X Subj: Cable cars, trolleys.

Caffey, Donna. *Yikes-lice!* ill. by Patrick Girouard. Albert Whitman, 1998. ISBN 0-8075-9374-5 Subj: Family life. Insects – lice. Rhyming text.

Cahill, Chris. *Bear magic* ill. by Mitchell Rose and Ruth Young. Schneider Educational, 1990. ISBN 1-877779-00-8 Subj: Animals – bears. Format, unusual – board books. Poetry. Puppets.

Bunny magic ill. by Mitchell Rose and Ruth Young. Schneider Educational, 1990. ISBN 1-877779-02-4 Subj: Animals – rabbits. Format, unusual – board books. Poetry. Puppets.

Spider magic ill. by Mitchell Rose and Ruth Young. Schneider Educational, 1990. ISBN 1-877779-03-2 Subj: Format, unusual. Format, unusual – board books. Puppets. Spiders.

Turtle magic ill. by Mitchell Rose and Ruth Young. Schneider Educational, 1990. ISBN 1-877779-01-6 Subj: Format, unusual. Format, unusual – board books. Puppets. Reptiles – turtles, tortoises.

Cain, Sheridan. *Look out for the big bad fish!* ill. by Tanya Linch. Little Tiger, 1998. ISBN 1-888444-27-4 Subj: Activities – jumping. Fish. Frogs and toads.

Why so sad, Brown Rabbit? ill. by Jo Kelly. Dutton, 1998. ISBN 0-525-45963-4 Subj: Animals – rabbits. Behavior – needing someone. Birds – ducks. Family life – mothers.

Caines, Jeannette. *Abby* ill. by Steven Kellogg. HarperCollins, 1973. ISBN 0-06-020922-4 Subj: Adoption. Ethnic groups in the U.S. – African Americans. Family life. Sibling rivalry.

Chilly stomach ill. by Pat Cummings. HarperCollins, 1986. ISBN 0-06-020977-1 Subj: Child abuse. Emotions – fear. Family life.

Daddy ill. by Ronald Himler. HarperCollins, 1977. ISBN 0-06-020924-0 Subj: Divorce. Ethnic groups in the U.S. – African Americans. Family life – fathers.

I need a lunch box ill. by Pat Cummings. HarperCollins, 1988. ISBN 0-06-020985-2 Subj: Emotions – envy, jealousy. Family life.

Just us women ill. by Pat Cummings. HarperCollins, 1982. ISBN 0-06-020942-9 Subj: Activities – traveling. Automobiles. Ethnic groups in the U.S. – African Americans.

Window wishing ill. by Kevin Brooks. HarperCollins, 1980. ISBN 0-06-020934-8 Subj: Family life – grandmothers.

Cairo, Jasmine. *Our brother has Down's syndrome: an introduction for children* (Cairo, Shelley)

Cairo, Shelley. *Our brother has Down's syndrome: an introduction for children* by Shelley, Jasmine and Tara Cairo; photos by Irene McNeil; designed by Helmut W. Weyerstrahs. Firefly, 1985. ISBN 0-920303-30-7 Subj: Family life. Handicaps.

Cairo, Tara. *Our brother has Down's syndrome: an introduction for children* (Cairo, Shelley)

Cakes and custard: *children's rhymes* comp. by Brian W. Alderson; ill. by Helen Oxenbury. Morrow, 1975, 1974. ISBN 0-688-32050-3 Subj: Nursery rhymes.

Calcagnino, Steve. *The body book* (Rotner, Shelley)

Caldecott, Randolph. *Panjandrum picture book* ill. by author. Warne, 1885. Subj: Nursery rhymes.

The Queen of Hearts ill. by author. Warne, 1881. Subj: Nursery rhymes.

The Randolph Caldecott treasury sel. and ed. by Elizabeth T. Billington; ill. by author. Warne, 1978. ISBN 0-7232-6139-3 Subj: Folk and fairy tales.

Randolph Caldecott's favorite nursery rhymes ill. by author. Castle Books, 1980. Subj: Nursery rhymes.

Randolph Caldecott's John Gilpin and other stories ill. by author. Warne, 1977. The diverting history of John Gilpin.—The house that Jack built.—The frog he would a-wooing go.—The milkmaid. Subj: Nursery rhymes.

Randolph Caldecott's picture book, no. 1 ill. by author. Warne, 1879. Subj: Nursery rhymes.

Randolph Caldecott's picture book, no. 2 ill. by author. Warne, 1879. Subj: Nursery rhymes.

Sing a song of sixpence (Mother Goose)

The three jovial huntsmen ill. by author. Warne, 1880. Subj: Nursery rhymes.

Calder, Lyn. *Walt Disney's Alice's tea party* ill. by Jesse Clay. Walt Disney, 1992. ISBN 1-56282-199-7 Subj: Activities – making things. Parties.

Calder, S. J. *If you were a bird* ill. by Cornelius Van Wright. Silver Pr., 1989. ISBN 0-671-68595-3 Subj: Birds – robins.

If you were a cat ill. by Cornelius Van Wright. Silver Pr., 1989. ISBN 0-671-68598-8 Subj: Animals – cats. Pets.

If you were a fish ill. by Cornelius Van Wright. Silver Pr., 1989. ISBN 0-671-68596-1 Subj: Aquariums. Fish.

If you were an ant ill. by Cornelius Van Wright. Silver Pr., 1989. ISBN 0-671-68597-X Subj: Insects – ants.

Calders, Pere. *Brush* trans. from Spanish by Marguerite Feitlowitz; ill. by Carme Solé Vendrell.

Kane/Miller, 1986. ISBN 0-916291-05-7 Subj: Crime. Family life. Imagination. Pets.

Caldwell, Mary. *Morning, rabbit, morning* ill. by Ann Schweninger. HarperCollins, 1982. ISBN 0-06-020940-2 Subj: Animals – rabbits. Morning.

Calhoun, Mary. *Audubon cat* ill. by Susan Bonners. Morrow, 1981. ISBN 0-688-32253-0 Subj: Animals – cats. Food. Problem solving.

Big Sixteen ill. by Trina Schart Hyman. Morrow, 1983. ISBN 0-688-02351-7 Subj: Ethnic groups in the U.S. – African Americans. Folk and fairy tales.

Blue-ribbon Henry ill. by Erick Ingraham. Morrow, 1998. ISBN 0-688-14675-9 Subj: Animals – cats. Character traits – helpfulness. Fairs.

Cross-country cat ill. by Erick Ingraham. Morrow, 1979. ISBN 0-688-32186-0 Subj: Animals – cats. Character traits – cleverness. Sports – skiing.

Euphonia and the flood ill. by Simms Taback. Parents, 1976. ISBN 0-819-30837-4 Subj: Animals. Boats, ships. Character traits – helpfulness. Weather – rain.

Flood! ill. by Erick Ingraham. Morrow, 1997. ISBN 0-688-13920-5 Subj: Family life. U.S. history. Weather – floods.

The goblin under the stairs ill. by Janet McCaffery. Morrow, 1968. Subj: Behavior – misbehavior. Folk and fairy tales. Mythical creatures – goblins.

Henry the sailor cat ill. by Erick Ingraham. Morrow, 1994. ISBN 0-688-10841-5 Subj: Animals – cats. Boats, ships. Sailors. Sea and seashore.

High-wire Henry ill. by Erick Ingraham. Morrow, 1991. ISBN 0-688-08984-4 Subj: Animals – cats. Animals – dogs. Emotions – envy, jealousy. Pets.

Hot-air Henry ill. by Erick Ingraham. Morrow, 1981. ISBN 0-688-00502-0 Subj: Activities – ballooning. Animals – cats.

Houn' dog ill. by Roger Antoine Duvoisin. Morrow, 1959. Subj: Animals – dogs. Animals – foxes. Sports – hunting.

The hungry leprechaun ill. by Roger Antoine Duvoisin. Harber, 1962. Subj: Food. Foreign lands – Ireland. Holidays – St. Patrick's Day. Mythical creatures – leprechauns.

Jack and the whoopee wind ill. by Dick Gackenbach. Morrow, 1987. ISBN 0-688-06138-9 Subj: Character traits – cleverness. Machines. Tall tales. Weather – wind.

Jack the wise and the Cornish cuckoos ill. by Tasha Tudor. Morrow, 1978. ISBN 0-688-32132-1 Subj: Character traits – helpfulness. Folk and fairy tales.

Mrs. Dog's own house ill. by Janet McCaffery. Morrow, 1972. Subj: Animals – dogs. Homes, houses.

The nine lives of Homer C. Cat ill. by Roger Antoine Duvoisin. Morrow, 1961. Subj: Animals – cats. Behavior – imitation. Humor.

Old man Whickutt's donkey ill. by Tomie de Paola. Parents, 1975. ISBN 0-819-30788-2 Subj: Animals – donkeys. Character traits – perseverance. Folk and fairy tales. Humor.

The pixy and the lazy housewife ill. by Janet McCaffery. Morrow, 1969. Subj: Behavior – trickery. Folk and fairy tales. Foreign lands – England. Mythical creatures – pixies.

The runaway brownie ill. by Janet McCaffery. Morrow, 1967. Subj: Character traits – pride. Folk and fairy tales. Foreign lands – Scotland. Mythical creatures – elves.

A shepherd's gift ill. by Raúl Colón. HarperCollins, 2001. ISBN 0-688-15177-9 Subj: Careers – shepherds. Gifts. Holidays – Christmas. Orphans. Religion – Nativity.

The thieving dwarfs ill. by Janet McCaffery. Morrow, 1967. Subj: Character traits – kindness. Dwarfs, midgets. Folk and fairy tales. Foreign lands – Germany.

Tonio's cat ill. by Ed Martinez. Morrow, 1996. ISBN 0-688-13315-0 Subj: Animals – cats. Ethnic groups in the U.S. – Mexican Americans. Friendship. Pets.

The traveling ball of string ill. by Janet McCaffery. Morrow, 1969. Subj: Behavior – saving things. Humor. String.

While I sleep ill. by Ed Young. Morrow, 1992. ISBN 0-688-08201-7 Subj: Bedtime. Sleep.

The witch of Hissing Hill ill. by Janet McCaffery. Morrow, 1964. ISBN 0-688-31762-6 Subj: Animals – cats. Holidays – Halloween. Witches.

The witch who lost her shadow ill. by Trinka Hakes Noble. HarperCollins, 1979. ISBN 0-06-020947-X Subj: Animals – cats. Character traits – loyalty. Emotions. Friendship. Witches.

The witch's pig: a Cornish folktale ill. by Tasha Tudor. Morrow, 1977. ISBN 0-688-32092-9 Subj: Animals – pigs. Folk and fairy tales. Foreign lands – England. Witches.

Wobble the witch cat ill. by Roger Antoine Duvoisin. Morrow, 1958. ISBN 0-688-31621-2 Subj: Animals – cats. Holidays – Halloween. Witches.

Callan, Elizabeth Koda. *Good luck pony* ill. by author. Workman, 1990. ISBN 0-89480-859-1 Subj: Animals – horses, ponies. Character traits – confidence. Character traits – luck. Emotions – fear.

Callen, Larry. *Dashiel and the night* ill. by Leslie Holt Morrill. Dutton, 1981. ISBN 0-525-28540-7 Subj: Bedtime. Dreams. Imagination. Insects – fireflies. Night.

Calloway, Northern J. *Northern J. Calloway presents Super-vroomer!* Written by Carol Hall; ill. by Sammis McLean; conceived by Northern J. Calloway. Doubleday, 1978. Written by Carol Hall; conceived by Northern J. Calloway. ISBN 0-385-14178-5 Subj: Ethnic groups in the U.S. – African Americans. Sports – racing.

Calmenson, Stephanie. *ABC: featuring Jim Henson's Sesame Street Muppets* ill. by John Nez. Western, in conjunction with Children's Television Workshop, 1986. At head of title: CTW Sesame Street. "Featuring Jim Henson's Sesame Street Muppets." ISBN 0-307-07016-6 Subj: ABC books. Puppets.

The after school book ill. by Beth Weiner Lipson. Grosset, 1984. ISBN 0-448-11227-2 Subj: Animals. School.

All aboard the goodnight train ill. by Normand Chartier. Grosset, 1984. ISBN 0-448-11226-4 Subj: Animals. Bedtime. Lullabies.

The birthday hat ill. by Susan Gantner. Grosset, 1983. ISBN 0-448-21705-8 Subj: Animals – hippopotamuses. Birthdays. Shopping.

The children's Æsop (Æsop)

Come to my party ill. by Beth Weiner Lipson. Parents, 1991. ISBN 0-8193-1195-2 Subj: Animals – raccoons. Birthdays. Counting, numbers.

Dinner at the Panda Palace ill. by Nadine Bernard Westcott. HarperCollins, 1991. ISBN 0-06-021011-7 Subj: Animals. Animals – pandas. Counting, numbers. Food. Rhyming text.

Engine, engine, number nine ill. by Paul Meisel. Hyperion, 1996. ISBN 0-7868-2127-2 Subj: Rhyming text. Trains.

Fido ill. by Maxie Chambliss. Scholastic, 1987. ISBN 0-590-40410-5 Subj: Animals – dogs. Careers.

Get well, gators! by Stephanie Calmenson and Joanna Cole; ill. by Lynn Munsinger. Morrow, 1998. Subj: Fairs. Illness. Reptiles – alligators, crocodiles.

Hotter than a hot dog! ill. by Elivia Savadier. Little, 1994. ISBN 0-316-12479-6 Subj: City. Family life – grandmothers. Sea and seashore. Seasons – summer. Weather.

It begins with an A ill. by Marisabina Russo. Hyperion, 1993. ISBN 1-56282-123-7 Subj: ABC books. Rhyming text. Riddles.

The kindergarten book ill. by Beth Weiner Lipson. Grosset, 1983. ISBN 0-448-14499-9 Subj: Activities. Animals. Emotions – fear. School. School – first day.

Kinderkittens, show-and-tell ill. by Diane de Groat. Scholastic, 1994. ISBN 0-590-46349-7 Subj: Anatomy – hands. Animals – cats. School. Shadows.

Kinderkittens, who took the cookie from the cookie jar? ill. by Diane de Groat. Scholastic, 1995. ISBN 0-590-46350-0 Subj: Animals – babies. Animals – cats. Food. School.

The little witch sisters ill. by R. W. Alley. Parents, 1993. ISBN 0-8368-0970-X Subj: Character traits – helpfulness. Family life – sisters. Magic. Witches.

Meet Penny ill. by Carolyn Bracken. Marvel, 1986. ISBN 0-8713-5152-8 Subj: Activities. Format, unusual – board books.

Meet Timmy ill. by Carolyn Bracken. Marvel, 1986. ISBN 0-8713-5151-X Subj: Activities. Format, unusual – board books.

My book of the seasons ill. by Eugenie. Golden Books, 1999. ISBN 0-307-68122-X Subj: Seasons. Senses.

Never take a pig to lunch and other funny poems about animals ill. by Hilary Knight. Doubleday, 1982. ISBN 0-385-15593-X Subj: Animals – pigs. Poetry.

No stage fright for me! ill. by Rose Mary Berlin. Western, 1988. ISBN 0-307-10284-X Subj: Emotions – fear. Theater.

One little monkey ill. by Ellen Appleby. Parents, 1994. ISBN 0-8368-0988-2 Subj: Animals. Animals – monkeys. Counting, numbers. Jungle. Rhyming text.

One red shoe (the other's blue!) ill. by Lisa McCue Karsten. Golden Books, 1987. ISBN 0-307-60908-1 Subj: Animals – rabbits. Clothing – shoes.

Pat-a-cake and other play rhymes (Cole, Joanna)

Pin the tail on the donkey and other party games (Cole, Joanna)

The principal's new clothes ill. by Denise Brunkus. Scholastic, 1989. ISBN 0-590-41822-X Subj: Careers – school principals. Careers – tailors. Character traits – pride. Character traits – vanity. Clothing. Folk and fairy tales. School.

Roller skates! ill. by True Kelley. Scholastic, 1992. ISBN 0-590-45716-0 Subj: Rhyming text. Sports – roller skating.

Rosie, a visiting dog's story ill. by Justin Sutcliffe. Clarion, 1994. ISBN 0-395-65477-7 Subj: Animals – dogs. Illness. Old age.

Shaggy, waggy dogs (and others) photos by Justin Sutcliffe. Clarion, 1998. ISBN 0-395-77605-8 Subj: Animals – dogs. Pets. Rhyming text.

The teeny tiny teacher ill. by Denis Roche. Scholastic, 1998. ISBN 0-590-37123-1 Subj: Careers – teachers. Folk and fairy tales. Ghosts. School.

Ten furry monsters ill. by Maxie Chambliss. Gareth Stevens, 1994. ISBN 0-8368-0989-0 Subj: Counting, numbers. Monsters. Rhyming text.

Wanted: warm, furry friend ill. by Amy Schwartz. Macmillan, 1990. ISBN 0-02-716390-3 Subj: Animals – rabbits. Friendship. Pen pals.

What am I? ill. by Karen Gundersheimer. HarperCollins, 1989. ISBN 0-06-020998-4 Subj: Riddles.

Where is Grandma Potamus? ill. by Susan Gantner. Grosset, 1983. ISBN 0-448-21706-6 Subj: Animals – hippopotamuses. Behavior – lost.

Where will the animals stay? ill. by Ellen Appleby. Parents, 1983. ISBN 0-819-31119-7 Subj: Animals. Homes, houses. Rhyming text. Zoos.

Why did the chicken cross the road? and other riddles, old and new (Cole, Joanna)

Zip, whiz, zoom! ill. by Dorothy Stott. Little, 1992. ISBN 0-316-12478-8 Subj: Activities – traveling. Birthdays. Family life – grandmothers. Transportation.

Calvert, Elinor H. *see* Lasell, Fen

Cameron, Alice. *The cat sat on the mat* ill. by Carol Jones. Houghton Mifflin, 1994. ISBN 0-395-68392-0 Subj: Animals – cats. Animals – mice. Format, unusual.

Cameron, Ann. *Harry (the monster)* ill. by Jeanette Winter. Pantheon, 1980. ISBN 0-394-94162-4 Subj: Bedtime. Character traits – bravery. Emotions – fear. Monsters.

Cameron, Elizabeth Jane. *see* Duncan, Jane

Cameron, John. *If mice could fly* ill. by author. Atheneum, 1979. ISBN 0-689-30731-4 Subj: Animals – cats. Animals – mice. Character traits – cleverness. Rhyming text.

Cameron, Polly. *The cat who thought he was a tiger* ill. by author. Coward, 1956. Subj: Animals – cats. Circus.

A child's book of nonsense ill. by author. Coward, 1960. Subj: Humor. Poetry.

"I can't," said the ant: a second book of nonsense ill. by author. Coward, 1961. Subj: Family life. Insects – ants. Participation. Poetry.

Camp, Lindsay. *The biggest bed in the world* ill. by Jonathan Langley. HarperCollins, 2000. ISBN 0-06-028687-3 Subj: Bedtime. Family life. Furniture – beds. Sleep.

Dinosaurs at the supermarket ill. by Clare Skilbeck. Viking, 1993. ISBN 0-670-84802-6 Subj: Dinosaurs. Imagination.

Keeping up with Cheetah ill. by Jill Newton. Lothrop, 1993. ISBN 0-688-12655-3 Subj: Animals – cheetahs. Animals – hippopotamuses. Friendship.

Why? ill. by Tony Ross. Putnam, 1998. ISBN 0-399-23396-2 Subj: Aliens. Character traits – questioning. Family life – fathers.

Campbell, Alison. *Are you asleep, rabbit?* by Alison Campbell and Julia Barton; ill. by Gill Scriven. Lothrop, 1990. ISBN 0-688-09491-0 Subj: Animals – rabbits. Bedtime.

Campbell, Ann. *Dora's box* ill. by Fabian Negrin. Knopf, 1998. ISBN 0-679-97642-6 Subj: Emotions. Folk and fairy tales. Mythical creatures. Witches.

Let's find out about boats ill. by author. Watts, 1967. Subj: Boats, ships.

Let's find out about color ill. by author. Watts, 1966. Subj: Concepts – color.

Campbell, M. Rudolph. *The talking crocodile* ill. by Judy Piussi-Campbell. Atheneum, 1968. Adapt. from Krokodil by Fyodor Dostoyevsky. Subj: Foreign lands – Russia. Reptiles – alligators, crocodiles.

Campbell, Rod. *Buster gets dressed* ill. by author. Barron's, 1988. ISBN 0-8120-5922-0 Subj: Clothing. Format, unusual – toy and movable books.

Buster keeps warm ill. by author. Barron's, 1988. ISBN 0-8120-5923-9 Subj: Clothing. Format, unusual – toy and movable books. Seasons – winter.

Buster's afternoon ill. by author. HarperCollins, 1984. ISBN 0-911745-74-2 Subj: Character traits – curiosity. Flowers. Format, unusual – toy and movable books. Nature.

Buster's morning ill. by author. HarperCollins, 1984. ISBN 0-911745-73-4 Subj: Character traits – curiosity. Format, unusual – toy and movable books. Homes, houses. Toys.

Dear zoo ill. by author. Four Winds, 1984. ISBN 0-02-716440-3 Subj: Animals. Format, unusual – toy and movable books. Zoos.

Funwheels with moving parts! ill. by author. Simon & Schuster, 1985. ISBN 0-671-54707-0 Subj: Automobiles. Format, unusual – toy and movable books.

Henry's busy day ill. by author. Viking, 1984. ISBN 0-670-80024-4 Subj: Animals – dogs. Behavior – misbehavior. Format, unusual.

It's mine ill. by author. Barron's, 1988. ISBN 0-8120-5921-2 Subj: Anatomy. Animals. Format, unusual – toy and movable books.

Look inside! All kinds of places ill. by author. HarperCollins, 1983. ISBN 0-911745-72-6 Subj: Format, unusual – board books. Wordless.

Look inside! Land, sea, air ill. by author. HarperCollins, 1983. ISBN 0-911745-71-8 Subj: Format, unusual – board books. Transportation. Wordless.

Misty's mischief ill. by author. Viking, 1985. ISBN 0-670-80149-6 Subj: Animals – cats. Behavior – misbehavior. Format, unusual.

My pop-up garden friends ill. by author. Aladdin, 1993. ISBN 0-689-71643-5 Subj: Animals. Format, unusual – toy and movable books. Gardens, gardening.

Oh dear! ill. by author. Four Winds, 1986. ISBN 0-590-07944-1 Subj: Eggs. Farms. Format, unusual – toy and movable books.

Playwheels with moving parts! ill. by author. Simon & Schuster, 1985. ISBN 0-671-54706-2 Subj: Format, unusual – toy and movable books. Trucks.

Campbell, Wayne. *What a catastrophe!* ill. by Eileen Christelow. Bradbury, 1987. ISBN 0-02-716420-9 Subj: Family life. Frogs and toads.

Can you see the red balloon? ill. by Debbie Harter. Orchard, 1998. ISBN 0-531-30077-3 Subj: Concepts – color.

Canfield, Jack. *Chicken soup for little souls: The best night out with Dad* (McCourt, Lisa)

Chicken soup for little souls: The Goodness Gorillas (McCourt, Lisa)

Chicken soup for little souls: The never-forgotten doll (McCourt, Lisa)

Della Splatnuk birthday girl (McCourt, Lisa)

The new kid and the cookie thief (McCourt, Lisa)

Canfield, Jane White. *The frog prince: a true story* ill. by Winn Smith. HarperCollins, 1970. Subj: Frogs and toads. Royalty – princes.

Swan cove ill. by Jo Polseno. HarperCollins, 1978. ISBN 0-06-020949-6 Subj: Birds – swans.

Canning, Kate. *A painted tale* ill. by author. Barron's, 1979. ISBN 0-8120-5358-3 Subj: Animals – tigers. Art. Behavior – imitation. Zoos.

Cannon, Annie. *The bat in the boot* ill. by author. Orchard, 1996. ISBN 0-531-08795-6 Subj: Animals – bats. Character traits – kindness to animals.

Cannon, Janell. *Stellaluna* ill. by author. Harcourt, 1993. ISBN 0-15-280217-7 Subj: Animals – bats. Birds. Character traits – being different. Family life – mothers. Friendship.

Stellaluna: a pop-up book and mobile ill. by author. Harcourt, 1997. ISBN 0-15-201530-2 Subj: Animals – bats. Birds. Character traits – being different. Family life – mothers. Format, unusual – toy and movable books. Friendship.

Trupp: a fuzzhead tale ill. by author. Harcourt, 1995. ISBN 0-15-200130-1 Subj: City. Homeless. Mythical creatures.

Verdi ill. by author. Harcourt, 1997. ISBN 0-15-201028-9 Subj: Behavior – growing up. Jungle. Reptiles – snakes.

Cantieni, Benita. *Little Elephant and Big Mouse* trans. by Oliver Gadsby; ill. by Fred Gächter. Alphabet Pr., 1981. Orig. title: Der Kleine Elefant und die Grosse Maus. ISBN 0-907234-09-7 Subj: Animals – elephants. Animals – mice. Concepts – size.

Caple, Kathy. *The biggest nose* ill. by author. Houghton Mifflin, 1985. ISBN 0-395-36894-4 Subj: Anatomy – noses. Animals – elephants. Character traits – being different. School.

The coolest place in town ill. by author. Houghton Mifflin, 1990. ISBN 0-395-51523-8 Subj: Animals – hippopotamuses. Family life – brothers and sisters.

Fox and bear ill. by author. Houghton Mifflin, 1992. ISBN 0-395-55634-1 Subj: Animals – bears. Animals – foxes. Friendship.

Harry's smile ill. by author. Houghton Mifflin, 1987. ISBN 0-395-43417-3 Subj: Friendship. Pen pals. Self-concept.

Inspector Aardvark and the perfect cake ill. by author. Windmill, 1980. ISBN 0-671-96108-X Subj: Animals – aardvarks. Careers – bakers.

The purse ill. by author. Houghton Mifflin, 1986. ISBN 0-395-41852-6 Subj: Activities – working. Family life. Money.

Starring Hillary ill. by author. Carolrhoda, 1999. ISBN 1-57505-261-X Subj: Animals – cats. Self-concept. Theater.

The wimp ill. by author. Houghton Mifflin, 1994. ISBN 0-395-63115-7 Subj: Animals – pigs. Behavior – bullying. Family life – brothers and sisters.

Cappetta, Cynthia. *Chairs, chairs, chairs!* ill. by Rick Stromoski. Children's, 1999. ISBN 0-516-21542-6 Subj: Furniture – chairs. Rhyming text.

Caprio, Annie De. *see* DeCaprio, Annie

Captain Kangaroo. *see* Keeshan, Robert

Capucilli, Alyssa Satin. *Bathtime for Biscuit* ill. by Pat Schories. HarperCollins, 1998. ISBN 0-06-027938-9 Subj: Activities – bathing. Animals – dogs. Pets.

Biscuit ill. by Pat Schories. HarperCollins, 1996. ISBN 0-06-026198-6 Subj: Animals – dogs. Bedtime.

Biscuit finds a friend ill. by Pat Schories. HarperCollins, 1997. ISBN 0-06-027413-1 Subj: Animals – dogs. Birds – ducks. Friendship.

Biscuit's picnic ill. by Pat Schories. HarperCollins, 1998. ISBN 0-06-028072-7 Subj: Activities – picnicking. Animals – dogs.

Good morning, pond ill. by Cynthia Jabar. Hyperion, 1994. ISBN 1-56282-675-1 Subj: Cumulative tales. Lakes, ponds. Morning. Nature.

Happy birthday, Biscuit! ill. by Pat Schories. HarperCollins, 1999. ISBN 0-06-028361-0 Subj: Animals – cats. Animals – dogs. Birthdays. Pets.

Hello, Biscuit! ill. by Pat Schories. HarperCollins, 1998. ISBN 0-06-028071-9 Subj: Animals – dogs. Names.

Inside a barn in the country: a rebus read-along story ill. by Tedd Arnold. Scholastic, 1993. ISBN 0-590-46999-1 Subj: Animals. Cumulative tales. Noise, sounds. Rebuses. Rhyming text.

Inside a house that is haunted: a rebus read-along story ill. by Tedd Arnold. Scholastic, 1998. ISBN 0-590-99716-5 Subj: Animals. Cumulative tales. Ghosts. Rebuses. Rhyming text.

Peekaboo bunny ill. by Mary Melcher. Scholastic, 1994. ISBN 0-590-46754-9 Subj: Animals – rabbits. Format, unusual – toy and movable books. Games. Rhyming text.

Caputo, Robert. *More than just pets: why people study animals* photos by author. Coward, 1980. ISBN 0-698-20460-3 Subj: Anatomy. Ecology.

Cardillo-Young, Donatella. *The yellow coat* ill. by Geoffrey Brittingham. Scythe, 1996. ISBN 1-55523-

729-0 Subj: Holidays – Christmas. Religion – Nativity.

Cardoza, Lois S. *see* Duncan, Lois

Carey, Bonnie. *Grasshopper to the rescue: a Georgian story* (Grasshopper to the rescue)

Carey, Helen H. *Adopted* (Greenberg, Judith E.)

Carey, Mary. *The owl who loved sunshine* ill. by Joe Giordano. Golden Pr., 1977. ISBN 0-307-13433-4 Subj: Birds – owls. Character traits – individuality. Character traits – kindness to animals.

Carey, Valerie Scho. *The devil and mother Crump* ill. by Arnold Lobel. HarperCollins, 1987. ISBN 0-06-020983-6 Subj: Behavior – trickery. Character traits – meanness. Devil. Folk and fairy tales.

Harriet and William and the terrible creature ill. by Lynne Cherry. Dutton, 1985. ISBN 0-525-44154-9 Subj: Animals – squirrels. Character traits – helpfulness. Monsters. Space and space ships.

Maggie Mab and the bogey beast ill. by Johanna Westerman. Arcade, 1992. ISBN 1-55970-155-2 Subj: Character traits – optimism. Folk and fairy tales. Poverty.

Quail song: a Pueblo Indian tale ill. by Ivan Barnett. Putnam, 1990. ISBN 0-399-21936-6 Subj: Animals – coyotes. Behavior – trickery. Birds – quail. Folk and fairy tales. Indians of North America – Pueblo.

Tsugele's broom ill. by Dirk Zimmer. HarperCollins, 1993. ISBN 0-06-020987-9 Subj: Character traits – individuality. Folk and fairy tales. Foreign lands – Poland.

Carigiet, Alois. *Anton the goatherd* ill. by author. Walck, 1966. Subj: Animals – goats. Behavior – lost.

The pear tree, the birch tree and the barberry bush ill. by author. Walck, 1967. Subj: Foreign lands – Switzerland. Trees.

Carle, Eric. *Do you want to be my friend?* ill. by author. Crowell, 1971. ISBN 0-690-24276-X Subj: Animals – mice. Friendship. Wordless.

Does a kangaroo have a mother, too? ill. by author. HarperCollins, 2000. ISBN 0-06-028767-5 Subj: Animals. Family life – mothers.

Dragons dragons and other creatures that never were ill. by author. Philomel, 1991. ISBN 0-399-22105-0 Subj: Dragons. Mythical creatures. Poetry.

Draw me a star ill. by author. Philomel, 1992. ISBN 0-399-21877-7 Subj: Activities – drawing. Circular tales.

From head to toe ill. by author. HarperCollins, 1997. ISBN 0-06-023516-0 Subj: Activities. Anatomy. Animals. Format, unusual – board books.

The grouchy ladybug ill. by author. Crowell, 1977. English title: The bad-tempered ladybird. ISBN 0-

690-01392-2 Subj: Behavior. Insects – ladybugs. Time.

Have you seen my cat? ill. by author. Watts, 1973. ISBN 0-531-02552-7 Subj: Animals – cats. Behavior – lost.

Hello, red fox ill. by author. Simon & Schuster, 1998. ISBN 0-689-81775-4 Subj: Animals. Art. Birthdays. Concepts – color. Frogs and toads. Holidays.

A house for Hermit Crab ill. by author. Picture Book Studio, 1988. ISBN 0-88708-056-1 Subj: Crustaceans. Sea and seashore.

I see a song ill. by author. Crowell, 1973. ISBN 0-690-43307-7 Subj: Music. Wordless.

Little cloud ill. by author. Philomel, 1996. ISBN 0-399-23034-3 Subj: Concepts – shape. Imagination. Sky. Weather – clouds. Weather – rain.

Little cloud, a board book ill. by author. 1st board book ed. Philomel, 1998. ISBN 0-399-23191-9 Subj: Concepts – shape. Format, unusual – board books. Imagination. Sky. Weather – clouds. Weather – rain.

The mixed-up chameleon ill. by author. Crowell, 1975; rev. ed. 1984. ISBN 0-690-00924-0 Subj: Character traits – being different. Concepts – color. Reptiles – lizards. Self-concept.

My apron: a story from my childhood ill. by author. Philomel, 1994. ISBN 0-399-22824-1 Subj: Careers – plasterers. Clothing – aprons. Family life – aunts, uncles.

My very first book of colors ill. by author. Harper-Collins, 1985. ISBN 0-694-00011-6 Subj: Concepts – color. Format, unusual.

My very first book of food ill. by author. Crowell, 1986. ISBN 0-694-00130-9 Subj: Food. Format, unusual – toy and movable books.

My very first book of growth ill. by author. Crowell, 1986. ISBN 0-694-00094-9 Subj: Behavior – growing up. Format, unusual.

My very first book of heads and tails ill. by author. Crowell, 1986. ISBN 0-694-00128-7 Subj: Anatomy. Format, unusual – toy and movable books.

My very first book of homes ill. by author. Crowell, 1986. ISBN 0-694-00092-2 Subj: Format, unusual. Homes, houses.

My very first book of motion ill. by author. Crowell, 1986. ISBN 0-694-00093-0 Subj: Concepts. Format, unusual.

My very first book of numbers ill. by author. Harper-Collins, 1985. ISBN 0-694-00012-4 Subj: Counting, numbers. Format, unusual.

My very first book of shapes ill. by author. Harper-Collins, 1985. ISBN 0-694-00013-2 Subj: Concepts – shape. Format, unusual.

My very first book of sounds ill. by author. Crowell, 1986. ISBN 0-694-00131-7 Subj: Format, unusual – toy and movable books. Noise, sounds.

My very first book of tools ill. by author. Crowell, 1986. ISBN 0-694-00129-5 Subj: Format, unusual – toy and movable books. Tools.

My very first book of touch ill. by author. Crowell, 1986. ISBN 0-694-00095-7 Subj: Format, unusual. Senses – touching.

My very first book of words ill. by author. Harper-Collins, 1985. ISBN 0-694-00014-0 Subj: Format, unusual. Language.

1, 2, 3 to the zoo: a counting book ill. by author. Philomel, 1996. ISBN 0-399-23013-0 Subj: Animals. Counting, numbers. Zoos.

Pancakes, pancakes ill. by author. Knopf, 1970. ISBN 0-394-90490-7 Subj: Cumulative tales. Food.

Papa, please get the moon for me ill. by author. Alphabet Pr., 1986. ISBN 0-88708-026-X Subj: Format, unusual – toy and movable books. Moon.

The rooster who set out to see the world ill. by author. Simon & Schuster, 1991. ISBN 0-8870-8178-9 Subj: Activities – traveling. Birds – chickens. Counting, numbers.

Rooster's off to see the world ill. by author. Picture Book Studio, 1987. ISBN 0-88708-042-1 Subj: Activities – traveling. Birds – chickens. Counting, numbers.

The secret birthday message ill. by author. Crowell, 1972. ISBN 0-690-72348-2 Subj: Birthdays. Format, unusual – toy and movable books.

The tiny seed ill. by author. Rev. ed. Picture Book Studio, 1987. ISBN 0-88708-015-4 Subj: Plants. Seasons. Seeds.

Today is Monday ill. by author. Philomel, 1993. ISBN 0-399-21966-8 Subj: Animals. Days of the week, months of the year. Food. Songs.

Twelve tales from Æsop ill. by adapt. Putnam, 1980. ISBN 0-399-61163-0 Subj: Folk and fairy tales.

The very busy spider ill. by author. Philomel, 1985. ISBN 0-399-21166-7 Subj: Animals. Spiders.

The very clumsy click beetle ill. by author. Philomel, 1999. ISBN 0-399-23201-X Subj: Character traits – perseverance. Insects – beetles.

The very hungry caterpillar ill. by author. Collins-World, 1979. ISBN 0-529-00776-2 Subj: Days of the week, months of the year. Format, unusual. Insects – butterflies, caterpillars. Metamorphosis.

The very lonely firefly ill. by author. Philomel, 1995. ISBN 0-399-22774-1 Subj: Format, unusual – toy and movable books. Insects – fireflies.

The very quiet cricket ill. by author. Putnam, 1990. ISBN 0-399-21885-8 Subj: Format, unusual. Insects – crickets. Noise, sounds.

Walter the baker ill. by author. Simon & Schuster, 1995. ISBN 0-689-80078-9 Subj: Activities – working. Careers – bakers. Food. Royalty.

Watch out! A giant! ill. by author. Collins-World, 1978. ISBN 0-529-05456-6 Subj: Format, unusual – toy and movable books. Giants.

Carleton, Barbee Oliver. *Benny and the bear* ill. by Dagmar Wilson. Follett, 1960. Subj: Animals – bears. Character traits – bravery.

Carling, Amelia Lau. *Mama and Papa have a store* ill. by author. Dial, 1998. ISBN 0-8037-2045-9 Subj: Careers – storekeepers. Family life. Foreign lands – Guatemala. Immigrants. Stores.

Carlisle, Clark. *see* Holding, James

Carlisle, Madelyn. *Bridges* (Carlisle, Norman)

Carlisle, Norman. *Bridges* by Norman and Madelyn Carlisle; ill. with photos. Childrens Pr., 1983. ISBN 0-516-01677-6 Subj: Bridges.

Carlson, Laurie M. *Boss of the plains: the hat that won the West* ill. by Holly Meade. DK, 1998. ISBN 0-7894-2479-7 Subj: Clothing – hats. U.S. history.

Carlson, Lori Marie. *Hurray for Three Kings' Day* ill. by Ed Martinez. Morrow, 1998. ISBN 0-688-16240-1 Subj: Ethnic groups in the U.S. – Hispanic Americans. Holidays. Religion.

Carlson, Maria. *Peter and the wolf* (Prokofiev, Sergei Sergeievitch)

Carlson, Melody. *King of the stable* ill. by Chris Ellison. Crossway, 1998. ISBN 1-58134-032-X Subj: Holidays – Christmas. Religion – Nativity.

What Nick and Holly found in grandpa's attic ill. by Jose Miralles. Gold'n'Honey, 1998. ISBN 1-57673-372-6 Subj: Family life – grandfathers. Holidays – Christmas. Religion – Nativity.

Carlson, Nancy L. *ABC, I like me!* ill. by author. Viking, 1997. ISBN 0-670-87458-2 Subj: ABC books. Language. Self-concept.

Arnie and the new kid ill. by author. Viking, 1990. ISBN 0-670-82499-2 Subj: Accidents. Animals. Friendship. Handicaps – physical handicaps. School.

Arnie and the skateboard gang ill. by author. Viking, 1995. ISBN 0-670-85722-X Subj: Animals. Animals – cats. Character traits – bravery. Character traits – foolishness. Sports – skateboarding.

Arnie and the stolen markers ill. by author. Puffin, 1989. ISBN 0-14-050707-8 Subj: Animals. Behavior – stealing. Crime.

Arnie goes to camp ill. by author. Viking, 1988. ISBN 0-670-81549-7 Subj: Activities. Animals. Animals – cats.

Bunnies and their hobbies ill. by author. Carolrhoda, 1984. ISBN 0-87614-257-9 Subj: Activities. Animals – rabbits.

Bunnies and their sports ill. by author. Viking, 1987. ISBN 0-670-81109-2 Subj: Animals – rabbits. Sports.

Harriet and the garden ill. by author. Carolrhoda, 1982. ISBN 0-87614-184-X Subj: Animals – dogs. Problem solving.

Harriet and the roller coaster ill. by author. Carolrhoda, 1982. ISBN 0-87614-183-1 Subj: Animals – dogs. Character traits – bravery.

Harriet and Walt ill. by author. Carolrhoda, 1982. ISBN 0-87614-185-8 Subj: Animals – dogs. Sibling rivalry.

Harriet's Halloween candy ill. by author. Carolrhoda, 1982. ISBN 0-87614-182-3 Subj: Animals – dogs. Behavior – greed.

Harriet's recital ill. by author. Carolrhoda, 1982. ISBN 0-87614-181-5 Subj: Animals – dogs. Emotions – fear.

How to lose all your friends ill. by author. Viking, 1994. ISBN 0-670-84906-5 Subj: Behavior – misbehavior. Character traits – meanness. Character traits – selfishness. Etiquette. Friendship.

I like me ill. by author. Viking, 1988. ISBN 0-670-82062-8 Subj: Character traits – individuality. Self-concept.

It's going to be perfect ill. by author. Viking, 1998. ISBN 0-670-87802-2 Subj: Dreams. Family life.

Life is fun ill. by author. Viking, 1993. ISBN 0-670-84206-0 Subj: Behavior. Emotions – happiness.

Look out kindergarten, here I come! ill. by author. Viking, 1999. ISBN 0-670-88378-6 Subj: Activities. Animals – mice. School – first day.

Louanne Pig in making the team ill. by author. Carolrhoda, 1985. ISBN 0-87614-281-1 Subj: Animals. Animals – pigs. Cheerleading. Friendship. School. Sports – football.

Louanne Pig in the mysterious valentine ill. by author. Carolrhoda, 1985. ISBN 0-87614-282-X Subj: Animals – pigs. Holidays – Valentine's Day.

Louanne Pig in the perfect family ill. by author. Carolrhoda, 1985. ISBN 0-87614-280-3 Subj: Animals – pigs. Family life. Sibling rivalry.

Loudmouth George and the big race ill. by author. Carolrhoda, 1983. ISBN 0-87614-215-3 Subj: Animals – rabbits. Behavior – boasting. Emotions – embarrassment.

Loudmouth George and the cornet ill. by author. Carolrhoda, 1983. ISBN 0-87614-214-5 Subj: Animals – rabbits. Behavior – boasting.

Loudmouth George and the fishing trip ill. by author. Carolrhoda, 1983. ISBN 0-87614-213-7 Subj: Animals – rabbits. Behavior – boasting.

Loudmouth George and the new neighbors ill. by author. Carolrhoda, 1983. ISBN 0-87614-216-1 Subj: Animals – rabbits. Behavior – boasting. Prejudice.

Loudmouth George and the sixth-grade bully ill. by author. Carolrhoda, 1983. ISBN 0-87614-217-X Subj: Animals – rabbits. Behavior – boasting. Behavior – bullying. Behavior – stealing.

Poor Carl ill. by author. Viking, 1989. ISBN 0-670-81774-0 Subj: Animals – dogs. Babies. Emotions – envy, jealousy.

Sit still! ill. by author. Viking, 1996. ISBN 0-670-85721-1 Subj: Behavior – fidgeting. School.

Snowden ill. by author. Viking, 1997. ISBN 0-670-88078-7 Subj: Friendship. Snowmen. Sports – ice skating.

Take time to relax ill. by author. Viking, 1991. ISBN 0-670-83287-1 Subj: Animals – beavers. Family life. Rhyming text. Weather – snow.

The talent show ill. by author. Carolrhoda, 1985. ISBN 0-87614-284-6 Subj: Animals. Theater.

A visit to grandma's ill. by author. Viking, 1991. ISBN 0-670-83288-X Subj: Animals – beavers. Family life – grandmothers. Holidays – Thanksgiving.

What if it never stops raining? ill. by author. Viking, 1992. ISBN 0-670-81775-9 Subj: Behavior – worrying. Weather – rain.

Witch lady ill. by author. Carolrhoda, 1985. ISBN 0-87614-283-8 Subj: Animals – pigs. Emotions – fear. Witches.

Carlson, Natalie Savage. *Marie Louise and Christophe at the carnival* ill. by José Aruego and Ariane Dewey. Scribners, 1981. ISBN 0-684-17014-0 Subj: Animals – mongooses. Reptiles – snakes.

Marie Louise's heyday ill. by José Aruego and Ariane Dewey. Scribners, 1975. ISBN 0-684-14360-7 Subj: Activities – babysitting. Animals – mongooses. Animals – possums.

Runaway Marie Louise ill. by José Aruego and Ariane Dewey. Scribners, 1977. ISBN 0-684-15045-X Subj: Animals – mongooses. Behavior – running away.

Spooky and the bad luck raven ill. by Andrew Glass. Lothrop, 1988. ISBN 0-688-07651-3 Subj: Animals – cats. Witches.

Spooky and the ghost cat ill. by Andrew Glass. Lothrop, 1985. ISBN 0-688-04317-8 Subj: Animals – cats. Holidays – Halloween. Magic.

Spooky and the witch's goat ill. by Andrew Glass. Lothrop, 1989. ISBN 0-688-08541-5 Subj: Animals – cats. Animals – goats. Magic. Witches.

Spooky and the wizard's bats ill. by Andrew Glass. Lothrop, 1986. ISBN 0-688-06281-4 Subj: Animals – bats. Animals – cats. Holidays – Halloween. Magic. Witches. Wizards.

Spooky night ill. by Andrew Glass. Lothrop, 1982. ISBN 0-688-00935-2 Subj: Animals – cats. Holidays – Halloween. Pets. Witches.

Surprise in the mountains ill. by Elise Primavera. HarperCollins, 1983. ISBN 0-06-021009-5 Subj: Animals. Holidays – Christmas. Seasons – winter.

Time for the white egret ill. by Charles Robinson. Scribners, 1978. ISBN 0-684-15990-2 Subj: Animals – bulls, cows. Birds – egrets. Farms.

Carlstrom, Nancy White. *Baby-O* ill. by Suçie Stevenson. Little, 1992. ISBN 0-316-12851-1 Subj: Cumulative tales. Family life. Foreign lands – Caribbean Islands. Stores.

Barney is best ill. by James Graham Hale. HarperCollins, 1994. ISBN 0-06-022876-8 Subj: Ethnic groups in the U.S. – Hispanic Americans. Family life. Hospitals. Illness – tonsillectomy. Toys.

Better not get wet, Jesse Bear ill. by Bruce Degen. Macmillan, 1988. ISBN 0-02-717280-5 Subj: Animals – bears. Rhyming text.

Blow me a kiss, Miss Lilly ill. by Amy Schwartz. HarperCollins, 1990. ISBN 0-06-021013-3 Subj: Death. Emotions – grief. Friendship. Old age.

Does God know how to tie shoes? ill. by Lori McElrath-Eslick. Eerdmans, 1993. ISBN 0-8028-5074-X Subj: Religion.

Fish and flamingo ill. by Lisa Desimini. Little, 1993. ISBN 0-316-12859-7 Subj: Birds – flamingos. Fish. Friendship.

Goodbye geese ill. by Ed Young. Putnam, 1991. ISBN 0-399-21832-7 Subj: Character traits – questioning. Family life – fathers. Rhyming text. Seasons – winter.

Graham cracker animals 1-2-3 ill. by John Sandford. Macmillan, 1989. ISBN 0-02-717270-8 Subj: Counting, numbers. Poetry.

Grandpappy ill. by Laurel Molk. Little, 1990. ISBN 0-316-12855-4 Subj: Family life – grandfathers.

Guess who's coming, Jesse Bear ill. by Bruce Degen. Simon & Schuster, 1998. ISBN 0-689-80702-3 Subj: Animals – bears. Family life – cousins. Rhyming text.

Happy birthday, Jesse Bear! ill. by Bruce Degen. Macmillan, 1994. ISBN 0-02-717277-5 Subj: Animals – bears. Birthdays. Parties. Rhyming text.

Heather hiding ill. by Dennis Nolan. Macmillan, 1990. ISBN 0-02-717370-4 Subj: Activities – playing. Family life.

How do you say it today, Jesse Bear? ill. by Bruce Degen. Macmillan, 1992. ISBN 0-02-717276-7 Subj: Animals – bears. Days of the week, months of the year. Rhyming text.

How does the wind walk? ill. by Deborah Kogan Ray. Macmillan, 1993. ISBN 0-02-717275-9 Subj: Seasons. Weather – wind.

I am Christmas ill. by Lori McElrath-Eslick. Eerdmans, 1995. ISBN 0-8028-5075-8 Subj: Foreign lands – Israel. Holidays – Christmas. Religion – Nativity.

I'm not moving, mama! ill. by Thor Wickstrom. Macmillan, 1990. ISBN 0-02-717286-4 Subj: Animals – mice. Moving.

It's about time, Jesse Bear ill. by Bruce Degen. Macmillan, 1990. ISBN 0-02-717351-8 Subj: Animals – bears. Rhyming text.

Jesse Bear, what will you wear? ill. by Bruce Degen. Macmillan, 1986. ISBN 0-02-717350-X Subj: Animals – bears. Clothing. Family life.

Jesse Bear's tra-la tub ill. by Bruce Degen. Aladdin, 1994. ISBN 0-689-71715-6 Subj: Activities – bathing. Animals – bears. Format, unusual – board books. Rhyming text.

Jesse Bear's tum-tum tickle ill. by Bruce Degen. Aladdin, 1994. ISBN 0-689-71716-4 Subj: Animals – bears. Format, unusual – board books. Rhyming text.

Jesse Bear's wiggle-jiggle jump-up ill. by Bruce Degen. Aladdin, 1994. ISBN 0-689-71717-2 Subj: Animals – bears. Clothing. Format, unusual – board books. Rhyming text.

Jesse Bear's yum-yum crumble ill. by Bruce Degen. Aladdin, 1994. ISBN 0-689-71718-0 Subj: Animals – bears. Character traits – cleanliness. Format, unusual – board books. Rhyming text.

Kiss your sister, Rose Marie ill. by Thor Wickstrom. Macmillan, 1992. ISBN 0-02-717271-6 Subj: Animals – rabbits. Babies. Family life – new sibling. Family life – sisters. Rhyming text. Sibling rivalry.

Let's count it out, Jesse Bear ill. by Bruce Degen. Simon & Schuster, 1996. ISBN 0-689-80478-4 Subj: Animals – bears. Counting, numbers. Rhyming text.

Midnight dance of the snowshoe hare: poems of Alaska ill. by Ken Kuroi. Philomel, 1998. ISBN 0-399-22746-6 Subj: Alaska. Animals. Animals – rabbits. Poetry. Seasons.

The moon came too ill. by Stella Ormai. Macmillan, 1987. ISBN 0-02-717380-1 Subj: Activities – vacationing. Behavior – collecting things. Family life – grandmothers. Rhyming text.

Moose in the garden ill. by Lisa Desimini. HarperCollins, 1990. ISBN 0-06-021014-1 Subj: Animals – moose. Food. Gardens, gardening.

No nap for Benjamin Badger ill. by Dennis Nolan. Macmillan, 1991. ISBN 0-02-717285-6 Subj: Animals – badgers. Rhyming text. Sleep.

Northern lullaby ill. by Leo and Diane Dillon. Putnam, 1992. ISBN 0-399-21806-8 Subj: Bedtime. Eskimos. Lullabies. Nature. Rhyming text.

Raven and river ill. by Jon Van Zyle. Little, 1997. ISBN 0-316-12894-5 Subj: Alaska. Animals. Birds – ravens. Rivers. Seasons – spring.

Rise and shine! ill. by Dominic Catalano. HarperCollins, 1993. ISBN 0-06-021452-X Subj: Animals. Farms. Rhyming text.

The snow speaks ill. by Jane Dyer. Little, 1992. ISBN 0-316-12861-9 Subj: Country. Seasons – winter. Weather – snow.

Swim the silver sea, Joshie Otter ill. by Ken Kuroi. Philomel, 1993. ISBN 0-399-21872-6 Subj: Animals – otters. Bedtime. Foreign lands – Arctic. Sea and seashore.

Ten Christmas sheep ill. by Cynthia Fisher. Eerdmans, 1996. ISBN 0-8028-5137-1 Subj: Animals – sheep. Format, unusual – toy and movable books. Holidays – Christmas. Rhyming text.

What a scare, Jesse Bear! ill. by Bruce Degen. Simon & Schuster, 1999. ISBN 0-689-81961-7 Subj: Animals – bears. Holidays – Halloween. Rhyming text.

What does the rain play? ill. by Henri Sorensen. Macmillan, 1993. ISBN 0-02-717273-2 Subj: Animals – cats. Family life. Weather – rain.

What would you do if you lived at the zoo? ill. by Lizi Boyd. Little, 1994. ISBN 0-316-12867-8 Subj: Animals. Format, unusual – toy and movable books. Rhyming text. Zoos.

Who gets the sun out of bed? ill. by David McPhail. Little, 1992. ISBN 0-316-12862-7 Subj: Animals – rabbits. Moon. Morning. Pets. Sun.

Who said boo? Halloween poems for the very young ill. by R. W. Alley. Simon & Schuster, 1995. ISBN 0-689-80308-7 Subj: Holidays – Halloween. Poetry.

Wild wild sunflower child Anna ill. by Jerry Pinkney. Macmillan, 1987. ISBN 0-02-717360-7 Subj: Ethnic groups in the U.S. – African Americans. Rhyming text.

Wishing at dawn in summer ill. by Diane Worfolk Allison. Little, 1993. ISBN 0-316-12854-6 Subj: Behavior – wishing. Family life – brothers and sisters. Sports – fishing.

Carmack, Lisa Jobe. *Philippe in Monet's garden* ill. by Lisa Canney Chesaux. Museum of Fine Arts, 1998. ISBN 0-8784-6456-5 Subj: Art. Frogs and toads. Museums. Rhyming text.

Carmi, Giora. *see* Karmi, Giora

Carmichael, Clay. *Bear at the beach* ill. by author. North-South, 1996. ISBN 1-558585-70-2 Subj: Animals – bears. Behavior – seeking better things. Friendship. Sea and seashore. Seasons – summer.

Used-up Bear ill. by author. North-South, 1998. ISBN 1-55858-902-3 Subj: Emotions – love. Self-concept. Toys – bears.

Carney, Margaret (Margaret Rose). *At Grandpa's sugar bush* ill. by Janet Wilson. Kids Can Pr., 1998. ISBN 1-55074-341-4 Subj: Careers – farmers. Food. Foreign lands – Canada. Trees.

Carney, Mary Lou. *Absolutely angels: poems for children and other believers* (Absolutely angels)

Carpenter, Mary-Chapin. *Dreamland: a lullaby* ill. by Julia Noonan. HarperCollins, 1996. ISBN 0-06-025403-3 Subj: Bedtime. Dreams. Lullabies. Sleep.

Halley came to Jackson ill. by Dan Andreasen. HarperCollins, 1998. ISBN 0-06-025400-1 Subj: Astronomy. Songs. Stars.

Carpenter, Stephen. *The three billy goats Gruff* (Asbjørnsen, P. C. [Peter Christen])

Carr, Jan. *Dark day, light night* ill. by James Ransome. Hyperion, 1995. ISBN 0-7868-2014-4 Subj: Character traits – meanness. Emotions – anger. Family life – aunts, uncles.

Frozen noses ill. by Dorothy Donohue. Holiday, 1999. ISBN 0823414620 Subj: Activities. Friendship. Seasons – winter. Sports.

The nature of the beast ill. by G. Brian Karas. Tambourine, 1996. ISBN 0-688-13597-8 Subj: Behavior – misbehavior. Monsters. Pets.

Carrick, Carol. *The accident* ill. by Donald Carrick. Seabury Pr., 1976. ISBN 0-8164-3172-8 Subj: Accidents. Animals – dogs. Death. Emotions – grief. Pets.

Banana beer ill. by Margot Apple. Albert Whitman, 1995. ISBN 0-8075-0568-4 Subj: Animals – orangutans. Family life. Illness – alcoholism.

Beach bird by Carol and Donald Carrick; ill. by Donald Carrick. Dial, 1973. Subj: Birds – seagulls. Sea and seashore.

Ben and the porcupine ill. by Donald Carrick. Houghton Mifflin, 1981. ISBN 0-395-30171-8 Subj: Animals – dogs. Animals – porcupines. Problem solving.

Big old bones: a dinosaur tale ill. by Donald Carrick. Houghton Mifflin, 1992. ISBN 0-395-61582-8 Subj: Dinosaurs.

The blue lobster: a life cycle by Carol and Donald Carrick; ill. by Donald Carrick. Dial, 1975. ISBN 0-8037-4483-8 Subj: Crustaceans. Science.

The brook by Carol and Donald Carrick; ill. by Donald Carrick. Macmillan, 1967. Subj: Rivers.

A clearing in the forest by Carol and Donald Carrick; ill. by Donald Carrick. Dial, 1970. Subj: Ecology. Forest, woods. Pets.

The climb ill. by Donald Carrick. Houghton Mifflin, 1980. ISBN 0-395-29431-2 Subj: Activities – babysitting. Sports.

The crocodiles still wait ill. by Donald Carrick. Houghton Mifflin, 1980. ISBN 0-395-29102-X Subj: Dinosaurs. Reptiles – alligators, crocodiles. Science.

Dark and full of secrets ill. by Donald Carrick. Houghton Mifflin, 1984. ISBN 0-89919-271-8 Subj: Emotions – fear. Sports – skin diving.

The foundling ill. by Donald Carrick. Seabury Pr., 1977. ISBN 0-816-43199-X Subj: Animals – dogs. Pets.

The highest balloon on the common by Carol and Donald Carrick; ill. by Donald Carrick. Greenwillow, 1977. ISBN 0-688-84100-7 Subj: Behavior – lost. Fairs. Toys – balloons.

In the moonlight, waiting ill. by Donald Carrick. Clarion, 1990. ISBN 0-89919-867-8 Subj: Animals. Birth. Farms.

Left behind ill. by Donald Carrick. Clarion, 1988. ISBN 0-89919-535-0 Subj: Behavior – lost. City. School.

Lost in the storm ill. by Donald Carrick. Greenwillow, 1981. ISBN 0-8164-3124-8 Subj: Animals – dogs. Islands. Pets. Weather – storms.

Melanie ill. by Alisher Dianov. Clarion, 1996. ISBN 0-395-66555-8 Subj: Birds – seagulls. Family life – grandfathers. Folk and fairy tales. Handicaps – blindness. Mythical creatures – trolls.

Norman fools the tooth fairy ill. by Lisa McCue. Scholastic, 1992. ISBN 0-590-42240-5 Subj: Behavior – trickery. Fairies. Monsters. Reptiles – alligators, crocodiles. Teeth.

Octopus ill. by Donald Carrick. Seabury Pr., 1978. ISBN 0-395-28777-4 Subj: Octopuses. Science.

The old barn ill. by Donald Carrick. Bobbs-Merrill, 1966. Subj: Barns. Seasons.

Old Mother Witch ill. by Donald Carrick. Seabury Pr., 1975. ISBN 0-816-43148-5 Subj: Behavior – misunderstanding. Character traits – meanness. Holidays – Halloween. Illness.

Patrick's dinosaurs ill. by Donald Carrick. Houghton Mifflin, 1983. ISBN 0-89919-189-4 Subj: Animals. Dinosaurs. Imagination. Science. Zoos.

Patrick's dinosaurs on the Internet ill. by David Milgrim. Clarion, 1999. ISBN 0-395-50949-1 Subj: Computers. Dinosaurs. Imagination. School. Space and space ships.

Paul's Christmas birthday ill. by Donald Carrick. Greenwillow, 1978. ISBN 0-688-84159-7 Subj: Birthdays. Holidays – Christmas.

A rabbit for Easter ill. by Donald Carrick. Greenwillow, 1979. ISBN 0-688-84195-3 Subj: Animals – rabbits. Behavior – carelessness. Holidays – Easter.

Sleep out ill. by Donald Carrick. Seabury Pr., 1973. ISBN 0-816-43094-2 Subj: Behavior – solitude. Camps, camping. Weather – rain.

Two coyotes ill. by Donald Carrick. Houghton Mifflin, 1982. ISBN 0-89919-078-2 Subj: Animals – coyotes. Science. Seasons – winter.

Two very little sisters ill. by Erika Weihs. Clarion, 1993. ISBN 0-395-60927-5 Subj: Character traits – being different. Circus. Little people.

Valentine ill. by Paddy Bouma. Clarion, 1995. ISBN 0-395-66554-X Subj: Animals – sheep. Family life – grandmothers. Family life – mothers. Holidays – Valentine's Day.

The washout ill. by Donald Carrick. Seabury Pr., 1978. ISBN 0-1864-3217-1 Subj: Activities – vacationing. Boats, ships. Weather – rain.

What happened to Patrick's dinosaurs? ill. by Donald Carrick. Houghton Mifflin, 1986. ISBN 0-89919-406-0 Subj: Dinosaurs. Imagination.

Carrick, Donald. *Beach bird* (Carrick, Carol)

The blue lobster: a life cycle (Carrick, Carol)

The brook (Carrick, Carol)

A clearing in the forest (Carrick, Carol)

The deer in the pasture ill. by author. Greenwillow, 1976. ISBN 0-688-84023-X Subj: Animals – bulls, cows. Animals – deer. Farms. Sports – hunting.

Harold and the giant knight ill. by author. Houghton Mifflin, 1982. ISBN 0-89919-060-X Subj: Farms. Humor. Knights.

Harold and the great stag ill. by author. Clarion, 1988. ISBN 0-89919-514-8 Subj: Animals – deer. Foreign lands – England. Forest, woods. Humor. Middle Ages. Sports – hunting.

The highest balloon on the common (Carrick, Carol)

Milk ill. by author. Greenwillow, 1985. ISBN 0-688-04823-4 Subj: Animals – bulls, cows. Farms. Food.

Morgan and the artist ill. by author. Clarion, 1985. ISBN 0-89919-300-5 Subj: Activities – painting. Art. Careers – artists.

Carrick, Malcolm. *The extraordinary hatmaker* ill. by author. Grosset, 1977. ISBN 0-448-13001-7 Subj: Clothing – hats.

I can squash elephants! a Masai tale about monsters ill. by author. Viking, 1978. ISBN 0-670-38983-8 Subj: Animals. Folk and fairy tales. Foreign lands – Africa. Insects – butterflies, caterpillars. Monsters.

Carrier, Lark. *A Christmas promise* ill. by author. Picture Book Studio, 1986. ISBN 0-88708-032-4 Subj: Animals. Friendship. Holidays – Christmas. Trees.

Scout and Cody ill. by author. Picture Book Studio, 1987. ISBN 0-88708-013-8 Subj: Activities – playing. Animals – dogs. Behavior – growing up. Imagination.

There was a hill . . . ill. by author. Picture Book Studio, 1985. ISBN 0-907234-70-4 Subj: Format, unusual. Imagination.

A tree's tale ill. by author. Dial, 1996. ISBN 0-8037-1203-0 Subj: Forest, woods. Trees. U.S. history.

Carrier, Roch. *The longest home run* ill. by Sheldon Cohen; trans. from French by Sheila Fischman. Tundra, 1993. ISBN 0-88776-312-X Subj: Foreign lands – Canada. Magic. Sports – baseball.

Carroll, Kathleen Sullivan. *One red rooster* ill. by Suzette Barbier. Houghton Mifflin, 1992. ISBN 0-395-60195-9 Subj: Animals. Concepts – color. Counting, numbers. Rhyming text.

Carroll, Latrobe. *Pet tale* (Carroll, Ruth)

Carroll, Lewis. *Jabberwocky* ill. by Graeme Base. Abrams, 1989. ISBN 0-8109-1150-7 Subj: Humor. Mythical creatures. Poetry.

Jabberwocky ill. from Disney archives. Walt Disney, 1992. ISBN 1-56282-246-2 Subj: Humor. Mythical creatures. Poetry.

Jabberwocky ill. by Jane Breskin Zalben. Warne, 1977. ISBN 0-723-26145-8 Subj: Humor. Mythical creatures. Poetry.

The nursery "Alice" intro. by Martin Gardner; ill. by Sir John Tenniel. McGraw-Hill, 1966. A facsimile of the 2d ed. (1890) of Carroll's adapt. of Alice's Adventures in Wonderland. Subj: Dreams. Imagination.

The walrus and the carpenter ill. by Julian Doyle. Merrimack, 1986. ISBN 0-88162-218-4 Subj: Humor. Poetry.

The walrus and the carpenter ill. by Jane Breskin Zalben. Holt, 1986. ISBN 0-8050-0071-2 Subj: Humor. Poetry.

Carroll, Ruth. *Old Mrs. Billups and the black cats* ill. by author. Walck, 1961. Subj: Animals – cats. Humor.

Pet tale by Ruth and Latrobe Carroll; ill. by Ruth Carroll. Oxford Univ. Pr., 1949. Subj: Pets.

What Whiskers did ill. by author. Walck, 1965. Subj: Animals – dogs. Animals – foxes. Animals – rabbits. Behavior – running away. Wordless.

Where's the bunny? ill. by author. Walck, 1950. Subj: Activities – playing. Animals – dogs. Animals – rabbits. Games. Participation. Wordless.

Carryl, Charles E. (Charles Edward). *A capital ship: or, The walloping window-blind* ill. by Paul Galdone. McGraw-Hill, 1963. Subj: Boats, ships. Music. Pirates. Songs.

The walloping window-blind adapt. and ill. by Jim LaMarche. Lothrop, 1994. ISBN 0-688-12518-2 Subj: Boats, ships. Pirates. Poetry.

The walloping window blind ill. by Ted Rand. Arcade, 1992. ISBN 1-55970-154-4 Subj: Boats, ships. Pirates. Poetry.

Cars and trucks ill. by Daisuke Yokoi. Simon & Schuster, 1984. ISBN 0-671-49879-7 Subj: Automobiles. Format, unusual – board books. Transportation. Trucks.

Cars and trucks and other vehicles created by Gallimard Jeunesse and Claude Delafosse; ill. by Sophie Kniffke. Scholastic, 1996. ISBN 0-590-62371-0 Subj: Automobiles. Format, unusual. Transportation. Trucks.

Carson, Jo. *The great shaking: an account of the earthquakes of 1811 and 1812* ill. by Robert Andrew Parker. Orchard, 1994. ISBN 0-531-08659-3 Subj: Animals – bears. Earth. Earthquakes. Weather – floods.

Pulling my leg ill. by Julie Downing. Orchard, 1990. ISBN 0-531-08417-5 Subj: Family life – aunts, uncles. Teeth.

You hold me and I'll hold you ill. by Annie Cannon. Orchard, 1992. ISBN 0-531-08495-7 Subj: Death. Emotions – grief. Family life.

Carter, Alden R. *Big brother Dustin* photos by Dan Young with Carol Carter. Albert Whitman, 1998. ISBN 0-8075-0715-6 Subj: Babies. Family life – brothers and sisters. Handicaps – Down syndrome. Names.

I'm tougher than asthma! by Alden R. Carter and Siri M. Carter; photos by Dan Young. Albert

Whitman, 1996. ISBN 0-8075-3474-9 Subj: Illness – asthma.

Seeing things my way photos by Carol S. Carter. Albert Whitman, 1998. ISBN 0-8075-7296-9 Subj: Handicaps. Illness.

Carter, Angela. *The sleeping beauty and other favourite fairy tales* ill. by Michael Foreman. Schocken, 1984. ISBN 0-8052-3921-9 Subj: Folk and fairy tales.

Carter, Anne. *Beauty and the beast* ill. by Binette Schroeder. Potter/Crown, 1986. A retelling of Belle et la bête by Madame Leprince de Beaumont. ISBN 0-517-56173-5 Subj: Character traits – appearance. Character traits – loyalty. Emotions – love. Folk and fairy tales. Magic.

Bella's secret garden ill. by John Butler. Crown, 1987. ISBN 0-517-56308-8 Subj: Animals – cats. Animals – rabbits. Behavior – greed. Character traits – kindness to animals.

The fisherwoman ill. by Louise Brierley. Lothrop, 1991. ISBN 0-688-09873-8 Subj: Behavior – seeking better things. Magic.

Molly in danger ill. by John Butler. Crown, 1987. ISBN 0-517-56534-X Subj: Animals – moles. Moving. Nature.

Ruff leaves home ill. by John Butler. Crown, 1986. ISBN 0-517-56068-2 Subj: Animals – foxes. Behavior – lost.

Scurry's treasure ill. by John Butler. Crown, 1987. ISBN 0-517-56535-8 Subj: Animals – squirrels. Nature.

Tall in the saddle ill. by David McPhail. Orca, 1999. ISBN 1-55143-154-8 Subj: Cowboys. Family life – fathers. Imagination.

The twelve dancing princesses (Grimm, Jacob)

Carter, David A. *How many bugs in a box?* ill. by author. Simon & Schuster, 1988. ISBN 0-671-64965-5 Subj: Format, unusual – toy and movable books. Insects.

I'm a little mouse (Carter, Noelle)

Carter, Debby L. *Clipper* ill. by author. Harper-Collins, 1981. ISBN 0-06-021128-8 Subj: Animals – dogs. Sea and seashore.

Carter, Donna Renee. *Music in the family* ill. by Cortrell J. Harris. Lindsey Pub., 1996. ISBN 1-885242-01-8 Subj: Family life. Foreign lands – Jamaica. Music.

Carter, Dorothy (Dorothy A.). *Wilhe'mina Miles after the stork night* ill. by Harvey Stevenson. Farrar, 1999. ISBN 0-374-33551-6 Subj: Behavior – growing up. Birth. Family life – mothers.

Carter, James. *see* Mayne, William

Carter, Katharine. *Houses* ill. with photos. Childrens Pr., 1982. ISBN 0-516-01672-5 Subj: Homes, houses.

Ships and seaports ill. with photos. Childrens Pr., 1982. ISBN 0-516-01656-3 Subj: Boats, ships.

Carter, Noelle. *I'm a little mouse* by Noelle and David A. Carter; ill. by David A. Carter. Holt, 1991. ISBN 0-8050-1420-9 Subj: Animals. Animals – mice. Behavior – lost. Format, unusual.

My house ill. by author. Viking, 1991. ISBN 0-670-83922-1 Subj: Animals. Format, unusual – toy and movable books. Homes, houses. Rhyming text.

My pet ill. by author. Viking, 1991. ISBN 0-670-83923-X Subj: Animals. Format, unusual – toy and movable books. Pets. Rhyming text.

Where's my squishy ball? ill. by author. Scholastic, 1993. ISBN 0-590-47385-9 Subj: Animals – cats. Animals – mice. Behavior – losing things. Format, unusual – toy and movable books.

Carter, Penny. *A new house for the Morrisons* ill. by author. Viking, 1993. ISBN 0-670-84567-1 Subj: Behavior – seeking better things. Family life. Homes, houses. Moving.

Carter, Peter. *My old grandad* (Harranth, Wolf)

The snowman who went for a walk (Lobe, Mira)

Valerie and the good-night swing (Lobe, Mira)

Carter, Phyllis Ann. *see* Eberle, Irmengarde

Carter, Siri M. *I'm tougher than asthma!* (Carter, Alden R.)

Cartlidge, Michelle. *Baby mice at home* ill. by author. Dutton, 1992. ISBN 0-525-44840-3 Subj: Animals – babies. Animals – mice. Format, unusual – board books.

Bear in the forest ill. by author. Dutton, 1991. ISBN 0-525-44674-5 Subj: Animals. Animals – bears. Forest, woods. Format, unusual – board books.

The bear's bazaar: a storycraft book ill. by author. Lothrop, 1980. ISBN 0-688-51922-9 Subj: Activities. Animals – bears.

Bears on the go ill. by author. Dutton, 1992. ISBN 0-525-44841-1 Subj: Animals – bears. Automobiles. Format, unusual – board books.

Bunny's birthday ill. by author. Dutton, 1992. ISBN 0-525-44843-8 Subj: Animals – rabbits. Birthdays. Format, unusual – board books. Parties.

Doggy days ill. by author. Dutton, 1992. ISBN 0-525-44844-6 Subj: Animals – dogs. Format, unusual – board books.

Duck in the pond ill. by author. Dutton, 1991. ISBN 0-525-44675-3 Subj: Animals. Birds – ducks. Format, unusual – board books. Lakes, ponds.

Elephant in the jungle ill. by author. Dutton, 1991. ISBN 0-525-44676-1 Subj: Animals. Animals – elephants. Format, unusual – board books. Jungle.

Fairy letters ill. by author. Campbell Books, 1993. ISBN 1-8529-2142-0 Subj: Animals – mice. Fairies.

Format, unusual – toy and movable books. Letters, cards.

Good night, Teddy ill. by author. Candlewick, 1992. ISBN 1-56402-076-2 Subj: Activities – bathing. Bedtime. Toys. Toys – bears.

A house for Lily Mouse ill. by author. Prentice-Hall, 1986. ISBN 0-13-395849-3 Subj: Animals – mice. Homes, houses. Moving.

Michelle Cartlidge's book of words ill. by author. Dutton, 1994. ISBN 0-525-45254-0 Subj: Animals – mice. Dictionaries. Language.

Mouse birthday ill. by author. Dutton, 1994. ISBN 0-525-45237-0 Subj: Animals – mice. Birthdays. Format, unusual – toy and movable books.

Mouse Christmas ill. by author. Dutton, 1996. ISBN 0-525-45684-8 Subj: Animals – mice. Format, unusual – toy and movable books. Holidays – Christmas.

Mouse in the house ill. by author. Dutton, 1991. ISBN 0-525-44678-8 Subj: Animals – mice. Format, unusual – board books. Homes, houses.

Mouse letters ill. by author. Dutton, 1993. ISBN 0-525-45089-0 Subj: Animals – mice. Format, unusual – toy and movable books. Letters, cards.

Mouse theater ill. by author. Dutton, 1992. ISBN 0-525-44980-9 Subj: Animals – mice. Format, unusual – toy and movable books. Theater.

Mouse time ill. by author. Dutton, 1991. ISBN 0-525-44766-0 Subj: Animals – mice. Format, unusual – toy and movable books. Time.

A mouse's diary ill. by author. Lothrop, 1982. ISBN 0-688-51987-3 Subj: Activities. Animals – mice.

Mouse's scrapbook ill. by author. Dutton, 1995. ISBN 0-525-45423-3 Subj: Animals – mice. Format, unusual – toy and movable books.

Pippin and Pod ill. by author. Pantheon, 1978. ISBN 0-394-93845-3 Subj: Activities – playing. Animals – mice. Behavior – lost. Behavior – misbehavior.

Teddy trucks ill. by author. Lothrop, 1982. ISBN 0-688-00905-0 Subj: Animals – bears. Careers – truck drivers. Trucks.

Teddy's cat ill. by author. Candlewick, 1996. ISBN 1-56402-944-1 Subj: Animals – cats. Toys – bears.

Teddy's Christmas ill. by author. Walker, 1986. ISBN 0-671-62912-3 Subj: Holidays – Christmas. Toys – bears.

Teddy's friends ill. by author. Candlewick, 1992. ISBN 1-56402-077-0 Subj: Activities – playing. Friendship. Toys – bears.

Carton, Lonnie Caming. *Mommies* ill. by Leslie Jacobs. Random House, 1960. Subj: Activities. Family life – mothers. Poetry.

Cartwright, Ann. *Norah's ark* ill. by Reg Cartwright. Simon & Schuster, 1984. ISBN 0-671-52540-9 Subj: Animals. Farms. Weather – floods. Weather – rain.

The winter hedgehog ill. by Reg Cartwright. Macmillan, 1990. ISBN 0-02-717775-0 Subj: Animals – hedgehogs. Helicopters. Seasons – winter. Weather – wind.

Cartwright, Reg. *The band over the hill* (Isherwood, Shirley)

Caseley, Judith. *Ada potato* ill. by author. Greenwillow, 1988. ISBN 0-688-07843-9 Subj: Character traits – cleverness. Music. School.

Annie's potty ill. by author. Greenwillow, 1990. ISBN 0-688-09066-4 Subj: Behavior – growing up. Toilet training.

Apple pie and onions ill. by author. Greenwillow, 1987. ISBN 0-688-06763-8 Subj: Ethnic groups in the U.S. Family life – grandmothers.

Cousins ill. by author. Greenwillow, 1990. ISBN 0-688-08434-6 Subj: Character traits – individuality. Family life – cousins.

Dear Annie ill. by author. Greenwillow, 1991. ISBN 0-688-10011-2 Subj: Activities – writing. Emotions – love. Family life – grandfathers. Letters, cards.

Grandpa's garden lunch ill. by author. Greenwillow, 1990. ISBN 0-688-08817-1 Subj: Family life – grandparents. Food. Gardens, gardening.

Harry and Willy and Carrothead ill. by author. Greenwillow, 1991. ISBN 0-688-09493-7 Subj: Character traits – confidence. Friendship. Handicaps – physical handicaps.

Mama, coming and going ill. by author. Greenwillow, 1994. ISBN 0-688-11442-3 Subj: Babies. Family life – mothers. Family life – new sibling.

Mickey's class play ill. by author. Greenwillow, 1998. ISBN 0-688-15406-9 Subj: Animals. Birds – ducks. School. Theater.

Mr. Green Peas ill. by author. Greenwillow, 1995. ISBN 0-688-12860-2 Subj: Pets. Reptiles – iguanas. School.

Molly Pink ill. by author. Greenwillow, 1985. ISBN 0-688-04005-5 Subj: Emotions – embarrassment. School. Songs.

Molly Pink goes hiking ill. by author. Greenwillow, 1985. ISBN 0-688-05700-4 Subj: Character traits – appearance. Sports.

My sister Celia ill. by author. Greenwillow, 1986. ISBN 0-688-06484-1 Subj: Family life – sisters. Weddings.

The noisemakers ill. by author. Greenwillow, 1992. ISBN 0-688-09395-7 Subj: Activities – playing. Behavior. Libraries. Noise, sounds.

Silly baby ill. by author. Greenwillow, 1988. ISBN 0-688-07356-5 Subj: Babies. Family life – new sibling. Sibling rivalry.

Slumber party! ill. by author. Greenwillow, 1996. ISBN 0-688-14016-5 Subj: Bedtime. Birthdays. Parties. Sleep. Sleepovers.

Sophie and Sammy's library sleepover ill. by author. Greenwillow, 1993. ISBN 0-688-10616-1 Subj: Activities – reading. Family life – brothers. Libraries. Sleep.

Three happy birthdays ill. by author. Greenwillow, 1989. ISBN 0-688-08180-0 Subj: Birthdays.

When Grandpa came to stay ill. by author. Greenwillow, 1986. ISBN 0-688-06129-X Subj: Death. Emotions – grief. Family life – grandfathers. Jewish culture.

Witch mama ill. by author. Greenwillow, 1996. ISBN 0-688-14458-6 Subj: Family life. Holidays – Halloween.

Casey, Denise. *The friendly prairie dog* photos by Tim W. Clark and others. Dodd, 1987. ISBN 0-396-08901-1 Subj: Animals – prairie dogs.

Casey, Patricia. *Beep! Beep! Oink! Oink! animals in the city* ill. by author. Candlewick, 1997. ISBN 0-7636-0306-6 Subj: Animals. City. Noise, sounds.

Cluck cluck ill. by author. Lothrop, 1988. ISBN 0-688-07768-4 Subj: Animals. Birds – chickens. Farms. Noise, sounds.

My cat Jack ill. by author. Candlewick, 1994. ISBN 1-56402-410-5 Subj: Animals – cats. Pets.

Quack quack ill. by author. Lothrop, 1988. ISBN 0-688-07765-X Subj: Birds – chickens. Birds – ducks. Eggs.

Casler, Leigh. *The boy who dreamed of an acorn* ill. by Shonto Begay. Philomel, 1994. ISBN 0-399-22547-1 Subj: Dreams. Indians of North America – Chinook. Self-concept. Trees.

Cass, Joan E. *The cat thief* ill. by William Stobbs. Abelard-Schuman, 1961. Subj: Animals – cats. Behavior – stealing. Crime. Night.

The cats go to market ill. by William Stobbs. Abelard-Schuman, 1969. ISBN 0-2007-1581-X Subj: Animals – cats. Shopping.

Cassedy, Sylvia. *The best cat suit of all* ill. by Rosekrans Hoffman. Dial, 1991. ISBN 0-8037-0517-4 Subj: Animals – cats. Friendship. Holidays – Halloween. Illness. Moving.

Moon-uncle, moon-uncle: rhymes from India sel. and trans. by Sylvia Cassedy and Parvathi Thampi; ill. by Susanne Suba. Doubleday, 1973. Subj: Foreign lands – India. Nursery rhymes.

Red dragonfly on my shoulder trans. by Sylvia Cassedy and Kunihiro Suetake; ill. by Molly Bang. HarperCollins, 1992. ISBN 0-06-022625-0 Subj: Animals. Foreign lands – Japan. Poetry.

Cassidy, Dianne. *Circus animals* ill. by author. Little, 1985. ISBN 0-316-13241-1 Subj: Animals. Circus. Format, unusual – board books. Format, unusual – toy and movable books. Rhyming text.

Circus people ill. by author. Little, 1985. ISBN 0-316-13243-8 Subj: Circus. Format, unusual – board books. Format, unusual – toy and movable books. Rhyming text.

Cassidy, Sheila. *The creation: the story of how God created the world* ill. by Emma Hunk. Crossroad, 1996. ISBN 0-8245-1506-4 Subj: Creation.

Castaneda, Omar S. *Abuela's weave* ill. by Enrique O. Sánchez. Lee & Low, 1993. ISBN 1-880000-00-8 Subj: Activities – weaving. Fairs. Family life – grandmothers. Foreign lands – Guatemala.

Castiglia, Julie. *Jill the pill* ill. by Steven Kellogg. Atheneum, 1979. ISBN 0-689-50105-6 Subj: Family life. Sibling rivalry.

Castilla, Julia Mercedes. *Family / familia* (Bertrand, Diane Gonzales)

Castillo, Violetta. *Animal babies* (Zoll, Max Alfred)

Castle, Caroline. *Grandpa Baxter and the photographs* ill. by Peter Bowman. Orchard, 1993. ISBN 0-531-08637-2 Subj: Activities – photographing. Family life. Family life – grandfathers. Toys – bears.

The hare and the tortoise (Æsop)

Herbert Binns and the flying tricycle ill. by Peter Weevers. Dial, 1987. ISBN 0-8037-0041-5 Subj: Animals. Animals – mice. Character traits – cleverness. Emotions – envy, jealousy.

Castle, Sue. *Face talk, hand talk, body talk* ill. by Frances McLaughlin-Gill. Doubleday, 1977. ISBN 0-385-11019-7 Subj: Anatomy. Emotions.

Caswell, Helen Rayburn. *God must like to laugh* ill. by author. Abingdon, 1987. ISBN 0-687-01869-2 Subj: Creation. Religion. Rhyming text.

Parable of the good Samaritan ill. by author. Abingdon, 1992. ISBN 0-687-30023-1 Subj: Character traits – kindness. Religion.

Catalano, Dominic. *The frog went a-courting: a musical play in six acts* (A frog he would a-wooing go [folk-song])

Catalanotto, Peter. *Christmas always . . .* ill. by author. Orchard, 1991. ISBN 0-531-08546-5 Subj: Bedtime. Holidays – Christmas. Santa Claus. Teeth.

Dad and me ill. by author. DK, 1999. ISBN 0-7894-2584-X Subj: Careers – astronauts. Family life – fathers. Imagination. Space and space ships.

Dylan's day out ill. by author. Orchard, 1989. ISBN 0-531-08429-9 Subj: Animals – dogs. Sports – soccer.

Mr. Mumble ill. by author. Orchard, 1990. ISBN 0-531-08480-9 Subj: Animals. Behavior – misunderstanding.

The painter ill. by author. Orchard, 1996. ISBN 0-531-08765-4 Subj: Activities – painting. Art. Family life – fathers.

Catchpole, Clive. *Deserts* ill. by Brian McIntyre. Dial, 1984. ISBN 0-8037-0035-0 Subj: Animals. Desert.

Grasslands ill. by Peter Snowball. Dial, 1984. ISBN 0-8037-0082-2 Subj: Animals.

Jungles ill. by Denise Finney. Dial, 1984. ISBN 0-8037-0034-2 Subj: Animals. Jungle.

Mountains ill. by Brian McIntyre. Dial, 1984. ISBN 0-8037-0086-5 Subj: Animals.

Cate, Rikki. *A cat's tale* ill. by Shirley Hughes. Harcourt, 1982. ISBN 0-15-215538-4 Subj: Animals – cats. Behavior – stealing. Foreign lands – Scotland. Rhyming text.

The caterpillar who turned into a butterfly. Simon & Schuster, 1980. ISBN 0-671-41347-3 Subj: Format, unusual – board books. Insects – butterflies, caterpillars. Metamorphosis.

Cathon, Laura E. *Tot Botot and his little flute* ill. by Arnold Lobel. Macmillan, 1970. Subj: Animals. Caldecott award honor books. Foreign lands – India. Music.

Caudill, Rebecca. *Contrary Jenkins* by Rebecca Caudill and James Sterling Ayars; ill. by Glen Rounds. Holt, 1969. ISBN 0-03-076295-2 Subj: Behavior. Country. Humor.

A pocketful of cricket ill. by Evaline Ness. Holt, 1964. Subj: Behavior – sharing. Caldecott award honor books. Farms. Insects – crickets. School.

Wind, sand and sky ill. by Donald Carrick. Dutton, 1976. ISBN 0-525-42899-2 Subj: Desert. Poetry.

Cauley, Lorinda Bryan. *The animal kids* ill. by author. Putnam, 1979. ISBN 0-399-20677-9 Subj: Animals. Behavior – imitation.

The bake-off ill. by author. Putnam, 1978. ISBN 0-399-61086-3 Subj: Activities – cooking. Animals.

Clap your hands ill. by author. Putnam, 1992. ISBN 0-399-22118-2 Subj: Activities. Activities – playing. Games. Nursery rhymes.

The cock, the mouse and the little red hen (The little red hen)

Goldilocks and the three bears (The three bears)

The goose and the golden coins ill. by adapt. Harcourt, 1981. ISBN 0-15-232206-X Subj: Birds – geese. Folk and fairy tales. Foreign lands – Italy. Humor.

Jack and the beanstalk (Jack and the beanstalk)

The pancake boy (The gingerbread boy)

Pease porridge hot: a Mother Goose cookbook ill. by author. Putnam, 1977. ISBN 0-399-20591-8 Subj: Activities – cooking. Food. Nursery rhymes.

Puss in boots (Perrault, Charles)

Treasure hunt ill. by author. Putnam, 1994. ISBN 0-399-22447-5 Subj: Activities – picnicking. Animals – bears. Rhyming text.

The trouble with Tyrannosaurus Rex ill. by author. Harcourt, 1988. ISBN 0-15-290880-3 Subj: Behavior – bullying. Character traits – cleverness. Dinosaurs.

Causley, Charles. *Dick Whittington: a story from England* (Dick Whittington and his cat)

Early in the morning ill. by Michael Foreman. Viking, 1987. ISBN 0-670-80810-5 Subj: Music. Nursery rhymes.

"Quack!" said the billy-goat ill. by Barbara Firth. Lippincott, 1986. ISBN 0-397-32192-9 Subj: Animals. Humor. Noise, sounds. Rhyming text.

Cavagnaro, David. *The pumpkin people* by David Cavagnaro and Maggie Cavagnaro; ill. with photos. Scribners, 1979. ISBN 0-684-16109-5 Subj: Gardens, gardening. Holidays – Halloween. Seasons – fall. Seasons – summer.

Cavagnaro, Maggie. *The pumpkin people* (Cavagnaro, David)

Cave, Joyce. *Airplanes* (Cave, Ron)

Automobiles (Cave, Ron)

Motorcycles (Cave, Ron)

Cave, Kathryn. *Out for the count* ill. by Chris Riddell. Simon & Schuster, 1992. ISBN 0-671-75591-9 Subj: Animals. Bedtime. Counting, numbers. Cumulative tales. Rhyming text.

Cave, Ron. *Airplanes* by Ron and Joyce Cave; ill. by David West and others. Watts, 1982. ISBN 0-531-04418-1 Subj: Airplanes, airports. Transportation.

Automobiles by Ron and Joyce Cave; ill. by David West and others. Watts, 1982. ISBN 0-531-04419-X Subj: Automobiles. Transportation.

Motorcycles by Ron and Joyce Cave; ill. by David West and others. Watts, 1982. ISBN 0-531-04420-3 Subj: Motorcycles. Transportation.

Cazet, Denys. *Are there any questions?* ill. by author. Orchard, 1992. ISBN 0-531-08601-1 Subj: Animals. Animals – cats. School.

Big shoe, little shoe ill. by author. Bradbury, 1984. ISBN 0-02-717820-X Subj: Activities – babysitting. Animals – rabbits. Family life – grandparents.

Born in the gravy ill. by author. Orchard, 1993. ISBN 0-531-08638-0 Subj: Ethnic groups in the U.S. – Mexican Americans. Family life. School – first day.

Christmas moon ill. by author. Bradbury, 1984. ISBN 0-02-717810-2 Subj: Animals – rabbits. Family life – grandfathers. Holidays – Christmas. Moon.

Dancing ill. by Craig Bond. Orchard, 1995. ISBN 0-531-08766-2 Subj: Activities – dancing. Activities – singing. Babies. Family life – fathers. Noise, sounds. Songs.

Daydreams ill. by author. Orchard, 1990. ISBN 0-531-08481-7 Subj: Dreams. Imagination. School.

December 24th ill. by author. Bradbury, 1986. ISBN 0-02-717950-8 Subj: Animals – rabbits. Birthdays. Family life – grandfathers. Holidays.

The duck with squeaky feet ill. by author. Bradbury, 1980. ISBN 0-87888-171-9 Subj: Animals. Birds – ducks. Reptiles – alligators, crocodiles. Theater.

A fish in his pocket ill. by author. Watts, 1987. ISBN 0-531-08313-6 Subj: Birthdays. Character traits – kindness. Death. School.

Frosted glass ill. by author. Bradbury, 1987. ISBN 0-02-717960-5 Subj: Animals. Animals – dogs. Art. School.

Good morning, Maxine! ill. by author. Bradbury, 1989. ISBN 0-02-717940-0 Subj: Animals – cats.

Great-Uncle Felix ill. by author. Watts, 1988. ISBN 0-531-08350-0 Subj: Animals – rhinoceros. Emotions – embarrassment. Family life – aunts, uncles.

I'm not sleepy ill. by author. Orchard, 1992. ISBN 0-531-08498-1 Subj: Bedtime. Family life – fathers. Sleep.

Lucky me ill. by author. Bradbury, 1983. ISBN 0-87888-192-1 Subj: Animals. Birds – chickens. Character traits – luck. Food.

Mother night ill. by author. Orchard, 1989. ISBN 0-531-08430-2 Subj: Animals. Bedtime. Night. Sleep.

Mud baths for everyone ill. by author. Bradbury, 1981. ISBN 0-8788-8178-6 Subj: Animals – pigs. Behavior – bullying. Emotions – fear.

Never spit on your shoes ill. by author. Orchard, 1990. ISBN 0-531-08447-7 Subj: Animals. Animals – cats. School – first day.

Night lights: 24 poems to sleep on ill. by author. Orchard, 1997. ISBN 0-531-33010-9 Subj: Bedtime. Poetry.

Nothing at all ill. by author. Orchard, 1994. ISBN 0-531-08672-0 Subj: Animals. Cumulative tales. Farms. Noise, sounds. Rhyming text. Scarecrows.

Saturday ill. by author. Bradbury, 1985. ISBN 0-02-717800-5 Subj: Animals – dogs. Family life – grandparents.

Sunday ill. by author. Bradbury, 1988. ISBN 0-02-717970-2 Subj: Animals. Family life.

You make the angels cry ill. by author. Bradbury, 1982. ISBN 0-02-717830-7 Subj: Animals – rabbits. Weather – rain.

Cazzola, Gus. *The bells of Santa Lucia* ill. by Pierr Morgan. Putnam, 1991. ISBN 0-399-21804-1 Subj: Animals – sheep. Death. Family life – grandmothers. Foreign lands – Italy.

Cech, John. *Django* ill. by Sharon McGinley-Nally. Macmillan, 1994. ISBN 0-02-765705-1 Subj: Ani-mals. Folk and fairy tales. Music. Weather – floods.

First snow, magic snow ill. by Sharon McGinley-Nally. Four Winds, 1992. ISBN 0-02-717971-0 Subj: Folk and fairy tales. Foreign lands – Russia. Seasons – winter. Weather – snow.

My grandmother's journey ill. by Sharon McGinley-Nally. Macmillan, 1991. ISBN 0-02-718135-9 Subj: Activities – traveling. Family life – grandmothers. Friendship.

The southernmost cat ill. by Kathy Osborn. Simon & Schuster, 1996. ISBN 0-689-80510-1 Subj: Activities – writing. Animals – cats. Animals – whales. Sports – fishing.

Cecil, Ivon. *Kirby Kelvin and the not laughing lessons* ill. by Judy Love. Whispering Coyote, 1998. ISBN 1-8790-8595-X Subj: Behavior. School.

Cecil, Laura. *The frog princess* ill. by Emma Chichester Clark. Greenwillow, 1995. ISBN 0-688-13506-4 Subj: Folk and fairy tales. Foreign lands – Italy. Frogs and toads. Magic. Middle Ages. Royalty – princes. Royalty – princesses.

Noah and the space ark ill. by Emma Chichester Clark. Carolrhoda, 1998. ISBN 1-57505-255-5 Subj: Animals. Ecology. Planets. Space and space ships.

Cecil, Mirabel. *Lottie's cats* ill. by Francesca Martin. Crown, 1990. ISBN 0-517-57707-0 Subj: Animals – cats. Holidays – Halloween.

Cendrars, Blaise. *Shadow* tr. and ill. by Marcia Brown. Scribners, 1982. ISBN 0-684-17226-7 Subj: Caldecott award books. Folk and fairy tales. Foreign lands – Africa. Poetry. Shadows.

Cerf, Bennett Alfred. *Bennett Cerf's book of animal riddles* ill. by Roy McKié. Random House, 1964. ISBN 0-394-80034-6 Subj: Humor. Riddles.

Bennett Cerf's book of laughs ill. by Carl Rose. Random House, 1959. ISBN 0-394-90011-1 Subj: Humor. Riddles.

Bennett Cerf's book of riddles ill. by Roy McKié. Random House, 1960. ISBN 0-394-90015-4 Subj: Humor. Riddles.

More riddles ill. by Roy McKié. Random House, 1961. Subj: Humor. Riddles.

Chacon, Michelle Netten. *How the Indians bought the farm* (Strete, Craig Kee)

Chadwick, Tim. *Cabbage moon* ill. by Piers Harper. Orchard, 1994. ISBN 0-531-06827-7 Subj: Animals – rabbits. Food. Moon.

Chafetz, Henry. *The legend of Befana* ill. by Ronni Solbert. Houghton Mifflin, 1958. Subj: Folk and fairy tales. Foreign lands – Italy. Holidays – Christmas.

Chaffin, Lillie D. *Tommy's big problem* ill. by Haris Petie. Lantern Pr., 1965. ISBN 0-8313-0016-7 Subj:

Babies. Behavior – growing up. Family life. Problem solving.

We be warm till springtime comes ill. by Lloyd Bloom. Macmillan, 1980. ISBN 0-02-717910-9 Subj: Character traits – bravery. Seasons – winter.

Chaikin, Miriam. *Esther* ill. by Vera Rosenberry. Jewish Publication Society, 1987. ISBN 0-8276-0272-3 Subj: Foreign lands – Persia. Holidays. Jewish culture.

Exodus ill. by Charles Mikolaycak. Holiday, 1987. ISBN 0-8234-0607-5 Subj: Jewish culture. Religion.

Hanukkah ill. by Ellen Weiss. Holiday, 1990. ISBN 0-8234-0816-7 Subj: Holidays – Hanukkah. Jewish culture.

On the little hearth (On the little hearth)

Chalk, Gary. *Mr. Frog went a-courting: discover the secret story* (A frog he would a-wooing go [folksong])

Yankee Doodle ill. by author. DK, 1993. ISBN 1-56458-202-7 Subj: Music. Songs. U.S. history.

Chall, Marsha Wilson. *Mattie* ill. by Barbara Lehman. Lothrop, 1992. ISBN 0-688-09730-8 Subj: Family life – brothers and sisters.

Rupa raises the sun ill. by Rosanne Litzinger. DK, 1998. ISBN 0-7894-2496-7 Subj: Humor. Morning. Sun. Superstition.

Up north at the cabin ill. by Steve Johnson. Lothrop, 1992. ISBN 0-688-09733-2 Subj: Activities – vacationing. Forest, woods. Nature.

Challoner, Jack. *The science book of numbers* ill. with photos. Harcourt, 1992. ISBN 0-15-200623-0 Subj: Counting, numbers. Science.

Chalmers, Audrey. *Fancy be good* ill. by author. Viking, 1941. Subj: Animals – cats. Behavior – misbehavior. Sibling rivalry.

Hector and Mr. Murfit ill. by author. Viking, 1953. Subj: Animals – dogs. Concepts – size.

Hundreds and hundreds of pancakes ill. by author. Viking, 1942. Subj: Animals. Food. Humor. Zoos.

Chalmers, Mary. *Be good, Harry* ill. by author. HarperCollins, 1967. ISBN 0-06-443027-8 Subj: Activities – babysitting. Animals – cats.

Boots finds a house ill. by author. HarperCollins, 1958. Subj: Animals – cats. Boats, ships.

The cat who liked to pretend ill. by author. HarperCollins, 1959. Subj: Animals – cats. Imagination.

A Christmas story ill. by author. Rev. ed. HarperCollins, 1987, 1956. ISBN 0-06-021191-1 Subj: Animals. Holidays – Christmas. Religion – Nativity. Trees.

Come for a walk with me ill. by author. HarperCollins, 1955. Subj: Animals – rabbits.

Come to the doctor, Harry ill. by author. HarperCollins, 1981. ISBN 0-06-021179-2 Subj: Animals – cats. Illness.

Easter parade ill. by author. HarperCollins, 1988. ISBN 0-06-021233-0 Subj: Animals. Holidays – Easter. Parades.

George Appleton ill. by author. HarperCollins, 1957. Subj: Animals – cats. Dragons.

A hat for Amy Jean ill. by author. HarperCollins, 1956. Subj: Birthdays. Character traits – generosity. Clothing – hats.

Here comes the trolley ill. by author. HarperCollins, 1955. Subj: Activities – picnicking. Activities – traveling. Cable cars, trolleys.

Kevin ill. by author. HarperCollins, 1957. Subj: Animals – rabbits. City.

Merry Christmas, Harry ill. by author. HarperCollins, 1977. ISBN 0-06-021183-0 Subj: Animals – cats. Holidays – Christmas. Santa Claus.

Mr. Cat's wonderful surprise ill. by author. HarperCollins, 1961. Subj: Activities – picnicking. Animals – cats. Family life.

Six dogs, twenty-three cats, forty-five mice, and one hundred sixteen spiders ill. by author. HarperCollins, 1986. ISBN 0-06-021189-X Subj: Humor. Parties. Pets.

Take a nap, Harry ill. by author. HarperCollins, 1964. ISBN 0-06-021244-6 Subj: Animals – cats. Family life. Sleep.

Throw a kiss, Harry ill. by author. HarperCollins, 1990. ISBN 0-06-021245-4 Subj: Animals – cats. Careers – firefighters.

Chamberlain, Margaret. *You can swim, Jim* (Umansky, Kay)

Chambers, Catherine. *Christmas* ill. by author. Raintree, 1997. ISBN 0-8172-4608-8 Subj: Holidays – Christmas.

Chambless, Jane. *Tucker and the bear* ill. by author. Simon & Schuster, 1989. ISBN 0-671-67357-2 Subj: Animals – bears. Friendship.

Chan, Chin-Yi. *Good luck horse* ill. by Plao Chan. Whittlesey House, 1943. Subj: Animals – horses, ponies. Caldecott award honor books.

Chandler, Edna Walker. *Cattle drive* ill. by Jack Merryweather. Benefic Pr., 1966. Subj: Cowboys. U.S. history – frontier and pioneer life.

Cowboy Andy ill. by Raymond Kinstler. Random House, 1959. Subj: Cowboys.

Pony rider ill. by Jack Merryweather. Benefic Pr., 1966. Subj: Animals – horses, ponies. Cowboys. U.S. history – frontier and pioneer life.

Secret tunnel ill. by Jack Merryweather. Benefic Pr., 1967. Subj: Cowboys. U.S. history – frontier and pioneer life.

Chandler, Robert. *Russian folk tales* (Afanas'ev, Aleksandr N.)

Chandoha, Walter. *A baby bunny for you* ill. by author. Collins, 1968. Subj: Animals – rabbits.

A baby goat for you ill. by author. Collins, 1968. Subj: Animals – goats.

A baby goose for you ill. by author. Collins, 1968. Subj: Birds – geese.

Chandra, Deborah. *A is for Amos* ill. by Keiko Narahashi. Farrar, 1999. ISBN 0-374-30001-1 Subj: ABC books. Animals – horses, ponies. Farms. Rhyming text. Toys – rocking horses.

Miss Mabel's table ill. by Max Grover. Harcourt, 1994. ISBN 0-15-276712-6 Subj: Activities – cooking. Counting, numbers. Cumulative tales. Rhyming text.

Chang, Margaret Scrogin. *The beggar's magic* ill. by David Johnson. Margaret K. McElderry, 1997. ISBN 0-689-81340-6 Subj: Character traits – selfishness. Folk and fairy tales. Foreign lands – China. Magic.

The cricket warrior by Margaret and Raymond Chang; ill. by Warwick Hutton. Margaret K. McElderry, 1994. ISBN 0-689-50605-8 Subj: Folk and fairy tales. Foreign lands – China. Insects – crickets. Royalty – emperors.

Chang, Raymond. *The cricket warrior* (Chang, Margaret Scrogin)

Chanin, Michael. *Chief's blanket* ill. by Kim Howard. H. J. Kramer, 1997. ISBN 0-915811-78-2 Subj: Activities – weaving. Family life – grandmothers. Illness. Indians of North America – Navajo.

Chanover, Alice. *Happy Hanukah everybody* (Chanover, Hyman)

Chanover, Hyman. *Happy Hanukah everybody* by Hyman and Alice Chanover; ill. by Maurice Sendak. United Synagogue Books, 1954. ISBN 0-8381-0712-5 Subj: Holidays – Hanukkah. Jewish culture. Music. Religion.

Chapin, Cynthia. *Squad car 55* ill. by Dale Fleming. Albert Whitman, 1966. Educational consultant: Jene Barr. Subj: Careers – police officers.

Chaplin, Susan Gibbons. *I can sign my ABCs* ill. by Laura McCaul. Gallaudet Univ. Pr., 1986. ISBN 0-930323-19-X Subj: ABC books. Handicaps – deafness. Language. Senses – hearing.

Chapman, Carol. *Barney Bipple's magic dandelions* ill. by Steven Kellogg. Dutton, 1988, 1977. ISBN 0-525-44449-1 Subj: Behavior – wishing. Flowers. Magic. Plants.

Herbie's troubles ill. by Kelly Oechsli. Dutton, 1981. ISBN 0-525-31645-0 Subj: Behavior – bullying. Behavior – misbehavior. Problem solving.

The tale of Meshka the Kvetch ill. by Arnold Lobel. Dutton, 1980. ISBN 0-525-40745-6 Subj: Behavior

– dissatisfaction. Folk and fairy tales. Jewish culture.

Chapman, Cheryl. *Pass the fritters, critters* ill. by Susan L. Roth. Bradbury, 1993. ISBN 0-02-717975-3 Subj: Animals. Etiquette. Rhyming text.

Snow on snow on snow ill. by Synthia Saint James. Dial, 1994. ISBN 0-8037-1457-2 Subj: Animals – dogs. Ethnic groups in the U.S. – African Americans. Family life. Language. Seasons – winter. Weather – snow.

Chapman, Elizabeth. *Suzy* ill. by Margery Gill. Salem House, 1987. ISBN 0-370-30375-X Subj: Character traits – being different. Handicaps – blindness. Senses – seeing.

Chapman, Gaynor. *Æsop* (Æsop)

The luck child ill. by author. Atheneum, 1968. Based on a story of the Brothers Grimm. Subj: Folk and fairy tales. Royalty.

Chapman, Jean. *Moon-Eyes* ill. by Astra Lacis. McGraw-Hill, 1980. ISBN 0-07-010648-7 Subj: Animals – cats. Folk and fairy tales. Foreign lands – Italy. Holidays – Christmas. Religion.

Chapman, Noralee. *The story of Barbara* ill. by Helen S. Hull. John Knox, 1963. Subj: Adoption.

Chapouton, Anne-Marie. *Ben finds a friend* trans. by Andrea Mernan; ill. by Ulises Wensell. Putnam, 1986. ISBN 0-399-21268-X Subj: City. Friendship. Pets.

Billy the brave trans. from French by Anthea Bell; ill. by Jean Claverie. Holt, 1986. ISBN 0-03-008019-3 Subj: Character traits – bravery. Monsters. Night.

Sebastian is always late ill. by Chantal van der Berghe. Holt, 1987. ISBN 0-8050-0487-4 Subj: Imagination. School.

Charbonnet, Gabrielle. *Boodil, my dog* (Lindenbaum, Pija)

Chardiet, Bernice. *C is for circus* ill. by Brinton Turkle. Walker, 1971. ISBN 0-8027-6083-X Subj: ABC books. Circus. Rhyming text.

Martin and the tooth fairy by Bernice Chardiet and Grace Maccarone; ill. by G. Brian Karas. Scholastic, 1991. ISBN 0-590-44396-8 Subj: Fairies. Money. School. Teeth.

Charles, Donald. *Calico Cat at school* ill. by author. Childrens Pr., 1981. ISBN 0-516-03445-6 Subj: Animals – cats. Rhyming text. School.

Calico Cat at the zoo ill. by author. Childrens Pr., 1981. ISBN 0-516-03443-X Subj: Animals. Animals – cats. Rhyming text. Zoos.

Calico Cat meets bookworm ill. by author. Childrens Pr., 1978. ISBN 0-516-03441-3 Subj: Animals – cats. Libraries. Rhyming text.

Calico Cat's exercise book ill. by author. Childrens Pr., 1982. ISBN 0-516-03457-X Subj: Animals – cats. Animals – mice. Health and fitness – exercise. Rhyming text.

Calico Cat's year ill. by author. Childrens Pr., 1984. ISBN 0-516-03461-8 Subj: Animals – cats. Days of the week, months of the year. Rhyming text. Seasons.

Chancay and the secret of fire ill. by author. Putnam, 1990. ISBN 0-399-22129-8 Subj: Fire. Folk and fairy tales. Foreign lands – Peru.

Shaggy dog's animal alphabet ill. by author. Childrens Pr., 1979. ISBN 0-516-03674-2 Subj: ABC books. Animals. Poetry.

Shaggy dog's birthday ill. by author. Childrens Pr., 1986. ISBN 0-516-03576-2 Subj: Animals – dogs. Birthdays. Etiquette.

Shaggy dog's Halloween ill. by author. Childrens Pr., 1984. ISBN 0-516-03575-4 Subj: Animals – dogs. Character traits – appearance. Holidays – Halloween.

Shaggy dog's tall tale ill. by author. Childrens Pr., 1980. ISBN 0-516-03616-5 Subj: Animals – dogs.

Time to rhyme with Calico Cat ill. by author. Childrens Pr., 1978. ISBN 0-516-03629-7 Subj: Animals – cats. Animals – dogs. Rhyming text.

Ugly bug ill. by author. Dial, 1994. ISBN 0-8037-1205-7 Subj: Character traits – appearance. Insects. Self-concept.

Charles, Faustin. *A Caribbean counting book* ill. by Roberta Arenson. Houghton Mifflin, 1996. ISBN 0-395-77944-8 Subj: Counting, numbers. Foreign lands – Caribbean Islands. Rhyming text.

Charles, N. N. *What am I? Looking through shapes at apples and grapes* ill. by Diane and Leo Dillon. Scholastic, 1994. ISBN 0-590-47891-5 Subj: Concepts – color. Concepts – shape. Format, unusual – toy and movable books. Riddles.

Charles, Nicholas. *see* Kuskin, Karla

Charles, R. H. (Robert Henry). *The roundabout turn* ill. by L. Leslie Brooke. Warne, 1930. Subj: Frogs and toads. Merry-go-rounds. Poetry.

Charles, Veronika Martenova. *The crane girl* ill. by author. Orchard, 1993. ISBN 0-531-05485-3 Subj: Behavior – running away. Birds – cranes. Family life. Folk and fairy tales. Foreign lands – Japan.

Charlip, Remy. *Arm in arm* ill. by author. Parents, 1969. Subj: Games. Humor.

Fortunately ill. by author. Parents, 1964. Subj: Humor. Participation.

Handtalk: an ABC of finger spelling and sign language by Remy Charlip, Mary Beth and George Ancona; ill. by George Ancona. Parents, 1974. ISBN 0-8193-0706-8 Subj: ABC books. Communication. Handicaps – deafness. Language. Senses – hearing.

Handtalk birthday: a number and story book in sign language photos by George Ancona. Four Winds, 1987. ISBN 0-02-718080-8 Subj: Birthdays. Handicaps – deafness. Language. Senses – hearing.

Harlequin and the gift of many colors by Remy Charlip and Burton Supree; ill. by Remy Charlip. Parents, 1973. ISBN 0-819-30495-6 Subj: Concepts – color. Folk and fairy tales. Foreign lands – France. Gifts.

Hooray for me! by Remy Charlip and Lilian Moore; ill. by Vera B. Williams. Rev. ed. Harcourt, 1995. ISBN 1-883672-43-0 Subj: Character traits – individuality. Family life. Self-concept.

"Mother, mother I feel sick" by Remy Charlip and Burton Supree; ill. by Remy Charlip. Four Winds, [1980] c1966. ISBN 0-590-07772-4 Subj: Careers – doctors. Humor. Illness.

Sleepytime rhyme ill. by author. Greenwillow, 1999. ISBN 0-688-16272-X Subj: Babies. Family life – mothers. Nursery rhymes. Rhyming text.

Thirteen by Remy Charlip and Jerry Joyner; ill. by Remy Charlip. Parents, 1975. ISBN 0-819-30808-0 Subj: Counting, numbers. Humor.

The tree angel (Martin, Judith)

Where is everybody? ill. by author. Addison-Wesley, 1957. Subj: Games. Weather – rain.

Charlot, Martin. *Felisa and the magic tikling bird* ill. by Martin Charlot from a story by Jodi Parry Belknap. Island Heritage, 1973. ISBN 0-8348-3015-9 Subj: Activities – dancing. Folk and fairy tales. Foreign lands – Philippines. Handicaps. Self-concept.

Sunnyside up ill. by author. Weatherhill, 1972. ISBN 0-8348-3000-0 Subj: Wordless.

Charlton, Elizabeth. *Jeremy and the ghost* ill. by Celia Reisman. Dandelion, 1979. ISBN 0-89799-118-4 Subj: Character traits – bravery. Ghosts. Holidays – Halloween.

Terrible tyrannosaurus ill. by Andrew Glass. Elsevier-Nelson, 1981. ISBN 0-525-66724-5 Subj: Behavior – bullying. Behavior – imitation. Dinosaurs.

Charlton, Nancy Lee. *Derek's dog days* ill. by Chris L. Demarest. Harcourt, 1996. ISBN 0-15-223219-2 Subj: Animals – dogs. Imagination. School – first day.

Charmatz, Bill. *The Troy St. bus* ill. by author. Macmillan, 1977. ISBN 0-02-718160-X Subj: Animals – horses, ponies. School.

Charosh, Mannis. *The ellipse* ill. by Leonard P. Kessler. Crowell, 1972. ISBN 0-690-25856-9 Subj: Concepts – shape. Science.

Number ideas through pictures ill. by Giulio Maestro. Crowell, 1975. ISBN 0-690-00156-8 Subj: Concepts. Counting, numbers.

Charters, Janet. *The general* by Janet Charters and Michael Foreman; ill. by Michael Foreman. Dutton, 1961. Subj: Violence, nonviolence.

Chase, Alice. *see* McHargue, Georgess

Chase, Catherine. *An alphabet book* ill. by June Goldsborough. Dandelion, 1979. ISBN 0-89799-087-0 Subj: ABC books.

Baby mouse goes shopping ill. by Jill Elgin. Elsevier-Nelson, 1981. ISBN 0-525-66742-3 Subj: Animals – mice. Shopping.

Baby mouse learns his ABC's ill. by Jill Elgin. Dandelion, 1979. ISBN 0-89799-089-7 Subj: ABC books. Animals – mice.

Feet ill. by Susan Reiss. Dandelion, 1979. ISBN 0-89799-104-4 Subj: Anatomy – feet. Concepts – left and right.

Hot and cold ill. by Gail Gibbons. Dandelion, 1979. ISBN 0-89799-110-9 Subj: Concepts.

The miracles at Cana ill. by Wayne Atkinson. Dandelion, 1979. ISBN 0-89799-124-9 Subj: Religion.

The mouse in my house ill. by Gail Gibbons. Dandelion, 1979. ISBN 0-89799-126-5 Subj: Animals – mice. Homes, houses.

My balloon ill. by Gail Gibbons. Dandelion, 1979. ISBN 0-89799-127-3 Subj: Toys – balloons.

The nightingale and the fool ill. by Judith Cheng. Dandelion, 1979. ISBN 0-89799-129-X Subj: Birds – nightingales. Folk and fairy tales. Foreign lands – India.

Noah's ark ill. by Elliot Ivenbaum. Dandelion, 1979. ISBN 0-89799-130-3 Subj: Animals. Boats, ships. Religion – Noah. Weather – floods. Weather – rain. Weather – rainbows.

Pete, the wet pet ill. by Gail Gibbons. Elsevier-Nelson, 1981. ISBN 0-525-66746-6 Subj: Animals – dogs. Family life.

Chase, Edith Newlin. *Secret dawn* ill. by Yolaine Lefebvre. Firefly, 1996. ISBN 1-55209-028-0 Subj: Morning. Poetry. Trees.

Chase, Jan Brinckerhoff. *The golden song* ill. by author. J.N. Townsend, 1993. ISBN 1-880158-01-9 Subj: Birds – canaries. Character traits – kindness to animals. Friendship. Pets.

Chase, Richard. *Billy Boy* (Billy Boy [folk-song])

Jack and the three sillies ill. by Joshua Tolford. Houghton Mifflin, 1950. Subj: Folk and fairy tales.

Chasek, Judith. *Have you seen Wilhelmina Krumpf?* ill. by Sal Murdocca. Lothrop, 1973. ISBN 0-688-51523-1 Subj: Foreign lands – Holland.

Chaucer, Geoffrey. *Chanticleer and the fox* adapt. and ill. by Barbara Cooney. Crowell, 1958. Adapt. of the "Nun's priest's tale" from the Canterbury tales. ISBN 0-690-18562-6 Subj: Animals – foxes.

Birds – chickens. Caldecott award books. Character traits – flattery. Farms. Folk and fairy tales.

Chausse, Sylvie. *The egg and I* ill. by François Crozat. Silver Pr., 1997. ISBN 0-382-39286-8 Subj: Character traits – luck. Dinosaurs. Eggs. Family life – cousins.

Chen, Tony. *Animals showing off* [Tony Chen, ill.; Jane R. McCauley, writer]. National Geographic, 1989. ISBN 0-87044-724-6 Subj: Animals. Format, unusual – toy and movable books.

Chenault, Nell. *Parsifal the Poddley* ill. by Vee Guthrie. Little, 1960. Subj: Emotions – loneliness. Mythical creatures. U.S. history.

Chenery, Janet. *Pickles and Jake* ill. by Lilian Obligado. Viking, 1975. ISBN 0-670-55335-2 Subj: Animals – cats. Animals – dogs. Pets.

The toad hunt ill. by Ben Shecter. HarperCollins, 1967. ISBN 0-06-021263-2 Subj: Frogs and toads. Science.

Wolfie ill. by Marc Simont. HarperCollins, 1969. ISBN 0-440-40496-7 Subj: Sibling rivalry. Spiders.

Cheng, Hou-Tien. *The Chinese New Year* ill. by author. Holt, 1976. ISBN 0-03-017511-9 Subj: Foreign lands – China. Holidays – Chinese New Year.

Chermayeff, Ivan. *Tomato and other colors* ill. by author. Prentice-Hall, 1981. ISBN 0-13-924753-X Subj: Concepts – color.

Chernoff, Goldie Taub. *Clay-dough, play-dough* ill. and photos by Margaret A. Hartelius. Walker, 1974. ISBN 0-8027-6178-X Subj: Activities.

Just a box? ill. by Margaret A. Hartelius. Walker, 1973. ISBN 0-8027-6138-0 Subj: Activities.

Pebbles and pods: a book of nature crafts ill. by Margaret A. Hartelius. Walker, 1973. ISBN 0-8027-6137-2 Subj: Activities.

Puppet party ill. by Margaret A. Hartelius. Walker, 1972. ISBN 0-8027-6100-3 Subj: Activities. Puppets.

Cherry, Lynne. *Archie, follow me* ill. by author. Dutton, 1990. ISBN 0-525-44647-8 Subj: Animals – cats. Forest, woods.

The armadillo from Amarillo ill. by author. Harcourt, 1994. ISBN 0-15-200359-2 Subj: Activities – flying. Animals – armadillos. Rhyming text.

The dragon and the unicorn ill. by author. Harcourt, 1995. ISBN 0-15-224193-0 Subj: Dragons. Ecology. Monsters. Mythical creatures – unicorns.

The great kapok tree: a tale of the Amazon rain forest ill. by author. Harcourt, 1990. ISBN 0-15-200520-X Subj: Animals. Ecology. Foreign lands – Brazil. Jungle. Trees.

Grizzly bear text and ed. by Lucia Monfried; ill. by author. Dutton, 1998. ISBN 0-525-45793-3 Subj: Animals – bears. Format, unusual – board books.

Orangutan text and ed. by Lucia Monfried; ill. by author. Dutton, 1998. ISBN 0-525-45794-1 Subj: Animals – orangutans. Format, unusual – board books.

A river ran wild ill. by author. Harcourt, 1992. ISBN 0-15-200542-0 Subj: Ecology. Nature. Rivers. U.S. history.

Seal text and ed. by Lucia Monfried; ill. by author. Dutton, 1998. ISBN 0-525-45796-8 Subj: Animals – seals. Format, unusual – board books.

Snow leopard text and ed. by Lucia Monfried; ill. by author. Dutton, 1998. ISBN 0-525-45797-6 Subj: Animals – leopards. Format, unusual – board books.

Who's sick today? ill. by author. Dutton, 1988. ISBN 0-525-44380-0 Subj: Animals. Illness. Rhyming text.

Chess, Victoria. *Alfred's alphabet walk* ill. by author. Greenwillow, 1979. ISBN 0-688-84223-2 Subj: ABC books. Behavior – misbehavior.

Poor Esmé ill. by author. Holiday, 1982. ISBN 0-8234-0455-2 Subj: Babies. Behavior – wishing. Emotions – loneliness. Family life – new sibling.

Chester, Jonathan. *Busy penguins* (Schindel, John)

Splash! a penguin counting book by Jonathan Chester and Kirsty Melville; ill. with photos. Tricycle, 1997. ISBN 1-883672-56-2 Subj: Birds – penguins. Counting, numbers. Foreign lands – Antarctic. Nature.

Chesworth, Michael. *Archibald Frisby* ill. by author. Farrar, 1994. ISBN 0-374-30392-4 Subj: Camps, camping. Rhyming text. Science.

Rainy day dream ill. by author. Farrar, 1992. ISBN 0-374-36177-0 Subj: Dreams. Umbrellas. Weather – storms. Wordless.

Chetwin, Grace. *Box and Cox* ill. by David Small. Bradbury, 1990. ISBN 0-02-718314-9 Subj: Careers – hatters. Careers – printers. Humor.

Mr. Meredith and the truly remarkable stone ill. by Catherine Stock. Bradbury, 1989. ISBN 0-02-718313-0 Subj: Rocks.

Chevalier, Christa. *The little bear who forgot* ed. by Kathleen Tucker; ill. by author. Albert Whitman, 1984. ISBN 0-8075-4571-6 Subj: Animals – bears. Family life.

Spence and the sleepytime monster ill. by author. Albert Whitman, 1984. ISBN 0-8075-7574-7 Subj: Bedtime. Imagination. Monsters.

Spence is small ill. by author. Albert Whitman, 1987. ISBN 0-8075-7567-4 Subj: Character traits – helpfulness. Character traits – smallness.

Spence isn't Spence anymore ill. by author. Albert Whitman, 1985. ISBN 0-8075-7565-8 Subj: Character traits – appearance.

Spence makes circles ill. by author. Albert Whitman, 1982. ISBN 0-8075-7570-4 Subj: Behavior – mistakes. Humor.

Chevalier, Joan. *Suzette and Nicholas and the seasons clock* (Mangin, Marie-France)

Chevance, Audrey. *Tutu* ill. by author. Dutton, 1991. ISBN 0-525-44769-5 Subj: Activities – dancing. Ballet. Careers – seamstresses.

Cheyette, Wendy. *see* Lewison, Wendy Cheyette

Chial, Debra. *M is for Minnesota* ed. by Helene Anderson and Julie Bach; ill. by author. Voyageur Pr., 1994. ISBN 0-8965-8234-5 Subj: ABC books. U.S. history.

Chiang, Ch'eng-an. *The legend of Mu Lan = La heroina Hua Mulan* (Chiang, Wei)

Chiang, Wei. *The legend of Mu Lan = La heroina Hua Mulan* written and ill. by Jiang, Wei and Gen, Xing. Victory, 1992. ISBN 1-878217-01-1 Subj: Folk and fairy tales. Foreign lands – China. Foreign languages. War.

Chichester Clark, Emma. *I love you, Blue Kangaroo!* ill. by author. Doubleday, 1999. ISBN 0-385-32638-6 Subj: Behavior – needing someone. Toys.

Little Miss Muffet's count-along surprise ill. by author. Bantam, 1997. ISBN 0-385-32517-7 Subj: Animals. Birthdays. Counting, numbers. Nursery rhymes. Parties.

Lunch with Aunt Augusta ill. by author. Dial, 1992. ISBN 0-8037-1104-2 Subj: Animals – lemurs. Family life – aunts, uncles. Food. Jungle.

More! ill. by author. Doubleday, 1999. ISBN 0-385-32630-0 Subj: Activities – playing. Behavior – greed. Behavior – seeking better things. Family life – mothers. Family life – sons. Imagination.

The story of Horrible Hilda and Henry ill. by author. Little, 1989. ISBN 0-316-14498-3 Subj: Animals – lions. Behavior – misbehavior. Zoos.

Chicken Little. *Chicken Licken* text by Kenneth McLeish; ill. by Jutta Ash. Bradbury, 1973. ISBN 0-582-16469-9 Subj: Animals. Behavior – gossip. Behavior – trickery. Birds – chickens. Cumulative tales. Folk and fairy tales.

Chicken Licken adapt. and ill. by Gavin Bishop. Oxford Univ. Pr., 1985. ISBN 0-19-558108-3 Subj: Animals. Behavior – gossip. Behavior – trickery. Birds – chickens. Cumulative tales. Folk and fairy tales.

Chicken Little ill. by Sally Hobson. Simon & Schuster, 1994. ISBN 0-671-89548-6 Subj: Animals. Behavior – gossip. Behavior – trickery. Birds – chickens. Cumulative tales. Folk and fairy tales.

Henny Penny retold by Harriet Ziefert; ill. by Emily Bolam. Viking, 1997. ISBN 0-670-86810-8 Subj: Animals. Behavior – gossip. Behavior – trickery. Birds – chickens. Cumulative tales. Folk and fairy tales.

Henny Penny ill. by Stephen Butler. Morrow, 1991. ISBN 0-688-09922-X Subj: Animals. Behavior – gossip. Behavior – trickery. Birds – chickens. Cumulative tales. Folk and fairy tales.

Henny Penny ill. by Paul Galdone. Seabury Pr., 1968. Subj: Animals. Behavior – gossip. Behavior – trickery. Birds – chickens. Cumulative tales. Folk and fairy tales.

Henny Penny ill. by William Stobbs. Follett, 1968. ISBN 0-3700-0780-8 Subj: Animals. Behavior – gossip. Behavior – trickery. Birds – chickens. Cumulative tales. Folk and fairy tales.

Henny-Penny retold and ill. by Jane Wattenberg. Scholastic, 2000. ISBN 0-439-07817-2 Subj: Animals. Behavior – gossip. Behavior – trickery. Birds – chickens. Cumulative tales. Folk and fairy tales.

The sky is falling Betty Miles; ill. by Cynthia Fisher. Simon & Schuster, 1998. ISBN 0-689-81790-8 Subj: Animals. Behavior – gossip. Behavior – trickery. Birds – chickens. Cumulative tales. Folk and fairy tales.

The story of Chicken Licken adapt. and ill. by Jan Ormerod. Lothrop, 1986. ISBN 0-688-06058-7 Subj: Animals. Behavior – gossip. Behavior – trickery. Birds – chickens. Cumulative tales. Folk and fairy tales.

Chiefari, Janet. *Kids are baby goats* ill. with photos. Dodd, 1984. ISBN 0-396-08316-1 Subj: Animals – goats. Fairs.

Chiemruom, Sothea. *Dara's Cambodian New Year* ill. by Dam Nang Pin. Modern Curriculum, 1992. ISBN 0-813-62256-5 Subj: Ethnic groups in the U.S. – Cambodian Americans. Holidays – New Year's.

Child, Lauren. *Clarice Bean, that's me* ill. by author. Candlewick, 1999. ISBN 0-7636-0961-7 Subj: Family life.

I want a pet ill. by author. Tricycle, 1999. ISBN 1-883672-82-1 Subj: Pets.

Child, Lydia Maria. *Over the river and through the wood* ill. by Brinton Turkle. Coward, 1974. First published in 1844 as The boy's Thanksgiving Day in the 2d vol. of the author's Flowers for children. ISBN 0-698-30553-1 Subj: Family life – grandparents. Farms. Holidays – Thanksgiving. Songs.

Child Study Association of America. *Brothers and sisters are like that!* (Brothers and sisters are like that!)

Children go where I send thee: *an American spiritual* ill. by Kathryn E. Shoemaker. Winston, 1980. ISBN 0-03-056673-8 Subj: Ethnic groups in the U.S. – African Americans. Music. Religion.

Children's prayers from around the world. Sadlier, 1981. Subj: Children as authors. Religion.

Children's Television Workshop. *ABC: featuring Jim Henson's Sesame Street Muppets* (Calmenson, Stephanie)

Muppets in my neighborhood ill. by Harry McNaught. Random House, 1977. ISBN 0-394-83593-X Subj: Format, unusual – board books. Puppets.

The Sesame Street book of letters (Sesame Street)

The Sesame Street book of numbers (Sesame Street)

The Sesame Street book of opposites with Zero Mostel (Mendoza, George)

The Sesame Street book of people and things (Sesame Street)

The Sesame Street book of shapes (Sesame Street)

The Sesame Street players present Mother Goose: featuring Jim Henson's Sesame Street Muppets (Mother Goose)

The Sesame Street song book (Raposo, Joe)

A visit to the Sesame Street firehouse: featuring Jim Henson's Sesame Street Muppets (Elliott, Dan)

Childress, Mark. *Joshua and Bigtooth* ill. by Rick Meyerowitz. Little, 1992. ISBN 0-316-14011-2 Subj: Activities – dancing. Parties. Pets. Reptiles – alligators, crocodiles.

Joshua and the big bad blue crabs ill. by Mary Barrett Brown. Little, 1996. ISBN 0-316-14118-6 Subj: Behavior – misbehavior. Crustaceans. Food.

A child's book of prayers ill. by Michael Hague. Holt, 1985. ISBN 0-03-001412-3 Subj: Religion.

A child's calendar ill. by Trina Schart Hyman. Holiday, 1999. ISBN 0-8234-1445-0 Subj: Caldecott award honor books. Days of the week, months of the year. Poetry.

A child's picture English-Hebrew dictionary ill. by Ita Meshi. Adama, 1985. ISBN 0-915361-07-8 Subj: ABC books. Dictionaries. Foreign languages. Jewish culture.

Chimaera. *see* Farjeon, Eleanor

Chin, Charlie. *China's bravest girl: the legend of Hua Mu Lan* ill. by Tomie Arai; trans. from Chinese by Wang Xing Chu. Childrens Book Pr., 1993. ISBN 0-89239-120-0 Subj: Careers – military. Folk and fairy tales. Foreign lands – China. Poetry.

Chin, Steven A. *Dragon Parade: a Chinese New Year story* ill. by Mou-Sien Tseng. Raintree, 1993. ISBN 0-8114-7215-9 Subj: Ethnic groups in the U.S. – Chinese Americans. Holidays – Chinese New Year.

Chinery, Michael. *Desert animals* ill. by Eric Robson and David Wright. Random House, 1992. ISBN 0-679-92048-X Subj: Animals. Desert.

Grassland animals ill. by John Butler and Brian McIntyre. Random House, 1992. ISBN 0-679-92045-5 Subj: Animals.

Ching. *The baboon's umbrella* ill. by author. Childrens Pr., 1991. ISBN 0-516-05131-8 Subj: Animals – baboons. Folk and fairy tales. Foreign lands – Africa. Umbrellas.

Ching, Simon. *The cricket's cage: a Chinese folktale* (Czernecki, Stefan)

Chin-Lee, Cynthia. *A is for Asia* ill. by Yumi Heo. Orchard, 1997. ISBN 0-531-33011-7 Subj: ABC books. Foreign lands – Asia.

Chinn, Karen. *Sam and the lucky money* ill. by Cornelius Van Wright and Ying-Hwa Hu. Lee & Low, 1995. ISBN 1-880000-13-X Subj: Character traits – generosity. Ethnic groups in the U.S. – Chinese Americans. Holidays – Chinese New Year. Homeless.

Chislett, Gail. *Melinda's no's cold* ill. by Hélène Desputeaux. Firefly, 1991. ISBN 1-55037-196-7 Subj: Careers – doctors. Illness. Language.

The rude visitors ill. by Barbara Di Lella. Firefly, 1984. Subj: Behavior – carelessness. Imagination.

Whump ill. by Vladyana Krykorka. Firefly, 1989. ISBN 1-55037-041-3 Subj: Bedtime. Family life. Sleep.

Chittum, Ida. *The cat's pajamas* ill. by Art Cumings. Parents, 1980. ISBN 0-8193-1030-1 Subj: Animals – cats. Pets.

Chlad, Dorothy. *Bicycles are fun to ride* ill. by Lydia Halverson. Childrens Pr., 1984. ISBN 0-516-01975-9 Subj: Safety. Sports – bicycling.

Matches, lighters, and firecrackers are not toys ill. by Lydia Halverson. Childrens Pr., 1982. ISBN 0-516-01982-1 Subj: Safety.

Poisons make you sick ill. by Lydia Halverson. Childrens Pr., 1984. ISBN 0-516-01976-1 Subj: Safety.

Strangers ill. by Lydia Halverson. Childrens Pr., 1982. ISBN 0-516-01984-8 Subj: Behavior – talking to strangers.

Chmielarz, Sharon. *Down at Angel's* ill. by Jill Kastner. Ticknor & Fields, 1994. ISBN 0-395-65993-0 Subj: Character traits – kindness. Friendship. Holidays – Christmas.

The pied piper of Hamelin (Browning, Robert)

Cho, Shinta. *The gas we pass: the story of farts* ill. by author; trans. by Amanda Mayer Stinchecum. Kane/Miller, 1994. ISBN 0-916291-52-9 Subj: Anatomy. Animals. Etiquette.

Chocolate, Deborah M. Newton. *Imani in the belly* ill. by Alex Boies. BridgeWater, 1994. ISBN 0-8167-3466-6 Subj: Animals. Character traits – bravery. Folk and fairy tales. Foreign lands – Africa.

Kente colors ill. by John Ward. Walker, 1996. ISBN 0-8027-8389-9 Subj: Clothing. Concepts – color. Foreign lands – Africa. Holidays – Kwanzaa.

Kwanzaa ill. by Melodye Rosales. Childrens Pr., 1990. ISBN 0-516-03991-1 Subj: Ethnic groups in the U.S. – African Americans. Family life. Holidays – Kwanzaa.

The piano man ill. by Eric Velasquez. Walker, 1998. ISBN 0-8027-8647-2 Subj: Careers – musicians. Ethnic groups in the U.S. – African Americans. Family life – grandparents. Music.

Choi, Sook Nyul. *Halmoni and the picnic* ill. by Karen Dugan. Houghton Mifflin, 1993. ISBN 0-395-61626-3 Subj: Ethnic groups in the U.S. – Korean Americans. Family life – grandmothers.

Yunmi and Halmoni's trip ill. by Karen Dugan. Houghton Mifflin, 1997. ISBN 0-395-81180-5 Subj: Ethnic groups in the U.S. – Korean Americans. Family life. Family life – grandmothers. Foreign lands – Korea.

Choi, Yangsook. *New cat* ill. by author. Farrar, 1999. ISBN 0-374-35512-6 Subj: Animals – cats. Animals – mice.

The sun girl and the moon boy retold and ill. by Yangsook Choi. Knopf, 1997. ISBN 0-679-98386-4 Subj: Animals – tigers. Behavior – talking to strangers. Folk and fairy tales. Foreign lands – Korea.

Choldenko, Gennifer. *Moonstruck: the true story of the cow that jumped over the moon* ill. by Paul Yalowitz. Hyperion, 1997. ISBN 0-7868-2130-2 Subj: Animals – bulls, cows. Animals – horses, ponies. Character traits – perseverance. Moon. Nursery rhymes.

Chönz, Selina. *A bell for Ursli* ill. by Alois Carigiet. Walck, 1950. Subj: Foreign lands – Switzerland. Rhyming text. Seasons – spring.

Florina and the wild bird trans. by Anne and Ian Serraillier; ill. by Alois Carigiet. Walck, 1966. Translation of Flurina und das Wildvöglein. Subj: Birds. Foreign lands – Switzerland. Rhyming text. Seasons – summer.

The snowstorm ill. by Alois Carigiet. Walck, 1958. Translated from the German. Subj: Foreign lands – Switzerland. Rhyming text. Seasons – winter. Weather – snow. Weather – storms.

Chorao, Kay. *Annie and cousin Precious* ill. by author. Dutton, 1994. ISBN 0-525-45238-9 Subj: Activities – playing. Animals – dogs. Family life – cousins.

The baby's bedtime book comp. and ill. by Kay Chorao. Dutton, 1984. ISBN 0-525-44149-2 Subj: Nursery rhymes. Poetry.

Baby's Christmas treasury ill. by author. Random House, 1991. ISBN 0-679-90198-1 Subj: Babies. Holidays – Christmas.

The baby's good morning book ill. by adapt. Dutton, 1986. ISBN 0-525-44257-X Subj: Babies. Morning. Poetry.

Carousel round and round ill. by author. Clarion, 1995. ISBN 0-395-63632-9 Subj: Animals. Merry-go-rounds. Rhyming text. Toys.

Cathedral mouse ill. by author. Dutton, 1988. ISBN 0-525-44400-9 Subj: Animals – mice. Homes, houses.

The cherry pie baby ill. by author. Dutton, 1989. ISBN 0-525-44435-1 Subj: Activities – trading. Animals – dogs. Babies.

The child's story book ill. by adapt. Dutton, 1987. ISBN 0-525-44328-2 Subj: Folk and fairy tales.

The Christmas story ill. by adapt. Holiday, 1996. ISBN 0-8234-1251-2 Subj: Holidays – Christmas. Religion – Nativity.

George told Kate ill. by author. Dutton, 1987. ISBN 0-525-44293-6 Subj: Animals – elephants. Sibling rivalry.

Ida and Betty and the secret eggs ill. by author. Houghton Mifflin, 1991. ISBN 0-395-52591-8 Subj: Animals – cats. Country. Eggs. Friendship.

Kate's box ill. by author. Dutton, 1982. ISBN 0-525-44010-0 Subj: Animals – elephants. Behavior – hiding.

Kate's car ill. by author. Dutton, 1982. ISBN 0-525-44011-9 Subj: Animals – elephants. Toys.

Kate's quilt ill. by author. Dutton, 1982. ISBN 0-525-44012-7 Subj: Animals – elephants. Quilts.

Kate's snowman ill. by author. Dutton, 1982. ISBN 0-525-44013-5 Subj: Animals – elephants. Snowmen.

Knock at the door and other baby action rhymes ill. by author. Dutton, 1999. ISBN 0-525-45969-3 Subj: Animals – cats. Babies. Nursery rhymes. Rhyming text.

Lemon moon ill. by author. Holiday, 1983. ISBN 0-8234-0490-0 Subj: Animals. Bedtime. Dreams. Family life – grandmothers.

Lester's overnight ill. by author. Dutton, 1977. ISBN 0-525-33480-7 Subj: Emotions – fear. Family life. Imagination. Sleep.

Little farm by the sea ill. by author. Holt, 1998. ISBN 0-8050-5053-1 Subj: Careers – farmers. Family life. Farms. Seasons.

Maudie's umbrella ill. by author. Dutton, 1975. ISBN 0-525-34770-4 Subj: Behavior – losing things. Umbrellas.

Molly's lies ill. by author. Seabury Pr., 1979. ISBN 0-816-43225-2 Subj: Behavior – losing things. Behavior – lying. Friendship. School – first day.

Molly's Moe ill. by author. Seabury Pr., 1976. ISBN 0-816-43171-X Subj: Behavior – losing things. Shopping. Toys.

Mother Goose magic ill. by author. Dutton, 1994. ISBN 0-525-45064-5 Subj: Nursery rhymes.

Number one number fun ill. by author. Holiday, 1995. ISBN 0-8234-1142-7 Subj: Animals. Circus. Counting, numbers. Rhyming text.

Peekaboo! Was it you? ill. by author. Random House, 1994. ISBN 0-679-84629-8 Subj: Activities. Format, unusual – board books. Games. Rhyming text.

Rock, rock, my baby ill. by author. Random House, 1993. ISBN 0-679-84333-7 Subj: Format, unusual – board books. Lullabies.

Chottin, Ariane. *Beaver gets lost* ill. by Marcelle Geneste; adapt. by Deborah Kovacs. Reader's Digest, 1992. ISBN 0-89577-419-4 Subj: Animals – beavers. Animals – squirrels. Behavior – lost. Character traits – ambition.

The curious little dolphin adapt. by Patricia Jensen; ill. by Olivier Raquois. Reader's Digest, 1992. ISBN 0-8957-7425-9 Subj: Animals – dolphins. Character traits – curiosity.

A home for Little Turtle ill. by Pascale Wirth; adapt. by Deborah Kovacs. Reader's Digest, 1992. ISBN 0895774208 Subj: Animals. Emotions – envy, jealousy. Reptiles – turtles, tortoises. Self-concept.

Little Goat's new horns adapt. by Patricia Jensen; ill. by Pascale Wirth. Reader's Digest, 1993. ISBN 0-8957-7544-1 Subj: Animals – goats. Emotions – envy, jealousy. Self-concept.

Little Kangaroo finds his way adapt. by Patricia Jensen; ill. by Catherine Fichaux. Reader's Digest, 1993. ISBN 0-8957-7543-3 Subj: Animals – kangaroos. Character traits – confidence.

Little Mouse's rescue adapt. by Patricia Jensen; ill. by Malgorzata Dzierzawska. Reader's Digest, 1993. ISBN 0-8957-7505-0 Subj: Animals – cats. Animals – mice. Friendship.

Chouinard, Mariko. *The amazing animal alphabet book* (Chouinard, Roger)

One magic box (Chouinard, Roger)

Chouinard, Roger. *The amazing animal alphabet book* by Roger and Mariko Chouinard; ill. by Roger Chouinard. Doubleday, 1988. ISBN 0-385-24029-5 Subj: ABC books. Animals.

One magic box by Roger and Mariko Chouinard; ill. by authors. Doubleday, 1989. ISBN 0-385-26204-3 Subj: Animals. Counting, numbers. Magic.

Chow, Octavio. *The invisible hunters* (Rohmer, Harriet)

Christelow, Eileen. *Don't wake up Mama! another five little monkeys story* ill. by author. Clarion, 1992. ISBN 0-395-60176-2 Subj: Activities – cooking. Animals – monkeys. Birthdays. Family life – mothers. Food.

Five little monkeys jumping on the bed ill. by author. Houghton Mifflin, 1991. ISBN 0-395-55701-1 Subj: Animals – monkeys. Bedtime. Behavior – misbehavior. Counting, numbers. Nursery rhymes. Poetry.

Five little monkeys sitting in a tree ill. by author. Houghton Mifflin, 1991. ISBN 0-395-54434-3 Subj: Activities – picnicking. Animals – monkeys. Behavior – misbehavior. Counting, numbers. Reptiles – alligators, crocodiles. Rhyming text.

Five little monkeys with nothing to do ill. by author. Clarion, 1996. ISBN 0-395-75830-0 Subj: Animals – monkeys. Behavior – boredom. Family life.

The five-dog night ill. by author. Clarion, 1993. ISBN 0-395-62399-5 Subj: Animals – dogs. Seasons – winter.

Gertrude, the bulldog detective ill. by author. Houghton Mifflin, 1992. ISBN 0-395-58701-8 Subj: Animals – dogs. Careers – detectives. Mystery stories.

Glenda Feathers casts a spell ill. by author. Houghton Mifflin, 1990. ISBN 0-395-51122-4 Subj: Animals. Witches.

The great pig escape ill. by author. Clarion, 1994. ISBN 0-395-66973-1 Subj: Animals – pigs. Behavior – running away. Careers – farmers.

Henry and the dragon ill. by author. Houghton Mifflin, 1984. ISBN 0-89919-220-3 Subj: Animals – rabbits. Bedtime. Dragons. Shadows.

Henry and the red stripes ill. by author. Houghton Mifflin, 1982. ISBN 0-89919-118-5 Subj: Animals – foxes. Animals – rabbits. Illness.

Jerome and the Witchcraft kids ill. by author. Clarion, 1988. ISBN 0-8991-9742-6 Subj: Activities – babysitting. Behavior – misbehavior. Holidays – Halloween. Reptiles – alligators, crocodiles.

Jerome camps out ill. by author. Clarion, 1998. ISBN 0-395-75831-9 Subj: Behavior – bullying. Camps, camping. Reptiles – alligators, crocodiles.

Jerome the babysitter ill. by author. Houghton Mifflin, 1985. ISBN 0-89919-331-5 Subj: Activities – babysitting. Behavior – trickery. Character traits – cleverness. Reptiles – alligators, crocodiles.

Mr. Murphy's marvelous invention ill. by author. Clarion, 1983. ISBN 0-89919-141-X Subj: Animals – pigs. Inventions.

Not until Christmas, Walter! ill. by author. Clarion, 1997. ISBN 0-395-82273-4 Subj: Animals – dogs. Holidays – Christmas.

Olive and the magic hat ill. by author. Clarion, 1987. ISBN 0-89919-513-X Subj: Animals. Behavior – trickery. Clothing – hats. Magic.

The robbery at the diamond dog diner ill. by author. Clarion, 1986. ISBN 0-89919-425-7 Subj: Animals. Behavior – secrets. Behavior – trickery. Birds. Crime. Restaurants.

What do authors do? ill. by author. Clarion, 1995. ISBN 0-395-71124-X Subj: Careers – artists. Careers – writers.

Christensen, Gardell Dano. *Mrs. Mouse needs a house* ill. by author. Holt, 1958. Subj: Animals.

Animals – mice. Homes, houses. Problem solving.

Christensen, Jack. *The forgotten rainbow* by Jack and Lee Christensen; ill. by authors. Morrow, 1960. Subj: Behavior – wishing. Folk and fairy tales.

Christensen, Lee. *The forgotten rainbow* (Christensen, Jack)

Christenson, Larry. *The wonderful way that babies are made* ill. by Dwight Walles. Bethany House, 1982. ISBN 0-87123-627-3 Subj: Babies. Birth. Family life. Science.

Christian, Frank P. *Dancin' in the kitchen* (Gelsanliter, Wendy)

Christian, Mary Blount. *Anna and the strangers* ill. by Charles T. Cox. Abingdon, 1981. ISBN 0-687-01529-4 Subj: Holidays – Christmas. Religion.

April fool ill. by Diane Dawson. Macmillan, 1982. ISBN 0-02-718280-0 Subj: Folk and fairy tales. Foreign lands – England. Holidays – April Fools' Day.

The bookstore mouse ill. by Gary A. Lippincott. Harcourt, 1995. ISBN 0-15-200203-0 Subj: Activities – reading. Animals – mice. Dragons. Stores.

Christmas reflections ill. by Arch Kirchhoff. Concordia, 1980. ISBN 0-570-03494-9 Subj: City. Country. Family life. Holidays – Christmas.

The devil take you, Barnabas Beane! ill. by Anne Burgess. Crowell, 1980. ISBN 0-690-03998-0 Subj: Behavior – greed. Character traits – generosity. Character traits – selfishness.

Devin and Goliath ill. by Normand Chartier. Addison-Wesley, 1974. ISBN 0-2010-1026-7 Subj: Pets. Reptiles – turtles, tortoises.

The doggone mystery ill. by Irene Trivas. Albert Whitman, 1980. ISBN 0-8075-1656-2 Subj: Behavior – stealing. Crime. Mystery stories.

Go west, swamp monsters ill. by Marc Brown. Dial, 1985. ISBN 0-8037-0144-6 Subj: Activities – picnicking. Behavior – misbehavior. Behavior – running away. Monsters.

Grandfathers, God's gift to children ill. by Susan Morris. Concordia, 1982. ISBN 0-570-04069-8 Subj: Family life – grandfathers. Religion.

Grandmothers, God's gift to children ill. by Susan Morris. Concordia, 1982. ISBN 0-570-04068-X Subj: Family life – grandmothers. Religion.

The green thumb thief ill. by Don Madden. Albert Whitman, 1982. ISBN 0-8075-3040-9 Subj: Animals – dogs. Behavior – stealing. Clubs, gangs. Plants.

No dogs allowed, Jonathan! ill. by Don Madden. Addison-Wesley, 1973. ISBN 0-2010-1028-3 Subj: Animals – dogs.

Nothing much happened today ill. by Don Madden. Addison-Wesley, 1973. ISBN 0-2010-1024-0 Subj: Cumulative tales. Humor.

The sand lot ill. by Dennis Kendrick. Harvey House, 1978. ISBN 0-8178-5827-X Subj: Activities – playing. Behavior – fighting, arguing. Sports – baseball.

Scarabee, the witch's cat ill. by Sybil McEntire. Steck-Vaughn, 1973. ISBN 0-8114-7750-9 Subj: Animals – cats. Witches.

Christian, Peggy. *Chocolate, a glacier grizzly* ill. by Carol Cottone-Kolthoff. Benefactory, 1997. ISBN 1-882728-63-7 Subj: Animals – bears. Careers – park rangers.

If you find a rock photos by Barbara Hirsch Lember. Harcourt, 2000. ISBN 0-15-239339-0 Subj: Rocks.

Christiana, David. *A Tooth Fairy's tale* ill. by author. Farrar, 1994. ISBN 0-374-37677-8 Subj: Fairies. Giants. Mythical creatures – sandman.

White nineteens ill. by author. Farrar, 1992. ISBN 0-374-38390-1 Subj: Animals. Fairies. Forest, woods. Seasons – winter.

Christiansen, C. B. *Mara in the morning* ill. by Catherine Stock. Macmillan, 1991. ISBN 0-689-31616-X Subj: Morning. Noise, sounds.

My mother's house, my father's house ill. by Irene Trivas. Macmillan, 1989. ISBN 0-689-31394-2 Subj: Divorce. Emotions. Family life.

Christiansen, Candace. *The ice horse* ill. by Thomas Locker. Dial, 1993. ISBN 0-8037-1401-7 Subj: Animals – horses, ponies. Family life – aunts, uncles. Seasons – winter.

A Christmas book trans. from Danish by Joan Tate; ill. by Svend Otto S. Larousse, 1982. ISBN 0-88332-286-2 Subj: Foreign lands – Denmark. Holidays – Christmas.

Christmas carols ill. by Diane Goode. Random House, 1983. ISBN 0-394-85723-2 Subj: Holidays – Christmas. Songs.

Christmas in the stable poems sel. and ill. by Beverly K. Duncan. Harcourt, 1990. ISBN 0-15-217758-2 Subj: Animals. Holidays – Christmas. Poetry. Religion – Nativity.

The Christmas story told through paintings from the Metropolitan Museum of Art with commentary by Richard Mühlberger. Harcourt, 1990. ISBN 0-15-200426-2 Subj: Art. Holidays – Christmas. Museums. Religion – Nativity.

Chukovskii, Kornei Ivanovich. *Good morning, chick* adapt. by Mirra Ginsburg; ill. by Byron Barton. Greenwillow, 1980. ISBN 0-688-84284-4 Subj: Birds – chickens. Noise, sounds.

The telephone adapt. from Russian by William Jay Smith in collaboration with Max Hayward; ill. by Blair Lent. Delacorte, 1977. ISBN 0-440-06040-0 Subj: Communication. Humor. Rhyming text.

Telephone ill. by Vladimir Radunsky; tr. and adapt. by Jamey Gambrell. North-South, 1996. ISBN 1-55858-481-1 Subj: Animals. Poetry. Telephone.

Church, Kristine. *My brother John* ill. by Kilmeny Niland. Morrow, 1991. ISBN 0-688-10801-6 Subj: Character traits – bravery. Emotions – fear. Family life – brothers and sisters. Monsters.

Chute, Beatrice Joy. *Journey to Christmas* ill. by Erik Blegvad. Dutton, 1958. Subj: Character traits – generosity. Holidays – Christmas.

Chwast, Seymour. *Alphabet parade* ill. by author. Harcourt, 1991. ISBN 0-15-200351-7 Subj: ABC books. Parades. Wordless.

Bushy bride: a Norwegian fairy tale ill. by reteller. Creative Ed., 1983. ISBN 0-87191-952-4 Subj: Emotions – envy, jealousy. Family life – step families. Folk and fairy tales. Foreign lands – Norway. Royalty – kings.

Mr. Merlin and the turtle ill. by author. Greenwillow, 1996. ISBN 0-688-14632-5 Subj: Animals. Format, unusual – toy and movable books. Magic. Pets. Reptiles – turtles, tortoises.

Moonride (Ziefert, Harriet)

Still another alphabet book by Seymour Chwast and Martin Stephen Moskof; ill. by authors. McGraw-Hill, 1969. Subj: ABC books. Wordless.

Still another children's book by Seymour Chwast and Martin Stephen Moskof; ill. by authors. McGraw-Hill, 1972. Subj: Dreams. Seasons – summer.

Still another number book by Seymour Chwast and Martin Stephen Moskof; ill. by authors. McGraw-Hill, 1971. Subj: Counting, numbers.

Tall city, wide country: a book to read forward and backward ill. by author. Viking, 1983. ISBN 0-670-69236-0 Subj: Activities – traveling. City. Country. Format, unusual.

Traffic jam ill. by author. Houghton Mifflin, 1999. ISBN 0-395-97495-X Subj: Animals – babies. Animals – cats. Careers – police officers. City. Format, unusual – toy and movable books. Traffic, traffic signs.

The twelve circus rings ill. by author. Harcourt, 1993. ISBN 0-15-200627-3 Subj: Animals. Circus. Counting, numbers.

Ciardi, John. *John J. Plenty and Fiddler Dan: a new fable of the grasshopper and the ant* ill. by Madeleine Gekiere. Lippincott, 1963. Subj: Behavior – saving things. Insects – ants. Insects – grasshoppers. Poetry.

The monster den: or, Look what happened at my house - and to it ill. by Edward Gorey. Lippincott, 1966. ISBN 1-878093-35-5 Subj: Monsters. Poetry.

Scrappy, the pup ill. by Jane Miller. Lippincott, 1960. Subj: Animals – dogs. Behavior – growing up. Sleep.

Cibula, Matt S. *The contrary kid* ill. by Brian Strassburg. Zino Pr., 1995. ISBN 1-55933-177-1 Subj: Character traits – being different. Rhyming text.

Slumgullion, the executive pig: a tale told in rhyme of a swine in his prime ill. by Tamara L. Boudreau. Zino Pr., 1994. ISBN 1-55933-149-6 Subj: Animals – pigs. Rhyming text. Self-concept.

What's up with you, Taquandra Fu? ill. by Brian Strassburg. Zino Pr., 1997. ISBN 1-55933-212-3 Subj: Behavior. Character traits – individuality. Humor. School.

Ciliotta, Claire. *"Why am I going to the hospital?"* by Claire Ciliotta and Carole Livingston; ill. by Dick Wilson. Lyle Stuart, 1982. ISBN 0-8184-0316-0 Subj: Hospitals. Illness.

Cimarusti, Marie Torres. *Peek-a-moo* ill. by Stephanie Peterson. Dutton, 1998. ISBN 0-525-46083-7 Subj: Activities – playing. Animals. Farms. Format, unusual – toy and movable books.

Cimino, Maria. *Who's there? Open the door* (Munari, Bruno)

Cisneros, Sandra. *Hairs = Pelitos* tr. and ill. by Terry Ybáñez. Knopf, 1994. ISBN 0-679-96171-2 Subj: Ethnic groups in the U.S. – Hispanic Americans. Family life. Foreign languages. Hair.

City ill. by Roser Capdevila. Firefly, 1986. ISBN 0-920303-45-5 Subj: City. Format, unusual – board books. Wordless.

Civardi, Anne. *Potty time* ill. by Jonathan Langley. Simon & Schuster, 1988. ISBN 0-671-65896-4 Subj: Behavior – growing up. Toilet training.

Things people do ill. by Stephen Cartwright; designed by Roger Priddy. Usborne, 1985. ISBN 0-86020-864-8 Subj: Activities – working. Careers. Games. Islands.

The wacky book of witches ill. by Graham Philpot. Cartwheel, 1991. ISBN 0-590-45094-8 Subj: Rhyming text. Witches.

Claret, Maria. *The chocolate rabbit* ill. by author. Barron's, 1985. ISBN 0-416-48260-0 Subj: Animals – rabbits. Behavior – carelessness. Eggs. Holidays – Easter.

Melissa Mouse ill. by author. Barron's, 1985. ISBN 0-8120-5623-X Subj: Animals – mice. Weddings.

Clark, Ann Nolan. *In my mother's house* ill. by Velino Herrera. Viking, 1941. Subj: Caldecott award honor books. Family life. Indians of North America – Tewa.

The little Indian basket maker ill. by Harrison Begay. Melmont, 1955. Subj: Activities – working. Indians of North America – Papago.

The little Indian pottery maker ill. by Don Perceval. Melmont, 1955. Subj: Activities – working. Indians of North America – Pueblo.

Tia Maria's garden ill. by Ezra Jack Keats. Viking, 1963. Subj: Desert.

Clark, Elizabeth. *Father Christmas and the donkey* ill. by Jan Ormerod. Viking, 1993. ISBN 0-670-84811-5 Subj: Animals – donkeys. Character traits – kindness to animals. Holidays – Christmas. Santa Claus.

Clark, Emma Chichester. *see* Chichester Clark, Emma

Clark, Garel. *see* Garelick, May

Clark, Gus. *How many days to my birthday?* ill. by author. Lothrop, 1992. ISBN 0-688-11237-4 Subj: Birthdays. Character traits – patience. Character traits – questioning. Days of the week, months of the year.

Clark, Harry. *The first story of the whale* ill. by author. Houghton Mifflin, 1938. Subj: Animals – whales. Games. Science.

Clark, Leonard. *Drums and trumpets: poetry for the youngest* ill. by Heather Copley. Bodley Head, 1979. ISBN 0-370-01010-X Subj: Nursery rhymes. Poetry.

Clark, Margaret. *The best of Æsop's fables* (Æsop)

Clark, Roberta. *Why?* ill. by Lois Axeman. Childrens Pr., 1983. ISBN 0-516-06594-7 Subj: Character traits – curiosity. Character traits – questioning.

Clark, Sue. *Bodies* ill. by author. Hyperion, 1994. ISBN 0-7868-0035-6 (set) Subj: Anatomy. Format, unusual – board books. Self-concept.

Clothes ill. by author. Hyperion, 1994. ISBN 0-7868-0035-6 (set) Subj: Clothing. Format, unusual – board books. Self-concept.

Faces ill. by author. Hyperion, 1994. ISBN 0-7868-0035-6 (set) Subj: Anatomy – faces. Format, unusual – board books. Self-concept.

Feelings ill. by author. Hyperion, 1994. ISBN 0-7868-0035-6 (set) Subj: Emotions. Format, unusual – board books. Self-concept.

Clarke, Gus. *Along came Eric* ill. by author. Lothrop, 1991. ISBN 0-688-10301-4 Subj: Babies. Family life – brothers. Family life – new sibling. Sibling rivalry.

Eddie and Teddy ill. by author. Lothrop, 1991. ISBN 0-688-10039-2 Subj: Friendship. School – first day. Toys – bears.

Ten green monsters ill. by author. Western, 1994. ISBN 0-307-17605-3 Subj: Counting, numbers. Format, unusual – toy and movable books. Monsters. Rhyming text.

Claude-Lafontaine, Pascale. *Monsieur Bussy, the celebrated hamster* ill. by Annick Delhumeau. McGraw-Hill, 1968. Delhumeau's name appeared first on the title page of the French ed. pub. under title: Bussy, le hamster doré. Subj: Animals – hamsters. Character traits – ambition.

Claverie, Jean. *The party* ill. by author. Crown, 1986. ISBN 0-517-56026-7 Subj: Behavior – misbehavior. Parties.

The picnic ill. by author. Crown, 1986. ISBN 0-517-56025-9 Subj: Activities – picnicking. Weather – rain.

Shopping ill. by author. Crown, 1986. ISBN 0-517-56024-0 Subj: Family life. Shopping.

Working ill. by author. Crown, 1986. ISBN 0-517-56021-6 Subj: Activities – working. Family life – fathers. Weather – snow.

Claxton, Ernest. *A child's grace* (Burdekin, Harold)

Clay, Helen. *Ants* (Clay, Pat)

Beetles (Clay, Pat)

Clay, Pat. *Ants* by Pat and Helen Clay; ill. with photos. Global Lib. Mktg. Serv., 1984. ISBN 0-7136-2386-1 Subj: Insects – ants. Nature. Science.

Beetles by Pat and Helen Clay; photos by authors. A & C Black, 1983. Subj: Insects – beetles. Science.

Clayton, Elaine. *Ella's trip to the museum* ill. by author. Crown, 1996. ISBN 0-517-70081-6 Subj: Activities – dancing. Art. Magic. Museums.

Pup in school ill. by author. Crown, 1993. ISBN 0-517-59086-7 Subj: Animals – dogs. Behavior – bullying. Character traits – meanness. Friendship. School.

The yeoman's daring daughter and the princes in the tower ill. by author. Crown, 1999. ISBN 0-517-70985-6 Subj: Behavior – running away. Foreign lands – England. Royalty – princes.

Clayton, Gordon. *Lamb* Written by Angela Royston; ill. by Jane Cradock-Watson; photos by Gordon Clayton. Lodestar, 1992. ISBN 0-525-67359-8 Subj: Animals – sheep. Behavior – growing up. Birth.

Clearman, Deborah. *The goose's tale* ill. by author. Whispering Coyote, 1996. ISBN 1-879085-85-2 Subj: Activities – flying. Birds – geese.

Cleary, Beverly. *The growing-up feet* ill. by DyAnne DiSalvo-Ryan. Morrow, 1987. ISBN 0-688-06620-8 Subj: Behavior – growing up. Family life. Multiple births – twins.

The hullabaloo ABC ill. by Ted Rand. Morrow, 1998. ISBN 0-688-15183-3 Subj: ABC books. Farms. Noise, sounds. Rhyming text.

The hullabaloo ABC ill. by Earl Thollander. Parnassus, 1960. ISBN 0-8746-6048-3 Subj: ABC books. Farms. Noise, sounds. Rhyming text.

Janet's thingamajigs ill. by DyAnne DiSalvo-Ryan. Morrow, 1987. ISBN 0-688-06618-6 Subj: Behavior – collecting things. Behavior – growing up. Family life. Sibling rivalry.

Lucky Chuck ill. by J. Winslow Higginbottom. Morrow, 1984. ISBN 0-688-02738-5 Subj: Behavior – carelessness. Motorcycles. Safety. Transportation.

Petey's bedtime story ill. by David Small. Morrow, 1993. ISBN 0-688-10661-7 Subj: Bedtime. Family life.

The real hole ill. by DyAnne DiSalvo-Ryan. Morrow, 1986. ISBN 0-688-05851-5 Subj: Activities – digging. Multiple births – twins. Problem solving. Trees.

Two dog biscuits ill. by DyAnne DiSalvo-Ryan. Morrow, 1986. ISBN 0-688-05848-5 Subj: Animals – cats. Animals – dogs. Multiple births – twins.

Cleaver, Elizabeth. *ABC* ill. by author. Atheneum, 1985. ISBN 0-689-31072-2 Subj: ABC books.

The enchanted caribou ill. by author. Atheneum, 1985. ISBN 0-689-31170-2 Subj: Animals – reindeer. Folk and fairy tales. Foreign lands – Canada. Indians of North America – Inuit. Magic. Puppets.

Clem, Tricia. *Great beginnings: the story of God's creation* (Foreman, Juli)

Clemens, Samuel. *see* Twain, Mark

Clément, Claude. *Be careful, Little Antelope* (Jensen, Patricia)

Be patient, Little Chick (Jensen, Patricia)

Gentle Little Lion (Jensen, Patricia)

Go to sleep, little groundhog (Jensen, Patricia)

The hungry duckling ill. by Marcelle Geneste. Reader's Digest, 1992. ISBN 0-89577-418-6 Subj: Animals. Birds – ducks. Character traits – being different. Food.

Kitty's special job (Jensen, Patricia)

Little Donkey learns to help (Jensen, Patricia)

Little Squirrel's special nest (Jensen, Patricia)

The man who lit the stars ill. by John Howe. Little, 1992. ISBN 0-316-14741-9 Subj: Homeless. Stars.

The painter and the wild swans ill. by Frédéric Clément. Dial, 1986. ISBN 0-8037-0268-X Subj: Birds – swans. Folk and fairy tales.

The voice of the wood ill. by Frédéric Clément. Dial, 1989. ISBN 0-8037-0635-9 Subj: Music. Trees.

Clement, Gary. *Just stay put: a Chelm story* ill. by author. Firefly, 1996. ISBN 0-88899-239-4 Subj: Folk and fairy tales. Foreign lands – Poland. Jewish culture.

Clement, Rod. *Frank's great museum adventure* ill. by author. HarperCollins, 1999. ISBN 0-06-027674-6 Subj: Animals – dogs. Museums.

Grandpa's teeth ill. by author. HarperCollins, 1998. ISBN 0-06-027671-1 Subj: Family life – grandfathers. Mystery stories. Teeth.

Just another ordinary day ill. by author. Harper-Collins, 1997. ISBN 0-06-027666-5 Subj: Animals. Humor. School.

Clements, Andrew. *The beast and the boy* (Mostacchi, Massimo)

Brave as a tiger (Palecek, Libuse)

Bright Christmas: an angel remembers ill. by Kate Kiesler. Clarion, 1996. ISBN 0-395-72096-6 Subj: Angels. Holidays – Christmas. Religion – Nativity.

The Christmas teddy bear (Gantschev, Ivan)

A dog's best friend (Mostacchi, Massimo)

Double trouble in Walla Walla ill. by Sal Murdocca. Millbrook, 1997. ISBN 0-7613-0275-1 Subj: Humor. Language. School.

Good morning, good night (Gantschev, Ivan)

Little pig, big trouble (Tharlet, Eve)

Mother Earth's counting book ill. by Lonni Sue Johnson. Picture Book Studio, 1990. ISBN 0-88708-138-X Subj: Counting, numbers. Earth.

Santa's secret helper ill. by Debrah Santini. Picture Book Studio, 1990. ISBN 0-88708-136-3 Subj: Character traits – helpfulness. Holidays – Christmas. Santa Claus.

Temple cat ill. by Kate Kiesler. Clarion, 1996. ISBN 0-395-69842-1 Subj: Animals – cats. Behavior – running away. Foreign lands – Egypt.

Temple cat ill. by Alan Marks. Picture Book Studio, 1991. ISBN 0-88708-184-3 Subj: Animals – cats. Behavior – running away. Foreign lands – Egypt.

Where is Mr. Mole? (Gantschev, Ivan)

Workshop ill. by David Wisniewski. Clarion, 1998. ISBN 0-395-85579-9 Subj: Merry-go-rounds. Tools.

Clemesha, David. *Trashy town* (Zimmerman, Andrea Griffing)

Clemson, David. *Patterns* (Bulloch, Ivan)

Clemson, Wendy. *Patterns* (Bulloch, Ivan)

Cleveland, David. *The April rabbits* ill. by Nurit Karlin. Coward, 1978. ISBN 0-698-20463-8 Subj: Animals – rabbits. Counting, numbers.

Cleveland-Peck, Patricia. *City cat, country cat* ill. by Gilly Marklew. Morrow, 1992. ISBN 0-688-11645-0 Subj: Animals – cats. Behavior – sharing. City. Country. Pets.

Clewes, Dorothy. *Happiest day* ill. by Sofia. Coward, 1959. Subj: Emotions – loneliness. School.

Henry Hare's boxing match ill. by Patricia W. Turner. Coward, 1950. Subj: Animals. Behavior – imitation.

Hide and seek ill. by Sofia. Coward, 1960. Subj: Farms.

The wild wood ill. by Irene Hawkins. Coward, 1948. Subj: Animals. Character traits – kindness to animals.

Clifford, David. *Your face is a picture* (Clifford, Eth)

Clifford, Eth. *A bear before breakfast* ill. by Kelly Oechsli. Putnam, 1962. Subj: Communication. Language.

Red is never a mouse ill. by Bill Heckler. Bobbs-Merrill, 1960. Subj: Concepts – color. Poetry.

Your face is a picture by Eth and David Clifford; photos by David Clifford; ed. consultant: Leo Fay. E. C. Seale, 1963. Subj: Emotions. Ethnic groups in the U.S.

Clifton, Lucille. *All us come cross the water* ill. by John Steptoe. Holt, 1973. ISBN 0-03-091976-2 Subj: Character traits – pride. Ethnic groups in the U.S. – African Americans. School.

Amifika ill. by Thomas di Grazia. Dutton, 1977. ISBN 0-525-25548-6 Subj: Emotions – fear. Ethnic groups in the U.S. – African Americans. Family life. Family life – fathers.

The boy who didn't believe in spring ill. by Brinton Turkle. Dutton, 1973. ISBN 0-525-27145-7 Subj: City. Ethnic groups in the U.S. – African Americans. Seasons – spring.

Don't you remember? ill. by Evaline Ness. Dutton, 1973. ISBN 0-525-28840-6 Subj: Birthdays. Ethnic groups in the U.S. – African Americans. Family life. Memories, memory.

Everett Anderson's Christmas coming ill. by Evaline Ness. Holt, 1971. ISBN 0-03-080219-9 Subj: City. Ethnic groups in the U.S. – African Americans. Holidays – Christmas. Poetry.

Everett Anderson's friend ill. by Ann Grifalconi. Holt, 1992. ISBN 0-8050-2246-5 Subj: Ethnic groups in the U.S. – African Americans. Friendship. Rhyming text.

Everett Anderson's goodbye ill. by Ann Grifalconi. Holt, 1988, 1983. ISBN 0-8050-0800-4 Subj: Death. Emotions – grief. Emotions – love. Ethnic groups in the U.S. – African Americans. Family life. Rhyming text.

Everett Anderson's nine months long ill. by Ann Grifalconi. Holt, 1987, 1970. ISBN 0-03-043536-6 Subj: Babies. Ethnic groups in the U.S. – African Americans. Family life – new sibling. Rhyming text.

Everett Anderson's 1-2-3 ill. by Ann Grifalconi. Holt, 1977. ISBN 0-03-017441-4 Subj: Ethnic groups in the U.S. – African Americans. Family life. Rhyming text.

Everett Anderson's year ill. by Ann Grifalconi. Holt, 1992. ISBN 0-8050-2310-0 Subj: Ethnic groups in the U.S. – African Americans. Rhyming text. Seasons.

Good, says Jerome ill. by Stephanie Douglas. Dutton, 1973. ISBN 0-525-30865-2 Subj: Emotions –

fear. Ethnic groups in the U.S. – African Americans. Family life. Moving.

My brother fine with me ill. by Moneta Barnett. Holt, 1975. ISBN 0-03-014171-0 Subj: Behavior – running away. Ethnic groups in the U.S. – African Americans. Family life. Sibling rivalry.

My friend Jacob ill. by Thomas di Grazia. Dutton, 1980. ISBN 0-525-35487-5 Subj: Character traits – helpfulness. Ethnic groups in the U.S. – African Americans. Friendship. Handicaps.

Some of the days of Everett Anderson ill. by Evaline Ness. Holt, 1987, 1970. ISBN 0-03-084404-5 Subj: Days of the week, months of the year. Ethnic groups in the U.S. – African Americans. Family life. Poetry.

Three wishes ill. by Stephanie Douglas. Viking, 1976. ISBN 0-670-71063-6 Subj: Behavior – wishing. Ethnic groups in the U.S. – African Americans. Friendship.

Three wishes ill. by Michael Hays. Doubleday, 1992. ISBN 0-385-30497-8 Subj: Behavior – wishing. Ethnic groups in the U.S. – African Americans. Friendship.

Climo, Lindee. *Chester's barn* ill. by author. Tundra, 1982. ISBN 0-88776-132-1 Subj: Barns. Farms. Foreign lands – Canada.

Clyde ill. by author. Tundra, 1986. ISBN 0-88776-185-2 Subj: Animals – horses, ponies. Behavior – seeking better things. Machines.

Climo, Shirley. *The adventure of Walter* ill. by Ingrid Fetz. Atheneum, 1965. Subj: Animals – whales. Character traits – curiosity.

The cobweb Christmas ill. by Joe Lasker. Crowell, 1982. ISBN 0-690-04216-7 Subj: Animals. Holidays – Christmas. Magic. Spiders.

The Egyptian Cinderella ill. by Ruth Heller. HarperCollins, 1989. ISBN 0-690-04824-6 Subj: Folk and fairy tales. Foreign lands – Egypt. Royalty. Sibling rivalry.

The Irish Cinderlad ill. by Loretta Krupinski. HarperCollins, 1996. ISBN 0-06-024397-X Subj: Animals – bulls, cows. Folk and fairy tales. Foreign lands – Ireland.

King of the birds ill. by Ruth Heller. HarperCollins, 1988. ISBN 0-690-04623-5 Subj: Birds. Character traits – cleverness. Royalty.

The Korean Cinderella ill. by Ruth Heller. HarperCollins, 1993. ISBN 0-06-020433-8 Subj: Folk and fairy tales. Foreign lands – Korea.

The little red ant and the great big crumb: a Mexican fable ill. by Francisco X. Mora. Clarion, 1995. ISBN 0-395-70732-3 Subj: Animals. Foreign lands – Mexico. Insects – ants. Self-concept.

The match between the winds ill. by Roni Shepherd. Macmillan, 1991. ISBN 0-02-719035-8 Subj: Folk and fairy tales. Foreign lands – Borneo. Weather – wind.

Stolen thunder: a Norse myth ill. by Alexander Koshkin. Clarion, 1994. ISBN 0-395-64368-6 Subj: Folk and fairy tales. Foreign lands. Mythical creatures. Weather – thunder.

Clinton, Susan. *I can be an architect.* Childrens Pr., 1986. ISBN 0-516-01890-6 Subj: Careers – architects.

Clise, Michele Durkson. *Ophelia's bedtime book* photos by Marsha Burns. Viking, 1994. ISBN 0-670-85310-0 Subj: Bedtime. Night. Poetry. Sleep. Toys – bears.

Clithero, Myrtle E. *see* Clithero, Sally

Clithero, Sally. *Beginning-to-read poetry* ill. by Erik Blegvad. Follett, 1967. Subj: Poetry.

Clymer, Eleanor Lowenton. *The tiny little house* ill. by Ingrid Fetz. Atheneum, 1964. Subj: Homes, houses.

A yard for John ill. by Mildred Boyle. McBride, 1943. Subj: Moving.

Clymer, Ted. *The horse and the bad morning* by Ted Clymer and Miska Miles; ill. by Leslie Holt Morrill. Dutton, 1982. ISBN 0-525-45103-X Subj: Animals. Behavior – dissatisfaction. Problem solving.

Coats, Laura Jane. *Alphabet garden* ill. by author. Macmillan, 1993. ISBN 0-02-719042-0 Subj: ABC books. Gardens, gardening.

City cat ill. by author. Macmillan, 1987. ISBN 0-02-719051-X Subj: Animals – cats. City.

Marcella and the moon ill. by author. Macmillan, 1986. ISBN 0-02-719050-1 Subj: Activities – painting. Birds – ducks. Moon.

Mr. Jordan in the park ill. by author. Macmillan, 1988. ISBN 0-02-719053-6 Subj: Behavior – growing up. Old age. Parks.

The oak tree ill. by author. Macmillan, 1987. ISBN 0-02-719052-8 Subj: Trees.

Ten little animals ill. by author. Macmillan, 1990. ISBN 0-02-719054-4 Subj: Animals. Counting, numbers. Rhyming text.

Coats, Lucy. *Bedtime for Rosie Rabbit* (Yee, Patrick)

One hungry baby: a bedtime counting rhyme ill. by Sue Hellard. Crown, 1994. ISBN 0-517-59887-6 Subj: Animals – babies. Babies. Bedtime. Counting, numbers. Rhyming text.

Coatsworth, Elizabeth. *The children come running: UNICEF greeting cards.* Golden Pr., 1961. The illustrations [by Roger Duvoisin and others] . . . first appeared as UNICEF greeting cards. Subj: Holidays – Christmas. Rhyming text. UNICEF.

The giant golden book of cat stories ill. by Feodor Rojankovsky. Simon & Schuster, 1953. Subj: Animals – cats. Folk and fairy tales. Rhyming text.

Good night ill. by José Aruego. Macmillan, 1972. Subj: Bedtime. Stars.

Lonely Maria ill. by Evaline Ness. Pantheon, 1960. Subj: Emotions – loneliness. Family life – grandfathers. Islands.

A peaceable kingdom, and other poems ill. by Fritz Eichenberg. Pantheon, 1958. Subj: Animals. Poetry.

Pika and the roses ill. by Kurt Wiese. Pantheon, 1959. Subj: Animals – rabbits. Character traits – cleverness.

Song of the camels: a Christmas poem ill. by Anna Vojtech. North-South, 1997. ISBN 1-55858-812-4 Subj: Animals – camels. Holidays – Christmas. Poetry. Religion.

Under the green willow ill. by Janina Domanska. Macmillan, 1971. ISBN 0-688-03846-8 Subj: Birds. Fish. Food.

Cobb, Annie. *Wheels!* ill. by Davy Jones. Random House, 1996. ISBN 0-679-96445-2 Subj: Rhyming text. Wheels.

Cobb, Vicki. *Feeding yourself* ill. by Marylin Hafner. HarperCollins, 1989. ISBN 0-397-32325-5 Subj: Behavior – growing up.

Getting dressed ill. by Marylin Hafner. HarperCollins, 1989. ISBN 0-397-32143-0 Subj: Behavior – growing up. Clothing.

How the doctor knows you're fine ill. by Anthony Ravielli. Lippincott, 1973. ISBN 0-397-31240-7 Subj: Careers – doctors. Health and fitness.

Keeping clean ill. by Marylin Hafner. HarperCollins, 1989. ISBN 0-397-32313-1 Subj: Character traits – cleanliness.

Lots of rot ill. by Brian Schatell. Lippincott, 1981. ISBN 0-397-31939-8 Subj: Science.

Writing it down ill. by Marylin Hafner. HarperCollins, 1989. ISBN 0-397-32327-1 Subj: Activities – writing.

Cobbett, Richard. *see* Pluckrose, Henry Arthur

Cober, Alan E. *Cober's choice* ill. by author. Dutton, 1979. ISBN 0-525-28065-0 Subj: Animals. Art.

Coburn, Jewell Reinhart. *Angkat: the Cambodian Cinderella* ill. by Eddie Flotte. Shen's Books, 1998. ISBN 1-885008-09-0 Subj: Family life – step families. Folk and fairy tales. Foreign lands – Cambodia. Royalty – princes. Sibling rivalry.

Jouanah: a Hmong Cinderella adapt. by Jewell Reinhart Coburn with Tzexa Cherta Lee; ill. by Anne Sibley O'Brien. Shen's Books, 1996. ISBN 1-885008-01-5 Subj: Family life – step families. Folk and fairy tales. Foreign lands. Royalty – princes. Sibling rivalry.

Cocagnac, A. M. (Augustin Maurice). *The three trees of the Samurai* adapt. from a Japanese no play; ill. by Alain Le Foll. Dial, 1970. ISBN 0-8252-0043-1 Subj: Folk and fairy tales. Foreign lands – Japan.

Cocca-Leffler, Maryann. *Ice-cold birthday* ill. by author. Grosset, 1992. ISBN 0-448-40381-1 Subj: Birthdays. Character traits – luck. Parties. Weather – snow. Weather – storms.

Missing: one stuffed rabbit ill. by author. Albert Whitman, 1998. ISBN 0-8075-5161-9 Subj: Animals – rabbits. Behavior – lost. School. Toys.

Mr. Tanen's ties ill. by author. Albert Whitman, 1999. ISBN 0-8075-5301-8 Subj: Careers – school principals. Clothing – neckties. School.

Wednesday is spaghetti day ill. by author. Scholastic, 1990. ISBN 0590428942 Subj: Activities – cooking. Animals – cats. Days of the week, months of the year. Food.

Cock Robin. *The courtship, merry marriage, and feast of Cock Robin and Jenny Wren: to which is added the doleful death of Cock Robin* ill. by Barbara Cooney. Scribners, 1965. Subj: Animals. Birds – robins. Birds – wrens. Death. Nursery rhymes. Weddings.

Who killed Cock Robin? ill. by William Stobbs. Oxford Univ. Pr., 1990. ISBN 0-19-279862-6 Subj: Animals. Birds – robins. Birds – wrens. Death. Format, unusual – board books. Nursery rhymes.

Coco, Eugene Bradley. *The fiddler's son* ill. by Robert James Sabuda. Green Tiger Pr., 1988. ISBN 0-88138-111-X Subj: Music.

The wishing well ill. by Robert James Sabuda. Green Tiger Pr., 1988. ISBN 0-88138-112-8 Subj: Behavior – greed. Behavior – wishing. Circular tales. Magic.

Coe, Lloyd. *Charcoal* ill. by author. Crowell, 1946. Subj: Animals – sheep.

Coerr, Eleanor. *The big balloon race* ill. by Carolyn Croll. HarperCollins, 1992. ISBN 0-06-021353-1 Subj: Activities – ballooning.

Chang's paper pony ill. by Deborah Kogan Ray. HarperCollins, 1988. ISBN 0-06-021329-9 Subj: Animals – horses, ponies. Ethnic groups in the U.S. – Chinese Americans.

The Josefina story quilt ill. by Bruce Degen. HarperCollins, 1986. ISBN 0-06-021349-3 Subj: Activities – traveling. Birds – chickens. Pets. Quilts.

Sadako ill. by Ed Young. Putnam, 1993. ISBN 0-399-21771-1 Subj: Birds – cranes. Death. Foreign lands – Japan. Illness. War.

Coffelt, Nancy. *The dog who cried woof* ill. by author. Harcourt, 1995. ISBN 0-15-200201-4 Subj: Animals – cats. Animals – dogs. Noise, sounds.

Dogs in space ill. by author. Harcourt, 1993. ISBN 0-15-200440-8 Subj: Animals – dogs. Science. Space and space ships.

Good night, Sigmund ill. by author. Harcourt, 1992. ISBN 0-15-200464-5 Subj: Activities – playing. Animals – cats. Pets.

Coffey, Maria. *A cat in a kayak* ill. by Eugenie Fernandes. Annick, 1998. ISBN 1-55037-509-1 Subj:

Animals. Animals – cats. Behavior – dissatisfaction. Pets.

A seal in the family ill. by Eugenie Fernandes. Annick, 1999. ISBN 1-55037-581-4 Subj: Animals – cats. Animals – seals. Careers – veterinarians. Character traits – kindness to animals.

Cohen, Barbara. *The binding of Isaac* ill. by Charles Mikolaycak. Lothrop, 1978. ISBN 0-688-51830-3 Subj: Religion.

The chocolate wolf ill. by David Ray. Philomel, 1996. ISBN 0-399-21961-7 Subj: Animals – rats. Animals – wolves. Behavior – running away.

The demon who would not die ill. by Anatoly Ivanov. Atheneum, 1982. ISBN 0-689-30917-1 Subj: Folk and fairy tales. Foreign lands – Russia. Monsters.

The donkey's story ill. by Susan Jeanne Cohen. Lothrop, 1988. ISBN 0-688-04105-1 Subj: Animals – donkeys. Religion.

Even higher ill. by Anatoly Ivanov. Lothrop, 1987. ISBN 0-688-06453-1 Subj: Character traits – generosity. Holidays. Jewish culture.

First fast ill. by Martin Lemelman. UAHC Pr., 1987. ISBN 0-8074-0354-7 Subj: Holidays – Yom Kippur. Jewish culture. Religion.

Gooseberries to oranges ill. by Beverly Brodsky McDermott. Lothrop, 1982. ISBN 0-688-00691-4 Subj: Jewish culture. Moving.

Here come the Purim players! ill. by Beverly Brodsky McDermott. Lothrop, 1984. ISBN 0-688-02108-5 Subj: Folk and fairy tales. Holidays – Purim. Jewish culture. Middle Ages.

Here come the Purim players! ill. by Shoshana Mekibel. UAHC Pr., 1998. ISBN 0-8074-0645-7 Subj: Foreign lands – Czechoslovakia. Holidays – Purim. Jewish culture. Religion.

Make a wish, Molly ill. by Jan Naimo Jones. Doubleday, 1994. ISBN 0-385-31079-X Subj: Behavior – misunderstanding. Birthdays. Ethnic groups in the U.S. – Russian Americans. Friendship. Jewish culture. Parties.

Cohen, Burton. *Nelson makes a face* ill. by William Schroder. Lothrop, 1978. ISBN 0-688-51850-8 Subj: Character traits – appearance.

Cohen, Carol L. *Wake up, groundhog!* ill. by author. Crown, 1975. ISBN 0-517-51693-4 Subj: Animals – groundhogs. Clocks, watches. Hibernation. Holidays – Groundhog Day. Seasons – spring.

Cohen, Caron Lee. *Bronco dogs* ill. by Roni Shepherd. Dutton, 1991. ISBN 0-525-44721-0 Subj: Animals – dogs. Cowboys. Crime. Ghosts. U.S. history – frontier and pioneer life.

The mud pony: a traditional Skidi Pawnee tale ill. by Shonto Begay. Scholastic, 1988. ISBN 0-590-41525-5 Subj: Animals – horses, ponies. Folk and fairy tales. Indians of North America – Pawnee.

Pigeon, pigeon ill. by G. Brian Karas. Dutton, 1992. ISBN 0-525-44866-7 Subj: Animals. Concepts – perspective. Zoos.

Renata, Whizbrain and the ghost ill. by Blanche Sims. Atheneum, 1987. ISBN 0-689-31271-1 Subj: Character traits – cleverness. Ghosts. Tall tales.

Sally Ann Thunder Ann Whirlwind Crockett ill. by Ariane Dewey. Greenwillow, 1985. ISBN 0-688-04007-1 Subj: Behavior – trickery. Tall tales.

Three yellow dogs ill. by Peter Sis. Greenwillow, 1986. ISBN 0-688-06231-8 Subj: Animals – dogs. Language.

Where's the fly? ill. by Nancy Barnet. Greenwillow, 1996. ISBN 0-688-14045-9 Subj: Concepts – perspective.

Whiffle Squeek ill. by Ted Rand. Dodd, 1987. ISBN 0-396-08999-2 Subj: Animals – cats. Monsters. Rhyming text. Sea and seashore.

Cohen, Daniel. *America's very own monsters* ill. by Tom Huffman. Dodd, 1982. ISBN 0-396-08069-3 Subj: Monsters.

Dinosaurs ill. by Jean Zallinger. Doubleday, 1987. ISBN 0-385-23415-5 Subj: Dinosaurs.

Cohen, Miriam. *Bee my Valentine!* ill. by Lillian Hoban. Greenwillow, 1978. ISBN 0-688-84129-5 Subj: Holidays – Valentine's Day. School.

Best friends ill. by Lillian Hoban. Aladdin, 1989, c1971. ISBN 0-689-71334-7 Subj: Friendship. School.

Don't eat too much turkey! ill. by Lillian Hoban. Greenwillow, 1987. ISBN 0-688-07142-2 Subj: Behavior – sharing. School.

Down in the subway ill. by Melanie Hope Greenberg. DK, 1998. ISBN 0-7894-2510-6 Subj: City. Foreign lands – Caribbean Islands. Imagination. Songs. Trains.

First grade takes a test ill. by Lillian Hoban. Greenwillow, 1980. ISBN 0-688-84265-8 Subj: Friendship. School.

It's George! ill. by Lillian Hoban. Greenwillow, 1988. ISBN 0-688-06813-8 Subj: Character traits – being different. School.

Jim meets the thing ill. by Lillian Hoban. Greenwillow, 1981. ISBN 0-688-00617-5 Subj: Behavior – growing up. Emotions – fear. Monsters. School.

Jim's dog Muffins ill. by Lillian Hoban. Greenwillow, 1984. ISBN 0-688-02565-X Subj: Animals – dogs. Death. Emotions – grief. Pets.

Liar, liar, pants on fire! ill. by Lillian Hoban. Greenwillow, 1985. ISBN 0-688-04245-7 Subj: Behavior – lying. Character traits – generosity. Friendship. School.

Lost in the museum ill. by Lillian Hoban. Greenwillow, 1979. ISBN 0-688-84187-2 Subj: Behavior – lost. Museums. School.

Mimmy and Sophie ill. by Thomas F. Yezerski. Farrar, 1998. ISBN 0-374-34988-6 Subj: Ethnic groups in the U.S. – Russian Americans. Family life. Family life – sisters. Immigrants.

The new teacher ill. by Lillian Hoban. Macmillan, 1972. ISBN 0-02-042390-X Subj: School.

No good in art ill. by Lillian Hoban. Greenwillow, 1980. ISBN 0-688-80234-6 Subj: Art. School. Self-concept.

The real-skin rubber monster mask ill. by Lillian Hoban. Greenwillow, 1990. ISBN 0-688-09123-7 Subj: Emotions – fear. Holidays – Halloween. Masks. School.

See you in second grade! ill. by Lillian Hoban. Greenwillow, 1989. ISBN 0-688-07139-2 Subj: Friendship. School. Sea and seashore.

See you tomorrow ill. by Lillian Hoban. Greenwillow, 1983. ISBN 0-688-01805-X Subj: Handicaps – blindness. School. Senses – seeing.

So what? ill. by Lillian Hoban. Greenwillow, 1982. ISBN 0-688-01203-5 Subj: School. Self-concept.

Starring first grade ill. by Lillian Hoban. Greenwillow, 1985. ISBN 0-688-04030-6 Subj: Behavior – misbehavior. School. Theater.

Tough Jim ill. by Lillian Hoban. Macmillan, 1974. ISBN 0-02-722760-X Subj: Behavior – bullying. Parties. School.

When will I read? ill. by Lillian Hoban. Greenwillow, 1977. ISBN 0-688-84073-6 Subj: Activities – reading. School.

Will I have a friend? ill. by Lillian Hoban. Macmillan, 1967. ISBN 0-689-71333-9 Subj: Ethnic groups in the U.S. Friendship. School – first day.

Cohen, Nora. *From apple to zipper* ill. by Donna Kern. Aladdin, 1993. ISBN 0-689-71708-3 Subj: ABC books. Rhyming text.

Cohen, Paul. *Creepy crawly critter riddles* (Bernstein, Joanne E.)

What was the wicked witch's real name? and other character riddles (Bernstein, Joanne E.)

Cohen, Peter Zachary. *Authorized autumn charts of the Upper Red Canoe River country* ill. by Tomie de Paola. Atheneum, 1972. Subj: ABC books. Boats, ships. Games. Seasons – fall.

Olson's meat pies trans. by Richard E. Fisher, ill. by Olof Landström. Farrar, 1989. ISBN 9-129-59180-5 Subj: Behavior – mistakes. Food.

Cohen, Ron. *My dad's baseball* ill. by author. Lothrop, 1994. ISBN 0-688-12391-0 Subj: Family life – fathers. Sports – baseball.

Cohn, Janice I. *I had a friend named Peter: talking to children about the death of a friend* ill. by Gail Owens. Morrow, 1987. ISBN 0-688-06686-0 Subj: Death. Emotions – grief. Friendship.

Molly's rosebush ill. by Gail Owens. Albert Whitman, 1994. ISBN 0-8075-5213-5 Subj: Babies. Death. Emotions – grief. Family life. Plants.

"Why did it happen?" helping young children cope in a violent world ill. by Gail Owens. Morrow, 1994. ISBN 0-688-12313-9 Subj: Behavior – stealing. Crime. Emotions – anger. Violence, nonviolence.

Cohn, Norma. *Brother and sister* ill. by author. Oxford Univ. Pr., 1942. Subj: Animals – cats. Sports – swimming.

Coker, Gylbert. *Naptime* ill. by author. Delacorte, 1978. ISBN 0-440-06304-3 Subj: School. Sleep.

Colby, C. B. (Carroll Burleigh). *Who lives there?* ill. by author. Atheneum, 1953. Subj: Animals. Birds. Homes, houses. Insects. Science.

Who went there? ill. by author. Atheneum, 1953. Subj: Animals. Birds. Reptiles. Science.

Coldrey, Jennifer. *Danger colors* (Oxford Scientific Films)

Hide and seek (Oxford Scientific Films)

Penguins photos by Douglas Allan and others. André Deutsch, 1983. ISBN 0-233-97524-1 Subj: Birds – penguins.

The world of chickens ill. with photos. Gareth Stevens, 1987. ISBN 1-55532-071-6 Subj: Birds – chickens. Science.

The world of crabs photos by Oxford Scientific Films. Gareth Stevens, 1986. ISBN 1-55532-063-5 Subj: Crustaceans. Science.

The world of frogs photos by Oxford Scientific Films. Gareth Stevens, 1986. ISBN 1-55532-024-4 Subj: Frogs and toads. Science.

The world of rabbits photos by Oxford Scientific Films. Gareth Stevens, 1986. ISBN 1-55532-064-3 Subj: Animals – rabbits. Science.

The world of squirrels photos by Oxford Scientific Films. Gareth Stevens, 1986. ISBN 1-55532-065-1 Subj: Animals – squirrels. Science.

Cole, Annette. *see* Steiner, Barbara (Annette)

Cole, Babette. *Babette Cole's beastly birthday book* by Babette Cole with Ron Van der Meer; ill. by Babette Cole. Doubleday, 1991. ISBN 0-385-41679-2 Subj: Birthdays. Format, unusual – toy and movable books. Rhyming text.

Babette Cole's brother ill. by author; paper engineered by Raphael Rangel. WH Books, 1997. ISBN 0-4348-0101-1 Subj: Family life – brothers. Format, unusual – toy and movable books. Rhyming text.

Babette Cole's ponies ill. by author; paper engineered by Bruce Reifel. Warner, 1995. ISBN 0-4469-1071-6 Subj: Animals – horses, ponies. Format, unusual – toy and movable books. Rhyming text.

The bad good manners book ill. by author. Dial, 1996. ISBN 0-8037-2006-8 Subj: Etiquette. Rhyming text.

Bad habits! or, The taming of Lucretzia Crum ill. by author. Dial, 1999. ISBN 0-8037-2432-2 Subj: Behavior – misbehavior. School.

Cupid ill. by author. Putnam, 1990. ISBN 0-399-22215-4 Subj: Emotions – love. Mythical creatures.

Dad ill. by author; paper engineered by Bruce Reifel. WH Books, 1997. ISBN 0-4348-0100-3 Subj: Family life – fathers. Format, unusual – toy and movable books. Rhyming text.

Dr. Dog ill. by author. Knopf, 1997. ISBN 0-679-86720-1 Subj: Animals – dogs. Character traits – cleanliness. Health and fitness. Hygiene.

Don't go out tonight ill. by author. Doubleday, 1982. Folding book; 31 x 127 cm. full size, folded to 31 cm. ISBN 0-385-18090-X Subj: Format, unusual – toy and movable books. Illness – measles. Witches.

The hairy book ill. by author. Random House, 1985. ISBN 0-394-97026-8 Subj: Hair. Rhyming text.

Hurray for Ethelyn ill. by author. Little, 1991. ISBN 0-316-15189-0 Subj: Animals – rats. Behavior – bullying. Emotions – envy, jealousy.

King Change-A-Lot ill. by author. Putnam, 1989. ISBN 0-399-21670-7 Subj: Behavior – dissatisfaction. Royalty – kings. Royalty – princes.

Mommy laid an egg! or where do babies come from? ill. by author. Chronicle, 1993. ISBN 0-8118-0350-3 Subj: Babies. Birth. Family life. Science.

Mum ill. by author; paper engineered by Renée Jablow. WH Books, 1997. ISBN 0-4348-0099-6 Subj: Family life – mothers. Format, unusual – toy and movable books. Rhyming text.

Nungu and the elephant ill. by author. McGraw-Hill, 1980. ISBN 0-07-011696-2 Subj: Animals – elephants. Foreign lands – Africa. Magic.

Nungu and the hippopotamus ill. by author. McGraw-Hill, 1979. ISBN 0-07-011695-4 Subj: Animals – hippopotamuses. Foreign lands – Africa.

Prince Cinders ill. by author. Putnam, 1988. ISBN 0-399-21502-6 Subj: Folk and fairy tales. Magic. Royalty – princes.

Princess Smartypants ill. by author. Putnam, 1987. ISBN 0-399-21409-7 Subj: Pets. Problem solving. Royalty – princesses.

Silly book ill. by author. Doubleday, 1990. ISBN 0-385-41238-X Subj: Friendship. Rhyming text.

The slimy book ill. by author. Random House, 1986. ISBN 0-394-98166-9 Subj: Dreams. Rhyming text.

The smelly book ill. by author. Simon & Schuster, 1988. ISBN 0-671-65670-8 Subj: Rhyming text. Senses – smelling.

Supermoo! ill. by author. Putnam, 1993. ISBN 0-399-22422-X Subj: Animals – bulls, cows. Ecology. Nature.

Tarzanna! ill. by author. Putnam, 1992. ISBN 0-399-21837-8 Subj: Animals. Behavior – misbehavior. Jungle. Language.

Three cheers for Errol! ill. by author. Putnam, 1989. ISBN 0-399-21671-5 Subj: Animals – rats. Sports.

The trouble with dad ill. by author. Putnam, 1986. ISBN 0-399-21206-X Subj: Activities – working. Family life – fathers. Robots.

The trouble with Gran ill. by author. Putnam, 1987. ISBN 0-399-21428-3 Subj: Family life – grandmothers. Space and space ships.

The trouble with grandad ill. by author. Putnam, 1988. ISBN 0-399-21545-X Subj: Concepts – size. Family life – grandfathers. Gardens, gardening.

The trouble with mom ill. by author. Coward, 1984. ISBN 0-698-20597-9 Subj: Family life – mothers. School. Witches.

The trouble with Uncle ill. by author. Little, 1992. ISBN 0-316-15190-4 Subj: Family life – aunts, uncles. Imagination. Pirates. Sea and seashore.

The un-wedding ill. by author. Knopf, 1997. ISBN 0-679-88898-5 Subj: Divorce. Family life.

Winni Allfours ill. by author. BridgeWater, 1993. ISBN 0-8167-3307-4 Subj: Animals – horses, ponies. Family life.

Cole, Barbara Hancock. *Texas star* ill. by Barbara Minton. Orchard, 1990. ISBN 0-531-08420-5 Subj: Family life. Quilts.

Cole, Brock. *The giant's toe* ill. by author. Farrar, 1986. ISBN 0-374-32559-6 Subj: Anatomy. Folk and fairy tales. Giants.

The king at the door ill. by author. Doubleday, 1979. ISBN 0-385-14719-8 Subj: Behavior – disbelief. Character traits – kindness. Foreign lands – England. Royalty – kings.

Nothing but a pig ill. by author. Doubleday, 1981. ISBN 0-385-17064-5 Subj: Animals – pigs. Behavior – imitation. Behavior – seeking better things. Friendship.

Cole, Davis. *see* Elting, Mary

Cole, Henry. *I took a walk* ill. by author. Greenwillow, 1998. ISBN 0-688-15116-7 Subj: Format, unusual – toy and movable books. Nature.

Jack's garden ill. by author. Greenwillow, 1995. ISBN 0-688-13501-3 Subj: Cumulative tales. Gardens, gardening. Plants.

Cole, Joanna. *Animal sleepyheads: one to ten* ill. by Jeni Bassett. Scholastic, 1988. ISBN 0-590-40919-0 Subj: Animals. Counting, numbers. Rhyming text.

Aren't you forgetting something, Fiona? ill. by Ned Delaney. Parents, 1984. ISBN 0-8193-1121-9 Subj: Animals – elephants. Behavior – forgetfulness.

Big Goof and Little Goof by Joanna and Philip Cole; ill. by M. K. Brown. Scholastic, 1989. ISBN 0-590-41591-3 Subj: Concepts – size. Pets. Seasons.

Bony-legs ill. by Dirk Zimmer. Four Winds, 1983. ISBN 0-590-07882-8 Subj: Folk and fairy tales. Foreign lands – Russia. Magic. Witches.

A calf is born photos by Jerome Wexler. Morrow, 1975. ISBN 0-688-32036-8 Subj: Animals – babies. Animals – bulls, cows. Birth. Science.

A chick hatches photos by Jerome Wexler. Morrow, 1976. ISBN 0-688-32087-2 Subj: Birds – chickens. Science.

The Clown-Arounds ill. by Jerry Smath. Gareth Stevens, 1994. ISBN 0-8368-0995-5 Subj: Clowns, jesters. Contests. Family life. Humor.

The Clown-Arounds go on vacation ill. by Jerry Smath. Parents, 1993. ISBN 0-8368-0966-1 Subj: Activities – vacationing. Behavior – lost. Clowns, jesters. Humor. Riddles.

The Clown-Arounds have a party ill. by Jerry Smath. Parents, 1995. ISBN 0-8368-0999-8 Subj: Clowns, jesters. Emotions – sadness. Family life.

Doctor Change ill. by Donald Carrick. Morrow, 1986. ISBN 0-688-06136-2 Subj: Character traits – cleverness. Folk and fairy tales.

Don't call me names! just right for 4's and 5's ill. by Lynn Munsinger. McKay, 1990. ISBN 0-679-90258-9 Subj: Behavior – bullying. Friendship. Frogs and toads.

Don't tell the whole world ill. by Kate Duke. HarperCollins, 1990. ISBN 0-690-04811-4 Subj: Behavior. Behavior – secrets. Folk and fairy tales. Money.

Evolution ill. by Aliki. Crowell, 1987. ISBN 0-690-04598-0 Subj: Animals. Plants. Science.

Find the hidden insect by Joanna Cole and Jerome Wexler; photos by Jerome Wexler. Morrow, 1979. ISBN 0-688-32203-4 Subj: Insects. Science.

A fish hatches photos by Jerome Wexler. Morrow, 1978. ISBN 0-688-32153-4 Subj: Fish. Science.

Fun on wheels ill. by Whitney Darrow, Jr. Morrow, 1977. ISBN 0-688-32102-X Subj: Activities. Rhyming text. Wheels.

Fun on wheels ill. by Don Gauthier. Delmar, 1990. ISBN 0-8273-4141-5 Subj: Activities. Rhyming text. Wheels.

Get well, Clown-Arounds! ill. by Jerry Smath. Parents, 1983. ISBN 0-8193-1096-4 Subj: Clowns, jesters. Humor. Illness. Riddles.

Get well, gators! (Calmenson, Stephanie)

A gift from Saint Francis: the first crèche ill. by Michèle Lemieux. Morrow, 1989. ISBN 0-688-06503-1 Subj: Character traits – kindness. Religion.

Golly Gump swallowed a fly (Little old lady who swallowed a fly)

How I was adopted: Samantha's story ill. by Maxie Chambliss. Morrow, 1995. ISBN 0-688-11930-1 Subj: Adoption. Family life.

How you were born photos by Margaret Miller. Rev. and expanded ed. Morrow, 1993. ISBN 0-688-12059-8 Subj: Babies. Birth. Family life. Science.

Hungry, hungry sharks ill. by Patricia Wynne. Random House, 1986. ISBN 0-394-97471-9 Subj: Fish – sharks. Science.

I'm a big brother ill. by Maxie Chambliss. Morrow, 1997. ISBN 0-688-14507-8 Subj: Babies. Family life – brothers.

I'm a big sister ill. by Maxie Chambliss. Morrow, 1997. ISBN 0-688-14509-4 Subj: Babies. Family life – sisters.

It's too noisy ill. by Kate Duke. HarperCollins, 1989. ISBN 0-690-04737-1 Subj: Animals. Folk and fairy tales. Humor. Jewish culture. Noise, sounds. Problem solving.

Large as life daytime animals ill. by Kenneth Lilly. Knopf, 1985. ISBN 0-394-97188-4 Subj: Animals.

Large as life nighttime animals ill. by Kenneth Lilly. Knopf, 1985. ISBN 0-394-97189-2 Subj: Animals. Night.

The magic school bus and the electric field trip ill. by Bruce Degen. Scholastic, 1997. ISBN 0-590-44682-7 Subj: Careers – electricians. School.

The magic school bus at the waterworks ill. by Bruce Degen. Scholastic, 1986. ISBN 0-590-40361-3 Subj: School. Water.

The magic school bus in the time of the dinosaurs ill. by Bruce Degen. Scholastic, 1994. ISBN 0-590-44688-6 Subj: Buses. Careers – teachers. Dinosaurs. Magic. School. Science.

The magic school bus inside a beehive ill. by Bruce Degen. Scholastic, 1990. ISBN 0-590-44684-3 Subj: Buses. Careers – teachers. Insects – bees. Magic. School. Science.

The magic school bus inside a hurricane ill. by Bruce Degen. Scholastic, 1995. ISBN 0-590-44686-X Subj: School. Science. Weather – hurricanes.

The magic school bus inside the earth ill. by Bruce Degen. Scholastic, 1987. ISBN 0-590-40759-7 Subj: Careers – geologists. Earth. Rocks. Science.

The magic school bus inside the human body ill. by Bruce Degen. Scholastic, 1989. ISBN 0-590-41426-7 Subj: Anatomy. School. Science.

The magic school bus lost in the solar system ill. by Bruce Degen. Scholastic, 1990. ISBN 0-590-41428-3 Subj: Buses. Careers – teachers. Magic. School. Science. Space and space ships.

The magic school bus on the ocean floor ill. by Bruce Degen. Scholastic, 1992. ISBN 0-590-41430-5 Subj: Buses. Careers – teachers. Magic. School. Science. Sea and seashore.

The magic school bus plants seeds: a book about how living things grow (Relf, Patricia)

The magic school bus shows and tells ill. by Bruce Degen. Scholastic, 1997. ISBN 0-590-92242-4 Subj: Careers – archaeologists. School. Science.

The missing tooth ill. by Marylin Hafner. Random House, 1988. ISBN 0-394-99279-2 Subj: Friendship. Teeth.

Mixed-up magic ill. by True Kelley. Hastings House, 1987. ISBN 0-8038-9298-5 Subj: Behavior – wishing. Magic. Mythical creatures – elves.

Monster and Muffin ill. by Karen Lee Schmidt. Grosset, 1996. ISBN 0-448-41146-6 Subj: Animals – dogs. Friendship. Rebuses.

Monster manners ill. by Jared D. Lee. Scholastic, 1995. ISBN 0-590-40926-3 Subj: Etiquette. Monsters.

My new kitten photos by Margaret Miller. Morrow, 1995. ISBN 0-688-12902-1 Subj: Animals – cats. Friendship.

My puppy is born photos by Margaret Miller. Morrow, 1991. ISBN 0-688-09771-5 Subj: Animals – dogs. Birth. Science.

The new baby at your house photos by Hella Hammid. Morrow, 1998. ISBN 0-688-05807-8 Subj: Babies. Emotions – envy, jealousy. Family life – new sibling. Sibling rivalry.

Norma Jean, jumping bean ill. by Lynn Munsinger. Random House, 1987. ISBN 0-394-98668-7 Subj: Activities – jumping. Animals – kangaroos. School.

Pat-a-cake and other play rhymes comp. by Joanna Cole and Stephanie Calmenson; ill. by Alan Tiegreen. Morrow, 1992. ISBN 0-688-11039-8 Subj: Nursery rhymes.

Pin the tail on the donkey and other party games comp. by Joanna Cole and Stephanie Calmenson; ill. by Alan Tiegreen. Morrow, 1993. ISBN 0-688-11892-5 Subj: Games. Parties.

Plants in winter ill. by Kazue Mizumura. Crowell, 1973. ISBN 0-690-62886-2 Subj: Plants. Science. Seasons – winter. Trees.

Riding Silver Star photos by Margaret Miller. Morrow, 1996. ISBN 0-688-13896-9 Subj: Animals – horses, ponies. Sports.

The secret box ill. by Joan Sandin. Morrow, 1971. Subj: Behavior – stealing.

Sweet dreams, Clown-Arounds! ill. by Jerry Smath. Gareth Stevens, 1993. ISBN 0-8193-0976-9 Subj: Bedtime. Clowns, jesters. Family life.

Why did the chicken cross the road? and other riddles, old and new comp. by Joanna Cole and Stephanie Calmenson; ill. by Alan Tiegreen. Morrow, 1994. ISBN 0-688-12203-5 Subj: Riddles.

You can't smell a flower with your ear: all about your 5 senses ill. by Mavis Smith. Grosset, 1994. ISBN 0-448-40469-9 Subj: Science. Senses.

Your insides ill. by Paul Meisel. Putnam, 1992. ISBN 0-399-22123-9 Subj: Anatomy. Science.

Your new potty ill. by Margaret Miller. Morrow, 1989. ISBN 0-688-06106-0 Subj: Behavior – growing up. Toilet training.

Cole, Julia. *My parents' divorce* ill. by Christopher O'Neill. Copper Beech, 1998. ISBN 0-7613-0869-5 Subj: Divorce. Family life.

Cole, Michael. *Head in the sand* ill. by Rowan Clifford. Carolrhoda, 1990. ISBN 0-87614-435-0 Subj: Animals. Behavior – hiding. Birds.

Cole, Philip (Philip A.). *Big Goof and Little Goof* (Cole, Joanna)

Cole, Sheila. *The hen that crowed* ill. by Barbara Rogoff. Lothrop, 1993. ISBN 0-688-10113-5 Subj: Animals. Birds – chickens.

When the rain stops ill. by Henri Sorensen. Lothrop, 1991. ISBN 0-688-07655-6 Subj: Country. Family life – fathers. Weather – rain.

When the tide is low ill. by Virginia Wright-Frierson. Lothrop, 1985. ISBN 0-688-04067-5 Subj: Animals. Sea and seashore.

Cole, William. *Aunt Bella's umbrella* ill. by Jacqueline Chwast. Doubleday, 1970. Subj: Character traits – helpfulness. Family life – aunts, uncles. Umbrellas. Weather – rain.

Frances face-maker ill. by Tomi Ungerer. Collins-World, 1963. Subj: Bedtime. Emotions. Family life. Participation. Rhyming text.

Have I got dogs! ill. by Margot Apple. Viking, 1993. ISBN 0-670-83070-4 Subj: Animals – dogs. Rhyming text.

I went to the animal fair ill. by Colette Rosselli. Collins-World, 1959. ISBN 0-529-03530-8 Subj: Animals. Poetry.

That pest Jonathan ill. by Tomi Ungerer. HarperCollins, 1970. Subj: Behavior – misbehavior. Family life. Rhyming text.

What's good for a four-year-old? ill. by Tomi Ungerer. Holt, 1967. Subj: Activities – playing. Rhyming text.

What's good for a six-year-old? ill. by Ingrid Fetz. Holt, 1965. Subj: Activities – playing. Rhyming text.

What's good for a three-year-old? ill. by Lillian Hoban. Holt, 1974. ISBN 0-03-007441-X Subj: Activities – babysitting. Birthdays. Rhyming text.

A zooful of animals ill. by Lynn Munsinger. Houghton Mifflin, 1992. ISBN 0-395-52278-1 Subj: Animals. Poetry.

Coleman, Evelyn. *The glass bottle tree* ill. by Gail Gordon Carter. Orchard, 1995. ISBN 0-531-08767-0 Subj: Communication. Ethnic groups in the U.S. – African Americans. Family life – grandmothers. Trees.

To be a drum ill. by Aminah Brenda Lynn Robinson. Albert Whitman, 1998. ISBN 0-8075-8006-6 Subj: Ethnic groups in the U.S. – African Americans. Foreign lands – Africa. Slavery. U.S. history.

White socks only ill. by Tyrone Geter. Albert Whitman, 1996. ISBN 0-8075-8955-1 Subj: Ethnic groups in the U.S. – African Americans. Prejudice. U.S. history.

Coleman, Michael. *Lazy Ozzie* ill. by Gwyneth Williamson. Little Tiger, 1996. ISBN 1-888444-02-9 Subj: Animals. Birds – owls. Character traits – laziness. Family life.

One, two, three, oops! ill. by Gwyneth Williamson. Little Tiger, 1998. ISBN 1-888444-45-2 Subj: Counting, numbers. Rhyming text.

Coleridge, Sara. *January brings the snow: a book of months* ill. by Jenni Oliver. Dial, 1986. ISBN 0-8037-0314-7 Subj: Days of the week, months of the year. Poetry. Seasons.

Coles, Alison. *Michael and the sea* ill. by Michael Charlton. E D C, 1985. ISBN 0-88110-268-7 Subj: Emotions – fear. Sea and seashore. Sports – swimming.

Michael in the dark ill. by Michael Charlton. E D C, 1985. ISBN 0-88110-267-9 Subj: Emotions – fear. Night.

Michael's first day ill. by Michael Charlton. E D C, 1985. ISBN 0-88110-266-0 Subj: Emotions – fear. School – first day.

Coles, Robert. *The story of Ruby Bridges* ill. by George Ford. Scholastic, 1995. ISBN 0-590-43967-7 Subj: Character traits – bravery. Ethnic groups in the U.S. – African Americans. Prejudice. School.

Coletta, Hallie. *From A to Z* (Coletta, Irene)

Coletta, Irene. *From A to Z* by Irene and Hallie Coletta; ill. by Hallie Coletta. Prentice-Hall, 1979. ISBN 0-13-331678-5 Subj: ABC books. Rebuses. Rhyming text.

Colette, Sidonie Gabrielle. *The boy and the magic* trans. by Christopher Fry; ill. by Gerard Hoffnung. Putnam, 1965. Subj: Behavior – misbehavior. Magic. Music.

Collard, Sneed B. *Creepy creatures* ill. by Kristin Kest. Rev. ed. of Do they scare you, 1992. Charlesbridge, 1997. ISBN 0-88106-837-3 Subj: Animals.

Cölle, Gisela. *The star tree* trans. by Rosemary Lanning; ill. by author. North-South, 1997. ISBN 1-55858-742-X Subj: Holidays – Christmas. Power failures. Stars.

Collicott, Sharleen. *Seeing stars* ill. by author. Dial, 1996. ISBN 0-8037-1523-4 Subj: Activities – flying. Animals. Sea and seashore. Space and space ships.

Toestomper and the caterpillars ill. by author. Houghton Mifflin, 1999. ISBN 0-395-91168-0 Subj: Animals. Behavior – bullying. Character traits – kindness to animals. Clubs, gangs. Insects – butterflies, caterpillars.

Collicutt, Paul. *This train* ill. by author. Farrar, 1999. ISBN 0-374-37493-7 Subj: Trains. Transportation.

Collier, Ethel. *I know a farm* ill. by Honoré Guilbeau. Addison-Wesley, 1960. Subj: Farms.

Who goes there in my garden? ill. by Honoré Guilbeau. Abelard-Schuman, 1963. Subj: Character traits – helpfulness. Gardens, gardening.

Collier, James Lincoln. *Danny goes to the hospital* ill. by Yale Joel. Norton, 1970. Subj: Hospitals.

Collier, John. *The backyard* ill. by author. Viking, 1993. ISBN 0-670-83609-5 Subj: Imagination.

Collier, Mary Jo. *The king's giraffe* by Mary Jo Collier and Peter Collier; ill. by Stéphane Poulin. Simon & Schuster, 1996. ISBN 0-671-88133-7 Subj: Animals – giraffes. Foreign lands – France. Royalty – kings.

Collier, Peter. *The king's giraffe* (Collier, Mary Jo)

Collington, Peter. *The angel and the soldier boy* ill. by author. Knopf, 1987. ISBN 0-394-98626-1 Subj: Angels. Behavior – stealing. Pirates. Toys – soldiers. Wordless.

Little pickle ill. by author. Dutton, 1986. ISBN 0-525-44230-8 Subj: Behavior – misbehavior. Dreams. Sleep. Wordless.

The midnight circus ill. by author. Knopf, 1992. ISBN 0-679-93262-3 Subj: Animals – horses, ponies. Circus. Dreams. Toys. Wordless.

My darling kitten ill. by author. Knopf, 1988. ISBN 0-394-89924-5 Subj: Animals – cats. Pets.

On Christmas eve ill. by author. Knopf, 1990. ISBN 0-679-90830-7 Subj: Fairies. Holidays – Christmas. Santa Claus. Wordless.

A small miracle ill. by author. Random House, 1997. ISBN 0-679-88725-3 Subj: Character traits – helpfulness. Holidays – Christmas. Old age. Wordless.

The tooth fairy ill. by author. Random House, 1995. ISBN 0-679-97168-8 Subj: Fairies. Teeth. Wordless.

Collins, Bonnie. *Rocks in my pocket* (Harshman, Marc)

Collins, Judith Graham. *Josh's scary dad* ill. by Diane Paterson. Abingdon, 1983. ISBN 0-687-20546-8 Subj: Character traits – appearance. Humor.

Collins, Pat Lowery. *Don't tease the guppies* ill. by Marylin Hafner. Putnam, 1994. ISBN 0-399-22530-7 Subj: Activities – reading. Aquariums. Family life – brothers.

I am an artist ill. by Robin Brickman. Millbrook, 1992. ISBN 1-56294-082-1 Subj: Art. Careers – artists.

My friend Andrew ill. by Howard Berelson. Prentice-Hall, 1981. ISBN 0-13-608844-9 Subj: Behavior – boasting. Imagination.

Taking care of Tucker ill. by Maxie Chambliss. Putnam, 1989. ISBN 0-399-21586-7 Subj: Behavior – misbehavior. Behavior – needing someone. Family life.

Tomorrow, up and away! ill. by Lynn Munsinger. Houghton Mifflin, 1990. ISBN 0-395-51524-6 Subj: Activities – flying. Animals. Animals – squirrels. Reptiles – turtles, tortoises.

Tumble, tumble, tumbleweed ill. by Charles Robinson. Albert Whitman, 1982. ISBN 0-8075-8122-4 Subj: Friendship. Pets.

Waiting for baby Joe ill. by Joan Whinham Dunn. Albert Whitman, 1990. ISBN 0-8075-8625-0 Subj: Babies. Family life – brothers and sisters. Family life – new sibling.

Collins, Ross. *What if?* (Thomas, Frances)

Collodi, Carlo. *The adventures of Pinocchio* adapt. by Stephanie Spinner; ill. by Diane Goode. Random House, 1983. ISBN 0-394-95910-8 Subj: Behavior – lying. Behavior – misbehavior. Character traits – loyalty. Folk and fairy tales. Puppets.

Pinocchio adapt. by Eric Metaxas; ill. by Brian Ajhar. Rabbit Ears, 1996. ISBN 0-689-80230-7 Subj: Behavior – lying. Behavior – misbehavior. Character traits – loyalty. Folk and fairy tales. Puppets.

Colman, Hila. *Peter's brownstone house* ill. by Leonard Weisgard. Morrow, 1963. Subj: City. Homes, houses.

Watch that watch ill. by Leonard Weisgard. Morrow, 1962. Subj: Animals. Clocks, watches. Time.

Colonius, Lillian. *At the zoo* by Lillian Colonius and Glen W. Schroeder; ill. by Glen W. Schroeder. Melmont, 1954. Subj: Zoos.

Coltman, Paul. *Tinker Jim* ill. by Gillian McClure. Farrar, 1992. ISBN 0-374-37611-5 Subj: Crime. Food. Foreign lands – England. Homeless. Poverty. Rhyming text.

Coman, Carolyn. *Losing things at Mr. Mudd's* ill. by Lance Hidy. Farrar, 1992. ISBN 0-374-34657-7 Subj: Behavior – losing things.

Come out to play ill. by Jeanette Winter. Knopf, 1986. ISBN 0-394-97742-4 Subj: City. Moon. Nursery rhymes.

Come to the circus. Simon & Schuster, 1980. ISBN 0-671-41479-8 Subj: Circus. Format, unusual – board books.

Comissiong, Lynette. *Mind me good now!* ill. by Marie Lafrance. Firefly, 1997. ISBN 1-55037-483-4 Subj: Folk and fairy tales. Foreign lands – Caribbean Islands. Witches.

Company González, Mercé. *Killian and the dragons* adapt. by Paula Franklin; ill. by Agustí Asensio Sauri. Silver Burdett, 1986. ISBN 0-382-09180-9 Subj: Dragons. Emotions – fear. Royalty.

Compton, Joanne. *Ashpet: an Appalachian tale* ill. by Kenn Compton. Holiday, 1994. ISBN 0-8234-1106-0 Subj: Character traits – kindness. Folk and fairy tales.

Granny Greenteeth and the noise in the night (Compton, Kenn)

Jack the giant chaser: an Appalachian tale (Compton, Kenn)

Little Rabbit's Easter surprise ill. by Kenn Compton. Holiday, 1992. ISBN 0-8234-0920-1 Subj: Animals – rabbits. Holidays – Easter.

Sody Sallyratus ill. by Kenn Compton. Holiday, 1995. ISBN 0-8234-1165-6 Subj: Animals – bears. Folk and fairy tales.

Compton, Kenn. *Granny Greenteeth and the noise in the night* by Kenn and Joanne Compton; ill. by Kenn Compton. Holiday, 1993. ISBN 0-8234-1051-X Subj: Bedtime. Cumulative tales. Emotions – fear. Folk and fairy tales. Noise, sounds.

Happy Christmas to all! ill. by author. Holiday, 1991. ISBN 0-8234-0890-6 Subj: Behavior – secrets. Holidays – Christmas. Mythical creatures – elves. Santa Claus.

Jack the giant chaser: an Appalachian tale by Kenn and Joanne Compton; ill. by Kenn Compton. Holiday, 1993. ISBN 0-8234-0998-8 Subj: Character traits – cleverness. Folk and fairy tales. Giants.

Conaway, Judith. *I'll get even* ill. by Mark Gubin. Raintree, 1977. ISBN 0-817-20964-6 Subj: Emotions – loneliness. Sibling rivalry.

Condra, Estelle. *See the ocean* ill. by Linda Crockett-Blassingame. Ideals, 1994. ISBN 1-57102-005-5 Subj: Family life. Handicaps – blindness. Sea and seashore.

Cone, Molly. *Squishy, misty, damp & muddy: the in-between world of wetlands* ill. by Molly Cone. Sierra Club, 1996. ISBN 0-87156-480-7 Subj: Animals. Ecology.

Conford, Ellen. *Eugene the brave* ill. by John M. Larrecq. Little, 1978. ISBN 0-316-15292-7 Subj: Animals – possums. Character traits – bravery. Emotions – fear. Night.

Impossible, possum ill. by Rosemary Wells. Little, 1971. Subj: Animals – possums. Character traits – individuality.

Just the thing for Geraldine ill. by John M. Larrecq. Little, 1974. ISBN 0-316-15304-4 Subj: Animals – possums. Character traits – perseverance.

Why can't I be William? ill. by Philip Wende. Little, 1972. Subj: Emotions – envy, jealousy. Family life. Family life – only child. Friendship.

Conger, Lesley. *Tops and bottoms* ill. by Imero Gobbato. Four Winds, 1970. Subj: Folk and fairy tales. Foreign lands – England. Monsters.

Conger, Marion. *The chipmunk that went to church* ill. by author. Simon & Schuster, 1952. Subj: Animals – chipmunks. Emotions – loneliness.

The little golden holiday book ill. by author. Simon & Schuster, 1951. Subj: Holidays.

Conklin, Gladys. *Cheetahs, the swift hunters* ill. by Charles Robinson. Holiday, 1976. ISBN 0-8234-0280-0 Subj: Animals – cheetahs. Science.

I caught a lizard ill. by Artur Marokvia. Holiday, 1967. Subj: Animals. Insects. Reptiles – lizards. Science. Spiders.

I like beetles ill. by Jean Zallinger. Holiday, 1975. ISBN 0-8234-0262-2 Subj: Insects – beetles. Science.

I like butterflies ill. by Barbara Latham. Holiday, 1960. Subj: Insects – butterflies, caterpillars. Science.

I like caterpillars ill. by Barbara Latham. Holiday, 1958. Subj: Insects – butterflies, caterpillars. Science.

I watch flies ill. by Jean Zallinger. Holiday, 1977. ISBN 0-8234-0290-8 Subj: Insects – flies. Science.

If I were a bird ill. by Artur Marokvia. Holiday, 1965. Subj: Birds. Science.

Journey of the gray whales ill. by Leonard Everett Fisher. Holiday, 1974. ISBN 0-8234-0244-4 Subj: Animals – whales. Science.

Little apes ill. by Joseph Cellini. Holiday, 1970. Subj: Animals – gorillas. Science.

Lucky ladybugs ill. by Glen Rounds. Holiday, 1968. Subj: Insects – ladybugs. Science.

Praying mantis: the garden dinosaur ill. by Glen Rounds. Holiday, 1978. ISBN 0-8234-0323-8 Subj: Insects – praying mantis. Science.

We like bugs ill. by Artur Marokvia. Holiday, 1962. Subj: Insects. Science.

When insects are babies ill. by Artur Marokvia. Holiday, 1969. Subj: Insects. Science.

Conover, Chris. *Froggie went a-courting* (A frog he would a-wooing go [folk-song])

Mother Goose and the sly fox ill. by author. Farrar, 1991. ISBN 0-374-35072-8 Subj: Animals – foxes. Behavior – talking to strangers. Birds – geese. Folk and fairy tales.

Sam Panda and Thunder Dragon ill. by author. Farrar, 1992. ISBN 0-374-36393-5 Subj: Animals – pandas. Dragons. Weather – rain.

Six little ducks ill. by author. Crowell, 1976. ISBN 0-690-01037-0 Subj: Birds – ducks. Counting, numbers. Music. Rhyming text. Songs.

The wizard's daughter: a Viking legend ill. by author. Little, 1984. ISBN 0-316-15314-1 Subj: Folk and fairy tales. Foreign lands – Denmark. Wizards.

Conrad, Pam. *Animal lingo* ill. by Barbara Bustetter Falk. HarperCollins, 1995. ISBN 0-06-023402-4 Subj: Animals. Foreign languages. Noise, sounds.

Animal lullabies ill. by Richard Cowdrey. Laura Geringer, 1997. ISBN 0-06-024719-3 Subj: Animals. Lullabies. Poetry.

Call me Ahnighito ill. by Richard Egielski. HarperCollins, 1995. ISBN 0-06-023323-0 Subj: Careers – explorers. Foreign lands – Greenland. Science.

Doll Face has a party! ill. by Brian Selznick. HarperCollins, 1994. ISBN 0-06-024263-9 Subj: Parties. Toys. Toys – dolls.

The lost sailor ill. by Richard Egielski. HarperCollins, 1992. ISBN 0-06-021696-4 Subj: Boats, ships. Careers – military. Character traits – luck. Sailors. Sea and seashore.

Molly and the strawberry day ill. by Mary Szilagyi. HarperCollins, 1993. ISBN 0-06-021370-1 Subj: Family life. Food.

The rooster's gift ill. by Eric Beddows. HarperCollins, 1996. ISBN 0-06-023604-3 Subj: Birds – chickens. Character traits – pride. Gifts. Morning.

This mess ill. by Elizabeth Sayles. Hyperion, 1998. ISBN 0-7868-2131-0 Subj: Character traits – cleanliness. Family life.

The Tub grandfather ill. by Richard Egielski. HarperCollins, 1993. ISBN 0-06-022896-2 Subj: Family life – grandfathers. Toys.

The Tub People ill. by Richard Egielski. HarperCollins, 1989. ISBN 0-06-021341-8 Subj: Activities – bathing. Toys.

The Tub People's Christmas ill. by Richard Egielski. Laura Geringer, 1999. ISBN 0-06-026029-7 Subj: Holidays – Christmas. Santa Claus. Toys. Trees.

Conran, Sebastian. *My first ABC book* ill. by author. Macmillan, 1988. ISBN 0-689-71198-0 Subj: ABC books.

Conroy, Jack. *The fast sooner hound* (Bontemps, Arna Wendell)

Conta, Marcia Maher. *Feelings between brothers and sisters* by Marcia Maher Conta and Maureen Reardon; photos by Jules M. Rosenthal. Raintree, 1974. ISBN 0-817-20039-8 Subj: Emotions. Family life. Sibling rivalry.

Feelings between friends by Marcia Maher Conta and Maureen Reardon; photos by Jules M. Rosenthal. Raintree, 1974. ISBN 0-817-20041-X Subj: Emotions. Friendship.

Feelings between kids and grownups by Marcia Maher Conta and Maureen Reardon; photos by Jules M. Rosenthal. Raintree, 1974. ISBN 0-817-20043-6 Subj: Emotions.

Feelings between kids and parents by Marcia Maher Conta and Maureen Reardon; photos by Jules M. Rosenthal. Raintree, 1974. ISBN 0-516-03002-7 Subj: Emotions. Family life.

Contos, Alexander. *Tanya and the tobo man = Tanya y el hombre tobo* (Koplow, Lesley)

Conway, Celeste. *Where is Papa now?* ill. by author. Boyds Mills, 1994. ISBN 1-56397-130-5 Subj: Activities – traveling. Boats, ships. Family life – fathers.

Conway, Diana Cohen. *Northern lights: a Hanukkah story* ill. by Shelly O. Haas. Kar-Ben Copies, 1994. ISBN 0-929371-79-8 Subj: Eskimos. Holidays – Hanukkah. Jewish culture.

Cook, Ann. *Lady Monster has a plan* (Blance, Ellen)

Lady Monster helps out (Blance, Ellen)

Monster and the magic umbrella (Blance, Ellen)

Monster and the mural (Blance, Ellen)

Monster and the surprise cookie (Blance, Ellen)

Monster at school (Blance, Ellen)

Monster buys a pet (Blance, Ellen)

Monster cleans his house (Blance, Ellen)

Monster comes to the city (Blance, Ellen)

Monster gets a job (Blance, Ellen)

Monster goes around the town (Blance, Ellen)

Monster goes to school (Blance, Ellen)

Monster goes to the beach (Blance, Ellen)

Monster goes to the circus (Blance, Ellen)

Monster goes to the hospital (Blance, Ellen)

Monster goes to the museum (Blance, Ellen)

Monster goes to the zoo (Blance, Ellen)

Monster has a party (Blance, Ellen)

Monster, Lady Monster and the bike ride (Blance, Ellen)

Monster looks for a friend (Blance, Ellen)

Monster looks for a house (Blance, Ellen)

Monster meets Lady Monster (Blance, Ellen)

Monster on the bus (Blance, Ellen)

Cook, Bernadine. *The little fish that got away* ill. by Crockett Johnson. Addison-Wesley, 1956. ISBN 0-590-41989-7 Subj: Fish. Sports – fishing.

Looking for Susie ill. by Judith Shahn. Addison-Wesley, 1959. ISBN 0-206-02241-4 Subj: Animals – cats. Family life. Farms.

Cook, Joel. *The rat's daughter* ill. by author. Boyds Mills, 1993. ISBN 1-56397-140-2 Subj: Animals – rats. Folk and fairy tales. Foreign lands – Japan.

Cook, Marion B. *Waggles and the dog catcher* ill. by Louis Darling. Morrow, 1951. Subj: Animals – dogs.

Cook, Scott. *The gingerbread boy* (The gingerbread boy)

Mother Goose (Mother Goose)

Cooke, Ann. *Giraffes at home* ill. by Robert M. Quackenbush. HarperCollins, 1972. ISBN 0-690-33083-9 Subj: Animals – giraffes. Science.

Cooke, Barbara. *see* Alexander, Anne (Anna Barbara Cooke)

Cooke, Trish. *Mr. Pam Pam and the Hullabazoo* ill. by Patrice Aggs. Candlewick, 1994. ISBN 1-56402-411-3 Subj: Ethnic groups in the U.S. – African Americans. Humor.

So much ill. by Helen Oxenbury. Candlewick, 1994. ISBN 1-56402-344-3 Subj: Babies. Birthdays. Cumulative tales. Family life.

When I grow bigger ill. by John Bendall-Brunello. Candlewick, 1994. ISBN 1-56402-430-X Subj: Behavior – growing up. Concepts – size. Family life. Sibling rivalry.

Coombs, Patricia. *Dorrie and the haunted schoolhouse* ill. by author. Clarion, 1992. ISBN 0-395-60116-9 Subj: School. Witches.

Lisa and the grompet ill. by author. Lothrop, 1970. Subj: Behavior – running away. Fairies. Family life.

The lost playground ill. by author. Lothrop, 1963. Subj: Behavior – losing things. Character traits – being different. Toys.

The magic pot ill. by author. Lothrop, 1977. ISBN 0-688-51792-7 Subj: Devil. Folk and fairy tales. Foreign lands – Denmark. Magic.

The magician and McTree ill. by author. Lothrop, 1984. ISBN 0-688-02111-5 Subj: Animals – cats. Behavior – secrets. Magic. Middle Ages.

Molly Mullett ill. by author. Lothrop, 1975. ISBN 0-688-51692-0 Subj: Character traits – bravery. Monsters.

Mouse Café ill. by author. Lothrop, 1972. Subj: Animals – mice. Character traits – selfishness. Restaurants. Weddings.

Tilabel ill. by author. Lothrop, 1978. ISBN 0-688-51831-1 Subj: Activities – weaving. Animals – groundhogs. Folk and fairy tales. Foreign lands – Germany. Royalty.

Cooner, Donna D. (Donna Danell). *I know an old Texan who swallowed a fly* ill. by Ann Hollis Rife. Hendrick-Long, 1996. ISBN 1-885777-14-0 Subj: Cumulative tales. Folk and fairy tales. Insects – flies. Songs.

The world God made ill. by Kim Simons. Word, 1994. ISBN 0-8499-1162-1 Subj: Creation. Cumulative tales. Nature. Religion. Rhyming text.

Cooney, Barbara. *Chanticleer and the fox* (Chaucer, Geoffrey)

Eleanor ill. by author. Viking, 1996. ISBN 0-670-86159-6 Subj: Family life. U.S. history.

A garland of games and other diversions: an alphabet book initial letters by Suzanne R. Morse; ill. by author. Holt, 1969. ISBN 0-03-081016-7 Subj: ABC books. Rhyming text.

Hattie and the wild waves ill. by author. Viking, 1990. ISBN 0-670-83056-9 Subj: Family life. Sea and seashore.

Island boy ill. by author. Viking, 1988. ISBN 0-670-81749-X Subj: Death. Emotions – grief. Family life. Islands.

Little brother and little sister ill. by author. Doubleday, 1982. ISBN 0-685-14583-7 Subj: Character traits – loyalty. Folk and fairy tales. Foreign lands – Germany. Royalty. Witches.

The little juggler ill. by author. Hastings House, 1982. Reprint of 1961 ed. ISBN 0-8038-4239-2 Subj: Holidays – Christmas.

A little prayer ill. by author. Hastings House, 1967. Subj: Religion.

Miss Ramphius ill. by author. Viking, 1982. ISBN 0-670-47958-6 Subj: Activities – traveling. Flowers.

Snow-White and Rose-Red (Grimm, Jacob)

The story of Christmas ill. by Loretta Krupinski. HarperCollins, 1995. ISBN 0-06-023434-2 Subj: Holidays. Holidays – Christmas. Religion – Nativity.

Cooney, Nancy Evans. *The blanket that had to go* ill. by Diane Dawson. Putnam, 1981. ISBN 0-399-20716-3 Subj: Behavior – growing up. Problem solving. School – first day.

Chatter-box Jamie ill. by Marylin Hafner. Putnam, 1993. ISBN 0-399-22208-1 Subj: Activities – playing. Character traits – shyness. School.

Donald says thumbs down ill. by Maxie Chambliss. Putnam, 1987. ISBN 0-399-21373-2 Subj: Behavior – growing up. Emotions – embarrassment. Problem solving. Thumb sucking.

Go away monsters, lickety split! ill. by Maxie Chambliss. Putnam, 1990. ISBN 0-399-21935-8 Subj: Emotions – fear. Monsters. Pets.

The wobbly tooth ill. by Marylin Hafner. Putnam, 1978. ISBN 0-399-20615-9 Subj: Teeth.

Coontz, Otto. *The quiet house* ill. by author. Little, 1978. ISBN 0-316-15533-0 Subj: Animals – dogs. Eggs. Emotions – loneliness. Friendship.

A real class clown ill. by author. Little, 1979. ISBN 0-316-15534-9 Subj: Circus. Clowns, jesters. School – first day.

Starring Rosa ill. by author. Little, 1980. ISBN 0-316-15535-7 Subj: Animals – pigs. Food. Humor.

Cooper, Ann (Ann C.). *In the forest* ill. by Dorothy Emerling. Denver Museum of Natural History Pr., 1996. ISBN 0-916278-71-9 Subj: Animals. Forest, woods. Nature.

Cooper, Elisha. *Ballpark* ill. by author. Greenwillow, 1998. ISBN 0-688-15755-6 Subj: Sports – baseball.

Building ill. by author. Greenwillow, 1999. ISBN 0-688-16494-3 Subj: Buildings. Careers – architects.

Country fair ill. by author. Greenwillow, 1997. ISBN 0-688-15531-6 Subj: Country. Fairs.

Cooper, Elizabeth K. *The fish from Japan* ill. by Beth and Joe Krush. Harcourt, 1969. Subj: Fish. Imagination. Kites. Pets.

Cooper, Floyd. *Coming home: from the life of Langston Hughes* ill. by author. Philomel, 1994. ISBN 0-399-22682-6 Subj: Ethnic groups in the U.S. – African Americans. Family life. Poetry.

Cooper, Helen (Helen F.). *The bear under the stairs* ill. by author. Dial, 1993. ISBN 0-8037-1279-0 Subj: Animals – bears. Emotions – fear. Imagination.

Little monster did it! ill. by author. Dial, 1996. ISBN 0-8037-1993-0 Subj: Babies. Behavior – misbehavior. Emotions – envy, jealousy. Family life. Sibling rivalry.

Pumpkin soup ill. by author. Farrar, 1999. ISBN 0-374-36164-9 Subj: Activities – cooking. Animals. Animals – cats. Animals – squirrels. Birds – ducks. Friendship.

Cooper, Jacqueline. *Angus and the Mona Lisa* ill. by author. Lothrop, 1981. ISBN 0-688-41972-0 Subj: Animals – cats. Behavior – stealing. Problem solving.

Cooper, Letice Ulpha. *The bear who was too big* ill. by Ruth Ives. Follett, 1963. Subj: Stores. Toys – bears.

Cooper, Melrose. *Gettin' through Thursday* ill. by Nneka Bennett. Lee & Low, 1998. ISBN 1-880000-67-9 Subj: Ethnic groups in the U.S. – African Americans. Family life.

I got a family ill. by Dale Gottlieb. Holt, 1993. ISBN 0-8050-1965-0 Subj: Family life. Rhyming text.

Pets! ill. by Yumi Heo. Holt, 1998. ISBN 0-8050-3893-0 Subj: Animals. Circus. Pets. Rhyming text.

Cooper, Patrick. *Never trust a squirrel* ill. by Catherine Walters. Dutton, 1999. ISBN 0-525-46009-8 Subj: Animals – guinea pigs. Animals – squirrels. Character traits – curiosity.

Cooper, Paulette. *Let's find out about Halloween* ill. by Errol Le Cain. Watts, 1972. ISBN 0-531-00075-3 Subj: Holidays – Halloween.

Cooper, Susan. *Danny and the Kings* ill. by Jos. A. Smith. Margaret K. McElderry, 1993. ISBN 0-689-50577-9 Subj: Character traits – helpfulness. Holidays – Christmas. Poverty. Trees.

Giff the scaredy bear (Gifford, Kathie Lee)

Giff's big game (Gifford, Kathie Lee)

Jethro and the jumbie ill. by Ashley Bryan. Atheneum, 1979. ISBN 0-689-50140-4 Subj: Emotions – anger. Foreign lands – Caribbean Islands. Mythical creatures.

Matthew's dragon ill. by Jos. A. Smith. Macmillan, 1991. ISBN 0-689-50512-4 Subj: Animals. Dragons. Dreams.

Moochie's surprise (Gifford, Kathie Lee)

The Selkie girl ill. by Warwick Hutton. Aladdin, 1991. ISBN 0-689-71467-X Subj: Animals – seals. Folk and fairy tales. Foreign lands – Ireland. Foreign lands – Scotland. Mythical creatures – selkies.

The silver cow: a Welsh tale ill. by Warwick Hutton. Atheneum, 1983. ISBN 0-689-50236-2 Subj: Behavior – greed. Character traits – smallness. Folk and fairy tales. Foreign lands – England.

Tam Lin ill. by Warwick Hutton. Macmillan, 1991. ISBN 0-689-50505-1 Subj: Folk and fairy tales. Foreign lands – Scotland. Mythical creatures – elves. Royalty – princesses.

Coopersmith, Jerome. *A Chanukah fable for Christmas* ill. by Syd Hoff. Putnam, 1969. Subj: Behavior – wishing. Holidays – Hanukkah. Jewish culture.

Cope, Dawn. *Humpty Dumpty's favorite nursery rhymes* comp. by Dawn and Peter Cope; ill. by Jessie M. King, Randolph Caldecott and others. Holt, 1981. ISBN 0-03-059907-5 Subj: Nursery rhymes.

Cope, Peter. *Humpty Dumpty's favorite nursery rhymes* (Cope, Dawn)

Copeland, Eric. *Milton, my father's dog* ill. by author. Tundra, 1994. ISBN 0-88776-339-1 Subj: Animals – dogs. Family life. Pets.

Copeland, Helen. *Meet Miki Takino* ill. by Kurt Werth. Lothrop, 1963. Subj: Ethnic groups in the U.S. – Japanese Americans. Family life – grandparents.

Coplans, Peta. *Cat and dog* ill. by author. Viking, 1996. ISBN 0-670-86766-7 Subj: Animals – cats. Animals – dogs. Counting, numbers. Sea and seashore.

Spaghetti for Suzy ill. by author. Houghton Mifflin, 1993. ISBN 0-395-65232-4 Subj: Animals. Character traits – stubbornness. Food.

Copp, Andrew James. *see* Copp, James (Andrew James)

Copp, James (Andrew James). *Martha Matilda O'Toole* ill. by Steven Kellogg. Bradbury, 1969. Originally appeared as a song in the author's phonorecord: Jim Copp tales. Subj: Behavior – forgetfulness. Humor. Rhyming text. School.

Copp, Jim. *see* Copp, James (Andrew James)

Corbalis, Judy. *The cuckoo bird* ill. by David Armitage. HarperCollins, 1991. ISBN 0-06-021698-0 Subj: Behavior – greed. Birds – cuckoos. Family life – grandmothers. Problem solving.

Porcellus, the flying pig ill. by Helen Craig. Dial, 1988. ISBN 0-8037-0486-0 Subj: Activities – flying. Animals – pigs. Character traits – being different.

Corbett, Grahame. *Guess who?* ill. by author. Dial, 1982. ISBN 0-8037-3036-5 Subj: Format, unusual – board books. Participation. Toys.

What number now? ill. by author. Dial, 1982. ISBN 0-8037-9735-4 Subj: Counting, numbers. Format, unusual – board books. Participation.

Who is hiding? ill. by author. Dial, 1982. ISBN 0-8037-9748-6 Subj: Format, unusual – board books. Participation. Toys.

Who is inside? ill. by author. Dial, 1982. ISBN 0-8037-9726-5 Subj: Format, unusual – board books. Participation. Toys.

Who is next? ill. by author. Dial, 1982. ISBN 0-8037-9759-1 Subj: Format, unusual – board books. Participation. Toys.

Corcos, Lucille. *The city book* ill. by author. Golden Pr., 1972. Subj: City.

Corddry, Thomas I. *Kibby's big feat* ill. by Quentin Blake. Follett, 1971. ISBN 0-695-80146-5 Subj: Bedtime. Behavior – lost. Jungle.

Córdova, Amy. *Abuelita's heart* ill. by author. Simon & Schuster, 1997. ISBN 0-689-80181-5 Subj: Desert. Ethnic groups in the U.S. Foreign languages.

Corey, Dorothy. *Everybody takes turns* ill. by Lois Axeman. Albert Whitman, 1979. Subj: Behavior – sharing.

A shot for baby bear ill. by Doug Cushman. Albert Whitman, 1988. ISBN 0-8075-7348-5 Subj: Animals. Careers – doctors.

Tomorrow you can ill. by Lois Axeman. Albert Whitman, 1977. ISBN 0-8075-8015-5 Subj: Behavior – growing up.

We all share ill. by Rondi Colette. Albert Whitman, 1980. ISBN 0-8075-8696-X Subj: Behavior – sharing.

Will it ever be my birthday? ill. by Eileen Christelow. Albert Whitman, 1986. ISBN 0-8075-9106-8 Subj: Animals. Birthdays. Emotions – envy, jealousy. Holidays – Halloween. Parties.

Will there be a lap for me? ill. by Nancy Poydar. Albert Whitman, 1992. ISBN 0-8075-9109-2 Subj:

Babies. Behavior – needing someone. Family life. Family life – new sibling. Sibling rivalry.

You go away ill. by Lois Axeman. Albert Whitman, 1976. ISBN 0-8075-9441-5 Subj: Behavior – needing someone. Concepts. Emotions – fear.

Cormack, M. Grant. *Animal tales from Ireland* ill. by Vana Earle. John Day, 1955. First published in England, 1954. Subj: Animals. Folk and fairy tales. Foreign lands – Ireland.

Cornelia. *see* Hale, Sarah Josepha Buell

Cornette. *Purple coyote* ill. by Rochette. Doubleday, 1999. ISBN 0-385-32664-5 Subj: Animals – coyotes. Character traits – curiosity.

Corney, Estelle. *Pa's top hat* ill. by Hilary Abrahams. Elsevier-Dutton, 1981. ISBN 0-233-97255-2 Subj: Sea and seashore. Trains.

Cornish, Sam. *Grandmother's pictures* ill. by Jeanne Johns. Bradbury, 1974. ISBN 0-912-84604-6 Subj: Family life. Family life – grandmothers.

Corrigan, Kathy. *Emily Umily* ill. by Vlasta van Kampen. Firefly, 1984. ISBN 0-920236-96-0 Subj: Emotions – embarrassment. Handicaps. School.

Corrin, Ruth. *Mister cat* ill. by John Hurford. Interlink, 1991. ISBN 0-940793-89-X Subj: Animals – cats. Birth. Pets.

Corrin, Sara. *Mrs. Fox's wedding* (Grimm, Jacob)

The pied piper of Hamelin (Browning, Robert)

Corrin, Stephen. *Mrs. Fox's wedding* (Grimm, Jacob)

The pied piper of Hamelin (Browning, Robert)

Cortesi, Wendy W. *Explore a spooky swamp* ill. by Joseph H. Bailey. National Geographic, 1979. ISBN 0-8704-4263-5 Subj: Animals. Birds. Frogs and toads. Reptiles.

Cosgrove, Margaret. *Wintertime for animals* ill. by author. Dodd, 1975. ISBN 0-396-07177-5 Subj: Animals. Science. Seasons – winter.

Cosgrove, Stephen (Edward). *Billy goats Gruff* (Asbjørnsen, P. C. [Peter Christen])

Sleepy time bunny by Stephen Cosgrove and Charles Reasoner. Price Stern Sloan, 1984. ISBN 0-8431-0997-1 Subj: Animals – rabbits. Bedtime. Format, unusual – board books. Night.

Cossi, Olga. *Gus the bus* ill. by Howie Schneider. Scholastic, 1989. ISBN 0-590-41616-2 Subj: Buses.

Costa, Nicoletta. *The birthday party, a board book* ill. by author. Grosset, 1984. Subj: Animals – cats. Birthdays. Family life. Format, unusual – board books. Parties.

The clever dog ill. by author. Macmillan, 1985. ISBN 0-02-724670-1 Subj: Animals – dogs. Character traits – cleverness.

Dressing up ill. by author. Grosset, 1984. ISBN 0-448-23401-7 Subj: Animals – cats. Format, unusual – board books.

A friend comes to play ill. by author. Grosset, 1984. ISBN 0-448-23403-3 Subj: Animals – cats. Format, unusual – board books. Friendship.

The grown-up dog ill. by author. Macmillan, 1985. ISBN 0-02-724680-9 Subj: Activities. Animals – dogs.

The mischievous princess ill. by author. Silver Burdett, 1986. ISBN 0-382-09179-5 Subj: Folk and fairy tales. Royalty – princesses.

The missing cat ill. by author. Grosset, 1984. ISBN 0-448-23402-5 Subj: Animals – cats. Format, unusual – board books.

Molly and Tom, the birthday party ill. by author. Grosset, 1984. ISBN 0-448-23404-1 Subj: Animals – cats. Birthdays. Family life. Parties.

The naughty puppy ill. by author. Macmillan, 1985. ISBN 0-02-724660-4 Subj: Animals – dogs. Behavior – misbehavior.

The new puppy ill. by author. Macmillan, 1985. ISBN 0-02-724650-7 Subj: Animals – dogs. Behavior – misbehavior.

Coste, Marion. *Honu* ill. by Cissy Gray. Univ. of Hawaii Pr., 1993. ISBN 0-8248-1507-6 Subj: Hawaii. Reptiles – turtles, tortoises.

Cote, Nancy. *Flip-flops* ill. by author. Albert Whitman, 1998. ISBN 0-8075-2504-9 Subj: Activities. Clothing – shoes. Sea and seashore.

Cotler, Joanna. *Sky above earth below* ill. by author. HarperCollins, 1990. ISBN 0-06-021366-3 Subj: Airplanes, airports.

Cottle, Joan. *Emily's shoes* ill. by author. Childrens Pr., 1999. ISBN 0-516-21585-X Subj: Activities – bathing. Clothing – shoes.

Cottringer, Anne. *Ella and the naughty lion* ill. by Russell Ayto. Houghton Mifflin, 1996. ISBN 0-395-79753-5 Subj: Animals – lions. Babies. Emotions – envy, jealousy. Family life – new sibling. Imagination – imaginary friends. Sibling rivalry.

Coulter, Hope Norman. *Uncle Chuck's truck* ill. by Rick Brown. Bradbury, 1993. ISBN 0-02-724825-9 Subj: Animals – bulls, cows. Family life – aunts, uncles. Farms. Trucks.

Counsel, June. *But Martin!* ill. by Carolyn Dinan. Faber, 1984. ISBN 0-571-13349-5 Subj: Character traits – being different. Space and space ships.

Count in the dark with Glo Worm ill. by Denise Fleming. Random House, 1985. ISBN 0-394-87273-8 Subj: Bedtime. Counting, numbers. Format, unusual. Rhyming text.

Count me in: *44 songs and rhymes about numbers.* Sterling, 1985. ISBN 0-7136-2622-4 Subj: Counting, numbers. Music. Rhyming text. Songs.

Counting rhymes ill. by Corinne Malvern. Simon & Schuster, 1946. Subj: Counting, numbers. Nursery rhymes.

Cousins, Lucy. *Count with Maisy* ill. by author. Candlewick, 1999. ISBN 0-7636-0234-5 Subj: Animals – mice. Counting, numbers. Format, unusual – board books.

Country animals ill. by author. Morrow, 1991. ISBN 0-688-10070-8 Subj: Animals. Country. Format, unusual – board books.

Farm animals ill. by author. Morrow, 1991. ISBN 0-688-10071-6 Subj: Animals. Farms. Format, unusual – board books.

Flower in the garden ill. by author. Candlewick, 1992. ISBN 1-56402-029-0 Subj: Flowers. Format, unusual. Wordless.

Garden animals ill. by author. Morrow, 1991. ISBN 0-688-10072-4 Subj: Animals. Format, unusual – board books.

Happy birthday, Maisy ill. by author; paper engineering by Lisa Boggiss. Candlewick, 1998. ISBN 0-7636-0577-8 Subj: Animals. Animals – mice. Birthdays. Format, unusual – toy and movable books.

Hen on the farm ill. by author. Candlewick, 1992. ISBN 1-56402-032-0 Subj: Birds – chickens. Farms. Format, unusual. Wordless.

Humpty Dumpty and other nursery rhymes ill. by author. Dutton, 1996. ISBN 0-525-45675-9 Subj: Format, unusual – board books. Nursery rhymes.

Jack and Jill: and other nursery rhymes ill. by selector. Dutton, 1996, c1989. ISBN 0-525-45676-7 Subj: Format, unusual – board books. Nursery rhymes.

Katy Cat and Beaky Boo ill. by author. Candlewick, 1996. ISBN 1-56402-884-4 Subj: Animals. Animals – cats. Concepts. Format, unusual – toy and movable books.

Kite in the park ill. by author. Candlewick, 1992. ISBN 1-56402-031-0 Subj: Format, unusual. Kites. Parks. Wordless.

Little Miss Muffet: and other nursery rhymes ill. by selector. Dutton, 1997. ISBN 0-525-45749-6 Subj: Format, unusual – board books. Nursery rhymes.

Maisy at the farm ill. by author; paper engineering by Lisa Boggiss. Candlewick, 1998. ISBN 0-7636-0576-X Subj: Animals – mice. Farms. Format, unusual – toy and movable books.

Maisy dresses up ill. by author. Candlewick, 1999. ISBN 0-7636-0885-8 Subj: Animals. Animals – mice. Clothing – costumes. Parties.

Maisy goes swimming ill. by author. Little, 1990. ISBN 0-316-15834-8 Subj: Animals – mice. Format, unusual – toy and movable books. Sports – swimming.

Maisy goes to bed ill. by author. Little, 1990. ISBN 0-316-15832-1 Subj: Animals – mice. Bedtime. Format, unusual – toy and movable books.

Maisy goes to school ill. by author. Candlewick, 1992. ISBN 1-56402-085-1 Subj: Animals – mice. Format, unusual – toy and movable books. School.

Maisy goes to the playground ill. by author. Candlewick, 1992. ISBN 1-56402-084-3 Subj: Activities – playing. Animals – mice. Format, unusual – toy and movable books.

Maisy makes gingerbread ill. by author. Candlewick, 1999. ISBN 0-7636-0887-4 Subj: Activities – cooking. Animals – mice. Food.

Maisy's ABC ill. by author. Candlewick, 1995. ISBN 1-56402-419-9 Subj: ABC books. Animals – mice. Format, unusual – toy and movable books.

Maisy's bedtime ill. by author. Candlewick, 1999. ISBN 0-7636-0884-X Subj: Animals. Animals – mice. Bedtime. Dreams. Toys – bears.

Maisy's colors ill. by author. Candlewick, 1997. ISBN 0-7636-0159-4 Subj: Animals – mice. Concepts – color.

Maisy's pool ill. by author. Candlewick, 1999. ISBN 0-7636-0886-6 Subj: Animals. Animals – mice. Sports – swimming.

Maisy's pop-up playhouse ill. by author. Candlewick, 1995. ISBN 1-56402-635-3 Subj: Animals – mice. Format, unusual – toy and movable books. Homes, houses.

Noah's ark ill. by author. Candlewick, 1993. ISBN 1-56402-213-7 Subj: Animals. Boats, ships. Religion – Noah. Weather – floods. Weather – rain. Weather – rainbows.

Pet animals ill. by author. Morrow, 1991. ISBN 0-688-10073-2 Subj: Animals. Format, unusual – board books. Pets.

Portly's hat ill. by author. Dutton, 1989. ISBN 0-525-44457-2 Subj: Birds. Birds – penguins. Clothing – hats.

Teddy in the house ill. by author. Candlewick, 1992. ISBN 1-56402-030-4 Subj: Format, unusual. Wordless.

Wee Willie Winkie and other nursery rhymes ill. by selector. Dutton, 1997. ISBN 0-525-45751-8 Subj: Format, unusual – board books. Nursery rhymes.

What can Pinky hear? ill. by author. Candlewick, 1997, c1991. ISBN 0-7636-0109-8 Subj: Animals – rabbits. Format, unusual – toy and movable books. Noise, sounds. Senses – hearing.

What can Pinky see? ill. by author. Candlewick, 1997, c1991. ISBN 0-7636-0110-1 Subj: Animals – rabbits. Format, unusual – toy and movable books. Senses – seeing.

What can rabbit hear? ill. by author. Morrow, 1991. ISBN 0-688-10455-X Subj: Animals. Animals – rabbits. Format, unusual – toy and movable books. Noise, sounds. Senses – hearing.

What can rabbit see? ill. by author. Morrow, 1991. ISBN 0-688-10454-1 Subj: Animals. Animals – rabbits. Format, unusual – toy and movable books. Glasses. Senses – seeing.

Za-Za's baby brother ill. by author. Candlewick, 1995. ISBN 1-56402-582-9 Subj: Animals – zebras. Family life. Nature. Sea and seashore. Sibling rivalry.

Cousteau Society. *Albatross* ill. with photos. Little Simon, 1993. ISBN 0-671-86565-X Subj: Birds – albatrosses. Nature. Sea and seashore.

Dolphins ill. with photos. Little Simon, 1992. ISBN 0-671-77062-4 Subj: Animals – dolphins. Nature. Sea and seashore.

Manatees ill. with photos. Little Simon, 1993. ISBN 0-671-86566-8 Subj: Animals – manatees. Nature. Sea and seashore.

Otters ill. with photos. Little Simon, 1993. ISBN 0-671-86567-6 Subj: Animals – otters. Nature. Sea and seashore.

Penguins ill. with photos. Little Simon, 1991. ISBN 0-671-77058-6 Subj: Birds – penguins. Nature. Sea and seashore.

Seals ill. with photos. Little Simon, 1992. ISBN 0-671-77061-6 Subj: Animals – seals. Nature. Sea and seashore.

Turtles ill. with photos. Little Simon, 1992. ISBN 0-671-77059-4 Subj: Nature. Reptiles – turtles, tortoises. Sea and seashore.

Whales ill. with photos. Little Simon, 1993. ISBN 0-671-86564-1 Subj: Animals – whales. Nature. Sea and seashore.

Coutant, Helen. *First snow* ill. by Vo-Dinh Mai. Knopf, 1974. ISBN 0-394-92831-8 Subj: Death. Emotions – grief. Family life – grandmothers. Seasons – winter.

Couture, Susan Arkin. *The biggest horse I ever did see* ill. by Claire Ewart. Laura Geringer, 1997. ISBN 0-06-023468-7 Subj: Animals – horses, ponies. Imagination. Rhyming text.

The block book ill. by Petra Mathers. HarperCollins, 1990. ISBN 0-06-020524-5 Subj: Behavior – collecting things. Rhyming text. Toys.

Melanie Jane ill. by Isabelle Dervaux. HarperCollins, 1996. ISBN 0-06-023392-3 Subj: Behavior – misbehavior. Emotions – anger.

Couvillon, Alice W. *Mimi and Jean-Paul's Cajun Mardi Gras* (Moore, Elizabeth)

Covault, Ruth M. *Pablo and Pimienta* ill. by Francisco Mora; trans. by Patricia Hinton Davison. Northland, 1994. ISBN 0-87358-588-7 Subj: Animals – coyotes. Careers – migrant workers. Ethnic groups in the U.S. – Mexican Americans. Foreign languages.

Coville, Bruce. *The foolish giant* by Bruce and Katherine Coville; ill. by Katherine Coville. Lippincott, 1978. ISBN 0-397-31800-6 Subj: Character traits – bravery. Character traits – kindness. Friendship. Giants. Magic.

My grandfather's house ill. by Henri Sorensen. BridgeWater, 1996. ISBN 0-816-73804-1 Subj: Death. Emotions – grief. Family life – grandfathers.

Sarah and the dragon ill. by Beth Peck. Lippincott, 1984. ISBN 0-397-32070-1 Subj: Character traits – kindness. Dragons. Folk and fairy tales. Magic. Mythical creatures. Witches.

Sarah's unicorn by Bruce and Katherine Coville; ill. by authors. Lippincott, 1979. ISBN 0-397-31873-1 Subj: Animals. Character traits – meanness. Mythical creatures – unicorns. Witches.

Coville, Katherine. *The foolish giant* (Coville, Bruce)

Sarah's unicorn (Coville, Bruce)

Cowan, Catherine. *My friend the piano* ill. by Kevin Hawkes. Lothrop, 1998. ISBN 0-688-13240-5 Subj: Family life – mothers. Music.

My life with the wave based on the story by Octavio Paz; tr. and adapt. for children by Catherine Cowan; ill. by Mark Buehner. Lothrop, 1997. ISBN 0-688-12661-8 Subj: Character traits – individuality. Sea and seashore.

Cowcher, Helen. *Jaguar* ill. by author. Scholastic, 1997. ISBN 0-590-29937-9 Subj: Animals – jaguars. Foreign lands – Venezuela. Sports – hunting.

Rain forest ill. by author. Farrar, 1988. ISBN 0-374-36167-3 Subj: Animals. Foreign lands – South America. Forest, woods. Machines.

Tigress ill. by author. Farrar, 1991. ISBN 0-374-37567-4 Subj: Animals – endangered animals. Animals – tigers. Character traits – kindness to animals.

Cowen-Fletcher, Jane. *Baby angels* ill. by author. Candlewick, 1996. ISBN 1-56402-666-3 Subj: Angels. Babies. Rhyming text.

Mama zooms ill. by author. Scholastic, 1993. ISBN 0-590-45774-8 Subj: Family life – mothers. Handicaps – physical handicaps.

Cowles, Kathleen. *Feelings* (Allington, Richard L.)

Hearing (Allington, Richard L.)

Looking (Allington, Richard L.)

Smelling (Allington, Richard L.)

Tasting (Allington, Richard L.)

Touching (Allington, Richard L.)

Cowley, Joy. *Big moon tortilla* ill. by Dyanne Strong-bow. Boyds Mills, 1998. ISBN 1-56397-601-3 Subj: Behavior – mistakes. Family life – grandmothers. Food. Indians of North America – Tohono O'Odham.

Gracias, the Thanksgiving turkey ill. by Joe Cepeda. Scholastic, 1996. ISBN 0-590-46976-2 Subj: Birds – turkeys. Careers – truck drivers. Ethnic groups in the U.S. – Puerto Rican Americans. Family life – fathers. Holidays – Thanksgiving.

The rusty, trusty tractor ill. by Olivier Dunrea. Boyds Mills, 1999. ISBN 1-56397-565-3 Subj: Careers – farmers. Family life – grandfathers. Tractors.

Singing down the rain ill. by Jan Spivey Gilchrist. HarperCollins, 1997. ISBN 0-06-027603-7 Subj: Activities – singing. Ethnic groups in the U.S. – African Americans. Weather – droughts. Weather – rain.

The video shop sparrow ill. by author. Boyds Mills, 1999. ISBN 1-56397-826-1 Subj: Birds – sparrows. Character traits – kindness to animals. Stores.

Cowley, Stewart. *Down Ladybug Lane* ill. by Susi Adams. Reader's Digest, 1993. ISBN 0-89577-481-X Subj: Animals. Counting, numbers. Format, unusual – board books.

Five little kittens ill. by Kate Davies. Reader's Digest, 1992. ISBN 0-89577-454-2 Subj: Animals – cats. Counting, numbers. Format, unusual – board books. Format, unusual – toy and movable books. Rhyming text.

From my window ill. by Caroline Fayne Church. Reader's Digest, 1994. ISBN 0-89577-595-6 Subj: Format, unusual – toy and movable books. Gardens, gardening.

Hide-and-seek puppies ill. by Kate Davies. Reader's Digest, 1991. ISBN 0-89577-455-0 Subj: Animals – dogs. Counting, numbers. Format, unusual – board books. Format, unusual – toy and movable books. Games. Rhyming text.

In dragonfly forest ill. by Elizabeth Gatt. Reader's Digest, 1993. ISBN 0-89577-479-8 Subj: Animals. Counting, numbers. Format, unusual – board books.

In songbird jungle ill. by Cindy Rosenheim. Reader's Digest, 1993. ISBN 0-89577-480-1 Subj: Animals. Counting, numbers. Format, unusual – board books.

Little bunny ill. by Susi Adams. Reader's Digest, 1996. ISBN 1-57584-006-5 Subj: Animals – rabbits. Format, unusual – board books. Rhyming text.

Little chick ill. by Susi Adams. Reader's Digest, 1996. ISBN 1-57584-007-3 Subj: Birds – chickens. Counting, numbers. Format, unusual – board books. Rhyming text.

Little lost rabbit ill. by Susi Adams. Reader's Digest, 1992. ISBN 0-89577-445-3 Subj: Animals – rabbits. Behavior – lost. Counting, numbers. Format, unusual – board books. Format, unusual – toy and movable books. Rhyming text.

The naughty ducklings ill. by Susi Adams. Reader's Digest, 1991. ISBN 0-89577-444-5 Subj: Behavior – misbehavior. Birds – ducks. Counting, numbers. Format, unusual – board books. Format, unusual – toy and movable books. Rhyming text.

On Butterfly Farm ill. by Elizabeth Gatt. Reader's Digest, 1993. ISBN 0-89577-478-X Subj: Animals. Counting, numbers. Format, unusual – board books.

"Tweet, tweet, tweet" ill. by Susan Nethery. Western, 1994. ISBN 0-307-17350-X Subj: Birds. Format, unusual – board books. Noise, sounds. Rhyming text.

What's that sound? ill. by Caroline Church. Reader's Digest, 1994. ISBN 0-89577-596-4 Subj: Animals. Format, unusual – board books. Noise, sounds. Pets. Stores.

Cox, David. *Ayu and the perfect moon* ill. by author. Bodley Head, 1984. ISBN 0-370-30533-7 Subj: Activities – dancing. Foreign lands – Bali.

Bossyboots ill. by author. Crown, 1987. ISBN 0-517-56491-2 Subj: Character traits – willfulness. Crime. Foreign lands – Australia.

Tin Lizzie and Little Nell ill. by author. Merrimack, 1984. ISBN 0-370-30922-7 Subj: Animals – horses, ponies. Foreign lands – Australia. Machines.

Cox, Judy. *Now we can have a wedding!* ill. by DyAnne DiSalvo-Ryan. Holiday, 1998. ISBN 0-8234-1342-X Subj: Ethnic groups in the U.S. Food. Weddings.

Rabbit pirates: a tale of the Spinach Main ill. by Emily Arnold McCully. Harcourt, 1999. ISBN 0-15-201832-8 Subj: Animals – foxes. Animals – rabbits. Behavior – trickery. Food. Foreign lands – France. Friendship.

The West Texas chili monster ill. by John O'Brien. BridgeWater, 1998. ISBN 0-8167-4546-3 Subj: Food. Space and space ships.

Cox, Lynn. *Crazy alphabet* ill. by Rodney McRae. Orchard, 1992. ISBN 0-531-08566-X Subj: ABC books. Cumulative tales.

Cox, Palmer. *Another Brownie book* ill. by author. McGraw-Hill, 1967. Re-publication of the orig. 1890 ed. Subj: Mythical creatures – elves.

The Brownies: their book ill. by author. McGraw-Hill, 1967. Re-publication of the orig. 1887 ed. Subj: Mythical creatures – elves. Poetry.

Cox, Paul. *The case of the botched book* ill. by author. Green Tiger Pr., 1992. ISBN 0-671-77586-3 Subj: Animals – badgers. Animals – koalas. Careers – detectives. Mystery stories.

The great eucalyptus mystery ill. by author. Green Tiger Pr., 1992. ISBN 0-671-77574-X Subj: Animals – badgers. Animals – koalas. Careers – detectives. Mystery stories.

The riddle of the floating island ill. by author. Green Tiger Pr., 1992. ISBN 0-671-77579-0 Subj: Animals

– badgers. Animals – koalas. Careers – detectives. Mystery stories.

Cox, Victoria. *Going my way?* (Applebaum, Stan)

Coxe, Molly. *Louella and the yellow balloon* ill. by author. Crowell, 1988. ISBN 0-690-04748-7 Subj: Circus. Toys – balloons.

6 sticks ill. by author. Random House, 1999. ISBN 0-679-98689-8 Subj: Animals – mice. Concepts – shape. Counting, numbers.

Whose footprints? ill. by author. HarperCollins, 1990. ISBN 0-690-04837-8 Subj: Animals. Family life. Farms. Seasons – winter.

Coxon, Michèle. *The cat who lost his purr* ill. by author. Peter Bedrick, 1991. ISBN 0-87226-453-X Subj: Animals – cats. Behavior – needing someone.

Coy, John. *Night driving* ill. by Peter McCarty. Holt, 1996. ISBN 0-805-02931-1 Subj: Activities – traveling. Automobiles. Family life – fathers. Night.

Coyne, Rachel. *Daughter, have I told you?* ill. by Virginia Halstead. Holt, 1998. ISBN 0-8050-5301-8 Subj: Family life – daughters. Family life – mothers. Poetry.

Crabtree, Judith. *The sparrow's story at the king's command* ill. by author. Oxford Univ. Pr., 1983. ISBN 0-19-554359-9 Subj: Birds – sparrows. Royalty – kings.

Craft, Ruth. *Carrie Hepple's garden* ill. by Irene Haas. Atheneum, 1979. ISBN 0-689-50099-8 Subj: Animals – cats. Character traits – bravery. Gardens, gardening.

The day of the rainbow ill. by Niki Daly. Viking, 1989. ISBN 0-670-82456-9 Subj: Behavior – losing things. City. Emotions – anger. Poetry. Seasons – summer. Weather – rainbows.

The winter bear ill. by Erik Blegvad. Atheneum, 1974. ISBN 0-00-195869-0 Subj: Rhyming text. Seasons – winter. Toys – bears.

Craig, Helen. *Charlie and Tyler at the seashore* ill. by author. Candlewick, 1995. ISBN 1-56402-573-X Subj: Animals – mice. Family life – cousins. Sea and seashore.

I see the moon, and the moon sees me: Helen Craig's book of nursery rhymes ill. by author. HarperCollins, 1993. ISBN 0-06-021454-6 Subj: Nursery rhymes.

The night of the paper bag monsters ill. by author. Knopf, 1985. ISBN 0-394-97307-0 Subj: Animals – pigs. Friendship. Monsters.

Susie and Alfred in a busy day in town ill. by author. Candlewick, 1994. ISBN 1-56402-380-X Subj: Animals – pigs. City. Family life – brothers and sisters.

Susie and Alfred in the knight, the princess and the dragon ill. by author. Knopf, 1985. ISBN 0-394-87212-6 Subj: Animals – pigs. Art. Imagination.

The town mouse and the country mouse (Æsop)

A welcome for Annie ill. by author. Knopf, 1994. ISBN 0-394-97954-0 Subj: Animals – pigs. Behavior – misbehavior. Behavior – trickery. Friendship.

Craig, Janet. *see* Palazzo-Craig, Janet

Craig, M. Jean. *Babar comes to America* (Brunhoff, Laurent de)

Boxes ill. by Joe Lasker. Norton, 1964. Subj: Concepts – shape. Concepts – size. Games. Participation. Toys.

Dinosaurs and more dinosaurs ill. by George Solonevich. Four Winds, 1968. Subj: Dinosaurs. Science.

The donkey prince (Grimm, Jacob)

The dragon in the clock box ill. by Kelly Oechsli. Norton, 1962. Subj: Dragons. Family life. Imagination.

The man whose name was not Thomas ill. by Diane Stanley. Doubleday, 1981. ISBN 0-385-15064-4 Subj: Careers – bakers. Humor.

Spring is like the morning ill. by Don Almquist. Putnam, 1965. Subj: Animals. Morning. Plants. Seasons – spring.

What did you dream? ill. by Margery Gill. Abelard-Schuman, 1964. Subj: Dreams. Morning.

Craighead, Charles. *The eagle and the river* photos by Tom Mangelsen. Macmillan, 1994. ISBN 0-02-762265-7 Subj: Animals. Birds – eagles. Ecology. Rivers. Seasons – winter.

Crampton, Patricia. *The beaver family book* (Kalas, Sybille)

The dragon with red eyes (Lindgren, Astrid)

The goose family book (Kalas, Sybille)

My nightingale is singing (Lindgren, Astrid)

The penguin family book (Somme, Lauritz)

Peter and the wolf (Prokofiev, Sergei Sergeievitch)

Crane, Alan. *Pepita bonita* ill. by author. Nelson, 1942. Subj: Birds – pelicans. Foreign lands – Mexico. Sea and seashore.

Crane, Donn. *Flippy and Skippy: the two flying squirrels* ill. by author. Winston, 1940. Subj: Animals – squirrels. Pets.

Crane, Lucy. *The frog prince* (Grimm, Jacob)

Crary, Elizabeth. *I'm frustrated* ill. by Jean Whitney. Parenting Pr., 1992. ISBN 0-943990-64-5 Subj: Emotions. Sports – roller skating.

I'm mad ill. by Jean Whitney. Parenting Pr., 1992. ISBN 0-943990-62-9 Subj: Emotions – anger. Weather – rain.

I'm proud ill. by Jean Whitney. Parenting Pr., 1992. ISBN 0-943990-66-1 Subj: Character traits – pride.

When you're mad and you know it by Elizabeth Crary and Shari Steelsmith; ill. by Mits Katayama. Parenting Pr., 1996. ISBN 1-884734-10-3 Subj: Emotions – anger. Format, unusual – board books.

Craven, Carolyn. *What the mailman brought* ill. by Tomie de Paola. Putnam, 1987. ISBN 0-399-21290-6 Subj: Activities – painting. Careers – postal workers. Emotions – loneliness. Illness. Imagination.

Craver, Mike. *Beaver ball at the bug club* ill. by Joan Kaghan. Farrar, 1992. ISBN 0-374-30662-1 Subj: Animals. Music. Parties. Songs.

Crawford, Elizabeth D. *Baby animals on the farm* (Isenbart, Hans-Heinrich)

Barry: the story of a brave St. Bernard (Hürlimann, Bettina)

Blackie and Marie (Kocí, Marta)

Hansel and Gretel (Grimm, Jacob)

The hare's race (Baumann, Hans)

Little Harry (Bröger, Achim)

Little red cap (Grimm, Jacob)

The seven ravens (Grimm, Jacob)

The three little pigs (The three little pigs)

Tiger cat (Wolski, Slawomir)

Traveling to Tripiti (Steger, Hans-Ulrich)

Crawford, Phyllis. *The blot: little city cat* ill. by Holling C. Holling. Jonathan Cape, 1930. Subj: Animals – cats.

Crawford, Ron. *Pet?* ill. by author. Green Tiger Pr., 1993. ISBN 0-671-79675-5 Subj: Animals. Pets.

Crawford, Sheryl Ann. *The baby who changed the world* ill. by Sonya Wilson. Faith Kids, 2000. ISBN 0-7814-3431-9 Subj: Animals. Animals – donkeys. Religion – Nativity.

Crayder, Teresa. *see* Colman, Hila

Crebbin, June. *Cows in the kitchen* ill. by Katharine McEwen. Candlewick, 1998. ISBN 0-7636-0645-6 Subj: Animals. Behavior – misbehavior. Careers – farmers. Rhyming text.

Fly by night ill. by Stephen Lambert. Candlewick, 1993. ISBN 1-56402-149-1 Subj: Activities – flying. Birds – owls. Night.

Into the castle ill. by John Bendall-Brunello. Candlewick, 1996. ISBN 1-56402-822-4 Subj: Castles. Monsters. Rhyming text.

Credle, Ellis. *Big fraid, little fraid: a folktale* ill. by author. Macmillan, 1964. Subj: Emotions – fear. Folk and fairy tales. Night.

Down, down the mountain ill. by author. Nelson, 1961, c1934. Subj: Clothing. Family life. Plants.

Creighton, Jill. *Maybe a monster* ill. by Ruth Ohi. Firefly, 1989. ISBN 1-55037-037-5 Subj: Activities – playing. Imagination.

One day there was nothing to do ill. by Ruth Ohi. Firefly, 1990. ISBN 1-55037-091-X Subj: Activities. Animals. Behavior – boredom. Imagination. Reptiles – snakes. Reptiles – turtles, tortoises.

Cremins, Robert. *My animal ABC* ill. by author. Crown, 1983. Subj: ABC books. Animals. Format, unusual – toy and movable books.

My animal Mother Goose ill. by author. Crown, 1983. Subj: Animals. Format, unusual – toy and movable books. Nursery rhymes.

Pop up baby brontosaurus ill. by author; paper engineering by Dick Dudley. Dial, 1989. ISBN 0-8037-0726-6 Subj: Dinosaurs. Format, unusual – toy and movable books.

Pop up baby coelophysis ill. by author; paper engineering by Dick Dudley. Dial, 1989. ISBN 0-8037-0735-5 Subj: Dinosaurs. Format, unusual – toy and movable books.

Pop up baby pteranodon ill. by author; paper engineering by Dick Dudley. Dial, 1989. ISBN 0-8037-0732-0 Subj: Dinosaurs. Format, unusual – toy and movable books.

Pop up baby stegosaurus ill. by author; paper engineering by Dick Dudley. Dial, 1989. ISBN 0-8037-0733-9 Subj: Dinosaurs. Format, unusual – toy and movable books.

Pop up baby triceratops ill. by author; paper engineering by Dick Dudley. Dial, 1989. ISBN 0-8037-0734-7 Subj: Dinosaurs. Format, unusual – toy and movable books.

Pop up baby tyrannosaurus rex ill. by author; paper engineering by Dick Dudley. Dial, 1989. ISBN 0-8037-0731-2 Subj: Dinosaurs. Format, unusual – toy and movable books.

Crespi, Francesca. *Little Bear and the oompah-pah* ill. by author. Dial, 1987. ISBN 0-8037-0394-5 Subj: Animals – bears. Holidays. Music.

Make a joyful noise: a pop-up book of Christmas carols ill. by author. Little Simon, 1997. ISBN 0-689-81526-3 Subj: Format, unusual – toy and movable books. Holidays – Christmas. Music.

Santa Claus is coming! ill. by author. Holt, 1987. ISBN 0-8050-0472-6 Subj: Format, unusual – toy and movable books. Holidays – Christmas. Santa Claus.

Silent night ill. by author. Holt, 1987. ISBN 0-8050-0471-8 Subj: Format, unusual – toy and movable books. Holidays – Christmas.

Crespo, George. *How the sea began: a Taino myth* ill. by Pané, Ramón, d. Clarion, 1993. ISBN 0-395-63033-9 Subj: Creation. Folk and fairy tales. Foreign lands – Puerto Rico. Indians of North America – Taino.

Cressey, James. *The dragon and George* ill. by Tamasin Cole. Prentice-Hall, 1979. ISBN 0-13-219154-7 Subj: Dragons. Foreign lands – England. Knights. Middle Ages.

Fourteen rats and a rat-catcher ill. by Tamasin Cole. Prentice-Hall, 1978. ISBN 0-13-329920-1 Subj: Animals – rats. Family life. Problem solving.

Max the mouse ill. by Tamasin Cole. Prentice-Hall, 1979. ISBN 0-13-566299-0 Subj: Animals – mice. Crime.

Pet parrot ill. by Tamasin Cole. Prentice-Hall, 1979. ISBN 0-13-661793-X Subj: Birds – parakeets, parrots. Crime.

Cresswell, Helen. *Two hoots and the king* ill. by Martine Blanc. Crown, 1978. ISBN 0-517-53494-0 Subj: Behavior – mistakes. Birds – owls.

Two hoots in the snow ill. by Martine Blanc. Crown, 1978. ISBN 0-517-53495-9 Subj: Behavior – mistakes. Birds – owls.

Cretan, Gladys Yessayan. *Lobo and Brewster* ill. by Patricia Coombs. Lothrop, 1971. Subj: Animals – cats. Animals – dogs. Emotions – envy, jealousy.

Ten brothers with camels ill. by Piero Ventura. Golden Pr., 1975. ISBN 0-307-15690-7 Subj: Counting, numbers. Desert.

Cretien, Paul D. *Sir Henry and the dragon* ill. by author. Follett, 1958. Subj: Animals – horses, ponies. Dragons. Knights. Royalty. Witches.

Crew, Gary. *Bright star* ill. by Anne Spudvilas. Kane/Miller, 1997. Originally published in Australia in 1996 by Thomas C. Lothian Pty. Ltd., Port Melbourne, Victoria, Australia. ISBN 0-916291-75-8 Subj: Astronomy. Careers – astronomers. Character traits – freedom. Dreams. Family life. Foreign lands – Australia.

Crewe, Sabrina. *The bear* ill. by Robert Morton. Raintree, 1997. ISBN 0-817-24367-4 Subj: Animals – bears. Nature.

The bee ill. with photos and illustrations. Raintree, 1997. ISBN 0-817-24362-3 Subj: Insects – bees. Nature.

Crews, Donald. *Bicycle race* ill. by author. Greenwillow, 1985. ISBN 0-688-05172-3 Subj: Counting, numbers. Sports – bicycling. Sports – racing.

Carousel ill. by author. Greenwillow, 1982. ISBN 0-688-00909-3 Subj: Merry-go-rounds.

Flying ill. by author. Greenwillow, 1986. ISBN 0-688-04319-4 Subj: Activities – flying. Airplanes, airports.

Freight train ill. by author. Greenwillow, 1978. ISBN 0-688-80165-X Subj: Caldecott award honor books. Trains.

Harbor ill. by author. Greenwillow, 1982. ISBN 0-688-00862-3 Subj: Boats, ships.

Light ill. by author. Greenwillow, 1981. ISBN 0-688-00310-9 Subj: Concepts. Lights.

Night at the fair ill. by author. Greenwillow, 1998. ISBN 0-688-11484-9 Subj: Fairs. Night.

Parade ill. by author. Greenwillow, 1983. ISBN 0-688-01996-X Subj: City. Parades.

Sail away ill. by author. Greenwillow, 1995. ISBN 0-688-11054-1 Subj: Boats, ships. Family life. Sailors. Sports – sailing. Weather – storms.

School bus ill. by author. Greenwillow, 1984. ISBN 0-688-02808-X Subj: Buses. School. Transportation.

Shortcut ill. by author. Greenwillow, 1992. ISBN 0-688-06436-1 Subj: Ethnic groups in the U.S. – African Americans. Trains.

Ten black dots ill. by author. Rev. ed. Greenwillow, 1986. ISBN 0-688-06068-4 Subj: Concepts – shape. Counting, numbers.

Truck ill. by author. Greenwillow, 1980. ISBN 0-688-84244-5 Subj: Caldecott award honor books. Transportation. Trucks. Wordless.

We read: A to Z ill. by author. Harper, 1984, c1967. Reprint. Originally published: New York: Harper & Row, [1967]. ISBN 0-688-03844-1 Subj: ABC books. Concepts.

Crews, Nina. *A high, low, near, far, loud, quiet story* ill. by author. Greenwillow, 1999. ISBN 0-688-16795-0 Subj: Activities. Concepts – opposites. Family life – brothers and sisters.

I'll catch the moon ill. by author. Greenwillow, 1996. ISBN 0-688-14135-8 Subj: Imagination. Moon. Night.

One hot summer day ill. by author. Greenwillow, 1995. ISBN 0-688-13394-0 Subj: City. Ethnic groups in the U.S. – African Americans. Seasons – summer.

Snowball ill. by author. Greenwillow, 1997. ISBN 0-688-14929-4 Subj: Activities – playing. Seasons – winter. Weather – snow.

You are here ill. by author. Greenwillow, 1998. ISBN 0-688-15753-X Subj: Ethnic groups in the U.S. – African Americans. Family life. Imagination. Weather – rain.

Crichton, Michael. *see* Douglas, Michael

Crimi, Carolyn. *Don't need friends* ill. by Lynn Munsinger. Doubleday, 1999. ISBN 0-385-32643-2 Subj: Animals. Animals – dogs. Animals – rats. Behavior – needing someone. Friendship.

Cristini, Ermanno. *In my garden* by Ermanno Cristini and Luigi Puricelli; ill. by authors. Alphabet Pr., [1985] c1981. Orig title: Falter, Blumen, Tierre und Ich. ISBN 0-907234-05-4 Subj: Gardens, gardening. Wordless.

In the pond by Ermanno Cristini and Luigi Puricelli; ill. by authors. Alphabet Pr., 1984. ISBN 0-907234-43-7 Subj: Animals. Insects. Plants. Reptiles.

In the woods by Ermanno Cristini and Luigi Puricelli; ill. by authors. Alphabet Pr., 1983. ISBN 0-907234-31-3 Subj: Animals. Birds. Forest, woods. Wordless.

Croft, Priscilla. *Dealing with jealousy* ill. by author. PowerKids, 1996. ISBN 0-8239-2326-6 Subj: Emotions – envy, jealousy. Sibling rivalry.

Croll, Carolyn. *The little snowgirl* ill. by author. Putnam, 1989. ISBN 0-399-21691-X Subj: Folk and fairy tales. Foreign lands – Russia. Holidays – Christmas. Weather – snow.

The three brothers ill. by author. Putnam, 1991. ISBN 0-399-22195-6 Subj: Family life – brothers. Family life – fathers. Farms. Folk and fairy tales. Foreign lands – Germany.

Too many babas ill. by author. HarperCollins, 1979. ISBN 0-06-021384-1 Subj: Behavior – sharing. Food.

Cromie, William J. *Steven and the green turtle* ill. by Tom Eaton. HarperCollins, 1970. ISBN 0-590-30904-8 Subj: Animals – endangered animals. Reptiles – turtles, tortoises. Science.

Crompton, Anne Eliot. *The lifting stone* ill. by Marcia Sewall. Holiday, 1978. ISBN 0-8234-0325-4 Subj: Character traits – cleverness. Folk and fairy tales.

The winter wife: an Abnaki folktale ill. by Robert Andrew Parker. Little, 1975. ISBN 0-316-16143-8 Subj: Character traits – loyalty. Folk and fairy tales. Indians of North America – Abnaki.

Crompton, Margaret. *The house where Jack lives* ill. by Margery Gill. Merrimack, 1980. ISBN 0-370-30027-0 Subj: Family life. Foreign lands – England. Homes, houses.

Cronin, Doreen. *Click, clack, moo: cows that type* ill. by Betsy Lewin. Simon & Schuster, 2000. ISBN 0-689-83213-3 Subj: Activities – writing. Animals – bulls, cows. Behavior – dissatisfaction. Birds. Caldecott award honor books. Careers – farmers. Farms.

Crook, Connie Brummel. *Maple moon* ill. by Scott Cameron. Stoddart Kids, 1997. ISBN 0-7737-3017-6 Subj: Food. Foreign lands – Canada. Indians of North America – Missisauga.

Crosby-Jones, Michael. *Goodbye Rune* (Kaldhol, Marit)

Cross, Diana Harding. *Some birds have funny names* ill. by Jan Brett. Crown, 1981. ISBN 0-517-54005-3 Subj: Birds. Names.

Some plants have funny names ill. by Jan Brett. Crown, 1983. ISBN 0-517-54840-2 Subj: Names. Plants.

Cross, Genevieve. *My bunny book* ill. by Charles Clement. Doubleday, 1952. Subj: Animals – rabbits. Holidays – Easter.

A trip to the yard ill. by Marjorie Hartwell and Rachel Dixon. Doubleday, 1952. Subj: Animals. Birds. Plants.

Cross, Verda. *Great-grandma tells of threshing day* ill. by Gail Owens. Albert Whitman, 1992. ISBN 0-8075-3042-5 Subj: Family life – great-grandparents. Farms.

Crossley-Holland, Kevin. *The green children* ill. by Margaret Gordon. Seabury Pr., 1968. Subj: Character traits – being different. Folk and fairy tales. Foreign lands – England.

The pedlar of Swaffham ill. by Margaret Gordon. Seabury Pr., 1971. ISBN 0-395-28786-3 Subj: Careers – peddlers. Folk and fairy tales.

Sleeping Nanna ill. by Peter Melnyczuk. Ideals, 1990. ISBN 0-8249-8458-7 Subj: Dreams. Islands. Senses. Sleep.

Croswell, Volney. *How to hide a hippopotamus* ill. by author. Dodd, 1958. Subj: Animals – hippopotamuses. Behavior – hiding things. Concepts – size.

Crothers, Samuel McChord. *Miss Muffet's Christmas party* ill. by Olive M. Long. Houghton Mifflin, 1929. Subj: Parties. Spiders.

Crowe, Robert L. *Clyde monster* ill. by Kay Chorao. Dutton, 1976. ISBN 0-525-28025-1 Subj: Emotions – fear. Monsters. Night.

Tyler Toad and the thunder ill. by Kay Chorao. Dutton, 1980. ISBN 0-525-41795-8 Subj: Animals. Noise, sounds. Weather – thunder.

Crowell, Maryalicia. *A horse in the house* ill. by Leonard P. Kessler. Addison-Wesley, 1957. Subj: City. Pets.

Crowley, Arthur. *Bonzo Beaver* ill. by Annie Gusman. Houghton Mifflin, 1980. ISBN 0-395-29081-3 Subj: Activities – babysitting. Animals – beavers. Rhyming text. Sibling rivalry.

The boogey man ill. by Annie Gusman. Houghton Mifflin, 1978. ISBN 0-395-26458-8 Subj: Behavior – dissatisfaction. Behavior – misbehavior. Family life. Monsters.

The ugly book ill. by Annie Gusman. Houghton Mifflin, 1982. ISBN 0-395-31858-0 Subj: Character traits – appearance.

The wagon man ill. by Annie Gusman. Houghton Mifflin, 1981. ISBN 0-395-30346-X Subj: Dreams. Rhyming text. Riddles.

Crowley, Michael. *New kid on Spurwick Ave.* ill. by Abby Carter. Little, 1992. ISBN 0-316-16230-2 Subj: Activities – making things. Clubs, gangs. Communities, neighborhoods. Friendship. Imagination.

Shack and back ill. by Abby Carter. Little, 1993. ISBN 0-316-16231-0 Subj: Clubs, gangs. Sports – bicycling. Sports – racing.

Crowther, Robert. *All the fun of the fair* ill. by author. Candlewick, 1992. ISBN 1-56402-001-0 Subj: Fairs. Format, unusual – toy and movable books.

Animal rap! ill. by author. Candlewick, 1993. ISBN 1-56402-207-2 Subj: Animals. Format, unusual – toy and movable books. Noise, sounds.

Animal snap! ill. by author. Candlewick, 1993. ISBN 1-56402-208-0 Subj: Animals. Format, unusual – toy and movable books.

Dump trucks and diggers ill. by author. Candlewick, 1996. ISBN 0-7636-0008-3 Subj: Activities – digging. Format, unusual – toy and movable books. Machines. Trucks.

Hide and seek counting book ill. by author. Viking, 1981. ISBN 0-670-48997-2 Subj: Counting, numbers. Format, unusual – toy and movable books.

The most amazing hide-and-seek alphabet book ill. by author. Viking, 1978. Subj: ABC books. Format, unusual – toy and movable books.

The most amazing hide-and-seek opposites book ill. by author. Viking, 1985. ISBN 0-670-80121-6 Subj: Concepts – opposites. Format, unusual – toy and movable books.

My pop-up surprise ABC ill. by author. Orchard, 1996. ISBN 0-531-30038-2 Subj: ABC books. Format, unusual – toy and movable books.

My pop-up surprise 1 2 3 ill. by author. Orchard, 1997. ISBN 0-531-30039-0 Subj: Counting, numbers. Format, unusual – toy and movable books.

Pop goes the weasel! 25 pop-up nursery rhymes comp. and ill. by Robert Crowther. Viking, 1987. ISBN 0-670-81815-1 Subj: Format, unusual – toy and movable books. Nursery rhymes.

Who lives in the country? ill. by author. Candlewick, 1992. ISBN 1-56402-090-8 Subj: Animals. Country. Format, unusual – toy and movable books.

Who lives in the garden? ill. by author. Candlewick, 1992. ISBN 1-56402-091-6 Subj: Animals. Format, unusual – toy and movable books. Gardens, gardening.

Who lives on the farm? ill. by author. Walker, 1989. ISBN 0-744-51504-1 Subj: Farms. Format, unusual – toy and movable books.

Croxford, Vera. *All kinds of animals* ill. by author. Grosset, 1972, c1968. Orig. title: All sorts of animals (Hamlyn Pub. Group, 1968). ISBN 0-448-03786-6 Subj: Animals.

Crozat, François. *I am a little cat* ill. by author. Barron's, 1992. ISBN 0-8120-6277-9 Subj: Animals – cats. Format, unusual – board books.

I am a little caterpillar ill. by author. Barron's, 1995. ISBN 0-8120-6485-2 Subj: Format, unusual – board books. Insects – butterflies, caterpillars. Metamorphosis. Science.

I am a little dog ill. by author. Barron's, 1992. ISBN 0-8120-6276-0 Subj: Animals – dogs. Format, unusual – board books.

Crume, Marion W. *Let me see you try* ill. by Jacques Rupp. Bowmar, 1968. Subj: Activities. Participation.

Listen! photos by Cliff Rowe and Judy Houston. Bowmar, 1968. Subj: Activities. Ethnic groups in the U.S. Participation.

What do you say? photos by Harvey Mandlin. Bowmar, 1967. Subj: Activities. Participation.

Crummel, Susan Stevens. *Cook-a-doodle-doo!* (Stevens, Janet)

My big dog (Stevens, Janet)

Crump, Donald J. *Creatures small and furry* ill. with photos. National Geographic, 1983. ISBN 0-87044-491-3 Subj: Animals.

Cuetara, Mittie. *The crazy crawler crane and other very short truck stories* ill. by author. Dutton, 1998. ISBN 0-525-45951-0 Subj: Rhyming text. Trucks.

Terrible Teresa and other very short stories ill. by author. Dutton, 1997. ISBN 0-525-45768-2 Subj: Behavior. Rhyming text.

Cullen, Lynn. *The mightiest heart* ill. by Laurel Long. Dial, 1998. ISBN 0-8037-2293-1 Subj: Animals – dogs. Character traits – loyalty. Folk and fairy tales. Foreign lands – Wales.

Cummings, Betty Sue. *Turtle* ill. by Susan Dodge. Atheneum, 1981. ISBN 0-689-30805-1 Subj: Behavior – lost. Pets. Reptiles – turtles, tortoises.

Cummings, E. E. (Edward Estlin). *Fairy tales* ill. by John Eaton. Harcourt, [1975] c1965. ISBN 0-15-629895-3 Subj: Folk and fairy tales. Imagination.

Hist whist ill. by Deborah Kogan Ray. Crown, 1989. ISBN 0-517-57258-3 Subj: Holidays – Halloween. Poetry.

In just-spring ill. by Heidi Goennel. Little, 1988. ISBN 0-316-16390-2 Subj: Poetry. Seasons – spring.

Little tree ill. by Deborah Kogan Ray. Crown, 1987. ISBN 0-517-56598-6 Subj: Holidays – Christmas. Poetry. Trees.

Little tree ill. by Mary C. Smith. Element Children's, 1999. ISBN 1-902618-55-6 Subj: Holidays – Christmas. Poetry. Trees.

Cummings, Pat. *C is for city* (Grimes, Nikki)

Carousel ill. by author. Bradbury, 1994. ISBN 0-02-725512-3 Subj: Animals. Birthdays. Emotions – anger. Ethnic groups in the U.S. – African Americans. Family life. Merry-go-rounds.

Clean your room, Harvey Moon! ill. by author. Bradbury, 1991. ISBN 0-02-725511-5 Subj: Character traits – cleanliness. Ethnic groups in the U.S. – African Americans. Rhyming text.

C.L.O.U.D.S. ill. by author. Lothrop, 1986. ISBN 0-688-04683-5 Subj: Weather – clouds.

Jimmy Lee did it ill. by author. Lothrop, 1985. ISBN 0-688-04633-9 Subj: Ethnic groups in the U.S. – African Americans. Family life – brothers. Imagination – imaginary friends. Problem solving. Rhyming text.

My aunt came back ill. by author. HarperCollins, 1998. ISBN 0-694-01059-6 Subj: Activities – traveling. Ethnic groups in the U.S. – African Americans. Family life – aunts, uncles. Rhyming text.

Petey Moroni's Camp Runamok diary ill. by author. Bradbury, 1992. ISBN 0-02-725513-1 Subj: Animals – raccoons. Camps, camping. Ethnic groups in the U.S.

Cummings, Phil. *Goodness gracious!* ill. by Craig Smith. Watts, 1992. ISBN 0-531-08567-8 Subj: Anatomy. Rhyming text.

Cummings, W. T. (Walter Thies). *The kid* ill. by author. McGraw-Hill, 1960. Subj: Animals – horses, ponies. Behavior – seeking better things. Emotions – loneliness. Music.

Miss Esta Maude's secret ill. by author. McGraw-Hill, 1961. Subj: Automobiles. Behavior – secrets. Careers – teachers.

Wickford of Beacon Hill ill. by author. McGraw-Hill, 1962. Subj: Birds – cockatoos.

Cummins, Julie. *The inside-outside book of libraries* (Munro, Roxie)

Cuneo, Diane. *Mary Louise loses her manners* ill. by Jack E. Davis. Doubleday, 1999. ISBN 0-385-32538-X Subj: Behavior. Etiquette.

Cuneo, Mary Louise. *How to grow a picket fence* ill. by Nadine Bernard Westcott. HarperCollins, 1993. ISBN 0-06-020864-3 Subj: Gardens, gardening. Imagination.

Inside a sandcastle and other secrets ill. by Jan Brett. Houghton Mifflin, 1979. ISBN 0-395-27805-8 Subj: Character traits – smallness.

What can a giant do? ill. by Benrei Huang. HarperCollins, 1994. ISBN 0-06-021217-9 Subj: Concepts – size. Giants. Imagination – imaginary friends. Rhyming text.

Cunliffe, John. *The king's birthday cake* ill. by Faith Jaques. Elsevier-Dutton, 1979. ISBN 0-233-96453-3 Subj: Activities – cooking. Birthdays. Cumulative tales. Royalty – kings.

Sara's giant and the upside down house ill. by Hilary Abrahams. Elsevier-Dutton, 1980. ISBN 0-233-97202-1 Subj: Giants.

Cunningham, David. *A crow's journey* ill. by author. Albert Whitman, 1996. ISBN 0-8075-1356-3 Subj: Birds – crows. Rivers. Water. Weather – snow.

Cunningham, Julia. *A mouse called Junction* ill. by Michael Hague. Pantheon, 1980. ISBN 0-394-94112-8 Subj: Animals – mice. Animals – rats. Emotions. Emotions – fear. Friendship.

The vision of François the fox ill. by Nicholas Angelo. Pantheon, 1969. Subj: Animals – foxes.

Curious George and the dinosaur ed. by Margret Rey and Alan J. Shalleck. Houghton Mifflin, 1989. ISBN 0-395-51942-X Subj: Animals – monkeys. Dinosaurs.

Curious George and the dump truck ill. from the Curious George film series. Houghton Mifflin, 1984. ISBN 0-395-36635-6 Subj: Animals – monkeys. Character traits – curiosity. Trucks.

Curious George and the dump truck ill. in the style of H. A. Rey by Vipah Interactive. Houghton Mifflin, 1999. The 1984 ed. of this title has a different story line. ISBN 0-395-97832-7 Subj: Animals – monkeys. Birds – ducks. Parks. Trucks.

Curious George and the hot air balloon ill. in the style of H. A. Rey by Vipah Interactive. Houghton Mifflin, 1998. ISBN 0-395-92338-7 Subj: Activities – ballooning. Animals – monkeys. Behavior.

Curious George and the pizza ill. from the Curious George film series. Houghton Mifflin, 1985. ISBN 0-395-39039-7 Subj: Animals – monkeys. Character traits – curiosity. Food.

Curious George and the puppies ill. in the style of H. A. Rey by Vipah Interactive. Houghton Mifflin, 1998. ISBN 0-395-92334-4 Subj: Animals – dogs. Animals – monkeys. Behavior.

Curious George at the fire station ill. from the Curious George film series. Houghton Mifflin, 1985. ISBN 0-395-39037-0 Subj: Animals – monkeys. Careers – firefighters. Character traits – curiosity.

Curious George goes camping ill. in the style of H. A. Rey by Vipah Interactive. Houghton Mifflin, 1999. ISBN 0-395-97831-9 Subj: Animals – monkeys. Camps, camping.

Curious George goes hiking ill. from the Curious George film series. Houghton Mifflin, 1985. ISBN 0-395-39038-9 Subj: Animals – monkeys. Character traits – curiosity. Sports – hiking.

Curious George goes sledding ill. from the Curious George film series. Houghton Mifflin, 1984. ISBN 0-395-36637-2 Subj: Animals – monkeys. Character traits – curiosity. Sports – sledding.

Curious George goes to a chocolate factory: *based on the original character by Margret and H. A. Rey* ill. in the style of H. A. Rey by Vipah Interactive. Houghton Mifflin, 1998. ISBN 0-395-91216-4 Subj: Animals – monkeys. Food.

Curious George goes to a movie: *based on the original character by Margret and H. A. Rey* ill. in the style of H. A. Rey by Vipah Interactive. Houghton Mifflin, 1998. ISBN 0-395-91901-0 Subj: Animals – monkeys. Behavior. Theater.

Curious George goes to an ice cream shop ed. by Margret Rey and Alan J. Shalleck. Houghton Mifflin, 1989. ISBN 0-395-51943-8 Subj: Animals – monkeys. Food.

Curious George goes to school ed. by Margret Rey and Alan J. Shalleck. Houghton Mifflin, 1989. ISBN 0-395-51944-6 Subj: Animals – monkeys. School.

Curious George goes to the aquarium ill. from the Curious George film series. Houghton Mifflin, 1984. ISBN 0-395-36634-8 Subj: Animals – monkeys. Aquariums. Character traits – curiosity. Fish.

Curious George goes to the circus ill. from the Curious George film series. Houghton Mifflin, 1984. ISBN 0-395-36636-4 Subj: Animals – monkeys. Character traits – curiosity. Circus.

Curious George goes to the dentist ed. by Margret Rey and Alan J. Shalleck. Houghton Mifflin, 1989. ISBN 0-395-51941-1 Subj: Animals – monkeys. Careers – dentists. Teeth.

Curious George in the snow: *based on the original character by Margret and H. A. Rey* ill. in the style of H. A. Rey by Vipah Interactive. Houghton Mifflin, 1998. ISBN 0-395-91902-9 Subj: Animals – monkeys. Weather – snow.

Curious George visits the zoo ill. from the Curious George film series. Houghton Mifflin, 1985. ISBN 0-395-39036-2 Subj: Animals – monkeys. Character traits – curiosity. Zoos.

Curle, Jock J. *The four good friends* ill. by Bernadette Watts. Holt, 1987. ISBN 0-8050-0231-6 Subj: Animals. Character traits – helpfulness. Character traits – kindness to animals.

Lucky Hans (Grimm, Jacob)

The sleepy owl (Pfister, Marcus)

The story of Jonah (Baumann, Kurt)

Currey, Anna. *Tickling tigers* ill. by author. Barron's, 1996. ISBN 0-8120-6594-8 Subj: Animals – mice. Animals – tigers. Behavior – boasting.

Curry, Jane Louise. *The Christmas knight* ill. by DyAnne DiSalvo-Ryan. Margaret K. McElderry, 1993. ISBN 0-689-50572-8 Subj: Behavior – sharing. Character traits – kindness. Holidays – Christmas. Knights. Middle Ages. Royalty – kings.

Little, little sister ill. by Erik Blegvad. Macmillan, 1989. ISBN 0-689-50459-4 Subj: Character traits – smallness. Family life. Family life – sisters. Farms.

Curry, Nancy. *The littlest house* ill. by Jacques Rupp. Bowmar, 1968. Subj: Family life. Homes, houses.

Curry, Peter. *Animals* ill. by author. Price Stern Sloan, 1984. ISBN 0-8431-0924-6 Subj: Animals.

Curti, Anna. *At home* ill. by author. Little, 1991. ISBN 0-316-16538-7 Subj: Family life.

Seasons ill. by author. Little, 1991. ISBN 0-316-16539-5 Subj: Animals – wolves. Format, unusual – board books. Seasons.

Curtis, Gavin. *The bat boy and his violin* ill. by E. B. Lewis. Simon & Schuster, 1998. ISBN 0-689-80099-1 Subj: Ethnic groups in the U.S. – African Americans. Music. Sports – baseball.

Grandma's baseball ill. by author. Crown, 1990. ISBN 0-517-57390-3 Subj: Emotions. Ethnic groups in the U.S. – African Americans. Family life – grandparents.

Curtis, Jamie Lee. *Tell me again about the night I was born* ill. by Laura Cornell. HarperCollins, 1996. ISBN 0-06-024529-8 Subj: Adoption. Babies. Family life.

Today I feel silly and other moods that make my day ill. by Laura Cornell. HarperCollins, 1998. ISBN 0-06-024561-1 Subj: Emotions. Family life. Format, unusual – toy and movable books. Rhyming text.

When I was little: a four-year-old's memoir of her youth ill. by Laura Cornell. HarperCollins, 1993. ISBN 0-06-021079-6 Subj: Babies. Behavior – growing up.

Curtis, Neil. *How paper is made* ill. by Peter Greenland. Lerner, 1992. ISBN 0-8225-2376-0 Subj: Activities – making things. Paper.

Curtis Brown, Beatrice. *see* Brown, Beatrice Curtis

Curtiss, A. B. *In the company of bears* ill. by Barbara Stone. Oldcastle, 1994. ISBN 0-932529-72-0 Subj: Activities. Animals – polar bears. Rhyming text.

Cushman, Doug. *The ABC mystery* ill. by author. HarperCollins, 1993. ISBN 0-06-021227-6 Subj: ABC books. Animals. Careers – detectives. Mystery stories. Rhyming text.

Giants comp. and ill. by Doug Cushman. Platt, 1980. ISBN 0-448-13623-6 Subj: Giants. Poetry.

Mouse and Mole and the Christmas walk ill. by author. Scientific American, 1994. ISBN 0-7167-6560-8 Subj: Animals – mice. Animals – moles. Ecology. Holidays – Christmas. Science. Trees.

The mystery of King Karfu ill. by author. HarperCollins, 1996. ISBN 0-06-024797-5 Subj: Animals – wombats. Careers – detectives. Foreign lands – Egypt. Mystery stories. Royalty – kings.

The mystery of the monkey's maze ill. by author. HarperCollins, 1999. ISBN 0-06-027720-3 Subj:

Animals. Careers – detectives. Foreign lands – Borneo. Mystery stories.

Nasty Kyle the crocodile ill. by author. Grosset, 1983. ISBN 0-448-16592-9 Subj: Behavior – dissatisfaction. Concepts. Reptiles – alligators, crocodiles.

Once upon a pig comp. and ill. by Doug Cushman. Grosset, 1982. ISBN 0-448-47492-1 Subj: Animals – pigs. Rhyming text.

Possum stew ill. by author. Dutton, 1990. ISBN 0-525-44566-8 Subj: Animals – possums. Behavior – trickery. Food.

Cushman, Jerome. *Marvella's hobby* ill. by Prue Theobalds. Abelard-Schuman, 1962. Subj: Animals – bulls, cows. Trains.

Cutler, Ebbitt. *Paulino* (Simons, Traute)

Cutler, Ivor. *The animal house* ill. by Helen Oxenbury. Morrow, 1977, 1976. ISBN 0-688-32110-0 Subj: Animals. Homes, houses. Zoos.

Doris ill. by Claudio Muñoz. Morrow, 1992. ISBN 0-688-11939-5 Subj: Birds. Songs.

Herbert: five stories ill. by Patrick Benson. Lothrop, 1988. ISBN 0-688-08148-7 Subj: Animals. Imagination.

Cutler, Jane. *Darcy and Gran don't like babies* ill. by Susannah Ryan. Scholastic, 1993. ISBN 0-590-44587-1 Subj: Babies. Emotions – envy, jealousy. Family life – grandmothers. Family life – new sibling. Sibling rivalry.

Mr. Carey's garden ill. by G. Brian Karas. Houghton Mifflin, 1996. ISBN 0-395-68191-X Subj: Animals – snails. Friendship. Gardens, gardening.

Cutts, David. *The gingerbread boy* (The gingerbread boy)

I can read about creatures of the night ill. by Janice Kinnealy; consultant, Kathy Carlstead. Troll, 1998. ISBN 0-8167-4345-2 Subj: Ghosts. Monsters. Night. Science.

Look . . . a butterfly ill. by Eulala Conner. Troll, 1982. ISBN 0-89375-662-8 Subj: Insects – butterflies, caterpillars. Metamorphosis. Science.

More about dinosaurs ill. by Gregory C. Wenzel. Troll, 1982. ISBN 0-89375-668-7 Subj: Dinosaurs.

Cuyler, Margery. *Baby Dot: a dinosaur story* ill. by Ellen Weiss. Houghton Mifflin, 1990. ISBN 0-395-51934-9 Subj: Dinosaurs. School.

The biggest, best snowman ill. by Will Hillenbrand. Scholastic, 1998. ISBN 0-590-13922-3 Subj: Animals. Concepts – size. Seasons – winter. Snowmen. Weather – snow.

Fat Santa ill. by Marsha Winborn. Holt, 1987. ISBN 0-8050-0423-8 Subj: Character traits – helpfulness. Dreams. Holidays – Christmas. Santa Claus.

Freckles and Jane ill. by Leslie Holt Morrill. Holt, 1989. ISBN 0-8050-0643-5 Subj: Animals – dogs. Friendship. Pets.

Freckles and Willie ill. by Marsha Winborn. Holt, 1986. ISBN 0-03-003772-7 Subj: Animals – dogs. Friendship.

From here to there ill. by Yu Cha Pak. Holt, 1999. ISBN 0-8050-3191-X Subj: Ethnic groups in the U.S. – Mexican Americans. Geography. Self-concept.

Shadow's baby ill. by Ellen Weiss. Houghton Mifflin, 1989. ISBN 0-89919-831-7 Subj: Animals – dogs. Babies. Family life.

Sir William and the pumpkin monster ill. by Marsha Winborn. Holt, 1984. ISBN 0-03-064032-6 Subj: Ghosts. Holidays – Halloween.

That's good! that's bad! ill. by David Catrow. Holt, 1991. ISBN 0-8050-1535-3 Subj: Animals. Zoos.

Cyrus, Kurt. *Slow train to Oxmox* ill. by author. Farrar, 1998. ISBN 0-374-37047-8 Subj: Behavior. Character traits – patience. Trains.

Czarnecki, Lois R. *The six wrinkled Woos* ill. by Laura Almada. Ohana Pr., 1992. ISBN 0-9627275-0-4 Subj: Animals – dogs.

Czernecki, Stefan. *The cricket's cage: a Chinese folktale* trans. by Simon Ching; ill. by author. Hyperion, 1997. ISBN 0-7868-2234-1 Subj: Buildings. Folk and fairy tales. Foreign lands – China. Insects – crickets.

The hummingbird's gift by Stefan Czernecki and Timothy Rhodes; ill. by Stefan Czernecki; weavings by Juliana Reyes de Silva and Juan Hilario Silva. Hyperion, 1994. ISBN 1-56282-605-0 Subj: Birds – humming birds. Foreign lands – Mexico. Gifts. Holidays – Day of the Dead. Indians of North America – Tarascan. Weather – droughts.

Pancho's piñata by Stefan Czernecki and Timothy Rhodes; ill. by Stefan Czernecki. Walt Disney, 1992. ISBN 1-56282-278-0 Subj: Emotions – happiness. Folk and fairy tales. Foreign lands – Mexico. Holidays – Christmas.

The singing snake by Stefan Czernecki and Timothy Rhodes; ill. by Stefan Czernecki. Hyperion, 1993. ISBN 1-56282-400-7 Subj: Activities – singing. Animals. Birds – larks. Folk and fairy tales. Foreign lands – Australia. Reptiles – snakes.

The sleeping bread by Stefan Czernecki and Timothy Rhodes; ill. by Stefan Czernecki. Hyperion, 1992. ISBN 1-56282-183-0 Subj: Activities – cooking. Food. Foreign lands – Guatemala. Poverty.

Zorah's magic carpet ill. by author. Hyperion, 1995. ISBN 0-7868-2066-7 Subj: Activities – traveling. Activities – weaving. Folk and fairy tales. Foreign lands – Morocco. Magic.

Dabcovich, Lydia. *Busy beavers* ill. by author. Dutton, 1988. ISBN 0-525-44384-3 Subj: Animals – beavers. Science.

Ducks fly ill. by author. Dutton, 1990. ISBN 0-525-44586-2 Subj: Activities – flying. Birds – ducks.

Follow the river ill. by author. Dutton, 1980. ISBN 0-525-30015-5 Subj: Rivers.

The keys to my kingdom ill. by author. Lothrop, 1992. ISBN 0-688-09775-8 Subj: Foreign languages. Nursery rhymes.

Mrs. Huggins and her hen Hannah ill. by author. Dutton, 1985. ISBN 0-525-44203-0 Subj: Birds – chickens. Death. Emotions – grief. Friendship.

The polar bear son: an Inuit tale ill. by reteller. Clarion, 1997. ISBN 0-395-72766-9 Subj: Animals – polar bears. Eskimos. Folk and fairy tales. Foreign lands – Arctic.

Sleepy bear ill. by author. Dutton, 1982. ISBN 0-525-39465-6 Subj: Animals – bears. Seasons – spring. Seasons – winter.

Dadey, Debbie. *Shooting star: Annie Oakley, the legend* ill. by Scott Goto. Walker, 1997. ISBN 0-8027-8485-2 Subj: Folk and fairy tales. Sports. U.S. history.

Will Rogers: larger than life ill. by Scott Goto. Walker, 1999. ISBN 0-8027-8682-0 Subj: Folk and fairy tales. U.S. history.

Daffis-Felicelli, Christine. *The little star of Bethlehem* ill. by author. Roman, 1993. ISBN 0-937739-20-0 Subj: Holidays – Christmas. Religion – Nativity. Stars.

Daghlian, Suzanne. *Babies help out* (Leonard, Marcia)

Favorite colors (Leonard, Marcia)

Dahl, Roald. *Dirty beasts* ill. by Rosemary Fawcett. Farrar, 1983. ISBN 0-374-31790-9 Subj: Bedtime. Dreams. Monsters. Poetry.

The enormous crocodile ill. by Quentin Blake. Knopf, 1978. ISBN 0-394-93594-2 Subj: Animals. Reptiles – alligators, crocodiles.

The giraffe and the pelly and me ill. by Quentin Blake. Farrar, 1985. ISBN 0-374-32602-9 Subj: Activities – working. Animals. Careers – window cleaners. Crime.

Dahl, Tessa. *Babies, babies, babies* ill. by Siobhan Dodds. Viking, 1991. ISBN 0-670-83921-3 Subj: Babies. Birth. Family life.

The same but different ill. by Arthur Robins. Viking, 1989. ISBN 0-670-82572-7 Subj: Activities. Family life.

Dahlbäck-Lutteman, Helena. *My sister Lotta and me* retold by Rika Lesser; ill. by Charlotte Ramel. Holt, 1993. ISBN 0-8050-2558-8 Subj: Activities – playing. Family life – sisters. Toys – dolls.

Daily, Don. *The twelve days of Christmas cats* ill. by author. Courage Books, 1998. ISBN 0-7624-0384-5 Subj: Animals – cats. Counting, numbers. Holidays – Christmas. Songs.

Dale, Elizabeth. *How long?* ill. by Alan Marks. Orchard, 1998. ISBN 0-531-30101-X Subj: Animals – dormice. Family life – mothers. Time.

Dale, Penny. *All about Alice* ill. by author. Candlewick, 1992. ISBN 1-56402-171-8 Subj: Activities – playing. Family life – sisters.

Bet you can't ill. by author. Lippincott, 1987. ISBN 0-397-32256-9 Subj: Bedtime. Character traits – orderliness. Ethnic groups in the U.S. – African Americans. Family life – brothers and sisters.

Big Brother, Little Brother ill. by author. Courage Books, 1997. ISBN 0-7636-0146-2 Subj: Family life – brothers.

Daisy Rabbit's tree house ill. by author. Candlewick, 1995. ISBN 1-56402-641-8 Subj: Animals. Animals – rabbits. Homes, houses. Night. Sleepovers. Trees.

The elephant tree ill. by author. Putnam, 1991. ISBN 0-399-22282-0 Subj: Animals. Animals – elephants. Jungle. Trees.

Ten out of bed ill. by author. Candlewick, 1994. ISBN 1-56402-322-2 Subj: Bedtime. Counting, numbers. Sleep. Toys.

Ten play hide-and-seek ill. by author. Candlewick, 1998. ISBN 0-7636-0654-5 Subj: Bedtime. Behavior – hiding. Toys.

Wake up, Mr. B.! ill. by author. Candlewick, 1992. ISBN 1-56402-104-1 Subj: Animals – dogs. Family life. Imagination. Morning. Pets.

Dale, Ruth Bluestone. *Benjamin . . . and Sylvester also* ill. by J. B. Handelsman. McGraw-Hill, 1960. Subj: Animals – dogs. Behavior – dissatisfaction. Country.

Daleo, Morgan Simone. *A spirited alphabet: from A to Z* ill. by Frank Riccio. Hampton Roads, 1999. ISBN 1-57174-148-8 Subj: ABC books.

Dalgliesh, Alice. *The little wooden farmer* ill. by Anita Lobel. Macmillan, 1988, c1930. ISBN 0-02-725590-5 Subj: Farms.

The Thanksgiving story ill. by Helen Moore Sewell. Scribners, [1987] c1954. ISBN 0-684-18999-2 Subj: Caldecott award honor books. Holidays – Thanksgiving. Pilgrims. U.S. history.

The turnip (Milhous, Katherine)

Dallas-Smith, Peter. *Trumpets in Grumpetland* ill. by Peter Cross. Random House, 1985. ISBN 0-394-97028-4 Subj: Music. Mythical creatures.

Dalmais, Anne-Marie. *And may the best animal win!* ill. by Doris Susan Smith. Golden Books, 1986. ISBN 0-307-15841-1 Subj: Activities – making things. Animals. Contests.

The Best bedtime stories of Mother Bear ill. by Violayne Hulné; English trans. by Diane Cohen. Derrydale Books, 1988, c1987. ISBN 0-517-66273-6 Subj: Animals – bears. Bedtime.

Best bedtime stories of Mother Cat ill. by Violayne Hulné; English trans. by Diane Cohen. Derrydale Books, 1988. ISBN 0-517-66272-8 Subj: Animals – cats. Bedtime.

Best bedtime stories of Mother Hen ill. by Violayne Hulné; English trans. by Diane Cohen. Derrydale Books, 1987. ISBN 0-517-65493-8 Subj: Bedtime. Birds – chickens.

Best bedtime stories of Mother Mouse ill. by Violayne Hulné; English trans. by Diane Cohen. Derrydale Books, 1987. ISBN 0-517-65492-X Subj: Animals – mice. Bedtime.

Best bedtime stories of Mother Pig ill. by Violayne Hulné; English trans. by Diane Cohen. Derrydale Books, 1988. ISBN 0-517-66276-0 Subj: Animals – pigs. Bedtime.

Best bedtime stories of Mother Sheep ill. by Violayne Hulné; English trans. by Diane Cohen. Derrydale Books, 1988, c1987. ISBN 0-517-66274-4 Subj: Animals – sheep. Bedtime.

Betsy the bunny ill. by Annie Bonhomme; English trans. by Diane Cohen. Derrydale Books, 1987. ISBN 0-517-65308-7 Subj: Animals – rabbits. Behavior – lost. Toys – dolls.

The butterfly book of birds ill. by Guy Michel. Two Continents, 1977. ISBN 0-8467-0226-6 Subj: Birds.

Danny the duck ill. by Annie Bonhomme; English trans. by Diane Cohen. Derrydale Books, 1987. ISBN 0-517-65309-5 Subj: Behavior – tardiness. Birds – ducks.

The Elephant's airplane and other machines ill. by Doris Susan Smith. Golden Books, 1984. ISBN 0-307-65579-2 Subj: Animals. Transportation.

Henry the hedgehog ill. by Annie Bonhomme; English trans. by Diane Cohen. Derrydale Books, 1987. ISBN 0-517-65310-9 Subj: Activities – vacationing. Animals – hedgehogs. Family life – grandparents.

In my garden: learning to count ill. by Genji. Two Continents, 1977. ISBN 0-8467-0219-3 Subj: Counting, numbers. Poetry.

Kelly the kitten ill. by Annie Bonhomme; English trans. by Diane Cohen. Derrydale Books, 1987. ISBN 0-517-65311-7 Subj: Animals – cats. Friendship. School.

Molly and Mimi the mouse twins ill. by Annie Bonhomme; English trans. by Diane Cohen. Derrydale Books, 1987. ISBN 0-517-65312-5 Subj: Animals – mice. Birthdays. Multiple births – twins.

Petey the puppy ill. by Annie Bonhomme; English trans. by Diane Cohen. Derrydale Books, 1987. ISBN 0-517-65313-3 Subj: Activities – making things. Animals – dogs. Homes, houses.

Dalton, Alene. *My new picture book of songs* scores by Reah Allen; ill. by Gini Bunnell. Osmond Pub., 1979. ISBN 0-89888-002-5 Subj: Music. Songs.

Dalton, Anne. *Prince Starr* ill. by author. Kaye & Ward, 1985. ISBN 071822101X Subj: Folk and fairy tales. Sky.

This is the way ill. by author. Scholastic, 1992. ISBN 0-590-45892-2 Subj: Family life. Nursery rhymes.

Daly, Kathleen N. *Daniel in the lions' den* (Bible. Old. Testament. Daniel)

Dinosaurs ill. by Tim and Greg Hildebrandt. Golden Pr., 1977. ISBN 0-307-11835-5 Subj: Dinosaurs.

The Giant little Golden Book of dogs ill. by Tibor Gergely. Simon & Schuster, 1957. Subj: Animals – dogs.

Jesus our friend ill. by Jim Cummins. Rand McNally, 1984. ISBN 0-528-82494-5 Subj: Format, unusual – board books. Religion.

Jonah and the great fish (Bible. Old Testament. Jonah)

Joseph and his brothers (Bible. Old Testament. Joseph)

The Macmillan picture wordbook ill. by John Wallner. Macmillan, 1982. ISBN 0-02-725600-6 Subj: Dictionaries.

Making friends ill. by Maryann Cocca-Leffler. Parker Brothers, 1984. ISBN 0-910-31327-X Subj: Friendship.

Noah and the ark (Bible. Old Testament. Noah)

Strawberry Shortcake and pets on parade ill. by Pat Sustendal. Parker Brothers, 1983. ISBN 0-910-31306-7 Subj: Pets. Theater.

The three bears (The three bears)

Today's biggest animals ill. by Tim and Greg Hildebrandt. Golden Pr., 1977. ISBN 0-307-61836-6 Subj: Animals. Science.

Unusual animals ill. by Tim and Greg Hildebrandt. Golden Pr., 1977. ISBN 0-307-61834-7 Subj: Animals. Science.

Daly, Maureen. *Patrick visits the library* ill. by Paul Lantz. Dodd, 1961. Subj: Animals – dogs. Birthdays. Libraries.

Daly, Niki. *Ben's gingerbread man* ill. by author. Viking, 1985. ISBN 0-670-80806-7 Subj: Family life – mothers. Food.

The boy on the beach ill. by author. Margaret K. McElderry, 1999. ISBN 0-689-82175-1 Subj: Behavior – lost. Family life. Foreign lands – South Africa. Rhyming text. Sea and seashore.

Bravo, Zan Angelo! a commedia dell'arte tale ill. by author. Farrar, 1998. ISBN 0-374-30953-1 Subj: Clowns, jesters. Fairs. Family life. Foreign lands – Italy. Theater.

The dinosaurs are back and it's all your fault, Edward! (Hartmann, Wendy)

Jamela's dress ill. by author. Farrar, 1999. ISBN 0-374-33667-9 Subj: Clothing – dresses. Foreign lands – South Africa.

Joseph's other red sock ill. by author. Atheneum, 1982. ISBN 0-689-50216-8 Subj: Clothing – socks.

Just like Archie ill. by author. Viking, 1986. ISBN 0-670-81253-6 Subj: Pets.

Look at me! ill. by author. Viking, 1986. ISBN 0-670-81252-8 Subj: Sibling rivalry.

Mama, papa and baby Joe ill. by author. Viking, 1991. ISBN 0-670-84161-7 Subj: Shopping.

Mary Malloy and the baby who wouldn't sleep ill. by author. Western, 1993. ISBN 0-307-17501-4 Subj: Foreign lands – Egypt. Moon. Reptiles – alligators, crocodiles. Sleep.

Monsters are like that ill. by author. Viking, 1985. ISBN 0-670-80807-5 Subj: Family life – brothers and sisters. Monsters.

My dad ill. by author. Margaret K. McElderry, 1995. ISBN 0-689-50620-1 Subj: Family life – fathers. Illness.

Not so fast Songololo ill. by author. Atheneum, 1986. ISBN 0-689-50367-9 Subj: City. Family life – grandmothers. Foreign lands – Africa. Foreign lands – South Africa. Shopping.

Papa Lucky's shadow ill. by author. Margaret K. McElderry, 1992. ISBN 0-689-50541-8 Subj: Activities – dancing. Family life – grandfathers.

Somewhere in Africa (Mennen, Ingrid)

Teddy's ear ill. by author. Viking, 1985. ISBN 0-670-80808-3 Subj: Family life – mothers. Toys – bears.

Thank you Henrietta ill. by author. Viking, 1986. ISBN 0-670-81254-4 Subj: Character traits – helpfulness.

Vim, the rag mouse ill. by author. Atheneum, 1979. ISBN 0-689-50141-2 Subj: Crime. Toys.

Why the sun and moon live in the sky ill. by author. Lothrop, 1995. ISBN 0-688-13332-0 Subj: Folk and fairy tales. Foreign lands – Nigeria. Moon. Sea and seashore. Sun.

Dame Wiggins of Lee and her seven wonderful cats ed. by John Ruskin; ill. by Robert Broomfield. McGraw-Hill, 1963. Ascribed to Richard Scrafton Sharpe and Mrs. Pearson. Endpapers: reproduction of Kate Greenaway drawings. Subj: Nursery rhymes.

Damjan, Mischa. *Atuk* ill. by Józef Wilkon. North-South, 1989. ISBN 1-55858-091-3 Subj: Animals – dogs. Animals – wolves. Eskimos. Foreign lands – Arctic.

The big squirrel and the little rhinoceros ill. by Hans de Beer; trans. by Lenny Hort. North-South, 1991. ISBN 1-55858-117-0 Subj: Animals. Behavior – wishing. Concepts – size.

The clown said no ill. by Józef Wilkon; trans. by Anthea Bell. North-South, 1986. ISBN 0-8050-0055-0 Subj: Behavior – seeking better things. Circus. Clowns, jesters.

December's travels ill. by Dusan Kállay. Dial, 1986. ISBN 0-8037-0257-4 Subj: Days of the week, months of the year. Holidays – Christmas.

The fake flamingos ill. by Józef Wilkon; trans. by Anthea Bell. North-South, 1987. ISBN 0-8050-0490-4 Subj: Birds – flamingos. Birds – storks. Self-concept.

Goodbye little bird trans. from German by Anthea Bell; ill. by Dorothée Duntze. Faber, 1983. ISBN 0-571-12520-4 Subj: Birds. Friendship.

How do Dinosaurs say goodnight? ill. by Mark Teague. Blue Sky, 2000. ISBN 0-590-31681-8 Subj: Bedtime. Dinosaurs. Family life – mothers.

The little prince and the tiger cat ill. by Ralph Steadman. McGraw-Hill, 1967. Subj: Animals – cats. Foreign lands – Japan. Royalty – princes.

The little sea horse ill. by Riccardo Bellettati. Faber, 1983. ISBN 0-571-12519-0 Subj: Fish. Imagination. Sea and seashore.

The wolf and the kid ill. by Max Velthuijs. McGraw-Hill, 1967. Subj: Animals – goats. Animals – wolves. Character traits – cleverness.

Damrell, Liz. *With the wind* ill. by Stephen Marchesi. Watts, 1991. ISBN 0-531-08482-5 Subj: Animals – horses, ponies. Handicaps – physical handicaps.

D'Andrea, Annette Cole. *see* Steiner, Barbara (Annette)

Daniel, Anne. *see* Steiner, Barbara (Annette)

Daniel, Doris Temple. *Pauline and the peacock* ill. by Barbara Brown Schoenewolf. E. C. Temple, 1980. ISBN 0-936650-00-1 Subj: Birds – peacocks, peahens. Family life. Farms. Science.

Daniel, Kira. *Teacher* ill. by Diane Paterson. Troll, 1989. ISBN 0-8167-1430-4 Subj: Careers – teachers.

Daniels, Guy. *The peasant's pea patch* (The peasant's pea patch)

The Tsar's riddles: or, the wise little girl ill. by Paul Galdone. McGraw-Hill, 1967. Subj: Character traits – cleverness. Folk and fairy tales. Foreign lands – Russia. Riddles.

D'Antonio, Nancy. *Our baby from China: an adoption story* ill. by author. Albert Whitman, 1997. ISBN 0-

8075-6162-2 Subj: Adoption. Ethnic groups in the U.S. – Chinese Americans. Family life. Foreign lands – China.

Dantzer-Rosenthal, Marya. *Some things are different, some things are the same* ill. by Miriam Nerlove. Albert Whitman, 1986. ISBN 0-8075-7535-6 Subj: Concepts.

Darby, Gene. *What is a bird?* ill. by Lucy and John Hawkinson. Benefic Pr., 1959. Subj: Birds. Science.

What is a butterfly? ill. by Lucy and John Hawkinson. Benefic Pr., 1958. Subj: Insects – butterflies, caterpillars. Metamorphosis. Science.

What is a fish? ill. by Lucy and John Hawkinson. Benefic Pr., 1958. Subj: Fish. Science.

What is a plant? ill. by Lucy and John Hawkinson. Benefic Pr., 1959. Subj: Plants. Science.

What is a turtle? ill. by Lucy and John Hawkinson. Benefic Pr., 1959. Subj: Reptiles – turtles, tortoises. Science.

Da Rif, Andrea. *The blueberry cake that little fox baked* ill. by author. Atheneum, 1984. ISBN 0-689-50307-5 Subj: Activities – cooking. Birthdays.

Darling, Abigail. *Teddy bears' picnic cookbook* ill. by Alexandra Day. Viking, 1991. ISBN 0-670-82947-1 Subj: Activities – cooking. Activities – picnicking. Food. Toys – bears.

Darling, Benjamin. *Valerie and the silver pear* ill. by Daniel Lane. Four Winds, 1992. ISBN 0-02-726100-X Subj: Activities – cooking. Family life – grandfathers.

Darling, Christina. *Mirror* (Day, Alexandra)

Darling, Harold. *The night before Christmas* (Moore, Clement C.)

Darling, Kathy (Mary Kathleen). *ABC cats* photos by Tara Darling. Walker, 1998. ISBN 0-8027-8667-7 Subj: ABC books. Animals – cats. Pets.

ABC dogs photos by Tara Darling. Walker, 1997. ISBN 0-8027-8635-9 Subj: ABC books. Animals – dogs. Pets.

Amazon A B C photos by Tara Darling. Lothrop, 1996. ISBN 0-688-13779-2 Subj: ABC books. Animals. Foreign lands – Amazon.

Arctic babies photos by Tara Darling. Walker, 1996. ISBN 0-8027-8414-3 Subj: Animals. Birds. Foreign lands – Arctic.

Bug circus ill. by Buck Brown. Garrard, 1976. ISBN 0-8116-4301-8 Subj: Circus. Insects.

Desert babies photos by Tara Darling. Walker, 1997. ISBN 0-8027-8480-1 Subj: Animals. Animals – babies. Desert.

The Easter bunny's secret ill. by Kelly Oechsli. Garrard, 1978. Subj: Animals – rabbits. Holidays – Easter.

The mystery in Santa's toyshop ill. by Lori Pierson. Garrard, 1978. Subj: Holidays – Christmas. Mystery stories. Santa Claus.

Pecos Bill finds a horse ill. by Lou Cunette. Garrard, 1979. ISBN 0-8116-4047-7 Subj: Animals. Animals – horses, ponies. Mythical creatures. Tall tales.

Rain forest babies photos by Tara Darling. Walker, 1996. ISBN 0-8027-8412-7 Subj: Animals. Foreign lands. Forest, woods.

Seashore babies photos by Tara Darling. Walker, 1997. ISBN 0-8027-8477-1 Subj: Animals. Sea and seashore.

Darling, Mary Kathleen. *see* Darling, Kathy (Mary Kathleen)

Dasent, George W. *The cat on the Dovrefell: a Christmas tale* (De Paola, Tomie [Thomas Anthony])

East o' the sun, west o' the moon trans. by George W. Dasent; ill. by Gillian Barlow. Putnam, 1988. ISBN 0-399-21570-0 Subj: Animals – polar bears. Folk and fairy tales. Foreign lands – Norway. Royalty – princes. Witches.

Daudet, Alphonse. *The brave little goat of Monsieur Séguin: a picture story from Provence* ill. by Chiyoko Nakatani. Collins-World, 1968. Translation and adaptation of La chèvre de M. Séguin. Subj: Animals – goats. Animals – wolves. Foreign lands – France.

Dauer, Rosamond. *Bullfrog builds a house* ill. by Byron Barton. Greenwillow, 1977. ISBN 0-688-84090-6 Subj: Friendship. Frogs and toads. Homes, houses.

Bullfrog grows up ill. by Byron Barton. Greenwillow, 1976. ISBN 0-688-84020-5 Subj: Animals – mice. Behavior – growing up. Frogs and toads.

My friend, Jasper Jones ill. by Jerry Joyner. Parents, 1977. ISBN 0-8193-0888-9 Subj: Behavior – misbehavior. Imagination – imaginary friends.

The 300 pound cat ill. by Skip Morrow. Holt, 1981. ISBN 0-03-049111-2 Subj: Animals – cats. Behavior – greed.

Daugherty, Charles Michael. *Wisher* ill. by James Henry Daugherty. Viking, 1960. Subj: Animals – cats. Behavior – wishing. Dreams.

Daugherty, James Henry. *Andy and the lion* ill. by author. Viking, 1938. ISBN 0-670-12433-8 Subj: Animals – lions. Caldecott award honor books. Character traits – kindness to animals. Humor. Libraries.

The picnic: a frolic in two colors and three parts ill. by author. Viking, 1958. Subj: Activities – picnicking. Animals – lions. Animals – mice.

Daugherty, Sonia (Medvedeva). *Vanka's donkey* ill. by James Henry Daugherty. Stokes, 1940. Subj: Animals – donkeys. Folk and fairy tales. Foreign lands – Russia.

Daughtry, Duanne. *What's inside?* photos by author. Knopf, 1984. ISBN 0-394-96249-4 Subj: Concepts – in and out. Wordless.

D'Aulaire, Edgar Parin. *see* Aulaire, Edgar Parin d'

D'Aulaire, Ingri Mortenson. *see* Aulaire, Ingri Mortenson d'

Dauphin, Francine Legrand. *A French A. B. C.* ill. by author. Coward, 1947. Subj: ABC books. Foreign lands – France. Foreign languages.

Davenier, Christine. *Leon and Albertine* ill. by author; trans. by Dominic Barth. Orchard, 1998. ISBN 0-531-30072-2 Subj: Animals. Animals – pigs. Birds – chickens. Emotions – love. Pets.

Davenport, Zoë. *Toys* ill. by author. Ticknor & Fields, 1995. ISBN 0-395-71539-3 Subj: Toys.

David, Eugene. *Crystal magic* ill. by Abner Graboff. Prentice-Hall, 1965. Subj: Science.

David, Lawrence. *The good little girl* ill. by Clément Oubrerie. Doubleday, 1998. ISBN 0-385-32614-9 Subj: Behavior – misbehavior. Behavior – needing someone. Character traits – meanness. Family life.

Davidson, Alice J. *The story of creation* ill. by Victoria Marshall. C.R. Gibson, 1984. ISBN 0-8378-5066-5 Subj: Creation. Religion.

Davidson, Amanda. *Teddy at the seashore* ill. by author. Holt, 1984. Originally published under title: Teddy at the seaside. ISBN 0-03-071026-X Subj: Foreign lands – England. Sea and seashore. Toys – bears.

Teddy goes outside ill. by author. Holt, 1985. ISBN 0-03-005004-9 Subj: Format, unusual – board books. Toys – bears. Weather.

Teddy in the garden ill. by author. Holt, 1986. ISBN 0-03-008502-0 Subj: Behavior – losing things. Gardens, gardening. Toys – bears.

Teddy's birthday ill. by author. Holt, 1985. ISBN 0-03-002887-6 Subj: Birthdays. Toys – bears.

Teddy's first Christmas ill. by author. Holt, 1982. ISBN 0-03-062616-1 Subj: Holidays – Christmas. Toys – bears.

Davidson, Jill A. *And that's what happened to little Lucy* ill. by Paul Meisel. Random House, 1989. ISBN 0-394-99945-2 Subj: Activities – trading. Activities – walking. Animals. Forest, woods.

Davies, Andrew. *Poonam's pets* ill. by Paul Dowling. Viking, 1990. ISBN 0-670-83321-5 Subj: Animals – lions. Pets. School.

Davies, Kay. *My apple* by Kay Davies and Wendy Oldfield; photos by Fiona Pragoff. Gareth Stevens, 1994. ISBN 0-8368-1114-3 Subj: Food. Nature. Science.

My balloon by Kay Davies and Wendy Oldfield; photos by Fiona Pragoff. Doubleday, 1990. ISBN 0-385-41199-5 Subj: Activities. Concepts – perspective. Science. Toys – balloons.

My drum by Kay Davies and Wendy Oldfield; photos by Pragoff, Fiona. Gareth Stevens, 1991. ISBN 0-8368-1116-X Subj: Music. Science.

My mirror by Kay Davies and Wendy Oldfield; photos by Fiona Pragoff. Doubleday, 1990. ISBN 0-385-41196-0 Subj: Activities. Concepts – perspective. Science.

Davies, Nicola. *Big blue whale* ill. by Nick Maland. Candlewick, 1997. ISBN 1-56402-895-X Subj: Animals – whales. Sea and seashore.

Davies, Sally. *When William went away* ill. by author. Carolrhoda, 1999. ISBN 1-57505-303-9 Subj: Friendship. Moving.

Davies, Sumiko. *see* Sumiko

Davis, Alice Vaught. *Timothy Turtle* ill. by Guy Brown Wiser. Harcourt, 1940. Subj: Character traits – helpfulness. Reptiles – turtles, tortoises.

Davis, Aubrey. *Bone button borscht* ill. by Dušan Petricic. Kids Can Pr., 1997. ISBN 1-55074-224-8 Subj: Character traits – generosity. Folk and fairy tales. Food. Homeless. Jewish culture.

The enormous potato ill. by Dušan Petricic. Kids Can Pr., 1998. ISBN 1-55074-386-4 Subj: Behavior – sharing. Cumulative tales. Farms. Folk and fairy tales. Food. Plants. Problem solving.

Sody salleratus ill. by Alan and Lea Daniel. Kids Can Pr., 1998. ISBN 1-55074-281-7 Subj: Animals – bears. Folk and fairy tales. Food.

Davis, Charles E. *Creatures at my feet* (Neidigh, Sherry)

Davis, Douglas F. *The lion's tail* ill. by Ronald Himler. Atheneum, 1980. ISBN 0-689-50153-6 Subj: Animals – lions. Folk and fairy tales. Foreign lands – Africa.

There's an elephant in the garage ill. by Steven Kellogg. Dutton, 1979. ISBN 0-525-41050-3 Subj: Animals. Animals – cats. Imagination. Toys – bears.

Davis, Gary. *Working at a TV station* ill. with photos. Childrens Pr., 1998. ISBN 0-516-20750-4 Subj: Careers. Television.

Davis, Gibbs. *Katy's first haircut* ill. by Linda Shute. Houghton Mifflin, 1985. ISBN 0-395-38942-9 Subj: Emotions – embarrassment. Hair.

The other Emily ill. by Linda Shute. Houghton Mifflin, 1984. ISBN 0-395-35482-X Subj: Behavior – sharing. Names.

Davis, Hubert J. *A January fog will freeze a hog: and other weather folklore* (A January fog will freeze a hog)

Davis, Jennifer. *Before you were born* ill. by Laura Cornell. Workman, 1997. ISBN 0-7611-1200-6 Subj: Babies. Birth. Family life. Format, unusual – toy and movable books.

Davis, Karen. *Star light, star bright* ill. by author. Green Tiger Pr., 1993. ISBN 0-671-79455-8 Subj: Behavior – wishing. Stars.

Davis, Katie (Katie I.). *I hate to go to bed!* ill. by author. Harcourt, 1999. ISBN 0-15-201920-0 Subj: Bedtime. Dreams. Family life. Parties.

Who hops? ill. by author. Harcourt, 1998. ISBN 0-15-201839-5 Subj: Animals.

Davis, Lavinia (Riker). *Roger and the fox* ill. by Hildegard Woodward. Doubleday, 1947. Subj: Animals – foxes. Caldecott award honor books.

The wild birthday cake ill. by Hildegard Woodward. Doubleday, 1949. Subj: Birthdays. Caldecott award honor books.

Davis, Lee. *The lifesize animal opposites book* ill. with photos. DK, 1994. ISBN 1-56458-720-7 Subj: Animals. Concepts. Rhyming text.

Davis, Maggie S. *The best way to Ripton* ill. by Stephen Gammell. Holiday, 1982. ISBN 0-8234-0459-5 Subj: Activities – traveling. Humor.

A garden of whales ill. by Jennifer Barrett O'Connell. Camden House, 1993. ISBN 0-944475-36-1 Subj: Animals – endangered animals. Animals – whales. Dreams. Gardens, gardening.

Grandma's secret letter ill. by John Wallner. Holiday, 1982. ISBN 0-8234-0382-3 Subj: Behavior – secrets. Character traits – kindness. Mythical creatures – elves.

Rickety witch ill. by Kay Chorao. Holiday, 1984. ISBN 0-8234-0521-4 Subj: Holidays – Halloween. Witches.

The rinky-dink café ill. by John Sandford. Simon & Schuster, 1988. ISBN 0-671-66408-5 Subj: Animals – pigs. Food. Restaurants. Rhyming text.

Something magic ill. by Mary O'Keefe Young. Simon & Schuster, 1991. ISBN 0-671-69627-0 Subj: Family life.

Davis, Reda. *Martin's dinosaur* ill. by Louis Slobodkin. Crowell, 1959. Subj: Dragons. Foreign lands – England.

Davison, Martine. *Kevin and the school nurse* ill. by Marylin Hafner. Random House, 1992. ISBN 0-679-91821-3 Subj: Careers – nurses. Food. School.

Maggie and the emergency room ill. by Marylin Hafner. Random House, 1992. ISBN 0-679-91818-3 Subj: Hospitals. Illness.

Rita goes to the hospital ill. by John Jones. Random House, 1992. ISBN 0-679-91820-5 Subj: Hospitals. Illness – tonsillectomy.

Robby visits the doctor ill. by Nancy Stevenson. Random House, 1992. ISBN 0679918191 Subj: Anatomy – ears. Careers – doctors. Illness.

Davison, Patricia Hinton. *Pablo and Pimienta* (Covault, Ruth M.)

Davol, Marguerite W. *Batwings and the curtain of night* ill. by Mary GrandPré. Orchard, 1997. ISBN 0-531-33005-2 Subj: Animals. Animals – bats. Bedtime. Creation. Dreams. Folk and fairy tales. Night.

Black, white, just right ill. by Irene Trivas. Albert Whitman, 1993. ISBN 0-8075-0785-7 Subj: Ethnic groups in the U.S. Family life. Marriage, interracial.

The heart of the wood ill. by Sheila Hamanaka. Simon & Schuster, 1992. ISBN 0-671-74778-9 Subj: Cumulative tales. Music. Rhyming text.

How snake got his hiss: an original tale ill. by Mercedes McDonald. Orchard, 1996. ISBN 0-531-08768-9 Subj: Animals. Cumulative tales. Foreign lands – Africa. Reptiles – snakes.

Davoll, Barbara. *Dusty Mole, private eye* ill. by Dennis Hockerman. Moody, 1992. ISBN 0-8024-2700-6 Subj: Animals. Animals – moles. Behavior – talking to strangers. Mystery stories.

Davy's scary journey ill. by Tim Warnes. Little Tiger, 1997. ISBN 1-888444-10-X Subj: Behavior – running away. Birds – ducks.

Dawson, Diane. *see* Hearn, Diane Dawson

Dawson, Linda. *Phoebe and the hot water bottles* (Furchgott, Terry)

Dawson, Zöe. *China* ill. with photos. Steck-Vaughn, 1996. ISBN 0-8172-4007-1 Subj: Foreign lands – China.

Japan ill. with photos. Steck-Vaughn, 1996. ISBN 0-81724-011-X Subj: Foreign lands – Japan.

Day, Alexandra. *Boswell wide-awake* ill. by author. Farrar, 1999. ISBN 0-374-39973-5 Subj: Activities. Animals – bears. Night.

Carl goes shopping ill. by author. Farrar, 1989. ISBN 0-374-31110-2 Subj: Animals – dogs. Shopping. Stores. Wordless.

Carl goes to daycare ill. by author. Farrar, 1993. ISBN 0-374-31093-9 Subj: Activities – playing. Animals – dogs. School.

Carl makes a scrapbook ill. by author. Farrar, 1994. ISBN 0-374-31129-3 Subj: Activities – babysitting. Activities – making things. Animals – dogs.

Carl pops up ill. by author. Simon & Schuster, 1994. ISBN 0-671-87105-6 Subj: Activities – babysitting. Animals – dogs. Format, unusual – toy and movable books. Wordless.

Carl's afternoon in the park ill. by author. Farrar, 1991. ISBN 0-374-31109-9 Subj: Activities – babysitting. Animals – dogs. Wordless.

Carl's birthday ill. by author. Farrar, 1995. ISBN 0-374-31144-7 Subj: Activities – babysitting. Animals – dogs. Behavior – misbehavior. Birthdays.

Carl's Christmas ill. by author. Farrar, 1990. ISBN 0-374-31114-5 Subj: Activities – babysitting. Animals – dogs. Holidays – Christmas. Wordless.

Carl's masquerade ill. by author. Farrar, 1992. ISBN 0-374-31094-7 Subj: Animals – dogs. Babies. Parties. Wordless.

The Christmas we moved to the barn by Alexandra Day and Cooper Edens; ill. by Alexandra Day. HarperCollins, 1997. ISBN 0-06-205149-0 Subj: Animals. Family life. Holidays – Christmas. Moving.

Follow Carl! ill. by author. Farrar, 1998. ISBN 0-374-34380-2 Subj: Activities – babysitting. Activities – playing. Animals – dogs. Wordless.

Frank and Ernest ill. by author. Scholastic, 1988. ISBN 0-590-41557-3 Subj: Animals – bears. Animals – elephants. Character traits – helpfulness. Language.

Frank and Ernest on the road ill. by author. Scholastic, 1994. ISBN 0-590-45048-4 Subj: Animals – bears. Animals – elephants. Careers – truck drivers. Language. Trucks.

Frank and Ernest play ball ill. by author. Scholastic, 1990. ISBN 0-590-42548-X Subj: Animals – bears. Animals – elephants. Dictionaries. Language. Sports – baseball.

Good dog, Carl ill. by author. Green Tiger Pr., 1985. ISBN 0-8813-8062-8 Subj: Activities – babysitting. Animals – dogs. Wordless.

Helping the animals by Alexandra Day and Cooper Edens; ill. by Alexandra Day. Green Tiger Pr., 1987. ISBN 0-8813-8085-7 Subj: Animals. Character traits – helpfulness. Format, unusual – board books.

Helping the flowers and trees by Alexandra Day and Cooper Edens; ill. by Alexandra Day. Green Tiger Pr., 1987. ISBN 0-8813-8086-5 Subj: Animals. Character traits – helpfulness. Flowers. Format, unusual – board books. Trees.

Helping the night by Alexandra Day and Cooper Edens; ill. by Alexandra Day. Green Tiger Pr., 1987. ISBN 0-8813-8084-9 Subj: Animals. Character traits – helpfulness. Format, unusual – board books. Night.

Helping the sun by Alexandra Day and Cooper Edens; ill. by Alexandra Day. Green Tiger Pr., 1987. ISBN 0-8813-8083-0 Subj: Animals. Character traits – helpfulness. Format, unusual – board books. Sun.

Mirror by Alexandra Day and Christina Darling; ill. by Alexander Day. Farrar, 1997. ISBN 0-374-34720-4 Subj: Imagination. Magic. Mirrors.

Paddy's pay-day ill. by author. Viking, 1989. ISBN 0-670-82598-0 Subj: Animals – dogs. Circus. Country. Money.

River parade ill. by author. Viking, 1990. ISBN 0-670-82946-3 Subj: Boats, ships. Family life – fathers. Rivers. Sports – swimming.

Day, Betsy. *Stefan and Olga* ill. by author. Dial, 1991. ISBN 0-8037-0817-3 Subj: Birds – geese. Farms. Friendship. Music. Pets.

Day, David. *King of the woods* ill. by Ken Brown. Four Winds, 1993. ISBN 0-02-726361-4 Subj: Animals. Birds. Cumulative tales. Forest, woods. Royalty – kings.

The swan children retold by David Day; ill. by Richard Evans. Ideals, 1991. ISBN 0-8249-8461-7 Subj: Birds – swans. Folk and fairy tales. Foreign lands – Ireland. Royalty.

Day, Edward C. *John Tabor's ride* ill. by Dirk Zimmer. Knopf, 1989. ISBN 0-394-98577-X Subj: Activities – traveling. Animals – whales. Humor. Tall tales.

Day, Marie. *Dragon in the rocks* ill. by author. Firefly, 1992. ISBN 0-920775-76-4 Subj: Animals. Careers – paleontologists. Character traits – persistence. Dragons.

Quennu and the cave bear: a prehistoric tale ill. by author. Owl Books, 1999. ISBN 1-895688-86-8 Subj: Activities – painting. Animals – bears. Caves.

Day, Michael E. *Berry Ripe Moon* ill. by Carol Whitmore. Tide Grass Pr., 1977. Subj: Indians of North America – Penobscot.

Day, Nancy Raines. *A kitten's year* ill. by Anne Mortimer. HarperCollins, 2000. ISBN 0-06-027231-7 Subj: Animals – cats. Days of the week, months of the year.

The lion's whiskers: an Ethiopian folktale ill. by Ann Grifalconi. Scholastic, 1995. ISBN 0-590-45803-5 Subj: Animals – lions. Family life – step families. Folk and fairy tales. Foreign lands – Ethiopia.

Day, Shirley. *Ruthie's big tree* ill. by author. Firefly, 1982. ISBN 0-920236-35-9 Subj: Character traits – perseverance. Trees.

Waldo's back yard ill. by author. Firefly, 1984. ISBN 0-920236-73-1 Subj: Behavior – dissatisfaction. Character traits – helpfulness. Picture puzzles.

Dayrell, Elphinstone. *Why the sun and the moon live in the sky: an African folktale* ill. by Blair Lent. Houghton Mifflin, 1968. First published in 1914 in the author's Folk stories from southern Nigeria, West Africa. Subj: Caldecott award honor books. Folk and fairy tales. Foreign lands – Africa. Moon. Sky. Sun.

Dayton, Laura. *LeRoy's birthday circus* ill. by Susan Huggins. Nelson, 1981. ISBN 0-525-66744-X Subj: Birthdays. Circus. Counting, numbers. Rhyming text.

Dayton, Mona. *Earth and sky* ill. by Roger Antoine Duvoisin. HarperCollins, 1969. Subj: Behavior – fighting, arguing. Earth. Sky.

Dean, Leigh. *Two special cards* (Lisker, Sonia O.)

De Angeli, Marguerite. *The book of nursery and Mother Goose rhymes* comp. and ill. by Marguerite De Angeli. Doubleday, 1954. ISBN 0-385-06246-X Subj: Caldecott award honor books. Nursery rhymes.

Yonie Wondernose: for three little Wondernoses, Nina, David and Kiki ill. by author. Doubleday, 1944. ISBN 0-8361-9083-1 Subj: Caldecott award honor books. Family life. Farms.

DeArmond, Dale. *The seal oil lamp* ill. by author. Little, 1988. ISBN 0-316-17786-5 Subj: Character traits – kindness. Death. Eskimos. Folk and fairy tales. Handicaps – blindness. Senses – seeing.

De Beer, Hans. *Ahoy there, little polar bear* ill. by author. Holt, 1988. ISBN 3-85539-006-1 Subj: Animals – polar bears.

Bernard Bear's amazing adventure trans. by Marianne Martens; ill. by author. North-South, 1994. ISBN 1-55858-295-9 Subj: Animals – bears. Animals – dormice. Hibernation. Seasons – winter.

Little polar bear ill. by author. Holt, 1987. ISBN 0-8050-0486-6 Subj: Animals – polar bears. Behavior – lost. Friendship.

Little polar bear and the brave little hare trans. by J. Alison James; ill. by author. North-South, 1992. ISBN 1-55858-180-4 Subj: Animals – polar bears. Animals – rabbits. Character traits – bravery. Foreign lands – Arctic. Friendship.

Little polar bear and the husky pup ill. by author; trans. by Rosemary Lanning. North-South, 1999. ISBN 0-7358-1155-5 Subj: Animals – dogs. Animals – polar bears. Character traits – kindness to animals.

Little polar bear finds a friend ill. by author. North-South, 1990. ISBN 1-55858-092-1 Subj: Animals – polar bears. Character traits – freedom. Foreign lands – Arctic. Friendship.

Little polar bear, take me home! trans. by J. Alison James; ill. by author. North-South, 1996. ISBN 1-55858-631-8 Subj: Activities – traveling. Animals – polar bears. Animals – tigers. Behavior – lost.

DeBoer, Jesslyn. *Follow the star* ill. by Nancy Munger. Zondervan, 1998. ISBN 0-310-97554-9 Subj: Format, unusual – toy and movable books. Holidays – Christmas. Stars.

Getting ready for Christmas ill. by Nancy Munger. Zondervan, 1998. ISBN 0-310-97561-1 Subj: Animals. Format, unusual – toy and movable books. Holidays – Christmas. Religion – Nativity.

De Brunhoff, Jean. *see* Brunhoff, Jean de

De Brunhoff, Laurent. *see* Brunhoff, Laurent de

De Bruyn, Monica. *Lauren's secret ring* ill. by author. Albert Whitman, 1980. ISBN 0-8075-4391-9 Subj: Friendship.

DeCaprio, Annie. *One, two* ill. by Seymour Nydorf. Grosset, 1965. Designed by David Krieger. Subj: Counting, numbers.

DeChristopher, Marlowe. *Greencoat and the swanboy* ill. by reteller. Putnam, 1991. ISBN 0-399-22165-4 Subj: Birds – swans. Folk and fairy tales. Royalty – princesses.

Decker, Dorothy W. *Stripe and the merbear* ill. by author. Dillon, 1986. ISBN 0-87518-329-8 Subj: Mythical creatures. Sea and seashore. Toys – bears.

Stripe visits New York ill. by author. Dillon, 1986. ISBN 0-87518-267-4 Subj: Activities – painting. Art. City. Toys – bears.

Dedieu, Thierry. *Baby clown* ill. by author; paper engineering by Jerome Bruandet. Hyperion, 1995. ISBN 0-7868-0075-5 Subj: Babies. Circus. Clowns, jesters. Format, unusual – toy and movable books.

The little Christmas soldier ill. by author; trans. from French by George Wen. Holt, 1993. ISBN 0-8050-2612-6 Subj: Holidays – Christmas. Toys.

Dee, Nicholas. *see* Aiken, Joan

Dee, Rosie. *see* Aiken, Joan

Dee, Ruby. *Tower to heaven* ill. by Jennifer Bent. Holt, 1991. ISBN 0-8050-1460-8 Subj: Folk and fairy tales. Foreign lands – Ghana. Sky.

Two ways to count to ten: a Liberian folktale ill. by Susan Meddaugh. Holt, 1988. ISBN 0-8050-0407-6 Subj: Character traits – cleverness. Folk and fairy tales. Foreign lands – Africa.

Deedy, Carmen Agra. *Agatha's feather bed: not just another wild goose story* ill. by Laura L. Seeley. Peachtree, 1991. ISBN 1-56145-008-1 Subj: Birds – geese. Furniture – beds. Problem solving.

The secret of Old Zeb ill. by Michael P. White. Peachtree, 1997. ISBN 1-56145-115-0 Subj: Boats, ships. Family life.

Deeter, Catherine. *Seymour Bleu* ill. by author. Simon & Schuster, 1998. ISBN 0-689-80137-8 Subj: Animals – cats. Art. Careers – artists. Concepts – color.

Deetlefs, Rene. *Tabu and the dancing elephants* ill. by Lyn Gilbert. Dutton, 1995. ISBN 0-525-45226-5 Subj: Activities – dancing. Animals – elephants. Behavior – lost. Family life. Folk and fairy tales. Foreign lands – South Africa.

DeFelice, Cynthia C. *Casey in the bath* ill. by Chris L. Demarest. Farrar, 1996. ISBN 0-374-31173-0 Subj: Activities – bathing.

Clever crow ill. by S. D. Schindler. Atheneum, 1998. ISBN 0-689-80671-X Subj: Behavior – trickery. Birds – crows. Character traits – cleverness. Rhyming text.

Three perfect peaches retold by the Wild Washerwomen Storytellers, Cynthia DeFelice and Mary DeMarsh; ill. by Irene Trivas. Orchard, 1995. ISBN 0-531-08722-0 Subj: Character traits – cleverness. Folk and fairy tales. Foreign lands – France. Royalty – princesses.

When Grampa kissed his elbow ill. by Karl Swanson. Macmillan, 1992. ISBN 0-02-726455-6 Subj: Country. Family life – grandfathers.

Willy's silly grandma ill. by Shelley Jackson. Orchard, 1997. ISBN 0-531-33012-5 Subj: Ethnic groups in the U.S. – African Americans. Family life – grandparents. Ghosts. Superstition.

DeForest, Charlotte B. *The prancing pony: nursery rhymes from Japan* adapt. into English verse for children, with "Kusa-e"; ill. by Keiko Hida. Walker, 1968. Subj: Foreign lands – Japan. Nursery rhymes.

Degen, Bruce. *Aunt Possum and the pumpkin man* ill. by author. HarperCollins, 1977. ISBN 0-06-021413-9 Subj: Animals – cats. Animals – possums. Family life – aunts, uncles. Holidays – Halloween. Wordless.

Goblin walk (Johnston, Tony)

Jamberry ill. by author. HarperCollins, 1983. ISBN 0-06-021417-1 Subj: Animals – bears. Food. Rhyming text.

The little witch and the riddle ill. by author. HarperCollins, 1980. ISBN 0-0602-1414-7 Subj: Friendship. Magic. Riddles. Witches.

Sailaway home ill. by author. Scholastic, 1996. ISBN 0-590-46443-4 Subj: Animals – pigs. Imagination. Rhyming text.

Teddy bear towers ill. by author. HarperCollins, 1991. ISBN 0-06-021430-9 Subj: Family life – brothers. Imagination. Rhyming text. Royalty – kings. Toys – bears.

De Gerez, Toni. *Louhi, witch of North Farm* ill. by Barbara Cooney. Viking, 1986. A story from Finlands's epic poem The Kalevala. ISBN 0-670-80556-4 Subj: Behavior – stealing. Folk and fairy tales. Foreign lands – Finland. Moon. Sun. Witches.

My song is a piece of jade: poems of ancient Mexico in English and Spanish ill. by William Stark. Little, 1984. ISBN 0-316-81088-6 Subj: Foreign lands – Mexico. Foreign languages. Poetry.

De Groat, Diane. *Alligator's toothache* ill. by author. Crown, 1977. ISBN 0-517-52805-3 Subj: Illness. Reptiles – alligators, crocodiles. Teeth. Wordless.

Happy Birthday to you, you belong in a zoo ill. by author. Morrow, 1999. ISBN 0-688-16545-1 Subj: Animals. Birthdays. Friendship. Gifts. Parties.

Roses are pink, your feet really stink ill. by author. Morrow, 1996. ISBN 0-688-13605-2 Subj: Animals. Behavior – misbehavior. Holidays – Valentine's Day. School.

Trick or treat, smell my feet ill. by author. Morrow, 1998. ISBN 0-688-15767-X Subj: Animals. Clothing – costumes. Family life – brothers and sisters. Holidays – Halloween. School.

DeGross, Monalisa. *Granddaddy's street songs* ill. by Floyd Cooper. Hyperion, 1999. ISBN 0-7868-2132-9 Subj: Activities – working. Careers – peddlers. Ethnic groups in the U.S. – African Americans. Family life – grandfathers.

De Hamel, Joan. *Hemi's pet* ill. by Christine Ross. Houghton Mifflin, 1987. ISBN 0-395-43665-6 Subj: Pets. School. Sibling rivalry.

DeJong, David Cornel. *Looking for Alexander* ill. by Harvey Weiss. Little, 1963. Subj: Animals – cats. Family life – grandmothers.

De Kay, Ormonde. *Rimes de la Mere Oie: Mother Goose rhymes* (Mother Goose)

Delacre, Lulu. *Arroz con leche: popular songs and rhymes from Latin America* ill. by author. Scholastic, 1989. ISBN 0-590-42442-4 Subj: Foreign languages. Games. Music. Poetry. Songs.

Good times with baby ill. by author. Grosset, 1989. ISBN 0-448-21014-2 Subj: Babies.

Nathan and Nicholas Alexander ill. by author. Scholastic, 1986. ISBN 0-590-33956-7 Subj: Animals – elephants. Animals – mice. Behavior – sharing.

Nathan's balloon adventure ill. by author. Scholastic, 1991. ISBN 0-590-44976-1 Subj: Activities – ballooning. Animals – elephants. Animals – mice.

Nathan's fishing trip ill. by author. Scholastic, 1988. ISBN 0-590-41281-7 Subj: Animals – elephants. Animals – mice. Friendship. Sports – fishing.

Las Navidades: popular Christmas songs from Latin America sel. by Lulu Delacre; trans. from Spanish by Elena Paz; arranged by Ana-Maria Rosado; ill. by selector. Scholastic, 1990. ISBN 0-590-43548-5 Subj: Foreign languages. Holidays – Christmas. Music. Poetry. Songs.

Peter Cottontail's Easter book ill. by author. Scholastic, 1991. ISBN 0-590-43338-5 Subj: Animals – rabbits. Holidays – Easter.

Time for school, Nathan! ill. by author. Scholastic, 1989. ISBN 0-590-41942-0 Subj: Animals – elephants. Friendship. School.

De La Fontaine, Jean. *see* La Fontaine, Jean de

Delafosse, Claude. *Cars and trucks and other vehicles* (Cars and trucks and other vehicles)

Houses (Houses)

DeLage, Ida. *ABC Christmas* ill. by Roger Beerworth. Garrard, 1978. ISBN 0-8116-4355-7 Subj: ABC books. Holidays – Christmas.

ABC Easter bunny ill. by Ellen Sloan. Garrard, 1979. ISBN 0-8116-4356-5 Subj: ABC books. Animals – rabbits. Holidays – Easter.

ABC fire dogs ill. by Ellen Sloan. Garrard, 1977. ISBN 0-8116-4351-4 Subj: ABC books. Animals – dogs. Careers – firefighters.

ABC Halloween witch ill. by Lou Cunette. Garrard, 1977. ISBN 0-8116-4353-0 Subj: ABC books. Holidays – Halloween. Witches.

ABC pigs go to market ill. by Kelly Oechsli. Garrard, 1977. ISBN 0-8116-4350-6 Subj: ABC books. Animals – pigs. Stores.

ABC pirate adventure ill. by Buck Brown. Garrard, 1977. ISBN 0-8116-4352-2 Subj: ABC books. Pirates.

ABC Santa Claus ill. by Judith Gwyn Brown. Garrard, 1978. ISBN 0-8116-4354-9 Subj: ABC books. Holidays – Christmas. Santa Claus.

ABC triplets at the zoo ill. by Lori Pierson. Garrard, 1980. ISBN 0-8116-4357-3 Subj: ABC books. Animals. Zoos.

Am I a bunny? ill. by Ellen Sloan. Garrard, 1978. ISBN 0-8116-6072-9 Subj: Animals – rabbits. Self-concept.

Beware! Beware! A witch won't share ill. by Ted Schroeder. Garrard, 1991. ISBN 0-7910-1473-8 Subj: Behavior – sharing. Witches.

A bunny ride ill. by Tracy McVay. Garrard, 1975. ISBN 0-8116-6065-6 Subj: Animals – rabbits. Emotions – envy, jealousy.

Bunny school ill. by Tracy McVay. Garrard, 1976. ISBN 0-8116-6071-0 Subj: Animals – rabbits. School.

Frannie's flower ill. by Ellen Sloan. Garrard, 1979. ISBN 0-8116-6076-1 Subj: Activities – playing. Flowers.

Good morning, lady ill. by Tracy McVay. Garrard, 1974. ISBN 0-8116-6051-6 Subj: Animals. Animals – possums. Careers – peddlers.

The old witch and her magic basket ill. by Ellen Sloan. Garrard, 1978. ISBN 0-8116-4063-9 Subj: Holidays – Halloween. Witches.

The old witch and the crows ill. by Marianne Smith. Garrard, 1983. ISBN 0-8116-4067-1 Subj: Birds – crows. Birds – owls. Night. Witches.

The old witch and the dragon ill. by Unada. Garrard, 1979. ISBN 0-8116-4064-7 Subj: Dragons. Witches.

The old witch and the ghost parade ill. by Jody Taylor. Garrard, 1978. ISBN 0-8116-4062-0 Subj: Ghosts. Witches.

The old witch and the snores ill. by Gil Miret. Chelsea, 1991. ISBN 0-7910-1479-7 Subj: Animals – bears. Caves. Hibernation. Noise, sounds. Witches.

The old witch and the wizard ill. by Mimi Korach. Chelsea, 1991, c1974. ISBN 0-7910-1480-0 Subj: Animals – cats. Witches. Wizards.

The old witch finds a new house ill. by Pat Paris. Garrard, 1979. ISBN 0-7910-1481-9 Subj: Moving. Witches.

The old witch gets a surprise ill. by Ellen Sloan. Chelsea, 1991, c1981. ISBN 0-7910-1482-7 Subj: Activities – ballooning. Witches.

The old witch goes to the ball ill. by Gustave E. Nebel. Chelsea, 1991, c1969. ISBN 0-7910-1483-5 Subj: Clothing – costumes. Holidays – Halloween. Witches.

The old witch's party ill. by Mimi Korach. Chelsea, 1991, c1976. ISBN 0-7910-1484-3 Subj: Holidays – Halloween. Parties. Witches.

Pilgrim children on the Mayflower ill. by Bert Dodson. Garrard, 1980. ISBN 0-8116-4315-8 Subj: Boats, ships. Pilgrims. U.S. history.

The squirrel's tree party ill. by Tracy McVay. Garrard, 1978. ISBN 0-8116-6073-7 Subj: Animals – squirrels. Parties. Trees.

Weeny witch ill. by Kelly Oechsli. Chelsea, 1991, c1968. ISBN 0-7910-1485-1 Subj: Fairies. Night. Witches.

What does a witch need? ill. by Ted Schroeder. Chelsea, 1991, c1971. ISBN 0-7910-1486-X Subj: Animals – dogs. Character traits – helpfulness. Witches.

The witchy broom ill. by Walt Peaver. Chelsea, 1991, c1969. ISBN 0-7910-1487-8 Subj: Magic. Witches.

Delamare, David. *The Christmas secret* ill. by author. Simon & Schuster, 1991. ISBN 0-671-74822-X Subj: Animals. Friendship. Holidays – Christmas. Santa Claus. Weather – storms.

De La Mare, Walter (Walter John). *Molly Whuppie* ill. by Errol Le Cain. Farrar, 1983. ISBN 0-374-35000-0 Subj: Character traits – bravery. Character traits – cleverness. Giants. Royalty.

Delaney, A. *The butterfly* ill. by author. Crown, 1977. ISBN 0-440-00891-3 Subj: Cumulative tales. Insects – butterflies, caterpillars.

The gunnywolf ill. by author. HarperCollins, 1988. ISBN 0-06-021595-X Subj: Animals – wolves. Behavior – misbehavior. Flowers. Foreign lands – Germany. Songs.

Monster tracks? ill. by author. HarperCollins, 1981. ISBN 0-06-021589-5 Subj: Imagination. Weather – snow.

Pearl's first prize plant ill. by author. HarperCollins, 1997. ISBN 0-06-027357-7 Subj: Fairs. Gardens, gardening. Plants.

Delaney, M. C. (Michael Clark). *The marigold monster* ill. by Ned Delaney. Dutton, 1983. ISBN 0-525-44023-2 Subj: Humor. Monsters. Riddles.

Delaney, Molly. *My sister* ill. by author. Atheneum, 1989. ISBN 0-689-31460-4 Subj: Family life – sisters. Sibling rivalry.

Delaney, Ned. *Bad dog!* ill. by author. Morrow, 1987. ISBN 0-688-06596-1 Subj: Animals – dogs. Behavior – lost. Behavior – misbehavior.

Bert and Barney ill. by author. Houghton Mifflin, 1979. ISBN 0-395-28377-9 Subj: Friendship.

Cosmic chickens ill. by author. HarperCollins, 1988. ISBN 0-06-021584-4 Subj: Birds – chickens. Farms. Space and space ships.

One dragon to another ill. by author. Houghton Mifflin, 1976. ISBN 0-395-24209-6 Subj: Character traits – individuality. Dragons. Games. Insects – butterflies, caterpillars. Metamorphosis.

Rufus the doofus ill. by author. Houghton Mifflin, 1978. ISBN 0-395-27153-3 Subj: Behavior – misbehavior. School.

Terrible things could happen ill. by author. Lothrop, 1983. ISBN 0-688-01284-1 Subj: Activities – working. Humor.

Two strikes, four eyes ill. by author. Houghton Mifflin, 1976. ISBN 0-395-24744-6 Subj: Animals – mice. Glasses. Sports – baseball.

A worm for dinner ill. by author. Houghton Mifflin, 1977. ISBN 0-395-25153-2 Subj: Animals – moles. Birds. Friendship.

Delaunay, Sonia. *Sonia Delaunay's alphabet* ill. by author. Crowell, 1972. ISBN 0-690-75228-X Subj: ABC books. Rhyming text.

Delessert, Etienne. *The endless party* trans. by Jeffrey Tabberner; ill. by author. Oxford Univ. Pr., 1981. ISBN 0-19-279753-0 Subj: Animals. Boats, ships. Parties. Religion – Noah. Weather – floods. Weather – rain.

How the mouse was hit on the head by a stone and so discovered the world text and ill. by Etienne Delessert in collaboration with Odie Mosimann; foreword by Jean Piaget; trans. by C. Ross Smith. Doubleday, 1971. Subj: Animals – mice. World.

A long long song ill. by author. Farrar, 1988. ISBN 0-374-34638-0 Subj: Imagination. Nursery rhymes. Songs.

Dellinger, Annetta. *You are special to Jesus* ill. by Jan Brett. Concordia, 1984. ISBN 0-570-04089-2 Subj: Character traits – appearance. Character traits – individuality. Religion.

Del Negro, Janice. *Lucy Dove* ill. by Leonid Gore. DK, 1998. ISBN 0-7894-2514-9 Subj: Folk and fairy tales. Foreign lands – Scotland. Monsters.

Delton, Judy. *Bear and Duck on the run* ill. by Lynn Munsinger. Albert Whitman, 1984. ISBN 0-8075-0594-3 Subj: Animals – bears. Birds – ducks.

The best mom in the world by Judy Delton and Elaine Knox-Wagner; ill. by John Faulkner. Albert Whitman, 1979. ISBN 0-8075-0665-6 Subj: Behavior – growing up. Family life – mothers.

Brimhall comes to stay ill. by Cyndy Szekeres. Lothrop, 1978. ISBN 0-688-51863-X Subj: Animals – bears. Family life.

Brimhall turns detective ill. by Cherie R. Wyman. Carolrhoda, 1983. ISBN 0-87614-203-X Subj: Animals – bears. Animals – rabbits. Weather – snow.

Brimhall turns to magic ill. by Bruce Degen. Lothrop, 1979. ISBN 0-688-51878-8 Subj: Animals – bears. Animals – rabbits. Magic.

Duck goes fishing ill. by Lynn Munsinger. Albert Whitman, 1983. ISBN 0-8075-1722-4 Subj: Animals – foxes. Birds – ducks. Birds – owls. Friendship. Sports – fishing.

The elephant in Duck's garden ill. by Lynn Munsinger. Albert Whitman, 1985. ISBN 0-8075-1959-6 Subj: Animals – bears. Animals – elephants. Behavior – worrying. Birds – ducks.

Groundhog's Day at the doctor ill. by Giulio Maestro. Parents, 1981. ISBN 0-8193-1042-5 Subj: Animals – groundhogs. Holidays – Groundhog Day. Illness.

Hired help for Rabbit ill. by Lisa McCue. Aladdin, 1992. ISBN 0-689-71522-6 Subj: Activities – working. Animals – rabbits.

I never win! ill. by Cathy Gilchrist. Carolrhoda, 1981. ISBN 0-87614-139-4 Subj: Character traits – luck. Games.

I'll never love anything ever again ill. by Rodney Pate. Albert Whitman, 1985. ISBN 0-8075-3521-4 Subj: Animals – dogs. Emotions – sadness. Pets.

I'm telling you now ill. by Lillian Hoban. Dutton, 1983. ISBN 0-525-44037-2 Subj: Activities. Behavior. Character traits – individuality.

It happened on Thursday ill. by June Goldsborough. Albert Whitman, 1978. ISBN 0-8075-3669-5 Subj: Character traits – luck. Family life. Illness.

Lee Henry's best friend ill. by John Faulkner. Albert Whitman, 1980. ISBN 0-8075-4417-5 Subj: Emotions – loneliness. Friendship. Moving.

My grandma's in a nursing home ill. by Charles Robinson. Albert Whitman, 1986. ISBN 0-8075-5333-6 Subj: Emotions – loneliness. Family life – grandmothers. Old age.

My mom hates me in January ill. by John Faulkner. Albert Whitman, 1977. ISBN 0-8075-5365-5 Subj: Behavior – boredom. Seasons – winter.

My mom made me go to camp ill. by Lisa McCue. Delacorte, 1990. ISBN 0-385-30040-9 Subj: Camps, camping. Family life – mothers.

My mom made me go to school ill. by Lisa McCue. Delacorte, 1991. ISBN 0-385-30330-0 Subj: Family life – mothers. School – first day.

My mom made me take piano lessons ill. by Lisa McCue. Doubleday, 1993. ISBN 0-385-31091-9 Subj: Family life – mothers. Music.

My mother lost her job today ill. by Irene Trivas. Albert Whitman, 1980. ISBN 0-8075-5359-X Subj: Activities – working. Character traits – optimism. Family life – mothers.

My Uncle Nikos ill. by Marc Simont. Crowell, 1983. ISBN 0-690-04165-9 Subj: Family life – aunts, uncles. Foreign lands – Greece.

The new girl at school ill. by Lillian Hoban. Dutton, 1979. ISBN 0-525-35780-7 Subj: School – first day.

No time for Christmas ill. by Anastasia Mitchell. Carolrhoda, 1988. ISBN 0-8761-4327-3 Subj: Animals – bears. Friendship. Gifts. Holidays – Christmas.

On a picnic ill. by Mamoru Funai. Doubleday, 1979. ISBN 0-385-12945-9 Subj: Activities – picnicking. Animals – gorillas. Animals – lions. Behavior – worrying. Birds – geese.

Penny wise, fun foolish ill. by Giulio Maestro. Crown, 1977. ISBN 0-517-52996-3 Subj: Animals – elephants. Behavior – saving things. Birds – ostriches. Fairs.

The perfect Christmas gift ill. by Lisa McCue. Macmillan, 1992. ISBN 0-02-728471-9 Subj: Animals. Birds – ducks. Friendship. Gifts. Holidays – Christmas.

A pet for Duck and Bear ill. by Lynn Munsinger. Albert Whitman, 1982. ISBN 0-8075-6522-9 Subj: Animals – bears. Birds – ducks. Friendship. Pets.

Rabbit finds a way ill. by Joe Lasker. Crown, 1975. ISBN 0-517-52030-3 Subj: Animals – bears. Animals – rabbits. Food.

Rabbit goes to night school ill. by Lynn Munsinger. Albert Whitman, 1986. ISBN 0-8075-6725-6 Subj: Animals – rabbits. Magic. School.

Three friends find spring ill. by Giulio Maestro. Crown, 1977. ISBN 0-517-52888-6 Subj: Animals – rabbits. Birds – ducks. Friendship. Seasons – spring. Seasons – winter.

Two good friends ill. by Giulio Maestro. Crown, 1974. ISBN 0-517-51401-X Subj: Animals – bears. Birds – ducks. Friendship.

A walk on a snowy night ill. by Ruth Rosner. HarperCollins, 1982. ISBN 0-06-021593-3 Subj: Night. Weather – snow. Weather – storms.

DeLuise, Dom. *Charlie the caterpillar* ill. by Christopher Santoro. Simon & Schuster, 1990. ISBN 0-671-69358-1 Subj: Animals – monkeys. Behavior – growing up. Insects – butterflies, caterpillars. Metamorphosis. Science.

Goldilocks (The three bears)

Hansel and Gretel (Grimm, Jacob)

King Bob's new clothes ill. by Christopher Santoro. Simon & Schuster, 1996. ISBN 0-671-89727-6 Subj: Character traits – pride. Character traits – vanity. Clothing. Folk and fairy tales. Imagination. Royalty – kings.

The nightingale (Andersen, H. C. [Hans Christian])

Del Vecchio, Ellen. *Big city port* (Maestro, Betsy)

De Lynam, Alicia Garcia. *It's mine!* ill. by author. Dial, 1988. ISBN 0-8037-0509-3 Subj: Behavior – sharing. Sibling rivalry. Toys.

Demarest, Chris L. *Benedict finds a home* ill. by author. Lothrop, 1982. ISBN 0-688-00586-1 Subj: Behavior – seeking better things. Birds.

Bus ill. by author. Harcourt, 1996. ISBN 0-15-200810-1 Subj: Buses. City. Format, unusual – board books. Rhyming text.

Clemens' kingdom ill. by author. Lothrop, 1983. ISBN 0-688-01657-X Subj: Animals – lions. Character traits – curiosity. Libraries.

The cowboy ABC ill. by author. Crown, 1976. ISBN 0-7894-2509-2 Subj: ABC books. Cowboys.

Fall ill. by author. Harcourt, 1996. ISBN 0-15-201026-2 Subj: Format, unusual – toy and movable books. Rhyming text. Seasons – fall.

Farmer Nat ill. by author. Harcourt, 1998. ISBN 0-15-200113-1 Subj: Animals. Careers – farmers. Farms. Format, unusual – toy and movable books. Noise, sounds. Rhyming text.

Honk! ill. by author. Boyds Mills, 1998. ISBN 1-56397-221-2 Subj: Birds – geese. Family life – mothers. Format, unusual – toy and movable books. Noise, sounds.

Kitman and Willy at sea ill. by author. Simon & Schuster, 1991. ISBN 0-671-65696-1 Subj: Animals. Animals – cats. Animals – mice. Problem solving.

Lindbergh ill. by author. Crown, 1993. ISBN 0-517-58719-X Subj: Activities – flying. Airplanes, airports. Transportation. U.S. history.

The lunatic adventure of Kitman and Willy ill. by author. Simon & Schuster, 1988. ISBN 0-671-65695-3 Subj: Animals – cats. Animals – mice. Moon. Space and space ships.

Morton and Sidney ill. by author. Macmillan, 1987. ISBN 0-02-728450-6 Subj: Behavior – sharing. Monsters.

My blue boat ill. by author. Harcourt, 1995. ISBN 0-15-200177-8 Subj: Activities – bathing. Boats, ships. Imagination. Sea and seashore. Toys.

My little red car ill. by author. Boyds Mills, 1992. ISBN 1-878093-86-X Subj: Activities – traveling. Automobiles. Imagination. Toys. Transportation.

No peas for Nellie ill. by author. Macmillan, 1988. ISBN 0-02-728460-3 Subj: Food. Imagination.

Orville's odyssey ill. by author. Prentice-Hall, 1986. ISBN 0-13-642851-7 Subj: Imagination. Sports – fishing. Wordless.

Plane ill. by author. Harcourt, 1995. ISBN 0-15-200268-5 Subj: Airplanes, airports. Format, unusual – board books. Rhyming text.

Ship ill. by author. Harcourt, 1995. ISBN 0-15-200267-7 Subj: Boats, ships. Rhyming text.

Spring ill. by author. Harcourt, 1997. ISBN 0-15-201390-3 Subj: Format, unusual – toy and movable books. Rhyming text. Seasons – spring.

Summer ill. by author. Harcourt, 1997. ISBN 0-15-201391-1 Subj: Format, unusual – toy and movable books. Rhyming text. Sea and seashore. Seasons – summer.

Train ill. by author. Harcourt, 1996. ISBN 0-15-200809-8 Subj: Format, unusual – board books. Rhyming text. Trains.

Winter ill. by author. Harcourt, 1996. ISBN 0-15-201027-0 Subj: Format, unusual – toy and movable books. Rhyming text. Seasons – winter.

De Marolles, Chantal. *The lonely wolf* ill. by Eleonore Schmid. Holt, 1986. ISBN 0-8050-0006-2 Subj: Animals – wolves. Character traits – kindness to animals. Foreign lands – Russia.

DeMarsh, Mary. *Three perfect peaches* (DeFelice, Cynthia C.)

Demas, Corinne. *see* Bliss, Corinne Demas

The littlest matryoshka ill. by Kathryn Brown. Hyperion, 1999. ISBN 0-7868-0153-0 Subj: Behavior – lost. Toys – dolls.

De Mejo, Oscar. *La Bella Magellona and the little cavalier* ill. by author. Putnam, 1992. ISBN 0-399-22138-7 Subj: Concepts – shape. Concepts – size. Emotions – love. Folk and fairy tales.

Oscar de Mejo's ABC ill. by author. HarperCollins, 1992. ISBN 0-06-020517-2 Subj: ABC books. Art.

Demi. *The adventures of Marco Polo* ill. by author. Holt, 1982. ISBN 0-03-061263-2 Subj: Activities – traveling. Foreign lands – China.

The artist and the architect ill. by author. Holt, 1991. ISBN 0-8050-1685-6 Subj: Careers – architects. Careers – artists. Emotions – envy, jealousy. Folk and fairy tales. Foreign lands – China.

Chen Ping and his magic axe ill. by author. Dodd, 1987. ISBN 0-396-08907-0 Subj: Character traits – honesty. Folk and fairy tales. Foreign lands – China. Magic.

A Chinese zoo: fables and proverbs ill. by adapt. Harcourt, 1987. ISBN 0-15-217510-5 Subj: Animals. Folk and fairy tales. Foreign lands – China.

Cuddly chick ill. by author. Grosset, 1988. ISBN 0-448-19154-7 Subj: Birds – chickens. Format, unusual – board books. Format, unusual – toy and movable books.

Demi's basket of books ill. by author. Grosset, 1989. ISBN 0-448-14975-3 Subj: Animals. Holidays – Easter. Seasons – spring.

Demi's Christmas surprise ill. by author. Grosset, 1990. ISBN 0-448-19167-9 Subj: Animals. Format, unusual – board books. Holidays – Christmas.

Demi's count the animals 1-2-3 ill. by author. Grosset, 1986. ISBN 0-448-18980-1 Subj: Animals. Counting, numbers. Rhyming text.

Demi's dragons and fantastic creatures ill. by author. Holt, 1993. ISBN 0-8050-2564-2 Subj: Animals. Dragons. Format, unusual – toy and movable books. Rhyming text.

Demi's find the animals A B C: an alphabet-game book ill. by author. Grosset, 1985. ISBN 0-448-18970-4 Subj: ABC books. Animals. Behavior – hiding things.

Demi's opposites: an animal game book ill. by author. Grosset, 1987. ISBN 0-448-18995-X Subj: Animals. Concepts – opposites. Games.

Demi's reflective fables ill. by author. Grosset, 1988. ISBN 0-448-09281-6 Subj: Folk and fairy tales. Foreign lands – China.

Downy duckling ill. by author. Grosset, 1988. ISBN 0-448-19153-9 Subj: Birds – ducks. Format, unusual – board books. Format, unusual – toy and movable books.

Dragon kites and dragonflies: a collection of Chinese nursery rhymes ill. by adapt. Harcourt, 1986. ISBN 0-15-224199-X Subj: Dragons. Foreign lands – China. Nursery rhymes.

The dragon's tale and other animal fables of the Chinese zodiac retold and ill. by Demi. Holt, 1996. ISBN 0-8050-3446-3 Subj: Dragons. Folk and fairy tales. Foreign lands – China. Zodiac.

The empty pot ill. by author. Holt, 1990. ISBN 0-8050-1217-6 Subj: Character traits – honesty. Folk and fairy tales. Foreign lands – China. Gardens, gardening. Royalty – emperors.

Find Demi's baby animals ill. by author. Grosset, 1990. ISBN 0-448-19169-5 Subj: Animals. Puzzles.

Find Demi's dinosaurs: an animal game book ill. by author. Grosset, 1989. ISBN 0-448-19020-6 Subj: Dinosaurs. Puzzles.

Find Demi's sea creatures: an animal game book ill. by author. Putnam, 1991. ISBN 0-399-22112-3 Subj: Animals. Fish. Puzzles.

The firebird (The firebird)

Fleecy bunny ill. by author. Grosset, 1987. ISBN 0-448-19151-2 Subj: Animals – rabbits. Format, unusual – board books.

Fleecy lamb ill. by author. Grosset, 1987. ISBN 0-448-19152-0 Subj: Animals – sheep. Format, unusual – board books.

Follow the line ill. by author. Holt, 1981. ISBN 0-03-059112-0 Subj: Wordless.

Fuzzy wuzzy puppy ill. by author. Grosset, 1986. ISBN 0-448-18985-2 Subj: Animals – dogs. Format, unusual – board books. Format, unusual – toy and movable books.

The greatest treasure ill. by author. Scholastic, 1998. ISBN 0-590-31339-8 Subj: Folk and fairy tales. Foreign lands – China.

The hallowed horse ill. by adapt. Dodd, 1987. ISBN 0-396-08908-9 Subj: Animals – horses, ponies. Folk and fairy tales. Foreign lands – India. Reptiles – snakes.

The leaky umbrella ill. by author. Prentice-Hall, 1980. ISBN 0-13-526962-8 Subj: Behavior – mistakes. Foreign lands – Japan. Umbrellas.

Liang and the magic paintbrush ill. by author. Holt, 1988. ISBN 0-8050-0801-2 Subj: Activities – painting. Foreign lands – China. Magic.

Little baby lamb ill. by author. Putnam, 1993. ISBN 0-448-40580-6 Subj: Animals – sheep. Format, unusual – board books. Seasons – spring.

Little bitty bunny ill. by author. Grosset, 1992. ISBN 0-448-41089-3 Subj: Animals – rabbits. Clothing – hats. Format, unusual – board books. Format, unusual – toy and movable books. Holidays – Easter.

Little chick chick ill. by author. Grosset, 1992. ISBN 0-448-41090-7 Subj: Birds – chickens. Eggs. Format, unusual – board books. Format, unusual – toy and movable books. Holidays – Easter.

Little lucky ducky ill. by author. Putnam, 1993. ISBN 0-448-40581-4 Subj: Birds – ducks. Format, unusual – board books.

The magic boat ill. by author. Holt, 1990. ISBN 0-8050-1141-2 Subj: Boats, ships. Folk and fairy tales. Foreign lands – China. Magic. Toys.

The magic tapestry ill. by adapt. Holt, 1994. ISBN 0-8050-2810-2 Subj: Folk and fairy tales. Foreign lands – China. Magic.

One grain of rice: a mathematical folktale ill. by author. Scholastic, 1997. ISBN 0-5909-3998-X Subj: Character traits – cleverness. Character traits – selfishness. Counting, numbers. Folk and fairy tales. Royalty – rajahs.

The peek-a-boo ABC ill. by author. Random House, 1982. ISBN 0-394-85418-7 Subj: ABC books. Format, unusual – toy and movable books.

So soft kitty ill. by author. Grosset, 1986. ISBN 0-448-18986-0 Subj: Animals – cats. Format, unusual – board books. Format, unusual – toy and movable books.

The stonecutter ill. by author. Crown, 1995. ISBN 0-517-59865-5 Subj: Behavior – wishing. Folk and fairy tales. Foreign lands – China.

Three little elephants ill. by author. Random House, 1981. ISBN 0-394-84760-1 Subj: Animals. Animals – elephants. Format, unusual – toy and movable books. Jungle.

Under the shade of the mulberry tree ill. by author. Prentice-Hall, 1979. ISBN 0-13-936476-5 Subj: Character traits – cleverness. Folk and fairy tales. Foreign lands – China.

Where is it? ill. by author. Doubleday, 1979. ISBN 0-385-14847-X Subj: Riddles.

Where is Willie Worm? ill. by author. Random House, 1981. ISBN 0-394-84759-8 Subj: Animals – worms. Format, unusual – toy and movable books.

De Montaño, Martha Kreipe. *Coyote in love with a star* ill. by Tom Coffin. National Museum of the American Indian, 1998. ISBN 0-7892-0162-3 Subj: Animals – coyotes. Folk and fairy tales. Indians of North America – Potawatomi. Stars.

DeMunn, Michael. *The earth is good: a chant in praise of nature* ill. by Jim McMullan. Scholastic, 1999. ISBN 0-590-35010-2 Subj: Earth. Nature.

Demuth, Patricia Brennan. *Achoo! all about colds* ill. by Maggie Smith. Grosset, 1997. ISBN 0-448-41348-5 Subj: Illness.

Busy at day care head to toe photos by Jack Demuth. Dutton, 1996. ISBN 0-525-45603-1 Subj: Rhyming text. School.

Max, the bad-talking parrot ill. by Bo Zaunders. Dodd, 1986. ISBN 0-396-08767-1 Subj: Behavior – misunderstanding. Birds – parakeets, parrots. Etiquette. Rhyming text.

Ornery morning ill. by Craig McFarland Brown. Dutton, 1991. ISBN 0-525-44688-5 Subj: Animals. Behavior – bad day. Careers – farmers. Cumulative tales. Farms.

Snakes ill. by Judith Moffatt. Grosset, 1993. ISBN 0448405148 Subj: Reptiles – snakes.

Denchfield, Nick. *Desmond the dog* by Nick Denchfield and Ant Parker; ill. by Ant Parker. Harcourt, 1997. ISBN 0-15-201340-7 Subj: Animals – dogs. Behavior – misbehavior. Family life – brothers and sisters.

Desmond the dog, a wag-the-tail pop-up book by Nick Denchfield and Ant Parker; ill. by Ant Parker. Macmillan, 1997. ISBN 0-33367-954-7 Subj: Animals – dogs. Behavior – misbehavior. Family life – brothers and sisters. Format, unusual – toy and movable books.

Denim, Sue. *The Dumb Bunnies* ill. by Dav Pilkey. Blue Sky, 1994. ISBN 0-590-47798-0 Subj: Animals – rabbits. Family life.

The Dumb Bunnies' Easter ill. by Dav Pilkey. Blue Sky, 1995. ISBN 0-590-20241-3 Subj: Animals – rabbits. Family life. Holidays – Christmas. Holidays – Easter.

The Dumb Bunnies go to the zoo ill. by Dav Pilkey. Blue Sky, 1997. ISBN 0-590-84735-X Subj: Animals. Animals – rabbits. Family life. Zoos.

Make way for Dumb Bunnies ill. by Dav Pilkey. Blue Sky, 1996. ISBN 0-590-58286-0 Subj: Activities. Animals – rabbits. Family life.

Denison, Carol. *A part-time dog for Nick* ill. by Jane Miller. Dodd, 1959. Subj: Animals – dogs. Family life.

Dennard, Deborah. *Do cats have nine lives? the strange things people say about animals around the* *house* ill. by Jackie Urbanovic. Carolrhoda, 1993. ISBN 0-87614-720-1 Subj: Animals. Pets.

Travis and the better mousetrap ill. by Theresa Burns. Cobblehill, 1996. ISBN 0-525-65178-0 Subj: Animals. Animals – mice. Family life – aunts, uncles. Inventions.

Dennis, Lynne. *Raymond Rabbit's early morning* ill. by author. Dutton, 1987. ISBN 0-525-44316-9 Subj: Animals – rabbits. Family life. Morning.

Dennis, Morgan. *Burlap* ill. by author. Viking, 1945. Subj: Animals – bears. Animals – dogs.

The pup himself ill. by author. Viking, 1943. Subj: Animals – dogs.

The sea dog ill. by author. Viking, 1958. Subj: Animals – dogs. Boats, ships. Weather – storms.

Skit and Skat ill. by author. Viking, 1952. Subj: Animals – cats. Animals – dogs.

Dennis, Suzanne E. *Answer me that* ill. by Owen Wood. Bobbs-Merrill, 1969. Subj: Animals. Humor. Poetry.

Dennis, Wesley. *Flip* ill. by author. Viking, 1941. ISBN 0-670-31876-0 Subj: Animals. Dreams. Farms.

Flip and the cows ill. by author. Viking, 1942. ISBN 0-208-02240-6 Subj: Animals – bulls, cows. Animals – horses, ponies. Farms.

Flip and the morning ill. by author. Viking, 1977, c1951. ISBN 0-670-31934-1 Subj: Animals – horses, ponies. Morning.

Tumble, the story of a mustang ill. by author. Hastings House, 1966. Subj: Animals – horses, ponies. Character traits – freedom.

Denslow, Sharon Phillips. *At Taylor's place* ill. by Nancy Carpenter. Bradbury, 1990. ISBN 0-02-728685-1 Subj: Careers – carpenters. Farms. Seasons – fall.

Bus riders ill. by Nancy Carpenter. Macmillan, 1993. ISBN 0-02-728682-7 Subj: Buses. Careers – bus drivers. Illness.

Hazel's circle ill. by Sharon McGinley-Nally. Four Winds, 1992. ISBN 0-02-728683-5 Subj: Birds – chickens. Communities, neighborhoods.

Night owls ill. by Jill Kastner. Bradbury, 1990. ISBN 0-02-728681-9 Subj: Activities. Night. Seasons – summer.

On the trail with Miss Pace ill. by G. Brian Karas. Simon & Schuster, 1995. ISBN 0-02-728688-6 Subj: Careers – teachers. Cowboys. Multiple births – twins.

Radio boy ill. by Alec Gillman. Simon & Schuster, 1994. ISBN 0-02-728684-3 Subj: Careers – inventors.

Riding with Aunt Lucy ill. by Nancy Carpenter. Bradbury, 1991. ISBN 0-02-728686-X Subj: Activities – traveling. Animals – pigs. Family life – aunts, uncles.

Woollybear good-bye ill. by Nancy Cote. Four Winds, 1994. ISBN 0-02-728687-8 Subj: Insects – butterflies, caterpillars. Moving. School.

Denslow, W. W. *Denslow's picture book treasury* ill. by author. Arcade, 1990. ISBN 1-55970-071-8 Subj: Nursery rhymes. Songs.

Denton, Kady MacDonald. *Christmas boot* ill. by author. Little, 1990. ISBN 0-316-18091-2 Subj: Clothing – shoes. Holidays – Christmas. Santa Claus.

Granny is a darling ill. by author. Macmillan, 1988. ISBN 0-689-50452-7 Subj: Bedtime. Family life – grandmothers. Monsters. Night.

The picnic ill. by author. Dutton, 1988. ISBN 0-525-44376-2 Subj: Activities – picnicking. Family life.

Denton, Terry. *Home is the sailor* ill. by author. Houghton Mifflin, 1989. ISBN 0-395-51525-4 Subj: Activities – traveling. Animals. Boats, ships. Sailors. Sea and seashore.

The school for laughter ill. by author. Houghton Mifflin, 1990. ISBN 0-395-53353-8 Subj: Behavior – losing things. School.

Denver, John. *The children and the flowers* ill. by Randi Gullerud. Green Tiger Pr., 1979. Subj: Flowers. Songs.

De Paola, Paula. *Rosie and the yellow ribbon* ill. by Janet Wolf. Little, 1992. ISBN 0-316-18100-5 Subj: Birthdays. City. Concepts – color. Friendship.

De Paola, Tomie (Thomas Anthony). *Andy (that's my name)* ill. by author. Prentice-Hall, 1973. ISBN 0-13-036731-1 Subj: Behavior – greed. Character traits – smallness. Friendship. Games. Names.

The art lesson ill. by author. Putnam, 1989. ISBN 0-399-21688-X Subj: Art. Family life. School.

The baby sister ill. by author. Putnam, 1996. ISBN 0-399-22908-6 Subj: Babies. Family life – grandmothers. Family life – new sibling. Family life – sisters.

Baby's first Christmas ill. by author. Putnam, 1988. ISBN 0-399-21591-3 Subj: Babies. Holidays – Christmas.

Big Anthony and the magic ring ill. by author. Harcourt, 1979. ISBN 0-15-207124-5 Subj: Character traits – appearance. Magic.

Big Anthony, his story ill. by author. Putnam, 1998. ISBN 0-399-23189-7 Subj: Folk and fairy tales. Foreign lands – Italy. Witches.

Bill and Pete ill. by author. Putnam, 1978. ISBN 0-399-20646-9 Subj: Birds – plovers. Foreign lands – Africa. Humor. Reptiles – alligators, crocodiles. School.

Bill and Pete go down the Nile ill. by author. Putnam, 1987. ISBN 0-399-21395-3 Subj: Behavior – stealing. Birds – plovers. Foreign lands – Egypt. Museums. Reptiles – alligators, crocodiles. School.

Bill and Pete to the rescue ill. by author. Putnam, 1998. ISBN 0-399-23208-7 Subj: Animals. Birds – plovers. Reptiles – alligators, crocodiles.

Bonjour, Mister Satie ill. by author. Putnam, 1991. ISBN 0-399-21782-7 Subj: Animals – cats. Art. Family life – aunts, uncles. Foreign lands – France.

The bubble factory ill. by author. Grosset, 1996. ISBN 0-448-41349-3 Subj: Bubbles. Family life – brothers and sisters. Family life – grandfathers. Multiple births – twins.

The cat on the Dovrefell: a Christmas tale trans. by George W. Dasent; ill. by author. Putnam, 1979. ISBN 0-399-20680-9 Subj: Holidays – Christmas. Mythical creatures – trolls.

Charlie needs a cloak ill. by author. Prentice-Hall, 1973. ISBN 0-13-128355-3 Subj: Animals – mice. Animals – sheep. Clothing – coats. Problem solving.

The Christmas pageant ill. by author. Winston, 1978. ISBN 0-03-046356-4 Subj: Holidays – Christmas. Religion – Nativity. Theater.

Christopher: the holy giant ill. by author. Holiday, 1994. ISBN 0-8234-0862-0 Subj: Religion.

The cloud book ill. by author. Holiday, 1975. ISBN 0-8234-0531-1 Subj: Weather – clouds.

The clown of God: an old story ill. by author. Harcourt, 1978. ISBN 0-15-219175-5 Subj: Foreign lands – Italy. Holidays – Christmas. Religion.

Country farm ill. by author. Putnam, 1984. ISBN 0-399-21056-3 Subj: Animals. Farms. Format, unusual. Wordless.

Criss-cross applesauce photos by B. A. King; ill. by the B. A. King children. Addison-Wesley, 1979. ISBN 0-89169-023-9 Subj: Children as illustrators.

An early American Christmas ill. by author. Holiday, 1987. ISBN 0-8234-0617-2 Subj: Holidays – Christmas. U.S. history.

The family Christmas tree book ill. by author. Holiday, 1980. ISBN 0-8234-0416-1 Subj: Family life. Holidays – Christmas. Trees.

Favorite nursery tales ill. by adapt. Putnam, 1986. ISBN 0-399-21319-8 Subj: Folk and fairy tales. Nursery rhymes.

Fight the night ill. by author. Lippincott, 1968. Subj: Bedtime. Sleep.

Fin M'Coul: the giant of Knockmany Hill ill. by author. Holiday, 1981. ISBN 0-8234-0384-X Subj: Folk and fairy tales. Foreign lands – Ireland. Giants.

Flicks ill. by author. Harcourt, 1979. ISBN 0-15-228487-7 Subj: Humor. Wordless.

Four stories for four seasons ill. by author. Prentice-Hall, 1977. ISBN 0-13-330175-3 Subj: Boats, ships. Gardens, gardening. Hibernation. Seasons.

Get dressed, Santa! ill. by author. Grosset, 1996. ISBN 0-448-41258-6 Subj: Format, unusual – board

books. Holidays – Christmas. Rhyming text. Santa Claus.

Haircuts for the Woolseys ill. by author. Putnam, 1989. ISBN 0-399-21662-6 Subj: Animals – sheep. Family life – grandmothers.

Helga's dowry ill. by author. Harcourt, 1977. ISBN 0-15-233701-6 Subj: Emotions – love. Mythical creatures – trolls. Poverty. Weddings.

The hunter and the animals ill. by author. Holiday, 1981. ISBN 0-8234-0397-1 Subj: Animals. Sports – hunting. Wordless.

Jamie O'Rourke and the big potato ill. by author. Putnam, 1992. ISBN 0-399-22257-X Subj: Character traits – laziness. Folk and fairy tales. Foreign lands – Ireland. Mythical creatures – leprechauns.

Jamie O'Rourke and the pooka ill. by author. Putnam, 2000. ISBN 0-399-23467-5 Subj: Character traits – laziness. Foreign lands – Ireland. Mythical creatures – goblins.

Jingle, the Christmas clown ill. by author. Putnam, 1992. ISBN 0-399-22338-X Subj: Animals. Circus. Clowns, jesters. Foreign lands – Italy. Holidays – Christmas.

Katie and Kit at the beach ill. by author. Little, 1987. ISBN 0-671-61722-2 Subj: Format, unusual – board books. Sea and seashore. Weather – rain.

Katie, Kit and cousin Tom ill. by author. Little, 1987. ISBN 0-671-61724-9 Subj: Activities – playing. Animals – cats. Behavior – bullying. Family life. Format, unusual – board books.

Katie's good idea ill. by author. Little, 1987. ISBN 0-671-61725-7 Subj: Behavior – growing up. Format, unusual – board books.

Kit and Kat ill. by author. Grosset, 1994. ISBN 0-448-40749-3 Subj: Animals – cats. Behavior – bullying. Clothing – pajamas. Family life – grandfathers. Sports – bicycling.

The knight and the dragon ill. by author. Putnam, 1980. ISBN 0-606-03327-0 Subj: Dragons. Knights. Libraries.

The Lady of Guadalupe ill. by author. Holiday, 1980. ISBN 0-8234-0373-4 Subj: Foreign lands – Mexico. Religion.

The legend of Old Befana ill. by author. Harcourt, 1980. ISBN 0-15-243816-5 Subj: Folk and fairy tales. Foreign lands – Italy. Religion.

The legend of the bluebonnet ill. by author. Putnam, 1983. ISBN 0-399-20937-9 Subj: Flowers. Folk and fairy tales. Indians of North America – Comanche.

The legend of the Indian paintbrush ill. by author. Putnam, 1987. ISBN 0-399-21534-4 Subj: Activities – painting. Flowers. Folk and fairy tales. Indians of North America – Great Plains.

The legend of the persian carpet ill. by Claire Ewart. Putnam, 1993. ISBN 0-399-22415-7 Subj: Folk and fairy tales. Foreign lands – Persia. Royalty – kings.

Little Grunt and the big egg: a prehistoric fairy tale ill. by author. Holiday, 1990. ISBN 0-8234-0730-6 Subj: Dinosaurs. Folk and fairy tales. Pets.

Marianna May and Nursey ill. by author. Holiday, 1983. ISBN 0-8234-0473-0 Subj: Character traits – cleanliness.

Merry Christmas, Strega Nona ill. by author. Harcourt, 1986. ISBN 0-15-253183-1 Subj: Foreign lands – Italy. Holidays – Christmas. Humor. Magic. Witches.

Michael Bird-Boy ill. by author. Prentice-Hall, 1975. ISBN 0-13-580803-0 Subj: Ecology.

My first Chanukah ill. by author. Putnam, 1989. ISBN 0-399-21780-0 Subj: Format, unusual – board books. Holidays – Hanukkah. Jewish culture. Religion.

My first Thanksgiving ill. by author. Putnam, 1992. ISBN 0-399-22327-4 Subj: Friendship. Holidays – Thanksgiving. U.S. history.

The mysterious giant of Barletta: an Italian folktale ill. by author. Harcourt, 1984. ISBN 0-15-256347-4 Subj: Folk and fairy tales. Foreign lands – Italy. Giants. War.

Nana upstairs and Nana downstairs ill. by author. Putnam, 1973. ISBN 0-399-60787-0 Subj: Death. Emotions – grief. Family life – grandmothers.

The night of Las Posadas ill. by author. Putnam, 1999. ISBN 0-399-23400-4 Subj: Holidays – Christmas. Religion. Theater.

Noah and the ark ill. by author. Winston, 1983. ISBN 0-86683-819-8 Subj: Animals. Boats, ships. Religion – Noah. Weather – floods. Weather – rain. Weather – rainbows.

Now one foot, now the other ill. by author. Putnam, 1981. ISBN 0-399-20774-0 Subj: Family life – grandfathers. Illness.

Oliver Button is a sissy ill. by author. Harcourt, 1979. ISBN 0-15-257852-8 Subj: Activities – dancing. Ballet. Character traits – individuality.

Pajamas for Kit ill. by author. Little, 1987. ISBN 0-671-61723-0 Subj: Bedtime. Clothing. Family life – grandparents. Format, unusual – board books.

Pancakes for breakfast ill. by author. Harcourt, 1978. ISBN 0-15-259455-8 Subj: Activities – cooking. Food. Wordless.

The parables of Jesus ill. by author. Holiday, 1987. ISBN 0-8234-0636-9 Subj: Religion.

Patrick: patron saint of Ireland ill. by author. Holiday, 1992. ISBN 0-8234-0924-4 Subj: Foreign lands – Ireland. Religion.

The popcorn book ill. by author. Holiday, 1978. ISBN 0-8234-0314-9 Subj: Activities – cooking. Food.

The Prince of the Dolomites ill. by author. Harcourt, 1980. ISBN 0-15-263528-9 Subj: Activities – storytelling. Folk and fairy tales. Foreign lands – Italy. Moon. Mythical creatures.

The quicksand book ill. by author. Holiday, 1977. ISBN 0-8234-0291-6 Subj: Behavior – carelessness.

Sing, Pierrot, sing: a picture book in mime ill. by author. Harcourt, 1983. ISBN 0-15-274988-8 Subj: Clowns, jesters. Theater. Wordless.

Songs of the fog maiden ill. by author. Holiday, 1979. ISBN 0-8234-0341-6 Subj: Rhyming text.

The story of the three wise kings ill. by author. Putnam, 1983. ISBN 0-399-20998-0 Subj: Holidays – Christmas. Religion – Nativity.

Strega Nona: an old tale ill. by author. Prentice-Hall, 1975. ISBN 0-13-851600-6 Subj: Behavior – forgetfulness. Caldecott award honor books. Humor. Magic. Witches.

Strega Nona meets her match ill. by author. Putnam, 1993. ISBN 0-399-22421-1 Subj: Folk and fairy tales. Humor. Magic. Witches.

Strega Nona takes a vacation ill. by author. Putnam, 2000. ISBN 0-399-23562-0 Subj: Activities – vacationing. Bubbles. Witches.

Strega Nona's magic lessons ill. by author. Harcourt, 1982. ISBN 0-15-281785-9 Subj: Behavior – carelessness. Humor. Magic. Witches.

Things to make and do for Valentine's Day ill. by author. Watts, 1976. ISBN 0-531-01187-9 Subj: Activities – cooking. Activities – making things. Games. Holidays – Valentine's Day.

Tom ill. by author. Putnam, 1993. ISBN 0-399-22417-3 Subj: Family life – grandfathers. Friendship. Names.

Tomie de Paola's Mother Goose ill. by sel. Putnam, 1985. ISBN 0-399-21258-2 Subj: Nursery rhymes.

Tony's bread ill. by author. Putnam, 1989. ISBN 0-399-21693-6 Subj: Careers – bakers. Folk and fairy tales. Food. Foreign lands – Italy.

Too many Hopkins ill. by author. Putnam, 1989. ISBN 0-399-21661-8 Subj: Animals – rabbits. Family life. Gardens, gardening.

The unicorn and the moon ill. by author. Silver Pr., 1995. ISBN 0-382-24659-4 Subj: Behavior – trickery. Moon. Mythical creatures – unicorns.

When everyone was fast asleep ill. by author. Holiday, 1976. ISBN 0-8234-0278-9 Subj: Sleep.

De Posadas Mane, Carmen. *Mister North Wind* adapt. by Joanne Fink; trans. from Spanish by Candido A. Valderrama; ill. by Alfonso Ruano. Silver Burdett, 1986. ISBN 0-382-09191-4 Subj: Animals. Character traits – bravery. Seasons – spring. Weather – wind.

Derby, Sally. *King Kenrick's splinter* ill. by Leonid Gore. Walker, 1994. ISBN 0-8027-8323-6 Subj: Character traits – bravery. Parades. Royalty – kings.

The mouse who owned the sun ill. by Friso Henstra. Four Winds, 1993. ISBN 0-02-766965-3 Subj: Activities – traveling. Animals – mice. Sun. World.

My steps ill. by Adjoa J. Burrowes. Lee & Low, 1996. ISBN 1-880000-40-7 Subj: Activities – playing. Ethnic groups in the U.S. – African Americans. Seasons.

De Regniers, Beatrice Schenk. *A bunch of poems and verses* ill. by Mary Jane Dunton. Seabury Pr., 1977. ISBN 0-8164-3185-X Subj: Poetry.

Catch a little fox: variations on a folk rhyme ill. by Brinton Turkle. Seabury Pr., 1979. ISBN 0-395-28821-5 Subj: Character traits – cleverness. Nursery rhymes. Sports – hunting.

Cats cats cats ill. by Bill Sokol. Pantheon, 1958. Subj: Animals – cats. Poetry.

Circus photos by Al Giese. Viking, 1966. Subj: Circus.

David and Goliath ill. by Scott Cameron. Orchard, 1996. ISBN 0-531-08796-4 Subj: Foreign lands – Israel. Giants. Religion – David.

David and Goliath ill. by Richard M. Powers. Viking, 1965. Subj: Foreign lands – Israel. Giants. Religion – David.

Everyone is good for something ill. by Margot Tomes. Houghton Mifflin, 1980. ISBN 0-395-28967-X Subj: Animals – cats. Folk and fairy tales. Foreign lands – Russia. Self-concept.

The giant story ill. by Maurice Sendak. HarperCollins, 1953. Subj: Family life. Giants.

Going for a walk ill. by Robert Knox. HarperCollins, 1993. Orig. title: The little book. ISBN 0-06-022957-8 Subj: Activities – walking. Animals. Farms. Friendship.

How Joe the bear and Sam the mouse got together ill. by Bernice Myers. Lothrop, 1990. ISBN 0-688-09080-X Subj: Animals – bears. Animals – mice. Friendship.

It does not say meow! ill. by Paul Galdone. Seabury Pr., 1972. ISBN 0-8164-3086-1 Subj: Animals. Participation. Poetry. Riddles.

Jack and the beanstalk (Jack and the beanstalk)

Jack the giant killer: Jack's first and finest adventure retold in verse as well as other useful information about giants including how to shake hands with a giant (Jack and the beanstalk)

Laura's story ill. by Jack Kent. Atheneum, 1979. ISBN 0-689-30677-6 Subj: Imagination.

A little house of your own ill. by Irene Haas. Harcourt, 1987, c1982. ISBN 0-15-245787-9 Subj: Family life. Homes, houses. Imagination.

Little Sister and the Month Brothers ill. by Margot Tomes. Lothrop, 1994. Orig. published by Seabury Pr., 1976. ISBN 0-688-05293-2 Subj: Days of the week, months of the year. Folk and fairy tales. Foreign lands.

May I bring a friend? ill. by Beni Montresor. Atheneum, 1964. ISBN 0-689-20615-1 Subj: Animals. Caldecott award books. Friendship. Humor. Rhyming text. Royalty.

Picture book theater: the mysterious stranger and the magic spell ill. by William Lahey Cummings. Seabury Pr., 1982. ISBN 0-89919-061-8 Subj: Animals – cats. Animals – mice. Theater. Wizards.

Red Riding Hood ill. by Edward Gorey. Atheneum, 1972. Retold in verse for boys and girls to read themselves. Subj: Animals – wolves. Behavior – talking to strangers. Folk and fairy tales. Rhyming text.

Sam and the impossible thing story by Tamara Kitt; ill. by Brinton Turkle. Norton, 1967. Subj: Activities – cooking. Food. Monsters. Rhyming text.

The shadow book ill. by Isabel Gordon. Harcourt, 1960. Subj: Shadows.

So many cats! ill. by Ellen Weiss. Clarion, 1985. ISBN 0-89919-322-6 Subj: Animals – cats. Counting, numbers. Rhyming text.

Something special ill. by Irene Haas. Harcourt, 1958. Subj: Rhyming text.

A special birthday party for someone very special ill. by Brinton Turkle. Norton, 1966. Subj: Animals – skunks. Birthdays.

Waiting for mama ill. by Victoria de Larrea. Clarion, 1984. ISBN 0-89919-222-X Subj: Imagination.

Was it a good trade? ill. by Irene Haas. Harcourt, 1956. Subj: Activities – trading. Rhyming text. Songs.

What can you do with a shoe? ill. by Maurice Sendak. HarperCollins, 1955. ISBN 0-06-024850-5 Subj: Games. Imagination.

Who likes the sun? ill. by Leona Pierce. Harcourt, 1961. Subj: Sun.

Willy O'Dwyer jumped in the fire: variations on a folk rhyme ill. by Beni Montresor. Atheneum, 1968. Subj: Fire. Moon. Nursery rhymes. Witches.

DeRubertis, Barbara. *Columbus Day: let's meet Christopher Columbus* ill. by Thomas Sperling. Phoenix Learning Resources, 1992. ISBN 0-7915-1904-X Subj: Boats, ships. Careers – explorers. Sea and seashore. U.S. history.

Janey Crane ill. by Eva Vágréti Cockrille. Kane, 1997. ISBN 1-57565-022-3 Subj: Language. Noise, sounds. Rhyming text.

Joey Goat ill. by Jan Pyk. Kane, 1997. ISBN 1-57565-025-8 Subj: Language. Noise, sounds. Rhyming text.

Suzy Mule ill. by Eva Vágréti Cockrille. Kane, 1997. ISBN 1-57565-026-6 Subj: Language. Noise, sounds. Rhyming text.

Tiny Tiger ill. by Eva Vágréti Cockrille. Kane, 1997. ISBN 1-57565-024-X Subj: Language. Noise, sounds. Rhyming text.

Zeely Zebra ill. by Eva Vágréti Cockrille. Kane, 1997. ISBN 1-57565-023-1 Subj: Language. Noise, sounds. Rhyming text.

DeSaix, Deborah Durland. *In the back seat* ill. by author. Farrar, 1993. ISBN 0-374-33639-3 Subj: Activities – traveling. Automobiles. Family life. Imagination.

DeSaix, Frank. *The girl who danced with dolphins* ill. by Debbi Durland DeSaix. Farrar, 1991. ISBN 0-374-32626-6 Subj: Animals – dolphins. Dreams. Sea and seashore.

DeSantis, Kenny. *A doctor's tools* photos by Patricia Agre. Dodd, 1985. ISBN 0-396-08516-4 Subj: Careers – doctors. Tools.

Desimini, Lisa. *All year round: a book to benefit children in need* (All year round)

I am running away today ill. by author. Walt Disney, 1992. ISBN 1-56282-121-0 Subj: Animals – cats. Behavior – running away.

Moon soup ill. by author. Hyperion, 1993. ISBN 1-56282-464-3 Subj: Food. Imagination. Moon.

My house ill. by author. Holt, 1994. ISBN 0-8050-3144-8 Subj: Homes, houses. Seasons.

Sun and moon: a giant love story ill. by author. Blue Sky, 1999. ISBN 0-590-18720-1 Subj: Friendship. Giants. Moon. Sun.

DeSpain, Pleasant. *The dancing turtle: a folktale from Brazil* ill. by David Boston. August House, 1998. ISBN 0-87483-502-X Subj: Behavior – trickery. Folk and fairy tales. Foreign lands – Brazil. Reptiles – turtles, tortoises.

Deutsch, Babette. *There comes a time* (Borchers, Elisabeth)

DeVajay, Szabolcs. *The animals' gift* ill. by Lilian Obligado. Simon & Schuster, 1994. ISBN 0-671-72962-4 Subj: Animals – donkeys. Animals – oxen. Holidays – Christmas. Religion – Nativity.

De Veaux, Alexis. *An enchanted hair tale* ill. by Cheryl Hanna. HarperCollins, 1987. ISBN 0-06-021624-7 Subj: Character traits – being different. Ethnic groups in the U.S. – African Americans. Hair. Imagination. Self-concept.

Na-ni ill. by author. HarperCollins, 1973. ISBN 0-06-021628-X Subj: Character traits – questioning. City. Emotions – sadness. Poverty.

Devlin, Harry. *Aunt Agatha, there's a lion under the couch!* (Devlin, Wende)

Cranberry autumn (Devlin, Wende)

Cranberry Christmas (Devlin, Wende)

Cranberry Easter (Devlin, Wende)

Cranberry summer (Devlin, Wende)

Cranberry Thanksgiving (Devlin, Wende)

Cranberry Valentine (Devlin, Wende)

Old Black Witch! (Devlin, Wende)

Old Witch and the polka-dot ribbon (Devlin, Wende)

Old Witch rescues Halloween (Devlin, Wende)

The walloping window blind: an old nautical tale ill. by author. Van Nostrand, 1968. Adapt. from an old sea tune. Subj: Boats, ships. Pirates. Songs.

Devlin, Wende. *Aunt Agatha, there's a lion under the couch!* by Wende and Harry Devlin; ill. by authors. Van Nostrand, 1968. Subj: Animals – lions. Emotions – fear. Family life – aunts, uncles. Furniture. Imagination.

Cranberry autumn by Wende and Harry Devlin; ill. by Hary Devlin. Four Winds, 1993. ISBN 0-02-729936-8 Subj: Character traits – helpfulness. Family life – grandmothers. Garage sales, rummage sales.

Cranberry Christmas by Wende and Harry Devlin; ill. by authors. Parents, 1976. ISBN 0-819-30845-5 Subj: Behavior – sharing. Character traits – helpfulness. Holidays – Christmas.

Cranberry Easter by Wende and Harry Devlin; ill. by Harry Devlin. Four Winds, 1990. ISBN 0-02-729935-X Subj: Behavior – worrying. Holidays – Easter.

Cranberry Halloween ill. by Harry Devlin. Four Winds, 1982. ISBN 0-590-07854-2 Subj: Behavior – stealing. Holidays – Halloween.

Cranberry summer by Wende and Harry Devlin; ill. by Harry Devlin. Four Winds, 1992. ISBN 0-02-729181-2 Subj: Animals – donkeys. Character traits – kindness to animals. Holidays – Fourth of July.

Cranberry Thanksgiving by Wende and Harry Devlin; ill. by Harry Devlin. Parents, 1971. ISBN 0-819-30499-9 Subj: Holidays – Thanksgiving.

Cranberry Valentine by Wende and Harry Devlin; ill. by authors. Four Winds, 1986. ISBN 0-02-729200-2 Subj: Character traits – shyness. Holidays – Valentine's Day.

Old Black Witch! by Wende and Harry Devlin; ill. by Harry Devlin. Four Winds, 1992. Orig. published by Encyclopaedia Brit., 1963. ISBN 0-02-729185-5 Subj: Activities – cooking. Witches.

Old Witch and the polka-dot ribbon by Wende and Harry Devlin; ill. by Harry Devlin. Parents, 1970. ISBN 0-819-30418-2 Subj: Activities – cooking. Fairs. Food. Witches.

Old Witch rescues Halloween by Wende and Harry Devlin; ill. by Harry Devlin. Parents, 1972. ISBN 0-819-30609-6 Subj: Activities – cooking. Holidays – Halloween. Witches.

De Vries, Maggie. *Once upon a golden apple* (Little, Jean)

Dewan, Ted. *The sorcerer's apprentice* ill. by author. Doubleday, 1998. ISBN 0-385-32537-1 Subj: Folk and fairy tales. Magic. Robots. Wizards.

Dewey, Ariane. *A crocodile's tale: a Philippine folk story* (Aruego, José)

Dorin and the dragon ill. by author. Greenwillow, 1982. ISBN 0-688-00911-5 Subj: Dragons. Dreams. Magic. Royalty.

Febold Feboldson ill. by author. Greenwillow, 1984. ISBN 0-688-02534-X Subj: Farms. Tall tales. Weather.

The fish Peri ill. by author. Macmillan, 1979. ISBN 0-02-730100-1 Subj: Folk and fairy tales. Foreign lands – Turkey. Magic. Problem solving.

Laffite, the pirate ill. by author. Greenwillow, 1985. ISBN 0-688-04230-9 Subj: Folk and fairy tales. Pirates. U.S. history.

Pecos Bill ill. by author. Greenwillow, 1983. ISBN 0-688-01412-7 Subj: Cowboys. Tall tales. U.S. history – frontier and pioneer life.

Rockabye crocodile: a folktale from the Philippines (Aruego, José)

The sky ill. by author. Green Tiger Pr., 1993. ISBN 0-671-77835-8 Subj: Sky.

The tea squall ill. by author. Greenwillow, 1988. ISBN 0-688-07493-6 Subj: Parties. Seasons – spring. Tall tales.

The thunder god's son: a Peruvian folktale ill. by author. Greenwillow, 1981. ISBN 0-688-84295-X Subj: Folk and fairy tales. Foreign lands – Peru. Magic.

We hide, you seek (Aruego, José)

Dewey, Jennifer Owings. *Stories on stone: rock art, images from the ancient ones* ill. by author. Little, 1996. ISBN 0-316-18211-7 Subj: Activities – writing. Art. Communication. Indians of North America – Pueblo.

DeWitt, Jamie. *Jamie's turn* ill. by Julie Brinckloe. Raintree, 1984. ISBN 0-940742-37-3 Subj: Farms. Illness.

DeWitt, Lyndia. *What will the weather be?* ill. by Carolyn Croll. HarperCollins, 1991. ISBN 0-06-021597-6 Subj: Weather.

Dexter, Alison. *Grandma* ill. by author. Harper-Collins, 1993. ISBN 0-06-021144-X Subj: Family life – grandmothers. Sea and seashore.

De Zutter, Hank. *Who says a dog goes bow-wow?* ill. by Suse MacDonald. Doubleday, 1993. ISBN 0-385-30659-8 Subj: Animals. Foreign languages. Noise, sounds.

Diakité, Baba Wagué. *The hunterman and the crocodiles* ill. by author. Scholastic, 1997. ISBN 0-590-89828-0 Subj: Behavior – lying. Folk and fairy tales. Foreign lands – Africa.

Diamond, Donna. *The Bremen town musicians* (Grimm, Jacob)

Rumpelstiltskin (Grimm, Jacob)

Dick Whittington and his cat. *Dick Whittington* retold by Kathleen Lines; ill. by Edward Ardiz-zone. Walck, 1970. ISBN 0-8098-1172-3 Subj: Activities – trading. Animals – cats. Folk and fairy tales. Foreign lands – England. Middle Ages.

Dick Whittington: a story from England retold by Charles Causley; ill. by Antony Maitland. Penguin, 1979. Subj: Activities – trading. Animals – cats. Folk and fairy tales. Foreign lands – England. Middle Ages.

Dick Whittington and his cat retold and ill. by Marcia Brown. Scribners, 1950. Subj: Activities – trading. Animals – cats. Caldecott award honor books. Folk and fairy tales. Foreign lands – England. Middle Ages.

Dick Whittington and his cat retold by Eva Moore; ill. by Kurt Werth. Seabury Pr., 1974. ISBN 0-8164-3126-4 Subj: Activities – trading. Animals – cats. Folk and fairy tales. Foreign lands – England. Middle Ages.

Dickens, Frank. *Boffo: the great motorcycle race* ill. by author. Parents, 1978. ISBN 0-8193-0957-5 Subj: Character traits – cleverness. Motorcycles. Sports – racing.

Dickens, Lucy. *At the beach* ill. by author. Viking, 1991. ISBN 0-670-83927-2 Subj: Activities – playing. Family life. Format, unusual – board books. Sea and seashore.

Dancing class ill. by author. Viking, 1992. ISBN 0-670-84484-5 Subj: Activities – dancing. Ethnic groups in the U.S.

Dirty Henry ill. by author. Viking, 1991. ISBN 0-670-83578-1 Subj: Activities – bathing. Animals – dogs.

Go fish ill. by author. Viking, 1991. ISBN 0-670-84164-1 Subj: Animals – polar bears. Emotions – fear.

Our day ill. by author. Viking, 1991. ISBN 0-670-83929-9 Subj: Activities – playing. Family life. Format, unusual – board books.

Outside ill. by author. Viking, 1991. ISBN 0-670-83928-0 Subj: Activities – playing. Family life. Format, unusual – board books.

Playtime ill. by author. Viking, 1991. ISBN 0-670-83926-4 Subj: Activities – playing. Family life. Format, unusual – board books.

Dickinson, Mary. *Alex and Roy* ill. by Charlotte Firmin. Elsevier-Dutton, 1981. ISBN 0-233-97347-8 Subj: Friendship. Imagination.

Alex's bed ill. by Charlotte Firmin. Elsevier-Dutton, 1980. ISBN 0-233-97207-2 Subj: Character traits – cleanliness. Furniture – beds. Problem solving.

Alex's outing ill. by Charlotte Firmin. Dutton, 1983. ISBN 0-233-97558-6 Subj: Activities – picnicking. Behavior – nagging. Country.

Dickinson, Mike. *My dad doesn't even notice* ill. by author. Elsevier-Dutton, 1982. ISBN 0-233-97385-0 Subj: Behavior – misunderstanding. Imagination.

Dietl, Ulla. *The plant-and-grow project book* ill. by author. Sterling, 1993. ISBN 0-806-90456-9 Subj: Gardens, gardening. Plants. Science.

DiFiori, Lawrence. *Baby animals* ill. by author. Macmillan, 1983. ISBN 0-02-730620-8 Subj: Animals. Format, unusual – board books.

The farm ill. by author. Macmillan, 1983. ISBN 0-02-730630-5 Subj: Farms. Format, unusual – board books.

If I had a little car ill. by author. Golden Pr., 1985. ISBN 0-307-12305-7 Subj: Automobiles. Format, unusual – board books. Imagination.

My first book ill. by author. Macmillan, 1983. ISBN 0-02-730610-0 Subj: Activities – reading. Format, unusual – board books.

My toys ill. by author. Macmillan, 1983. ISBN 0-02-730600-3 Subj: Format, unusual – board books. Toys.

D'Ignazio, Fred. *Katie and the computer* ill. by Stan Gilliam. Creative Computing, 1980. ISBN 0-916688-11-9 Subj: Computers. Imagination.

Dijs, Carla. *Are you my daddy?* ill. by author. Simon & Schuster, 1990. ISBN 0-671-70227-0 Subj: Animals. Format, unusual – toy and movable books.

Are you my mommy? ill. by author. Simon & Schuster, 1990. ISBN 0-671-70226-2 Subj: Animals. Format, unusual – toy and movable books.

Big and small ill. by author. Grosset, 1989. ISBN 0-448-09075-9 Subj: Concepts – opposites. Format, unusual – toy and movable books.

How many? ill. by author. Grosset, 1989. ISBN 0-448-09076-7 Subj: Counting, numbers. Format, unusual – toy and movable books.

Mommy, would you love me if . . . ? ill. by author. Simon & Schuster, 1996. ISBN 0-689-80813-5 Subj: Animals. Family life – mothers. Format, unusual – toy and movable books.

Pretend you're a hippo ill. by author. Simon & Schuster, 1992. ISBN 0-671-76057-2 Subj: Animals – hippopotamuses. Format, unusual – toy and movable books. Imagination. Jungle. Rhyming text.

Diller, Harriett. *Big band sound* ill. by Andrea Shine. Boyds Mills, 1996. ISBN 1-56397-129-1 Subj: Music. Noise, sounds.

The faraway drawer ill. by Andrea Shine. Boyds Mills, 1996. ISBN 1-56397-190-9 Subj: Clothing – sweaters. Family life – great-grandparents. Imagination.

Grandaddy's highway ill. by Henri Sorensen. Caroline House, 1993. ISBN 1-878093-63-0 Subj: Activities – traveling. Family life – grandfathers. Trucks.

The waiting day ill. by Chi Chung. Green Tiger Pr., 1994. ISBN 0-671-86579-X Subj: Boats, ships. Folk and fairy tales. Foreign lands – China. Poverty.

Dilley, Becki. *Sixty fingers, sixty toes: see how the Dilley sextuplets grow!* by Becki and Keith Dilley; photos by E. Anthony Valainis. Walker, 1998. ISBN 0-8027-8614-6 Subj: Babies. Family life – brothers and sisters. Multiple births – sextuplets.

Dilley, Keith. *Sixty fingers, sixty toes: see how the Dilley sextuplets grow!* (Dilley, Becki)

Dillon, Barbara. *The beast in the bed* ill. by Chris Conover. Morrow, 1981. ISBN 0-688-22254-4 Subj: Furniture – beds. Imagination – imaginary friends. Monsters.

Dillon, Eilis. *The cats' opera* ill. by Kveta Vanecek. Bobbs-Merrill, 1963. Subj: Animals – cats. Music.

Dillon, Jana. *Jeb Scarecrow's pumpkin patch* ill. by author. Houghton Mifflin, 1992. ISBN 0-395-57578-8 Subj: Birds – crows. Holidays – Halloween. Scarecrows.

Lucky O'Leprechaun ill. by author. Pelican, 1998. ISBN 1-56554-333-5 Subj: Character traits – luck. Holidays – St. Patrick's Day. Mythical creatures – leprechauns.

Din dan don, it's Christmas ill. by Janina Domanska. Greenwillow, 1975. Text is a rendition of an anonymous Polish Christmas carol. ISBN 0-688-84003-5 Subj: Foreign lands – Poland. Holidays – Christmas. Religion. Songs.

Dinan, Carolyn. *The lunch box monster* ill. by author. Faber, 1983. ISBN 0-571-13153-0 Subj: Imagination – imaginary friends. Monsters.

Say cheese! ill. by author. Viking, 1986. ISBN 0-670-80954-3 Subj: Character traits – being different. School. Teeth.

Dinardo, Jeffrey. *Timothy and the night noises* ill. by author. Prentice-Hall, 1986. ISBN 0-13-922048-8 Subj: Emotions – fear. Frogs and toads. Night. Noise, sounds.

The wolf who cried boy ill. by author. Grosset, 1989. ISBN 0-448-09314-6 Subj: Animals – wolves. Behavior – lying. Behavior – trickery. Folk and fairy tales.

Dineen, Jacqueline. *Frédéric Chopin* ill. by author. Carolrhoda, 1996. ISBN 1-57505-248-2 Subj: Careers – composers. Music.

Dines, Glen. *Gilly and the wicharoo* ill. by author. Lothrop, 1968. Subj: Behavior – trickery. Character traits – cleverness. Foreign lands – England.

Pitadoe, the color maker ill. by author. Macmillan, 1959. Subj: Concepts – color. Wizards.

A tiger in the cherry tree ill. by author. Macmillan, 1958. Subj: Animals – tigers. Behavior – forgetfulness. Character traits – shyness. Foreign lands – Japan. Magic.

Dinosaurs and monsters ill. by Louise Nevett. Watts, 1984. ISBN 0-531-04770-9 Subj: Activities. Dinosaurs. Monsters.

Dionetti, Michelle V. *Coal mine peaches* ill. by Anita Riggio. Watts, 1991. ISBN 0-531-08548-1 Subj: Character traits – optimism. Ethnic groups in the U.S. – Italian Americans. Family life – grandfathers.

The day Eli went looking for bear ill. by Joyce Audy Dos Santos. Addison-Wesley, 1980. ISBN 0-201-02663-5 Subj: Animals. Family life – mothers. Seasons – winter. Sports – hunting.

Painting the wind ill. by Kevin Hawkes. Little, 1996. ISBN 0-316-18602-3 Subj: Activities – painting. Art.

Thalia Brown and the blue bug ill. by James Calvin. Addison-Wesley, 1979. ISBN 0-201-01399-1 Subj: Art. Character traits – pride. Ethnic groups in the U.S. – African Americans.

Dionne, Wanda. *Little Thumb* ill. by Jana Dillon. Pelican, 2000. ISBN 1-56554-754-3 Subj: Rhyming text. Thumb sucking.

Diot, Alain. *Better, best, bestest* ill. by Joel Naprstek. Dial, 1977. ISBN 0-8252-0478-X Subj: Behavior – boasting. Family life – fathers.

DiSalvo-Ryan, DyAnne. *City green* ill. by author. Morrow, 1994. ISBN 0-688-12787-8 Subj: City. Communities, neighborhoods. Gardens, gardening.

A dog like Jack ill. by author. Holiday, 1999. ISBN 0-8234-1369-1 Subj: Animals – dogs. Death. Emotions – grief. Pets.

Disher, Garry. *Switch cat* ill. by Andrew McLean. Ticknor & Fields, 1995. ISBN 0-395-71643-8 Subj: Animals – cats. Moving. Rhyming text.

Diska, Pat. *Andy says . . . Bonjour!* ill. by Chris Jenkyns. Vanguard, 1954. Subj: Animals – cats. Foreign lands – France. Foreign languages.

Diviny, Sean. *Snow inside the house* ill. by Joe Rocco. HarperCollins, 1998. ISBN 0-06-027354-2 Subj: Imagination. Nature. Rhyming text. Weather – snow.

DiVito, Anna. *Elephants on ice* ill. by author. Dial, 1991. ISBN 0-8037-0798-3 Subj: Animals – elephants. Sports – ice skating.

Dixon, Ann. *The blueberry shoe* ill. by Evon Zerbetz. Alaska Northwest, 1999. ISBN 0-88240-518-7 Subj: Alaska. Animals. Behavior – losing things. Clothing – shoes. Cumulative tales. Family life. Food.

How raven brought light to people ill. by James Watts. Macmillan, 1992. ISBN 0-689-50536-1 Subj: Birds – ravens. Folk and fairy tales. Indians of North America – Tlingit.

Dixon, Chuck. *Batman: the joker's apprentice* ill. by John Calmette and Todd Winter. Little, 1996. ISBN 0-316-17798-9 Subj: Crime.

Dixon, Ruth. *see* Barrows, Marjorie Wescott

Dobbs, Rose. *More once-upon-a-time stories* ill. by Flavia Gág. Random House, 1961. Subj: Folk and fairy tales.

Once-upon-a-time story book ill. by Walter Hodges. Random House, 1958. Subj: Folk and fairy tales.

Dobkin, Bonnie. *Everybody says* ill. by Keith Neely. Childrens Pr., 1993. ISBN 0-516-02019-6 Subj: Character traits – individuality. Ethnic groups in the U.S. – African Americans. Friendship.

Dobrin, Arnold Jack. *Josephine's 'magination* ill. by author. Four Winds, 1973. ISBN 0-590-43494-2 Subj: Foreign lands – Caribbean Islands. Imagination. Toys.

Dobson, Clive. *Fred's TV* ill. by author. Firefly, 1989. ISBN 0-920668-60-7 Subj: Birds. Character traits – kindness to animals. Seasons – winter. Television.

Dobson, David. *Can we save them? endangered species of North America* ill. by James M. Needham. Charlesbridge, 1997. ISBN 0-88106-824-1 Subj: Animals – endangered animals. Ecology. Plants. Science.

Dodd, Anne Westcott. *Footprints and shadows* ill. by Henri Sorensen. Simon & Schuster, 1992. ISBN 0-671-78716-0 Subj: Shadows.

The story of the sea glass ill. by Mary Beth Owens. Down East, 1999. ISBN 0-8927-2416-1 Subj: Family life – grandmothers. Sea and seashore.

Dodd, Lynley. *The apple tree* ill. by author. Gareth Stevens, 1985. ISBN 0-918831-08-3 Subj: Animals – possums. Behavior – stealing. Food. Trees.

A dragon in a wagon ill. by author. Gareth Stevens, 2000. ISBN 0-8368-2687-6 Subj: Animals – dogs. Imagination. Rhyming text.

Find me a tiger ill. by author. Gareth Stevens, 2001. ISBN 0-8368-2781-3 Subj: Animals. Behavior – hiding. Rhyming text.

Hairy Maclary from Donaldson's dairy ill. by author. Gareth Stevens, 1985. ISBN 0-918831-05-9 Subj: Animals – cats. Animals – dogs. Cumulative tales. Emotions – fear. Rhyming text.

Hairy Maclary, Scattercat ill. by author. Gareth Stevens, 1988. ISBN 1-555-32123-2 Subj: Animals – cats. Animals – dogs. Behavior – bullying. Rhyming text.

Hairy Maclary, sit ill. by author. Gareth Stevens, 1998. ISBN 0-8368-2093-2 Subj: Animals – dogs. Rhyming text.

Hairy Maclary's bone ill. by author. Gareth Stevens, 1985. ISBN 0-918331-06-7 Subj: Animals – dogs. Character traits – cleverness. Cumulative tales. Rhyming text.

Hairy Maclary's caterwaul caper ill. by author. Gareth Stevens, 2000. ISBN 0-8368-2690-6 Subj: Animals – cats. Animals – dogs. Rhyming text. Trees.

Hairy Maclary's rumpus at the vet ill. by author. Gareth Stevens, 2000. ISBN 0-8368-2691-4 Subj: Animals – dogs. Behavior – misbehavior. Careers – veterinarians. Rhyming text.

Hairy Maclary's showbusiness ill. by author. Gareth Stevens, 1992. ISBN 0-8368-0763-4 Subj: Animals – cats. Animals – dogs. Rhyming text.

The minister's cat: ABC ill. by author. Gareth Stevens, 1994. ISBN 0-8368-1073-2 Subj: ABC books. Animals – cats.

The nickle nackle tree ill. by author. Macmillan, 1976. ISBN 0-241-89330-5 Subj: Counting, numbers. Rhyming text.

Schnitzel von Krumm forget-me-not ill. by author. Gareth Stevens, 1998. ISBN 0-8368-2094-0 Subj: Activities – vacationing. Animals – dogs. Behavior – forgetfulness. Rhyming text.

Schnitzel von Krumm's basketwork ill. by author. Gareth Stevens, 2001. ISBN 0-8368-2783-X Subj: Animals – dogs. Emotions – happiness. Rhyming text.

Slinky Malinki ill. by author. Gareth Stevens, 2001. ISBN 0-8368-2784-8 Subj: Animals – cats. Crime. Rhyming text.

Slinky Malinki catflaps ill. by author. Gareth Stevens, 1999. ISBN 0-8368-2249-8 Subj: Animals – cats. Rhyming text.

Slinky Malinki, open the door ill. by author. Gareth Stevens, 2001. ISBN 0-8368-2785-6 Subj: Animals – cats. Behavior – misbehavior. Birds. Rhyming text.

The smallest turtle ill. by author. Gareth Stevens, 1985. ISBN 0-918831-07-5 Subj: Reptiles – turtles, tortoises. Science. Sea and seashore.

Wake up, bear ill. by author. Gareth Stevens, 1988. ISBN 1-555-32124-0 Subj: Animals. Animals – bears. Seasons – spring. Sleep.

Dodds, Dayle Ann. *The color box* ill. by Giles Laroche. Little, 1992. ISBN 0-316-18820-4 Subj: Animals – monkeys. Concepts – color. Format, unusual – toy and movable books.

Do bunnies talk? ill. by Arlene Dubanevich. HarperCollins, 1992. ISBN 0-06-020249-1 Subj: Animals. Animals – rabbits. Language. Noise, sounds. Rhyming text.

The Great Divide ill. by Tracy Mitchell. Candlewick, 1999. ISBN 0-7636-0442-9 Subj: Counting, numbers. Rhyming text. Sports – racing.

The shape of things ill. by Julie Lacome. Candlewick, 1994. ISBN 1-56402-224-2 Subj: Concepts – shape.

Sing, Sophie! ill. by Rosanne Litzinger. Candlewick, 1997. ISBN 0-7636-0131-4 Subj: Activities – singing. Family life. Rhyming text. Weather – storms.

Wheel away! ill. by Thacher Hurd. HarperCollins, 1991. ISBN 0-06-021689-1 Subj: Circular tales. Format, unusual. Rhyming text.

Dodds, Siobhan. *Charles Tiger* ill. by author. Little, 1988. ISBN 0-316-18817-4 Subj: Animals. Animals – tigers. Behavior – losing things.

Elizabeth Hen ill. by author. Little, 1988. ISBN 0-316-18818-2 Subj: Animals. Birds – chickens. Counting, numbers. Eggs. Farms.

Grandpa Bud ill. by author. Candlewick, 1993. ISBN 1-56402-175-0 Subj: Activities – cooking. Cumulative tales. Family life – grandfathers. Toys.

Ting-a-ling! ill. by author. DK, 1999. ISBN 0-7894-4841-6 Subj: Activities – bathing. Family life – mothers. Telephone. Toys.

Words and pictures ill. by author. Candlewick, 1992. ISBN 1-56402-042-8 Subj: Activities. Dictionaries. Rebuses.

Dodge, Mary Mapes. *Mary Anne* ill. by June Amos Grammer. Lothrop, 1983. ISBN 0-688-02089-5 Subj: Rhyming text. Toys – dolls.

Dodgson, Charles Lutwidge. *see* Carroll, Lewis

The dog writes on the window with his nose, and other poems coll. by David Kherdian; ill. by Nonny Hogrogian. Four Winds, 1977. ISBN 0-590-07448-2 Subj: Poetry.

Doherty, Berlie. *The midnight man* ill. by Ian Andrew. Candlewick, 1998. ISBN 0-7636-0700-2 Subj: Dreams. Moon. Night. Stars.

Paddiwak and cozy ill. by Alison Bartlett. Orchard, 1991. ISBN 0-531-30180-X Subj: Animals – cats. Emotions – envy, jealousy.

Paddiwak and cozy ill. by Teresa O'Brien. Dial, 1989. ISBN 0-8037-0483-6 Subj: Animals – cats. Emotions – envy, jealousy.

Snowy ill. by Keith Bowen. Dial, 1993. ISBN 0-8037-1343-6 Subj: Animals – horses, ponies. Boats, ships. Family life. School.

Domanska, Janina. *A was an angler* ill. by author. Greenwillow, 1991. ISBN 0-688-06991-6 Subj: ABC books. Nursery rhymes.

The best of the bargain ill. by author. Greenwillow, 1977. ISBN 0-688-84062-0 Subj: Animals – foxes. Animals – hedgehogs. Behavior – trickery. Character traits – cleverness. Folk and fairy tales. Foreign lands – Poland. Gardens, gardening.

Busy Monday morning ill. by author. Greenwillow, 1985. ISBN 0-688-03834-4 Subj: Folk and fairy tales. Foreign lands – Poland. Music. Songs.

I saw a ship a-sailing ill. by author. Macmillan, 1972. Subj: Boats, ships. Holidays – Christmas. Nursery rhymes.

If all the seas were one sea ill. by author. Macmillan, 1971. ISBN 0-02-732540-7 Subj: Caldecott award honor books. Nursery rhymes. Sea and seashore.

King Krakus and the dragon ill. by author. Greenwillow, 1979. ISBN 0-688-84189-9 Subj: Character traits – cleverness. Dragons. Folk and fairy tales. Foreign lands – Poland. Royalty – kings.

Look, there is a turtle flying ill. by author. Macmillan, 1968. Subj: Folk and fairy tales. Foreign lands – Poland. Reptiles – turtles, tortoises. Royalty.

Marek, the little fool ill. by author. Greenwillow, 1982. ISBN 0-688-00913-1 Subj: Folk and fairy tales. Foreign lands.

Palmiero and the ogre ill. by author. Macmillan, 1967. Subj: Behavior – forgetfulness. Folk and fairy tales. Magic. Mythical creatures – ogres.

A scythe, a rooster and a cat ill. by author. Greenwillow, 1981. ISBN 0-688-84308-5 Subj: Folk and fairy tales. Foreign lands – Russia.

Spring is ill. by author. Greenwillow, 1976. ISBN 0-688-84026-4 Subj: Animals – dogs. Character traits – curiosity. Seasons.

The tortoise and the tree ill. by author. Greenwillow, 1978. ISBN 0-688-84132-5 Subj: Folk and fairy tales. Foreign lands – Africa. Reptiles – turtles, tortoises.

The turnip ill. by author. Macmillan, 1969. Subj: Cumulative tales. Farms. Folk and fairy tales. Foreign lands – Russia. Plants. Problem solving.

What do you see? ill. by author. Macmillan, 1974. ISBN 0-02-732830-9 Subj: Animals. Rhyming text. World.

What happens next? ill. by author. Greenwillow, 1983. ISBN 0-688-01749-5 Subj: Tall tales.

Why so much noise? ill. by author. HarperCollins, 1965. Adapt. of the tale entitled 'The elephant has a bet with the tiger,' [as recorded] by Walter William Skeat. Subj: Animals – elephants. Animals – tigers. Character traits – cleverness. Folk and fairy tales. Foreign lands – India. Noise, sounds.

Domestic animals ill. with photos. Imported Pubs., 1983. ISBN 0-8285-2429-7 Subj: Animals. Format, unusual – board books. Wordless.

Dominguez, Angel. *Diary of a Victorian mouse* ill. by author. Arcade, 1991. ISBN 1-55970-121-8 Subj: Animals – mice. Foreign lands – England.

Donaldson, Joan. *The real pretend* ill. by Tasha Tudor. Checkerboard, 1992. ISBN 1-56288-158-2 Subj: Activities – playing. Behavior – misunderstanding. Family life – brothers.

Donaldson, Julia. *The gruffalo* ill. by Axel Scheffler. Dial, 1999. ISBN 0-8037-2386-5 Subj: Animals. Animals – mice. Monsters. Rhyming text.

Donaldson, Lois. *Karl's wooden horse* ill. by Annie Bergmann. Albert Whitman, 1970. ISBN 0-8075-4107-9 Subj: Dreams. Holidays – Christmas. Night. Toys – rocking horses.

Donnelly, Liza. *Dinosaur beach* ill. by author. Scholastic, 1991. ISBN 0-590-42175-1 Subj: City. Dinosaurs. Sea and seashore.

Dinosaur garden ill. by author. Scholastic, 1991. ISBN 0-590-43172-2 Subj: City. Dinosaurs. Gardens, gardening.

Dinosaurs' Halloween ill. by author. Scholastic, 1987. ISBN 0-590-41025-3 Subj: City. Dinosaurs. Holidays – Halloween.

Donohue, Dorothy. *Big and little on the farm* ill. by author. Golden Books, 1999. ISBN 0-307-10225-4 Subj: Animals. Animals – babies. Concepts – size. Farms.

Donovan, Mary Lee. *Bedtime* (Bedtime)

Won't you come and play with me? ill. by Cynthia Jabar. Houghton Mifflin, 1998. ISBN 0-395-84630-7 Subj: Activities – playing. Music. Nursery rhymes. Songs.

Don't tell the scarecrow: and other Japanese poems by Issa, Yayu, Kikaku and other Japanese poets; ill. by Talivaldis Stubis. Four Winds, 1970. Subj: Foreign lands – Japan. Poetry. Seasons.

Dooley, Norah. *Everybody bakes bread* ill. by Peter J. Thornton. Carolrhoda, 1996. ISBN 0-87614-864-X Subj: Activities – cooking. Communities, neighborhoods. Ethnic groups in the U.S. Food.

Everybody cooks rice ill. by Peter J. Thornton. Carolrhoda, 1991. ISBN 0-87614-412-1 Subj: Ethnic groups in the U.S. Family life. Food.

Dooley, Virginia. *Tubes in my ears: my trip to the hospital* ill. by Miriam Katin. Mondo, 1996. ISBN 1-57255-118-6 Subj: Hospitals. Illness.

Doolittle, Eileen. *The ark in the attic: an alphabet adventure* photos by Starr Ockenga. Godine, 1987. ISBN 0-87923-648-1 Subj: ABC books. Rebuses. Riddles.

World of wonders: a trip through numbers photos by Starr Ockenga; ill. by author. Houghton Mifflin, 1988. ISBN 0-325-48726-9 Subj: Counting, numbers. Imagination. Rhyming text.

Dorian, Marguerite. *When the snow is blue* ill. by author. Lothrop, 1960. Subj: Animals – bears. Imagination. Weather – snow.

Dornbusch, Erica. *Finding Kate's shoes* ill. by author. Firefly, 2001. ISBN 1-55037-671-3 Subj: Behavior – losing things. Clothing – shoes. Family life – mothers. Imagination. Wordless.

Doro, Ann. *Twin pickle* ill. by Clare Mackie. Holt, 1996. ISBN 0-8050-3802-7 Subj: Multiple births – twins. Rhyming text.

Dörrie, Doris. *Lottie's princess dress* ill. by Julia Kaergel. Dial, 1999. ISBN 0-8037-2388-1 Subj: Clothing – dresses. Family life – daughters. Family life – mothers.

Dorros, Arthur. *Abuela* ill. by Elisa Kleven. Dutton, 1991. ISBN 0-525-44750-4 Subj: Activities – flying. City. Ethnic groups in the U.S. Family life – grandmothers. Foreign languages.

Alligator shoes ill. by author. Dutton, 1982. ISBN 0-525-44001-1 Subj: Reptiles – alligators, crocodiles.

Ant cities ill. by author. Crowell, 1987. ISBN 0-690-04570-0 Subj: Insects – ants. Science.

Feel the wind ill. by author. HarperCollins, 1989. ISBN 0-690-04741-X Subj: Weather – wind.

Follow the water from brook to ocean ill. by author. HarperCollins, 1991. ISBN 0-06-021599-2 Subj: Science. Water.

Me and my shadow ill. by author. Scholastic, 1990. ISBN 0-590-42772-5 Subj: Shadows.

Pretzels ill. by author. Greenwillow, 1981. ISBN 0-688-00669-8 Subj: Boats, ships. Humor.

Radio Man/Don Radio: a story in English and Spanish trans. by Sandra Dorros. HarperCollins, 1993. Text in English and Spanish. ISBN 0-06-021548-8 Subj: Careers – migrant workers. Communication. Ethnic groups in the U.S. – Mexican Americans. Farms. Radio.

This is my house ill. by author. Scholastic, 1992. ISBN 0-590-45302-5 Subj: Foreign lands. Homes, houses.

Tonight is carnaval ill. with photos of arpilleras sewn by the Club de Madres Virgen del Carmen of Lima, Peru. Dutton, 1991. ISBN 0-525-44641-9 Subj: Fairs. Farms. Foreign lands – Peru.

Dorros, Sandra Marulanda. *Radio Man/Don Radio: a story in English and Spanish* (Dorros, Arthur)

Dorsky, Blanche. *Harry, a true story* ill. by Muriel Batherman. Prentice-Hall, 1977. ISBN 0-13-384198-7 Subj: Animals – rabbits. School.

Dos Santos, Joyce Audy. *The diviner* ill. by author. Lippincott, 1980. ISBN 0-397-31910-X Subj: Character traits – cleverness. Folk and fairy tales. Foreign lands – Canada. Royalty.

Henri and the Loup-Garou ill. by author. Pantheon, 1982. ISBN 0-394-94950-1 Subj: Folk and fairy tales. Foreign lands – Canada. Monsters.

Sand dollar, sand dollar ill. by author. Lippincott, 1980. ISBN 0-397-31894-4 Subj: Sea and seashore.

Dostoyevsky, Fyodor. *The talking crocodile* (Campbell, M. Rudolph)

Dotlich, Rebecca Kai. *Lemonade sun: and other summer poems* ill. by Jan Spivey Gilchrist. Wordsong, 1998. ISBN 1-56397-660-9 Subj: Poetry. Seasons – summer.

What is round? photos by Maria Ferrari. Harper-Festival, 1999. ISBN 0-694-01208-4 Subj: Concepts – shape. Rhyming text.

What is square? photos by Maria Ferrari. Harper-Festival, 1999. ISBN 0-694-01207-6 Subj: Concepts – shape. Rhyming text.

Doty, Roy. *Eye fooled you: the big book of optical illusions* ill. by author. Macmillan, 1983. ISBN 0-02-042980-0 Subj: Optical illusions.

Old-one-eye meets his match ill. by author. Lothrop, 1978. ISBN 0-688-51825-7 Subj: Animals – mice. Animals – rats.

Doubilet, Anne. *Under the sea from A to Z* photos by David Doubilet. Crown, 1991. ISBN 0-517-57837-9 Subj: ABC books. Sea and seashore.

Doucet, Sharon Arms. *Why Lapin's ears are long and other stories of the Louisiana bayou* ill. by David Catrow. Orchard, 1997. ISBN 0-531-33041-9 Subj: Animals – rabbits. Folk and fairy tales.

Doughtie, Charles. *Gabriel Wrinkles, the bloodhound who couldn't smell* ill. by Charles D. Saxon. Dodd, 1959. Subj: Animals – dogs. Senses – smelling.

High Henry . . . the cowboy who was too tall to ride a horse ill. by Don Gregg. Dodd, 1960. Subj: Animals – giraffes. Cowboys. U.S. history – frontier and pioneer life.

Douglas, Michael. *Round, round world* ill. by author. Golden Pr., 1960. Subj: Animals – cats. Foreign lands. World.

Douglas, Richardo Keens. *The nutmeg princess* ill. by Annouchka Galouchko. Firefly, 1992. ISBN 1-55037-239-4 Subj: Character traits – bravery. Character traits – selfishness. Foreign lands – Caribbean Islands. Gardens, gardening.

Douglas, Robert W. *John Paul II: the Pilgrim Pope* ill., map and photos. Childrens Pr., 1979. ISBN 0-516-03563-0 Subj: Religion.

Douglass, Ann. *Baby science: how babies really work!* photos by Hélène Desputeaux. Owl Books, 1998. ISBN 1-895688-83-3 Subj: Babies. Behavior – growing up. Family life.

Douglass, Barbara. *The chocolate chip cookie contest* ill. by Eric Jon Nones. Lothrop, 1985. ISBN 0-688-04044-6 Subj: Activities – cooking. Clowns, jesters.

Good as new ill. by Patiences Brewster. Lothrop, 1982. ISBN 0-688-51983-0 Subj: Behavior – misbehavior. Family life – grandfathers. Toys – bears.

Douzou, Olivier. *Wolf's lunch* ill. by author. Chronicle, 1997. ISBN 0-8118-1806-3 Subj: Animals – wolves. Format, unusual – board books.

Dow, Katharine. *My time of year* ill. by Walter Erhard. Walck, 1961. Subj: Seasons.

Dowdy, Mrs. Regera. see Gorey, Edward (St. John)

Dowers, Patrick. *One day scene through a leaf* ill. by author. Green Tiger Pr., 1981. ISBN 0-914676-55-5 Subj: Poetry.

Dowling, Paul. *Are you sleepy, Puff?* ill. by author. Hyperion, 1993. ISBN 1-56282-393-0 Subj: Animals – cats. Bedtime. Sleep.

Happy birthday, Owl ill. by author. Walt Disney, 1992. ISBN 1-56282-253-5 Subj: Animals. Birds – owls. Birthdays. Parties.

Jimmy's snowy book ill. by author. Bantam, 1994. ISBN 0-553-09649-4 Subj: Animals – dogs. Format, unusual – toy and movable books. Weather – snow.

Meg and Jack are moving ill. by author. Houghton Mifflin, 1990. ISBN 0-395-53514-X Subj: Family life. Moving.

Meg and Jack's new friends ill. by author. Houghton Mifflin, 1990. ISBN 0-395-53513-1 Subj: Behavior – sharing. Friendship. Moving. Toys.

The night journey ill. by author. Delacorte, 1997. ISBN 0-385-32287-9 Subj: Format, unusual – toy and movable books. Night.

Splodger ill. by author. Houghton Mifflin, 1991. ISBN 0-395-57443-9 Subj: Bedtime. Behavior – misbehavior. Imagination.

Where are you going, Jimmy? ill. by author. Thomasson-Grant, 1993. ISBN 1-56566-026-9 Subj: Activities – walking. Animals. Communities, neighborhoods.

You can do it, Rabbit ill. by author. Walt Disney, 1992. ISBN 1-56282-252-7 Subj: Animals – rabbits. Character traits – helpfulness. Sports – bicycling.

You need a bath, Mustard ill. by author. Hyperion, 1993. ISBN 1-56282-392-2 Subj: Activities – bathing. Animals. Animals – bears.

Downes, Belinda. *Every little angel's handbook* words and embroideries by Belinda Downes. Dial, 1997. ISBN 0-8037-2264-8 Subj: Angels. Religion.

Downey, Lynn. *Sing, Henrietta! Sing!* ill. by Tony Sansevero. Ideals, 1997. ISBN 1-57102-103-5 Subj: Activities – singing. Food. Friendship. Gardens, gardening.

Downie, Jill. *Alphabet puzzle* ill. by author. Lothrop, 1988. ISBN 0-688-08044-8 Subj: ABC books. Rebuses. Riddles.

Downing, Joan. *Baseball is our game* ill. by Tony Freeman. Childrens Pr., 1982. ISBN 0-516-03402-2 Subj: Sports – baseball.

Doyle, Charlotte Lackner. *Where's Bunny's mommy?* ill. by Rick Brown. Simon & Schuster, 1995. ISBN 0-671-88984-8 Subj: Animals – rabbits. Family life – mothers. School.

You can't catch me ill. by Rosanne Litzinger. HarperFestival, 1998. ISBN 0-694-01038-3 Subj: Activities – playing. Rhyming text.

Doyle, Donovan. *see* Boegehold, Betty

Doyle, Malachy. *Jody's beans* ill. by Judith Allibone. Candlewick, 1999. ISBN 0-7636-0687-1 Subj: Family life – grandfathers. Food. Gardens, gardening.

Dragon poems comp. by John Foster and Korky Paul; ill. by Korky Paul. Oxford Univ. Pr., 1992. ISBN 0-19-276096-3 Subj: Dragons. Poetry.

Dragonwagon, Crescent. *Alligator arrived with apples: a potluck alphabet feast* ill. by José Aruego and Ariane Dewey. Macmillan, 1987. ISBN 0-02-733090-7 Subj: ABC books. Animals. Holidays – Thanksgiving. Reptiles – alligators, crocodiles.

Alligators and others all year long! a book of months ill. by José Aruego and Ariane Dewey. Macmillan, 1993. ISBN 0-02-733091-5 Subj: Animals. Days of the week, months of the year. Poetry.

Always, always ill. by Arieh Zeldich. Macmillan, 1984. ISBN 0-02-733080-X Subj: Divorce.

Annie flies the birthday bike ill. by Emily Arnold McCully. Macmillan, 1993. ISBN 0-02-733155-5 Subj: Birthdays. Rhyming text. Sports – bicycling.

Bat in the dining room ill. by S. D. Schindler. Cavendish, 1997. ISBN 0-7614-5007-6 Subj: Animals – bats. Character traits – kindness to animals. Rhyming text.

Coconut ill. by Nancy Tafuri. HarperCollins, 1984. ISBN 0-06-021760-X Subj: Behavior – wishing. Birds – parakeets, parrots.

Diana, maybe ill. by Deborah Kogan Ray. Macmillan, 1987. ISBN 0-02-733180-6 Subj: Behavior – wishing. Family life.

Half a moon and one whole star ill. by Jerry Pinkney. Macmillan, 1986. ISBN 0-02-733120-2 Subj: Dreams. Night. Rhyming text.

Home place ill. by Jerry Pinkney. Macmillan, 1990. ISBN 0-02-733190-3 Subj: Ethnic groups in the U.S. – African Americans. Family life. Homes, houses.

I hate my brother Harry ill. by Dick Gackenbach. HarperCollins, 1983. ISBN 0-06-021758-8 Subj: Sibling rivalry.

I hate my sister Maggie ill. by Leslie Holt Morrill. Macmillan, 1989. ISBN 0-02-733150-4 Subj: Sibling rivalry.

If you call my name ill. by David Palladini. Harper, 1981. ISBN 0-06-021744-8 Subj: Imagination.

The itch book ill. by Joseph Mahler. Macmillan, 1990. ISBN 0-02-733121-0 Subj: Rhyming text. Seasons – summer.

Jemima remembers ill. by Troy Howell. Macmillan, 1984. ISBN 0-02-733070-2 Subj: Farms. Memories, memory. Rhyming text. Seasons.

Katie in the morning ill. by Betsy Day. HarperCollins, 1983. ISBN 0-06-021730-8 Subj: Behavior – solitude. Morning.

Margaret Ziegler is horse-crazy ill. by Peter Elwell. Macmillan, 1988. ISBN 0-02-733230-6 Subj: Animals – horses, ponies.

Rainy day together ill. by Lillian Hoban. Harper-Collins, 1971. ISBN 0-06-024688-X Subj: Emotions. Family life. Family life – only child. Weather – rain.

Strawberry dress escape ill. by Lillian Hoban. Scribners, 1975. ISBN 0-684-13912-X Subj: School. Seasons – spring.

The sun begun ill. by Terea Shaffer. Atheneum, 1999. ISBN 0-689-81159-4 Subj: Family life. Family life – fathers. Rhyming text.

This is the bread I baked for Ned ill. by Isadore Seltzer. Macmillan, 1989. ISBN 0-02-733220-9 Subj: Activities – cooking. Cumulative tales. Food. Rhyming text.

When light turns into night ill. by Robert Andrew Parker. HarperCollins, 1975. ISBN 0-06-021740-5 Subj: Behavior – solitude. Night.

Will it be okay? ill. by Ben Shecter. Harper, 1977. ISBN 0-06-021738-3 Subj: Emotions – fear. Family life – mothers.

Wind Rose ill. by Ronald Himler. HarperCollins, 1976. ISBN 0-06-021742-1 Subj: Babies. Emotions – love. Names.

Drake, Jane. *Farming* (Love, Ann)

Fishing (Love, Ann)

Drake, John. *The beginning of the river: Herman's quest* ill. by Kelly Kortekaas. Little Turtle, 1992. ISBN 0-9633574-0-9 Subj: Animals – cats. Rhyming text. Rivers.

Drawson, Blair. *Flying Dimitri* ill. by author. Orchard, 1997. ISBN 0-531-30037-4 Subj: Activities – flying. Birthdays. Emotions – loneliness. Family life – fathers. Imagination.

Mary Margaret's tree ill. by author. Orchard, 1996. ISBN 0-531-08871-5 Subj: Imagination. Nature. Seasons. Trees.

Drdek, Richard E. *Horace the friendly octopus* ill. by Joseph Veno. Allyn & Bacon, 1965. Reading consultants: William D. Sheldon and Mary C. Austin. Subj: Friendship. Octopuses.

Dreamer, Sue. *Circus ABC* ill. by author. Little, 1985. ISBN 0-316-19196-5 Subj: ABC books. Circus. Format, unusual – board books.

Circus 1, 2, 3 ill. by author. Little, 1985. ISBN 0-316-19195-7 Subj: Circus. Counting, numbers. Format, unusual – board books.

Dreier, Ted. *Moozie's kind adventure* ill. by Jane Labik. Best Friends Books, 1999. ISBN 0-9662268-1-X Subj: Animals – bulls, cows. Birds – ducks. Farms.

Dreifus, Miriam W. *Brave Betsy* ill. by Sheila Greenwald. Putnam, 1961. Subj: Character traits – bravery. School. Toys – dolls.

Drescher, Henrik. *The boy who ate around* ill. by author. Hyperion, 1994. ISBN 0-7868-2011-X Subj: Food. Monsters.

Klutz ill. by author. Hyperion, 1996. ISBN 0-7868-2182-5 Subj: Circus. Clowns, jesters. Family life.

Look-alikes ill. by author. Lothrop, 1985. ISBN 0-688-05817-5 Subj: Animals – monkeys. Toys.

Looking for Santa Claus ill. by author. Lothrop, 1984. ISBN 0-688-02999-X Subj: Animals – bulls, cows. Holidays – Christmas. Imagination. Santa Claus.

Pat the beastie: a pull-and-poke book ill. by author; paper engineering by Dennis K. Meyer. Hyperion, 1993. ISBN 1-5628-2407-4 Subj: Format, unusual – toy and movable books. Monsters.

Simon's book ill. by author. Lothrop, 1983. ISBN 0-688-02086-0 Subj: Dreams. Monsters.

The strange appearance of Howard Cranebill, Jr. ill. by author. Lothrop, 1982. ISBN 0-688-00962-X Subj: Babies. Birds – storks. Character traits – being different. Family life.

The yellow umbrella ill. by author. Bradbury, 1987. ISBN 0-02-733240-3 Subj: Animals – monkeys. Jungle. Umbrellas. Wordless. Zoos.

Drescher, Joan E. *The birth-order blues* ill. by author. Viking, 1993. ISBN 0-670-83621-4 Subj: Family life. Sibling rivalry.

I'm in charge! ill. by author. Little, 1981. ISBN 0-316-19330-5 Subj: Behavior – growing up. Family life.

The marvelous mess ill. by author. Houghton Mifflin, 1980. ISBN 0-395-28160-7 Subj: Family life. Sibling rivalry.

Max and Rufus ill. by author. Houghton Mifflin, 1982. ISBN 0-395-32435-1 Subj: Animals – dogs. Humor.

My mother's getting married ill. by author. Dial, 1986. ISBN 0-8037-0176-4 Subj: Emotions – envy, jealousy. Family life – mothers. Weddings.

Your family, my family ill. by author. Walker, 1980. ISBN 0-8027-6382-0 Subj: Family life.

Drew, Patricia. *Spotter Puff* ill. by author. Merrimack, 1979. ISBN 0-686-25198-9 Subj: Birds – puffins. Character traits – kindness to animals.

Driscoll, Debbie. *Baby comes home* ill. by Barbara Samuels. Simon & Schuster, 1993. ISBN 0-671-75540-4 Subj: Babies. Family life – brothers and sisters. Family life – new sibling.

Driscoll, Laura. *The bravest cat! the true story of Scarlett* ill. by DyAnne DiSalvo-Ryan. Grosset, 1997. ISBN 0-448-41720-0 Subj: Animals – cats. Character traits – bravery. Fire.

Driz, Ovsei. *The boy and the tree* trans. by Joachim Neugroschel; ill. by Victor Pivovarov. Prentice-Hall, 1978. ISBN 0-13-080929-2 Subj: Poetry.

Drucker, Malka. *Grandma's latkes* ill. by Eve Chwast. Harcourt, 1992. ISBN 0-15-200468-8 Subj: Family life – grandmothers. Food. Holidays – Hanukkah. Jewish culture. Religion.

A Jewish holiday ABC ill. by Rita Pocock. Harcourt, 1992. ISBN 0-15-200482-3 Subj: ABC books. Holidays. Jewish culture. Religion.

Drummond, Allan. *Moby Dick* ill. by adapt. Farrar, 1997. ISBN 0-374-34997-5 Subj: Animals – whales. Careers – whalers. Sea and seashore. Sports – hunting.

The willow pattern story ill. by author. North-South, 1992. ISBN 1-55858-172-3 Subj: Emotions – love. Folk and fairy tales. Foreign lands – China.

Drummond, Violet H. *The flying postman* ill. by author. Walck, 1964. Subj: Careers – postal workers. Foreign lands – England. Helicopters.

Phewtus the squirrel ill. by author. Lothrop, 1987. ISBN 0-688-07013-2 Subj: Animals – squirrels. Behavior – lost. Toys.

Drury, Tim. *When I'm big* by Tim Drury and Nila Aye; ill. by Nila Aye. Orchard, 1999. ISBN 0-531-30189-3 Subj: Imagination. Rhyming text. Weather – rain.

Dryden, Emma. *Good morning - good night* ill. by Richard Max Kolding. Random House, 1990. ISBN 0-679-80066-2 Subj: Animals. Format, unusual. Morning. Night.

Dubanevich, Arlene. *Calico cows* ill. by author. Viking, 1993. ISBN 0-670-84436-5 Subj: Animals – bulls, cows. Behavior – lost.

Pig William ill. by author. Bradbury, 1985. ISBN 0-02-733200-4 Subj: Activities – picnicking. Animals – pigs. Behavior – indifference. Sibling rivalry. Weather – rain.

The piggest show on earth ill. by author. Watts, 1989. ISBN 0-531-05789-5 Subj: Animals – pigs. Circus.

Pigs at Christmas ill. by author. Bradbury, 1986. ISBN 0-02-733160-1 Subj: Animals – pigs. Character traits – being different. Holidays – Christmas.

Pigs in hiding ill. by author. Four Winds, 1983. ISBN 0-590-07872-0 Subj: Animals – pigs. Behavior – hiding. Games.

Tom's tail ill. by author. Viking, 1990. ISBN 0-670-83021-6 Subj: Animals – cats. Animals – mice. Poetry. Rhyming text.

Dubois, Claude K. *He's my jumbo!* ill. by author. Viking, 1990. ISBN 0-670-83029-1 Subj: Animals – bears. Behavior – sharing. Sibling rivalry. Wordless.

Looking for Ginny ill. by author. Viking, 1990. ISBN 0-670-83030-5 Subj: Animals – bears. Family life – brothers and sisters. Pets. Wordless.

DuBois, Ivy. *Baby Jumbo* ill. by Elsie Wrigley. Grosset, 1977. ISBN 0-448-14289-9 Subj: Animals – elephants.

Mother fox ill. by Elsie Wrigley. Grosset, 1977. ISBN 0-448-14278-3 Subj: Animals – foxes.

Du Bois, William Pène. *Bear circus* ill. by author. Viking, 1971. ISBN 0-670-15073-8 Subj: Animals. Animals – koalas. Character traits – helpfulness. Circus. Insects – grasshoppers.

Bear party ill. by author. Viking, 1951. ISBN 0-14-050793-0 Subj: Animals. Animals – koalas. Caldecott award honor books. Emotions – anger. Parties.

Elisabeth, the cow ghost ill. by author. Viking, 1964. Subj: Animals – bulls, cows. Ghosts.

Giant Otto ill. by author. Viking, n.d. Subj: Animals – dogs. Giants.

The hare and the tortoise and the tortoise and the hare: La liebre y la tortuga and La tortuga y la liebre by William Pène Du Bois and Lee Po; ill. by William Pène Du Bois. Doubleday, 1972. Subj: Animals – rabbits. Folk and fairy tales. Foreign languages. Reptiles – turtles, tortoises.

Lazy Tommy pumpkinhead ill. by author. HarperCollins, 1966. Subj: Character traits – laziness. Machines.

Lion ill. by author. Viking, 1957. ISBN 0-670-42950-3 Subj: Animals – lions. Caldecott award honor books.

Otto and the magic potatoes ill. by author. Viking, 1970. ISBN 0-670-52986-9 Subj: Activities – vacationing. Animals – dogs. Fire. Giants.

Otto at sea ill. by author. Viking, 1936. Subj: Animals – dogs. Boats, ships. Giants.

Otto in Africa ill. by author. Viking, 1961. Subj: Animals – dogs. Foreign lands – Africa. Giants.

Otto in Texas ill. by author. Viking, 1959. Subj: Animals – dogs. Giants.

Dubov, Christine Salac. *Aleksandra, where are your toes?* photos by Josef Schneider. St. Martin's, 1986. ISBN 0-312-01717-0 Subj: Anatomy – toes. Format, unusual – board books.

Aleksandra, where is your nose? photos by Josef Schneider. St. Martin's, 1986. ISBN 0-312-01719-7 Subj: Anatomy – noses. Format, unusual – board books.

Ding dong! and other sounds ill. by Elizabeth Hathon. Morrow, 1991. ISBN 0-688-10162-3 Subj: Format, unusual – board books. Noise, sounds.

Knock! and other sounds ill. by Elizabeth Hathon. Morrow, 1991. ISBN 0-688-10161-5 Subj: Format, unusual – board books. Noise, sounds.

Oink! and other sounds ill. by Elizabeth Hathon. Morrow, 1991. ISBN 0-688-10102-X Subj: Animals. Format, unusual – board books. Noise, sounds.

Dubowski, Cathy East. *A cake for Jake* ill. by Mark Dubowski. Checkerboard, 1989. ISBN 0-02-898251-7 Subj: Animals – dogs. Birthdays. Parties. Pets.

Cave boy by Cathy East Dubowski and Mark Dubowski; ill. by Mark Dubowski. Random House, 1988. ISBN 0-394-99571-6 Subj: Birthdays. Gifts. Inventions. Wheels.

The Christmas Santa almost missed ill. by Nan Pollard. McClanahan, 1990. ISBN 1-878624-48-2 Subj: Holidays – Christmas. Mythical creatures – elves. Santa Claus.

Dumpy the dump truck ill. by Mark Samuels. McClanahan, 1990. ISBN 1-878624-32-6 Subj: Trucks.

Fire engine to the rescue ill. by Shirley Beckes. McClanahan, 1990. ISBN 1-878624-37-7 Subj: Careers – firefighters. Fire. Trucks.

Megan's messy room ill. by Mark Dubowski. Star Bright, 1997. ISBN 1-887734-20-1 Subj: Character traits – orderliness. Family life – daughters. Family life – mothers.

Picky Nicky by Cathy East Dubowski and Mark Dubowski; ill. by Mark Dubowski. Grosset, 1996. ISBN 0-448-41295-0 Subj: Food. Rebuses.

Snug Bug by Cathy East Dubowski and Mark Dubowski; ill. by Mark Dubowski. Grosset, 1995. ISBN 0-448-40850-3 Subj: Bedtime. Insects. Rhyming text.

Snug Bug's play day by Cathy East Dubowski and Mark Dubowski; ill. by Mark Dubowski. Grosset, 1997. ISBN 0-448-41642-5 Subj: Activities – playing. Behavior – sharing. Insects. Rhyming text.

Dubowski, Mark. *Cave boy* (Dubowski, Cathy East)

Picky Nicky (Dubowski, Cathy East)

Snug Bug (Dubowski, Cathy East)

Snug Bug's play day (Dubowski, Cathy East)

Duchess of York. *Budgie at Bendick's Point* ill. by John Richardson. Simon & Schuster, 1989. ISBN 0-671-67684-9 Subj: Airplanes, airports. Helicopters.

Budgie the little helicopter ill. by John Richardson. Simon & Schuster, 1989. ISBN 0-671-67683-0 Subj: Airplanes, airports. Helicopters.

Dudley, Dick. *Pop up baby brontosaurus* (Cremins, Robert)

Pop up baby coelophysis (Cremins, Robert)

Pop up baby pteranodon (Cremins, Robert)

Pop up baby stegosaurus (Cremins, Robert)

Pop up baby triceratops (Cremins, Robert)

Pop up baby tyrannosaurus rex (Cremins, Robert)

Duerrstein, Richard. *In . . . out: a Disney book of opposites = Dentro fuera: un libro Disney de opuestos* trans. by Daniel Santacruz; ill. by author. Walt Disney, 1993. Text in English and Spanish. ISBN 1-56282-266-7 Subj: Concepts – in and out. Foreign languages.

Mickey is happy: a Disney book of feelings ill. by author. Walt Disney, 1992. ISBN 1-56282-267-5 Subj: Emotions. Format, unusual – board books.

One Mickey Mouse: a Disney book of numbers = Un Ratón Mickey: un libro Disney de números trans. by Daniel Santacruz; ill. by author. Walt Disney, 1993. Text in English and Spanish. ISBN 1-56282-460-0 Subj: Counting, numbers. Foreign languages.

Duff, Maggie (Margaret K.). *Dancing turtle* ill. by Maria Horvath. Macmillan, 1981. ISBN 0-02-733010-9 Subj: Animals. Behavior – trickery. Folk and fairy tales.

The princess and the pumpkin: from a Majorcan tale ill. by Catherine Stock. Macmillan, 1980. ISBN 0-02-783000-1 Subj: Folk and fairy tales. Foreign lands – Spain. Illness.

Rum pum pum ill. by José Aruego and Ariane Dewey. Macmillan, 1978. ISBN 0-02-732950-X Subj: Birds – blackbirds. Folk and fairy tales. Foreign lands – India.

Duffy, Dee Dee (Deborah). *Barnyard tracks* ill. by Janet Perry Marshall. Boyds Mills, 1992. ISBN 1-878093-66-5 Subj: Animals. Games.

Dugan, Barbara. *Leaving home with a pickle jar* ill. by Karen Lee Baker. Greenwillow, 1993. ISBN 0-688-10837-7 Subj: Activities – traveling. Friendship. Insects – grasshoppers. Moving.

Loop the loop ill. by James Stevenson. Greenwillow, 1992. ISBN 0-688-09648-4 Subj: Friendship. Illness. Old age. Toys.

Dukas, P. (Paul Abraham). *The sorcerer's apprentice* adapt. by Makoto Oishi; trans. by Ann Brannen; ill. by Ryohei Yanagihara. Gakken, 1971. Subj: Folk and fairy tales. Magic.

Duke, Kate. *Archaeologists dig for clues* ill. by author. HarperCollins, 1997. ISBN 0-06-027056-X Subj: Activities – digging. Careers – archaeologists.

Aunt Isabel makes trouble ill. by author. Dutton, 1996. ISBN 0-525-45496-9 Subj: Animals – mice. Family life – aunts, uncles.

Aunt Isabel tells a good one ill. by author. Dutton, 1992. ISBN 0-525-44835-7 Subj: Animals. Animals – mice. Bedtime. Family life – aunts, uncles. Royalty.

Bedtime ill. by author. Dutton, 1986. ISBN 0-525-44207-3 Subj: Animals – guinea pigs. Bedtime. Family life. Format, unusual – board books.

Clean-up day ill. by author. Dutton, 1986. ISBN 0-525-44208-1 Subj: Activities – working. Animals – guinea pigs. Family life. Format, unusual – board books.

The guinea pig ABC ill. by author. Dutton, 1983. ISBN 0-525-44058-5 Subj: ABC books. Animals – guinea pigs.

Guinea pigs far and near ill. by author. Dutton, 1984. ISBN 0-525-44112-3 Subj: Animals – guinea pigs. Concepts.

If you walk down this road ill. by author. Dutton, 1993. ISBN 0-525-45072-6 Subj: Animals. Communities, neighborhoods. Family life.

The playground ill. by author. Dutton, 1986. ISBN 0-525-44206-5 Subj: Activities – playing. Animals – guinea pigs. Family life. Format, unusual – board books.

Seven froggies went to school ill. by author. Dutton, 1985. ISBN 0-525-44160-3 Subj: Frogs and toads. Rhyming text. School.

What bounces? ill. by author. Dutton, 1986. ISBN 0-525-44209-X Subj: Animals – guinea pigs. Concepts. Family life. Format, unusual – board books.

Dulcken, H. W. *The fir tree* (Andersen, H. C. [Hans Christian])

Dumas, Philippe. *Caesar, cock of the village* ill. by author. Prentice-Hall, 1979. ISBN 0-13-110189-7 Subj: Birds – chickens. Foreign lands – France.

Laura, Alice's new puppy ill. by author. David & Charles, 1979. ISBN 0-575-02568-9 Subj: Animals – dogs.

Laura and the bandits ill. by author. David & Charles, 1980. ISBN 96-86-79851-1 Subj: Animals – dogs. Crime.

Laura loses her head ill. by author. David & Charles, 1982. ISBN 0-575-03016-X Subj: Animals – dogs. Family life – grandfathers. Foreign lands – France.

Laura on the road ill. by author. David & Charles, 1979. ISBN 0-575-02712-6 Subj: Animals – dogs.

Lucy, a tale of a donkey ill. by author. Prentice-Hall, 1977. ISBN 0-13-541169-6 Subj: Animals – donkeys. Behavior – running away.

The story of Edward ill. by author. Parents, 1977. ISBN 0-8193-0869-2 Subj: Animals – donkeys. Foreign lands – France.

Dumbleton, Mike. *Dial-a-croc* ill. by Ann James. Watts, 1991. ISBN 0-531-08545-7 Subj: Activities – working. Foreign lands – Australia. Reptiles – alligators, crocodiles.

Dunbar, Fiona. *You'll never guess!* ill. by author. Dial, 1991. ISBN 0-8037-0871-8 Subj: Concepts – shape. Games.

Dunbar, James. *Tick-tock* ill. by author. Carolrhoda, 1998. ISBN 1-57505-251-2 Subj: Clocks, watches. Concepts – measurement. Time.

Dunbar, Joyce. *Baby bird* ill. by Russell Ayto. Candlewick, 1998. ISBN 0-7636-0322-8 Subj: Activities – flying. Animals. Birds. Rhyming text.

A cake for Barney ill. by Emilie Boon. Watts, 1988. ISBN 0-531-08335-7 Subj: Animals – bears. Character traits – assertiveness.

Eggday ill. by Jane Cabrera. Holiday, 1999. ISBN 0-8234-1510-4 Subj: Animals. Birds. Contests. Eggs.

Gander's pond ill. by Helen Craig. Candlewick, 1999. ISBN 0-76360-722-3 Subj: Animals – pandas. Behavior – sharing. Birds – geese.

Indigo and the whale ill. by Geoffrey Patterson. BridgeWater, 1996. ISBN 0-816-73802-5 Subj: Animals – whales. Careers – fishermen. Concepts – color. Family life – fathers. Music.

Lollopy ill. by Susan Varley. Macmillan, 1992. ISBN 0-02-733195-4 Subj: Animals – rabbits. Toys.

The pig who wished ill. by Selina Young. DK, 1999. ISBN 0-7894-3487-3 Subj: Animals – pigs. Behavior – wishing.

The sand children ill. by Mark Edwards. Crocodile Books, 1999. ISBN 1-56656-309-7 Subj: Dreams. Giants. Sea and seashore.

The secret friend ill. by Helen Craig. Candlewick, 1999. ISBN 0-7636-0720-7 Subj: Animals – pandas. Birds – geese. Friendship. Letters, cards.

Tell me something happy before I go to sleep ill. by Debi Gliori. Harcourt, 1998. ISBN 0-15-201795-X Subj: Animals – rabbits. Bedtime. Dreams. Family life – brothers and sisters.

When I was young ill. by author. Carolrhoda, 1999. ISBN 1-57505-359-4 Subj: Family life. Family life – grandparents. Genealogy.

Why is the sky up? ill. by James Dunbar. Houghton Mifflin, 1991. ISBN 0-395-57580-X Subj: Character traits – questioning. Family life. Nature.

Duncan, Alice Faye. *Miss Viola and Uncle Ed Lee* ill. by Catherine Stock. Atheneum, 1999. ISBN 0-689-80476-8 Subj: Character traits – orderliness. Ethnic groups in the U.S. – African Americans. Friendship. Old age.

Duncan, Beverly K. *Christmas in the stable* (Christmas in the stable)

Duncan, Gregory. *see* McClintock, Marshall

Duncan, Jane. *Brave Janet Reachfar* ill. by Mairi Hedderwick. Seabury Pr., 1975. ISBN 0-8164-3130-2 Subj: Animals – sheep. Character traits – bravery. Weather – snow. Weather – storms.

Janet Reachfar and Chickabird ill. by Mairi Hedderwick. Seabury Pr., 1978. ISBN 0-8164-3203-1 Subj: Behavior – bad day. Farms. Foreign lands – Scotland.

Janet Reachfar and the kelpie ill. by Mairi Hedderwick. Seabury Pr., 1976. ISBN 0-8164-3169-8 Subj: Monsters. Mythical creatures – kelpies.

Duncan, Lois. *Birthday moon* ill. by Susan Davis. Viking, 1989. ISBN 0-670-82238-8 Subj: Birthdays. Moon. Rhyming text.

Giving away Suzanne ill. by Leonard Weisgard. Dodd, 1964. Subj: Sibling rivalry.

Horses of dreamland ill. by Donna Diamond. Little, 1985. ISBN 0-316-19554-5 Subj: Animals – horses, ponies. Dreams. Night.

The longest hair in the world ill. by Jon McIntosh. Doubleday, 1998. ISBN 0-385-32113-9 Subj: Behavior – wishing. Birthdays. Hair.

The magic of Spider Woman ill. by Shonto Begay. Scholastic, 1996. ISBN 0-590-46155-9 Subj: Activities – weaving. Folk and fairy tales. Indians of North America – Navajo.

Songs from dreamland ill. by Kay Chorao. Knopf, 1989. ISBN 0-394-99904-5 Subj: Lullabies. Music. Poetry. Songs.

Duncan, Riana. *A nutcracker in a tree: a book of riddles* ill. by author. Delacorte, 1981. ISBN 0-385-28733-X Subj: Animals. Riddles.

When Emily woke up angry ill. by author. Barron's, 1989. ISBN 0-8120-5985-9 Subj: Animals. Emotions – anger.

Dunham, Meredith. *Colors: how do you say it?* ill. by author. Lothrop, 1987. ISBN 0-688-06949-5 Subj: Concepts – color. Foreign languages. Language.

Numbers: how do you say it? ill. by author. Lothrop, 1987. ISBN 0-688-06951-7 Subj: Counting, numbers. Foreign languages. Language.

Picnic: how do you say it? ill. by author. Lothrop, 1987. ISBN 0-688-07097-3 Subj: Activities – picnicking. Foreign languages. Language.

Shapes: how do you say it? ill. by author. Lothrop, 1987. ISBN 0-688-06953-3 Subj: Concepts – shape. Foreign languages. Language.

Dunn, Judy. *The animals of Buttercup Farm* photos by Phoebe Dunn. Random House, 1981. ISBN 0-394-94798-3 Subj: Animals. Farms.

The little duck ill. by Phoebe Dunn. Random House, 1978. ISBN 0-394-83247-7 Subj: Birds – ducks.

The little goat ill. by Phoebe Dunn. Random House, 1978. ISBN 0-394-93872-0 Subj: Animals – goats. Pets.

The little lamb ill. by Phoebe Dunn. Random House, 1977. ISBN 0-394-83455-0 Subj: Animals – sheep. Character traits – kindness to animals. Farms.

The little puppy photos by Phoebe Dunn. Random House, 1984. ISBN 0-394-96595-7 Subj: Animals – dogs. Pets.

The little rabbit photos by Phoebe Dunn. Random House, 1980. ISBN 0-394-94377-5 Subj: Animals – rabbits. Holidays – Easter. Pets.

Dunn, Phoebe. *Baby's animal friends* photos by author. Random House, 1988. ISBN 0-394-89583-5 Subj: Animals. Babies. Format, unusual – board books.

Busy, busy toddlers photos by author. Random House, 1987. ISBN 0-394-88604-6 Subj: Activities. Babies. Format, unusual – board books.

I'm a baby! photos by author. Random House, 1987. ISBN 0-394-88605-4 Subj: Babies. Format, unusual – board books.

Dunphy, Madeleine. *Here is the Arctic winter* ill. by Alan James Robinson. Hyperion, 1993. ISBN 1-56282-337-X Subj: Animals. Cumulative tales. Foreign lands – Arctic. Rhyming text. Seasons – winter.

Here is the coral reef ill. by Tom Leonard. Hyperion, 1998. ISBN 0-7868-2135-3 Subj: Cumulative tales. Ecology. Sea and seashore.

Here is the southwestern desert ill. by Anne Coe. Hyperion, 1995. ISBN 0-7868-2038-1 Subj: Cumulative tales. Desert. Ecology. Poetry.

Here is the tropical rain forest ill. by Michael Rothman. Hyperion, 1994. ISBN 1-56282-637-9 Subj: Animals. Forest, woods. Plants. Weather.

Dunrea, Olivier. *Deep down underground* ill. by author. Macmillan, 1989. ISBN 0-02-732861-9 Subj: Animals. Counting, numbers. Cumulative tales.

Eddy B, pigboy ill. by author. Atheneum, 1983. ISBN 0-689-50277-X Subj: Animals – pigs. Farms.

Fergus and Bridey ill. by author. Holiday, 1985. ISBN 0-8234-0554-0 Subj: Animals – dogs. Boats, ships. Friendship.

The painter who loved chickens ill. by Olivier Dunrea. Farrar, 1995. ISBN 0-374-35729-3 Subj: Careers – artists. Character traits – ambition. City. Farms.

Ravena ill. by author. Dell, 1992. ISBN 0-8234-0487-0 Subj: Mythical creatures.

The trow-wife's treasure ill. by author. Farrar, 1998. ISBN 0-374-37792-8 Subj: Behavior – losing things. Careers – farmers. Eggs. Foreign lands – Europe. Mythical creatures – trolls.

Dupasquier, Philippe. *A busy day at the garage* ill. by author. Candlewick, 1996. ISBN 1-56402-590-X Subj: Activities – working. Automobiles. Careers – mechanics. Communities, neighborhoods.

Dear Daddy . . . ill. by author. Bradbury, 1985. ISBN 0-02-733170-9 Subj: Boats, ships. Careers. Family life – fathers. Sea and seashore.

The great escape ill. by author. Houghton Mifflin, 1988. ISBN 0-395-46806-X Subj: Behavior – running away. Prisons. Wordless.

I can't sleep ill. by author. Watts, 1989. ISBN 0-531-08474-4 Subj: Family life. Night. Sleep. Wordless.

Jack at sea ill. by author. Prentice-Hall, 1987. ISBN 0-13-509209-4 Subj: Boats, ships. Sea and seashore. War.

Our house on the hill ill. by author. Viking, 1988. ISBN 0-670-81971-9 Subj: Seasons. Wordless.

A robot named chip ill. by author. Viking, 1991. ISBN 0-670-83574-9 Subj: Robots.

Duplaix, Georges. *see* Ariane

Dupré, Judith. *The mouse bride* ill. by Fabricio Vandenbroeck. Knopf, 1993. ISBN 0-679-93273-9 Subj: Animals – mice. Folk and fairy tales. Foreign lands – Mexico. Indians of Central America – Maya. Indians of North America – Chol.

Dupré, Ramona Dorrel. *Too many dogs* ill. by Howard Baer. Follett, 1960. Subj: Animals – dogs.

Dupré, Rick. *Agassu: legend of the leopard king* ill. by author. Carolrhoda, 1993. ISBN 0-87614-764-3 Subj: Ethnic groups in the U.S. – African Americans. Folk and fairy tales. Foreign lands – Africa. Slavery.

The wishing chair ill. by author. Carolrhoda, 1993. ISBN 0-87614-774-0 Subj: Behavior – wishing. Ethnic groups in the U.S. – African Americans. Family life – grandmothers. U.S. history.

Duquennoy, Jacques. *The ghosts in the cellar* ill. by author. Harcourt, 1998. ISBN 0-15-201775-5 Subj: Castles. Ghosts.

Operation ghost ill. by author. Harcourt, 1999. ISBN 0-15-202182-5 Subj: Clocks, watches. Ghosts. Illness. Illness – measles.

Du Quette, Keith. *Hotel Animal* ill. by author. Viking, 1994. ISBN 0-670-85056-X Subj: Animals. Concepts – size. Hotels. Reptiles – lizards.

The house book ill. by author. Putnam, 1999. ISBN 0-399-231838- Subj: Homes, houses. Rhyming text.

Ripping day for a picnic ill. by author. Viking, 1990. ISBN 0-670-08331-8 Subj: Activities – picnicking. Animals. Food.

Duran, Bonté. *The adventures of Arthur and Edmund: a tale of two seals* ill. by Quentin Blake. Atheneum, 1984. ISBN 0-689-50295-8 Subj: Animals – seals.

Durant, Alan. *Mouse party* ill. by Sue Heap. Candlewick, 1995. ISBN 1-56402-584-5 Subj: Animals. Animals – elephants. Animals – mice. Homes, houses. Parties.

Snake supper ill. by Ant Parker. Western, 1994. ISBN 0-307-17519-7 Subj: Animals. Food. Format, unusual. Noise, sounds. Reptiles – snakes.

Durell, Ann. *The Diane Goode book of American folk tales and songs* coll. by Ann Durell; ill. by Diane Goode. Dutton, 1989. ISBN 0-525-44458-0 Subj: Folk and fairy tales. Music. Songs.

Dürr, Gisela. *The secret of Trembleton Hall* (Dürr, Ursula)

Dürr, Ursula. *The secret of Trembleton Hall* by Ursula Dürr and Gisela Dürr; ill. by Gisela Dürr. North-South, 1995. ISBN 1-55858-433-1 Subj: Castles. Dreams. Format, unusual. Ghosts. Mythical creatures – elves. School.

Durrell, Julie. *Mouse tails* ill. by author. Crown, 1985. ISBN 0-517-55592-1 Subj: Animals. Animals – mice.

Dussling, Jennifer. *Bugs! bugs! bugs!* ill. with photos. DK, 1998. ISBN 0-7894-3762-7 Subj: Insects.

Stars ill. by Mavis Smith. Grosset, 1996. ISBN 0-448-41149-0 Subj: Astronomy. Stars.

Dutton, Sandra. *The cinnamon hen's autumn day* ill. by author. Atheneum, 1988. ISBN 0-689-31414-0 Subj: Animals – rabbits. Birds – chickens. Seasons – fall.

Duvall, Jill. *Who keeps the water clean? Ms. Schindler!* photos by Lili Duvall. Childrens Pr., 1997. ISBN 0-516-20315-0 Subj: Careers – plumbers. Water.

Duvoisin, Roger Antoine. *A for the ark* ill. by author. Lothrop, 1952. Subj: ABC books. Animals. Boats, ships. Religion – Noah. Weather – floods. Weather – rain.

The Christmas whale ill. by author. Knopf, 1945. Subj: Animals – whales. Holidays – Christmas. Illness. Santa Claus.

The crocodile in the tree ill. by author. Knopf, 1973. ISBN 0-394-92516-5 Subj: Animals. Farms. Friendship. Reptiles – alligators, crocodiles.

Crocus ill. by author. Knopf, 1977. ISBN 0-394-93583-7 Subj: Careers – dentists. Character traits – pride. Farms. Reptiles – alligators, crocodiles. Teeth.

Day and night ill. by author. Knopf, 1960. Subj: Animals – dogs. Birds – owls.

Donkey-donkey ill. by author. Parents, 1968. Subj: Animals – donkeys.

Easter treat ill. by author. Knopf, 1954. Subj: Holidays – Easter.

The happy hunter ill. by author. Lothrop, 1961. Subj: Character traits – kindness to animals. Ecology. Sports – hunting. Violence, nonviolence. Weapons.

The house of four seasons ill. by author. Lothrop, 1956. Subj: Activities – painting. Concepts – color. Seasons.

Jasmine ill. by author. Knopf, 1973. ISBN 0-394-92444-4 Subj: Animals. Character traits – individuality. Clothing. Farms.

Lonely Veronica ill. by author. Knopf, 1963. Subj: Animals – hippopotamuses. City. Progress.

The missing milkman ill. by author. Knopf, 1967. Subj: Behavior – running away. Dreams. Night.

One thousand Christmas beards ill. by author. Knopf, 1955. Subj: Holidays – Christmas. Santa Claus.

Our Veronica goes to Petunia's farm ill. by author. Knopf, 1962. ISBN 0-394-91469-4 Subj: Animals. Animals – hippopotamuses. Character traits – being different. Farms. Humor.

Periwinkle ill. by author. Knopf, 1976. ISBN 0-394-93298-6 Subj: Animals – giraffes. Emotions – loneliness. Etiquette. Friendship. Frogs and toads.

Petunia ill. by author. Knopf, 1950. ISBN 0-394-90865-1 Subj: Activities – reading. Animals. Birds – geese. Character traits – pride. Farms. Friendship. Humor.

Petunia and the song ill. by author. Knopf, 1951. Subj: Animals. Birds – geese. Crime. Farms. Friendship. Humor. Noise, sounds. Songs.

Petunia, beware! ill. by author. Knopf, 1958. ISBN 0-394-90867-8 Subj: Animals. Behavior – dissatisfaction. Birds – geese. Farms. Humor.

Petunia, I love you ill. by author. Knopf, 1965. Subj: Animals – raccoons. Behavior – trickery. Birds – geese. Birds – vultures. Farms. Friendship. Humor.

Petunia takes a trip ill. by author. Knopf, 1953. ISBN 0-394-90869-4 Subj: Activities – flying. Activities – vacationing. Animals. Birds – geese. Humor.

Petunia, the silly goose: stories ill. by author. Knopf, 1987. ISBN 0-394-98292-4 Subj: Animals. Birds – geese. Farms. Humor.

Petunia's Christmas ill. by author. Knopf, 1952. ISBN 0-394-90868-6 Subj: Birds – geese. Holidays – Christmas. Humor.

Petunia's treasure ill. by author. Knopf, 1975. Subj: Animals. Birds – geese. Farms. Friendship. Humor.

See what I am ill. by author. Lothrop, 1974. ISBN 0-688-50058-7 Subj: Behavior – boasting. Concepts – color.

Snowy and Woody ill. by author. Knopf, 1979. ISBN 0-394-94241-8 Subj: Animals – bears. Animals – polar bears. Birds – seagulls. Friendship.

Two lonely ducks ill. by author. Knopf, 1955. Subj: Birds – ducks. Counting, numbers. Farms.

Veronica ill. by author. Knopf, 1961. Subj: Animals – hippopotamuses. Character traits – being different. City. Farms.

Veronica and the birthday present ill. by author. Knopf, 1971. ISBN 0-394-92282-4 Subj: Animals – cats. Animals – hippopotamuses. Birthdays. Farms.

Veronica's smile ill. by author. Knopf, 1964. Subj: Animals – hippopotamuses. Behavior – boredom.

Dwight, Laura. *We can do it!* ill. with photos. Checkerboard, 1992. ISBN 1-56288-301-1 Subj: Activities. Handicaps.

Dwyer, Mindy. *Coyote in love* ill. by reteller. Alaska Northwest, 1997. ISBN 0-88240-485-7 Subj: Activities – storytelling. Animals – coyotes. Creation. Folk and fairy tales. Indians of North America – Coquelle.

Dyjak, Elisabeth. *Bertha's garden* ill. by Janet Wilkins. Houghton Mifflin, 1995. ISBN 0-395-68715-2 Subj: Animals – rabbits. Animals – wolves. Gardens, gardening.

Dyke, John. *Pigwig* ill. by author. Methuen, 1978. ISBN 0-416-87110-0 Subj: Animals – pigs. Behavior – stealing. Character traits – bravery. Emotions – love.

Pigwig and the pirates ill. by author. Methuen, 1979. ISBN 0-416-30121-5 Subj: Animals – pigs. Pirates. Sea and seashore.

Dynely, James. *see* Mayne, William

Dyssegaard, Elisabeth Kallick. *Andrei's search* (Lindgren, Barbro)

Benny's had enough (Lindgren, Barbro)

Do you know Pippi Longstocking? (Lindgren, Astrid)

The little house from the sea (Gedin, Birgitta)

Will gets a haircut (Landström, Olof)

Will goes to the post office (Landström, Olof)

Eachus, Jennifer. *I'm sorry* (McBratney, Sam)

Eagle, Ellen. *Gypsy's cleaning day* ill. by author. Morrow, 1990. ISBN 0-688-07392-1 Subj: Animals – dogs. Behavior – losing things. Character traits – cleanliness.

Eagle, Kin. *Rub a dub dub* ill. by Rob Gilbert. Whispering Coyote, 1998. ISBN 1-58089-008-3 Subj: Nursery rhymes.

Earle, Olive L. *Squirrels in the garden* ill. by author. Morrow, 1963. Subj: Animals – squirrels.

Easter babies ill. by Roma Bishop; paper engineering by Ruth Mawdsley. Simon & Schuster, 1996. ISBN 0-689-80611-6 Subj: Animals. Format, unusual – toy and movable books. Holidays – Easter.

Easterling, Bill. *Prize in the snow* ill. by Mary Beth Owens. Little, 1994. ISBN 0-316-22489-8 Subj: Animals – rabbits. Character traits – kindness to animals. Seasons – winter.

Eastman, David. *The story of dinosaurs* ill. by Joel Snyder. Troll, 1982. ISBN 0-89375-648-2 Subj: Dinosaurs.

The velveteen rabbit: or, How toys became real (Bianco, Margery Williams)

What is a fish? ill. by Lynn Sweat. Troll, 1982. ISBN 0-89375-660-1 Subj: Fish. Science.

Eastman, P. D. (Philip D.). *The alphabet book* ill. by author. Random House, 2000. ISBN 0-375-80603-2 Subj: ABC books.

Are you my mother? ill. by author. Random House, 1960. ISBN 0-394-90018-9 Subj: Behavior – misbehavior. Birds. Family life – mothers.

The cat in the hat dictionary (Seuss, Dr.)

Flap your wings ill. by author. Random House, 1969. ISBN 0-394-90839-2 Subj: Birds. Eggs. Reptiles – alligators, crocodiles.

Go, dog, go! ill. by author. Random House, 1961. ISBN 0-394-90020-0 Subj: Animals – dogs.

Sam and the firefly ill. by author. Random House, 1958. ISBN 0-394-90006-5 Subj: Birds – owls. Insects – fireflies.

Snow (McKié, Roy)

Eastman, Patricia. *Sometimes things change* ill. by Seymour Fleishman. Childrens Pr., 1983. ISBN 0-516-02044-7 Subj: Science.

Easton, Violet. *Elephants never jump* ill. by Carme Solé Vendrell. Little, 1986. ISBN 0-87113-049-1 Subj: Activities – jumping. Animals. Animals – elephants. Humor.

Eastwick, Ivy O. *Cherry stones! Garden swings! poems* ill. by Robert Jones. Abingdon, 1962. Subj: Poetry.

Rainbow over all ill. by Anne Siberell. McKay, 1970. Subj: Poetry.

Easwaran, Eknath. *The monkey and the mango: stories of my granny* ill. by Ilka Jerabek. Nilgiri Press, 1996. ISBN 0-915132-82-6 Subj: Family life – grandmothers. Folk and fairy tales. Foreign lands – India. Religion.

Eaton, Deborah. *The rainy day grump* photos by Dorothy Handelman. Millbrook, 1998. ISBN 0-7613-2018-0 Subj: Activities – playing. Family life – brothers and sisters. Nature. Sports – baseball. Weather – rain.

Eaton, Su. *Punch and Judy in the rain* by Su Eaton and Martin Bridle; ill. by authors. Hamish Hamilton, 1985. ISBN 0-241-11222-2 Subj: Puppets.

Eberle, Irmengarde. *Fawn in the woods* photos by Lilo Hess. Crowell, 1962. Subj: Animals – deer.

Eberstadt, Frederick. *What is for my birthday?* (Eberstadt, Isabel [Nash])

Eberstadt, Isabel (Nash). *What is for my birthday?* by Isabel and Frederick Eberstadt; ill. by Leonard Weisgard. Little, 1961. Subj: Birthdays. Illness. Rhyming text.

Eccles, Jane. *Maxwell's birthday* ill. by author. Tambourine, 1991. ISBN 0-688-11037-1 Subj: Birthdays. Family life – mothers. Imagination. Monsters.

Eckert, Horst. *see* Janosch

Eco, Umberto. *The bomb and the general* ill. by Eugenio Carmi. Harcourt, 1989. ISBN 0-15-209700-7 Subj: War.

The three astronauts ill. by Eugenio Carmi. Harcourt, 1989. ISBN 0-15-286383-4 Subj: Careers – astronauts. Character traits – appearance. Space and space ships.

Economakis, Olga. *Oasis of the stars* ill. by Blair Lent. Coward, 1965. Subj: Foreign lands – Africa. Problem solving.

Edelman, Elaine. *Boom-de-boom* ill. by Karen Gundersheimer. Pantheon, 1980. ISBN 0-394-94341-4 Subj: Activities – dancing. Old age. Rhyming text.

I love my baby sister (most of the time) ill. by Wendy Watson. Lothrop, 1984. ISBN 0-688-02247-2 Subj: Babies. Family life – sisters. Sibling rivalry.

Edens, Cooper. *An ABC of fashionable animals* by Cooper Edens, Alexandra Day, Welleran Poltarnees. Green Tiger Pr., 1991. ISBN 0-671-75201-4 Subj: ABC books. Animals. Art.

A child's garden of verses (Stevenson, Robert Louis)

The Christmas we moved to the barn (Day, Alexandra)

The glorious Mother Goose (Mother Goose)

Helping the animals (Day, Alexandra)

Helping the flowers and trees (Day, Alexandra)

Helping the night (Day, Alexandra)

Helping the sun (Day, Alexandra)

Nicholi ill. by A. Scott Banfill. Simon & Schuster, 1996. ISBN 0-671-50545-9 Subj: Holidays – Christmas. Magic. Santa Claus.

The night before Christmas (Moore, Clement C.)

A present for Rose ill. by Molly Hashimoto. Sasquatch, 1993. ISBN 0-912365-89-7 Subj: Folk and fairy tales. Foreign lands – Japan. Seasons.

Edgett, Ken. *Touchdown Mars! an ABC adventure* (Wethered, Peggy)

Edman, Polly. *Red thread riddles* (Jensen, Virginia Allen)

Edmund and the White Witch adapt. from The chronicles by C. S. Lewis; ill. by Deborah Maze. HarperCollins, 1997. ISBN 0-06-027517-0 Subj: Imagination. Magic. Witches.

Eduar, Gilles. *Dream journey* ill. by author. Orchard, 1999. ISBN 0-531-30202-4 Subj: Animals – camels. Dreams. Rhyming text.

Jooka saves the day ill. by author. Orchard, 1997. ISBN 0-531-30036-6 Subj: Character traits – individuality. Dragons. Reptiles – alligators, crocodiles.

Edwards, Al. *see* Nourse, Alan Edward

Edwards, Becky. *My brother Sammy* by Becky Edwards and David Armitage; ill. by David Armitage. Millbrook, 1999. ISBN 0-7613-1417-2 Subj: Family life – brothers. Handicaps – autism.

Edwards, Dorothy. *A wet Monday* by Dorothy Edwards and Jenny Williams; ill. by Jenny Williams. Morrow, 1976. ISBN 0-688-32081-3 Subj: Birds – chickens. Character traits – pride. Weather – rain.

Edwards, Frank B. *Is the spaghetti ready?* ill. by John Bianchi. Bungalo, 1998. ISBN 0-921285-67-1 Subj: Activities – cooking. Food.

Melody Mooner stayed up all night ill. by John Bianchi. Firefly, 1991. ISBN 0-921285-03-5 Subj: Animals – pigs. Bedtime. Night.

Mortimer Mooner stopped taking a bath ill. by John Bianchi. Firefly, 1990. ISBN 0-921285-21-3 Subj: Activities – bathing. Animals – pigs. Character traits – cleanliness. Family life.

Troubles with bubbles ill. by John Bianchi. Bungalo, 1998. ISBN 0-921285-63-9 Subj: Activities – bathing. Bubbles.

Edwards, Linda Strauss. *The downtown day* ill. by author. Pantheon, 1983. ISBN 0-694-95407-6 Subj: Shopping.

Edwards, Lisa. *Disney's Beauty and the beast, a book of manners.* Walt Disney, 1993. ISBN 1-56282-130-X Subj: Character traits – appearance. Character traits – loyalty. Emotions – love. Etiquette. Folk and fairy tales. Magic.

Edwards, Michelle. *Alef-bet: a Hebrew alphabet book* ill. by author. Lothrop, 1992. ISBN 0-688-09725-1 Subj: ABC books. Family life. Foreign languages. Handicaps – physical handicaps. Jewish culture.

A baker's portrait ill. by author. Lothrop, 1991. ISBN 0-688-09713-8 Subj: Careers – artists. Careers – bakers. Family life – aunts, uncles. Jewish culture.

Chicken Man ill. by author. Lothrop, 1991. ISBN 0-688-09709-X Subj: Birds – chickens. Communities, neighborhoods. Foreign lands – Israel.

Dora's book ill. by author. Carolrhoda, 1990. ISBN 0-87614-411-3 Subj: Careers – printers. Careers – writers.

Eve and Smithy: an Iowa tale ill. by author. Lothrop, 1994. ISBN 0-688-11826-7 Subj: Careers – artists. Character traits – helpfulness. Friendship. Gardens, gardening.

Edwards, Pamela Duncan. *Barefoot: escape on the underground railroad* ill. by Henry Cole. HarperCollins, 1997. ISBN 0-06-027137-X Subj: Behavior – running away. Ethnic groups in the U.S. – African Americans. Slavery. U.S. history.

Dinorella: a prehistoric fairy tale ill. by Henry Cole. Hyperion, 1997. ISBN 0-7868-2249-X Subj: Dinosaurs. Folk and fairy tales.

Ed and Fred Flea ill. by Henry Cole. Hyperion, 1999. ISBN 0-7868-2410-7 Subj: Animals – dogs. Behavior – greed. Insects – fleas. Rhyming text.

Four famished foxes and Fosdyke ill. by Henry Cole. HarperCollins, 1995. ISBN 0-06-024926-9 Subj: Activities – cooking. Animals – foxes. Family life – brothers. Food.

The grumpy morning ill. by Darcia Labrosse. Hyperion, 1998. ISBN 0-7868-2279-1 Subj: Animals. Behavior – tardiness. Farms. Rhyming text.

Honk! ill. by Henry Cole. Hyperion, 1998. ISBN 0-7868-2384-4 Subj: Activities – dancing. Ballet. Birds – swans.

Livingstone Mouse ill. by Henry Cole. HarperCollins, 1996. ISBN 0-06-025870-5 Subj: Activities – trading. Animals – mice. Careers – explorers.

Some smug slug ill. by Henry Cole. HarperCollins, 1996. ISBN 0060247924 Subj: Animals. Animals – slugs.

The wacky wedding: a book of alphabet antics ill. by Henry Cole. Hyperion, 1999. ISBN 0-7868-2248-1 Subj: ABC books. Insects. Insects – ants. Weddings.

Warthogs in the kitchen: a sloppy counting book ill. by Henry Cole. Hyperion, 1998. ISBN 0-7868-2351-8 Subj: Activities – cooking. Animals – warthogs. Counting, numbers. Rhyming text.

The worrywarts ill. by Henry Cole. HarperCollins, 1999. ISBN 0-06-028150-2 Subj: Activities – walking. Animals. Behavior – worrying.

Edwards, Patricia Kier. *Chester and Uncle Willoughby* ill. by Diane Worfolk Allison. Little, 1987. ISBN 0-316-21173-7 Subj: Family life – aunts, uncles. Imagination. Sleep.

Edwards, Richard. *Copy me, Copycub* ill. by Susan Winter. HarperCollins, 1999. ISBN 0-06-028571-0 Subj: Animals – bears. Family life – mothers. Seasons.

Fly with the birds ill. by Satoshi Kitamura. Orchard, 1996. ISBN 0-531-09491-X Subj: Activities. Format, unusual – toy and movable books. Language. Rhyming text.

The forest child ill. by Peter Malone. Orchard, 1995. ISBN 0-531-09463-4 Subj: Animals. Character traits – meanness. Forest, woods.

Moon frog ill. by Sarah Fox-Davies. Candlewick, 1993. ISBN 1-56402-116-5 Subj: Animals. Poetry.

Ten tall oaktrees ill. by Caroline Crossland. Tambourine, 1993. ISBN 0-688-04621-5 Subj: Counting, numbers. Rhyming text. Trees.

Edwards, Roberta. *Anna Bear's first winter* ill. by Laura Lydecker. Random House, 1986. ISBN 0-394-88199-0 Subj: Animals – bears. Format, unusual – board books. Sleep.

Five silly fishermen ill. by Sylvie Wickstrom. Random House, 1989. ISBN 0-679-90092-6 Subj: Careers – fishermen. Counting, numbers. Folk and fairy tales.

Edwards, Roland. *Tigers* ill. by Judith Riches. Tambourine, 1992. ISBN 0-688-11686-8 Subj: Animals – tigers. Imagination. Night. Rhyming text.

Efron, Marshall. *Gabby the shrew* (Olsen, Alfa-Betty)

Egan, Tim. *The blunder of the Rogues* ill. by author. Houghton Mifflin, 1999. ISBN 0-395-91007-2 Subj: Animals. Crime. Sports – bowling.

Chestnut Cove ill. by author. Houghton Mifflin, 1995. ISBN 0-395-69823-5 Subj: Character traits – selfishness. Food.

Distant Feathers ill. by author. Houghton Mifflin, 1998. ISBN 0-395-85808-9 Subj: Birds. Humor. Weather – hurricanes.

Friday night at Hodges' café ill. by author. Houghton Mifflin, 1994. ISBN 0-395-68076-X Subj: Animals. Animals – tigers. Birds – ducks. Restaurants.

Metropolitan cow ill. by author. Houghton Mifflin, 1996. ISBN 0-395-73096-1 Subj: Animals. Behavior. Behavior – running away. Friendship. Prejudice.

Eggs ill. by Esmé Eve. Grosset, 1971. Subj: Eggs.

Egielski, Richard. *Buz* ill. by author. Laura Geringer, 1995. ISBN 0-06-023567-5 Subj: Health and fitness. Insects.

The gingerbread boy (The gingerbread boy)

Jazper ill. by author. Laura Geringer, 1998. ISBN 0-06-027817-X Subj: Insects. Magic.

Ehlert, Lois. *Circus* ill. by author. HarperCollins, 1992. ISBN 0-06-020253-X Subj: Circus.

Color farm ill. by author. HarperCollins, 1990. ISBN 0-397-32441-3 Subj: Concepts – color. Concepts – shape. Format, unusual.

Color zoo ill. by author. HarperCollins, 1990. ISBN 0-397-32260-7 Subj: Caldecott award honor books. Concepts – color. Concepts – shape. Format, unusual.

Cuckoo: a Mexican folktale = Cucú: un cuento folklórico mexicano tr. into Spanish by Gloria de Aragón Andujar; ill. by author. Harcourt, 1997. ISBN 0-15-200274-X Subj: Birds. Birds – cuckoos. Character traits – bravery. Fire. Folk and fairy tales. Foreign lands – Mexico. Foreign languages. Indians of Central America – Maya.

Eating the alphabet ill. by author. Harcourt, 1996. ISBN 0-15-201036-X Subj: ABC books. Food.

Feathers for lunch ill. by author. Harcourt, 1990. ISBN 0-15-230550-5 Subj: Animals – cats. Birds. Rhyming text.

Fish eyes: a book you can count on ill. by author. Harcourt, 1990. ISBN 0-15-201618-X Subj: Concepts – color. Counting, numbers. Fish. Rhyming text.

Growing vegetable soup ill. by author. Harcourt, 1987. ISBN 0-15-232575-1 Subj: Food. Gardens, gardening.

Hands ill. by author. Harcourt, 1997. ISBN 0-15-201506-X Subj: Activities – making things. Anatomy – hands. Family life. Format, unusual – toy and movable books.

Mole's hill: a woodland tale ill. by author. Harcourt, 1994. ISBN 0-15-255116-6 Subj: Animals – foxes. Animals – moles. Folk and fairy tales. Indians of North America – Seneca.

Moon rope: Un lazo a la luna ill. by adapt. Harcourt, 1992. ISBN 0-15-255343-6 Subj: Animals – foxes. Animals – moles. Folk and fairy tales. Foreign lands – Peru. Foreign languages. Moon.

Nuts to you! ill. by author. Harcourt, 1993. ISBN 0-15-257647-9 Subj: Animals – squirrels. Rhyming text.

Planting a rainbow ill. by author. Harcourt, 1988. ISBN 0-15-262609-3 Subj: Flowers. Gardens, gardening.

Red leaf, yellow leaf ill. by author. Harcourt, 1991. ISBN 0-15-266197-2 Subj: Seasons. Trees.

Snowballs ill. by author. Harcourt, 1995. ISBN 0-15-200074-7 Subj: Seasons – winter. Snowmen.

Top cat ill. by author. Harcourt, 1998. ISBN 0-15-201739-9 Subj: Animals – cats. Behavior – sharing. Rhyming text.

Ehrhardt, Reinhold. *Kikeri: or, The proud red rooster* ill. by Bernadette Watts. Collins, 1969. Subj: Birds – chickens. Character traits – pride.

Ehrlich, Amy. *Bunnies all day long* ill. by Marie H. Henry. Dial, 1985. ISBN 0-8037-0185-3 Subj: Activities. Animals – rabbits.

Bunnies and their grandma ill. by Marie H. Henry. Dial, 1985. ISBN 0-8037-0186-1 Subj: Animals – rabbits. Family life – grandmothers.

Bunnies at Christmastime ill. by Marie H. Henry. Dial, 1986. ISBN 0-8037-0321-X Subj: Animals – rabbits. Family life. Family life – aunts, uncles. Holidays – Christmas. Parties. Santa Claus. Sibling rivalry.

Bunnies on their own ill. by Marie H. Henry. Dial, 1986. ISBN 0-8037-0256-6 Subj: Animals – rabbits. Family life. Sibling rivalry.

Cinderella (Perrault, Charles)

Emma's new pony photos by Richard Brown. Random House, 1988. ISBN 0-394-99210-5 Subj: Animals – horses, ponies.

The everyday train ill. by Martha G. Alexander. Dial, 1977. ISBN 0-8037-2192-7 Subj: Behavior – solitude. Trains.

Leo, Zack and Emmie ill. by Steven Kellogg. Dial, 1981. ISBN 0-8037-4761-6 Subj: Friendship. School.

Leo, Zack, and Emmie together again ill. by Steven Kellogg. Dial, 1987. ISBN 0-8037-0382-1 Subj: Friendship. School.

Lucy's winter tale ill. by Troy Howell. Dial, 1992. ISBN 0-8037-0661-8 Subj: Animals. Circus.

Maggie and Silky and Joe ill. by Robert Blake. Viking, 1994. ISBN 0-670-83387-8 Subj: Animals – dogs. Death. Farms.

Parents in the pigpen, pigs in the tub ill. by Steven Kellogg. Dial, 1993. ISBN 0-8037-0928-5 Subj: Animals. Careers – farmers. Farms.

Pome and Peel ill. by László Gál. Dial, 1990. ISBN 0-8037-0288-4 Subj: Folk and fairy tales. Foreign lands – Italy. Magic.

Rapunzel (Grimm, Jacob)

The snow queen (Andersen, H. C. [Hans Christian])

The story of Hannukkah ill. by Ori Sherman. Dial, 1989. ISBN 0-8037-0616-2 Subj: Jewish culture. Religion.

Thumbelina (Andersen, H. C. [Hans Christian])

The wild swans (Andersen, H. C. [Hans Christian])

Zeek Silver Moon ill. by Robert Andrew Parker. Dial, 1972. ISBN 0-8037-9826-1 Subj: Family life. Indians of North America.

Ehrlich, Bettina Bauer. *see* Bettina (Bettina Ehrlich)

Ehrlich, H. M. *Louie's goose* ill. by Emily Bolam. Houghton Mifflin, 2000. ISBN 0-618-03023-9 Subj: Sea and seashore. Toys.

Eichenberg, Fritz. *Ape in cape* ill. by author. Harcourt, 1952. ISBN 0-15-203722-5 Subj: ABC books. Caldecott award honor books.

Dancing in the moon ill. by author. Harcourt, 1955. ISBN 0-15-221443-7 Subj: Animals. Counting, numbers. Rhyming text.

Eisen, Armand. *Goldilocks and the three bears* (The three bears)

Eisenberg, Ann. *Bible heroes I can be* ill. by Rosalyn Schanzer. Kar-Ben Copies, 1990. ISBN 0-929371-09-7 Subj: Religion.

I can celebrate ill. by Rosalyn Schanzer. Kar-Ben Copies, 1989. ISBN 0-930494-93-8 Subj: Format,

unusual – board books. Holidays. Jewish culture. Religion.

Eisenberg, Lisa. *Batty riddles* (McMullan, Kate [Hall])

Bunny riddles (McMullan, Kate [Hall])

Chickie riddles (McMullan, Kate [Hall])

Creepy riddles (McMullan, Kate [Hall])

Dinosaur riddles (McMullan, Kate [Hall])

Fishy riddles (McMullan, Kate [Hall])

Hearty har har: Valentine riddles you'll love (McMullan, Kate [Hall])

Kitty riddles (McMullan, Kate [Hall])

Mummy riddles (McMullan, Kate [Hall])

Puppy riddles (McMullan, Kate [Hall])

Sheepish riddles (McMullan, Kate [Hall])

Snakey riddles (McMullan, Kate [Hall])

Spacey riddles (McMullan, Kate [Hall])

Trick or eeek! and other ha ha Halloween riddles (McMullan, Kate [Hall])

Eisenberg, Phyllis Rose. *A mitzvah is something special* ill. by Susan Jeschke. HarperCollins, 1978. ISBN 0-06-021808-8 Subj: Family life – grandmothers. Family life – grandparents. Jewish culture.

You're my Nikki ill. by Jill Kastner. Dial, 1992. ISBN 0-8037-1129-8 Subj: Activities – working. Emotions – love. Family life – mothers.

Eisenstein, Marilyn. *Periwinkle isn't Paris* ill. by Rudolf Stüssi. Tundra, 1999. ISBN 0-88776-451-7 Subj: Activities – traveling. Behavior – running away. Emotions. Foreign lands – France. Friendship.

Eisler, Colin. *Cats know best* ill. by Lesley Anne Ivory. Dial, 1988. ISBN 0-8037-0560-3 Subj: Animals – cats.

Eisman, Carol. *I wish I had a big, big tree* (Sato, Satoru)

Ekker, Ernest A. *What is beyond the hill?* ill. by Hilde Heyduck-Huth. Lippincott, 1986. ISBN 0-397-32167-8 Subj: Activities – traveling. Imagination. World.

Ekoomiak, Normee. *Arctic memories* ill. by author. Holt, 1990, 1988. ISBN 0-8050-1256-0 Subj: Careers – artists. Eskimos. Indians of North America – Cree. Indians of North America – Inuk. Memories, memory.

Elbling, Peter. *Aria* ill. by Sophy Williams. Viking, 1994. ISBN 0-670-85062-4 Subj: Birds. Character traits – kindness to animals. Communication. Jungle.

Elborn, Andrew. *Big Al* ill. by Yoshi. Picture Book Studio, 1988. ISBN 0-88708-075-8 Subj: Character traits – appearance. Fish. Friendship.

Bird Adalbert ill. by Susi Bohdal. Alphabet Pr., 1983. ISBN 0-907234-45-3 Subj: Behavior – dissatisfaction. Behavior – wishing. Birds. Character traits – appearance. Character traits – vanity. Rhyming text.

Noah and the ark and the animals ill. by Ivan Gantschev. Picture Book Studio, 1984. ISBN 0-907234-58-5 Subj: Animals. Animals – horses, ponies. Boats, ships. Religion – Noah. Weather – floods. Weather – rain. Weather – rainbows.

Elgar, Rebecca. *Tiger and the new baby* (French, Vivian)

Tiger and the temper tantrum (French, Vivian)

Elias, Joyce. *Whose toes are those?* ill. by Cathy Sturm. Barron's, 1992. ISBN 0-8120-6215-9 Subj: Anatomy – toes. Animals. Format, unusual. Poetry. Riddles.

Eliot, T. S. (Thomas Stearns). *Mr. Mistoffelees with Mungojerrie and Rumpelteazer* ill. by Errol Le Cain. Harcourt, 1991. ISBN 0-15-256230-3 Subj: Animals – cats. Poetry.

Elkin, Benjamin. *Gillespie and the guards* ill. by James Henry Daugherty. Viking, 1956. Subj: Anatomy. Behavior – trickery. Caldecott award honor books. Character traits – cleverness. Royalty.

The king who could not sleep ill. by Victoria Chess. Parents, 1975. ISBN 0-819-30776-9 Subj: Cumulative tales. Rhyming text. Royalty – kings. Sleep.

The king's wish and other stories ill. by Leonard W. Shortall. Random House, 1960. Subj: Folk and fairy tales. Royalty – kings.

Lucky and the giant ill. by Katherine Evans. Childrens Pr., 1962. Subj: Character traits – cleverness. Character traits – luck. Character traits – selfishness. Giants.

Six foolish fishermen ill. by Katherine Evans. Childrens Pr., 1957. Based on a folktale in Ashton's Chap-Books of the 18th century. ISBN 0-516-03601-7 Subj: Counting, numbers. Folk and fairy tales. Sports – fishing.

Such is the way of the world ill. by Yoko Mitsuhashi. Parents, 1968. Subj: Animals – monkeys. Cumulative tales. Folk and fairy tales. Foreign lands – Africa. Problem solving.

Why the sun was late ill. by James Snyder. Parents, 1966. Subj: Animals. Cumulative tales. Insects – flies. Sun.

The wisest man in the world: a legend of ancient Israel retold by Benjamin Elkin; ill. by Anita Lobel. Parents, 1968. Subj: Folk and fairy tales. Foreign lands – Israel. Riddles. Royalty.

Elks, Wendy. *Charles B. Wombat and the very strange thing* ill. by author. David & Charles, 1989. ISBN 0-

09-168910-4 Subj: Animals – wombats. Circus. Reptiles – turtles, tortoises.

Ellen, Barbara. *Phillip the flower-eating phoenix* (Todaro, John)

Ellentuck, Shan. *Did you see what I said?* ill. by author. Doubleday, 1967. Subj: Humor. Language.

A sunflower as big as the sun ill. by author. Doubleday, 1968. Subj: Behavior – boasting. Flowers. Humor. Plants.

Elliot, David. *An alphabet of rotten kids!* ill. by Oscar de Mejo. Putnam, 1991. ISBN 0-399-22260-X Subj: ABC books. Behavior. Poetry.

Elliott, Dan. *Ernie's little lie* ill. by Joseph Mathieu. Random House, 1983. ISBN 0-394-95440-8 Subj: Art. Behavior – lying. Puppets.

A visit to the Sesame Street firehouse: featuring Jim Henson's Sesame Street Muppets ill. by Joseph Mathieu. Random House, 1983. ISBN 0-394-96029-7 Subj: Careers – firefighters. Fire. Puppets.

Elliott, Ingrid Glatz. *Hospital roadmap: a book to help explain the hospital experience to young children* ill. by author. Resources for Children in Hospitals, 1982. ISBN 0-9608150-0-7 Subj: Hospitals. Illness.

Elliott, Robert. *see* Allen, Robert

Ellis, Anne Leo. *Dabble Duck* ill. by Sue Truesdell. HarperCollins, 1984. ISBN 0-06-021818-5 Subj: Birds – ducks. City. Emotions – loneliness. Friendship.

Ellwand, David. *Alfred's camera: a collection of picture puzzles* ill. by author. Dutton, 1998. ISBN 0-525-45978-2 Subj: Animals – dogs. Behavior – losing things.

Elson, Raymond. *Clothes* ill. by Sonia Canals. Larousse, 1996. ISBN 1-85697-660-2 Subj: Clothing. Format, unusual – toy and movable books.

Pets ill. by Sonia Canals. Larousse, 1996. ISBN 1-85697-653-X Subj: Format, unusual – toy and movable books. Pets.

Toys ill. by Sonia Canals. Larousse, 1996. ISBN 1-85697-659-9 Subj: Format, unusual – toy and movable books. Toys.

Elting, Mary. *The big book of real boats and ships* ill. by George J. Zaffo. Grosset, 1951. Subj: Boats, ships.

The Hopi way ill. by Louis Mofsie. Lippincott, 1970. Subj: Indians of North America – Hopi.

Q is for duck: an alphabet guessing game by Mary Elting and Michael Folsom; ill. by Jack Kent. Houghton Mifflin, 1980. ISBN 0-395-29437-1 Subj: ABC books. Animals. Games. Participation.

Elves, fairies and gnomes: *poems* sel. by Lee Bennett Hopkins; ill. by Rosekrans Hoffman. Knopf, 1980. ISBN 0-394-94351-1 Subj: Fairies. Mythical creatures – elves. Mythical creatures – gnomes. Poetry.

Elwell, Peter. *The king of the pipers* ill. by author. Macmillan, 1984. ISBN 0-02-733460-0 Subj: Devil. Folk and fairy tales.

Elya, Susan Middleton. *Say hola to Spanish* ill. by Loretta Lopez. Lee & Low, 1996. ISBN 1-880000-29-6 Subj: Foreign languages.

Elzbieta. *Brave Babette and sly Tom* ill. by author. Dial, 1989. ISBN 0-8037-0633-2 Subj: Animals – cats. Animals – mice. Birds. Family life.

Dikou and the baby star ill. by author. Crowell, 1988. ISBN 0-690-04721-5 Subj: Character traits – kindness. Stars.

Dikou and the mysterious moon sheep ill. by author. Crowell, 1988. ISBN 0-690-04694-4 Subj: Behavior – running away. Dreams. Family life. Imagination.

Dikou and the Snivelly Snoak ill. by author. Barron's, 1984. ISBN 0-8120-5622-1 Subj: Behavior – running away. Folk and fairy tales. Foreign lands – France. Monsters.

Dikou the little troon who walks at night ill. by author. Barron's, 1985. ISBN 0-8120-5621-3 Subj: Behavior – lying. Character traits – kindness. Mythical creatures.

Jon-Jon and Annette ill. by author. Holt, 1994. ISBN 0-8050-3299-1 Subj: Animals – rabbits. Emotions – love. War.

Emberley, Barbara. *Drummer Hoff* ill. by Ed Emberley. Prentice-Hall, 1967. Adapt. from a folk verse. ISBN 0-13-220822-9 Subj: Caldecott award books. Careers – military. Cumulative tales. Poetry. Weapons.

Night's nice by Barbara and Ed Emberley; ill. by Ed Emberley. Doubleday, 1963. Subj: Night. Poetry.

One wide river to cross ill. by Ed Emberley. Prentice-Hall, 1966. Includes unacc. melody. Adapt. of the American folk song. ISBN 0-316-23445-1 Subj: Animals. Caldecott award honor books. Folk and fairy tales. Poetry. Religion – Noah. Songs. Weather – floods. Weather – rain.

Simon's song ill. by Ed Emberley. Prentice-Hall, 1969. Includes unacc. melody. Adapt. of the folk song Simple Simon. Subj: Nursery rhymes. Songs.

The story of Paul Bunyan ill. with woodcuts by Ed Emberley. Half Moon, 1994. ISBN 0-671-88557-X Subj: Animals – oxen. Careers – lumberjacks. Tall tales.

Emberley, Ed (Edward Randolph). *Animals* ill. by author. Little, 1987. ISBN 0-316-23428-1 Subj: Animals. Format, unusual – board books.

Cars, boats, and planes ill. by author. Little, 1987. ISBN 0-316-23430-3 Subj: Airplanes, airports. Automobiles. Boats, ships. Format, unusual – board books. Transportation.

Ed Emberley's ABC ill. by author. Little, 1978. ISBN 0-316-23408-7 Subj: ABC books.

Ed Emberley's amazing look through book ill. by author. Little, 1979. ISBN 0-316-23407-9 Subj: Concepts. Format, unusual. Participation. Riddles.

Ed Emberley's big green drawing book ill. by author. Little, 1979. ISBN 0-316-23595-4 Subj: Art. Wordless.

Ed Emberley's big orange drawing book ill. by author. Little, 1980. ISBN 0-316-23418-4 Subj: Art.

Ed Emberley's big purple drawing book ill. by author. Little, 1981. ISBN 0-316-23422-2 Subj: Art.

Ed Emberley's crazy mixed-up face game ill. by author. Little, 1981. ISBN 0-316-23420-6 Subj: Anatomy – faces. Art. Games.

Ed Emberley's drawing book: make a world ill. by author. Little, 1972. ISBN 0-316-23598-9 Subj: Art.

Glad monster, sad monster: a book about feelings ill. by author. Little, 1997. ISBN 0-316-57395-7 Subj: Emotions. Format, unusual – toy and movable books. Masks. Monsters.

Go away, big green monster! ill. by author. Little, 1992. ISBN 0-316-23653-5 Subj: Bedtime. Emotions – fear. Format, unusual – toy and movable books. Monsters.

Green says go ill. by author. Little, 1968. ISBN 0-316-23599-7 Subj: Communication. Concepts – color.

Home ill. by author. Little, 1987. ISBN 0-316-23433-8 Subj: Format, unusual – board books. Homes, houses.

Klippity klop ill. by author. Little, 1974. ISBN 0-316-23607-1 Subj: Dragons. Games. Knights. Participation.

Night's nice (Emberley, Barbara)

The parade book ill. by author. Little, 1962. Subj: Parades.

Rosebud ill. by author. Little, 1966. Subj: Character traits – being different. Problem solving. Reptiles – turtles, tortoises.

Sounds ill. by author. Little, 1987. ISBN 0-316-23431-1 Subj: Format, unusual – board books. Noise, sounds.

Emberley, Michael. *More dinosaurs! and other prehistoric beasts* ill. by author. Little, 1983. ISBN 0-316-23424-9 Subj: Art. Dinosaurs.

The present ill. by author. Little, 1991. ISBN 0-316-23411-7 Subj: Birthdays. Character traits – generosity.

Ruby ill. by author. Little, 1990. ISBN 0-316-23643-8 Subj: Animals – cats. Animals – mice. Behavior – talking to strangers. City.

Welcome back, Sun ill. by author. Little, 1993. ISBN 0-316-23647-0 Subj: Family life. Foreign lands – Norway. Seasons – spring. Sun.

Emberley, Rebecca. *City sounds* ill. by author. Little, 1989. ISBN 0-316-23635-7 Subj: City. Noise, sounds.

Drawing with numbers and letters ill. by author. Little, 1981. ISBN 0-316-23406-0 Subj: Art.

Jungle sounds ill. by author. Little, 1989. ISBN 0-316-23636-5 Subj: Jungle. Noise, sounds.

My mother's secret life ill. by author. Little, 1998. ISBN 0-316-23496-6 Subj: Behavior – secrets. Circus. Dreams. Family life – mothers.

Three cool kids ill. by author. Little, 1995. ISBN 0-316-23666-7 Subj: Animals – goats. Animals – rats. City. Folk and fairy tales.

Embry, Margaret. *The blue-nosed witch* ill. by Carl Rose. Holiday, 1956. ISBN 0-8234-0011-5 Subj: Holidays – Halloween. Witches.

Emecheta, Buchi. *Nowhere to play* ill. by Peter Archer. Schocken, 1981. ISBN 0-8052-8058-8 Subj: Activities – playing. Foreign lands – England. Safety.

Emerman, Ellen. *Just right: the story of a Jewish home* ill. by Sarah Kranz. Hachai, 1999. ISBN 0-922613-91-5 Subj: Family life. Homes, houses. Jewish culture.

Emerson, Sally. *The Kingfisher nursery rhyme songbook* music arranged by Mary Frank; ill. by Moira and Cohn Maclean. Kingfisher, 1992. ISBN 1-85697-823-0 Subj: Music. Nursery rhymes. Songs.

The nursery treasury ill. by Moira and Colin Maclean. Doubleday, 1988. ISBN 0-385-24650-1 Subj: Nursery rhymes.

Emerson, Scott. *The magic boots* by Scott Emerson and Howard Post; ill. by Howard Post. Gibbs Smith, 1994. ISBN 0-87905-603-7 Subj: Clothing – boots. Imagination.

Emmett, Fredrick Rowland. *New world for Nellie* ill. by author. Harcourt, 1952. Subj: Trains.

Emmons, Ramona Ware. *Your world: let's visit the hospital* (Pope, Billy N.)

Empress Michiko of Japan. *The animals* (Mado, Michio)

Encking, Louise F. *The little gardeners* (Morgenstern, Elizabeth)

The toy maker: how a tree becomes a toy village (Thelen, Gerda)

Enderle, Judith (Ann) Ross. *Francis, the earthquake dog* by Judith Ross Enderle and Stephanie Gordon Tessler; ill. by Brooke Scudder. Chronicle, 1996. ISBN 0-8118-0630-8 Subj: Animals – dogs. Earthquakes.

Good junk ill. by Gail Gibbons. Elsevier-Nelson, 1981. ISBN 0-525-66720-2 Subj: Behavior – collecting things.

The good-for-something dragon by Judith Ross Enderle and Stephanie Gordon Tessler; ill. by Les Gray. Caroline House, 1993. ISBN 1-56397-214-X Subj: Dragons.

Nell Nugget and the cow caper by Judith Ross Enderle and Stephanie Gordon Tessler; ill. by Paul Yalowitz. Simon & Schuster, 1995. ISBN 0-689-80502-0 Subj: Behavior – stealing. Cowboys. U.S. history – frontier and pioneer life.

A pile of pigs by Judith Ross Enderle and Stephanie Gordon Tessler; ill. by Charles Jordan. Bell Books, 1993. ISBN 1-878093-88-6 Subj: Animals. Animals – pigs.

Six creepy sheep by Judith Ross Enderle and Stephanie Gordon Tessler; ill. by John O'Brien. Caroline House, 1992. ISBN 0-56397-092-9 Subj: Animals – sheep. Counting, numbers. Holidays – Halloween. Parties.

Six sandy sheep by Judith Ross Enderle and Stephanie Gordon Tessler; ill. by John O'Brien. Boyds Mills, 1997. ISBN 1-56397-582-3 Subj: Animals – sheep. Counting, numbers. Sea and seashore.

Six snowy sheep by Judith Ross Enderle and Stephanie Gordon Tessler; ill. by John O'Brien. Boyds Mills, 1995. ISBN 1-56397-138-0 Subj: Animals. Counting, numbers. Holidays – Christmas. Weather – snow.

Upstairs by Judith Ross Enderle and Stephanie Gordon Tessler; ill. by Kate Salley Palmer. Boyds Mills, 1998. ISBN 1-56397-466-5 Subj: Animals. City. Homes, houses.

What would Mama do? by Judith Ross Enderle and Stephanie Gordon Tessler; ill. by Chris L. Demarest. Boyds Mills, 1995. ISBN 1-56397-418-5 Subj: Animals – foxes. Birds – geese. Concepts – measurement. Concepts – weight. Shopping.

Where are you, little Zack? by Judith Ross Enderle and Stephanie Gordon Tessler; ill. by Brian Floca. Houghton Mifflin, 1997. ISBN 0-395-73092-9 Subj: Behavior – lost. Birds – ducks. City. Counting, numbers.

Enell, Trinka. *Roll over, Rosie* ill. by Dick Gackenbach. Clarion, 1992. ISBN 0-395-59340-9 Subj: Animals – dogs. Pets.

Engdahl, Sylvia. *Our world is earth* ill. by Don Sibley. Atheneum, 1979. ISBN 0-689-30678-4 Subj: Communication. Earth. Science.

Engel, Diana. *Circle song* ill. by author. Cavendish, 1999. ISBN 0-7614-5040-8 Subj: Bedtime. Concepts – shape. Ethnic groups in the U.S. – African Americans. Family life – fathers. Rhyming text.

Eleanor, Arthur, and Claire ill. by author. Macmillan, 1992. ISBN 0-02-733462-7 Subj: Animals – mice. Death. Family life – grandparents.

Fishing ill. by author. Macmillan, 1993. ISBN 0-02-733463-5 Subj: Ethnic groups in the U.S. – African Americans. Family life – grandfathers. Moving. Sports – fishing.

Gino Badino ill. by author. Morrow, 1991. ISBN 0-688-09503-8 Subj: Animals – mice. Family life. Food.

Josephina hates her name ill. by author. Morrow, 1989. ISBN 0-688-07796-X Subj: Family life. Names. Reptiles – alligators, crocodiles.

Josephina, the great collector ill. by author. Morrow, 1988. ISBN 0-688-07543-6 Subj: Behavior – collecting things. Sibling rivalry.

The little lump of clay ill. by author. Morrow, 1989. ISBN 0-688-08407-9 Subj: Activities – making things.

The shelf-paper jungle ill. by author. Morrow, 1991. ISBN 0-02-733464-3 Subj: Activities – drawing. Friendship. Jungle. Paper.

Engelbrektson, Sune. *Gravity at work and play* ill. by Eric Carle. Holt, 1963. Subj: Science.

The sun is a star ill. by Eric Carle. Holt, 1963. Subj: Science. Sun.

England, Linda. *The old cotton blues* ill. by Teresa Flavin. Margaret K. McElderry, 1998. ISBN 0-689-81074-1 Subj: Careers – musicians. Emotions. Ethnic groups in the U.S. – African Americans.

3 kids dreamin' ill. by Dena Schutzer. Margaret K. McElderry, 1997. ISBN 0-689-80866-6 Subj: Careers – musicians. Music.

Engle, Joanna. *Cap'n kid goes to the South Pole* ill. by Pat Paris. Random House, 1983. ISBN 0-394-85643-0 Subj: Animals – whales.

English, Jennifer. *My mommy's special* ill. with photos. Childrens Pr., 1985. ISBN 0-516-03861-3 Subj: Family life – mothers. Handicaps.

English, Karen. *Big wind coming!* ill. by Cedric Lucas. Albert Whitman, 1996. ISBN 0-8075-0726-1 Subj: Ethnic groups in the U.S. – African Americans. Farms. Toys – dolls. Weather – storms.

Just right stew ill. by Anna Rich. Boyds Mills, 1998. ISBN 1-56397-487-8 Subj: Activities – cooking. Ethnic groups in the U.S. – African Americans. Family life. Food.

Nadia's hands ill. by Jonathan Weiner. Boyds Mills, 1999. ISBN 1-56397-667-6 Subj: Ethnic groups in the U.S. – Pakistani Americans. Family life. Self-concept. Weddings.

Neeny coming, Neeny going ill. by Synthia Saint James. BridgeWater, 1996. ISBN 0-8167-3796-7 Subj: Emotions. Ethnic groups in the U.S. – African Americans. Family life – cousins. Friendship. Islands.

Engvick, William. *Lullabies and night songs* ed. by William Engvick; music by Alec Wilder; ill. by Maurice Sendak. HarperCollins, 1965. ISBN 0-06-021820-7 Subj: Bedtime. Lullabies. Music.

Enright, Elizabeth. *Zeee* ill. by Susan Gaber. Harcourt, 1993. ISBN 0-15-299958-2 Subj: Behavior – misbehavior. Emotions – anger. Fairies.

Ephron, Delia. *Santa and Alex* ill. by Elise Primavera. Little, 1983. ISBN 0-3162-4300-0 Subj: Holidays – Christmas. Santa Claus.

Erdoes, Richard. *Policemen around the world* ill. by author. McGraw-Hill, 1968. Subj: Careers – police officers.

Erdrich, Louise. *Grandmother's pigeon* ill. by Jim LaMarche. Hyperion, 1996. ISBN 0-7868-2137-X Subj: Birds – pigeons. Family life – grandmothers.

Erickson, Karen. *Do I have to go home?* ill. by Maureen Roffey. Viking, 1989. ISBN 0-670-82673-1 Subj: Behavior.

I like to help ill. by Maureen Roffey. Viking, 1989. ISBN 0-670-82675-8 Subj: Character traits – helpfulness.

I was so mad ill. by Maureen Roffey. Viking, 1987. ISBN 0-670-81573-X Subj: Emotions – anger.

I'll try ill. by Maureen Roffey. Viking, 1987. ISBN 0-670-81572-1 Subj: Character traits – perseverance.

I'm brave! by Karen Erickson and Maureen Roffey; ill. by Maureen Roffey. Viking, 1989. ISBN 0-670-82676-6 Subj: Character traits – bravery.

It's dark – but I'm not scared ill. by Maureen Roffey. Viking, 1987. ISBN 0-670-81571-3 Subj: Emotions – fear. Night.

No one is perfect ill. by Maureen Roffey. Viking, 1987. ISBN 0-670-81570-5 Subj: Behavior – mistakes.

Waiting my turn ill. by Maureen Roffey. Viking, 1989. ISBN 0-670-82674-X Subj: Character traits – patience.

Erickson, Phoebe. *Just follow me* ill. by author. Follett, 1960. Subj: Animals – dogs. Behavior – lost. Homes, houses.

Erickson, Russell E. *Warton and the traders* ill. by Lawrence DiFiori. Lothrop, 1979. ISBN 0-688-51886-9 Subj: Animals – rats. Character traits – cleverness. Character traits – generosity. Frogs and toads.

Warton's Christmas eve adventure ill. by Lawrence DiFiori. Lothrop, 1977. ISBN 0-688-51822-2 Subj: Animals. Frogs and toads. Holidays – Christmas.

Ericsson, Jennifer A. *No milk!* ill. by Ora Eitan. Tambourine, 1993. ISBN 0-688-11306-0 Subj: Animals – bulls, cows. Behavior – misunderstanding.

Eriksson, Ake. *Joel, Jasper, and Julia* ill. by author. Carolrhoda, 1990. ISBN 0-87614-419-9 Subj: Animals – pigs. Farms.

Eriksson, Eva. *Hocus-pocus* ill. by author; trans. from Swedish by Barbro Eriksson Roehrdanz. Carolrhoda, 1985. ISBN 0-87614-235-8 Subj: Bedtime. Friendship.

Jealousy ill. by author; trans. from Swedish by Barbro Eriksson Roehrdanz. Carolrhoda, 1985. ISBN 0-87614-237-4 Subj: Emotions – envy, jealousy. Friendship. Illness.

Mimi and the biscuit factory (Sundvall, Viveca)

One short week ill. by author; trans. from Swedish by Barbro Eriksson Roehrdanz. Carolrhoda, 1985. ISBN 0-87614-234-X Subj: Behavior – boredom. Birthdays. Friendship.

The tooth trip ill. by author; trans. from Swedish by Barbro Eriksson Roehrdanz. Carolrhoda, 1985. ISBN 0-87614-236-6 Subj: Behavior – losing things. Friendship. Teeth.

Erlbruch, Wolf. *Leonard* ill. by author. Orchard, 1995. ISBN 0-531-08782-4 Subj: Animals – dogs. Behavior – wishing. Emotions – fear. Fairies.

Mrs. Meyer, the bird adapt. from German by Sabina Magyar and Susan Rich; ill. by author. Orchard, 1997. ISBN 0-531-33017-6 Subj: Activities – flying. Behavior – worrying. Birds.

Ernst, Kathryn F. *Danny and his thumb* ill. by Tomie de Paola. Prentice-Hall, 1973. ISBN 0-13-196725-8 Subj: Behavior – growing up. School. Thumb sucking.

Ernst, Lisa Campbell. *Breakfast time!* (Ziefert, Harriet)

Bubba and Trixie ill. by author. Simon & Schuster, 1997. ISBN 0-689-81357-0 Subj: Friendship. Insects – butterflies, caterpillars. Insects – ladybugs. Metamorphosis. Self-concept.

Bye-bye, daddy! (Ziefert, Harriet)

A colorful adventure of the bee who left home one Monday morning and what he found along the way ill. by Lee Ernst. Lothrop, 1986. ISBN 0-688-05564-8 Subj: Concepts – color. Insects – bees.

Duke, the Dairy Delight dog ill. by author. Simon & Schuster, 1996. ISBN 0-689-80750-3 Subj: Animals – dogs. Character traits – cleanliness.

Ginger jumps ill. by author. Bradbury, 1990. ISBN 0-02-733565-8 Subj: Animals – dogs. Circus.

Good morning, sun! (Ziefert, Harriet)

Hamilton's art show ill. by author. Lothrop, 1986. ISBN 0-688-04121-3 Subj: Activities – painting. Animals. Art. Gardens, gardening.

Let's get dressed! (Ziefert, Harriet)

The letters are lost! ill. by author. Viking, 1996. ISBN 0-670-86336-X Subj: ABC books. Toys.

Little Red Riding Hood: a newfangled prairie tale ill. by author. Simon & Schuster, 1995. ISBN 0-689-80145-9 Subj: Activities – cooking. Animals – wolves. Behavior – talking to strangers. Family life – grandmothers. Folk and fairy tales.

Miss Penny and Mr. Grubbs ill. by author. Bradbury, 1991. ISBN 0-02-733563-1 Subj: Animals – rabbits. Emotions – envy, jealousy. Fairs. Gardens, gardening.

Nattie Parsons' good-luck lamb ill. by author. Viking, 1988. ISBN 0-670-81778-3 Subj: Activities – weaving. Animals – sheep.

The prize pig surprise ill. by author. Lothrop, 1984. ISBN 0-688-03798-4 Subj: Animals – pigs. Behavior – greed. Character traits – cleverness.

The rescue of Aunt Pansy ill. by author. Viking, 1987. ISBN 0-670-81716-3 Subj: Animals – cats. Animals – mice. Family life – aunts, uncles. Format, unusual. Friendship. Toys.

Sam Johnson and the blue ribbon quilt ill. by author. Lothrop, 1983. ISBN 0-688-01517-4 Subj: Activities. Gender roles. Quilts.

Squirrel Park ill. by author. Bradbury, 1993. ISBN 0-02-733562-3 Subj: Animals – squirrels. Ecology. Family life – fathers. Parks. Trees.

Stella Louella's runaway book ill. by author. Simon & Schuster, 1998. ISBN 0-689-81883-1 Subj: Behavior – losing things. Cumulative tales. Libraries.

Up to ten and down again ill. by author. Lothrop, 1986. ISBN 0-688-04542-1 Subj: Activities – picnicking. Counting, numbers.

Walter's tail ill. by author. Bradbury, 1992. ISBN 0-02-733564-X Subj: Animals – dogs. Pets.

When Bluebell sang ill. by author. Bradbury, 1989. ISBN 0-02-733561-5 Subj: Animals – bulls, cows. Theater.

Zinnia and Dot ill. by author. Viking, 1992. ISBN 0-670-83091-7 Subj: Animals – weasels. Behavior – fighting, arguing. Birds – chickens. Eggs.

Erskine, Jim. *Bedtime story* ill. by Ann Schweninger. Crown, 1982. ISBN 0-417-54540-3 Subj: Bedtime. Dreams. Night.

Bert and Susie's messy tale ill. by author. Crown, 1979. ISBN 0-517-53475-4 Subj: Activities. Animals – pigs.

The snowman ill. by author. Crown, 1978. ISBN 0-517-53202-6 Subj: Snowmen.

Esbensen, Barbara Juster. *Dance with me* ill. by Megan Lloyd. HarperCollins, 1995. ISBN 0-06-022823-7 Subj: Activities – dancing. Nature. Poetry.

The dream mouse: a lullaby tale from Old Latvia ill. by Judith Mitchell. Little, 1995. ISBN 0-316-24975-0 Subj: Animals – mice. Dreams. Night. Sleep.

Echoes for the eye: poems to celebrate patterns in nature ill. by Helen K. Davie. HarperCollins, 1996. ISBN

0-06-024399-6 Subj: Concepts – shape. Nature. Poetry.

The great buffalo race: how the buffalo got its hump; a Seneca tale ill. by Helen K. Davie. Little, 1994. ISBN 0-316-24982-3 Subj: Animals – buffaloes. Folk and fairy tales. Indians of North America – Seneca.

Jumping day ill. by Maryann Cocca-Leffler. Boyds Mills, 1999. ISBN 1-56397-709-5 Subj: Activities – jumping. Rhyming text.

Ladder to the sky: how the gift of healing came to the Ojibway nation ill. by Helen K. Davie. Little, 1989. ISBN 0-316-24952-1 Subj: Folk and fairy tales. Indians of North America – Ojibwa. Rhyming text.

Sponges are skeletons ill. by Holly Keller. Harper-Collins, 1993. ISBN 0-06-021037-0 Subj: Anatomy – skeletons. Animals – sponges. Sea and seashore.

The star maiden: an Ojibway tale ill. by Helen K. Davie. Little, 1988. ISBN 0-316-24951-3 Subj: Folk and fairy tales. Indians of North America – Ojibwa. Rhyming text.

Who shrank my grandmother's house? ill. by Eric Beddows. HarperCollins, 1992. ISBN 0-06-021828-2 Subj: Behavior – growing up. Poetry.

Escudie, René. *Paul and Sebastian* trans. by Roderick Townley; ill. by Ulises Wensell. Kane/Miller, 1988. ISBN 0-916291-19-7 Subj: Behavior – lost. Character traits – being different. Family life. Friendship. Prejudice.

Espenscheid, Gertrude E. *The oh ball* ill. by author. Crown, 1966. Subj: Royalty. Toys – balls.

Esterl, Arnica. *The fine round cake* trans. from German by Pauline Hejl; ill. by Andrej Dugin and Olga Dugina. Four Winds, 1991. An adaptation of *Johnny cake* by Joseph Jacobs. ISBN 0-02-733568-2 Subj: Cumulative tales. Folk and fairy tales. Food. Foreign lands – England.

Estes, Kristyn Rehling. *Manuela's gift* ill. by Claire Cotts. Chronicle, 1999. ISBN 0-811-82085-8 Subj: Birthdays. Family life. Foreign lands – Mexico. Gifts.

Etherington, Frank. *The spaghetti word race* ill. by Gina Calleja. Firefly, 1982. ISBN 0-920236-11-1 Subj: Imagination. Sibling rivalry.

Ets, Marie Hall. *Another day* ill. by author. Viking, 1953. Subj: Animals. Forest, woods. Parades. Theater.

Bad boy, good boy ill. by author. Crowell, 1967. Subj: Behavior. Ethnic groups in the U.S. – Mexican Americans. Family life. School.

Beasts and nonsense ill. by author. Viking, 1952. Subj: Animals. Humor. Poetry.

The cow's party ill. by author. Viking, 1958. Subj: Animals – bulls, cows. Behavior – dissatisfaction. Behavior – sharing. Parties.

Elephant in a well ill. by author. Viking, 1972. ISBN 0-670-29169-2 Subj: Animals. Animals – elephants. Character traits – helpfulness. Cumulative tales.

Gilberto and the wind ill. by author. Viking, 1978, c1963. ISBN 0-670-34025-1 Subj: Ethnic groups in the U.S. – Mexican Americans. Weather – wind.

In the forest ill. by author. Viking, 1944. ISBN 0-670-39687-7 Subj: Activities – picnicking. Animals. Caldecott award honor books. Forest, woods. Imagination. Parades.

Just me ill. by author. Viking, 1978, c1965. ISBN 0-670-41109-4 Subj: Animals. Caldecott award honor books. Participation.

Little old automobile ill. by author. Viking, 1948. Subj: Automobiles.

Mister Penny ill. by author. Viking, 1935. Subj: Animals. Caldecott award honor books. Farms.

Mister Penny's circus ill. by author. Viking, 1961. Subj: Animals. Circus.

Mr. Penny's race horse ill. by author. Viking, 1956. Subj: Animals – horses, ponies. Caldecott award honor books. Fairs. Farms.

Mr. T. W. Anthony Woo ill. by author. Viking, 1951. Subj: Animals – cats. Animals – dogs. Animals – mice. Caldecott award honor books.

Nine days to Christmas ill. by author. Viking, 1959. ISBN 0-670-51350-4 Subj: Caldecott award books. Ethnic groups in the U.S. – Mexican Americans. Foreign lands – Mexico. Holidays – Christmas. Parties.

Play with me ill. by author. Viking, 1955. ISBN 0-670-55977-6 Subj: Activities – playing. Animals. Behavior. Caldecott award honor books.

Talking without words ill. by author. Viking, 1968. ISBN 0-670-69218-2 Subj: Communication. Participation.

Eugenie. *see* Fernandes, Eugenie

Euvremer, Teryl. *After dark* ill. by author. Crown, 1989. ISBN 0-517-57104-8 Subj: Rhyming text.

Sun's up ill. by author. Crown, 1987. ISBN 0-517-56432-7 Subj: Activities – working. Farms. Sun. Wordless.

The thieves of Peck's pocket ill. by author. Crown, 1990. ISBN 0-517-57538-8 Subj: Animals. Behavior – stealing. Crime. Plants.

Triple whammy ill. by author. HarperCollins, 1993. ISBN 0-06-021061-3 Subj: Behavior – trickery. Character traits – meanness. Monsters. Weddings. Witches.

Evans, Dilys. *Monster soup and other spooky poems* (Monster soup and other spooky poems)

Weird pet poems (Weird pet poems)

Evans, Eva Knox. *Sleepy time* ill. by Reed Champion. Houghton Mifflin, 1962. Subj: Animals. Cumulative tales. Hibernation. Sleep.

That lucky Mrs. Plucky ill. by Jo Ann Stover. McKay, 1961. Subj: Animals – cats. Behavior – collecting things.

Where do you live? ill. by Beatrice Darwin. Golden Pr., 1960. Subj: Animals.

Evans, Katherine. *The boy who cried wolf* ill. by author. Albert Whitman, 1960. Subj: Animals – wolves. Behavior – lying. Behavior – trickery. Folk and fairy tales.

A bundle of sticks ill. by author. Albert Whitman, 1962. A retelling of an Æsop fable. Subj: Folk and fairy tales.

The maid and her pail of milk ill. by author. Albert Whitman, 1959. Subj: Behavior – greed. Folk and fairy tales. Humor.

The man, the boy and the donkey ill. by author. Albert Whitman, 1958. Subj: Animals – donkeys. Character traits – practicality. Folk and fairy tales. Humor.

Evans, Katie. *Hunky Dory ate it* ill. by Janet M. Stoeke. Dutton, 1992. ISBN 0-525-44847-0 Subj: Animals – dogs. Food. Rhyming text.

Evans, Lezlie. *Can you count ten toes? count to 10 in 10 different languages* ill. by Denis Roche. Houghton Mifflin, 1999. ISBN 0-395-90499-4 Subj: Counting, numbers. Foreign languages. Rhyming text.

If I were the wind ill. by Victoria Lisi. Ideals, 1997. ISBN 1-57102-096-9 Subj: Family life – mothers. Imagination. Rhyming text.

Rain song ill. by Cynthia Jabar. Houghton Mifflin, 1995. ISBN 0-395-69865-0 Subj: Poetry. Weather – rain.

Evans, Mari. *Singing black* ill. by Ramon Price. Third World Pr., 1978. ISBN 0-940975-80-7 Subj: Ethnic groups in the U.S. – African Americans. Nursery rhymes.

Evans, Mark. *Guinea pigs* ill. with photos. DK, 1992. ISBN 1-56458-125-X Subj: Animals – guinea pigs. Pets.

Kitten ill. with photos. DK, 1992. ISBN 1-56458-126-8 Subj: Animals – cats. Pets.

Puppy ill. with photos. DK, 1992. ISBN 1-56458-127-6 Subj: Animals – dogs. Pets.

Rabbit ill. by author. DK, 1992. ISBN 1-56458-128-4 Subj: Animals – rabbits. Pets.

Evans, Mel. *The tiniest sound* ill. by Ed Young. Doubleday, 1969. Subj: Noise, sounds. Poetry.

Evans, Nate. *The mixed-up zoo of professor Yahoo* ill. by author. Junior League of Kansas City Mo., 1992. ISBN 0-9607076-3-8 Subj: Rhyming text. Royalty – queens. Zoos.

Evans, Richard Paul. *The Christmas candle* ill. by Jacob Collins. Simon & Schuster, 1998. ISBN 0-689-82319-3 Subj: Character traits – generosity. Holidays – Christmas. Magic.

The dance ill. by Jonathan Linton. Simon & Schuster, 1999. ISBN 0-689-82351-7 Subj: Activities – dancing. Family life – fathers.

Everett, Gwen. *Li'l Sis and Uncle Willie: a story based on the life and paintings of William H. Johnson* ill. with photos of paintings by William H. Johnson. Rizzoli, 1992. ISBN 0-8478-1462-9 Subj: Art. Careers – artists. Ethnic groups in the U.S. – African Americans. Family life – aunts, uncles. Museums. U.S. history.

Everett, Percival L. *The one that got away* ill. by Dirk Zimmer. Clarion, 1992. ISBN 0-395-56437-9 Subj: Counting, numbers. Cowboys. Language. U.S. history – frontier and pioneer life.

Everitt, Betsy. *Mean soup* ill. by author. Harcourt, 1992. ISBN 0-15-253146-7 Subj: Activities – cooking. Behavior – bad day. Emotions – anger. Food. School.

Eversole, Robyn Harbert. *The gift stone* ill. by Allen Garns. Knopf, 1998. ISBN 0-679-98684-7 Subj: Careers – miners. Family life – grandparents. Foreign lands – Australia.

The magic house ill. by Peter Palagonia. Orchard, 1992. ISBN 0-531-08524-4 Subj: Activities – dancing. Ballet. Family life – sisters. Imagination.

Red berry wool ill. by Tim Coffey. Albert Whitman, 1999. ISBN 0-8075-0654-0 Subj: Animals – sheep. Careers – shepherds.

Everton, Macduff. *El circo magico modelo: Finding the magic circus* ill. by author. Carolrhoda, 1979. ISBN 0-87614-106-8 Subj: Activities – vacationing. Circus. Foreign lands – Mexico. Foreign languages.

Ezra, Mark. *The sleepy dormouse* ill. by Gavin Rowe. Crocodile Books, 1994. ISBN 1-56656-153-1 Subj: Animals – dormice. Animals – mice. Animals – weasels. Gardens, gardening.

Fabiny, Sarah. *My first pop-up book of dinosaurs* (Bishop, Roma)

Facklam, Margery. *The big bug book* ill. by Paul Facklam. Little, 1994. ISBN 0-316-27389-9 Subj: Concepts – size. Insects.

But not like mine ill. by Jeni Bassett. Harcourt, 1988. ISBN 0-15-200419-X Subj: Anatomy. Animals. Format, unusual – toy and movable books.

I eat dinner ill. by Anita Riggio. Little, 1987. ISBN 0-316-27374-0 Subj: Animals. Food.

I go to sleep ill. by Anita Riggio. Little, 1987. ISBN 0-316-27375-9 Subj: Animals. Bedtime. Sleep.

Only a star ill. by Nancy Carpenter. Eerdmans, 1996. ISBN 0-8028-5122-3 Subj: Animals. Holidays – Christmas. Nature. Poetry. Stars.

So can I ill. by Jeni Bassett. Harcourt, 1988. ISBN 0-15-200419-X Subj: Activities. Animals. Format, unusual – toy and movable books.

Factor, Jane. *Summer* ill. by Alison Lester. Viking, 1988. ISBN 0-670-81157-2 Subj: Family life. Foreign lands – Australia. Holidays – Christmas. Rhyming text. Seasons – summer.

Fagan, Cary. *Gogol's coat* ill. by Regolo Ricci. Tundra, 1998. ISBN 0-88776-429-0 Subj: Behavior – stealing. Clothing – coats.

Fain, James W. *Rodeos* ill. with photos. Childrens Pr., 1983. ISBN 0-516-01685-7 Subj: Animals – horses, ponies. Cowboys.

Fain, Moira. *Snow day* ill. by author. Walker, 1996. ISBN 0-8027-8410-0 Subj: Activities – drawing. Activities – writing. School. Weather – snow.

Fair, David. *The fabulous four skunks* ill. by Bruce Koscielniak. Houghton Mifflin, 1996. ISBN 0-395-73572-6 Subj: Animals – skunks. Music. Senses – smelling.

Fair, Sylvia. *The bedspread* ill. by author. Morrow, 1982. ISBN 0-688-00877-1 Subj: Activities. Sibling rivalry.

Fairclough, Chris. *Take a trip to China* photos by author. Watts, 1981. ISBN 0-531-04317-7 Subj: Activities – traveling. Foreign lands – China.

Take a trip to England photos by author. Watts, 1982. ISBN 0-531-04416-5 Subj: Activities – traveling. Foreign lands – England.

Take a trip to Holland photos by author. Watts, 1982. ISBN 0-531-04417-3 Subj: Activities – traveling. Foreign lands – Holland.

Take a trip to Israel photos by author. Watts, 1981. ISBN 0-531-04318-5 Subj: Activities – traveling. Foreign lands – Israel.

Take a trip to Italy photos by author. Watts, 1981. ISBN 0-531-04219-3 Subj: Activities – traveling. Foreign lands – Italy.

Take a trip to West Germany photos by author. Watts, 1981. ISBN 0-531-04320-7 Subj: Activities – traveling. Foreign lands – Germany.

Fairfield, Flora. *see* Alcott, Louisa May

Fairy poems for the very young ill. by Beverlie Manson. Doubleday, 1982. ISBN 0-385-17542-6 Subj: Fairies. Poetry.

Faison, Eleanora. *Becoming* ill. by Cecelia Ercin. Patterson Pr., 1981. ISBN 0-9607432-0-0 Subj: Behavior – growing up.

Falconer, Ian. *Olivia* ill. by author. Atheneum, 2000. ISBN 0-689-82953-1 Subj: Activities. Animals – pigs. Behavior. Caldecott award honor books.

Falda, Dominique. *The treasure chest* trans. by Rosemary Lanning; ill. by author. North-South, 1999. ISBN 0-7358-1050-8 Subj: Animals. Animals – squirrels. Friendship.

Falk, Barbara Bustetter. *Grusha* ill. by author. HarperCollins, 1993. ISBN 0-06-021300-0 Subj: Animals – bears. Character traits – kindness to animals. Circus. Foreign lands – Russia.

Falla, Dominique. *Woodlore* (Miller, Cameron)

Falloon, Jane. *Thumbelina* (Andersen, H. C. [Hans Christian])

Falls, C. B. (Charles Buckles). *ABC book* ill. by author. Morrow, 1998. ISBN 0-688-14712-7 Subj: ABC books.

Falwell, Cathryn. *Christmas for 10* ill. by author. Clarion, 1998. ISBN 0-395-85581-0 Subj: Counting, numbers. Ethnic groups in the U.S. – African Americans. Holidays – Christmas. Rhyming text.

Clowning around ill. by author. Watts, 1991. ISBN 0-531-08552-X Subj: Circus. Concepts – shape. Language.

Dragon tooth ill. by author. Clarion, 1996. ISBN 0-395-56916-8 Subj: Dragons. Family life – fathers. Teeth.

Feast for ten ill. by author. Clarion, 1993. ISBN 0-395-62037-6 Subj: Activities – cooking. Counting, numbers. Ethnic groups in the U.S. – African Americans. Family life. Rhyming text.

Nicky and Alex ill. by author. Houghton Mifflin, 1992. ISBN 0-395-56915-X Subj: Activities – making things. Activities – playing. Babies. Family life – brothers. Format, unusual.

Nicky and grandpa ill. by author. Houghton Mifflin, 1991. ISBN 0-395-56917-6 Subj: Activities – playing. Babies. Family life – grandfathers. Format, unusual.

Nicky loves daddy ill. by author. Houghton Mifflin, 1992. ISBN 0-395-60820-1 Subj: Activities – walking. Babies. Family life – fathers. Format, unusual. Senses.

Nicky, 1-2-3 ill. by author. Houghton Mifflin, 1991. ISBN 0-395-56913-3 Subj: Babies. Counting, numbers. Format, unusual.

Nicky's walk ill. by author. Houghton Mifflin, 1991. ISBN 0-395-56914-1 Subj: Activities – walking. Babies. Concepts – color. Family life – mothers. Format, unusual.

P.J. & Puppy ill. by author. Clarion, 1997. ISBN 0-395-56918-4 Subj: Animals – dogs. Family life – mothers. Pets. Toilet training.

Shape space ill. by author. Clarion, 1992. ISBN 0-395-61305-1 Subj: Concepts – shape. Rhyming text.

We have a baby ill. by author. Clarion, 1993. ISBN 0-395-62038-4 Subj: Babies. Family life.

Where's Nicky? ill. by author. Houghton Mifflin, 1991. ISBN 0-395-56936-2 Subj: Activities – playing. Babies. Format, unusual. Games.

Word wizard ill. by author. Clarion, 1998. ISBN 0-395-85580-2 Subj: Imagination. Language.

Fancher, Lou. *The quest for the One Big Thing* ill. by Steve Johnson and Lou Fancher. Disney Pr., 1998. ISBN 0-7868-5091-4 Subj: Counting, numbers. Insects – ants.

Fanelli, Sara. *Button* ill. by author. Little, 1994. ISBN 0-316-27393-7 Subj: Circular tales. Clothing.

The doggy book ill. by author. Running Pr., 1998. ISBN 0-7624-0345-4 Subj: Animals – dogs.

Fanshawe, Elizabeth. *Rachel* ill. by Michael Charlton. Dutton, 1975. ISBN 0-370-10783-7 Subj: Handicaps. School.

Farber, Erica. *Ooey gooey* by Erica Farber and J. R. Sansevere. Random House, 1998. ISBN 0-679-98991-9 Subj: Food. Pirates. Rhyming text. Teeth.

Farber, Norma. *All those mothers at the manger* ill. by Megan Lloyd. Harper, 1985. ISBN 0-06-021870-3 Subj: Animals. Birth. Family life – mothers. Holidays – Christmas. Religion – Nativity. Rhyming text.

As I was crossing Boston Common ill. by Arnold Lobel. Dutton, 1975. ISBN 0-525-25960-0 Subj: ABC books. Animals. Poetry.

The boy who longed for a lift ill. by Brian Selznick. Laura Geringer, 1997. ISBN 0-06-027109-4 Subj: Behavior – needing someone. Behavior – running away. Family life. Rhyming text.

How does it feel to be old? ill. by Trina Schart Hyman. Dutton, 1988, 1979. ISBN 0-525-44367-3 Subj: Family life – grandparents. Old age.

How the hibernators came to Bethlehem ill. by Barbara Cooney. Walker, 1980. ISBN 0-8027-8313-9 Subj: Animals. Holidays – Christmas. Poetry. Religion.

How the left-behind beasts built Ararat ill. by Antonio Frasconi. Walker, 1978. ISBN 0-8027-6314-6 Subj: Animals. Boats, ships. Poetry. Problem solving. Religion – Noah. Weather – floods. Weather – rain.

How to ride a tiger ill. by Claire Schumacher. Houghton Mifflin, 1983. ISBN 0-395-34553-7 Subj: Animals. Animals – tigers. Poetry.

I swim an ocean in my sleep ill. by Elivia Savadier. Holt, 1997. ISBN 0-8050-3381-5 Subj: Dreams. Rhyming text. Sea and seashore.

Never say ugh to a bug ill. by José Aruego. Greenwillow, 1979. ISBN 0-688-84140-6 Subj: Insects. Poetry.

Return of the shadows ill. by Andrea Baruffi. HarperCollins, 1992. ISBN 0-06-020518-0 Subj: Behavior – running away. Holidays – Groundhog Day. Shadows.

Small wonders ill. by Kazue Mizumura. Coward, 1979. ISBN 0-698-20484-0 Subj: Poetry.

There goes feathertop! ill. by Marc Brown. Unicorn-Dutton, 1979. ISBN 0-525-29667-0 Subj: Behavior – imitation. Poetry. Scarecrows.

There once was a woman who married a man ill. by Lydia Dabcovich. Addison-Wesley, 1978. ISBN 0-20-101947-7 Subj: Humor. Noise, sounds. Poetry.

Up the down elevator ill. by Annie Gusman. Addison-Wesley, 1979. ISBN 0-201-01924-8 Subj: Counting, numbers. Elevators, escalators. Poetry.

When it snowed that night ill. by Petra Mathers. HarperCollins, 1993. ISBN 0-06-021708-1 Subj: Animals. Holidays – Christmas. Poetry. Religion.

Where's Gomer? ill. by William Pène Du Bois. Dutton, 1974. ISBN 0-525-42590-X Subj: Behavior – lost. Boats, ships. Poetry. Religion – Noah. Weather – floods. Weather – rain.

Without wings, mother, how can I fly? ill. by Keiko Narahashi. Holt, 1998. ISBN 0-8050-3380-7 Subj: Animals. Family life – mothers. Rhyming text.

Farber, Werner. *Night lion* trans. from German by Jane Fior; ill. by Barbara Mossman. Houghton Mifflin, 1991. ISBN 0-395-57816-7 Subj: Emotions – fear. Night. Sleep. Toys.

Farge, Phyllis La. *see* La Farge, Phyllis

Farge, Sheila La. *see* La Farge, Sheila

Farjeon, Eleanor. *Around the seasons: poems* ill. by Jane Paton. Walck, 1969. ISBN 0-8098-1143-X Subj: Poetry. Seasons.

Between the earth and sun ill. by Catherine Deeter. HarperCollins, 1996. ISBN 0-06-020796-5 Subj: Nature. Poetry.

Cats ill. by T. Lewis. Contemporary Books, 1989. ISBN 0-8092-4354-7 Subj: Animals – cats. Format, unusual – board books. Poetry.

Cats sleep anywhere. ill. by Mary Price Jenkins. Lippincott, 1990. ISBN 0-397-32464-2 Subj: Animals – cats. Poetry.

Cats sleep anywhere ill. by Anne Mortimer. HarperCollins, 1996. ISBN 0-06-027335-6 Subj: Animals – cats. Poetry.

Mr. Garden ill. by Jane Paton. Walck, 1966. Subj: Gardens, gardening. Seasons – summer.

Morning has broken ill. by Tim Ladwig. Eerdmans, 1996. ISBN 0-8028-5127-4 Subj: Family life – grandfathers. Morning. Songs.

Mrs. Malone ill. by Edward Ardizzone. Walck, 1962. Subj: Character traits – generosity. Rhyming text.

Farley, Carol J. *Mr. Pak buys a story* Ill. by Benrei Huang. Albert Whitman, 1997. ISBN 0-8075-5178-3 Subj: Activities – storytelling. Folk and fairy tales. Foreign lands – Korea.

Farley, Jacqui. *Giant hiccups* ill. by Pamela Venus. Gareth Stevens, 1998. ISBN 0-8368-2090-8 Subj: Giants. Hiccups.

Farley, Walter. *Black stallion: an easy-to-read adaptation* ill. by Sandy Rabinowitz. Random House, 1986. ISBN 0-394-96876-X Subj: Animals – horses, ponies. Islands.

Farm animals photos by Philip Dowell and others. Macmillan, 1991. ISBN 0-689-71403-3 Subj: Animals. Farms.

Farm animals photos sel. by Debby Slier. Macmillan, 1988. ISBN 0-02-688752-5 Subj: Animals. Format, unusual – board books.

Farm house ill. by Zokeisha; ed. by Kate Klimo. Simon & Schuster, 1983. ISBN 0-671-46130-3 Subj: Animals. Farms. Format, unusual – board books. Homes, houses.

A farmer boy birthday adapt. from the Little house books by Laura Ingalls Wilder; ill. by Jody Wheeler. HarperCollins, 1998. ISBN 0-06-027477-8 Subj: Birthdays. Careers – farmers. U.S. history – frontier and pioneer life.

The farmer in the dell. *The farmer in the dell* ill. by John O'Brien. Boyds Mills, 2000. ISBN 1-56397-775-3 Subj: Careers – farmers. Farms. Games. Music. Songs.

The farmer in the dell ed. by Ann Fay; ill. by Kathy Parkinson. Albert Whitman, 1988. ISBN 0-8075-2271-6 Subj: Careers – farmers. Farms. Games. Music. Songs.

The farmer in the dell ill. by Mary Maki Rae. Viking, 1988. ISBN 0-670-81853-4 Subj: Careers – farmers. Farms. Games. Music. Songs.

The farmer in the dell ill. by Diane Stanley. Little, 1978. ISBN 0-316-98889-8 Subj: Careers – farmers. Farms. Games. Music. Songs.

The farmer in the dell ill. by Alexandra Wallner. Holiday, 1998. ISBN 0-8234-1382-9 Subj: Careers – farmers. Farms. Games. Music. Songs.

Farmer, Nancy. *Runnery granary* ill. by Jos. A. Smith. Greenwillow, 1996. ISBN 0-688-14188-3 Subj: Behavior – stealing. Family life – grandmothers. Mythical creatures – gnomes.

Farmer, Patti. *What's he doing now?* ill. by Janet Wilson. Firefly, 1998. ISBN 1-55209-220-8 Subj: Family life – brothers and sisters.

Farris, Pamela J. *Young Mouse and Elephant* ill. by Valeri Gorbachev. Houghton Mifflin, 1996. ISBN 0-395-73977-2 Subj: Animals. Animals – elephants. Animals – mice. Behavior – boasting. Folk and fairy tales. Foreign lands – Africa.

Fass, David E. *The shofar that lost its voice* ill. by Marlene Lobell Ruthen. UAHC Pr., 1982. ISBN 0-8074-0168-4 Subj: Jewish culture. Religion.

Fassler, David. *What's a virus, anyway? the kids' book about aids* ill. by Kelly McQueen. Waterfront Bks., 1990. ISBN 0-914525-14-X Subj: Health and fitness. Illness.

Fassler, Joan. *All alone with daddy* ill. by Dorothy Lake Gregory. Behavioral, 1969. ISBN 0-87705-009-0 Subj: Family life – fathers.

Boy with a problem ill. by Stuart [i.e. Stewart] Kranz. Behavioral, 1971. ISBN 0-87705-054-6 Subj: Friendship. Problem solving.

Don't worry dear ill. by Stuart [i.e. Stewart] Kranz. Behavioral, 1971. ISBN 0-87705-055-4 Subj: Behavior – growing up. Ethnic groups in the U.S. – African Americans.

Howie helps himself ill. by Joe Lasker. Albert Whitman, 1975. ISBN 0-8075-3422-6 Subj: Handicaps.

The man of the house ill. by Peter Landa. Behavioral, 1969. ISBN 0-87705-010-4 Subj: Behavior – growing up. Dragons. Family life – mothers. Monsters.

My grandpa died today ill. by Stuart [i.e. Stewart] Kranz. Behavioral, 1971. ISBN 0-87705-053-8 Subj: Death. Emotions – grief. Family life – grandfathers. Jewish culture. Old age.

One little girl ill. by M. Jane Smyth. Behavioral, 1969. ISBN 0-87705-008-2 Subj: Family life. Handicaps – mental handicaps.

Fast rolling fire trucks ill. by Carolyn Bracken. Grosset, 1984. ISBN 0-448-09876-8 Subj: Careers – firefighters. Format, unusual – board books. Trucks.

Fast rolling work trucks ill. by Alan Singer. Grosset, 1984. ISBN 0-448-09877-6 Subj: Format, unusual – board books. Trucks.

The fat cat ill. by Jack Kent. Parents, 1971. Translated from the Danish by Jack Kent. ISBN 0-819-30454-9 Subj: Animals – cats. Cumulative tales.

Fatio, Louise. *Anna, the horse* ill. by Roger Antoine Duvoisin. Atheneum, 1951. Subj: Animals – horses, ponies. Holidays – Christmas.

The happy lion ill. by Roger Antoine Duvoisin. McGraw-Hill, 1954. ISBN 0-07-020044-0 Subj: Animals – lions. Foreign lands – France. Friendship. Zoos.

The happy lion and the bear ill. by Roger Antoine Duvoisin. McGraw-Hill, 1964. Subj: Animals – bears. Animals – lions. Character traits – appearance. Foreign lands – France. Zoos.

The happy lion in Africa ill. by Roger Antoine Duvoisin. McGraw-Hill, 1955. Subj: Animals –

lions. Foreign lands – Africa. Foreign lands – France. Zoos.

The happy lion roars ill. by Roger Antoine Duvoisin. McGraw-Hill, 1957. Subj: Animals – lions. Emotions – loneliness. Foreign lands – France. Zoos.

The happy lion's quest ill. by Roger Antoine Duvoisin. McGraw-Hill, 1961. Subj: Animals – lions. Foreign lands – France.

The happy lion's rabbits ill. by Roger Antoine Duvoisin. McGraw-Hill, 1974. ISBN 0-07-020068-9 Subj: Animals – lions. Animals – rabbits. Character traits – kindness. Foreign lands – France. Zoos.

The happy lion's treasure ill. by Roger Antoine Duvoisin. McGraw-Hill, 1970. Subj: Animals – lions. Emotions – love. Foreign lands – France. Zoos.

The happy lion's vacation ill. by Roger Antoine Duvoisin. McGraw-Hill, 1967. Subj: Activities – vacationing. Animals – lions.

Hector and Christina ill. by Roger Antoine Duvoisin. McGraw-Hill, 1977. ISBN 0-07-020073-4 Subj: Birds – penguins. Character traits – freedom. Friendship. Zoos.

Hector penguin ill. by Roger Antoine Duvoisin. McGraw-Hill, 1973. ISBN 0-07-020066-1 Subj: Birds – penguins. Character traits – individuality.

Marc and Pixie and the walls in Mrs. Jones's garden ill. by Roger Antoine Duvoisin. McGraw-Hill, 1975. ISBN 0-07-020039-4 Subj: Animals – cats. Gardens, gardening.

The red bantam ill. by Roger Antoine Duvoisin. McGraw-Hill, 1963. Subj: Animals – foxes. Birds – chickens. Character traits – bravery. Farms.

The three happy lions ill. by Roger Antoine Duvoisin. McGraw-Hill, 1959. Subj: Animals – lions. Foreign lands – France. Zoos.

Faulkner, Anne Irvin. *see* Faulkner, Nancy

Faulkner, Keith. *Amble has a dream* ill. by Jonathan Lambert. Price Stern Sloan, 1994. ISBN 0-8431-3653-7 Subj: Dinosaurs. Dreams. Format, unusual – toy and movable books.

Basil Rattlebones ill. by Jonathan Lambert. Barron's, 1997. ISBN 0-8120-6604-9 Subj: Anatomy – skeletons.

Bertie's big blue binoculars ill. by Jo Davies. Barron's, 1996. ISBN 0-8120-6568-9 Subj: Birthdays. Format, unusual – toy and movable books. Senses – seeing.

Butterfly ill. by Jonathan Lambert. HarperFestival, 1993. ISBN 0-694-00463-4 Subj: Format, unusual – toy and movable books. Insects – butterflies, caterpillars.

David dreaming of dinosaurs ill. by Jonathan Lambert. W. J. Fantasy, 1992. ISBN 1-56021-182-2 Subj: Dinosaurs. Format, unusual – toy and movable books. Museums. Rhyming text.

Frog ill. by Jonathan Lambert. HarperFestival, 1993. ISBN 0-694-00464-2 Subj: Format, unusual – toy and movable books. Frogs and toads.

Hector Specter ill. by Jonathan Lambert. Barron's, 1997. ISBN 0-8120-6605-7 Subj: Friendship. Ghosts.

The long-nosed pig: a pop-up book ill. by Jonathan Lambert. Dial, 1998. ISBN 0-8037-2296-6 Subj: Anatomy – noses. Animals – pigs. Format, unusual – toy and movable books.

The monster in my bathroom ill. by Jonathan Lambert. Price Stern Sloan, 1993. ISBN 0-8431-3482-8 Subj: Behavior – misbehavior. Family life. Monsters.

The monster in my toybox ill. by Jonathan Lambert. Price Stern Sloan, 1993. ISBN 0-8431-3481-X Subj: Behavior – misbehavior. Family life. Monsters. Toys.

Munch looks for lunch ill. by Jonathan Lambert. Price Stern Sloan, 1994. ISBN 0-8431-3652-9 Subj: Dinosaurs. Format, unusual – toy and movable books.

My first one hundred words in French and English ill. by Paul Johnson. Simon & Schuster, 1993. ISBN 0-671-86447-5 Subj: Foreign languages. Format, unusual – toy and movable books.

My pets ill. by Jonathan Lambert. St. Martin's, 1987. ISBN 0-312-00968-2 Subj: Animals. Format, unusual – toy and movable books. Pets.

The puzzled penguin ill. by Jonathan Lambert. Millbrook, 1999. ISBN 0-7613-1042-8 Subj: Birds – penguins. Foreign lands – Antarctic. Format, unusual – toy and movable books. Self-concept. Weather – cold.

Rumble frightens himself ill. by Jonathan Lambert. Price Stern Sloan, 1994. ISBN 0-8431-3650-2 Subj: Dinosaurs. Format, unusual – toy and movable books.

Sam at the seaside ill. by Jonathan Lambert. Macmillan, 1988. ISBN 0-689-71183-2 Subj: Format, unusual – toy and movable books. Sea and seashore.

Sam helps out ill. by Jonathan Lambert. Macmillan, 1988. ISBN 0-689-71182-4 Subj: Format, unusual – toy and movable books. Shopping.

The snake's mistake ill. by Jonathan Lambert. Price Stern Sloan, 1988. ISBN 0-8431-2370-2 Subj: Reptiles – snakes. Rhyming text.

Swoop flies too high ill. by Jonathan Lambert. Price Stern Sloan, 1994. ISBN 0-8431-3651-0 Subj: Dinosaurs. Format, unusual – toy and movable books.

This is me ill. by Jonathan Lambert. St. Martin's, 1987. ISBN 0-312-00967-4 Subj: Anatomy. Format, unusual – toy and movable books.

Velma Vampire ill. by Jonathan Lambert. Barron's, 1997. ISBN 0-8120-6606-5 Subj: Monsters.

The wide-mouthed frog ill. by Jonathan Lambert. Dial, 1996. ISBN 0-8037-1875-6 Subj: Animals. Food. Format, unusual – toy and movable books. Frogs and toads.

Faulkner, Matt. *The amazing voyage of Jackie Grace* ill. by author. Scholastic, 1987. ISBN 0-590-40713-9 Subj: Activities – bathing. Boats, ships. Imagination. Pirates. Weather – storms.

Faulkner, Nancy. *Small clown* ill. by Paul Galdone. Doubleday, 1960. Subj: Clowns, jesters.

Faulkner, William J. *Brer Tiger and the big wind* ill. by Roberta Wilson. Morrow, 1995. ISBN 0-688-12986-2 Subj: Behavior – greed. Ethnic groups in the U.S. – African Americans. Folk and fairy tales.

Faunce-Brown, Daphne. *Snuffles' house* ill. by Frances Thatcher. Childrens Pr., 1983. ISBN 0-516-08943-9 Subj: Activities. Animals – cats.

Fay, Ann. *Boot weather* (Vigna, Judith)

The farmer in the dell (The farmer in the dell)

I wish my daddy didn't drink so much (Vigna, Judith)

Ooops! (Kline, Suzy)

Fay, Hermann. *My zoo* ill. by author. Hubbard Sci., 1972. ISBN 0-833-10013-8 Subj: Animals. Zoos.

Fayon, Lavinia. *see* Russ, Lavinia

Fazio, Brenda Lena. *Grandfather's story* ill. by author. Sasquatch, 1996. ISBN 1-57061-028-2 Subj: Dreams. Family life – grandfathers. Foreign lands – Japan.

Fazzi, Maura. *The circus of mystery* written and ill. by Maura Fazzi and Peter Kühner; trans. by Rosemary Lanning. North-South, 1999. ISBN 0-7358-1169-5 Subj: Anatomy – noses. Circus. Clowns, jesters. Imagination.

Fearnley, Jan. *Little Robin's Christmas* ill. by author. Little Tiger, 1998. ISBN 1-888444-40-1 Subj: Animals. Birds – robins. Character traits – generosity. Clothing. Holidays – Christmas. Santa Claus.

Fechner, Amrei. *I am a little dog* trans. from German by Robert Kimber; ill. by author. Barron's, 1983. ISBN 0-8120-5514-4 Subj: Animals – dogs. Format, unusual – board books.

I am a little elephant ill. by author. Barron's, 1983. ISBN 0-8120-5512-2 Subj: Animals – elephants. Format, unusual – board books.

I am a little lion ill. by author. Barron's, 1983. ISBN 0-8120-5516-0 Subj: Animals – lions. Format, unusual – board books.

Feczko, Kathy. *Halloween party* ill. by Blanche Sims. Troll, 1985. ISBN 0-8167-0354-X Subj: Holidays – Halloween. Parties.

Umbrella parade ill. by Deborah Borgo. Troll, 1985. ISBN 0-8167-0356-6 Subj: Animals. Parades. Umbrellas.

Feder, Harriet K. *Not yet, Elijah!* ill. by Joan Halpern. Kar-Ben Copies, 1989. ISBN 0-930494-95-4 Subj: Holidays – Passover. Jewish culture. Religion. Rhyming text.

What can you do with a bagel? ill. by Sally Springer. Kar-Ben Copies, 1992. ISBN 0-929371-59-3 Subj: Activities – cooking. Food. Jewish culture.

Feder, Jane. *Beany* ill. by Karen Gundersheimer. Pantheon, 1979. ISBN 0-394-93734-1 Subj: Animals – cats.

Table, chair, bear: a book in many languages ill. by author. Ticknor & Fields, 1995. ISBN 0-395-65938-8 Subj: Foreign languages.

Feder, Paula Kurzband. *Where does the teacher live?* ill. by Lillian Hoban. Dutton, 1979. ISBN 0-525-42586-1 Subj: Careers – teachers. Homes, houses. Problem solving. School.

Feelings, Muriel. *Jambo means hello: Swahili alphabet book* ill. by Tom Feelings. Dial, 1974. ISBN 0-8037-4346-7 Subj: ABC books. Caldecott award honor books. Foreign lands – Africa. Foreign languages.

Menjo means one: Swahili counting book ill. by Tom Feelings. Dial, 1972. ISBN 0-8037-5711-5 Subj: Caldecott award honor books. Counting, numbers. Foreign lands – Africa. Foreign languages.

Feelings Tom. *Something on my mind* (Grimes, Nikki)

Feeney, Stephanie. *Hawaii is a rainbow* photos by Jeff Reese. Kolowalu Books, 1985. ISBN 0-8248-1007-4 Subj: Concepts – color.

Fehlner, Paul. *Dog and cat* ill. by Maxie Chambliss. Childrens Pr., 1990. ISBN 0-516-05353-1 Subj: Animals – cats. Animals – dogs. Rhyming text.

Feiffer, Jules. *Bark, George* ill. by author. Harper-Collins, 1999. ISBN 0-06-205185-7 Subj: Animals – dogs. Humor. Noise, sounds.

I lost my bear ill. by author. Morrow, 1998. ISBN 0-688-15148-5 Subj: Behavior – losing things. Family life. Toys. Toys – bears.

Meanwhile . . . ill. by author. HarperCollins, 1997. ISBN 0-06-205155-5 Subj: Activities – reading. Imagination.

Feilen, John. *see* May, Julian

Feinberg, Harold S. *Snail in the woods* (Ryder, Joanne)

Feistel, Sally. *The guinea pigs that went to school* (Meshover, Leonard)

The monkey that went to school (Meshover, Leonard)

Feitlowitz, Marguerite. *Brush* (Calders, Pere)

Feldman, Barbara. *Going, going* ill. by author. Firefly, 1989. ISBN 1-55037-045-6 Subj: Activities – traveling. Automobiles. Family life – mothers.

Stephen's frog ill. by author. Firefly, 1991. ISBN 1-55037-200-9 Subj: Family life – grandparents. Farms. Frogs and toads. Pets. Wordless.

Feldman, Eve B. *Animals don't wear pajamas* ill. by Mary Beth Owens. Holt, 1992. ISBN 0-8050-1710-0 Subj: Animals. Bedtime. Ethnic groups in the U.S. Sleep.

Birthdays! celebrating life around the world ill. with children's art provided by Paintbrush Diplomacy. BridgeWater, 1996. ISBN 0-8167-3494-1 Subj: Art. Birthdays. Children as illustrators. Foreign lands.

Feldman, Jacqueline. *The lavender box* ill. by Nannette Hoffman. Ellicott, 1990. ISBN 0-9623903-0-5 Subj: Poetry.

Feldman, Judy. *The alphabet in nature* ill. with photos. Childrens Pr., 1991. ISBN 0-516-05101-6 Subj: ABC books. Nature. Wordless.

Shapes in nature ill. with photos. Childrens Pr., 1991. ISBN 0-516-05102-4 Subj: Concepts – shape. Nature. Wordless.

Felicelli, Christine. *see* Daffis-Felicelli, Christine

Félix, Monique. *The further adventures of the little mouse trapped in a book* ill. by author. Green Tiger Pr., 1984. ISBN 0-88138-009-1 Subj: Animals – mice. Imagination. Wordless.

The story of a little mouse trapped in a book ill. by author. Green Tiger Pr., 1980. ISBN 0-914676-52-0 Subj: Animals – mice. Imagination. Wordless.

Fellows, Rebecca Nevers. *A lei for Tutu* ill. by Linda Finch. Albert Whitman, 1998. ISBN 0-8075-4426-4 Subj: Family life – grandmothers. Flowers. Hawaii.

Felt, Sue. *Hello-goodbye* ill. by author. Doubleday, 1960. Subj: Friendship. Moving.

Rosa-too-little ill. by author. Doubleday, 1950. Subj: Activities – writing. Behavior – growing up. Ethnic groups in the U.S. – Mexican Americans. Family life. Libraries.

Felton, Harold W. *Pecos Bill and the mustang* ill. by Leonard W. Shortall. Prentice-Hall, 1965. ISBN 0-13-655597-7 Subj: Animals – horses, ponies. Cowboys. Tall tales. U.S. history – frontier and pioneer life.

Fender, Kay. *Odette! a bird in Paris* ill. by Philippe Dumas. Prentice-Hall, 1978. ISBN 0-13-630525-3 Subj: Birds. Foreign lands – France. Old age.

Fenner, Carol. *Christmas tree on the mountain* ill. by author. Harcourt, 1966. Subj: Holidays – Christmas. Trees.

Tigers in the cellar ill. by author. Harcourt, 1963. Subj: Animals – tigers. Imagination. Night.

Fenton, Edward. *The big yellow balloon* ill. by Ib Spang Olsen. Doubleday, 1967. Subj: Cumulative tales. Humor. Toys – balloons.

Fierce John ill. by William Pène Du Bois. Doubleday, 1969, c1959. ISBN 0-03-072925-4 Subj: Family life. Imagination.

Fenton, Stephen H. *Who will pick me up when I fall?* (Molnar, Dorothy E.)

Ferguson, Alane. *That new pet!* ill. by Catherine Stock. Lothrop, 1986. ISBN 0-688-05516-8 Subj: Babies. Emotions – envy, jealousy. Pets.

Ferguson, Don. *Winnie the Pooh's A to Zzzz* ill. by Bill Langley and Diana Wakeman. Walt Disney, 1992. ISBN 1-56282-015-X Subj: ABC books. Format, unusual – toy and movable books. Rhyming text. Toys – bears.

Ferguson, Richard. *Bruce the balding moose* (Mellor, Corinne)

Fern, Eugene. *Birthday presents* ill. by author. Farrar, 1967. Includes the song Sing me (2 p.). Subj: Birthdays. Gifts. Songs.

The king who was too busy ill. by author. Ariel, 1966. Subj: Royalty – kings.

The most frightened hero ill. by author. Coward, 1961. Subj: Character traits – bravery. Foreign lands – Scotland.

Pepito's story ill. by author. Ariel, 1960. ISBN 1-878274-04-X Subj: Activities – dancing. Character traits – being different. Illness.

What's he been up to now? ill. by author. Dial, 1961. Subj: Animals – elephants. Friendship.

Fernandes, Eugenie. *A difficult day* ill. by author. Kids Can Pr., 1999. ISBN 0-921103-17-4 Subj: Behavior – bad day.

Fernandes, Kim. *One gray mouse* (Burton, Katherine)

Visiting granny photos by Pat Lacroix; ill. by author. Firefly, 1990. ISBN 1-55037-077-4 Subj: Family life – grandmothers. Food.

Ferns, Ronald. *Osbert and Lucy* ill. by author. HarperCollins, 1989. ISBN 0-06-021836-3 Subj: Animals – dogs. Animals – rabbits. Behavior – running away. Friendship.

Ferraro, Renato. *Alex, the amazing juggler* (Gianni, Peg)

Ferro, Beatriz. *Caught in the rain* ill. by Michele Sambin. Doubleday, 1980. ISBN 0-385-15625-1 Subj: Weather – rain.

Fichter, George S. *Bees, wasps, and ants* ill. by Kristin Kest. Western, 1993. ISBN 0-307-61434-4 Subj: Insects – ants. Insects – bees. Insects – wasps.

Fiday, Beverly. *Time to go* by Beverly and David Fiday; ill. by Thomas B. Allen. Harcourt, 1990. ISBN 0-15-200608-7 Subj: Family life. Farms. Moving.

Fiday, David. *Time to go* (Fiday, Beverly)

Fiddle-i-fee: *a traditional American chant* ill. by Diane Stanley. Little, 1979. ISBN 0-316-81040-0 Subj: Animals. Cumulative tales. Folk and fairy tales.

Field, Edward. *Magic words: poems* based on songs and stories of the Netsilik Inuit, collected by Knud Rasmussen; ill. by Stefano Vitale. Harcourt, 1998. ISBN 0-15-201498-5 Subj: Creation. Folk and fairy tales. Indians of North America – Inuit. Poetry.

Field, Eugene. *The gingham dog and the calico cat* ill. by Janet Street. Philomel, 1990. ISBN 0-399-22151-4 Subj: Animals – cats. Animals – dogs. Behavior – fighting, arguing. Poetry. Toys.

The gingham dog and the calico cat ill. by Johanna Westerman. North-South, 1994. ISBN 1-55858-292-4 Subj: Animals – cats. Animals – dogs. Behavior – fighting, arguing. Poetry. Toys.

Wynken, Blynken and Nod ill. by Barbara Cooney. Hastings House, 1964. ISBN 0-80388-046-4 Subj: Poetry. Sea and seashore. Sleep.

Wynken, Blynken and Nod ill. by Susan Jeffers. Dutton, 1982. ISBN 0-525-44022-4 Subj: Poetry. Sea and seashore. Sleep.

Wynken, Blynken and Nod ill. by Holly Johnson. Warne, 1973. ISBN 0-723-26100-8 Subj: Poetry. Sea and seashore. Sleep.

Wynken, Blynken and Nod ill. by Johanna Westerman. North-South, 1995. ISBN 1-55858-423-4 Subj: Poetry. Sea and seashore. Sleep.

Field, Rachel Lyman. *General store* ill. by Giles Laroche. Little, 1988. ISBN 0-316-28163-8 Subj: Poetry. Stores.

General store ill. by Nancy Winslow Parker. Greenwillow, 1988. ISBN 0-688-07354-9 Subj: Poetry. Stores.

If once you have slept on an island ill. by Iris Van Rynbach. Boyds Mills, 1993. ISBN 1-56397-106-2 Subj: Islands. Poetry.

Prayer for a child ill. by Elizabeth Orton Jones. Macmillan, 1944. ISBN 0-02-735190-4 Subj: Caldecott award books. Religion.

A road might lead to anywhere ill. by Giles Laroche. Little, 1990. ISBN 0-316-28178-6 Subj: Activities – traveling. Animals – mice. Dreams. Rhyming text. Roads.

Field, Susan. *The sun, the moon, and the silver baboon* ill. by author. HarperCollins, 1993. ISBN 0-06-022991-8 Subj: Animals – baboons. Concepts – color. Night. Stars. Sun.

Fields, Sadie. *Hidden numbers* (Holmes, Stephen)

Fife, Dale. *Adam's ABC* ill. by Don Robertson. Coward, 1971. Subj: ABC books. City. Ethnic groups in the U.S. – African Americans.

Empty lot ill. by Jim Arnosky. Little, 1991. ISBN 0-316-28167-0 Subj: Nature. Progress.

The little park ill. by Janet LaSalle. Albert Whitman, 1973. ISBN 0-8075-4634-8 Subj: Animals. Ecology. Parks. Progress.

Rosa's special garden ill. by Marie DeJohn. Albert Whitman, 1985. ISBN 0-8075-7115-6 Subj: Ethnic groups in the U.S. – Mexican Americans. Gardens, gardening. Sibling rivalry.

Fifield, Flora. *Pictures for the palace* ill. by Nola Langner. Vanguard, 1957. Subj: Art. Foreign lands – Japan.

Figley, Marty Rhodes. *Noah's wife* ill. by Anita Riggio. Eerdmans, 1998. ISBN 0-8028-5107-X Subj: Boats, ships. Family life. Religion – Noah. Weather – floods. Weather – rain.

The story of Zacchaeus ill. by Cat Bowman Smith. Eerdmans, 1995. ISBN 0-8028-5092-8 Subj: Foreign lands – Middle East. Religion.

Figueredo, D. H. *When this world was new* ill. by Enrique O. Sánchez. Lee & Low, 1999. ISBN 1-880000-86-5 Subj: Emotions – fear. Ethnic groups in the U.S. – Hispanic Americans. Family life. Immigrants. Moving. Weather – snow.

Fillingham, David. *Such a noise!* (Brodmann, Aliana)

Fine, Anne. *Poor Monty* ill. by Clara Vulliamy. Houghton Mifflin, 1992. ISBN 0-395-60472-9 Subj: Behavior – needing someone. Careers – doctors. Family life – mothers. Gender roles. Illness – chicken pox.

Fine, Edith Hope. *Under the lemon moon* ill. by René King Moreno. Lee & Low, 1999. ISBN 1-880000-69-5 Subj: Behavior – stealing. Character traits – generosity. Foreign lands – Mexico.

Fine, Judith. *Princess Lily* (Bazilian, Barbara)

Finfer, Celentha. *Grandmother dear* by Celentha Finfer, Esther Wasserberg and Florence Weinberg; ill. by Roy Mathews. Follett, 1968. Subj: Activities – babysitting. Family life – grandmothers. Poetry.

Fink, Dale Borman. *Mr. Silver and Mrs. Gold* ill. by Shirley Chan. Human Sciences Pr., 1980. ISBN 0-87705-447-9 Subj: Friendship. Old age.

Fink, Joanne. *Mister North Wind* (De Posadas Mane, Carmen)

Finsand, Mary Jane. *The town that moved* ill. by Reg Sandland. Carolrhoda, 1983. ISBN 0-87614-200-5 Subj: City. Moving.

Finzel, Julia. *Large as life* ill. by author. Lothrop, 1991. ISBN 0-688-10653-6 Subj: Animals. Concepts – size. Games. Insects – ladybugs.

Fior, Jane. *The lazy beaver* (Gallo, Giovanni)

Night lion (Farber, Werner)

Fire ill. by Michael Ricketts. Grosset, 1972. ISBN 0-448-09659-5 Subj: Fire.

The firebird retold by Selina Hastings; ill. by Reg Cartwright. Holt, 1994. ISBN 1-56402-096-7 Subj: Ballet. Behavior – stealing. Folk and fairy tales. Foreign lands – Russia. Magic. Royalty – princes.

The firebird retold by Margaret Greaves; ill. by Francesca Crespi. Dial, 1986. ISBN 0-8037-0265-5 (set) Subj: Ballet. Behavior – stealing. Folk and fairy tales. Foreign lands – Russia. Magic. Royalty – princes.

The firebird retold and ill. by Demi. Holt, 1994. ISBN 0-8050-3244-4 Subj: Ballet. Behavior – stealing. Folk and fairy tales. Foreign lands – Russia. Magic. Royalty – princes.

The firebird adapt. and ill. by Rachel Isadora. Putnam, 1994. ISBN 0-399-22510-2 Subj: Ballet. Behavior – stealing. Folk and fairy tales. Foreign lands – Russia. Magic. Royalty – princes.

The firebird retold and ill. by Moira Kemp. Godine, 1984. ISBN 0-87923-486-5 Subj: Ballet. Behavior – stealing. Folk and fairy tales. Foreign lands – Russia. Magic. Royalty – princes.

The firebird adapt. by Robert D. San Souci; ill. by Kris Waldherr. Dial, 1992. ISBN 0-8037-0800-9 Subj: Ballet. Behavior – stealing. Folk and fairy tales. Foreign lands – Russia. Magic. Royalty – princes.

The firebird: *and other Russian fairy tales* ill. by Boris Zvorykin; ed. by Jacqueline Onassis. Viking, 1978. ISBN 0-670-31544-3 Subj: Ballet. Behavior – stealing. Folk and fairy tales. Foreign lands – Russia. Magic. Royalty – princes.

Firehouse ed. by Kate Klimo; ill. by Zokeisha. Simon & Schuster, 1983. ISBN 0-671-46128-1 Subj: Careers – firefighters. Fire. Format, unusual – board books. Homes, houses.

Firmin, Peter. *Basil Brush and the windmills* ill. by author. Prentice-Hall, 1980. ISBN 0-13-066720-X Subj: Animals – foxes. Animals – moles. Ecology.

Chicken stew ill. by author. Merrimack, 1982. ISBN 0-7207-1299-8 Subj: Animals – wolves. Birds – chickens. Gardens, gardening.

Noggin and the whale (Postgate, Oliver)

Noggin the king (Postgate, Oliver)

First graces ill. by Tasha Tudor. Walck, 1989, c1955. ISBN 0-394-94409-7 Subj: Poetry. Religion.

First prayers ill. by Anna Maria Magagna. Macmillan, 1983. ISBN 0-02-762120-0 Subj: Poetry. Religion.

First prayers ill. by Tasha Tudor. Random House, 1989, c1980. ISBN 0-394-84429-1 Subj: Poetry. Religion.

Fischer, Alexandra E. *Look how a baby grows* (Mantegazza, Giovanna)

Look inside a farm (Mantegazza, Giovanna)

Look inside a rainforest (Mantegazza, Giovanna)

Fischer, Hans. *The birthday* ill. by author. Harcourt, 1954. Subj: Animals. Birthdays.

Puss in boots (Perrault, Charles)

Fischer, Vera Kistiakowsky. *One way is down: a book about gravity* ill. by Ward Brackett. Little, 1967. Subj: Concepts – weight. Science.

Fischer-Nagel, Andreas. *A kitten is born* (Fischer-Nagel, Heiderose)

A puppy is born (Fischer-Nagel, Heiderose)

Fischer-Nagel, Heiderose. *A kitten is born* by Heiderose and Andreas Fischer-Nagel; trans. from German by Andrea Mernan; photos by authors. Putnam, 1983. ISBN 0-399-20961-1 Subj: Animals – cats. Birth. Science.

A puppy is born by Heiderose and Andreas Fischer-Nagel; trans. from German by Andrea Mernan; photos by authors. Putnam, 1985. ISBN 0-399-21234-5 Subj: Animals – dogs. Birth. Science.

Fischetto, Laura. *All pigs on deck: Christopher Columbus's second marvelous voyage* ill. by Letizia Galli. Delacorte, 1991. ISBN 0-385-30440-4 Subj: Animals – pigs. Boats, ships. U.S. history.

Inside Noah's ark ill. by Letizia Galli. Viking, 1989. ISBN 0-670-83028-3 Subj: Animals. Boats, ships. Religion – Noah. Weather – floods. Weather – rain. Weather – rainbows.

The jungle is my home ill. by Letizia Galli. Viking, 1991. ISBN 0-670-83550-1 Subj: Animals. Ecology. Foreign lands – South America. Jungle.

Fischman, Sheila. *The longest home run* (Carrier, Roch)

Fischtrom, Harvey. *see* Zemach, Harve

Fish, Hans. *Pitschi, the kitten who always wanted to do something else* ill. by author. North-South, 1996. ISBN 1-55858-645-8 Subj: Animals – cats. Behavior – dissatisfaction.

Fish, Helen Dean. *Four and twenty blackbirds* ill. by Robert Lawson. Stokes, 1937. Subj: Caldecott award honor books. Nursery rhymes.

When the root children wake up ill. by Sibylle Von Olfers. Lippincott, 1930. ISBN 0-397-30075-1 Subj: Mythical creatures. Seasons – spring.

When the root children wake up ill. by Sibylle Von Olfers. Green Tiger Pr., 1988. ISBN 0-88138-103-9 Subj: Mythical creatures. Seasons – spring.

Fisher, Aileen Lucia. *And a sunflower grew* ill. by Trina Schart Hyman; lettering by Paul Taylor. Noble, 1977. ISBN 0-8372-2394-6 Subj: Flowers. Plants. Rhyming text. Science.

Anybody home? ill. by Susan Bonners. Crowell, 1980. ISBN 0-690-04055-5 Subj: Animals. Character traits – curiosity. Rhyming text.

Arbor day ill. by Nonny Hogrogian. Crowell, 1965. Subj: Holidays. Trees.

As the leaves fall down ill. by Barbara Smith. Noble, 1977. ISBN 0-8372-2397-0 Subj: Plants. Science. Seasons. Trees.

Best little house ill. by Arnold Spilka. Crowell, 1966. Subj: Homes, houses. Moving. Poetry.

Do bears have mothers too? ill. by Eric Carle. Crowell, 1973. ISBN 0-690-00167-3 Subj: Animals. Family life – mothers. Poetry.

Going barefoot ill. by Adrienne Adams. Crowell, 1960. Subj: Rhyming text. Seasons.

The house of a mouse ill. by Joan Sandin. Harper-Collins, 1988. ISBN 0-06-021849-5 Subj: Animals – mice. Homes, houses. Poetry.

I like weather ill. by Janina Domanska. Crowell, 1963. Subj: Animals – dogs. Poetry. Weather.

I wonder how, I wonder why ill. by Carol Barker. Abelard-Schuman, 1963. Subj: Poetry.

In one door and out the other: a book of poems ill. by Lillian Hoban. Crowell, 1969. Subj: Family life. Poetry.

In the middle of the night ill. by Adrienne Adams. Crowell, 1965. Subj: Night. Poetry.

Like nothing at all ill. by Leonard Weisgard. Crowell, 1962. ISBN 0-690-49379-7 Subj: Nature. Poetry. Science. Seasons.

Listen, rabbit ill. by Symeon Shimin. Crowell, 1964. Subj: Animals – rabbits. Poetry.

My first Hanukkah book ill. by Priscilla Kiedrowski. Childrens Pr., 1985. ISBN 0-516-42905-1 Subj: Holidays – Hanukkah. Jewish culture. Poetry.

My mother and I ill. by Kazue Mizumura. Crowell, 1967. Subj: Family life – mothers. Poetry. Seasons – spring.

Mysteries in the garden ill. by Ati Forberg; lettering by Paul Taylor. Noble, 1977. ISBN 0-8372-2392-0 Subj: Gardens, gardening. Plants. Poetry. Science.

Now that spring is here ill. by Symeon Shimin; lettering by Paul Taylor. Noble, 1977. ISBN 0-8372-2396-2 Subj: Plants. Rhyming text. Science. Seasons – spring.

Petals yellow and petals red ill. by Albert John Pucci; lettering by Paul Taylor. Noble, 1977. ISBN 0-8372-2395-4 Subj: Flowers. Rhyming text. Science.

Plant magic ill. by Barbara Cooney; lettering by Paul Taylor. Noble, 1977. Subj: Plants. Rhyming text. Science.

Prize performance ill. by Margot Tomes. Noble, 1977. ISBN 0-8372-2398-9 Subj: Plants. Rhyming text. Science.

Rabbits, rabbits ill. by Gail Niemann. Harper-Collins, 1983. ISBN 0-06-021896-7 Subj: Animals – rabbits. Poetry.

Seeds on the go ill. by Hans Zander; lettering by Paul Taylor. Noble, 1977. ISBN 0-8372-2400-4 Subj: Plants. Rhyming text. Science.

Sing, little mouse ill. by Symeon Shimin. Crowell, 1969. Subj: Animals – mice. Rhyming text.

Skip around the year ill. by Gioia Fiammenghi. Crowell, 1967. Subj: Holidays. Poetry.

The story of Easter ill. by Stefano Vitale. Harper-Collins, 1997. ISBN 0-06-027297-X Subj: Holidays – Easter. Religion. Seasons – spring.

Swords and daggers ill. by James Higa; lettering by Paul Taylor. Noble, 1977. ISBN 0-8372-2393-8 Subj: Plants. Rhyming text. Science.

We went looking ill. by Marie Angel. Crowell, 1968. Subj: Animals. Birds. Insects – ladybugs. Plants. Poetry.

When it comes to bugs ill. by Chris and Bruce Degen. HarperCollins, 1986. ISBN 0-06-021822-3 Subj: Insects. Poetry. Spiders.

Where does everyone go? ill. by Adrienne Adams. Crowell, 1961. Subj: Animals. Hibernation. Poetry. Seasons – winter.

Fisher, Iris L. *Katie-Bo: an adoption story* ill. by Miriam Schaer. Watts, 1988. ISBN 0-915361-91-4 Subj: Adoption. Babies. Ethnic groups in the U.S. Family life – new sibling. Sibling rivalry.

Fisher, Leonard Everett. *The ABC exhibit* ill. by author. Macmillan, 1991. ISBN 0-02-735251-X Subj: ABC books.

Boxes! Boxes! ill. by author. Viking, 1984. ISBN 0-670-18334-2 Subj: Concepts. Concepts – color. Counting, numbers. Rhyming text.

Cyclops ill. by author. Holiday, 1991. ISBN 0-8234-0891-4 Subj: Folk and fairy tales. Mythical creatures.

David and Goliath adapt. from the Bible and ill. by Leonard Everett Fisher. Holiday, 1993. ISBN 0-8234-0997-X Subj: Giants. Religion – David.

Gutenberg ill. by author. Macmillan, 1993. ISBN 0-02-735238-2 Subj: Careers – printers. Communication. Inventions.

A head full of hats ill. by author. Dial, 1962. Subj: Clothing – hats.

Look around! a book about shapes ill. by author. Viking, 1987. ISBN 0-670-80869-5 Subj: Concepts – shape. Games.

Pumpers, boilers, hooks and ladders: a book of fire engines ill. by author. Dial, 1961. Subj: Careers – firefighters. Trucks.

The seven days of creation ill. by author. Holiday, 1981. Adapt. from the Bible. ISBN 0-8234-0398-X Subj: Creation. Religion.

Star signs ill. by author. Holiday, 1983. ISBN 0-8234-0491-9 Subj: Folk and fairy tales. Zodiac.

Stars and stripes: our national flag ill. by author. Holiday, 1993. ISBN 0-8234-1053-6 Subj: U.S. history.

Theseus and the minotaur ill. by author. Holiday, 1988. ISBN 0-8234-0703-9 Subj: Folk and fairy tales. Mythical creatures. Royalty.

William Tell ill. by author. Farrar, 1996. ISBN 0-374-38436-3 Subj: Folk and fairy tales. Foreign lands – Switzerland. Sports – archery.

Fisher, Richard E. *The boy and the dog* (Widerberg, Siv)

Mrs. Pepperpot and the moose (Prøysen, Alf)

Olson's meat pies (Cohen, Peter Zachary)

Shorty takes off (Lindgren, Barbro)

Will's new cap (Landström, Olof)

Fishman, Cathy Goldberg. *On Hanukkah* ill. by Melanie W. Hall. Atheneum, 1998. ISBN 0-689-80643-4 Subj: Holidays – Hanukkah. Jewish culture. Religion.

On Passover ill. by Melanie W. Hall. Atheneum, 1997. ISBN 0-689-80528-4 Subj: Holidays – Passover. Jewish culture. Religion.

On Rosh Hashanah and Yom Kippur ill. by Melanie W. Hall. Atheneum, 1997. ISBN 0-689-80526-8 Subj: Holidays – Rosh Hashanah. Holidays – Yom Kippur. Jewish culture. Religion.

Fitch, Florence Mary. *A book about God* ill. by Henri Sorensen. Lothrop, 1999. ISBN 0-688-16129-4 Subj: Religion.

Fitzhugh, Louise. *Bang, bang, you're dead* by Louise Fitzhugh and Sandra Scoppetone; ill. by Louise Fitzhugh. HarperCollins, 1969. ISBN 0-06-021914-9 Subj: Activities – playing. Cowboys. Violence, nonviolence. War. Weapons.

I am five ill. by author. Delacorte, 1978. ISBN 0-440-03953-3 Subj: Self-concept.

I am three ill. by Susanna Natti. Delacorte, 1982. ISBN 0-440-04039-6 Subj: Self-concept.

Fitzpatrick, Jean Grasso. *Animals of the forest* (Mora, Emma)

Gideon, the little bear cub (Mora, Emma)

Fitzsimons, Cecilia. *My first birds* ill. by author. HarperCollins, 1985. ISBN 0-06-021892-4 Subj: Birds. Format, unusual – board books.

My first butterflies ill. by author. HarperCollins, 1985. ISBN 0-06-021893-2 Subj: Format, unusual – board books. Insects – butterflies, caterpillars.

Five little pumpkins ill. by Dan Yaccarino. Harper-Festival, 1998. ISBN 0-694-01177-0 Subj: Format, unusual – board books. Holidays – Halloween. Plants. Rhyming text.

Flack, Marjorie. *Angus and the cat* ill. by author. Doubleday, [1989], c1931. ISBN 0-685-01488-6 Subj: Animals – cats. Animals – dogs. Character traits – completing things. Character traits – curiosity.

Angus and the ducks ill. by author. Doubleday, 1930. ISBN 0-385-07213-9 Subj: Animals – dogs. Birds – ducks. Character traits – conceit. Character traits – curiosity.

Angus lost ill. by author. Doubleday, [1989], c1932. ISBN 0-385-07214-7 Subj: Animals – dogs. Behavior – lost. Seasons – winter.

Ask Mr. Bear ill. by author. Macmillan, 1932. ISBN 0-02-735390-7 Subj: Animals. Animals – bears. Birthdays. Emotions – love. Family life – mothers.

The boats on the river ill. by author. Viking, 1946. ISBN 0-670-83918-3 Subj: Boats, ships. Caldecott award honor books. Rivers.

The restless robin ill. by author. Houghton Mifflin, 1937. Subj: Birds – robins. Music.

The story about Ping by Marjorie Flack and Kurt Wiese; ill. by Kurt Wiese. Viking, 1933. Subj: Behavior – misbehavior. Birds – ducks. Foreign lands – China.

Tim Tadpole and the great bullfrog ill. by author. Doubleday, 1934. Subj: Frogs and toads.

Wait for William ill. by Marjorie Flack and Richard A. Holberg. Houghton Mifflin, 1934. ISBN 0-395-15484-7 Subj: Circus. Family life. Parades.

William and his kitten ill. by author. Houghton Mifflin, 1938. ISBN 0-395-20212-4 Subj: Animals – cats.

Flanagan, Alice K. *Coach John and his soccer team* photos by Christine Osinski. Childrens Pr., 1998. ISBN 0-516-20777-6 Subj: Careers – coaches. Communities, neighborhoods. Sports – soccer.

A day in court with Mrs. Trinh photos by Christine Osinski. Childrens Pr., 1997. ISBN 0-516-20008-9 Subj: Careers – judges. Careers – lawyers.

Here comes Mr. Eventoff with the mail! photos by Christine Osinski. Childrens Pr., 1998. ISBN 0-516-20776-8 Subj: Careers – postal workers. Communities, neighborhoods.

Ms. Murphy fights fires photos by Christine Osinski. Childrens Pr., 1997. ISBN 0-516-20494-7 Subj:

Careers – firefighters. Communities, neighborhoods.

Officer Brown keeps neighborhoods safe photos by Christine Osinski. Childrens Pr., 1998. ISBN 0-516-20780-6 Subj: Careers – police officers. Communities, neighborhoods.

Riding the school bus with Mrs. Kramer photos by Christine Osinski. Childrens Pr., 1998. ISBN 0-516-20779-2 Subj: Careers – bus drivers. Communities, neighborhoods.

A visit to the Gravesens' farm photos by Christine Osinski. Childrens Pr., 1998. ISBN 0-516-20778-4 Subj: Careers – farmers. Communities, neighborhoods. Family life. Farms.

The Wilsons, a house-painting team photos by Christine Osinski. Childrens Pr., 1996. ISBN 0-516-20216-2 Subj: Activities – painting. Careers – painters. Homes, houses.

Flanders, Michael. *Creatures great and small* ill. by Marcello Minale. Holt, 1965. Subj: Animals. Birds. Poetry.

The hippopotamus song: a muddy love story ill. by Nadine Bernard Westcott; music by Donald Swann and Michael Flanders. Little, 1991. ISBN 0-316-28557-9 Subj: Animals – hippopotamuses. Emotions – love. Music. Songs.

Flather, Lisa. *Ten silly dogs* ill. by author. Orchard, 1999. ISBN 0-531-33192-X Subj: Animals – dogs. Counting, numbers. Rhyming text.

Flatt, Lizann. *My first nature treasury* ill. by Allan Cormack and Deborah Drew-Brook. Sierra Club, 1995. ISBN 0-87156-362-2 Subj: Nature.

Fleetwood, Jenni. *While shepherds watched* ill. by Peter Melnyczuk. Rev. ed. Broadman & Holman, 1999. ISBN 0-688-11598-5 Subj: Animals – sheep. Birthdays. Holidays – Christmas. Religion – Nativity.

Fleischman, Paul. *The animal hedge* ill. by Lydia Dabcovich. Dutton, 1983. ISBN 0-525-44002-X Subj: Activities – working. Farms. Folk and fairy tales.

The birthday tree ill. by Marcia Sewall. HarperCollins, 1979. ISBN 0-06-021916-5 Subj: Birthdays. Trees.

Rondo in C ill. by Janet Wentworth. HarperCollins, 1988. ISBN 0-06-021857-6 Subj: Imagination. Music. Rhyming text.

Time train ill. by Claire Ewart. HarperCollins, 1991. ISBN 0-06-021710-3 Subj: Dinosaurs. School. Time. Trains.

Fleischman, Sid. *Kate's secret riddle* ill. by Barbara Bottner. Watts, 1977. ISBN 0-531-01334-0 Subj: Illness. Riddles.

Longbeard the wizard ill. by Charles Bragg. Little, 1970. Subj: Royalty. Wizards.

The scarebird ill. by Peter Sis. Mulberry, 1994. ISBN 0-688-13105-0 Subj: Character traits – kindness. Farms. Friendship. Scarecrows.

Fleisher, Robbin. *Quilts in the attic* ill. by Ati Forberg. Macmillan, 1978. ISBN 0-02-735420-2 Subj: Family life. Games. Quilts.

Fleishman, Seymour. *Too hot in Potzburg* ill. by author. Walker, 1981. ISBN 0-8075-8024-4 Subj: Animals – bears. Machines.

Fleming, Bill. *Kitten training and critters, too!* (Petersen-Fleming, Judy)

Puppy training and critters, too! (Petersen-Fleming, Judy)

Fleming, Candace. *A big cheese for the White House: the true tale of a tremendous cheddar* ill. by S. D. Schindler. DK, 1999. ISBN 0-7894-2573-4 Subj: Food. U.S. history.

Gabriella's song ill. by Giselle Potter. Atheneum, 1997. ISBN 0-689-80973-5 Subj: Foreign lands – Italy. Music. Songs.

The hatmaker's sign: a story by Benjamin Franklin retold by Candace Fleming; ill. Robert Andrew Parker. Orchard, 1998. ISBN 0-531-33075-3 Subj: Careers – storekeepers. Clothing. Stores. U.S. history.

Madame LaGrande and her so high, to the sky, uproarious pompadour ill. by S. D. Schindler. Knopf, 1996. ISBN 0-679-95835-5 Subj: Character traits – vanity. Foreign lands – France. Hair.

Professor Fergus Fahrenheit and his wonderful weather machine ill. by Don Weller. Simon & Schuster, 1994. ISBN 0-671-87047-5 Subj: Machines. Weather – droughts. Weather – rain.

Westward ho, Carlotta! ill. by David Catrow. Atheneum, 1998. ISBN 0-689-81063-6 Subj: Activities – singing. Careers – opera singers. U.S. history – frontier and pioneer life.

When Agnes caws ill. by Giselle Potter. Atheneum, 1999. ISBN 0-689-81471-2 Subj: Birds. Foreign lands – Himalayas. Noise, sounds.

Fleming, Denise. *Barnyard banter* ill. by author. Holt, 1994. ISBN 0-8050-1957-X Subj: Animals. Farms. Noise, sounds. Rhyming text.

Count! ill. by author. Holt, 1992. ISBN 0-8050-1595-7 Subj: Animals. Counting, numbers.

In the small, small pond ill. by author. Holt, 1993. ISBN 0-8050-2264-3 Subj: Animals. Caldecott award honor books. Frogs and toads. Lakes, ponds. Rhyming text. Seasons.

In the tall, tall grass ill. by author. Holt, 1991. ISBN 0-8050-1635-X Subj: Insects – butterflies, caterpillars. Nature.

Lunch ill. by author. Holt, 1992. ISBN 0-8050-1636-8 Subj: Animals – mice. Concepts – color. Food.

Mama cat has three kittens ill. by author. Holt, 1998. ISBN 0-8050-5745-5 Subj: Animals – babies.

Animals – cats. Character traits – being different. Family life – brothers and sisters.

Time to sleep ill. by author. Holt, 1997. ISBN 0-8050-3762-4 Subj: Animals – bears. Hibernation. Seasons – winter.

Where once there was a wood ill. by author. Holt, 1996. ISBN 0-8050-3761-6 Subj: Animals. Nature. Plants.

Fleming, Virginia M. *Be good to Eddie Lee* ill. by Floyd Cooper. Philomel, 1993. ISBN 0-399-21993-5 Subj: Friendship. Handicaps – Down syndrome. Nature.

Fletcher, Claire. *The seashell song* (Jenkin-Pearce, Susie)

Fletcher, Elizabeth. *The little goat* ill. by Deborah and Kilmeny Niland. Grosset, 1977. ISBN 0-448-14287-2 Subj: Animals – goats. Behavior – lost.

What am I? ill. by Deborah and Kilmeny Niland. Grosset, 1977. ISBN 0-448-14280-5 Subj: Animals. Riddles.

Fletcher, Jane Cowen. *see* Cowen-Fletcher, Jane

Fletcher, Ralph J. *Twilight comes twice* ill. by Kate Kiesler. Clarion, 1997. ISBN 0-395-84826-1 Subj: Poetry. Twilight.

Flint, Russ. *Let's build a house* ill. by author. Ideals, 1990. ISBN 0-8249-8432-3 Subj: Activities – making things. Homes, houses.

Floca, Brian. *Five trucks* ill. by author. DK, 1999. ISBN 0-7894-2561-0 Subj: Airplanes, airports. Trucks.

The frightful story of Harry Walfish ill. by author. Orchard, 1997. ISBN 0-531-33008-7 Subj: Animals. Behavior – misbehavior. Museums.

Flöethe, Louise Lee. *The Indian and his pueblo* ill. by Richard Flöethe. Scribners, 1960. Subj: Indians of North America.

Flood, Bo. *I'll go to school if . . .* ill. by Ronnie Shipman. Fairview, 1997. ISBN 1-57749-024-X Subj: Emotions – fear. School – first day.

Flora. *Feathers like a rainbow* ill. by author. HarperCollins, 1989. ISBN 0-06-021838-X Subj: Birds. Concepts – color. Folk and fairy tales. Foreign lands – South America. Indians of South America.

Flora, James. *The day the cow sneezed* ill. by author. Harcourt, 1975, c1957. ISBN 0-15-624213-3 Subj: Animals. Cumulative tales. Humor.

Fishing with dad ill. by author. Harcourt, 1967. ISBN 0-15-228100-2 Subj: Boats, ships. Careers – fishermen.

Grandpa's farm: 4 tall tales ill. by author. Harcourt, 1965. Subj: Family life – grandfathers. Farms. Humor.

Grandpa's ghost stories ill. by author. Atheneum, 1978. ISBN 0-689-50112-9 Subj: Family life – grandfathers. Ghosts. Witches.

Leopold, the see-through crumbpicker ill. by author. Harcourt, 1961. Subj: Monsters. Zoos.

My friend Charlie ill. by author. Harcourt, 1964. Subj: Friendship.

Sherwood walks home ill. by author. Harcourt, 1966. Subj: Toys – bears.

Florian, Douglas. *Airplane ride* ill. by author. Crowell, 1984. ISBN 0-690-04365-1 Subj: Activities – flying. Airplanes, airports.

At the zoo ill. by author. Greenwillow, 1992. ISBN 0-688-09629-8 Subj: Animals. Zoos.

An auto mechanic ill. by author. Greenwillow, 1991. ISBN 0-688-10636-6 Subj: Automobiles. Careers – mechanics.

Beach day ill. by author. Greenwillow, 1990. ISBN 0-688-09105-9 Subj: Sea and seashore.

Beast feast ill. by author. Harcourt, 1994. ISBN 0-15-295178-4 Subj: Animals. Poetry.

A bird can fly ill. by author. Greenwillow, 1980. ISBN 0-688-84266-6 Subj: Animals. Science.

A carpenter ill. by author. Greenwillow, 1991. ISBN 0-688-09761-8 Subj: Careers – carpenters.

A chef ill. by author. Greenwillow, 1992. ISBN 0-688-11109-2 Subj: Activities – cooking. Careers – chefs, cooks.

The city ill. by author. Crowell, 1982. ISBN 0-690-04167-5 Subj: City. Wordless.

City street ill. by author. Greenwillow, 1990. ISBN 0-688-09544-5 Subj: City.

A fisher ill. by author. Greenwillow, 1994. ISBN 0-688-13130-1 Subj: Careers – fishermen.

In the swim ill. by author. Harcourt, 1997. ISBN 0-15-201307-5 Subj: Animals. Poetry. Sea and seashore.

Insectlopedia ill. by author. Harcourt, 1998. ISBN 0-15-201306-7 Subj: Insects. Poetry.

Monster Motel ill. by author. Harcourt, 1993. ISBN 0-15-255320-7 Subj: Monsters. Poetry.

Nature walk ill. by author. Greenwillow, 1989. ISBN 0-688-08269-6 Subj: Activities – walking. Nature.

On the wing: bird poems and paintings ill. by author. Harcourt, 1996. ISBN 0-15-200497-1 Subj: Birds. Poetry.

A painter ill. by author. Greenwillow, 1993. ISBN 0-688-11873-9 Subj: Activities – painting. Art. Careers – artists.

People working ill. by author. Crowell, 1983. ISBN 0-690-04264-7 Subj: Activities – working. Careers.

A potter ill. by author. Greenwillow, 1991. ISBN 0-688-10101-1 Subj: Activities – making things. Activities – working. Art. Rhyming text.

A summer day ill. by author. Greenwillow, 1988. ISBN 0-688-07565-7 Subj: Activities – vacationing. Counting, numbers. Family life.

Turtle day ill. by author. HarperCollins, 1989. ISBN 0-690-04745-2 Subj: Reptiles – turtles, tortoises.

Vegetable garden ill. by author. Harcourt, 1991. ISBN 0-15-293383-2 Subj: Gardens, gardening. Rhyming text.

A winter day ill. by author. Greenwillow, 1987. ISBN 0-688-07352-2 Subj: Family life. Rhyming text. Seasons – winter.

A year in the country ill. by author. Greenwillow, 1989. ISBN 0-688-08187-8 Subj: Country. Farms. Seasons.

Flory, Jane. *The bear on the doorstep* ill. by Carolyn Croll. Houghton Mifflin, 1980. ISBN 0-395-29239-5 Subj: Animals – bears. Animals – rabbits. Homes, houses.

The unexpected grandchildren ill. by Carolyn Croll. Houghton Mifflin, 1977. ISBN 0-395-25797-2 Subj: Behavior – sharing. Family life – grandparents.

We'll have a friend for lunch ill. by Carolyn Croll. Houghton Mifflin, 1974. ISBN 0-395-18448-7 Subj: Animals – cats. Food. Friendship.

Flot, Jeannette B. *Princess Kalina and the hedgehog* adapt. by Frances Marshall; ill. by Dorothée Duntze. Faber, 1981. ISBN 0-571-11844-5 Subj: Animals – hedgehogs. Character traits – cleanliness. Folk and fairy tales. Magic. Royalty – princesses.

Flournoy, Valerie. *The best time of day* ill. by George Ford. Random House, 1979. ISBN 0-394-93799-6 Subj: Activities. Ethnic groups in the U.S. – African Americans. Family life.

The patchwork quilt ill. by Jerry Pinkney. Dial, 1985. ISBN 0-8037-0098-9 Subj: Ethnic groups in the U.S. – African Americans. Family life – grandmothers. Quilts.

Flower, Phyllis. *Barn owl* ill. by Cherryl Pape. HarperCollins, 1978. ISBN 0-06-021921-1 Subj: Birds – owls. Science.

Floyd, Lucy. *Agatha's alphabet, with her very own dictionary* by Lucy Floyd and Kathryn Lasky; ill. by Dora Leder. Rand McNally, 1975. ISBN 0-528-80149-X Subj: ABC books. Dictionaries.

Flugge, Klauss. *Hey Presto! You're a bear!* (Janosch)

Foa, Maryclare. *Songs are thoughts* ill. by author. Orchard, 1995. ISBN 0-531-06893-5 Subj: Foreign lands – Arctic. Indians of North America – Inuit. Poetry.

Foley, Bernice Williams. *The gazelle and the hunter: a folk tale from Persia* ill. by Diana Magnuson. Childrens Pr., 1980. ISBN 0-516-06480-0 Subj: Folk and fairy tales. Foreign lands – Persia.

A walk among clouds: a folk tale from China ill. by Mina Gow McLean. Childrens Pr., 1980. ISBN 0-516-06484-3 Subj: Folk and fairy tales. Foreign lands – China.

Folsom, Marcia. *Easy as pie: a guessing game of sayings* by Marcia and Michael Folsom; ill. by Jack Kent. Houghton Mifflin, 1985. ISBN 0-89919-303-X Subj: Humor. Language.

Folsom, Michael. *Easy as pie: a guessing game of sayings* (Folsom, Marcia)

Q is for duck: an alphabet guessing game (Elting, Mary)

Fontaine, Jan. *The spaghetti tree* ill. by Anne Marshall Runyon. Talespinner, 1980. ISBN 0-934926-00-X Subj: Food. Gardens, gardening. Imagination.

Fontaine, Jean de La. *see* La Fontaine, Jean de

Fontane, Theodor. *Nick Ribbeck of Ribbeck of Havelland* trans. from German by Anthea Bell; ill. by Marta Kočí. Picture Book Studio, 1990. ISBN 0-88708-149-5 Subj: Character traits – generosity. Poetry.

Sir Ribbeck of Ribbeck of Havelland trans. from German by Elizabeth Shub; ill. by Nonny Hogrogian. Macmillan, 1971, c1969. ISBN 0-20-071750-2 Subj: Character traits – generosity. Poetry.

Fontenot, Mary Alice. *Tah-Tye: the last 'possum in the pouch* ill. by Scott R. Blazek. Blue Heron, 1996. ISBN 1-884725-10-4 Subj: Animals – possums. Behavior – growing up. Family life.

Fonteyn, Margot, Dame. *Coppélia* as told by Margot Fonteyn; ill. by Steve Johnson and Lou Fancher. Harcourt, 1998. ISBN 0-15-200428-9 Subj: Activities – dancing. Ballet. Emotions – envy, jealousy. Toys – dolls.

Foord, Jo. *The book of babies* photos by author. Random House, 1991. ISBN 0-679-90955-9 Subj: Activities. Babies. Rhyming text.

Foote, Dan. *The cobbler, the princess, and the newborn King* ill. by author. Chariot Victor, 1999. ISBN 0-7814-3079-8 Subj: Holidays – Christmas. Religion – Nativity.

For laughing out louder: *more poems to tickle your funnybone* sel. by Jack Prelutsky; ill. by Marjorie Priceman. Knopf, 1995. ISBN 0-679-87063-6 Subj: Poetry.

Ford, Bernette G. *Bright eyes, brown skin* (Hudson, Cheryl Willis)

Ford, Christine. *Snow!* ill. by Candace Whitman. HarperCollins, 1999. ISBN 0-694-01199-1 Subj: Activities – playing. Family life. Seasons – winter. Weather – snow.

Ford, George Cephas. *Walk on!* (Williamson, Mel)

Ford, June. *A child's garden of verses* (Stevenson, Robert Louis)

Ford, Juwanda G. *K is for Kwanzaa: a Kwanzaa alphabet book* ill. by Ken Wilson-Max. Scholastic, 1997. ISBN 0-590-92200-9 Subj: ABC books. Ethnic groups in the U.S. – African Americans. Holidays – Kwanzaa.

Ford, Lauren. *The ageless story* ill. by author. Dodd, 1939. Subj: Caldecott award honor books.

Ford, Miela. *Follow the leader* photos by author. Greenwillow, 1996. ISBN 0-688-14655-4 Subj: Activities – playing. Animals – polar bears.

Mom and me ill. by author. Greenwillow, 1998. ISBN 0-688-15890-0 Subj: Activities – playing. Animals – polar bears. Family life – mothers. Foreign lands – Arctic.

My day in the garden ill. by Anita Lobel. Greenwillow, 1999. ISBN 0-688-15542-1 Subj: Activities – playing. Clothing – costumes. Imagination. Theater. Weather – rain.

Sunflower ill. by Sally Noll. Greenwillow, 1995. ISBN 0-688-13302-9 Subj: Flowers. Gardens, gardening. Nature. Plants.

Watch us play ill. by author. Greenwillow, 1998. ISBN 0-688-15667-X Subj: Activities. Animals – lions. Zoos.

Foreman, Juli. *Great beginnings: the story of God's creation* by Juli Foreman and Tricia Clem; ill. by Kevin Foreman. Thomas More, 1995. ISBN 0-88347-307-0 Subj: Creation. Religion.

Foreman, Michael. *The angel and the wild animal* ill. by author. Atheneum, 1989. ISBN 0-689-31492-2 Subj: Behavior. Family life.

Ben's baby ill. by author. HarperCollins, 1988. ISBN 0-06-021844-4 Subj: Babies. Family life – new sibling.

Cat and canary ill. by author. Dial, 1985. ISBN 0-8037-0137-3 Subj: Animals – cats. Birds – canaries.

Cat in the manger ill. by author. Holt, 2001. ISBN 0-8050-6677-2 Subj: Animals – cats. Holidays – Christmas. Memories, memory. Religion.

Dad! I can't sleep ill. by author. Harcourt, 1995. ISBN 0-15-200307-X Subj: Animals – pandas. Bedtime. Counting, numbers. Family life – fathers. Sleep.

The general (Charters, Janet)

Grandfather's pencil and the room of stories ill. by author. Harcourt, 1994. ISBN 0-15-200061-5 Subj: Activities – storytelling. Activities – writing. Family life – grandfathers.

Jack's fantastic voyage ill. by author. Harcourt, 1992. ISBN 0-15-239496-6 Subj: Boats, ships. Dreams. Family life – grandfathers. Sea and seashore. Weather – storms.

Land of dreams ill. by author. Holt, 1982. ISBN 0-03-062053-8 Subj: Dreams.

The little reindeer ill. by author. Dial, 1997. ISBN 0-8037-2184-6 Subj: Activities – flying. Animals – reindeer. Holidays – Christmas.

Look! Look! ill. by author. Andersen, 1998. ISBN 0-86264-758-4 Subj: Animals. Animals – pandas. Crime.

Moose ill. by author. Pantheon, 1972. Subj: Animals – bears. Animals – moose. Birds – eagles. Violence, nonviolence.

One world ill. by author. Arcade, 1991. ISBN 1-55970-108-0 Subj: Ecology. Sea and seashore.

Panda and the bunyips ill. by author. Schocken, 1987, c1984. ISBN 0-8052-4041-1 Subj: Animals – pandas. Foreign lands – Australia. Mythical creatures.

Panda and the bushfire ill. by author. Prentice-Hall, 1986. ISBN 0-13-648395-X Subj: Animals. Animals – pandas. Fire. Foreign lands – Australia. Mythical creatures.

Panda's puzzle, and his voyage of discovery ill. by author. Bradbury, 1978. ISBN 0-8788-8127-1 Subj: Animals – pandas. Self-concept.

The perfect present ill. by author. Coward McCann, 1967. Subj: Buses. Holidays – Christmas. Santa Claus.

Seal surfer ill. by author. Harcourt, 1996. ISBN 0-15-201399-7 Subj: Animals – seals. Birth. Family life – grandfathers. Handicaps. Sea and seashore.

Surprise! Surprise! ill. by author. Harcourt, 1995. ISBN 0-15-200038-0 Subj: Animals – pandas. Birthdays. Emotions – fear. Family life – mothers.

The two giants ill. by author. Pantheon, 1967. Subj: Behvior – fighting, arguing. Giants.

War and peas ill. by author. Crowell, 1974. ISBN 0-690-00629-2 Subj: Royalty. War.

Forest, Charlotte B. De. *see* DeForest, Charlotte B.

Forest, Heather. *The baker's dozen* ill. by Susan Graber. Harcourt, 1988. ISBN 0-15-200412-2 Subj: Careers – bakers. Folk and fairy tales.

Stone soup retold by Heather Forest; ill. by Susan Gaber. August House, 1998. ISBN 0-8748-3498-8 Subj: Behavior – sharing. Character traits – cleverness. Folk and fairy tales. Food.

The woman who flummoxed the fairies ill. by Susan Gaber. Harcourt, 1990. ISBN 0-15-299150-6 Subj: Fairies. Folk and fairy tales. Food. Foreign lands – Scotland.

Forrester, Victoria. *The magnificent moo* ill. by author. Atheneum, 1983. ISBN 0-689-30954-6 Subj: Animals – bulls, cows. Animals – cats. Noise, sounds.

Oddward ill. by author. Atheneum, 1982. ISBN 0-689-30912-0 Subj: Holidays. Reptiles – snakes.

Poor Gabriella: a Christmas story ill. by Susan Boulet. Atheneum, 1986. ISBN 0-689-31266-0

Subj: Animals – bulls, cows. Holidays – Christmas. Religion.

The touch said hello ill. by author. Atheneum, 1982. ISBN 0-689-30947-3 Subj: Seasons – spring.

Words to keep against the night ill. by author. Atheneum, 1983. ISBN 0-689-30984-8 Subj: Poetry.

Fort, Patrick. *Redbird* ill. by author. Watts, 1988. ISBN 0-531-05746-1 Subj: Activities – flying. Airplanes, airports. Format, unusual.

Forward, Toby. *Ben's Christmas carol* ill. by Ruth Brown. Dutton, 1996. ISBN 0-525-45593-0 Subj: Animals – mice. Behavior – greed. Behavior – sharing. Holidays – Christmas.

Fosberg, John. *Cookie shapes* ill. by author. Simon & Schuster, 1997. ISBN 0-689-81288-4 Subj: Concepts – shape. Format, unusual – board books.

Ice cream colors ill. by author. Little Simon, 1997. ISBN 0-689-81287-6 Subj: Concepts – color. Format, unusual – board books.

Foster, Doris Van Liew. *A pocketful of seasons* ill. by Talivaldis Stubis. Lothrop, 1961. Subj: Behavior – saving things. Seasons.

Tell me, Mr. Owl ill. by Helen Stone. Lothrop, 1957. Subj: Birds – owls. Holidays – Halloween.

Foster, John. *Dragon poems* (Dragon poems)

Foster, Karen Sharp. *Good night my little chicks = Buenas noches mis pollitos* adapt. and ill. by Karen Sharp Foster. First Story Pr., 1997. ISBN 1-890326-12-7 Subj: Bedtime. Birds – chickens. Family life. Foreign languages.

Foster, Marian Curtis. *see* Mariana

Foster, Sally. *A pup grows up* photos by author. Dodd, 1984. ISBN 0-396-08314-5 Subj: Animals – dogs. Pets.

Foulds, Elfrida Vipont. *The elephant and the bad baby* ill. by Raymond Briggs. Coward, 1986, 1969. ISBN 0-698-20039-X Subj: Animals – elephants. Babies. Behavior – stealing. Cumulative tales.

Fournier, Catharine. *The coconut thieves* ill. by Janina Domanska. Scribners, 1964. Subj: Animals. Folk and fairy tales. Foreign lands – Africa.

Fowler, Allan. *The biggest animal ever* ill. with photos. Childrens Pr., 1992. ISBN 0-516-06001-5 Subj: Animals – whales. Sea and seashore.

The biggest animal on land ill. by author. Childrens Pr., 1996. ISBN 0-516-06050-3 Subj: Animals – elephants. Animals – endangered animals.

Corn . . . on and off the cob ill. with photos. Childrens Pr., 1994. ISBN 0-516-06027-9 Subj: Food. Plants.

Cubs and colts and calves and kittens ill. with photos. Childrens Pr., 1991. ISBN 0-516-04913-5 Subj: Animals. Science.

Feeling things ill. with photos. Childrens Pr., 1991. ISBN 0-516-04908-9 Subj: Senses – touching.

Friendly dolphins ill. by author. Childrens Pr., 1997. ISBN 0-516-20428-9 Subj: Animals – dolphins. Animals – whales. Sea and seashore.

Hard-to-see animals ill. by author. Childrens Pr., 1997. ISBN 0-516-20548-X Subj: Animals. Concepts – color.

Hearing things ill. with photos. Childrens Pr., 1991. ISBN 0-516-04909-7 Subj: Senses – hearing.

It could still be a bird ill. with photos. Childrens Pr., 1990. ISBN 0-516-04901-1 Subj: Birds.

Seeing things ill. with photos. Childrens Pr., 1991. ISBN 0-516-04910-0 Subj: Senses – seeing.

Smelling things ill. with photos. Childrens Pr., 1991. ISBN 0-516-04912-7 Subj: Senses – smelling.

So that's how the moon changes shape! ill. by author. Childrens Pr., 1991. ISBN 0-516-04917-8 Subj: Moon. Science.

Spiders are not insects ill. by author. Childrens Pr., 1996. ISBN 0-516-06054-6 Subj: Science. Spiders.

Tasting things ill. with photos. Childrens Pr., 1991. ISBN 0-516-04911-9 Subj: Senses – tasting.

What do you see in a cloud? ill. by author. Childrens Pr., 1996. ISBN 0-516-06056-2 Subj: Concepts – shape. Games. Imagination. Participation. Science. Weather – clouds.

What's the weather today? ill. with photos. Childrens Pr., 1991. ISBN 0-516-04918-6 Subj: Weather.

Fowler, Richard. *Cat's cake* ill. by author. Barron's, 1987. ISBN 0-8120-5878-X Subj: Animals. Behavior – dissatisfaction. Food.

Cat's car ill. by author. Barron's, 1988. ISBN 0-81205-920-4 Subj: Animals. Automobiles.

Cat's story ill. by author. Grosset, 1985. ISBN 0-448-07851-1 Subj: Animals – cats. Format, unusual – board books. Rhyming text.

Happy birthday, Mouse! by Richard Fowler and David Wood; ill. by Richard Fowler. Grosset, 1990. ISBN 0-448-19023-0 Subj: Animals. Animals – mice. Birthdays. Counting, numbers. Format, unusual. Parties.

Honeybee's busy day ill. by author. Harcourt, 1994. ISBN 0-15-200055-0 Subj: Format, unusual – toy and movable books. Insects – bees.

Inspector Smart gets the message! ill. by author. Little, 1983. ISBN 0-316-28983-3 Subj: Birthdays. Mystery stories.

Ladybug on the move ill. by author. Harcourt, 1993. ISBN 0-15-200475-0 Subj: Format, unusual – toy and movable books. Insects – ladybugs.

Little Chick's big adventure ill. by author. Harcourt, 1996. ISBN 0-15-201040-8 Subj: Animals. Behavior – lost. Birds – chickens. Format, unusual – toy and movable books.

Mr. Little's noisy car ill. by author. Grosset, 1986. ISBN 0-448-18977-1 Subj: Animals. Automobiles. Format, unusual – toy and movable books. Noise, sounds.

Mr. Little's noisy fire engine ill. by author. Grosset, 1990. ISBN 0-448-40042-1 Subj: Animals. Careers – firefighters. Format, unusual – toy and movable books. Noise, sounds. Trucks.

Mr. Little's noisy truck ill. by author. Grosset, 1989. ISBN 0-448-19021-4 Subj: Animals. Format, unusual – toy and movable books. Noise, sounds. Trucks.

Pop-up trucks ill. by author. Harcourt, 1998. ISBN 0-15-201681-3 Subj: Format, unusual – toy and movable books. Trucks.

Fowler, Susi Gregg. *Beautiful* ill. by Jim Fowler. Greenwillow, 1998. ISBN 0-688-15112-4 Subj: Death. Emotions – love. Family life – aunts, uncles. Gardens, gardening. Illness.

Circle of thanks ill. by Peter Catalanotto. Scholastic, 1998. ISBN 0-590-10066-1 Subj: Alaska. Animals. Character traits – kindness to animals.

Fog ill. by Jim Fowler. Greenwillow, 1992. ISBN 0-688-10594-7 Subj: Activities – singing. Family life. Music. Weather – fog.

I'll see you when the moon is full ill. by Jim Fowler. Greenwillow, 1994. ISBN 0-688-10830-X Subj: Activities – trading. Family life – fathers. Moon.

When Joel comes home ill. by Jim Fowler. Greenwillow, 1993. ISBN 0-688-11065-7 Subj: Adoption. Babies. Friendship.

When summer ends ill. by Marisabina Russo. Greenwillow, 1989. ISBN 0-688-07606-8 Subj: Seasons.

Fowles, John. *Cinderella* (Perrault, Charles)

Fox, Charles Philip. *Come to the circus* photos by author. Reilly & Lee, 1960. Subj: Circus.

A fox in the house photos by author. Reilly & Lee, 1960. Subj: Animals – foxes.

Mr. Stripes the gopher photos by author. Reilly & Lee, 1962. Subj: Animals. Family life. Seasons.

Fox, Dorothea Warren. *Follow me the leader* ill. by author. Parents, 1968. Subj: Games. Poetry.

Fox, Louisa. *Every Monday in the mailbox* ill. by Jan Naimo Jones. Eerdmans, 1995. ISBN 0-8028-3792-1 Subj: Death. Emotions – grief. Friendship. Letters, cards. Old age.

Fox, Mem. *Because of the bloomers* ill. by Terry Denton. Harcourt, 1998. ISBN 0-15-200250-2 Subj: Animals – bulls, cows. Clothing. Foreign lands – Australia.

A bedtime story ill. by Elivia Savadier. Mondo, 1996. ISBN 1-57255-136-4 Subj: Activities – reading. Bedtime. Family life. Toys.

Boo to a goose ill. by David Miller. Dial, 1998. ISBN 0-8037-2274-5 Subj: Birds – geese. Rhyming text.

Feathers and fools ill. by Nicholas Wilton. Harcourt, 1996. ISBN 0-15-200473-4 Subj: Behavior – sharing. Birds – peacocks, peahens. Birds – swans. War.

Guess what? ill. by Vivienne Goodman. Harcourt, 1990. ISBN 0-15-200452-1 Subj: Witches.

Hattie and the fox ill. by Patricia Mullins. Bradbury, 1987. ISBN 0-02-735470-9 Subj: Animals. Birds – chickens. Cumulative tales. Farms.

Koala Lou ill. by Pamela Lofts. Harcourt, 1989. ISBN 0-15-200502-1 Subj: Animals – koalas. Emotions – love. Family life – mothers.

Night noises ill. by Terry Denton. Harcourt, 1989. ISBN 0-15-200543-9 Subj: Animals – dogs. Birthdays. Night. Noise, sounds. Sleep.

Possum magic ill. by Julie Vivas. Abingdon, 1987. ISBN 0-687-31732-0 Subj: Activities – traveling. Animals – possums. Behavior – wishing. Food. Foreign lands – Australia.

Shoes from grandpa ill. by Patricia Mullins. Watts, 1990. ISBN 0-531-08448-5 Subj: Behavior – growing up. Clothing. Cumulative tales. Family life – grandfathers. Rhyming text.

Sleepy bears ill. by Kerry Argent. Harcourt, 1999. ISBN 0-15-202016-0 Subj: Animals – bears. Lullabies. Rhyming text. Sleep.

Sophie ill. by Aminah Brenda Lynn Robinson. Harcourt, 1994. ISBN 0-15-277160-3 Subj: Birth. Death. Emotions – love. Family life – grandfathers.

The straight line wonder ill. by Marc Rosenthal. Mondo, 1996. ISBN 1-57255-206-9 Subj: Self-concept.

Time for bed ill. by Jane Dyer. Harcourt, 1993. ISBN 0-15-288183-2 Subj: Animals. Bedtime. Family life. Rhyming text.

Tough Boris ill. by Kathryn Brown. Harcourt, 1994. ISBN 0-15-289612-0 Subj: Birds – parakeets, parrots. Pirates.

Wilfrid Gordon McDonald Partridge ill. by Julie Vivas. Kane/Miller, 1985. ISBN 0-916291-04-9 Subj: Behavior – forgetfulness. Old age.

With love, at Christmas ill. by Gary Lippincott. Abingdon, 1988. ISBN 0-687-45863-3 Subj: Character traits – generosity. Death. Holidays – Christmas.

Wombat divine ill. by Kerry Argent. Harcourt, 1996. ISBN 0-15-201416-0 Subj: Animals. Animals – wombats. Holidays – Christmas. Theater.

Zoo-looking ill. by Candace Whitman. Mondo, 1996. ISBN 1-57255-010-4 Subj: Animals. Rhyming text. Zoos.

Fox, Perla. *The Wooodles: stretching your imagination* by Perla Fox and Deborah Lieberman; ill. by Perla Fox. Full Court, 1996. ISBN 0-9645887-5-7 Subj: Activities – making things. Rhyming text.

Fox, Siv Cedering. *The blue horse and other night poems* ill. by Donald Carrick. Seabury Pr., 1979. ISBN 0-8614-3226-0 Subj: Bedtime. Poetry.

The fox went out on a chilly night ill. by Peter Spier. Doubleday, 1961. ISBN 0-385-00231-9 Subj: Animals – foxes. Caldecott award honor books. Folk and fairy tales. Songs.

Fradon, Dana. *Sir Dana - a knight: as told by his trusty armor* ill. by author. Dutton, 1988. ISBN 0-525-44424-6 Subj: Knights. Middle Ages. Museums.

Franceschelli, Christopher. *The bear's cave* (Schindler, Regina)

Francia, Silvia. *Roberta's vacation* ill. by author. Kane/Miller, 1998. ISBN 0-916291-83-9 Subj: Animals – dogs. Friendship. Sea and seashore.

Francis, Anna B. *Pleasant dreams* ill. by author. Holt, 1983. ISBN 0-03-060574-1 Subj: Dreams. Monsters. Toys.

Francis, Frank. *The magic wallpaper* ill. by author. Abelard-Schuman, 1970. ISBN 0-20-071651-4 Subj: Animals. Behavior – lost. Dreams. Imagination.

Natasha's new doll ill. by author. O'Hara, 1971. Subj: Folk and fairy tales. Foreign lands – Russia. Toys – dolls. Witches.

Françoise. *see* Seignobosc, Françoise

Frank, John. *Odds 'n' Ends Alvy* ill. by G. Brian Karas. Four Winds, 1993. ISBN 0-02-735675-2 Subj: Inventions. School.

Frank, Josette. *More poems to read to the very young* ill. by Dagmar Wilson. Random House, 1968. Subj: Poetry.

Poems to read to the very young ill. by Dagmar Wilson. Random House, 1988. ISBN 0-394-99768-9 Subj: Poetry.

Frank, Mary. *The Kingfisher nursery rhyme songbook* (Emerson, Sally)

Frank, Penny. *In the beginning* ill. by Tony Morris. Reader's Digest, 1992. ISBN 0-7459-2608-8 Subj: Creation. Religion.

Frankel, Ben. *Tertius and Pliny* ill. by Emma Chichester Clark. Harcourt, 1992. ISBN 0-15-200604-4 Subj: Friendship. Toys.

Frankel, Bernice. *Half-As-Big and the tiger* ill. by Leonard Weisgard. Watts, 1961. Subj: Animals – deer. Animals – tigers. Character traits – cleverness.

Frankenberg, Lloyd. *Wings of rhyme* ill. by Alan Benjamin. Funk & Wagnalls, 1967. Subj: Nursery rhymes. Poetry.

Franklin, Jonathan. *Don't wake the baby* ill. by author. Farrar, 1991. ISBN 0-374-31826-3 Subj: Babies. Family life – brothers and sisters. Family life – new sibling. Imagination. Sibling rivalry.

Franklin, Kristine L. *The gift* ill. by Barbara Lavallee. Chronicle, 1999. ISBN 0-8118-0447-X Subj: Animals – whales. Old age. Sports – fishing.

The old, old man and the very little boy ill. by Terea D. Shaffer. Atheneum, 1992. ISBN 0-689-31735-2 Subj: Foreign lands – Africa. Friendship. Old age.

When the monkeys came back ill. by Robert Roth. Atheneum, 1994. ISBN 0-689-31807-3 Subj: Animals – monkeys. Ecology. Foreign lands – Costa Rica. Forest, woods. Trees.

Franklin, Paula. *Killian and the dragons* (Company González, Mercé)

Franklin, Sheila. *Egyptian art from the Brooklyn Museum: ABC* (Mayers, Florence Cassen)

The Museum of Fine Arts, Boston: ABC (Mayers, Florence Cassen)

The Museum of Modern Art, New York: ABC (Mayers, Florence Cassen)

The National Air and Space Museum: ABC (Mayers, Florence Cassen)

Frascino, Edward. *My cousin the king* ill. by author. Prentice-Hall, 1985. ISBN 0-13-608423-0 Subj: Animals. Animals – cats. Character traits – cleverness. Character traits – vanity.

Nanny Noony and the dust queen ill. by author. Pippin Pr., 1990. ISBN 0-945912-09-9 Subj: Animals – cats. Farms. Magic. Weather – droughts. Witches.

Nanny Noony and the magic spell ill. by author. Pippin Pr., 1988. ISBN 0-945912-00-5 Subj: Animals – cats. Birds – crows. Farms. Magic. Witches.

Frasconi, Antonio. *See again, say again: a picture book in four languages* ill. by author. Harcourt, 1964. Subj: Foreign languages.

See and say: a picture book in four languages ill. by author. Harcourt, 1955. Subj: Foreign languages.

The snow and the sun = la nieve y el sol: a South American folk rhyme in two languages ill. by author. Harcourt, 1961. ISBN 0-15-276565-4 Subj: Folk and fairy tales. Foreign lands – South America. Foreign languages. Poetry.

Fraser, Ferrin. *Jungle animals* (Buck, Frank)

Fraser, James Howard. *Los Posadas: a Christmas story* ill. by Nick De Grazia. Northland, 1963. Subj: Ethnic groups in the U.S. – Mexican Americans. Foreign lands – Mexico. Holidays – Christmas. Religion.

Fraser, Kathleen. *Adam's world, San Francisco* by Kathleen Fraser and Miriam F. Levy; ill. by Helen D. Hipshman. Albert Whitman, 1971. ISBN 0-8075-0174-3 Subj: City. Ethnic groups in the U.S. – African Americans. Family life.

Fraser, Mary Ann. *Forest fire!* ill. by author. Fulcrum Kids, 1996. ISBN 1-55591-251-6 Subj: Ecology. Fire. Forest, woods.

Fraser, Phyllis Maurine. *Mother Goose* (Mother Goose)

Mother Goose: or, the old nursery rhymes (Mother Goose)

Frasier, Debra. *On the day you were born* ill. by author. Harcourt, 1991. ISBN 0-15-257995-8 Subj: Babies. Birth. Poetry.

Out of the ocean ill. by author. Harcourt, 1998. ISBN 0-15-258849-3 Subj: Family life – mothers. Sea and seashore.

Freedman, Florence B. *Brothers: a Hebrew legend* ill. by Robert Andrew Parker. HarperCollins, 1985. ISBN 0-06-021872-X Subj: Emotions – love. Family life – brothers. Folk and fairy tales. Jewish culture.

Freedman, Russell. *Farm babies* photos by author. Holiday, 1981. ISBN 0-8234-0426-9 Subj: Animals. Farms.

Hanging on: how animals carry their young ill. by author. Holiday, 1977. ISBN 0-8234-0292-4 Subj: Animals. Science.

Tooth and claw: a look at animal weapons photos by author. Holiday, 1980. ISBN 0-8234-0406-4 Subj: Animals. Science.

When winter comes ill. by Pamela Johnson. Dutton, 1981. ISBN 0-525-42583-7 Subj: Animals. Science. Seasons – winter.

Freedman, Sally. *Devin's new bed* ill. by Robin Oz. Albert Whitman, 1986. ISBN 0-8075-1565-5 Subj: Bedtime. Behavior – growing up. Furniture – beds.

Monster birthday party ill. by Diane Dawson. Albert Whitman, 1983. ISBN 0-8075-5259-3 Subj: Birthdays. Monsters. Parties.

Freeman, David. *The nutcracker* (Hoffmann, E. T. A.)

Freeman, Don. *Add-a-line alphabet* ill. by author. Golden Gate, 1968. Subj: ABC books. Animals.

Beady Bear ill. by author. Viking, 1954. ISBN 0-670-15056-8 Subj: Behavior – running away. Toys – bears.

Bearymore ill. by author. Viking, 1976. ISBN 0-670-15174-2 Subj: Animals – bears. Circus. Hibernation.

The chalk box story ill. by author. Lippincott, 1976. ISBN 0-397-31699-2 Subj: Activities – painting. Concepts – color.

Come again, pelican ill. by author. Viking, 1961. Subj: Birds – pelicans. Sea and seashore.

Corduroy ill. by author. Viking, 1968. ISBN 0-670-24133-4 Subj: Clothing. Emotions – love. Ethnic groups in the U.S. – African Americans. Stores. Toys – bears.

Corduroy's birthday (Hennessy, B. G. [Barbara G.])

Corduroy's busy street and Corduroy goes to the doctor ill. by author. Live Oak Media, 1989. ISBN 0-87499-133-1 Subj: Careers – doctors. Communities, neighborhoods. Format, unusual – board books. Toys – bears.

Corduroy's Christmas (Hennessy, B. G. [Barbara G.])

Corduroy's Easter (Hennessy, B. G. [Barbara G.])

Corduroy's Halloween (Hennessy, B. G. [Barbara G.])

Corduroy's party ill. by Lisa McCue. Viking, 1985. ISBN 0-670-80520-3 Subj: Birthdays. Format, unusual – board books. Parties. Toys. Toys – bears.

Cyrano the crow ill. by author. Viking, 1960. Subj: Birds – crows.

Dandelion ill. by author. Viking, 1964. ISBN 0-670-25532-7 Subj: Animals – lions. Character traits – appearance. Parties. Weather – rain.

The day is waiting ill. by author; words by Linda Z. Knab. Viking, 1980. ISBN 0-670-71820-3 Subj: Activities. Rhyming text.

Fly high, fly low ill. by author. Viking, 1957. Subj: Birds. Caldecott award honor books. City.

Forever laughter ill. by author. Golden Gate, 1970. ISBN 0-8746-4058-X Subj: Clowns, jesters. Humor. Royalty. Wordless.

The guard mouse ill. by author. Viking, 1967. ISBN 0-670-35639-5 Subj: Animals – mice. Birthdays. City. Foreign lands – England.

Hattie the backstage bat ill. by author. Viking, 1970. ISBN 0-670-36253-0 Subj: Animals – bats. Theater.

Mop Top ill. by author. Viking, 1955. Subj: Birthdays. Careers – barbers. Hair. Rhyming text.

The night the lights went out ill. by author. Viking, 1958. Subj: Careers. Night. Power failures. Seasons – winter.

Norman the doorman ill. by author. Viking, 1981, c1959. ISBN 0-14-050588-2 Subj: Animals – mice. Art. Museums.

The paper party ill. by author. Viking, 1974. ISBN 0-670-53804-3 Subj: Imagination. Parties. Puppets.

Pet of the Met (Freeman, Lydia)

A pocket for Corduroy ill. by author. Viking, 1978. ISBN 0-670-56172-X Subj: Clothing. Ethnic groups in the U.S. – African Americans. Laundry. Toys – bears.

Quiet! There's a canary in the library ill. by author. Golden Gate, 1969. ISBN 0-516-08737-1 Subj: Birds – canaries. Emotions – embarrassment. Imagination. Libraries.

A rainbow of my own ill. by author. Viking, 1966. ISBN 0-570-58928-4 Subj: Concepts – color. Weather – rainbows.

The seal and the slick ill. by author. Viking, 1974. ISBN 0-670-62659-7 Subj: Animals – seals. Character traits – kindness to animals. Ecology. Oil.

Ski pup ill. by author. Viking, 1963. Subj: Animals – dogs. Foreign lands – Switzerland. Sports – skiing.

Space witch ill. by author. Viking, 1959. ISBN 0-670-65995-9 Subj: Holidays – Halloween. Space and space ships. Witches.

Tilly Witch ill. by author. Viking, 1969. ISBN 0-670-71303-1 Subj: Character traits – meanness. Holidays – Halloween. Witches.

The turtle and the dove ill. by author. Viking, 1964. Subj: Birds – doves. Reptiles – turtles, tortoises.

Will's quill ill. by author. Viking, 1975. ISBN 0-670-76922-3 Subj: Birds – geese. Foreign lands – England. Shakespeare. Theater.

Freeman, Ira Maximilian. *The sun, the moon and the stars* (Freeman, Mae Blacker)

You will go to the moon (Freeman, Mae Blacker)

Freeman, Jean Todd. *Cynthia and the unicorn* ill. by Leonard Weisgard. Norton, 1967. Subj: Holidays – Christmas. Mythical creatures – unicorns. Poetry.

Freeman, Lydia. *Corduroy's day* ill. by Lisa McCue. Viking, 1985. ISBN 0-670-80521-1 Subj: Counting, numbers. Format, unusual – board books. Toys – bears.

Pet of the Met ill. by Don Freeman. Viking, 1953. ISBN 0-670-54875-8 Subj: Animals – mice. Music. Theater.

Freeman, Mae Blacker. *The sun, the moon and the stars* by Mae and Ira Freeman; ill. by René Martin. Rev. ed. Random House, 1979. ISBN 0-394-90110-X Subj: Moon. Science. Stars. Sun.

You will go to the moon by Mae and Ira Freeman; ill. by Lee J. Ames. Rev. ed. Random House, 1971. ISBN 0-394-92340-5 Subj: Moon. Space and space ships.

Freeman, Mylo. *Shanti* (Padt, Maartje)

Fregosi, Claudia. *The happy horse* ill. by author. Greenwillow, 1977. ISBN 0-688-84087-6 Subj: Animals – horses, ponies. Seasons – fall.

The pumpkin sparrow: adapt. from a Korean folktale ill. by author. Morrow, 1977. Subj: Birds – sparrows. Folk and fairy tales. Foreign lands – Korea.

Snow maiden ill. by author. Prentice-Hall, 1979. ISBN 0-13-815340-X Subj: Folk and fairy tales. Foreign lands – Russia.

French, Fiona. *Anancy and Mr. Dry-Bone* ill. by author. Little, 1991. ISBN 0-316-29298-2 Subj: Animals. Clothing. Folk and fairy tales.

The blue bird ill. by author. Walck, 1972. ISBN 0-8098-1194-4 Subj: Birds.

Hunt the thimble ill. by author. Oxford Univ. Pr., 1978. ISBN 0-19279-719-0 Subj: Games. Participation.

King of another country ill. by author. Scholastic, 1993. ISBN 0-590-46369-1 Subj: Folk and fairy tales. Foreign lands – Africa. Royalty – kings.

Little Inchkin ill. by author. Dial, 1994. ISBN 0-8037-1478-5 Subj: Concepts – size. Folk and fairy tales. Foreign lands – Japan. Little people.

Lord of the animals: a Miwok Indian creation myth ill. by author. Millbrook, 1997. ISBN 0-7613-0112-7 Subj: Animals – coyotes. Creation. Folk and fairy tales. Indians of North America – Miwok.

Rise and shine ill. by adapt. Little, 1989. ISBN 0-316-29299-0 Subj: Boats, ships. Religion – Noah. Songs. Weather – floods. Weather – rain.

Snow White in New York ill. by author. Oxford Univ. Pr., 1987. ISBN 0-19-279808-1 Subj: City. Crime. Dwarfs, midgets. Family life – step families.

French, Paul. *see* Asimov, Isaac

French, Vivian. *Caterpillar, caterpillar* ill. by Charlotte Voake. Candlewick, 1995. ISBN 1-56402-206-4 Subj: Family life – grandfathers. Insects – butterflies, caterpillars. Metamorphosis.

Christmas kitten ill. by Chris Fisher. Shaw's Candlewick Pr., 1996. ISBN 0-7636-0046-6 Subj: Animals – cats. Holidays – Christmas. Santa Claus.

A Christmas star called Hannah ill. by Anne Yvonne Gilbert. Candlewick, 1997. ISBN 0-7636-0397-X Subj: Family life – brothers and sisters. Holidays – Christmas. School. Theater.

It's a go-to-the-park day ill. by Clive Scruton. Simon & Schuster, 1992. ISBN 0-671-74477-1 Subj: Animals – moles. Behavior – running away.

Lazy Jack ill. by Russell Ayto. Candlewick, 1995. ISBN 1-56402-130-0 Subj: Behavior. Folk and fairy tales.

Little Ghost ill. by John Prater. Candlewick, 1994. ISBN 1-56402-394-X Subj: Activities – flying. Activities – playing. Ghosts.

Little Tiger finds a friend ill. by Andy Cooke. Candlewick, 1996. ISBN 0-7636-0070-9 Subj: Animals – tigers. Friendship. Kites.

Little Tiger goes shopping ill. by Andy Cooke. Candlewick, 1994. ISBN 1-56402-263-3 Subj: Animals. Animals – tigers. Behavior – sharing.

Molly in the middle ill. by Venice Shone. Candlewick, 1996. ISBN 1-56402-945-X Subj: Concepts – size. Family life – brothers and sisters.

Oh no, Anna! ill. by Alex Ayliffe. Peachtree, 1997. ISBN 1-56145-125-8 Subj: Accidents. Concepts – color. Format, unusual – toy and movable books.

Oliver's fruit salad ill. by Alison Bartlett. Orchard, 1998. ISBN 0-531-30087-0 Subj: Family life – grandfathers. Food.

Oliver's vegetables ill. by Alison Bartlett. Orchard, 1995. ISBN 0-531-09462-6 Subj: Family life – grandparents. Food. Gardens, gardening.

Once upon a picnic (Prater, John)

Once upon a time (Prater, John)

One ballerina two ill. by Jan Ormerod. Lothrop, 1991. ISBN 0-688-10334-0 Subj: Activities – dancing. Ballet. Counting, numbers.

Red Hen and Sly Fox ill. by Sally Hobson. Simon & Schuster, 1995. ISBN 0-689-80010-X Subj: Animals – foxes. Birds – chickens. Character traits – cleverness. Folk and fairy tales.

A song for little toad ill. by Barbara Firth. Candlewick, 1998. ISBN 1-56402-614-0 Subj: Family life. Frogs and toads. Lullabies.

Spider watching ill. by Alison Wisenfeld. Candlewick, 1995. ISBN 1-56402-543-8 Subj: Family life – cousins. Spiders.

The thistle princess ill. by Elizabeth Harbour. Candlewick, 1998. ISBN 0-7636-0307-4 Subj: Folk and fairy tales. Royalty – princesses.

Tiger and the new baby by Vivian French and Rebecca Elgar; ill. by Rebecca Elgar. Kingfisher, 1999. ISBN 0-7534-5198-0 Subj: Animals – tigers. Babies. Family life – brothers and sisters.

Tiger and the temper tantrum by Vivian French and Rebecca Elgar; ill. by Rebecca Elgar. Kingfisher, 1999. ISBN 0-7534-5197-2 Subj: Animals – tigers. Behavior. Emotions – anger. Family life.

Whale journey ill. by Lisa Flather. Zero to Ten, 1998. ISBN 1-84089-022-3 Subj: Animals – whales. Sea and seashore.

Why the sea is salt ill. by Patrice Aggs. Candlewick, 1993. ISBN 1-56402-183-1 Subj: Character traits – generosity. Folk and fairy tales. Foreign lands – Norway. Magic. Sea and seashore.

Freschet, Berniece. *The ants go marching* ill. by Stefan Martin. Scribners, 1973. ISBN 0-684-13250-8 Subj: Activities – picnicking. Counting, numbers. Insects – ants. Poetry.

Bear mouse ill. by Donald Carrick. Scribners, 1973. ISBN 0-684-13320-2 Subj: Animals – mice. Science.

Bernard of Scotland Yard ill. by Gina Freschet. Scribners, 1978. ISBN 0-684-15931-7 Subj: Animals – mice. Foreign lands – England. Mystery stories.

Elephant and friends ill. by Glen Rounds. Scribners, 1978. ISBN 0-684-15530-3 Subj: Animals – elephants. Character traits – cleverness.

Five fat raccoons ill. by Irene Brady. Scribners, 1980. ISBN 0-684-16253-9 Subj: Animals – raccoons.

Furlie Cat ill. by Betsy Lewin. Lothrop, 1986. ISBN 0-688-05918-X Subj: Animals – cats. Behavior – bullying. Emotions – fear.

The little woodcock ill. by Leonard Weisgard. Scribners, 1967. Subj: Birds. Science.

Moose baby ill. by Jim Arnosky. Putnam, 1979. ISBN 0-399-61146-0 Subj: Animals – moose. Science.

The old bullfrog ill. by Roger Antoine Duvoisin. Scribners, 1968. ISBN 0-24101-684-3 Subj: Frogs and toads.

Owl in the garden ill. by Carol Newsom. Lothrop, 1985. ISBN 0-688-04048-9 Subj: Animals. Behavior – stealing. Birds. Birds – owls. Seasons – fall.

Possum baby ill. by Jim Arnosky. Putnam, 1978. ISBN 0-399-61105-3 Subj: Animals – possums.

Turtle pond ill. by Donald Carrick. Scribners, 1971. ISBN 0-684-12326-6 Subj: Reptiles – turtles, tortoises.

The watersnake ill. by Susanne Suba. Scribners, 1979. ISBN 0-684-16112-5 Subj: Reptiles – snakes.

The web in the grass ill. by Roger Antoine Duvoisin. Scribners, 1972. ISBN 0-684-12956-6 Subj: Spiders.

Where's Henrietta's hen? ill. by Lorinda Bryan Cauley. Putnam, 1980. ISBN 0-399-20669-8 Subj: Animals. Birds – chickens. Counting, numbers. Farms.

Wood duck baby ill. by Jim Arnosky. Putnam, 1983. ISBN 0-399-61191-6 Subj: Birds – ducks. Science.

Freudberg, Judy. *Some, more, most* ill. by Richard Hefter. Larousse, 1976. ISBN 0-8847-0023-2 Subj: Concepts.

Susan and Gordon adopt a baby by Judy Freudberg and Tony Geiss; ill. by Joseph Mathieu. Random House, 1992. ISBN 0-394-98341-6 Subj: Adoption. Family life. Puppets.

Fribourg, Marjorie G. *Ching-Ting and the ducks* ill. by Artur Marokvia. Sterling, 1957. Subj: Behavior – growing up. Birds – ducks. Foreign lands – China.

Frieden, Sarajo. *The care and feeding of fish* ill. by author. Houghton Mifflin, 1996. ISBN 0-395-71251-3 Subj: Character traits – being different. Fish.

Friedman, Aileen. *The king's commissioners* ill. by Susan Guevara. Scholastic, 1994. ISBN 0-590-48989-5 Subj: Counting, numbers. Royalty – kings.

Friedman, Ina R. *How my parents learned to eat* ill. by Allen Say. Houghton Mifflin, 1984. ISBN 0-395-35379-3 Subj: Family life. Sailors.

Friedrich, Elizabeth. *Leah's pony* ill. by Michael Garland. Boyds Mills, 1996. ISBN 1-56397-189-5 Subj: Careers – farmers. Poverty. U.S. history. Weather – droughts.

Friedrich, Otto. *The Easter bunny that overslept* (Friedrich, Priscilla)

The marshmallow ghosts (Friedrich, Priscilla)

The wishing well in the woods (Friedrich, Priscilla)

Friedrich, Priscilla. *The Easter bunny that overslept* by Priscilla and Otto Friedrich; ill. by Adrienne Adams. Lothrop, 1957. ISBN 0-688-01541-7 Subj: Holidays – Easter.

The marshmallow ghosts by Priscilla and Otto Friedrich; ill. by Louis Slobodkin. Lothrop, 1960. Subj: Ghosts. Holidays – Halloween.

The wishing well in the woods by Priscilla and Otto Friedrich; ill. by Roger Antoine Duvoisin. Lothrop, 1961. Subj: Animals. Behavior – wishing.

The friendly beasts ill. by Sarah Chamberlain. Dutton, 1991. ISBN 0-525-44773-3 Subj: Animals. Holidays – Christmas. Music. Religion.

The friendly beasts and a partridge in a pear tree ill. by Virginia Parsons; calligraphy by Sheila Waters. Doubleday, 1966. Subj: Holidays – Christmas. Music. Poetry. Religion. Songs.

Friskey, Margaret (Margaret Richards). *Birds we know* ill. with photos. Childrens Pr., 1981. ISBN 0-516-01609-1 Subj: Birds. Science.

Chicken Little, count-to-ten ill. by Katherine Evans. Childrens Pr., 1946. Subj: Counting, numbers.

Indian Two Feet and his eagle feather ill. by John and Lucy Hawkinson. Childrens Pr., 1967. ISBN 0-516-03503-7 Subj: Indians of North America.

Indian Two Feet and his horse ill. by Katherine Evans. Childrens Pr., 1959. ISBN 0-516-03501-0 Subj: Animals – horses, ponies. Indians of North America.

Indian Two Feet and the wolf cubs ill. by John Hawkinson. Childrens Pr., 1971. ISBN 0-516-03506-1 Subj: Animals – wolves. Indians of North America.

Indian Two Feet rides alone ill. by John Hawkinson. Childrens Pr., 1980. ISBN 0-516-03523-1 Subj: Character traits – pride. Indians of North America.

Mystery of the gate sign ill. by Katherine Evans. Childrens Pr., 1958. Subj: Activities – reading. Animals – rabbits.

The perky little pumpkin ill. by Tom Dunnington. Childrens Pr., 1990. ISBN 0-516-03564-9 Subj: Holidays – Halloween.

Seven diving ducks ill. by Jean Morey. Childrens Pr., 1965. ISBN 0-516-03605-X Subj: Birds – ducks. Counting, numbers.

Three sides and the round one ill. by Mary Gehr. Childrens Pr., 1973. ISBN 0-516-03627-0 Subj: Concepts – shape.

Frissen. *Yann and the whale* (Hanze)

Frith, Michael K. *I'll teach my dog 100 words* ill. by P. D. Eastman. Random House, 1973. ISBN 0-394-92692-7 Subj: Animals – dogs. Humor. Rhyming text.

Some of us walk, some fly, some swim ill. by author. Random House, 1971. ISBN 0-394-92325-1 Subj: Animals. Science.

Fritz, Jean. *The good giants and the bad Pukwudgies* ill. by Tomie de Paola. Putnam, 1982. ISBN 0-399-20870-4 Subj: Folk and fairy tales. Giants. Indians of North America – Wampanoag.

Froese, Deborah L. *The wise washerman* ill. by Wang Kui. Hyperion, 1996. ISBN 0-7868-2232-5 Subj: Animals – elephants. Folk and fairy tales. Foreign lands – Burma. Royalty – kings.

A frog he would a-wooing go (folk-song). *Frog went a-courtin'* retold by John Langstaff; ill. by Feodor Rojankovsky. Harcourt, 1955. ISBN 0-15-230214-X Subj: Animals. Caldecott award books. Frogs and toads. Songs.

The frog went a-courting: a musical play in six acts adapt. and ill. by Dominic Catalano. Boyds Mills, 1998. ISBN 1-56397-637-4 Subj: Animals. Foreign lands – Scotland. Frogs and toads. Music. Songs. Theater. Weddings.

Froggie went a courting adapt. and ill. by Marjorie Priceman. Little, 1999. ISBN 0-316-71227-2 Subj: Animals. Frogs and toads. Songs. Weddings.

Froggie went a-courting retold and ill. by Chris Conover. Farrar, 1986. ISBN 0-374-32466-2 Subj: Animals. Frogs and toads. Music. Songs. Weddings.

Mr. Frog went a-courting: discover the secret story adapt. and ill. by Gary Chalk. DK, 1994. ISBN 1-56458-622-7 Subj: Animals. Foreign lands – England. Frogs and toads. Music. Songs. Weddings.

Wendy Watson's frog went a-courting ill. by Wendy Watson. Lothrop, 1990. ISBN 0-688-06540-6 Subj: Animals. Frogs and toads. Music. Songs. Weddings.

Froissart, Bénédicte. *Uncle Henry's dinner guests* ill. by Pierre Pratt. Firefly, 1990. ISBN 1-55037-141-X Subj: Birds – chickens. Clothing. Family life – aunts, uncles.

From King Boggen's hall to nothing-at-all: *a collection of improbable houses and unusual places found in traditional rhymes and limericks* ill. by Blair Lent. Little, 1967. Subj: Animals. Nursery rhymes.

From morn to midnight sel. by Elaine Moss; ill. by Satomi Ichikawa. Crowell, 1977. ISBN 0-690-01394-9 Subj: Poetry.

Froman, Robert. *Angles are easy as pie* ill. by Byron Barton. Crowell, 1976. ISBN 0-690-00916-X Subj: Concepts.

A game of functions ill. by Enrico Arno. Crowell, 1975. ISBN 0-690-00545-8 Subj: Concepts.

Froment, Eugène. *The story of a round loaf* adapt. and ill. by Kathleen Rebek. Prentice-Hall, 1979. ISBN 0-13-850834-8 Subj: Behavior – misbehavior. Foreign lands – France.

Fromm, Lilo. *Muffel and Plums* ill. by author. Macmillan, 1972. Subj: Animals. Wordless.

Frost, Erica. *see* Supraner, Robyn

Frost, Robert. *The runaway* ill. by Glenna Lang. Godine, 1996. ISBN 1-56792-006-3 Subj: Animals – horses, ponies. Emotions – fear. Poetry. Weather – snow.

Stopping by woods on a snowy evening ill. by Susan Jeffers. Dutton, 1978. ISBN 0-525-40115-6 Subj: Forest, woods. Poetry. Seasons – winter.

Fry, Christopher. *The boat that mooed* ill. by Leonard Weisgard. Macmillan, 1965. Subj: Boats, ships. Weather – fog.

The boy and the magic (Colette, Sidonie Gabrielle)

Frye, Dean. *Days of sunshine, days of rain* ill. by Roger Antoine Duvoisin. McGraw-Hill, 1965. Subj: Theater. Weather.

Fuchs, Erich. *Journey to the moon* ill. by author. Delacorte, 1969. Translation of Hier Apollo 11. Subj: Moon. Space and space ships. Wordless.

Fuchshuber, Annegert. *Giant story – Mouse tale: a half picture book* ill. by author. Carolrhoda, 1988. ISBN 0-87614-319-2 Subj: Animals – dormice. Character traits – bravery. Format, unusual – toy and movable books. Friendship. Giants.

Two peas in a pod ill. by author. Millbrook, 1998. ISBN 0-7613-0410-X Subj: Animals. Animals – babies. Birth. Character traits – individuality. Counting, numbers. Multiple births – twins.

The wishing hat ill. by author. Morrow, 1977. Translation of Korbinian mit dem Wunschhut by Elizabeth D. Crawford. ISBN 0-688-32100-3 Subj: Behavior – wishing. Humor. Magic.

Fuge, Charles. *What is stuck* (Hayles, Karen)

Fuhr, Ute. *Bees* (Bees)

Native Americans (Native Americans)

Whales (Whales)

Fujikawa, Gyo. *Are you my friend today?* ill. by author. Random House, 1988. ISBN 0-394-99031-5 Subj: Friendship.

Baby Mother Goose ill. by author. Random House, 1989. ISBN 0-394-89032-9 Subj: Nursery rhymes.

Gyo Fujikawa's A to Z picture book ill. by author. Grosset, 1974. ISBN 0-448-13205-2 Subj: ABC books.

Let's grow a garden ill. by author. Grosset, 1978. ISBN 0-448-14613-4 Subj: Format, unusual – board books. Gardens, gardening.

Millie's secret ill. by author. Grosset, 1978. ISBN 0-448-14726-2 Subj: Animals – dogs. Format, unusual – board books. Wordless.

My favorite thing ill. by author. Grosset, 1978. ISBN 0-448-14727-0 Subj: Activities. Format, unusual – board books. Wordless.

Sam's all-wrong day ill. by author. Grosset, 1982. ISBN 0-448-11755-X Subj: Behavior – bad day.

See what I can be! ill. by author. Grosset, 1990. ISBN 0-448-09257-3 Subj: Format, unusual – board books. Imagination. Self-concept.

Shags finds a kitten ill. by author. Grosset, 1983. ISBN 0-448-16465-5 Subj: Animals – cats. Animals – dogs. Emotions – loneliness.

Surprise! Surprise! ill. by author. Grosset, 1978. ISBN 0-448-14557-X Subj: Activities. Format, unusual – board books.

Ten little babies ill. by author. Random House, 1989. ISBN 0-394-89033-7 Subj: Babies. Counting, numbers. Rhyming text.

That's not fair! ill. by author. Grosset, 1983. ISBN 0-448-16466-3 Subj: Activities – playing. Seasons – winter.

Fujita, Miho. *The little choo-choo: sounds, sights and opposites* ill. by author. Doubleday, 1988. ISBN 0-385-24426-6 Subj: Concepts – opposites. Format, unusual – board books. Noise, sounds. Toys – trains.

Fujita, Tamao. *The boy and the bird* trans. from Japanese by Kiyoko Tucker; ill. by Chiyo Ono. HarperCollins, 1972. Subj: Birds. Character traits – freedom. Foreign lands – Japan. Pets.

Fuller, Ted. *Barney the bus* ill. by Pam DeVito. Windswept House, 1989. ISBN 0-932433-49-9 Subj: Buses.

Funai, Mamoru. *Moke and Poki in the rain forest* ill. by author. HarperCollins, 1972. ISBN 0-060-21927-0 Subj: Hawaii. Mythical creatures – menehunes.

Funakoshi, Canna. *One Christmas* ill. by Yohji Izawa. Picture Book Studio, 1990. ISBN 0-88708-140-1 Subj: Holidays – Christmas.

One evening tr. and ill. by Yohji Izawa. Picture Book Studio, 1988. ISBN 0-88708-063-4 Subj: Night. Seasons – winter. Weather – snow.

One morning ill. by Yohji Izawa. Picture Book Studio, 1986. ISBN 0-88707-033-2 Subj: Animals – cats. Morning.

Funazaki, Yasuko. *Baby owl* ill. by Shuji Tateishi. Methuen, 1980. ISBN 0-416-30721-3 Subj: Birds – owls. Emotions – loneliness.

Funk, Tom (Thompson). *I read signs* ill. by author. Holiday, 1962. Subj: Activities – reading.

Furchgott, Terry. *Phoebe and the hot water bottles* by Terry Furchgott and Linda Dawson; ill. by Terry Furchgott. Elsevier-Dutton, 1979. ISBN 0-233-96860-1 Subj: Animals – dogs. Character traits – bravery. Pets.

Furtado, Jo. *Sorry, Miss Folio!* ill. by Frederic Joos. Kane/Miller, 1988. ISBN 0-916291-18-9 Subj: Activities – reading. Imagination. Libraries.

Fussenegger, Gertrud. *Noah's ark* ill. by Annegert Fuchshuber; trans. by Anthea Bell. Lippincott, 1987. Tr. of Die Arche Noah by Anthea Bell. ISBN 0-397-32242-9 Subj: Animals. Boats, ships. Religion – Noah. Weather – floods. Weather – rain. Weather – rainbows.

Futamata, Eigoro. *How not to catch a mouse* ill. by author. Weatherhill, 1972. Translation of Nezumi wa tsukamaru ka. ISBN 0-8348-2007-2 Subj: Animals. Animals – mice.

Fyleman, Rose. *A fairy went a-marketing* ill. by Jamichael Henterly. Dutton, 1986. ISBN 0-525-44258-8 Subj: Character traits – kindness. Fairies. Poetry. Shopping.

Gabel, Susan L. *Where the sun kisses the sea* ill. by Joanne Bowring. Perspectives Pr., 1989. ISBN 0-944934-00-5 Subj: Adoption. Ethnic groups in the U.S. – Asian Americans. Orphans.

Gabler, Mirko. *The alphabet soup* ill. by author. Holt, 1992. ISBN 0-8050-2049-7 Subj: ABC books. Activities – cooking. Food. Multiple births – twins. Witches.

Brakus, Krakus . . . Or the incredible adventure of Mr. Skola's Tourist Club ill. by author. Holt, 1993. ISBN 0-8050-1963-4 Subj: Castles. Ghosts. Magic. School.

Gackenbach, Dick. *Alice's special room* ill. by author. Houghton Mifflin, 1991. ISBN 0-395-54433-5 Subj: Family life – mothers.

Annie and the mud monster ill. by author. Lothrop, 1982. ISBN 0-688-00792-9 Subj: Parties.

Arabella and Mr. Crack ill. by author. Macmillan, 1982. A retelling of Joseph Jacob's Master of all masters. ISBN 0-02-735770-8 Subj: Behavior – misunderstanding. Folk and fairy tales.

A bag full of pups ill. by author. Houghton Mifflin, 1981. ISBN 0-395-30081-9 Subj: Animals – dogs.

Barker's crime ill. by author. Harcourt, 1996. ISBN 0-15-200628-1 Subj: Animals – dogs. Behavior – greed. Food. Senses – smelling. Shadows.

Beauty, brave and beautiful ill. by author. Clarion, 1990. ISBN 0-395-52000-2 Subj: Animals – dogs. Character traits – bravery.

Binky gets a car ill. by author. Houghton Mifflin, 1983. ISBN 0-89919-144-4 Subj: Behavior – carelessness. Birthdays.

Claude and Pepper ill. by author. Coward, 1976. ISBN 0-816-43157-4 Subj: Animals – dogs. Behavior – running away.

Claude has a picnic ill. by author. Clarion, 1993. ISBN 0-395-61161-X Subj: Activities – picnicking. Animals – dogs. Communities, neighborhoods.

Claude the dog ill. by author. Seabury Pr., 1974. ISBN 0-816-43116-7 Subj: Animals – dogs. Behavior – sharing. Holidays – Christmas.

Crackle, Gluck and the sleeping toad ill. by author. Seabury Pr., 1979. ISBN 0-816-43227-9 Subj: Behavior – lying. Farms. Frogs and toads.

The dog and the deep dark woods ill. by author. HarperCollins, 1984. ISBN 0-06-021978-5 Subj: Animals – dogs. Character traits – pride.

Dog for a day ill. by author. Clarion, 1987. ISBN 0-899-19452-4 Subj: Animals – dogs. Machines.

Harry and the terrible whatzit ill. by author. Seabury Pr., 1977. ISBN 0-816-43182-5 Subj: Emotions – fear. Imagination. Monsters.

Harvey, the foolish pig ill. by author. Clarion, 1988. ISBN 0-89919-540-7 Subj: Animals – pigs. Animals – wolves. Character traits – foolishness. Character traits – luck. Royalty – kings.

Hattie be quiet, Hattie be good ill. by author. HarperCollins, 1977. ISBN 0-06-021952-1 Subj: Animals – rabbits. Behavior. Illness.

Hattie rabbit ill. by author. HarperCollins, 1976. ISBN 0-06-021940-8 Subj: Animals – rabbits. Behavior – wishing.

Hurray for Hattie Rabbit! ill. by author. HarperCollins, 1986. ISBN 0-06-021983-1 Subj: Animals – pigs. Animals – rabbits. Family life – mothers.

Ida Fanfanny ill. by author. HarperCollins, 1978. ISBN 0-06-021954-8 Subj: Magic. Seasons. Weather.

King Wacky ill. by author. Crown, 1984. ISBN 0-517-55265-5 Subj: Behavior – misunderstanding. Royalty – kings.

Little bug ill. by author. Houghton Mifflin, 1981. ISBN 0-395-30080-0 Subj: Behavior – seeking better things. Insects.

Mag the magnificent ill. by author. Clarion, 1985. ISBN 0-89919-339-0 Subj: Imagination. Monsters.

Mighty tree ill. by author. Harcourt, 1992. ISBN 0-15-200519-6 Subj: Nature. Trees.

Mr. Wink and his shadow, Ned ill. by author. HarperCollins, 1983. ISBN 0-06-021974-2 Subj: Shadows.

Mother Rabbit's son Tom ill. by author. Harper-Collins, 1978. ISBN 0-06-021948-3 Subj: Animals – rabbits. Behavior – dissatisfaction. Food. Pets.

Pepper and all the legs ill. by author. Seabury Pr., 1978. ISBN 0-8164-3221-X Subj: Animals – dogs. Behavior – misbehavior.

The perfect mouse: a Japanese tale ill. by author. Macmillan, 1984. ISBN 0-02-736760-6 Subj: Animals – mice. Folk and fairy tales. Foreign lands – Japan.

The pig who saw everything ill. by author. Seabury Pr., 1978. ISBN 0-816-43205-8 Subj: Animals – pigs. Character traits – curiosity. Farms. Humor.

Poppy the panda ill. by author. Houghton Mifflin, 1984. ISBN 0-89919-276-9 Subj: Bedtime. Clothing. Toys.

Supposes ill. by author. Harcourt, 1989. ISBN 0-15-200594-3 Subj: Animals. Imagination. Riddles.

Tiny for a day ill. by author. Clarion, 1993. ISBN 0-395-65616-8 Subj: Concepts – size. Inventions.

What's Claude doing? ill. by author. Houghton Mifflin, 1984. ISBN 0-89919-244-6 Subj: Animals – dogs. Illness.

Where are Momma, Poppa, and Sister June? ill. by author. Clarion, 1994. ISBN 0-395-67323-2 Subj: Behavior – worrying. Family life.

With love from Gran ill. by author. Houghton Mifflin, 1989. ISBN 0-89919-842-2 Subj: Activities – traveling. Family life – grandmothers.

Gadsby, Oliver. *Little Elephant and Big Mouse* (Cantieni, Benita)

The moon lake (Gantschev, Ivan)

Gaeddert, LouAnn Bigge. *Noisy Nancy Norris* ill. by Gioia Fiammenghi. Doubleday, 1965. Subj: Behavior. Noise, sounds.

Gaffington, Urslan Judith. *Silver berries and Christmas magic* ill. by Steven Morris. RiverMoon Books, 1996. ISBN 0-9647811-0-7 Subj: Holidays – Christmas. Magic. Santa Claus.

Gaffney, Michael. *Secret forests* ill. by author. Western, 1994. ISBN 0-307-17505-7 Subj: Animals. Forest, woods. Insects.

Gág, Flavia. *Chubby's first year* ill. by author. Holt, 1960. Subj: Animals – cats. Days of the week, months of the year.

Gág, Wanda. *ABC bunny* ill. by author; hand lettered by Howard Gág. Coward, 1978, c1933. ISBN 0-698-20465-4 Subj: ABC books. Animals – rabbits. Rhyming text.

The earth gnome (Grimm, Jacob)

The funny thing ill. by author. Coward, 1929. ISBN 0-698-30087-1 Subj: Dragons. Food. Monsters.

Gone is gone ill. by author. Coward, 1935. ISBN 0-698-30179-X Subj: Activities – working. Behavior – mistakes. Gender roles.

Jorinda and Joringel (Grimm, Jacob)

Millions of cats ill. by author. Coward, 1928. ISBN 0-698-20091-8 Subj: Animals – cats. Character traits – practicality. Cumulative tales.

Nothing at all ill. by author. Coward, 1941. ISBN 0-698-30264-8 Subj: Animals – dogs. Caldecott award honor books. Emotions – loneliness. Magic.

The six swans (Grimm, Jacob)

Snippy and Snappy ill. by author. Coward, 1931. ISBN 0-698-30319-9 Subj: Animals – mice.

The sorcerer's apprentice ill. by Margot Tomes. Coward, 1979. ISBN 0-698-20481-6 Subj: Behavior – misbehavior. Folk and fairy tales. Magic.

Gage, Wilson. *Anna's garden songs* ill. by Lena Castell Anderson. Greenwillow, 1989. ISBN 0-688-08218-1 Subj: Gardens, gardening. Plants. Poetry.

Anna's summer songs ill. by Lena Castell Anderson. Greenwillow, 1988. ISBN 0-688-07181-3 Subj: Plants. Poetry. Seasons – summer.

The crow and Mrs. Gaddy ill. by Marylin Hafner. Greenwillow, 1984. ISBN 0-688-02536-6 Subj: Behavior – trickery. Birds – crows.

Cully Cully and the bear ill. by James Stevenson. Greenwillow, 1983. ISBN 0-688-01769-X Subj: Animals – bears. Sports – hunting.

Down in the boondocks ill. by Glen Rounds. Greenwillow, 1977. ISBN 0-688-84085-X Subj: Crime. Handicaps – deafness. Rhyming text.

Mrs. Gaddy and the fast-growing vine ill. by Marylin Hafner. Greenwillow, 1985. ISBN 0-688-04232-5 Subj: Animals – goats. Behavior – seeking better things. Gardens, gardening.

Mrs. Gaddy and the ghost ill. by Marylin Hafner. Greenwillow, 1979. ISBN 0-688-84179-1 Subj: Ghosts. Imagination.

Gál, László. *The parrot: an Italian folktale* retold and ill. by László and Raffaella Gál. Groundwood, 1997. ISBN 0-8889-9287-4 Subj: Birds – parakeets, parrots. Folk and fairy tales. Foreign lands – Italy. Royalty – princes. Royalty – princesses.

Gál, Raffaella. *The parrot: an Italian folktale* (Gál, László)

Galassi, Jonathan. *A boy named Giotto* (Guarnieri, Paolo)

Galbraith, Kathryn Osebold. *Katie did!* ill. by Ted Ramsey. Atheneum, 1982. ISBN 0-689-50237-0 Subj: Behavior – misbehavior. Family life. Sibling rivalry.

Laura Charlotte ill. by Floyd Cooper. Putnam, 1990. ISBN 0-399-21613-8 Subj: Family life – mothers. Toys.

Look! Snow! ill. by Nina Montezinos. Margaret K. McElderry, 1992. ISBN 0-689-50551-5 Subj: Weather – snow.

Roommates ill. by Mark Graham. Macmillan, 1990. ISBN 0-689-50487-X Subj: Babies. Behavior – growing up. Family life – sisters. Sibling rivalry.

Spots are special ill. by Diane Dawson. Atheneum, 1976. ISBN 0-689-50038-6 Subj: Illness. Imagination.

Waiting for Jennifer ill. by Irene Trivas. Macmillan, 1987. ISBN 0-689-50430-6 Subj: Babies. Behavior – secrets. Family life – new sibling. Family life – sisters.

Galbraith, Richard. *Reuben runs away* ill. by author. Watts, 1989. ISBN 0-531-08390-X Subj: Behavior – running away. Toys – bears.

Galchutt, David. *There was magic inside* ill. by author. Simon & Schuster, 1993. ISBN 0-671-75978-7 Subj: Careers – fishermen. Dragons. Folk and fairy tales. Magic.

Galdone, Joanna. *Amber day* ill. by Paul Galdone. McGraw-Hill, 1978. ISBN 0-07-022686-5 Subj: Devil. Folk and fairy tales.

Gertrude, the goose who forgot ill. by Paul Galdone. Watts, 1975. ISBN 0-531-02735-X Subj: Behavior – forgetfulness. Birds – geese. Rhyming text.

Honeybee's party ill. by Paul Galdone. Watts, 1972. Subj: Insects – bees. Parties. Spiders.

The little girl and the big bear ill. by Paul Galdone. Houghton Mifflin, 1980. ISBN 0-395-29029-5 Subj: Animals – bears. Folk and fairy tales.

The tailypo: a ghost story ill. by Paul Galdone. Seabury Pr., 1977. ISBN 0-8164-3191-4 Subj: Ghosts.

Galdone, Paul. *The amazing pig: an old Hungarian tale* ill. by author. Houghton Mifflin, 1981. ISBN 0-395-29101-1 Subj: Animals – pigs. Folk and fairy tales. Royalty.

Androcles and the lion ill. by author. McGraw-Hill, 1970. Subj: Animals – lions. Character traits – helpfulness. Character traits – kindness to animals. Folk and fairy tales. Foreign lands – Italy.

Cat goes fiddle-i-fee ill. by adapt. Clarion, 1985. ISBN 0-89919-336-6 Subj: Animals. Cumulative tales. Farms. Noise, sounds. Nursery rhymes.

Counting carnival (Ziner, Feenie)

The first seven days ill. by author. Crowell, 1962. Subj: Religion.

The frog prince (Grimm, Jacob)

The greedy old fat man: an American folk tale ill. by author. Houghton Mifflin, 1983. ISBN 0-89919-188-6 Subj: Cumulative tales. Folk and fairy tales.

Hans in luck (Grimm, Jacob)

King of the cats: a ghost story by Joseph Jacobs; ill. by adapt. Houghton Mifflin, 1980. ISBN 0-395-29100-3 Subj: Animals – cats. Folk and fairy tales. Ghosts.

The life of Jack Sprat, his wife and his cat (Jack Sprat)

Little Bo-Peep ill. by author. Ticknor & Fields, 1986. ISBN 0-89919-395-1 Subj: Animals – sheep. Nursery rhymes.

The magic porridge pot ill. by author. Seabury Pr., 1976. ISBN 0-816-43173-6 Subj: Behavior – forgetfulness. Behavior – sharing. Folk and fairy tales. Food. Magic.

The monkey and the crocodile: a Jataka tale from India ill. by author. Seabury Pr., 1969. ISBN 0-395-28806-1 Subj: Animals – monkeys. Character traits – cleverness. Folk and fairy tales. Foreign lands – India. Reptiles – alligators, crocodiles.

The monster and the tailor: a ghost story ill. by author. Houghton Mifflin, 1982. An adaptation of Joseph Jacobs' The sprightly tailor. ISBN 0-89919-116-9 Subj: Careers – tailors. Ghosts. Monsters. Royalty.

Obedient Jack ill. by author. Watts, 1971. ISBN 0-531-01970-5 Subj: Behavior – mistakes. Family life. Folk and fairy tales.

Over in the meadow: an old nursery counting rhyme (Over in the meadow)

Rumpelstiltskin (Grimm, Jacob)

A strange servant: a Russian folktale trans. by Blanche Ross; ill. by author. Knopf, 1977. ISBN 0-394-93453-9 Subj: Animals – rabbits. Behavior – trickery. Folk and fairy tales. Foreign lands – Russia.

The table, the donkey and the stick (Grimm, Jacob)

The teeny-tiny woman: a ghost story ill. by adapt. Clarion, 1984. ISBN 0-89919-270-X Subj: Emotions. Folk and fairy tales. Ghosts.

The three sillies (Jacobs, Joseph)

What's in fox's sack? ill. by author. Houghton Mifflin, 1982. ISBN 0-89919-062-6 Subj: Character traits – cleverness. Folk and fairy tales.

Galea'i Fa'apouli, Sano M. *My days are made of butterflies* (Martin, Bill [William Ivan])

Galinsky, Ellen. *The baby cardinal* photos by author. Putnam, 1977. ISBN 0-399-20596-9 Subj: Birds – cardinals.

Gallant, Kathryn. *The flute player of Beppu* ill. by Kurt Wiese. Coward, 1960. Subj: Character traits – honesty.

Gallaudet Pre-school Signed English Project. *Nursery rhymes from Mother Goose in signed English* (Mother Goose)

Gallaz, Christophe. *Threadbear* ill. by Gabrielle Vincent; trans. by Martin Sokolinsky. Creative Ed., 1993. ISBN 0-88682-630-6 Subj: Careers – toy makers. Emotions. Toys – bears.

Galli, Letizia. *Mona Lisa: the secret of the smile* ill. by author; trans. from Italian by Nicholas B. A. Nicholson. Delacorte, 1996. ISBN 0-385-32108-2 Subj: Art. Careers – artists.

Gallimard Jeunesse (Publisher). *All about time* (Verdet, Andre)

Bees (Bees)

Cars and trucks and other vehicles (Cars and trucks and other vehicles)

Houses (Houses)

Native Americans (Native Americans)

Trains (Trains)

Whales (Whales)

Gallo, Giovanni. *The lazy beaver* ill. by Ermanno Samsa; trans. from Italian by Jane Fior. Putnam, 1983. ISBN 0-399-20965-4 Subj: Activities – working. Animals – beavers.

Gallwey, Kay. *Dancing Daisy* ill. by author. Gollancz, 1994. ISBN 0-575-05843-9 Subj: Activities – dancing. Ballet. Theater.

Galouchko, Annouchka. *Shô and the demons of the deep* ill. by author. Annick, 1995. ISBN 1-55037-398-6 Subj: Bedtime. Dreams. Foreign lands – Japan. Kites.

Gambill, Henrietta D. *Little Christmas animals* ill. by author. Standard, 1994. ISBN 0-7847-0274-8 Subj: Animals. Holidays – Christmas. Religion – Nativity.

Self-control ill. by Kathryn Hutton. Rev. ed. Childrens Pr., 1982. ISBN 0-516-06528-9 Subj: Behavior. Ethnic groups in the U.S. – African Americans.

Gambrell, Jamey. *The story of a boy named Will, who went sledding down the hill* (Kharms, Daniil)

Telephone (Chukovskii, Kornei Ivanovich)

Gamgee, John. *Journey through France* ill. by Martin Camm. Troll, 1994. ISBN 0-8167-2759-7 Subj: Foreign lands – France.

Gammell, Stephen. *Git along, old Scudder* ill. by author. Lothrop, 1983. ISBN 0-688-01677-4 Subj: Old age.

Is that you, winter? ill. by author. Silver Whistle, 1997. ISBN 0-15-201415-2 Subj: Behavior – bad day. Seasons – winter. Weather – snow.

Once upon MacDonald's farm ill. by author. Four Winds, 1981. ISBN 0-590-07792-9 Subj: Animals. Farms.

The story of Mr. and Mrs. Vinegar ill. by author. Lothrop, 1982. ISBN 0-688-00889-5 Subj: Character traits – foolishness. Folk and fairy tales.

Wake up, bear . . . It's Christmas! ill. by author. Morrow, 1990. ISBN 0-688-09934-3 Subj: Animals – bears. Hibernation. Holidays – Christmas. Santa Claus.

Ganeri, Anita. *Animal hideaways* ill. by Halli Verrinder. Little Simon, 1996. ISBN 0-689-80265-X Subj: Animals. Behavior – hiding. Format, unusual – toy and movable books.

The hunt for food ill. by Graham Austin. Millbrook, 1997. ISBN 0-7613-0304-9 Subj: Animals. Food. Nature.

The longest and tallest ill. by Anita Ganeri. Barron's, 1992. ISBN 0-8120-6293-0 Subj: Concepts – measurement.

The story of Christmas ill. by author. DK, 1995. ISBN 0-7894-0146-0 Subj: Holidays – Christmas. Religion – Nativity.

Ganly, Helen. *Jyoti's journey* ill. by author. Dutton, 1986. ISBN 0-233-97899-2 Subj: Family life. Foreign lands – England. Foreign lands – India. Weddings.

Gannett, Ruth Stiles. *Katie and the sad noise* ill. by Ellie Simmons. Random House, 1961. Subj: Animals – dogs. Character traits – kindness. Holidays – Christmas. Noise, sounds.

Gans, Roma. *How do birds find their way?* ill. by Paul Mirocha. HarperCollins, 1996. ISBN 0-06-020225-4 Subj: Activities – traveling. Birds. Nature.

Hummingbirds in the garden ill. by Grambs Miller. Crowell, 1969. Subj: Birds. Gardens, gardening. Seasons – summer.

Let's go rock collecting ill. by Holly Keller. HarperCollins, 1997. ISBN 0-06-027283-X Subj: Behavior – collecting things. Rocks.

Rock collecting ill. by Holly Keller. Crowell, 1984. ISBN 0-690-04266-3 Subj: Behavior – collecting things. Rocks. Science.

When birds change their feathers ill. by Felicia Bond. Crowell, 1980. ISBN 0-690-03948-4 Subj: Birds. Science.

Gant, Elizabeth. *Little Red Riding Hood* (Grimm, Jacob)

Gant, Katherine. *Little Red Riding Hood* (Grimm, Jacob)

Gantos, Jack (John, Jr.). *Aunt Bernice* ill. by Nicole Rubel. Houghton Mifflin, 1978. ISBN 0-395-26461-8 Subj: Behavior – carelessness. Family life – aunts, uncles.

Back to school for Rotten Ralph ill. by Nicole Rubel. HarperCollins, 1998. ISBN 0-06-027532-4 Subj: Animals – cats. Character traits – selfishness. Emotions – envy, jealousy. Emotions – fear. Friendship. School – first day.

Greedy Greeny ill. by Nicole Rubel. Doubleday, 1979. ISBN 0-385-14686-8 Subj: Dreams. Monsters.

Happy birthday, Rotten Ralph ill. by Nicole Rubel. Houghton Mifflin, 1990. ISBN 0-395-53766-5 Subj: Animals – cats. Behavior – misbehavior. Birthdays.

Not so Rotten Ralph ill. by Nicole Rubel. Houghton Mifflin, 1994. ISBN 0-395-62302-2 Subj: Animals – cats. Behavior – misbehavior. School.

The perfect pal ill. by Nicole Rubel. Houghton Mifflin, 1979. ISBN 0-395-28380-9 Subj: Animals. Pets.

Rotten Ralph ill. by Nicole Rubel. Houghton Mifflin, 1976. ISBN 0-395-24276-2 Subj: Animals – cats. Behavior – misbehavior.

Rotten Ralph's Halloween howl ill. by Nicole Rubel. HarperFestival, 1998. ISBN 0-694-00985-7 Subj: Animals – cats. Holidays – Halloween. Monsters.

Rotten Ralph's rotten Christmas ill. by Nicole Rubel. Houghton Mifflin, 1984. ISBN 0-395-35380-7 Subj: Animals – cats. Character traits – meanness. Emotions – envy, jealousy. Holidays – Christmas.

Rotten Ralph's rotten romance ill. by Nicole Rubel. Houghton Mifflin, 1997. ISBN 0-395-73978-0 Subj: Animals – cats. Behavior – misbehavior. Holidays – Valentine's Day. Parties.

Rotten Ralph's show and tell ill. by Nicole Rubel. Houghton Mifflin, 1989. ISBN 0-395-44312-1 Subj: Animals – cats. Character traits – meanness. School.

Rotten Ralph's trick or treat ill. by Nicole Rubel. Houghton Mifflin, 1986. ISBN 0-395-38943-7 Subj: Animals – cats. Character traits – meanness. Holidays – Halloween.

Swampy alligator ill. by Nicole Rubel. Windmill, 1980. ISBN 0-671-96092-X Subj: Birthdays. Character traits – cleanliness. Reptiles – alligators, crocodiles.

Wedding bells for Rotten Ralph ill. by Nicole Rubel. HarperCollins, 1999. ISBN 0-06-027534-0 Subj: Animals – cats. Behavior – misbehavior. Weddings.

The werewolf family ill. by Nicole Rubel. Houghton Mifflin, 1980. ISBN 0-395-28760-X Subj: Monsters.

Worse than Rotten Ralph ill. by Nicole Rubel. Houghton Mifflin, 1978. ISBN 0-395-28106-1 Subj: Animals – cats. Behavior – misbehavior. Character traits – meanness.

Gantschev, Ivan. *The Christmas teddy bear* adapt. by Andrew Clements; ill. by Ivan Gantschev. North-South, 1994. ISBN 1-55858-348-3 Subj: Behavior – lost. Family life – grandfathers. Holidays – Christmas. Toys – bears. Weather – snow. Weather – storms.

The Christmas train ill. by author; trans. from German by Karen M. Klockner. Little, 1984. ISBN 0-316-30346-1 Subj: Character traits – bravery. Holidays – Christmas. Trains.

Good morning, good night ill. by author; adapt. by Andrew Clements. Picture Book Studio, 1991. ISBN 0-88708-183-5 Subj: Friendship. Moon. Sun.

Journey of the storks ill. by author. Alphabet Pr., 1983. ISBN 0-907234-27-5 Subj: Birds – storks.

The moon lake trans. by Oliver Gadsby; ill. by author. Alphabet Pr., 1981. ISBN 0-907234-08-9 Subj: Behavior – greed. Careers – shepherds. Lakes, ponds. Moon.

Otto the bear trans. from German by Karen M. Klockner; ill. by author. Little, 1986. ISBN 0-316-30348-8 Subj: Animals – bears. Character traits – kindness to animals.

RumpRump ill. by author. Alphabet Pr., 1984. ISBN 0-907234-53-4 Subj: Animals – bears. Food. Friendship.

Santa's favorite story (Aoki, Hisako)

The train to Grandma's ill. by author. Picture Book Studio, 1987. ISBN 0-88708-053-7 Subj: Activities – traveling. Family life – grandparents. Format, unusual. Islands. Trains.

Where is Mr. Mole? adapt. by Andrew Clements; ill. by author. Picture Book Studio, 1989. ISBN 0-88708-109-6 Subj: Animals – moles. Behavior – seeking better things. Birds – owls. Format, unusual.

Where the moon lives ill. by author. North-South, 1998. ISBN 1-55858-921-X Subj: Behavior – sharing. Birds – ducks. Birds – swans. Format, unusual – toy and movable books. Moon.

Gantz, David. *Captain Swifty counts to 50* ill. by author. Doubleday, 1982. ISBN 0-385-17527-2 Subj: Counting, numbers.

The genie bear with the light brown hair word book ill. by author. Doubleday, 1982. ISBN 0-385-17528-0 Subj: ABC books. Animals – bears. Animals – mice.

Ganz, Yaffa. *The story of Mimmy and Simmy* ill. by Harvey Klineman. Feldheim, 1985. ISBN 0-87306-385-6 Subj: Behavior – seeking better things. Emotions – envy, jealousy. Jewish culture.

Garaway, Margaret Kahn. *Ashkii and his grandfather* ill. by Harry Warren. Treasure Chest, 1989. ISBN 0-918080-41-X Subj: Careers – shepherds. Family life – grandfathers. Indians of North America – Navajo.

Garay, Luis. *The long road* ill. by author. Tundra, 1997. ISBN 0-88776-408-8 Subj: Activities – traveling. Foreign lands – Canada. Immigrants.

Pedrito's day ill. by author. Orchard, 1997. ISBN 0-531-09522-3 Subj: Foreign lands – Latin America. Poverty. Toys.

Garbutt, Bernard. *Roger, the rosin back* ill. by author. Hastings House, 1961. Subj: Animals – horses, ponies. Circus.

Garcia, Carolyn. *Moonboy* ill. by author. Beyond Words, 1999. ISBN 1-885223-81-1 Subj: Character traits – being different. Friendship. Moon.

García, Cheo. *Pick a pet* (Rotner, Shelley)

García Lorca, Federico. *The Lieutenant Colonel and the gypsy* tr. and ill. by Marc Simont. Doubleday, 1971. Subj: Foreign lands – Spain. Gypsies. Poetry.

Gardam, Catharine. *The animals' Christmas* ill. by Gavin Rowe. Macmillan, 1990. ISBN 0-689-50502-7 Subj: Animals. Holidays – Christmas.

Gardella, Tricia. *Just like my dad* ill. by Margot Apple. HarperCollins, 1993. ISBN 0-06-021938-6 Subj: Cowboys. Family life – fathers.

Gardner, Beau. *Can you imagine . . . ? a counting book* ill. by author. Dodd, 1987. ISBN 0-396-09001-X Subj: Animals. Counting, numbers.

Guess what? ill. by author. Lothrop, 1985. ISBN 0-688-04983-4 Subj: Animals. Concepts – shape. Games.

Have you ever seen . . . ? an ABC book ill. by author. Dodd, 1986. ISBN 0-396-08825-2 Subj: ABC books. Humor.

The look again . . . and again, and again, and again book ill. by author. Lothrop, 1984. ISBN 0-688-03806-9 Subj: Optical illusions.

The turn about, think about, look about book ill. by author. Lothrop, 1980. ISBN 0-688-51969-5 Subj: Optical illusions.

What is it? ill. by author. Putnam, 1989. ISBN 0-399-21664-2 Subj: Concepts – shape. Format, unusual – toy and movable books. Games.

Whooo's a fright on Halloween night? ill. by author. Putnam, 1990. ISBN 0-399-22212-X Subj: Format, unusual – toy and movable books. Holidays – Halloween. Rhyming text.

Gardner, Jane Mylum. *Henry Moore: from bones and stones to sketches and sculptures* ill. by author. Four Winds, 1993. ISBN 0-02-735812-7 Subj: Art. Careers – artists.

Gardner, Martin. *Never make fun of a turtle, my son* ill. by John Alcorn. Simon & Schuster, 1969. ISBN 0-671-65033-5 Subj: Etiquette. Poetry.

Gardner, Mercedes. *Scooter and the magic star* by Mercedes and Jean Shannon Smith; ill. by Bob Johnson. Atheneum, 1980. ISBN 0-89742-033-0 Subj: Fairies.

Garelick, May. *Down to the beach* ill. by Barbara Cooney. Four Winds, 1973. Subj: Sea and seashore. Seasons – summer.

Just my size ill. by William Pène du Bois. HarperCollins, 1990. ISBN 0-06-022419-3 Subj: Behavior – growing up. Clothing – coats. Toys – dolls.

Look at the moon ill. by Barbara Garrison. Mondo, 1996. ISBN 1-57255-142-9 Subj: Animals. Moon. Rhyming text.

Look at the moon ill. by Leonard Weisgard. Addison-Wesley, 1969. Subj: Animals. Moon. Rhyming text.

Sounds of a summer night ill. by Beni Montresor. Addison-Wesley, 1963. Subj: Night. Noise, sounds.

The tremendous tree book (Brenner, Barbara A.)

Two orphan cubs (Brenner, Barbara A.)

Where does the butterfly go when it rains? ill. by Leonard Weisgard. Addison-Wesley, 1961. Subj: Insects – butterflies, caterpillars. Rhyming text. Weather – rain.

Where does the butterfly go when it rains? ill. by Nicholas Wilton. Mondo, 1997. ISBN 1-57255-165-8 Subj: Insects – butterflies, caterpillars. Rhyming text. Weather – rain.

Garfinkel, Bernard. *see* Allen, Robert

Garland, Michael. *Angel cat* ill. by author. Boyds Mills, 1998. ISBN 1-56397-726-5 Subj: Angels. Animals – cats. Death. Fires. Pets.

Circus girl ill. by author. Dutton, 1993. ISBN 0-525-45069-6 Subj: Activities – working. Circus. Clowns, jesters. Family life.

The mouse before Christmas ill. by author. Dutton, 1997. ISBN 0-525-45578-7 Subj: Animals – mice. Holidays – Christmas. Rhyming text.

My cousin Katie ill. by author. HarperCollins, 1989. ISBN 0-690-04740-1 Subj: Family life. Farms.

Garland, Sarah. *All gone!* ill. by author. Viking, 1990. ISBN 0-670-83074-7 Subj: Babies. Concepts.

Billy and Belle ill. by author. Viking, 1992. ISBN 0-670-84396-2 Subj: Animals. Babies. Family life – new sibling. Family life – sisters. Pets. School.

Going shopping ill. by author. Little, 1985. ISBN 0-87113-001-7 Subj: Family life. Shopping.

Having a picnic ill. by author. Little, 1985. ISBN 0-87113-002-5 Subj: Activities – picnicking. Birds – ducks. Family life.

Oh, no! ill. by author. Viking, 1990. ISBN 0-670-83075-5 Subj: Babies. Behavior – misbehavior.

Polly's puffin ill. by author. Greenwillow, 1989. ISBN 0-688-08749-3 Subj: Babies. Behavior – losing things. City.

Seeing red ill. by Tony Ross. Kane/Miller, 1996. ISBN 0-916291-64-2 Subj: Clothing. Concepts – color. Folk and fairy tales. Foreign lands – England.

Garland, Sherry. *Goodnight, cowboy* ill. by John Kanzler. Scholastic, 1999. ISBN 0-590-98831-X Subj: Bedtime. Cowboys.

The lotus seed ill. by Tatsuro Kiuchi. Harcourt, 1993. ISBN 0-15-249465-0 Subj: Ethnic groups in the U.S. – Vietnamese Americans. Family life – grandmothers. Foreign lands – Vietnam. War.

My father's boat ill. by Ted Rand. Scholastic, 1998. ISBN 0-590-47867-2 Subj: Boats, ships. Careers – fishermen. Ethnic groups in the U.S. – Vietnamese Americans.

Summer sands ill. by Robert J. Lee. Harcourt, 1995. ISBN 0-15-282492-8 Subj: Ecology. Sand. Sea and seashore.

Why ducks sleep on one leg ill. by Jean and Mou-sien Tseng. Scholastic, 1993. ISBN 0-590-45697-0 Subj: Birds – ducks. Folk and fairy tales. Foreign lands – Vietnam.

Garne, S. T. *By a blazing blue sea* ill. by Lori Lohstoeter. Harcourt, 1999. ISBN 0-15-201780-1 Subj: Careers – fishermen. Concepts – color. Foreign lands – Caribbean Islands. Rhyming text.

Garner, Alan. *Little red hen* (The little red hen)

Once upon a time, though it wasn't in your time, and it wasn't in my time, and it wasn't in anybody else time . . . ill. by Norman Messenger. DK, 1993. ISBN 1-56458-381-3 Subj: Folk and fairy tales.

Garrett, Ann. *Keeper of the swamp* ill. by Karen Chandler. Turtle Books, 1999. ISBN 1-890515-12-4 Subj: Ecology. Family life – grandfathers. Reptiles – alligators, crocodiles. Swamps.

What's for lunch? by Ann Garrett and Gene-Michael Higney; ill. by Stephanie Peterson. Dutton, 1999. ISBN 0-525-46251-1 Subj: Animals. Food. Format, unusual – toy and movable books. Rhyming text.

Garrett, Jennifer. *The queen who stole the sky* ill. by Linda Hendry. North Winds, 1986. ISBN 0-590-71524-0 Subj: Character traits – selfishness. Character traits – stubbornness. Royalty – queens.

Garrison, Barbara. *Josiah True and the art maker* (Littlesugar, Amy)

Garrison, Christian. *The dream eater* ill. by Diane Goode. Dutton, 1978. ISBN 0-8788-8134-4 Subj: Dragons. Dreams. Foreign lands – Japan.

Little pieces of the west wind ill. by Diane Goode. Dutton, 1975. ISBN 0-8788-8105-0 Subj: Cumulative tales. Weather – wind.

Garten, Jan. *The alphabet tale* ill. by Muriel Batherman. Greenwillow, 1994. ISBN 0-688-12703-7 Subj: ABC books. Animals. Participation. Poetry.

Gascoigne, Bamber. *Why the rope went tight* ill. by Christina Gascoigne. Lothrop, 1981. ISBN 0-688-00590-X Subj: Circus.

Gaston, Susan. *New boots for Salvador* ill. by Lydia Schwartz. Ritchie, 1972. ISBN 0-378-62659-0 Subj: Animals – horses, ponies.

Gates, Frieda. *Owl eyes* ill. by Yoshi Miyake. Lothrop, 1994. ISBN 0-688-12473-9 Subj: Birds – owls. Creation. Folk and fairy tales. Indians of North America – Mohawk.

Gauch, Patricia Lee. *Bravo, Tanya* ill. by Satomi Ichikawa. Putnam, 1992. ISBN 0-399-22145-X Subj: Activities – dancing. Ballet. Toys – bears.

Christina Katerina and Fats and the Great Neighborhood War ill. by Stacey Schuett. Putnam, 1997. ISBN 0-399-22651-6 Subj: Communities, neighborhoods. Friendship.

Christina Katerina and the great bear train ill. by Elise Primavera. Putnam, 1990. ISBN 0-399-21623-5 Subj: Babies. Family life – sisters. Toys – bears.

Christina Katerina and the time she quit the family ill. by Elise Primavera. Putnam, 1987. ISBN 0-399-21408-9 Subj: Behavior – needing someone. Family life. Sibling rivalry.

Dance, Tanya ill. by Satomi Ichikawa. Putnam, 1989. ISBN 0-399-21521-2 Subj: Activities – dancing. Ballet. Behavior – imitation. Toys – bears.

The little friar who flew ill. by Tomie de Paola. Putnam, 1980. ISBN 0-399-20714-7 Subj: Folk and fairy tales. Magic. Religion.

Noah ill. by Jonathan Green. Philomel, 1994. ISBN 0-399-22548-X Subj: Animals. Boats, ships. Religion – Noah. Weather – floods. Weather – rain. Weather – rainbows.

On to Widecombe Fair ill. by Trina Schart Hyman. Putnam, 1978. ISBN 0-399-20563-2 Subj: Fairs. Folk and fairy tales. Foreign lands – England.

Once upon a Dinkelsbühl ill. by Tomie de Paola. Putnam, 1977. ISBN 0-399-20560-8 Subj: War.

Presenting Tanya, the Ugly Duckling ill. by Satomi Ichikawa. Philomel, 1999. ISBN 0-399-23200-1 Subj: Activities – dancing. Ballet. Self-concept.

Tanya and Emily in a dance for two ill. by Satomi Ichikawa. Philomel, 1994. ISBN 0-399-22688-5 Subj: Activities – dancing. Ballet. Friendship.

Tanya and the magic wardrobe ill. by Satomi Ichikawa. Philomel, 1997. ISBN 0-399-22940-X Subj: Activities – dancing. Ballet. Clothing – costumes. Theater.

Tanya steps out ill. by Satomi Ichikawa. Philomel, 1996. ISBN 0-399-22936-1 Subj: Activities – dancing. Ballet. Format, unusual – toy and movable books.

Uncle Magic ill. by Deborah Kogan Ray. Holiday, 1992. ISBN 0-8234-0937-6 Subj: Family life – aunts, uncles. Magic.

Gauthier, Bertrand. *Animal capers* (Paré, Roger)

Circus days (Paré, Roger)

Play time (Paré, Roger)

Summer days (Paré, Roger)

Gay, Marie-Louise. *Moonbeam on a cat's ear* ill. by author. Silver Burdett, 1986. ISBN 0-385-09162-0 Subj: Animals – cats. Animals – mice. Bedtime. Dreams. Moon. Night. Rhyming text.

Rainy day magic ill. by author. Albert Whitman, 1989. ISBN 0-8075-6767-1 Subj: Family life. Illness. Imagination. Rhyming text. Weather – rain.

Gay, Michel. *Bibi takes flight* ill. by author. Morrow, 1988. ISBN 0-688-06829-4 Subj: Activities – flying. Airplanes, airports. Birds – penguins.

Bibi's birthday surprise ill. by author. Morrow, 1987. ISBN 0-688-06978-9 Subj: Animals. Birds – penguins. Parties. Royalty. Toys.

The Christmas wolf ill. by author. Greenwillow, 1983. ISBN 0-688-02291-X Subj: Animals – wolves. Holidays – Christmas.

Little auto ill. by author. Macmillan, 1986. ISBN 0-02-737900-0 Subj: Automobiles. Sea and seashore.

Little boat ill. by author. Macmillan, 1985. ISBN 0-02-737540-4 Subj: Boats, ships.

Little helicopter ill. by author. Macmillan, 1986. ISBN 0-02-737920-5 Subj: Character traits – smallness. Helicopters.

Little plane ill. by author. Macmillan, 1985. ISBN 0-02-737500-5 Subj: Airplanes, airports.

Little shoe ill. by author. Macmillan, 1986. ISBN 0-02-737890-X Subj: Behavior – losing things. Clothing – shoes.

Little truck ill. by author. Macmillan, 1985. ISBN 0-02-737520-X Subj: Transportation. Trucks.

Night ride ill. by author. Morrow, 1987. ISBN 0-688-07287-9 Subj: Activities – traveling. Animals. Circus. Family life – fathers. Night.

Rabbit express ill. by author. Morrow, 1985. ISBN 0-688-04648-7 Subj: Animals – cats. Animals – rabbits. Friendship.

Take me for a ride ill. by author. Morrow, 1985. ISBN 0-688-04136-1 Subj: Behavior – lost.

Gay, Tenner Ottley. *Dinosaurs and their relatives in action* ill. by Jean Cassels. Macmillan, 1990. ISBN 0-689-71434-3 Subj: Dinosaurs. Format, unusual – toy and movable books.

Sharks in action ill. by Jean Cassels. Macmillan, 1990. ISBN 0-689-71435-1 Subj: Fish – sharks. Format, unusual – toy and movable books.

Gay, Zhenya. *I'm tired of lions* ill. by author. Viking, 1961. Subj: Animals – lions. Behavior – dissatisfaction.

Look! ill. by author. Viking, 1952. Subj: Animals. Libraries. Poetry.

Small one ill. by author. Viking, 1958. Subj: Animals – rabbits. Behavior – lost.

Who's afraid? ill. by author. Viking, 1965. Subj: Emotions – fear.

Gebert, Warren. *The old ball and the sea* ill. by author. Bradbury, 1988. ISBN 0-02-735821-6 Subj: Activities – playing. Sea and seashore.

Geddes, Anne. *Shapes* ill. by author. Cedco, 1997. ISBN 0-7683-2023-2 Subj: Babies. Clothing – costumes. Concepts – shape.

Gedin, Birgitta. *The little house from the sea* trans. by Elisabeth Kallick Dyssegaard; ill. by Petter Pettersson. Farrar, 1988. ISBN 91-29-58770-0 Subj: Boats, ships. Homes, houses. Sea and seashore. Weather – storms.

Geeslin, Campbell. *How Nanita learned to make flan* ill. by Petra Mathers. Atheneum, 1999. ISBN 0-689-81546-8 Subj: Activities – cooking. Clothing – shoes. Food. Foreign lands – Mexico.

Geis, Jacqueline. *Where the buffalo roam* ill. by adapt. Ideals, 1992. ISBN 0-8249-8584-2 Subj: Animals. Desert. Plants. Poetry.

Geisel, Theodor Seuss. *see* Seuss, Dr.

Geisert, Arthur. *After the flood* ill. by author. Houghton Mifflin, 1994. ISBN 0-395-66611-2 Subj: Animals. Boats, ships. Religion. Weather – rainbows.

The ark ill. by author. Houghton Mifflin, 1988. ISBN 0-395-43078-X Subj: Animals. Boats, ships. Religion – Noah. Weather – floods. Weather – rain.

Oink ill. by author. Houghton Mifflin, 1991. ISBN 0-395-55329-6 Subj: Animals – pigs. Behavior – misbehavior. Noise, sounds.

Oink oink ill. by author. Houghton Mifflin, 1993. ISBN 0-395-64048-2 Subj: Animals – pigs. Behavior – misbehavior. Family life – mothers.

Pigs from 1 to 10 ill. by author. Houghton Mifflin, 1992. ISBN 0-395-58519-8 Subj: Animals – pigs. Counting, numbers. Puzzles.

Prairie town (Geisert, Bonnie)

Geisert, Bonnie. *Prairie town* by Bonnie and Arthur Geisert; ill. by Arthur Geisert. Houghton Mifflin, 1998. ISBN 0-395-85907-7 Subj: City. Communities, neighborhoods. Country. Seasons.

Geiss, Tony. *Susan and Gordon adopt a baby* (Freudberg, Judy)

Gekiere, Madeleine. *The frilly lily and the princess* ill. by author. Lippincott, 1960. Subj: Behavior – fighting, arguing. Royalty – princesses.

Gelbard, Jane. *My bye-bye bottle book* by Jane Gelbard and Betsy Bober Polivy; photos by Arthur J. Klonsky. Grosset, 1989. ISBN 0-448-21526-8 Subj: Babies. Behavior – growing up. Format, unusual – board books. Rhyming text.

My dressing book by Jane Gelbard and Betsy Bober Polivy; photos by Arthur J. Klonsky. Grosset, 1989. ISBN 0-448-21527-6 Subj: Babies. Behavior –

growing up. Clothing. Format, unusual – board books. Rhyming text.

My eating book by Jane Gelbard and Betsy Bober Polivy; photos by Arthur J. Klonsky. Grosset, 1989. ISBN 0-448-21528-4 Subj: Babies. Behavior – growing up. Food. Format, unusual – board books. Rhyming text.

My sharing book by Jane Gelbard and Betsy Bober Polivy; photos by Arthur J. Klonsky. Grosset, 1989. ISBN 0-448-21529-2 Subj: Babies. Behavior – growing up. Behavior – sharing. Format, unusual – board books. Rhyming text.

Gellman, Ellie. *It's Chanukah!* ill. by Katherine Janus Kahn. Kar-Ben Copies, 1985. ISBN 0-930494-51-2 Subj: Format, unusual – board books. Holidays – Hanukkah. Jewish culture.

It's Rosh Hashanah! ill. by Katherine Janus Kahn. Kar-Ben Copies, 1985. ISBN 0-930494-50-4 Subj: Format, unusual – board books. Holidays – Rosh Hashanah. Jewish culture.

Shai's Shabbat walk ill. by Chari R. McLean. Kar-Ben Copies, 1985. ISBN 0-930494-49-0 Subj: Format, unusual – board books. Holidays. Jewish culture.

Gelman, Amy. *Little big feet* (Schubert, Ingrid)

Gelman, Rita Golden. *Hey, kid* ill. by Carol Nicklaus. Watts, 1977. ISBN 0-531-01333-2 Subj: Humor. Rhyming text.

A koala grows up ill. by Gioia Fiammenghi. Scholastic, 1986. ISBN 0-590-30563-8 Subj: Animals – koalas. Foreign lands – Australia. Science.

Splash! all about baths (Buxbaum, Susan Kovacs)

Gelsanliter, Wendy. *Dancin' in the kitchen* by Wendy Gelsanliter and Frank Christian; ill. by Marjorie Priceman. Putnam, 1988. ISBN 0-399-23035-1 Subj: Activities – cooking. Activities – dancing. Family life. Rhyming text.

Gemme, Leila Boyle. *T-ball is our game* photos by Richard Marshall. Childrens Pr., 1978. ISBN 0-516-03630-0 Subj: Sports – T-ball.

Gemming, Elisabeth. *Sandy at the children's zoo* (Bolliger, Max)

Gentieu, Penny. *Baby! Talk!* ill. by author. Crown, 1999. ISBN 0-517-80028-4 Subj: Activities. Babies.

Grow! babies! ill. by author. Crown, 2000. ISBN 0-517-80029-2 Subj: Babies. Behavior – growing up.

Geoghegan, Adrienne. *Dogs don't wear glasses* ill. by author. Crocodile Books, 1996. ISBN 1-56656-208-2 Subj: Animals – dogs. Glasses. Pets. Senses – seeing.

There's a wardrobe in my monster! ill. by Adrian Johnson. Carolrhoda, 1999. ISBN 1-57505-414-0 Subj: Behavior – boredom. Monsters. Pets.

George, Jean Craighead. *All upon a stone* ill. by Don Bolognese. Crowell, 1971. ISBN 0-690-05533-1 Subj: Insects. Science. Spiders.

Arctic son ill. by Wendell Minor. Hyperion, 1997. ISBN 0-7868-2255-4 Subj: Eskimos. Foreign lands – Arctic. Indians of North America – Inuit.

Dear Katie, the volcano is a girl ill. by Daniel Powers. Hyperion, 1998. ISBN 0-7868-2254-6 Subj: Family life – grandmothers. Hawaii. Mythical creatures. Volcanoes.

Dear Rebecca, winter is here ill. by Loretta Krupinski. HarperCollins, 1993. ISBN 0-06-021140-7 Subj: Family life – grandmothers. Nature. Seasons. Seasons – winter.

Everglades ill. by Wendell Minor. HarperCollins, 1995. ISBN 0-06-021229-2 Subj: Ecology. Nature. Rivers.

The first Thanksgiving ill. by Thomas Locker. Philomel, 1993. ISBN 0-399-21991-9 Subj: Holidays – Thanksgiving. Pilgrims. U.S. history.

Giraffe trouble ill. by Anna Vojtech. Disney Pr., 1998. ISBN 0-7868-3167-7 Subj: Animals – giraffes. Animals – lions.

Gorilla gang ill. by Stacey Schuett. Disney Pr., 1998. ISBN 0-7868-3166-9 Subj: Animals – gorillas.

The grizzly bear with the golden ears ill. by Tom Catania. HarperCollins, 1982. ISBN 0-06-021966-1 Subj: Animals – bears.

Look to the north: a wolf pup diary ill. by Lucia Washburn. HarperCollins, 1997. ISBN 0-06-023640-X Subj: Animals – babies. Animals – wolves. Behavior – growing up. Seasons.

Morning, noon, and night ill. by Wendell Minor. HarperCollins, 1999. ISBN 0-06-023628-0 Subj: Activities. Animals. Day.

Rhino romp ill. by Stacey Schuett. Disney Pr., 1998. ISBN 0-7868-5068-X Subj: Animals – rhinoceros. Behavior – lost.

Snow bear ill. by Wendell Minor. Hyperion, 1999. ISBN 0-7868-0456-4 Subj: Activities – playing. Animals – polar bears. Eskimos. Foreign lands – Arctic. Weather – snow.

To climb a waterfall ill. by Thomas Locker. Philomel, 1995. ISBN 0-399-22673-7 Subj: Sports – mountain climbing. Water.

The wentletrap trap ill. by Symeon Shimin. Dutton, 1978. ISBN 0-525-42310-9 Subj: Ethnic groups in the U.S. – African Americans. Foreign lands – Caribbean Islands. Sea and seashore.

George, Kristine O'Connell. *The great frog race and other poems* ill. by Kate Kiesler. Clarion, 1997. ISBN 0-395-77607-4 Subj: Counting, numbers. Nature. Poetry.

Old Elm speaks ill. by Kate Kiesler. Clarion, 1998. ISBN 0-395-87611-7 Subj: Poetry. Seasons. Trees.

George, Lindsay Barrett. *Around the pond: who's been here?* ill. by author. Greenwillow, 1996. ISBN

0-688-14377-6 Subj: Animals. Lakes, ponds. Nature. Seasons – summer.

Beaver at Long Pond (George, William T.)

In the woods: who's been here? ill. by author. Greenwillow, 1995. ISBN 0-688-12319-8 Subj: Activities – walking. Animals. Forest, woods. Nature. Problem solving. Seasons – fall.

William and Boomer ill. by author. Greenwillow, 1987. ISBN 0-688-06641-0 Subj: Birds – geese. Pets. Sports – swimming.

George, William T. *Beaver at Long Pond* by William T. and Lindsay Barrett George; ill. by Lindsay Barrett George. Greenwillow, 1988. ISBN 0-688-07107-4 Subj: Animals – beavers. Nature. Night.

Box turtle at Long Pond ill. by Lindsay Barrett George. Greenwillow, 1989. ISBN 0-688-08185-1 Subj: Nature. Reptiles – turtles, tortoises.

Christmas at Long Pond ill. by Lindsay Barrett George. Greenwillow, 1992. ISBN 0-688-09215-2 Subj: Animals. Family life – fathers. Forest, woods. Holidays – Christmas. Nature. Seasons – winter. Trees.

Fishing at Long Pond ill. by Lindsay Barrett George. Greenwillow, 1991. ISBN 0-688-09402-3 Subj: Animals. Family life – grandfathers. Sports – fishing.

Georgiady, Nicholas P. *Gertie the duck* ill. by Dagmar Wilson. Follett, 1959. ISBN 0-695-83363-4 Subj: Birds – ducks. Character traits – kindness to animals.

Geraghty, Paul. *The giraffe who got in a knot* (Bush, John)

The great green forest ill. by author. Hutchinson, 1992. ISBN 0-09-176420-3 Subj: Animals. Forest, woods. Noise, sounds.

The hunter ill. by author. Crown, 1994. ISBN 0-517-59693-8 Subj: Animals – elephants. Character traits – kindness to animals. Foreign lands – Africa. Sports – hunting.

Look out, Patrick! ill. by author. Macmillan, 1990. ISBN 0-02-735822-4 Subj: Animals – mice. Character traits – luck.

Over the steamy swamp ill. by author. Harcourt, 1989. ISBN 0-15-200561-7 Subj: Animals. Insects. Nature.

Slobcat ill. by author. Macmillan, 1991. ISBN 0-02-735825-9 Subj: Animals – cats. Character traits – laziness.

Solo ill. by author. Crown, 1995. ISBN 0-517-70909-0 Subj: Birds – penguins. Foreign lands – Antarctic.

Stop that noise! ill. by author. Crown, 1992. ISBN 0-517-59158-8 Subj: Animals. Animals – mice. Jungle. Noise, sounds.

Geraty, Virginia Mixson. *Gullah night before Christmas* ill. by James Rice. Pelican, 1998. ISBN 1-56554-330-0 Subj: Foreign languages. Holidays – Christmas. Poetry.

Gerber, Carole. *Arctic dreams* ill. by Marty Husted. Whispering Coyote, 1999. ISBN 1-58089-021-0 Subj: Animals. Eskimos. Family life – mothers. Foreign lands – Arctic. Sleep.

Hush! a Gaelic lullaby ill. by Marty Husted. Whispering Coyote, 1997. ISBN 1-879085-57-7 Subj: Foreign lands – Ireland. Foreign languages. Lullabies.

Gerez, Toni De. *see* De Gerez, Toni

Gergely, Tibor. *Wheel on the chimney* (Brown, Margaret Wise)

Geringer, Laura. *The cow is mooing anyhow* ill. by Dirk Zimmer. HarperCollins, 1991. ISBN 0-06-021987-4 Subj: ABC books. Animals. Rhyming text.

Look out, look out, it's coming! ill. by Sue Truesdell. HarperCollins, 1992. ISBN 0-06-021712-X Subj: Imagination – imaginary friends. Monsters.

Molly's new washing machine ill. by Petra Mathers. HarperCollins, 1986. ISBN 0-06-022151-8 Subj: Activities – dancing. Animals – rabbits. Behavior – mistakes. Machines.

A three hat day ill. by Arnold Lobel. HarperCollins, 1985. ISBN 0-06-021989-0 Subj: Behavior – collecting things. Clothing – hats.

Yours 'til the ice cracks: a book of Valentines ill. by Andrea Baruffi. HarperCollins, 1992. ISBN 0-06-020399-4 Subj: Holidays – Valentine's Day.

Gerrard, Jean. *Matilda Jane* ill. by Roy Gerrard. Farrar, 1983. ISBN 0-374-34865-0 Subj: Foreign lands – England. Sea and seashore.

Gerrard, Roy. *Croco'nile* ill. by author. Farrar, 1994. ISBN 0-374-31659-7 Subj: Foreign lands – Egypt. Reptiles – alligators, crocodiles. Rhyming text. Rivers.

The Favershams ill. by author. Farrar, 1983. ISBN 0-374-32292-9 Subj: Rhyming text.

Jocasta Carr, movie star ill. by author. Farrar, 1992. ISBN 0-374-33654-7 Subj: Activities – flying. Activities – traveling. Animals – dogs. Careers – actors. Crime. Foreign lands. Rhyming text.

Mik's mammoth ill. by author. Farrar, 1990. ISBN 0-374-31891-3 Subj: Animals. Character traits – individuality. Rhyming text.

A pocket full of posies ill. by author. Farrar, 1991. ISBN 0-374-36032-4 Subj: Format, unusual – toy and movable books. Nursery rhymes.

The Roman twins ill. by author. Farrar, 1998. ISBN 0-374-36339-0 Subj: Foreign lands – Italy. Multiple births – twins. Rhyming text. Slavery.

Rosie and the rustlers ill. by author. Farrar, 1989. ISBN 0-374-36345-5 Subj: Cowboys. Crime. Rhyming text. U.S. history – frontier and pioneer life.

Sir Cedric ill. by author. Farrar, 1984. ISBN 0-374-36959-3 Subj: Knights. Middle Ages. Rhyming text.

Sir Cedric rides again ill. by author. Farrar, 1987. ISBN 0-374-36961-5 Subj: Knights. Middle Ages. Rhyming text.

Sir Francis Drake: his daring deeds ill. by author. Farrar, 1988. ISBN 0-374-36962-3 Subj: Boats, ships. Foreign lands. Poetry. Sea and seashore.

Wagons west! ill. by author. Farrar, 1996. ISBN 0-374-38249-2 Subj: Activities – traveling. U.S. history. U.S. history – frontier and pioneer life.

Gershator, David. *Palampam Day* by David and Phillis Gershator; ill. by Enrique O. Sánchez. Cavendish, 1997. ISBN 0-7614-5002-5 Subj: Food. Foreign lands – Caribbean Islands. Foreign languages.

Gershator, Phillis. *Honi and his magic circle* ill. by Shay Rieger. Jewish Publication Society, 1980. ISBN 0-8276-0167-0 Subj: Jewish culture.

Palampam Day (Gershator, David)

Sweet, sweet fig banana ill. by Fritz Millvoix. Albert Whitman, 1996. ISBN 0-8075-7693-X Subj: Foreign lands – Caribbean Islands. Gardens, gardening. Shopping.

When it starts to snow ill. by Martin Matje. Holt, 1998. ISBN 0-8050-5404-9 Subj: Animals. Rhyming text. Seasons – winter. Weather – snow.

Zzzng! zzzng! zzzng! a Yoruba tale ill. by Theresa Smith. Orchard, 1998. ISBN 0-531-08873-1 Subj: Folk and fairy tales. Foreign lands – Africa. Insects – mosquitoes.

Gerson, Corinne. *Good dog, bad dog* ill. by Emily Arnold McCully. Atheneum, 1983. ISBN 0-689-30986-4 Subj: Animals – dogs. Behavior – misbehavior. Pets.

Gerson, Mary-Joan. *Why the sky is far away* ill. by Carla Golembe. Little, 1992. ISBN 0-316-30852-8 Subj: Behavior – greed. Folk and fairy tales. Foreign lands – Nigeria. Sky.

Gerstein, Mordicai. *The absolutely awful alphabet* ill. by author. Harcourt, 1999. ISBN 0-15-201494-2 Subj: ABC books. Animals. Monsters.

Anytime Mapleson and the hungry bears ill. by Susan Yard Harris. HarperCollins, 1990. ISBN 0-06-022415-0 Subj: Animals – bears.

Bedtime, everybody! ill. by author. Hyperion, 1996. ISBN 0-7868-2138-8 Subj: Bedtime. Toys.

Daisy's garden by Mordicai Gerstein and Susan Yard Harris; ill. by authors. Hyperion, 1995. ISBN 0-7868-2080-2 Subj: Animals. Gardens, gardening. Rhyming text. Seasons.

Follow me! ill. by author. Morrow, 1983. ISBN 0-688-01856-4 Subj: Birds – ducks.

The gigantic baby ill. by Arnie Levin. Harper-Collins, 1991. ISBN 0-06-022106-2 Subj: Babies.

Concepts – shape. Concepts – size. Family life – brothers and sisters.

Guess what? by Mordicai Gerstein and Susan Yard Harris; ill. by Mordicai Gerstein. Crown, 1991. ISBN 0-517-58217-1 Subj: Birthdays. Counting, numbers. Format, unusual – toy and movable books. Gifts.

Jonah and the two great fish ill. by author. Simon & Schuster, 1997. ISBN 0-689-81373-2 Subj: Animals – whales. Religion – Jonah.

The mountains of Tibet ill. by author. Harper-Collins, 1987. ISBN 0-06-022149-6 Subj: Death. Kites.

The new creatures ill. by author. HarperCollins, 1991. ISBN 0-06-022167-4 Subj: Animals – cats. Animals – dogs. Family life – grandfathers.

Noah and the great flood ill. by author. Simon & Schuster, 1999. ISBN 0-689-81371-6 Subj: Animals. Boats, ships. Religion – Noah. Weather – floods. Weather – rain.

Prince Sparrow ill. by author. Four Winds, 1984. ISBN 0-590-07907-7 Subj: Birds – sparrows. Emotions – love.

Queen Esther the morning star ill. by author. Simon & Schuster, 2000. ISBN 0-689-81372-4 Subj: Holidays – Purim. Jewish culture. Religion.

Roll over! ill. by author. Crown, 1984. ISBN 0-517-55209-4 Subj: Counting, numbers. Nursery rhymes.

The room ill. by author. Harper, 1984. ISBN 0-06-021999-8 Subj: Homes, houses.

The seal mother ill. by author. Dial, 1986. ISBN 0-8037-0303-1 Subj: Animals – seals. Folk and fairy tales. Seasons – summer.

The shadow of a flying bird: a legend of the Kurdistani Jews ill. by reteller. Hyperion, 1994. ISBN 0-7868-2012-8 Subj: Death. Folk and fairy tales. Foreign lands – Kurdistan. Jewish culture. Religion – Moses.

Stop those pants! ill. by author. Harcourt, 1998. ISBN 0-15-201495-0 Subj: Behavior – misbehavior. Clothing. Clothing – pants. Problem solving.

The story of May ill. by author. HarperCollins, 1993. ISBN 0-06-022288-3 Subj: Days of the week, months of the year. Seasons.

The sun's day ill. by author. HarperCollins, 1989. ISBN 0-06-022405-3 Subj: Sun. Time.

The wild boy ill. by author. Farrar, 1998. ISBN 0-374-38431-2 Subj: Character traits – kindness. Character traits – patience. Homeless.

William, where are you? ill. by author. Crown, 1985. ISBN 0-517-55644-8 Subj: Animals. Bedtime. Behavior – hiding. Format, unusual – toy and movable books.

Gervais, Bernadette. *Voyage under the stars* by Bernadette Gervais and Francisco Pittau; ill. by Bernadette Gervais. Lothrop, 1992. ISBN 0-688-

11329-X Subj: Animals. Behavior – sharing. Birds – geese. Night.

Getz, Arthur. *Humphrey, the dancing pig* ill. by author. Dial, 1980. ISBN 0-8037-4497-8 Subj: Activities – dancing. Animals – pigs. Behavior – dissatisfaction.

Gewing, Lisa. *Mama, daddy, baby and me* ill. by Donna Larimer. Spirit Pr., 1989. ISBN 0-944296-04-1 Subj: Babies. Family life – new sibling. Rhyming text. Sibling rivalry.

Gezi, Kal. *The mystery at Misty Falls* (Bradford, Ann)

The mystery in the secret club house (Bradford, Ann)

The mystery of the blind writer (Bradford, Ann)

The mystery of the live ghosts (Bradford, Ann)

The mystery of the midget clown (Bradford, Ann)

The mystery of the missing dogs (Bradford, Ann)

The mystery of the missing raccoon (Bradford, Ann)

The mystery of the square footsteps (Bradford, Ann)

The mystery of the tree house (Bradford, Ann)

Ghazi, Suhaib Hamid. *Ramadan* ill. by Omar Rayyan. Holiday, 1996. ISBN 0-8234-1254-7 Subj: Holidays – Ramadan. Religion.

Ghigna, Charles. *Good cats/Bad cats* ill. by David Catrow. Walt Disney, 1992. ISBN 1-56282-293-4 Subj: Animals – cats. Behavior – misbehavior. Format, unusual. Poetry.

Good dogs/Bad dogs ill. by David Catrow. Walt Disney, 1992. ISBN 1-56282-291-8 Subj: Animals – dogs. Behavior – misbehavior. Format, unusual. Poetry.

Mice are nice ill. by Jon Goodell. Random House, 1999. ISBN 0-679-98929-3 Subj: Animals – mice. Pets. Rhyming text.

Gianni, Peg. *Alex, the amazing juggler* by Peg Gianni and Renato Ferraro; ill. by Peg Gianni. Holt, 1981. ISBN 0-03-059891-5 Subj: Behavior – running away. Royalty.

Giannini, Enzo. *Little Parsley* ill. by author. Simon & Schuster, 1990. ISBN 0-671-67197-9 Subj: Folk and fairy tales. Foreign lands – Italy. Witches.

Giasullo, Cresent. *Gia and the one hundred dollars worth of bubblegum* (Asch, Frank)

Gibbon, David. *Kittens* ill. with photos. Crescent Books, 1979. ISBN 84-499-5052-X Subj: Animals – cats.

Gibbons, Faye. *Mama and me and the Model-T* ill. by Ted Rand. Morrow, 1999. ISBN 0-688-15299-6 Subj: Activities – driving. Automobiles. Family life – mothers. Gender roles.

Mountain wedding ill. by Ted Rand. Morrow, 1996. ISBN 0-688-11349-4 Subj: Country. Family life – step families. Insects – bees. Weddings.

Gibbons, Gail. *The art box* ill. by author. Holiday, 1998. ISBN 0-8234-1386-1 Subj: Art. Careers – artists. Tools.

Boat book ill. by author. Holiday, 1983. ISBN 0-8234-0478-1 Subj: Boats, ships.

Cats ill. by author. Holiday, 1996. ISBN 0-8234-1253-9 Subj: Animals – cats.

Check it out! the book about libraries ill. by author. Harcourt, 1985. ISBN 0-15-216400-6 Subj: Libraries.

Clocks and how they go ill. by author. Crowell, 1979. ISBN 0-690-03974-3 Subj: Clocks, watches. Time.

County fair ill. by author. Little, 1994. ISBN 0-316-30951-6 Subj: Country. Fairs.

Deadline! from news to newspaper ill. by author. HarperCollins, 1987. ISBN 0-690-04602-2 Subj: Activities – working. Paper.

Department store ill. by author. Crowell, 1984. ISBN 0-690-04367-8 Subj: Stores.

Dinosaurs ill. by author. Holiday, 1987. ISBN 0-8234-0657-1 Subj: Dinosaurs.

Dogs ill. by author. Holiday, 1996. ISBN 0-8234-1226-1 Subj: Animals – dogs.

Easter ill. by author. Holiday, 1989. ISBN 0-8234-0737-3 Subj: Holidays – Easter.

Emergency! ill. by author. Holiday, 1994. ISBN 0-8234-1128-1 Subj: Careers. Character traits – helpfulness. Trucks.

Farming ill. by author. Holiday, 1988. ISBN 0-8234-0682-2 Subj: Careers. Farms. Seasons.

Fill it up! all about service stations ill. by author. Crowell, 1985. ISBN 0-690-04440-2 Subj: Automobiles. Careers.

Fire! Fire! ill. by author. Crowell, 1984. ISBN 0-690-04416-X Subj: Careers – firefighters.

Flying ill. by author. Holiday, 1986. ISBN 0-8234-0599-0 Subj: Activities – ballooning. Activities – flying. Airplanes, airports.

Frogs ill. by author. Holiday, 1993. ISBN 0-8234-1052-8 Subj: Frogs and toads.

From seed to plant ill. by author. Holiday, 1991. ISBN 0-8234-0872-8 Subj: Plants. Science. Seeds.

Halloween ill. by author. Holiday, 1984. ISBN 0-8234-0524-9 Subj: Holidays – Halloween.

Happy birthday! ill. by author. Holiday, 1986. ISBN 0-8234-0614-8 Subj: Birthdays.

How a house is built ill. by author. Holiday, 1990. ISBN 0-8234-0841-8 Subj: Activities – making things. Homes, houses.

Knights in shining armor ill. by author. Little, 1995. ISBN 0-316-30948-6 Subj: Knights. Middle Ages.

The milk makers ill. by author. Macmillan, 1985. ISBN 0-02-736640-5 Subj: Farms. Food.

The missing maple syrup sap mystery: or, How maple syrup is made ill. by author. Warne, 1979. ISBN 0-7232-6167-9 Subj: Activities. Food. Mystery stories. Trees.

Monarch butterfly ill. by author. Holiday, 1989. ISBN 0-8234-0773-X Subj: Insects – butterflies, caterpillars. Metamorphosis. Science.

Nature's green umbrella: tropical rain forests ill. by author. Morrow, 1994. ISBN 0-688-12353-8 Subj: Animals. Ecology. Forest, woods. Plants.

New road! ill. by author. Crowell, 1983. ISBN 0-690-04343-0 Subj: Transportation.

Paper, paper everywhere ill. by author. Harcourt, 1983. ISBN 0-15-259488-4 Subj: Paper.

Penguins! ill. by author. Holiday, 1998. ISBN 0-8234-1388-8 Subj: Birds – penguins. Foreign lands – Antarctic.

Pigs ill. by author. Holiday, 1999. ISBN 0-8234-1441-8 Subj: Animals – pigs.

The planets ill. by author. Holiday, 1993. ISBN 0-8234-1040-4 Subj: Astronomy. Planets.

Playgrounds ill. by author. Holiday, 1985. ISBN 0-8234-0553-2 Subj: Activities – playing.

The post office book: mail and how it moves ill. by author. Crowell, 1982. ISBN 0-690-04199-3 Subj: Careers – postal workers. Communication. Post office.

The pottery place ill. by author. Harcourt, 1987. ISBN 0-15-263265-4 Subj: Careers.

Prehistoric animals ill. by author. Holiday, 1988. ISBN 0-8234-0707-1 Subj: Animals. Science.

Puff - flash - bang! a book about signals ill. by author. Morrow, 1993. ISBN 0-688-07378-6 Subj: Communication.

The reasons for seasons ill. by author. Holiday, 1995. ISBN 0-8234-1174-5 Subj: Seasons.

Recycle! ill. by author. Little, 1992. ISBN 0-316-30971-0 Subj: Ecology.

Say woof! the day of a country veterinarian ill. by author. Macmillan, 1992. ISBN 0-02-736781-9 Subj: Animals. Careers – veterinarians. Illness.

The seasons of Arnold's apple tree ill. by author. Harcourt, 1988. ISBN 0-15-271246-1 Subj: Food. Seasons. Trees.

Sharks ill. by author. Holiday, 1992. ISBN 0-8234-0960-0 Subj: Fish – sharks. Science.

Soaring with the wind: the bald eagle ill. by author. Morrow, 1998. ISBN 0-688-13731-8 Subj: Birds – eagles. Science.

Spiders ill. by author. Holiday, 1993. ISBN 0-8234-1006-4 Subj: Spiders.

Stargazers ill. by author. Holiday, 1992. ISBN 0-8234-0983-X Subj: Astronomy. Stars.

Sun up, sun down ill. by author. Harcourt, 1983. ISBN 0-15-282781-1 Subj: Science. Sun.

Surrounded by sea ill. by author. Little, 1991. ISBN 0-316-30961-3 Subj: Careers – fishermen. Islands. Sports – fishing.

Thanksgiving Day ill. by author. Holiday, 1983. ISBN 0-8234-0489-7 Subj: Holidays – Thanksgiving. Pilgrims.

The too-great bread bake book ill. by author. Warne, 1980. ISBN 0-7232-6182-2 Subj: Activities – cooking.

Tool book ill. by author. Holiday, 1982. ISBN 0-8234-0444-7 Subj: Tools.

Trains ill. by author. Holiday, 1987. ISBN 0-8234-0640-7 Subj: Trains.

Trucks ill. by author. Crowell, 1981. ISBN 0-690-04119-5 Subj: Trucks.

Tunnels ill. by author. Holiday, 1984. ISBN 0-8234-0507-9 Subj: Activities – digging.

Up goes the skyscraper! ill. by author. Four Winds, 1986. ISBN 0-02-736780-0 Subj: Buildings. City.

Valentine's Day ill. by author. Holiday, 1985. ISBN 0-8234-0572-9 Subj: Holidays – Valentine's Day.

Weather words and what they mean ill. by author. Holiday, 1990. ISBN 0-8234-0805-1 Subj: Language. Weather.

Whales ill. by author. Holiday, 1991. ISBN 0-8234-0900-7 Subj: Animals – whales.

Yippee-yay! a book about cowboys and cowgirls ill. by author. Little, 1998. ISBN 0-316-30944-3 Subj: Animals – bulls, cows. Cowboys. Rodeos. U.S. history – frontier and pioneer life.

Zoo ill. by author. Crowell, 1987. ISBN 0-690-04633-2 Subj: Activities – working. Animals. Zoos.

Giblin, James Cross. *George Washington: a picture book biography* ill. by Michael Dooling. Scholastic, 1992. ISBN 0-59-042550-1 Subj: U.S. history.

Gibson, Betty. *The story of Little Quack* ill. by Kady MacDonald Denton. Little, 1991. ISBN 0-316-30966-4 Subj: Birds – ducks. Farms. Pets.

Gibson, Josephine. *see* Joslin, Sesyle

Gibson, Kari Smalley. *Mooki's secret* by Kari Smalley Gibson with Gary Smalley; ill. by Richard Bernal. Gold'n'Honey, 1998. ISBN 1-57673-266-5 Subj: Animals – beavers. Orphans. Self-concept.

Gibson, Myra Tomback. *What is your favorite thing to touch?* ill. by author. Grosset, 1965. Subj: Poetry. Senses – touching.

Giesen, Rosemary. *Famous planes* (Thompson, Brenda)

Pirates (Thompson, Brenda)

Gifaldi, David. *The boy who spoke colors* ill. by C. Shana Greger. Houghton Mifflin, 1993. ISBN 0-395-65025-9 Subj: Behavior – greed. Folk and fairy tales. Language. Royalty – kings.

Giff, Patricia Reilly. *The almost awful play* ill. by Susanna Natti. Viking, 1984. ISBN 0-670-11458-8 Subj: Theater.

The beast in Ms. Rooney's room ill. by Blanche Sims. Dell, 1984. ISBN 0-440-40485-1 Subj: Activities – reading. School.

Good luck, Ronald Morgan ill. by Susanna Natti. Viking, 1996. ISBN 0-670-86303-3 Subj: Animals – cats. Animals – dogs. Pets.

Happy birthday, Ronald Morgan! ill. by Susanna Natti. Viking, 1986. ISBN 0-670-80741-9 Subj: Birthdays. Friendship. School.

I love Saturday ill. by Frank Remkiewicz. Viking, 1989. ISBN 0-670-81409-1 Subj: Behavior – secrets. City. Days of the week, months of the year.

Next year I'll be special ill. by Marylin Hafner. Dutton, 1980. ISBN 0-525-35810-2 Subj: Behavior – seeking better things. Dreams. School.

Ronald Morgan goes to bat ill. by Susanna Natti. Viking, 1988. ISBN 0-670-81457-1 Subj: Sports – baseball.

Ronald Morgan goes to camp ill. by Susanna Natti. Viking, 1995. ISBN 0-670-86195-2 Subj: Activities. Camps, camping. Friendship.

Today was a terrible day ill. by Susanna Natti. Viking, 1980. ISBN 0-670-81830-0 Subj: Behavior – bad day. School.

Watch out, Ronald Morgan! ill. by Susanna Natti. Viking, 1985. ISBN 0-670-80433-9 Subj: Glasses. School. Senses – seeing.

Giffard, Hannah. *Fast car* ill. by Hannah Giffard. Tambourine, 1993. ISBN 0-688-12444-5 Subj: Automobiles. Concepts – opposites. Format, unusual – board books. Trucks.

Hens say cluck ill. by author. Tambourine, 1993. ISBN 0-688-12442-9 Subj: Animals. Format, unusual – board books. Noise, sounds.

Red bus ill. by author. Tambourine, 1993. ISBN 0-688-12443-7 Subj: Buses. Concepts – color. Format, unusual – board books.

Red Fox ill. by author. Dial, 1991. ISBN 0-8037-0869-6 Subj: Animals – foxes. Food.

Red Fox on the move ill. by author. Dial, 1992. ISBN 0-8037-1057-7 Subj: Animals – foxes. Family life. Moving.

Striped zebra ill. by author. Tambourine, 1993. ISBN 0-688-12441-0 Subj: Animals. Format, unusual – board books.

Gifford, Kathie Lee. *Giff the scaredy bear* by Kathie Lee Gifford, Paul Taublieb, and Susan Cooper; ill. by Debbie Young. Random House, 1997. ISBN 0-679-88504-8 Subj: Animals – bears. Emotions – fear. Sports – roller skating.

Giff's big game by Kathie Lee Gifford, Paul Taublieb, and Susan Cooper; ill. by Debbie Young. Random House, 1997. ISBN 0-679-88495-5 Subj: Animals – bears. Sports – football. Sportsmanship.

Moochie's surprise by Kathie Lee Gifford, Paul Taublieb, and Susan Cooper; ill. by Debbie Young. Random House, 1997. ISBN 0-679-88496-3 Subj: Animals – mice. Friendship. Self-concept.

Giganti, Paul. *Each orange had eight slices* ill. by Donald Crews. Greenwillow, 1992. ISBN 0-688-10429-0 Subj: Counting, numbers.

How many snails? a counting book by Paul Giganti, Jr.; ill. by Donald Crews. Greenwillow, 1988. ISBN 0-688-06370-5 Subj: Counting, numbers.

Gikow, Louise. *Baby Kermit's Christmas* ill. by Lauren Attinello. Muppet Pr., 1993. ISBN 0-307-13722-8 Subj: Babies. Holidays – Christmas. Puppets.

Boober Fraggle's ghosts ill. by Lawrence DiFiori. Holt, 1985. ISBN 0-03-004549-5 Subj: Emotions – fear. Ghosts. Puppets.

Bye-bye, pacifier ill. by Tom Cooke. Muppet Pr., 1992. ISBN 0-307-12330-8 Subj: Animals – pigs. Babies. Behavior – growing up. Format, unusual – board books. Puppets.

Count with me ill. by David Prebenna. Grolier, 1992. ISBN 0-717-28283-X Subj: Counting, numbers. Puppets.

Follow that Fraggle! ill. by Barbara Lanza. Holt, 1985. ISBN 0-03-004558-4 Subj: Activities – traveling. Animals – dogs. Puppets.

For every child, a better world by Kermit the Frog; in cooperation with the United Nations; as told to Louise Gikow and Ellen Weiss; ill. by Bruce McNally. Western, 1993. ISBN 0-307-65628-4 Subj: Puppets. World.

I am Kermit ill. by Joe Ewers. Muppet Pr., 1993. ISBN 0-307-12170-4 Subj: Format, unusual – board books. Frogs and toads. Puppets.

Jim Henson's Muppets in Rowlf's big test: a book about listening to your conscience ill. by Dave Prebenna. Grolier, 1993. ISBN 0-717-28331-3 Subj: Character traits – honesty. Puppets. School.

Jim Henson's Muppets in What's fair is fair: a book about sharing ill. by Tom Leigh. Grolier, 1992. ISBN 0-717-28269-4 Subj: Behavior – sharing. Fairs. Friendship. Puppets.

Sprocket's Christmas tale ill. by Lisa McCue. Holt, 1984. ISBN 0-03-000708-9 Subj: Holidays – Christmas. Puppets.

Gilbert, Helen Earle. *Dr. Trotter and his big gold watch* ill. by Margaret Bradfield. Abingdon, 1948. Subj: Careers – doctors. Clocks, watches.

Mr. Plum and the little green tree ill. by Margaret Bradfield. Abingdon, 1946. Subj: Careers – shoemakers. Trees.

Gilbert, Lisa Weedn. *The elephant prince* (Weedn, Flavia)

The enchanted tree (Weedn, Flavia)

The giant's garden (Weedn, Flavia)

The little snow bear (Weedn, Flavia)

The magic cap (Weedn, Flavia)

The moon maiden (Weedn, Flavia)

The ragged peddler (Weedn, Flavia)

The star gift (Weedn, Flavia)

Gilbert, Suzie. *Hawk Hill* ill. by Sylvia Long. Chronicle, 1996. ISBN 0-8118-0839-4 Subj: Animals. Birds – hawks. Character traits – kindness to animals. Friendship. Illness.

Gilbert, Yvonne. *Baby's book of lullabies and cradle songs* ill. by author. Dial, 1990. ISBN 0-8037-0795-9 Subj: Lullabies. Music. Songs.

Gilchrist, Jan Spivey. *Indigo and moonlight gold* ill. by author. Black Butterfly, 1993. ISBN 0-86316-210-X Subj: Ethnic groups in the U.S. – African Americans. Family life – mothers. Night.

Gilchrist, Theo E. *Halfway up the mountain* ill. by Glen Rounds. Lippincott, 1978. ISBN 0-397-31805-7 Subj: Activities – cooking. Behavior – fighting, arguing. Rhyming text.

Gile, John. *Oh, how I wished I could read!* ill. by Frank Fiorello. John Gile Communications, 1995. ISBN 0-910941-10-6 Subj: Activities – reading. Dreams. Rhyming text.

Gili, Phillida. *Fanny and Charles: a regency escapade or, The trick that went wrong* ill. by author. Viking, 1983. ISBN 0-670-30697-5 Subj: Activities – vacationing. Animals – mice. Sibling rivalry.

Gilks, Helen. *Bears* ill. by Andrew Bale. Ticknor & Fields, 1993. ISBN 0-395-66899-9 Subj: Animals – bears.

Gill, Bob. *A balloon for a blunderbuss* by Bob Gill and Alastair Reid; ill. by Bob Gill. HarperCollins, 1961. Subj: Activities – trading.

Gill, Janet. *Basket Weaver and Catches Many Mice* ill. by Yangsook Choi. Random House, 1999. ISBN 0-679-98922-6 Subj: Activities – weaving. Animals – cats. Folk and fairy tales. Royalty.

Gill, Joan. *Hush, Jon!* ill. by Tracy Sugarman. Doubleday, 1968. Subj: Babies. Emotions – envy, jealousy. Ethnic groups in the U.S. – African Americans. Family life.

Gill, Madelaine. *The spring hat* ill. by author. Simon & Schuster, 1993. ISBN 0-671-75664-8 Subj: Animals – rabbits. Clothing – hats. Wordless.

Gill, Shelley. *The big buck adventure* by Shelley Gill and Deborah Tobola; ill. by Grace Lin. Charlesbridge, 2000. ISBN 0-88106-294-4 Subj: Counting, numbers. Money. Shopping.

Gilleo, Alma. *Learning about monsters* ill. by Joe Van Severen. Childrens Pr., 1982. ISBN 0-516-06535-1 Subj: Folk and fairy tales. Monsters. Mythical creatures.

Gillerlain, Gayle. *Reverend Thomas's false teeth* ill. by Dena Schutzer. BridgeWater, 1994. ISBN 0-8167-3303-1 Subj: Behavior – losing things. Careers – preachers. Teeth.

Gillham, Bill. *Can you see it?* photos by Fiona Horne. Putnam, 1986. ISBN 0-399-21323-6 Subj: Games.

The early words picture book photos by Sam Grainger. Coward, 1983. ISBN 0-698-20583-9 Subj: Activities – reading.

Let's look for colors by Bill Gillham and Susan Hulme; photos by Jan Siegieda. Putnam, 1984. ISBN 0-698-20612-6 Subj: Concepts – color.

Let's look for numbers by Bill Gillham and Susan Hulme; photos by Jan Siegieda. Putnam, 1984. ISBN 0-698-20613-4 Subj: Counting, numbers.

Let's look for opposites by Bill Gillham and Susan Hulme; photos by Jan Siegieda. Putnam, 1984. ISBN 0-698-20614-2 Subj: Concepts – opposites.

Let's look for shapes by Bill Gillham and Susan Hulme; photos by Jan Siegieda. Putnam, 1984. ISBN 0-698-20615-0 Subj: Concepts – shape.

What can you do? photos by Fiona Horne. Putnam, 1986. ISBN 0-399-21324-4 Subj: Games. Imagination.

What's the difference? photos by Fiona Horne. Putnam, 1986. ISBN 0-399-21321-X Subj: Concepts – opposites. Games.

Where does it go? photos by Fiona Horne. Putnam, 1986. ISBN 0-399-21322-8 Subj: Concepts. Games.

Gilliland, Judith Heide. *The day of Ahmed's secret* (Heide, Florence Parry)

River ill. by Joyce Powzyk. Houghton Mifflin, 1993. ISBN 0-395-55963-4 Subj: Foreign lands – Amazon. Forest, woods. Rivers.

Sami and the time of the troubles (Heide, Florence Parry)

Gillmor, Don. *The fabulous song* ill. by Marie-Louise Gay. Kane/Miller, 1998. ISBN 0-916291-80-4 Subj: Careers – musicians. Family life.

Gilmore, Rachna. *Lights for Gita* ill. by Alice Priestley. Tilbury House, 1994. ISBN 0-88448-150-6 Subj: Ethnic groups in the U.S. – East Indian

Americans. Holidays – Divali. Moving. Religion – Hinduism.

Gilmour, H. B. *Why Wembley Fraggle couldn't sleep* ill. by Barbara McClintock. Holt, 1985. ISBN 0-03-004557-6 Subj: Puppets. Sleep.

The gingerbread boy. *Gingerbread baby* retold and ill. by Jan Brett. Putnam, 1999. ISBN 0-399-23444-6 Subj: Behavior – running away. Cumulative tales. Folk and fairy tales. Food. Format, unusual – toy and movable books.

The gingerbread boy retold by Harriet Ziefert; ill. by Emily Bolam. Viking, 1995. ISBN 0-670-86052-2 Subj: Behavior – running away. Cumulative tales. Folk and fairy tales.

The gingerbread boy retold and ill. by Scott Cook. Knopf, 1987. ISBN 0-394-98698-9 Subj: Behavior – running away. Cumulative tales. Folk and fairy tales.

The gingerbread boy retold and ill. by Richard Egielski. Laura Geringer, 1997. ISBN 0-06-026031-9 Subj: Behavior – running away. Cumulative tales. Folk and fairy tales. Food.

The gingerbread boy ill. by Paul Galdone. Seabury Pr., 1975. ISBN 0-8164-3132-9 Subj: Behavior – running away. Cumulative tales. Folk and fairy tales. Food. Rhyming text.

The gingerbread boy retold by David Cutts; ill. by Joan Elizabeth Goodman. Troll, 1979. ISBN 0-89375-122-7 Subj: Behavior – running away. Cumulative tales. Folk and fairy tales. Food.

The gingerbread boy ill. by William Curtis Holdsworth. Farrar, 1968. Subj: Behavior – running away. Cumulative tales. Folk and fairy tales. Food.

The gingerbread man retold by Eric A. Kimmel; ill. by Megan Lloyd. Holiday, 1993. ISBN 0-8234-0824-8 Subj: Behavior – running away. Cumulative tales. Folk and fairy tales.

The gingerbread man retold by Jim Aylesworth; ill. by Barbara McClintock. Scholastic, 1998. ISBN 0-590-97219-7 Subj: Behavior – running away. Cumulative tales. Folk and fairy tales. Food.

The gingerbread man retold by Barbara Ireson; ill. by Gerald Rose. Norton, 1963. Subj: Behavior – running away. Cumulative tales. Folk and fairy tales. Food.

The pancake boy adapt. and ill. by Lorinda Bryan Cauley. Putnam, 1988. ISBN 0-399-21505-0 Subj: Behavior – running away. Cumulative tales. Folk and fairy tales. Food.

Whiff, sniff, nibble and chew: The Gingerbread boy retold by Charlotte Pomerantz; ill. by Monica Incisa. Greenwillow, 1984. ISBN 0-688-02552-8 Subj: Behavior – running away. Cumulative tales. Folk and fairy tales. Rhyming text.

Ginolfi, Arthur. *The tiny star: the greatest star the world has ever seen!* ill. by Pat Schories. Tommy Nelson, 1997. ISBN 0-8499-1510-4 Subj: Holidays – Christmas. Religion – Nativity. Stars.

Ginsburg, Mirra. *Across the stream* ill. by Nancy Tafuri. Greenwillow, 1982. ISBN 0-688-01206-X Subj: Animals – foxes. Birds – chickens. Birds – ducks. Dreams.

Asleep, asleep ill. by Nancy Tafuri. Greenwillow, 1992. ISBN 0-688-09154-7 Subj: Bedtime. Lullabies. Night.

The chick and the duckling ill. by José Aruego and Ariane Dewey. Macmillan, 1972. Translation of Tsyplenok i utenok by Vladimir Grigorévich Suteyev. ISBN 0-02-735940-9 Subj: Birds – chickens. Birds – ducks. Sports – swimming.

The Chinese mirror ill. by Margot Zemach. Harcourt, 1988. ISBN 0-15-200420-3 Subj: Character traits – appearance. Folk and fairy tales. Foreign lands – Korea.

Clay boy ill. by Jos. A. Smith. Greenwillow, 1997. Adapt. from a Russian folk tale. ISBN 0-688-14410-1 Subj: Activities – making things. Folk and fairy tales. Foreign lands – Russia.

The fisherman's son ill. by Tony Chen. Greenwillow, 1979. ISBN 0-688-84216-X Subj: Character traits – cleverness. Folk and fairy tales. Foreign lands – Russia.

Four brave sailors ill. by Nancy Tafuri. Greenwillow, 1987. ISBN 0-688-06515-5 Subj: Animals – mice. Boats, ships. Dreams. Pirates. Rhyming text. Sailors. Sea and seashore. Toys. Weather.

The fox and the hare ill. by Victor Nolden. Crown, 1969. Subj: Animals. Animals – foxes. Animals – rabbits. Folk and fairy tales. Foreign lands – Russia. Friendship.

Good morning, chick (Chukovskii, Kornei Ivanovich)

How the sun was brought back to the sky adapt. from a Slovenian folk tale; ill. by José Aruego and Ariane Dewey. Macmillan, 1975. ISBN 0-02-735750-3 Subj: Folk and fairy tales. Foreign lands – Czechoslovakia. Sun.

The king who tried to fry an egg on his head ill. by Will Hillenbrand. Macmillan, 1994. ISBN 0-02-736242-6 Subj: Character traits – foolishness. Folk and fairy tales. Foreign lands – Russia. Royalty – kings.

Kitten from one to ten ill. by Giulio Maestro. Crown, 1980. ISBN 0-517-53972-1 Subj: Animals – cats. Counting, numbers. Rhyming text.

Mushroom in the rain ill. by José Aruego and Ariane Dewey. Macmillan, 1988, 1974. Adapt. from the Russian of Valdimir Grigorévich Suteyev. ISBN 0-02-736241-8 Subj: Animals. Animals – foxes. Plants. Weather – rain.

The old man and his birds ill. by Donna Ruff. Greenwillow, 1994. ISBN 0-688-04604-5 Subj: Birds. Days of the week, months of the year. Magic. Seasons.

Ookie-Spooky ill. by Emily Arnold McCully. Crown, 1979. ISBN 0-517-53610-2 Subj: Monsters.

Pampalche of the silver teeth ill. by Rocco Negri. Crown, 1976. ISBN 0-517-52241-1 Subj: Folk and fairy tales. Foreign lands – Russia. Witches.

Striding slippers: an Udmurt tale ill. by Sal Murdocca. Macmillan, 1978. ISBN 0-02-736370-8 Subj: Behavior – stealing. Folk and fairy tales. Magic.

The strongest one of all ill. by José Aruego and Ariane Dewey. Greenwillow, 1977. ISBN 0-688-84081-7 Subj: Animals – sheep. Character traits – bravery. Foreign lands – Russia.

The sun's asleep behind the hill ill. by Paul O. Zelinsky. Greenwillow, 1982. ISBN 0-688-00825-9 Subj: Night. Rhyming text.

Three kittens trans. from the Russian of V. Suteyev; ill. by Lisa McCue. Random House, 1992. ISBN 0-679-93254-2 Subj: Animals – cats. Concepts – color.

Two greedy bears ill. by José Aruego and Ariane Dewey. Macmillan, 1976. ISBN 0-02-736450-X Subj: Animals – bears. Animals – foxes. Behavior – greed. Foreign lands – Hungary. Sibling rivalry.

We adopted you, Benjamin Koo ill. by Linda Shute. Albert Whitman, 1985. ISBN 0-8075-8694-3 Subj: Adoption. Ethnic groups in the U.S. – Korean Americans. Family life.

Where does the sun go at night? ill. by José Aruego and Ariane Dewey. Greenwillow, 1980. ISBN 0-688-84245-3 Subj: Night. Sun.

Which is the best place? ill. by Roger Antoine Duvoisin. Macmillan, 1976. Tr. from Gde luchshe by Pyotr Dubochkin. ISBN 0-02-735980-8 Subj: Bedtime. Foreign lands – Russia.

Giovanni, Nikki. *The genie in the jar* ill. by Christopher Raschka. Holt, 1996. ISBN 0-8050-4118-4 Subj: Activities. Ethnic groups in the U.S. – African Americans. Family life – mothers. Poetry.

Spin a soft black song ill. by George Martins. Rev. ed. Hill & Wang, 1985. ISBN 0-8090-8796-0 Subj: Ethnic groups in the U.S. – African Americans. Poetry.

The sun is so quiet ill. by Ashley Bryan. Holt, 1996. ISBN 0-8050-4119-2 Subj: Ethnic groups in the U.S. – African Americans. Nature. Poetry.

Gipson, Morrell. *Favorite nursery tales* ill. by S. D. Schindler. Doubleday, 1983. ISBN 0-385-17961-8 Subj: Nursery rhymes.

Hello, Peter ill. by Clement Hurd. Doubleday, 1948. Subj: Activities.

Whose tracks are these? adapt. by Morrell Gipson; story and ill. by Paul Mangold. Garrett Educational Corp., 1990. ISBN 0-944483-93-3 Subj: Animals. Seasons – winter. Weather – snow.

Girard, Linda Walvoord. *Adoption is for always* ill. by Judi Friedman. Albert Whitman, 1986. ISBN 0-8075-0185-9 Subj: Adoption. Family life.

At Daddy's on Saturdays ill. by Judith Friedman. Albert Whitman, 1987. ISBN 0-8075-0475-0 Subj: Divorce. Emotions – love. Family life.

Jeremy's first haircut ill. by Maryjane Begin. Albert Whitman, 1986. ISBN 0-8075-3805-1 Subj: Emotions – fear. Hair.

My body is private ill. by Rodney Pate. Albert Whitman, 1984. ISBN 0-8075-5320-4 Subj: Safety. Self-concept.

Who is a stranger, and what should I do? ill. by Helen Cogancherry. Albert Whitman, 1985. ISBN 0-8075-9014-2 Subj: Behavior – talking to strangers. Safety.

You were born on your very first birthday ill. by Christa Kieffer. Albert Whitman, 1983. ISBN 0-8075-9455-5 Subj: Babies. Birth. Science.

Girion, Barbara. *The boy with the special face* ill. by Heidi Palmer. Abingdon, 1978. ISBN 0-687-03909-6 Subj: Character traits – appearance.

Giuliano, Katie. *All the way to God* by Katie and Michael Giuliano; ill. by the Giuliano children. Golden Books, 1999. ISBN 0-307-10223-8 Subj: Children as illustrators. Concepts – distance. Emotions – love. Family life – fathers. Religion.

Giuliano, Michael. *All the way to God* (Giuliano, Katie)

Givens, Janet Eaton. *Just two wings* ill. by Susan Dodge. Atheneum, 1984. ISBN 0-689-31001-3 Subj: Birds.

Something wonderful happened ill. by Susan Dodge. Atheneum, 1982. ISBN 0-689-30904-X Subj: Flowers.

Givens, Terryl. *Dragon scales and willow leaves* ill. by Andrew Portwood. Putnam, 1997. ISBN 0-399-22619-2 Subj: Family life – brothers and sisters. Imagination. Multiple births – twins.

Givon, Hannah Gelman. *We shake in a quake* ill. by David Uttal. Tricycle, 1996. ISBN 1-883672-25-2 Subj: Earthquakes.

Glaser, Byron. *Action alphabet* (Neumeier, Marty)

Glaser, Linda. *Beautiful bats* ill. by Sharon Lane Holm. Millbrook, 1997. ISBN 0-7613-0254-9 Subj: Animals – bats.

The borrowed Hanukkah latkes ill. by Nancy Cote. Albert Whitman, 1997. ISBN 0-8075-0841-1 Subj: Behavior – sharing. Friendship. Holidays – Hanukkah. Jewish culture. Old age.

Compost! growing gardens from your garbage ill. by Anca Hariton. Millbrook, 1996. ISBN 1-56294-659-5 Subj: Gardens, gardening. Nature.

Keep your socks on, Albert! ill. by Sally G. Ward. Dutton, 1992. ISBN 0-525-44838-1 Subj: Animals – possums. Clothing – socks. Emotions – fear. Family life – sisters.

Spectacular spiders ill. by Gay W. Holland. Millbrook, 1998. ISBN 0-7613-0353-7 Subj: Gardens, gardening. Spiders.

Stop that garbage truck! ill. by Karen Lee Schmidt. Albert Whitman, 1993. ISBN 0-8075-7626-3 Subj: Careers – sanitation workers. Character traits – shyness. Ethnic groups in the U.S. – African Americans.

Wonderful worms ill. by Loretta Krupinski. Millbrook, 1992. ISBN 1-56294-062-7 Subj: Animals – worms. Insects – butterflies, caterpillars. Metamorphosis. Nature. Science.

Glass, Andrew. *Charles T. McBiddle* ill. by author. Doubleday, 1993. ISBN 0-385-30554-0 Subj: Character traits – persistence. Sports – bicycling.

Chickpea and the talking cow ill. by author. Lothrop, 1987. ISBN 0-688-06175-3 Subj: Animals – bulls, cows. Character traits – smallness. Emotions – love. Family life. Farms. Royalty.

My brother tries to make me laugh ill. by author. Lothrop, 1984. ISBN 0-688-02259-6 Subj: Imagination. Space and space ships.

The sweetwater run: the story of Buffalo Bill Cody and the Pony Express ill. by author. Doubleday, 1996. ISBN 0-385-32220-8 Subj: Animals – horses, ponies. Careers – postal workers. U.S. history – frontier and pioneer life.

Glass, Marvin. *What happened today, Freddy Groundhog?* ill. by author. Crown, 1989. ISBN 0-517-57140-4 Subj: Animals – groundhogs. Holidays – Groundhog Day.

Glasscock, Sarah. *My prairie summer* ill. by Ed Martinez. Steck-Vaughn, 1998. ISBN 0-8172-7284-4 Subj: Animals – buffaloes. Farms. U.S. history – frontier and pioneer life.

Glassman, Peter. *My working mom* ill. by Tedd Arnold. Morrow, 1994. ISBN 0-688-12260-4 Subj: Family life – mothers. Magic. Witches.

The wizard next door ill. by Steven Kellogg. Morrow, 1993. ISBN 0-688-10646-3 Subj: Imagination. Magic. Wizards.

Glazer, Lee. *Cookie Becker casts a spell* ill. by Margot Apple. Little, 1980. ISBN 0-316-31582-6 Subj: Character traits – meanness. Magic.

Gleeson, Brian. *Anansi* ill. by Steven Guarnaccia. Picture Book Studio, 1991. ISBN 0-88708-230-0 Subj: Folk and fairy tales. Foreign lands – Jamaica. Spiders.

Finn McCoul ill. by Peter de Sève. Rabbit Ears, 1995. ISBN 0-689-80201-3 Subj: Folk and fairy tales. Foreign lands – Ireland. Giants. Tall tales.

Koi and the kola nuts ill. by Reynold Ruffins. Picture Book Studio, 1992. ISBN 0-88708-281-5 Subj: Character traits – kindness to animals. Folk and fairy tales. Foreign lands – Liberia.

Paul Bunyan ill. by Rick Meyerowitz. Rabbit Ears, 1993. ISBN 0-8870-8302-1 Subj: Careers – lumber-jacks. Tall tales. U.S. history – frontier and pioneer life.

The Savior is born ill. by Robert Van Nutt. Rabbit Ears, 1992. ISBN 0-88708-283-1 Subj: Holidays – Christmas. Religion.

The tiger and the Brahmin ill. by Kurt Vargo. Rabbit Ears, 1992. ISBN 0-8870-8232-7 Subj: Animals. Animals – tigers. Folk and fairy tales. Foreign lands – India.

Gleiter, Jan. *Paul Revere* by Jan Gleiter and Kathleen Thompson; ill. by Francis Balistreri. Raintree, 1995. ISBN 0-8172-2644-3 Subj: U.S. history. War.

Sacagawea by Jan Gleiter and Kathleen Thompson; ill. by Yoshi Miyake. Raintree, 1987. ISBN 0-8172-2651-6 Subj: Indians of North America – Shoshone. U.S. history.

Glen, Maggie. *Ruby* ill. by author. Putnam, 1991. ISBN 0-399-22281-2 Subj: Prejudice. Toys – bears.

Ruby to the rescue ill. by author. Putnam, 1992. ISBN 0-399-22149-2 Subj: School. Self-concept.

Glennon, Karen M. *Miss Eva and the red balloon* ill. by Hans Poppel. Simon & Schuster, 1990. ISBN 0-671-68854-5 Subj: Careers – teachers. Magic. Toys – balloons.

Gliori, Debi. *A lion at bedtime* ill. by author. Barron's, 1994. ISBN 0-8120-6379-1 Subj: Animals – lions. Bedtime. Emotions – fear.

Mr. Bear babysits ill. by author. Golden Books, 1994. ISBN 0-307-17506-5 Subj: Activities. Activities – babysitting. Animals – bears. Behavior – misbehavior.

Mr. Bear says, "Are you there, Baby Bear?" ill. by author. Orchard, 1999. ISBN 0-531-30182-6 Subj: Animals. Animals – bears. Behavior – lost. Format, unusual – toy and movable books. Rhyming text.

Mr. Bear says peek-a-boo ill. by author. Golden Books, 1996. ISBN 0-689-81516-6 Subj: Activities – playing. Animals – bears. Format, unusual – board books. Games.

Mr. Bear's new baby ill. by author. Orchard, 1999. ISBN 0-531-30152-4 Subj: Animals – bears. Babies. Family life.

Mr. Bear's picnic ill. by author. Golden Books, 1995. ISBN 0-615-00266-8 Subj: Activities – picnicking. Animals – bears.

My little brother ill. by author. Candlewick, 1992. ISBN 1-56402-079-7 Subj: Family life – brothers and sisters.

New big house ill. by author. Candlewick, 1992. ISBN 1-56402-036-3 Subj: Activities – making things. Family life. Homes, houses.

New big sister ill. by author. Bradbury, 1991. ISBN 0-02-735995-6 Subj: Babies. Birth. Family life – new sibling. Multiple births – twins.

No matter what ill. by author. Harcourt, 1999. ISBN 0-15-202061-6 Subj: Animals – foxes. Emotions – love. Family life. Rhyming text.

A present for Big Pig ill. by Kate Simpson. Candlewick, 1995. ISBN 1-56402-460-1 Subj: Animals – pigs. Gifts.

The princess and the pirate king ill. by author. Kingfisher, 1996. ISBN 0-7534-5023-2 Subj: Family life. Pirates. Royalty – princesses.

The snow lambs ill. by author. Scholastic, 1996. ISBN 0-590-20304-5 Subj: Animals – dogs. Animals – sheep. Weather – snow. Weather – storms.

The snowchild ill. by author. Bradbury, 1994. ISBN 0-02-735997-2 Subj: Activities – playing. Emotions – loneliness. Friendship. Weather – snow.

What can I give him? ill. by author. Holiday, 1998. ISBN 0-8234-1392-6 Subj: Gifts. Holidays – Christmas. Religion – Nativity. Rhyming text.

When I'm big ill. by author. Candlewick, 1994. ISBN 1-56402-241-2 Subj: Bedtime. Concepts – size. Imagination.

Willie Bear and the Wish Fish ill. by author. Macmillan, 1995. ISBN 0-02-736021-0 Subj: Animals – bears. Behavior – wishing. Fish. Weather.

Glyman, Caroline A. *Learning your ABC's of nutrition* ill. by Dee Biser. Forest House, 1992. ISBN 1-878363-75-1 Subj: ABC books. Food. Health and fitness.

What's above the sky? a book about the planets ill. by Dee Biser. Forest House, 1992. ISBN 1-878363-76-X Subj: Planets. Sky. Stars.

Go tell Aunt Rhody. *Go tell Aunt Rhody* ill. by Aliki. Macmillan, 1974. ISBN 0-02-700410-4 Subj: Family life – aunts, uncles. Folk and fairy tales. Games. Songs.

Go tell Aunt Rhody ill. by Robert M. Quackenbush. Lippincott, 1973. ISBN 0-397-31459-0 Subj: Family life – aunts, uncles. Games. Music. Songs.

Gobhai, Mehlli. *Lakshmi, the water buffalo who wouldn't* ill. by author. Hawthorn, 1969. Subj: Animals – water buffaloes. Foreign lands – India.

Usha, the mouse-maiden ill. by author. Hawthorn, 1969. Subj: Family life. Folk and fairy tales. Foreign lands – India.

Goble, Paul. *Adopted by the eagles: a Plains Indian story of friendship and treachery* ill. by author. Bradbury, 1994. ISBN 0-02-736575-1 Subj: Animals – horses, ponies. Birds – eagles. Folk and fairy tales. Indians of North America – Lakota (Sioux).

Beyond the ridge ill. by author. Bradbury, 1988. ISBN 0-02-736581-6 Subj: Death. Indians of North America – Great Plains.

Buffalo woman ill. by author. Bradbury, 1984. ISBN 0-02-737720-2 Subj: Folk and fairy tales. Indians of North America.

Crow chief: a Plains Indian story ill. by author. Orchard, 1992. ISBN 0-531-08547-3 Subj: Birds – crows. Folk and fairy tales. Indians of North America – Crow.

Death of the iron horse ill. by author. Bradbury, 1987. ISBN 0-02-737830-6 Subj: Indians of North America – Cheyenne (Sioux). Trains. War.

The dream wolf ill. by author. Rev. ed. of The friendly wolf. Bradbury, 1990. ISBN 0-02-736585-9 Subj: Folk and fairy tales. Indians of North America – Great Plains.

The friendly wolf ill. by author. Dutton, 1974. ISBN 0-87888-104-2 Subj: Animals – wolves. Behavior – lost. Indians of North America – Great Plains.

The gift of the sacred dog ill. by author. Bradbury, 1980. ISBN 0-87888-165-4 Subj: Animals – horses, ponies. Folk and fairy tales. Gifts. Indians of North America – Great Plains.

The girl who loved wild horses ill. by author. Dutton, 1978. ISBN 0-87888-121-2 Subj: Animals – horses, ponies. Caldecott award books. Indians of North America.

The great race of the birds and animals ill. by author. Bradbury, 1991. ISBN 0-689-71452-1 Subj: Animals. Birds. Creation. Folk and fairy tales. Indians of North America – Cheyenne (Sioux).

Her seven brothers ill. by author. Bradbury, 1988. ISBN 0-02-737960-4 Subj: Animals – buffaloes. Folk and fairy tales. Indians of North America – Cheyenne (Sioux).

I sing for the animals ill. by author. Bradbury, 1991. ISBN 0-02-737725-3 Subj: Activities – singing. Creation. Nature.

Iktomi and the berries: a Plains Indian story ill. by author. Orchard, 1989. ISBN 0-531-08419-1 Subj: Folk and fairy tales. Indians of North America – Great Plains.

Iktomi and the boulder ed. by Richard Jackson; ill. by author. Watts, 1988. ISBN 0-531-08360-8 Subj: Birthdays. Character traits – conceit. Folk and fairy tales. Indians of North America – Dakota (Sioux). Indians of North America – Great Plains. Rocks.

Iktomi and the buffalo skull: a Plains Indian story ill. by author. Orchard, 1991. ISBN 0-531-08511-2 Subj: Behavior – trickery. Character traits – conceit. Folk and fairy tales. Indians of North America – Great Plains.

Iktomi and the buzzard ill. by author. Orchard, 1994. ISBN 0-531-08662-3 Subj: Behavior – trickery. Birds – buzzards. Folk and fairy tales. Indians of North America – Dakota (Sioux).

Iktomi and the coyote: a Plains Indian story ill. by author. Orchard, 1998. ISBN 0-531-33108-3 Subj: Behavior – trickery. Folk and fairy tales. Indians of North America – Great Plains. Mythical creatures.

Iktomi and the ducks: a Plains Indian story ill. by author. Orchard, 1990. ISBN 0-531-08483-3 Subj:

Animals – coyotes. Behavior – trickery. Birds – ducks. Folk and fairy tales. Indians of North America – Great Plains.

The legend of the White Buffalo Woman ill. by author. National Geographic, 1998. ISBN 0-7922-7074-6 Subj: Folk and fairy tales. Indians of North America – Lakota (Sioux).

The lost children: the boys who were neglected ill. by author. Bradbury, 1993. ISBN 0-02-736555-7 Subj: Character traits – meanness. Folk and fairy tales. Indians of North America – Blackfoot. Indians of North America – Siksika. Orphans. Stars.

Love flute ill. by author. Bradbury, 1992. ISBN 0-02-736261-2 Subj: Character traits – shyness. Emotions – love. Folk and fairy tales. Indians of North America – Dakota (Sioux).

Remaking the earth: a creation story from the Great Plains of North America ill. by author. Orchard, 1996. ISBN 0-531-08874-X Subj: Creation. Folk and fairy tales. Indians of North America – Great Plains. Weather – floods.

The return of the buffaloes: a Plains Indian story about famine and renewal of the earth ill. by author. National Geographic, 1996. ISBN 0-7922-2714-X Subj: Animals – buffaloes. Folk and fairy tales. Food. Indians of North America – Lakota (Sioux).

Star boy ill. by author. Bradbury, 1983. ISBN 0-02-722660-3 Subj: Activities – dancing. Character traits – appearance. Folk and fairy tales. Indians of North America – Siksika.

Godard, Alex. *Idora* trans. by Laura McKenna; ill. by author. Kane/Miller, 1999. ISBN 0-916291-89-8 Subj: Animals. Animals – giraffes. Emotions – loneliness.

Goddard, Carrie Lou. *Isn't it a wonder!* ill. by Leigh Grant. Abingdon, 1976. ISBN 0-687-19715-5 Subj: Religion.

Godfrey, Jane. *see* Bowden, Joan Chase

Godkin, Celia. *What about ladybugs?* ill. by author. Sierra Club, 1995. ISBN 0-87156-549-8 Subj: Ecology. Gardens, gardening. Insects – ladybugs. Nature.

Godwin, Laura. *Little white dog* ill. by Dan Yaccarino. Hyperion, 1998. ISBN 0-7868-2256-2 Subj: Animals. Concepts – color. Concepts – shape. Imagination. Rhyming text.

Goennel, Heidi. *The circus* ill. by author. Morrow, 1992. ISBN 0-688-10884-9 Subj: Circus.

Colors ill. by author. Little, 1990. ISBN 0-316-31843-4 Subj: Concepts – color.

Heidi's zoo: an un-alphabet book ill. by author. Tambourine, 1993. ISBN 0-688-12110-1 Subj: ABC books. Animals.

I pretend ill. by author. Tambourine, 1995. ISBN 0-688-13593-5 Subj: Imagination.

If I were a penguin . . . ill. by author. Little, 1989. ISBN 0-316-31841-8 Subj: Animals. Imagination.

It's my birthday ill. by author. Tambourine, 1992. ISBN 0-688-11422-9 Subj: Birthdays. Parties.

My day ill. by author. Little, 1988. ISBN 0-316-31839-6 Subj: Activities.

My dog ill. by author. Orchard, 1989. ISBN 0-531-08434-5 Subj: Animals – dogs. Pets.

Odds and evens ill. by author. Tambourine, 1994. ISBN 0-688-12919-6 Subj: Counting, numbers.

Seasons ill. by author. Little, 1986. ISBN 0-316-31836-1 Subj: Seasons.

Sometimes I like to be alone ill. by author. Little, 1989. ISBN 0-316-31842-6 Subj: Activities. Behavior – solitude.

When I grow up . . . ill. by author. Little, 1987. ISBN 0-316-31838-8 Subj: Behavior – growing up.

While I am little ill. by author. Tambourine, 1993. ISBN 0-688-12372-4 Subj: Activities. Behavior – growing up.

Goff, Beth. *Where's daddy? the story of a divorce* ill. by Susan Perl. Beacon, 1969. ISBN 0-8070-2388-4 Subj: Divorce.

Goffe, Toni. *The story of creation* ill. by author. Standard, 1997. ISBN 0-7847-0629-9 Subj: Creation.

Toby's animal rescue service ill. by author. David & Charles, 1982. ISBN 0-241-10580-3 Subj: Activities – ballooning. Animals.

Goffin, Josse. *The Christmas story* ill. by author. Ticknor & Fields, 1994. ISBN 0-395-70929-6 Subj: Holidays – Christmas. Religion – Nativity.

Oh! ill. by author. Abrams, 1991. ISBN 0-8109-3660-7 Subj: Format, unusual – toy and movable books. Wordless.

Silent Christmas ill. by author. Boyds Mills, 1991. ISBN 1-878093-08-8 Subj: Holidays – Christmas. Religion – Nativity. Wordless.

Who is the boss? ill. by author. Houghton Mifflin, 1992. ISBN 0-395-61192-X Subj: Behavior – fighting, arguing.

Yes ill. by author. Lothrop, 1993. ISBN 0-688-12376-7 Subj: Animals. Eggs.

Goffstein, M. B. (Marilyn Brooke). *Across the sea* ill. by author. Farrar, 1968. Subj: Foreign lands.

An actor ill. by author. HarperCollins, 1987. ISBN 0-06-022169-0 Subj: Activities – working. Careers. Theater.

An artist ill. by author. Harper, 1980. ISBN 0-06-022013-9 Subj: Art. Careers – artists.

Artists' helpers enjoy the evening ill. by author. HarperCollins, 1987. ISBN 0-06-022182-8 Subj: Art. Concepts – color. Foreign lands – France.

Family scrapbook ill. by author. Farrar, 1978. ISBN 0-374-32269-4 Subj: Family life.

Fish for supper ill. by author. Dial, 1976. ISBN 0-8037-2572-8 Subj: Caldecott award honor books. Family life – grandmothers. Old age. Sports – fishing.

A house, a home photos by author. HarperCollins, 1989. ISBN 0-06-022437-1 Subj: Homes, houses.

Laughing latkes ill. by author. Farrar, 1981. ISBN 0-374-34364-0 Subj: Holidays – Hanukkah. Jewish culture.

A little Schubert ill. by author. HarperCollins, 1972. ISBN 0-8792-3540-3 Subj: Music.

Me and my captain ill. by author. Farrar, 1974. ISBN 0-374-34901-0 Subj: Toys – dolls.

My Noah's ark ill. by author. HarperCollins, 1978. ISBN 0-06-022023-6 Subj: Boats, ships. Religion – Noah. Weather – floods. Weather – rain.

Natural history ill. by author. Farrar, 1979. ISBN 0-374-35498-7 Subj: Animals. Character traits – kindness to animals.

Neighbors ill. by author. HarperCollins, 1979. ISBN 0-06-022019-4 Subj: Character traits – shyness. Emotions – loneliness.

Our prairie home: a picture album ill. by author. HarperCollins, 1988. ISBN 0-06-022291-3 Subj: Country. Family life. Toys – dolls.

Our snowman ill. by author. HarperCollins, 1986. ISBN 0-06-022153-4 Subj: Activities – playing. Family life. Snowmen.

School of names ill. by author. HarperCollins, 1986. ISBN 0-06-021985-8 Subj: Names. School. World.

Sleepy people ill. by author. Farrar, 1966. Subj: Bedtime.

A writer ill. by author. HarperCollins, 1984. ISBN 0-06-022143-7 Subj: Activities – working. Careers – writers.

Gold, Julie. *From a distance* ill. by Jane Ray. Dutton, 1998. ISBN 0-525-45872-7 Subj: Activities – singing. War.

Goldblatt, Eli. *Leo loves round* ill. by Wendy Osterweil. Harbinger House, 1990. ISBN 0-943173-49-3 Subj: Concepts – shape. Rhyming text.

The golden goose ill. by William Stobbs. McGraw-Hill, 1967. Subj: Birds – chickens. Cumulative tales. Folk and fairy tales. Humor. Royalty.

Golden tales from long ago: *Like Grandpa, Only birds, The three kittens.* Delacorte, 1980. Anonymous stories published by Ernest Nister in London near the turn of the century. ISBN 0-440-03015-3 Subj: Format, unusual.

Goldfrank, Helen Colodny Kay. *see* Kay, Helen

Goldhor, Susan Henne. *What's so terrible about swallowing an apple seed?* (Lerner, Harriet Goldhor)

Goldie-Morrison, Karen. *Danger colors* (Oxford Scientific Films)

Hide and seek (Oxford Scientific Films)

Goldin, Augusta. *Ducks don't get wet* ill. by Leonard P. Kessler. Crowell, 1989. ISBN 0-690-04782-7 Subj: Birds – ducks. Science.

Salt ill. by Robert Galster. Crowell, 1966. ISBN 0-690-71815-2 Subj: Science.

The shape of water ill. by Demi. Doubleday, 1979. ISBN 0-385-02385-5 Subj: Science.

Spider silk ill. by Joseph Low. Crowell, 1964. Subj: Science. Spiders.

Straight hair, curly hair ill. by Ed Emberley. Crowell, 1966. ISBN 0-690-77921-6 Subj: Hair. Science.

Where does your garden grow? ill. by Helen Borten. Crowell, 1967. ISBN 0-690-88358-7 Subj: Gardens, gardening. Science.

Goldin, Barbara Diamond. *Cakes and miracles: a Purim tale* ill. by Erika Weihs. Viking, 1991. ISBN 0-670-83047-X Subj: Activities – cooking. Food. Handicaps – blindness. Jewish culture. Religion. Self-concept.

Just enough is plenty: a Hannukkah tale ill. by Seymour Chwast. Viking, 1988. ISBN 0-670-81852-6 Subj: Behavior – sharing. Holidays – Hanukkah. Jewish culture.

World's birthday ill. by Jeanette Winter. Harcourt, 1990. ISBN 0-15-299648-6 Subj: Birthdays. Holidays – Rosh Hashanah. Jewish culture.

Golding, Kim. *Alphababies* ill. by author. DK, 1998. ISBN 0-7894-2529-7 Subj: ABC books. Babies. Rhyming text.

Goldman, Dara. *There's no such thing!* ill. by author. Putnam, 1990. ISBN 0-399-22193-X Subj: Animals – bears. Behavior – trickery. Character traits – cleverness.

Goldman, Molly Rose. *How to take your grandmother to the museum* (Wyse, Lois)

Goldman, Susan. *Cousins are special* ill. by author. Albert Whitman, 1978. ISBN 0-8075-1317-2 Subj: Family life.

Grandma is somebody special ed. by Caroline Rubin; ill. by author. Albert Whitman, 1976. ISBN 0-8075-3034-4 Subj: Family life – grandmothers.

Goldner, Kathryn Allen. *The dangers of strangers* (Vogel, Carole Garbuny)

Goldsmith, Cathy. *Did I ever tell you how high you can count?* (Hayward, Linda)

I can add upside down! (Hayward, Linda)

Oh, the things you can count from 1-10 (Hayward, Linda)

Wet foot, dry foot, low foot, high foot (Hayward, Linda)

Goldsmith, Howard. *Little lost dog* ill. by Ulises Wensell. Santillana, 1983. ISBN 0-88272-179-8 Subj: Animals – dogs. Behavior – lost. Character traits – honesty. Friendship. Illness.

Sleepy little owl ill. by Denny Bond. Learning Triangle Pr., 1997. ISBN 0-07-024543-6 Subj: Animals. Bedtime. Birds – owls. Dreams.

Toto the timid turtle ill. by Shirley Chan. Human Sciences Pr., 1981. ISBN 0-87705-525-7 Subj: Reptiles – turtles, tortoises.

Goldstein, Bobbye S. *Bear in mind: a book of bear poems* ill. by William Pène du Bois. Viking, 1989. ISBN 0-670-81907-7 Subj: Animals – bears. Poetry.

Birthday rhymes, special times sel. by Bobbye S. Goldstein; ill. by José Aruego and Ariane Dewey. Delacorte, 1993. ISBN 0-385-30418-8 Subj: Birthdays. Poetry.

Inner chimes: poems on poetry sel. by Bobbye S. Goldstein; ill. by Jane Breskin Zalben. Boyds Mills, 1992. ISBN 1-56397-040-6 Subj: Poetry.

What's on the menu? ill. by Chris L. Demarest. Viking, 1992. ISBN 0-670-83031-3 Subj: Food. Poetry.

Goldstone, Bruce. *The beastly feast* ill. by Blair Lent. Holt, 1998. ISBN 0-8050-3867-1 Subj: Activities – picnicking. Animals. Food.

Gold-Vukson, Marji. *The colors of my Jewish Year* ill. by author. Kar-Ben Copies, 1998. ISBN 1-58013-011-9 Subj: Concepts – color. Format, unusual – board books. Jewish culture. Religion.

Golembe, Carla. *Annabelle's big move* ill. by author. Houghton Mifflin, 1999. ISBN 0-395-91543-0 Subj: Animals – dogs. Emotions – loneliness.

Gollub, Matthew. *The twenty-five Mixtec cats* ill. by Leovigildo Martinez. Tambourine, 1993. ISBN 0-688-11640-X Subj: Animals – cats. Folk and fairy tales. Foreign lands – Mexico. Magic.

Gomboli, Mario. *Look inside a house* trans. by Denice Patrick; ill. by author. Putnam, 1989. ISBN 0-448-19351-5 Subj: Format, unusual – board books. Homes, houses.

Look inside a ship trans. by Denice Patrick; ill. by author. Putnam, 1989. ISBN 0-448-19352-3 Subj: Boats, ships. Format, unusual – board books.

Gomi, Taro. *The big book of boxes* ill. by author. Chronicle, 1991. ISBN 0-8118-0067-9 Subj: Concepts – shape.

Bus stop ill. by author. Chronicle, 1988. ISBN 0-87701-551-1 Subj: Activities -- traveling. Buses. Transportation.

Coco can't wait! ill. by author. Morrow, 1984. ISBN 0-688-02790-3 Subj: Family life – grandmothers.

The crocodile and the dentist ill. by author. Millbrook, 1994. ISBN 1-56294-555-6 Subj: Careers – dentists. Reptiles – alligators, crocodiles. Teeth.

First comes Harry ill. by author. Morrow, 1987. ISBN 0-688-06732-8 Subj: Behavior – hurrying.

Guess what? ill. by author. Chronicle, 1992. ISBN 0-8118-0015-6 Subj: Concepts. Format, unusual – board books.

Guess who? ill. by author. Chronicle, 1991. ISBN 0-8118-0021-0 Subj: Animals. Format, unusual – board books. Games. Toys.

Hi, butterfly! ill. by author. Morrow, 1985. ISBN 0-688-04138-8 Subj: Format, unusual. Insects – butterflies, caterpillars.

My friends ill. by author. Chronicle, 1990. ISBN 0-87701-688-7 Subj: Activities. Animals.

Santa through the window ill. by author. Millbrook, 1995. ISBN 1-56294-454-1 Subj: Animals. Format, unusual – toy and movable books. Gifts. Holidays – Christmas. Santa Claus.

Seeing, saying, doing, playing ill. by author. Chronicle, 1991. ISBN 0-87701-859-6 Subj: Activities. Language.

Spring is here ill. by author. Chronicle, 1989. ISBN 0-87701-626-7 Subj: Animals – bulls, cows. Seasons.

Toot! ill. by author. Morrow, 1986. ISBN 0-688-06421-3 Subj: Illness. Music. Rhyming text.

Where's the fish? ill. by author. Morrow, 1986. ISBN 0-688-06242-3 Subj: Behavior – hiding. Fish.

Who ate it? ill. by author. Millbrook, 1991. ISBN 1-56294-010-4 Subj: Games.

Who hid it? ill. by author. Millbrook, 1991. ISBN 1-56294-011-2 Subj: Games.

The good-hearted youngest brother: *an Hungarian folktale* trans. by Emöke de Papp Severo; ill. by Diane Goode. Bradbury, 1981. ISBN 0-87888-141-7 Subj: Character traits – kindness to animals. Folk and fairy tales. Foreign lands – Hungary. Magic.

Good, Merle. *Amos and Susie: an Amish story* ill. by Cheryl Benner. Good Books, 1993. ISBN 1-56148-088-6 Subj: Activities. Ethnic groups in the U.S. – Amish. Religion. Rhyming text. Seasons.

Reuben and the fire ill. by P. Buckley Moss. Good Books, 1993. ISBN 1-56148-091-6 Subj: Ethnic groups in the U.S. – Amish. Family life. Fire.

Good, Phyllis Pellman. *Plain Pig's ABCs: a day on Plain Pig's Amish farm* ill. by Cheryl Benner. Good Books, 1998. ISBN 1-56148-251-X Subj: ABC books. Animals – pigs. Ethnic groups in the U.S. – Amish. Farms.

Goodall, Daphne Machin. *Zebras* ill. with photos. Raintree, 1978. Subj: Animals – zebras.

Goodall, Jane. *Dr. White* ill. by Julie Wintz-Litty. North-South, 1999. ISBN 0-7358-1064-8 Subj: Animals – pigs. Hospitals. Illness.

Goodall, John S. *The adventures of Paddy Pork* ill. by author. Harcourt, 1968. ISBN 0-15-201589-2 Subj: Animals – pigs. Behavior – running away. Circus. Format, unusual. Wordless.

The ballooning adventures of Paddy Pork ill. by author. Harcourt, 1969. Subj: Animals – pigs. Format, unusual. Wordless.

Creepy castle ill. by author. Rev. jacket ed. Margaret K. McElderry, 1998. ISBN 0-689-82205-7 Subj: Animals – mice. Format, unusual. Knights. Monsters. Wordless.

An Edwardian Christmas ill. by author. Atheneum, 1978. ISBN 0-689-50106-4 Subj: Foreign lands – England. Format, unusual. Holidays – Christmas. Wordless.

An Edwardian summer ill. by author. Atheneum, 1976. ISBN 0-689-50062-9 Subj: Foreign lands – England. Format, unusual. Seasons – summer. Wordless.

Great days of a country house ill. by author. Margaret K. McElderry, 1992. ISBN 0-689-50545-0 Subj: Foreign lands – England. Homes, houses.

Jacko ill. by author. Harcourt, 1971. ISBN 0-15-239494-X Subj: Animals – monkeys. Boats, ships. Format, unusual. Wordless.

The midnight adventures of Kelly, Dot and Esmeralda ill. by author. Margaret K. McElderry, 1999. ISBN 0-689-82564-1 Subj: Format, unusual. Wordless.

Naughty Nancy ill. by author. Rev. jacket ed. Margaret K. McElderry, 1999. ISBN 0-689-82358-4 Subj: Behavior – misbehavior. Format, unusual. Weddings. Wordless.

Naughty Nancy goes to school ill. by author. Margaret K. McElderry, 1999. ISBN 0-689-82563-3 Subj: Animals – mice. Behavior – misbehavior. Format, unusual. School – first day. Wordless.

Paddy goes traveling ill. by author. Atheneum, 1982. ISBN 0-689-50239-7 Subj: Activities – traveling. Animals – pigs. Format, unusual. Wordless.

Paddy Pork: odd jobs ill. by author. Atheneum, 1983. ISBN 0-689-50293-1 Subj: Activities – working. Animals – pigs. Format, unusual. Wordless.

Paddy Pork's holiday ill. by author. Atheneum, 1976. ISBN 0-689-50043-2 Subj: Activities – vacationing. Animals – pigs. Format, unusual. Wordless.

Paddy to the rescue ill. by author. Atheneum, 1986. ISBN 0-689-50330-X Subj: Animals – pigs. Behavior – stealing. Character traits – bravery. Crime. Wordless.

Paddy under water ill. by author. Atheneum, 1984. ISBN 0-689-50297-4 Subj: Animals – pigs. Format, unusual. Sea and seashore. Wordless.

Paddy's evening out ill. by author. Atheneum, 1973. ISBN 8-689-30412-9 Subj: Animals – pigs. Format, unusual. Theater. Wordless.

Paddy's new hat ill. by author. Atheneum, 1980. ISBN 0-689-50172-2 Subj: Animals – pigs. Careers – police officers. Format, unusual. Wordless.

Puss in boots (Perrault, Charles)

Shrewbettina's birthday ill. by author. Rev. jacket ed. Margaret K. McElderry, 1998. ISBN 0-689-82206-5 Subj: Animals – shrews. Birthdays. Format, unusual. Wordless.

The story of a castle ill. by author. Macmillan, 1986. ISBN 0-689-50405-5 Subj: Foreign lands – England. Format, unusual. Wordless.

The story of a farm ill. by author. Macmillan, 1988. ISBN 0-689-50479-9 Subj: Farms. Foreign lands – England. Format, unusual. Wordless.

The story of a main street ill. by author. Macmillan, 1987. ISBN 0-233-98070-9 Subj: City. Format, unusual. Roads. Wordless.

The story of an English village ill. by author. Atheneum, 1979. ISBN 0-689-50125-0 Subj: City. Foreign lands – England. Format, unusual. Progress. Wordless.

The surprise picnic ill. by author. Rev. jacket ed. Margaret K. McElderry, 1999. ISBN 0-689-82359-2 Subj: Activities – picnicking. Animals – cats. Food. Format, unusual. Wordless.

Goode, Diane. *Cinderella* (Perrault, Charles)

Diane Goode's book of silly stories & songs ill. by author. Dutton, 1992. ISBN 0-525-44967-1 Subj: Folk and fairy tales. Humor. Music. Songs.

The dinosaur's new clothes ill. by author. Blue Sky, 1999. ISBN 0-590-38360-4 Subj: Character traits – pride. Character traits – vanity. Clothing. Dinosaurs. Folk and fairy tales. Imagination. Royalty – emperors.

The fir tree (Andersen, H. C. [Hans Christian])

I hear a noise ill. by author. Dutton, 1988. ISBN 0-525-44353-3 Subj: Bedtime. Dragons. Emotions – fear. Monsters. Night.

The little book of farm friends ill. by author. Dutton, 1993. ISBN 0-525-45157-9 Subj: Animals. Farms. Nursery rhymes.

Mama's perfect present ill. by author. Dutton, 1996. ISBN 0-525-45493-4 Subj: Animals – dogs. Birthdays. Family life – brothers and sisters. Family life – mothers. Foreign lands – France.

Where's our mama? ill. by author. Dutton, 1991. ISBN 0-525-44770-9 Subj: Behavior – lost. Family life – mothers. Foreign lands – France.

Goode, Molly. *Mama loves* ill. by Lisa McCue. Random House, 1999. ISBN 0-679-99462-9 Subj: Animals. Animals – babies. Birds. Family life – mothers. Rhyming text.

Goodenow, Earle. *The last camel* ill. by author. Walck, 1968. Subj: Animals – camels. Foreign lands – Egypt.

The owl who hated the dark ill. by author. Walck, 1969. ISBN 0-8098-1145-6 Subj: Birds – owls. Emotions – fear. Night.

Goodhart, Pippa. *Noah makes a boat* ill. by Bernard Lodge. Houghton Mifflin, 1997. ISBN 0-395-86957-9 Subj: Animals. Boats, ships. Religion – Noah. Weather – floods. Weather – rain. Weather – rainbows.

Row, row, row your boat ill. by Stephen Lambert. Crown, 1997. ISBN 0-517-70970-8 Subj: Animals. Animals – lions. Boats, ships. Dreams. Islands. Music. Songs. Toys.

Goodman, Joan Elizabeth. *Bernard's bath* ill. by Dominic Catalano. Boyds Mills, 1996. ISBN 1-56397-323-5 Subj: Activities – bathing. Animals – elephants. Family life.

Bernard's nap ill. by Dominic Catalano. Boyds Mills, 1999. ISBN 1-56397-728-1 Subj: Animals – elephants. Bedtime. Dreams. Sleep.

Goodman, Louise. *Ida's doll* ill. by Debby L. Carter. HarperCollins, 1989. ISBN 0-06-022276-X Subj: Family life – grandmothers. Family life – sisters. Poverty. Toys – dolls.

Goodsell, Jane. *Katie's magic glasses* ill. by Barbara Cooney. Houghton Mifflin, 1965. ISBN 0-395-20108-X Subj: Careers – doctors. Glasses. Senses – seeing.

Toby's toe ill. by Gioia Fiammenghi. Morrow, 1986. ISBN 0-688-06162-1 Subj: Character traits – kindness. Character traits – meanness. Toys – balloons.

Goodspeed, Peter. *Hugh and Fitzhugh* ill. by Carol Nicklaus. Platt, 1974. ISBN 0-8228-7575-6 Subj: Animals – dogs. Language.

A rhinoceros wakes me up in the morning: a bedtime tale ill. by Dennis Panek. Bradbury, 1982. ISBN 0-87888-201-4 Subj: Animals. Bedtime. Rhyming text.

Goor, Nancy. *All kinds of feet* (Goor, Ron)

In the driver's seat (Goor, Ron)

Shadows: here, there and everywhere (Goor, Ron)

Signs (Goor, Ron)

Goor, Ron. *All kinds of feet* by Ron and Nancy Goor; photos by authors. Crowell, 1984. ISBN 0-690-04385-6 Subj: Anatomy – feet. Animals.

In the driver's seat by Ron and Nancy Goor; photos by authors. Crowell, 1982. ISBN 0-690-04177-2 Subj: Activities. Machines.

Shadows: here, there and everywhere by Ron and Nancy Goor; photos by authors. Crowell, 1981. ISBN 0-690-04133-0 Subj: Shadows.

Signs by Ron and Nancy Goor; photos by authors. Crowell, 1983. ISBN 0-690-04355-4 Subj: Activities – reading. Communication.

Gorbachev, Valeri. *The Fool of the world and the flying ship: a Ukrainian folk tale* ill. by adapt. Star Bright, 1998. ISBN 1-887734-19-8 Subj: Activities – flying. Boats, ships. Character traits – cleverness. Folk and fairy tales. Foreign lands – Ukraine. Royalty – tsars.

Nicky and the big, bad wolves ill. by author. North-South, 1998. ISBN 1-55858-918-X Subj: Animals – rabbits. Animals – wolves. Bedtime. Dreams. Emotions – fear.

Where is the apple pie? ill. by author. Philomel, 1999. ISBN 0-399-23385-7 Subj: Animals. Character traits – questioning. Circular tales. Tall tales.

Gorbaty, Norman. *Get up and go, little dinosaur!* ill. by author. Random House, 1990. ISBN 0-679-80693-8 Subj: Dinosaurs. Format, unusual – board books.

Tow truck ill. by author. Grosset, 1993. ISBN 0-448-40597-0 Subj: Format, unusual – toy and movable books. Trucks.

Gordon, Gaelyn. *Duckat* ill. by Chris Gaskin. Scholastic, 1992. ISBN 0-590-45455-2 Subj: Animals – cats. Birds – ducks. Self-concept.

Gordon, Jeffie Ross. *Six sleepy sheep* ill. by John O'Brien. Boyds Mills, 1991. ISBN 1-878093-06-1 Subj: Animals – sheep. Language. Tongue twisters.

Two badd babies ill. by Chris L. Demarest. Boyds Mills, 1992. ISBN 1-878093-85-1 Subj: Bedtime. Multiple births – twins. Rhyming text.

Gordon, Lynn. *The witch's revenge* ill. by Val Martino. Simon & Schuster, 1997. ISBN 0-689-81679-0 Subj: Format, unusual – toy and movable books. Holidays – Halloween. Witches.

Gordon, Margaret. *Frogs' holiday* ill. by author. Viking, 1987. ISBN 0-670-80854-7 Subj: Activities – babysitting. Frogs and toads.

The supermarket mice ill. by author. Dutton, 1984. ISBN 0-525-44145-X Subj: Animals – cats. Animals – mice. Problem solving. Stores.

Wilberforce goes on a picnic ill. by author. Morrow, 1982. ISBN 0-688-01481-X Subj: Activities – picnicking. Animals – bears.

Wilberforce goes to a party ill. by author. Viking, 1985. ISBN 0-670-80148-8 Subj: Animals – bears. Behavior – misbehavior. Birthdays. Etiquette. Parties.

Gordon, Ruth. *Feathers* ill. by Lydia Dabcovich. Macmillan, 1993. ISBN 0-02-736511-5 Subj: Character traits – foolishness. Folk and fairy tales. Foreign lands – Poland. Jewish culture.

Gordon, Sharon. *Christmas surprise* ill. by John Magine. Troll, 1980. ISBN 0-89375-273-8 Subj: Animals – bears. Holidays – Christmas.

Dinosaurs in trouble ill. by Paul Harvey. Troll, 1980. ISBN 0-89375-274-6 Subj: Dinosaurs.

Dolphins and porpoises ill. by June Goldsborough. Troll, 1985. ISBN 0-8167-0340-X Subj: Animals – dolphins. Sea and seashore.

Easter Bunny's lost egg ill. by John Magine. Troll, 1980. ISBN 0-89375-375-0 Subj: Animals – rabbits. Eggs. Holidays – Easter.

Friendly snowman ill. by John Magine. Troll, 1980. ISBN 0-89375-377-7 Subj: Snowmen.

Pete the parakeet ill. by Paul Harvey. Troll, 1980. ISBN 0-89075-384-X Subj: Birds – parakeets, parrots.

Play ball, Kate! ill. by Don Page. Troll, 1981. ISBN 0-89375-525-7 Subj: Sports – baseball.

Sam the scarecrow ill. by Don Silverstein. Troll, 1980. ISBN 0-89375-387-4 Subj: Scarecrows.

Three little witches ill. by Deborah Sims. Troll, 1980. ISBN 0-89375-390-4 Subj: Witches.

Tick tock clock ill. by Don Page. Troll, 1982. ISBN 0-89375-676-8 Subj: Clocks, watches. Time.

Trees ill. by Irene Trivas. Troll, 1983. ISBN 0-89375-801-5 Subj: Trees.

What a dog! ill. by Deborah Sims. Troll, 1980. ISBN 0-89375-393-9 Subj: Animals – dogs.

Gordon, Shirley. *Grandma zoo* ill. by Whitney Darrow, Jr. HarperCollins, 1978. ISBN 0-06-022050-3 Subj: Animals. Family life – grandmothers. Zoos.

Gore, Sheila. *My shadow* photos by Fiona Pragoff. Doubleday, 1990. ISBN 0-385-41198-7 Subj: Activities. Concepts – perspective. Science. Shadows.

Gorey, Edward (St. John). *The tunnel calamity* ill. by author. Putnam, 1984. ISBN 0-399-21055-5 Subj: Format, unusual. Monsters. Wordless.

Gorham, Michael. *see* Elting, Mary

Gorog, Judith. *Zilla Sasparilla and the mud baby* ill. by Amanda Harvey. Candlewick, 1995. ISBN 1-56402-295-1 Subj: Babies. Behavior – worrying. Family life – grandmothers. Family life – mothers. Rivers.

Gorsline, Douglas W. *North American Indians* (Gorsline, Marie)

Gorsline, Marie. *North American Indians* by Marie and Douglas W. Gorsline; ill. by authors. Random House, 1978. ISBN 0-394-93702-3 Subj: Indians of North America. U.S. history.

Nursery rhymes (Mother Goose)

Goss, Linda. *The frog who wanted to be a singer* ill. by Cynthia Jabar. Orchard, 1995. ISBN 0-531-08745-X Subj: Activities – singing. Frogs and toads. Music.

Gottlieb, Dale. *Seeing Eye Willie* ill. by author. Knopf, 1992. ISBN 0-679-92449-3 Subj: Character traits – curiosity. Homeless. Imagination.

Where Jamaica go? ill. by author. Orchard, 1996. ISBN 0-531-08875-8 Subj: Foreign lands – Caribbean Islands. Rhyming text.

Goudey, Alice E. *The day we saw the sun come up* ill. by Adrienne Adams. Scribners, 1961. Subj: Caldecott award honor books. Family life. Sun.

The good rain ill. by Nora Spicer Unwin. Dutton, 1950. Subj: Weather – rain.

Houses from the sea ill. by Adrienne Adams. Scribners, 1959. Subj: Caldecott award honor books. Sea and seashore.

Red legs ill. by Marie Nonnast. Scribners, 1966. Subj: Insects.

Gould, Deborah. *Aaron's shirt* ill. by Cheryl Harness. Bradbury, 1989. ISBN 0-02-736351-1 Subj: Behavior – growing up. Clothing – shirts.

Brendan's best-timed birthday ill. by Jacqueline Rogers. Bradbury, 1988. ISBN 0-02-737390-8 Subj: Behavior – sharing. Birthdays. Clocks, watches. Parties.

Camping in the Temple of the Sun ill. by Diane Paterson. Bradbury, 1992. ISBN 0-02-736355-4 Subj: Camps, camping. Family life. Weather.

Grandpa's slide show ill. by Cheryl Harness. Lothrop, 1987. ISBN 0-688-06973-8 Subj: Death. Dreams. Emotions – grief. Family life – grandparents.

Goundaud, Karen Jo. *A very mice joke book* ill. by Lynn Munsinger. Houghton Mifflin, 1981. ISBN 0-395-30445-8 Subj: Animals – mice. Riddles.

Gove, Doris. *My mother talks to trees* ill. by Marilynn H. Mallory. Peachtree, 1999. ISBN 1-56145-166-5 Subj: Activities. Family life – mothers. Trees.

Goyder, Alice. *Holiday in Catland* ill. by author. Crowell, 1979. ISBN 0-690-03932-8 Subj: Activities – vacationing. Animals – cats.

Party in Catland ill. by author. Crowell, 1979. ISBN 0-690-03930-1 Subj: Animals – cats. Parties.

Grabianski, Janusz. *Cats* ill. by author. Watts, 1966. Subj: Animals – cats.

Grabianski's wild animals ill. by author. Watts, 1969. Translation of Tiere der Wildnis. Subj: Animals.

Horses ill. by author. Watts, 1966. Subj: Animals – horses, ponies.

Graeber, Charlotte Towner. *Nobody's Dog* ill. by Barry Root. Hyperion, 1998. ISBN 0-7868-2093-4 Subj: Animals – dogs. Behavior – needing someone.

Graeber, Jean B. *Bantie and her chicks* ill. by June Hendrickson. Melmont, 1959. Subj: Birds – chickens. School. Science.

Graff, Nancy Price. *In the hush of the evening* ill. by G. Brian Karas. HarperCollins, 1998. ISBN 0-06-022099-6 Subj: Bedtime. Concepts – color. Noise, sounds.

Graham, Al. *Timothy Turtle* ill. by Tony Palazzo. Walck, 1946. Subj: Caldecott award honor books. Character traits – ambition. Character traits – helpfulness. Friendship. Reptiles – turtles, tortoises.

Graham, Amanda. *Picasso, the green tree frog* ill. by John Siow. Gareth Stevens, 1987. ISBN 1-55532-152-6 Subj: Concepts – color. Frogs and toads.

Who wants Arthur? ill. by Donna Gynell. Gareth Stevens, 1987. ISBN 1-55532-153-4 Subj: Animals – dogs. Behavior – imitation. Stores.

Graham, Bob. *Benny* ill. by author. Candlewick, 1999. ISBN 0-7636-0813-0 Subj: Animals – dogs. Careers – magicians.

Crusher is coming! ill. by author. Viking, 1987. ISBN 0-670-82081-4 Subj: Babies. Friendship.

First there was Frances ill. by author. Bradbury, 1986. ISBN 0-02-737030-5 Subj: Animals. Family life. Moving.

Greetings from Sandy Beach ill. by author. Kane/ Miller, 1992. ISBN 0-916291-40-5 Subj: Activities – vacationing. Camps, camping. Family life. Sea and seashore.

Has anyone here seen William? ill. by author. Little, 1989. ISBN 0-316-32313-6 Subj: Behavior – misbehavior.

Libby, Oscar and me ill. by author. HarperCollins, 1985. ISBN 0-911745-89-0 Subj: Activities – picnicking. Animals – cats. Animals – dogs.

Pete and Roland ill. by author. Viking, 1984. ISBN 0-670-54912-6 Subj: Birds – parakeets, parrots. Character traits – kindness to animals.

Queenie, one of the family ill. by author. Candlewick, 1997. ISBN 0-7636-0359-7 Subj: Birds – chickens. Character traits – kindness to animals. Family life.

The red woolen blanket ill. by author. Little, 1988. ISBN 0-316-32310-1 Subj: Behavior – growing up. Concepts – color.

Rose meets Mr. Wintergarten ill. by author. Candlewick, 1992. ISBN 1-56402-039-8 Subj: Friendship. Old age.

Spirit of Hope ill. by author. Mondo, 1996. ISBN 1-57255-202-6 Subj: Family life. Homes, houses. Moving.

The wild ill. by author. HarperCollins, 1987. ISBN 0-87226-139-5 Subj: Family life. Nature. Pets.

Graham, Charlotte. *see* Bowden, Joan Chase

Graham, Georgia. *The strongest man this side of Cremona* ill. by author. Red Deer Pr., 1998. ISBN 0-88995-182-9 Subj: Emotions – love. Family life – fathers. Farms. Weather – storms.

Graham, Hugh. *see* Barrows, Marjorie Wescott

Graham, Ian. *The best book of spaceships* ill. by author. Kingfisher, 1998. ISBN 0-7534-5133-6 Subj: Space and space ships.

Graham, Joan Bransfield. *Flicker flash* ill. by Nancy Davis. Houghton Mifflin, 1999. ISBN 0-395-90501-X Subj: Lights. Poetry.

Graham, John. *A crowd of cows* ill. by Feodor Rojankovsky. Harcourt, 1968. Subj: Animals. Noise, sounds.

I love you, mouse ill. by Tomie de Paola. Harcourt, 1976. ISBN 0-15-238005-1 Subj: Animals. Animals – mice.

Graham, Lorenz B. *David he no fear* ill. by Ann Grifalconi. Crowell, 1971. ISBN 0-690-23265-9 Subj: Religion.

Every man heart lay down ill. by Colleen Browning. Crowell, 1970. ISBN 0-690-27134-4 Subj: Religion – Nativity.

God wash the world and start again ill. by Clare Romano. Crowell, 1971. ISBN 0-690-33295-5 Subj: Boats, ships. Religion – Noah. Weather – floods. Weather – rain.

Hongry catch the foolish boy ill. by James Brown, Jr. Crowell, 1973. Story first appeared in the author's How God fix Jonah, published in 1946. ISBN 0-690-40112-4 Subj: Religion.

A road down in the sea ill. by Gregorio Prestopino. Crowell, 1970. ISBN 0-690-70500-X Subj: Religion.

Song of the boat ill. by Leo and Diane Dillon. Crowell, 1975. ISBN 0-690-75232-6 Subj: Foreign lands – Africa. Rhyming text.

Graham, Margaret Bloy. *Be nice to spiders* ill. by author. HarperCollins, 1967. ISBN 0-06-022073-2 Subj: Spiders. Zoos.

Benjy and his friend Fifi ill. by author. HarperCollins, 1988. ISBN 0-06-022253-0 Subj: Animals – dogs. Character traits – helpfulness. Emotions – fear.

Benjy and the barking bird ill. by author. HarperCollins, 1971. ISBN 0-06-022079-1 Subj: Animals – dogs. Birds – parakeets, parrots. Emotions – envy, jealousy.

Benjy's boat trip ill. by author. HarperCollins, 1977. ISBN 0-06-022093-7 Subj: Animals – dogs. Boats, ships.

Benjy's dog house ill. by author. HarperCollins, 1973. ISBN 0-06-022084-8 Subj: Animals – dogs.

Graham, Mary Stuart (Campbell). *The pirates' bridge* ill. by Winifred Lubell. Lothrop, 1960. Subj: Pirates.

Graham, Richard. *Jack and the monster* ill. by Susan Varley. Houghton Mifflin, 1989. ISBN 0-395-49680-2 Subj: Babies. Emotions – envy, jealousy. Family life – new sibling. Sibling rivalry.

Graham, Steve. *Dear old Donegal* music by author; ill. by John O'Brien. Clarion, 1996. ISBN 0-395-68187-1 Subj: Foreign lands – Ireland. Music. Songs.

Graham, Thomas. *Mr. Bear's boat* ill. by author. Dutton, 1988. ISBN 0-525-44375-4 Subj: Activities – picnicking. Animals – bears. Boats, ships.

Mr. Bear's chair ill. by author. Dutton, 1987. ISBN 0-525-44300-2 Subj: Activities – making things. Animals – bears. Family life. Furniture – chairs.

Grahame, Kenneth. *Duck song* ill. by Joung Un Kim. HarperFestival, 1998. ISBN 0-694-01163-0 Subj: Birds – ducks. Format, unusual – board books. Rhyming text.

The open road ill. by Beverley Gooding. Scribners, 1980. ISBN 0-684-16471-X Subj: Activities – traveling. Animals.

The wind in the willows: home sweet home ill. by Val Biro. Wanderer, 1987. ISBN 0-671-63629-4 Subj: Animals. Holidays – Christmas. Homes, houses.

The wind in the willows: the open road ill. by Val Biro. Wanderer, 1987. ISBN 0-671-63626-X Subj: Activities – traveling. Animals.

The wind in the willows: the river bank ill. by Val Biro. Wanderer, 1987. ISBN 0-671-63627-8 Subj: Animals. Rivers.

The wind in the willows: the wild wood ill. by Val Biro. Wanderer, 1987. ISBN 0-671-63628-6 Subj: Animals. Forest, woods.

Gralley, Jean. *Hogula, dread pig of night* ill. by author. Holt, 1999. ISBN 0-8050-5700-5 Subj: Animals – pigs. Friendship. Monsters – vampires.

Gramatky, Hardie. *Bolivar* ill. by author. Putnam, 1961. Subj: Animals – donkeys. Foreign lands – South America.

Hercules ill. by author. Putnam, 1940. ISBN 0-399-60240-2 Subj: Careers – firefighters. Fire. Museums. Trucks.

Homer and the circus train ill. by author. Putnam, 1957. Subj: Circus. Trains.

Little Toot ill. by author. Putnam, 1939. Subj: Boats, ships. Character traits – ambition.

Little Toot and the Loch Ness monster ill. by Hardie and Dorothea Cooke Gramatky. Putnam, 1989. ISBN 0-399-21684-7 Subj: Boats, ships. Foreign lands – Scotland. Monsters.

Little Toot on the Mississippi ill. by author. Putnam, 1973. Subj: Boats, ships. Rivers.

Little Toot on the Thames ill. by author. Putnam, 1964. Subj: Boats, ships. Foreign lands – England.

Little Toot through the Golden Gate ill. by author. Putnam, 1975. Subj: Boats, ships. Character traits – individuality. City.

Loopy ill. by author. Putnam, 1941. Subj: Activities – flying. Airplanes, airports.

Nikos and the sea god ill. by author. Putnam, 1963. Subj: Careers – fishermen. Folk and fairy tales. Mythical creatures. Religion.

Sparky: the story of a little trolley car ill. by author. Putnam, 1952. Subj: Cable cars, trolleys. Transportation.

Grambling, Lois G. *Can I have a Stegosaurus, Mom? Can I? Please!?* ill. by H. B. Lewis. BridgeWater, 1994. ISBN 0-8167-3386-4 Subj: Dinosaurs. Pets.

Daddy will be there ill. by Walter Gaffney-Kessell. Greenwillow, 1998. ISBN 0-688-14984-7 Subj: Activities. Family life – fathers.

Night sounds ill. by Randall R. Ray. Rayve, 1996. ISBN 1-877810-77-0 Subj: Bedtime. Night. Noise, sounds. Sleep.

Granfield, Linda. *The legend of the panda* ill. by Song Nan Zhang. Tundra, 1998. ISBN 0-88776-421-5 Subj: Animals – pandas. Folk and fairy tales. Foreign lands – China.

Silent night: the song from heaven ill. by Nelly and Ernst Hofer. Tundra, 1997. ISBN 0-88776-395-2 Subj: Holidays – Christmas. Music. Songs.

Granowsky, Alvin. *The dinosaurs' last days* ill. by Paul Lopez. Steck-Vaughn, 1992. ISBN 0-8114-3250-5 Subj: Dinosaurs. Science.

Meat-eating dinosaurs ill. by Carol Inouye. Steck-Vaughn, 1992. ISBN 0-8114-3254-8 Subj: Dinosaurs. Science.

The three billy goats Gruff (Asbjørnsen, P. C. [Peter Christen])

Granström, Brita. *Honk! honk!* (Manning, Mick)

My body, your body (Manning, Mick)

Grant, Joan. *The monster that grew small* ill. by Jill K. Schwarz. Lothrop, 1987. ISBN 0-688-06809-X Subj: Character traits – bravery. Character traits – kindness to animals. Emotions – fear. Folk and fairy tales. Foreign lands – Egypt. Monsters.

Grant, Matthew G. *see* May, Julian

Grasshopper to the rescue: *a Georgian story* trans. from Russian by Bonnie Carey; ill. by Tasha Tudor. Morrow, 1979. Subj: Character traits – bravery. Cumulative tales. Insects – grasshoppers. Rivers.

Graves, Helen. *The brave little kittens* (Wilkon, Piotr)

Graves, Keith. *Frank was a monster who wanted to dance* ill. by author. Chronicle, 1999. ISBN 0-8118-2169-2 Subj: Activities – dancing. Monsters. Rhyming text.

Gray, Catherine. *Tammy and the gigantic fish* by Catherine and James Gray; ill. by William Joyce. HarperCollins, 1983. Subj: Family life. Sports – fishing.

Gray, Genevieve. *How far, Felipe?* ill. by Ann Grifalconi. HarperCollins, 1978. Subj: Activities – traveling. Animals – donkeys. Character traits – perseverance.

Send Wendell ill. by Symeon Shimin. McGraw-Hill, 1974. Subj: Character traits – helpfulness. Ethnic groups in the U.S. – African Americans. Family life.

Gray, James. *Tammy and the gigantic fish* (Gray, Catherine)

Gray, Jenny. *see* Gray, Genevieve

Gray, Libba Moore. *Is there room on the feather bed?* ill. by Nadine Bernard Westcott. Orchard, 1997. ISBN 0-531-33013-3 Subj: Animals. Animals – skunks. Cumulative tales. Farms. Rhyming text. Weather – storms.

The little black truck ill. by Elizabeth Sayles. Simon & Schuster, 1994. ISBN 0-671-78105-7 Subj: Trucks.

Miss Tizzy ill. by Jada Rowland. Simon & Schuster, 1993. ISBN 0-671-77590-1 Subj: Communities, neighborhoods. Ethnic groups in the U.S. – African Americans. Friendship. Illness.

My mama had a dancing heart ill. by Raúl Colón. Orchard, 1995. ISBN 0-531-08770-0 Subj: Activities – dancing. Ballet. Family life – mothers. Seasons.

Small green snake ill. by Holly Meade. Orchard, 1994. ISBN 0-531-08694-1 Subj: Reptiles – snakes. Rhyming text.

When Uncle took the fiddle ill. by Lloyd Bloom. Orchard, 1999. ISBN 0-531-33137-7 Subj: Family life – aunts, uncles. Music.

Gray, Nigel. *A balloon for grandad* ill. by Jane Ray. Watts, 1988. ISBN 0-531-08355-1 Subj: Family life – fathers. Family life – grandfathers. Toys – balloons.

A country far away ill. by Philippe Dupasquier. Watts, 1989. ISBN 0-531-08392-6 Subj: Family life. Foreign lands.

The dog show by Nigel Gray and Margaret Wilson; ill. by Margaret Wilson. Cygnet Books, 1996. ISBN 1-875560-63-7 Subj: Animals – cats. Animals – dogs. Contests.

Fly ill. by Craig Smith. Cygnet Books, 1994. ISBN 1-875560-39-4 Subj: Insects – flies. Rhyming text.

The frog prince ill. by Allan Langoulant. Cygnet Books, 1996. ISBN 1-8755-6068-8 Subj: Folk and fairy tales. Frogs and toads. Royalty – princes. Royalty – princesses.

The grocer's daughter ill. by David Mackintosh. Univ. of Queensland Pr., 1994. ISBN 0-7022-2703-X Subj: Behavior. Rhyming text.

I'll take you to Mrs. Cole! ill. by Michael Foreman. Kane/Miller, 1992. ISBN 0-916291-39-1 Subj: Behavior – running away. Ethnic groups in the U.S. – African Americans.

It'll all come out in the wash ill. by Edward Frascino. HarperCollins, 1979. Subj: Family life.

Little pig's tale ill. by Mary Rees. Macmillan, 1990. ISBN 0-02-736942-0 Subj: Animals – pigs. Birthdays. Family life.

Pigs can't fly ill. by Carme Solé Vendrell. Andersen, 1990. ISBN 0-8626-4272-8 Subj: Animals – pigs. Concepts – size.

Running away from home ill. by Gregory Rogers. Crown, 1996. ISBN 0-517-70923-6 Subj: Behavior – running away. Family life – fathers.

Grayson, Laura. *see* Wilson, Barbara Ker

Grayson, Marion F. *Let's count and count out* (Let's count and count out)

Greaves, Margaret. *The firebird* (The firebird)

Henry's wild morning ill. by Teresa O'Brien. Dial, 1991. ISBN 0-8037-0907-2 Subj: Animals – cats. Character traits – ambition.

Kate Crackernuts ill. by Francesca Crespi. Dial, 1985. ISBN 0-8037-0225-6 (set) Subj: Folk and fairy tales. Foreign lands – England. Magic. Royalty – princesses. Royalty – queens. Witches.

Little Bear and the Papagini circus ill. by Francesca Crespi. Dial, 1986. ISBN 0-8037-0264-7 Subj: Animals – bears. Circus. Family life.

The lucky coin (Underhill, Liz)

The mice of Nibbling Village ill. by Jane Pinkney. Dutton, 1986. ISBN 0-525-44277-4 Subj: Animals – mice. Rhyming text.

Mother Cuspen ill. by Francesca Crespi. Dial, 1985. ISBN 0-8037-0225-6 (set) Subj: Folk and fairy tales. Foreign lands – England. Witches.

The naming ill. by Pauline Baynes. Harcourt, 1993. ISBN 0-15-200534-X Subj: Animals. Mythical creatures – unicorns. Names.

Once there were no pandas ill. by Beverley Gooding. Dutton, 1985. ISBN 0-525-44211-1 Subj: Animals – pandas. Character traits – bravery.

Petrushka ill. by Francesca Crespi. Dial, 1986. ISBN 0-8037-0265-5 (set) Subj: Ballet. Folk and fairy tales. Foreign lands – Russia. Puppets.

Sarah's lion ill. by Honey de Lacey. Barron's, 1992. ISBN 0-8120-6279-5 Subj: Animals – lions. Behavior. Royalty – princesses.

The star horse ill. by Jan Nesbitt. Barron's, 1992. ISBN 0-8120-6294-9 Subj: Animals – horses, ponies. Behavior – wishing. Merry-go-rounds.

The witch cat ill. by Francesca Crespi. Dial, 1985. ISBN 0-8037-0225-6 (set) Subj: Animals – cats. Folk and fairy tales. Foreign lands – England. Witches.

The witch's servant ill. by Francesca Crespi. Dial, 1985. ISBN 0-8037-0225-6 (set) Subj: Folk and fairy tales. Foreign lands – England. Witches.

Greeley, Valerie. *The acorn's story* ill. by author. Macmillan, 1994. ISBN 0-02-736916-1 Subj: Rhyming text. Seeds. Trees.

Animals ill. by author. Peter Bedrick, 1990. ISBN 0-8722-6435-1 Subj: Animals. Format, unusual – board books.

Farm animals ill. by author. HarperCollins, 1984. Subj: Animals. Farms. Format, unusual – board books. Wordless.

Field animals ill. by author. HarperCollins, 1984. Subj: Animals. Format, unusual – board books. Wordless.

Pets ill. by author. HarperCollins, 1984. Subj: Animals. Format, unusual – board books. Pets. Wordless.

Where's my share? ill. by author. Macmillan, 1990. ISBN 0-02-736761-4 Subj: Animals. Birds. Circular tales. Food. Nursery rhymes.

White is the moon ill. by author. Macmillan, 1991. ISBN 0-02-736915-3 Subj: Animals. Concepts – color. Nature. Rhyming text.

Zoo animals ill. by author. HarperCollins, 1984. Subj: Animals. Format, unusual – board books. Wordless. Zoos.

Green, Adam. *see* Weisgard, Leonard

Green, Donna. *My little artist* ill. by author. Smithmark, 1999. ISBN 0-7651-1742-8 Subj: Careers – artists. Family life – grandmothers.

The green grass grows all around: *a traditional folk song* ill. by Hilde Hoffmann. Macmillan, 1968. Subj: Plants. Poetry. Songs.

Green, Jen. *Our new baby* ill. by Christopher O'Neill. Copper Beech, 1998. ISBN 0-7613-0871-7 Subj: Babies. Family life – brothers and sisters.

Green, Marion. *The magician who lived on the mountain* ill. by John Dyke. Childrens Pr., 1978. Subj: Art. Magic.

Green, Mary McBurney. *Everybody has a house and everybody eats* ill. by Louis Klein. Abelard-Schuman, 1944. Subj: Farms. Homes, houses.

Is it hard? Is it easy? ill. by Lucienne Bloch. Abelard-Schuman, 1948. Subj: Concepts.

Green, Melinda. *Bembelman's bakery* ill. by Barbara Seuling. Parents, 1978. ISBN 0-8193-0914-1 Subj: Careers – bakers.

Green, Norma B. *The hole in the dike* ill. by Eric Carle. Crowell, 1974. ISBN 0-690-00676-4 Subj: Character traits – helpfulness. Foreign lands – Holland.

Green, Phyllis. *Bagdad ate it* ill. by Joel Schick. Watts, 1980. ISBN 0-531-02855-0 Subj: Animals – dogs. Behavior – greed.

Uncle Roland, the perfect guest ill. by Marybeth Farrell. Four Winds, 1983. ISBN 0-590-07885-2 Subj: Family life – aunts, uncles.

Green-Armytage, Stephen. *Dudley, the little terrier that could* ill. by author. Abrams, 1999. ISBN 0-8109-4098-1 Subj: Animals – dogs. Concepts – size. Self-concept.

Greenaway, Kate. *A apple pie* ill. by author. Warne, 1886. ISBN 0-7232-1801-3 Subj: ABC books.

Marigold garden ill. by author. Warne, 1885. Subj: Poetry.

Under the window ill. by author. Warne, 1880?. Subj: Poetry.

Greenaway, Shirley. *Forests* ill. with photos. Newington, 1991. ISBN 1-878137-08-5 Subj: Animals. Forest, woods. Nature.

Jungles ill. with photos. Newington, 1991. ISBN 1-878137-09-3 Subj: Animals. Jungle. Nature.

Greenberg, Barbara. *The bravest babysitter* ill. by Diane Paterson. Dial, 1977. ISBN 0-8037-0364-3 Subj: Activities – babysitting. Babies. Emotions – fear. Weather.

Greenberg, Dan. *The bed who ran away from home* ill. by John Wallner. HarperCollins, 1991. ISBN 0-06-022280-8 Subj: Bedtime. Behavior – running away. Furniture – beds. Multiple births – twins. Rhyming text.

Greenberg, David (David T.). *Bugs!* ill. by Lynn Munsinger. Little, 1997. ISBN 0-316-32574-0 Subj: Insects. Rhyming text.

Slugs ill. by Victoria Chess. Little, 1983. ISBN 0-316-32658-5 Subj: Animals – snails. Rhyming text.

Greenberg, Judith E. *Adopted* by Judith E. Greenberg and Helen H. Carey; photos by Barbara Kirk. Watts, 1987. ISBN 0-531-10290-4 Subj: Adoption. Babies.

What is the sign for friend? photos by Gayle Rothschild. Watts, 1985. ISBN 0-531-04939-6 Subj: Handicaps – deafness. Language. Senses – hearing.

Greenberg, Melanie Hope. *At the beach* ill. by author. Dutton, 1989. ISBN 0-525-44474-2 Subj: Sea and seashore.

My father's luncheonette ill. by author. Dutton, 1991. ISBN 0-525-44725-3 Subj: Activities – cooking. Careers. City. Family life – fathers.

Greenberg, Polly. *Oh, Lord, I wish I was a buzzard* ill. by Aliki. Macmillan, 1968. Subj: Behavior – wishing. Ethnic groups in the U.S. – African Americans. Farms. Plants.

Greenblat, Rodney Alan. *Aunt Ippy's museum of junk* ill. by author. HarperCollins, 1991. ISBN 0-06-022512-2 Subj: Behavior – collecting things. Family life – aunts, uncles.

Thunder Bunny ill. by author. HarperCollins, 1997. ISBN 0-06-026434-9 Subj: Activities – drawing. Activities – traveling. Activities – writing. Animals – rabbits. Imagination. Weather – clouds.

Uncle Wizzmo's new used car ill. by author. HarperCollins, 1990. ISBN 0-06-022098-8 Subj: Automobiles. Family life – aunts, uncles.

Greenburg, Dan. *Great-Grandpa's in the litter box* ill. by Jack E. Davis. Grosset, 1996. ISBN 0-448-41289-6 Subj: Animals – cats. Family life – great-grandparents. Imagination.

Through the medicine cabinet ill. by Jack E. Davis. Grosset, 1996. ISBN 0-448-41291-8 Subj: Imagination. Self-concept.

Greene, Carla. *Doctors and nurses: what do they do?* ill. by Leonard P. Kessler. HarperCollins, 1963. ISBN 0-06-022076-7 Subj: Careers – doctors. Careers – nurses.

I want to be a carpenter ill. by Frances Eckart. Childrens Pr., 1959. Subj: Careers – carpenters.

A motor holiday ill. by Harold L. Van Pelt. Melmont, 1956. Subj: Activities – traveling. Automobiles.

Greene, Carol. *Astronauts work in space* ill. with photos. Child's World, 1998. ISBN 1-56766-406-7 Subj: Careers – astronauts. Space and space ships.

A computer went a-courting: a love song for Valentine's Day ill. by Tom Dunnington. Childrens Pr., 1983. ISBN 0-516-08232-9 Subj: Animals – mice. Computers. Holidays – Valentine's Day. Music. Songs.

God's good creation ill. by Michelle Dorenkamp. Concordia, 1994. ISBN 0-570-09040-7 Subj: Creation. Religion.

The golden locket ill. by Marcia Sewall. Harcourt, 1992. ISBN 0-15-231220-X Subj: Behavior – worrying. Emotions – love. Problem solving.

Hi, clouds ill. by Gene Sharp. Grosset, 1989. ISBN 0-516-02036-6 Subj: Weather – clouds.

Hinny Winny Bunco ill. by Jeanette Winter. HarperCollins, 1982. ISBN 0-06-022129-1 Subj: Music. Sibling rivalry. Songs.

I can be a baseball player ill. with photos. Childrens Pr., 1985. ISBN 0-516-01845-0 Subj: Careers. Sports – baseball.

I can be a forest ranger ill. with photos. Childrens Pr., 1989. ISBN 0-516-41924-2 Subj: Careers – park rangers. Forest, woods. Nature.

I can be a librarian ill. with photos. Childrens, 1988. ISBN 0-516-01913-9 Subj: Careers – librarians.

I can be a model ill. with photos. Childrens Pr., 1985. ISBN 0-516-01887-6 Subj: Careers – models.

The insignificant elephant ill. by Susan Gantner. Harcourt, 1985. ISBN 0-15-238730-7 Subj: Animals – elephants. Animals – rabbits.

Katherine Dunham: black dancer ill. by author. Childrens Pr., 1992. ISBN 0-516-04252-1 Subj: Activities – dancing. Ethnic groups in the U.S. – African Americans.

Margaret Wise Brown, author of Goodnight moon ill. by author. Childrens Pr., 1993. ISBN 0-516-04254-8 Subj: Activities – writing.

Margarete Steiff, toy maker ill. by author. Childrens Pr., 1993. ISBN 0-516-04257-2 Subj: Toys – bears.

The old ladies who liked cats ill. by Loretta Krupinski. HarperCollins, 1991. ISBN 0-06-022105-4 Subj: Animals – cats. Ecology. Islands. Old age.

Please, wind? ill. by Gene Sharp. Childrens Pr., 1982. ISBN 0-516-02033-1 Subj: Weather – wind.

Rain! Rain! ill. by Larry Frederick. Childrens Pr., 1982. ISBN 0-516-42034-8 Subj: Weather – rain.

Reading about the gray wolf ill. by author. Enslow, 1993. ISBN 0-89490-427-2 Subj: Animals – endangered animals. Animals – wolves.

Reading about the peregrine falcon ill. by author. Enslow, 1993. ISBN 0-89490-422-1 Subj: Animals – endangered animals. Birds – falcons.

Reading about the river otter ill. by author. Enslow, 1993. ISBN 0-89490-425-6 Subj: Animals – endangered animals. Animals – otters. Rivers.

Robots ill. with photos. Childrens Pr., 1983. ISBN 0-516-01684-9 Subj: Robots.

Shine, sun! ill. by Gene Sharp. Childrens Pr., 1983. ISBN 0-516-02038-2 Subj: Sun.

Snow Joe ill. by Paul Sharp. Childrens Pr., 1982. ISBN 0-516-02035-8 Subj: Weather – snow.

Sunflower Island ill. by Leonard Jenkins. HarperCollins, 1999. ISBN 0-06-027327-5 Subj: Boats, ships. Islands. Rivers.

Teachers help us learn photos. by Phil Martin. Child's World, 1998. ISBN 1-56766-404-0 Subj: Careers – teachers.

The thirteen days of Halloween ill. by Tom Dunnington. Childrens Pr., 1983. ISBN 0-516-08231-0 Subj: Holidays – Halloween. Music. Songs. Witches.

Where is that cat? ill. by Loretta Krupinski. Hyperion, 1999. ISBN 0-7868-2399-2 Subj: Animals – cats. Behavior – hiding.

The world's biggest birthday cake ill. by Tom Dunnington. Childrens Pr., 1985. ISBN 0-516-08233-7 Subj: Birthdays. Food. Music. Rhyming text.

Greene, Ellin. *Billy Beg and his bull* ill. by Kimberly Bulcken Root. Holiday, 1994. ISBN 0-8234-1100-1 Subj: Animals – bulls, cows. Folk and fairy tales. Foreign lands – Ireland. Magic. Royalty – princes. Royalty – princesses.

The legend of the Christmas rose (Lagerlöf, Selma)

The legend of the cranberry: a Paleo-Indian tale ill. by Brad Sneed. Simon & Schuster, 1993. ISBN 0-671-75975-2 Subj: Animals. Folk and fairy tales. Indians of North America – Delaware.

Ling-li and the phoenix fairy ill. by Zong-Zhou Wang. Clarion, 1996. ISBN 0-395-71528-8 Subj: Birds. Clothing. Flowers. Folk and fairy tales. Foreign lands – China. Mythical creatures – phoenix. Weddings.

The pumpkin giant ill. by Trina Schart Hyman. Lothrop, 1970. Orig. story by Mary E. Wilkins. Subj: Food. Giants. Holidays – Halloween.

Greene, Graham. *The little fire engine* ill. by Edward Ardizzone. Doubleday, 1973. ISBN 0-385-08908-2 Subj: Fire. Progress.

The little train ill. by Edward Ardizzone. Doubleday, 1973. ISBN 0-385-08907-4 Subj: Behavior – running away. Trains.

Greene, Jacqueline Dembar. *Butchers and bakers, rabbis and kings* ill. by Marilyn Hirsh. Kar-Ben Copies, 1984. ISBN 0-930494-27-X Subj: Jewish culture.

What his father did ill. by John O'Brien. Houghton Mifflin, 1992. ISBN 0-395-55042-4 Subj: Folk and fairy tales. Food. Jewish culture. Poverty.

Greene, Laura. *Change: getting to know about ebb and flow* ill. by Gretchen Will Mayo. Human Sciences Pr., 1981. ISBN 0-898540-10-0 Subj: Concepts.

Help: getting to know about needing and giving ill. by Gretchen Will Mayo. Human Sciences Pr., 1981. ISBN 0-87705-401-0 Subj: Character traits – helpfulness.

Greene, Rhonda Gowler. *Barnyard song* ill. by Robert Bender. Atheneum, 1997. ISBN 0-689-80758-9 Subj: Animals. Farms. Illness. Noise, sounds. Rhyming text.

Greene, Roberta. *Two and me makes three* ill. by Paul Galdone. Coward, 1970. Subj: Ethnic groups in the U.S.

Greenfield, Eloise. *Africa dream* ill. by Carole M. Byard. John Day, 1977. ISBN 0-381-90061-4 Subj: Dreams. Foreign lands – Africa.

Angels ill. by Jan Spivey Gilchrist. Jump at the Sun, 1998. ISBN 0-7868-0442-4 Subj: Angels. Ethnic groups in the U.S. – African Americans. Poetry.

Big friend, little friend ill. by Jan Spivey Gilchrist. Black Butterfly, 1991. ISBN 0-86316-204-5 Subj: Activities – playing. Ethnic groups in the U.S. – African Americans. Format, unusual – board books. Friendship. Poetry.

Daddy and I ill. by Jan Spivey Gilchrist. Black Butterfly, 1991. ISBN 0-86316-206-1 Subj: Ethnic groups in the U.S. – African Americans. Family life – fathers. Format, unusual – board books. Poetry.

Daydreamers ill. by Tom Feelings. Dial, 1981. ISBN 0-8037-2134-X Subj: Ethnic groups in the U.S. – African Americans. Poetry.

Easter parade ill. by Jan Spivey Gilchrist. Hyperion, 1997. ISBN 0-7868-0326-6 Subj: Ethnic groups in the U.S. – African Americans. Family life – cousins. Holidays – Easter. Parades. U.S. history. War.

First pink light ill. by Moneta Barnett. Crowell, 1976. ISBN 0-690-01087-7 Subj: Ethnic groups in the U.S. – African Americans. Family life – fathers.

Grandpa's face ill. by Floyd Cooper. Putnam, 1988. ISBN 0-399-21525-5 Subj: Character traits – appearance. Family life – grandfathers.

I can do it by myself (Little, Lessie Jones)

I make music ill. by Jan Spivey Gilchrist. Black Butterfly, 1991. ISBN 0-86316-205-3 Subj: Ethnic groups in the U.S. – African Americans. Family life. Format, unusual – board books. Music. Poetry.

Kia Tanisha ill. by Jan Spivey Gilchrist. HarperCollins, 1997. ISBN 0-694-00847-8 Subj: Activities – running. Ethnic groups in the U.S. – African Americans. Rhyming text.

Kia Tanisha drives her car ill. by Jan Spivey Gilchrist. HarperCollins, 1997. ISBN 0-694-00848-6 Subj: Activities – driving. Automobiles. Toys.

Lisa's daddy and daughter day ill. by Jan Spivey Gilchrist. Sundance, 1991. ISBN 0-88741-918-6 Subj: Ethnic groups in the U.S. – African Americans. Family life – daughters. Family life – fathers.

Me and Nessie ill. by Moneta Barnett. Crowell, 1975. ISBN 0-690-00715-9 Subj: Ethnic groups in the U.S. – African Americans. Family life. Imagination – imaginary friends.

My doll, Keshia ill. by Jan Spivey Gilchrist. Black Butterfly, 1991. ISBN 0-86316-203-7 Subj: Activities – playing. Ethnic groups in the U.S. – African Americans. Format, unusual – board books. Poetry. Toys – dolls.

Nathaniel talking ill. by Jan Spivey Gilchrist. Black Butterfly, 1988. ISBN 0-86316-200-2 Subj: Ethnic groups in the U.S. – African Americans. Poetry.

Night on Neighborhood Street ill. by Jan Spivey Gilchrist. Dial, 1991. ISBN 0-8037-0778-9 Subj: City. Communities, neighborhoods. Ethnic groups in the U.S. – African Americans. Night. Poetry.

On my horse ill. by Jan Spivey Gilchrist. HarperFestival, 1995. ISBN 0-694-00583-5 Subj: Animals – horses, ponies. Ethnic groups in the U.S. – African Americans. Imagination. Rhyming text.

She come bringing me that little baby girl ill. by John Steptoe. Lippincott, 1974. ISBN 0-397-31586-4 Subj: Babies. Emotions – envy, jealousy. Ethnic groups in the U.S. – African Americans. Family life – new sibling. Sibling rivalry.

Sweet baby coming ill. by Jan Spivey Gilchrist. HarperCollins, 1994. ISBN 0-694-00578-9 Subj: Babies. Ethnic groups in the U.S. – African Americans. Family life – new sibling. Format, unusual – board books.

Under the Sunday tree ill. by Amos Ferguson. HarperCollins, 1988. ISBN 0-06-022257-3 Subj: Foreign lands – Caribbean Islands. Islands. Poetry.

Water, water ill. by Jan Spivey Gilchrist. HarperFestival, 1999. ISBN 0-694-01247-5 Subj: Ethnic groups in the U.S. – African Americans. Rhyming text. Water.

William and the good old days ill. by Jan Spivey Gilchrist. HarperCollins, 1993. ISBN 0-06-021094-X Subj: Ethnic groups in the U.S. – African Americans. Family life – grandmothers. Illness.

Greenfield, Karen R. *Sister Yessa's story* ill. by Claire Ewart. HarperCollins, 1992. ISBN 0-06-020279-3 Subj: Activities – walking. Animals. Religion – Noah. Weather – rain. Weather – storms.

Greenfield, Monica. *The baby* ill. by Jan Spivey Gilchrist. HarperCollins, 1994. ISBN 0-694-00577-0 Subj: Babies. Ethnic groups in the U.S. – African Americans. Family life. Format, unusual – board books.

Waiting for Christmas ill. by Jan Spivey Gilchrist. Scholastic, 1996. ISBN 0-590-52700-2 Subj: Ethnic groups in the U.S. – African Americans. Family life. Holidays – Christmas.

Greenleaf, Ann. *No room for Sarah* ill. by author. Dodd, 1983. ISBN 0-396-08213-0 Subj: Bedtime. Toys.

Greenlee, Sharon. *When someone dies* ill. by Bill Drath. Peachtree, 1992. ISBN 1-56145-044-8 Subj: Death. Emotions – grief.

Greenstein, Elaine. *Emily and the crows* ill. by author. Picture Book Studio, 1992. ISBN 0-88708-238-6 Subj: Animals – bulls, cows. Birds – crows. Imagination.

Mrs. Rose's garden ill. by author. Simon & Schuster, 1996. ISBN 0-88708-264-5 Subj: Fairs. Gardens, gardening.

Greenway, Jennifer. *The three billy goats Gruff* (Asbjørnsen, P. C. [Peter Christen])

Greenway, Shirley. *Animal homes: burrows* photos by Oxford Scientific Films. Newington, 1991. ISBN 1-87813-711-5 Subj: Animals. Homes, houses.

Can you see me? photos by Oxford Scientific Films. Ideals, 1992. ISBN 0-8249-8575-3 Subj: Animals. Nature.

Color me bright photos by Oxford Scientific Films. Whispering Coyote, 1992. ISBN 1-879085-53-4 Subj: Animals. Concepts – color. Format, unusual – board books. Nature.

Here's ears photos by Oxford Scientific Films. Whispering Coyote, 1992. ISBN 1-879085-50-X Subj: Anatomy – ears. Animals. Format, unusual – board books. Nature.

How big am I? photos by Oxford Scientific Films. Ideals, 1993. ISBN 0-8249-8625-3 Subj: Animals. Concepts – size.

How do I move? photos by Oxford Scientific Films. Ideals, 1992. ISBN 0-8249-8578-8 Subj: Animals. Nature.

Legs and all photos by Oxford Scientific Films. Whispering Coyote, 1992. ISBN 1-879085-52-6 Subj: Anatomy – legs. Animals. Format, unusual – board books. Nature.

A tale of tails photos by Oxford Scientific Films. Whispering Coyote, 1992. ISBN 1-879085-51-8 Subj: Anatomy – tails. Animals. Format, unusual – board books. Nature.

Two's company . . . photos by Oxford Scientific Films. Charlesbridge, 1997. ISBN 0-88106-964-7 Subj: Animals. Concepts.

What do I eat? photos by Oxford Scientific Films. Ideals, 1993. ISBN 0-8249-8627-X Subj: Animals. Food.

Where do I live? photos by Oxford Scientific Films. Ideals, 1992. ISBN 0-8249-8576-1 Subj: Animals. Ecology. Nature.

Whose baby am I? photos by Oxford Scientific Films. Ideals, 1992. ISBN 0-8249-8577-X Subj: Animals. Nature.

Greenwood, Ann. *A pack of dreams* ill. by Bernard Colonna and Mary Elizabeth Gordon. Prentice-Hall, 1979. ISBN 0-13-647784-4 Subj: Dreams. Rhyming text.

Greeson, Janet. *An American army of two* ill. by Patricia Rose Mulvihill. Carolrhoda, 1992. ISBN 0-87614-664-7 Subj: Character traits – cleverness. Family life – sisters. U.S. history. War.

The stingy baker ill. by David LaRochelle. Carolrhoda, 1989. ISBN 0-87614-378-8 Subj: Angels. Careers – bakers. Folk and fairy tales. Magic. Witches.

Gregg, Andy. *Great Rabbit and the long-tailed Wildcat* ill. by Cat Bowman Smith. Albert Whitman, 1993. ISBN 0-8075-3047-6 Subj: Anatomy – tails. Animals – cougars. Folk and fairy tales. Indians of North America – Algonquian.

Gregoire, Caroline. *Uglypuss* ill. by author; trans. from French by George Wen. Holt, 1994. ISBN 0-8050-3300-9 Subj: Animals – dogs. Pets.

Gregor, Arthur S. *Animal babies* (Ylla)

The little elephant (Ylla)

1, 2, 3, 4, 5 ill. by Robert Doisneau. Lippincott, 1956. Subj: Counting, numbers.

Gregorich, Barbara. *My friend goes left* ill. by Joyce John; ed. by Joan Hoffman. School Zone Pub., 1984. ISBN 0-88743-008-2 Subj: Poetry. Riddles.

Gregorowski, Christopher. *Fly, eagle, fly! an African fable* ill. by Niki Daly. Margaret K. McElderry, 2000. ISBN 0-689-82398-3 Subj: Activities – flying. Birds – eagles. Folk and fairy tales. Foreign lands – Africa. Self-concept.

Gregory, Nan. *How Smudge came* ill. by Ron Lightburn. Walker, 1997. ISBN 0-88995-143-8 Subj: Animals – dogs. Character traits – loyalty. Handicaps – Down syndrome. Pets.

Gregory, Valiska. *Babysitting for Benjamin* ill. by Lynn Munsinger. Little, 1993. ISBN 0-316-32785-9 Subj: Ethnic groups in the U.S. – Amish. Poetry. Weddings.

Kate's giants ill. by Virginia Austin. Candlewick, 1995. ISBN 1-56402-299-4 Subj: Bedtime. Emotions – fear. Giants. Night.

Looking for angels ill. by Leslie A. Baker. Simon & Schuster, 1996. ISBN 0-671-50546-7 Subj: Angels.

The oatmeal cookie giant ill. by Jeni Bassett. Four Winds, 1987. ISBN 0-02-738070-X Subj: Animals – dogs. Family life – aunts, uncles. Old age.

Riddle soup ill. by Jeni Bassett. Four Winds, 1987. ISBN 0-02-738090-4 Subj: Activities – cooking. Animals – dogs.

Sunny side up ill. by Jeni Bassett. Four Winds, 1986. ISBN 0-02-738050-5 Subj: Animals – dogs. Character traits – optimism.

Terribly wonderful ill. by Jeni Bassett. Four Winds, 1986. ISBN 0-02-738110-1 Subj: Animals – dogs. Character traits – optimism.

Through the mickle woods ill. by Barry Moser. Little, 1992. ISBN 0-316-32779-4 Subj: Animals – bears. Death. Folk and fairy tales. Forest, woods. Royalty – kings.

A valentine for Norman Noggs ill. by Martha Winborn. HarperCollins, 1999. ISBN 0-06-027657-6 Subj: Animals – hamsters. Holidays – Valentine's Day. School. Self-concept.

When stories fell like shooting stars ill. by Stefano Vitale. Simon & Schuster, 1996. ISBN 0-689-80012-6 Subj: Animals. Behavior – greed. Character traits – responsibility. Moon. Sun.

Greifenstein, Sandra. *The fish* (Bruna, Dick)

Greisman, Joan. *Things I hate!* (Wittels, Harriet)

Grejniec, Michael. *Albert's nap* ill. by author. North-South, 1995. ISBN 1-55858-280-0 Subj: Animals – hippopotamuses. Insects – flies. Sleep.

Good morning, good night ill. by author. North-South, 1993. ISBN 1-55858-174-X Subj: Activities. Concepts – opposites. Friendship.

Look ill. by author. North-South, 1993. ISBN 1-55858-213-4 Subj: Communities, neighborhoods. Friendship. Illness.

What do you like? ill. by author. North-South, 1992. ISBN 1-55858-176-6 Subj: Character traits – individuality.

When I open my eyes ill. by author. Holt, 1990. ISBN 0-8050-1417-9 Subj: Animals – sheep. Imagination.

Who is my neighbor? ill. by author. Knopf, 1994. ISBN 0-679-95801-0 Subj: Careers – magicians. Communities, neighborhoods. Power failures.

Gretz, Susanna. *Duck takes off* ill. by author. Four Winds, 1991. ISBN 0-02-737472-6 Subj: Activities – playing. Animals. Birds – ducks. Friendship.

Frog, duck, and rabbit ill. by author. Four Winds, 1992. ISBN 0-02-737327-4 Subj: Animals. Clothing – costumes. Parades.

Frog in the middle ill. by author. Four Winds, 1991. ISBN 0-02-737471-8 Subj: Animals. Behavior – secrets. Birthdays. Emotions – envy, jealousy. Friendship. Frogs and toads.

Hide-and-seek ill. by author. Macmillan, 1986. ISBN 0-02-737400-9 Subj: Bedtime. Behavior – hiding. Emotions – fear. Format, unusual – board books. Games. Night. Toys – bears.

I'm not sleepy ill. by author. Macmillan, 1986. ISBN 0-02-737470-X Subj: Bedtime. Format, unusual – board books. Games. Sleep. Toys – bears.

It's your turn, Roger ill. by author. Dial, 1985. ISBN 0-8037-0198-5 Subj: Animals – pigs. Behavior – sharing. Food.

Rabbit food ill. by author. Candlewick, 1999. ISBN 0-7636-0731-2 Subj: Animals – rabbits. Family life – aunts, uncles. Food.

Rabbit rambles on ill. by author. Four Winds, 1992. ISBN 0-02-737325-8 Subj: Animals. Animals – rabbits. Behavior – boasting. Character traits – honesty. Friendship.

Ready for bed ill. by author. Macmillan, 1986. ISBN 0-02-737460-2 Subj: Bedtime. Format, unusual – board books.

Roger loses his marbles! ill. by author. Dial, 1988. ISBN 0-8037-0565-4 Subj: Animals – pigs. Birthdays. Character traits – practicality.

Roger takes charge! ill. by author. Dial, 1987. ISBN 0-8037-0121-7 Subj: Activities – babysitting. Animals – pigs. Behavior – bullying.

Teddy bears ABC ill. by author. Follett, 1975. ISBN 0-695-40540-3 Subj: ABC books. Counting, numbers. Toys – bears.

Teddy bears at the seaside by Susanna Gretz and Alison Sage; ill. by Susanna Gretz. 1st Four Winds Press ed. Four Winds, 1989. First published in . . . 1972 . . . under title The bears who went to the seaside. ISBN 0-02-738141-2 Subj: Animals – dogs. Sea and seashore. Toys – bears.

Teddy bears cure a cold by Susanna Gretz and Alison Sage; ill. by Susanna Gretz. Four Winds, 1985. ISBN 0-590-07949-2 Subj: Illness. Toys – bears.

Teddy bears go shopping ill. by author. Four Winds, 1982. ISBN 0-590-07861-5 Subj: Shopping. Toys – bears.

Teddy bears' moving day ill. by author. Four Winds, 1981. ISBN 0-590-07819-4 Subj: Moving. Toys – bears.

Teddy bears 1 - 10 ill. by author. Four Winds, 1986, 1969. ISBN 0-02-738140-4 Subj: Counting, numbers. Toys – bears.

Teddy bears stay indoors by Susanna Gretz and Alison Sage; ill. by Susanna Gretz. 2nd American ed. with new text. Four Winds, 1987. Rev. ed. of: The bears who stayed indoors. ISBN 0-02-738150-1 Subj: Activities – playing. Food. Toys – bears.

Teddy bears take the train by Susanna Gretz and Alison Sage; ill. by Susanna Gretz. Four Winds, 1987. ISBN 0-02-738170-6 Subj: Activities – traveling. Toys – bears. Trains.

Teddybears cookbook by Susanna Gretz and Alison Sage; ill. by Susanna Gretz. Doubleday, 1978. ISBN 0-385-14415-6 Subj: Activities – cooking. Toys – bears.

Too dark! ill. by author. Macmillan, 1986. ISBN 0-02-737410-6 Subj: Bedtime. Emotions – fear. Format, unusual – board books. Night. Toys – bears.

Greve, Andreas. *Christopher's dream car* ill. by author. Firefly, 1991. ISBN 1-55037-169-X Subj: Automobiles. Family life – grandparents. Imagination.

Greydanus, Rose. *Animals at the zoo* ill. by Susan Hall. Troll, 1980. ISBN 0-89375-371-8 Subj: Animals. Zoos.

Bedtime story ill. by Doug Cushman. Troll, 1988. ISBN 0-8167-0996-3 Subj: Animals – bears. Bedtime. Family life – fathers.

Big red fire engine ill. by Paul Harvey. Troll, 1980. ISBN 0-89375-372-6 Subj: Careers – firefighters. Trucks.

Changing seasons ill. by Susan Hall. Troll, 1983. ISBN 0-89375-802-3 Subj: Seasons.

Climb aboard ill. by George Ulrich. Troll, 1988. ISBN 0-8167-1099-6 Subj: Animals – bears. Animals – rabbits. Sports – sailing.

Freddie the frog ill. by Tom Garcia. Troll, 1980. ISBN 0-89375-376-9 Subj: Frogs and toads.

Horses ill. by Joel Snyder. Troll, 1983. ISBN 0-89375-900-7 Subj: Animals – horses, ponies.

Let's get a pet ill. by Lynn Sweat. Troll, 1988. ISBN 0-8167-0986-6 Subj: Pets.

Let's pretend ill. by Marsha Winborn. Troll, 1981. ISBN 0-8937-5545-1 Subj: Imagination.

My secret hiding place ill. by Paul Harvey. Troll, 1980. ISBN 0-89375-383-1 Subj: Behavior – hiding.

Someone's baby-sitting ill. by Don Page. Troll, 1981. ISBN 0-8937-5515-X Subj: Holidays – Valentine's Day.

Susie goes shopping ill. by Margot Apple. Troll, 1980. ISBN 0-89375-389-0 Subj: Shopping.

Tree house fun ill. by Chris L. Demarest. Troll, 1980. ISBN 0-89375-391-2 Subj: Homes, houses. Trees.

Trouble in space ill. by Don Page. Troll, 1981. ISBN 0-8937-5517-6 Subj: Space and space ships. Toys – bears.

Willie the slowpoke ill. by Andrea Eberbach. Troll, 1980. ISBN 0-89375-394-7 Subj: Behavior – hurrying.

Grieg, E. H. (Edvard Hagerup). *E. H. Grieg's Peer Gynt* adapt. by Makoto Oishi; trans. by Ann Brannen; ill. by Yoshiharu Suzuki. Gakken, 1971. Subj: Folk and fairy tales. Foreign lands – Norway.

Griese, Arnold A. *Anna's Athabaskan summer* ill. by Charles Ragins. Boyds Mills, 1995. ISBN 1-56397-232-8 Subj: Alaska. Family life. Foreign lands – Arctic. Indians of North America – Athabascan. Seasons – summer.

Griessman, Annette. *Jenny's prayer* ill. by Mary Anne Lard. Morehouse, 1998. ISBN 0-8192-1746-8 Subj: Animals – cats. Pets. Religion.

Griest, Lisa. *Lost at the White House: a 1909 Easter story* ill. by Andrea Shine. Carolrhoda, 1994. ISBN 0-87614-726-0 Subj: Holidays – Easter. U.S. history.

Griest, Virginia. *In between* ill. by Monica Wellington. Dutton, 1989. ISBN 0-525-44521-8 Subj: Concepts.

Grifalconi, Ann. *The bravest flute: a story of courage in the Mayan tradition* ill. by author. Little, 1994. ISBN 0-316-32878-2 Subj: Foreign lands – Mexico. Holidays – New Year's. Indians of Central America – Maya.

City rhythms ill. by author. Bobbs-Merrill, 1965. Subj: City. Ethnic groups in the U.S. – African Americans.

Darkness and the butterfly ill. by author. Little, 1987. ISBN 0-316-32863-4 Subj: Emotions – fear. Foreign lands – Africa. Insects – butterflies, caterpillars. Night.

Electric Yancy ill. by author. Lothrop, 1997. ISBN 0-688-13188-3 Subj: Activities – reading. Ethnic groups in the U.S. – African Americans. Imagination.

Flyaway girl ill. by author. Little, 1992. ISBN 0-316-32866-9 Subj: Behavior – growing up. Foreign lands – Africa. Rivers.

Kinda blue ill. by author. Little, 1993. ISBN 0-316-32869-3 Subj: Emotions. Ethnic groups in the U.S. – African Americans. Family life – aunts, uncles. Farms.

Osa's pride ill. by author. Little, 1990. ISBN 0-316-32865-0 Subj: Character traits – pride. Family life – grandmothers. Foreign lands – Africa.

Tiny's hat ill. by author. HarperCollins, 1999. ISBN 0-06-027655-X Subj: Clothing – hats. Emotions – grief. Ethnic groups in the U.S. – African Americans. Family life – fathers.

The toy trumpet ill. by author. Little, 1995. ISBN 0-316-32858-8 Subj: Foreign lands – Mexico. Music. Toys.

The village of round and square houses ill. by author. Little, 1986. ISBN 0-316-32862-6 Subj: Caldecott award honor books. Folk and fairy tales. Foreign lands – Africa. Volcanoes.

Griffen, Elizabeth. *A dog's book of bugs* ill. by Peter Parnall. Atheneum, 1967. Subj: Insects.

Griffith, Helen V. *Alex and the cat* ill. by Joseph Low. Greenwillow, 1982. ISBN 0-688-00421-0 Subj: Animals – cats. Animals – dogs.

Alex remembers ill. by Donald Carrick. Greenwillow, 1983. ISBN 0-688-01801-7 Subj: Animals – cats. Animals – dogs. Memories, memory. Moon. Seasons – fall.

Dream meadow ill. by Nancy Barnet. Greenwillow, 1994. ISBN 0-688-12294-9 Subj: Animals – dogs. Death. Old age.

Emily and the enchanted frog ill. by Susan Condie Lamb. Greenwillow, 1989. ISBN 0-688-08484-2 Subj: Behavior – wishing. Crustaceans. Frogs and toads.

Georgia music ill. by James Stevenson. Greenwillow, 1986. ISBN 0-688-06072-2 Subj: Family life – grandfathers. Gardens, gardening. Music. Nature. Old age. Seasons – summer.

Grandaddy's place ill. by James Stevenson. Greenwillow, 1987. ISBN 0-688-06254-7 Subj: Animals. Country. Family life – grandfathers. Sports – fishing.

Grandaddy's stars ill. by James Stevenson. Greenwillow, 1995. ISBN 0-688-13655-9 Subj: City. Family life – grandfathers.

How many candles? ill. by Sonja Lamut. Greenwillow, 1999. ISBN 0-688-16259-2 Subj: Animals. Birthdays. Old age.

Mine will, said John ill. by Muriel Batherman. Greenwillow, 1980. ISBN 0-688-84267-4 Subj: Animals – dogs. Family life. Pets.

More Alex and the cat ill. by Donald Carrick. Greenwillow, 1983. ISBN 0-688-02292-8 Subj: Animals – cats. Animals – dogs.

Nata ill. by Nancy Tafuri. Greenwillow, 1985. ISBN 0-688-04977-X Subj: Behavior – bad day. Fairies.

Pluck's dreams ill. by Susan Condie Lamb. Greenwillow, 1990. ISBN 0-688-08813-9 Subj: Animals – dogs. Dreams.

Grigg, Carol. *The singing snow bear* ill. by author. Houghton Mifflin, 1999. ISBN 0-395-94223-3 Subj: Activities – singing. Animals – polar bears. Animals – whales. Foreign lands – Arctic. Music.

Grimes, Nikki. *At break of day* ill. by Paul Morin. Eerdmans, 1995. ISBN 0-8028-5104-5 Subj: Creation. Religion.

Baby's bedtime ill. by Sylvia Walker. Western, 1995. ISBN 0-307-12872-5 Subj: Babies. Bedtime. Ethnic groups in the U.S. – African Americans. Format, unusual – board books. Rhyming text.

C is for city by Nikki Grimes and Pat Cummings; ill. by Pat Cummings. Lothrop, 1994. ISBN 0-688-11809-7 Subj: ABC books. City. Rhyming text.

Come Sunday ill. by Michael Bryant. Eerdmans, 1996. ISBN 0-8028-5108-8 Subj: Ethnic groups in the U.S. – African Americans. Family life. Poetry. Religion.

Danitra Brown leaves town ill. by Floyd Cooper. Lothrop, 1996. ISBN 0-688-13156-5 Subj: City. Country. Ethnic groups in the U.S. – African Americans. Friendship. Poetry.

From a child's heart ill. by Brenda Joysmith. Just Us Books, 1993. ISBN 0-940975-44-0 Subj: Ethnic groups in the U.S. – African Americans. Poetry. Religion.

Is it far to Zanzibar? poems about Tanzania ill. by Betsy Lewin. Lothrop, 2000. ISBN 0-688-13158-1 Subj: Foreign lands – Tanzania. Foreign lands – Zanzibar. Poetry.

It's raining laughter photos by Myles C. Pinkney. Dial, 1997. ISBN 0-8037-2004-1 Subj: Behavior – growing up. Ethnic groups in the U.S. – African Americans. Poetry.

Meet Danitra Brown ill. by Floyd Cooper. Lothrop, 1994. ISBN 0-688-12074-1 Subj: City. Ethnic groups in the U.S. – African Americans. Family life. Friendship. Poetry.

Minnie's new friend ill. by Peter Emslie and Darren Hunt. Western, 1992. ISBN 0-307-11524-0 Subj: Animals. Friendship.

Someone's baby-sitting ill. by Sue DiCicco. Golden Books, 1997. ISBN 0-307-12634-X Subj: Activities – babysitting. Behavior. Toys.

Someone's fighting ill. by Darrell Baker. Golden Books, 1997. ISBN 0-307-12635-8 Subj: Behavior – fighting, arguing. Friendship. Toys.

Something on my mind by Nikki Grimes and Tom Feelings; ill. by Tom Feelings. Dial, 1978. ISBN 0-8037-8225-X Subj: Behavior – growing up. Emotions. Poetry.

Wild, wild hair ill. by George Ford. Scholastic, 1996. ISBN 0-590-26590-3 Subj: Ethnic groups in the U.S. – African Americans. Hair. Rhyming text.

Grimm, Jacob. *Battle of the beasts: a tale of epic proportions from the brothers Grimm* (Wallis, Diz)

The bear and the kingbird by Jacob and Wilhelm Grimm; trans. by Lore Segal; ill. by Chris Conover. Farrar, 1979. ISBN 0-374-30618-4 Subj: Animals – bears. Birds. Folk and fairy tales.

The bearskinner by Jacob and Wilhelm Grimm; ill. by Felix Hoffmann. Atheneum, 1978. Translation of Der Bärenhäuter. ISBN 0-689-50123-4 Subj: Devil. Folk and fairy tales.

The brave little tailor by Jacob and Wilhelm Grimm; ill. by Mark Corcoran. Troll, 1979. ISBN 0-89375-137-5 Subj: Careers – tailors. Character traits – bravery. Folk and fairy tales. Giants.

The brave little tailor by Jacob and Wilhelm Grimm; adapt. by Robert D. San Souci; ill. by Daniel San Souci. Doubleday, 1982. ISBN 0-385-17570-1 Subj: Careers – tailors. Character traits – bravery. Folk and fairy tales. Giants.

The brave little tailor by Jacob and Wilhelm Grimm; trans. by Anthea Bell; ill. by Svend Otto S. Larousse, 1979. ISBN 0-88332-116-5 Subj: Careers – tailors. Character traits – bravery. Folk and fairy tales. Giants.

The brave little tailor by Jacob and Wilhelm Grimm; trans. by Anthea Bell; ill. by Eve Tharlet. Picture Book Studio, 1989. ISBN 0-88708-091-X Subj: Careers – tailors. Character traits – bravery. Folk and fairy tales. Giants.

The brave little tailor by Jacob and Wilhelm Grimm; retold by Peggy Thomson; ill. by James Warhola. Simon & Schuster, 1992. ISBN 0-671-73736-8 Subj: Careers – tailors. Character traits – bravery. Folk and fairy tales. Giants.

The Bremen town band retold and ill. by Brian Wildsmith. Oxford Univ. Pr., 1999. ISBN 0-19-279034-X Subj: Animals. Crime. Folk and fairy tales. Old age.

The Bremen town musicians by Jacob and Wilhelm Grimm; retold and ill. by Donna Diamond. Delacorte, 1981. ISBN 0-440-00827-1 Subj: Animals. Crime. Folk and fairy tales. Old age.

The Bremen town musicians by Jacob and Wilhelm Grimm; trans. by Elizabeth Shub; ill. by Janina Domanska. Greenwillow, 1980. ISBN 0-688-84233-X Subj: Animals. Crime. Folk and fairy tales. Old age.

The Bremen town musicians by Jacob and Wilhelm Grimm; ill. by Paul Galdone. McGraw-Hill, 1968. Tr. of Der Bremer Stadtmusikanten. Subj: Animals. Crime. Folk and fairy tales. Old age.

The Bremen town musicians by Jacob and Wilhelm Grimm; retold and ill. by David Johnson. Macmillan, 1997. ISBN 0-689-80236-6 Subj: Animals. Folk and fairy tales. Old age.

Bremen town musicians by Jacob and Wilhelm Grimm; trans. by Anthea Bell; ill. by Josef Palecek. Picture Book Studio, 1988. ISBN 0-88708-071-5 Subj: Animals. Crime. Folk and fairy tales. Old age.

The Bremen town musicians by Jacob and Wilhelm Grimm; retold and ill. by Ilse Plume. Doubleday, 1980. ISBN 0-385-15162-4 Subj: Animals. Caldecott award honor books. Crime. Folk and fairy tales. Old age.

The Bremen town musicians by Jacob and Wilhelm Grimm; retold and ill. by Janet Stevens. Holiday, 1992. ISBN 0-8234-0939-2 Subj: Animals. Folk and fairy tales. Old age.

The Bremen town musicians by Jacob and Wilhelm Grimm; trans. by Anthea Bell; ill. by Bernadette Watts. North-South, 1992. ISBN 1-55858-148-0 Subj: Animals. Crime. Folk and fairy tales. Old age.

Cinderella by Jacob and Wilhelm Grimm; retold and ill. by Nonny Hogrogian. Greenwillow, 1981. ISBN 0-688-84299-2 Subj: Family life – step families. Folk and fairy tales. Royalty – princes. Sibling rivalry.

Cinderella by Jacob and Wilhelm Grimm; trans. by Anne Rogers; ill. by Svend Otto S. Larousse, 1978. ISBN 0-88332-093-2 Subj: Family life – step families. Folk and fairy tales. Royalty – princes. Sibling rivalry.

Clever Kate by Jacob and Wilhelm Grimm; adapt. by Elizabeth Shub; ill. by Anita Lobel. Macmillan, 1973. ISBN 0-02-782490-X Subj: Folk and fairy tales. Humor.

The devil with the green hairs by Jacob and Wilhelm Grimm; retold and ill. by Nonny Hogrogian. Knopf, 1983. ISBN 0-394-95560-9 Subj: Devil. Folk and fairy tales.

Dick Bruna's Little Red Riding Hood (Bruna, Dick)

Dick Bruna's Snow-White and the seven dwarfs (Bruna, Dick)

The donkey prince by Jacob and Wilhelm Grimm; adapt. by M. Jean Craig; ill. by Barbara Cooney. Doubleday, 1977. ISBN 0-385-11295-5 Subj: Animals – donkeys. Folk and fairy tales. Magic. Royalty – princes. Wizards.

The earth gnome by Jacob and Wilhelm Grimm; trans. by Wanda Gág; ill. by Margot Tomes. Coward, 1985. ISBN 0-698-20618-5 Subj: Folk and fairy tales. Magic. Mythical creatures – gnomes. Royalty.

The elves and the shoemaker by Jacob and Wilhelm Grimm; retold by Marcia Leonard; ill. by Doug Cushman. Silver Pr., 1990. ISBN 0-671-69347-6 Subj: Careers – shoemakers. Character traits – helpfulness. Folk and fairy tales. Foreign lands – Germany. Mythical creatures – elves. Picture puzzles.

The elves and the shoemaker by Jacob and Wilhelm Grimm; ill. by Paul Galdone. Clarion, 1984. Based on Lucy Crane's tr. from the German. Adaption of Wichtelmänner. ISBN 0-89919-226-2 Subj: Careers – shoemakers. Character traits – helpfulness. Folk and fairy tales. Foreign lands – Germany. Mythical creatures – elves.

The elves and the shoemaker by Jacob and Wilhelm Grimm; ill. by Margaret Walty. Barefoot, 1998. ISBN 1-901223-69-8 Subj: Careers – shoemakers. Character traits – helpfulness. Folk and fairy tales. Foreign lands – Germany. Mythical creatures – elves.

The elves and the shoemaker by Jacob and Wilhelm Grimm; adapt. and ill. by Bernadette Watts. Holt, 1986. ISBN 0-03-008022-3 Subj: Careers – shoemakers. Character traits – helpfulness. Folk and fairy tales. Foreign lands – Germany. Mythical creatures – elves.

The falling stars by Jacob and Wilhelm Grimm; ill. by Eugen Sopko. Holt, 1985. ISBN 0-03-005742-6 Subj: Character traits – generosity. Clothing. Folk and fairy tales.

The fisherman and his wife retold by Rosemary Wells; ill. by Eleanor Hubbard. Dial, 1998. ISBN 0-8037-1851-9 Subj: Animals – cats. Behavior – greed. Folk and fairy tales.

The fisherman and his wife by Jacob and Wilhelm Grimm; trans. by Elizabeth Shub; ill. by Monika Laimgruber. Greenwillow, 1979. ISBN 0-688-86003-6 Subj: Behavior – greed. Folk and fairy tales.

The fisherman and his wife by Jacob and Wilhelm Grimm; trans. from German by Anthea Bell; ill. by Alan Marks. Picture Book Studio, 1989. ISBN 0-88708-072-3 Subj: Behavior – greed. Folk and fairy tales.

The fisherman and his wife by Jacob and Wilhelm Grimm; ill. by Laurinda Spear. Rizzoli, 1992. ISBN 0-8478-1370-3 Subj: Behavior – greed. Folk and fairy tales.

The fisherman and his wife by Jacob and Wilhelm Grimm; adapt. by John Warren Stewig; ill. by Margot Tomes. Holiday, 1988. ISBN 0-8234-0714-4 Subj: Behavior – greed. Folk and fairy tales.

The fisherman and his wife by Jacob and Wilhelm Grimm; trans. by Randall Jarrell; ill. by Margot Zemach. Farrar, 1980. ISBN 0-374-32340-2 Subj: Behavior – greed. Folk and fairy tales.

Fitcher's bird photos by Cindy Sherman. Rizzoli, 1992. ISBN 0-8478-1567-6 Subj: Folk and fairy tales. Magic.

The four clever brothers by Jacob and Wilhelm Grimm; ill. by Felix Hoffmann. Harcourt, 1967. ISBN 0-15-229100-8 Subj: Character traits – cleverness. Dragons. Folk and fairy tales.

The four gallant sisters (Kimmel, Eric A.)

The frog prince trans. by Lucy Crane; adapt. and ill. by Paul Galdone. McGraw-Hill, 1974. An adaptation of the story that appeared in Household Stories by the Brothers Grimm, translated by Lucy Crane. ISBN 0-07-022689-X Subj: Folk and fairy tales. Frogs and toads. Royalty – princes. Royalty – princesses.

The frog prince: or Iron Henry trans. from German by Naomi Lewis; ill. by Binette Schroeder. North-South, 1989. ISBN 1-55858-015-8 Subj: Folk and

fairy tales. Frogs and toads. Royalty – princes. Royalty – princesses.

The glass mountain adapt. by Diane Wolkstein; ill. by Louisa Bauer. Morrow, 1999. Adapt. from the Grimm Brothers' story Old Rinkrank, also known as The glass mountain. ISBN 0-688-14848-4 Subj: Folk and fairy tales. Mythical creatures – trolls.

The glass mountain by Jacob and Wilhelm Grimm; adapt. and ill. by Nonny Hogrogian. Knopf, 1985. Originally titled The raven. ISBN 0-394-96724-0 Subj: Folk and fairy tales. Giants.

Godfather Cat and Mousie by Jacob and Wilhelm Grimm; adapt. by Doris Orgel; ill. by Ann Schweninger. Macmillan, 1986. ISBN 0-02-768690-6 Subj: Animals – cats. Animals – mice. Folk and fairy tales.

The golden bird by Jacob and Wilhelm Grimm; retold by Neil Philip; ill. by Isabelle Brent. Little, 1995. ISBN 0-316-70522-5 Subj: Animals – foxes. Behavior – greed. Birds. Folk and fairy tales. Royalty – kings. Royalty – princes.

The golden bird: and other fairy tales by Jacob and Wilhelm Grimm; trans. by Randall Jarrell; ill. by Sandro Nardini. Macmillan, 1962. Subj: Animals – foxes. Behavior – greed. Birds. Folk and fairy tales. Royalty – kings. Royalty – princes.

The golden goose by Jacob and Wilhelm Grimm; trans. by Anthea Bell; ill. by Dorothée Duntze. Holt, 1988. ISBN 3-85539-004-5 Subj: Character traits – kindness. Folk and fairy tales. Humor. Royalty – princesses.

The golden goose by Jacob and Wilhelm Grimm; adapt. by Susan Saunders; ill. by Isadore Seltzer. Scholastic, 1988. ISBN 0-590-41544-1 Subj: Character traits – kindness. Folk and fairy tales. Humor. Royalty – princesses.

The golden goose by Jacob and Wilhelm Grimm; ill. by Martin Ursell; text by Linda M. Jennings. Silver Burdett, 1985. ISBN 0-382-09147-7 Subj: Character traits – kindness. Folk and fairy tales. Humor. Royalty – princesses.

The goose girl by Jacob and Wilhelm Grimm; trans. by Anthea Bell; ill. by Sabine Bruntjen. Holt, 1988. ISBN 3-85539-003-7 Subj: Folk and fairy tales. Royalty. Weddings.

The goose girl: a story from the Brothers Grimm retold by Eric A. Kimmel; ill. by Robert Sauber. Holiday, 1995. ISBN 0-8234-1074-9 Subj: Folk and fairy tales. Royalty. Weddings.

Grimm Tom Thumb (Tom Thumb)

Hans in luck by Jacob and Wilhelm Grimm; retold and ill. by Paul Galdone. Parents, 1979. Translation of Hans in Glück. ISBN 0-8193-1011-5 Subj: Character traits – foolishness. Character traits – luck. Folk and fairy tales.

Hans in luck by Jacob and Wilhelm Grimm; ed. and ill. by Felix Hoffmann. Atheneum, 1975. Translation of Hans in Glück. ISBN 0-689-50020-3

Subj: Character traits – foolishness. Character traits – luck. Folk and fairy tales.

Hansel and Gretel by Jacob and Wilhelm Grimm; trans. by Charles Scribner, Jr.; ill. by Adrienne Adams. Scribners, 1975. ISBN 0-684-14422-X Subj: Folk and fairy tales. Forest, woods. Witches.

Hansel and Gretel by Jacob and Wilhelm Grimm; ill. by Anthony Browne. Watts, 1982. ISBN 0-531-04062-3 Subj: Folk and fairy tales. Forest, woods. Witches.

Hansel and Gretel by Jacob and Wilhelm Grimm; ill. by Susan Jeffers. Dial, 1980. ISBN 0-8037-3491-3 Subj: Folk and fairy tales. Forest, woods. Witches.

Hansel and Gretel by Jacob and Wilhelm Grimm; ill. by Winslow P. Pels. Scholastic, 1988. ISBN 0-590-41793-2 Subj: Behavior – lost. Folk and fairy tales. Forest, woods. Witches.

Hansel and Gretel by Jacob and Wilhelm Grimm; retold and ill. by Jane Ray. Candlewick, 1997. ISBN 0-7636-0358-9 Subj: Folk and fairy tales. Forest, woods. Witches.

Hansel and Gretel by Jacob and Wilhelm Grimm; trans. from Spanish by Leland Northam; adapt. by M. Eulalia Valeri; ill. by Conxita Rodriguez. Silver Burdett, 1985. ISBN 0-392-09072-1 Subj: Folk and fairy tales. Forest, woods. Witches. Wordless.

Hansel and Gretel by Jacob and Wilhelm Grimm; retold by Dom DeLuise; ill. by Christopher Santoro. Simon & Schuster, 1997. ISBN 0-689-81202-7 Subj: Folk and fairy tales. Forest, woods. Witches.

Hansel and Gretel by Jacob and Wilhelm Grimm; ill. by John Wallner. Prentice-Hall, 1985. ISBN 0-13-383654-1 Subj: Folk and fairy tales. Forest, woods. Witches.

Hansel and Gretel by Jacob and Wilhelm Grimm; retold by Rika Lesser; ill. by Paul O. Zelinsky. Dodd, 1984. ISBN 0-396-08449-4 Subj: Caldecott award honor books. Folk and fairy tales. Forest, woods. Witches.

Hansel and Gretel by Jacob and Wilhelm Grimm; trans. from German by Elizabeth D. Crawford; ill. by Lisbeth Zwerger. Morrow, 1980. ISBN 0-688-32198-4 Subj: Folk and fairy tales. Forest, woods. Witches.

The horse, the fox, and the lion by Jacob and Wilhelm Grimm; ill. by Paul Galdone. Seabury Pr., 1968. Adapt. from The fox and the horse [Der Fuchs und das Pferd]. Subj: Animals – dogs. Animals – foxes. Animals – horses, ponies. Animals – lions. Behavior – trickery. Folk and fairy tales. Old age.

Iron Hans by Jacob and Wilhelm Grimm; ill. by Marilee Heyer. Viking, 1993. ISBN 0-670-81741-4 Subj: Folk and fairy tales. Foreign lands – Germany. Royalty – kings. Royalty – princes.

Iron John by Jacob and Wilhelm Grimm; adapt. by Eric A. Kimmel; ill. by Trina Schart Hyman. Holiday, 1994. ISBN 0-8234-1073-0 Subj: Folk and fairy tales. Foreign lands – Germany. Royalty – kings. Royalty – princes.

Iron John by Jacob and Wilhelm Grimm; as told by Marianna Mayer; ill. by Winslow Pels. Morrow, 1998. ISBN 0-688-11555-1 Subj: Folk and fairy tales. Foreign lands – Germany. Royalty – kings. Royalty – princes.

Jack in luck by Jacob and Wilhelm Grimm; tr. and adapt. by Anthea Bell; ill. by Eve Tharlet. Picture Book Studio, 1992. ISBN 0-88708-249-1 Subj: Character traits – foolishness. Folk and fairy tales.

Jorinda and Joringel by Jacob and Wilhelm Grimm; trans. by Elizabeth Shub; ill. by Adrienne Adams. Scribners, 1968. Subj: Folk and fairy tales. Witches.

Jorinda and Joringel by Jacob and Wilhelm Grimm; adapt. by Naomi Lewis; ill. by Jutta Ash. David & Charles, 1987. ISBN 0-86264-064-4 Subj: Folk and fairy tales. Witches.

Jorinda and Joringel by Jacob and Wilhelm Grimm; retold by Wanda Gág; ill. by Margot Tomes. Coward, 1978. ISBN 0-698-20440-9 Subj: Folk and fairy tales. Witches.

King Grisly-Beard by Jacob and Wilhelm Grimm; trans. by Edgar Taylor; ill. by Maurice Sendak. Farrar, 1973. 1823 translation. ISBN 0-374-34134-6 Subj: Character traits – conceit. Folk and fairy tales. Royalty. Theater.

Little brother and little sister by Jacob and Wilhelm Grimm; tr. and adapt. by Anthea Bell; ill. by Bernadette Watts. North-South, 1996. ISBN 1-55858-589-3 Subj: Character traits – loyalty. Family life – step families. Folk and fairy tales.

Little red cap by Jacob and Wilhelm Grimm; trans. from German by Elizabeth D. Crawford; ill. by Lisbeth Zwerger. Morrow, 1983. ISBN 0-688-01715-0 Subj: Animals – wolves. Behavior – talking to strangers. Folk and fairy tales.

Little Red Riding Hood by Jacob and Wilhelm Grimm; adapt. by Elizabeth and Katherine Gant; ill. by Frank E. Aloise. Abingdon, 1969. Adapt. and music based on retelling of Rotkäppchen. Incl. melodies with texts, with piano acc. Subj: Animals – wolves. Behavior – talking to strangers. Folk and fairy tales.

Little Red Riding Hood by Jacob and Wilhelm Grimm; adapt. by Margaret Hillert; ill. by Gwen Connelly. Follett, 1982. ISBN 0-695-41543-3 Subj: Animals – wolves. Behavior – talking to strangers. Folk and fairy tales.

Little Red Riding Hood by Jacob and Wilhelm Grimm; ill. by Paul Galdone. McGraw-Hill, 1974. Adapt. from the retelling of Rotkäppchen. ISBN 0-07-022732-2 Subj: Animals – wolves. Behavior – talking to strangers. Folk and fairy tales.

Little Red Riding Hood by Jacob and Wilhelm Grimm; ill. by John S. Goodall. Macmillan, 1988. ISBN 0-689-50457-8 Subj: Animals. Animals – mice. Animals – wolves. Behavior – talking to strangers. Folk and fairy tales. Format, unusual. Wordless.

Little Red Riding Hood by Jacob and Wilhelm Grimm; retold and ill. by Trina Schart Hyman. Holiday, 1983. ISBN 0-8234-0470-6 Subj: Animals – wolves. Behavior – talking to strangers. Caldecott award honor books. Folk and fairy tales.

Little Red Riding Hood by Jacob and Wilhelm Grimm; adapt. and ill. by Mireille Levert. Firefly, 1996. ISBN 0-88899-226-2 Subj: Animals – wolves. Behavior – talking to strangers. Folk and fairy tales.

Little Red Riding Hood: a fairy tale by Grimm ill. by Jean-François Martin. Abbeville, 1998. ISBN 0-7892-0421-5 Subj: Animals – wolves. Behavior – talking to strangers. Folk and fairy tales.

Little Red Riding Hood by Jacob and Wilhelm Grimm; retold and ill. by David M. McPhail. Scholastic, 1995. ISBN 0-590-48116-9 Subj: Animals – wolves. Behavior – talking to strangers. Folk and fairy tales.

Little Red Riding Hood by Jacob and Wilhelm Grimm; ill. by Bernadette Watts. Collins-World, 1969. Subj: Animals – wolves. Behavior – talking to strangers. Folk and fairy tales.

Lucky Hans by Jacob and Wilhelm Grimm; trans. by Jock J. Curle; ill. by Eugen Sopko. Holt, 1986. ISBN 0-8050-0009-7 Subj: Character traits – foolishness. Character traits – luck. Folk and fairy tales.

Mother Holly by Jacob and Wilhelm Grimm; ill. by Bernadette Watts. Crowell, 1972. Based on the Grimm brothers' Frau Holle. ISBN 0-690-56364-7 Subj: Behavior – greed. Character traits – helpfulness. Character traits – laziness. Folk and fairy tales.

Mrs. Fox's wedding by Jacob and Wilhelm Grimm; retold by Sara and Stephen Corrin; ill. by Errol Le Cain. Doubleday, 1980. ISBN 0-385-15762-2 Subj: Animals – foxes. Counting, numbers. Folk and fairy tales. Weddings.

The musicians of Bremen by Jacob and Wilhelm Grimm; retold by Jane Yolen; ill. by John Segal. Simon & Schuster, 1996. ISBN 0-689-51117-3 Subj: Animals. Folk and fairy tales. Old age.

The musicians of Bremen by Jacob and Wilhelm Grimm; trans. by Anne Rogers; ill. by Svend Otto S. Larousse, 1974. ISBN 0-88332-060-6 Subj: Animals. Folk and fairy tales. Old age.

The musicians of Bremen by Jacob and Wilhelm Grimm; ill. by Martin Ursell; text by Linda M. Jennings. Silver Burdett, 1985. ISBN 0-382-09155-8 Subj: Animals. Folk and fairy tales. Old age.

Nanny goat and the seven little kids by Jacob and Wilhelm Grimm; retold by Eric A. Kimmel; ill. by Janet Stevens. Holiday, 1990. An adaptation of: The wolf and the seven little kids. ISBN 0-8234-0789-6 Subj: Animals – goats. Animals – wolves. Folk and fairy tales.

One gift deserves another by Jacob and Wilhelm Grimm; adapt. by Joanne Oppenheim; ill. by Bo Zaunders. Dutton, 1992. ISBN 0-525-44975-2 Subj: Behavior – greed. Character traits – generosity. Family life – brothers. Gifts.

Ouch! a tale from Grimm (Babbitt, Natalie)

The princess and the frog by Jacob and Wilhelm Grimm; retold and ill. by Rachel Isadora. Greenwillow, 1989. ISBN 0-688-06374-8 Subj: Character traits – willfulness. Folk and fairy tales. Frogs and toads. Royalty – princesses.

Rapunzel by Jacob and Wilhelm Grimm; retold and ill. by Jutta Ash. Holt, 1982. ISBN 0-03-061219-5 Subj: Folk and fairy tales. Hair. Royalty – princes. Witches.

Rapunzel by Jacob and Wilhelm Grimm; retold by Marianna Mayer; ill. by Sheilah Beckett. Western, 1991. ISBN 0-307-00207-1 Subj: Folk and fairy tales. Hair. Royalty – princes. Witches.

Rapunzel by Jacob and Wilhelm Grimm; ill. by Bert Dodson. Troll, 1979. ISBN 0-89375-135-9 Subj: Folk and fairy tales. Hair. Royalty – princes. Witches.

Rapunzel: a fairy tale by Jacob and Wilhelm Grimm; ill. by Maja Dusíková; trans. by Anthea Bell. North-South, 1997. ISBN 1-55858-685-7 Subj: Folk and fairy tales. Hair. Royalty – princes. Witches.

Rapunzel by Jacob and Wilhelm Grimm; ill. by Michael Hague. Creative Ed., 1984. ISBN 0-87191-936-2 Subj: Folk and fairy tales. Hair. Royalty – princes. Witches.

Rapunzel by Jacob and Wilhelm Grimm; retold by Barbara Rogasky; ill. by Trina Schart Hyman. Holiday, 1982. ISBN 0-8234-0454-4 Subj: Folk and fairy tales. Hair. Royalty – princes. Witches.

Rapunzel by Jacob and Wilhelm Grimm; retold by Amy Ehrlich; ill. by Kris Waldherr. Dial, 1989. ISBN 0-8037-0655-3 Subj: Folk and fairy tales. Hair. Royalty – princes. Witches.

Rapunzel by Jacob and Wilhelm Grimm; adapt. and ill. by Bernadette Watts. HarperCollins, 1975. ISBN 0-690-00980-1 Subj: Folk and fairy tales. Hair. Royalty – princes. Witches.

Rapunzel by Jacob and Wilhelm Grimm; retold and ill. by Paul O. Zelinsky. Dutton, 1997. ISBN 0-525-45607-4 Subj: Caldecott award books. Folk and fairy tales. Hair. Royalty – princes. Witches.

Rose Red and the bear prince by Jacob and Wilhelm Grimm; adapt. and ill. by Dan Andreasen. HarperCollins, 2000. ISBN 0-06-027967-2 Subj: Animals – bears. Dwarfs, midgets. Folk and fairy tales. Magic. Royalty – princes.

Rumpelstiltskin by Jacob and Wilhelm Grimm; ill. by Jacqueline Ayer. Harcourt, 1967. ISBN 0-89375-140-5 Subj: Folk and fairy tales. Magic. Riddles. Royalty. Weddings.

Rumpelstiltskin by Jacob and Wilhelm Grimm; retold and ill. by Donna Diamond. Holiday, 1983. ISBN 0-8234-0488-9 Subj: Folk and fairy tales. Magic. Riddles. Royalty. Weddings.

Rumpelstiltskin by Jacob and Wilhelm Grimm; adapt. and ill. by Paul Galdone. Houghton Mifflin, 1985. ISBN 0-89919-266-1 Subj: Folk and fairy tales. Magic. Riddles. Royalty. Weddings.

Rumpelstiltskin by Jacob and Wilhelm Grimm; retold and ill. by Jonathan Langley. HarperCollins, 1992. ISBN 0-06-020199-1 Subj: Folk and fairy tales. Magic. Riddles. Royalty. Weddings.

Rumpelstiltskin by Jacob and Wilhelm Grimm; retold by Alison Sage; ill. by Gennady Spirin. Dial, 1991. ISBN 0-8037-0908-0 Subj: Folk and fairy tales. Magic. Riddles. Royalty. Weddings.

Rumpelstiltskin by Jacob and Wilhelm Grimm; ill. by John Wallner. Prentice-Hall, 1984. ISBN 0-13-783747-X Subj: Folk and fairy tales. Magic. Riddles. Royalty. Weddings.

Rumpelstiltskin by Jacob and Wilhelm Grimm; trans. by Anthea Bell; ill. by Bernadette Watts. North-South, 1993. ISBN 1-55858-189-8 Subj: Folk and fairy tales. Magic. Riddles. Royalty. Weddings.

Rumpelstiltskin by Jacob and Wilhelm Grimm; adapt. and ill. by Paul O. Zelinsky. Dutton, 1986. ISBN 0-525-44265-0 Subj: Folk and fairy tales. Magic. Riddles. Royalty. Weddings.

Seven at one blow: a tale from the Brothers Grimm retold by Eric A. Kimmel; ill. by Megan Lloyd. Holiday, 1998. ISBN 0-8234-1383-7 Subj: Careers – tailors. Character traits – bravery. Folk and fairy tales. Foreign lands – Germany. Giants.

The seven ravens by Jacob and Wilhelm Grimm; ill. by Felix Hoffmann. Harcourt, 1963. ISBN 0-06-023552-7 Subj: Birds – ravens. Folk and fairy tales. Magic.

The seven ravens by Jacob and Wilhelm Grimm; trans. from German by Elizabeth D. Crawford; ill. by Lisbeth Zwerger. Morrow, 1981. ISBN 0-688-00372-9 Subj: Birds – ravens. Folk and fairy tales. Magic.

The shoemaker and the elves by Jacob and Wilhelm Grimm; ill. by Adrienne Adams. Macmillan, 1972. ISBN 0-684-12982-5 Subj: Careers – shoemakers. Character traits – helpfulness. Folk and fairy tales. Foreign lands – Germany. Mythical creatures – elves.

The shoemaker and the elves by Jacob and Wilhelm Grimm; ill. by Cynthia and William Birrer. Lothrop, 1983. Adapt. of Wichtelmänner. ISBN 0-688-01989-7 Subj: Careers – shoemakers. Character traits – helpfulness. Folk and fairy tales. Foreign lands – Germany. Mythical creatures – elves.

The shoemaker and the elves by Jacob and Wilhelm Grimm; retold and ill. by Ilse Plume. Harcourt, 1991. ISBN 0-15-274050-3 Subj: Careers – shoemakers. Character traits – helpfulness. Folk and fairy tales. Foreign lands – Germany. Mythical creatures – elves.

The six servants by Jacob and Wilhelm Grimm; ill. by Sergei Goloshapov; trans. by Anthea Bell. North-South, 1996. ISBN 1-55858-476-5 Subj: Folk and fairy tales. Magic. Royalty – princesses. Royalty – queens.

The six swans by Jacob and Wilhelm Grimm; ill. by Dorothée Duntze; trans. by Anthea Bell. North-South, 1998. ISBN 1-55858-983-X Subj: Birds – swans. Folk and fairy tales. Magic.

The six swans by Jacob and Wilhelm Grimm; retold by Robert D. San Souci; ill. by Daniel San Souci. Simon & Schuster, 1989. ISBN 0-671-65848-4 Subj: Birds – swans. Family life – brothers and sisters. Folk and fairy tales. Magic.

The six swans by Jacob and Wilhelm Grimm; retold by Wanda Gág; ill. by Margot Tomes. Coward, 1982. ISBN 0-689-20552-9 Subj: Birds – swans. Folk and fairy tales. Magic.

The sleeping beauty by Jacob and Wilhelm Grimm; retold and ill. by Warwick Hutton. Atheneum, 1979. ISBN 0-689-50131-5 Subj: Folk and fairy tales.

The sleeping beauty by Jacob and Wilhelm Grimm; retold and ill. by Trina Schart Hyman. Little, 1977. ISBN 0-316-38702-9 Subj: Folk and fairy tales.

The sleeping beauty by Jacob and Wilhelm Grimm; ill. by Monika Laimgruber; trans. by Anthea Bell. North-South, 1995. ISBN 1-55858-400-5 Subj: Folk and fairy tales.

The sleeping beauty by Jacob and Wilhelm Grimm; adapt. and ill. by Mercer Mayer. Macmillan, 1984. ISBN 0-02-765340-4 Subj: Folk and fairy tales.

Sleeping Beauty by Jacob and Wilhelm Grimm; trans. from Spanish by Leland Northam; adapt. by M. Eulalia Valeri; ill. by Fina Rifa. Silver Burdett, 1985. ISBN 0-382-09068-3 Subj: Folk and fairy tales. Wordless.

The sleeping beauty by Jacob and Wilhelm Grimm; adapt. by Jane Yolen; ill. by Ruth Sanderson. Knopf, 1986. ISBN 0-394-55431-0 Subj: Folk and fairy tales.

Sleeping Beauty by Jacob and Wilhelm Grimm; adapt. and ill. by John Wallner. Viking, 1987. ISBN 0-670-81708-2 Subj: Folk and fairy tales. Format, unusual – toy and movable books. Rebuses.

Snow White by Jacob and Wilhelm Grimm; trans. from German by Paul Heins; ill. by Trina Schart Hyman. Little, 1975. ISBN 0-316-35450-3 Subj: Dwarfs, midgets. Emotions – envy, jealousy. Folk and fairy tales. Magic. Witches.

Snow White by Jacob and Wilhelm Grimm; ill. by Bernadette Watts. Faber, 1983. ISBN 0-571-12518-2 Subj: Dwarfs, midgets. Emotions – envy, jealousy. Folk and fairy tales. Magic. Witches.

Snow White and Rose Red by Jacob and Wilhelm Grimm; trans. by Wayne Andrews; ill. by Adrienne Adams. Scribners, 1964. Subj: Animals – bears. Dwarfs, midgets. Folk and fairy tales. Magic. Weddings.

Snow-White and Rose-Red adapt. and ill. by Barbara Cooney. Dial, 1966. Subj: Animals – bears. Folk and fairy tales.

Snow White and Rose Red by Jacob and Wilhelm Grimm; trans. by Andrew Lang; ill. by John Wallner. Prentice-Hall, 1984. ISBN 0-13-815234-9 Subj: Animals – bears. Dwarfs, midgets. Folk and fairy tales. Magic. Weddings.

Snow White and Rose Red by Jacob and Wilhelm Grimm; adapt. and ill. by Bernadette Watts. Holt, 1988. ISBN 0-8050-0738-5 Subj: Animals – bears. Dwarfs, midgets. Folk and fairy tales. Magic. Weddings.

Snow White and the seven dwarfs by Jacob and Wilhelm Grimm; ill. by Wanda Gág. Coward, 1938. Subj: Caldecott award honor books. Dwarfs, midgets. Folk and fairy tales.

Snow White and the seven dwarves by Jacob and Wilhelm Grimm; adapt. by Anthea Bell; ill. by Chihiro Iwasaki. Picture Book Studio, 1985. ISBN 0-88708-012-X Subj: Dwarfs, midgets. Emotions – envy, jealousy. Folk and fairy tales. Magic. Witches.

The table, the donkey and the stick adapt. and ill. by Paul Galdone. McGraw-Hill, 1976. Adapt. from a retelling of Das tapfere Schneiderlein. ISBN 0-07-022701-2 Subj: Cumulative tales. Folk and fairy tales. Furniture – tables.

Three Grimms' fairy tales: The fox and the geese; The magic porridge pot; The silver pennies by Jacob and Wilhelm Grimm; ill. by Bernadette Watts. Little, 1981. ISBN 0-316-32885-5 Subj: Folk and fairy tales.

Tom Thumb (Tom Thumb)

The traveling musicians of Bremen by Jacob and Wilhelm Grimm; retold by P. K. Page; ill. by Kady MacDonald Denton. Little, 1992. ISBN 0-316-68836-3 Subj: Animals. Folk and fairy tales. Old age. Rhyming text.

The twelve dancing princesses by Jacob and Wilhelm Grimm; retold by Marianna Mayer; ill. by Kinuko Y. Craft. Morrow, 1989. ISBN 0-688-02026-7 Subj: Activities – dancing. Folk and fairy tales. Royalty – princesses.

The twelve dancing princesses by Jacob and Wilhelm Grimm; retold by Anne Carter; ill. by Anne Dalton. HarperCollins, 1989. ISBN 0-397-32373-5 Subj: Activities – dancing. Folk and fairy tales. Royalty – princesses.

The twelve dancing princesses by Jacob and Wilhelm Grimm; ill. by Dennis Hockerman. Troll, 1979. ISBN 0-89375-139-1 Subj: Activities – dancing. Folk and fairy tales. Royalty – princesses.

The twelve dancing princesses by Jacob and Wilhelm Grimm; ill. by Errol Le Cain. Viking, 1978. ISBN 0-670-73358-X Subj: Activities – dancing. Folk and fairy tales. Royalty – princesses.

The twelve dancing princesses by Jacob and Wilhelm Grimm; retold by Marianna Mayer; ill. by Gerald McDermott. Morrow, 1988. Subj: Activities – dancing. Folk and fairy tales. Royalty – princesses.

The twelve dancing princesses by Jacob and Wilhelm Grimm; retold and ill. by Jane Ray. Dutton, 1996. ISBN 0-525-45595-7 Subj: Activities – dancing. Folk and fairy tales. Royalty – princesses.

The twelve dancing princesses by Jacob and Wilhelm Grimm; trans. by Elizabeth Shub; ill. by Uri Shulevitz. Scribners, 1966. Subj: Activities – dancing. Folk and fairy tales. Royalty – princesses.

The twelve dancing princesses by Jacob and Wilhelm Grimm; retold and ill. by Suçie Stevenson. Yearling, 1995. ISBN 0-385-32167-8 Subj: Activities – dancing. Folk and fairy tales. Royalty – princesses.

The valiant little tailor by Jacob and Wilhelm Grimm; ill. by Victor G. Ambrus. Oxford Univ. Pr., 1980. First pub. in 1971. ISBN 0-19-279727-1 Subj: Careers – tailors. Character traits – bravery. Folk and fairy tales. Giants.

Walt Disney's Snow White and the seven dwarfs (Walt Disney Productions)

The water of life (Rogasky, Barbara)

The wishing table by Jacob and Wilhelm Grimm; trans. by Anthea Bell; ill. by Eve Tharlet. Picture Book Studio, 1988. ISBN 0-88708-064-2 Subj: Cumulative tales. Folk and fairy tales. Furniture – tables.

The wolf and the seven kids by Jacob and Wilhelm Grimm; ill. by Kinuko Y. Craft. Troll, 1979. ISBN 0-89375-138-3 Subj: Animals – goats. Animals – wolves. Folk and fairy tales.

The wolf and the seven little kids by Jacob and Wilhelm Grimm; trans. by Anne Rogers; ill. by Svend Otto S. Larousse, 1977. ISBN 0-88332-080-0 Subj: Animals – goats. Animals – wolves. Folk and fairy tales.

The wolf and the seven little kids by Jacob and Wilhelm Grimm; adapt. by Linda M. Jennings; ill. by Martin Ursell. Silver Burdett, 1986. ISBN 0-382-09306-2 Subj: Animals – goats. Animals – wolves. Folk and fairy tales.

Grimm, Wilhelm. *Battle of the beasts: a tale of epic proportions from the brothers Grimm* (Wallis, Diz)

The bear and the kingbird (Grimm, Jacob)

The bearskinner (Grimm, Jacob)

The brave little tailor (Grimm, Jacob)

The Bremen town band (Grimm, Jacob)

The Bremen town musicians (Grimm, Jacob)

Cinderella (Grimm, Jacob)

Clever Kate (Grimm, Jacob)

Dear Mili trans. by Ralph Manheim; ill. by Maurice Sendak. Farrar, 1988. ISBN 0-374-31762-3 Subj: Death. Folk and fairy tales. War.

The devil with the green hairs (Grimm, Jacob)

Dick Bruna's Little Red Riding Hood (Bruna, Dick)

Dick Bruna's Snow-White and the seven dwarfs (Bruna, Dick)

The donkey prince (Grimm, Jacob)

The earth gnome (Grimm, Jacob)

The elves and the shoemaker (Grimm, Jacob)

The falling stars (Grimm, Jacob)

The fisherman and his wife (Grimm, Jacob)

Fitcher's bird (Grimm, Jacob)

The four clever brothers (Grimm, Jacob)

The four gallant sisters (Kimmel, Eric A.)

The frog prince (Grimm, Jacob)

The frog prince: or Iron Henry (Grimm, Jacob)

The glass mountain (Grimm, Jacob)

Godfather Cat and Mousie (Grimm, Jacob)

The golden bird: and other fairy tales (Grimm, Jacob)

The golden bird (Grimm, Jacob)

The golden goose (Grimm, Jacob)

The goose girl (Grimm, Jacob)

The goose girl: a story from the Brothers Grimm (Grimm, Jacob)

Grimm Tom Thumb (Tom Thumb)

Hans in luck (Grimm, Jacob)

Hansel and Gretel (Grimm, Jacob)

The horse, the fox, and the lion (Grimm, Jacob)

Iron Hans (Grimm, Jacob)

Iron John (Grimm, Jacob)

Jack in luck (Grimm, Jacob)

Jorinda and Joringel (Grimm, Jacob)

King Grisly-Beard (Grimm, Jacob)

Little brother and little sister (Grimm, Jacob)

Little red cap (Grimm, Jacob)

Little Red Riding Hood (Grimm, Jacob)

Little Red Riding Hood: a fairy tale by Grimm (Grimm, Jacob)

Lucky Hans (Grimm, Jacob)

Mother Holly (Grimm, Jacob)

Mrs. Fox's wedding (Grimm, Jacob)

The musicians of Bremen (Grimm, Jacob)

Nanny goat and the seven little kids (Grimm, Jacob)

One gift deserves another (Grimm, Jacob)

Ouch! a tale from Grimm (Babbitt, Natalie)

The princess and the frog (Grimm, Jacob)

Rapunzel (Grimm, Jacob)

Rapunzel: a fairy tale (Grimm, Jacob)

Rose Red and the bear prince (Grimm, Jacob)

Rumpelstiltskin (Grimm, Jacob)

Seven at one blow: a tale from the Brothers Grimm (Grimm, Jacob)

The seven ravens (Grimm, Jacob)

The shoemaker and the elves (Grimm, Jacob)

The six servants (Grimm, Jacob)

The six swans (Grimm, Jacob)

The sleeping beauty (Grimm, Jacob)

Snow White (Grimm, Jacob)

Snow White and Rose Red (Grimm, Jacob)

Snow White and the seven dwarves (Grimm, Jacob)

The table, the donkey and the stick (Grimm, Jacob)

Three Grimms' fairy tales: The fox and the geese; The magic porridge pot; The silver pennies (Grimm, Jacob)

Tom Thumb (Tom Thumb)

The traveling musicians of Bremen (Grimm, Jacob)

The twelve dancing princesses (Grimm, Jacob)

The ugly duckling (Andersen, H. C. [Hans Christian])

The valiant little tailor (Grimm, Jacob)

Walt Disney's Snow White and the seven dwarfs (Walt Disney Productions)

The water of life (Rogasky, Barbara)

The wishing table (Grimm, Jacob)

The wolf and the seven kids (Grimm, Jacob)

The wolf and the seven little kids (Grimm, Jacob)

Grimsdell, Jeremy. *Kalinzu* ill. by author. Kingfisher, 1993. ISBN 1-85697-886-9 Subj: Animals – buffaloes. Animals – hyenas. Behavior – lost. Foreign lands – Africa.

Grindley, Sally. *A flag for Grandma* ill. by Jason Cockcroft. DK, 1998. ISBN 0-7894-3490-3 Subj: Family life – grandfathers. Family life – grandmothers. Memories, memory. Sea and seashore.

Four black puppies ill. by Clive Scruton. Lothrop, 1987. ISBN 0-688-07266-6 Subj: Animals – dogs. Behavior – misbehavior.

I don't want to! ill. by Carol Thompson. Little, 1990. ISBN 0-316-32893-6 Subj: Behavior. School.

Knock, knock! Who's there? ill. by Anthony Browne. Knopf, 1986. ISBN 0-394-98400-5 Subj: Bedtime. Family life – fathers. Games. Monsters. Toys – bears.

Little Elephant Thunderfoot ill. by John Butler. Peachtree, 1999. ISBN 1-56145-180-0 Subj: Animals – babies. Animals – elephants.

Little Sibu: an orangutan tale ill. by John Butler. Peachtree, 1999. ISBN 1-56145-196-7 Subj: Animals – orangutans. Behavior – growing up. Forest, woods.

Peter's place ill. by Michael Foreman. Harcourt, 1996. ISBN 0-15-200916-7 Subj: Ecology. Sea and seashore. Water.

Polar Star ill. by John Butler. Peachtree, 1998. ISBN 1-56145-181-9 Subj: Animals – babies. Animals – polar bears. Foreign lands – Arctic.

Shhh! ill. by Peter Utton. Little, 1992. ISBN 0-316-32899-5 Subj: Format, unusual. Giants.

Silly Goose and Dizzy Duck play hide-and-seek ill. by Adrian Reynolds. DK, 1999. ISBN 0-7894-4844-0 Subj: Animals – foxes. Birds – ducks. Birds – geese. Games.

Too big bear ill. by Peter Utton; paper engineering by José R. Seminario. Orchard, 1995. ISBN 1-8521-3931-5 Subj: Concepts – size. Format, unusual – toy and movable books. Toys – bears.

Wake up, dad! ill. by Siobhan Dodds. Doubleday, 1989. ISBN 0-385-26018-0 Subj: Family life. Furniture – beds. Morning.

What are friends for? ill. by Penny Dann. Kingfisher, 1998. ISBN 0-7534-5108-5 Subj: Animals – bears. Animals – foxes. Friendship.

What will I do without you? ill. by Penny Dann. Kingfisher, 1999. ISBN 0-7534-5110-7 Subj: Animals – bears. Animals – foxes. Animals – squirrels. Friendship. Hibernation. Seasons – winter.

Why is the sky blue? ill. by Susan Varley. Simon & Schuster, 1997. ISBN 0-689-81486-0 Subj: Animals – donkeys. Animals – rabbits. Character traits – patience.

Groat, Diane. *see* De Groat, Diane

Grode, Redway. *see* Gorey, Edward (St. John)

Groening, Maggie. *Maggie Simpson's alphabet book* by Maggie and Matt Groening. HarperCollins, 1991. ISBN 0-06-020236-X Subj: ABC books.

Maggie Simpson's book of animals by Maggie and Matt Groening; ill. by Matt Groening. HarperCollins, 1991. ISBN 0-06-020237-8 Subj: Animals. Zoos.

Maggie Simpson's book of colors and shapes by Maggie and Matt Groening; ill. by Matt Groening. HarperCollins, 1991. ISBN 0-06-020235-1 Subj: Concepts – color. Concepts – shape.

Maggie Simpson's counting book by Maggie and Matt Groening. HarperCollins, 1991. ISBN 0-06-020238-6 Subj: Counting, numbers.

Groening, Matt. *Maggie Simpson's alphabet book* (Groening, Maggie)

Maggie Simpson's book of animals (Groening, Maggie)

Maggie Simpson's book of colors and shapes (Groening, Maggie)

Maggie Simpson's counting book (Groening, Maggie)

Grohmann, Susan. *The dust under Mrs. Merriweather's bed* ill. by author. Whispering Coyote, 1994. ISBN 1-879085-82-8 Subj: Character traits – orderliness. Seasons. Weather.

Groner, Judyth Saypol. *All about Hanukkah* by Judyth Groner and Madeline Wikler; ill. by Rosalyn Schanzer. Kar-Ben Copies, 1988. ISBN 0-930494-81-4 Subj: Holidays – Hanukkah. Jewish culture. Religion.

All about Sukkot by Judyth Groner and Madeline Wikler; ill. by Kinny Kreiswirth. Kar-Ben Copies, 1998. ISBN 1-58013-018-6 Subj: Folk and fairy tales. Holidays – Sukkot. Jewish culture. Religion.

Let's build a Sukkah (Wikler, Madeline)

My first seder (Wikler, Madeline)

My very own Jewish community by Judyth Groner and Madeline Wikler; photos by Madeline Wikler. Kar-Ben Copies, 1984. ISBN 0-930494-32-6 Subj: Communities, neighborhoods. Jewish culture.

The Purim parade (Wikler, Madeline)

Thank you, God! a Jewish child's book of prayers by Judyth Groner and Madeline Wikler; ill. by Shelly O. Haas. Kar-Ben Copies, 1993. ISBN 0-929371-65-8 Subj: Jewish culture. Religion.

Where is the Afikomen? by Judyth Groner and Madeline Wikler; ill. by Chari R. McLean. Kar-Ben Copies, 1985. ISBN 0-930494-52-0 Subj: Format, unusual – board books. Holidays. Jewish culture.

Gross, Alan. *Sometimes I worry . . .* ill. by Mike Venezia. Childrens Pr., 1978. ISBN 0-516-03670-X Subj: Behavior – worrying.

What if the teacher calls on me? ill. by Mike Venezia. Childrens Pr., 1980. ISBN 0-516-03671-8 Subj: Behavior – worrying. School.

Gross, Michael. *The fable of the fig tree* ill. by Mila Lazarevich. Walck, 1975. ISBN 0-8098-1228-2 Subj: Folk and fairy tales. Jewish culture.

Gross, Ruth Belov. *Alligators and other crocodilians* ill. with photos. Four Winds, 1978. ISBN 0-590-07556-X Subj: Reptiles – alligators, crocodiles. Science.

A book about your skeleton ill. by Deborah Robison. Hastings House, 1979. ISBN 0-8038-0794-5 Subj: Anatomy – skeletons. Health and fitness.

The emperor's new clothes (Andersen, H. C. [Hans Christian])

The girl who wouldn't get married ill. by Jack Kent. Four Winds, 1983. ISBN 0-590-07908-5 Subj: Animals – horses, ponies. Folk and fairy tales. Weddings.

What's on my plate? ill. by Isadore Seltzer. Macmillan, 1990. ISBN 0-02-737000-3 Subj: Food.

Grossbart, Francine. *A big city* ill. by author. HarperCollins, 1966. Subj: ABC books. City.

Grossblatt, Ruby M. *Who's that sleeping on my sofabed?* ill. by Sara Kranz. Hachai, 1999. ISBN 0-922613-90-7 Subj: Family life. Furniture – beds. Furniture – couches, sofas. Jewish culture.

Grossman, Bill. *The banging book* ill. by Robert Zimmerman. HarperCollins, 1995. ISBN 0-06-024498-4 Subj: Activities – making things. Noise, sounds. Rhyming text.

The bear whose bones were Jezebel Jones ill. by Jonathan Allen. Dial, 1997. ISBN 0-8037-1743-1 Subj: Anatomy – skin. Animals. Animals – bears. Rhyming text. Zoos.

Cowboy Ed ill. by Florence Wint. HarperCollins, 1993. ISBN 0-06-021571-2 Subj: Cowboys. Rhyming text. U.S. history – frontier and pioneer life.

Donna O'Neeshuck was chased by some cows ill. by Sue Truesdell. HarperCollins, 1988. ISBN 0-06-022159-3 Subj: Cumulative tales. Rhyming text.

The guy who was five minutes late ill. by Judy Glasser. HarperCollins, 1990. ISBN 0-06-022269-7 Subj: Behavior – tardiness. Rhyming text.

My little sister ate one hare ill. by Kevin Hawkes. Crown, 1996. ISBN 0-517-59601-6 Subj: Counting, numbers. Rhyming text.

Tommy at the grocery store ill. by Victoria Chess. HarperCollins, 1989. ISBN 0-06-022409-6 Subj: Animals – pigs. Behavior – lost. Rhyming text. Shopping. Stores.

Grossman, Patricia. *The night ones* ill. by Lydia Dabcovich. Harcourt, 1991. ISBN 0-15-257438-7 Subj: Activities – working. Careers. Night.

Saturday market by Patricia Grossman and Enrique O. Sánchez; ill. by Enrique O. Sánchez. Lothrop, 1994. ISBN 0-688-12177-2 Subj: Foreign lands – Mexico. Indians of North America – Zapotec. Shopping.

Grossman, Virginia. *Ten little rabbits* ill. by Sylvia Long. Chronicle, 1991. ISBN 0-87701-552-X Subj: Animals – rabbits. Counting, numbers. Indians of North America. Rhyming text.

Grosvenor, Donna. *Pandas* photos by author; ill. by George Founds. National Geographic, 1973. ISBN 0-87044-143-4 Subj: Animals – pandas. Science.

Zoo babies ill. by author. National Geographic, 1979. ISBN 0-8704-4262-7 Subj: Animals. Zoos.

Grosz, Peter. *The special gifts* ill. by Giuliano Lunelli; trans. by Rosemary Lanning. North-South, 1998. ISBN 1-55858-962-7 Subj: Behavior – sharing. Gifts. Homes, houses. Old age.

Groth-Fleming, Candace. *see* Fleming, Candace

Grover, Eulalie Osgood. *Mother Goose* (Mother Goose)

Mother Goose (Mother Goose)

Grover, Max. *The accidental zucchini: an unexpected alphabet* ill. by author. Browndeer, 1993. ISBN 0-15-277695-8 Subj: ABC books. Language.

Groves-Raines, Antony. *The tidy hen* ill. by author. Harcourt, 1961. Subj: Birds – chickens. Character traits – cleanliness.

Gruber, Ruth. *see* Michaels, Ruth

Gruelle, Johnny. *How Raggedy Ann got her candy heart* (How Raggedy Ann got her candy heart)

My first Raggedy Ann, Raggedy Ann and Andy and the camel with the wrinkled knees (My first Raggedy Ann, Raggedy Ann and Andy and the camel with the wrinkled knees)

My first Raggedy Ann, Raggedy Ann and Andy and the nice police officer (My first Raggedy Ann, Raggedy Ann and Andy and the nice police officer)

My first Raggedy Ann, Raggedy Ann's wishing pebble (My first Raggedy Ann, Raggedy Ann's wishing pebble)

Gruenberg, Hannah Coale. *Felix's hat* (Bancroft, Catherine)

Grunwald, Lisa. *Now, soon, later* ill. by Jane Johnson. Greenwillow, 1995. ISBN 0-688-13946-9 Subj: Character traits – patience. Time.

Grupper, Jonathan. *Destination, rain forest* ill. with photos. National Geographic, 1997. ISBN 0-7922-7018-5 Subj: Ecology. Forest, woods. Nature.

Gryspeerdt, Rebecca. *Counting friends* ill. by author. Trafalgar Square, 1993. ISBN 1-85681-092-5 Subj: Animals. Counting, numbers. Friendship. Rhyming text.

Guarino, Deborah. *Is your mama a llama?* ill. by Steven Kellogg. Scholastic, 1989. ISBN 0-590-41387-2 Subj: Animals. Animals – llamas. Rhyming text.

Guarnieri, Paolo. *A boy named Giotto* ill. by Bimba Landmann; trans. by Jonathan Galassi. Farrar, 1999. ISBN 0-374-30931-0 Subj: Careers – artists. Careers – shepherds. Foreign lands – Italy.

Guback, Georgia. *Luka's quilt* ill. by author. Greenwillow, 1994. ISBN 0-688-12155-1 Subj: Family life – grandmothers. Hawaii. Quilts.

Gueritz, Caroline. *Bruno takes a trip* (Bröger, Achim)

Guettier, Bénédicte. *The father who had ten children* ill. by author. Dial, 1999. ISBN 0-8037-2446-2 Subj: Counting, numbers. Family life – fathers.

Guggenmos, Josef. *Franz, der Drache. Dragon Franz* (Shub, Elizabeth)

Gugler, Laurel Dee. *Facing the day* ill. by Deidre Betteridge. Annick, 1999. ISBN 1-55037-577-6 Subj: Emotions. Family life. Rhyming text.

Guiberson, Brenda Z. *Cactus hotel* ill. by Megan Lloyd. Holt, 1991. ISBN 0-8050-1333-4 Subj: Desert. Ecology. Plants.

Into the sea ill. by Alix Berenzy. Holt, 1996. ISBN 0-8050-2263-5 Subj: Nature. Reptiles – turtles, tortoises. Sea and seashore.

Lobster boat ill. by Megan Lloyd. Holt, 1993. ISBN 0-8050-1756-9 Subj: Careers – fishermen. Crustaceans. Sea and seashore.

Spoonbill swamp ill. by Megan Lloyd. Holt, 1992. ISBN 0-8050-1583-3 Subj: Birds – spoonbills. Nature. Reptiles – alligators, crocodiles.

Guilfoile, Elizabeth. *Have you seen my brother?* ill. by Mary Stevens. Follett, 1962. Subj: Behavior – lost. Careers – police officers. City.

Nobody listens to Andrew ill. by Mary Stevens. Follett, 1957. Subj: Animals – bears. Behavior – needing someone.

Valentine's Day ill. by Gordon Laite. Garrard, 1965. Subj: Holidays – Valentine's Day.

Guitar, Jeremy. *Tidy pig* (McQueen, Lucinda)

Gukova, Julia. *Mole's daughter: an adaptation of a Korean folktale* ill. by author. Annick, 1998. ISBN 1-55037-525-3 Subj: Animals – moles. Folk and fairy tales. Foreign lands – Korea.

Gullikson, Sandy. *Trouble for breakfast* ill. by author. Dial, 1990. ISBN 0-8037-0776-2 Subj: Animals. Behavior – misbehavior. Food. Illness.

Gullo, Stephen V. *When people die* (Bernstein, Joanne E.)

Gundersheimer, Karen. *A B C, say with me* ill. by author. HarperCollins, 1984. ISBN 0-06-022175-5 Subj: ABC books.

Colors to know ill. by author. HarperCollins, 1986. ISBN 0-06-022196-8 Subj: Animals. Concepts – color.

Find cat, wear hat ill. by author. Scholastic, 1995. ISBN 0-590-48061-8 Subj: Activities – playing. Format, unusual – board books. Noise, sounds. Rhyming text. School.

Happy winter ill. by author. HarperCollins, 1982. ISBN 0-06-022173-9 Subj: Rhyming text. Seasons – winter.

1, 2, 3, play with me ill. by author. HarperCollins, 1984. ISBN 0-06-022177-1 Subj: Animals – mice. Counting, numbers.

Shapes to show ill. by author. HarperCollins, 1986. ISBN 0-06-022197-6 Subj: Animals – mice. Concepts – shape. Toys.

Splish splash bang crash! ill. by author. Scholastic, 1995. ISBN 0-590-48060-X Subj: Activities – playing. Noise, sounds. Rhyming text. School.

Gunning, Monica. *The two Georges: Los dos Jorges* ill. by Veronica Mary Miracle. Blaine-Ethridge, 1976. ISBN 0-8791-7049-2 Subj: ABC books. Foreign languages.

Gunther, Louise. *Anna's snow day* ill. by Paul Frame. Garrard, 1979. ISBN 0-8116-4310-7 Subj: Weather – snow.

A tooth for the tooth fairy ill. by Jim Cummins. Garrard, 1978. ISBN 0-8116-4308-5 Subj: Fairies. Teeth.

Gunthrop, Karen. *Adam and the wolf* ill. by Attilio Cassinelli. Doubleday, 1967. Translation of Il pulcino e il lupo. Subj: Animals – wolves. Behavior – disbelief. Food.

Rina at the farm ill. by Attilio Cassinelli. Doubleday, 1968. Subj: Farms.

Guthrie, Donna. *Grandpa doesn't know it's me* ill. by Katy Keck Arnsteen. Human Sciences Pr., 1986. ISBN 0-89885-308-7 Subj: Behavior – forgetfulness. Behavior – losing things. Behavior – lost. Family life – grandfathers. Illness – Alzheimer's. Old age.

Mrs. Gigglebelly is coming for tea ill. by Katy Keck Arnsteen. Simon & Schuster, 1989. ISBN 0-671-67937-6 Subj: Family life – mothers. Imagination – imaginary friends. Parties.

Nobiah's well: a modern African folk tale ill. by Robert Roth. Ideals, 1993. ISBN 0-8249-8631-8 Subj: Animals. Folk and fairy tales. Foreign lands – Africa. Water. Weather – droughts.

Not for babies ill. by Katy Keck Arnsteen. Simon & Schuster, 1993. ISBN 0-671-79362-4 Subj: Night.

One hundred and two steps ill. by Meg Kelleher Aubrey. Cool Kids, 1995. ISBN 1-56790-522-6 Subj: Behavior – secrets. Family life – aunts, uncles. Memories, memory.

A rose for Abby ill. by Dennis Hockerman. Abingdon, 1988. ISBN 0-687-36586-4 Subj: City. Ethnic groups in the U.S. – African Americans. Homeless.

The secret admirer ill. by Tony Sansevero. Ideals, 1996. ISBN 1-57102-045-4 Subj: Family life – great-grandparents. Holidays – Valentine's Day. Old age.

This little pig stayed home ill. by Katy Keck Arnsteen. Price Stern Sloan, 1987. ISBN 0-8431-1820-2 Subj: Animals – pigs. Animals – wolves. Careers – chefs, cooks.

The witch has an itch ill. by Katy Keck Arnsteen. Little Simon, 1990. ISBN 0-671-70346-3 Subj: Magic. Witches.

The witch who lives down the hall ill. by Amy Schwartz. Harcourt, 1985. ISBN 0-15-298610-3 Subj: Holidays – Halloween. Magic. Witches.

Guthrie, Feliz. *African animal tales* (Barbosa, Rogério Andrade)

Guthrie, Marjorie Mazia. *Woody's 20 grow big songs* (Guthrie, Woody)

Guthrie, Woody. *This land is your land* music by author; ill. by Kathy Jakobsen; with a tribute by Pete Seeger. Little, 1998. ISBN 0-316-39215-4 Subj: Music. Songs.

Woody's 20 grow big songs by Woody Guthrie and Marjorie Mazia Guthrie; ill. by Woody Guthrie. HarperCollins, 1992. ISBN 0-06-020283-1 Subj: Music. Songs.

Guy, Ginger Foglesong. *Black crow, black crow* ill. by Nancy Winslow Parker. Greenwillow, 1991. ISBN 0-688-08957-7 Subj: Birds – crows. Imagination.

Fiesta! ill. by Rene King Moreno. Greenwillow, 1996. ISBN 0-688-14332-6 Subj: Counting, numbers. Fairs. Foreign lands – Mexico. Foreign languages.

Guy, Rosa. *Billy the Great* ill. by Caroline Binch. Delacorte, 1992. ISBN 0-385-30666-0 Subj: Character traits – individuality. Ethnic groups in the U.S. – African Americans. Family life. Friendship.

Caribbean carnival: songs of the West Indies (Burgie, Irving)

Mother crocodile ill. by John Steptoe. Delacorte, 1981. ISBN 0-440-06406-6 Subj: Animals – monkeys. Folk and fairy tales. Foreign lands – Africa. Reptiles – alligators, crocodiles.

Guy, Suzanne. *The music box: the story of Cristofori* by Suzanne Guy and Donna Lacy; ill. by Donna Lacy. Brunswick, 1998. ISBN 1-55618-172-8 Subj: Foreign lands – Italy. Music.

Guzzo, Sandra E. *Fox and Heggie* ill. by Kathy Parkinson. Albert Whitman, 1983. ISBN 0-8075-2546-4 Subj: Animals – foxes. Animals – hedgehogs. Shopping.

Gwynne, Fred. *A chocolate moose for dinner* ill. by author. Messner, 1981. ISBN 0-671-43706-2 Subj: Imagination. Language.

Easy to see why ill. by author. Simon & Schuster, 1993. ISBN 0-671-79776-X Subj: Animals – dogs. Behavior. Pets.

A little pigeon toad ill. by author. Simon & Schuster, 1988. ISBN 0-671-66659-2 Subj: Imagination. Language.

Pondlarker ill. by author. Simon & Schuster, 1992. ISBN 0-671-70846-5 Subj: Frogs and toads. Royalty – princesses. Self-concept.

Haarhoff, Dorian. *Desert December* ill. by Leon Vermeulen. Houghton Mifflin, 1992. Subj: Babies. Desert. Family life – new sibling. Foreign lands – Namibia. Foreign lands – South Africa. Holidays – Christmas.

Haas, Dorothy. *My first communion* photos by William Franklin McMahon. Albert Whitman, 1987. ISBN 0-8075-5331-X Subj: Religion.

Haas, Irene. *The Maggie B* ill. by author. Atheneum, 1975. Subj: Behavior – wishing. Boats, ships. Rhyming text. Sea and seashore.

A summertime song ill. by author. Margaret K. McElderry, 1997. ISBN 0-689-50549-3 Subj: Animals. Birthdays. Family life – grandparents. Imagination. Seasons – summer.

Haas, Jessie. *Busybody Brandy* ill. by Yossi Abolafia. Greenwillow, 1994. ISBN 0-688-12793-2 Subj: Animals – dogs. Character traits – responsibility. Farms.

Chipmunk! ill. by Jos. A. Smith. Greenwillow, 1993. ISBN 0-688-11875-5 Subj: Animals – cats. Animals – chipmunks. Behavior – carelessness.

Getting ready to drive a horse and cart ill. by Christine Erickson. Storey Communications, 1995. ISBN 0-88266-381-X Subj: Animals – horses, ponies. Transportation.

Mowing ill. by Jos. A. Smith. Greenwillow, 1994. ISBN 0-688-11681-7 Subj: Character traits – kindness to animals. Family life – grandfathers. Farms.

No foal yet ill. by Jos. A. Smith. Greenwillow, 1995. ISBN 0-688-12926-9 Subj: Animals – horses, ponies. Birth. Family life – grandparents. Farms.

Sugaring ill. by Jos. A. Smith. Greenwillow, 1996. ISBN 0-688-14201-X Subj: Animals – horses, ponies. Family life – grandparents. Food. Trees.

Haas, Merle. *Babar and Father Christmas* (Brunhoff, Jean de)

Babar and his children (Brunhoff, Jean de)

Babar and Zephir (Brunhoff, Jean de)

Babar the king (Brunhoff, Jean de)

Babar the king (Brunhoff, Jean de)

Babar visits another planet (Brunhoff, Laurent de)

Babar's castle (Brunhoff, Laurent de)

Babar's cousin, that rascal Arthur (Brunhoff, Laurent de)

Babar's fair will be opened next Sunday (Brunhoff, Laurent de)

The story of Babar, the little elephant (Brunhoff, Jean de)

The travels of Babar (Brunhoff, Jean de)

Haddon, Mark. *At home* ill. by author. Western, 1994. ISBN 0-307-17575-8 Subj: Activities. Dinosaurs. Format, unusual – board books.

At playgroup ill. by author. Western, 1994. ISBN 0-307-17576-6 Subj: Activities. Dinosaurs. Format, unusual – board books.

Gilbert's gobstopper ill. by author. Dial, 1988. ISBN 0-8037-0506-9 Subj: Behavior – losing things.

In the garden ill. by author. Western, 1994. ISBN 0-307-17578-2 Subj: Activities. Dinosaurs. Format, unusual – board books. Gardens, gardening.

On vacation ill. by author. Western, 1994. ISBN 0-307-17577-4 Subj: Activities. Activities – vacationing. Dinosaurs. Format, unusual – board books.

The Sea of Tranquillity ill. by Christian Birmingham. Harcourt, 1996. ISBN 0-15-201285-0 Subj: Moon. Space and space ships.

Toni and the tomato soup ill. by author. Harcourt, 1989. ISBN 0-15-200610-9 Subj: Behavior – wishing. Food.

Hader, Berta Hoerner. *The big snow* by Berta and Elmer Hader; ill. by authors. Macmillan, 1948. Subj: Caldecott award books. Weather – snow.

Cock-a-doodle doo: the story of a little red rooster by Berta and Elmer Hader; ill. by authors. Macmillan, 1939. Subj: Birds – chickens. Birds – ducks. Caldecott award honor books. Farms.

Lost in the zoo by Berta and Elmer Hader; ill. by authors. Macmillan, 1951. Subj: Behavior – lost. Zoos.

The mighty hunter by Berta and Elmer Hader; ill. by authors. Macmillan, 1943. Subj: Caldecott award honor books. Ecology. Indians of North America. School. Sports – hunting.

Mister Billy's gun by Berta and Elmer Hader; ill. by authors. Macmillan, 1960. Subj: Birds. Character traits – kindness to animals. Gardens, gardening. Violence, nonviolence. Weapons.

The story of Pancho and the bull with the crooked tail by Berta and Elmer Hader; ill. by authors. Oxford Univ. Pr., 1933. Subj: Animals – bulls, cows. Foreign lands – Mexico.

Hader, Elmer. *The big snow* (Hader, Berta Hoerner)

Cock-a-doodle doo: the story of a little red rooster (Hader, Berta Hoerner)

Lost in the zoo (Hader, Berta Hoerner)

The mighty hunter (Hader, Berta Hoerner)

Mister Billy's gun (Hader, Berta Hoerner)

The story of Pancho and the bull with the crooked tail (Hader, Berta Hoerner)

Hafner, Marylin. *Mommies don't get sick* ill. by author. Candlewick, 1995. ISBN 1-56402-287-0 Subj: Family life – mothers. Illness.

A year with Molly and Emmett ill. by author. Candlewick, 1997. ISBN 1-56402-966-2 Subj: Activities. Animals – cats. Friendship. Pets.

Haggerty, Mary Elizabeth. *A crack in the wall* ill. by Rubén De Anda. Lee & Low, 1993. ISBN 1-880000-03-2 Subj: Family life – mothers. Imagination. Poverty.

Hague, Kathleen. *Alphabears: an ABC book* ill. by Michael Hague. Holt, 1984. Subj: ABC books. Rhyming text. Toys – bears.

Bear hugs ill. by Michael Hague. Holt, 1989. ISBN 0-8050-0512-9 Subj: Poetry. Toys – bears.

Calendarbears: a book of months ill. by Michael Hague. Holt, 1997. ISBN 0-8050-3818-3 Subj: Animals – bears. Days of the week, months of the year. Rhyming text.

East of the sun and west of the moon retold by Kathleen and Michael Hague; ill. by Michael Hague. Harcourt, 1980. ISBN 0-15-224702-5 Subj: Folk and fairy tales. Foreign lands – Norway. Royalty – princes.

The legend of the Veery bird ill. by Michael Hague. Harcourt, 1985. ISBN 0-15-243824-6 Subj: Birds. Character traits – helpfulness. Folk and fairy tales. Forest, woods.

The man who kept house by Kathleen and Michael Hague; ill. by Michael Hague. Harcourt, 1981. Subj: Family life. Folk and fairy tales. Foreign lands – Norway.

Numbears: a counting book ill. by Michael Hague. Holt, 1986. ISBN 0-03-007194-1 Subj: Counting, numbers. Toys – bears.

Out of the nursery, into the night ill. by Michael Hague. Holt, 1986. ISBN 0-8050-0088-7 Subj: Dreams. Night. Rhyming text. Toys – bears.

Ten little bears: a counting rhyme ill. by Michael Hague. Morrow, 1999. ISBN 0-688-16383-1 Subj: Animals – bears. Counting, numbers. Rhyming text.

Hague, Michael. *Æsop's fables* (Æsop)

Deck the halls ill. by author. Holt, 1991. ISBN 0-8050-1007-6 Subj: Holidays – Christmas. Music.

East of the sun and west of the moon (Hague, Kathleen)

The little mermaid (Andersen, H. C. [Hans Christian])

The man who kept house (Hague, Kathleen)

Michael Hague's world of unicorns ill. by author. Holt, 1986. ISBN 0-8050-0070-4 Subj: Format, unusual. Mythical creatures – unicorns.

Mother Goose: a collection of classic nursery rhymes (Mother Goose)

The perfect present ill. by author. Morrow, 1996. ISBN 0-688-10880-6 Subj: Animals – kangaroos. Format, unusual – toy and movable books. Gifts. Holidays – Christmas.

Teddy bear, teddy bear: a classic action rhyme ill. by author. Morrow, 1993. ISBN 0-688-12085-7 Subj: Games. Nursery rhymes. Toys – bears.

Hahn, Deborah. *The swineherd* (Andersen, H. C. [Hans Christian])

Hahn, Hannelore. *Take a giant step* ill. by Margot Zemach. Little, 1960. Subj: Games.

Haidle, Elizabeth. *Elmer the grump* ill. by author. Landmark, 1989. ISBN 0-933849-20-6 Subj: Children as authors. Children as illustrators. Friendship. Mythical creatures – elves.

Haines, Gail Kay. *Fire* ill. by Jacqueline Chwast. Morrow, 1975. Subj: Fire. Science.

Hains, Harriet. *My baby brother* ill. by author. DK, 1992. ISBN 1-879431-76-9 Subj: Babies. Family life – brothers and sisters. Family life – new sibling.

My new puppy ill. by author. DK, 1992. ISBN 1-879431-77-7 Subj: Animals – dogs. Pets.

My new school ill. by author. DK, 1992. ISBN 1-56458-116-0 Subj: School – first day.

Our new kitten ill. by author. DK, 1992. ISBN 1-56458-117-9 Subj: Animals – cats. Pets.

Hair ill. by Christine Sharr. Wonder Books, 1971. Subj: Hair.

Haiz, Danah. *Jonah's journey* ill. by H. Hechtkopf. Lerner, 1973. Subj: Animals – whales. Religion – Jonah.

Halak, Glenn. *A grandmother's story* ill. by author. Green Tiger Pr., 1992. ISBN 0-671-74953-6 Subj: Boats, ships. Family life – grandmothers. Sea and seashore.

Haldane, Suzanne. *Teddies and machines* ill. by Maude Salinger. Dutton, 1996. ISBN 0-525-45401-2 Subj: Format, unusual – board books. Machines. Toys – bears.

Teddies and trucks ill. by Maude Salinger. Dutton, 1996. ISBN 0-525-45400-4 Subj: Format, unusual – board books. Machines. Toys – bears.

Hale, Irina. *Boxman* ill. by author. Viking, 1992. ISBN 0-670-84287-7 Subj: Disguises. Family life.

Brown bear in a brown chair ill. by author. Atheneum, 1983. Subj: Character traits – appearance. Furniture – chairs. Toys – bears.

Chocolate mouse and sugar pig ill. by author. Atheneum, 1979. Subj: Animals – mice. Animals – pigs. Behavior – running away. Food. Toys.

Donkey's dreadful day ill. by author. Atheneum, 1982. Subj: Animals – donkeys. Circus. Dreams.

How I found a friend ill. by author. Viking, 1992. ISBN 0-670-84286-9 Subj: Friendship. Toys – bears.

The lost toys ill. by author. Atheneum, 1985. ISBN 0-689-50328-8 Subj: Activities – trading. Behavior – forgetfulness. Toys.

The naughty crow ill. by author. Margaret K. McElderry, 1992. ISBN 0689505469 Subj: Birds – crows. Foreign lands – Ukraine. Pets.

Small big bad boy ill. by author. Viking, 1991. ISBN 0-670-83818-7 Subj: Behavior – growing up. Behavior – wishing.

Hale, Kathleen. *Orlando and the water cats* ill. by author. Merrimack, 1979. ISBN 0-224-00662-2 Subj: Activities – vacationing. Animals – cats. Family life.

Orlando buys a farm ill. by author. Merrimack, 1980. Subj: Animals – cats. Farms.

Orlando, the frisky housewife ill. by author. Merrimack, 1979. ISBN 0-224-00753-X Subj: Animals – cats. Stores.

Hale, Linda. *The glorious Christmas soup party* ill. by author. Viking, 1962. Subj: Animals – mice. Food. Holidays – Christmas.

Hale, Lucretia. *The lady who put salt in her coffee* adapt. and ill. by Amy Schwartz. Harcourt, 1989. ISBN 0-15-243475-5 Subj: Family life. Humor.

Hale, Michael. *Shoemaker Martin* (Tolstoy, Aleksey Nikolayevich)

Hale, Sarah Josepha Buell. *Mary had a little lamb* as told and ill. by Iza Trapani. Gareth Stevens, 1999. ISBN 0-8368-2488-1 Subj: Animals – sheep. Farms. Humor. Music. Nursery rhymes. Songs.

Mary had a little lamb ill. by Tomie de Paola. Holiday, 1984. ISBN 0-8234-0509-5 Subj: Animals – sheep. Music. Nursery rhymes. School.

Mary had a little lamb photos by Bruce McMillan. Scholastic, 1990. ISBN 0-590-43773-9 Subj: Animals – sheep. Music. Nursery rhymes. School.

Mary had a little lamb ill. by Salley Mavor. Orchard, 1995. ISBN 0-531-08725-5 Subj: Animals – sheep. Nursery rhymes. School.

Mary had a little lamb ill. by Ann Schweninger. Western, 1992. ISBN 0-307-06139-6 Subj: Animals – sheep. Music. Nursery rhymes. School.

Mary had a little lamb ill. by Suzanne Vasilak. Modern Pub., 1993. ISBN 1-56144-351-4 Subj: Animals – sheep. Music. Nursery rhymes. School.

Haley, Alex. *Young Martin's promise* (Myers, Walter Dean)

Haley, Gail E. *Birdsong* ill. by author. Crown, 1984. ISBN 0-517-55051-2 Subj: Birds. Character traits – helpfulness. Folk and fairy tales.

Dream peddler ill. by author. Dutton, 1993. ISBN 0-525-45153-6 Subj: Activities – reading. Careers – peddlers. Dreams. Foreign lands – England.

Go away, stay away ill. by author. Scribners, 1977. ISBN 0-684-15272-X Subj: Mythical creatures – goblins. Seasons.

The green man ill. by author. Scribners, 1980. ISBN 0-684-16338-1 Subj: Knights. Seasons.

Jack and the bean tree ill. by author. Crown, 1986. ISBN 0-517-55717-7 Subj: Folk and fairy tales. Giants. Magic.

Jack and the fire dragon ill. by author. Crown, 1988. ISBN 0-517-56814-4 Subj: Character traits – bravery. Dragons. Folk and fairy tales.

Jack Jouett's ride ill. by author. Viking, 1973. ISBN 0-670-40466-7 Subj: U.S. history.

Noah's ark ill. by author. Atheneum, 1971. ISBN 0-689-20659-3 Subj: Animals. Boats, ships. Ecology. Religion – Noah. Weather – floods. Weather – rain. Weather – rainbows.

The post office cat ill. by author. Scribners, 1976. ISBN 0-684-14653-3 Subj: Animals – cats. Careers – postal workers. Foreign lands – England. Post office.

Puss in boots (Perrault, Charles)

Sea tale ill. by author. Dutton, 1990. ISBN 0-525-44567-6 Subj: Folk and fairy tales. Mythical creatures – mermaids, mermen. Sea and seashore.

A story, a story ill. by author. Aladdin, 1988, c1970. ISBN 0-689-71201-4 Subj: Caldecott award books. Folk and fairy tales. Foreign lands – Africa.

Two bad boys: a very old Cherokee tale ill. by author. Dutton, 1996. ISBN 0-525-45311-3 Subj: Activities – working. Creation. Indians of North America – Cherokee.

Haley, Patrick. *The little person* ill. by Jonna Kool. East Eagle, 1981. ISBN 0-9605738-0-1 Subj: Activities – traveling.

Hall, Amanda. *The gossipy wife* ill. by author. HarperCollins, 1984. ISBN 0-911745-19-X Subj: Folk and fairy tales. Foreign lands – Russia.

Hall, Bill. *Fish tale* ill. by John E. Johnson. Norton, 1967. Subj: Fish. Sports – fishing.

Hall, Carol. *Northern J. Calloway presents Supervroomer!* (Calloway, Northern J.)

Hall, Derek. *Baby animals: five stories of endangered species* ill. by John Butler. Candlewick, 1992. ISBN 1-56402-004-5 Subj: Animals – endangered animals.

Elephant bathes ill. by John Butler. Sierra Club, 1985. ISBN 0-394-96529-9 Subj: Activities – bathing. Animals – elephants. Behavior – growing up. Family life.

Gorilla builds ill. by John Butler. Sierra Club, 1985. ISBN 0-394-96530-2 Subj: Animals – gorillas. Behavior – growing up. Family life.

Otter swims ill. by John Butler. Sierra Club, 1984. ISBN 0-394-96503-5 Subj: Animals – otters. Emotions – fear. Sports – swimming.

Panda climbs ill. by John Butler. Sierra Club, 1984. ISBN 0-394-96502-7 Subj: Animals – pandas. Emotions – fear. Trees.

Polar bear leaps ill. by John Butler. Sierra Club, 1985. ISBN 0-394-96531-0 Subj: Animals – polar bears. Behavior – growing up. Family life.

Tiger runs ill. by John Butler. Sierra Club, 1984. ISBN 0-394-96504-3 Subj: Animals – tigers. Emotions – fear. Sports – racing.

Hall, Donald. *Andrew the lion farmer* ill. by Jane Miller. Watts, 1959. Subj: Animals. Humor.

I am the dog, I am the cat ill. by Barry Moser. Dial, 1994. ISBN 0-8037-1505-6 Subj: Animals – cats. Animals – dogs. Pets.

Lucy's Christmas ill. by Michael McCurdy. Harcourt, 1994. ISBN 0-15-276870-X Subj: Activities – making things. Family life. Holidays – Christmas. U.S. history.

Lucy's summer ill. by Michael McCurdy. Harcourt, 1995. ISBN 0-15-276873-4 Subj: Family life. Farms. Seasons – summer. U.S. history.

The man who lived alone ill. by Mary Azarian. Godine, 1984. ISBN 0-87923-538-1 Subj: Behavior – solitude.

The milkman's boy ill. by Greg Shed. Walker, 1997. ISBN 0-8027-8465-8 Subj: Careers – farmers. Food.

The ox-cart man ill. by Barbara Cooney. Viking, 1979. ISBN 0-670-53328-9 Subj: Activities – working. Caldecott award books. Farms. Seasons.

Hall, Fergus. *Groundsel* ill. by author. Merrimack, 1983. ISBN 0-224-01938-4 Subj: Gardens, gardening. Seasons.

Hall, Kathy. *see* McMullan, Kate (Hall)

Hall, Malcolm. *And then the mouse . . .* ill. by Stephen Gammell. Four Winds, 1980. ISBN 0-590-07618-3 Subj: Animals – mice. Folk and fairy tales.

CariCATures ill. by Bruce Degen. Coward, 1978. ISBN 0-698-30685-6 Subj: Animals. Riddles.

The friends of Charlie Ant Bear ill. by Alexandra Wallner. Coward, 1980. ISBN 0-398-30711-9 Subj: Animals – anteaters. Character traits – optimism.

Hall, Pam. *On the edge of the eastern ocean* ill. by author. Silver Burdett, 1982. ISBN 0-88874-055-7 Subj: Birds – puffins. Poetry.

Hall, Richard. *Humphrey the lost whale: a true story* (Tokuda, Wendy)

Hall, Zoe. *The apple pie tree* ill. by Shari Halpern. Scholastic, 1996. ISBN 0-590-62382-6 Subj: Food. Nature. Seasons. Trees.

It's pumpkin time! ill. by Shari Halpern. Scholastic, 1994. ISBN 0-590-47833-8 Subj: Holidays – Halloween. Plants.

The surprise garden ill. by Shari Halpern. Blue Sky, 1998. ISBN 0-590-10075-0 Subj: Gardens, gardening. Seeds.

Hallensleben, Georg. *Pauline* ill. by author. Farrar, 1999. ISBN 0-374-35758-7 Subj: Animals – elephants. Animals – weasels. Friendship.

Haller, Danita Ross. *Not just any ring* ill. by Deborah Kogan Ray. Knopf, 1982. ISBN 0-394-95082-8 Subj: Magic.

Hallinan, P. K. (Patrick K.). *For the love of our earth* ill. by author. Forest House, 1992. ISBN 1-878363-73-5 Subj: Ecology. Nature.

I know I belong ill. by author. Hazelden, 1991. ISBN 0-89486-782-2 Subj: Rhyming text. Self-concept.

I know who I am ill. by author. Hazelden, 1991. ISBN 0-89486-781-4 Subj: Rhyming text. Self-concept.

I'm glad to be me ill. by author. Childrens Pr., 1977. ISBN 0-516-03509-6 Subj: Activities. Family life – only child. Self-concept.

I'm thankful each day! ill. by author. Childrens Pr., 1981. ISBN 0-8249-8008-5 Subj: Folk and fairy tales.

Just being alone ill. by author. Childrens Pr., 1976. ISBN 0-516-03516-9 Subj: Activities. Behavior – solitude. Family life – only child.

Just open a book ill. by author. Childrens Pr., 1981. ISBN 0-516-03521-5 Subj: Activities – reading. Rhyming text.

Let's care about sharing! ill. by author. Ideals, 1997. ISBN 1-57102-105-1 Subj: Behavior – sharing.

Let's learn all we can! ill. by author. Ideals, 1999. ISBN 1-57102-156-6 Subj: Rhyming text. School.

Let's play as a team ill. by author. Ideals, 1996. ISBN 1-57102-099-3 Subj: Activities – playing. Rhyming text.

My dentist, my friend ill. by author. Ideals, 1996. ISBN 1-57102-086-1 Subj: Careers – dentists. Rhyming text. Teeth.

My doctor, my friend ill. by author. Ideals, 1996. ISBN 1-57102-071-3 Subj: Careers – doctors. Illness. Rhyming text.

My teacher's my friend ill. by author. Childrens Pr., 1989. ISBN 0-516-09217-0 Subj: Careers – teachers. Friendship. School.

A rainbow of friends ill. by author. Ideals, 1994. ISBN 0-8249-8657-1 Subj: Character traits – individuality. Friendship. Rhyming text.

The small town children's Easter ill. by author. Ideals, 1988. ISBN 0-8249-8319-X Subj: Holidays – Easter. Religion. Rhyming text.

That's what a friend is ill. by author. Childrens Pr., 1977. ISBN 0-516-03628-9 Subj: Friendship. Rhyming text.

Three freckles past a hair: a grandfather's legacy of love ill. by author. Forest House, 1994. ISBN 1-56674-105-X Subj: Death. Emotions – grief. Family life – grandfathers. Sea and seashore.

Today is Easter! ill. by author. Ideals, 1993. ISBN 1-878363-94-8 Subj: Family life – brothers and sisters. Holidays – Easter. Rhyming text.

Today is Halloween ill. by author. Ideals, 1992. ISBN 1-878363-95-6 Subj: Holidays – Halloween. Rhyming text.

Today is Valentine's Day! ill. by author. Ideals, 1994. ISBN 1-57102-129-9 Subj: Friendship. Holidays – Valentine's Day. Rhyming text. School.

Today is your birthday! ill. by author. Ideals, 1990. ISBN 1-878363-29-8 Subj: Birthdays.

We're very good friends, my aunt and I ill. by author. Childrens Pr., 1989. ISBN 0-516-03655-6 Subj: Family life – aunts, uncles. Friendship. Rhyming text.

When I grow up ill. by author. Ideals, 1995. ISBN 1-57102-061-6 Subj: ABC books. Careers. Rhyming text.

Where's Michael? ill. by author. Childrens Pr., 1978. ISBN 0-516-03668-8 Subj: Behavior – imitation. Self-concept.

Hallworth, Grace. *Down by the river* ill. by Caroline Binch. Scholastic, 1996. ISBN 0-590-69320-4 Subj: Activities – playing. Foreign lands – Caribbean Islands. Poetry. Songs.

Halperin, Wendy Anderson. *Once upon a company* ill. by author. Orchard, 1998. ISBN 0-531-33089-3 Subj: Activities – making things. Careers.

When chickens grow teeth: a story from the French of Guy de Maupassant retold and ill. by Wendy Anderson Halperin. Orchard, 1996. ISBN 0-531-08876-6 Subj: Birds – chickens. Eggs. Family life. Illness.

Halpern, Shari. *Hush little baby* (Hush little baby)

I have a pet! ill. by author. Macmillan, 1994. ISBN 0-02-741982-7 Subj: Pets.

Moving from one to ten ill. by author. Macmillan, 1993. ISBN 0-02-741981-9 Subj: Counting, numbers. Moving.

My river ill. by author. Macmillan, 1992. ISBN 0-02-741980-0 Subj: Animals. Ecology. Rivers.

What shall we do when we all go out? text adapt. by Philip H. Bailey; ill. by Shari Halpern. North-South, 1995. ISBN 1-55858-425-0 Subj: Activities – playing. Music. Songs.

Halsey, Megan. *Jump for joy* ill. by author. Bradbury, 1994. ISBN 0-02-742040-X Subj: Days of the week, months of the year.

Halsey, William D. *The magic world of words: a very first dictionary* ed. by William D. Halsey and Christopher G. Morris; ill. by Dora Leder, Angela Adams, and John Hamberger. Macmillan, 1977. ISBN 0-02-578770-5 Subj: Dictionaries.

Hamanaka, Sheila. *I look like a girl* ill. by author. Morrow, 1999. ISBN 0-688-14626-0 Subj: Animals. Imagination. Rhyming text.

Screen of frogs ill. by reteller. Orchard, 1993. ISBN 0-531-08614-3 Subj: Ecology. Folk and fairy tales. Foreign lands – Japan. Frogs and toads.

Hamberger, John. *The day the sun disappeared* ill. by author. Norton, 1964. Subj: Animals. Ecology. Science. Sun.

Hazel was an only pet ill. by author. Norton, 1968. Subj: Animals – dogs. Family life – only child. Pets.

The lazy dog ill. by author. Four Winds, 1971. Subj: Animals – dogs. Toys – balls. Wordless.

The peacock who lost his tail ill. by author. Norton, 1967. Subj: Birds – peacocks, peahens. Character traits – pride.

This is the day ill. by author. Grosset, 1971. ISBN 0-448-21424-5 Subj: Animals – groundhogs. Holidays – Groundhog Day.

Hamil, Thomas Arthur. *Brother Alonzo* ill. by author. Macmillan, 1957. Subj: Religion.

Hamilton, DeWitt. *Sad days, glad days* ill. by Gail Owens. Albert Whitman, 1995. ISBN 0-8075-7200-4 Subj: Animals – cats. Family life. Family life – mothers. Illness.

Hamilton, Emily. *My name is Emily* (Hamilton, Morse)

Hamilton, Morse. *Belching Hill* ill. by Forest Rogers. Greenwillow, 1997. ISBN 0-688-14049-1 Subj: Folk and fairy tales. Foreign lands – Japan. Mythical creatures – ogres.

Big sisters are bad witches ill. by Marylin Hafner. Greenwillow, 1981. ISBN 0-688-84268-2 Subj: Sibling rivalry. Witches.

The black hen, or, The underground inhabitants by Antony Pogorelsky; retold by Morse Hamilton; ill. by Tatyana Yuditskaya. Cobblehill, 1994. ISBN 0-525-65133-0 Subj: Birds – chickens. Folk and fairy tales. Foreign lands – Russia.

How do you do, Mr. Birdsteps? ill. by Patience Brewster. Avon, 1983. ISBN 0-380-82875-8 Subj: Character traits – shyness.

Little sister for sale ill. by Gioia Fiammenghi. Dutton, 1992. ISBN 0-525-65078-4 Subj: Family life – sisters. Sibling rivalry.

My name is Emily by Morse and Emily Hamilton; ill. by Jenni Oliver. Greenwillow, 1979. ISBN 0-688-84181-3 Subj: Behavior – running away. Sibling rivalry.

Who's afraid of the dark? ill. by Patience Brewster. Avon, 1983. ISBN 0-380-82883-9 Subj: Emotions – fear. Night.

Hamilton, Virginia. *Drylongso* ill. by Jerry Pinkney. Harcourt, 1992. ISBN 0-15-224241-4 Subj: Ecology. Ethnic groups in the U.S. – African Americans. Farms. Weather – droughts. Weather – wind.

Jaguarundi ill. by Floyd Cooper. Blue Sky, 1995. ISBN 0-590-47366-2 Subj: Animals. Animals – endangered animals. Animals – jaguars. Behavior – seeking better things. Ecology.

Hamilton-Merritt, Jane. *My first days of school* photos by author. Simon & Schuster, 1982. ISBN 0-671-44417-4 Subj: School – first day.

Our new baby photos by author. Simon & Schuster, 1982. ISBN 0-671-44416-6 Subj: Babies. Family life – new sibling.

Hamley, Dennis. *Tigger and friends* ill. by Meg Rutherford. Lothrop, 1989. ISBN 0-688-08605-5 Subj: Animals – cats. Pets.

Hamm, Diane Johnston. *Grandma drives a motor bed* ill. by Charles Robinson. Albert Whitman, 1987. ISBN 0-8075-3025-5 Subj: Family life – grandmothers. Family life – grandparents. Furniture – beds. Handicaps. Illness. Old age.

How many feet in the bed? ill. by Kate Salley Palmer. Simon & Schuster, 1991. ISBN 0-671-72638-2 Subj: Anatomy – feet. Bedtime. Counting, numbers. Family life.

Laney's lost momma ill. by Sally G. Ward. Albert Whitman, 1991. ISBN 0-8075-4340-3 Subj: Behavior – lost. Family life – mothers. Shopping. Stores.

Rock-a-bye farm ill. by Rick Brown. Simon & Schuster, 1992. ISBN 0-671-74773-8 Subj: Animals. Babies. Bedtime. Careers – farmers. Farms. Night. Sleep.

Hammar, Asa. *Fit for pigs* ill. by Johanna Moller. Checkerboard, 1992. ISBN 1-56288-265-1 Subj: Animals – pigs. Careers – firefighters. Fire. Homes, houses.

Hammarberg, Dyan. *Jessie the chicken* (Pursell, Margaret Sanford)

Polly the guinea pig (Pursell, Margaret Sanford)

Rusty the Irish setter (Overbeck, Cynthia)

Shelley the sea gull (Pursell, Margaret Sanford)

Sprig the tree frog (Pursell, Margaret Sanford)

Hammerschlag, Carl A. *The go away doll* ill. by author. Turtle Island Pr., 1998. ISBN 1-889166-22-7 Subj: Activities – traveling. Friendship. Toys – dolls.

Hammerstein, Oscar. *A real nice clambake* (Rodgers, Richard)

Hammond, Anna. *This home we have made* by Anna Hammond and Joe Matunis; trans. from English by Olga Karman Mendell. Crossroad, 1993. ISBN 0-517-59339-4 Subj: Art. Foreign languages. Homeless.

Hample, Stoo. *Stoo Hample's silly joke book* ill. by author. Delacorte, 1978. ISBN 0-440-08160-2 Subj: Humor. Riddles.

Yet another big fat funny silly book ill. by author. Delacorte, 1980. ISBN 0-440-09797-5 Subj: Poetry. Riddles.

Hampshire, Susan. *Rosie's ballet slippers* ill. by Maria Teresa Meloni. HarperCollins, 1996. ISBN 0-06-026504-3 Subj: Activities – dancing. Ballet. Clothing – shoes.

Hamsa, Bobbie. *Animal babies* ill. by Renée Mansfield. Delmar, 1991. ISBN 0-8273-4495-3 Subj: Animals – babies.

Dirty Larry ill. by Paul Sharp. Childrens Pr., 1983. ISBN 0-516-02040-4 Subj: Character traits – cleanliness.

Fast-draw Freddie ill. by Susan Miller. Rev. ed. Childrens Pr., 2000. ISBN 0-516-22153-1 Subj: Activities – drawing. Rhyming text.

Polly wants a cracker ill. by Jerry Warshaw. Childrens Pr., 1986. ISBN 0-516-02071-4 Subj: Birds – parakeets, parrots. Counting, numbers. Rhyming text.

Your pet bear ill. by Tom Dunnington. Childrens Pr., 1980. ISBN 0-516-03351-4 Subj: Animals – bears. Imagination.

Your pet beaver ill. by Tom Dunnington. Childrens Pr., 1980. ISBN 0-516-03352-2 Subj: Animals – beavers. Imagination.

Your pet camel ill. by Tom Dunnington. Childrens Pr., 1980. ISBN 0-516-03362-X Subj: Animals – camels. Imagination.

Your pet elephant ill. by Tom Dunnington. Childrens Pr., 1980. ISBN 0-516-03353-0 Subj: Animals – elephants. Imagination.

Your pet giraffe ill. by Tom Dunnington. Childrens Pr., 1982. ISBN 0-516-03355-7 Subj: Animals – giraffes. Imagination.

Your pet kangaroo ill. by Tom Dunnington. Childrens Pr., 1980. ISBN 0-516-03363-8 Subj: Animals – kangaroos. Imagination.

Your pet penguin ill. by Tom Dunnington. Childrens Pr., 1980. ISBN 0-516-03364-6 Subj: Birds – penguins. Imagination.

Your pet sea lion ill. by Tom Dunnington. Childrens Pr., 1982. ISBN 0-516-03356-5 Subj: Animals – sea lions. Imagination.

Han, Oki S. *Kongi and Potgi: a Cinderella story from Korea* adapt. by Oki S. Han and Stephanie Haboush Plunkett; pictures by Oki S. Han. Dial, 1994. ISBN 0-8037-1572-2 Subj: Animals. Character traits – helpfulness. Family life – step families. Folk and fairy tales. Foreign lands – Korea. Royalty – princes.

Sir Whong and the golden pig adapt. by Oki S. Han and Stephanie Haboush Plunkett; pictures by Oki S. Han. Dial, 1993. ISBN 0-8037-1345-2 Subj: Behavior – trickery. Folk and fairy tales. Foreign lands – Korea.

Hancock, Joy Elizabeth. *The loudest little lion* ill. by Eileen Christelow. Albert Whitman, 1988. ISBN 0-8075-4773-5 Subj: Animals – lions. Bedtime. Noise, sounds.

Hancock, Sibyl. *Esteban and the ghost* ill. by Dirk Zimmer. Dial, 1983. Adapt. from The tinker and the ghost by Ralph Steele Boggs and Mary Gould Davis. ISBN 0-8037-2411-X Subj: Ghosts.

Freaky Francie ill. by Leonard W. Shortall. Prentice-Hall, 1979. ISBN 0-13-330563-5 Subj: Problem solving.

Old Blue ill. by Erick Ingraham. Putnam, 1980. ISBN 0-399-61141-X Subj: Animals – bulls, cows. Cowboys. U.S. history – frontier and pioneer life.

Handelman, Dorothy. *Babies help out* (Leonard, Marcia)

Peek-a-boo, baby! (Leonard, Marcia)

Handford, Martin. *Find Waldo now* ill. by author. Little, 1994. ISBN 0-316-34232-7 Subj: Activities – traveling. Games. Picture puzzles. Time.

The great Waldo search ill. by author. Little, 1989. ISBN 0-316-34282-3 Subj: Activities – traveling. Games. Picture puzzles.

Where's Waldo? ill. by author. Candlewick, 1997. ISBN 0-7636-0310-4 Subj: Activities – traveling. Behavior – losing things. Foreign lands. Games. Picture puzzles.

Where's Waldo? In Hollywood ill. by author. Candlewick, 1993. ISBN 1-56402-294-3 Subj: Activities – traveling. Games.

Where's Waldo now? ill. by author. Candlewick, 1997. ISBN 0-7636-0308-2 Subj: Activities – traveling. Games. Time.

Where's Waldo? The fantastic journey ill. by author. Candlewick, 1997. ISBN 0-7636-0309-0 Subj: Activities – traveling. Games. Imagination.

Where's Waldo? The wonder book ill. by author. Candlewick, 1997. ISBN 0-7636-0312-0 Subj: Activities – traveling. Behavior – losing things. Games.

Handforth, Thomas. *Mei Li* ill. by author. Doubleday, 1938. ISBN 0-385-07401-8 Subj: Caldecott award books. Foreign lands – China. Holidays – Chinese New Year.

Hands, Hargrave. *Bunny sees* ill. by author. Grosset, 1985. ISBN 0-488-10577-2 Subj: Animals – rabbits. Format, unusual – board books. Nature.

Duckling sees ill. by author. Grosset, 1985. ISBN 0-448-10579-9 Subj: Animals. Format, unusual – board books.

Little lamb sees ill. by author. Grosset, 1985. ISBN 0-448-10576-4 Subj: Animals. Format, unusual – board books.

Hänel, Wolfram. *The gold at the end of the rainbow* trans. by Anthea Bell; ill. by Loek Koopmans. North-South, 1997. ISBN 1-55858-693-8 Subj: Character traits – generosity. Family life – grandfathers. Folk and fairy tales. Foreign lands – Ireland. Mythical creatures – leprechauns.

Mia the beach cat ill. Kirsten Hocker; translated by J. Alison James. North-South, 1994. ISBN 1-55858-314-9 Subj: Activities – vacationing. Animals – cats. Pets. Sea and seashore.

Hanhart, Brigitte. *Shoemaker Martin* (Tolstoy, Aleksey Nikolayevich)

Hanklin, Rebecca. *I can be a doctor* ill. with photos. Childrens Pr., 1985. ISBN 0-516-01846-9 Subj: Careers – doctors.

I can be a fire fighter ill. with photos. Childrens Pr., 1985. ISBN 0-516-01847-7 Subj: Careers – firefighters.

Hanlon, Emily. *What if a lion eats me and I fall into a hippopotamus' mud hole?* ill. by Leigh Grant. Delacorte, 1975. ISBN 0-440-05951-8 Subj: Emotions – fear. Imagination. Zoos.

Hanly, Shelia. *Toddler's book of fun things to do* photos by Steve Shott. DK, 1999. ISBN 0-7894-3979-4 Subj: Activities.

Hann, Jacquie. *Crybaby* ill. by author. Four Winds, 1979. ISBN 0-590-07609-4 Subj: Emotions.

Follow the leader ill. by author. Crown, 1982. ISBN 0-517-54603-5 Subj: Activities – playing. Games.

Up day, down day ill. by author. Four Winds, 1978. ISBN 0-590-07519-5 Subj: Character traits – luck. Sports – fishing.

Hanna, Jack. *Jungle Jack Hanna's safari adventure* by Jack Hanna and Rick A. Prebeg; photos by Rick A. Prebeg. Scholastic, 1996. ISBN 0-590-67322-X Subj: Animals. Foreign lands – Africa.

The petting zoo ill. by Neil Brennan. Doubleday, 1992. ISBN 0-385-41694-6 Subj: Animals. Format, unusual – toy and movable books. Zoos.

Hannan, Peter. *The battle of Sillyville: live silly or die!* ill. by author. Knopf, 1991. ISBN 0-679-90286-4 Subj: Behavior. Humor.

Escape from Camp Wannabarf ill. by author. Knopf, 1991. ISBN 0-679-90287-2 Subj: Camps, camping. Humor.

School after dark ill. by author. Knopf, 1991. ISBN 0-679-80288-0 Subj: Humor. Night. School.

Sillyville or bust ill. by author. Knopf, 1991. ISBN 0-679-90285-6 Subj: Activities – traveling. Automobiles. Behavior – boredom. Humor.

Hannant, Judith Stuller. *Doorknob collection of nursery rhymes* ill. by author. Little, 1991. ISBN 0-316-34343-9 Subj: Format, unusual. Format, unusual – board books. Nursery rhymes.

The doorknob collection of pets and pals ill. by author. Little, 1994. ISBN 0-316-34387-0 Subj: Animals. Format, unusual – board books. Nursery rhymes.

Three little kittens ill. by author. Little, 1995. ISBN 0-316-34413-3 Subj: Animals – cats. Format, unusual – board books. Nursery rhymes.

Hanrahan, Barbara. *My sisters love my clothes* ill. by Lise Stork. Perry Heights Pr., 1992. ISBN 0-9630181-0-8 Subj: Clothing. Family life – sisters.

Hansard, Peter. *I like monkeys because . . .* ill. by Patricia Casey. Candlewick, 1993. ISBN 1-56402-196-3 Subj: Animals – monkeys.

Wag, wag, wag ill. by Barbara Firth. Candlewick, 1994. ISBN 1-56402-301-X Subj: Animals – dogs.

Hansen, Biruta Akerbergs. *Parading with piglets* ill. by author. National Geographic, 1996. ISBN 0-7922-2711-5 Subj: ABC books. Animals. Format, unusual – toy and movable books.

Hansen, Carla. *Barnaby Bear builds a boat* by Carla and Vilhelm Hansen; ill. by authors. Random House, 1979. ISBN 0-394-84247-2 Subj: Animals – bears. Boats, ships.

Barnaby Bear visits the farm by Carla and Vilhelm Hansen; ill. by authors. Random House, 1979. ISBN 0-394-84248-0 Subj: Animals – bears. Farms.

Hansen, Jeff. *Being a fire fighter isn't just squirtin' water* ill. by author. Vantage Pr., 1978. ISBN 0-533-03498-1 Subj: Careers – firefighters.

Hansen, Mark Victor. *Chicken soup for little souls: The best night out with Dad* (McCourt, Lisa)

Chicken soup for little souls: The Goodness Gorillas (McCourt, Lisa)

Chicken soup for little souls: The never-forgotten doll (McCourt, Lisa)

Della Splatnuk birthday girl (McCourt, Lisa)

The new kid and the cookie thief (McCourt, Lisa)

Hansen, Vilhelm. *Barnaby Bear builds a boat* (Hansen, Carla)

Barnaby Bear visits the farm (Hansen, Carla)

Hanson, Joan. *I don't like Timmy* ill. by author. Carolrhoda, 1972. ISBN 0-8761-4028-2 Subj: Babies. Family life – brothers. Family life – new sibling.

I won't be afraid ill. by author. Carolrhoda, 1974. ISBN 0-8761-4050-9 Subj: Behavior – growing up. Emotions – fear.

I'm going to run away ill. by author. Platt, 1978. ISBN 0-448-46522-1 Subj: Behavior – running away.

Hanson, Mary Elizabeth. *Snug* ill. by Cheryl Munro Taylor. Simon & Schuster, 1998. ISBN 0-689-81164-0 Subj: Animals – bears. Behavior. Family life – mothers.

Hanson, Regina. *The face at the window* ill. by Linda Saport. Clarion, 1997. ISBN 0-395-78625-8 Subj: Emotions – fear. Foreign lands – Japan. Illness.

The tangerine tree ill. by Harvey Stevenson. Clarion, 1995. ISBN 0-395-68963-5 Subj: Behavior – worrying. Careers – migrant workers. Emotions – sadness. Family life – fathers. Foreign lands – Jamaica.

Hanze. *Yann and the whale* ill. by Hanze; story by Frissen. Kane/Miller, 1997. ISBN 0-916291-71-5 Subj: Animals – whales. Sea and seashore. Sports – fishing.

Hapgood, Miranda. *Martha's mad day* ill. by Emily Arnold McCully. Crown, 1977. ISBN 0-517-52997-1 Subj: Emotions – anger.

Harada, Joyce. *It's the ABC book* ill. by author. Heian Intl., 1982. ISBN 0-89346-157-1 Subj: ABC books.

It's the 0-1-2-3 book ill. by author. Heian Intl., 1985. ISBN 0-89346-252-7 Subj: Counting, numbers.

Harber, Frances. *The brothers' promise* ill. by Thor Wickstrom. Albert Whitman, 1998. ISBN 0-8075-0900-0 Subj: Behavior. Family life – brothers. Jewish culture. Religion.

My king has donkey ears ill. by Maryann Kovalski. North Winds, 1986. ISBN 0-590-71522-4 Subj: Folk and fairy tales. Problem solving. Royalty – kings.

Harbour, Elizabeth. *A first picture book of nursery rhymes* ill. by author. Viking, 1995. ISBN 0-670-85030-6 Subj: Nursery rhymes.

Harder, Dan (Dan Wymbs). *Colliding with Chris* ill. by Kevin O'Malley. Hyperion, 1997. ISBN 0-7868-2098-5 Subj: Accidents. Rhyming text. Sports – bicycling.

Hardy, Tad. *Lost cat* ill. by David Goldin. Houghton Mifflin, 1996. ISBN 0-395-73574-2 Subj: Animals – cats. Behavior – lost. Pets. Rhyming text.

Hare, Lorraine. *Who needs her?* ill. by author. Atheneum, 1983. ISBN 0-689-50268-0 Subj: Character traits – cleanliness.

Hare, Norma Q. *Mystery at mouse house* ill. by Stella Ormai. Garrard, 1980. ISBN 0-8116-6412-0 Subj: Behavior – stealing. Mystery stories.

Haring, Keith. *Big* ill. by author. Hyperion, 1998. ISBN 0-7868-0390-8 Subj: Clothing. Concepts – color. Concepts – size. Format, unusual – board books.

10 ill. by author. Hyperion, 1998. ISBN 0-7868-0391-6 Subj: Counting, numbers. Foreign languages. Format, unusual – board books.

Hariton, Anca. *Butterfly story* ill. by author. Dutton, 1995. ISBN 0-525-45212-5 Subj: Insects – butterflies, caterpillars. Metamorphosis. Science.

Egg story ill. by author. Dutton, 1992. ISBN 0-525-44861-6 Subj: Birds – chickens. Birth. Eggs.

Harley, Bill. *Nothing happened* ill. by Ann Miya. Tricycle, 1995. ISBN 1-883672-09-0 Subj: Bedtime. Emotions. Family life. Family life – brothers. Night.

Harlow, Joan Hiatt. *Shadow bear* ill. by Jim Arnosky. Doubleday, 1981. ISBN 0-385-15067-9 Subj: Animals – polar bears. Emotions – fear. Eskimos.

Harmer, Juliet. *Prayers for children* ill. by author. Viking, 1990. ISBN 0-670-83348-7 Subj: Days of the week, months of the year. Religion.

Harms, D. *The merry starlings* (Marshak, S. [Samuil])

Harms, John, II. *The saving of Sly Manatee* ill. by Robin Lee Makowski. Frederick, 1998. ISBN 0-9653871-3-5 Subj: Animals – manatees.

Harness, Cheryl. *Mark Twain and the queens of the Mississippi* ill. by author. Simon & Schuster, 1998. ISBN 0-689-81542-5 Subj: Boats, ships. Careers – writers. Rivers. U.S. history.

Midnight in the cemetery: a spooky search-and-find alphabet book ill. by Robin Brickman. Simon & Schuster, 1999. ISBN 0-689-80873-9 Subj: ABC books. Ghosts. Rhyming text.

Papa's Christmas gift: around the world on the night before Christmas ill. by author. Simon & Schuster, 1995. ISBN 0-689-80344-3 Subj: Holidays – Christmas. Poetry.

The queen with bees in her hair ill. by author. Holiday, 1993. ISBN 0-8050-1715-1 Subj: Folk and fairy tales. Royalty – kings. Royalty – queens. Seasons – spring.

Three young pilgrims ill. by author. Bradbury, 1992. ISBN 0-02-742643-2 Subj: Pilgrims. U.S. history.

Harold, Jerdine Nolen. *Harvey Potter's balloon farm* ill. by Mark Buehner. Lothrop, 1994. ISBN 0-688-07888-5 Subj: Farms. Magic. Tall tales. Toys – balloons.

Harper, Anita. *How we live* ill. by Christine Roche. HarperCollins, 1977. ISBN 0-060-22223-9 Subj: Homes, houses.

How we work ill. by Christine Roche. HarperCollins, 1977. ISBN 0-06-022225-5 Subj: Activities – working. Careers.

It's not fair! ill. by Susan Hellard. Putnam, 1986. ISBN 0-399-21365-1 Subj: Animals – kangaroos. Babies. Family life – new sibling. Sibling rivalry.

Harper, Dan. *Telling time with Big Mama Cat* ill. by Barry and Cara Moser. Harcourt, 1998. ISBN 0-15-201738-0 Subj: Animals – cats. Clocks, watches. Format, unusual – toy and movable books. Time.

Harper, Isabelle. *My dog Rosie* ill. by Barry Moser. Blue Sky, 1994. ISBN 0-590-47619-X Subj: Animals – dogs. Children as authors. Family life – grandfathers.

Our new puppy ill. by Barry Moser. Silver Burdett, 1996. ISBN 0-590-56926-0 Subj: Animals – dogs. Family life – grandfathers. Family life – sisters.

Harper, Jessica. *I forgot my shoes* ill. by Kathy Osborn. Putnam, 1999. ISBN 0-399-23149-8 Subj: Clothing – shoes. Memories, memory. Rhyming text.

Harper, Jo. *Jalapeno Hal* ill. by Jennifer Beck Harris. Four Winds, 1993. ISBN 0-02-742645-9 Subj: Food. U.S. history – frontier and pioneer life. Weather – droughts. Weather – rain.

Prairie dog pioneers by Jo and Josephine Harper; ill. by Craig Spearing. Turtle Books, 1998. ISBN 1-890515-10-8 Subj: Behavior – misunderstanding. Family life. Family life – daughters. Moving. U.S. history – frontier and pioneer life.

Harper, Josephine. *Prairie dog pioneers* (Harper, Jo)

Harper, Piers. *How the world was saved and other Native American tales* ill. by author. Western, 1994. ISBN 0-307-17507-3 Subj: Creation. Folk and fairy tales. Indians of North America.

If you love a bear ill. by author. Candlewick, 1998. ISBN 0-7636-0371-6 Subj: Activities. Animals – bears.

Harper, Wilhelmina. *The gunniwolf* ill. by William Wiesner. Dutton, 1967. Subj: Animals – wolves. Behavior – misbehavior. Flowers. Foreign lands – Germany.

Harranth, Wolf. *The flute concert* ill. by Romulus Candea. Blackbirch, 1998. ISBN 1-56711-803-8 Subj: Behavior – losing things. Careers – musicians. Music.

My old grandad trans. from German by Peter Carter; ill. by Christina Oppermann-Dimow. Merrimack, 1984. ISBN 0-19-279787-5 Subj: Death. Emotions – grief. Emotions – loneliness. Family life – grandfathers. Farms.

Harriott, Ted. *Coming home: a dog's true story* ill. by Lisa Kopper. David & Charles, 1985. ISBN 0-575-03583-8 Subj: Animals – dogs. Character traits – kindness to animals. Death. Emotions – grief.

Harris, Dorothy Joan. *Four seasons for Toby* ill. by Vlasta van Kampen. North Winds, 1987. ISBN 0-590-71677-8 Subj: Reptiles – turtles, tortoises. Seasons.

Goodnight Jeffrey ill. by Nancy Hannans. Warne, 1983. ISBN 0-7232-6224-1 Subj: Bedtime.

Harris, Jim. *Jack and the giant: a story full of beans* ill. by author. Rising Moon, 1997. ISBN 0873586808 Subj: Folk and fairy tales. Giants. Plants.

Harris, Joel Chandler. *Brer Rabbit and Boss Lion* (Kessler, Brad)

Hello, house! (Hayward, Linda)

Jump! the adventures of Brer Rabbit adapt. by Van Dyke Parks and Malcolm Jones; ill. by Barry Moser. Harcourt, 1986. ISBN 0-15-241350-2 Subj: Animals. Folk and fairy tales.

Jump again! more adventures of Brer Rabbit adapt. by Van Dyke Parks; ill. by Barry Moser. Harcourt, 1987. ISBN 0-15-241352-9 Subj: Animals. Folk and fairy tales.

Harris, John. *A is for artist: a Getty Museum alphabet* (J. Paul Getty Museum)

Harris, Lee. *Never let your cat make lunch for you* ill. by Debbie Tilley. Tricycle, 1999. ISBN 1-883672-80-5 Subj: Activities – cooking. Animals – cats. Food.

Harris, Leon A. *The great diamond robbery* ill. by Joseph Schindelman. Atheneum, 1985. ISBN 0-689-31188-5 Subj: Animals – mice. Character traits – bravery. Crime. Songs. Stores.

The great picture robbery ill. by Joseph Schindelman. Atheneum, 1963. Subj: Animals – mice. Art. Crime. Foreign lands – France.

Harris, Louise Dyer. *Flash, the life of a firefly* by Louise Dyer Harris and Norman Dyer Harris; ill. by Henry B. Kane. Little, 1966. Subj: Insects – fireflies. Science.

Harris, Marian. *Tuesday in Arizona* ill. by Jim Harris. Pelican, 1998. ISBN 1-56554-233-9 Subj: Animals – rats. Careers – miners.

Harris, Norman Dyer. *Flash, the life of a firefly* (Harris, Louise Dyer)

Harris, Pamela. *Hot, cold, shy, bold: looking at opposites* photos by author. Kids Can Pr., 1995. ISBN 1-55074-153-5 Subj: Concepts – opposites. Rhyming text.

Harris, Robie H. *Don't forget to come back* ill. by Tony DeLuna. Atheneum, 1963. ISBN 0-394-83849-1 Subj: Activities – babysitting. Behavior. Family life.

Hot Henry ill. by Nicole Hollander. St. Martin's, 1987. ISBN 0-312-01041-9 Subj: Clothing. Family life.

I hate kisses ill. by Diane Paterson. Knopf, 1981. ISBN 0-394-94324-4 Subj: Behavior – growing up.

Messy Jessie ill. by Nicole Hollander. St. Martin's, 1987. ISBN 0-312-01067-2 Subj: Behavior – carelessness. Family life.

Harris, Steven Michael. *This is my trunk* ill. by Norma Welliver. Atheneum, 1985. ISBN 0-689-31128-1 Subj: Careers. Circus. Clowns, jesters.

Harris, Susan. *Creatures that look alike* ill. by Don Forrest. Watts, 1980. ISBN 0-531-01375-8 Subj: Animals. Science.

Reptiles ill. by Jim Robins. Watts, 1978. ISBN 0-531-01335-9 Subj: Reptiles. Science.

Harris, Susan Yard. *Daisy's garden* (Gerstein, Mordicai)

Guess what? (Gerstein, Mordicai)

Harrison, Carol. *Dinosaurs everywhere!* ill. by Richard Courtney. Scholastic, 1998. ISBN 0-590-00089-6 Subj: Dinosaurs.

Harrison, David Lee. *The animals' song* ill. by Chris L. Demarest. Boyds Mills, 1997. ISBN 1-56397-144-5 Subj: Animals. Cumulative tales. Music. Noise, sounds. Rhyming text. Songs.

The boy who counted stars ill. by Betsy Lewin. Wordsong, 1994. ISBN 1-56397-125-9 Subj: Humor. Poetry.

The case of Og, the missing frog ill. by Jerry Warshaw. Rand McNally, 1972. ISBN 0-528-82635-2 Subj: Frogs and toads. Rhyming text.

Detective Bob and the great ape escape ill. by Ned Delaney. Parents, 1980. ISBN 0-819-31032-8 Subj: Animals – gorillas. Careers – detectives. Mystery stories. Zoos.

Little boy soup ill. by Toni Goffe. Ladybird, 1990. ISBN 0-7214-5267-1 Subj: Character traits – cleverness. Witches.

Little turtle's big adventure ill. by J. P. Miller. Random House, 1985, c1978. ISBN 0-394-96345-8 Subj: Character traits – kindness to animals. Progress. Reptiles – turtles, tortoises.

A thousand cousins, poems of family life ill. by Betsy Lewin. Wordsong, 1996. ISBN 1-56397-131-3 Subj: Family life. Poetry.

Wake up, sun! ill. by Hans Wilhelm. Random House, 1986. ISBN 0-394-88256-8 Subj: Animals. Morning. Sun.

When cows come home ill. by Chris L. Demarest. Caroline House, 1994. ISBN 1-56397-143-7 Subj: Animals – bulls, cows. Homes, houses. Rhyming text.

Harrison, Joanna. *Dear bear* ill. by author. Carolrhoda, 1994. ISBN 0-87614-839-9 Subj: Activities – writing. Animals – bears. Emotions – fear. Letters, cards. Toys – bears.

Harrison, Michael. *Bright star shining: poems for Christmas* (Bright star shining)

Harrison, Sarah. *In granny's garden* ill. by Mike Wilks. Holt, 1980. ISBN 0-03-050876-2 Subj: Animals. Dinosaurs. Rhyming text.

Harrison, Ted. *A northern alphabet: A is for arctic* ill. by author. Tundra, 1982. ISBN 0-88776-209-3 Subj: ABC books.

O Canada ill. by author. Ticknor & Fields, 1993. ISBN 0-395-66075-0 Subj: Foreign lands – Canada.

Harrison, Troon. *Aaron's awful allergies* ill. by Eugenie Fernandes. Kids Can Pr., 1998. ISBN 1-55074-299-X Subj: Illness – allergies. Pets.

Don't dig so deep, Nicholas! ill. by Gary Clement. Owl Books, 1997. ISBN 1-895688-51-5 Subj: Activities – digging. Animals. Foreign lands – Australia. Sea and seashore.

The dream collector ill. by Alan and Lea Daniel. Kids Can Pr., 1999. ISBN 1-55074-437-2 Subj: Animals – dogs. Dreams. Imagination.

Lavender Moon ill. by Eugenie Fernandes. Annick, 1997. ISBN 1-55037-455-9 Subj: Activities – traveling. Careers – bus drivers. Careers – chefs, cooks.

Harrop, Beatrice. *Sing hey diddle diddle: 66 nursery rhymes with their traditional tunes* (Mother Goose)

Harsh, Fred. *Alfie* ill. by author. Ideals, 1991. ISBN 0-685-48862-4 Subj: Animals – dogs. Birds – crows. Self-concept.

Harshman, Marc. *All the way to morning* ill. by Felipe Dávalos. Cavendish, 1999. ISBN 0-7614-5042-4 Subj: Bedtime. Night. Noise, sounds. Sleep.

A little excitement ill. by Ted Rand. Cobblehill, 1989. ISBN 0-525-65001-6 Subj: Behavior – wishing. Character traits – bravery. Country. Farms. Fire. Seasons – winter.

Moving days ill. by Wendy Popp. Cobblehill, 1994. ISBN 0-525-65135-7 Subj: Emotions. Family life. Moving.

Only one ill. by Barbara Garrison. Cobblehill, 1993. ISBN 0-525-65116-0 Subj: Counting, numbers. Fairs.

Rocks in my pocket by Marc Harshman and Bonnie Collins; ill. by Toni Goffe. Dutton, 1991. ISBN 0-525-65055-5 Subj: Folk and fairy tales. Rocks.

Snow company ill. by Leslie W. Bowman. Dutton, 1990. ISBN 0-525-65029-6 Subj: Weather – snow. Weather – storms.

The storm ill. by Mark Mohr. Cobblehill, 1995. ISBN 0-525-65150-0 Subj: Emotions – anger. Emotions – fear. Farms. Handicaps – physical handicaps. Weather – storms.

Uncle James ill. by Michael Dooling. Cobblehill, 1993. ISBN 0-525-65110-1 Subj: Behavior – boasting. Death. Family life – aunts, uncles. Farms. Illness. Poverty.

Harshman, Terry Webb. *Porcupine's pajama party* ill. by Doug Cushman. HarperCollins, 1988. ISBN 0-06-022249-2 Subj: Animals – otters. Animals – porcupines. Bedtime. Birds – owls. Monsters. Parties. Sleep. Sleepovers.

Hart, Jeanne McGahey. *Scareboy* ill. by Gerhardt Hurt. Parnassus, 1957. ISBN 0-395-27660-8 Subj: Humor. Scarecrows.

Hart, Rebecca. *Tortillas and lullabies = Tortillas y cancioncitas* (Tortillas and lullabies = Tortillas y cancioncitas)

Hartelius, Margaret A. *The chicken's child* ill. by author. Doubleday, 1975. ISBN 0-385-07370-4 Subj: Birds – chickens. Reptiles – alligators, crocodiles. Wordless.

Harter, Debbie. *Walking through the jungle* ill. by author. Orchard, 1997. ISBN 0-531-30035-8 Subj: Animals. Jungle.

Hartley, Deborah. *Up north in the winter* ill. by Lydia Dabcovich. Dutton, 1986. ISBN 0-525-44268-5 Subj: Animals – foxes. Family life – grandfathers. Seasons – winter.

Hartman, Bob. *Aunt Mabel's table* ill. by Richard Max Kolding. Standard, 1994. ISBN 0-7847-0178-4 Subj: Etiquette. Family life – aunts, uncles. Food.

The birthday of a king ill. by Michael McGuire. Victor Books, 1993. ISBN 1-56476-043-X Subj: Birthdays. Holidays – Christmas. Religion.

Lobster for lunch ill. by Jo Ellen McAllister Stammen. Down East, 1992. ISBN 0-89272-302-5 Subj: Crustaceans. Family life. Food. Friendship.

The morning of the world ill. by Michael McGuire. Victor Books, 1993. ISBN 1-56476-040-5 Subj: Creation. Religion.

A night the stars danced for joy ill. by Tim Jonke. Lion, 1996. ISBN 0-7459-3684-9 Subj: Holidays – Christmas. Religion.

The one and only Delgado Cheese: a tale of talent, fame and friendship ill. by Donna Kae Nelson. Lion, 1993. ISBN 0-7459-2405-0 Subj: Family life – aunts, uncles. School. Self-concept. Theater.

Who brought the bread? ill. by author. Standard, 1994. ISBN 0-7847-0188-1 Subj: Careers – bakers. Food. Religion.

Who wrecked the roof? ill. by Terri Steiger. Standard, 1994. ISBN 0-7847-0189-X Subj: Family life – fathers. Family life – sons. Religion.

Hartman, Gail. *As the crow flies* ill. by Harvey Stevenson. Bradbury, 1991. ISBN 0-02-743005-7 Subj: Animals. Maps.

As the roadrunner runs: a first book of maps ill. by Cathy Bobak. Bradbury, 1994. ISBN 0-02-743092-8 Subj: Animals. Maps.

For sand castles or seashells ill. by Ellen Weiss. Bradbury, 1990. ISBN 0-02-743091-X Subj: Activities – playing. Concepts.

For strawberry jam or fireflies ill. by Ellen Weiss. Bradbury, 1989. ISBN 0-02-742990-3 Subj: Concepts. Language.

Hartmann, Wendy. *All the magic in the world* ill. by Niki Daly. Dutton, 1993. ISBN 0-525-45092-0 Subj: Careers – sanitation workers. Communities, neighborhoods. Imagination. Magic.

The dinosaurs are back and it's all your fault, Edward! by Wendy Hartmann and Niki Daly; ill. by Niki Daly. Margaret K. McElderry, 1997. ISBN 0-689-81152-7 Subj: Dinosaurs. Eggs. Family life – brothers.

One sun rises: an African wildlife counting book ill. by Nicolaas Maritz. Dutton, 1994. ISBN 0-525-45225-7 Subj: Animals. Counting, numbers. Foreign lands – Africa.

Harvey, Amanda. *Stormy weather* ill. by author. Lothrop, 1992. ISBN 0-688-10608-0 Subj: Behavior – fighting, arguing. Family life. Seasons – winter.

Harvey, Brett. *Cassie's journey: going West in the 1860s* ill. by Deborah Kogan Ray. Holiday, 1988. ISBN 0-8234-0684-9 Subj: Activities – traveling. Family life. U.S. history – frontier and pioneer life.

Immigrant girl: Becky of Eldridge Street ill. by Deborah Kogan Ray. Holiday, 1987. ISBN 0-8234-0638-5 Subj: City. Family life. Jewish culture.

My prairie Christmas ill. by Deborah Kogan Ray. Holiday, 1990. ISBN 0-8234-0827-2 Subj: Holidays – Christmas. Weather – storms.

My prairie year: based on the diary of Elenore Plaisted ill. by Deborah Kogan Ray. Holiday, 1986. ISBN 0-8234-0604-0 Subj: Activities – working. Farms. U.S. history – frontier and pioneer life.

Harwick, B. L. *see* Keller, Beverly

Haseley, Dennis. *The cave of snores* ill. by Eric Beddows. HarperCollins, 1987. ISBN 0-06-022215-8 Subj: Animals. Folk and fairy tales. Magic. Sleep. Wizards.

Crosby ill. by Jonathan Green. Harcourt, 1996. ISBN 0-15-200829-2 Subj: Ethnic groups in the U.S. – African Americans. Friendship. Kites.

Ghost catcher ill. by Lloyd Bloom. HarperCollins, 1991. ISBN 0-06-022247-6 Subj: Death. Emotions – love. Ghosts. Shadows.

Horses with wings ill. by Lynn Curlee. HarperCollins, 1993. ISBN 0-06-022886-5 Subj: Activities – ballooning. Foreign lands – France. War.

Kite flier ill. by David Wiesner. Four Winds, 1986. ISBN 0-02-743110-X Subj: Family life – fathers. Kites.

My father doesn't know about the woods and me ill. by Michael Hays. Atheneum, 1988. ISBN 0-689-31365-9 Subj: Family life – fathers. Forest, woods. Imagination.

The old banjo ill. by Stephen Gammell. Macmillan, 1983. ISBN 0-02-743100-2 Subj: Farms. Music.

The pirate who tried to capture the moon ill. by Sue Truesdell. HarperCollins, 1983. ISBN 0-06-022227-1 Subj: Pirates.

The soap bandit ill. by Jane Chambless. Warne, 1984. ISBN 0-7232-6216-0 Subj: Character traits – cleanliness.

The thieves' market ill. by Lisa Desimini. Harper-Collins, 1991. ISBN 0-06-022493-2 Subj: Crime. Imagination. Night. Stores.

Haskins, Francine. *I remember "121"* ill. by author. Childrens Pr., 1991. ISBN 0-89239-100-6 Subj: Communities, neighborhoods. Ethnic groups in the U.S. – African Americans. Family life. Memories, memory.

Haskins, Ilma. *Color seems* ill. by author. Vanguard, 1973. Subj: Concepts – color.

Haskins, Jim (James). *Count your way through Africa* ill. by Barbara Knutson. Carolrhoda, 1989. ISBN 0-87614-347-8 Subj: Counting, numbers. Foreign lands – Africa. Foreign languages.

Count your way through Brazil by Jim Haskins and Kathleen Benson; ill. by Liz Brenner Dodson. Carolrhoda, 1996. ISBN 0-87614-873-9 Subj: Counting, numbers. Foreign languages.

Count your way through Canada ill. by Steve Michaels. Carolrhoda, 1989. ISBN 0-87614-350-8 Subj: Counting, numbers. Foreign lands – Canada.

Count your way through China ill. by Dennis Hockerman. Carolrhoda, 1987. ISBN 0-87614-302-8 Subj: Counting, numbers. Foreign lands – China.

Count your way through France ill. by Andrea Shine. Carolrhoda, 1996. ISBN 0-87614-874-7 Subj: Counting, numbers. Foreign lands – France. Foreign languages.

Count your way through Germany ill. by Helen Byers. Carolrhoda, 1992. ISBN 0-87614-407-5 Subj: Counting, numbers. Foreign lands – Germany. Foreign languages.

Count your way through Greece ill. by Janice Lee Porter. Carolrhoda, 1996. ISBN 0-87614-875-5 Subj: Counting, numbers. Foreign lands – Greece. Foreign languages.

Count your way through India ill. by Liz Brenner Dodson. Carolrhoda, 1990. ISBN 0-87614-414-8 Subj: Counting, numbers. Foreign lands – India. Foreign languages.

Count your way through Ireland ill. by Beth Wright. Carolrhoda, 1996. ISBN 0-87614-872-0 Subj: Counting, numbers. Foreign lands – Ireland.

Count your way through Israel ill. by Rick Hanson. Carolrhoda, 1990. ISBN 0-87614-415-6 Subj: Counting, numbers. Foreign lands – Israel. Foreign languages.

Count your way through Italy ill. by Beth Wright. Carolrhoda, 1990. ISBN 0-87614-406-7 Subj: Counting, numbers. Foreign lands – Italy. Foreign languages.

Count your way through Japan ill. by Martin Skoro. Carolrhoda, 1987. ISBN 0-87614-301-X Subj: Counting, numbers. Foreign lands – Japan.

Count your way through Korea ill. by Dennis Hockerman. Carolrhoda, 1989. ISBN 0-87614-348-6 Subj: Counting, numbers. Foreign lands – Korea. Foreign languages.

Count your way through Mexico ill. by Helen Byers. Carolrhoda, 1989. ISBN 0-87614-349-4 Subj: Counting, numbers. Foreign lands – Mexico. Foreign languages.

Count your way through Russia ill. by Vera Mednikov. Carolrhoda, 1987. ISBN 0-87614-303-6 Subj: Counting, numbers. Foreign lands – Russia.

Count your way through the Arab world ill. by Dana Gustafson. Carolrhoda, 1987. ISBN 0-87616-304-4 Subj: Counting, numbers. Foreign lands – Arabia.

The Statue of Liberty: America's proud lady ill. with photos. Lerner, 1986. ISBN 0-8225-1706-X Subj: Art. U.S. history.

Hasler, Eveline. *The giantess* ill. by Renate Seelig; trans. by Laura McKenna. Kane/Miller, 1997. ISBN 0-916291-76-6 Subj: Clothing – costumes. Giants. Self-concept.

Martin is our friend ill. by Dorothea Desmarowitz. Abingdon, 1981. ISBN 0-687-23650-9 Subj: Animals – horses, ponies. Character traits – kindness. Handicaps.

Winter magic ill. by Michèle Lemieux. Morrow, 1985. ISBN 0-688-05258-4 Subj: Animals – cats. Night. Seasons – winter.

Hassett, Ann M. *Cat up a tree* (Hassett, John)

Junior: a little loon tale (Hassett, John)

Hassett, John. *Cat up a tree* by John and Ann Hassett; ill. by authors. Houghton Mifflin, 1998. ISBN 0-395-88415-2 Subj: Animals – cats. Behavior – needing someone. Character traits – helpfulness. Counting, numbers.

Junior: a little loon tale by John and Ann Hassett; ill. by John Hassett. Down East, 1993. ISBN 0-89272-322-X Subj: Behavior – losing things. Behavior – lost. Birds – loons. Ecology.

Hastings, Evelyn Beilhart. *The department store* ill. by Lewis A. Ogan. Melmont, 1956. Subj: Shopping. Stores.

Hastings, Selina. *The firebird* (The firebird)

The man who wanted to live forever ill. by Reg Cartwright. Holt, 1988. ISBN 0-8050-0572-2 Subj: Death. Folk and fairy tales.

Peter and the wolf (Prokofiev, Sergei Sergeievitch)

The singing ringing tree ill. by Louise Brierley. Holt, 1988. ISBN 0-8050-0573-0 Subj: Character traits – kindness. Folk and fairy tales. Magic. Royalty – princes. Royalty – princesses.

Haswell, Peter. *Pog* ill. by author. Watts, 1989. ISBN 0-531-08443-4 Subj: Animals – pigs. Character traits – questioning.

Pog climbs Mount Everest ill. by author. Watts, 1990. ISBN 0-531-08473-6 Subj: Animals – pigs. Sports – mountain climbing.

Hatcher, Charles. *What shape is it?* ill. by Gareth Adamson. Duell, 1966. Subj: Concepts – shape.

Hathon, Elizabeth. *We go to school* photos by author. Random House, 1992. ISBN 0-679-83377-3 Subj: Format, unusual – board books. Format, unusual – toy and movable books. School.

We go to the zoo photos by author. Random House, 1992. ISBN 0-679-83376-5 Subj: Format, unusual – board books. Format, unusual – toy and movable books. Zoos.

Hathorn, Libby (Elizabeth). *Freya's fantastic surprise* ill. by Sharon Thompson. Scholastic, 1989. ISBN 0-86896-381-X Subj: Babies. Character traits – honesty. Emotions – envy, jealousy. Family life – new sibling. Friendship. School.

Sky sash so blue ill. by Benny Andrews. Simon & Schuster, 1998. ISBN 0-689-81090-3 Subj: Ethnic groups in the U.S. – African Americans. Rhyming text. Slavery.

The tram to Bondi beach ill. by Julie Vivas. Kane/Miller, 1989. ISBN 0-916291-20-0 Subj: Foreign lands – Australia. Trains.

The wonder thing ill. by Peter Gouldthorpe. Houghton Mifflin, 1996. ISBN 0-395-71541-5 Subj: Nature. Riddles. Water.

Haubensak-Tellenbach, Margrit. *The story of Noah's ark* ill. by Erna Emhardt. Crown, 1983. ISBN 0-517-55050-4 Subj: Animals. Boats, ships. Religion – Noah. Weather – floods. Weather – rain. Weather – rainbows.

Haugaard, Erik Christian. *The emperor's nightingale* (Andersen, H. C. [Hans Christian])

Prince Boghole ill. by Julie Downing. Macmillan, 1987. ISBN 0-02-743440-0 Subj: Folk and fairy tales. Foreign lands – Ireland. Royalty – princes.

Princess Horrid ill. by Diane Dawson Hearn. Macmillan, 1990. ISBN 0-02-743445-1 Subj: Behavior. Folk and fairy tales. Royalty – princesses. Witches.

Thumbelina (Andersen, H. C. [Hans Christian])

Hauptmann, Tatjana. *A day in the life of Petronella Pig* ill. by author. Holt, 1982. ISBN 0-03-057794-2 Subj: Animals – pigs. Format, unusual. Wordless.

Haus, Felice. *Beep! Beep! I'm a jeep: a toddler's book of "let's pretend"* ill. by Norman Gorbaty. Random House, 1986. ISBN 0-394-88000-5 Subj: Activities – playing. Format, unusual – board books. Imagination. Toys.

Hausherr, Rosmarie. *My first kitten* photos by author. Four Winds, 1985. ISBN 0-02-743420-6 Subj: Animals – cats. Pets.

My first puppy photos by author. Four Winds, 1986. ISBN 0-02-743410-9 Subj: Animals – dogs. Pets.

Hausman, Bonnie. *A to Z, do you ever feel like me?* photos by Sandi Fellman. Dutton, 1999. ISBN 0-525-46216-3 Subj: ABC books. Emotions.

Hausman, Gerald. *Coyote walks on two legs* ill. by Floyd Cooper. Philomel, 1993. ISBN 0-399-22018-6 Subj: Animals – coyotes. Behavior – greed. Behavior – trickery. Character traits – vanity. Folk and fairy tales. Indians of North America – Navajo.

Doctor Bird ill. by Ashley Wolff. Philomel, 1998. ISBN 0-399-22744-X Subj: Birds – humming birds. Folk and fairy tales. Foreign lands – Jamaica.

Eagle boy ill. by Cara and Barry Moser. Harper-Collins, 1996. ISBN 0-06-021101-6 Subj: Birds – eagles. Folk and fairy tales. Indians of North America – Navajo.

How Chipmunk got tiny feet ill. by Ashley Wolff. HarperCollins, 1995. ISBN 0-06-022907-1 Subj: Animals. Folk and fairy tales. Indians of North America.

The story of Blue Elk ill. by Kristina Rodanas. Clarion, 1998. ISBN 0-395-84512-2 Subj: Animals – elk. Folk and fairy tales. Indians of North America – Pueblo. Magic.

Turtle Island ABC: a gathering of Native American symbols ill. by Cara and Barry Moser. Harper-Collins, 1994. ISBN 0-06-021308-6 Subj: ABC books. Indians of North America.

Hautzig, Deborah. *Beauty and the beast* ill. by Kathy Mitchell. Random House, 1995. ISBN 0-679-95296-9 Subj: Character traits – loyalty. Emotions – love. Folk and fairy tales. Magic.

Big Bird at the beach ill. by Carol Nicklaus; featuring Jim Henson's Sesame Street Muppets. Random House, 1990. ISBN 0-679-80159-6 Subj: Family life – grandmothers. Puppets. Sea and seashore.

The Christmas story: from the Gospels according to Saint Matthew and Saint Luke ill. by Yoshi Miyake. Random House, 1994. ISBN 0-679-86153-X Subj: Holidays – Christmas. Religion – Nativity.

Ernie and Bert's new kitten ill. by Joe Mathieu; featuring Jim Henson's Sesame Street Muppets. Random House, 1990. ISBN 0-679-90420-4 Subj: Animals – cats. Pets. Puppets.

Get well, Granny Bird ill. by Joseph Mathieu. Random House, 1989. ISBN 0-394-92247-6 Subj: Birds. Family life – grandmothers. Illness.

Grover's bad dream ill. by Joe Mathieu. Random House, 1990. ISBN 0-679-90898-6 Subj: Birthdays. Emotions – envy, jealousy. Parties. Puppets.

It's not fair! ill. by Tom Leigh. Random House, 1986. ISBN 0-394-98151-0 Subj: Activities – working. Behavior – dissatisfaction. Puppets.

The little mermaid (Andersen, H. C. [Hans Christian])

Little Witch goes to school ill. by Sylvie Wickstrom. Random House, 1998. ISBN 0-679-98738-X Subj: School – first day. Witches.

Little Witch's bad dream ill. by Sylvie Wickstrom. Random House, 2000. ISBN 0-679-97342-7 Subj: Behavior. Family life – cousins. Witches.

The nutcracker (Hoffmann, E. T. A.)

Thumbelina (Andersen, H. C. [Hans Christian])

A visit to the Sesame Street hospital ill. by Joseph Mathieu. Random House, 1985. ISBN 0-394-87062-X Subj: Hospitals. Puppets.

A visit to the Sesame Street library: featuring Jim Henson's Sesame Street Muppets ill. by Joe Mathieu. Random House, 1986. ISBN 0-394-97744-0 Subj: Libraries. Puppets.

Why are you so mean to me? ill. by Tom Cooke. Random House, 1986. ISBN 0-394-98060-3 Subj: Emotions – anger.

Hautzig, Esther (Rudomin). *At home: a visit in four languages* ill. by Aliki. Macmillan, 1969. Subj: Family life. Foreign lands – France. Foreign lands – Russia. Foreign lands – Spain. Foreign languages.

In the park: an excursion in four languages ill. by Ezra Jack Keats. Macmillan, 1968. Subj: Foreign lands – France. Foreign lands – Russia. Foreign lands – Spain. Foreign languages. Parks.

Havard, Christian. *The fox, playful prowler* ill. with photos by Viäl Jacana. Charlesbridge, 1995. ISBN 0-88106-434-3 Subj: Animals – foxes.

Haviland, Virginia. *The talking pot* ill. by Melissa Sweet. Little, 1990. ISBN 0-316-35060-5 Subj: Folk and fairy tales. Foreign lands – Denmark.

Havill, Juanita. *Embarcadero upset* ill. by author. Lothrop, 1999. ISBN 0-688-13058-5 Subj: Sports – skateboarding.

I love you more ill. by Amy Aitken. Golden Books, 1990. ISBN 0-307-10177-0 Subj: Emotions – love.

Jamaica and Brianna ill. by Anne Sibley O'Brien. Houghton Mifflin, 1993. ISBN 0-395-64489-5 Subj: Clothing – boots. Emotions – envy, jealousy. Ethnic groups in the U.S. – African Americans. Ethnic groups in the U.S. – Asian Americans. Friendship.

Jamaica and the substitute teacher ill. by Anne Sibley O'Brien. Houghton Mifflin, 1999. ISBN 0-395-90503-6 Subj: Behavior – misbehavior. Careers – teachers. School.

Jamaica Tag-Along ill. by Anne Sibley O'Brien. Houghton Mifflin, 1989. ISBN 0-395-49602-0 Subj: Activities – playing. Ethnic groups in the U.S. – African Americans. Family life – brothers and sisters. Friendship.

Jamaica's blue marker ill. by Anne Sibley O'Brien. Houghton Mifflin, 1995. ISBN 0-395-72036-2 Subj: Emotions – sadness. Ethnic groups in the U.S. – African Americans. Moving.

Jamaica's find ill. by Anne Sibley O'Brien. Houghton Mifflin, 1986. ISBN 0-395-39376-0 Subj: Behavior – losing things. Character traits – honesty. Ethnic groups in the U.S. – African Americans.

Kentucky troll ill. by Bert Dodson. Lothrop, 1993. ISBN 0-688-10458-4 Subj: Folk and fairy tales. Mythical creatures – trolls.

Magic fort ill. by Linda Shute. Houghton Mifflin, 1991. ISBN 0-395-50067-2 Subj: Behavior – misbehavior. Family life – brothers. Trees.

Sato and the elephants ill. by Jean and Mou-Sien Tseng. Lothrop, 1993. ISBN 0-688-11156-4 Subj: Animals – elephants. Animals – endangered animals. Careers – artists.

Treasure nap ill. by Elivia Savadier. Houghton Mifflin, 1992. ISBN 0-395-57817-5 Subj: Ethnic groups in the U.S. – Mexican Americans. Family life. Weather.

Hawcock, David. *Ant* by David Hawcock and Lee Montgomery; design and paper engineering by David Hawcock; ill. by Lee Montgomery. Random House, 1994. ISBN 0-679-85469-X Subj: Format, unusual – toy and movable books. Insects – ants.

Bee by David Hawcock and Lee Montgomery; design and paper engineering by David Hawcock; ill. by Lee Montgomery. Random House, 1994. ISBN 0-679-85470-3 Subj: Format, unusual – toy and movable books. Insects – bees.

Beetle by David Hawcock and Lee Montgomery; design and paper engineering by David Hawcock; ill. by Lee Montgomery. Random House, 1996. ISBN 0-679-87566-2 Subj: Format, unusual – toy and movable books. Insects – beetles.

Brontosaurus ill. by author. Holt, 1993. ISBN 0-8050-2361-5 Subj: Dinosaurs. Format, unusual – toy and movable books.

Dinosaur hunt design and paper engineering by David Hawcock; ill. by Philip Hood. Putnam & Grosset, 1995. ISBN 0-399-22777-6 Subj: Careers – paleontologists. Dinosaurs. Format, unusual – toy and movable books.

Fly by David Hawcock and Lee Montgomery; design and paper engineering by David Hawcock; ill. by Lee Montgomery. Random House, 1996. ISBN 0-679-87567-0 Subj: Format, unusual – toy and movable books. Insects – flies.

Spider by David Hawcock and Lee Montgomery; design and paper engineering by David Hawcock; ill. by Lee Montgomery. Random House, 1994. ISBN 0-679-85471-1 Subj: Format, unusual – toy and movable books. Spiders.

Stegosaurus ill. by author. Holt, 1993. ISBN 0-8050-2362-3 Subj: Dinosaurs. Format, unusual – toy and movable books.

Triceratops ill. by author. Holt, 1993. ISBN 0-8050-2364-X Subj: Dinosaurs. Format, unusual – toy and movable books.

Tyrannosaurus ill. by author. Holt, 1993. ISBN 0-8050-2363-1 Subj: Dinosaurs. Format, unusual – toy and movable books.

Wasp by David Hawcock and Lee Montgomery; design and paper engineering by David Hawcock; ill. by Lee Montgomery. Random House, 1996. ISBN 0-679-87565-4 Subj: Format, unusual – toy and movable books. Insects – wasps.

Whose coat? ill. by author. Little Simon, 1993. ISBN 0-671-79163-X Subj: Anatomy – skin. Animals. Format, unusual – toy and movable books.

Whose home? ill. by author. Little Simon, 1993. ISBN 0-671-79164-8 Subj: Animals. Format, unusual – toy and movable books. Homes, houses.

Whose nose? ill. by author. Little Simon, 1993. ISBN 0-671-79162-1 Subj: Anatomy – noses. Animals. Format, unusual – toy and movable books.

Hawes, Judy. *Fireflies in the night* ill. by Ellen Alexander. Rev. ed. HarperCollins, 1991. ISBN 0-06-022484-3 Subj: Family life – grandparents. Farms. Insects – fireflies. Night. Science.

Ladybug, ladybug, fly away home ill. by Ed Emberley. Crowell, 1968. Subj: Insects – ladybugs. Science.

My daddy longlegs ill. by Walter Lorraine. Crowell, 1972. ISBN 0-690-56656-5 Subj: Spiders.

Shrimps ill. by Joseph Low. Crowell, 1967. Subj: Fish. Science.

Spring peepers ill. by Graham Booth. Crowell, 1975. ISBN 0-690-00522-9 Subj: Frogs and toads. Science.

Watch honeybees with me ill. by Helen Stone. Crowell, 1964. Subj: Insects – bees. Science.

Why frogs are wet ill. by Don Madden. Crowell, 1968. Subj: Frogs and toads. Science.

Hawkes, Kevin. *His Royal Buckliness* ill. by author. Lothrop, 1992. ISBN 0-688-11063-0 Subj: Giants. Rhyming text. Seasons.

Then the troll heard the squeak ill. by author. Lothrop, 1991. ISBN 0-688-09757-X Subj: Behavior – misbehavior. Mythical creatures – trolls. Rhyming text.

Hawkesworth, Jenny. *The lonely skyscraper* ill. by Emanuel Schongut. Doubleday, 1980. ISBN 0-385-15948-X Subj: City. Country.

Hawkins, Colin. *Boo! Who?* by Colin and Jacqui Hawkins; ill. by authors. Holt, 1984. ISBN 0-03-063929-8 Subj: Rhyming text.

Busy ABC by Colin and Jacqui Hawkins; ill. by authors. Viking, 1987. ISBN 0-670-81153-X Subj: ABC books. Activities.

Come for a ride on the ghost train by Colin and Jacqui Hawkins; ill. by Jacqui Hawkins. Candlewick, 1993. ISBN 1-56402-236-6 Subj: Format, unusual – toy and movable books. Ghosts. Monsters. Trains.

Dip, dip, dip ill. by author. Little, 1986. ISBN 0-87113-087-4 Subj: Activities – playing. Animals – bears. Bedtime. Toys – bears.

The elephant by Colin and Jacqui Hawkins; ill. by authors. Viking, 1986. ISBN 0-670-80314-6 Subj: Animals – elephants. Format, unusual – toy and movable books.

Hey diddle diddle by Colin and Jacqui Hawkins; ill. by authors. Candlewick, 1992. ISBN 1-56402-014-2 Subj: Format, unusual – board books. Nursery rhymes.

I'm not sleepy! by Colin and Jacqui Hawkins; ill. by authors. Crown, 1986. ISBN 0-517-55973-0 Subj: Animals – bears. Bedtime.

Incy wincy spider by Colin and Jacqui Hawkins; ill. by authors. Viking, 1986. ISBN 0-670-80317-0 Subj: Format, unusual – toy and movable books. Games. Spiders.

Jen the hen by Colin and Jacqui Hawkins; ill. by Colin Hawkins. Putnam, 1985. ISBN 0-399-21207-8 Subj: Birds – chickens. Birthdays. Format, unusual – toy and movable books. Rhyming text.

Max and the magic word by Colin and Jacqui Hawkins; ill. by authors. Viking, 1986. ISBN 0-670-80853-9 Subj: Animals. Etiquette.

Mig the pig by Colin and Jacqui Hawkins; ill. by Colin Hawkins. Putnam, 1984. ISBN 0-399-21061-X Subj: Animals – pigs. Format, unusual – toy and movable books. Rhyming text.

Old Mother Hubbard (Martin, Sarah Catherine)

One finger, one thumb ill. by author. Little, 1986. ISBN 0-87113-088-2 Subj: Activities – playing. Animals – bears. Bedtime. Toys – bears.

Oops-a-Daisy ill. by author. Little, 1986. ISBN 0-87113-086-6 Subj: Activities – playing. Animals – bears. Bedtime. Toys – bears.

Pat the cat by Colin and Jacqui Hawkins; ill. by Colin Hawkins. Putnam, 1983. ISBN 0-399-20957-3 Subj: Animals – cats.

Round the garden by Colin and Jacqui Hawkins; ill. by authors. Viking, 1986. ISBN 0-670-80315-4 Subj: Format, unusual – toy and movable books. Games. Gardens, gardening.

Snap! Snap! by Colin and Jacqui Hawkins; ill. by Colin Hawkins. Putnam, 1984. ISBN 0-399-21163-2 Subj: Emotions – fear. Monsters. Night. Rhyming text.

Take away monsters ill. by author. Putnam, 1984. ISBN 0-399-20962-X Subj: Counting, numbers. Format, unusual – toy and movable books. Monsters. Rhyming text.

There was an old lady who swallowed a fly (Little old lady who swallowed a fly)

This little pig by Colin and Jacqui Hawkins; ill. by authors. Viking, 1986. ISBN 0-670-80316-2 Subj: Anatomy – toes. Animals – pigs. Format, unusual – toy and movable books. Games.

Tog the dog by Colin and Jacqui Hawkins; ill. by authors. Putnam, 1986. ISBN 0-399-21338-4 Subj: Animals – dogs. Behavior – lost. Format, unusual – toy and movable books. Language. Rhyming text.

What time is it, Mr. Wolf? ill. by author. Putnam, 1983. ISBN 0-399-20959-X Subj: Animals – wolves. Format, unusual – toy and movable books. Time.

Where's bear? ill. by author. Little, 1986. ISBN 0-87113-090-4 Subj: Activities – playing. Animals – bears. Bedtime. Toys – bears.

Where's my mommy? by Colin and Jacqui Hawkins; ill. by authors. Crown, 1986. ISBN 0-517-55974-9 Subj: Animals. Behavior – needing someone. Family life – mothers.

Hawkins, Jacqui. *Boo! Who?* (Hawkins, Colin)

Busy ABC (Hawkins, Colin)

Come for a ride on the ghost train (Hawkins, Colin)

The elephant (Hawkins, Colin)

Hey diddle diddle (Hawkins, Colin)

I'm not sleepy! (Hawkins, Colin)

Incy wincy spider (Hawkins, Colin)

Jen the hen (Hawkins, Colin)

Max and the magic word (Hawkins, Colin)

Mig the pig (Hawkins, Colin)

Old Mother Hubbard (Martin, Sarah Catherine)

Pat the cat (Hawkins, Colin)

Round the garden (Hawkins, Colin)

Snap! Snap! (Hawkins, Colin)

This little pig (Hawkins, Colin)

Tog the dog (Hawkins, Colin)

Where's my mommy? (Hawkins, Colin)

Hawkins, Mark. *A lion under her bed* ill. by Jean Vallario. Holt, 1978. ISBN 0-03-040381-2 Subj: Animals – lions. Bedtime. Furniture – beds.

Hawkinson, John. *Birds in the sky* (Hawkinson, Lucy [Ozone])

The old stump ill. by author. Albert Whitman, 1965. Subj: Animals – mice. Trees.

Robins and rabbits by John and Lucy Hawkinson; ill. by John Hawkinson. Albert Whitman, 1960. Subj: Animals. Birds – robins.

Where the wild apples grow ill. by author. Albert Whitman, 1967. Subj: Animals – horses, ponies. Character traits – freedom.

Hawkinson, Lucy (Ozone). *Birds in the sky* by Lucy and John Hawkinson; ill. by authors. Childrens Pr., 1966. Subj: Birds. Science.

Dance, dance, Amy-Chan! ill. by author. Albert Whitman, 1964. Subj: Ethnic groups in the U.S. – Japanese Americans.

Robins and rabbits (Hawkinson, John)

Hawthorne, Nathaniel. *King Midas and the golden touch* (Hewitt, Kathryn)

Hawxhurst, Joan C. *Bubbe and Gram, my two grandmothers* ill. by Jane K. Bynum. Dovetail, 1996. ISBN 0-9661284-2-3 Subj: Family life – grandmothers. Holidays – Christmas. Holidays – Easter. Holidays – Hanukkah. Holidays – Passover. Jewish culture. Religion.

Hay, Dean. *I see a lot of things* ill. by author. Lion, 1966. Subj: Senses – seeing.

Now I can count ill. by author. Lion, 1968. Subj: Counting, numbers. Time.

Hay, Timothy. *see* Brown, Margaret Wise

Hayashi, Akiko. *Aki and the fox* ill. by author. Doubleday, 1991. ISBN 0-385-41948-1 Subj: Activities – traveling. Family life – grandmothers. Toys. Trains.

Hayden, Kate. *Baby animals* (Lilly, Kenneth)

Hayden, Lea. *Sunny day - rainy day* ill. by Joe Ewers. Random House, 1990. ISBN 0-679-80068-9 Subj: Format, unusual. Weather. Weather – rain.

Hayes, Ann. *Meet the Marching Smithereens* ill. by Karmen Thompson. Harcourt, 1995. ISBN 0-15-253158-0 Subj: Animals. Music. Parades.

Meet the orchestra ill. by Karmen Thompson. Harcourt, 1991. ISBN 0-15-200526-9 Subj: Animals. Music.

Hayes, Geoffrey. *Bear by himself* ill. by author. HarperCollins, 1976. ISBN 0-06-022263-8 Subj: Behavior – solitude. Toys – bears.

Christmas in Puttyville ill. by author. Random House, 1985. ISBN 0-394-97286-4 Subj: Animals – bears. Character traits – generosity. Holidays – Christmas.

Elroy and the witch's child ill. by author. HarperCollins, 1982. ISBN 0-06-022259-X Subj: Animals – cats. Witches.

The mystery of the pirate ghost ill. by author. Random House, 1985. ISBN 0-394-97220-1 Subj: Ghosts. Mystery stories. Pirates.

Patrick and his grandpa ill. by author. Random House, 1986. ISBN 0-394-87287-8 Subj: Animals – bears. Family life – grandfathers. Format, unusual – board books.

Patrick and Ted ill. by author. Four Winds, 1984. ISBN 0-590-07902-6 Subj: Animals – bears. Behavior – growing up.

The secret inside ill. by author. HarperCollins, 1980. ISBN 0-06-022274-3 Subj: Animals – bears. Dreams.

Hayes, Joe. *A spoon for every bite* ill. by Rebecca Leer. Orchard, 1996. ISBN 0-531-08799-9 Subj: Behavior – boasting. Ethnic groups in the U.S. – Hispanic Americans. Indians of North America.

Hayes, Sarah. *Away in a manger* ill. by Inga Moore. Little Simon, 1987. ISBN 0-671-64311-8 Subj: Holidays – Christmas. Religion – Nativity.

Bad egg: the true story of Humpty Dumpty ill. by Charlotte Voake. Little, 1987. ISBN 0-316-35184-9 Subj: Behavior – misbehavior. Nursery rhymes. Royalty.

A bad start for Santa ill. by Jamie Charteris. Joy Street, 1986. ISBN 0-316-35183-0 Subj: Behavior – losing things. Holidays – Christmas. Santa Claus.

The cats of Tiffany Street ill. by author. Candlewick, 1992. ISBN 1-56402-094-0 Subj: Animals – cats.

Clap your hands: finger rhymes ill. by Toni Goffe. Lothrop, 1988. ISBN 0-688-07693-9 Subj: Games. Nursery rhymes.

Eat up, Gemma ill. by Jan Ormerod. Lothrop, 1988. ISBN 0-688-08149-5 Subj: Babies. Ethnic groups in the U.S. – African Americans. Food.

The grumpalump ill. by Barbara Firth. Clarion, 1991. ISBN 0-89919-871-6 Subj: Activities – ballooning. Animals. Rhyming text.

Happy Christmas, Gemma ill. by Jan Ormerod. Lothrop, 1986. ISBN 0-688-06508-2 Subj: Ethnic groups in the U.S. – African Americans. Family life. Family life – grandmothers. Holidays – Christmas.

Mary Mary ill. by Helen Craig. Macmillan, 1990. ISBN 0-689-50514-0 Subj: Behavior – needing someone. Character traits – being different. Giants.

Nine ducks nine ill. by author. Lothrop, 1990. ISBN 0-688-09535-6 Subj: Animals – foxes. Birds – ducks. Character traits – cleverness. Rhyming text.

This is the bear ill. by Helen Craig. Lippincott, 1986. ISBN 0-397-32171-6 Subj: Behavior – lost. Behavior – secrets. Rhyming text. Toys – bears.

This is the bear and the bad little girl ill. by Helen Craig. Candlewick, 1995. ISBN 1-56402-648-5 Subj: Animals – dogs. Character traits – helpfulness. Toys.

This is the bear and the picnic lunch ill. by Helen Craig. Little, 1989. ISBN 0-316-35248-9 Subj: Activities – picnicking. Animals – dogs. Rhyming text. Toys – bears.

This is the bear and the scary night ill. by Helen Craig. Little, 1992. ISBN 0-316-35250-0 Subj: Character traits – bravery. Night. Rhyming text. Toys – bears.

Hayles, Karen. *What is stuck* by Karen Hayles and Charles Fuge; ill. by Charles Fuge. Simon & Schuster, 1993. ISBN 0-671-86587-0 Subj: Animals. Animals – whales. Foreign lands – Arctic. Sea and seashore.

Haynes, Max. *Dinosaur island* ill. by author. Lothrop, 1991. ISBN 0-688-10330-8 Subj: Dinosaurs. Islands.

Sparky's rainbow repair photos and ill. by author. Lothrop, 1992. ISBN 0-688-11194-7 Subj: Games. Weather – rainbows.

Ticklemonster and me ill. by author. Doubleday, 1999. ISBN 0-385-32582-7 Subj: Family life – mothers. Games. Monsters.

Haynes, Robert. *The elephant that ga-lumped* (Ward, Nanda Weedon)

Hays, Daniel. *Charley sang a song* (Hays, Hoffman Reynolds)

Hays, Hoffman Reynolds. *Charley sang a song* by Hoffman and Daniel Hays; ill. by Uri Shulevitz. HarperCollins, 1964. Subj: Activities – flying.

Hays, Wilma Pitchford. *Little Yellow Fur* ill. by Richard Cuffari. Coward, 1973. ISBN 0-698-30503-5 Subj: Indians of North America – Dakota (Sioux).

Hayward, Linda. *All stuck up* ill. by Normand Chartier. McKay, 1990. ISBN 0-379-90216-3 Subj: Animals – foxes. Animals – rabbits. Behavior – trickery. Folk and fairy tales.

Alphabet School ill. by Ann Schweninger. Random House, 1989. ISBN 0-394-92226-3 Subj: ABC books. Animals – cats. School.

Baby Moses ill. by Barb Henry. Random House, 1989. ISBN 0-394-99410-8 Subj: Babies. Foreign lands – Egypt. Religion – Moses.

Baker, baker, cookie maker ill. by Tom Brannon. Random House, 1998. ISBN 0-679-98379-1 Subj: Careers – bakers. Puppets. Rhyming text.

The biggest cookie in the world ill. by Joe Ewers. Random House, 1995. ISBN 0-679-97146-7 Subj: Careers – bakers. Puppets.

The case of the missing Duckie ill. by Maggie Swanson. Western, 1992. ISBN 0-307-23124-0 Subj: Behavior – losing things. Mystery stories. Puppets.

The city worm and the country worm ill. by Carol Nicklaus. Western, 1993. ISBN 0-307-23144-5 Subj: Animals – worms. City. Country.

D is for doll ill. by Denise Fleming. Random House, 1988. ISBN 0-394-89635-1 Subj: ABC books. Rebuses. Rhyming text.

A day in the life of Oscar the Grouch: featuring Jim Henson's Sesame Street Muppets ill. by Bill Davis. Western, 1981. ISBN 0-307-23138-0 Subj: Behavior. Puppets.

Did I ever tell you how high you can count? adapt. by Linda Hayward and Cathy Goldsmith from the works of Dr. Seuss. Random House, 1996. ISBN 0-679-87081-4 Subj: Counting, numbers.

Elmo goes to day camp ill. by Carol Nicklaus. Random House, 1990. ISBN 0-679-80158-8 Subj: Camps, camping. Puppets.

Ernie and Bert's summer project ill. by Carol Nicklaus. Random House, 1991. ISBN 0-679-81051-X Subj: Behavior – collecting things. Museums. Puppets. Seasons – summer.

Goldilocks and the three bears (The three bears)

Grover's summer vacation ill. by Ronald Fritz. Random House, 1989. ISBN 0-394-83969-2 Subj: Activities – vacationing. Puppets.

Hello, house! ill. by Lynn Munsinger. Random House, 1988. Adapt. of: Heyo house by Joel Chandler Harris. ISBN 0-394-98864-7 Subj: Animals – rabbits. Animals – wolves. Behavior – trickery. Ethnic groups in the U.S. – African Americans. Folk and fairy tales. Homes, houses.

I can add upside down! by Linda Hayward and Cathy Goldsmith from the works of Dr. Seuss. Random House, 1995. ISBN 0-679-86754-6 Subj: Counting, numbers.

I can count to ten and back again ill. by Maggie Swanson. Western, 1992. ISBN 0-307-23116-X Subj: Counting, numbers. Puppets.

Noah's ark ill. by Amy Flynn. Random House, 1993. ISBN 0-679-83600-4 Subj: Boats, ships. Religion – Noah. Weather – floods. Weather – rain.

Oh, the things you can count from 1-10 adapt. by Linda Hayward and Cathy Goldsmith from the works of Dr. Seuss. Random House, 1995. ISBN 0-679-86753-8 Subj: Counting, numbers.

The runaway Christmas toy ill. by Loretta Krupinski. Random House, 1994. ISBN 0-679-86173-4 Subj: Behavior – running away. Holidays – Christmas. Santa Claus. Toys. Trains.

Sunny Day Bunny ill. by Lucinda McQueen. Grosset, 1986. ISBN 0-448-10452-0 Subj: Animals – rabbits. Family life – grandmothers. Format, unusual – board books. Weather.

The three little pigs (The three little pigs)

Wet foot, dry foot, low foot, high foot by Linda Hayward and Cathy Goldsmith from the works of Dr. Seuss. Random House, 1996. ISBN 0-679-87086-5 Subj: Concepts. Language.

Hayward, Max. *The telephone* (Chukovskii, Kornei Ivanovich)

Haywood, Carolyn. *A Christmas fantasy* ill. by Glenys and Victor G. Ambrus. Morrow, 1972. ISBN 0-688-30094-4 Subj: Holidays – Christmas. Santa Claus.

Hello, star ill. by Julie Durrell. Morrow, 1987. ISBN 0-688-06651-8 Subj: Animals. Family life – grandparents. Farms. Seasons – summer.

How the reindeer saved Santa ill. by Victor G. Ambrus. Morrow, 1986. ISBN 0-688-05904-X Subj: Animals – reindeer. Character traits – loyalty. Holidays – Christmas. Santa Claus.

The king's monster ill. by Victor G. Ambrus. Morrow, 1980. ISBN 0-688-32214-X Subj: Monsters. Royalty – kings.

Santa Claus forever! ill. by Glenys and Victor G. Ambrus. Morrow, 1983. ISBN 0-688-02345-2 Subj: Behavior – bad day. Holidays – Christmas. Santa Claus.

Hazelaar, Cor. *Dogs everywhere* ill. by author. Knopf, 1995. ISBN 0-679-95439-2 Subj: Animals – dogs. City. Pets.

Zoo dreams ill. by author. Farrar, 1997. ISBN 0-374-39730-9 Subj: Animals. Bedtime. Dreams. Sleep. Zoos.

Hazelton, Elizabeth Baldwin. *Sammy, the crow who remembered* ill. by Ann Atwood. Scribners, 1969. Subj: Birds – crows. Family life. Memories, memory.

Hazen, Barbara Shook. *Digby* ill. by Barbara J. Phillips-Duke. HarperCollins, 1997. ISBN 0-06-026254-0 Subj: Animals – dogs. Old age.

Even if I did something awful ill. by Nancy Kincade. Atheneum, 1981. ISBN 0-689-30843-4 Subj: Emotions – love. Family life.

Fang ill. by Leslie Holt Morrill. Atheneum, 1987. ISBN 0-689-31307-1 Subj: Animals – dogs. Character traits – bravery. Emotions – fear.

The Fat Cats, Cousin Scraggs and the monster mice ill. by Lonni Sue Johnson. Atheneum, 1985. ISBN 0-689-31092-7 Subj: Animals – cats. Animals – mice. Behavior – dissatisfaction. Character traits – cleverness.

Good-bye/Hello ill. by Michael Bryant. Atheneum, 1995. ISBN 0-689-31665-8 Subj: Emotions. Moving. Rhyming text.

The gorilla did it! ill. by Ray Cruz. Atheneum, 1974. ISBN 0-689-30138-3 Subj: Animals – gorillas. Imagination – imaginary friends.

Gorilla wants to be the baby ill. by Jacqueline Bardner Smith. Atheneum, 1978. ISBN 0-689-30654-7 Subj: Animals – gorillas. Imagination – imaginary friends.

Happy, sad, silly, mad: a beginning book about emotions ill. by Elizabeth Dauber; ed. consultant: Mary Elting. Grosset, 1971. ISBN 0-448-03622-3 Subj: Emotions.

If it weren't for Benjamin (I'd always get to lick the icing spoon) ill. by Laura Hartman. Human Sciences Pr., 1979. ISBN 0-87705-384-7 Subj: Sibling rivalry.

The knight who was afraid of the dark ill. by Tony Ross. Dial, 1988. ISBN 0-8037-0668-5 Subj: Emotions – fear. Knights. Middle Ages. Night.

The knight who was afraid to fight ill. by Toni Goffe. Dial, 1994. ISBN 0-8037-1592-7 Subj: Emotions – fear. Knights. Middle Ages.

The me I see ill. by Ati Forberg. Abingdon, 1978. ISBN 0-687-23910-9 Subj: Activities – bathing. Anatomy.

Mommy's office ill. by David Soman. Atheneum, 1992. ISBN 0-689-31601-1 Subj: Activities – working. Careers. Family life – mothers.

The new dog ill. by R. W. Alley. Dial, 1996. ISBN 0-8037-1813-6 Subj: Animals – dogs. Behavior. Character traits – bravery.

Santa clues ill. by Simon Galkin. Longmeadow, 1995. ISBN 0-681-00682-X Subj: Character traits – questioning. Holidays – Christmas. Rhyming text. Santa Claus.

The sorcerer's apprentice ill. by Tomi Ungerer. Lancelot Pr., 1969. Subj: Folk and fairy tales. Magic.

Stay, Fang ill. by Leslie Holt Morrill. Atheneum, 1990. ISBN 0-689-31599-6 Subj: Animals – dogs. Pets.

The story of Santa Claus ill. by Carolyn Bracken. Western, 1989. ISBN 0-307-62097-2 Subj: Santa Claus.

Tight times ill. by Trina Schart Hyman. Viking, 1979. ISBN 0-670-71287-6 Subj: Animals – cats. Family life. Family life – only child. Poverty.

Turkey in the straw ill. by Brad Sneed. Dial, 1993. ISBN 0-8037-1299-5 Subj: Activities – dancing. Careers – farmers. Farms.

Two homes to live in ill. by Peggy Luks. Human Sciences Pr., 1978. ISBN 0-8770-5313-8 Subj: Divorce. Emotions.

Wally the worry-warthog ill. by Janet Stevens. Houghton Mifflin, 1990. ISBN 0-89919-896-1 Subj: Animals – warthogs. Behavior – worrying. Emotions – fear.

Where do bears sleep? ill. by Mary Morgan Van Royen. HarperCollins, 1998. ISBN 0-694-01037-5 Subj: Animals. Rhyming text. Sleep.

Where do bears sleep? ill. by Ian E. Staunton. Addison-Wesley, 1970. Subj: Animals. Rhyming text. Sleep.

Why couldn't I be an only kid like you, Wigger? ill. by Leigh Grant. Atheneum, 1975. ISBN 0-689-30488-9 Subj: Babies. Emotions – envy, jealousy. Family life – only child. Sibling rivalry.

Why did Grandpa die? a book about death ill. by Pat Schories. Childrens Pr., 1985. ISBN 0-307-62484-6 Subj: Death. Emotions – grief. Family life – grandfathers. Old age.

World, world, what can I do? ill. by Margaret Leibold. Morehouse, 1991. ISBN 0-8192-1537-6 Subj: Ecology. Rhyming text.

Heap, Sue. *Cowboy Baby* ill. by author. Candlewick, 1998. ISBN 0-7636-0437-2 Subj: Babies. Bedtime. Cowboys. Family life – fathers. Toys.

Hearn, Diane Dawson. *Anna in the garden* ill. by author. Silver Moon Pr., 1994. ISBN 1-881889-57-2 Subj: Flowers. Gardens, gardening.

Bad luck Boswell ill. by author. Simon & Schuster, 1995. ISBN 0-689-80303-6 Subj: Animals – cats. Character traits – luck. Witches.

Dad's dinosaur day ill. by author. Macmillan, 1993. ISBN 0-02-743485-0 Subj: Dinosaurs. Family life – fathers.

Hearn, Lafcadio. *The funny little woman* (Mosel, Arlene)

Hearn, Michael Patrick. *The porcelain cat* ill. by Leo and Diane Dillon. Little, 1985. ISBN 0-316-35330-2 Subj: Animals – cats. Animals – rats. Cumulative tales. Folk and fairy tales. Magic.

Hearne, Betsy Gould. *Seven brave women* ill. by Bethanne Andersen. Greenwillow, 1997. ISBN 0-688-14503-5 Subj: Character traits – bravery. Family life. Immigrants. U.S. history. War.

Heath, Amy. *Sofie's role* ill. by Sheila Hamanaka. Four Winds, 1992. ISBN 0-02-743505-9 Subj: Activities – cooking. Careers – bakers. Ethnic groups in the U.S. – African Americans. Family life. Holidays – Christmas.

Heatwole, Marsha. *Jambo, watoto!* ill. by author; text by Elizabeth Massie and Barbara Spilman Lawson. Creative Art Pr., 1998. ISBN 0-9642712-3-0 Subj: Animals. Animals – cheetahs. Family life – mothers. Foreign lands – Africa.

Heck, Elisabeth. *The black sheep* trans. by Karen M. Klockner; ill. by Sita Jucker. Little, 1986. ISBN 0-316-35402-3 Subj: Animals – sheep. Behavior – running away. Holidays – Christmas. Religion.

Heckman, Philip. *The moon is following me* ill. by Mary O'Keefe Young. Atheneum, 1991. ISBN 0-689-31565-1 Subj: Activities – traveling. Moon.

Waking upside down ill. by Dwight Been. Atheneum, 1996. ISBN 0-689-31930-4 Subj: Dreams. Family life. Imagination. Sibling rivalry.

Hedderwick, Mairi. *Katie Morag and the big boy cousins* ill. by author. Little, 1987. ISBN 0-316-35403-1 Subj: Behavior – misbehavior. Family life. Family life – grandmothers. Foreign lands – Scotland. Islands.

Katie Morag and the tiresome Ted ill. by author. Little, 1986. ISBN 0-316-35401-5 Subj: Babies. Behavior – misbehavior. Emotions – envy, jealousy. Family life – new sibling. Foreign lands – Scotland. Islands. Sibling rivalry.

Katie Morag and the two grandmothers ill. by author. Little, 1986. ISBN 0-316-35400-7 Subj: Activities – bathing. Animals – sheep. Fairs. Family life – grandmothers. Foreign lands – Scotland. Islands.

Katie Morag delivers the mail ill. by author. Little, 1987, 1984. ISBN 0-316-35405-8 Subj: Behavior – misbehavior. Careers – postal workers. Family life – grandmothers. Foreign lands – Scotland. Islands. Post office.

P. D. Pebbles' summer or winter book ill. by author. Little, 1989. ISBN 0-316-35406-6 Subj: Family life. Format, unusual. Seasons – summer. Seasons – winter.

Hefter, Richard. *The strawberry book of shapes* ill. by author. Larousse, 1976. ISBN 0-8847-0021-6 Subj: Concepts – shape.

Heide, Florence Parry. *The bigness contest* ill. by Victoria Chess. Joy Street, 1994. ISBN 0-316-35444-9 Subj: Animals – hippopotamuses. Concepts. Self-concept.

The day of Ahmed's secret by Florence Parry Heide and Judith Heide Gilliland; ill. by Ted Lewin. Lothrop, 1990. ISBN 0-688-08895-3 Subj: Activities – working. Activities – writing. Behavior – secrets. Foreign lands – Egypt.

Grim and ghastly goings-on ill. by Victoria Chess. Lothrop, 1992. ISBN 0-688-08322-6 Subj: Monsters. Poetry.

A monster is coming! A monster is coming! by Florence Parry Heide and Roxanne Heide; ill. by Rachi Farrow. Watts, 1980. ISBN 0-531-03449-6 Subj: Monsters.

Oh, grow up! poems to help you survive parents, chores, school, and other afflictions by Florence Parry Heide and Roxanne Heide Pierce; ill. by Nadine Bernard Westcott. Orchard, 1996. ISBN 0-531-08771-9 Subj: Behavior – dissatisfaction. Behavior – growing up. Poetry. Sibling rivalry.

Sami and the time of the troubles by Florence Parry Heide and Judith Heide Gilliland; ill. by Ted Lewin. Clarion, 1992. ISBN 0-395-55964-2 Subj: Family life. Foreign lands – Lebanon. War.

Timothy Twinge by Florence Parry Heide and Roxanne Heide Pierce; ill. by Barbara Lehman. Lothrop, 1993. ISBN 0-688-10763-X Subj: Behavior – worrying. Character traits – bravery. Emotions – fear. Rhyming text.

Heide, Roxanne. *A monster is coming! A monster is coming!* (Heide, Florence Parry)

Heilbroner, Joan. *Robert the rose horse* ill. by Philip Eastman. Random House, 1962. ISBN 0-394-90025-1 Subj: Animals – horses, ponies. Flowers. Humor.

This is the house where Jack lives ill. by Aliki. HarperCollins, 1962. ISBN 0-06-022286-7 Subj: Cumulative tales. Participation.

Tom the TV cat ill. by Sal Murdocca. Random House, 1984. ISBN 0-394-96708-9 Subj: Animals – cats. Behavior – seeking better things. Television.

Heiligman, Deborah. *From caterpillar to butterfly* ill. by Bari Weissman. HarperCollins, 1996. ISBN 0-06-024268-X Subj: Insects – butterflies, caterpillars. Metamorphosis. Science.

Into the night ill. by Melissa Sweet. HarperCollins, 1990. ISBN 0-06-026382-2 Subj: Bedtime. Family life – mothers. Rhyming text.

Mike Swan, sink or swim ill. by Chris Demarest. First Choice Chapter Book, 1998. ISBN 0-385-32522-3 Subj: Emotions. Family life. Food. Sports – swimming.

On the move ill. by Lizzy Rockwell. HarperCollins, 1996. ISBN 0-06-024742-8 Subj: Activities. Animals.

Pockets ill. by Suzanne Duranceau. Hyperion, 1995. ISBN 0-7868-2141-8 Subj: Clothing. Family life. Family life – grandfathers.

Heine, Helme. *The boxer and the princess* ill. by author. Margaret K. McElderry, 1998. ISBN 0-689-82195-6 Subj: Animals – rhinoceros. Emotions – love. Royalty – princesses.

Friends ill. by author. Atheneum, 1982. ISBN 0-689-50256-7 Subj: Animals. Friendship. Sports – bicycling.

Friends go adventuring ill. by author. Margaret K. McElderry, 1995. ISBN 0-689-80463-6 Subj: Animals. Friendship.

King Bounce the 1st ill. by author. Alphabet Pr., 1982. ISBN 0-907234-11-9 Subj: Royalty – kings. Sleep.

The marvelous journey through the night trans. by Ralph Manheim; ill. by author. Farrar, 1990. ISBN 0-374-38478-9 Subj: Dreams. Night. Sleep.

Merry-go-round ill. by author. Barron's, 1980. ISBN 0-8120-5393-1 Subj: Activities – working.

Mr. Miller, the dog ill. by author. Atheneum, 1980. ISBN 0-689-50174-9 Subj: Animals – dogs. Behavior – imitation.

Mollywoop trans. by Ralph Manheim; ill. by author. Farrar, 1991. ISBN 0-374-35001-9 Subj: Animals. Birds – chickens. Friendship. Rhyming text.

The most wonderful egg in the world ill. by author. Atheneum, 1983. ISBN 0-689-50280-X Subj: Birds – chickens. Character traits – appearance. Royalty.

One day in paradise ill. by adapt. Atheneum, 1986. ISBN 0-689-50394-6 Subj: Religion.

The pigs' wedding ill. by author. Atheneum, 1979. ISBN 0-689-50127-7 Subj: Animals – pigs. Weddings.

Prince Bear ill. by author. Macmillan, 1989. ISBN 0-689-50484-5 Subj: Animals – bears. Progress. Royalty – princes. Royalty – princesses.

Superhare ill. by author. Barron's, 1979. ISBN 0-8120-5357-5 Subj: Animals – rabbits. Character traits – being different.

Three little friends: the alarm clock ill. by author. Atheneum, 1985. ISBN 0-689-71043-7 Subj: Animals. Birds – chickens. Friendship. Night.

Three little friends: the racing cart ill. by author. Atheneum, 1985. ISBN 0-689-71045-3 Subj: Animals. Birds – chickens. Friendship. Sports – racing.

Three little friends: the visitor ill. by author. Atheneum, 1985. ISBN 0-689-71044-5 Subj: Animals. Birds – chickens. Friendship.

Heins, Ethel L. *The cat and the cook and other fables of Krylov* ill. by Anita Lobel. Greenwillow, 1995. ISBN 0-688-12311-2 Subj: Folk and fairy tales. Foreign lands – Russia.

Heins, Paul. *Snow White* (Grimm, Jacob)

Heinst, Marie. *My first number book* photos by author. DK, 1992. ISBN 1-879431-74-2 Subj: Concepts – shape. Counting, numbers. Ethnic groups in the U.S. Games.

Heinz, Brian J. *The monsters' test* scary pictures by Sal Murdocca. Millbrook, 1996. ISBN 0-7613-0095-3 Subj: Holidays – Halloween. Monsters. Rhyming text. Witches.

Nanuk, lord of the ice ill. by Gregory Manchess. Dial, 1998. ISBN 0-8037-2195-1 Subj: Animals – polar bears. Eskimos. Foreign lands – Arctic. Indians of North America – Inuit. Sports – hunting.

The wolves ill. by Bernie Fuchs. Dial, 1996. ISBN 0-8037-1736-9 Subj: Animals – endangered animals. Animals – wolves. Nature.

Heitler, Susan M. (Susan McCrensky). *David decides, no more thumb-sucking* photos by Paula Singer. Avon, 1993. Previously published: David decides about thumbsucking. 1st U.S. ed. Denver, CO: Reading Matters, 1985. ISBN 0-380-76852-6 Subj: Behavior – growing up. Problem solving. Thumb sucking.

Hejl, Pauline. *The fine round cake* (Esterl, Arnica)

The Helen Oxenbury nursery rhyme book chosen by Brian W. Alderson; ill. by Helen Oxenbury. Morrow, 1987. ISBN 0-688-06899-5 Subj: Nursery rhymes.

Helena, Ann. *The lie* ill. by Ellen Pizer. Raintree, 1977. ISBN 0-8172-0958-1 Subj: Behavior – lying. Emotions. Friendship.

Hellard, Susan. *Baby lemur* ill. by author. Holt, 1999. ISBN 0-8050-6142-8 Subj: Animals – babies. Animals – lemurs. Behavior – growing up. Family life – mothers.

Billy goats Gruff (Asbjørnsen, P. C. [Peter Christen])

Eleanor and the babysitter ill. by author. Little, 1991. ISBN 0-316-35459-7 Subj: Activities – babysitting. Animals – anteaters. Animals – koalas. Monsters.

Froggie goes a-courting ill. by adapt. Putnam, 1988. ISBN 0-399-21508-5 Subj: Frogs and toads.

This little piggy ill. by author. Putnam, 1989. ISBN 0-399-21625-1 Subj: Animals – pigs. Format, unusual. Nursery rhymes.

Time to get up ill. by author. Putnam, 1990. ISBN 0-399-21948-X Subj: Animals. Format, unusual – toy and movable books. Morning. Rhyming text.

Helldorfer, M. C. (Mary Claire). *Cabbage Rose* ill. by Julie Downing. Bradbury, 1993. ISBN 0-02-743513-X Subj: Activities – painting. Folk and fairy tales. Royalty.

Carnival ill. by Dan Yaccarino. Viking, 1996. ISBN 0-670-86687-3 Subj: Activities. Fairs.

Clap clap! ill. by Sandra Speidel. Viking, 1993. ISBN 0-670-85155-8 Subj: Creation. Religion.

Daniel's gift ill. by Julie Downing. Bradbury, 1987. ISBN 0-02-743511-3 Subj: Animals – sheep. Gifts. Holidays – Christmas. Religion – Nativity.

The darling boys ill. by Megan Halsey. Bradbury, 1992. ISBN 0-02-743516-4 Subj: Behavior – stealing. Careers – bakers. Character traits – cleverness. Family life – brothers and sisters.

Gather up, gather in ill. by Judy Pedersen. Viking, 1994. ISBN 0-670-84752-6 Subj: Seasons.

Harmonica night ill. by Alexi Natchev. Atheneum, 1997. ISBN 0-689-80532-2 Subj: Family life. Family life – grandmothers. Night. Sea and seashore.

Jack, Skinny Bones, and the golden pancakes ill. by Elise Primavera. Viking, 1996. ISBN 0-670-86006-9 Subj: Behavior – trickery. Character traits – cleverness. Devil. Tall tales.

The mapmaker's daughter ill. by Jonathan Hunt. Bradbury, 1991. ISBN 0-02-743515-6 Subj: Character traits – bravery. Magic. Maps. Royalty – princes. Witches.

Night of the white stag ill. by Yvonne Gilbert. Random House, 1999. ISBN 0-385-32261-5 Subj: Animals – deer. Folk and fairy tales. Forest, woods. Holidays – Christmas. Night.

Sailing to the sea ill. by Loretta Krupinski. Viking, 1991. ISBN 0-670-83520-X Subj: Boats, ships. Family life – aunts, uncles. Sailors.

Silver Rain Brown ill. by Teresa Flavin. Houghton Mifflin, 1999. ISBN 0-395-73093-7 Subj: Birth. City. Communities, neighborhoods. Ethnic groups in the U.S. – African Americans. Family life. Seasons – summer. Weather – rain.

Hellen, Nancy. *Animals of the jungle* ill. by author. Peter Bedrick, 1991. ISBN 0-87226-458-0 Subj: Animals. Jungle.

Bus stop ill. by author. Watts, 1988. ISBN 0-531-05765-8 Subj: Buses. Character traits – patience. Format, unusual. Transportation.

Circle farm ill. by author. Bantam, 1994. ISBN 0-553-09635-4 Subj: Animals. Farms. Format, unusual – toy and movable books.

Circle zoo ill. by author. Bantam, 1994. ISBN 0-553-09634-6 Subj: Format, unusual – toy and movable books. Zoos.

Creatures of the ocean ill. by author. Peter Bedrick, 1991. ISBN 0-87226-457-2 Subj: Sea and seashore.

A visit to the farm ill. by author. Peter Bedrick, 1990. ISBN 0-87226-432-7 Subj: Animals. Farms. Format, unusual – toy and movable books.

A visit to the zoo ill. by author. Peter Bedrick, 1990. ISBN 0-87226-431-9 Subj: Animals. Format, unusual – toy and movable books. Zoos.

Heller, George. *Hiroshi's wonderful kite* ill. by Kyuzo Tsugami. Silver Burdett, 1968. Subj: Crime. Foreign lands – Japan. Kites.

Heller, Julek. *Jack and the beanstalk* (Jack and the beanstalk)

Heller, Linda. *Alexis and the golden ring* ill. by author. Macmillan, 1980. ISBN 0-02-743540-7 Subj: Folk and fairy tales. Foreign lands – Russia. Magic.

The castle on Hester Street ill. by author. Jewish Publication Society, 1982. ISBN 0-8276-0206-5 Subj: Family life – grandparents.

Lily at the table ill. by author. Macmillan, 1979. ISBN 0-02-743530-X Subj: Family life. Food. Furniture – tables. Wordless.

Heller, Nicholas. *An adventure at sea* ill. by author. Greenwillow, 1988. ISBN 0-688-07847-8 Subj: Imagination. Sea and seashore. Sibling rivalry.

A book for Woody ill. by author. Greenwillow, 1995. ISBN 0-688-13378-9 Subj: Activities – reading. Animals – pigs.

The front hall carpet ill. by author. Greenwillow, 1990. ISBN 0-688-05273-8 Subj: Imagination.

The giant ill. by Jos. A. Smith. Greenwillow, 1997. ISBN 0-688-15225-2 Subj: Careers – artists. Family life – grandfathers. Giants.

Goblins in green ill. by Jos. A. Smith. Greenwillow, 1995. ISBN 0-688-12803-3 Subj: ABC books. Mythical creatures – goblins.

Happy birthday, Moe dog ill. by author. Greenwillow, 1988. ISBN 0-688-07671-8 Subj: Animals – dogs. Birthdays.

Mathilda the dream bear ill. by author. Greenwillow, 1989. ISBN 0-688-08239-4 Subj: Animals. Animals – bears. Dreams.

The monster in the cave ill. by author. Greenwillow, 1987. ISBN 0-688-07314-X Subj: Family life. Holidays – Christmas. Monsters. Parties.

Ogres! ogres! ogres! a feasting frenzy from A to Z ill. by Jos. A. Smith. Greenwillow, 1999. ISBN 0-688-16987-2 Subj: Food. Monsters. Mythical creatures – ogres.

Peas ill. by author. Greenwillow, 1993. ISBN 0-688-12407-0 Subj: Dreams. Food. Toys – trains.

Ten old pails ill. by Yossi Abolafia. Greenwillow, 1994. ISBN 0-688-12420-8 Subj: Behavior – collecting things. Concepts.

This little piggy ill. by Sonja Lamut. Greenwillow, 1997. ISBN 0-688-15175-2 Subj: Bedtime. Family life – grandmothers. Nursery rhymes.

The tooth tree ill. by author. Greenwillow, 1991. ISBN 0-688-09393-0 Subj: Fairies. Teeth. Trees.

A troll story ill. by author. Greenwillow, 1990. ISBN 0-688-08971-2 Subj: Imagination. Mythical creatures – trolls.

Up the wall ill. by author. Greenwillow, 1992. ISBN 0-688-10634-X Subj: Behavior – running away. Family life. Imagination.

Woody ill. by author. Greenwillow, 1994. ISBN 0-688-12805-X Subj: Animals – pigs. Behavior – wishing.

Heller, Ruth. *Animals born alive and well* ill. by author. Grosset, 1982. ISBN 0-448-01822-5 Subj: Animals.

A cache of jewels and other collective nouns ill. by author. Grosset, 1989. ISBN 0-448-19211-X Subj: Language. Rhyming text.

Chickens aren't the only ones ill. by author. Grosset, 1981. ISBN 0-448-01872-1 Subj: Eggs. Science.

Color, color, color, color ill. by author. Putnam & Grosset, 1995. ISBN 0-399-22815-2 Subj: Concepts – color. Rhyming text.

Fantastic! wow! and unreal! a book about interjections and conjunctions ill. by author. Grosset, 1998. ISBN 0-448-41862-2 Subj: Language. Rhyming text.

How to hide a butterfly: and other insects ill. by author. Grosset, 1985. ISBN 0-488-10478-4 Subj: Behavior – hiding. Insects. Insects – butterflies, caterpillars. Rhyming text.

How to hide a crocodile and other reptiles ill. by author. Grosset, 1986. ISBN 0-448-19028-1 Subj: Disguises. Reptiles. Reptiles – alligators, crocodiles. Rhyming text.

How to hide a gray treefrog and other amphibians ill. by author. Grosset, 1986. ISBN 0-448-19026-5 Subj: Animals. Disguises. Frogs and toads. Rhyming text.

How to hide a parakeet and other birds ill. by author. Grosset, 1995. ISBN 0-448-40964-X Subj: Birds. Birds – parakeets, parrots. Disguises. Rhyming text.

How to hide a polar bear: and other mammals ill. by author. Grosset, 1985. ISBN 0-488-10477-6 Subj: Animals. Animals – polar bears. Behavior – hiding. Rhyming text.

How to hide a whip-poor-will and other birds ill. by author. Grosset, 1986. ISBN 0-448-19027-3 Subj: Birds. Disguises. Rhyming text.

How to hide an octopus: and other sea creatures ill. by author. Grosset, 1985. ISBN 0-488-10476-8 Subj: Animals. Crustaceans. Octopuses. Rhyming text.

Kites sail high: a book about verbs ill. by author. Grosset, 1988. ISBN 0-448-10480-6 Subj: Language. Rhyming text.

Many luscious lollipops: a book about adjectives ill. by author. Sandcastle Books, 1992. ISBN 0-448-03151-5 Subj: Language. Rhyming text.

Merry-go-round ill. by author. Sandcastle Books, 1992. ISBN 0-448-40085-5 Subj: Language. Rhyming text.

Mine, all mine: a book about pronouns ill. by author. Grosset, 1997. ISBN 0-448-41606-9 Subj: Language. Rhyming text.

Plants that never ever bloom ill. by author. Grosset, 1984. ISBN 0-448-18964-X Subj: Plants.

The reason for a flower ill. by author. Grosset, 1983. ISBN 0-448-14495-6 Subj: Flowers. Rhyming text.

Heller, Wendy. *Clementine and the cage* ill. by Rex J. Irvine. Kalimát, 1980. ISBN 0-922770-12-X Subj: Behavior – running away. Birds – canaries.

Hellings, Colette. *Too little, too big* ill. by Dominique Maes. Chronicle, 1993. ISBN 0-8118-0530-1 Subj: Animals – mice. Concepts – size. Self-concept.

Hello, baby photos sel. by Debby Slier. Macmillan, 1988. ISBN 0-02-688750-9 Subj: Babies. Format, unusual – board books.

Hellsing, Lennart. *The wonderful pumpkin* ill. by Svend Otto S. Atheneum, 1976, 1975. Translation of Der underbara pumpan. ISBN 0-689-50056-4 Subj: Animals – bears. Food. Holidays – Halloween.

Hellums, Julia Pemberton. *Hold the anchovies!* (Rotner, Shelley)

Helman, Andrea. *Northwest animal babies* (Wolfe, Art)

1, 2, 3 moose (Wolfe, Art)

Helmer, Marilyn. *Mr. McGratt and the ornery cat* ill. by Martine Gourbault. Kids Can Pr., 1999. ISBN 1-55074-564-6 Subj: Animals – cats. Behavior – misbehavior.

Helmering, Doris Wild. *I have two families* ill. by Heidi Palmer. Abingdon, 1981. ISBN 0-687-18507-6 Subj: Family life – step families.

We're going to have a baby by Doris and John William Helmering; ill. by Robert H. Cassell. Abingdon, 1978. ISBN 0-687-44446-2 Subj: Babies. Family life – new sibling. Sibling rivalry.

Helmering, John William. *We're going to have a baby* (Helmering, Doris Wild)

Helweg, Hans. *Farm animals* ill. by author. Random House, 1978. ISBN 0-394-93733-3 Subj: Animals. Birds. Farms.

Hendershot, Judith. *In coal country* ill. by Thomas B. Allen. Knopf, 1987. ISBN 0-394-98190-1 Subj: Family life. Family life – fathers.

Up the tracks to Grandma's ill. by Thomas B. Allen. Knopf, 1993. ISBN 0-679-91964-3 Subj: Country. Family life – grandmothers.

Henderson, Douglas. *Dinosaur tree* ill. by author. Bradbury, 1994. ISBN 0-02-743547-4 Subj: Dinosaurs. Plants. Time. Trees.

Henderson, Kathy. *The baby dances* ill. by Tony Kerins. Candlewick, 1999. ISBN 0-7636-0374-0 Subj: Babies. Behavior – growing up.

The baby's book of babies photos by Anthea Sieveking. Dial, 1989. ISBN 0-8037-0634-0 Subj: Babies.

Bounce, bounce, bounce ill. by Carol Thompson. Candlewick, 1994. ISBN 1-56402-311-7 Subj: Activities – playing. Rhyming text.

Bumpety bump ill. by Carol Thompson. Candlewick, 1994. ISBN 1-56402-312-5 Subj: Babies. Family life. Rhyming text.

Counting farm ill. by author. Shaw's Candlewick Pr., 1996. Cover title: Shaw's counting farm. ISBN 1-56402-758-9 Subj: Animals. Counting, numbers. Farms.

Disney's Bambi: the winter trail penciled by David Pacheco; painted by Valeria Turati. Mouse Works, 1996. ISBN 1-57082-427-4 Subj: Animals – deer. Seasons – winter. Weather – snow.

Disney's Pooh's grand adventure: the search for Christopher Robin adapt. by Kathy Henderson and Victoria Saxon; penciled by Sparky Moore. Mouse Works, 1997. ISBN 1-57082-671-4 Subj: Behavior – lost. Toys – bears.

Don't interrupt! ill. by Susan Hellard. Barron's, 1988. ISBN 0-8120-5785-6 Subj: Family life. Format, unusual – toy and movable books. Rhyming text.

I can be a basketball player ill. by author. Childrens Pr., 1991. ISBN 0-516-01963-5 Subj: Sports – basketball.

I can be a farmer ill. with photos. Childrens Pr., 1989. ISBN 0-516-01923-6 Subj: Careers – farmers. Farms.

I can be a rancher ill. by author. Childrens Pr., 1990. ISBN 0-516-01962-7 Subj: Animals. Careers – ranchers.

In the middle of the night ill. by Jennifer Eachus. Macmillan, 1992. ISBN 0-02-743545-8 Subj: Activities – working. City. Night.

The little boat ill. by Patrick Benson. Candlewick, 1995. ISBN 1-56402-420-2 Subj: Boats, ships. Sea and seashore. Toys.

Newborn ill. by Caroline Binch. Dial, 1999. ISBN 0-8037-2434-9 Subj: Babies. Family life.

The storm ill. by author. Candlewick, 1999. ISBN 0-7636-0904-8 Subj: Sea and seashore. Weather – storms. Weather – wind.

A year in the city ill. by Paul Howard. Candlewick, 1996. ISBN 1-56402-872-0 Subj: City. Days of the week, months of the year. Seasons.

Hendra, Sue. *Oliver's wood* ill. by author. Candlewick, 1996. ISBN 1-56402-932-8 Subj: Animals. Bedtime. Birds – owls. Sun.

Hendrick, Mary Jean. *If anything ever goes wrong at the zoo* ill. by Jane Dyer. Harcourt, 1993. ISBN 0-15-238007-8 Subj: Animals. Weather – floods. Zoos.

Hendrickson, Karen. *Baby and I can play* ill. by Marina Megale. Parenting Pr., 1986. ISBN 0-943990-13-0 Subj: Activities – playing. Babies. Family life – brothers and sisters.

Fun with toddlers ill. by Marina Megale. Parenting Pr., 1986. ISBN 0-943990-14-9 Subj: Activities – playing. Babies. Family life.

Hendry, Diana. *Back soon!* ill. by Carol Thompson. BridgeWater, 1993. ISBN 0-8167-3487-9 Subj: Animals – cats. Character traits – individuality. Family life.

Dog Donovan ill. by Margaret Chamberlain. Candlewick, 1995. ISBN 1-56402-537-3 Subj: Animals – dogs. Character traits – kindness to animals. Emotions – fear.

Not anywhere house ill. by Thor Wickstrom. Lothrop, 1991. ISBN 0-688-10194-1 Subj: Family life. Moving.

Henkes, Kevin. *All alone* ill. by author. Greenwillow, 1981. ISBN 0-688-00605-1 Subj: Behavior – solitude.

Bailey goes camping ill. by author. Greenwillow, 1985. ISBN 0-688-05702-0 Subj: Animals – rabbits. Camps, camping. Family life.

The biggest boy ill. by Nancy Tafuri. Greenwillow, 1995. ISBN 0-688-12830-0 Subj: Concepts – shape. Concepts – size.

Chester's way ill. by author. Greenwillow, 1988. ISBN 0-688-07608-4 Subj: Animals – mice. Behavior – bullying.

Chrysanthemum ill. by author. Greenwillow, 1991. ISBN 0-688-09700-6 Subj: Animals. Names. School.

Circle dogs ill. by Dan Yaccarino. Greenwillow, 1998. ISBN 0-688-15447-6 Subj: Animals – dogs. Concepts – shape.

Clean enough ill. by author. Greenwillow, 1982. ISBN 0-688-00829-1 Subj: Activities – bathing.

Good-bye, Curtis ill. by Marisabina Russo. Greenwillow, 1995. ISBN 0-688-12828-9 Subj: Careers – postal workers. Communities, neighborhoods.

Grandpa and Bo ill. by author. Greenwillow, 1986. ISBN 0-688-04957-5 Subj: Family life – grandfathers. Seasons – summer.

Jessica ill. by author. Greenwillow, 1989. ISBN 0-688-07830-3 Subj: Friendship. Imagination – imaginary friends. School – first day.

Julius, the baby of the world ill. by author. Greenwillow, 1990. ISBN 0-688-08944-5 Subj: Family life. Sibling rivalry.

Lilly's purple plastic purse ill. by author. Greenwillow, 1996. ISBN 0-688-12898-X Subj: Animals – mice. Careers – teachers. Emotions – anger. School.

Oh! ill. by Laura Dronzek. Greenwillow, 1999. ISBN 0-688-17054-4 Subj: Activities – playing. Animals. Rhyming text. Seasons – winter. Weather – snow.

Once around the block ill. by Victoria Chess. Greenwillow, 1987. ISBN 0-688-04955-9 Subj: Behavior – boredom. Communities, neighborhoods.

Owen ill. by author. Greenwillow, 1993. ISBN 0-688-11450-4 Subj: Animals – mice. Behavior – growing up. Caldecott award honor books.

Sheila Rae, the brave ill. by author. Greenwillow, 1987. ISBN 0-688-07156-2 Subj: Animals – mice. Behavior – lost. Character traits – bravery. Family life – sisters.

Shhhh ill. by author. Greenwillow, 1989. ISBN 0-688-07986-5 Subj: Family life. Morning. Sleep.

A weekend with Wendell ill. by author. Greenwillow, 1986. ISBN 0-688-06326-8 Subj: Activities – playing. Animals – mice. Behavior – misbehavior. Character traits – selfishness.

Henkle, Henrietta. *see* Buckmaster, Henrietta

Henley, Claire. *At the zoo* ill. by author. Walt Disney, 1992. ISBN 1-56282-152-0 Subj: Activities. Animals. Zoos.

Dinnertime ill. by author. Grosset, 1994. ISBN 0-448-40826-0 Subj: Animals. Food. Format, unusual – board books.

Farm day ill. by author. Dial, 1991. ISBN 0-8037-0954-4 Subj: Animals. Careers – farmers. Farms.

I'm a baby, too! ill. by author. Grosset, 1994. ISBN 0-448-40825-2 Subj: Animals – babies. Babies. Format, unusual – board books.

In the ocean ill. by author. Walt Disney, 1992. ISBN 1-56282-154-7 Subj: Animals. Fish. Sea and seashore.

Joe's pool ill. by author. Hyperion, 1994. ISBN 1-56282-432-5 Subj: Counting, numbers. Sports – swimming.

Jungle day ill. by author. Dial, 1991. ISBN 0-8037-0959-5 Subj: Animals. Jungle.

Playtime ill. by author. Grosset, 1994. ISBN 0-448-40827-9 Subj: Activities – playing. Animals. Format, unusual – board books.

Quack, quack ill. by author. Grosset, 1994. ISBN 0-448-40828-7 Subj: Animals. Birds. Format, unusual – board books. Noise, sounds.

Stormy day ill. by author. Hyperion, 1993. ISBN 1-56282-343-4 Subj: Weather – storms. Weather – thunder.

Sunny day ill. by author. Hyperion, 1993. ISBN 1-56282-341-8 Subj: Sea and seashore. Seasons – summer. Sun.

Henley, Karyn. *Hatch!* ill. by Susan Kennedy. Carolrhoda, 1980. ISBN 0-87614-122-X Subj: Animals.

Hennessy, B. G. (Barbara G.). *A, B, C, D, tummy, toes, hands, knee* ill. by Wendy Watson. Viking, 1989. ISBN 0-670-81703-1 Subj: Concepts. Family life. Rhyming text.

Busy Dinah Dinosaur ill. by Ana Martin Larrañaga. Candlewick, 2000. ISBN 0-7636-1140-9 Subj: Activities. Dinosaurs.

Corduroy's birthday ill. by Lisa McCue. Viking, 1997. Based on the character by Don Freeman. ISBN 0-670-87065-X Subj: Birthdays. Format, unusual – toy and movable books. Parties. Toys – bears.

Corduroy's Christmas ill. by Lisa McCue. Viking, 1992. Based on the character by Don Freeman. ISBN 0-670-84477-2 Subj: Format, unusual – toy and movable books. Holidays – Christmas. Toys – bears.

Corduroy's Easter ill. by Lisa McCue. Viking, 1998. Based on the character by Don Freeman. ISBN 0-670-88101-5 Subj: Format, unusual – toy and movable books. Holidays – Easter. Toys – bears.

Corduroy's Halloween ill. by Lisa McCue. Viking, 1995. Based on the character by Don Freeman. ISBN 0-670-86193-6 Subj: Format, unusual – toy and movable books. Holidays – Halloween. Toys – bears.

The dinosaur who lived in my backyard ill. by Susan Davis. Viking, 1988. ISBN 0-670-81685-X Subj: Dinosaurs. Imagination.

Eeney, Meeney, Miney, Mo ill. by Letizia Galli. Viking, 1995. ISBN 0-670-82864-5 Subj: Animals. Jungle. Rhyming text.

The first night ill. by Steve Johnson with Lou Fancher. Viking, 1993. ISBN 0-670-83026-7 Subj: Holidays – Christmas. Religion.

Jake baked the cake ill. by Mary Morgan. Viking, 1990. ISBN 0-670-82237-X Subj: Food. Rhyming text. Weddings.

Meet Dinah Dinosaur ill. by Ana Martin Larrañaga. Candlewick, 2000. ISBN 0-7636-1133-6 Subj: Dinosaurs.

Meet Winslow whale ill. by Joyce Howell. Viking, 1994. ISBN 0-670-85632-0 Subj: Animals – whales. Character traits – being different. Friendship.

The missing tarts ill. by Tracey Campbell Pearson. Viking, 1989. ISBN 0-670-82039-3 Subj: Behavior – stealing. Nursery rhymes. Rhyming text. Royalty – queens.

Olympics! ill. by Michael Chesworth. Viking, 1996. ISBN 0-670-86522-2 Subj: Sports – Olympics.

One little, two little, three little pilgrims ill. by Lynne Cravath. Viking, 1999. ISBN 0-670-87779-4 Subj: Counting, numbers. Indians of North America – Wampanoag. Pilgrims.

Road builders ill. by Simms Taback. Viking, 1994. ISBN 0-670-83390-8 Subj: Careers – construction workers. Machines. Roads.

School days ill. by Tracey Campbell Pearson. Viking, 1990. ISBN 0-670-83025-9 Subj: Rhyming text. School.

Sleep tight ill. by Anthony Carnabuci. Viking, 1992. ISBN 0-670-83567-6 Subj: Bedtime. Rhyming text. Sleep.

When you were just a little girl ill. by Jeanne Arnold. Viking, 1991. ISBN 0-670-83998-6 Subj: Family life – grandmothers. Rhyming text.

Henri, Adrian. *The postman's palace* ill. by Simon Henwood. Atheneum, 1990. ISBN 0-689-31667-4 Subj: Buildings. Careers – postal workers. Dreams. Post office.

Henrietta. *A mouse in the house* ill. with photos. DK, 1991. ISBN 1-879431-26-2 Subj: Animals – mice. Birthdays. Games. Rhyming text.

Henriod, Lorraine. *Grandma's wheelchair* ill. by Christa Chevalier. Albert Whitman, 1982. ISBN 0-8075-3035-2 Subj: Family life – grandmothers. Handicaps. Sibling rivalry.

Henrioud, Charles. *Mr. Noah and the animals: Monsieur Noé et les animaux* ill. by author. Walck, 1960. Subj: Boats, ships. Religion – Noah. Weather – floods. Weather – rain. Weather – rainbows.

Henry, Lenny. *Charlie and the big chill* ill. by Chris Burke. Trafalgar Square, 1997. ISBN 0-575-05938-9 Subj: Imagination.

Charlie, queen of the desert ill. by Chris Burke. Trafalgar Square, 1997. ISBN 0-575-05939-7 Subj: Foreign lands – Australia. Imagination.

Henry, O. *The gift of the Magi* ill. by Lisbeth Zwerger. Picture Book Studio, 1982. ISBN 0-907234-17-8 Subj: Character traits – generosity. Gifts. Holidays – Christmas.

Henson, Jim. *ABC: featuring Jim Henson's Sesame Street Muppets* (Calmenson, Stephanie)

Baby Piggy and giant bubble (Anastasio, Dina)

Big Bird at the beach (Hautzig, Deborah)

Ernie and Bert's new kitten (Hautzig, Deborah)

Jim Henson's Muppets in Rowlf's big test: a book about listening to your conscience (Gikow, Louise)

Jim Henson's Muppets in What's fair is fair: a book about sharing (Gikow, Louise)

A visit to the Sesame Street library: featuring Jim Henson's Sesame Street Muppets (Hautzig, Deborah)

Henstra, Friso. *Wait and see* ill. by author. Addison-Wesley, 1978. ISBN 0-201-03077-2 Subj: Machines.

Henwood, Simon. *The clock shop* ill. by author. Farrar, 1989. ISBN 0-674-31380-6 Subj: Careers – clockmakers. Clocks, watches. Time.

The hidden jungle ill. by author. Farrar, 1992. ISBN 0-374-33070-0 Subj: City. Ecology. Trees.

A piece of luck ill. by author. Farrar, 1990. ISBN 0-374-35925-3 Subj: Behavior – greed. Behavior – hiding things. Character traits – luck.

The troubled village ill. by author. Farrar, 1991. ISBN 0-374-37780-4 Subj: Communities, neighborhoods. Problem solving.

The view (Yoaker, Harry)

Heo, Yumi. *Father's rubber shoes* ill. by author. Orchard, 1995. ISBN 0-531-08723-9 Subj: Careers – storekeepers. Clothing – shoes. Ethnic groups in the U.S. – Korean Americans. Family life – fathers.

The green frogs ill. by author. Houghton Mifflin, 1996. ISBN 0-395-68378-5 Subj: Behavior – misbehavior. Folk and fairy tales. Foreign lands – Korea. Frogs and toads.

One afternoon ill. by author. Orchard, 1994. ISBN 0-531-08695-X Subj: City. Communities, neighborhoods. Family life – mothers. Noise, sounds.

One Sunday morning ill. by author. Orchard, 1999. ISBN 0-531-33156-3 Subj: City. Family life – fathers. Noise, sounds. Parks.

Hepworth, Catherine. *ANTics! an alphabetical anthology* ill. by author. Putnam, 1992. ISBN 0-399-21862-9 Subj: ABC books. Insects – ants.

Bug off! a swarm of insect words ill. by author. Putnam, 1998. ISBN 0-399-22640-0 Subj: Insects. Language.

Herford, Oliver. *The most timid in the land* ill. by Sylvia Long. Chronicle, 1992. ISBN 0-87701-862-6 Subj: Animals – rabbits. Middle Ages. Poetry.

Hergé. *Explorers on the moon* ill. by author. Joy Street, 1992. ISBN 0-316-35860-6 Subj: Format, unusual – toy and movable books. Moon. Space and space ships.

Herman, Bill. *Jenny's magic wand* by Bill and Helen Herman; photos by Don Perdue. Watts, 1988. ISBN 0-531-10292-0 Subj: Handicaps – blindness. Senses – seeing.

Herman, Charlotte. *My mother didn't kiss me goodnight* ill. by Bruce Degen. Dutton, 1980. ISBN 0-525-35495-6 Subj: Behavior – worrying.

Herman, Emily. *Hubknuckles* ill. by Deborah Kogan Ray. Crown, 1985. ISBN 0-517-55646-4 Subj: Ghosts. Holidays – Halloween.

Herman, Gail. *Double-header* ill. by Jerry Smath. Grosset, 1993. ISBN 0-448-40156-8 Subj: Monsters. Sports – baseball.

Fievel's big showdown ill. by Beverly Lazor-Bahr; based on characters created by David Kirschner.

Grosset, 1992. ISBN 0-448-40379-X Subj: Activities – reading. Animals – cats. Animals – mice. Character traits – bravery.

Flower girl ill. by Paige Billin-Frye. Grosset, 1996. ISBN 0-448-41107-5 Subj: Behavior – dissatisfaction. Family life – sisters. Weddings.

The haunted house ill. by Carol Nicklaus. Random House, 1989. ISBN 0-394-82717-1 Subj: Animals – cats. Ghosts. Homes, houses.

Ice cream soup adapt. by Gail Herman; based on a story by Jack Kent; ill. by R. W. Alley. Random House, 1990. ISBN 0-679-80790-X Subj: Behavior – tardiness.

The lion and the mouse (Æsop)

The littlest duckling ill. by Ann Schweninger. Viking, 1996. ISBN 0-670-85113-2 Subj: Birds – ducks. Family life. Sports – swimming.

Make way for trucks: big machines on wheels ill. by Christopher Santoro. McKay, 1990. ISBN 0-679-90110-8 Subj: Trucks.

My dog talks ill. by Ron Fritz. Scholastic, 1995. ISBN 0-590-22196-5 Subj: Animals – dogs. Pets.

Otto the cat ill. by Norman Gorbaty. Grosset, 1995. ISBN 0-448-40968-2 Subj: Animals – cats. Animals – dogs. Rebuses.

Pizza cats ill. by Louie del Carmen and James Peters. Simon Spotlight/Nickelodeon, 1999. ISBN 0-689-82391-6 Subj: Animals – cats. Restaurants.

The puppy who went to school ill. by Betina Ogden. Platt, 1992. ISBN 0-448-40481-8 Subj: Animals – dogs. Pets. School.

Teddy bear for sale ill. by Doug Cushman. Scholastic, 1995. ISBN 0-590-25943-1 Subj: Behavior – running away. Toys – bears.

There is a town ill. by Katy Bratun. Random House, 1995. ISBN 0-679-96439-8 Subj: Birthdays. Parties. Toys.

What a hungry puppy! ill. by Norman Gorbaty. Grosset, 1993. ISBN 0-448-40537-7 Subj: Animals – dogs. Behavior – losing things.

Herman, Helen. *Jenny's magic wand* (Herman, Bill)

Herman, R. A. (Ronnie Ann). *Pal the pony* ill. by Betina Ogden. Grosset, 1996. ISBN 0-448-41257-8 Subj: Animals – horses, ponies. Character traits – ambition. Concepts – size.

Hermes, Patricia. *When snow lay soft on the mountain* ill. by Leslie Baker. Little, 1996. ISBN 0-316-36005-8 Subj: Behavior – wishing. Family life – aunts, uncles. Family life – fathers. Illness. Quilts. Toys – dolls.

Hern, Lafcadio. *The voice of the great bell* (Hodges, Margaret)

Herold, Ann Bixby. *The helping day* ill. by Victoria de Larrea. Coward, 1980. ISBN 0-698-20492-1 Subj: Character traits – helpfulness.

Herrick, Amy. *Kimbo's marble* ill. by Edward S. Gazsi. HarperCollins, 1993. ISBN 0-06-020374-9 Subj: Family life – brothers and sisters. Folk and fairy tales. Mythical creatures – trolls.

Herring, Ann (King). *Peter and the wolf* (Prokofiev, Sergei Sergeievitch)

Suho and the white horse: a legend of Mongolia (Otsuka, Yuzo)

Herriot, James. *Blossom comes home* ill. by Ruth Brown. St. Martin's, 1988. ISBN 0-312-02169-0 Subj: Animals – bulls, cows. Behavior – needing someone. Farms. Old age.

Bonny's big day ill. by Ruth Brown. St. Martin's, 1987. ISBN 0-312-01000-1 Subj: Animals – horses, ponies. Fairs. Farms.

Christmas Day kitten ill. by Ruth Brown. St. Martin's, 1986. ISBN 0-312-13407-X Subj: Animals – cats. Character traits – kindness to animals. Holidays – Christmas. Wordless.

Moses the kitten ill. by Peter Barrett. St. Martin's, 1984. ISBN 0-312-54905-9 Subj: Animals – cats. Careers – veterinarians.

Only one woof ill. by Peter Barrett. St. Martin's, 1985. ISBN 0-312-58583-7 Subj: Animals. Animals – dogs. Careers – veterinarians.

Herrmann, Dagmar. *My father always embarrasses me* (Shalev, Meir)

Nobody has time for me (Skutina, Vladimir)

Herrmann, Frank. *The giant Alexander* ill. by George Him. McGraw-Hill, 1965. Subj: Foreign lands – England. Giants.

The giant Alexander and the circus ill. by George Him. McGraw-Hill, 1966. Subj: Circus. Foreign lands – England. Giants.

Hershenhorn, Esther. *There goes Lowell's party!* ill. by Jacqueline Rogers. Holiday, 1998. ISBN 0-8234-1313-6 Subj: Birthdays. Family life. Weather – rain. Weather – storms.

Hershey, Kathleen. *Cotton mill town* ill. by Jeanette Winter. Dutton, 1993. ISBN 0-525-44966-3 Subj: Family life – grandmothers. Nature.

Hersom, Donald. *The copycat* (Hersom, Kathleen)

Hersom, Kathleen. *The copycat* by Kathleen and Donald Hersom; ill. by Catherine Stock. Atheneum, 1989. ISBN 0-689-31448-5 Subj: Animals. Behavior – imitation. Noise, sounds. Rhyming text.

Herter, Jonina. *Eighty-eight kisses* ill. with photos. Boss Books, 1978. ISBN 0-932430-02-3 Subj: Babies. Family life – great-grandparents.

Hertz, Ole. *Tobias catches trout* trans. from Danish by Tobi Tobias; ill. by author. Carolrhoda, 1984. ISBN 0-87614-263-3 Subj: Foreign lands – Greenland. Sports – fishing.

Tobias goes ice fishing trans. from Danish by Tobi Tobias; ill. by author. Carolrhoda, 1984. ISBN 0-87614-260-9 Subj: Foreign lands – Greenland. Seasons – winter. Sports – fishing.

Tobias goes seal hunting trans. from Danish by Tobi Tobias; ill. by author. Carolrhoda, 1984. ISBN 0-87614-262-5 Subj: Foreign lands – Greenland. Sports – hunting.

Tobias has a birthday trans. from Danish by Tobi Tobias; ill. by author. Carolrhoda, 1984. ISBN 0-87614-261-7 Subj: Birthdays. Foreign lands – Greenland.

Herzig, Alison Cragin. *Bronco busters* ill. by Kimberly Bulcken Root. Putnam, 1998. ISBN 0-399-22917-5 Subj: Animals – horses, ponies. Cowboys.

Hess, Edith. *Peter and Susie find a family* trans. from German by Miriam Moore; ill. by Jacqueline Blass. Abingdon, 1985. ISBN 0-687-30848-8 Subj: Adoption. Family life.

Hess, Paul. *Farmyard animals* ill. by author. De Agostini, 1996. ISBN 1-899883-34-7 Subj: Animals. Farms. Poetry.

Polar animals ill. by author. De Agostini, 1996. ISBN 1-899883-36-3 Subj: Animals. Foreign lands – Arctic. Poetry.

Rainforest animals ill. by author. De Agostini, 1996. ISBN 1-899883-37-1 Subj: Animals. Foreign lands. Forest, woods. Poetry.

Safari animals ill. by author. De Agostini, 1996. ISBN 1-899883-35-5 Subj: Animals. Foreign lands – Africa. Poetry.

Hesse, Karen. *Come on, rain* ill. by Jon J. Muth. Scholastic, 1999. ISBN 0-590-33125-6 Subj: Activities – dancing. Ethnic groups in the U.S. – African Americans. Family life – daughters. Family life – mothers. Seasons – summer. Weather – rain.

Lavender ill. by Andrew Glass. Holt, 1993. ISBN 0-8050-2528-6 Subj: Babies. Family life – aunts, uncles. Family life – cousins. Friendship. Quilts.

Lester's dog ill. by Nancy Carpenter. Crown, 1993. ISBN 0-517-58358-5 Subj: Animals – cats. Animals – dogs. Emotions – fear. Handicaps – deafness.

Poppy's chair ill. by Kay Life. Macmillan, 1993. ISBN 0-02-743705-1 Subj: Death. Emotions – grief. Family life – grandparents.

Hessell, Jenny. *Staying at Sam's* ill. by Jenny Williams. HarperCollins, 1990. ISBN 0-397-32433-2 Subj: Family life.

Hest, Amy. *The babies are coming!* ill. by Chloë Cheese. Crown, 1997. ISBN 0-517-70944-9 Subj: Activities – storytelling. Babies. Libraries.

Baby Duck and the bad eyeglasses ill. by Jill Barton. Candlewick, 1996. ISBN 1-56402-680-9 Subj: Birds – ducks. Family life – grandfathers. Glasses.

Best-ever good-bye party ill. by DyAnne DiSalvo-Ryan. Morrow, 1989. ISBN 0-688-07326-3 Subj: Friendship. Moving.

The crack-of-dawn walkers ill. by Amy Schwartz. Macmillan, 1984. ISBN 0-02-743710-8 Subj: Family life – grandfathers.

Fancy Aunt Jess ill. by Amy Schwartz. Morrow, 1990. ISBN 0-688-08097-9 Subj: Family life – aunts, uncles. Jewish culture. Weddings.

Gabby growing up ill. by Amy Schwartz. Simon & Schuster, 1998. ISBN 0-689-80573-X Subj: Birthdays. Family life – grandparents. Family life – parents. Hair. Holidays.

The go-between ill. by DyAnne DiSalvo-Ryan. Four Winds, 1992. ISBN 0-02-743632-2 Subj: Emotions – love. Family life – grandmothers. Friendship. Weddings.

How to get famous in Brooklyn ill. by Linda Dalal Sawaya. Simon & Schuster, 1993. ISBN 0-02-743655-1 Subj: Activities. Communities, neighborhoods.

In the rain with Baby Duck ill. by Jill Barton. Candlewick, 1995. ISBN 1-56402-532-2 Subj: Babies. Behavior – secrets. Birds – ducks. Family life – grandfathers. Weather – rain.

Jamaica Louise James ill. by Sheila White Samton. Candlewick, 1996. ISBN 1-56402-348-6 Subj: Activities – painting. Birthdays. Ethnic groups in the U.S. – African Americans. Family life – grandmothers.

The midnight eaters ill. by Karen Gundersheimer. Four Winds, 1989. ISBN 0-02-743630-6 Subj: Family life – grandmothers. Night. Old age.

The mommy exchange ill. by DyAnne DiSalvo-Ryan. Four Winds, 1988. ISBN 0-02-743650-0 Subj: Behavior – dissatisfaction. Family life – mothers.

Nana's birthday party ill. by Amy Schwartz. Morrow, 1993. ISBN 0-688-07498-7 Subj: Birthdays. Careers – artists. City. Family life – cousins. Family life – grandmothers.

Nannies for hire ill. by Irene Trivas. Morrow, 1994. ISBN 0-688-12528-X Subj: Activities – babysitting. Babies. Friendship.

Off to school, Baby Duck ill. by Jill Barton. Candlewick, 1999. ISBN 0-7636-0244-2 Subj: Babies. Birds – ducks. Emotions – fear. Family life – grandfathers. School – first day.

The purple coat ill. by Amy Schwartz. Four Winds, 1986. ISBN 0-02-743640-3 Subj: Careers – tailors. Clothing – coats. Concepts – color. Family life. Family life – grandfathers.

The ring and the window seat ill. by Deborah Haeffele. Scholastic, 1990. ISBN 0-590-41350-3 Subj: Careers – carpenters. Family life. War.

Rosie's fishing trip ill. by Paul Howard. Candlewick, 1994. ISBN 1-56402-296-X Subj: Family life – grandfathers. Sports – fishing.

Ruby's storm ill. by Nancy Cote. Four Winds, 1994. ISBN 0-02-743160-6 Subj: City. Family life – grandfathers. Seasons – spring. Weather – storms.

A sort-of sailor ill. by Lizzy Rockwell. Four Winds, 1990. ISBN 0-02-743641-1 Subj: Boats, ships. Emotions – fear. Sailors.

Weekend girl ill. by Harvey Stevenson. Morrow, 1993. ISBN 0-688-09690-5 Subj: Activities – photographing. Activities – picnicking. City. Family life – grandparents.

You're the boss, Baby Duck ill. by Jill Barton. Candlewick, 1997. ISBN 1-56402-667-1 Subj: Babies. Birds – ducks. Emotions – envy, jealousy. Family life – brothers and sisters. Family life – grandfathers. Self-concept.

Hetfield, Jamie. *The Yoruba of West Africa* ill. with photos. Rosen, 1996. ISBN 0-8239-2332-0 Subj: Foreign lands – Africa.

Heuck, Sigrid. *Pony and Bear are friends* ill. by author. Knopf, 1990. ISBN 0-394-92311-1 Subj: Animals – bears. Animals – horses, ponies. Friendship. Rebuses.

Who stole the apples? ill. by author. Knopf, 1986. ISBN 0-394-98371-8 Subj: Activities – traveling. Animals. Behavior – sharing. Rebuses.

Hewetson, Sarah. *My first pop-up book of prehistoric animals* (Bishop, Roma)

Hewett, Anita. *The tale of the turnip* ill. by Margery Gill. McGraw-Hill, 1961. Subj: Cumulative tales. Participation. Plants.

Hewett, Joan. *Fly away free* photos by Richard Hewett. Walker, 1981. ISBN 0-8027-6403-7 Subj: Birds – pelicans. Careers – veterinarians. Illness.

The mouse and the elephant photos by Richard Hewett. Little, 1977. ISBN 0-316-35966-1 Subj: Animals – elephants. Animals – mice.

Rosalie ill. by Donald Carrick. Lothrop, 1987. ISBN 0-688-06229-6 Subj: Animals – dogs. Character traits – kindness to animals. Old age.

Tiger, tiger, growing up photos by Richard Hewett. Clarion, 1993. ISBN 0-395-61583-6 Subj: Animals – tigers. Zoos.

Hewitt, Kathryn. *King Midas and the golden touch* by Nathaniel Hawthorne; adapt. and ill. by Kathryn Hewitt. Harcourt, 1987. ISBN 0-15-242800-3 Subj: Behavior – greed. Folk and fairy tales. Royalty – kings.

The three sillies (Jacobs, Joseph)

Two by two: the untold story ill. by author. Harcourt, 1984. ISBN 0-15-291801-9 Subj: Boats, ships. Religion – Noah. Weather – floods. Weather – rain. Weather – rainbows.

Heyduck-Huth, Hilde. *The starfish: a treasure chest story* ill. by author. Macmillan, 1987. ISBN 0-689-50434-9 Subj: Behavior – collecting things. Crustaceans. Sea and seashore.

The strawflower: a treasure chest story ill. by author. Macmillan, 1987. ISBN 0-689-50435-7 Subj: Behavior – collecting things. Flowers. Seasons.

Heyer, Carol. *Dinosaurs! strange and wonderful* ill. by Carol Heyer. Boyds Mills, 1995. ISBN 1-878093-16-9 Subj: Dinosaurs.

Robin Hood ill. by author. Ideals, 1993. ISBN 0-8249-8648-2 Subj: Behavior – greed. Character traits – bravery. Character traits – honesty. Folk and fairy tales.

Heyer, Marilee. *The weaving of a dream: a Chinese folktale* ill. by author. Viking, 1986. ISBN 0-670-80555-6 Subj: Activities – weaving. Folk and fairy tales. Foreign lands – China.

Heymans, Annemie. *The princess in the kitchen garden* written and ill. by Annemie and Margriet Heymans; trans. from Dutch by Johanna H. Prins and Johanna W. Prins. Farrar, 1993. ISBN 0-374-36122-3 Subj: Death. Emotions – grief. Family life. Family life – brothers and sisters.

Heymans, Margriet. *Pippin and Robber Grumblecroak's big baby* ill. by author. Addison-Wesley, 1973. Subj: Crime. Puppets.

The princess in the kitchen garden (Heymans, Annemie)

Heyward, Du Bose. *The country bunny and the little gold shoes* ill. by Marjorie Flack. Houghton Mifflin, 1974, c1939. ISBN 0-395-18557-2 Subj: Animals – rabbits. Character traits – kindness. Holidays – Easter.

Hiatt, Fred. *Baby talk* ill. by Mark Graham. Margaret K. McElderry, 1999. ISBN 0-689-82146-8 Subj: Babies. Family life – brothers. Language.

If I were queen of the world ill. by Mark Graham. Margaret K. McElderry, 1997. ISBN 0-689-80700-7 Subj: Family life – brothers and sisters. Imagination. Royalty – queens.

Hickcox, Ruth. *Great-Grandmother's treasure* ill. by David Soman. Dial, 1998. ISBN 0-8037-1514-5 Subj: Death. Family life – great-grandparents. Memories, memory. Old age.

Hickman, Martha Whitmore. *And God created squash: how the world began* ill. by Giuliano Ferri. Albert Whitman, 1993. ISBN 0-8075-0340-1 Subj: Creation.

Eeps creeps, it's my room! ill. by Mary Alice Baer. Abingdon, 1984. ISBN 0-687-11527-2 Subj: Character traits – cleanliness.

My friend William moved away ill. by Bill Myers. Abingdon, 1979. ISBN 0-687-27540-7 Subj: Friendship. Moving.

Robert lives with his grandparents ill. by Tim Hinton. Albert Whitman, 1995. ISBN 0-8075-7084-2 Subj: Divorce. Family life – grandparents. School.

When Andy's father went to prison ill. by Larry Raymond. Albert Whitman, 1990. Rev. ed. of: When can daddy come home? c1983. ISBN 0-8075-8874-1 Subj: Crime. Family life. Prisons.

Hickox, Rebecca. *see* Ayers, Rebecca Hickox

The golden sandal ill. by Will Hillenbrand. Holiday, 1998. ISBN 0-8234-1331-4 Subj: Clothing. Family life – step families. Folk and fairy tales. Foreign lands – Iraq.

Hicks, Eleanor B. *see* Coerr, Eleanor

Hidaka, Masako. *Girl from the snow country* trans. from Japanese by Amanda Mayer Stinchecum; ill. by author. Kane/Miller, 1986. ISBN 0-916291-06-5 Subj: Flowers. Folk and fairy tales. Foreign lands – Japan. Weather – snow.

Hide-and-seek bunnies ill. by Judith Moffatt. Grosset, 1996. ISBN 0-448-41283-7 Subj: Animals – rabbits. Format, unusual – toy and movable books. Rhyming text.

Higgs, Liz Curtis. *Go away, dark night* ill. by Nancy Munger. WaterBrook, 1998. ISBN 1-57856-129-9 Subj: Emotions – fear. Night. Religion.

The parable of the lily ill. by Nancy Munger. Nelson, 1997. ISBN 0-7852-7231-3 Subj: Gardens, gardening. Gifts. Holidays – Easter.

High, Linda Oatman. *Barn savers* ill. by Ted Lewin. Boyds Mills, 1999. ISBN 1-56397-403-7 Subj: Barns. Family life – fathers.

Beekeepers ill. by Doug Chayka. Boyds Mills, 1998. ISBN 1-56397-486-X Subj: Family life – grandfathers. Insects – bees.

A Christmas Star ill. by Ronald Himler. Holiday, 1997. ISBN 0-8234-1301-2 Subj: Crime. Gifts. Holidays – Christmas. Trees.

Higham, Jon Atlas. *Aardvark's picnic* ill. by author. Little, 1987. ISBN 0-316-36085-6 Subj: Activities – picnicking. Animals. Animals – aardvarks.

Highlights for Children, Inc. *The Timbertoes ABC alphabet book* (The Timbertoes ABC alphabet book)

The Timbertoes 1 2 3 counting book (The Timbertoes 1 2 3 counting book)

Hightower, Susan. *Twelve snails to one lizard: a tale of mischief and measurement* ill. by Matt Novak. Simon & Schuster, 1997. ISBN 0-689-80452-0 Subj: Animals. Animals – snails. Concepts – measurement. Reptiles – lizards.

Highwater, Jamake. *Moonsong lullaby* photos by Marcia Keegan. Lothrop, 1981. ISBN 0-688-00428-8 Subj: Lullabies. Night. Rhyming text.

Higney, Gene-Michael. *What's for lunch?* (Garrett, Ann)

Hill, Donna. *Ms. Glee was waiting* ill. by Diane Dawson. Atheneum, 1978. ISBN 0-689-30618-0 Subj: School.

Hill, Elizabeth Starr. *Evan's corner* ill. by Sandra Speidel. Rev. ed. Viking, 1991. ISBN 0-670-82830-0 Subj: Character traits – helpfulness. Ethnic groups in the U.S. – African Americans. Family life.

Hill, Eric. *At home* ill. by author. Random House, 1983. ISBN 0-394-85638-4 Subj: Animals – bears. Family life. Wordless.

Baby Bear's bedtime ill. by author. Random House, 1984. ISBN 0-394-96572-8 Subj: Animals – bears. Bedtime.

Good morning, baby bear ill. by author. Random House, 1984. ISBN 0-394-96571-X Subj: Animals – bears. Morning.

My pets ill. by author. Random House, 1983. ISBN 0-394-85637-6 Subj: Animals – bears. Pets.

The park ill. by author. Random House, 1983. ISBN 0-394-85636-8 Subj: Activities – walking. Parks. Wordless.

Puppy love ill. by author. Putnam, 1982. ISBN 0-399-20939-5 Subj: Animals – dogs. Emotions – love. Format, unusual – board books.

Spot and friends dress up ill. by author. Putnam, 1996. ISBN 0-399-23031-9 Subj: Animals – dogs. Clothing. Format, unusual – toy and movable books. Friendship.

Spot and friends play ill. by author. Putnam, 1996. ISBN 0-399-23032-7 Subj: Activities – playing. Animals – dogs. Format, unusual – toy and movable books. Friendship.

Spot at home ill. by author. Putnam, 1991. ISBN 0-399-21774-6 Subj: Animals – dogs. Format, unusual – board books.

Spot at play ill. by author. Putnam, 1985. ISBN 0-399-21228-0 Subj: Activities – playing. Animals. Animals – dogs.

Spot at the fair ill. by author. Putnam, 1985. ISBN 0-399-21229-9 Subj: Animals. Animals – dogs. Fairs. Format, unusual – board books.

Spot bakes a cake ill. by author. Putnam, 1994. ISBN 0-399-22701-6 Subj: Activities – cooking. Animals – dogs. Birthdays. Food. Format, unusual – toy and movable books.

Spot counts from 1 to 10 ill. by author. Putnam, 1989. ISBN 0-399-21672-3 Subj: Animals. Animals – dogs. Counting, numbers. Format, unusual – board books.

Spot goes on holiday ill. by author. Heinemann, 1985. ISBN 0-434-94260-X Subj: Activities – vacationing. Animals – dogs. Format, unusual – toy and movable books. Sea and seashore.

Spot goes to a party ill. by author. Putnam, 1992. ISBN 0-399-22409-2 Subj: Animals – dogs. Cowboys. Format, unusual – toy and movable books. Parties.

Spot goes to school ill. by author. Putnam, 1984. ISBN 0-399-21073-3 Subj: Animals – dogs. Format,

unusual – toy and movable books. School – first day.

Spot goes to the beach ill. by author. Putnam, 1985. ISBN 0-399-21247-7 Subj: Activities – playing. Animals – dogs. Family life. Format, unusual – toy and movable books. Sea and seashore.

Spot goes to the circus ill. by author. Putnam, 1986. ISBN 0-399-21317-1 Subj: Animals – dogs. Circus. Format, unusual – board books.

Spot goes to the farm ill. by author. Putnam, 1987. ISBN 0-399-21434-8 Subj: Animals. Animals – dogs. Farms. Format, unusual – board books. Machines.

Spot goes to the park ill. by author. Putnam, 1991. ISBN 0-399-21833-5 Subj: Activities – playing. Animals – dogs. Format, unusual – toy and movable books. Parks.

Spot in the garden ill. by author. Putnam, 1991. ISBN 0-399-21772-X Subj: Animals – dogs. Format, unusual – board books. Gardens, gardening.

Spot looks at colors ill. by author. Putnam, 1986. ISBN 0-399-21349-X Subj: Animals – dogs. Concepts – color. Format, unusual – board books.

Spot looks at opposites ill. by author. Putnam, 1989. ISBN 0-399-21681-2 Subj: Animals – dogs. Concepts – opposites. Format, unusual – board books.

Spot looks at shapes ill. by author. Putnam, 1986. ISBN 0-399-21350-3 Subj: Animals – dogs. Concepts – shape. Format, unusual – board books.

Spot looks at weather ill. by author. Putnam, 1989. ISBN 0-399-21673-1 Subj: Animals – dogs. Format, unusual – board books. Weather.

Spot on the farm ill. by author. Putnam, 1985. ISBN 0-399-21230-2 Subj: Animals. Animals – dogs. Farms. Format, unusual – board books.

Spot sleeps over ill. by author. Putnam, 1990. ISBN 0-399-21815-7 Subj: Activities – playing. Animals – dogs. Format, unusual – toy and movable books. Friendship. Sleepovers.

Spot visits his grandparents ill. by author. Putnam, 1996. ISBN 0-399-23033-5 Subj: Animals – dogs. Family life – grandparents. Format, unusual – board books.

Spot visits the hospital ill. by author. Putnam, 1987. ISBN 0-399-21397-X Subj: Animals – dogs. Behavior – misbehavior. Hospitals.

Spot's baby sister ill. by author. Putnam, 1989. ISBN 0-399-21640-5 Subj: Animals – dogs. Animals – hippopotamuses. Format, unusual – toy and movable books. Reptiles – alligators, crocodiles.

Spot's big book of colors, shapes and numbers; El libro grande de Spot: colores, formas ye numeros ill. by author. Putnam, 1994. ISBN 0-399-22782-2 Subj: Animals – dogs. Concepts – color. Concepts – shape. Counting, numbers. Foreign languages.

Spot's big book of colours, shapes, and numbers ill. by author. F. Warne, 1994. ISBN 0-399-22679-6 Subj:

Animals – dogs. Concepts – color. Concepts – shape. Counting, numbers.

Spot's big book of words; El libro grande de las palabras de Spot ill. by author. Rev. ed. Putnam, 1989. ISBN 0-399-21689-8 Subj: Animals – dogs. Foreign languages. Language.

Spot's birthday party ill. by author. Putnam, 1982. ISBN 0-399-20903-4 Subj: Birthdays. Folk and fairy tales. Format, unusual – toy and movable books.

Spot's favorite baby animals ill. by author. Putnam, 1997. ISBN 0-399-23157-9 Subj: Animals. Animals – dogs. Format, unusual – board books.

Spot's favorite colors ill. by author. Putnam, 1997. ISBN 0-399-23177-3 Subj: Animals – dogs. Concepts – color. Format, unusual – board books.

Spot's favorite numbers ill. by author. Putnam, 1997. ISBN 0-399-23155-2 Subj: Animals – dogs. Counting, numbers. Format, unusual – board books.

Spot's favorite words ill. by author. Putnam, 1997. ISBN 0-399-23156-0 Subj: Animals – dogs. Format, unusual – board books. Language.

Spot's first Christmas ill. by author. Putnam, 1983. ISBN 0-399-20963-8 Subj: Animals – dogs. Format, unusual – toy and movable books. Holidays – Christmas.

Spot's first Easter ill. by author. Putnam, 1988. ISBN 0-399-21435-6 Subj: Animals – dogs. Eggs. Format, unusual – toy and movable books. Holidays – Easter.

Spot's first 1, 2, 3 frieze ill. by author. F. Warne, 1994. ISBN 0-72324-176-7 Subj: Animals – dogs. Counting, numbers. Format, unusual.

Spot's first picnic ill. by author. Putnam, 1987. ISBN 0-399-21398-8 Subj: Activities – picnicking. Animals – dogs. Behavior – misbehavior.

Spot's first walk ill. by author. Putnam, 1981. ISBN 0-399-20838-0 Subj: Activities – walking. Animals – dogs. Format, unusual – toy and movable books.

Spot's first words ill. by author. Putnam, 1986. ISBN 0-399-21348-1 Subj: Animals – dogs. Format, unusual – board books. Language.

Spot's magical Christmas ill. by author. Putnam, 1995. ISBN 0-399-22912-4 Subj: Animals – dogs. Format, unusual – board books. Holidays – Christmas. Santa Claus.

Spot's toy box ill. by author. Putnam, 1991. ISBN 0-399-21773-8 Subj: Animals – dogs. Format, unusual – board books. Toys.

Spot's walk in the woods ill. by author. Viking, 1993. ISBN 0-670-85080-2 Subj: Activities – playing. Animals – dogs. Forest, woods. Format, unusual – toy and movable books. Rebuses.

Up there ill. by author. Random House, 1983. ISBN 0-394-85635-X Subj: Activities – flying. Animals – bears. Wordless.

Where's Spot? ill. by author. Putnam, 1980. ISBN 0-399-20758-9 Subj: Behavior – lost. Folk and fairy tales. Format, unusual – toy and movable books.

Hill, Lee Sullivan. *Schools help us learn* ill. with photos. Carolrhoda, 1998. ISBN 1-57505-092-7 Subj: School.

Hill, Mary Lou. *My dad's a park ranger* ill. by Tom De Hart. Childrens Pr., 1978. ISBN 0-516-07635-3 Subj: Careers – park rangers. Parks.

My dad's a smokejumper ill. by Don Hendricks. Childrens Pr., 1978. ISBN 0-516-07636-1 Subj: Careers – firefighters. Forest, woods.

Hill, Monica. *see* Watson, Jane Werner

Hill, Susan. *Beware, beware* ill. by Angela Barrett. Candlewick, 1993. ISBN 1-56402-245-5 Subj: Family life – mothers. Imagination. Night. Rhyming text. Seasons – winter.

Can it be true? ill. by Angela Barrett. Viking, 1988. ISBN 0-670-82517-4 Subj: Holidays – Christmas. Rhyming text.

Go away, bad dreams! ill. by Vanessa Julian-Ottie. Random House, 1985. ISBN 0-394-97222-8 Subj: Dreams. Emotions – fear. Family life. Night.

King of kings ill. by John Lawrence. Candlewick, 1993. ISBN 1-56402-210-2 Subj: Babies. Holidays – Christmas. Old age.

Simba's A-Z ill. by Doug Hart. Disney Pr., 1998. ISBN 0-7868-3168-5 Subj: ABC books. Animals. Animals – lions. Foreign lands – Africa. Language. Rhyming text.

Hille-Brandts, Lene. *The little black hen* tr. and adapt. by Marion Koenig; ill. by Sigrid Heuck. Childrens Pr., 1968. Translation of Die Henne Gudula. Subj: Behavior – dissatisfaction. Birds – chickens.

Hiller, Catherine. *Abracatabby* ill. by Victoria De Larrea. Coward, 1981. ISBN 0-698-30727-5 Subj: Animals – cats. Magic.

Argentaybee and the boonie ill. by Cyndy Szekeres. Coward, 1979. ISBN 0-698-20441-7 Subj: Behavior – misbehavior. Imagination – imaginary friends.

Hillerich, Robert L. *Rand McNally picturebook dictionary: a thousand words to see and say* (Rand McNally picturebook dictionary)

Hillert, Margaret. *The birthday car* ill. by Kelly Oechsli. Follett, 1966. ISBN 0-8136-5031-3 Subj: Birthdays. Toys.

The funny baby ill. by Hertha Depper. Follett, 1966. The tale of The Ugly Duckling by H. C. Andersen. ISBN 0-695-83300-6 Subj: Birds – ducks. Birds – swans. Character traits – appearance. Character traits – being different. Folk and fairy tales.

Happy birthday, dear dragon ill. by Carl Kock. Follett, 1977. ISBN 0-695-40743-0 Subj: Birthdays. Dragons.

The little cowboy and the big cowboy ill. by Dan Siculan. Follett, 1980. ISBN 0-695-41453-4 Subj: Cowboys. Family life – fathers.

Little Red Riding Hood (Grimm, Jacob)

The little runaway ill. by Irv Anderson. Follett, 1966. ISBN 0-8136-5052-6 Subj: Animals – cats. Behavior – running away.

The magic beans ill. by Mel Pekarsky. Follett, 1966. The tale of Jack and the beanstalk. ISBN 0-8136-5053-4 Subj: Folk and fairy tales. Giants. Plants.

Merry Christmas, dear dragon ill. by Carl Kock. Follett, 1980. ISBN 0-695-41359-7 Subj: Dragons. Holidays – Christmas.

Play ball ill. by Dick Martin. Follett, 1978. ISBN 0-695-40879-8 Subj: Activities – playing. Games. Sports – baseball.

The three bears ill. by Irma Wilde. Follett, 1963. Subj: Animals – bears. Folk and fairy tales.

The three goats ill. by Mel Pekarsky. Follett, 1963. The tale of The three billy goats Gruff. ISBN 0-695-48720-5 Subj: Animals – goats. Character traits – cleverness. Cumulative tales. Folk and fairy tales. Mythical creatures – trolls.

The three little pigs (The three little pigs)

Tom Thumb (Tom Thumb)

Up, up and away ill. by Robert Masheris. Modern Curriculum, 1981. ISBN 0-8136-5096-8 Subj: Moon. Space and space ships.

What is it? ill. by Kinuko Y. Craft. Follett, 1978. ISBN 0-695-40882-8 Subj: Activities – playing. Animals – dogs. Imagination. Rhyming text.

The yellow boat ill. by Ed Young. Follett, 1966. ISBN 0-8136-5033-X Subj: Boats, ships.

Hillman, Elizabeth. *Min-Yo and the moon dragon* ill. by John Wallner. Harcourt, 1992. ISBN 0-15-254230-2 Subj: Dragons. Folk and fairy tales. Foreign lands – China. Moon. Stars.

Hillman, Priscilla. *A Merry-Mouse book of favorite poems* ill. by author. Doubleday, 1981. ISBN 0-385-17104-8 Subj: Animals – mice. Poetry.

A Merry-Mouse book of months ill. by author. Doubleday, 1980. ISBN 0-385-15595-6 Subj: Animals – mice. Days of the week, months of the year. Format, unusual – toy and movable books. Rhyming text.

A Merry-Mouse book of nursery rhymes comp. and ill. by Priscilla Hillman. Doubleday, 1981. ISBN 0-385-17103-X Subj: Animals – mice. Nursery rhymes.

The Merry-Mouse book of opposites ill. by author. Doubleday, 1983. ISBN 0-385-17918-9 Subj: Animals – mice. Concepts – opposites. Poetry.

The Merry-Mouse book of prayers and graces ill. by author. Doubleday, 1983. ISBN 0-385-18337-2 Subj: Religion. Rhyming text.

The Merry-Mouse book of toys ill. by author. Doubleday, 1983. ISBN 0-385-17916-2 Subj: Animals – mice. Poetry. Toys.

A Merry-Mouse Christmas A B C ill. by author. Doubleday, 1980. ISBN 0-385-15597-2 Subj: ABC books. Animals – mice. Holidays – Christmas. Poetry.

The Merry-Mouse counting and colors book ill. by author. Doubleday, 1983. Subj: Animals – mice. Concepts – color. Counting, numbers.

The Merry-Mouse schoolhouse ill. by author. Doubleday, 1982. ISBN 0-385-17107-2 Subj: Animals – mice. School – first day.

Hilton, Nette. *Andrew Jessup* ill. by Cathy Wilcox. Ticknor & Fields, 1993. ISBN 0-395-66900-6 Subj: Friendship. Moving.

Dirty Dave ill. by Roland Harvey. Watts, 1990. ISBN 0-531-08461-2 Subj: Careers – tailors. Clothing. Crime. Foreign lands – Australia.

The long red scarf ill. by Margaret Power. Carolrhoda, 1990. ISBN 0-87614-399-0 Subj: Activities – knitting. Clothing. Family life – grandfathers. Gender roles.

Prince Lachlan ill. by Ann James. Watts, 1990. ISBN 0-531-08463-9 Subj: Behavior – misbehavior. Royalty. Royalty – princes.

A proper little lady ill. by Cathy Wilcox. Watts, 1990. ISBN 0-531-08460-4 Subj: Clothing.

Himler, Ronald. *The girl on the yellow giraffe* ill. by author. HarperCollins, 1976. ISBN 0-06-022318-9 Subj: City. Imagination.

Wake up, Jeremiah ill. by author. HarperCollins, 1979. ISBN 0-06-022324-3 Subj: Morning.

Himmelman, John. *Amanda and the magic garden* ill. by author. Viking, 1987. ISBN 0-670-80823-7 Subj: Animals. Gardens, gardening. Magic. Witches.

Amanda and the witch switch ill. by author. Viking, 1985. ISBN 0-670-11531-2 Subj: Behavior – misbehavior. Behavior – wishing. Character traits – meanness. Frogs and toads. Witches.

The Clover County carrot contest ill. by author. Silver Pr., 1991. ISBN 0-671-69637-8 Subj: Animals – beavers. Careers – inventors. Contests. Family life. Gardens, gardening.

A dandelion's life ill. by author. Childrens Pr., 1998. ISBN 0-516-21177-3 Subj: Flowers. Plants. Seeds.

The day-off machine ill. by author. Silver Pr., 1990. ISBN 0-671-69635-1 Subj: Activities – making things. Animals – beavers. Weather – snow.

Ellen and the goldfish ill. by author. HarperCollins, 1990. ISBN 0-06-022417-7 Subj: Activities – painting. Fish. Friendship.

The great leaf blast-off ill. by author. Silver Pr., 1990. ISBN 0-671-69634-3 Subj: Activities – making things. Animals – beavers. Family life. Trees.

A guest is a guest ill. by author. Dutton, 1991. ISBN 0-525-44720-2 Subj: Animals. Etiquette. Farms.

Honest Tulio ill. by author. BridgeWater, 1997. ISBN 0-8167-3812-2 Subj: Character traits – honesty. Cumulative tales.

Ibis: a true whale story ill. by author. Scholastic, 1990. ISBN 0-590-42848-9 Subj: Animals – whales. Character traits – kindness to animals.

J.J. versus the babysitter ill. by author. BridgeWater, 1996. ISBN 0-8167-3800-9 Subj: Activities – babysitting. Family life – brothers. Multiple births – twins.

Lights out! ill. by author. Troll, 1995. ISBN 0-8167-3450-X Subj: Bedtime. Camps, camping. Emotions – fear. Imagination. Night.

A luna moth's life ill. by author. Childrens Pr., 1998. ISBN 0-516-20821-7 Subj: Insects – moths.

Montigue on the high seas ill. by author. Viking, 1988. ISBN 0-670-81861-5 Subj: Animals. Animals – mice. Animals – moles.

Simpson Snail sings ill. by author. Dutton, 1992. ISBN 0-525-44978-7 Subj: Activities – singing. Animals – snails. Friendship.

The super camper caper ill. by author. Silver Pr., 1991. ISBN 0-671-69636-X Subj: Animals – beavers. Camps, camping. Careers – inventors.

Talester the lizard ill. by author. Dial, 1982. ISBN 0-8037-8788-X Subj: Reptiles – lizards.

The talking tree: or Don't believe everything you hear ill. by author. Viking, 1986. ISBN 0-670-80775-3 Subj: Animals – dogs. Trees.

Wanted: perfect parents ill. by author. BridgeWater, 1993. ISBN 0-8167-3028-8 Subj: Behavior. Family life.

A wood frog's life ill. by author. Childrens Pr., 1998. ISBN 0-516-21178-1 Subj: Forest, woods. Frogs and toads. Nature.

Hindley, Judy. *The best thing about a puppy* ill. by Pat Casey. Candlewick, 1998. ISBN 0-7636-0596-4 Subj: Animals – babies. Animals – dogs. Pets.

The big red bus ill. by William Benedict. Candlewick, 1995. ISBN 1-56402-639-6 Subj: Accidents. Buses. Format, unusual – toy and movable books. Rhyming text. Roads.

Crazy ABC ill. by Nick Sharratt. Candlewick, 1996. ISBN 1-56402-682-5 Subj: ABC books.

Eyes, nose, fingers and toes ill. by Brita Granström. Candlewick, 1999. ISBN 0-7636-0440-2 Subj: Anatomy. Rhyming text.

Funny walks ill. by Alex Ayliffe. BridgeWater, 1994. ISBN 0-8167-3313-9 Subj: Activities – walking. Animals.

How many twos? ill. by Stephen Bland. Doubleday, 1992. ISBN 0-385-30661-X Subj: Counting, numbers.

Into the jungle ill. by Melanie Epps. Candlewick, 1994. ISBN 1-56402-423-7 Subj: Activities – walking. Animals. Jungle.

Little and big ill. by Nick Sharratt. Candlewick, 1996. ISBN 1-56402-677-9 Subj: Concepts – size. Rhyming text.

The little train ill. by Robert Kendall. Watts, 1990. ISBN 0-531-08450-7 Subj: Activities – making things. Old age. Toys – trains.

Maybe it's a pirate ill. by Selina Young. Thomasson-Grant, 1992. ISBN 1-56566-016-1 Subj: Bedtime. Emotions – fear. Imagination.

Mrs. Mary Malarky's seven cats ill. by Denise Teasdale. Watts, 1990. ISBN 0-531-08422-1 Subj: Activities – babysitting. Animals – cats.

One by one ill. by Nick Sharratt. Candlewick, 1996. ISBN 1-56402-678-7 Subj: Animals. Counting, numbers. Rhyming text.

A piece of string is a wonderful thing ill. by Margaret Chamberlain. Candlewick, 1993. ISBN 1-56402-147-5 Subj: String.

The sleepy book: a lullaby ill. by Patrice Aggs. Orchard, 1992. ISBN 0-531-08571-6 Subj: Bedtime. Lullabies. Night. Sleep.

Soft and noisy ill. by Patrice Aggs. Walt Disney, 1992. ISBN 1-56282-225-X Subj: Noise, sounds. Senses – hearing.

A song of colors ill. by Mike Bostock. Candlewick, 1998. ISBN 0-7636-0320-1 Subj: Concepts – color. Poetry.

Ten bright eyes ill. by Alison Bartlett. Peachtree, 1998. ISBN 1-56145-173-8 Subj: Animals. Birds. Concepts – shape. Counting, numbers. Format, unusual – toy and movable books.

The tree ill. by Alison Wisenfeld. C.N. Potter, 1990. ISBN 0-517-57630-9 Subj: Trees.

Uncle Harold and the green hat ill. by Peter Utton. Farrar, 1991. ISBN 0-374-38030-9 Subj: Clothing – hats. Family life – aunts, uncles. Humor. Imagination. Magic. Rhyming text.

The wheeling and whirling-around book ill. by Margaret Chamberlain. Candlewick, 1994. ISBN 1-56402-490-3 Subj: Concepts – shape. Wheels.

Hine, Sesyle Joslin. *see* Joslin, Sesyle

Hines, Anna Grossnickle. *All by myself* ill. by author. Clarion, 1985. ISBN 0-89919-293-9 Subj: Behavior – growing up. Self-concept.

Bethany for real ill. by author. Greenwillow, 1985. ISBN 0-688-04009-8 Subj: Activities – playing. Imagination.

Big help ill. by author. Clarion, 1995. ISBN 0-395-68702-0 Subj: Family life – brothers and sisters.

Big like me ill. by author. Greenwillow, 1989. ISBN 0-688-08355-2 Subj: Babies. Behavior – growing up. Family life.

Come to the meadow ill. by author. Houghton Mifflin, 1984. ISBN 0-89919-227-0 Subj: Activities – picnicking. Family life – grandmothers.

Daddy makes the best spaghetti ill. by author. Clarion, 1986. ISBN 0-89919-388-9 Subj: Family life. Family life – fathers. Gender roles.

Don't worry, I'll find you ill. by author. Dutton, 1986. ISBN 0-525-44228-6 Subj: Behavior – lost. Shopping. Toys – dolls.

Even if I spill my milk? ill. by author. Clarion, 1994. ISBN 0-395-65010-0 Subj: Character traits – questioning. Emotions. Family life.

Gramma's walk ill. by author. Greenwillow, 1993. ISBN 0-688-11481-4 Subj: Family life – grandmothers. Handicaps – physical handicaps. Imagination. Nature. Sea and seashore.

Grandma gets grumpy ill. by author. Clarion, 1988. ISBN 0-89919-529-6 Subj: Activities – babysitting. Family life – grandmothers.

The greatest picnic in the world ill. by author. Clarion, 1991. ISBN 0-395-55266-4 Subj: Activities – picnicking. Rhyming text. Weather – rain.

I'll tell you what they say ill. by author. Greenwillow, 1987. ISBN 0-688-06487-6 Subj: Animals. Animals – dogs. Farms. Toys – bears.

It's just me, Emily ill. by author. Clarion, 1987. ISBN 0-89919-487-7 Subj: Activities – playing. Family life – mothers. Rhyming text.

Jackie's lunch box ill. by author. Greenwillow, 1991. ISBN 0-688-09694-8 Subj: Family life – sisters.

Keep your old hat ill. by author. Dutton, 1987. ISBN 0-525-44299-5 Subj: Activities – playing. Toys – dolls.

Maybe a band-aid will help ill. by author. Dutton, 1984. ISBN 0-525-44115-8 Subj: Family life – mothers. Problem solving. Toys – dolls.

Mean old Uncle Jack ill. by author. Clarion, 1990. ISBN 0-395-52137-8 Subj: Behavior. Family life – aunts, uncles. Holidays – Fourth of July.

Miss Emma's wild garden ill. by author. Greenwillow, 1997. ISBN 0-688-14693-7 Subj: Animals. Birds. Flowers. Gardens, gardening. Insects. Plants.

Moompa, Toby, and Bomp ill. by author. Clarion, 1993. ISBN 0-395-61301-9 Subj: Behavior – losing things. Family life – grandfathers. Toys – dolls.

Moon's wish ill. by author. Houghton Mifflin, 1992. ISBN 0-395-58114-1 Subj: Behavior – wishing. Family life. Moon.

My own big bed ill. by Mary Watson. Greenwillow, 1998. ISBN 0-688-15600-2 Subj: Emotions – fear. Furniture – beds.

Remember the butterflies ill. by author. Dutton, 1991. ISBN 0-525-44679-6 Subj: Death. Emotions – grief. Family life – grandfathers. Insects – butterflies, caterpillars. Memories, memory.

Rumble thumble boom! ill. by author. Greenwillow, 1992. ISBN 0-688-10912-8 Subj: Bedtime. Emotions – fear. Weather – storms. Weather – thunder.

The secret keeper ill. by author. Greenwillow, 1990. ISBN 0-688-08946-1 Subj: Behavior – secrets. Family life. Holidays – Christmas.

Sky all around ill. by author. Clarion, 1989. ISBN 0-89919-801-5 Subj: Family life – daughters. Family life – fathers. Night. Sky. Stars.

Taste the raindrops ill. by author. Greenwillow, 1983. ISBN 0-688-01423-2 Subj: Weather – rain.

They really like me! ill. by author. Greenwillow, 1989. ISBN 0-688-07734-X Subj: Activities – playing. Family life. Sibling rivalry.

What can you do in the rain? ill. by Thea Kliros. Greenwillow, 1999. ISBN 0-688-16077-8 Subj: Activities. Format, unusual – board books. Weather – rain.

What can you do in the snow? ill. by Thea Kliros. Greenwillow, 1999. ISBN 0-688-16078-6 Subj: Activities. Format, unusual – board books. Weather – snow.

What can you do in the sun? ill. by Thea Kliros. Greenwillow, 1999. ISBN 0-688-16080-8 Subj: Activities. Format, unusual – board books. Sun. Weather. Weather – rainbows.

What can you do in the wind? ill. by Thea Kliros. Greenwillow, 1999. ISBN 0-688-16079-4 Subj: Activities. Format, unusual – board books. Games. Weather – wind.

What Joe saw ill. by author. Greenwillow, 1994. ISBN 0-688-13124-7 Subj: Behavior – tardiness. Character traits – individuality.

When the goblins came knocking ill. by author. Greenwillow, 1995. ISBN 0-688-13736-9 Subj: Holidays – Halloween. Memories, memory. Rhyming text.

When we married Gary ill. by author. Greenwillow, 1996. ISBN 0-688-14277-X Subj: Emotions – love. Family life – step families.

Hines, Gary. *A Christmas tree in the White House* ill. by Alexandra Wallner. Holt, 1998. ISBN 0-8050-5076-0 Subj: Ecology. Holidays – Christmas. Trees. U.S. history.

The day of the high climber ill. by Anna Grossnickle Hines. Greenwillow, 1994. ISBN 0-688-11495-4 Subj: Careers – lumberjacks. Family life. Forest, woods. Trees.

A ride in the crummy ill. by Anna Grossnickle Hines. Greenwillow, 1991. ISBN 0-688-09692-1 Subj: Family life – grandfathers. Memories, memory. Trains.

Hines, Stephen W. *Laura Ingalls Wilder's fairy poems* (Wilder, Laura Ingalls)

Hines-Stephens, Sarah. *Bean's games* ill. by Anna Grossnickle Hines. Harcourt, 1998. ISBN 0-15-201606-6 Subj: Activities – playing. Animals – cats.

Hinton, S. E. *Big David, Little David* ill. by Alan Daniel. Doubleday, 1995. ISBN 0-385-31093-5 Subj: Family life – fathers. Names. School.

Hippel, Ursula Von. *see* Von Hippel, Ursula

Hippely, Hilary Horder. *Adventure on Klickitat Island* ill. by Barbara Upton. Dutton, 1998. ISBN 0-525-45293-1 Subj: Animals. Night. Rhyming text. Toys. Weather – storms.

The crimson ribbon ill. by Jo Ellen McAllister Stammen. Putnam, 1994. ISBN 0-399-22542-0 Subj: Behavior – needing someone. Family life.

A song for Lena ill. by Leslie A. Baker. Simon & Schuster, 1996. ISBN 0-689-80763-5 Subj: Activities – cooking. Family life – grandmothers. Food. Foreign lands – Hungary.

Hippopotamus, Eugene H. *see* Kraus, Robert

The Hippopotamus's birthday and other poems about animals and birds ill. by Roger Hughes; compiled by Linda M. Jennings. Hodder & Stoughton, 1987. ISBN 0-340-38681-9 Subj: Animals. Foreign lands – England. Poetry.

Hirano, Cathy. *The fox's egg* (Isami, Ikuyo)

Hirschberg, J. Cotter. *My friend the babysitter* (Watson, Jane Werner)

My friend the dentist (Watson, Jane Werner)

My friend the doctor (Watson, Jane Werner)

Sometimes a family has to move (Watson, Jane Werner)

Sometimes a family has to split up (Watson, Jane Werner)

Sometimes I get angry (Watson, Jane Werner)

Sometimes I'm afraid (Watson, Jane Werner)

Sometimes I'm jealous (Watson, Jane Werner)

Hirschi, Ron. *Faces in the forest* photos by Thomas D. Mangelsen. Cobblehill, 1997. ISBN 0-525-65224-8 Subj: Animals. Birds. Forest, woods.

Fall photos by Thomas D. Mangelsen. Dutton, 1991. ISBN 0-525-65053-9 Subj: Animals. Seasons – fall.

Forest ill. by Barbara Bash. Bantam, 1991. ISBN 0-553-07469-5 Subj: Animals. Ecology. Forest, woods.

Harvest song ill. by Deborah Haeffele. Cobblehill, 1991. ISBN 0-525-65067-9 Subj: Country. Family life – grandmothers. Farms.

Hungry little frog (Kuhn, Dwight)

Loon lake photos by Daniel J. Cox. Dutton, 1991. ISBN 0-525-65046-6 Subj: Animals. Birds – loons. Nature.

Mountain ill. by Barbara Bash. Bantam, 1992. ISBN 0-553-07998-0 Subj: Animals. Mountains.

Ocean ill. by Barbara Bash. Bantam, 1991. ISBN 0-553-07470-9 Subj: Animals. Fish. Sea and seashore.

Seya's song ill. by Constance R. Bergum. Sasquatch, 1992. ISBN 0-912365-62-5 Subj: Indians of North America – Clallam. Language. Seasons.

Spring photos by Thomas D. Mangelsen. Dutton, 1990. ISBN 0-525-65037-7 Subj: Animals. Seasons – spring.

Summer photos by Thomas D. Mangelsen. Dutton, 1991. ISBN 0-525-65054-7 Subj: Animals. Nature. Seasons – summer.

A time for babies photos by Thomas D. Mangelsen. Cobblehill, 1993. ISBN 0-525-65095-4 Subj: Animals. Animals – babies.

A time for playing photos by Thomas D. Mangelsen. Cobblehill, 1994. ISBN 0-525-65159-4 Subj: Activities – playing. Animals.

A time for singing photos by Thomas D. Mangelsen. Cobblehill, 1994. ISBN 0-525-65096-2 Subj: Activities – singing. Animals. Communication. Noise, sounds.

A time for sleeping photos by Thomas D. Mangelsen. Cobblehill, 1993. ISBN 0-525-65128-4 Subj: Animals. Sleep.

What is a bird? photos by Galen Burrell. Walker, 1987. ISBN 0-8027-6721-4 Subj: Birds. Science.

What is a cat? photos by Linda Quartman Younker. Walker, 1991. ISBN 0-8027-8123-3 Subj: Animals – cats.

What is a horse? photos by Linda Quartman Yonker and author. Walker, 1989. ISBN 0-8027-6877-6 Subj: Animals – horses, ponies.

Where are my bears? photos by Erwin and Peggy Bauer. Bantam, 1992. ISBN 0-553-07805-4 Subj: Animals – bears. Animals – endangered animals.

Where are my prairie dogs and black-footed ferrets? photos by Erwin and Peggy Bauer. Bantam, 1992. ISBN 0-553-07802-X Subj: Animals – endangered animals. Animals – ferrets. Animals – prairie dogs.

Where are my puffins, whales, and seals? photos by Erwin and Peggy Bauer. Bantam, 1992. ISBN 0-553-07803-8 Subj: Animals – endangered animals. Animals – seals. Animals – whales. Birds – puffins.

Where are my swans, whooping cranes, and singing loons? photos by Erwin and Peggy Bauer. Bantam, 1992. ISBN 0-553-07801-1 Subj: Animals – endangered animals. Birds – cranes. Birds – loons. Birds – swans.

Where do birds live? photos by Galen Burrell. Walker, 1987. ISBN 0-8027-6723-0 Subj: Birds. Science.

Where do horses live? photos by Linda Quartman Yonker and author. Walker, 1989. ISBN 0-8027-6879-2 Subj: Animals – horses, ponies.

Who lives in . . . Alligator Swamp? photos by Galen Burrell. Dodd, 1987. ISBN 0-396-09123-7 Subj: Animals. Forest, woods. Reptiles – alligators, crocodiles. Science.

Who lives in . . . the forest? photos by Galen Burrell. Dodd, 1987. ISBN 0-396-09121-0 Subj: Animals. Birds. Forest, woods.

Winter photos by Thomas D. Mangelsen. Dutton, 1990. ISBN 0-525-65026-1 Subj: Animals. Seasons – winter.

Hirschmann, Linda. *In a lick of a flick of a tongue* ill. by Jeni Bassett. Dodd, 1980. ISBN 0-396-07833-8 Subj: Anatomy. Animals.

Hirsh, Marilyn. *Captain Jiri and Rabbi Jacob: from a Jewish folktale* ill. by author. Holiday, 1976. ISBN 0-8234-0279-7 Subj: Folk and fairy tales. Jewish culture.

Could anything be worse? a Yiddish tale ill. by author. Holiday, 1974. ISBN 0-8234-0239-8 Subj: Humor. Jewish culture.

Deborah the dybbuk: a ghost story ill. by author. Holiday, 1978. ISBN 0-8234-0315-7 Subj: Behavior – misbehavior. Character traits – kindness to animals. Ghosts.

I love Hanukkah ill. by author. Holiday, 1984. ISBN 0-8234-0525-7 Subj: Holidays – Hanukkah. Jewish culture.

I love Passover ill. by author. Holiday, 1985. ISBN 0-8234-0549-4 Subj: Holidays – Passover. Jewish culture. Religion.

Joseph who loved the Sabbath ill. by Devis Grebu. Viking, 1986. ISBN 0-670-81194-7 Subj: Folk and fairy tales. Jewish culture. Religion.

Leela and the watermelon by Marilyn Hirsh and Maya Narayan; ill. by Marilyn Hirsh. Crown, 1971. Subj: Babies. Food. Foreign lands – India.

One little goat: a Passover song ill. by author. Holiday, 1979. ISBN 0-8234-0345-9 Subj: Folk and fairy tales. Holidays – Passover. Jewish culture. Songs.

The pink suit ill. by author. Crown, 1970. Subj: Activities – trading. Emotions – embarrassment. Family life. Jewish culture.

Potato pancakes all around: a Hanukkah tale ill. by author. Bonim Books, 1978. ISBN 0-88482-762-3 Subj: Food. Holidays – Hanukkah. Jewish culture. Religion.

The Rabbi and the twenty-nine witches ill. by author. Holiday, 1976. ISBN 0-8234-0270-3 Subj: Character traits – cleverness. Jewish culture. Witches.

Where is Yonkela? ill. by author. Crown, 1969. Subj: Babies. Behavior – lost. Jewish culture.

Hirst, Robin. *My place in space* by Robin and Sally Hirst; ill. by Roland Harvey and Joe Levine. Watts, 1990. ISBN 0-531-08459-0 Subj: Astronomy. Buses. Science. Space and space ships.

Hirst, Sally. *My place in space* (Hirst, Robin)

Hiser, Berniece T. *The adventure of Charlie and his wheat-straw hat* ill. by Mary Szilagyi. Dodd, 1986. ISBN 0-396-08772-8 Subj: Character traits – bravery. Clothing – hats. Family life – grandmothers. U.S. history.

Hiskey, Iris. *Cassandra who?* ill. by Normand Chartier. Simon & Schuster, 1992. ISBN 0-671-70574-1 Subj: Animals – cats. Animals – pigs. Clothing. Parties.

I like a snack on an iceberg by Iris Hiskey Arno; ill. by John Sandford. HarperFestival, 1999. ISBN 0-694-01176-2 Subj: Animals. Food. Rhyming text.

Hissey, Jane. *Hoot* ill. by author. Random House, 1997. Subj: Bedtime. Birds – owls. Night. Toys.

Jolly snow ill. by author. Putnam, 1991. ISBN 0-399-22131-X Subj: Activities – playing. Toys. Toys – bears. Weather – snow.

Jolly Tall ill. by author. Putnam, 1990. ISBN 0-399-21827-0 Subj: Activities – knitting. Toys. Toys – bears.

Little Bear lost ill. by author. Putnam, 1989. ISBN 0-399-21743-6 Subj: Behavior – losing things. Games. Toys. Toys – bears.

Little bear's bedtime ill. by author. Random House, 1992. ISBN 0-679-84176-8 Subj: Bedtime. Format, unusual – board books. Rhyming text. Toys – bears.

Little Bear's day ill. by author. Random House, 1993. ISBN 0-679-84175-X Subj: Format, unusual – board books. Rhyming text. Toys – bears.

Little Bear's trousers: an Old Bear story ill. by author. Putnam, 1990. ISBN 0-399-21493-3 Subj: Clothing – pants. Toys – bears.

Old Bear ill. by author. Philomel, 1986. ISBN 0-399-21401-1 Subj: Friendship. Toys. Toys – bears.

Old bear, a board book ill. by author. 1st American board book ed. Philomel, 1997. ISBN 0-399-23205-2 Subj: Format, unusual – board books. Friendship. Toys. Toys – bears.

Old Bear, a pop-up book ill. by author; paper engineering by Dennis K. Meyer. Hutchinson, 1995. ISBN 0-09-176506-4 Subj: Format, unusual – toy and movable books. Toys. Toys – bears.

Ruff ill. by author. Random House, 1994. ISBN 0-679-86042-8 Subj: Birthdays. Parties. Toys.

Hitz, Demi. *see* Demi

Ho, Minfong. *Brother Rabbit: a Cambodian tale* ill. by Jennifer Hewitson. Lothrop, 1997. ISBN 0-688-12553-0 Subj: Animals. Animals – rabbits. Folk and fairy tales. Foreign lands – Cambodia.

Hush! a Thai lullaby ill. by Holly Meade. Orchard, 1996. ISBN 0-531-08850-2 Subj: Animals. Caldecott award honor books. Family life – mothers. Foreign lands – Thailand. Lullabies. Noise, sounds.

Maples in the mist: children's poems from the Tang Dynasty ill. by Jean and Mou-sien Tseng; trans. by Minfong Ho. Lothrop, 1996. ISBN 0-688-12044-X Subj: Foreign lands – China. Poetry.

The two brothers by Minfong Ho and Saphan Ros; ill. by Jean and Mou-sien Tseng. Lothrop, 1995. ISBN 0-688-12551-4 Subj: Behavior – growing up. Folk and fairy tales. Foreign lands – Cambodia.

Hoban, Brom. *Skunk Lane* ill. by author. Harper-Collins, 1983. ISBN 0-06-022348-0 Subj: Animals – skunks. Behavior – growing up. Songs.

Hoban, Julia. *Amy loves the rain* ill. by Lillian Hoban. HarperCollins, 1989. ISBN 0-06-022358-8 Subj: Family life. Weather – rain.

Amy loves the snow ill. by Lillian Hoban. Harper-Collins, 1989. ISBN 0-06-022395-2 Subj: Family life. Snowmen. Weather – snow.

Amy loves the sun ill. by Lillian Hoban. Harper-Collins, 1988. ISBN 0-06-022397-9 Subj: Family life. Flowers.

Amy loves the wind ill. by Lillian Hoban. Harper-Collins, 1988. ISBN 0-06-022403-7 Subj: Seasons – fall. Weather – wind.

Buzby to the rescue ill. by John Himmelman. HarperCollins, 1993. ISBN 0-06-021024-9 Subj: Activities – working. Animals – cats. Behavior – mistakes. Mystery stories.

Quick chick ill. by Lillian Hoban. Dutton, 1989. ISBN 0-525-44490-4 Subj: Animals. Birds – chickens. Farms. Names.

Hoban, Lillian. *Arthur's back to school day* ill. by author. HarperCollins, 1996. ISBN 0-06-024956-0 Subj: Animals – chimpanzees. Family life – brothers and sisters. Food. Safety. School.

Arthur's Christmas cookies ill. by author. Harper-Collins, 1972. ISBN 0-06-022368-5 Subj: Activities – cooking. Animals – chimpanzees. Holidays – Christmas.

Arthur's funny money ill. by author. HarperCollins, 1981. ISBN 0-06-022344-8 Subj: Animals – chimpanzees. Money. Problem solving.

Arthur's great big Valentine ill. by author. Harper-Collins, 1989. ISBN 0-06-022407-X Subj: Animals – chimpanzees. Emotions – anger. Friendship. Holidays – Valentine's Day.

Arthur's pen pal ill. by author. HarperCollins, 1976. ISBN 0-06-022372-3 Subj: Activities – writing. Animals – chimpanzees. Sibling rivalry.

Arthur's prize reader ill. by author. HarperCollins, 1978. ISBN 0-06-022380-4 Subj: Activities – reading. Animals – chimpanzees. Family life.

Big Little Otter ill. by author. HarperCollins, 1997. ISBN 0-694-00850-8 Subj: Animals – otters. Behav-

ior – growing up. Format, unusual – board books.

The case of the two masked robbers ill. by author. HarperCollins, 1986. ISBN 0-06-022299-9 Subj: Animals. Animals – raccoons. Eggs. Masks. Mystery stories.

Harry's song ill. by author. Greenwillow, 1980. ISBN 0-688-84220-8 Subj: Animals – rabbits. Songs.

Here come raccoons ill. by author. Holt, 1977. ISBN 0-03-017781-2 Subj: Animals – raccoons. Multiple births – twins.

It's really Christmas ill. by author. Greenwillow, 1982. ISBN 0-688-00831-3 Subj: Animals – mice. Behavior – wishing. Holidays – Christmas.

The laziest robot in zone one by Lillian and Phoebe Hoban; ill. by Lillian Hoban. HarperCollins, 1983. ISBN 0-06-022352-9 Subj: Animals – dogs. Behavior – lost. Robots.

Mr. Pig and family ill. by author. HarperCollins, 1980. ISBN 0-06-022384-7 Subj: Animals – pigs. Family life.

Mr. Pig and Sonny too ill. by author. Harper-Collins, 1977. ISBN 0-06-022341-3 Subj: Animals – pigs. Sports – ice skating. Weddings.

No, no, Sammy Crow ill. by author. Greenwillow, 1981. ISBN 0-688-84297-6 Subj: Birds. Character traits – bravery. Family life – brothers and sisters.

Silly Tilly and the Easter bunny ill. by author. HarperCollins, 1987. ISBN 0-06-022693-6 Subj: Animals – moles. Holidays – Easter. Humor.

Silly Tilly's Valentine ill. by author. HarperCollins, 1998. ISBN 0-06-027401-8 Subj: Animals – moles. Holidays – Valentine's Day. Memories, memory. Weather – snow.

Stick-in-the-mud turtle ill. by author. Greenwillow, 1977. ISBN 0-688-84045-0 Subj: Behavior – dissatisfaction. Poverty. Reptiles – turtles, tortoises.

The sugar snow spring ill. by author. Harper-Collins, 1973. ISBN 0-06-022334-0 Subj: Animals – mice. Seasons – spring. Weather – cold. Weather – snow.

Turtle spring ill. by author. Greenwillow, 1978. ISBN 0-688-84136-8 Subj: Reptiles – turtles, tortoises. Seasons – spring.

Hoban, Phoebe. *The laziest robot in zone one* (Hoban, Lillian)

Hoban, Russell. *Ace Dragon Ltd.* ill. by Quentin Blake. Merrimack, 1981. ISBN 0-224-01706-3 Subj: Activities – flying. Dragons.

Arthur's new power ill. by Byron Barton. Crowell, 1978. ISBN 0-690-01371-X Subj: Progress. Reptiles – alligators, crocodiles.

A baby sister for Frances ill. by Lillian Hoban. HarperCollins, 1964. ISBN 0-06-022336-7 Subj: Animals – badgers. Behavior – running away.

Emotions – envy, jealousy. Family life. Sibling rivalry.

A bargain for Frances ill. by Lillian Hoban. Harper, 1992. ISBN 0-06-022330-8 Subj: Animals – badgers. Friendship.

The battle of Zormla ill. by Colin McNaughton. Putnam, 1982. ISBN 0-399-61200-9 Subj: Sibling rivalry.

Bedtime for Frances ill. by Garth Williams. HarperCollins, 1995. ISBN 0-06-022351-0 Subj: Animals – badgers. Bedtime. Emotions – fear.

Best friends for Frances ill. by Lillian Hoban. HarperCollins, 1994. ISBN 0-06-022328-6 Subj: Animals – badgers. Family life – brothers. Family life – sisters. Friendship.

Big John Turkle ill. by Martin Baynton. Holt, 1984. ISBN 0-03-069499-X Subj: Character traits – meanness.

A birthday for Frances ill. by Lillian Hoban. HarperCollins, 1995. ISBN 0-06-022339-1 Subj: Animals – badgers. Birthdays. Emotions – envy, jealousy.

Bread and jam for Frances ill. by Lillian Hoban. HarperCollins, 1993. ISBN 0-06-022360-X Subj: Animals – badgers. Food. School.

Charlie Meadows ill. by Martin Baynton. Holt, 1984. ISBN 0-03-069502-3 Subj: Activities – dancing. Animals – mice. Birds – owls.

Charlie the tramp ill. by Lillian Hoban. Four Winds, 1967. Subj: Activities – working. Animals – beavers.

La corona and the tin frog ill. by Nicola Bayley. Merrimack, 1981. ISBN 0-224-01397-1 Subj: Emotions. Toys.

The dancing tigers ill. by David Gentleman. Merrimack, 1981. ISBN 0-224-01374-2 Subj: Activities – dancing. Animals – tigers. Sports – hunting.

Dinner at Alberta's ill. by James Marshall. Crowell, 1975. ISBN 0-690-23993-9 Subj: Behavior. Etiquette. Food. Reptiles – alligators, crocodiles.

Emmet Otter's jug-band Christmas ill. by Lillian Hoban. Parents, 1971. ISBN 0-819-30405-0 Subj: Animals – otters. Character traits – generosity. Holidays – Christmas. Music.

Flat cat ill. by Clive Scruton. Putnam, 1980. ISBN 0-399-61159-2 Subj: Animals – cats. Animals – mice. Animals – rats.

The flight of Bembel Rudzuk ill. by Colin McNaughton. Putnam, 1982. ISBN 0-399-61198-3 Subj: Imagination.

Goodnight ill. by Lillian Hoban. Norton, 1966. Subj: Bedtime. Emotions – fear. Imagination. Poetry.

The great gum drop robbery ill. by Colin McNaughton. Putnam, 1982. ISBN 0-399-61184-3 Subj: Imagination. Sibling rivalry.

Harvey's hideout ill. by Lillian Hoban. Four Winds, 1980, c1969. ISBN 0-590-07767-8 Subj: Animals – muskrats. Behavior – fighting, arguing. Family life – brothers. Family life – sisters.

How Tom beat Captain Najork and his hired sportsmen ill. by Quentin Blake. Atheneum, 1974. ISBN 0-689-30441-2 Subj: Behavior – misbehavior. Games.

Jim Frog ill. by Martin Baynton. Holt, 1984. ISBN 0-03-069501-5 Subj: Frogs and toads. Insects – beetles.

Lavina bat ill. by Martin Baynton. Holt, 1984. ISBN 0-03-069502-1 Subj: Animals – bats.

The little Brute family ill. by Lillian Hoban. Macmillan, 1966. ISBN 0-02-744110-5 Subj: Character traits – meanness. Etiquette.

The marzipan pig ill. by Quentin Blake. Farrar, 1987. ISBN 0-374-34859-6 Subj: Animals. Circular tales. Emotions. Food.

The mole family's Christmas ill. by Lillian Hoban. Four Winds, 1980, c1969. ISBN 0-590-07774-0 Subj: Animals – moles. Character traits – generosity. Holidays – Christmas.

Monsters ill. by Quentin Blake. Scholastic, 1989. ISBN 0-590-43422-5 Subj: Activities – drawing. Imagination. Monsters.

A near thing for Captain Najork ill. by Quentin Blake. Atheneum, 1976. ISBN 0-689-30503-6 Subj: Humor. Self-concept.

Nothing to do ill. by Lillian Hoban. HarperCollins, 1964. Subj: Animals – possums. Behavior – boredom.

The rain door ill. by Quentin Blake. Crowell, 1987. ISBN 0-690-04577-8 Subj: Animals – horses, ponies. Animals – lions. Imagination. Weather – rain.

Some snow said hello ill. by Lillian Hoban. HarperCollins, 1963. Subj: Seasons – winter. Sibling rivalry. Weather – snow.

The sorely trying day ill. by Lillian Hoban. HarperCollins, 1964. Subj: Behavior – bad day. Behavior – fighting, arguing.

The stone doll of Sister Brute ill. by Lillian Hoban. Macmillan, 1968. Subj: Animals – dogs. Emotions. Toys – dolls.

Ten what? a mystery counting book by Russell Hoban and Sylvie Selig; ill. by authors. Scribners, 1974. ISBN 0-684-13400-4 Subj: Counting, numbers.

They came from Aargh! ill. by Colin McNaughton. Putnam, 1981. ISBN 0-399-61182-7 Subj: Family life. Sibling rivalry.

Tom and the two handles ill. by Lillian Hoban. HarperCollins, 1965. ISBN 0-06-022431-2 Subj: Behavior – fighting, arguing.

Hoban, Tana. *A B See!* photos by author. Greenwillow, 1982. ISBN 0-688-00833-X Subj: ABC books.

All about where photos by author. Greenwillow, 1991. ISBN 0-688-09698-0 Subj: Concepts. Language.

Big ones, little ones ill. by author. Greenwillow, 1976. ISBN 0-688-84040-X Subj: Animals. Concepts – size. Wordless.

Black on white photos by author. Greenwillow, 1993. ISBN 0-688-11918-2 Subj: Concepts. Wordless.

A children's zoo photos by author. Greenwillow, 1985. ISBN 0-688-05204-5 Subj: Animals. Birds. Zoos.

Circles, triangles, and squares ill. by author. Macmillan, 1974. ISBN 0-02-744830-4 Subj: Concepts – shape. Wordless.

Colors everywhere photos by author. Greenwillow, 1994. ISBN 0-688-12763-0 Subj: Concepts – color. Wordless.

Construction zone ill. by author. Greenwillow, 1997. ISBN 0-688-12285-X Subj: Activities – making things. Machines.

Count and see ill. by author. Macmillan, 1972. ISBN 0-02-744800-2 Subj: Counting, numbers.

Dig, drill, dump, fill ill. by author. Greenwillow, 1975. ISBN 0-688-84016-7 Subj: Activities – digging. Machines. Wordless.

Dots, spots, speckles, and stripes photos by author. Greenwillow, 1987. ISBN 0-688-06863-4 Subj: Concepts. Concepts – color. Concepts – shape.

Exactly the opposite photos by author. Greenwillow, 1990. ISBN 0-688-08862-7 Subj: Concepts – opposites. Wordless.

I read signs photos by author. Greenwillow, 1983. ISBN 0-688-02318-5 Subj: Activities – reading. Communication.

I read symbols photos by author. Greenwillow, 1983. ISBN 0-688-02332-0 Subj: Activities – reading. Communication.

I walk and read photos by author. Greenwillow, 1984. ISBN 0-688-02576-5 Subj: Activities – reading. Activities – walking.

Is it larger? Is it smaller? photos by author. Greenwillow, 1985. ISBN 0-688-04028-4 Subj: Concepts – size. Wordless.

Is it red? Is it yellow? Is it blue? photos by author. Greenwillow, 1978. ISBN 0-688-84171-6 Subj: City. Concepts – color. Concepts – shape. Concepts – size. Wordless.

Is it rough? Is it smooth? Is it shiny? photos by author. Greenwillow, 1984. ISBN 0-688-03824-7 Subj: Concepts. Wordless.

Just look photos by author. Greenwillow, 1996. ISBN 0-688-14041-6 Subj: Format, unusual – toy and movable books. Wordless.

Let's count photos by author. Greenwillow, 1999. ISBN 0-688-16009-3 Subj: Counting, numbers.

Look again photos by author. Macmillan, 1971. ISBN 0-02-744050-8 Subj: Participation. Senses – seeing. Wordless.

Look book photos by author. Greenwillow, 1997. ISBN 0-688-14972-3 Subj: Format, unusual – toy and movable books. Nature. Wordless.

Look! Look! Look! photos by author. Greenwillow, 1988. ISBN 0-688-07240-2 Subj: Concepts. Format, unusual. Wordless.

Look up, look down photos by author. Greenwillow, 1992. ISBN 0-688-10578-5 Subj: Concepts – up and down.

More, fewer, less photos by author. Greenwillow, 1998. ISBN 0-688-15694-0 Subj: Concepts. Counting, numbers. Wordless.

More than one photos by author. Greenwillow, 1981. ISBN 0-688-00597-7 Subj: Language.

Of colors and things photos by author. Greenwillow, 1989. ISBN 0-688-07535-5 Subj: Concepts – color.

One little kitten photos by author. Greenwillow, 1979. ISBN 0-688-80222-2 Subj: Animals – cats. Rhyming text.

1, 2, 3 photos by author. Greenwillow, 1985. ISBN 0-688-02579-X Subj: Counting, numbers. Format, unusual – board books. Wordless.

Over, under and through photos by author. Aladdin, 1987. ISBN 0-689-71111-5 Subj: Concepts.

Panda, panda ill. by author. Greenwillow, 1986. ISBN 0-688-06564-3 Subj: Animals – pandas. Format, unusual – board books.

Push-pull, empty-full: a book of opposites ill. by author. Collier, 1976, c1972. ISBN 0-02-043600-9 Subj: Concepts – opposites.

Red, blue, yellow shoe photos by author. Greenwillow, 1986. ISBN 0-688-06563-5 Subj: Concepts – color. Format, unusual – board books.

Round and round and round photos by author. Greenwillow, 1983. ISBN 0-688-01814-9 Subj: Concepts – shape.

Shadows and reflections photos by author. Greenwillow, 1990. ISBN 0-688-07090-6 Subj: Shadows. Wordless.

Shapes and things ill. by author. Macmillan, 1970. ISBN 0-02-744060-5 Subj: Concepts – shape. Wordless.

Shapes, shapes, shapes photos by author. Greenwillow, 1985. ISBN 0-688-05833-7 Subj: Concepts – shape. Wordless.

So many circles, so many squares photos by author. Greenwillow, 1998. ISBN 0-688-15166-3 Subj: Concepts – shape. Wordless.

Spirals, curves, fanshapes and lines photos by author. Greenwillow, 1992. ISBN 0-688-11229-3 Subj: Concepts – shape. Concepts – size. Wordless.

Take another look photos by author. Greenwillow, 1981. ISBN 0-688-84298-4 Subj: Concepts. Wordless.

26 letters and 99 cents photos by author. Greenwillow, 1987. ISBN 0-688-06362-4 Subj: ABC books. Counting, numbers. Format, unusual.

What is it? photos by author. Greenwillow, 1985. ISBN 0-688-02577-3 Subj: Format, unusual – board books. Wordless.

What is that? photos by author. Greenwillow, 1994. ISBN 0-688-12920-X Subj: Format, unusual – board books. Wordless.

Where is it? ill. by author. Macmillan, 1974. ISBN 0-02-744070-2 Subj: Animals – rabbits. Participation. Rhyming text.

White on black photos by author. Greenwillow, 1993. ISBN 0-688-11919-0 Subj: Concepts. Format, unusual – board books.

Who are they? photos by author. Greenwillow, 1994. ISBN 0-688-12921-8 Subj: Animals. Format, unusual – board books. Wordless.

Hobbie, Holly. *Toot and Puddle* ill. by author. Little, 1997. ISBN 0-316-36552-1 Subj: Activities – traveling. Animals – pigs. Friendship. Letters, cards.

Toot and Puddle, a present for Toot ill. by author. Little, 1998. ISBN 0-316-36556-4 Subj: Animals – pigs. Birthdays. Gifts.

Toot and Puddle, I'll be home for Christmas ill. by author. Little, 2001. ISBN 0-316-36623-4 Subj: Activities – traveling. Animals – pigs. Holidays – Christmas. Weather – blizzards. Weather – snow. Weather – storms.

Toot and Puddle, Puddle's ABC ill. by author. Little, 2000. ISBN 0-316-36593-9 Subj: ABC books. Animals – pigs.

Toot and Puddle, you are my sunshine ill. by author. Little, 1999. ISBN 0-316-36562-9 Subj: Animals – pigs. Emotions. Friendship. Weather – storms. Weather – thunder.

Hobbs, Will. *Beardream* ill. by Jill Kastner. Atheneum, 1997. ISBN 0-689-31973-8 Subj: Activities – dancing. Animals – bears. Folk and fairy tales. Hibernation. Indians of North America – Ute.

Howling Hill ill. by Jill Kastner. Morrow, 1998. ISBN 0-688-15430-1 Subj: Animals – bears. Animals – wolves. Behavior – growing up. Behavior – lost. Emotions – loneliness.

Hoberman, Mary Ann. *And to think that we thought that we'd never be friends* ill. by Kevin Hawkes. Crown, 1999. ISBN 0-517-80070-5 Subj: Family life – brothers and sisters. Friendship. Rhyming text.

The cozy book ill. by Tony Chen. Viking, 1982. ISBN 0-670-24447-3 Subj: Poetry.

Fathers, mothers, sisters, brothers ill. by Marylin Hafner. Little, 1991. ISBN 0-316-36736-2 Subj: Family life. Poetry.

A fine fat pig and other animal poems ill. by Malcah Zeldis. HarperCollins, 1991. ISBN 0-06-022426-6 Subj: Animals. Poetry.

A house is a house for me ill. by Betty Fraser. Viking, 1978. ISBN 0-670-38016-4 Subj: Homes, houses. Rhyming text.

How do I go? by Mary Ann and Norman Hoberman; ill. by authors. Little, 1958. Subj: Transportation.

I like old clothes ill. by Jacqueline Chwast. Knopf, 1976. ISBN 0-394-93092-4 Subj: Clothing. Rhyming text.

Miss Mary Mack ill. by Nadine Bernard Westcott. Little, 1998. ISBN 0-316-93118-7 Subj: Animals – elephants. Nursery rhymes.

Mr. and Mrs. Muddle ill. by Catharine O'Neill. Little, 1988. ISBN 0-316-36735-4 Subj: Animals – horses, ponies. Sports.

Nuts to you and nuts to me: an alphabet of poems ill. by Ronni Solbert. Knopf, 1974. ISBN 0-394-92742-7 Subj: ABC books. Poetry.

One of each ill. by Marjorie Priceman. Little, 1997. ISBN 0-316-36731-1 Subj: Animals – dogs. Behavior – sharing. Friendship. Rhyming text.

Hoberman, Norman. *How do I go?* (Hoberman, Mary Ann)

Hobson, Bruce. *see* Mwenye Hadithi

Hobson, Laura Z. *"I'm going to have a baby!"* ill. by May Kirkham. John Day, 1967. Subj: Babies. Birth. Family life – new sibling.

Hobzek, Mildred. *We came a-marching . . . 1, 2, 3* ill. by William Pène Du Bois. Parents, 1978. ISBN 0-8193-0975-3 Subj: Folk and fairy tales. Songs.

Hodeir, André. *Warwick's 3 bottles* by André Hodeir and Tomi Ungerer; ill. by Tomi Ungerer. Grove Pr., 1966. Subj: Behavior – misbehavior. Country. Reptiles – alligators, crocodiles.

Hodge, Deborah. *Beavers* ill. by Pat Stephens. Kids Can Pr., 1998. ISBN 1-55074-429-1 Subj: Animals – beavers.

Deer, moose, elk and caribou ill. by Pat Stephens. Kids Can Pr., 1998. ISBN 1-55074-435-6 Subj: Animals. Animals – deer. Animals – elk. Animals – moose. Animals – reindeer.

Wild cats: cougars, bobcats and lynx ill. by Nancy Gray Ogle. Kids Can Pr., 1997. ISBN 1-55074-267-1 Subj: Animals – bobcats. Animals – cats. Animals – cougars. Animals – lynx.

Hodges, Margaret. *Buried moon* ill. by Jamichael Henterly. Little, 1990. ISBN 0-316-36793-1 Subj: Folk and fairy tales. Forest, woods. Moon.

Comus adapt. by Margaret Hodges from A masque at Ludlow Castle by John Milton; ill. by Trina Schart Hyman. Holiday, 1996. ISBN 0-8234-1146-X Subj: Careers – magicians. Family life – brothers and sisters. Folk and fairy tales. Forest, woods. Magic. Mythical creatures. Theater.

The fire bringer: a Paiute Indian legend ill. by Peter Parnall. Little, 1972. ISBN 0-316-36783-4 Subj: Folk and fairy tales. Indians of North America – Paiute.

The golden deer ill. by Daniel San Souci. Scribners, 1992. ISBN 0-684-19218-7 Subj: Animals – deer. Character traits – kindness to animals. Foreign lands – India. Religion. Sports – hunting.

The hero of Bremen ill. by Charles Mikolaycak. Holiday, 1993. ISBN 0-8234-0934-1 Subj: Careers – shoemakers. Folk and fairy tales. Foreign lands – Germany. Handicaps – physical handicaps. Knights. War.

Hidden in sand ill. by Paul Birling. Scribners, 1994. ISBN 0-684-19559-3 Subj: Character traits – persistence. Folk and fairy tales. Foreign lands – India.

The kitchen knight ill. by Trina Schart Hyman. Holiday, 1990. ISBN 0-8234-0787-X Subj: Behavior – fighting, arguing. Emotions – love. Folk and fairy tales. Knights. Middle Ages.

Molly Limbo ill. by Elizabeth J. Miles. Atheneum, 1996. ISBN 0-689-80581-0 Subj: Foreign lands – England. Ghosts. Homes, houses.

Moses ill. by Mike Wimmer. Harcourt, 1999. ISBN 0-15-200946-9 Subj: Religion – Moses.

Saint Christopher ill. by Richard Jesse Watson. Eerdmans, 1997. ISBN 0-8028-5077-4 Subj: Religion.

Saint George and the dragon ill. by Trina Schart Hyman. Little, 1984. ISBN 0-316-36789-3 Subj: Caldecott award books. Dragons. Folk and fairy tales. Foreign lands – England. Middle Ages.

St. Jerome and the lion ill. by Barry Moser. Orchard, 1991. ISBN 0-531-08538-4 Subj: Animals – lions. Character traits – kindness to animals. Folk and fairy tales. Religion.

Saint Patrick and the peddler ill. by Paul Brett Johnson. Orchard, 1993. ISBN 0-531-05489-6 Subj: Character traits – generosity. Character traits – luck. Folk and fairy tales. Foreign lands – Ireland. Ghosts.

Silent night: the song and its story ill. by Tim Ladwig. Eerdmans, 1997. ISBN 0-8028-5138-X Subj: Family life. Holidays – Christmas. Music. Songs.

Up the chimney ill. by Amanda Harvey. Holiday, 1998. ISBN 0-8234-1354-3 Subj: Family life – sisters. Folk and fairy tales. Foreign lands – England. Witches.

The voice of the great bell by Lafcadio Hearn; retold by Margaret Hodges; ill. by Ed Young. Little, 1989. ISBN 0-316-36791-5 Subj: Folk and fairy tales. Foreign lands – China.

The wave ill. by Blair Lent. Houghton Mifflin, 1964. ISBN 0-395-06817-7 Subj: Caldecott award honor books. Folk and fairy tales. Foreign lands – Japan. Tsunamis.

Hodgetts, Blake Christopher. *Dream of the dinosaurs* ill. by Victoria Hodgetts. Doubleday, 1978. ISBN 0-385-12139-3 Subj: Dinosaurs. Dreams.

Hoestlandt, Jo. *Star of fear, star of hope* ill. by Johanna Kang; trans. from French by Mark Polizzotti. Walker, 1995. ISBN 0-8027-8374-0 Subj: Foreign lands – France. Friendship. Holocaust. Jewish culture. War.

Hoff, Carol. *The four friends* ill. by Jim Ponter. Follett, 1958. Subj: Animals. Animals – mice.

Hoff, Syd. *Albert the albatross* ill. by author. HarperCollins, 1961. ISBN 0-06-022446-0 Subj: Birds – albatrosses. Sea and seashore.

Arturo's baton ill. by author. Clarion, 1995. ISBN 0-395-71020-0 Subj: Behavior – losing things. Careers – musicians. Music.

Barkley ill. by author. HarperCollins, 1975. ISBN 0-06-022448-7 Subj: Animals – dogs. Circus. Old age.

Bernard on his own ill. by author. Clarion, 1993. ISBN 0-395-65226-X Subj: Animals – bears. Behavior – lost.

Captain Cat ill. by author. HarperCollins, 1993. ISBN 0-06-020528-8 Subj: Animals – cats. Careers – military.

Chester ill. by author. HarperCollins, 1961. ISBN 0-06-022456-8 Subj: Animals – horses, ponies.

Danny and the dinosaur go to camp ill. by author. HarperCollins, 1996. ISBN 0-06-026440-3 Subj: Camps, camping. Dinosaurs.

Grizzwold ill. by author. HarperCollins, 1963. ISBN 0-06-022481-9 Subj: Animals – bears. Ecology.

Happy birthday, Danny and the dinosaur! ill. by author. HarperCollins, 1995. ISBN 0-06-026438-1 Subj: Birthdays. Dinosaurs. Friendship.

Happy birthday, Henrietta! ill. by author. Garrard, 1983. ISBN 0-8116-4423-5 Subj: Animals – goats. Animals – pigs. Birds – chickens. Birthdays.

Henrietta, circus star ill. by author. Garrard, 1978. ISBN 0-8116-4413-8 Subj: Birds – chickens. Circus.

Henrietta goes to the fair ill. by author. Garrard, 1979. ISBN 0-8116-4416-2 Subj: Birds – chickens. Fairs.

Henrietta, the early bird ill. by author. Garrard, 1978. ISBN 0-8116-4410-3 Subj: Behavior – mistakes. Birds – chickens. Time.

Henrietta's Halloween ill. by author. Garrard, 1980. ISBN 0-8116-4421-9 Subj: Birds – chickens. Holidays – Halloween. Parties.

The horse in Harry's room ill. by author. HarperCollins, 1970. ISBN 0-06-022483-5 Subj: Animals – horses, ponies. Imagination – imaginary friends.

Julius ill. by author. HarperCollins, 1959. ISBN 0-06-022490-8 Subj: Animals – gorillas.

Lengthy ill. by author. Putnam, 1964. ISBN 0-399-20704-X Subj: Animals – dogs.

The lighthouse children ill. by author. HarperCollins, 1994. ISBN 0-06-022959-4 Subj: Birds – seagulls. Lighthouses.

The littlest leaguer ill. by author. Dutton, 1976. ISBN 0-525-61536-9 Subj: Character traits – smallness. Games. Sports – baseball.

Merry Christmas, Henrietta! ill. by author. Garrard, 1980. ISBN 0-8116-4419-7 Subj: Birds – chickens. Holidays – Christmas. Stores.

Mrs. Brice's mice ill. by author. HarperCollins, 1988. ISBN 0-06-022452-5 Subj: Animals – mice. Character traits – being different. Pets.

My Aunt Rosie ill. by author. HarperCollins, 1972. ISBN 0-06-022503-3 Subj: Family life – aunts, uncles.

Oliver ill. by author. HarperCollins, 1960. ISBN 0-06-022516-5 Subj: Animals – elephants. Character traits – optimism. Circus.

Sammy the seal ill. by author. HarperCollins, 1959. ISBN 0-06-022526-2 Subj: Animals – seals. Zoos.

Santa's moose ill. by author. HarperCollins, 1988, 1979. ISBN 0-06-022506-8 Subj: Animals – moose. Holidays – Christmas. Santa Claus.

Slithers ill. by author. Putnam, 1968. Subj: Reptiles – snakes.

Slugger Sal's slump ill. by author. Dutton, 1979. ISBN 0-525-61590-3 Subj: Character traits – perseverance. Sports – baseball.

Stanley ill. by author. HarperCollins, 1992. ISBN 0-06-022536-X Subj: Cavemen. Character traits – confidence. Homes, houses.

A walk past Ellen's house ill. by author. McGraw-Hill, 1973. ISBN 0-07-029176-4 Subj: Emotions – embarrassment.

Walpole ill. by author. HarperCollins, 1977. ISBN 0-06-022544-0 Subj: Animals – walruses.

When will it snow? ill. by Mary Chalmers. HarperCollins, 1971. ISBN 0-06-022554-8 Subj: Seasons – winter. Weather – snow.

Where's Prancer? ill. by author. HarperCollins, 1997. ISBN 0-06-027601-0 Subj: Animals – reindeer. Holidays – Christmas. Santa Claus.

Who will be my friends? ill. by author. HarperCollins, 1960. ISBN 0-06-022556-4 Subj: Friendship. Moving.

Hoffman, Alice. *Fireflies* ill. by Wayne McLoughlin. Hyperion, 1997. ISBN 0-7868-2180-9 Subj: Animals – wolves. Handicaps. Insects – fireflies. Seasons – winter.

Hoffman, Christine. *Sewing by hand* ill. by Harriett Barton. HarperCollins, 1994. ISBN 0-06-021147-4 Subj: Activities – sewing.

Hoffman, Joan. *My friend goes left* (Gregorich, Barbara)

Hoffman, Mary. *Amazing Grace* ill. by Caroline Binch. Dial, 1991. ISBN 0-8037-1040-2 Subj: Ethnic groups in the U.S. – African Americans. School. Self-concept. Theater.

An angel just like me ill. by Cornelius Van Wright and Ying-Hwa Hu. Dial, 1997. ISBN 0-8037-2265-6 Subj: Angels. Ethnic groups in the U.S. – African Americans. Holidays – Christmas.

Animals in the wild: elephant ill. by author. Random House, 1984. ISBN 0-394-86553-7 Subj: Animals – elephants. Science.

Animals in the wild: monkey ill. by author. Random House, 1984. ISBN 0-394-86554-5 Subj: Animals – monkeys. Science.

Animals in the wild: panda ill. by author. Random House, 1984. ISBN 0-394-86555-3 Subj: Animals – pandas. Science.

Animals in the wild: tiger ill. by author. Random House, 1984. ISBN 0-394-86556-1 Subj: Animals – tigers. Science.

Clever Katya ill. by Marie Cameron. Barefoot, 1998. ISBN 1-901223-64-7 Subj: Animals – horses, ponies. Folk and fairy tales. Foreign lands – Russia. Riddles. Royalty – tsars.

Grace and family ill. by Caroline Binch. Frances Lincoln, 1995. ISBN 0-7112-0868-9 Subj: Ethnic groups in the U.S. – African Americans. Family life. Foreign lands – Gambia.

Henry's baby ill. by Susan Winter. DK, 1993. ISBN 1-56458-196-9 Subj: Babies. Clubs, gangs. Family life – brothers.

Three wise women ill. by Lynne Russell. Fogelman, 1999. ISBN 0-8037-2466-7 Subj: Holidays – Christmas. Religion – Nativity. Stars.

Hoffman, Phyllis. *Baby's first year* ill. by Sarah Wilson. HarperCollins, 1988. ISBN 0-06-022552-1 Subj: Babies. Behavior – growing up.

Meatball ill. by Emily Arnold McCully. HarperCollins, 1991. ISBN 0-06-022564-5 Subj: Ethnic groups in the U.S. Friendship. School.

Steffie and me ill. by Emily Arnold McCully. HarperCollins, 1970. Subj: Ethnic groups in the U.S. – African Americans. Family life. Friendship. School.

The ugly duckling (Andersen, H. C. [Hans Christian])

We play ill. by Sarah Wilson. HarperCollins, 1990. ISBN 0-06-022558-0 Subj: Activities – playing. Rhyming text. School.

Hoffman, Rosekrans. *Sister Sweet Ella* ill. by author. Morrow, 1981. ISBN 0-688-00866-6 Subj: Babies. Emotions – envy, jealousy. Family life – brothers and sisters. Family life – new sibling. Magic.

Hoffmann, E. T. A. *The nutcracker* retold by Jean Richardson; ill. by Francesca Crespi. Arcade, 1990. ISBN 1-55970-105-6 Subj: Activities – dancing. Animals – mice. Ballet. Careers – toy makers. Folk and fairy tales. Holidays – Christmas. Imagination. Royalty.

The nutcracker retold by Deborah Hautzig; ill. by Carolyn Ewing. Random House, 1992. ISBN 0-679-92385-3 Subj: Activities – dancing. Animals – mice. Ballet. Careers – toy makers. Folk and fairy tales. Holidays – Christmas. Imagination. Royalty.

The nutcracker retold and ill. by Rachel Isadora. Macmillan, 1981. Adapt. of Nussknacker und Mausekönig. ISBN 0-02-747470-4 Subj: Activities – dancing. Animals – mice. Ballet. Careers – toy makers. Fairies. Folk and fairy tales. Holidays – Christmas. Imagination.

The nutcracker retold by David Freeman; ill. by Joanna Isles. Pavilion, 1996. ISBN 1-85793-545-4 Subj: Activities – dancing. Animals – mice. Ballet. Careers – toy makers. Folk and fairy tales. Holidays – Christmas. Imagination. Royalty.

The nutcracker trans. by Ralph Manheim; ill. by Maurice Sendak. Crown, 1984. ISBN 0-517-55285-X Subj: Activities – dancing. Animals – mice. Ballet. Careers – toy makers. Fairies. Folk and fairy tales. Holidays – Christmas. Imagination. Theater.

The nutcracker retold by Anthea Bell; ill. by Lisbeth Zwerger. Picture Book Studio, 1987. ISBN 0-88708-051-0 Subj: Activities – dancing. Animals – mice. Ballet. Careers – toy makers. Folk and fairy tales. Holidays – Christmas. Imagination. Royalty.

The nutcracker ballet retold and ill. by Vladimir Vasil'evich Vagin. Scholastic, 1995. ISBN 0-590-47220-8 Subj: Activities – dancing. Animals – mice. Ballet. Folk and fairy tales. Holidays – Christmas. Imagination. Royalty.

The strange child tr. and adapt. by Anthea Bell; ill. by Lisbeth Zwerger. Picture Book Studio, 1984. Adapt. of Das fremde Kind. ISBN 0-907234-60-7 Subj: Death. Emotions – grief. Family life. Folk and fairy tales. Magic.

Hoffmann, Felix. *Hans in luck* (Grimm, Jacob)

The story of Christmas ill. by author. Atheneum, 1975. ISBN 0-689-50031-9 Subj: Holidays – Christmas. Religion – Nativity.

Hofmeyr, Dianne. *The stone: a Persian legend of the Magi* ill. by Jude Daly. Farrar, 1998. ISBN 0-374-37198-9 Subj: Folk and fairy tales. Foreign lands – Iran. Religion – Nativity.

Hofsepian, Sylvia A. *Why not?* ill. by Friso Henstra. Four Winds, 1991. ISBN 0-02-743980-1 Subj: Animals – cats. Emotions – loneliness.

Hofstrand, Mary. *Albion pig* ill. by author. Knopf, 1984. ISBN 0-394-96255-9 Subj: Animals – pigs. Rhyming text.

By the sea ill. by author. Atheneum, 1989. ISBN 0-689-31421-3 Subj: Animals – pigs. Family life. Rhyming text. Sea and seashore.

Hogan, Bernice. *My grandmother died but I won't forget her* ill. by Nancy Munger. Abingdon, 1983. ISBN 0-687-27548-2 Subj: Death. Emotions – grief. Family life – grandmothers.

Hogan, Inez. *About Nono, the baby elephant* ill. by author. Dutton, 1947. Subj: Animals – elephants. Behavior – misbehavior. Names.

Hogan, Kirk. *The hospital scares me* (Hogan, Paula Z.)

Hogan, Paula Z. *The black swan* ill. by Kinuko Y. Craft. Raintree, 1979. ISBN 0-8172-1254-X Subj: Birds – swans. Science.

The butterfly ill. by Geri K. Strigenz. Raintree, 1979. ISBN 0-8172-1252-3 Subj: Insects – butterflies, caterpillars. Metamorphosis. Science.

The dandelion ill. by Yoshi Miyake. Raintree, 1979. ISBN 0-8172-1250-7 Subj: Plants. Science.

The frog ill. by Geri K. Strigenz. Raintree, 1979. ISBN 0-8172-1253-1 Subj: Frogs and toads. Science.

The honeybee ill. by Geri K. Strigenz. Raintree, 1979. ISBN 0-8172-1256-6 Subj: Insects – bees. Science.

The hospital scares me by Paula Z. Hogan and Kirk Hogan; ill. by Mary Thelen. Raintree, 1980. ISBN 0-8172-1351-1 Subj: Ethnic groups in the U.S. Ethnic groups in the U.S. – African Americans. Hospitals. Illness.

The oak tree ill. by Kinuko Y. Craft. Raintree, 1979. ISBN 0-8172-1251-5 Subj: Science. Trees.

The penguin ill. by Geri K. Strigenz. Raintree, 1979. ISBN 0-8172-1257-4 Subj: Birds – penguins. Science.

The salmon ill. by Yoshi Miyake. Raintree, 1979. ISBN 0-8172-1255-8 Subj: Fish. Science.

Högner, Franz. *From blueprint to house* ill. by author. Carolrhoda, 1986. ISBN 0-87614-295-1 Subj: Homes, houses.

Hogrogian, Nonny. *Carrot cake* ill. by author. Greenwillow, 1977. ISBN 0-688-84061-2 Subj: Animals – rabbits. Behavior. Character traits – compromising. Character traits – shyness. Weddings.

The cat who loved to sing ill. by author. Knopf, 1988. ISBN 0-394-99004-8 Subj: Animals – cats. Cumulative tales. Folk and fairy tales. Songs.

Cinderella (Grimm, Jacob)

The contest ill. by author. Greenwillow, 1976. ISBN 0-688-84042-6 Subj: Caldecott award honor books. Crime. Folk and fairy tales. Foreign lands – Armenia.

The devil with the green hairs (Grimm, Jacob)

The first Christmas ill. by author. Greenwillow, 1995. ISBN 0-688-13580-3 Subj: Holidays – Christmas. Religion – Nativity.

The glass mountain (Grimm, Jacob)

The hermit and Harry and me ill. by author. Little, 1972. Subj: Behavior – indifference. Friendship.

Noah's ark ill. by author. Knopf, 1986. ISBN 0-394-98191-X Subj: Animals. Boats, ships. Religion – Noah. Weather – floods. Weather – rain. Weather – rainbows.

One fine day ill. by Nonny Hogrogian. Macmillan, 1971. ISBN 0-606-01196-X Subj: Animals – foxes. Caldecott award books. Cumulative tales.

Rooster brother ill. by author. Macmillan, 1974. ISBN 0-02-743990-9 Subj: Behavior – stealing. Character traits – cleverness. Crime. Folk and fairy tales.

Hoguet, Susan Ramsay. *I unpacked my grandmother's trunk: a picture book game* ill. by author. Dutton, 1983. ISBN 0-525-44069-0 Subj: ABC books. Cumulative tales. Games.

Hoke, Helen L. *The biggest family in the town* ill. by Vance Locke. McKay, 1947. Subj: Family life.

Hol, Coby. *Henrietta saves the show* ill. by author. North-South, 1991. ISBN 1-55858-102-2 Subj: Animals – horses, ponies. Circus.

Lisa and the snowman ill. by author. North-South, 1989. ISBN 1-55858-022-0 Subj: Seasons – winter. Snowmen.

Niki's little donkey ill. by author; trans. by J. Alison James. North-South, 1993. ISBN 1-55858-183-9 Subj: Animals – donkeys. Character traits – kindness to animals. Family life – grandmothers. Foreign lands – Greece.

Tippy Bear and little Sam ill. by author. North-South, 1992. Tr. of: Taps, der Bär, besucht den kleinen Jan. ISBN 1-55858-149-9 Subj: Animals – bears. Babies. Family life.

Tippy Bear goes to a party ill. by author. North-South, 1991. ISBN 1-55858-129-4 Subj: Animals – bears. Parties.

Tippy Bear hunts for honey ill. by author. North-South, 1991. ISBN 1-55858-128-6 Subj: Animals – bears. Character traits – helpfulness.

Tippy Bear's Christmas ill. by author. North-South, 1992. ISBN 1-55858-157-X Subj: Animals. Animals – bears. Holidays – Christmas.

A visit to the farm ill. by author. North-South, 1989. ISBN 1-55858-000-X Subj: Animals. Farms.

Holabird, Katharine. *Alexander and the dragon* ill. by Helen Craig. Potter/Crown, 1988. ISBN 0-517-56996-5 Subj: Bedtime. Behavior – fighting, arguing. Dragons. Friendship.

Alexander and the magic boat ill. by Helen Craig. Crown, 1990. ISBN 0-517-58149-3 Subj: Activities – traveling. Boats, ships. Family life. Imagination.

Angelina and Alice ill. by Helen Craig. Potter/Crown, 1987. ISBN 0-517-56074-7 Subj: Animals – mice. Friendship. School.

Angelina and the princess ill. by Helen Craig. Crown, 1984. ISBN 0-517-55273-6 Subj: Activities – dancing. Animals – mice. Ballet.

Angelina at the fair ill. by Helen Craig. Crown, 1985. ISBN 0-517-55744-4 Subj: Animals – mice. Fairs. Friendship.

Angelina ballerina ill. by Helen Craig. Crown, 1983. ISBN 0-517-55083-0 Subj: Activities – dancing. Animals – mice. Ballet.

Angelina dances ill. by Helen Craig. Random House, 1992. ISBN 0-679-83484-2 Subj: Activities – dancing. Animals – mice. Ballet. Format, unusual – board books.

Angelina ice skates ill. by Helen Craig. Pleasant Co., 2001. ISBN 1-58485-146-5 Subj: Animals – mice. Holidays – New Year's. Sports – ice skating. Theater.

Angelina on stage ill. by Helen Craig. Crown, 1986. ISBN 0-517-56073-9 Subj: Activities – dancing. Animals – mice. Ballet. Theater.

Angelina's baby sister ill. by Helen Craig. Pleasant Co., 2000. ISBN 1-58485-132-5 Subj: Animals – mice. Babies. Family life – new sibling. Family life – sisters. Sibling rivalry.

Angelina's birthday surprise ill. by Helen Craig. Crown, 1989. ISBN 0-517-57325-3 Subj: Animals – mice. Birthdays. Sports – bicycling.

Angelina's Christmas ill. by Helen Craig. Crown, 1986. ISBN 0-517-55823-8 Subj: Animals – mice. Careers – postal workers. Family life – cousins. Holidays – Christmas.

Christmas with Angelina ill. by Helen Craig. Random House, 1992. ISBN 0-679-83485-0 Subj: Animals – mice. Holidays – Christmas.

The little mouse ABC ill. by Helen Craig. Simon & Schuster, 1983. ISBN 0-671-47733-1 Subj: ABC books. Animals – mice.

Holbrook, Stewart. *America's Ethan Allen* ill. by Lynd Ward. Houghton Mifflin, 1949. ISBN 0-395-24449-8 Subj: Caldecott award honor books. U.S. history. War.

Holcomb, Nan. *Leah's night of wonder* ill. by Dot Yoder. Jason and Nordic, 1999. ISBN 0-944727-35-2 Subj: Religion – Nativity.

Patrick and Emma Lou ill. by Dot Yoder. Jason & Nordic, 1989. ISBN 0-944727-03-4 Subj: Family life – brothers and sisters. Handicaps – physical handicaps.

Holden, Edith. *The hedgehog feast* ill. by Edith Holden; words by Rowena Stott. Dutton, 1978. ISBN 0-525-61580-2 Subj: Animals – hedgehogs. Food.

Holden, Robert. *The pied piper of Hamelin* (Browning, Robert)

Holder, Heidi. *Æsop's fables* (Æsop)

Carmine the crow ill. by author. Farrar, 1992. ISBN 0-374-31119-6 Subj: Animals. Behavior – sharing. Birds – crows. Forest, woods. Old age.

Crows: an old rhyme ill. by author. Farrar, 1987. ISBN 0-374-31660-0 Subj: Animals – minks. Animals – weasels. Birds – crows. Counting, numbers. Nursery rhymes.

Holder, Mig. *The fourth wise man* ill. by Tony Morris. Augsburg, 1995. ISBN 0-8066-2713-1 Subj: Holidays – Christmas. Religion – Nativity.

Holding, James. *The lazy little Zulu* ill. by Aliki. Morrow, 1962. Subj: Character traits – laziness. Foreign lands – Africa.

Holl, Adelaide. *The ABC of cars, trucks and machines* ill. by William Dugan. American Heritage, 1970. ISBN 0-8281-5019-2 Subj: ABC books. Automobiles. Machines. Trucks.

Most-of-the-time Maxie ill. by Hilary Knight. Xerox Family Education Services, 1974. ISBN 0-88375-202-6 Subj: Activities – reading. Imagination.

A mouse story: Minnikin, Midgie and Moppet ill. by Priscilla Hillman. Golden Pr., 1977. ISBN 0-307-62362-9 Subj: Animals – mice. City. Country.

Mrs. McGarrity's peppermint sweater ill. by Abner Graboff. Lothrop, 1966. Subj: Activities – knitting. Circus. Rhyming text.

My father and I (Ringi, Kjell [Arne Sorensen])

The rain puddle ill. by Roger Antoine Duvoisin. Lothrop, 1965. ISBN 0-688-51096-5 Subj: Animals. Weather – rain.

The remarkable egg ill. by Roger Antoine Duvoisin. Lothrop, 1968. ISBN 0-688-51090-6 Subj: Toys – balls.

The runaway giant ill. by Mamoru Funai. Lothrop, 1967. Subj: Behavior – gossip. Snowmen.

Sir Kevin of Devon ill. by Leonard Weisgard. Lothrop, 1963. Subj: Character traits – bravery. Knights. Rhyming text.

Small Bear builds a playhouse ill. by Cyndy Szekeres. Garrard, 1978. ISBN 0-8116-4454-5 Subj: Animals. Animals – bears. Homes, houses.

Small Bear solves a mystery ill. by Lorinda Bryan Cauley. Garrard, 1979. ISBN 0-8116-4456-1 Subj: Animals – bears. Food. Illness. Mystery stories.

Holland, Cheri. *Maccabee jamboree: a Hanukkah countdown* ill. by Roz Schanzer. Kar-Ben Copies, 1998. ISBN 1-58013-019-4 Subj: Counting, numbers. Holidays – Hanukkah. Jewish culture. Religion.

Holland, Isabelle. *Kevin's hat* ill. by Leonard B. Lubin. Lothrop, 1984. ISBN 0-688-02360-6 Subj: Clothing – hats. Reptiles – alligators, crocodiles.

Holland, Janice. *You never can tell* ill. by adapt. Scribners, 1963. Adapt. from the tr. by Arthur W.

Hummel from the book of Huai-nan tzu, written before 122 B.C. Subj: Character traits – luck. Folk and fairy tales. Foreign lands – China.

Holland, Kevin Crossley. *see* Crossley-Holland, Kevin

Holland, Viki. *We are having a baby* ill. by author. Scribners, 1972. ISBN 0-684-12809-8 Subj: Babies. Family life – new sibling.

Holleyman, Sonia. *Mona the vampire* ill. by author. Delacorte, 1991. ISBN 0-385-30299-1 Subj: Activities – reading. Imagination. Monsters – vampires.

Holling, Holling C. (Holling Clancy). *Paddle-to-the-sea* ill. by author. Houghton Mifflin, 1941. ISBN 0-395-15082-5 Subj: Caldecott award honor books. Foreign lands – Canada. Rivers.

Hollow, Elizabeth. *In this night* (Lucht, Irmgard)

Hollyer, Belinda. *Daniel in the lions' den* (Bible. Old Testament. Daniel)

David and Goliath (Bible. Old Testament. David)

Jonah and the great fish (Bible. Old Testament. Jonah)

Hollyn, Lynn. *Lynn Hollyn's Christmas toyland* ill. by Lori Anzalone. Knopf, 1985. ISBN 0-394-97631-2 Subj: Fairies. Holidays – Christmas. Toys.

Holm, Mayling Mack. *A forest Christmas* ill. by author. HarperCollins, 1977. ISBN 0-06-022573-4 Subj: Animals. Holidays – Christmas.

Holman, Felice. *Victoria's castle* ill. by Lillian Hoban. Norton, 1966. Subj: Birds – parakeets, parrots. Humor. Imagination.

Holman, Sandy Lynne. *Grandpa, is everything black bad?* ill. by Lela Kometiani. Culture Coop, 1995. ISBN 0-9644655-0-7 Subj: Ethnic groups in the U.S. – African Americans. Family life – grandfathers. Self-concept.

Holmes, Anita. *The 100-year-old cactus* ill. by Carol Lerner. Four Winds, 1983. ISBN 0-590-07634-5 Subj: Desert. Plants. Science.

Holmes, Efner Tudor. *Amy's goose* ill. by Tasha Tudor. Crowell, 1977. ISBN 0-690-03801-1 Subj: Birds – geese. Character traits – helpfulness. Character traits – kindness to animals.

Carrie's gift ill. by Tasha Tudor. Collins-World, 1978. ISBN 0-529-05429-9 Subj: Animals – dogs. Character traits – kindness to animals. Gifts.

The Christmas cat ill. by Tasha Tudor. Crowell, 1976. ISBN 0-690-01268-3 Subj: Animals – cats. Holidays – Christmas.

Deer in the hollow ill. by Marlowe deChristopher. Philomel, 1993. ISBN 0-399-21735-5 Subj: Animals. Animals – deer. Forest, woods. Holidays – Christmas.

Holmes, Olivia. *The saint and the circus* (Piumini, Roberto)

Holmes, Stephen. *Hidden numbers* text by Sadie Fields; ill. by author. Harcourt, 1990. ISBN 0-15-200469-6 Subj: Counting, numbers. Format, unusual – toy and movable books. Games.

Holsonback, Anita. *Monkey see, monkey do: an animal exercise book for you!* by Anita Holsonback, with rhymes by Deb Adamson; ill. by Leo Timmers. Millbrook, 1997. ISBN 0-7613-0260-3 Subj: Animals. Rhyming text.

Holub, Joan. *Pen pals* ill. by author. Grosset, 1997. ISBN 0-448-41613-1 Subj: Letters, cards. Pen pals. School.

Holzenthaler, Jean. *My feet do* ill. by George Ancona. Dutton, 1979. ISBN 0-525-35485-9 Subj: Activities. Anatomy – feet.

My hands can ill. by Nancy Tafuri. Dutton, 1978. ISBN 0-525-35490-5 Subj: Activities. Anatomy – hands.

Homel, David. *Animal capers* (Paré, Roger)

Circus days (Paré, Roger)

A friend like you (Paré, Roger)

Play time (Paré, Roger)

Summer days (Paré, Roger)

Homme, Bob. *The friendly giant's birthday* ill. by Kim LaFave and Carol Snelling. CBC Merchandising, 1982. ISBN 0-88794-099-4 Subj: Birthdays. Giants. Songs.

The friendly giant's book of fire engines ill. by Kim LaFave and Carol Snelling. CBC Merchandising, 1981. ISBN 0-88794-100-1 Subj: Careers – firefighters. Giants. Trucks.

Honda, Tetsuya. *Wild horse winter* ill. by author. Chronicle, 1992. ISBN 0-8118-0251-5 Subj: Animals – horses, ponies. Foreign lands – Japan. Seasons – winter. Weather – snow.

Honeycutt, Natalie. *Whistle home* ill. by Annie Cannon. Orchard, 1993. ISBN 0-531-08640-2 Subj: Activities – whistling. Animals – dogs. Emotions – fear. Family life – aunts, uncles.

Hong, Lily Toy. *How the ox star fell from heaven* ill. by author. Albert Whitman, 1990. ISBN 0-8075-3428-5 Subj: Animals – oxen. Folk and fairy tales. Food. Foreign lands – China.

Hood, Susan. *The new kid* photos by Dorothy Handelman. Millbrook, 1998. ISBN 0-7613-2014-8 Subj: Behavior. Friendship. Rhyming text. School.

Hood, Thomas. *Before I go to sleep* ill. by Maryjane Begin-Callanan. Morrow, 1999. ISBN 0-688-12424-0 Subj: Animals. Bedtime. Imagination. Rhyming text.

Hooker, Ruth. *At Grandma and Grandpa's house* ill. by Ruth Rosner. Albert Whitman, 1986. ISBN 0-8075-0477-7 Subj: Family life. Family life – grandparents.

Matthew the cowboy ill. by Cat Bowman Smith. Albert Whitman, 1990. ISBN 0-8075-4999-1 Subj: Cowboys. Imagination. U.S. history – frontier and pioneer life.

Sara loves her big brother ill. by Margot Apple. Albert Whitman, 1987. ISBN 0-8075-7244-6 Subj: Behavior – sharing. Family life – brothers. Family life – new sibling. Sibling rivalry.

Hooks, Bell. *Happy to be nappy* ill. by Chris Raschka. Hyperion, 1999. ISBN 0-7868-2377-1 Subj: Ethnic groups in the U.S. – African Americans. Hair.

Hooks, William H. *A dozen dizzy dogs* ill. by Gary Baseman. Gareth Stevens, 1997. ISBN 0-8368-1748-6 Subj: Animals – dogs. Counting, numbers. Rhyming text.

Feed me! an Æsop fable ill. by Doug Cushman. Gareth Stevens, 1996. ISBN 0-8368-1616-1 Subj: Birds. Folk and fairy tales.

The Gruff brothers ill. by Pierre Cornuel. Gareth Stevens, 1997. ISBN 0-8368-1749-4 Subj: Animals – goats. Character traits – cleverness. Folk and fairy tales. Mythical creatures – trolls. Rebuses.

How do you make a bubble? by William H. Hooks, Joanne Oppenheim, and Barbara A. Brenner; ill. by Doug Cushman. Bantam, 1992. ISBN 0-553-07887-9 Subj: Activities. Bubbles. Rhyming text.

The legend of the Christmas rose ill. by Richard Williams. HarperCollins, 1998. ISBN 0-06-027103-5 Subj: Family life – brothers and sisters. Flowers – roses. Foreign lands – Sweden. Holidays – Christmas. Religion – Nativity.

Lion and Lamb (Brenner, Barbara A.)

The mighty Santa Fe ill. by Angela Trotta Thomas. Macmillan, 1993. ISBN 0-02-744432-5 Subj: Emotions – fear. Family life – great-grandparents. Holidays – Christmas. Toys – trains.

Mr. Baseball ill. by Paul Meisel. Gareth Stevens, 1998. ISBN 0-8368-1765-6 Subj: Family life – brothers. Sports – baseball.

Mr. Dinosaur ill. by Paul Meisel. Gareth Stevens, 1997. ISBN 0-8368-1755-9 Subj: Dinosaurs. Eggs. Family life – brothers. Reptiles – lizards.

Mr. Garbage ill. by Kate Duke. Gareth Stevens, 1997. ISBN 0-8368-1756-7 Subj: Ecology.

Mr. Monster ill. by Paul Meisel. Gareth Stevens, 1998. ISBN 0-8368-1774-5 Subj: Family life – brothers. Monsters. Toys.

The monster from the sea ill. by Angela Trotta Thomas. Gareth Stevens, 1997. ISBN 0-8368-1694-3 Subj: Behavior – talking to strangers. Islands. Royalty – princesses.

Moss gown ill. by Donald Carrick. Clarion, 1987. ISBN 0-89919-460-5 Subj: Family life – fathers. Folk and fairy tales. Magic.

The mystery of the missing tooth ill. by Nancy Poydar. Gareth Stevens, 1998. ISBN 0-8368-1758-3 Subj: Fairies. Teeth.

No way, Slippery Slick! a child's first book about drugs (Oppenheim, Joanne)

Peach boy ill. by June Otani. Bantam, 1992. ISBN 0-553-07621-3 Subj: Behavior – fighting, arguing. Character traits – bravery. Folk and fairy tales. Foreign lands – Japan. Monsters.

The rainbow ribbon by William H. Hooks and Betty Boegehold; ill. by Lynn Munsinger. Viking, 1991. ISBN 0-670-82866-1 Subj: Behavior – running away. Behavior – stealing. Character traits – selfishness.

Read-a-rebus by William H. Hooks, Joanne Oppenheim, Betty D. Boegehold; ill. by Lynn Munsinger. Random House, 1986. ISBN 0-394-95833-0 Subj: Anatomy. Concepts – color. Counting, numbers. Rebuses. Rhyming text.

Rough, tough, Rowdy ill. by Lynn Munsinger. Viking, 1992. ISBN 0-670-82868-8 Subj: Animals. Animals – rabbits. Behavior – bullying. Family life – brothers and sisters.

Snowbear Whittington, an Appalachian Beauty and the Beast ill. by Victoria Lisi. Macmillan, 1994. ISBN 0-02-744355-8 Subj: Animals – bears. Folk and fairy tales. Monsters. Witches.

The three little pigs and the fox (The three little pigs)

Three rounds with rabbit ill. by Lissa McLaughlin. Lothrop, 1984. ISBN 0-688-02364-9 Subj: Animals – rabbits. Character traits – cleverness.

Where's Lulu? ill. by R. W. Alley. Bantam, 1991. ISBN 0-553-07093-2 Subj: Animals – dogs. Ethnic groups in the U.S. – African Americans. Toys – balls.

Hooper, Meredith. *A cow, a bee, a cookie, and me* ill. by Alison Bartlett. Kingfisher, 1997. ISBN 0-7534-5067-4 Subj: Activities – baking. Family life – grandparents.

Seven eggs ill. by Terry McKenna. HarperCollins, 1985. ISBN 0-06-022586-6 Subj: Counting, numbers. Cumulative tales. Days of the week, months of the year. Eggs. Format, unusual.

Tom's rabbit: a surprise on the way to Antarctica ill. by Bert Kitchen. National Geographic, 1998. ISBN 0-7922-7070-3 Subj: Animals – rabbits. Boats, ships. Foreign lands – Antarctic. Holidays – Christmas.

Hooper, Patricia. *A bundle of beasts* ill. by Mark Steele. Houghton Mifflin, 1987. ISBN 0-395-44259-1 Subj: ABC books. Animals. Language. Poetry.

How the sky's housekeeper wore her scarves ill. by Susan L. Roth. Little, 1995. ISBN 0-316-37255-2 Subj: Weather – rainbows.

Hoopes, Lyn Littlefield. *Daddy's coming home* ill. by Bruce Degen. HarperCollins, 1984. ISBN 0-06-022569-6 Subj: Family life.

Half a button ill. by Trish Parcell Watts. Harper, 1989. ISBN 0-06-024018-0 Subj: Boats, ships. Family life – grandfathers. Gifts. Memories, memory.

Mommy, daddy, me ill. by Ruth Lercher Bornstein. HarperCollins, 1988. ISBN 0-06-022550-5 Subj: Family life. Islands. Nature. Rhyming text.

My own home ill. by Ruth Richardson. Harper-Collins, 1991. ISBN 0-06-022571-8 Subj: Animals. Birds – owls. Nature.

Nana ill. by Arieh Zeldich. HarperCollins, 1981. ISBN 0-06-022575-0 Subj: Death. Emotions – grief. Family life – grandmothers.

The unbeatable bread ill. by Brad Sneed. Dial, 1996. ISBN 0-8037-1612-5 Subj: Activities – cooking. Food. Poetry.

When I was little ill. by Marcia Sewall. Dutton, 1983. ISBN 0-525-44053-4 Subj: Emotions – love. Seasons – winter. Sibling rivalry.

Wing-a-ding ill. by Stephen Gammell. Little, 1990. ISBN 0-316-37237-4 Subj: Cumulative tales. Poetry. Toys. Trees.

Hoose, Hannah. *Hey little ant* (Hoose, Philip M.)

Hoose, Philip M. *Hey little ant* by Philip and Hannah Hoose; ill. by Debbie Tilley. Tricycle, 1998. ISBN 1-883672-54-6 Subj: Character traits – kindness to animals. Insects – ants. Music. Songs.

Hoover, Roseanna. *The fireflies* (Bolliger, Max)

The golden apple (Bolliger, Max)

Hopkins, Lee Bennett. *All God's children: a book of prayers* ill. by Amanda Schaffer. Harcourt, 1998. ISBN 0-15-201499-3 Subj: Poetry. Religion.

And God bless me: prayers, lullabies and dream-poems ill. by Patricia Henderson Lincoln. Knopf, 1982. ISBN 0-394-94624-3 Subj: Lullabies. Poetry. Religion.

Animals from Mother Goose: a question book ill. by Kathryn Hewitt. Harcourt, 1989. ISBN 0-15-200406-8 Subj: Animals. Character traits – questioning. Nursery rhymes.

April, bubbles, chocolate: an ABC of poetry ill. by Barry Root. Simon & Schuster, 1994. ISBN 0-671-75911-6 Subj: ABC books. Poetry.

Best friends ill. by James Watts. HarperCollins, 1986. ISBN 0-06-022562-9 Subj: Friendship. Poetry.

Blast off! poems about space ill. by Melissa Sweet. HarperCollins, 1995. ISBN 0-06-024261-2 Subj: Poetry. Space and space ships.

Circus! Circus! ill. by John O'Brien. Knopf, 1982. ISBN 0-394-95342-8 Subj: Circus. Poetry.

Click, rumble, roar: poems about machines photos by Anna Held Audette. Crowell, 1987. ISBN 0-690-04589-1 Subj: Machines. Poetry.

Climb into my lap: poems to read together ill. by Kathryn Brown. Simon & Schuster, 1998. ISBN 0-689-80715-5 Subj: Poetry.

Creatures ill. by Stella Ormai. Harcourt, 1985. ISBN 0-15-220875-5 Subj: Monsters. Poetry.

Crickets and bullfrogs and whispers of thunder (Behn, Harry)

Dinosaurs ill. by Murray Tinkelman. Harcourt, 1987. ISBN 0-15-223495-0 Subj: Dinosaurs. Poetry.

A dog's life ill. by Linda Rochester Richards. Harcourt, 1983. ISBN 0-05-223937-5 Subj: Animals – dogs. Poetry.

Easter buds are springing ill. by Tomie de Paola. Harcourt, 1979. ISBN 0-15-224705-X Subj: Holidays – Easter. Poetry. Seasons – spring.

Elves, fairies and gnomes: poems (Elves, fairies and gnomes)

Flit, flutter, fly! poems about bugs and other crawly creatures ill. by Peter Palagonia. Doubleday, 1992. ISBN 0-385-41468-4 Subj: Insects. Poetry.

Go to bed! a book of bedtime poems ill. by Rosekrans Hoffman. Knopf, 1979. ISBN 0-394-93869-0 Subj: Bedtime. Poetry.

Good books, good times ill. by Harvey Stevenson. HarperCollins, 1990. ISBN 0-06-022528-9 Subj: Activities – reading. Poetry.

Good rhymes, good times ill. by Frané Lessac. HarperCollins, 1995. ISBN 0-06-023500-4 Subj: Poetry.

Happy birthday ill. by Hilary Knight. Simon & Schuster, 1991. ISBN 0-671-70973-9 Subj: Birthdays. Poetry.

How do you make an elephant float? and other delicious riddles ill. by Rosekrans Hoffman. Albert Whitman, 1983. ISBN 0-8075-3415-3 Subj: Food. Riddles.

I loved Rose Ann ill. by Ingrid Fetz. Knopf, 1976. ISBN 0-394-93100-0 Subj: Behavior – misunderstanding. Emotions.

I think I saw a snail: young poems for city seasons ill. by Harold James. Crown, 1969. Subj: City. Ethnic groups in the U.S. – African Americans. Poetry.

It's about time ill. by Matt Novak. Simon & Schuster, 1993. ISBN 0-671-78512-5 Subj: Friendship. Poetry. Time.

Merrily comes our harvest in: poems for Thanksgiving ill. by Ben Shecter. Harcourt, 1978. ISBN 0-15-253179-3 Subj: Holidays – Thanksgiving. Poetry. Seasons – fall.

On the farm ill. by Laurel Molk. Little, 1991. ISBN 0-316-37274-9 Subj: Farms. Poetry.

People from Mother Goose: a question book ill. by Kathryn Hewitt. Harcourt, 1989. ISBN 0-15-200558-7 Subj: Character traits – questioning. Nursery rhymes.

Questions ill. by Carolyn Croll. HarperCollins, 1992. ISBN 0-06-022413-4 Subj: Character traits – questioning. Poetry.

Ragged shadows: poems of Halloween night ill. by Giles Laroche. Little, 1993. ISBN 0-316-37276-5 Subj: Holidays – Halloween. Poetry.

Ring out, wild bells ill. by Karen Baumann. Harcourt, 1992. ISBN 0-15-267100-5 Subj: Holidays. Poetry. Seasons.

School supplies ill. by Renee Flower. Simon & Schuster, 1996. ISBN 0-671-51172-6 Subj: Poetry. School.

The sea is calling me ill. by Walter Gaffney-Kessell. Harcourt, 1986. ISBN 0-15-271155-4 Subj: Poetry. Sea and seashore.

The sky is full of song ill. by Dirk Zimmer. HarperCollins, 1983. ISBN 0-06-022583-1 Subj: Poetry.

Song and dance ill. by Cheryl Munro Taylor. Simon & Schuster, 1997. ISBN 0-689-80159-9 Subj: Poetry.

A song in stone: city poems photos by Anna Held Audette. Crowell, 1983. ISBN 0-690-04270-1 Subj: City. Poetry.

Still as a star ill. by Karen Milone. Little, 1989. ISBN 0-316-37272-2 Subj: Poetry. Sleep.

Through our eyes: poems and pictures about growing up ill. by Jeffrey Dunn. Little, 1992. ISBN 0-316-19654-1 Subj: Behavior – growing up. Poetry.

To the zoo ill. by John Wallner. Little, 1992. ISBN 0-316-37273-0 Subj: Animals. Poetry. Zoos.

Hopkins, Margaret. *Sleepytime for baby mouse* ill. by Karen Lee Schmidt. Platt, 1985. ISBN 0-448-49875-9 Subj: Animals – mice. Bedtime. Family life. Format, unusual – board books.

Hopkins, Marjorie. *Three visitors* ill. by Anne F. Rockwell. Parents, 1967. Subj: Eskimos.

Hopkinson, Deborah. *Birdie's lighthouse* ill. by Kimberly Bulcken Root. Atheneum, 1997. ISBN 0-689-81052-0 Subj: Family life – fathers. Lighthouses. Sea and seashore. Weather – storms.

Maria's comet ill. by Deborah Lanino. Atheneum, 1999. ISBN 0-689-81501-8 Subj: Careers – astronomers. Family life. Sky.

Sweet Clara and the freedom quilt ill. by author. Knopf, 1993. ISBN 0-679-92311-X Subj: Activities – sewing. Behavior – seeking better things. Slavery.

Hoppe, Matthias. *Mouse and elephant* ill. by Jan Lenica. Little, 1991. ISBN 0-316-37284-6 Subj: Animals. Animals – elephants. Animals – mice. Friendship.

Horace. *Two Roman mice* (Roach, Marilynne K.)

Horenstein, Henry. *A is for – ? a photographer's alphabet of animals* photos by author. Harcourt, 1999. ISBN 0-15-201582-5 Subj: ABC books. Animals. Picture puzzles.

Arf! beg! catch! dogs from A to Z photos by author. Scholastic, 1999. ISBN 0-590-03380-8 Subj: ABC books. Animals – dogs. Language.

Sam goes trucking photos by author. Houghton Mifflin, 1989. ISBN 0-395-44313-X Subj: Careers – truck drivers. Family life – fathers. Trucks.

Horio, Seishi. *The monkey and the crab* by Saru Kani; retold by Seishi Horio; trans. by D. T. Ooka; ill. by Tsutomu Murakami. Heian Intl., 1985. ISBN 0-89346-246-2 Subj: Animals – monkeys. Crustaceans. Death.

Horn, Peter. *When I grow up –* ill. by Cristina Kadmon; trans. by Rosemary Lanning. North-South, 1999. ISBN 0-7358-1149-0 Subj: Behavior – growing up. Family life – fathers. Reptiles – turtles, tortoises.

Horner, Althea J. *Little big girl* ill. by Patricia Rosamilia. Human Sciences Pr., 1983. ISBN 0-89885-098-3 Subj: Behavior – growing up.

Horowitz, Ruth. *Bat time* ill. by Susan Avishai. Four Winds, 1991. ISBN 0-02-744541-0 Subj: Animals – bats. Bedtime. Family life – fathers.

Mommy's lap ill. by Henri Sorensen. Lothrop, 1993. ISBN 0-688-07236-4 Subj: Babies. Family life – brothers and sisters. Family life – new sibling.

Horse, Harry. *A friend for Little Bear* ill. by author. Candlewick, 1996. ISBN 1-56402-876-3 Subj: Behavior – collecting things. Friendship. Islands. Toys – bears.

Hort, Lenny. *The big squirrel and the little rhinoceros* (Damjan, Mischa)

The boy who held back the sea ill. by Thomas Locker. Dial, 1987. Adapt. of Hans Brinker, or The Silver Skates by Mary Mapes Dodge. ISBN 0-8037-0407-0 Subj: Behavior – misbehavior. Character traits – bravery. Folk and fairy tales.

How many stars in the sky ill. by James E. Ransome. Morrow, 1991. ISBN 0-688-10104-6 Subj: Ethnic groups in the U.S. – African Americans. Family life – fathers. Night. Stars.

The tale of the unicorn (Preussler, Otfried)

Horton, Barbara Savadge. *What comes in spring?* ill. by Ed Young. Knopf, 1992. ISBN 0-679-90268-6 Subj: Babies. Birth. Family life. Seasons.

Horvath, Betty F. *Be nice to Josephine* ill. by Pat Grant Porter. Watts, 1970. ISBN 0-531-01939-X Subj: Behavior. Family life.

The cheerful quiet ill. by Jo Ann Stover. Watts, 1969. Subj: Noise, sounds. Problem solving.

Hooray for Jasper ill. by Fermin Rocker. Watts, 1966. Subj: Character traits – smallness. Ethnic groups in the U.S. – African Americans.

Jasper and the hero business ill. by Don Bolognese. Watts, 1977. ISBN 0-531-01317-0 Subj: Character traits – bravery. Ethnic groups in the U.S. – African Americans.

Jasper makes music ill. by Fermin Rocker. Watts, 1967. Subj: Activities – working. Ethnic groups in the U.S. – African Americans. Music.

Will the real Tommy Wilson please stand up? ill. by Charles Robinson. Watts, 1969. Subj: Character traits – individuality. Emotions. Friendship.

Horwitz, Elinor Lander. *Sometimes it happens* ill. by Susan Jeschke. HarperCollins, 1981. ISBN 0-06-022597-1 Subj: Character traits – ambition. Imagination.

When the sky is like lace ill. by Barbara Cooney. Lippincott, 1975. ISBN 0-397-31550-3 Subj: Night.

Hot cross buns, and other old street cries sel. by John M. Langstaff; ill. by Nancy Winslow Parker. Atheneum, 1978. ISBN 0-689-50103-X Subj: Music. Poetry. Songs.

Houck, Eric L. *Rabbit surprise* by Eric L. Houck, Jr.; ill. by Dominic Catalano. Crown, 1993. ISBN 0-517-58778-5 Subj: Animals – foxes. Animals – rabbits. Holidays – Fourth of July. Magic.

Houghton, Eric. *The backwards watch* ill. by Simone Abel. Orchard, 1992. ISBN 0-531-08568-6 Subj: Activities – playing. Family life – grandfathers.

The crooked apple tree ill. by Caroline Gold. Barefoot, 1999. ISBN 1-902283-59-7 Subj: Activities – playing. Family life. Games. Trees.

Walter's magic wand ill. by Denise Teasdale. Watts, 1990. ISBN 0-531-08451-5 Subj: Libraries. Magic.

Houk, Randy. *Chessie, the travelin' man* ill. by Paula Bartlett. Benefactory, 1997. ISBN 1-882728-56-4 Subj: Activities – traveling. Animals – manatees. Rhyming text.

Rico's hawk ill. by Nancy Lane. Benefactory, 1998. ISBN 1-58021-029-5 Subj: Birds – hawks. Character traits – kindness to animals. Farms. Illness – mental illness. Rhyming text.

Ruffle, Coo and Hoo Doo ill. by author. Benefactory, 1993. ISBN 1-882728-02-5 Subj: Birds – owls. Birds – parakeets, parrots. Rhyming text.

House mouse photos by David Thompson. Putnam, 1978. ISBN 0-399-20620-5 Subj: Animals – mice. Science.

The house that Jack built. *The house that Jack built* ill. by Randolph Caldecott. G. Routledge, 1878. Subj: Cumulative tales. Nursery rhymes.

The house that Jack built ill. by Seymour Chwast. Random House, 1973. ISBN 0-394-82647-7 Subj: Cumulative tales. Format, unusual – toy and movable books. Nursery rhymes. Participation.

The house that Jack built: la maison que Jacques a batie ill. by Antonio Frasconi. Harcourt, 1958. Subj: Caldecott award honor books. Cumulative tales. Foreign languages. Nursery rhymes.

The house that Jack built ill. by Rodney Peppé. Delacorte, 1970. Subj: Cumulative tales. Nursery rhymes.

The house that Jack built: a Mother Goose nursery rhyme ill. by Janet Stevens. Holiday, 1985. ISBN 0-8234-0548-6 Subj: Circus. Cumulative tales. Nursery rhymes.

The house that Jack built ill. by Jenny Stow. Dial, 1992. ISBN 0-8037-1090-9 Subj: Cumulative tales. Nursery rhymes.

The house that Jack built ill. by Nadine Bernard Westcott. Little, 1991. ISBN 0-316-93138-1 Subj: Cumulative tales. Format, unusual – toy and movable books. Nursery rhymes. Participation.

The house that Jack built retold and ill. by Jeanette Winter. Dial, 2000. ISBN 0-8037-2524-8 Subj: Cumulative tales. Nursery rhymes. Rebuses.

This is the house that Jack built ill. by Liz Underhill. Holt, 1987. ISBN 0-8050-0339-8 Subj: Cumulative tales. Nursery rhymes.

Houselander, Caryll. *Petook: an Easter story* ill. by Tomie de Paola. Holiday, 1988. ISBN 0-8234-0681-4 Subj: Birds – chickens. Holidays – Easter. Religion.

Houses created by Gallimard Jeunesse and Claude Delafosse; ill. by Donald Grant. Scholastic, 1998. ISBN 0-590-38152-0 Subj: Homes, houses.

Houston, Gloria. *But no candy* ill. by Lloyd Bloom. Philomel, 1992. ISBN 0-399-22142-5 Subj: Family life – aunts, uncles. Food. Stores. U.S. history. War.

My Great-Aunt Arizona ill. by Susan Condie Lamb. HarperCollins, 1992. ISBN 0-06-022607-2 Subj: Careers – teachers. Family life – aunts, uncles.

The year of the perfect Christmas tree: an Appalachian story ill. by Barbara Cooney. Dial, 1988. ISBN 0-8037-0300-7 Subj: Family life. Holidays – Christmas. Trees.

Houston, James. *Kiviok's magic journey: an Eskimo legend* ill. by author. Atheneum, 1973. ISBN 0-689-30419-6 Subj: Birds – geese. Eskimos. Folk and fairy tales.

Houston, John A. *The bright yellow rope* ill. by Winnie Fitch. Addison-Wesley, 1973. ISBN 0-201-02995-2 Subj: Behavior – sharing. Character traits – generosity. Character traits – helpfulness. Problem solving. Rhyming text. Songs.

A mouse in my house ill. by Winnie Fitch. Addison-Wesley, 1973. ISBN 0-201-02989-X Subj: Animals – mice. Cumulative tales. Problem solving. Songs.

A room full of animals ill. by Winnie Fitch. Addison-Wesley, 1973. ISBN 0-201-12997-9 Subj: Animals. Songs.

How big is the ocean? *first questions and answers about the beach.* Time-Life, 1994. ISBN 0-7835-0897-2 Subj: Sea and seashore.

How Raggedy Ann got her candy heart adapt. from stories by Johnny Gruelle; ill. by Jan Palmer. Simon & Schuster, 1998. ISBN 0-689-81119-5 Subj: Accidents. Kites. Toys – dolls.

How the cock wrecked the manor trans. from Lithuanian by Olimpija Armalyte; ill. by Albina Makunaite. Imported Pubs., 1982. ISBN 0-8285-2228-6 Subj: Folk and fairy tales. Magic.

Howard, Arthur. *Cosmo zooms* ill. by author. Harcourt, 1999. ISBN 0-15-201788-7 Subj: Animals – dogs. Self-concept. Sports – skateboarding.

When I was five ill. by author. Harcourt, 1996. ISBN 0-15-200261-8 Subj: Behavior – growing up. Friendship.

Howard, Elizabeth Fitzgerald. *Aunt Flossie's hats (and crab cakes later)* ill. by James E. Ransome. Houghton Mifflin, 1991. ISBN 0-395-54682-6 Subj: Clothing – hats. Ethnic groups in the U.S. – African Americans. Family life – aunts, uncles.

Chita's Christmas tree ill. by Floyd Cooper. Bradbury, 1989. ISBN 0-02-744621-2 Subj: Ethnic groups in the U.S. – African Americans. Holidays – Christmas.

Mac and Marie and the train toss surprise ill. by Gail Gordon Carter. Four Winds, 1993. ISBN 0-02-744640-9 Subj: Ethnic groups in the U.S. – African Americans. Family life – brothers and sisters. Trains.

Papa tells Chita a story ill. by Floyd Cooper. Simon & Schuster, 1995. ISBN 0-02-744623-9 Subj: Character traits – bravery. Ethnic groups in the U.S. – African Americans. Family life – daughters. Family life – fathers. War.

The train to Lulu's ill. by Robert Casilla. Bradbury, 1988. ISBN 0-02-744620-4 Subj: Activities – traveling. Family life – sisters.

What's in Aunt Mary's room? ill. by Cedric Lucas. Clarion, 1996. ISBN 0-395-69845-6 Subj: Ethnic groups in the U.S. – African Americans. Family life – aunts, uncles. Family life – sisters.

When will Sarah come? ill. by Nina Crews. Greenwillow, 1999. ISBN 0-688-16181-2 Subj: Ethnic groups in the U.S. – African Americans. Family life – brothers and sisters. Family life – grandmothers. Noise, sounds.

Howard, Ellen. *The big seed* ill. by Lillian Hoban. Simon & Schuster, 1993. ISBN 0-671-73956-5 Subj: Behavior – growing up. Family life. Family life – step families. Gardens, gardening. School. Seeds.

The log cabin quilt ill. by Ronald Himler. Holiday, 1996. ISBN 0-8234-1247-4 Subj: Family life – grandmothers. Quilts. U.S. history – frontier and pioneer life.

Murphy and Kate ill. by Mark Graham. Simon & Schuster, 1995. ISBN 0-671-79775-1 Subj: Animals – dogs. Death. Emotions – grief.

Howard, Jane R. *When I'm hungry* ill. by Teri Sloat. Dutton, 1992. ISBN 0-525-44983-3 Subj: Animals. Food.

When I'm sleepy ill. by Lynne Cherry. Dutton, 1985. ISBN 0-525-44204-9 Subj: Imagination. Sleep.

Howard, Jean G. *Of mice and mice* ill. by author. Tidal Pr., 1978. ISBN 0-930954-03-3 Subj: Animals – mice.

Howard, Katherine. *Do you know colors?* (Miller, J. P. [John Parr])

I can count to 100 . . . can you? ill. by Michael J. Smollin. Random House, 1979. ISBN 0-394-84090-9 Subj: Counting, numbers.

My first picture dictionary ill. by Huck Scarry. Random House, 1978. ISBN 0-394-93486-5 Subj: Dictionaries.

Howard, Kim. *In wintertime* ill. by author. Lothrop, 1994. ISBN 0-688-11379-6 Subj: Family life – grandmothers. Foreign lands – Norway. Seasons – winter.

Howard-Gibbon, Amelia Frances. *An illustrated comic alphabet* ill. by author. Walck, 1967. Subj: ABC books.

Howe, Caroline Walton. *Counting penguins* ill. by author. HarperCollins, 1983. ISBN 0-06-022619-6 Subj: Birds – penguins. Counting, numbers.

Teddy Bear's bird and beast band ill. by author. Windmill, 1980. ISBN 0-671-96116-0 Subj: Music. Toys – bears.

Howe, James. *Bunnicula escapes! a pop-up adventure* ill. by Alan and Lea Daniel; paper engineering by Vicki Teague-Cooper. Morrow, 1995. ISBN 0-688-13212-X Subj: Animals – rabbits. Behavior – running away. Format, unusual – toy and movable books.

The case of the missing mother ill. by William Cleaver. Random House, 1983. ISBN 0-394-85729-1 Subj: Holidays – Mother's Day. Puppets.

Creepy-crawly birthday ill. by Leslie Holt Morrill. Morrow, 1991. ISBN 0-688-09688-3 Subj: Animals – cats. Animals – dogs. Birthdays. Pets.

The day the teacher went bananas ill. by Lillian Hoban. Dutton, 1984. ISBN 0-525-44107-7 Subj: Animals – gorillas. School. Zoos.

Horace and Morris but mostly Dolores ill. by Amy Walrod. Atheneum, 1999. ISBN 0-689-31874-X Subj: Animals – mice. Clubs, gangs. Friendship.

Hot fudge ill. by Leslie Holt Morrill. Morrow, 1990. ISBN 0-688-09701-4 Subj: Animals. Food.

I wish I were a butterfly ill. by Ed Young. Harcourt, 1987. ISBN 0-15-200470-X Subj: Behavior – wishing. Emotions – envy, jealousy.

Rabbit-Cadabra! ill. by Alan Daniel. Morrow, 1993. ISBN 0-688-10403-7 Subj: Animals – cats. Animals – dogs. Animals – rabbits. Careers – magicians.

Scared silly ill. by Leslie Holt Morrill. Morrow, 1989. ISBN 0-688-07667-X Subj: Animals – cats. Animals – dogs. Animals – rabbits. Holidays – Halloween. Witches.

There's a dragon in my sleeping bag ill. by David S. Rose. Atheneum, 1994. ISBN 0-689-31873-1 Subj: Dragons. Family life – brothers. Imagination – imaginary friends.

There's a monster under my bed ill. by David S. Rose. Atheneum, 1986. ISBN 0-689-31178-8 Subj: Emotions – fear. Furniture – beds. Monsters. Night.

When you go to kindergarten photos by Betsy Imershein. Morrow, 1994. ISBN 0-688-12913-7 Subj: School – first day.

Howe, John. *Jack and the beanstalk* (Jack and the beanstalk)

Rip Van Winkle (Irving, Washington)

Howell, Lynn. *Winifred's new bed* by Lynn and Richard Howell; ill. by authors. Knopf, 1985. ISBN 0-394-87772-1 Subj: Animals – cats. Days of the week, months of the year. Format, unusual. Furniture – beds. Toys.

Howell, Richard. *Winifred's new bed* (Howell, Lynn)

Howell, Ruth. *Everything changes* photos by Arline Strong. Atheneum, 1968. Subj: Seasons.

Splash and flow photos by Arline Strong. Atheneum, 1973. ISBN 0-689-30101-4 Subj: Science.

Howell, Troy. *The ugly duckling* (Andersen, H. C. [Hans Christian])

Howell, Will C. *I call it sky* ill. by John Ward. Walker, 1999. ISBN 0-8027-8678-2 Subj: Friendship. Nature. Seasons. Weather.

Howells, Mildred. *The woman who lived in Holland* ill. by William Curtis Holdsworth. Farrar, 1973. Text originally published in 1898 in St. Nicholas magazine under title: Going too far. ISBN 0-374-38460-6 Subj: Character traits – cleanliness. Foreign lands – Holland. Rhyming text.

Howland, Naomi. *ABCDrive!* ill. by author. Clarion, 1994. ISBN 0-395-66414-4 Subj: ABC books. Activities – traveling. Automobiles.

Latkes, latkes, good to eat: a Chanukah story ill. by author. Clarion, 1999. ISBN 0-395-89903-6 Subj: Folk and fairy tales. Foreign lands – Russia. Holidays – Hanukkah. Jewish culture. Magic.

Hoyt-Goldsmith, Diane. *Celebrating Chinese New Year* photos by Lawrence Migdale. Holiday, 1998. ISBN 0-8234-1393-4 Subj: Ethnic groups in the

U.S. – Chinese Americans. Holidays – Chinese New Year.

Hru, Dakari. *Joshua's Masai mask* ill. by Anna Rich. Lee & Low, 1993. ISBN 1-880000-02-4 Subj: Behavior – wishing. Ethnic groups in the U.S. – African Americans. Magic. Masks.

The magic moonberry jump ropes ill. by E. B. Lewis. Dial, 1996. ISBN 0-8037-1755-5 Subj: Activities – playing. Family life – sisters. Friendship. Sports – jumping rope.

Hubbard, Patricia. *My crayons talk* ill. by G. Brian Karas. Holt, 1996. ISBN 0-8050-3529-X Subj: Concepts – color. Rhyming text.

Trick or treat countdown ill. by Michael Letzig. Holiday, 1999. ISBN 0-8234-1367-5 Subj: Counting, numbers. Holidays – Halloween. Rhyming text.

Hubbard, Woodleigh Marx. *C is for curious: an ABC of feelings* ill. by author. Chronicle, 1990. ISBN 0-8770-1679-8 Subj: ABC books. Emotions.

2 is for dancing: a 1 2 3 of actions ill. by author. Chronicle, 1991. ISBN 0-8770-1895-2 Subj: Activities. Animals. Counting, numbers.

Hubbell, Patricia. *Camel caravan* (Roberts, Bethany)

Pots and pans ill. by Diane de Groat. HarperFestival, 1998. ISBN 0-694-01072-3 Subj: Activities – playing. Format, unusual – board books. Noise, sounds. Rhyming text.

Sidewalk trip ill. by Mari Takabayashi. HarperFestival, 1999. ISBN 0-694-01174-6 Subj: Activities – walking. City. Communities, neighborhoods. Family life – mothers. Rhyming text.

Wrapping paper romp ill. by Jennifer Plecas. HarperFestival, 1998. ISBN 0-694-01098-7 Subj: Animals – cats. Babies. Format, unusual – board books. Gifts. Holidays – Halloween. Rhyming text.

Huck, Charlotte S. *A creepy countdown* ill. by Jos. A. Smith. Greenwillow, 1998. ISBN 0-688-15461-1 Subj: Counting, numbers. Holidays – Halloween. Rhyming text.

Princess Furball ill. by Anita Lobel. Greenwillow, 1989. ISBN 0-688-07838-9 Subj: Character traits – cleverness. Folk and fairy tales. Royalty – princesses.

Secret places poems sel. by Charlotte Huck; ill. by Lindsay Barrett George. Greenwillow, 1993. ISBN 0-688-11670-1 Subj: Behavior – solitude. Poetry.

Hudson, Cheryl Willis. *Animal sounds for baby* ill. by George Ford. Scholastic, 1995. ISBN 0-590-48029-4 Subj: Animals. Babies. Ethnic groups in the U.S. – African Americans. Format, unusual – board books. Noise, sounds. Rhyming text.

Bright eyes, brown skin by Cheryl Willis Hudson and Bernette G. Ford; ill. by George Ford. Just Us Books, 1990. ISBN 0-940975-10-6 Subj: Ethnic groups in the U.S. – African Americans. Poetry.

Good morning baby ill. by George Ford. Scholastic, 1992. ISBN 0-590-45760-8 Subj: Babies. Ethnic groups in the U.S. – African Americans. Format, unusual – board books. Morning. Rhyming text.

Good night baby ill. by George Ford. Scholastic, 1992. ISBN 0-590-45761-6 Subj: Babies. Bedtime. Ethnic groups in the U.S. – African Americans. Format, unusual – board books. Night. Rhyming text.

Let's count, baby ill. by George Ford. Scholastic, 1995. ISBN 0-590-48028-6 Subj: Counting, numbers. Ethnic groups in the U.S. – African Americans. Format, unusual – board books. Rhyming text.

Hudson, Eleanor. *A whale of a rescue* ill. by Pat Paris. Random House, 1983. ISBN 0-394-85642-2 Subj: Animals – whales.

Hudson, Wade. *Afro-bets kids I'm gonna be* ill. by Culverson Blair. Just Us Books, 1992. ISBN 0-940975-40-8 Subj: ABC books. Ethnic groups in the U.S. – African Americans.

I love my family ill. by Cal Massey. Scholastic, 1993. ISBN 0-590-45764-0 Subj: Ethnic groups in the U.S. – African Americans. Family life. Farms.

Jamal's busy day ill. by George Ford. Just Us Books, 1991. ISBN 0-940975-21-1 Subj: Careers – accountants. Careers – architects. Family life – fathers. Family life – mothers. School.

Pass it on: African-American poetry for children ill. by Floyd Cooper. Scholastic, 1993. ISBN 0-590-45770-5 Subj: Ethnic groups in the U.S. – African Americans. Poetry.

Huff, Barbara A. *Once inside the library* ill. by Iris Van Rynbach. Little, 1990. ISBN 0-316-37967-0 Subj: Activities – reading. Libraries.

Huff, Vivian. *Let's make paper dolls* photos by author. HarperCollins, 1978. ISBN 0-06-022644-7 Subj: Activities – making things. Paper. Toys – dolls.

Huffaker, Alice. *That first Christmas day* ill. by Keith Neely. Moody, 1989. ISBN 0-8024-2637-9 Subj: Holidays – Christmas. Religion – Nativity. Rhyming text.

Hughes, Langston. *Carol of the brown king: nativity poems* ill. by Ashley Bryan. Atheneum, 1998. ISBN 0-689-81877-7 Subj: Ethnic groups in the U.S. – African Americans. Holidays – Christmas. Poetry. Religion – Nativity.

The sweet and sour animal book ill. by students from the Harlem School of the Arts. Oxford Univ. Pr., 1994. ISBN 0-19-509185-X Subj: ABC books. Animals. Art. Children as illustrators. Poetry.

Hughes, Monica. *A handful of seeds* ill. by Luis Garay. Orchard, 1996. ISBN 0-531-09498-7 Subj: Behavior – sharing. Ethnic groups in the U.S. – Hispanic Americans. Food. Gardens, gardening. Homeless.

Little Fingerling ill. by Brenda Clark. Ideals, 1992. ISBN 0-8249-8553-2 Subj: Character traits – bravery. Character traits – cleverness. Family life. Folk and fairy tales. Foreign lands – Japan. Little people.

Hughes, Peter. *The emperor's oblong pancake* ill. by Gerald Rose. Abelard-Schuman, 1961. Subj: Concepts – shape. Food. Royalty – emperors.

The king who loved candy ill. by Gerald Rose. Abelard-Schuman, 1964. Subj: Food. Royalty – kings. War.

Hughes, Richard. *Gertrude's child* ill. by Rick Schreiter. Crown, 1966. Subj: Behavior – needing someone. Behavior – running away. Toys.

Hughes, Shirley. *Abel's moon* ill. by author. DK, 1999. ISBN 0-7894-4601-4 Subj: Activities – traveling. Activities – writing. Emotions – loneliness. Family life – fathers. Imagination. Moon.

Alfie and the birthday surprise ill. by author. Lothrop, 1998. ISBN 0-688-15187-6 Subj: Animals – cats. Birthdays. Gifts. Parties.

Alfie gets in first ill. by author. Lothrop, 1982. ISBN 0-688-00849-6 Subj: Cumulative tales. Homes, houses.

Alfie gives a hand ill. by author. Lothrop, 1984. ISBN 0-688-02387-8 Subj: Behavior – needing someone. Birthdays. Parties.

Alfie's ABC ill. by author. Lothrop, 1998. ISBN 0-688-16126-X Subj: ABC books. Family life – brothers and sisters.

Alfie's feet ill. by author. Lothrop, 1983. ISBN 0-688-01660-X Subj: Activities – playing.

All shapes and sizes ill. by author. Lothrop, 1986. ISBN 0-688-04205-8 Subj: Concepts – shape. Concepts – size. Rhyming text.

Angel Mae ill. by author. Lothrop, 1989. ISBN 0-688-08539-3 Subj: Babies. Family life – new sibling. Holidays – Christmas. Theater.

Bathwater's hot ill. by author. Lothrop, 1985. ISBN 0-688-04202-3 Subj: Activities – bathing. Concepts – opposites. Family life. Foreign lands – England. Rhyming text.

Being together ill. by author. Candlewick, 1997. ISBN 0-7636-0399-6 Subj: Babies. Family life. Format, unusual – board books.

The big concrete lorry ill. by author. Lothrop, 1990. ISBN 0-688-08535-0 Subj: Activities – making things. City. Ethnic groups in the U.S. Homes, houses.

Bouncing ill. by author. Candlewick, 1993. ISBN 1-56402-128-9 Subj: Activities.

Chatting ill. by author. Candlewick, 1994. ISBN 1-56402-340-0 Subj: Communication. Communities, neighborhoods. Family life.

Colors ill. by author. Lothrop, 1986. ISBN 0-688-04206-6 Subj: Concepts – color. Rhyming text.

David and dog ill. by author. Prentice-Hall, 1978. Edition of 1977 published under title: Dogger. ISBN 0-13-197301-0 Subj: Activities – trading. Family life. Toys.

Dogger ill. by author. Lothrop, 1988, 1977. 1978 Prentice-Hall edition published under title David and dog. ISBN 0-688-07981-4 Subj: Activities – trading. Family life. Toys.

An evening at Alfie's ill. by author. Lothrop, 1985. ISBN 0-688-04123-X Subj: Activities – babysitting. Family life. Problem solving.

George the babysitter ill. by author. Prentice-Hall, 1978. ISBN 0-13-352682-8 Subj: Activities – babysitting.

Giving ill. by author. Candlewick, 1993. ISBN 1-56402-129-7 Subj: Character traits – generosity. Family life.

Hiding ill. by author. Candlewick, 1994. ISBN 1-56402-342-7 Subj: Behavior – hiding.

Lucy and Tom's A.B.C. ill. by author. Viking, 1986. ISBN 0-670-81256-0 Subj: ABC books. Family life. Foreign lands – England.

Lucy and Tom's Christmas ill. by author. Viking, 1986. ISBN 0-670-81255-2 Subj: Family life. Foreign lands – England. Holidays – Christmas. Religion.

Lucy and Tom's 1, 2, 3 ill. by author. Viking, 1987. ISBN 0-670-81763-5 Subj: Concepts. Counting, numbers. Family life.

Moving Molly ill. by author. Prentice-Hall, 1979. ISBN 0-13-604587-1 Subj: Emotions – loneliness. Family life. Friendship. Moving.

Noisy ill. by author. Lothrop, 1985. ISBN 0-688-04203-1 Subj: Family life. Foreign lands – England. Noise, sounds. Rhyming text.

Out and about ill. by author. Lothrop, 1988. ISBN 0-688-07691-2 Subj: Family life. Foreign lands – England. Rhyming text.

Playing ill. by author. Candlewick, 1997. ISBN 0-7636-0400-3 Subj: Activities – playing. Format, unusual – board books.

Rhymes for Annie Rose ill. by author. Lothrop, 1995. ISBN 0-688-14220-6 Subj: Family life – brothers and sisters. Rhyming text.

Sally's secret ill. by author. Merrimack, 1980. ISBN 0-370-02010-3 Subj: Behavior – secrets. Homes, houses.

The snow lady ill. by author. Lothrop, 1990. ISBN 0-688-09875-4 Subj: Behavior – misbehavior. Foreign lands – England. Old age. Snowmen. Weather – snow.

Two shoes, new shoes ill. by author. Lothrop, 1986. ISBN 0-688-04207-4 Subj: Clothing – shoes. Rhyming text.

Up and up ill. by author. Lothrop, 1986. First published by Prentice-Hall, 1979. ISBN 0-688-

06261-X Subj: Activities – flying. Imagination. Wordless.

Wheels ill. by author. Lothrop, 1991. ISBN 0-688-09880-0 Subj: Birthdays. Friendship. Sports – bicycling.

When we went to the park ill. by author. Lothrop, 1985. ISBN 0-688-04204-X Subj: Counting, numbers. Family life. Family life – grandfathers. Foreign lands – England. Parks. Rhyming text.

Hulbert, Jay. *Armando asked "Why?"* by Jay Hulbert and Sid Kantor; ill. by Pat Hoggan. Raintree, 1990. ISBN 0-8172-3576-0 Subj: Character traits – questioning. Ethnic groups in the U.S. – African Americans. Libraries.

Hulme, Joy N. *Bubble trouble* ill. by Mike Cressy. Childrens Pr., 1999. ISBN 0-516-21584-1 Subj: Activities – playing. Bubbles. Rhyming text.

Eerie feary feeling: a hairy scary pop-up book ill. by Paul Ely. Orchard, 1998. ISBN 0-531-30086-2 Subj: Emotions. Format, unusual – toy and movable books.

Sea squares ill. by Carol Schwartz. Walt Disney, 1991. ISBN 1-56282-080-X Subj: Animals. Counting, numbers. Rhyming text. Sea and seashore.

Sea sums ill. by Carol Schwartz. Hyperion, 1996. ISBN 0-7868-2142-6 Subj: Counting, numbers. Rhyming text. Sea and seashore.

What if? just wondering poems ill. by Valeri Gorbachev. Boyds Mills, 1993. ISBN 1-56397-186-0 Subj: Animals. Poetry.

Hulme, Susan. *Let's look for colors* (Gillham, Bill)

Let's look for numbers (Gillham, Bill)

Let's look for opposites (Gillham, Bill)

Let's look for shapes (Gillham, Bill)

Hulpach, Vladimir. *Ahaiyute and Cloud Eater* ill. by Marek Zawadzki. Harcourt, 1996. ISBN 0-15-201237-0 Subj: Character traits – bravery. Folk and fairy tales. Indians of North America – Zuni. Magic. Monsters.

Hulse, Gillian. *Morris, where are you?* ill. by author. Oxford Univ. Pr., 1988. ISBN 0-19-520646-0 Subj: Animals – cats. Behavior – hiding. Problem solving.

Humphries, Tudor. *Hiding* ill. by author. Orchard, 1997. ISBN 0-5313-0056-0 Subj: Behavior – hiding. Behavior – misbehavior. Family life.

Hundley, David H. *Bruises* photos by author. Rourke, 1998. ISBN 1-57103-254-1 Subj: Illness.

Hunt, Angela Elwell. *The tale of three trees* ill. by Tim Jonke. Lion, 1989. ISBN 0-7459-1743-7 Subj: Folk and fairy tales. Religion. Trees.

Hunt, Bernice Kohn. *Your ant is a which* ill. by Jan Pyk. Harcourt, 1975. ISBN 0-15-299880-2 Subj: Language.

Hunt, Francesca. *see* Holland, Isabelle

Hunt, Jonathan. *Leif's saga* ill. by author. Simon & Schuster, 1996. ISBN 0-02-745780-X Subj: Boats, ships. Careers – boat builders. Careers – explorers. Family life. Folk and fairy tales. Sea and seashore.

One is a mouse by Jonathan and Lisa Hunt; ill. by authors. Macmillan, 1995. ISBN 0-02-745781-8 Subj: Animals. Counting, numbers. Rhyming text.

Hunt, Joyce. *A first look at bird nests* (Selsam, Millicent E.)

A first look at caterpillars (Selsam, Millicent E.)

A first look at cats (Selsam, Millicent E.)

A first look at dinosaurs (Selsam, Millicent E.)

A first look at dogs (Selsam, Millicent E.)

A first look at flowers (Selsam, Millicent E.)

A first look at kangaroos, koalas and other animals with pouches (Selsam, Millicent E.)

A first look at monkeys (Selsam, Millicent E.)

A first look at owls, eagles and other hunters of the sky (Selsam, Millicent E.)

A first look at rocks (Selsam, Millicent E.)

A first look at seashells (Selsam, Millicent E.)

A first look at sharks (Selsam, Millicent E.)

A first look at spiders (Selsam, Millicent E.)

A first look at the world of plants (Selsam, Millicent E.)

A first look at whales (Selsam, Millicent E.)

Keep looking! (Selsam, Millicent E.)

Hunt, Lisa. *One is a mouse* (Hunt, Jonathan)

Hunt, Nan. *Families are funny* ill. by Deborah Niland. Orchard, 1992. ISBN 0-531-08569-4 Subj: Family life.

Hunter, Anne. *Possum and the peeper* ill. by author. Houghton Mifflin, 1998. ISBN 0-395-84631-5 Subj: Animals. Animals – possums. Frogs and toads. Seasons – spring.

Possum's harvest moon ill. by author. Houghton Mifflin, 1996. ISBN 0-395-73575-0 Subj: Animals. Animals – possums. Moon. Parties. Seasons.

Hunter, C. W. *The green gourd* ill. by Tony Griego. Putnam, 1992. ISBN 0-399-22278-2 Subj: Folk and fairy tales. Magic.

Hunter, Norman. *Professor Branestawm's building bust-up* ill. by Gerald Rose. Merrimack, 1982. ISBN 0-370-30457-8 Subj: Homes, houses. Humor. Machines.

Hunter, Ryan Ann. *Cross a bridge* ill. by Edward Miller. Holiday, 1998. ISBN 0-8234-1340-3 Subj: Bridges.

Into the sky ill. by Edward Miller. Holiday, 1998. ISBN 0-8234-1372-1 Subj: Buildings. Careers – architects.

Hurd, Edith Thacher. *The black dog who went into the woods* ill. by Emily Arnold McCully. Harper-Collins, 1980. ISBN 0-06-022684-6 Subj: Animals – dogs. Death. Pets.

Caboose ill. by Clement Hurd. Lothrop, 1950. Subj: Rhyming text. Trains.

Christmas eve ill. by Clement Hurd. Harper, 1962. Subj: Animals. Holidays – Christmas.

Come and have fun ill. by Clement Hurd. Harper-Collins, 1962. ISBN 0-06-022681-1 Subj: Animals – cats. Animals – mice. Rhyming text.

The day the sun danced ill. by Clement Hurd. HarperCollins, 1965. ISBN 0-06-022692-7 Subj: Seasons. Seasons – spring. Sun.

Dinosaur, my darling ill. by Don Freeman. Harper-Collins, 1978. ISBN 0-06-022744-3 Subj: Dinosaurs.

Engine, engine no. 9 ill. by Clement Hurd. Lothrop, 1940. Subj: Trains.

Five little firemen (Brown, Margaret Wise)

Hurry, hurry! ill. by Clement Hurd. Harper-Collins, 1960. Subj: Activities – babysitting. Behavior – hurrying.

I dance in my red pajamas ill. by Emily Arnold McCully. HarperCollins, 1982. ISBN 0-06-022700-1 Subj: Activities – dancing. Family life – grandparents.

Johnny Lion's bad day ill. by Clement Hurd. HarperCollins, 1970. ISBN 0-06-022708-7 Subj: Animals – lions. Illness.

Johnny Lion's book ill. by Clement Hurd. Harper-Collins, 1965. ISBN 0-06-022706-0 Subj: Activities – reading. Animals – lions.

Johnny Lion's rubber boots ill. by Clement Hurd. HarperCollins, 1972. ISBN 0-06-022710-9 Subj: Animals – lions. Weather – rain.

Last one home is a green pig ill. by Clement Hurd. HarperCollins, 1959. ISBN 0-06-022716-8 Subj: Animals – monkeys. Birds – ducks. Games. Sports – racing.

Little dog, dreaming by Edith Thacher Hurd and Thacher Hurd; ill. by Clement Hurd. Harper-Collins, 1967. Subj: Animals – dogs. Dreams.

Look for a bird ill. by Clement Hurd. Harper-Collins, 1977. ISBN 0-06-022720-6 Subj: Birds. Nature. Science.

The mother chimpanzee ill. by Clement Hurd. Little, 1978. ISBN 0-316-38327-9 Subj: Animals – chimpanzees. Family life – mothers.

The mother kangaroo ill. by Clement Hurd. Little, 1976. ISBN 0-316-38326-0 Subj: Animals – kangaroos. Family life. Science.

No funny business ill. by Clement Hurd. Harper-Collins, 1962. Subj: Activities – picnicking. Animals – cats.

Sandpipers ill. by Lucienne Bloch. Crowell, 1961. Subj: Birds – sandpipers. Science.

The so-so cat ill. by Clement Hurd. HarperCollins, 1964. Subj: Animals – cats. Holidays – Halloween. Witches.

Starfish ill. by Lucienne Bloch. Crowell, 1962. ISBN 0-690-77069-3 Subj: Science. Sea and seashore.

Stop, stop ill. by Clement Hurd. HarperCollins, 1961. Subj: Activities – babysitting. Character traits – cleanliness.

Under the lemon tree ill. by Clement Hurd. Little, 1980. ISBN 0-316-38328-7 Subj: Animals – donkeys. Animals – foxes. Character traits – loyalty. Farms.

What whale? Where? ill. by Clement Hurd. Harper-Collins, 1966. Subj: Animals – whales. Boats, ships.

The white horse ill. by Tony Chen. HarperCollins, 1970. Subj: Imagination.

Wilson's world ill. by Clement Hurd. Harper-Collins, 1971. ISBN 0-06-022750-8 Subj: Art. Ecology.

Hurd, Thacher. *Art dog* ill. by author. Harper-Collins, 1996. ISBN 0-06-024425-9 Subj: Activities – painting. Animals – dogs. Art. Museums. Mystery stories.

Axle the freeway cat ill. by author. HarperCollins, 1988. ISBN 0-06-443173-8 Subj: Animals – cats. Friendship.

Blackberry ramble ill. by author. Crown, 1989. ISBN 0-517-57105-6 Subj: Animals – mice. Farms. Seasons – spring.

Hobo dog ill. by author. Scholastic, 1980. ISBN 0-590-31283-9 Subj: Activities – traveling. Animals – dogs. Trains.

Little dog, dreaming (Hurd, Edith Thacher)

Little Mouse's big Valentine ill. by author. Harper-Collins, 1990. ISBN 0-06-026193-5 Subj: Animals – mice. Holidays – Valentine's Day.

Little Mouse's birthday cake ill. by author. Harper-Collins, 1992. ISBN 0-06-020216-5 Subj: Animals – mice. Birthdays.

Mama don't allow ill. by author. HarperCollins, 1984. ISBN 0-06-022690-0 Subj: Animals – possums. Music. Reptiles – alligators, crocodiles.

Mystery on the docks ill. by author. HarperCollins, 1983. ISBN 0-06-022702-8 Subj: Animals – rats. Behavior – bad day. Mystery stories.

A night in the swamp: a movable book ill. by author. HarperCollins, 1987. ISBN 0-694-00177-5 Subj: Animals. Format, unusual – toy and movable books. Night.

The pea patch jig ill. by author. Crown, 1986. ISBN 0-517-56307-X Subj: Animals – mice. Gardens, gardening. Music.

The quiet evening ill. by author. Greenwillow, 1978. ISBN 0-688-84166-X Subj: Night.

Santa Mouse and the ratdeer ill. by author. Harper-Collins, 1998. ISBN 0-06-027694-0 Subj: Accidents. Animals – mice. Behavior – bad day. Holidays – Christmas. Santa Claus.

Tomato soup ill. by author. Crown, 1992. ISBN 0-517-58238-4 Subj: Animals – cats. Animals – mice. Farms. Illness.

Zoom City ill. by author. HarperCollins, 1998. ISBN 0-694-01057-X Subj: Automobiles. City.

Hurford, John. *The dormouse* ill. by author. Associated Booksellers, 1986. ISBN 0-907349-25-0 Subj: Animals. Animals – mice.

Huriet, Genevieve. *Dandelion's vanishing vegetable garden* ill. by Loic Jouannigot. Gareth Stevens, 1991. ISBN 0-8368-0526-7 Subj: Animals – rabbits. Gardens, gardening.

Hürlimann, Bettina. *Barry: the story of a brave St. Bernard* ill. by Paul Nussbaumer; trans. by Elizabeth D. Crawford. Harcourt, 1968. Subj: Animals – dogs. Character traits – bravery. Character traits – helpfulness.

Hürlimann, Ruth. *The mouse with the daisy hat* ill. by author. White, 1971. ISBN 0-8725-0245-7 Subj: Animals – mice. Clothing – hats. Weddings.

The proud white cat trans. by Anthea Bell; ill. by author. Morrow, 1977. Translation of Der stolze weisse Kater. ISBN 0-688-32095-3 Subj: Animals – cats. Character traits – pride. Folk and fairy tales. Foreign lands – Germany.

Hurst, Brian Seth. *A pig tale* (Newton-John, Olivia)

Hurwitz, Johanna. *A dream come true* photos by Michael Craine. R.C. Owen, 1998. ISBN 1-57274-193-7 Subj: Careers – writers.

New shoes for Silvia ill. by Jerry Pinkney. Morrow, 1993. ISBN 0-688-05287-8 Subj: Clothing – shoes. Foreign lands – Latin America.

Hush little baby. *Hush little baby: a folk lullaby* ill. by Aliki. Prentice-Hall, 1968. ISBN 0-13-448167-4 Subj: Babies. Character traits – generosity. Cumulative tales. Lullabies. Music.

Hush little baby ill. by Shari Halpern. North-South, 1997. ISBN 1-55858-808-6 Subj: Babies. Character traits – generosity. Cumulative tales. Lullabies. Music.

Hush little baby ill. by Jeanette Winter. Pantheon, 1984. ISBN 0-394-96325-3 Subj: Babies. Character traits – generosity. Cumulative tales. Folk and fairy tales. Lullabies. Music.

Hush little baby ill. by Margot Zemach. Dutton, 1976. ISBN 0-525-32510-7 Subj: Babies. Character traits – generosity. Cumulative tales. Lullabies. Music.

Huss, Sally. *I love you with all my hearts: the many ways a mother loves her daughter* ill. by author. Tommy Nelson, 1998. ISBN 0-8499-5886-5 Subj: Emotions – love. Family life – mothers. Rhyming text.

Hutchings, Tony. *Things that go word book* ill. by author. Rand McNally, 1977. ISBN 0-528-82040-0 Subj: Machines.

Hutchins, H. J. (Hazel J.). *Ben's snow song* ill. by Lisa Smith. Firefly, 1987. ISBN 0-920303-91-9 Subj: Sports – skiing. Weather – snow.

The catfish palace ill. by Ruth Ohi. Firefly, 1993. ISBN 1-55037-316-1 Subj: Character traits – kindness to animals. Fish.

It's raining, Yancy and Bear ill. by Ruth Ohi. Firefly, 1998. ISBN 1-55037-529-6 Subj: Toys – bears. Weather – rain.

Katie's babbling brother ill. by Ruth Ohi. Firefly, 1991. ISBN 1-55037-153-3 Subj: Family life. Noise, sounds. Sibling rivalry.

Leanna builds a genie trap ill. by Catharine O'Neill. Firefly, 1986. ISBN 0-920303-54-4 Subj: Behavior – losing things. Furniture.

Nicholas at the library ill. by Ruth Ohi. Firefly, 1990. ISBN 1-55037-134-7 Subj: Activities – reading. Imagination. Libraries.

Norman's snowball ill. by Ruth Ohi. Firefly, 1989. ISBN 1-55037-053-7 Subj: Activities – playing. Behavior – losing things. Family life. Weather – snow.

One duck ill. by Ruth Ohi. Firefly, 1999. ISBN 1-55037-561-X Subj: Birds – ducks. Careers – farmers. Character traits – kindness to animals. Farms.

Hutchins, Pat. *Changes, changes* ill. by author. Macmillan, 1971. ISBN 0-02-745870-9 Subj: Toys – blocks. Wordless.

Clocks and more clocks ill. by author. Macmillan, 1994. ISBN 0-02-745921-7 Subj: Clocks, watches. Humor. Time.

Don't forget the bacon! ill. by author. Greenwillow, 1975. ISBN 0-688-84019-1 Subj: Behavior – forgetfulness. Cumulative tales. Food. Humor. Shopping.

The doorbell rang ill. by author. Greenwillow, 1986. ISBN 0-688-05252-5 Subj: Behavior – sharing. Family life. Friendship.

Good night owl ill. by author. Macmillan, 1991. ISBN 0-689-71541-2 Subj: Birds – owls. Cumulative tales. Noise, sounds. Participation. Sleep.

Happy birthday, Sam ill. by author. Greenwillow, 1978. ISBN 0-688-84160-0 Subj: Birthdays. Family life – grandfathers.

It's my birthday! ill. by author. Greenwillow, 1999. ISBN 0-688-09664-6 Subj: Behavior – sharing. Birthdays. Family life. Gifts. Monsters.

King Henry's palace ill. by author. Greenwillow, 1983. ISBN 0-688-02295-2 Subj: Birthdays. Holidays – Christmas. Royalty – kings.

Little pink pig ill. by author. Greenwillow, 1994. ISBN 0-688-12015-6 Subj: Animals. Animals – pigs. Bedtime. Behavior – tardiness.

My best friend ill. by author. Greenwillow, 1993. ISBN 0-688-11486-5 Subj: Ethnic groups in the U.S. – African Americans. Friendship.

One-eyed Jake ill. by author. Greenwillow, 1979. ISBN 0-688-84183-X Subj: Pirates.

1 hunter ill. by author. Greenwillow, 1982. ISBN 0-688-00615-9 Subj: Animals. Counting, numbers.

Our baby is best ill. by author. Greenwillow, 1991. Subj: Adoption. Babies. Family life – new sibling. Family life – sisters.

Rosie's walk ill. by author. Macmillan, 1968. ISBN 0-02-745850-4 Subj: Animals – foxes. Birds – chickens. Farms. Humor.

Rosie's walk, a board book ill. by author. 1st Little Simon board book ed. Little Simon, 1998. ISBN 0-689-82231-6 Subj: Animals. Animals – foxes. Birds – chickens. Farms. Format, unusual – board books.

Shrinking mouse ill. by author. Greenwillow, 1997. ISBN 0-688-13962-0 Subj: Animals. Concepts – perspective. Concepts – size.

Silly Billy! ill. by author. Greenwillow, 1992. ISBN 0-688-10818-0 Subj: Family life – brothers and sisters. Monsters.

The silver Christmas tree ill. by author. Macmillan, 1974. ISBN 0-02-745920-7 Subj: Animals. Holidays – Christmas. Trees.

The surprise party ill. by author. Macmillan, 1986, 1969. ISBN 0-02-745930-6 Subj: Animals. Behavior – gossip. Parties.

The tale of Thomas Mead ill. by author. Greenwillow, 1980. ISBN 0-688-84282-8 Subj: Activities – reading. Rhyming text.

Three-star Billy ill. by author. Greenwillow, 1994. ISBN 0-688-13079-8 Subj: Behavior – misbehavior. Monsters. School.

Tidy Titch ill. by author. Greenwillow, 1991. ISBN 0-688-09964-5 Subj: Behavior. Family life. Toys.

Titch ill. by author. Macmillan, 1971. Subj: Concepts – size. Cumulative tales. Family life. Plants.

Titch and Daisy ill. by author. Greenwillow, 1996. ISBN 0-688-13960-4 Subj: Behavior – hiding. Character traits – shyness. Friendship. Parties.

The very worst monster ill. by author. Greenwillow, 1985. ISBN 0-688-04011-X Subj: Monsters. Sibling rivalry.

What game shall we play? ill. by author. Greenwillow, 1990. ISBN 0-688-09197-0 Subj: Animals. Games.

Where's the baby? ill. by author. Greenwillow, 1988. ISBN 0-688-05934-1 Subj: Babies. Behavior – lost. Behavior – misbehavior. Character traits – cleanliness. Monsters.

Which witch is which? ill. by author. Greenwillow, 1989. ISBN 0-688-06358-6 Subj: Games. Holidays – Halloween. Multiple births – twins. Parties. Rhyming text.

The wind blew ill. by author. Macmillan, 1974. ISBN 0-02-745910-1 Subj: Rhyming text. Weather – wind.

You'll soon grow into them, Titch ill. by author. Greenwillow, 1983. ISBN 0-688-01771-1 Subj: Clothing. Family life.

Huth, Holly Young. *Darkfright* ill. by Jenny Stow. Atheneum, 1996. ISBN 0-689-80188-2 Subj: Emotions – fear. Foreign lands – Caribbean Islands. Night.

Hutton, Warwick. *Adam and Eve: the Bible story* ill. by adapt. Macmillan, 1987. ISBN 0-689-50433-0 Subj: Religion.

Beauty and the beast retold and ill. by Warwick Hutton. Atheneum, 1985. ISBN 0-689-50316-4 Subj: Character traits – appearance. Character traits – loyalty. Emotions – love. Folk and fairy tales. Magic.

Jonah and the great fish ill. by adapt. Atheneum, 1984. ISBN 0-689-50283-4 Subj: Animals – whales. Religion – Jonah.

Moses in the bulrushes ill. by reteller. Aladin, 1992. ISBN 0-689-71553-6 Subj: Babies. Foreign lands – Egypt. Jewish culture. Religion – Moses.

Noah and the great flood ill. by author. Atheneum, 1977. ISBN 0-689-50098-X Subj: Animals. Boats, ships. Religion – Noah. Weather – floods. Weather – rain. Weather – rainbows.

The nose tree ill. by adapt. Atheneum, 1981. ISBN 0-689-50166-8 Subj: Anatomy – noses. Character traits – cleverness. Folk and fairy tales. Friendship. Witches.

Persephone ill. by author. Margaret K. McElderry, 1994. ISBN 0-689-50600-7 Subj: Foreign lands – Greece. Mythical creatures. Religion. Seasons.

Perseus ill. by author. Margaret K. McElderry, 1993. ISBN 0-689-50565-5 Subj: Folk and fairy tales. Mythical creatures.

The sleeping beauty (Grimm, Jacob)

Theseus and the Minotaur ill. by author. Margaret K. McElderry, 1989. ISBN 0-689-50473-X Subj: Death. Foreign lands – Greece. Monsters. Mythical creatures. Religion.

The Trojan horse ill. by author. Margaret K. McElderry, 1992. ISBN 0-689-50542-6 Subj: Folk and fairy tales. Foreign lands – Greece. War.

Hyatt, Christine. *Erik and the Christmas horse* (Peterson, Hans)

Erik has a squirrel (Peterson, Hans)

Hyman, Inge. *Casper and the rainbow bird* (Hyman, Robin)

Hyman, Robin. *Casper and the rainbow bird* by Robin and Inge Hyman; ill. by Yutaka Sugita. Barron's, 1979. ISBN 0-8120-5253-6 Subj: Behavior – running away. Birds – crows. Birds – parakeets, parrots.

Hyman, Trina Schart. *The enchanted forest* ill. by author. Putnam, 1984. ISBN 0-399-21057-1 Subj: Forest, woods. Format, unusual. Wordless.

A little alphabet ill. by author. Little, 1980. ISBN 0-316-38705-3 Subj: ABC books.

Little Red Riding Hood (Grimm, Jacob)

The sleeping beauty (Grimm, Jacob)

Hymes, James L. *Oodles of noodles and other rhymes* (Hymes, Lucia)

Hymes, Lucia. *Oodles of noodles and other rhymes* by Lucia and James L. Hymes, Jr.; ill. by authors. Addison-Wesley, 1964. Subj: Poetry.

Hynard, Julia. *Percival's party* ill. by Frances Thatcher. Childrens Pr., 1983. ISBN 0-516-08941-2 Subj: Activities. Parties.

Hynard, Stephen. *Snowy the rabbit* ill. by Frances Thatcher. Childrens Pr., 1983. ISBN 0-516-08942-0 Subj: Activities. Animals – rabbits.

Ichikawa, Satomi. *A child's book of seasons* ill. by author. Parents, 1976. Subj: Folk and fairy tales. Seasons.

Fickle Barbara ill. by author. Philomel, 1993. ISBN 0-399-22020-8 Subj: Character traits – loyalty. Friendship. Toys – bears.

The first bear in Africa! ill. by author. Philomel, 2001. ISBN 0-399-23485-3 Subj: Behavior – losing things. Foreign lands – Africa. Toys – bears.

Isabela's ribbons ill. by author. Philomel, 1995. ISBN 0-399-22772-5 Subj: Activities – playing. Foreign lands – Puerto Rico. Friendship. Imagination. Islands.

Let's play ill. by author. Philomel, 1981. ISBN 0-399-61186-X Subj: Activities – playing.

Nora's castle ill. by author. Philomel, 1986. ISBN 0-399-21302-3 Subj: Animals. Homes, houses. Parties. Toys.

Nora's duck ill. by author. Putnam, 1991. ISBN 0-399-21805-X Subj: Animals. Birds – ducks. Character traits – kindness to animals.

Nora's roses ill. by author. Philomel, 1993. ISBN 0-399-21968-4 Subj: Behavior – boredom. Flowers. Illness.

Nora's stars ill. by author. Putnam, 1989. ISBN 0-399-21616-2 Subj: Family life – grandmothers. Sky. Stars. Toys.

Nora's surprise ill. by author. Philomel, 1994. ISBN 0-399-22535-8 Subj: Activities – picnicking. Animals – sheep. Birds – geese. Etiquette. Parties.

Sun through small leaves: poems of spring comp. and ill. by Satomi Ichikawa. Collins-World, 1980. ISBN 0-529-05572-4 Subj: Folk and fairy tales. Seasons – spring.

Suzanne and Nicholas at the market ill. by author. Watts, 1977. Translation by Denise Sheldon of Suzette et Nicolas au marché. ISBN 0-85166-669-8 Subj: Family life. Foreign lands – France. Shopping.

Suzanne and Nicholas in the garden ill. by author. St. Martin's, 1978. Translation by Denise Sheldon of Suzette et Nicolas dans leur jardin. ISBN 0-312-77982-8 Subj: Activities – playing. Ecology. Family life. Flowers. Foreign lands – France. Gardens, gardening.

If dragon flies made honey: *poems* col. by David Kherdian; ill. by José Aruego and Ariane Dewey. Greenwillow, 1977. ISBN 0-688-80101-3 Subj: Poetry.

If you ever meet a whale: *poems* sel. by Myra Cohn Livingston; ill. by Leonard Everett Fisher. Holiday, 1992. ISBN 0-8234-0940-6 Subj: Animals – whales. Poetry.

Ife, Elaine. *The childhood of Jesus* ill. by Eric Rowe. Rourke, 1983. ISBN 0-86625-223-1 Subj: Religion.

Moses in the bulrushes ill. by Eric Rowe. Rourke, 1983. ISBN 0-86625-217-7 Subj: Babies. Foreign lands – Egypt. Jewish culture. Religion – Moses.

Noah and the ark ill. by Russell Lee. Rourke, 1983. ISBN 0-86625-224-X Subj: Animals. Boats, ships. Religion – Noah. Weather – floods. Weather – rain. Weather – rainbows.

Stories Jesus told ill. by Russell Lee. Rourke, 1983. ISBN 0-86625-221-5 Subj: Religion.

Ignatowicz, Nina. *At the frog pond* (Michels, Tilde)

Leo the lion (Wagener, Gerda)

Igus, Toyomi. *Two Mrs. Gibsons* ill. by Daryl Wells. Children's Book Pr., 1996. ISBN 0-89239-135-9 Subj: Ethnic groups in the U.S. – African Americans. Ethnic groups in the U.S. – Japanese Americans. Family life – grandmothers. Family life – mothers. Marriage, interracial.

When I was little ill. by Higgins Bond. Just Us Books, 1992. ISBN 0-940975-33-5 Subj: Ethnic groups in the U.S. – African Americans. Family life – grandfathers. Sports – fishing.

Iké, Jane Hori. *A Japanese fairy tale* by Jane Hori Iké and Baruch Zimmerman; ill. by Jane Hori Iké. Warne, 1982. ISBN 0-7232-6208-X Subj: Character traits – appearance. Folk and fairy tales. Foreign lands – Japan.

Ikeda, Daisaku. *The cherry tree* trans. from Japanese by Geraldine McCaughrean; ill. by Brian Wildsmith. Knopf, 1992. ISBN 0-679-92669-0 Subj: Foreign lands – Japan. Hope. Trees. War.

Kanta and the deer ill. by Christina Sun. Weatherhill, 1997. ISBN 0-8348-0406-9 Subj: Animals – deer. Character traits – kindness to animals. Foreign lands – Japan.

Over the deep blue sea ill. by Geraldine McCaughrean. Knopf, 1992. ISBN 0-679-94184-3 Subj: Friendship. Islands. Prejudice.

The princess and the moon ill. by Brian Wildsmith; trans. from Japanese by Geraldine McCaughrean. Knopf, 1992. ISBN 0-679-93620-3 Subj: Animals – rabbits. Behavior. Emotions – anger. Moon.

The snow country prince trans. from Japanese by Geraldine McCaughrean; ill. by Brian Wildsmith. Knopf, 1991. ISBN 0-679-91965-1 Subj: Character traits – kindness to animals. Folk and fairy tales. Foreign lands – Japan. Royalty – princes.

Illyés, Gyula. *Matt the gooseherd: a story from Hungary* ill. by Károly Reich. Penguin, 1979. ISBN 0-14-030803-2 Subj: Birds – geese. Folk and fairy tales. Foreign lands – Hungary.

Ilsley, Velma. *A busy day for Chris* ill. by author. Lippincott, 1957. Subj: ABC books. Poetry.

M is for moving ill. by author. Walck, 1966. Subj: ABC books. Moving.

The pink hat ill. by author. Lippincott, 1956. Subj: Behavior – carelessness. Poetry.

Imagine that! poems of never-was sel. by Jack Prelutsky; ill. by Kevin Hawkes. Knopf, 1998. ISBN 0-679-98206-X Subj: Imagination. Poetry.

Imai, Miko. *Lilly's secret* ill. by author. Candlewick, 1994. ISBN 1-56402-232-3 Subj: Animals – cats. Character traits – being different. Friendship.

Little Lumpty ill. by author. Candlewick, 1994. ISBN 1-56402-233-1 Subj: Eggs. Family life – mothers.

Imershein, Betsy. *Finding red, finding yellow* photos by author. Harcourt, 1989. ISBN 0-15-200453-X Subj: Concepts – color. Format, unusual. Wordless.

Imoto, Yoko. *Skipper at the beach* ill. by author. Grosset, 1989. ISBN 0-448-09293-X Subj: Animals – cats. Family life. Sea and seashore.

Skipper is the daddy ill. by author. Grosset, 1989. ISBN 0-448-09294-8 Subj: Animals – cats. Family life.

Impey, Rose. *The ankle grabber* ill. by Moira Kemp. Barron's, 1989. ISBN 0-8120-5973-5 Subj: Emotions – fear. Monsters. Night.

The flat man ill. by Moira Kemp. Barron's, 1988. ISBN 0-8120-5975-1 Subj: Bedtime. Emotions – fear. Monsters. Mythical creatures – goblins. Night.

Joe's café ill. by Sue Porter. Little, 1991. ISBN 0-316-41777-7 Subj: Activities – babysitting. Activities – playing. Family life – brothers and sisters. Restaurants.

Jumble Joan ill. by Moira Kemp. Carolrhoda, 1998. ISBN 1-57505-295-4 Subj: Emotions – fear. Family life – brothers and sisters.

My mom and our dad ill. by Maureen Galvani. Viking, 1991. ISBN 0-670-83663-X Subj: Family life – fathers. Family life – mothers. Multiple births – twins.

Scare yourself to sleep ill. by Moira Kemp. Barron's, 1988. ISBN 0-8120-5974-3 Subj: Emotions – fear. Family life – cousins. Monsters. Night.

Who's a bright girl? ill. by André Amstutz. Barron's, 1989. ISBN 0-8120-6144-6 Subj: Pirates. Sex roles.

Imsand, Marcel. *The fir tree* (Andersen, H. C. [Hans Christian])

In daddy's arms I am tall ill. by Javaka Steptoe. Lee & Low, 1997. ISBN 1-8800003-1-8 Subj: Ethnic groups in the U.S. – African Americans. Family life – fathers. Poetry.

Ingle, Annie. *The big city book* ill. by Tim and Greg Hildebrandt. Platt, 1976. ISBN 0-8228-7616-7 Subj: City.

Ingman, Bruce. *Lost property* ill. by author. Houghton Mifflin, 1998. ISBN 0-395-88900-6 Subj: Animals – dogs. Behavior – losing things. Family life.

A night on the tiles ill. by author. Houghton Mifflin, 1999. ISBN 0-395-93655-1 Subj: Activities. Animals – cats. Foreign lands – France. Night.

Ingoglia, Gina. *The art class* ill. by Ed Rodriguez. Walt Disney, 1992. ISBN 1-56282-227-6 Subj: Art. Character traits – assertiveness. School.

The big book of real airplanes ill. by George Guzzi. Putnam, 1987. ISBN 0-448-19179-2 Subj: Airplanes, airports. Helicopters. Transportation.

Ingpen, Robert. *The idle bear* ill. by author. HarperCollins, 1987. ISBN 0-87226-159-X Subj: Toys – bears.

Inkiow, Dimiter. *Me and Clara and Baldwin the pony* trans. from German by Paula McGuire; ill. by Traudl and Walter Reiner. Pantheon, 1980. ISBN 0-694-94434-8 Subj: Animals – horses, ponies. Behavior – misbehavior.

Me and Clara and Casimir the cat trans. from German by Paula McGuire; ill. by Traudl and Walter Reiner. Pantheon, 1979. ISBN 0-394-94124-1 Subj: Animals – cats.

Me and Clara and Snuffy the dog trans. from German by Paula McGuire; ill. by Traudl and Walter Reiner. Pantheon, 1980. ISBN 0-394-94433-X Subj: Animals – dogs. Behavior – misbehavior.

Me and my sister Clara trans. from German by Paula McGuire; ill. by Traudl and Walter Reiner. Pantheon, 1979. ISBN 0-394-94123-3 Subj: Behavior – misbehavior.

Inkpen, Mick. *Anything cuddly will do!* ill. by author; paper engineering by Dennis K. Meyer. Orchard, 1993. ISBN 1-8521-3608-1 Subj: Animals. Format, unusual – toy and movable books. Pets. Rhyming text.

Arnold ill. by author. Harcourt, 1998. ISBN 0-15-202289-9 Subj: Animals – dogs. Animals – pigs. Thumb sucking.

Billy's beetle ill. by author. Harcourt, 1992. ISBN 0-15-200427-0 Subj: Animals. Behavior – losing things. Cumulative tales. Insects – beetles.

The blue balloon ill. by author. Little, 1990. ISBN 0-316-41886-2 Subj: Format, unusual. Imagination. Toys – balloons.

Butterfly ill. by author. Harcourt, 1999. ISBN 0-15-202409-3 Subj: Animals – dogs. Insects – butterflies, caterpillars.

Crocodile! ill. by author. Orchard, 1993. ISBN 1-8521-3609-X Subj: Format, unusual – toy and movable books. Reptiles – alligators, crocodiles. Rhyming text.

Field day (Butterworth, Nick)

The great pet sale ill. by author. Orchard, 1999. ISBN 0-531-30130-3 Subj: Animals. Money. Pets.

Gumboot's chocolatey day ill. by author. Doubleday, 1991. ISBN 0-385-41490-0 Subj: Animals – pigs. Birds – ducks. Food.

Hissss! ill. by author. Harcourt, 2000. ISBN 0-15-202415-8 Subj: Animals – dogs. Seasons – summer.

Honk! ill. by author. Harcourt, 1998. ISBN 0-15-202284-8 Subj: Animals – dogs. Birds – geese. Noise, sounds.

The house on the rock (Butterworth, Nick)

If I had a pig ill. by author. Little, 1988. ISBN 0-316-41887-0 Subj: Animals – pigs. Friendship. Imagination.

If I had a sheep ill. by author. Little, 1988. ISBN 0-316-41888-9 Subj: Animals – sheep. Friendship. Imagination.

Jasper's beanstalk (Butterworth, Nick)

Kipper ill. by author. Little, 1992. ISBN 0-316-41883-8 Subj: Animals – dogs. Behavior – imitation. Sleep.

Kipper's A to Z: an alphabet adventure ill. by author. Harcourt, 2000. ISBN 0-15-202594-4 Subj: ABC books. Animals. Animals – dogs. Animals – pigs.

Kipper's bathtime ill. by author. Harcourt, 1999. ISBN 0-15-202694-0 Subj: Activities – bathing. Animals – dogs. Format, unusual – toy and movable books. Toys.

Kipper's bedtime ill. by author. Harcourt, 1999. ISBN 0-15-202403-4 Subj: Animals – dogs. Bedtime. Format, unusual – toy and movable books.

Kipper's birthday ill. by author. Harcourt, 1993. ISBN 0-15-200503-X Subj: Animals – dogs. Behavior – mistakes. Birthdays. Parties.

Kipper's book of colors ill. by author. Harcourt, 1995. ISBN 0-15-200647-8 Subj: Animals – dogs. Concepts – color.

Kipper's book of counting ill. by author. Hodder & Stoughton, 1994. ISBN 0-340-59848-4 Subj: Animals. Animals – dogs. Counting, numbers.

Kipper's book of numbers ill. by author. Harcourt, 1995. ISBN 0-15-200646-X Subj: Animals. Animals – dogs. Counting, numbers.

Kipper's book of opposites ill. by author. Harcourt, 1995. ISBN 0-15-200668-0 Subj: Animals – dogs. Concepts – opposites. Language.

Kipper's book of weather ill. by author. Harcourt, 1995. ISBN 0-15-200644-3 Subj: Animals – dogs. Weather.

Kipper's Christmas Eve ill. by author. Harcourt, 1999. ISBN 0-15-202660-6 Subj: Animals – dogs. Friendship. Holidays – Christmas.

Kipper's playtime ill. by author. Harcourt, 1999. ISBN 0-15-202421-2 Subj: Activities – playing. Animals – dogs. Format, unusual – toy and movable books.

Kipper's snacktime ill. by author. Harcourt, 1999. ISBN 0-15-202433-6 Subj: Animals – dogs. Food. Format, unusual – toy and movable books.

Kipper's snowy day ill. by author. Harcourt, 1996. ISBN 0-15-201362-8 Subj: Activities – playing. Animals – dogs. Friendship. Toys. Weather – snow.

Kipper's toybox ill. by author. Harcourt, 1992. ISBN 0-15-200501-3 Subj: Animals – dogs. Animals – mice. Counting, numbers. Toys.

Lullabyhullaballoo! ill. by author. Artists & Writers Guild, 1994. ISBN 0-307-17509-X Subj: Bedtime. Format, unusual – toy and movable books. Imagination. Noise, sounds. Royalty – princesses.

Meow! ill. by author. Harcourt, 2000. ISBN 0-15-202666-5 Subj: Animals. Animals – cats. Animals – dogs.

The Nativity play (Butterworth, Nick)

Nice or nasty (Butterworth, Nick)

Nothing ill. by author. Orchard, 1998. ISBN 0-531-30076-5 Subj: Names. Self-concept. Toys.

One bear at bedtime ill. by author. Little, 1988. ISBN 0-316-41889-7 Subj: Animals. Bedtime. Counting, numbers. Imagination. Toys – bears.

Penguin small ill. by author. Harcourt, 1993. ISBN 0-15-200567-6 Subj: Activities – trading. Animals – polar bears. Birds – penguins. Emotions – fear. Foreign lands – Antarctic. Foreign lands – Arctic. Format, unusual – toy and movable books. Snowmen.

Picnic ill. by author. Harcourt, 2001. ISBN 0-15-216319-0 Subj: Activities – picnicking. Animals. Animals – dogs.

Sandcastle ill. by author. Harcourt, 1998. ISBN 0-15-202296-1 Subj: Sand. Sea and seashore.

The school trip (Butterworth, Nick)

Splosh! ill. by author. Harcourt, 1998. ISBN 0-15-202299-6 Subj: Animals. Animals – dogs. Weather – rain.

Swing! ill. by author. Harcourt, 2000. ISBN 0-15-202672-X Subj: Activities – playing. Animals – dogs. Friendship.

Thing ill. by author. Harcourt, 2001. ISBN 0-15-216326-3 Subj: Animals – dogs. Bubbles. Toys.

This troll, that troll ill. by author; paper engineering by José R. Seminario. Orchard, 1993. ISBN 1-8521-3607-3 Subj: Format, unusual – toy and movable books. Mythical creatures – trolls. Rhyming text.

Threadbear ill. by author. Little, 1991. ISBN 0-316-41884-6 Subj: Format, unusual. Toys – bears.

The very good dinosaur ill. by author; paper engineering by Rodger Smith. Orchard, 1993. ISBN 1-8521-3610-3 Subj: Dinosaurs. Format, unusual – toy and movable books. Rhyming text.

Where, oh where, is Kipper's bear? a pop-up book with light! ill. by author. Harcourt, 1995. ISBN 0-15-200394-0 Subj: Animals – dogs. Behavior – losing things. Format, unusual – toy and movable books. Rhyming text. Toys – bears.

Wibbly Pig can dance! ill. by author. Golden Books, 1995. ISBN 0-307-16626-0 Subj: Activities – dancing. Activities – playing. Animals – pigs. Bedtime.

Wibbly Pig can make a tent ill. by author. Golden Books, 1995. ISBN 0-307-16628-7 Subj: Activities – making things. Activities – playing. Animals – pigs. Camps, camping. Format, unusual – board books.

Wibbly Pig is upset ill. by author. Golden Books, 1995. ISBN 0-307-16629-5 Subj: Animals – pigs. Emotions. Format, unusual – board books.

Wibbly Pig likes bananas ill. by author. Golden Books, 1995. ISBN 0-307-16630-9 Subj: Animals – pigs. Food. Format, unusual – board books.

Wibbly Pig makes pictures ill. by author. Golden Books, 1995. ISBN 0-307-16625-2 Subj: Activities – drawing. Animals – pigs. Format, unusual – board books.

Wibbly Pig opens his presents ill. by author. Golden Books, 1995. ISBN 0-307-16627-9 Subj: Animals – pigs. Format, unusual – board books. Gifts.

Intrater, Roberta Grobel. *Peek-a-boo!* ill. by author. Scholastic, 1997. ISBN 0-590-05896-7 Subj: Babies. Family life. Format, unusual – board books. Games.

Smile! ill. by author. Scholastic, 1997. ISBN 0-590-05899-1 Subj: Babies. Family life. Format, unusual – board books.

Two eyes, a nose, and a mouth ill. by author. Scholastic, 1995. ISBN 0-590-48247-5 Subj: Anatomy – faces. Rhyming text.

Inwald, Robin. *Cap it off with a smile: a guide for making friends* ill. by author. Hilson Press, 1994. ISBN 1-8857-3800-5 Subj: Behavior. Friendship. Rhyming text.

Ipcar, Dahlov. *Animal hide and seek* ill. by author. Addison-Wesley, 1947. Subj: Animals.

The biggest fish in the sea ill. by author. Viking, 1972. ISBN 0-670-16541-7 Subj: Concepts – size. Fish. Sports – fishing.

Black and white ill. by author. Knopf, 1963. Subj: Animals – dogs. Dreams. Rhyming text.

Bright barnyard ill. by author. Knopf, 1966. Subj: Animals. Birds. Farms.

Brown cow farm: a counting book ill. by author. Doubleday, 1959. Subj: Animals. Counting, numbers. Farms.

Bug city ill. by author. Holiday, 1975. ISBN 0-8234-0258-4 Subj: Insects.

The calico jungle ill. by author. Knopf, 1965. Subj: Animals. Bedtime. Quilts.

The cat at night ill. by author. Doubleday, 1969. Subj: Animals – cats. Night.

The cat came back ill. by author. Knopf, 1971. ISBN 0-394-82291-9 Subj: Animals – cats. Music. Rhyming text. Songs.

A flood of creatures ill. by author. Holiday, 1973. ISBN 0-8234-0224-X Subj: Animals. Weather – floods.

Hard scrabble harvest ill. by author. Doubleday, 1976. ISBN 0-385-00777-9 Subj: Farms. Holidays – Thanksgiving. Plants. Rhyming text.

I like animals ill. by author. Knopf, 1960. Subj: Animals. Careers.

I love my anteater with an A ill. by author. Knopf, 1964. ISBN 0-394-91267-5 Subj: ABC books. Animals.

The land of flowers ill. by author. Viking, 1974. ISBN 0-670-41754-8 Subj: Animals – sheep. Concepts – size. Flowers. Gardens, gardening.

Lost and found: a hidden animal book ill. by author. Doubleday, 1981. ISBN 0-385-15171-3 Subj: Animals. Participation.

My wonderful Christmas tree ill. by author. Down East, 1999. ISBN 0-89272-475-7 Subj: Animals. Counting, numbers. Holidays – Christmas. Rhyming text.

One horse farm ill. by author. Doubleday, 1950. Subj: Animals – horses, ponies. Farms. Machines. Progress.

Sir Addlepate and the unicorn ill. by author. Doubleday, 1971. Subj: Knights. Mythical creatures – unicorns.

"The song of the day birds" and "The song of the night birds" ill. by author. Doubleday, 1967. Subj: Birds. Music. Night. Songs.

Stripes and spots ill. by author. Doubleday, 1953. Subj: Animals – leopards. Animals – tigers.

Ten big farms ill. by author. Knopf, 1958. Subj: Counting, numbers. Farms.

Wild and tame animals ill. by author. Doubleday, 1962. Subj: Animals.

World full of horses ill. by author. Doubleday, 1955. Subj: Animals – horses, ponies.

Irbinskas, Heather. *How Jackrabbit got his very long ears* ill. by Ken Spengler. Northland, 1994. ISBN 0-87358-566-6 Subj: Anatomy – ears. Animals. Animals – rabbits. Behavior. Desert. Folk and fairy tales. Self-concept.

Ireson, Barbara. *The gingerbread man* (The gingerbread boy)

Iribarren, Elena. *Nina Bonita* (Machado, Ana Maria)

Irvine, Georgeanne. *Bo the orangutan* photos by Ron Garrison. Childrens Pr., 1983. ISBN 0-516-09307-X Subj: Animals – monkeys. Zoos.

Elmer the elephant photos by Ron Garrison. Childrens Pr., 1983. ISBN 0-516-09310-X Subj: Animals – elephants. Zoos.

Georgie the giraffe photos by Ron Garrison. Childrens Pr., 1983. ISBN 0-516-09308-8 Subj: Animals – giraffes. Zoos.

Lindi the leopard photos by Ron Garrison. Childrens Pr., 1983. ISBN 0-516-09309-6 Subj: Animals – leopards. Zoos.

The nursery babies photos by Ron Garrison. Childrens Pr., 1983. ISBN 0-516-09311-8 Subj: Animals. Zoos.

Sasha the cheetah photos by Ron Garrison. Childrens Pr., 1982. ISBN 0-516-09303-7 Subj: Animals – cheetahs. Zoos.

Sydney the koala photos by Ron Garrison. Childrens Pr., 1982. ISBN 0-516-09304-5 Subj: Animals – koalas. Zoos.

Tully the tree kangaroo photos by Ron Garrison. Childrens Pr., 1983. ISBN 0-516-09312-6 Subj: Animals. Zoos.

Irving, Washington. *The headless horseman* (Standiford, Natalie)

The legend of Sleepy Hollow (San Souci, Robert D.)

The legend of Sleepy Hollow (Wolkstein, Diane)

Rip Van Winkle adapt. and ill. by John Howe. Little, 1988. ISBN 0-316-37578-0 Subj: Behavior – lost. Folk and fairy tales. Mythical creatures – elves. Sleep.

Rip Van Winkle adapt. and ill. by Thomas Locker. Little, 1988. ISBN 0-8037-0521-2 Subj: Behavior – lost. Folk and fairy tales. Mythical creatures – elves. Sleep.

Rip Van Winkle adapt. by Catherine Storr; ill. by Peter Wingham. Raintree, 1984. ISBN 0-8172-2108-5 Subj: Behavior – lost. Folk and fairy tales. Mythical creatures – elves. Sleep.

Washington Irving's Rip Van Winkle (Bergen, Lara Rice)

Isaacs, Anne. *Cat up a tree* ill. by Stephen Mackey. Dutton, 1998. ISBN 0-525-45994-4 Subj: Animals – cats. Poetry.

Swamp Angel ill. by Paul O. Zelinsky. Dutton, 1994. ISBN 0-525-45271-0 Subj: Caldecott award honor books. Tall tales. U.S. history – frontier and pioneer life.

Isaacs, Gwynne L. *Baby face: a mirror book* ill. by Evelyn Clarke Mott. Random House, 1994. ISBN 0-679-84981-5 Subj: Anatomy – faces. Babies. Format, unusual – toy and movable books. Rhyming text.

Isadora, Rachel. *ABC pop!* ill. by author. Viking, 1999. ISBN 0-670-88329-8 Subj: ABC books. Art.

At the crossroads ill. by author. Greenwillow, 1991. ISBN 0-688-05271-1 Subj: Emotions. Family life. Foreign lands – South Africa.

Babies ill. by author. Greenwillow, 1990. ISBN 0-688-08032-4 Subj: Activities. Babies.

Ben's trumpet ill. by author. Greenwillow, 1979. ISBN 0-688-80194-3 Subj: Caldecott award honor books. Ethnic groups in the U.S. – African Americans. Music.

Bring on that beat ill. by author. Putnam, 2001. ISBN 0-399-23232-X Subj: Ethnic groups in the U.S. – African Americans. Music. Rhyming text.

Caribbean dream ill. by author. Putnam, 1998. ISBN 0-399-23230-3 Subj: Dreams. Foreign lands – Caribbean Islands. Islands.

City seen from A to Z ill. by author. Greenwillow, 1983. ISBN 0-688-01803-3 Subj: ABC books. City.

The firebird (The firebird)

Friends ill. by author. Greenwillow, 1990. ISBN 0-688-08265-3 Subj: Activities. Friendship.

I hear ill. by author. Greenwillow, 1985. ISBN 0-688-04062-4 Subj: Babies. Family life. Noise, sounds. Senses – hearing.

I see ill. by author. Greenwillow, 1985. ISBN 0-688-04060-8 Subj: Babies. Family life. Senses – seeing.

I touch ill. by author. Greenwillow, 1985. ISBN 0-688-04256-2 Subj: Senses – touching.

Jesse and Abe ill. by author. Greenwillow, 1981. ISBN 0-688-84302-6 Subj: Family life – grandfathers. Theater.

Lili at ballet ill. by author. Putnam, 1993. ISBN 0-399-22423-8 Subj: Activities – dancing. Ballet.

Lili on stage ill. by author. Putnam, 1995. ISBN 0-399-22637-0 Subj: Activities – dancing. Ballet. Careers – dancers. Theater.

Listen to the city ill. by author. Putnam, 2000. ISBN 0-399-23047-5 Subj: City. Noise, sounds.

The little mermaid (Andersen, H. C. [Hans Christian])

Max ill. by author. Macmillan, 1976. ISBN 0-02-747450-7 Subj: Activities – dancing. Ballet. Sports – baseball.

My ballet class ill. by author. Greenwillow, 1980. ISBN 0-688-84253-4 Subj: Activities – dancing. Ballet.

My ballet diary ill. by author. Putnam, 1995. ISBN 0-399-22620-6 Subj: Activities – dancing. Ballet.

No, Agatha! ill. by author. Greenwillow, 1980. ISBN 0-688-84274-7 Subj: Activities – traveling. Boats, ships.

The nutcracker (Hoffmann, E. T. A.)

123 pop! ill. by author. Viking, 2000. ISBN 0-670-88859-1 Subj: Counting, numbers.

Opening night ill. by author. Greenwillow, 1984. ISBN 0-688-02727-X Subj: Activities – dancing. Theater.

Over the green hills ill. by author. Greenwillow, 1992. ISBN 0-688-10510-6 Subj: Activities – traveling. Communities, neighborhoods. Family life – grandmothers. Foreign lands – South Africa.

The pirates of Bedford Street ill. by author. Greenwillow, 1988. ISBN 0-688-05208-8 Subj: Imagination. Pirates.

The Potters' kitchen ill. by author. Greenwillow, 1977. ISBN 0-688-84089-2 Subj: Moving.

The princess and the frog (Grimm, Jacob)

Sophie skates ill. by author. Putnam, 1999. ISBN 0-399-23046-7 Subj: Sports – ice skating.

A South African night ill. by author. Greenwillow, 1998. ISBN 0-688-11390-7 Subj: Animals. Foreign lands – Africa. Foreign lands – South Africa. Jungle. Night.

The steadfast tin soldier (Andersen, H. C. [Hans Christian])

Willaby ill. by author. Macmillan, 1977. ISBN 0-02-747746-0 Subj: School.

Isami, Ikuyo. *The fox's egg* trans. from Japanese by Cathy Hirano; ill. by author. Carolrhoda, 1989. ISBN 0-87614-339-7 Subj: Animals – foxes. Birds – chickens. Eggs.

Isele, Elizabeth. *The frog princess: a Russian tale retold* ill. by Michael Hague. HarperCollins, 1984. ISBN 0-690-04218-3 Subj: Folk and fairy tales. Foreign lands – Russia. Frogs and toads. Magic. Royalty – princesses. Witches.

Pooks ill. by Chris L. Demarest. Lippincott, 1983. ISBN 0-397-32045-0 Subj: Activities – traveling. Animals – dogs. Music.

Isenbart, Hans-Heinrich. *Baby animals on the farm* trans. from German by Elizabeth D. Crawford; photos by Ruth Rau. Putnam, 1984. ISBN 0-399-20960-3 Subj: Animals. Farms.

A duckling is born trans. by Catherine Edwards Sadler; photos by Othmar Baumli. Putnam, 1981. ISBN 0-399-20778-3 Subj: Birds – ducks. Birth. Science.

Isenberg, Barbara. *The adventures of Albert, the running bear* by Barbara Isenberg and Susan Wolf; ill. by Dick Gackenbach. Houghton Mifflin, 1982. ISBN 0-89919-113-4 Subj: Animals – bears. Behavior – running away. Sports – racing. Zoos.

Albert the running bear gets the jitters by Barbara Isenberg and Susan Wolf; ill. by Diane de Groat. Clarion, 1987. ISBN 0-89919-532-6 Subj: Animals – bears. Behavior – bullying. Behavior – trickery. Sports – racing.

Albert the running bear's exercise book by Barbara Isenberg and Marjorie Jaffe; ill. by Diane de Groat. Houghton Mifflin, 1984. ISBN 0-89919-294-7 Subj: Animals – bears. Health and fitness – exercise.

Isherwood, Shirley. *The band over the hill* by Shirley Isherwood and Reg Cartwright; ill. by Reg Cartwright. Hutchinson, 1997. ISBN 0-09-176753-9 Subj: Animals – bears. Careers – musicians. Music.

Flora the frog ill. by Anna C. Leplar. Peachtree, 2000. ISBN 1-56145-223-8 Subj: Frogs and toads. School. Theater.

Something for James ill. by Neil Reed. Dial, 1996. ISBN 0-8037-1914-0 Subj: Animals. Mystery stories. Toys.

Ishii, Momoko. *The tongue-cut sparrow* trans. from Japanese by Katherine Paterson; ill. by Suekichi Akaba. Lodestar, 1987. Tr. of Sita-kiri suzume. ISBN 0-525-67199-4 Subj: Behavior – greed. Birds

– sparrows. Character traits – kindness to animals. Folk and fairy tales. Foreign lands – Japan.

Isom, Joan Shaddox. *The first starry night* ill. by author. Whispering Coyote, 1997. ISBN 1-8790-8596-8 Subj: Art. Careers – artists.

Israel, Marion Louise. *The tractor on the farm* ill. by Robert Dranko. Melmont, 1958. Subj: Farms. Tractors.

It feels like Christmas! *It feels like Christmas! a book of surprises to touch, see, and sniff* ill. by Denise Fleming. Random House, 1984. ISBN 0-394-86862-5 Subj: Format, unusual – toy and movable books. Holidays – Christmas. Senses.

Ivanov, Anatoly. *Ol' Jake's lucky day* ill. by author. Lothrop, 1984. ISBN 0-688-02867-5 Subj: Behavior – seeking better things. Character traits – luck. Folk and fairy tales. Foreign lands – Russia. Imagination.

I've been working on the railroad ill. by Nadine Bernard Westcott. Hyperion, 1996. ISBN 0-7868-2041-1 Subj: Folk and fairy tales. Music. Songs. Trains.

Iverson, Diane. *Discover the seasons* ill. by author. Dawn Pub., 1996. ISBN 1-883220-43-2 Subj: Activities. Activities – making things. Nature. Seasons.

Iverson, Genie. *I want to be big* ill. by David McPhail. Dutton, 1979. ISBN 0-525-32539-5 Subj: Behavior – growing up.

Ives, Penny. *The golden angel* ill. by author. Tango, 1995. ISBN 1-8570712-6-3 Subj: Angels. Format, unusual – toy and movable books.

Mrs. Santa Claus ill. by author. Delacorte, 1991. ISBN 0-385-30303-3 Subj: Family life. Gender roles. Holidays – Christmas. Illness. Problem solving. Santa Claus.

On Christmas eve: a three-dimensional celebration ill. by author; paper engineering by David Hawcock. Putnam, 1992. ISBN 0-399-22148-4 Subj: Format, unusual – toy and movable books. Holidays – Christmas.

The snow angel: a pop-up ornament book ill. by author; paper engineering by David Hawcock. Tango, 1995. ISBN 1-8570712-5-5 Subj: Angels. Format, unusual – toy and movable books. Weather – snow.

Ivimey, John William. *The complete story of the three blind mice* ill. by Paul Galdone. Clarion, 1987. ISBN 0-89919-481-8 Subj: Animals – mice. Music. Nursery rhymes. Songs.

The complete version of ye three blind mice ill. by Walton Corbould. Warne, 1909. ISBN 0-7232-2256-8 Subj: Animals – mice. Music. Nursery rhymes. Songs.

Three blind mice ill. by Lorinda Bryan Cauley. Putnam, 1991. ISBN 0-399-21775-4 Subj: Animals – mice. Music. Nursery rhymes. Songs.

Three blind mice ill. by Victoria Chess. Little, 1990. ISBN 0-316-13867-3 Subj: Animals – mice. Music. Nursery rhymes. Songs.

Ivory, Lesley Anne. *The birthday cat* ill. by author. HarperCollins, 1993. ISBN 0-8037-1622-2 Subj: Animals – cats. Animals – rabbits. Behavior – hiding things. Birthdays. Toys.

Cats in the sun ill. by author. Dial, 1991. ISBN 0-8037-0955-2 Subj: Animals – cats. Sun.

A day in London ill. by author. Burke, 1982. ISBN 0-222-00785-0 Subj: City. Foreign lands – England.

A day in New York ill. by author. Burke, 1982. ISBN 0-222-00788-5 Subj: City.

Meet my cats ill. by author. Dial, 1989. ISBN 0-8037-0602-2 Subj: Animals – cats. Pets.

Iwamatsu, Jun. *see* Yashima, Taro

Iwamura, Kazuo. *The fourteen forest mice and the harvest moon watch* ill. by author. Gareth Stevens, 1991. ISBN 0-8368-0497-X Subj: Animals – mice. Forest, woods. Moon. Seasons – fall.

The fourteen forest mice and the spring meadow picnic ill. by author. Gareth Stevens, 1991. ISBN 0-8368-0498-8 Subj: Activities – picnicking. Animals – mice. Forest, woods. Seasons – spring.

The fourteen forest mice and the summer laundry day ill. by author. Gareth Stevens, 1991. ISBN 0-8368-0576-3 Subj: Animals – mice. Forest, woods. Laundry. Seasons – summer.

The fourteen forest mice and the winter sledding day ill. by author. Gareth Stevens, 1991. ISBN 0-8368-0499-6 Subj: Animals – mice. Forest, woods. Seasons – winter. Sports – sledding.

Tan Tan's hat ill. by author. Bradbury, 1983. ISBN 0-02-747490-9 Subj: Animals – monkeys. Clothing – hats.

Tan Tan's suspenders ill. by author. Bradbury, 1983. ISBN 0-02-747500-X Subj: Animals – monkeys. Clothing.

Ton and Pon: big and little ill. by author. Bradbury, 1984. ISBN 0-02-747480-1 Subj: Animals – dogs. Concepts – size. Friendship.

Ton and Pon: two good friends ill. by author. Bradbury, 1984. ISBN 0-02-747510-7 Subj: Animals – dogs. Friendship.

Iwasaki, Chihiro. *The birthday wish* ill. by author. McGraw-Hill, 1974, 1972. ISBN 0-07032-073-X Subj: Behavior – wishing. Birthdays. Weather – snow.

Staying home alone on a rainy day ill. by author. McGraw-Hill, 1968. Subj: Family life. Family life – only child. Weather – rain.

What's fun without a friend? ill. by author. McGraw-Hill, 1972. ISBN 0-07-032089-6 Subj: Animals – dogs. Sea and seashore.

Will you be my friend? ill. by author. McGraw-Hill, 1970. ISBN 0-07-032077-2 Subj: Friendship.

Izawa, Yohji. *One evening* (Funakoshi, Canna)

J. Paul Getty Museum. *A is for artist: a Getty Museum alphabet* (John Harris, writer and editor). J. P. Getty Museum, 1997. ISBN 0-89236-377-0 Subj: ABC books. Art. Museums.

Jabar, Cynthia. *Bored blue? Think what you can do!* ill. by author. Little, 1991. ISBN 0-316-43458-2 Subj: Activities. Rhyming text.

Party day! ill. by author. Little, 1987. ISBN 0-316-43456-6 Subj: Animals – rabbits. Birthdays. Counting, numbers.

Shimmy shake earthquake: don't forget to dance poems ed. and ill. by Cynthia Jabar. Little, 1992. ISBN 0-316-43459-0 Subj: Activities – dancing. Poetry.

Jack and the beanstalk. *The history of Mother Twaddle and the marvelous achievements of her son Jack* ill. by Paul Galdone. Seabury Pr., 1974. A verse version of Jack and the beanstalk, written by Basil T. Blackwood [B.A.T.] and pub. in 1807 by J. Harris, London. ISBN 0-8164-3112-4 Subj: Folk and fairy tales. Giants. Plants. Rhyming text.

Jack and the beanstalk retold and ill. by Val Biro. Oxford Univ. Pr., 1990. ISBN 0-19-278008-5 Subj: Folk and fairy tales. Giants. Plants.

Jack and the beanstalk adapt. and ill. by Lorinda Bryan Cauley. Putnam, 1983. ISBN 0-399-20901-8 Subj: Folk and fairy tales. Giants. Plants.

Jack and the beanstalk adapt. by Sindy McKay; ill. by Lydia Halverson. Treasure Bay, 1997. ISBN 1-891327-00-3 Subj: Folk and fairy tales. Giants. Plants.

Jack and the beanstalk ill. by Julek Heller. Doubleday, 1992. ISBN 0-385-30693-8 Subj: Folk and fairy tales. Giants. Plants.

Jack and the beanstalk retold and ill. by John Howe. Little, 1989. ISBN 0-316-37579-9 Subj: Folk and fairy tales. Giants. Plants.

Jack and the beanstalk retold and ill. by Steven Kellogg. Morrow, 1991. ISBN 0-688-10251-4 Subj: Folk and fairy tales. Giants. Plants.

Jack and the beanstalk ill. by Ed Parker. Troll, 1979. ISBN 0-89375-125-1 Subj: Folk and fairy tales. Giants. Plants.

Jack and the beanstalk adapt. and ill. by Tony Ross. Delacorte, 1981. ISBN 0-440-04174-0 Subj: Folk and fairy tales. Giants. Plants.

Jack and the beanstalk retold by Richard Walker; ill. by Niamh Sharkey. Barefoot, 1999. ISBN 1-902283-13-9 Subj: Folk and fairy tales. Giants. Plants.

Jack and the beanstalk retold by Ann Keay Beneduce; ill. by Gennady Spirin. Philomel, 1999. ISBN 0-399-23118-8 Subj: Folk and fairy tales. Giants. Plants.

Jack and the beanstalk ill. by William Stobbs. Dial, 1966. Subj: Folk and fairy tales. Giants. Plants.

Jack and the beanstalk retold by Susan Pearson; ill. by James Warhola. Simon & Schuster, 1989. ISBN 0-671-67196-0 Subj: Folk and fairy tales. Giants. Plants.

Jack and the beanstalk retold by Beatrice Schenk De Regniers; ill. by Anne Wilsdorf. Atheneum, 1985. ISBN 0-689-31174-5 Subj: Folk and fairy tales. Giants. Plants. Rhyming text.

Jack and the beanstalk / Juan y los frijoles magicos by Francesc Bofill; ill. by Arnal Ballester. Chronicle, 1998. ISBN 0-8118-1843-8 Subj: Folk and fairy tales. Foreign languages. Giants. Plants.

Jack the giant killer: Jack's first and finest adventure retold in verse as well as other useful information about giants including how to shake hands with a giant retold by Beatrice Schenk De Regniers; ill. by Anne Wilsdorf. Atheneum, 1987. ISBN 0-689-31218-0 Subj: Folk and fairy tales. Giants. Plants. Rhyming text.

Jack the giantkiller adapt. and ill. by Tony Ross. David & Charles, 1987. ISBN 0-862-64060-1 Subj: Folk and fairy tales. Giants. Plants.

Jack Sprat. *The life of Jack Sprat, his wife and his cat* retold and ill. by Paul Galdone. McGraw-Hill, 1969. Subj: Animals – cats. Family life. Food. Nursery rhymes.

Jacka, Martin. *Waiting for Billy* ill. by author. Watts, 1991. ISBN 0-531-08533-3 Subj: Animals – dogs. Animals – dolphins. Animals – horses, ponies. Foreign lands – Australia.

Jackson, Alison. *I know an old lady who swallowed a pie* ill. by Judith Byron Schachner. Dutton, 1997. ISBN 0-525-45645-7 Subj: Cumulative tales. Folk and fairy tales. Food. Holidays – Thanksgiving. Humor. Rhyming text.

Jackson, Bobby L. *Little Red Ronnika* ill. by Rhonda Mitchell. Multicultural Pub., 1998. ISBN 1-884242-80-4 Subj: Ethnic groups in the U.S. – African Americans. Family life – grandmothers. Folk and fairy tales.

Makimba's animal world ill. by Julienne Jones. Multicultural Pub., 1994. ISBN 0-9634932-9-9 Subj: Animals. Foreign lands – Africa. Language.

Jackson, Carolyn. *The flying ark* ill. by Graham Bardell. Stoddart, 1995. ISBN 0-7737-5711-2 Subj: Activities – flying. Animals.

Jackson, Ellen B. *Ants can't dance* ill. by Frank Remkiewicz. Macmillan, 1991. ISBN 0-02-747661-8 Subj: Behavior – disbelief.

The bear in the bathtub ill. by Margot Apple. Addison-Wesley, 1981. ISBN 0-201-04701-2 Subj: Activities – bathing. Animals – bears. Character traits – cleanliness.

The book of slime ill. by Jan Davey Ellis. Millbrook, 1997. ISBN 0-7613-0042-2 Subj: Anatomy. Nature.

Boris the boring boar ill. by Normand Chartier. Macmillan, 1992. ISBN 0-02-747662-6 Subj: Animals – pigs. Animals – wolves. Emotions – loneliness.

Brown cow, green grass, yellow mellow sun ill. by Victoria Raymond. Hyperion, 1995. ISBN 0-7868-2006-3 Subj: Circular tales. Concepts – color. Farms. Food. Nature.

Cinder Edna ill. by Kevin O'Malley. Lothrop, 1994. ISBN 0-688-12323-6 Subj: Folk and fairy tales. Royalty – princes.

The impossible riddle ill. by Alison Winfield. Whispering Coyote, 1995. ISBN 1-879085-93-3 Subj: Character traits – cleverness. Food. Foreign lands – Russia. Riddles. Royalty – kings.

Monsters in my mailbox ill. by Maxie Chambliss. Troll, 1995. ISBN 0-8167-3631-6 Subj: Activities – playing. Clubs, gangs. Monsters.

The precious gift: a Navaho creation myth ill. by Woodleigh Marx Hubbard. Simon & Schuster, 1996. ISBN 0-689-80480-6 Subj: Animals. Animals – snails. Creation. Gifts. Indians of North America – Navajo. Water.

The wacky witch war ill. by Denise Brunkus. WhistleStop, 1996. ISBN 0-8167-3717-7 Subj: School. Witches.

Jackson, Isaac. *Somebody's new pajamas* ill. by David Soman. Dial, 1996. ISBN 0-8037-1549-8 Subj: Clothing – pajamas. Ethnic groups in the U.S. – African Americans. Family life. Friendship. Sleepovers.

Jackson, Jacqueline. *Chicken ten thousand* ill. by Barbara Morrow. Little, 1968. Subj: Birds – chickens. Science.

Jackson, Jean. *Big lips and hairy arms: a monster story* ill. by Vera Rosenberry. DK, 1998. ISBN 0-7894-2521-1 Subj: Emotions – fear. Monsters. Telephone.

Mrs. Piccolo's easy chair ill. by Diane Greenseid. DK, 1999. ISBN 0-7894-2580-7 Subj: Furniture – chairs. Stores.

Thorndike and Nelson ill. by Vera Rosenberry. DK, 1997. ISBN 0-7894-2452-5 Subj: Behavior. Friendship. Monsters.

Jackson, Richard. *Iktomi and the boulder* (Goble, Paul)

Jackson, Shelley. *The old woman and the wave* ill. by author. DK, 1998. ISBN 0-7894-2484-3 Subj: Character traits – bravery. Emotions – fear. Nature. Sea and seashore. Water.

Jackson, Woody. *Counting cows* ill. by author. Harcourt, 1995. ISBN 0-15-220165-3 Subj: Animals – bulls, cows. Counting, numbers. Nature.

Jacobs, Daniel. *What does it do? inventions then and now* ill. with photos. Raintree, 1990. ISBN 0-8172-3586-8 Subj: Machines.

Jacobs, Howard. *Cajun night before Christmas* (Trosclair)

Jacobs, Joseph. *The crock of gold: being "The pedlar of Swaffham"* ill. by William Stobbs. Follett, 1971. ISBN 0-695-80213-5 Subj: Careers – peddlers. Dreams. Folk and fairy tales. Foreign lands – England.

Hereafterthis ill. by Paul Galdone. McGraw-Hill, 1973. ISBN 0-07022-691-1 Subj: Animals. Behavior – mistakes. Crime. Farms. Folk and fairy tales.

Hudden and Dudden and Donald O'Neary ill. by Doris Burn. Coward, 1968. Subj: Behavior – greed. Folk and fairy tales. Foreign lands – Ireland.

Johnny-cake ill. by Emma Lillian Brock. Putnam, 1933. Subj: Cumulative tales. Folk and fairy tales. Food.

Johnny-cake ill. by William Stobbs. Viking, 1973, c1972. ISBN 0-670-40826-3 Subj: Cumulative tales. Folk and fairy tales. Food.

King of the cats: a ghost story (Galdone, Paul)

Lazy Jack (Lazy Jack)

Master of all masters ill. by Anne F. Rockwell. Grosset, 1972. ISBN 0-448-26210-X Subj: Folk and fairy tales.

Old Mother Wiggle-Waggle ill. by William Stobbs. Bodley Head, 1980. ISBN 0-370-02048-0 Subj: Folk and fairy tales.

Tattercoats ill. by Margot Tomes. Putnam, 1989. ISBN 0-399-21584-0 Subj: Emotions – love. Family life – grandfathers. Folk and fairy tales. Foreign lands – England. Royalty – princes.

The three sillies retold and ill. by Paul Galdone. Houghton Mifflin, 1981. ISBN 0-395-30172-6 Subj: Folk and fairy tales.

The three sillies retold and ill. by Kathryn Hewitt. Harcourt, 1986. ISBN 0-15-286855-0 Subj: Animals. Animals – pigs. Character traits – foolishness. Folk and fairy tales.

The three sillies adapt. and ill. by Steven Kellogg. Candlewick, 1999. ISBN 0-7636-0811-4 Subj: Animals. Animals – pigs. Character traits – foolishness. Folk and fairy tales.

Jacobs, Kate. *A sister's wish* ill. by Nancy Carpenter. Hyperion, 1996. ISBN 0-7868-2112-4 Subj: Behavior – needing someone. Behavior – wishing. Family life – brothers. Rhyming text. Sibling rivalry.

Jacobs, Laurie A. *So much in common* ill. by Valeri Gorbachev. Caroline House, 1994. ISBN 1-56397-115-1 Subj: Activities – cooking. Animals – goats. Animals – hippopotamuses. Friendship. Gardens, gardening.

Jacobs, Leland B. (Leland Blair). *Belling the cat and other stories* (Belling the cat and other stories)

Is somewhere always far away? ill. by John E. Johnson. Holt, 1967. Subj: Activities – traveling. Character traits – questioning. Poetry.

Is somewhere always far away? poems about places ill. by Jeff Kaufman. Holt, 1995. ISBN 0-8050-2677-0 Subj: Activities – traveling. Character traits – questioning. Poetry.

Just around the corner: poems about the seasons ill. by Jeff Kaufman. Holt, 1993. ISBN 0-8050-2676-2 Subj: Poetry. Seasons.

Jacobs, Shannon K. *The boy who loved morning* ill. by Michael Hays. Little, 1993. ISBN 0-316-45556-3 Subj: Folk and fairy tales. Indians of North America. Morning. Names.

Jacobson, Jennifer Richard. *Moon sandwich mom* ill. by Benrei Huang. Albert Whitman, 1999. ISBN 0-8075-4071-4 Subj: Animals. Animals – foxes. Family life – mothers.

A net of stars ill. by Greg Shed. Dial, 1998. ISBN 0-8037-2088-2 Subj: Emotions – fear. Fairs. Night. Sky.

Jacoby-Nelson, Frank. *In this night* (Lucht, Irmgard)

The red poppy (Lucht, Irmgard)

Jaffe, Marjorie. *Albert the running bear's exercise book* (Isenberg, Barbara)

Jaffe, Nina. *The golden flower: a Taino myth from Puerto Rico* ill. by Enrique O. Sánchez. Simon & Schuster, 1996. ISBN 0-02-747585-9 Subj: Creation. Folk and fairy tales. Foreign lands – Puerto Rico. Indians of North America – Taino.

In the month of Kislev: a story for Hanukkah ill. by Louise August. Viking, 1992. ISBN 0-670-82863-7 Subj: Folk and fairy tales. Holidays – Hanukkah. Jewish culture.

Older brother, younger brother ill. by Wenhai Ma. Viking, 1995. ISBN 0-670-85645-2 Subj: Family life – brothers. Folk and fairy tales. Foreign lands – Korea.

The way meat loves salt: a Cinderella tale from the Jewish tradition ill. by Louise August. Holt, 1998. ISBN 0-8050-4384-5 Subj: Emotions – love. Family life – fathers. Folk and fairy tales. Foreign lands – Europe. Jewish culture. Weddings.

Jaffe, Rona. *Last of the wizards* ill. by Erik Blegvad. Simon & Schuster, 1961. Subj: Behavior – wishing. Character traits – cleverness.

Jaffrey, Madhur. *Market days* (Shohet, Marti)

Jagendorf, Moritz A. *Kwi-na the eagle: and other Indian tales* ill. by Jack Endewelt; consultant: Carolyn W. Field. Silver Burdett, 1968. Subj: Folk and fairy tales. Indians of North America.

Jahn-Clough, Lisa. *My friend and I* ill. by author. Houghton Mifflin, 1999. ISBN 0-395-93545-8 Subj: Friendship. Toys.

My happy birthday book ill. by author. Houghton Mifflin, 1996. ISBN 0-395-77260-5 Subj: Birthdays. Friendship.

1 2 3 yippie ill. by author. Houghton Mifflin, 1998. ISBN 0-395-87003-8 Subj: Animals. Counting, numbers. Parties.

Jakes, John. *Susanna of the Alamo* ill. by Paul Bacon. Harcourt, 1986. ISBN 0-15-200595-1 Subj: Character traits – bravery. U.S. history – frontier and pioneer life.

Jakob, Donna. *My bike* ill. by Nelle Davis. Hyperion, 1994. ISBN 1-56282-455-4 Subj: Rhyming text. Sports – bicycling. Time.

My new sandbox ill. by Julia Gorton. Hyperion, 1996. ISBN 0-7868-2144-2 Subj: Activities – playing. Animals. Behavior – sharing.

Tiny toes ill. by Mireille Levert. Hyperion, 1995. ISBN 0-7868-2009-8 Subj: Activities – playing. Anatomy – toes.

Jam, Teddy. *Night cars* ill. by Eric Beddows. Orchard, 1989. ISBN 0-531-08393-4 Subj: Babies. City. Family life – fathers. Night. Rhyming text.

The year of fire ill. by Ian Wallace. Margaret K. McElderry, 1993. ISBN 0-689-50566-3 Subj: Country. Family life – grandfathers. Fire. Foreign lands – Canada. Forest, woods.

James, Betsy. *The dream stair* ill. by Richard Jesse Watson. HarperCollins, 1990. ISBN 0-06-022788-5 Subj: Dreams. Ethnic groups in the U.S. Family life – grandmothers. Sleep.

Flashlight ill. by Stacey Schuett. Knopf, 1997. ISBN 0-679-97970-0 Subj: Emotions – fear. Family life – grandparents. Night.

He wakes me ill. by Helen K. Davie. Watts, 1991. ISBN 0-531-08554-6 Subj: Animals – cats. Pets.

Mary Ann ill. by author. Dutton, 1994. ISBN 0-525-45077-7 Subj: Friendship. Insects – praying mantis. Moving.

The mud family ill. by Paul Morin. Putnam, 1994. ISBN 0-399-22549-8 Subj: Family life. Indians of North America – Anasazi. Toys – dolls. Weather – droughts. Weather – floods. Weather – rain.

Tadpoles ill. by author. Dutton, 1999. ISBN 0-525-46197-3 Subj: Animals – babies. Behavior. Frogs and toads.

James, J. Alison. *The birthday bear* (Schneider, Antonie)

The Christmas star (Pfister, Marcus)

Danny, the angry lion (Lachner, Dorothea)

The dream house (Vainio, Pirkko)

The drums of Noto Hanto ill. by Tsukushi. DK, 1999. ISBN 0-7894-2574-2 Subj: Character traits – bravery. Foreign lands – Japan. Music. War.

The elf's hat (Weninger, Brigitte)

Eucalyptus wings ill. by Demi. Atheneum, 1995. ISBN 0-689-31886-3 Subj: Activities – flying. Friendship. Magic.

Fabian Youngpig sails the world (Ostheeren, Ingrid)

Good-bye, Vivi! (Schneider, Antonie)

The happy hedgehog (Pfister, Marcus)

How Leo learned to be king (Pfister, Marcus)

The little green goose (Sansone, Adele)

Little polar bear and the brave little hare (De Beer, Hans)

Little polar bear, take me home! (De Beer, Hans)

Luke the Lionhearted (Schneider, Antonie)

Martin and the Pumpkin Ghost (Ostheeren, Ingrid)

Meet the Molesons (Bos, Burny)

Meredith, the witch who wasn't (Lachner, Dorothea)

Meredith's mixed-up magic (Lachner, Dorothea)

Mia the beach cat (Hänel, Wolfram)

The moon man (Scheidl, Gerda Marie)

The new dog (Ostheeren, Ingrid)

Niki's little donkey (Hol, Coby)

Not now, Sara! (Voigt, Hannelore)

Rainbow fish and the big blue whale (Pfister, Marcus)

Rainbow fish to the rescue! (Pfister, Marcus)

Wake up, Grizzly! (Bittner, Wolfgang)

Wake up, Santa Claus! (Pfister, Marcus)

James, Shirley Kerby. *Going to a horse farm* ill. by Laura Jacques. Charlesbridge, 1992. ISBN 0-88106-477-7 Subj: Animals – horses, ponies. Farms.

James, Simon. *Dear Mr. Blueberry* ill. by author. Macmillan, 1991. ISBN 0-689-50529-9 Subj: Animals – whales. Careers – teachers. Imagination. Letters, cards.

Leon and Bob ill. by author. Candlewick, 1997. ISBN 1-56402-991-3 Subj: Foreign lands – England. Friendship. Imagination – imaginary friends.

My friend whale ill. by author. Bantam, 1991. ISBN 0-553-07065-7 Subj: Animals – whales.

Sally and the limpet ill. by author. Macmillan, 1991. ISBN 0-689-50528-0 Subj: Crustaceans. Ecology. Sea and seashore.

The wild woods ill. by author. Candlewick, 1993. ISBN 1-56402-219-6 Subj: Animals – squirrels. Family life – grandfathers. Nature.

Jameson, Cynthia. *The house of five bears* ill. by Lorinda Bryan Cauley. Putnam, 1978. ISBN 0-399-61122-3 Subj: Character traits – cleverness. Folk and fairy tales. Foreign lands – Russia.

Janice. *Angélique* ill. by Roger Antoine Duvoisin. McGraw-Hill, 1960. Subj: Animals – dogs. Behavior – bullying. Birds – ducks.

Little Bear marches in the St. Patrick's Day parade ill. by Mariana. Lothrop, 1967. Subj: Animals – bears. Holidays – St. Patrick's Day. Parades.

Little Bear's Christmas ill. by Mariana. Lothrop, 1964. ISBN 0-688-51076-0 Subj: Animals – bears. Character traits – generosity. Hibernation. Holidays – Christmas.

Little Bear's New Year's party ill. by Mariana. Lothrop, 1973. ISBN 0-688-50002-1 Subj: Animals – bears. Holidays – New Year's. Parties.

Little Bear's pancake party ill. by Mariana. Lothrop, 1960. Subj: Animals – bears. Food. Parties. Seasons – spring.

Little Bear's Sunday breakfast ill. by Mariana. Lothrop, 1958. Subj: Animals – bears. Food.

Little Bear's Thanksgiving ill. by Mariana. Lothrop, 1967. ISBN 0-688-51078-7 Subj: Animals – bears. Holidays – Thanksgiving.

Minette ill. by Alain. McGraw-Hill, 1959. Subj: Animals – cats.

Mr. and Mrs. Button's wonderful watchdogs ill. by Roger Antoine Duvoisin. Lothrop, 1978. ISBN 0-688-51848-6 Subj: Animals – dogs. Crime.

Janisch, Heinz. *Noah's ark* ill. by Lisbeth Zwerger. North-South, 1997. ISBN 1-55858-785-3 Subj: Animals. Boats, ships. Religion – Noah. Weather – floods. Weather – rain. Weather – rainbows.

Janosch. *Dear snowman* ill. by author. Collins, 1969. Subj: Seasons – winter. Snowmen. Weather – snow.

Hey Presto! You're a bear! trans. by Klauss Flugge; ill. by author. Little, 1980. ISBN 0-316-45765-5 Subj: Imagination.

Joshua and the magic fiddle ill. by author. Collins, 1967. Subj: Magic. Moon. Music.

Just one apple trans. by Refna Wilkin; ill. by author. Walck, 1966. Subj: Behavior – wishing. Dragons.

The magic auto ill. by author. Crown, 1971. Translation of Das Regenauto. Subj: Automobiles. Magic.

Tonight at nine ill. by author. Walck, 1967. Translation of Heute um neune hinter der Scheune. Subj: Animals. Music. Rhyming text.

The trip to Panama trans. by Anthea Bell; ill. by author. Little, 1978. Translation of Oh, wie schon ist Panama. ISBN 0-316-45766-3 Subj: Activities – traveling. Foreign lands – Panama.

Janovitz, Marilyn. *Baa baa, black sheep* (Mother Goose)

Bowl patrol! ill. by author. North-South, 1996. ISBN 1-55858-637-7 Subj: Animals – dogs. Rhyming text.

Can I help? ill. by author. North-South, 1996. ISBN 1-55858-576-1 Subj: Animals – wolves. Character traits – helpfulness. Family life – fathers. Gardens, gardening. Rhyming text.

Hey diddle diddle (Mother Goose)

Hickory dickory dock (Mother Goose)

Is it time? ill. by author. North-South, 1994. ISBN 1-55858-332-7 Subj: Activities – bathing. Animals – wolves. Bedtime. Family life – fathers. Rhyming text. Sleep.

Little Fox ill. by author. North-South, 1999. ISBN 0-7358-1161-X Subj: Animals – foxes.

Look out, bird! ill. by author. North-South, 1994. ISBN 1-55858-250-9 Subj: Animals. Animals – snails. Birds. Circular tales.

Pat-a-cake (Mother Goose)

What could be keeping Santa? ill. by author. North-South, 1997. ISBN 1-55858-820-5 Subj: Animals – reindeer. Holidays – Christmas. Rhyming text. Santa Claus.

A January fog will freeze a hog: *and other weather folklore* comp. and ed. by Hubert Davis; ill. by John Wallner. Crown, 1977. ISBN 0-517-52811-8 Subj: Folk and fairy tales. Weather.

Jaques, Faith. *Tilly's house* ill. by author. Atheneum, 1979. ISBN 0-689-50138-2 Subj: Homes, houses. Toys – dolls.

Tilly's rescue ill. by author. Atheneum, 1981. ISBN 0-689-50175-7 Subj: Behavior – lost. Character traits – bravery. Friendship. Holidays – Christmas. Toys – dolls.

Jaquith, Priscilla. *Bo Rabbit smart for true: tall tales from the Gullah* ill. by Ed Young. Philomel, 1995. ISBN 0-399-22668-0 Subj: Animals – rabbits. Ethnic groups in the U.S. – African Americans. Folk and fairy tales. Noise, sounds. Reptiles – alligators, crocodiles. Reptiles – snakes.

Jaramillo, Raquel. *Ride, baby, ride!* ill. with photos. Little Simon, 1998. ISBN 0-689-82027-5 Subj: Activities – playing. Babies. Format, unusual – board books.

Jarrell, Mary. *The knee baby* ill. by Symeon Shimin. Farrar, 1973. ISBN 0-374-34246-6 Subj: Babies. Family life. Family life – grandmothers.

Jarrell, Randall. *A bat is born* ill. by John Schoenherr. Doubleday, 1977, c1964. ISBN 0-385-12224-1 Subj: Animals – bats. Birth. Poetry.

The fisherman and his wife (Grimm, Jacob)

The golden bird: and other fairy tales (Grimm, Jacob)

The rabbit catcher and other fairy tales (Bechstein, Ludwig)

Jaspersohn, William. *My hometown library* ill. by author. Houghton Mifflin, 1994. ISBN 0-395-55723-2 Subj: Libraries.

Timber! ill. by author. Little, 1996. ISBN 0-316-45825-2 Subj: Forest, woods. Paper. Trees.

Jauck, Andrea. *Assateague: island of the wild ponies* by Andrea Jauck and Larry Points; ill. with photos. Macmillan, 1993. ISBN 0-02-774695-X Subj: Animals – horses, ponies. Islands. Seasons.

Jay, Betsy. *Swimming lessons* ill. by Lori Osiecki. Rising Moon, 1998. ISBN 0-8735-8685-9 Subj: Children as authors. Emotions – fear. Sports – swimming.

Jaynes, Ruth M. *Benny's four hats* photos. by Harvey Mandlin. Bowmar, 1967. Subj: Clothing – hats. Ethnic groups in the U.S. Participation. Weather.

The biggest house ill. by Jacques Rupp. Bowmar, 1968. Subj: Homes, houses.

Friends! friends! friends! photos. by Harvey Mandlin. Bowmar, 1967. Subj: Ethnic groups in the U.S. Friendship. School.

Melinda's Christmas stocking photos by Richard George. Bowmar, 1968. Subj: Ethnic groups in the U.S. – Mexican Americans. Holidays – Christmas. Senses – hearing. Senses – seeing. Senses – smelling. Senses – tasting. Senses – touching.

Tell me please! What's that? photos. by Harvey Mandlin. Bowmar, 1968. Subj: Animals. Ethnic groups in the U.S. Ethnic groups in the U.S. – Mexican Americans. Foreign languages.

That's what it is! photos. by Harvey Mandlin. Bowmar, 1968. Subj: Ethnic groups in the U.S. Ethnic groups in the U.S. – Mexican Americans. Insects.

Three baby chicks photos. by Harvey Mandlin. Bowmar, 1967. Subj: Birds – chickens. School.

What is a birthday child? photos. by Harvey Mandlin. Bowmar, 1967. Subj: Birthdays. Character traits – individuality. Ethnic groups in the U.S. Ethnic groups in the U.S. – Mexican Americans.

Jeake, Samuel. *see* Aiken, Conrad Potter

Jefferds, Vincent. *Disney's elegant ABC book.* Simon & Schuster, 1983. ISBN 0-671-45571-0 Subj: ABC books.

Disney's elegant book of manners. Simon & Schuster, 1985. ISBN 0-671-60507-0 Subj: Etiquette. Rhyming text.

Jeffers, Susan. *All the pretty horses* ill. by author. Macmillan, 1974. ISBN 0-02-747680-4 Subj: Animals – horses, ponies. Bedtime. Sleep.

Forest of dreams (Wells, Rosemary)

The three jovial huntsmen (Mother Goose)

Wild Robin ill. by author. Dutton, 1976. Based on a tale in Little Prudy's fairy book by R. S. Clarke. ISBN 0-525-42787-2 Subj: Behavior – misbehavior. Foreign lands – Scotland.

Jeffery, Graham. *Thomas the tortoise* ill. by author. Crown, 1988. ISBN 0-517-57043-2 Subj: Character traits – individuality. Character traits – kindness to animals. Reptiles – turtles, tortoises.

Jekyll, Walter. *I have a news: rhymes from the Caribbean* comp. by Walter Jekyll and Neil Philip; ill. by Jacqueline Mair. Lothrop, 1994. ISBN 0-688-13367-3 Subj: Foreign lands – Caribbean Islands. Islands. Nursery rhymes. Poetry.

Jendresen, Erik. *The first story ever told* by Erik Jendresen and Alberto Villoldo; ill. by Yoshi. Simon & Schuster, 1996. ISBN 0-689-80515-2 Subj: Careers – explorers. Creation. Dreams. Indians of South America – Incas.

Jenkin-Pearce, Susie. *The babies of Cockle Bay* (McAllister, Angela)

Bad Boris and the new kitten ill. by author. Macmillan, 1987. ISBN 0-02-747620-0 Subj: Animals – cats. Animals – elephants. Emotions – envy, jealousy.

Bad Boris goes to school ill. by author. Macmillan, 1989. ISBN 0-02-747621-9 Subj: Animals. Animals – elephants. School – first day.

Boris's big ache ill. by author. Dial, 1989. ISBN 0-8037-0551-4 Subj: Animals – elephants. Behavior – growing up. Teeth.

The enchanted garden ill. by author. Oxford Univ. Pr., 1989. ISBN 0-19-279845-6 Subj: Gardens, gardening. Imagination.

Percy Short and Cuthbert ill. by author. Viking, 1991. ISBN 0-670-82803-3 Subj: Animals – hippopotamuses. Behavior – dissatisfaction. Birds – pelicans. Friendship.

The seashell song by Susie Jenkin-Pearce and Claire Fletcher; ill. by authors. Lothrop, 1992. ISBN 0-688-11726-0 Subj: Rhyming text. Sea and seashore.

Jenkins, Christopher N. H. *The little weaver of Thái-Yên Village* (Trân-Khánh-Tuyê)

Jenkins, Jessica. *Thinking about colors* ill. by author. Dutton, 1992. ISBN 0-525-44908-6 Subj: Concepts – color. Emotions. Ethnic groups in the U.S.

Jenkins, Jordan. *Learning about love* ill. by Gene Ruggles. Childrens Pr., 1979. ISBN 0-516-02020-X Subj: Emotions – love. Family life – mothers. Illness.

Jenkins, Martin. *Chameleons are cool* ill. by Sue Shields. Candlewick, 1998. ISBN 0-7636-0144-6 Subj: Nature. Reptiles – lizards.

Fly traps! plants that bite back ill. by David Parkins. Candlewick, 1996. ISBN 1-56402-896-8 Subj: Insects – flies. Plants.

Wings, stings, and wriggly things ill. by author. Candlewick, 1996. ISBN 0-7636-0036-9 Subj: Format, unusual. Insects.

Jenkins, Priscilla Belz. *Falcons nest on skyscrapers* ill. by Megan Lloyd. HarperCollins, 1996. ISBN 0-06-021105-9 Subj: Animals – endangered animals. Birds – falcons. City.

A nest full of eggs ill. by Lizzy Rockwell. HarperCollins, 1995. ISBN 0-06-023442-3 Subj: Birds – robins. Eggs. Science.

Jenkins, Steve. *Big and little* ill. by author. Houghton Mifflin, 1996. ISBN 0-395-72664-6 Subj: Animals. Concepts – size.

Biggest, strongest, fastest ill. by author. Ticknor & Fields, 1995. ISBN 0-395-69701-8 Subj: Animals. Concepts.

Duck's breath and mouse pie: a collection of animal superstitions ill. by author. Ticknor & Fields, 1994. ISBN 0-395-69688-7 Subj: Animals. Folk and fairy tales. Superstition.

Jennings, Linda M. *The brave little bunny* ill. by Catherine Walters. Dutton, 1995. ISBN 0-525-45364-4 Subj: Animals – rabbits. Pets.

Coppelia ill. by Krystyna Turska. Silver Burdett, 1984. ISBN 0-382-09241-4 Subj: Activities – dancing. Ballet. Folk and fairy tales. Toys – dolls.

Crispin and the dancing piglet ill. by Krystyna Turska. Silver Burdett, 1986. ISBN 0-382-09242-2 Subj: Activities – dancing. Animals – pigs. Behavior – seeking better things.

Easy peasy! ill. by Tanya Linch. Farrar, 1997. ISBN 0-374-31949-9 Subj: Animals. Animals – cats.

Franklin's neighborhood ill. by Brenda Clark. Kids Can Pr., 1999. ISBN 1-55074-729-0 Subj: Activities – drawing. Animals. Communities, neighborhoods. Reptiles – turtles, tortoises.

The golden goose (Grimm, Jacob)

The Hippopotamus's birthday and other poems about animals and birds (The Hippopotamus's birthday and other poems about animals and birds)

The musicians of Bremen (Grimm, Jacob)

The sleeping beauty: the story of the ballet ill. by Francesca Crespi. David & Charles, 1987. ISBN 0-340-33518-1 Subj: Activities – dancing. Ballet. Folk and fairy tales.

Tom's tail ill. by Tim Warnes. Little, 1995. ISBN 0-316-13341-8 Subj: Animals – pigs. Farms. Self-concept.

The wolf and the seven little kids (Grimm, Jacob)

Jennings, Michael. *The bears who came to breakfix* ill. by Tom Dunnington. Childrens Pr., 1977. ISBN 0-516-03411-1 Subj: Animals – bears. Dreams. Family life – mothers. Moving.

Robin Goodfellow and the giant dwarf ill. by Tomie de Paola. McGraw-Hill, 1981. ISBN 0-07-032451-4 Subj: Behavior – trickery. Dwarfs, midgets. Giants.

Jennings, Sharon. *Franklin's class trip* (Bourgeois, Paulette)

When Jeremiah found Mrs. Ming ill. by Mireille Levert. Firefly, 1992. ISBN 1-55037-237-8 Subj: Activities. Behavior – boredom.

Jenny, Anne. *The fantastic story of King Brioche the First* ill. by Joycelyne Pache. Lothrop, 1970. Translation by Catherine Barton from La fantastique histoire d roi Brioche Ier. Subj: Activities – flying. Birds.

Jensen, Helen Zane. *When Panda came to our house* ill. by author. Dial, 1985. ISBN 0-8037-0236-1 Subj: Activities. Animals – pandas. Foreign lands – China.

Jensen, Patricia. *Be careful, Little Antelope* by Claude Clément; adapt. by Patricia Jensen; ill. by Pio. Reader's Digest, 1993. Adapt. of: Un petit chamois bien maladroit by Claude Clément. ISBN 0-89577-504-2 Subj: Animals – antelopes. Family life – fathers.

Be patient, Little Chick by Claude Clément; adapt. by Patricia Jensen; ill. by Erost. Reader's Digest, 1993. Adapt. of: Petit poussin pressé by Claude Clément. ISBN 0-8957-7503-4 Subj: Animals – babies. Behavior – growing up. Birds – chickens. Character traits – patience. Concepts – size.

The curious little dolphin (Chottin, Ariane)

Gentle Little Lion by Claude Clément; adapt. by Patricia Jensen; ill. by Marcelle Geneste. Reader's Digest, 1994. Adapt. of: Un Petit Lion si mignon! by Claude Clément. ISBN 0-89577-562-X Subj: Animals – lions. Behavior – growing up. Noise, sounds.

Go to sleep, little groundhog by Claude Clément; adapt. by Patricia Jensen; ill. by Catherine Nouvelle. Reader's Digest, 1992. Adapt. of: Trotte marmotte by Claude Clément. ISBN 0-89577-424-0 Subj: Animals – groundhogs. Sleep.

Kitty's special job by Claude Clément; adapt. by Patricia Jensen; ill. by Olivier Raquois. Reader's Digest, 1992. Adapt. of: Gare à toi, le chat! by Claude Clément. ISBN 0-89577-427-5 Subj: Animals – cats. Animals – mice. Careers. Farms.

Little Donkey learns to help by Claude Clément; adapt. by Patricia Jensen; ill. by Pascal Robin. Reader's Digest, 1993. Adapt. of: Es-tu têtu, Petit Âne? by Claude Clément. ISBN 0-89577-502-6 Subj: Animals – donkeys. Behavior – needing someone. Character traits – helpfulness.

Little Goat's new horns (Chottin, Ariane)

Little Kangaroo finds his way (Chottin, Ariane)

Little Mouse's rescue (Chottin, Ariane)

Little Squirrel's special nest by Claude Clément; adapt. by Patricia Jensen; ill. by Bernadette Pons Fudym. Reader's Digest, 1993. Rev. translation of: Trésor d'Ecureuil by Claude Clément. ISBN 0-89577-542-5 Subj: Animals. Animals – squirrels. Character traits – helpfulness.

The mess ill. by Molly Delaney. Childrens Pr., 1990. ISBN 0-516-05357-4 Subj: Activities – playing. Behavior – messy. Rhyming text.

Jensen, Virginia Allen. *Cat alley* (Olsen, Ib Spang)

Catching: a book for blind and sighted children with pictures to feel as well as to see ill. by author. Putnam, 1984. ISBN 0-399-20997-2 Subj: Concepts – shape. Format, unusual. Handicaps – blindness. Senses – seeing.

Red thread riddles by Virginia Allen Jensen and Polly Edman; ill. by authors. Putnam, 1980. ISBN 0-529-05604-6 Subj: Format, unusual. Handicaps – blindness. Riddles. Senses – seeing.

Sara and the door ill. by Ann Strugnell. Addison-Wesley, 1977. ISBN 0-201-03446-8 Subj: Character traits – perseverance. Clothing. Ethnic groups in the U.S. – African Americans.

What's that? ill. by Dorcas Woodbury Haller. Collins-World, 1979. ISBN 0-529-05500-7 Subj: Concepts. Handicaps – blindness. Senses – seeing.

Jeram, Anita. *All together now* ill. by author. Candlewick, 1999. ISBN 0-7636-0846-7 Subj: Animals – mice. Animals – rabbits. Birds – ducks. Orphans.

Bill's belly button ill. by author. Little, 1991. ISBN 0-316-46114-8 Subj: Anatomy. Animals – elephants. Behavior – losing things. Zoos.

Birthday happy, Contrary Mary ill. by author. Candlewick, 1998. ISBN 0-7636-0448-8 Subj: Animals – mice. Behavior. Birthdays. Parties.

Bunny, my Honey ill. by author. Candlewick, 1999. ISBN 0-7636-0710-X Subj: Animals – mice. Animals – rabbits. Behavior – lost. Birds – ducks. Family life – mothers.

Contrary Mary ill. by author. Candlewick, 1995. ISBN 1-56402-644-2 Subj: Animals – mice. Behavior. Character traits – individuality.

Daisy Dare ill. by author. Candlewick, 1995. ISBN 1-56402-645-0 Subj: Animals – mice. Character traits – being different. Character traits – bravery.

It was Jake ill. by author. Little, 1991. ISBN 0-316-46120-2 Subj: Animals – dogs. Behavior – lying. Behavior – misbehavior. Pets.

Jerome, Judson. *I never saw . . .* ill. by Helga Aichinger. Albert Whitman, 1974. ISBN 0-8075-3514-1 Subj: Poetry.

Jeschke, Susan. *Angela and Bear* ill. by author. Holt, 1979. ISBN 0-03-044511-6 Subj: Animals – bears. Imagination – imaginary friends. Magic.

The devil did it ill. by author. Holt, 1979. ISBN 0-03-014506-6 Subj: Animals – bears. Imagination – imaginary friends.

Firerose ill. by author. Holt, 1974. ISBN 0-03-011991-X Subj: Careers – fortune tellers. Dragons. Humor. Magic.

Lucky's choice ill. by author. Scholastic, 1987. ISBN 0-590-40520-9 Subj: Animals – cats. Behavior – needing someone. Behavior – running away. Friendship.

Mia, Grandma and the genie ill. by author. Holt, 1978. ISBN 0-03-028586-0 Subj: Fairies. Family life – grandmothers. Magic.

Perfect the pig ill. by author. Holt, 1981. ISBN 0-03-058622-4 Subj: Activities – flying. Animals – pigs.

Rima and Zeppo ill. by author. Dutton, 1976. ISBN 0-525-61524-3 Subj: Magic. Witches.

Tamar and the tiger ill. by author. Holt, 1980. ISBN 0-03-052176-9 Subj: Imagination.

Jessell, Camilla. *The kitten book* ill. by author. Candlewick, 1992. ISBN 1-56402-020-7 Subj: Animals – cats. Birth.

The puppy book ill. by author. Candlewick, 1992. ISBN 1-56402-021-5 Subj: Animals – dogs. Birth.

Jessell, Tim. *Amorak* ill. by author. Creative Ed., 1994. ISBN 0-88682-662-4 Subj: Animals – reindeer. Animals – wolves. Eskimos. Family life – grandfathers. Folk and fairy tales. Foreign lands – Canada.

Jessup, Harley. *Grandma summer* ill. by author. Viking, 1999. ISBN 0-670-88260-7 Subj: Family life – grandmothers. Sea and seashore. Seasons – summer.

Jewell, Nancy. *ABC cat* ill. by Ann Schweninger. HarperCollins, 1983. ISBN 0-06-022848-2 Subj: ABC books. Animals – cats. Rhyming text.

Bus ride ill. by Ronald Himler. HarperCollins, 1978. ISBN 0-06-022842-3 Subj: Buses.

Christmas lullaby ill. by Stefano Vitale. Clarion, 1994. ISBN 0-395-66586-8 Subj: Animals. Religion – Nativity. Rhyming text.

Five little kittens ill. by Elizabeth Sayles. Clarion, 1999. ISBN 0-395-77517-5 Subj: Animals – cats. Rhyming text.

Sailor song ill. by Stefano Vitale. Clarion, 1999. ISBN 0-395-82511-3 Subj: Activities – singing. Careers – military. Sailors.

The snuggle bunny ill. by Mary Chalmers. HarperCollins, 1972. ISBN 0-06-022834-2 Subj: Animals – rabbits. Emotions – love.

Time for Uncle Joe ill. by Joan Sandin. HarperCollins, 1981. ISBN 0-06-022844-X Subj: Death. Emotions – grief. Family life – aunts, uncles.

Try and catch me ill. by Leonard Weisgard. HarperCollins, 1972. ISBN 0-06-022832-6 Subj: Activities – playing. Ecology. Friendship. Imagination.

Jijii, Hanasaka. *The old man who made the trees bloom* (Shibano, Tamizo)

Jitodai, Hitomi. *I wish I had a big, big tree* (Sato, Satoru)

Jocelyn, Marthe. *Hannah and the seven dresses* ill. by author. Dutton, 1999. ISBN 0-525-46113-2 Subj: Birthdays. Clothing – dresses.

Joerns, Consuelo. *The foggy rescue* ill. by author. Four Winds, 1980. ISBN 0-590-07744-9 Subj: Animals – mice. Behavior – lost. Boats, ships.

The forgotten bear ill. by author. Four Winds, 1978. ISBN 0-590-07560-8 Subj: Behavior – lost. Toys – bears.

The lost and found house ill. by author. Four Winds, 1979. ISBN 0-590-07627-2 Subj: Animals – mice. Homes, houses.

Oliver's escape ill. by author. Four Winds, 1981. ISBN 0-590-07817-8 Subj: Animals. Animals – dogs. Behavior – running away. Friendship.

Johansen, K. V. (Krista V.). *Pippin takes a bath* ill. by Bernice Lum. Kids Can Pr., 1999. ISBN 1-55074-627-8 Subj: Activities – bathing. Animals – dogs.

John, Naomi. *Roadrunner* ill. by Peter and Virginia Parnall. Dutton, 1980. ISBN 0-525-38485-5 Subj: Birds. Desert.

Johns, Linda. *Sarah's secret plan* ill. by Denise Brunkus. Troll, 1995. ISBN 0-816-73693-6 Subj: Behavior – tardiness. Clocks, watches. Family life.

Johnson, Angela. *The aunt in our house* ill. by David Soman. Orchard, 1996. ISBN 0-531-08852-9 Subj: Emotions – sadness. Ethnic groups in the U.S. Family life – aunts, uncles.

Casey Jones ill. by Loren Long. Simon & Schuster, 2000. ISBN 0-689-82609-5 Subj: Careers – farmers. Ethnic groups in the U.S. – African Americans. Family life – fathers. Farms. Trains.

Daddy calls me man ill. by Rhonda Mitchell. Orchard, 1997. ISBN 0-531-33042-7 Subj: Careers – artists. Ethnic groups in the U.S. – African Americans. Family life. Poetry.

Do like Kyla ill. by James E. Ransome. Watts, 1990. ISBN 0-531-08452-3 Subj: Ethnic groups in the U.S. – African Americans. Family life – brothers and sisters.

Down the winding road ill. by Shane Evans. DK, 2000. ISBN 0-7894-2596-3 Subj: Country. Ethnic groups in the U.S. – African Americans. Family life. Friendship.

The girl who wore snakes ill. by James E. Ransome. Orchard, 1993. ISBN 0-531-08641-0 Subj: Animals. Ethnic groups in the U.S. – African Americans. Family life – aunts, uncles. Pets. Reptiles – snakes.

Joshua by the sea ill. by Rhonda Mitchell. Orchard, 1994. ISBN 0-531-06846-3 Subj: Ethnic groups in the U.S. – African Americans. Format, unusual – board books. Sea and seashore.

Joshua's night whispers ill. by Rhonda Mitchell. Orchard, 1994. ISBN 0-531-06847-1 Subj: Ethnic groups in the U.S. – African Americans. Family life – fathers. Format, unusual – board books. Night. Noise, sounds.

Julius ill. by Dav Pilkey. Orchard, 1993. ISBN 0-531-08615-1 Subj: Animals – pigs. Ethnic groups in the U.S. – African Americans. Family life – grandfathers. Pets.

The leaving morning ill. by David Soman. Orchard, 1992. ISBN 0-531-08592-9 Subj: Emotions. Ethnic groups in the U.S. – African Americans. Family life. Moving.

Mama bird, baby birds ill. by Rhonda Mitchell. Orchard, 1994. ISBN 0-531-06848-X Subj: Birds. Ethnic groups in the U.S. – African Americans. Format, unusual – board books. Rhyming text.

One of three ill. by David Soman. Watts, 1991. ISBN 0-531-08555-4 Subj: Ethnic groups in the U.S. – African Americans. Family life – sisters.

Rain feet ill. by Rhonda Mitchell. Orchard, 1994. ISBN 0-531-06849-8 Subj: Ethnic groups in the U.S. – African Americans. Format, unusual – board books. Weather – rain.

The Rolling Store ill. by Peter Catalanotto. Orchard, 1997. ISBN 0-531-33015-X Subj: Careers – peddlers. Ethnic groups in the U.S. – African Americans. Family life – grandfathers. Memories, memory. Stores.

Shoes like Miss Alice's ill. by Ken Page. Orchard, 1995. ISBN 0-531-08664-X Subj: Activities – babysitting. Clothing – shoes. Ethnic groups in the U.S. – African Americans.

Tell me a story, mama ill. by David Soman. Watts, 1989. ISBN 0-531-08394-2 Subj: Family life – mothers.

Those building men ill. by Mike Benny. Blue Sky, 1999. ISBN 0-590-66521-9 Subj: Activities – making things. Careers – construction workers.

The wedding ill. by David Soman. Orchard, 1999. ISBN 0-531-33139-3 Subj: Ethnic groups in the U.S. – African Americans. Family life – sisters. Weddings.

When I am old with you ill. by David Soman. Watts, 1990. ISBN 0-531-08484-1 Subj: Ethnic groups in the U.S. – African Americans. Family life – grandfathers. Old age.

When mules flew on Magnolia Street ill. by John Ward. Knopf, 2000. ISBN 0-679-99077-1 Subj: Ethnic groups in the U.S. – African Americans. Family life – brothers and sisters. Friendship.

Johnson, B. J. *A hat like that* by B. J. Johnson and Susan Aiello; ill. by authors. St. Martin's, 1986. ISBN 0-312-36416-4 Subj: Clothing – hats. Format, unusual – toy and movable books. Imagination. Rhyming text.

My blanket Burt by B. J. Johnson and Susan Aiello; ill. by authors. St. Martin's, 1986. ISBN 0-312-55600-4 Subj: Behavior – losing things. Format, unusual – toy and movable books. Rhyming text.

Johnson, Bruce H. *Apples, alligators, and also alphabets* (Johnson, Odette)

One prickly porcupine (Johnson, Odette)

Johnson, Crockett. *The blue ribbon puppies* ill. by author. HarperCollins, 1958. ISBN 0-590-40626-4 Subj: Animals – dogs. Imagination. Toys.

Ellen's lion ill. by author. HarperCollins, 1959. Subj: Imagination. Toys.

The emperor's gifts ill. by author. Holt, 1965. Subj: Character traits. Character traits – generosity. Gifts. Royalty – emperors.

The frowning prince ill. by author. Harper, 1959. ISBN 0-912846-09-7 Subj: Royalty – princes.

Harold and the purple crayon ill. by author. HarperCollins, 1955. ISBN 0-06-022936-5 Subj: Art. Humor. Imagination.

Harold at the North Pole ill. by author. HarperCollins, 1958. ISBN 0-06-028074-3 Subj: Holidays – Christmas. Humor. Imagination. Santa Claus.

Harold's ABC: another purple crayon adventure ill. by author. HarperCollins, 1963. ISBN 0-606-02127-2 Subj: ABC books. Humor. Imagination.

Harold's circus ill. by author. HarperCollins, 1959. ISBN 0-06-022966-7 Subj: Circus. Humor. Imagination.

Harold's fairy tale: further adventures with the purple crayon ill. by author. HarperCollins, 1956. ISBN 0-06-022976-4 Subj: Folk and fairy tales. Humor. Imagination.

Harold's trip to the sky ill. by author. HarperCollins, 1957. ISBN 0-06-022986-1 Subj: Humor. Imagination. Space and space ships.

A picture for Harold's room ill. by author. HarperCollins, 1960. ISBN 0-06-023006-1 Subj: Art. Humor. Imagination.

Terrible terrifying Toby ill. by author. HarperCollins, 1957. Subj: Animals – dogs.

Time for spring ill. by author. HarperCollins, 1957. Subj: Seasons – spring. Snowmen.

Upside down ill. by author. Albert Whitman, 1969. ISBN 0-8075-8345-6 Subj: Animals – kangaroos. Concepts – up and down. World.

We wonder what will Walter be? When he grows up ill. by author. Holt, 1964. Subj: Animals. Behavior – growing up.

Will spring be early or will spring be late? ill. by author. Crowell, 1959. ISBN 0-690-89423-6 Subj: Animals – groundhogs. Holidays – Groundhog Day. Seasons – spring.

Johnson, D. B. (Donald B.). *Henry hikes to Fitchburg* ill. by author. Houghton Mifflin, 2000. ISBN 0-395-96867-4 Subj: Activities – walking. Sports – hiking. U.S. history.

Johnson, David. *The Bremen town musicians* (Grimm, Jacob)

Oh, that Nuzzle! ill. by Tom Brannon. Grosset, 1997. ISBN 0-448-41299-3 Subj: Animals – dogs. Food.

Johnson, Diana F. *Princesa and Friskie* ill. by Ernesto López. Interkids, 1997. Based on Princesa's true story as told by Ricardo Allende. ISBN 0-9657928-0-3 Subj: Animals – cats. Animals – dogs. Foreign languages. Friendship.

Johnson, Dinah. *All around town* photos by Richard Samuel Roberts. Holt, 1998. ISBN 0-8050-5456-1 Subj: Activities – photographing. Careers – photographers. Ethnic groups in the U.S. – African Americans. U.S. history.

Sunday week ill. by Tyrone Geter. Holt, 1999. ISBN 0-8050-4911-8 Subj: City. Days of the week, months of the year. Ethnic groups in the U.S. – African Americans. Poetry. Religion.

Johnson, Dolores. *The best bug to be* ill. by author. Macmillan, 1992. ISBN 0-02-747842-4 Subj: Ethnic groups in the U.S. – African Americans. School. Theater.

Grandma's hands ill. by author. Cavendish, 1998. ISBN 0-7614-5025-4 Subj: Emotions – love. Ethnic groups in the U.S. – African Americans. Family life – grandmothers. Farms.

My mom is my show-and-tell ill. by author. Cavendish, 1999. ISBN 0-7614-5041-6 Subj: Ethnic groups in the U.S. – African Americans. Family life – mothers. School.

Now let me fly: the story of a slave family ill. by author. Macmillan, 1993. ISBN 0-02-747699-5 Subj: Ethnic groups in the U.S. – African Americans. Slavery. U.S. history.

Papa's stories ill. by author. Macmillan, 1994. ISBN 0-02-747847-5 Subj: Activities – reading. Ethnic groups in the U.S. – African Americans. Family life – fathers.

Seminole diary: remembrances of a slave ill. by author. Macmillan, 1994. ISBN 0-02-747848-3

Subj: Behavior – running away. Ethnic groups in the U.S. – African Americans. Indians of North America – Seminole. Slavery. U.S. history.

What kind of baby-sitter is this? ill. by author. Macmillan, 1991. ISBN 0-02-747846-7 Subj: Activities – babysitting. Ethnic groups in the U.S. – African Americans.

What will mommy do when I'm at school? ill. by author. Macmillan, 1990. ISBN 0-02-747845-9 Subj: Ethnic groups in the U.S. – African Americans. Family life – mothers.

Your dad was just like you ill. by author. Macmillan, 1993. ISBN 0-02-747838-6 Subj: Ethnic groups in the U.S. – African Americans. Family life – fathers. Family life – grandfathers.

Johnson, Donna Kay. *Brighteyes* ill. by author. Holt, 1978. ISBN 0-03-044651-1 Subj: Animals – raccoons. Handicaps – blindness. Senses – seeing.

Johnson, Doug. *Never babysit the hippopotamuses!* ill. by Abby Carter. Holt, 1993. ISBN 0-8050-1873-5 Subj: Activities – babysitting. Animals – hippopotamuses.

Johnson, Elizabeth. *All in free but Janey* ill. by Trina Schart Hyman. Little, 1968. Subj: Games. Imagination.

Johnson, Evelyne. *The cow in the kitchen: a folk tale* ill. by Anthony Rao. Simon & Schuster, 1983. ISBN 0-671-46004-8 Subj: Behavior – dissatisfaction. Character traits – foolishness.

Johnson, James Weldon. *The Creation* ill. by James Ransome. Holiday, 1994. ISBN 0-8234-1069-2 Subj: Creation. Ethnic groups in the U.S. – African Americans. Poetry. Religion.

Lift ev'ry voice and sing ill. by Jan Spivey Gilchrist. Scholastic, 1995. ISBN 0-590-46982-7 Subj: Ethnic groups in the U.S. – African Americans. Slavery. Songs.

Johnson, Jane. *Bertie on the beach* ill. by author. Four Winds, 1981. ISBN 0-590-07822-4 Subj: Circus. Dreams. Sea and seashore.

My dear Noel: the story of a letter from Beatrix Potter ill. by author. Dial, 1999. ISBN 0-8037-2051-3 Subj: Animals – rabbits. Careers – writers. Letters, cards.

Sybil and the blue rabbit ill. by author. Doubleday, 1980. ISBN 0-385-15758-4 Subj: Imagination. Toys.

Today I thought I'd run away ill. by author. Dutton, 1986. ISBN 0-525-44193-X Subj: Bedtime. Behavior – running away. Monsters.

Johnson, Janet P. *How Mr. Dog got tame: an African-American legend* ill. by Charles Reasoner. Troll, 1998. ISBN 0-8167-4350-9 Subj: Animals – dogs. Animals – wolves. Ethnic groups in the U.S. – African Americans. Folk and fairy tales.

Keelboat Annie: an African-American legend ill. by Charles Reasoner. Troll, 1998. ISBN 0-8167-4347-9

Subj: Ethnic groups in the U.S. – African Americans. Folk and fairy tales.

Johnson, Janice (Janice Kay). *Rosamund* ill. by Deborah Haeffele. Simon & Schuster, 1994. ISBN 0-671-79329-2 Subj: Names. Plants.

Johnson, Jean. *Teachers A to Z* photos by author. Walker, 1987. ISBN 0-8027-6677-3 Subj: ABC books. Careers – teachers. School.

Johnson, John Emil. *My first book of things* ill. by author. Random House, 1979. ISBN 0-394-84128-X Subj: Format, unusual – board books.

Johnson, Julie. *How do I feel about my stepfamily* ill. by Christopher O'Neill. Copper Beech, 1998. ISBN 0-7613-0868-7 Subj: Emotions. Family life – step families.

Johnson, Lindsay Lee. *Hurricane Henrietta* ill. by Wally Neibart. Dial, 1998. ISBN 0-8037-1977-9 Subj: Hair. Humor.

Johnson, Louise. *Malunda* ill. by Edward Durose. Carolrhoda, 1982. ISBN 0-87614-177-7 Subj: Animals – rhinoceros. Illness. Zoos.

Johnson, Mildred D. *Wait, skates!* ill. by Tom Dunnington. Childrens Pr., 1983. ISBN 0-516-02039-0 Subj: Activities – playing. Sports – roller skating.

Johnson, Neil. *Big-top circus* ill. by author. Dial, 1995. ISBN 0-8037-1603-6 Subj: Circus.

Fire and silk: flying in a hot air balloon photos by author. Little, 1991. ISBN 0-316-46959-9 Subj: Activities – ballooning. Activities – flying.

Jack Creek cowboy ill. by author. Dial, 1993. ISBN 0-8037-1229-4 Subj: Cowboys. Friendship. Seasons – summer.

Johnson, Odette. *Apples, alligators, and also alphabets* by Odette and Bruce H. Johnson; ill. by authors. Oxford Univ. Pr., 1991. ISBN 0-19-540757-1 Subj: ABC books.

One prickly porcupine by Odette and Bruce H. Johnson; ill. by authors. Oxford Univ. Pr., 1992. ISBN 0-19-540834-9 Subj: Birthdays. Counting, numbers. Giants. Tongue twisters.

Johnson, Pamela. *A mouse's tale* ill. by author. Harcourt, 1991. ISBN 0-15-256032-7 Subj: Animals – mice. Behavior – collecting things. Boats, ships. Sea and seashore.

Johnson, Paul Brett. *The cow who wouldn't come down* ill. by author. Orchard, 1993. ISBN 0-531-08631-3 Subj: Activities – flying. Animals – bulls, cows. Farms.

Farmers' market ill. by author. Orchard, 1997. ISBN 0-531-33014-1 Subj: Careers – farmers. Farms. Stores.

Frank Fister's hidden talent ill. by author. Orchard, 1994. ISBN 0-531-08663-1 Subj: Crime. Magic.

Lost ill. by Celeste Lewis. Orchard, 1996. ISBN 0-531-08851-0 Subj: Animals – dogs. Behavior – lost. Camps, camping. Desert. Pets.

A perfect pork stew ill. by author. Orchard, 1998. ISBN 0-531-33070-2 Subj: Animals – pigs. Behavior – trickery. Witches.

The pig who ran a red light ill. by author. Orchard, 1999. ISBN 0-531-33136-9 Subj: Activities. Animals – pigs. Behavior.

Johnson, Russell. *Trouble at Christmas* ill. by Bernadette Watts. North-South, 1991. ISBN 1-55858-116-2 Subj: Animals. Holidays – Christmas. Santa Claus.

Johnson, Ryerson. *Kenji and the magic geese* ill. by Jean and Mou-sien Tseng. Simon & Schuster, 1992. ISBN 0-671-75974-4 Subj: Art. Birds – geese. Foreign lands – Japan.

Let's walk up the wall ill. by Eva Cellini. Holiday, 1967. Subj: Participation.

Upstairs and downstairs ill. by Lisl Weil. Crowell, 1962. Subj: Concepts.

Johnson, Stephen T. *Alphabet city* ill. by author. Viking, 1995. ISBN 0-670-85631-2 Subj: ABC books. Caldecott award honor books. City. Concepts.

City by numbers ill. by author. Viking, 1998. ISBN 0-670-87251-2 Subj: Counting, numbers.

Johnson, Walter Ryerson. *see* Johnson, Ryerson

Johnson-Petrov, Arden. *The Lost Tooth Club* ill. by author. Tricycle, 1998. ISBN 1-883672-55-4 Subj: Clubs, gangs. Teeth.

Johnston, Deborah. *Mathew Michael's beastly day* ill. by Seymour Chwast. Harcourt, 1992. ISBN 0-15-200521-8 Subj: Animals. Behavior – bad day. Family life. Imagination. Morning. School. Self-concept.

Johnston, Johanna. *Penguin's way* ill. by Leonard Weisgard. Doubleday, 1962. Subj: Birds – penguins. Science.

Sugarplum ill. by Marvin Bileck. Knopf, 1955. Subj: Character traits – smallness. Toys – dolls.

Whale's way ill. by Leonard Weisgard. Doubleday, 1965. Subj: Animals – whales. Science.

Johnston, Marianne. *Dealing with anger* ill. by author. PowerKids, 1996. ISBN 0-8239-2325-8 Subj: Behavior. Emotions – anger.

Dealing with bullying ill. by author. PowerKids, 1996. ISBN 0-8239-2374-6 Subj: Behavior – bullying. Emotions.

Johnston, Mary Anne. *Sing me a song* ill. by John Magine. Childrens Pr., 1977. ISBN 0-913778-81-8 Subj: Animals – rabbits. Songs.

Johnston, Tony. *Alice Nizzy Nazzy, the Witch of Santa Fe* ill. by Tomie de Paola. Putnam, 1995. ISBN 0-399-22788-1 Subj: Behavior – trickery. Folk and fairy tales. Foreign lands – Russia. Witches.

Amber on the mountain ill. by Robert Duncan. Dial, 1994. ISBN 0-8037-1219-7 Subj: Activities – reading. Family life. Friendship. Roads.

The badger and the magic fan ill. by Tomie de Paola. Putnam, 1990. ISBN 0-399-21945-5 Subj: Anatomy – noses. Animals – badgers. Behavior – trickery. Folk and fairy tales. Foreign lands – Japan. Magic.

The barn owls ill. by Deborah Kogan Ray. Charlesbridge, 2000. ISBN 0-88106-981-7 Subj: Barns. Birds – owls. Poetry.

Big red apple ill. by Judith Hoffman Corwin. Scholastic, 1999. ISBN 0-439-09860-2 Subj: Circular tales. Plants. Trees.

Bigfoot Cinderrrrrella ill. by James Warhola. Putnam, 1998. ISBN 0-399-23021-1 Subj: Folk and fairy tales. Forest, woods. Mythical creatures.

The bull and the fire truck ill. by R. W. Alley. Scholastic, 1996. ISBN 0-590-47597-5 Subj: Animals – bulls, cows. Concepts – color. Trucks.

The Chizzywink and the Alamagoozlum ill. by Robert Bender. Holiday, 1998. ISBN 0-8234-1359-4 Subj: Insects – mosquitoes. Night. Sleep.

The cowboy and the black-eyed pea ill. by Ludwig Warren. Putnam, 1992. ISBN 0-399-22330-4 Subj: Cowboys. Folk and fairy tales. U.S. history – frontier and pioneer life. Weddings.

Day of the Dead ill. by Jeanette Winter. Harcourt, 1997. ISBN 0-15-222863-2 Subj: Foreign lands – Mexico. Holidays – Day of the Dead.

Desert song ill. by Ed Young. Sierra Club, 2000. ISBN 0-8715-6491-2 Subj: Animals. Desert. Night.

Farmer Mack measures his pig ill. by Megan Lloyd. HarperCollins, 1986. ISBN 0-06-023018-5 Subj: Animals – pigs. Behavior – boasting. Farms.

Fishing Sunday ill. by Barry Root. Tambourine, 1996. ISBN 0-688-13538-2 Subj: Ethnic groups in the U.S. – Japanese Americans. Family life – grandfathers. Sports – fishing.

Four scary stories ill. by Tomie de Paola. Putnam, 1978. ISBN 0-399-20614-0 Subj: Ghosts. Monsters. Mythical creatures – goblins.

The ghost of Nicholas Greebe ill. by S. D. Schindler. Dial, 1996. ISBN 0-8037-1649-4 Subj: Anatomy – skeletons. Animals – dogs. Ghosts.

Goblin walk by Tony Johnston and Bruce Degen; ill. by Bruce Degen. Putnam, 1991. ISBN 0-399-22238-3 Subj: Animals. Emotions – fear. Family life – grandmothers. Humor. Mythical creatures – goblins.

Grandpa's song ill. by Brad Sneed. Dial, 1991. ISBN 0-8037-0802-5 Subj: Family life – grandfathers. Old age. Songs.

How many miles to Jacksonville? ill. by Bart Forbes. Putnam, 1995. ISBN 0-399-22615-X Subj: City. Trains.

The iguana brothers, a perfect day ill. by Mark Teague. Blue Sky, 1995. ISBN 0-590-47468-5 Subj: Family life – brothers. Foreign lands – Mexico. Reptiles – iguanas.

I'm gonna tell mama I want an iguana ill. by Lillian Hoban. Putnam, 1990. ISBN 0-399-21931-X Subj: Family life. Poetry. Sibling rivalry.

Isabel's house of butterflies ill. by Susan Guevara. Sierra Club, 1997. ISBN 0-8715-6409-2 Subj: Foreign lands – Mexico. Insects – butterflies, caterpillars. Trees.

The last snow of winter ill. by Friso Henstra. Tambourine, 1993. ISBN 0-688-10750-8 Subj: Art. Circular tales. Friendship. Seasons – winter. Weather – snow.

Little bear sleeping ill. by Lillian Hoban. Putnam, 1991. ISBN 0-399-22157-3 Subj: Animals – bears. Bedtime. Rhyming text.

Little Rabbit goes to sleep ill. by Harvey Stevenson. HarperCollins, 1994. ISBN 0-06-021241-1 Subj: Animals – rabbits. Bedtime. Emotions – fear. Family life – grandfathers. Night. Sleep.

Little wild parrot ill. by Ora Eitan. Tambourine, 1995. ISBN 0-688-13536-6 Subj: Birds – parakeets, parrots.

Lorenzo the naughty parrot ill. by Leo Politi. Harcourt, 1992. ISBN 0-15-249350-6 Subj: Behavior – misbehavior. Birds – parakeets, parrots. Foreign lands – Mexico. Holidays – Christmas. Parties.

Mole and Troll trim the tree ill. by Wallace Tripp. Putnam, 1974. ISBN 0-399-60909-1 Subj: Animals – moles. Behavior – sharing. Holidays – Christmas. Mythical creatures – trolls. Seasons – winter. Trees.

My Mexico = México mío ill. by F. John Sierra. Putnam, 1996. ISBN 0-399-22275-8 Subj: Foreign lands – Mexico. Foreign languages. Poetry.

The old lady and the birds ill. by Stephanie Garcia. Harcourt, 1994. ISBN 0-15-257769-6 Subj: Animals – cats. Birds. Foreign lands – Mexico. Foreign languages. Gardens, gardening.

Once in the country: poems of a farm ill. by Thomas B. Allen. Putnam, 1996. ISBN 0-399-22644-3 Subj: Farms. Nature. Poetry. Seasons.

Pages of music ill. by Tomie de Paola. Putnam, 1988. ISBN 0-399-21436-4 Subj: Activities – painting. Islands. Music.

The promise ill. by Pamela Keavney. Harper, 1992. ISBN 0-06-023020-7 Subj: Animals – bulls, cows. Farms.

The quilt story ill. by Tomie de Paola. Putnam, 1984. ISBN 0-399-21009-1 Subj: Family life. Moving. Quilts.

Slither McCreep and his brother, Joe ill. by Victoria Chess. Harcourt, 1992. ISBN 0-15-276100-4 Subj:

Family life – brothers. Reptiles – snakes. Sibling rivalry.

Soup bone ill. by Margot Tomes. Harcourt, 1990. ISBN 0-15-277255-3 Subj: Anatomy – skeletons. Friendship. Holidays – Halloween.

Sparky and Eddie, the first day of school ill. by Susannah Ryan. Scholastic, 1997. ISBN 0-590-47978-4 Subj: Friendship. School – first day.

Sparky and Eddie, trouble with bugs ill. by Susannah Ryan. Scholastic, 1998. Subj: Friendship. Insects. School. Science.

Sparky and Eddie, trouble with rats ill. by Susannah Ryan. Scholastic, 1998. ISBN 0-590-47980-6 Subj: Animals – rats. Friendship. School. Science.

Sparky and Eddie, wild, wild rodeo! ill. by Susannah Ryan. Scholastic, 1998. ISBN 0-590-47984-9 Subj: Cowboys. Friendship. School. Sports.

The tale of Rabbit and Coyote ill. by Tomie de Paola. Putnam, 1994. ISBN 0-399-22258-8 Subj: Animals – coyotes. Animals – rabbits. Folk and fairy tales. Foreign lands – Mexico. Indians of North America – Zapotec.

Three little bikers ill. by G. Brian Karas. Knopf, 1994. ISBN 0-679-94701-9 Subj: Animals – sheep. Sports – bicycling.

Uncle rain cloud ill. by Fabricio Vandenbroeck. Charlesbridge, 2000. ISBN 0-88106-371-1 Subj: Ethnic groups in the U.S. – Mexican Americans. Family life – aunts, uncles. Language.

The vanishing pumpkin ill. by Tomie de Paola. Putnam, 1983. ISBN 0-3992-0991-3 Subj: Holidays – Halloween. Witches.

The wagon ill. by James E. Ransome. Tambourine, 1996. ISBN 0-688-13537-4 Subj: Ethnic groups in the U.S. – African Americans. Slavery. U.S. history.

We love the dirt ill. by Alexa Brandenberg. Scholastic, 1997. ISBN 0-590-92953-4 Subj: Earth. Farms.

Whale song ill. by Ed Young. Putnam, 1987. ISBN 0-399-21402-X Subj: Animals – whales. Counting, numbers.

The witch's hat ill. by Margot Tomes. Putnam, 1984. ISBN 0-399-21010-5 Subj: Clothing – hats. Magic. Witches.

Yonder ill. by Lloyd Bloom. Dial, 1988. ISBN 0-8037-0278-7 Subj: Cumulative tales. Seasons.

Jolin, Dominique. *It's not fair!* ill. by Dominique Jolin. Crossing Pr., 1996. ISBN 0-89594-780-3 Subj: Behavior – dissatisfaction. Family life – fathers.

Jolley, Mike. *Grunter, a pig with an attitude!* ill. by Deborah Allwright. Millbrook, 1999. ISBN 0-7613-1308-7 Subj: Animals – pigs. Behavior. Birthdays. Format, unusual – toy and movable books.

Jolliffe, Anne. *From pots to plastics* ill. by author. Hawthorn, 1965. Subj: Science.

Water, wind and wheels ill. by author. Hawthorn, 1965. Subj: Science. Water.

Joly, Fanny. *Mr. Fine, porcupine* ill. by Rémi Saillard. Chronicle, 1997. ISBN 0-8118-1842-X Subj: Animals – porcupines. Character traits – appearance. Hair. Self-concept.

Joly-Berbesson, Fanny. *Marceau Bonappetit* ill. by Agnès Mathieu. Carolrhoda, 1989. ISBN 0-87614-369-9 Subj: Animals – mice. Behavior – seeking better things. Food.

Jonas, Ann. *Aardvarks, disembark!* ill. by author. Greenwillow, 1990. ISBN 0-688-07207-0 Subj: ABC books. Animals. Animals – endangered animals. Boats, ships. Religion – Noah. Weather – floods. Weather – rain.

Bird talk ill. by author. Greenwillow, 1999. ISBN 0-688-14173-0 Subj: Birds. Noise, sounds. Songs.

Color dance ill. by author. Greenwillow, 1989. ISBN 0-688-05990-2 Subj: Activities – dancing. Concepts – color.

Holes and peeks ill. by author. Greenwillow, 1984. ISBN 0-688-02538-2 Subj: Caldecott award honor books. Emotions – fear. Problem solving.

Now we can go ill. by author. Greenwillow, 1986. ISBN 0-688-04803-X Subj: Toys.

The quilt ill. by author. Greenwillow, 1984. ISBN 0-688-03826-3 Subj: Bedtime. Dreams. Quilts.

Reflections ill. by author. Greenwillow, 1987. ISBN 0-688-06141-9 Subj: Concepts. Format, unusual.

Round trip ill. by author. Greenwillow, 1983. ISBN 0-688-01781-9 Subj: Activities – traveling. City.

Splash! ill. by author. Greenwillow, 1995. ISBN 0-688-11052-5 Subj: Animals. Counting, numbers. Ethnic groups in the U.S. – African Americans. Fish.

The thirteenth clue ill. by author. Greenwillow, 1992. ISBN 0-688-09742-1 Subj: Birthdays. Format, unusual. Mystery stories. Parties.

The trek ill. by author. Greenwillow, 1985. ISBN 0-688-04799-8 Subj: Activities – walking. Animals. Games. Imagination.

Two bear cubs ill. by author. Greenwillow, 1982. ISBN 0-688-01408-9 Subj: Animals – bears. Behavior – lost. Family life – mothers.

Watch William walk ill. by author. Greenwillow, 1997. ISBN 0-688-14175-7 Subj: Activities – walking. Animals – dogs. Birds – ducks. Language.

When you were a baby ill. by author. Greenwillow, 1982. ISBN 0-688-00864-X Subj: Activities. Behavior – growing up.

Where can it be? ill. by author. Greenwillow, 1986. ISBN 0-688-05246-0 Subj: Behavior – losing things. Format, unusual – toy and movable books.

Jonasson, Dianne. *Tuan* (Boholm-Olsson, Eva)

Jonell, Lynne. *I need a snake* ill. by Petra Mathers. Putnam, 1998. ISBN 0-399-23176-5 Subj: Family life – mothers. Pets. Reptiles – snakes.

It's my birthday, too! ill. by Petra Mathers. Putnam, 1999. ISBN 0-399-23323-7 Subj: Animals – dogs. Birthdays. Family life – brothers. Parties. Sibling rivalry.

Mommy go away! ill. by Petra Mathers. Putnam, 1997. ISBN 0-399-23001-7 Subj: Activities – bathing. Concepts – size. Family life – mothers. Imagination.

Jones, Bill T. *Dance* by Bill T. Jones and Susan Kuklin; photos by Susan Kuklin. Hyperion, 1998. ISBN 0-7868-2307-0 Subj: Activities – dancing. Rhyming text.

Jones, Brian. *Space: a three-dimensional journey* ill. by Richard Clifton-Day. Dial, 1991. ISBN 0-8037-0759-2 Subj: Astronomy. Science. Space and space ships.

Jones, Carol. *The hare and the tortoise* (Æsop)

The lion and the mouse (Æsop)

This old man ill. by author. Houghton Mifflin, 1990. ISBN 0-395-54699-0 Subj: Counting, numbers. Farms. Format, unusual. Music. Songs.

Town mouse, country mouse (Æsop)

What's the time, Mr. Wolf? ill. by author. Houghton Mifflin, 1999. ISBN 0-395-95800-8 Subj: Animals. Animals – wolves. Clocks, watches. Format, unusual – toy and movable books. Time.

Jones, Chuck. *William the backwards skunk* ill. by author. Crown, 1987. ISBN 0-517-56063-1 Subj: Animals – skunks. Behavior – imitation. Forest, woods.

Jones, Diana Wynne. *Yes, dear* ill. by Graham Philpot. Greenwillow, 1992. ISBN 0-688-11195-5 Subj: Behavior – unnoticed, unseen. Family life – grandmothers. Imagination. Magic.

Jones, Harold. *Tales from Æsop* (Æsop)

There and back again ill. by author. Atheneum, 1977. ISBN 0-689-50095-5 Subj: Toys.

Jones, Hettie. *The trees stand shining: poetry of the North American Indians* ill. by Robert Andrew Parker. Dial, 1971. ISBN 0-8037-9084-8 Subj: Indians of North America. Poetry.

Jones, Jennifer Berry. *Heetunka's harvest: a tale of the Plains Indians* ill. by Shannon Keegan. Roberts Rinehart, 1994. ISBN 1-879373-17-3 Subj: Animals – mice. Folk and fairy tales. Indians of North America – Dakota (Sioux).

Jones, Jessie Mae Orton. *A little child: the Christmas miracle told in Bible verses* ill. by Elizabeth Orton Jones. Viking, 1946. Subj: Holidays – Christmas. Religion.

Small rain: verses from the Bible ill. by Elizabeth Orton Jones. Viking, 1943. ISBN 0-670-05088-1 Subj: Caldecott award honor books. Poetry. Religion.

Jones, Joy. *Tambourine moon* ill. by Terry Widener. Simon & Schuster, 1999. ISBN 0-689-80648-5 Subj: Ethnic groups in the U.S. – African Americans. Family life – grandfathers. Moon. Night.

Jones, Kathryn D. *Carnival* (Burden-Patmon, Denise)

Jones, Malcolm. *Jump! the adventures of Brer Rabbit* (Harris, Joel Chandler)

Jones, Maurice. *I'm going on a dragon hunt* ill. by Charlotte Firmin. Four Winds, 1987. ISBN 0-02-748000-3 Subj: Dragons. Sports – hunting.

Jones, Michael. *see* Crosby-Jones, Michael

Jones, Penelope. *I didn't want to be nice* ill. by Rosalie Orlando. Bradbury, 1977. ISBN 0-87888-111-5 Subj: Animals – squirrels. Birthdays. Parties.

I'm not moving! ill. by Amy Aitken. Bradbury, 1980. ISBN 0-87888-156-5 Subj: Family life. Moving.

Jones, Rebecca C. *The biggest (and best) flag that ever flew* ill. by Charles Geer. Cornell Maritime Pr., 1988. ISBN 0-317-67910-4 Subj: U.S. history. War.

The biggest, meanest, ugliest dog in the whole wide world ill. by Wendy Watson. Macmillan, 1982. ISBN 0-02-747800-9 Subj: Animals – dogs. Character traits – meanness. Friendship.

Down at the bottom of the deep dark sea ill. by Virginia Wright-Frierson. Bradbury, 1991. ISBN 0-02-747901-3 Subj: Emotions – fear. Sand. Sea and seashore.

Great Aunt Martha ill. by Shelley Jackson. Dutton, 1995. ISBN 0-525-45257-5 Subj: Family life – aunts, uncles. Old age.

Matthew and Tilly ill. by Beth Peck. Dutton, 1991. ISBN 0-525-44684-2 Subj: City. Ethnic groups in the U.S. – African Americans. Friendship.

Jong, David Cornel De. *see* DeJong, David Cornel

Joos, Françoise. *The golden snowflake* ill. by author. Little, 1991. ISBN 0-316-47328-6 Subj: Snowmen. Weather – snow.

Joosse, Barbara M. *Better with two* ill. by Catherine Stock. HarperCollins, 1988. ISBN 0-06-023077-0 Subj: Animals – dogs. Death. Pets.

Dinah's mad, bad wishes ill. by Emily Arnold McCully. HarperCollins, 1989. ISBN 0-06-023099-1 Subj: Emotions – anger. Family life – mothers.

Fourth of July ill. by Emily Arnold McCully. Knopf, 1985. ISBN 0-394-95195-6 Subj: Behavior – growing up. Holidays – Fourth of July. Parades.

I love you the purplest ill. by Mary Whyte. Chronicle, 1996. ISBN 0-8118-0718-5 Subj: Family life – brothers. Family life – mothers. Sibling rivalry. Sports – fishing.

Jam day ill. by Emily Arnold McCully. HarperCollins, 1987. ISBN 0-06-023097-5 Subj: Family life. Family life – grandparents.

Lewis and papa: adventure on the Santa Fe Trail ill. by Jon Van Zyle. Chronicle, 1998. ISBN 0-8118-1959-0 Subj: Activities – traveling. Family life – fathers. Family life – sons. U.S. history – frontier and pioneer life.

Mama, do you love me? ill. by Barbara Lavallee. Chronicle, 1991. ISBN 0-87701-759-X Subj: Emotions – love. Eskimos. Family life – mothers.

The morning chair ill. by Marcia Sewall. Clarion, 1995. ISBN 0-395-62337-5 Subj: City. Ethnic groups in the U.S. – Dutch Americans. Furniture – chairs. Immigrants.

Nugget and Darling ill. by Sue Truesdell. Clarion, 1997. ISBN 0-395-64571-9 Subj: Animals – cats. Animals – dogs. Character traits – kindness to animals. Emotions – envy, jealousy.

Snow day! ill. by Jennifer Plecas. Clarion, 1995. ISBN 0-395-66588-4 Subj: Family life. Weather – snow.

Spiders in the fruit cellar ill. by Kay Chorao. Knopf, 1983. ISBN 0-394-95327-4 Subj: Emotions – fear. Spiders.

The thinking place ill. by Kay Chorao. Knopf, 1982. ISBN 0-394-94908-0 Subj: Behavior – misbehavior. Imagination – imaginary friends.

Jordan, Helene J. (Helene Jamieson). *How a seed grows* ill. by Loretta Krupinski. Rev. ed. HarperCollins, 1992. ISBN 0-06-020185-1 Subj: Gardens, gardening. Nature. Science. Seeds.

Seeds of wind and water ill. by Nils Hogner. Crowell, 1962. Subj: Plants.

Jordan, Jennifer. *Albert goes to town* ill. by Shannon McNeill. Chronicle, 1997. ISBN 0-8118-0860-2 Subj: Automobiles. Imagination.

Jordan, June. *Kimako's story* ill. by Kay Burford. Houghton Mifflin, 1981. ISBN 0-395-31604-9 Subj: Animals – dogs. City. Family life. Pets.

Jordan, Martin. *Amazon alphabet* by Martin and Tanis Jordan; ill. by Tanis Jordan. Kingfisher, 1996. ISBN 1-85697-666-1 Subj: ABC books. Animals. Foreign lands – South America. Jungle.

Jungle days, jungle nights by Martin and Tanis Jordan; ill. by Tanis Jordan. Kingfisher, 1993. ISBN 1-85697-885-0 Subj: Animals. Foreign lands – South America. Jungle.

Jordan, Sandra. *Christmas tree farm* ill. by author. Orchard, 1993. ISBN 0-531-08649-6 Subj: Ecology. Family life. Farms. Holidays – Christmas. Seasons. Trees.

Down on Casey's farm ill. by author. Orchard, 1996. ISBN 0-531-08853-7 Subj: Animals. Farms. Imagination. Noise, sounds.

Jordan, Tanis. *Amazon alphabet* (Jordan, Martin)

Jungle days, jungle nights (Jordan, Martin)

Jorgensen, Gail. *Crocodile Beat* ill. by Patricia Mullins. Bradbury, 1989. ISBN 0-02-748010-0 Subj: Animals. Rhyming text.

Joseph, Daniel M. *All dressed up and nowhere to go* by Daniel M. Joseph and Lydia J. Mendel; ill. by Normand Chartier. Houghton Mifflin, 1993. ISBN 0-395-60196-7 Subj: Clothing. Family life – grandparents. Holidays – Christmas.

Joseph, Lynn. *Coconut kind of day* ill. by Sandra Speidel. Lothrop, 1992. ISBN 0-688-09120-2 Subj: Foreign lands – Trinidad. Islands. Poetry.

Fly, Bessie, fly ill. by Yvonne Buchanan. Simon & Schuster, 1998. ISBN 0-689-81339-2 Subj: Airplanes, airports. Careers – airplane pilots. Ethnic groups in the U.S. – African Americans.

An island Christmas ill. by Catherine Stock. Clarion, 1992. ISBN 0-395-58761-1 Subj: Foreign lands – Trinidad. Holidays – Christmas.

Jasmine's parlour day ill. by Ann Grifalconi. Lothrop, 1994. ISBN 0-688-11488-1 Subj: Activities – working. Family life – mothers. Foreign lands – Trinidad. Islands. Sea and seashore.

Jump up time: a Trinidad Carnival story ill. by Linda Saport. Clarion, 1998. ISBN 0-395-65012-7 Subj: Emotions – envy, jealousy. Fairs. Family life – sisters. Foreign lands – Trinidad.

Josephs, Rhoda. *The baby bubble book* ill. by Emily Arnold McCully. Grosset, 1988. ISBN 0-448-09256-5 Subj: Activities – bathing. Babies. Bubbles. Format, unusual – board books.

Joslin, Mary. *The goodbye boat* ill. by Claire St. Louis Little. Eerdmans, 1998. ISBN 0-8028-5186-X Subj: Death. Emotions – grief. Family life.

The tale of the heaven tree ill. by Meilo So. Eerdmans, 1999. ISBN 0-8028-5190-8 Subj: Ecology. Gardens, gardening. Trees.

Joslin, Sesyle. *Baby elephant and the secret wishes* ill. by Leonard Weisgard. Harcourt, 1962. Subj: Animals – elephants. Holidays – Christmas.

Baby elephant goes to China ill. by Leonard Weisgard. Harcourt, 1963. Subj: Animals – elephants. Foreign languages. Sea and seashore.

Baby elephant's trunk ill. by Leonard Weisgard. Harcourt, 1961. Subj: Animals – elephants. Foreign lands – France. Foreign languages.

Brave Baby Elephant ill. by Leonard Weisgard. Harcourt, 1960. Subj: Animals – elephants. Bedtime.

Dear dragon: and other useful letter forms for young ladies and gentlemen engaged in everyday correspon-

dence ill. by Irene Haas. Harcourt, 1962. Subj: Activities – writing. Communication. Dragons. Etiquette.

Señor Baby Elephant, the pirate ill. by Leonard Weisgard. Harcourt, 1962. Subj: Animals – elephants. Foreign languages. Pirates.

What do you do, dear? ill. by Maurice Sendak. Addison-Wesley, 1985, c1961. ISBN 0-06-023075-4 Subj: Etiquette. Humor.

What do you say, dear? ill. by Maurice Sendak. Harper, 1986, c1958. ISBN 0-06-023074-6 Subj: Caldecott award honor books. Etiquette. Humor.

Joyce, Irma. *Never talk to strangers* ill. by George Buckett. Western, 1990. ISBN 0-307-12609-9 Subj: Behavior – talking to strangers. Humor. Safety.

Joyce, James. *The cat and the devil* ill. by Richard Erdoes. Dodd, 1965. Subj: Behavior – trickery. Devil.

Joyce, Susan. *ABC animal riddles* ill. by D. C. DuBosque. Peel Productions, 1999. ISBN 0-939217-51-1 Subj: ABC books. Animals. Rhyming text. Riddles.

Alphabet riddles ill. by Doug DuBosque. Peel Productions, 1998. ISBN 0-939217-50-3 Subj: ABC books. Rhyming text. Riddles.

Joyce, William. *Baseball Bob* ill. by author. 1st board book ed. Laura Geringer, 1999. ISBN 0-694-01180-0 Subj: Format, unusual – board books. Sports – baseball.

Bently and egg ill. by author. HarperCollins, 1992. ISBN 0-06-020386-2 Subj: Birds – ducks. Character traits – helpfulness. Eggs. Frogs and toads. Reptiles – turtles, tortoises.

A day with Wilbur Robinson ill. by author. HarperCollins, 1990. ISBN 0-06-022968-3 Subj: Family life.

Dinosaur Bob: and his adventures with the family Lazardo ill. by author. Expanded ed. HarperCollins, 1995. ISBN 0-06-021075-3 Subj: Activities – vacationing. Dinosaurs. Family life. Pets.

George shrinks ill. by author. HarperCollins, 1985. ISBN 0-06-023071-1 Subj: Activities – babysitting. Concepts – size. Family life.

The Leaf Men and the brave good bugs ill. by author. HarperCollins, 1996. ISBN 0-06-027238-4 Subj: Character traits – helpfulness. Gardens, gardening. Insects. Mythical creatures – elves. Old age. Toys.

Life with Bob ill. by author. Laura Geringer, 1998. ISBN 0-694-01181-9 Subj: Dinosaurs. Format, unusual – board books.

Rolie Polie Olie ill. by author. Laura Geringer, 1999. ISBN 0-06-027164-7 Subj: Concepts – shape. Rhyming text. Robots.

Rolie Polie Olie, how many howdys? computer imaging by Nelvana Ltd. Mouse Works, 1999. ISBN 0-

7364-0165-2 Subj: Counting, numbers. Format, unusual – board books. Robots.

Santa calls ill. by author. HarperCollins, 1993. ISBN 0-06-021134-2 Subj: Activities – flying. Family life – brothers and sisters. Friendship. Santa Claus. Sibling rivalry.

Snowie Rolie ill. by author. Laura Geringer, 2000. ISBN 0-06-029286-5 Subj: Robots. Snowmen. Weather – snow.

Joyner, Jerry. *Thirteen* (Charlip, Remy)

Jüchen, Aurel von. *The Holy Night: the story of the first Christmas* trans. from German by Cornelia Schaeffer; ill. by Celestino Piatti. Atheneum, 1968. Subj: Holidays – Christmas. Religion.

Jukes, Mavis. *I'll see you in my dreams* ill. by Stacey Schuett. Knopf, 1993. ISBN 0-679-92690-9 Subj: Activities – flying. Death. Family life – aunts, uncles. Illness.

Jung, Minna. *William's ninth life* ill. by Vera Rosenberry. Orchard, 1993. ISBN 05-31-08642-9 Subj: Animals – cats. Old age.

Jungman, Ann. *When the people are away* ill. by Linda Birch. Boyds Mills, 1992. ISBN 1-56397-202-6 Subj: Animals – cats. Parties. Pets.

Justice, Jennifer. *The tiger* ill. by Graham Allen. Watts, 1979. ISBN 0-531-09154-6 Subj: Animals – tigers. Science.

Kadono, Eiko. *Grandpa's soup* ill. by Satomi Ichikawa. Eerdmans, 1999. ISBN 0-8028-5195-9 Subj: Behavior – sharing. Emotions – grief. Emotions – loneliness. Family life – grandfathers. Food.

Kahl, Virginia. *Away went Wolfgang* ill. by author. Scribners, 1954. Subj: Animals – dogs. Foreign lands – Austria.

The Baron's booty ill. by author. Scribners, 1963. Subj: Middle Ages. Rhyming text. Royalty.

Droopsi ill. by author. Scribners, 1958. Subj: Foreign lands – Germany. Music.

The Duchess bakes a cake ill. by author. Scribners, 1955. Subj: Activities – cooking. Food. Middle Ages. Rhyming text. Royalty.

Giants, indeed! ill. by author. Scribners, 1974. ISBN 0-684-13659-7 Subj: Giants. Monsters.

How do you hide a monster? ill. by author. Scribners, 1971. ISBN 0-684-12318-5 Subj: Monsters. Rhyming text. Sports – hunting.

Maxie ill. by author. Scribners, 1956. Subj: Animals – dogs. Character traits – perseverance. Foreign lands – Germany. Old age.

The perfect pancake ill. by author. Scribners, 1960. Subj: Character traits – selfishness. Food. Rhyming text.

Plum pudding for Christmas ill. by author. Scribners, 1956. Subj: Food. Holidays – Christmas. Rhyming text. Royalty.

Whose cat is that? ill. by author. Scribners, 1979. ISBN 0-684-16097-8 Subj: Animals – cats. Cumulative tales.

Kahn, Joan. *Hi, Jock, run around the block* ill. by Whitney Darrow, Jr. HarperCollins, 1978. ISBN 0-06-023079-7 Subj: City. Rhyming text.

Seesaw ill. by Crosby Newell Bonsall. HarperCollins, 1964. Subj: Games. Toys.

Kahn, Katherine Janus. *The shofar calls to us* ill. by author. Kar-Ben Copies, 1992. ISBN 0-929371-61-5 Subj: Format, unusual – board books. Holidays – Rosh Hashanah. Jewish culture. Religion.

Kahn, Michèle. *My everyday Spanish word book* trans. from French by Michael Mahler and Gwen Marsh; ill. by Benvenuti. Barron's, 1982. ISBN 0-8120-5429-6 Subj: Foreign languages.

Kahn, Rosemary. *Grandma's hat* ill. by Terry Milne. Viking, 1991. ISBN 0-670-84023-8 Subj: Clothing – hats. Family life – grandmothers. Foreign lands – South Africa.

Kahng, Kim. *The loathsome dragon* (Wiesner, David)

Kaiser Johnson, Lee. *If I ran the family* by Lee and Sue Kaiser Johnson; ill. by Roberta Collier-Morales. Free Spirit, 1992. ISBN 0-915793-41-5 Subj: Emotions. Ethnic groups in the U.S. Family life. Rhyming text. Self-concept.

Kaiser Johnson, Sue. *If I ran the family* (Kaiser Johnson, Lee)

Kaizuki, Kiyonori. *A calf is born* ill. by author. Orchard, 1990. ISBN 0-531-08462-0 Subj: Animals – babies. Animals – bulls, cows. Birth. Science.

Kajikawa, Kimiko. *Sweet dreams: how animals sleep* ill. by author. Holt, 1999. ISBN 0-8050-5890-7 Subj: Animals. Sleep.

Kajpust, Melissa. *A dozen silk diapers* ill. by Veselina Tomova. Hyperion, 1993. ISBN 1-56282-457-0 Subj: Clothing. Holidays – Christmas. Religion. Spiders.

The peacock's pride ill. by Jo'Anne Kelly. Hyperion, 1997. ISBN 0-7868-2233-3 Subj: Behavior – boasting. Birds – peacocks, peahens. Character traits – vanity. Folk and fairy tales. Foreign lands – India.

Kalan, Robert. *Blue sea* ill. by Donald Crews. Greenwillow, 1979. ISBN 0-688-84184-8 Subj: Concepts – size. Fish.

Jump, frog, jump! ill. by Byron Barton. Greenwillow, 1981. ISBN 0-688-84271-2 Subj: Cumulative tales. Frogs and toads.

Moving day ill. by Yossi Abolafia. Greenwillow, 1996. ISBN 0-688-13949-3 Subj: Crustaceans. Cumulative tales. Moving. Rhyming text.

Rain ill. by Donald Crews. Greenwillow, 1978. ISBN 0-688-84139-2 Subj: Weather – rain.

Stop, thief! ill. by Yossi Abolafia. Greenwillow, 1993. ISBN 0-688-11877-1 Subj: Animals. Circular tales.

Kalas, Klaus. *The beaver family book* (Kalas, Sybille)

Kalas, Sybille. *The beaver family book* by Sybille and Klaus Kalas; photos by Sybille Kalas; trans. by Patricia Crampton. Picture Book Studio, 1987. ISBN 0-88708-050-2 Subj: Animals – beavers. Science.

The goose family book trans. by Patricia Crampton; preface by Konrad Lorenz; ill. with photos. Picture Book Studio, 1986. Tr. of Das gänse-kinder-buch. ISBN 0-88708-019-7 Subj: Birds – geese.

The penguin family book (Somme, Lauritz)

Kaldhol, Marit. *Goodbye Rune* trans. by Michael Crosby-Jones; adapt. by Catherine Maggs; ill. by Wenche Øyen. Kane/Miller, 1987. Tr. of Farvel, Rune. ISBN 0-916291-11-1 Subj: Death. Emotions – grief. Friendship.

Kallen, Stuart A. *Brontosaurus* ill. by Kristen Copham. Abdo, 1994. ISBN 1-56239-286-7 Subj: Dinosaurs.

Stegosaurus ill. by Kristen Copham. Abdo, 1994. ISBN 1-56239-285-9 Subj: Dinosaurs.

Triceratops ill. by Kristen Copham. Abdo, 1994. ISBN 1-56239-288-3 Subj: Dinosaurs.

Kalman, Benjamin. *Animals in danger: poems from no man's valley* ill. by Cécile Curtis and Michael Jupp. Random House, 1982. ISBN 0-394-95454-8 Subj: Animals – endangered animals. Ecology. Poetry.

Kalman, Bobbie. *Celebrating the powwow* ill. with photos. Crabtree, 1997. ISBN 0-8650-5640-4 Subj: Fairs. Indians of North America.

A koala is not a bear! (Sotzek, Hannelore)

Kalman, Maira. *Hey Willy, see the pyramids!* ill. by author. Puffin, 1990, c1988. ISBN 0-14-050840-6 Subj: Bedtime. Family life – sisters. Imagination.

Sayonara, Mrs. Kackleman ill. by author. Viking, 1989. ISBN 0-670-82945-5 Subj: Activities – traveling. Foreign lands – Japan.

Kamal, Aleph. *The bird who was an elephant* ill. by Frané Lessac. Lippincott, 1990. ISBN 0-397-32446-4 Subj: Birds. Foreign lands – India.

Kamen, Gloria. *"Paddle," said the swan* ill. by author. Atheneum, 1989. ISBN 0-689-31330-6 Subj: Animals. Bedtime. Rhyming text.

The ringdoves: from the fables of Bidpai ill. by adapt. Atheneum, 1988. ISBN 0-689-31312-8 Subj: Animals. Friendship. Sports – hunting.

Second-hand cat ill. by author. Atheneum, 1992. ISBN 0-689-31631-3 Subj: Animals – cats.

Kamish, Daniel. *The night scary beasties popped out of my head* by Daniel and David Kamish; ill. by Daniel Kamish. Random House, 1998. ISBN 0-679-99039-9 Subj: Activities – drawing. Bedtime. Children as illustrators. Dreams. Family life. Monsters. Night. Sleep.

Kamish, David. *The night scary beasties popped out of my head* (Kamish, Daniel)

Kanagy, Ruth A. *The park bench* (Takeshita, Fumiko)

Kanao, Keiko. *Kitten up a tree* ill. by author. Knopf, 1987. ISBN 0-394-88817-0 Subj: Animals – cats. Character traits – curiosity. Family life – mothers.

Kandell, Alice. *Max, the music-maker* (Stecher, Miriam B.)

Kandoian, Ellen. *Is anybody up?* ill. by author. Putnam, 1989. ISBN 0-399-21749-5 Subj: Etiquette. Food.

Maybe she forgot ill. by author. Dutton, 1990. ISBN 0-525-65031-8 Subj: Behavior – growing up. Family life – mothers.

Molly's seasons ill. by author. Dutton, 1992. ISBN 0-525-65076-8 Subj: Seasons.

Under the sun ill. by author. Dodd, 1987. ISBN 0-396-09059-1 Subj: Morning. Night. Sun.

Kane, Henry B. *Wings, legs, or fins* photos and ill. by author. Knopf, 1966. Subj: Animals. Science.

Kangas, Juli. *Fluffy Bunny's friend* ill. by author. Putnam, 1992. ISBN 0-448-40140-1 Subj: Animals – rabbits. Format, unusual – board books. Friendship.

Ginger Kitten's surprise ill. by author. Putnam, 1992. ISBN 0-448-40139-8 Subj: Animals – cats. Format, unusual – board books. Friendship.

Hello, Honey Bear ill. by author. Putnam, 1992. ISBN 0-448-40141-X Subj: Animals – bears. Format, unusual – board books. Friendship.

Kani, Saru. *The monkey and the crab* (Horio, Seishi)

Kannapell, Barbara M. *The night before Christmas in signed English* (Moore, Clement C.)

Kanome, Kayoko. *Little Mop lost* ill. by author; trans. from Japanese by Prudence Moodie. Carolrhoda, 1992. ISBN 0-87614-738-4 Subj: Animals – dogs. Behavior – lost. City.

Kantor, MacKinlay. *The preposterous week* ill. by Kurt Wiese. Putnam, 1942. Subj: Food. Humor.

Kantor, Sid. *Armando asked "Why?"* (Hulbert, Jay)

Kantrowitz, Mildred. *I wonder if Herbie's home yet* ill. by Tony DeLuna. Parents, 1971. ISBN 0-819-30466-2 Subj: Friendship.

When Violet died ill. by Emily Arnold McCully. Parents, 1973. ISBN 0-719-30691-6 Subj: Birds. Death. Emotions – grief.

Willy Bear ill. by Nancy Winslow Parker. Parents, 1976. ISBN 0-819-30884-6 Subj: School – first day. Sleep. Toys – bears.

Kaplan, Boche. *Sweet Betsy from Pike* (Abisch, Roz)

Kaplan, John. *Mom and me* photos by author. Scholastic, 1996. ISBN 0-590-47294-1 Subj: Family life – mothers.

Kapp, Paul. *Cock-a-doodle-doo! Cock-a-doodle-dandy!* ill. by Anita Lobel. HarperCollins, 1966. Subj: Music. Songs.

Karas, G. Brian. *Home on the bayou* ill. by author. Simon & Schuster, 1996. ISBN 0-689-80516-4 Subj: Behavior – bullying. Cowboys. Family life. Moving.

I know an old lady (Little old lady who swallowed a fly)

The windy day ill. by author. Simon & Schuster, 1998. ISBN 0-689-81449-6 Subj: Weather – wind.

Karas, Jacqueline. *The doll house* ill. by Judith Riches. Tambourine, 1993. ISBN 0-688-12481-X Subj: Emotions. Friendship. Toys – dolls.

Karim, Roberta. *Kindle me a riddle: a pioneer story* ill. by Bethanne Andersen. Greenwillow, 1999. ISBN 0-688-16203-7 Subj: Family life. Riddles. U.S. history – frontier and pioneer life.

Mandy Sue Day ill. by Karen Ritz. Clarion, 1994. ISBN 0-395-66155-2 Subj: Animals – horses, ponies. Family life. Farms. Handicaps – blindness.

This is a hospital, not a zoo! ill. by Sue Truesdell. Clarion, 1998. ISBN 0-395-72099-0 Subj: Animals. Careers – nurses. Hospitals. Humor. Illness. Imagination.

Kark, Nina Mary. *see* Bawden, Nina

Karkowsky, Nancy. *Grandma's soup* ill. by Shelly O. Haas. Kar-Ben Copies, 1989. ISBN 0-930494-98-9 Subj: Family life – grandmothers. Illness – Alzheimer's. Jewish culture. Old age.

Karlin, Barbara. *Cinderella* (Perrault, Charles)

Karlin, Nurit. *The blue frog* ill. by author. Coward, 1983. ISBN 0-698-20577-4 Subj: Character traits – being different. Frogs and toads.

The dream factory ill. by author. Lippincott, 1988. ISBN 0-397-32212-7 Subj: Dreams. Sleep.

The fat cat sat on the mat ill. by author. HarperCollins, 1996. ISBN 0-06-026674-0 Subj: Animals – cats. Animals – rats. Rhyming text. Witches.

I see, you saw ill. by author. HarperCollins, 1997. ISBN 0-06-026678-3 Subj: Animals. Language.

Little big mouse ill. by author. HarperCollins, 1991. ISBN 0-06-021608-5 Subj: Animals – mice. Concepts – size. Self-concept.

Ten little bunnies ill. by author. Simon & Schuster, 1994. ISBN 0-671-88026-8 Subj: Animals – rabbits. Counting, numbers. Rhyming text.

The tooth witch ill. by author. Lippincott, 1985. ISBN 0-397-32120-1 Subj: Character traits – kindness. Fairies. Witches.

A train for the king ill. by author. Coward, 1983. ISBN 0-698-20578-2 Subj: Royalty – kings. Self-concept.

Karlins, Mark. *Music over Manhattan* ill. by Jack E. Davis. Doubleday, 1998. ISBN 0-385-32225-9 Subj: City. Family life. Music. Weddings.

Karlinsky, Ruth Schild. *My first book of Mitzvos* photos by Isaiah Karlinsky. Feldheim, 1986. ISBN 0-87306-388-0 Subj: Jewish culture. Religion.

Karmi, Giora. *And Shira imagined* ill. by author. Jewish Publication Society, 1988. ISBN 0-8276-0288-X Subj: Activities – traveling. Family life. Foreign lands – Israel. Imagination.

Karn, George. *Circus big and small* ill. by author. Little, 1986. ISBN 0-316-30342-9 Subj: Circus. Concepts – opposites. Format, unusual – board books.

Circus colors ill. by author. Little, 1986. ISBN 0-316-30343-7 Subj: Circus. Concepts – color. Format, unusual – board books.

Karon, Jan. *Miss Fannie's hat* ill. by Toni Goffe. Augsburg, 1998. ISBN 0-8066-3526-6 Subj: Behavior – sharing. Clothing – hats. Religion.

Karpin, Florence Baker. *Tree spirits* ill. by author. Countryman Pr., 1992. ISBN 0-88150-248-0 Subj: Ecology. Trees.

Karsunke, Yaak. *Hello Irina* (Blech, Dietlind)

Kasperson, James. *Little brother moose* ill. by Karlyn Holman. Dawn Pub., 1995. ISBN 1-883220-34-3 Subj: Animals – moose. Birds – geese. Senses.

Kassirer, Sue. *Joseph and his coat of many colors* ill. by Danuta Jarecka. Simon & Schuster, 1997. ISBN 0-689-81227-2 Subj: Clothing – coats. Religion. Sibling rivalry.

Kastner, Jill. *Barnyard big top* ill. by author. Simon & Schuster, 1997. ISBN 0-689-80484-9 Subj: Animals. Circus. Family life. Farms.

Snake hunt ill. by author. Four Winds, 1993. ISBN 0-02-749395-4 Subj: Family life – grandfathers. Reptiles – snakes. Sports – hunting.

Kasza, Keiko. *Don't laugh, Joe* ill. by author. Putnam, 1997. ISBN 0-399-23036-X Subj: Animals – bears. Animals – possums. Behavior.

Dorothy and Mikey ill. by author. Putnam, 2000. ISBN 0-399-23356-3 Subj: Activities – playing. Animals – hippopotamuses. Friendship.

Grandpa Toad's last secret ill. by author. Putnam, 1995. ISBN 0-399-22610-9 Subj: Family life – grandfathers. Frogs and toads. Monsters.

The mightiest ill. by author. Putnam, 2001. ISBN 0-399-23586-8 Subj: Animals – bears. Animals – elephants. Animals – lions. Giants.

A mother for Choco ill. by author. Putnam, 1992. ISBN 0-399-21841-6 Subj: Adoption. Animals. Birds. Emotions – love. Family life – mothers.

The pigs' picnic ill. by author. Putnam, 1988. ISBN 0-399-21543-3 Subj: Activities – picnicking. Animals – pigs. Character traits – appearance.

The rat and the tiger ill. by author. Putnam, 1993. ISBN 0-399-22404-1 Subj: Animals – rats. Animals – tigers. Behavior – bullying. Behavior – sharing. Friendship.

When the elephant walks ill. by author. Putnam, 1990. ISBN 0-399-21755-X Subj: Animals. Cumulative tales. Emotions – fear.

The wolf's chicken stew ill. by author. Putnam, 1987. ISBN 0-399-21400-3 Subj: Animals – wolves. Birds – chickens. Character traits – generosity. Food.

Kates, Bobbi Jane. *We're different, we're the same: featuring Jim Henson's Sesame Street Muppets* ill. by Joe Mathieu. Random House, 1992. ISBN 0-679-83227-0 Subj: Anatomy. Puppets. Rhyming text.

Katz, Avner. *The little pickpocket* ill. by author. Simon & Schuster, 1996. ISBN 0-689-80494-6 Subj: Animals – kangaroos. Bedtime. Foreign lands – Australia. Sleep.

Tortoise solves a problem ill. by author. HarperCollins, 1993. ISBN 0-06-020799-X Subj: Homes, houses. Reptiles – turtles, tortoises.

Katz, Bobbi. *The creepy crawly book* ill. by S. D. Schindler. Random House, 1989. ISBN 0-394-82709-0 Subj: Animals. Insects.

Tick-tock, let's read the clock ill. by Carol Nicklaus. Random House, 1988. ISBN 0-394-89399-9 Subj: Clocks, watches. Poetry. Time.

Katz, Karen. *The colors of us* ill. by author. Holt, 1999. ISBN 0-8050-5864-8 Subj: Character traits – individuality. Concepts – color. Ethnic groups in the U.S.

Katz, Michael Jay. *Ten potatoes in a pot and other counting rhymes* ill. by June Otani. HarperCollins,

1990. ISBN 0-06-023107-6 Subj: Counting, numbers. Poetry.

Kauffman, Lois. *What's that noise?* ill. by Allan Eitzen. Lothrop, 1965. Subj: Family life – fathers. Night. Noise, sounds.

Kaufman, Curt. *Hotel boy* by Curt and Gita Kaufman; photos by Curt Kaufman. Atheneum, 1987. ISBN 0-689-31287-3 Subj: Activities. City. Ethnic groups in the U.S. – African Americans. Family life.

Rajesh by Curt and Gita Kaufman; photos by Curt Kaufman. Atheneum, 1985. ISBN 0-689-31074-9 Subj: Handicaps. School.

Kaufman, Gita. *Hotel boy* (Kaufman, Curt)

Rajesh (Kaufman, Curt)

Kaufman, Jeff. *Milk rock* ill. by author. Holt, 1994. ISBN 0-8050-2814-5 Subj: Careers – farmers. Farms. Magic. Rocks.

Kaufmann, John. *Birds are flying* ill. by author. Crowell, 1979. ISBN 0-690-03942-5 Subj: Birds. Science.

Flying giants of long ago ill. by author. Crowell, 1984. ISBN 0-690-04219-1 Subj: Activities – flying. Animals. Birds. Insects. Science.

Kaune, Merriman B. *My own little house* ill. by author. Follett, 1957. Subj: Homes, houses.

Kavanaugh, James J. *The crooked angel* ill. by Elaine Havelock. Nash, 1970. ISBN 0-8402-1157-0 Subj: Angels. Rhyming text.

Kay, Helen. *An egg is for wishing* ill. by Yaroslava. Abelard-Schuman, 1966. Subj: Behavior – animals, dislike of. Behavior – wishing. Eggs. Foreign lands – Ukraine. Holidays – Easter.

One mitten Lewis ill. by Kurt Werth. Lothrop, 1955. Subj: Behavior – losing things. Clothing – gloves, mittens.

A stocking for a kitten ill. by Yaroslava. Abelard-Schuman, 1965. Subj: Animals – cats. Family life – grandmothers.

Kay, Ormonde De. *see* De Kay, Ormonde

Kay, Verla. *Covered wagons, bumpy trails* ill. by S. D. Schindler. Putnam, 2000. ISBN 0-399-22928-0 Subj: Activities – traveling. Homes, houses. Rhyming text. U.S. history.

Gold fever ill. by S.D. Schindler. Putnam, 1999. ISBN 0-399-23027-0 Subj: Careers – miners. Rhyming text. U.S. history – frontier and pioneer life.

Iron horses ill. by Michael McCurdy. Putnam, 1999. ISBN 0-399-23119-6 Subj: Rhyming text. Trains. U.S. history.

Kaye, Buddy. *A you're adorable* (Lippman, Sidney)

Kaye, Geraldine. *The sea monkey: a picture story from Malaysia* ill. by Gay Galsworthy. Collins-World, 1968. ISBN 0-582-16571-1 Subj: Animals – monkeys. Foreign lands – Malaysia.

Kaye, Marilyn. *The real tooth fairy* ill. by Helen Cogancherry. Harcourt, 1990. ISBN 0-15-265780-0 Subj: Fairies. Teeth.

Kazeroid, Sibylle. *Make a wish, Honey Bear!* (Pfister, Marcus)

Meg's wish (Recknagel, Friedrich)

Keams, Geri. *Snail girl brings water: a Navajo story* ill. by Richard Ziehler-Martin. Rising Moon, 1998. ISBN 0-8735-8662-X Subj: Creation. Folk and fairy tales. Indians of North America – Navajo. Water.

Keaney, Leonie. *Zoo day* (Brennan, John)

Keats, Ezra Jack. *Apt. 3* ill. by author. Macmillan, 1971. ISBN 0-689-71059-3 Subj: City. Ethnic groups in the U.S. – African Americans. Family life. Handicaps – blindness. Music. Senses – seeing.

Clementina's cactus ill. by author. Viking, 1999. ISBN 0-670-88545-2 Subj: Desert. Plants. Weather – storms. Wordless.

Dreams ill. by author. Macmillan, 1974. ISBN 0-02-749610-4 Subj: Dreams. Ethnic groups in the U.S. – African Americans. Imagination. Night. Sleep.

God is in the mountain ill. by author. Holt, 1994. ISBN 0-8050-3168-5 Subj: Religion.

Goggles ill. by author. Macmillan, 1969. ISBN 0-02-749590-6 Subj: Behavior – bullying. Caldecott award honor books. City. Ethnic groups in the U.S. – African Americans. Problem solving.

Hi, cat! ill. by author. Viking, 1999. ISBN 0-670-88546-0 Subj: Animals – cats. City. Ethnic groups in the U.S. – African Americans.

Jennie's hat ill. by author. HarperCollins, 1966. ISBN 0-06-023114-9 Subj: Behavior – dissatisfaction. Character traits – kindness to animals. Clothing – hats.

John Henry ill. by author. HarperCollins, 1965. ISBN 0-394-99052-8 Subj: Character traits – perseverance. Character traits – pride. Ethnic groups in the U.S. – African Americans. Folk and fairy tales.

Kitten for a day ill. by author. Watts, 1974. ISBN 0-531-02714-7 Subj: Animals – cats. Animals – dogs. Wordless.

A letter to Amy ill. by author. HarperCollins, 1968. ISBN 0-06-023109-2 Subj: Ethnic groups in the U.S. – African Americans. Friendship. Letters, cards. Parties. Weather – rain. Weather – wind.

The little drummer boy ill. by author. Aladdin, 1987, c1968. Words and music by Katherine Davis, Henry Onorati and Harry Simeonne. ISBN 0-689-

71158-1 Subj: Holidays – Christmas. Music. Religion. Songs.

Louie ill. by author. Greenwillow, 1975. ISBN 0-688-84002-7 Subj: Character traits – shyness. Ethnic groups in the U.S. – African Americans. Puppets.

Louie's search ill. by author. Four Winds, 1989, c1980. ISBN 0-689-71354-1 Subj: Behavior – needing someone. Family life.

Maggie and the pirate ill. by author. Four Winds, 1979. ISBN 0-590-07602-7 Subj: Death. Pets. Pirates.

My dog is lost! ill. by Ezra Jack Keats. Viking, 1999. ISBN 0-670-88550-9 Subj: Animals – dogs. Behavior – lost. Careers – police officers. Ethnic groups in the U.S. Ethnic groups in the U.S. – Puerto Rican Americans. Foreign languages.

One red sun: a counting book ill. by author. Viking, 1999. ISBN 0-670-88478-2 Subj: Counting, numbers. Format, unusual – board books.

Pet show! ill. by author. Aladdin, 1987, c1972. ISBN 0-689-71159-X Subj: Animals. Ethnic groups in the U.S. – African Americans. Pets.

Peter's chair ill. by author. HarperCollins, 1967. ISBN 0-06-023112-2 Subj: Babies. Behavior – sharing. Ethnic groups in the U.S. – African Americans. Family life – new sibling. Friendship. Furniture – chairs. Self-concept.

Pssst! doggie ill. by author. Watts, 1973. ISBN 0-531-02598-5 Subj: Animals – cats. Animals – dogs. Wordless.

Regards to the man in the moon ill. by author. Four Winds, 1981. ISBN 0-590-07820-8 Subj: Imagination. Space and space ships.

Skates ill. by author. Four Winds, 1981, c1972. ISBN 0-590-07812-7 Subj: Activities – playing. Animals – dogs. Ethnic groups in the U.S. – African Americans. Humor. Wordless.

The snowy day ill. by author. Viking, 1962. Subj: Activities – playing. Caldecott award books. Ethnic groups in the U.S. – African Americans. Seasons – winter. Weather – snow.

The snowy day ill. by author. Viking, 1996. ISBN 0-670-86733-0 Subj: Activities – playing. Caldecott award books. Ethnic groups in the U.S. – African Americans. Format, unusual – board books. Weather – snow.

The trip ill. by author. Greenwillow, 1978. ISBN 0-688-84123-6 Subj: Emotions – loneliness. Ethnic groups in the U.S. – African Americans. Holidays – Halloween. Imagination. Moving.

Whistle for Willie ill. by author. Viking, 1964. Subj: Activities – whistling. Animals – dogs. Ethnic groups in the U.S. – African Americans. Problem solving. Self-concept.

Keenan, Martha. *The mannerly adventures of Little Mouse* ill. by Meri Shardin. Crown, 1977. ISBN 0-517-52845-2 Subj: Animals – mice. Etiquette.

Keenen, George. *The preposterous week* ill. by Stanley Mack. Dial, 1971. ISBN 0-8037-7072-3 Subj: Behavior – losing things. Character traits – foolishness. Days of the week, months of the year. Humor. Problem solving.

Keens-Douglas, Richardo. *The Miss Meow pageant* ill. by Marie Lafrance. Annick, 1998. ISBN 1-55037-537-7 Subj: Animals – cats. Character traits – individuality.

Keeping, Charles. *Alfie finds the other side of the world* ill. by author. Watts, 1968. Subj: City. Foreign lands – England. Rivers. Weather – fog:

Joseph's yard ill. by author. Watts, 1969. Subj: Gardens, gardening. Poverty.

Molly o' the moors: the story of a pony ill. by author. Collins, 1966. Subj: Animals – horses, ponies. Old age.

Through the window ill. by author. Watts, 1970. ISBN 0-531-01868-7 Subj: City. Foreign lands – England.

Willie's fire-engine ill. by author. Oxford Univ. Pr., 1980. ISBN 0-19-279728-X Subj: Activities – playing. Careers – firefighters. Imagination.

Keeshan, Robert. *Alligator in the basement* ill. by Kyle Corkum. Fairview, 1996. ISBN 0-925190-90-X Subj: Animals – monkeys. Family life – grandfathers. Imagination. Reptiles – alligators, crocodiles.

Itty Bitty Kitty ill. by Jane Maday. Fairview, 1997. ISBN 1-57749-017-7 Subj: Animals – cats. Format, unusual – board books.

Itty Bitty Kitty makes a big splash ill. by Jane Maday. Fairview, 1997. ISBN 1-57749-018-5 Subj: Accidents. Animals – cats. Format, unusual – board books. Hotels. Sports – swimming.

She loves me, she loves me not ill. by Maurice Sendak. HarperCollins, 1963. Subj: Games. Holidays – Valentine's Day. Mythical creatures.

Kehoe, Michael. *Road closed* photos by author. Carolrhoda, 1982. ISBN 0-87614-192-0 Subj: Roads.

The rock quarry book photos by author. Carolrhoda, 1981. ISBN 0-87614-142-4 Subj: Rocks.

Keigwin, R. P. *Thumbelina* (Andersen, H. C. [Hans Christian])

The ugly duckling (Andersen, H. C. [Hans Christian])

Keillor, Garrison. *Cat, you better come home* ill. by Steve Johnson and Lou Fancher. Viking, 1995. ISBN 0-670-85112-4 Subj: Animals – cats. Behavior – seeking better things. Rhyming text.

The old man who loved cheese ill. by Anne Wilsdorf. Little, 1996. ISBN 0-316-48615-9 Subj: Food. Rhyming text. Senses – smelling.

Katz, Douglas. *Fernando's gift = El regalo de Fernando* ill. with photos. Sierra Club, 1995. ISBN 0-87156-

414-9 Subj: Ecology. Family life. Foreign lands – Costa Rica. Foreign languages. Forest, woods. Gifts. Trees.

Keith, Adrienne. *Fairies from A to Z* ill. by Wendy Wallin Malinow. Tricycle, 1994. ISBN 1-883672-10-4 Subj: ABC books. Fairies. Rhyming text.

Keith, Eros. *Bedita's bad day* ill. by author. Harper-Collins, 1973. ISBN 0-878-88036-4 Subj: Behavior – bad day. Witches.

Nancy's backyard ill. by author. HarperCollins, 1973. ISBN 0-06-023123-8 Subj: Dreams. Weather – rain.

Rrra-ah ill. by author. Bradbury, 1969. ISBN 0-13-783456-X Subj: Frogs and toads. Pets.

Keller, Beverly. *Fiona's bee* ill. by Diane Paterson. Coward, 1975. ISBN 0-698-30595-7 Subj: Character traits – shyness. Insects – bees.

Pimm's place ill. by Jacqueline Chwast. Coward, 1978. ISBN 0-698-30689-9 Subj: Behavior – solitude. Character traits – bravery. Emotions – fear.

When mother got the flu ill. by Maxie Chambliss. Coward, 1984. ISBN 0-698-30743-7 Subj: Behavior – misbehavior. Family life – mothers. Illness.

Keller, Charles. *School daze* ill. by Sam Q. Weissman. Prentice-Hall, 1979. ISBN 0-13-793620-6 Subj: Humor. Riddles.

Tongue twisters ill. by Ron Fritz. Simon & Schuster, 1989. ISBN 0-671-67123-5 Subj: Poetry. Tongue twisters.

Keller, Holly. *A bear for Christmas* ill. by author. Greenwillow, 1986. ISBN 0-688-05989-9 Subj: Behavior – misbehavior. Family life. Gifts. Holidays – Christmas. Toys – bears.

A bed full of cats ill. by author. Harcourt, 1999. ISBN 0-15-202331-3 Subj: Animals – cats. Behavior – losing things. Pets.

The best present ill. by author. Greenwillow, 1989. ISBN 0-688-07320-4 Subj: Family life – grandmothers. Hospitals.

Brave Horace ill. by author. Greenwillow, 1998. ISBN 0-688-15408-5 Subj: Animals – leopards. Character traits – bravery. Emotions – fear. Parties.

Cromwell's glasses ill. by author. Greenwillow, 1982. ISBN 0-688-00835-6 Subj: Animals – rabbits. Family life. Glasses. Senses – seeing.

Furry ill. by author. Greenwillow, 1992. ISBN 0-688-10520-3 Subj: Animals. Illness. Pets. School.

Geraldine and Mrs. Duffy ill. by author. Greenwillow, 2000. ISBN 0-688-16888-4 Subj: Activities – babysitting. Animals – pigs. Family life – brothers and sisters.

Geraldine first ill. by author. Greenwillow, 1996. ISBN 0-688-14150-1 Subj: Animals – pigs. Family life. Sibling rivalry.

Geraldine's baby brother ill. by author. Greenwillow, 1994. ISBN 0-688-12006-7 Subj: Animals – pigs. Babies. Emotions – envy, jealousy. Family life – new sibling. Sibling rivalry.

Geraldine's big snow ill. by author. Greenwillow, 1988. ISBN 0-688-07514-2 Subj: Animals – pigs. Weather – snow.

Geraldine's blanket ill. by author. Greenwillow, 1984. ISBN 0-688-02540-4 Subj: Animals – pigs. Family life. Toys – dolls.

Goodbye, Max ill. by author. Greenwillow, 1987. ISBN 0-688-06562-7 Subj: Animals – dogs. Death. Emotions – grief. Pets.

Grandfather's dream ill. by author. Greenwillow, 1994. ISBN 0-688-12340-6 Subj: Birds – cranes. Family life – grandfathers. Foreign lands – Vietnam.

Harry and Tuck ill. by author. Greenwillow, 1993. ISBN 0-688-11463-6 Subj: Character traits – individuality. Family life – brothers. Multiple births – twins. School – first day.

Henry's Fourth of July ill. by author. Greenwillow, 1985. ISBN 0-688-04013-6 Subj: Activities – picnicking. Animals – possums. Holidays – Fourth of July.

Henry's happy birthday ill. by author. Greenwillow, 1990. ISBN 0-688-09451-1 Subj: Birthdays. Parties.

Horace ill. by author. Greenwillow, 1991. ISBN 0-688-09832-0 Subj: Adoption. Animals – leopards. Character traits – being different. Self-concept.

Island baby ill. by author. Greenwillow, 1992. ISBN 0-688-10580-7 Subj: Birds – flamingos. Character traits – kindness to animals. Family life – grandfathers. Islands.

Jacob's tree ill. by author. Greenwillow, 1999. ISBN 0-688-15996-6 Subj: Animals – bears. Behavior – growing up. Concepts – size. Family life.

Lizzie's invitation ill. by author. Greenwillow, 1987. ISBN 0-688-06125-7 Subj: Birthdays. Emotions. Friendship.

Maxine in the middle ill. by author. Greenwillow, 1989. ISBN 0-688-08151-7 Subj: Animals – rabbits. Behavior – running away. Family life – brothers and sisters.

Merry Christmas, Geraldine ill. by author. Greenwillow, 1997. ISBN 0-688-14501-9 Subj: Animals – pigs. Character traits – stubbornness. Holidays – Christmas.

The new boy ill. by author. Greenwillow, 1991. ISBN 0-688-09828-2 Subj: Animals – mice. Behavior. School.

Rosata ill. by author. Greenwillow, 1995. ISBN 0-688-05321-1 Subj: Clothing – hats. Friendship.

Ten sleepy sheep ill. by author. Greenwillow, 1983. ISBN 0-688-02307-X Subj: Bedtime.

That's mine, Horace ill. by author. Greenwillow, 2000. ISBN 0-688-17159-1 Subj: Animals. Behavior. Character traits – honesty. School.

Too big ill. by author. Greenwillow, 1983. ISBN 0-688-01999-4 Subj: Animals. Sibling rivalry.

What Alvin wanted ill. by author. Greenwillow, 1990. ISBN 0-688-08934-8 Subj: Activities – babysitting. Babies. Family life – brothers and sisters.

What I see ill. by author. Harcourt, 1999. ISBN 0-15-201996-0 Subj: Rhyming text. Senses – seeing.

When Francie was sick ill. by author. Greenwillow, 1985. ISBN 0-688-05434-X Subj: Family life – mothers. Illness.

Will it rain? ill. by author. Greenwillow, 1984. ISBN 0-688-03840-9 Subj: Animals. Weather – rain. Weather – storms.

Keller, Irene. *Benjamin Rabbit and the stranger danger* ill. by Dick Keller. Dodd, 1985. ISBN 0-396-08655-1 Subj: Animals – rabbits. Behavior – talking to strangers. School.

The Thingumajig book of manners ill. by Dick Keller. Ideals, 1981. ISBN 0-8249-8010-7 Subj: Character traits – appearance. Etiquette.

Keller, John G. *Krispin's fair* ill. by Ed Emberley. Little, 1976. ISBN 0-316-48652-3 Subj: Etiquette. Friendship.

Keller, Laurie. *The scrambled states of America* ill. by author. Holt, 1998. ISBN 0-8050-5802-8 Subj: Maps. U.S. history.

Kelley, Anne. *Daisy's discovery* ill. by Metin Salih. Barron's, 1985. ISBN 0-8120-5676-0 Subj: Animals – dogs. Behavior – losing things. Birthdays. Family life.

Kelley, Marty. *Fall is not easy* ill. by author. Zino Pr., 1998. ISBN 1-55933-234-4 Subj: Nursery rhymes. Seasons. Trees.

Kelley, True. *Buggly Bear's hiccup cure* ill. by author. Gareth Stevens, 1994. ISBN 0-8368-0982-3 Subj: Animals – bears. Animals – moose. Hiccups.

Day-care teddy bear ill. by author. Random House, 1990. ISBN 0-394-94305-8 Subj: Emotions – fear. Toys – bears.

Hammers and mops, pencils and pots: a first book of tools and gadgets we use around the house ill. by author. Crown, 1994. ISBN 0-517-59626-1 Subj: Dictionaries. Format, unusual – board books. Tools.

I've got chicken pox ill. by author. Dutton, 1994. ISBN 0-525-45185-4 Subj: Illness – chicken pox.

Let's eat ill. by author. Dutton, 1989. ISBN 0-525-44482-3 Subj: Food.

Look again at funny animals ill. by author. Candlewick, 1996. ISBN 1-56402-791-0 Subj: Animals. Senses – seeing.

Look again at my funny family ill. by author. Candlewick, 1996. ISBN 1-56402-790-2 Subj: Family life.

Look, baby! Listen, baby! Do, baby! ill. by author. Dutton, 1987. ISBN 0-525-44320-7 Subj: Activities. Anatomy. Babies. Noise, sounds.

A valentine for Fuzzboom ill. by author. Houghton Mifflin, 1981. ISBN 0-395-30446-6 Subj: Animals – rabbits. Holidays – Valentine's Day.

Kellogg, Steven (Stephen). *A-hunting we will go!* ill. by author. Morrow, 1998. ISBN 0-688-14945-6 Subj: Bedtime. Songs.

Aster Aardvark's alphabet adventures ill. by author. Morrow, 1987. ISBN 0-688-07257-7 Subj: ABC books. Animals. Animals – aardvarks. Birds.

A beasty story (Martin, Bill [William Ivan])

Best friends ill. by author. Dial, 1986. ISBN 0-8037-0101-2 Subj: Animals – dogs. Emotions – envy, jealousy. Friendship.

Can I keep him? ill. by author. Dial, 1971. ISBN 0-8037-0989-7 Subj: Family life. Pets.

Chicken Little ill. by author. Morrow, 1985. ISBN 0-688-05691-1 Subj: Animals. Behavior – trickery. Birds – chickens. Folk and fairy tales.

The Christmas witch ill. by author. Dial, 1992. ISBN 0-8037-1269-3 Subj: Holidays – Christmas. Witches.

Give the dog a bone ill. by author. SeaStar, 2000. ISBN 1-58717-002-7 Subj: Animals – dogs. Counting, numbers. Songs.

I was born about 10,000 years ago: a tall tale ill. by author. Morrow, 1996. ISBN 0-688-13412-2 Subj: Folk and fairy tales. Songs. Tall tales.

The island of the skog ill. by author. Dial, 1973. ISBN 0-8037-3840-4 Subj: Animals – mice. Boats, ships. Islands. Monsters.

Jack and the beanstalk (Jack and the beanstalk)

Johnny Appleseed: a tall tale ill. by author. Morrow, 1988. ISBN 0-688-06418-3 Subj: Activities – traveling. Folk and fairy tales. Trees. U.S. history.

Mike Fink: a tall tale ill. by author. Morrow, 1992. ISBN 0-688-07004-3 Subj: Boats, ships. Rivers. Tall tales. U.S. history.

The mysterious tadpole ill. by author. Dial, 1977. ISBN 0-8037-6246-1 Subj: Frogs and toads. Monsters. Pets.

The mystery of the flying orange pumpkin ill. by author. Dial, 1980. ISBN 0-8037-6116-3 Subj: Holidays – Halloween. Mystery stories.

The mystery of the magic green ball ill. by author. Dial, 1978. ISBN 0-8037-6215-1 Subj: Behavior – losing things. Gypsies. Mystery stories. Toys – balls.

The mystery of the missing red mitten ill. by author. Dial, 2000. Re-worked edition of: The mystery of the missing red mitten. 1974. ISBN 0-8037-2566-3

Subj: Behavior – losing things. Clothing – gloves, mittens. Mystery stories. Snowmen.

The mystery of the stolen blue paint ill. by author. Dial, 1982. ISBN 0-8037-5659-3 Subj: Mystery stories.

Paul Bunyan: a tall tale ill. by reteller. Morrow, 1984. ISBN 0-688-03850-6 Subj: Careers – lumberjacks. Tall tales. U.S. history – frontier and pioneer life.

Pecos Bill ill. by adapt. Morrow, 1986. ISBN 0-688-05872-8 Subj: Cowboys. Tall tales. U.S. history – frontier and pioneer life.

A penguin pup for Pinkerton ill. by author. Dial, 2001. ISBN 0-8037-2536-1 Subj: Animals – dogs. Birds – penguins. Eggs.

Pinkerton, behave! ill. by author. Dial, 1979. ISBN 0-8037-6575-4 Subj: Animals – dogs.

Prehistoric Pinkerton ill. by author. Dial, 1987. ISBN 0-8037-0323-6 Subj: Animals – dogs. Behavior – misbehavior. Dinosaurs. Museums.

Ralph's secret weapon ill. by author. Dial, 1983. ISBN 0-8037-7087-1 Subj: Activities – vacationing. Imagination.

A rose for Pinkerton ill. by author. Dial, 1981. ISBN 0-8037-7503-2 Subj: Animals – cats. Animals – dogs. Behavior – imitation.

Sally Ann Thunder Ann Whirlwind Crockett ill. by author. Morrow, 1995. ISBN 0-688-14043-2 Subj: Tall tales. U.S. history – frontier and pioneer life.

Tallyho, Pinkerton! ill. by author. Dial, 1982. ISBN 0-8037-8743-X Subj: Animals – cats. Animals – dogs. Sports – hunting.

There was an old woman (Little old lady who swallowed a fly)

The three little pigs (The three little pigs)

The three sillies (Jacobs, Joseph)

Yankee Doodle ill. by author. Four Winds, 1980, c1976. ISBN 0-590-07782-1 Subj: Music. Songs. U.S. history.

Kelly, Irene. *Ebbie and Flo* ill. by author. Smith & Kraus, 1997. ISBN 1-57525-115-9 Subj: Fish. Science.

Kelly, Sheila M. *The A.D.D. book for kids* (Rotner, Shelley)

Lots of moms (Rotner, Shelley)

Kemp, Anthea. *Mr. Percy's magic greenhouse* ill. by Penny Metcalfe. David & Charles, 1988. ISBN 0-575-03870-5 Subj: Animals. Gardens, gardening. Jungle. Magic.

Kemp, Moira. *The firebird* (The firebird)

Humpty Dumpty (Mother Goose)

I'm a little teapot ill. by author. Lodestar, 1992. ISBN 0-525-67394-6 Subj: Format, unusual – board books. Rhyming text. Songs.

Knock at the door ill. by author. Lodestar, 1992. ISBN 0-525-67396-2 Subj: Format, unusual – board books. Games. Nursery rhymes. Rhyming text.

Lift-the-flap chick ill. by author. Lodestar, 1998. ISBN 0-525-67565-5 Subj: Animals. Behavior – lost. Birds – chickens. Format, unusual – toy and movable books.

Lift-the-flap kitten ill. by author. Lodestar, 1998. ISBN 0-525-67564-7 Subj: Animals. Animals – cats. Format, unusual – toy and movable books. Sleep.

Lift-the-flap mouse ill. by author. Lodestar, 1998. ISBN 0-525-67563-9 Subj: Animals – mice. Format, unusual – toy and movable books.

Lift-the-flap puppy ill. by author. Lodestar, 1998. ISBN 0-525-67566-3 Subj: Animals – dogs. Format, unusual – toy and movable books.

Round and round the garden ill. by author. Lodestar, 1992. ISBN 0-525-67395-4 Subj: Format, unusual – board books. Gardens, gardening. Rhyming text. Sports – roller skating. Toys – bears.

Kendrick, Dennis. *The three billy goats Gruff* (Asbjørnsen, P. C. [Peter Christen])

Kennaway, Adrienne. *Awful aardvark* (Mwalimu)

Bushbaby ill. by author. Little, 1991. ISBN 0-316-48890-9 Subj: Animals – bushbabies. Food. Foreign lands – Africa. Reptiles – monitor lizards.

Little elephant's walk ill. by author. HarperCollins, 1992. ISBN 0-06-020378-1 Subj: Animals. Animals – elephants. Foreign lands – Africa.

Kennedy, Jimmy. *The teddy bears' Christmas* adapt. and ill. by Prue Theobalds. Benford, 1999. ISBN 1-56649-241-6 Subj: Holidays – Christmas. Parties. Poetry. Toys – bears.

The teddy bears' picnic ill. by Alexandra Day. Green Tiger Pr., 1983. ISBN 0-88138-010-5 Subj: Activities – picnicking. Toys – bears.

The teddy bears' picnic ill. by Michael Hague. Holt, 1992. ISBN 0-8050-1008-4 Subj: Activities – picnicking. Poetry. Songs. Toys – bears.

The teddy bears' picnic ill. by Prue Theobalds. HarperCollins, 1987. ISBN 0-87226-153-0 Subj: Activities – picnicking. Poetry. Toys – bears.

Kennedy, Kim. *Mr. Bumble* ill. by Doug Kennedy. Hyperion, 1997. ISBN 0-7868-2293-7 Subj: Fairies. Insects – bees.

Napoleon ill. by Kim and Doug Kennedy. Viking, 1995. ISBN 0-670-86404-8 Subj: Activities – playing. Animals – dogs. Weather – rain.

Kennedy, Richard. *The contests at Cowlick* ill. by Marc Simont. Little, 1975. Subj: Character traits

– cleverness. Cowboys. Humor. U.S. history – frontier and pioneer life.

The leprechaun's story ill. by Marcia Sewall. Dutton, 1979. ISBN 0-525-33472-6 Subj: Foreign lands – Ireland. Mythical creatures – leprechauns.

The lost kingdom of Karnica ill. by Uri Shulevitz. Sierra Club, 1979. ISBN 0-684-16164-8 Subj: Behavior – greed. Royalty.

The porcelain man ill. by Marcia Sewall. Little, 1976. ISBN 0-316-48901-8 Subj: Magic.

Kennedy, X. J. *The beasts of Bethlehem* drawings by Michael McCurdy. Margaret K. McElderry, 1992. ISBN 0-689-50561-2 Subj: Animals. Holidays – Christmas. Poetry. Religion.

Uncle Switch: loony limericks ill. by John O'Brien. Margaret K. McElderry, 1997. ISBN 0-689-80967-0 Subj: Humor. Poetry.

Kenny, Kathryn. *see* Bowden, Joan Chase

Kent, Jack. *The biggest shadow in the zoo* ill. by author. Parents, 1992. ISBN 0-8368-0874-6 Subj: Animals – elephants. Shadows.

The caterpillar and the polliwog ill. by author. Prentice-Hall, 1982. ISBN 0-13-120469-6 Subj: Frogs and toads. Insects – butterflies, caterpillars. Metamorphosis.

The Christmas piñata ill. by author. Parents, 1975. ISBN 0-8193-0816-1 Subj: Foreign lands – Mexico. Holidays – Christmas.

Clotilda ill. by author. Random House, 1969. ISBN 0-394-93911-5 Subj: Character traits – kindness. Fairies.

The egg book ill. by author. Macmillan, 1975. ISBN 0-02-750200-7 Subj: Eggs. Wordless.

Hoddy doddy ill. by author. Greenwillow, 1979. ISBN 0-688-84192-9 Subj: Foreign lands – Denmark. Humor.

Jack Kent's happy-ever-after book ill. by author. Random House, 1976. ISBN 0-394-93135-1 Subj: Folk and fairy tales.

Jack Kent's hokus pokus bedtime book ill. by author. Random House, 1979. ISBN 0-394-94217-5 Subj: Folk and fairy tales.

Joey ill. by author. Prentice-Hall, 1984. ISBN 0-13-510348-7 Subj: Activities – playing. Animals – kangaroos. Family life – mothers.

Joey runs away ill. by author. Prentice-Hall, 1985. ISBN 0-13-510462-9 Subj: Animals. Animals – kangaroos. Behavior – running away. Behavior – seeking better things. Family life.

Knee-high Nina ill. by author. Doubleday, 1981. ISBN 0-385-15128-4 Subj: Behavior – wishing.

Little Peep ill. by author. Prentice-Hall, 1981. ISBN 0-13-537746-3 Subj: Animals. Birds – chickens. Farms.

Mrs. Mooley ill. by author. Artists & Writers Guild, 1993. ISBN 0-307-17550-2 Subj: Animals – bulls, cows. Character traits – perseverance.

The once-upon-a-time dragon ill. by author. Harcourt, 1982. ISBN 0-15-257885-4 Subj: Bedtime. Behavior – imitation. Dragons.

Piggy Bank Gonzalez ill. by author. Parents, 1979. ISBN 0-8193-0998-2 Subj: Animals – pigs. Money. Toys.

Round Robin ill. by author. Prentice-Hall, 1982. ISBN 0-13-783332-6 Subj: Birds – robins.

The scribble monster ill. by author. Harcourt, 1981. ISBN 0-15-271031-0 Subj: Behavior – misbehavior.

Silly goose ill. by author. Prentice-Hall, 1983. ISBN 0-13-809947-2 Subj: Animals – foxes. Birds – geese.

Socks for supper ill. by author. Parents, 1978. ISBN 0-8193-0965-6 Subj: Friendship.

There's no such thing as a dragon ill. by author. Golden Pr., 1975. ISBN 0-307-12525-4 Subj: Behavior – needing someone. Dragons.

Kent, Lorna. *No, no, Charlie Rascal!* ill. by author. Viking, 1989. ISBN 0-670-82512-3 Subj: Animals – cats. Behavior – misbehavior. Format, unusual.

Keo, Ena. *The crane wife* ill. by Cheryl Kirk Noll. Steck-Vaughn, 1998. ISBN 0-817-27258-5 Subj: Activities – weaving. Birds – cranes. Character traits – kindness to animals. Folk and fairy tales. Foreign lands – Japan.

Keown, Elizabeth. *Emily's snowball* ill. by Irene Trivas. Atheneum, 1992. ISBN 0-689-31518-X Subj: Activities – playing. Weather – snow.

Kepes, Juliet. *Cock-a-doodle-doo* ill. by author. Pantheon, 1978. ISBN 0-394-93494-6 Subj: Animals – tigers. Birds – chickens.

Five little monkeys ill. by author. Houghton Mifflin, 1952. Subj: Animals. Animals – monkeys. Caldecott award honor books.

Frogs, merry ill. by author. Pantheon, 1961. Subj: Frogs and toads. Hibernation.

Lady bird, quickly ill. by author. Little, 1964. Subj: Insects – ladybugs. Nursery rhymes.

Run little monkeys, run, run, run ill. by author. Pantheon, 1974. ISBN 0-394-92795-8 Subj: Animals – leopards. Animals – monkeys. Participation.

The seed that peacock planted ill. by author. Little, 1967. Subj: Birds – peacocks, peahens. Magic. Music. Plants.

The story of a bragging duck ill. by author. Houghton Mifflin, 1983. ISBN 0-395-32863-2 Subj: Behavior – boasting. Birds – ducks. Character traits – vanity.

Kerins, Tony (Anthony). *The brave ones* ill. by author. Candlewick, 1996. ISBN 1-56402-812-7

Subj: Animals. Character traits – bravery. Forest, woods. Noise, sounds. Toys.

Tat Rabbit's treasure ill. by author. Margaret K. McElderry, 1993. ISBN 0-689-50553-1 Subj: Clothing. Toys.

Kern, Noris. *I love you with all my heart* ill. by author. Chronicle, 1998. ISBN 0-8118-2031-9 Subj: Animals – polar bears. Emotions – love. Family life – mothers.

Kerr, Judith. *Mog and bunny* ill. by author. Knopf, 1989. ISBN 0-394-92249-2 Subj: Animals – cats. Family life. Pets. Toys.

Mog's Christmas ill. by author. Collins-World, 1976. ISBN 0-529-05376-4 Subj: Animals – cats. Holidays – Christmas.

Kerr, Phyllis Forbes. *I tricked you* ill. by author. Simon & Schuster, 1990. ISBN 0-671-69408-1 Subj: Animals – mice. Behavior. School.

Kerrigan, Anthony. *Mother Goose in Spanish: Poesias de la Madre Oca* (Mother Goose)

Kerry, Lois. *see* Duncan, Lois

Kershen, L. Michael (Lloyd Michael). *Why buffalo roam* ill. by Monica Hansen. Stemmer House, 1993. ISBN 0-88-045043-6 Subj: Animals – buffaloes. Children as authors. Indians of North America – Comanche.

Ker Wilson, Barbara. *see* Wilson, Barbara Ker

Keselman, Gabriela. *The gift* ill. by Pep Montserrat; trans. by Laura McKenna. Kane/Miller, 1999. ISBN 0-916291-91-X Subj: Birthdays. Family life. Gifts.

Kesselman, Judi R. *I can use tools* by Judi R. Kesselman and Franklynn Peterson; ill. by Tomás Gonzales. Elsevier-Nelson, 1981. ISBN 0-525-66725-3 Subj: Tools.

Kesselman, Wendy Ann. *Angelita* ill. by Norma Holt. Hill & Wang, 1970. ISBN 0-8090-2662-7 Subj: City. Emotions – loneliness. Ethnic groups in the U.S. Ethnic groups in the U.S. – Puerto Rican Americans.

Emma ill. by Barbara Cooney. Doubleday, 1980. ISBN 0-385-13462-2 Subj: Art. Emotions – loneliness.

Sand in my shoes ill. by Ronald Himler. Hyperion, 1995. ISBN 0-7868-2045-4 Subj: Rhyming text. Sea and seashore. Seasons – summer.

There's a train going by my window ill. by Tony Chen. Doubleday, 1982. ISBN 0-385-15670-7 Subj: Activities – traveling.

Time for Jody ill. by Gerald Dumas. HarperCollins, 1975. ISBN 0-06-023139-4 Subj: Animals – groundhogs. Hibernation. Holidays – Groundhog Day. Seasons – spring.

Kessler, Brad. *Brer Rabbit and Boss Lion* coll. by Joel Chandler Harris; written by Brad Kessler; ill. by Bill Mayer. Rabbit Ears, 1996. ISBN 0-88708-273-4 Subj: Animals. Ethnic groups in the U.S. – African Americans. Folk and fairy tales.

Moses in Egypt ill. by Phil Huling. Simon & Schuster, 1997. ISBN 0-689-80226-9 Subj: Jewish culture. Religion – Moses.

Kessler, Cristina. *One night: a story from the desert* ill. by Ian Schoenherr. Philomel, 1995. ISBN 0-399-22726-1 Subj: Animals – goats. Behavior – growing up. Desert. Foreign lands – Africa. Night.

Kessler, Ethel. *Are there hippos on the farm?* by Ethel and Len Kessler; ill. by authors. Simon & Schuster, 1987. ISBN 0-671-62066-5 Subj: Animals. Farms. Format, unusual – board books.

Are there seals in the sandbox? by Ethel and Len Kessler; ill. by Leonard P. Kessler. Simon & Schuster, 1990. ISBN 0-671-70539-3 Subj: Animals – seals. Format, unusual – board books. Parks.

Do baby bears sit in chairs? by Ethel and Leonard P. Kessler; ill. by authors. Doubleday, 1961. Subj: Animals. Furniture – chairs. Rhyming text.

Is there a gorilla in the band? by Ethel and Len Kessler; ill. by Leonard P. Kessler. Simon & Schuster, 1994. ISBN 0-671-88303-8 Subj: Animals – gorillas. Format, unusual – board books. Music.

Is there a horse in your house? by Ethel and Len Kessler; ill. by Leonard P. Kessler. Little Simon, 1990. ISBN 0-671-70540-7 Subj: Animals – horses, ponies. Format, unusual – board books.

Is there a penguin at your party? by Ethel and Len Kessler; ill. by Leonard P. Kessler. Simon & Schuster, 1994. ISBN 0-671-88302-X Subj: Birds – penguins. Birthdays. Format, unusual – board books. Parties.

Is there an elephant in your kitchen? by Ethel and Len Kessler; ill. by authors. Simon & Schuster, 1987. ISBN 0-671-62065-7 Subj: Animals. Format, unusual – board books. Homes, houses.

Two, four, six, eight: a book about legs by Ethel and Leonard P. Kessler; ill. by Leonard P. Kessler. Dodd, 1980. ISBN 0-396-07842-7 Subj: Counting, numbers.

Kessler, Jascha. *Rose of Mother-of-Pearl* (Olujic, Grozdana)

Kessler, Leonard P. *Are there hippos on the farm?* (Kessler, Ethel)

Are there seals in the sandbox? (Kessler, Ethel)

Are we lost, daddy? ill. by author. Grosset, 1967. Subj: Activities – vacationing. Behavior – lost. Family life. Family life – fathers.

The big mile race ill. by author. Greenwillow, 1983. ISBN 0-688-01421-6 Subj: Animals. Sports – racing.

Do baby bears sit in chairs? (Kessler, Ethel)

Do you have any carrots? ill. by Lori Pierson. Garrard, 1979. ISBN 0-8116-6074-5 Subj: Animals. Food.

Hey diddle diddle (Mother Goose)

Hickory dickory dock (Mother Goose)

Is there a gorilla in the band? (Kessler, Ethel)

Is there a horse in your house? (Kessler, Ethel)

Is there a penguin at your party? (Kessler, Ethel)

Is there an elephant in your kitchen? (Kessler, Ethel)

Mr. Pine's mixed-up signs ill. by author. Grosset, 1961. Subj: Glasses. Senses – seeing.

Mr. Pine's purple house ill. by author. Grosset, 1965. Subj: Activities – painting. Concepts – color.

Mrs. Pine takes a trip ill. by author. Grosset, 1966. Subj: Activities – traveling.

The pirates' adventure on Spooky Island ill. by author. Garrard, 1979. ISBN 0-8116-4414-6 Subj: Islands. Pirates.

The silly Mother Goose ill. by author. Garrard, 1980. ISBN 0-8116-7401-0 Subj: Nursery rhymes.

Soup for the king ill. by author. Grosset, 1969. Subj: Careers – bakers. Food. Royalty – kings.

That's not Santa! ill. by author. Scholastic, 1994. ISBN 0-590-48140-1 Subj: Clothing – costumes. Holidays – Christmas. Santa Claus.

Two, four, six, eight: a book about legs (Kessler, Ethel)

Ketcham, Sallie. *Bach's big adventure* ill. by Timothy Bush. Orchard, 1999. ISBN 0-531-33140-7 Subj: Careers – organists. Music.

Ketner, Mary Grace. *Ganzy remembers* ill. by Barbara Sparks. Atheneum, 1991. ISBN 0-689-31610-0 Subj: Family life – grandmothers. Family life – great-grandparents. Hospitals. Memories, memory. Old age.

Ketteman, Helen. *Aunt Hilarity's bustle* ill. by James Warhola. Simon & Schuster, 1992. ISBN 0-671-73958-1 Subj: Clothing. Family life – aunts, uncles.

Bubba the cowboy prince: a fractured Texas tale ill. by James Warhola. Scholastic, 1997. ISBN 0-590-25506-1 Subj: Animals – bulls, cows. Cowboys. Folk and fairy tales. Humor. Parties.

Grandma's cat ill. by Marsha Lynn Winborn. Houghton Mifflin, 1996. ISBN 0-395-73094-5 Subj: Animals – cats. Family life – grandmothers. Rhyming text.

Heat wave ill. by Scott Goto. Walker, 1998. ISBN 0-8027-8645-6 Subj: Farms. Tall tales. Weather.

I remember papa ill. by Greg Shed. Dial, 1998. ISBN 0-8037-1849-7 Subj: Behavior – losing things. Careers – farmers. Family life – fathers. Sports – baseball.

Not yet, Yvette ill. by Irene Trivas. Albert Whitman, 1992. ISBN 0-8075-5771-4 Subj: Birthdays. Character traits – patience. Ethnic groups in the U.S. – African Americans. Family life – fathers. Family life – mothers.

Shoeshine Whittaker ill. by Scott Goto. Walker, 1999. ISBN 0-8027-8715-0 Subj: Careers. Tall tales. U.S. history – frontier and pioneer life.

The year of no more corn ill. by Robert Andrew Parker. Orchard, 1993. ISBN 0-531-08550-3 Subj: Farms. Plants. Weather – floods. Weather – wind.

Kettner, Christine. *An ordinary cat* ill. by author. HarperCollins, 1991. ISBN 0-06-023173-4 Subj: Animals – cats. Behavior. Pets.

Keven, Elisa. *Ernest* ill. by author. Dutton, 1989. ISBN 0-525-44515-3 Subj: Character traits – questioning. Reptiles – alligators, crocodiles.

Key, Francis Scott. *The Star-Spangled Banner* ill. by Paul Galdone. Crowell, 1966. ISBN 0-690-77281-5 Subj: Songs. U.S. history.

The Star-Spangled Banner ill. by Peter Spier. Doubleday, 1973. ISBN 0-385-07746-7 Subj: Songs. U.S. history.

Keyser, Marcia. *Roger on his own* ill. by Diane Dawson. Crown, 1982. ISBN 0-517-54476-8 Subj: Animals – dogs. Behavior – solitude.

Keyworth, C. L. *New day* ill. by Carolyn Bracken. Morrow, 1986. ISBN 0-688-05922-8 Subj: Moving.

Khalsa, Dayal Kaur. *How pizza came to Queens* ill. by author. Tundra, 1989. ISBN 0-88776-231-X Subj: Emotions – loneliness. Food.

I want a dog ill. by author. Crown, 1987. ISBN 0-517-56532-3 Subj: Animals – dogs. Behavior – growing up. Family life.

My family vacation ill. by author. Potter/Crown, 1988. ISBN 0-517-56697-4 Subj: Activities – vacationing. Family life.

Sleepers ill. by author. Crown, 1988. ISBN 0-517-56917-5 Subj: Bedtime. Sleep.

The snow cat ill. by author. Potter/Crown, 1992. ISBN 0-517-59183-9 Subj: Animals – cats. Imagination – imaginary friends. Sports – ice skating. Sports – swimming.

Tales of a gambling grandma ill. by author. Crown, 1986. ISBN 0-517-56137-9 Subj: Family life – grandmothers. Games.

Khan, Rukhsana. *Bedtime ba-a-a-lk* ill. by Kristi Frost. Stoddart Kids, 1998. ISBN 0-7737-3068-0 Subj: Bedtime. Dreams. Lullabies. Sleep.

The roses in my carpets ill. by Ronald Himler. Holiday, 1998. ISBN 0-8234-1399-3 Subj: Activities – weaving. Foreign lands – Afghanistan. Homeless. War.

Kharms, Daniil. *First, second* ill. by Marc Rosenthal; trans. from Russian by Richard Pevear. Farrar,

1996. ISBN 0-374-32339-9 Subj: Counting, numbers. Cumulative tales.

The story of a boy named Will, who went sledding down the hill ill. by Vladimir Radunsky; trans. by Jamey Gambrell. North-South, 1993. ISBN 1-55858-215-0 Subj: Animals. Cumulative tales. Rhyming text. Sports – sledding. Weather – snow.

Khdir, Kate. *Little ghost* ill. by Caroline Church. Barron's, 1991. ISBN 0-8120-6203-5 Subj: Ghosts. Holidays – Halloween. School.

Kherdian, David. *The animal* ill. by Nonny Hogrogian. Knopf, 1984. ISBN 0-394-95597-8 Subj: Animals.

By myself ill. by Nonny Hogrogian. Holt, 1993. ISBN 0-8050-2386-0 Subj: Imagination – imaginary friends. Nature. School.

The cat's midsummer jamboree ill. by Nonny Hogrogian. Putnam, 1990. ISBN 0-399-22222-7 Subj: Animals. Animals – cats. Music.

Country cat, city cat ill. by Nonny Hogrogian. Four Winds, 1978. ISBN 0-590-07482-2 Subj: Animals – cats. Poetry.

The dog writes on the window with his nose, and other poems (The dog writes on the window with his nose, and other poems)

The golden bracelet ill. by Nonny Hogrogian. Holiday, 1998. ISBN 0-8234-1362-4 Subj: Activities – weaving. Careers. Folk and fairy tales. Foreign lands – Armenia. Royalty – kings. Wizards.

If dragon flies made honey: poems (If dragon flies made honey)

Lullaby for Emily ill. by Nonny Hogrogian. Holt, 1995. ISBN 0-8050-2957-5 Subj: Lullabies.

Right now ill. by Nonny Hogrogian. Knopf, 1983. ISBN 0-394-95596-X Subj: Emotions.

Kibbey, Marsha. *My grammy* ill. by Karen Ritz. Carolrhoda, 1988. ISBN 0-87614-328-1 Subj: Character traits – patience. Family life – grandmothers. Illness. Old age.

Kidd, Bruce. *Hockey showdown* ill. by Leoung O'Young. Lorimer, 1980. ISBN 0-88862-525-X Subj: Character traits – meanness. Sports – hockey.

Kidd, Nina. *June Mountain secret* ill. by author. HarperCollins, 1991. ISBN 0-06-023168-8 Subj: Family life – fathers. Sports – fishing.

Kidd, Richard. *Almost famous Daisy!* ill. by author. Simon & Schuster, 1996. ISBN 0-689-80390-7 Subj: Activities – painting. Activities – traveling. Art.

Monsieur Thermidor: a fantastic fishy tale ill. by Lindsey Kidd. Blackbirch, 1998. ISBN 1-56711-800-3 Subj: Activities – cooking. Animals. Careers – chefs, cooks. Crustaceans.

Kightley, Rosalinda. *ABC* ill. by author. Little, 1986. ISBN 0-316-49930-7 Subj: ABC books.

The farmer ill. by author. Macmillan, 1988. ISBN 0-02-750290-2 Subj: Careers – farmers. Farms.

Opposites ill. by author. Little, 1986. ISBN 0-316-49931-5 Subj: Concepts – opposites.

The postman ill. by author. Macmillan, 1988. ISBN 0-02-750270-8 Subj: Careers – postal workers. City. Post office.

Shapes ill. by author. Little, 1986. ISBN 0-316-54005-6 Subj: Concepts – shape.

Kilborne, Sarah S. *Peach and Blue* ill. by Steve Johnson and Lou Fancher. Knopf, 1994. ISBN 0-679-93929-6 Subj: Food. Friendship. Frogs and toads.

Kilburn, Greta. *The Christmas carp* (Tornqvist, Rita)

Killilea, Marie (Marie Lyons). *Newf* ill. by Ian Schoenherr. Philomel, 1992. ISBN 0-399-21875-0 Subj: Animals – cats. Animals – dogs. Friendship.

Killingback, Julia. *Busy Bears at the fire station* ill. by author. Oxford Univ. Pr., 1988. ISBN 0-19-520653-3 Subj: Animals – bears. Careers – firefighters.

Busy Bears' picnic ill. by author. Oxford Univ. Pr., 1988. ISBN 0-19-520654-1 Subj: Activities – picnicking. Animals – bears.

Monday is washing day ill. by author. Morrow, 1985. ISBN 0-688-04077-2 Subj: Activities – working. Animals – bears. Family life.

What time is it, Mrs. Bear? ill. by author. Morrow, 1985. ISBN 0-688-04076-4 Subj: Animals – bears. Family life. Time.

Kilreon, Beth. *see* Walker, Barbara K. (Barbara Kerlin)

Kilroy, Sally. *Animal noises* ill. by author. Four Winds, 1983. ISBN 0-590-07915-8 Subj: Animals. Format, unusual – board books. Noise, sounds. Wordless.

Babies' bodies ill. by author. Scholastic, 1983. ISBN 0-590-07914-X Subj: Anatomy. Babies. Format, unusual – board books.

Babies' homes ill. by author. Scholastic, 1984. ISBN 0-590-07945-X Subj: Format, unusual – board books. Homes, houses.

Babies' outings ill. by author. Scholastic, 1984. ISBN 0-590-07946-8 Subj: Format, unusual – board books.

Babies' zoo ill. by author. Scholastic, 1984. ISBN 0-590-07947-6 Subj: Animals. Format, unusual – board books. Zoos.

Baby colors ill. by author. Four Winds, 1983. ISBN 0-590-07917-4 Subj: Babies. Concepts – color. Format, unusual – board books.

The baron's hunting party ill. by author. Viking, 1987. ISBN 0-670-81313-3 Subj: Sports – hunting.

Busy babies ill. by author. Scholastic, 1984. ISBN 0-590-07948-4 Subj: Activities. Babies. Format, unusual – board books.

Copycat drawing book ill. by author. Dial, 1981. ISBN 0-8037-1116-6 Subj: Art.

Grandpa's garden ill. by author. Viking, 1986. ISBN 0-670-80338-3 Subj: Family life – grandparents. Gardens, gardening.

Market day ill. by author. Viking, 1986. ISBN 0-670-80339-1 Subj: Family life – fathers. Shopping.

Noisy homes ill. by author. Scholastic, 1983. ISBN 0-590-07916-6 Subj: Format, unusual – board books. Noise, sounds.

On the road ill. by author. Viking, 1986. ISBN 0-670-80337-5 Subj: Activities – traveling. Buses. Family life – mothers.

What a week! ill. by author. Viking, 1986. ISBN 0-670-80336-7 Subj: Family life.

Kimber, Robert. *I am a little cat* (Spanner, Helmut)

I am a little dog (Fechner, Amrei)

Kimmel, Eric A. *Anansi and the magic stick* ill. by Janet Stevens. Holiday, 2001. ISBN 0-8234-1443-4 Subj: Animals – hyenas. Folk and fairy tales. Foreign lands – Africa. Magic. Spiders.

Anansi and the moss-covered rock ill. by Janet Stevens. Holiday, 1990. ISBN 0-8234-0689-X Subj: Animals. Behavior – trickery. Folk and fairy tales. Spiders.

Anansi and the talking melon ill. by Janet Stevens. Holiday, 1994. ISBN 0-8234-1104-4 Subj: Animals. Animals – elephants. Behavior – trickery. Folk and fairy tales. Foreign lands – Africa. Spiders.

Anansi goes fishing ill. by Janet Stevens. Holiday, 1992. ISBN 0-8234-0918-X Subj: Behavior – trickery. Folk and fairy tales. Foreign lands – Africa. Reptiles – turtles, tortoises. Spiders.

Asher and the capmakers ill. by Will Hillenbrand. Holiday, 1993. ISBN 0823410315 Subj: Fairies. Folk and fairy tales. Holidays – Hanukkah. Jewish culture.

Baba Yaga ill. by Megan Lloyd. Holiday, 1991. ISBN 0-8234-0854-X Subj: Behavior – trickery. Folk and fairy tales. Foreign lands – Russia. Witches.

Bearhead ill. by Charles Mikolaycak. Holiday, 1991. ISBN 0-8234-0902-3 Subj: Animals – bears. Folk and fairy tales. Foreign lands – Russia. Witches.

Bernal and Florinda ill. by Robert Rayevsky. Holiday, 1994. ISBN 0-8234-1089-7 Subj: Folk and fairy tales. Foreign lands – Spain.

Billy Lazroe and the King of the Sea: a tale of the Northwest ill. by Michael Steirnagle. Browndeer, 1996. ISBN 0-15-200108-5 Subj: Careers – military. Folk and fairy tales. Mythical creatures. Sailors. Sea and seashore.

The birds' gift: a Ukrainian Easter story ill. by Katya Krénina. Holiday, 1999. ISBN 0-8234-1384-5 Subj: Birds. Character traits – kindness to animals. Eggs. Folk and fairy tales. Foreign lands – Ukraine. Holidays – Easter.

Boots and his brothers ill. by Kimberly Bulcken Root. Holiday, 1992. ISBN 0-8234-0886-8 Subj: Folk and fairy tales. Foreign lands – Norway. Magic.

The Chanukkah guest ill. by Giora Karmi. Holiday, 1990. ISBN 0-8234-0788-8 Subj: Holidays – Hanukkah. Jewish culture. Religion.

The Chanukkah tree ill. by Giyora Karmi. Holiday, 1988. ISBN 0-8234-0705-5 Subj: Folk and fairy tales. Holidays – Hanukkah. Jewish culture. Religion.

Charlie drives the stage ill. by Glen Rounds. Holiday, 1989. ISBN 0-8234-0738-1 Subj: Transportation. U.S. history – frontier and pioneer life.

Count Silvernose ill. by Omar Rayyan. Holiday, 1996. ISBN 0-8234-1216-4 Subj: Character traits – cleverness. Folk and fairy tales. Foreign lands – Italy.

Easy work! an old tale ill. by Andrew Glass. Holiday, 1998. ISBN 0-8234-1349-7 Subj: Folk and fairy tales. Foreign lands – Norway.

Four dollars and fifty cents ill. by Glen Rounds. Holiday, 1990. ISBN 0-8234-0817-5 Subj: Cowboys. Crime. Humor. Money. U.S. history – frontier and pioneer life.

The four gallant sisters adapt. from the Brothers Grimm; ill. by Tatyana Yuditskaya. Holt, 1992. ISBN 0-8050-1901-4 Subj: Character traits – bravery. Dragons. Folk and fairy tales. Foreign lands – Germany. Royalty.

The gingerbread man (The gingerbread boy)

The goose girl: a story from the Brothers Grimm (Grimm, Jacob)

The greatest of all ill. by Giora Karmi. Holiday, 1991. ISBN 0-8234-0885-X Subj: Animals – mice. Folk and fairy tales. Foreign lands – Japan. Weddings.

Grizz! ill. by Andrew Glass. Holiday, 2000. ISBN 0-8234-1469-8 Subj: Cowboys. Devil. Folk and fairy tales.

Hershel and the Hanukkah goblins ill. by Trina Schart Hyman. Holiday, 1989. ISBN 0-8234-0769-1 Subj: Caldecott award honor books. Holidays – Hanukkah. Jewish culture. Mythical creatures – goblins. Religion.

I took my frog to the library ill. by Blanche Sims. Viking, 1990. ISBN 0-670-82418-6 Subj: Animals. Libraries. Pets.

Iron John (Grimm, Jacob)

The magic dreidels ill. by Katya Krénina. Holiday, 1996. ISBN 0-8234-1256-3 Subj: Folk and fairy tales. Holidays – Hanukkah. Jewish culture.

Nanny goat and the seven little kids (Grimm, Jacob)

The old woman and her pig (The old woman and her pig)

One Eye, Two Eyes, Three Eyes: a Hutzul tale ill. by Dirk Zimmer. Holiday, 1996. ISBN 0-8234-1183-4 Subj: Animals – goats. Folk and fairy tales. Foreign lands – Ukraine. Royalty – princes. Witches.

One winter night: a Hanukkah story ill. by Jon Goodell. Doubleday, 2000. ISBN 0-385-32652-1 Subj: Holidays – Hanukkah. Jewish culture. Religion.

Onions and garlic ill. by Katya Arnold. Holiday, 1996. ISBN 0-8234-1222-9 Subj: Activities – trading. Behavior – greed. Folk and fairy tales. Jewish culture.

Rimonah of the Flashing Sword ill. by Omar Rayyan. Holiday, 1995. ISBN 0-8234-1093-5 Subj: Emotions – envy, jealousy. Folk and fairy tales. Foreign lands – Egypt. Royalty – princesses.

Robin Hook, pirate hunter! ill. by Michael Dooling. Scholastic, 2001. ISBN 0-590-68199-0 Subj: Pirates.

The rooster's antlers: a story of the Chinese zodiac ill. by YongSheng Xuan. Holiday, 1999. ISBN 0-8234-1385-3 Subj: Animals. Birds – chickens. Creation. Dragons. Zodiac.

The runaway tortilla ill. by Randy Cecil. Winslow, 2000. ISBN 1-890817-18-X Subj: Behavior – running away. Cumulative tales. Folk and fairy tales.

Seven at one blow: a tale from the Brothers Grimm (Grimm, Jacob)

Sirko and the wolf: a Ukrainian tale ill. by Robert Sauber. Holiday, 1997. ISBN 0-8234-1257-1 Subj: Animals – dogs. Animals – wolves. Folk and fairy tales. Foreign lands – Ukraine.

Squash it! a true and ridiculous tale ill. by Robert Rayevsky. Holiday, 1997. ISBN 0-8234-1299-7 Subj: Folk and fairy tales. Foreign lands – Spain. Insects – fleas. Royalty – kings.

The tale of Aladdin and the wonderful lamp: a story from the Arabian Nights (Arabian Nights)

The tale of Ali Baba and the forty thieves: a story from the Arabian nights retold by Eric A. Kimmel; ill. by Will Hillenbrand. Holiday, 1996. ISBN 0-8234-1258-X Subj: Behavior – stealing. Folk and fairy tales. Foreign lands – Middle East.

Ten suns: a Chinese legend ill. by YongSheng Xuan. Holiday, 1998. ISBN 0-8234-1317-9 Subj: Animals – cats. Concepts – shape. Concepts – size. Holidays – Hanukkah. Jewish culture. Religion.

The three princes ill. by Leonard Everett Fisher. Holiday, 1994. ISBN 0-8234-1115-X Subj: Folk and fairy tales. Foreign lands – Arabia. Royalty – princes. Royalty – princesses.

Three sacks of truth ill. by Robert Rayevsky. Holiday, 1993. ISBN 0-8234-0921-X Subj: Folk and fairy tales. Foreign lands – France. Royalty – kings.

The two mountains: an Aztec legend ill. by Leonard Everett Fisher. Holiday, 2000. ISBN 0-8234-1504-X Subj: Folk and fairy tales. Foreign lands – Mexico. Indians of North America – Aztec. Mountains. Volcanoes.

The valiant red rooster: a story from Hungary ill. by Katya Arnold. Holt, 1994. ISBN 0-8050-2781-5 Subj: Birds – chickens. Folk and fairy tales. Foreign lands – Hungary. Royalty – sultans.

Why worry? ill. by Beth Cannon. Pantheon, 1979. ISBN 0-394-94010-5 Subj: Insects – crickets. Insects – grasshoppers. Music. Songs.

The witch's face: a Mexican tale ill. by Fabricio Vandenbroeck. Holiday, 1993. ISBN 0-8234-1038-2 Subj: Folk and fairy tales. Foreign lands – Mexico. Witches.

Kimmel, Margaret Mary. *Magic in the mist* ill. by Trina Schart Hyman. Atheneum, 1975. ISBN 0-689-50026-2 Subj: Dragons. Magic. Wizards.

Kimmelman, Leslie. *Frannie's fruits* ill. by Petra Mathers. HarperCollins, 1989. ISBN 0-06-023143-2 Subj: Animals – dogs. Careers – storekeepers. Family life.

Hanukkah lights, Hanukkah nights ill. by John Himmelman. HarperCollins, 1992. ISBN 0-06-020369-2 Subj: Family life. Holidays – Hanukkah. Jewish culture. Religion.

Hooray! it's Passover! ill. by John Himmelman. HarperCollins, 1996. ISBN 0-06-024674-X Subj: Family life. Holidays – Passover. Jewish culture. Religion.

Me and Nana ill. by Marilee Robin Burton. HarperCollins, 1990. ISBN 0-06-023163-7 Subj: Family life – grandmothers. Friendship.

The runaway latkes ill. by Paul Yalowitz. Albert Whitman, 2000. ISBN 0-8075-7176-8 Subj: Behavior – running away. Holidays – Hanukkah. Jewish culture. Religion.

Sound the shofar! a story for Rosh Hashanah and Yom Kippur ill. by John Himmelman. HarperCollins, 1998. ISBN 0-06-027498-0 Subj: Family life – aunts, uncles. Holidays – Rosh Hashanah. Holidays – Yom Kippur. Jewish culture. Religion.

Kimpton, Diana. *The bear Santa Claus forgot* ill. by Anna Kiernan. Scholastic, 1994. ISBN 0-590-26564-4 Subj: Holidays – Christmas. Santa Claus. Toys – bears.

Kimura, Yasuko. *Fergus and the sea monster* ill. by author. McGraw-Hill, 1978. ISBN 0-07-034559-7 Subj: Animals – dogs. Friendship. Monsters. Sea and seashore.

Kincaid, Lucy. *The three billygoats Gruff* (Asbjørnsen, P. C. [Peter Christen])

Kinerk, Robert. *Slim and Miss Prim* ill. by Jim Harris. Rising Moon, 1998. ISBN 0-8735-8689-1 Subj: Cowboys. Crime. Emotions – love. Rhyming text.

Kines, Pat Decker. *see* Tapio, Pat Decker

King, B. A. *The very best Christmas tree* ill. by Michael McCurdy. Godine, 1984. ISBN 0-87923-539-X Subj: Holidays – Christmas. Trees.

King, Bob. *Sitting on the farm* ill. by Bill Slavin. Orchard, 1992. ISBN 0-531-08585-6 Subj: Activities – picnicking. Animals. Cumulative tales. Music. Songs. Telephone.

King, Christopher L. *The boy who ate the moon* ill. by John Wallner. Putnam, 1988. ISBN 0-399-21459-3 Subj: Activities – flying. Moon.

The vegetables go to bed ill. by Mary GrandPré. Crown, 1994. ISBN 0-517-59126-X Subj: Bedtime. Food. Rhyming text.

King, Dave. *Counting book* photos by author. DK, 1998. ISBN 0-7894-3448-2 Subj: Counting, numbers. Picture puzzles.

King, Deborah. *Cloudy* ill. by author. Putnam, 1990. ISBN 0-399-22242-1 Subj: Animals – cats.

Custer: the true story of a horse ill. by author. Putnam, 1992. ISBN 0-399-22147-6 Subj: Animals – horses, ponies. Friendship.

The flight of the snow geese ill. by author. Orchard, 1998. ISBN 0-531-30088-9 Subj: Birds – geese. Seasons – winter.

Sirius and Saba ill. by author. David & Charles, 1982. ISBN 0-241-10599-4 Subj: Animals – dogs. Islands.

King, Elizabeth. *Backyard sunflower* photos by author. Dutton, 1993. ISBN 0-525-45082-3 Subj: Flowers. Gardens, gardening. Seeds.

Pumpkin patch photos by author. Dutton, 1990. ISBN 0-525-44640-0 Subj: Gardens, gardening. Holidays – Halloween.

King, Larry L. *Because of Lozo Brown* ill. by Amy Schwartz. Viking, 1988. ISBN 0-670-81031-2 Subj: Friendship. Imagination. Rhyming text.

King, Patricia. *Mable the whale* ill. by Katherine Evans. Follett, 1958. ISBN 0-695-35443-4 Subj: Animals – whales.

King, Stephen Michael. *Henry and Amy (right-way-round and upside down)* ill. by author. Walker, 1998. ISBN 0-8027-8687-1 Subj: Character traits – individuality. Concepts – opposites. Friendship.

Kingman, Lee. *Catch the baby!* ill. by Susanna Natti. Viking, 1989. ISBN 0-670-81751-1 Subj: Family life. Rhyming text.

Peter's long walk ill. by Barbara Cooney. Doubleday, 1953. Subj: Activities – walking. Animals. Country. Friendship.

Pierre Pigeon ill. by Arnold Edwin Bare. Houghton Mifflin, 1943. Subj: Birds – pigeons. Caldecott award honor books.

Kingsland, Robin. *Bus stop bop* ill. by Alex Ayliffe. Viking, 1991. ISBN 0-670-83919-1 Subj: Activities – dancing. Buses. Music.

King-Smith, Dick. *All pigs are beautiful* ill. by Anita Jeram. Candlewick, 1993. ISBN 1-56402-148-3 Subj: Animals – pigs.

Cuckoobush farm ill. by Kazuko. Greenwillow, 1988. ISBN 0-688-07681-5 Subj: Farms. Multiple births – twins. Seasons.

Dick King-Smith's Alphabeasts ill. by Quentin Blake. Macmillan, 1992. ISBN 0-02-750720-3 Subj: ABC books. Language. Poetry.

Farmer Bungle forgets ill. by Martin Honeysett. Atheneum, 1987. ISBN 0-689-31370-5 Subj: Behavior – forgetfulness. Farms. Humor.

I love guinea pigs ill. by Anita Jeram. Candlewick, 1995. ISBN 1-56402-389-3 Subj: Animals – guinea pigs. Pets.

A mouse called Wolf ill. by Jon Goodell. Crown, 1997. ISBN 0-517-70974-0 Subj: Animals – cats. Animals – mice. Illness. Music.

Puppy love ill. by Anita Jeram. Candlewick, 1997. ISBN 0-7636-0116-0 Subj: Animals – dogs. Emotions – love. Pets.

The spotty pig ill. by Mary Wormell. Farrar, 1997. ISBN 0-374-37154-7 Subj: Animals – pigs. Self-concept.

Kinnell, Galway. *How the alligator missed breakfast* ill. by Lynn Munsinger. Houghton Mifflin, 1982. ISBN 0-395-32436-X Subj: Reptiles – alligators, crocodiles.

Kinney, Jean. *What does the sun do?* ill. by Cle Kinney. W. R. Scott, 1967. Subj: Sun.

Kinsey, Elizabeth. *see* Clymer, Eleanor Lowenton

Kinsey, Helen. *The bear that heard crying* (Kinsey-Warnock, Natalie)

Kinsey-Warnock, Natalie. *The bear that heard crying* by Natalie Kinsey-Warnock and Helen Kinsey; ill. by Ted Rand. Cobblehill, 1993. ISBN 0-525-65103-9 Subj: Animals – bears. Behavior – lost. U.S. history – frontier and pioneer life.

The fiddler of the Northern Lights ill. by Leslie W. Bowman. Cobblehill, 1996. ISBN 0-525-65143-8 Subj: Family life – grandfathers. Folk and fairy tales. Foreign lands – Canada. Music.

On a starry night ill. by David McPhail. Orchard, 1994. ISBN 0-531-08670-4 Subj: Emotions – fear. Family life. Nature. Night.

The summer of Stanley ill. by Donald Gates. Cobblehill, 1997. ISBN 0-525-65177-2 Subj: Animals – goats. Birthdays. Family life – brothers and sisters. Farms.

When spring comes ill. by Stacey Schuett. Dutton, 1993. ISBN 0-525-45008-4 Subj: Family life – fathers. Farms. Seasons – spring.

The wild horses of Sweetbriar ill. by Ted Rand. Dutton, 1990. ISBN 0-525-65015-6 Subj: Animals – horses, ponies. Islands. Seasons – winter.

Wilderness cat ill. by Mark Graham. Cobblehill, 1992. ISBN 0-525-65068-7 Subj: Animals – cats. Foreign lands – Canada. Moving.

Kinter, Judith. *King of magic, man of glass* ill. by Dirk Zimmer. Clarion, 1998. ISBN 0-395-79730-6 Subj: Behavior – greed. Folk and fairy tales. Foreign lands – Germany.

Kipling, Rudyard. *The beginning of the armadillos* ill. by Lorinda Bryan Cauley. Harcourt, 1985. ISBN 0-15-206380-3 Subj: Animals – armadillos.

The beginning of the armadillos ill. by Charles Keeping. HarperCollins, 1983. ISBN 0-911745-03-3 Subj: Animals – armadillos.

The crab that played with the sea ill. by Michael Foreman. HarperCollins, 1983. ISBN 0-911745-06-8 Subj: Crustaceans. Sea and seashore.

The elephant's child ill. by Louise Brierley. HarperCollins, 1985. ISBN 0-87226-030-5 Subj: Animals. Animals – elephants. Character traits – curiosity. Foreign lands – Africa.

The elephant's child ill. by Lorinda Bryan Cauley. Harcourt, 1983. ISBN 0-15-225385-8 Subj: Animals. Animals – elephants. Character traits – curiosity. Foreign lands – Africa.

The elephant's child ill. by Tim Raglin. Knopf, 1986. ISBN 0-394-88401-9 Subj: Animals. Animals – elephants. Character traits – curiosity. Foreign lands – Africa.

The elephant's child ill. by John A. Rowe. North-South, 1995. ISBN 1-55858-370-X Subj: Animals. Animals – elephants. Character traits – curiosity. Foreign lands – Africa. Reptiles – alligators, crocodiles.

How the camel got his hump ill. by Quentin Blake. HarperCollins, 1985. ISBN 0-87226-029-1 Subj: Animals. Animals – camels. Foreign lands – Africa.

How the camel got his hump ill. by Tim Raglin. Rabbit Ears, 1989. ISBN 0-88708-096-0 Subj: Animals. Animals – camels. Foreign lands – Africa.

How the leopard got his spots ill. by Caroline Ebborn. HarperCollins, 1986. ISBN 0-87226-072-0 Subj: Animals – leopards.

How the leopard got his spots ill. by Lori Lohstoeter. Picture Book Studio, 1989. ISBN 0-88708-112-6 Subj: Animals – leopards.

How the rhinoceros got his skin ill. by Leonard Weisgard. Walker, 1974. ISBN 0-8027-6150-X Subj: Anatomy – skin. Animals – rhinoceros.

The miracle of the mountain adapt. by Aroline Arnett Beecher Leach; ill. by Willi Baum. Addison-Wesley, 1969. Adapt. from The Miracle of Purun Bhagat, by Rudyard Kipling. Subj: Animals. Foreign lands – India. Religion.

Rikki-tikki-tavi ill. by Lambert Davis. Harcourt, 1992. ISBN 0-15-267015-7 Subj: Animals – mongooses. Character traits – cleverness. Foreign lands – India. Reptiles – snakes.

The sing-song of old man kangaroo ill. by Michael C. Taylor. HarperCollins, 1986. ISBN 0-87226-073-9 Subj: Animals – kangaroos. Foreign lands – Australia.

Kirby, David K. *The bear who came to stay* (Woodman, Allen)

Cows are going to Paris by David Kirby and Allen Woodman; ill. by Chris L. Demarest. Boyds Mills, 1991. ISBN 0-878093-11-8 Subj: Animals – bulls, cows. Foreign lands – France. Trains.

Kirk, Barbara. *Grandpa, me and our house in the tree* ill. by author. Macmillan, 1978. ISBN 0-02-750750-5 Subj: Family life – grandfathers. Homes, houses. Trees.

Kirk, Daniel. *Bigger* ill. by author. Putnam, 1998. ISBN 0-399-23127-7 Subj: Behavior – growing up. Concepts – size. Self-concept.

Breakfast at the Liberty Diner ill. by author. Hyperion, 1997. ISBN 0-7868-2243-0 Subj: Handicaps – physical handicaps. Restaurants. Trains. U.S. history.

Hush, little alien ill. by author. Hyperion, 1999. ISBN 0-7868-2469-7 Subj: Aliens. Bedtime. Lullabies.

Lucky's twenty-four hour garage ill. by author. Hyperion, 1996. ISBN 0-7868-2168-X Subj: Automobiles. Careers – mechanics.

Moondogs ill. by author. Putnam, 1999. ISBN 0-399-23128-5 Subj: Animals – dogs. Moon. Rhyming text. Space and space ships.

Trash trucks! ill. by author. Putnam, 1997. ISBN 0-399-22927-2 Subj: Careers – sanitation workers. Rhyming text. Trucks.

Kirk, David. *Little Miss Spider* ill. by author. Scholastic, 1999. ISBN 0-439-08389-3 Subj: Emotions – love. Family life – mothers. Rhyming text. Spiders.

Little Miss Spider at Sunny Patch School ill. by author. Scholastic, 2000. ISBN 0-439-08727-9 Subj: Insects. Rhyming text. School – first day. Spiders.

Miss Spider's ABC ill. by author. Scholastic, 1998. ISBN 0-590-28279-4 Subj: ABC books. Birthdays. Insects. Rhyming text. Spiders.

Miss Spider's new car ill. by author. Scholastic, 1997. ISBN 0-590-30713-4 Subj: Automobiles. Insects. Rhyming text. Spiders.

Miss Spider's tea party ill. by author. Scholastic, 1994. ISBN 0-590-47724-2 Subj: Emotions – fear. Parties. Rhyming text. Spiders.

Kirkpatrick, Rena K. *Leaves* ill. by Annabel Milne and Peter Stebbing. Raintree, 1991. Rev. ed. of: Look at leaves. ISBN 0-8172-2353-3 Subj: Plants. Science.

Look at flowers ill. by Annabel Milne and Peter Stebbing. Raintree, 1978. ISBN 0-8393-0061-1 Subj: Flowers. Science.

Magnets ill. by Ann Knight. Raintree, 1985. Rev. ed. of: Look at magnets. ISBN 0-8172-2354-1 Subj: Science.

Pond life ill. by Annabel Milne and Peter Stebbing. Raintree, 1985. Rev. ed. of: Look at pond life. ISBN 0-8172-2355-X Subj: Science.

Rainbow colors ill. by Anna Barnard. Raintree, 1978. Rev. ed. of: Look at rainbow colors. ISBN 0-8172-2356-8 Subj: Concepts – color. Science. Weather – rainbows.

Seeds and weeds ill. by Debbie King. Raintree, 1985. ISBN 0-8172-2357-6 Subj: Plants. Science.

Trees ill. by Jo Worth and Ann Knight. Raintree, 1985. Rev. ed. of: Look at trees. ISBN 0-8172-2359-2 Subj: Science. Trees.

Weather ill. by Janetta Lewin. Raintree, 1985. Rev. ed. of: Look at weather. ISBN 0-8172-2360-6 Subj: Science. Weather.

Kirn, Ann. *Beeswax catches a thief: from a Congo folktale* ill. by author. Norton, 1968. Subj: Animals. Ethnic groups in the U.S. – African Americans.

I spy ill. by author. Norton, 1965. Subj: Birds – owls. Crime.

The tale of a crocodile: from a Congo folktale ill. by author. Norton, 1968. Subj: Animals – rabbits. Fire. Folk and fairy tales. Foreign lands – Africa. Reptiles – alligators, crocodiles.

Kirschner, David. *Fievel's big showdown* (Herman, Gail)

Kirstein, Lincoln. *Puss in boots* (Perrault, Charles)

Kirtland, G. B. *see* Joslin, Sesyle

Kiser, Kevin. *The birthday thing* (Kiser, SuAnn)

Buzzy Widget ill. by John O'Brien. Cavendish, 1999. ISBN 0-7614-5057-2 Subj: Activities – making things. Behavior – needing someone. Emotions. Robots.

Sherman the sheep ill. by Rowan Barnes-Murphy. Macmillan, 1994. ISBN 0-02-750825-0 Subj: Animals – sheep.

Kiser, SuAnn. *The birthday thing* by SuAnn and Kevin Kiser; ill. by Yossi Abolafia. Greenwillow, 1989. ISBN 0-688-07773-0 Subj: Activities – making things. Birthdays. Family life.

The catspring somersault flying one-handed flip-flop ill. by Peter Catalanotto. Orchard, 1993. ISBN 0-531-08643-7 Subj: Behavior – running away. Family life. Farms. Sibling rivalry.

The hog call to end all! ill. by John Steven Gurney. Orchard, 1994. ISBN 0-531-08676-3 Subj: Animals – pigs. Country. Fairs. Farms.

Kishida, Eriko. *The hippo boat* ill. by Chiyoko Nakatani. Collins, 1967. Subj: Animals – hippopotamuses. Weather – floods. Weather – rain. Zoos.

The lion and the bird's nest ill. by Chiyoko Nakatani. Crowell, 1972. Subj: Animals – lions. Birds. Character traits – helpfulness. Friendship.

Kismaric, Carole. *A gift from Saint Nicholas* (Timmermans, Felix)

The rumor of Pavel and Paali: a Ukrainian folktale ill. by Charles Mikolaycak. HarperCollins, 1988. ISBN 0-06-023278-1 Subj: Behavior – greed. Character traits – meanness. Folk and fairy tales. Multiple births – twins.

Kitamura, Satoshi. *Captain Toby* ill. by author. Dutton, 1988. ISBN 0-525-44414-9 Subj: Animals – cats. Family life – grandparents. Sea and seashore. Weather – storms.

From acorn to zoo and everything in between in alphabetical order ill. by author. Farrar, 1992. ISBN 0-374-32470-0 Subj: ABC books.

Lily takes a walk ill. by author. Dutton, 1987. ISBN 0-525-44333-9 Subj: Animals – dogs. Emotions – fear. Imagination.

Sheep in wolves' clothing ill. by author. Farrar, 1996. ISBN 0-374-36780-9 Subj: Animals – sheep. Animals – wolves. Behavior – trickery. Careers – detectives. Mystery stories.

What's inside? ill. by author. Farrar, 1985. ISBN 0-374-38306-5 Subj: ABC books.

When sheep cannot sleep ill. by author. Farrar, 1986. ISBN 0-374-38311-1 Subj: Animals – sheep. Bedtime. Counting, numbers.

Kitchen, Bert. *And so they build* ill. by author. Candlewick, 1993. ISBN 1-56402-217-X Subj: Animals. Homes, houses.

Animal alphabet ill. by author. Dial, 1984. ISBN 0-8037-0117-9 Subj: ABC books. Animals. Wordless.

Animal numbers ill. by author. Dial, 1987. ISBN 0-8037-0459-3 Subj: Animals. Counting, numbers.

Pig in a barrow ill. by author. Dial, 1991. ISBN 0-8037-0943-9 Subj: Animals. Rhyming text.

Somewhere today ill. by author. Candlewick, 1992. ISBN 1-56402-074-6 Subj: Activities. Animals.

Tenrec's twigs ill. by author. Putnam, 1989. ISBN 0-399-21720-7 Subj: Animals. Foreign lands – Africa. Jungle.

When hunger calls ill. by author. Candlewick, 1994. ISBN 1-56402-316-8 Subj: Animals. Food. Nature.

Kite, L. Patricia. *Dandelion adventures* ill. by Anca Hariton. Millbrook, 1998. ISBN 0-7613-0037-6 Subj: Plants. Seasons – spring. Seeds.

Down in the sea. The jellyfish ill. by author. Albert Whitman, 1993. ISBN 0-8075-1712-7 Subj: Fish. Sea and seashore.

Down in the sea. The octopus ill. by author. Albert Whitman, 1993. ISBN 0-8075-1715-1 Subj: Octopuses. Sea and seashore.

Kitt, Tamara. *see* De Regniers, Beatrice Schenk

Klages, Simone. *Now, now Markus* (Auer, Martin)

Klein, Arthur Luce. *Puss in boots* (Perrault, Charles)

Klein, Leonore. *Henri's walk to Paris* ill. by Saul Bass. Addison-Wesley, 1962. Subj: Activities – walking. Foreign lands – France.

Just like you ill. by Audrey Walters. Harvey House, 1968. Subj: Ethnic groups in the U.S.

Old, older, oldest ill. by Leonard P. Kessler. Hastings House, 1983. ISBN 0-8038-5396-3 Subj: Old age.

Klein, Norma. *Girls can be anything* ill. by Roy Doty. Dutton, 1973. ISBN 0-525-30662-5 Subj: Careers.

Visiting Pamela ill. by Kay Chorao. Dial, 1979. ISBN 0-8037-9308-1 Subj: Behavior – sharing. Friendship.

Klein, Robin. *Thing* ill. by Alison Lester. Oxford Univ. Pr., 1983. ISBN 0-19-554330-0 Subj: Dinosaurs. Pets.

Klein, Suzanne. *An elephant in my bed* ill. by Sharleen Pederson. Follett, 1974. ISBN 0-695-40476-8 Subj: Animals – elephants. Furniture – beds.

Kleven, Elisa. *The lion and the little red bird* ill. by author. Dutton, 1992. ISBN 0-525-44898-5 Subj: Animals – lions. Birds. Careers – artists. Concepts – color.

A monster in the house ill. by author. Dutton, 1998. ISBN 0-525-45973-1 Subj: Babies. Family life – brothers. Monsters.

The paper princess ill. by author. Dutton, 1994. ISBN 0-525-45231-1 Subj: Activities – drawing. Activities – flying. Paper. Royalty – princesses.

Kleven, Sandy. *The right touch: a read aloud story to help prevent child sexual abuse* ill. by Jody Bergsma. Illumination Arts, 1997. ISBN 0-935699-10-4 Subj: Child abuse. Family life.

Klimo, Kate. *Farm house* (Farm house)

Firehouse (Firehouse)

Gerald McBoing Boing (Seuss, Dr.)

Mother Goose house (Mother Goose)

Mouse house (Mouse house)

Sing a song of sixpence (Mother Goose)

Klimowicz, Barbara. *The strawberry thumb* ill. by Gloria Kamen. Abingdon, 1968. Subj: Problem solving. Puppets. Rhyming text. Thumb sucking.

Kline, Suzy. *Don't touch!* ill. by Dora Leder. Albert Whitman, 1985. ISBN 0-8075-1707-0 Subj: Activities – playing. Behavior – misbehavior.

Ooops! ed. by Ann Fay; ill. by Dora Leder. Albert Whitman, 1988. ISBN 0-8075-6122-3 Subj: Behavior – bad day. Behavior – carelessness.

Shhhh! ill. by Dora Leder. Albert Whitman, 1984. ISBN 0-8075-7321-3 Subj: Noise, sounds.

Klinting, Lars. *Regal the golden eagle* trans. by Alan Bernstein; ill. by author. Farrar, 1988. ISBN 91-2958-774-3 Subj: Behavior – growing up. Birds – eagles. Emotions – fear.

Klockner, Karen M. *The black sheep* (Heck, Elisabeth)

The Christmas train (Gantschev, Ivan)

Otto the bear (Gantschev, Ivan)

Klove, Lars. *I see a sign* photos by author. Simon & Schuster, 1996. ISBN 0-689-80800-3 Subj: Communication. Concepts.

Klugmann, Judith. *The happy apple* (Bruna, Dick)

Klyce, Katherine P. *Kenya, jambo!* (McLean, Virginia O.)

Knab, Linda Z. *The day is waiting* (Freeman, Don)

Knaff, Jean Christian. *Manhattan* ill. by author. Knopf, 1989. ISBN 0-571-14653-8 Subj: Emotions – loneliness. Friendship. Imagination.

Knapp, Jennifer. *The go go dogs* ill. by author. Chronicle, 1998. ISBN 0-8118-2028-9 Subj: Activities – traveling. Animals – dogs.

Knapp, John, II. *A pillar of pepper and other Bible nursery rhymes* ill. by Dianne Turner Deckert. Cook, 1982. ISBN 0-89191-559-1 Subj: Nursery rhymes. Religion.

Kneen, Maggie. *"Too many cooks . . ." and other proverbs* ill. by author. Green Tiger Pr., 1992. ISBN 0-671-78120-0 Subj: Proverbs.

When you're not looking ill. by author. Simon & Schuster, 1996. ISBN 0-689-80026-6 Subj: Counting, numbers. Puzzles.

Knight, Bertram T. *Working at a zoo* ill. with photos. Childrens Pr., 1998. ISBN 0-516-20751-2 Subj: Animals. Careers – zoo keepers. Zoos.

Knight, David C. *Dinosaur days* ill. by Joel Schick. McGraw-Hill, 1977. ISBN 0-07035-102-3 Subj: Dinosaurs. Science.

Knight, Hilary. *Angels and berries and candy canes* ill. by author. HarperCollins, 1963. Subj: Angels. Holidays – Christmas. Santa Claus.

A firefly in a fir tree ill. by author. HarperCollins, 1963. ISBN 0-06-023190-4 Subj: Insects – fireflies.

Hilary Knight's Cinderella ill. by author. Random House, 1978. ISBN 0-394-93759-7 Subj: Family life – step families. Folk and fairy tales. Royalty – princes. Sibling rivalry.

Hilary Knight's the owl and the pussy-cat ill. by author. Macmillan, 1983. Based on The owl and the pussy-cat by Edward Lear. ISBN 0-02-750900-1 Subj: Imagination. Magic. Poetry.

Sylvia the sloth ill. by author. HarperCollins, 1969. Subj: Animals – sloths. Concepts – up and down.

Where's Wallace? ill. by author. HarperCollins, 1964. ISBN 0-06-023171-8 Subj: Animals – monkeys. Behavior – running away. Zoos.

Knight, Joan. *Bon appetit, Bertie!* ill. by Penny Dann. DK, 1993. ISBN 1-56458-195-0 Subj: Behavior – misunderstanding. Family life. Food. Foreign lands – France. Hotels.

Opal in the closet ill. by Pau Estrada. Simon & Schuster, 1992. ISBN 0-88708-174-6 Subj: Babies. Emotions. Family life – new sibling. Sibling rivalry.

Tickle-toe rhymes ill. by John Wallner. Watts, 1988. ISBN 0-531-08373-X Subj: Games. Nursery rhymes. Poetry.

Knight, Margy Burns. *Talking walls* ill. by Anne Sibley O'Brien. Tilbury House, 1992. ISBN 0-88448-102-6 Subj: Foreign lands.

Welcoming babies ill. by Anne Sibley O'Brien. Tilbury House, 1994. ISBN 0-88448-123-9 Subj: Babies. Family life.

Knotts, Howard. *Great-grandfather, the baby and me* ill. by author. Atheneum, 1978. ISBN 0-689-30656-3 Subj: Family life – great-grandparents.

The lost Christmas ill. by author. Harcourt, 1978. ISBN 0-15-249361-1 Subj: Dreams. Holidays – Christmas. Illness.

The summer cat ill. by author. HarperCollins, 1981. ISBN 0-06-023179-3 Subj: Animals – cats. Seasons – summer.

The winter cat ill. by author. HarperCollins, 1972. ISBN 0-06-023167-X Subj: Animals – cats. Seasons – winter.

Knowles, Sheena. *Edward the emu* ill. by Rod Clement. HarperTrophy, 1998. ISBN 0-06-443499-0 Subj: Animals. Birds – emus. Character traits – individuality. Zoos.

Knowlton, Laurie Lazzaro. *The Nativity: Mary remembers* ill. by Kasi Kubiak. Boyds Mills, 1998. ISBN 1-56397-714-1 Subj: Babies. Holidays – Christmas. Religion – Nativity.

Knox-Wagner, Elaine. *The best mom in the world* (Delton, Judy)

My grandpa retired today ill. by Charles Robinson. Albert Whitman, 1982. ISBN 0-8075-5334-4 Subj: Emotions. Family life – grandfathers. Old age.

The oldest kid ill. by Gail Owens. Albert Whitman, 1981. ISBN 0-8075-5986-5 Subj: Activities – picnicking. Sibling rivalry.

Knüppel, Helga. *The adventures of Christabel Crocodile* ill. by author. Interlink, 1991. ISBN 0-940793-74-1 Subj: Animals. Behavior – lost. Reptiles – alligators, crocodiles.

Christabel Crocodile's birthday egg ill. by author. Crocodile Books, 1992. ISBN 1-56656-113-2 Subj: Animals – rats. Behavior – lost. Birds – penguins. Birthdays. Eggs. Reptiles – alligators, crocodiles.

Knutson, Barbara. *How the guinea fowl got her spots: a Swahili tale of friendship* ill. by adapt. Carolrhoda, 1990. ISBN 0-87614-416-4 Subj: Animals. Birds – guinea fowl. Folk and fairy tales. Friendship.

Why the crab has no head: an African tale ill. by author. Carolrhoda, 1987. ISBN 0-87614-322-2 Subj: Behavior – boasting. Crustaceans. Folk and fairy tales. Foreign lands – Africa. Foreign lands – Zaire.

Knutson, Kimberley. *Beach babble* ill. by author. Cavendish, 1998. ISBN 0-7614-5026-2 Subj: Noise, sounds. Sea and seashore.

Bed bouncers ill. by author. Macmillan, 1995. ISBN 0-02-750871-4 Subj: Bedtime. Furniture – beds. Rhyming text.

Jungle jamboree ill. by author. Cavendish, 1998. ISBN 0-7614-5032-7 Subj: Imagination. Music. Rhyming text. Weather – rain.

Muddigush ill. by author. Macmillan, 1992. ISBN 0-02-750843-9 Subj: Activities – playing. Rhyming text. Weather – rain.

Ska-tat! ill. by author. Macmillan, 1993. ISBN 0-02-750846-3 Subj: Noise, sounds. Seasons – fall. Senses – smelling.

Kobayashi, Masako Matsuno. *see* Matsuno, Masako

Kobayashi, Robert. *Maria Mazaretti loves spaghetti* ill. by author. Knopf, 1991. ISBN 0-679-91659-8 Subj: Animals. Careers – butchers. Food. Magic.

Kobayashi, Yuji. *Miss Josephine's secret walk* ill. by author. Green Tiger Pr., 1991. ISBN 0-88138-096-2 Subj: Activities – playing. Animals.

Kobrin, Janet. *Coyote goes hunting for fire: a California Indian myth* (Bernstein, Margery)

Earth namer: a California Indian myth (Bernstein, Margery)

The first morning: an African myth (Bernstein, Margery)

How the sun made a promise and kept it: a Canadian Indian myth (Bernstein, Margery)

Koch, Dorothy Clarke. *Gone is my goose* ill. by Doris Lee. Holiday, 1956. Subj: Birds – geese.

I play at the beach ill. by Feodor Rojankovsky. Random House, 1955. Subj: Family life. Games. Sea and seashore.

When the cows got out ill. by Paul Lantz. Holiday, 1958. Subj: Animals – bulls, cows. Farms.

Koch, Michelle. *By the sea* ill. by author. Greenwillow, 1991. ISBN 0-688-09550-X Subj: Concepts – opposites. Language. Sea and seashore.

Hoot, howl, hiss ill. by author. Greenwillow, 1991. ISBN 0-688-09652-2 Subj: Animals. Nature. Noise, sounds.

Just one more ill. by author. Greenwillow, 1989. ISBN 0-688-08128-2 Subj: Counting, numbers. Language.

World water watch ill. by author. Greenwillow, 1993. ISBN 0-688-11465-2 Subj: Ecology. Water.

Kocí, Marta. *Blackie and Marie* trans. from German by Elizabeth D. Crawford; ill. by author. Morrow, 1981. ISBN 0-688-00236-6 Subj: Animals – dogs. Friendship.

Katie's kitten ill. by author. Alphabet Pr., 1982. ISBN 0-907234-21-6 Subj: Animals – cats. Behavior – lost.

Sarah's bear ill. by author. Picture Book Studio, 1987. ISBN 0-88708-038-3 Subj: Emotions – love. Toys – bears.

Koehler, Phoebe. *The day we met you* ill. by author. Bradbury, 1990. ISBN 0-02-750901-X Subj: Adoption. Babies. Family life.

Making room ill. by author. Bradbury, 1993. ISBN 0-02-750875-7 Subj: Animals – cats. Animals – dogs. Babies. Behavior – sharing. Family life.

Koelling, Caryl. *Animal mix and match* ill. by Roger Beerworth. Delacorte, 1980. ISBN 0-440-00015-7 Subj: Animals. Format, unusual – board books.

Mad monsters mix and match ill. by Linda Griffith. Delacorte, 1980. ISBN 0-440-05141-X Subj: Format, unusual – board books. Monsters.

Silly stories mix and match ill. by Carroll Andrus. Delacorte, 1980. ISBN 0-440-07845-8 Subj: Format, unusual – board books. Humor.

Koenig, Marion. *The little black hen* (Hille-Brandts, Lene)

Poor fish (Beisert, Heide Helene)

The tale of fancy Nancy: a Spanish folktale ill. by Klaus Ensikat. Merrimack, 1979. ISBN 0-7011-5100-5 Subj: Animals – cats. Animals – mice. Folk and fairy tales.

The wonderful world of night ill. by David Parry. Grosset, 1969. Subj: Animals – cats. Behavior – misbehavior. Night.

Koenner, Alfred. *Be quite quiet beside the lake* trans. from German by Georgia Peet; ill. by Karl-Heinz Appelmann. Imported Pubs., 1981. ISBN 0-8285-1837-8 Subj: Format, unusual – board books. Noise, sounds.

High flies the ball by Alfred Koenner and Siegfried Linke; trans. from German by Georgia Peet; ill.

by Siegfried Linke. Imported Pubs., 1983. ISBN 0-8285-2553-6 Subj: Format, unusual – board books. Poetry.

Koffler, Camilla. *see* Ylla

Kohlenberg, Sherry. *Sammy's mommy has cancer* ill. by Lauri Crow. Gareth Stevens, 1994. ISBN 0-8368-1071-6 Subj: Emotions – love. Family life – mothers. Illness – cancer.

Koide, Tan. *May we sleep here tonight?* ill. by Yasuko Koide. Atheneum, 1983. ISBN 0-689-50261-3 Subj: Animals. Bedtime.

Koike, Kay. *Left or right?* (Rehm, Karl)

Kojima, Naomi. *The flying grandmother* ill. by author. Crowell, 1981. ISBN 0-690-04143-8 Subj: Activities – flying. Behavior – wishing. Family life – grandmothers. Imagination.

Kolar, Bob. *Stomp, stomp!* ill. by author. North-South, 1997. ISBN 1-55858-633-4 Subj: Animals. Dinosaurs. Family life – mothers. Rhyming text.

Koller, Jackie French. *Bouncing on the bed* ill. by Anna Gossnickle Hines. Orchard, 1999. ISBN 0-531-33138-5 Subj: Activities. Rhyming text.

Fish fry tonight ill. by Catharine O'Neill. Crown, 1992. ISBN 0-517-57815-8 Subj: Animals. Animals – mice. Food. Friendship. Rhyming text. Sports – fishing.

Mole and Shrew ill. by Stella Ormai. Atheneum, 1991. ISBN 0-689-31611-9 Subj: Animals – moles. Animals – shrews. Friendship. Homes, houses. Moving.

Mole and Shrew are two ill. by Anne Reas. Random House, 2000. ISBN 0-375-90690-8 Subj: Animals – moles. Animals – shrews. Friendship.

Mole and Shrew step out ill. by Stella Ormai. Atheneum, 1992. ISBN 0-689-31713-1 Subj: Animals. Animals – moles. Animals – shrews. Friendship. Parties.

Nickommoh! a Thanksgiving celebration ill. by Marcia Sewall. Atheneum, 1999. ISBN 0-689-81094-6 Subj: Holidays – Thanksgiving. Indians of North America – Narragansett. Seasons – fall.

No such thing ill. by Betsy Lewin. Boyds Mills, 1997. ISBN 1-56397-490-8 Subj: Bedtime. Emotions – fear. Family life – mothers. Monsters.

One monkey too many ill. by Lynn Munsinger. Harcourt, 1999. ISBN 0-15-200006-2 Subj: Animals – monkeys. Counting, numbers. Rhyming text.

Komaiko, Leah. *Annie Bananie* ill. by Laura Cornell. HarperCollins, 1987. ISBN 0-06-023261-7 Subj: Friendship. Moving. Rhyming text.

Aunt Elaine does the dance from Spain ill. by Petra Mathers. Doubleday, 1992. ISBN 0-385-30674-1 Subj: Activities – dancing. Careers – dancers. Rhyming text. Theater.

Broadway Banjo Bill ill. by Franz Spohn. Doubleday, 1993. ISBN 0-385-30524-9 Subj: Birthdays. Careers – musicians. Music. Rhyming text.

Earl's too cool for me ill. by Laura Cornell. HarperCollins, 1988. ISBN 0-06-023282-X Subj: Behavior – misunderstanding. Friendship. Rhyming text.

Fritzi Fox flew in from Florida ill. by Thacher Hurd. HarperCollins, 1995. ISBN 0-060-21507-0 Subj: Animals – foxes. Magic. Rhyming text.

Great Aunt Ida and her Great Dane, Doc ill. by S. D. Schindler. Doubleday, 1994. ISBN 0-385-30682-2 Subj: Activities – walking. Animals – dogs. Family life – aunts, uncles. Rhyming text.

I like the music ill. by Barbara Westman. HarperCollins, 1987. ISBN 0-06-023272-2 Subj: Music. Rhyming text.

Just my dad and me ill. by Jeffrey Greene. HarperCollins, 1995. ISBN 0-06-024574-3 Subj: Family life – fathers. Fish. Rhyming text. Sea and seashore.

Lenora O'Grady ill. by Laura Cornell. HarperCollins, 1992. ISBN 0-06-021767-7 Subj: Homeless. Rhyming text.

A million moms and mine written and ill. by Leah Komaiko and kids. L. Claiborne, 1992. ISBN 0-9634893-0-5 Subj: Activities – working. Children as authors. Children as illustrators. Family life – mothers.

My perfect neighborhood ill. by Barbara Westman. HarperCollins, 1990. ISBN 0-06-023288-9 Subj: Communities, neighborhoods. Rhyming text.

On Sally Perry's farm ill. by Cat Bowman Smith. Simon & Schuster, 1996. ISBN 0-689-80083-5 Subj: Activities – working. Farms. Gardens, gardening.

Shoeshine Shirley ill. by Franz Spohn. Doubleday, 1993. ISBN 0-385-30526-5 Subj: Clothing – shoes. Rhyming text.

Where can Daniel be? ill. by Denys Cazet. Orchard, 1994. ISBN 0-531-08700-X Subj: Babies. Behavior – lost. Behavior – worrying. Family life – brothers and sisters.

Komoda, Beverly. *Simon's soup* ill. by author. Parents, 1978. ISBN 0-8193-0951-6 Subj: Animals – cats. Animals – monkeys. Food.

The too hot day ill. by author. HarperCollins, 1991. ISBN 0-06-021612-3 Subj: Animals – rabbits. Family life. Seasons – summer.

The winter day ill. by author. HarperCollins, 1991. ISBN 0-06-023302-8 Subj: Animals – rabbits. Illness. Seasons – winter. Snowmen.

Komori, Atsushi. *Animal mothers* ill. by Masayuki Yabuuchi. Putnam, 1983. ISBN 0-399-20980-8 Subj: Animals. Science.

Konigsburg, E. L. (Elaine Lobl). *Amy Elizabeth explores Bloomingdale's* ill. by author. Atheneum, 1992. ISBN 0-689-31766-2 Subj: Activities. City. Family life – grandmothers.

Samuel Todd's book of great colors ill. by author. Atheneum, 1990. ISBN 0-689-31593-7 Subj: Concepts – color.

Samuel Todd's book of great inventions ill. by author. Atheneum, 1991. ISBN 0-689-31680-1 Subj: Family life.

Kooharian, David. *Sammy's story* ill. by author. DK, 1997. ISBN 0-7894-2466-5 Subj: Death. Family life. Illness.

Koontz, Robin Michal. *Chicago and the cat* ill. by author. Cobblehill, 1993. ISBN 0-525-65097-0 Subj: Animals – cats. Animals – rabbits. Friendship.

Chicago and the cat, the camping trip ill. by author. Cobblehill, 1994. ISBN 0-525-65137-3 Subj: Animals – cats. Animals – rabbits. Camps, camping. Friendship.

Chicago and the cat, the family reunion ill. by author. Cobblehill, 1996. ISBN 0-525-65202-7 Subj: Animals – cats. Animals – rabbits. Family life. Friendship. Parties.

Dinosaur dream ill. by author. Putnam, 1988. ISBN 0-399-21669-3 Subj: Dinosaurs. Dreams. Wordless.

I see something you don't see ill. by author. Dutton, 1992. ISBN 0-525-65077-6 Subj: Riddles.

Pussycat ate the dumplings: cat rhymes from Mother Goose ill. by author. Dodd, 1987. ISBN 0-396-08899-6 Subj: Animals – cats. Nursery rhymes.

This old man: the counting song ill. by author. Putnam, 1988. ISBN 0-396-09120-2 Subj: Counting, numbers. Farms. Music. Songs.

Koopmans, Loek. *The woodcutter's mitten* ill. by author. Interlink, 1990. ISBN 0-940793-67-9 Subj: Animals. Clothing.

Kopczynski, Anna. *Jerry and Ami* ill. by author. Scribners, 1963. Subj: Animals – dogs. Friendship.

Koplow, Lesley. *Tanya and the tobo man = Tanya y el hombre tobo* tr. into Spanish by Alexander Contos; ill. by Eric Velasquez. Magination Pr., 1991. ISBN 0-945354-34-7 Subj: Ethnic groups in the U.S. – African Americans. Foreign languages. Illness.

Kopper, Lisa. *Daisy knows best* ill. by author. Dutton, 1999. ISBN 0-525-45915-4 Subj: Activities – bathing. Animals – babies. Animals – dogs. Babies.

Daisy thinks she is a baby ill. by author. Knopf, 1994. ISBN 0-679-94723-X Subj: Animals – dogs. Babies.

An elephant came to swim (Lewin, Hugh)

I'm a baby, you're a baby ill. by author. Viking, 1995. ISBN 0-670-85813-7 Subj: Animals – babies. Babies. Language.

Ten little babies ill. by author. Dutton, 1990. ISBN 0-525-44643-5 Subj: Babies. Counting, numbers. Format, unusual – toy and movable books. Rhyming text.

Koralek, Jenny. *The boy and the cloth of dreams* ill. by James Mayhew. Candlewick, 1994. ISBN 1-56402-349-4 Subj: Dreams. Emotions – fear. Family life – grandmothers. Night. Quilts. Sleep.

Cat and Kit ill. by Patricia MacCarthy. Hyperion, 1994. ISBN 0-7868-2030-6 Subj: Animals – cats. Behavior – growing up. City. Farms.

The cobweb curtain: a Christmas story ill. by Pauline Baynes. Holt, 1989. Based on a legend told by William Barclay. ISBN 0-8050-1051-3 Subj: Behavior – hiding. Holidays – Christmas. Spiders.

The friendly fox ill. by Beverley Gooding. Little, 1988. ISBN 0-316-50179-4 Subj: Animals. Animals – foxes. Farms. Friendship.

Hanukkah: the festival of lights ill. by Juan Wijngaard. Lothrop, 1990. ISBN 0-688-09329-9 Subj: Holidays – Hanukkah. Jewish culture. Religion.

Night ride to Nanna's ill. by Mandy Sutcliffe. Candlewick, 2000. ISBN 0-7636-1192-1 Subj: Activities – traveling. Automobiles. Family life – grandmothers.

Koren, Edward. *Behind the wheel* ill. by author. Holt, 1972. ISBN 0-03-080232-6 Subj: Transportation.

Kornblatt, Marc. *Eli and the Dimplemeyers* ill. by Jack Ziegler. Macmillan, 1994. ISBN 0-02-750947-8 Subj: Family life. Imagination – imaginary friends.

Korth-Sander, Irmtraut. *Will you be my friend?* trans. from German by Rosemary Lanning; ill. by author. Holt, 1986. ISBN 0-8050-0039-9 Subj: Animals – pigs. Friendship.

Koscielniak, Bruce. *Bear and Bunny grow tomatoes* ill. by author. Knopf, 1993. ISBN 0-679-93687-4 Subj: Animals – bears. Animals – rabbits. Character traits – laziness. Gardens, gardening.

Euclid Bunny delivers the mail ill. by author. Knopf, 1991. ISBN 0-679-91069-7 Subj: Animals. Animals – rabbits. Behavior – carelessness. Careers – postal workers. Post office.

Geoffrey Groundhog predicts the weather ill. by author. Houghton Mifflin, 1995. ISBN 0-395-70933-4 Subj: Animals – groundhogs. Holidays – Groundhog Day. Seasons – spring. Weather.

Hector and Prudence ill. by author. Knopf, 1990. ISBN 0-394-94514-X Subj: Animals – pigs. Family life.

Hector and Prudence - all aboard! ill. by author. Knopf, 1990. ISBN 0-679-90486-7 Subj: Animals – pigs. Holidays – Christmas. Trains.

Koski, Mary. *Impatient Pamela calls 9-1-1* ill. by Dan Brown. Trellis Pub., 1998. ISBN 0-9663281-9-1 Subj: Character traits – patience. Telephone.

Kosowsky, Cindy. *Wordless counting book* ill. by author. Greene Bark Press, 1992. ISBN 1-880851-00-8 Subj: Counting, numbers. Wordless.

Kotzwinkle, William. *The day the gang got rich* ill. by Joe Servello. Viking, 1970. ISBN 0-670-25943-8 Subj: Clubs, gangs. Friendship.

The nap master ill. by Joe Servello. Harcourt, 1979. ISBN 0-15-256704-6 Subj: Bedtime. Dreams. Sleep.

Up the alley with Jack and Joe ill. by Joe Servello. Macmillan, 1974. ISBN 0-02-750940-0 Subj: Friendship.

Kouts, Anne. *Kenny's rat* ill. by Betty Fraser. Viking, 1970. ISBN 0-670-41263-5 Subj: Animals – rats. Pets.

Kovacs, Deborah. *Beaver gets lost* (Chottin, Ariane)

A home for Little Turtle (Chottin, Ariane)

Moonlight on the river ill. by William Shattuck. Viking, 1993. ISBN 0-670-84463-2 Subj: Boats, ships. Family life – brothers. Night. Rivers. Sports – fishing. Weather – storms.

Kovalski, Maryann. *Brenda and Edward* ill. by author. Kids Can Pr., 1984. ISBN 0-919964-77-X Subj: Animals – dogs. Behavior – lost. Friendship.

Jingle bells ill. by adapt. Little, 1988. Originally published in 1859 as "Jingle bells or the one horse open sleigh, song and chorus," by J. Pierpont. ISBN 0-316-50258-8 Subj: City. Holidays – Christmas. Music. Seasons – winter. Songs. Weather – snow.

Pizza for breakfast ill. by author. Kids Can Pr., 1991. ISBN 0-688-10410-X Subj: Behavior – wishing. Food.

Queen Nadine ill. by author. Orca, 1998. ISBN 1-55143-093-2 Subj: Animals – bulls, cows. Farms.

Take me out to the ball game ill. by author. Scholastic, 1992. ISBN 0-590-45638-5 Subj: Family life – grandmothers. Songs. Sports – baseball.

The wheels on the bus ill. by author. Little, 1987. ISBN 0-316-50256-1 Subj: Buses. Family life – grandmothers. Music. Songs.

Kowall, Barbara. *Squaps the moonling* (Ziegler, Ursina)

Kozielski, Dolores. *On Halloween night* (Wolff, Ferida)

Krahn, Fernando. *Amanda and the mysterious carpet* ill. by author. Clarion, 1985. ISBN 0-89919-258-0 Subj: Imagination. Magic. Wordless.

April fools ill. by author. Dutton, 1974. ISBN 0-525-25825-6 Subj: Holidays – April Fools' Day. Humor. Wordless.

Arthur's adventure in the abandoned house ill. by author. Dutton, 1981. ISBN 0-525-25945-7 Subj: Mystery stories. Wordless.

The biggest Christmas tree on earth ill. by author. Little, 1978. ISBN 0-316-50309-6 Subj: Animals. Holidays – Christmas. Toys – balls. Trees. Wordless.

Catch that cat! ill. by author. Dutton, 1978. ISBN 0-525-27555-X Subj: Animals – cats. Wordless.

The creepy thing ill. by author. Houghton Mifflin, 1982. ISBN 0-89919-099-5 Subj: Imagination – imaginary friends. Wordless.

A funny friend from heaven ill. by author. Lippincott, 1977. ISBN 0-397-31760-3 Subj: Angels. Clowns, jesters. Wordless.

The great ape: being the true version of the famous saga of adventure and friendship newly discovered ill. by author. Viking, 1978. ISBN 0-670-34840-6 Subj: Animals – gorillas. Friendship. Islands. Wordless.

Here comes Alex Pumpernickel! ill. by author. Little, 1981. ISBN 0-316-50311-8 Subj: Behavior – bad day. Wordless.

How Santa Claus had a long and difficult journey delivering his presents ill. by author. Delacorte, 1970. Holidays - Christmas. Subj: Gifts. Santa Claus. Wordless.

Little love story ill. by author. Lippincott, 1976. ISBN 0-397-31700-X Subj: Holidays – Valentine's Day. Wordless.

Mr. Top ill. by author. Morrow, 1983. ISBN 0-688-02369-X Subj: Crime. Traffic, traffic signs.

The mystery of the giant footprints ill. by author. Dutton, 1977. ISBN 0-525-35595-2 Subj: Cumulative tales. Monsters. Mystery stories. Wordless.

Robot-bot-bot ill. by author. Dutton, 1979. ISBN 0-525-38545-2 Subj: Activities – playing. Activities – working. Robots. Wordless.

Sebastian and the mushroom ill. by author. Delacorte, 1976. ISBN 0-440-07695-1 Subj: Dreams. Wordless.

The secret in the dungeon ill. by author. Houghton Mifflin, 1983. ISBN 0-89919-148-7 Subj: Behavior – secrets. Dragons. Wordless.

Sleep tight, Alex Pumpernickel ill. by author. Little, 1982. ISBN 0-316-50312-6 Subj: Bedtime. Sleep. Wordless.

Who's seen the scissors? ill. by author. Dutton, 1975. ISBN 0-525-42710-4 Subj: Wordless.

Krajnc, Anton C. *For the sake of a cake* (Nobisso, Josephine)

Kramer, Anthony Penta. *Numbers on parade: 0 to 10* ill. by author. Lothrop, 1987. ISBN 0-688-05555-9 Subj: Animals. Counting, numbers.

Kramer, Sydelle. *Wagon train* ill. by Deborah Kogan Ray. Grosset, 1997. ISBN 0-448-41335-3 Subj: Family life. U.S. history – frontier and pioneer life.

Kramlich, Carolyn Walz. *Mary's treasure box* ill. by Walter Porter. Nelson, 1998. ISBN 0-8499-5834-2 Subj: Memories, memory. Religion – Nativity.

Kramsky, Jerry. *The cranky sun* ill. by Lorenzo Mattotti. Little, 1995. ISBN 0-316-50361-4 Subj: Bedtime. Clocks, watches. Sun.

Kranendonk, Anke. *Just a minute* ill. by Jung-Hee Spetter. Front Street, 1998. ISBN 1-886910-29-4 Subj: Animals – pigs. Behavior – misbehavior. Family life – mothers.

Krasilovsky, Phyllis. *The cow who fell in the canal* ill. by Peter Spier. Doubleday, 1957. ISBN 0-385-07740-8 Subj: Animals – bulls, cows. Cumulative tales. Foreign lands – Holland.

The girl who was a cowboy ill. by Cyndy Szekeres. Doubleday, 1965. Subj: Clothing. Cowboys.

The man who cooked for himself ill. by Mamoru Funai. Parents, 1994. ISBN 0-8368-0984-X Subj: Activities – cooking. Food.

The man who didn't wash his dishes ill. by Barbara Cooney. Doubleday, 1950. Subj: Character traits – cleanliness. Character traits – laziness.

The man who entered a contest ill. by Yuri Salzman. Doubleday, 1980. ISBN 0-385-13352-9 Subj: Activities – cooking. Behavior – misbehavior.

The man who tried to save time ill. by Marcia Sewall. Doubleday, 1979. ISBN 0-385-12999-8 Subj: Character traits – laziness. Time.

The man who was too lazy to fix things ill. by John Emil Cymerman. Morrow, 1992. ISBN 0-688-10395-2 Subj: Character traits – laziness.

Scaredy cat ill. by Ninon. Macmillan, 1959. ISBN 0-02-750930-3 Subj: Animals – cats.

The shy little girl ill. by Trina Schart Hyman. Houghton Mifflin, 1970. Subj: Character traits – shyness. Friendship.

The very little boy ill. by Karen Gundersheimer. Scholastic, 1992. ISBN 0-590-44762-9 Subj: Activities. Babies. Behavior – growing up. Family life. Family life – new sibling.

The very little girl ill. by Karen Gundersheimer. Scholastic, 1992. ISBN 0-590-44761-0 Subj: Babies. Behavior – growing up. Family life – new sibling.

The very tall little girl ill. by Olivia Cole. Doubleday, 1969. Subj: Character traits – being different. Family life.

The woman who saved things ill. by John Emil Cymerman. Tambourine, 1993. ISBN 0-688-11163-7 Subj: Behavior – collecting things. Old age.

Kratka, Suzanne C. *Hi, new baby: a book to help your child learn about the new baby* (Andry, Andrew C.)

Kratky, Lada Josefa. *Arriba y abajo: Over and under* (Matthias, Catherine)

Demasiados globos: Too many balloons (Matthias, Catherine)

Sal y entra: Out the door (Matthias, Catherine)

Kraus, Bruce. *The detective of London* (Kraus, Robert)

Kraus, Robert. *The adventures of Wise Old Owl* ill. by author. Troll, 1993. ISBN 0-8167-2943-3 Subj: Activities – writing. Animals. Birds – owls.

All my chickens ill. by author. Western, 1993. ISBN 0-307-30125-7 Subj: Animals – foxes. Birds – chickens.

Animal families ill. by José Aruego and Ariane Dewey. Windmill, 1980. ISBN 0-671-41532-8 Subj: Animals. Family life. Format, unusual – board books.

Another mouse to feed ill. by José Aruego and Ariane Dewey. Simon & Schuster, 1989. ISBN 0-671-66522-7 Subj: Animals – mice. Family life.

Big brother ill. by author. Parents, 1973. ISBN 0-8193-0649-5 Subj: Animals – rabbits. Babies. Family life.

Big Squeak, Little Squeak ill. by Kevin O'Malley. Orchard, 1996. ISBN 0-531-08774-3 Subj: Animals – cats. Animals – mice. Character traits – cleverness. Food.

Boris bad enough ill. by José Aruego and Ariane Dewey. Simon & Schuster, 1988. ISBN 0-671-66894-3 Subj: Animals – elephants. Behavior – misbehavior. Careers – doctors.

Buggy Bear cleans up ill. by author. Silver Pr., 1989. ISBN 0-671-68608-9 Subj: Animals. Animals – bears. Character traits – cleanliness. Emotions – love. School.

The Christmas cookie sprinkle snitcher ill. by author. Windmill, 1980. ISBN 0-671-41199-3 Subj: Character traits – meanness. Food. Holidays – Christmas. Rhyming text.

Come out and play, little mouse ill. by José Aruego and Ariane Dewey. Delmar, 1991. ISBN 0-8273-4504-6 Subj: Activities – playing. Animals – cats. Animals – mice. Behavior – trickery.

Daddy Long Ears ill. by author. Little Simon, 1990. ISBN 0-671-67415-3 Subj: Animals – rabbits. Family life – fathers. Holidays – Easter.

Dance, Spider, dance! ill. by author. Western, 1993. ISBN 0-307-65656-X Subj: Activities – dancing. Spiders.

The detective of London by Robert and Bruce Kraus; ill. by Robert Byrd. Windmill, 1978. ISBN 0-525-61568-7 Subj: Animals – dogs. Careers – detectives. Crime. Mystery stories.

Dr. Mouse, Bungle Jungle doctor ill. by author. Western, 1992. ISBN 0-307-69550-6 Subj: Animals – mice. Careers – doctors.

Ella the bad speller ill. by author. Silver Pr., 1989. ISBN 0-671-68606-2 Subj: Animals. Animals – elephants. Language. School.

The first robin ill. by author. Windmill, 1965. ISBN 0-671-44565-0 Subj: Birds – robins. Character traits – kindness. Illness. Seasons – spring.

Freddy, the fire engine ill. by author. Grosset, 1985. ISBN 0-448-10219-6 Subj: Fire. Format, unusual – board books. Trucks.

Good morning, Miss Gator ill. by author. Silver Pr., 1989. ISBN 0-671-68605-4 Subj: Animals. Careers – teachers. Reptiles – alligators, crocodiles. School.

Good night little one by Robert Kraus and N. M. Bodecker; ill. by N. M. Bodecker. Dutton, 1972. ISBN 0-525-61500-8 Subj: Bedtime. Counting, numbers. Night. Sleep.

Good night Richard Rabbit by Robert Kraus and N. M. Bodecker; ill. by N. M. Bodecker. Dutton, 1972. ISBN 0-525-61502-4 Subj: Animals – rabbits. Bedtime. Counting, numbers. Night. Sleep.

Here comes Tardy Toad ill. by author. Silver Pr., 1989. ISBN 0-671-68607-0 Subj: Animals. Behavior – tardiness. Frogs and toads. School.

Herman the helper ill. by José Aruego and Ariane Dewey. Simon & Schuster, 1987. ISBN 0-671-66270-8 Subj: Character traits – helpfulness. Octopuses. Sea and seashore.

How Spider saved Easter ill. by author. Scholastic, 1988. ISBN 0-590-41092-X Subj: Animals. Holidays – Easter. Insects – flies. Insects – ladybugs. Spiders.

How Spider saved Halloween ill. by author. Simon & Schuster, 1988. ISBN 0-671-66888-9 Subj: Holidays – Halloween. Insects. Spiders.

How Spider saved Turkey ill. by author. Windmill, 1991. ISBN 0-590-44411-5 Subj: Birds – turkeys. Friendship. Holidays – Thanksgiving. Spiders.

How Spider saved Valentine's Day ill. by author. Scholastic, 1986. ISBN 0-590-33743-2 Subj: Friendship. Holidays – Valentine's Day. Insects. Spiders.

I, Mouse ill. by author. Windmill, 1978. Subj: Animals – mice.

Jack O'Lantern's scary Halloween ill. by author. Western, 1993. ISBN 0-307-10016-2 Subj: Holidays – Halloween.

The king's trousers ill. by Fred Gwynne. Windmill, 1981. ISBN 0-671-42259-6 Subj: Behavior – trickery. Clothing – pants. Royalty – kings.

Klunky Monkey, new kid in class ill. by author. Silver Pr., 1990. ISBN 0-671-70853-8 Subj: Animals. Animals – monkeys. Food. School.

Ladybug, ladybug! ill. by author. Windmill, 1977. ISBN 0-525-62326-4 Subj: Behavior – misunderstanding. Friendship. Insects – ladybugs. Rhyming text.

Leo the late bloomer ill. by José Aruego. Simon & Schuster, 1987. ISBN 0-671-96078-4 Subj: Animals – tigers. Behavior – growing up.

The little giant ill. by author. Windmill, 1977. ISBN 0-525-62322-1 Subj: Concepts – size. Giants.

Little Louie the baby bloomer ill. by José Aruego and Ariane Dewey. HarperCollins, 1998. ISBN 0-06-026294-X Subj: Animals – tigers. Family life – brothers.

The littlest rabbit ill. by author. HarperCollins, 1961. Subj: Animals – rabbits. Character traits – smallness.

Ludwig the dog who snored symphonies ill. by author. Windmill, 1981. ISBN 0-671-43411-X Subj: Animals – dogs. Music.

Mert the blurt ill. by José Aruego and Ariane Dewey. Simon & Schuster, 1989. ISBN 0-671-66537-5 Subj: Behavior – gossip. Frogs and toads.

Milton the early riser ill. by José Aruego and Ariane Dewey. Simon & Schuster, 1987. ISBN 0-671-66272-4 Subj: Animals – pandas. Sleep.

Mouse work ill. by author. Windmill, 1980. Subj: Animals – mice. Format, unusual – board books. Rhyming text.

Mummy knows best ill. by author. Warner, 1988. ISBN 1-55782-057-0 Subj: Ghosts. Mystery stories.

Musical Max ill. by José Aruego and Ariane Dewey. Simon & Schuster, 1990. ISBN 0-671-68681-X Subj: Animals – hippopotamuses. Music.

Noel the coward ill. by José Aruego and Ariane Dewey. Simon & Schuster, 1988. ISBN 0-671-66845-5 Subj: Emotions – fear.

Owliver ill. by José Aruego and Ariane Dewey. Prentice-Hall, 1987, 1974. ISBN 0-13-647538-8 Subj: Birds – owls. Careers. Character traits – individuality.

The phantom of Creepy Hollow ill. by author. Warner, 1988. ISBN 1-5578-2060-0 Subj: Monsters.

Phil the ventriloquist ill. by author. Greenwillow, 1989. ISBN 0-688-07988-1 Subj: Animals – rabbits. Family life.

Rebecca Hatpin ill. by Robert Byrd. Dutton, 1974. ISBN 0-525-61520-2 Subj: Careers – nurses. Character traits – helpfulness. Character traits – selfishness. Family life – grandmothers.

Robert Kraus' a sunny day in Babytown ill. by author. Little Simon, 1987. ISBN 0-671-63300-7 Subj: Animals. Babies. Family life. Format, unusual – board books.

Robert Kraus' Babytown express ill. by author. Little Simon, 1987. ISBN 0-671-63301-5 Subj: Babies. Country. Format, unusual – board books.

Robert Kraus' meet the babies ill. by author. Little Simon, 1987. ISBN 0-671-63299-X Subj: Babies. Format, unusual – board books.

Robert Kraus' welcome to Babytown ill. by author. Little Simon, 1987. ISBN 0-671-63298-1 Subj: Babies. Format, unusual – board books.

Screamy Mimi ill. by Hilary Knight. Simon & Schuster, 1987. ISBN 0-671-44471-9 Subj: Activities – singing. Noise, sounds.

See the Christmas lights ill. by Pam Kraus. Windmill, 1981. ISBN 0-671-44407-7 Subj: Format, unusual – toy and movable books. Holidays – Christmas. Poetry.

See the moon ill. by author. Windmill, 1980. ISBN 0-671-41206-X Subj: Format, unusual – toy and movable books. Moon. Night. Sleep.

Springfellow ill. by Sam Savitt. Dutton, 1978. ISBN 0-525-61577-6 Subj: Activities – playing. Animals – horses, ponies.

Springfellow's parade ill. by author. Windmill, 1982. ISBN 0-671-44564-2 Subj: Animals. Animals – horses, ponies. Parades. Seasons – spring.

Squirmy's big secret ill. by author. Silver Pr., 1990. ISBN 0-671-70851-1 Subj: Animals. Animals – worms. Names. School.

Strudwick, a sheep in wolf's clothing ill. by author. Viking, 1995. ISBN 0-670-85887-0 Subj: Animals – sheep. Animals – wolves. Behavior – trickery. Clothing. Disguises.

The three friends ill. by José Aruego and Ariane Dewey. Windmill, 1980. ISBN 0-671-96061-X Subj: Animals. Friendship.

Tony, the tow truck ill. by author. Grosset, 1985. ISBN 0-448-10220-X Subj: Format, unusual – board books. Friendship. Trucks.

The tree that stayed up until next Christmas ill. by Edna Eicke. Windmill, 1977. ISBN 0-525-61001-4 Subj: Holidays – Christmas. Toys. Trees.

The trouble with spider ill. by author. Harper-Collins, 1962. Subj: Friendship. Insects – flies. Spiders.

Where are you going, little mouse? ill. by José Aruego and Ariane Dewey. Greenwillow, 1986. ISBN 0-688-04295-3 Subj: Animals – mice. Behavior – running away. Behavior – seeking better things.

Whose mouse are you? ill. by José Aruego. Aladdin, 1986. ISBN 0-02-751190-1 Subj: Animals – mice. Rhyming text.

Wise Old Owl's canoe trip adventure ill. by author. Troll, 1993. ISBN 0-8167-2947-6 Subj: Birds – owls. Canoes and canoeing. Reptiles – turtles, tortoises.

Wise Old Owl's Christmas adventure ill. by Robert and Pamela Kraus. Troll, 1994. ISBN 0-8167-2945-X Subj: Animals. Birds – owls. Holidays – Christmas.

Krause, Ute. *Nora and the great bear* ill. by author. Dial, 1989. ISBN 0-8037-0685-5 Subj: Animals – bears. Behavior – lost. Sports – hunting.

Pig surprise ill. by author. Dial, 1989. ISBN 0-8037-0714-2 Subj: Animals – pigs. Behavior – misbehavior. Behavior – misunderstanding. Pets.

Krauss, Ronnie. *Take a look, it's in a book* photos by Christopher Hornsby. Walker, 1997. ISBN 0-8027-8489-5 Subj: Television. Theater.

Krauss, Ruth. *The backward day* ill. by Marc Simont. HarperCollins, 1950. Subj: Family life.

Bears ill. by Phyllis Rowand. HarperCollins, 1948. Subj: Animals – bears. Poetry.

Big and little ill. by Mary Szilagyi. Scholastic, 1988. ISBN 0-590-41707-X Subj: Concepts – size. Emotions – love.

A bouquet of littles ill. by Jane Flora. HarperCollins, 1963. Subj: Concepts – size. Poetry.

The bundle book ill. by Helen Stone. HarperCollins, 1951. Subj: Emotions. Family life – mothers. Games.

The carrot seed ill. by Crockett Johnson. Scholastic, 1974, c1945. ISBN 0-06-023351-6 Subj: Character traits – optimism. Gardens, gardening. Plants. Self-concept.

Charlotte and the white horse ill. by Maurice Sendak. HarperCollins, 1955. ISBN 0-06-023361-3 Subj: Animals – horses, ponies.

Everything under a mushroom ill. by Margot Tomes. Four Winds, 1974. Subj: Imagination. Little people. Rhyming text.

Eyes, nose, fingers, toes ill. by Elizabeth Schneider. HarperCollins, 1964. Subj: Anatomy.

A good man and his good wife ill. by Marc Simont. Harper, 1962. Subj: Behavior – boredom. Friendship.

The growing story ill. by Helen Oxenbury. HarperCollins, 2000. ISBN 0-06-024717-7 Subj: Behavior – growing up.

The happy day ill. by Marc Simont. HarperCollins, 1949. ISBN 0-06-023396-6 Subj: Caldecott award honor books. Hibernation. Seasons – spring. Seasons – winter. Weather – snow.

The happy egg ill. by Crockett Johnson. O'Hara, 1967. ISBN 0-8795-5701-X Subj: Birds. Eggs.

A hole is to dig: a first book of first definitions ill. by Maurice Sendak. HarperCollins, 1952. ISBN 0-06-023406-7 Subj: Activities – digging. Language.

I can fly ill. by Mary Blair. Golden Books, 1999. ISBN 0-307-20320-4 Subj: Activities – flying. Activities – playing. Format, unusual – board books. Imagination. Rhyming text.

I write it ill. by Mary Chalmers. HarperCollins, 1970. Subj: Activities – writing.

I'll be you and you be me ill. by Maurice Sendak. HarperCollins, 1954. ISBN 0-06-023431-8 Subj: Friendship. Humor.

Mama, I wish I was snow. Child, you'd be very cold ill. by Ellen Raskin. Atheneum, 1962. Subj: Behavior – wishing. Games.

A moon or a button ill. by Remy Charlip. HarperCollins, 1959. Subj: Imagination.

Open house for butterflies ill. by Maurice Sendak. HarperCollins, 1960. ISBN 0-06-023446-6 Subj: Imagination.

Somebody else's nut tree, and other tales from children ill. by Maurice Sendak. Linnet Books, 1990. ISBN 0-208-02264-3 Subj: Children as authors. Imagination.

This thumbprint ill. by author. HarperCollins, 1967. Subj: Humor. Imagination.

A very special house ill. by Maurice Sendak. HarperCollins, 1953. ISBN 0-06-023456-3 Subj: Caldecott award honor books. Homes, houses. Imagination.

You're just what I need ill. by Julia Noonan. HarperCollins, 1998. ISBN 0-06-027515-4 Subj: Emotions. Family life – mothers. Games.

Krauze, Andrzej. *What's so special about today?* ill. by author. Lothrop, 1984. ISBN 0-688-02835-7 Subj: Animals. Birthdays. Character traits – questioning.

Krementz, Jill. *Benjy goes to a restaurant* photos by author. Crown, 1986. ISBN 0-517-56166-2 Subj: Careers – waiters, waitresses. Family life. Format, unusual – board books. Restaurants.

Jack goes to the beach photos by author. Random House, 1986. ISBN 0-394-88001-3 Subj: Family life. Format, unusual – board books. Sand. Sea and seashore.

Jamie goes on an airplane photos by author. Random House, 1986. ISBN 0-394-88196-6 Subj: Activities – traveling. Airplanes, airports. Careers – airplane pilots. Format, unusual – board books.

Katharine goes to nursery school photos by author. Random House, 1986. ISBN 0-394-88195-8 Subj: Activities. Format, unusual – board books. School – first day.

Lily goes to the playground photos by author. Random House, 1986. ISBN 0-394-87999-6 Subj: Activities – playing. Family life. Format, unusual – board books.

Taryn goes to the dentist photos by author. Crown, 1986. ISBN 0-517-56168-9 Subj: Careers – dentists. Family life. Format, unusual – board books.

A very young actress photos by author. Knopf, 1991. ISBN 0-679-40637-9 Subj: Careers – actors. Theater.

A very young gardener photos by author. Dial, 1991. ISBN 0-8037-0875-0 Subj: Gardens, gardening.

A very young musician photos by author. Simon & Schuster, 1991. ISBN 0-671-72687-0 Subj: Careers – musicians. Music.

A very young skier photos by author. Dial, 1990. ISBN 0-8037-0823-8 Subj: Seasons – winter. Sports – skiing.

A visit to Washington, D.C. photos by author. Scholastic, 1987. ISBN 0-500-40582-9 Subj: Activities – traveling. City. Museums.

Krensky, Stephen. *The big time bears* ill. by Maryann Cocca-Leffler. Little, 1989. ISBN 0-316-50375-4 Subj: Animals – bears. Time.

Breaking into print: before and after the invention of the printing press ill. by Bonnie Christensen. Little, 1996. ISBN 0-316-50376-2 Subj: Activities – reading. Careers – printers. Libraries.

Children of the wind and water: five stories about Native American children ill. by James Watling. Scholastic, 1994. ISBN 0-590-46963-0 Subj: Behavior – growing up. Indians of North America.

Dinosaurs, beware! a safety guide (Brown, Marc Tolon)

Fraidy Cats ill. by Betsy Lewin. Scholastic, 1993. ISBN 0-590-46438-8 Subj: Animals – cats. Bedtime. Emotions – fear. Imagination. Night. Rhyming text.

A good knight's sleep ill. by Renée Williams-Andriani. Candlewick, 1996. ISBN 1-56402-769-4 Subj: Behavior – wishing. Knights.

How Santa got his job ill. by S. D. Schindler. Simon & Schuster, 1998. ISBN 0-689-80697-3 Subj: Careers. Holidays – Christmas. Santa Claus.

How Santa lost his job ill. by S. D. Schindler. Simon & Schuster, 2001. ISBN 0-689-83173-0 Subj: Careers. Holidays – Christmas. Mythical creatures – elves. Santa Claus.

The lion upstairs ill. by Leigh Grant. Atheneum, 1983. ISBN 0-689-30969-4 Subj: Imagination – imaginary friends.

The missing Mother Goose ill. by Chris L. Demarest. Doubleday, 1991. ISBN 0-385-26273-6 Subj: Nursery rhymes.

My first dictionary ill. by George Ulrich. Houghton Mifflin, 1980. ISBN 0-395-29210-7 Subj: Dictionaries.

My loose tooth ill. by Hideko Takahashi. Random House, 1998. ISBN 0-679-98847-5 Subj: Rhyming text. Teeth.

My teacher's secret life ill. by JoAnn Adinolfi. Simon & Schuster, 1996. ISBN 0-689-80271-4 Subj: Careers – teachers. Communities, neighborhoods. School.

Perfect pigs: an introduction to manners (Brown, Marc Tolon)

The pizza book ill. by R. W. Alley. Scholastic, 1992. ISBN 0-590-44844-7 Subj: Activities – cooking. Food.

We just moved! ill. by Larry DiFiori. Scholastic, 1998. ISBN 0-590-33127-2 Subj: Castles. Middle Ages. Moving.

What a mess! ill. by Joe Mathieu. Random House, 2001. ISBN 0-375-90220-1 Subj: Character traits – cleanliness.

Kress, Camille. *Tot Shabbat* ill. by author. UAHC Pr., 1996. ISBN 0-8074-0607-4 Subj: Format, unusual – board books. Holidays. Jewish culture.

Kreye, Walter. *The giant from the little island* ill. by Tomek Bogacki. North-South, 1990. ISBN 1-55858-085-9 Subj: Activities – making things. Behavior – wishing. Friendship. Giants.

Krings, Antoon. *Oliver's bicycle* ill. by author. Walt Disney, 1992. ISBN 1-56282-161-X Subj: Animals – koalas. Sports – bicycling. Weather – rain.

Oliver's pool ill. by author. Walt Disney, 1992. ISBN 1-56282-161-X Subj: Animals – koalas. Sports – swimming.

Oliver's strawberry patch ill. by author. Walt Disney, 1992. ISBN 1-56282-163-6 Subj: Animals – koalas. Food. Gardens, gardening. Plants.

Krisher, Trudy. *Kathy's hats: a story of hope* ill. by Nadine Bernard Westcott. Albert Whitman, 1992. ISBN 0-8075-4116-8 Subj: Clothing – hats. Hair. Illness – cancer.

Kroll, Steven. *Amanda and the giggling ghost* ill. by Dick Gackenbach. Holiday, 1980. ISBN 0-8234-0408-0 Subj: Behavior – stealing. Ghosts.

Annie's four grannies ill. by Eileen Christelow. Holiday, 1986. ISBN 0-8234-0605-9 Subj: Family life – grandmothers. Family life – step families. Rhyming text.

Are you pirates? ill. by Marylin Hafner. Pantheon, 1982. ISBN 0-394-93936-0 Subj: Imagination. Pirates.

The big bunny and the Easter eggs ill. by Janet Stevens. Holiday, 1982. ISBN 0-8234-0436-6 Subj: Animals – rabbits. Holidays – Easter. Illness.

The big bunny and the magic show ill. by Janet Stevens. Holiday, 1986. ISBN 0-8234-0589-3 Subj: Animals – rabbits. Holidays – Easter. Magic.

Big Jeremy ill. by Donald Carrick. Holiday, 1989. ISBN 0-8234-0759-4 Subj: Friendship. Giants.

Branigan's cat and the Halloween ghost ill. by Carolyn Ewing. Holiday, 1990. ISBN 0-8234-0822-1 Subj: Animals – cats. Ghosts. Holidays – Halloween.

By the dawn's early light: the story of the Star spangled banner ill. by Dan Andreasen. Scholastic, 1994. ISBN 0-590-45054-9 Subj: Music. Songs. U.S. history.

The candy witch ill. by Marylin Hafner. Holiday, 1979. ISBN 0-8234-0359-9 Subj: Behavior – unnoticed, unseen. Holidays – Halloween. Magic. Witches.

Doctor on an elephant ill. by Michael Chesworth. Holt, 1994. ISBN 0-8050-2876-5 Subj: Animals – elephants. Careers – doctors. Foreign lands – India. Weather – rain.

Don't get me in trouble ill. by Marvin Glass. Crown, 1987. ISBN 0-517-56724-5 Subj: Animals – dogs. Friendship.

Fat magic ill. by Tomie de Paola. Holiday, 1978. ISBN 0-823-40327-0 Subj: Magic. Royalty.

The goat parade ill. by Tim Kirk. Parents, 1983. ISBN 0-8193-1100-6 Subj: Animals – goats. Parades.

The hand-me-down doll ill. by Evaline Ness. Holiday, 1983. ISBN 0-8234-0495-1 Subj: Toys – dolls.

Happy Father's Day ill. by Marylin Hafner. Holiday, 1987. ISBN 0-5234-0671-7 Subj: Family life – fathers. Holidays – Father's Day.

Happy Mother's Day ill. by Marylin Hafner. Holiday, 1985. ISBN 0-8234-0504-4 Subj: Family life. Holidays – Mother's Day.

The Hokey-Pokey man ill. by Deborah Kogan Ray. Holiday, 1989. ISBN 0-8234-0728-4 Subj: Food.

Howard and Gracie's luncheonette ill. by Michael Sours. Holt, 1991. ISBN 0-8050-1305-9 Subj: Activities – working. Careers.

I love spring! ill. by Kathryn E. Shoemaker. Holiday, 1987. ISBN 0-8234-0634-2 Subj: Seasons – spring.

If I could be my grandmother ill. by Tasha Tudor. Pantheon, 1977. ISBN 0-394-93554-3 Subj: Family life – grandmothers.

It's April Fools' Day! ill. by Jeni Bassett. Holiday, 1990. ISBN 0-8234-0747-0 Subj: Animals – cats. Behavior – bullying. Holidays – April Fools' Day.

It's Groundhog Day! ill. by Jeni Bassett. Holiday, 1987. ISBN 0-8234-0643-1 Subj: Activities – picnicking. Animals. Holidays – Groundhog Day.

Lewis and Clark: explorers of the American West ill. by Richard Williams. Holiday, 1994. ISBN 0-8234-1034-X Subj: Careers – explorers. U.S. history.

Looking for Daniela ill. by Anita Lobel. Holiday, 1988. ISBN 0-8234-0695-4 Subj: Crime. Foreign lands – Italy. Problem solving.

Loose tooth ill. by Tricia Tusa. Holiday, 1984. ISBN 0-8234-0518-4 Subj: Fairies. Teeth.

The magic rocket ill. by Will Hillenbrand. Holiday, 1992. ISBN 0-8234-0916-3 Subj: Animals – dogs. Imagination. Space and space ships. Toys.

Mary McLean and the St. Patrick's Day parade ill. by Michael Dooling. Scholastic, 1991. ISBN 0-590-43701-1 Subj: City. Ethnic groups in the U.S. – Irish Americans. Holidays – St. Patrick's Day. Parades.

Oh, Tucker! ill. by Scott Nash. Candlewick, 1998. ISBN 0-7636-0429-1 Subj: Animals – dogs. Character traits – clumsiness.

Oh, what a Thanksgiving! ill. by S. D. Schindler. Scholastic, 1988. ISBN 0-590-40613-2 Subj: Holidays – Thanksgiving. Imagination. U.S. history.

One tough turkey: a Thanksgiving story ill. by John Wallner. Holiday, 1982. ISBN 0-8234-0457-9 Subj: Birds – turkeys. Holidays – Thanksgiving. Pilgrims. Sports – hunting.

Otto ill. by Ned Delaney. Parents, 1983. ISBN 0-8193-1106-5 Subj: Behavior – misbehavior. Robots.

Patches: an art story ill. by Barry Gott. Winslow, 2001. ISBN 1-8908-1753-8 Subj: Activities – drawing. Animals – guinea pigs. Behavior – losing things. Children as authors. Children as illustrators.

The pigrates clean up ill. by Jeni Bassett. Holt, 1993. ISBN 0-8050-2368-2 Subj: Activities – bathing. Animals – pigs. Boats, ships. Character traits – cleanliness. Pirates. Rhyming text. Weddings.

Pigs in the house ill. by Tim Kirk. Parents, 1983. ISBN 0-8193-1111-1 Subj: Animals – pigs. Behavior – misbehavior. Homes, houses. Rhyming text.

Princess Abigail and the wonderful hat ill. by Patience Brewster. Holiday, 1991. ISBN 0-8234-0853-1 Subj: Clothing – hats. Folk and fairy tales. Royalty – princesses.

Queen of the May ill. by Patience Brewster. Holiday, 1993. ISBN 0-8234-1004-8 Subj: Animals. Character traits – kindness to animals. Fairs. Family life – step families. Folk and fairy tales.

Santa's crash-bang Christmas ill. by Tomie de Paola. Holiday, 1977. ISBN 0-8234-0302-5 Subj: Holidays – Christmas. Santa Claus.

The squirrels' Thanksgiving ill. by Jeni Bassett. Holiday, 1991. ISBN 0-8234-0823-X Subj: Animals – squirrels. Family life. Holidays – Thanksgiving. Sibling rivalry.

Toot! Toot! ill. by Anne F. Rockwell. Holiday, 1983. ISBN 0-8234-0471-4 Subj: Family life – grandparents. Imagination. Toys – trains. Trains.

The tyrannosaurus game ill. by Tomie de Paola. Holiday, 1976. ISBN 0-8234-0275-4 Subj: Cumulative tales. Dinosaurs. Games. Imagination.

Will you be my valentine? ill. by Lillian Hoban. Holiday, 1993. ISBN 0-8234-0925-2 Subj: Activities – making things. Behavior – indifference. Holidays – Valentine's Day. School.

Woof, woof! ill. by Nicole Rubel. Dial, 1983. ISBN 0-8037-9651-X Subj: Animals – dogs. Crime.

Kroll, Virginia L. *Africa brothers and sisters* ill. by Vanessa French. Four Winds, 1993. ISBN 0-02-751166-9 Subj: Ethnic groups in the U.S. – African Americans. Family life – fathers. Foreign lands – Africa.

Beginnings: how families come to be ill. by Stacey Schuett. Albert Whitman, 1994. ISBN 0-8075-0602-8 Subj: Adoption. Family life.

Butterfly boy ill. by Gerardo Suzán. Boyds Mills, 1997. ISBN 1-56397-371-5 Subj: Family life – grandfathers. Foreign lands – Mexico. Illness. Insects – butterflies, caterpillars.

Can you dance, Dalila? ill. by Nancy Carpenter. Simon & Schuster, 1996. ISBN 0-689-80551-9 Subj: Activities – dancing. Ballet. Ethnic groups in the U.S. – African Americans.

A carp for Kimiko ill. by Katherine Roundtree. Charlesbridge, 1993. ISBN 0-8810-6413-0 Subj:

Family life. Fish. Foreign lands – Japan. Holidays. Kites. Sex roles.

The Christmas cow ill. by author. Players Pr., 1996. ISBN 0-8873-4481-X Subj: Animals – bulls, cows. Holidays – Christmas. Religion – Nativity. Self-concept.

Faraway drums ill. by Floyd Cooper. Little, 1998. ISBN 0-316-50449-1 Subj: City. Ethnic groups in the U.S. – African Americans. Family life – sisters. Foreign lands – Africa. Imagination.

Fireflies, peach pies, and lullabies ill. by Nancy Cote. Simon & Schuster, 1995. ISBN 0-02-751001-8 Subj: Death. Family life. Illness – Alzheimer's. Memories, memory. Old age.

Girl, you're amazing! ill. by Mélisande Potter. Albert Whitman, 2001. ISBN 0-8075-2930-3 Subj: Rhyming text. Sex roles.

Hands! ill. by Cathryn Falwell. Boyds Mills, 1997. ISBN 1-56397-051-1 Subj: Anatomy – hands.

Helen the fish ill. by Teri Weidner. Albert Whitman, 1992. ISBN 0-8075-3194-4 Subj: Death. Family life – brothers. Fish. Pets.

Jaha and Jamil went down the hill: an African Mother Goose ill. by Katherine Roundtree. Charlesbridge, 1995. ISBN 0-88106-867-5 Subj: Foreign lands – Africa. Nursery rhymes.

Lunching and munching ill. by Jesse Sweetwater. Simon & Schuster, 1999. ISBN 0-689-81564-6 Subj: Animals. Food. Rhyming text.

Masai and I ill. by Nancy Carpenter. Four Winds, 1992. ISBN 0-02-751165-0 Subj: Ethnic groups in the U.S. – African Americans. Family life. Foreign lands – Africa.

Motherlove ill. by Lucia Washburn. Dawn, 1998. ISBN 1-8832-2080-7 Subj: Animals – babies. Family life – mothers. Rhyming text.

My sister, then and now ill. by Mary Worcester. Carolrhoda, 1992. ISBN 0-8761-4718-X Subj: Family life – sisters. Illness.

Naomi knows it's springtime ill. by Jill Kastner. Caroline House, 1993. ISBN 1-56397-006-6 Subj: Handicaps – blindness. Seasons – spring.

New friends, true friends, stuck-like-glue friends ill. by Rose Rosely. Eerdmans, 1994. ISBN 0-8028-5085-5 Subj: Ethnic groups in the U.S. Friendship. Rhyming text.

Pink paper swans ill. by Nancy L. Clouse. Eerdmans, 1994. ISBN 0-8028-5081-2 Subj: Ethnic groups in the U.S. – Japanese Americans. Illness. Paper.

The seasons and someone ill. by Tatsuro Kiuchi. Harcourt, 1994. ISBN 0-15-271233-X Subj: Eskimos. Foreign lands – Arctic. Indians of North America. Names. Seasons.

She is born: a celebration of daughters ill. by John Rowe. Beyond Words, 1999. ISBN 1-8852-2394-3 Subj: Babies. Family life – daughters.

Sweet Magnolia ill. by Laura Jacques. Charlesbridge, 1995. ISBN 0-8810-6416-5 Subj: Animals. Birds. Character traits – kindness to animals. Ethnic groups in the U.S. – African Americans. Family life – grandmothers.

Wood-hoopoe Willie ill. by Katherine Roundtree. Charlesbridge, 1992. ISBN 0-88106-410-6 Subj: Birds – wood-hoopoe. Ethnic groups in the U.S. – African Americans. Family life. Holidays – Kwanzaa. Music.

Kroninger, Stephen. *If I crossed the road* ill. by author. Atheneum, 1997. ISBN 0-689-81190-X Subj: Imagination. Roads.

Krudop, Walter Lyon. *Blue claws* ill. by author. Atheneum, 1993. ISBN 0-689-31787-5 Subj: Crustaceans. Family life – grandfathers. Sports – fishing.

The man who caught fish ill. by author. Farrar, 2000. ISBN 0-374-34786-7 Subj: Behavior – greed. Folk and fairy tales. Foreign lands – Thailand. Royalty – kings. Sports – fishing.

Something is growing ill. by author. Atheneum, 1995. ISBN 0-689-31940-1 Subj: Behavior – unnoticed, unseen. City. Gardens, gardening.

Krudwig, Vickie Leigh. *Cucumber soup* ill. by Craig McFarland Brown. Fulcrum Kids, 1998. ISBN 1-55591-380-6 Subj: Counting, numbers. Food. Insects.

Krull, Kathleen. *Autumn* (Allington, Richard L.)

It's my earth too ill. by Melanie Hope Greenberg. Doubleday, 1992. ISBN 0-385-42088-9 Subj: Ecology. Nature.

Maria Molina and the Days of the Dead ill. by Enrique O. Sánchez. Macmillan, 1994. ISBN 0-02-750999-0 Subj: Family life. Foreign lands – Mexico. Holidays – Day of the Dead.

Measuring (Allington, Richard L.)

Reading (Allington, Richard L.)

Science (Allington, Richard L.)

Songs of praise ill. by Kathryn Hewitt. Harcourt, 1989. ISBN 0-15-277108-5 Subj: Music. Religion. Seasons. Songs.

Spring (Allington, Richard L.)

Summer (Allington, Richard L.)

Talking (Allington, Richard L.)

Thinking (Allington, Richard L.)

Time (Allington, Richard L.)

Winter (Allington, Richard L.)

Words (Allington, Richard L.)

Writing (Allington, Richard L.)

Krum, Charlotte. *The four riders* ill. by Katherine Evans. Follett, 1953. Subj: Animals – horses, ponies.

Krupinski, Loretta. *Best friends* ill. by author. Hyperion, 1998. ISBN 0-7868-0332-0 Subj: Friendship. Indians of North America – Nez Perce. Toys – dolls. U.S. history.

Celia's island journal (Thaxter, Celia)

Into the woods: a woodland scrapbook ill. by author. HarperCollins, 1997. ISBN 0-06-026444-6 Subj: Activities – walking. Forest, woods. Nature. Science.

Lost in the fog (Bacheller, Irving)

A New England scrapbook: a journey through poetry, prose, and pictures ill. by author. HarperCollins, 1994. ISBN 0-06-022951-9 Subj: Poetry.

Krupp, E. C. *The comet and you* ill. by Robin Rector Krupp. Macmillan, 1985. ISBN 0-02-751250-9 Subj: Science.

Krupp, Robin Rector. *Get set to wreck!* ill. by author. Macmillan, 1988. ISBN 0-02-751140-5 Subj: Activities – playing. Imagination. Language.

Let's go traveling in Mexico ill. by author. Morrow, 1996. ISBN 0-688-12368-6 Subj: Foreign lands – Mexico. Mythical creatures. Seasons.

Krüss, James. *Johnny Longnose* by James Krüss and Naomi Lewis; ill. by Stasys Eidrigevicius. North-South, 1990. ISBN 1-55858-023-9 Subj: Anatomy – noses. Poetry.

3 X 3: Three by three ill. by Eva Johanna Rubin; English text by Geoffrey Strachan. Macmillan, 1963. Subj: Animals. Counting, numbers. Poetry.

Krylov, Ivan Andreevich. *The cat and the cook and other fables of Krylov* (Heins, Ethel L.)

Kubler, Susanne. *The three friends* ill. by author. Macmillan, 1985. ISBN 0-02-751150-2 Subj: Animals. Friendship.

Kübler-Ross, Elisabeth. *Remember the secret* ill. by Heather Preston. Celestial Arts, 1982. Subj: Death. Memories, memory.

Kuchalla, Susan. *All about seeds* ill. by Jane McBee. Troll, 1982. Subj: Plants. Science. Seeds.

Baby animals ill. by Joel Snyder. Troll, 1982. Subj: Animals.

Bears ill. by Kathie Kelleher. Troll, 1982. Subj: Animals – bears.

Birds ill. by Gary Britt. Troll, 1982. Subj: Birds.

What is a reptile? ill. by Paul Harvey. Troll, 1982. Subj: Reptiles.

Kudler, David. *The Seven Gods of Luck* ill. by Linda Finch. Houghton Mifflin, 1997. ISBN 0-395-78830-7 Subj: Family life – brothers and sisters. Folk

and fairy tales. Foreign lands – Japan. Holidays – New Year's. Poverty.

Kudrna, C. Imbior. *To bathe a boa* ill. by author. Carolrhoda, 1986. ISBN 0-87614-306-0 Subj: Activities – bathing. Behavior – hiding. Reptiles – snakes. Rhyming text.

Kuei, Ye Ping. *Monkey and the white bone demon* (Shi, Zhang Xiu)

Kuhn, Dwight. *Hungry little frog* photos by Dwight Kuhn; text by Ron Hirschi. Cobblehill, 1992. ISBN 0-525-65109-8 Subj: Animals. Counting, numbers. Frogs and toads.

Kühner, Peter. *The circus of mystery* (Fazzi, Maura)

Kuklin, Susan. *Dance* (Jones, Bill T.)

From head to toe: how a doll is made photos by author. Hyperion, 1994. ISBN 1-56282-667-0 Subj: Activities – making things. Toys – dolls.

Going to my ballet class photos by author. Bradbury, 1989. ISBN 0-02-751235-5 Subj: Activities – dancing. Ballet.

Going to my gymnastics class photos by author. Bradbury, 1991. ISBN 0-02-751236-3 Subj: Sports – gymnastics.

Going to my nursery school photos by author. Bradbury, 1990. ISBN 0-02-751237-1 Subj: School.

How my family lives in America photos by author. Bradbury, 1992. ISBN 0-02-751239-8 Subj: Ethnic groups in the U.S. Family life.

Lighting fires photos by author. Bradbury, 1993. ISBN 0-02-751238-X Subj: Careers – firefighters. Fire. Trucks.

Taking my dog to the vet photos by author. Bradbury, 1988. ISBN 0-02-751234-7 Subj: Animals. Careers – veterinarians. Pets.

Thinking big: the story of a young dwarf photos by author. Lothrop, 1986. ISBN 0-688-05827-2 Subj: Character traits – being different. Handicaps.

When I see my dentist photos by author. Bradbury, 1988. ISBN 0-02-751231-2 Subj: Careers – dentists. Health and fitness.

When I see my doctor photos by author. Bradbury, 1988. ISBN 0-02-751232-0 Subj: Careers – doctors.

Kulling, Monica. *Waiting for Amos* ill. by Vicky Lowe. Bradbury, 1993. ISBN 0-02-751245-2 Subj: Animals. Character traits – patience. Friendship. Frogs and toads. Reptiles – turtles, tortoises.

Kulman, Andrew. *Red light stop, green light go* ill. by author. Simon & Schuster, 1993. ISBN 0-671-79493-0 Subj: Concepts. Traffic, traffic signs.

Kumin, Maxine W. *The beach before breakfast* ill. by Leonard Weisgard. Putnam, 1964. Subj: Sea and seashore.

Eggs of things ill. by Leonard W. Shortall. Putnam, 1963. Subj: Eggs. Frogs and toads. Humor. Science.

Follow the fall ill. by Artur Marokvia. Putnam, 1961. Subj: Holidays. Imagination. Rhyming text. Seasons – fall.

Joey and the birthday present by Maxine W. Kumin and Anne Sexton; ill. by Evaline Ness. McGraw-Hill, 1971. Subj: Animals – mice. Birthdays.

Mittens in May ill. by Eliott Gilbert. Putnam, 1962. Subj: Birds. Character traits – kindness to animals. Clothing – gloves, mittens.

Sebastian and the dragon ill. by William D. Hayes. Putnam, 1960. Subj: Character traits – smallness. Dragons. Rhyming text.

Speedy digs downside up ill. by Ezra Jack Keats. Putnam, 1964. Subj: Activities – digging. Character traits – ambition. Humor. Rhyming text.

What color is Caesar? ill. by Evaline Ness. McGraw-Hill, 1978. Subj: Animals – dogs. Concepts – color.

A winter friend ill. by Artur Marokvia. Putnam, 1961. Subj: Poetry. Seasons – winter.

Kunhardt, Dorothy. *Billy the barber* ill. by William Pène Du Bois. HarperCollins, 1961. Subj: Careers – barbers. Hair. Old age.

Kitty's new doll ill. by Lucinda McQueen. Golden Pr., 1984. Subj: Animals – cats. Toys – dolls.

Kunhardt, Edith. *Danny and the Easter egg* ill. by author. Greenwillow, 1989. ISBN 0-688-08036-7 Subj: Holidays – Easter. Reptiles – alligators, crocodiles.

Danny's birthday ill. by author. Greenwillow, 1986. ISBN 0-688-06177-X Subj: Birthdays. Parties. Reptiles – alligators, crocodiles.

Danny's Christmas star ill. by author. Greenwillow, 1989. ISBN 0-688-07906-7 Subj: Activities – making things. Holidays – Christmas. Reptiles – alligators, crocodiles.

Danny's mystery Valentine ill. by author. Greenwillow, 1987. ISBN 0-688-06854-5 Subj: Family life – grandmothers. Holidays – Valentine's Day. Reptiles – alligators, crocodiles.

I'm going to be a farmer photos by author. Scholastic, 1996. Originally published: I want to be a farmer. New York: Grosset & Dunlap, c1989. ISBN 0-590-25482-0 Subj: Careers – farmers. Farms.

I'm going to be a fire fighter photos by author. Scholastic, c1989, (1995 printing). Originally published: I want to be a fire fighter. New York: Grosset & Dunlap, 1989. ISBN 0-590-25483-9 Subj: Careers – firefighters.

I'm going to be a police officer photos by author. Scholastic, 1995. Originally published: I want to be a police officer. New York: Grosset & Dunlap, 1989. ISBN 0-590-25485-5 Subj: Careers – police officers.

I'm going to be a vet photos by author. Scholastic, 1996. ISBN 0-590-25484-7 Subj: Animals. Careers – veterinarians.

Pat the cat ill. by author. Golden Pr., 1984. Subj: Animals – cats. Format, unusual – toy and movable books. Pets.

Pat the puppy ill. by author. Western, 1993. ISBN 0-307-12004-X Subj: Animals – dogs. Family life – grandparents. Format, unusual – toy and movable books.

Red day, green day ill. by Marylin Hafner. Greenwillow, 1992. ISBN 0-688-09400-7 Subj: Concepts – color. School. Weather – rainbows.

Trick or treat, Danny! ill. by author. Greenwillow, 1988. ISBN 0-688-07311-5 Subj: Holidays – Halloween. Illness. Reptiles – alligators, crocodiles.

Where's Peter? ill. by author. Greenwillow, 1988. ISBN 0-688-07205-4 Subj: Babies. Family life. Games.

Which one would you choose? ill. by author. Greenwillow, 1989. ISBN 0-688-07908-3 Subj: Activities. Participation.

Which pig would you choose? ill. by author. Greenwillow, 1990. ISBN 0-688-08982-8 Subj: Activities. Farms. Participation.

Kunnas, Mauri. *The nighttime book* by Mauri Kunnas with Tarja Kunnas; trans. from Finnish by Tim Steffa; ill. by author. Crown, 1985. ISBN 0-517-55819-X Subj: Activities. Night.

One spooky night and other scary stories by Mauri Kunnas with Tarja Kunnas; trans. by Tim Steffa; ill. by author. Crown, 1986. ISBN 0-517-56253-7 Subj: Ghosts. Holidays – Halloween. Monsters.

Santa Claus and his elves by Mauri Kunnas; assisted by Tarja Kunnas; ill. by authors. Harmony, 1982. Translation of Joulupukki. Subj: Holidays – Christmas. Mythical creatures – elves. Santa Claus.

Twelve gifts for Santa Claus by Mauri and Tarja Kunnas; trans. by Tim Steffa; ill. by authors. Crown, 1988. ISBN 0-517-56631-1 Subj: Character traits – generosity. Gifts. Holidays – Christmas. Mythical creatures – elves. Santa Claus.

Kunnas, Tarja. *The nighttime book* (Kunnas, Mauri)

One spooky night and other scary stories (Kunnas, Mauri)

Santa Claus and his elves (Kunnas, Mauri)

Twelve gifts for Santa Claus (Kunnas, Mauri)

Kunstler, James Howard. *Annie Oakley* ill. by Fred Warter. Rabbit Ears, 1996. ISBN 0-689-80605-1 Subj: U.S. history – frontier and pioneer life.

Kupfer, Andrew. *Night city* (Wellington, Monica)

Kuratomi, Chizuko. *Mr. Bear and the robbers* ill. by Kozo Kakimoto. Dial, 1970. Subj: Animals – bears. Animals – rabbits.

Kurjian, Judi. *In my own backyard* ill. by David Wagner. Charlesbridge, 1993. ISBN 0-88106-443-2 Subj: Imagination.

Kurokawa, Mitsuhiro. *Dinosaur valley* ill. by author. Chronicle, 1992. ISBN 0-8118-0257-4 Subj: Dinosaurs. Format, unusual – toy and movable books.

Kurt, Kemal. *The five fingers and the moon* ill. by Aljoscha Blau; trans. by Anthea Bell. North-South, 1997. ISBN 1-55858-802-7 Subj: Magic. Moon. Mythical creatures.

Kurtz, Christopher. *Only a pigeon* (Kurtz, Jane)

Kurtz, Jane. *Fire on the mountain* ill. by E. B. Lewis. Simon & Schuster, 1994. ISBN 0-671-88268-6 Subj: Family life – brothers and sisters. Folk and fairy tales. Foreign lands – Ethiopia.

Miro in the kingdom of the sun ill. with woodcuts by David Frampton. Houghton Mifflin, 1996. ISBN 0-395-69181-8 Subj: Character traits – bravery. Folk and fairy tales. Indians of South America – Incas. Magic. Royalty.

Only a pigeon by Jane and Christopher Kurtz; ill. by E. B. Lewis. Simon & Schuster, 1997. ISBN 0-689-80077-0 Subj: Birds – pigeons. Foreign lands – Ethiopia. Pets. Sports – racing.

River friendly, river wild ill. by Neil Brennan. Simon & Schuster, 2000. ISBN 0-689-82049-6 Subj: Family life. Rivers. U.S. history. Weather – floods.

Kuskin, Karla. *ABCDEFGHIJKLMNOPQRSTU-VWXYZ* ill. by author. HarperCollins, 1963. Subj: ABC books.

All sizes of noises ill. by author. HarperCollins, 1962. Subj: Concepts. Noise, sounds. Poetry.

The animals and the ark ill. by author. Harper-Collins, 1958. Subj: Animals. Boats, ships. Poetry. Religion – Noah. Weather – floods. Weather – rain.

A boy had a mother who bought him a hat ill. by author. Houghton Mifflin, 1976. Subj: Cumulative tales. Rhyming text.

City dog ill. by author. Clarion, 1994. ISBN 0-395-66138-2 Subj: Animals – dogs. Country. Rhyming text. Sea and seashore.

City noise ill. by Renee Flower. HarperCollins, 1994. ISBN 0-06-021076-1 Subj: City. Noise, sounds. Poetry.

The Dallas Titans get ready for bed ill. by Marc Simont. HarperCollins, 1986. ISBN 0-06-023563-2 Subj: Bedtime. Clothing. Sports – football.

A great miracle happened there: a Chanukah story Robert Andrew Parker ill. by Robert Andrew Parker. Willa Perlman Books, 1993. ISBN 0-06-023618-3 Subj: Family life. Holidays – Hanukkah. Jewish culture. Religion.

Herbert hated being small ill. by author. Houghton Mifflin, 1979. ISBN 0-395-26462-6 Subj: Character traits – smallness. Concepts – size. Rhyming text.

I am me ill. by Dyanna Wolcott. Simon & Schuster, 2000. ISBN 0-689-81473-9 Subj: Character traits – individuality. Family life. Sea and seashore.

In the flaky frosty morning ill. by author. Harper-Collins, 1969. Subj: Rhyming text. Seasons – winter. Snowmen. Weather – snow.

James and the rain ill. by author. HarperCollins, 1957. ISBN 0-671-88808-0 Subj: Animals. Rhyming text. Weather – rain.

Jerusalem, shining still ill. by David Frampton. HarperCollins, 1987. ISBN 0-06-023549-7 Subj: City. Foreign lands – Israel. Religion.

Just like everyone else ill. by author. HarperCollins, 1959. ISBN 0-06-443032-4 Subj: Activities – flying.

Night again ill. by author. Little, 1981. ISBN 0-316-50721-0 Subj: Bedtime.

Patchwork island ill. by Petra Mathers. Harper-Collins, 1994. ISBN 0-06-021284-5 Subj: Activities – sewing. Poetry. Quilts.

Paul ill. by Milton Avery. HarperCollins, 1994. ISBN 0-06-023573-X Subj: Family life – grandmothers. Imagination. Magic. Songs.

The Philharmonic gets dressed ill. by Marc Simont. HarperCollins, 1982. ISBN 0-06-023622-1 Subj: Clothing.

Roar and more ill. by author. HarperCollins, 1956. ISBN 0-06-023619-1 Subj: Animals. Noise, sounds. Participation. Rhyming text.

Sand and snow ill. by author. HarperCollins, 1965. Subj: Poetry. Sea and seashore. Seasons – summer. Seasons – winter.

The sky is always in the sky ill. by Isabelle Dervaux. Laura Geringer, 1998. ISBN 0-06-027084-5 Subj: Poetry.

Soap soup and other verses ill. by author. Harper-Collins, 1992. ISBN 0-06-023572-1 Subj: Poetry.

Something sleeping in the hall ill. by author. Harper-Collins, 1985. ISBN 0-06-023634-5 Subj: Animals. Pets. Poetry.

A space story ill. by Marc Simont. HarperCollins, 1978. ISBN 0-06-023542-X Subj: Bedtime. Space and space ships. Stars.

The upstairs cat ill. by Howard Fine. Clarion, 1997. ISBN 0-395-70146-5 Subj: Animals – cats. Poetry.

Watson, the smartest dog in the U.S.A. ill. by author. HarperCollins, 1968. Subj: Activities – reading. Animals – dogs.

What did you bring me? ill. by author. Harper-Collins, 1973. ISBN 0-06-023653-1 Subj: Animals – mice. Behavior – greed. Self-concept. Witches.

Which horse is William? ill. by author. Greenwillow, 1992. ISBN 0-688-10638-2 Subj: Character traits – individuality. Imagination.

Kusugak, Michael. *A promise is a promise* (Munsch, Robert N.)

Kutner, Merrily. *Z is for zombie* ill. by John Manders. Albert Whitman, 1999. ISBN 0-8075-9490-3 Subj: ABC books. Holidays – Halloween. Rhyming text.

Kvasnosky, Laura McGee. *One, two, three, play with me!* ill. by author. Dutton, 1994. ISBN 0-525-45234-6 Subj: Activities – playing. Counting, numbers. Format, unusual – board books. Poetry.

Pink, red, blue, what are you? ill. by author. Dutton, 1994. ISBN 0-525-45233-8 Subj: Animals. Concepts – color. Format, unusual – board books. Poetry.

What shall I dream? ill. by Judith Byron Schachner. Dutton, 1996. ISBN 0-525-45207-9 Subj: Dreams. Royalty – princes.

Zelda and Ivy ill. by author. Candlewick, 1998. ISBN 0-7636-0469-0 Subj: Animals – foxes. Family life – sisters.

Zelda and Ivy and the boy next door ill. by author. Candlewick, 1999. ISBN 0-7636-0672-3 Subj: Animals – foxes. Family life – sisters.

Zelda and Ivy one Christmas ill. by author. Candlewick, 2000. ISBN 0-7636-1000-3 Subj: Animals – foxes. Character traits – generosity. Family life – sisters. Holidays – Christmas. Old age.

Kwitz, Mary DeBall. *Little chick's breakfast* ill. by Bruce Degen. HarperCollins, 1983. ISBN 0-06-023675-2 Subj: Birds – chickens. Farms. Food.

Little chick's story ill. by Cyndy Szekeres. Harper-Collins, 1978. ISBN 0-06-023666-3 Subj: Birds – chickens. Eggs.

Mouse at home ill. by author. HarperCollins, 1966. Subj: Animals – mice. Seasons.

Rabbits' search for a little house ill. by Lorinda Bryan Cauley. Crown, 1977. ISBN 0-517-52867-3 Subj: Animals – rabbits. Homes, houses.

When it rains ill. by author. Follett, 1974. ISBN 0-695-40411-3 Subj: Animals. Rhyming text. Weather – rain. Weather – rainbows.

Kwon, Holly H. *The moles and the mireuk: a Korean folktale* ill. by Woodleigh Hubbard. Houghton Mifflin, 1993. ISBN 0-395-64347-3 Subj: Animals – moles. Behavior – seeking better things. Folk and fairy tales. Foreign lands – Korea.

Kyte, Dennis. *Mattie and Cataragus* ill. by author. Doubleday, 1988. ISBN 0-385-24404-5 Subj: Animals – cats. Friendship.

L. M. C. *see* Child, Lydia Maria

Lacapa, Michael. *Antelope Woman: an Apache folktale* ill. by author. Northland, 1992. ISBN 0-87358-543-7 Subj: Animals – antelopes. Folk and fairy tales. Indians of North America – Apache. Sports – hunting.

Lachner, Dorothea. *Andrew's angry words* ill. by The Tjong-Khing. North-South, 1995. ISBN 1-55858-436-6 Subj: Communication. Emotions – anger. Language.

Danny, the angry lion ill. by Gusti; trans. by J. Alison James. North-South, 2000. ISBN 0-7358-1387-6 Subj: Emotions – anger.

The gift from Saint Nicholas ill. by Maja Dusíková. North-South, 1995. ISBN 1-55858-457-9 Subj: Holidays – Christmas. Weather – snow.

Look out, Cinder! ill. by Eugen Sopko; trans. by Rosemary Lanning. North-South, 1996. ISBN 1-55858-521-4 Subj: Animals – cats. Emotions – loneliness. Friendship.

Meredith, the witch who wasn't ill. by Christa Unzner; trans. by J. Alison James. North-South, 1997. ISBN 1-55858-781-0 Subj: Character traits – individuality. Magic. Witches.

Meredith's mixed-up magic ill. by Christa Unzner; trans. by J. Alison James. North-South, 2000. ISBN 0-7358-1190-3 Subj: Magic. Witches.

Smoky's special Easter present ill. by Christa Unzner; trans. by Marianne Martens. North-South, 1996. ISBN 1-55858-574-5 Subj: Activities. Animals – rabbits. Holidays – Easter. Pets.

Lacoe, Addie. *Just not the same* ill. by Pau Estrada. Houghton Mifflin, 1992. ISBN 0-395-59347-6 Subj: Behavior – sharing. Birthdays. Multiple births – triplets. Sibling rivalry.

Lacome, Julie. *Funny business* ill. by author. Morrow, 1991. ISBN 0-688-10159-3 Subj: Animals – dogs. Circus. Clowns, jesters. Concepts – color. Concepts – shape. Format, unusual – toy and movable books.

Garden ill. by author. Candlewick, 1995. ISBN 1-56402-478-4 Subj: Animals. Format, unusual – toy and movable books. Gardens, gardening.

Hocus pocus ill. by author. Morrow, 1991. ISBN 0-688-10158-5 Subj: Animals – rabbits. Format, unusual – toy and movable books. Magic.

I'm a jolly farmer ill. by author. Candlewick, 1994. ISBN 1-56402-318-4 Subj: Activities – playing. Animals – dogs. Imagination. Rhyming text.

My first book of words ill. by author. 2nd ed. Candlewick, 1996. ISBN 1-56402-749-1 Subj: Language.

On the farm ill. by author. Candlewick, 1995. ISBN 1-56402-706-6 Subj: Farms.

Ruthie's big old coat ill. by author. Candlewick, 2000. ISBN 0-7636-0969-2 Subj: Activities – playing. Animals – rabbits. Clothing – coats.

Seashore ill. by author. Candlewick, 1995. ISBN 1-56402-479-2 Subj: Animals. Format, unusual – board books. Sea and seashore.

Walking through the jungle ill. by author. Candlewick, 1993. ISBN 1-56402-137-8 Subj: Animals. Jungle. Noise, sounds. Nursery rhymes.

Lacy, Donna. *The music box: the story of Cristofori* (Guy, Suzanne)

Laden, Nina. *Peek-a-who?* ill. by author. Chronicle, 2000. ISBN 0-8118-2602-3 Subj: Format, unusual – board books. Rhyming text.

Private I. Guana, the case of the missing chameleon ill. by author. Chronicle, 1995. ISBN 0-8118-0940-4 Subj: Humor. Mystery stories. Reptiles – chameleons. Reptiles – iguanas. Reptiles – lizards.

When Pigasso met Mootisse ill. by author. Chronicle, 1998. ISBN 0-8118-1121-2 Subj: Animals – bulls, cows. Animals – pigs. Careers – artists.

Ladwig, Tim. *The Lord's prayer* (Bible. New Testament)

Psalm twenty-three (Bible. Old Testament. Psalms)

Lady Eden's School. *Just how stories* ill. by Derek Steele. Merrimack, 1981. ISBN 0-224-01713-6 Subj: Animals. Children as authors.

Ladybug, ladybug, and other nursery rhymes ill. by Eloise Wilkin. Random House, 1979. ISBN 0-394-84282-0 Subj: Format, unusual. Nursery rhymes.

La Farge, Phyllis. *Joanna runs away* ill. by Trina Schart Hyman. Holt, 1973. ISBN 0-03-091306-3 Subj: Animals – horses, ponies. Behavior – running away.

La Farge, Sheila. *The boy who ate more than the giant and other Swedish folktales* (Löfgren, Ulf)

Peter's adventures in Blueberry Land (Beskow, Elsa Maartman)

La Fontaine, Jean de. *The fox and the stork* (McDermott, Gerald)

The hare and the tortoise ill. by Brian Wildsmith. Watts, 1963. Subj: Animals – rabbits. Folk and fairy tales. Reptiles – turtles, tortoises. Sports – racing.

The lion and the rat ill. by Brian Wildsmith. Oxford Univ. Pr., 1984 printing, c1963. ISBN 0-19-279607-0 Subj: Animals – lions. Animals – rats. Character traits – helpfulness. Folk and fairy tales.

The miller, the boy and the donkey adapt. and ill. by Brian Wildsmith. Watts, 1969. Based on a fable by La Fontaine. ISBN 0-19-279652-6 Subj: Animals – donkeys. Character traits – practicality. Folk and fairy tales. Humor.

The north wind and the sun ill. by Brian Wildsmith. Watts, 1964. ISBN 0-19-272168-2 Subj: Folk and fairy tales. Sun. Weather – wind.

The turtle and the two ducks: animal fables (Plante, Patricia)

Lafontaine, Pascale Claude. *see* Claude-Lafontaine, Pascale

Lage, Ida De. *see* DeLage, Ida

Lager, Claude. *A tale of two rats* ill. by Nicole Rutten. Stewart, Tabori & Chang, 1991. ISBN 1-55670-228-0 Subj: Animals – rats. Careers – artists. Foreign lands – Italy. Friendship.

Lagercrantz, Rose. *Brave little Pete of Geranium Street* by Rose and Samuel Lagercrantz; trans. by Jack Prelutsky; ill. by Eva Eriksson. Greenwillow, 1986. ISBN 0-688-06181-8 Subj: Behavior – bullying. Character traits – bravery. Rhyming text.

Lagercrantz, Samuel. *Brave little Pete of Geranium Street* (Lagercrantz, Rose)

Lagerlöf, Selma. *The changeling* trans. from Swedish by Susanna Stevens; ill. by Jeanette Winter. Knopf, 1992. ISBN 0-679-91035-2 Subj: Babies. Emotions – love. Fairies. Format, unusual – toy and movable books. Mythical creatures – trolls.

The legend of the Christmas rose retold by Ellin Greene; ill. by Charles Mikolaycak. Holiday, 1990. ISBN 0-8234-8021-3 Subj: Flowers. Folk and fairy tales. Holidays – Christmas.

Laidlaw, Ken. *The amazing I spy ABC* ill. by author. Dial, 1996. ISBN 0-8037-1992-2 Subj: ABC books. Format, unusual – toy and movable books. Picture puzzles.

Laimgruber, Monika. *Susannah and the Sandman: a good-night story* ill. by author. North-South, 1996. ISBN 1-55858-602-4 Subj: Bedtime. Dreams. Mythical creatures – sandman. Sleep.

Laird, Donivee Martin. *The three little Hawaiian pigs and the magic shark* ill. by Carol Jossem. Bess Pr., 1981. ISBN 0-940350-01-7 Subj: Animals – pigs. Fish – sharks. Hawaii.

Laird, Elizabeth. *A book of promises* ill. by Michael Frith. DK, 2000. ISBN 0-7894-2547-5 Subj: Emotions – love. Family life.

The day Patch stood guard ill. by Colin Reeder. Morrow, 1991. ISBN 0-688-10240-9 Subj: Animals

– dogs. Farms. Foreign lands – England. Tractors.

The day Sidney ran off ill. by Colin Reeder. Morrow, 1991. ISBN 0-688-10242-5 Subj: Animals – pigs. Farms. Foreign lands – England. Tractors.

The day the ducks went skating ill. by Colin Reeder. Morrow, 1991. ISBN 0-688-10247-6 Subj: Animals. Birds – ducks. Careers – farmers. Character traits – kindness to animals. Farms. Tractors.

The day Veronica was nosy ill. by Colin Reeder. Morrow, 1991. ISBN 0-688-10249-2 Subj: Animals. Careers – farmers. Farms. Insects – hornets. Tractors.

Lake, Mary Dixon. *The royal drum: an Ashanti tale* ill. by Carol O'Malia. Mondo, 1996. ISBN 1-57255-125-9 Subj: Animals. Folk and fairy tales. Foreign lands – Ghana. Spiders.

Lakin, Pat (Patricia). *Aware and alert* ill. by Doug Cushman. Raintree, 1995. ISBN 0-8114-8261-8 Subj: Careers – police officers. Communities, neighborhoods. Crime. Safety.

Dad and me in the morning ill. by Robert G. Steele. Albert Whitman, 1994. ISBN 0-8075-1419-5 Subj: Family life – fathers. Family life – sons. Handicaps – physical handicaps. Morning. Sea and seashore.

Don't forget ill. by Ted Rand. Tambourine, 1994. ISBN 0-688-12076-8 Subj: Behavior – secrets. Birthdays. Holocaust. Jewish culture.

Don't touch my room ill. by Patience Brewster. Little, 1985. ISBN 0-316-51230-3 Subj: Babies. Behavior – sharing. Emotions – fear. Family life – new sibling. Sibling rivalry.

Family: around the world ill. by author. Blackbirch, 1995. ISBN 1-56711-143-2 Subj: Family life. World.

A good sport ill. by Doug Cushman. Raintree, 1995. ISBN 0-8114-3870-8 Subj: Behavior. Sports – soccer.

Grandparents: around the world ill. by author. Blackbirch, 1999. ISBN 1-56711-146-7 Subj: Family life – grandparents. Old age. World.

Growing up: around the world ill. by author. Blackbirch, 1995. ISBN 1-56711-144-0 Subj: Behavior – growing up. Behavior – sharing. Family life.

Hurricane! ill. by Vanessa Lubach. Millbrook, 2000. ISBN 0-7613-1616-7 Subj: Family life – fathers. Weather – hurricanes.

Information, please ill. by Doug Cushman. Raintree, 1995. ISBN 0-8114-8260-X Subj: Careers – librarians. Communities, neighborhoods.

Jet black pickup truck ill. by Rosekrans Hoffman. Orchard, 1990. ISBN 0-531-08485-X Subj: Family life – grandmothers. Rhyming text. Trucks.

Just like me ill. by Patience Brewster. Little, 1989. ISBN 0-316-51233-8 Subj: Family life – brothers. School.

The mystery illness ill. by Doug Cushman. Raintree, 1995. ISBN 0-8114-3867-8 Subj: Careers – nurses. Illness. School.

Oh, brother! ill. by Patience Brewster. Little, 1987. ISBN 0-316-51231-1 Subj: Family life. Sibling rivalry. Trees.

The palace of stars ill. by Kimberly Bulcken Root. Tambourine, 1993. ISBN 0-688-11177-7 Subj: Family life – aunts, uncles. Friendship. Theater.

Play: around the world ill. by author. Blackbirch, 1995. ISBN 1-56711-141-6 Subj: Activities – playing.

Red letter day ill. by Doug Cushman. Raintree, 1995. ISBN 0-8114-8264-2 Subj: Careers – postal workers. Communities, neighborhoods. School.

Snow day! ill. by Scott Nash. Dial, 2002. ISBN 0-8037-2642-2 Subj: School. Weather – snow.

Subway sonata ill. by Heather Harms Maione. Millbrook, 2001. ISBN 0-7613-1464-4 Subj: Careers – artists. City. Trains.

Trash and treasure ill. by Doug Cushman. Raintree, 1995. ISBN 0-8114-3865-1 Subj: Behavior – losing things. Careers – custodians, janitors. School.

Up a tree ill. by Doug Cushman. Raintree, 1995. ISBN 0-8114-3868-6 Subj: Careers – bus drivers. Pets. School.

Lakota, Philomine. *Shota and the star quilt* (Bateson-Hill, Margaret)

Lalicki, Barbara. *If there were dreams to sell* ill. by Margot Tomes. 2nd ed. Four Winds, 1994. ISBN 0-02-751251-7 Subj: ABC books. Poetry.

Lalli, Judy. *Feelings alphabet: an album of emotions from A to Z* photos by Douglas L. Mason-Fry. Jalmar, 1984. ISBN 0-935266-15-1 Subj: ABC books. Emotions.

LaMarche, Jim. *The walloping window-blind* (Carryl, Charles E. [Charles Edward])

La Mare, Walter De. *see* De La Mare, Walter (Walter John)

Lambert, Paulette Livers. *Evening: an Appalachian lullaby* ill. by adapt. Roberts Rinehart, 1995. ISBN 1-57098-012-8 Subj: Lullabies. Music. Songs.

Lamborn, Florence. *Christmas in noisy village* (Lindgren, Astrid)

Laminack, Lester L. *The sunsets of Miss Olivia Wiggins* ill. by Constance R. Bergum. Peachtree, 1998. ISBN 1-56145-139-8 Subj: Family life – grandparents. Memories, memory. Old age.

Trevor's wiggly-wobbly tooth ill. by Kathi Garry McCord. Peachtree, 1998. ISBN 1-56145-175-4 Subj: Emotions – fear. Family life – grandmothers. School. Teeth.

Lamm, C. Drew. *Anniranni and Mollymishi, the wild-haired doll* ill. by Ruth Ohi. Firefly, 1990. ISBN 1-55037-105-3 Subj: Animals – dogs. Toys – dolls.

Screech Owl at Midnight Hollow ill. by Joel Snyder. Soundprints Pr., 1996. ISBN 1-56899-265-3 Subj: Birds – owls. Family life. Nature.

Lamont, Priscilla. *Out to lunch* ill. by author. Kingfisher, 1995. ISBN 1-85697-564-9 Subj: Animals – dogs. Behavior – tardiness.

The troublesome pig (The old woman and her pig)

Lampert, Emily. *A little touch of monster* ill. by Victoria Chess. Atlantic Monthly, 1986. ISBN 0-87113-022-X Subj: Character traits – individuality. Family life.

Lamstein, Sarah Marwil. *Annie's Shabbat* ill. by Cecily Lang. Albert Whitman, 1997. ISBN 0-8075-0376-2 Subj: Jewish culture. Religion.

I like your buttons! ill. by Nancy Cote. Albert Whitman, 1999. ISBN 0-8075-3510-9 Subj: Character traits – kindness. School.

Landa, Norbert. *Cubs* by Norbert Landa, Ona Pans, Victoria Seix. Barron's, 2000. ISBN 0-7641-1480-8 Subj: Animals – babies.

How does it feel? ill. by Karin Littlewood. Thomasson-Grant, 1993. ISBN 1-56566-032-3 Subj: Imagination.

Kittens by Norbert Landa and Ona Pans. Barron's, 2000. ISBN 0-7641-1481-6 Subj: Animals – babies. Animals – cats.

Little Bear's Christmas ill. by Marlis Scharff-Kniemeyer; trans. by Anna Trenter. Little Tiger, 1999. ISBN 1-888444-60-6 Subj: Animals – bears. Holidays – Christmas. Santa Claus. Weather – snow.

Puppies by Norbert Landa, Ona Pans, Victoria Seix. Barron's, 2000. ISBN 0-7641-1482-4 Subj: Animals – babies. Animals – dogs.

Rabbit and chicken count eggs ill. by Hanne Türk. Tambourine, 1992. ISBN 0-688-09971-8 Subj: Animals – rabbits. Birds – chickens. Counting, numbers. Eggs. Format, unusual – board books. Friendship.

Rabbit and chicken find a box ill. by Hanne Türk. Morrow, 1992. ISBN 0-688-09968-8 Subj: Animals – rabbits. Birds – chickens. Character traits – helpfulness. Format, unusual – board books. Friendship.

Rabbit and chicken play hide and seek ill. by Hanne Türk. Morrow, 1992. ISBN 0-688-09970-X Subj: Activities – playing. Animals – rabbits. Birds – chickens. Friendship. Games.

Rabbit and chicken play with colors ill. by Hanne Türk. Tambourine, 1992. ISBN 0-688-09969-6 Subj: Animals – rabbits. Birds – chickens. Concepts – color. Eggs. Format, unusual – board books. Friendship. Holidays – Easter.

Landalf, Helen. *The secret night world of cats* ill. by author. Smith & Kraus, 1997. ISBN 1-57525-117-5 Subj: Animals – cats. Magic. Night.

Landau, Terry. *Butterflies and rainbows* (Berger, Judith)

Landshoff, Ursula. *Cats are good company* ill. by author. HarperCollins, 1983. ISBN 0-06-023677-9 Subj: Animals – cats. Pets. Science.

Landström, Lena. *Boo and Baa at sea* (Landström, Olof)

Boo and Baa in a party mood (Landström, Olof)

Boo and Baa in windy weather (Landström, Olof)

Boo and Baa on a cleaning spree (Landström, Olof)

Will gets a haircut (Landström, Olof)

Will goes to the beach (Landström, Olof)

Will goes to the post office (Landström, Olof)

Will's new cap (Landström, Olof)

Landström, Olof. *Boo and Baa at sea* written and ill. by Olof and Lena Landström; trans. by Joan Sandin. R&S Books, 1997. ISBN 91-29-63921-2 Subj: Animals – sheep. Boats, ships. Sea and seashore.

Boo and Baa in a party mood written and ill. by Olof and Lena Landström; trans. by Joan Sandin. Farrar, 1996. ISBN 91-29-63918-2 Subj: Activities – dancing. Animals – sheep. Birthdays. Parties.

Boo and Baa in windy weather written and ill. by Olof and Lena Landström; trans. by Joan Sandin. Farrar, 1996. ISBN 91-29-63920-4 Subj: Animals – sheep. Food. Weather – snow. Weather – storms.

Boo and Baa on a cleaning spree written and ill. by Olof and Lena Landström; trans. by Joan Sandin. R&S Books, 1997. ISBN 91-29-63919-0 Subj: Animals – sheep. Character traits – cleanliness.

Will gets a haircut written and ill. by Olof and Lena Landström; trans. by Elizabeth Dyssegaard. R&S Books, 1993. ISBN 91-29-62075-9 Subj: Hair.

Will goes to the beach written and ill. by Olof and Lena Landström. R&S Books, 1995. ISBN 91-29-65305-3 Subj: Sea and seashore.

Will goes to the post office written and ill. by Olof and Lena Landström; trans. by Elisabeth Dyssegaard. Farrar, 1994. ISBN 91-29-62950-0 Subj: Post office.

Will's new cap written and ill. by Olof and Lena Landström; trans. by Richard E. Fisher. Farrar, 1992. ISBN 91-29-62062-7 Subj: Clothing – hats.

Lane, Judith. *Buster, where are you?* ill. by Nancy Lane. Benefactory, 1998. ISBN 1-58021-019-8 Subj: Animals – dogs. Behavior – lost.

Lane, Marcia. *Christoph wants a party* (Lobe, Mira)

Lane, Margaret. *The frog* ill. by Grahame Corbett. Dial, 1981. ISBN 0-8037-2711-9 Subj: Frogs and toads. Science.

The squirrel ill. by Kenneth Lilly. Dial, 1981. ISBN 0-8037-8230-6 Subj: Animals – squirrels. Science.

Lane, Megan Halsey. *Something to crow about* ill. by author. Dial, 1990. ISBN 0-8037-0698-7 Subj: Birds – chickens. Gender roles. Self-concept.

Lang, Andrew. *The flying ship* ill. by Dennis McDermott. Morrow, 1995. ISBN 0-688-11405-9 Subj: Activities – flying. Boats, ships. Folk and fairy tales. Foreign lands – Russia. Royalty – kings. Royalty – princesses.

Nursery rhyme book (Mother Goose)

Snow White and Rose Red (Grimm, Jacob)

Langford, Sondra Gordon. *Mishka and Plishka* ill. by Debrah Santini. Simon & Schuster, 1995. ISBN 0-689-80244-7 Subj: Careers – bakers. Foreign lands – Russia. Money.

Langham, Tony. *The amazing adventures of Teddy Tum Tum* (Breese, Gillian)

Langley, Jonathan. *Rumpelstiltskin* (Grimm, Jacob)

The three billy goats Gruff (Asbjørnsen, P. C. [Peter Christen])

Langner, Nola. *By the light of the silvery moon* ill. by author. Lothrop, 1983. ISBN 0-688-01663-4 Subj: Behavior – running away. Imagination – imaginary friends. Royalty.

Freddy my grandfather ill. by author. Four Winds, 1979. ISBN 0-890-07577-2 Subj: Family life – grandfathers.

Langreuter, Jutta. *Little Bear and the big fight* by Jutta Langreuter and Vera Sobat; ill. by Vera Sobat. Millbrook, 1998. ISBN 0-7613-0403-7 Subj: Animals – bears. Behavior – misbehavior. Emotions – anger. Friendship. School.

Little Bear brushes his teeth by Jutta Langreuter and Vera Sobat; ill. by Vera Sobat. Millbrook, 1997. ISBN 0-7613-0190-9 Subj: Animals – bears. Family life. Hygiene.

Little Bear goes to kindergarten by Jutta Langreuter and Vera Sobat; ill. by Vera Sobat. Millbrook, 1997. ISBN 0-7613-0191-7 Subj: Animals – bears. Friendship. School – first day.

Langsen, Richard C. *When someone in the family drinks too much* ill. by Nicole Rubel. Dial, 1996. ISBN 0-8037-1687-7 Subj: Animals – bears. Family life. Illness – alcoholism.

Langstaff, John M. *Frog went a-courtin'* (A frog he would a-wooing go [folk-song])

Hot cross buns, and other old street cries (Hot cross buns, and other old street cries)

Oh, a-hunting we will go ill. by Nancy Winslow Parker. Atheneum, 1974. ISBN 0-689-50007-6 Subj: Folk and fairy tales. Music. Songs. Sports – hunting.

Ol' Dan Tucker ill. by Joe Krush. Harcourt, 1963. Subj: Folk and fairy tales. Music. Songs.

On Christmas day in the morning ill. by Antony Groves-Raines. Harcourt, 1959. Piano settings by Marshall Woodbridge. Subj: Folk and fairy tales. Holidays – Christmas. Music. Songs.

Over in the meadow ill. by Feodor Rojankovsky. Harcourt, 1957. Includes Over in the meadow (for voice and piano) by Marshall Woodbridge. ISBN 0-15-258854-X Subj: Animals. Counting, numbers. Folk and fairy tales. Songs.

Soldier, soldier, won't you marry me? ill. by Anita Lobel. Doubleday, 1972. Subj: Careers – military. Folk and fairy tales. Music. Songs.

The swapping boy ill. by Beth and Joe Krush. Harcourt, 1960. ISBN 0-15-283358-7 Subj: Activities – trading. Folk and fairy tales. Music. Songs.

The two magicians ill. by Fritz Eichenberg. Atheneum, 1973. Adapt. by John Langstaff from an ancient ballad. ISBN 0-689-30319-X Subj: Folk and fairy tales. Magic. Music. Songs. Witches.

What a morning! the Christmas story in Black spirituals (What a morning!)

Langstaff, Nancy. *A tiny baby for you* ill. by Suzanne Szasz. Harcourt, 1955. Subj: Babies.

Langston, Laura. *The fox's kettle* ill. by Victor Bosson. Orca, 1998. ISBN 1-55143-132-7 Subj: Animals – foxes. Folk and fairy tales. Foreign lands – Japan. Magic.

Langton, Jane. *The hedgehog boy: a Latvian folktale* ill. by Ilse Plume. HarperCollins, 1985. ISBN 0-06-023697-3 Subj: Character traits – honesty. Folk and fairy tales. Foreign lands – Latvia. Royalty. Weddings.

The queen's necklace: a Swedish folktale ill. by Ilse Plume. Hyperion, 1994. ISBN 0-7868-2007-1 Subj: Birds. Folk and fairy tales. Foreign lands – Sweden. Jewelry. Royalty.

Salt: from a Russian folktale (Afanas'ev, Aleksandr N.)

Lankford, Mary D. *Is it dark? Is it light?* ill. by Stacey Schuett. Knopf, 1991. ISBN 0-679-91579-6 Subj: Concepts – opposites. Moon.

Lanning, Rosemary. *Annie's dancing day* (Moers, Hermann)

The bear's Christmas (Moret, Brigitte Frey)

The blue monster (Ostheeren, Ingrid)

Camomile heads for home (Moers, Hermann)

Can we help you, Saint Nicholas? (Scheidl, Gerda Marie)

The Christmas visitor (Lussert, Anneliese)

The circus of mystery (Fazzi, Maura)

Coriander's Easter adventure (Ostheeren, Ingrid)

Happy birthday, Davy (Weninger, Brigitte)

Hopper hunts for spring (Pfister, Marcus)

Hopper's treetop adventure (Pfister, Marcus)

I'm the real Santa Claus! (Ostheeren, Ingrid)

Jonathan Mouse (Ostheeren, Ingrid)

Jonathan Mouse and the baby bird (Ostheeren, Ingrid)

Jonathan Mouse and the magic box (Ostheeren, Ingrid)

Jonathan Mouse, detective (Ostheeren, Ingrid)

Laura (Schroeder, Binette)

Little Man's lucky day (Velthuijs, Max)

Little polar bear and the husky pup (De Beer, Hans)

Look out, Cinder! (Lachner, Dorothea)

Lullaby for a newborn king (Wilkon, Józef)

Merry Christmas, Davy! (Weninger, Brigitte)

Penguin Pete and Little Tim (Pfister, Marcus)

Pickle and Patch (Scheidl, Gerda Marie)

Snail started it! (Reider, Katja)

The special gifts (Grosz, Peter)

The squirrel and the moon (Schmid, Eleonore)

The star tree (Cölle, Gisela)

What's the matter, Davy? (Weninger, Brigitte)

When I grow up – (Horn, Peter)

Why are you fighting, Davy? (Weninger, Brigitte)

Will you be my friend? (Korth-Sander, Irmtraut)

Will you mind the baby, Davy? (Weninger, Brigitte)

Lansdown, Brenda. *Galumph* ill. by Ernest Crichlow. Houghton Mifflin, 1963. Subj: Animals – cats. Ethnic groups in the U.S. Ethnic groups in the U.S. – African Americans. Pets.

Lansky, Bruce. *Sweet dreams* ill. by Vicki Wehrman. Meadowbrook Press, 1996. ISBN 0-671-53479-3 Subj: Bedtime. Lullabies. Songs.

Lansky, Vicki. *It's not your fault, KoKo Bear: a read-together book for parents and young children during divorce* ill. by Jane Prince. Book Peddlers, 1998. ISBN 0-916-77346-9 Subj: Animals – bears. Divorce. Family life.

Lanteigne, Helen. *The seven chairs* ill. by Maryann Kovalski. Orchard, 1998. ISBN 0-531-30110-9 Subj: Activities – making things. Furniture – chairs.

Lanton, Sandy. *Daddy's chair* ill. by Shelly O. Haas. Kar-Ben Copies, 1991. ISBN 0-929371-51-8 Subj: Death. Emotions – grief. Family life – fathers. Furniture – chairs.

Lapp, Carolyn. *The dentists' tools* ill. by George Overlie. Lerner, 1961. Subj: Careers – dentists.

Lapp, Eleanor. *The blueberry bears* ill. by Margot Apple. Albert Whitman, 1983. ISBN 0-8075-0796-2 Subj: Animals – bears. Food.

In the morning mist ill. by David Cunningham. Albert Whitman, 1978. ISBN 0-8075-3634-2 Subj: Family life – grandfathers. Morning. Sports – fishing.

The mice came in early this year ill. by David Cunningham. Albert Whitman, 1976. ISBN 0-8075-5111-2 Subj: Animals. Farms. Seasons – fall. Seasons – winter.

La Prise, Larry. *The hokey pokey* by Larry La Prise, Charles P. Macak, and Taftt Baker; ill. by Sheila Hamanaka. Simon & Schuster, 1996. ISBN 0-689-80519-5 Subj: Activities – dancing. Music.

Lapsley, Susan. *I am adopted* ill. by Michael Charlton. Bradbury, 1974. ISBN 0-8788-8075-5 Subj: Adoption. Family life.

Larios, Julie Hofstrand. *On the stairs* ill. by Mary Hofstrand Cornish. Front Street, 1999. ISBN 1-886910-34-0 Subj: Animals – mice. Counting, numbers. Rhyming text.

Laroche, Michel. *The snow rose* ill. by Sandra Laroche. Holiday, 1986. ISBN 0-8234-0594-X Subj: Character traits – cleverness. Folk and fairy tales. Royalty – princesses.

LaRochelle, David. *A Christmas guest* ill. by Martin Skoro. Carolrhoda, 1988. ISBN 0-87614-325-7 Subj: Character traits – kindness. Holidays – Christmas. Rhyming text.

The evening king ill. by Catherine Stock. Atheneum, 1993. ISBN 0-689-31640-2 Subj: Activities – playing. Imagination.

LaRose, Linda. *Jessica takes charge* ill. by Leanne Franson. Annick, 1999. ISBN 1-55037-563-6 Subj: Emotions – fear. Family life. Monsters. Night.

Larrick, Nancy. *Cats are cats* ill. by Ed Young. Putnam, 1988. ISBN 0-399-21517-4 Subj: Animals – cats. Poetry.

When the dark comes dancing: a bedtime poetry book ill. by John Wallner. Putnam, 1983. ISBN 0-399-20807-0 Subj: Bedtime. Night. Poetry.

Larry, Charles. *Peboan and Seegwun* ill. by author. Farrar, 1993. ISBN 0-374-35773-0 Subj: Folk and fairy tales. Indians of North America – Ojibwa. Seasons – spring. Seasons – winter.

Larsen, Hanne. *Don't forget Tom* ill. with photos. Crowell, 1978. ISBN 0-381-99554-2 Subj: Handicaps.

Lasell, Fen. *Fly away goose* ill. by author. Houghton Mifflin, 1965. Subj: Birds – geese. Eggs. Imagination.

Michael grows a wish ill. by author. Houghton Mifflin, 1974. ISBN 0-395-06880-0 Subj: Animals – horses, ponies. Behavior – wishing. Birthdays.

Laser, Michael. *The rain* ill. by Jeffrey Greene. Simon & Schuster, 1997. ISBN 0-689-80506-3 Subj: Memories, memory. Weather – rain.

Lasher, Faith B. *Hubert Hippo's world* ill. by Leonard Lee Rue, III. Childrens Pr., 1971. ISBN 0-516-03489-8 Subj: Animals – hippopotamuses.

Lasker, David. *The boy who loved music* ill. by Joe Lasker. Viking, 1979. ISBN 0-670-18385-7 Subj: Music. Royalty.

Lasker, Joe. *The do-something day* ill. by author. Viking, 1982. ISBN 0-670-27503-4 Subj: Behavior – running away.

He's my brother ill. by author. Albert Whitman, 1974. ISBN 0-8075-3218-5 Subj: Character traits – loyalty. Family life. Handicaps.

Lentil soup ill. by author. Albert Whitman, 1977. ISBN 0-8075-4438-8 Subj: Activities – cooking. Counting, numbers. Days of the week, months of the year. Food.

Mothers can do anything ill. by author. Albert Whitman, 1972. ISBN 0-8075-5287-9 Subj: Activities – working. Careers. Family life – mothers.

Nick joins in ill. by author. Albert Whitman, 1980. ISBN 0-8075-5612-2 Subj: Handicaps – physical handicaps. School – first day.

Rabbit finds a way (Delton, Judy)

A tournament of knights ill. by author. Crowell, 1986. ISBN 0-690-04542-5 Subj: Behavior – fighting, arguing. Knights.

Laskin, Pamela L. *Wish upon a star: a story for children with a parent who is mentally ill* by Pamela L. Laskin and Addie Alexander Moskowitz; ill. by Margo Lemieux. Magination Pr., 1991. ISBN 0-945354-30-4 Subj: Emotions. Family life. Illness.

Laskowski, Janina Domanska. *see* Domanska, Janina

Laskowski, Jerzy. *Master of the royal cats* ill. by Janina Domanska. Seabury Pr., 1965. Subj: Animals – cats. Animals – dogs. Foreign lands – Africa. Foreign lands – Egypt. Royalty.

Lasky, Kathryn. *Agatha's alphabet, with her very own dictionary* (Floyd, Lucy)

A baby for Max photos by Christopher G. Knight. Scribners, 1984. ISBN 0-684-18064-2 Subj: Babies. Family life – new sibling. Sibling rivalry.

Baby love ill. by Jennifer Plecas. Candlewick, 2001. ISBN 1-56402-679-5 Subj: Babies.

The emperor's old clothes ill. by David Catrow. Harcourt, 1999. ISBN 0-15-200384-3 Subj: Careers – farmers. Clothing. Folk and fairy tales. Humor. Royalty – emperors.

Fourth of July bear ill. by Helen Cogancherry. Morrow, 1991. ISBN 0-688-08288-2 Subj: Animals – bears. Friendship. Holidays – Fourth of July. Parades.

The Gates of the Wind ill. by Janet Stevens. Harcourt, 1995. ISBN 0-15-204264-4 Subj: Activities – traveling. Mountains. Weather – wind.

I have an aunt on Marlborough Street ill. by Susan Guevara. Macmillan, 1992. ISBN 0-02-751701-2 Subj: City. Family life – aunts, uncles. Friendship.

I have four names for my grandfather ill. by Christopher G. Knight. Little, 1976. ISBN 0-316-51520-5 Subj: Emotions – love. Family life – grandfathers.

Lunch bunnies ill. by Marylin Hafner. Little, 1996. ISBN 0-316-51525-6 Subj: Animals – rabbits. Behavior – worrying. School – first day.

Marven of the Great North Woods ill. by Kevin Hawkes. Harcourt, 1997. ISBN 0-15-200104-2 Subj: Careers – accountants. Careers – lumberjacks. Forest, woods. Friendship. Illness.

My island grandma ill. by Emily Arnold McCully. Warne, 1979. ISBN 0-7232-6159-8 Subj: Family life – grandmothers. Islands. Seasons – summer.

My island grandma ill. by Amy Schwartz. Morrow, 1993. ISBN 0-688-07948-2 Subj: Family life – grandmothers. Islands. Seasons – summer.

Pond year ill. by Mike Bostock. Candlewick, 1995. ISBN 1-56402-187-4 Subj: Activities – playing. Friendship. Lakes, ponds. Nature.

Science fair bunnies ill. by Marylin Hafner. Candlewick, 2000. ISBN 0-7636-0729-0 Subj: Animals – rabbits. Fairs. School. Science.

Sea swan ill. by Catherine Stock. Macmillan, 1988. ISBN 0-02-751700-4 Subj: Behavior – seeking better things. Old age. Sports – swimming.

Show and tell bunnies ill. by Marylin Hafner. Candlewick, 1998. ISBN 0-7636-0396-1 Subj: Animals – rabbits. School. Spiders.

The solo ill. by Bobette McCarthy. Macmillan, 1994. ISBN 0-02-751664-4 Subj: Activities – dancing. Character traits – confidence. Friendship. School.

Sophie and Rose ill. by Wendy Anderson Halperin. Candlewick, 1998. ISBN 0-7636-0459-3 Subj: Family life. Toys – dolls.

Starring Lucille ill. by Marylin Hafner. Crown, 2001. ISBN 0-517-80038-1 Subj: Activities – dancing. Animals – pigs. Ballet. Birthdays. Family life – brothers and sisters.

The tantrum ill. by Bobette McCarthy. Macmillan, 1993. ISBN 0-02-751661-X Subj: Emotions – anger. Family life.

Laslett, Stephanie. *The monster party: with six spooky holograms* ill. by Nigel McMullen. Dutton, 1996. ISBN 0-525-45691-0 Subj: Monsters. Parties. Witches.

Lass, Bonnie. *Who took the cookies from the cookie jar?* by Bonnie Lass and Philemon Sturges; ill. by Ashley Wolff. Little, 2000. ISBN 0-316-82016-4 Subj: Animals. Food. Insects – ants. Mystery stories. Rhyming text.

Lassen, Cary Pillo. *The big busy building* (Reasoner, Charles)

Lasson, Robert. *Orange Oliver: the kitten who wore glasses* ill. by Chuck Hayden. McKay, 1957. Subj: Animals – cats. Farms. Glasses. Senses – seeing.

Latham, Hugh. *Mother Goose in French: Poesies de la vraie Mere Oie* (Mother Goose)

Lathrop, Dorothy Pulis. *An angel in the woods* ill. by author. Macmillan, 1947. Subj: Angels. Holidays – Christmas.

Puppies for keeps ill. by author. Macmillan, 1943. Subj: Animals – dogs. Pets.

Who goes there? ill. by author. Macmillan, 1935. Subj: Activities – picnicking. Animals. Character traits – kindness to animals. Seasons – winter.

Latimer, Jim. *The fox under first base* ill. by Lisa McCue. Scribners, 1991. ISBN 0-684-19053-2 Subj: Animals – bears. Animals – foxes. Careers – detectives. Sports – baseball.

Going the moose way home ill. by Donald Carrick. Scribners, 1988. ISBN 0-684-18890-2 Subj: Animals – moose. Forest, woods. Friendship.

The Irish piper ill. by John O'Brien. Scribners, 1991. ISBN 0-684-19130-X Subj: Animals – rats. Behavior – trickery. Folk and fairy tales. Foreign lands – Germany. Poetry.

James Bear and the goose gathering ill. by Betsy Franco-Feeney. Scribners, 1994. ISBN 0-684-19526-7 Subj: Activities – singing. Animals. Animals – bears. Behavior – trickery. Birds – geese.

James Bear's pie ill. by Betsy Franco-Feeney. Scribners, 1992. ISBN 0-684-19226-8 Subj: Activities – cooking. Animals – bears. Animals – skunks. Birds – crows.

Moose and friends ill. by C. S. Ewing. Scribners, 1993. ISBN 0-684-19335-3 Subj: Animals. Animals – moose.

Snail and Buffalo ill. by Tom Curry. Orchard, 1995. ISBN 0-531-08790-5 Subj: Animals – buffaloes. Animals – snails. Character traits – individuality.

When moose was young ill. by Donald Carrick. Scribners, 1990. ISBN 0-684-18932-1 Subj: Animals. Animals – moose.

Lattimore, Deborah Nourse. *Cinderhazel: the Cinderella of Halloween* ill. by author. Scholastic, 1997. ISBN 0-590-20232-4 Subj: Character traits – cleanliness. Royalty – princes. Witches.

The dragon's robe ill. by author. HarperCollins, 1990. ISBN 0-06-023723-6 Subj: Activities – weaving. Character traits – generosity. Character traits – selfishness. Dragons. Folk and fairy tales. Foreign lands – China.

Frida Maria: a story of the Old Southwest ill. by author. Browndeer, 1994. ISBN 0-15-276636-7 Subj: Family life. Sex roles.

I wonder what's under there? ill. by author; paper engineering by David A. Carter. Browndeer, 1998. ISBN 0-15-276652-9 Subj: Clothing. Format, unusual – toy and movable books.

The lady with the ship on her head ill. by author. Harcourt, 1990. ISBN 0-15-243525-5 Subj: Clothing – hats. Contests. Humor.

The prince and the golden ax: a Minoan tale ill. by author. HarperCollins, 1988. ISBN 0-06-023716-3 Subj: Character traits – willfulness. Folk and fairy tales. Royalty – princes.

Punga the goddess of ugly ill. by author. Harcourt, 1993. ISBN 0-15-292862-6 Subj: Activities – dancing. Behavior – misbehavior. Family life – sisters. Folk and fairy tales. Foreign lands – New Zealand. Multiple births – twins.

The sailor who captured the sea: a story of the Book of Kells ill. by author. HarperCollins, 1991. ISBN 0-06-023711-2 Subj: Activities – reading. Activities – writing. Character traits – persistence. Foreign lands – Ireland. Religion. Sailors.

Why there is no arguing in heaven: a Mayan myth ill. by author. Harper, 1989. ISBN 0-06-023718-X Subj: Creation. Folk and fairy tales. Indians of Central America – Maya.

Lattin, Anne. *Peter's policeman* ill. by Gertrude E. Espenscheid. Follett, 1958. Subj: Careers – police officers.

Lauber, Patricia. *Be a friend to trees* ill. by Holly Keller. HarperCollins, 1994. ISBN 0-06-021529-1 Subj: Ecology. Science. Trees.

Get ready for robots! ill. by True Kelley. HarperCollins, 1987. ISBN 0-690-04578-6 Subj: Robots.

How we learned the earth is round ill. by Megan Lloyd. Crowell, 1990. ISBN 0-690-04863-3 Subj: Earth. Science.

An octopus is amazing ill. by Holly Keller. Crowell, 1990. ISBN 0-690-04862-9 Subj: Octopuses.

Snakes are hunters ill. by Holly Keller. HarperCollins, 1988. ISBN 0-690-04630-8 Subj: Reptiles – snakes. Science.

What's hatching out of that egg? ill. with photos. Crown, 1979. ISBN 0-517-53724-9 Subj: Eggs. Science.

Who eats what? ill. by Holly Keller. HarperCollins, 1995. ISBN 0-06-022982-9 Subj: Ecology. Food. Science.

You're aboard spaceship Earth ill. by Holly Keller. HarperCollins, 1996. ISBN 0-06-024408-9 Subj: Earth. Space and space ships.

Laurence, Margaret. *The Christmas birthday story* ill. by Helen Lucas. Knopf, 1980. ISBN 0-394-94361-9 Subj: Birthdays. Holidays – Christmas. Religion – Nativity.

Laurencin, Geneviève. *I wish I were* trans. from German by Andrea Mernan; ill. by Ulises Wensell. Putnam, 1987. ISBN 0-399-21416-X Subj: Animals. Behavior – bullying. Behavior – wishing.

Laurin, Anne. *Little things* ill. by Marcia Sewall. Atheneum, 1978. ISBN 0-689-30623-7 Subj: Activities – knitting. Character traits – patience. Humor.

Perfect crane ill. by Charles Mikolaycak. Harper-Collins, 1981. ISBN 0-06-023744-9 Subj: Birds – cranes. Foreign lands – Japan. Magic.

Lauture, Denizé. *Father and son* ill. by Jonathan Green. Philomel, 1992. ISBN 0-399-21867-X Subj: Ethnic groups in the U.S. – African Americans. Family life – fathers. Family life – sons. Poetry.

Running the road to ABC ill. by Reynold Ruffins. Simon & Schuster, 1996. ISBN 0-689-80507-1 Subj: ABC books. Foreign lands – Haiti. School.

Lavies, Bianca. *Lily pad pond* photos by author. Dutton, 1989. ISBN 0-525-44483-1 Subj: Animals. Nature. Trees.

Tree trunk traffic photos by author. Dutton, 1989. ISBN 0-525-44495-5 Subj: Animals. Insects. Nature. Trees.

Lavis, Steve. *Cock-a-doodle-doo: a farmyard counting book* ill. by author. Dutton, 1997. ISBN 0-525-67542-6 Subj: Animals. Counting, numbers. Noise, sounds.

Jump! ill. by author. Lodestar, 1998. ISBN 0-525-67578-7 Subj: Activities. Animals. Behavior – imitation. Birds.

Lawlor, Laurie. *The biggest pest on Eighth Avenue* ill. by Cynthia Fisher. Holiday, 1997. ISBN 0-8234-1321-7 Subj: Family life – brothers and sisters. Theater.

Second-grade dog ill. by Gioia Fiammenghi. Albert Whitman, 1990. ISBN 0-8075-7280-2 Subj: Animals – dogs. Behavior – boredom. School.

Lawrence, James. *Binky Brothers and the fearless four* ill. by Leonard P. Kessler. HarperCollins, 1970. Subj: Careers – detectives. Multiple births – twins. Mystery stories.

Binky Brothers, detectives ill. by Leonard P. Kessler. HarperCollins, 1968. ISBN 0-06-023759-7 Subj: Careers – detectives. Multiple births – twins. Mystery stories.

Lawrence, John. *The giant of Grabbist* ill. by author. White, 1969. Subj: Foreign lands – England. Giants.

Pope Leo's elephant ill. by author. Collins-World, 1970, 1969. Subj: Animals – elephants. Fire. Foreign lands – Vatican City.

Rabbit and pork: rhyming talk ill. by author. Crowell, 1976. ISBN 0-690-00973-9 Subj: Animals – cats. Animals – pigs. Animals – rabbits. Rhyming text.

Lawrence, Michael (Michael C.). *Baby loves* ill. by Adrian Reynolds. DK, 1999. ISBN 0-7894-3410-5 Subj: Babies. Emotions – love. Format, unusual – board books.

Lawson, Annetta. *The lucky yak* ill. by Allen Say. Houghton Mifflin, 1980. ISBN 0-395-29523-8 Subj: Activities – babysitting. Animals – yaks. Birds – puffins.

Lawson, Barbara Spilman. *Jambo, watoto!* (Heatwole, Marsha)

Lawson, Carol. *Teddy bear, teddy bear* ill. by author. Dial, 1991. ISBN 0-8037-0970-6 Subj: Activities. Nursery rhymes. Toys – bears.

Lawson, Julie. *Bear on the train* ill. by Brian Dienes. Kids Can Pr., 1999. ISBN 1-55074-560-3 Subj: Animals – bears. Hibernation. Trains.

The dragon's pearl ill. by Paul Morin. Clarion, 1993. ISBN 0-395-63623-X Subj: Dragons. Folk and fairy tales. Foreign lands – China.

Emma and the silk train ill. by Paul Mombourquette. Kids Can Pr., 1998. ISBN 1-55074-388-0 Subj: Accidents. Trains. Transportation.

Midnight in the mountains ill. by Sheena Lott. Orca, 1999. ISBN 1-55143-113-0 Subj: Activities – vacationing. Family life. Mountains. Noise, sounds. Seasons – winter.

Lawson, Robert. *They were strong and good* ill. by author. Viking, 1940. ISBN 0-670-69949-7 Subj: Caldecott award books. Family life. U.S. history – frontier and pioneer life.

Lawston, Lisa. *Can you hop?* ill. by Ed Vere. Orchard, 1999. ISBN 0-53130-131-1 Subj: Activities. Animals – rabbits. Friendship. Frogs and toads.

A pair of red sneakers ill. by B. B. Sams. Orchard, 1998. ISBN 0-531-33104-0 Subj: Clothing – shoes. Rhyming text.

Layton, Aviva. *The squeakers* ill. by Louise Scott. Mosaic Pr., 1982. Subj: Animals – mice. Family life. Theater.

Layton, Neal. *Smile if you're human* ill. by author. Dial, 1998. ISBN 0-8037-2381-4 Subj: Aliens. Animals. Animals – gorillas. Family life.

Lazard, Naomi. *What Amanda saw* ill. by Paul O. Zelinsky. Greenwillow, 1981. ISBN 0-688-84272-0 Subj: Activities – vacationing. Animals. Parties.

Lazy Jack. *Lazy Jack* ill. by Bert Dodson. Troll, 1979. ISBN 0-89375-123-5 Subj: Character traits – laziness. Cumulative tales. Folk and fairy tales.

Lazy Jack ill. by Tony Ross. Dial, 1986. ISBN 0-8037-0275-2 Subj: Character traits – laziness. Cumulative tales. Folk and fairy tales.

Lazy Jack ill. by Kurt Werth. Viking, 1970. ISBN 0-670-42146-4 Subj: Character traits – laziness. Cumulative tales. Folk and fairy tales.

Lazy Jack ill. by Barry Wilkinson. World, 1969. Story from Joseph Jacob's English fairy tales. Subj: Character traits – foolishness. Character traits – laziness. Folk and fairy tales.

Leach, Aroline Arnett Beecher. *The miracle of the mountain* (Kipling, Rudyard)

Leach, Michael. *Rabbits* ill. with photos. Global Lib. Mktg. Serv., 1984. ISBN 0-7136-2387-X Subj: Animals – rabbits. Nature. Science.

Leach, Norman. *My wicked stepmother* ill. by Jane Browne. Macmillan, 1993. ISBN 0-02-754700-0 Subj: Behavior – misbehavior. Family life – step families. Folk and fairy tales.

Leaf, Margaret. *Eyes of the dragon* ill. by Ed Young. Lothrop, 1987. ISBN 0-688-06156-7 Subj: Activities – painting. Careers – artists. Character traits – stubbornness. Dragons. Foreign lands – China.

Leaf, Munro. *Boo, who used to be scared of the dark* ill. by author. Random House, 1948. Subj: Bedtime. Emotions – fear. Night.

A flock of watchbirds ill. by author. Lippincott, 1946. Subj: Behavior – misbehavior. Etiquette.

Gordon, the goat ill. by author. Lippincott, 1944. Subj: Animals – goats.

Grammar can be fun ill. by author. Lippincott, 1934. Subj: Language.

Health can be fun ill. by author. Stokes, 1943. Subj: Health and fitness.

How to behave and why ill. by author. Lippincott, 1946. Subj: Etiquette.

Manners can be fun ill. by author. 3rd ed. Lippincott, 1985. ISBN 0-397-32118-X Subj: Etiquette.

Noodle ill. by author. Four Winds, 1965. Subj: Animals – dogs. Self-concept.

Robert Francis Weatherbee ill. by author. Lippincott, 1935. ISBN 0-208-02211-2 Subj: School.

Safety can be fun ill. by author. 3rd ed. Lippincott, 1961. ISBN 0-06-443111-8 Subj: Safety.

The story of Ferdinand the bull ill. by Robert Lawson. Viking, 1936. Subj: Animals – bulls, cows. Character traits – individuality. Foreign lands – Spain. Violence, nonviolence.

Wee Gillis ill. by Robert Lawson. Puffin, 1985, c1938. ISBN 0-14-050535-0 Subj: Caldecott award honor books. Foreign lands – Scotland.

Leander, Ed. *Q is for crazy* ill. by Józef Sumichrast. Dial-Delacorte, 1977. ISBN 0-8252-7512-1 Subj: ABC books.

Lear, Edward. *A was once an apple pie* ill. by Julie Lacome. Candlewick, 1992. ISBN 1-56402-000-2 Subj: ABC books. Poetry.

ABC ill. by author. McGraw-Hill, 1965. Subj: ABC books. Poetry.

A book of nonsense ill. by author. Metropolitan Museum of Art-Viking, 1980. ISBN 0-670-18011-4 Subj: Humor. Poetry.

The dong with a luminous nose ill. by Edward Gorey. Adama, 1986. ISBN 0-915-36146-9 Subj: Humor. Poetry.

An Edward Lear alphabet ill. by Carol Newsom. Lothrop, 1983. ISBN 0-688-00965-4 Subj: ABC books. Poetry.

An Edward Lear alphabet ill. by Vladimir Radunsky. HarperCollins, 1999. ISBN 0-06-028114-6 Subj: ABC books. Poetry.

Edward Lear's ABC: alphabet rhymes for children ill. by Carol Pike. Merrimack, 1986. ISBN 0-88162-219-2 Subj: ABC books. Poetry.

Edward Lear's nonsense book ill. by Tony Palazzo. Doubleday, 1956. Subj: Humor. Music. Poetry.

Hilary Knight's the owl and the pussy-cat (Knight, Hilary)

The jumblies ill. by Emma Crosby. Merrimack, 1986. ISBN 0-88162-185-4 Subj: Poetry.

The jumblies ill. by Ted Rand. Putnam, 1989. ISBN 0-399-21632-4 Subj: Poetry.

A Learical lexicon comp. by Myra Cohn Livingston; ill. by Joseph Low. Atheneum, 1985. ISBN 0-689-50318-0 Subj: Humor. Poetry.

Lear's nonsense verses ill. by Tomi Ungerer. Grosset, 1967. Subj: Humor. Poetry.

Limericks ill. by Lois Ehlert. Collins-World, 1965. Subj: Poetry.

The new vestments ill. by DeLoss McGraw. Simon & Schuster, 1995. ISBN 0-671-50089-9 Subj: Clothing. Food. Poetry.

Nonsense alphabet ill. by Richard Scarry. Doubleday, 1962. Subj: ABC books. Poetry.

The nutcrackers and the sugar-tongs ill. by Marcia Sewall. Little, 1978. ISBN 0-316-78181-9 Subj: Humor. Poetry.

Of pelicans and pussycats ill. by Jill Newton. Dial, 1990. ISBN 0-8037-0728-2 Subj: Animals – cats. Birds – pelicans. Clothing – hats. Poetry.

The owl and the pussy cat ill. by Ian Beck. Atheneum, 1996. ISBN 0-689-81032-6 Subj: Animals – cats. Birds – owls. Poetry.

The owl and the pussycat ill. by Jan Brett. Putnam, 1991. ISBN 0-399-21925-0 Subj: Animals – cats. Birds – owls. Poetry.

The owl and the pussycat ill. by Lorinda Bryan Cauley. Putnam, 1986. ISBN 0-399-21254-X Subj: Animals – cats. Birds – owls. Poetry.

The owl and the pussy-cat ill. by Barbara Cooney. Little, 1969. First pub. in 1961. Subj: Animals – cats. Birds – owls. Poetry.

The owl and the pussycat ill. by Emma Crosby. Merrimack, 1986. ISBN 0-88162-183-8 Subj: Animals – cats. Birds – owls. Poetry.

The owl and the pussy-cat ill. by William Pène Du Bois. Doubleday, 1961. Subj: Animals – cats. Birds – owls. Poetry.

The owl and the pussycat ill. by Lori Farbanish. Putnam, 1988. ISBN 0-448-10229-3 Subj: Animals – cats. Birds – owls. Poetry.

The owl and the pussy-cat ill. by Gwen Fulton. Atheneum, 1977. ISBN 0-224-01400-5 Subj: Animals – cats. Birds – owls. Poetry.

The owl and the pussycat ill. by Paul Galdone. Houghton Mifflin, 1987. ISBN 0-89919-505-9 Subj: Animals – cats. Birds – owls. Poetry.

The owl and the pussy-cat ill. by Elaine Muis. Grosset, 1977. ISBN 0-448-13006-8 Subj: Animals – cats. Birds – owls. Poetry.

The owl and the pussycat ill. by Erica Rutherford. Tundra, 1986. ISBN 0-88776-181-X Subj: Animals – cats. Birds – owls. Poetry.

The owl and the pussycat ill. by Janet Stevens. Holiday, 1983. ISBN 0-8231-0474-9 Subj: Animals – cats. Birds – owls. Poetry.

The owl and the pussycat ill. by Louise Voce. Lothrop, 1991. ISBN 0-688-09537-2 Subj: Animals – cats. Birds – owls. Poetry.

The owl and the pussycat ill. by Colin West. Warne, 1988. ISBN 0-7232-3541-4 Subj: Animals – cats. Birds – owls. Poetry.

The owl and the pussy-cat: and other nonsense ill. by Owen Wood. Viking, 1979. ISBN 0-670-53314-9 Subj: Animals – cats. Birds – owls. Poetry.

The pelican chorus ill. by Harold Berson. Parents, 1967. Subj: Birds – pelicans. Humor. Music. Poetry. Songs.

The pelican chorus and the quangle wangle's hat ill. by Kevin W. Maddison. Viking, 1981. ISBN 0-670-54613-5 Subj: Birds – pelicans. Humor. Music. Poetry. Songs.

The pobble who has no toes ill. by Emma Crosby. Merrimack, 1986. ISBN 0-88162-184-6 Subj: Humor. Poetry.

The pobble who has no toes ill. by Kevin W. Maddison. Viking, 1977. ISBN 0-904-06912-5 Subj: Humor. Poetry.

The quangle wangle's hat ill. by Emma Crosby. Merrimack, 1986. ISBN 0-88162-182-X Subj: Clothing – hats. Humor. Poetry.

The quangle wangle's hat ill. by Helen Oxenbury. Watts, 1969. ISBN 0-434-95596-5 Subj: Clothing – hats. Humor. Poetry.

The quangle wangle's hat ill. by Janet Stevens. Harcourt, 1988. ISBN 0-15-264450-4 Subj: Clothing – hats. Humor. Poetry.

Two laughable lyrics: The pobble who has no toes, [and] The quangle wangle's hat ill. by Paul Galdone. Putnam, 1966. Subj: Clothing – hats. Humor. Poetry.

Whizz! ill. by Janina Domanska. Macmillan, 1973. Completed by Ogden Nash. Subj: Cumulative tales. Humor. Poetry.

Lears, Laurie. *Ian's walk: a story about autism* ill. by Karen Ritz. Albert Whitman, 1998. ISBN 0-8075-3480-3 Subj: Behavior – lost. Family life – brothers and sisters. Handicaps – autism. Senses.

Waiting for Mr. Goose ill. by Karen Ritz. Albert Whitman, 1999. ISBN 0-8075-8628-5 Subj: Birds – geese. Character traits – kindness to animals. Handicaps.

Leatham, E. Rutter (Mrs.). *A child's grace* (Burdekin, Harold)

Leavitt, Melvin. *Grena and the magic pomegranate* ill. by Beth Wright. Carolrhoda, 1994. ISBN 0-87614-760-0 Subj: Folk and fairy tales. Food.

Leavy, Una. *Good-bye, Papa* ill. by Jennifer Eachus. Orchard, 1996. ISBN 0-531-09545-2 Subj: Death. Emotions – grief. Family life – grandfathers.

Harry's stormy night ill. by Peter Utton. Margaret K. McElderry, 1995. ISBN 0-689-50625-2 Subj: Activities. Power failures. Rhyming text. Weather – storms.

Lebentritt, Julia. *The Kooken* by Julia Lebentritt and Richard Ploetz; ill. by Clément Oubrerie. Holt, 1992. ISBN 0-8050-1749-6 Subj: Animals – dogs. Family life – grandparents. Music. Problem solving.

Leblanc, Anne. *Benjamin finds a friend* ill. by author. Sterling, 1999. ISBN 0-8069-1923-X Subj: Animals – bears. Friendship. Toys – bears.

Benjamin in the snow ill. by author. Sterling, 1999. ISBN 0-8069-1931-0 Subj: Animals – bears. Family life – fathers. Format, unusual – board books. Weather – snow.

Benjamin takes care of Mommy ill. by author. Sterling, 1999. ISBN 0-8069-1933-7 Subj: Animals – bears. Family life – mothers. Format, unusual – board books.

Benjamin's busy day ill. by author. Sterling, 1999. ISBN 0-8069-1935-3 Subj: Activities. Animals – bears. Format, unusual – board books.

Shopping with Benjamin ill. by author. Sterling, 1997. ISBN 0-8069-0395-3 Subj: Food. Format, unusual – board books. Shopping. Toys – bears.

Lebrun, Claude. *Little Brown Bear does not want to eat* ill. by Danièle Bour. Childrens Pr., 1995. ISBN 0-516-07823-2 Subj: Animals – bears. Behavior – growing up. Behavior – sharing. Food.

Little Brown Bear learns to share ill. by Danièle Bour. Childrens, 1995. ISBN 0-516-07822-4 Subj: Activities – playing. Animals – bears. Behavior – growing up. Behavior – sharing.

Lecher, Doris. *Angelita's magic yarn* ill. by author. Farrar, 1992. ISBN 0-374-30332-0 Subj: Activities – knitting. Character traits – luck. Magic.

Lechner, Susan. *Followers of the north star: rhymes about African American heroes, heroines, and historical times* (Altman, Susan)

Lecourt, Nancy. *Abracadabra to zigzag* ill. by Barbara Lehman. Lothrop, 1991. ISBN 0-688-09481-3 Subj: ABC books.

Lee, Dennis. *Alligator pie* ill. by Frank Newfeld. Houghton Mifflin, 1975. ISBN 0-395-21596-X Subj: Nursery rhymes. Poetry.

Lee, Hector Viveros. *I had a hippopotamus* ill. by author. Lee & Low, 1996. ISBN 1-880000-28-8 Subj: Animals – hippopotamuses. Food.

Lee, Jeanne M. *Ba-Nam* ill. by author. Holt, 1987. ISBN 0-8050-0169-7 Subj: Character traits – kindness. Foreign lands – Vietnam. Weather – storms.

I once was a monkey: stories Buddha told ill. by author. Farrar, 1999. ISBN 0-374-33548-6 Subj: Animals. Folk and fairy tales. Religion.

Legend of the Li River: an ancient Chinese tale ill. by author. Holt, 1983. ISBN 0-03-063523-3 Subj: Folk and fairy tales. Foreign lands – China. Rocks.

The legend of the milky way ill. by author. Holt, 1982. ISBN 0-03-060439-7 Subj: Folk and fairy tales. Foreign lands – China. Stars.

Silent lotus ill. by author. Farrar, 1991. ISBN 0-374-36911-9 Subj: Activities – dancing. Foreign lands – Cambodia. Handicaps – deafness. Handicaps – physical handicaps.

The song of Mu Lan ill. by author. Front Street, 1995. ISBN 1-886910-00-6 Subj: Careers – military. Character traits – bravery. Folk and fairy tales. Foreign lands – China.

Toad is the uncle of heaven: a Vietnamese folk tale ill. by reteller. Holt, 1985. ISBN 0-03-004652-1 Subj: Animals. Folk and fairy tales. Frogs and toads. Royalty. Weather – rain.

Lee, Milly. *Nim and the war effort* ill. by Yangsook Choi. Farrar, 1997. ISBN 0-374-22262-2 Subj: Ethnic groups in the U.S. – Chinese Americans. Family life. U.S. history. War.

Lee, Sandra. *Giant pandas* ill. by author. Child's World, 1993. ISBN 1-56766-009-6 Subj: Animals – endangered animals. Animals – pandas.

Lee, Tzexa Cherta. *Jouanah: a Hmong Cinderella* (Coburn, Jewell Reinhart)

Leech, Bryan Jeffery. *John Jeremy Colton designed and ill.* by Byron Glaser and Sandra Higashi.

Hyperion, 1994. ISBN 1-56282-651-4 Subj: Character traits – being different. Fire. Rhyming text.

Leech, Jay. *Bright Fawn and me* by Jay Leech and Zane Spencer; ill. by Glo Coalson. Crowell, 1979. ISBN 0-690-03938-7 Subj: Fairs. Family life – sisters. Indians of North America – Cheyenne (Sioux). Sibling rivalry.

Leedahl, Shelley A. (Shelley Ann). *The bone talker* ill. by Bill Slavin. Red Deer Pr., 1999. ISBN 0-88995-214-0 Subj: Family life – grandmothers. Memories, memory. Old age. Quilts.

Leedy, Loreen. *Blast off to Earth!* ill. by author. Holiday, 1992. ISBN 0-8234-0973-2 Subj: Activities – traveling. School. Space and space ships.

The bunny play ill. by author. Holiday, 1988. ISBN 0-8234-0679-2 Subj: Animals – rabbits. Theater.

A dragon Christmas: things to make and do ill. by author. Holiday, 1988. ISBN 0-8234-0716-0 Subj: Activities. Activities – making things. Dragons. Holidays – Christmas. Rhyming text.

The dragon Halloween party ill. by author. Holiday, 1986. ISBN 0-8234-0611-3 Subj: Dragons. Holidays – Halloween. Parties. Rhyming text.

The dragon Thanksgiving feast ill. by author. Holiday, 1990. ISBN 0-8234-0828-0 Subj: Dragons. Food. Holidays – Thanksgiving. Rhyming text.

The edible pyramid: good eating every day ill. by author. Holiday, 1994. ISBN 0-8234-1126-5 Subj: Food. Health and fitness.

Fraction action ill. by author. Holiday, 1994. ISBN 0-8234-1109-5 Subj: Animals. Counting, numbers. School.

The Furry News ill. by author. Holiday, 1990. ISBN 0-8234-0793-4 Subj: Activities – writing. Animals. Careers – journalists. Communication. Communities, neighborhoods.

The great trash bash ill. by author. Holiday, 1991. ISBN 0-8234-0869-8 Subj: Animals. Ecology.

How humans make friends ill. by author. Holiday, 1996. ISBN 0-8234-1223-7 Subj: Friendship. Space and space ships.

Messages in the mailbox ill. by author. Holiday, 1991. ISBN 0-8234-0889-2 Subj: Activities – writing. Letters, cards. School.

Mission – addition ill. by author. Holiday, 1997. ISBN 0-8234-1307-1 Subj: Animals. Counting, numbers. School.

The monster money book ill. by author. Holiday, 1992. ISBN 0-8234-0922-8 Subj: Clubs, gangs. Money. Monsters.

A number of dragons ill. by author. Holiday, 1985. ISBN 0-8234-0568-0 Subj: Counting, numbers. Dragons. Rhyming text.

Pingo the plaid panda ill. by author. Holiday, 1989. ISBN 0-8234-0727-6 Subj: Animals – pandas. Character traits – being different. Friendship.

Postcards from Pluto ill. by author. Holiday, 1993. ISBN 0-8234-1000-5 Subj: Astronomy. Space and space ships.

The potato party and other troll tales ill. by author. Holiday, 1989. ISBN 0-8234-0761-6 Subj: Mythical creatures – trolls.

The race ill. by author. Scott Foresman, 1993. ISBN 0-673-80337-6 Subj: Animals – rabbits. Animals – raccoons. Sports – racing.

There's a frog in my throat: 312 animal sayings from the horse's mouth by Loreen Leedy and Pat Street; ill. by Loreen Leedy. Winslow, 2001. ISBN 1-89081-724-4 Subj: Animals. Language.

Tracks in the sand ill. by author. Doubleday, 1993. ISBN 0-385-30658-X Subj: Eggs. Reptiles – turtles, tortoises. Sea and seashore.

2 x 2 = boo! a set of spooky multiplication stories ill. by author. Holiday, 1995. ISBN 0-8234-1190-7 Subj: Counting, numbers. Holidays – Halloween. Witches.

Who's who in my family? ill. by author. Holiday, 1995. ISBN 0-8234-1151-6 Subj: Animals. Family life.

Leemis, Ralph. *Mister Momboo's hat* ill. by Jeni Bassett. Dutton, 1991. ISBN 0-525-65045-8 Subj: Animals – hippopotamuses. Circular tales. Clothing – hats. Rhyming text. Weather – wind.

Smart dog ill. by Chris L. Demarest. Caroline House, 1993. ISBN 1-56397-109-7 Subj: Animals – dogs. Behavior – wishing. Imagination.

Leeton, Will C. *The Tower of Babel* ill. by Jeffrey K. Lindberg. Dandelion, 1979. ISBN 0-89799-141-9 Subj: Language. Religion.

Le Gallienne, Eva. *The little mermaid* (Andersen, H. C. [Hans Christian])

The nightingale (Andersen, H. C. [Hans Christian])

The snow queen (Andersen, H. C. [Hans Christian])

Legg, Gerald. *From caterpillar to butterfly* ill. by Carolyn Scrace; created and designed by David Salariya. Watts, 1998. ISBN 0-531-14493-3 Subj: Insects – butterflies, caterpillars. Metamorphosis.

From egg to chicken ill. by Carolyn Scrace; created and designed by David Salariya. Watts, 1998. ISBN 0-531-14490-9 Subj: Birds – chickens. Eggs. Science.

From seed to sunflower ill. by Carolyn Scrace; created and designed by David Salariya. Watts, 1998. ISBN 0-531-14492-5 Subj: Flowers. Gardens, gardening. Science. Seeds.

From tadpole to frog ill. by Carolyn Scrace; created and designed by David Salariya. Watts, 1998. ISBN 0-531-15335-5 Subj: Frogs and toads.

Legge, David. *Bamboozled* ill. by author. Scholastic, 1994. ISBN 0-5904-7989-X Subj: Family life – grandfathers.

Le Guin, Ursula K. *Fish soup* ill. by Patrick Wynne. Atheneum, 1992. ISBN 0-689-31733-6 Subj: Family life. Gender roles. Imagination. Prejudice.

A ride on the red mare's back ill. by Julie Downing. Watts, 1992. ISBN 0-531-08591-0 Subj: Animals – horses, ponies. Character traits – bravery. Family life – brothers and sisters. Folk and fairy tales. Mythical creatures – trolls.

Solomon Leviathan's nine hundred and thirty-first trip around the world ill. by Alicia Austin. Putnam, 1988. ISBN 0-399-21491-7 Subj: Animals – giraffes. Animals – whales. Behavior – seeking better things. Reptiles – snakes.

Tom Mouse ill. by Julie Downing. DK, 1998. ISBN 0-7894-2554-8 Subj: Animals – mice. Trains.

A visit from Dr. Katz ill. by Ann Barrow. Atheneum, 1988. ISBN 0-689-31332-2 Subj: Animals – cats. Illness.

Lehan, Daniel. *This is not a book about dodos* ill. by author. Dutton, 1992. ISBN 0-525-44878-0 Subj: Art. Birds – dodos. Careers – artists.

Lehn, Barbara. *What is a scientist?* photos by Carol Krauss. Millbrook, 1998. ISBN 0-7613-1272-2 Subj: Careers – scientists. Science.

Leichman, Seymour. *Shaggy dogs and spotty dogs and shaggy and spotty dogs* ill. by author. Harcourt, 1973. ISBN 0-15-278020-3 Subj: Animals – dogs. Rhyming text.

The wicked wizard and the wicked witch ill. by author. Harcourt, 1972. ISBN 0-15-296455-X Subj: Magic. Rhyming text. Witches. Wizards.

Leigh, Oretta. *The merry-go-round* ill. by Kathryn E. Shoemaker. Holiday, 1985. ISBN 0-8234-0544-3 Subj: Animals. Merry-go-rounds. Rhyming text.

Leighton, Maxinne Rhea. *An Ellis Island Christmas* ill. by Dennis Nolan. Viking, 1992. ISBN 0-670-83182-4 Subj: Activities – traveling. Ethnic groups in the U.S. – Polish Americans. Holidays – Christmas. Moving.

Leiner, Katherine. *Both my parents work* photos by Steve Sax. Watts, 1986. ISBN 0-531-10101-0 Subj: Activities – working. Family life.

Halloween ill. with photos sel. by author. Atheneum, 1993. ISBN 0-689-31769-7 Subj: Clothing. Holidays – Halloween.

Leisk, David Johnson. *see* Johnson, Crockett

Leister, Mary. *The silent concert* ill. by Yoko Mitsuhashi. Bobbs-Merrill, 1970. Subj: Forest, woods. Noise, sounds.

Lemaître, Pascal. *Emily the giraffe* ill. by author. Hyperion, 1993. ISBN 1-56282-404-X Subj: Animals – giraffes. Character traits – bravery. Fire.

Zelda's secret ill. by author. BridgeWater, 1994. ISBN 0-8167-3309-0 Subj: Activities – dancing. Animals. Animals – elephants. Ballet. Behavior – secrets.

Leman, Jill. *Ten little pussy cats* ill. by Martin Leman. Trafalgar Square, 1996. ISBN 0-575-05979-6 Subj: Animals – cats. Counting, numbers.

Lember, Barbara Hirsch. *A book of fruit* ill. by author. Ticknor & Fields, 1994. ISBN 0-395-66989-8 Subj: Concepts. Food. Plants.

Lemberg, Stephen H. *Scaredy dog* ill. by Cat Bowman Smith. Knopf, 1994. ISBN 0-679-93175-9 Subj: Animals – dogs. Birds – swans. Emotions – fear. Seasons – summer.

Lemerise, Bruce. *Sheldon's lunch* ill. by author. Parents, 1980. ISBN 0-8193-1026-3 Subj: Activities – cooking. Food. Reptiles – snakes.

Lemieux, Margo. *The fiddle ribbon* ill. by Francis Livingston. Silver Pr., 1996. ISBN 0-382-39096-2 Subj: Activities – dancing. Family life – grandparents. Farms. Music.

Lemieux, Michèle. *What's that noise?* ill. by author. Morrow, 1985. ISBN 0-688-04140-X Subj: Animals – bears. Noise, sounds.

Lemke, Horst. *Places and faces* ill. by author. Scroll Pr., 1971. Translation of Vielerlei aus Stadt und Land. ISBN 0-87592-041-1 Subj: Wordless.

Lenski, Lois. *Animals for me* ill. by author. Walck, 1941. Subj: Animals.

At our house ill. by author. Walck, 1959. Music by Clyde Robert Bulla. Subj: Family life. Music. Songs.

Big little Davy ill. by author. Walck, 1956. Subj: Animals.

Cowboy Small ill. by author. Walck, 1960, c1949. ISBN 0-8098-1021-2 Subj: Cowboys.

Davy and his dog ill. by author. Walck, 1957. Subj: Animals – dogs. Music. Songs.

Davy goes places ill. by author. Walck, 1961. Subj: Activities – traveling. Music. Songs. Transportation.

Debbie and her dolls ill. by author. Walck, 1970. ISBN 0-8098-1159-6 Subj: Animals – dogs. Toys – dolls.

Debbie and her family ill. by author. Walck, 1969. ISBN 0-8098-1156-1 Subj: Family life.

Debbie and her grandma ill. by author. Walck, 1967. Subj: Family life – grandmothers. Music. Songs.

Debbie goes to nursery school ill. by author. Walck, 1970. ISBN 0-8098-1161-8 Subj: School.

A dog came to school ill. by author. Oxford Univ. Pr., 1955. Subj: Animals – dogs. Music. School. Songs.

I like winter ill. by author. Walck, 1950. Subj: Music. Poetry. Seasons – winter. Songs.

I went for a walk ill. by author. Walck, 1958. Subj: Activities – walking. Music. Songs.

Let's play house ill. by author. Walck, 1961, c1944. Subj: Activities – playing. Toys – dolls.

The life I live: collected poems ill. by author. Walck, 1966. Subj: Poetry. Songs.

The little airplane ill. by author. Walck, 1959, c1938. ISBN 0-8098-1004-2 Subj: Airplanes, airports.

The little auto ill. by author. Oxford Univ. Pr., 1934. ISBN 0-8098-1001-8 Subj: Automobiles.

The little family ill. by author. Doubleday, 1932. Subj: Family life.

The little farm ill. by author. Walck, 1959, c1942. ISBN 0-8098-1009-3 Subj: Farms.

The little fire engine ill. by author. Oxford Univ. Pr., 1946. Subj: Careers – firefighters.

The little train ill. by author. Oxford Univ. Pr., 1960, c1940. Subj: Careers – railroad engineers. Trains.

Lois Lenski's big book of Mr. Small ill. by author. Walck, 1979. ISBN 0-8098-6026-0 Subj: Careers. Transportation.

Mr. and Mrs. Noah ill. by author. Crowell, 1948. ISBN 0-690-54562-2 Subj: Boats, ships. Religion – Noah. Weather – floods. Weather – rain.

Now it's fall ill. by author. Walck, 1948. Subj: Poetry. Seasons – fall.

On a summer day ill. by author. Oxford Univ. Pr., 1953. Subj: Poetry. Seasons – summer.

Papa Small ill. by author. Walck, 1959, c1951. Subj: Family life. Family life – fathers.

Policeman Small ill. by author. Walck, 1962. ISBN 0-8098-1082-4 Subj: Careers – police officers. City.

Sing a song of people ill. by Giles Laroche. Little, 1987. ISBN 0-316-52074-8 Subj: City. Format, unusual. Rhyming text.

Spring is here ill. by author. Walck, 1960, c1945. Subj: Poetry. Seasons – spring.

A surprise for Davy ill. by author. Walck, 1959, c1947. Subj: Birthdays. Parties.

Susie Mariar ill. by author. Walck, 1968, c1967. First pub. in 1939. Subj: Cumulative tales. Folk and fairy tales. Poetry.

Lenssen, Ann. *A rainbow balloon* photos by author. Cobblehill, 1992. ISBN 0-525-65093-8 Subj: Activities – ballooning. Language.

Lent, Blair. *Bayberry Bluff* ill. by author. Houghton Mifflin, 1987. ISBN 0-395-35384-X Subj: City. Islands.

John Tabor's ride ill. by author. Little, 1966. Subj: Animals – whales. Folk and fairy tales. Humor. Tall tales.

Molasses flood ill. by author. Houghton Mifflin, 1992. ISBN 0-395-45314-3 Subj: City. Food. U.S. history.

Pistachio ill. by author. Little, 1964. Subj: Animals – bulls, cows. Circus. Clowns, jesters.

Ruby and Fred ill. by author. Holt, 2000. ISBN 0-8050-6117-7 Subj: Animals – cats. Animals – dogs. Birds.

Leodhas, Sorche Nic. *see* Alger, Leclaire Gowans

Leonard, Alain. *Barnaby and the big gorilla* ill. by author. Morrow, 1992. ISBN 0-688-11292-7 Subj: Animals – rabbits. Character traits – bravery. Toys.

Leonard, Marcia. *Alphabet bandits: an ABC book* ill. by Maryann Cocca-Leffler. Troll, 1990. ISBN 0-8167-1718-4 Subj: ABC books. Animals – raccoons. Food.

Angry ill. by Wendy Watson. Fitzgerald, 1998. ISBN 1-887238-13-1 Subj: Emotions – anger. Family life.

Animal talk photos by Dorothy Handelman. HarperFestival, 2000. ISBN 0-694-01363-3 Subj: Animals. Noise, sounds.

Babies help out by Marcia Leonard, Dorothy Handelman; ed. by Suzanne Daghlian; photos by Dorothy Handelman. HarperCollins, 2001. ISBN 0-694-01369-2 Subj: Babies.

Bear's busy year: a book about seasons ill. by Bari Weissman. Troll, 1990. ISBN 0-8167-1720-6 Subj: Animals – bears. Seasons.

Best friends photos by Dorothy Handelman. Millbrook, 1999. ISBN 0-7613-2064-4 Subj: Character traits – individuality. Friendship. Rhyming text.

The best snowman ever ill. by Nancy Rainsford, Pistone. Troll, 1989. ISBN 0-8167-1488-6 Subj: Format, unusual – toy and movable books. Holidays – Christmas. Snowmen.

Big Ben photos by Dorothy Handelman. Millbrook, 1998. ISBN 0-7613-2013-X Subj: Careers – musicians. Rhyming text.

Birthday in a bathtub ill. by John Wallner. Silver Pr., 1989. ISBN 0-671-08588-0 Subj: Animals – pigs. Birthdays. Problem solving. Rhyming text.

Busy babies photos by Dorothy Handelman. HarperFestival, 2000. ISBN 0-694-01364-1 Subj: Activities. Babies.

Bye-bye, Baby-boo ill. by Dana Regan. C.R. Gibson, 1992. ISBN 0-8378-2521-1 Subj: Activities – traveling. Babies. Format, unusual – board books.

Counting kangaroos: a book about numbers ill. by Diane Palmisciano. Troll, 1990. ISBN 0-8167-1722-2 Subj: Animals – kangaroos. Counting, numbers.

Dan and Dan photos by Dorothy Handelman. Millbrook, 1998. ISBN 0-7613-2003-2 Subj: Family life – grandfathers. Rhyming text.

Dress-up photos by Dorothy Handelman. Millbrook, 1999. ISBN 0-7613-2053-9 Subj: Activities – playing. Imagination. Rhyming text.

The elves and the shoemaker (Grimm, Jacob)

Favorite colors by Marcia Leonard, Dorothy Handleman; ed. by Suzanne Daghlian; photos by Dorothy Handelman. HarperCollins, 2001. ISBN 0-694-01370-6 Subj: Concepts – color.

Food is fun! pictures by Dorothy Handelman. HarperFestival, 2000. ISBN 0-694-01366-8 Subj: Activities – cooking. Food.

Get the ball, Slim photos by Dorothy Handelman. Millbrook, 1998. ISBN 0-7613-2000-8 Subj: Animals – dogs. Ethnic groups in the U.S. – African Americans. Family life – brothers and sisters. Multiple births – twins.

Getting dressed ill. by Deborah Michel. Bantam, 1988. ISBN 0-553-05467-8 Subj: Clothing. Family life.

Goldilocks and the three bears (The three bears)

Gregory and Mr. Grump ill. by Maxie Chambliss. Silver Pr., 1990. ISBN 0-671-70402-8 Subj: Gardens, gardening. Old age.

Hannah the hamster hunter ill. by Maxie Chambliss. Silver Pr., 1990. ISBN 0-671-70399-4 Subj: Animals – hamsters. School – first day.

Hop, skip, run photos by Dorothy Handelman. Millbrook, 1998. ISBN 0-7613-2015-6 Subj: Activities – playing. Rhyming text.

I like mess photos by Dorothy Handelman. Millbrook, 1998. ISBN 0-7613-2002-4 Subj: Character traits – orderliness. Family life – mothers. Rhyming text.

Jeffrey Lee, future fireman ill. by Ann Iosa. Silver Pr., 1990. ISBN 0-671-70403-6 Subj: Careers – firefighters.

King Lionheart's castle ill. by Alexandra Wallner. Silver Pr., 1992. ISBN 0-671-72974-8 Subj: Animals. Castles. Participation. Royalty – kings.

The kitten twins ill. by Maryann Cocca-Leffler. Troll, 1990. ISBN 0-8167-1724-9 Subj: Animals – cats. Concepts – opposites. Multiple births – twins.

Laura Jean the yard sale queen ill. by Ann Iosa. Silver Pr., 1990. ISBN 0-671-70401-X Subj: Animals – dogs.

Little owl leaves the nest ill. by Carol Newsom. Bantam, 1984. ISBN 0-533-15266-1 Subj: Birds – owls. Problem solving.

My camp-out photos by Dorothy Handelman. Millbrook, 1999. ISBN 0-7613-2052-0 Subj: Camps, camping. Ethnic groups in the U.S. – African Americans. Family life – mothers. Rhyming text.

My pal Al photos by Dorothy Handelman. Millbrook, 1998. ISBN 0-7613-2001-6 Subj: Ethnic groups in the U.S. – African Americans. Rhyming text. Toys.

Night-night, Baby-boo ill. by Dana Regan. C.R. Gibson, 1992. ISBN 0-8378-2522-9 Subj: Babies. Bedtime.

No new pants! photos by Dorothy Handelman. Millbrook, 1999. ISBN 0-7613-2063-6 Subj: Clothing. Family life – mothers. Rhyming text. Shopping.

Noisy neighbors ill. by Bari Weissman. Troll, 1990. ISBN 0-8167-1726-5 Subj: Animals. Noise, sounds.

The opposite of stop is go photos by Dorothy Handelman. HarperCollins, 2000. ISBN 0-694-01368-4 Subj: Concepts – opposites.

Paintbox penguins: a book about colors ill. by Diane Palmisciano. Troll, 1990. ISBN 0-8167-1716-8 Subj: Activities – painting. Birds – penguins. Concepts – color.

Peek-a-boo, baby! by Marcia Leonard, Dorothy Handelman; ed. by Mary-Alice Moore; photos by Dorothy Handelman. HarperCollins, 2000. ISBN 0-694-01373-0 Subj: Babies. Games.

The pet vet photos by Dorothy Handelman. Millbrook, 1999. ISBN 0-7613-2050-4 Subj: Careers – veterinarians. Rhyming text.

Rainboots for breakfast ill. by John Himmelman. Silver Pr., 1989. ISBN 0-671-68587-2 Subj: Food. Frogs and toads.

Shopping for snowflakes ill. by John Himmelman. Silver Pr., 1989. ISBN 0-671-68590-2 Subj: Animals – rabbits. Shopping.

Spots photos by Dorothy Handelman. Millbrook, 1998. ISBN 0-7613-2016-4 Subj: Concepts. Multiple births – twins. Rhyming text.

Swimming in the sand ill. by John Wallner. Silver Pr., 1989. ISBN 0-671-68589-9 Subj: Animals – hippopotamuses. Sea and seashore.

The three little pigs (The three little pigs)

The tin can man photos by Dorothy Handelman. Millbrook, 1998. ISBN 0-7613-2012-1 Subj: Family life – daughters. Family life – fathers. Parades. Rhyming text.

Violet and the pirates ill. by John Wallner. Silver Pr., 1992. ISBN 0-671-72975-6 Subj: Activities – sewing. Animals – cats. Boats, ships. Pirates.

What's that, Baby-boo? ill. by Dana Regan. C.R. Gibson, 1992. ISBN 0-8378-2519-9 Subj: Animals. Babies. Format, unusual – board books.

Where's Baby-boo? ill. by Dana Regan. C.R. Gibson, 1992. ISBN 0-8378-2520-2 Subj: Babies. Format, unusual – board books. Games.

Lepon, Shoshana. *Hillel builds a house* ill. by Marilynn G. Barr. Kar-Ben Copies, 1993. ISBN 0-92937-141-0 Subj: Holidays – Sukkot. Homes, houses. Jewish culture. Religion.

Lerman, Rory S. *Charlie's checklist* ill. by Alison Bartlett. Orchard, 1997. ISBN 0-531-30001-3 Subj: Animals – dogs. City. Farms. Foreign lands – England.

Lerner, Carol. *Flowers of a woodland spring* ill. by author. Morrow, 1979. ISBN 0-688-32190-9 Subj: Flowers. Forest, woods. Seasons – spring.

Lerner, Harriet Goldhor. *What's so terrible about swallowing an apple seed?* by Harriet Goldhor Lerner and Susan Henne Goldhor; ill. by Catharine O'Neill. HarperCollins, 1996. ISBN 0-06-024524-7 Subj: Behavior – worrying. Family life – sisters. Seeds. Sibling rivalry.

Lerner, Marguerite Rush. *Dear little mumps child* ill. by George Overlie. Lerner, 1959. ISBN 0-8225-0003-5 Subj: Illness – mumps. Rhyming text.

Doctors' tools ill. by George Overlie. Rev. 2nd ed. Lerner, 1960. Subj: Careers – doctors. Tools.

Lefty, the story of left-handedness ill. by Rov André. Lerner, 1960. Subj: Character traits – being different. Left-handedness.

Michael gets the measles ill. by George Overlie. Lerner, 1959. Subj: Illness.

Peter gets the chickenpox ill. by George Overlie. Lerner, 1959. ISBN 0-8225-0002-7 Subj: Illness.

Lerner, Sharon. *Big Bird's copycat day* featuring Jim Henson's Sesame Street Muppets; ill. by Jean-Pierre Jacquet. Random House, 1984. ISBN 0-394-86912-5 Subj: Puppets.

Follow the monsters! ill. by Tom Cooke. Random House, 1985. ISBN 0-394-97126-4 Subj: Monsters. Puppets. Rhyming text.

LeRoy, Gen. *Billy's shoes* ill. by J. Winslow Higginbottom. McGraw-Hill, 1981. ISBN 0-07-037201-2 Subj: Clothing – shoes. Sibling rivalry.

Lucky stiff! ill. by J. Winslow Higginbottom. McGraw-Hill, 1981. ISBN 0-07-037203-9 Subj: Humor. Sibling rivalry.

LeSieg, Theo. *see* Seuss, Dr.

Lesikin, Joan. *Down the road* ill. by author. Prentice-Hall, 1978. ISBN 0-13-218909-7 Subj: Behavior – sharing. Reptiles – snakes. Reptiles – turtles, tortoises.

Leslie, Amanda. *Animal noises* ill. by author. Candlewick, 1995. ISBN 1-56402-702-3 Subj: Animals. Noise, sounds.

Are chickens stripy? ill. by author. Handprint Books, 2000. ISBN 1-929766-09-2 Subj: Animals. Birds – chickens. Format, unusual – toy and movable books.

Do crocodiles moo? ill. by author. Handprint Books, 2000. ISBN 1-929766-08-4 Subj: Animals. Concepts – color. Format, unusual – toy and movable books. Noise, sounds.

Flappy, waggy, wiggly ill. by author. Dutton, 1999. ISBN 0-525-46182-5 Subj: Animals. Format, unusual – toy and movable books.

Hidden toys ill. by author. Dial, 1989. ISBN 0-8037-0568-9 Subj: Games. Toys.

Let's look inside the red car ill. by author. Candlewick, 1997. ISBN 0-7636-0089-X Subj: Automobiles. Format, unusual – toy and movable books.

Let's look inside the yellow truck ill. by author. Candlewick, 1997. ISBN 0-7636-0104-7 Subj: Format, unusual – toy and movable books. Trucks.

Play kitten play ill. by author. Candlewick, 1992. ISBN 1-56402-088-6 Subj: Animals. Animals – cats. Format, unusual – toy and movable books. Games.

Play puppy play ill. by author. Candlewick, 1992. ISBN 1-56402-087-8 Subj: Animals. Animals – dogs. Format, unusual – toy and movable books. Games.

Lessac, Frané. *Caribbean canvas* comp. and ill. by Frané Lessac. Wordsong, 1994, 1989. ISBN 1-56397-390-1 Subj: Art. Foreign lands – Caribbean Islands. Poetry.

My little island ill. by author. Lippincott, 1985. ISBN 0-397-32115-5 Subj: Foreign lands – Caribbean Islands. Islands.

Lesser, Carolyn. *The goodnight circle* ill. by Lorinda Bryan Cauley. Harcourt, 1984. ISBN 0-15-232158-6 Subj: Animals. Bedtime. Night.

Great crystal bear ill. by William Noonan. Harcourt, 1996. ISBN 0-15-200667-2 Subj: Animals – polar bears. Seasons.

What a wonderful day to be a cow ill. by Melissa Bay Mathis. Knopf, 1995. ISBN 0-679-92430-2 Subj: Animals. Days of the week, months of the year. Farms. Poetry. Seasons.

Lesser, Rika. *Hansel and Gretel* (Grimm, Jacob)

My sister Lotta and me (Dahlbäck-Lutteman, Helena)

Lester, Alison. *Alice and Aldo* ill. by author. Houghton Mifflin, 1997. ISBN 0-395-87092-5 Subj: ABC books. Activities – playing.

Celeste sails to Spain ill. by author. Houghton Mifflin, 1999. ISBN 0-395-97395-3 Subj: Activities. Character traits – individuality. Imagination.

Clive eats alligators ill. by author. Houghton Mifflin, 1986. ISBN 0-395-40775-3 Subj: Activities. Character traits – individuality.

Ernie dances to the didgeridoo ill. by author. Houghton Mifflin, 2001. ISBN 0-618-10442-9 Subj: Australian aborigines. Foreign lands – Australia. Letters, cards.

Imagine ill. by author. Houghton Mifflin, 1990. ISBN 0-395-53753-3 Subj: Animals.

Isabella's bed ill. by author. Houghton Mifflin, 1993. ISBN 0-395-65565-X Subj: Dreams. Family life – grandmothers. Imagination. Magic. Songs.

The journey home ill. by author. Houghton Mifflin, 1991. ISBN 0-395-53355-4 Subj: Activities – traveling. Family life – brothers and sisters.

Magic beach ill. by author. Little, 1992. ISBN 0-316-52177-9 Subj: Activities – vacationing. Family life. Imagination. Rhyming text. Sea and seashore.

My farm ill. by author. Houghton Mifflin, 1994. ISBN 0-395-68193-6 Subj: Family life. Farms. Foreign lands – Australia.

Rosie sips spiders ill. by author. Houghton Mifflin, 1989. ISBN 0-395-51526-2 Subj: Family life. Foreign lands – Australia.

Ruby ill. by author. Houghton Mifflin, 1988. ISBN 0-395-46477-3 Subj: Bedtime. Dreams.

Tessa snaps snakes ill. by author. Houghton Mifflin, 1991. ISBN 0-395-59505-3 Subj: Activities. Character traits – individuality.

When Frank was four ill. by author. Houghton Mifflin, 1996. ISBN 0-395-74275-7 Subj: Behavior – growing up. Counting, numbers.

Yikes! in seven wild adventures, who would you be? ill. by author. Houghton Mifflin, 1995. ISBN 0-395-71252-1 Subj: Activities. Rhyming text.

Lester, Helen. *Author: a true story* ill. by author. Houghton Mifflin, 1997. ISBN 0-395-82744-2 Subj: Careers – writers. Handicaps.

Help! I'm stuck! ill. by Paulette Bogan. Celebration Pr., 1996. ISBN 0-673-75716-1 Subj: Activities – storytelling. Family life – brothers and sisters. Pets.

Hooway for Wodney Wat ill. by Lynn Munsinger. Houghton Mifflin, 1999. ISBN 0-395-92392-1 Subj: Animals. Animals – rats. Behavior – bullying. Handicaps. School.

It wasn't my fault ill. by Lynn Munsinger. Houghton Mifflin, 1985. ISBN 0-395-35629-6 Subj: Animals. Cumulative tales.

Lin's backpack ill. by Lynn Munsinger. Scott Foresman, 1993. ISBN 0-673-80339-2 Subj: Animals. Sports – hiking.

Listen, Buddy ill. by Lynn Munsinger. Houghton Mifflin, 1995. ISBN 0-395-72361-2 Subj: Animals – rabbits.

Me first ill. by Lynn Munsinger. Houghton Mifflin, 1992. ISBN 0-395-58706-9 Subj: Animals – pigs. Behavior. Character traits – selfishness. Witches.

Pookins gets her way ill. by Lynn Munsinger. Houghton Mifflin, 1987. ISBN 0-395-42636-7 Subj: Character traits – willfulness. Mythical creatures – gnomes.

A porcupine named Fluffy ill. by Lynn Munsinger. Houghton Mifflin, 1986. ISBN 0-395-36895-2 Subj: Animals – porcupines. Names.

Princess Penelope's parrot ill. by Lynn Munsinger. Houghton Mifflin, 1996. ISBN 0-395-78320-8 Subj: Birds – parakeets, parrots. Character traits – selfishness. Emotions – anger. Royalty – princes. Royalty – princesses.

The revenge of the magic chicken ill. by Lynn Munsinger. Houghton Mifflin, 1990. ISBN 0-395-50929-7 Subj: Birds – chickens. Magic.

Roy Foy's special name (Lester, Robin)

The shy people's picnic ill. by Nadine Bernard Westcott. Celebration Pr., 1996. ISBN 0-673-75739-0 Subj: Character traits – shyness.

Tacky and the Emperor ill. by Lynn Munsinger. Houghton Mifflin, 2000. ISBN 0-395-98120-4 Subj: Birds – penguins. Clothing.

Tacky in trouble ill. by Lynn Munsinger. Houghton Mifflin, 1998. ISBN 0-395-86113-6 Subj: Animals – elephants. Behavior. Birds – penguins.

Tacky the penguin ill. by Lynn Munsinger. Houghton Mifflin, 1988. ISBN 0-395-45536-7 Subj: Animals – wolves. Birds – penguins. Character traits – individuality.

Three cheers for Tacky ill. by Lynn Munsinger. Houghton Mifflin, 1994. ISBN 0-395-66841-7 Subj: Birds – penguins. Character traits – individuality. Cheerleading. Friendship. School.

The wizard, the fairy and the magic chicken ill. by Lynn Munsinger. Houghton Mifflin, 1983. ISBN 0-395-33885-9 Subj: Behavior – sharing. Birds – chickens. Fairies. Friendship. Wizards.

Wuzzy takes off (Lester, Robin)

Lester, Julius. *Albidaro and the mischievous dream* ill. by Jerry Pinkney. Fogelman, 2000. ISBN 0-8037-1987-6 Subj: Animals. Behavior. Dreams.

Black cowboy, wild horses: a true story ill. by Jerry Pinkney. Dial, 1998. ISBN 0-8037-1788-1 Subj: Animals – horses, ponies. Cowboys. Ethnic groups in the U.S. – African Americans.

John Henry ill. by Jerry Pinkney. Dial, 1994. ISBN 0-8037-1607-9 Subj: Caldecott award honor books. Character traits – perseverance. Character traits – pride. Ethnic groups in the U.S. – African Americans. Folk and fairy tales.

The knee-high man and other tales ill. by Ralph Pinto. Dial, 1972. ISBN 0-8037-4593-1 Subj: Ethnic groups in the U.S. – African Americans. Folk and fairy tales.

Sam and the tigers: a new telling of Little Black Sambo ill. by Jerry Pinkney. Dial, 1996. ISBN 0-8037-2029-7 Subj: Animals – tigers. Clothing. Family life.

Shining ill. by Terea Shaffer. Silver Whistle, 2000. ISBN 0-15-200773-3 Subj: Foreign lands – Africa. Handicaps.

What a truly cool world ill. by Joe Cepeda. Scholastic, 1999. ISBN 0-590-86468-8 Subj: Angels. Creation. Ethnic groups in the U.S. – African Americans. Religion.

Lester, Mike. *A is for salad* ill. by author. Putnam, 2000. ISBN 0-399-23388-1 Subj: ABC books. School – first day.

Lester, Robin. *Roy Foy's special name* by Robin and Helen Lester; ill. by Diana Cain Bluthenthal. Candlewick, 1996. ISBN 1-56402-798-8 Subj: Names. School.

Wuzzy takes off by Robin and Helen Lester; ill. by Miko Imai. Candlewick, 1995. ISBN 1-56402-498-9 Subj: Moon. Toys – bears.

Lesynski, Loris. *Night school* ill. by author. Firefly, 2001. ISBN 1-55037-585-7 Subj: Bedtime. Night. School.

Le-Tan, Pierre. *The afternoon cat* ill. by author. Pantheon, 1977. ISBN 0-394-93095-9 Subj: Activities. Animals – cats.

Timothy's dream book ill. by author. Farrar, 1978. ISBN 0-374-37598-4 Subj: Careers. Imagination.

Visit to the North Pole ill. by author. Crown, 1983. ISBN 0-517-54893-3 Subj: Dreams. Imagination. Toys – bears.

Le Tord, Bijou. *A bird or two: a story about Henri Matisse* ill. by author. Eerdmans, 1999. ISBN 0-8028-5184-3 Subj: Art. Careers – artists. Concepts – color. Foreign lands – France.

A brown cow ill. by author. Little, 1989. ISBN 0-316-52166-3 Subj: Animals – bulls, cows.

The deep blue sea ill. by author. Orchard, 1990. ISBN 0-531-08453-1 Subj: Creation. Religion.

God's little seeds: a book of parables ill. by author. Eerdmans, 1998. ISBN 0-8028-5169-X Subj: Activities – storytelling. Religion. Seeds.

Good wood bear ill. by author. Bradbury, 1985. ISBN 0-02-756440-1 Subj: Animals – bears. Birds – geese. Homes, houses.

Joseph and Nellie ill. by author. Bradbury, 1986. ISBN 0-02-756450-9 Subj: Careers – fishermen. Sea and seashore.

My Grandma Leonie ill. by author. Bradbury, 1987. ISBN 0-02-756490-8 Subj: Death. Emotions – grief. Family life – grandmothers.

Noah's trees ill. by author. HarperCollins, 1999. ISBN 0-06-028527-3 Subj: Animals. Boats, ships. Religion – Noah. Trees. Weather – floods. Weather – rain.

Picking and weaving ill. by author. Four Winds, 1980. ISBN 0-590-07642-6 Subj: Activities – weaving. Plants.

Rabbit seeds ill. by author. Four Winds, 1984. ISBN 0-590-07797-X Subj: Animals – rabbits. Gardens, gardening.

The river and the rain: the Lord's prayer ill. by author. Doubleday, 1994. ISBN 0-385-32034-5 Subj: Ecology. Forest, woods. Religion.

Sing a new song: a book of Psalms ill. by author. Eerdmans, 1997. ISBN 0-8028-5139-8 Subj: Gardens, gardening. Religion. Seeds.

Let's count and count out comp. by Marion F. Grayson; ill. by Deborah Derr McClintock. Luce, 1975. ISBN 0-8833-1073-2 Subj: Counting, numbers. Games. Poetry.

Leuck, Laura. *My baby brother has ten tiny toes* ill. by Clara Vulliamy. Albert Whitman, 1997. ISBN 0-8075-5310-7 Subj: Babies. Counting, numbers. Family life – brothers and sisters. Rhyming text.

My monster mama loves me so ill. by Mark Buehner. Lothrop, 1999. ISBN 0-688-16867-1 Subj: Family life – mothers. Monsters. Rhyming text.

Leupold, Nancy S. *Little ghost Godfry* (Sandberg, Inger)

Leutscher, Alfred. *Earth* ill. by John Butler. Dial, 1983. ISBN 0-8037-2109-9 Subj: Earth. Science.

Water ill. by Nick Hardcastle. Dial, 1983. ISBN 0-8037-9390-1 Subj: Ecology. Science. Water.

Levens, George. *Kippy the koala* ill. by Crosby Newell Bonsall. HarperCollins, 1960. Subj: Animals – koalas. Poetry. Seasons – spring.

Levenson, George. *Pumpkin circle: the story of a garden* photos by Shmuel Thaler. Tricycle, 1999. ISBN 1-58246-004-3 Subj: Gardens, gardening. Rhyming text.

Leventhal, Debra. *What is your language?* song by Debra Leventhal; ill. by Monica Wellington. Dutton, 1994. ISBN 0-525-45133-1 Subj: Activities – traveling. Foreign languages. Songs.

Leverich, Kathleen. *The hungry fox and the foxy duck* ill. by Paul Galdone. Parents, 1979. ISBN 0-8193-0988-5 Subj: Animals – foxes. Birds – ducks. Character traits – cleverness.

Levert, Mireille. *Little Red Riding Hood* (Grimm, Jacob)

Levete, Sarah. *Being jealous* ill. by Christopher O'Neill. Copper Beech, 1999. ISBN 0-7613-0911-X Subj: Emotions – envy, jealousy.

Looking after myself ill. by author. Copper Beech, 1998. ISBN 0-7613-0809-1 Subj: Emotions. Health and fitness. Safety.

Making friends ill. by author. Copper Beech, 1998. ISBN 0-7613-0808-3 Subj: Emotions – loneliness. Friendship.

When people die ill. by Chrisopher O'Neill. Copper Beech, 1998. ISBN 0-7613-0870-9 Subj: Death. Emotions – grief.

Levi, Dorothy Hoffman. *A very special sister* ill. by Ethel Gold. Gallaudet Univ. Pr., 1992. ISBN 0-930323-96-3 Subj: Babies. Family life – new sibling. Family life – sisters. Handicaps – deafness. Multiple births – twins. Sibling rivalry.

Levin, Isadora. *The scarlet flower* (Aksakov, Sergei)

Levin, Miriam Ramsfelder. *In the beginning* ill. by Katherine Janus Kahn. Kar-Ben Copies, 1996. ISBN 0-929371-94-1 Subj: Creation. Emotions – loneliness.

Levine, Abby. *Gretchen Groundhog, it's your day!* ill. by Nancy Cote. Albert Whitman, 1998. ISBN 0-8075-3058-1 Subj: Animals – groundhogs. Holidays – Groundhog Day.

Ollie knows everything ill. by Lynn Munsinger. Albert Whitman, 1994. ISBN 0-8075-6020-0 Subj: Activities – trading. Animals – rabbits. Behavior – lost. Sibling rivalry.

Sometimes I wish I were Mindy by Abby and Sarah Levine; ill. by Blanche Sims. Albert Whitman, 1986. ISBN 0-8075-7542-9 Subj: Emotions – envy, jealousy.

This is the pumpkin ill. by Paige Billin-Frye. Albert Whitman, 1997. ISBN 0-8075-7886-X Subj: Cumulative tales. Holidays – Halloween. Rhyming text.

This is the turkey ill. by Paige Billin-Frye. Albert Whitman, 2000. ISBN 0-8075-7888-6 Subj: Family life. Holidays – Thanksgiving. Rhyming text.

Too much mush! ill. by Kathy Parkinson. Albert Whitman, 1989. ISBN 0-8075-8025-2 Subj: Folk and fairy tales. Food. Magic. Poverty.

What did mommy do before you? ill. by DyAnne DiSalvo-Ryan. Albert Whitman, 1988. ISBN 0-8075-8819-9 Subj: Babies. Behavior – growing up. Family life – mothers.

You push, I ride ill. by Margot Apple. Albert Whitman, 1989. ISBN 0-8075-9444-X Subj: Animals – pigs. Family life. Rhyming text.

Levine, Arthur A. *All the lights in the night* ill. by James E. Ransome. Morrow, 1991. ISBN 0-688-10108-9 Subj: Family life – brothers. Foreign lands – Russia. Holidays – Hanukkah. Jewish culture. Religion.

The boardwalk princess ill. by Susan Guevara. Tambourine, 1993. ISBN 0-688-10307-3 Subj: Animals – mice. Family life – brothers and sisters. Folk and fairy tales. Witches.

Bono and Nonno ill. by Judy Lanfredi. Tambourine, 1995. ISBN 0-688-13234-0 Subj: Animals. Family life – grandfathers. Rhyming text.

The boy who drew cats ill. by Frédéric Clément. Dial, 1994. ISBN 0-8037-1173-5 Subj: Activities – drawing. Animals – cats. Careers – artists. Folk and fairy tales. Foreign lands – Japan. Religion.

On Cat Mountain (Richard, Françoise)

Pearl Moscowitz's last stand ill. by Robert Roth. Tambourine, 1993. ISBN 0-688-10754-0 Subj: City. Trees.

Sheep dreams ill. by Judy Lanfredi. Dial, 1993. ISBN 0-8037-1195-6 Subj: Animals – sheep. Character traits – shyness. Theater.

Levine, Ellen. *I hate English!* ill. by Steve Björkman. Scholastic, 1989. ISBN 0-590-42305-3 Subj: Ethnic groups in the U.S. – Chinese Americans. Language.

Levine, Evan. *Not the piano, Mrs. Medley!* ill. by S. D. Schindler. Watts, 1991. ISBN 0-531-08556-2 Subj: Animals – dogs. Family life – grandmothers. Music. Sea and seashore.

Levine, Joan. *A bedtime story* ill. by Gail Owens. Dutton, 1975. ISBN 0-525-26290-3 Subj: Bedtime.

Levine, Rhoda. *Harrison loved his umbrella* ill. by Karla Kuskin. Atheneum, 1964. Subj: Character traits – being different. Character traits – individuality. Umbrellas.

Levine, Sarah. *Sometimes I wish I were Mindy* (Levine, Abby)

Levinson, Nancy Smiler. *Clara and the bookwagon* ill. by Carolyn Croll. HarperCollins, 1988. ISBN 0-06-023838-0 Subj: Activities – reading. Libraries.

Levinson, Riki. *Country dawn to dusk* ill. by Kay Chorao. Dutton, 1992. ISBN 0-525-44957-4 Subj: Animals – dogs. Concepts – color. Country. Pets.

The emperor's new clothes (Andersen, H. C. [Hans Christian])

Grandpa's hotel ill. by David Soman. Orchard, 1995. ISBN 0-531-08775-1 Subj: Family life. Family life – grandparents. Hotels.

I go with my family to Grandma's ill. by Diane Goode. Dutton, 1990. ISBN 0-525-44261-8 Subj: Activities – photographing. Family life. Family life – grandmothers. Transportation.

Me baby! ill. by Marylin Hafner. Dutton, 1991. ISBN 0-525-44693-1 Subj: Babies. Behavior – unnoticed, unseen. Family life. Family life – new sibling. Sibling rivalry.

Our home is the sea ill. by Dennis Luzak. Dutton, 1988. ISBN 0-525-44406-8 Subj: City. Family life. Foreign lands – China.

Soon, Annala ill. by Julie Downing. Orchard, 1993. ISBN 0-531-08644-5 Subj: Ethnic groups in the U.S. – Polish Americans. Immigrants. Jewish culture. Language.

Touch! Touch! ill. by True Kelley. Dutton, 1987. ISBN 0-525-44309-6 Subj: Behavior – misbehavior. Family life.

Watch the stars come out ill. by Diane Goode. Dutton, 1985. ISBN 0-525-44205-7 Subj: Family life. Family life – grandmothers. U.S. history.

Levitin, Sonia. *All the cats in the world* ill. by Charles Robinson. Harcourt, 1982. ISBN 0-15-202396-8 Subj: Animals – cats. Character traits – kindness to animals.

Boom town ill. Cat Bowman Smith. Orchard, 1998. ISBN 0-531-33043-5 Subj: Careers – bakers. Careers – miners.

The man who kept his heart in a bucket ill. by Jerry Pinkney. Dial, 1991. ISBN 0-8037-1030-5 Subj: Emotions – love.

Nine for California ill. Cat Bowman Smith. Orchard, 1996. ISBN 0-531-08877-4 Subj: Activities – traveling. Family life. U.S. history – frontier and pioneer life.

Nobody stole the pie ill. by Fernando Krahn. Harcourt, 1980. ISBN 0-15-257469-7 Subj: Activities – cooking. Crime. Food.

A piece of home ill. by Juan Wijngaard. Dial, 1996. ISBN 0-8037-1626-5 Subj: Behavior – worrying. Ethnic groups in the U.S. – Russian Americans. Family life – cousins.

A single speckled egg ill. by John M. Larrecq. Parnassus, 1976. ISBN 0-874-66075-0 Subj: Behavior – worrying. Eggs. Farms.

Taking charge ill. by Cat Bowman Smith. Orchard, 1999. ISBN 0-531-33149-0 Subj: Babies. U.S. history – frontier and pioneer life.

Who owns the moon? ill. by John M. Larrecq. Parnassus, 1973. ISBN 0-395-27656-X Subj: Behavior – fighting, arguing. Moon. Problem solving.

Levoy, Myron. *The Hanukkah of Great-Uncle Otto* ill. by Donna Ruff. Jewish Publication Society, 1984. ISBN 0-8276-0242-1 Subj: Family life – aunts, uncles. Holidays – Hanukkah. Jewish culture.

Levy, Elizabeth. *Cleo and the coyote* ill. by Diana Bryer. HarperCollins, 1996. ISBN 0-06-024272-8 Subj: Animals – coyotes. Animals – dogs. Desert. Friendship.

Nice little girls ill. by Mordicai Gerstein. Delacorte, 1974. ISBN 0-440-06193-8 Subj: School.

Levy, Janice. *Abuelito eats with his fingers* ill. by Layne Johnson. Eakin Pr., 1998. ISBN 1-57168-177-9 Subj: Ethnic groups in the U.S. – Mexican Americans. Family life – grandfathers.

Totally uncool ill. by Chris Monroe. Carolrhoda, 1999. ISBN 1-57505-306-3 Subj: Ethnic groups in the U.S. Family life – fathers. Friendship.

Levy, Miriam F. *Adam's world, San Francisco* (Fraser, Kathleen)

Levy, Sara G. *Mother Goose rhymes for Jewish children* ill. by Jessie B. Robinson. Bloch, 1945. ISBN 0-8197-0254-4 Subj: Jewish culture. Nursery rhymes.

Lewin, Betsy. *Animal snackers* ill. by author. Dodd, 1980. ISBN 0-396-07782-X Subj: Animals. Food. Poetry.

Booby hatch ill. by author. Clarion, 1995. ISBN 0-395-68703-9 Subj: Birds – boobys. Islands. Nature.

Cat count ill. by author. Dodd, 1981. ISBN 0-396-07928-8 Subj: Animals – cats. Counting, numbers. Poetry.

Chubbo's pool ill. by author. Clarion, 1996. ISBN 0-395-72807-X Subj: Animals – elephants. Animals

– hippopotamuses. Character traits – selfishness. Foreign lands – Botswana.

Groundhog day ill. by author. Scholastic, 2000. ISBN 0-439-10802-0 Subj: Animals – groundhogs. Holidays – Groundhog Day. Shadows.

Hip, hippo, hooray! ill. by author. Dodd, 1982. ISBN 0-396-08032-4 Subj: Animals – hippopotamuses. Counting, numbers. Illness. Weather.

What's the matter, Habibi? ill. by author. Clarion, 1997. ISBN 0-395-85816-X Subj: Animals – camels. Foreign lands – Egypt.

Wiley learns to spell ill. by author. Scholastic, 1998. ISBN 0-590-10835-2 Subj: Language. Monsters.

Lewin, Hugh. *An elephant came to swim* by Hugh Lewin and Lisa Kopper; ill. by authors. David & Charles, 1986. ISBN 0-241-11432-2 Subj: Animals – elephants. Foreign lands – Africa.

Jafta ill. by Lisa Kopper. Carolrhoda, 1983. ISBN 0-87614-207-2 Subj: Emotions. Family life. Foreign lands – Africa.

Jafta and the wedding ill. by Lisa Kopper. Carolrhoda, 1983. ISBN 0-87614-210-2 Subj: Family life. Foreign lands – Africa. Weddings.

Jafta - the homecoming ill. by Lisa Kopper. Knopf, 1994. ISBN 0-679-84722-7 Subj: Emotions. Family life – fathers. Foreign lands – South Africa.

Jafta - the journey ill. by Lisa Kopper. Carolrhoda, 1984. ISBN 0-87614-265-X Subj: Activities – traveling. Emotions. Foreign lands – Africa.

Jafta - the town ill. by Lisa Kopper. Carolrhoda, 1984. ISBN 0-87614-266-8 Subj: City. Emotions. Foreign lands – Africa.

Jafta's father ill. by Lisa Kopper. Carolrhoda, 1983. ISBN 0-87614-209-9 Subj: Family life – fathers. Foreign lands – Africa.

Jafta's mother ill. by Lisa Kopper. Carolrhoda, 1983. ISBN 0-87614-208-0 Subj: Family life – mothers. Foreign lands – Africa.

Lewin, Ted. *Amazon boy* ill. by author. Macmillan, 1993. ISBN 0-02-757383-4 Subj: Birthdays. Boats, ships. City. Ecology. Foreign lands – Brazil. Rivers.

Fair! ill. by author. Lothrop, 1997. ISBN 0-688-12851-3 Subj: Country. Fairs.

Market! ill. by author. Lothrop, 1996. ISBN 0-688-12162-4 Subj: Foreign lands. Stores.

Nilo and the tortoise ill. by author. Scholastic, 1999. ISBN 0-590-96004-0 Subj: Animals. Boats, ships. Careers – fishermen. Emotions – loneliness. Foreign lands – Galapagos Islands. Islands.

The storytellers ill. by author. Lothrop, 1998. ISBN 0-688-15179-5 Subj: Activities – storytelling. Foreign lands – Morocco.

When the rivers go home ill. by author. Macmillan, 1992. ISBN 0-02-757382-6 Subj: Animals. Ecology. Foreign lands – Brazil.

Lewis, Bobby. *Home before midnight: a traditional verse;* retold and ill. by Bobby Lewis. Lothrop, 1984. ISBN 0-688-00731-7 Subj: Animals – pigs. Cumulative tales.

Lewis, C. S. (Clive Staples). *Edmund and the White Witch* (Edmund and the White Witch)

Lucy steps through the wardrobe (Lucy steps through the wardrobe)

Lewis, Claudia Louise. *When I go to the moon* ill. by Leonard Weisgard. Macmillan, 1961. Subj: Earth. Moon.

Lewis, Eils Moorhouse. *The snug little house* ill. by Elise Primavera. Atheneum, 1981. ISBN 0-689-50177-3 Subj: Character traits – helpfulness. Homes, houses.

Lewis, J. Patrick. *At the wish of the fish* ill. by Katya Krénina. Atheneum, 1999. ISBN 0-689-81336-8 Subj: Behavior – wishing. Fish. Folk and fairy tales. Foreign lands – Russia.

The boat of many rooms ill. by Reg Cartwright. Atheneum, 1997. ISBN 0-689-80118-1 Subj: Animals. Boats, ships. Religion – Noah. Rhyming text. Weather – floods. Weather – rain.

The bookworm's feast ill. by John O'Brien. Dial, 1999. ISBN 0-8037-1693-1 Subj: Games. Humor. Poetry.

The Christmas of the reddle moon ill. by Gary Kelley. Dial, 1994. ISBN 0-8037-1567-6 Subj: Behavior – lost. Foreign lands – England. Holidays – Christmas. Imagination. Magic. Santa Claus.

Doodle dandies: poems that take shape ill. by Lisa Desimini. Atheneum, 1998. ISBN 0-689-81075-X Subj: Poetry.

The Fat-Cats at sea ill. by Victoria Chess. Knopf, 1994. ISBN 0-679-82639-4 Subj: Animals – cats. Boats, ships. Poetry.

The frog princess ill. by Gennady Spirin. Dial, 1994. ISBN 0-8037-1624-9 Subj: Folk and fairy tales. Foreign lands – Russia. Frogs and toads. Magic. Royalty – princesses. Witches.

A hippopotamusn't ill. by Victoria Chess. Dial, 1990. ISBN 0-8037-0519-0 Subj: Animals. Poetry.

The house of Boo ill. by Katya Krénina. Atheneum, 1998. ISBN 0-689-80356-7 Subj: Ghosts. Holidays – Halloween. Rhyming text.

Isabella Abnormella and the very, very finicky Queen of Trouble ill. by Kyrsten Brooker. DK, 2000. ISBN 0-7894-2605-6 Subj: Furniture – beds. Rhyming text. Royalty – queens. Sleep.

July is a mad mosquito ill. by Melanie W. Hall. Atheneum, 1994. ISBN 0-689-31813-8 Subj: Days of the week, months of the year. Nature. Poetry. Seasons.

The la-di-da hare ill. by Diana Cain Bluthenthal. Atheneum, 1997. ISBN 0-689-31925-8 Subj: Activities – picnicking. Animals. Islands. Poetry.

The little buggers: insect and spider poems ill. by Victoria Chess. Dial, 1998. ISBN 0-8037-1770-9 Subj: Insects. Poetry. Spiders.

Long was the winter road they traveled: a tale of the nativity ill. by Drew Bairley. Dial, 1997. ISBN 0-8037-1815-2 Subj: Animals. Holidays – Christmas. Poetry. Religion – Nativity.

The moonbow of Mr. B. Bones ill. by Dirk Zimmer. Knopf, 1992. ISBN 0-394-95365-7 Subj: Careers – peddlers. Magic. Moon.

The night of the goat children ill. by Alexi Natchev. Dial, 1999. ISBN 0-8037-1871-3 Subj: Animals – goats. Crime. Disguises. Royalty – princesses.

Riddle-icious ill. by Debbie Tilley. Knopf, 1996. ISBN 0-679-94011-1 Subj: Poetry. Riddles.

Riddle-lightful: oodles of little riddle-poems ill. by Debbie Tilley. Knopf, 1998. ISBN 0-679-98760-6 Subj: Rhyming text. Riddles.

The tsar and the amazing cow ill. by Friso Henstra. Dial, 1988. ISBN 0-8037-0411-9 Subj: Behavior – greed. Folk and fairy tales. Old age.

Two-legged, four-legged, no-legged rhymes ill. by Pamela Paparone. Knopf, 1991. ISBN 0-679-90771-8 Subj: Animals. Poetry.

Lewis, Kevin. *Chugga-chugga choo-choo* ill. by Daniel Kirk. Hyperion, 1999. ISBN 0-7868-2379-8 Subj: Rhyming text. Toys – trains.

Lewis, Kim. *Emma's lamb* ill. by author. Four Winds, 1991. ISBN 0-02-758821-1 Subj: Animals – sheep. Behavior – needing someone. Farms.

First snow ill. by author. Candlewick, 1993. ISBN 1-56402-194-7 Subj: Animals – dogs. Animals – sheep. Behavior – losing things. Farms. Toys – bears. Weather – snow.

Floss ill. by author. Candlewick, 1992. ISBN 1-56402-010-X Subj: Activities – playing. Activities – working. Animals – dogs.

Friends ill. by author. Candlewick, 1997. ISBN 0-7636-0346-5 Subj: Emotions – anger. Farms. Friendship.

Just like Floss ill. by author. Candlewick, 1998. ISBN 0-7636-0684-7 Subj: Animals – babies. Animals – dogs. Farms.

The last train ill. by author. Candlewick, 1994. ISBN 1-56402-343-5 Subj: Family life. Foreign lands – England. Imagination. Trains.

Little Baa ill. by author. Candlewick, 2001. ISBN 0-7636-1447-5 Subj: Animals – babies. Animals – sheep. Farms.

Little calf ill. by author. Candlewick, 2000. ISBN 0-7636-0899-8 Subj: Animals – babies. Animals – bulls, cows. Farms.

Little lamb ill. by author. Candlewick, 2000. ISBN 0-7636-0900-5 Subj: Animals – babies. Animals – sheep. Farms.

Little puppy ill. by author. Candlewick, 2000. ISBN 0-7636-0901-3 Subj: Animals – babies. Animals – dogs. Farms.

My friend Harry ill. by author. Candlewick, 1995. ISBN 1-56402-617-5 Subj: Animals – elephants. School. Toys.

One summer day ill. by author. Candlewick, 1996. ISBN 1-56402-883-6 Subj: Activities – walking. Country. Seasons – summer. Tractors.

The shepherd boy ill. by author. Four Winds, 1990. ISBN 0-02-758581-6 Subj: Animals – sheep. Careers – shepherds.

Lewis, Lucia Z. *see* Anderson, Lucia Z.

Lewis, Naomi. *The butterfly collector* ill. by Fulvio Testa. Prentice-Hall, 1979. ISBN 0-13-108852-1 Subj: Behavior – collecting things. Insects – butterflies, caterpillars. Rhyming text. Riddles.

The frog prince: or Iron Henry (Grimm, Jacob)

Hare and badger go to town ill. by Tony Ross. David & Charles, 1987. ISBN 0-905478-94-0 Subj: Animals. Ecology.

Johnny Longnose (Krüss, James)

Jorinda and Joringel (Grimm, Jacob)

Leaves ill. by Fulvio Testa. HarperCollins, 1983. ISBN 0-911-74501-7 Subj: Plants. Seasons. Trees.

The nightingale (Andersen, H. C. [Hans Christian])

Once upon a rainbow ill. by Gabriele Eichenauer. Jonathan Cape, 1981. ISBN 0-224-01842-6 Subj: Concepts – color. Rhyming text. Toys – bears.

Puffin ill. by Deborah King. Lothrop, 1984. ISBN 0-688-03783-6 Subj: Birds – puffins. Foreign lands – Scotland.

Puss in boots (Perrault, Charles)

The snow queen (Andersen, H. C. [Hans Christian])

The snow queen (Andersen, H. C. [Hans Christian])

The steadfast tin soldier (Andersen, H. C. [Hans Christian])

The stepsister ill. by Allison Reed. Dial, 1987. ISBN 0-8037-0430-5 Subj: Animals – cats. Family life – step families.

Swan ill. by Deborah King. Lothrop, 1986. ISBN 0-688-05535-4 Subj: Birds – swans. Nature. Science.

The tale of the vanishing rainbow (Rupprecht, Siegfried P.)

The wild swans (Andersen, H. C. [Hans Christian])

Lewis, Paul Owen. *Frog girl* ill. by author. Gareth Stevens, 1999. ISBN 0-8368-2228-5 Subj: Character traits – kindness to animals. Ecology. Folk and fairy tales. Frogs and toads. Indians of North America – Tlingit. Volcanoes.

Storm boy ill. by author. Gareth Stevens, 1999. ISBN 0-8368-2229-3 Subj: Animals – whales. Sea and seashore. Weather – storms.

Lewis, Richard. *In a spring garden* ill. by Ezra Jack Keats. Dial, 1965. A collection of haiku. ISBN 0-8037-4024-7 Subj: Poetry.

In the night, still dark ill. by Ed Young. Atheneum, 1988. ISBN 0-689-31310-1 Subj: Hawaii. Poetry.

Lewis, Robin Baird. *Aunt Armadillo* ill. by author. Firefly, 1985. ISBN 0-920303-38-2 Subj: Animals – armadillos. Family life – aunts, uncles. Libraries.

Friska, the sheep that was too small ill. by author. Farrar, 1988. ISBN 0-374-32461-1 Subj: Animals – sheep. Animals – wolves. Character traits – bravery.

Hello, Mr. Scarecrow ill. by author. Farrar, 1987. ISBN 0-374-32947-8 Subj: Days of the week, months of the year. Scarecrows.

Lewis, Shari. *Baby Lamb Chop loves animals* ill. by Cathy Beylon. Random House, 1991. ISBN 0-679-81723-9 Subj: Animals. Format, unusual – board books. Puppets.

Baby Lamb Chop loves numbers ill. by Cathy Beylon. Random House, 1991. ISBN 0-679-81724-7 Subj: Counting, numbers. Format, unusual – board books. Puppets.

Baby Lamb Chop loves nursery school ill. by Cathy Beylon. Random House, 1991. ISBN 0-679-81725-5 Subj: Format, unusual – board books. Puppets. School.

Baby Lamb Chop loves the beach ill. by Cathy Beylon. Random House, 1991. ISBN 0-679-81726-3 Subj: Format, unusual – board books. Puppets. Sea and seashore.

Baby Lamb Chop loves words ill. by Cathy Beylon. Random House, 1991. ISBN 0-679-81722-0 Subj: Format, unusual – board books. Language. Puppets.

Lewis, Sharon. *Orca! the killer whale* ill. by Linda Roberts. HarperCollins, 1990. ISBN 0-694-00295-X Subj: Animals – whales.

Tiger! ill. by Linda Roberts. HarperCollins, 1990. ISBN 0-694-00296-8 Subj: Animals – tigers.

Lewis, Stephen. *Zoo city* ill. by author. Greenwillow, 1976. ISBN 0-688-86000-1 Subj: Animals. City. Format, unusual. Imagination. Wordless. Zoos.

Lewis, Thomas P. *Call for Mr. Sniff* ill. by Beth Weiner Lipson. HarperCollins, 1981. ISBN 0-06-023815-1 Subj: Animals – dogs. Birthdays. Mystery stories.

Clipper ship ill. by Joan Sandin. HarperCollins, 1978. ISBN 0-06-023809-7 Subj: Activities – traveling. Boats, ships.

Hill of fire ill. by Joan Sandin. HarperCollins, 1971. ISBN 0-06-023803-8 Subj: Foreign lands – Mexico. Volcanoes.

Mr. Sniff and the motel mystery ill. by Beth Weiner Lipson. HarperCollins, 1984. ISBN 0-06-023825-9 Subj: Animals – dogs. Mystery stories.

Lewis, Zoe. *Disney's Beauty and the beast teacup mix-up* ill. by Phil Wilson. Walt Disney, 1994. ISBN 0-7868-3013-1 Subj: Concepts.

Lewison, Wendy Cheyette. *Baby has a boo-boo* ill. by Bettina Paterson. Grosset, 1994. ISBN 0-448-40583-0 Subj: Babies. Format, unusual – board books. Illness.

Baby's first Mother Goose (Mother Goose)

"Buzz," said the bee ill. by Hans Wilhelm. Scholastic, 1992. ISBN 0-590-44185-X Subj: Animals. Cumulative tales. Noise, sounds. Rhyming text.

Bye-bye, baby ill. by True Kelley. Scholastic, 1992. ISBN 0-590-45172-3 Subj: Babies. Format, unusual – toy and movable books.

Don't wake the baby! ill. by Jerry Smath. Grosset, 1996. ISBN 0-448-41293-4 Subj: Babies. Rebuses.

Going to sleep on the farm ill. by Juan Wijngaard. Dial, 1992. ISBN 0-8037-1097-6 Subj: Animals. Bedtime. Cumulative tales. Farms. Rhyming text. Sleep.

Happy Thanksgiving! ill. by Mary Morgan. Grosset, 1993. ISBN 0-448-40552-0 Subj: Animals – mice. Format, unusual – board books. Rhyming text.

Hello, snow! ill. by Maryann Cocca-Leffler. Grosset, 1994. ISBN 0-448-40486-9 Subj: Rhyming text. Weather – snow.

I am a flower girl photos by Elizabeth Hathon. Grosset, 1999. ISBN 0-448-41956-4 Subj: Family life – aunts, uncles. Weddings.

I wear my tutu everywhere! ill. by Mary Morgan. Grosset, 1996. ISBN 0-448-40877-5 Subj: Activities – dancing. Ballet.

Mud ill. by Maryann Cocca-Leffler. Random House, 2001. ISBN 0-679-80251-7 Subj: Activities – playing. Rhyming text.

My baby brother ill. by Stephen Cartwright. Warner, 1990. ISBN 1-55782-102-X Subj: Family life – brothers and sisters. Format, unusual – toy and movable books.

My favorite doll ill. by Stephen Cartwright. Warner, 1990. ISBN 1-55782-116-X Subj: Bedtime. Format, unusual – toy and movable books. Toys – dolls.

My new puppy ill. by Stephen Cartwright. Warner, 1990. ISBN 1-55782-119-4 Subj: Animals – dogs. Format, unusual – toy and movable books.

Nighty-night ill. by Giulia Orecchia. Grosset, 1992. ISBN 0-448-40391-9 Subj: Format, unusual – board books. Moon. Night. Rhyming text.

Our new baby ill. by Nancy Sheehan. Grosset, 1996. ISBN 0-448-41147-4 Subj: Babies. Family life – brothers and sisters. Family life – new sibling.

The princess and the potty ill. by Rick Brown. Simon & Schuster, 1994. ISBN 0-671-87284-2 Subj: Royalty – princesses. Toilet training.

The rooster who lost his crow ill. by Thor Wickstrom. Dial, 1995. ISBN 0-8037-1546-3 Subj: Animals. Birds – chickens. Farms.

Say thank you, Theodore: a book about manners ill. by Juli Kangas. Platt, 1992. ISBN 0-448-40476-1 Subj: Animals – rabbits. Etiquette. Family life – brothers and sisters.

Shy Vi ill. by Stephen John Smith. Simon & Schuster, 1993. ISBN 0-671-76968-5 Subj: Animals – mice. Character traits – individuality. Character traits – shyness. Theater.

So many boots ill. by Tony Griego. Scholastic, 2000. ISBN 0-439-09865-3 Subj: Clothing – boots. Insects. Rhyming text. Weather – rain.

Ten little ballerinas ill. by Joan Holub. Grosset, 1996. ISBN 0-448-41491-0 Subj: Activities – dancing. Ballet. Format, unusual – toy and movable books. Rhyming text.

A trip to the firehouse ill. by Elizabeth Hathon. Grosset, 1998. ISBN 0-448-41740-5 Subj: Careers – firefighters. Communities, neighborhoods.

Uh oh, baby ill. by True Kelley. Scholastic, 1992. ISBN 0-590-45171-5 Subj: Babies. Format, unusual – toy and movable books.

Where is Sammy's smile? ill. by Katy Bratun. Grosset, 1989. ISBN 0-448-40150-9 Subj: Animals – raccoons. Format, unusual.

Where's baby? ill. by True Kelley. Scholastic, 1992. ISBN 0-590-45170-7 Subj: Babies. Format, unusual – toy and movable books.

Where's my teddy? ill. by Stephen Cartwright. Warner, 1990. ISBN 1-55782-052-X Subj: Behavior – losing things. Format, unusual – toy and movable books. Toys – bears.

Lewiton, Mina. *see* Simon, Mina Lewiton

Lexau, Joan M. *Benjie* ill. by Don Bolognese. Dial, 1964. Subj: Character traits – shyness. Ethnic groups in the U.S. – African Americans. Family life. Family life – grandmothers. Problem solving.

Benjie on his own ill. by Don Bolognese. Dial, 1970. Subj: City. Ethnic groups in the U.S. – African Americans. Family life – grandmothers. Illness. Problem solving.

Cathy is company ill. by Aliki. Dial, 1961. Subj: Etiquette. Friendship.

Come here, cat ill. by Steven Kellogg. Harper-Collins, 1973. ISBN 0-06-024558-1 Subj: Animals – cats. City.

Crocodile and hen ill. by Joan Sandin. Harper-Collins, 1969. Adapt. of Why the crocodile does not eat the hen, from Notes on the folklore of the Fjort (French Congo), by R. E. Dennett. Subj: Birds – chickens. Cumulative tales. Folk and fairy tales. Foreign lands – Africa. Reptiles – alligators, crocodiles.

The dog food caper ill. by Marylin Hafner. Dial, 1985. ISBN 0-8037-0108-X Subj: Animals – dogs. Animals – mice. Mystery stories. Witches.

Every day a dragon ill. by Ben Shecter. Harper-Collins, 1967. Subj: Family life. Family life – fathers. Games.

Finders keepers, losers weepers ill. by Tomie de Paola. Lippincott, 1967. Subj: Babies. Behavior – losing things. Behavior – lying. Family life.

Go away, dog ill. by Crosby Newell Bonsall. HarperCollins, 1963. ISBN 0-06-024556-5 Subj: Animals – dogs. Birthdays. Character traits – persistence.

Go away, dog ill. by Paul Meisel. HarperCollins, 1997. ISBN 0-06-027503-0 Subj: Animals – dogs. Birthdays. Character traits – persistence.

The homework caper ill. by Syd Hoff. Harper-Collins, 1966. ISBN 0-06-023856-9 Subj: Sibling rivalry.

A house so big ill. by Syd Hoff. HarperCollins, 1968. Subj: Character traits – generosity. Emotions – love. Family life – mothers. Imagination.

I hate red rover ill. by Gail Owens. Dutton, 1979. ISBN 0-525-32527-1 Subj: Behavior – growing up. Games.

I should have stayed in bed ill. by Syd Hoff. Harper-Collins, 1965. Subj: Behavior – bad day. Emotions – embarrassment. Ethnic groups in the U.S. – African Americans.

I'll tell on you ill. by Gail Owens. Dutton, 1981. ISBN 0-525-32542-5 Subj: Animals – dogs. Behavior – misbehavior. Sports – baseball.

It all began with a drip, drip, drip ill. by Joan Sandin. McCall, 1970. ISBN 0-8415-2019-4 Subj: Behavior – mistakes. Character traits – bravery. Folk and fairy tales. Foreign lands – India.

Me day ill. by Robert Weaver. Dial, 1971. Subj: Birthdays. City. Divorce. Ethnic groups in the U.S. – African Americans. Family life. Family life – fathers.

Millicent's ghost ill. by Ben Shecter. Dial, 1962. Subj: Ghosts. Night.

More beautiful than flowers ill. by Don Bolognese. Lippincott, 1966. Subj: Poetry. Religion.

Olaf reads ill. by Harvey Weiss. Dial, 1961. ISBN 0-8037-6559-2 Subj: Activities – reading.

The rooftop mystery ill. by Syd Hoff. HarperCollins, 1968. ISBN 0-06-023865-8 Subj: Ethnic groups in the U.S. – African Americans. Moving. Mystery stories. Toys – dolls.

Who took the farmer's hat? ill. by Fritz Siebel. HarperCollins, 1963. ISBN 0-06-024566-2 Subj: Clothing – hats. Farms. Weather – wind.

L'Hommedieu, Arthur John. *Working at a museum* ill. with photos. Childrens Pr., 1998. ISBN 0-516-20748-2 Subj: Careers – museum workers. Museums.

Liatsos, Sandra Olson. *Bicycle riding and other poems* ill. by Karen Dugan. Wordsong, 1997. ISBN 1-56397-235-2 Subj: Activities. Poetry. Sports.

Lichtenheld, Tom. *Everything I know about pirates* ill. by author. Simon & Schuster, 2000. ISBN 0-689-82625-7 Subj: Pirates.

Lichtveld, Noni. *I lost my arrow in a kankan tree* ill. by author. Lothrop, 1993. ISBN 0-688-12748-7 Subj: Activities – trading. Circular tales. Foreign lands – Suriname.

Liddell, Janice. *Imani and the Flying Africans* ill. by Linda Nickens. Africa World, 1994. ISBN 0-86543-365-8 Subj: Activities – flying. Activities – traveling. Ethnic groups in the U.S. – African Americans. Folk and fairy tales.

Lidz, Jane. *Zak, the one-of-a-kind dog* ill. by author. Abrams, 1997. ISBN 0-8109-3995-9 Subj: Animals – dogs. Character traits – individuality.

Lieberman, Deborah. *The Wooodles: stretching your imagination* (Fox, Perla)

Lieberman, Syd. *The wise shoemaker of Studena* ill. by Martin Lemelman. Jewish Publication Society, 1994. ISBN 0-8276-0509-9 Subj: Behavior – misbehavior. Careers – shoemakers. Character traits – appearance. Character traits – cleverness. Foreign lands – Hungary. Jewish culture.

Liebler, John. *Frog counts to ten* ill. by author. Millbrook, 1994. ISBN 1-56294-436-3 Subj: Counting, numbers. Frogs and toads. Sports – bicycling.

Liebman, Daniel. *I want to be a cowboy* ill. with photos. Firefly, 1999. ISBN 1-55209-447-2 Subj: Careers. Cowboys.

I want to be a firefighter ill. with photos. Firefly, 1999. ISBN 1-55209-448-0 Subj: Careers – firefighters. Communities, neighborhoods. Fire.

I want to be a police officer ill. with photos. Firefly, 2000. ISBN 1552094677 Subj: Careers – police officers. Communities, neighborhoods.

Liersch, Anne. *A house is not a home* ill. by Christa Unzner; trans. by J. Alison James. North-South, 1999. ISBN 0-7358-1157-1 Subj: Animals. Animals – badgers. Behavior – bullying. Friendship. Homes, houses.

Lies, Brian. *Hamlet and the enormous Chinese dragon kite* ill. by author. Houghton Mifflin, 1994. ISBN 0-395-68391-2 Subj: Activities – flying. Animals – pigs. Animals – porcupines. Friendship. Kites.

Lifton, Betty Jean. *Goodnight orange monster* ill. by Cyndy Szekeres. Atheneum, 1972. Subj: Bedtime. Emotions – fear. Monsters. Night.

Joji and the Amanojaku ill. by Eiichi Mitsui. Norton, 1965. Subj: Birds. Foreign lands – Japan. Mythical creatures – goblins. Scarecrows.

Joji and the dragon ill. by Eiichi Mitsui. Morrow, 1989, c1957. Reprint. Originally published: New York: Morrow, 1957. ISBN 0-208-02245-7 Subj: Birds. Dragons. Foreign lands – Japan. Scarecrows.

Joji and the fog ill. by Eiichi Mitsui. Morrow, 1959. Subj: Birds. Scarecrows. Weather – fog.

The many lives of Chio and Goro ill. by Yasuo Segawa. Norton, 1968. Subj: Animals – foxes. Birds – chickens. Foreign lands – Japan.

The rice-cake rabbit ill. by Eiichi Mitsui. Norton, 1966. Subj: Animals – rabbits. Foreign lands – Japan. Moon.

The secret seller ill. by Etienne Delessert and Norma Holt. Norton, 1967. Subj: Behavior – secrets. Imagination.

Tell me a real adoption story ill. by Claire A. Nivola. Knopf, 1993. ISBN 0-679-90629-0 Subj: Activities – dancing. Insects. Parties. Rhyming text.

Lillegard, Dee. *The Big Bug Ball* ill. by Rex Barron. Putnam, 1999. ISBN 0-399-23121-8 Subj: Activities – dancing. Parties. Rhyming text.

The day the daisies danced ill. by Rex Barron. Putnam, 1996. ISBN 0-399-22661-3 Subj: Flowers. Rhyming text. Weddings.

The hee-haw river ill. by Allan Eitzen. Holt, 1995. ISBN 0-8050-2375-5 Subj: Animals. Noise, sounds. Rivers.

Hello school! ill. by Don Carter. Knopf, 2001. ISBN 0-375-91020-4 Subj: Poetry. School.

I can be a baker ill. with photos. Childrens Pr., 1986. ISBN 0-516-01892-2 Subj: Careers – bakers.

I can be a carpenter ill. with photos. Childrens Pr., 1986. ISBN 0-516-01884-1 Subj: Careers – carpenters.

I can be a welder by Dee Lillegard and Wayne Stoker. Childrens Pr., 1986. ISBN 0-516-01895-7 Subj: Careers – welders.

I can be an electrician ill. with photos. Childrens Pr., 1986. ISBN 0-516-01896-5 Subj: Careers – electricians.

My yellow ball ill. by Sarah Chamberlain. Dutton, 1993. ISBN 0-525-45078-5 Subj: Animals. Animals – dogs. Behavior – wishing. Toys – balls.

Sitting in my box ill. by Jon Agee. Dutton, 1989. ISBN 0-525-44528-5 Subj: Activities – reading. Animals. Cumulative tales.

Tortoise brings the mail ill. by Jillian Lund. Dutton, 1997. ISBN 0-525-45156-0 Subj: Animals. Careers – postal workers. Letters, cards. Reptiles – turtles, tortoises.

Wake up house! rooms full of poems ill. by Don Carter. Knopf, 2000. ISBN 0-679-98351-1 Subj: Furniture. Homes, houses. Poetry.

The wild bunch ill. by Rex Barron. Putnam, 1997. ISBN 0-399-22826-8 Subj: Food. Poetry.

Lillie, Patricia. *Everything has a place* ill. by Nancy Tafuri. Greenwillow, 1993. ISBN 0-688-10083-X Subj: Character traits – orderliness.

Floppy teddy bear ill. by Karen Lee Baker. Greenwillow, 1995. ISBN 0-688-12570-0 Subj: Emotions – anger. Family life – sisters. Sibling rivalry. Toys – bears.

Jake and Rosie ill. by author. Greenwillow, 1989. ISBN 0-688-07625-4 Subj: Animals – cats. Ethnic groups in the U.S. – African Americans. Friendship.

One very, very quiet afternoon ill. by author. Greenwillow, 1986. ISBN 0-688-04323-2 Subj: ABC books. Behavior – misbehavior. Parties.

When the rooster crowed ill. by Nancy Winslow Parker. Greenwillow, 1991. ISBN 0-688-09379-5 Subj: Animals. Cumulative tales. Farms. Noise, sounds.

When this box is full ill. by Donald Crews. Greenwillow, 1993. ISBN 0-688-12017-2 Subj: Behavior – collecting things. Days of the week, months of the year.

Lilly, Kenneth. *Animal builders* ill. by author. Random House, 1984. ISBN 0-394-86373-9 Subj: Activities. Animals. Format, unusual – board books. Science.

Animal climbers ill. by author. Random House, 1984. ISBN 0-394-86374-7 Subj: Activities. Animals. Format, unusual – board books. Science.

Animal jumpers ill. by author. Random House, 1984. ISBN 0-394-86375-5 Subj: Activities. Animals. Format, unusual – board books. Science.

Animal runners ill. by author. Random House, 1984. ISBN 0-394-86376-3 Subj: Activities. Animals. Format, unusual – board books. Science.

Animal swimmers ill. by author. Random House, 1984. ISBN 0-394-86377-1 Subj: Activities. Animals. Format, unusual – board books. Science.

Animals at the zoo ill. by author. Simon & Schuster, 1982. ISBN 0-671-45152-9 Subj: Animals. Format, unusual – board books. Zoos.

Animals in the country ill. by author. Simon & Schuster, 1982. ISBN 0-671-45153-7 Subj: Animals. Format, unusual – board books. Wordless.

Animals in the jungle ill. by author. Simon & Schuster, 1982. ISBN 0-671-45154-5 Subj: Animals. Format, unusual – board books. Jungle.

Animals of the ocean ill. by author. Simon & Schuster, 1982. ISBN 0-671-45155-3 Subj: Animals – dolphins. Animals – polar bears. Animals – seals. Animals – whales. Birds – penguins. Format, unusual – board books. Sea and seashore.

Animals on the farm ill. by author. Simon & Schuster, 1982. ISBN 0-671-45151-0 Subj: Animals. Farms. Format, unusual – board books.

Baby animals text by Kate Hayden; ill. by Kenneth Lilly. Candlewick, 1996. ISBN 0-7636-0067-9 Subj: Animals – babies.

Limb, Sue. *Come back, Grandma* ill. by Claudio Muñoz. Knopf, 1993. ISBN 0-679-84720-0 Subj: Death. Emotions – grief. Family life. Family life – grandmothers.

Lin, Grace. *The ugly vegetables* ill. by author. Charlesbridge, 1999. ISBN 0-88106-336-3 Subj: Ethnic groups in the U.S. – Chinese Americans. Flowers. Food. Gardens, gardening.

Linch, Elizabeth Johanna. *Samson* ill. by author. HarperCollins, 1964. Subj: Animals – mice. Holidays – Christmas. Seasons – winter.

Lind, Mecka. *Cackle goes a-courting* ill. by Lars Rudebjer. Carolrhoda, 1992. ISBN 0-87614-715-5 Subj: Animals. Birds – chickens.

Lindbergh, Anne. *Tidy lady* ill. by Susan Ramsay Hoguet. Harcourt, 1989. ISBN 0-15-287150-0 Subj: Character traits – cleanliness. Cumulative tales.

Lindbergh, Reeve. *The awful aardvarks go to school* ill. by Tracey Campbell Pearson. Viking, 1997. ISBN 0-670-85920-6 Subj: ABC books. Animals – aardvarks. Behavior – misbehavior. Rhyming text. School.

The awful aardvarks shop for school ill. by Tracey Campbell Pearson. Viking, 2000. ISBN 0-670-88763-3 Subj: Animals – aardvarks. Behavior – misbehavior. Rhyming text. Shopping.

Benjamin's barn ill. by Susan Jeffers. Dial, 1990. ISBN 0-8037-0614-6 Subj: Animals. Barns. Farms. Imagination. Rhyming text.

The circle of days ill. by Cathie Felstead. Candlewick, 1998. ISBN 0-7636-0357-0 Subj: Creation. Religion.

The day the goose got loose ill. by Steven Kellogg. Dial, 1990. ISBN 0-8037-0409-7 Subj: Animals. Behavior – misbehavior. Birds – geese. Farms.

Grandfather's lovesong ill. by Rachel Isadora. Viking, 1993. ISBN 0-670-84842-5 Subj: Emotions – love. Family life – grandfathers. Poetry.

The hippie grandmother ill. by Aby Carter. Candlewick, 2002. ISBN 0-7636-0671-5 Subj: Family life – grandmothers. Rhyming text.

If I'd known then what I know now ill. by Bulcken Root Kimberly. Viking, 1994. ISBN 0-670-85351-8 Subj: Behavior – mistakes. Family life – fathers. Homes, houses. Rhyming text.

Johnny Appleseed ill. by Kathy Jakobsen. Little, 1990. ISBN 0-316-52618-5 Subj: Activities – traveling. Folk and fairy tales. Rhyming text. Trees. U.S. history.

Midnight farm ill. by Susan Jeffers. Dial, 1987. ISBN 0-8037-0333-3 Subj: Animals. Counting, numbers. Farms. Night.

Nobody owns the sky: the story of "brave Bessie" Coleman ill. by Pamela Paparone. Candlewick, 1996. ISBN 1-56402-533-0 Subj: Activities – flying. Airplanes, airports. Ethnic groups in the U.S. – African Americans. Rhyming text.

North country spring ill. by Liz Sivertson. Houghton Mifflin, 1997. ISBN 0-395-82819-8 Subj: Animals. Nature. Rhyming text. Seasons – spring.

There's a cow in the road! ill. by Tracey Campbell Pearson. Dial, 1993. ISBN 0-8037-1336-3 Subj: Animals. Rhyming text.

A view from the air: Charles Lindbergh's earth and sky photos by Richard Brown. Viking, 1992. ISBN 0-670-84660-0 Subj: Careers – airplane pilots. Ecology. Nature. Rhyming text.

What is the sun? ill. by Stephen Lambert. Candlewick, 1994. ISBN 1-56402-146-7 Subj: Character traits – questioning. Moon. Sun. Weather – rain. Weather – wind.

Lindbloom, Steven. *Let's give kitty a bath!* ill. by True Kelley. Addison-Wesley, 1982. ISBN 0-201-10712-0 Subj: Activities – bathing. Animals – cats.

Linden, Ann Marie. *One smiling grandma* ill. by Lynne Russell. Dial, 1992. ISBN 0-8037-1132-8 Subj: Counting, numbers. Family life – grandmothers. Foreign lands – Caribbean Islands.

Linden, Madelaine Gill. *Under the blanket* ill. by author. Little, 1987. ISBN 0-316-52626-6 Subj: Rhyming text. Toys.

Lindenbaum, Pija. *Boodil, my dog* retold by Gabrielle Charbonnet; ill. by author. Holt, 1992. ISBN 0-8050-2444-1 Subj: Animals – dogs. Character traits – appearance.

Else-Marie and her seven little daddies ill. by author. Holt, 1991. ISBN 0-8050-1752-6 Subj: Behavior – worrying. Family life – fathers.

Lindgren, Astrid. *A calf for Christmas* trans. from Swedish by Barbara Lucas; ill. by Marit Tornqvist. Farrar, 1991. ISBN 91-29-59920-2 Subj: Animals – bulls, cows. Foreign lands – Sweden. Holidays – Christmas.

Christmas in noisy village by Astrid Lindgren and Ilon Wikland; trans. by Florence Lamborn; ill. by Ilon Wikland. Viking, 1964. ISBN 0-670-22106-6 Subj: Foreign lands – Sweden. Holidays – Christmas.

Christmas in the stable ill. by Harald Wiberg. Coward, 1962. ISBN 0-698-20677-0 Subj: Foreign lands – Sweden. Holidays – Christmas. Religion – Nativity.

Do you know Pippi Longstocking? ill. by Ingrid Nyman; trans. by Elisabeth Kallick Dyssegaard. R&S Books, 1999. ISBN 91-29-64661-8 Subj: Foreign lands – Sweden. Friendship. Humor.

The dragon with red eyes ill. by Ilon Wikland; trans. by Patricia Crampton. Viking, 1987. ISBN 0-670-81620-5 Subj: Dragons. Farms.

The ghost of Skinny Jack ill. by Ilon Wikland. Viking, 1988. ISBN 0-670-81913-1 Subj: Emotions – fear. Family life – grandmothers. Folk and fairy tales. Ghosts.

I want a brother or sister trans. from Swedish by Barbara Lucas; ill. by Ilon Wikland. Farrar, 1988. ISBN 91-29-58778-6 Subj: Babies. Emotions – envy, jealousy. Family life – new sibling. Sibling rivalry.

I want to go to school too trans. by Barbara Lucas; ill. by Ilon Wikland. Farrar, 1987. ISBN 91-29-58328-4 Subj: School. Sibling rivalry.

Lotta's Christmas surprise ill. by Ilon Wikland. Farrar, 1990. ISBN 91-29-59782-X Subj: Foreign lands – Sweden. Holidays – Christmas. Trees.

My nightingale is singing trans. by Patricia Crampton; ill. by Svend Otto S. Viking, 1986. ISBN 0-670-80997-7 Subj: Behavior – seeking better things. Emotions – sadness. Poverty.

Of course Polly can do almost everything ill. by Ilon Wikland. Follett, 1978. ISBN 0-695-40967-0 Subj: Character traits – optimism. Character traits – perseverance. Holidays – Christmas. Trees.

Pippi Longstocking's after-Christmas party ill. by Michael Chesworth. Viking, 1996. ISBN 0-679-86790-X Subj: Character traits – assertiveness. Foreign lands – Sweden. Holidays – Christmas. Parties.

The tomten ill. by Harald Wiberg. Coward, 1961. Adapt. from a poem by Victor Rydberg. ISBN 0-698-20147-7 Subj: Farms. Foreign lands – Sweden. Mythical creatures – trolls. Seasons – winter.

The tomten and the fox adapt. from a poem by Karl-Erik Forsslund; ill. by Harald Wiberg. Coward, 1965. ISBN 0-698-30371-7 Subj: Animals – foxes. Foreign lands – Sweden. Mythical creatures – trolls. Seasons – winter.

Lindgren, Barbro. *Andrei's search* ill. by Eva Eriksson; trans. by Elisabeth Kallick Dyssegaard. R&S Books, 2000. ISBN 91-29-64756-8 Subj: Behavior – needing someone. Foreign lands – Russia.

Benny's had enough ill. by Olof Landström; trans. by Elisabeth Kallick Dyssegaard. R&S Books, 1999. ISBN 91-29-64563-8 Subj: Animals – pigs. Behavior – running away. Family life – mothers.

Rosa ill. by Eva Eriksson. Firefly, 1996. ISBN 1-55054-241-9 Subj: Activities – playing. Animals – dogs.

Rosa goes to daycare ill. by Eva Eriksson. Douglas & McIntyre, 2000. ISBN 0-88899-391-9 Subj: School.

Sam's ball ill. by Eva Eriksson. Morrow, 1983. ISBN 0-688-02359-2 Subj: Animals – cats. Toys – balls.

Sam's bath ill. by Eva Eriksson. Morrow, 1983. ISBN 0-688-02362-2 Subj: Activities – bathing. Animals – dogs.

Sam's car ill. by Eva Eriksson. Morrow, 1982. ISBN 0-688-01263-9 Subj: Behavior – sharing. Toys.

Sam's cookie ill. by Eva Eriksson. Morrow, 1982. ISBN 0-688-01267-1 Subj: Behavior – sharing. Pets.

Sam's lamp ill. by Eva Eriksson. Morrow, 1983. ISBN 0-688-02356-8 Subj: Safety.

Sam's potty ill. by Eva Eriksson. Morrow, 1986. ISBN 0-688-06603-8 Subj: Behavior – growing up. Toilet training.

Sam's teddy bear ill. by Eva Eriksson. Morrow, 1982. ISBN 0-688-01270-1 Subj: Toys – bears.

Sam's wagon ill. by Eva Eriksson. Morrow, 1986. ISBN 0-688-05803-5 Subj: Animals – dogs. Toys.

Shorty takes off trans. by Richard E. Fisher; ill. by Olof Landström. Farrar, 1990. ISBN 91-29-59770-6 Subj: Activities – flying. Character traits – smallness.

The wild baby adapt. from Swedish by Jack Prelutsky; ill. by Eva Eriksson. Greenwillow, 1981. ISBN 0-688-00601-9 Subj: Behavior – misbehavior. Family life – mothers. Rhyming text.

The wild baby gets a puppy ill. by Eva Eriksson; adapt. from the Swedish by Jack Prelutsky. Greenwillow, 1988. ISBN 0-688-06712-3 Subj: Animals – dogs. Dreams. Family life – mothers. Night. Rhyming text.

The wild baby goes to sea adapt. from Swedish by Jack Prelutsky; ill. by Eva Eriksson. Greenwillow, 1983. ISBN 0-688-01931-7 Subj: Activities – playing. Family life – mothers. Imagination. Toys.

A worm's tale ill. by Cecilia Torudd. Farrar, 1988. ISBN 91-29-59068-X Subj: Animals – worms. Friendship.

Lindman, Maj. *Flicka, Ricka, Dicka and a little dog* ill. by author. Albert Whitman, 1995. ISBN 0-8075-2486-7 Subj: Animals – dogs. Family life. Foreign lands – Sweden. Multiple births – triplets.

Flicka, Ricka, Dicka and the big red hen ill. by author. Albert Whitman, 1995. ISBN 0-8075-2493-X Subj: Birds – chickens. Family life. Farms. Multiple births – triplets.

Flicka, Ricka, Dicka and the new dotted dress ill. by author. Albert Whitman, 1994. ISBN 0-8075-2494-8 Subj: Character traits – helpfulness. Family life. Foreign lands – Sweden. Multiple births – triplets.

Flicka, Ricka, Dicka and the three kittens ill. by author. Albert Whitman, 1994. ISBN 0-8075-2500-6 Subj: Animals – cats. Family life. Multiple births – triplets.

Flicka, Ricka, Dicka bake a cake ill. by author. Albert Whitman, 1995. ISBN 0-8075-2480-8 Subj: Activities – cooking. Birthdays. Family life. Foreign lands – Sweden. Multiple births – triplets.

Sailboat time ill. by author. Albert Whitman, 1951. Subj: Boats, ships. Foreign lands – Sweden.

Snipp, Snapp, Snurr and the buttered bread ill. by author. Albert Whitman, 1995. ISBN 0-8075-7504-6 Subj: Cumulative tales. Family life. Farms. Foreign lands – Sweden. Multiple births – triplets.

Snipp, Snapp, Snurr and the magic horse ill. by author. Albert Whitman, 1935. Subj: Family life. Foreign lands – Sweden. Magic. Multiple births – triplets. Toys – rocking horses.

Snipp, Snapp, Snurr and the red shoes ill. by author. Albert Whitman, 1994. ISBN 0-8075-7496-1 Subj: Activities – vacationing. Birthdays. Character traits – generosity. Character traits – helpfulness. Family life. Foreign lands – Lapland. Multiple births – triplets. Sports – skiing.

Snipp, Snapp, Snurr and the reindeer ill. by author. Albert Whitman, 1995. ISBN 0-8075-7497-X Subj: Animals – deer. Family life. Foreign lands – Sweden. Multiple births – triplets.

Snipp, Snapp, Snurr and the seven dogs ill. by author. Albert Whitman, 1959. Subj: Animals – dogs. Family life. Foreign lands – Sweden. Multiple births – triplets.

Snipp, Snapp, Snurr and the yellow sled ill. by author. Albert Whitman, 1995. ISBN 0-8075-7499-6 Subj: Animals – dogs. Family life. Foreign lands – Sweden. Multiple births – triplets. Sports – ice skating.

Lindsay, Elizabeth. *A letter for Maria* ill. by Alex de Wolf. Watts, 1988. ISBN 0-531-08375-6 Subj: Activities – painting. Toys – bears.

Lindsay, Jeanne Warren. *Do I have a daddy?* ill. by Jami Moffett. Morning Glory Pr., 2000. ISBN 1-885356-62-5 Subj: Family life. Family life – fathers. Family life – mothers.

Lindsey, Treska. *When Batistine made bread* ill. by author. Macmillan, 1985. ISBN 0-02-759120-4 Subj: Activities – cooking. Activities – working. Food.

Lines, Kathleen. *Dick Whittington* (Dick Whittington and his cat)

Lavender's blue: a book of nursery rhymes (Mother Goose)

The old ballad of the babes in the woods (The babes in the woods)

Once in royal David's city: a picture book of the Nativity, retold from the Gospels ill. by Harold Jones. Watts, 1956. Subj: Holidays – Christmas. Religion.

Ling, Mary. *Butterfly* ill. by Kim Taylor. DK, 1992. ISBN 1-56458-112-8 Subj: Insects – butterflies, caterpillars.

Calf photos by Gordon Clayton. DK, 1993. ISBN 1-564582-05-1 Subj: Animals – bulls, cows. Farms.

Foal photos by Gordon Clayton. DK, 1992. ISBN 1-56458-113-6 Subj: Animals – horses, ponies. Farms.

Fox photos by Jane Burton. DK, 1992. ISBN 1-56458-114-4 Subj: Animals – foxes. Nature.

Pig photos by Bill Ling. DK, 1993. ISBN 1-56458-204-3 Subj: Animals – pigs. Farms.

Lingo, Susan L. *Do you see the star?* (Nappa, Mike)

Link, Martin A. *The goat in the rug* (Blood, Charles L.)

Linke, Siegfried. *High flies the ball* (Koenner, Alfred)

Linn, Margot. *A trip to the dentist* ill. by Catherine Siracusa. HarperCollins, 1988. ISBN 0-06-025834-9 Subj: Careers – dentists.

A trip to the doctor ill. by Catherine Siracusa. HarperCollins, 1988. ISBN 0-06-025843-8 Subj: Careers – doctors.

Linscott, Jody. *Once upon A to Z* ill. by Claudia Porges Holland. Doubleday, 1991. ISBN 0-385-41907-4 Subj: ABC books. Careers – musicians.

Linzer, Jeff. *The fire station book* (Bundt, Nancy)

Lionni, Leo. *Alexander and the wind-up mouse* ill. by author. Pantheon, 1969. ISBN 0-394-90914-3 Subj: Animals – mice. Caldecott award honor books. Emotions – envy, jealousy. Friendship. Toys.

The biggest house in the world ill. by author. Pantheon, 1968. ISBN 0-394-90944-5 Subj: Animals. Behavior – greed.

A busy year ill. by author. Knopf, 1992. ISBN 0-679-92464-7 Subj: Animals – mice. Nature. Seasons. Trees.

A color of his own ill. by author. Delmar, 1990. ISBN 0-8273-4114-8 Subj: Character traits – individuality. Concepts – color. Reptiles – lizards.

Colors to talk about ill. by author. Pantheon, 1985. ISBN 0-394-87003-4 Subj: Animals – mice. Concepts – color. Format, unusual – board books.

Cornelius ill. by author. Pantheon, 1983. ISBN 0-394-95419-X Subj: Character traits – being different. Reptiles – alligators, crocodiles.

An extraordinary egg ill. by author. Knopf, 1994. ISBN 0-679-95840-1 Subj: Eggs. Friendship. Frogs and toads. Reptiles – alligators, crocodiles.

Fish is fish ill. by author. Pantheon, 1970. ISBN 0-394-90440-0 Subj: Behavior – misunderstanding. Fish. Friendship. Frogs and toads.

Frederick ill. by author. Random House, 1973, c1967. ISBN 0-394-82614-0 Subj: Animals – mice. Caldecott award honor books. Music.

Frederick's fables ill. by author. Pantheon, 1985. ISBN 0-394-87710-1 Subj: Animals.

Geraldine, the music mouse ill. by author. Pantheon, 1979. ISBN 0-394-94238-8 Subj: Animals – mice. Music.

The greentail mouse ill. by author. Pantheon, 1973. ISBN 0-394-92678-1 Subj: Animals – mice. Mardi Gras.

In the rabbitgarden ill. by author. Pantheon, 1975. ISBN 0-394-93089-4 Subj: Animals – foxes. Animals – mice. Reptiles – snakes.

Inch by inch ill. by author. Astor-Honor, 1960. ISBN 0-8392-3010-9 Subj: Birds. Caldecott award honor books. Concepts – measurement. Insects.

It's mine! a fable ill. by author. Knopf, 1986. ISBN 0-394-97000-X Subj: Behavior – fighting, arguing. Frogs and toads.

Let's make rabbits ill. by author. Knopf, 1992. Originally published: New York: Pantheon Books, c1982. ISBN 0-679-82640-8 Subj: Activities. Animals – rabbits. Art. Imagination.

Letters to talk about ill. by author. Pantheon, 1985. ISBN 0-394-87001-8 Subj: ABC books. Animals – mice. Format, unusual – board books.

Little blue and little yellow ill. by author. Mulberry, 1994. ISBN 0-688-13285-5 Subj: Concepts – color. Friendship.

Matthew's dream ill. by author. Knopf, 1991. ISBN 0-679-91075-1 Subj: Animals – mice. Careers – artists. Museums.

Mr. McMouse ill. by author. Knopf, 1992. ISBN 0-679-93890-7 Subj: Animals – mice. Friendship. Self-concept.

Mouse days ill. by author. Pantheon, 1981. ISBN 0-394-84548-X Subj: Animals – mice. Seasons.

Nicholas, where have you been? ill. by author. Knopf, 1987. ISBN 0-394-98370-X Subj: Animals – mice. Friendship.

Numbers to talk about ill. by author. Pantheon, 1985. ISBN 0-394-87002-6 Subj: Animals – mice. Counting, numbers. Format, unusual – board books.

On my beach there are many pebbles ill. by author. Astor-Honor, 1961. ISBN 0-8392-3024-9 Subj: Rocks. Sea and seashore.

Pezzettino ill. by author. Pantheon, 1975. ISBN 0-394-93156-4 Subj: Character traits – individuality. Concepts – shape. Self-concept.

Six crows ill. by author. Knopf, 1988. ISBN 0-394-99572-4 Subj: Birds – crows. Birds – owls. Farms.

Swimmy ill. by author. Random House, 1973, c1963. ISBN 0-394-82620-5 Subj: Caldecott award honor books. Fish. Sea and seashore.

Theodore and the talking mushroom ill. by author. Pantheon, 1971. ISBN 0-394-82312-5 Subj: Animals – mice. Character traits – optimism.

Tico and the golden wings ill. by author. Knopf, 1975, c1964. ISBN 0-394-83078-4 Subj: Birds. Character traits – generosity. Character traits – individuality. Character traits – questioning. Folk and fairy tales.

Tillie and the wall ill. by author. Knopf, 1989. ISBN 0-394-92155-0 Subj: Animals – mice. Behavior – seeking better things.

What? pictures to talk about ill. by author. Pantheon, 1983. ISBN 0-394-86031-4 Subj: Animals – mice. Format, unusual – board books. Senses – hearing. Senses – seeing. Senses – smelling. Senses – tasting. Senses – touching. Wordless.

When? ill. by author. Pantheon, 1983. ISBN 0-394-86032-2 Subj: Animals – mice. Format, unusual – board books. Night. Seasons. Wordless.

Where? pictures to talk about ill. by author. Pantheon, 1983. ISBN 0-394-86033-0 Subj: Animals – mice. Format, unusual – board books. Humor. Wordless.

Who? pictures to talk about ill. by author. Pantheon, 1983. ISBN 0-394-86030-6 Subj: Animals – mice. Format, unusual – board books. Wordless.

Words to talk about ill. by author. Pantheon, 1985. ISBN 0-394-87004-2 Subj: Animals – mice. Format, unusual – board books. Language.

Lipkind, William. *Billy the kid* by William Lipkind and Nicolas Mordvinoff; ill. by Nicolas Mordvinoff. Harcourt, 1964. Subj: Animals – goats.

The boy and the forest by William Lipkind and Nicolas Mordvinoff; ill. by Nicolas Mordvinoff. Harcourt, 1964. Subj: Animals. Character traits – kindness to animals. Forest, woods. Magic.

Chaga by William Lipkind and Nicolas Mordvinoff; ill. by Nicolas Mordvinoff. Harcourt, 1955. Subj: Animals – elephants. Concepts – size.

The Christmas bunny by William Lipkind and Nicolas Mordvinoff; ill. by Nicolas Mordvinoff. Harcourt, 1953. Subj: Animals – foxes. Animals – rabbits. Holidays – Christmas. Parties.

Circus rucus by William Lipkind and Nicolas Mordvinoff; ill. by Nicolas Mordvinoff. Harcourt, 1954. Subj: Circus.

Even Steven by William Lipkind and Nicolas Mordvinoff; ill. by Nicolas Mordvinoff. Harcourt, 1952. Subj: Animals – dogs. Character traits – selfishness.

Finders keepers by William Lipkind and Nicolas Mordvinoff; ill. by Nicolas Mordvinoff. Harcourt, 1951. ISBN 0-15-227529-0 Subj: Animals – dogs. Caldecott award books. Character traits – selfishness.

Four-leaf clover by William Lipkind and Nicolas Mordvinoff; ill. by Nicolas Mordvinoff. Harcourt, 1959. Subj: Ethnic groups in the U.S. – African Americans.

The little tiny rooster by William Lipkind and Nicolas Mordvinoff; ill. by Nicolas Mordvinoff. Harcourt, 1960. ISBN 0-15-247578-8 Subj: Animals – foxes. Birds – chickens. Character traits – smallness. Self-concept.

The magic feather duster by William Lipkind and Nicolas Mordvinoff; ill. by Nicolas Mordvinoff.

Harcourt, 1958. Subj: Character traits – kindness. Folk and fairy tales. Magic.

Nubber bear ill. by Roger Antoine Duvoisin. Harcourt, 1966. Subj: Animals – bears. Behavior – misbehavior.

Professor Bull's umbrella by William Lipkind and Georges Schreiber; ill. by Georges Schreiber. Viking, 1954. Subj: Umbrellas.

Russet and the two reds by William Lipkind and Nicolas Mordvinoff; ill. by Nicolas Mordvinoff. Harcourt, 1962. Subj: Animals – cats.

Sleepyhead by William Lipkind and Nicolas Mordvinoff; ill. by Nicolas Mordvinoff. Harcourt, 1957. Subj: Activities – playing. Games. Rhyming text.

The two reds by William Lipkind and Nicolas Mordvinoff; ill. by Nicolas Mordvinoff. Harcourt, 1950. Subj: Animals – cats. Caldecott award honor books. Friendship.

Lipniacka, Ewa. *To bed . . . or else!* ill. by Basia Bogdanowicz. Interlink, 1992. ISBN 0-940793-85-7 Subj: Bedtime. Friendship. Night. Sleepovers.

Lippman, Peter. *The Know-It-Alls go to sea* ill. by author. Doubleday, 1982. ISBN 0-385-17396-2 Subj: Behavior – misbehavior. Boats, ships.

The Know-It-Alls help out ill. by author. Doubleday, 1982. ISBN 0-385-17397-0 Subj: Behavior – misbehavior. Homes, houses.

The Know-It-Alls mind the store ill. by author. Doubleday, 1982. ISBN 0-385-17399-7 Subj: Behavior – misbehavior. Stores.

The Know-It-Alls take a winter vacation ill. by author. Doubleday, 1982. ISBN 0-385-17398-9 Subj: Activities – vacationing. Behavior – misbehavior.

New at the zoo ill. by author. HarperCollins, 1969. Subj: Animals. Bedtime. Zoos.

Peter Lippman's numbers ill. by author. Grosset, 1988. ISBN 0-448-19105-9 Subj: Counting, numbers. Format, unusual – toy and movable books.

Peter Lippman's opposites ill. by author. Grosset, 1988. ISBN 0-448-19106-7 Subj: Concepts – opposites. Format, unusual – toy and movable books.

Lippman, Sidney. *A you're adorable* words and music by Sidney Lippman, Buddy Kaye, and Fred Wise; ill. by Martha Alexander. Candlewick, 1994. ISBN 1-56402-237-4 Subj: ABC books. Babies. Ethnic groups in the U.S. Music. Songs.

Lipson, Beth Weiner. *Benjamin's perfect solution* ill. by author. Warner, 1979. ISBN 0-7232-6160-1 Subj: Animals – porcupines. Animals – possums. Behavior – mistakes. Self-concept.

Lipson, Michael. *How the wind plays* ill. by Daniel Kirk. Hyperion, 1994. ISBN 1-56282-326-4 Subj: Weather – wind.

Lishak, Anthony. *Row your boat* ill. by Graham Percy. DK, 1999. ISBN 0-7894-3489-X Subj: Animals. Birthdays. Format, unusual – toy and movable books. Songs. Transportation.

Lisker, Sonia O. *Lost* ill. by author. Harcourt, 1975. ISBN 0-15-249363-8 Subj: Behavior – lost. Wordless. Zoos.

Two special cards by Sonia O. Lisker and Leigh Dean; ill. by Sonia O. Lisker. Harcourt, 1976. Subj: Divorce. Family life.

Lisowski, Gabriel. *How Tevye became a milkman* ill. by author. Holt, 1976. ISBN 0-03-016636-5 Subj: Foreign lands – Ukraine. Jewish culture.

Roncalli's magnificent circus ill. by author. Doubleday, 1980. ISBN 0-685-14856-9 Subj: Animals – bears. Behavior – running away. Circus.

Listen to the storyteller: *a trio of musical tales from around the world* ill. by Kristen Balouch. Viking, 1999. ISBN 0-670-88054-X Subj: Folk and fairy tales. Foreign lands. Music.

Litchfield, Ada B. *A button in her ear* ill. by Eleanor Mill. Albert Whitman, 1976. ISBN 0-8075-0987-6 Subj: Handicaps – deafness. Senses – hearing.

A cane in her hand ill. by Eleanor Mill. Albert Whitman, 1977. ISBN 0-8075-1056-4 Subj: Handicaps – blindness. Senses – seeing.

Litowinsky, Olga. *Boats for bedtime* ill. by Melanie Hope Greenberg. Clarion, 1999. ISBN 0-395-89128-0 Subj: Bedtime. Boats, ships.

A little ABC book. Simon & Schuster, 1980. ISBN 0-671-41342-2 Subj: ABC books. Format, unusual – board books.

The little book of cats ill. by Diane Goode. Dutton, 1993. ISBN 0-525-45160-9 Subj: Animals – cats. Nursery rhymes.

A little book of colors. Simon & Schuster, 1982. ISBN 0-671-45570-2 Subj: Concepts – color. Format, unusual – board books.

The Little book of mice ill. by Diane Goode. Dutton, 1993. ISBN 0-525-45158-7 Subj: Animals – mice. Nursery rhymes.

A little book of numbers. Simon & Schuster, 1980. ISBN 0-671-41346-5 Subj: Counting, numbers. Format, unusual – board books.

The Little book of pigs ill. by Diane Goode. Dutton, 1993. ISBN 0-525-45159-5 Subj: Animals – pigs. Nursery rhymes.

Little book of prayers ill. by Roma Bishop. Little, 1987. ISBN 0-316-09660-1 Subj: Religion.

Little, Debbie. *The potluck adventures of Mrs. Marmalade* (Swendson, Patsy)

Little, Emily. *David and the giant* (Bible. Old Testament. David)

Little, Jean. *Bats about baseball* by Jean Little and Clair Mackay; ill. by Kim LaFave. Viking, 1995. ISBN 0-670-85270-8 Subj: Family life – grandmothers. Language. Sports – baseball.

Gruntle Piggle takes off ill. by Johnny Wales. Viking, 1996. ISBN 0-670-86340-8 Subj: Activities – reading. Animals – pigs. City. Family life – grandfathers. Farms.

Jess was the brave one ill. by Janet Wilson. Viking, 1992. ISBN 0-670-83495-5 Subj: Behavior – bullying. Character traits – bravery. Emotions – fear. Family life – sisters. Toys – bears.

Once upon a golden apple by Jean Little and Maggie De Vries; ill. by Phoebe Gilman. Viking, 1991. ISBN 0-670-82963-3 Subj: Activities – picnicking. Activities – reading. Folk and fairy tales.

Revenge of the small Small ill. by Janet Wilson. Viking, 1992. ISBN 0-670-84471-3 Subj: Concepts – size. Family life – brothers and sisters. Sibling rivalry.

Little, Lessie Jones. *Children of long ago* ill. by Jan Spivey Gilchrist. Putnam, 1988. ISBN 0-399-21473-9 Subj: Ethnic groups in the U.S. – African Americans. Poetry.

I can do it by myself by Lessie Jones Little and Eloise Greenfield; ill. by Carole M. Byard. Crowell, 1978. ISBN 0-690-03851-8 Subj: Birthdays. Character traits – bravery. Plants.

Little, Mary E. *ABC for the library* ill. by author. Atheneum, 1975. ISBN 0-689-30467-6 Subj: ABC books. Libraries.

Ricardo and the puppets ill. by author. Scribners, 1958. Subj: Animals – mice. Libraries. Puppets.

Little, Mimi Otey. *Blue moon soup spoon* ill. by author. Farrar, 1993. ISBN 0-374-30851-9 Subj: Moon. Rhyming text.

Daddy has a pair of striped shorts ill. by author. Farrar, 1990. ISBN 0-374-31675-9 Subj: Clothing. Family life – fathers.

Yoshiko and the foreigner ill. by author. Farrar, 1996. ISBN 0-374-32448-4 Subj: Careers – military. Ethnic groups in the U.S. – African Americans. Foreign lands – Japan. Weddings.

Little old lady who swallowed a fly. *Fancy that!* retold and ill. by Jan Pienkowski. Orchard, 1989. ISBN 1-8521-3345-7 Subj: Cumulative tales. Folk and fairy tales. Foreign lands – England. Format, unusual – toy and movable books. Insects – flies. Songs.

Golly Gump swallowed a fly retold by Joanna Cole; ill. by Bari Weisman. Gareth Stevens, 1992. ISBN 0-8368-0881-9 Subj: Cumulative tales. Folk and fairy tales. Insects – flies. Songs.

I know an old lady retold by Rose Bonne; ill. by Abner Graboff; music by Alan Mills. Rand McNally, 1961. Subj: Cumulative tales. Folk and fairy tales. Foreign lands – Canada. Insects – flies. Music. Songs.

I know an old lady retold and ill. by G. Brian Karas. Scholastic, 1994. ISBN 0-590-46575-9 Subj: Cumulative tales. Folk and fairy tales. Foreign lands – England. Insects – flies. Rhyming text. Songs. Witches.

I know an old lady adapt. by Amy Bauman and Margaret Snyder; ill. by Steve McInturff. Western, 1993. ISBN 0-307-74818-9 Subj: Cumulative tales. Folk and fairy tales. Foreign lands – England. Format, unusual – toy and movable books. Insects – flies. Songs.

I know an old lady retold and ill. by Albert Miller. Rand McNally, 1961. Subj: Cumulative tales. Folk and fairy tales. Insects – flies. Songs.

I know an old lady who swallowed a fly retold and ill. by Glen Rounds. Holiday, 1990. ISBN 0-8234-0814-0 Subj: Cumulative tales. Folk and fairy tales. Foreign lands – England. Insects – flies. Songs.

I know an old lady who swallowed a fly retold by Rose Bonne; ill. by William Stobbs. Oxford Univ. Pr., 1987. ISBN 0-19-279837-5 Subj: Cumulative tales. Folk and fairy tales. Foreign lands – Canada. Insects – flies. Songs.

I know an old lady who swallowed a fly retold and ill. by Nadine Bernard Westcott. Little, 1980. ISBN 0-316-93128-4 Subj: Cumulative tales. Folk and fairy tales. Foreign lands – England. Insects – flies. Songs.

There was an old lady retold and ill. by Nick Bantock. Viking, 1990. ISBN 0-670-83194-8 Subj: Cumulative tales. Folk and fairy tales. Foreign lands – England. Format, unusual – toy and movable books. Insects – flies. Songs.

There was an old lady who swallowed a fly ill. by Pam Adams. Child's Play, 1990. ISBN 0-85953-021-3 Subj: Cumulative tales. Folk and fairy tales. Foreign lands – Canada. Format, unusual – toy and movable books. Insects – flies. Songs.

There was an old lady who swallowed a fly retold and ill. by Colin Hawkins. Putnam, 1987. ISBN 0-399-21484-4 Subj: Cumulative tales. Folk and fairy tales. Foreign lands – England. Format, unusual – toy and movable books. Insects – flies. Songs.

There was an old lady who swallowed a fly retold and ill. by Simms Taback. Viking, 1997. ISBN 0-670-86939-2 Subj: Caldecott award honor books. Cumulative tales. Folk and fairy tales. Format, unusual. Insects – flies. Rhyming text. Songs.

There was an old woman retold and ill. by Steven Kellogg. Four Winds, 1980, 1974. ISBN 0-590-07779-1 Subj: Cumulative tales. Folk and fairy tales. Insects – flies. Songs.

The little red hen. *The cock, the mouse and the little red hen* adapt. and ill. by Lorinda Bryan Cauley. Putnam, 1982. ISBN 0-399-20740-6 Subj: Animals. Character traits – cleverness. Folk and fairy tales.

The cock, the mouse and the little red hen ill. by Graham Percy. Candlewick, 1992. ISBN 1-56402-008-8 Subj: Animals. Birds – chickens. Character traits

– laziness. Cumulative tales. Farms. Folk and fairy tales. Plants.

The little red hen ill. by Byron Barton. HarperCollins, 1993. ISBN 0-06-021676-X Subj: Animals. Birds – chickens. Character traits – laziness. Cumulative tales. Farms. Folk and fairy tales. Plants.

The little red hen retold by Harriet Ziefert; ill. by Emily Bolam. Viking, 1995. ISBN 0-670-86050-6 Subj: Animals. Birds – chickens. Character traits – laziness. Cumulative tales. Farms. Folk and fairy tales. Plants.

The little red hen ill. by Janina Domanska. Macmillan, 1973. ISBN 0-02-732820-1 Subj: Animals. Birds – chickens. Character traits – laziness. Cumulative tales. Farms. Folk and fairy tales. Plants.

The little red hen ill. by Paul Galdone. Seabury Pr., 1973. ISBN 0-8164-3099-3 Subj: Animals. Birds – chickens. Character traits – laziness. Cumulative tales. Farms. Folk and fairy tales. Plants.

The little red hen by Patricia C. and Fredrick McKissack; ill. by Dennis Hockerman. Childrens Pr., 1985. ISBN 0-516-02363-2 Subj: Animals. Birds – chickens. Character traits – laziness. Cumulative tales. Farms.

Little red hen by Alan Garner; ill. by Norman Messenger. DK, 1997. ISBN 0-7894-1171-1 Subj: Animals. Birds – chickens. Character traits – laziness. Cumulative tales. Farms. Folk and fairy tales. Plants.

The little red hen retold by Jean Horton Berg; reading consultant: Morton Betel; ill. by Mel Pekarsky. Follett, 1963. Subj: Animals. Birds – chickens. Character traits – laziness. Cumulative tales. Farms. Folk and fairy tales. Plants.

The little red hen adapt. and ill. by William Stobbs. Oxford Univ. Pr., 1985. ISBN 0-19-279807-3 Subj: Animals. Birds – chickens. Character traits – laziness. Cumulative tales. Farms. Folk and fairy tales. Plants.

The little red hen: an old story retold and ill. by Margot Zemach. Farrar, 1983. ISBN 0-374-34621-6 Subj: Animals. Birds – chickens. Character traits – laziness. Cumulative tales. Farms. Folk and fairy tales. Plants.

The Little Red Hen makes a pizza retold by Philemon Sturges; ill. by Amy Walrod. Dutton, 1999. ISBN 0-525-45953-7 Subj: Animals. Birds – chickens. Character traits – laziness. Cumulative tales. Farms. Folk and fairy tales.

Little Robin Redbreast: *a Mother Goose rhyme* ill. by Shari Halpern. North-South, 1994. ISBN 1-55858-248-7 Subj: Animals – cats. Birds – robins. Nursery rhymes.

Little Tom Tucker ill. by Paul Galdone. McGraw-Hill, 1970. This version was published by J. Kendrew, York, England, ca. 1820. Subj: Nursery rhymes.

Little Tuppen: *an old tale* ill. by Paul Galdone. Seabury Pr., 1967. ISBN 0-395-28804-5 Subj: Birds – chickens. Cumulative tales. Folk and fairy tales.

Littledale, Freya. *The farmer in the soup* ill. by Molly Delaney. Scholastic, 1987. ISBN 0-590-40194-7 Subj: Behavior – sharing. Farms. Folk and fairy tales.

The little mermaid (Andersen, H. C. [Hans Christian])

The magic plum tree ill. by Enrico Arno. Crown, 1981. ISBN 0-517-54166-1 Subj: Character traits – individuality. Plants. Royalty.

Peter and the north wind ill. by Troy Howell. Scholastic, 1988. ISBN 0-590-40756-2 Subj: Folk and fairy tales. Weather – wind.

The snow child ill. by Leon Steinmetz. Scholastic, 1978. Subj: Behavior – wishing. Old age. Seasons – winter.

Littlefield, William. *The whiskers of Ho Ho* ill. by Vladimir Bobri. Lothrop, 1958. Subj: Animals – rabbits. Birds – chickens. Folk and fairy tales. Foreign lands – China. Holidays – Easter.

Littlesugar, Amy. *Jonkonnu: a story from the sketchbook of Winslow Homer* ill. by Ian Schoenherr. Philomel, 1997. ISBN 0-399-22831-4 Subj: Careers – artists. Ethnic groups in the U.S. – African Americans. Prejudice.

Josiah True and the art maker by Amy Littlesugar and Barbara Garrison; ill. by Barbara Garrison. Simon & Schuster, 1995. ISBN 0-671-88354-2 Subj: Activities – drawing. Art. Careers – artists.

Marie in fourth position: the story of Degas's "The little dancer" ill. by Ian Schoenherr. Philomel, 1996. ISBN 0-399-22794-6 Subj: Art. Ballet. Careers – artists. Careers – models.

Shake Rag: from the life of Elvis Presley ill. by Floyd Cooper. Philomel, 1998. ISBN 0-399-23005-X Subj: Careers – singers. Ethnic groups in the U.S. – African Americans. Music.

Tree of hope ill. by Floyd Cooper. Philomel, 1999. ISBN 0-399-23300-8 Subj: Careers – actors. Ethnic groups in the U.S. – African Americans. Poverty. Theater. U.S. history.

Littlewood, Valerie. *The season clock* ill. by author. Viking, 1987. ISBN 0-670-81433-4 Subj: Behavior – misbehavior. Character traits – bravery. Seasons. Time.

Litzinger, Rosanne. *The old woman and her pig* (The old woman and her pig)

Lively, Penelope. *The cat, the crow, and the banyan tree* ill. by Terry Milne. Candlewick, 1994. ISBN 1-56402-325-7 Subj: Animals – cats. Birds – crows. Imagination.

Good night, sleep tight ill. by Adriano Gon. Candlewick, 1995. ISBN 1-56402-417-2 Subj: Bedtime. Night. Sleep. Toys.

One, two, three, jump! ill. by Jan Ormerod. Margaret K. McElderry, 1999. ISBN 0-689-82201-4 Subj: Character traits – helpfulness. Frogs and toads. Insects – dragonflies.

Livermore, Elaine. *Find the cat* ill. by author. Houghton Mifflin, 1973. ISBN 0-395-14756-5 Subj: Animals – cats. Games.

Follow the fox ill. by author. Houghton Mifflin, 1981. ISBN 0-395-31672-3 Subj: Animals – foxes. Behavior – lost. Behavior – needing someone.

Looking for Henry ill. by author. Houghton Mifflin, 1988. ISBN 0-395-44240-0 Subj: Animals – leopards. Behavior – hiding. Sports – hunting.

Lost and found ill. by author. Houghton Mifflin, 1975. ISBN 0-395-20279-5 Subj: Behavior – losing things. Games.

One to ten, count again ill. by author. Houghton Mifflin, 1973. ISBN 0-395-17514-3 Subj: Counting, numbers. Games.

Three little kittens lost their mittens ill. by author. Houghton Mifflin, 1979. ISBN 0-395-28379-5 Subj: Animals – cats. Behavior – losing things. Games. Nursery rhymes.

Livingston, Carole. *"Why am I going to the hospital?"* (Ciliotta, Claire)

"Why was I adopted?" ill. by Arthur Robins; designed by Paul Walter. Lyle Stuart, 1978. ISBN 0-8184-0257-1 Subj: Adoption. Family life.

Livingston, Myra Cohn. *Abraham Lincoln: a man for all the people* ill. by Samuel Byrd. Holiday, 1993. ISBN 0-8234-1049-8 Subj: Poetry. U.S. history.

B is for baby: an alphabet of verses photos by Steel Stillman. Margaret K. McElderry, 1996. ISBN 0-689-80950-6 Subj: ABC books. Babies. Poetry.

Birthday poems ill. by Margot Tomes. Holiday, 1989. ISBN 0-8234-0783-7 Subj: Birthdays. Poetry.

Cat poems ill. by Trina Schart Hyman. Holiday, 1987. ISBN 0-8234-0631-8 Subj: Animals – cats. Poetry.

Celebrations ill. by Leonard Everett Fisher. Holiday, 1985. ISBN 0-8234-0550-8 Subj: Holidays. Poetry.

Dog poems ill. by Leslie Holt Morrill. Holiday, 1990. ISBN 0-8234-0776-4 Subj: Animals – dogs. Poetry.

Festivals ill. by Leonard Everett Fisher. Holiday, 1996. ISBN 0-8234-1217-2 Subj: Fairs. Poetry.

Higgledy-Piggledy: verses and pictures by Myra Cohn Livingston and Peter Sis; ill. by Peter Sis. Macmillan, 1986. ISBN 0-689-50407-1 Subj: Behavior. Rhyming text.

If you ever meet a whale: poems (If you ever meet a whale)

Keep on singing: a ballad of Marian Anderson ill. by Samuel Byrd. Holiday, 1994. ISBN 0-8234-1098-6

Subj: Ethnic groups in the U.S. – African Americans. Poetry. U.S. history.

A Learical lexicon (Lear, Edward)

Poems for brothers, poems for sisters ill. by Jean Zallinger. Holiday, 1991. ISBN 0-8234-0861-2 Subj: Family life – brothers and sisters. Poetry.

Poems for fathers ill. by Robert Casilla. Holiday, 1989. ISBN 0-5234-0729-2 Subj: Family life – fathers. Holidays – Father's Day. Poetry.

Poems for mothers ill. by Deborah Kogan Ray. Holiday, 1988. ISBN 0-8234-0678-4 Subj: Family life – mothers. Holidays – Mother's Day. Poetry.

Valentine poems ill. by Patience Brewster. Holiday, 1987. ISBN 0-8234-0587-7 Subj: Animals. Holidays – Valentine's Day.

Llewellyn, Claire. *My first book of time* ill. by Julie Carpenter; photos by Paul Bricknell. DK, 1992. ISBN 1-879431-78-5 Subj: Clocks, watches. Days of the week, months of the year. Format, unusual – toy and movable books. Seasons. Time.

Some bugs glow in the dark ill. by Myke Taylor, Rob Shone, and Jo Moore. Copper Beech, 1997. ISBN 0-7613-0562-9 Subj: Insects. Nature. Spiders.

Spiders have fangs ill. by Myke Taylor and Jo Moore. Copper Beech, 1997. ISBN 0-7613-0610-2 Subj: Spiders.

Lloyd, David. *Air* ill. by Peter Visscher. Dial, 1982. ISBN 0-8037-0143-8 Subj: Science.

Cat and dog ill. by Clive Scruton. Lothrop, 1987. ISBN 0-688-07268-2 Subj: Animals – cats. Animals – dogs.

Duck ill. by Charlotte Voake. Lippincott, 1988. ISBN 0-397-32275-5 Subj: Animals. Birds – ducks. Family life – grandmothers.

Grandma and the pirate ill. by Gill Tomblin. Crown, 1986. ISBN 0-517-56023-2 Subj: Family life – grandmothers. Imagination. Pirates. Sand. Sea and seashore.

Hello, goodbye ill. by Louise Voce. Lothrop, 1988. ISBN 0-688-07699-8 Subj: Animals. Trees. Weather – rain.

The ridiculous story of Gammer Gurton's needle ill. by Charlotte Voake. Potter/Crown, 1987. ISBN 0-517-56513-7 Subj: Behavior – lying. Folk and fairy tales. Humor.

The stopwatch ill. by Penny Dale. Lippincott, 1986. ISBN 0-397-32193-7 Subj: Clocks, watches. Family life – grandmothers. Sibling rivalry.

Lloyd, Errol. *Nandy's bedtime* ill. by author. Merrimack, 1983. ISBN 0-370-30395-4 Subj: Bedtime. Night.

Nini at carnival ill. by author. Crowell, 1979. ISBN 0-690-03892-5 Subj: Character traits – helpfulness. Clothing.

Lloyd, Megan. *Chicken tricks* ill. by author. HarperCollins, 1983. ISBN 0-06-023985-9 Subj: Birds – chickens. Eggs. Humor. Rhyming text.

Lobato, Arcadio. *The greatest treasure* ill. by author. Picture Book Studio, 1991. Originally published in Spanish. ISBN 0-88708-093-6 Subj: Animals – whales. Friendship. Royalty – queens. Sea and seashore. Witches.

Just one wish ill. by author. Picture Book Studio, 1989. ISBN 0-88708-134-7 Subj: Behavior – wishing. Magic.

Paper bird ill. by Emilio Urberuaga. Carolrhoda, 1994. ISBN 0-87614-817-8 Subj: Activities – flying. Art. Birds. Kites. Paper.

Lobe, Mira. *Christoph wants a party* retold by Marcia Lane, ill. by Winfried Opgenoorth. Kane/Miller, 1995. ISBN 0-916291-59-6 Subj: Birthdays. Parties.

The snowman who went for a walk trans. from German by Peter Carter; ill. by Winfried Opgenoorth. Morrow, 1984. ISBN 0-688-03866-2 Subj: Activities – walking. Snowmen.

Valerie and the good-night swing trans. from German by Peter Carter; ill. by Winfried Opgenoorth. Oxford Univ. Pr., 1983. ISBN 0-19-279769-7 Subj: Bedtime. Rhyming text.

Lobel, Anita. *Alison's zinnia* ill. by author. Greenwillow, 1990. ISBN 0-688-08866-X Subj: ABC books. Flowers.

Away from home ill. by author. Greenwillow, 1994. ISBN 0-688-10355-3 Subj: ABC books. Activities – traveling.

A birthday for the princess ill. by author. HarperCollins, 1973. ISBN 0-06-023944-1 Subj: Behavior – needing someone. Birthdays. Royalty – princesses.

The dwarf giant ill. by author. Greenwillow, 1996. ISBN 0-688-14407-1 Subj: Dwarfs, midgets. Folk and fairy tales. Foreign lands – Japan. Giants.

King Rooster, Queen Hen ill. by author. Greenwillow, 1975. ISBN 0-688-84008-6 Subj: Animals. Birds – chickens. Foreign lands – Denmark.

One lighthouse, one moon ill. by author. Greenwillow, 2000. ISBN 0-688-15540-5 Subj: Animals – cats. Counting, numbers. Days of the week, months of the year. Lighthouses.

The pancake ill. by author. Greenwillow, 1978. ISBN 0-688-84125-2 Subj: Cumulative tales. Food.

Pierrot's ABC garden ill. by author. Western, 1993. ISBN 0-307-17551-0 Subj: ABC books. Clowns, jesters. Gardens, gardening.

Potatoes, potatoes ill. by author. Greenwillow, 1967. Subj: Violence, nonviolence.

The straw maid ill. by author. Greenwillow, 1983. ISBN 0-688-00330-3 Subj: Character traits – cleverness. Crime.

Sven's bridge ill. by author. Greenwillow, 1992. Newly illustrated. ISBN 0-688-11252-8 Subj: Bridges. Royalty.

The troll music ill. by author. HarperCollins, 1966. Subj: Magic. Music. Mythical creatures – trolls.

Lobel, Arnold. *Days with Frog and Toad* ill. by author. HarperCollins, 1979. ISBN 0-06-023964-6 Subj: Friendship. Frogs and toads.

Fables ill. by author. HarperCollins, 1980. ISBN 0-06-023974-3 Subj: Animals. Caldecott award books.

Frog and Toad all year ill. by author. Harper-Collins, 1976. ISBN 0-06-023951-4 Subj: Friendship. Frogs and toads. Seasons.

Frog and Toad are friends ill. by author. Harper-Collins, 1970. ISBN 0-06-023958-1 Subj: Caldecott award honor books. Friendship. Frogs and toads.

The frog and toad pop-up book ill. by author. HarperCollins, 1986. ISBN 0-06-023986-7 Subj: Format, unusual – toy and movable books. Frogs and toads.

Frog and Toad together ill. by author. Harper-Collins, 1971. ISBN 0-06-023959-X Subj: Friendship. Frogs and toads.

Giant John ill. by author. HarperCollins, 1964. ISBN 0-06-022946-2 Subj: Giants.

Grasshopper on the road ill. by author. Harper-Collins, 1978. ISBN 0-06-023962-X Subj: Insects. Insects – grasshoppers.

The great blueness and other predicaments ill. by author. HarperCollins, 1968. ISBN 0-06-023938-7 Subj: Concepts – color. Wizards.

Gregory Griggs and other nursery rhyme people (Mother Goose)

A holiday for Mister Muster ill. by author. Harper-Collins, 1963. ISBN 0-06-023956-5 Subj: Animals. Illness. Zoos.

How the rooster saved the day ill. by Anita Lobel. Greenwillow, 1977. ISBN 0-688-84063-9 Subj: Birds – chickens. Character traits – cleverness. Crime.

Lucille ill. by author. HarperCollins, 1964. ISBN 0-06-023966-2 Subj: Animals – horses, ponies. Humor.

The man who took the indoors out ill. by author. HarperCollins, 1974. ISBN 0-06-023947-6 Subj: Behavior – running away.

Martha, the movie mouse ill. by author. Harper-Collins, 1966. Subj: Animals – mice. Rhyming text. Theater.

Ming Lo moves the mountain ill. by author. Greenwillow, 1982. ISBN 0-688-00611-6 Subj: Foreign lands – China. Moving.

Mouse soup ill. by author. HarperCollins, 1977. ISBN 0-06-023968-9 Subj: Animals – mice. Animals – weasels. Character traits – cleverness.

Mouse tales ill. by author. HarperCollins, 1972. ISBN 0-06-023942-5 Subj: Animals – mice. Humor. Tall tales.

On Market Street ill. by Anita Lobel. Greenwillow, 1981. ISBN 0-688-84309-3 Subj: ABC books. Caldecott award honor books. Rhyming text. Shopping. Stores.

On the day Peter Stuyvesant sailed into town ill. by author. HarperCollins, 1971. ISBN 0-06-023972-7 Subj: Problem solving. Rhyming text. U.S. history.

Owl at home ill. by author. HarperCollins, 1975. ISBN 0-06-023949-2 Subj: Birds – owls.

Prince Bertram the bad ill. by author. Harper-Collins, 1963. ISBN 0-06-023976-X Subj: Behavior – misbehavior. Dragons. Royalty – princes. Witches.

The rose in my garden ill. by Anita Lobel. 1st Mulberry ed. Mulberry, 1993. ISBN 0-688-12265-5 Subj: Animals – cats. Animals – mice. Cumulative tales. Flowers. Gardens, gardening. Insects – bees. Rhyming text.

Small pig ill. by author. HarperCollins, 1969. ISBN 0-06-023932-8 Subj: Animals – pigs. Behavior – running away. Farms.

A treeful of pigs ill. by Anita Lobel. Greenwillow, 1979. ISBN 0-688-84177-5 Subj: Animals – pigs. Character traits – laziness. Farms. Humor.

The turnaround wind ill. by author. HarperCollins, 1988. ISBN 0-06-023988-3 Subj: Weather – wind.

Uncle Elephant ill. by author. HarperCollins, 1981. ISBN 0-06-023980-8 Subj: Animals – elephants. Behavior – lost. Family life – aunts, uncles. Sea and seashore.

Whiskers and rhymes ill. by author. Greenwillow, 1985. ISBN 0-688-03836-0 Subj: Animals – cats. Poetry.

A zoo for Mister Muster ill. by author. Harper-Collins, 1962. ISBN 0-06-023991-3 Subj: Animals. Zoos.

Locker, Thomas. *Anna and the bagpiper* ill. by author. Philomel, 1994. ISBN 0-399-22546-3 Subj: Music. Senses – hearing.

Cloud dance ill. by author. Harcourt, 2000. ISBN 0-15-202231-7 Subj: Weather – clouds.

Family farm ill. by author. Dial, 1988. ISBN 0-8037-0490-9 Subj: Farms.

The land of gray wolf ill. by author. Dial, 1991. ISBN 0-8037-0937-4 Subj: Ecology. Indians of North America. Nature.

The man who paints nature photos by Tim Holmstrom. R.C. Owen, 1999. ISBN 1-57274-328-X Subj: Careers – artists. Careers – illustrators. Nature.

The mare on the hill ill. by author. Dial, 1985. ISBN 0-8037-0208-6 Subj: Animals – horses, ponies. Family life – grandfathers. Farms.

Miranda's smile ill. by author. Dial, 1994. ISBN 0-8037-1689-3 Subj: Careers – artists. Family life – daughters. Family life – fathers.

Rip Van Winkle (Irving, Washington)

Sailing with the wind ill. by author. Dial, 1986. ISBN 0-8037-0312-0 Subj: Activities – traveling. Boats, ships. Sailors.

Sky tree ill. by Candice Christiansen. Harper-Collins, 1995. ISBN 0-06-024884-X Subj: Science. Seasons. Trees.

Where the river begins ill. by author. Dial, 1984. ISBN 0-8937-0090-3 Subj: Family life – grandfathers. Rivers.

The young artist ill. by author. Dial, 1989. ISBN 0-8037-0627-8 Subj: Careers – artists. Royalty.

Lockwood, Primrose. *Cat boy!* ill. by Clara Vulliamy. Houghton Mifflin, 1991. ISBN 0-395-55208-7 Subj: Animals – cats.

Cissy Lavender ill. by Emma Chichester Clark. Little, 1989. ISBN 0-316-14497-5 Subj: Activities – working. Activities – writing.

One winter's night ill. by Elaine Mills. Macmillan, 1991. ISBN 0-02-759235-9 Subj: Animals – dogs. Pets.

Lodge, Bernard. *Cloud Cuckoo Land (and other odd spots)* ill. by author. Houghton Mifflin, 1999. ISBN 0-395-96318-4 Subj: Activities – traveling. Humor. Rhyming text.

Door to door ill. by Maureen Roffey. Lothrop, 1980. ISBN 0-688-41966-6 Subj: Foreign lands – England. Format, unusual.

Mouldylocks ill. by author. Houghton Mifflin, 1998. ISBN 0-395-90945-7 Subj: Birthdays. Magic. Parties. Witches.

Rhyming Nell ill. by Maureen Roffey. Lothrop, 1979. ISBN 0-688-51898-2 Subj: Format, unusual. Rhyming text. Witches.

Loewen, Nancy. *Bicycle safety* ill. by Penny Dann. Child's World, 1997. ISBN 1-56766-260-9 Subj: Safety. Sports – bicycling.

Emergencies ill. by Penny Dann. Child's World, 1997. ISBN 1-56766-259-5 Subj: Accidents. Safety.

School safety ill. by Penny Dann. Child's World, 1997. ISBN 1-56766-255-2 Subj: Health and fitness. Safety. School.

Traffic safety ill. by Penny Dann. Child's World, 1997. ISBN 1-56766-254-4 Subj: Safety. Traffic, traffic signs.

Lofa, Denize (pseud.). *see* Lauture, Denizé

Löfgren, Ulf. *Alvin the Knight* ill. by author. Carolrhoda, 1992. ISBN 0-8761-4698-1 Subj: Knights. Middle Ages. Museums.

Alvin the pirate ill. by author. Carolrhoda, 1990. ISBN 0-87614-402-4 Subj: Imagination. Pirates.

Alvin the zookeeper ill. by author. Carolrhoda, 1991. ISBN 0-87614-689-2 Subj: Animals. Careers – zoo keepers. Zoos.

The boy who ate more than the giant and other Swedish folktales trans. from Swedish by Sheila La Farge; ill. by author. Collins-World, 1978. ISBN 0-529-05451-5 Subj: Folk and fairy tales. Giants. Humor.

The color trumpet ill. by author. Addison-Wesley, 1973. English text by Alison Winn; adapt. by Ray Broekel. ISBN 0-340-17649-0 Subj: Concepts – color.

The flying orchestra ill. by author. Addison-Wesley, 1973. English text by Alison Winn; adapt. by Ray Broekel. ISBN 0-340-17650-4 Subj: Music.

One-two-three ill. by author. Addison-Wesley, 1973. English text by Alison Winn; adapt. by Ray Brockel. Subj: Animals. Counting, numbers. Participation.

The traffic stopper that became a grandmother visitor ill. by author. Addison-Wesley, 1973. English text by Alison Winn; adapt. by Ray Broekel. Subj: Animals – elephants. Automobiles. Machines.

The wonderful tree ill. by author. Delacorte, 1969. Subj: Imagination. Trees.

Logue, Christopher. *The magic circus* ill. by Wayne Anderson. Viking, 1979. ISBN 0-670-44809-5 Subj: Character traits – cleverness. Circus. Monsters.

Lohans, Alison. *Sundog rescue* ill. by Vladyana Krykorka. Annick, 1999. ISBN 1-55037-571-7 Subj: Animals – dogs. Family life – grandparents.

Lohf, Sabine. *Things I can make with buttons* ill. by author. Chronicle, 1990. ISBN 0-87701-687-9 Subj: Activities – making things.

Things I can make with cloth ill. by author. Chronicle, 1989. ISBN 0-87701-666-6 Subj: Activities – making things.

Things I can make with cork ill. by author. Chronicle, 1990. ISBN 0-87701-726-3 Subj: Activities – making things.

Things I can make with paper ill. by author. Chronicle, 1989. ISBN 0-87701-671-2 Subj: Activities – making things. Paper.

Lomas Garza, Carmen. *In my family* ill. by author. Children's Book Pr., 1996. ISBN 0-8923-9138-3 Subj: Ethnic groups in the U.S. – Hispanic Americans. Family life. Foreign languages.

LoMonaco, Palmyra. *Night letters* ill. by Normand Chartier. Dutton, 1995. ISBN 0-525-45387-3 Subj: Communication. Nature. Night.

London, Jonathan. *Ali, child of the desert* ill. by Ted Lewin. Lothrop, 1997. ISBN 0-688-12561-1 Subj: Behavior – lost. Desert. Foreign lands – Morocco. Shopping. Weather – sandstorms.

At the edge of the forest ill. by Barbara Frith. Candlewick, 1998. ISBN 0-7636-0014-8 Subj: Animals –

coyotes. Animals – sheep. Family life – fathers. Family life – sons. Farms.

Baby whale's journey ill. by Jon Van Zyle. Chronicle, 1999. ISBN 0-8118-2496-9 Subj: Animals – babies. Animals – whales.

Candystore man ill. by Malcolm Brown. Lothrop, 1999. ISBN 0-688-13242-1 Subj: Food. Rhyming text. Stores.

Condor's egg ill. by James Chaffee. Chronicle, 1994. ISBN 0-8118-0260-4 Subj: Animals – endangered animals. Birds – condors. Eggs.

Crunch munch ill. by Michael Rex. Silver Whistle, 2001. ISBN 0-15-202603-7 Subj: Animals. Food.

Dream weaver ill. by Rocco Baviera. Silver Whistle, 1997. ISBN 0-15200-944-2 Subj: Nature. Spiders.

The eyes of Gray Wolf ill. by Jon Van Zyle. Chronicle, 1993. ISBN 0-8118-0285-X Subj: Animals – wolves.

Fall rap ill. by author. Lothrop, 1995. ISBN 0-688-13995-5 Subj: Poetry. Seasons – fall.

Fire race: a Karuk coyote tale about how fire came to the people ill. by Sylvia Long. Chronicle, 1993. ISBN 0-8118-0241-8 Subj: Animals – coyotes. Fire. Folk and fairy tales. Indians of North America – Karok.

Fireflies, fireflies, light my way ill. by Linda Messier. Viking, 1996. ISBN 0-670-85442-5 Subj: Animals. Indians of North America. Lullabies. Night. Rhyming text.

Froggy gets dressed ill. by Frank Remkiewicz. Viking, 1992. ISBN 0-670-84249-4 Subj: Clothing. Frogs and toads. Hibernation. Seasons – winter. Weather – snow.

Froggy goes to bed ill. by Frank Remkiewicz. Viking, 2000. ISBN 0-670-88860-5 Subj: Bedtime. Frogs and toads.

Froggy goes to school ill. by Frank Remkiewicz. Viking, 1996. ISBN 0-670-86726-8 Subj: Clothing. Dreams. Frogs and toads. School – first day.

Froggy learns to swim ill. by Frank Remkiewicz. Viking, 1995. ISBN 0-670-85551-0 Subj: Emotions – fear. Frogs and toads. Sports – swimming.

Froggy plays soccer ill. by Frank Remkiewicz. Viking, 1999. ISBN 0-670-88257-7 Subj: Animals. Frogs and toads. Sports – soccer.

Froggy's first Christmas ill. by Frank Remkiewicz. Viking, 2000. ISBN 0-670-89220-3 Subj: Animals. Frogs and toads. Holidays – Christmas.

Froggy's first kiss ill. by Frank Remkiewicz. Viking, 1998. ISBN 0-670-87064-1 Subj: Emotions – love. Frogs and toads. Holidays – Valentine's Day. School.

Froggy's Halloween ill. by Frank Remkiewicz. Viking, 1999. ISBN 0-670-88449-9 Subj: Clothing – costumes. Frogs and toads. Holidays – Halloween.

Gray fox ill. by Robert Sauber. Viking, 1993. ISBN 0-670-84490-X Subj: Animals – foxes. Death. Nature.

Hip cat ill. by Woodleigh Hubbard. Chronicle, 1993. ISBN 0-8118-0315-5 Subj: Activities – working. Animals – cats. Careers – musicians. City.

Honey Paw and Lightfoot ill. by Jon Van Zyle. Chronicle, 1994. ISBN 0-8118-0533-6 Subj: Animals – bears. Nature.

Hurricane! ill. by Henri Sorensen. Lothrop, 1998. ISBN 0-688-12978-1 Subj: Family life. Foreign lands – Puerto Rico. Weather – hurricanes.

I see the moon and the moon sees me adapt. and expanded by Jonathan London; ill. by Peter Fiore. Viking, 1996. ISBN 0-670-85918-4 Subj: Nature. Nursery rhymes. Rhyming text.

Ice Bear and Little Fox ill. by Daniel San Souci. Dutton, 1998. ISBN 0-525-45907-3 Subj: Animals – foxes. Animals – polar bears. Foreign lands – Arctic. Indians of North America – Inuit.

If I had a horse ill. by Brooke Scudder. Chronicle, 1997. ISBN 0-8118-1112-3 Subj: Animals – horses, ponies. Imagination.

Into this night we are rising ill. by G. Brian Karas. Viking, 1993. ISBN 0-670-84905-7 Subj: Dreams. Folk and fairy tales. Jewish culture. Night. Religion.

Jackrabbit ill. by Deborah Kogan Ray. Crown, 1996. ISBN 0-517-59658-X Subj: Animals – rabbits. Character traits – kindness to animals.

A koala for Katie: an adoption story ill. by Cynthia Jabar. Albert Whitman, 1993. ISBN 0-8075-4209-1 Subj: Adoption. Animals – koalas. Emotions – love. Family life. Zoos.

Let the lynx come in ill. by Patrick Benson. Candlewick, 1996. ISBN 1-56402-531-4 Subj: Animals – lynx. Imagination. Night.

Let's go, Froggy! ill. by Frank Remkiewicz. Viking, 1994. ISBN 0-670-85055-1 Subj: Activities – picnicking. Behavior – losing things. Frogs and toads. Sports – bicycling.

Like butter on pancakes ill. by G. Brian Karas. Viking, 1995. ISBN 0-670-85130-2 Subj: Farms. Sun.

The lion who had asthma ill. by Nadine Bernard Westcott. Albert Whitman, 1992. ISBN 0-8075-4559-7 Subj: Illness – asthma. Imagination.

Liplap's wish ill. by Sylvia Long. Chronicle, 1994. ISBN 0-8118-0505-0 Subj: Animals – rabbits. Death. Emotions – grief. Family life – grandmothers. Stars.

Little Red Monkey ill. by Frank Remkiewicz. Dutton, 1997. ISBN 0-525-45642-2 Subj: Animals – monkeys. Circus. Jungle. Rhyming text.

Loon Lake ill. by Susan Ford. Chronicle, 2001. ISBN 0-8118-2003-3 Subj: Animals. Birds – loons. Canoes and canoeing. Family life – fathers. Family life – sons. Lakes, ponds.

Moshi moshi ill. by Yoshi Miyake. Millbrook, 1998. ISBN 0-76130-110-0 Subj: Activities – traveling. Family life – brothers. Foreign lands – Japan.

Mustang canyon ill. by Daniel San Souci. Dutton, 2000. ISBN 0-525-45596-5 Subj: Animals – horses, ponies.

Old salt, young salt ill. by Todd L. W. Doney. Lothrop, 1997. ISBN 0-688-12976-5 Subj: Behavior – growing up. Boats, ships. Family life – fathers. Sports – fishing.

The owl who became the moon ill. by Ted Rand. Dutton, 1993. ISBN 0-525-45054-8 Subj: Animals. Birds – owls. Night. Trains.

Park beat: rhyming through the seasons ill. by Woodleigh Hubbard. HarperCollins, 2000. ISBN 0-688-13995-7 Subj: Rhyming text. Seasons.

Phantom of the prairie: year of the black footed ferret ill. by Barbara Bash. Sierra Club, 1997. ISBN 0-8715-6387-8 Subj: Animals – ferrets. Nature.

Puddles ill. by G. Brian Karas. Viking, 1997. ISBN 0-670-87218-0 Subj: Activities – playing. Clothing – boots. Weather – rain.

Red wolf country ill. by Daniel San Souci. Dutton, 1996. ISBN 0-525-45191-9 Subj: Animals – wolves. Nature.

Shawn and Keeper and the birthday party ill. by Renée Williams-Andriani. Dutton, 1999. ISBN 0-525-46115-9 Subj: Animals – dogs. Birthdays. Food. Parties.

Shawn and Keeper: show-and-tell ill. by Renée Williams-Andriani. Dutton, 2000. ISBN 0-525-46114-0 Subj: Animals – dogs. Behavior – misbehavior. Friendship. School.

Snuggle wuggle ill. by Michael Rex. Silver Whistle, 2000. ISBN 0-15-202159-0 Subj: Animals – babies.

The sugaring-off party ill. by Gilles Pelletier. Dutton, 1995. ISBN 0-525-45187-0 Subj: Family life – grandmothers. Food. Foreign lands – Canada. Trees.

Tell me a story photos by Sherry Shahan. R.C. Owen, 1998. ISBN 1-57274-194-5 Subj: Careers – writers.

Thirteen moons on turtle's back (Bruchac, Joseph)

The village basket weaver ill. by George Crespo. Dutton, 1996. ISBN 0-525-45314-8 Subj: Activities – weaving. Family life – grandfathers. Foreign lands – Belize. Indians of Central America – Black Carib.

The waterfall ill. by Jill Kastner. Viking, 1999. ISBN 0-670-87617-8 Subj: Camps, camping. Family life. Sports – hiking. Sports – rock climbing.

What do you love? ill. by Karen Lee Schmidt. Silver Whistle, 2000. ISBN 0-15-201919-7 Subj: Emotions – love. Rhyming text.

What Newt could do for Turtle ill. by Louise Voce. Candlewick, 1996. ISBN 1-56402-259-5 Subj: Friendship. Reptiles – lizards. Reptiles – turtles, tortoises. Seasons. Swamps.

White water ill. by Jill Kastner. Viking, 2001. ISBN 0-670-89286-6 Subj: Rivers. Sports.

Who bop ill. by Henry Cole. HarperCollins, 2000. ISBN 0-06-027918-4 Subj: Activities – dancing. Animals. Rhyming text.

Wiggle, waggle ill. by Michael Rex. Harcourt, 1999. ISBN 0-15-201940-5 Subj: Activities – walking. Animals. Noise, sounds.

London, Sara. *Firehouse Max* ill. by Ann Arnold. HarperCollins, 1997. ISBN 0-06-205094-X Subj: Animals – horses, ponies. Careers – peddlers. Music. Problem solving.

Long, Claudia. *Albert's story* ill. by Judy Glasser. Delacorte, 1978. ISBN 0-440-00080-7 Subj: Dragons. Imagination.

Long, Earlene. *Gone fishing* ill. by Richard Eric Brown. Houghton Mifflin, 1984. ISBN 0-395-35570-2 Subj: Concepts – size. Family life – fathers. Sports – fishing.

Johnny's egg photos by Neal Slavin and Charles Mikolaycak. Addison-Wesley, 1980. ISBN 0-201-04153-7 Subj: Activities – cooking. Eggs.

Long, Jan Freeman. *The bee and the dream* ill. by Kaoru Ono. Dutton, 1996. ISBN 0-525-45287-7 Subj: Character traits – luck. Folk and fairy tales. Foreign lands – Japan. Insects – bees.

Long, Kathy. *Hallelujah the clown: a story of blessing and discovery* ill. by Joe Boddy. Augsburg, 1992. ISBN 0-8066-2560-0 Subj: Clowns, jesters. Religion.

Longfellow, Henry Wadsworth. *Hiawatha* ill. by Susan Jeffers. Dial, 1983. ISBN 0-8037-0014-8 Subj: Indians of North America – Iroquois. Poetry.

Hiawatha's childhood ill. by Errol Le Cain. Farrar, 1984. ISBN 0-374-33065-4 Subj: Indians of North America – Iroquois. Poetry.

Paul Revere's ride ill. by Paul Galdone. Crowell, 1963. Subj: Poetry. U.S. history.

Paul Revere's ride ill. by Nancy Winslow Parker. Mulberry, 1993. ISBN 0-688-12387-2 Subj: Poetry. U.S. history.

Longfellow, Layne. *Imaginary menagerie* ill. by Woodleigh Marx Hubbard. Chronicle, 1997. ISBN 0-8118-0797-5 Subj: Animals. Format, unusual – toy and movable books. Imagination. Rhyming text.

Lööf, Jan. *Uncle Louie's fantastic sea voyage* ill. by author. Random House, 1978. ISBN 0-394-93860-7 Subj: Activities – traveling. Boats, ships. Family life – aunts, uncles. Zoos.

Look, Lenore. *Love as strong as ginger* ill. by Stephen T. Johnson. Atheneum, 1999. ISBN 0-689-81248-5 Subj: Activities – working. Ethnic groups in the U.S. – Chinese Americans. Family life – grandmothers.

Loomans, Diane. *The lovables in the kingdom of self-esteem* ill. by Kim Howard. Starseed Pr., 1991. ISBN 0-915811-25-1 Subj: Animals. Rhyming text. Self-concept.

Loomis, Christine. *Across America, I love you* ill. by Kate Kiesler. Hyperion, 2000. ISBN 0-7868-2314-3 Subj: Family life. Nature. U.S. history.

Astro Bunnies ill. by Ora Eitan. Putnam, 1998. ISBN 0-399-23175-7 Subj: Animals – rabbits. Rhyming text. Space and space ships.

At the laundromat ill. by Nancy Poydar. Scholastic, 1993. ISBN 0-590-72830-X Subj: Activities. Clothing. Communities, neighborhoods. Rhyming text.

At the library ill. by Nancy Poydar. Scholastic, 1993. ISBN 0-590-72829-6 Subj: Libraries. Rhyming text.

At the mall ill. by Nancy Poydar. Scholastic, 1994. ISBN 0-590-72832-6 Subj: Communities, neighborhoods. Shopping. Stores.

The cleanup surprise ill. by Julie Brillhart. Scholastic, 1993. ISBN 0-590-72774-5 Subj: Character traits – cleanliness. Ecology. Rhyming text. Robots. School.

Cowboy bunnies ill. by Ora Eitan. Putnam, 1997. ISBN 0-399-22625-7 Subj: Activities – playing. Animals – rabbits. Country. Cowboys. Rhyming text.

The Hippo Hop ill. by Nadine Bernard Westcott. Houghton Mifflin, 1995. ISBN 0-395-69702-6 Subj: Animals. Jungle. Parties. Rhyming text.

In the diner ill. by Nancy Poydar. Scholastic, 1994. ISBN 0-590-46716-6 Subj: Activities – cooking. Careers – chefs, cooks. Careers – waiters, waitresses. Friendship. Restaurants.

My new baby-sitter photos by George Ancona. Morrow, 1991. ISBN 0-688-09626-3 Subj: Activities – babysitting.

One cow coughs: a counting book for the sick and miserable ill. by Pat Dypold. Ticknor & Fields, 1994. ISBN 0-395-67899-4 Subj: Animals. Counting, numbers. Illness. Rhyming text.

Rush hour ill. by Mari Takabayashi. Houghton Mifflin, 1996. ISBN 0-395-69129-X Subj: Activities – working. City. Rhyming text. Transportation.

We're going on a trip ill. by Maxie Chambliss. Morrow, 1994. ISBN 0-688-10173-9 Subj: Activities – traveling. Activities – vacationing. Airplanes, airports. Automobiles. Trains.

Loomis, Jennifer A. *A duck in a tree* photos by author. Stemmer House, 1996. ISBN 0-88045-136-X Subj: Birds – ducks. Nature.

Lopez, Loretta. *The birthday swap* ill. by author. Lee & Low, 1997. ISBN 1-880000-47-4 Subj: Birthdays. Ethnic groups in the U.S. – Mexican Americans. Family life. Parties.

Lopshire, Robert. *The biggest, smallest, fastest, tallest things you've ever heard of* ill. by author. Crowell, 1980. ISBN 0-690-04014-8 Subj: Concepts.

How to make snop snappers and other fine things ill. by author. Greenwillow, 1977. ISBN 0-688-84066-3 Subj: Activities – making things. Games.

I am better than you ill. by author. HarperCollins, 1968. ISBN 0-06-023997-2 Subj: Behavior – boasting. Reptiles – lizards.

I want to be somebody new! ill. by author. Random House, 1986. ISBN 0-394-97616-9 Subj: Behavior – seeking better things. Character traits – individuality. Rhyming text.

It's magic ill. by author. Macmillan, 1969. Subj: Magic.

New tricks I can do! ill. by author. Beginner Books, 1996. ISBN 0-679-97715-5 Subj: Activities – playing. Animals – dogs. Circus. Concepts – color. Concepts – shape. Rhyming text.

Put me in the zoo ill. by author. Random House, 1960. ISBN 0-394-90017-0 Subj: Animals – dogs. Circus. Concepts – color. Rhyming text.

Lorbiecki, Marybeth. *Sister Anne's hands* ill. by K. Wendy Popp. Dial, 1998. ISBN 0-8037-2039-4 Subj: Careers – teachers. Ethnic groups in the U.S. – African Americans. Prejudice. Rhyming text. School.

Lorca, Federico García. *see* García Lorca, Federico

Lord, Beman. *The days of the week* ill. by Walter Erhard. Walck, 1968. Subj: Days of the week, months of the year. Nursery rhymes. Poetry. Songs.

Lord, John Vernon. *Mr. Mead and his garden* ill. by author. Houghton Mifflin, 1975. ISBN 0-395-20278-7 Subj: Animals – snails. Gardens, gardening. Rhyming text.

Lord, Nancy. *see* Titus, Eve

Loredo, Elizabeth. *Boogie Bones* ill. by Kevin Hawkes. Putnam, 1997. ISBN 0-399-22763-6 Subj: Activities – dancing. Anatomy – skeletons. Contests.

Lorenz, Konrad. *The goose family book* (Kalas, Sybille)

Lorenz, Lee. *Big Gus and Little Gus* ill. by author. Prentice-Hall, 1982. ISBN 0-03-077875-3 Subj: Character traits – laziness. Cumulative tales. Folk and fairy tales.

Dinah's egg ill. by author. Simon & Schuster, 1990. ISBN 0-671-68685-2 Subj: Dinosaurs. Eggs.

The feathered ogre ill. by author. Prentice-Hall, 1983. ISBN 0-13-308296-2 Subj: Character traits – cleverness. Folk and fairy tales. Magic. Mythical creatures – ogres. Royalty.

Hugo and the spacedog ill. by author. Prentice-Hall, 1983. ISBN 0-13-444497-3 Subj: Animals. Animals – dogs. Farms. Space and space ships.

Pinchpenny John ill. by author. Prentice-Hall, 1981. ISBN 0-13-676254-9 Subj: Behavior – greed. Folk and fairy tales.

Scornful Simkin ill. by author. Prentice-Hall, 1980. ISBN 0-13-796664-4 Subj: Folk and fairy tales.

A weekend in the city ill. by author. Pippin Pr., 1991. ISBN 0-945912-15-3 Subj: Animals. City. Country.

A weekend in the country ill. by author. Prentice-Hall, 1984. ISBN 0-13-947961-9 Subj: Animals – pigs. Birds – ducks. Country.

Lorenzini, Carlo. *see* Collodi, Carlo

Loretan, Sylvia. *Bob the snowman* ill. by Jan Lenica. Viking, 1991. ISBN 0-670-83677-X Subj: Snowmen. Weather – snow.

Lorian, Nicole. *A birthday present for Mama* ill. by J. P. Miller. Random House, 1984. ISBN 0-394-96755-0 Subj: Animals. Animals – rabbits. Birthdays.

Lorimer, Janet. *The biggest bubble in the world* ill. by Diane Paterson. Watts, 1982. ISBN 0-531-04378-9 Subj: Behavior – misbehavior. Bubbles.

Lorimer, Lawrence T. *Noah's ark* (Martin, Charles E.)

Loriot. *Peter and the wolf* (Prokofiev, Sergei Sergeievitch)

Losi, Carol A. *The 512 ants on Sullivan Street* ill. by Jerry Zimmerman; math activities by Marilyn Burns. Scholastic, 1997. ISBN 0-590-30876-9 Subj: Activities – picnicking. Counting, numbers. Cumulative tales. Food. Insects – ants.

Losordo, Stephen. *Cow moo me* ill. by Jane Conteh-Morgan. HarperFestival, 1998. ISBN 0-694-01108-8 Subj: Animals. Format, unusual – board books. Noise, sounds. Rhyming text.

Lottridge, Celia B. (Celia Barker). *Music for the Tsar of the Sea* ill. by Harvey Chan. Douglas & McIntyre, 1998. ISBN 0-88899-328-5 Subj: Folk and fairy tales. Foreign lands – Russia. Music. Royalty – tsars.

Something might be hiding ill. by Jill Zwolak. Douglas & McIntyre, 1994. ISBN 0-88899-176-2 Subj: Emotions – fear. Family life. Monsters. Moving.

Lotz, Karen E. *Can't sit still* ill. by Colleen Browning. Dutton, 1993. ISBN 0-525-45066-1 Subj: City. Ethnic groups in the U.S. – African Americans. Family life. Seasons. Weather.

Snowsong whistling ill. by Ehsa Kleven. Dutton, 1993. ISBN 0-525-45145-5 Subj: Noise, sounds. Rhyming text. Seasons – fall. Seasons – winter.

Louie, Ai-Ling. *Yeh Shen: a Cinderella story from China* ill. by Ed Young. Putnam, 1990. ISBN 0-399-20900-X Subj: Folk and fairy tales. Foreign lands – China.

Lourie, Helen. *see* Storr, Catherine (Cole)

Love, Ann. *Farming* by Ann Love with Jane Drake; ill. by Pat Cupples. Kids Can Pr., 1998. ISBN 1-55074-451-8 Subj: Careers – farmers. Farms. Machines.

Fishing by Ann Love with Jane Drake; ill. by Pat Cupples. Kids Can Pr., 1999. ISBN 1-55074-457-7 Subj: Activities – working. Careers – fishermen. Fish. U.S. history.

Ice cream at the castle ill. by Toni Goffe. Child's Play, 1999. ISBN 0-8595-3677-7 Subj: Castles. Food. Money. Royalty – kings. Royalty – princes.

The prince who wrote a letter ill. by Toni Goffe. Child's Play, 1992. ISBN 0-85953-398-0 Subj: Behavior – gossip. Royalty – kings. Royalty – princesses.

Loverseed, Amanda. *The thunder king: a Peruvian folk tale* ill. by author. Peter Bedrick, 1991. ISBN 0-87226-450-5 Subj: Folk and fairy tales. Foreign lands – Peru.

Tikkatoo's journey ill. by author. Peter Bedrick, 1990. ISBN 0-87226-420-3 Subj: Eskimos. Folk and fairy tales.

Low, Alice. *The charge of the mouse brigade* (Stone, Bernard)

David's windows ill. by Tomie de Paola. Putnam, 1974. ISBN 0-399-60883-4 Subj: Animals – horses, ponies. City. Family life – grandmothers.

Taro and the bamboo shoot: a Japanese tale (Matsuno, Masako)

The witch who was afraid of witches ill. by Karen Gundersheimer. Pantheon, 1978. ISBN 0-394-93718-X Subj: Holidays – Halloween. Sibling rivalry. Witches.

Witch's holiday ill. by Tony Walton. Pantheon, 1971. ISBN 0-394-92165-8 Subj: Holidays – Halloween. Rhyming text. Witches.

Low, Joseph. *Adam's book of odd creatures* ill. by author. Atheneum, 1962. Subj: ABC books. Animals. Names. Poetry.

Benny rabbit and the owl ill. by author. Greenwillow, 1978. ISBN 0-688-84117-1 Subj: Birds – geese. Character traits – bravery. Emotions – fear. Farms.

Boo to a goose ill. by author. Atheneum, 1975. ISBN 0-689-50009-2 Subj: Birds – geese. Character traits – bravery. Emotions – fear. Farms.

The Christmas grump ill. by author. Atheneum, 1977. ISBN 0-689-50092-0 Subj: Animals – mice. Emotions – happiness. Emotions – sadness. Holidays – Christmas.

Don't drag your feet . . . ill. by author. Atheneum, 1983. ISBN 0-689-50271-0 Subj: Behavior. Dreams. Toys.

Five men under one umbrella ill. by author. Macmillan, 1975. ISBN 0-02-761460-3 Subj: Riddles.

A mad wet hen and other riddles ill. by author. Greenwillow, 1977. ISBN 0-688-84082-5 Subj: Riddles.

Mice twice ill. by author. Aladdin, 1986, c1980. ISBN 0-689-71060-7 Subj: Animals – mice. Caldecott award honor books.

My dog, your dog ill. by author. Macmillan, 1978. ISBN 0-02-761400-X Subj: Animals – dogs. Behavior.

What if . . . ? fourteen encounters - some frightful, some frivolous - that might happen to anyone ill. by author. Atheneum, 1976. ISBN 0-689-50064-5 Subj: Problem solving.

Low, Robert. *Peoples of the Arctic* ill. by author. Rosen, 1996. ISBN 0-8239-2294-4 Subj: Foreign lands – Arctic.

Peoples of the rain forest ill. by author. Rosen, 1996. ISBN 0-8239-2297-9 Subj: Foreign lands. Forest, woods.

Low, William. *Chinatown* ill. by author. Holt, 1997. ISBN 0-8050-4214-8 Subj: Communities, neighborhoods. Ethnic groups in the U.S. – Chinese Americans. Family life – grandmothers. Holidays – Chinese New Year.

Lowell, Susan. *The bootmaker and the elves* ill. by Tom Curry. Orchard, 1997. ISBN 0-531-33044-3 Subj: Careers – shoemakers. Character traits – helpfulness. Clothing – boots. Cowboys. Folk and fairy tales. Humor. Mythical creatures – elves. U.S. history – frontier and pioneer life.

Cindy Ellen: a wild western Cinderella ill. by Jane Manning. HarperCollins, 2000. ISBN 0-06-027447-6 Subj: Fairies. Family life – step families. Folk and fairy tales. U.S. history – frontier and pioneer life.

Dusty Locks and the three bears ill. by Randy Cecil. Holt, 2001. ISBN 0-8050-5862-1 Subj: Animals – bears. U.S. history – frontier and pioneer life.

Little Red Cowboy Hat ill. by Randy Cecil. Holt, 1997. ISBN 0-8050-3508-7 Subj: Animals – bulls, cows. Animals – wolves. Clothing – hats. Family life – grandmothers. Folk and fairy tales.

The three little javelinas ill. by Jim Harris. Northland, 1992. ISBN 0-87358-542-9 Subj: Animals – coyotes. Animals – pigs. Character traits – cleverness. Folk and fairy tales.

The tortoise and the jackrabbit ill. by Jim Harris. Northland, 1994. ISBN 0-87358-586-0 Subj: Animals. Animals – rabbits. Desert. Folk and fairy tales. Reptiles – turtles, tortoises. Sports – racing.

Lowitz, Anson. *The pilgrims' party* (Lowitz, Sadyebeth)

Lowitz, Sadyebeth. *The pilgrims' party* by Sadyebeth and Anson Lowitz; ill. by Anson Lowitz. Lerner, 1967, c1931. Subj: Holidays – Thanksgiving. Pilgrims. U.S. history.

Lowrey, Janette Sebring. *Six silver spoons* ill. by Robert M. Quackenbush. HarperCollins, 1971. Subj: Birthdays. U.S. history.

Lubach, Peter. *Harry and the singing fish* ill. by author. Walt Disney, 1992. ISBN 1-56282-159-8 Subj: Fish. Songs. Theater. Wordless.

Lubell, Cicil. *Rosalie, the bird market turtle* (Lubell, Winifred)

Lubell, Winifred. *Here comes daddy: a book for twos and threes* ill. by author. Addison-Wesley, 1944. Subj: Family life – fathers.

I wish I had another name (Williams, Jay)

Rosalie, the bird market turtle by Winifred and Cicil Lubell; ill. by Winifred Lubell. Rand McNally, 1962. Subj: Behavior – lost. Birds. Foreign lands – France. Reptiles – turtles, tortoises.

Lubin, Leonard B. *Christmas gift-bringers* ill. by author. Lothrop, 1989. ISBN 0-688-07020-5 Subj: Animals – mice. Gifts. Holidays – Christmas. Santa Claus.

Lucado, Max. *Alabaster's song: Christmas through the eyes of an angel* ill. by Michael Garland. Word Pub., 1996. ISBN 0-8499-1307-1 Subj: Activities – singing. Angels. Holidays – Christmas.

Jacob's gift ill. by Robert Hunt. Nelson, 1998. ISBN 0-8499-5830-X Subj: Careers – carpenters. Religion – Nativity.

Lucas, Barbara (Barbara M.). *A calf for Christmas* (Lindgren, Astrid)

Cats by Mother Goose (Mother Goose)

I want a brother or sister (Lindgren, Astrid)

I want to go to school too (Lindgren, Astrid)

Sleeping over ill. by Stella Ormai. Macmillan, 1986. ISBN 0-02-761360-7 Subj: Animals – bears. Frogs and toads. Sleep. Sleepovers.

Snowed in ill. by Catherine Stock. Bradbury, 1993. ISBN 0-02-761465-4 Subj: Family life. Farms. School. Seasons – winter. Weather – snow.

Lucas, Victoria. see Plath, Sylvia

Lucht, Irmgard. *In this night* ill. by author; trans. by Frank Jacoby-Nelson; adapt. by Elizabeth Hollow. Hyperion, 1993. ISBN 1-56282-408-2 Subj: Night. Seasons – spring.

The red poppy ill. by author; trans. by Frank Jacoby-Nelson. Hyperion, 1995. ISBN 0-7868-2043-8 Subj: Flowers. Nature.

Lucy steps through the wardrobe adapt. from The chronicles by C. S. Lewis; ill. by Deborah Maze. HarperCollins, 1997. ISBN 0-06-027451-4 Subj: Imagination. Magic. Witches.

Ludwig, Warren. *Good morning, Granny Rose: an Arkansas folktale* ill. by reteller. Putnam, 1990. ISBN 0-399-21950-1 Subj: Animals – bears. Animals – dogs. Folk and fairy tales. Hibernation. Weather – snow.

Old Noah's elephants ill. by adapt. Putnam, 1991. ISBN 0-399-22256-1 Subj: Animals – elephants. Boats, ships. Folk and fairy tales. Religion – Noah. Weather – floods. Weather – rain. Weather – rainbows.

Ludy, Mark. *The farmer* ill. by author. Green Pastures, 1999. ISBN 0-9664276-0-2 Subj: Careers – farmers. Character traits – helpfulness. Character traits – patience. Character traits – perseverance. Farms.

Luenn, Nancy. *The dragon kite* ill. by Michael Hague. Harcourt, 1982. ISBN 0-15-224196-5 Subj: Folk and fairy tales. Foreign lands – Japan. Kites.

A gift for Abuelita: celebrating the Day of the Dead ill. by Robert Chapman. Rising Moon, 1998. ISBN 0-8735-8688-3 Subj: Death. Ethnic groups in the U.S. – Mexican Americans. Family life – grandmothers. Foreign languages. Holidays – Day of the Dead.

Miser on the mountain: a Nisqually legend of Mount Rainier ill. by Pierr Morgan. Sasquatch, 1997. ISBN 1-57061-082-7 Subj: Behavior – greed. Folk and fairy tales. Indians of North America – Nisqually. Mountains.

Mother earth ill. by Neil Waldman. Atheneum, 1992. ISBN 0-689-31668-2 Subj: Earth. Ecology.

Nessa's fish ill. by Neil Waldman. Atheneum, 1990. ISBN 0-689-31477-9 Subj: Eskimos. Family life – grandmothers. Indians of North America. Sports – fishing.

Nessa's story ill. by Neil Waldman. Atheneum, 1994. ISBN 0-689-31782-4 Subj: Eskimos. Family life – grandmothers. Foreign lands – Arctic. Imagination.

Otter play ill. by Anna Vojtech. Atheneum, 1998. ISBN 0-689-81126-8 Subj: Activities – playing. Animals – otters.

Song for the ancient forest ill. by Jill Kastner. Atheneum, 1993. ISBN 0-689-31719-0 Subj: Behavior – trickery. Birds – ravens. Ecology. Forest, woods.

Squish! a wetland walk ill. by Ronald Himler. Atheneum, 1994. ISBN 0-689-31842-1 Subj: Activities – walking. Ecology. Nature.

Lukesová, Milena. *Julian in the autumn woods* ill. by Jan Kudláček. Holt, 1977. ISBN 0-03-021151-4 Subj: Forest, woods.

The little girl and the rain ill. by Jan Kudláček. Holt, 1978. ISBN 0-03-021146-8 Subj: Emotions – loneliness. Weather – rain.

Lullaby and goodnight coll. and ill. by Ilse Plume. HarperCollins, 1994. ISBN 0-06-023502-0 Subj: Bedtime. Lullabies. Poetry. Songs.

Lum, Kate. *What! cried Granny* ill. by Adrian Johnson. Dial, 1999. ISBN 0-8037-2382-2 Subj: Activities – making things. Bedtime. Family life – grandmothers. Furniture – beds.

Lumley, Katheryn Wentzel. *I can be an animal doctor.* Childrens Pr., 1985. ISBN 0-516-01836-1 Subj: Careers – veterinarians.

Lund, Doris Herold. *The paint-box sea* ill. by Symeon Shimin. McGraw-Hill, 1971. ISBN 0-07-039098-3 Subj: Rhyming text. Sea and seashore. Seasons – summer.

You ought to see Herbert's house ill. by Steven Kellogg. McGraw-Hill, 1973. ISBN 0-531-02595-0 Subj: Behavior – boasting. Friendship.

Lund, Jillian. *Two cool coyotes* ill. by author. Dutton, 1999. ISBN 0-525-46151-5 Subj: Animals – coyotes. Emotions – loneliness. Friendship.

Lundell, Margo. *The furry bedtime book: Lovey Bear's story* ill. by David McPhail. Scholastic, 1996. ISBN 0-590-86371-1 Subj: Animals – bears. Bedtime. Format, unusual – toy and movable books. Rhyming text.

Teddy bear's birthday ill. by Dee deRosa. Platt, 1985. ISBN 0-448-40876-7 Subj: Birthdays. Format, unusual – board books. Toys – bears.

Lunge-Larsen, Lise. *The legend of the lady slipper: an Ojibwe tale* ill. by Andrea Arroyo. Houghton Mifflin, 1999. ISBN 0-395-90512-5 Subj: Character traits – bravery. Clothing – shoes. Flowers. Folk and fairy tales. Indians of North America – Ojibwa.

Lunn, Carolyn. *A buzz is part of a bee* ill. by Tom Dunnington. Childrens Pr., 1990. ISBN 0-516-02062-5 Subj: Rhyming text.

Lunn, Janet Louise Swoboda. *Amos's sweater* ill. by Kim LaFave. Firefly, 1991. ISBN 0-88899-074-X Subj: Animals – sheep. Clothing – sweaters.

Come to the fair ill. by Gilles Pelletier. Tundra, 1997. ISBN 0-88776-409-6 Subj: Careers – farmers. Country. Fairs.

Duck cakes for sale ill. by Kim LaFave. Firefly, 1991. ISBN 0-88899-094-4 Subj: Birds – ducks.

Lurie, Morris. *The story of Imelda, who was small* ill. by Terry Denton. Houghton Mifflin, 1988, c1984. ISBN 0-395-48863-7 Subj: Character traits – smallness. Food.

Lussert, Anneliese. *The Christmas visitor* ill. by Loek Koopmans; trans. by Rosemary Lanning. North-South, 1995. ISBN 1-55858-450-1 Subj: Character traits – generosity. Holidays – Christmas. Religion – Nativity.

The farmer and the moon trans. by Anthea Bell; ill. by Józef Wilkon. Holt, 1987. ISBN 0-8050-0281-2 Subj: Behavior – greed. Magic. Moon.

Lustig, Esther. *Willy Whyner, cloud designer* (Lustig, Michael)

Lustig, Michael. *Willy Whyner, cloud designer* by Michael and Esther Lustig; ill. by Michael Lustig. Four Winds, 1994. ISBN 0-02-761365-8 Subj: Careers – inventors. Machines. Weather – clouds.

Lüton, Mildred. *Little chicks' mothers and all the others* ill. by Mary Maki Rae. Viking, 1983. ISBN 0-670-43113-3 Subj: Animals. Farms. Poetry.

Lutteman, Helena. *see* Dahlbäck-Lutteman, Helena

Luttrell, Ida. *Be nice to Marilyn* ill. by Lonni Sue Johnson. Atheneum, 1992. ISBN 0-689-31716-6 Subj: Family life – cousins. Farms.

Lonesome Lester ill. by Megan Lloyd. Harper-Collins, 1984. ISBN 0-06-024030-X Subj: Animals – prairie dogs. Behavior – solitude. Emotions – loneliness.

Mattie and the chicken thief ill. by Thacher Hurd. Putnam, 1988. ISBN 0-396-09126-1 Subj: Animals. Behavior – misbehavior. Birds – chickens.

Mattie's little possum pet ill. by Betsy Lewin. Atheneum, 1993. ISBN 0-689-31786-7 Subj: Animals – cats. Animals – dogs. Animals – possums. Farms. Pets.

Milo's toothache ill. by Enzo Giannini. Dial, 1992. ISBN 0-8037-1035-6 Subj: Animals – pigs. Careers – dentists. Teeth.

Ottie Slockett ill. by Ute Krause. Dial, 1990. ISBN 0-8037-0711-8 Subj: Behavior. Friendship.

The star counters ill. by Korinna Pretro. Tambourine, 1994. ISBN 0-688-12150-0 Subj: Animals. Behavior – greed. Counting, numbers. Royalty – kings. Stars.

Three good blankets ill. by Michael McDermott. Atheneum, 1990. ISBN 0-689-31586-4 Subj: Animals. Behavior – sharing.

Lyfick, Warren. *Animal tales* ill. by Joe Kohl. Harvey House, 1980. ISBN 0-933258-01-1 Subj: Animals. Riddles.

The little book of fowl jokes ill. by Chris Cummings. Harvey House, 1980. ISBN 0-8178-5198-7 Subj: Birds. Riddles.

Lynch, Marietta. *Mommy and daddy are divorced* (Perry, Patricia)

Lyndon, Kerry Raines. *A birthday for Blue* ill. by Michael Hays. Albert Whitman, 1989. ISBN 0-8075-0774-1 Subj: Activities – traveling. Birthdays. Family life. U.S. history – frontier and pioneer life.

Lyne, Alice. *A, my name is . . .* ill. by Lynne Cravath. Whispering Coyote, 1997. ISBN 1-879085-40-2 Subj: ABC books. Activities – jumping. Names. Rhyming text.

Lynn, Patricia. *see* Watts, Mabel (Pizzey)

Lynn, Sara. *Big animals* ill. by author. Aladdin, 1987. ISBN 0-689-71098-4 Subj: Animals. Format, unusual – board books.

Clothes ill. by author. Macmillan, 1986. ISBN 0-689-71095-X Subj: Clothing. Format, unusual – board books.

Colors ill. by author. Little, 1986. ISBN 0-316-54002-1 Subj: Clowns, jesters. Concepts – color.

Farm animals ill. by author. Aladdin, 1987. ISBN 0-689-71100-X Subj: Animals. Format, unusual – board books.

Food ill. by author. Candlewick, 1996. ISBN 1-56402-766-X Subj: Food. Format, unusual – board books.

Garden animals ill. by author. Aladdin, 1987. ISBN 0-689-71101-8 Subj: Animals. Format, unusual – board books. Gardens, gardening.

Home ill. by author. Macmillan, 1986. ISBN 0-689-71097-6 Subj: Format, unusual – board books. Homes, houses.

Jungle friends ill. by author. Candlewick, 1996. ISBN 0-7636-0042-3 Subj: Animals. Format, unusual – board books. Jungle.

1 2 3 ill. by author. Little, 1986. ISBN 0-316-54004-8 Subj: Animals. Counting, numbers.

Small animals ill. by author. Aladdin, 1987. ISBN 0-689-71099-2 Subj: Animals. Format, unusual – board books.

Toys ill. by author. Macmillan, 1986. ISBN 0-689-71096-8 Subj: Format, unusual – board books. Toys.

Wheels ill. by author. Candlewick, 1996. ISBN 1-56402-947-6 Subj: Format, unusual – board books. Wheels.

Lyon, David. *The biggest truck* ill. by author. Lothrop, 1988. ISBN 0-688-05514-1 Subj: Activities – working. Night. Trucks.

The brave little computer ill. by R. W. Alley. Simon & Schuster, 1984. ISBN 0-671-52455-0 Subj: Computers. Problem solving.

The crumbly coast ill. by author. Doubleday, 1995. ISBN 0-385-32079-5 Subj: Animals – bears. Animals – minks. Food. Orphans.

The runaway duck ill. by author. Lothrop, 1985. ISBN 0-688-04002-0 Subj: Toys.

Lyon, George Ella. *A B Cedar: an alphabet of trees* designed and ill. by Tom Parker. Watts, 1989. ISBN 0-531-08395-0 Subj: ABC books. Trees.

Ada's pal ill. by Marguerite Casparian. Orchard, 1996. ISBN 0-531-08878-2 Subj: Animals – dogs. Death. Emotions – grief. Pets.

Basket ill. by Mary Szilagyi. Watts, 1990. ISBN 0-531-08486-8 Subj: Behavior – losing things. Family life – grandfathers.

Book ill. by Peter Catalanotto. DK, 1999. ISBN 0-7894-2560-2 Subj: Activities – reading. Poetry.

Cecil's story ill. by Peter Catalanotto. Watts, 1991. ISBN 0-531-08512-0 Subj: Emotions – fear. Family life. Illness. U.S. history. War.

Come a tide ill. by Stephen Gammell. Watts, 1990. ISBN 0-531-08454-X Subj: Family life. Weather – floods.

Counting on the woods photos by Ann W. Olson. DK, 1998. ISBN 0-7894-2480-0 Subj: Counting, numbers. Forest, woods. Nature. Poetry.

A day at damp camp ill. by Peter Catalanotto. Orchard, 1996. ISBN 0-531-08854-5 Subj: Camps, camping. Friendship. Rhyming text.

Dreamplace ill. by Peter Catalanotto. Orchard, 1993. ISBN 0-531-08616-X Subj: Dreams. Indians of North America – Pueblo. Poetry.

Father Time and the day boxes ill. by Robert Andrew Parker. Bradbury, 1985. ISBN 0-02-761370-4 Subj: Time.

Five live bongos ill. by author. Scholastic, 1994. ISBN 0-590-44993-1 Subj: Family life. Music. Noise, sounds.

Mama is a miner ill. by Peter Catalanotto. Orchard, 1994. ISBN 0-531-08703-4 Subj: Activities – working. Careers – miners. Family life – mothers. Gender roles. Rhyming text.

One lucky girl ill. by Irene Trivas. DK, 2000. ISBN 0-7894-2613-7 Subj: Family life. Homes, houses. Weather – tornadoes.

The outside inn ill. by Vera Rosenberry. Watts, 1991. ISBN 0-531-08536-8 Subj: Food. Nature. Rhyming text.

A regular rolling Noah ill. by Stephen Gammell. Bradbury, 1986. ISBN 0-02-761330-5 Subj: Activities – traveling. Animals. Trains.

A sign ill. by Chris K. Soentpiet. Orchard, 1998. ISBN 0-531-33073-7 Subj: Activities. Careers – writers. Memories, memory. Poetry.

Together ill. by Vera Rosenberry. Watts, 1989. ISBN 0-531-08431-0 Subj: Friendship. Poetry.

A traveling cat ill. by Paul Brett Johnson. Orchard, 1998. ISBN 0-531-33102-4 Subj: Activities – traveling. Animals – cats.

Who came down that road? ill. by Peter Catalanotto. Orchard, 1992. ISBN 0-531-08587-2 Subj: Imagination. Roads.

Lystad, Mary H. *That new boy* ill. by Emily Arnold McCully. Crown, 1973. ISBN 0-517-50259-3 Subj: Character traits – individuality. Friendship. Moving.

M. M. D. *see* Dodge, Mary Mapes

Maass, Robert. *Garbage* ill. by author. Holt, 2000. ISBN 0-8050-5951-2 Subj: Careers – sanitation workers. Ecology.

Garden ill. by author. Holt, 1998. ISBN 0-8050-5477-4 Subj: Gardens, gardening. Plants.

Tugboats ill. by author. Holt, 1997. ISBN 0-8050-3116-2 Subj: Boats, ships. Sailors. Transportation.

When autumn comes photos by author. Holt, 1990. ISBN 0-8050-1259-1 Subj: Seasons – fall.

When spring comes photos by author. Holt, 1994. ISBN 0-8050-2085-3 Subj: Seasons – spring.

When summer comes photos by author. Holt, 1993. ISBN 0-8050-2087-X Subj: Seasons – summer.

When winter comes photos by author. Holt, 1993. ISBN 0-8050-2086-1 Subj: Seasons – winter.

Mabey, Richard. *Oak and company* ill. by Clare Roberts. Greenwillow, 1983. ISBN 0-688-01993-5 Subj: Ecology. Science. Trees.

McAfee, Annalena. *Kirsty knows best* ill. by Anthony Browne. Knopf, 1987. ISBN 0-394-99478-7 Subj: Imagination. Rhyming text.

The visitors who came to stay ill. by Anthony Browne. Viking, 1985. ISBN 0-670-74714-9 Subj: Behavior – trickery. Family life – fathers. Sea and seashore.

Macak, Charles P. *The hokey pokey* (La Prise, Larry)

McAlinden, Paul. *Old MacDonald had a farm* (Old MacDonald had a farm)

McAllister, Angela. *The babies of Cockle Bay* by Angela McAllister and Susie Jenkin-Pearce; ill. by Susie Jenkin-Pearce. Barron's, 1994. ISBN 0-8120-6424-0 Subj: Activities – babysitting. Babies. Pirates.

The battle of Sir Cob and Sir Filbert ill. by author. Crown, 1992. ISBN 0-517-58730-0 Subj: Behavior – sharing. Emotions – envy, jealousy. Middle Ages. War.

The Christmas wish ill. by Susie Jenkin-Pearce. Viking, 1991. ISBN 0-670-84107-2 Subj: Behavior – wishing. Holidays – Christmas.

The clever cowboy ill. by Katherine Lodge. DK, 1998. ISBN 0-7894-3491-1 Subj: Cowboys. Family life – brothers and sisters. Tall tales.

The enchanted flute ill. by Margaret Chamberlain. Delacorte, 1991. ISBN 0-385-30327-0 Subj: Birthdays. Magic. Music. Self-concept.

The ice palace ill. by Angela Barrett. Putnam, 1994. ISBN 0-399-22784-9 Subj: Concepts – cold and heat. Dreams. Family life – fathers. Illness.

Jessie's journey ill. by Anne Magill. Macmillan, 1992. ISBN 0-02-765366-8 Subj: Activities – traveling. Imagination. Trains. Transportation.

Matepo ill. by Jill Newton. Dial, 1991. ISBN 0-8037-0838-6 Subj: Activities – trading. Animals. Animals – monkeys. Circular tales. Jungle.

Nesta, the little witch ill. by Susie Jenkin-Pearce. Viking, 1990. ISBN 0-670-83376-2 Subj: School. Witches.

Sleepy Ella ill. by Susan Winter. Delacorte, 1994. ISBN 0-385-32050-7 Subj: Bedtime. Behavior – wishing. Imagination. Rhyming text.

Snail's birthday problem ill. by Susie Jenkin-Pearce. Viking, 1989. ISBN 0-670-82991-9 Subj: Animals – snails. Birthdays. Parties.

The snow angel ill. by Claire Fletcher. Lothrop, 1993. ISBN 0-688-04569-3 Subj: Angels. Family life – brothers and sisters. Weather – snow.

The whales' tale ill. by Michaela Bloomfield. Aurum, 1990. ISBN 1-85406-053-8 Subj: Animals – whales.

The wind garden ill. by Claire Fletcher. Lothrop, 1995. ISBN 0-688-13280-4 Subj: Family life – grandparents. Gardens, gardening. Weather – wind.

MacArthur-Onslow, Annette Rosemary. *Minnie* ill. by author. Rand McNally, 1971. ISBN 0-528-82278-0 Subj: Animals – cats.

Macaulay, David. *Black and white* ill. by author. Houghton Mifflin, 1990. ISBN 0-395-52151-3 Subj: Animals – bulls, cows. Caldecott award books. Family life. Trains.

Castle ill. by author. Houghton Mifflin, 1977. ISBN 0-395-25784-0 Subj: Caldecott award honor books.

Cathedral ill. by author. Houghton Mifflin, 1973. ISBN 0-395-17513-5 Subj: Caldecott award honor books.

Why the chicken crossed the road ill. by author. Houghton Mifflin, 1987. ISBN 0-395-44241-9 Subj: Cumulative tales. Humor.

MacBean, Dilla Wittemore. *Picture book dictionary* ill. by Pauline B. Adams. Childrens Pr., 1962. Subj: Dictionaries.

MacBeth, George. *Jonah and the Lord* ill. by Margaret Gordon. Holt, 1970. ISBN 0-03-081612-2 Subj: Folk and fairy tales. Religion – Jonah.

Noah's journey ill. by Margaret Gordon. Viking, 1966. Subj: Boats, ships. Religion – Noah. Rhym-

ing text. Weather – floods. Weather – rain. Weather – rainbows.

McBratney, Sam. *The caterpillow fight* ill. by Jill Barton. Candlewick, 1996. ISBN 1-56402-804-6 Subj: Bedtime. Behavior – misbehavior. Insects – butterflies, caterpillars. Rhyming text.

The dark at the top of the stairs ill. by Ivan Bates. Candlewick, 1996. ISBN 1-56402-640-X Subj: Animals – cats. Animals – mice. Bedtime. Character traits – curiosity. Emotions – fear.

Guess how much I love you ill. by Anita Jeram. Candlewick, 1995. ISBN 1-56402-473-3 Subj: Animals – rabbits. Bedtime. Emotions – love. Family life – fathers.

I'll always be your friend ill. by Kim Lewis. HarperCollins, 2001. ISBN 0-06-029485-X Subj: Animals – foxes. Emotions – anger. Family life – mothers.

I'm sorry by Sam McBratney and Jennifer Eachus; ed. by Robert Warren; ill. by Jennifer Eachus. HarperCollins, 2000. ISBN 0-06-028686-5 Subj: Behavior – fighting, arguing. Emotions – anger. Friendship. School.

Just one! ill. by Ivan Bates. Candlewick, 1997. ISBN 0-7636-0223-X Subj: Animals – squirrels. Character traits – generosity.

Just you and me ill. by Ivan Bates. Candlewick, 1998. ISBN 0-7636-0436-4 Subj: Animals. Birds – geese. Weather – storms.

McCain, Becky R. (Becky Ray). *Grandmother's dreamcatcher* ill. by Stacey Schuett. Albert Whitman, 1998. ISBN 0-8075-3031-X Subj: Activities – making things. Dreams. Family life – grandmothers. Indians of North America – Chippewa.

Nobody knew what to do: a story about bullying ill. by Todd Leonard. Albert Whitman, 2001. ISBN 0-8075-5711-0 Subj: Behavior – bullying. School.

Maccarone, Grace. *Baby visits grandma and grandpa* ill. by Carol Hudson. Scholastic, 1999. ISBN 0-590-43092-0 Subj: Babies. Family life – grandparents. Format, unusual – board books.

Baby's toys ill. by Carol Hudson. Scholastic, 1990. ISBN 0-590-43098-X Subj: Babies. Format, unusual – board books. Toys.

Cars! Cars! Cars! ill. by David A. Carter. Scholastic, 1995. ISBN 0-590-47572-X Subj: Automobiles. Rhyming text.

A child was born ill. by Sam Williams. Scholastic, 2000. ISBN 0-439-18296-4 Subj: Holidays – Christmas. Religion – Nativity. Rhyming text.

A child's good night prayer ill. by Sam Williams. Scholastic, 2001. ISBN 0-439-23505-7 Subj: Bedtime. Religion.

The class trip ill. by Besty Lewin. Scholastic, 1999. ISBN 0-439-06755-3 Subj: Animals. Behavior – lost. Rhyming text. School. Zoos.

The classroom pet ill. by Betsy Lewin. Scholastic, 1995. ISBN 0-590-26264-5 Subj: Crustaceans. Pets. Rhyming text. School.

Dinosaurs ill. by Richard Courtney. Scholastic, 2001. ISBN 0-439-20060-1 Subj: Dinosaurs.

I have a cold ill. by Betsy Lewin. Scholastic, 1998. ISBN 0-590-39638-2 Subj: Illness – cold (disease). Rhyming text.

I shop with my daddy ill. by Denise Brunkus. Scholastic, 1998. ISBN 0-590-50196-8 Subj: Family life. Rhyming text. Shopping.

Itchy, itchy chicken pox ill. by Betsy Lewin. Scholastic, 1992. ISBN 0-590-44948-6 Subj: Illness – chicken pox. Rhyming text.

The lunch box surprise ill. by Betsy Lewin. Scholastic, 1995. ISBN 0-590-26267-X Subj: Emotions. Food. School.

Martin and the tooth fairy (Chardiet, Bernice)

My tooth is about to fall out ill. by Betsy Lewin. Scholastic, 1995. ISBN 0-590-48376-5 Subj: Behavior – growing up. Teeth.

Oink! moo! how do you do? ill. by Hans Wilhelm. Scholastic, 1994. ISBN 0-590-48161-4 Subj: Animals. Careers – farmers. Farms. Noise, sounds. Rhyming text.

Pizza party ill. by Emily Arnold McCully. Cartwheel, 1994. ISBN 0-590-47563-0 Subj: Activities – cooking. Food. Rhyming text.

Pumpkin faces ill. by author. Scholastic, 1997. ISBN 0-590-13454-X Subj: Animals. Concepts – opposites. Format, unusual – toy and movable books. Holidays – Halloween. Plants.

Sharing time troubles ill. by Betsy Lewin. Cartwheel, 1996. ISBN 0-590-73879-8 Subj: Behavior – sharing. Family life – brothers. Rhyming text. School.

McCarthy, Bobette. *Buffalo girls* ill. by author. Crown, 1987. ISBN 0-517-65568-4 Subj: Animals – buffaloes. Music. Songs.

Dreaming ill. by author. Candlewick, 1994. ISBN 1-56402-184-X Subj: Animals. Bedtime. Boats, ships. Dreams. Rhyming text. Sleep.

Happy hiding hippos ill. by author. Bradbury, 1994. ISBN 0-02-765446-X Subj: Animals – hippopotamuses. Behavior – hiding. Games.

See you later, alligator ill. by author. Macmillan, 1995. ISBN 0-02-765447-8 Subj: Moving. Reptiles – alligators, crocodiles. Rhyming text.

Ten little hippos ill. by author. Bradbury, 1992. ISBN 0-02-765445-1 Subj: Animals – hippopotamuses. Counting, numbers. Rhyming text.

MacCarthy, Patricia. *Herds of words* ill. by author. Dial, 1991. ISBN 0-8037-0892-0 Subj: Language.

McCarthy, Ruth. *Katie and the smallest bear* ill. by Emilie Boon. Knopf, 1986. ISBN 0-394-97855-2 Subj: Activities – playing. Animals – bears. Zoos.

McCarty, Peter. *Little bunny on the move* ill. by author. Holt, 1999. ISBN 0-8050-4620-8 Subj: Activities – traveling. Animals. Animals – rabbits. Homes, houses.

McCaughrean, Geraldine. *The cherry tree* (Ikeda, Daisaku)

Grandma Chickenlegs ill. by Moira Kemp. Carolrhoda, 2000. ISBN 1-57505-415-9 Subj: Family life – step families. Folk and fairy tales. Foreign lands – Russia. Magic. Witches.

The princess and the moon (Ikeda, Daisaku)

Saint George and the dragon ill. by Nicki Palin. Doubleday, 1989. ISBN 0-385-26529-8 Subj: Dragons. Folk and fairy tales.

The snow country prince (Ikeda, Daisaku)

The story of Noah and the ark ill. by Helen Ward. Ideals, 1989. ISBN 0-8249-8403-X Subj: Animals. Boats, ships. Religion – Noah. Weather – floods. Weather – rain. Weather – rainbows.

The story of the Nativity conceived and ill. by Ruth Wickings. Doubleday, 1998. ISBN 0-385-32631-9 Subj: Holidays – Christmas. Religion – Nativity.

Unicorns! Unicorns! ill. by Sophie Windham. Holiday, 1997. ISBN 0-8234-1319-5 Subj: Folk and fairy tales. Imagination. Mythical creatures – unicorns. Religion – Noah.

McCauley, Jane R. *Animals showing off* (Chen, Tony)

Baby birds and how they grow ill. with photos. National Geographic, 1983. ISBN 0-87044-492-1 Subj: Birds. Science.

The way animals sleep ill. with photos. National Geographic, 1983. ISBN 0-87044-494-8 Subj: Animals. Sleep.

McClenathan, Louise. *The Easter pig* ill. by Rosekrans Hoffman. Morrow, 1982. ISBN 0-688-01446-1 Subj: Animals – pigs. Character traits – generosity. Holidays – Easter.

My mother sends her wisdom ill. by Rosekrans Hoffman. Morrow, 1979. ISBN 0-688-32193-3 Subj: Behavior – greed. Character traits – cleverness.

McClintock, Barbara. *Animal fables from Æsop* (Æsop)

The battle of Luke and Longnose ill. by author. Houghton Mifflin, 1994. ISBN 0-395-65751-2 Subj: Animals – cats. Dreams. Magic. Theater. Toys.

The fantastic drawings of Danielle ill. by author. Houghton Mifflin, 1996. ISBN 0-395-73980-2 Subj: Activities – drawing. Activities – painting. Activities – photographing. Careers – artists. Imagination.

Molly and the magic wishbone ill. by author. Farrar, 2000. ISBN 0-374-34999-1 Subj: Behavior – wishing. Fairies. Family life – brothers and sisters.

McClintock, Marshall. *A fly went by* ill. by Fritz Siebel. Random House, 1958. ISBN 0-394-90003-0 Subj: Behavior – misunderstanding. Cumulative tales. Insects – flies.

Stop that ball ill. by Fritz Siebel. Random House, 1959. ISBN 0-394-90010-3 Subj: Toys – balls.

What have I got? ill. by Leonard P. Kessler. HarperCollins, 1961. ISBN 0-06-024141-1 Subj: Clothing. Imagination. Poetry.

McClintock, Mike. *see* McClintock, Marshall

McCloskey, Kevin. *Mrs. Fitz's flamingos* ill. by author. Lothrop, 1992. ISBN 0-688-10474-6 Subj: Birds – flamingos. City. Emotions – love.

McCloskey, Robert. *Bert Dow, deep-water man: a tale of the sea in the classic tradition* ill. by author. Viking, 1963. Subj: Animals – whales. Boats, ships. Sea and seashore.

Blueberries for Sal ill. by author. Viking, 1948. ISBN 0-670-17591-9 Subj: Animals – bears. Behavior – lost. Caldecott award honor books. Family life. Food.

Lentil ill. by author. Viking, 1940. ISBN 0-670-42357-2 Subj: Music. Noise, sounds. Problem solving.

Make way for ducklings ill. by author. Viking, 1941. ISBN 0-670-45149-5 Subj: Birds – ducks. Caldecott award books. Careers – police officers. City.

One morning in Maine ill. by author. Viking, 1952. ISBN 0-670-52627-4 Subj: Caldecott award honor books. Family life. Sea and seashore. Teeth.

Time of wonder ill. by author. Viking, 1957. ISBN 0-670-71512-3 Subj: Caldecott award books. Islands. Sea and seashore. Seasons – summer. Weather.

McClung, Robert. *How animals hide* ill. with photos. National Geographic, 1973. ISBN 0-87044-144-2 Subj: Animals. Behavior – hiding. Science.

Sphinx: the story of a caterpillar ill. by Carol Lerner. Rev. ed. Morrow, 1981. ISBN 0-688-00465-2 Subj: Insects – butterflies, caterpillars. Metamorphosis. Science.

McClure, Gillian. *Fly home McDoo* ill. by author. Dutton, 1980. ISBN 0-233-97108-4 Subj: Behavior – running away. Birds – pigeons.

Prickly pig ill. by author. Elsevier-Dutton, 1980. ISBN 0-233-96780-X Subj: Animals – hedgehogs. Hibernation.

Selkie ill. by author. Farrar, 1999. ISBN 0-374-36709-4 Subj: Animals – seals. Character traits – kindness to animals. Folk and fairy tales. Islands. Mythical creatures – selkies. Sea and seashore.

What's the time, Rory Wolf? ill. by author. Dutton, 1982. Subj: Animals – wolves. Emotions – loneliness. Friendship.

McConnachie, Brian. *Elmer and the chickens vs. the big league* ill. by Harvey Stevenson. Crown, 1992.

ISBN 0-517-57617-1 Subj: Birds – chickens. Farms. Imagination. Sports – baseball.

Flying boy ill. by Jack Ziegler. Crown, 1988. ISBN 0-517-55980-3 Subj: Activities – flying. Character traits – helpfulness. Character traits – individuality.

Lily of the forest ill. by Jack Ziegler. Crown, 1987. ISBN 0-517-56595-1 Subj: Animals. Behavior – boredom. Behavior – running away. Family life. Forest, woods.

McCord, David. *Every time I climb a tree* ill. by Marc Simont. Little, 1967. ISBN 0-316-55514-2 Subj: Activities – playing. Poetry. Trees.

The star in the pail ill. by Marc Simont. Little, 1976. ISBN 0-316-55515-0 Subj: Poetry.

McCormack, John E. *Rabbit tales* ill. by Jenni Oliver. Dutton, 1980. ISBN 0-525-38005-1 Subj: Animals – rabbits. Character traits – cleverness. Character traits – individuality. Character traits – vanity. Friendship. Imagination.

Rabbit travels ill. by Lynne Cherry. Dutton, 1984. ISBN 0-525-44087-9 Subj: Activities – traveling. Animals – rabbits. Friendship.

McCormick, Wendy. *Daddy, will you miss me?* ill. by Jennifer Eachus. Simon & Schuster, 1999. ISBN 0-689-81898-X Subj: Behavior – needing someone. Emotions – loneliness. Family life – fathers. Foreign lands – Africa.

McCourt, Lisa. *Chicken soup for little souls: The best night out with Dad* story adapt. by Lisa McCourt; ill. by Bert Dodson. Health Communications, 1997. Based on the . . . best-selling series Chicken soup for the soul by Jack Canfield and Mark Victor Hansen. ISBN 1-55874-508-4 Subj: Character traits – generosity. Circus. Family life – fathers.

Chicken soup for little souls: The Goodness Gorillas story adapt. by Lisa McCourt; ill. by Pat Grant Porter. Health Communications, 1997. Based on the . . . best-selling series Chicken soup for the soul by Jack Canfield and Mark Victor Hansen. ISBN 1-55874-505-X Subj: Character traits – kindness. Clubs, gangs. School.

Chicken soup for little souls: The never-forgotten doll story adapt. by Lisa McCourt; ill. by Mary O'Keefe Young. Health Communications, 1997. Based on the . . . best-selling series Chicken soup for the soul by Jack Canfield and Mark Victor Hansen. ISBN 1-55874-507-6 Subj: Activities – babysitting. Behavior – losing things. Birthdays. Character traits – kindness. Gifts.

Della Splatnuk birthday girl ill. by Pat Grant Porter. Health Communications, 1999. Based on the . . . best-selling series Chicken soup for the soul by Jack Canfield and Mark Victor Hansen. ISBN 1-55874-600-5 Subj: Birthdays. Friendship. Parties. Prejudice.

I love you, Stinky Face ill. by Cyd Moore. Troll, 1997. ISBN 0-8167-4392-4 Subj: Bedtime. Emotions – love. Family life – mothers. Imagination.

The long and short of it (Nathan, Cheryl)

The new kid and the cookie thief ill. by Mary O'Keefe Young. Health Communications, 1998. Inspired by . . . 'Chicken soup for the soul' by Jack Canfield and Mark Victor Hansen. ISBN 1-55874-588-2 Subj: Character traits – shyness. Friendship. School.

The rainforest counts! ill. by Cheryl Nathan. Troll, 1997. ISBN 0-8167-4388-6 Subj: Animals. Counting, numbers. Forest, woods.

McCoy, Karen Kawamoto. *Bon Odori dancer* ill. by Carolina Yao. Polychrome Pub., 1998. ISBN 1-879965-16-X Subj: Activities – dancing. Ethnic groups in the U.S. – Japanese Americans.

McCrea, James. *The king's procession* by James and Ruth McCrea; ill. by authors. Atheneum, 1963. Subj: Animals – donkeys. Character traits – loyalty. Poverty. Royalty – kings.

The magic tree by James and Ruth McCrea; ill. by authors. Atheneum, 1965. Subj: Character traits – meanness. Emotions. Emotions – happiness. Royalty.

The story of Olaf by James and Ruth McCrea; ill. by authors. Atheneum, 1964. Subj: Dragons. Knights. Wizards.

McCrea, Lilian. *Mother hen* ill. by Edda Reinl. Picture Book Studio, 1987. ISBN 0-88708-037-5 Subj: Animals. Birds – chickens. Counting, numbers. Eggs. Farms.

McCrea, Ruth. *The king's procession* (McCrea, James)

The magic tree (McCrea, James)

The story of Olaf (McCrea, James)

McCready, Lady. *see* Tudor, Tasha

McCready, Tasha Tudor. *see* Tudor, Tasha

McCue, Lisa. *Corduroy's party* ill. by author. Viking, 1985. Subj: Birthdays. Format, unusual – board books. Toys – bears. Wordless.

Corduroy's toys ill. by author. Viking, 1985. ISBN 0-670-80522-X Subj: Format, unusual – board books. Toys. Toys – bears. Wordless.

The little chick ill. by author. Random House, 1986. ISBN 0-394-88017-X Subj: Birds – chickens. Farms. Format, unusual – board books.

McCully, Emily Arnold. *The ballot box battle* ill. by author. Knopf, 1996. ISBN 0-679-97938-7 Subj: Behavior – growing up. Character traits – persistence. U.S. history.

The Christmas gift ill. by author. HarperCollins, 1988. ISBN 0-06-024212-4 Subj: Animals – mice. Family life – grandfathers. Gifts. Holidays – Christmas. Toys. Wordless.

Crossing the new bridge ill. by author. Putnam, 1994. ISBN 0-399-22618-4 Subj: Bridges. Emotions – happiness.

The evil spell ill. by author. HarperCollins, 1992. ISBN 0-06-024154-3 Subj: Animals – bears. Emotions – fear. Theater.

First snow ill. by author. HarperCollins, 1985. ISBN 0-06-024129-2 Subj: Activities – playing. Animals – mice. Seasons – winter. Weather – snow. Wordless.

Four hungry kittens ill. by author. Dial, 2001. ISBN 0-8037-2505-1 Subj: Animals – cats. Wordless.

The grandma mix-up ill. by author. HarperCollins, 1988. ISBN 0-06-024202-7 Subj: Activities – babysitting. Family life – grandmothers.

Little Kit, or, The Industrious Flea Circus girl ill. by author. Dial, 1995. ISBN 0-8037-1674-5 Subj: Character traits – meanness. Circus. Insects – fleas. Orphans.

Mirette and Bellini cross Niagara Falls ill. by author. Putnam, 2000. ISBN 0-399-23348-2 Subj: Careers – aerialists. Ethnic groups in the U.S. – French Americans. Immigrants.

Mirette on the high wire ill. by author. Putnam, 1992. ISBN 0-399-22130-1 Subj: Caldecott award books. Emotions – fear. Foreign lands – France.

Monk camps out ill. by author. Scholastic, 2000. ISBN 0-439-09976-5 Subj: Animals – mice. Camps, camping. Family life.

Mouse practice ill. by author. Scholastic, 1999. ISBN 0-590-68220-2 Subj: Animals – mice. Character traits – persistence. Sports – baseball.

My real family ill. by author. Browndeer, 1994. ISBN 0-15-277698-2 Subj: Adoption. Animals – bears. Animals – sheep. Behavior – running away. Family life. Theater.

New baby ill. by author. HarperCollins, 1988. ISBN 0-06-024131-4 Subj: Animals – mice. Sibling rivalry. Wordless.

The orphan singer ill. by author. Scholastic, 2001. ISBN 0-439-19274-9 Subj: Activities – singing. Foreign lands – Italy. Music. Orphans.

An outlaw Thanksgiving ill. by author. Dial, 1998. ISBN 0-8037-2198-6 Subj: Crime. Holidays – Thanksgiving. Trains. U.S. history. Weather – snow.

Picnic ill. by author. HarperCollins, 1984. ISBN 0-06-024099-7 Subj: Activities – picnicking. Animals – mice. Behavior – lost. Wordless.

The pirate queen ill. by author. Putnam, 1995. ISBN 0-399-22657-5 Subj: Boats, ships. Foreign lands – Ireland. Pirates.

Popcorn at the palace ill. by author. Browndeer, 1997. ISBN 0-15-277699-0 Subj: Family life – fathers. Food. Foreign lands – England.

School ill. by author. HarperCollins, 1987. ISBN 0-06-024133-0 Subj: Animals – mice. School. Wordless.

Speak up, Blanche! ill. by author. HarperCollins, 1991. ISBN 0-06-024228-0 Subj: Animals – bears. Animals – sheep. Character traits – shyness. Theater.

Zaza's big break ill. by author. HarperCollins, 1989. ISBN 0-06-024224-8 Subj: Animals – bears. Careers – actors. Television. Theater.

McCunn, Ruthanne L. *Pie-Biter* ill. by You-Shah Tang. Design Ent., 1983. ISBN 0-932538-09-6 Subj: Activities – working. Behavior – seeking better things. Ethnic groups in the U.S. – Chinese Americans.

McCurdy, Michael. *The devils who learned to be good* ill. by author. Little, 1987. ISBN 0-316-55527-4 Subj: Character traits – cleverness. Devil. Folk and fairy tales.

The old man and the fiddle ill. by author. Putnam, 1992. ISBN 0-399-21812-2 Subj: Music. Rhyming text.

The sailor's alphabet ill. by author. Houghton Mifflin, 1998. ISBN 0-395-84167-4 Subj: ABC books. Poetry. Sailors. Sea and seashore.

McCutcheon, John. *Happy adoption day!* lyrics by John McCutcheon; ill. by Julie Paschkis. Little, 1996. ISBN 0-316-55455-3 Subj: Adoption. Family life. Songs.

McCutcheon, Marc. *Grandfather's Christmas camp* ill. by Kate Kiesler. Clarion, 1995. ISBN 0-395-69626-7 Subj: Animals – dogs. Camps, camping. Family life – grandfathers. Holidays – Christmas. Weather – snow.

McDaniel, Becky Bring. *Katie did it* ill. by Lois Axeman. Childrens Pr., 1983. ISBN 0-516-02043-9 Subj: Sibling rivalry.

McDermott, Beverly Brodsky. *The crystal apple: a Russian tale* ill. by author. Viking, 1974. ISBN 0-670-25052-X Subj: Folk and fairy tales. Foreign lands – Russia. Imagination.

The dreamtime ill. by author. Blue Sky, 1995. ISBN 0-590-48518-0 Subj: Creation. Folk and fairy tales. Foreign lands – Australia.

The Golem: a Jewish legend ill. by author. Lippincott, 1976. ISBN 0-397-31674-7 Subj: Folk and fairy tales. Jewish culture.

Jonah: an Old Testament story ill. by author. Lippincott, 1977. ISBN 0-397-31711-6 Subj: Animals – whales. Religion – Jonah.

McDermott, Gerald. *Anansi the spider: a tale from the Ashanti* ill. by author. Holt, 1972. ISBN 0-03080-236-9 Subj: Caldecott award honor books. Folk and fairy tales. Foreign lands – Africa. Moon. Spiders.

Arrow to the sun: a Pueblo Indian tale ill. by author. Viking, 1974. ISBN 0-670-13369-8 Subj: Caldecott award books. Folk and fairy tales. Indians of North America – Pueblo.

The Brambleberrys animal book of colors (Mayer, Marianna)

Coyote: a trickster tale from the American Southwest ill. by author. Harcourt, 1994. ISBN 0-15-220724-4 Subj: Activities – flying. Animals – coyotes. Birds – crows. Folk and fairy tales. Indians of North America – Southwest.

Daniel O'Rourke: an Irish tale ill. by author. Viking, 1986. ISBN 0-670-80924-1 Subj: Dreams. Folk and fairy tales. Foreign lands – Ireland. Mythical creatures – pooka spirit.

Daughter of earth: a Roman myth ill. by author. Delacorte, 1984. ISBN 0-385-29295-3 Subj: Folk and fairy tales. Seasons.

The fox and the stork retold from La Fontaine's fable and ill. by Gerald McDermott. Harcourt, 1999. ISBN 0-15-202343-7 Subj: Animals – foxes. Birds – storks. Folk and fairy tales.

The light of the world: the story of the Nativity ill. by author. Simon & Schuster, 1998. ISBN 0-689-80707-4 Subj: Holidays – Christmas. Religion – Nativity.

The magic tree: a tale from the Congo ill. by author. Holt, 1994. ISBN 0-8050-3080-8 Subj: Character traits – appearance. Magic. Multiple births – twins.

Musicians of the sun ill. by author. Simon & Schuster, 1997. ISBN 0-689-80706-6 Subj: Folk and fairy tales. Foreign lands – Mexico. Indians of North America – Aztec. Music. Sun.

Papagayo, the mischief maker ill. by author. Windmill, 1980. ISBN 0-671-96084-9 Subj: Birds – parakeets, parrots. Moon.

Raven: a trickster tale from the Pacific Northwest ill. by author. Harcourt, 1993. ISBN 0-15-265661-8 Subj: Behavior – trickery. Birds – ravens. Caldecott award honor books. Folk and fairy tales. Indians of North America.

The stonecutter: a Japanese folk tale ill. by author. Viking, 1975. ISBN 0-670-67074-X Subj: Behavior – dissatisfaction. Folk and fairy tales. Foreign lands – Japan.

Tim O'Toole and the wee folk ill. by author. Viking, 1990. ISBN 0-670-80393-6 Subj: Behavior – trickery. Folk and fairy tales. Magic.

The voyage of Osiris: a myth of ancient Egypt ill. by author. Windmill, 1977. ISBN 0-525-61567-9 Subj: Folk and fairy tales. Foreign lands – Egypt. Religion. Royalty.

Zomo the rabbit ill. by author. Harcourt, 1992. ISBN 0-15-299967-1 Subj: Animals – rabbits. Behavior – trickery. Foreign lands – Africa.

MacDonald, Alan. *Beware of the bears!* ill. by Gwyneth Williamson. Little Tiger, 1998. ISBN 1-888444-

28-2 Subj: Animals – bears. Character traits – orderliness.

The not-so-wise man ill. by Andrew Rowland. Eerdmans, 1999. ISBN 0-8028-5196-7 Subj: Holidays – Christmas. Religion – Nativity. Royalty – kings.

MacDonald, Allan. *The pig in a wig* ill. by Paul Hess. Peachtree, 1999. ISBN 1-56145-197-5 Subj: Animals – pigs. Hair. Self-concept.

MacDonald, Amy. *Cousin Ruth's tooth* ill. by Marjorie Priceman. Houghton Mifflin, 1996. ISBN 0-395-71253-X Subj: Behavior – growing up. Behavior – losing things. Family life. Rhyming text. Teeth.

Let's do it ill. by Maureen Roffey. Candlewick, 1992. ISBN 1-56402-024-X Subj: Activities. Format, unusual – board books. Games.

Let's go ill. by Maureen Roffey. Candlewick, 1994. ISBN 1-56402-202-1 Subj: Activities – playing. Format, unusual – board books.

Let's make a noise ill. by Maureen Roffey. Candlewick, 1992. ISBN 1-56402-025-8 Subj: Format, unusual – board books. Noise, sounds.

Let's play ill. by Maureen Roffey. Candlewick, 1992. ISBN 1-56402-023-1 Subj: Activities – playing. Format, unusual – board books. Toys.

Let's pretend ill. by Maureen Roffey. Candlewick, 1994. ISBN 1-56402-201-3 Subj: Activities – playing. Format, unusual – board books. Imagination.

Let's try ill. by Maureen Roffey. Candlewick, 1992. ISBN 1-56402-022-3 Subj: Activities. Format, unusual – board books.

Little Beaver and the echo ill. by Sarah Fox-Davies. Putnam, 1990. ISBN 0-399-22203-0 Subj: Animals – beavers. Cumulative tales. Friendship. Noise, sounds.

Please, Malese! a trickster tale from Haiti ill. by Emily Lisker. DK, 2001. ISBN 0-7894-2647-1 Subj: Behavior – trickery. Folk and fairy tales. Foreign lands – Haiti.

Rachel Fister's blister ill. by Marjorie Priceman. Houghton Mifflin, 1990. ISBN 0-395-52152-1 Subj: Illness. Rhyming text.

The spider who created the world ill. by G. Brian Karas. Orchard, 1996. ISBN 0-531-08855-3 Subj: Creation. Spiders.

MacDonald, Elizabeth. *Dilly-Dally and the nine secrets* ill. by Ken Brown. Dutton, 1999. ISBN 0-525-46006-3 Subj: Animals – babies. Birds – ducks. Counting, numbers. Rivers.

John's picture ill. by David McTaggart. Viking, 1991. ISBN 0-670-83579-X Subj: Art.

Mike's kite ill. by Robert Kendall. Watts, 1990. ISBN 0-531-08476-0 Subj: Counting, numbers. Cumulative tales. Kites.

Miss Poppy and the honey cake ill. by Claire Smith. Dial, 1989. ISBN 0-8037-0578-6 Subj: Activities – cooking. Animals – pigs. Rhyming text.

Mr. Badger's birthday pie ill. by Claire Smith. Dial, 1989. ISBN 0-8037-0579-4 Subj: Activities – cooking. Animals – badgers. Birthdays.

Mr. MacGregor's breakfast egg ill. by Alex Ayliffe. Viking, 1990. ISBN 0-670-83256-1 Subj: Eggs. Food.

My aunt and the animals by Elizabeth MacDonald and Annie Owen; ill. by Annie Owen. Barron's, 1985. ISBN 0-8120-5641-8 Subj: Animals. Counting, numbers. Days of the week, months of the year. Family life – aunts, uncles.

The very windy day ill. by Lesley Summers. Tambourine, 1992. ISBN 0-688-11045-2 Subj: Circular tales. Weather – wind.

The wolf is coming! ill. by Ken Brown. Dutton, 1998. ISBN 0-525-45952-9 Subj: Animals. Animals – rabbits. Animals – wolves. Cumulative tales.

MacDonald, George. *The light princess* ill. by Maurice Sendak. Farrar, 1969. ISBN 0-374-34455-8 Subj: Folk and fairy tales.

The light princess adapt. by Robin McKinley; ill. by Katie Thamer Treherne. Harcourt, 1987. ISBN 0-15-245300-8 Subj: Concepts – weight. Folk and fairy tales. Royalty – princesses. Witches.

Little Daylight ill. by Dorothée Duntze. Holt, 1987. ISBN 0-8050-0493-9 Subj: Fairies. Folk and fairy tales. Magic. Royalty – princes. Royalty – princesses.

McDonald, Golden. *see* Brown, Margaret Wise

MacDonald, Greville. *see* MacDonald, George

McDonald, Jamie. *see* Heide, Florence Parry

MacDonald, Margaret Read. *The girl who wore too much* Thai text by Supaporn Vathanaprida; ill. by Yvonne LeBrun Davis. August House, 1998. ISBN 0-8748-3503-8 Subj: Character traits – vanity. Clothing. Folk and fairy tales. Foreign lands – Thailand.

The old woman who lived in a vinegar bottle ill. by Nancy Dunaway Fowlkes. August House, 1995. ISBN 0-87483-415-5 Subj: Behavior – dissatisfaction. Folk and fairy tales. Foreign lands – England.

Pickin' peas ill. by Pat Cummings. HarperCollins, 1998. ISBN 0-06-027970-2 Subj: Animals – rabbits. Behavior – trickery. Ethnic groups in the U.S. – African Americans. Folk and fairy tales. Gardens, gardening.

Slop! a Welsh folktale ill. by Yvonne LeBrun Davis. Fulcrum Kids, 1997. ISBN 1-55591-352-0 Subj: Character traits – kindness. Fairies. Folk and fairy tales. Foreign lands – Wales.

McDonald, Mary Ann. *Leopards* photos by author. Child's World, 1996. ISBN 1-56766-211-0 Subj: Animals – leopards.

Macdonald, Maryann. *Ben at the beach* ill. by David McTaggart. Viking, 1991. ISBN 0-670-83920-5 Subj: Family life – brothers and sisters. Sand. Sea and seashore.

Hedgehog bakes a cake ill. by Lynn Munsinger. Gareth Stevens, 1996. ISBN 0-8368-1619-6 Subj: Activities – baking. Animals. Animals – hedgehogs. Food.

Little Hippo gets glasses ill. by Anna King. Dial, 1992. ISBN 0-8037-0964-1 Subj: Animals – hippopotamuses. Glasses. Senses – seeing.

Little Hippo starts school ill. by Anna King. Dial, 1990. ISBN 0-8037-0720-7 Subj: Animals – hippopotamuses. School – first day.

The pink party ill. by Abby Carter. Hyperion, 1994. ISBN 1-56282-621-2 Subj: Concepts – color. Emotions – envy, jealousy. Friendship.

Rabbit's birthday kite ill. by Lynn Munsinger. Bantam, 1991. ISBN 0-553-05876-2 Subj: Animals – hedgehogs. Animals – rabbits. Birthdays. Kites.

Rosie and the poor rabbits ill. by Melissa Sweet. Atheneum, 1994. ISBN 0-689-31832-4 Subj: Animals – rabbits. Behavior – sharing. Character traits – generosity. Dreams.

Rosie runs away ill. by Melissa Sweet. Atheneum, 1990. ISBN 0-689-31625-9 Subj: Animals – rabbits. Behavior – running away. Family life.

Rosie's baby tooth ill. by Melissa Sweet. Atheneum, 1991. ISBN 0-689-31626-7 Subj: Animals – rabbits. Fairies. Teeth.

Sam's worries ill. by Judith Riches. Walt Disney, 1991. ISBN 1-56282-082-6 Subj: Behavior – worrying. Toys – bears.

McDonald, Megan. *Ant and Honey Bee* ill. by Tom Payne. Candlewick, 2001. ISBN 0-7636-1265-0 Subj: Clothing – costumes. Insects – ants. Insects – bees. Parties.

Bedbugs ill. by Paul Brett Johnson. Orchard, 1999. ISBN 0-531-33193-8 Subj: Activities – bathing. Bedtime. Emotions – fear. Family life – fathers. Imagination. Insects. Monsters. Rhyming text.

The bone keeper ill. by G. Brian Karas. DK, 1999. ISBN 0-7894-2559-9 Subj: Anatomy – skeletons. Animals – wolves. Desert. Magic. Mythical creatures.

The great pumpkin switch ill. by Ted Lewin. Watts, 1992. ISBN 0-531-08600-3 Subj: Family life – grandfathers. Mystery stories. Plants.

Insects are my life ill. by Paul Brett Johnson. Orchard, 1995. ISBN 0-531-08724-7 Subj: Behavior – collecting things. Family life. Insects. School.

Is this a house for Hermit Crab? ill. by S. D. Schindler. Watts, 1990. ISBN 0-531-08455-8 Subj: Crustaceans. Sea and seashore.

Lucky star ill. by Andrea Wallace. St. Martin's, 2000. ISBN 0-307-46329-X Subj: Activities – reading. Friendship.

My house has stars ill. by Peter Catalanotto. Orchard, 1996. ISBN 0-531-08879-0 Subj: Foreign lands. Homes, houses. Night. Stars.

The night Iguana left home ill. by Ponder Goembel. DK, 1999. ISBN 0-7894-2581-5 Subj: Activities – traveling. Behavior – dissatisfaction. Friendship. Reptiles – iguanas.

The potato man ill. by Ted Lewin. Watts, 1991. ISBN 0-531-08514-7 Subj: Careers – peddlers. Family life – grandfathers.

Tundra mouse ill. by S. D. Schindler. Orchard, 1997. ISBN 0-531-33047-8 Subj: Activities – storytelling. Animals – mice. Eskimos. Indians of North America – Yupik.

Whoo-oo is it? ill. by S. D. Schindler. Watts, 1992. ISBN 0-531-08574-0 Subj: Birds – owls. Night. Noise, sounds.

MacDonald, Suse. *Alphabatics* ill. by author. Bradbury, 1986. ISBN 0-02-761520-0 Subj: ABC books. Caldecott award honor books.

Elephants on board ill. by author. Harcourt, 1999. ISBN 0-15-200951-5 Subj: Animals – elephants. Circus. Machines. Rhyming text. Transportation. Trucks.

Look whooo's counting ill. by author. Scholastic, 2000. ISBN 0-590-68320-9 Subj: Animals. Counting, numbers. Picture puzzles.

Nanta's lion ill. by author. Morrow, 1995. ISBN 0-688-13125-5 Subj: Animals. Animals – lions. Foreign lands – Africa. Format, unusual. Jungle. Sports – hunting.

Numblers by Suse MacDonald and Bill Oakes; ill. by authors. Dial, 1988. ISBN 0-8037-0548-4 Subj: Counting, numbers.

Once upon another by Suse MacDonald and Bill Oakes; ill. by authors. Dial, 1990. ISBN 0-8037-0787-8 Subj: Folk and fairy tales. Format, unusual.

Peck, slither and slide ill. by author. Harcourt, 1997. ISBN 0-15-200079-8 Subj: Animals. Behavior. Picture puzzles.

Sea shapes ill. by author. Harcourt, 1997. ISBN 0-15-201700-3 Subj: Animals. Concepts – shape. Sea and seashore.

Space spinners ill. by author. Dial, 1991. ISBN 0-8037-1009-7 Subj: Space and space ships. Spiders.

McDonnell, Flora. *Flora McDonnell's ABC* ill. by author. Candlewick, 1997. ISBN 0-7636-0118-7 Subj: ABC books.

I love animals ill. by author. Candlewick, 1994. ISBN 1-56402-387-7 Subj: Animals. Character traits – kindness to animals. Farms.

I love boats ill. by author. Candlewick, 1995. ISBN 1-56402-539-X Subj: Activities – bathing. Boats, ships. Toys.

Splash! ill. by author. Candlewick, 1999. ISBN 0-7636-0481-X Subj: Animals. Animals – elephants. Water.

McDonough, Yona Zeldis. *Eve and her sisters: women of the Old Testament* by Yona Zeldis McDonough and Malcah Zeldis; ill. by Malcah Zeldis. Greenwillow, 1994. ISBN 0-688-12513-1 Subj: Religion.

McFall, Gardner. *Jonathan's cloud* ill. by Steven Guarnaccia. HarperCollins, 1986. ISBN 0-06-024124-1 Subj: Weather – clouds.

Naming the animals ill. by Steven Guarnaccia. Viking, 1994. ISBN 0-670-84814-X Subj: Animals. Creation. Names.

MacFarland, Cynthia. *Cows in the parlor* photos by author. Atheneum, 1990. ISBN 0-689-31584-8 Subj: Animals – bulls, cows. Farms.

McFarland, John. *The exploding frog and other fables from Æsop* retold by John McFarland; ill. by James Marshall. Little, 1981. ISBN 0-316-55576-2 Subj: Folk and fairy tales.

McFarland, Lyn Rossiter. *The pirate's parrot* ill. by Jim McFarland. Tricycle, 2000. ISBN 1-58246-014-0 Subj: Behavior – fighting, arguing. Behavior – mistakes. Birds – parakeets, parrots. Pirates. Toys – bears.

McFarlane, Sheryl. *Eagle dreams* ill. by Ron Lightburn. Philomel, 1994. ISBN 0-399-22695-8 Subj: Animals – endangered animals. Birds – eagles. Character traits – kindness to animals.

Going to the fair ill. by Sheena Lott. Orca, 1996. ISBN 1-55143-062-2 Subj: Fairs.

Waiting for the whales ill. by Ron Lightburn. Philomel, 1993. ISBN 0-399-22515-3 Subj: Animals – whales. Death. Family life – grandfathers.

McGee, Barbara. *Counting sheep* ill. by author. Firefly, 1991. ISBN 1-55037-157-6 Subj: Animals – sheep. Counting, numbers.

McGee, Marni. *The quiet farmer* ill. by Lynne Dennis. Atheneum, 1991. ISBN 0-689-31678-X Subj: Animals. Farms. Noise, sounds.

McGee, Shelagh. *I'm a little teapot* ill. by author. Doubleday, 1992. ISBN 0-385-30324-6 Subj: Games. Nursery rhymes. Songs.

McGeorge, Constance W. *Boomer goes to school* ill. by Mary Whyte. Chronicle, 1996. ISBN 0-8118-1117-4 Subj: Animals – dogs. Pets. School.

Boomer's big day ill. by Mary Whyte. Chronicle, 1994. ISBN 0-8118-0526-3 Subj: Animals – dogs. Moving. Pets.

Boomer's big surprise ill. by Mary Whyte. Chronicle, 1999. ISBN 0-8118-1977-9 Subj: Animals – babies. Animals – dogs. Emotions – envy, jealousy.

McGill, Alice. *Molly Bannaky* ill. by Chris K. Soentpiet. Houghton Mifflin, 1999. ISBN 0-395-72287-X Subj: Activities – reading. Ethnic groups in the U.S. – African Americans. Farms. Immigrants. Marriage, interracial. Slavery. U.S. history.

MacGill-Callahan, Sheila. *And still the turtle watched* ill. by Barry Moser. Dial, 1991. ISBN 0-8037-0932-3 Subj: Art. Family life – grandfathers. Folk and fairy tales. Indians of North America – Delaware. Progress. Reptiles – turtles, tortoises.

The children of Lir ill. by Gennady Spirin. Dial, 1993. ISBN 0-8037-1122-0 Subj: Birds – swans. Folk and fairy tales. Foreign lands – Ireland. Magic. Royalty – kings.

Finn MacCool and the talking fish ill. by John Thompson. Dial, 1998. ISBN 0-8037-1537-4 Subj: Fish. Folk and fairy tales. Foreign lands – Ireland.

The last snake in Ireland ill. by Will Hillenbrand. Holiday, 1999. ISBN 0-8234-1425-6 Subj: Folk and fairy tales. Foreign lands – Ireland. Reptiles – snakes. Tall tales.

The seal prince ill. by Kris Waldherr. Dial, 1995. ISBN 0-8037-1487-4 Subj: Animals – seals. Folk and fairy tales. Foreign lands – Scotland. Mythical creatures – selkies.

To capture the wind ill. by Gregory Manchess. Dial, 1997. ISBN 0-8037-1542-0 Subj: Boats, ships. Folk and fairy tales. Foreign lands – Ireland. Inventions. Pirates.

When Solomon was king ill. by Stephen T. Johnson. Dial, 1995. ISBN 0-8037-1590-0 Subj: Animals. Folk and fairy tales. Jewish culture. Royalty – kings.

McGillicuddy, Mr. *see* Abisch, Roz

McGinley, Phyllis. *All around the town* ill. by Helen Stone. Lippincott, 1948. Subj: ABC books. Caldecott award honor books. City. Rhyming text.

The horse who lived upstairs ill. by Helen Stone. Lippincott, 1944. Subj: Animals – horses, ponies. Behavior – dissatisfaction.

How Mrs. Santa Claus saved Christmas ill. by Kurt Werth. Lippincott, 1963. Subj: Holidays – Christmas. Rhyming text. Santa Claus.

Lucy McLockett ill. by Helen Stone. Lippincott, 1958. Subj: Behavior – losing things. Family life. Rhyming text. Teeth.

The most wonderful doll in the world ill. by Helen Stone. Lippincott, 1950. ISBN 0-590-43476-4 Subj: Caldecott award honor books. Toys – dolls.

Wonderful time ill. by John Alcorn. Lippincott, 1966. Subj: Clocks, watches. Rhyming text. Time.

McGinnis, Lila Sprague. *If Daddy only knew me* ill. by Diane Paterson. Albert Whitman, 1995. ISBN 0-8075-3537-0 Subj: Behavior – needing someone. Family life – fathers. Family life – sisters.

McGough, Roger. *Counting by numbers* ill. by Marketa Prachaticka. Viking, 1990. ISBN 0-670-82671-5 Subj: Counting, numbers. Rhyming text.

Until I met Dudley: how everyday things really work ill. by Chris Riddell. Walker, 1997. ISBN 0-8027-8624-3 Subj: Animals – dogs. Homes, houses. Machines.

McGovern, Ann. *Black is beautiful* photos by Hope Wurmfeld. Four Winds, 1969. Subj: Ethnic groups in the U.S. – African Americans.

Eggs on your nose ill. by Maxie Chambliss. Macmillan, 1987. ISBN 0-02-765750-7 Subj: Eggs. Food. Rhyming text.

Feeling mad, feeling sad, feeling bad, feeling glad photos by Hope Wurmfeld. Walker, 1977. ISBN 0-8027-6295-6 Subj: Emotions. Poetry.

Mr. Skinner's skinny house ill. by Mort Gerberg. Four Winds, 1980. ISBN 0-590-07620-5 Subj: Character traits – being different. Emotions – loneliness. Homes, houses.

Nicholas Bentley Stoningpot III ill. by Tomie de Paola. Holiday, 1982. ISBN 0-8234-0443-9 Subj: Behavior – boredom. Boats, ships. Emotions – loneliness. Islands.

Too much noise ill. by Simms Taback. Houghton Mifflin, 1967. ISBN 0-590-02435-3 Subj: Humor. Noise, sounds.

Zoo, where are you? ill. by Ezra Jack Keats. HarperCollins, 1965. Subj: Zoos.

McGowan, Alan. *Sailing ships* by Alan McGowan and Ron van der Meer; ill. by Borje Svensson. Viking, 1984. ISBN 0-670-61529-3 Subj: Boats, ships. Format, unusual – toy and movable books.

McGowen, Tom (Thomas). *The only glupmaker in the U.S. Navy* ill. by author. Albert Whitman, 1966. Subj: Activities – working. Careers – military.

MacGregor, Ellen. *Mr. Pingle and Mr. Buttonhouse* ill. by Paul Galdone. McGraw-Hill, 1957. Subj: Friendship.

Theodor Turtle ill. by Paul Galdone. McGraw-Hill, 1955. Subj: Behavior – forgetfulness. Participation. Reptiles – turtles, tortoises.

MacGregor, Marilyn. *Baby takes a trip* ill. by author. Macmillan, 1985. ISBN 0-02-761940-0 Subj: Babies. Character traits – curiosity. Wordless.

Helen the hungry bear ill. by author. Four Winds, 1987. ISBN 0-02-761950-8 Subj: Activities – picnicking. Animals – bears. Family life. Food.

On top ill. by author. Morrow, 1988. ISBN 0-688-07491-X Subj: Animals – sheep. Character traits – individuality. Wordless.

McGuire, Leslie. *Baby night owl* ill. by Mary Szilagyi. Random House, 1989. ISBN 0-394-99986-X Subj: Bedtime. Birds – owls.

Who will play with Little Dinosaur? ill. by Norman Gorbaty. Random House, 1989. ISBN 0-394-82129-7 Subj: Dinosaurs.

McGuire, Paula. *Me and Clara and Baldwin the pony* (Inkiow, Dimiter)

Me and Clara and Casimir the cat (Inkiow, Dimiter)

Me and Clara and Snuffy the dog (Inkiow, Dimiter)

Me and my sister Clara (Inkiow, Dimiter)

McGuire, Richard. *Night becomes day* ill. by author. Viking, 1994. ISBN 0-670-85547-2 Subj: Time.

The orange book ill. by author. Rizzoli, 1992. ISBN 0-8478-1465-3 Subj: Counting, numbers. Food.

What goes around comes around ill. by author. Viking, 1995. ISBN 0-670-86396-3 Subj: Behavior – misbehavior. Circular tales. Toys – dolls.

What's wrong with this book? ill. by author. Viking, 1997. ISBN 0-670-86852-3 Subj: Clowns, jesters. Format, unusual – toy and movable books. Picture puzzles. Rhyming text.

McGuire-Turcotte, Casey A. *How Honu the turtle got his shell* ill. by Dick Sakahara. Raintree, 1991. ISBN 0-8172-2783-0 Subj: Folk and fairy tales. Hawaii. Reptiles – turtles, tortoises.

McGuirk, Leslie. *Tucker flips!* ill. by author. Dutton, 1999. ISBN 0-525-46259-7 Subj: Activities – playing. Animals – dogs. Weather – snow.

McGurn, Patty. *Me and Marie* ill. by author. Crown, 1989. ISBN 0-517-57218-4 Subj: Animals – cats. Pets.

Machado, Ana Maria. *Nina Bonita* ill. by Rosana Faria; trans. from Spanish by Elena Iribarren. Kane/Miller, 1996. ISBN 0-916291-63-4 Subj: Animals – rabbits. Character traits – being different. Foreign lands – Brazil.

McHale, Ethel Kharasch. *Son of thunder: an old Lapp tale* ill. by Ruth Lercher Bornstein. Childrens Pr., 1974. ISBN 0-516-08856-4 Subj: Folk and fairy tales. Foreign lands – Lapland.

McHargue, Georgess. *Private zoo* ill. by Michael Foreman. Viking, 1975. ISBN 0-670-57859-2 Subj: Imagination. Shadows.

Machetanz, Fred. *A puppy named Gia* (Machetanz, Sara)

Machetanz, Sara. *A puppy named Gia* by Sara and Fred Machetanz; ill. by Fred Machetanz. Scribners, 1957. Subj: Animals – dogs. Eskimos.

Machotka, Hana. *Breathtaking noses* photos by author. Morrow, 1992. ISBN 0-688-09527-5 Subj: Anatomy – noses. Animals. Games.

Outstanding outsides ill. by author. Morrow, 1993. ISBN 0-688-11753-8 Subj: Anatomy – skin. Animals.

Pasta factory ill. by author. Houghton Mifflin, 1992. ISBN 0-395-60197-5 Subj: Food. Machines.

Terrific tails ill. by author. Morrow, 1994. ISBN 0-688-04563-4 Subj: Anatomy – tails. Animals.

What do you do at a petting zoo? photos by author. Morrow, 1990. ISBN 0-688-08738-8 Subj: Animals. Zoos.

What neat feet! photos by author. Morrow, 1990. ISBN 0-688-09475-9 Subj: Anatomy – feet. Animals. Games.

McIntire, Alta. *Follett beginning to read picture dictionary* ill. by Janet La Salle. Follett, 1959. Subj: Dictionaries.

Mack, Gail. *Yesterday's snowman* ill. by Erik Blegvad. Pantheon, 1979. ISBN 0-394-93662-0 Subj: Family life. Snowmen.

Mack, Stanley (Stan). *Ten bears in my bed: a good-night countdown* ill. by author. Pantheon, 1974. ISBN 0-394-92902-0 Subj: Animals – bears. Bedtime. Counting, numbers. Songs.

Mackall, Dandi Daley. *Off to Bethlehem!* ill. by R. W. Alley. HarperCollins, 2002. ISBN 0-694-01505-9 Subj: Religion – Nativity. Rhyming text.

McKaughan, Larry. *Why are your fingers cold?* ill. by Joy Dunn Keenan. Herald Pr., 1992. ISBN 0-8361-3604-7 Subj: Character traits – questioning. Family life.

Mackay, Claire. *Bats about baseball* (Little, Jean)

McKay, George. *Marny's ride with the wind* (McKay, Louise)

McKay, Hilary. *Where's bear?* ill. by Alex Ayliffe. Margaret K. McElderry, 1998. ISBN 0-689-82271-5 Subj: Character traits – cleanliness. Family life. Toys – bears.

MacKay, Jed. *The big secret* ill. by Heather Collins. Firefly, 1984. ISBN 0-920236-88-X Subj: Adoption. Family life. Parties.

McKay, Lawrence. *Caravan* ill. by Darryl Ligasan. Lee & Low, 1995. ISBN 1-880000-23-7 Subj: Activities – trading. Activities – traveling. Family life – fathers. Family life – sons. Foreign lands – Afghanistan.

Journey home ill. by Dom and Keunhee Lee. Lee & Low, 1998. ISBN 1-880000-65-2 Subj: Activities – traveling. Ethnic groups in the U.S. – Vietnamese Americans. Family life – mothers. Foreign lands – Vietnam. Orphans.

McKay, Louise. *Marny's ride with the wind* by Louise and George McKay; ill. by Margaret Smetana. New Harbinger, 1979. Subj: Friendship. Weather – wind.

McKay, Sindy. *Jack and the beanstalk* (Jack and the beanstalk)

McKean, Thomas. *Hooray for Grandma Jo!* ill. by Chris L. Demarest. Crown, 1994. ISBN 0-517-57843-3 Subj: Animals – lions. Behavior – losing things. Crime. Family life – grandmothers. Glasses. Zoos.

McKee, David. *The day the tide went out and out and out* ill. by author. Abelard-Schuman, 1975. Subj: Animals – camels. Desert. Sea and seashore.

Elmer ill. by author. Lothrop, 1989. ISBN 0-688-09172-5 Subj: Animals – elephants. Character traits – being different.

Elmer again ill. by author. Lothrop, 1991. ISBN 0-688-11597-7 Subj: Animals – elephants. Behavior – boredom.

Elmer and the kangaroo ill. by author. HarperCollins, 2000. ISBN 0-688-17951-7 Subj: Animals – elephants. Animals – kangaroos. Self-concept.

Elmer and the lost teddy ill. by author. Lothrop, 1999. ISBN 0-688-16912-0 Subj: Animals – elephants. Behavior – losing things. Toys – bears.

Elmer and the wind ill. by author. Lothrop, 1998. Subj: Activities – flying. Animals – elephants. Weather – wind.

Elmer and Wilbur ill. by author. Lothrop, 1996. ISBN 0-688-14934-0 Subj: Animals – elephants. Behavior – lost. Friendship.

Elmer in the snow ill. by author. Lothrop, 1995. ISBN 0-688-14596-5 Subj: Activities – playing. Animals – elephants. Friendship. Weather – snow.

Elmer takes off ill. by author. Lothrop, 1998. ISBN 0-688-15785-8 Subj: Activities – flying. Animals – elephants. Weather – wind.

Elmer's colors ill. by author. Lothrop, 1994. ISBN 0-688-13762-8 Subj: Animals – elephants. Concepts – color. Format, unusual – board books.

Elmer's day ill. by author. Lothrop, 1994. ISBN 0-688-13759-8 Subj: Animals – elephants. Format, unusual – board books.

Elmer's friends ill. by author. Lothrop, 1994. ISBN 0-688-13761-X Subj: Animals. Animals – elephants. Format, unusual – board books. Friendship.

Elmer's weather ill. by author. Lothrop, 1994. ISBN 0-688-13760-1 Subj: Animals – elephants. Format, unusual – board books. Weather.

The hill and the rock ill. by author. Ticknor & Fields, 1985. ISBN 0-89919-341-2 Subj: Behavior – seeking better things. Rocks.

I can too! an Elmer pop-up book ill. by author. Lothrop, 1997. ISBN 0-688-15547-2 Subj: Animals. Animals – elephants. Format, unusual – toy and movable books.

King Rollo and the birthday ill. by author. Little, 1979. Subj: Birthdays. Royalty – kings.

King Rollo and the bread ill. by author. Little, 1979. Subj: Food. Royalty – kings.

King Rollo and the new shoes ill. by author. Little, 1979. Subj: Clothing – shoes. Royalty – kings.

The man who was going to mind the house: a Norwegian folk-tale ill. by author. Abelard-Schuman, 1973. ISBN 0-200-71946-7 Subj: Folk and fairy tales.

The monster and the teddy bear ill. by author. Trafalgar Square, 1998. ISBN 0-86264-762-2 Subj: Behavior – wishing. Monsters. Toys – bears.

123456789 Benn ill. by author. McGraw-Hill, 1970. Subj: Crime. Mystery stories. Prisons.

Prince Peter and the teddy bear ill. by author. Farrar, 1997. ISBN 0-374-36123-1 Subj: Birthdays. Family life – fathers. Family life – mothers. Gifts. Royalty – princes. Toys – bears.

The sad story of Veronica who played the violin ill. by author. Kane/Miller, 1991. ISBN 0-916291-37-5 Subj: Animals. Careers – musicians. Music.

The school bus comes at eight o'clock ill. by author. Hyperion, 1994. ISBN 1-56282-663-8 Subj: Clocks, watches. Family life. Time.

Snow woman ill. by author. Lothrop, 1988. ISBN 0-688-07675-0 Subj: Family life. Snowmen.

Tusk tusk ill. by author. Kane/Miller, 1990, c1978. ISBN 0-916291-28-6 Subj: Animals – elephants. Behavior – fighting, arguing. War.

Two can toucan ill. by author. Abelard-Schuman, 1964. Subj: Birds – toucans. Names.

Two monsters ill. by author. Bradbury, 1986. ISBN 0-02-765760-4 Subj: Behavior – fighting, arguing. Monsters.

Zebra's hiccups ill. by author. Simon & Schuster, 1993. ISBN 0-671-79440-X Subj: Animals. Animals – zebras. Hiccups.

McKee, Douglas. *Good night, Veronica* (Trez, Denise)

Maila and the flying carpet (Trez, Denise)

The royal hiccups (Trez, Denise)

MacKeen, Leslie Ann. *Who can fix it?* ill. by author. Landmark Editions, 1989. ISBN 0-933849-19-2 Subj: Animals. Automobiles. Children as authors. Children as illustrators.

McKeever, Katherine. *A family for Minerva* photos by author. Greey de Pencier Books, 1981. ISBN 0-910872-50-6 Subj: Birds – owls. Science.

McKelvey, David. *Bobby the mostly silky* ill. by author. Corona, 1984. ISBN 0-931722-28-4 Subj: Birds – chickens. Character traits – being different.

Macken, JoAnn Early. *Cats on Judy* ill. by Judith DuFour Love. Whispering Coyote, 1997. ISBN 1-879085-73-9 Subj: Animals – cats. Emotions – love. Pets.

McKenna, Laura. *The giantess* (Hasler, Eveline)

The gift (Keselman, Gabriela)

Idora (Godard, Alex)

McKenna, Virginia. *Back to the blue* ill. by Ian Andrew. Millbrook, 1998. ISBN 0-7613-0409-6 Subj: Animals – dolphins. Character traits – freedom. Sea and seashore.

McKenzie, Ellen Kindt. *The perfectly orderly house* ill. by Megan Lloyd. Holt, 1994. ISBN 0-8050-1946-4 Subj: ABC books. Character traits – orderliness.

Mackie, Maron. *see* McNeely, Jeannette

McKié, Roy. *Noah's ark* ill. by author. Random House, 1984. ISBN 0-394-96584-1 Subj: Animals. Boats, ships. Religion – Noah. Weather – floods. Weather – rain. Weather – rainbows.

The riddle book ill. by author. Random House, 1978. ISBN 0-394-93732-5 Subj: Humor. Riddles.

Snow by Roy McKié and P. D. Eastman; ill. by P. D. Eastman. Random House, 1962. ISBN 0-394-90027-8 Subj: Activities. Rhyming text. Weather – snow.

McKinley, Robin. *The light princess* (MacDonald, George)

My father is in the Navy ill. by Martine Gourbault. Greenwillow, 1992. ISBN 0-688-10640-4 Subj: Careers – military. Family life – fathers. Sailors.

Rowan ill. by Donna Ruff. Greenwillow, 1992. ISBN 0-688-10683-8 Subj: Animals – dogs. Pets.

MacKinnon, Debbie. *All about me* photos by Anthea Sieveking. Barron's, 1994. ISBN 0-8120-6348-1 Subj: Anatomy.

Baby's first year photos by Anthea Sieveking. Barron's, 1993. ISBN 0-8120-6334-1 Subj: Babies. Behavior – growing up.

Billy's boots photos by Anthea Sieveking. Dial, 1996. ISBN 0-8037-1905-1 Subj: Behavior – losing things. Clothing – boots. Format, unusual – toy and movable books.

Cathy's cake photos by Anthea Sieveking. Dial, 1996. ISBN 0-8037-1904-3 Subj: Behavior – losing things. Birthdays. Food. Format, unusual – toy and movable books. Parties.

Daniel's duck photos by Anthea Sieveking. Dial, 1997. ISBN 0-8037-2102-1 Subj: Activities – bathing. Birds – ducks. Format, unusual – toy and movable books. Toys.

Eye spy colors photos by Anthea Sieveking. Charlesbridge, 1998. ISBN 0-88106-334-7 Subj: Concepts – color. Format, unusual.

Eye spy shapes photos by Anthea Sieveking. Charlesbridge, 2000. ISBN 0-8810-6135-2 Subj: Concepts – shape. Format, unusual.

Find monkey! photos by Anthea Sieveking. Frances Lincoln, 1996. ISBN 0-7112-0923-5 Subj: Bedtime. Format, unusual – toy and movable books. Toys.

Find my boots! photos by Anthea Sieveking. Frances Lincoln, 1996. ISBN 0-7112-0922-7 Subj: Babies. Clothing. Format, unusual – toy and movable books.

Find my cake! photos by Anthea Sieveking. Frances Lincoln, 1996. ISBN 0-7112-0920-0 Subj: Birthdays. Food. Format, unusual – toy and movable books. Parties.

How many? photos by Anthea Sieveking. Dial, 1993. ISBN 0-8037-1253-7 Subj: Counting, numbers.

Ken's kitten photos by Anthea Sieveking. Dial, 1996. ISBN 0-8037-1903-5 Subj: Animals – cats. Behavior – losing things. Format, unusual – toy and movable books.

Let's play: I can do it! photos by Anthea Sieveking; paper engineered by Ania Mochlinska. Little, 1999. ISBN 0-316-64897-3 Subj: Activities – playing. Family life. Format, unusual – toy and movable books.

Meg's monkey photos by Anthea Sieveking. Dial, 1996. ISBN 0-8037-1907-8 Subj: Animals – monkeys. Behavior – losing things. Format, unusual – toy and movable books.

My day: I can do it! photos by Anthea Sieveking; paper engineered by Ania Mochlinska. Little, 1999. ISBN 0-316-64898-1 Subj: Activities. Format, unusual – toy and movable books.

My first ABC photos by Anthea Sieveking. Barron's, 1992. ISBN 0-8120-6331-7 Subj: ABC books. Ethnic groups in the U.S.

My kitty! photos by Anthea Sieveking. Frances Lincoln, 1996. ISBN 0-7112-0921-9 Subj: Animals – cats. Format, unusual – toy and movable books. Games.

Pippa's puppy photos by Anthea Sieveking. Dial, 1997. ISBN 0-8037-2104-8 Subj: Animals – dogs. Format, unusual – toy and movable books.

Sarah's shovel photos by Anthea Sieveking. Dial, 1997. ISBN 0-8037-2101-3 Subj: Format, unusual – toy and movable books. Sea and seashore. Toys.

The seasons: spring, summer, autumn, winter photos by Anthea Sieveking. Barron's, 1995. ISBN 0-8120-6422-4 Subj: Seasons.

Tom's train photos by Anthea Sieveking. Dial, 1997. ISBN 0-8037-2105-6 Subj: Family life – brothers. Format, unusual – toy and movable books. Multiple births – twins. Trains.

What am I? photos by Anthea Sieveking. Dial, 1996. ISBN 0-8037-1826-8 Subj: Activities – playing. Careers. Toys.

What noise? photos by Anthea Sieveking. Dial, 1994. ISBN 0-8037-1510-2 Subj: Noise, sounds.

What shape? photos by Anthea Sieveking. Dial, 1992. ISBN 0-8037-1244-8 Subj: Concepts – shape. Concepts – size.

What size? photos by Anthea Sieveking. Dial, 1995. ISBN 0-8037-1745-8 Subj: Concepts – size.

McKissack, Fredrick. *Ada, la desordenada: Messy Bessey* (McKissack, Patricia C.)

Big bug book of counting (McKissack, Patricia C.)

Big bug book of opposites (McKissack, Patricia C.)

Big bug book of places to go (McKissack, Patricia C.)

Big bug book of the alphabet (McKissack, Patricia C.)

Booker T. Washington: leader and educator (McKissack, Patricia C.)

Cinderella (McKissack, Patricia C.)

Country mouse and city mouse (McKissack, Patricia C.)

King Midas and his gold (McKissack, Patricia C.)

The king's new clothes (McKissack, Patricia C.)

The little red hen (The little red hen)

Messy Bessey (McKissack, Patricia C.)

Messy Bessey and the birthday overnight (McKissack, Patricia C.)

Messy Bessey's closet (McKissack, Patricia C.)

Messy Bessey's holidays (McKissack, Patricia C.)

My Bible ABC book (McKissack, Patricia C.)

Paul Robeson: a voice to remember (McKissack, Patricia C.)

Three billy goats Gruff (Asbjørnsen, P. C. [Peter Christen])

The ugly little duck (Andersen, H. C. [Hans Christian])

Who is coming? (McKissack, Patricia C.)

McKissack, Patricia C. *Ada, la desordenada: Messy Bessey* by Patricia C. and Fredrick McKissack; ill. by Richard Hackney. Childrens Pr., 1988. ISBN 0-516-32083-1 Subj: Behavior – messy. Character traits – cleanliness. Ethnic groups in the U.S. – African Americans. Foreign languages.

Big bug book of counting by Patricia C. and Fredrick McKissack; ill. by Bartholomew. Milliken, 1987. ISBN 0-88335-762-3 Subj: Counting, numbers. Insects.

Big bug book of opposites by Patricia C. and Fredrick McKissack; ill. by Bartholomew. Milliken, 1987. ISBN 0-88335-763-1 Subj: Concepts – opposites. Insects.

Big bug book of places to go by Patricia C. and Fredrick McKissack; ill. by Bartholomew. Milliken, 1987. ISBN 0-88335-765-8 Subj: Activities – traveling. Insects.

Big bug book of the alphabet by Patricia C. and Fredrick McKissack; ill. by Bartholomew. Milliken, 1987. ISBN 0-88335-764-X Subj: ABC books. Insects.

Booker T. Washington: leader and educator by Patricia C. and Fredrick McKissack; photos by Michael Bryant. Enslow, 1992. ISBN 0-89490-314-4 Subj: Careers – preachers. Careers – teachers. Ethnic groups in the U.S. – African Americans. U.S. history.

Cinderella by Patricia C. and Fredrick McKissack; ill. by Tom Dunnington. Childrens Pr., 1985. ISBN 0-516-02361-6 Subj: Family life – step families. Folk and fairy tales. Royalty – princes. Sibling rivalry.

Country mouse and city mouse by Patricia C. and Fredrick McKissack; ill. by Anne Sikorski. Childrens Pr., 1985. ISBN 0-516-02362-4 Subj: Animals – mice. City. Country.

Flossie and the fox ill. by Rachel Isadora. Dial, 1986. ISBN 0-8037-0251-5 Subj: Animals – foxes. Ethnic groups in the U.S. – African Americans.

King Midas and his gold by Patricia C. and Fredrick McKissack; ill. by Tom Dunnington. Childrens Pr., 1986. ISBN 0-516-03984-9 Subj: Behavior – greed. Behavior – wishing. Royalty – kings.

The king's new clothes by Patricia C. and Fredrick McKissack; ill. by Gwen Connelly. Childrens Pr., 1987. ISBN 0-516-02365-9 Subj: Character traits – pride. Character traits – vanity. Clothing. Humor. Imagination. Royalty – kings.

The little red hen (The little red hen)

Ma Dear's aprons ill. by Floyd Cooper. Atheneum, 1997. ISBN 0-689-81051-2 Subj: Careers – housekeepers. Clothing – aprons. Ethnic groups in the U.S. – African Americans.

Messy Bessey by Patricia C. and Frederick McKissack; ill. by Dana Regan. Childrens Pr., 1999. ISBN 0-516-21650-3 Subj: Behavior – messy. Character traits – cleanliness. Character traits – orderliness. Ethnic groups in the U.S. – African Americans.

Messy Bessey and the birthday overnight by Patricia C. and Fredrick McKissack; ill. by Dana Regan. Childrens Pr., 1998. ISBN 0-516-20828-4 Subj: Birthdays. Character traits – cleanliness. Character traits – helpfulness. Friendship. Rhyming text. Sleepovers.

Messy Bessey's closet by Patricia C. and Fredrick McKissack; ill. by Richard Hackney. Childrens Pr., 1989. ISBN 0-516-02091-9 Subj: Behavior – messy. Ethnic groups in the U.S. – African Americans. Rhyming text.

Messy Bessey's holidays by Patricia C. and Fredrick McKissack; ill. by Dana Regan. Childrens Pr., 1999. ISBN 0-516-20829-2 Subj: Activities – baking. Character traits – cleanliness. Ethnic groups in the U.S. – African Americans. Holidays – Christmas. Holidays – Hanukkah. Holidays – Kwanzaa. Rhyming text.

A million fish . . . more or less ill. by Dena Schutzer. Knopf, 1992. ISBN 0-679-90692-4 Subj: Folk and fairy tales. Sports – fishing. Tall tales.

Mirandy and brother wind ill. by Jerry Pinkney. Knopf, 1988. ISBN 0-394-88765-4 Subj: Activities – dancing. Caldecott award honor books. Ethnic groups in the U.S. – African Americans. Folk and fairy tales.

My Bible ABC book by Patricia C. and Fredrick McKissack; ill. by Reed Merrill. Augsburg, 1987. ISBN 0-8066-2271-7 Subj: ABC books. Religion.

Nettie Jo's friends ill. by Scott Cook. Knopf, 1989. ISBN 0-394-99158-3 Subj: Clothing. Family life. Toys – dolls.

Paul Robeson: a voice to remember by Patricia C. and Fredrick McKissack; photos by Michael David Biegel. Enslow, 1992. ISBN 0-89490-310-1 Subj: Careers – actors. Careers – singers. Ethnic groups in the U.S. – African Americans. U.S. history.

Three billy goats Gruff (Asbjørnsen, P. C. [Peter Christen])

The ugly little duck (Andersen, H. C. [Hans Christian])

Who is coming? by Patricia C. and Fredrick McKissack; ill. by Clovis Martin. Childrens Pr., 1986. Prepared under the direction of Robert Hillerick. ISBN 0-516-02073-0 Subj: Animals – monkeys. Behavior – running away. Foreign lands – Africa. Safety.

Who is who? ill. by Elizabeth M. Allen. Childrens Pr., 1983. ISBN 0-516-02042-0 Subj: Multiple births – twins.

MacLachlan, Patricia. *All the places to love* ill. by Mike Wimmer. HarperCollins, 1994. ISBN 0-06-021099-0 Subj: Babies. Birth. Country. Family life. Farms.

Mama one, Mama two ill. by Ruth Lercher Bornstein. HarperCollins, 1982. ISBN 0-06-024082-2 Subj: Family life – mothers. Illness.

Moon, stars, frogs and friends ill. by Tomie de Paola. Pantheon, 1980. ISBN 0-394-94138-1 Subj: Friendship. Frogs and toads. Witches.

Three names ill. by Alexander Pertzoff. HarperCollins, 1991. ISBN 0-06-024036-9 Subj: Animals – dogs. Family life – great-grandparents. Names. School.

What you know first ill. with engravings by Barry Moser. HarperCollins, 1995. ISBN 0-06-024414-3 Subj: Country. Emotions. Farms. Moving. U.S. history – frontier and pioneer life.

McLaughlin, Lissa. *Why won't winter go?* ill. by author. Lothrop, 1983. ISBN 0-688-02381-9 Subj: Behavior – boredom. Seasons – winter.

McLean, Janet. *Dog tales* ill. by Andrew McLean. Ticknor & Fields, 1995. ISBN 0-395-72288-8 Subj: Animals – dogs. Rhyming text.

McLean, Virginia O. *Kenya, jambo!* by Virginia O. McLean and Katherine P. Klyce; ill. with photos and black-and-white drawings. Redbird Pr., 1989. Accompanying cassette by Regina and Evans Okuth. ISBN 0-9606046-4-2 Subj: Foreign lands – Kenya.

McLeish, Kenneth. *Chicken Licken* (Chicken Little)

McLenighan, Valjean. *I know you cheated* photos by Brent Jones. Raintree, 1977. ISBN 0-8172-0962-X Subj: Character traits – honesty. School.

One whole doughnut, one doughnut hole ill. by Steven Roger Cole. Childrens Pr., 1982. ISBN 0-516-02031-5 Subj: Activities – reading.

Stop-go, fast-slow ill. by Margrit Fiddle. Childrens Pr., 1982. ISBN 0-516-03617-3 Subj: Concepts – opposites.

Three strikes and you're out ill. by Laurie Hamilton. Follett, 1980. ISBN 0-695-41462-3 Subj: Behavior – greed. Magic.

Turtle and rabbit ill. by Vernon McKissack. Follett, 1980. ISBN 0-695-41461-5 Subj: Animals – rabbits. Folk and fairy tales. Reptiles – turtles, tortoises. Sports – racing.

What you see is what you get ill. by Dev Appleyard. Four Winds, 1980. ISBN 0-695-41370-8 Subj: Character traits – pride. Clothing. Folk and fairy tales. Humor. Imagination. Royalty.

You are what you are ill. by Jack Reilly. Follett, 1977. ISBN 0-695-40748-1 Subj: Folk and fairy tales. Frogs and toads. Royalty.

You can go jump ill. by Jared D. Lee. Follett, 1977. ISBN 0-695-40744-9 Subj: Emotions – envy, jealousy. Folk and fairy tales. Magic. Mythical creatures. Witches.

MacLeod, Elizabeth. *I heard a little baa* ill. by Louise Phillips. Kids Can Pr., 1998. ISBN 1-55074-496-8 Subj: Animals. Noise, sounds. Rhyming text. Toys – bears.

McLeod, Emilie Warren. *The bear's bicycle* ill. by David McPhail. Little, 1975. ISBN 0-316-56203-3 Subj: Safety. Sports – bicycling. Toys – bears.

One snail and me: a book of numbers and animals and a bathtub ill. by Walter Lorraine. Little, 1961. ISBN 0-316-56198-3 Subj: Activities – bathing. Animals. Counting, numbers. Imagination.

McLerran, Alice. *Dreamsong* ill. by Valery Vasiliev. Morrow, 1992. ISBN 0-688-10106-2 Subj: Dreams. Songs.

The ghost dance ill. by Paul Morin. Clarion, 1995. ISBN 0-395-63168-8 Subj: Activities – dancing. Indians of North America. Religion.

Hugs ill. by Mary Morgan. Scholastic, 1993. ISBN 0-590-44637-1 Subj: Emotions. Rhyming text.

I want to go home ill. by Jill Kastner. Morrow, 1992. ISBN 0-688-10145-3 Subj: Animals – cats. Moving.

Kisses ill. by Mary Morgan. Scholastic, 1993. ISBN 0-590-44711-4 Subj: Kissing. Rhyming text.

The mountain that loved a bird ill. by Eric Carle. Alphabet Pr., 1985. ISBN 0-88708-000-6 Subj: Behavior – needing someone. Birds. Character traits – loyalty. Emotions – sadness.

Roxaboxen ill. by Barbara Cooney. Lothrop, 1991. ISBN 0-688-07593-2 Subj: Activities – playing. Desert. Imagination.

The year of the ranch ill. by Kimberly Bulcken Root. Viking, 1996. ISBN 0-670-85131-0 Subj: Desert. Dreams. Family life. U.S. history – frontier and pioneer life.

McMahon, Patricia. *Listen for the bus: David's story* photos by John Godt. Boyds Mills, 1995. ISBN 1-56397-368-5 Subj: Buses. Handicaps – blindness. School – first day.

McMillan, Bruce. *The alphabet symphony: an ABC book* photos by author. Greenwillow, 1977. ISBN 0-688-84112-0 Subj: ABC books. Music.

Beach ball - left, right photos by author. Holiday, 1992. ISBN 0-8234-0946-5 Subj: Concepts – left and right. Toys – balls.

Becca backward, Becca forward photos by author. Lothrop, 1986. ISBN 0-688-06283-0 Subj: Concepts. Concepts – opposites.

Counting wildflowers ill. by author. Lothrop, 1986. ISBN 0-688-02860-8 Subj: Counting, numbers. Flowers. Science.

Dry or wet? photos by author. Lothrop, 1988. ISBN 0-688-07101-5 Subj: Concepts.

Eating fractions photos by author. Scholastic, 1991. ISBN 0-590-43770-4 Subj: Counting, numbers.

Fire engine shapes photos by author. Lothrop, 1988. ISBN 0-688-07843-5 Subj: Concepts – shape.

Ghost doll ill. by author. Houghton Mifflin, 1983. ISBN 0-395-33073-4 Subj: Ghosts. Toys – dolls.

Gletta the foal ill. by author. Cavendish, 1998. ISBN 0-7614-5039-4 Subj: Animals – horses, ponies. Foreign lands – Iceland. Noise, sounds.

Going on a whale watch ill. by author. Scholastic, 1992. ISBN 0-590-45768-3 Subj: Animals – whales. Boats, ships.

Grandfather's trolley photos by author. Candlewick, 1995. ISBN 1-56402-633-7 Subj: Cable cars, trolleys. Family life – grandfathers.

Growing colors photos by author. Lothrop, 1988. ISBN 0-688-07845-1 Subj: Concepts – color.

Here a chick, there a chick photos by author. Lothrop, 1983. ISBN 0-688-02001-1 Subj: Concepts – opposites.

Jelly beans for sale photos by author. Scholastic, 1996. ISBN 0-590-86584-6 Subj: Counting, numbers. Money.

Kitten can . . . photos by author. Lothrop, 1984. ISBN 0-688-02669-9 Subj: Animals – cats.

Mouse views: what the class pet saw ill. by author. Holiday, 1993. ISBN 0-8234-1008-0 Subj: Animals – mice. Picture puzzles. School.

Nights of the pufflings photos by author. Houghton Mifflin, 1995. ISBN 0-395-70810-9 Subj: Birds – puffins. Character traits – kindness to animals. Foreign lands – Iceland.

One sun: a book of terse verse photos by author. Holiday, 1990. ISBN 0-8234-0810-8 Subj: Language. Poetry. Sea and seashore.

One, two, one pair! photos by author. Scholastic, 1991. ISBN 0-590-43767-4 Subj: Concepts. Counting, numbers.

Play day: a book of terse verse photos by author. Holiday, 1991. ISBN 0-8234-0894-9 Subj: Activities – playing. Language. Poetry.

Puffins climb, penguins rhyme photos by author. Harcourt, 1995. ISBN 0-15-200362-2 Subj: Birds – penguins. Birds – puffins. Rhyming text.

Sense suspense: a guessing game for the five senses photos by author. Scholastic, 1994. ISBN 0-590-47904-0 Subj: Concepts. Foreign lands – Caribbean Islands. Senses.

Step by step photos by author. Lothrop, 1987. ISBN 0-688-07234-8 Subj: Activities. Babies.

Super, super, superwords photos by author. Lothrop, 1989. ISBN 0-688-08099-5 Subj: Language.

Time to . . . photos by author. Lothrop, 1989. ISBN 0-688-08856-2 Subj: Clocks, watches. Time.

McMullen, Jim. *No no Jo* (McMullen, Kate [Hall])

McMullen, Kate (Hall). *Batty riddles* by Katy Hall and Lisa Eisenberg; ill. by Nicole Rubel. Dial, 1993. ISBN 0-8037-1218-9 Subj: Animals – bats. Riddles.

Bunny riddles by Katy Hall and Lisa Eisenberg; ill. by Nicole Rubel. Dial, 1997. ISBN 0-8037-1521-8 Subj: Animals – rabbits. Riddles.

Chickie riddles by Katy Hall and Lisa Eisenberg; ill. by Thor Wickstrom. Dial, 1997. ISBN 0-8037-1779-2 Subj: Birds – chickens. Riddles.

Creepy riddles by Katy Hall and Lisa Eisenberg; ill. by S. D. Schindler. Dial, 1998. ISBN 0-8037-1685-0 Subj: Ghosts. Monsters. Riddles. Witches.

Dinosaur riddles by Katy Hall and Lisa Eisenberg; ill. by Nicole Rubel. Dial, 1999. ISBN 0-8037-2239-7 Subj: Dinosaurs. Riddles.

Fishy riddles by Katy Hall and Lisa Eisenberg; ill. by Simms Taback. Puffin, 1993. ISBN 0-14-036546-X Subj: Fish. Riddles.

Good night, Stella ill. by Emma Chichester Clark. Candlewick, 1994. ISBN 1-56402-065-7 Subj: Bedtime. Emotions – fear. Imagination. Sleep.

Hearty har har: Valentine riddles you'll love by Katy Hall and Lisa Eisenberg; ill. by R. W. Alley. HarperFestival, 1997. ISBN 0-694-00691-2 Subj: Format, unusual – toy and movable books. Holidays – Valentine's Day. Riddles.

Hey, Pipsqueak! ill. by Jim McMullan. HarperCollins, 1995. ISBN 0-06-205101-6 Subj: Behavior – bullying. Mythical creatures – trolls. Parties.

If you were my bunny ill. by David McPhail. Scholastic, 1996. ISBN 0-590-52749-5 Subj: Animals – babies. Babies. Bedtime. Family life – mothers. Lullabies.

Kitty riddles by Katy Hall and Lisa Eisenberg; ill. by R. W. Alley. Dial, 2000. ISBN 0-8037-2121-8 Subj: Animals – cats. Riddles.

Mummy riddles by Katy Hall and Lisa Eisenberg; ill. by Nicole Rubel. Dial, 1997. ISBN 0-8037-1847-0 Subj: Foreign lands – Egypt. Riddles.

No no Jo by Kate and Jim McMullan; ill. by Jim McMullan. HarperCollins, 1997. ISBN 0-694-00904-0 Subj: Animals – cats. Character traits – helpfulness. Format, unusual – toy and movable books.

Noel the first ill. by Jim McMullan. HarperCollins, 1996. ISBN 0-06-205142-3 Subj: Activities – dancing. Ballet. Character traits – pride.

The noisy giant's tea party ill. by Jim McMullan. HarperCollins, 1992. ISBN 0-06-205018-4 Subj: Dreams. Imagination. Sleep.

Nutcracker Noel ill. by Jim McMullan. HarperCollins, 1993. ISBN 0-06-205040-0 Subj: Activities – dancing. Ballet. Careers – toy makers. Emotions – envy, jealousy.

Papa's song ill. by Jim McMullan. Farrar, 2000. ISBN 0-374-35732-3 Subj: Animals – bears. Babies. Family life – fathers. Sleep.

Puppy riddles by Katy Hall and Lisa Eisenberg; ill. by Thor Wickstrom. Dial, 1998. ISBN 0-8037-2129-3 Subj: Animals – dogs. Riddles.

Sheepish riddles by Katy Hall and Lisa Eisenberg; ill. by R. W. Alley. Dial, 1996. ISBN 0-8037-1536-6 Subj: Animals – sheep. Riddles.

Skeletons! Skeletons! All about bones ill. by Paige Billin-Frye. Grosset, 1991. ISBN 0-448-40108-8 Subj: Anatomy – skeletons.

Snakey riddles by Katy Hall and Lisa Eisenberg; ill. by Simms Taback. Dial, 1990. ISBN 0-8037-0670-7 Subj: Reptiles – snakes. Riddles.

Spacey riddles by Katy Hall and Lisa Eisenberg; ill. by Simms Taback. Dial, 1992. ISBN 0-8037-0815-7 Subj: Riddles. Space and space ships.

Trick or eeek! and other ha ha Halloween riddles by Katy Hall and Lisa Eisenberg; ill. by R. W. Alley. HarperFestival, 1996. ISBN 0-694-00693-9 Subj: Format, unusual – toy and movable books. Holidays – Halloween. Riddles.

McMullen, Eunice. *Dragon for breakfast* by Eunice and Nigel McMullen; ill. by authors. Carolrhoda, 1990. ISBN 0-87614-650-7 Subj: Dragons. Royalty – kings.

McMullen, Nigel. *Dragon for breakfast* (McMullen, Eunice)

McNally, Darcie. *In a cabin in a wood* ill. by Robin Michal Koontz. Dutton, 1991. ISBN 0-525-65035-0 Subj: Animals. Character traits – kindness to animals. Music. Songs.

McNaught, Harry. *Baby animals* ill. by author. Random House, 1976. ISBN 0-394-83241-8 Subj: Animals. Format, unusual – board books.

The truck book ill. by author. Random House, 1978. ISBN 0-394-93703-1 Subj: Transportation. Trucks.

Words to grow on ill. by author. Random House, 1984. ISBN 0-394-96103-X Subj: Language.

McNaughton, Colin. *At home* ill. by author. Putnam, 1982. ISBN 0-399-20878-X Subj: Concepts – opposites. Format, unusual – board books.

At playschool ill. by author. Putnam, 1982. ISBN 0-399-20875-5 Subj: Concepts – opposites. Format, unusual – board books. School.

At the park ill. by author. Putnam, 1982. ISBN 0-399-20879-8 Subj: Concepts – opposites. Format, unusual – board books. Parks.

At the party ill. by author. Putnam, 1982. ISBN 0-399-20877-1 Subj: Concepts – opposites. Format, unusual – board books. Parties.

At the stores ill. by author. Putnam, 1982. ISBN 0-399-20876-3 Subj: Concepts – opposites. Format, unusual – board books. Stores.

Autumn ill. by author. Dutton, 1983. ISBN 0-8037-0043-1 Subj: Activities. Format, unusual – board books. Seasons – fall.

Big bad pig (Ahlberg, Allan)

Boo! ill. by author. Harcourt, 1996. ISBN 0-15-200834-9 Subj: Animals – pigs. Disguises.

Captain Abdul's pirate school ill. by author. Candlewick, 1994. ISBN 1-56402-429-6 Subj: Behavior – misbehavior. Pirates. School.

Don't step on the crack! ill. by author. Dial, 2001. ISBN 0-8037-2611-2 Subj: Superstition.

Fee fi fo fum (Ahlberg, Allan)

Guess who's just moved in next door? ill. by author. Random House, 1991. ISBN 0-679-81802-2 Subj: Family life. Folk and fairy tales. Format, unusual. Moving.

Happy worm (Ahlberg, Allan)

Help! (Ahlberg, Allan)

Here come the aliens! ill. by author. Candlewick, 1995. ISBN 1-56402-642-6 Subj: Aliens. Space and space ships.

If dinosaurs were cats and dogs ill. by author. Four Winds, 1991. ISBN 0-02-765785-X Subj: Animals. Dinosaurs. Rhyming text.

Jolly Roger and the pirates of Captain Abdul ill. by author. Candlewick, 1995. ISBN 1-56402-512-8 Subj: Pirates.

Little boo! ill. by author. Harcourt, 2000. ISBN 0-15-202671-1 Subj: Animals – pigs.

Little goal! ill. by author. Harcourt, 2001. ISBN 0-15-202525-1 Subj: Animals – pigs.

Little oops! ill. by author. Harcourt, 2001. ISBN 0-15-202537-5 Subj: Animals – pigs.

Little suddenly! ill. by author. Harcourt, 2000. ISBN 0-15-202531-6 Subj: Animals – pigs.

Oomph! ill. by author. Harcourt, 2001. ISBN 0-15-216463-4 Subj: Animals – pigs. Animals – wolves. Emotions – love. Sea and seashore.

Oops! ill. by author. Harcourt, 1997. ISBN 0-15-201588-4 Subj: Animals – pigs. Animals – wolves. Character traits – cleverness.

Preston's goal! ill. by author. Harcourt, 1998. ISBN 0-15-201816-6 Subj: Animals – pigs. Animals – wolves. Character traits – clumsiness. Humor. Sports – soccer.

The rat race: the amazing adventures of Anton B. Stanton ill. by author. Doubleday, 1978. ISBN 0-385-13620-X Subj: Animals – rats. Royalty. Sports – racing.

Shh! (Don't tell Mr. Wolf!) ill. by author. Harcourt, 1999. ISBN 0-15-202341-0 Subj: Animals – pigs. Animals – wolves. Behavior – hiding. Format, unusual – toy and movable books.

Spring ill. by author. Dial, 1984. ISBN 0-8037-0044-X Subj: Format, unusual – board books. Seasons – spring.

Suddenly! ill. by author. Harcourt, 1995. ISBN 0-15-200308-8 Subj: Animals – pigs. Animals – wolves. Humor.

Summer ill. by author. Dial, 1984. ISBN 0-8037-0042-3 Subj: Format, unusual – board books. Seasons – summer.

Walk rabbit walk by Colin McNaughton and Elizabeth Attenborough; ill. by Colin McNaughton. Tambourine, 1992. ISBN 0-688-11375-3 Subj: Activities – walking. Animals – rabbits. Transportation.

Who's that banging on the ceiling? ill. by author. Candlewick, 1992. ISBN 1-56402-105-X Subj: Format, unusual – toy and movable books. Homes, houses. Imagination. Noise, sounds.

Winter ill. by author. Dutton, 1983. ISBN 0-8037-0040-7 Subj: Activities. Format, unusual – board books. Seasons – winter.

Yum! ill. by author. Harcourt, 1999. ISBN 0-15-202064-0 Subj: Animals – pigs. Animals – wolves. Careers.

McNeal, Laura. *The dog who lost his Bob* (McNeal, Tom)

McNeal, Tom. *The dog who lost his Bob* by Tom and Laura McNeal; ill. by John Sandford. Albert Whitman, 1996. ISBN 0-8075-1662-7 Subj: Activities – bathing. Animals – dogs. Behavior – running away.

McNeely, Jeannette. *Where's Izzy?* ill. by Bill Morrison. Follett, 1972. ISBN 0-695-40318-4 Subj: Behavior – losing things. Pets. Reptiles – lizards.

McNeer, May Yonge. *Little Baptiste* ill. by Lynd Ward. Houghton Mifflin, 1954. Subj: Animals. Farms.

My friend Mac: the story of Little Baptiste and the moose ill. by Lynd Ward. Houghton Mifflin, 1960. ISBN 0-395-24371-8 Subj: Animals – moose. Emotions – loneliness.

McNeill, Janet. *The giant's birthday* ill. by Walter Erhard. Walck, 1964. Subj: Birthdays. Giants.

McNulty, Faith. *The lady and the spider* ill. by Bob Marstall. HarperCollins, 1986. ISBN 0-06-024192-6 Subj: Character traits – kindness to animals. Spiders.

Mouse and Tim ill. by Marc Simont. HarperCollins, 1978. ISBN 0-06-024157-8 Subj: Animals – mice. Character traits – kindness to animals. Pets.

When a boy wakes up in the morning ill. by Leonard Weisgard. Knopf, 1962. Subj: Activities – playing. Morning. Noise, sounds.

Woodchuck ill. by Joan Sandin. HarperCollins, 1974. ISBN 0-06-024167-5 Subj: Animals – groundhogs. Science.

McPartland, Suzy. *Good morning, sun* ill. by William Neeper. Simon & Schuster, 1994. ISBN 0-689-71747-4 Subj: Format, unusual – toy and movable books. Morning. Rhyming text. Sun.

Sleepy-time moon ill. by William Neeper. Simon & Schuster, 1994. ISBN 0-689-71748-2 Subj: Bedtime. Format, unusual – toy and movable books. Moon. Night. Rhyming text. Sleep.

Toy-shop surprise ill. by William Neeper. Simon & Schuster, 1994. ISBN 0-689-71749-0 Subj: Format, unusual – toy and movable books. Rhyming text. Stores. Toys.

Zoom, car, zoom ill. by William Neeper. Simon & Schuster, 1994. ISBN 0-689-71740-4 Subj: Automobiles. Country. Format, unusual – toy and movable books. Rhyming text.

McPhail, David M. *Adam's smile* ill. by author. Dutton, 1987. ISBN 0-525-44327-4 Subj: Dreams. Illness. Night.

Alligators are awful (and they have terrible manners, too) ill. by author. Doubleday, 1980. ISBN 0-385-13583-1 Subj: Humor. Reptiles – alligators, crocodiles.

Andrew's bath ill. by author. Little, 1984. ISBN 0-316-56319-6 Subj: Activities – bathing. Animals. Behavior – misbehavior.

Animals A to Z ill. by author. Scholastic, 1988. ISBN 0-590-40715-5 Subj: ABC books. Animals.

Annie and Co. ill. by author. Holt, 1991. ISBN 0-8050-1686-4 Subj: Activities – working.

The bear's toothache ill. by author. Puffin, 1978, c1972. ISBN 0-14-050263-7 Subj: Animals – bears. Character traits – kindness to animals. Illness. Teeth.

Big brown bear ill. by author. Harcourt, 1999. ISBN 0-15-201999-5 Subj: Accidents. Activities – painting. Animals – bears. Concepts – color. Rhyming text.

Big Pig and Little Pig ill. by author. Harcourt, 2001. ISBN 0-15-216516-9 Subj: Animals – pigs. Friendship.

A bug, a bear, and a boy ill. by author. Scholastic, 1998. ISBN 0-590-14904-0 Subj: Activities. Animals – bears. Concepts – size. Friendship. Insects.

A bug, a bear, and a boy go to school ill. by author. Scholastic, 1999. ISBN 0-439-07783-4 Subj: Animals – bears. Insects. School.

Captain Toad and the motorbike ill. by author. Atheneum, 1978. ISBN 0-689-50118-8 Subj: Frogs and toads. Motorcycles.

The cereal box ill. by author. Little, 1974. ISBN 0-316-56313-7 Subj: Family life. Humor. Imagination. Shopping.

The day the dog said, "Cock-a-doodle doo!" ill. by author. Scholastic, 1996. ISBN 0-590-73887-9 Subj: Animals. Noise, sounds. Weather – wind.

Drawing lessons from a bear ill. by author. Little, 2000. ISBN 0-316-56345-5 Subj: Activities – drawing. Animals – bears. Careers – artists.

The dream child ill. by author. Dutton, 1985. ISBN 0-525-44109-3 Subj: Bedtime. Dreams. Night. Sleep. Toys – bears.

Ed and me ill. by author. Harcourt, 1990. ISBN 0-15-224888-9 Subj: Country. Family life – fathers. Trucks.

Edward and the pirates ill. by author. Little, 1997. ISBN 0-316-56344-7 Subj: Activities – reading. Imagination. Pirates.

Edward in the jungle ill. by author. Little, 2001. ISBN 0-316-56391-9 Subj: Animals. Imagination. Jungle.

Emma's pet ill. by author. Dutton, 1987. ISBN 0-525-44210-3 Subj: Activities – vacationing. Animals – bears. Behavior – needing someone. Family life. Pets.

Emma's vacation ill. by author. Dutton, 1987. ISBN 0-525-44315-0 Subj: Activities – vacationing. Animals – bears. Family life.

Farm boy's year ill. by author. Atheneum, 1992. ISBN 0-689-31679-8 Subj: Farms. U.S. history.

Farm morning ill. by author. Harcourt, 1985. ISBN 0-15-227299-2 Subj: Animals. Birds. Farms.

First flight ill. by author. Little, 1987. ISBN 0-316-56323-4 Subj: Activities – flying. Airplanes, airports. Toys – bears.

Fix-it ill. by author. Dutton, 1984. ISBN 0-525-44093-3 Subj: Activities – reading. Television.

A girl, a goat, and a goose ill. by author. Scholastic, 2000. ISBN 0-439-09978-1 Subj: Activities. Animals – goats. Birds – geese. Friendship.

The Glerp ill. by author. Silver Pr., 1995. ISBN 0-382-24668-3 Subj: Animals. Monsters.

Goldilocks and the three bears (The three bears)

Great cat ill. by author. Dutton, 1982. ISBN 0-525-45102-1 Subj: Animals – cats. Behavior – needing someone. Islands.

The great race ill. by author. Scholastic, 1997. ISBN 0-590-84909-3 Subj: Animals. Sports – racing.

Henry Bear's Christmas ill. by author. Atheneum, 2001. ISBN 0-689-82198-0 Subj: Animals – bears. Animals – raccoons. Holidays – Christmas. Trees.

Henry Bear's park ill. by author. Atheneum, 2001. ISBN 0-689-83967-7 Subj: Activities – ballooning. Animals – bears. Family life – fathers. Parks.

Little Red Riding Hood (Grimm, Jacob)

Lorenzo ill. by author. Doubleday, 1984. ISBN 0-385-15591-3 Subj: Activities – painting. Animals. Homes, houses.

Lost ill. by author. Little, 1990. ISBN 0-316-56329-3 Subj: Animals – bears. Behavior – lost.

The magical drawings of Moony B. Finch ill. by author. Doubleday, 1978. ISBN 0-385-12104-0 Subj: Art. Magic.

Mistletoe ill. by author. Dutton, 1978. ISBN 0-525-35040-3 Subj: Dreams. Holidays – Christmas. Imagination. Santa Claus. Toys.

Mole music ill. by author. Holt, 1999. ISBN 0-8050-2819-6 Subj: Animals – moles. Music.

Moony B. Finch, fastest draw in the West ill. by author. Artists & Writers Guild, 1994. ISBN 0-307-17554-5 Subj: Activities – drawing. Crime. Imagination. Magic. Trains.

The party ill. by author. Little, 1990. ISBN 0-316-56330-7 Subj: Animals. Family life – fathers. Parties. Toys.

Pig Pig and the magic photo album ill. by author. Dutton, 1986. ISBN 0-525-44238-3 Subj: Activities – photographing. Animals – pigs. Imagination.

Pig Pig gets a job ill. by author. Dutton, 1990. ISBN 0-525-44619-2 Subj: Activities – working. Animals – pigs. Careers.

Pig Pig goes to camp ill. by author. Dutton, 1983. ISBN 0-525-44064-X Subj: Animals – pigs. Camps, camping.

Pig Pig grows up ill. by author. Dutton, 1980. ISBN 0-525-37027-7 Subj: Animals – pigs. Behavior – growing up.

Pig Pig rides ill. by author. Dutton, 1982. ISBN 0-525-44024-0 Subj: Activities – playing. Animals – pigs. Imagination.

Pigs ahoy ill. by author. Dutton, 1995. ISBN 0-525-45334-2 Subj: Animals – pigs. Boats, ships. Rhyming text.

Pigs aplenty, pigs galore! ill. by author. Dutton, 1993. ISBN 0-525-45079-3 Subj: Animals – pigs. Food. Rhyming text.

The puddle ill. by author. Farrar, 1998. ISBN 0-374-36148-7 Subj: Animals. Toys. Weather – rain.

Santa's book of names ill. by author. Little, 1993. ISBN 0-316-56335-8 Subj: Activities – reading. Character traits – helpfulness. Holidays – Christmas. Santa Claus.

Sisters ill. by author. Harcourt, 1984. ISBN 0-15-275319-2 Subj: Emotions – love. Sibling rivalry.

Snow lion ill. by author. Parents, 1983. ISBN 0-8193-1097-2 Subj: Weather – snow.

Something special ill. by author. Little, 1988. ISBN 0-316-56324-2 Subj: Activities – painting. Animals – raccoons.

Stanley: Henry Bear's friend ill. by author. Little, 1979. ISBN 0-316-56318-8 Subj: Animals – bears. Animals – raccoons. Behavior – running away. Crime.

Those can-do pigs ill. by author. Dutton, 1996. ISBN 0-525-45495-0 Subj: Activities. Animals – pigs. Rhyming text.

The three little pigs (The three little pigs)

Tinker and Tom and the Star Baby ill. by author. Little, 1998. ISBN 0-316-56349-8 Subj: Aliens. Animals – bears. Imagination. Space and space ships.

The train ill. by author. Little, 1977. ISBN 0-316-56316-1 Subj: Dreams. Imagination. Toys – trains. Trains.

Where can an elephant hide? ill. by author. Doubleday, 1979. ISBN 0-385-12941-6 Subj: Animals. Animals – elephants. Behavior – hiding.

A wolf story ill. by author. Scribners, 1981. ISBN 0-684-16713-1 Subj: Animals – wolves. Character traits – freedom. Character traits – kindness to animals.

McQuade, Jacqueline. *At preschool with Teddy Bear* ill. by author. Dial, 1999. ISBN 0-8037-2394-6 Subj: Family life – fathers. Format, unusual – board books. School – first day. Toys – bears.

At the petting zoo with Teddy Bear ill. by author. Dial, 1999. ISBN 0-8037-2395-4 Subj: Animals. Format, unusual – board books. Toys – bears. Zoos.

Christmas with Teddy Bear ill. by author. Dial, 1996. ISBN 0-8037-2075-0 Subj: Holidays – Christmas. Toys – bears.

Good times with Teddy Bear ill. by author. Dial, 1997. ISBN 0-8037-2076-9 Subj: Activities. Animals – cats. Family life. Toys – bears.

McQueen, John Troy. *A world full of monsters* ill. by Marc Brown. Crowell, 1986. ISBN 0-690-04546-8

Subj: Family life – grandmothers. Monsters. Night.

McQueen, Lucinda. *Tidy pig* by Lucinda McQueen and Jeremy Guitar; ill. by authors. Random House, 1989. ISBN 0-394-90573-3 Subj: Animals – pigs. Character traits – cleanliness.

Macsolis. *Baile de luna: Dance moon* ill. by author. Donars Spanish Books, 1991. ISBN 84-261-2583-2 Subj: Animals – cats. Foreign languages. Moon.

McToots, Rudi. *The kid's book of games for cars, trains and planes* ill. by author. Bantam, 1980. ISBN 0-553-01230-4 Subj: Activities – traveling. Games.

Madden, Don. *Lemonade serenade, or, the thing in the garden* ill. by author. Albert Whitman, 1966. Subj: Noise, sounds.

The Wartville wizard ill. by author. Macmillan, 1986. ISBN 0-02-762100-6 Subj: Character traits – cleanliness. Wizards.

Maddern, Eric. *Curious clownfish* ill. by Adrienne Kennaway. Little, 1990. ISBN 0-316-48894-1 Subj: Fish. Sea and seashore.

The fire children: a West African creation tale ill. by Frané Lessac. Dial, 1993. ISBN 0-8037-1477-7 Subj: Creation. Folk and fairy tales. Foreign lands – Africa.

Madenski, Melissa. *Some of the pieces* ill. by Deborah Kogan Ray. Little, 1991. ISBN 0-316-54324-1 Subj: Death. Emotions – grief. Family life – fathers.

Madgwick, Wendy. *Animaze! a collection of amazing nature mazes* ill. by Lorna Hussey. Knopf, 1992. ISBN 0-679-92665-8 Subj: Animals. Mazes.

Up in the air ill. by author. Raintree, 1999. ISBN 0-8172-5325-4 Subj: Science.

Water play ill. by author. Raintree, 1999. ISBN 0-8172-5326-2 Subj: Science. Water.

Mado, Michio. *The animals* trans. by The Empress Michiko of Japan; ill. by Mitsumasa Anno. Macmillan, 1992. ISBN 0-689-50574-4 Subj: Animals. Poetry.

The magic pocket trans. by Empress Michiko of Japan; ill. by Mitsumasa Anno. Margaret K. McElderry, 1998. ISBN 0-689-82137-9 Subj: Foreign lands – Japan. Foreign languages. Poetry.

Madrigal, Antonio Hernandez. *Erandi's braids* ill. by Tomie de Paola. Putnam, 1999. ISBN 0-399-23212-5 Subj: Birthdays. Family life – mothers. Foreign lands – Mexico. Hair.

Maestro, Betsy. *All aboard overnight* ill. by Giulio Maestro. Houghton Mifflin, 1992. ISBN 0-395-51120-8 Subj: Language. Trains.

Around the clock with Harriet: a book about telling time ill. by Giulio Maestro. Crown, 1984. ISBN 0-517-55118-7 Subj: Animals – elephants. Clocks, watches. Time.

Bats ill. by Giulio Maestro. Scholastic, 1994. ISBN 0-590-46150-8 Subj: Animals – bats.

Big city port by Betsy Maestro and Ellen Del Vecchio; ill. by Giulio Maestro. Four Winds, 1983. ISBN 0-590-07869-0 Subj: Boats, ships. City.

Bike trip ill. by Giulio Maestro. HarperCollins, 1992. ISBN 0-06-022732-X Subj: Family life. Safety. Sports – bicycling.

Busy day: a book of action words by Betsy and Giulio Maestro; ill. by Giulio Maestro. Crown, 1978. ISBN 0-517-53288-3 Subj: Activities. Circus.

Camping out: a book of action words by Betsy and Giulio Maestro; ill. by authors. Crown, 1985. ISBN 0-517-55119-5 Subj: Camps, camping. Language.

Coming to America ill. by Susannah Ryan. Scholastic, 1996. ISBN 0-590-44151-5 Subj: Ethnic groups in the U.S.

Delivery van ill. by Giulio Maestro. Houghton Mifflin, 1990. ISBN 0-395-51119-4 Subj: City. Country. Language.

Dollars and cents for Harriet ill. by Giulio Maestro. Crown, 1988. ISBN 0-517-56958-2 Subj: Counting, numbers. Money.

Fat polka-dot cat and other haiku ill. by Giulio Maestro. Dutton, 1976. ISBN 0-525-29625-5 Subj: Poetry.

Ferryboat by Betsy and Giulio Maestro; ill. by authors. Crowell, 1986. ISBN 0-690-04520-4 Subj: Activities – traveling. Boats, ships.

The guessing game ill. by Giulio Maestro. Grosset, 1983. ISBN 0-488-21701-5 Subj: Animals – pigs. Problem solving.

Harriet at home ill. by Giulio Maestro. Crown, 1984. ISBN 0-517-55417-8 Subj: Animals – elephants. Format, unusual – board books. Homes, houses.

Harriet at play ill. by Giulio Maestro. Crown, 1984. ISBN 0-517-55420-8 Subj: Activities – playing. Animals – elephants. Format, unusual – board books.

Harriet at school ill. by Giulio Maestro. Crown, 1984. ISBN 0-517-55419-4 Subj: Animals – elephants. Format, unusual – board books. School.

Harriet at work ill. by Giulio Maestro. Crown, 1984. ISBN 0-517-55418-6 Subj: Activities – working. Animals – elephants. Format, unusual – board books.

Harriet goes to the circus by Betsy and Giulio Maestro; ill. by Giulio Maestro. Crown, 1977. ISBN 0-517-52844-4 Subj: Animals – elephants. Circus. Counting, numbers.

Harriet reads signs and more signs ill. by Giulio Maestro. Crown, 1981. ISBN 0-517-54167-X Subj: Activities – reading. Animals – elephants.

How do apples grow? ill. by Giulio Maestro. HarperCollins, 1992. ISBN 0-06-020056-1 Subj: Food. Science. Trees.

On the go: a book of adjectives by Betsy and Giulio Maestro; ill. by authors. Crown, 1979. ISBN 0-517-53596-3 Subj: Animals – elephants. Language.

On the town: a book of clothing words by Betsy and Giulio Maestro; ill. by authors. Crown, 1983. ISBN 0-517-54749-X Subj: Animals – elephants. Character traits – appearance. Clothing.

The pandas take a vacation ill. by Giulio Maestro. Western, 1986. ISBN 0-307-68258-7 Subj: Activities – vacationing. Animals – pandas.

The perfect picnic ill. by Giulio Maestro. Western, 1986. ISBN 0-307-10266-1 Subj: Activities – picnicking.

The story of the Statue of Liberty by Betsy and Giulio Maestro; ill. by Giulio Maestro. Lothrop, 1986. ISBN 0-688-05773-X Subj: Art. U.S. history.

Taxi ill. by Giulio Maestro. Clarion, 1989. ISBN 0-89919-528-8 Subj: City. Language. Taxis.

Temperature and you ill. by Giulio Maestro. Dutton, 1990. ISBN 0-525-67271-0 Subj: Concepts. Weather.

Through the year with Harriet by Betsy and Giulio Maestro; ill. by authors. Crown, 1985. ISBN 0-517-55613-8 Subj: Animals – elephants. Days of the week, months of the year. Seasons. Weather.

Traffic: a book of opposites by Betsy and Giulio Maestro; ill. by authors. Crown, 1981. ISBN 0-517-54427-X Subj: Concepts – opposites. Traffic, traffic signs.

Where is my friend? ill. by Giulio Maestro. Crown, 1976. ISBN 0-517-55304-X Subj: Animals – elephants. Concepts.

Why do leaves change color? ill. by Loretta Krupinski. HarperCollins, 1994. ISBN 0-06-022874-1 Subj: Nature. Science. Seasons – fall. Trees.

Maestro, Giulio. *Busy day: a book of action words* (Maestro, Betsy)

Camping out: a book of action words (Maestro, Betsy)

Ferryboat (Maestro, Betsy)

Geese find the missing piece (Maestro, Marco)

Halloween howls: riddles that are a scream ill. by author. Dutton, 1983. ISBN 0-525-44059-3 Subj: Holidays – Halloween. Riddles.

Harriet goes to the circus (Maestro, Betsy)

Just enough Rosie ill. by author. Grosset, 1983. ISBN 0-448-21702-3 Subj: Animals – rhinoceros. Humor.

Leopard is sick ill. by author. Greenwillow, 1978. ISBN 0-688-84162-7 Subj: Animals. Animals – leopards. Friendship. Illness.

On the go: a book of adjectives (Maestro, Betsy)

On the town: a book of clothing words (Maestro, Betsy)

One more and one less ill. by author. Crown, 1974. ISBN 0-517-51575-X Subj: Animals. Counting, numbers.

A raft of riddles ill. by author. Dutton, 1982. ISBN 0-525-44017-8 Subj: Humor. Riddles.

The remarkable plant in apartment 4 ill. by author. Bradbury, 1973. Subj: City. Humor. Plants.

Riddle romp ill. by author. Houghton Mifflin, 1983. ISBN 0-89919-180-0 Subj: Riddles.

The story of the Statue of Liberty (Maestro, Betsy)

Through the year with Harriet (Maestro, Betsy)

The tortoise's tug of war ill. by author. Bradbury, 1971. ISBN 0-8788-8030-5 Subj: Animals – tapirs. Animals – whales. Folk and fairy tales. Foreign lands – South America. Games. Reptiles – turtles, tortoises.

Traffic: a book of opposites (Maestro, Betsy)

Maestro, Marco. *Geese find the missing piece* by Marco and Giulio Maestro; ill. by Giulio Maestro. HarperCollins, 1999. ISBN 0-06-026221-4 Subj: Animals. Rhyming text. Riddles. School.

What do you hear when cows sing? and other silly riddles ill. by Giulio Maestro. HarperCollins, 1996. ISBN 0-06-024949-8 Subj: Riddles.

Magdanz, James S. *Go home, river* ill. by Dianne Widom. Alaska Northwest, 1996. ISBN 0-88240-476-8 Subj: Alaska. Eskimos. Family life. Rivers. U.S. history.

Magee, Doug. *All aboard ABC* by Doug Magee and Robert Newman; photos by authors. Dutton, 1990. ISBN 0-525-65036-9 Subj: ABC books. Trains.

Let's fly from A to Z by Doug Magee and Robert Newman; ill. by Robert Newman. Cobblehill, 1992. ISBN 0-525-65105-5 Subj: ABC books. Airplanes, airports. Language.

Trucks you can count on photos by author. Dodd, 1985. ISBN 0-396-08507-5 Subj: Counting, numbers. Trucks.

Maggs, Catherine. *Goodbye Rune* (Kaldhol, Marit)

Magnus, Erica. *Around me* ill. by author. Lothrop, 1992. ISBN 0-688-09753-7 Subj: Concepts. Format, unusual.

The boy and the devil ill. by author. Carolrhoda, 1986. ISBN 0-87614-305-2 Subj: Behavior – trickery. Devil. Folk and fairy tales. Foreign lands – Norway.

My secret place ill. by author. Lothrop, 1994. ISBN 0-688-11860-7 Subj: Imagination. Toys – bears.

Old Lars ill. by author. Carolrhoda, 1984. ISBN 0-87614-253-6 Subj: Folk and fairy tales. Foreign lands – Norway.

Magorian, Michelle. *Who's going to take care of me?* ill. by James Graham Hale. HarperCollins, 1990.

ISBN 0-06-024106-3 Subj: Behavior – worrying. Family life – brothers and sisters. School.

Maguire, Gregory. *Lucas Fishbone* ill. by Frank Gargiulo. HarperCollins, 1990. ISBN 0-06-024090-3 Subj: Death. Emotions – grief. Family life – grandmothers. Gardens, gardening. Rhyming text.

Magyar, Sabina. *Mrs. Meyer, the bird* (Erlbruch, Wolf)

Mahiri, Jabari. *The day they stole the letter J* ill. by Dorothy Carter. Third World Pr., 1981. Subj: Behavior – misbehavior. Careers – barbers. Magic.

Mahler, Michael. *My everyday Spanish word book* (Kahn, Michèle)

Mählqvist, Stefan. *I'll take care of the crocodiles* ill. by Tord Nygren. Atheneum, 1979. ISBN 0-689-50124-2 Subj: Bedtime. Dreams.

Mahony, Elizabeth Winthrop. *see* Winthrop, Elizabeth

Mahood, Kenneth. *The laughing dragon* ill. by author. Scribners, 1970. Subj: Dragons. Fire. Humor. Royalty.

Why are there more questions than answers, Grandad? ill. by author. Bradbury, 1974. ISBN 0-87888-101-8 Subj: Character traits – questioning. Family life – grandfathers.

Mahurin, Tim. *Jeremy Kooloo* ill. by author. Dutton, 1995. ISBN 0-525-45203-6 Subj: ABC books. Animals – cats.

Mahy, Margaret. *Beaten by a balloon* ill. by Jonathan Allen. Viking, 1998. ISBN 0-670-87697-6 Subj: Behavior – bullying. Crime. Emotions – anger. Emotions – fear. Humor.

Boom Baby boom, boom ill. by Patricia MacCarthy. Viking, 1997. ISBN 0-670-87314-4 Subj: Animals. Babies. Family life – mothers. Food. Noise, sounds.

The boy who was followed home ill. by Steven Kellogg. Watts, 1975. ISBN 0-531-02834-8 Subj: Animals – hippopotamuses. Humor. Witches.

The boy with two shadows ill. by Jenny Williams. Lippincott, 1988, 1971. ISBN 0-397-32271-2 Subj: Behavior – misbehavior. Character traits – meanness. Shadows. Witches.

A busy day for a good grandmother ill. by Margaret Chamberlain. Margaret K. McElderry, 1993. ISBN 0-689-50595-7 Subj: Activities – traveling. Babies. Family life – grandmothers. Food. Transportation.

The Christmas tree tangle ill. by Anthony Kerins. Margaret K. McElderry, 1994. ISBN 0-689-50616-3 Subj: Animals. Animals – cats. Cumulative tales. Holidays – Christmas. Rhyming text. Trees.

Down the dragon's tongue ill. by Patricia MacCarthy. Orchard, 2000. ISBN 0-531-30272-5 Subj: Family life – fathers. Multiple births – twins. Parks.

The dragon of an ordinary family ill. by Helen Oxenbury. Watts, 1969. ISBN 0-434-95000-9 Subj: Dragons.

The great white man-eating shark ill. by Jonathan Allen. Dial, 1990. ISBN 0-8037-0749-5 Subj: Behavior – trickery. Fish – sharks.

The horrendous hullabaloo ill. by Patricia MacCarthy. Viking, 1992. ISBN 0-670-84547-7 Subj: Birds – parakeets, parrots. Family life – aunts, uncles. Pirates.

Jam: a true story ill. by Helen Craig. Atlantic Monthly, 1986. ISBN 0-87113-048-3 Subj: Family life. Food.

Keeping house ill. by Wendy Smith. Macmillan, 1991. ISBN 0-689-50515-9 Subj: Character traits – cleanliness.

A lion in the meadow ill. by Jenny Williams. Watts, 1969. ISBN 0-87951-446-9 Subj: Animals – lions. Dragons.

Making friends ill. by Wendy Smith. Macmillan, 1990. ISBN 0-689-50498-5 Subj: Animals – dogs. Friendship.

The man whose mother was a pirate ill. by Margaret Chamberlain. Viking, 1986. ISBN 0-670-81070-3 Subj: Behavior – seeking better things. Pirates. Sea and seashore.

Mrs. Discombobulous ill. by Jan Brychta. Watts, 1969. ISBN 0-460-05796-0 Subj: Behavior – nagging. Family life. Gypsies.

Pillycock's shop ill. by Carol Baker. Watts, 1969. ISBN 0-234-77473-8 Subj: Fairies. Values.

The pumpkin man and the crafty creeper ill. by Helen Craig. Lothrop, 1991. ISBN 0-688-10347-2 Subj: Gardens, gardening. Plants.

The queen's goat ill. by Emma Chichester Clark. Dial, 1991. ISBN 0-8037-0938-2 Subj: Animals – goats. Pets. Royalty – queens.

The rattlebang picnic ill. by Steven Kellogg. Dial, 1994. ISBN 0-8037-1319-3 Subj: Activities – picnicking. Automobiles. Family life.

Rooms for rent ill. by Jenny Williams. Watts, 1974. ISBN 0-531-02590-X Subj: Behavior – greed. Hotels.

Sailor Jack and the twenty orphans ill. by Robert Bartelt. Watts, 1970. ISBN 0-531-01863-6 Subj: Boats, ships. Careers – military. Orphans. Pirates. Sailors. Sea and seashore.

The seven Chinese brothers ill. by Jean and Mou-sien Tseng. Scholastic, 1990. ISBN 0-590-42055-0 Subj: Character traits – cleverness. Family life. Folk and fairy tales. Foreign lands – China.

17 kings and 42 elephants ill. by Patricia Mac-Carthy. Dial, 1987. ISBN 0-8037-0458-5 Subj: Animals. Jungle. Rhyming text. Royalty – kings.

Simply delicious! ill. by Jonathan Allen. Orchard, 1999. ISBN 0-531-33181-4 Subj: Animals. Food. Jungle. Tongue twisters.

A summery Saturday morning ill. by Selina Young. Viking, 1998. ISBN 0-670-87943-6 Subj: Animals. Birds – geese. Humor. Rhyming text. Sea and seashore. Seasons – summer.

The three-legged cat ill. by Jonathan Allen. Viking, 1993. ISBN 0-670-85015-2 Subj: Activities – traveling. Animals – cats. Humor.

When the king rides by ill. by Betina Ogden. Mondo, 1995. ISBN 1-57255-003-1 Subj: Animals. Cumulative tales. Parades. Rhyming text. Royalty – kings.

Mainwaring, Jane. *My feather* photos by Fiona Pragoff. Doubleday, 1990. ISBN 0-385-41197-9 Subj: Activities. Concepts – perspective. Science.

Maiorano, Robert. *Backstage* ill. by Rachel Isadora. Greenwillow, 1978. ISBN 0-688-84130-9 Subj: Theater.

Francisco ill. by Rachel Isadora. Macmillan, 1978. ISBN 0-02-762170-7 Subj: Foreign lands – South America. Poverty. Problem solving.

A little interlude ill. by Rachel Isadora. Coward, 1980. ISBN 0-698-20496-4 Subj: Activities – dancing. Ballet. Behavior – sharing. Music.

Maisner, Heather. *Find Mouse in the house* ill. by Charlotte Hard. Candlewick, 1994. ISBN 1-56402-351-6 Subj: Animals – mice. Behavior – lost. Format, unusual – toy and movable books.

Find Mouse in the yard ill. by Charlotte Hard. Candlewick, 1994. ISBN 1-56402-350-8 Subj: Animals – mice. Format, unusual – toy and movable books. Games.

Planet monster ill. by Alan Rowe. Candlewick, 1996. ISBN 0-763-60057-1 Subj: Concepts – color. Concepts – shape. Counting, numbers. Space and space ships.

Save Brave Ted ill. by Charlotte Hard. Candlewick, 1996. ISBN 1-56402-878-X Subj: Monsters. Picture puzzles. Toys. Toys – bears.

Maitland, Antony. *Idle Jack* ill. by author. Farrar, 1979. ISBN 0-374-33628-8 Subj: Character traits – foolishness. Folk and fairy tales.

Maitland, Barbara. *The bear who didn't like honey* ill. by Odilon Moraes. Orchard, 1997. ISBN 0-531-09546-0 Subj: Animals – bears. Character traits – bravery. Emotions – fear. Night.

The bookstore ghost ill. by Nadine Bernard Westcott. Dutton, 1998. ISBN 0-525-46049-7 Subj: Animals – cats. Animals – mice. Ghosts. Stores.

My bear and me ill. by Lisa Flather. Margaret K. McElderry, 1999. ISBN 0-689-82085-2 Subj: Activities. Bedtime. Toys – bears.

Maizlish, Lisa. *The ring* photos by author. Greenwillow, 1996. ISBN 0-688-14217-6 Subj: Activities – flying. City. Imagination. Wordless.

Majewski, Joe. *A friend for Oscar Mouse* ill. by Maria Majewska. Dial, 1988. ISBN 0-8037-0348-1 Subj: Animals – mice. Friendship.

Major, Beverly. *Playing sardines* ill. by Andrew Glass. Scholastic, 1988. ISBN 0-590-41153-5 Subj: Activities – playing. Behavior – hiding. Games. Twilight.

Makower, Sylvia. *Samson's breakfast* ill. by author. Watts, 1961. Subj: Animals – lions.

Malecki, Maryann. *Mom and dad and I are having a baby!* ill. by author. Pennypress, 1982. ISBN 0-937604-03-8 Subj: Babies. Family life – new sibling.

Maley, Anne. *Have you seen my mother?* ill. by Yutaka Sugita. Carolrhoda, 1969. ISBN 0-8761-4001-0 Subj: Circus. Family life – mothers. Toys – balls.

Malfatti, Patrizia. *Look inside an airplane* (Mantegazza, Giovanna)

Malkovych, Ivan. *The cat and the rooster* ill. by Kost' Lavro; trans. by Motria Onyschuk. Knopf, 1995. ISBN 0-679-86964-6 Subj: Animals – cats. Animals – foxes. Birds – chickens. Folk and fairy tales. Foreign lands – Soviet Union. Foreign lands – Ukraine.

Mallat, Kathy. *Brave bear* ill. by author. Walker, 1999. ISBN 0-8027-8705-3 Subj: Animals – bears. Birds. Character traits – bravery. Emotions – fear.

Seven stars, more! ill. by author. Walker, 1998. ISBN 0-8027-8676-6 Subj: Animals – sheep. Bedtime. Counting, numbers. Sleep. Stars.

Mallett, Anne. *Here comes Tagalong* ill. by Steven Kellogg. Parents, 1971. ISBN 0-8193-0496-4 Subj: Family life. Friendship. Sibling rivalry.

Mallett, David. *Inch by inch: the garden song* ill. by Ora Eitan. HarperCollins, 1995. ISBN 0-06-024304-X Subj: Gardens, gardening. Music. Songs.

Mallory, Kenneth. *Families of the deep blue sea* ill. by Marshall H. Peck, III. Charlesbridge, 1995. ISBN 0-88106-887-X Subj: Animals. Fish. Sea and seashore.

Malloy, Judy. *Bad Thad* ill. by Martha G. Alexander. Dutton, 1980. ISBN 0-525-26148-6 Subj: Behavior – misbehavior. Family life. School.

Malone, Nola Langner. *A home* ill. by author. Bradbury, 1988. ISBN 0-02-751440-4 Subj: Friendship. Homes, houses. Moving.

Maloney, Peter. *The magic hockey stick* by Peter Maloney and Felicia Zekauskas; ill. by authors. Dial, 1999. ISBN 0-8037-2476-X Subj: Rhyming text. Sports – hockey.

Redbird at Rockefeller Center by Peter Maloney and Felicia Zekauskas; ill. by authors. Dial, 1997. ISBN 0-8037-2257-5 Subj: Birds – cardinals. Holidays – Christmas. Magic. Rhyming text. Santa Claus. Trees.

Malotki, Ekkehart. *The magic hummingbird* ill. by Michael Lomatuway'ma. Kiva, 1996. ISBN 1-885772-04-1 Subj: Folk and fairy tales. Indians of North America – Hopi. Weather – droughts.

Mamchur, Carolyn Marie. *The popcorn tree* ill. by Laurie McGaw. Stoddart Kids, 1998. ISBN 0-7737-2896-1 Subj: Holidays – Christmas. Trees.

Mamin-Sibiryak, D. N. *Grey Neck* adapt. and trans. from Russian by Marguerita Rudolph; ill. by Leslie Shuman Kronz. Stemmer House, 1988. ISBN 0-88045-068-1 Subj: Birds – ducks. Character traits – kindness to animals. Folk and fairy tales. Seasons – winter.

Mammano, Julie. *Rhinos who skateboard* ill. by author. Chronicle, 1999. ISBN 0-8118-2356-3 Subj: Animals – rhinoceros. Sports – skateboarding.

Mandel, Peter. *Say hey: a song of Willie Mays* ill. by Don Tate. Hyperion, 2000. ISBN 0-7868-2417-4 Subj: Ethnic groups in the U.S. – African Americans. Rhyming text. Sports – baseball.

Mandry, Kathy. *The cat and the mouse and the mouse and the cat* ill. by Joe Toto. Pantheon, 1972. ISBN 0-394-92401-0 Subj: Animals – cats. Animals – mice. Friendship.

Manes, Esther. *The bananas move to the ceiling* by Esther and Stephen Manes; ill. by Barbara Samuels. Watts, 1983. ISBN 0-531-04517-X Subj: Family life. Humor.

Manes, Stephen. *The bananas move to the ceiling* (Manes, Esther)

Mangan, Anne. *Browny, the smallest bear of all* ill. by Joanne Moss. Crocodile Books, 1998. ISBN 1-56656-266-X Subj: Animals – bears. Concepts – size. Self-concept.

Mangas, Brian. *A nice surprise for Father Rabbit* ill. by Sidney Levitt. Simon & Schuster, 1989. ISBN 0-671-67194-4 Subj: Animals – rabbits. Emotions – love. Family life – fathers.

Mangin, Marie-France. *Suzette and Nicholas and the seasons clock* trans. from French by Joan Chevalier; ill. by Satomi Ichikawa. Putnam, 1982. ISBN 0-399-20832-1 Subj: Activities. Seasons.

Mangold, Paul. *Whose tracks are these?* (Gipson, Morrell)

Manheim, Ralph. *Dear Mili* (Grimm, Wilhelm)

The marvelous journey through the night (Heine, Helme)

Mollywoop (Heine, Helme)

The nutcracker (Hoffmann, E. T. A.)

Mann, Pamela. *The frog princess?* ill. by author. Gareth Stevens, 1995. ISBN 0-83681-352-9 Subj: Careers – librarians. Folk and fairy tales. Frogs and toads. Royalty – princes.

Mann, Peggy. *King Laurence, the alarm clock* ill. by Ray Cruz. Doubleday, 1976. ISBN 0-385-04972-2 Subj: Animals. Animals – lions. Illness. Morning.

Manna, Anthony L. *Mr. Semolina-Semolinus* retold by Anthony L. Manna and Christodoula Mitakidou; ill. by Giselle Potter. Atheneum, 1997. ISBN 0-689-81093-8 Subj: Emotions – love. Folk and fairy tales. Foreign lands – Greece. Magic.

Manniche, Lise. *The prince who knew his fate: an ancient Egyptian tale* (The prince who knew his fate)

Manning, Linda. *Animal hours* ill. by Vlasta van Kampen. Oxford Univ. Pr., 1991. ISBN 0-19-540771-7 Subj: Animals. Cumulative tales. Rhyming text. Time.

Dinosaur days ill. by Vlasta van Kampen. BridgeWater, 1994. ISBN 0-8167-3315-5 Subj: Behavior – misbehavior. Days of the week, months of the year. Dinosaurs.

Manning, Mick. *Honk! honk!* by Mick Manning and Brita Granström; ill. by authors. Kingfisher, 1997. ISBN 0-7534-5103-4 Subj: Birds – geese. Dreams. Migration.

My body, your body by Mick Manning and Brita Granström; ill. by authors. Watts, 1997. ISBN 0-531-14486-0 Subj: Anatomy. Animals. Character traits – individuality.

A ruined house ill. by author. Candlewick, 1994. ISBN 1-56402-453-9 Subj: Foreign lands – Scotland. Homes, houses. Nature.

Mansell, Dom. *If dinosaurs came to town* ill. by author. Little, 1991. ISBN 0-316-54584-8 Subj: Dinosaurs. Imagination.

My old teddy ill. by author. Candlewick, 1992. ISBN 1-56402-035-5 Subj: Toys – bears.

Manson, Beverlie. *The fairies' alphabet book* ill. by author. Doubleday, 1982. ISBN 0-385-17544-2 Subj: ABC books. Fairies.

Manson, Christopher. *The crab prince* ill. by reteller. Holt, 1991. ISBN 0-8050-1215-X Subj: Crustaceans. Folk and fairy tales. Foreign lands – Italy. Royalty – princes. Witches.

A farmyard song ill. by author. North-South, 1992. ISBN 1-55858-170-7 Subj: Animals. Cumulative tales. Farms. Noise, sounds. Nursery rhymes. Songs.

A gift for the king ill. by author. Holt, 1989. ISBN 0-8050-0951-5 Subj: Folk and fairy tales. Foreign lands – Persia. Gifts. Royalty – kings.

Here begins the tale of the marvellous blue mouse ill. by author. Holt, 1992. ISBN 0-8050-1622-8 Subj: Animals – mice. Behavior – greed. Behavior – trickery. Foreign lands – France. Middle Ages. Problem solving. Royalty – emperors.

The tree in the wood: an old nursery song ill. by adapt. North-South, 1993. ISBN 1-55858-193-6 Subj: Cumulative tales. Folk and fairy tales. Songs. Trees.

Two travelers ill. by author. Holt, 1990. ISBN 0-8050-1214-1 Subj: Activities – traveling. Animals – elephants. Friendship.

Mantegazza, Giovanna. *The cat* ill. by Cristina Mesturini. Boyds Mills, 1992. ISBN 1-56397-032-5 Subj: Animals – cats. Format, unusual – board books.

The hippopotamus ill. by Cristina Mesturini. Boyds Mills, 1992. ISBN 1-56397-033-3 Subj: Animals – hippopotamuses. Foreign lands – Africa. Format, unusual – board books.

Look how a baby grows trans. from Italian by Alexandra E. Fischer; ill. by Anna Curti. Grosset, 1995. ISBN 0-448-40925-9 Subj: Babies. Birth. Format, unusual – board books. Format, unusual – toy and movable books.

Look inside a car trans. from Italian by Alexandra E. Fischer; ill. by Gianna Ronco. Grosset, 1996. ISBN 0-448-41315-9 Subj: Automobiles. Format, unusual – toy and movable books. Transportation.

Look inside a farm trans. from Italian by Alexandra E. Fischer; ill. by Cristina Mesturini. Grosset, 1994. ISBN 0-448-40958-5 Subj: Farms. Format, unusual – toy and movable books.

Look inside a rainforest trans. from Italian by Alexandra E. Fischer; ill. by Carlo A. Michelini. Grosset, 1993. ISBN 0-448-40489-3 Subj: Ecology. Forest, woods. Format, unusual – toy and movable books.

Look inside an airplane trans. from Italian by Patrizia Malfatti; ill. by Carlo A. Michelini. Grosset, 1994. ISBN 0-448-40543-1 Subj: Airplanes, airports. Transportation.

Mantinband, Gerda. *Blabbermouths* ill. by Paul Borovsky. Greenwillow, 1992. ISBN 0-688-10602-1 Subj: Behavior – gossip. Folk and fairy tales. Money.

Three clever mice ill. by Martine Gourbault. Greenwillow, 1993. ISBN 0-688-11370-2 Subj: Animals – mice. Character traits – cleverness.

Manuel, Lynn. *Lucy Maud and the Cavendish cat* ill. by Janet Wilson. Tundra, 1997. ISBN 0-88776-397-9 Subj: Animals – cats. Careers – authors.

The night the moon blew kisses ill. by Robin Spowart. Houghton Mifflin, 1996. ISBN 0-395-73979-9 Subj: Activities – walking. Family life – grandmothers. Moon. Seasons – winter. Weather – snow.

Manushkin, Fran. *Baby* ill. by Ronald Himler. HarperCollins, 1972. ISBN 0-06-024062-8 Subj: Babies. Family life.

Baby, come out! ill. by Ronald Himler. HarperCollins, 1972. Orig. entitled Baby. ISBN 0-06-024062-8 Subj: Babies. Birth.

Be brave, baby rabbit ill. by Diane de Groat. Crown, 1990. ISBN 0-517-57574-4 Subj: Animals – rabbits. Character traits – bravery. Family life – brothers and sisters. Holidays – Halloween.

The best toy of all ill. by Robin Ballard. Dutton, 1992. ISBN 0-525-44897-7 Subj: Activities – playing. Family life. Seasons. Toys.

Bubblebath! ill. by Ronald Himler. HarperCollins, 1974. ISBN 0-06-024059-8 Subj: Activities – bathing. Bubbles. Family life.

Hocus and Pocus at the circus ill. by Geoffrey Hayes. HarperCollins, 1983. ISBN 0-06-024092-X Subj: Character traits – meanness. Holidays – Halloween. Witches.

Hooray for Hanukkah! ill. by author. Random House, 2001. ISBN 0-375-91043-3 Subj: Holidays – Hanukkah. Jewish culture. Religion.

Latkes and applesauce ill. by Robin Spowart. Scholastic, 1990. ISBN 0-590-42261-8 Subj: Holidays – Hanukkah. Jewish culture. Religion.

Let's go riding in our strollers ill. by Benrei Huang. Hyperion, 1993. ISBN 1-56282-391-4 Subj: City. Rhyming text.

Little rabbit's baby brother ill. by Diane de Groat. Crown, 1986. ISBN 0-517-56251-0 Subj: Animals – rabbits. Babies. Emotions – envy, jealousy. Family life – new sibling. Sibling rivalry.

The matzah that Papa brought home ill. by Ned Bittinger. Scholastic, 1995. ISBN 0-590-47146-5 Subj: Cumulative tales. Food. Holidays – Passover. Jewish culture. Religion.

Miriam's cup: a Passover story ill. by Bob Dacey. Scholastic, 1998. ISBN 0-590-67720-9 Subj: Holidays – Passover. Jewish culture. Religion.

Moon dragon ill. by Geoffrey Hayes. Macmillan, 1982. ISBN 0-02-762210-X Subj: Animals – mice. Dragons. Food. Moon.

My Christmas safari ill. by R. W. Alley. Dial, 1993. ISBN 0-8037-1295-2 Subj: Animals. Counting, numbers. Cumulative tales. Foreign lands – Africa. Holidays – Christmas. Music.

Peeping and sleeping ill. by Jennifer Plecas. Clarion, 1994. ISBN 0-395-64339-2 Subj: Family life – fathers. Frogs and toads. Night. Noise, sounds.

The perfect Christmas picture ill. by Karen Ann Weinhaus. HarperCollins, 1980. ISBN 0-06-024069-5 Subj: Activities – photographing. Family life. Holidays – Christmas.

Shirleybird ill. by Carl Stuart. HarperCollins, 1975. ISBN 0-06-024064-4 Subj: Character traits – individuality.

Starlight and candles: the joys of the Sabbath ill. by Jacqueline Chwast. Simon & Schuster, 1995. ISBN 0-671-88333-X Subj: Family life. Jewish culture. Religion.

Swinging and swinging ill. by Thomas di Grazia. HarperCollins, 1976. ISBN 0-06-024067-9 Subj: Activities – playing. Activities – swinging. Weather – clouds.

Walt Disney's one hundred one dalmations ill. by Russell Hicks. Walt Disney, 1991. ISBN 1-56282-032-X Subj: Animals – dogs. Counting, numbers.

Maple, Marilyn J. *On the wings of a butterfly: a story about life and death* ill. by Sandy Haight. Parenting Pr., 1992. ISBN 0-943990-69-6 Subj: Death. Emotions – grief. Illness – cancer. Insects – butterflies, caterpillars. Metamorphosis.

Marceau, Marcel. *The Marcel Marceau counting book* (Mendoza, George)

The story of Bip ill. by author. HarperCollins, 1976. ISBN 0-06-024053-9 Subj: Clowns, jesters. Imagination.

Marcellino, Fred. *I, crocodile* ill. by author. HarperCollins, 1999. ISBN 0-06-205199-7 Subj: Food. Foreign lands – Egypt. Foreign lands – France. Humor. Reptiles – alligators, crocodiles. Royalty – emperors.

Marcin, Marietta. *A zoo in her bed* ill. by Sofia. Coward, 1963. Subj: Bedtime. Rhyming text. Toys.

Marcus, Susan. *Casey visits the doctor* ill. by Deborah Drew-Brook. CBC Merchandising, 1982. ISBN 0-88794-101-X Subj: Careers – doctors. Health and fitness.

The missing button adventure ill. by Hajime Sawada. CBC Merchandising, 1981. ISBN 0-88794-102-8 Subj: Behavior – losing things. Character traits – helpfulness. Toys – bears.

Mare, Walter De La. *see* De La Mare, Walter (Walter John)

Margalit, Avishai. *The Hebrew alphabet book: Me-Alef'ad Tav* ill. by author. Funk & Wagnalls, 1968. Subj: ABC books. Jewish culture.

Margolis, Matthew. *Some swell pup: or Are you sure you want a dog?* (Sendak, Maurice)

Margolis, Richard J. *Big bear, spare that tree* ill. by Jack Kent. Greenwillow, 1980. ISBN 0-688-80248-6 Subj: Animals – bears. Birds – bluejays. Ecology. Trees.

Secrets of a small brother ill. by Donald Carrick. Macmillan, 1984. ISBN 0-02-762280-0 Subj: Poetry. Sibling rivalry.

Margret and H. A. Rey's Curious George and the puppies ill. in the style of H. A. Rey by Vipah

Interactive. Houghton Mifflin, 1998. ISBN 0-395-91217-2 Subj: Animals. Animals – monkeys. Behavior – misbehavior.

Mari, Iela. *Eat and be eaten* ill. by author. Barron's, 1980. ISBN 0-8120-5396-6 Subj: Animals. Format, unusual. Sports – hunting. Wordless.

The magic balloon ill. by author. S. G. Phillips, 1970. Subj: Toys – balloons. Wordless.

Mariana. *Doki, the lonely papoose* ill. by author. Lothrop, 1955. Subj: Indians of North America.

The journey of Bangwell Putt ill. by author. Lothrop, 1965. Subj: Holidays – Christmas. Toys – dolls.

Marie, Geraldine. *The magic box* ill. by Michele Chessare. Elsevier-Nelson, 1981. ISBN 0-525-66721-0 Subj: Animals – dogs. Birthdays. Magic. Problem solving.

Maril, Lee. *Mr. Bunny paints the eggs* ill. by Irena Lorentowicz. Roy Pub., 1945. Subj: Animals – rabbits. Concepts – color. Holidays – Easter. Music. Songs.

Marino, Barbara Pavis. *Eric needs stitches* photos by Richard Rudinski. Addison-Wesley, 1979. ISBN 0-201-04401-3 Subj: Hospitals.

Marino, Dorothy. *Buzzy Bear and the rainbow* ill. by author. Watts, 1962. Subj: Animals – bears. Weather – rainbows.

Buzzy Bear goes camping ill. by author. Watts, 1964. Subj: Animals – bears. Camps, camping.

Buzzy Bear in the garden ill. by author. Watts, 1963, 1961. Subj: Animals – bears. Gardens, gardening.

Buzzy Bear's busy day ill. by author. Watts, 1965. Subj: Animals – bears.

Edward and the boxes ill. by author. Lippincott, 1957. Subj: Activities – playing. Sleep.

Good-bye thunderstorm ill. by author. Lippincott, 1958. Subj: Weather – rain. Weather – storms. Weather – thunder.

Mario, Heidi Stetson. *I'd rather have an iguana* ill. by author. Charlesbridge, 1999. ISBN 0-88106-357-6 Subj: Babies. Emotions – envy, jealousy. Family life – brothers and sisters. Family life – new sibling.

Marion, Jeff Daniel. *Hello, Crow* ill. by Leslie Bowman. Orchard, 1992. ISBN 0-531-08575-9 Subj: Birds – crows.

Mariotti, Mario. *Hand games* photos by author. Kane/Miller, 1992. ISBN 0-916291-43-X Subj: Sports – Olympics.

Hands off! photos by Roberto Marchiori. Kane/Miller, 1990. ISBN 0-916291-29-4 Subj: Imagination.

Hanimations photos by Roberto Marchiori. Kane/Miller, 1989. Original title: Rimani. ISBN 0-916291-22-7 Subj: Imagination.

Maris, Ron. *Are you there, bear?* ill. by author. Greenwillow, 1984. ISBN 0-688-03998-7 Subj: Behavior – lost. Toys. Toys – bears.

Bernard's boring day ill. by author. Delacorte, 1990. ISBN 0-385-29948-6 Subj: Animals. Behavior – boredom. Format, unusual – toy and movable books. Mythical creatures – gnomes. Sports – fishing.

Better move on, frog! ill. by author. Watts, 1982. ISBN 0-531-04575-7 Subj: Animals. Frogs and toads. Homes, houses. Nature.

Ducks quack ill. by author. Candlewick, 1992. ISBN 1-56402-080-0 Subj: Animals. Farms. Format, unusual – board books. Noise, sounds. Scarecrows.

Frogs jump ill. by author. Candlewick, 1992. ISBN 1-56402-081-9 Subj: Animals. Format, unusual – board books. Frogs and toads.

Hold tight, bear! ill. by author. Delacorte, 1989. ISBN 0-440-50152-0 Subj: Animals – bears. Animals – donkeys. Forest, woods. Problem solving. Toys – dolls. Wordless.

I wish I could fly ill. by author. Greenwillow, 1986. ISBN 0-688-06655-0 Subj: Animals. Behavior – wishing. Reptiles – turtles, tortoises.

In my garden ill. by author. Greenwillow, 1988. ISBN 0-688-07631-9 Subj: Activities – picnicking. Animals. Counting, numbers. Flowers. Gardens, gardening.

Is anyone home? ill. by author. Greenwillow, 1985. ISBN 0-688-05899-X Subj: Family life – grandparents. Farms. Format, unusual – toy and movable books.

My book ill. by author. Watts, 1983. ISBN 0-531-04610-9 Subj: Animals – cats. Bedtime.

Runaway rabbit ill. by author. Delacorte, 1989. ISBN 0-385-29764-5 Subj: Animals. Animals – rabbits. Behavior – running away.

Mark, Jan. *Fun with Mrs. Thumb* ill. by Nicola Bayley. Candlewick, 1993. ISBN 1-56402-247-1 Subj: Animals – cats. Rhyming text. Toys. Toys – dolls.

Fur ill. by Charlotte Voake. Walker, 1986. ISBN 0-7445-0478-3 Subj: Animals – cats. Birth. Pets.

The Midas touch ill. by Juan Wijngaard. Candlewick, 1999. ISBN 0-7636-0488-7 Subj: Behavior – greed. Behavior – wishing. Folk and fairy tales. Royalty – kings.

The tale of Tobias ill. by Rachel Merriman. Candlewick, 1996. ISBN 1-56402-692-2 Subj: Folk and fairy tales. Religion.

Markle, Sandra. *Outside and inside alligators* ill. by author. Atheneum, 1998. ISBN 0-689-81457-7 Subj: Anatomy. Reptiles – alligators, crocodiles.

Outside and inside bats ill. by author. Atheneum, 1997. ISBN 0-689-81165-9 Subj: Anatomy. Animals – bats.

Outside and inside you ill. by Susan Kuklin. Bradbury, 1991. ISBN 0-02-762311-4 Subj: Anatomy.

Markoe, Merrill. *The day my dogs became guys* ill. by Eric Brace. Viking, 1999. ISBN 0-670-85344-5 Subj: Animals – dogs. Astronomy. Behavior. Sun.

Marks, Alan. *Nowhere to be found* ill. by author. Picture Book Studio, 1988. ISBN 0-88708-062-6 Subj: Behavior – losing things. Behavior – lost. Language.

Marks, Burton. *Animals* ill. by Paul Harvey. Troll, 1991. ISBN 0-8167-2415-6 Subj: Animals.

Colors and numbers ill. by Paul Harvey. Troll, 1991. ISBN 0-8167-2411-3 Subj: Concepts – color. Counting, numbers.

Marks, J. *see* Highwater, Jamake

Marks, Marcia Bliss. *Swing me, swing tree* ill. by David Berger. Little, 1959. Subj: Activities – swinging. Poetry.

Marokvia, Merelle. *A French school for Paul* ill. by Artur Marokvia. Lippincott, 1963. Subj: Circus. Foreign lands – France. School.

Marol, Jean-Claude. *Vagabul and his shadow* ill. by author. Creative Ed., 1983. ISBN 0-87191-889-7 Subj: Shadows. Wordless.

Vagabul escapes ill. by author. Creative Ed., 1983. ISBN 0-87191-888-9 Subj: Behavior – running away. Wordless.

Vagabul goes skiing ill. by author. Creative Ed., 1983. ISBN 0-87191-886-2 Subj: Sports – skiing. Wordless.

Vagabul in the clouds ill. by author. Creative Ed., 1983. ISBN 0-87191-887-0 Subj: Weather – clouds. Wordless.

Marron, Carol A. *Gretchen's grandma* (Root, Phyllis)

No trouble for Grandpa ill. by Chaya M. Burstein. Raintree, 1983. ISBN 0-940742-27-6 Subj: Family life – grandfathers. Handicaps. Sibling rivalry.

Marsh, Gwen. *My everyday Spanish word book* (Kahn, Michèle)

Marsh, Jeri. *Hurrah for Alexander* ill. by Joan Hanson. Carolrhoda, 1977. ISBN 0-8761-4092-4 Subj: Character traits – persistence. Humor.

Marsh, T. J. *Somewhere in the ocean* (Ward, Jennifer)

Way out in the desert by T. J. Marsh and Jennifer Ward; ill. by Kenneth J. Spengler. Rising Moon, 1998. ISBN 0-8735-8687-5 Subj: Animals. Animals – babies. Counting, numbers. Desert. Picture puzzles. Rhyming text.

Marshak, S. (Samuil). *The absentminded fellow* trans. from Russian by Richard Pevear; ill. by Marc Rosenthal. Farrar, 1999. ISBN 0-374-30013-5 Subj: Behavior – forgetfulness. Humor. Memories, memory. Rhyming text.

Hail to mail trans. from Russian by Richard Pevear; ill. by Vladimir Radunsky. Holt, 1990. ISBN 0-8050-1132-3 Subj: Careers – postal workers. Poetry. Post office.

In the van trans. from Russian by Margaret Wettlin; ill. by V. Lebedev. Imported Pubs., 1983. ISBN 0-8285-2289-8 Subj: Animals – dogs. Moving. Poetry.

The merry starlings by Samuel Marshak with D. Harms; trans. from Russian by Dorian Rottenberg; ill. by Arieh Zeldich. HarperCollins, 1983. Subj: Birds. Nursery rhymes. Poetry.

The Month-Brothers: a Slavic tale trans. from Russian by Thomas P. Whitney; ill. by Diane Stanley. Morrow, 1983. ISBN 0-688-01510-7 Subj: Foreign lands – Czechoslovakia. Rhyming text. Seasons. Weather.

The pup grew up! trans. by Richard Pevear; ill. by Vladimir Radunsky. Holt, 1989. ISBN 0-8050-0952-3 Subj: Activities – traveling. Animals – dogs. Behavior – growing up. Behavior – losing things. Rhyming text. Trains.

The tale of a hero nobody knows trans. from Russian by Peter Tempest; ill. by Vassili Shulzhenko. Imported Pubs., 1983. ISBN 0-8285-2291-X Subj: Character traits – bravery. Foreign lands – Russia. Poetry.

Marshall, Douglas. *see* McClintock, Marshall

Marshall, Edward. *Four on the shore* ill. by James Marshall. Dial, 1985. ISBN 0-8037-0142-X Subj: Monsters. Sibling rivalry.

Fox all week ill. by James Marshall. Dial, 1984. ISBN 0-8037-0066-0 Subj: Animals. Animals – foxes. Friendship.

Fox and his friends ill. by James Marshall. Dial, 1982. ISBN 0-8037-2669-4 Subj: Animals – foxes. Behavior – misbehavior.

Fox at school ill. by James Marshall. Dial, 1983. ISBN 0-8037-2675-9 Subj: Animals – foxes. Humor. School.

Fox in love ill. by James Marshall. Dial, 1982. ISBN 0-8037-2433-0 Subj: Animals – foxes. Emotions – love.

Fox on wheels ill. by James Marshall. Dial, 1983. ISBN 0-8037-0002-4 Subj: Animals – foxes. Behavior – misbehavior. Sports – racing.

Space case ill. by James Marshall. Dial, 1980. ISBN 0-8037-8007-9 Subj: Holidays – Halloween. Robots. Space and space ships.

Three by the sea ill. by James Marshall. Dial, 1981. ISBN 0-8037-8671-9 Subj: Activities – picnicking. Friendship.

Troll country ill. by James Marshall. Dial, 1980. ISBN 0-8037-6211-9 Subj: Forest, woods. Mythical creatures – trolls.

Marshall, Frances. *Princess Kalina and the hedgehog* (Flot, Jeannette B.)

Marshall, James. *The Cut-Ups* ill. by author. Viking, 1984. ISBN 0-670-25195-X Subj: Behavior – misbehavior. Humor. Toys.

The Cut-Ups at Camp Custer ill. by author. Viking, 1989. ISBN 0-670-82051-2 Subj: Behavior – misbehavior. Camps, camping. Humor.

The Cut-Ups carry on ill. by author. Viking, 1990. ISBN 0-670-81645-0 Subj: Activities – dancing. Contests. Humor.

The Cut-Ups crack up ill. by author. Viking, 1992. ISBN 0-670-84486-1 Subj: Automobiles. Behavior – misbehavior. Humor. School.

The Cut-Ups cut loose ill. by author. Viking, 1987. ISBN 0-670-80740-0 Subj: Behavior – misbehavior. Friendship. Humor. School.

Four little troubles ill. by author. Houghton Mifflin, 1975. ISBN 0-395-19880-1 Subj: Animals. Problem solving.

Fox on the job ill. by author. Dial, 1988. ISBN 0-8037-0351-1 Subj: Activities – working. Animals – foxes. Behavior – misbehavior.

George and Martha ill. by author. Houghton Mifflin, 1972. ISBN 0-395-13732-2 Subj: Animals – hippopotamuses. Friendship.

George and Martha back in town ill. by author. Houghton Mifflin, 1984. ISBN 0-395-35386-6 Subj: Animals – hippopotamuses. Behavior – misbehavior. Friendship.

George and Martha encore ill. by author. Houghton Mifflin, 1973. ISBN 0-395-17512-7 Subj: Activities – dancing. Animals – hippopotamuses. Friendship.

George and Martha one fine day ill. by author. Houghton Mifflin, 1978. ISBN 0-395-27154-1 Subj: Animals – hippopotamuses. Friendship.

George and Martha rise and shine ill. by author. Houghton Mifflin, 1976. ISBN 0-395-24738-1 Subj: Animals – hippopotamuses. Friendship.

George and Martha 'round and 'round ill. by author. Houghton Mifflin, 1988. ISBN 0-395-46763-2 Subj: Activities – vacationing. Animals – hippopotamuses. Friendship. Imagination.

George and Martha, tons of fun ill. by author. Houghton Mifflin, 1980. ISBN 0-395-29524-6 Subj: Animals – hippopotamuses. Character traits – vanity.

Goldilocks and the three bears (The three bears)

The guest ill. by author. Houghton Mifflin, 1975. ISBN 0-395-20277-9 Subj: Animals – moose. Animals – snails. Friendship.

Hansel and Gretel ill. by reteller. Dial, 1990. ISBN 0-8037-0828-9 Subj: Folk and fairy tales. Forest, woods. Witches.

Hey, diddle, daddle ill. by author. Heath, 1989. ISBN 0-669-13293-4 Subj: Animals. Animals – horses, ponies. Format, unusual. Frogs and toads. Rhyming text. Sea and seashore.

Hey, diddle, diddle ill. by author. Farrar, 1994. ISBN 0-374-33061-1 Subj: Format, unusual – toy and movable books. Nursery rhymes.

Merry Christmas, space case ill. by author. Dial, 1986. ISBN 0-8037-0216-7 Subj: Holidays – Christmas. Space and space ships.

Miss Dog's Christmas ill. by author. Houghton Mifflin, 1973. ISBN 0-395-18154-2 Subj: Animals – dogs. Food. Holidays – Christmas.

Miss Nelson is back (Allard, Harry)

Miss Nelson is missing! (Allard, Harry)

Pocketful of nonsense ill. by author. Artists & Writers Guild, 1993. ISBN 0-307-17552-9 Subj: Poetry.

Portly McSwine ill. by author. Houghton Mifflin, 1979. ISBN 0-395-28003-6 Subj: Animals – pigs. Behavior – worrying.

Rapscallion Jones ill. by author. Viking, 1983. ISBN 0-670-58965-9 Subj: Animals – foxes. Behavior – seeking better things.

Red Riding Hood ill. by adapt. Dial, 1987. ISBN 0-8037-0345-7 Subj: Animals – wolves. Behavior – talking to strangers. Folk and fairy tales.

Speedboat ill. by author. Houghton Mifflin, 1976. ISBN 0-395-24384-X Subj: Animals – dogs. Boats, ships. Friendship.

The Stupids have a ball (Allard, Harry)

The Stupids take off (Allard, Harry)

Swine lake ill. by Maurice Sendak. HarperCollins, 1999. ISBN 0-06-205171-7 Subj: Activities – dancing. Animals – pigs. Animals – wolves. Ballet. Theater.

The three little pigs (The three little pigs)

Three up a tree ill. by author. Dutton, 1986. ISBN 0-8037-0329-5 Subj: Activities – playing. Imagination. Monsters. Trees.

What's the matter with Carruthers? ill. by author. Houghton Mifflin, 1972. ISBN 0-395-13895-7 Subj: Animals – bears. Bedtime. Character traits – helpfulness. Friendship. Hibernation.

Willis ill. by author. Houghton Mifflin, 1974. ISBN 0-395-19494-6 Subj: Animals. Friendship. Glasses.

Wings: a tale of two chickens ill. by author. Viking, 1986. ISBN 0-670-80961-6 Subj: Activities – reading. Animals – foxes. Birds – chickens.

Yummers! ill. by author. Houghton Mifflin, 1973. ISBN 0-395-14757-3 Subj: Animals – pigs. Food. Illness.

Yummers too: the second course ill. by author. Houghton Mifflin, 1986. ISBN 0-395-38990-9 Subj: Animals – pigs. Behavior – greed. Food. Reptiles – turtles, tortoises.

Marshall, Janet Perry. *Banana moon* ill. by author. Greenwillow, 1998. ISBN 0-688-15768-8 Subj: Food. Format, unusual – toy and movable books. Sea and seashore. Sports – sailing.

A honey of a day ill. by author. Greenwillow, 2000. ISBN 0-688-16917-1 Subj: Animals. Flowers. Weddings.

My camera: at the zoo ill. by author. Little, 1989. ISBN 0-316-54687-9 Subj: Activities – photographing. Animals. Games. Zoos.

Ohmygosh, my pocket ill. by author. Boyds Mills, 1992. ISBN 1-56397-044-9 Subj: Clothing. Rhyming text. School.

Marshall, Lyn. *Yoga for your children* ill. with photos. Schocken, 1979. ISBN 0-8052-0630-2 Subj: Health and fitness. Religion.

Marshall, Margaret. *Mike* ill. by Lorraine Spiro. Merrimack, 1983. ISBN 0-370-30934-0 Subj: Bedtime. Problem solving.

Marshall, Ray. *Pop-up numbers #1* by Ray Marshall and Korky Paul; ill. by authors. Dutton, 1984. ISBN 0-525-44088-7 Subj: Counting, numbers. Format, unusual – toy and movable books.

Pop-up numbers #2 by Ray Marshall and Korky Paul; ill. by authors. Dutton, 1984. ISBN 0-525-44089-5 Subj: Counting, numbers. Format, unusual – toy and movable books.

Pop-up numbers #3 by Ray Marshall and Korky Paul; ill. by authors. Dutton, 1984. ISBN 0-525-44090-9 Subj: Counting, numbers. Format, unusual – toy and movable books.

Pop-up numbers #4 by Ray Marshall and Korky Paul; ill. by authors. Dutton, 1984. ISBN 0-525-44091-7 Subj: Counting, numbers. Format, unusual – toy and movable books.

The train: watch it work by operating the moving diagrams! ill. by John Bradley. Viking, 1986. ISBN 0-670-81134-3 Subj: Format, unusual – toy and movable books. Trains.

Marston, Elsa. *Cynthia and the runaway gazebo* ill. by Friso henstra. Tambourine, 1992. ISBN 0-688-10283-2 Subj: Boats, ships. Pirates. Sea and seashore.

The fox maiden ill. by Tatsuro Kiuchi. Simon & Schuster, 1996. ISBN 0-689-80107-6 Subj: Animals – foxes. Folk and fairy tales. Foreign lands – Japan. Magic.

A griffin in the garden ill. by Larry Daste. Tambourine, 1993. ISBN 0-688-10982-9 Subj: Gardens, gardening. Mythical creatures – griffins. Rocks.

Marston, Hope Irvin. *Big rigs* ill. with photos. Dodd, 1979. ISBN 0-396-07785-4 Subj: Transportation. Trucks.

Fire trucks ill. with photos. Dodd, 1984. ISBN 0-396-08451-6 Subj: Careers – firefighters. Trucks.

Martchenko, Michael. *Bird feeder banquet* ill. by author. Firefly, 1990. ISBN 1-55037-147-9 Subj: Birds. Character traits – assertiveness. Character traits – kindness to animals. Food. Seasons – winter.

Martel, Cruz. *Yagua days* ill. by Jerry Pinkney. Dial, 1976. ISBN 0-8037-9766-4 Subj: Family life. Foreign lands – Puerto Rico.

Martens, Marianne. *Bernard Bear's amazing adventure* (De Beer, Hans)

Evie to the rescue! (Moers, Hermann)

Katie and the big, brave bear (Moers, Hermann)

Milo and the magical stones (Pfister, Marcus)

Smoky's special Easter present (Lachner, Dorothea)

Martin, Ann M. *Fire truck to the rescue* ill. by Steven James Petruccio. Scholastic, 1994. ISBN 0-590-48854-6 Subj: Careers – firefighters. Trucks.

Leo the Magnificat ill. by Emily Arnold McCully. Scholastic, 1996. ISBN 0-590-48498-2 Subj: Animals – cats. Homeless. Religion.

Rachel Parker, kindergarten show-off ill. by Nancy Poydar. Holiday, 1992. ISBN 0-8234-0935-X Subj: Character traits – conceit. Emotions – envy, jealousy. Ethnic groups in the U.S. – African Americans. Friendship. School.

Martin, Antoinette Truglio. *Famous seaweed soup* ill. by Nadine Bernard Westcott. Albert Whitman, 1993. ISBN 0-8075-2263-5 Subj: Character traits – laziness. Food. Sea and seashore.

Martin, Bernard H. *Brave little Indian* (Martin, Bill [William Ivan])

Chicken Chuck (Martin, Bill [William Ivan])

Smoky Poky (Martin, Bill [William Ivan])

Martin, Bill (William Ivan). *Adam, Adam, what do you see?* by Bill Martin, Jr. and Michael Sampson; ill. by Cathie Felstead. Nelson, 2000. ISBN 0-8499-7614-6 Subj: Religion. Rhyming text.

Barn dance! ill. by Ted Rand. Holt, 1986. ISBN 0-8050-0089-5 Subj: Activities – dancing. Barns. Country. Dreams. Night. Rhyming text. Scarecrows.

A beasty story by Bill Martin, Jr. and Steven Kellogg; ill. by Steven Kellogg. Harcourt, 1999. ISBN 0-15-201683-X Subj: Animals – mice. Forest, woods. Monsters.

A beautiful feast for a big king cat (Archambault, John)

Brave little Indian by Bill Martin, Jr. and Bernard H. Martin; ill. by Bernard H. Martin. Holt, 1967, c1951. Subj: Indians of North America. Participation.

Brown bear, brown bear, what do you see? ill. by Eric Carle. Holt, 1992. ISBN 0-8050-1744-5 Subj: Animals – bears. Concepts – color. Cumulative tales. Rhyming text.

Chicka chicka boom boom by Bill Martin, Jr. and John Archambault; ill. by Lois Ehlert. Simon & Schuster, 1989. ISBN 0-617-67949-X Subj: ABC books. Rhyming text. Trees.

Chicka chicka sticka sticka: an ABC sticker book by Bill Martin, Jr. and John Archambault; ill. by Lois Ehlert. Little Simon, 1995. ISBN 0-689-80096-7 Subj: ABC books. Format, unusual – toy and movable books. Rhyming text. Trees.

Chicken Chuck by Bill Martin, Jr. and Bernard H. Martin; ill. by Steven Salerno. Winslow, 2000. ISBN 1-8908-1731-7 Subj: Animals. Animals – horses, ponies. Birds – chickens. Character traits – individuality. Circus. Farms.

Fire! Fire! said Mrs. McGuire ill. by Richard Egielski. Harcourt, 1996. ISBN 0-15-227562-2 Subj: Birthdays. Careers – firefighters. Fire. Nursery rhymes.

The happy hippopotami ill. by Betsy Everitt. Harcourt, 1990, c1970. ISBN 0-15-233380-0 Subj: Animals – hippopotamuses. Rhyming text.

Here are my hands by Bill Martin, Jr. and John Archambault; ill. by Ted Rand. Holt, 1998. ISBN 0-8050-5911-3 Subj: Anatomy. Rhyming text.

Knots on a counting rope by Bill Martin, Jr. and John Archambault; ill. by Ted Rand. Holt, 1987. ISBN 0-8050-0571-4 Subj: Character traits – bravery. Emotions – love. Family life – grandfathers. Handicaps – blindness. Indians of North America. Senses – seeing.

Listen to the rain by Bill Martin, Jr. and John Archambault; ill. by James R. Endicott. Holt, 1988. ISBN 0-8050-0682-6 Subj: Rhyming text. Weather – rain.

The little squeegy bug by Bill Martin, Jr. and Michael Sampson; ill. by Pat Corrigan. Winslow, 2001. ISBN 1-8908-1790-2 Subj: Insects.

Maestro plays ill. by Vladimir Radunsky. Holt, 1994. ISBN 0-8050-1746-1 Subj: Careers – musicians. Rhyming text.

The magic pumpkin by Bill Martin, Jr. and John Archambault; ill. by Robert J. Lee. Holt, 1989. ISBN 0-8050-1134-X Subj: Holidays – Halloween. Magic. Rhyming text.

My days are made of butterflies adapt. by William Ivan Martin, Jr.; written by Sano M. Galea'i Fa'apouli; ill. by Vic Herman. Holt, 1970. ISBN 0-030-84599-8 Subj: Foreign lands – Mexico.

Old devil wind ill. by Barry Root. Harcourt, 1993. ISBN 0-15-257768-8 Subj: Cumulative tales. Ghosts. Holidays – Halloween. Weather – wind.

Polar bear, polar bear, what do you hear? ill. by Eric Carle. Holt, 1991. ISBN 0-8050-1759-3 Subj: Animals. Noise, sounds. Rhyming text. Zoos.

Rock it, sock it, number line by Bill Martin, Jr. and Michael Sampson; ill. by Heather Cahoon. Holt, 2001. ISBN 0-8050-6304-8 Subj: Counting, numbers. Food. Parties. Plants. Royalty.

Smoky Poky by Bill Martin, Jr. and Bernard H. Martin; ill. by Bernard H. Martin. Tell-Well Pr., 1947. Subj: Animals – elephants. Trains.

Sounds around the clock comp. by Bill Martin, Jr. in collaboration with Peggy Brogan; ill. by various authors and artists. Holt, 1972. ISBN 0-03-086194-2 Subj: Noise, sounds. Poetry.

Sounds I remember comp. by Bill Martin, Jr. in collaboration with Peggy Brogan; ill. by various artists. Holt, 1974. ISBN 0-03-089259-7 Subj: Counting, numbers. Memories, memory. Noise, sounds. Nursery rhymes.

Sounds of home comp. by Bill Martin, Jr. in collaboration with Peggy Brogan; ill. by various authors and artists. Holt, 1972. ISBN 0-03-083351-5 Subj: Noise, sounds. Poetry.

Sounds of laughter comp. by Bill Martin, Jr. in collaboration with Peggy Brogan; ill. by various artists. Holt, 1972. ISBN 0-03-086195-0 Subj: Folk and fairy tales. Humor. Noise, sounds. Poetry.

Sounds of numbers comp. by Bill Martin, Jr. in collaboration with Peggy Brogan; ill. by various artists. Holt, 1972. ISBN 0-03-086193-4 Subj: Counting, numbers. Noise, sounds. Poetry.

Swish! by Bill Martin, Jr. and Michael Sampson; ill. by Michael Chesworth. Holt, 1997. ISBN 0-8050-4498-1 Subj: Sports – basketball.

The turning of the year ill. by Greg Shed. Harcourt, 1998. ISBN 0-15-201085-8 Subj: Days of the week, months of the year. Rhyming text. Seasons.

Up and down on the merry-go-round by Bill Martin, Jr. and John Archambault; ill. by Ted Rand. Holt, 1988. ISBN 0-8050-0681-8 Subj: Merry-go-rounds.

White Dynamite and Curly Kidd by Bill Martin, Jr. and John Archambault; ill. by Ted Rand. Holt, 1986. ISBN 0-03-008399-0 Subj: Animals – bulls, cows. Family life. Sports.

The wizard ill. by Alex Schaefer. Harcourt, 1994. ISBN 0-15-298926-9 Subj: Magic. Rhyming text. Wizards.

Words by Bill Martin, Jr. and John Archambault; ill. by Lois Ehlert. Little Simon, 1993. ISBN 0-671-87174-9 Subj: Language.

Martin, C. L. G. *The blueberry train* ill. by Angela Trotta Thomas. Atheneum, 1995. ISBN 0-689-80304-4 Subj: Activities – traveling. Behavior – growing up. Family life. Trains. Transportation.

Down Dairy Farm Road ill. by Diane Dawson Hearn. Macmillan, 1994. ISBN 0-02-762450-1 Subj: Animals. Careers – veterinarians. Family life – grandfathers. Farms.

The dragon nanny ill. by Robert Rayevsky. Aladdin, 1991. ISBN 0-689-71451-3 Subj: Activities – babysitting. Dragons. Royalty – kings.

Three brave women ill. by Peter Elwell. Macmillan, 1991. ISBN 0-02-762445-5 Subj: Emotions – fear. Family life – grandmothers. Family life – mothers.

Martin, Charles E. *Dunkel takes a walk* ill. by author. Greenwillow, 1983. ISBN 0-688-01816-5 Subj: Animals – dogs. Character traits – cleverness.

For rent ill. by author. Greenwillow, 1986. ISBN 0-688-05717-9 Subj: Activities – painting. Islands. School. Seasons – summer.

Island rescue ill. by author. Greenwillow, 1985. ISBN 0-688-04258-9 Subj: Hospitals. Islands. Seasons – spring.

Island winter ill. by author. Greenwillow, 1984. ISBN 0-688-02592-7 Subj: Islands. Seasons – winter.

Noah's ark retold by Lawrence T. Lorimer; ill. by Charles E. Martin. Random House, 1978. ISBN 0-394-93861-5 Subj: Boats, ships. Religion – Noah. Weather – floods. Weather – rain. Weather – rainbows.

Sam saves the day ill. by author. Greenwillow, 1987. ISBN 0-688-06815-4 Subj: Activities – traveling. Activities – vacationing. Seasons – summer.

Martin, Claire. *Boots and the glass mountain* ill. by Gennady Spirin. Dial, 1992. ISBN 0-8037-1111-5 Subj: Folk and fairy tales. Foreign lands – Norway. Mythical creatures – trolls. Royalty – princesses.

The race of the golden apples ill. by Leo and Diane Dillon. Dial, 1991. ISBN 0-8037-0249-3 Subj: Animals – bears. Folk and fairy tales. Royalty – princesses.

Martin, David. *Five little piggies* ill. by Susan Meddaugh. Candlewick, 1998. ISBN 1-56402-918-2 Subj: Animals – pigs. Family life. Shopping.

Little Chicken Chicken ill. by Sue Heap. Candlewick, 1996. ISBN 1-56402-381-8 Subj: Birds – chickens. Imagination. Weather – storms. Weather – thunder.

Lizzie and her dolly ill. by Debi Gliori. Candlewick, 1993. ISBN 1-56402-060-6 Subj: Games. Rhyming text. Toys – dolls.

Lizzie and her friend ill. by Debi Gliori. Candlewick, 1993. ISBN 1-56402-061-4 Subj: Activities – playing. Friendship. Rhyming text. Water.

Lizzie and her kitty ill. by Debi Gliori. Candlewick, 1993. ISBN 1-56402-058-4 Subj: Animals – cats. Rhyming text.

Lizzie and her puppy ill. by Debi Gliori. Candlewick, 1993. ISBN 1-56402-059-2 Subj: Activities – playing. Animals – dogs. Rhyming text.

Monkey business ill. by Scott Nash. Candlewick, 2000. ISBN 0-7636-1178-6 Subj: Animals – monkeys. Birthdays. Family life – mothers.

Monkey trouble ill. by Scott Nash. Candlewick, 2000. ISBN 0-7636-1179-4 Subj: Animals – monkeys. Behavior – misbehavior.

Piggy and Dad ill. by Frank Remkiewicz. Candlewick, 2001. ISBN 0-7636-1326-6 Subj: Activities. Animals – pigs. Family life – fathers.

Martin, Diane. *Mister Mole* (Murschetz, Luis)

Martin, Francesca. *Clever Tortoise: a traditional African tale* ill. by author. Candlewick, 2000. ISBN 0-7636-0506-9 Subj: Animals. Folk and fairy tales. Foreign lands – Tanzania. Reptiles – turtles, tortoises.

The honey hunters ill. by reteller. Candlewick, 1992. ISBN 1-56402-086-X Subj: Animals. Behavior – fighting, arguing. Folk and fairy tales. Foreign lands – Africa.

Martin, Jacqueline Briggs. *Bizzy Bones and Moosemouse* ill. by Stella Ormai. Lothrop, 1986. ISBN 0-688-05746-2 Subj: Animals – mice. Behavior – lost. Friendship.

Bizzy Bones and the lost quilt ill. by Stella Ormai. Lothrop, 1988. ISBN 0-688-07408-1 Subj: Animals – mice. Behavior – losing things. Friendship. Quilts.

Bizzy Bones and Uncle Ezra ill. by Stella Ormai. Lothrop, 1984. ISBN 0-688-03782-8 Subj: Animals – mice. Emotions – fear. Family life – aunts, uncles.

Button, bucket, sky ill. by Vicki Jo Redenbaugh. Carolrhoda, 1998. ISBN 1-57505-244-X Subj: Gardens, gardening. Seeds. Trees.

The finest horse in town ill. by Susan Gaber. HarperCollins, 1992. ISBN 0-06-024152-7 Subj: Animals – horses, ponies. Family life – sisters. Memories, memory.

Good times on Grandfather Mountain ill. by Susan Gaber. Watts, 1992. ISBN 0-531-08577-5 Subj: Activities – making things. Character traits – optimism.

Grandmother Bryant's pocket ill. by Petra Mathers. Houghton Mifflin, 1996. ISBN 0-395-68984-8 Subj: Dreams. Emotions – fear. Emotions – grief. Family life – grandparents. Fire. Pets. Sleep.

The green truck garden giveaway: a neighborhood story and almanac ill. by Alec Gillman. Simon & Schuster, 1997. ISBN 0-689-80498-9 Subj: City. Communities, neighborhoods. Gardens, gardening.

Snowflake Bentley ill. by Mary Azarian. Houghton Mifflin, 1998. ISBN 0-395-86162-4 Subj: Caldecott award books. Careers – photographers. Careers – scientists. Nature. U.S. history. Weather – snow.

Washing the willow tree loon ill. by Nancy Carpenter. Simon & Schuster, 1995. ISBN 0-02-762442-0 Subj: Birds – loons. Character traits – kindness to animals. Ecology.

The water gift and the pig of the pig ill. by Linda Wingerter. Houghton Mifflin, 2002. ISBN 0-618-07436-8 Subj: Animals – pigs. Family life – grandfathers. Orphans.

Martin, Jane Read. *Now everybody really hates me* by Jane Read Martin and Patricia Marx; ill. by Roz Chast. HarperCollins, 1993. ISBN 0-06-021294-2 Subj: Behavior – bad day. Character traits – selfishness. Sibling rivalry.

Now I will never leave the dinner table by Jane Read Martin and Patricia Marx; ill. by Roz Chast. HarperCollins, 1996. ISBN 0-06-024795-9 Subj: Behavior – bad day. Sibling rivalry.

Martin, Janet. *see* Allen, Robert

Martin, Jerome. *Carrot/parrot* ill. by author. Simon & Schuster, 1991. ISBN 0-671-69555-X Subj: Format, unusual. Language. Rhyming text.

Mitten/kitten ill. by author. Simon & Schuster, 1991. ISBN 0-671-69556-8 Subj: Format, unusual. Language. Rhyming text.

Martin, Judith. *The tree angel* by Judith Martin and Remy Charlip; ill. by Remy Charlip. Knopf, 1962. ISBN 0-440-40726-7 Subj: Angels. Holidays – Christmas. Theater.

Martin, Linda. *When dinosaurs go to school* ill. by author. Chronicle, 1999. ISBN 0-8118-2089-0 Subj: Dinosaurs. Rhyming text. School.

Martin, Mary Jane. *From Anne to Zach* ill. by Michael Grejniec. Boyds Mills, 1996. ISBN 1-56397-573-4 Subj: ABC books. Names. Rhyming text.

Martin, Nora. *The stone dancers* ill. by Jill Kastner. Atheneum, 1995. ISBN 0-689-80312-5 Subj: Activities – dancing. Character traits – kindness.

Martin, Patricia Miles. *see* Miles, Miska

Martin, Rafe. *The eagle's gift* ill. by Tatsuro Kiuchi. Putnam, 1997. ISBN 0-399-22923-X Subj: Alaska. Birds – eagles. Eskimos. Folk and fairy tales. Indians of North America – Inuit.

Foolish rabbit's big mistake ill. by Ed Young. Putnam, 1985. ISBN 0-399-21178-0 Subj: Animals – rabbits. Behavior – mistakes. Folk and fairy tales.

The hungry tigress: and other traditional Asian tales ill. by Richard Wehrman. Shambhala, 1984. ISBN 0-394-53698-3 Subj: Folk and fairy tales.

The monkey bridge ill. by Fahimeh Amiri. Knopf, 1997. ISBN 0-679-98106-3 Subj: Animals – monkeys. Character traits – bravery. Foreign lands – India. Royalty – kings.

The rough-face girl ill. by David Shannon. Putnam, 1992. ISBN 0-399-21859-9 Subj: Family life – sisters. Folk and fairy tales. Indians of North America – Algonquian.

Will's mammoth ill. by Stephen Grammell. Putnam, 1989. ISBN 0-399-21627-8 Subj: Animals. Imagination.

Martin, Sarah Catherine. *The comic adventures of Old Mother Hubbard and her dog* ill. by Arnold Lobel. Bradbury, 1968. Subj: Animals – dogs. Nursery rhymes.

Old Mother Hubbard adapt. by Colin and Jacqui Hawkins; ill. by Colin Hawkins. Putnam, 1985. ISBN 0-399-21162-4 Subj: Animals – dogs. Format, unusual – toy and movable books. Nursery rhymes.

Old Mother Hubbard and her dog ill. by Lisa Amoroso. Knopf, 1987. ISBN 0-394-98922-8 Subj: Animals – dogs. Nursery rhymes.

Old Mother Hubbard and her dog ill. by Paul Galdone. McGraw-Hill, 1960. Subj: Animals – dogs. Nursery rhymes.

Old Mother Hubbard and her dog ill. by Evaline Ness. Holt, 1972. ISBN 0-03-091360-8 Subj: Animals – dogs. Nursery rhymes.

Old Mother Hubbard and her wonderful dog ill. by James Marshall. Farrar, 1991. ISBN 0-374-35621-1 Subj: Animals – dogs. Nursery rhymes.

Martinez, Alba Nora. *Delicious hullabaloo = Pachanga deliciosa* (Mora, Pat)

Martinez, Ruth. *Mrs. McDockerty's knitting* ill. by Catherine O'Neill. Houghton Mifflin, 1990. ISBN 0-395-51591-2 Subj: Activities – knitting. Animals – cats. Animals – dogs. Animals – pigs. Cumulative tales. Problem solving.

Martín Larrañaga, Ana. *The big wide-mouthed frog* ill. by author. Candlewick, 1999. ISBN 0-7636-0807-6 Subj: Frogs and toads. Self-concept.

Woo! ill. by author. Levine, 2000. ISBN 0-439-16958-5 Subj: Behavior – running away. Ghosts.

Marton, Jirina. *Flowers for mom* ill. by author. Firefly, 1991. ISBN 1-55037-155-X Subj: Behavior – bullying. Character traits – generosity. Flowers.

I'll do it myself ill. by author. Firefly, 1989. ISBN 1-55037-063-4 Subj: Dreams. Family life – mothers. Hair.

Midnight visit at Molly's house ill. by author. Firefly, 1988. ISBN 0-920303-99-4 Subj: Dreams. Moon. Night.

Marx, Patricia (Patricia A.). *Meet my staff* ill. by Roz Chast. HarperCollins, 1998. ISBN 0-06-027485-9 Subj: Imagination – imaginary friends.

Now everybody really hates me (Martin, Jane Read)

Now I will never leave the dinner table (Martin, Jane Read)

Marzollo, Claudio. *Jed and the space bandits* (Marzollo, Jean)

Jed's junior space patrol (Marzollo, Jean)

Marzollo, Jean. *Amy goes fishing* ill. by Ann Schweninger. Dial, 1980. ISBN 0-8037-0109-8 Subj: Family life – fathers. Sports – fishing.

Christmas cats ill. by Hans Wilhelm. Scholastic, 1997. ISBN 0-590-37212-2 Subj: Animals – cats. Holidays – Christmas. Rhyming text.

Close your eyes ill. by Susan Jeffers. Dial, 1978. ISBN 0-8037-1610-9 Subj: Bedtime. Family life – fathers. Lullabies.

Do you know new? ill. by Mari Takabayashi. HarperCollins, 1997. ISBN 0-694-00870-2 Subj: Babies. Format, unusual – board books. Rhyming text.

Home sweet home ill. by Ashley Wolff. HarperCollins, 1997. ISBN 0-06-027353-4 Subj: Animals. Homes, houses. Nature. Rhyming text.

I love you: a rebus poem ill. by Suse MacDonald. Scholastic, 2000. ISBN 0-590-37656-X Subj: Concepts. Emotions – love. Poetry. Rebuses.

I spy Christmas: a book of picture riddles (Wick, Walter)

I spy extreme challenger: a book of picture riddles (Wick, Walter)

I spy fantasy: a book of picture riddles (Wick, Walter)

I spy gold challenger! a book of picture riddles (Wick, Walter)

I spy little animals photos by Walter Wick. Scholastic, 1998. ISBN 0-590-11711-4 Subj: Animals. Format, unusual – board books. Picture puzzles. Rhyming text.

I spy little book photos by Walter Wick. Scholastic, 1997. ISBN 0-590-34129-4 Subj: Format, unusual – board books. Picture puzzles. Rhyming text.

I spy little Christmas photos by Walter Wick. Scholastic, 1999. ISBN 0-439-08331-1 Subj: Holidays – Christmas. Picture puzzles. Rhyming text.

I spy little letters photos by Walter Wick. Scholastic, 2000. ISBN 0-439-11496-9 Subj: ABC books. Picture puzzles. Rhyming text.

I spy little numbers photos by Walter Wick. Scholastic, 1999. ISBN 0-590-68714-X Subj: Counting, numbers. Picture puzzles. Rhyming text.

I spy little wheels photos by Walter Wick. Scholastic, 1998. ISBN 0-590-04706-X Subj: Format, unusual – board books. Picture puzzles. Rhyming text. Toys.

I spy, mystery photos by Walter Wick. Scholastic, 1993. ISBN 0-590-46294-6 Subj: Picture puzzles. Rhyming text. Riddles.

I spy school days (Wick, Walter)

I spy spooky night: a book of picture riddles (Wick, Walter)

I spy super challenger! (Wick, Walter)

I spy treasure hunt (Wick, Walter)

I'm a caterpillar ill. by Judith Moffatt. Scholastic, 1997. ISBN 0-590-84779-1 Subj: Insects – butterflies, caterpillars. Metamorphosis. Science.

I'm a seed ill. by Judith Moffatt. Scholastic, 1996. ISBN 0-590-26586-5 Subj: Flowers. Plants. Seeds.

Jed and the space bandits by Jean and Claudio Marzollo; ill. by Peter Sis. Dial, 1987. ISBN 0-8037-0136-5 Subj: Crime. Pets. Robots. Space and space ships.

Jed's junior space patrol by Jean and Claudio Marzollo; ill. by David S. Rose. Dial, 1982. ISBN 0-8037-4288-6 Subj: Robots. Space and space ships. Toys – bears.

Mama, Mama ill. by Laura Regan. HarperFestival, 1999. ISBN 0-694-01245-9 Subj: Animals. Family life – mothers. Format, unusual – board books. Rhyming text.

Papa, papa ill. by Simone Kaplan. HarperFestival, 2000. ISBN 0-694-01246-7 Subj: Animals. Family life – fathers. Format, unusual – board books. Rhyming text.

Pretend you're a cat ill. by Jerry Pinkney. Dial, 1990. ISBN 0-8037-0774-6 Subj: Animals. Behavior – imitation. Imagination. Rhyming text.

The rebus treasury ill. by Carol D. Carson. Dial, 1986. ISBN 0-8037-0255-8 Subj: Nursery rhymes. Rebuses.

The silver bear ill. by Susan Meddaugh. Dial, 1987. ISBN 0-8037-0369-4 Subj: Imagination.

Snow angel ill. by Jacqueline Rogers. Scholastic, 1995. ISBN 0-590-48748-5 Subj: Angels. Behavior – lost. Weather – snow.

Sun song ill. by Laura Regan. HarperCollins, 1995. ISBN 0-06-020788-4 Subj: Animals. Plants. Rhyming text. Sun.

The teddy bear book ill. by Ann Schweninger. Dial, 1989. ISBN 0-8037-0632-4 Subj: Poetry. Toys – bears.

Ten cats have hats: a counting book ill. by David McPhail. Scholastic, 1994. ISBN 0-590-46968-1 Subj: Animals. Counting, numbers. Rhyming text.

Thanksgiving cats ill. by Hans Wilhelm. Scholastic, 1999. ISBN 0-590-03714-5 Subj: Animals – cats. Holidays – Thanksgiving. Rhyming text.

The three little kittens (Mother Goose)

Uproar on Hollercat Hill ill. by Steven Kellogg. Dial, 1980. ISBN 0-8037-9028-7 Subj: Animals – cats. Behavior – misbehavior. Rhyming text.

Valentine cats ill. by Hans Wilhelm. Scholastic, 1996. ISBN 0-590-47596-7 Subj: Animals – cats. Holidays – Valentine's Day. Rhyming text.

Welcome to the Shanna show ill. by Shane Evans. Hyperion, 2001. ISBN 0-7868-2549-9 Subj: Rhyming text. Royalty – princesses.

What's the matter with Mother Goose? ill. by Irene Trivas. HarperCollins, 2000. ISBN 0-06-027277-5 Subj: Accidents. Animals. Rhyming text.

Maschler, Fay. *T. G. and Moonie go shopping* ill. by Sylvie Selig. Doubleday, 1978. ISBN 0-385-14148-3 Subj: Animals – cats. Birds – owls. Shopping. Stores.

T. G. and Moonie have a baby ill. by Sylvie Selig. Doubleday, 1979. ISBN 0-385-15333-3 Subj: Animals – cats. Birds – owls. Family life.

T. G. and Moonie move out of town ill. by Sylvia Selig. Doubleday, 1978. ISBN 0-395-14146-7 Subj: Animals – cats. Birds – owls. Moving.

Masks and puppets ill. by Louise Nevett. Watts, 1984. ISBN 0-531-04771-7 Subj: Activities. Masks. Puppets.

Mason, Ann Maree. *The weird things in Nanna's house* ill. by Cathy Wilcox. Watts, 1992. ISBN 0-531-08570-8 Subj: Family life – grandmothers. Homes, houses.

Mason, Jane B. *The flying horse: the story of Pegasus* ill. by Susan Swan. Grosset, 1999. ISBN 0-448-42051-1 Subj: Folk and fairy tales. Foreign lands – Greece. Monsters. Mythical creatures – Pegasus.

Hello, two-wheeler! ill. by David Monteith. Grosset, 1995. ISBN 0-448-40854-6 Subj: Behavior – growing up. Sports – bicycling.

River day ill. by Henri Sorensen. Macmillan, 1994. ISBN 0-02-762869-8 Subj: Birds – eagles. Canoes and canoeing. Family life – grandfathers.

The shadow stealer ill. by Aristides Ruiz. Scholastic, 1996. ISBN 0-590-50205-0 Subj: Mystery stories.

The wee puppy who wouldn't go to sleep ill. by Karen Lee Schmidt. Grosset, 1995. ISBN 0-448-40485-0 Subj: Animals – dogs. Bedtime.

Mason, Lura. *A book of boxes* ill. by author. Simon & Schuster, 1989. ISBN 0-671-67801-9 Subj: Format, unusual – toy and movable books. Holidays.

Massey, Ed. *Milton* ill. by Kristy Chu. RDR/Wetlands, 1996. ISBN 1-57143-047-4 Subj: Art. Imagination.

Massey, Jeanne. *The littlest witch* ill. by Adrienne Adams. Knopf, 1959. Subj: Holidays – Halloween. Witches.

Massie, Diane Redfield. *The baby beebee bird* ill. by author. HarperCollins, 1963. Subj: Animals. Birds. Noise, sounds. Sleep.

Cockle stew and other rhymes ill. by author. Atheneum, 1967. Subj: Poetry.

Tiny pin ill. by author. HarperCollins, 1964. Subj: Animals – porcupines. Behavior – growing up. Poetry.

Walter was a frog ill. by author. Simon & Schuster, 1970. ISBN 0-671-65158-7 Subj: Behavior – dissatisfaction. Frogs and toads.

Massie, Elizabeth. *Jambo, watoto!* (Heatwole, Marsha)

Masurel, Claire. *Christmas is coming* ill. by Marie H. Henry. Chronicle, 1998. ISBN 0-8118-2106-4 Subj: Behavior – sharing. Holidays – Christmas. Toys.

No, no, Titus! ill. by Shari Halpern. North-South, 1999. ISBN 1-55858-726-8 Subj: Animals – dogs. Behavior. Farms.

Ten dogs in the window ill. by Pamela Paparone. North-South, 1997. ISBN 1-55858-755-1 Subj: Animals – dogs. Counting, numbers. Pets. Rhyming text.

Too big! ill. by Hanako Wakiyama. Chronicle, 1999. ISBN 0-8118-2090-4 Subj: Concepts – size. Dinosaurs. Toys.

Mathers, Petra. *A cake for Herbie* ill. by author. Atheneum, 2000. ISBN 0-689-83017-3 Subj: Animals. Birds – ducks. Contests. Poetry.

Dodo gets married ill. by author. Atheneum, 2001. ISBN 0-689-83018-1 Subj: Birds – dodos. Weddings.

Lottie's new beach towel ill. by author. Atheneum, 1998. ISBN 0-689-81606-5 Subj: Birds – chickens. Character traits – cleverness. Gifts. Sea and seashore.

Lottie's new friend ill. by author. Atheneum, 1999. ISBN 0-689-82014-3 Subj: Birds. Emotions – envy, jealousy. Friendship.

Maria Theresa ill. by author. HarperCollins, 1992. ISBN 0-06-443282-3 Subj: Birds – chickens. City.

Sophie and Lou ill. by author. HarperCollins, 1991. ISBN 0-06-024072-5 Subj: Activities – dancing. Animals – mice. Character traits – shyness.

Theodor and Mr. Balbini ill. by author. HarperCollins, 1988. ISBN 0-06-024144-6 Subj: Animals – dogs. Pets.

Mathews, Judith. *An egg and seven socks* ill. by Marylin Hafner. HarperCollins, 1993. ISBN 0-06-020208-4 Subj: Clothing – socks. Dragons. Family life – sisters.

Nathaniel Willy, scared silly retold by Judith Mathews and Fay Robinson; ill. by Alexi Natchev. Bradbury, 1994. ISBN 0-02-765285-8 Subj: Animals. Bedtime. Emotions – fear. Family life – grandmothers. Folk and fairy tales. Rhyming text.

There's nothing to d-o-o-o! ill. by Kurt Cyrus. Harcourt, 1999. ISBN 0-15-201647-3 Subj: Animals – bulls, cows. Behavior – lost.

Tuti, Blue Horse, and the Nipnope Man ill. by Daniel Powers. Albert Whitman, 1993. ISBN 0-8075-8130-5 Subj: Behavior – lost. Toys.

Mathews, Louise. *Bunches and bunches of bunnies* ill. by Jeni Bassett. Dodd, 1978. ISBN 0-396-07601-7 Subj: Animals – rabbits. Counting, numbers. Rhyming text.

Cluck one ill. by Jeni Bassett. Dodd, 1982. ISBN 0-396-08029-4 Subj: Animals – weasels. Birds – chickens. Counting, numbers. Eggs.

The great take-away ill. by Jeni Bassett. Dodd, 1980. ISBN 0-396-07846-X Subj: Animals – pigs. Character traits – laziness. Counting, numbers. Crime.

Mathias, Beverly. *Reader's Digest children's book of poetry* (Reader's Digest children's book of poetry)

Mathiesen, Egon. *Oswald, the monkey* adapt. from Danish by Nancy and Edward Maze; ill. by author. Astor-Honor, 1959. Subj: Animals – monkeys.

Mathis, Melissa Bay. *Animal house* ill. by author. Simon & Schuster, 1999. ISBN 0-689-81594-8 Subj: Animals. Homes, houses. Rhyming text. Trees.

Matje, Martin. *Celeste: a day in the park* ill. by author. Simon & Schuster, 1999. ISBN 0-689-82100-X Subj: Activities – picnicking. Birds – ducks. Parks. Toys – bears.

Matsui, Susan. *The bears' autumn* (Tejima, Keizaburo)

The sea and I (Nakawatari, Harutaka)

Matsuno, Masako. *A pair of red clogs* ill. by Kazue Mizumura. Philomel, 1981, c1960. ISBN 0-399-20796-1 Subj: Character traits – honesty. Clothing – shoes. Foreign lands – Japan.

Taro and the bamboo shoot: a Japanese tale ill. by Yasuo Segawa; adapt. from the Japanese by Alice Low. Pantheon, 1964. ISBN 0-394-91727-8 Subj: Folk and fairy tales. Foreign lands – Japan.

Taro and the Tofu ill. by Kazue Mizumura. Collins-World, 1962. Subj: Character traits – honesty. Foreign lands – Japan.

Matsutani, Miyoko. *The fisherman under the sea* English version by Alvin Tresselt; ill. by Chihiro Iwasaki. Parents, 1969. Translation of Urashima Tarō. Subj: Careers – fishermen. Folk and fairy tales. Foreign lands – Japan. Reptiles – turtles, tortoises. Royalty. Sea and seashore.

How the withered trees blossomed ill. by Yasuo Segawa. Lippincott, 1969. Subj: Behavior – greed. Foreign lands – Japan. Foreign languages.

The witch's magic cloth English version by Alvin Tresselt; ill. by Yasuo Segawa. Parents, 1969. Subj: Character traits – bravery. Folk and fairy tales. Foreign lands – Japan. Witches.

Mattern, Joanne. *Safety at school* ill. by author. ABCO Pub., 1999. ISBN 1-57765-070-0 Subj: Safety. School.

Safety in public places ill. by author. ABCO Pub., 1999. ISBN 1-57765-074-3 Subj: Accidents. Safety.

Safety in the water ill. by author. ABCO Pub., 1999. ISBN 1-57765-072-7 Subj: Safety. Sports – swimming. Water.

Matthews, Caitlin. *The blessing seed: a creation myth for the new millennium* ill. by Alison Dexter. Barefoot, 1998. ISBN 1-901223-28-0 Subj: Creation. Religion.

Matthews, Wendy. *The gift of a traveler* ill. by Robert Van Nutt. BridgeWater, 1995. ISBN 0-8167-3656-1 Subj: Family life – great-grandparents. Foreign lands – Romania. Holidays – Christmas.

Matthias, Catherine. *Arriba y abajo: Over and under* trans. from English by Lada Josefa Kratky; ill. by Gene Sharp. Childrens Pr., 1989. ISBN 0-516-32048-3 Subj: Concepts. Foreign languages.

Demasiados globos: Too many balloons trans. from English by Lada Josefa Kratky; ill. by Gene Sharp. Childrens Pr., 1989. ISBN 0-516-33633-9 Subj: Foreign languages. Toys – balloons.

I can be a computer operator ill. with photos. Childrens Pr., 1985. ISBN 0-516-01838-8 Subj: Careers. Computers.

I love cats ill. by Tom Dunnington. Childrens Pr., 1983. ISBN 0-516-02041-2 Subj: Animals – cats.

Out the door ill. by Eileen Mueller Neill. Childrens Pr., 1982. ISBN 0-516-03560-6 Subj: Buses. School.

Over-under ill. by Gene Sharp. Childrens Pr., 1984. ISBN 0-516-02048-X Subj: Concepts – opposites.

Sal y entra: Out the door trans. from English by Lada Josefa Kratky; ill. by Eileen Mueller Neill. Childrens Pr., 1989. ISBN 0-516-33560-X Subj: Concepts – in and out. Concepts – up and down. Foreign languages.

Too many balloons ill. by Gene Sharp. Childrens Pr., 1982. ISBN 0-516-03633-5 Subj: Counting, numbers. Toys – balloons. Zoos.

Matthiesen, Thomas. *Things to see: a child's world of familiar objects* photos by author. Platt, 1968. ISBN 0-448-41051-6 Subj: Concepts. Senses – seeing.

Mattingley, Christobel. *The angel with a mouth-organ* ill. by Astra Lacis. Holiday, 1984. ISBN 0-8234-0593-1 Subj: Death. Holidays – Christmas. War.

Matunis, Joe. *This home we have made* (Hammond, Anna)

Matura, Mustapha. *Moon jump* ill. by Jane Gifford. Knopf, 1988. ISBN 0-394-91976-9 Subj: Bedtime. Imagination. Moon.

Matus, Greta. *Where are you, Jason?* ill. by author. Lothrop, 1974. ISBN 0-688-51584-3 Subj: Behavior – hiding. Imagination. Night.

Matze, Claire Sidhom. *The stars in my Geddoh's sky* ill. by Bill Farnsworth. Albert Whitman, 1999. ISBN 0-8075-5332-8 Subj: Family life – grandfathers. Foreign lands – Middle East.

Maugham, W. Somerset (William Somerset). *Princess September and the nightingale* ill. by Richard C. Jones. Oxford Univ. Pr., 1998. ISBN 0-19-512480-4 Subj: Birds – nightingales. Character traits – freedom. Folk and fairy tales. Foreign lands – Thailand. Royalty – princesses.

Maupassant, Guy de. *When chickens grow teeth: a story from the French of Guy de Maupassant* (Halperin, Wendy Anderson)

Maurer-Mathison, Diane V. *Make your own spectacular Valentines* photos by Michael Grand. Little, 1995. ISBN 0-316-45447-0 Subj: Activities – making things. Holidays – Valentine's Day.

Maury, Inez. *My mother the mail carrier: Mi mama la cartera* trans. by Norah E. Alemany; ill. by Tasha Tudor. Feminist Pr., 1976. ISBN 0-91267-023-1 Subj: Careers – postal workers. Foreign languages. Post office.

Mauver, Judy A. *Dusty wants to help* (Sandberg, Inger)

Mavor, Salley. *You and me: poems of friendship* (You and me)

Mawdsley, Ruth. *My first pop-up book of dinosaurs* (Bishop, Roma)

My first pop-up book of prehistoric animals (Bishop, Roma)

Maxfield, Christine. *Christmas in Water Village* ill. by Jean Colquhoun. Prima Design, 1989. ISBN 0-9621029-0-3 Subj: Holidays – Christmas. U.S. history.

Maxner, Joyce. *Lady Bugatti* ill. by Kevin Hawkes. Lothrop, 1991. ISBN 0-688-10341-3 Subj: Insects. Parties. Rhyming text.

Nicholas Cricket ill. by William Joyce. HarperCollins, 1989. ISBN 0-06-024222-1 Subj: Animals. Insects – crickets. Music. Rhyming text.

May, Charles Paul. *High-noon rocket* ill. by Brinton Turkle. Holiday, 1966. Subj: Activities – traveling. Science. Space and space ships. Time.

May, Daryl. *Rachael's splendifilous adventure* (Bansemer, Roger)

May, Julian. *Why people are different colors* ill. by Symeon Shimin. Holiday, 1971. ISBN 0-8234-0180-4 Subj: Ethnic groups in the U.S.

May, Kara. *Big brave brother Ben* ill. by Gus Clarke. Lothrop, 1992. ISBN 0-688-11235-8 Subj: Behavior – boasting. Character traits – bravery. Family life – brothers and sisters.

Creepy crawly caterpillar ill. by Emily Bolam. Doubleday, 1995. ISBN 0-385-32166-X Subj: Behavior – dissatisfaction. Insects – butterflies, caterpillars. Metamorphosis.

May, Robert Lewis. *Rudolph the red-nosed reindeer* ill. by Diana Magnuson. Four Winds, 1980. ISBN 0-

695-81471-0 Subj: Animals – reindeer. Holidays – Christmas. Mythical creatures – elves. Santa Claus. Weather – fog.

Mayer, Gina. *This is my family* ill. by Mercer Mayer. Western, 1992. ISBN 0-307-00137-7 Subj: Family life.

Mayer, Marianna. *Alley oop!* ill. by Gerald McDermott. Holt, 1985. ISBN 0-03-070496-0 Subj: Animals – mice. Counting, numbers. Reptiles – alligators, crocodiles.

Baba Yaga and Vasilisa the Brave ill. by K. Y. Craft. Morrow, 1994. ISBN 0-688-08501-6 Subj: Folk and fairy tales. Foreign lands – Russia. Royalty. Toys – dolls. Witches.

Beauty and the beast ill. by Mercer Mayer. SeaStar, 2000. ISBN 1-58717-018-3 Subj: Animals. Character traits – appearance. Character traits – loyalty. Emotions – love. Folk and fairy tales. Magic.

The black horse ill. by Katie Thamer. Dial, 1984. ISBN 0-8037-0076-8 Subj: Animals – horses, ponies. Behavior – trickery. Folk and fairy tales. Magic. Royalty.

The Brambleberrys animal alphabet ill. by Gerald McDermott. Boyds Mills, 1991. ISBN 1-878093-78-9 Subj: ABC books. Animals.

The Brambleberrys animal book of big and small shapes ill. by Gerald McDermott. Boyds Mills, 1991. ISBN 1-878093-77-0 Subj: Animals. Concepts – shape. Concepts – size.

The Brambleberrys animal book of colors by Marianna Mayer and Gerald McDermott; ill. by Gerald McDermott. St. Martin's, 1991. ISBN 1-8780-9376-2 Subj: Animals. Animals – pandas. Concepts – color.

The Brambleberrys animal book of counting ill. by Gerald McDermott. Boyds Mills, 1991. ISBN 1-878093-75-4 Subj: Animals. Counting, numbers.

Iron John (Grimm, Jacob)

The little jewel box ill. by Margot Tomes. Dial, 1986. ISBN 0-8037-0149-7 Subj: Animals. Birds. Character traits – kindness. Character traits – luck. Folk and fairy tales. Magic.

Marcel the pastry chef ill. by Gerald McDermott. Bantam, 1991. ISBN 0-553-05192-X Subj: Activities – cooking. Animals – hippopotamuses. Careers – bakers. Royalty – kings. Weddings.

Mine! (Mayer, Mercer)

My first book of nursery tales: five favorite bedtime tales ill. by William Joyce. Random House, 1983. ISBN 0-394-95396-7 Subj: Folk and fairy tales.

One frog too many (Mayer, Mercer)

Pegasus ill. by K. Y. Craft. Morrow, 1998. ISBN 0-688-13382-7 Subj: Folk and fairy tales. Foreign lands – Greece. Monsters. Mythical creatures – Pegasus.

Perseus ill. by Joel Spector. Fogelman, 2002. ISBN 0-8037-2619-8 Subj: Folk and fairy tales. Foreign lands – Greece. Religion.

The prince and the pauper adapt. by Marianna Mayer from the Mark Twain novel; ill. by Gary A. Lippincott. Dial, 1999. ISBN 0-8037-2099-8 Subj: Behavior – growing up. Behavior – misunderstanding. Character traits – individuality. Royalty – kings.

Rapunzel (Grimm, Jacob)

The spirit of the blue light ill. by Gerald McDermott. Macmillan, 1990. ISBN 0-02-765350-1 Subj: Behavior – wishing. Folk and fairy tales. Foreign lands – Germany. Magic. Royalty.

The twelve dancing princesses (Grimm, Jacob)

The ugly duckling (Andersen, H. C. [Hans Christian])

The unicorn alphabet ill. by Michael Hague. Dial, 1989. ISBN 0-8037-0373-2 Subj: ABC books. Mythical creatures – unicorns.

The unicorn and the lake ill. by Michael Hague. Dial, 1982. ISBN 0-8037-9338-3 Subj: Character traits – bravery. Mythical creatures – unicorns.

Mayer, Mercer. *Ah-choo* ill. by author. Dial, 1976. ISBN 0-8037-4895-7 Subj: Animals – elephants. Illness. Wordless.

Appelard and Liverwurst ill. by Steven Kellogg. Four Winds, 1978. ISBN 0-590-07506-3 Subj: Animals. Behavior – misbehavior. Farms.

Astronaut critter ill. by author. Simon & Schuster, 1986. ISBN 0-671-61142-9 Subj: Format, unusual – board books. Space and space ships.

A boy, a dog, a frog and a friend ill. by author. Dial, 1971. ISBN 0-8037-0755-X Subj: Animals – dogs. Friendship. Frogs and toads. Sports – fishing. Wordless.

A boy, a dog and a frog ill. by author. Dial, 1967. ISBN 0-8037-0767-3 Subj: Animals – dogs. Friendship. Frogs and toads. Sports – fishing. Wordless.

Bubble bubble ill. by author. Four Winds, 1980, c1973. ISBN 0-590-07759-7 Subj: Bubbles. Imagination. Wordless.

Cowboy critter ill. by author. Simon & Schuster, 1986. ISBN 0-671-61141-0 Subj: Cowboys. Format, unusual – board books.

Fireman critter ill. by author. Simon & Schuster, 1986. ISBN 0-671-61143-7 Subj: Careers – firefighters. Format, unusual – board books.

Frog goes to dinner ill. by author. Dial, 1974. ISBN 0-8037-3381-X Subj: Food. Frogs and toads. Wordless.

Frog on his own ill. by author. Dial, 1973. ISBN 0-8037-2695-3 Subj: Frogs and toads. Wordless.

Frog, where are you? ill. by author. Dial, 1969. ISBN 0-8037-2732-1 Subj: Friendship. Frogs and toads. Wordless.

The great cat chase ill. by author. Four Winds, 1974. ISBN 0-590-07400-8 Subj: Animals – cats. Wordless.

Hiccup ill. by author. Dial, 1976. ISBN 0-8037-3592-8 Subj: Animals – hippopotamuses. Illness. Wordless.

How the trollusk got his hat ill. by author. Golden Pr., 1979. ISBN 0-307-13733-3 Subj: Character traits – appearance. Character traits – honesty.

I am a hunter ill. by author. Dial, 1969. Subj: Imagination.

Just for you ill. by author. Golden Pr., 1975. ISBN 0-307-12542-4 Subj: Character traits – helpfulness. Emotions – love. Family life – mothers.

Just me and my dad ill. by author. Golden Pr., 1977. ISBN 0-307-61839-0 Subj: Camps, camping. Family life – fathers.

Little Monster at home ill. by author. Golden Pr., 1978. ISBN 0-307-61846-3 Subj: Homes, houses. Monsters.

Little Monster at school ill. by author. Golden Pr., 1978. ISBN 0-307-11845-2 Subj: Monsters. School.

Little Monster at work ill. by author. Golden Pr., 1978. ISBN 0-307-63736-0 Subj: Careers. Family life – grandfathers. Monsters.

Little Monster's alphabet book ill. by author. Golden Pr., 1978. ISBN 0-307-11847-9 Subj: ABC books. Monsters.

Little Monster's bedtime book ill. by author. Golden Pr., 1978. ISBN 0-307-61848-X Subj: Bedtime. Monsters. Poetry.

Little Monster's counting book ill. by author. Golden Pr., 1978. ISBN 0-307-61844-7 Subj: Counting, numbers. Monsters.

Little Monster's neighborhood ill. by author. Golden Pr., 1978. ISBN 0-307-61849-8 Subj: City. Monsters.

Liverwurst is missing ill. by Steven Kellogg. Four Winds, 1981. ISBN 0-590-07793-7 Subj: Character traits – bravery. Circus. Crime.

Liza Lou and the Yeller Belly Swamp ill. by author. Parents, 1976. ISBN 0-81-930802-1 Subj: Character traits – bravery. Ethnic groups in the U.S. – African Americans. Monsters.

Mine! by Mercer and Marianna Mayer; ill. by Mercer Mayer. Simon & Schuster, 1970. ISBN 0-671-65146-5 Subj: Concepts. Emotions.

Mrs. Beggs and the wizard ill. by author. Parents, 1973. ISBN 0-819-30693-2 Subj: Magic. Monsters. Wizards.

One frog too many by Mercer and Marianna Mayer; ill. by Mercer Mayer. Dial, 1975. ISBN 0-8037-4858-2 Subj: Emotions – envy, jealousy. Frogs and toads. Wordless.

Oops ill. by author. Dial, 1977. ISBN 0-8037-6567-3 Subj: Animals – hippopotamuses. Behavior – carelessness. Wordless.

The pied piper of Hamelin adapt. and ill. by Mercer Mayer. Macmillan, 1987. Adapt. of the poem The pied piper of Hamelin by Robert Browning. ISBN 0-02-765361-7 Subj: Animals – rats. Behavior – trickery. Folk and fairy tales. Foreign lands – Germany.

Policeman critter ill. by author. Simon & Schuster, 1986. ISBN 0-671-61140-2 Subj: Careers – police officers. Format, unusual – board books.

The queen always wanted to dance ill. by author. Simon & Schuster, 1971. ISBN 0-671-65143-9 Subj: Activities – dancing. Humor. Music. Royalty – queens.

Shibumi and the kitemaker ill. by author. Cavendish, 1999. ISBN 0-7614-5054-8 Subj: Family life – fathers. Foreign lands – Japan. Kites. Royalty – emperors. Royalty – princesses.

The sleeping beauty (Grimm, Jacob)

A special trick ill. by author. Dial, 1976. ISBN 0-8037-8103-2 Subj: Magic.

Terrible troll ill. by author. Dial, 1968. ISBN 0-8037-8621-2 Subj: Imagination. Knights. Monsters. Mythical creatures. Mythical creatures – trolls.

There's a nightmare in my closet ill. by author. Dial, 1990. ISBN 0-8037-0843-2 Subj: Bedtime. Emotions – fear. Monsters.

There's an alligator under my bed ill. by author. Dial, 1987. ISBN 0-8037-0375-9 Subj: Bedtime. Emotions – fear. Reptiles – alligators, crocodiles.

There's something in my attic ill. by author. Dial, 1988. ISBN 0-8037-0415-1 Subj: Dreams. Emotions – fear. Night.

Two moral tales ill. by author. Four Winds, 1974. Bear's new clothes / Bird's new hat. ISBN 0-590-07366-4 Subj: Animals – bears. Birds. Clothing. Clothing – hats. Wordless.

What do you do with a kangaroo? ill. by author. Four Winds, 1973. ISBN 0-590-72851-2 Subj: Animals. Humor. Problem solving.

Whinnie the lovesick dragon ill. by Diane Dawson Hearn. Macmillan, 1986. ISBN 0-02-765180-0 Subj: Behavior – needing someone. Dragons. Emotions – love. Magic. Middle Ages.

You're the scaredy cat ill. by author. Parents, 1974. ISBN 0-8193-0763-7 Subj: Camps, camping. Emotions – fear. Night.

Mayers, Florence Cassen. *Egyptian art from the Brooklyn Museum: ABC* designed by Florence Cassen Mayers; ed. by Sheila Franklin. Abrams, 1988. ISBN 0-8109-1888-3 Subj: ABC books. Art. Foreign lands – Egypt. Museums.

The Museum of Fine Arts, Boston: ABC designed by Florence Cassen Mayers; ed. by Sheila Franklin. Abrams, 1986. ISBN 0-8109-1847-1 Subj: ABC books. Art. Museums.

The Museum of Modern Art, New York: ABC designed by Florence Cassen Mayers; ed. by Sheila Franklin. Abrams, 1986. ISBN 0-8109-1849-8 Subj: ABC books. Art. Museums.

The National Air and Space Museum: ABC designed by Florence Cassen Mayers; ed. by Sheila Franklin. Abrams, 1988. ISBN 0-8109-1859-5 Subj: ABC books. Museums. Space and space ships.

Mayers, Patrick. *Just one more block* ill. by Lucy Hawkinson. Albert Whitman, 1970. ISBN 0-8075-4081-1 Subj: Activities – playing. Emotions. Sibling rivalry. Toys – blocks.

Mayhew, James. *Katie and the dinosaurs* ill. by author. Bantam, 1992. ISBN 0-553-08129-2 Subj: Dinosaurs. Museums.

Katie and the Mona Lisa ill. by author. Orchard, 1999. ISBN 0-531-30177-X Subj: Art. Careers – artists. Museums.

Katie meets the Impressionists ill. by author. Orchard, 1999. ISBN 0-531-30151-6 Subj: Art. Careers – artists. Museums.

Mayle, Peter. *Divorce can happen to the nicest people* ill. by Arthur Robins. Macmillan, 1980. ISBN 0-02-582500-3 Subj: Divorce. Family life.

Why are we getting a divorce? ill. by Arthur Robins. Crown, 1988. ISBN 0-517-56527-7 Subj: Divorce. Family life.

Maynard, Bill. *Incredible Ned* ill. by Frank Remkiewicz. Putnam, 1997. ISBN 0-399-23023-8 Subj: Careers – artists. Rhyming text.

Quiet, Wyatt! ill. by Frank Remkiewicz. Putnam, 1999. ISBN 0-399-23217-6 Subj: Language. Noise, sounds. Rhyming text.

Santa's time off ill. by Tom Browning. Putnam, 1997. ISBN 0-399-23138-2 Subj: Activities – vacationing. Rhyming text. Santa Claus.

Maynard, Joyce. *Camp-out* ill. by Steve Bethel. Harcourt, 1985. ISBN 0-15-214077-8 Subj: Camps, camping. Family life.

New house ill. by Steve Bethel. Harcourt, 1987. ISBN 0-15-257042-X Subj: Activities – working. Homes, houses. Trees.

Mayne, William. *Barnabas walks* ill. by Barbara Firth. Prentice-Hall, 1987. ISBN 0-13-057001-X Subj: Animals – guinea pigs. School.

The blue book of Hob stories ill. by Patrick Benson. Putnam, 1984. ISBN 0-399-20137-7 Subj: Character traits – helpfulness. Mythical creatures.

Come, come to my corner ill. by Kenneth Lilly. Prentice-Hall, 1987. ISBN 0-13-152497-6 Subj: Animals. Animals – rabbits.

The green book of Hob stories ill. by Patrick Benore. Putnam, 1984. ISBN 0-399-21039-3 Subj: Character traits – helpfulness. Fairies. Mythical creatures.

A house in town ill. by Sarah Fox-Davies. Prentice-Hall, 1988. ISBN 0-13-395880-9 Subj: Animals – foxes.

Lady Muck ill. by Jonathan Heale. Houghton Mifflin, 1997. ISBN 0-395-75281-7 Subj: Animals – pigs. Behavior – greed.

Mousewing ill. by Martin Baynton. Prentice-Hall, 1988. ISBN 0-13-604240-6 Subj: Animals – mice.

Pandora ill. by Dietlind Blech. Knopf, 1995. ISBN 0-679-94183-5 Subj: Animals – cats. Behavior – running away. Emotions – envy, jealousy.

The patchwork cat ill. by Nicola Bayley. Knopf, 1981. ISBN 0-394-95021-6 Subj: Animals – cats. Behavior – saving things. Emotions – love.

The red book of Hob stories ill. by Patrick Benson. Putnam, 1984. ISBN 0-399-21047-4 Subj: Character traits – helpfulness. Fairies. Mythical creatures.

Tibber ill. by Jonathan Heale. Prentice-Hall, 1987. ISBN 0-13-921214-0 Subj: Animals – cats. Farms.

The yellow book of Hob stories ill. by Patrick Benson. Putnam, 1984. ISBN 0-399-21050-4 Subj: Character traits – helpfulness. Fairies. Mythical creatures.

Mayper, Monica. *After good-night* ill. by Peter Sis. HarperCollins, 1987. ISBN 0-06-024121-7 Subj: Bedtime. Dreams. Family life.

Come and see: a Christmas story ill. by Stacey Schuett. HarperCollins, 1999. ISBN 0-06-023527-6 Subj: Holidays – Christmas. Religion – Nativity.

Oh snow ill. by June Otani. HarperCollins, 1991. ISBN 0-06-024204-3 Subj: Activities – playing. Rhyming text. Weather – snow.

Maze, Edward. *Oswald, the monkey* (Mathiesen, Egon)

Maze, Nancy. *Oswald, the monkey* (Mathiesen, Egon)

Mazer, Anne. *The Fixits* ill. by Paul Meisel. Hyperion, 1998. ISBN 0-7868-2202-3 Subj: Behavior – misbehavior. Careers – handymen. Family life – brothers and sisters. Humor.

The No-Nothings and their baby ill. by Ross Collins. Levine, 2000. ISBN 0-590-68051-X Subj: Babies. Family life. Humor.

The salamander room ill. by Steve Johnson. Knopf, 1991. ISBN 0-394-92945-4 Subj: Ecology. Imagination. Pets. Reptiles – salamanders.

Watch me ill. by Stacey Schuett. Knopf, 1990. ISBN 0-394-92946-2 Subj: Activities. Family life.

The yellow button ill. by Judy Pedersen. Knopf, 1990. ISBN 0-394-92935-7 Subj: Concepts.

Mazzola, Frank. *Counting is for the birds* ill. by author. Charlesbridge, 1997. ISBN 0-88106-952-3 Subj: Birds. Counting, numbers. Rhyming text.

M'Bane, Phumla. *see* Phumla

Mead, Alice. *Billy and Emma* ill. by Christy Hale. Farrar, 2000. ISBN 0-374-30705-9 Subj: Birds. Birds – macaws. Crime. Friendship. Zoos.

Mead, Katherine. *How spiders got eight legs* ill. by Carol O'Malia. Steck-Vaughn, 1998. ISBN 0-8172-7272-0 Subj: Anatomy – legs. Folk and fairy tales. Spiders.

Meade, Holly. *John Willy and Freddy McGee* ill. by author. Cavendish, 1998. ISBN 0-7614-5033-5 Subj: Animals – guinea pigs. Behavior – running away. Character traits – freedom.

Meddaugh, Susan. *Beast* ill. by author. Houghton Mifflin, 1981. ISBN 0-395-30349-4 Subj: Character traits – kindness. Monsters.

The best place ill. by author. Houghton Mifflin, 1999. ISBN 0-395-97994-3 Subj: Animals. Animals – wolves. Behavior – dissatisfaction. Homes, houses.

Cinderella's rat ill. by author. Houghton Mifflin, 1997. ISBN 0-395-86833-5 Subj: Animals – rats. Family life – brothers and sisters. Humor. Magic.

Hog-eye ill. by author. Houghton Mifflin, 1995. ISBN 0-395-74276-5 Subj: Activities – cooking. Activities – reading. Animals – pigs. Animals – wolves.

Martha and Skits ill. by author. Houghton Mifflin, 2000. ISBN 0-618-05776-5 Subj: Animals – dogs. Behavior – growing up.

Martha blah blah ill. by author. Houghton Mifflin, 1996. ISBN 0-395-79755-1 Subj: Animals – dogs. Food.

Martha calling ill. by author. Houghton Mifflin, 1994. ISBN 0-395-69825-1 Subj: Activities – vacationing. Animals – dogs.

Martha speaks ill. by author. Houghton Mifflin, 1992. ISBN 0-395-63313-3 Subj: Animals – dogs.

Martha walks the dog ill. by author. Houghton Mifflin, 1998. ISBN 0-395-90494-3 Subj: Animals – dogs. Behavior – bullying. Birds – parakeets, parrots.

Maude and Claude go abroad ill. by author. Houghton Mifflin, 1980. ISBN 0-395-29162-3 Subj: Activities – traveling. Animals – foxes. Boats, ships. Foreign lands – France.

Too short Fred ill. by author. Houghton Mifflin, 1978. ISBN 0-395-27155-X Subj: Animals – cats. Character traits – smallness.

Tree of birds ill. by author. Houghton Mifflin, 1990. ISBN 0-395-53147-0 Subj: Birds. Character traits – kindness to animals.

The witches' supermarket ill. by author. Houghton Mifflin, 1991. ISBN 0-395-57034-4 Subj: Animals – dogs. Holidays – Halloween. Stores. Witches.

Medearis, Angela Shelf. *The adventures of Sugar and Junior* ill. by Nancy Poydar. Holiday, 1995. ISBN 0-8234-1182-6 Subj: Ethnic groups in the U.S. – African Americans. Ethnic groups in the U.S. – Hispanic Americans. Friendship.

Annie's gifts ill. by Anna Rich. Just Us Books, 1994. ISBN 0-940975-30-0 Subj: Ethnic groups in the U.S. – African Americans. Gifts. Self-concept.

Barry and Bennie ill. by Pat Cummings. Celebration Pr., 1996. ISBN 0-673-75753-6 Subj: Animals. Animals – bats. Animals – bears.

Best friends in the snow ill. by Ken Wilson-Max. Scholastic, 1999. ISBN 0-590-52284-1 Subj: Friendship. Rhyming text. Weather – snow.

Bye-bye, babies! ill. by Patrice Aggs. Candlewick, 1995. ISBN 1-56402-258-7 Subj: Babies. Format, unusual – board books. Rhyming text.

Dancing with the Indians ill. by Samuel Byrd. Holiday, 1991. ISBN 0-8234-0893-0 Subj: Activities – dancing. Ethnic groups in the U.S. – African Americans. Indians of North America – Seminole. Rhyming text.

Eat, babies, eat! ill. by Patrice Aggs. Candlewick, 1995. ISBN 1-56402-257-9 Subj: Babies. Food. Format, unusual – board books.

The freedom riddle ill. by John Ward. Dutton, 1995. ISBN 0-525-67469-1 Subj: Ethnic groups in the U.S. – African Americans. Folk and fairy tales. Riddles. Slavery. U.S. history.

The friendship garden ill. by Marcy Ramsey. Celebration Pr., 1996. ISBN 0-673-75742-0 Subj: Gardens, gardening.

The ghost of Sifty-Sifty Sam ill. by Jacqueline Rogers. Scholastic, 1997. ISBN 0-590-48290-4 Subj: Careers – chefs, cooks. Ethnic groups in the U.S. – African Americans. Ghosts. Homes, houses. Rhyming text.

Here comes the snow ill. by Maxie Chambliss. Scholastic, 1996. ISBN 0-590-26266-1 Subj: Activities – playing. Rhyming text. Weather – snow.

Kyle's first Kwanzaa ill. by Gershom Griffith. Celebration Pr., 1996. ISBN 0-673-75745-5 Subj: Ethnic groups in the U.S. – African Americans. Holidays – Kwanzaa.

The 100th day of school ill. by Joan Holub. Scholastic, 1996. ISBN 0-590-25944-X Subj: Counting, numbers. Rhyming text. School.

Our people ill. by Michael Bryant. Atheneum, 1994. ISBN 0-689-31826-X Subj: Ethnic groups in the U.S. – African Americans. Family life – fathers.

Picking peas for a penny ill. by author. State House Press, 1990. ISBN 0-938349-54-6 Subj: Activities – working. Ethnic groups in the U.S. – African Americans. Farms. U.S. history.

Poppa's itchy Christmas ill. by John Ward. Holiday, 1998. ISBN 0-8234-1298-9 Subj: Clothing. Holidays – Christmas. Sports – ice skating.

Poppa's new pants ill. by John Ward. Holiday, 1995. ISBN 0-8234-1155-9 Subj: Behavior – mistakes. Clothing. Ethnic groups in the U.S. – African Americans.

Rum-a-tum-tum ill. by James Ransome. Holiday, 1997. ISBN 0-8234-1143-5 Subj: Communities, neighborhoods. Ethnic groups in the U.S. – African Americans. Noise, sounds. Rhyming text.

Seeds grow ill. by Jill Dubin. Scholastic, 1999. ISBN 0-590-37974-7 Subj: Flowers. Plants. Rhyming text. Seeds.

Seven spools of thread: a Kwanzaa story ill. by Daniel Minter. Albert Whitman, 2000. ISBN 0-8075-7315-9 Subj: Activities – weaving. Folk and fairy tales. Foreign lands – Ghana. Holidays – Kwanzaa.

The singing man: adapted from a West African folktale ill. by Terea Shaffer. Holiday, 1994. ISBN 0-8234-1103-6 Subj: Folk and fairy tales. Foreign lands – Nigeria. Music.

Tailypo: a newfangled tall tale ill. by Sterling Brown. Holiday, 1996. ISBN 0-8234-1249-0 Subj: Ethnic groups in the U.S. – African Americans. Folk and fairy tales. Monsters.

Too much talk ill. by Stefano Vitale. Candlewick, 1995. ISBN 1-56402-323-0 Subj: Cumulative tales. Folk and fairy tales. Foreign lands – Ghana. Royalty – kings.

We eat dinner in the bathtub ill. by Jacqueline Rogers. Scholastic, 1996. ISBN 0-590-73886-0 Subj: Friendship. Homes, houses.

We play on a rainy day ill. by Sylvia Walker. Scholastic, 1995. ISBN 0-590-26265-3 Subj: Activities – playing. Rhyming text. Weather – rain.

The zebra-riding cowboy ill. by María Cristina Brusca. Holt, 1992. ISBN 0-8050-1712-7 Subj: Animals – horses, ponies. Cowboys. Ethnic groups in the U.S. Music. Songs. U.S. history – frontier and pioneer life.

Medicine Crow, Joseph. *Brave Wolf and the Thunderbird* ill. by Linda R. Martin. National Museum of the American Indian, 1998. Developed under the auspices of the Smithsonian's National Museum of the American Indian. ISBN 0-7892-0160-7 Subj: Folk and fairy tales. Indians of North America – Crow. Monsters. Mythical creatures.

Medina, Nina. *Have you ever noticed that rabbits don't sing?* ill. by author. Harpswell Pr., 1989. ISBN 0-88448-061-5 Subj: Activities – dancing. Animals – rabbits. Poetry.

Mee, Charles L. *Noah* ill. by Ken Munowitz. HarperCollins, 1978. ISBN 0-06-024184-5 Subj: Boats, ships. Religion – Noah. Weather – floods. Weather – rain. Weather – rainbows.

Meeker, Clare Hodgson. *A tale of two rice birds: a folktale from Thailand* ill. by Christine Lamb. Sasquatch, 1994. ISBN 1-57061-008-8 Subj: Birds. Death. Emotions – love. Royalty – princesses.

Who wakes rooster? ill. by Megan Halsey. Simon & Schuster, 1996. ISBN 0-689-80541-1 Subj: Animals. Birds – chickens. Farms. Morning. Sun.

Meeks, Esther K. *The curious cow* ill. by Mel Pekarsky. Follett, 1960. Also published in German as "Die neugierige Kuh"; in French as "La vache curieuse"; and in Spanish as "La Vaca curiosa." Subj: Animals – bulls, cows. Character traits – curiosity.

Friendly farm animals. Follett, 1965. Subj: Animals. Farms.

The hill that grew ill. by Lazlo Roth. Follett, 1959. Subj: Activities – playing.

One is the engine ill. by Ernie King. Follett, 1956. Subj: Counting, numbers. Trains.

One is the engine: a counting book ill. by Joe Rogers. Follett, 1947, 1972. ISBN 0-695-40236-6 Subj: Counting, numbers. Trains.

Playland pony ill. by Mary Miller Salem. Follett, 1951. Subj: Animals – horses, ponies.

Something new at the zoo ill. by Hazel Hoecker. Follett, 1957. Subj: Animals. Zoos.

Meeuwissen, Tony. *Remarkable animals: 1,000 amazing amalgamations* ill. by author. Orchard, 1998. ISBN 0-531-30066-8 Subj: Animals. Format, unusual – toy and movable books. Humor.

Meggendorfer, Lothar. *The genius of Lothar Meggendorfer* ill. by Jim Deesing. Random House, 1985. ISBN 0-394-54690-3 Subj: Format, unusual – toy and movable books. Rhyming text. Toys.

Meigs, Mildred Plew. *Moon song* ill. by Chris Conover. Morrow, 1990. ISBN 0-688-08707-8 Subj: Lullabies.

Meijer, Marie. *The bake-a-cake book* ill. by Charlotte Ramel. Chronicle, 1994. ISBN 0-8118-0693-6 Subj: Activities – cooking. Food. Format, unusual.

Meister, Cari. *Tiny goes to the library* ill. by Rich Davis. Viking, 2000. ISBN 0-670-88556-8 Subj: Activities – reading. Animals – dogs. Concepts – size. Libraries.

Tiny's bath ill. by Rich Davis. Viking, 1998. ISBN 0-670-87962-2 Subj: Activities – bathing. Animals – dogs. Concepts – size.

When Tiny was tiny ill. by Rich Davis. Viking, 1999. ISBN 0-670-88058-2 Subj: Animals – dogs. Behavior – growing up. Concepts – size.

Melcher, Mary. *Mommy, who does God love?* ill. by Mary Melcher. Little Simon, 1997. ISBN 0-689-81036-9 Subj: Format, unusual – toy and movable books. Religion.

Mellings, Joan. *It's fun to go to school* ill. by Sandra Laroche. Lippincott, 1986. ISBN 0-694-00125-2 Subj: Rhyming text. School.

Mellor, Corinne. *Bruce the balding moose* ill. by Jonathan Allen; paper engineering by Richard Ferguson. Dial, 1996. ISBN 0-8037-2064-5 Subj: Activities – dancing. Animals. Animals – moose. Format, unusual – toy and movable books. Friendship.

Clark the toothless shark ill. by Jonathan Allen. Western, 1994. ISBN 0-307-17606-1 Subj: Fish – sharks. Format, unusual – toy and movable books. Teeth.

Melmed, Laura Krauss. *The first song ever sung* ill. by Ed Young. Lothrop, 1993. ISBN 0-688-08231-9 Subj: Bedtime. Foreign lands – Japan. Poetry. Songs.

I love you as much . . . ill. by Henri Sorensen. 1st Tupelo board books ed. Tupelo, 1998. ISBN 0-688-15978-8 Subj: Animals. Family life – mothers. Format, unusual – board books. Rhyming text.

Jumbo's lullaby ill. by Henri Sorensen. Lothrop, 1999. ISBN 0-688-16996-1 Subj: Animals – elephants. Bedtime. Dreams. Foreign lands – Africa. Lullabies. Rhyming text.

Little Oh ill. by Jim LaMarche. Lothrop, 1997. ISBN 0-688-14209-5 Subj: Behavior – lost. Family life. Paper.

The Marvelous Market on Mermaid ill. by Maryann Kovalski. Lothrop, 1995. ISBN 0-688-13054-2 Subj: Careers – storekeepers. Cumulative tales. Family life – grandmothers. Rhyming text. Stores.

Moishe's miracle: a Hanukkah story ill. by David Slonim. HarperCollins, 2000. ISBN 0-688-14683-X Subj: Folk and fairy tales. Holidays – Hanukkah. Jewish culture. Magic.

1-2-3 Thanksgiving ill. by Robin Kramer. Harper-Collins, 2000. ISBN 0-688-14555-8 Subj: Counting, numbers. Holidays – Thanksgiving. Poetry. U.S. history.

Prince Nautilus ill. by Henri Sorensen. Lothrop, 1994. ISBN 0-688-04567-7 Subj: Character traits – laziness. Folk and fairy tales.

The rainbabies ill. by Jim LaMarche. Lothrop, 1992. ISBN 0-688-10756-7 Subj: Babies. Folk and fairy tales.

Meltzer, Lisa. *The three billy goats Gruff* (Asbjørnsen, P. C. [Peter Christen])

Melville, Herman. *Catskill eagle* ill. by Thomas Locker. Putnam, 1991. ISBN 0-399-21857-2 Subj: Birds – eagles.

Melville, Kristy. *Splash! a penguin counting book* (Chester, Jonathan)

Memling, Carl. *What's in the dark?* ill. by John E. Johnson. Parent's, 1971. ISBN 0-8193-0445-X Subj: Monsters. Night.

Mendel, Lydia J. *All dressed up and nowhere to go* (Joseph, Daniel M.)

Mendell, Olga Karman. *This home we have made* (Hammond, Anna)

Mendelson, S. T. *Stupid Emilien* ill. by author. Stewart, Tabori & Chang, 1991. ISBN 1-55670-213-2 Subj: Animals – rabbits. Folk and fairy tales. Foreign lands – Russia.

Mendoza, George. *The alphabet boat: a seagoing alphabet book* ill. by author. American Heritage, 1972. ISBN 0-07-041425-4 Subj: ABC books. Boats, ships.

Alphabet sheep ill. by Kathleen Reidy. Grosset, 1982. ISBN 0-448-12220-0 Subj: ABC books. Animals – sheep. Behavior – lost.

The gillygoofang ill. by Mercer Mayer. Dial, 1982. ISBN 0-8037-2875-1 Subj: Fish.

Henri Mouse ill. by Joelle Boucher. Viking, 1985. ISBN 0-670-36689-7 Subj: Animals – mice. Art.

Henri Mouse, the juggler ill. by Joelle Boucher. Viking, 1986. ISBN 0-670-80945-4 Subj: Animals – mice. Foreign lands – France. Magic.

The hunter I might have been photos by De Wayne Dalrymple. Astor-Honor, 1968. ISBN 0-8392-3064-8 Subj: Death. Emotions – grief. Poetry. Sports – hunting.

The Marcel Marceau counting book photos by Milton H. Greene. Doubleday, 1971. Subj: Clowns, jesters.

Need a house? Call Ms. Mouse ill. by Doris Susan Smith. Grosset, 1981. ISBN 0-448-16575-9 Subj: Animals. Animals – mice. Homes, houses.

Norman Rockwell's Americana ABC ill. by Norman Rockwell. Abrams, 1975. ISBN 0-440-05944-5 Subj: ABC books.

The scribbler ill. by Robert M. Quackenbush. Holt, 1971. ISBN 0-03-086359-7 Subj: Birds – sandpipers. Poetry. Sea and seashore.

The Sesame Street book of opposites with Zero Mostel photos by Sheldon Secunda; book design by Nicole Sekora-Mendoza. Platt, 1974. ISBN 0-8228-7701-5 Subj: Concepts – opposites.

Silly sheep and other sheepish rhymes ill. by Kathleen Reidy. Grosset, 1982. ISBN 0-448-12219-7 Subj: Animals – sheep. Nursery rhymes.

Traffic jam ill. by David Stoltz. Stewart, Tabori & Chang, 1990. ISBN 1-55670-135-7 Subj: Animals. Automobiles. Rhyming text. Traffic, traffic signs.

Were you a wild duck, where would you go? ill. by Jane Osborn-Smith. Stewart, Tabori & Chang, 1990. ISBN 1-55670-136-5 Subj: Birds – ducks. Ecology. Rhyming text.

Mennen, Ingrid. *Somewhere in Africa* by Ingrid Mennen and Niki Daly; ill. by Nicolaas Maritz. Dutton, 1992. ISBN 0-525-44848-9 Subj: City. Foreign lands – South Africa.

Menter, Ian. *The Albany Road mural* photos by Will Guy. David & Charles, 1984. ISBN 0-241-11032-7 Subj: Activities – painting. Art.

Carnival photos by Will Guy. David & Charles, 1983. ISBN 0-241-10833-0 Subj: Foreign lands – England. Holidays.

Meredith, Carol. *Jamie Anderson wouldn't . . .* ill. by Lorrie Szekat. Annick, 1998. ISBN 1-55037-457-5 Subj: Emotions – fear. Family life – fathers. Illness. School – first day.

Meredith, Lucy. *The princess on the nut: or, the curious courtship of the son of the princess on the pea* (Nikly, Michelle)

Mernan, Andrea. *Ben finds a friend* (Chapouton, Anne-Marie)

I wish I were (Laurencin, Geneviève)

A kitten is born (Fischer-Nagel, Heiderose)

A puppy is born (Fischer-Nagel, Heiderose)

A walk in the rain (Scheffler, Ursel)

Meroux, Felix. *The prince of the rabbits* ill. by Cooper Edens. Green Tiger Pr., 1985. ISBN 0-88138-030-X Subj: Animals – rabbits. Behavior – boredom.

Merriam, Eve. *Bam, bam, bam* ill. by Dan Yaccarino. Holt, 1995. ISBN 0-8050-3527-3 Subj: Buildings. City. Machines. Poetry.

The birthday cow ill. by Guy Michel. Knopf, 1978. ISBN 0-394-93808-9 Subj: Animals. Humor. Poetry.

The birthday door ill. by Peter J. Thornton. Morrow, 1986. ISBN 0-688-06194-X Subj: Animals – cats. Birthdays. Homes, houses. Problem solving.

Blackberry ink ill. by Hans Wilhelm. Morrow, 1985. ISBN 0-688-04151-5 Subj: Poetry.

Boys and girls, girls and boys ill. by Harriet Sherman. Holt, 1972. ISBN 0-03-005716-7 Subj: Activities – playing. Ethnic groups in the U.S. Friendship.

Christmas (Bruna, Dick)

The Christmas box ill. by David Small. Morrow, 1985. ISBN 0-688-05256-8 Subj: Family life. Holidays – Christmas.

Epaminondas ill. by Trina Schart Hyman. Follett, 1968. Originally published in 1938 as "Epaminondas and his Aunty" by Sara Cone Bryant. Subj: Ethnic groups in the U.S. – African Americans. Family life – aunts, uncles. Folk and fairy tales. Humor.

Fighting words ill. by David Small. Morrow, 1992. ISBN 0-688-09677-8 Subj: Behavior – fighting, arguing. Behavior – name calling. City. Country.

Goodnight to Annie ill. by Carol Schwartz. Four Winds, 1992. ISBN 1-56282-206-3 Subj: ABC books. Animals. Bedtime. Lullabies. Sleep.

Goodnight to Annie ill. by John Wallner. Four Winds, 1980. ISBN 0-590-07485-7 Subj: ABC books. Bedtime.

Halloween ABC ill. by Lane Smith. Macmillan, 1987. ISBN 0-02-766870-3 Subj: ABC books. Holidays – Halloween. Poetry.

Higgle wiggle ill. by Hans Wilhelm. Morrow, 1994. ISBN 0-688-11949-2 Subj: Poetry.

The hole story designed and ill. by Ivan Chermayeff. Simon & Schuster, 1995. ISBN 0-671-88353-4 Subj: Format, unusual – board books. Poetry.

Low song ill. by Pam Paparone. Margaret K. McElderry, 2001. ISBN 0-689-82820-9 Subj: Nature. Rhyming text.

Mommies at work ill. by Eugenie Fernandes. Simon & Schuster, 1989. ISBN 0-671-64386-X Subj: Activities – working. Careers. Family life – mothers.

On my street ill. by Melanie Hope Greenberg. HarperCollins, 2000. ISBN 0-694-01258-0 Subj: City. Communities, neighborhoods. Family life – mothers. Rhyming text.

A poem for a pickle: funnybone verses ill. by Sheila Hamanaka. Morrow, 1989. ISBN 0-688-08138-X Subj: Poetry.

Ten rosy roses ill. by Julia Gorton. HarperCollins, 1999. ISBN 0-06-027888-9 Subj: Counting, numbers. Flowers. Rhyming text.

Train leaves the station ill. by Dale Gottlieb. Holt, 1992. ISBN 0-8050-1934-0 Subj: Counting, numbers. Rhyming text. Time. Toys – trains.

12 ways to get to 11 ill. by Bernie Karlin. Simon & Schuster, 1993. ISBN 0-671-75544-7 Subj: Counting, numbers.

What in the world? ill. by Barbara J. Phillips-Duke. HarperCollins, 1997. ISBN 0-694-01036-7 Subj: Animals. Format, unusual – toy and movable books. Rhyming text.

Where is everybody? ill. by Diane de Groat. Simon & Schuster, 1989. ISBN 0-671-64964-7 Subj: ABC books. Animals.

Where's that cat? by Eve Merriam and Pam Pollack; ill. by Joanna Harrison. Margaret K. McElderry, 2000. ISBN 0-689-82904-3 Subj: Animals – cats. Parks. Rhyming text.

Merrick, Patrick. *Easter bunnies* ill. by author. Child's World, 1999. ISBN 1-56766-639-6 Subj: Animals – rabbits. Eggs. Holidays – Easter.

Merrill, Bob. *How much is that doggie in the window?* (Trapani, Iza)

Merrill, Jean. *Emily Emerson's moon* by Jean Merrill and Ronni Solbert; ill. by Ronni Solbert. Little, 1960. Subj: Family life. Moon.

The girl who loved caterpillars ill. by Floyd Cooper. Philomel, 1992. ISBN 0-399-21871-8 Subj: Foreign lands – Japan. Insects – butterflies, caterpillars. Nature. Science.

How many kids are hiding on my block? by Jean Merrill and Frances Gruse Scott; ill. by Frances Gruse Scott. Albert Whitman, 1970. ISBN 0-807-53418-8 Subj: Counting, numbers. Ethnic groups in the U.S. Games.

Tell about the cowbarn, Daddy ill. by Lili Cassel-Wronker. Addison-Wesley, 1963. Subj: Animals – bulls, cows. Barns. Farms.

Merritt, Jane Hamilton. *see* Hamilton-Merritt, Jane

Meryl, Debra. *Baby's peek-a-boo album* ill. by True Kelley. Putnam, 1989. ISBN 0-448-15375-0 Subj: Activities – playing. Format, unusual – toy and movable books. Games.

Meshover, Leonard. *The guinea pigs that went to school* by Leonard Meshover and Sally Feistel; photos by Eve Hoffmann. Follett, 1968. Subj: Animals – guinea pigs. School. Science.

The monkey that went to school by Leonard Meshover and Sally Feistel; photos by Eve Hoffmann. Follett, 1978. ISBN 0-695-40878-X Subj: Animals – monkeys. School. Science.

Messenger, Jannat. *Lullabies and baby songs* ill. by author. Dial, 1988. ISBN 0-8037-0491-7 Subj: Lullabies. Poetry.

Metaxas, Eric. *Bible ABC* ill. by Jim Harris. Tommy Nelson, 1998. ISBN 0-8499-1524-4 Subj: ABC books. Religion. Rhyming text.

The birthday ABC by Eric Metaxas and Tim Raglin; ill. by Tim Raglin. Simon & Schuster, 1995. ISBN 0-671-88306-2 Subj: ABC books. Animals. Birthdays. Rhyming text.

The boy and the whale: a Christmas fairy tale ill. by Paul Lopez. Third Story Books, 1994. ISBN 1-884506-15-1 Subj: Animals – whales. Fairies. Folk and fairy tales. Holidays – Christmas. Lighthouses.

David and Goliath ill. by Douglas Fraser. Rabbit Ears, 1996. ISBN 0-88708-294-7 Subj: Foreign lands – Israel. Jewish culture. Religion. Royalty – kings.

The emperor's new clothes (Andersen, H. C. [Hans Christian])

The fool and the flying ship ill. by Henrik Drescher. Rabbit Ears, 1997. ISBN 0-689-81582-4 Subj: Activities – flying. Boats, ships. Character traits – cleverness. Folk and fairy tales. Foreign lands – Russia. Royalty – tsars.

The gardener's apprentice ill. by Rodica Prato. Creative Ed., 1997. ISBN 1-56846-154-2 Subj: Animals – horses, ponies. Folk and fairy tales. Foreign lands – Romania. Magic.

The monkey people ill. by Diana Bryan. Rabbit Ears, 1995. ISBN 0-689-80191-2 Subj: Animals – monkeys. Character traits – laziness. Folk and fairy

tales. Foreign lands – Colombia. Indians of South America.

Pinocchio (Collodi, Carlo)

Princess Scargo and the birthday pumpkin ill. by Karen Barbour. Rabbit Ears, 1996. ISBN 0-689-80231-5 Subj: Fish. Indians of North America – Nobscusset. Royalty – princesses. Weather – droughts.

Puss in boots ill. by Pierre Le-Tan. Rabbit Ears, 1992. ISBN 0-88708-285-8 Subj: Animals – cats. Character traits – cleverness. Folk and fairy tales. Royalty – kings.

Stormalong, the legendary sea captain ill. by Don Vanderbeek. Rabbit Ears, 1995. ISBN 0-689-80194-7 Subj: Boats, ships. Sailors. Sea and seashore. Tall tales.

Uncle Mugsy and the terrible twins of Christmas ill. by Tim Raglin. Madison Square Pr., 1995. ISBN 0-942604-53-9 Subj: Holidays – Christmas. Multiple births – twins. Rhyming text.

The white cat ill. by Barbara McClintock. Simon & Schuster, 2000. ISBN 0-689-80140-8 Subj: Animals – cats. Folk and fairy tales. Royalty – princes.

Metcalf, Paula. *Norma No Friends* ill. by author. Barefoot, 1999. ISBN 1-902283-87-2 Subj: Character traits – shyness. Friendship.

Métral, Yvette. *The turtle* ill. by Charlotte Knox. Rourke, 1983. ISBN 0-86592-856-8 Subj: Reptiles – turtles, tortoises.

Metropolitan Museum of Art. *The Christmas story* (The Christmas story)

Meyer, Dennis K. *Anything cuddly will do!* (Inkpen, Mick)

Pat the beastie: a pull-and-poke book (Drescher, Henrik)

Meyer, Eleanor Walsh. *The keeper of ugly sounds* ill. by Vlad Guzner. Winslow, 1998. ISBN 1-890817-02-3 Subj: Behavior. Noise, sounds.

Meyer, Elizabeth C. *The blue china pitcher* ill. by author. Abingdon, 1974. ISBN 0-687-03625-9 Subj: Holidays. Parties.

Meyer, June. *see* Jordan, June

Meyer, Linda D. *Safety zone* ill. by Marina Megale. Chas. Franklin Pr., 1984. ISBN 0-960-35168-X Subj: Behavior – talking to strangers. Safety.

Meyer, Louis A. *The clean air and peaceful contentment dirigible airline* ill. by author. Little, 1972. Subj: Ecology. Humor. Noise, sounds.

Meyers, Susan. *The truth about gorillas* ill. by John Hamberger. Dutton, 1980. ISBN 0-525-41564-5 Subj: Animals – gorillas. Science.

Michael, Emory H. *Androcles and the lion* ill. by Mia Hatchem. Winston-Derek, 1988. ISBN 1-55523-

132-2 Subj: Animals – lions. Character traits – helpfulness. Character traits – kindness to animals. Folk and fairy tales. Foreign lands – Italy. Religion.

Michaels, Ruth. *The family that grew* (Rondell, Florence)

Michaels, William. *Clare and her shadow* ill. by author. Linnet Books, 1991. ISBN 0-208-02301-1 Subj: Family life – grandfathers. Shadows.

Michel, Anna. *Little wild lion cub* ill. by Tony Chen. Pantheon, 1981. ISBN 0-394-84352-5 Subj: Animals – lions.

Michels, Tilde. *At the frog pond* trans. by Nina Ignatowicz; ill. by Reinhard Michl. Lippincott, 1989. ISBN 0-397-32315-8 Subj: Ecology. Frogs and toads. Science.

Rabbit spring ill. by Käthi Bhend. Harcourt, 1989. ISBN 0-15-200568-4 Subj: Animals – rabbits. Nature.

What a beautiful day! ill. by Thomas Müller. Carolrhoda, 1992. ISBN 0-87614-739-2 Subj: Nature. Seasons – summer.

Who's that knocking at my door? ill. by Reinhard Michl. Barron's, 1986. ISBN 0-8120-5732-5 Subj: Animals. Rhyming text. Seasons – winter. Sports – hunting.

Michelson, Richard. *Animals that ought to be: poems about imaginary pets* ill. by Leonard Baskin. Simon & Schuster, 1996. ISBN 0-689-80635-3 Subj: Animals. Imagination. Poetry.

Did you say ghosts? ill. by Leonard Baskin. Macmillan, 1993. ISBN 0-02-766915-7 Subj: Bedtime. Emotions – fear. Ghosts. Monsters. Night. Rhyming text.

Michl, Reinhard. *A day on the river* ill. by author. Barron's, 1986. ISBN 0-8120-5715-5 Subj: Rivers.

Micklethwait, Lucy. *Spot a cat* ill. by author. DK, 1995. ISBN 0-7894-0144-4 Subj: Animals – cats. Art. Behavior – hiding things.

Spot a dog ill. by author. DK, 1995. ISBN 0-789-40145-2 Subj: Animals – dogs. Art. Behavior – hiding things.

Micucci, Charles. *A little night music* ill. by author. Morrow, 1989. ISBN 0-688-07901-6 Subj: Animals – cats. Music. Night.

Midge, Tiffany. *Buffalo* retold by Tiffany Midge; additional text and book design by Vic Warren; ill. by Diana Magnuson. Scholastic, 1995. ISBN 0-590-22489-1 Subj: Animals – buffaloes. Folk and fairy tales. Indians of North America.

Mike, Jan M. *The bird maiden* ill. by Dave Albers. Troll, 1996. ISBN 0-8167-4023-2 Subj: Folk and fairy tales. Foreign lands – Serbia. Magic. Royalty – princes. Royalty – princesses. Witches.

Clever Karlis ill. by Charles Reasoner. Troll, 1996. ISBN 0-8167-4024-0 Subj: Folk and fairy tales. Foreign lands – Latvia. Royalty – princesses.

Gift of the Nile: an Ancient Egyptian legend ill. by Charles Reasoner. Troll, 1993. ISBN 0-8167-2813-5 Subj: Folk and fairy tales. Foreign lands – Egypt. Royalty – pharaohs.

Juan Bobo and the horse of seven colors ill. by Charles Reasoner. Troll, 1995. ISBN 0-8167-3745-2 Subj: Behavior – wishing. Character traits – foolishness. Folk and fairy tales. Foreign lands – Puerto Rico. Royalty – princesses.

Opossum and the great firemaker ill. by Charles Reasoner. Troll, 1993. ISBN 0-8167-3055-5 Subj: Fire. Folk and fairy tales. Foreign lands – Mexico. Indians of North America – Cora.

Miklowitz, Gloria D. *Bearfoot boy* ill. by Jim Collins. Follett, 1964. Subj: Birthdays. Clothing.

Save that raccoon! ill. by St. Tamara. Harcourt, 1978. ISBN 0-15-270241-5 Subj: Animals – raccoons. Character traits – kindness to animals. Fire. Forest, woods.

The zoo that moved ill. by Don Madden. Follett, 1968. Subj: Animals. Zoos.

Miles, Betty. *Around and around . . . love* ill. with photos. Knopf, 1975. ISBN 0-394-93111-4 Subj: Emotions – love. Poetry.

Having a friend ill. by Erik Blegvad. Knopf, 1958. Subj: Friendship.

A house for everyone ill. by Jo Lowery. Knopf, 1958. Subj: Homes, houses.

The sky is falling (Chicken Little)

The three little pigs (The three little pigs)

Miles, Calvin. *Calvin's Christmas wish* ill. by Dolores Johnson. Viking, 1993. ISBN 0-670-84295-8 Subj: Ethnic groups in the U.S. – African Americans. Family life. Farms. Holidays – Christmas. Santa Claus.

Miles, Miska. *Apricot ABC* ill. by Peter Parnall. Little, 1969. Subj: ABC books. Rhyming text. Trees.

Chicken forgets ill. by Jim Arnosky. Little, 1976. ISBN 0-316-56972-0 Subj: Behavior – forgetfulness. Birds – chickens. Humor.

The fox and the fire ill. by John Schoenherr. Little, 1966. Subj: Animals – foxes. Fire. Forest, woods.

Friend of Miguel ill. by Genia. Rand McNally, 1967. Subj: Animals – horses, ponies. Foreign lands – Mexico.

The horse and the bad morning (Clymer, Ted)

Jump frog jump ill. by Earl Thollander. Putnam, 1965. Subj: Fairs. Frogs and toads.

Mouse six and the happy birthday ill. by Leslie Holt Morrill. Dutton, 1978. ISBN 0-525-35230-9 Subj: Animals – mice. Birthdays. Family life – mothers.

No, no, Rosina ill. by Earl Thollander. Putnam, 1964. Subj: Boats, ships. Careers – fishermen. Character traits – smallness. City. Sports – fishing.

Noisy gander ill. by Leslie Holt Morrill. Dutton, 1978. ISBN 0-525-36026-3 Subj: Animals. Birds – ducks. Farms. Noise, sounds.

The pointed brush . . . ill. by Roger Antoine Duvoisin. Lothrop, 1959. Subj: Activities – writing. Foreign lands – China.

Rabbit garden ill. by John Schoenherr. Little, 1967. Subj: Animals – rabbits. Ecology. Gardens, gardening.

The raccoon and Mrs. McGinnis ill. by Leonard Weisgard. Putnam, 1961. ISBN 0-399-60530-4 Subj: Animals – raccoons. Barns. Crime.

The rice bowl pet ill. by Ezra Jack Keats. Crowell, 1962. Subj: Pets.

Rolling the cheese ill. by Alton Raible. Atheneum, 1966. Subj: City. Games.

Show and tell . . . ill. by Thomas Arthur Hamil. Putnam, 1962. Subj: Animals – dogs. School.

Small rabbit ill. by Jim Arnosky. Little, 1977. ISBN 0-316-56973-9 Subj: Animals – rabbits.

Somebody's dog ill. by John Schoenherr. Little, 1973. ISBN 0-316-56965-8 Subj: Animals – dogs. Pets.

Sylvester Jones and the voice in the forest ill. by Leonard Weisgard. Lothrop, 1958. Subj: Animals. Forest, woods.

This little pig ill. by Leslie Holt Morrill. Dutton, 1980. ISBN 0-525-41145-3 Subj: Animals – pigs. Behavior – lost. Behavior – running away. Farms.

Wharf rat ill. by John Schoenherr. Little, 1972. Subj: Animals – rats.

Miles, Sally. *Alfi and the dark* ill. by Errol Le Cain. Chronicle, 1988. ISBN 0-87701-527-9 Subj: Bedtime. Friendship. Night.

Milgram, Mary. *Brothers are all the same* ill. by Rosmarie Hausherr. Dutton, 1978. ISBN 0-525-27243-7 Subj: Adoption. Family life. Sibling rivalry.

Milgrim, David. *Cows can't fly* ill. by author. Viking, 1998. ISBN 0-670-87475-2 Subj: Animals – bulls, cows. Imagination. Rhyming text.

Dog brain ill. by author. Viking, 1996. ISBN 0-670-86935-X Subj: Animals – dogs. Behavior – misbehavior.

Here in space ill. by author. BridgeWater, 1997. ISBN 0-8167-4393-2 Subj: Earth. Rhyming text.

Why Benny barks ill. by author. Random House, 1994. ISBN 0-679-86157-2 Subj: Animals – dogs. Noise, sounds. Rhyming text.

Milgrom, Harry. *Egg-ventures: first science experiments* ill. by Giulio Maestro. Dutton, 1974. ISBN 0-525-29160-1 Subj: Eggs. Science.

Milhous, Katherine. *The egg tree* ill. by author. Aladdin, 1992, c1950. ISBN 0-689-71568-4 Subj: Caldecott award books. Eggs. Holidays – Easter.

The turnip by Katherine Milhouse and Alice Dalgliesh; ill. by Pierr Morgan. Putnam, 1990. From: Once on a time by Katherine Milhouse and Alice Dalgliesh (1938). ISBN 0-399-22229-4 Subj: Cumulative tales. Farms. Folk and fairy tales. Foreign lands – Russia. Plants. Problem solving.

Milich, Melissa. *Can't scare me!* ill. by Tyrone Geter. Doubleday, 1995. ISBN 0-385-31052-8 Subj: Emotions – fear. Ethnic groups in the U.S. – African Americans. Ghosts.

Miz Fannie Mae's fine new Easter hat ill. by Yong Chen. Little, 1997. ISBN 0-316-57159-8 Subj: City. Clothing – hats. Ethnic groups in the U.S. – African Americans. Family life – fathers. Family life – mothers. Holidays – Easter.

Milios, Rita. *Sneaky Pete* ill. by Clovis Martin. Childrens Pr., 1989. ISBN 0-516-02092-7 Subj: Behavior – hiding. Rhyming text.

Yo soy = I am ill. by Clovis Martin. Childrens Pr., 1990. ISBN 0-516-32081-5 Subj: Activities. Concepts – opposites. Foreign languages. Self-concept.

Milius, Winifred. *see* Lubell, Winifred

Mill, Garrett. *see* Miller, Margaret

Millais, Raoul. *Elijah and Pin-Pin* ill. by author. Simon & Schuster, 1992. ISBN 0-671-75543-9 Subj: Animals – hedgehogs. Animals – moles. Friendship. Parties.

Millen, C. M. *The low-down laundry line blues* ill. by Christine Davenier. Houghton Mifflin, 1999. ISBN 0-395-87497-1 Subj: Emotions. Family life – sisters. Sports.

Miller, Albert. *see* Mills, Alan

I know an old lady (Little old lady who swallowed a fly)

Miller, Alice P. *The little store on the corner* ill. by John Lawrence. Abelard-Schuman, 1961. Subj: Stores.

The mouse family's blueberry pie ill. by Carol Bloch. Elsevier-Nelson, 1981. ISBN 0-525-66745-8 Subj: Activities – cooking. Animals – mice.

Miller, Cameron. *Woodlore* by Cameron Miller and Dominique Falla; ill. by authors. Ticknor & Fields, 1995. ISBN 0-395-72034-6 Subj: Activities – making things.

Miller, Debbie S. *A caribou journey* ill. by Jon Van Zyle. Little, 1994. ISBN 0-316-57380-9 Subj: Alaska. Animals – reindeer. Nature.

Miller, Edna. *Jumping bean* ill. by author. Prentice-Hall, 1980. ISBN 0-13-512384-4 Subj: Science.

Mousekin finds a friend ill. by author. Prentice-Hall, 1967. ISBN 0-13-604413-1 Subj: Animals – mice. Friendship.

Mousekin takes a trip ill. by author. Prentice-Hall, 1976. ISBN 0-13-604363-1 Subj: Activities – traveling. Animals – mice.

Mousekin's ABC ill. by author. Prentice-Hall, 1972. ISBN 0-136-04389-5 Subj: ABC books. Animals – mice. Forest, woods. Rhyming text.

Mousekin's Christmas eve ill. by author. Prentice-Hall, 1965. ISBN 0-13-604454-9 Subj: Animals – mice. Holidays – Christmas.

Mousekin's close call ill. by author. Prentice-Hall, 1978. ISBN 0-13-604207-4 Subj: Animals – mice. Forest, woods.

Mousekin's Easter basket ill. by author. Prentice-Hall, 1987. ISBN 0-13-604141-8 Subj: Animals – mice. Holidays – Easter. Seasons – spring.

Mousekin's fables ill. by author. Prentice-Hall, 1982. ISBN 0-13-604165-5 Subj: Animals – mice. Folk and fairy tales. Seasons.

Mousekin's family ill. by author. Prentice-Hall, 1969. ISBN 0-13-604462-X Subj: Animals – mice. Family life.

Mousekin's frosty friend ill. by author. Simon & Schuster, 1990. ISBN 0-671-70445-1 Subj: Animals – mice. Character traits – kindness to animals. Food. Snowmen.

Mousekin's golden house ill. by author. Prentice-Hall, 1964. ISBN 0-13-604232-5 Subj: Animals – mice. Hibernation. Holidays – Halloween. Seasons – winter.

Mousekin's lost woodland ill. by author. Simon & Schuster, 1992. ISBN 0-671-74938-2 Subj: Animals – mice. Ecology. Forest, woods.

Mousekin's mystery ill. by author. Prentice-Hall, 1983. ISBN 0-13-604330-5 Subj: Animals – mice. Mystery stories.

Mousekin's Thanksgiving ill. by author. Prentice-Hall, 1985. ISBN 0-13-604299-6 Subj: Animals – mice. Forest, woods. Holidays – Thanksgiving.

Patches finds a new home ill. by author. Simon & Schuster, 1989. ISBN 0-671-66266-X Subj: Animals – cats. Nature.

Pebbles, a pack rat ill. by author. Prentice-Hall, 1976. ISBN 0-13-655399-0 Subj: Animals – pack rats. Scarecrows.

Scamper: a gray tree squirrel ill. by author. Pippin Pr., 1991. ISBN 0-915912-12-9 Subj: Animals – squirrels. Nature.

Miller, Edward. *The curse of Claudia* ill. by author. Crown, 1989. ISBN 0-517-57409-8 Subj: Character traits – cleanliness. Emotions – happiness. Monsters.

Frederick Ferdinand Fox ill. by author. Crown, 1987. ISBN 0-517-56356-8 Subj: Animals – foxes. War.

Miller, Elizabeth I. *Just like home = Como en mi tierra* ill. by Mira Reisberg; Spanish trans. by Teresa Mlawer. Albert Whitman, 1999. ISBN 0-8075-4068-4 Subj: Ethnic groups in the U.S. – Hispanic Americans. Foreign languages. Homes, houses. Immigrants.

Miller, J. P. (John Parr). *Do you know colors?* by J. P. Miller and Katherine Howard; ill. by J. P. Miller. Random House, 1979. ISBN 0-394-93957-3 Subj: Concepts – color.

Farmer John's animals ill. by author. Random House, 1979. ISBN 0-394-84270-7 Subj: Animals. Farms.

Good night, Little Rabbit ill. by author. Random House, 1986. ISBN 0-394-87992-9 Subj: Animals – rabbits. Bedtime. Family life. Format, unusual – board books.

Learn about colors with Little Rabbit ill. by author. Random House, 1984. ISBN 0-394-86671-1 Subj: Concepts – color.

Learn to count with Little Rabbit ill. by author. Random House, 1984. ISBN 0-394-96149-8 Subj: Animals – rabbits. Counting, numbers.

Miller, Jane. *Farm alphabet book* photos by author. Prentice-Hall, 1984. ISBN 0-13-304767-9 Subj: ABC books. Farms.

Farm counting book photos by author. Prentice-Hall, 1983. ISBN 0-13-304790-3 Subj: Counting, numbers. Farms.

Farm noises photos by author. Simon & Schuster, 1989. ISBN 0-671-67450-1 Subj: Animals. Farms. Noise, sounds.

Seasons on the farm ill. by author. Prentice-Hall, 1986. ISBN 0-13-797275-X Subj: Animals. Farms. Seasons.

Miller, Judith Ransom. *Nabob and the geranium* ill. by Marilyn Neuhart. Golden Gate, 1967. Subj: Plants. Science.

Miller, Kathryn Ann. *Did my first mother love me? a story for an adopted child, with a special section for adoptive parents* ill. by Jami Moffett. Morning Glory Pr., 1994. ISBN 0-930934-85-7 Subj: Adoption. Emotions. Family life.

Miller, M. L. *Dizzy from fools* ill. by Eve Tharlet. Alphabet Pr., 1985. ISBN 0-88708-004-9 Subj: Character traits – questioning. Clowns, jesters. Royalty. Royalty – princesses.

The enormous snore ill. by Kevin Hawkes. Putnam, 1995. ISBN 0-399-22650-8 Subj: Behavior – lost. Character traits – helpfulness. Noise, sounds. Royalty – kings. Sleep.

Those Bottles! ill. by Barry Root. Putnam, 1994. ISBN 0-399-22607-9 Subj: Family life. Prejudice. Weather – floods.

Miller, Margaret. *At my house* ill. by author. Crowell, 1989. ISBN 0-694-00276-3 Subj: Babies. Family life. Format, unusual – board books.

At the shore photos by author. Little Simon, 1996. ISBN 0-689-80052-5 Subj: Format, unusual – board books. Sea and seashore.

Baby faces ill. by author. Little Simon, 1998. ISBN 0-689-81911-0 Subj: Anatomy – faces. Babies. Format, unusual – board books.

Big and little ill. by author. Greenwillow, 1998. ISBN 0-688-14749-6 Subj: Concepts – opposites. Concepts – size.

Can you guess? ill. by author. Greenwillow, 1993. ISBN 0-688-11181-5 Subj: Character traits – questioning.

Every day photos by author. HarperCollins, 1991. ISBN 0-694-00304-2 Subj: Activities. Format, unusual – board books. Language.

Family time photos by author. Little Simon, 1996. ISBN 0-689-80051-7 Subj: Family life. Format, unusual – board books.

Guess who? photos by author. Little Simon, 1996. ISBN 0-688-12784-3 Subj: Format, unusual – board books.

Happy days photos by author. Little Simon, 1996. ISBN 0-689-80050-9 Subj: Activities. Format, unusual – board books.

Here we go! ill. by author. Simon, 1998. ISBN 0-689-80041-X Subj: Format, unusual – board books. Sports.

I can help ill. by author. Little Simon, 1998. ISBN 0-689-80044-4 Subj: Family life. Format, unusual – board books.

I can make it! ill. by author. Little Simon, 1997. ISBN 0-689-80048-7 Subj: Activities – making things. Format, unusual – board books.

I love colors ill. by author. Little Simon, 1999. ISBN 0-689-82356-8 Subj: Animals. Babies. Concepts – color. Family life. Format, unusual – board books.

I'm grown up! ill. by author. Little Simon, 1998. ISBN 0-689-80043-6 Subj: Family life. Format, unusual – board books. Language.

In my room ill. by author. Crowell, 1989. ISBN 0-694-00271-2 Subj: Babies. Family life. Format, unusual – board books.

Let's play! ill. by author. Little Simon, 1997. ISBN 0-689-80047-9 Subj: Activities – playing. Format, unusual – board books.

Let's pretend! ill. by author. Little Simon, 1998. ISBN 0-689-80042-8 Subj: Format, unusual – board books. Imagination.

Me and my bear ill. by author. Little Simon, 1999. ISBN 0-689-82355-X Subj: Animals – babies. Animals – bears. Concepts – color. Format, unusual – board books.

My best friends photos by author. Little Simon, 1996. ISBN 0-689-80049-5 Subj: Format, unusual – board books. Pets.

My birthday photos by author. HarperCollins, 1991. ISBN 0-694-00302-6 Subj: Birthdays. Format, unusual – board books. Language. Parties.

My first words: me and my clothes ill. by author. Crowell, 1989. ISBN 0-694-00272-0 Subj: Babies. Clothing. Family life. Format, unusual – board books.

My five senses photos by author. Simon & Schuster, 1994. ISBN 0-671-79168-0 Subj: Senses.

Now I'm big photos by author. Greenwillow, 1996. ISBN 0-688-14078-5 Subj: Babies. Concepts – size. School.

On my street photos by author. HarperCollins, 1991. ISBN 0-694-00303-4 Subj: Communities, neighborhoods. Format, unusual – board books. Language.

Playtime photos by author. HarperCollins, 1991. ISBN 0-694-00301-8 Subj: Activities – playing. Concepts – opposites. Format, unusual – board books. Language.

Time to eat ill. by author. Crowell, 1989. ISBN 0-87449-618-7 Subj: Babies. Family life. Food. Format, unusual – board books.

Water play ill. by author. Little Simon, 1997. ISBN 0-689-80046-0 Subj: Activities – playing. Format, unusual – board books. Sports. Water.

What's on my head? ill. by author. Little Simon, 1998. ISBN 0-689-81912-9 Subj: Anatomy – heads. Clothing – hats. Format, unusual – board books.

Wheels go 'round ill. by author. Little Simon, 1997. ISBN 0-689-80045-2 Subj: Format, unusual – board books. Wheels.

Where does it go? photos by author. Greenwillow, 1992. ISBN 0-688-10929-2 Subj: Character traits – orderliness. Clothing. Toys.

Where's Jenna? photos by author. Simon & Schuster, 1994. ISBN 0-671-79167-2 Subj: Activities – bathing. Language.

Who uses this? photos by author. Greenwillow, 1990. ISBN 0-688-08279-3 Subj: Careers. Tools.

Whose hat? photos by author. Greenwillow, 1988. ISBN 0-688-06907-X Subj: Careers. Clothing – hats.

Whose shoe? photos by author. Greenwillow, 1991. ISBN 0-688-10009-0 Subj: Clothing – shoes. Games.

Miller, Michaela. *Guinea pigs* ill. with photos. Heinemann, 1998. ISBN 1-57572-575-4 Subj: Animals – guinea pigs. Pets.

Miller, Moira. *The moon dragon* ill. by Ian Deuchar. Dial, 1989. ISBN 0-8037-0566-2 Subj: Behavior – boasting. Folk and fairy tales. Foreign lands – China. Kites.

Oscar Mouse finds a home ill. by Maria Majewska. Dial, 1985. ISBN 0-8037-0229-9 Subj: Animals – mice. Behavior – seeking better things.

The proverbial mouse ill. by Ian Deuchar. Dial, 1987. ISBN 0-8037-0195-0 Subj: Animals – mice. Rhyming text. Toys.

The search for spring ill. by Ian Deuchar. Dial, 1988. ISBN 0-8037-0445-3 Subj: Seasons.

Miller, Robert H. (Robert Henry). *The story of Nat Love* by Robert Miller and Michael Bryant; ill. by Michael Bryant. Silver Pr., 1995. ISBN 0-382-24389-7 Subj: Cowboys. Slavery. U.S. history – frontier and pioneer life.

Miller, Ruth. *I went to the bay* ill. by Martine Gourbault. Kids Can Pr., 1998. ISBN 1-55074-498-4 Subj: Animals. Boats, ships. Frogs and toads. Sea and seashore.

Miller, Thomas Patton. *Can a coal scuttle fly?* by Tomas Patton Miller and Camay Calloway Murphy; ill. by Tomas Patton Miller. Maryland Historical Society, 1996. ISBN 0-938420-55-0 Subj: Art. Concepts – color. Ethnic groups in the U.S. – African Americans.

Miller, Virginia. *Be gentle!* ill. by author. Candlewick, 1997. ISBN 0-7636-0251-5 Subj: Animals – bears. Animals – cats. Pets.

Eat your dinner! ill. by author. Candlewick, 1992. ISBN 1-56402-121-1 Subj: Animals – bears. Food.

Go to bed! ill. by author. Candlewick, 1993. ISBN 1-56402-244-7 Subj: Animals – bears. Bedtime.

I love you just the way you are ill. by author. Candlewick, 1998. ISBN 0-7636-0664-2 Subj: Animals – bears. Behavior – bad day.

In a minute! ill. by author. Candlewick, 2000. ISBN 0-7636-1270-7 Subj: Activities – playing. Animals – bears.

On your potty! ill. by author. Greenwillow, 1991. ISBN 0-688-10618-8 Subj: Animals – bears. Behavior – growing up. Etiquette. Toilet training.

Miller, Warren. *The goings on at Little Wishful* ill. by Edward Sorel. Little, 1959. Subj: Behavior – boasting. Emotions – envy, jealousy.

Pablo paints a picture ill. by Edward Sorel. Little, 1959. Subj: Activities – painting. Careers – artists.

Miller, William. *The bus ride* ill. by John Ward; intro. by Rosa Parks. Lee & Low, 1998. ISBN 1-880000-60-1 Subj: Ethnic groups in the U.S. – African Americans. Prejudice. U.S. history.

The conjure woman ill. by Terea D. Shaffer. Atheneum, 1996. ISBN 0-689-31962-2 Subj: Ethnic groups in the U.S. – African Americans. Illness. Magic.

Frederick Douglass: the last day of slavery ill. by Cedric Lucas. Lee & Low, 1995. ISBN 1-880000-17-2 Subj: Ethnic groups in the U.S. – African Americans. Slavery. U.S. history.

A house by the river ill. by Cornelius Van Wright and Ying-Hwa Hu. Lee & Low, 1997. ISBN 1-880000-48-2 Subj: Emotions – fear. Ethnic groups in the U.S. – African Americans. Family life – mothers. Homes, houses. Weather – storms.

Jenny and the peddler ill. by Rod Brown. Dial, 2000. ISBN 0-8037-2046-7 Subj: Careers – peddlers. Country. Ethnic groups in the U.S. – African Americans. Jewish culture.

The knee-high man ill. by Roberta Glidden. Gibbs Smith, 1996. ISBN 0-8790-5634-7 Subj: Character traits – foolishness. Ethnic groups in the U.S. – African Americans. Folk and fairy tales.

Night golf ill. by Cedric Lucas. Lee & Low, 1999. ISBN 1-880000-79-2 Subj: Ethnic groups in the U.S. – African Americans. Prejudice. Sports – golf.

The piano ill. by Susan Keeter. Lee & Low, 2000. ISBN 1-880000-98-9 Subj: Ethnic groups in the U.S. – African Americans. Music. Old age. Piano.

Richard Wright and the library card ill. by Gregory Christie. Lee & Low, 1997. ISBN 1-880000-57-1 Subj: Activities – reading. Ethnic groups in the U.S. – African Americans. Libraries.

Millhouse, Nicholas. *Blue-footed booby: bird of the Galápagos* ill. by Margret Bowman. Walker, 1986. ISBN 0-8027-6629-3 Subj: Animals. Birds. Islands. Science.

Millman, Isaac. *Moses goes to a concert* ill. by author. Farrar, 1998. ISBN 0-374-35067-1 Subj: Handicaps – deafness. Language. Music. School.

Mills, Alan. *The hungry goat* ill. by Abner Graboff. Rand McNally, 1964. Subj: Animals – goats. Humor. Music. Songs.

I know an old lady (Little old lady who swallowed a fly)

Mills, Claudia. *One small lost sheep* ill. by Walter Lyon Krudop. Farrar, 1997. ISBN 0-374-35649-1 Subj: Animals – sheep. Careers – shepherds. Religion – Nativity.

Phoebe's parade ill. by Carolyn Ewing. Macmillan, 1994. ISBN 0-02-767012-0 Subj: Family life – brothers and sisters. Parades. Sibling rivalry.

A visit to Amy-Claire ill. by Sheila Hamanaka. Macmillan, 1992. ISBN 0-02-766991-2 Subj: Emotions – envy, jealousy. Family life. Family life – sisters. Sibling rivalry.

Mills, Joyce C. *Gentle Willow: a story for children about dying* ill. by Michael Chesworth. Gareth Stevens, 1994. ISBN 0-8368-1070-8 Subj: Animals – squirrels. Death. Trees.

Little Tree: a story for children with serious medical problems ill. by Michael Chesworth. Magination Pr., 1992. ISBN 0-945354-52-5 Subj: Illness. Self-concept. Trees.

Mills, Judith Christine. *The stonehook schooner* ill. by author. Key Porter Books, 1995. ISBN 1-55013-

653-4 Subj: Boats, ships. Lakes, ponds. Rocks. Sailors. U.S. history.

Mills, Lauren A. *The dog prince* ill. by Lauren Mills and Dennis Nolan. Little, 1996. ISBN 0-316-57417-1 Subj: Animals – dogs. Behavior. Magic. Monsters. Royalty – princes.

Fairy wings ill. by Lauren Mills and Dennis Nolan. Little, 1995. ISBN 0-316-57397-3 Subj: Activities – flying. Fairies. Folk and fairy tales. Mythical creatures – trolls. Royalty – princes.

The goblin baby ill. by author. Dial, 1999. ISBN 0-8037-2172-2 Subj: Babies. Emotions – envy, jealousy. Family life – brothers and sisters. Family life – new sibling. Imagination.

The rag coat ill. by author. Little, 1991. ISBN 0-316-57407-4 Subj: Behavior – sharing. Clothing. Friendship. Poverty.

Tatterhood and the hobgoblins: a Norwegian folktale ill. by reteller. Little, 1993. ISBN 0-316-57406-6 Subj: Character traits – individuality. Folk and fairy tales. Foreign lands – Norway. Mythical creatures – goblins. Royalty – princesses.

Mills, Patricia. *On an island in the bay* photos by author. North-South, 1994. ISBN 1-55858-334-3 Subj: Careers – fishermen. Islands. Sea and seashore.

Millward, David Wynn. *Jenny and Bob* ill. by Kady MacDonald Denton. Delacorte, 1991. ISBN 0-385-30431-5 Subj: Emotions. Family life.

Milne, A. A. (Alan Alexander). *Disney's Pooh's grand adventure: the search for Christopher Robin* (Henderson, Kathy)

House at Pooh corner [a pop-up book] with ill. after the style of Ernest H. Shepard. Dutton, 1986. ISBN 0-525-44245-6 Subj: Format, unusual – toy and movable books. Homes, houses. Toys – bears.

Pooh and some bees ill. by Robert Cremins. Dutton, 1987. ISBN 0-525-44339-8 Subj: Format, unusual – toy and movable books. Insects. Toys – bears.

Pooh goes visiting ill. by Robert Cremins. Dutton, 1987. ISBN 0-525-44337-1 Subj: Format, unusual – toy and movable books. Toys – bears.

Pooh's alphabet book ill. by E. H. Shepard. Dutton, 1976. ISBN 0-525-37370-5 Subj: ABC books. Toys – bears.

Pooh's counting book ill. by E. H. Shepard. Dutton, 1982. ISBN 0-525-44016-X Subj: Counting, numbers. Toys – bears.

Pooh's quiz book ill. by E. H. Shepard. Dutton, 1977. ISBN 0-525-37485-X Subj: Games. Hungry. Toys – bears.

Prince Rabbit: and, The princess who could not laugh ill. by Mary Shepard. Dutton, 1966. Subj: Animals – rabbits. Folk and fairy tales. Royalty – princes.

Winnie-the-Pooh: a pop-up book ill. by Chuck Murphy; engineering by Keith Moseley. Dutton, 1984. ISBN 0-525-44119-0 Subj: Character traits – bravery. Format, unusual – toy and movable books. Toys – bears.

Winnie-the-Pooh's ABC (Shepard, E. H. [Ernest Howard])

Milord, Jerry. *Maggie and the goodbye gift* (Milord, Sue)

Milord, Sue. *Maggie and the goodbye gift* by Sue and Jerry Milord; ill. by authors. Lothrop, 1979. ISBN 0-688-51912-1 Subj: Family life. Gifts. Moving.

Milstein, Linda Breiner. *Amanda's perfect hair* ill. by Susan Meddaugh. Tambourine, 1993. ISBN 0-688-11154-8 Subj: Behavior – dissatisfaction. Hair.

Coconut mon ill. by Cheryl Munro Taylor. Tambourine, 1995. ISBN 0-688-12862-9 Subj: Counting, numbers. Ethnic groups in the U.S. – African Americans. Foreign lands – Caribbean Islands.

Grandma's jewelry box ill. by Jean Hirashima. Random House, 1992. ISBN 0-679-81973-8 Subj: Family life – grandmothers. Format, unusual – toy and movable books.

Miami-Nanny stories ill. by Oki S. Han. Tambourine, 1994. ISBN 0-688-11152-1 Subj: Family life – grandmothers. Jewish culture.

Milton, John. *Comus* (Hodges, Margaret)

Milton, Joyce. *Big cats* ill. by Silvia Duran. Grosset, 1994. ISBN 0-448-40565-2 Subj: Animals – cheetahs. Animals – cougars. Animals – jaguars. Animals – leopards. Animals – lions. Animals – tigers.

Dinosaur days ill. by Richard Roe. Random House, 1985. ISBN 0-394-97023-3 Subj: Dinosaurs.

Milton, Nancy. *The giraffe that walked to Paris* ill. by Roger Roth. Crown, 1992. ISBN 0-517-58133-7 Subj: Activities – traveling. Animals – giraffes. Foreign lands – France. Royalty – kings.

Min, Laura. *Mrs. Sato's hens* ill. by Benrei Huang. Scott Foresman, 1994. ISBN 0-673-36193-4 Subj: Birds – chickens. Counting, numbers. Days of the week, months of the year. Eggs. Ethnic groups in the U.S. – Asian Americans.

Min, Willemien. *Peter's patchwork dream* ill. by author. Barefoot, 1999. ISBN 1-902283-45-7 Subj: Friendship. Illness. Imagination. Quilts.

Minarik, Else Holmelund. *Am I beautiful?* ill. by Yossi Abolafia. Greenwillow, 1992. ISBN 0-688-09912-2 Subj: Animals. Animals – hippopotamuses. Family life – mothers. Self-concept.

Cat and dog ill. by Fritz Siebel. HarperCollins, 1960. ISBN 0-06-024221-3 Subj: Animals – cats. Animals – dogs.

Father Bear comes home ill. by Maurice Sendak. HarperCollins, 1959. ISBN 0-06-024231-0 Subj: Animals – bears. Family life – fathers.

It's spring! ill. by Margaret Bloy Graham. Greenwillow, 1989. ISBN 0-688-07620-3 Subj: Animals – cats. Seasons – spring.

A kiss for Little Bear ill. by Maurice Sendak. HarperCollins, 1959. ISBN 0-06-024299-X Subj: Animals – bears.

Little Bear ill. by Maurice Sendak. HarperCollins, 1957. ISBN 0-06-024241-8 Subj: Animals – bears. Birthdays.

Little Bear's friend ill. by Maurice Sendak. HarperCollins, 1960. ISBN 0-06-024256-6 Subj: Animals – bears. Friendship.

Little Bear's visit ill. by Maurice Sendak. HarperCollins, 1961. ISBN 0-06-024266-3 Subj: Animals – bears. Caldecott award honor books. Family life – grandparents.

The little giant girl and the elf boys ill. by Garth Williams. HarperCollins, 1963. Subj: Giants. Mythical creatures – elves.

The little girl and the dragon ill. by Martine Gourbault. Greenwillow, 1991. ISBN 0-688-09914-9 Subj: Animals. Behavior – bullying. Character traits – stubbornness. Dragons.

No fighting, no biting! ill. by Maurice Sendak. HarperCollins, 1958. ISBN 0-06-024291-4 Subj: Behavior – fighting, arguing. Reptiles – alligators, crocodiles.

Percy and the five houses ill. by James Stevenson. Greenwillow, 1989. ISBN 0-688-08105-3 Subj: Animals – beavers. Homes, houses.

Minier, Nelson. *see* Baker, Laura Nelson

Minsberg, David. *The book monster* ill. by Shelley Matheis. Littlebee Pr., 1982. ISBN 0-940674-00-9 Subj: Activities – reading. Monsters.

Minters, Frances. *Cinder-Elly* ill. by G. Brian Karas. Viking, 1994. ISBN 0-670-84417-9 Subj: Folk and fairy tales. Rhyming text. Royalty – princes. Sibling rivalry.

Sleepless Beauty ill. by G. Brian Karas. Viking, 1996. ISBN 0-670-87033-1 Subj: Folk and fairy tales. Rhyming text. Witches.

Too big, too small, just right ill. by Janie Bynum. Harcourt, 2001. ISBN 0-15-202157-4 Subj: Animals – rabbits. Concepts – opposites. Rhyming text.

Mintzberg, Yvette. *Sally, where are you?* ill. by author. David & Charles, 1988. ISBN 0-434-95158-7 Subj: Behavior – hiding. Family life.

Mintzer, Jo. *Con mi hermano = With my brother* (Roe, Eileen)

Miranda, Anne. *Baby talk* ill. by Dorothy M. Stott. Dutton, 1987. ISBN 0-525-44319-3 Subj: Babies. Family life. Format, unusual – toy and movable books.

Baby walk ill. by Dorothy M. Stott. Dutton, 1988. ISBN 0-525-44421-1 Subj: Activities – playing. Babies. Format, unusual.

Baby-sit ill. by Dorothy M. Stott. Little, 1990. ISBN 0-316-57454-6 Subj: Activities – babysitting. Family life – mothers. Format, unusual – toy and movable books.

Beep! beep! ill. by David Murphy. Turtle Books, 1999. ISBN 1-890515-14-0 Subj: Automobiles. Imagination. Noise, sounds. Rhyming text. Trucks.

Cownting ill. by Barbara Leonard Gibson. Time-Life, 1994. ISBN 0-7835-4502-9 Subj: Animals – bulls, cows. Birthdays. Counting, numbers. Rhyming text.

Does a mouse have a house? ill. by author. Bradbury, 1994. ISBN 0-02-767251-4 Subj: Animals. Homes, houses. Insects. Rhyming text.

The elephant at the Waldorf ill. by Don Vanderbeek. BridgeWater, 1995. ISBN 0-8167-3452-6 Subj: Animals – elephants. Circus. Rhyming text.

Monster math ill. by Polly Powell. Harcourt, 1999. ISBN 0-15-201835-2 Subj: Birthdays. Counting, numbers. Monsters. Parties. Rhyming text.

Night songs ill. by author. Bradbury, 1993. ISBN 0-02-767250-6 Subj: Lullabies. Night. Noise, sounds.

Pignic ill. by Rosekrans Hoffman. Boyds Mills, 1996. ISBN 1-56397-558-0 Subj: ABC books. Activities – picnicking. Animals – pigs.

To market, to market ill. by Janet Stevens. Harcourt, 1997. ISBN 0-15-200035-6 Subj: Animals. Animals – pigs. Nursery rhymes. Stores.

Vroom, chugga, vroom-vroom ill. by David Murphy. Turtle Books, 1998. ISBN 1-8905-1507-8 Subj: Automobiles. Counting, numbers. Sports – racing. Transportation.

Mirkovic, Irene. *The greedy shopkeeper* ill. by Harold Berson. Harcourt, 1980. Translated and adapt. from a Serbian folk tale. ISBN 0-15-232551-4 Subj: Behavior – trickery. Careers – judges. Folk and fairy tales.

Miryam. *The happy man and his dump truck* ill. by Tibor Gergely. Golden Books, 1999. ISBN 0-307-10218-1 Subj: Animals. Emotions – happiness. Trucks.

Mitakidou, Christodoula. *Mr. Semolina-Semolinus* (Manna, Anthony L.)

Mitchell, Adrian. *Nobody rides the unicorn* ill. by Stephen Lambert. Levine, 2000. ISBN 0-439-11204-4 Subj: Mythical creatures – unicorns. Royalty – kings.

Our mammoth ill. by Priscilla Lamont. Harcourt, 1987. ISBN 0-15-258838-8 Subj: Animals. Humor.

Twice my size ill. by Daniel Pudles. Millbrook, 1999. ISBN 0-7613-1423-7 Subj: Animals. Birds. Concepts – size. Insects. Rhyming text.

Mitchell, Barbara. *Down Buttermilk Lane* ill. by John Sandford. Lothrop, 1993. ISBN 0-688-10115-1 Subj: Ethnic groups in the U.S. – Amish.

Red Bird ill. by Todd L. W. Doney. Lothrop, 1996. ISBN 0-688-10860-1 Subj: Fairs. Family life. Indians of North America – Nanticoke.

Waterman's child ill. by Daniel San Souci. Lothrop, 1997. ISBN 0-688-10862-8 Subj: Careers – fishermen. Family life. U.S. history.

Mitchell, Cynthia. *Halloweena Hecatee* ill. by Eileen Browne. Crowell, 1979. ISBN 0-690-03926-3 Subj: Activities – playing. Games. Poetry.

Here a little child I stand: poems of prayer and praise for children ill. by Satomi Ichikawa. Putnam, 1985. ISBN 0-399-21244-2 Subj: Foreign lands. Poetry. Religion.

Playtime ill. by Satomi Ichikawa. Collins-World, 1978. ISBN 0-434-94364-9 Subj: Activities – playing. Emotions. Poetry.

Under the cherry tree ill. by Satomi Ichikawa. Collins-World, 1979. ISBN 0-529-05544-9 Subj: Poetry.

Mitchell, Joyce Slayton. *My mommy makes money* ill. by True Kelley. Little, 1984. ISBN 0-316-57501-1 Subj: Activities – working. Careers. Family life – mothers.

Tractor-trailer trucker: a powerful truck book photos by Steven Borns. Tricycle, 2000. ISBN 1-58246-010-8 Subj: Careers – truck drivers. Trucks.

Mitchell, Lori. *Different just like me* ill. by author. Charlesbridge, 1999. ISBN 0-88106-975-2 Subj: Character traits – individuality. Family life – grandmothers.

Mitchell, Lucy Sprague. *The taxi that hurried* by Lucy Sprague Mitchell, Irma Simonton Black, and Jessie Stanton; ill. by Tibor Gergely. Western, 1992. ISBN 0-307-00144-X Subj: Taxis. Traffic, traffic signs.

Mitchell, Margaree King. *Granddaddy's gift* ill. by Larry Johnson. BridgeWater, 1996. ISBN 0-8167-4010-0 Subj: Character traits – bravery. Ethnic groups in the U.S. – African Americans. Family life – grandfathers. U.S. history.

Susie Mae ill. by Melodye Benson Rosales. Lothrop, 2000. ISBN 0-688-15222-8 Subj: Ethnic groups in the U.S. – African Americans. Prejudice. School.

Uncle Jed's barbershop ill. by James Ransome. Simon & Schuster, 1993. ISBN 0-671-76969-3 Subj: Careers – barbers. Character traits – perseverance. Ethnic groups in the U.S. – African Americans. Family life – aunts, uncles.

Mitchell, Rhonda. *The talking cloth* ill. by author. Orchard, 1997. ISBN 0-531-33004-4 Subj: Ethnic groups in the U.S. – African Americans. Family life – aunts, uncles. Foreign lands – Africa.

Mitgutsch, Ali. *From gold to money* ill. by author. Carolrhoda, 1985. ISBN 0-87614-230-7 Subj: Science.

From graphite to pencil ill. by author. Carolrhoda, 1985. ISBN 0-87614-231-5 Subj: Science.

From lemon to lemonade ill. by author. Carolrhoda, 1986. ISBN 0-87614-298-6 Subj: Food.

From rubber tree to tire ill. by author. Carolrhoda, 1986. ISBN 0-87614-297-8 Subj: Automobiles.

From sea to salt ill. by author. Carolrhoda, 1985. ISBN 0-87614-232-3 Subj: Science.

From swamp to coal ill. by author. Carolrhoda, 1985. ISBN 0-87614-233-1 Subj: Science.

From wood to paper ill. by author. Carolrhoda, 1986. ISBN 0-87614-296-X Subj: Paper.

Mitra, Annie. *Penguin moon* ill. by author. Holiday, 1989. ISBN 0-8234-0749-7 Subj: Behavior – wishing. Birds – penguins. Moon.

Tusk! Tusk! ill. by author. Holiday, 1990. ISBN 0-8234-0819-1 Subj: Animals – elephants. Careers – dentists. Teeth.

Mitton, Jacqueline. *Zoo in the sky: a book of animal constellations* ill. by Christina Balit; star maps by Wil Tirion. National Geographic, 1998. ISBN 0-7922-7069-X Subj: Stars.

Mitton, Tony. *Flashing fire engines* by Tony Mitton and Ant Parker; ill. by Ant Parker. Kingfisher, 1998. ISBN 0-7534-5104-2 Subj: Careers – firefighters. Noise, sounds. Rhyming text. Trucks.

Miyoshi, Sekiya. *Singing David* ill. by author. Watts, 1969. ISBN 0-531-01936-5 Subj: Religion.

Mizumura, Kazue. *If I built a village* ill. by author. Crowell, 1971. ISBN 0-690-42903-7 Subj: Character traits – kindness. City. Ecology. Homes, houses.

If I were a cricket . . . ill. by author. Crowell, 1973. ISBN 0-690-00076-6 Subj: Animals. Emotions – love. Insects – crickets. Poetry.

If I were a mother ill. by author. Crowell, 1967. Subj: Family life – mothers.

Mlawer, Teresa. *Just like home = Como en mi tierra* (Miller, Elizabeth I.)

Moak, Allan. *A big city ABC* ill. by author. Tundra, 1984. ISBN 0-88776-161-5 Subj: ABC books. City. Foreign lands – Canada.

Mobley, Jane. *The star husband* ill. by Anna Vojtech. Doubleday, 1979. ISBN 0-385-14283-8 Subj: Folk and fairy tales. Indians of North America – Great Plains. Stars.

Moché, Dinah L. *The astronauts* ill. with photos from NASA. Random House, 1979. ISBN 0-394-93901-8 Subj: Moon. Science. Space and space ships.

Mochizuki, Ken. *Baseball saved us* ill. by Dom Lee. Lee & Low, 1993. ISBN 1-880000-01-6 Subj: Ethnic groups in the U.S. – Japanese Americans. Sports – baseball. U.S. history. War.

Heroes ill. by Dom Lee. Lee & Low, 1995. ISBN 1-880000-16-4 Subj: Ethnic groups in the U.S. – Japanese Americans. U.S. history. War.

Mockford, Caroline. *What's this?* ill. by author. Barefoot, 2000. ISBN 1-84148-018-5 Subj: Flowers. Gardens, gardening. Seeds.

Modarressi, Mitra. *The beastly visits* ill. by author. Orchard, 1996. ISBN 0-531-09530-4 Subj: Behavior – bullying. Character traits – being different. Friendship. Monsters.

The dream pillow ill. by author. Orchard, 1994. ISBN 0-531-08705-0 Subj: Birthdays. Character traits – conceit. Dreams. Friendship.

The parent thief ill. by author. Orchard, 1995. ISBN 0-531-08776-X Subj: Behavior – boredom. Behavior – running away. Boats, ships. Family life. Sea and seashore.

Yard sale ill. by author. DK, 2000. ISBN 0-7894-2651-X Subj: Communities, neighborhoods. Magic. Stores.

Modell, Frank. *Goodbye old year, hello new year* ill. by author. Greenwillow, 1984. ISBN 0-688-03939-1 Subj: Holidays – New Year's.

Ice cream soup ill. by author. Greenwillow, 1988. ISBN 0-688-07771-4 Subj: Birthdays. Parties.

Look out, it's April Fools' Day ill. by author. Greenwillow, 1985. ISBN 0-688-04017-9 Subj: Holidays – April Fools' Day. Riddles.

One zillion valentines ill. by author. Greenwillow, 1981. ISBN 0-688-00569-1 Subj: Character traits – practicality. Holidays – Valentine's Day.

Seen any cats? ill. by author. Greenwillow, 1979. ISBN 0-688-84229-1 Subj: Animals – cats. Circus.

Skeeter and the computer ill. by author. Greenwillow, 1988. ISBN 0-688-03706-2 Subj: Animals – dogs. Computers.

Tooley! Tooley! ill. by author. Greenwillow, 1979. ISBN 0-688-84092-2 Subj: Animals – dogs. Behavior – lost. Humor.

Modesitt, Jeanne. *It's Hanukkah!* ill. by Robin Spowart. Holiday, 1999. ISBN 0-8234-1451-5 Subj: Animals – mice. Holidays – Hanukkah. Jewish culture. Religion.

Little Bunny's Easter surprise ill. by Robin Spowart. Simon & Schuster, 1999. ISBN 0-689-82491-2 Subj: Animals – rabbits. Behavior – hiding things. Holidays – Easter.

Lunch with Milly ill. by Robin Spowart. BridgeWater, 1995. ISBN 0-8167-3388-0 Subj: Activities – working. Animals. Food. Sea and seashore.

Mama, if you had a wish ill. by Robin Spowart. Green Tiger Pr., 1993. ISBN 0-671-75437-8 Subj: Animals – rabbits. Behavior – wishing. Character traits – individuality. Family life – mothers.

The night call ill. by Robin Spowart. Viking, 1989. ISBN 0-670-82500-X Subj: Animals. Night. Stars. Toys.

Sometimes I feel like a mouse: a book about feelings ill. by Robin Spowart. Scholastic, 1992. ISBN 0-590-44835-8 Subj: Emotions. Imagination.

Songs of Chanukah ill. by Robin Spowart; music arranged by Uri Ophir. Little, 1992. ISBN 0-316-57739-1 Subj: Holidays – Hanukkah. Jewish culture. Music. Religion. Songs.

The story of Z ill. by Lonni Sue Johnson. Picture Book Studio, 1990. ISBN 0-88708-105-3 Subj: Emotions.

Vegetable soup ill. by Robin Spowart. Macmillan, 1991. ISBN 0-689-71523-4 Subj: Animals. Animals – rabbits. Communities, neighborhoods. Food.

Moe, J. E. *The man who kept house* (Asbjørnsen, P. C. [Peter Christen])

Moeri, Louise. *Star Mother's youngest child* ill. by Trina Schart Hyman. Houghton Mifflin, 1975. ISBN 0-395-21406-8 Subj: Folk and fairy tales. Holidays – Christmas.

The unicorn and the plow ill. by Diane Goode. Dutton, 1982. ISBN 0-525-45116-1 Subj: Character traits – luck. Farms. Mythical creatures – unicorns.

Moers, Hermann. *Annie's dancing day* ill. by Christa Unzner-Fischer; trans. by Rosemary Lanning. North-South, 1992. ISBN 1-55858-161-8 Subj: Activities – dancing. Ballet. Behavior – lost. Imagination.

Camomile heads for home trans. by Rosemary Lanning; ill. by Marcus Pfister. Holt, 1987. ISBN 0-8050-0280-4 Subj: Animals – bulls, cows. Behavior – growing up.

Evie to the rescue! ill. by Gusti; trans. by Marianne Martens. North-South, 1997. ISBN 1-55858-794-2 Subj: Animals – lions. Dreams. Foreign lands – Africa.

Hugo's baby brother ill. by Józef Wilkon. North-South, 1991. ISBN 1-55858-146-4 Subj: Animals – lions. Family life. Sibling rivalry.

Katie and the big, brave bear ill. by Józef Wilkon; trans. by Marianne Martens. North-South, 1995. ISBN 1-55858-398-X Subj: Animals – bears. Emotions – fear. Friendship. Imagination – imaginary friends.

Little Ben ill. by Jean-Pierre Corderoch; trans. by Rosemary Lanning. North-South, 1991. ISBN 1-55858-105-7 Subj: Behavior – growing up. Concepts – size.

Lullaby for a newborn king (Wilkon, Józef)

Moffatt, Judith. *Christmas lights* ill. by author. Little Simon, 1999. ISBN 0-689-82269-3 Subj: Format, unusual. Holidays – Christmas.

Halloween frights ill. by author. Little Simon, 1999. ISBN 0-689-82270-7 Subj: Format, unusual. Holidays – Halloween.

The pumpkin man ill. by author. Scholastic, 1998. ISBN 0-590-63865-3 Subj: Holidays – Halloween. Rhyming text.

Trick-or-treat faces: a glowing book you can read in the dark! ill. by author. Scholastic, 2000. ISBN 0-439-18299-9 Subj: Format, unusual. Holidays – Halloween. Monsters. Rhyming text.

Who stole the cookies? ill. by author. Grosset, 1996. ISBN 0-448-41127-X Subj: Animals. Behavior – stealing. Food. Rhyming text.

Moffett, Martha A. *A flower pot is not a hat* ill. by Susan Perl. Dutton, 1972. ISBN 0-525-29920-3 Subj: Activities – playing. Humor.

Mogensen, Jan. *The forty-six little men* ill. by author. Greenwillow, 1991. ISBN 0-688-09284-5 Subj: Imagination. Little people. Wordless.

The Land of the Big ill. by author. Crocodile Books, 1992. ISBN 1-56656-111-6 Subj: Concepts – size. Family life – aunts, uncles. Insects.

Lost and found Teddy ill. by author. Gareth Stevens, 1990. ISBN 0-8368-0432-5 Subj: Behavior – lost. Toys – bears. Trains.

Teddy and the Chinese dragon ill. by author. Gareth Stevens, 1985. ISBN 1-55532-002-3 Subj: Dragons. Toys – bears.

Teddy in the undersea kingdom ill. by author. Gareth Stevens, 1985. ISBN 1-55532-000-7 Subj: Crustaceans. Sea and seashore. Toys – bears.

Teddy runs away ill. by author. Gareth Stevens, 1990. ISBN 0-8368-0371-X Subj: Behavior – running away. Toys. Toys – bears.

Teddy's birthday bugle ill. by author. Gareth Stevens, 1990. ISBN 0-8368-0372-8 Subj: Animals. Birthdays. Toys. Toys – bears.

Teddy's Christmas gift ill. by author. Gareth Stevens, 1985. ISBN 1-55532-004-X Subj: Character traits – kindness to animals. Gifts. Holidays – Christmas. Santa Claus. Toys – bears.

The tiger's breakfast ill. by author. Interlink, 1991. ISBN 0-940793-83-0 Subj: Animals – elephants. Animals – mice. Behavior – trickery. Character traits – cleverness.

When Teddy woke early ill. by author. Gareth Stevens, 1985. ISBN 1-55532-006-6 Subj: Behavior – lost. Toys – bears.

Mohr, Joseph. *Silent night* verses by Joseph Mohr; ill. by Susan Jeffers. Dutton, 1984. Orig. title: Stille Nacht, heilige Nacht. ISBN 0-525-44144-1 Subj: Holidays – Christmas. Songs.

Molarsky, Osmond. *A sky full of kites* ill. by Helen D. Hipshman. Tricycle, 1996. ISBN 1-883672-26-0 Subj: Activities – painting. Ethnic groups in the U.S. – Asian Americans. Kites.

Mole, John. *Copy cat* ill. by Bee Willey. Kingfisher, 1997. ISBN 0-7534-5008-9 Subj: Animals – cats. Behavior – imitation.

Molk, Laurel. *Good job, Oliver!* ill. by author. Crown, 1999. ISBN 0-517-70976-7 Subj: Animals – rabbits. Gardens, gardening.

Mollel, Tololwa M. (Tololwa Marti). *Ananse's feast: an Ashanti tale* ill. by Andrew Glass. Clarion, 1997. ISBN 0-395-67402-6 Subj: Behavior – trickery. Country. Folk and fairy tales. Foreign lands – Ghana. Reptiles – turtles, tortoises. Spiders.

Big boy ill. by E. B. Lewis. Clarion, 1995. ISBN 0-395-67403-4 Subj: Behavior – wishing. Folk and fairy tales. Foreign lands – Tanzania. Giants.

Dume's roar ill. by Kathy Blankley Roman. Stoddart Kids, 1998. ISBN 0-7737-3003-6 Subj: Animals. Animals – lions. Folk and fairy tales. Foreign lands – Africa. Royalty – kings.

The flying tortoise: an Igbo tale ill. by Barbara Spurll. Oxford Univ. Pr., 1993. ISBN 0-395-68845-0 Subj: Behavior – greed. Behavior – trickery. Folk and fairy tales. Foreign lands – Nigeria. Reptiles – turtles, tortoises.

Kele's secret ill. by Catherine Stock. Dutton, 1997. ISBN 0-525-67500-0 Subj: Birds – chickens. Family life – grandparents. Foreign lands – Tanzania.

The king and the tortoise ill. by Kathy Blankley. Clarion, 1993. ISBN 0-395-64480-1 Subj: Animals. Folk and fairy tales. Foreign lands – Cameroon. Reptiles – turtles, tortoises. Royalty – kings.

Kitoto the mighty ill. by Kristi Frost. Stoddart Kids, 1998. ISBN 0-7737-3019-2 Subj: Animals – mice. Folk and fairy tales. Foreign lands – Africa.

My rows and piles of coins ill. by E. B. Lewis. Clarion, 1999. ISBN 0-395-75186-1 Subj: Foreign lands – Tanzania. Money. Sports – bicycling.

Orphan boy ill. by Paul Morin. Clarion, 1991. ISBN 0-89919-985-2 Subj: Folk and fairy tales. Foreign lands – Kenya. Magic. Orphans.

The princess who lost her hair: an Akamba legend ill. by Charles Reasoner. Troll, 1993. ISBN 0-816-72815-1 Subj: Character traits – selfishness. Folk and fairy tales. Foreign lands – Africa. Hair. Royalty – princesses.

A promise to the sun ill. by Beatriz A. Vidal. Little, 1992. ISBN 0-316-57813-4 Subj: Animals – bats. Birds. Foreign lands – Kenya. Sun. Weather.

Rhinos for lunch and elephants for supper ill. by Barbara Spurll. Houghton Mifflin, 1992. ISBN 0-395-60734-5 Subj: Animals. Cumulative tales. Emotions – fear. Foreign lands – Kenya.

Shadow dance ill. by Donna Perrone. Clarion, 1998. ISBN 0-395-82909-7 Subj: Behavior – trickery. Folk and fairy tales. Foreign lands – Tanzania. Reptiles – alligators, crocodiles.

Song bird ill. by Rosanne Litzinger. Clarion, 1999. ISBN 0-395-82908-9 Subj: Birds. Folk and fairy tales. Foreign lands – Tanzania. Magic. Monsters.

Subira subira ill. by Linda Saport. Clarion, 2000. ISBN 0-395-91809-X Subj: Character traits – patience. Folk and fairy tales. Foreign lands – Tanzania.

To dinner, for dinner ill. by Synthia Saint James. Holiday, 2000. ISBN 0-8234-1527-9 Subj: Animals. Animals – leopards. Animals – rabbits. Foreign lands – Africa.

Molnar, Dorothy E. *Who will pick me up when I fall?* by Dorothy E. Molnar and Stephan H. Fenton; ill. by Irene Trivas. Albert Whitman, 1991. ISBN 0-8075-9072-X Subj: Days of the week, months of the year. Family life.

Molnar, Joe. *Graciela: a Mexican-American child tells her story* photos by author. Watts, 1972. ISBN 0-531-02023-1 Subj: Ethnic groups in the U.S. – Mexican Americans.

Molnar-Fenton, Stephan. *An Mei's strange and wondrous journey* ill. by Vivienne Flesher. DK, 1998. ISBN 0-7894-2477-0 Subj: Adoption. Ethnic groups in the U.S. – Chinese Americans.

Moncure, Jane Belk. *Happy healthkins* ill. by Lois Axeman. Childrens Pr., 1982. ISBN 0-516-06314-6 Subj: Health and fitness. Rhyming text.

The healthkin food train ill. by Lois Axeman. Childrens Pr., 1982. ISBN 0-516-06311-1 Subj: Health and fitness. Rhyming text.

Healthkins exercise! ill. by Lois Axeman. Childrens Pr., 1982. ISBN 0-516-06312-X Subj: Health and fitness – exercise. Rhyming text.

Healthkins help ill. by Lois Axeman. Childrens Pr., 1982. ISBN 0-516-06313-8 Subj: Health and fitness. Rhyming text.

The look book ill. by Lois Axeman. Childrens Pr., 1982. ISBN 0-516-03251-8 Subj: Senses – seeing.

Now I am five! ill. by Helen Endes. Childrens Pr., 1984. ISBN 0-516-01879-5 Subj: Activities. Behavior – growing up.

Now I am four! ill. by Kathryn Hutton. Childrens Pr., 1984. ISBN 0-516-01878-7 Subj: Activities. Behavior – growing up.

Now I am three! ill. by Linda Hohag. Childrens Pr., 1984. ISBN 0-516-01877-9 Subj: Activities. Behavior – growing up.

Riddle me a riddle ill. by Marc Belenchia. Childrens Pr., 1977. ISBN 0-913778-80-X Subj: Animals. Magic. Riddles.

Sounds all around ill. by Lois Axeman. Childrens Pr., 1982. ISBN 0-516-03252-6 Subj: Senses – hearing.

The talking tabby cat: a folk tale from France ill. by Helen Endres. Childrens Pr., 1980. ISBN 0-516-06483-5 Subj: Animals – cats. Folk and fairy tales.

A tasting party ill. by Viki Woodworth. Child's World, 1998. ISBN 1-56766-283-8 Subj: Food. Senses – tasting.

The touch book ill. by Lois Axeman. Childrens Pr., 1982. ISBN 0-516-03254-2 Subj: Senses – touching.

What your nose knows! ill. by Lois Axeman. Childrens Pr., 1982. ISBN 0-516-03255-0 Subj: Anatomy – noses. Senses – smelling.

Where? ill. by Lois Axeman. Childrens Pr., 1983. ISBN 0-516-06593-9 Subj: Character traits – curiosity. Character traits – questioning.

Word Bird's fall words ill. by Linda Hohag. Childrens Pr., 1985. ISBN 0-89565-308-7 Subj: Language. Seasons – fall.

Word Bird's spring words ill. by Vera Gohman. Childrens Pr., 1985. ISBN 0-89565-310-9 Subj: Language. Seasons – spring.

Word Bird's summer words ill. by Linda Hohag. Childrens Pr., 1985. ISBN 0-89565-311-7 Subj: Language. Seasons – summer.

Word Bird's winter words ill. by Vera Gohman. Childrens Pr., 1985. ISBN 0-89565-309-5 Subj: Language. Seasons – winter.

Monfried, Lucia. *Baby's world* ill. by Stephen Shott. Dutton, 1990. ISBN 0-525-44617-6 Subj: Babies. Format, unusual. Language.

The Daddies Boat ill. by Michele Chessare. Dutton, 1990. ISBN 0-525-44584-6 Subj: Activities – vacationing. Boats, ships. Family life – mothers. Islands.

Dishes all done ill. by Jon Agee. Dutton, 1989. ISBN 0-525-44433-5 Subj: Activities. Format, unusual – toy and movable books. Rhyming text.

Grizzly bear (Cherry, Lynne)

Orangutan (Cherry, Lynne)

Seal (Cherry, Lynne)

Snow leopard (Cherry, Lynne)

Monjo, F. N. *The drinking gourd: a story of the underground railroad* ill. by Fred Brenner. HarperCollins, 1993. ISBN 0-06-024330-9 Subj: Ethnic groups in the U.S. – African Americans. Slavery. U.S. history.

The one bad thing about father ill. by Rocco Negri. HarperCollins, 1970. ISBN 0-06-024334-1 Subj: Family life – fathers. U.S. history.

Poor Richard in France ill. by Brinton Turkle. Holt, 1973. ISBN 0-03-088597-3 Subj: U.S. history.

Rudi and the distelfink ill. by George Kraus. Windmill, 1972. ISBN 0-525-61002-2 Subj: Family life.

Monks, Lydia. *The cat barked?* ill. by author. Dial, 1999. ISBN 0-8037-2338-5 Subj: Animals – cats. Animals – dogs. Rhyming text. Self-concept.

Monsell, Helen Albee. *Paddy's Christmas* ill. by Kurt Wiese. Knopf, 1942. Subj: Animals – bears. Holidays – Christmas.

Monsell, Mary Elise. *Armadillo* ill. by Sylvie Wickstrom. Macmillan, 1991. ISBN 0-689-31676-3 Subj: Animals – armadillos. Friendship.

Crackle Creek ill. by Kathleen Garry McCord. Atheneum, 1990. ISBN 0-689-31564-3 Subj: Animals – mice. Careers – printers. Character traits – helpfulness. Paper.

Underwear! ill. by Lynn Munsinger. Albert Whitman, 1988. ISBN 0-8075-8308-1 Subj: Animals. Clothing. Humor.

Monson, A. M. *Wanted . . . best friend* ill. by Lynn Munsinger. Dial, 1997. ISBN 0-8037-1485-8 Subj: Animals – cats. Animals – mice. Friendship. Games.

Monster poems ed. by Daisy Wallace; ill. by Kay Chorao. Holiday, 1976. ISBN 0-8234-0268-1 Subj: Monsters. Poetry. Tongue twisters.

Monster soup and other spooky poems ill. by Jacqueline Rogers; comp. by Dilys Evans. Scholastic, 1992. ISBN 0-590-45208-8 Subj: Monsters. Poetry.

Montenegro, Laura Nyman. *One stuck drawer* ill. by author. Houghton Mifflin, 1991. ISBN 0-395-57319-X Subj: Furniture – dressers.

Sweet Tooth ill. by author. Houghton Mifflin, 1995. ISBN 0-395-68078-6 Subj: Animals – lions. Character traits – loyalty. Circus. Friendship.

Montgomerie, Norah. *This little pig went to market: play rhymes* ill. by Margery Gill. Watts, 1967. Subj: Games. Nursery rhymes. Participation.

Montgomery, Lee. *Ant* (Hawcock, David)

Bee (Hawcock, David)

Beetle (Hawcock, David)

Fly (Hawcock, David)

Spider (Hawcock, David)

Wasp (Hawcock, David)

Montgomery, Michael. *'Night, America* ill. by author. Contemporary Books, 1989. ISBN 0-8092-4397-0 Subj: Bedtime. Night. Rhyming text.

Montresor, Beni. *A for angel: Beni Montresor's ABC picture-stories* ill. by author. Knopf, 1969. ISBN 0-394-90883-X Subj: ABC books.

Bedtime! ill. by author. HarperCollins, 1978. ISBN 0-06-024354-6 Subj: Bedtime. Dreams.

The witches of Venice ill. by author. Doubleday, 1989. ISBN 0-385-26355-4 Subj: Dreams. Flowers. Royalty. Witches.

Moodie, Fiona. *Nabulela: a South African folk tale* ill. by reteller. Farrar, 1997. ISBN 0-374-35486-3 Subj: Emotions – envy, jealousy. Foreign lands – South Africa. Monsters.

Moodie, Prudence. *Little Mop lost* (Kanome, Kayoko)

Moon, Carl. *One little Indian* (Moon, Grace Purdie)

Moon, Cliff. *Pigs on the farm* ill. by Anna Jupp. Watts, 1983. ISBN 0-531-04696-6 Subj: Animals – pigs. Farms.

Moon, Dolly M. *My very first book of cowboy songs: 21 favorite songs in easy piano arrangements* ill. by Frederic Remington. Dover, 1982. ISBN 0-486-24311-7 Subj: Cowboys. Folk and fairy tales. Songs.

Moon, Grace Purdie. *One little Indian* by Grace and Carl Moon; ill. by Carl Moon. Albert Whitman, 1950. Subj: Birthdays. Indians of North America.

Moon, Nicola. *Alligator tails and crocodile cakes* ill. by Andy Ellis. Kingfisher, 1997. ISBN 0-7534-5080-1 Subj: Activities – baking. Character traits – cleanliness. Friendship. Games. Reptiles – alligators, crocodiles.

At the beginning of a pig ill. by Andy Ellis. Kingfisher, 1994. ISBN 1-85697-977-6 Subj: Anatomy. Animals. Format, unusual – toy and movable books.

Lucy's picture ill. by Alex Ayliffe. Dial, 1995. ISBN 0-8037-1833-0 Subj: Activities – making things. Art. Family life – grandfathers. Handicaps – blindness.

Something special ill. by Alex Ayliffe. Peachtree, 1997. ISBN 1-56145-137-1 Subj: Babies. Family life – brothers and sisters. School.

Moon, Pat. *This is the earth* ill. by Lisa Flather. Viking, 1994. ISBN 0-670-85488-3 Subj: Cumulative tales. Ecology. Poetry.

The moon's the north wind's cooky: *night poems* comp. and ill. by Susan Russo. Lothrop, 1979. ISBN 0-688-51879-6 Subj: Bedtime. Night. Poetry.

Moorat, Joseph. *Thirty old-time nursery songs* (Mother Goose)

Moore, Chevelle. *Getting dressed* (Moore, Dessie)

Good morning (Moore, Dessie)

Good night (Moore, Dessie)

Let's pretend (Moore, Dessie)

Moore, Christopher J. *Ishtar and Tammuz: a Babylonian myth of the seasons* ill. by Christina Balit. Kingfisher, 1996. ISBN 0-7534-5012-7 Subj: Mythical creatures. Seasons.

Moore, Clement C. *The night before Christmas* ill. by Jan Brett. Putnam, 1998. ISBN 0-399-23190-0 Subj: Holidays – Christmas. Poetry. Santa Claus.

The night before Christmas ill. by Tomie de Paola. Holiday, 1980. ISBN 0-8234-0414-5 Subj: Holidays – Christmas. Poetry. Santa Claus.

The night before Christmas comp. by Cooper Edens and Harold Darling; ill. by various 19th- and 20th-century artists. A classic illustrated ed. Chronicle, 1998. ISBN 0-8118-1712-1 Subj: Holidays – Christmas. Poetry. Santa Claus.

The night before Christmas ill. by Michael Foreman. Viking, 1988. ISBN 0-670-82388-0 Subj: Holidays – Christmas. Poetry. Santa Claus.

The night before Christmas ill. by Gyo Fujikawa. Grosset, 1961. ISBN 0-448-02935-9 Subj: Holidays – Christmas. Poetry. Santa Claus.

The night before Christmas ill. by Scott Gustafson. Knopf, 1985. ISBN 0-394-54809-4 Subj: Holidays – Christmas. Poetry. Santa Claus.

The night before Christmas ill. by Cheryl Harness. Random House, 1990. ISBN 0-394-92698-6 Subj: Holidays – Christmas. Poetry. Santa Claus.

The night before Christmas ill. by Loretta Krupinski. Hyperion, 1998. ISBN 0-7868-2252-X Subj: Animals – mice. Holidays – Christmas. Poetry. Santa Claus.

The night before Christmas ill. by Anita Lobel. Knopf, 1984. ISBN 0-394-96863-8 Subj: Holidays – Christmas. Poetry. Santa Claus.

The night before Christmas ill. by James Marshall. Scholastic, 1989. ISBN 0-590-33805-6 Subj: Holidays – Christmas. Poetry. Santa Claus.

The night before Christmas ill. by Jacqueline Rogers. Platt, 1987. ISBN 0-448-19097-4 Subj: Holidays – Christmas. Poetry. Santa Claus.

The night before Christmas ill. by Robin Spowart. Dodd, 1986. ISBN 0-396-08798-1 Subj: Holidays – Christmas. Poetry. Santa Claus.

The night before Christmas ill. by Gustaf Tenggren. Simon & Schuster, 1951. Subj: Holidays – Christmas. Poetry. Santa Claus.

The night before Christmas ill. by Tasha Tudor. Rand McNally, 1975. ISBN 0-5288-0144-9 Subj: Holidays – Christmas. Poetry. Santa Claus.

The night before Christmas ill. by Wendy Watson. Houghton Mifflin, 1990. ISBN 0-395-53624-3 Subj: Holidays – Christmas. Poetry. Santa Claus.

The night before Christmas ill. by Jody Wheeler. Ideals, 1988. ISBN 0-8249-8279-7 Subj: Holidays – Christmas. Poetry. Santa Claus.

The night before Christmas in signed English ill. by Ralph R. Miller, Sr. Prepated under the supervision of the staff of the Pre-School Signed English Project by Barbara M. Kannapell. Gallaudet Univ. Pr., 1973. ISBN 0-913580-15-5 Subj: Handicaps – deafness. Holidays – Christmas. Languages. Poetry. Santa Claus.

The teddy bears' night before Christmas photos by Monica Stevenson. Scholastic, 1999. ISBN 0-590-03243-7 Subj: Holidays – Christmas. Poetry. Santa Claus. Toys. Toys – bears.

A visit from St. Nicholas: 'Twas the night before Christmas ill. by Paul Galdone. McGraw-Hill, 1968. Subj: Holidays – Christmas. Poetry. Santa Claus.

Moore, Dessie. *Getting dressed* by Dessie and Chevelle Moore; ill. by Chevelle Moore. Harper-Collins, 1994. ISBN 0-694-00590-8 Subj: Clothing. Ethnic groups in the U.S. – African Americans. Format, unusual – board books.

Good morning by Dessie and Chevelle Moore; ill. by Chevelle Moore. HarperCollins, 1994. ISBN 0-694-00593-2 Subj: Ethnic groups in the U.S. – African Americans. Format, unusual – board books. Morning.

Good night by Dessie and Chevelle Moore; ill. by Chevelle Moore. HarperCollins, 1994. ISBN 0-694-00592-4 Subj: Ethnic groups in the U.S. – African Americans. Format, unusual – board books. Night.

Let's pretend by Dessie and Chevelle Moore; ill. by Chevelle Moore. HarperCollins, 1994. ISBN 0-694-00591-6 Subj: Ethnic groups in the U.S. – African Americans. Format, unusual – board books. Rhyming text.

Moore, Elaine. *Deep river* ill. by Henri Sorensen. Simon & Schuster, 1994. ISBN 0-671-87278-8 Subj: Family life – grandfathers. Sports – fishing.

Good morning, city ill. by William Low. BridgeWater, 1995. ISBN 0-8167-3654-5 Subj: Careers. City. Morning.

Grammy, do you love me? ill. by Kathy Wilburn. Longmeadow, 1994. ISBN 0-681-00442-8 Subj: Animals – rabbits. Emotions – love. Family life – grandmothers.

Grandma's garden ill. by Dan Andreasen. Lothrop, 1990. ISBN 0-688-08694-2 Subj: Family life – grandmothers. Gardens, gardening. Seasons – spring. Weather.

Grandma's house ill. by Elise Primavera. Lothrop, 1985. ISBN 0-688-04116-7 Subj: Animals. Country. Family life – grandmothers. Seasons – summer.

Grandma's promise ill. by Elise Primavera. Lothrop, 1988. ISBN 0-688-06741-7 Subj: Country. Family life – grandmothers. Seasons – winter.

Grandma's smile ill. by Dan Andreasen. Lothrop, 1995. ISBN 0-688-11076-2 Subj: Fairs. Family life – grandmothers. Seasons – fall.

Roly-poly puppies ill. by Jacqueline Rogers. Scholastic, 1996. ISBN 0-590-46665-8 Subj: Animals – dogs. Counting, numbers. Rhyming text.

Moore, Elizabeth. *Mimi and Jean-Paul's Cajun Mardi Gras* by Elizabeth Moore and Alice W. Couvillon; ill. by Marilyn Carter Rougelot. Pelican, 1996. ISBN 1-56554-069-7 Subj: Mardi Gras.

Moore, Eva. *Dick Whittington and his cat* (Dick Whittington and his cat)

Moore, Inga. *Aktil's big swim* ill. by author. Oxford Univ. Pr., 1981. ISBN 0-19-554250-9 Subj: Animals – rats. Sports – swimming.

A big day for Little Jack ill. by author. Candlewick, 1994. ISBN 1-56402-418-0 Subj: Animals – rabbits. Character traits – shyness. Emotions – fear. Parties.

Fifty red night-caps ill. by Linda Moore. Chronicle, 1988. ISBN 0-87701-520-1 Subj: Animals – monkeys. Behavior – imitation. Behavior – stealing. Clothing – hats. Forest, woods.

Little dog lost ill. by author. Macmillan, 1991. ISBN 0-02-767648-X Subj: Animals – dogs. Behavior – running away. Country. Friendship. Moving.

Oh, little Jack ill. by author. Candlewick, 1992. ISBN 1-56402-028-2 Subj: Animals – rabbits. Character traits – smallness. Family life.

Rose and the nightingale ill. by author. Knopf, 1990. ISBN 0-679-80197-9 Subj: Birds – nightingales. Character traits – kindness to animals.

Six dinner Sid ill. by author. Simon & Schuster, 1991. ISBN 0-671-73199-8 Subj: Animals – cats. Pets.

The sorcerer's apprentice ill. by author. Macmillan, 1989. ISBN 0-02-767645-5 Subj: Folk and fairy tales. Magic.

The truffle hunter ill. by author. Kane/Miller, 1987. ISBN 0-916291-09-X Subj: Animals – pigs. Behavior – seeking better things. Country. Foreign lands – France.

The vegetable thieves ill. by author. Viking, 1984. ISBN 0-670-74380-1 Subj: Animals – mice. Gardens, gardening. Orphans.

Moore, John. *Granny Stickleback* by John Moore and Martin Wright; ill. by authors. Hamish Hamilton, 1982. ISBN 0-241-10635-4 Subj: Animals. Crime. Sports – racing.

Moore, Julia. *While you sleep* ill. by Lyn Gilbert. Dutton, 1996. ISBN 0-525-45462-4 Subj: Babies. Bedtime. Rhyming text. Sleep.

Moore, Karen Ann. *The baby king: fun fur to touch!* ill. by Bev Luedecke. Chariot Victor, 1999. ISBN 0-7814-3253-7 Subj: Animals. Format, unusual – toy and movable books. Holidays – Christmas. Religion – Nativity.

Moore, Lilian. *Adam Mouse's book of poems* ill. by Kathleen Garry-McCord. Atheneum, 1992. ISBN 0-689-31765-4 Subj: Animals – mice. Nature. Poetry.

Hooray for me! (Charlip, Remy)

I feel the same way ill. by Robert M. Quackenbush. Atheneum, 1967. Subj: Poetry.

I never did that before ill. by Lillian Hoban. Atheneum, 1995. ISBN 0-689-31889-8 Subj: Poetry.

I'm small and other verses ill. by Jill McElmurry. Candlewick, 2001. ISBN 0-7636-1169-7 Subj: Poetry.

Little Raccoon and no trouble at all ill. by Gioia Fiammenghi. McGraw-Hill, 1972. ISBN 0-07-042909-X Subj: Activities – babysitting. Animals – chipmunks. Animals – raccoons. Multiple births – twins.

Little Raccoon and the outside world ill. by Gioia Fiammenghi. McGraw-Hill, 1965. Subj: Animals – raccoons.

Little Raccoon and the thing in the pool ill. by Gioia Fiammenghi. McGraw-Hill, 1963. Subj: Animals – raccoons. Emotions – fear.

Papa Albert ill. by Gioia Fiammenghi. Atheneum, 1964. Subj: Careers – taxi drivers. Family life. Foreign lands – France. Foreign languages. Taxis.

See my lovely poison ivy, and other verses about witches, ghosts and things ill. by Diane Dawson. Atheneum, 1975. ISBN 0-689-30468-4 Subj: Animals – cats. Monsters. Poetry. Witches.

The ugly duckling (Andersen, H. C. [Hans Christian])

Moore, Mary-Alice. *Peek-a-boo, baby!* (Leonard, Marcia)

Moore, Miriam. *Peter and Susie find a family* (Hess, Edith)

Moore, Sheila. *Samson Svenson's baby* ill. by Karen Ann Weinhaus. HarperCollins, 1983. ISBN 0-06-022613-7 Subj: Birds – ducks. Character traits – appearance. Character traits – kindness to animals.

Moorman, Margaret. *Light the lights!* ill. by author. Scholastic, 1994. ISBN 0-590-47003-5 Subj: Family life. Holidays – Christmas. Holidays – Hanukkah. Religion.

Mooser, Stephen. *The fat cat* by Stephen Mooser and Lin Oliver; ill. by Susan Day. Warner, 1988. ISBN 1-55782-022-8 Subj: Animals – cats.

Funnyman and the penny dodo ill. by Tomie de Paola. Watts, 1984. ISBN 0-531-04393-2 Subj: Crime. Humor. Mystery stories.

Funnyman meets the monster from outer space ill. by Maxie Chambliss. Scholastic, 1987. ISBN 0-590-33959-1 Subj: Aliens. Monsters. Space and space ships.

Funnyman's first case ill. by Tomie de Paola. Watts, 1981. ISBN 0-531-04300-2 Subj: Careers – waiters, waitresses. Mystery stories. Riddles.

The ghost with the Halloween hiccups ill. by Tomie de Paola. Watts, 1977. ISBN 0-531-01316-2 Subj: Ghosts. Holidays – Halloween.

Mora, Emma. *Animals of the forest* trans. from Italian by Jean Grasso Fitzpatrick; ill. by Kennedy. Barron's, 1986. ISBN 0-8120-5722-8 Subj: Animals. Forest, woods.

Gideon, the little bear cub trans. from Italian by Jean Grasso Fitzpatrick; ill. by Kennedy. Barron's, 1986. ISBN 0-8120-5728-7 Subj: Forest, woods. Rhyming text. Seasons.

Mora, Jo. *Budgee Budgee Cottontail* ill. by author. D.R. Stoecklein, 1995. ISBN 0-922029-23-7 Subj: Animals – rabbits. Behavior – running away. Cowboys. Holidays – Christmas.

Mora, Pat. *A birthday basket for Tía* ill. by Cecily Lang. Macmillan, 1992. ISBN 0-02-767400-2 Subj: Animals – cats. Birthdays. Ethnic groups in the U.S. – Mexican Americans. Family life – aunts, uncles. Gifts.

Confetti ill. by Enrique O. Sánchez. Lee & Low, 1996. ISBN 1-880000-25-3 Subj: Ethnic groups in the U.S. – Mexican Americans. Foreign languages. Poetry.

Delicious hullabaloo = Pachanga deliciosa ill. by Francisco X. Mora; Spanish trans. by Alba Nora Martinez and Pat Mora. Piñata Books, 1998. ISBN 1-55885-246-8 Subj: Animals. Desert. Foreign languages. Night. Parties. Poetry. Reptiles – lizards.

The desert is my mother = El desierto es mi madre ill. by Daniel Lechón. Piñata Books, 1994. ISBN 1-55885-121-6 Subj: Desert. Foreign languages. Poetry.

The gift of the poinsettia = El regalo de la flor de nochebuena by Pat Mora and Charles Ramírez Berg; ill. by Charles Ramírez Berg. Piñata Books, 1995. ISBN 1-55885-137-2 Subj: Foreign lands – Mexico. Foreign languages. Gifts. Holidays – Christmas.

Listen to the desert = Oye al desierto ill. by Francisco X. Mora. Clarion, 1994. ISBN 0-395-67292-9 Subj: Animals. Desert. Foreign languages. Noise, sounds. Poetry.

The night the moon fell: a Maya myth retold ill. by Domi. Douglas & McIntyre, 2000. ISBN 0-88899-398-6 Subj: Folk and fairy tales. Foreign lands – Mexico. Indians of Central America – Maya. Moon.

Pablo's tree ill. by Cecily Lang. Macmillan, 1994. ISBN 0-02-767401-0 Subj: Adoption. Birthdays. Ethnic groups in the U.S. – Mexican Americans. Family life – grandfathers.

The race of toad and deer ill. by Maya Itzna Brooks. Orchard, 1995. ISBN 0-531-08777-8 Subj: Animals. Behavior – trickery. Folk and fairy tales. Foreign lands – Guatemala. Foreign languages. Sports – racing.

The rainbow tulip ill. by Elizabeth Sayles. Viking, 1999. ISBN 0-670-87291-1 Subj: Character traits – being different. Ethnic groups in the U.S. – Mexican Americans. Holidays – May Day. Parades. School.

This big sky ill. by Steve Jenkins. Scholastic, 1998. ISBN 0-590-37120-7 Subj: Animals. Desert. Poetry.

Tomás and the library lady ill. by Raúl Colón. Knopf, 1997. ISBN 0-679-90401-8 Subj: Activities – reading. Careers – librarians. Careers – migrant workers. Ethnic groups in the U.S. – Mexican Americans. Libraries.

Uno, dos, tres = One, two, three ill. by Barbara Lavallee. Clarion, 1996. ISBN 0-395-67294-5 Subj: Birthdays. Counting, numbers. Foreign languages. Rhyming text.

Moran, George. *Imagine me on a sit-ski!* ill. by Nadine Bernard Westcott. Albert Whitman, 1995. ISBN 0-8075-3618-0 Subj: Handicaps – cerebral palsy. Handicaps – physical handicaps. Sports – skiing.

Morck, Irene. *Tyler's new boots* ill. by Georgia Graham. Chronicle, 1998. ISBN 0-8118-2248-6 Subj: Animals – bulls, cows. Clothing – boots. Cowboys.

Mordvinoff, Nicolas. *Billy the kid* (Lipkind, William)

The boy and the forest (Lipkind, William)

Chaga (Lipkind, William)

The Christmas bunny (Lipkind, William)

Circus ruckus (Lipkind, William)

Coral Island ill. by author. Doubleday, 1957. Subj: Behavior – growing up. Foreign lands – South Sea Islands. Islands.

Even Steven (Lipkind, William)

Finders keepers (Lipkind, William)

Four-leaf clover (Lipkind, William)

The little tiny rooster (Lipkind, William)

The magic feather duster (Lipkind, William)

Russet and the two reds (Lipkind, William)

Sleepyhead (Lipkind, William)

The two reds (Lipkind, William)

More, Caroline. *see* Cone, Molly

Morehead, Debby. *A special place for Charlee: a child's companion through pet loss* ill. by Karen Cannon. Partners in Publishing, 1996. ISBN 0-9654049-0-0 Subj: Animals. Death. Emotions – grief. Pets.

Moreillon, Judi. *Sing down the rain* ill. by Michael Chiago. Kiva, 1997. ISBN 1-885772-07-6 Subj: Desert. Indians of North America – Pima. Plants. Rhyming text.

Morel, Eve. *Fairy tales* ill. by Gyo Fujikawa. Grosset, 1980. ISBN 0-448-13144-7 Subj: Folk and fairy tales.

Fairy tales and fables ill. by Gyo Fujikawa. Grosset, 1970. Subj: Folk and fairy tales.

Moremen, Grace E. *No, no, Natalie* photos by Geoffrey P. Fulton. Childrens Pr., 1973. ISBN 0-516-07624-8 Subj: Animals – rabbits. Behavior – misbehavior. School.

Moret, Brigitte Frey. *The bear's Christmas* ill. by Alexander Reichstein; trans. by Rosemary Lanning. North-South, 1998. ISBN 1-55858-972-4 Subj: Animals – bears. Hibernation. Holidays – Christmas. Religion – Nativity.

Moreton, Daniel. *La Cucaracha Martina: a Caribbean folktale* ill. by reteller. Turtle Books, 1997. ISBN 1-890515-03-5 Subj: Animals. City. Folk and fairy tales. Foreign lands – Caribbean Islands. Foreign languages. Insects – cockroaches. Noise, sounds.

Morgan, Allen. *Matthew and the midnight ball game* ill. by Michael Martchenko. Stoddart Kids, 1997. ISBN 0-7737-5853-4 Subj: Birds – turkeys. Careers – postal workers. Sports – baseball.

Matthew and the midnight firemen ill. by Michael Martchenko. Stoddart Kids, 2000. ISBN 0-7737-6090-3 Subj: Careers – firefighters.

Matthew and the midnight flood ill. by Michael Martchenko. Stoddart Kids, 1998. ISBN 0-7737-5941-7 Subj: Careers – plumbers. Weather – floods.

Matthew and the midnight hospital ill. by Michael Martchenko. Stoddart Kids, 1999. ISBN 0-7737-6014-8 Subj: Health and fitness. Hospitals.

Matthew and the midnight money van ill. by Michael Martchenko. Firefly, 1987. ISBN 0-920303-75-7 Subj: Behavior – losing things. Holidays – Mother's Day.

Matthew and the midnight pilot ill. by Michael Martchenko. Stoddart Kids, 1997. ISBN 0-7737-5852-6 Subj: Airplanes, airports. Careers – airplane pilots.

Matthew and the midnight pirates ill. by Michael Martchenko. Stoddart Kids, 1998. ISBN 0-7737-5940-9 Subj: Pirates.

Matthew and the midnight tow truck ill. by Michael Martchenko. Annick, 1984. ISBN 0-920303-00-5 Subj: Trucks.

Matthew and the midnight turkeys ill. by Michael Martchenko. Annick, 1985. ISBN 0-920303-36-6 Subj: Birds – turkeys.

Matthew and the midnight wrestlers ill. by Michael Martchenko. Stoddart Kids, 2000. ISBN 0-7737-6053-9 Subj: Sports – wrestling.

Molly and Mr. Maloney ill. by Maryann Kovalski. Kids Can Pr., 1982. ISBN 0-919964-41-9 Subj: Animals – raccoons. Behavior – misbehavior. Pets.

Nicole's boat ill. by Jirina Marton. Firefly, 1986. ISBN 0-920303-60-9 Subj: Bedtime. Boats, ships. Dreams. Family life – fathers. Sea and seashore.

Sadie and the snowman ill. by Brenda Clark. Kids Can Pr., 1985. ISBN 0-919964-86-9 Subj: Seasons – winter. Snowmen.

Morgan, Justina. *see* Freeman, Jean Todd

Morgan, Mary. *see* Morgan-Vanroyen, Mary

Morgan, Michaela. *Dinostory* ill. by True Kelley. Dutton, 1991. ISBN 0-525-44726-1 Subj: Dinosaurs.

Edward gets a pet ill. by Sue Porter. Dutton, 1987. ISBN 0-525-44349-5 Subj: Animals. Imagination. Pets.

Helpful Betty solves a mystery ill. by Moira Kemp. Carolrhoda, 1994. ISBN 0-87614-832-1 Subj: Animals – hippopotamuses. Character traits – helpfulness. Jungle. Mystery stories.

Helpful Betty to the rescue ill. by Moira Kemp. Carolrhoda, 1994. ISBN 0-87614-831-3 Subj: Animals – hippopotamuses. Animals – monkeys. Behavior – misunderstanding. Character traits – foolishness. Character traits – helpfulness. Jungle.

Visitors for Edward ill. by Sue Porter. Dutton, 1988. ISBN 0-525-44354-1 Subj: Family life – grandparents. Imagination.

Morgan-Vanroyen, Mary. *Benjamin's bugs* ill. by author. Bradbury, 1994. ISBN 0-02-767450-9 Subj: Animals – porcupines. Insects.

Curious Rosie ill. by author. Hyperion, 2000. ISBN 0-7868-0477-7 Subj: Animals – mice. Character traits – curiosity.

Gentle Rosie ill. by author. Hyperion, 1999. ISBN 0-7868-0474-2 Subj: Animals – mice. Behavior.

Guess who I love? ill. by author. Grosset, 1992. ISBN 0-448-40313-7 Subj: Animals – mice. Emotions – love. Family life. Format, unusual – board books. Rhyming text.

Night ride ill. by author. Atheneum, 1997. ISBN 0-689-80545-4 Subj: Family life – grandfathers. Night. Seasons – spring. Sports – bicycling.

Patient Rosie ill. by author. Hyperion, 2000. ISBN 0-7868-0476-9 Subj: Animals – mice. Character traits – patience.

The Pudgy merry Christmas book ill. by author. Grosset, 1989. ISBN 0-448-02262-1 Subj: Animals – mice. Format, unusual – board books. Holidays – Christmas.

Wild Rosie ill. by author. Hyperion, 1999. ISBN 0-7868-0475-0 Subj: Activities – playing. Animals – mice. Behavior.

Morgenstern, Aliyah. *The wedding of Brown Bear and White Bear* (Beck, Martine)

Morgenstern, Christian. *Lullabies, lyrics and gallows songs* ill. by Lisbeth Zwerger; trans. by Anthea Bell. North-South, 1995. ISBN 1-55858-365-3 Subj: Lullabies. Poetry. Songs.

Morgenstern, Constance. *Good night, feet* ill. by Cat Bowman Smith. Holt, 1991. ISBN 0-8050-1453-5 Subj: Anatomy – feet. Bedtime. Rhyming text.

Morgenstern, Elizabeth. *The little gardeners* trans. from German by Elizabeth Morgenstern; retold by Louise F. Encking; ill. by Marigard Bantzer. Albert Whitman, 1933. Subj: Foreign lands – Germany. Gardens, gardening.

Morice, Dave. *Dot town* ill. by author. Toothpaste Pr., 1982. ISBN 0-915124-38-6 Subj: Poetry.

The happy birthday handbook ill. by author. Coffee House, 1982. ISBN 0-915-12467-X Subj: Birthdays.

A visit from St. Alphabet ill. by author. Coffee House, 1980. ISBN 0-915-12447-5 Subj: ABC books. Poetry.

Morimoto, Isao. *The two bullies* (Morimoto, Junko)

Morimoto, Junko. *The inch boy* ill. by author. Viking, 1986. ISBN 0-670-80955-1 Subj: Family life. Folk and fairy tales. Little people.

Mouse's marriage ill. by author. Viking, 1986. ISBN 0-670-81071-1 Subj: Animals – mice. Folk and fairy tales.

My Hiroshima ill. by author. Viking, 1990. ISBN 0-670-83181-6 Subj: War.

The two bullies trans. from an original Japanese story by Isao Morimoto; ill. by Junko Morimoto. Crown, 1999. ISBN 0-517-80062-4 Subj: Behavior – bullying. Folk and fairy tales. Foreign lands – China. Foreign lands – Japan.

Morley, Carol. *Dots and spots* ill. by author. Willa Perlman Books, 1993. ISBN 0-06-021527-5 Subj: Witches.

Farmyard song ill. by author. Simon & Schuster, 1995. ISBN 0-671-89551-6 Subj: Animals. Cumulative tales. Farms. Music. Noise, sounds. Nursery rhymes. Songs.

A spider and a pig ill. by author. Little, 1993. ISBN 0-316-58405-3 Subj: Animals – pigs. Behavior – lost. Folk and fairy tales. Islands. Spiders. Weather – storms.

Moroney, Lynn. *Baby Rattlesnake* (Ata, Te)

The boy who loved bears: adapt. from a traditional Pawnee tale ill. by Charles W. Chapman. Childrens Pr., 1994. ISBN 0-516-05142-3 Subj: Animals – bears. Folk and fairy tales. Indians of North America – Pawnee.

Elinda who danced in the sky: an Estonian folktale ill. by Veg Reisberg. Children's Book Pr., 1990. ISBN 0-89239-066-2 Subj: Folk and fairy tales. Foreign lands – Estonia. Sky.

Moontellers: myths of the moon from around the world ill. by Gred Shed. Northland, 1995. ISBN 0-87358-601-8 Subj: Folk and fairy tales. Moon.

Morozumi, Atsuko. *Helping daddy* ill. by author. Knopf, 2000. ISBN 0-375-80593-1 Subj: Family life. Format, unusual – board books.

In the park ill. by author. Knopf, 2000. ISBN 0-375-80591-5 Subj: Format, unusual – board books. Parks.

My friend gorilla ill. by author. Farrar, 1998. ISBN 0-374-35458-8 Subj: Animals – gorillas. Foreign lands – Africa. Friendship. Pets. Zoos.

One gorilla ill. by author. Farrar, 1990. ISBN 0-374-35644-0 Subj: Animals. Animals – gorillas. Counting, numbers.

Playing ill. by author. Knopf, 2000. ISBN 0-375-80592-3 Subj: Activities – playing. Format, unusual – board books.

Time for bed ill. by author. Knopf, 2000. ISBN 0-375-80594-X Subj: Bedtime. Format, unusual – board books.

Morpurgo, Michael. *Jo-Jo the melon donkey* ill. by Chris Molan. Prentice-Hall, 1988. ISBN 0-13-510009-7 Subj: Animals – donkeys. Foreign lands – Italy. Weather – floods.

Wombat goes walkabout ill. by Christian Birmingham. Candlewick, 2000. ISBN 0-7636-1168-9 Subj: Animals. Animals – wombats. Behavior – lost. Foreign lands – Australia.

Morris, Ann. *The animal book* ill. by author. Silver Pr., 1996. ISBN 0-382-24702-7 Subj: Animals.

The baby book photos by Ken Heyman. Silver Pr., 1996. ISBN 0-382-24699-3 Subj: Babies. Family life.

Bread, bread, bread photos by Ken Heyman. Lothrop, 1989. ISBN 0-688-06335-7 Subj: Food.

The Cinderella rebus book ill. by Ljiljana Rylands. Orchard, 1989. ISBN 0-531-08361-6 Subj: Fairies. Folk and fairy tales. Foreign lands – France. Rebuses. Royalty – princes.

Cuddle up ill. by Maureen Roffey. HarperCollins, 1986. ISBN 0-694-00072-8 Subj: Bedtime. Family life – mothers. Night.

The daddy book photos by Ken Heyman. Silver Pr., 1996. ISBN 0-382-24696-9 Subj: Family life – fathers.

Eleanora Mousie catches a cold ill. by Ruth Young. Macmillan, 1987. ISBN 0-02-767500-9 Subj: Animals – mice. Illness.

Eleanora Mousie in the dark ill. by Ruth Young. Macmillan, 1987. ISBN 0-02-767530-0 Subj: Animals – mice. Monsters. Night.

Eleanora Mousie makes a mess ill. by Ruth Young. Macmillan, 1987. ISBN 0-02-767520-3 Subj: Animals – mice. Character traits – cleanliness.

Eleanora Mousie's gray day ill. by Ruth Young. Macmillan, 1987. ISBN 0-02-767510-6 Subj: Animals – mice. Behavior – bad day. Friendship.

Families ill. with photos. HarperCollins, 2000. ISBN 0-688-17199-0 Subj: Character traits – individuality. Family life.

The grandma book photos by Ken Heyman. Silver Pr., 1999. ISBN 0-382-39838-6 Subj: Family life – grandmothers.

The grandpa book photos by Ken Heyman. Silver Pr., 1999. ISBN 0-382-39841-6 Subj: Family life – grandfathers.

Hats, hats, hats photos by Ken Heyman. Lothrop, 1989. ISBN 0-688-06339-X Subj: Clothing – hats.

Hello Peter = Bonjour, Rémy ill. by Deborah Melmon. Celebration Pr., 1996. ISBN 0-673-75895-8 Subj: Animals – cats. Foreign lands – France. Foreign languages.

Houses and homes photos by Ken Heyman. Lothrop, 1992. ISBN 0-688-10169-0 Subj: Foreign lands. Homes, houses.

I am six photos by Nancy Sheehan. Silver Burdett, 1995. ISBN 0-382-24759-0 Subj: School.

Karate boy ill. by David Katzenstein. Dutton, 1996. ISBN 0-525-45337-7 Subj: Sports – karate.

Kiss time ill. by Maureen Roffey. HarperCollins, 1986. ISBN 0-694-00073-6 Subj: Bedtime. Night.

Light the candle! Bang the drum! ill. by Peter Linenthal. Dutton, 1997. ISBN 0-525-45639-2 Subj: Holidays.

Little ballerinas photos by Nancy Sheehan. Grosset, 1997. ISBN 0-448-41607-7 Subj: Activities – dancing. Ballet.

The Little Red Riding Hood rebus book ill. by Ljiljana Rylands. Orchard, 1987. ISBN 0-531-08330-6 Subj: Animals – wolves. Behavior – talking to strangers. Folk and fairy tales. Rebuses.

Little skaters photos by Nancy Sheehan. Grosset, 1997. ISBN 0-448-41734-0 Subj: Sports – ice skating.

Loving photos by Ken Heyman. Lothrop, 1990. ISBN 0-688-06341-1 Subj: Emotions – love. Family life. Foreign lands.

The mommy book photos by Ken Heyman. Silver Pr., 1996. ISBN 0-382-24693-4 Subj: Family life – mothers.

Night counting ill. by Maureen Roffey. HarperCollins, 1986. ISBN 0-694-00074-4 Subj: Bedtime. Counting, numbers. Night.

On the go photos by Ken Heyman. Lothrop, 1990. ISBN 0-688-06337-3 Subj: Foreign lands. Transportation.

Play photos by Ken Heyman. Lothrop, 1998. ISBN 0-688-14553-1 Subj: Activities – playing. Foreign lands. Imagination.

700 kids on Grandpa's farm photos by Ken Heyman. Dutton, 1994. ISBN 0-525-45162-5 Subj: Animals – goats. Family life – grandfathers. Farms.

Shoes, shoes, shoes ill. by author. Lothrop, 1995. ISBN 0-688-13667-2 Subj: Clothing – shoes. Rhyming text.

Sleepy, sleepy ill. by Maureen Roffey. HarperCollins, 1986. ISBN 0-694-00075-2 Subj: Bedtime. Night.

This little baby goes out (Breeze, Lynn)

This little baby's bedtime (Breeze, Lynn)

This little baby's morning (Breeze, Lynn)

Tools photos by Ken Heyman. Lothrop, 1992. ISBN 0-688-10171-2 Subj: Tools.

Weddings photos by Ken Heyman. Lothrop, 1995. ISBN 0-688-13273-1 Subj: Clothing. Weddings.

Work photos by Ken Heyman. Lothrop, 1998. ISBN 0-688-14867-0 Subj: Activities – working. Careers. Foreign lands.

Morris, Christopher G. *The magic world of words: a very first dictionary* (Halsey, William D.)

Morris, Jill. *The boy who painted the sun* ill. by Geoff Hocking. Viking, 1984. ISBN 0-7226-6052-9 Subj: Activities – painting. Behavior – solitude. City. Moving.

Monkey creates havoc in heaven (P'an, Ts'ai-ying)

Morris, Linda Lowe. *Morning milking* ill. by David DeRan. Picture Book Studio, 1991. ISBN 0-88708-173-8 Subj: Animals. Animals – bulls, cows. Farms.

Morris, Neil. *Find the canary* by Neil and Ting Morris; ill. by Anna Clarke. Little, 1983. ISBN 0-316-58375-8 Subj: Games.

Hide and seek by Neil and Ting; Morris ill. by Anna Clarke. Little, 1983. ISBN 0-316-58376-6 Subj: Games.

Search for Sam by Neil and Ting Morris; ill. by Anna Clarke. Little, 1983. ISBN 0-316-58377-4 Subj: Games.

Where's my hat? by Neil and Ting Morris; ill. by Anna Clarke. Little, 1983. ISBN 0-316-58378-2 Subj: Clothing – hats. Games.

Morris, Terry Nell. *Good night, dear monster!* ill. by author. Knopf, 1980. ISBN 0-394-94221-3 Subj: Bedtime. Imagination – imaginary friends. Monsters.

Lucky puppy! Lucky boy! ill. by author. Knopf, 1980. ISBN 0-394-84220-0 Subj: Animals – dogs. Behavior – needing someone.

Morris, Ting. *Find the canary* (Morris, Neil)

Hide and seek (Morris, Neil)

Search for Sam (Morris, Neil)

Where's my hat? (Morris, Neil)

Morris, Winifred. *The future of Yen-Tzu* ill. by Friso Henstra. Atheneum, 1992. ISBN 0-689-31501-5 Subj: Folk and fairy tales. Foreign lands – China. Royalty – emperors.

Just listen ill. by Patricia Cullen-Clark. Atheneum, 1990. ISBN 0-689-31588-0 Subj: Family life – grandmothers. Noise, sounds. Senses – hearing.

The magic leaf ill. by Ju-Hong Chen. Atheneum, 1987. ISBN 0-689-31358-6 Subj: Folk and fairy tales. Foreign lands – China.

What if the shark wears tennis shoes? ill. by Betsy Lewin. Atheneum, 1990. ISBN 0-689-31587-2 Subj: Bedtime. Emotions – fear. Imagination.

Morrison, Bill. *Louis James hates school* ill. by author. Houghton Mifflin, 1978. ISBN 0-395-27156-8 Subj: Careers. School.

Squeeze a sneeze ill. by author. Houghton Mifflin, 1977. ISBN 0-395-25151-6 Subj: Poetry.

Morrison, Gordon. *Bald eagle* ill. by author. Houghton Mifflin, 1998. ISBN 0-395-87328-2 Subj: Birds – eagles.

Morrison, Sean. *Is that a happy hippopotamus?* ill. by Aliki. Crowell, 1966. Subj: Animals. Humor. Noise, sounds. Poetry.

Morrison, Taylor. *Cheetah* ill. by author. Holt, 1998. ISBN 0-8050-5121-X Subj: Animals – cheetahs. Foreign lands – Africa.

Morrow, Barbara. *Edward's portrait* ill. by author. Macmillan, 1991. ISBN 0-02-767591-2 Subj: Activities – photographing. Family life. U.S. history.

Help for Mr. Peale ill. by author. Macmillan, 1990. ISBN 0-02-767590-4 Subj: Moving. Museums.

Morrow, Elizabeth Cutter. *The painted pig* ill. by René d'Harnoncourt. Knopf, 1930. Subj: Foreign lands – Mexico.

Morrow, Suzanne Stark. *Inatuck's friend* ill. by Ellen Raskin. Little, 1968. Subj: Eskimos. Friendship.

Morse, Samuel French. *All in a suitcase* ill. by Barbara Cooney. Little, 1966. Subj: ABC books. Animals.

Sea sums ill. by Fuku Akino. Little, 1970. Subj: Counting, numbers. Poetry. Sea and seashore. Weather – fog.

Morton, Christine. *Picnic farm* ill. by Sarah Barringer. Holiday, 1998. ISBN 0-8234-1332-2 Subj: Activities – picnicking. Animals. Farms.

Mosel, Arlene. *The funny little woman* ill. by Blair Lent. Dutton, 1972. Based on The old woman and her dumpling by Lafcadio Hearn. ISBN 0-525-30265-4 Subj: Caldecott award books. Foreign lands – Japan. Monsters.

Tikki Tikki Tembo ill. by Blair Lent. Holt, 1968. ISBN 0-8050-0662-1 Subj: Folk and fairy tales. Foreign lands – China. Names.

Moseley, Keith. *Big creatures from the past* (Watson, Claire)

Dinosaurs: a lost world ill. by Robert Cremins. Putnam, 1984. ISBN 0-399-21063-6 Subj: Dinosaurs. Format, unusual – toy and movable books. Science.

Prehistoric mammals (Berger, Melvin)

Winnie-the-Pooh: a pop-up book (Milne, A. A. [Alan Alexander])

Moser, Barry. *Tucker Pfeffercorn: an old story retold* ill. by author. Little, 1994. ISBN 0-316-58542-4 Subj: Activities. Folk and fairy tales. Names.

Moser, Erwin. *The crow in the snow and other bedtime stories* trans. from German by Joel Agee; ill. by author. Adama, 1986. ISBN 0-915361-49-3 Subj: Animals. Imagination.

Wilma the elephant ill. by author. Adama, 1986. ISBN 0-915361-45-0 Subj: Animals – elephants. Behavior – lost. Behavior – needing someone.

Moser, Madeline. *Ever heard of an aardwolf?* ill. by Barry Moser. Harcourt, 1996. ISBN 0-15-200474-2 Subj: Animals. Character traits – being different.

Moses, Amy. *At the hospital* ill. by Penny Dann; photos by Phil Martin. Child's World, 1998. ISBN 1-56766-291-9 Subj: Hospitals.

At the zoo ill. by Penny Dann; photos by Phil Martin. Child's World, 1998. ISBN 1-56766-287-0 Subj: Animals. Zoos.

Moses, Will. *Silent night* ill. by author. Philomel, 1997. ISBN 0-399-23100-5 Subj: Babies. Family life. Holidays – Christmas. Songs.

Mosimann, Odile. *How the mouse was hit on the head by a stone and so discovered the world* (Delessert, Etienne)

Moskin, Marietta D. *Lysbet and the fire kittens* ill. by Margot Tomes. Coward, 1973. ISBN 0-698-30522-1 Subj: Animals – cats. Behavior – carelessness. Fire. U.S. history.

Moskof, Martin Stephen. *Still another alphabet book* (Chwast, Seymour)

Still another children's book (Chwast, Seymour)

Still another number book (Chwast, Seymour)

Moskowitz, Addie Alexander. *Wish upon a star: a story for children with a parent who is mentally ill* (Laskin, Pamela L.)

Mosley, Francis. *The dinosaur eggs* ill. by author. Barron's, 1988. ISBN 0-8120-5910-7 Subj: Dinosaurs. Family life.

Moss, Elaine. *From morn to midnight* (From morn to midnight)

Polar ill. by Jeannie Baker. Elsevier-Dutton, 1979. ISBN 0-233-96695-1 Subj: Activities – playing. Illness. Safety. Toys – bears.

Moss, Jeffrey. *The Sesame Street ABC storybook* featuring Jim Henson's Muppets; by Jeffrey Moss, Norman Stiles and Daniel Wilcox; ill. by Peter Cross and others. Random House, 1974. ISBN 0-394-92921-7 Subj: ABC books. Puppets.

The Sesame Street song book (Raposo, Joe)

The songs of Sesame Street in poems and pictures by Jeffrey Moss and others; ill. by Normand Chartier. Random House, 1983. ISBN 0-394-95245-6 Subj: Poetry. Puppets. Songs.

Moss, Lloyd. *Our marching band* ill. by Diana Cain Bluthenthal. Putnam, 2001. ISBN 0-399-23335-0 Subj: Music. Rhyming text.

Zin! zin! zin! A violin ill. by Marjorie Priceman. Simon & Schuster, 1995. ISBN 0-671-88239-2 Subj: Caldecott award honor books. Counting, numbers. Music. Rhyming text.

Moss, Marissa. *After-school monster* ill. by author. Lothrop, 1991. ISBN 0-688-10117-8 Subj: Character traits – assertiveness. Character traits – bravery. Emotions – fear. Ethnic groups in the U.S. Monsters.

But not Kate ill. by author. Lothrop, 1992. ISBN 0-688-10601-3 Subj: Animals – mice. Character traits – individuality. Magic. School. Self-concept.

In America ill. by author. Dutton, 1994. ISBN 0-525-45152-8 Subj: Activities – traveling. Ethnic groups in the U.S. – Lithuanian Americans. Family life – aunts, uncles. Family life – grandfathers. Jewish culture.

Knick knack paddywack ill. by author. Houghton Mifflin, 1992. ISBN 0-395-54701-6 Subj: Activities – making things. Animals – dogs. Counting, numbers. Cumulative tales. Songs. Space and space ships.

Mel's diner ill. by author. BridgeWater, 1994. ISBN 0-8167-3460-7 Subj: Activities – cooking. Careers – chefs, cooks. Careers – waiters, waitresses. Ethnic groups in the U.S. – African Americans. Family life. Restaurants.

Regina's big mistake ill. by author. Houghton Mifflin, 1990. ISBN 0-395-55330-X Subj: Activities – drawing. Art. Careers – artists. School. Self-concept.

True heart ill. by C. F. Payne. Silver Whistle, 1999. ISBN 0-15-201344-X Subj: Careers – engineers. Sex roles. Trains.

The ugly menorah ill. by author. Farrar, 1996. ISBN 0-374-38927-9 Subj: Family life – grandparents. Holidays – Hanukkah. Jewish culture. Religion.

Want to play? ill. by author. Houghton Mifflin, 1990. ISBN 0-395-52022-3 Subj: Activities – playing. Sibling rivalry. Toys.

Who was it? ill. by author. Houghton Mifflin, 1989. ISBN 0-395-49699-3 Subj: Behavior – misbehavior. Character traits – honesty. Family life – mothers.

Moss, P. Buckley (Pat Buckley). *Reuben and the quilt* text by Merle Good; ill. by author. Good Books, 1999. ISBN 1-56148-234-X Subj: Crime. Ethnic groups in the U.S. – Amish. Quilts.

Moss, Thylias. *I want to be* ill. by Jerry Pinkney. Dial, 1993. ISBN 0-8037-1287-1 Subj: Behavior – growing up. Ethnic groups in the U.S. – African Americans.

Most, Bernard. *ABC T-Rex* ill. by author. Harcourt, 2000. ISBN 0-15-202007-1 Subj: ABC books. Dinosaurs.

Boo! ill. by author. Prentice-Hall, 1980. ISBN 0-13-079780-4 Subj: Emotions – fear. Monsters.

Catbirds and dogfish ill. by author. Harcourt, 1995. ISBN 0-15-292844-8 Subj: Animals. Names.

Catch me if you can! ill. by author. Harcourt, 1999. ISBN 0-15-202001-2 Subj: Dinosaurs. Family life – grandfathers.

Cock-a-doodle-moo! ill. by author. Harcourt, 1996. ISBN 0-15-201252-4 Subj: Animals. Birds – chickens. Careers – farmers. Farms. Morning.

The cow that went oink ill. by author. Harcourt, 1990. ISBN 0-15-220195-5 Subj: Animals. Noise, sounds.

Dinosaur cousins? ill. by author. Harcourt, 1987. ISBN 0-15-223497-7 Subj: Animals. Dinosaurs.

A dinosaur named after me ill. by author. Harcourt, 1991. ISBN 0-15-223494-2 Subj: Dinosaurs. Names.

Dinosaur questions ill. by author. Harcourt, 1995. ISBN 0-15-292885-5 Subj: Dinosaurs.

Four and twenty dinosaurs ill. by author. HarperCollins, 1990. ISBN 0-06-024377-5 Subj: Dinosaurs. Nursery rhymes. Poetry.

Happy holidaysaurus! ill. by author. Harcourt, 1992. ISBN 0-15-233386-X Subj: Dinosaurs. Holidays.

Hippopotamus hunt ill. by author. Harcourt, 1994. ISBN 0-15-234520-5 Subj: Animals – hippopotamuses. Jungle. Language.

How big were the dinosaurs? ill. by author. Harcourt, 1994. ISBN 0-15-236800-0 Subj: Concepts – size. Dinosaurs.

If the dinosaurs came back ill. by author. Harcourt, 1995. ISBN 0-15-238020-5 Subj: Dinosaurs. Imagination.

The littlest dinosaurs ill. by author. Harcourt, 1989. ISBN 0-15-248125-7 Subj: Dinosaurs.

Moo-ha! ill. by author. Harcourt, 1997. ISBN 0-15-201248-6 Subj: Animals – bulls, cows. Format, unusual – board books.

My very own octopus ill. by author. Harcourt, 1980. ISBN 0-05-256641-4 Subj: Octopuses. Pets.

Oink-ha! ill. by author. Harcourt, 1997. ISBN 0-15-201249-4 Subj: Animals – pigs. Format, unusual – board books.

A pair of protoceratops ill. by author. Harcourt, 1998. ISBN 0-15-201443-8 Subj: Activities. Dinosaurs.

Peek-a-moo! ill. by author. Harcourt, 1998. ISBN 0-15-201251-6 Subj: Animals. Animals – bulls, cows. Format, unusual – toy and movable books. Games.

Pets in trumpets and other word-play riddles ill. by author. Harcourt, 1991. ISBN 0-15-261210-6 Subj: Language. Pets. Riddles.

Row, row, row your goat ill. by author. Harcourt, 1998. ISBN 0-15-201250-8 Subj: Animals. Boats, ships. Songs.

There's an ant in Anthony ill. by author. Morrow, 1980. ISBN 0-688-62226-3 Subj: Activities – reading.

There's an ape behind the drape ill. by author. Morrow, 1981. ISBN 0-688-00381-8 Subj: Animals – gorillas. Games. Language.

A trio of triceratops ill. by author. Harcourt, 1998. ISBN 0-15-201448-9 Subj: Activities. Dinosaurs.

The very boastful kangaroo ill. by author. Harcourt, 1999. ISBN 0-15-202349-6 Subj: Activities – jumping. Animals – kangaroos. Contests.

Whatever happened to the dinosaurs? ill. by author. Harcourt, 1995. ISBN 0-15-200378-9 Subj: Dinosaurs.

Where to look for a dinosaur ill. by author. Harcourt, 1993. ISBN 0-15-295616-6 Subj: Dinosaurs. Science.

Zoodles ill. by author. Harcourt, 1992. ISBN 0-15-299969-8 Subj: Animals. Birds. Riddles.

Z-Z-Zoink! ill. by author. Harcourt, 1999. ISBN 0-15-292845-6 Subj: Animals – pigs. Birds – owls. Noise, sounds. Sleep.

Mostacchi, Massimo. *The beast and the boy* ill. by Monica Miceli; adapt. by Andrew Clements. North-South, 1995. ISBN 1-55858-444-7 Subj: Animals – lions. Behavior – running away. Prejudice.

A dog's best friend ill. by Monica Miceli; adapt. by Andrew Clements. North-South, 1995. ISBN 1-55858-498-6 Subj: Animals – dogs. Behavior – running away. Friendship.

Mostel, Zero. *The Sesame Street book of opposites with Zero Mostel* (Mendoza, George)

Mother Goose. *A child's book of old nursery rhymes* ill. by Joan Walsh Anglund. Atheneum, 1973. ISBN 0-689-30413-7 Subj: Nursery rhymes.

ABC rhymes ill. by Lulu Delacre. Simon & Schuster, 1984. ISBN 0-671-49685-9 Subj: ABC books. Format, unusual – board books. Nursery rhymes.

Animals from Mother Goose: a question book (Hopkins, Lee Bennett)

The annotated Mother Goose: nursery rhymes old and new arranged and explained by William S. and Ceil Baring-Gould; chapter decorations by E. M. Simon; ill. by Walter Crane and others. Potter/Crown, 1962. Subj: Nursery rhymes.

As I was going up and down: and other nonsense rhymes ill. by Nicola Bayley. Lothrop, 1986. ISBN 0-02-708590-2 Subj: Nursery rhymes.

The authentic Mother Goose fairy tales and nursery rhymes (Barchilon, Jacques)

Baa baa, black sheep adapt. and ill. by Marilyn Janovitz. Hyperion, 1991. ISBN 1-56282-086-9 Subj: Animals – dogs. Animals – sheep. Nursery rhymes.

Baa, baa, black sheep ill. by Moira Kemp. Lodestar, 1994. ISBN 0-525-67443-8 Subj: Animals – sheep. Format, unusual – board books. Nursery rhymes.

Baa baa black sheep ill. by Sue Porter. Peter Bedrick, 1984. ISBN 0-911745-26-2 Subj: Format, unusual – board books. Nursery rhymes.

Baa baa black sheep ill. by Ferelith Eccles Williams. David & Charles, 1985. ISBN 0-437-86003-5 Subj: Format, unusual – board books. Nursery rhymes.

Baby's first Mother Goose ill. by Mary Morgan; comp. by Wendy Lewison. Western, 1993. ISBN 0-307-06143-4 Subj: Format, unusual – board books. Nursery rhymes.

The baby's lap book ill. by Kay Chorao. Dutton, 1977. ISBN 0-525-26100-1 Subj: Nursery rhymes.

Beatrix Potter's nursery rhyme book ill. by Beatrix Potter. Warne, 1984. ISBN 0-7232-3254-7 Subj: Nursery rhymes.

Blessed Mother Goose: favorite nursery rhymes for today's children ill. by Kaye Luke. House-Warven, 1951. Subj: Nursery rhymes.

Brian Wildsmith's Mother Goose ill. by Brian Wildsmith. Watts, 1964. Subj: Nursery rhymes.

Carolyn Wells' edition of Mother Goose ill. by Margeria Cooper and others. Doubleday, 1946. Subj: Nursery rhymes.

Cats by Mother Goose sel. by Barbara Lucas; ill. by Carol Newsom. Lothrop, 1986. ISBN 0-688-04635-5 Subj: Animals – cats. Nursery rhymes.

The Charles Addams Mother Goose ill. by Charles Addams. Harper, 1967. Subj: Nursery rhymes.

The Chinese Mother Goose rhymes sel. and ed. by Robert Wyndham; ill. by Ed Young. Putnam, 1982. Orig. pub. by World, 1968. ISBN 0-399-20866-6 Subj: Nursery rhymes.

The city and country Mother Goose ill. by Hilda Hoffmann. American Heritage, 1969. ISBN 0-8281-5007-9 Subj: Nursery rhymes.

The comic adventures of Old Mother Hubbard and her dog (Martin, Sarah Catherine)

Frank Baber's Mother Goose sel. by Ruth Spriggs; ill. by Frank Baber. Crown, 1976. ISBN 0-517-52819-3 Subj: Nursery rhymes.

The gay Mother Goose ill. by Françoise Seignobosc. Scribners, 1938. Subj: Nursery rhymes.

The glorious Mother Goose sel. by Cooper Edens; ill. by the best artists from the past. Atheneum, 1988. ISBN 0-689-31434-5 Subj: Nursery rhymes.

The golden goose (The golden goose)

The golden goose book ill. by L. Leslie Brooke. Warne, 1977, 1905. ISBN 0-7232-1979-6 Subj: Birds – geese. Folk and fairy tales. Humor. Royalty.

Grafa' Grig had a pig: and other rhymes without reason from Mother Goose ill. by Wallace Tripp. Little, 1976. ISBN 0-316-85282-1 Subj: Nursery rhymes.

Gray goose and gander and other Mother Goose rhymes coll. and ill. by Anne F. Rockwell. Crowell, 1980. ISBN 0-690-04049-0 Subj: Nursery rhymes.

Gregory Griggs and other nursery rhyme people sel. and ill. by Arnold Lobel. Greenwillow, 1978. ISBN 0-688-84128-7 Subj: Nursery rhymes.

Here's a ball for baby: finger rhymes for young children (Williams, Jenny [Jennifer])

Hey, diddle, diddle (Marshall, James)

Hey diddle diddle adapt. and ill. by Marilyn Janovitz. Walt Disney, 1992. ISBN 1-56282-169-5 Subj: Animals. Music. Nursery rhymes.

Hey diddle, diddle ill. by Moira Kemp. Lodestar, 1994. ISBN 0-525-67445-4 Subj: Animals. Format, unusual – board books. Moon. Nursery rhymes.

Hey diddle diddle adapt. by Leonard P. Kessler; ill. by Marc Mongeau. Delmar, 1991. ISBN 0-8273-4503-8 Subj: Nursery rhymes.

Hey diddle diddle ill. by Nita Sowter. Peter Bedrick, 1984. ISBN 0-911745-27-0 Subj: Format, unusual – board books. Nursery rhymes.

Hey diddle diddle ill. by Eleanor Wasmuth. Simon & Schuster, 1986. ISBN 0-671-61726-5 Subj: Format, unusual – board books. Nursery rhymes.

Hey diddle diddle, and Baby bunting ill. by Randolph Caldecott. Warne, 1882. Subj: Nursery rhymes.

Hey diddle diddle picture book ill. by Randolph Caldecott. Warne, 1883. Subj: Nursery rhymes.

Hickory dickory dock adapt. by Leonard P. Kessler; ill. by Doug Cushman. Garrard, 1980. ISBN 0-8116-7400-2 Subj: Animals – cats. Animals – mice. Clocks, watches.

Hickory, dickory, dock adapt. by Robin Muller; ill. by Suzanne Duranceau. Scholastic, 1994. ISBN 0-590-47278-X Subj: Animals. Clocks, watches. Parties. Rhyming text.

Hickory dickory dock adapt. and ill. by Marilyn Janovitz. Hyperion, 1991. ISBN 1-56282-084-2 Subj: Animals – cats. Animals – mice. Clocks, watches. Nursery rhymes.

Hickory, dickory, dock ill. by Moira Kemp. Lodestar, 1993. ISBN 0-525-67444-6 Subj: Animals – mice. Clocks, watches. Format, unusual – board books. Nursery rhymes.

Hickory dickory dock and other nursery rhymes ill. by Carol Jones. Houghton Mifflin, 1992. ISBN 0-395-60834-1 Subj: Format, unusual. Nursery rhymes.

Humpty Dumpty: five fingerwiggle nursery rhymes ill. by Colin and Jacqui Hawkins. Candlewick, 1992. ISBN 1-56402-015-0 Subj: Format, unusual – board books. Nursery rhymes.

Humpty Dumpty ill. by Moira Kemp; paper engineering by Steve Augarde; designed by Herman

Lelie. Lodestar, 1996. ISBN 0-525-67540-X Subj: Eggs. Format, unusual – toy and movable books. Nursery rhymes.

Humpty Dumpty and other first rhymes ill. by Betty Ferrell Youngs. Bodley Head, 1980. ISBN 0-370-30025-4 Subj: Nursery rhymes.

Humpty Dumpty and other rhymes ed. by Iona Opie; ill. by Rosemary Wells. Candlewick, 1997. ISBN 0-7636-0353-8 Subj: Format, unusual – board books. Nursery rhymes.

Hurrah, we're outward bound! ill. by Peter Spier. Doubleday, 1968. ISBN 0-440-40715-X Subj: Nursery rhymes.

Hush-a-bye baby: and other bedtime rhymes ill. by Nicola Bayley. Lothrop, 1986. ISBN 0-02-708610-0 Subj: Bedtime. Nursery rhymes.

Ian Penney's book of nursery rhymes ill. by Ian Penney. H.N. Abrams, 1994. ISBN 0-8109-3733-6 Subj: Nursery rhymes.

In a pumpkin shell ill. by Joan Walsh Anglund. Harcourt, 1960. ISBN 0-15-238269-0 Subj: ABC books. Nursery rhymes.

Jack and Jill ill. by Eleanor Wasmuth. Simon & Schuster, 1986. ISBN 0-671-61729-X Subj: Format, unusual – board books. Nursery rhymes.

Jack and Jill: and other nursery rhymes (Cousins, Lucy)

Jack Kent's merry Mother Goose ill. by Jack Kent. Golden Pr., 1977. ISBN 0-307-65798-1 Subj: Nursery rhymes.

James Marshall's Mother Goose ill. by James Marshall. Farrar, 1979. ISBN 0-374-33653-9 Subj: Nursery rhymes.

Kate Greenaway's Mother Goose ill. by Kate Greenaway. Dial, 1988. ISBN 0-8037-0479-8 Subj: Format, unusual – board books. Nursery rhymes.

Kitten rhymes ill. by Lulu Delacre. Simon & Schuster, 1984. ISBN 0-671-49687-5 Subj: Animals – cats. Format, unusual – board books. Nursery rhymes.

The Larousse book of nursery rhymes ed. by Robert Owen; ill. with photos. Larousse, 1984. Ill. are full color photos. of tile pictures, painted during the late 19th and early 20th cents., created by the Royal Doulton Co., designed by Margaret Thompson, William Rowe and John H. McLennan. ISBN 0-88332-371-0 Subj: Nursery rhymes.

Lavender's blue: a book of nursery rhymes comp. by Kathleen Lines; ill. by Harold Jones. Oxford Univ. Pr., 1982. ISBN 0-19-279537-6 Subj: Nursery rhymes.

Little Boy Blue ill. by Nita Sowter. Peter Bedrick, 1984. ISBN 0-911745-28-9 Subj: Format, unusual – board books. Nursery rhymes.

Little Boy Blue and other rhymes ed. by Iona Opie; ill. by Rosemary Wells. Candlewick, 1997. ISBN 0-7636-0354-6 Subj: Format, unusual – board books. Nursery rhymes.

Little Miss Muffet ill. by Mary Morgan. Publications International, 1998. ISBN 0-7853-2633-2 Subj: Format, unusual – toy and movable books. Nursery rhymes.

Little Miss Muffet: and other nursery rhymes (Cousins, Lucy)

The little Mother Goose ill. by Jessie Willcox Smith. Dodd, 1918. Subj: Nursery rhymes.

Little Robin Redbreast: a Mother Goose rhyme (Little Robin Redbreast)

London Bridge is falling down ill. by Ed Emberley. Little, 1967. Subj: Folk and fairy tales. Foreign lands – England. Games. Nursery rhymes. Songs.

London Bridge is falling down ill. by Peter Spier. Doubleday, 1989, c1967. ISBN 0-385-08025-5 Subj: Folk and fairy tales. Foreign lands – England. Games. Nursery rhymes. Songs.

The Margaret Tarrant nursery rhyme book (Tarrant, Margaret)

Michael Foreman's Mother Goose ill. by Michael Foreman. Harcourt, 1991. ISBN 0-15-255820-9 Subj: Nursery rhymes.

Mother Goose sel. and ill. by Scott Cook. Knopf, 1994. ISBN 0-679-90949-4 Subj: Nursery rhymes.

Mother Goose: a comprehensive collection of the rhymes comp. by William Rose Benét; ill. by Roger Antoine Duvoisin. Heritage Pr., 1943. Subj: Nursery rhymes.

Mother Goose sel. by Phyllis Maurine Fraser; ill. by Miss Elliott. Simon & Schuster, 1942. Subj: Nursery rhymes.

Mother Goose ill. by C. B. Falls. Doubleday, 1924. Subj: Nursery rhymes.

Mother Goose ill. by Gyo Fujikawa. Grosset, 1967. ISBN 0-448-01810-1 Subj: Nursery rhymes.

Mother Goose: as told by Kellogg's singing lady ill. by Vernon Grant. Kellogg Co., 1933. Subj: Nursery rhymes.

Mother Goose: or, the old nursery rhymes sel. by Phyllis Maurine Fraser; ill. by Kate Greenaway. Routledge, 1881. Illustrated as originally engraved and printed by Edmund Evans. Subj: Nursery rhymes.

Mother Goose: a collection of classic nursery rhymes sel. and ill. by Michael Hague. Holt, 1984. ISBN 0-03-070723-4 Subj: Nursery rhymes.

Mother Goose: sixty-seven favorite rhymes ill. by Violet La Mont. Simon & Schuster, 1957. Subj: Nursery rhymes.

Mother Goose: the old nursery rhymes ill. by Arthur Rackham. Century, 1913. Subj: Nursery rhymes.

Mother Goose arranged and ed. by Eulalie Osgood Grover; ill. by Frederick Richardson. The Volland ed. Volland, 1915. ISBN 0-517-43619-1 Subj: Nursery rhymes.

Mother Goose re-arranged and ed. in this form by Eulalie Osgood Grover; ill. by Frederick Richardson. The classic Volland ed. Rand McNally, 1976. Reprint of the 1971 ed. published by Hubbard Press, Northbrook, Ill. ISBN 0-528-88559-6 Subj: Nursery rhymes.

Mother Goose ill. by Gustaf Tenggren. Little, 1940. Subj: Nursery rhymes.

Mother Goose: seventy-seven verses ill. by Tasha Tudor. Walck, 1944. Subj: Caldecott award honor books. Nursery rhymes.

Mother Goose abroad: nursery rhymes (Tucker, Nicholas)

Mother Goose and nursery rhymes ill. with wood engravings by Philip Reed. Regnery/Gateway, 1979, c1963. ISBN 0-8952-6098-0 Subj: Caldecott award honor books. Nursery rhymes.

A Mother Goose book ill. by Joan Walsh Anglund. Harcourt, 1991. ISBN 0-15-200529-3 Subj: Nursery rhymes.

The Mother Goose book ill. by Alice and Martin Provensen. Random House, 1976. ISBN 0-394-92122-4 Subj: Nursery rhymes.

The Mother Goose book gathered from many sources; ill. by Sonia Roetter. Peter Pauper Pr., 1985, 1946. ISBN 0-8808-8759-1 Subj: Nursery rhymes.

Mother Goose house ill. by Zokeisha; ed. by Kate Klimo. Simon & Schuster, 1983. ISBN 0-671-46127-3 Subj: Format, unusual – board books. Homes, houses. Nursery rhymes.

Mother Goose in French: Poesies de la vraie Mere Oie trans. by Hugh Latham; ill. by Barbara Cooney. Crowell, 1964. Subj: Foreign languages. Nursery rhymes.

Mother Goose in hieroglyphics ill. by George S. Appleton. Houghton Mifflin, 1962. Reproduction of the 1st ed. published in 1849. ISBN 0-486-20745-5 Subj: Games. Hieroglyphics. Nursery rhymes. Rebuses.

Mother Goose in prose (Baum, L. Frank [Lyman Frank])

Mother Goose in Spanish: Poesias de la Madre Oca trans. by Alastair Reid and Anthony Kerrigan; ill. by Barbara Cooney. Crowell, 1968. Subj: Foreign languages. Nursery rhymes.

Mother Goose melodies intro. and bib. note by E. F. Bleiler; ill. with engravings. Facsimile ed. of the Munroe and Francis c.1833 version. Dover, 1970. ISBN 0-486-22659-X Subj: Nursery rhymes.

Mother Goose nursery rhymes ill. by Arthur Rackham. Watts, 1969. Reprint of the 1913 ed. Subj: Nursery rhymes.

Mother Goose nursery rhymes ill. by Arthur Rackham. Viking, 1975. ISBN 0-670-49003-2 Subj: Nursery rhymes.

Mother Goose rhymes ed. by Watty Piper; ill. by Eulalie M. Banks and Lois Lenski. Platt, 1947, 1956. Subj: Nursery rhymes.

The Mother Goose songbook ill. by Jacqueline Sinclair. David & Charles, 1985. ISBN 0-434-92841-0 Subj: Music. Nursery rhymes. Songs.

The Mother Goose treasury ill. by Raymond Briggs. Coward, 1966. ISBN 0-698-20094-2 Subj: Nursery rhymes.

Mother Goose's melodies: or, songs for the nursery ed. by William A. Wheeler. Houghton Mifflin, 189?. Subj: Nursery rhymes. Songs.

Mother Goose's melody: or, sonnets for the cradle. Facsimile of John Newbery's collection of Mother Goose rhymes, reproduced from the earliest known perfect copy of the 1794 printing. Frederic G. Melcher, 1945. Subj: Nursery rhymes.

Mother Goose's nursery rhymes ill. by Allen Atkinson. Knopf, 1984. ISBN 0-394-53699-1 Subj: Nursery rhymes.

Mother Goose's rhymes and melodies ill. by J. L. Webb; music and melodies by E. I. Lane. Cassell, 1888. Subj: Music. Nursery rhymes.

The movable Mother Goose (Sabuda, Robert James)

My first real Mother Goose board book ill. by Blanche Fisher Wright. Scholastic, 2000. ISBN 0-439-14671-2 Subj: Format, unusual – board books. Nursery rhymes.

Nursery rhyme book ed. by Andrew Lang; ill. by L. Leslie Brooke. Warne, 1897. Subj: Nursery rhymes.

Nursery rhymes sel. by Marie Gorsline; ill. by Douglas W. Gorsline. Random House, 1977. ISBN 0-394-83550-6 Subj: Nursery rhymes.

Nursery rhymes ill. by Eloise Wilkin. Random House, 1979. ISBN 0-394-94129-8 Subj: Nursery rhymes.

Nursery rhymes from Mother Goose in signed English Prepared under the supervision of the staff of the Pre-School Signed English Project: Barbara M. Kanapell and others. Gallaudet Univ. Pr., 1972. Subj: Handicaps – deafness. Nursery rhymes.

Old Mother Hubbard and her dog (Martin, Sarah Catherine)

Old Mother Hubbard and her dog (Martin, Sarah Catherine)

The old woman in a shoe ill. by Eleanor Wasmuth. Simon & Schuster, 1986. ISBN 0-671-61728-1 Subj: Format, unusual – board books. Nursery rhymes.

One I love, two I love, and other loving Mother Goose rhymes ill. by Nonny Hogrogian. Dutton, 1972. ISBN 0-525-36420-X Subj: Nursery rhymes.

One misty moisty morning: rhymes from Mother Goose ill. by Mitchell Miller. Farrar, 1971. ISBN 0-374-35647-5 Subj: Nursery rhymes.

1, 2 buckle my shoe ill. by Sherry Neidigh. Publications International, 1997. ISBN 0-7853-2364-3 Subj: Counting, numbers. Format, unusual – toy and movable books. Nursery rhymes.

One, two, buckle my shoe: counting rhymes for young children (Williams, Jenny [Jennifer])

The only true Mother Goose melodies intro. by Edward Everett Hale. Lothrop, 1905. An exact and full-size reproduction of the original edition published and copyrighted in Boston in the year 1833 by Munroe and Francis. Subj: Nursery rhymes.

Over the moon: a book of nursery rhymes ill. by Charlotte Voake. Crown, 1985. ISBN 0-517-55873-4 Subj: Nursery rhymes.

Pat-a-cake adapt. and ill. by Marilyn Janovitz. Walt Disney, 1992. ISBN 1-56282-171-7 Subj: Animals. Birthdays. Music. Nursery rhymes.

Pat-a-cake, pat-a-cake ill. by Moira Kemp. Lodestar, 1992. ISBN 0-525-67393-8 Subj: Format, unusual – board books. Games. Nursery rhymes.

People from Mother Goose: a question book (Hopkins, Lee Bennett)

The piper's son ill. by Emily Newton Barto. Longman, 1942. Subj: Nursery rhymes.

A pocket full of posies ill. by Marguerite De Angeli. Doubleday, 1961. First pub. in 1954. Subj: Nursery rhymes.

A pocket full of posies (Gerrard, Roy)

The pudgy book of Mother Goose (The pudgy book of Mother Goose)

Pussy cat, pussy cat ill. by Ferelith Eccles Williams. David & Charles, 1985. ISBN 0-437-86009-4 Subj: Format, unusual – board books. Nursery rhymes.

Pussycat ate the dumplings: cat rhymes from Mother Goose (Koontz, Robin Michal)

Pussycat, pussycat and other rhymes ed. by Iona Opie; ill. by Rosemary Wells. Candlewick, 1997. ISBN 0-7636-0355-4 Subj: Format, unusual – board books. Nursery rhymes.

The rainbow Mother Goose ed. with an intro. by May Lamberton Becker; ill. by Lili Cassel-Wronker. Collins-World, 1947. Subj: Nursery rhymes.

The real Mother Goose ill. by Blanche Fisher Wright. Rand McNally, 1916. Subj: Nursery rhymes.

The real Mother Goose board book ill. by Diane Muldrow. Scholastic, 1998. ISBN 0-590-00368-2 Subj: Format, unusual – board books. Nursery rhymes.

The real Mother Goose clock book ill. by Jane Chambless. Rand McNally, 1984. ISBN 0-528-82329-9 Subj: Clocks, watches. Nursery rhymes. Time.

Richard Scarry's best Mother Goose ever ill. by Richard Scarry. Golden Pr., 1970. ISBN 0-307-15578-1 Subj: Nursery rhymes.

Richard Scarry's favorite Mother Goose rhymes ill. by Richard Scarry. Golden Pr., 1964. Subj: Nursery rhymes.

Ride a cock-horse (Williams, Sarah)

Ride a cockhorse: animal rhymes for young children (Williams, Jenny [Jennifer])

Rimes de la Mere Oie: Mother Goose rhymes rendered into French by Ormonde De Kay, Jr.; ill. by Seymour Chwast, Milton Glaser, and Barry Zaid. Little, 1971. Subj: Foreign languages. Nursery rhymes.

Ring around a rosy: action rhymes for young children (Williams, Jenny [Jennifer])

Ring o' roses ill. by L. Leslie Brooke. Warne, 1923. ISBN 0-7232-1980-X Subj: Nursery rhymes.

The Sesame Street players present Mother Goose: featuring Jim Henson's Sesame Street Muppets ill. by Michael J. Smollin. Random House, 1982. ISBN 0-394-95223-5 Subj: Nursery rhymes. Puppets.

Sing a song of Mother Goose ill. by Barbara Reid. North Winds, 1987. ISBN 0-590-71781-2 Subj: Nursery rhymes.

Sing a song of sixpence comp. and ill. by Randolph Caldecott. Barron's, 1988. Reprint of 1888 ed. ISBN 0-8120-5900-X Subj: Nursery rhymes.

Sing a song of sixpence ill. by Randolph Caldecott. New ed. Hart, 1977. Reprint of orig. Warne pub. between 1876 and 1886. ISBN 0-8055-0359-5 Subj: Nursery rhymes.

Sing a song of sixpence ill. by Margaret Chamberlain. Peter Bedrick, 1984. ISBN 0-911745-29-7 Subj: Format, unusual – board books. Nursery rhymes.

Sing a song of sixpence ill. by Leonard B. Lubin. Lothrop, 1987. ISBN 0-688-00545-4 Subj: Nursery rhymes. Royalty.

Sing a song of sixpence ed. by Kate Klimo; ill. by Ray Marshall and Korky Paul. Simon & Schuster, 1983. ISBN 0-671-46237-7 Subj: Format, unusual – toy and movable books. Nursery rhymes.

Sing a song of sixpence ill. by Ferelith Eccles Williams. David & Charles, 1985. ISBN 0-437-86002-7 Subj: Format, unusual – board books. Nursery rhymes.

Sing hey diddle diddle: 66 nursery rhymes with their traditional tunes comp. by Beatrice Harrop; ill. by Frank Francis and Bernard Cheese. Sterling, 1983. ISBN 0-7136-2334-9 Subj: Music. Nursery rhymes.

Songs for Mother Goose ill. by Maginel Wright Enright Barney; set to music by Sidney Homer. Macmillan, 1920. Subj: Nursery rhymes.

The tall Mother Goose ill. by Feodor Rojankovsky. HarperCollins, 1942. Subj: Nursery rhymes.

Thirty old-time nursery songs ed. by Joseph Moorat; ill. by Paul Woodroffe. Norton, 1980. Orig. pub.

in 1912. ISBN 0-500-01242-3 Subj: Music. Nursery rhymes. Songs.

This little pig: a Mother Goose favorite ill. by Leonard B. Lubin. Lothrop, 1985. ISBN 0-688-04089-6 Subj: Animals – pigs. Nursery rhymes.

This little pig ill. by Eleanor Wasmuth. Simon & Schuster, 1986. ISBN 0-671-61727-3 Subj: Format, unusual – board books. Nursery rhymes.

This little pig went to market ill. by L. Leslie Brooke. Warne, 1922. Subj: Animals – pigs. Nursery rhymes.

This little pig went to market ill. by Denise Fleming. Random House, 1985. ISBN 0-394-87030-1 Subj: Format, unusual – toy and movable books. Nursery rhymes.

This little pig went to market ill. by Ferelith Eccles Williams. David & Charles, 1985. ISBN 0-437-86004-3 Subj: Format, unusual – board books. Games. Nursery rhymes.

This little piggy ill. by Moira Kemp. Lodestar, 1993. ISBN 0-525-67446-2 Subj: Animals – pigs. Format, unusual – board books. Nursery rhymes.

The three jovial huntsmen ill. by Susan Jeffers. Bradbury, 1973. ISBN 0-8788-8023-2 Subj: Caldecott award honor books. Nursery rhymes.

Three little kittens (Siomades, Lorianne)

The three little kittens ill. by Lorinda Bryan Cauley. Putnam, 1982. ISBN 0-399-20855-0 Subj: Animals – cats. Behavior – losing things. Games. Nursery rhymes.

The three little kittens ill. by Paul Galdone. Clarion, 1986. ISBN 0-89919-426-5 Subj: Animals – cats. Behavior – losing things. Nursery rhymes.

The three little kittens ill. by Dorothy Stott. Putnam, 1984. ISBN 0-448-10216-1 Subj: Animals – cats. Behavior – losing things. Format, unusual – board books. Nursery rhymes.

The three little kittens adapt. by Jean Marzollo; ill. by Shelley Thornton. Scholastic, 1986. ISBN 0-590-33370-4 Subj: Animals – cats. Behavior – losing things. Games. Nursery rhymes.

To market! To market! ill. by Emma Lillian Brock. Knopf, 1930. Subj: Nursery rhymes. Shopping.

To market! To market! ill. by Peter Spier. Doubleday, 1989, c1967. ISBN 0-385-05352-5 Subj: Nursery rhymes.

Tom, Tom the piper's son ill. by Paul Galdone. McGraw-Hill, 1964. Subj: Nursery rhymes.

Tomie de Paola's Mother Goose (De Paola, Tomie [Thomas Anthony])

Twenty nursery rhymes ill. by Philip Van Aver. Grabhorn-Hoyem, 1970. Subj: Nursery rhymes.

Vernon Grant's Mother Goose ill. by Vernon Grant. Abrams, 1998. ISBN 0-8109-4128-7 Subj: Nursery rhymes.

Wee Willie Winkie and other nursery rhymes (Cousins, Lucy)

Wee Willie Winkie and other rhymes ed. by Iona Opie; ill. by Rosemary Wells. Candlewick, 1997. ISBN 0-7636-0356-2 Subj: Format, unusual – board books. Nursery rhymes.

Wendy Watson's Mother Goose ill. by Wendy Watson. Lothrop, 1989. ISBN 0-688-05708-X Subj: Nursery rhymes.

Willy Pogany's Mother Goose ill. by Willy Pogany. Nelson, 1928. Subj: Nursery rhymes.

Motomora, Mitchell. *Specs: the true story of baseball player George Toporcer* ill. by Nina Barbaresi. Raintree, 1990. ISBN 0-8172-3585-X Subj: Glasses. Sports – baseball.

Mott, Evelyn Clarke. *Balloon ride* ill. by author. Walker, 1991. ISBN 0-8027-8126-8 Subj: Activities – ballooning.

Cool cat ill. by author. Random House, 1996. ISBN 0-679-86956-5 Subj: Animals – cats. Format, unusual – board books. Rhyming text.

Dancing rainbows: a Pueblo boy's story photos by author. Cobblehill, 1996. ISBN 0-525-65216-7 Subj: Fairs. Family life – grandfathers. Food. Indians of North America – Twa.

Hot dog ill. by author. Random House, 1996. ISBN 0-679-86955-7 Subj: Animals – dogs. Format, unusual – board books. Pets. Rhyming text.

Steam train ride ill. by author. Walker, 1991. ISBN 0-8027-6996-9 Subj: Trains.

Motyka, Sally Mitchell. *An ordinary day* ill. by Donna Ayers. Simon & Schuster, 1989. ISBN 0-671-67118-9 Subj: Activities. Family life.

Mouse house ed. by Kate Klimo; ill. by Zokeisha. Simon & Schuster, 1983. ISBN 0-671-46129-X Subj: Animals – mice. Format, unusual – board books. Homes, houses.

The moving adventures of Old Dame Trot and her comical cat ill. by Paul Galdone. McGraw-Hill, 1973. ISBN 0-07-022692-X Subj: Animals – cats. Nursery rhymes.

Mower, Nancy. *I visit my Tūtū and Grandma* ill. by Patricia A. Wozniak. Press Pacifica, 1984. ISBN 0-916630-41-2 Subj: Family life – grandmothers. Hawaii.

Moxley, Susan. *Abdul's treasure* ill. by author. David & Charles, 1988. ISBN 0-340-38918-4 Subj: Careers – fishermen. Folk and fairy tales. Royalty.

Moyer, Marshall M. *Rollo Bones, canine hypnotist* ill. by author. Tricycle, 1998. ISBN 1-883672-65-1 Subj: Animals – dogs. Behavior – running away.

Mozelle, Shirley. *The pig is in the pantry, the cat is on the shelf* ill. by Jennifer Plecas. Clarion, 2000. ISBN 0-395-78627-4 Subj: Animals. Behavior – misbehavior. Farms. Homes, houses. Pets.

Mozley, Charles. *The first book of tales of ancient Araby* (Arabian Nights)

Mudd-Ruth, Maria. *The beetle* ill. by Wendy Smith-Griswold. Stewart, Tabori & Chang, 1992. ISBN 1-55670-255-8 Subj: Format, unusual – toy and movable books. Insects – beetles.

The ultimate ocean book ill. by Virge Kask and Beverly E. Benner. Artists & Writers Guild, 1995. ISBN 0-307-17628-2 Subj: Animals. Fish. Format, unusual – toy and movable books. Sea and seashore.

Mude, O. *see* Gorey, Edward (St. John)

Mueller, Evelyn. *I'm deaf and it's okay* (Aseltine, Lorraine)

Mueller, Virginia. *A Halloween mask for Monster* ill. by Lynn Munsinger. Albert Whitman, 1986. ISBN 0-8075-3134-0 Subj: Holidays – Halloween. Masks. Monsters.

In the morning ill. by Diane Jaquith. Houghton Mifflin, 1991. ISBN 0-395-55018-1 Subj: Birds – chickens. Morning.

Monster and the baby ill. by Lynn Munsinger. Albert Whitman, 1985. ISBN 0-8075-5253-4 Subj: Activities – babysitting. Babies. Monsters.

Monster can't sleep ill. by Lynn Munsinger. Albert Whitman, 1986. ISBN 0-8075-5261-5 Subj: Bedtime. Monsters. Sleep.

Monster goes to school ill. by Lynn Munsinger. Albert Whitman, 1991. ISBN 0-8075-5264-X Subj: Clocks, watches. Monsters. School. Time.

Monster's birthday hiccups ill. by Lynn Munsinger. Albert Whitman, 1991. ISBN 0-8075-5267-4 Subj: Birthdays. Illness. Monsters. Parties.

A playhouse for Monster ill. by Lynn Munsinger. Albert Whitman, 1985. ISBN 0-8075-6541-5 Subj: Activities – playing. Monsters.

Mühlberger, Richard. *The Christmas story* (The Christmas story)

Muller, Gerda. *Around the oak* ill. by author. Dutton, 1994. ISBN 0-525-45239-7 Subj: Careers – park rangers. Forest, woods. Seasons. Trees.

Circle of seasons ill. by author. Dutton, 1995. ISBN 0-525-45394-6 Subj: Seasons.

The garden in the city ill. by author. Dutton, 1992. ISBN 0-525-44697-4 Subj: City. Gardens, gardening.

Muller, Robin. *Hickory, dickory, dock* (Mother Goose)

Little Wonder ill. by author. North Winds, 1994. ISBN 0-590-24225-3 Subj: Animals – dogs.

The lucky old woman. Kids Can Pr., 1987. ISBN 0-921103-07-7 Subj: Folk and fairy tales.

The magic paintbrush ill. by author. Viking, 1990. ISBN 0-670-83167-0 Subj: Activities – painting. Behavior – greed. Magic. Royalty – kings.

Mollie Whuppie and the giant ill. by reteller. Scholastic, 1993. ISBN 0-590-74036-9 Subj: Behavior – trickery. Folk and fairy tales. Foreign lands – England. Giants.

The sorcerer's apprentice ill. by author. Silver Burdett, 1986. ISBN 0-382-09382-8 Subj: Folk and fairy tales. Magic. Royalty.

Mullins, Edward S. *Animal limericks* ill. by author. Follett, 1966. Subj: Animals. Poetry.

Mullins, Patricia. *Dinosaur encore* ill. by author. HarperCollins, 1993. ISBN 0-06-021073-7 Subj: Dinosaurs. Format, unusual – toy and movable books.

One horse waiting for me ill. by author. Simon & Schuster, 1998. ISBN 0-689-81381-3 Subj: Animals – horses, ponies. Counting, numbers.

The Sea-Breeze Hotel (Vaughan, Marcia Kapok)

V for vanishing: an alphabet of endangered animals ill. by author. HarperCollins, 1994. ISBN 0-06-023557-8 Subj: ABC books. Animals – endangered animals.

Munari, Bruno. *ABC* ill. by author. Collins-World, 1960. Subj: ABC books.

Animals for sale ill. by author. W. Collins, 1980, c1959. ISBN 0-529-05567-8 Subj: Animals.

The birthday present ill. by author. Collins, 1980, c1959. ISBN 0-529-05565-1 Subj: Birthdays. Games. Transportation.

Bruno Munari's zoo ill. by author. Collins-World, 1963. Subj: Animals. Birds. Zoos.

The circus in the mist ill. by author. Collins, 1968. Subj: Circus. Format, unusual. Weather – fog.

The elephant's wish ill. by author. Collins, 1959. First pub. in 1945. ISBN 0-529-05562-7 Subj: Animals. Behavior – wishing. Format, unusual – toy and movable books.

Jimmy has lost his cap ill. by author. Collins, 1980, c1959. ISBN 0-529-05563-5 Subj: Behavior – losing things. Format, unusual – toy and movable books.

Tic, Tac and Toc ill. by author. Collins-World, 1980, c1957. ISBN 0-529-05564-3 Subj: Birds. Format, unusual – toy and movable books.

Who's there? Open the door trans. by Maria Cimino; ill. by author. Collins-World, 1980, c1957. ISBN 0-529-05568-6 Subj: Animals. Format, unusual – toy and movable books.

Munro, Roxie. *Christmastime in New York City* ill. by author. Dodd, 1987. ISBN 0-396-08909-7 Subj: City. Holidays – Christmas.

The inside-outside book of libraries ill. by author; text by Julie Cummins. Dutton, 1996. ISBN 0-525-45608-2 Subj: Libraries.

The inside-outside book of London ill. by author. Dutton, 1989. ISBN 0-525-44522-6 Subj: City. Foreign lands – England.

The inside-outside book of New York City ill. by author. Dodd, 1985. ISBN 0-396-08513-X Subj: City.

The inside-outside book of Paris ill. by author. Dutton, 1992. ISBN 0-525-44863-2 Subj: City. Foreign lands – France.

The inside-outside book of Washington, D.C. ill. by author. Dutton, 1987. ISBN 0-525-44298-7 Subj: Activities – traveling. City. Museums.

Munsch, Robert N. *Aaron's hair* ill. by Alan and Lea Daniel. Scholastic, 2000. ISBN 0-439-19258-7 Subj: Behavior – running away. Emotions. Hair.

Alligator baby ill. by Michael Martchenko. Scholastic, 1997. ISBN 0-590-21101-3 Subj: Animals. Babies. Family life – brothers and sisters. Family life – new sibling. Zoos.

Andrew's loose tooth ill. by Michael Martchenko. Scholastic, 1998. ISBN 0-590-21102-1 Subj: Behavior – growing up. Fairies. Teeth.

Angela's airplane ill. by Michael Martchenko. Firefly, 1988. ISBN 1-55037-027-8 Subj: Activities – flying. Airplanes, airports. Behavior – misbehavior.

David's father ill. by Michael Martchenko. Firefly, 1983. ISBN 0-920236-62-6 Subj: Character traits – kindness. Giants.

The fire station ill. by Michael Martchenko. Firefly, 1991. ISBN 1-55037-170-3 Subj: Careers – firefighters.

From far away by Robert Munsch and Saoussan Askar; ill. by Michael Martchenko. Firefly, 1995. ISBN 1-55037-397-8 Subj: Foreign lands – Canada. Foreign lands – Lebanon. Moving. Names. School. War.

Get me another one! ill. by Shawn Steffler. Doubleday Canada, 1992. ISBN 0-385-25337-0 Subj: Family life – fathers. Foreign lands – Canada. Sports – fishing.

Get out of bed! ill. by Alan Daniel. Scholastic, 1998. ISBN 0-590-21103-X Subj: School. Sleep.

Good families don't ill. by Alan Daniel. Doubleday Canada, 1990. ISBN 0-385-25267-6 Subj: Anatomy. Behavior – misbehavior. Etiquette. Family life. Foreign lands – Canada.

I have to go! ill. by Michael Martchenko. Firefly, 1987. ISBN 0-920303-77-3 Subj: Behavior – growing up. Family life.

Jonathan cleaned up - then he heard a sound: or, blackberry subway jam ill. by Michael Martchenko. Firefly, 1981. ISBN 0-920236-22-7 Subj: Machines. Problem solving. Trains.

Love you forever ill. by Sheila McGraw. Firefly, 1994, 1986. ISBN 0-920668-36-4 Subj: Emotions – love. Family life – mothers. Foreign lands – Canada.

Millicent and the wind ill. by Suzanne Duranceau. Firefly, 1984. ISBN 0-920236-98-7 Subj: Behavior – needing someone. Behavior – wishing. Friendship. Weather – wind.

Mmm, cookies! ill. by Michael Martchenko. Scholastic, 2000. ISBN 0-590-89603-2 Subj: Behavior – trickery. Family life. Food. School.

Moira's birthday ill. by Michael Martchenko. Firefly, 1987. ISBN 0-920303-85-4 Subj: Behavior – misbehavior. Birthdays. Parties.

Mortimer ill. by Michael Martchenko. Firefly, 1985. ISBN 0-920303-12-9 Subj: Bedtime. Noise, sounds. Songs.

Mud puddle ill. by author. Firefly, 1982. ISBN 0-920236-47-2 Subj: Activities – playing. Character traits – cleanliness. Foreign lands – Canada. Weather – rain.

Murmel, Murmel, Murmel ill. by Michael Martchenko. Firefly, 1982. ISBN 0-920236-33-2 Subj: Foreign lands – Canada. Friendship.

The paper bag princess ill. by Michael Martchenko. Firefly, 1980. ISBN 0-920236-82-0 Subj: Character traits – appearance. Dragons.

Pigs ill. by Michael Martchenko. Firefly, 1989. ISBN 1-550370-39-1 Subj: Animals – pigs.

A promise is a promise by Robert N. Munsch and Michael Kusugak; ill. by Vladyana Krykorka. Firefly, 1988. ISBN 1-55037-009-X Subj: Eskimos. Folk and fairy tales. Foreign lands – Canada. Sea and seashore.

Purple, green and yellow ill. by Hélène Desputeaux. Firefly, 1992. ISBN 1-55037-255-6 Subj: Concepts – color.

Ribbon rescue ill. by Eugenie Fernandes. Scholastic, 1999. ISBN 0-590-89012-3 Subj: Character traits – generosity. Clothing – dresses. Weddings.

Show-and-tell ill. by Michael Martchenko. Firefly, 1991. ISBN 1-55037-195-9 Subj: School.

Something good ill. by Michael Martchenko. Firefly, 1990. ISBN 1-55037-099-5 Subj: Family life – fathers. Shopping. Stores.

Stephanie's ponytail ill. by Michael Martchenko. Firefly, 1996. ISBN 1-55037-485-0 Subj: Behavior – imitation. Character traits – appearance. Cumulative tales. Hair. School.

Thomas' snowsuit ill. by Michael Martchenko. Firefly, 1985. ISBN 0-920303-32-3 Subj: Careers – teachers. Clothing. Foreign lands – Canada. School. Seasons – winter. Weather – snow.

Up, up, down! ill. by Michael Martchenko. Scholastic, 2001. ISBN 0-439-18770-2 Subj: Activities. Trees.

Wait and see ill. by Michael Martchenko. Firefly, 1993. ISBN 1-55037-335-8 Subj: Behavior – wishing. Birthdays. Foreign lands – Canada. Friendship.

We share everything! ill. by Michael Martchenko. Scholastic, 1999. ISBN 0-590-89600-8 Subj: Behavior – sharing. School.

Where is Gah-Ning? ill. by Hélène Desputeaux. Annick, 1994. ISBN 1-55037-982-8 Subj: Family life – fathers. Foreign lands – Canada. Shopping. Toys – balloons.

Munsterberg, Peggy. *Beastly banquet: tasty treats for animal appetites* ill. by Tracy Gallup. Dial, 1997. ISBN 0-8037-1482-3 Subj: Animals. Food. Poetry.

Muntean, Michaela. *Alligator's garden* ill. by Nicole Rubel. Dial, 1984. ISBN 0-8037-0025-3 Subj: Gardens, gardening. Reptiles – alligators, crocodiles.

Bicycle bear ill. by Doug Cushman. Parents, 1983. ISBN 0-8193-1103-0 Subj: Animals – bears. Rhyming text. Sports – bicycling.

Bicycle Bear rides again ill. by Doug Cushman. Gareth Stevens, 1995. ISBN 0-8368-0964-5 Subj: Animals – bears. Family life – aunts, uncles. Rhyming text. Sports – bicycling.

The house that bear built ill. by Nicole Rubel. Dial, 1984. ISBN 0-8037-0026-1 Subj: Animals – bears. Homes, houses.

Kermit and Robin's scary story ill. by Tom Leigh. Viking, 1995. ISBN 0-670-86106-5 Subj: Bedtime. Careers – writers. Family life – aunts, uncles. Frogs and toads. Puppets.

Mokey and the festival of the bells ill. by Michael Adams. Holt, 1985. ISBN 0-03-004553-3 Subj: Character traits – generosity. Puppets.

Muppet babies through the year ill. by Bruce McNally. Random House, 1984. ISBN 0-394-86544-8 Subj: Puppets. Seasons.

The very bumpy bus ride ill. by Bernard Wiseman. Gareth Stevens, 1993. ISBN 0-8368-0980-7 Subj: Buses. Fairs.

Munthe, Adam John. *I believe in unicorns* ill. by Elizabeth Falconer. Merrimack, 1980. ISBN 0-7011-2437-7 Subj: Emotions – loneliness. Mythical creatures – unicorns.

The Muppet Show book ill. by Tudor Banus. Abrams, 1978. ISBN 0-8109-1328-3 Subj: Puppets.

Murdocca, Sal (Salvatore). *Baby wants the moon* ill. by author. Lothrop, 1994. ISBN 0-688-13665-6 Subj: Babies. Family life – brothers and sisters. Family life – new sibling.

Christmas bear ill. by author. Simon & Schuster, 1987. ISBN 0-671-64565-X Subj: Animals – bears. Holidays – Christmas. Santa Claus.

Lucy takes a holiday ill. by author. Mondo, 1998. ISBN 1-57255-560-2 Subj: Activities – vacationing. Animals – dogs.

Tuttle's shell ill. by author. Mondo, 1999. ISBN 1-57255-643-9 Subj: Animals. Behavior – losing things. Reptiles – turtles, tortoises.

Murphey, Sara. *The animal hat shop* reading consultant: Morton Botel; ill. by Mel Pekarsky. Follett, 1964. Subj: Animals – cats. Birds – chickens. Clothing – hats.

The roly poly cookie reading consultant: Morton Botel; ill. by Leonard W. Shortall. Follett, 1963. Subj: Cumulative tales. Food.

Murphy, Camay Calloway. *Can a coal scuttle fly?* (Miller, Thomas Patton)

Murphy, Chuck. *Black cat, white cat: a pop up book of opposites* ill. by author. Little Simon, 1998. ISBN 0-689-81415-1 Subj: Animals – cats. Concepts – opposites. Format, unusual – toy and movable books.

Chuck Murphy's alphabet magic ill. by author. Little Simon, 1997. ISBN 0-689-81286-8 Subj: ABC books. Format, unusual – toy and movable books.

Colors ill. by author. Little Simon, 1997. ISBN 0-689-81497-6 Subj: Concepts – color. Format, unusual – board books.

Murphy, Elspeth Campbell. *Do you see me God? prayers for young children* ill. by Bill Duca. David C. Cook, 1989. ISBN 1-55513-457-2 Subj: Poetry. Religion.

Murphy, Jill. *All for one* ill. by author. Candlewick, 1999. ISBN 0-7636-0785-1 Subj: Activities – playing. Friendship. Monsters.

All in one piece ill. by author. Putnam, 1987. ISBN 0-399-21433-X Subj: Animals – elephants. Behavior – misbehavior. Family life.

Five minutes' peace ill. by author. Putnam, 1986. ISBN 0-399-21354-6 Subj: Animals – elephants. Family life.

The last noo-noo ill. by author. Candlewick, 1995. ISBN 1-56402-581-0 Subj: Babies. Behavior – growing up. Family life. Monsters.

Peace at last ill. by author. Dial, 1980. ISBN 0-8037-6758-7 Subj: Animals – bears. Noise, sounds. Sleep.

A piece of cake ill. by author. Candlewick, 1997. ISBN 0-7636-0572-7 Subj: Animals – elephants. Food. Self-concept.

A quiet night in ill. by author. Candlewick, 1994. ISBN 1-56402-248-X Subj: Animals – elephants. Bedtime. Family life.

What next, baby bear! ill. by author. Dial, 1984. ISBN 0-8037-0027-X Subj: Animals – bears. Bedtime. Imagination. Night. Space and space ships.

Murphy, Jim. *Backyard bear* ill. by Jeffrey Greene. Scholastic, 1993. ISBN 0-590-44375-5 Subj: Animals – bears. Night.

The call of the wolves ill. by Mark Alan Weatherby. Scholastic, 1989. ISBN 0-590-41941-2 Subj: Animals – wolves.

Dinosaur for a day ill. by Mark Alan Weatherby. Scholastic, 1992. ISBN 0-590-42866-7 Subj: Dinosaurs.

Murphy, Mary. *Caterpillar's wish* ill. by author. DK, 1999. ISBN 0-7894-2593-9 Subj: Behavior – wishing. Insects – butterflies, caterpillars. Metamorphosis.

Here comes spring, and summer and fall and winter ill. by author. DK, 1999. ISBN 0-7894-3484-9 Subj: Animals – dogs. Seasons.

I feel happy, and sad, and angry, and glad ill. by author. DK, 2000. ISBN 0-7894-2680-3 Subj: Animals – dogs. Emotions.

My puffer train ill. by author. Houghton Mifflin, 1999. ISBN 0-395-97105-5 Subj: Animals. Birds – penguins. Noise, sounds. Rhyming text. Trains.

Please be quiet! ill. by author. Houghton Mifflin, 1999. ISBN 0-395-97113-6 Subj: Birds – penguins. Family life – mothers. Noise, sounds.

You smell and taste and feel and see and hear ill. by author. DK, 1997. ISBN 0-7894-2471-1 Subj: Animals – dogs. Senses.

Murphy, Pat. *Pigasus* ill. by Graham Percy. Dial, 1996. ISBN 0-8037-1588-9 Subj: Activities – flying. Animals – pigs. Behavior – stealing. Birds – blackbirds. Character traits – being different.

Murphy, Shirley Rousseau. *Tattie's river journey* ill. by Tomie de Paola. Dial, 1983. ISBN 0-8037-8770-7 Subj: Homes, houses. Rivers. Weather – rain.

Valentine for a dragon ill. by Kay Chorao. Atheneum, 1984. ISBN 0-689-31016-1 Subj: Dragons. Emotions – loneliness. Holidays – Valentine's Day. Monsters.

Wind child ill. by Leo and Diane Dillon. HarperCollins, 1999. ISBN 0-06-024904-8 Subj: Activities – weaving. Folk and fairy tales. Royalty – princes. Weather – wind.

Murphy, Stuart J. *Animals on board* ill. by R. W. Alley. HarperCollins, 1998. ISBN 0-06-027443-3 Subj: Animals. Counting, numbers. Merry-go-rounds. Rhyming text.

Beep beep, vroom vroom! ill. by Chris Demarest. HarperCollins, 2000. ISBN 0-06-028017-4 Subj: Automobiles. Counting, numbers.

The best bug parade ill. by Holly Keller. HarperCollins, 1996. ISBN 0-06-025872-1 Subj: Counting, numbers. Insects.

The best vacation ever ill. by Nadine Bernard Westcott. HarperCollins, 1997. ISBN 0-06-026767-4 Subj: Activities – vacationing. Family life. Problem solving. Rhyming text.

Betcha! ill. by S. D. Schindler. HarperCollins, 1997. ISBN 0-06-026769-0 Subj: Counting, numbers. Friendship.

Bug dance ill. by Christopher Santoro. Harper-Collins, 2002. ISBN 0-06-446252-8 Subj: Counting, numbers. Insects.

Captain Invincible and the space shapes ill. by Rémy Simard. HarperCollins, 2001. ISBN 0-06-028023-9 Subj: Concepts – shape. Counting, numbers.

Circus shapes ill. by Edward Miller. HarperCollins, 1998. ISBN 0-06-027437-9 Subj: Circus. Concepts – shape. Rhyming text.

Dave's down-to-earth rock shop ill. by Cat Bowman Smith. HarperCollins, 2000. ISBN 0-06-028019-0 Subj: Counting, numbers.

Elevator magic ill. by G. Brian Karas. Harper-Collins, 1997. ISBN 0-06-446709-0 Subj: Counting, numbers. Elevators, escalators. Rhyming text.

Every buddy counts ill. by Fiona Dunbar. Harper-Collins, 1997. ISBN 0-06-026773-9 Subj: Counting, numbers. Rhyming text.

A fair bear share ill. by John Speirs. HarperCollins, 1998. ISBN 0-06-446714-7 Subj: Activities – cooking. Animals – bears. Counting, numbers. Food.

Get up and go! ill. by Diane Greenseid. Harper-Collins, 1996. ISBN 0-06-025882-9 Subj: Animals – dogs. Morning. Rhyming text. School. Time.

Give me half! ill. by G. Brian Karas. HarperCollins, 1996. ISBN 0-06-025874-8 Subj: Behavior – sharing. Counting, numbers. Friendship. Sibling rivalry.

The greatest gymnast of all ill. by Cynthia Jabar. HarperCollins, 1998. ISBN 0-06-027609-6 Subj: Concepts. Counting, numbers.

Henry the fourth ill. by Scott Nash. HarperCollins, 1999. ISBN 0-06-027611-8 Subj: Animals – dogs. Counting, numbers.

Just enough carrots ill. by Frank Remkiewicz. HarperCollins, 1997. ISBN 0-06-026779-8 Subj: Animals – rabbits. Counting, numbers. Food. Shopping. Stores.

Missing mittens ill. by G. Brian Karas. Harper-Collins, 2001. ISBN 0-06-028027-1 Subj: Concepts. Counting, numbers.

Monster musical chairs ill. by Scott Nash. Harper-Collins, 2000. ISBN 0-06-028021-2 Subj: Counting, numbers. Games.

A pair of socks ill. by Lois Ehlert. HarperCollins, 1996. ISBN 0-06-025880-2 Subj: Clothing – socks.

The penny pot ill. by Lynne Cravath. Harper-Collins, 1998. ISBN 0-06-027607-X Subj: Counting, numbers. Fairs. Money. School.

Rabbit's pajama party ill. by Frank Remkiewicz. HarperCollins, 1999. ISBN 0-06-027617-7 Subj: Animals – rabbits. Family life – mothers. Rhyming text. Sleepovers.

Ready, set, hop! ill. by John Buller. HarperCollins, 1996. ISBN 0-06-025878-0 Subj: Activities – jumping. Counting, numbers. Frogs and toads.

Too many kangaroo things to do! ill. by Kevin O'Malley. HarperCollins, 1996. ISBN 0-06-025884-5 Subj: Animals – kangaroos. Birthdays. Counting, numbers. Parties.

Murray, Marjorie Dennis. *The stars are waiting* ill. by Jacqueline Rogers. Cavendish, 1998. ISBN 0-7614-5024-6 Subj: Animals. Bedtime. Night. Rhyming text.

Murrow, Liza Ketchum. *Good-bye, Sammy* ill. by Gail Owens. Holiday, 1989. ISBN 0-8234-0726-8 Subj: Behavior – losing things. Toys.

Murschetz, Luis. *Mister Mole* trans. by Diane Martin; ill. by author. Prentice-Hall, 1976. Translation of Der Maulwurf Grabowski. ISBN 0-13-585976-X Subj: Animals – moles. Ecology. Progress.

Musgrave, Susan. *Dreams are more real than bathtubs* ill. by Marie-Louise Gay. Orca, 1998. ISBN 1-55143-107-6 Subj: Dreams. Emotions. School – first day.

Musgrove, Margaret. *Ashanti to Zulu* ill. by Leo and Diane Dillon. Dial, 1976. ISBN 0-8037-0358-9 Subj: ABC books. Caldecott award books. Foreign lands – Africa.

Musicant, Elke. *The night vegetable eater* by Elke and Ted Musicant; ill. by Jeni Bassett. Dodd, 1981. ISBN 0-396-07923-7 Subj: Animals. Gardens, gardening. Mystery stories.

Musicant, Ted. *The night vegetable eater* (Musicant, Elke)

Muzik, Katharine. *At home in the coral reef* ill. by Katherine Brown-Wing. Charlesbridge, 1992. ISBN 0-88106-487-4 Subj: Ecology. Fish. Sea and seashore.

Mwalimu. *Awful aardvark* by Mwalimu and Adrienne Kennaway; ill. by Adrienne Kennaway. Little, 1989. ISBN 0-316-59218-8 Subj: Animals – aardvarks. Animals – mongooses. Folk and fairy tales. Foreign lands – Africa. Night. Sleep.

Mwenye Hadithi. *Crafty chameleon* ill. by Adrienne Kennaway. Little, 1987. ISBN 0-316-33723-4 Subj: Animals. Behavior – bullying. Behavior – unnoticed, unseen.

Greedy zebra ill. by Adrienne Kennaway. Little, 1984. ISBN 0-316-33721-8 Subj: Animals – zebras. Behavior – greed. Clothing. Folk and fairy tales. Foreign lands – Africa.

Hot hippo ill. by Adrienne Kennaway. Little, 1986. ISBN 0-316-33722-6 Subj: Animals – hippopotamuses. Foreign lands – Africa. Rivers.

Lazy lion ill. by Adrienne Kennaway. Little, 1990. ISBN 0-316-33725-0 Subj: Animals. Animals – lions. Character traits – laziness.

Tricky tortoise ill. by Adrienne Kennaway. Little, 1988. ISBN 0-316-33724-2 Subj: Animals. Behavior – bullying. Jungle.

My body ill. by Sue Porter. HarperCollins, 1985. ISBN 0-911745-96-3 Subj: Anatomy. Format, unusual – board books. Wordless.

My first book of baby animals ill. by Karen Lee Schmidt. Platt, 1986. ISBN 0-448-10826-7 Subj: Animals. Format, unusual – board books.

My first nursery rhymes ill. by Bruce Whatley. HarperFestival, 1999. ISBN 0-694-01205-X Subj: Nursery rhymes.

My first Raggedy Ann, Raggedy Ann and Andy and the camel with the wrinkled knees adapt. from the story by Johnny Gruelle; ill. by Jan Palmer. Simon & Schuster, 1998. ISBN 0-689-81120-9 Subj: Pirates. Toys. Toys – dolls.

My first Raggedy Ann, Raggedy Ann and Andy and the nice police officer adapt. from the story by Johnny Gruelle; ill. by Jan Palmer. Simon & Schuster, 1999. ISBN 0-689-82174-3 Subj: Careers – magicians. Careers – police officers. Toys – dolls.

My first Raggedy Ann, Raggedy Ann's wishing pebble adapt. from the story by Johnny Gruelle; ill. by Jan Palmer. Simon & Schuster, 1999. ISBN 0-689-82173-5 Subj: Behavior – stealing. Behavior – wishing. Toys – dolls.

My first songs ill. by Jane Manning. HarperFestival, 1998. ISBN 0-694-00983-0 Subj: Nursery rhymes. Songs.

Myers, Amy. *I know a monster* ill. by author. Addison-Wesley, 1979. ISBN 0-201-04990-2 Subj: Character traits – appearance. Games. Monsters.

Myers, Arthur. *Kids do amazing things* ill. by Anthony Rao. Random House, 1980. ISBN 0-394-94271-X Subj: Activities.

Myers, Bernice. *Charlie's birthday present* ill. by author. Scholastic, 1981. ISBN 0-590-31992-2 Subj: Birthdays. Trees.

The flying shoes ill. by author. Lothrop, 1992. ISBN 0-688-10696-X Subj: Activities – flying. Animals. Clothing – shoes. Magic. Royalty – queens.

The gold watch ill. by author. Lothrop, 1991. ISBN 0-688-09889-4 Subj: Careers. Clocks, watches. Family life – fathers.

Herman and the bears and the giants ill. by author. Scholastic, 1978. Subj: Animals – bears. Circus. Sports – bicycling.

It happens to everyone ill. by author. Lothrop, 1990. ISBN 0-688-09082-6 Subj: Behavior – hurrying. Careers – teachers.

The millionth egg ill. by author. Lothrop, 1991. ISBN 0-688-09886-X Subj: Birds – chickens. Eggs.

Sidney Rella and the glass sneaker ill. by author. Macmillan, 1985. ISBN 0-02-767790-7 Subj: Behavior – wishing. Fairies. Sports – football.

Myers, Christopher A. *Sparrows* ill. by author. Hyperion, 2001. ISBN 0-7868-2373-9 Subj: Birds. Birds – sparrows. City. Ethnic groups in the U.S. – African Americans. Homeless.

Turnip soup by Christopher A. Myers and Lynne Born Myers; ill. by Katie Keller. Hyperion, 1994. ISBN 1-56282-446-5 Subj: Emotions – fear. Food. Reptiles – Komodo dragons. Reptiles – lizards.

Wings ill. by author. Scholastic, 2000. ISBN 0-590-03377-8 Subj: Activities – flying. Character traits – being different. Wings.

Myers, Edward. *Forri the baker* ill. by Alexi Natchev. Dial, 1995. ISBN 0-8037-1397-5 Subj: Activities – cooking. Careers – chefs, cooks. Character traits – cleverness. Food. War.

Myers, Lynne Born. *Turnip soup* (Myers, Christopher A.)

Myers, Walter Dean. *The blues of Flats Brown* ill. by Nina Laden. Holiday, 2000. ISBN 0-8234-1480-9 Subj: Animals – dogs. Music.

Brown angels ill. with photos. HarperCollins, 1993. ISBN 0-06-022918-7 Subj: Angels. Ethnic groups in the U.S. – African Americans. Poetry.

The dragon takes a wife ill. by Fiona French. Scholastic, 1995. ISBN 0-590-46693-3 Subj: Dragons. Fairies. Folk and fairy tales. Knights.

Glorious angels: a celebration of children ill. with photos. HarperCollins, 1995. ISBN 0-06-024823-8 Subj: Angels. Ethnic groups in the U.S. – African Americans. Poetry.

The golden serpent ill. by Alice and Martin Provensen. Viking, 1980. ISBN 0-670-34445-1 Subj: Folk and fairy tales. Foreign lands – India. Problem solving. Royalty.

Harlem: a poem ill. by Christopher Myers. Scholastic, 1997. ISBN 0-590-54340-7 Subj: Caldecott award honor books. Careers – authors. Careers – illustrators. City. Ethnic groups in the U.S. – African Americans. Poetry.

How Mr. Monkey saw the whole world ill. by Synthia Saint James. Doubleday, 1996. ISBN 0-385-32057-4 Subj: Activities – flying. Animals – monkeys. Birds – buzzards. Emotions – fear. Food.

The story of the three kingdoms ill. by Ashley Bryan. HarperCollins, 1995. ISBN 0-06-024287-6 Subj: Animals. Nature.

Young Martin's promise ill. by Barbara Higgins Bond; Alex Haley, general editor. Raintree, 1993. ISBN 0-8114-7210-8 Subj: Ethnic groups in the U.S. – African Americans. U.S. history.

Myller, Lois. *No! No!* ill. by Cyndy Szekeres. Simon & Schuster, 1971. ISBN 0-671-65186-2 Subj: Animals – hedgehogs. Behavior. Behavior – misbehavior. Etiquette. Family life. Safety.

Myller, Rolf. *How big is a foot?* ill. by author. Atheneum, 1962. ISBN 0-689-20298-9 Subj: Birthdays. Concepts – measurement. Humor. Royalty – kings.

Rolling round ill. by author. Atheneum, 1963. Subj: Royalty. Wheels.

A very noisy day ill. by author. Atheneum, 1981. ISBN 0-689-30853-1 Subj: Animals – dogs. Crime. Noise, sounds.

Myrick, Jean Lockwood. *Ninety-nine pockets* ill. by Haris Petie. Lantern Pr., 1966. ISBN 0-8313-0079-5 Subj: Birthdays. Clothing. Problem solving.

Nagel, Andreas Fischer. *see* Fischer-Nagel, Andreas

Nagel, Heiderose Fischer. *see* Fischer-Nagel, Heiderose

Nail, James T. *Whose tracks are these? a clue book of familiar forest animals* ill. by Hyla Skudder. Roberts Rinehart, 1994. ISBN 1-879373-89-0 Subj: Animals. Forest, woods. Games.

Nakabayashi, Ei. *The rainy day puddle* ill. by author. Random House, 1989. ISBN 0-394-82095-9 Subj: Animals. Concepts – size. Weather – rain.

Nakano, Hirotaka. *Elephant blue* trans. by Fukuinkan Shoten; ill. by author. Bobbs-Merrill, 1970. Subj: Animals. Animals – elephants. Character traits – helpfulness.

Nakao, Naomi Löw. *The adventures of Chester the chest* (Ayal, Ora)

Ugbu (Ayal, Ora)

Nakatani, Chiyoko. *The day Chiro was lost* ill. by author. Collins-World, 1969. ISBN 0-370-01501-0 Subj: Animals – dogs. Behavior – lost.

Fumio and the dolphins ill. by author. Addison-Wesley, 1970. First published in Japan by Fukuinkan-Shoten, Tokyo, 1969. ISBN 0-370-01519-3 Subj: Animals – dolphins. Character traits – kindness to animals. Foreign lands – Japan. Sea and seashore.

My day on the farm ill. by author. Crowell, 1976. ISBN 0-690-01075-3 Subj: Farms.

The zoo in my garden ill. by author. Crowell, 1973. Translation of Boku no uchi no dōbutsuen. ISBN 0-690-95905-2 Subj: Animals.

Nakawatari, Harutaka. *The sea and I* trans. by Susan Matsui; ill. by author. Farrar, 1992. ISBN 0-374-36428-1 Subj: Boats, ships. Careers – fishermen. Sea and seashore.

Namioka, Lensey. *The laziest boy in the world* ill. by YongSheng Xuan. Holiday, 1998. ISBN 0-8234-1330-6 Subj: Character traits – laziness. Family life. Foreign lands – China.

The loyal cat ill. by Aki Sogabe. Harcourt, 1995. ISBN 0-15-200092-5 Subj: Animals – cats. Character traits – bravery. Emotions – fear. Folk and fairy tales. Foreign lands – Japan. Magic. Poverty. Religion.

Namm, Diane. *Bunny's bedtime* ill. by Kathy Wilburn. Grolier, 1991. ISBN 0-7172-8247-3 Subj: Animals – rabbits. Bedtime. Rhyming text.

Favorite nursery rhymes comp. by Diane Namm; ill. by Delana Bettoli. Little, 1986. ISBN 0-671-60264-0 Subj: Nursery rhymes.

Little bear ill. by Lisa McCue. Childrens Pr., 1990. ISBN 0-516-05356-6 Subj: Animals – bears. Poetry.

Monsters! ill. by Maxie Chambliss. Childrens Pr., 1990. ISBN 0-516-05358-2 Subj: Counting, numbers. Monsters.

Nanao, Jun. *Contemplating your bellybutton* ill. by Tomako Hasegawa. Kane/Miller, 1995. ISBN 0-916291-60-X Subj: Anatomy. Babies. Birth.

Napoli, Guillier. *Adventure at Mont-Saint-Michel* ill. by author. McGraw-Hill, 1966. Subj: Careers – fishermen. Character traits – curiosity. Foreign lands – France. Sea and seashore.

Nappa, Mike. *Do you see the star?* by Mike Nappa and Susan L. Lingo; ill. by Tony Griego. Group Pub., 1996. ISBN 1-55945-617-5 Subj: Format, unusual – toy and movable books. Religion – Nativity. Rhyming text. Stars.

Narahashi, Keiko. *I have a friend* ill. by author. Margaret K. McElderry, 1987. ISBN 0-689-50432-2 Subj: Shadows.

Is that Josie? ill. by author. Margaret K. McElderry, 1994. ISBN 0-689-50606-6 Subj: Activities – playing. Animals. Imagination.

Two girls can! ill. by author. Margaret K. McElderry, 2000. ISBN 0-689-82618-4 Subj: Friendship.

Narayan, Maya. *Leela and the watermelon* (Hirsh, Marilyn)

Nash, Ogden. *The adventures of Isabel* ill. by Walter Lorraine. Little, 1963. Subj: Animals – bears. Character traits – bravery. Emotions – fear. Giants. Poetry. Witches.

The adventures of Isabel ill. by James Marshall. Little, 1991. ISBN 0-316-59874-7 Subj: Animals – bears. Character traits – bravery. Emotions – fear. Giants. Poetry. Witches.

The animal garden ill. by Hilary Knight. Lippincott, 1965. Subj: Humor. Plants. Poetry.

A boy is a boy ill. by Arthur Shilstone. Watts, 1960. Subj: Humor. Poetry.

Custard the dragon ill. by Linell Nash. Little, 1961. ISBN 0-316-59841-0 Subj: Animals. Character traits – bravery. Dragons. Pirates. Poetry.

Custard the dragon and the wicked knight ill. by Lynn Munsinger. Little, 1996. ISBN 0-316-59882-8 Subj: Character traits – bravery. Dragons. Knights. Poetry.

Custard the dragon and the wicked knight ill. by Linell Nash. Little, 1959. Subj: Character traits – bravery. Dragons. Knights. Poetry.

Nast, Elsa Ruth. *see* Watson, Jane Werner

Nathan, Cheryl. *Bugs and beasties ABC* ill. by author. Cool Kids, 1995. ISBN 1-56790-516-1 Subj: ABC books. Animals. Insects.

The long and short of it by Cheryl Nathan and Lisa McCourt; ill. by Cheryl Nathan. BridgeWater, 1998. ISBN 0-8167-4545-5 Subj: Animals. Concepts – size.

Native Americans created by Gallimard Jeunesse, Ute Fuhr and Raoul Sautai; ill. by Ute Fuhr and Raoul Sautai. Scholastic, 1998. ISBN 0-590-38153-9 Subj: Indians of North America.

Nave, Yolanda. *Goosebumps and butterflies* ill. by author. Watts, 1990. ISBN 0-531-08504-X Subj: Emotions. Poetry.

Nayer, Judy. *Bath* ill. by author. McClanahan, 1996. ISBN 1-56293-912-2 Subj: Activities – bathing. Babies. Format, unusual – board books.

The eight nights of Hanukka ill. by Yuri Salzman. Troll, 1998. ISBN 0-8167-4550-1 Subj: Holidays – Hanukkah. Jewish culture. Religion.

Funny bunnies ill. by Steve Henry. McClanahan, 1994. ISBN 1-56293-436-8 Subj: Animals – rabbits. Counting, numbers. Format, unusual – toy and movable books.

Games ill. by author. McClanahan, 1996. ISBN 1-56293-911-4 Subj: Babies. Games.

The happy little engine ill. by Roz Schanzer. McClanahan, 1990. ISBN 1-878624-43-1 Subj: Activities – traveling. Automobiles. Family life.

Jungle life ill. by Grace Goldberg. McClanahan, 1992. ISBN 1-56293-221-7 Subj: Animals. Format, unusual – board books. Jungle.

Little bear's first Christmas ill. by author. McClanahan, 1994. ISBN 1-56293-498-8 Subj: Animals – bears. Holidays – Christmas.

Mice are nice ill. by Paul Harvey. McClanahan, 1994. ISBN 1-56293-434-1 Subj: Animals – mice. Format, unusual – toy and movable books. Language.

Night animals ill. by Grace Goldberg. McClanahan, 1992. ISBN 1-56293-223-3 Subj: Animals. Format, unusual – board books. Night.

Pig in a wig ill. by Paul Harvey. McClanahan, 1994. ISBN 1-56293-433-3 Subj: Animals – pigs.

Format, unusual – toy and movable books. Language.

Reptiles ill. by Grace Goldberg. Margaret K. McElderry, 1992. ISBN 1-56293-220-9 Subj: Format, unusual – board books. Reptiles.

Rhymes ill. by author. McClanahan, 1996. ISBN 1-56293-910-6 Subj: Babies. Nursery rhymes.

Sea creatures ill. by Grace Goldberg. Margaret K. McElderry, 1992. ISBN 1-56293-222-5 Subj: Animals. Fish. Format, unusual – board books. Sea and seashore.

Toys ill. by author. McClanahan, 1996. ISBN 1-56293-913-0 Subj: Babies. Toys.

Tricky puppies ill. by Steve Henry. Margaret K. McElderry, 1994. ISBN 1-56293-435-X Subj: Animals – dogs. Counting, numbers. Format, unusual – toy and movable books.

Naylor, Phyllis Reynolds. *The baby, the bed, and the rose* ill. by Mary Szilagyi. Clarion, 1987. ISBN 0-899-19459-1 Subj: Babies. Emotions – love. Family life – brothers and sisters.

Ducks disappearing ill. by Tony Maddox. Atheneum, 1997. ISBN 0-689-31902-9 Subj: Behavior – lost. Birds – ducks. Counting, numbers. Hotels.

"I can't take you anywhere!" ill. by Jef Kaminsky. Atheneum, 1997. ISBN 0-689-31966-5 Subj: Character traits – clumsiness. Family life – aunts, uncles. Weddings.

Jennifer Jean, the Cross-Eyed Queen ill. by Karen Ritz. Carolrhoda, 1994. ISBN 0-8761-4791-0 Subj: Anatomy – eyes. Handicaps. School.

Keeping a Christmas secret ill. by Lena Shiffman. Macmillan, 1993. ISBN 0-689-71760-1 Subj: Behavior – secrets. Gifts. Holidays – Christmas.

King of the playground ill. by Nola Langner Malone. Atheneum, 1991. ISBN 0-689-31558-9 Subj: Activities – playing. Behavior – bullying. Friendship.

Old Sadie and the Christmas bear ill. by Patricia Montgomery Newton. Atheneum, 1984. ISBN 0-689-31052-8 Subj: Animals – bears. Holidays – Christmas.

The picnic ill. by Ana Escriva Lopez. Atheneum, 2002. ISBN 0-689-82561-7 Subj: Activities – picnicking. Animals. Sea and seashore. Toys – bears.

Sweet strawberries ill. by Rosalind Charney Kaye. Atheneum, 1999. ISBN 0-689-81338-4 Subj: Behavior. Food. Stores.

Neale, J. M. (John Mason). *Good King Wenceslas* ill. by Jamichael Henterly. Dutton, 1988. ISBN 0-525-44420-3 Subj: Folk and fairy tales. Holidays – Christmas. Music. Songs.

Neasi, Barbara J. *Just like me* ill. by Lois Axeman. Childrens Pr., 1984. ISBN 0-516-02047-1 Subj: Multiple births – twins.

Listen to me ill. by Gene Sharp. Childrens Pr., 1986. ISBN 0-516-02072-2 Subj: Family life – grandmothers.

Neidigh, Sherry. *Creatures at my feet* ill. by author; text by Charles E. Davis. Northland, 1993. ISBN 0-8735-8560-7 Subj: Anatomy – feet. Animals. Clothing – shoes. Poetry.

Neitzel, Shirley. *The bag I'm taking to Grandma's* ill. by Nancy Winslow Parker. Greenwillow, 1995. ISBN 0-688-12961-7 Subj: Activities – traveling. Cumulative tales. Rebuses. Rhyming text.

The dress I'll wear to the party ill. by Nancy Winslow Parker. Greenwillow, 1992. ISBN 0-688-09960-2 Subj: Clothing. Cumulative tales. Rebuses. Rhyming text.

From the land of the white birch ill. by Daniel Powers. River Road Pub., 1997. ISBN 0-938682-44-X Subj: Creation. Folk and fairy tales. Indians of North America – Ojibwa.

The house I'll build for the wrens ill. by Nancy Winslow Parker. Greenwillow, 1997. ISBN 0-688-14974-X Subj: Activities – making things. Birds. Cumulative tales. Homes, houses. Rebuses. Rhyming text. Tools.

I'm not feeling well today ill. by Nancy Winslow Parker. Greenwillow, 2001. ISBN 0-688-17381-0 Subj: Cumulative tales. Illness. Rebuses. Rhyming text. School.

I'm taking a trip on my train ill. by Nancy Winslow Parker. Greenwillow, 1999. ISBN 0-688-15834-X Subj: Activities – playing. Cumulative tales. Imagination. Rebuses. Rhyming text. Trains.

The jacket I wear in the snow ill. by Nancy Winslow Parker. Greenwillow, 1989. ISBN 0-688-08030-8 Subj: Clothing. Cumulative tales. Rhyming text.

We're making breakfast for mother ill. by Nancy Winslow Parker. Greenwillow, 1997. ISBN 0-688-14576-0 Subj: Family life – mothers. Food. Rebuses. Rhyming text.

Nelson, Brenda. *Mud for sale* ill. by Richard Eric Brown. Houghton Mifflin, 1984. ISBN 0-395-36175-3 Subj: Activities. Friendship.

Nelson, Esther L. *The funny songbook* ill. by Joyce Behr. Sterling, 1984. Subj: Music. Songs.

Holiday singing and dancing games photos by Shirley Zeiberg. Sterling, 1980. ISBN 0-8069-4630-X Subj: Activities – dancing. Games. Music. Songs.

The silly songbook ill. by Joyce Behr. Sterling, 1982. ISBN 0-8069-4651-2 Subj: Music. Songs.

Nelson, Nan Ferring. *My day with Anka* ill. by Bill Farnsworth. Lothrop, 1996. ISBN 0-688-11059-2 Subj: Activities – babysitting. Activities – cooking. Ethnic groups in the U.S. – Czechoslovakian Americans. Friendship.

Nelson, S. D. *Gift horse: a Lakota story* ill. by author. Abrams, 1999. ISBN 0-8109-4127-9 Subj: Animals – horses, ponies. Behavior – growing up. Indians of North America – Dakota (Sioux).

Nelson, Vaunda Micheaux. *Always Gramma* ill. by Kimanne Uhler. Putnam, 1988. ISBN 0-399-21542-5 Subj: Family life. Family life – grandmothers. Illness – Alzheimer's. Old age.

Nerlove, Miriam. *Christmas* ill. by author. Albert Whitman, 1990. ISBN 0-8075-1148-X Subj: Holidays – Christmas. Rhyming text.

Easter ill. by author. Albert Whitman, 1989. ISBN 0-8075-1871-9 Subj: Family life. Holidays – Easter. Religion. Rhyming text.

Flowers on the wall ill. by author. Margaret K. McElderry, 1996. ISBN 0-689-50614-7 Subj: Activities – painting. Foreign lands – Poland. Holocaust. Jewish culture. War.

Halloween ill. by author. Albert Whitman, 1989. ISBN 0-8075-3131-6 Subj: Holidays – Halloween. Rhyming text.

Hanukkah ill. by author. Albert Whitman, 1989. ISBN 0-8075-3143-X Subj: Holidays – Hanukkah. Jewish culture. Religion. Rhyming text.

I made a mistake ill. by author. Atheneum, 1985. ISBN 0-689-50327-X Subj: Animals. Rhyming text.

I meant to clean my room today ill. by author. Macmillan, 1988. ISBN 0-689-50438-1 Subj: Character traits – cleanliness. Imagination. Rhyming text.

If all the world were paper ill. by author. Albert Whitman, 1990. ISBN 0-8075-3535-4 Subj: Activities – painting. Imagination. Rhyming text.

Just one tooth ill. by author. Macmillan, 1989. ISBN 0-689-50465-9 Subj: Rhyming text. Teeth.

Passover ill. by author. Albert Whitman, 1989. ISBN 0-8075-6360-9 Subj: Jewish culture. Religion. Rhyming text.

Purim ill. by author. Albert Whitman, 1992. ISBN 0-8075-6682-9 Subj: Holidays – Purim. Jewish culture. Religion.

Shabbat ill. by author. Albert Whitman, 1998. ISBN 0-8075-7324-8 Subj: Jewish culture. Religion.

The Ten Commandments for Jewish children ill. by author. Albert Whitman, 1999. ISBN 0-8075-7770-7 Subj: Jewish culture. Religion.

Thanksgiving ill. by author. Albert Whitman, 1990. ISBN 0-8075-7818-5 Subj: Holidays – Thanksgiving. Rhyming text.

Valentine's Day ill. by author. Albert Whitman, 1992. ISBN 0-8075-8454-1 Subj: Holidays – Valentine's Day. Rhyming text.

Nesbit, Edith. *Beauty and the beast* ill. by Julia Christie. Warne, 1988. ISBN 0-7232-3540-6 Subj: Character traits – appearance. Character traits – loyalty. Emotions – love. Folk and fairy tales. Magic.

Cockatoucan ill. by Elory Hughes. Dial, 1988. ISBN 0-8037-0474-7 Subj: Birds. Imagination.

The ice dragon ill. by Carole Gray. Dial, 1988. ISBN 0-8037-0475-5 Subj: World.

The last of the dragons ill. by Peter Firmin. McGraw-Hill, 1980. ISBN 0-07-046285-2 Subj: Character traits – kindness. Dragons. Folk and fairy tales. Royalty.

Melisande ill. by P. J. Lynch. Harcourt, 1989. ISBN 0-15-253164-5 Subj: Fairies. Folk and fairy tales. Hair. Magic. Royalty – princesses.

Ness, Evaline. *Do you have the time, Lydia?* ill. by author. Dutton, 1971. ISBN 0-525-28790-6 Subj: Birds – seagulls. Character traits – completing things. Problem solving. Time.

Exactly alike ill. by author. Scribners, 1964. Subj: Family life.

Fierce: the lion ill. by author. Holiday, 1980. ISBN 0-8234-0412-9 Subj: Animals – lions. Circus.

The girl and the goatherd: or, this and that and thus and so ill. by author. Dutton, 1970. ISBN 0-52530-657-9 Subj: Character traits – appearance. Folk and fairy tales.

Josefina February ill. by author. Scribners, 1963. Subj: Animals – donkeys. Birthdays. Character traits – generosity. Foreign lands – Caribbean Islands.

Pavo and the princess ill. by author. Scribners, 1964. Subj: Birds. Character traits – helpfulness. Emotions. Royalty – princesses.

Sam, Bangs, and moonshine ill. by author. Holt, 1966. ISBN 0-606-01326-1 Subj: Caldecott award books. Imagination. Sports – fishing.

Nestrick, Nova. *Pelle's new suit* (Beskow, Elsa Maartman)

Nethery, Mary. *Hannah and Jack* ill. by Mary Morgan. Atheneum, 1996. ISBN 0-689-80533-0 Subj: Activities – vacationing. Activities – working. Animals – cats. Family life – grandmothers.

Mary Veronica's egg ill. by Paul Yalowitz. Orchard, 1999. ISBN 0-531-33134-2 Subj: Birds – ducks. Eggs.

Orange cat goes to market ill. by author. Candlewick, 1997. ISBN 0-7636-0028-8 Subj: Animals – cats. Shopping.

Neugebauer, Charise. *The real winner* ill. by Barbara Nascimbeni. North-South, 2000. ISBN 0-7358-1253-5 Subj: Animals – hippopotamuses. Animals – raccoons. Contests.

Santa's gift ill. by Barbara Nascimbeni. North-South, 1999. ISBN 0-7358-1146-6 Subj: Animals. Gifts. Holidays – Christmas. Santa Claus.

Neugroschel, Joachim. *The boy and the tree* (Driz, Ovsei)

Neuhaus, David. *His finest hour* ill. by author. Viking, 1984. ISBN 0-670-37260-9 Subj: Friendship. Sports – racing.

Neumeier, Marty. *Action alphabet* by Marty Neumeier and Byron Glaser; ill. by authors. Greenwillow, 1985. ISBN 0-688-05704-7 Subj: ABC books. Activities.

Neumeyer, Peter F. *Mischa and his brothers* (Baumann, Hans)

Sleep well, little bear (Buchholz, Quint)

Neuschwander, Cindy. *Amanda Bean's amazing dream* ill. by Liza Woodruff; math activities by Marilyn Burns. Scholastic, 1998. ISBN 0-590-30012-1 Subj: Counting, numbers. Dreams. School.

Neville, Emily Cheney. *The bridge* ill. by Ronald Himler. HarperCollins, 1988. ISBN 0-06-024386-4 Subj: Bridges. Family life. Machines.

Neville, Mary. *The Christmas tree ride* ill. by Megan Lloyd. Holiday, 1992. ISBN 0-8234-0956-2 Subj: Family life. Friendship. Holidays – Christmas. Trees.

Newberry, Clare Turlay. *April's kittens* ill. by author. HarperCollins, 1940. ISBN 0-06-024401-1 Subj: Animals – cats. Caldecott award honor books. Pets.

Barkis ill. by author. HarperCollins, 1938. Subj: Animals – dogs. Caldecott award honor books. Pets.

Cousin Toby ill. by author. HarperCollins, 1939. Subj: Babies.

Herbert the lion ill. by author. HarperCollins, 1956. First pub. in 1931. Subj: Animals – lions. Pets.

The kittens' ABC verse and pictures by Clare Turlay Newberry. New and rev. ed.; completely redrawn. HarperCollins, 1965. Subj: ABC books. Animals – cats. Rhyming text.

Marshmallow ill. by author. HarperCollins, 1942. Subj: Animals – cats. Animals – rabbits. Caldecott award honor books. Friendship.

Pandora ill. by author. HarperCollins, 1944. Subj: Animals – cats.

Percy, Polly and Pete ill. by author. HarperCollins, 1952. Subj: Animals – cats. Behavior – growing up. Character traits – kindness to animals. Pets.

Smudge ill. by author. HarperCollins, 1948. Subj: Animals – cats.

T-Bone, the baby-sitter story and pictures by author. HarperCollins, 1950. Subj: Activities – babysitting. Animals – cats. Babies. Caldecott award honor books.

Widget ill. by author. HarperCollins, 1958. Subj: Animals – cats.

Newbolt, Henry John, Sir. *Rilloby-rill* ill. by Susanna Gretz. O'Hara, 1973. ISBN 0-8795-5707-9 Subj: Fairies. Insects – grasshoppers. Music. Songs.

Newcome, Zita. *Animal fun* ill. by author. Candlewick, 1999. ISBN 0-7636-0803-3 Subj: Behavior – imitation. Health and fitness – exercise. Rhyming text.

Rosie goes exploring ill. by author. Trafalgar Square, 1992. ISBN 1-85681-170-0 Subj: Animals. Imagination. Plants.

Rosie goes shopping ill. by author. Trafalgar Square, 1992. ISBN 1-85681-160-3 Subj: Family life – mothers. Foreign lands – England. Shopping.

Toddlerobics ill. by author. Candlewick, 1996. ISBN 1-56402-809-7 Subj: Activities – playing. Health and fitness – exercise. Rhyming text. Sports – gymnastics.

Newell, Crosby. *see* Bonsall, Crosby Newell

Newell, Peter. *Topsys and turvys* ill. by author. Dover, 1965. Subj: Format, unusual. Humor.

Newfield, Marcia. *Iggy* ill. by Jacqueline Chwast. Houghton Mifflin, 1972. ISBN 0-395-13898-1 Subj: Pets. Reptiles – iguanas.

Newland, Mary Reed. *Good King Wenceslas: a legend in music and pictures* ill. by author. Seabury Pr., 1980. ISBN 0-8164-0474-7 Subj: Holidays – Christmas. Music. Songs.

Newman, Lesléa. *Belinda's bouquet* ill. by Michael Willhoite. Alyson Wonderland, 1991. ISBN 1-55583-154-0 Subj: Character traits – individuality. Flowers. Health and fitness.

Cats, cats, cats ill. by Erika Oller. Simon & Schuster, 2001. ISBN 0-689-83077-7 Subj: Animals – cats. Night. Rhyming text.

Heather has two mommies ill. by Diana Souza. Alyson Wonderland, 2000. ISBN 1-55583-570-8 Subj: Family life – daughters. Family life – mothers. Homosexuality.

Matzo ball moon ill. by Elaine Greenstein. Clarion, 1998. ISBN 0-395-71530-X Subj: Family life – grandmothers. Food. Holidays – Passover. Jewish culture. Religion.

Remember that ill. by Karen Ritz. Clarion, 1996. ISBN 0-395-66589-2 Subj: Family life – grandmothers. Memories, memory. Old age.

Saturday is Pattyday ill. by Annette Hegel. New Victoria, 1993. ISBN 0-934678-52-9 Subj: Divorce. Family life – mothers. Family life – sons. Homosexuality.

Too far away to touch ill. by Catherine Stock. Clarion, 1995. ISBN 0-395-68968-6 Subj: Death. Emotions – grief. Family life – aunts, uncles. Illness – AIDS. Stars.

Newman, Nanette. *There's a bear in the bath!* ill. by Michael Foreman. Harcourt, 1994. ISBN 0-15-285512-2 Subj: Animals – bears.

Newman, Robert. *All aboard ABC* (Magee, Doug)

Let's fly from A to Z (Magee, Doug)

Newman, Shirlee. *Tell me, grandma; tell me, grandpa* ill. by Joan E. Drescher. Houghton Mifflin, 1979. ISBN 0-395-27815-5 Subj: Family life – grandparents.

Newsham, Ian. *The monster hunt* (Newsham, Wendy)

Newsham, Wendy. *The monster hunt* by Wendy and Ian Newsham; ill. by authors. Hamish Hamilton, 1983. ISBN 0-241-10859-4 Subj: Monsters.

Newsome, Effie Lee. *Wonders: the best children's poems of Effie Lee Newsome* ill. by Lois Mailou Jones; comp. by Rudine Sims Bishop. Wordsong, 1999. ISBN 1-56397-788-5 Subj: Poetry.

Newsome, Jill. *Shadow* ill. by Claudio Muñoz. DK, 1999. ISBN 0-7894-2631-5 Subj: Animals – rabbits. Friendship. Moving.

Newth, Philip. *Roly goes exploring: a book for blind and sighted children, in Braille and standard type, with pictures to feel as well as see.* Putnam, 1981. ISBN 0-399-20815-1 Subj: Concepts – shape. Format, unusual. Handicaps – blindness. Senses – seeing.

Newton, James R. *A forest is reborn* ill. by Susan Bonners. Crowell, 1982. ISBN 0-690-04232-9 Subj: Fire. Forest, woods. Science.

Forest log ill. by Irene Brady. Crowell, 1980. ISBN 0-690-04008-3 Subj: Ecology. Forest, woods. Science. Trees.

Newton, Jill. *Cat-fish* ill. by author. Lothrop, 1992. ISBN 0-688-11424-5 Subj: Animals – cats. Behavior – dissatisfaction. Fish. Sea and seashore.

Don't sit there! ill. by author. Lothrop, 1994. ISBN 0-688-13309-6 Subj: Family life. Furniture – couches, sofas.

Polar bear scare ill. by author. Lothrop, 1992. ISBN 0-688-11233-1 Subj: Animals – polar bears. Animals – rabbits. Foreign lands – Arctic.

Newton, Laura P. *Me and my aunts* ill. by Robin Oz. Albert Whitman, 1986. ISBN 0-8075-5029-9 Subj: Emotions – love. Family life – aunts, uncles.

William the vehicle king ill. by Jacqueline Rogers. Bradbury, 1987. ISBN 0-02-768230-7 Subj: Automobiles. Imagination. Toys. Trucks.

Newton, Pam. *see* Newton, Patricia Montgomery

Newton, Patricia Montgomery. *The five sparrows* ill. by author. Atheneum, 1982. ISBN 0-689-30936-8 Subj: Character traits – kindness. Folk and fairy tales. Foreign lands – Japan.

The frog who drank the waters of the world ill. by author. Atheneum, 1983. ISBN 0-689-30993-7 Subj: Animals. Birds – bluejays. Frogs and toads. Reptiles – snakes.

The stonecutter ill. by reteller. Putnam, 1990. ISBN 0-399-22187-5 Subj: Folk and fairy tales. Foreign lands – India.

Vacation surprise ill. by author. Atheneum, 1986. ISBN 0-689-31264-4 Subj: Activities – vacationing. Animals – pigs.

Newton-John, Olivia. *A pig tale* by Olivia Newton-John and Brian Seth Hurst; ill. by Sal Murdocca. Simon & Schuster, 1993. ISBN 0-671-78778-0 Subj: Animals – pigs. Ecology. Family life – fathers. Rhyming text.

Nez, Redwing T. *Forbidden talent* ill. by Kathryn Wilder. Northland, 1995. ISBN 0-87358-605-0 Subj: Activities – painting. Art. Family life – grandfathers. Indians of North America – Navajo.

Nic Leodhas, Sorche. *see* Alger, Leclaire Gowans

Nichol, B. P. *Once: a lullaby* ill. by Anita Lobel. Greenwillow, 1986. ISBN 0-688-04285-6 Subj: Animals. Bedtime. Lullabies. Music. Night. Sleep.

Nichol, Barbara. *Biscuits in the cupboard* ill. by Philippe Béha. Stoddard Kids, 1997. ISBN 0-7737-3025-7 Subj: Animals – dogs. Foreign lands – Canada. Poetry.

Nicholls, Judith. *Someone I like: poems about people* comp. by Judith Nicholls; ill. by Giovanni Manna. Barefoot, 2000. ISBN 1-84148-004-5 Subj: Emotions. Family life. Friendship. Poetry.

Nichols, Cathy. *Tuxedo Sam: a penguin of a different color* ill. by Haruo Takahashi. Random House, 1983. ISBN 0-394-86107-8 Subj: Birds – penguins. City.

Nichols, Grace. *Asana and the animals: a book of pet poems* ill. by Sarah Adams. Candlewick, 1997. ISBN 0-7636-0145-4 Subj: Animals. Nursery rhymes. Poetry. Rhyming text.

No hickory no dickory no dock: Caribbean nursery rhymes (Agard, John)

Nichols, Paul. *Big Paul's school bus* ill. by William Marshall. Prentice-Hall, 1981. ISBN 0-13-076091-9 Subj: Buses. Careers. School.

Nicholson, Nicholas B. A. *Little girl in a red dress with cat and dog* ill. by Cynthia von Buhler. Viking, 1998. ISBN 0-670-87183-4 Subj: Animals. Art. Careers – artists. Family life. Farms. U.S. history.

Mona Lisa: the secret of the smile (Galli, Letizia)

Nicholson, William, Sir. *Clever Bill* ill. by author. Doubleday, 1961. Subj: Toys – soldiers.

Nickens, Bessie. *Walking the log* ill. by author. Rizzoli, 1994. ISBN 0-8478-1794-6 Subj: Careers – artists. Ethnic groups in the U.S. – African Americans. Poverty. U.S. history.

Nickl, Peter. *Ra ta ta tam: the strange story of a little engine* by Peter Nickl and Binette Schroeder; ill.

by authors. Merrimack, 1984. ISBN 0-224-00974-5 Subj: Character traits – meanness. Format, unusual – board books. Trains.

Nickle, John. *The ant bully* ill. by author. Scholastic, 1999. ISBN 0-590-39591-2 Subj: Behavior – bullying. Concepts – size. Insects – ants.

Nicolai, Margaret. *Kitaq goes ice fishing* ill. by David Rubin. Alaska Northwest, 1998. ISBN 0-88240-504-7 Subj: Alaska. Eskimos. Family life – grandfathers. Sports – fishing.

Nicolas. *see* Mordvinoff, Nicolas

Nicoll, Helen. *Meg and Mog* by Helen Nicoll and Jan Pienkowski; ill. by Jan Pienkowski. Atheneum, 1972. ISBN 0-434-95420-9 Subj: Animals – cats. Holidays – Halloween. Magic. Witches.

Meg at sea by Helen Nicoll and Jan Pienkowski; ill. by Jan Pienkowski. Harvey House, 1974. ISBN 0-8178-5281-6 Subj: Animals – cats. Birds – owls. Magic. Sea and seashore. Witches.

Meg on the moon by Helen Nicoll and Jan Pienkowski; ill. by Jan Pienkowski. Harvey House, 1974. ISBN 0-8178-5271-9 Subj: Animals – cats. Magic. Moon. Witches.

Meg's eggs by Helen Nicoll and Jan Pienkowski ill. by Jan Pienkowski. Atheneum, 1972. ISBN 0-434-95421-7 Subj: Animals – cats. Birds – owls. Dinosaurs. Eggs. Magic. Witches.

Mog's box ill. by Jan Pienkowski. David & Charles, 1987. ISBN 0-434-95658-9 Subj: Animals – cats. Magic. Witches.

Nielsen, Laura F. *Jeremy's muffler* ill. by Christine M. Schneider. Bradbury, 1994. ISBN 0-02-768135-1 Subj: Clothing. Family life – aunts, uncles.

Night time written and ill. by the first grade students of Nancy Dutil at Richmond Elementary School, Richmond, Vermont. Willowisp Pr., 1995. Kids are authors award. ISBN 0-87406-800-2 Subj: Children as authors. Children as illustrators. Night.

Nightingale, Sandy. *Cat's knees and bee's whiskers* ill. by author. Harcourt, 1993. ISBN 0-15-215364-0 Subj: Animals – cats. Witches.

Cider apples ill. by author. Harcourt, 1996. ISBN 0-15-201244-3 Subj: Fairies. Family life – grandmothers. Magic. Trees.

A giraffe on the moon ill. by author. Harcourt, 1992. ISBN 0-15-230950-0 Subj: Dreams. Rhyming text.

I'm a little monster ill. by author. Harcourt, 1995. ISBN 0-15-200309-6 Subj: Birthdays. Imagination. Monsters.

Pink pigs aplenty ill. by author. Harcourt, 1992. ISBN 0-15-261882-1 Subj: Animals – pigs. Circus. Counting, numbers.

The witch's spell ill. by author. Andersen, 1998. ISBN 0-86264-739-8 Subj: Behavior – dissatisfaction. Magic. Seasons. Witches.

Nikly, Michelle. *The emperor's plum tree* trans. from French by Elizabeth Shub; ill. by author. Greenwillow, 1982. ISBN 0-688-01244-2 Subj: Friendship. Royalty – emperors. Trees.

The perfume of memory ill. by Jean Claverie. Levine, 1998. ISBN 0-439-08206-4 Subj: Behavior – forgetfulness. Senses – smelling.

The princess on the nut: or, the curious courtship of the son of the princess on the pea trans. by Lucy Meredith; ill. by Jean Claverie. Faber, 1981. ISBN 0-571-11846-1 Subj: Folk and fairy tales. Royalty – princesses.

Nikola-Lisa, W. *America: my land, your land, our land* ill. by 14 outstanding American artists. Lee & Low, 1997. ISBN 1-880000-37-7 Subj: Ethnic groups in the U.S. Poetry. U.S. history.

Bein' with you this way ill. by Michael Bryant. Lee & Low, 1994. ISBN 1-880000-05-9 Subj: Activities – playing. Ethnic groups in the U.S. Ethnic groups in the U.S. – African Americans. Friendship. Poetry.

Can you top that? ill. by Hector Viveros Lee. Lee & Low, 2000. ISBN 1-880000-99-7 Subj: Activities – drawing. Animals. Counting, numbers.

The dancin' fox ill. by Marcia Sewall. Atheneum, 2000. ISBN 0-689-82621-4 Subj: Animals – foxes. Behavior – trickery. Birds – turkeys. Folk and fairy tales.

Hallelujah! a Christmas celebration ill. by Synthia Saint James. Atheneum, 1999. ISBN 0-689-81673-1 Subj: Ethnic groups in the U.S. – African Americans. Holidays – Christmas. Religion – Nativity.

Night is coming ill. by Jamichael Henterly. Dutton, 1991. ISBN 0-525-44687-7 Subj: Country. Family life – grandfathers. Night. Noise, sounds.

No babies asleep ill. by Peter Palagonia. Atheneum, 1994. ISBN 0-689-31841-3 Subj: Animals. Babies. Counting, numbers. Rhyming text.

One hole in the road ill. by Dan Yaccarino. Holt, 1996. ISBN 0-8050-4285-7 Subj: Counting, numbers. Machines. Roads.

One, two, three Thanksgiving! ill. by Robin Kramer. Albert Whitman, 1991. ISBN 0-8075-6109-6 Subj: Counting, numbers. Family life. Holidays – Thanksgiving.

Shake dem Halloween bones ill. by Mike Reed. Houghton Mifflin, 1997. ISBN 0-395-73095-3 Subj: Holidays – Halloween. Parties. Rhyming text.

Storm ill. by Michael Hays. Atheneum, 1993. ISBN 0-689-31704-2 Subj: Country. Weather – storms. Weather – thunder.

Tangletalk ill. by Jessica Clerk. Dutton, 1997. ISBN 0-525-45399-7 Subj: Humor. Rhyming text.

Till year's good end: a calendar of medieval labors ill. by Christopher Manson. Atheneum, 1997. ISBN 0-689-80020-7 Subj: Country. Days of the week, months of the year. Farms. Foreign lands – England.

Wheels go round ill. by Jane Conteh-Morgan. Doubleday, 1994. ISBN 0-385-32069-8 Subj: Animals – bulls, cows. Fairs. Rhyming text. Transportation. Wheels.

Niland, Deborah. *ABC of monsters* ill. by author. McGraw-Hill, 1978. ISBN 0-07-046560-6 Subj: ABC books. Monsters.

Niland, Kilmeny. *A bellbird in a flame tree* ill. by author. Morrow, 1991. ISBN 0-688-10798-2 Subj: Foreign lands – Australia. Holidays – Christmas. Music. Songs.

Nilsén, Anna. *Drive your car* ill. by Tony Wells. Candlewick, 1996. ISBN 1-56402-921-2 Subj: Automobiles. Format, unusual.

Drive your tractor ill. by Tony Wells. Candlewick, 1996. ISBN 1-56402-920-4 Subj: Farms. Format, unusual. Tractors.

Let's all hang and dangle ill. by Ann Axworthy. Zero to Ten, 1998. ISBN 1-84089-002-9 Subj: Animals. Format, unusual.

Where are Percy's friends? ill. by Dom Mansell. Candlewick, 1996. ISBN 0-76360-017-2 Subj: Animals. Animals – dogs. Format, unusual – toy and movable books. Friendship.

Where is Percy's dinner? ill. by Dom Mansell. Candlewick, 1996. ISBN 0-76360-019-9 Subj: Animals. Animals – dogs. Food. Format, unusual – toy and movable books.

Nilsson, Ulf. *Little sister rabbit* ill. by Eva Eriksson. Little, 1985. ISBN 0-87113-009-2 Subj: Activities – babysitting. Animals – rabbits. Family life.

Nims, Bonnie Larkin. *Just beyond reach and other riddle poems* photos by George Ancona. Scholastic, 1992. ISBN 0-590-44077-2 Subj: Poetry. Riddles.

Where is the bear? ill. by John Wallner. Albert Whitman, 1988. ISBN 0-8075-8933-0 Subj: Behavior – lost. Rhyming text. Toys – bears.

Where is the bear at school? ill. by Madelaine Gill. Albert Whitman, 1989. ISBN 0-8075-8935-7 Subj: Games. Picture puzzles. Rhyming text. School. Toys – bears.

Where is the bear in the city? ill. by Madelaine Gill. Albert Whitman, 1992. ISBN 0-8075-8937-3 Subj: Animals – bears. Behavior – hiding. City. Rhyming text.

Nishikawa, Osamu. *Alexander and the blue ghost* ill. by author. Morrow, 1986. ISBN 0-688-06267-9 Subj: Character traits – bravery. Ghosts. Royalty.

Nister, Ernest. *Little tales from long ago: Cat's cradle, The tale of a dog, Three friends, Three little maids* ill.

by author. Delacorte, 1979. ISBN 0-440-04968-6 Subj: Folk and fairy tales.

Nivola, Claire A. *Elisabeth* ill. by author. Farrar, 1997. ISBN 0-374-32085-3 Subj: Ethnic groups in the U.S. – German Americans. Family life. Immigrants. Jewish culture. Toys – dolls. War.

Nixon, Joan Lowery. *Beats me, Claude* ill. by Tracey Campbell Pearson. Viking, 1986. ISBN 0-670-80781-8 Subj: Activities – cooking. Humor.

Bigfoot makes a movie ill. by Syd Hoff. Putnam, 1979. ISBN 0-399-20684-1 Subj: Behavior – misunderstanding. Folk and fairy tales. Monsters.

Fat chance, Claude ill. by Tracey Campbell Pearson. Viking, 1987. ISBN 0-670-81459-8 Subj: Careers – miners.

If you say so, Claude ill. by Lorinda Bryan Cauley. Warne, 1980. ISBN 0-7232-6183-0 Subj: Activities – traveling. Behavior – seeking better things. U.S. history – frontier and pioneer life.

If you were a writer ill. by Bruce Degen. Four Winds, 1988. ISBN 0-02-768210-2 Subj: Activities – writing.

The Thanksgiving mystery ill. by Jim Cummins. Albert Whitman, 1980. ISBN 0-8075-7820-7 Subj: Ghosts. Holidays – Thanksgiving. Mystery stories.

That's the spirit, Claude ill. by Tracey Campbell Pearson. Viking, 1992. ISBN 0-670-83434-3 Subj: Adoption. Holidays – Christmas. Humor. Santa Claus. U.S. history – frontier and pioneer life.

The Valentine mystery ill. by Jim Cummins. Albert Whitman, 1979. ISBN 0-8075-8450-9 Subj: Holidays – Valentine's Day. Mystery stories.

When I am eight ill. by Dick Gackenbach. Dial, 1994. ISBN 0-8037-1499-8 Subj: Birthdays. Family life – brothers. Imagination. Sibling rivalry.

Will you give me a dream? ill. by Bruce Degen. Four Winds, 1994. ISBN 0-02-768211-0 Subj: Bedtime. Dreams. Family life – mothers.

You bet your britches, Claude ill. by Tracey Campbell Pearson. Viking, 1989. ISBN 0-670-82310-4 Subj: Adoption. Family life. Humor. U.S. history – frontier and pioneer life.

Njeng, Pierre Yves. *Vacation in the village: a story from West Africa* ill. by author. Boyds Mills, 1999. ISBN 1-56397-768-0 Subj: Activities – vacationing. Foreign lands – Cameroon. Friendship. Seasons – summer.

Nobens, C. A. *Montgomery's time zone* ill. by author. Carolrhoda, 1990. ISBN 0-87614-398-2 Subj: Dreams. Time.

Nobisso, Josephine. *For the sake of a cake* by Josephine Nobisso and Anton C. Krajnc. Rizzoli, 1993. ISBN 0-8478-1685-0 Subj: Animals – koalas. Character traits – laziness. Reptiles – alligators, crocodiles. Rhyming text.

Grandma's scrapbook ill. by Maureen Hyde. Green Tiger Pr., 1991. ISBN 0-671-74976-5 Subj: Family life – grandmothers. Memories, memory.

Grandpa loved ill. by Maureen Hyde. 2nd ed. Gingerbread House, 2000. ISBN 0-940112-01-9 Subj: Death. Emotions – grief. Emotions – love. Family life – grandfathers.

Hot-cha-cha! ill. by Joan Holub. Winslow, 1998. ISBN 1-890817-00-7 Subj: Activities – playing. Rhyming text.

Shh! the whale is smiling ill. by Maureen Hyde. Green Tiger Pr., 1992. ISBN 0-671-74908-0 Subj: Animals – whales. Bedtime. Night. Sea and seashore.

The yawn ill. by Glo Coalson. Orchard, 2001. ISBN 0-531-33319-1 Subj: Sleep.

Noble, June. *Two homes for Lynn* ill. by Yuri Salzman. Holt, 1979. ISBN 0-03-046186-3 Subj: Behavior – sharing. Divorce. Family life. Imagination – imaginary friends.

Noble, Kate. *The blue elephant* ill. by Rachel Bass. Silver Seahorse, 1994. ISBN 0-9631798-3-7 Subj: Animals – elephants. Zoos.

Bubble gum ill. by Rachel Bass. Silver Seahorse, 1995. ISBN 0-9631798-0-2 Subj: Animals. Animals – baboons. Foreign lands – Africa.

The dragon of Navy Pier ill. by Rachel Bass. Silver Seahorse, 1996. ISBN 0-9631798-5-3 Subj: Dragons. Merry-go-rounds.

Oh look, it's a nosserus ill. by Rachel Bass. Silver Seahorse, 1993. ISBN 0-96317-982-9 Subj: Animals. Animals – rhinoceros. Foreign lands – Africa.

Noble, Trinka Hakes. *Apple tree Christmas* ill. by author. Dial, 1984. ISBN 0-8037-0103-9 Subj: Farms. Holidays – Christmas. Trees. Weather – storms.

The day Jimmy's boa ate the wash ill. by Steven Kellogg. Dial, 1980. ISBN 0-8037-1724-5 Subj: Activities. Humor. Reptiles – snakes. School.

Hansy's mermaid ill. by author. Dial, 1983. ISBN 0-8037-3606-1 Subj: Character traits – kindness. Mythical creatures – mermaids, mermen.

Jimmy's boa and the big splash birthday bash ill. by Steven Kellogg. Dial, 1989. ISBN 0-8037-0540-9 Subj: Birthdays. Humor. Pets. Reptiles – snakes.

Jimmy's boa bounces back ill. by Steven Kellogg. Dial, 1984. ISBN 0-8037-0049-0 Subj: Humor. Reptiles – snakes.

The king's tea ill. by author. Dial, 1979. ISBN 0-8037-4520-3 Subj: Cumulative tales. Royalty – kings.

Meanwhile back at the ranch ill. by Tony Ross. Dial, 1987. ISBN 0-8037-0354-6 Subj: Behavior – boredom. Humor.

Nodar, Carmen Santiago. *Abuelita's paradise* ill. by Diane Paterson. Albert Whitman, 1992. ISBN 0-

8075-0129-8 Subj: Death. Emotions – grief. Family life – grandmothers. Farms. Foreign lands – Puerto Rico.

Nodset, Joan L. *see* Lexau, Joan M.

Noguere, Suzanne. *Little raccoon* ill. by Tony Chen. Holt, 1981. ISBN 0-03-054826-8 Subj: Animals – raccoons.

Nolan, Dennis. *Androcles and the lion* (Æsop)

The castle builder ill. by author. Macmillan, 1987. ISBN 0-02-768240-4 Subj: Dragons. Imagination. Knights. Sand. Sea and seashore.

Dinosaur dream ill. by author. Aladdin, 1994. ISBN 0-689-71832-2 Subj: Dinosaurs. Dreams.

Witch Bazooza ill. by author. Prentice-Hall, 1979. ISBN 0-13-961573-3 Subj: Holidays – Halloween. Homes, houses. Witches.

Wizard McBean and his flying machine ill. by author. Prentice-Hall, 1977. ISBN 0-139-61607-1 Subj: Airplanes, airports. Cumulative tales. Magic. Rhyming text. Wizards.

Nolan, Lucy A. *The Lizard Man of Crabtree County* ill. by Jill Kastner. Cavendish, 1999. ISBN 0-7614-5049-1 Subj: Communities, neighborhoods. Country. Humor. Monsters.

Nolan, Madeena Spray. *My daddy don't go to work* ill. by Jim LaMarche. Carolrhoda, 1978. ISBN 0-8761-4093-2 Subj: Ethnic groups in the U.S. – African Americans. Family life. Family life – fathers. Poverty.

Nolen, Jerdine. *Big Jabe* ill. by Kadir Nelson. Lothrop, 2000. ISBN 0-688-13663-X Subj: Ethnic groups in the U.S. – African Americans. Slavery. Tall tales.

In my momma's kitchen ill. by Colin Bootman. Lothrop, 1999. ISBN 0-688-12761-4 Subj: Activities – cooking. Family life. Homes, houses.

Raising dragons ill. by Elise Primavera. Silver Whistle, 1998. ISBN 0-15-201288-5 Subj: Careers. Dragons. Eggs. Farms. Friendship.

Noll, Sally. *I have a loose tooth* ill. by author. Greenwillow, 1992. ISBN 0-688-11192-0 Subj: Behavior – growing up. Family life – grandmothers. Teeth.

Jiggle wiggle prance ill. by author. Greenwillow, 1987. ISBN 0-688-06761-1 Subj: Activities. Animals.

Lucky morning ill. by author. Greenwillow, 1994. ISBN 0-688-12475-5 Subj: Activities – vacationing. Animals. Family life – grandfathers. Sports – fishing.

Off and counting ill. by author. Greenwillow, 1984. ISBN 0-688-02796-2 Subj: Counting, numbers. Frogs and toads. Rhyming text. Toys.

Surprise! ill. by author. Greenwillow, 1997. ISBN 0-688-15171-X Subj: Animals – cats. Birthdays. Counting, numbers. Holidays.

That bothered Kate ill. by author. Greenwillow, 1991. ISBN 0-688-10096-1 Subj: Behavior – growing up. Behavior – imitation. Family life – sisters. Sibling rivalry.

Watch where you go ill. by author. Greenwillow, 1990. ISBN 0-688-08499-0 Subj: Animals – mice. Optical illusions.

Nomura, Noriko S. *I am Shinto* photos by author. Rosen, 1996. ISBN 0-8239-2380-0 Subj: Religion.

Nomura, Takaaki. *Grandpa's town* ill. by author; trans. by Amanda Mayer Stinchecum. Kane/Miller, 1991. ISBN 0-916291-57-X Subj: Activities – bathing. Emotions – loneliness. Family life – grandfathers. Foreign lands – Japan. Foreign languages. Friendship.

Nones, Eric Jon. *Angela's wings* ill. by author. Farrar, 1995. ISBN 0-374-30331-2 Subj: Activities – flying. Character traits – being different.

Caleb's friend ill. by author. Farrar, 1993. ISBN 0-374-31017-3 Subj: Friendship. Mythical creatures – mermaids, mermen.

Canary prince ill. by author. Farrar, 1991. ISBN 0-374-31029-7 Subj: Birds – canaries. Folk and fairy tales. Foreign lands – Italy. Magic. Royalty – princes. Royalty – princesses.

Wendell ill. by author. Farrar, 1989. ISBN 0-374-38266-2 Subj: Animals – cats. Behavior – misbehavior. Family life. Mythical creatures.

Norac, Carl. *Hello, sweetie pie* ill. by Claude K. Dubois. Random House, 2000. ISBN 0-385-32733-1 Subj: Animals – hamsters. Names. School.

I love you so much ill. by Claude K. Dubois. Doubleday, 1997. ISBN 0-385-32512-6 Subj: Animals – hamsters. Emotions – love. Family life.

Norby, Lisa. *The Herself the elf storybook.* Scholastic, 1983. ISBN 0-590-32911-1 Subj: Magic. Mythical creatures – elves.

Nordlicht, Lillian. *I love to laugh* ill. by Allen Davis. Raintree, 1980. ISBN 0-8172-1364-3 Subj: Behavior – growing up. Character traits – being different.

Nordqvist, Sven. *Festus and Mercury go camping* ill. by author. Carolrhoda, 1993. ISBN 0-87614-802-X Subj: Animals – cats. Birds – chickens. Camps, camping. Humor.

Festus and Mercury: ruckus in the garden ill. by author. Carolrhoda, 1991. ISBN 0-87614-678-7 Subj: Animals – cats. Gardens, gardening. Seasons – spring.

Festus and Mercury wishing to go fishing ill. by author. Carolrhoda, 1991. ISBN 0-87614-658-2 Subj: Animals – cats. Humor. Old age. Sports – fishing.

The fox hunt ill. by author. Morrow, 1988. ISBN 0-688-06882-0 Subj: Animals – cats. Animals – foxes. Behavior – trickery. Careers – farmers.

Pancake pie ill. by author. Morrow, 1985. ISBN 0-688-04142-6 Subj: Animals – cats. Food.

Porker finds a chair ill. by author. Carolrhoda, 1989. ISBN 0-87614-367-2 Subj: Animals – bears. Behavior – misunderstanding. Furniture – chairs.

Porker's taxi ill. by author. Carolrhoda, 1992. ISBN 0-87614-744-9 Subj: Animals – bears. Taxis.

Willie in the big world: adventures with numbers ill. by author. Morrow, 1986. ISBN 0-688-06143-5 Subj: Activities – traveling. Counting, numbers.

Norman, Charles. *The hornbean tree and other poems* ill. by Ted Rand. Holt, 1988. ISBN 0-8050-0417-3 Subj: Animals. Birds. Nature. Poetry.

Norman, Howard A. *The owl-scatterer* ill. by Michael McCurdy. Atlantic Monthly, 1986. ISBN 0-87113-058-0 Subj: Behavior – disbelief. Birds – owls. Foreign lands – Canada.

Who-Paddled-Backward-With-Trout ill. by Ed Young. Little, 1987. ISBN 0-316-61182-4 Subj: Folk and fairy tales. Foreign lands – Canada. Indians of North America – Cree. Names.

Norman, Philip Ross. *The carrot war* ill. by author. Little, 1992. ISBN 0-316-61200-6 Subj: Animals – rabbits. Food. War.

Dancing dogs ill. by author. Little, 1995. ISBN 0-316-61208-1 Subj: Activities – dancing. Animals – cats. Animals – dogs.

A mammoth imagination ill. by author. Little, 1992. ISBN 0-316-61201-4 Subj: Animals. Imagination. Weather – snow.

Norris, Lori P. (Peters). *D is for divorce* ill. by author. Health Communications, 1991. ISBN 1-55874-140-2 Subj: Divorce.

North, George, Captain. *see* Stevenson, Robert Louis

Northam, Leland. *Hansel and Gretel* (Grimm, Jacob)

Sleeping Beauty (Grimm, Jacob)

The ugly duckling (Andersen, H. C. [Hans Christian])

Northrup, Mili. *The watch cat* ill. by Adrina Zanazanian; designed by Kent Salisbury. Bobbs-Merrill, 1968. Subj: Animals – cats. Foreign lands – Thailand.

Northway, Jennifer. *Get lost, Laura!* ill. by author. Artists & Writers Guild, 1995. ISBN 0-307-17520-0 Subj: Activities – playing. Family life – cousins. Family life – sisters. Sibling rivalry.

Lucy's day trip ill. by author. André Deutsch, 1991. ISBN 0-233-98423-2 Subj: Family life – cousins. Foreign lands – England. Marriage, interracial.

Norton, Natalie. *A little old man* ill. by Will Huntington. Rand McNally, 1959. Subj: Emotions – loneliness.

Norworth, Jack. *Take me out to the ballgame* ill. by Alec Gillman. Four Winds, 1993. ISBN 0-02-735991-3 Subj: Songs. Sports – baseball.

Nourse, Alan Edward. *Lumps, bumps and rashes: a look at kids' diseases.* Watts, 1990. ISBN 0-531-10865-1 Subj: Illness.

Novak, Matt. *Claude and Sun* ill. by author. Bradbury, 1987. ISBN 0-02-768151-3 Subj: Friendship. Sun.

Elmer Blunt's open house ill. by author. Orchard, 1992. ISBN 0-531-08598-8 Subj: Behavior – carelessness. Homes, houses.

Gertie and Gumbo ill. by author. Orchard, 1995. ISBN 0-531-08778-6 Subj: Emotions – loneliness. Family life – fathers. Music. Reptiles – alligators, crocodiles. Sports – wrestling.

Jazzbo and Googy ill. by author. Hyperion, 2000. ISBN 0-7868-2340-2 Subj: Animals – bears. Animals – pigs. Friendship. Toys – bears.

Jazzbo goes to school ill. by author. Hyperion, 1999. ISBN 0-7868-2339-9 Subj: Animals – bears. School – first day.

The last Christmas present ill. by author. Orchard, 1993. ISBN 0-531-08645-3 Subj: Holidays – Christmas. Mythical creatures – elves. Santa Claus.

Mr. Floop's lunch ill. by author. Watts, 1990. ISBN 0-531-08426-4 Subj: Animals. Behavior – sharing. Character traits – kindness to animals.

Mouse TV ill. by author. Orchard, 1994. ISBN 0-531-08706-9 Subj: Animals – mice. Family life. Television.

No zombies allowed ill. by author. Atheneum, 2001. ISBN 0-689-84130-2 Subj: Holidays – Halloween. Parties. Witches.

The Pillow War ill. by author. Orchard, 1998. ISBN 0-531-33048-6 Subj: Animals – dogs. Behavior – fighting, arguing. Family life – brothers and sisters. Rhyming text. Sleep.

The Robobots ill. by author. DK, 1999. ISBN 0-7894-2566-1 Subj: Communities, neighborhoods. Robots.

Rolling ill. by author. Bradbury, 1986. ISBN 0-02-768150-5 Subj: Weather – thunder.

While the shepherd slept ill. by author. Watts, 1991. ISBN 0-531-08515-5 Subj: Animals – sheep. Sleep. Theater.

Noyes, Alfred. *The highwayman* ill. by Neil Waldman. Harcourt, 1990. ISBN 0-15-234340-7 Subj: Crime. Emotions – love. Poetry. Royalty – kings.

Numeroff, Laura Joffe. *Amy for short* ill. by author. Macmillan, 1976. ISBN 0-02-768180-7 Subj: Character traits – appearance. Friendship.

The Chicken sisters ill. by Sharleen Collicott. Laura Geringer, 1997. ISBN 0-06-026680-5 Subj: Animals. Birds – chickens. Family life – sisters. Farms.

Chimps don't wear glasses ill. by Joseph Mathieu. Simon & Schuster, 1995. ISBN 0-671-87007-6 Subj: Activities. Animals. Imagination. Rhyming text.

Emily's bunch by Laura Joffe Numeroff and Alice Numeroff Richter; ill. by Laura Joffe Numeroff. Macmillan, 1978. ISBN 0-02-768430-X Subj: Holidays – Halloween.

If you give a moose a muffin ill. by Felicia Bond. HarperCollins, 1991. ISBN 0-06-024406-2 Subj: Animals – moose. Character traits – kindness to animals. Circular tales.

If you give a mouse a cookie ill. by Felicia Bond. HarperCollins, 1985. ISBN 0-06-024587-5 Subj: Animals – mice. Behavior – imitation. Character traits – kindness to animals. Circular tales.

If you give a pig a pancake ill. by Felicia Bond. Laura Geringer, 1998. ISBN 0-06-026687-2 Subj: Animals – pigs. Character traits – kindness to animals. Circular tales.

If you take a mouse to the movies ill. by Felicia Bond. Laura Geringer, 2000. ISBN 0-06-027868-4 Subj: Activities. Animals – mice. Holidays – Christmas.

Monster munchies ill. by Nate Evans. Random House, 1998. ISBN 0-679-99163-8 Subj: Counting, numbers. Monsters. Rhyming text.

Phoebe Dexter has Harriet Peterson's sniffles ill. by author. Greenwillow, 1977. ISBN 0-688-84091-4 Subj: Illness.

What daddies do best ill. by Lynn Munsinger. Simon & Schuster, 2002. ISBN 0-689-82554-4 Subj: Animals – foxes. Buildings. City. Family life – fathers. Sex roles.

What mommies do best ill. by Lynn Munsinger. Simon & Schuster, 1998. ISBN 0-689-80577-2 Subj: Activities – picnicking. Animals – mice. Sex roles.

Why a disguise? ill. by David McPhail. Simon & Schuster, 1996. ISBN 0-671-87006-8 Subj: Character traits – appearance.

You can't put braces on spaces (Richter, Alice Numeroff)

Nunes, Susan Miho. *Coyote dreams* ill. by Ronald Himler. Aladdin, 1994. ISBN 0-689-71804-7 Subj: Animals – coyotes. Desert. Dreams. Imagination.

The last dragon ill. by Chris K. Soentpiet. Clarion, 1995. ISBN 0-395-67020-9 Subj: Dragons. Ethnic groups in the U.S. – Chinese Americans. Family life – aunts, uncles.

Tiddalick the frog ill. by Ju-Hong chen. Atheneum, 1989. ISBN 0-689-31502-3 Subj: Folk and fairy tales. Foreign lands – Australia. Frogs and toads.

Nursery rhymes ill. by Gertrude Elliott. Simon & Schuster, 1948. Subj: Nursery rhymes.

Nussbaumer, Mares. *Away in a manger: a story of the Nativity* by Mares and Paul Nussbaumer; ill. by Paul Nussbaumer. Harcourt, 1965. Translation of Ihr Kinderlein kommet. ISBN 0-15-204735-2 Subj: Holidays – Christmas. Music. Religion – Nativity.

Nussbaumer, Paul. *Away in a manger: a story of the Nativity* (Nussbaumer, Mares)

Nye, Naomi Shihab. *Benito's dream bottle* ill. by Yu Cha Pak. Simon & Schuster, 1995. ISBN 0-02-768467-9 Subj: Dreams. Family life – grandmothers. Poetry.

Come with me: poems for a journey ill. by Dan Yaccarino. Greenwillow, 2000. ISBN 0-688-15947-8 Subj: Poetry.

Lullaby raft ill. by Vivienne Flesher. Simon & Schuster, 1997. ISBN 0-689-80521-7 Subj: Animals. Family life – mothers. Lullabies. Night.

Sitti's secrets ill. by Nancy Carpenter. Four Winds, 1994. ISBN 0-02-768460-1 Subj: Ethnic groups in the U.S. – Arab Americans. Family life – grandmothers. Foreign lands – Palestine. Foreign languages.

Nygaard, Elizabeth. *Snake alley band* ill. by Betsy Lewin. Doubleday, 1998. ISBN 0-385-32323-9 Subj: Animals. Music. Noise, sounds. Reptiles – snakes.

Nygren, Tord. *The red thread* ill. by author. Farrar, 1988. ISBN 91-29-59005-1 Subj: Imagination. Wordless.

O Christmas tree ill. by Michael Hague. Holt, 1991. ISBN 0-8050-1538-8 Subj: Holidays – Christmas. Songs. Trees.

Oakes, Bill. *Numblers* (MacDonald, Suse)

Once upon another (MacDonald, Suse)

Oakley, Graham. *The church cat abroad* ill. by author. Atheneum, 1973. ISBN 0-333-14825-8 Subj: Animals – cats. Animals – mice. Foreign lands – England.

The church mice adrift ill. by author. Atheneum, 1976. ISBN 0-689-30562-1 Subj: Animals – mice. Animals – rats. Rivers.

The church mice and the moon ill. by author. Atheneum, 1974. ISBN 0-689-30437-4 Subj: Animals – cats. Animals – mice. Foreign lands – England. Moon.

The church mice and the ring ill. by author. Atheneum, 1992. ISBN 0-689-31790-5 Subj: Animals –

cats. Animals – dogs. Animals – mice. Friendship. Homes, houses.

The church mice at bay ill. by author. Atheneum, 1978. ISBN 0-333-23235-6 Subj: Animals – cats. Animals – mice. Foreign lands – England.

The church mice at Christmas ill. by author. Atheneum, 1980. ISBN 0-689-30797-7 Subj: Animals – mice. Holidays – Christmas.

The church mice in action ill. by author. Atheneum, 1983. ISBN 0-689-30949-X Subj: Animals – mice. Problem solving.

The church mice spread their wings ill. by author. Atheneum, 1975. ISBN 0-689-30496-X Subj: Animals – cats. Animals – mice. Foreign lands – England.

The church mouse ill. by author. Aladdin, 1987, c1972. ISBN 0-689-70475-5 Subj: Animals – cats. Animals – mice. Foreign lands – England.

The diary of a church mouse ill. by author. Atheneum, 1987. ISBN 0-689-31334-9 Subj: Activities – writing. Animals – cats. Animals – mice.

Graham Oakley's magical changes ill. by author. Atheneum, 1980. ISBN 0-689-30732-2 Subj: Format, unusual – toy and movable books. Imagination. Wordless.

Hetty and Harriet ill. by author. Atheneum, 1982. ISBN 0-689-30888-4 Subj: Behavior – running away. Birds – chickens.

Oana, Kay D. *Robbie and the raggedy scarecrow* ill. by Jackie Stephens. Oddo, 1978. ISBN 0-87783-154-8 Subj: Birds. Scarecrows. Trees.

Shasta and the shebang machine ill. by Jackie Stephens. Oddo, 1978. ISBN 0-87783-152-1 Subj: Animals – cats. Behavior – misbehavior.

Oates, Eddie Hershel. *Making music: 6 instruments you can create* ill. by Michael Koelsch. Harper-Collins, 1995. ISBN 0-06-021479-1 Subj: Activities – making things. Music. Noise, sounds.

Oates, Joyce Carol. *Come meet Muffin!* ill. by Mark Graham. Ecco, 1998. ISBN 0-88001-556-X Subj: Animals – cats. Animals – deer. Behavior – lost.

Oberman, Sheldon. *The always prayer shawl* ill. by Ted Lewin. Boyds Mills, 1994. ISBN 1-878093-22-3 Subj: Clothing. Family life – grandfathers. Immigrants. Jewish culture.

By the Hanukkah light ill. by Neil Waldman. Boyds Mills, 1997. ISBN 1-56397-658-7 Subj: Family life – grandfathers. Holidays – Hanukkah. Holocaust. War.

King Solomon, Sheba, and the hoopoe bird ill. by Neil Waldman. Boyds Mills, 2000. ISBN 1-56397-816-4 Subj: Character traits – responsibility. Jewish culture. Religion. Royalty – kings.

Sound of the shofar ill. by Neil Waldman. Boyds Mills, 1997. ISBN 1-56397-557-2 Subj: Jewish culture. Religion.

The white stone in the castle wall ill. by Les Tait. Tundra, 1995. ISBN 0-88776-333-2 Subj: Castles. Foreign lands – Canada.

Obligado, Lilian. *Faint frogs feeling feverish and other terrifically tantalizing tongue twisters* ill. by author. Viking, 1983. ISBN 0-670-30477-8 Subj: ABC books. Animals. Tongue twisters.

O'Book, Irene. *Maybe my baby* photos by Paula Hible. HarperCollins, 1997. ISBN 0-694-00872-9 Subj: Babies. Careers. Rhyming text.

O'Brien, Anne Sibley. *Come play with us* ill. by author. Holt, 1985. ISBN 0-03-005008-1 Subj: Activities. Format, unusual – board books. School.

I want that! ill. by author. Holt, 1985. ISBN 0-03-005012-X Subj: Behavior – sharing. Format, unusual – board books.

I'm not tired ill. by author. Holt, 1985. ISBN 0-03-005009-X Subj: Character traits – stubbornness. Format, unusual – board books.

Where's my truck? ill. by author. Holt, 1985. ISBN 0-03-005013-8 Subj: Behavior – losing things. Format, unusual – board books.

O'Brien, Claire. *Sam's sneaker search* ill. by Charles Fuge. Simon & Schuster, 1997. ISBN 0-689-80169-6 Subj: Activities. Animals. Behavior – losing things.

O'Brien, John. *The farmer in the dell* (The farmer in the dell)

O'Brien, John (1953-). *Mother Hubbard's Christmas* ill. by author. Boyds Mills, 1996. ISBN 1-56397-139-9 Subj: Animals – dogs. Holidays – Christmas. Rhyming text.

Poof! ill. by author. Boyds Mills, 1999. ISBN 1-56397-815-6 Subj: Babies. Family life. Magic. Witches. Wizards.

Sam and Spot ill. by author. Cool Kids, 1995. ISBN 1-56790-500-5 Subj: Animals – dogs. Language.

O'Brien, Mary. *Counting sheep to sleep* ill. by Bobette McCarthy. Little, 1992. ISBN 0-316-62206-0 Subj: Animals – sheep. Bedtime. Counting, numbers. Farms. Sleep.

O'Brien, Patrick. *Gigantic! how big were the dinosaurs?* ill. by author. Holt, 1999. ISBN 0-8050-5738-2 Subj: Concepts – size. Dinosaurs.

Obrist, Jürg. *Bear business* ill. by author. Atheneum, 1986. ISBN 0-689-31149-4 Subj: Animals – bears. Behavior – misbehavior. Multiple births – twins.

Fluffy: the story of a cat ill. by author. Atheneum, 1981. ISBN 0-689-30722-5 Subj: Animals – cats. Moving.

The miser who wanted the sun ill. by author. Atheneum, 1984. ISBN 0-689-50294-X Subj: Behavior – greed. Character traits – cleverness. Sun.

They do things right in Albern ill. by author. Atheneum, 1978. ISBN 0-689-30671-7 Subj: Animals – moles. Problem solving.

O'Callahan, Jay. *Herman and Marguerite* ill. by Laura O'Callahan. Peachtree, 1996. ISBN 1-56145-103-7 Subj: Animals – worms. Friendship. Insects – butterflies, caterpillars.

Orange cheeks ill. by Patricia Raine. Peachtree, 1993. ISBN 1-56145-073-1 Subj: Behavior. Family life – grandmothers.

Tulips ill. by Debrah Santini. Picture Book Studio, 1992. ISBN 0-88708-223-8 Subj: Behavior – trickery. Family life – grandmothers. Flowers. Foreign lands – France. Gardens, gardening.

O'Connor, Francine M. *The ABC's of Christmas* ill. by Bartholomew. Liguori Pub., 1994. ISBN 0-8924-3581-X Subj: Holidays – Christmas. Religion – Nativity. Rhyming text.

O'Connor, Jane. *Benny's big bubble* ill. by Tomie de Paola. Grosset, 1997. ISBN 0-448-41303-5 Subj: Bubbles. Rebuses.

Kate skates ill. by DyAnne DiSalvo-Ryan. Grosset, 1995. ISBN 0-448-40936-4 Subj: Behavior – sharing. Family life – sisters. Sports – ice skating.

Nina, Nina and the copycat ballerina ill. by DyAnne DiSalvo-Ryan. Grosset, 2000. ISBN 0-448-42152-6 Subj: Activities – dancing. Ballet. Behavior – imitation.

Nina, Nina ballerina ill. by DyAnne DiSalvo-Ryan. Grosset, 1993. ISBN 0-448-40512-1 Subj: Accidents. Activities – dancing. Ballet.

Nina, Nina, star ballerina ill. by DyAnne DiSalvo-Ryan. Grosset, 1997. ISBN 0-448-41611-5 Subj: Activities – dancing. Ballet. Character traits – honesty.

The teeny tiny woman ill. by R. W. Alley. Random House, 1986. ISBN 0-394-98320-3 Subj: Folk and fairy tales. Ghosts.

O'Cuilleanain, Eilis Dillon. *see* Dillon, Eilis

O'Donnell, Elizabeth Lee. *I can't get my turtle to move* ill. by Maxie Chambliss. Morrow, 1989. ISBN 0-688-07324-7 Subj: Counting, numbers. Pets. Reptiles – turtles, tortoises.

Maggie doesn't want to move ill. by Amy Schwartz. Four Winds, 1987. ISBN 0-02-768830-5 Subj: Behavior – dissatisfaction. Behavior – running away. Emotions. Family life. Moving.

Patrick's day ill. by Jacqueline Rogers. Morrow, 1994. ISBN 0-688-07854-0 Subj: Birthdays. Foreign lands – Ireland. Holidays – St. Patrick's Day. Parades. Self-concept.

Sing me a window ill. by Melissa Sweet. Morrow, 1993. ISBN 0-688-09501-1 Subj: Bedtime. Family life – fathers. Poetry. Toys – bears.

The twelve days of summer ill. by Karen Lee Schmidt. Morrow, 1991. ISBN 0-688-08203-3 Subj: Counting, numbers. Poetry. Sea and seashore. Seasons – summer.

Winter visitors ill. by Carol Schwartz. Morrow, 1997. ISBN 0-688-13064-X Subj: Animals. Counting, numbers. Rhyming text. Seasons – winter.

O'Donnell, Peter. *Carnegie's excuse* ill. by author. Scholastic, 1992. ISBN 0-590-46435-3 Subj: Animals. Animals – tigers. Behavior – tardiness. Parks. School.

Dizzy ill. by author. Scholastic, 1992. ISBN 0-590-45475-7 Subj: Airplanes, airports. Animals – elephants.

Moonlit journey ill. by author. Scholastic, 1991. ISBN 0-590-44655-X Subj: Animals. Emotions – fear. Forest, woods. Night. Toys – bears.

Oscar ill. by author. ABC, 1992. ISBN 1-8540-6135-6 Subj: Animals – elephants. City. Jungle.

Pinkie goes south ill. by author. ABC, 1991. ISBN 1-8540-6120-8 Subj: Birds – penguins. Friendship.

Odoyevsky, Vladimir. *Old Father Frost* trans. from Russian by James Riordan; ill. by Vassili Shulzhenko. Imported Pubs., 1983. ISBN 0-8285-2216-2 Subj: Folk and fairy tales. Foreign lands – Russia. Seasons – winter.

Oechsli, Helen. *Fly away!* by Helen and Kelly Oechsli; ill. by Kelly Oechsli. Macmillan, 1992. ISBN 0-02-768520-9 Subj: Activities – traveling. Airplanes, airports. Family life – grandparents.

In my garden: a child's gardening book by Helen and Kelly Oechsli; ill. by Kelly Oechsli. Macmillan, 1985. ISBN 0-02-768510-1 Subj: Gardens, gardening.

Oechsli, Kelly. *Fly away!* (Oechsli, Helen)

In my garden: a child's gardening book (Oechsli, Helen)

Offen, Hilda. *As quiet as a mouse* ill. by author. Dutton, 1994. ISBN 0-525-45309-1 Subj: Animals. Noise, sounds. Rhyming text.

Elephant pie ill. by author. Dutton, 1993. ISBN 0-525-45123-4 Subj: Animals – elephants. Behavior – lost. Food. Reptiles – alligators, crocodiles.

A fox got my socks ill. by author. Dutton, 1993. ISBN 0-525-44991-4 Subj: Animals. Clothing. Rhyming text.

Good girl, Gracie Growler! ill. by author. Gareth Stevens, 1996. ISBN 0-8368-1624-2 Subj: Animals – tigers. Babies. Family life – brothers and sisters. Sibling rivalry.

Nice work, little wolf! ill. by author. Dutton, 1992. ISBN 0-525-44880-2 Subj: Animals – pigs. Animals – wolves.

The sheep made a leap ill. by author. Dutton, 1994. ISBN 0-525-45174-9 Subj: Activities – playing. Animals. Games. Rhyming text.

Ogburn, Jacqueline K. *The jukebox man* ill. by James Ransome. Dial, 1998. ISBN 0-8037-1430-0 Subj: Family life – grandfathers. Music.

The magic nesting doll ill. by Laurel Long. Dial, 2000. ISBN 0-8037-2414-4 Subj: Family life – grandmothers. Folk and fairy tales. Magic. Royalty – tsars. Toys – dolls.

The Masked Maverick ill. by Nancy Carlson. Lothrop, 1994. ISBN 0-688-11050-9 Subj: Character traits – individuality. Sports – wrestling.

Noise lullaby ill. by John Sandford. Lothrop, 1994. ISBN 0-688-10453-3 Subj: Bedtime. Lullabies. Noise, sounds.

The reptile ball ill. by John O'Brien. Dial, 1997. ISBN 0-8037-1732-6 Subj: Frogs and toads. Parties. Poetry. Reptiles.

Scarlett Angelina Wolverton-Manning ill. by Brian Ajhar. Dial, 1994. ISBN 0-8037-1377-0 Subj: Crime. Mythical creatures – werewolves.

Ogle, Lucille. *A B See* by Lucille Ogle and Tina Thoburn; ill. by Ralph Stobart. McGraw-Hill, 1973. ISBN 0-07-047498-2 Subj: ABC books.

I hear by Lucille Ogle and Tina Thoburn; ill. by Eloise Wilkin. American Heritage, 1971. ISBN 0-07-047543-1 Subj: Noise, sounds. Participation. Senses – hearing.

I spy ill. by Joe Kaufman. American Heritage, 1970. ISBN 0-07-047549-0 Subj: Senses – seeing. Wordless.

O'Hagan, Caroline. *It's easy to have a caterpillar visit you* ill. by Judith Allan. Lothrop, 1980. ISBN 0-688-51847-4 Subj: Insects – butterflies, caterpillars. Metamorphosis. Pets.

It's easy to have a snail visit you ill. by Judith Allan. Lothrop, 1980. ISBN 0-688-51848-2 Subj: Animals – snails. Pets.

It's easy to have a worm visit you ill. by Judith Allan. Lothrop, 1980. ISBN 0-688-51846-6 Subj: Animals – worms. Pets.

O'Hare, Colette. *What do you feed your donkey on? rhymes from a Belfast childhood* (What do you feed your donkey on?)

O'Hearn, Michael. *Hercules the harbor tug* ill. by Mela Lyman. Charlesbridge, 1994. ISBN 0-88106-890-X Subj: Boats, ships.

O Huigin, Sean. *King of the birds* ill. by Tim Dixon. Firefly, 1991. ISBN 0-88753-168-7 Subj: Birds. Folk and fairy tales. Giants. Poetry.

Oishi, Makoto. *E. H. Grieg's Peer Gynt* (Grieg, E. H. [Edvard Hagerup])

The sorcerer's apprentice (Dukas, P. [Paul Abraham])

O'Keefe, Susan Heyboer. *Angel prayer* ill. by Sofia Suzán. Boyds Mills, 1999. ISBN 1-56397-683-8 Subj: Religion. Rhyming text.

Good night, God bless ill. by Hideko Takahashi. Holt, 1999. ISBN 0-8050-6008-1 Subj: Bedtime. Religion. Rhyming text.

One hungry monster ill. by Lynn Munsinger. Little, 1989. ISBN 0-316-63385-2 Subj: Counting, numbers. Food. Monsters. Poetry.

O'Kelley, Mattie Lou. *Circus!* ill. by author. Atlantic Monthly, 1986. ISBN 0-87113-094-7 Subj: Behavior – misbehavior. Circus. Family life. Farms.

Moving to town ill. by author. Little, 1991. ISBN 0-316-63805-6 Subj: Activities – traveling. City. Moving.

Okimoto, Jean Davies. *Blumpoe the grumpoe meets Arnold the cat* ill. by Howie Schneider. Little, 1990. ISBN 0-316-62811-0 Subj: Animals – cats.

No dear, not here ill. by Celeste Henriquez. Sasquatch, 1995. ISBN 1-57061-019-3 Subj: Birds. Homes, houses.

A place for Grace ill. by Doug Keith. Sasquatch, 1993. ISBN 0-912365-73-0 Subj: Animals – dogs. Character traits – helpfulness. Handicaps – deafness.

Okrend, Elise. *Blintzes for Blitzen* ill. by Alice L. Oglesby. MixedBlessings, 1996. ISBN 0-9651475-0-9 Subj: Animals – reindeer. Food. Holidays – Christmas. Holidays – Hanukkah.

Oksner, Robert M. *The incompetent wizard* ill. by Janet McCaffery. Morrow, 1965. Subj: Dragons. Magic. Wizards.

Olaleye, Isaac. *Bikes for rent!* ill. by Chris Demarest. Orchard, 2001. ISBN 0-531-33290-X Subj: Foreign lands – Nigeria. Sports – bicycling.

Bitter bananas ill. by Ed Young. Caroline House, 1994. ISBN 1-56397-039-2 Subj: Animals – baboons. Character traits – cleverness. Food. Foreign lands – Africa. Foreign lands – Nigeria. Problem solving.

The distant talking drum ill. by Frané Lessac. Wordsong, 1995. ISBN 1-56397-095-3 Subj: Foreign lands – Nigeria. Poetry.

In the Rainfield: who is the greatest? ill. by Ann Grifalconi. Blue Sky, 2000. ISBN 0-590-48363-3 Subj: Contests. Folk and fairy tales. Foreign lands – Nigeria. Nature. Weather – rain. Weather – wind.

Lake of the Big Snake ill. by Claudia Shepard. Boyds Mills, 1998. ISBN 1-56397-096-1 Subj: Foreign lands – Africa. Forest, woods. Reptiles – snakes.

Old MacDonald had a farm. *E I E I O: the story of Old MacDonald, who had a farm* ill. by Gus Clarke. Lothrop, 1993. ISBN 0-688-12215-9 Subj: Animals. Careers – farmers. Cumulative tales. Farms. Music. Songs.

Old MacDonald retold and ill. by Rosemary Wells. Scholastic, 1998. ISBN 0-590-76985-5 Subj: Animals. Careers – farmers. Cumulative tales. Farms. Songs.

Old MacDonald had a farm ill. by Holly Berry. North-South, 1994. ISBN 1-55858-282-7 Subj: Animals. Careers – farmers. Cumulative tales. Farms. Music. Songs.

Old MacDonald had a farm ill. by Lorinda Bryan Cauley. Putnam, 1989. ISBN 0-399-21628-6 Subj: Animals. Careers – farmers. Cumulative tales. Farms. Music. Songs.

Old MacDonald had a farm ill. by Mel Crawford. Golden Pr., 1967. Subj: Animals. Careers – farmers. Cumulative tales. Farms. Music. Songs.

Old MacDonald had a farm ill. by Tracey English. Western, 1993. ISBN 0-307-17601-1 Subj: Animals. Careers – farmers. Cumulative tales. Farms. Music. Songs.

Old MacDonald had a farm ill. by David Frankland. Merrill, 1980. ISBN 0-675-01065-9 Subj: Animals. Careers – farmers. Cumulative tales. Farms. Music. Songs.

Old MacDonald had a farm ill. by Abner Graboff. Four Winds, 1970. Subj: Animals. Careers – farmers. Cumulative tales. Farms. Music. Songs.

Old MacDonald had a farm ill. by Nancy Hellen. Watts, 1990. ISBN 0-531-05872-7 Subj: Animals. Careers – farmers. Cumulative tales. Farms. Music. Songs.

Old MacDonald had a farm ill. by Carol Jones. Houghton Mifflin, 1989. ISBN 0-395-49212-2 Subj: Animals. Careers – farmers. Cumulative tales. Farms. Format, unusual. Music. Songs.

Old MacDonald had a farm ill. by Tracey Campbell Pearson. Dial, 1984. ISBN 0-8037-0070-9 Subj: Animals. Careers – farmers. Cumulative tales. Farms. Music. Songs.

Old MacDonald had a farm ill. by Robert M. Quackenbush. Lippincott, 1972. ISBN 0-397-31218-0 Subj: Animals. Careers – farmers. Cumulative tales. Farms. Music. Songs.

Old MacDonald had a farm ill. by Glen Rounds. Holiday, 1989. ISBN 0-8234-0739-X Subj: Animals. Careers – farmers. Cumulative tales. Farms. Music. Songs.

Old MacDonald had a farm retold and ill. by Jessica Souhami; designed by Paul McAlinden. Orchard, 1996. ISBN 0-531-09493-6 Subj: Animals. Careers – farmers. Cumulative tales. Farms. Format, unusual – toy and movable books. Songs. Transportation.

Old MacDonald had a farm ill. by William Stobbs. Oxford Univ. Pr., 1986. ISBN 0-19-279817-0 Subj: Animals. Careers – farmers. Cumulative tales. Farms. Music. Songs.

Old MacDonald had a farm ill. by Prue Theobalds. Peter Bedrick, 1991. ISBN 0-87226-452-1 Subj: Animals. Careers – farmers. Cumulative tales. Farms. Music. Songs.

Old, Wendie C. *Stacy had a little sister* ill. by Judith Friedman. Albert Whitman, 1995. ISBN 0-8075-7598-4 Subj: Babies. Death. Emotions – grief. Family life – new sibling. Family life – sisters.

The old woman and her pig. *The old woman and her pig* ill. by Paul Galdone. McGraw-Hill, 1960. Subj: Cumulative tales. Folk and fairy tales.

The old woman and her pig adapt. by Eric A. Kimmel; ill. by Giora Karmi. Holiday, 1992. ISBN 0-8234-0970-8 Subj: Cumulative tales. Folk and fairy tales.

The old woman and her pig retold and ill. by Rosanne Litzinger. Harcourt, 1993. ISBN 0-15-257802-1 Subj: Cumulative tales. Folk and fairy tales.

The troublesome pig retold and ill. by Priscilla Lamont. Crown, 1985. ISBN 0-517-55546-8 Subj: Cumulative tales. Folk and fairy tales.

The old-fashioned children's storybook. Wanderer, 1980. ISBN 0-671-41540-9 Subj: Folk and fairy tales.

Oldfield, Pamela. *Melanie Brown climbs a tree* ill. by Carolyn Dinan. Faber, 1980. ISBN 0-571-11488-1 Subj: Behavior – misbehavior. Foreign lands – England.

Oldfield, Wendy. *My apple* (Davies, Kay)

My balloon (Davies, Kay)

My drum (Davies, Kay)

My mirror (Davies, Kay)

Olds, Elizabeth. *Feather mountain* ill. by author. Houghton Mifflin, 1951. Subj: Birds. Caldecott award honor books.

Little Una ill. by author. Scribners, 1963. Subj: City.

Plop plop ploppie ill. by author. Scribners, 1962. Subj: Animals – sea lions. Clowns, jesters.

Olds, Helen Diehl. *Miss Hattie and the monkey* ill. by Dorothy Marino. Follett, 1958. Subj: Animals – monkeys. Careers – seamstresses.

Oleson, Claire. *For Pipita, an orange tree* ill. by Margot Tomes. Doubleday, 1967. Subj: Foreign lands – Spain. Plants.

Oleson, Jens. *Snail* photos by Bo Jarner. Silver Burdett, 1986. ISBN 0-382-09289-9 Subj: Animals – snails. Science.

Oliver, Dexter. *I want to be . . .* by Dexter and Patricia Oliver; photos by Dexter Oliver. Third World Pr., 1974. ISBN 0-8837-8041-0 Subj: ABC books. Careers.

Oliver, Lin. *The fat cat* (Mooser, Stephen)

Oliver, Patricia. *I want to be . . .* (Oliver, Dexter)

Oliver, Stephen. *Clothes* photos by Steve Gorton. Random House, 1991. ISBN 0-679-81806-5 Subj: Clothing.

My first look at colors photos by author. McKay, 1990. ISBN 0-679-80535-4 Subj: Concepts – color.

My first look at numbers photos by author. McKay, 1990. ISBN 0-679-80533-8 Subj: Counting, numbers.

My first look at shapes photos by author. McKay, 1990. ISBN 0-679-80534-6 Subj: Concepts – shape.

My first look at sizes photos by author. McKay, 1990. ISBN 0-679-80532-X Subj: Concepts – size.

Nature photos by Steve Gorton. Random House, 1991. ISBN 0-679-81805-7 Subj: Nature.

Opposites photos by author. Random House, 1990. ISBN 0-679-80620-2 Subj: Concepts – opposites.

Seasons photos by author. Random House, 1990. ISBN 0-679-80621-0 Subj: Seasons.

Shopping photos by Steve Gorton. Random House, 1991. ISBN 0-679-81803-0 Subj: Shopping. Stores.

Things that go photos by Steve Gorton. Random House, 1991. ISBN 0-679-81804-9 Subj: Toys. Transportation.

Touch photos by author. Random House, 1990. ISBN 0-679-80623-7 Subj: Senses – touching.

Oliver, Sy. *The Sesame Street song book* (Raposo, Joe)

Oliviero, Jamie. *The day Sun was stolen* ill. by Sharon Hitchcock. Hyperion, 1995. ISBN 0-7868-2026-8 Subj: Animals – bears. Creation. Folk and fairy tales. Indians of North America – Haida.

The fish skin ill. by Brent Morriseau. Hyperion, 1993. ISBN 1-56282-402-3 Subj: Folk and fairy tales. Indians of North America – Cree. Sun. Weather – clouds. Weather – droughts. Weather – rain.

Som See and the magic elephant ill. by Jo'Anne Kelly. Hyperion, 1995. ISBN 0-7868-2020-9 Subj: Death. Emotions – grief. Family life – aunts, uncles. Foreign lands – Thailand.

Olivo, Richard. *Close, closer, closest* (Rotner, Shelley)

Olney, Ross R. *Construction giants* ill. with photos. Atheneum, 1984. ISBN 0-689-31067-6 Subj: Machines.

Farm giants ill. with photos. Atheneum, 1982. ISBN 0-689-30937-6 Subj: Farms. Machines.

Olofsdotter, Marie. *Frej the fearless: the secret world of Frej* ill. by Marie Olofsdotter. Free Spirit, 1995. ISBN 0-915793-86-5 Subj: Activities – babysitting. Behavior – secrets. Imagination.

Sofia and the Heartmender ill. by author. Free Spirit, 1993. ISBN 0-915793-50-4 Subj: Emotions – fear. Monsters. Night. Shadows.

Olschewski, Alfred. *We fly* ill. by author. Little, 1967. Subj: Airplanes, airports.

The wheel rolls over ill. by author. Little, 1962. Subj: Transportation. Wheels.

Olsen, Alfa-Betty. *Gabby the shrew* by Alfa-Betty Olsen and Marshall Efron; ill. by Roz Chast. Random House, 1994. ISBN 0-679-94467-2 Subj: Animals – shrews. Behavior – dissatisfaction. Character traits – individuality. Noise, sounds.

Olsen, Ib Spang. *The boy in the moon* ill. by author. Parents, 1977. Tr. of Dregen i manen from the Danish by Virginia Allen Jensen. ISBN 0-8193-0734-3 Subj: Moon.

Cat alley trans. by Virginia Allen Jensen; ill. by author. Coward, 1971. Translation of Kattehuset. Subj: Behavior – lost. City.

The grown-up trap ill. by author. Thomasson-Grant, 1992. ISBN 0-934738-96-3 Subj: Behavior – needing someone. Emotions – loneliness. Family life. Imagination. Rhyming text.

Olson, Arielle North. *Hurry home, Grandma!* ill. by Lydia Dabcovich. Dutton, 1984. ISBN 0-525-44113-1 Subj: Family life – grandmothers. Holidays – Christmas.

The lighthouse keeper's daughter ill. by Elaine Wentworth. Little, 1987. ISBN 0-316-65053-6 Subj: Character traits – bravery. Flowers. Islands. Lighthouses. Weather – storms.

Noah's cats and the devil's fire ill. by Barry Moser. Watts, 1992. ISBN 0-531-08584-8 Subj: Animals – cats. Animals – mice. Boats, ships. Devil. Folk and fairy tales. Foreign lands – Romania. Religion – Noah. Weather – floods. Weather – rain.

Olson, Helen Kronberg. *The strange thing that happened to Oliver Wendell Iscovitch* ill. by Betsy Lewin. Dodd, 1983. ISBN 0-396-08147-9 Subj: Behavior – misbehavior. Ghosts. Humor.

Olujic, Grozdana. *Rose of Mother-of-Pearl* trans. from Serbo-Croatian by Grozdana Olujic and Jascha Kessler; ill. by Kathy Jacobi. Toothpaste Pr., 1983. ISBN 0-915124-90-4 Subj: Behavior – dissatisfaction. Sea and seashore.

Olyff, Clotilde. *1,2,3. One, two, three* ill. by author. Ticknor & Fields, 1994. ISBN 0-395-70736-6 Subj: Counting, numbers. Format, unusual – toy and movable books.

O'Malley, Kevin. *The box* ill. by author. Stewart, Tabori & Chang, 1993. ISBN 1-55670-275-2 Subj: Activities – playing. Imagination. Toys – bears. Wordless.

Bud ill. by author. Walker, 2000. ISBN 0-8027-8719-3 Subj: Animals – rhinoceros. Character traits – orderliness. Family life – grandfathers. Gardens, gardening.

Carl caught a flying fish ill. by author. Simon & Schuster, 1996. ISBN 0-689-80098-3 Subj: Behavior – misbehavior. Fish. Rhyming text. School.

Leo Cockroach . . . toy tester ill. by author. Walker, 1999. ISBN 0-8027-8690-1 Subj: Insects – cockroaches. Toys.

Roller coaster ill. by author. Lothrop, 1995. ISBN 0-688-13972-8 Subj: Fairs.

Velcome ill. by author. Walker, 1997. ISBN 0-8027-8629-4 Subj: Activities – storytelling. Holidays – Halloween. Monsters.

Who killed Cock Robin? ill. by Keevin O'Malley. Lothrop, 1993. ISBN 0-688-12431-3 Subj: Birds – owls. Birds – robins. Birds – wrens. Careers – detectives. Crime. Mystery stories. Picture puzzles. Rhyming text.

On the little hearth trans. by Miriam Chaikin; ill. by Gabriel Lisowski; score by Mark Warshawski. Holt, 1978. ISBN 0-03-039931-9 Subj: Foreign languages. Jewish culture. Music. Songs.

Onassis, Jacqueline. *The firebird: and other Russian fairy tales* (The firebird)

Once I was . . . ill. by Woodleigh Marx Hubbard. Putnam, 1999. ISBN 0-399-23105-6 Subj: Behavior – growing up. Concepts. Rhyming text.

100 words about transportation ill. by Richard Eric Brown. Harcourt, 1987. ISBN 0-15-200551-X Subj: Language. Transportation.

100 words about working ill. by Richard Eric Brown. Harcourt, 1988. ISBN 0-15-200553-6 Subj: Activities – working. Careers. Language.

One rubber duckie: *a Sesame Street counting book* photos by John E. Barrett. Random House, 1982. ISBN 0-394-85309-1 Subj: Counting, numbers. Puppets.

One, two, buckle my shoe: *a book of counting rhymes* comp. and ill. by Rowan Barnes-Murphy. Simon & Schuster, 1988. ISBN 0-671-63791-6 Subj: Counting, numbers. Nursery rhymes.

One, two, buckle my shoe ill. by Gail E. Haley. Doubleday, 1964. Subj: Counting, numbers. Nursery rhymes.

One, two, skip a few! *first number rhymes* ill. by Roberta Arenson. Barefoot, 1998. ISBN 1-901223-99-X Subj: Counting, numbers. Nursery rhymes. Rhyming text.

O'Neil, Amanda. *I wonder why spiders spin webs: and other questions about creepy crawlies* ill. by author. Kingfisher, 1995. ISBN 1-85697-643-2 Subj: Insects. Spiders.

O'Neill, Alexis. *Loud Emily* ill. by Nancy Carpenter. Simon & Schuster, 1998. ISBN 0-689-81078-4 Subj: Animals – whales. Boats, ships. Noise, sounds. Sailors.

O'Neill, Catharine. *Mrs. Dunphy's dog* ill. by author. Viking, 1987. ISBN 0-670-81135-1 Subj: Activities – reading. Animals – dogs.

O'Neill, Mary. *Big red hen* ill. by Judy Piussi-Campbell. Doubleday, 1971. Subj: Birds – chickens. Eggs. Rhyming text.

O'Neill, Rachael. *The Christmas story* (Butterfield, Moira)

Onyefulu, Ifeoma. *Grandfather's work: a traditional healer in Nigeria* ill. with photos. Millbrook, 1998. ISBN 0-7613-0412-6 Subj: Family life – grandfathers. Foreign lands – Nigeria. Health and fitness.

Ogbo: sharing life in an African village ill. by author. Gulliver, 1996. ISBN 0-15-200498-X Subj: Foreign lands – Nigeria.

Onyefulu, Obi. *Chinye* ill. by Evie Safarewicz. Viking, 1994. ISBN 0-670-85115-9 Subj: Folk and fairy tales. Foreign lands – Africa.

Onyschuk, Motria. *The cat and the rooster* (Malkovych, Ivan)

Ooka, D. T. *The monkey and the crab* (Horio, Seishi)

The old man who made the trees bloom (Shibano, Tamizo)

Wally the whale who loved balloons (Watanabe, Yuichi)

Ophir, Uri. *Songs of Chanukah* (Modesitt, Jeanne)

Opie, Iona A. *Humpty Dumpty and other rhymes* (Mother Goose)

Little Boy Blue and other rhymes (Mother Goose)

Pussycat, pussycat and other rhymes (Mother Goose)

Wee Willie Winkie and other rhymes (Mother Goose)

Oppenheim, Joanne. *The Christmas witch* ill. by Annie Mitra. Gareth Stevens, 1997. ISBN 0-8368-1697-8 Subj: Folk and fairy tales. Holidays – Christmas. Religion – Nativity. Witches.

Could it be? ill. by S. D. Schindler. Gareth Stevens, 1998. ISBN 0-8368-1770-2 Subj: Animals – bears. Noise, sounds. Seasons – spring.

Do you like cats? ill. by Carol Newsom. Gareth Stevens, 1998. ISBN 0-8368-1757-5 Subj: Animals – cats. Rhyming text.

Donkey's tale ill. by Chris L. Demarest. Bantam, 1991. ISBN 0-553-07090-8 Subj: Animals – donkeys. Character traits – practicality. Folk and fairy tales. Humor. Rhyming text.

The eency weency spider ill. by S. D. Schindler. Bantam, 1991. ISBN 0-553-07316-8 Subj: Games. Songs. Spiders.

Have you seen birds? ill. by Barbara Reid. Scholastic, 1986. ISBN 0-590-40585-3 Subj: Birds.

Have you seen bugs? ill. by Ron Broda. Scholastic, 1997. ISBN 0-590-05963-7 Subj: Insects. Rhyming text. Spiders.

Have you seen roads? ill. by Gerard Nook. Addison-Wesley, 1969. Subj: Poetry. Transportation.

Have you seen trees? ill. by Irwin Rosenhouse. Addison-Wesley, 1967. Subj: Poetry. Seasons. Trees.

Have you seen trees? ill. by Jean and Mou-sien Tseng. Scholastic, 1995. ISBN 0-590-46691-7 Subj: Poetry. Seasons. Trees.

How do you make a bubble? (Hooks, William H.)

James will never die ill. by True Kelley. Dodd, 1982. ISBN 0-396-08067-7 Subj: Activities – playing.

Left and right ill. by Rosanne Litzinger. Harcourt, 1989. ISBN 0-15-200505-6 Subj: Careers – shoe-makers. Concepts – left and right. Family life – brothers.

Mrs. Peloki's class play ill. by Joyce Audy dos San-tos. Dodd, 1984. ISBN 0-396-08178-9 Subj: School. Theater.

Mrs. Peloki's snake ill. by Joyce Audy dos Santos. Dodd, 1980. ISBN 0-396-07810-9 Subj: Reptiles – snakes. School.

Mrs. Peloki's substitute ill. by Joyce Audy Zarins. Dodd, 1987. ISBN 0-396-08918-6 Subj: Behavior – trickery. School.

No way, Slippery Slick! a child's first book about drugs by Joanne Oppenheim, Barbara A. Brenner, and William H. Hooks; ill. by Joan Auclair. Harper-Collins, 1991. ISBN 0-06-107437-3 Subj: Animals – cats. Illness – alcoholism. Illness – drug addiction.

"Not now!" said the cow ill. by Chris L. Demarest. Bantam, 1989. ISBN 0-553-34691-1 Subj: Animals. Birds – crows. Character traits – laziness. Cumu-lative tales. Farms.

On the other side of the river ill. by Aliki. Watts, 1972. Subj: Behavior – needing someone. Bridges. Careers.

One gift deserves another (Grimm, Jacob)

Read-a-rebus (Hooks, William H.)

Rooter remembers ill. by Lynn Munsinger. Viking, 1991. ISBN 0-670-82865-3 Subj: Family life. Memo-ries, memory.

The story book prince ill. by Rosanne Litzinger. Har-court, 1987. ISBN 0-15-200590-0 Subj: Bedtime. Rhyming text. Royalty – princes. Sleep.

"Uh-oh!" said the crow ill. by Chris L. Demarest. Gareth Stevens, 1997. ISBN 0-8368-1753-2 Subj: Animals. Barns. Emotions – fear. Noise, sounds.

You can't catch me! ill. by Andrew Shachat. Houghton Mifflin, 1986. ISBN 0-395-41452-0 Subj: Animals. Behavior – boasting. Cumulative tales. Insects – flies. Rhyming text.

Oppenheim, Shulamith Levey. *And the earth trem-bled: the creation of Adam and Eve* ill. by Neil Wald-man. Harcourt, 1996. ISBN 0-15-200025-9 Subj: Creation. Religion – Islam.

Fireflies for Nathan ill. by John Ward. Tambourine, 1994. ISBN 0-688-12148-9 Subj: Ethnic groups in the U.S. – African Americans. Family life – grandparents. Insects – fireflies.

The hundredth name ill. by Michael Hays. Boyds Mills, 1995. ISBN 1-56397-183-6 Subj: Animals – camels. Behavior – secrets. Foreign lands – Egypt. Names. Religion.

I love you, Bunny Rabbit ill. by Cyd Moore. Boyds Mills, 1995. ISBN 1-56397-322-7 Subj: Emotions – love. Toys.

Iblis ill. by Ed Young. Harcourt, 1994. ISBN 0-15-238016-7 Subj: Creation. Devil. Religion.

The lily cupboard ill. by Ronald Himler. Harper-Collins, 1992. ISBN 0-06-024670-7 Subj: Behavior – hiding. Character traits – bravery. Emotions – fear. Foreign lands – Holland. Friendship. Holo-caust. Jewish culture. War.

Waiting for Noah ill. by Lillian Hoban. Harper, 1999. ISBN 0-06-024634-0 Subj: Babies. Birth. Birthdays. Family life – grandmothers.

What is the full moon full of? ill. by Cyd Moore. Boyds Mills, 1997. ISBN 1-56397-479-7 Subj: Ani-mals. Bedtime. Moon. Night.

Yanni rubbish ill. by Doug Chayka. Boyds Mills, 1999. ISBN 1-56397-668-4 Subj: Animals – don-keys. Careers. Family life – fathers. Foreign lands – Greece.

Oram, Hiawyn. *Angry Arthur* ill. by Satoshi Kita-mura. Farrar, 1997. ISBN 0-374-40386-4 Subj: Emotions – anger.

Baba Yaga and the wise doll ill. by Ruth Brown. Dutton, 1998. ISBN 0-525-45947-2 Subj: Behavior – trickery. Folk and fairy tales. Foreign lands – Russia. Toys – dolls. Witches.

Badger's bad mood ill. by Susan Varley. Levine, 1998. ISBN 0-590-18920-4 Subj: Animals. Animals – badgers. Animals – moles. Behavior – bad day. Friendship.

Badger's bring something party ill. by Susan Varley. Lothrop, 1995. ISBN 0-688-14082-3 Subj: Animals. Animals – badgers. Friendship. Parties.

A boy wants a dinosaur ill. by Satoshi Kitamura. Farrar, 1991. ISBN 0-374-30939-6 Subj: Dinosaurs. Dreams. Family life – grandfathers. Pets.

Gerda the goose ill. by David Melling. Barron's, 2000. ISBN 0-7641-1484-0 Subj: Birds – geese.

In the attic ill. by Satoshi Kitamura. Holt, 1985. ISBN 0-03-002462-5 Subj: Activities – playing. Behavior – boredom. Imagination.

Jenna and the troublemaker ill. by Tony Ross. Holt, 1986. ISBN 0-8050-0025-9 Subj: Behavior – dissatis-faction. Mythical creatures.

Just Dog ill. by Lisa Flather. Chronicle, 1998. ISBN 0-8118-2247-8 Subj: Animals – cats. Animals – dogs. Self-concept.

Mine! ill. by Mary Rees. Barron's, 1992. ISBN 0-8120-6303-1 Subj: Behavior – sharing. Friendship.

Mole's moon ill. by Susan Varley. Andersen, 1997. ISBN 0-8626-4694-4 Subj: Animals. Animals – moles. Moon.

Ned and the Joybaloo ill. by Satoshi Kitamura. David & Charles, 1989, c1983. ISBN 0-86264-048-2 Subj: Behavior – misbehavior. Character traits – individuality. Imagination – imaginary friends.

Princess Chamomile gets her way ill. by Susan Varley. Dutton, 1999. ISBN 0-525-46148-5 Subj: Animals – mice. Character traits – freedom. Crime. Royalty – princesses.

Reckless Ruby ill. by Tony Ross. Crown, 1992. ISBN 0-517-58744-0 Subj: Behavior – carelessness. Family life.

The second princess ill. by Tony Ross. Artists & Writers Guild, 1994. ISBN 0-307-17513-8 Subj: Family life – sisters. Royalty – princesses. Sibling rivalry.

Skittlewonder and the wizard ill. by Jenny Rodwell. Dial, 1980. ISBN 0-8037-7834-1 Subj: Folk and fairy tales. Games. Gypsies. Royalty. Witches. Wizards.

Where are you hiding, little lamb? ill. by Jonathan Langley. Barron's, 1999. ISBN 0-7641-5196-7 Subj: Animals – sheep. Behavior – hiding.

Orbach, Ruth. *Apple pigs* ill. by author. Collins-World, 1977. ISBN 0-529-05332-2 Subj: Food. Rhyming text. Trees.

Please send a panda ill. by author. Collins-World, 1978. ISBN 0-00-183749-4 Subj: Behavior – wishing. Family life – grandmothers. Pets.

O'Reilly, Edward. *Brown pelican at the pond* ill. by Florence Strange. Manzanita, 1979. ISBN 0-931644-01-1 Subj: Birds – pelicans. Children as authors.

Orgel, Doris. *Button soup* ill. by Pau Estrada. Gareth Stevens, 1998. ISBN 0-8368-1761-3 Subj: Folk and fairy tales. Food. Foreign lands – France.

The flower of Sheba by Doris Orgel and Ellen Schecter; ill. by Laura Kelly. Bantam, 1994. ISBN 0-553-09041-0 Subj: Jewish culture. Religion. Royalty.

Godfather Cat and Mousie (Grimm, Jacob)

The lion and the mouse and other Æsop fables (Æsop)

Little John by Theodor Storm; retold from the German by Doris Orgel; ill. by Anita Lobel. Farrar, 1972. ISBN 0-374-34620-8 Subj: Bedtime. Dreams.

Merry merry FIBruary ill. by Arnold Lobel. Parents, 1978. ISBN 0-8193-0901-X Subj: Poetry.

On the sand dune ill. by Leonard Weisgard. HarperCollins, 1968. Subj: Character traits – smallness. Sea and seashore.

Two crows counting ill. by Judith Moffatt. Bantam, 1995. ISBN 0-553-37573-3 Subj: Birds – crows. Counting, numbers. Rhyming text.

Ormerod, Jan. *Ben goes swimming* ill. by author. HarperCollins, 1999. ISBN 0-688-17714-X Subj: Format, unusual – toy and movable books. Imagination. Sports – swimming.

Bend and stretch ill. by author. Lothrop, 1987. ISBN 0-688-07272-0 Subj: Babies. Family life – mothers. Sports.

Come back, kittens ill. by author. Lothrop, 1992. ISBN 0-688-09134-2 Subj: Animals – cats. Counting, numbers. Format, unusual.

Come back, puppies ill. by author. Lothrop, 1992. ISBN 0-688-09135-0 Subj: Animals – dogs. Counting, numbers. Format, unusual.

Dad's back ill. by author. Lothrop, 1985. ISBN 0-688-04126-4 Subj: Babies. Clothing. Family life – fathers.

Emily dances ill. by author. Tupelo, 1999. ISBN 0-688-17713-1 Subj: Activities – dancing. Format, unusual – toy and movable books.

Joe can count ill. by author. Mulberry, 1993. ISBN 0-688-04588-X Subj: Animals. Counting, numbers.

Just like me ill. by author. Lothrop, 1986. ISBN 0-688-04211-2 Subj: Babies. Character traits – appearance.

Kitten day ill. by author. Lothrop, 1989. ISBN 0-688-08537-7 Subj: Animals – cats. Pets.

Making friends ill. by author. Lothrop, 1987. ISBN 0-688-07270-4 Subj: Babies. Family life – mothers. Toys – dolls.

Messy baby ill. by author. Lothrop, 1985. ISBN 0-688-04128-0 Subj: Babies. Family life – fathers. Toys.

Midnight pillow fight ill. by author. Candlewick, 1993. ISBN 1-56402-169-6 Subj: Activities – playing. Night.

Miss Mouse takes off ill. by author. HarperCollins, 2001. ISBN 0-688-17871-5 Subj: Activities – traveling. Airplanes, airports. Toys – dolls.

Mom's home ill. by author. Lothrop, 1987. ISBN 0-688-07274-7 Subj: Babies. Family life – mothers.

Moonlight ill. by author. Lothrop, 1982. ISBN 0-688-00847-X Subj: Bedtime. Family life. Sleep. Wordless.

Ms. MacDonald has a class ill. by author. Clarion, 1996. ISBN 0-395-77611-2 Subj: Animals. Cumulative tales. Farms. School. Songs.

101 things to do with a baby ill. by author. Turtleback, 1993. ISBN 0-606-06153-3 Subj: Babies. Behavior – sharing. Sibling rivalry.

Our Ollie ill. by author. Lothrop, 1986. ISBN 0-688-04208-2 Subj: Babies. Character traits – appearance.

Reading ill. by author. Lothrop, 1985. ISBN 0-688-04127-2 Subj: Activities – reading. Family life – fathers.

Rock-a-baby ill. by author. Dutton, 1998. ISBN 0-525-45935-9 Subj: Babies. Format, unusual – toy and movable books. Rhyming text.

The saucepan game ill. by author. Lothrop, 1989. ISBN 0-688-08519-9 Subj: Activities – playing. Animals – cats. Babies. Imagination.

Silly goose ill. by author. Lothrop, 1986. ISBN 0-688-04209-0 Subj: Babies. Character traits – appearance.

Sleeping ill. by author. Lothrop, 1985. ISBN 0-688-04129-9 Subj: Babies. Family life – fathers. Sleep.

The story of Chicken Licken (Chicken Little)

Sunshine ill. by author. Lothrop, 1981. ISBN 0-688-00553-5 Subj: Morning. Sun. Wordless.

This little nose ill. by author. Lothrop, 1987. ISBN 0-688-07276-3 Subj: Anatomy – noses. Babies. Family life – mothers. Illness.

To baby with love ill. by author. Lothrop, 1994. ISBN 0-688-12559-X Subj: Games. Nursery rhymes.

When we went to the zoo ill. by author. Lothrop, 1991. ISBN 0-688-09879-7 Subj: Animals. Zoos.

Who's whose? ill. by author. Lothrop, 1998. ISBN 0-688-14679-1 Subj: Activities. Family life.

Young Joe ill. by author. Lothrop, 1986. ISBN 0-688-04210-4 Subj: Babies. Counting, numbers.

Ormondroyd, Edward. *Broderick* ill. by John M. Larrecq. Parnassus, 1969. ISBN 0-686-86580-4 Subj: Activities – reading. Animals – mice. Sports – surfing.

Johnny Castleseed ill. by Diana Thewlis. Houghton Mifflin, 1985. ISBN 0-395-38355-2 Subj: Sand. Sea and seashore.

Theodore ill. by John M. Larrecq. Parnassus, 1966. ISBN 0-87466-028-9 Subj: Character traits – appearance. Character traits – kindness. Laundry. Toys – bears.

Theodore's rival ill. by John M. Larrecq. Parnassus, 1971. ISBN 0-8746-6001-7 Subj: Emotions – envy, jealousy. Sibling rivalry. Toys – bears.

Ormsby, Virginia H. *Twenty-one children plus ten* ill. by author. Lippincott, 1971. Subj: Ethnic groups in the U.S. – Mexican Americans. School.

Orstadius, Brita. *The dolphin journey* trans. from Swedish by Eric Bibb; ill. by Lennart Didoff. Farrar, 1989. ISBN 9-12-959138-4 Subj: Animals – dolphins. Character traits – kindness to animals. Foreign lands.

Ortiz, Simon. *The people shall continue* ill. by Sharol Graves. Children's Book Pr., 1988. ISBN 0-89239-041-7 Subj: Creation. Indians of North America. U.S. history.

Osborne, Mary Pope. *Kate and the beanstalk* ill. by Giselle Potter. Atheneum, 2000. ISBN 0-689-82550-1 Subj: Folk and fairy tales. Giants. Plants.

Molly and the prince ill. by Elizabeth Sayles. Knopf, 1994. ISBN 0-679-91941-4 Subj: Animals – dogs. Forest, woods. Mythical creatures. Royalty – princes.

Moonhorse ill. by David McPhail. Knopf, 1988. ISBN 0-394-98960-0 Subj: Activities – flying. Animals – horses, ponies. Behavior – wishing. Night. Sky.

Moonhorse ill. by S. M. Saelig. Knopf, 1991. ISBN 0-679-86709-0 Subj: Activities – flying. Animals – horses, ponies. Behavior – wishing. Night. Sky. Space and space ships.

Osborne, Valerie. *One big yo to go* ill. by Jiri Tibor Novak. Oxford Univ. Pr., 1981. ISBN 0-19-554265-7 Subj: Rhyming text.

Osborne, Victor. *Rex, the most special car in the world* ill. by Scoular Anderson. Carolrhoda, 1989. ISBN 0-87614-357-5 Subj: Automobiles.

O'Shell, Marcia. *Alphabet Annie announces an all-American album* by Marcia O'Shell and Susan Purviance; ill. by Ruth Brunner-Strosser. Houghton Mifflin, 1988. ISBN 0-395-48070-1 Subj: ABC books. City.

Osofsky, Audrey. *Dreamcatcher* ill. by Ed Young. Watts, 1992. ISBN 0-531-08588-0 Subj: Babies. Dreams. Family life. Folk and fairy tales. Indians of North America – Ojibwa.

My buddy ill. by Ted Rand. Holt, 1992. ISBN 0-8050-1747-X Subj: Animals – dogs. Camps, camping. Handicaps – physical handicaps. Illness – muscular dystrophy.

Ostheeren, Ingrid. *The blue monster* ill. by Christa Unzner; trans. by Rosemary Lanning. North-South, 1996. ISBN 1-55858-557-5 Subj: Animals – dogs. Birthdays. Family life. Pets.

Coriander's Easter adventure ill. by Jean-Pierre Corderoc'h; trans. by Rosemary Lanning. North-South, 1992. ISBN 1-55858-150-2 Subj: Animals – rabbits. Behavior – wishing. Holidays – Easter.

Fabian Youngpig sails the world ill. by Serena Romanelli; trans. by J. Alison James. North-South, 1992. ISBN 1-55858-145-6 Subj: Animals – pigs. Boats, ships. Sea and seashore.

I'm the real Santa Claus! ill. by Christa Unzner-Fischer; trans. by Rosemary Lanning. North-South, 1994. ISBN 1-55858-318-1 Subj: Behavior – imitation. Holidays – Christmas. Santa Claus.

Jonathan Mouse ill. by Agnès Mathieu; trans. by Rosemary Lanning. Holt, 1986. ISBN 0-03-005848-1 Subj: Animals – mice. Concepts – color. Magic.

Jonathan Mouse and the baby bird trans. from German by Rosemary Lanning; ill. by Agnès Mathieu. North-South, 1991. ISBN 1-55858-108-1 Subj: Animals – mice. Birds – sparrows. Farms.

Jonathan Mouse and the magic box trans. by Rosemary Lanning; ill. by Agnès Mathieu. North-South, 1990. ISBN 1-55858-087-5 Subj: Animals – mice. Magic.

Jonathan Mouse at the circus ill. by Agnès Mathieu. North-South, 1988. ISBN 3-85539-001-0 Subj: Animals – mice. Circus.

Jonathan Mouse, detective ill. by Agnès Mathieu; trans. by Rosemary Lanning. North-South, 1993. ISBN 1-55858-164-2 Subj: Animals. Animals – mice. Careers – detectives. Mystery stories.

Martin and the Pumpkin Ghost ill. by Christa Unzner-Fischer; tr. and adapt. by J. Alison James. North-South, 1994. ISBN 1-55858-268-1 Subj: Emotions – fear. Ghosts.

The new dog ill. by Christa Unzner-Fischer; tr. and adapt. by J. Alison James. North-South, 1993. ISBN 1-55858-219-3 Subj: Animals – dogs. Farms. Foreign lands – Switzerland. Pets.

Ostrovsky, Vivian. *Mumps!* ill. by Rose Ostrovsky. Holt, 1978. ISBN 0-03-042126-8 Subj: Illness – mumps.

Ostrow, Vivian. *My brother is from outer space: the book of proof* ill. by Eric Brace. Albert Whitman, 1996. ISBN 0-8075-5325-5 Subj: Character traits – being different. Sibling rivalry. Space and space ships.

Otey, Mimi. *see* Little, Mimi Otey

Otfinoski, Steven. *The truth about three billy goats Gruff* (Asbjørnsen, P. C. [Peter Christen])

Otsuka, Yuzo. *Suho and the white horse: a legend of Mongolia* trans. by Ann Herring; ill. by Suekichi Akaba. Viking, 1981. ISBN 0-670-68149-0 Subj: Animals – horses, ponies. Emotions – love. Sports – racing.

Ott, John. *Peter Pumpkin* originated by Peter Coley; ill. by Ivan Chermayeff. Doubleday, 1963. Subj: Holidays – Halloween. Holidays – Thanksgiving. Seasons – fall.

Otten, Charlotte F. *January rides the wind: a book of months* ill. by Todd L. W. Doney. Lothrop, 1997. ISBN 0-688-12557-3 Subj: Days of the week, months of the year. Poetry.

Ottley, Matt. *What Faust saw* ill. by author. Dutton, 1996. ISBN 0-525-45650-3 Subj: Animals – dogs. Imagination. Night. Space and space ships.

Otto, Carolyn. *Dinosaur chase* ill. by Thacher Hurd. HarperCollins, 1991. ISBN 0-06-021614-X Subj: Bedtime. Dinosaurs. Poetry.

Ducks, ducks, ducks ill. by Molly Coxe. HarperCollins, 1991. ISBN 0-06-024639-1 Subj: Birds – ducks. City. Poetry.

I can tell by touching ill. by Nadine Bernard Westcott. HarperCollins, 1994. ISBN 0-06-023325-7 Subj: Senses – touching.

Our puppies are growing ill. by Mary Morgan. HarperCollins, 1998. ISBN 0-06-027272-4 Subj: Animals – babies. Animals – dogs. Behavior – growing up.

Pioneer church ill. by Megan Lloyd. Holt, 1999. ISBN 0-8050-2554-5 Subj: Buildings. Religion. U.S. history.

That sky, that rain ill. by Megan Lloyd. HarperCollins, 1990. ISBN 0-690-04765-7 Subj: Family life – grandfathers. Farms. Sky. Weather – rain.

What color is camouflage? ill. by Megan Lloyd. HarperCollins, 1996. ISBN 0-06-027099-3 Subj: Animals. Character traits – appearance.

Otto, Margaret Glover. *The little brown horse* ill. by Barbara Cooney. Knopf, 1959. Subj: Animals – cats. Animals – horses, ponies. Birds – chickens.

Oughton, Jerrie. *How the stars fell into the sky* ill. by Lisa Desimini. Houghton Mifflin, 1992. ISBN 0-395-58798-0 Subj: Folk and fairy tales. Indians of North America – Navajo. Sky. Stars.

The magic weaver of rugs ill. by Lisa Desimini. Houghton Mifflin, 1994. ISBN 0-395-66140-4 Subj: Activities – weaving. Folk and fairy tales. Indians of North America – Navajo.

Our house ill. by Roser Capdevila. Firefly, 1985. ISBN 0-920303-10-2 Subj: City. Format, unusual – board books. Homes, houses.

Ovenell-Carter, Julie. *Adam's daycare* ill. by Ruth Ohi. Firefly, 1997. ISBN 1-55037-445-1 Subj: Activities – babysitting. Family life.

Over in the Grasslands ill. by Alison Bartlett. Little, 2000. ISBN 0-316-93910-2 Subj: Animals. Counting, numbers. Foreign lands – Africa.

Over in the meadow: *an old nursery counting rhyme* adapt. and ill. by Paul Galdone. Prentice-Hall, 1986. ISBN 0-13-646654-0 Subj: Animals. Counting, numbers. Nursery rhymes.

Over in the meadow ill. by Ezra Jack Keats. Four Winds, 1971. Subj: Animals. Counting, numbers. Folk and fairy tales. Rhyming text. Songs.

Overbeck, Cynthia. *Rusty the Irish setter* rev. English text by Cynthia Overbeck; original French text by Anne Marie Pajot; trans. by Dyan Hammarberg; photos by Antoinette Barrère; ill. by L'Enc Matte. Carolrhoda, 1977. Original ed. published under title: Jimmy, le grand chien. ISBN 0-8761-4080-0 Subj: Animals – dogs.

The winds that blow (Thompson, Brenda)

Overend, Jenni. *Welcome with love* ill. by Julie Vivas. Kane/Miller, 2000. ISBN 0-916291-96-0 Subj: Babies. Birth. Family life.

Owen, Annie. *Bumper to bumper* ill. by author. Knopf, 1991. ISBN 0-679-91448-X Subj: Activities – traveling. Automobiles. Birthdays. Noise, sounds.

From snowflakes to sandcastles ill. by author. Millbrook, 1996. ISBN 1-56294-086-4 Subj: Counting, numbers. Days of the week, months of the year. Language. Puzzles.

Goodnight bear! ill. by author. Grisewood & Dempsey, 1994. ISBN 1-85697-945-8 Subj: Animals – bears. Bedtime. Format, unusual – board books. Night.

Hungry panda ill. by author. Grisewood & Dempsey, 1994. ISBN 1-85697-946-6 Subj: Animals – pandas. Food. Format, unusual – board books.

My aunt and the animals (MacDonald, Elizabeth)

Playtime duck ill. by author. Grisewood & Dempsey, 1994. ISBN 1-85697-947-4 Subj: Activities – playing. Birds – ducks. Format, unusual – board books.

Wake up Frog! ill. by author. Grisewood & Dempsey, 1994. ISBN 1-85697-948-2 Subj: Format, unusual – board books. Frogs and toads.

Owen, Robert. *The Larousse book of nursery rhymes* (Mother Goose)

Owen, Roy. *The ibis and the egret* ill. by Robert Sabuda. Philomel, 1993. ISBN 0-399-22504-8 Subj: Birds – herons. Birds – ibis. Seasons.

My night forest ill. by Amy Córdova. Four Winds, 1994. ISBN 0-02-769005-9 Subj: Animals. Bedtime. Forest, woods. Sleep.

Owens, Mary Beth. *A caribou alphabet* ill. by Mark McCollough. Farrar, 1990. ISBN 0-374-41043-7 Subj: ABC books. Animals – reindeer. Rhyming text.

Counting cranes ill. by author. Little, 1993. ISBN 0-316-67719-1 Subj: Birds – cranes. Counting, numbers.

Oxenbury, Helen. *All fall down* ill. by author. Macmillan, 1987. ISBN 0-02-769040-7 Subj: Activities – playing. Babies. Format, unusual – board books. Games.

Beach day ill. by author. Dial, 1982. ISBN 0-8037-0439-9 Subj: Family life. Format, unusual – board books. Sea and seashore. Wordless.

The birthday party ill. by author. Dial, 1983. ISBN 0-8037-0717-7 Subj: Birthdays.

The car trip ill. by author. Dial, 1983. ISBN 0-8037-0009-1 Subj: Automobiles. Behavior – bad day. Behavior – misbehavior.

The checkup ill. by author. Dial, 1983. ISBN 0-8037-0010-5 Subj: Careers – doctors. Health and fitness.

Clap hands ill. by author. Macmillan, 1987. ISBN 0-02-769030-X Subj: Activities – playing. Babies. Format, unusual – board books.

The dancing class ill. by author. Dial, 1983. ISBN 0-8037-1651-6 Subj: Activities – dancing. Ballet.

Dressing ill. by author. Simon & Schuster, 1981. ISBN 0-671-42113-1 Subj: Clothing. Format, unusual – board books.

Eating out ill. by author. Dial, 1983. ISBN 0-8037-2203-6 Subj: Food.

Family ill. by author. Simon & Schuster, 1981. ISBN 0-671-42110-7 Subj: Family life. Format, unusual – board books.

First day of school ill. by author. Dial, 1983. ISBN 0-8037-0012-1 Subj: Friendship. School – first day.

Friends ill. by author. Simon & Schuster, 1981. ISBN 0-671-42111-5 Subj: Animals. Format, unusual – board books. Friendship.

Good night, good morning ill. by author. Dial, 1982. ISBN 0-8037-2980-4 Subj: Bedtime. Morning. Wordless.

Grandma and Grandpa ill. by author. Dial, 1984. ISBN 0-8037-0128-4 Subj: Activities – playing. Family life – grandparents.

Helen Oxenbury's ABC of things ill. by author. Watts, 1971. ISBN 0-434-95598-1 Subj: ABC books.

I can ill. by author. Random House, 1985. ISBN 0-394-87482-X Subj: Activities. Babies. Format, unusual – board books.

I hear ill. by author. Random House, 1985. ISBN 0-394-87481-1 Subj: Babies. Format, unusual – board books. Noise, sounds. Senses – hearing.

I see ill. by author. Random House, 1985. ISBN 0-394-87479-X Subj: Babies. Format, unusual – board books. Senses – seeing.

I touch ill. by author. Random House, 1985. ISBN 0-394-87480-3 Subj: Babies. Format, unusual – board books. Senses – touching.

The important visitor ill. by author. Dial, 1984. ISBN 0-8037-0125-X Subj: Behavior – misbehavior.

It's my birthday ill. by author. Candlewick, 1994. ISBN 1-56402-412-1 Subj: Activities – cooking. Animals. Birthdays. Cumulative tales. Food.

Monkey see, monkey do ill. by author. Dial, 1982. ISBN 0-8037-5436-1 Subj: Animals. Wordless. Zoos.

Mother's helper ill. by author. Dial, 1982. ISBN 0-8037-5425-6 Subj: Character traits – helpfulness. Family life – mothers. Wordless.

Numbers of things ill. by author. Watts, 1968. Subj: Counting, numbers.

Our dog ill. by author. Dial, 1984. ISBN 0-8037-0127-6 Subj: Activities – walking. Animals – dogs. Family life. Pets.

Pig tale ill. by author. Morrow, 1974. ISBN 0-688-30092-8 Subj: Animals – pigs. Rhyming text.

Pippo gets lost ill. by author. Macmillan, 1989. ISBN 0-689-71336-3 Subj: Animals. Behavior – losing things. Toys.

Playing ill. by author. Wanderer, 1981. ISBN 0-671-42109-3 Subj: Activities – playing. Babies. Format, unusual – board books. Toys.

The queen and Rosie Randall by Helen Oxenbury from an idea by Jill Butterfield-Campbell; ill. by author. Morrow, 1979. ISBN 0-688-32171-2 Subj: Foreign lands – England. Games. Parties. Royalty – queens.

Say goodnight ill. by author. Macmillan, 1987. ISBN 0-02-769010-5 Subj: Activities – playing. Babies. Format, unusual – board books. Sleep.

729 curious creatures ill. by author. HarperCollins, 1980. ISBN 0-06-024598-5 Subj: Animals. Format, unusual – board books. Imagination.

729 merry mix-ups ill. by author. HarperCollins, 1980. ISBN 0-06-024599-3 Subj: Animals. Format, unusual – board books. Imagination.

729 puzzle people ill. by author. HarperCollins, 1980. ISBN 0-06-024597-7 Subj: Format, unusual – board books. Imagination.

The shopping trip ill. by author. Dial, 1982. ISBN 0-8037-7939-9 Subj: Format, unusual – board books. Shopping. Wordless.

Tickle, tickle ill. by author. Macmillan, 1987. ISBN 0-02-769020-2 Subj: Activities – playing. Babies. Format, unusual – board books.

Tiny Tim: verses for children chosen by Jill Bennett; ill. by author. Delacorte, 1982. ISBN 0-440-08970-7 Subj: Humor. Poetry.

Tom and Pippo and the dog ill. by author. Macmillan, 1989. ISBN 0-689-71338-X Subj: Activities – playing. Animals – dogs. Animals – monkeys. Friendship. Toys.

Tom and Pippo go shopping ill. by author. Macmillan, 1989. ISBN 0-689-71278-2 Subj: Animals – monkeys. Shopping. Toys.

Tom and Pippo in the garden ill. by author. Macmillan, 1989. ISBN 0-689-71275-8 Subj: Animals – monkeys. Gardens, gardening. Toys.

Tom and Pippo on the beach ill. by author. Candlewick, 1993. ISBN 1-56402-181-5 Subj: Animals – monkeys. Sea and seashore. Toys.

Tom and Pippo see the moon ill. by author. Macmillan, 1989. ISBN 0-689-71277-4 Subj: Animals – monkeys. Moon. Space and space ships. Toys.

Tom and Pippo's day ill. by author. Macmillan, 1989. ISBN 0-689-71276-6 Subj: Activities. Animals – monkeys. Toys.

Oxford Scientific Films. *Danger colors* ed. by Jennifer Coldrey and Karen Goldie-Morrison. Putnam, 1986. ISBN 0-399-21341-4 Subj: Behavior – hiding. Concepts – color.

Grey squirrel photos by George Bernard and John Paling. Putnam, 1982. ISBN 0-399-20906-9 Subj: Animals – squirrels. Science.

Hide and seek ed. by Jennifer Coldrey and Karen Goldie-Morrison. Putnam, 1986. ISBN 0-399-21342-2 Subj: Behavior – hiding. Concepts – color.

The spider's web photos by John Cooke. Putnam, 1978. ISBN 0-399-20621-4 Subj: Science. Spiders.

Pace, David. *Shouting Sharon* ill. by author. Western, 1995. ISBN 0-307-17518-9 Subj: Behavior. Counting, numbers. Cumulative tales. Poetry.

Pace, Elizabeth. *Chris gets ear tubes* ill. by Kathryn Hutton. Gallaudet Univ. Pr., 1987. ISBN 0-930323-36-X Subj: Handicaps – deafness. Hospitals. Illness. Senses – hearing.

Pacheco, Miguel Angel. *Kangaroo* (Sanchez, Jose Louis Garcia)

Pacini, Kathy. *In a meadow, two hares hide* (Bartoli, Jennifer)

Pack, Robert. *How to catch a crocodile* ill. by Nola Langner. Knopf, 1964. ISBN 0-394-91251-9 Subj: Character traits – laziness. Imagination. Poetry. Reptiles – alligators, crocodiles.

Then what did you do? ill. by Nola Langner. Macmillan, 1961. Subj: Animals. Cumulative tales. Humor. Poetry.

Packard, Edward. *Big numbers: and pictures that show just how big they are!* ill. by Sal Murdocca. Millbrook, 2000. ISBN 0-7613-1570-5 Subj: Concepts – size. Counting, numbers.

Packard, Mary. *Bubble trouble* ill. by Elena Kuckarik. Scholastic, 1995. ISBN 0-590-48513-X Subj: Activities – playing. Bubbles. Rhyming text.

The kite ill. by Benrei Huang. Childrens Pr., 1990. ISBN 0-516-05355-8 Subj: Kites. Rhyming text.

We are monsters ill. by John Magine. Scholastic, 1996. ISBN 0-590-68995-9 Subj: Bedtime. Emotions – fear. Monsters. Rhyming text.

When I am big ill. by Laura Rader. Reader's Digest, 1999. ISBN 1-57584-294-7 Subj: Behavior – growing up. Behavior – imitation. Family life – brothers.

Where is Jake? ill. by Carolyn Ewing. Childrens Pr., 1990. ISBN 0-516-05361-2 Subj: Activities – playing. Games.

Pacovská, Kveta. *Flying* ill. by author. North-South, 1995. ISBN 1-55858-496-X Subj: Activities – flying. Animals.

One, five, many ill. by author. Houghton Mifflin, 1990. ISBN 0-395-54997-3 Subj: Counting, numbers. Format, unusual. Rhyming text.

Padt, Maartje. *Shanti* by Maartje Padt and Mylo Freeman; ill. by Mylo Freeman. DK, 1998. ISBN 0-7894-2520-3 Subj: Animals – zebras. Birth. Foreign lands – Africa. Format, unusual.

Paek, Min. *Aekyung's dream* ill. by author. Childrens Book Pr., 1989. ISBN 0-89239-042-5 Subj: Character traits – being different. Ethnic groups in the U.S. Ethnic groups in the U.S. – Korean Americans. School.

Page, Eleanor. *see* Coerr, Eleanor

Page, P. K. (Patricia Kathleen). *The traveling musicians of Bremen* (Grimm, Jacob)

Page, Robin. *The alphabet sticker book* ill. by author. Houghton Mifflin, 1995. ISBN 0-395-71543-1 Subj: ABC books. Format, unusual.

Paige, Rob. *Some of my best friends are monsters* ill. by Paul Yalowitz. Bradbury, 1988. ISBN 0-02-769640-5 Subj: Monsters.

Paine, Penelope Colville. *My way Sally* (Bingham, Mindy)

Pajot, Anne Marie. *Rusty the Irish setter* (Overbeck, Cynthia)

Pak, Soyung. *Dear Juno* ill. by Susan Kathleen Hartung. Viking, 1999. ISBN 0-670-88252-6 Subj: Ethnic groups in the U.S. – Korean Americans. Family life – grandmothers. Foreign languages. Letters, cards.

Paker, Josephine. *I wonder why flutes have holes* ill. by author. Kingfisher, 1995. ISBN 1-85697-583-5 Subj: Music.

Palacios, Argentina. *A Christmas surprise for Chabelita* ill. by Lori Lohstoeter. BridgeWater, 1993. ISBN 0-8167-3131-4 Subj: Family life – grandparents. Family life – mothers. Foreign lands – Panama. School.

This can lick a lollipop: body riddles for kids; esto goza chupando un caramelo: las partes del cuerpo en adivinanzas infantiles (Rothman, Joel)

Paladino, Catherine. *Our vanishing farm animals* ill. with photos. Little, 1992. ISBN 0-316-68891-6 Subj: Animals – endangered animals. Farms.

Palatini, Margie. *Bedhead* ill. by Jack E. Davis. Simon & Schuster, 2000. ISBN 0-689-82397-5 Subj: Hair. School.

Ding dong ding dong ill. by Howard Fine. Hyperion, 1999. ISBN 0-7868-2367-4 Subj: Animals – gorillas. Careers – salesmen. Humor.

Good as Goldie ill. by author. Hyperion, 2000. ISBN 0-7868-2435-2 Subj: Behavior – dissatisfaction. Family life – brothers and sisters. Sibling rivalry.

Moosetache ill. by Henry Cole. Hyperion, 1997. ISBN 0-7868-2246-5 Subj: Animals – moose. Hair.

Piggie pie ill. by Howard Fine. Clarion, 1995. ISBN 0-395-71691-8 Subj: Animals – pigs. Animals – wolves. Character traits – appearance. Holidays – Halloween. Witches.

Zak's lunch ill. by Howard Fine. Clarion, 1998. ISBN 0-395-81674-2 Subj: Family life – mothers. Food. Imagination.

Zoom Broom ill. by Howard Fine. Hyperion, 1998. ISBN 0-7868-0322-3 Subj: Animals – foxes. Witches.

Palazzo, Tony (Anthony D.). *Animal babies* ill. by author. Doubleday, 1960. Subj: Animals.

Animals 'round the mulberry bush ill. by author. Doubleday, 1958. Subj: Animals. Nursery rhymes.

Noah's ark ill. by author. Doubleday, 1955. Subj: Boats, ships. Religion – Noah. Weather – floods. Weather – rain. Weather – rainbows.

Waldo the woodchuck ill. by author. Duell, 1964. Subj: Animals – groundhogs. Holidays – Groundhog Day. Picture puzzles.

Palazzo-Craig, Janet. *Ballet dancer* ill. by Barbara Todd. Troll, 1988. ISBN 0-8167-1434-7 Subj: Activities – dancing. Ballet.

Little Danny Dinosaur ill. by Paul Harvey. Troll, 1988. ISBN 0-8167-1229-8 Subj: Animals. Concepts – size. Dinosaurs.

Muffy and Fluffy: the kittens who didn't agree ill. by Susan Hall. Troll, 1988. ISBN 0-8167-1227-1 Subj: Animals – cats. Behavior – sharing.

Our friend the sun ill. by Susan Hall. Troll, 1982. ISBN 0-89375-650-4 Subj: Science. Sun.

Turtles ill. by Kathie Kelleher. Troll, 1982. ISBN 0-89375-664-4 Subj: Reptiles – turtles, tortoises. Science.

What makes the weather ill. by Paul Harvey. Troll, 1982. ISBN 0-89375-654-7 Subj: Weather.

What's under the ocean? ill. by Paul Harvey. Troll, 1982. ISBN 0-89375-652-0 Subj: Sea and seashore.

Palecek, Libuse. *Brave as a tiger* ill. by Josef Palecek; English adapt. by Andrew Clements. North-South, 1995. ISBN 1-55858-396-3 Subj: Animals – tigers. Character traits – bravery. Emotions – fear. Family life – mothers. Illness.

Palecek, Phyllis. *The ugly duckling* (Andersen, H. C. [Hans Christian])

Pallandt, Nicholas van. *The butterfly night of Old Brown Bear* ill. by author. Farrar, 1992. ISBN 0-374-31009-2 Subj: Animals – bears. Dreams. Insects – butterflies, caterpillars.

Pallotta, Jerry. *The airplane alphabet book* by Jerry Pallotta and Fred Stillwell; ill. by Rob Bolster. Charlesbridge, 1997. ISBN 0-8810-6908-6 Subj: ABC books. Airplanes, airports.

The crayon counting book (Ryan, Pam Muñoz)

The dory story ill. by David Biedrzycki. Talewinds, 2000. ISBN 0-8810-6075-5 Subj: Activities – bathing. Animals. Boats, ships. Fish. Imagination. Nature. Sea and seashore.

Going lobstering ill. by Rob Bolster. Charlesbridge, 1990. ISBN 0-88106-475-0 Subj: Careers – fishermen. Sea and seashore.

The palm of my heart: *poetry by African American children* ed. by Davida Adedjouma; ill. by Gregory Christie. Lee & Low, 1996. ISBN 1-880000-41-5 Subj: Children as authors. Ethnic groups in the U.S. – African Americans. Poetry.

Palmer, Carole. *Why does it fly?* (Arvetis, Chris)

Why does it thunder and lightning? (Arvetis, Chris)

Why is it dark? (Arvetis, Chris)

Palmer, Mary Babcock. *No-sort-of-animal* ill. by Abner Graboff. Houghton Mifflin, 1964. Subj: Animals. Behavior – dissatisfaction. Self-concept.

Palmer, Todd Starr. *Rhino and Mouse* ill. by Judy Lanfredi. Dial, 1994. ISBN 0-8037-1323-1 Subj: Animals – mice. Animals – rhinoceros. Friendship.

Palmisciano, Diane. *Garden partners* ill. by author. Atheneum, 1989. ISBN 0-689-31415-9 Subj: Family life – grandmothers. Gardens, gardening.

P'an, Ts'ai-ying. *Monkey creates havoc in heaven* adapt. by Pan Cai Ying from the novel The pilgrimage to the West by Wu Cheng En; ill. by Xin Kuan Liang . . . et al.; translated by Ye Pin Kuei and revised by Jill Morris. Viking, 1989. ISBN 0-670-81805-4 Subj: Animals – monkeys. Folk and fairy tales. Foreign lands – China.

Pancheri, Jan. *The twelve poodle princess* ill. by author. Hutchinson, 1995. ISBN 0-09-176710-5 Subj: Activities – dancing. Animals – dogs. Folk and fairy tales. Royalty – princesses.

Pandell, Karen. *I love you sun, I love you moon* ill. by Tomie de Paola. Putnam, 1994. ISBN 0-399-22628-1 Subj: Ecology. Nature.

Panek, Dennis. *Ba ba sheep wouldn't go to sleep* ill. by author. Watts, 1988. ISBN 0-531-08376-4 Subj: School. Sleep.

Catastrophe Cat ill. by author. Bradbury, 1978. ISBN 0-8788-8130-1 Subj: Animals – cats. Behavior – carelessness.

Catastrophe Cat at the zoo ill. by author. Bradbury, 1979. ISBN 0-8788-8147-6 Subj: Animals – cats. Wordless. Zoos.

Detective Whoo ill. by author. Bradbury, 1981. ISBN 0-87888-183-2 Subj: Birds – owls. Careers – detectives. Circus. Mystery stories. Noise, sounds.

Matilda Hippo has a big mouth ill. by author. Bradbury, 1980. ISBN 0-8788-8161-1 Subj: Animals – hippopotamuses. Behavior.

Pans, Ona. *Cubs* (Landa, Norbert)

Kittens (Landa, Norbert)

Puppies (Landa, Norbert)

Paola, Tomie (Thomas Anthony) de. *see* De Paola, Tomie (Thomas Anthony)

Papajani, Janet. *Museums* ill. with photos. Childrens Pr., 1983. ISBN 0-516-01682-2 Subj: Museums.

Paparone, Pamela. *Five little ducks* ill. by author. North-South, 1995. ISBN 1-55858-474-9 Subj: Birds – ducks. Counting, numbers. Nursery rhymes.

Papas, William. *Taresh the tea planter* ill. by author. Collins-World, 1968. ISBN 0-19-279643-7 Subj: Character traits – laziness. Foreign lands – India.

Pape, D. L. (Donna Lugg). *Doghouse for sale* ill. by Tom Eaton. Garrard, 1979. ISBN 0-8116-4415-4 Subj: Animals – dogs. Homes, houses.

Snoino mystery ill. by William Hutchinson. Garrard, 1980. ISBN 0-8116-6410-4 Subj: Mystery stories.

Where is my little Joey? ill. by Tom Eaton. Garrard, 1978. ISBN 0-8116-4411-1 Subj: Animals – kangaroos.

A paper of pins ill. by Margaret Gordon. Seabury Pr., 1975. ISBN 0-8164-3131-0 Subj: Folk and fairy tales. Money. Songs.

Paradis, Susan. *My Daddy* ill. by author. Front Street, 1998. ISBN 1-886910-30-8 Subj: Activities. Family life – fathers.

Paraskevas, Betty. *Cecil Bunions and the midnight train* ill. by Michael Paraskevas. Harcourt, 1996. ISBN 0-15-292884-7 Subj: Dreams. Monsters. Night. Rhyming text. Trains.

The ferocious beast with the polka-dot hide ill. by Michael Paraskevas. Harcourt, 1996. ISBN 0-15-200838-1 Subj: Animals – pigs. Behavior – greed. Food. Rhyming text.

Gracie Graves and the kids from room 402 ill. by Michael Paraskevas. Harcourt, 1995. ISBN 0-15-200321-5 Subj: Careers – teachers. Poetry. School.

Hoppy and Joe ill. by Michael Paraskevas. Simon & Schuster, 1999. ISBN 0-689-82199-9 Subj: Animals – dogs. Birds – seagulls. Friendship. Sea and seashore. Seasons – summer.

Junior Kroll and Company ill. by Michael Paraskevas. Harcourt, 1994. ISBN 0-15-292855-3 Subj: Animals. Birds. Music. Poetry.

Maggie and the Ferocious Beast, the big carrot ill. by Michael Paraskevas. Simon & Schuster, 2000. ISBN 0-689-82490-4 Subj: Activities – digging. Animals – rabbits. Character traits – helpfulness. Gardens, gardening. Monsters.

Maggie and the Ferocious Beast, the big scare ill. by Michael Paraskevas. Simon & Schuster, 1999. ISBN 0-689-82489-0 Subj: Animals – mice. Animals – pigs. Emotions – fear. Monsters.

Monster Beach ill. by Michael Paraskevas. Harcourt, 1995. ISBN 0-15-292882-0 Subj: Family life – grandfathers. Monsters. Sea and seashore.

On the day the tall ships sailed ill. by Michael Paraskevas. Simon & Schuster, 2000. ISBN 0-689-82864-0 Subj: Birds – eagles. Boats, ships. Holidays – Fourth of July. Music. U.S. history.

The tangerine bear ill. by Michael Paraskevas. HarperCollins, 1997. ISBN 0-06-205146-6 Subj: Behavior – needing someone. Character traits – appearance. Family life. Stores. Toys – bears.

A very Kroll Christmas ill. by Michael Paraskevas. Harcourt, 1994. ISBN 0-15-292883-9 Subj: Animals – dogs. Holidays – Christmas. Holidays – Thanksgiving. Poetry.

Paré, Roger. *Animal capers* by Roger Paré with Bertrand Gauthier; trans. by David Homel; ill. by Roger Paré. Firefly, 1992. ISBN 1-55037-243-2 Subj: Animals. Poetry.

Circus days by Roger Paré with Bertrand Gauthier; trans. by David Homel; ill. by Roger Paré. Firefly, 1988. ISBN 1-55037-021-9 Subj: Animals. Circus. Poetry.

A friend like you trans. by David Homel; ill. by author. Firefly, 1984. ISBN 0-920303-04-8 Subj: Animals – cats. Friendship.

Play time by Roger Paré with Bertrand Gauthier; trans. by David Homel; ill. by Roger Paré. Firefly, 1990. ISBN 1-55037-087-1 Subj: Animals. Poetry.

Summer days by Roger Paré with Bertrand Gauthier; trans. by David Homel; ill. by Roger Paré. Firefly, 1989. ISBN 1-55037-043-X Subj: Activities – playing. Animals. Poetry.

Parenteau, Shirley. *I'll bet you thought I was lost* ill. by Lorna Tomei. Lothrop, 1981. ISBN 0-688-00259-5 Subj: Behavior – lost.

Parillo, Tony. *Michelangelo's surprise* ill. by author. Farrar, 1998. ISBN 0-374-34961-4 Subj: Careers – artists. Foreign lands – Italy. Snowmen. Weather – snow.

Paris, Lena. *Mom is single* ill. by Mark Christianson. Childrens Pr., 1980. ISBN 0-516-01477-3 Subj: Divorce. Family life – fathers. Family life – mothers.

Parish, Herman. *Good driving, Amelia Bedelia* ill. by Lynn Sweat. Greenwillow, 1995. ISBN 0-688-13359-2 Subj: Automobiles.

Parish, Peggy. *Be ready at eight* ill. by Leonard P. Kessler. Macmillan, 1979. ISBN 0-02-769830-0 Subj: Behavior – forgetfulness. Birthdays.

The cats' burglar ill. by Lynn Sweat. Greenwillow, 1983. ISBN 0-688-01826-2 Subj: Animals – cats. Crime.

Dinosaur time ill. by Arnold Lobel. HarperCollins, 1974. ISBN 0-06-024654-5 Subj: Dinosaurs. Science.

Good hunting, Blue Sky ill. by James Watts. HarperCollins, 1988. ISBN 0-06-024662-6 Subj: Indians of North America. Sports – hunting.

Good hunting, Little Indian ill. by Leonard Weisgard. Addison-Wesley, 1962. Subj: Indians of North America.

Granny and the desperadoes ill. by Steven Kellogg. Macmillan, 1970. ISBN 0-689-80878-X Subj: Crime. Family life – grandmothers. Humor.

Granny and the Indians ill. by Brinton Turkle. Macmillan, 1969. Subj: Family life – grandmothers. Humor. Indians of North America.

Granny, the baby and the big gray thing ill. by Lynn Sweat. Macmillan, 1972. Subj: Animals – wolves. Babies. Family life – grandmothers. Humor. Indians of North America.

I can - can you? ill. by Marylin Hafner. Greenwillow, 1984. Set of 4 books: levels 1-4. ISBN 0-688-03888-2 Subj: Activities. Behavior – growing up. Format, unusual – board books.

Jumper goes to school ill. by Cyndy Szekeres. Simon & Schuster, 1969. ISBN 0-671-65076-9 Subj: Animals – chimpanzees. School.

Little Indian ill. by John E. Johnson. Simon & Schuster, 1968. Subj: Indians of North America. Names.

Mind your manners ill. by Marylin Hafner. Greenwillow, 1978. ISBN 0-688-84157-0 Subj: Etiquette.

No more monsters for me! ill. by Marc Simont. HarperCollins, 1981. ISBN 0-06-024658-8 Subj: Monsters. Pets.

Ootah's lucky day ill. by Mamoru Funai. HarperCollins, 1970. Subj: Eskimos. Sports – hunting.

Scruffy ill. by Kelly Oechsli. HarperCollins, 1988. ISBN 0-06-024660-X Subj: Animals – cats. Birthdays. Pets.

Snapping turtle's all wrong day ill. by John E. Johnson. Simon & Schuster, 1970. ISBN 0-671-65094-7 Subj: Birthdays. Indians of North America.

Too many rabbits ill. by Leonard P. Kessler. Macmillan, 1974. ISBN 0-02-769850-5 Subj: Animals – rabbits.

Zed and the monsters ill. by Paul Galdone. Doubleday, 1979. ISBN 0-385-12949-1 Subj: Character traits – cleverness. Monsters.

Park, Barbara. *Junie B. Jones and some sneaky peeky spying* ill. by Denise Brunkus. Random House, 1994. ISBN 0-679-95101-6 Subj: Careers – teachers. Mystery stories. School.

Psssst! It's me . . . the Bogeyman ill. by Stephen Kroninger. Atheneum, 1998. ISBN 0-689-81667-7 Subj: Emotions – fear. Monsters.

Park, Frances. *My freedom trip* by Frances Park and Ginger Park; ill. by Debra Reid Jenkins. Boyds Mills, 1998. ISBN 1-56397-468-1 Subj: Character traits – freedom. Foreign lands – Korea (North). Immigrants.

The royal bee by Frances Park and Ginger Park; ill. by Christopher Zhong-Yuan Zhang. Boyds Mills, 2000. ISBN 1-56397-614-5 Subj: Contests. Foreign lands – Korea. Poverty. School.

Park, Ginger. *My freedom trip* (Park, Frances)

The royal bee (Park, Frances)

Park, Ruth. *When the wind changed* ill. by Deborah Niland. Coward, 1981. ISBN 0-698-20525-1 Subj: Character traits – appearance.

Park, W. B. *Bakery business* ill. by author. Little, 1983. ISBN 0-316-69078-3 Subj: Animals. Birthdays.

The costume party ill. by author. Little, 1983. ISBN 0-316-69077-5 Subj: Animals. Emotions – loneliness. Parties.

Parke, Margaret B. *Young reader's color-picture dictionary* ill. by Cynthia and Alvin Koehler. Grosset, 1958. Subj: Dictionaries.

Parker, Ant. *Desmond the dog* (Denchfield, Nick)

Desmond the dog, a wag-the-tail pop-up book (Denchfield, Nick)

Flashing fire engines (Mitton, Tony)

Parker, Dorothy D. *Liam's catch* ill. by Robert Andrew Parker. Viking, 1972. ISBN 0-670-42744-6 Subj: Careers – fishermen. Foreign lands – Ireland. Sports – fishing.

Parker, Ed. *Jack and the beanstalk* (Jack and the beanstalk)

Parker, Kristy. *My dad the magnificent* ill. by Lillian Hoban. Dutton, 1987. ISBN 0-525-44314-2 Subj: Behavior – boasting. Family life – fathers.

Parker, Nancy Winslow. *Bugs* by Nancy Winslow Parker and Joan Richards Wright; ill. by Nancy Winslow Parker. Greenwillow, 1987. ISBN 0-688-06624-0 Subj: Insects. Science.

The Christmas camel ill. by author. Dodd, 1983. ISBN 0-396-08220-3 Subj: Animals – camels. Holidays – Christmas.

Cooper, the McNallys' big black dog ill. by author. Dodd, 1981. ISBN 0-396-07914-8 Subj: Animals – dogs. Behavior – misbehavior. Character traits – helpfulness.

The crocodile under Louis Finneberg's bed ill. by author. Dodd, 1978. ISBN 0-396-07542-8 Subj: Behavior – running away. Behavior – trickery. Furniture – beds. Reptiles – alligators, crocodiles.

Love from Aunt Betty ill. by author. Dodd, 1983. ISBN 0-396-08135-5 Subj: Activities – cooking. Family life – aunts, uncles. Monsters.

Love from Uncle Clyde ill. by author. Dodd, 1977. ISBN 0-396-07426-X Subj: Animals – hippopotamuses. Birthdays. Family life – aunts, uncles.

Poofy loves company ill. by author. Dodd, 1980. ISBN 0-396-00783-8 Subj: Animals – dogs. Behavior – misbehavior.

Puddums, the Cathcarts' orange cat ill. by author. Atheneum, 1980. ISBN 0-689-50159-5 Subj: Animals – cats. Behavior.

Working frog ill. by author. Greenwillow, 1992. ISBN 0-688-09919-X Subj: Animals. Frogs and toads. Zoos.

Parker, Steve. *I wonder why tunnels are round* ill. by author. Kingfisher, 1995. ISBN 1-85697-641-6 Subj: Activities – making things. Buildings. Character traits – curiosity. Concepts – shape. Machines.

Parkin, Rex. *The red carpet* ill. by author. Macmillan, 1988, 1948. ISBN 0-02-770010-0 Subj: Hotels. Humor.

Parkinson, Kathy. *The enormous turnip* ill. by adapt. Albert Whitman, 1985. ISBN 0-8075-2062-4 Subj: Behavior – sharing. Cumulative tales. Folk and fairy tales.

The paper chain (Blake, Claire)

Parkison, Jami. *Amazing Mallika* ill. by Itoko Maeno. MarshMedia, 1996. ISBN 1-55942-087-1 Subj: Animals – tigers. Emotions – anger. Family life – mothers. Foreign lands – India.

Parks, Van Dyke. *Jump! the adventures of Brer Rabbit* (Harris, Joel Chandler)

Jump again! more adventures of Brer Rabbit (Harris, Joel Chandler)

Parnall, Peter. *Alfalfa Hill* ill. by author. Doubleday, 1975. ISBN 0-385-02448-7 Subj: Animals. Birds. Seasons – winter. Weather – snow.

The great fish ill. by author. Doubleday, 1973. ISBN 0-385-07863-3 Subj: Ecology. Fish. Folk and fairy tales. Indians of North America.

The rock ill. by author. Macmillan, 1991. ISBN 0-02-770181-6 Subj: Ecology. Forest, woods. Rocks.

Winter barn ill. by author. Macmillan, 1986. ISBN 0-02-770170-0 Subj: Animals. Barns. Seasons – winter.

Parr, Letitia. *A man and his hat* ill. by Paul Terrett; photos by Bob Peters. Putnam, 1991. ISBN 0-399-22255-3 Subj: Behavior – losing things. Clothing – hats. Rhyming text.

Parr, Todd. *Do's and don'ts* ill. by author. Little, 1999. ISBN 0-316-69213-1 Subj: Behavior. Etiquette.

The okay book ill. by author. Little, 1999. ISBN 0-316-69220-4 Subj: Character traits – individuality. Self-concept.

Things that make you feel good, things that make you feel bad ill. by author. Little, 1999. ISBN 0-316-69270-0 Subj: Emotions.

This is my hair ill. by author. Little, 1999. ISBN 0-316-69236-0 Subj: Hair.

Parry, Marian. *King of the fish* ill. by author. Macmillan, 1977. ISBN 0-02-770200-6 Subj: Animals – rabbits. Character traits – cleverness. Fish. Folk and fairy tales. Foreign lands – Korea. Reptiles – turtles, tortoises.

Parsons, Alexandra. *Amazing birds* photos by Jerry Young. Knopf, 1990. ISBN 0-679-90223-6 Subj: Birds. Science.

Amazing mammals photos by Jerry Young. Knopf, 1990. ISBN 0-679-90224-4 Subj: Animals. Science.

Amazing snakes photos by Jerry Young. Knopf, 1990. ISBN 0-679-90225-2 Subj: Reptiles – snakes. Science.

Amazing spiders photos by Jerry Young. Knopf, 1990. ISBN 0-679-90226-0 Subj: Science. Spiders.

Parsons, Virginia. *Pinocchio and Gepetto* ill. by adapt. McGraw-Hill, 1979. ISBN 0-07-048531-3 Subj: Behavior – lying. Behavior – misbehavior. Character traits – loyalty. Folk and fairy tales. Puppets.

Pinocchio and the money tree ill. by adapt. McGraw-Hill, 1979. ISBN 0-07-048533-X Subj: Folk and fairy tales. Puppets.

Pinocchio goes on the stage ill. by adapt. McGraw-Hill, 1979. ISBN 0-07-048532-1 Subj: Folk and fairy tales. Puppets.

Pinocchio plays truant ill. by adapt. McGraw-Hill, 1979. ISBN 0-07-048530-5 Subj: Folk and fairy tales. Puppets.

Partch, Virgil Franklin. *The Christmas cookie sprinkle snitcher* ill. by author. Windmill, 1969. ISBN 0-67-166513-8 Subj: Crime. Holidays – Christmas. Rebuses. Rhyming text.

Partis, Joanne. *Stripe* ill. by author. Carolrhoda, 2000. ISBN 1-57505-450-7 Subj: Animals – babies. Animals – tigers. Behavior – misbehavior.

Parton, Dolly. *Coat of many colors* ill. by Judith Sutton. HarperCollins, 1994. ISBN 0-06-023413-X Subj: Clothing – coats. Family life – mothers. Poverty. Religion. Songs.

Partridge, Jenny. *Colonel Grunt* ill. by author. Holt, 1982. ISBN 0-03-061511-9 Subj: Animals.

Grandma Snuffles ill. by author. Holt, 1983. ISBN 0-03-062974-8 Subj: Animals. Clothing.

Hopfellow ill. by author. Holt, 1982. ISBN 0-03-061512-7 Subj: Animals. Boats, ships. Frogs and toads. Problem solving.

Mr. Squint ill. by author. Holt, 1982. ISBN 0-03-061509-7 Subj: Animals. Problem solving.

Peterkin Pollensnuff ill. by author. Holt, 1982. ISBN 0-03-061508-9 Subj: Animals. Character traits – helpfulness. Problem solving.

Parvathi, Thampi. *Moon-uncle, moon-uncle: rhymes from India* (Cassedy, Sylvia)

Paschkis, Julie. *Play all day* ill. by author. Little, 1998. ISBN 0-316-69043-0 Subj: Activities – playing. Rhyming text.

So happy/So sad ill. by author. Holt, 1995. ISBN 0-8050-3862-0 Subj: Animals. Emotions – happiness. Emotions – sadness. Format, unusual.

Pascoe, Gwen. *Deep in a rainforest* ill. by Veronica Jefferis. Gareth Stevens, 1999. ISBN 0-8368-2149-1 Subj: Concepts – color. Ecology. Forest, woods. Science.

Passen, Lisa. *Fat, fat Rose Marie* ill. by author. Holt, 1991. ISBN 0-8050-1653-8 Subj: Behavior – bullying. Character traits – being different. Friendship.

Grammy and Sammy ill. by author. Holt, 1990. ISBN 0-8050-1415-2 Subj: Animals – cats. Family life – grandmothers.

Patent, Dorothy Hinshaw. *Babies!* photos by author. Holiday, 1988. ISBN 0-8234-0685-7 Subj: Babies.

Bold and bright, black-and-white animals ill. by Kendahl Jan Jubb. Walker, 1998. ISBN 0-8027-8673-1 Subj: Animals. Concepts – color.

Maggie, a sheep dog photos by William Muñoz. Dodd, 1986. ISBN 0-396-08617-9 Subj: Animals – dogs. Animals – sheep.

Paterson, A. B. (Andrew Barton). *The man from Ironbark* ill. by Quentin Hole. Collins-World, 1975. ISBN 0-529-05262-8 Subj: Character traits – cleverness. Poetry.

Mulga Bill's bicycle ill. by Kilmeny and Deborah Niland. Parents, 1975. ISBN 0-8193-0778-5 Subj: Animals – horses, ponies. Foreign lands – Australia. Poetry. Sports – bicycling.

Waltzing Matilda ill. by Desmund Digby. Holt, 1970. ISBN 0-03-086749-5 Subj: Foreign lands – Australia. Songs.

Paterson, Bettina. *Bun and Mrs. Tubby* ill. by author. Watts, 1987. ISBN 0-531-08300-4 Subj: Activities – babysitting. Animals – elephants.

Bun's birthday ill. by author. Watts, 1988. ISBN 0-531-08336-5 Subj: Animals – elephants. Behavior – sharing. Birthdays. Parties.

In my house ill. by author. Holt, 1992. ISBN 0-8050-1882-4 Subj: Format, unusual – board books.

In my yard ill. by author. Holt, 1992. ISBN 0-8050-1881-6 Subj: Format, unusual – board books.

My clothes ill. by author. Holt, 1992. ISBN 0-8050-1884-0 Subj: Clothing. Format, unusual – board books.

My first wild animals ill. by author. HarperCollins, 1991. ISBN 0-690-04773-8 Subj: Animals.

My toys ill. by author. Holt, 1992. ISBN 0-8050-1883-2 Subj: Format, unusual – board books. Toys.

Paterson, Diane. *The bathtub ocean* ill. by author. Dial, 1979. ISBN 0-8037-0462-3 Subj: Activities – bathing. Imagination.

Eat ill. by author. Dial, 1975. ISBN 0-8037-4831-0 Subj: Food. Humor.

Hey, cowboy! ill. by author. Knopf, 1983. ISBN 0-394-95341-X Subj: Family life – grandfathers. Sibling rivalry.

If I were a toad ill. by author. Dial, 1977. ISBN 0-8037-4804-3 Subj: Animals. Behavior – wishing. Participation.

Smile for auntie ill. by author. Dial, 1976. ISBN 0-8037-8067-2 Subj: Family life – aunts, uncles. Humor.

Soap and suds ill. by author. Knopf, 1984. ISBN 0-394-96131-5 Subj: Activities – working. Behavior – misbehavior.

Wretched Rachel ill. by author. Dial, 1978. ISBN 0-8037-9695-1 Subj: Behavior. Emotions – love. Family life.

Paterson, Katherine. *The angel and the donkey* ill. by Alexander Koshkin. Clarion, 1996. ISBN 0-395-68969-4 Subj: Angels. Religion – Moses. Royalty – kings.

Celia and the sweet, sweet water ill. by Vladimir Vagin. Clarion, 1998. ISBN 0-525-67481-0 Subj: Animals – dogs. Character traits – kindness. Family life – mothers. Friendship. Water.

The crane wife (Yagawa, Sumiko)

The tale of the Mandarin ducks ill. by Leo and Diane Dillon. Dutton, 1990. ISBN 0-525-67283-4 Subj: Birds – ducks. Folk and fairy tales. Foreign lands – Japan.

The tongue-cut sparrow (Ishii, Momoko)

Patkau, Karen. *In the sea* ill. by author. Firefly, 1989. ISBN 1-55037-067-7 Subj: Sea and seashore.

Paton, Priscilla. *Howard and the sitter surprise* ill. by Paul Meisel. Houghton Mifflin, 1996. ISBN 0-395-71814-7 Subj: Activities – babysitting. Activities –

storytelling. Animals – bears. Behavior – misbehavior.

Paton Walsh, Jill. *see* Walsh, Jill Paton

Patrick, Denise Lewis. *Look inside a house* (Gomboli, Mario)

Look inside a ship (Gomboli, Mario)

No diapers for baby! ill. by Sylvia Walker. Western, 1995. ISBN 0-307-12870-9 Subj: Ethnic groups in the U.S. – African Americans. Format, unusual – board books. Toilet training.

Patron, Susan. *Burgoo stew* ill. by Mike Shenon. Watts, 1991. ISBN 0-531-08516-3 Subj: Activities – cooking. Character traits – cleverness. Folk and fairy tales. Food. Foreign lands – France.

Dark cloud strong breeze ill. by Peter Catalanotto. Orchard, 1994. ISBN 0-531-08665-8 Subj: Automobiles. Cumulative tales. Family life – fathers. Rhyming text. Weather – rain. Weather – wind.

Five bad boys, Billy Que, and the dustdobbin ill. by Mike Shenon. Orchard, 1992. ISBN 0-531-05989-8 Subj: Character traits – generosity. Concepts – size.

Patterson, Elizabeth Burman. *Whose eyes are these?* ill. by author. Tommy Nelson, 1997. ISBN 0-8499-1464-7 Subj: Anatomy – eyes. Animals. Games. Nature. Rhyming text. Science.

Patterson, Geoffrey. *Jonah and the whale* ill. by author. Lothrop, 1992. ISBN 0-688-11239-0 Subj: Animals – whales. Religion – Jonah.

The lion and the gypsy ill. by author. Doubleday, 1991. ISBN 0-385-41536-2 Subj: Animals. Gypsies. Music.

The naughty boy and the strawberry horse ill. by author. Hutchinson, 1997. ISBN 0-09-176547-1 Subj: Animals – horses, ponies. Behavior. Etiquette.

A pig's tale ill. by author. Dutton, 1983. ISBN 0-233-97477-6 Subj: Animals – pigs. Behavior – running away. Farms.

Patterson, José. *Mazal-Tov: a Jewish wedding* photos by Liba Taylor. David & Charles, 1988. ISBN 0-241-12269-4 Subj: Jewish culture. Weddings.

Patterson, Pat. *Hickory dickory duck: a book of very funny rhymes and picture puzzles* by Pat Patterson and Joe Weissmann. Greey de Pencier Books, 1982. ISBN 0-919872-72-7 Subj: Games. Nursery rhymes.

Pattison, Darcy. *The river dragon* ill. by Jean and Mou-Sien Tseng. Lothrop, 1991. ISBN 0-688-10427-4 Subj: Dragons. Folk and fairy tales. Foreign lands – China.

Patton, Don. *Armadillos* ill. by author. Child's World, 1996. ISBN 1-56766-182-3 Subj: Animals – armadillos.

Pythons ill. with photos. Child's World, 1996. ISBN 1-56766-180-7 Subj: Reptiles – snakes.

Sea turtles ill. with photos. Child's World, 1996. ISBN 1-56766-188-2 Subj: Reptiles – turtles, tortoises.

Patz, Nancy. *Gina Farina and the Prince of Mintz* ill. by author. Harcourt, 1986. ISBN 0-15-230815-6 Subj: Activities – traveling. Character traits – meanness. Character traits – persistence. Royalty – princes. Theater.

Moses supposes his toeses are roses and 7 other silly old rhymes ill. by author. Harcourt, 1983. ISBN 0-15-255690-7 Subj: Nursery rhymes. Poetry.

No thumpin' no bumpin' no rumpus tonight! ill. by author. Atheneum, 1990. ISBN 0-689-31510-4 Subj: Animals – elephants. Birthdays. Family life – mothers. Food. Imagination – imaginary friends.

Pumpernickel tickle and mean green cheese ill. by author. Watts, 1978. ISBN 0-531-02221-8 Subj: Animals – elephants. Behavior – forgetfulness. Humor. Shopping. Tongue twisters.

Sarah Bear and Sweet Sidney ill. by author. Four Winds, 1989. ISBN 0-02-770270-7 Subj: Animals – bears. Hibernation. Poetry. Seasons – spring. Seasons – winter.

To Annabella Pelican from Thomas Hippopotamus ill. by author. Four Winds, 1991. ISBN 0-02-770280-4 Subj: Animals – hippopotamuses. Birds – pelicans. Friendship. Moving.

Paul, Ann Whitford. *Eight hands round* ill. by Jeanette Winter. HarperCollins, 1991. ISBN 0-06-024704-5 Subj: ABC books. Quilts.

Everything to spend the night . . . from A to Z ill. by Maggie Smith. DK, 1999. ISBN 0-7894-2511-4 Subj: ABC books. Bedtime. Family life – grandfathers. Rhyming text.

Hello toes! Hello feet! ill. by Nadine Bernard Westcott. DK, 1998. ISBN 0-7894-2481-9 Subj: Activities – playing. Anatomy – feet. Anatomy – toes. Animals – dogs. Clothing – shoes.

Paul, Anthony. *The tiger who lost his stripes* ill. by Michael Foreman. Harcourt, 1982. ISBN 0-15-287681-2 Subj: Animals – tigers. Character traits – cleverness. Forest, woods.

Paul, Jan S. *Hortense* ill. by Madelaine Gill Linden. HarperCollins, 1984. ISBN 0-690-04371-6 Subj: Animals. Behavior – lost. Farms.

Paul, Korky. *Dragon poems* (Dragon poems)

Pop-up numbers #1 (Marshall, Ray)

Pop-up numbers #2 (Marshall, Ray)

Pop-up numbers #3 (Marshall, Ray)

Pop-up numbers #4 (Marshall, Ray)

Winnie flies again by Korky Paul and Valerie Thomas; ill. by Valerie Thomas. Kane/Miller,

2000. ISBN 0-916291-94-4 Subj: Glasses. Humor. Witches.

Winnie in winter by Korky Paul and Valerie Thomas; ill. by Valerie Thomas. Oxford Univ. Pr., 1996. ISBN 0-19-279004-8 Subj: Animals. Nature. Seasons – winter. Witches.

Paul, Sherry. *2-B and the rock 'n roll band* ill. by Bob Miller. Childrens Pr., 1981. ISBN 0-516-02355-1 Subj: Character traits – helpfulness. Robots.

2-B and the space visitor ill. by Bob Miller. Childrens Pr., 1981. ISBN 0-516-02356-X Subj: Holidays – Halloween. Robots. Space and space ships.

Paulsen, Gary. *Canoe days* ill. by Ruth Wright Paulsen. Doubleday, 1999. ISBN 0-385-32524-X Subj: Birds. Canoes and canoeing. Fish. Insects. Seasons – summer.

Worksong ill. by Ruth Wright Paulsen. Harcourt, 1997. ISBN 0-15-200980-9 Subj: Activities – working. Careers. Rhyming text.

Pavey, Peter. *I'm Taggarty Toad* ill. by author. Bradbury, 1980. ISBN 0-87888-172-7 Subj: Behavior – boasting. Frogs and toads. Imagination.

One dragon's dream ill. by author. Bradbury, 1979. ISBN 0-87888-148-4 Subj: Counting, numbers. Dragons. Dreams. Rhyming text.

Paxton, Tom. *Androcles and the lion: and other Æsop fables* (Æsop)

Belling the cat and other Æsop fables ill. by Robert Rayevsky. Morrow, 1990. ISBN 0-688-08159-2 Subj: Animals. Folk and fairy tales.

Engelbert the elephant ill. by Steven Kellogg. Morrow, 1990. ISBN 0-688-08936-4 Subj: Activities – dancing. Animals – elephants. Etiquette. Parties. Royalty – queens.

Going to the zoo ill. by Karen Schmidt. Morrow, 1996. ISBN 0-688-13801-2 Subj: Animals. Music. Songs. Zoos.

Jennifer's rabbit ill. by Donna Ayers. Morrow, 1988. ISBN 0-688-07432-4 Subj: Behavior – running away. Dreams. Poetry.

The jungle baseball game ill. by Karen Schmidt. Morrow, 1999. ISBN 0-688-13980-9 Subj: Animals – hippopotamuses. Animals – monkeys. Sports – baseball.

The marvelous toy ill. by Elizabeth Sayles. Morrow, 1996. ISBN 0-688-13879-9 Subj: Family life – fathers. Rhyming text. Songs. Toys.

The story of Santa Claus ill. by Michael Dooling. Morrow, 1995. ISBN 0-688-11365-6 Subj: Folk and fairy tales. Holidays – Christmas. Santa Claus.

The story of the Tooth Fairy ill. by Robert Sauber. Morrow, 1996. ISBN 0-688-12988-9 Subj: Fairies. Folk and fairy tales. Friendship. Teeth.

Payne, Emmy. *Katy no-pocket* ill. by Hans Augusto Rey. Houghton Mifflin, 1944. ISBN 0-395-52141-6

Subj: Animals – kangaroos. Clothing – aprons. Problem solving.

Payne, Joan Balfour. *The stable that stayed* ill. by author. Ariel, 1952. Subj: Animals. Careers – artists. Country.

Payne, Sherry Neuwirth. *A contest* ill. by Jeff Kyle. Carolrhoda, 1982. ISBN 0-87614-176-9 Subj: Character traits – being different. Handicaps – cerebral palsy. School.

Paz, Elena. *Las Navidades: popular Christmas songs from Latin America* (Delacre, Lulu)

Paz, Octavio. *My life with the wave* (Cowan, Catherine)

Peaceable kingdom: *the Shaker abecedarius* ill. by Alice and Martin Provensen. Viking, 1978. ISBN 0-670-54500-7 Subj: ABC books. Animals. Poetry.

Peacock, Carol Antoinette. *Mommy far, Mommy near* ill. by Shawn Costello Brownell. Albert Whitman, 2000. ISBN 0-8075-5234-8 Subj: Adoption. Emotions. Ethnic groups in the U.S. – Chinese Americans. Family life.

Pearce, Philippa. *Emily's own elephant* ill. by John Lawrence. Greenwillow, 1988. ISBN 0-688-07679-3 Subj: Animals – elephants. Family life. Pets.

Pearce, Q. L. *In the African grasslands* by Q. L. and W. J. Pearce; ill. by Delana Bettoli. Silver Pr., 1990. ISBN 0-671-68827-8 Subj: Animals. Foreign lands – Africa.

In the desert by Q. L. and W. J. Pearce; ill. by Delana Bettoli. Silver Pr., 1990. ISBN 0-671-68825-1 Subj: Animals. Desert.

Pearce, W. J. *In the African grasslands* (Pearce, Q. L.)

In the desert (Pearce, Q. L.)

Pearson, Kit. *The singing basket* ill. by Ann Blades. Firefly, 1990. ISBN 0-88899-104-5 Subj: Behavior – lying. Folk and fairy tales. Foreign lands – Canada.

Pearson, Susan. *Baby and the bear* ill. by Nancy Carlson. Viking, 1987. ISBN 0-670-81299-4 Subj: Format, unusual – board books. Toys – bears.

Everybody knows that! ill. by Diane Paterson. Dial, 1978. ISBN 0-8037-2418-7 Subj: Friendship. School. Sex roles.

Happy birthday, Grampie ill. by Ronald Himler. Dial, 1987. ISBN 0-8037-3457-3 Subj: Birthdays. Family life – grandfathers.

Jack and the beanstalk (Jack and the beanstalk)

Karin's Christmas walk ill. by Trinka Hakes Noble. Dial, 1980. ISBN 0-8037-4432-3 Subj: Family life – aunts, uncles. Holidays – Christmas.

Lenore's big break ill. by Nancy Carlson. Viking, 1992. ISBN 0-670-83474-2 Subj: Birds. Self-concept. Theater.

My favorite time of year ill. by John Wallner. HarperCollins, 1988. ISBN 0-06-024682-0 Subj: Seasons.

Saturday, I ran away ill. by Susan Jeschke. HarperCollins, 1981. ISBN 0-397-31958-4 Subj: Behavior – running away. Family life.

Silver morning ill. by David Christiana. Harcourt, 1998. ISBN 0-15-274786-9 Subj: Activities – walking. Family life – mothers. Weather – fog.

That's enough for one day! ill. by Kay Chorao. Dial, 1977. ISBN 0-8037-8567-4 Subj: Activities – playing. Activities – reading.

Well, I never! ill. by James Warhola. Simon & Schuster, 1990. ISBN 0-671-69199-6 Subj: Farms.

When baby went to bed ill. by Nancy Carlson. Viking, 1987. ISBN 0-670-81300-1 Subj: Babies. Bedtime. Counting, numbers. Format, unusual – board books.

Pearson, Tracey Campbell. *A apple pie* ill. by author. Dial, 1986. ISBN 0-8037-0252-3 Subj: ABC books. Format, unusual – toy and movable books. Nursery rhymes. Poetry.

The howling dog ill. by author. Farrar, 1991. ISBN 0-374-33502-8 Subj: Animals – dogs. Behavior – misbehavior. Emotions – loneliness. Night. Noise, sounds.

The purple hat ill. by author. Farrar, 1997. ISBN 0-374-36153-3 Subj: Birds. Clothing – hats. Forest, woods.

Sing a song of sixpence ill. by author. Dial, 1985. ISBN 0-8037-0152-7 Subj: Behavior – misbehavior. Humor. Nursery rhymes.

The storekeeper ill. by author. Dial, 1988. ISBN 0-8037-0371-6 Subj: Animals – cats. Careers – storekeepers. Stores.

Where does Joe go? ill. by author. Farrar, 1999. ISBN 0-374-38319-7 Subj: Restaurants. Rhyming text. Santa Claus. Seasons – winter.

The peasant's pea patch trans. by Guy Daniels; ill. by Robert M. Quackenbush. Delacorte, 1971. Subj: Birds – cranes. Folk and fairy tales. Foreign lands – Russia.

Peavy, Linda. *Allison's grandfather* ill. by Ronald Himler. Scribners, 1981. ISBN 0-684-17017-5 Subj: Death. Emotions – grief. Family life – grandfathers.

Peck, Jan. *The giant carrot* ill. by Barry Root. Dial, 1998. ISBN 0-8037-1824-1 Subj: Behavior – sharing. Folk and fairy tales. Food. Foreign lands – Russia.

Peck, Robert Newton. *Hamilton* ill. by Laura Lydecker. Little, 1976. ISBN 0-316-69653-6 Subj:

Animals – pigs. Animals – wolves. Farms. Rhyming text.

Peddle, Daniel. *Snow day* ill. by author. Doubleday, 2000. ISBN 0-385-32693-9 Subj: Nature. Snowmen. Weather – snow. Wordless.

Pedersen, Judy. *Out in the country* ill. by author. Knopf, 1991. ISBN 0-679-90630-4 Subj: Country. Family life. Homes, houses. Moving.

The tiny patient ill. by author. Knopf, 1989. ISBN 0-394-90170-3 Subj: Birds. Character traits – kindness to animals. Illness.

When night time comes near ill. by author. Viking, 2000. ISBN 0-670-88259-3 Subj: Bedtime. Communities, neighborhoods. Night.

Peek, Merle. *The balancing act: a counting book* ill. by author. Clarion, 1987. ISBN 0-89919-458-3 Subj: Animals. Animals – elephants. Counting, numbers. Music. Rhyming text. Songs.

Mary wore her red dress and Henry wore his green sneakers ill. by adapt. Clarion, 1985. ISBN 0-89919-324-2 Subj: Animals. Animals – bears. Birthdays. Concepts – color. Songs.

Peet, Bill (William Bartlett). *The ant and the elephant* ill. by author. Little, 1972. ISBN 0-395-13734-9 Subj: Animals. Animals – elephants. Character traits – helpfulness. Character traits – selfishness. Cumulative tales. Insects – ants.

Big bad Bruce ill. by author. Houghton Mifflin, 1977. ISBN 0-395-25150-8 Subj: Animals – bears. Behavior – bullying. Forest, woods. Humor. Witches.

Bill Peet: an autobiography ill. by author. Houghton Mifflin, 1989. ISBN 0-395-50932-7 Subj: Caldecott award honor books.

Buford the little bighorn ill. by author. Houghton Mifflin, 1967. Subj: Animals – sheep. Character traits – individuality. Humor. Sports – hunting. Sports – skiing.

The caboose who got loose ill. by author. Houghton Mifflin, 1971. ISBN 0-395-12578-2 Subj: Behavior – dissatisfaction. Ecology. Trains.

Chester the worldly pig ill. by author. Houghton Mifflin, 1965. Subj: Animals – pigs. Circus. Humor. World.

Cock-a-doodle Dudley ill. by author. Houghton Mifflin, 1990. ISBN 0-395-55331-8 Subj: Animals. Birds – chickens. Farms. Sun.

Countdown to Christmas ill. by author. Houghton Mifflin, 1972. ISBN 0-8746-4199-3 Subj: Holidays – Christmas. Humor. Magic. Progress. Santa Claus.

Cowardly Clyde ill. by author. Houghton Mifflin, 1979. ISBN 0-395-27802-3 Subj: Animals – horses, ponies. Character traits – bravery. Humor. Knights.

Cyrus the unsinkable sea serpent ill. by author. Houghton Mifflin, 1975. ISBN 0-395-20272-8 Subj:

Character traits – helpfulness. Monsters. Mythical creatures. Sea and seashore.

Eli ill. by author. Houghton Mifflin, 1978. ISBN 0-606-03378-5 Subj: Animals – lions. Birds – vultures. Friendship. Humor.

Ella ill. by author. Houghton Mifflin, 1964. ISBN 0-395-17577-1 Subj: Animals – elephants. Behavior – lost. Character traits – conceit. Circus. Rhyming text.

Encore for Eleanor ill. by author. Houghton Mifflin, 1981. ISBN 0-395-29860-1 Subj: Animals – elephants. Art.

Farewell to Shady Glade ill. by author. Houghton Mifflin, 1966. ISBN 0-395-18975-6 Subj: Animals. Ecology. Progress.

Fly, Homer, fly ill. by author. Houghton Mifflin, 1969. Subj: Birds – pigeons. City. Ecology.

The gnats of knotty pine ill. by author. Houghton Mifflin, 1975. ISBN 0-395-21405-X Subj: Animals. Ecology. Insects – gnats. Sports – hunting.

How Droofus the dragon lost his head ill. by author. Houghton Mifflin, 1971. ISBN 0-395-15085-X Subj: Dragons. Knights. Royalty – kings.

Hubert's hair-raising adventures ill. by author. Houghton Mifflin, 1959. Subj: Animals – lions. Careers – barbers. Humor. Rhyming text.

Huge Harold ill. by author. Houghton Mifflin, 1961. ISBN 0-395-32923-X Subj: Animals – rabbits. Character traits – kindness to animals. Concepts – size. Humor. Rhyming text.

Jennifer and Josephine ill. by author. Houghton Mifflin, 1967. ISBN 0-395-18225-5 Subj: Animals – cats. Automobiles. Humor.

Jethro and Joel were a troll ill. by author. Houghton Mifflin, 1987. ISBN 0-395-43081-X Subj: Humor. Magic. Mythical creatures – trolls.

Kermit the hermit ill. by author. Houghton Mifflin, 1965. ISBN 0-395-15084-1 Subj: Behavior – greed. Crustaceans. Humor. Poetry. Sea and seashore.

The kweeks of Kookatumdee ill. by author. Houghton Mifflin, 1985. ISBN 0-395-37902-4 Subj: Activities – flying. Behavior – greed. Birds. Rhyming text.

The luckiest one of all ill. by author. Houghton Mifflin, 1982. ISBN 0-395-31863-7 Subj: Behavior – dissatisfaction. Emotions – envy, jealousy. Rhyming text.

Merle the high flying squirrel ill. by author. Houghton Mifflin, 1974. ISBN 0-395-18452-5 Subj: Activities – flying. Animals – squirrels. Humor. Kites. Trees.

No such things ill. by author. Houghton Mifflin, 1983. ISBN 0-395-33888-3 Subj: Animals. Mythical creatures. Rhyming text.

Pamela Camel ill. by author. Houghton Mifflin, 1984. ISBN 0-395-35975-9 Subj: Animals – camels. Behavior – running away. Self-concept.

The pinkish, purplish, bluish egg ill. by author. Houghton Mifflin, 1963. ISBN 0-395-18472-X Subj: Birds. Birds – doves. Eggs. Mythical creatures. Rhyming text. Violence, nonviolence.

Randy's dandy lions ill. by author. Houghton Mifflin, 1964. ISBN 0-395-18507-6 Subj: Animals – lions. Circus. Humor. Rhyming text.

Smokey ill. by author. Houghton Mifflin, 1962. ISBN 0-395-15992-X Subj: Old age. Rhyming text. Trains.

The spooky tail of Prewitt Peacock ill. by author. Houghton Mifflin, 1973. ISBN 0-395-15494-4 Subj: Birds – peacocks, peahens. Character traits – being different. Character traits – individuality.

The Whingdingdilly ill. by author. Houghton Mifflin, 1970. ISBN 0-395-24729-2 Subj: Animals – dogs. Behavior – dissatisfaction. Character traits – optimism. Witches.

The wump world ill. by author. Houghton Mifflin, 1970. ISBN 0-395-19841-0 Subj: Ecology. Progress. Space and space ships.

Zella, Zack, and Zodiac ill. by author. Houghton Mifflin, 1986. ISBN 0-395-40567-5 Subj: Animals – zebras. Behavior – needing someone. Birds – ostriches. Rhyming text.

Peet, Georgia. *Be quite quiet beside the lake* (Koenner, Alfred)

High flies the ball (Koenner, Alfred)

Peguero, Leone. *Lionel and Amelia* ill. by Adrian Peguero and Gerard Peguero. Mondo, 1996. ISBN 1-57255-197-6 Subj: Animals – mice. Character traits – orderliness. Friendship.

Pelham, David. *A is for animals* ill. by author. Simon & Schuster, 1991. ISBN 0-671-72495-9 Subj: ABC books. Animals. Format, unusual – toy and movable books.

Crawlies creep ill. by author. Dutton, 1996. ISBN 0525455760 Subj: Animals. Format, unusual – toy and movable books.

Sam's pizza ill. by author. Dutton, 1996. ISBN 0-525-45594-9 Subj: Activities – cooking. Family life – brothers and sisters. Food. Format, unusual – toy and movable books. Rhyming text. Sibling rivalry.

Sam's sandwich ill. by author. Dutton, 1991. ISBN 0-525-44751-2 Subj: Family life – brothers and sisters. Food. Format, unusual – toy and movable books. Rhyming text.

Worms wiggle ill. by Michael Foreman. Simon & Schuster, 1989. ISBN 0-671-67218-5 Subj: Activities. Animals. Format, unusual – toy and movable books.

Pellegrini, Nina. *Families are different* ill. by author. Holiday, 1991. ISBN 0-8234-0887-6 Subj: Adoption. Ethnic groups in the U.S. Ethnic groups in the U.S. – Korean Americans. Family life.

Pelletier, David. *The graphic alphabet* ill. by author. Orchard, 1996. ISBN 0-531-36001-6 Subj: ABC books. Caldecott award honor books. Concepts.

Pellowski, Anne. *The nine crying dolls: a story from Poland* ill. by Charles Mikolaycak. Philomel, 1980. ISBN 0-399-61162-2 Subj: Folk and fairy tales. Foreign lands – Poland. Toys – dolls.

Stairstep farm: Anna Rose's story ill. by Wendy Watson. Putnam, 1981. ISBN 0-399-20814-3 Subj: Behavior – growing up. Family life. Farms.

Pellowski, Michael. *Clara joins the circus* ill. by True Kelley. Parents, 1981. ISBN 0-8193-1058-1 Subj: Animals – bulls, cows. Circus. Clowns, jesters.

Pender, Lydia. *Barnaby and the horses* ill. by Alie Evers. Oxford Univ. Pr., 1980. ISBN 0-19-554216-9 Subj: Animals – horses, ponies. Behavior – carelessness. Country.

Pendery, Rosemary. *A home for Hopper* ill. by Robert M. Quackenbush. Morrow, 1971. Subj: Frogs and toads.

Pendziwol, Jean. *No dragons for tea: fire safety for kids (and dragons)* ill. by Martine Gourbault. Kids Can Pr., 1999. ISBN 1-55074-569-7 Subj: Dragons. Fire. Friendship. Rhyming text. Safety.

Pène Du Bois, William. *see* Du Bois, William Pène

Penn, Ruth Bonn. *see* Clifford, Eth

Penner, Fred. *Proud* ill. by Vickey Bolling. Longstreet, 1997. ISBN 1-56352-441-4 Subj: Behavior – collecting things. Poetry.

Penner, Lucille Recht. *Dinosaur babies* ill. by Peter Barrett. Random House, 1991. ISBN 0-679-91207-X Subj: Dinosaurs. Science.

Monster bugs ill. by Pamela Johnson. Random House, 1996. ISBN 0-679-96974-8 Subj: Insects. Science. Spiders.

Penney, Ian. *Ian Penney's ABC* ill. by author. Abrams, 1998. ISBN 0-8109-4350-6 Subj: ABC books. Foreign lands – England.

Ian Penney's book of fairy tales comp. and ill. by Ian Penney. Abrams, 1995. ISBN 0-8109-3740-9 Subj: Folk and fairy tales.

Ian Penney's book of nursery rhymes (Mother Goose)

Pennington, Daniel. *Itse selu: Cherokee harvest festival* ill. by Don Stewart. Charlesbridge, 1994. ISBN 0-88106-852-7 Subj: Holidays. Indians of North America – Cherokee.

Penrose, Gordon. *More science surprises from Dr. Zed* ill. with photos; ed. by Marilyn Baillie. Simon & Schuster, 1992. ISBN 0-671-77810-2 Subj: Science.

Peppé, Rodney. *The alphabet book* ill. by author. Four Winds, 1968. Subj: ABC books.

Cat and mouse: a book of rhymes comp. and ill. by Rodney Peppé. Holt, 1973. ISBN 0-03-010321-5 Subj: Animals – cats. Animals – mice. Nursery rhymes. Poetry.

Circus numbers: a counting book ill. by author. Delacorte, 1969. ISBN 0-440-01288-0 Subj: Circus. Counting, numbers.

The color catalog ill. by author. Peter Bedrick, 1992. ISBN 0-87226-472-6 Subj: Animals – cats. Character traits – vanity. Concepts – color.

Hey riddle diddle ill. by author. Holt, 1971. ISBN 0-03-086233-7 Subj: Nursery rhymes. Riddles.

The kettleship pirates ill. by author. Lothrop, 1983. ISBN 0-688-02077-1 Subj: Animals – mice. Birthdays. Boats, ships. Imagination. Pirates.

Little circus ill. by author. Viking, 1984. ISBN 0-670-43134-6 Subj: Animals. Circus. Format, unusual – board books. Toys.

Little dolls ill. by author. Viking, 1984. ISBN 0-670-43182-6 Subj: Clothing. Format, unusual – board books. Toys.

Little games ill. by author. Viking, 1984. ISBN 0-670-43187-7 Subj: Format, unusual – board books. Games. Toys.

Little numbers ill. by author. Viking, 1984. ISBN 0-670-43248-2 Subj: Counting, numbers. Format, unusual – board books. Toys.

Little wheels ill. by author. Viking, 1984. ISBN 0-670-43417-5 Subj: Automobiles. Format, unusual – board books. Toys. Trucks.

The magic toy box ill. by author. Candlewick, 1996. ISBN 0-7636-0010-5 Subj: Magic. Toys.

The mice and the clockwork bus ill. by author. Lothrop, 1987. ISBN 0-688-06543-0 Subj: Animals – mice. Animals – rats. Buses.

The mice and the flying basket ill. by author. Lothrop, 1985. ISBN 0-688-04252-X Subj: Activities – ballooning. Animals – mice. Animals – rats. Behavior – greed.

The mice who lived in a shoe ill. by author. Lothrop, 1982. ISBN 0-688-00844-5 Subj: Animals – mice. Homes, houses.

Odd one out ill. by author. Viking, 1974. ISBN 0-670-52029-2 Subj: Concepts. Games.

Rodney Peppé's puzzle book ill. by author. Viking, 1977. ISBN 0-722-65274-7 Subj: Concepts. Games.

Thumbprint circus ill. by author. Delacorte, 1989. ISBN 0-440-50154-7 Subj: Circus.

Percy, Graham. *Elephants never forget* comp. and ill. by Graham Percy. Chronicle, 1992. ISBN 0-8118-0239-6 Subj: Animals – elephants. Nursery rhymes.

24 strange little animals in a haunted house ill. by author. Chronicle, 1996. ISBN 0-8118-1035-6 Subj: Animals. Character traits – individuality. Night.

Perera, Lydia. *Frisky* ill. by Oscar Liebman. Random House, 1966. Subj: City. Merry-go-rounds.

Peretz, Isaac Loeb. *The magician* (Shulevitz, Uri)

Perez, Carla. *Your turn, doctor* (Robison, Deborah)

Periwinkle, Tribulation. *see* Alcott, Louisa May

Perkins, Al. *The digging-est dog* ill. by Eric Gurney. Random House, 1967. Subj: Activities – digging. Animals – dogs. Poetry.

Don and Donna go to bat ill. by Barney Tobey. Random House, 1968. Subj: Multiple births – twins. Sports – baseball.

The ear book ill. by William O'Brian. Random House, 1968. ISBN 0-394-91199-7 Subj: Anatomy – ears. Rhyming text. Senses – hearing.

Hand, hand, fingers, thumb ill. by Eric Gurney. Random House, 1969. ISBN 0-394-91076-1 Subj: Anatomy – hands. Rhyming text.

King Midas and the golden touch ill. by Harold Berson. Random House, 1970. Subj: Behavior – greed. Behavior – wishing. Royalty – kings.

The nose book ill. by Roy McKié. Random House, 1970. ISBN 0-394-80623-9 Subj: Anatomy – noses. Rhyming text. Senses – smelling.

Tubby and the lantern ill. by Rowland B. Wilson. Random House, 1971. ISBN 0-394-92297-2 Subj: Animals – elephants. Birthdays. Foreign lands – China. Pirates.

Tubby and the Poo-Bah ill. by Rowland B. Wilson. Random House, 1972. ISBN 0-394-92469-X Subj: Animals – elephants. Boats, ships.

Perkins, Charles. *Swinging on a rainbow* ill. by Thomas Hamilton. Africa World, 1993. ISBN 0-86543-286-4 Subj: Ethnic groups in the U.S. – African Americans. Imagination. Rhyming text.

Perkins, Lynne Rae. *Clouds for dinner* ill. by author. Greenwillow, 1997. ISBN 0-688-14904-9 Subj: Character traits – orderliness. Family life. Family life – aunts, uncles.

Home lovely ill. by author. Greenwillow, 1995. ISBN 0-688-13688-5 Subj: Family life. Gardens, gardening.

Perlman, Janet. *The Emperor Penguin's new clothes* ill. by author. Viking, 1995. ISBN 0-670-85864-1 Subj: Birds – penguins. Character traits – pride. Character traits – vanity. Clothing. Folk and fairy tales. Imagination. Royalty – emperors.

Perrault, Charles. *Cinderella* adapt. by John Fowles; ill. by Sheilah Beckett. Little, 1974. Adapt. from Perrault's Cendrillon of 1697. ISBN 0-316-29101-3 Subj: Family life – step families. Folk and fairy tales. Royalty – princes. Sibling rivalry.

Cinderella: or, The little glass slipper ill. by Marcia Brown. Aladdin, 1988, c1954. ISBN 0-689-71261-8 Subj: Caldecott award books. Family life – step families. Folk and fairy tales. Royalty – princes. Sibling rivalry.

Cinderella ill. by Paul Galdone. McGraw-Hill, 1978. ISBN 0-07-022684-9 Subj: Family life – step families. Folk and fairy tales. Royalty – princes. Sibling rivalry.

Cinderella tr. and ill. by Diane Goode. Knopf, 1988. ISBN 0-394-99603-8 Subj: Family life – step families. Folk and fairy tales. Royalty – princes. Sibling rivalry.

Cinderella retold by Amy Ehrlich; ill. by Susan Jeffers. Dial, 1985. ISBN 0-8037-0206-X Subj: Family life – step families. Folk and fairy tales. Royalty – princes. Sibling rivalry.

Cinderella ill. by Loek Koopmans; trans. by Anthea Bell. North-South, 1999. ISBN 0-7358-1052-4 Subj: Family life – step families. Folk and fairy tales. Royalty – princes. Sibling rivalry.

Cinderella: the story of Rossini's opera adapt. by Alan Blyth; ill. by Emanuele Luzzati. Watts, 1982. ISBN 0-531-04061-5 Subj: Family life – step families. Folk and fairy tales. Music. Royalty – princes. Sibling rivalry.

Cinderella retold by Barbara Karlin; ill. by James Marshall. Little, 1989. ISBN 0-316-54654-2 Subj: Family life – step families. Folk and fairy tales. Royalty – princes. Sibling rivalry.

Cinderella ill. by Phil Smith. Troll, 1979. ISBN 0-89375-120-0 Subj: Family life – step families. Folk and fairy tales. Royalty – princes. Sibling rivalry.

Dick Bruna's Cinderella (Bruna, Dick)

Puss in boots a free translation from the French; ill. by Marcia Brown. Scribners, 1952. Subj: Animals – cats. Caldecott award honor books. Character traits – cleverness. Folk and fairy tales. Royalty – kings.

Puss in boots adapt. and ill. by Lorinda Bryan Cauley. Harcourt, 1986. ISBN 0-15-264227-7 Subj: Animals – cats. Character traits – cleverness. Folk and fairy tales. Royalty – kings.

Puss in boots retold by Kurt Baumann; ill. by Jean Claverie. Faber, 1982. ISBN 0-571-12511-5 Subj: Animals – cats. Character traits – cleverness. Folk and fairy tales. Royalty – kings.

Puss in boots ill. by Andrea Da Rif. Farrar, 1990. ISBN 0-89375-130-8 Subj: Animals – cats. Character traits – cleverness. Folk and fairy tales. Royalty – kings.

Puss in boots ill. by Stasys Eidrigevicius; trans. by Naoma Lewis. North-South, 1994. ISBN 1-55858-120-0 Subj: Animals – cats. Character traits – cleverness. Folk and fairy tales. Royalty – kings.

Puss in boots adapt. and ill. by Hans Fischer. Harcourt, 1959. Subj: Animals – cats. Character traits – cleverness. Folk and fairy tales. Royalty – kings.

Puss in boots ill. by Paul Galdone. Seabury Pr., 1976. ISBN 0-8164-3159-0 Subj: Animals – cats. Character traits – cleverness. Folk and fairy tales. Royalty – kings.

Puss in boots retold and ill. by John S. Goodall. Macmillan, 1990. ISBN 0-689-50521-3 Subj: Animals – cats. Character traits – cleverness. Folk and fairy tales. Royalty – kings. Wordless.

Puss in boots retold and ill. by Gail E. Haley. Dutton, 1991. ISBN 0-525-44740-7 Subj: Animals – cats. Character traits – cleverness. Folk and fairy tales. Royalty – kings.

Puss in boots retold by Kurt Baumann; trans. by Anthea Bell; ill. by Giuliano Lunelli. North-South, 1999. ISBN 0-7358-1159-8 Subj: Animals – cats. Character traits – cleverness. Folk and fairy tales. Royalty – kings.

Puss in boots ill. by Fred Marcellino; trans. by Malcolm Arthur. Farrar, 1990. ISBN 0-374-36160-6 Subj: Animals – cats. Caldecott award honor books. Character traits – cleverness. Folk and fairy tales. Royalty – kings.

Puss in boots ill. by Fred Marcellino; trans. by Malcolm Arthur. Farrar, 1998. ISBN 0-374-46034-5 Subj: Animals – cats. Character traits – cleverness. Folk and fairy tales. Royalty – kings.

Puss in boots adapt. by Arthur Luce Klein; ill. by Julia Noonan. Doubleday, 1970. Adapt. of Le Chat botté. Subj: Animals – cats. Character traits – cleverness. Folk and fairy tales. Foreign lands – France. Royalty – kings.

Puss in boots: the story of a sneaky cat adapt. and ill. by Tony Ross. Delacorte, 1981. ISBN 0-440-07157-7 Subj: Animals – cats. Character traits – cleverness. Folk and fairy tales. Royalty – kings.

Puss in boots ill. by William Stobbs. McGraw-Hill, 1975. A retelling of Maître Chat. ISBN 0-07-061581-0 Subj: Animals – cats. Character traits – cleverness. Folk and fairy tales. Royalty – kings.

Puss in boots trans. by Anthea Bell; ill. by Yan Thomas. Kingfisher, 1995. ISBN 1-85697-624-6 Subj: Animals – cats. Character traits – cleverness. Folk and fairy tales. Royalty – kings.

Puss in boots retold by Lincoln Kirstein; ill. by Alain Vaës. Little, 1992. ISBN 0-316-89506-7 Subj: Animals – cats. Character traits – cleverness. Folk and fairy tales. Royalty – kings.

Puss in boots ill. by Barry Wilkinson. Collins-World, 1969. Subj: Animals – cats. Character traits – cleverness. Folk and fairy tales. Royalty – kings.

The sleeping beauty tr. and ill. by David Walker. Crowell, 1977. ISBN 0-690-01279-9 Subj: Folk and fairy tales.

Tom Thumb: a tale (Tom Thumb)

Perrine, Mary. *Salt boy* ill. by Leonard Weisgard. Houghton Mifflin, 1968. ISBN 0-395-17450-3 Subj: Indians of North America – Navajo.

Perrow, Angeli. *Captain's castaway* ill. by Emily Harris. Down East, 1998. ISBN 0-8927-2419-6 Subj: Accidents. Animals – dogs. Friendship. Lighthouses. Sea and seashore.

Perry, Patricia. *Mommy and daddy are divorced* by Patricia Perry and Marietta Lynch; ill. by authors. Dial, 1978. ISBN 0-8037-5771-9 Subj: Divorce.

Perry, Sarah. *If . . .* ill. by author. J.P. Getty Museum, 1995. ISBN 0-89236-321-5 Subj: Imagination.

Pershall, Mary K. *Hello, Barney!* ill. by Mark Wilson. Viking, 1989. ISBN 0-670-82406-2 Subj: Birds – cockatoos. Foreign lands – Australia. Pets.

Petach, Heidi. *Goldilocks and the three hares* ill. by author. Putnam, 1995. ISBN 0-399-22828-4 Subj: Animals – rabbits. Folk and fairy tales.

Peter, Beate. *The adventures of Marco and Polo* (Wiesmüller, Dieter)

Peters, Andrew. *Salt is sweeter than gold* ill. by Zdena Kabátová-Táborská. Barefoot, 1994. ISBN 1-56957-933-4 Subj: Folk and fairy tales. Foreign lands – Czechoslovakia. Royalty – kings. Royalty – princesses.

Peters, Lisa Westberg. *Cold little duck, duck, duck* ill. by Sam Williams. Greenwillow, 2000. ISBN 0-688-16179-0 Subj: Birds – ducks. Imagination. Seasons – spring.

Good morning, river! ill. by Deborah Kogan Ray. Arcade, 1990. ISBN 1-55970-011-4 Subj: Old age. Rivers. Seasons.

The hayloft ill. by K. D. Plum. Dial, 1995. ISBN 0-8037-1491-2 Subj: Animals. Animals – cats. Farms. Seasons – summer.

Meg and dad discover treasure in the air ill. by Deborah Durland DeSaix. Holt, 1995. ISBN 0-8050-2418-2 Subj: Forest, woods. Nature. Rocks.

October smiled back ill. by Ed Young. Holt, 1996. ISBN 0-8050-1776-3 Subj: Days of the week, months of the year. Rhyming text.

Purple delicious blackberry jam ill. by Barbara McGregor. Arcade, 1992. ISBN 1-55970-167-6 Subj: Family life – grandmothers. Food.

The sun, the wind and the rain ill. by Ted Rand. Holt, 1988. ISBN 0-8050-0699-0 Subj: Nature. Science. Sea and seashore. Weather.

This way home ill. by Normand Chartier. Holt, 1994. ISBN 0-8050-1368-7 Subj: Activities – traveling. Birds. Nature.

Water's way ill. by Ted Rand. Arcade, 1991. ISBN 1-55970-062-9 Subj: Nature. Science. Water. Weather.

Peters, Sharon. *Animals at night* ill. by Paul Harvey. Troll, 1983. ISBN 0-89375-903-1 Subj: Animals. Night.

Fun at camp ill. by Irene Trivas. Troll, 1980. ISBN 0-89375-378-5 Subj: Camps, camping.

Happy birthday ill. by Paul Harvey. Troll, 1980. ISBN 0-89375-379-3 Subj: Birthdays.

Happy Jack ill. by Paul Harvey. Troll, 1980. ISBN 0-89375-380-7 Subj: Careers – waiters, waitresses.

Messy Mark ill. by Bill Morrison. Troll, 1980. ISBN 0-89375-381-5 Subj: Character traits – cleanliness.

Puppet show ill. by Alana Lee. Troll, 1980. ISBN 0-89375-385-8 Subj: Puppets.

Ready, get set, go! ill. by Irene Trivas. Troll, 1980. ISBN 0-89375-386-6 Subj: Animals – rabbits.

Stop that rabbit ill. by Don Silverstein. Troll, 1980. ISBN 0-89375-388-2 Subj: Animals – rabbits.

Trick or treat Halloween ill. by Susan Hall. Troll, 1980. ISBN 0-89375-392-0 Subj: Holidays – Halloween.

Petersen, David. *Dinosaur National Monument* ill. by author. Childrens Pr., 1995. ISBN 0-516-01074-3 Subj: Dinosaurs.

Petersen-Fleming, Judy. *Kitten training and critters, too!* by Judy Peterson-Fleming and Bill Fleming; photos by Darryl Bush. Tambourine, 1996. ISBN 0-688-13387-8 Subj: Animals – cats. Pets.

Puppy training and critters, too! by Judy Peterson-Fleming and Bill Fleming; photos by Darryl Bush. Tambourine, 1996. ISBN 0-688-13385-1 Subj: Animals – dogs. Pets.

Petersham, Maud. *An American ABC* by Maud and Miska Petersham; ill. by authors. Macmillan, 1941. Subj: ABC books. Caldecott award honor books. U.S. history.

The circus baby by Maud and Miska Petersham; ill. by authors. Aladdin, 1989, c1950. ISBN 0-689-71295-2 Subj: Animals – elephants. Circus. Clowns, jesters. Etiquette.

Off to bed: 7 stories for wide-awakes by Maud and Miska Petersham; ill. by authors. Macmillan, 1954. Subj: Bedtime.

The rooster crows by Maud and Miska Petersham; ill. by authors. Macmillan, 1945. ISBN 0-02-773100-6 Subj: Caldecott award books. Nursery rhymes.

Petersham, Miska. *An American ABC* (Petersham, Maud)

The circus baby (Petersham, Maud)

Off to bed: 7 stories for wide-awakes (Petersham, Maud)

The rooster crows (Petersham, Maud)

Peterson, Cris. *Extra cheese, please!* photos by Alvis Upitis. Boyds Mills, 1994. ISBN 1-56397-177-1 Subj: Animals – bulls, cows. Careers – farmers. Farms. Food.

Horsepower: the wonder of draft horses photos by Alvis Upitis. Boyds Mills, 1997. ISBN 1-56397-626-9 Subj: Activities – working. Animals – horses, ponies.

Peterson, Esther Allen. *Frederick's alligator* ill. by Susanna Natti. Crown, 1979. ISBN 0-517-53597-1 Subj: Animals. Behavior – boasting. Reptiles – alligators, crocodiles.

Penelope gets wheels ill. by Susanna Natti. Crown, 1982. ISBN 0-517-54467-9 Subj: Birthdays. Sports.

Peterson, Franklynn. *I can use tools* (Kesselman, Judi R.)

Peterson, Hans. *Erik and the Christmas horse* trans. from Swedish by Christine Hyatt; ill. by Ilon Wikland. Lothrop, 1970. Translation of Magnus, Lindberg och hästen Mari. Subj: Character traits – kindness. Foreign lands – Sweden. Holidays – Christmas.

Erik has a squirrel trans. from Swedish by Christine Hyatt; ill. by Ilon Wikland. Farrar, 1989. ISBN 9-12-959140-6 Subj: Animals – squirrels. Friendship.

Peterson, Jeanne Whitehouse. *My mama sings* ill. by Sandra Speidel. HarperCollins, 1994. ISBN 0-06-023859-3 Subj: Activities – singing. Ethnic groups in the U.S. – African Americans. Family life – mothers. Music.

Sometimes I dream horses ill. by Eleanor Schick. HarperCollins, 1987. ISBN 0-06-024713-4 Subj: Animals – horses, ponies. Family life – grandmothers.

That is that ill. by Deborah Kogan Ray. HarperCollins, 1979. ISBN 0-06-024709-6 Subj: Divorce.

Peterson, Julienne. *Caterina, the clever farm girl* ill. by Enzo Giannini. Dial, 1996. ISBN 0-8037-1182-4 Subj: Character traits – cleverness. Folk and fairy tales. Foreign lands – Italy. Royalty – kings.

Peterson, Scott K. *What's your name? jokes about names* ill. by Joan Hanson. Lerner, 1987. ISBN 0-8225-0994-6 Subj: Names. Riddles.

Petie, Haris. *Billions of bugs* ill. by author. Prentice-Hall, 1975. ISBN 0-13-076240-7 Subj: Counting, numbers. Insects. Rhyming text.

The seed the squirrel dropped ill. by author. Prentice-Hall, 1976. ISBN 0-13-799627-6 Subj: Activities – cooking. Cumulative tales. Food. Plants. Rhyming text. Seeds. Trees.

Petrides, Heidrun. *Hans and Peter* ill. by author. Harcourt, 1962. Subj: Activities – working. Character traits – completing things.

Petrie, Catherine. *Hot Rod Harry* ill. by Paul Sharp. Childrens Pr., 1982. ISBN 0-516-03493-6 Subj: Automobiles.

Joshua James likes trucks ill. by Jerry Warshaw. Childrens Pr., 1982. ISBN 0-516-43525-6 Subj: Toys. Trucks.

Pets ill. with photos. Macmillan, 1991. ISBN 0-689-71404-1 Subj: Nature. Pets.

Pettigrew, Eileen. *Night-time* ill. by William Kimber. Firefly, 1992. ISBN 1-55037-235-1 Subj: Family life – fathers. Night.

Pettit, Henry. *The authentic Mother Goose fairy tales and nursery rhymes* (Barchilon, Jacques)

Petty, Kate. *Being careful with strangers* ill. by Lisa Kopper. Watts, 1988. ISBN 0-531-17107-8 Subj: Behavior – talking to strangers. Safety.

Dinosaurs ill. by Alan Baker. Watts, 1984. ISBN 0-531-04811-X Subj: Dinosaurs.

Gerbils photos by George Thompson. Watts, 1989. ISBN 0-531-17158-2 Subj: Animals – gerbils. Pets.

Hamsters photos by George Thompson. Watts, 1989. ISBN 0-531-17159-0 Subj: Animals – hamsters. Pets.

On a plane ill. by Aline Riquier. Watts, 1984. ISBN 0-531-04716-4 Subj: Activities – traveling. Airplanes, airports. Foreign lands – England.

Rabbits photos by George Thompson. Watts, 1989. ISBN 0-531-17160-4 Subj: Animals – rabbits. Pets.

Petty, Roberta. *see* Petie, Haris

Pevear, Richard. *The absentminded fellow* (Marshak, S. [Samuil])

First, second (Kharms, Daniil)

Hail to mail (Marshak, S. [Samuil])

Mister Cat-and-a-Half ill. by Robert Rayevsky. Macmillan, 1986. ISBN 0-02-773910-4 Subj: Animals. Animals – cats. Animals – foxes. Folk and fairy tales.

Our king has horns! ill. by Robert Rayevsky. Macmillan, 1987. ISBN 0-02-773920-1 Subj: Behavior – secrets. Folk and fairy tales. Foreign lands – Russia. Royalty – kings.

The pup grew up! (Marshak, S. [Samuil])

Peyo. *The Smurfs and their woodland friends* ill. by author. Random House, 1983. ISBN 0-394-85370-9 Subj: Animals. Forest, woods. Insects.

What do smurfs do all day? ill. by author. Random House, 1983. ISBN 0-394-96078-5 Subj: Activities. Rhyming text.

Pfanner, Louise. *Louise builds a boat* ill. by author. Watts, 1990. ISBN 0-531-08488-4 Subj: Activities – making things. Boats, ships.

Louise builds a house ill. by author. Watts, 1989. ISBN 0-531-08396-9 Subj: Activities – making things. Homes, houses. Imagination.

Pfeffer, Wendy. *From tadpole to frog* ill. by Holly Keller. HarperCollins, 1994. ISBN 0-06-023117-3 Subj: Frogs and toads. Nature. Science.

Marta's magnets ill. by Gail Piazza. Silver Pr., 1995. ISBN 0-382-24930-5 Subj: Behavior – collecting things. Friendship.

What's it like to be a fish? ill. by Holly Keller. HarperCollins, 1996. ISBN 0-06-024429-1 Subj: Fish. Pets.

Pfister, Marcus. *Chris and Croc* ill. by author. North-South, 1994. ISBN 1-55858-274-6 Subj: Activities – playing. Friendship. Toys.

The Christmas star ill. by author; trans. by J. Alison James. North-South, 1993. ISBN 1-55858-204-5 Subj: Holidays – Christmas. Religion – Nativity. Stars.

Dazzle the dinosaur ill. by J. Alison James. North-South, 1994. ISBN 1-55858-338-6 Subj: Dinosaurs.

Hang on, Hopper! ill. by Rosemary Lanning. North-South, 1995. ISBN 1-55858-404-8 Subj: Animals – rabbits. Safety. Sports – swimming.

The happy hedgehog ill. by author; trans. by J. Alison James. North-South, 2000. ISBN 0-7358-1165-2 Subj: Animals – hedgehogs. Family life – grandfathers.

Hopper ill. by author. North-South, 1991. ISBN 1-55858-106-5 Subj: Animals – rabbits. Seasons – spring. Seasons – winter.

Hopper hunts for spring ill. by author; trans. by Rosemary Lanning. North-South, 1992. ISBN 1-55858-139-1 Subj: Animals. Animals – rabbits. Frogs and toads. Seasons – spring.

Hopper's treetop adventure ill. by author; trans. by Rosemary Lanning. North-South, 1997. ISBN 1-55858-681-4 Subj: Animals – rabbits. Animals – squirrels. Nature. Trees.

How Leo learned to be king ill. by author; trans. by J. Alison James. North-South, 1998. ISBN 1-55858-914-7 Subj: Animals. Animals – lions. Behavior. Royalty – kings.

I see the moon: good-night poems and lullabies comp. and ill. by Marcus Pfister. North-South, 1991. ISBN 1-55858-119-7 Subj: Bedtime. Lullabies. Moon. Night. Poetry. Songs.

Make a wish, Honey Bear! ill. by author; trans. by Sibylle Kazeroid. North-South, 1999. ISBN 0-7358-1244-6 Subj: Animals – bears. Behavior – wishing. Birthdays.

Milo and the magical stones ill. by author; trans. by Marianne Martens. North-South, 1997. ISBN 1-55858-682-2 Subj: Animals – mice. Behavior. Format, unusual – toy and movable books. Magic.

Penguin Pete and Little Tim ill. by author; trans. by Rosemary Lanning. North-South, 1994. ISBN 1-55858-302-5 Subj: Activities – walking. Birds – penguins. Family life – fathers. Weather – snow.

The rainbow fish ill. by author. North-South, 1992. ISBN 1-55858-010-7 Subj: Behavior – sharing. Character traits – appearance. Emotions – loneliness. Fish.

Rainbow fish and the big blue whale ill. by author; trans. by J. Alison James. North-South, 1998. ISBN 0-7358-1010-9 Subj: Animals – whales. Behavior – fighting, arguing. Fish.

Rainbow fish to the rescue! ill. by author; trans. by J. Alison James. North-South, 1995. ISBN 1-55858-487-0 Subj: Character traits – appearance. Emotions – fear. Fish. Fish – sharks. Friendship.

The sleepy owl trans. from German by Jock J. Curle; ill. by author. Holt, 1986. ISBN 0-03-008023-1 Subj: Birds – owls. Friendship. Sleep.

Wake up, Santa Claus! ill. by author; trans. by J. Alison James. North-South, 1996. ISBN 1-55858-606-7 Subj: Behavior – hurrying. Dreams. Holidays – Christmas. Santa Claus.

Where is my friend? ill. by author. Holt, 1986. ISBN 0-03-008033-9 Subj: Animals – porcupines. Format, unusual – board books. Friendship.

Pfloog, Jan. *Kittens* ill. by author. Random House, 1977. ISBN 0-394-83590-5 Subj: Animals – cats. Format, unusual – board books.

Puppies ill. by author. Random House, 1979. ISBN 0-394-84132-8 Subj: Animals – dogs. Format, unusual – board books.

Phang, Ruth. *Patchwork tales* (Roth, Susan L.)

Phifer, Martha Nelson. *The colors of Christmas* ill. by Judy I. Roberts. Herald Pr., 1995. ISBN 0-8361-9029-7 Subj: Concepts – color. Holidays – Christmas. Religion – Nativity. Rhyming text.

Philip, Neil. *The golden bird* (Grimm, Jacob)

I have a news: rhymes from the Caribbean (Jekyll, Walter)

The snow queen (Andersen, H. C. [Hans Christian])

Phillips, Jack. *see* Sandburg, Carl (Charles August)

Phillips, Joan. *Lucky bear* ill. by J. P. Miller. Random House, 1986. ISBN 0-394-97987-7 Subj: Toys – bears.

My new boy ill. by Lynn Munsinger. Random House, 1986. ISBN 0-394-98277-0 Subj: Animals – dogs. Pets.

Peek-a-boo! I see you! ill. by Kathy Wilburn. Putnam, 1983. ISBN 0-488-03092-6 Subj: Animals – bears. Format, unusual – board books. Rhyming text.

Phillips, Louis. *The brothers Wrong and Wrong Again* ill. by J. Winslow Higginbottom. McGraw-Hill, 1979. ISBN 0-07-049805-9 Subj: Character traits – foolishness. Dragons. Middle Ages. War.

The upside down riddle book ill. by Beau Gardner. Lothrop, 1982. ISBN 0-688-00932-8 Subj: Humor. Rhyming text. Riddles.

Phillips, Mildred. *And the cow said, "moo"!* ill. by Sonja Lamut. Greenwillow, 2000. ISBN 0-688-16803-5 Subj: Animals. Farms. Noise, sounds.

The sign in Mendel's window ill. by Margot Zemach. Macmillan, 1985. ISBN 0-02-774600-3 Subj: Folk and fairy tales. Jewish culture.

Phillips, Tamara. *Day care ABC* ill. by Dora Leder. Albert Whitman, 1989. ISBN 0-8075-1483-7 Subj: ABC books. School.

Philothea. *see* Child, Lydia Maria

Philpot, Graham. *Amazing Anthony Ant* (Philpot, Lorna)

Fabulous fairy tale follies ill. by author. Random House, 1994. ISBN 0-679-85316-2 Subj: Careers – actors. Folk and fairy tales. Games. Theater.

Philpot, Lorna. *Amazing Anthony Ant* by Lorna and Graham Philpot; ill. by authors. Orion Children's Books, 1993. ISBN 1-8588-1005-1 Subj: Counting, numbers. Format, unusual – toy and movable books. Insects – ants. Songs.

Phumla. *Nomi and the magic fish: a story from Africa* ill. by Carole M. Byard. Doubleday, 1973. Subj: Children as authors. Folk and fairy tales. Foreign lands – Africa. Magic.

Piatti, Celestino. *Celestino Piatti's animal ABC* English text by Jon Reid; ill. by author. Atheneum, 1966. Subj: ABC books. Animals. Poetry.

The happy owls ill. by author. Atheneum, 1964. ISBN 0-689-20337-3 Subj: Birds – owls. Character traits – optimism. Emotions – happiness.

Pickett, Carla. *Calvin Crocodile and the terrible noise* ill. by Carroll Dolezal. Steck-Vaughn, 1972. ISBN 0-8114-7736-3 Subj: Noise, sounds. Reptiles – alligators, crocodiles.

Pickthall, Marjorie L. C. (Marjorie Lowry Christie). *The worker in sandalwood: a Christmas eve miracle* ill. by Frances Tyrrell. Dutton, 1994. ISBN 0-525-45332-6 Subj: Careers – carpenters. Foreign lands – Canada. Holidays – Christmas.

Pienkowski, Jan. *Colors* ill. by author. Harvey House, 1974. ISBN 0-8178-5232-8 Subj: Concepts – color.

Easter ill. by author. Knopf, 1989. ISBN 0-394-82455-5 Subj: Holidays – Easter. Religion.

Faces ill. by author. Simon & Schuster, 1991. ISBN 0-671-72846-6 Subj: Anatomy – faces. Format, unusual – board books.

Fancy that! (Little old lady who swallowed a fly)

Farm ill. by author. David & Charles, 1985. ISBN 0-434-95651-1 Subj: Animals. Farms.

Food ill. by author. Simon & Schuster, 1991. ISBN 0-671-72845-8 Subj: Food. Format, unusual – board books.

Good night, a pop-up lullaby ill. by author; paper engineering by Helen Balmer and Martin Taylor. Candlewick, 1999. ISBN 0-7636-0763-0 Subj: Format, unusual – toy and movable books. Lullabies.

Homes ill. by author. Messner, 1983. ISBN 0-671-46935-5 Subj: Animals. Homes, houses.

Meg and Mog (Nicoll, Helen)

Meg at sea (Nicoll, Helen)

Meg on the moon (Nicoll, Helen)

Meg's eggs (Nicoll, Helen)

Numbers ill. by author. Harvey House, 1975. ISBN 0-8178-5241-7 Subj: Counting, numbers.

Shapes ill. by author. Harvey House, 1975. ISBN 0-671-44455-7 Subj: Concepts – shape.

Sizes ill. by author. Messner, 1983. Orig. pub. by Harvey House, 1974. ISBN 0-671-46936-3 Subj: Concepts – size.

Time ill. by author. Messner, 1980. ISBN 0-671-46933-9 Subj: Clocks, watches. Time.

Weather ill. by author. Messner, 1983. ISBN 0-671-46934-7 Subj: Weather.

Zoo ill. by author. David & Charles, 1985. ISBN 0-434-95652-X Subj: Animals. Zoos.

Pierce, Jack. *The freight train book* photos by author. Carolrhoda, 1980. ISBN 0-87614-123-8 Subj: Trains.

Pierce, Roxanne Heide. *Oh, grow up! poems to help you survive parents, chores, school, and other afflictions* (Heide, Florence Parry)

Timothy Twinge (Heide, Florence Parry)

Pierpont, James. *Jingle bells* ill. by Michael Hague. Holt, 1990. ISBN 0-8050-1413-6 Subj: Holidays – Christmas. Music. Songs.

Piers, Helen. *Grasshopper and butterfly* ill. by Pauline Baynes. McGraw-Hill, 1975. Subj: Hibernation. Insects – butterflies, caterpillars. Insects – grasshoppers.

Is there room on the bus? ill. by Hannah Giffard. Simon & Schuster, 1996. ISBN 0-689-80610-8 Subj: Activities – traveling. Animals. Buses. Counting, numbers. Cumulative tales.

The mouse book photos by author. Watts, 1968. Subj: Animals – mice.

Puppy's ABC photos by author. Oxford Univ. Pr., 1987. ISBN 0-19-520606-1 Subj: ABC books. Animals – dogs.

Who's in my bed? ill. by Dave Saunders. Cavendish, 1999. ISBN 0-7614-5046-7 Subj: Animals. Bedtime. Character traits – orderliness. Cumulative tales. Farms. Format, unusual – toy and movable books.

Pierson, Judith Patterson. *The always moon* ill. by Karen Stormer Brooks. First Story Pr., 1998. ISBN

1-890326-17-8 Subj: Bedtime. Dreams. Moon. Night.

Pike, Carol. *The nutty queen* ill. by author. Trafalgar Square, 1990. ISBN 0-09-173795-8 Subj: Rhyming text. Royalty – queens. Toys – bears.

Pike, Debi. *Like me and you* (Raffi)

Pike, Norman. *The peach tree* ill. by Robin and Patricia DeWitt. Stemmer House, 1983. ISBN 0-88045-014-2 Subj: Gardens, gardening. Trees.

Pilegard, Virginia Walton. *The warlord's puzzle* ill. by Nicolas Debon. Pelican, 2000. ISBN 1-56554-495-1 Subj: Concepts – shape. Folk and fairy tales. Foreign lands – China.

Pilkey, Dav. *Dragon's fat cat* ill. by author. Orchard, 1992. ISBN 0-531-08582-1 Subj: Animals – cats. Dragons.

Dragon's merry Christmas ill. by author. Orchard, 1991. ISBN 0-531-08557-0 Subj: Character traits – generosity. Dragons. Holidays – Christmas.

A friend for Dragon ill. by author. Orchard, 1991. ISBN 0-531-05934-0 Subj: Dragons. Emotions – loneliness. Friendship. Reptiles – snakes.

The Hallo-wiener ill. by author. Blue Sky, 1995. ISBN 0-590-41703-7 Subj: Animals – dogs. Family life. Holidays – Halloween.

The Moonglow Roll-O-Rama ill. by author. Orchard, 1995. ISBN 0-531-08726-3 Subj: Animals. Night. Rhyming text. Sports – roller skating.

The paperboy ill. by author. Orchard, 1996. ISBN 0-531-08856-1 Subj: Activities – working. Caldecott award honor books. Morning.

The Silly Gooses ill. by author. Blue Sky, 1997. ISBN 0-590-94733-8 Subj: Behavior. Birds – geese. Humor. Weddings.

The Silly Gooses build a house ill. by author. Blue Sky, 1998. ISBN 0-590-94741-9 Subj: Activities – making things. Behavior – mistakes. Birds – geese. Homes, houses. Humor.

'Twas the night before Thanksgiving ill. by author. Watts, 1990. ISBN 0-531-08505-8 Subj: Birds – turkeys. Holidays – Thanksgiving. Rhyming text.

When cats dream ill. by author. Watts, 1992. ISBN 0-531-08597-X Subj: Animals – cats. Art. Dreams.

Pillar, Marjorie. *Join the band!* photos by author. HarperCollins, 1992. ISBN 0-06-021829-0 Subj: Music. School.

Pizza man photos by author. HarperCollins, 1990. ISBN 0-690-04836-X Subj: Careers – chefs, cooks. Food.

Pincus, Harriet. *Minna and Pippin* ill. by author. Farrar, 1972. ISBN 0-374-34991-6 Subj: Toys – dolls.

Pinczes, Elinor J. *Arctic fives arrive* ill. by Holly Berry. Houghton Mifflin, 1996. ISBN 0-395-73577-7 Subj: Counting, numbers. Foreign lands – Arctic. Rhyming text.

A remainder of one ill. by Bonnie MacKain. Houghton Mifflin, 1995. ISBN 0-395-69455-8 Subj: Counting, numbers. Insects. Rhyming text.

Pingry, Patricia. *Joseph's story* ill. by George Hinke. CandyCane, 1998. ISBN 0-8249-4092-X Subj: Family life – fathers. Holidays – Christmas. Religion – Nativity.

Pinkney, Andrea Davis. *Alvin Ailey* ill. by J. Brian Pinkney. Hyperion, 1993. ISBN 1-56282-414-7 Subj: Activities – dancing. Careers – dancers. Ethnic groups in the U.S. – African Americans.

Bill Pickett, rodeo ridin' cowboy ill. by J. Brian Pinkney. Harcourt, 1996. ISBN 0-15-200100-X Subj: Cowboys. Ethnic groups in the U.S. – African Americans.

Dear Benjamin Banneker ill. by J. Brian Pinkney. Harcourt, 1994. ISBN 0-15-200417-3 Subj: Careers – astronomers. Ethnic groups in the U.S. – African Americans. Slavery. U.S. history.

Duke Ellington: the piano prince and his orchestra ill. by Brian Pinkney. Hyperion, 1998. ISBN 0-7868-2150-7 Subj: Caldecott award honor books. Careers – musicians. Ethnic groups in the U.S. – African Americans. Music.

Pinkney, Gloria Jean. *Back home* ill. by Jerry Pinkney. Dial, 1992. ISBN 0-8037-1169-7 Subj: Ethnic groups in the U.S. – African Americans. Family life. Farms.

The Sunday outing ill. by Jerry Pinkney. Dial, 1994. ISBN 0-8037-1199-9 Subj: Activities – traveling. Ethnic groups in the U.S. – African Americans. Family life. Farms. Trains.

Pinkney, J. Brian. *The adventures of sparrowboy* ill. by author. Simon & Schuster, 1997. ISBN 0-689-81071-7 Subj: Activities – flying. Behavior – bullying. Communities, neighborhoods. Ethnic groups in the U.S. – African Americans. Humor.

Cosmo and the robot ill. by author. Greenwillow, 2000. ISBN 0-688-15941-9 Subj: Monsters. Planets. Robots. Space and space ships.

Jojo's flying side kick ill. by author. Simon & Schuster, 1995. ISBN 0-671-88111-6 Subj: Character traits – perseverance. Family life. Sports – Tae Kwon Do.

Pinkney, Jerry. *The ugly duckling* (Andersen, H. C. [Hans Christian])

Pinkwater, Daniel Manus. *At the Hotel Larry* ill. by Jill Pinkwater. Cavendish, 1997. ISBN 0-7614-5005-X Subj: Animals – polar bears. Careers – lifeguards. Hotels. Humor.

Aunt Lulu ill. by author. Macmillan, 1988. ISBN 0-02-774661-5 Subj: Animals – dogs. Careers – librarians. Family life – aunts, uncles.

The bear's picture ill. by author. Dutton, 1984. ISBN 0-525-44102-6 Subj: Animals – bears. Art. Careers – artists. Concepts – color.

The big orange splot ill. by author. Hastings House, 1977. ISBN 0-8038-0777-5 Subj: Activities – painting. Character traits – individuality. Concepts – color. Homes, houses.

Bongo Larry ill. by Jill Pinkwater. Cavendish, 1998. ISBN 0-7614-5020-3 Subj: Animals – polar bears. Careers – musicians. Humor.

Devil in the drain ill. by author. Dutton, 1984. ISBN 0-525-44092-5 Subj: Character traits – curiosity. Devil.

Doodle flute ill. by author. Macmillan, 1991. ISBN 0-02-774635-6 Subj: Behavior – sharing. Friendship. Music.

The Frankenbagel monster ill. by author. Dutton, 1986. ISBN 0-525-44260-X Subj: Careers – bakers. Monsters.

Guys from space ill. by author. Macmillan, 1989. ISBN 0-02-774672-0 Subj: Aliens. Space and space ships.

I was a second grade werewolf ill. by author. Dutton, 1983. ISBN 0-525-44038-0 Subj: Imagination. Monsters.

The phantom of the lunch wagon ill. by author. Macmillan, 1992. ISBN 0-02-774641-0 Subj: Animals – cats. Food. Ghosts.

Pickle creature ill. by author. Four Winds, 1979. ISBN 0-590-07579-9 Subj: Imagination – imaginary friends.

Rainy morning ill. by Jill Pinkwater. Atheneum, 1998. ISBN 0-689-81143-8 Subj: Animals. Character traits – kindness to animals. Circus. Food. Homes, houses. Weather – rain.

Roger's umbrella ill. by James Marshall. Dutton, 1982. ISBN 0-525-38555-X Subj: Animals – cats. Umbrellas.

Tooth-gnasher superflash ill. by author. Four Winds, 1981. ISBN 0-590-07624-8 Subj: Automobiles. Imagination.

Wallpaper from space ill. by author. Atheneum, 1996. ISBN 0-689-80764-3 Subj: Dreams. Space and space ships.

Wempires ill. by author. Macmillan, 1991. ISBN 0-02-774411-6 Subj: Family life. Imagination.

Wolf Christmas ill. by Jill Pinkwater. Cavendish, 1998. ISBN 0-7614-5030-0 Subj: Animals – wolves. Holidays – Christmas.

Young Larry ill. by Jill Pinkwater. Cavendish, 1997. ISBN 0-7614-5004-1 Subj: Animals – polar bears. Behavior – growing up. Humor.

Piper, Watty. *The little engine that could* ill. by George and Doris Hauman. Platt, 1990. Retold from The pony engine, by Mable C. Bragg. This version first pub. in 1955. 60th anniversary ed. ISBN 0-448-40041-3 Subj: Character traits – perseverance. Trains.

Mother Goose rhymes (Mother Goose)

Pirani, Felix. *Abigail at the beach* ill. by Christine Roche. Dial, 1989. ISBN 0-8037-0561-1 Subj: Activities – playing. Imagination. Sea and seashore.

Triplets ill. by Christine Roche. Viking, 1991. ISBN 0-670-83375-4 Subj: Multiple births – triplets.

Pirner, Connie White. *Even little kids get diabetes* ill. by Nadine Bernard Westcott. Albert Whitman, 1991. ISBN 0-8075-2158-2 Subj: Hospitals. Illness – diabetes.

Pirotta, Saviour. *Little bird* ill. by Stephen Butler. Morrow, 1992. ISBN 0-688-11290-0 Subj: Activities. Activities – flying. Animals. Birds.

Pitcher, Caroline. *Animals* ill. by Louise Nevett. Watts, 1983. ISBN 0-531-04656-7 Subj: Activities. Animals. Wordless.

Cars and boats ill. by Louise Nevett. Watts, 1983. ISBN 0-531-04657-5 Subj: Activities. Automobiles. Boats, ships. Wordless.

Mariana and the merchild: a folk tale from Chile ill. by Jackie Morris. Eerdmans, 2000. ISBN 0-8028-5204-1 Subj: Folk and fairy tales. Foreign lands – Chile. Mythical creatures – mermaids, mermen.

Run with the wind ill. by Jane Chapman. Little Tiger, 1998. ISBN 1-888444-29-0 Subj: Animals – horses, ponies. Behavior – growing up. Family life – mothers.

The snow whale ill. by Jackie Morris. Sierra Club, 1996. ISBN 0-87156-915-9 Subj: Animals – whales. Family life – brothers and sisters. Water. Weather – snow.

The time of the lion ill. by Jackie Morris. Beyond Words, 1998. ISBN 1-885223-83-8 Subj: Animals – lions. Family life – fathers. Foreign lands – Africa. Friendship.

Pitre, Felix. *Paco and the witch* ill. by Christy Hale. Lodestar, 1995. ISBN 0-525-67501-9 Subj: Folk and fairy tales. Foreign lands – Puerto Rico. Names. Witches.

Pittau, Francisco. *Voyage under the stars* (Gervais, Bernadette)

Pittaway, Margaret. *The rainforest children: a story set in tropical Australia* ill. by Heather Philpott. Oxford Univ. Pr., 1980. ISBN 0-19-554238-X Subj: Behavior – running away. Behavior – seeking better things. Foreign lands – Australia.

Pittman, Helena Clare. *The angel tree* ill. by Jo Ellen McAllister Stammen. Dial, 1998. ISBN 0-8037-1941-8 Subj: Angels. Communities, neighborhoods. Friendship. Holidays – Christmas. Trees.

A dinosaur for Gerald ill. by author. Carolrhoda, 1990. ISBN 0-87614-431-8 Subj: Birthdays. Dinosaurs. Pets.

The gift of the willows ill. by author. Carolrhoda, 1988. ISBN 0-87614-354-0 Subj: Folk and fairy tales. Foreign lands – Japan.

A grain of rice ill. by author. Hastings House, 1986. ISBN 0-8038-9289-6 Subj: Character traits – cleverness. Folk and fairy tales. Foreign lands – China. Royalty.

Miss Hindy's cats ill. by author. Carolrhoda, 1990. ISBN 0-87614-368-0 Subj: ABC books. Animals – cats.

Once when I was scared ill. by Ted Rand. Dutton, 1988. ISBN 0-525-44407-6 Subj: Animals. Emotions – fear. Imagination. Night.

Still-life stew ill. by Victoria Raymond. Hyperion, 1998. ISBN 0-7868-2206-6 Subj: Activities – painting. Art. Food. Gardens, gardening.

Sunrise ill. by Michael Rex. Silver Whistle, 1998. ISBN 0-15-201684-8 Subj: Counting, numbers. Morning. Rhyming text.

Uncle Phil's diner ill. by author. Carolrhoda, 1998. ISBN 1-57505-083-8 Subj: Family life – fathers. Food. Restaurants. Seasons – winter.

Piumini, Roberto. *The saint and the circus* trans. from Italian by Olivia Holmes; ill. by Barrett V. Root. Morrow, 1991. ISBN 0-688-10377-4 Subj: Circus.

Pizer, Abigail. *Charlie the puppy* ill. by author. Carolrhoda, 1989. ISBN 0-87614-363-X Subj: Animals – dogs. Farms. Seasons.

Harry's night out ill. by author. Dial, 1987. ISBN 0-8037-0055-5 Subj: Activities. Animals – cats. Night.

Hattie the goat ill. by author. Carolrhoda, 1989. ISBN 0-87614-364-8 Subj: Animals – goats. Farms. Seasons.

It's a perfect day ill. by author. Lippincott, 1990. ISBN 0-397-32420-0 Subj: Animals. Farms. Noise, sounds. Rebuses.

Loppylugs ill. by author. Viking, 1990. ISBN 0-670-83209-X Subj: Animals – rabbits. Behavior – running away.

Nosey Gilbert ill. by author. Dial, 1987. ISBN 0-8037-0081-4 Subj: Animals – cats. Animals – dogs. Birds – geese. Emotions – fear. Insects – bees.

Penelope pig ill. by author. Carolrhoda, 1989. ISBN 0-87614-366-4 Subj: Animals – pigs. Farms. Seasons.

Percy the duck ill. by author. Carolrhoda, 1989. ISBN 0-87614-365-6 Subj: Birds – ducks. Farms. Seasons.

Planes ill. with photos. DK, 1993. ISBN 1-56458-135-7 Subj: Airplanes, airports.

Plante, Patricia. *The turtle and the two ducks: animal fables* retold from La Fontaine by Patricia Plante and David Bergman; ill. by Anne F. Rockwell.

HarperCollins, 1981. ISBN 0-690-04147-0 Subj: Animals. Folk and fairy tales.

Plath, Sylvia. *The bed book* ill. by Emily Arnold McCully. HarperCollins, 1976. ISBN 0-06-024747-9 Subj: Bedtime. Poetry. Sleep.

Please, Mr. Crocodile! comp. by Tessa Strickland; ill. by Rosslyn Moran. Barefoot, 1999. ISBN 1-902283-62-7 Subj: Animals. Poetry.

Ploetz, Richard. *The Kooken* (Lebentritt, Julia)

Plotz, Helen. *A week of lullabies* comp. and ed. by Helen Plotz; ill. by Marisabina Russo. Greenwillow, 1988. ISBN 0-688-06653-4 Subj: Bedtime. Days of the week, months of the year. Lullabies. Poetry.

Plourde, Lynn. *Pigs in the mud in the middle of the rud* ill. by John Schoenherr. Blue Sky, 1997. ISBN 0-590-56863-9 Subj: Animals – pigs. Character traits – stubbornness. Humor. Poetry. Roads. Weather – rain.

Wild child ill. by Greg Couch. Simon & Schuster, 1999. ISBN 0-689-81552-2 Subj: Bedtime. Mythical creatures. Rhyming text. Seasons – fall.

Winter waits ill. by Greg Couch. Simon & Schuster, 2001. ISBN 0-689-83268-0 Subj: Mythical creatures. Rhyming text. Seasons – winter. Time.

Pluckrose, Henry Arthur. *Ants* ill. by Tony Swift and David Cook. Watts, 1981. ISBN 0-531-03452-6 Subj: Insects – ants. Science.

Bears ill. by Richard Orr. Watts, 1979. ISBN 0-531-03403-8 Subj: Animals – bears. Animals – pandas. Animals – polar bears. Science.

Bees and wasps ill. by Tony Swift and Norman Weaver. Watts, 1981. ISBN 0-531-03453-4 Subj: Insects – bees. Insects – wasps. Science.

Beginnings and endings photos by Steve Shott. Childrens Pr., 1996. ISBN 0-516-08236-1 Subj: Concepts.

Big and little photos by Chris Fairclough. Watts, 1987. ISBN 0-531-10373-0 Subj: Concepts – size.

Butterflies and moths ill. by Norman Weaver and others. Watts, 1981. ISBN 0-531-03454-2 Subj: Insects – butterflies, caterpillars. Insects – moths. Science.

Counting photos by Chris Fairclough. Watts, 1988. ISBN 0-531-10524-5 Subj: Counting, numbers.

Elephants ill. by Peter Barrett. Watts, 1979. ISBN 0-531-03404-6 Subj: Animals – elephants. Science.

Floating and sinking photos by Chris Fairclough. Watts, 1987. ISBN 0-531-10294-7 Subj: Science.

Fur and feathers ill. with photos. Watts, 1989. ISBN 0-531-10720-5 Subj: Anatomy. Animals.

Hearing photos by Chris Fairclough. G. Stevens, 1995. ISBN 0-8368-1287-5 Subj: Senses – hearing.

Horses ill. by Peter Barrett and Maurice Wilson. Watts, 1979. ISBN 0-531-03405-4 Subj: Animals – horses, ponies. Science.

Hot and cold photos by Chris Fairclough. Watts, 1987. ISBN 0-531-10295-5 Subj: Science.

Join it! ill. with photos. Watts, 1989. ISBN 0-531-10730-2 Subj: Activities. Language.

Lions and tigers ill. by Eric Tenny and Maurice Wilson. Archon Pr., 1979. ISBN 0-531-03410-0 Subj: Animals – lions. Animals – tigers.

Numbers photos by Chris Fairclough. Watts, 1988. ISBN 0-531-10453-2 Subj: Counting, numbers.

On the farm photos by Teri Gower. Watts, 1998. ISBN 0-531-14496-8 Subj: Farms. Machines.

On the move photos by Teri Gower. Watts, 1998. ISBN 0-531-14497-6 Subj: Machines. Transportation.

Paws and claws ill. with photos. Watts, 1989. ISBN 0-531-10721-3 Subj: Anatomy. Animals.

Reptiles ill. by Gary Hincks and others. Watts, 1981. ISBN 0-531-03455-0 Subj: Reptiles. Science.

Seeing photos by Chris Fairclough. G. Stevens, 1995. ISBN 0-8368-1288-3 Subj: Senses – seeing.

Shape photos by Chris Fairclough. Watts, 1987. ISBN 0-531-10374-9 Subj: Concepts – shape.

Skin, shell and scale ill. with photos. Watts, 1989. ISBN 0-531-10722-7 Subj: Anatomy – skin. Animals.

Smelling photos by Chris Fairclough. G. Stevens, 1995. ISBN 0-8368-1289-1 Subj: Senses – smelling.

Tasting photos by Chris Fairclough. G. Stevens, 1995. ISBN 0-8368-1290-5 Subj: Senses – tasting.

Things we cut ill. by G. W. Hales. Watts, 1976. ISBN 0-531-01216-6 Subj: Tools.

Things we hear ill. by G. W. Hales. Watts, 1976. ISBN 0-531-00363-9 Subj: Senses – hearing.

Things we see ill. by G. W. Hales. Watts, 1976. ISBN 0-531-01217-4 Subj: Senses – seeing.

Things we touch ill. by G. W. Hales. Watts, 1976. ISBN 0-531-00364-7 Subj: Senses – touching.

Time photos by Chris Fairclough. Watts, 1988. ISBN 0-531-10452-4 Subj: Time.

Touching photos by Chris Fairclough. G. Stevens, 1995. ISBN 0-8368-1291-3 Subj: Senses – touching.

Walls photos by Steve Shott. Childrens Pr., 1996. ISBN 0-516-08239-6 Subj: Buildings.

Weight photos by Chris Fairclough. Watts, 1988. ISBN 0-531-10525-3 Subj: Concepts – weight.

Whales ill. by Norman Weaver. Watts, 1979. ISBN 0-531-03406-2 Subj: Animals – whales. Science.

Plume, Alice. *Salt: from a Russian folktale* (Afanas'ev, Aleksandr N.)

Plume, Ilse. *The Bremen town musicians* (Grimm, Jacob)

Lullaby and goodnight (Lullaby and goodnight)

The shoemaker and the elves (Grimm, Jacob)

The story of Befana: an Italian Christmas tale ill. by adapt. Godine, 1981. ISBN 0-87923-420-2 Subj: Folk and fairy tales. Foreign lands – Italy. Holidays – Christmas.

Plummer, David. *Counting kittens* by David Plummer and John Archambault; ill. by Liisa Chauncy Guida. Silver Pr., 1997. ISBN 0-382-39649-9 Subj: Animals – babies. Animals – cats. Counting, numbers. Rhyming text.

Plunkett, Stephanie Haboush. *Kongi and Potgi: a Cinderella story from Korea* (Han, Oki S.)

Sir Whong and the golden pig (Han, Oki S.)

Po, Lee. *The hare and the tortoise and the tortoise and the hare: La liebre y la tortuga and La tortuga y la liebre* (Du Bois, William Pène)

Pochocki, Ethel. *Rosebud and red flannel* ill. by Mary Beth Owens. Down East, 1999. ISBN 0-8927-2474-9 Subj: Clothing. Emotions – love.

A Pocketful of stars: *poems about the night* ill. by Emma Shaw-Smith. Barefoot, 2000. ISBN 1-902283-84-8 Subj: Night. Poetry.

Pocock, Rita. *Annabelle and the big slide* ill. by author. Harcourt, 1989. ISBN 0-15-200407-6 Subj: Activities – playing. Character traits – confidence.

Podendorf, Illa. *Color* ill. by Wayne Stuart. Childrens Pr., 1971. ISBN 0-516-01572-9 Subj: Concepts – color.

Shapes, sides, curves and corners ill. by Frank Rakoncay. Childrens Pr., 1970. ISBN 0-516-01555-9 Subj: Concepts – shape.

Space ill. with photos. Childrens Pr., 1982. ISBN 0-516-01650-4 Subj: Space and space ships.

Podwal, Mark H. *Golem: a giant made of mud* ill. by author. Greenwillow, 1995. ISBN 0-688-13811-X Subj: Folk and fairy tales. Giants. Jewish culture.

The menorah story ill. by author. Greenwillow, 1998. ISBN 0-688-15759-9 Subj: Holidays – Hanukkah. Jewish culture. Religion.

Poems go clang! *a collection of noisy verse* ill. by Debi Gliori. Candlewick, 1997. ISBN 0-76360-148-9 Subj: Noise, sounds. Poetry.

Pogorelsky, Antony. *The black hen, or, The underground inhabitants* (Hamilton, Morse)

Pohrt, Tom. *Coyote goes walking* ill. by author. Farrar, 1995. ISBN 0-374-31628-7 Subj: Animals – coyotes. Creation. Folk and fairy tales. Indians of North America – Great Plains.

Having a wonderful time ill. by author. Farrar, 1999. ISBN 0-374-32898-6 Subj: Activities – vacationing. Animals – cats. Desert. Foreign lands – Africa.

Points, Larry. *Assateague: island of the wild ponies* (Jauck, Andrea)

Pokornik, Brigitte. *Circus* (Blume, Karin)

My new friends (Blume, Karin)

POLA. *see* Watson, Pauline

Polacco, Patricia. *Appelemando's dreams* ill. by author. Putnam, 1991. ISBN 0-399-21800-9 Subj: Dreams. Imagination.

Aunt Chip and the great Triple Creek dam affair ill. by author. Philomel, 1996. ISBN 0-399-22943-4 Subj: Activities – reading. Libraries. Television.

Babushka's doll ill. by author. Simon & Schuster, 1990. ISBN 0-671-68343-8 Subj: Toys – dolls.

Babushka's Mother Goose ill. by author. Philomel, 1995. ISBN 0-399-22747-4 Subj: Family life – grandmothers. Folk and fairy tales. Foreign lands – Russia. Nursery rhymes.

The butterfly ill. by author. Philomel, 2000. ISBN 0-399-23170-6 Subj: Behavior – hiding. Behavior – secrets. Character traits – freedom. Foreign lands – France. Insects – butterflies, caterpillars. War.

Chicken Sunday ill. by author. Putnam, 1992. ISBN 0-399-22133-6 Subj: Eggs. Ethnic groups in the U.S. – African Americans. Family life – grandmothers. Friendship. Holidays – Easter. Religion.

I can hear the sun ill. by author. Philomel, 1996. ISBN 0-399-22520-X Subj: Birds – geese. Character traits – being different. Ethnic groups in the U.S. – African Americans. Homeless. Sun.

In Enzo's splendid gardens ill. by author. Philomel, 1997. ISBN 0-399-23107-2 Subj: Accidents. Cumulative tales. Food. Humor. Insects – bees. Restaurants.

Just plain Fancy ill. by author. Bantam, 1990. ISBN 0-553-07062-2 Subj: Birds – peacocks, peahens. Eggs. Farms.

The keeping quilt ill. by author. Simon & Schuster, 1998. ISBN 0-689-82090-9 Subj: Immigrants. Jewish culture. Quilts.

Luba and the wren ill. by author. Philomel, 1999. ISBN 0-399-23168-4 Subj: Behavior – wishing. Birds – wrens. Folk and fairy tales. Foreign lands – Soviet Union. Magic.

Meteor! ill. by author. Dodd, 1987. ISBN 0-396-08910-0 Subj: Country. Science.

Mrs. Katz and Tush ill. by author. Bantam, 1992. ISBN 0-553-08122-5 Subj: Animals – cats. Ethnic groups in the U.S. – African Americans. Friendship. Jewish culture. Pets.

My ol' man ill. by author. Philomel, 1995. ISBN 0-399-22822-5 Subj: Family life – fathers. Imagination. Magic. Rocks.

My rotten redheaded older brother ill. by author. Simon & Schuster, 1994. ISBN 0-671-72751-6 Subj: Family life – brothers and sisters. Family life – grandparents. Sibling rivalry.

Picnic at Mudsock Meadow ill. by author. Putnam, 1992. ISBN 0-399-21811-4 Subj: Activities – picnicking. Holidays – Halloween.

Rechenka's eggs ill. by author. Putnam, 1988. ISBN 0-399-21501-8 Subj: Birds – geese. Eggs. Folk and fairy tales.

Some birthday! ill. by author. Simon & Schuster, 1991. ISBN 0-671-72750-8 Subj: Birthdays. Family life – fathers. Monsters. Parties.

Thank you, Mr. Falker ill. by author. Philomel, 1998. ISBN 0-399-23166-8 Subj: Activities – reading. Careers – teachers. Handicaps. School.

Thunder cake ill. by author. Putnam, 1990. ISBN 0-399-22231-6 Subj: Emotions – fear. Family life – grandmothers. Weather – storms. Weather – thunder.

Tikvah means hope ill. by author. Doubleday, 1994. ISBN 0-385-32059-0 Subj: Animals – cats. Fire. Holidays – Sukkot. Jewish culture.

Welcome Comfort ill. by author. Philomel, 1999. ISBN 0-399-23169-2 Subj: Holidays – Christmas. Orphans. Santa Claus. School.

Polette, Nancy. *The little old woman and the hungry cat* ill. by Frank Modell. Greenwillow, 1989. ISBN 0-688-08315-3 Subj: Animals – cats. Cumulative tales.

Polhamus, Jean Burt. *Dinosaur do's and don'ts* ill. by Steve O'Neill. Prentice-Hall, 1975. ISBN 0-13-214643-6 Subj: Dinosaurs. Etiquette.

Doctor Dinosaur ill. by Steve O'Neill. Prentice-Hall, 1981. ISBN 0-13-217083-3 Subj: Careers – veterinarians. Dinosaurs. Illness.

Policoff, Stephen Phillip. *Cesar's amazing journey* ill. by David Catrow. Viking, 1999. ISBN 0-670-88753-6 Subj: Frogs and toads. Spiders. Zoos.

Polisar, Barry Louis. *Don't do that! a child's guide to bad manners, ridiculous rules, and inadequate etiquette* ill. by David Clark. Rainbow Morning Music, 1994. ISBN 0-938663-20-8 Subj: Etiquette.

The haunted house party ill. by David Clark. Rainbow Morning Music, 1995. ISBN 0-938663-21-6 Subj: Ghosts. Holidays – Halloween. Homes, houses. Monsters. Parties. Rhyming text.

The trouble with Ben ill. by David Clark. Rainbow Morning Music, 1992. ISBN 0-938663-13-5 Subj: Animals – bears. Character traits – being different. School. Self-concept.

Politi, Leo. *Emmet* ill. by author. Scribners, 1971. ISBN 0-684-12320-7 Subj: Animals – dogs. Crime.

Juanita ill. by author. Scribners, 1948. Subj: Caldecott award honor books. Ethnic groups in the U.S. – Mexican Americans.

Lito and the clown ill. by author. Scribners, 1964. Subj: Animals – cats. Clowns, jesters. Foreign lands – Mexico. Pets.

Little Leo ill. by author. Scribners, 1951. Subj: Clothing. Family life. Foreign lands – Italy.

Moy Moy ill. by author. Scribners, 1960. Subj: Ethnic groups in the U.S. – Chinese Americans. Holidays – Chinese New Year.

The nicest gift ill. by author. Scribners, 1973. ISBN 0-684-13383-0 Subj: Animals – dogs. Behavior – lost. Gifts. Holidays – Christmas.

Pedro, the angel of Olvera Street ill. by author. Scribners, 1946. Subj: Caldecott award honor books. Ethnic groups in the U.S. – Mexican Americans. Holidays – Christmas.

Rosa ill. by author. Scribners, 1963. Subj: Babies. Foreign lands – Mexico. Holidays – Christmas. Sibling rivalry. Toys – dolls.

Song of the swallows ill. by author. Scribners, 1949. ISBN 0-684-18831-7 Subj: Birds – swallows. Caldecott award books. Ethnic groups in the U.S. – Mexican Americans. Missions.

Polivy, Betsy Bober. *My bye-bye bottle book* (Gelbard, Jane)

My dressing book (Gelbard, Jane)

My eating book (Gelbard, Jane)

My sharing book (Gelbard, Jane)

Polizzotti, Mark. *Star of fear, star of hope* (Hoestlandt, Jo)

Pollack, Eileen. *Whisper whisper Jesse, whisper whisper Josh* ill. by Bruce Gilfoy. Advantage/Aurora, 1992. ISBN 0-9624828-4-6 Subj: Death. Emotions – grief. Family life – aunts, uncles. Illness – AIDS.

Pollack, Pamela. *Where's that cat?* (Merriam, Eve)

Pollock, Penny. *Emily's tiger* ill. by author. Paulist Pr., 1985. ISBN 0-8091-6554-6 Subj: Pets. Toys.

The turkey girl: a Zuni Cinderella story ill. by Ed Young. Little, 1996. ISBN 0-316-71314-7 Subj: Birds – turkeys. Character traits – loyalty. Folk and fairy tales. Indians of North America – Zuni.

Water is wet photos by Barbara Beirne. Putnam, 1985. ISBN 0-399-21180-2 Subj: Activities – playing. Water.

Polushkin, Maria. *Baby brother blues* ill. by Ellen Weiss. Bradbury, 1987. ISBN 0-02-774780-8 Subj: Babies. Family life – new sibling. Sibling rivalry.

Bubba and Babba: based on a Russian folktale ill. by Diane de Groat. Crown, 1976. ISBN 0-517-52435-X Subj: Animals – bears. Character traits – cleanliness. Folk and fairy tales.

Here's that kitten ill. by Betsy Lewin. Bradbury, 1990. ISBN 0-02-774741-7 Subj: Animals – cats.

Kitten in trouble ill. by Betsy Lewin. Bradbury, 1988. ISBN 0-02-774740-9 Subj: Animals – cats. Behavior – misbehavior.

The little hen and the giant ill. by Yuri Salzman. HarperCollins, 1977. Subj: Birds – chickens. Character traits – bravery. Folk and fairy tales. Foreign lands – Russia. Giants.

Morning ill. by Bill Morrison. Four Winds, 1983. ISBN 0-590-07871-2 Subj: Farms. Morning.

Mother, Mother, I want another ill. by Diane Dawson. Crown, 1978. ISBN 0-517-53401-0 Subj: Animals – mice. Behavior – misunderstanding. Family life – mothers. Sleep.

Who said meow? ill. by Giulio Maestro. Crown, 1975. An adaptation of Vladimir Grigorévich Suteev's Kto skazal "Miau"? ISBN 0-517-51846-5 Subj: Animals – cats. Animals – dogs. Noise, sounds.

Who said meow? ill. by Ellen Weiss. Bradbury, 1988. An adaptation of Vladimir Grigorévich Suteev's Kto skazal "Miau"? ISBN 0-02-774770-0 Subj: Animals – cats. Animals – dogs. Noise, sounds.

Pomeranc, Marion Hess. *The American Wei* ill. by DyAnne DiSalvo-Ryan. Albert Whitman, 1998. ISBN 0-8075-0312-6 Subj: Ethnic groups in the U.S. – Chinese Americans. Fairies. Immigrants.

The can-do Thanksgiving ill. by Nancy Cote. Albert Whitman, 1998. ISBN 0-8075-1054-8 Subj: Food. Holidays – Thanksgiving. School.

Pomerantz, Charlotte. *All asleep* ill. by Nancy Tafuri. Greenwillow, 1984. ISBN 0-688-03762-3 Subj: Bedtime. Lullabies. Poetry.

The ballad of the long-tailed rat ill. by Marian Parry. Macmillan, 1975. ISBN 0-02-774890-1 Subj: Animals – cats. Animals – rats. Character traits – pride. Rhyming text.

The birthday letters ill. by JoAnn Adinolfi. Greenwillow, 2000. ISBN 0-688-16336-X Subj: Animals. Parties. Pets.

Buffy and Albert ill. by Yossi Abolafia. Greenwillow, 1982. ISBN 0-688-00921-2 Subj: Animals – cats. Family life – grandfathers. Old age.

The chalk doll ill. by Frané Lessac. HarperCollins, 1989. ISBN 0-397-32319-0 Subj: Family life – mothers. Toys – dolls.

Flap your wings and try ill. by Nancy Tafuri. Greenwillow, 1989. ISBN 0-688-08020-0 Subj: Activities – flying. Birds. Rhyming text.

The half-birthday party ill. by DyAnne DiSalvo-Ryan. Houghton Mifflin, 1984. ISBN 0-89919-273-4 Subj: Birthdays.

Here comes Henny ill. by Nancy Winslow Parker. Greenwillow, 1994. ISBN 0-688-12356-2 Subj: Birds – chickens. Rhyming text.

How many trucks can a tow truck tow? ill. by R. W. Alley. Random House, 1987. ISBN 0-394-88775-1 Subj: Rhyming text. Trucks.

If I had a Paka: poems of eleven languages ill. by Nancy Tafuri. Greenwillow, 1982. ISBN 0-688-00837-2 Subj: Foreign languages. Poetry.

Mangaboom ill. by Anita Lobel. Greenwillow, 1997. ISBN 0-688-12957-9 Subj: Giants. Trees.

The mango tooth ill. by Marylin Hafner. Greenwillow, 1977. ISBN 0-688-84070-1 Subj: Family life. Teeth.

One duck, another duck ill. by José Aruego and Ariane Dewey. Greenwillow, 1984. ISBN 0-688-03745-3 Subj: Birds – ducks. Counting, numbers.

The outside dog ill. by Jennifer Plecas. HarperCollins, 1993. ISBN 0-06-024783-5 Subj: Animals – dogs. Family life – grandfathers. Foreign lands – Puerto Rico.

The piggy in the puddle ill. by James Marshall. Macmillan, 1974. ISBN 0-02-774900-2 Subj: Animals – pigs. Rhyming text. Tongue twisters.

Posy ill. by Catherine Stock. Greenwillow, 1983. ISBN 0-688-02299-5 Subj: Bedtime. Family life.

Serena Katz ill. by R. W. Alley. Macmillan, 1992. ISBN 0-02-774901-0 Subj: Activities. Friendship.

The tamarindo puppy and other poems ill. by Byron Barton. Greenwillow, 1980. ISBN 0-688-84251-8 Subj: Foreign languages. Poetry.

Timothy Tall Feather ill. by Catherine Stock. Greenwillow, 1986. ISBN 0-688-04247-3 Subj: Family life – grandfathers. Imagination. Indians of North America.

Where's the bear? ill. by Byron Barton. Greenwillow, 1984. ISBN 0-688-01753-3 Subj: Animals – bears.

Whiff, sniff, nibble and chew: The Gingerbread boy (The gingerbread boy)

You're not my best friend anymore ill. by David Soman. Dial, 1998. ISBN 0-8037-1560-9 Subj: Birthdays. Friendship. Gifts.

Pomeroy, Diana. *One potato* ill. by author. Harcourt, 1996. ISBN 0-15-200300-2 Subj: Counting, numbers. Food.

Ponti, Claude. *Adele's album* ill. by author. Dutton, 1988. ISBN 0-525-44412-2 Subj: Imagination. Wordless.

Poole, Amy Lowry. *How the rooster got his crown* ill. by author. Holiday, 1999. ISBN 0-8234-1389-6 Subj: Birds – chickens. Creation. Folk and fairy tales. Foreign lands – China.

Poole, Josephine. *Joan of Arc* ill. by Angela Barrett. Knopf, 1998. ISBN 0-679-99041-0 Subj: Foreign lands – France. Religion. War.

Poole, Valerie. *Obadiah Coffee and the music contest* ill. by author. HarperCollins, 1991. ISBN 0-06-

021620-4 Subj: Animals. Animals – rabbits. Careers – musicians. Music.

Pope, Billy N. *Your world: let's visit the hospital* by Billy N. Pope and Ramona Ware Emmons. Taylor, 1971. ISBN 0-8783-3023-2 Subj: Hospitals.

Pope, Geraldine. *The empty creel* ill. by Dennis Cunningham. Godine, 1995. ISBN 1-56792-044-6 Subj: Family life – grandfathers. Sports – fishing.

Popov, Nikolai. *Why?* ill. by author. North-South, 1996. ISBN 1-55858-535-4 Subj: Animals – mice. Frogs and toads. War. Wordless.

Porazinska, Janina. *The enchanted book: a tale from Krakow* ill. by Jan Brett; trans. by Bozena Smith. Harcourt, 1987. ISBN 0-15-225950-3 Subj: Activities – reading. Family life – sisters. Folk and fairy tales. Foreign lands – Poland.

The porcupine ill. by Patrick Oxenham. Rourke, 1983. ISBN 0-86592-852-5 Subj: Animals – porcupines.

Porte, Barbara Ann. *Chickens! Chickens!* ill. by Greg Henry. Orchard, 1995. ISBN 0-531-08727-1 Subj: Art. Birds – chickens. Careers – artists.

Harry in trouble ill. by Yossi Abolafia. Greenwillow, 1989. ISBN 0-688-07722-6 Subj: Careers – librarians. Character traits – helpfulness.

Harry's dog ill. by Yossi Abolafia. Greenwillow, 1983. ISBN 0-688-02556-0 Subj: Animals – dogs. Family life – fathers. Illness.

Harry's mom ill. by Yossi Abolafia. Greenwillow, 1985. ISBN 0-688-04818-8 Subj: Death. Emotions – grief. Family life. Family life – fathers. Family life – grandparents. Family life – mothers. School.

Harry's visit ill. by Yossi Abolafia. Greenwillow, 1983. ISBN 0-688-01208-6 Subj: Behavior – sharing. Sports – basketball.

When Aunt Lucy rode a mule and other stories ill. by Maxie Chambliss. Orchard, 1994. ISBN 0-531-08666-6 Subj: Family life – aunts, uncles. Family life – sisters.

Porter, David Lord. *Mine!* ill. by author. Houghton Mifflin, 1981. ISBN 0-395-31607-3 Subj: Behavior – greed.

Porter, Sue. *Little Wolf and the giant* ill. by author. Simon & Schuster, 1990. ISBN 0-671-70363-3 Subj: Animals – wolves. Forest, woods. Giants.

My little rabbit tale ill. by author. DK, 1994. ISBN 1-56458-339-2 Subj: Animals – rabbits.

One potato ill. by author. Bradbury, 1989. ISBN 0-02-774910-X Subj: Animals. Food.

Parsnip ill. by author. DK, 1997. ISBN 0-7894-2470-3 Subj: Animals – babies. Animals – sheep. Format, unusual – toy and movable books. Seasons – winter.

Parsnip and the pink blanket ill. by author. DK, 2000. ISBN 0-7894-5619-2 Subj: Animals – babies.

Animals – horses, ponies. Animals – sheep. Behavior – losing things. Format, unusual – toy and movable books.

Parsnip and the runaway tractor ill. by author. DK, 1999. ISBN 0-7894-2494-0 Subj: Accidents. Animals – babies. Animals – sheep. Format, unusual – toy and movable books. Tractors.

Porter-Gaylord, Laurel. *I love my daddy because . . .* ill. by Ashley Wolff. Dutton, 1991. ISBN 0-525-44624-9 Subj: Animals. Emotions – love. Family life – fathers.

I love my mommy because . . . ill. by Ashley Wolff. Dutton, 1991. ISBN 0-525-44625-7 Subj: Animals. Emotions – love. Family life – mothers.

Portlock, Rob. *Someone's trying to cut off my head* ill. by author. InterVarsity, 1992. ISBN 0-8308-1902-9 Subj: Careers – barbers. Hair. Imagination.

Portnoy, Mindy Avra. *Ima on the Bima: my mommy is a Rabbi* ill. by Steffi Karen Rubin. Kar-Ben Copies, 1986. ISBN 0-930494-55-5 Subj: Careers. Family life – mothers. Jewish culture.

Matzah ball: a Passover story ill. by Katherine Janus Kahn. Kar-Ben Copies, 1994. ISBN 0-929-37168-2 Subj: Food. Holidays – Passover. Jewish culture. Sports – baseball.

Mommy never went to Hebrew school ill. by Shelly O. Haas. Kar-Ben Copies, 1989. ISBN 0-930494-96-2 Subj: Family life. Jewish culture.

Posada, Mia. *Dandelions, stars in the grass* ill. by author. Carolrhoda, 2000. ISBN 1-575-05383-7 Subj: Flowers. Plants. Science.

Posey, Lee. *Night rabbits* ill. by Michael Montgomery. Peachtree, 1999. ISBN 1-56145-164-9 Subj: Animals – rabbits. Family life – fathers. Homes, houses. Night. Seasons – summer.

Poskanzer, Susan Cornell. *Dairy farmer* ill. by George Ulrich. Troll, 1989. ISBN 0-8167-1426-6 Subj: Animals – bulls, cows. Careers – farmers. Farms.

Puppeteer ill. by Diane Paterson. Troll, 1989. ISBN 0-8167-1432-0 Subj: Careers – puppeteers. Family life – grandmothers. Puppets.

Riddles about Hannukah photos by Rob Gray. Silver Pr., 1990. ISBN 0-671-70553-9 Subj: Holidays – Hanukkah. Rhyming text. Riddles.

What's it like to be a chef? ill. by Karen E. Pellaton. Troll, 1990. ISBN 0-8167-1797-4 Subj: Careers – chefs, cooks.

Post, Howard. *The magic boots* (Emerson, Scott)

Postgate, Oliver. *Noggin and the whale* by Oliver Postgate and Peter Firmin; ill. by Peter Firmin. White, 1967. Subj: Animals – whales. Humor. Royalty – kings.

Noggin the king by Oliver Postgate and Peter Firmin; ill. by Peter Firmin. White, 1965. Subj:

Birds. Character traits – kindness. Humor. Royalty – kings.

Postma, Lidia. *The stolen mirror* ill. by author. McGraw-Hill, 1976. Translation of De gestolen Spiegel. ISBN 0-07-050534-9 Subj: Imagination. Magic. Sibling rivalry.

Tom Thumb: a tale (Tom Thumb)

Poston, Elizabeth. *Baby's song book* ill. by William Stobbs. Crowell, 1971. Subj: Music. Songs.

Potok, Chaim. *The sky of now* ill. by Tony Auth. Knopf, 1995. ISBN 0-679-86021-5 Subj: Activities – flying. Emotions – fear. Family life – aunts, uncles.

Potter, Beatrix. *Appley Dapply's nursery rhymes* ill. by author. Warne, 1917. ISBN 0-7232-0613-9 Subj: Animals. Nursery rhymes.

Beatrix Potter's nursery rhyme book (Mother Goose)

Cecily Parsley's nursery rhymes ill. by author. Warne, 1922. ISBN 0-7232-0614-7 Subj: Animals. Nursery rhymes.

The complete adventures of Peter Rabbit ill. by author. Warne, 1982. ISBN 0-7232-6165-2 Subj: Animals – rabbits. Behavior – misbehavior.

Ginger and Pickles ill. by author. Warne, 1937. First pub. in 1909. Subj: Animals. Stores.

More tales from Beatrix Potter ill. by author. Warne, 1987. ISBN 0-7232-3366-7 Subj: Animals.

Peter Rabbit's ABC ill. by author. Warne, 1999, c1987. ISBN 0-7232-3423-X Subj: ABC books. Animals.

Peter Rabbit's one two three ill. by author. Warne, 1999, c1988. ISBN 0-7232-3424-8 Subj: Animals – rabbits. Counting, numbers.

The pie and the patty-pan ill. by author. Warne, 1933. First pub. in 1905. Subj: Animals – cats. Animals – dogs. Behavior – trickery.

Rolly-polly pudding ill. by author. Warne, 1936. First pub. in 1908. Subj: Animals – cats.

The sly old cat ill. by author. Warne, 1971. ISBN 0-7232-1420-4 Subj: Animals – cats. Animals – rats. Character traits – cleverness. Etiquette. Parties.

The story of fierce bad rabbit ill. by author. Warne, 1906. Subj: Animals – rabbits.

The story of Miss Moppet ill. by author. Warne, 1906. ISBN 0-7232-0612-0 Subj: Animals – cats. Behavior – trickery.

The tailor of Gloucester ill. by author. Warne, 1931. Subj: Animals – mice. Careers – tailors. Character traits – helpfulness.

The tale of Benjamin Bunny ill. by author. Warne, 1904. ISBN 0-7232-0595-7 Subj: Animals – rabbits. Behavior – misbehavior.

The tale of Jemima Puddle-Duck ill. by author. Warne, 1936. First pub. in 1910. Subj: Birds – ducks. Eggs.

The tale of Jemima Puddle-Duck and other farmyard tales: The tale of Mr. Jeremy Fisher; The tale of Mrs. Tiggy-Winkle; The tale of Pigling Bland ill. by author. Large format ed. Warne, 1987. ISBN 0-7232-3425-6 Subj: Animals. Birds.

The tale of Johnny Town-Mouse ill. by author. Warne, 1918. ISBN 0-7232-0604-X Subj: Animals – mice.

The tale of Little Pig Robinson ill. by author. Warne, 1930. Subj: Animals – pigs. Behavior – talking to strangers. Boats, ships. Shopping.

The tale of Mr. Jeremy Fisher ill. by author. Warne, 1934. ISBN 0-7232-6231-4 Subj: Frogs and toads. Sports – fishing.

The tale of Mr. Jeremy Fisher ill. by David Jorgensen. Picture Book Studio, 1989. ISBN 0-88708-094-4 Subj: Frogs and toads. Sports – fishing.

The tale of Mr. Tod ill. by author. Warne, 1939. First pub. in 1911. Subj: Animals – badgers. Animals – foxes. Animals – rabbits.

The tale of Mrs. Tiggy-Winkle ill. by author. Warne, 1905. Subj: Animals – hedgehogs. Clothing.

The tale of Mrs. Tittlemouse ill. by author. Warne, 1910. ISBN 0-7232-6235-7 Subj: Animals – mice. Character traits – cleanliness.

The tale of Mrs. Tittlemouse and other mouse stories: The tale of Johnny Town-Mouse; The tale of two bad mice; The tailor of Gloucester ill. by author. Large format ed. Warne, 1985. ISBN 0-7232-3324-1 Subj: Animals – mice.

The tale of Peter Rabbit ill. by Margot Apple. Troll, 1979. ISBN 0-89375-124-3 Subj: Animals – rabbits. Behavior – misbehavior.

The tale of Peter Rabbit ill. by author. Warne, 1902. ISBN 0-7232-0592-2 Subj: Animals – rabbits. Behavior – misbehavior. Farms.

The tale of Peter Rabbit and other stories ill. by Allen Atkinson. Knopf, 1982. ISBN 0-394-52845-X Subj: Animals.

The tale of Pigling Bland ill. by author. Warne, 1941, 1913. ISBN 0-7232-0606-6 Subj: Animals – pigs.

The tale of Squirrel Nutkin ill. by author. Warne, 1903. ISBN 0-7232-0593-0 Subj: Animals – squirrels. Birds – owls. Riddles. Seasons – fall.

The tale of the faithful dove ill. by Marie Angel. Warne, 1970. Subj: Birds – doves. Character traits – loyalty.

The tale of the Flopsy Bunnies ill. by author. Warne, 1909, 1937. ISBN 0-7232-0601-5 Subj: Animals – rabbits. Character traits – cleverness.

The tale of Timmy Tiptoes ill. by author. Warne, 1911, 1939. ISBN 0-7232-0603-1 Subj: Animals – squirrels.

The tale of Tom Kitten ill. by author. Warne, 1907. ISBN 0-7232-0599-X Subj: Animals – cats. Humor.

The tale of Tuppeny ill. by Marie Angel. Warne, 1971. Subj: Animals – guinea pigs.

The tale of two bad mice ill. by author. Warne, 1904, 1934. Subj: Animals – mice. Behavior – misbehavior. Toys.

A treasury of Peter Rabbit and other stories ill. by author. Watts, 1978. Subj: Animals.

The two bad mice: pop-up book ill. by author. Warne, 1986. ISBN 0-7232-3360-8 Subj: Animals – mice. Behavior – misbehavior. Format, unusual – toy and movable books.

Where's Peter Rabbit? ill. by Colin Twinn. Warne, 1988. ISBN 0-7232-3519-8 Subj: Animals – rabbits. Behavior – misbehavior. Format, unusual.

Yours affectionately, Peter Rabbit: miniature letters ill. by author. Warne, 1984. ISBN 0-7232-3178-8 Subj: Animals. Communication.

Potter, Stephen. *Squawky, the adventures of a clasper-choice* ill. by George Him. Lippincott, 1964. Subj: Birds – parakeets, parrots.

Potter, Tessa. *Digger, the story of a mole in the fall* ill. by Ken Lilly. Raintree, 1997. ISBN 0-8172-4623-1 Subj: Animals – moles. Seasons – fall. Weather – rain.

Potter, Tony. *See how it works: cars* ill. by Robin Lawrie. Aladdin, 1989. ISBN 0-689-71303-7 Subj: Automobiles. Format, unusual.

See how it works: earth movers ill. by Robin Lawrie. Aladdin, 1989. ISBN 0-689-71302-9 Subj: Format, unusual. Machines.

See how it works: planes ill. by Robin Lawrie. Aladdin, 1989. ISBN 0-689-71304-5 Subj: Airplanes, airports. Format, unusual.

See how it works: trucks ill. by Robin Lawrie. Aladdin, 1989. ISBN 0-689-71301-0 Subj: Format, unusual. Trucks.

Poulin, Stéphane. *Benjamin and the pillow saga* ill. by author. Firefly, 1989. ISBN 1-55037-069-3 Subj: Magic. Music.

Can you catch Josephine? ill. by author. Tundra, 1987. ISBN 0-88776-198-4 Subj: Animals – cats. Behavior – misbehavior. Foreign lands – Canada. School.

Have you seen Josephine? ill. by author. Tundra, 1986. ISBN 0-88776-180-1 Subj: Animals – cats. Behavior – running away. Foreign lands – Canada.

My mother's loves: stories and lies from my childhood ill. by author. Firefly, 1990. ISBN 1-55037-149-5 Subj: Behavior – growing up. Family life.

Travels for two ill. by author. Firefly, 1991. ISBN 1-55037-205-X Subj: Activities – traveling. Family life. Islands. Sea and seashore.

Pouyanne, Rési. *What I see hidden by the pond* ill. by Gerda Muller. Two Continents, 1977. Subj: Animals. Plants. Science.

Pouyanne, Thérèse. *The hippo* ill. by Caroline Binch. Rourke, 1983. ISBN 0-86592-855-X Subj: Animals – hippopotamuses.

Powell, Consie. *A bold carnivore* ill. by author. Roberts Rinehart, 1995. ISBN 1-57098-023-3 Subj: ABC books. Animals. Birds. Nature.

Old dog Cora and the Christmas tree ill. by author. Albert Whitman, 1999. ISBN 0-8075-5968-7 Subj: Animals – dogs. Family life. Holidays – Christmas. Old age. Trees.

Powell, E. Sandy. *A chance to grow* ill. by Zulma Davila. Carolrhoda, 1992. ISBN 0-87614-741-4 Subj: Family life. Homeless. Poverty.

Powell, Jillian. *Eggs* ill. by author. Raintree, 1997. ISBN 0-8172-4759-9 Subj: Activities – cooking. Eggs. Food.

Jumpers photos by author. Carolrhoda, 1992. ISBN 0-87614-702-3 Subj: Activities – jumping. Animals.

Powell, Polly. *Just dessert* ill. by author. Harcourt, 1996. ISBN 0-15-200383-5 Subj: Emotions – fear. Food. Imagination. Night.

Powell, Roxanne Dyer. *Cat, mouse and moon* ill. by Will Hillenbrand. Houghton Mifflin, 1994. ISBN 0-395-59348-4 Subj: Animals – cats. Animals – mice. Moon. Night.

Power, Barbara. *I wish Laura's mommy was my mommy* ill. by Marylin Hafner. Lippincott, 1979. ISBN 0-397-31838-3 Subj: Behavior – growing up. Behavior – wishing. Family life – mothers.

Powers, Daniel. *Jiro's pearl* ill. by author. Candlewick, 1997. ISBN 1-56402-631-0 Subj: Family life – grandmothers. Folk and fairy tales. Foreign lands – Japan. Illness.

Powers, Mary E. *Our teacher's in a wheelchair* photos by author. Albert Whitman, 1986. ISBN 0-8075-6240-8 Subj: Careers – teachers. Handicaps. School.

Powzyk, Joyce Ann. *Tasmania: a wildlife journey* ill. by author. Lothrop, 1987. ISBN 0-688-06460-4 Subj: Animals. Foreign lands – Australia. Nature. Science.

Poydar, Nancy. *Busy Bea* ill. by author. Margaret K. McElderry, 1994. ISBN 0-689-50592-2 Subj: Behavior – losing things. Ethnic groups in the U.S. – African Americans. Family life – grandmothers. School.

Cool Ali ill. by author. Margaret K. McElderry, 1996. ISBN 0-689-80755-4 Subj: Activities – drawing. City. Concepts – shape. Concepts – size. Seasons – summer.

First day, hooray! ill. by author. Holiday, 1999. ISBN 0-8234-1437-X Subj: School – first day.

Mailbox magic ill. by author. Holiday, 2000. ISBN 0-8234-1525-2 Subj: Character traits – patience. Letters, cards.

Snip, snip . . . snow! ill. by author. Holiday, 1997. ISBN 0-8234-1328-4 Subj: Activities – playing. Nature. School. Seasons – winter. Weather – snow.

Prager, Annabelle. *The baseball birthday party* ill. by Marilyn Mets. Random House, 1995. ISBN 0-679-94171-1 Subj: Behavior – mistakes. Ethnic groups in the U.S. Parties. Sports – baseball.

The spooky Halloween party ill. by Tomie de Paola. Pantheon, 1981. ISBN 0-394-94370-8 Subj: Holidays – Halloween. Parties.

The surprise party ill. by Tomie de Paola. Random House, 1988. ISBN 0-394-93235-8 Subj: Birthdays. Parties.

Pragoff, Fiona. *It's fun to be one* photos by author. Aladdin, 1994. ISBN 0-689-71813-6 Subj: Activities – playing. Babies.

It's great to be two photos by author. Aladdin, 1994. ISBN 0-689-71814-4 Subj: Activities – playing. Babies.

Let's find Teddy photos by author. Random House, 1992. ISBN 0-679-83501-6 Subj: Concepts. Games.

Odd one out ill. by author. Doubleday, 1989. ISBN 0-385-26410-0 Subj: Concepts. Format, unusual – board books. Games.

Opposites ill. by author. Doubleday, 1989. ISBN 0-385-26409-7 Subj: Concepts – opposites. Format, unusual – board books.

Shapes ill. by author. Doubleday, 1989. ISBN 0-385-26408-9 Subj: Concepts – shape. Concepts – size. Format, unusual – board books.

Prall, Jo. *My sister's special* ill. with photos. Childrens Pr., 1985. ISBN 0-516-03862-1 Subj: Family life – sisters. Handicaps.

Prater, John. *Along came Tom* ill. by author. Trafalgar Square, 1992. ISBN 0-370-31411-5 Subj: Family life.

The gift ill. by author. Viking, 1986. ISBN 0-670-80952-7 Subj: Behavior – wishing. Gifts. Wordless.

The greatest show on earth ill. by author. Candlewick, 1995. ISBN 1-56402-563-2 Subj: Circus. Clowns, jesters. Family life. Self-concept.

"No!" said Joe ill. by author. Candlewick, 1992. ISBN 1-56402-037-1 Subj: Behavior – misbehavior. Rhyming text. Shopping.

On Friday something funny happened ill. by author. Random House, 1988. ISBN 0-370-30449-7 Subj: Behavior – misbehavior. Days of the week, months of the year.

On top of the world ill. by author. Mondo, 1998. ISBN 1-57255-649-8 Subj: Animals. Night. Toys.

Once upon a picnic conceived and ill. by John Prater; text by Vivian French. Candlewick, 1996. ISBN 1-56402-810-0 Subj: Activities – picnicking. Imagination. Rhyming text.

Once upon a time conceived and ill. by John Prater; text by Vivian French. Candlewick, 1993. ISBN 1-56402-177-7 Subj: Imagination. Rhyming text.

The perfect day ill. by author. Dutton, 1987. ISBN 0-525-44282-0 Subj: Behavior – bad day. Sea and seashore.

You can't catch me! ill. by author. Salem House, 1986. ISBN 0-370-30594-9 Subj: Behavior – misbehavior. Behavior – running away.

Prather, Ray. *Double dog dare* ill. by author. Macmillan, 1975. ISBN 0-02-775040-X Subj: Animals – dogs. Humor.

The ostrich girl ill. by author. Scribners, 1978. ISBN 0-684-15889-2 Subj: Folk and fairy tales. Foreign lands – Africa. Forest, woods. Reptiles – snakes. Witches.

Pratt, Kristin Joy. *A fly in the sky* ill. by author. Dawn Pub., 1996. ISBN 1-883220-40-8 Subj: ABC books. Animals. Birds. Insects. Insects – flies.

A swim through the sea ill. by author. Dawn Pub., 1994. ISBN 1-883220-03-3 Subj: ABC books. Crustaceans. Fish. Sea and seashore.

Prebeg, Rick A. *Jungle Jack Hanna's safari adventure* (Hanna, Jack)

Precek, Katharine Wilson. *Penny in the road* ill. by Patricia Cullen-Clark. Macmillan, 1989. ISBN 0-02-774970-3 Subj: Behavior – losing things. U.S. history.

Preiss, Byron. *The first crazy word book: verbs* by Byron Preiss and Ralph Reese; ill. by Ralph Reese. Watts, 1982. ISBN 0-531-04439-4 Subj: Language.

Preller, James. *Cardinal and sunflower* ill. by Huy Voun Lee. HarperCollins, 1998. ISBN 0-06-026223-0 Subj: Birds – cardinals. Flowers. Nature.

Prelutsky, Jack. *The baby uggs are hatching* ill. by James Stevenson. Greenwillow, 1982. ISBN 0-688-00923-9 Subj: Humor. Imagination. Monsters. Poetry.

Beneath a blue umbrella ill. by Garth Williams. Greenwillow, 1990. ISBN 0-688-06429-9 Subj: Animals. Poetry.

Brave little Pete of Geranium Street (Lagercrantz, Rose)

Circus ill. by Arnold Lobel. Macmillan, 1974. ISBN 0-02-775060-4 Subj: Circus. Poetry.

For laughing out louder: more poems to tickle your funnybone (For laughing out louder)

Imagine that! poems of never-was (Imagine that! poems of never-was)

The mean old mean hyena ill. by Arnold Lobel. Greenwillow, 1978. ISBN 0-688-84163-5 Subj: Animals – hyenas. Character traits – meanness. Rhyming text.

Monday's troll ill. by Peter Sis. Greenwillow, 1996. ISBN 0-688-09644-1 Subj: Fairies. Mythical creatures – trolls. Poetry. Witches.

The pack rat's day and other poems ill. by Margaret Bloy Graham. Macmillan, 1974. ISBN 0-02-775050-7 Subj: Animals. Poetry.

The queen of Eene ill. by Victoria Chess. Greenwillow, 1978. ISBN 0-688-84144-9 Subj: Humor. Poetry.

Rainy rainy Saturday ill. by Marylin Hafner. Greenwillow, 1980. ISBN 0-688-84252-6 Subj: Poetry. Weather – rain.

The Random House book of poetry for children ill. by Arnold Lobel. Random House, 1983. ISBN 0-394-95010-0 Subj: Humor. Poetry.

Read-aloud rhymes for the very young ill. by Marc Brown. Knopf, 1986. ISBN 0-394-97218-X Subj: Poetry.

Ride a purple pelican ill. by Garth Williams. Greenwillow, 1986. ISBN 0-688-04031-4 Subj: Imagination. Poetry.

The snopp on the sidewalk and other poems ill. by Byron Barton. Greenwillow, 1977. ISBN 0-688-84084-1 Subj: Humor. Imagination. Poetry.

The terrible tiger ill. by Arnold Lobel. Macmillan, 1970. ISBN 0-689-71300-2 Subj: Animals – tigers. Cumulative tales. Rhyming text.

Tyrannosaurus was a beast ill. by Arnold Lobel. Greenwillow, 1988. ISBN 0-688-06443-4 Subj: Dinosaurs. Poetry.

The wild baby (Lindgren, Barbro)

The wild baby gets a puppy (Lindgren, Barbro)

The wild baby goes to sea (Lindgren, Barbro)

Presencer, Alain. *Roaring lion tales* ill. by Ron Van der Meer. HarperCollins, 1984. ISBN 0-216-91606-2 Subj: Animals – lions. Folk and fairy tales. Format, unusual – toy and movable books.

Preston, Edna Mitchell. *Horrible Hepzibah* ill. by Ray Cruz. Viking, 1971. ISBN 0-670-37877-1 Subj: Behavior – misbehavior. Humor.

Monkey in the jungle ill. by Clement Hurd. Viking, 1968. Subj: Animals – monkeys. Bedtime. Night. Sleep.

One dark night ill. by Kurt Werth. Viking, 1969. ISBN 0-670-52585-5 Subj: Cumulative tales. Holidays – Halloween.

Pop Corn and Ma Goodness ill. by Robert Andrew Parker. Viking, 1969. Subj: Caldecott award honor books. Humor. Rhyming text. Songs. Weather – rain.

Squawk to the moon, little goose ill. by Barbara Cooney. Viking, 1974. ISBN 0-670-66609-2 Subj: Animals – foxes. Behavior – misbehavior. Birds – geese. Moon.

Preussler, Otfried. *The tale of the unicorn* trans. by Lenny Hort; ill. by Gennady Spirin. Dial, 1989. ISBN 0-8037-0583-2 Subj: Folk and fairy tales. Mythical creatures – unicorns.

Price, Christine. *One is God: two old counting songs* ill. by author. Warne, 1970. Subj: Counting, numbers. Religion. Songs.

Price, Dorothy E. *Speedy gets around* ill. by Betsy Warren. Steck-Vaughn, 1965. Subj: Animals – chipmunks. Camps, camping.

Price, Hope Lynne. *These hands* ill. by Bryan Collier. Hyperion, 1999. ISBN 0-7868-2320-8 Subj: Anatomy – hands. Ethnic groups in the U.S. – African Americans. Family life – mothers. Rhyming text.

Price, Leontyne. *Aïda* ill. by Leo and Diane Dillon. Harcourt, 1990. Retells the story of Giuseppe Verdi's opera. ISBN 0-15-200405-X Subj: Emotions – love. Foreign lands – Egypt. Music. Royalty.

Price, Mathew. *Do you see what I see?* ill. by Sue Porter. HarperCollins, 1986. ISBN 0-694-00002-7 Subj: Animals. Behavior – losing things. Circus. Format, unusual.

Don't worry, Alfie ill. Emma Chichester Clark. Orchard, 1999. ISBN 0-531-30127-3 Subj: Animals. Animals – bears. Family life – mothers.

Dumbo ill. by Atsuko Morozumi. Disney Pr., 2000. ISBN 0-7868-3274-6 Subj: Animals – elephants. Circus.

Have you seen my sister? ill. by Errol Le Cain. Harcourt, 1992. ISBN 0-15-200467-X Subj: Family life – sisters. Format, unusual. Friendship. Imagination. Toys.

Patch and the rabbits ill. Emma Chichester Clark. Orchard, 2000. ISBN 0-531-30265-2 Subj: Animals – dogs. Animals – rabbits. Dreams. Format, unusual – toy and movable books.

Patch finds a friend ill. Emma Chichester Clark. Orchard, 2000. ISBN 0-531-30264-4 Subj: Animals – cats. Animals – dogs. Friendship.

Peekaboo! ill. by Jean Claverie. Knopf, 1985. ISBN 0-394-87142-1 Subj: Family life. Format, unusual – toy and movable books.

Where's Alfie? ill. Emma Chichester Clark. Orchard, 1999. ISBN 0-531-30126-5 Subj: Animals – bears. Behavior – hiding. Family life – mothers.

Price, Michelle. *Mean Melissa* ill. by author. Bradbury, 1977. ISBN 0-87888-126-3 Subj: Character traits – meanness. School.

Price, Roger. *The last little dragon* ill. by Mamoru Funai. HarperCollins, 1969. Subj: Behavior – dissatisfaction. Dragons.

Priceman, Marjorie. *Emeline at the circus* ill. by author. Knopf, 1999. ISBN 0-679-87685-5 Subj: Careers – teachers. Circus. School.

Friend or frog ill. by author. Houghton Mifflin, 1989. ISBN 0-395-44523-X Subj: Friendship. Frogs and toads.

Froggie went a courting (A frog he would a-wooing go [folk-song])

How to make an apple pie and see the world ill. by author. Knopf, 1994. ISBN 0-679-93705-6 Subj: Activities – cooking. Activities – traveling. Food.

My nine lives / by Clio ill. by author. Atheneum, 1998. ISBN 0-689-81135-7 Subj: Animals – cats. Memories, memory.

Price-Thomas, Brian. *The magic ark* ill. by author. Crown, 1987. ISBN 0-517-56705-9 Subj: Animals. Imagination.

Priddy, Roger. *Baby's book of nature* ill. by author. DK, 1995. ISBN 0-7894-0003-0 Subj: Concepts – color. Concepts – shape. Nature.

Priest, Robert. *The old pirate of Central Park* ill. by author. Houghton Mifflin, 1999. ISBN 0-395-90505-2 Subj: Activities – playing. Boats, ships. Toys.

Priestley, Alice. *Someone is reading this book* ill. by author. Firefly, 1998. ISBN 1-55037-448-6 Subj: Activities – flying. Format, unusual – toy and movable books. Giants. Royalty – princes.

Prigger, Mary Skillings. *Aunt Minnie McGranahan* ill. by Betsy Lewin. Clarion, 1999. Subj: Character traits – orderliness. Family life – aunts, uncles. Family life – brothers and sisters. Orphans.

Primavera, Elise. *Basil and Maggie* ill. by author. Lippincott, 1983. ISBN 0-397-32028-0 Subj: Animals – horses, ponies. Character traits – appearance.

Plantpet ill. by author. Putnam, 1994. ISBN 0-399-22627-3 Subj: Gardens, gardening. Pets. Plants.

Prince, Pamela. *The secret world of teddy bears* photos by Elaine Faris Keenan. Crown, 1983. ISBN 0-517-55022-9 Subj: Poetry. Toys – bears.

The prince who knew his fate: *an ancient Egyptian tale* trans. from hieroglyphs and ill. by Lise Manniche. Putnam, 1982. ISBN 0-399-20850-X Subj: Folk and fairy tales. Foreign lands – Egypt. Hieroglyphics. Magic. Royalty – princes.

Pringle, Laurence P. *Everybody has a bellybutton: your life before you were born* ill. by Clare Wood. Boyds Mills, 1997. ISBN 1-56397-009-0 Subj: Birth. Family life.

Jesse builds a road ill. by Leslie Holt Morrill. Macmillan, 1989. ISBN 0-02-775311-5 Subj: Imagination. Machines. Roads.

Naming the cat ill. by Katherine Potter. Walker, 1997. ISBN 0-8027-8622-7 Subj: Animals – cats. Names. Pets.

Octopus hug ill. by Kate Salley Palmer. Boyds Mills, 1993. ISBN 1-56397-034-1 Subj: Activities – playing. Family life.

Prins, Johanna H. *The princess in the kitchen garden* (Heymans, Annemie)

Prins, Johanna W. *The princess in the kitchen garden* (Heymans, Annemie)

Proimos, James. *Joe's wish* ill. by author. Harcourt, 1998. ISBN 0-15-201831-X Subj: Behavior – wishing. Family life – grandfathers. Old age.

The loudness of Sam ill. by author. Harcourt, 1999. ISBN 0-15-202087-X Subj: City. Emotions. Family life – aunts, uncles.

Prokofiev, Sergei Sergeievitch. *Peter and the wolf* adapt. by Selina Hastings; ill. by Reg Cartwright. Holt, 1987. ISBN 0-8050-0408-4 Subj: Animals – wolves. Character traits – cleverness. Folk and fairy tales. Foreign lands – Russia.

Peter and the wolf ill. by Warren Chappell; foreword by Serge Koussevitsky; calligraphy by Hollis Holland. Schocken, 1981, c1940. ISBN 0-8052-0684-1 Subj: Animals – wolves. Character traits – cleverness. Folk and fairy tales. Foreign lands – Russia. Music.

Peter and the wolf ill. by Barbara Cooney. Viking, 1986. ISBN 0-670-80849-0 Subj: Animals – wolves. Character traits – cleverness. Folk and fairy tales. Foreign lands – Russia. Format, unusual – toy and movable books. Music.

Peter and the wolf adapt. by Gerlinde Wiencirz; ill. by Julia Gukova; trans. by Anthea Bell. North-South, 1999. ISBN 0-7358-1189-X Subj: Animals – wolves. Character traits – cleverness. Folk and fairy tales. Foreign lands – Russia. Music.

Peter and the wolf ill. by Frans Haacken. Watts, 1961. Subj: Animals – wolves. Character traits – cleverness. Folk and fairy tales. Foreign lands – Russia. Music.

Peter and the wolf ill. by Alan Howard. Transatlantic, 1954. Subj: Animals – wolves. Character traits – cleverness. Folk and fairy tales. Foreign lands – Russia. Music.

Peter and the wolf trans. by Maria Carlson; ill. by Charles Mikolaycak. Viking, 1982. ISBN 0-670-54919-3 Subj: Animals – wolves. Character traits – cleverness. Folk and fairy tales. Foreign lands – Russia. Music.

Peter and the wolf adapt. by Loriot; ill. by Jörg Müller. Knopf, 1986. Book-cassette included. ISBN 0-394-88417-5 Subj: Animals – wolves. Character traits – cleverness. Folk and fairy tales. Foreign lands – Russia. Music.

Peter and the wolf trans. by Patricia Crampton; ill. by Josef Palecek. Picture Book Studio, 1987. ISBN 0-88708-049-9 Subj: Animals – wolves. Character traits – cleverness. Folk and fairy tales. Foreign lands – Russia. Music.

Peter and the wolf retold by Ann Herring; ill. by Kozo Shimizu; photos by Yasugi Yajima. Gakken, 1971. Subj: Animals – wolves. Character traits – cleverness. Folk and fairy tales. Foreign lands – Russia. Music.

Peter and the wolf retold and ill. by Vladimir Vagin. Scholastic, 2000. ISBN 0-590-38608-5 Subj: Animals – wolves. Character traits – cleverness. Folk and fairy tales. Foreign lands – Russia. Music.

Peter and the wolf ill. by Erna Voigt. Godine, 1980. ISBN 0-87923-331-1 Subj: Animals – wolves. Character traits – cleverness. Folk and fairy tales. Foreign lands – Russia. Music.

Propp, James. *Tuscanini* ill. by Ellen Weiss. Bradbury, 1992. ISBN 0-02-774911-8 Subj: Animals – elephants. Crime. Zoos.

Prose, Francine. *The angel's mistake: stories of Chelm* ill. by Mark Podwal. Greenwillow, 1997. ISBN 0-688-14906-5 Subj: Angels. Behavior – mistakes. Folk and fairy tales. Jewish culture.

Dybbuk ill. by Mark Podwal. Greenwillow, 1996. ISBN 0-688-14308-3 Subj: Angels. Folk and fairy tales. Jewish culture. Weddings.

You never know: a legend of the Lamed-Vavniks ill. by Mark Podwal. Greenwillow, 1998. ISBN 0-688-15807-2 Subj: Behavior – secrets. Careers – shoemakers. Folk and fairy tales. Jewish culture.

Provensen, Alice. *A book of seasons* by Alice and Martin Provensen; ill. by authors. Random House, 1976. ISBN 0-394-83242-6 Subj: Seasons.

The glorious flight: across the channel with Louis Blériot by Alice and Martin Provensen; ill. by authors. Viking, 1983. ISBN 0-14-050729-9 Subj: Activities – flying. Airplanes, airports. Caldecott award books.

Karen's opposites by Alice and Martin Provensen; ill. by authors. Golden Pr., 1963. Subj: Concepts – opposites. Rhyming text.

My little hen by Alice and Martin Provensen; ill. by authors. Random House, 1973. ISBN 0-394-92684-6 Subj: Birds – chickens.

Our animal friends at Maple Hill Farm by Alice and Martin Provensen; ill. by authors. Random House, 1992, 1974. ISBN 0-394-92123-2 Subj: Animals. Farms.

An owl and three pussycats by Alice and Martin Provensen; ill. by authors. Browndeer, 1994. ISBN 0-15-200183-2 Subj: Family life. Farms. Pets.

Punch in New York ill. by author. Viking, 1991. ISBN 0-670-82790-8 Subj: Behavior – misbehavior. City. Puppets.

Shaker Lane by Alice and Martin Provensen; ill. by authors. Viking, 1987. ISBN 0-670-81568-3 Subj: City. Moving. Poverty.

Town and country by Alice and Martin Provensen; ill. by authors. Crown, 1984. ISBN 0-15-200182-4 Subj: City. Country.

The year at Maple Hill Farm by Alice and Martin Provensen; ill. by authors. Atheneum, 1978. ISBN 0-689-20494-9 Subj: Animals. Days of the week, months of the year. Farms. Seasons.

Provensen, Martin. *A book of seasons* (Provensen, Alice)

The glorious flight: across the channel with Louis Blériot (Provensen, Alice)

Karen's opposites (Provensen, Alice)

My little hen (Provensen, Alice)

Our animal friends at Maple Hill Farm (Provensen, Alice)

An owl and three pussycats (Provensen, Alice)

Shaker Lane (Provensen, Alice)

Town and country (Provensen, Alice)

The year at Maple Hill Farm (Provensen, Alice)

Prøysen, Alf. *Christmas eve at Santa's* ill. by author. Farrar, 1992. ISBN 91-29-62066-X Subj: Careers – carpenters. Family life. Holidays – Christmas. Santa Claus.

Mrs. Pepperpot and the moose trans. from Swedish by Richard E. Fisher; ill. by Björn Berg. Farrar, 1991. ISBN 91-29-59924-5 Subj: Animals – moose. Character traits – smallness. Concepts – size.

Prunier, James. *Trains* (Trains)

Prusski, Jeffrey. *Bring back the deer* ill. by Neil Waldman. Harcourt, 1988. ISBN 0-15-200418-1 Subj: Animals – deer. Animals – wolves. Family life. Forest, woods. Indians of North America. Seasons – winter. Sports – hunting.

Pryor, Ainslie. *The baby blue cat and the dirty dog brothers* ill. by author. Viking, 1987. ISBN 0-670-81781-3 Subj: Activities – bathing. Animals – cats. Animals – dogs.

The baby blue cat and the smiley worm doll ill. by author. Viking, 1990. ISBN 0-670-83531-5 Subj: Animals – cats. Behavior – losing things. Toys – dolls.

The baby blue cat and the whole batch of cookies ill. by author. Viking, 1989. ISBN 0-670-81782-1 Subj: Behavior – losing things. Toys – dolls.

The baby blue cat who said no ill. by author. Viking, 1988. ISBN 0-670-81780-5 Subj: Animals – cats. Bedtime.

Pryor, Bonnie. *Amanda and April* ill. by Diane de Groat. Morrow, 1986. ISBN 0-688-05870-1 Subj: Animals – pigs. Family life – sisters. Parties. Sibling rivalry.

The beaver boys ill. by Karen Lee Baker. Morrow, 1991. ISBN 0-688-08703-5 Subj: Animals – beavers. Homes, houses. Moving.

The dream jar ill. by Mark Graham. Morrow, 1996. ISBN 0-688-13062-3 Subj: Activities – working. City. Ethnic groups in the U.S. – Russian Americans. Family life. Immigrants.

Greenbrook farm ill. by Mark Graham. Simon & Schuster, 1991. ISBN 0-671-69205-4 Subj: Animals. Babies. Farms.

The house on Maple Street ill. by Beth Peck. Morrow, 1987. ISBN 0-688-06381-0 Subj: U.S. history.

Lottie's dream ill. by Mark Graham. Simon & Schuster, 1992. ISBN 0-671-74774-6 Subj: Farms. Sea and seashore. U.S. history – frontier and pioneer life.

Louie and Dan are friends ill. by Elizabeth J. Miles. Morrow, 1997. ISBN 0-688-08561-X Subj: Animals – mice. Family life – brothers. Friendship.

Merry Christmas, Amanda and April ill. by Diane de Groat. Morrow, 1990. ISBN 0-688-07545-2 Subj: Animals – pigs. Family life – sisters. Holidays – Christmas.

Mr. Munday and the rustlers ill. by Wallop Manyum. Prentice-Hall, 1988. ISBN 0-13-604737-8 Subj: Crime. Farms.

Mr. Munday and the space creatures ill. by Lee Lorenz. Simon & Schuster, 1989. ISBN 0-671-67114-6 Subj: Aliens. Careers – postal workers. Space and space ships.

The porcupine mouse ill. by Maryjane Begin. Morrow, 1988. ISBN 0-688-07154-6 Subj: Animals – mice. Character traits – bravery. Emotions – fear. Sibling rivalry.

The pudgy book of babies ill. by Kathy Wilburn. Putnam, 1984. ISBN 0-448-10207-2 Subj: Babies. Format, unusual – board books.

The pudgy book of farm animals ill. by Julie Durrell. Putnam, 1984. ISBN 0-448-10211-0 Subj: Animals. Farms. Format, unusual – board books.

The pudgy book of here we go ill. by Beth Weiner Lipson. Putnam, 1984. ISBN 0-448-10208-0 Subj: Format, unusual – board books.

The pudgy book of make-believe ill. by Andrea Brooks. Putnam, 1984. ISBN 0-448-10209-9 Subj: Format, unusual – board books. Imagination.

The pudgy book of Mother Goose ill. by Richard Walz. Putnam, 1984. ISBN 0-448-10212-9 Subj: Format, unusual – board books. Nursery rhymes.

The pudgy book of toys ill. by Julie Durrell. Grosset, 1983. ISBN 0-448-10201-3 Subj: Format, unusual – board books. Toys.

The pudgy bunny book ill. by Ruth Sanderson. Putnam, 1984. ISBN 0-448-10210-2 Subj: Animals – rabbits. Format, unusual – board books.

The pudgy fingers counting book ill. by Doug Cushman. Grosset, 1983. ISBN 0-448-10202-1 Subj: Birthdays. Counting, numbers. Format, unusual – board books.

The pudgy pals ill. by Kathy Wilburn. Grosset, 1983. Subj: Format, unusual – board books.

The pudgy pat-a-cake book ill. by Terri Super. Grosset, 1983. ISBN 0-448-10204-8 Subj: Format, unusual – board books. Games.

The pudgy peek-a-boo book ill. by Amye Rosenberg. Grosset, 1983. ISBN 0-448-10205-6 Subj: Format, unusual – board books. Games.

The pudgy rock-a-bye book ill. by Kathy Wilburn. Grosset, 1983. ISBN 0-448-10206-4 Subj: Format, unusual – board books.

Pulsifer, Marjorie P. *Bikes* (Baugh, Dolores M.)

Let's go (Baugh, Dolores M.)

Let's see the animals (Baugh, Dolores M.)

Let's take a trip (Baugh, Dolores M.)

Slides (Baugh, Dolores M.)

Supermarket (Baugh, Dolores M.)

Swings (Baugh, Dolores M.)

Trucks and cars to ride (Baugh, Dolores M.)

Pulver, Robin. *Alicia's tutu* ill. by Mark Graham. Dial, 1997. ISBN 0-8037-1933-7 Subj: Activities – dancing. Ballet. Behavior – wishing. Family life. Family life – grandmothers. Furniture – beds.

Axle Annie ill. by Tedd Arnold. Dial, 1999. ISBN 0-8037-2096-3 Subj: Careers – bus drivers. School. Weather – snow.

Homer and the house next door ill. by Annie Levin. Four Winds, 1994. ISBN 0-02-775457-X Subj: Animals – dogs. Moving.

Mrs. Toggle and the dinosaur ill. by R. W. Alley. Four Winds, 1991. ISBN 0-02-775452-9 Subj: Careers – teachers. Dinosaurs. School.

Mrs. Toggle's beautiful blue shoe ill. by R. W. Alley. Four Winds, 1991. ISBN 0-02-775456-1 Subj: Careers – teachers. Clothing – shoes. School.

Mrs. Toggle's zipper ill. by R. W. Alley. Four Winds, 1990. ISBN 0-02-775451-0 Subj: Careers – teachers. Clothing – coats. Humor. School.

Nobody's mother is in second grade ill. by Brian G. Karas. Dial, 1992. ISBN 0-8037-1211-1 Subj: Family life – mothers. Plants. School.

Way to go, Alex! ill. by Elizabeth Wolf. Albert Whitman, 1999. ISBN 0-8075-1583-3 Subj: Family life – brothers and sisters. Handicaps. Sports – Special Olympics.

Puner, Helen Walker. *Daddys, what they do all day* ill. by Roger Antoine Duvoisin. Lothrop, 1946. Subj: Activities – working. Careers. Family life – fathers. Rhyming text.

The sitter who didn't sit ill. by Roger Antoine Duvoisin. Lothrop, 1949. Subj: Activities – babysitting. Humor. Rhyming text.

Puppies and kittens photos by Walter Chandoha. Platt, 1983. ISBN 0-448-40874-0 Subj: Animals – cats. Animals – dogs. Format, unusual – board books. Rhyming text.

Purcell, John Wallace. *African animals* ill. with photos. Rev. ed. Childrens Pr., 1982. ISBN 0-516-01665-2 Subj: Animals. Foreign lands – Africa.

Purdy, Carol. *Iva Dunnit and the big wind* ill. by Steven Kellogg. Dial, 1985. ISBN 0-8037-0184-5 Subj: Family life. Weather – wind.

Least of all ill. by Tim Arnold. Macmillan, 1987. ISBN 0-689-50404-7 Subj: Activities – reading. Activities – working. Family life. Self-concept.

Mrs. Merriwether's musical cat ill. by Petra Mathers. Putnam, 1994. ISBN 0-399-22543-9 Subj: Animals – cats. Music.

Puricelli, Luigi. *In my garden* (Cristini, Ermanno)

In the pond (Cristini, Ermanno)

In the woods (Cristini, Ermanno)

Pursell, Margaret Sanford. *Jessie the chicken* orig. trans. by Dyan Hammarberg; photos by Claudie Fayn-Rodriguez; ill. by L'Enc Matte. Carolrhoda, 1977. Based on Anne Marie Pajot's Picota la poule. ISBN 0-8761-4074-6 Subj: Birds – chickens. Eggs.

A look at birth ill. by Maria S. Forrai. Lerner, 1976. ISBN 0-8225-1307-2 Subj: Babies. Birth. Science.

A look at divorce ill. by Maria S. Forrai. Lerner, 1976. ISBN 0-8225-1301-3 Subj: Divorce. Emotions.

Polly the guinea pig orig. trans. by Dyan Hammarberg; photos by Antoinette Barrère; ill. by L'Enc Matte. Carolrhoda, 1977. Original ed. published under title: Amilcar le cochon d'Inde. ISBN 0-8761-4077-0 Subj: Animals – guinea pigs. Pets. Science.

Shelley the sea gull trans. by Dyan Hammarberg; photos by Jean Christian David, Guy Dhuit, and Claudie Fayn-Rodriguez. Carolrhoda, 1977. Original ed. published under title: Gwelan le goeland. ISBN 0-8761-4083-5 Subj: Birds – seagulls. Pets. Science.

Sprig the tree frog trans. by Dyan Hammarberg; ill. by Yves Vial. Carolrhoda, 1976. ISBN 0-8761-4064-9 Subj: Eggs. Frogs and toads. Science.

Purviance, Susan. *Alphabet Annie announces an all-American album* (O'Shell, Marcia)

Pushkin, Aleksandr Sergeevich. *The tale of Tsar Saltan* ill. by Gennady Spirin. Dial, 1996. ISBN 0-8037-2001-7 Subj: Emotions – envy, jealousy. Folk and fairy tales. Foreign lands – Russia. Royalty.

Pyle, Howard. *The Swan Maiden* ill. by Robert Sauber. Holiday, 1994. ISBN 0-8234-1088-9 Subj: Behavior – stealing. Birds – swans. Folk and fairy tales. Royalty – princes. Trees.

Quackenbush, Robert M. *Batbaby* ill. by author. Random House, 1997. ISBN 0-679-98541-7 Subj: Animals – bats. Animals – squirrels. Bedtime. Weather – storms.

Batbaby finds a home ill. by author. Random House, 2001. ISBN 0-375-80430-7 Subj: Animals – bats. Homes, houses.

Chuck lends a paw ill. by author. Clarion, 1986. ISBN 0-89919-363-3 Subj: Animals – mice. Character traits – helpfulness.

City trucks ill. by author. Albert Whitman, 1981. ISBN 0-8075-1163-3 Subj: City. Trucks.

Clementine ill. by author. Lippincott, 1974. ISBN 0-397-31506-6 Subj: Folk and fairy tales. Music. Songs. U.S. history.

First grade jitters ill. by author. Lippincott, 1982. ISBN 0-397-31981-9 Subj: Animals – rabbits. School – first day.

Funny bunnies ill. by author. Houghton Mifflin, 1984. ISBN 0-8991-9267-X Subj: Animals – rabbits. Humor.

Funny bunnies on the run ill. by author. Clarion, 1989. ISBN 0-89919-771-X Subj: Animals – rabbits. Family life. Parties. Power failures.

Henry babysits ill. by author. Parents, 1983. ISBN 0-8193-1107-3 Subj: Activities – babysitting. Birds – ducks.

Henry's world tour ill. by author. Doubleday, 1992. ISBN 0-385-42010-2 Subj: Activities – traveling. Birds – ducks. Family life. Foreign lands.

I don't want to go, I don't know how to act ill. by author. Lippincott, 1983. ISBN 0-397-32034-5 Subj: Animals – koalas. Behavior. Etiquette. Family life.

The man on the flying trapeze: the circus life of Emmett Kelly, Sr., told with pictures and song! ill. by author. Lippincott, 1975. ISBN 0-397-31643-7 Subj: Circus. Clowns, jesters. Music. Songs.

Mouse feathers ill. by author. Clarion, 1988. ISBN 0-89919-527-X Subj: Behavior – misbehavior. Family life.

No mouse for me ill. by author. Watts, 1981. ISBN 0-531-04303-7 Subj: Cumulative tales. Pets.

Pete Pack Rat ill. by author. Lothrop, 1976. ISBN 0-688-51763-3 Subj: Animals. Animals – pack rats. Cowboys. Humor. U.S. history – frontier and pioneer life.

Pop! goes the weasel and Yankee Doodle: New York in 1776 and today ill. by author. HarperCollins, 1988, 1976. ISBN 0-397-32265-8 Subj: Music. Songs. U.S. history.

She'll be comin' 'round the mountain ill. by author. Lippincott, 1973. ISBN 0-397-31480-9 Subj: Folk and fairy tales. Music. Songs.

Sheriff Sally Gopher and the Thanksgiving caper ill. by author. Lothrop, 1982. ISBN 0-688-01293-0 Subj: Holidays – Thanksgiving.

Skip to my Lou ill. by author. Lippincott, 1975. ISBN 0-397-31613-5 Subj: Folk and fairy tales. Music. Songs.

There'll be a hot time in the old town tonight: the great Chicago fire of 1871 ill. by author. HarperCollins, 1988, 1974. ISBN 0-397-32267-4 Subj: Fire. Folk and fairy tales. Music. Songs. U.S. history.

Quattlebaum, Mary. *In the beginning* ill. by Bryn Barnard. Time-Life, 1995. ISBN 0-7835-4627-0 Subj: Creation. Religion.

Underground train ill. by Cat Bowman Smith. Doubleday, 1997. ISBN 0-385-32204-6 Subj: Activities – traveling. Trains. Transportation.

Quattrocki, Carolyn. *The little drummer boy* ill. by Susan Spellman. Publications International, 1992. ISBN 1-56674-023-1 Subj: Gifts. Holidays – Christmas. Music. Religion – Nativity.

Quigley, Lillian Fox. *The blind men and the elephant* ill. by Janice Holland. Scribners, 1959. Subj: Animals – elephants. Folk and fairy tales. Foreign lands – India. Handicaps – blindness. Senses – seeing.

Quindlen, Anna. *The tree that came to stay* ill. by Nancy Carpenter. Crown, 1992. ISBN 0-517-58146-9 Subj: Family life. Holidays – Christmas. Trees.

Quin-Harkin, Janet. *Benjamin's balloon* ill. by Robert Censoni. Parents, 1979. ISBN 0-8193-0977-X Subj: Activities – ballooning. Character traits – willfulness.

Helpful Hattie ill. by Susanna Natti. Harcourt, 1983. ISBN 0-15-233756-3 Subj: Birthdays. Hair. Parties. Teeth.

Peter Penny's dance ill. by Anita Lobel. Dial, 1976. ISBN 0-8037-7184-3 Subj: Activities – dancing. Weddings. World.

Quinlan, Patricia. *Anna's red sled* ill. by Lindsay Grater. Firefly, 1989. ISBN 1-55037-073-1 Subj: Family life – mothers. Seasons – winter. Toys.

Emma's sea journey ill. by Jirina Marton. Firefly, 1991. ISBN 1-55037-179-7 Subj: Activities – playing. Sea and seashore.

My dad takes care of me ill. by Vlasta van Kampen. Firefly, 1987. ISBN 0-920303-79-X Subj: Activities – working. Family life – fathers. Family life – mothers.

Quinsey, Mary Beth. *Why does that man have such a big nose?* photos by Wilson Chan. Parenting Pr., 1986. ISBN 0-943990-25-4 Subj: Character traits – appearance. Character traits – being different.

Quintero-Spongberg, Emily. *Hannibal and the king* ill. by Tim Spongberg. Rainbow House, 1999. ISBN 1-893659-00-3 Subj: Animals – donkeys. Friendship. Religion.

R. F. *see* Fyleman, Rose

Ra, Carol F. *The sun is up* (Smith, William Jay)

Trot, trot to Boston: play rhymes for baby ill. by Catherine Stock. Lothrop, 1987. ISBN 0-688-06191-5 Subj: Games. Poetry.

Rabe, Berniece. *The balancing girl* ill. by Lillian Hoban. Dutton, 1981. ISBN 0-525-26160-5 Subj: Handicaps. School.

The first Christmas candy cane ill. by Kathy Wilburn. Longmeadow, 1994. ISBN 0-681-00441-X Subj: Food. Holidays – Christmas. Religion – Nativity.

A smooth move ill. by Linda Shute. Albert Whitman, 1987. ISBN 0-8075-7486-4 Subj: Activities – traveling. Moving.

Where's Chimpy? photos by Diane Schmidt. Albert Whitman, 1988. ISBN 0-8075-8928-4 Subj: Behavior – losing things. Family life – fathers. Handicaps. Toys.

Rabinowitz, Sandy. *A colt named mischief* ill. by author. Doubleday, 1979. ISBN 0-385-14629-9 Subj: Animals – horses, ponies. Behavior – misbehavior.

What's happening to Daisy? ill. by author. HarperCollins, 1977. ISBN 0-06-024835-1 Subj: Animals – horses, ponies. Birth. Science.

Racioppo, Larry. *Halloween* photos by author. Scribners, 1980. ISBN 0-684-16708-5 Subj: Holidays – Halloween.

Raczek, Linda Theresa. *The night the grandfathers danced* ill. by Katalin Olah Ehling. Northland, 1995. ISBN 0-87358-610-7 Subj: Activities – danc-

ing. Family life – grandfathers. Indians of North America – Ute.

Radcliffe, Theresa. *Bashi, elephant baby* ill. by John Butler. Viking, 1997. ISBN 0-670-87054-4 Subj: Animals – babies. Animals – elephants. Family life – mothers. Foreign lands – Africa.

The snow leopard ill. by Theresa Radcliffe. Viking, 1994. ISBN 0-670-85052-7 Subj: Animals – leopards.

Radford, Derek. *Building machines and what they do* ill. by author. Candlewick, 1992. ISBN 1-56402-006-1 Subj: Machines.

Cargo machines and what they do ill. by author. Candlewick, 1992. ISBN 1-56402-005-3 Subj: Machines.

Harry at the garage ill. by author. Candlewick, 1995. ISBN 1-56402-564-0 Subj: Animals – hippopotamuses. Automobiles. Careers – mechanics.

Harry builds a house ill. by author. Aladdin, 1990. ISBN 0-689-71439-4 Subj: Activities – making things. Homes, houses.

Radin, Ruth Yaffe. *High in the mountains* ill. by Ed Young. Macmillan, 1989. ISBN 0-02-775650-5 Subj: Family life – grandfathers. Nature.

A winter place ill. by Mattie Lou O'Kelley. Little, 1982. ISBN 0-316-73218-4 Subj: Seasons – winter. Sports – ice skating.

Radlauer, Ruth Shaw. *Breakfast by Molly* ill. by Emily Arnold McCully. Prentice-Hall, 1988. ISBN 0-671-66165-5 Subj: Birthdays. Family life – mothers. Food.

Molly ill. by Emily Arnold McCully. Prentice-Hall, 1987. ISBN 0-13-599762-3 Subj: Activities – picnicking. Activities – walking.

Molly at the library ill. by Emily Arnold McCully. Prentice-Hall, 1988. ISBN 0-671-66166-3 Subj: Activities – reading. Family life – fathers. Libraries.

Molly goes hiking ill. by Emily Arnold McCully. Prentice-Hall, 1987. ISBN 0-13-599770-4 Subj: Activities – picnicking. Activities – walking.

Of course, you're a horse! ill. by Abner Graboff and Sheila Greenwald. Abelard-Schuman, 1959. Subj: Health and fitness. Imagination.

Radley, Gail. *The night Stella hid the stars* ill. by John Wallner. Crown, 1978. ISBN 0-517-53256-5 Subj: Imagination. Stars.

Rainy day rhymes ill. by Ellen Kandoian. Houghton Mifflin, 1992. ISBN 0-395-59967-9 Subj: Poetry. Weather – rain.

The spinner's gift ill. by Paige Miglio. North-South, 1994. ISBN 1-55858-326-2 Subj: Activities – weaving. Clothing. Ecology. Gifts. Quilts. Royalty.

Radunsky, Eugenia. *Square, triangle, round, skinny* ill. by Vladimir Radunsky. Holt, 1992. ISBN 0-

8050-2205-8 Subj: Concepts – shape. Format, unusual.

Yucka Drucka Droni by Eugenia Radunsky and Vladimir Radunsky; ill. by Vladimir Radunsky. Scholastic, 1998. ISBN 0-590-09837-3 Subj: Family life – brothers and sisters. Tongue twisters.

Radunsky, Vladimir. *Yucka Drucka Droni* (Radunsky, Eugenia)

Raebeck, Lois. *Who am I?* ill. by June Goldsborough. Follett, 1970. Subj: Activities – playing. Games. Songs.

Rael, Elsa. *When Zaydeh danced on Eldridge Street* ill. by Marjorie Priceman. Simon & Schuster, 1997. ISBN 0-689-80451-2 Subj: Emotions – fear. Family life – grandfathers. Jewish culture. Religion.

Rael, Rick. *Baseball brothers* (Rubin, Jeff)

Raffi. *Baby beluga* ill. by Ashley Wolff. Crown, 1990. ISBN 0-517-57840-9 Subj: Animals – endangered animals. Animals – whales. Foreign lands – Arctic. Music. Songs.

Down by the bay ill. by Nadine Bernard Westcott. Crown, 1987. ISBN 0-517-56644-3 Subj: Music. Songs.

Everything grows photos by Bruce McMillan. Crown, 1989. ISBN 0-517-57275-3 Subj: Music. Songs.

Like me and you words and music by Raffi and Debi Pike; ill. by Lillian Hoban. Crown, 1994. ISBN 0-517-59588-5 Subj: Foreign lands. Letters, cards. Music. Songs.

One light, one sun ill. by Eugenie Fernandes. Crown, 1988. ISBN 0-517-56785-7 Subj: Family life. Music. Songs.

Rise and shine words and music by Raffi, Bonnie Simpson, and Bert Simpson; ill. by Eugenie Fernandes. Crown, 1996. ISBN 0-517-70940-6 Subj: Morning. Music. Songs.

Shake my sillies out ill. by David Allender. Crown, 1987. ISBN 0-517-56646-X Subj: Music. Songs.

Wheels on the bus ill. by Sylvie Wickstrom. Crown, 1988. ISBN 0-517-56784-9 Subj: Foreign lands – France. Music. Songs.

Raglin, Tim. *The birthday ABC* (Metaxas, Eric)

Raglus, Jeff. *Schnorky the wave puncher* ill. by author. Crown, 1996. ISBN 0-517-70924-4 Subj: Character traits – bravery. Islands. Sports – surfing. Weather – storms.

Ragz, M. M. *Lost little angel* ill. by Jane Manning. Simon & Schuster, 1998. ISBN 0-689-81067-9 Subj: Angels. Behavior – lost. Humor. Religion.

Rahaman, Vashanti. *O Christmas tree* ill. by Frané Lessac. Boyds Mills, 1996. ISBN 1-56397-237-9 Subj: Foreign lands – Caribbean Islands. Foreign lands – West Indies. Holidays – Christmas. Islands.

Read for me, Mama ill. by Lori McElrath-Eslick. Boyds Mills, 1997. ISBN 1-56397-313-8 Subj: Activities – reading. Family life – mothers. Libraries.

Rahn, Joan Elma. *Holes* photos by author. Houghton Mifflin, 1984. ISBN 0-395-35389-0 Subj: Concepts.

Rand, Ann. *Little 1* by Ann and Paul Rand; ill. by Paul Rand. Abrams, 1991. ISBN 0-8109-3558-9 Subj: Counting, numbers.

Sparkle and spin: a book about words by Ann and Paul Rand; ill. by Paul Rand. Harcourt, 1957. ISBN 0-8109-3822-7 Subj: Language.

Rand, Gloria. *Aloha, Salty!* ill. by Ted Rand. Holt, 1996. ISBN 0-8050-3429-3 Subj: Animals – dogs. Boats, ships. Hawaii. Sea and seashore. Weather – storms.

Baby in a basket ill. by Ted Rand. Cobblehill, 1997. ISBN 0-525-65233-7 Subj: Accidents. Alaska. Babies. Family life. U.S. history.

The cabin key ill. by Ted Rand. Harcourt, 1994. ISBN 0-15-213884-6 Subj: Activities – vacationing. Family life. Nature.

Prince William ill. by Ted Rand. Holt, 1992. ISBN 0-8050-1841-7 Subj: Alaska. Animals – mice. Ecology. Oil.

Salty dog ill. by Ted Rand. Holt, 1989. ISBN 0-8050-0837-3 Subj: Animals – dogs. Boats, ships. Careers – boat builders. Character traits – individuality.

Salty sails north ill. by Ted Rand. Holt, 1990. ISBN 0-8050-1160-9 Subj: Alaska. Animals – dogs. Boats, ships. Sea and seashore.

Salty takes off ill. by Ted Rand. Holt, 1991. ISBN 0-8050-1159-5 Subj: Airplanes, airports. Alaska. Animals – dogs.

Willie takes a hike ill. by Ted Rand. Harcourt, 1996. ISBN 0-15-200272-3 Subj: Animals – mice. Behavior – lost. Safety. Sports – hiking.

Rand McNally picturebook dictionary: *a thousand words to see and say* comp. by Robert L. Hillerich and others; ill. by Dan Siculan. Rand McNally, 1971. Subj: Dictionaries.

Rand, Paul. *Little 1* (Rand, Ann)

Sparkle and spin: a book about words (Rand, Ann)

Raney, Ken. *Stick horse* ill. by author. Green Tiger Pr., 1991. ISBN 0-9625261-4-2 Subj: Activities – playing. Activities – traveling. Toys. Wordless.

Rankin, Joan. *The little cat and the greedy old woman* ill. by author. Margaret K. McElderry, 1995. ISBN 0-689-50611-2 Subj: Animals – cats. Behavior – sharing. Character traits – selfishness. Emotions – anger.

Wow! It's great being a duck ill. by author. Margaret K. McElderry, 1998. ISBN 0-689-81756-8 Subj: Animals – foxes. Birds – ducks.

You're somebody special, Walliwigs! ill. by author. Margaret K. McElderry, 1999. ISBN 0-689-82230-8 Subj: Animals. Birds – chickens. Birds – parakeets, parrots. Character traits – being different. Character traits – individuality. Emotions – love.

Rankin, Laura. *The handmade counting book* ill. by author. Dial, 1998. ISBN 0-8037-2311-3 Subj: Counting, numbers. Handicaps – deafness. Language.

Ransom, Candice F. *The Christmas dolls* ill. by Moira Fain. Walker, 1998. ISBN 0-8027-8661-8 Subj: Family life – mothers. Holidays – Christmas. Toys – dolls.

The promise quilt ill. by Ellen Beier. Walker, 1999. ISBN 0-8027-8695-2 Subj: Activities – making things. Activities – sewing. Quilts. U.S. history.

When the whippoorwill calls ill. by Kimberly Bulcken Root. Tambourine, 1995. ISBN 0-688-12730-4 Subj: Emotions. Family life. Moving.

Ransome, Arthur. *The fool of the world and the flying ship* ill. by Uri Shulevitz. Farrar, 1968. ISBN 0-374-32442-5 Subj: Activities – flying. Boats, ships. Caldecott award books. Character traits – cleverness. Folk and fairy tales. Foreign lands – Ukraine. Royalty – tsars.

Ranville, Myralene. *Tex* ill. by author. Firefly, 1999. ISBN 1-55209-294-1 Subj: Animals – dogs. Behavior – needing someone.

Raphael, Elaine. *Donkey and Carlo* by Elaine Raphael and Don Bolognese; ill. by authors. HarperCollins, 1978. ISBN 0-06-020553-9 Subj: Animals – donkeys. Farms. Friendship.

Donkey, it's snowing by Elaine Raphael and Don Bolognese; ill. by authors. HarperCollins, 1981. ISBN 0-06-020555-5 Subj: Animals – donkeys. Farms. Weather – snow.

Turnabout by Elaine Raphael and Don Bolognese; ill. by authors. Viking, 1980. ISBN 0-670-73281-8 Subj: Animals – bears. Behavior – boasting. Family life. Folk and fairy tales. Rhyming text.

Raposo, Joe. *The Sesame Street song book* words and music by Joe Raposo and Jeffrey Moss; arrangements by Sy Oliver; ill. by Loretta Trezzo. Simon & Schuster, 1971. Published in conjunction with Children's Television Workshop. Subj: Music. Songs.

Rappaport, Doreen. *Journey of Meng* ill. by Yang Ming-Yi. Dial, 1991. ISBN 0-8037-0896-3 Subj: Death. Folk and fairy tales. Foreign lands – China.

The long-haired girl ill. by Yang Ming-Yi. Dial, 1995. ISBN 0-8037-1412-2 Subj: Behavior – secrets. Character traits – bravery. Folk and fairy tales. Foreign lands – China. Weather – droughts.

The new king ill. by E. B. Lewis. Dial, 1995. ISBN 0-8037-1461-0 Subj: Death. Emotions – grief. Family life – fathers. Folk and fairy tales. Foreign lands – Madagascar. Royalty.

Rappus, Gerhard. *When the sun was shining* ill. by author. Imported Pubs., 1986. ISBN 0-8285-2269-3 Subj: Activities – picnicking. Animals – goats. Behavior – misbehavior. Wordless.

Rascal. *Oregon's journey* ill. by Louis Joos. Bridge-Water, 1993. ISBN 0-816-73305-8 Subj: Animals – bears. Character traits – freedom. Circus. Clowns, jesters. Dwarfs, midgets.

Orson ill. by Mario Ramos. Lothrop, 1995. ISBN 0-688-13799-7 Subj: Animals – bears. Friendship. Hibernation. Toys – bears.

Socrates ill. by Gert Bogaerts. Chronicle, 1992. ISBN 0-8118-0314-7 Subj: Animals – dogs. Glasses. Homeless.

Raschka, Christopher. *Arlene sardine* ill. by author. Orchard, 1998. ISBN 0-531-33111-3 Subj: Fish. Food. Self-concept.

The blushful hippopotamus ill. by author. Orchard, 1996. ISBN 0-531-08882-0 Subj: Animals – hippopotamuses. Emotions – embarrassment. Family life – brothers and sisters. Sibling rivalry.

Can't sleep ill. by author. Orchard, 1995. ISBN 0-531-08779-4 Subj: Animals – dogs. Bedtime. Emotions – fear. Moon. Night.

Charlie Parker played be bop ill. by author. Watts, 1992. ISBN 0-531-08599-6 Subj: Careers – musicians. Ethnic groups in the U.S. – African Americans. Music.

Elizabeth imagined an iceberg ill. by author. Orchard, 1994. ISBN 0-531-08667-4 Subj: Behavior – talking to strangers. Imagination.

Moosey Moose ill. by author. Hyperion, 2000. ISBN 0-7868-0581-1 Subj: Animals. Animals – moose. Clothing – pants.

Mysterious Thelonious ill. by author. Orchard, 1997. ISBN 0-531-33057-5 Subj: Careers – musicians. Concepts – color. Ethnic groups in the U.S. – African Americans.

Ring! Yo? ill. by author. DK, 2000. ISBN 0-7894-2614-5 Subj: Emotions. Friendship. Telephone.

Simple gifts: a Shaker hymn (Simple gifts)

Sluggy Slug ill. by author. Hyperion, 2000. ISBN 0-7868-0584-6 Subj: Animals – slugs.

Whaley Whale ill. by author. Hyperion, 2000. ISBN 0-7868-0583-8 Subj: Animals – whales. Behavior – hiding.

Wormy Worm ill. by author. Hyperion, 2000. ISBN 0-7868-0582-X Subj: Animals – worms.

Yo! Yes? ill. by author. Orchard, 1993. ISBN 0-531-08619-4 Subj: Caldecott award honor books. Emotions. Ethnic groups in the U.S. – African Americans. Friendship.

Raskin, Ellen. *A & The: or, William T. C. Baumgarten comes to town* ill. by author. Atheneum, 1970. Subj: Friendship. Names.

And it rained ill. by author. Atheneum, 1969. Subj: Animals. Weather – rain.

Franklin Stein ill. by author. Atheneum, 1972. Subj: City. Friendship. Humor. Imagination.

Ghost in a four-room apartment ill. by author. Atheneum, 1969. ISBN 0-689-20354-3 Subj: Cumulative tales. Family life. Ghosts. Rhyming text.

Nothing ever happens on my block ill. by author. Atheneum, 1966. ISBN 0-689-20588-0 Subj: Behavior – boredom. City. Humor.

Spectacles ill. by author. Atheneum, 1968. ISBN 0-689-20352-7 Subj: Glasses. Imagination. Senses – seeing.

Who, said Sue, said whoo? ill. by author. Atheneum, 1973. Subj: Animals. Noise, sounds. Rhyming text.

Rasmussen, Knud. *Magic words: poems* (Field, Edward)

Rassmus, Jens. *Farmer Enno and his cow* ill. by author. Orchard, 1998. ISBN 0-531-30081-1 Subj: Boats, ships. Dreams. Farms.

Rathmann, Peggy. *Good night, Gorilla* ill. by author. Putnam, 1994. ISBN 0-399-22445-9 Subj: Animals. Careers – zoo keepers. Night. Zoos.

Officer Buckle and Gloria ill. by author. Putnam, 1995. ISBN 0-399-22616-8 Subj: Animals – dogs. Behavior – sharing. Caldecott award books. Careers – police officers. School.

Ruby the copycat ill. by author. Scholastic, 1991. ISBN 0-590-43747-X Subj: Animals – cats. Behavior – imitation. School.

10 minutes till bedtime ill. by author. Putnam, 1998. ISBN 0-399-23103-X Subj: Animals – hamsters. Bedtime. Pets.

Ratnett, Michael. *Jenny's bear* ill. by June Goulding. Putnam, 1992. ISBN 0-399-22325-8 Subj: Animals – bears. Behavior – wishing. Imagination. Toys – bears.

Marmaduke and the scary story ill. by June Goulding. Trafalgar Square, 1992. ISBN 0-09-174084-3 Subj: Animals – rabbits. Emotions – fear.

Rattigan, Jama Kim. *The woman in the moon* ill. by Carla Golembe. Little, 1996. ISBN 0-316-73446-2 Subj: Folk and fairy tales. Foreign languages. Hawaii. Moon.

Ratz de Tagyos, Paul. *A coney tale* ill. by author. Houghton Mifflin, 1992. ISBN 0-395-58834-0 Subj: Animals – rabbits. Communities, neighborhoods.

Rau, Dana Meachen. *The secret code* ill. by Bari Weissman. Childrens Pr., 1998. ISBN 0-516-20700-8 Subj: Activities – reading. Handicaps – blindness.

Rauch, Hans-Georg. *The lines are coming: a book about drawing* ill. by author. Scribners, 1978. ISBN 0-684-15989-9 Subj: Art.

Rauch, Jennifer. *see* Davis, Jennifer

Rauzon, Mark J. *Eyes and ears* ill. by author. Lothrop, 1994. ISBN 0-688-10238-7 Subj: Anatomy – ears. Anatomy – eyes. Animals. Senses – hearing. Senses – seeing.

Feet, flippers, hooves, and hands ill. by author. Lothrop, 1994. ISBN 0-688-10235-2 Subj: Anatomy. Anatomy – feet. Anatomy – hands. Animals.

Water, water everywhere by Mark J. Rauzon and Cynthia Overbeck Bix; ill. with photos. Sierra Club, 1994. ISBN 0-87156-598-6 Subj: Water.

Raven, Margot. *Angels in the dust* ill. by Roger Essley. BridgeWater, 1997. ISBN 0-8167-3806-8 Subj: Family life. Farms. Friendship. Memories, memory. U.S. history.

Ravilious, Robin. *The runaway chick* ill. by author. Macmillan, 1987. ISBN 0-02-775640-8 Subj: Behavior – running away. Birds – chickens. Character traits – curiosity.

Two in a pocket ill. by author. Little, 1991. ISBN 0-316-73449-7 Subj: Animals – dormice. Birds – wrens. Friendship.

Rawlins, Donna. *Digging to China* ill. by author. Watts, 1989. ISBN 0-531-08414-0 Subj: Activities – digging. Old age.

Ray, Deborah Kogan. *The cloud* ill. by author. HarperCollins, 1984. ISBN 0-06-024847-5 Subj: Activities – walking. Weather – clouds.

Fog drift morning ill. by author. HarperCollins, 1983. ISBN 0-06-023198-X Subj: Morning. Sea and seashore.

Stargazing sky ill. by author. Crown, 1991. ISBN 0-517-57838-7 Subj: Family life – mothers. Night. Stars.

Sunday morning we went to the zoo ill. by author. HarperCollins, 1981. ISBN 0-06-024842-4 Subj: Family life. Sibling rivalry. Zoos.

Ray, Jane. *Hansel and Gretel* (Grimm, Jacob)

The twelve dancing princesses (Grimm, Jacob)

Ray, Karen. *Sleep song* ill. by Rhonda Mitchell. Orchard, 1995. ISBN 0-531-08728-X Subj: Activities. Bedtime. Games. Rhyming text.

Ray, Mary Lyn. *Basket moon* ill. by Barbara Cooney. Little, 1999. ISBN 0-316-73521-3 Subj: Activities – making things. Careers. Family life – fathers. Mountains.

Mud ill. by Lauren Stringer. Harcourt, 1996. ISBN 0-15-256263-X Subj: Poetry. Seasons – spring.

Pianna ill. by Bobbie Henba. Harcourt, 1994. ISBN 0-15-261357-9 Subj: Careers – musicians. Music. U.S. history.

Pumpkins ill. by Barry Root. Harcourt, 1992. ISBN 0-15-252252-2 Subj: Ecology. Gardens, gardening. Plants. Progress.

Shaker boy ill. by Jeanette Winter. Harcourt, 1994. ISBN 0-15-276921-8 Subj: Ethnic groups in the U.S. – Shakers. Music. Religion. Songs. U.S. history.

Rayevsky, Inna. *The talking tree* ill. by Robert Rayevsky. Putnam, 1990. ISBN 0-399-21631-6 Subj: Folk and fairy tales. Foreign lands – Italy. Trees.

Rayner, Mary. *Crocodarling* ill. by author. Bradbury, 1986. ISBN 0-02-775770-6 Subj: Behavior – bullying. Behavior – needing someone. School. Toys.

Garth Pig and the ice cream lady ill. by author. Atheneum, 1977. ISBN 0-33-322040-4 Subj: Animals – pigs. Animals – wolves.

Marathon and Steve ill. by author. Dutton, 1989. ISBN 0-525-44456-4 Subj: Animals – dogs. Pets. Sports.

Mr. and Mrs. Pig's evening out ill. by author. Atheneum, 1976. ISBN 0-689-30530-3 Subj: Activities – babysitting. Animals – pigs. Animals – wolves.

Mrs. Pig gets cross and other stories ill. by author. Dutton, 1987. ISBN 0-525-44280-4 Subj: Animals – pigs. Family life.

Mrs. Pig's bulk buy ill. by author. Atheneum, 1981. ISBN 0-689-30831-0 Subj: Animals – pigs. Food.

One by one: Garth Pig's rain song ill. by author. Dutton, 1994. ISBN 0-525-45240-0 Subj: Animals – pigs. Counting, numbers. Music. Songs. Weather – rain.

The rain cloud ill. by author. Atheneum, 1980. ISBN 0-689-30763-2 Subj: Character traits – helpfulness. Weather – clouds.

Ten pink piglets: Garth Pig's wall song ill. by author. Dutton, 1994. ISBN 0-525-45241-9 Subj: Animals – pigs. Counting, numbers. Music. Songs.

Rayner, Shoo. *My first picture joke book* ill. by author. Viking, 1990. ISBN 0-670-82450-X Subj: Animals. Humor.

Raynor, Dorka. *Grandparents around the world* ed. by Caroline Rubin; photos by author. Albert Whitman, 1977. ISBN 0-8075-3037-9 Subj: Family life – grandparents.

Rea, Jesus Guerrero. *Atariba and Niguayona: a story from the Taino people of Puerto Rico* (Rohmer, Harriet)

Reader, Dennis. *Butterfingers* ill. by author. Houghton Mifflin, 1991. ISBN 0-395-57581-8 Subj: Babies. Behavior – carelessness. Family life – brothers and sisters. Family life – new sibling.

I want one! ill. by author. Ideals, 1990. ISBN 0-8249-8442-0 Subj: Character traits – selfishness.

Reader's Digest children's book of poetry sel. by Beverly Mathias; ill. by Alan Snow. Reader's Digest, 1992. ISBN 0-895-77442-9 Subj: Poetry.

Reardon, Maureen. *Feelings between brothers and sisters* (Conta, Marcia Maher)

Feelings between friends (Conta, Marcia Maher)

Feelings between kids and grownups (Conta, Marcia Maher)

Feelings between kids and parents (Conta, Marcia Maher)

Reasoner, Charles. *The big busy building* by Chuck Reasoner and Cary Pillo Lassen; ill. by authors. Price Stern Sloan, 1994. ISBN 0-8431-3659-6 Subj: Buildings. Elevators, escalators. Format, unusual – board books. Format, unusual – toy and movable books. Wordless.

Sleepy time bunny (Cosgrove, Stephen [Edward])

Who drives this? ill. by author. Price Stern Sloan, 1996. ISBN 0-8431-3939-0 Subj: Animals. Automobiles. Careers. Format, unusual – toy and movable books. Transportation. Trucks.

Who pretends? ill. by author. Price Stern Sloan, 1996. ISBN 0-8431-3940-4 Subj: Activities. Foreign languages. Format, unusual – toy and movable books. Imagination.

Reavin, Sam. *Hurray for Captain Jane!* ill. by Emily Arnold McCully. Parents, 1971. ISBN 0-8193-0511-1 Subj: Activities – bathing. Boats, ships. Imagination.

Rebek, Kathleen. *The story of a round loaf* (Froment, Eugène)

Recknagel, Friedrich. *Meg's wish* ill. by Ilse van Garderen; trans. by Sibylle Kazeroid. North-South, 1999. ISBN 0-7358-1117-2 Subj: Behavior – wishing. Dreams. Friendship.

Reddix, Valerie. *Dragon kite of the autumn moon* ill. by Jean and Mou-sien Tseng. Lothrop, 1992. ISBN 0-688-11031-2 Subj: Dragons. Family life – grandfathers. Foreign lands – Taiwan. Kites.

Millie and the mudhole ill. by Thor Wickstrom. Lothrop, 1992. ISBN 0-688-10213-1 Subj: Animals. Animals – pigs. Farms. Noise, sounds. Rhyming text.

Redies, Rainer. *The cats' party* ill. by Gerta Melle. Barron's, 1986. ISBN 0-8120-5720-1 Subj: Animals – cats. Character traits – individuality. Family life. Parties.

Reece, Colleen L. *What?* ill. by Lois Axeman. Childrens Pr., 1983. ISBN 0-516-06591-2 Subj: Character traits – curiosity. Character traits – questioning.

Reed, Allison. *Genesis: the story of creation* ill. by author. Schocken, 1981. ISBN 0-8052-3778-X Subj: Creation. Religion.

Reed, Jonathan. *Do armadillos come in houses?* ill. by Carol Nicklaus. Atheneum, 1981. ISBN 0-689-30858-2 Subj: Emotions – fear.

Reed, Kit. *When we dream* ill. by Yutaka Sugita. Hawthorn, 1966. Subj: Behavior – wishing. Dreams.

Reed, Lillian Craig. *see* Reed, Kit

Reed, Lynn Rowe. *Pedro, his perro, and the alphabet sombrero* ill. by author. Hyperion, 1995. ISBN 0-7868-2058-6 Subj: ABC books. Animals – dogs. Birthdays. Clothing – hats. Foreign languages.

Reed, Mary M. *Biddy and the ducks* (Sondergaard, Arensa)

Reed-Jones, Carol. *The tree in the ancient forest* ill. by Christopher Canyon. Dawn Pub., 1995. ISBN 1-883220-32-7 Subj: Ecology. Forest, woods. Trees.

Rees, Mary. *Ten in a bed* ill. by adapt. Little, 1988. ISBN 0-316-73708-9 Subj: Bedtime. Counting, numbers. Family life.

Reese, Ralph. *The first crazy word book: verbs* (Preiss, Byron)

Reesink, Marijke. *The golden treasure* ill. by Jaap Tol. Harcourt, 1968. Translation of Het vrouwtje van Stavoren. Subj: Boats, ships. Character traits – selfishness. Folk and fairy tales. Foreign lands – Holland.

The princess who always ran away ill. by Françoise Trésy. McGraw-Hill, 1981. ISBN 0-07-051714-2 Subj: Behavior – solitude. Character traits – being different. Folk and fairy tales. Royalty – princesses. Sibling rivalry.

Reeves, Howard W. *There was an old witch* ill. by David Catrow. Hyperion, 1998. ISBN 0-7868-2387-9 Subj: Holidays – Halloween. Rhyming text. Witches.

Reeves, James. *Ragged Robin: poems from A to Z* ill. by Emma Chichester Clark. Little, 1990. ISBN 0-316-73829-8 Subj: ABC books. Poetry.

Reeves, Mona Rabun. *I had a cat* ill. by Julie Downing. Bradbury, 1989. ISBN 0-02-775731-5 Subj: Animals. Rhyming text.

The spooky eerie night noise ill. by Paul Yalowitz. Bradbury, 1989. ISBN 0-02-775732-3 Subj: Animals – skunks. Emotions – fear. Night. Rhyming text.

Regan, Dian Curtis. *Daddies* ill. by Mary Morgan-Vanroyen. Scholastic, 1996. ISBN 0-590-47973-3 Subj: Activities. Family life – fathers. Rhyming text.

Regniers, Beatrice De. *see* De Regniers, Beatrice Schenk

Rehm, Karl. *Left or right?* by Karl Rehm and Kay Koike; photos by authors. Houghton Mifflin, 1991. ISBN 0-395-58080-3 Subj: Concepts – left and right.

Rehnman, Mats. *The clay flute* ill. by author. Farrar, 1989. ISBN 91-29-59184-8 Subj: Foreign lands. Magic. Music. Witches.

Reich, Hanns. *Animal babies* (Zoll, Max Alfred)

Reichmeier, Betty. *Potty time!* ill. by author. Random House, 1988. ISBN 0-394-89403-0 Subj: Behavior – growing up. Toilet training.

Reid, Alastair. *A balloon for a blunderbuss* (Gill, Bob)

Mother Goose in Spanish: Poesias de la Madre Oca (Mother Goose)

Supposing ill. by Abe Birnbaum. Little, 1960. Subj: Humor. Imagination.

Reid, Barbara. *The party* ill. by author. Scholastic, 1999. ISBN 0-590-97801-2 Subj: Family life. Parties. Rhyming text.

Reid, Jon. *Celestino Piatti's animal ABC* (Piatti, Celestino)

Reid, Rob. *Wave goodbye* ill. by Lorraine Williams. Lee & Low, 1996. ISBN 1-880000-30-X Subj: Activities – playing. Rhyming text.

Reidel, Marlene. *Jacob and the robbers* ill. by author. Atheneum, 1967. Subj: Crime. Night. Sleep.

Reider, Katja. *Snail started it!* by Katja Reider and Angela von Roehl; ill. by Angela von Roehl; trans. by Rosemary Lanning. North-South, 1999. ISBN 1-55858-707-1 Subj: Animals. Animals – snails. Behavior. Cumulative tales.

Reidy, Hannah. *Crazy creature contrasts* ill. by Clare Mackie. Stewart, Tabori & Chang, 1996. ISBN 1-899883-44-4 Subj: Animals. Character traits – being different. Format, unusual – board books.

Reimold, Mary Gallagher. *My mom is a runner* photos by Sid Dorris. Abingdon, 1987. ISBN 0-687-27545-8 Subj: Family life – mothers. Sports – racing.

Reinl, Edda. *The little snake* ill. by author. Alphabet Pr., 1982. ISBN 0-907234-15-1 Subj: Emotions – love. Reptiles – snakes.

Reiser, Lynn. *Any kind of dog* ill. by author. Greenwillow, 1992. ISBN 0-688-10915-2 Subj: Animals – dogs. Family life – mothers. Imagination. Pets. Toys.

Bedtime cat ill. by author. Greenwillow, 1991. ISBN 0-688-10026-0 Subj: Animals – cats. Bedtime.

Best friends think alike ill. by author. Greenwillow, 1997. ISBN 0-688-15200-7 Subj: Activities – playing. Concepts – color. Friendship. Imagination.

Cherry pies and lullabies ill. by author. Greenwillow, 1998. ISBN 0-688-13392-4 Subj: Activities – cooking. Family life – grandmothers. Family life – great-grandparents. Family life – mothers.

Christmas counting ill. by author. Greenwillow, 1992. ISBN 0-688-10677-3 Subj: Counting, numbers. Cumulative tales. Holidays – Christmas. Trees.

Dog and cat ill. by author. Greenwillow, 1991. ISBN 0-688-09893-2 Subj: Animals – cats. Animals – dogs.

Earthdance ill. by author. Greenwillow, 1999. ISBN 0-688-16327-0 Subj: Earth. Plants. School.

Little clam ill. by author. Greenwillow, 1998. ISBN 0-688-15909-5 Subj: Activities – storytelling. Animals. Bedtime. Sea and seashore.

Night thunder and the Queen of the Wild Horses ill. by author. Greenwillow, 1995. ISBN 0-688-11792-9 Subj: Animals. Bedtime. Noise, sounds. Sleep. Weather – thunder.

The surprise family ill. by author. Greenwillow, 1994. ISBN 0-688-11672-8 Subj: Birds – chickens. Birds – ducks. Emotions – love.

Two mice in three fables ill. by author. Greenwillow, 1995. ISBN 0-688-13390-8 Subj: Animals – mice. Friendship.

Reiss, John J. *Colors* ill. by author. Aladdin, 1987, c1969. ISBN 0-689-71119-0 Subj: Concepts – color.

Numbers ill. by author. Aladdin, 1987, c1971. ISBN 0-689-71120-4 Subj: Counting, numbers.

Shapes ill. by author. Aladdin, 1974. ISBN 0-689-71121-2 Subj: Concepts – shape.

Reit, Seymour. *The king who learned to smile* ill. by Gordon Laite. Golden Pr., 1960. Subj: Behavior – boredom. Royalty – kings.

Rebus bears ill. by Kenneth Smith. Bantam, 1989. ISBN 0-553-34689-X Subj: Animals – bears. Folk and fairy tales. Rebuses.

Round things everywhere photos by Carol Basen. McGraw-Hill, 1969. Subj: Concepts – shape. Ethnic groups in the U.S.

Reitveld, Jane Klatt. *Monkey island* ill. by author. Viking, 1963. Subj: Animals – monkeys. Zoos.

Relf, Patricia. *The magic school bus plants seeds: a book about how living things grow* ill. John Speirs. Scholastic, 1995. Based on The magic school bus series written by Joanna Cole and illustrated by Bruce Degen. TV tie-in book adaptation by Patricia Relf ; TV script written by Ronnie Krauss, Brian Meehl, and Joycelyn Stevenson. ISBN 0-590-22296-1 Subj: Plants. Science. Seeds.

Tonka big book of trucks ill. by Thomas LaPadula. Scholastic, 1996. ISBN 0-590-84572-1 Subj: Toys. Trucks.

Remkiewicz, Frank. *Greedyanna* ill. by author. Lothrop, 1992. ISBN 0-688-10295-6 Subj: Behavior. Character traits – selfishness. Family life.

The last time I saw Harris ill. by author. Lothrop, 1991. ISBN 0-688-10292-1 Subj: Behavior – lost. Birds – parakeets, parrots. Pets.

Renberg, Dalia Hardof. *Hello, clouds!* ill. by Alona Frankel. HarperCollins, 1985. ISBN 0-06-024839-4 Subj: Imagination. Weather – clouds.

King Solomon and the bee ill. by Ruth Heller. HarperCollins, 1994. ISBN 0-06-022902-0 Subj: Folk and fairy tales. Insects – bees. Jewish culture. Religion.

Reneaux, J. J. *Why Alligator hates Dog* ill. by Donnie Lee Green. August House, 1995. ISBN 0-87483-412-0 Subj: Animals – dogs. Character traits – cleverness. Reptiles – alligators, crocodiles.

Repchuk, Caroline. *The forgotten garden* ill. by Ian Andrew. Millbrook, 1997. ISBN 0-7613-0141-0 Subj: Family life – fathers. Gardens, gardening. Memories, memory.

Ressmeyer, Roger. *Astronaut to zodiac: a young stargazer's alphabet* photos by author. Crown, 1992. ISBN 0-517-58806-4 Subj: ABC books. Astronomy.

Ressner, Phil. *August explains* ill. by Crosby Newell Bonsall. HarperCollins, 1963. Subj: Animals – bears.

Dudley Pippin ill. by Arnold Lobel. HarperCollins, 1965. Subj: City. Imagination.

Retan, Walter. *The snowplow that tried to go south* by Walter Retan [i.e. George Walters]; ill. by John Resko. Atheneum, 1950. Subj: Machines. Seasons – winter. Weather – snow.

The steam shovel that wouldn't eat dirt ill. by Roger Antoine Duvoisin. Atheneum, 1948. Subj: Food. Machines.

Rettich, Margret. *The voyage of the jolly boat* trans. from German by Joy Backhouse; ill. by author. Methuen, 1981. ISBN 0-416-30791-4 Subj: Boats, ships. Careers – fishermen. Weather – storms.

Reuter, Margaret. *My mother is blind* ill. by Philip Lanier. Childrens Pr., 1979. ISBN 0-516-02021-8 Subj: Family life – mothers. Handicaps – blindness. Senses – seeing.

Rex, Michael. *My fire engine* ill. by author. Holt, 1999. ISBN 0-8050-5391-3 Subj: Careers – firefighters. Fire. Imagination. Safety. Trucks.

Who builds? ill. by author. HarperFestival, 1999. ISBN 0-694-01249-1 Subj: Buildings. Careers – construction workers. Format, unusual – toy and movable books.

Who digs? ill. by author. HarperFestival, 1999. ISBN 0-694-01254-8 Subj: Activities – digging. Animals. Careers – construction workers. Format, unusual – toy and movable books.

Rey, H. A. (Hans Augusto). *Anybody at home?* ill. by author. Houghton Mifflin, 1942. Subj: Format, unusual. Homes, houses.

Billy's picture (Rey, Margret [Margret Elisabeth Waldstein])

Cecily G and the nine monkeys ill. by author. Houghton Mifflin, 1989, c1942. ISBN 0-395-18430-4 Subj: Animals – giraffes. Animals – monkeys. Humor.

Curious George ill. by author. Houghton Mifflin, 1941. Subj: Animals – monkeys. Careers – firefighters. Character traits – curiosity. Humor.

Curious George and the dump truck (Curious George and the dump truck)

Curious George and the hot air balloon (Curious George and the hot air balloon)

Curious George and the puppies (Curious George and the puppies)

Curious George gets a medal ill. by author. Houghton Mifflin, 1957. Subj: Animals – monkeys. Character traits – curiosity. Humor. Space and space ships.

Curious George goes camping (Curious George goes camping)

Curious George goes to a chocolate factory: based on the original character by Margret and H. A. Rey (Curious George goes to a chocolate factory)

Curious George goes to a movie: based on the original character by Margret and H. A. Rey (Curious George goes to a movie)

Curious George goes to the hospital (Rey, Margret [Margret Elisabeth Waldstein])

Curious George in the snow: based on the original character by Margret and H. A. Rey (Curious George in the snow)

Curious George learns the alphabet ill. by author. Houghton Mifflin, 1963. ISBN 0-395-16031-6 Subj: ABC books. Animals – monkeys. Character traits – curiosity.

Curious George rides a bike ill. by author. Houghton Mifflin, 1952. ISBN 0-395-16964-X Subj: Animals – monkeys. Character traits – curiosity. Circus. Humor. Sports – bicycling.

Curious George takes a job ill. by author. Houghton Mifflin, 1947. Subj: Animals – monkeys. Careers – window cleaners. Character traits – curiosity. Humor. Zoos.

Elizabite: adventures of a carnivorous plant ill. by author. Houghton Mifflin, 1999. ISBN 0-395-97702-9 Subj: Humor. Plants. Rhyming text.

Elizabite, adventures of a carnivorous plant ill. by author. HarperCollins, 1942. Subj: Humor. Plants. Rhyming text.

Feed the animals ill. by author. Houghton Mifflin, 1944. Subj: Rhyming text. Zoos.

How do you get there? ill. by author. Houghton Mifflin, 1941. Subj: Format, unusual. Transportation.

Humpty Dumpty and other Mother Goose songs ill. by author. HarperCollins, 1943. Subj: Music. Nursery rhymes. Songs.

Look for the letters ill. by author. HarperCollins, 1942. Subj: ABC books.

Margret and H. A. Rey's Curious George and the puppies (Margret and H. A. Rey's Curious George and the puppies)

The original Curious George ill. by author. Houghton Mifflin, 1998. Printed from H.A. Rey's original watercolors. ISBN 0-395-92272-0 Subj: Animals – monkeys. Careers – firefighters. Character traits – curiosity. Humor.

See the circus ill. by author. Houghton Mifflin, 1956. Subj: Circus. Format, unusual. Rhyming text.

Tit for tat ill. by author. HarperCollins, 1942. Subj: Animals. Humor.

Where's my baby? ill. by author. Houghton Mifflin, 1943. Subj: Animals. Format, unusual. Rhyming text.

Rey, Margret (Margret Elisabeth Waldstein). *Billy's picture* by Margret and Hans Augusto Rey; ill. by Hans Augusto Rey. HarperCollins, 1948. Subj: Animals. Art. Humor.

Curious George and the dinosaur (Curious George and the dinosaur)

Curious George and the dump truck (Curious George and the dump truck)

Curious George and the hot air balloon (Curious George and the hot air balloon)

Curious George and the puppies (Curious George and the puppies)

Curious George flies a kite ill. by Hans Augusto Rey. Houghton Mifflin, 1958. Subj: Animals – monkeys. Character traits – curiosity. Humor. Kites. Sports – fishing.

Curious George goes camping (Curious George goes camping)

Curious George goes to a chocolate factory: based on the original character by Margret and H. A. Rey (Curious George goes to a chocolate factory)

Curious George goes to a movie: based on the original character by Margret and H. A. Rey (Curious George goes to a movie)

Curious George goes to an ice cream shop (Curious George goes to an ice cream shop)

Curious George goes to school (Curious George goes to school)

Curious George goes to the dentist (Curious George goes to the dentist)

Curious George goes to the hospital by Margret and Hans Augusto Rey in collaboration with the Children's Hospital Medical Center, Boston; ill. by Hans Augusto Rey. Houghton Mifflin, 1966. Subj: Animals – monkeys. Behavior – lost. Character traits – curiosity. Hospitals. Humor.

Curious George in the snow: based on the original character by Margret and H. A. Rey (Curious George in the snow)

Margret and H. A. Rey's Curious George and the puppies (Margret and H. A. Rey's Curious George and the puppies)

Pretzel ill. by Hans Augusto Rey. HarperCollins, 1941. Subj: Animals – dogs.

Pretzel and the puppies ill. by Hans Augusto Rey. HarperCollins, 1946. Subj: Animals – dogs.

Spotty ill. by Hans Augusto Rey. Houghton Mifflin, 1997. ISBN 0-395-83736-7 Subj: Animals – rabbits. Character traits – being different.

Reyher, Rebecca (Hourwich). *My mother is the most beautiful woman in the world* ill. by Ruth S. Gannett. Lothrop, 1945. Subj: Caldecott award honor books. Family life – mothers.

Reynolds, Jan. *Amazon* photos by author. Harcourt, 1993. ISBN 0-15-202832-3 Subj: Foreign lands – South America. Indians of South America. Rivers.

Down under photos by author. Harcourt, 1992. ISBN 0-15-224182-5 Subj: Foreign lands – Australia.

Far north photos by author. Harcourt, 1992. ISBN 0-15-227178-3 Subj: Foreign lands – Arctic. Foreign lands – Lapland. Foreign lands – Norway.

Himalaya photos by author. Harcourt, 1991. ISBN 0-15-234465-9 Subj: Foreign lands – Nepal.

Sahara photos by author. Harcourt, 1991. ISBN 0-15-269959-7 Subj: Desert. Foreign lands – Sahara Desert.

Reynolds, Marilynn. *The new land: a first year on the prairie* ill. by Stephen McCallum. Orca, 1997. ISBN 1-55143-069-X Subj: Family life. Farms. Immigrants. U.S. history – frontier and pioneer life.

The prairie fire ill. by Don Kilby. Orca, 1999. ISBN 1-55143-137-8 Subj: Farms. Fire. U.S. history – frontier and pioneer life.

Rheingrover, Jean Sasso. *Veronica's first year* ill. by Kay Life. Albert Whitman, 1996. ISBN 0-8075-8474-6 Subj: Babies. Family life – new sibling. Family life – sisters. Handicaps – Down syndrome.

Rhodes, Timothy. *The hummingbird's gift* (Czernecki, Stefan)

Pancho's piñata (Czernecki, Stefan)

The singing snake (Czernecki, Stefan)

The sleeping bread (Czernecki, Stefan)

Rice, Eve. *Aren't you coming too?* ill. by Nancy Winslow Parker. Greenwillow, 1988. ISBN 0-688-06447-7 Subj: Activities. Family life – grandfathers.

At Grammy's house ill. by Nancy Winslow Parker. Greenwillow, 1990. ISBN 0-688-08875-9 Subj: Family life – grandparents.

Benny bakes a cake ill. by author. Greenwillow, 1993. ISBN 0-688-11580-2 Subj: Activities – cooking. Animals – dogs. Behavior – misbehavior. Birthdays.

City night ill. by Peter Sis. Greenwillow, 1987. ISBN 0-688-06857-X Subj: City. Family life. Night. Poetry.

Ebbie ill. by author. Greenwillow, 1975. ISBN 0-688-84017-5 Subj: Family life. Names.

Goodnight, goodnight ill. by author. Greenwillow, 1980. ISBN 0-688-84254-2 Subj: Bedtime. Night.

New blue shoes ill. by author. Macmillan, 1975. ISBN 0-02-775960-1 Subj: Clothing – shoes. Family life – mothers. Shopping.

Once in a wood: ten tales from Æsop (Æsop)

Papa's lemonade and other stories ill. by author. Greenwillow, 1976. ISBN 0-688-84041-8 Subj: Animals – dogs. Family life.

Peter's pockets ill. by Nancy Winslow Parker. Greenwillow, 1989. ISBN 0-688-07242-9 Subj: Clothing – pants. Problem solving.

Sam who never forgets ill. by author. Greenwillow, 1977. ISBN 0-688-84088-4 Subj: Animals. Food. Zoos.

Swim! ill. by Marisabina Russo. Greenwillow, 1996. ISBN 0-688-14275-3 Subj: Family life – fathers. Sports – swimming.

What Sadie sang ill. by author. Greenwillow, 1976. ISBN 0-688-84038-8 Subj: Babies. Emotions – happiness.

Rice, Inez. *A long long time* ill. by Robert M. Quackenbush. Lothrop, 1964. Subj: Character traits – optimism. Imagination.

The March wind ill. by Vladimir Bobri. Lothrop, 1957. Subj: Clothing. Imagination. Weather – wind.

Rice, James. *Cajun alphabet* ill. by author. Pelican, 1991. ISBN 0-88289-822-1 Subj: ABC books.

Gaston goes to Texas ill. by author. Pelican, 1978. ISBN 0-88289-204-5 Subj: Reptiles – alligators, crocodiles. Rhyming text.

Rich, Scharlotte. *Who made the wild woods?* ill. by Anna Currey. WaterBrook, 1999. ISBN 1-57856-027-6 Subj: Animals. Creation. Forest, woods. Plants. Religion.

Rich, Susan. *Mrs. Meyer, the bird* (Erlbruch, Wolf)

Richard, Françoise. *On Cat Mountain* adapt. by Arthur A. Levine; ill. by Anne Buguet. Putnam, 1994. ISBN 0-399-22608-7 Subj: Animals – cats. Character traits – kindness. Folk and fairy tales. Foreign lands – Japan.

Richards, Jane. *A horse grows up* ill. by Bert Hardy. Walker, 1972. ISBN 0-8027-6104-6 Subj: Animals – horses, ponies. Science.

Richards, Jon. *Jetliners* ill. by Simon Tegg and Mike Saunders. Copper Beech, 1998. ISBN 0-7613-0744-3 Subj: Airplanes, airports. Transportation.

Trains ill. with photos. Copper Beech, 1998. ISBN 0-7613-0824-5 Subj: Trains. Transportation.

Richards, Kitty. *It's about time, Max!* ill. by Gioia Fiammenghi. Kane Pr., 2000. ISBN 1-57565-088-6 Subj: Clocks, watches. Time.

Merry Christmas, Rugrats! ill. by Barry Goldberg. Simon Spotlight, 1998. ISBN 0-689-82179-4 Subj: Babies. Format, unusual – toy and movable books. Holidays – Christmas.

Richardson, Jack E. *Six in a mix* by Jack E. Richardson, Jr., and others; ill. by Carlos Alfonso and others. Benziger, 1971. Subj: Language.

Richardson, Jean. *The bear who went to the ballet* ill. by Susan Winter. DK, 1995. ISBN 0-7894-0318-8 Subj: Activities – dancing. Ballet. Toys – bears.

Clara's dancing feet ill. by Joanna Carey. Putnam, 1987. ISBN 0-399-21388-0 Subj: Activities – dancing. Ballet. Character traits – shyness.

The nutcracker (Hoffmann, E. T. A.)

The sleeping beauty: the story of Tchaikovsky's ballet ill. by Francesca Crespi. Arcade, 1991. ISBN 1-55970-142-0 Subj: Activities – dancing. Ballet. Folk and fairy tales.

Stephen's feast ill. by Alice Englander. Little, 1991. ISBN 0-316-74435-2 Subj: Holidays – Christmas. Middle Ages. Music. Songs.

Tall inside ill. by Alice Englander. Putnam, 1988. ISBN 0-399-21486-0 Subj: Clowns, jesters. Self-concept.

Thomas's sitter ill. by Dawn Holmes. Four Winds, 1991. ISBN 0-02-776146-0 Subj: Activities – babysitting. Behavior – misbehavior. Gender roles.

Richardson, John. *Ten bears in a bed* ill. by author. Hyperion, 1992. ISBN 1-56282-157-1 Subj: Animals. Animals – bears. Bedtime. Counting, numbers. Format, unusual – toy and movable books.

Where's Jack? a Christmas pop-up book ill. by author; paper engineering by David Hawcock. Aladdin, 1993. ISBN 0-689-71713-X Subj: Format, unusual – toy and movable books. Holidays – Christmas. Toys.

Richardson, Judith Benét. *Old winter* ill. by R. W. Alley. Orchard, 1996. ISBN 0-531-08883-9 Subj: Seasons – spring. Seasons – winter. Sleep.

The way home ill. by Salley Mavor. Macmillan, 1991. ISBN 0-02-776145-2 Subj: Animals – elephants. Sea and seashore.

Riches, Judith. *Giraffes have more fun* ill. by author. Morrow, 1992. ISBN 0-688-11043-6 Subj: Animals – giraffes. Imagination.

Richmond Elementary School (Richmond, Vt.). *Night time* (Night time)

Richter, Alice Numeroff. *Emily's bunch* (Numeroff, Laura Joffe)

You can't put braces on spaces by Alice Numeroff Richter and Laura Joffe Numeroff; ill. by Laura Joffe Numeroff. Greenwillow, 1979. ISBN 0-688-84190-2 Subj: Careers – dentists. Teeth.

Richter, Mischa. *Eric and Matilda* ill. by author. HarperCollins, 1967. Subj: Birds – ducks. Parades.

Quack? ill. by author. Harper, 1978. ISBN 0-06-025020-8 Subj: Animals. Birds – ducks. Noise, sounds. Wordless.

To bed, to bed! ill. by author. Prentice-Hall, 1981. ISBN 0-03-922922-1 Subj: Bedtime. Royalty.

Rickard, Graham. *Let's look at tractors* ill. by Clifford Meadway. Watts, 1990. ISBN 0-531-18256-8 Subj: Tractors.

Ricketts, Michael. *Rain* ill. by author. Wonder Books, 1971. Subj: Weather – rain.

Teeth ill. by author. Grosset, 1971. Subj: Teeth.

Ricklen, Neil. *My clothes = Mi ropa* ill. by author. Aladdin, 1994. ISBN 0-689-71773-3 Subj: Clothing. Foreign languages. Format, unusual – board books.

My colors = Mis colores ill. by author. Aladdin, 1994. ISBN 0-689-71772-5 Subj: Concepts – color. Foreign languages. Format, unusual – board books.

My family = Mi familia photos by author. Aladdin, 1994. ISBN 0-689-71771-7 Subj: Family life. Foreign languages. Format, unusual – board books.

My numbers = Mi numeros photos by author. Aladdin, 1994. ISBN 0-689-71770-9 Subj: Counting, numbers. Foreign languages. Format, unusual – board books.

Riddell, Chris. *The bear dance* ill. by author. Simon & Schuster, 1990. ISBN 0-671-70974-7 Subj: Activities – dancing. Animals – bears.

Ben and the bear ill. by author. Lippincott, 1986. ISBN 0-397-32194-5 Subj: Animals – bears. Behavior – sharing.

Bird's new shoes ill. by author. Holt, 1987. ISBN 0-8050-0326-6 Subj: Animals. Behavior – imitation. Character traits – being different. Clothing – shoes. Cumulative tales.

Mr. Underbed ill. by author. Holt, 1986. ISBN 0-8050-0026-7 Subj: Bedtime. Humor. Monsters. Night. Toys.

The trouble with elephants ill. by author. Lippincott, 1988. ISBN 0-397-32273-9 Subj: Animals – elephants.

The wish factory ill. by author. Ideals, 1990. ISBN 0-8249-8482-X Subj: Behavior – wishing. Dreams. Monsters. Sleep.

Riddell, Edwina. *My first day at preschool* ill. by author. Barron's, 1992. ISBN 0-8120-6261-2 Subj: School – first day.

One hundred first words ill. by author. Barron's, 1988. ISBN 0-8120-5786-4 Subj: Language.

Riddle, Tohby. *Careful with that ball, Eugene!* ill. by author. Watts, 1991. ISBN 0-531-08517-1 Subj: Imagination. Sports.

The great escape from City Zoo ill. by author. Farrar, 1999. ISBN 0-374-32776-9 Subj: Animals. Character traits – freedom. Disguises. Zoos.

Rider, Alex. *A la ferme = At the farm: learn-a-language book in French and English* ill. by Paul Davis. Doubleday, 1962. Subj: Farms. Foreign lands – France. Foreign languages.

Chez nous = At our house: learn-a-language book in French and English ill. by Isadore Seltzer. Doubleday, 1962. Subj: Family life. Foreign lands – France. Foreign languages.

Rider, Joanne. *First grade valentines* ill. by Betsy Lewin. Troll, 1993. ISBN 0-8167-3004-0 Subj: Character traits – kindness. Holidays – Valentine's Day. School.

Ridlon, Marcia. *Kittens and more kittens* ill. by Elizabeth Dauber. Follett, 1967. Subj: Animals – cats. Pets.

Riecken, Nancy. *Today is the day* ill. by Catherine Stock. Houghton Mifflin, 1996. ISBN 0-395-73917-9 Subj: Careers – farmers. Family life – fathers. Farms. Foreign lands – Mexico.

Riehecky, Janet. *Apatosaurus* ill. by Lydia Halverson. Child's World, 1988. ISBN 0-89565-423-7 Subj: Dinosaurs.

Rigby, Rodney. *Hello, this is your penguin speaking* ill. by author. Walt Disney, 1992. ISBN 1-56282-232-2 Subj: Activities – flying. Birds – penguins. Character traits – persistence.

There's a building on Sixth Avenue ill. by author. Walt Disney, 1992. ISBN 1-56282-156-3 Subj: Poetry.

Rigby, Shirley Lincoln. *Smaller than most* ill. by Debby L. Carter. HarperCollins, 1985. ISBN 0-06-025028-3 Subj: Animals – pandas. Babies. Character traits – smallness. Family life. Family life – grandfathers.

Riggio, Anita. *Beware the Brindlebeast* ill. by author. Caroline House, 1994. ISBN 1-56397-133-X Subj: Folk and fairy tales. Foreign lands – England. Holidays – Halloween. Monsters.

Secret signs: along the underground railroad ill. by author. Boyds Mills, 1997. ISBN 1-56397-555-6 Subj: Behavior – secrets. Ethnic groups in the U.S. – African Americans. Slavery. U.S. history.

Wake up, William! ill. by author. Atheneum, 1987. ISBN 0-689-31344-6 Subj: Family life. Sleep.

Rikys, Bodel. *Red bear* ill. by author. Dial, 1992. ISBN 0-8037-1048-8 Subj: Animals – bears. Concepts – color.

Riley, James Whitcomb. *Little Orphan Annie* ill. by Diane Stanley. Putnam, 1983. ISBN 0-399-20904-2 Subj: Poetry.

Riley, Linda Capus. *Elephants swim* ill. by Steve Jenkins. Houghton Mifflin, 1995. ISBN 0-395-73654-4 Subj: Animals. Sports – swimming. Water.

Riley, Linnea Asplind. *Mouse mess* ill. by author. Blue Sky, 1997. ISBN 0-590-10048-3 Subj: Animals – mice. Behavior – messy. Food. Night.

Rinder, Lenore. *A big mistake* ill. by Susan Horn. Gareth Stevens, 1994. ISBN 0-8368-0674-3 Subj: Activities – painting. Behavior – mistakes. Imagination. Rhyming text.

Ring, Elizabeth. *Lucky mouse* ill. by Dwight Kuhn. Millbrook, 1995. ISBN 1-56294-344-8 Subj: Animals – mice. Nature.

Some stuff ill. by Anne Canevari Green. Millbrook, 1995. ISBN 1-56294-466-5 Subj: Activities – playing. Behavior – sharing. Emotions – loneliness. Rhyming text.

Tiger lilies and other beastly plants ill. by Barbara Bash. Walker, 1996. ISBN 0-8027-7454-7 Subj: Character traits – appearance. Plants.

Ringgold, Faith. *Bonjour, Lonnie* ill. by author. Hyperion, 1996. ISBN 0-7868-2062-4 Subj: Birds. Ethnic groups in the U.S. – African Americans. Family life. Foreign lands – France. Imagination.

Dinner at Aunt Connie's house ill. by author. Hyperion, 1993. ISBN 1-56282-426-0 Subj: Art. Ethnic groups in the U.S. – African Americans. Family life. Food. U.S. history.

My dream of Martin Luther King ill. by author. Crown, 1995. ISBN 0-517-59977-5 Subj: Dreams. Ethnic groups in the U.S. – African Americans. U.S. history.

Tar Beach ill. by author. Crown, 1991. ISBN 0-517-58031-4 Subj: Activities – flying. Caldecott award honor books. City. Dreams. Ethnic groups in the U.S. – African Americans. Quilts.

Ringi, Kjell (Arne Sorensen). *My father and I* by Kjell Ringi and Adelaide Holl; ill. by Kjell Ringi. Watts, 1972. ISBN 0-531-02560-8 Subj: Character traits – ambition. Family life – fathers. Imagination.

The sun and the cloud ill. by author. HarperCollins, 1971. ISBN 0-06-025032-1 Subj: Plants. Sun. Weather – clouds.

The winner ill. by author. HarperCollins, 1969. Subj: Behavior. Wordless.

Riordan, James. *The coming of Night: a Yoruba tale from West Africa* ill. by Jenny Stow. Millbrook, 1999. ISBN 0-7613-1358-3 Subj: Creation. Folk and fairy tales. Foreign lands – Africa. Night.

Little Bunny Bobkin ill. by Tim Warnes. Little Tiger, 1999. ISBN 1-8884-4438-X Subj: Animals – foxes. Animals – rabbits. Counting, numbers.

Old Father Frost (Odoyevsky, Vladimir)

The Snowmaiden ill. by Stephen Lambert. Trafalgar Square, 1992. ISBN 0-09-173861-X Subj: Folk and fairy tales. Foreign lands – Russia.

The three magic gifts ill. by Errol le Cain. Oxford Univ. Pr., 1980. ISBN 0-19-520194-9 Subj: Character traits – perseverance. Folk and fairy tales. Gifts. Magic. Sibling rivalry.

Thumbelina (Andersen, H. C. [Hans Christian])

Ripley, Catherine. *Two dozen dinosaurs* ill. by Bo-Kim Louie. Firefly, 1992. ISBN 0-920775-55-1 Subj: Dinosaurs. Games.

Why do stars twinkle? and other nighttime questions ill. by Scot Ritchie. Firefly, 1996. ISBN 1-895688-42-6 Subj: Bedtime. Character traits – questioning. Night.

Why is soap so slippery? and other bathtime stories ill. by Scot Ritchie. Firefly, 1995. ISBN 1-895688-34-5 Subj: Activities – bathing. Character traits – questioning.

Rippon, Penelope. *My day* ill. by author. Viking, 1990. ISBN 0-670-83459-9 Subj: Babies. Family life.

Rister, Claude. *see* Marshall, James

Rix, Jamie. *The last chocolate cookie* ill. by Arthur Robins. Candlewick, 1998. ISBN 0-7636-0411-9 Subj: Aliens. Etiquette. Food. Humor. Monsters.

Roach, Marilynne K. *Dune fox* ill. by author. Little, 1977. ISBN 0-316-74870-6 Subj: Animals – foxes. Ecology. Sand. Seasons.

Two Roman mice by Horace (Quintus Horatius Flaccus); ill. by reteller. Crowell, 1975. Based on a version of Æsop's fable about the country mouse and the city mouse as it appeared in Horace's Satirae II, 6. ISBN 0-690-00771-X Subj: Animals – mice. City. Country.

Robart, Rose. *The cake that Mack ate* ill. by Maryann Kovalski. Little, 1987. ISBN 0-87113-121-8 Subj: Cumulative tales. Farms. Food.

Robb, Brian. *My grandmother's djinn* ill. by author. Parents, 1978. ISBN 0-8193-0918-4 Subj: Family life. Foreign lands. Mythical creatures. Problem solving.

Robb, Laura. *Snuffles and snouts* ill. by Steven Kellogg. Dial, 1995. ISBN 0-8037-1598-6 Subj: Animals – pigs. Poetry.

Robbins, Ken. *Autumn leaves* ill. by author. Scholastic, 1998. ISBN 0-590-29879-8 Subj: Plants. Seasons – fall. Trees.

Beach days photos by author. Viking, 1987. ISBN 0-670-80138-0 Subj: Sand. Sea and seashore.

City/country: a car trip in photographs photos by author. Viking, 1985. ISBN 0-670-80743-5 Subj: Activities – traveling. Automobiles.

Trucks of every sort photos by author. Crown, 1981. ISBN 0-517-54164-5 Subj: Trucks.

Robbins, Ruth. *Baboushka and the three kings* ill. by Nicolas Sidjakov; verse by Edith R. Thomas; music by Mary Clement Sanks. Parnassus, 1960. Adapt. from a Russian folk tale. ISBN 0-395-27672-1 Subj: Caldecott award books. Folk and fairy tales. Foreign lands – Russia. Holidays – Christmas. Music. Rhyming text. Songs.

The harlequin and Mother Goose: or, The magic stick ill. by Nicolas Sidjakov. Parnassus, 1965. Subj: Nursery rhymes.

How the first rainbow was made ill. by author. Houghton Mifflin, 1980. ISBN 0-395-29082-1 Subj: Folk and fairy tales. Indians of North America. Weather – rain. Weather – rainbows.

Robbins, Sandra. *The firefly star* ill. by Iku Oseki. See-More's Workshop, 1995. ISBN 1-882601-23-8 Subj: Animals – horses, ponies. Animals – mice. Foreign lands – Latin America. Holidays. Insects – fireflies. Insects – ladybugs. Stars.

Roberts, Bethany. *Camel caravan* by Bethany Roberts and Patricia Hubbell; ill. by Cheryl Munro Taylor. Tambourine, 1996. ISBN 0-688-13940-X Subj: Activities – traveling. Animals – camels. Behavior – dissatisfaction. Desert. Rhyming text.

Valentine mice! ill. by Doug Cushman. Clarion, 1997. ISBN 0-395-77518-3 Subj: Animals. Animals – mice. Holidays – Valentine's Day. Rhyming text.

Waiting-for-Christmas stories ill. by Sarah Stapler. Clarion, 1994. ISBN 0-395-67324-0 Subj: Animals – rabbits. Bedtime. Holidays – Christmas.

Waiting-for-Papa stories ill. by Sarah Stapler. HarperCollins, 1990. ISBN 0-06-025051-8 Subj: Animals – rabbits. Family life – fathers.

Waiting-for-spring stories ill. by William Joyce. HarperCollins, 1984. ISBN 0-06-025062-3 Subj: Animals – rabbits. Seasons – winter.

Roberts, Cliff. *The dot* ill. by author. Watts, 1960. Subj: Concepts – shape.

Start with a dot ill. by author. Watts, 1968, c1960. Subj: Concepts – shape. Rhyming text.

Roberts, Sarah. *Bert and the missing mop mix-up* ill. by Joseph Mathieu. Random House, 1983. ISBN 0-394-95752-0 Subj: Behavior – misunderstanding. Puppets.

Ernie's big mess ill. by Joseph Mathieu. Random House, 1981. ISBN 0-394-94847-5 Subj: Behavior – carelessness. Puppets.

I want to go home! ill. by Joseph Mathieu. Random House, 1985. ISBN 0-394-97027-6 Subj: Behavior – needing someone. Family life – grandmothers. Puppets. Sea and seashore.

Roberts, Thom. *Pirates in the park* ill. by Harold Berson. Crown, 1973. ISBN 0-517-50257-7 Subj: Imagination. Parks. Pirates. Toys – rocking horses.

Roberts, Tom. *The three billy goats Gruff* (Asbjørnsen, P. C. [Peter Christen])

Robertson, Janet. *Oscar's spots* ill. by author. BridgeWater, 1993. ISBN 0-8167-3133-0 Subj: Animals – leopards. Magic. Self-concept.

Robertson, Joanne. *Sea witches* ill. by László Gál. Dial, 1991. ISBN 0-8037-1070-4 Subj: Family life – grandmothers. Folk and fairy tales. Foreign lands – Scotland. Poetry. Witches.

Robertson, Lilian. *Picnic woods* ill. by author. Harcourt, 1949. Subj: Activities – picnicking.

Runaway rocking horse ill. by author. Harcourt, 1948. Subj: Toys – rocking horses.

Robertus, Polly M. *The dog who had kittens* ill. by Janet Stevens. Holiday, 1991. ISBN 0-8234-0860-4 Subj: Animals – cats. Animals – dogs.

Robins, Arthur. *The teeny tiny woman: a traditional tale* ill. by author. Candlewick, 1998. ISBN 0-7636-0444-5 Subj: Folk and fairy tales. Foreign lands – England. Ghosts.

Robins, Joan. *Addie meets Max* ill. by Sue Truesdell. HarperCollins, 1985. ISBN 0-06-025064-X Subj: Animals – dogs. Friendship.

Addie runs away ill. by Sue Truesdell. HarperCollins, 1989. ISBN 0-06-025081-X Subj: Behavior – running away. Camps, camping. Seasons – summer.

Addie's bad day ill. by Sue Truesdell. HarperCollins, 1993. ISBN 0-06-021298-5 Subj: Behavior – bad day. Birthdays. Friendship. Hair.

My brother, Will ill. by Marylin Hafner. Greenwillow, 1986. ISBN 0-688-05223-1 Subj: Babies. Family life – brothers. Family life – new sibling. Sibling rivalry.

Robinson, Adjai. *Femi and old grandaddie* ill. by Jerry Pinkney. Coward, 1972. ISBN 0-698-20189-2 Subj: Folk and fairy tales. Foreign lands – Africa.

Robinson, Aminah Brenda Lynn. *A street called home* ill. by author. Harcourt, 1997. ISBN 0-15-201465-9 Subj: Careers. Communities, neighborhoods. Ethnic groups in the U.S. – African Americans. Format, unusual – toy and movable books. U.S. history.

Robinson, Earl. *Black and white* (Arkin, Alan)

Robinson, Fay. *Nathaniel Willy, scared silly* (Mathews, Judith)

Where did all the dragons go? ill. by Victor Lee. BridgeWater, 1996. ISBN 0-8167-3808-4 Subj: Dragons. Folk and fairy tales. Rhyming text.

Robinson, Irene Bowen. *Picture book of animal babies* by Irene and W. W. Robinson; ill. by Irene Bowen Robinson. Macmillan, 1947. Subj: Animals.

Robinson, Nancy K. *Firefighters!* ill. with photos. Scholastic, 1979. Subj: Careers – firefighters.

Robinson, Thomas P. *Buttons* ill. by Peggy Bacon. Viking, 1938. Subj: Animals – cats.

Robinson, W. W. (William Wilcox). *On the farm* ill. by Irene Bowen Robinson. Macmillan, 1939. Subj: Animals. Farms.

Picture book of animal babies (Robinson, Irene Bowen)

Robison, Deborah. *Bye-bye, old buddy* ill. by author. Houghton Mifflin, 1983. ISBN 0-89919-185-1 Subj: Problem solving.

No elephants allowed ill. by author. Houghton Mifflin, 1981. ISBN 0-395-30078-9 Subj: Bedtime. Emotions – fear. Problem solving.

Your turn, doctor by Deborah Robison and Carla Perez; ill. by Deborah Robison. Dial, 1982. ISBN 0-8037-9788-5 Subj: Behavior – misbehavior. Careers – doctors.

Robison, Nancy. *Ten tall soldiers* ill. by Hilary Knight. Holt, 1991. ISBN 0-8050-0768-7 Subj: Monsters. Royalty – kings. Shadows.

UFO kidnap ill. by Edward Frascino. Lothrop, 1978. ISBN 0-688-51853-2 Subj: Space and space ships.

Roche, A. K. *see* Abisch, Roz

Roche, A. K. *see* Kaplan, Boche

Roche, Hannah. *Corey's kite* ill. by Pierre Pratt. Stewart, Tabori & Chang, 1996. ISBN 1-899883-48-7 Subj: Kites. Weather – wind.

Sandra's sun hat ill. by Pierre Pratt. Stewart, Tabori & Chang, 1996. ISBN 1-899883-47-9 Subj: Clothing – hats. Sun. Weather.

Roche, Harriet. *Pete's puddles* ill. by Pierre Pratt. Stewart, Tabori & Chang, 1996. ISBN 1-899883-46-0 Subj: Activities – playing. Clothing – boots. Weather – rain.

Roche, P. K. (Patrick K.). *Good-bye, Arnold!* ill. by author. Dial, 1979. ISBN 0-8037-3032-2 Subj: Animals – mice. Family life. Sibling rivalry.

Jump all the morning: a child's day in verses ill. by author. Viking, 1984. ISBN 0-670-41057-8 Subj: Poetry.

Plaid bear and the rude rabbit gang ill. by author. Dial, 1982. ISBN 0-8037-6990-3 Subj: Behavior – bullying. Toys.

Webster and Arnold go camping ill. by author. Viking, 1989. ISBN 0-670-81993-X Subj: Animals – mice. Camps, camping. Family life – brothers.

Rochelle, Belinda. *Jewels* ill. by Cornelius Van Wright and Ying-Hua Hwa. Lodestar, 1998. ISBN 0-525-67502-7 Subj: Activities – storytelling. Ethnic groups in the U.S. – African Americans. Family life – great-grandparents. Memories, memory. Slavery. U.S. history.

Rockwell, Anne F. *The acorn tree and other folktales* ill. by author. Greenwillow, 1995. ISBN 0-688-13723-7 Subj: Folk and fairy tales.

Apples and pumpkins ill. by Lizzy Rockwell. Macmillan, 1989. ISBN 0-02-777270-5 Subj: Food. Holidays – Halloween.

At the beach ill. by Harlow Rockwell. Macmillan, 1987. ISBN 0-02-777940-8 Subj: Activities – playing. Sea and seashore.

Bafana: a Christmas story ill. by author. Atheneum, 1974. ISBN 0-689-30417-X Subj: Folk and fairy tales. Holidays – Christmas.

A bear, a bobcat and three ghosts ill. by author. Macmillan, 1977. ISBN 0-02-777460-0 Subj: Animals – bears. Animals – bobcats. Careers – peddlers. Ghosts. Holidays – Halloween.

Bear Child's book of hours ill. by author. Crowell, 1987. ISBN 0-690-04551-4 Subj: Animals – bears. Time.

Big bad goat ill. by author. Dutton, 1982. ISBN 0-525-45100-5 Subj: Animals. Character traits – helpfulness. Insects – bees.

Big boss ill. by author. Macmillan, 1975. ISBN 0-02-777570-4 Subj: Animals – foxes. Animals – tigers. Character traits – cleverness. Frogs and toads.

Big wheels ill. by author. Dutton, 1986. ISBN 0-525-44226-X Subj: Machines.

Bikes ill. by author. Dutton, 1987. ISBN 0-525-44287-1 Subj: Sports – bicycling.

Blackout by Anne F. and Harlow Rockwell; ill. by authors. Macmillan, 1979. ISBN 0-02-777610-7 Subj: Family life. Power failures. Weather.

Boats ill. by author. Dutton, 1982. ISBN 0-525-44004-6 Subj: Animals – bears. Boats, ships.

The boy who wouldn't obey: a Mayan legend ill. by author. Greenwillow, 2000. ISBN 0-688-14881-6 Subj: Behavior – misbehavior. Folk and fairy tales. Indians of Central America – Maya.

Bumblebee, bumblebee, do you know me? a garden guessing game ill. by author. HarperCollins, 1999. ISBN 0-06-028212-6 Subj: Flowers. Insects. Insects – bees.

The bump in the night ill. by author. Greenwillow, 1979. ISBN 0-688-84180-5 Subj: Character traits – cleverness. Character traits – helpfulness.

Buster and the bogeyman ill. by author. Four Winds, 1978. ISBN 0-590-07531-4 Subj: Bedtime. Dreams. Mythical creatures.

Can I help? by Anne F. and Harlow Rockwell; ill. by authors. Macmillan, 1982. ISBN 0-02-777720-0 Subj: Character traits – helpfulness.

Career day ill. by Lizzy Rockwell. HarperCollins, 2000. ISBN 0-06-027566-9 Subj: Careers. School.

Cars ill. by author. Dutton, 1984. ISBN 0-525-44079-8 Subj: Automobiles.

Come to town ill. by author. Crowell, 1987. ISBN 0-690-04646-4 Subj: Animals – bears. City.

Ducklings and pollywogs ill. by Lizzy Rockwell. Macmillan, 1994. ISBN 0-02-777452-X Subj: Family life – fathers. Lakes, ponds. Seasons.

The emergency room by Anne and Harlow Rockwell; ill. by authors. Macmillan, 1985. ISBN 0-02-777300-0 Subj: Hospitals. Illness.

Ferryboat ride! ill. by Maggie Smith. Crown, 1999. ISBN 0-517-70959-7 Subj: Boats, ships. Islands. Sea and seashore. Transportation.

Fire engines ill. by author. Dutton, 1986. ISBN 0-525-44259-6 Subj: Animals – dogs. Careers – firefighters. Trucks.

First comes spring ill. by author. Crowell, 1985. ISBN 0-690-04455-0 Subj: Animals – bears. Seasons.

The first snowfall by Anne and Harlow Rockwell; ill. by authors. Macmillan, 1987. ISBN 0-02-777770-7 Subj: Seasons – winter. Weather – snow.

Gogo's pay day ill. by author. Doubleday, 1978. ISBN 0-385-13046-5 Subj: Character traits – generosity. Clowns, jesters. Money.

The gollywhopper egg ill. by author. Macmillan, 1974. ISBN 0-02-777470-8 Subj: Behavior – trickery. Eggs. Farms.

The good llama ill. by author. World, 1963. Subj: Animals. Animals – llamas. Foreign lands – South America.

Halloween day ill. by Lizzy Rockwell. HarperCollins, 1997. ISBN 0-06-027568-5 Subj: Clothing – costumes. Holidays – Halloween. School.

Handy Hank will fix it ill. by author. Holt, 1988. ISBN 0-8050-0697-4 Subj: Careers – handymen. Character traits – helpfulness.

Happy birthday to me by Anne F. and Harlow Rockwell; ill. by authors. Macmillan, 1981. ISBN 0-02-777680-8 Subj: Birthdays.

Honk honk! ill. by author. Dutton, 1980. ISBN 0-525-32120-9 Subj: Animals. Behavior – misbehavior. Birds. Cumulative tales.

How my garden grew by Anne F. and Harlow Rockwell; ill. by authors. Macmillan, 1982. ISBN 0-02-777660-3 Subj: Gardens, gardening.

Hugo at the park ill. by author. Macmillan, 1990. ISBN 0-02-777301-9 Subj: Animals – dogs. Parks.

Hugo at the window ill. by author. Macmillan, 1988. ISBN 0-02-777330-2 Subj: Animals – dogs. Birthdays. City.

I like the library ill. by author. Dutton, 1977. ISBN 0-525-32528-X Subj: Libraries.

I love my pets by Anne F. and Harlow Rockwell; ill. by authors. Macmillan, 1982. ISBN 0-02-777710-3 Subj: Pets.

I play in my room by Anne F. and Harlow Rockwell; ill. by authors. Macmillan, 1981. ISBN 0-02-777670-0 Subj: Activities – playing.

In our house ill. by author. Crowell, 1985. ISBN 0-690-04488-7 Subj: Activities. Animals – bears. Family life.

Long ago yesterday ill. by author. Greenwillow, 1999. ISBN 0-688-14411-X Subj: Babies. Family life.

Machines by Anne F. and Harlow Rockwell; ill. by Harlow Rockwell. Macmillan, 1972. ISBN 0-02-777520-8 Subj: Machines.

The Mother Goose cookie-candy book ill. by author. Random House, 1983. ISBN 0-394-95500-5 Subj: Activities – cooking. Food.

My back yard by Anne F. and Harlow Rockwell; ill. by authors. Macmillan, 1984. ISBN 0-02-777690-5 Subj: Activities – playing.

My barber by Anne F. and Harlow Rockwell; ill. by authors. Macmillan, 1981. ISBN 0-02-777630-1 Subj: Careers – barbers. Hair.

My spring robin ill. by Harlow Rockwell and Lizzy Rockwell. Macmillan, 1989. ISBN 0-02-777611-5 Subj: Birds – robins. Flowers. Seasons – spring.

Nice and clean by Anne F. and Harlow Rockwell; ill. by authors. Macmillan, 1984. ISBN 0-02-777290-X Subj: Character traits – cleanliness. Homes, houses.

The night we slept outside by Anne F. and Harlow Rockwell; ill. by authors. Macmillan, 1983. ISBN 0-02-777450-3 Subj: Camps, camping. Night.

No! No! No! ill. by author. Macmillan, 1995. ISBN 0-02-777782-0 Subj: Behavior – bad day. Family life.

The old woman and her pig and 10 other stories ill. by adapt. Crowell, 1979. ISBN 0-390-03928-X Subj: Folk and fairy tales.

On our vacation ill. by author. Dutton, 1989. ISBN 0-525-44487-7 Subj: Activities – vacationing. Animals – bears. Camps, camping. Islands.

Once upon a time this morning ill. by Suçie Stevenson. Greenwillow, 1997. ISBN 0-688-14707-0 Subj: Babies. Family life.

One bean ill. by Megan Halsey. Walker, 1998. ISBN 0-8027-8649-9 Subj: Plants. Science. Seeds.

The one-eyed giant and other monsters from the Greek Myths ill. by author. Greenwillow, 1996. ISBN 0-688-13810-1 Subj: Monsters. Mythical creatures.

Our garage sale ill. by Harlow Rockwell. Greenwillow, 1984. ISBN 0-688-84278-X Subj: Garage sales, rummage sales.

Our yard is full of birds ill. by Lizzy Rockwell. Macmillan, 1992. ISBN 0-02-777273-X Subj: Birds.

Planes by Anne and Harlow Rockwell; ill. by authors. Dutton, 1985. ISBN 0-525-44159-X Subj: Airplanes, airports. Transportation.

Poor Goose: a French folktale ill. by author. Crowell, 1976. ISBN 0-690-01014-1 Subj: Animals. Birds – geese. Cumulative tales. Folk and fairy tales. Foreign lands – France.

Pumpkin day, pumpkin night ill. by Megan Halsey. Walker, 1999. ISBN 0-8027-8697-9 Subj: Family life – mothers. Holidays – Halloween. Plants.

Romulus and Remus ill. by author. Simon & Schuster, 1997. ISBN 0-689-81291-4 Subj: Animals – wolves. Folk and fairy tales. Foreign lands – Italy. Multiple births – twins.

Root-a-toot-toot ill. by author. Macmillan, 1991. ISBN 0-02-777272-1 Subj: Animals. Cumulative tales. Noise, sounds.

Show and tell day ill. by Lizzy Rockwell. Harper-Collins, 1997. ISBN 0-06-027301-1 Subj: Character traits – individuality. School.

Sick in bed by Anne F. and Harlow Rockwell; ill. by authors. Macmillan, 1982. ISBN 0-02-777730-8 Subj: Illness.

Space vehicles by Anne F. Rockwell and David Brion; ill. by authors. Dutton, 1994. ISBN 0-525-45270-2 Subj: Animals – cats. Space and space ships.

The stolen necklace: a picture story from India ill. by author. Collins-World, 1968. Based on a tale from the Jataka. Subj: Animals – monkeys. Character traits – cleverness. Foreign lands – India.

The storm ill. by Robert Sauber. Hyperion, 1994. ISBN 0-7868-2013-6 Subj: Family life. Sea and seashore. Weather – storms.

The story snail ill. by author. Macmillan, 1974. ISBN 0-02-777560-7 Subj: Animals – snails. Magic.

The supermarket by Anne F. and Harlow Rockwell; ill. by authors. Macmillan, 1979. ISBN 0-02-777580-1 Subj: Shopping. Stores.

Thanksgiving Day ill. by Lizzy Rockwell. Harper-Collins, 1999. ISBN 0-06-027795-5 Subj: Holidays – Thanksgiving. School. Theater.

Things that go ill. by author. Dutton, 1986. ISBN 0-525-44266-9 Subj: Transportation.

The three bears and 15 other stories ill. by author. Crown, 1975. ISBN 0-690-00598-9 Subj: Folk and fairy tales.

Thump thump thump! ill. by author. Dutton, 1981. ISBN 0-525-41300-6 Subj: Folk and fairy tales. Monsters.

Toad by Anne F. and Harlow Rockwell; ill. by authors. Doubleday, 1972. Subj: Frogs and toads.

The toolbox by Anne F. and Harlow Rockwell; ill. by Harlow Rockwell. Macmillan, 1971. ISBN 0-02-777540-2 Subj: Tools.

Trains ill. by author. Dutton, 1988. ISBN 0-525-44377-0 Subj: Trains. Transportation.

Trucks ill. by author. Dutton, 1984. ISBN 0-525-44147-6 Subj: Trucks.

The way to Captain Yankee's ill. by author. Macmillan, 1994. ISBN 0-02-777271-3 Subj: Animals – cats. Maps.

What we like ill. by author. Macmillan, 1992. ISBN 0-02-777274-8 Subj: Activities – making things. Concepts. Language.

When Hugo went to school ill. by author. Macmillan, 1991. ISBN 0-02-777305-1 Subj: Animals – dogs. School.

When I go visiting by Anne F. and Harlow Rockwell; ill. by authors. Macmillan, 1984. ISBN 0-02-777740-5 Subj: Family life – grandmothers. Family life – grandparents.

Willy can count ill. by author. Little, 1989. ISBN 1-55970-013-0 Subj: Activities – walking. Counting, numbers. Country. Family life – mothers.

Willy runs away ill. by author. Dutton, 1978. ISBN 0-525-42795-3 Subj: Animals – dogs. Behavior – running away.

The wolf who had a wonderful dream ill. by author. Crowell, 1973. ISBN 0-690-89724-3 Subj: Animals – wolves. Dreams. Folk and fairy tales. Food. Foreign lands – France.

The wonderful eggs of Furicchia: a picture story from Italy ill. by author. Collins-World, 1969. Subj: Birds – chickens. Eggs. Folk and fairy tales. Foreign lands – Italy. Magic.

Rockwell, Harlow. *Blackout* (Rockwell, Anne F.)

Can I help? (Rockwell, Anne F.)

The compost heap ill. by author. Doubleday, 1974. ISBN 0-385-08989-9 Subj: Gardens, gardening. Plants.

The emergency room (Rockwell, Anne F.)

The first snowfall (Rockwell, Anne F.)

Happy birthday to me (Rockwell, Anne F.)

How my garden grew (Rockwell, Anne F.)

I did it ill. by author. Macmillan, 1974. ISBN 0-02-777550-X Subj: Activities.

I love my pets (Rockwell, Anne F.)

I play in my room (Rockwell, Anne F.)

Look at this ill. by author. Macmillan, 1978. ISBN 0-02-777590-9 Subj: Activities.

Machines (Rockwell, Anne F.)

My back yard (Rockwell, Anne F.)

My barber (Rockwell, Anne F.)

My dentist ill. by author. Greenwillow, 1975. ISBN 0-688-84004-3 Subj: Careers – dentists. Teeth.

My doctor ill. by author. Macmillan, 1973. ISBN 0-02-777480-5 Subj: Careers – doctors. Health and fitness.

My kitchen ill. by author. Greenwillow, 1980. ISBN 0-688-84236-4 Subj: Food.

My nursery school ill. by author. Greenwillow, 1976. ISBN 0-688-84025-6 Subj: School.

Nice and clean (Rockwell, Anne F.)

The night we slept outside (Rockwell, Anne F.)

Planes (Rockwell, Anne F.)

Sick in bed (Rockwell, Anne F.)

The supermarket (Rockwell, Anne F.)

Toad (Rockwell, Anne F.)

The toolbox (Rockwell, Anne F.)

When I go visiting (Rockwell, Anne F.)

Rockwell, Lizzy. *Hello baby!* ill. by author. Crown, 1999. ISBN 0-517-80012-8 Subj: Babies. Birth. Family life – brothers and sisters. Family life – new sibling.

Rockwell, Norman. *Norman Rockwell's counting book* sel. by Glorina Taborin; ill. by author. Harmony, 1977. ISBN 0-517-53205-0 Subj: Counting, numbers. Games. Holidays – April Fools' Day.

Rodanas, Kristina. *The dragonfly's tale* ill. by author. Houghton Mifflin, 1992. ISBN 0-395-57003-4 Subj: Folk and fairy tales. Indians of North America – Zuni. Insects – dragonflies.

Follow the stars: a native American woodlands tale ill. by reteller. Little, 1998. ISBN 0-7614-5029-7 Subj: Creation. Folk and fairy tales. Indians of North America – Ojibwa.

The story of Wali Dâd ill. by author. Lothrop, 1988. ISBN 0-688-07363-1 Subj: Character traits – generosity. Foreign lands – India.

Rodda, Emily. *Power and glory* ill. by Geoff Kelly. Greenwillow, 1996. ISBN 0-688-14215-X Subj: Birthdays. Games. Television.

Yay! ill. by Craig Smith. Greenwillow, 1997. ISBN 0-688-15255-4 Subj: Activities – vacationing. Family life. Foreign lands – Australia. Parks.

Roddie, Shen. *Animal stew* ill. by Patrick J. Gallagher. Houghton Mifflin, 1992. ISBN 0-395-

57582-6 Subj: Animals. Cumulative tales. Format, unusual. Giants.

Hatch, egg, hatch! ill. by Frances Cony. Little, 1991. ISBN 0-316-75345-9 Subj: Babies. Birds – chickens. Birth. Eggs. Format, unusual – toy and movable books.

Help, Mama, help! ill. by Frances Cony. Little, 1995. ISBN 0-316-75357-2 Subj: Birds – chickens. Emotions – fear. Family life – mothers. Format, unusual – toy and movable books.

Toes are to tickle ill. by Kady MacDonald. Tricycle, 1997. ISBN 1-883672-49-X Subj: Activities – playing. Babies. Family life – brothers and sisters. Games.

Rodell, Susanna. *Dear Fred* ill. by Kim Gamble. Ticknor & Fields, 1995. ISBN 0-395-71544-X Subj: Animals – mice. Behavior – needing someone. Divorce. Family life – brothers and sisters. Letters, cards. Moving.

Rodgers, Frank. *Who's afraid of the ghost train?* ill. by author. Harcourt, 1989. ISBN 0-15-200642-7 Subj: Emotions – fear. Family life – grandfathers. Ghosts. Imagination. Trains.

Rodgers, Richard. *A real nice clambake* by Richard Rodgers and Oscar Hammerstein; ill. by Nadine Bernard Westcott. Little, 1992. ISBN 0-316-75422-6 Subj: Activities – picnicking. Music. Sea and seashore. Songs.

Rodriguez, Anita. *Jamal and the angel* ill. by author. Crown, 1992. ISBN 0-517-59115-4 Subj: Activities – working. Angels. Behavior – wishing. Ethnic groups in the U.S. – African Americans.

Rodriguez, Bobbie. *Sarah's sleepover* ill. by Mark Graham. Viking, 2000. ISBN 0-670-87750-6 Subj: Family life – cousins. Games. Handicaps – blindness. Night. Power failures. Sleepovers.

Roe, Eileen. *All I am* ill. by Helen Cogancherry. Bradbury, 1990. ISBN 0-02-777372-8 Subj: Selfconcept.

Con mi hermano = With my brother tr. to Spanish by Jo Mintzer; ill. by Robert Casilla. Bradbury, 1991. ISBN 0-02-777373-6 Subj: Ethnic groups in the U.S. – Mexican Americans. Family life – brothers. Foreign languages.

Staying with Grandma ill. by Jacqueline Rogers. Bradbury, 1989. ISBN 0-02-777371-X Subj: Country. Family life – grandmothers.

Roe, Richard. *Animal ABC* ill. by author. Random House, 1984. ISBN 0-394-96864-6 Subj: ABC books. Animals.

Roehl, Angela von. *Snail started it!* (Reider, Katja)

Roehrdanz, Barbro Eriksson. *Hocus-pocus* (Eriksson, Eva)

Jealousy (Eriksson, Eva)

One short week (Eriksson, Eva)

The tooth trip (Eriksson, Eva)

Roennfeldt, Robert. *A day on the avenue* ill. by author. Viking, 1984. ISBN 0-670-25940-3 Subj: Roads. Wordless.

Roffey, Maureen. *Bathtime* ill. by author. Four Winds, 1989. ISBN 0-02-777161-X Subj: Activities – bathing. Family life.

Family scramble ill. by author. Dutton, 1987. ISBN 0-525-44290-1 Subj: Family life. Format, unusual.

Here, kitty kitty! ill. by author. Houghton Mifflin, 1991. ISBN 0-395-57584-2 Subj: Animals – cats. Family life. Format, unusual. Pets.

Home sweet home ill. by author. Coward, 1983. ISBN 0-698-20595-2 Subj: Format, unusual – toy and movable books. Homes, houses.

I spy at the zoo ill. by author. Four Winds, 1988. ISBN 0-02-777150-4 Subj: Animals. Zoos.

I spy on vacation ill. by author. Four Winds, 1988. ISBN 0-02-777160-1 Subj: Activities – vacationing. Sea and seashore.

I'm brave! (Erickson, Karen)

Look, there's my hat! ill. by author. Putnam, 1985. ISBN 0-399-21192-6 Subj: Behavior – greed. Format, unusual.

Mealtime ill. by author. Four Winds, 1989. ISBN 0-02-777151-2 Subj: Activities – picnicking. Birthdays. Family life. Food.

Quick, catch Dan! ill. by author. Houghton Mifflin, 1991. ISBN 0-395-57583-4 Subj: Animals – dogs. Family life. Format, unusual. Pets.

Rogasky, Barbara. *Rapunzel* (Grimm, Jacob)

The water of life ill. by Trina Schart Hyman. Holiday, 1986. Adapt. of Das Wasser des Lebens by Jacob and Wilhelm Grimm. ISBN 0-8234-0552-4 Subj: Character traits – pride. Folk and fairy tales. Magic. Royalty. Sibling rivalry.

Rogers, Anne. *Cinderella* (Grimm, Jacob)

The musicians of Bremen (Grimm, Jacob)

The wolf and the seven little kids (Grimm, Jacob)

Rogers, Edmund. *Elephants* ill. with photos. Raintree, 1978. ISBN 0-8172-1076-8 Subj: Animals – elephants.

Rogers, Emma. *Quacky Duck* (Rogers, Paul [Patrick])

Rogers, Fred. *Adoption* photos by Jim Judkis. Putnam, 1994. ISBN 0-399-22432-7 Subj: Adoption. Emotions. Family life.

Divorce photos by Jim Judkis. Putnam, 1998. ISBN 0-399-22449-1 Subj: Divorce. Family life.

Extraordinary friends photos by Jim Judkis. Putnam, 2000. ISBN 0-399-23146-3 Subj: Friendship. Handicaps.

Going on an airplane photos by Jim Judkis. Putnam, 1989. ISBN 0-399-21635-9 Subj: Activities – traveling. Airplanes, airports.

Going to day care photos by Jim Judkis. Putnam, 1985. ISBN 0-399-21235-3 Subj: School.

Going to the doctor photos by Jim Judkis. Putnam, 1986. ISBN 0-399-21298-1 Subj: Careers – doctors.

Going to the hospital photos by Jim Judkis. Putnam, 1988. ISBN 0-399-21503-4 Subj: Hospitals. Illness.

Going to the potty photos by Jim Judkis. Putnam, 1986. ISBN 0-399-21296-5 Subj: Behavior – growing up. Toilet training.

If we were all the same ill. by Pat Sustendal. Random House, 1988. ISBN 0-394-98778-0 Subj: Character traits – individuality.

Making friends photos by Jim Judkis. Putnam, 1987. ISBN 0-399-21382-1 Subj: Activities – playing. Emotions. Friendship.

Moving photos by Jim Judkis. Putnam, 1987. ISBN 0-399-21383-X Subj: Communities, neighborhoods. Emotions. Family life. Friendship. Moving.

The new baby photos by Jim Judkis. Putnam, 1985. ISBN 0-399-21236-1 Subj: Babies. Family life – new sibling. Sibling rivalry.

When a pet dies photos by Jim Judkis. Putnam, 1988. ISBN 0-399-21504-2 Subj: Death. Emotions – grief. Pets.

Rogers, Helen Spelman. *Morris and his brave lion* ill. by Glo Coalson. McGraw-Hill, 1975. ISBN 0-07-053502-7 Subj: Divorce.

Rogers, Jacqueline. *Tiptoe into kindergarten* ill. by author. Scholastic, 1999. ISBN 0-590-46653-4 Subj: Family life – brothers and sisters. School.

Rogers, Jean. *Runaway mittens* ill. by Rie Munoz. Greenwillow, 1988. ISBN 0-688-07054-X Subj: Behavior – losing things. Clothing – gloves, mittens.

Rogers, Margaret. *Green is beautiful* by Margaret Rogers and Bernadette Watts; ill. by Bernadette Watts. State Mutual Books, 1982. ISBN 0-905478-17-7 Subj: Concepts – color. Folk and fairy tales.

Rogers, Paul (Patrick). *Don't blame me!* ill. by Robin Bell Corfield. Trafalgar Square, 1992. ISBN 0-370-31204-X Subj: Activities – painting. Circular tales. Foreign lands – England.

Forget-me-not ill. by Celia Berridge. Viking, 1984. ISBN 0-670-32365-9 Subj: Behavior – forgetfulness. Behavior – losing things.

From me to you ill. by Jane Johnson. Watts, 1988. ISBN 0-531-08332-2 Subj: Family life – grandmothers. Rhyming text.

Lily's picnic ill. by John Prater. Bodley Head, 1988. ISBN 0-370-31098-5 Subj: Activities – picnicking. Family life.

Quacky Duck by Paul and Emma Rogers; ill. by Barbara Mullarney. Little, 1995. ISBN 0-316-37647-7 Subj: Animals. Birds – ducks. Farms. Noise, sounds.

The shapes game ill. by Sian Tucker. Holt, 1990. ISBN 0-8050-1280-X Subj: Concepts – shape.

Sheepchase ill. by Celia Berridge. Viking, 1986. ISBN 0-670-80599-8 Subj: Animals – sheep. Behavior – running away. Rhyming text.

Somebody's awake ill. by Robin Bell Corfield. Atheneum, 1988. ISBN 0-689-31490-6 Subj: Family life. Food. Morning.

Somebody's sleepy ill. by Robin Bell Corfield. Atheneum, 1988. ISBN 0-689-31491-4 Subj: Bedtime. Family life.

Tumbledown ill. by Robin Bell Corfield. Atheneum, 1988. ISBN 0-689-31392-6 Subj: City. Royalty – princes.

What can you see? ill. by Kazuko. Doubleday, 1998. ISBN 0-385-32603-3 Subj: Activities – ballooning. Animals – dogs. Picture puzzles.

What will the weather be like today? ill. by Kazuko. Greenwillow, 1990. ISBN 0-688-08951-8 Subj: Rhyming text. Weather.

Rogow, Zak. *Oranges* ill. by Mary Szilagyi. Watts, 1988. ISBN 0-531-08343-8 Subj: Food. Trees.

Rohmann, Eric. *The cinder-eyed cats* ill. by author. Crown, 1997. ISBN 0-517-70897-3 Subj: Animals – cats. Bedtime. Boats, ships. Dreams. Islands. Night.

Time flies ill. by author. Crown, 1994. ISBN 0-517-59599-0 Subj: Birds. Caldecott award honor books. Dinosaurs. Museums. Time. Wordless.

Rohmer, Harriet. *Atariba and Niguayona: a story from the Taino people of Puerto Rico* adapt. by Harriet Rohmer and Jesus Guerrero Rea; ill. by Consuelo Mendez. Children's Book Pr., 1988. ISBN 0-89239-026-3 Subj: Character traits – kindness. Foreign lands – Puerto Rico. Illness.

How we came to the fifth world: a creation story from Ancient Mexico adapt. by Harriet Rohmer and Mary Anchondo; ill. by Graciela Carrillo. Children's Book Pr., 1988. ISBN 0-89239-024-7 Subj: Creation. Folk and fairy tales. Foreign lands – Mexico.

The invisible hunters by Harriet Rohmer, Octavio Chow and Morris Vidaure; ill. by Joe Sam. Children's Book Pr., 1987. ISBN 0-89239-031-X Subj: Behavior – greed. Folk and fairy tales. Foreign lands – Nicaragua. Sports – hunting.

Mother scorpion country by Harriet Rohmer and Dorminster Wilson; ill. by Virginia Stearns. Children's Book Pr., 1987. ISBN 0-89239-032-8 Subj: Emotions – love. Folk and fairy tales. Foreign lands – Nicaragua.

Rojankovsky, Feodor. *ABC, an alphabet of many things* ill. by author. Golden Pr., 1970. Subj: ABC books.

Animals in the zoo ill. by author. Random House, 1973, c1962. ISBN 0-394-82622-1 Subj: ABC books. Animals. Zoos.

Animals on the farm ill. by author. Knopf, 1967. Subj: Animals. Farms. Wordless.

The great big animal book ill. by author. Simon & Schuster, 1950. Subj: Animals. Farms.

The great big wild animal book ill. by author. Simon & Schuster, 1951. Subj: Animals.

Roll over! *a counting song* ill. by Merle Peek. Houghton Mifflin, 1981. ISBN 0-395-29438-X Subj: Counting, numbers. Songs.

Rollings, Susan. *New shoes, red shoes* ill. by author. Orchard, 2000. ISBN 0-531-30268-7 Subj: Birthdays. Clothing – shoes. Parties. Rhyming text.

Romanek, Enid Warner. *Teddy* ill. by author. Scribners, 1978. ISBN 0-684-15811-6 Subj: Toys – bears.

Romanelli, Serena. *Little Bobo saves the day* ill. by Hans De Beer. North-South, 1997. ISBN 1-55858-787-X Subj: Activities – painting. Animals – orangutans. Illness. Kites.

Romanoli, Robert. *What's so funny?!!* ill. by Jerry Zimmerman. Grosset, 1978. ISBN 0-448-16400-0 Subj: Riddles.

Ronay, Jadja. *Ginger* ill. by Anthony Accardo. Magnolia, 1981. ISBN 0-943516-00-5 Subj: Folk and fairy tales. Magic.

Ronco, Gianna. *Look inside a car* (Mantegazza, Giovanna)

Rondell, Florence. *The family that grew* by Florence Rondell and Ruth Michaels. Crown, 1965. Subj: Adoption.

Roop, Connie. *Going buggy!* (Roop, Peter)

Let's celebrate! jokes about holidays (Roop, Peter)

Stick out your tongue! (Roop, Peter)

Roop, Peter. *The buffalo jump* ill. by Bill Farnsworth. Northland, 1996. ISBN 0-87358-616-6 Subj: Animals – buffaloes. Emotions – envy, jealousy. Indians of North America – Blackfoot. Sports – hunting.

Going buggy! by Peter and Connie Roop; ill. by Joan Hanson. Lerner, 1986. ISBN 0-8225-0988-1 Subj: Insects. Riddles.

Let's celebrate! jokes about holidays by Peter and Connie Roop; ill. by Joan Hanson. Lerner, 1986. ISBN 0-8225-0989-X Subj: Holidays. Riddles.

Stick out your tongue! by Peter and Connie Roop; ill. by Joan Hanson. Lerner, 1986. ISBN 0-8225-0990-3 Subj: Careers – doctors. Riddles.

Roosevelt, Michelle Chopin. *Zoo animals* ill. by author. Random House, 1983. ISBN 0-394-85285-0 Subj: Format, unusual – board books. Zoos.

Root, Phyllis. *Aunt Nancy and Cousin Lazybones* ill. by David Parkins. Candlewick, 1998. ISBN 1-56402-425-3 Subj: Character traits – laziness. Family life – cousins.

Aunt Nancy and Old Man Trouble ill. by David Parkins. Candlewick, 1996. ISBN 1-56402-347-8 Subj: Behavior – trickery. Folk and fairy tales.

Contrary bear ill. by Laura Cornell. HarperCollins, 1996. ISBN 0-06-025086-0 Subj: Behavior – mistakes. Family life – fathers. Toys – bears.

Grandmother Winter ill. by Beth Krommes. Houghton Mifflin, 1999. ISBN 0-395-88399-7 Subj: Birds – geese. Folk and fairy tales. Foreign lands – Germany. Seasons – winter. Weather – snow.

Gretchen's grandma by Phyllis Root and Carol A. Marron; ill. by Deborah Kogan Ray. Raintree, 1983. ISBN 0-940742-16-0 Subj: Birthdays. Family life – grandmothers. Language.

The hungry monster ill. by Sue Heap. Candlewick, 1997. ISBN 0-7636-0060-1 Subj: Food. Monsters. Space and space ships.

Moon tiger ill. by Ed Young. Holt, 1985. ISBN 0-03-000042-4 Subj: Animals. Animals – tigers. Imagination. Sibling rivalry.

Mrs. Potter's pig ill. by Russell Ayto. Candlewick, 1996. ISBN 1-56402-924-7 Subj: Animals – pigs. Babies. Character traits – cleanliness. Character traits – orderliness.

The old red rocking chair ill. by John Sanford. Little, 1992. ISBN 1-55970-063-7 Subj: Circular tales. Furniture – chairs.

One duck stuck ill. by Jane Chapman. Candlewick, 1998. ISBN 0-7636-0334-1 Subj: Animals. Birds – ducks. Counting, numbers. Rhyming text.

One windy Wednesday ill. by Helen Craig. Candlewick, 1996. ISBN 0-7636-0054-7 Subj: Animals. Farms. Noise, sounds. Weather – wind.

Rosie's fiddle ill. Kevin O'Malley. Lothrop, 1997. ISBN 0-688-12853-X Subj: Contests. Devil. Music. Tall tales.

Sam, who was swallowed by a shark ill. by Axel Scheffler. Candlewick, 1994. ISBN 1-56402-198-X Subj: Animals – rats. Boats, ships. Character traits – ambition. Sea and seashore.

Soup for supper ill. by Sue Truesdell. HarperCollins, 1986. ISBN 0-06-025071-2 Subj: Folk and fairy tales. Food. Friendship. Giants. Music. Songs.

Turnover Tuesday ill. by Helen Craig. Candlewick, 1998. ISBN 0-7636-0447-X Subj: Activities – cooking. Food.

What Baby wants ill. by Jill Barton. Candlewick, 1998. ISBN 0-7636-0207-8 Subj: Babies. Family life. Farms. Lullabies.

Ros, Saphan. *The two brothers* (Ho, Minfong)

Rosa-Casanova, Sylvia. *Mama Provi and the pot of rice* ill. by Robert Roth. Atheneum, 1997. ISBN 0-689-31932-0 Subj: Character traits – helpfulness. Ethnic groups in the U.S. Food. Illness – chicken pox.

Rosado, Ana-Maria. *Las Navidades: popular Christmas songs from Latin America* (Delacre, Lulu)

Rosales, Melodye Benson. *Double Dutch and the voodoo shoes* ill. by author. Childrens Pr., 1992. ISBN 0-516-05133-4 Subj: Ethnic groups in the U.S. – African Americans. Games. Magic.

Leola and the honeybears ill. by author. Scholastic, 1999. An African-American retelling of Goldilocks and the Three Bears. ISBN 0-590-38358-2 Subj: Animals – bears. Ethnic groups in the U.S. – African Americans. Folk and fairy tales.

'Twas the night b'fore Christmas: an African-American version ill. by author. Scholastic, 1996. Based on the original poem, A visit from St. Nicholas, by Clement C. Moore. ISBN 0-590-73944-1 Subj: Ethnic groups in the U.S. – African Americans. Holidays – Christmas. Poetry. Santa Claus.

Rosario, Idalia. *Idalia's project ABC: an urban alphabet book in English and Spanish* ill. by author. Holt, 1981. ISBN 0-03-044141-2 Subj: ABC books. City. Foreign languages.

Roscoe, William. *The butterfly's ball and the grasshopper's feast* ill. by Don Bolognese. McGraw-Hill, 1967. Subj: Animals. Insects – butterflies, caterpillars. Poetry.

Rose, Agatha. *Hide-and-seek in the yellow house* ill. by Kate Spohn. Viking, 1992. ISBN 0-670-84383-0 Subj: Animals – cats.

Rose, Anne K. *Akimba and the magic cow: a folktale from Africa* ill. by Hope Meryman. Four Winds, 1979. ISBN 0-590-07492-X Subj: Folk and fairy tales. Foreign lands – Africa. Magic.

As right as right can be ill. by Arnold Lobel. Dial, 1976. ISBN 0-8037-0296-5 Subj: Behavior – seeking better things. Money.

How does a czar eat potatoes? ill. by Janosch. Lothrop, 1973. ISBN 0-688-51531-2 Subj: Poverty. Rhyming text. Royalty.

Pot full of luck ill. by Margot Tomes. Lothrop, 1982. ISBN 0-688-00393-1 Subj: Folk and fairy tales. Foreign lands – Africa.

Spider in the sky ill. by Gail Owens. HarperCollins, 1978. Based on the story How the Sun came from American Indian mythology by Alice Marriott and Carol K. Rachlin. ISBN 0-06-025074-7 Subj: Animals. Creation. Folk and fairy tales. Indians of North America. Spiders.

The talking turnip ill. by Paul Galdone. Parents, 1979. ISBN 0-8193-1006-9 Subj: Cumulative tales. Folk and fairy tales.

The triumphs of Fuzzy Fogtop ill. by Tomie de Paola. Dial, 1979. ISBN 0-8037-8647-6 Subj: Folk and fairy tales.

Rose, David S. *It hardly seems like Halloween* ill. by author. Lothrop, 1983. ISBN 0-688-02093-3 Subj: Holidays – Halloween.

Rose, Deborah Lee. *Meredith's mother takes the train* ill. by Irene Trivas. Albert Whitman, 1990. ISBN 0-8075-5061-2 Subj: Activities – working. Family life – mothers. Rhyming text.

Rose, Emma. *Ballet magic* ill. by Jan Palmer. Scholastic, 1996. ISBN 0-590-26242-4 Subj: Activities – dancing. Ballet. Format, unusual – toy and movable books.

Rose, Gerald. *The bird garden* ill. by author. Salem House, 1987. ISBN 0-370-30690-2 Subj: Birds. Language. Royalty.

The hare and the tortoise (Æsop)

The lion and the mouse (Æsop)

PB takes a holiday ill. by author. Bodley Head, 1981. ISBN 0-370-30314-8 Subj: Activities – traveling. Animals – polar bears.

The raven and the fox (Æsop)

Scruff ill. by author. Salem House, 1985. ISBN 0-370-30619-8 Subj: Animals – dogs. Senses – smelling.

The tiger-skin rug ill. by author. Prentice-Hall, 1979. ISBN 0-13-921585-9 Subj: Animals – tigers. Crime.

Trouble in the ark ill. by author. Morehouse, 1989. ISBN 0-8192-1511-2 Subj: Animals. Behavior – fighting, arguing. Boats, ships. Religion – Noah. Weather – floods. Weather – rain.

Wolf! Wolf! (Æsop)

Rose, Mitchell. *Norman* ill. by author. Simon & Schuster, 1970. ISBN 0-671-65107-2 Subj: Animals – dogs. Theater.

Rosen, Anne. *A family Passover* by Anne Rosen and others; photos by Laurence Salzmann. Jewish Publication Society, 1980. ISBN 0-8276-0169-7 Subj: Holidays – Passover. Jewish culture.

Rosen, Michael (1946-). *Crow and Hawk* ill. by John Clementson. Harcourt, 1995. ISBN 0-15-200257-X Subj: Behavior – running away. Birds – crows. Birds – hawks. Folk and fairy tales. Indians of North America – Pueblo.

How the animals got their colors: animal myths from around the world ill. by John Clementson. Harcourt, 1992. ISBN 0-15-236783-7 Subj: Animals. Concepts – color. Folk and fairy tales. Poetry.

Little rabbit Foo Foo ill. by Arthur Robins. Simon & Schuster, 1990. ISBN 0-671-70968-2 Subj: Animals. Animals – rabbits.

Mission Ziffoid ill. by Arthur Robins. Candlewick, 1999. ISBN 0-7636-0805-X Subj: Aliens. Space and space ships.

Smelly jelly smelly fish ill. by Quentin Blake. Prentice-Hall, 1987. ISBN 0-13-814567-9 Subj: Humor. Poetry.

A Thanksgiving wish ill. by John Thompson. Blue Sky, 1999. ISBN 0-590-25563-0 Subj: Communities, neighborhoods. Death. Family life – grandparents. Holidays – Thanksgiving.

This is our house ill. by Bob Graham. Candlewick, 1996. ISBN 1-56402-870-4 Subj: Behavior – sharing. Character traits – selfishness. Homes, houses. Prejudice.

Under the bed: the bedtime book ill. by Quentin Blake. Prentice-Hall, 1986. ISBN 0-13-935412-3 Subj: Bedtime. Furniture – beds. Poetry.

We're going on a bear hunt ill. by Helen Oxenbury. Macmillan, 1989. ISBN 0-689-50476-4 Subj: Animals – bears. Games. Participation. Sports – hunting.

You can't catch me! ill. by Quentin Blake. Elsevier-Dutton, 1982. ISBN 0-233-97345-1 Subj: Humor. Poetry.

Rosen, Michael J. (1954-). *All eyes on the pond* ill. by Tom Leonard. Hyperion, 1994. ISBN 1-56282-476-7 Subj: Animals. Lakes, ponds. Nature.

Avalanche ill. by David Butler. Candlewick, 1998. ISBN 0-7636-0589-1 Subj: ABC books. Animals – dogs. Rhyming text. Weather – snow.

Bonesy and Isabel ill. by James Ransome. Harcourt, 1995. ISBN 0-15-209813-5 Subj: Adoption. Animals – dogs. Death. Emotions – grief. Farms. Pets.

The dog who walked with God ill. by Stan Fellows. Candlewick, 1998. ISBN 0-7636-0470-4 Subj: Animals – dogs. Creation. Indians of North America – Kato. Weather – floods.

Elijah's angel ill. by Aminah Brenda Lynn Robinson. Harcourt, 1992. ISBN 0-15-225394-7 Subj: Careers – woodcarvers. Ethnic groups in the U.S. – African Americans. Friendship. Holidays – Christmas. Holidays – Hanukkah. Jewish culture.

Home: a collaboration of thirty authors and illustrators to aid the homeless. HarperCollins, 1992. ISBN 0-06-021789-8 Subj: Homeless.

With a dog like that, a kid like me . . . ill. by Ted Rand. Dial, 2000. ISBN 0-8037-2059-9 Subj: Animals. Animals – dogs. Imagination.

Rosen, Sidney. *How far is a star?* ill. by Dean Lindberg. Carolrhoda, 1992. ISBN 0-87614-684-1 Subj: Concepts – distance. Space and space ships. Stars.

Where does the moon go? ill. by Dean Lindberg. Carolrhoda, 1992. ISBN 0-87614-685-X Subj: Moon. Space and space ships.

Where's the big dipper? ill. by Dean Lindberg. Carolrhoda, 1995. ISBN 0-87614-883-6 Subj: Astronomy. Sky. Stars.

Rosen, Winifred. *Dragons hate to be discreet* ill. by Edward Koren. Knopf, 1978. ISBN 0-394-95377-2 Subj: Dragons. Imagination.

Henrietta and the day of the iguana ill. by Kay Chorao. Four Winds, 1978. ISBN 0-590-07471-7 Subj: Behavior – wishing. Pets. Reptiles – iguanas.

Henrietta and the gong from Hong Kong ill. by Kay Chorao. Four Winds, 1981. ISBN 0-590-07657-4 Subj: Family life – grandparents. Sibling rivalry.

Rosenberg, David. *see* Clifford, David

Rosenberg, Ethel. *see* Clifford, Eth

Rosenberg, Liz. *Adelaide and the night train* ill. by Lisa Desimini. HarperCollins, 1989. ISBN 0-06-025103-4 Subj: Bedtime. Night. Sleep. Trains.

A big and little alphabet ill. by Vera Rosenberry. Orchard, 1997. ISBN 0-531-33050-8 Subj: ABC books. Animals.

The carousel ill. by Jim LaMarche. Harcourt, 1995. ISBN 0-15-200853-5 Subj: Animals – horses, ponies. Death. Emotions – grief. Family life – mothers. Family life – sisters. Imagination. Merry-go-rounds.

Grandmother and the runaway shadow ill. by Beth Peck. Harcourt, 1996. ISBN 0-15-200948-5 Subj: Activities – traveling. Ethnic groups in the U.S. – Russian Americans. Family life – grandmothers. Jewish culture. Shadows.

Mama Goose: a new Mother Goose ill. by Janet Street. Philomel, 1994. ISBN 0-399-22348-7 Subj: Nursery rhymes.

The scrap doll ill. by Robin Ballard. HarperCollins, 1991. ISBN 0-06-024865-3 Subj: Activities – making things. Toys – dolls.

The silence in the mountains ill. by Chris Soentpiet. Orchard, 1999. ISBN 0-531-33084-2 Subj: Family life – grandparents. Immigrants. Noise, sounds.

Window, mirror, moon ill. by Ruth Richardson. HarperCollins, 1990. ISBN 0-06-025076-3 Subj: Babies. Circular tales. Moon. Night. Rhyming text.

Rosenberg, Maxine B. *Being adopted* photos by George Ancona. Lothrop, 1984. ISBN 0-688-02673-7 Subj: Adoption. Ethnic groups in the U.S. Family life.

Brothers and sisters photos by George Ancona. Houghton Mifflin, 1991. ISBN 0-395-51121-6 Subj: Family life – brothers and sisters.

Mommy's in the hospital having a baby photos by Robert Maass. Clarion, 1997. ISBN 0-395-71813-9 Subj: Babies. Birth. Family life – new sibling. Hospitals.

My friend Leslie: the story of a handicapped child photos by George Ancona. Lothrop, 1983. ISBN 0-688-01691-X Subj: Handicaps. School.

Rosenberg, Nancy Sherman. *see* Sherman, Nancy

Rosenberry, Vera. *Run, jump, whiz, splash* ill. by author. Holiday, 1999. ISBN 0-8234-1378-0 Subj: Activities. Seasons.

Vera's first day of school ill. by author. Holt, 1999. ISBN 0-8050-5936-9 Subj: Character traits – shyness. Emotions – fear. School – first day.

When Vera was sick ill. by author. Holt, 1998. ISBN 0-8050-5405-7 Subj: Illness – chicken pox.

Rosenbloom, Joseph. *Deputy Dan and the bank robbers* ill. by Tim Raglin. Random House, 1985. ISBN 0-394-97045-4 Subj: Crime.

The funniest joke book ever! ill. by Hans Wilhelm. Sterling, 1986. ISBN 0-8069-4724-1 Subj: Riddles.

Rosenblum, Richard. *Journey to the golden land* ill. by author. Jewish Publication Society, 1992. ISBN 0-8276-0405-X Subj: Activities – traveling. Ethnic groups in the U.S. – Russian Americans. Family life. Foreign lands – Russia. Jewish culture.

The old synagogue ill. by author. Jewish Publication Society, 1989. ISBN 0-8276-0322-3 Subj: City. Jewish culture. Religion.

Rosenthal, Marya. *see* Dantzer-Rosenthal, Marya

Rosman, Steven M. *Deena the damselfly* ill. by Giyora Karmi. UAHC Pr., 1992. ISBN 0-8074-0477-2 Subj: Behavior – growing up. Insects – damselflies. Nature.

Rosner, Ruth. *Arabba gah zee, Marissa and Me!* ill. by author. Albert Whitman, 1987. ISBN 0-8075-0442-4 Subj: Activities – playing. Friendship. Imagination.

Nattie witch ill. by author. HarperCollins, 1989. ISBN 0-06-025099-2 Subj: Witches.

Ross, Anna. *I did it!* ill. by Norman Gorbaty. Random House, 1990. ISBN 0-394-86019-5 Subj: Behavior – growing up. Character traits – pride. Puppets.

I have to go ill. by Norman Gorbaty. Random House, 1990. ISBN 0-394-86051-9 Subj: Behavior – growing up. Puppets.

Naptime ill. by Norman Gorbaty. Random House, 1990. ISBN 0-394-85828-X Subj: Puppets. Sleep.

Say the magic word, please ill. by Norman Gorbaty. Random House, 1990. ISBN 0-394-85857-3 Subj: Etiquette. Puppets.

Ross, Blanche. *A strange servant: a Russian folktale* (Galdone, Paul)

Ross, Christine. *Lily and the bears* ill. by author. Houghton Mifflin, 1991. ISBN 0-395-55332-6 Subj: Animals – bears. Behavior – imitation. Zoos.

Lily and the present ill. by author. Houghton Mifflin, 1992. ISBN 0-395-61127-X Subj: Babies. Character traits – generosity. Family life – new sibling. Shopping. Toys – balloons.

Ross, Dave (David). *A book of friends* ill. by Laura Rader. HarperCollins, 1999. ISBN 0-06-028170-7 Subj: Friendship.

A book of hugs ill. by Laura Rader. HarperCollins, 1999. ISBN 0-06-028147-2 Subj: Emotions.

A book of kisses ill. by Laura Rader. HarperCollins, 2000. ISBN 0-06-028453-6 Subj: Emotions.

Gorp and the space pirates ill. by author. Walker, 1983. ISBN 0-8037-6494-0 Subj: Monsters. Pirates. Space and space ships.

More hugs! ill. by author. Crowell, 1984. ISBN 0-694-00147-3 Subj: Emotions.

Space monster ill. by author. Walker, 1981. Subj: Monsters. Space and space ships.

Space Monster Gorp and the runaway computer ill. by author. Walker, 1984. Subj: Computers. Monsters. Space and space ships.

Ross, Diana. *The story of the little red engine* ill. by Leslie Wood. Transatlantic, 1947. Subj: Foreign lands – England. Trains.

Ross, Eileen. *The Halloween showdown* ill. by Lynn Rowe Reed. Holiday, 1999. ISBN 0-8234-1395-0 Subj: Animals. Animals – cats. Holidays – Halloween. Witches.

Ross, Gayle. *How Turtle's back was cracked* ill. by Murv Jacob. Dial, 1995. ISBN 0-8037-1729-6 Subj: Animals – wolves. Behavior – boasting. Folk and fairy tales. Indians of North America – Cherokee. Reptiles – turtles, tortoises.

The legend of the Windigo: a tale from native North America ill. by Murv Jacob. Dial, 1996. ISBN 0-8037-1898-5 Subj: Folk and fairy tales. Indians of North America – Algonquian. Indians of North America – Windigos. Insects – mosquitoes. Monsters.

Ross, George Maxim. *When Lucy went away* ill. by Ingrid Fetz. Dutton, 1976. Subj: Animals – cats. Pets.

Ross, H. L. *Not counting monsters* ill. by Doug Cushman. Platt, 1978. Subj: Activities. Counting, numbers. Monsters.

Ross, Jessica. *Ms. Klondike* ill. by author. Viking, 1977. Subj: Activities – working. Careers – taxi drivers. Taxis.

Ross, Joel. *Your first airplane trip* (Ross, Pat)

Ross, Katharine (1950-). *When you were a baby* photos by Phoebe Dunn. Random House, 1988. ISBN 0-394-89897-4 Subj: Babies. Behavior – growing up. Family life.

Ross, Lillian Hammer. *Buba Leah and her paper children* ill. by Mary Morgan. Jewish Publication Society, 1991. ISBN 0-8276-0375-4 Subj: Jewish culture. Letters, cards. Moving.

The little old man and his dreams ill. by Deborah Healy. HarperCollins, 1990. ISBN 0-06-025095-X Subj: Dreams. Jewish culture. Old age. Weddings.

Ross, Pat. *Meet M and M* ill. by Marylin Hafner. Pantheon, 1980. Subj: Friendship.

Molly and the slow teeth ill. by Jerry Milord. Lothrop, 1980. Subj: School. Teeth.

Your first airplane trip by Pat and Joel Ross; ill. by Lynn Wheeling. Lothrop, 1981. Subj: Activities – flying. Airplanes, airports. Emotions – fear.

Ross, Stacey. *The magic dogs of the volcanoes* (Argueta, Manlio)

Ross, Tom. *Eggbert, the slightly cracked egg* ill. by Rex Barron. Putnam, 1994. ISBN 0-399-22416-5 Subj: Careers – artists. Character traits – individuality. Eggs.

Ross, Tony. *The boy who cried wolf* ill. by author. Dial, 1991. ISBN 0-8037-0193-4 Subj: Animals – wolves. Behavior – lying. Behavior – trickery. Folk and fairy tales.

The enchanted pig: an old Rumanian tale ill. by author. HarperCollins, 1983. ISBN 0-911745-00-9 Subj: Animals – pigs. Folk and fairy tales. Magic. Witches.

A fairy tale ill. by author. Little, 1992. ISBN 0-316-75750-0 Subj: Fairies. Friendship.

Goldilocks and the three bears (The three bears)

The greedy little cobbler ill. by author. Barron's, 1980. ISBN 0-8120-5389-3 Subj: Behavior – greed. Careers – shoemakers.

Hansel and Gretel ill. by author. Trafalgar Square, 1990. ISBN 0-86264-210-8 Subj: Folk and fairy tales. Forest, woods. Witches.

Happy blanket ill. by author. Farrar, 1990. ISBN 0-374-32843-9 Subj: Emotions – fear. Format, unusual.

Hugo and Oddsock ill. by author. Rourke, 1982. ISBN 0-8659-2123-7 Subj: Animals – mice. Imagination – imaginary friends.

Hugo and the bureau of holidays ill. by author. Follett, 1982. ISBN 0-86592-129-6 Subj: Animals – mice. Holidays.

Hugo and the man who stole colors ill. by author. Follett, 1982. ISBN 0-86592-121-0 Subj: Animals – mice. Behavior – stealing. Concepts – color.

I want a cat ill. by author. Farrar, 1989. ISBN 0-374-33621-0 Subj: Animals – cats. Character traits – persistence. Pets.

I want my potty ill. by author. Kane/Miller, 1986. ISBN 0-916291-08-1 Subj: Behavior – growing up. Toilet training.

I'm coming to get you! ill. by author. Dial, 1984. ISBN 0-8037-0119-5 Subj: Emotions – fear. Monsters. Space and space ships.

Jack and the beanstalk (Jack and the beanstalk)

Jack the giantkiller (Jack and the beanstalk)

Oscar got the blame ill. by author. Dial, 1988. ISBN 0-8037-0499-2 Subj: Behavior – misbehavior.

The pied piper of Hamelin retold and ill. by Tony Ross. Lothrop, 1978. ISBN 0-688-51824-9 Subj: Animals – rats. Folk and fairy tales. Foreign lands – Germany.

Puss in boots: the story of a sneaky cat (Perrault, Charles)

Stone soup ill. by author. Dial, 1987. ISBN 0-8037-0401-1 Subj: Animals – wolves. Birds – chickens. Character traits – cleverness. Folk and fairy tales.

This old man: a musical counting book ill. by author; paper engineering by Rodger Smith. Collins, 1990. ISBN 0-00-184559-4 Subj: Animals – dogs. Counting, numbers. Format, unusual – toy and movable books. Music. Songs.

Towser and the terrible thing ill. by author. Pantheon, 1984. ISBN 0-394-96541-8 Subj: Animals – dogs. Monsters. Royalty.

Treasure of Cozy Cove ill. by author. Farrar, 1990. ISBN 0-374-37744-8 Subj: Activities. Animals – cats. Pirates.

Rosselson, Leon. *Where's my mom?* ill. by Priscilla Lamont. Candlewick, 1994. ISBN 1-56402-392-3 Subj: Family life – mothers. Rhyming text.

Rossetti, Christina Georgina. *Color* ill. by Mary Teichman. HarperCollins, 1992. ISBN 0-06-022650-1 Subj: Concepts – color. Poetry.

Fly away, fly away over the sea ill. by Bernadette Watts. North-South, 1991. ISBN 1-55858-101-4 Subj: Birds. Poetry.

What is pink? ill. by José Aruego. Macmillan, 1971. Subj: Birds – flamingos. Concepts – color. Poetry.

Rossiter, Nan Parson. *The way home* ill. by author. Dutton, 1999. ISBN 0-525-45767-4 Subj: Birds – geese. Character traits – kindness to animals. Farms. Illness.

Rossner, Judith. *What kind of feet does a bear have?* ill. by Irwin Rosenhouse. Bobbs-Merrill, 1963. Subj: Humor.

Rotenberg, Lisa. *Rodeo pup* ill. by author. Firefly, 1998. ISBN 1-55209-245-3 Subj: Animals – dogs. Sports.

Roth, Carol. *Little Bunny's sleepless night* ill. by Valeri Gorbachev. North-South, 1999. ISBN 0-

7358-1070-2 Subj: Animals – rabbits. Behavior – dissatisfaction. Friendship. Sleep.

Ten dirty pigs / Ten clean pigs ill. by Pamela Paparone. North-South, 1999. ISBN 0-7358-1090-7 Subj: Animals – pigs. Bedtime. Counting, numbers. Format, unusual.

Roth, Harold. *Autumn days* photos by author. Grosset, 1986. ISBN 0-448-10680-9 Subj: Format, unusual – board books. Seasons – fall.

A checkup photos by author. Grosset, 1986. ISBN 0-448-10683-3 Subj: Format, unusual – board books. Health and fitness.

Let's look all around the farm photos by author. Putnam, 1988. ISBN 0-448-10687-6 Subj: Farms. Format, unusual – toy and movable books.

Let's look all around the house photos by author. Putnam, 1988. ISBN 0-448-10685-X Subj: Format, unusual – toy and movable books. Homes, houses.

Let's look all around the town photos by author. Putnam, 1988. ISBN 0-448-10684-1 Subj: City. Format, unusual – toy and movable books.

Let's look for surprises all around photos by author. Putnam, 1988. ISBN 0-448-10686-8 Subj: Format, unusual – toy and movable books.

Nursery school photos by author. Grosset, 1986. ISBN 0-448-10682-5 Subj: Format, unusual – board books. School.

Winter days photos by author. Grosset, 1986. ISBN 0-448-10681-7 Subj: Format, unusual – board books. Seasons – winter.

Roth, Roger. *Fishing for Methuselah* ill. by author. HarperCollins, 1998. ISBN 0-06-027592-8 Subj: Friendship. Sports – fishing. Tall tales.

The sign painter's dream ill. by author. Crown, 1993. ISBN 0-517-58921-4 Subj: Activities – painting. Careers – sign painters. Character traits – generosity. Dreams.

Roth, Susan L. *Another Christmas* ill. by author. Morrow, 1992. ISBN 0-688-09943-2 Subj: Death. Emotions – grief. Family life. Family life – grandmothers. Foreign lands – Puerto Rico. Holidays – Christmas.

The biggest frog in Australia ill. by author. Simon & Schuster, 1996. ISBN 0-689-80490-3 Subj: Foreign lands – Australia. Frogs and toads. Tall tales.

Brave Martha and the dragon ill. by author. Dial, 1996. ISBN 0-8037-1853-5 Subj: Character traits – bravery. Dragons. Folk and fairy tales.

Cinnamon's day out: a gerbil adventure ill. by author. Dial, 1998. ISBN 0-8037-2323-7 Subj: Animals – gerbils. Behavior – running away.

Fire came to the earth people: a Dahomean folktale ill. by adapt. St. Martin's, 1988. ISBN 0-312-01723-5 Subj: Fire. Folk and fairy tales. Foreign lands – Africa.

Kanahena: a Cherokee story ill. by adapt. St. Martin's, 1988. ISBN 0-312-01722-7 Subj: Animals – wolves. Folk and fairy tales. Indians of North America – Cherokee.

Night-time numbers: a scary counting book ill. by author. Barefoot, 1999. ISBN 1-84148-001-0 Subj: Bedtime. Counting, numbers. Night. Rhyming text.

Patchwork tales by Susan L. Roth and Ruth Phang; ill. by authors. Atheneum, 1984. ISBN 0-689-31053-6 Subj: Family life – grandmothers.

The story of light ill. by author. Morrow, 1990. ISBN 0-688-08677-2 Subj: Folk and fairy tales. Indians of North America – Cherokee. Sun.

We'll ride elephants through Brooklyn ill. by author. Farrar, 1990. ISBN 0-374-38258-1 Subj: Family life – grandfathers. Illness. Parades.

Rothenberg, Joan. *Inside-out grandma* ill. by author. Hyperion, 1995. ISBN 0-7868-2092-6 Subj: Clothing. Family life – grandmothers. Folk and fairy tales. Holidays – Hanukkah. Jewish culture. Religion.

Matzah ball soup ill. by author. Hyperion, 1999. ISBN 0-7868-2170-1 Subj: Family life – sisters. Food. Holidays – Passover. Jewish culture.

Rothman, Joel. *This can lick a lollipop: body riddles for kids; esto goza chupando un caramelo: las partes del cuerpo en adivinanzas infantiles* English by Joel Rothman, Spanish by Argentina Palacios; photos by Patricia Ruben. Doubleday, 1979. ISBN 0-385-13072-4 Subj: Anatomy. Foreign languages.

Rotner, Shelley. *The A.D.D. book for kids* by Shelley Rotner and Sheila Kelly; photos by Shelley Rotner. Millbrook, 2000. ISBN 0-7613-1722-8 Subj: Behavior. Handicaps – ADD.

Boats afloat photos by author. Orchard, 1998. ISBN 0-531-33112-1 Subj: Boats, ships. Transportation.

The body book by Shelley Rotner and Steve Calcagnino; photos by Shelley Rotner. Orchard, 2000. ISBN 0-531-33256-X Subj: Anatomy.

Changes (Allen, Marjorie N.)

Citybook photos by Ken Kreisler. Orchard, 1994. ISBN 0-531-06837-4 Subj: City. Rhyming text.

Close, closer, closest by Shelley Rotner and Richard Olivo; photos by Shelley Rotner. Atheneum, 1997. ISBN 0-689-80762-7 Subj: Concepts – perspective. Concepts – size.

Faces photos by Ken Kreisler. Macmillan, 1994. ISBN 0-02-777887-8 Subj: Anatomy – faces. Character traits – individuality.

Hold the anchovies! by Shelley Rotner and Julia Pemberton Hellums; photos by Shelley Rotner. Orchard, 1996. ISBN 0-531-08857-X Subj: Activities – cooking. Food.

Lots of moms by Shelley Rotner and Sheila M. Kelly; photos by Shelley Rotner. Dial, 1996. ISBN

0-8037-1892-6 Subj: Ethnic groups in the U.S. Family life – mothers.

Pick a pet by Shelley Rotner and Cheo García; photos by Shelley Rotner. Orchard, 1999. ISBN 0-531-33147-4 Subj: Animals. Pets.

Wheels around photos by author. Houghton Mifflin, 1995. ISBN 0-395-71815-5 Subj: Wheels.

Rottenberg, Dorian. *The merry starlings* (Marshak, S. [Samuil])

Roughsey, Dick. *The giant devil-dingo* ill. by author. Macmillan, 1975. ISBN 0-02-777840-1 Subj: Animals. Folk and fairy tales. Foreign lands – Australia.

Round, Graham. *Hangdog* ill. by author. Dial, 1987. ISBN 0-8037-0448-8 Subj: Animals – dogs. Animals – tigers. Boats, ships. Friendship. Islands. Sea and seashore.

Rounds, Glen. *The boll weevil* Ill. by author. Golden Gate, 1967. Subj: Folk and fairy tales. Insects. Music. Songs.

Casey Jones: the story of a brave engineer ill. by author. Golden Gate, 1968. Subj: Folk and fairy tales. Music. Songs. Trains.

Cowboys ill. by author. Holiday, 1991. ISBN 0-8234-0867-1 Subj: Cowboys. U.S. history – frontier and pioneer life.

The day the circus came to Lone Tree ill. by author. Holiday, 1973. ISBN 0-8234-0232-0 Subj: Circus. Humor.

I know an old lady who swallowed a fly (Little old lady who swallowed a fly)

Once we had a horse ill. by author. Holiday, 1996. ISBN 0-8234-1241-5 Subj: Animals – horses, ponies.

Sod houses on the Great Plains ill. by author. Holiday, 1995. ISBN 0-8234-1162-1 Subj: Family life. Homes, houses. U.S. history – frontier and pioneer life.

The strawberry roan comp. and ill. by Glen Rounds. Golden Gate, 1970. ISBN 0-8746-4160-8 Subj: Animals – horses, ponies. Music. Songs.

Sweet Betsy from Pike comp. and ill. by Glen Rounds. Childrens Pr., 1973. ISBN 0-516-08855-6 Subj: Folk and fairy tales. Music. Songs.

The three billy goats Gruff (Asbjørnsen, P. C. [Peter Christen])

The three little pigs and the big bad wolf (The three little pigs)

Washday on Noah's ark ill. by author. Holiday, 1985. ISBN 0-8234-0555-9 Subj: Animals. Boats, ships. Character traits – cleanliness. Religion – Noah. Tall tales. Weather – floods. Weather – rain.

Rouss, Sylvia A. *Sammy Spider's first Passover* ill. by Katherine Janus Kahn. Kar-Ben Copies, 1995.

ISBN 0-929371-81-X Subj: Holidays – Passover. Jewish culture. Religion. Spiders.

Sammy Spider's first Shabbat ill. by Katherine Janus Kahn. Kar-Ben Copies, 1997. ISBN 1-58013-007-0 Subj: Jewish culture. Religion. Spiders.

Routh, Jonathan. *The Nuns go to Africa* ill. by author. Bobbs-Merrill, 1971. Subj: Careers – nuns. Foreign lands – Africa.

Rovetch, Lissa. *Trigwater did it* ill. by author. Morrow, 1989. ISBN 0-688-08058-8 Subj: Behavior – misbehavior. Imagination – imaginary friends.

Rowan, James P. *I can be a zoo keeper.* Childrens Pr., 1985. ISBN 0-516-01889-2 Subj: Animals. Careers. Zoos.

Rowand, Phyllis. *Every day in the year* ill. by author. Little, 1959. Subj: Emotions – love. Holidays – Christmas.

George ill. by author. Little, 1956. Subj: Animals – dogs.

George goes to town ill. by author. Little, 1958. Subj: Animals – dogs.

It is night ill. by author. HarperCollins, 1953. Subj: Night. Sleep.

Rowe, Jeanne A. *City workers.* Watts, 1969. Subj: Careers. City.

A trip through a school. Watts, 1969. Subj: School.

Rowe, Jeannette. *Whose ears?* ill. by author. Little, 1998. ISBN 0-316-75932-5 Subj: Anatomy – ears. Animals. Format, unusual – toy and movable books.

Whose feet? ill. by author. Little, 1998. ISBN 0-316-75934-1 Subj: Anatomy – feet. Animals. Format, unusual – toy and movable books.

Whose nose? ill. by author. Little, 1998. ISBN 0-316-75933-3 Subj: Anatomy – noses. Animals. Format, unusual – toy and movable books.

Rowe, John A. *Baby Crow* ill. by author. North-South, 1994. ISBN 1-55858-278-9 Subj: Birds – crows. Food.

Monkey trouble ill. by author. North-South, 1999. ISBN 0-7358-1034-6 Subj: Animals – monkeys. Behavior – mistakes.

Rabbit moon ill. by author. Picture Book Studio, 1992. ISBN 0-8870-8246-7 Subj: Animals – rabbits. Moon.

Smudge ill. by author. North-South, 1997. ISBN 1-55858-789-6 Subj: Animals. Animals – rats. Birds. Family life – mothers. Memories, memory.

Rowinski, Kate. *Cats in the dark* ill. by Bonnie Bishop. Down East, 1998. ISBN 0-8927-2427-7 Subj: Animals – cats. Lighthouses. Night. Noise, sounds. Rhyming text.

L. L. Bear's island adventure ill. by Dawn Peterson. Down East, 1992. ISBN 0-89272-320-3 Subj: Activities – picnicking. Animals. Animals – bears. Sea and seashore. Seasons – winter. Weather – storms.

Roy, Indrapramit. *The very hungry lion* (Wolf, Gita)

Roy, Ronald. *Breakfast with my father* ill. by Troy Howell. Houghton Mifflin, 1980. ISBN 0-395-29430-4 Subj: Divorce. Family life.

A thousand pails of water ill. by Vo-Dinh Mai. Knopf, 1978. ISBN 0-394-93752-X Subj: Animals – whales. Character traits – kindness to animals. Foreign lands – Japan.

Three ducks went wandering ill. by Paul Galdone. Seabury Pr., 1979. ISBN 0-8164-3231-7 Subj: Behavior – indifference. Birds – ducks. Humor.

Whose hat is that? ill. by Rosmarie Hausherr. Clarion, 1987. ISBN 0-89919-446-X Subj: Clothing – hats.

Whose shoes are these? photos by Rosmarie Hausherr. Clarion, 1988. ISBN 0-89919-445-1 Subj: Clothing – shoes.

Royston, Angela. *Baby animals* photos by Steve Shott; additional photos by Jane Burton; ill. by Jane Cradock-Watson and Dave Hopkins. Aladdin, 1992. ISBN 0-689-71563-3 Subj: Animals.

Big machines ill. by Terry Pastor. Little, 1994. ISBN 0-316-76070-6 Subj: Machines. Trucks.

Cars ill. by Jane Cradock-Watson and Dave Hopkins; photos by Tim Ridley. Macmillan, 1991. ISBN 0-689-71517-X Subj: Automobiles. Format, unusual – board books.

Chick (Burton, Jane)

Cow ill. by Bob Bampton. Watts, 1990. ISBN 0-531-19077-3 Subj: Animals – bulls, cows. Farms.

Diggers and dump trucks ill. by Jane Cradock-Watson and Dave Hopkins; photos by Tim Ridley. Macmillan, 1991. ISBN 0-689-71516-1 Subj: Activities – digging. Machines. Trucks.

Dinosaurs ill. by Jane Cradock-Watson and Dave Hopkins; photos by Colin Keates. Macmillan, 1991. ISBN 0-689-71518-8 Subj: Dinosaurs.

Duck (Watts, Barrie)

Fire fighters ill. with photos. DK, 1998. ISBN 0-7894-2960-8 Subj: Careers – firefighters. Fires. Safety.

Frog (Taylor, Kim)

The goat ill. by Eric Robson. Watts, 1990. ISBN 0-531-19078-1 Subj: Animals – goats. Farms.

The hen ill. by Dave Cook. Watts, 1990. ISBN 0-531-19079-X Subj: Birds – chickens. Farms.

Jungle animals ill. by Martine Blaney and Dave Hopkins; photos by Philip Dowell. Macmillan, 1991. ISBN 0-689-71519-6 Subj: Animals. Jungle.

Kitten (Burton, Jane)

Lamb (Clayton, Gordon)

Monster road builders ill. by Graham Thompson. Barron's, 1989. ISBN 0-8120-6126-8 Subj: Machines. Roads.

Mouse (Watts, Barrie)

My body ill. by Richard Manning. DK, 1991. ISBN 1-879431-22-X Subj: Anatomy.

Night-time animals photos by Dave King. Aladdin, 1992. ISBN 0-689-71646-X Subj: Animals. Night.

The pig ill. by Jim Channel. Watts, 1990. ISBN 0-531-19080-3 Subj: Animals – pigs. Farms.

Planes photos by Tim Ridley. Aladdin, 1992. ISBN 0-689-71564-1 Subj: Airplanes, airports.

The pony ill. by Bob Bampton. Watts, 1990. ISBN 0-531-19081-1 Subj: Animals – horses, ponies. Farms.

Puppy (Burton, Jane)

Rabbit (Watts, Barrie)

Sea animals photos by Steve Shott; ill. by Jane Cradock-Watson and Dave Hopkins. Aladdin, 1992. ISBN 0-689-71565-X Subj: Animals. Crustaceans. Fish. Sea and seashore.

The sheep ill. by Josephine Martin. Watts, 1990. ISBN 0-531-19082-X Subj: Animals – sheep. Farms.

Shells ill. by Richard Manning. DK, 1991. ISBN 1-879431-25-4 Subj: Format, unusual. Sea and seashore.

Ships and boats photos by Tim Ridley. Aladdin, 1992. ISBN 0-689-71566-8 Subj: Boats, ships.

Small animals ill. by Richard Manning. DK, 1991. ISBN 1-879431-24-6 Subj: Animals. Format, unusual. Nature.

Toys ill. by Richard Manning. DK, 1991. ISBN 1-879431-23-8 Subj: Toys.

Truck trouble ill. with photos. DK, 1998. ISBN 0-7894-2958-6 Subj: Careers – truck drivers. Trucks.

Rubel, Nicole. *Bruno Brontosaurus* ill. by author. Camelot, 1983. ISBN 0-380-81562-1 Subj: Dinosaurs.

The ghost family meets its match ill. by author. Dial, 1992. ISBN 0-8037-1094-1 Subj: Ghosts.

Goldie ill. by author. HarperCollins, 1989. ISBN 0-06-025097-6 Subj: Birds – chickens. Shopping. Stores.

Goldie's nap ill. by author. HarperCollins, 1991. ISBN 0-06-025107-7 Subj: Behavior – misbehavior. Birds – chickens. School. Sleep.

It came from the swamp ill. by author. Dial, 1988. ISBN 0-8037-0515-8 Subj: Behavior – lost. Humor. Reptiles – alligators, crocodiles.

Me and my kitty ill. by author. Macmillan, 1983. ISBN 0-02-777880-0 Subj: Activities. Animals – cats.

Sam and Violet are twins ill. by author. Camelot, 1981. ISBN 0-380-76919-0 Subj: Animals – cats. Character traits – individuality. Multiple births – twins.

Sam and Violet go camping ill. by author. Camelot, 1981. ISBN 0-380-76927-1 Subj: Animals – cats. Camps, camping. Character traits – individuality. Multiple births – twins.

Uncle Henry and Aunt Henrietta's honeymoon ill. by author. Dial, 1986. ISBN 0-8037-0247-7 Subj: Activities – babysitting. Boats, ships. Family life – aunts, uncles.

Ruben, Patricia. *Apples to zippers: an alphabet book* ill. by author. Doubleday, 1976. ISBN 0-385-11443-5 Subj: ABC books.

True or false? ill. by author. Lippincott, 1978. ISBN 0-397-31791-3 Subj: Concepts.

Rubin, Caroline. *Grandma is somebody special* (Goldman, Susan)

Grandparents around the world (Raynor, Dorka)

Snow on bear's nose: a story of a Japanese moon bear cub (Bartoli, Jennifer)

Tell them my name is Amanda (Wold, Jo Anne)

Wild Bill Hiccup's riddle book (Bishop, Ann)

Rubin, Cynthia Elyce. *ABC Americana from the National Gallery of Art* photos by Carleton Palmer. Harcourt, 1989. ISBN 0-15-200660-5 Subj: ABC books. Art.

Rubin, Jeff. *Baseball brothers* by Jeff Rubin and Rick Rael; ill. by Sandy Kossin. Lothrop, 1976. ISBN 0-688-51744-7 Subj: Friendship. Sports – baseball.

Rubinetti, Donald. *Cappy the lonely camel* ill. by Liisa Chauncy Guida. Silver Pr., 1996. ISBN 0-382-39151-9 Subj: Animals – camels. Character traits – being different. Prejudice.

Ruby-Spears Enterprises. *The puppy's new adventures: hide and seek* ill. by Ruby-Spears Enterprises. Antioch, 1983. ISBN 0-89954-228-X Subj: Animals – dogs. Crime. Format, unusual – toy and movable books.

Rucki, Ani. *When the Earth wakes* ill. by author. Scholastic, 1998. ISBN 0-590-05951-3 Subj: Animals – bears. Earth. Nature. Seasons.

Ruck-Pauquèt, Gina. *Little hedgehog* ill. by Marianne Richter. Hastings House, 1959. Subj: Animals – hedgehogs.

Mumble bear trans. by Anthea Bell; ill. by Erika Dietzsch-Capelle. Putnam, 1980. ISBN 0-399-20712-0 Subj: Animals – bears. Character traits – individuality.

Oh, that koala! ill. by Anna Mossakowska. McGraw-Hill, 1979. ISBN 0-07-054192-2 Subj: Animals – koalas. Behavior – misbehavior.

Rudin, Ellen. *The three billy goats Gruff* (Asbjørnsen, P. C. [Peter Christen])

Rudolph, Marguerita. *The good stepmother* (Zakhoder, Boris Vladimirovich)

Grey Neck (Mamin-Sibiryak, D. N.)

How a piglet crashed the Christmas party (Zakhoder, Boris Vladimirovich)

How a shirt grew in the field adapt. from the Russian of Konstantin Ushinsky; ill. by Erika Weihs. Clarion, 1992. ISBN 0-395-59761-7 Subj: Clothing – shirts. Foreign lands – Ukraine. Plants.

How a shirt grew in the field adapt. from the Russian of Konstantin Ushinsky; ill. by Yaroslava. McGraw-Hill, 1967. Subj: Clothing – shirts. Foreign lands – Ukraine. Plants.

Rosachok (Zakhoder, Boris Vladimirovich)

Rudomin, Esther. *see* Hautzig, Esther (Rudomin)

Ruffins, Reynold. *My brother never feeds the cat* ill. by author. Scribners, 1979. ISBN 0-684-16211-3 Subj: Family life.

Rukeyser, Muriel. *More night* ill. by Symeon Shimin. HarperCollins, 1981. ISBN 0-06-025128-X Subj: Activities. Night.

Uncle Eddie's moustache (Brecht, Bertolt)

Rumford, James. *The cloudmakers* ill. by author. Houghton Mifflin, 1996. ISBN 0-395-76505-6 Subj: Activities – making things. Family life – grandfathers. Folk and fairy tales. Foreign lands – China. Paper.

The Island-below-the-star ill. by author. Houghton Mifflin, 1998. ISBN 0-395-85159-9 Subj: Activities – traveling. Boats, ships. Family life – brothers. Hawaii. Islands.

Runcie, Jill. *Cock-a-doodle-doo* ill. by Lee Lorenz. Simon & Schuster, 1991. ISBN 0-671-72602-1 Subj: Animals. Circular tales. Farms. Noise, sounds.

Rupprecht, Siegfried P. *The tale of the vanishing rainbow* trans. by Naomi Lewis; ill. by Józef Wilkon. North-South, 1989. ISBN 1-55858-001-8 Subj: Animals. War. Weather – rainbows.

Ruschak, Lynette. *The counting zoo* ill. by May Rousseau. Aladdin, 1992. ISBN 0-689-71619-2 Subj: Animals. Counting, numbers. Format, unusual – toy and movable books.

Rush, Ken. *Friday's journey* ill. by author. Orchard, 1994. ISBN 0-531-08671-2 Subj: Activities – traveling. City. Divorce. Family life – fathers. Imagination. Trains.

Ruskin, John. *Dame Wiggins of Lee and her seven wonderful cats* (Dame Wiggins of Lee and her seven wonderful cats)

Rusling, Albert. *The mouse and Mrs. Proudfoot* ill. by author. Prentice-Hall, 1985. ISBN 0-13-604265-1 Subj: Animals. Homes, houses. Humor.

Russ, Lavinia. *Alec's sand castle* ill. by James Stevenson. HarperCollins, 1972. ISBN 0-06-020150-9 Subj: Activities – playing. Imagination. Sea and seashore.

Russell, Betty. *Big store, funny door* ill. by Mary Gehr. Albert Whitman, 1955. Subj: Character traits – luck. Shopping.

Run sheep run ill. by Mary Gehr. Albert Whitman, 1952. Subj: Animals – sheep.

Russell, Janice. *Goldilocks* (The three bears)

Russell, Naomi. *The stream* ill. by author. Dutton, 1991. ISBN 0-525-44729-6 Subj: Nature. Rivers. Water.

The tree ill. by author. Dutton, 1989. ISBN 0-525-44468-8 Subj: Format, unusual. Nature. Trees.

Russell, P. Craig. *Fairy tales of Oscar Wilde: The selfish giant, and The star child* (Wilde, Oscar)

Russell, Pamela. *Do you have a secret? how to get help for scary secrets* by Pamela Russell and Beth Stone; ill. by Mary McKee. CompCare, 1986. ISBN 0-89638-098-X Subj: Behavior – secrets. Safety.

Russell, Sandra Joanne. *A farmer's dozen* ill. by author. HarperCollins, 1982. ISBN 0-06-025144-1 Subj: Farms. Rhyming text.

Russell, Solveig Paulson. *What good is a tail?* ill. by Ezra Jack Keats. Bobbs-Merrill, 1962. Subj: Animals. Science.

Russo, Marisabina. *The big brown box* ill. by author. Greenwillow, 2000. ISBN 0-688-17097-8 Subj: Activities – playing. Behavior – sharing. Family life – brothers. Games. Imagination. Sibling rivalry.

Grandpa Abe ill. by author. Greenwillow, 1996. ISBN 0-688-14098-X Subj: Death. Emotions – grief. Family life – grandfathers.

Hannah's baby sister ill. by author. Greenwillow, 1998. ISBN 0-688-15832-3 Subj: Babies. Family life – brothers and sisters. Family life – new sibling.

The line up book ill. by author. Greenwillow, 1986. ISBN 0-688-06205-9 Subj: Activities – playing. Family life. Games.

Mama talks too much ill. by author. Greenwillow, 1999. ISBN 0-688-16412-9 Subj: City. Communities, neighborhoods. Family life – mothers. Shopping.

Only six more days ill. by author. Greenwillow, 1988. ISBN 0-688-07072-8 Subj: Birthdays. Sibling rivalry.

Under the table ill. by author. Greenwillow, 1997. ISBN 0-688-14603-1 Subj: Activities – drawing. Behavior – misbehavior. Family life.

A visit to Oma ill. by author. Greenwillow, 1991. ISBN 0-688-09624-7 Subj: Family life – great-grandparents.

Waiting for Hannah ill. by author. Greenwillow, 1989. ISBN 0-688-08016-2 Subj: Babies. Birth. Family life – mothers. Gardens, gardening.

When mama gets home ill. by author. Greenwillow, 1998. ISBN 0-688-14986-3 Subj: Family life. Family life – mothers.

Where is Ben? ill. by author. Greenwillow, 1990. ISBN 0-688-08013-8 Subj: Activities – playing. Games.

Why do grownups have all the fun? ill. by author. Greenwillow, 1987. ISBN 0-688-06626-7 Subj: Bedtime. Behavior – dissatisfaction. Family life. Imagination.

Russo, Susan. *The ice cream ocean and other delectable poems of the sea* ill. by author. Lothrop, 1984. ISBN 0-688-02123-9 Subj: Poetry. Sea and seashore.

The moon's the north wind's cooky: night poems (The moon's the north wind's cooky)

Rutherford, Meg. *Animal poems* ill. by Polly Richardson. Barron's, 1992. ISBN 0-8120-6283-3 Subj: Animals. Poetry.

Ruthstrom, Dorotha. *The big kite contest* ill. by Lillian Hoban. Pantheon, 1980. ISBN 0-394-94430-5 Subj: Kites. Sibling rivalry.

Ryan, Cheli Durán. *Hildilid's night* ill. by Arnold Lobel. Macmillan, 1986, c1971. ISBN 0-02-777260-8 Subj: Caldecott award honor books. Night.

Ryan, Pam Muñoz. *Amelia and Eleanor go for a ride* ill. by Brian Selznick. Scholastic, 1999. ISBN 0-590-96075-X Subj: Activities – flying. Airplanes, airports. U.S. history.

Armadillos sleep in dugouts: and other places animals live ill. by Diane De Groat. Hyperion, 1997. ISBN 0-7868-2222-8 Subj: Animals. Homes, houses. Rhyming text.

The crayon counting book by Pam Muñoz Ryan and Jerry Pallotta; ill. by Frank Mazzola, Jr. Charlesbridge, 1996. ISBN 0-88106-955-8 Subj: Concepts – color. Counting, numbers. Rhyming text.

The flag we love ill. by Ralph Masiello. Charlesbridge, 1996. ISBN 0-88106-846-2 Subj: Poetry. U.S. history.

One hundred is a family ill. by Benrei Huang. Hyperion, 1994. ISBN 1-56282-673-5 Subj: Counting, numbers. Family life. Rhyming text.

A pinky is a baby mouse, and other baby animal names ill. by Diane DeGroat. Hyperion, 1997. ISBN 0-7868-2190-6 Subj: Animals – babies. Names. Rhyming text.

Rydell, Katy. *Wind says good night* ill. by David Jorgensen. Houghton Mifflin, 1994. ISBN 0-395-60474-5 Subj: Bedtime. Cumulative tales. Night.

Ryden, Hope. *The raggedy red squirrel* photos by author. Dutton, 1992. ISBN 0-525-67400-4 Subj: Animals – squirrels.

Wild animals of Africa ABC photos by author. Dutton, 1989. ISBN 0-525-67290-7 Subj: ABC books. Foreign lands – Africa.

Ryder, Eileen. *Winklet goes to school* ill. by Stephanie Lang. John Godon Burke, 1982. ISBN 0-222-00732-X Subj: School.

Winston's new cap ill. by Stephanie Lang. John Godon Burke, 1982. ISBN 0-222-00735-4 Subj: Behavior – losing things. Clothing – hats.

Ryder, Joanne. *Beach party* ill. by Diane Stanley. Warne, 1982. ISBN 0-7232-6198-9 Subj: Animals – sheep. Family life. Sea and seashore.

Bears out there ill. by Jo Ellen McAllister Stammen. Atheneum, 1995. ISBN 0-689-31780-8 Subj: Animals – bears. Imagination. Seasons – summer.

Catching the wind ill. by Michael Rothman. Morrow, 1989. ISBN 0-688-07171-6 Subj: Birds – geese. Nature.

Chipmunk song ill. by Lynne Cherry. Dutton, 1987. ISBN 0-525-67191-9 Subj: Animals – chipmunks. Nature. Rhyming text.

Dancers in the garden ill. by Judith Lopez. Sierra Club, 1992. ISBN 0-87156-578-1 Subj: Birds – humming birds. Gardens, gardening. Nature.

Fireflies ill. by Don Bolognese. HarperCollins, 1977. ISBN 0-06-025154-9 Subj: Insects – fireflies. Science.

First grade ladybugs ill. by Betsy Lewin. Troll, 1993. ISBN 0-8167-3006-7 Subj: Gardens, gardening. Insects – ladybugs. School.

Fog in the meadow ill. by Gail Owens. HarperCollins, 1979. ISBN 0-06-025149-2 Subj: Animals. Weather – fog.

Hello, first grade ill. by Betsy Lewin. Troll, 1993. ISBN 0-8167-3008-3 Subj: Animals – rabbits. Puppets. School.

Hello, tree! ill. by Michael Hays. Dutton, 1991. ISBN 0-525-67310-5 Subj: Nature. Rhyming text. Trees.

A house by the sea ill. by Melissa Sweet. Morrow, 1994. ISBN 0-688-12676-6 Subj: Animals. Homes, houses. Rhyming text. Sea and seashore.

Jaguar in the rain forest ill. by Michael Rothman. Morrow, 1996. ISBN 0-688-12991-9 Subj: Animals – jaguars. Foreign lands – French Guiana. Forest, woods.

Lizard in the sun ill. by Michael Rothman. Morrow, 1990. ISBN 0-688-07173-2 Subj: Nature. Reptiles – lizards.

Mockingbird morning ill. by Dennis Nolan. Four Winds, 1989. ISBN 0-02-777961-0 Subj: Birds – mockingbirds. Nature. Poetry.

My father's hands ill. by Mark Graham. Morrow, 1994. ISBN 0-688-09190-3 Subj: Anatomy – hands. Family life – fathers. Gardens, gardening. Insects.

The night flight ill. by Amy Schwartz. Four Winds, 1985. ISBN 0-02-778020-1 Subj: Animals. City. Dreams. Night.

Rainbow wings ill. by Victor Lee. Morrow, 2000. ISBN 0-688-14129-3 Subj: Activities – flying. Science.

Snail in the woods by Joanne Ryder with the assistance of Harold S. Feinberg; ill. by Jo Polseno. HarperCollins, 1979. ISBN 0-06-025169-7 Subj: Animals – snails. Science.

The snail's spell ill. by Lynne Cherry. Warne, 1982. ISBN 0-7232-6197-0 Subj: Animals – snails. Night.

The spiders dance ill. by Robert J. Blake. HarperCollins, 1981. ISBN 0-06-025134-4 Subj: Science. Spiders.

Step into the night ill. by Dennis Nolan. Four Winds, 1988. ISBN 0-02-777951-3 Subj: Nature. Night. Poetry.

Tyrannosaurus time ill. by Michael Rothman. Morrow, 1999. ISBN 0-688-13683-4 Subj: Dinosaurs. Imagination.

Under your feet ill. by Dennis Nolan. Macmillan, 1990. ISBN 0-02-777955-6 Subj: Nature. Poetry. Seasons.

A wet and sandy day ill. by Donald Carrick. HarperCollins, 1977. ISBN 0-06-025159-X Subj: Sea and seashore. Weather – rain.

Where butterflies grow ill. by Lynne Cherry. Dutton, 1989. ISBN 0-525-67284-2 Subj: Insects – butterflies, caterpillars. Metamorphosis. Nature. Science.

White bear, ice bear ill. by Michael Rothman. Morrow, 1989. ISBN 0-688-07175-9 Subj: Animals – polar bears. Foreign lands – Arctic. Nature.

Winter whale ill. by Michael Rothman. Morrow, 1991. ISBN 0-688-07177-5 Subj: Animals – whales. Nature. Seasons – winter.

Rylant, Cynthia. *All I see* ill. by Peter Catalanotto. Watts, 1988. ISBN 0-531-08377-2 Subj: Activities – painting. Art. Friendship.

Appalachia: the voices of sleeping birds ill. by Barry Moser. Harcourt, 1991. ISBN 0-15-201605-8 Subj: Country.

Bear day ill. by Jennifer Selby. Harcourt, 1998. ISBN 0-15-201090-4 Subj: Animals – bears. Rhyming text.

Best wishes photos by Carlo Ontal. R.C. Owen, 1992. ISBN 1-878450-20-4 Subj: Activities – writing. Careers – writers. Family life.

The bird house ill. by Barry Moser. Blue Sky, 1998. ISBN 0-590-47345-X Subj: Birds. Homes, houses. Orphans.

Birthday presents ill. by Suçie Stevenson. Watts, 1987. ISBN 0-531-08305-5 Subj: Behavior – sharing. Birthdays. Family life. Gifts.

Bless us all: a child's yearbook of blessings ill. by author. Simon & Schuster, 1998. ISBN 0-689-82370-3 Subj: Days of the week, months of the year. Religion. Rhyming text.

The bookshop dog ill. by author. Blue Sky, 1996. ISBN 0-590-54331-8 Subj: Animals – dogs. Character traits – kindness to animals. Friendship. Weddings.

Bunny bungalow ill. by author. Harcourt, 1999. ISBN 0-15-201092-0 Subj: Animals – rabbits. Family life. Homes, houses. Rhyming text.

The cookie-store cat ill. by author. Blue Sky, 1999. ISBN 0-590-54329-6 Subj: Activities – cooking. Animals – cats. Careers – bakers.

Dog Heaven ill. by author. Blue Sky, 1995. ISBN 0-590-41701-0 Subj: Angels. Animals – dogs. Death.

Give me grace: a child's daybook of prayers ill. by author. Simon & Schuster, 1999. ISBN 0-689-82293-6 Subj: Days of the week, months of the year. Religion. Rhyming text.

Miss Maggie ill. by Thomas di Grazia. Dutton, 1983. ISBN 0-525-44048-8 Subj: Character traits – curiosity. Friendship.

Mr. Griggs' work ill. by Julie Downing. Watts, 1989. ISBN 0-531-08369-1 Subj: Activities – working. Careers – postal workers. Character traits – pride. Post office.

Mr. Putter and Tabby bake the cake ill. by Arthur Howard. Harcourt, 1994. ISBN 0-15-200205-7 Subj: Activities – cooking. Animals – cats. Food. Holidays – Christmas. Old age.

Mr. Putter and Tabby pick the pears ill. by Arthur Howard. Harcourt, 1995. ISBN 0-15-200245-6 Subj: Animals – cats. Food. Friendship. Old age.

Mr. Putter and Tabby pour the tea ill. by Arthur Howard. Harcourt, 1994. ISBN 0-15-256255-9 Subj: Animals – cats. Emotions – loneliness. Old age.

Mr. Putter and Tabby walk the dog ill. by Arthur Howard. Harcourt, 1994. ISBN 0-15-256259-1 Subj: Animals – cats. Animals – dogs. Character traits – helpfulness. Old age.

Night in the country ill. by Mary Szilagyi. Bradbury, 1986. ISBN 0-02-777210-1 Subj: Animals. Country. Night.

The relatives came ill. by Stephen Gammell. Bradbury, 1985. ISBN 0-02-777220-9 Subj: Activities – traveling. Caldecott award honor books. Family life.

Scarecrow ill. by Lauren Stringer. Harcourt, 1998. ISBN 0-15-201084-X Subj: Country. Farms. Scarecrows.

Silver packages: an Appalachian Christmas story ill. by Chris K. Soentpiet. Orchard, 1997. ISBN 0-531-33051-6 Subj: Accidents. Careers – doctors. Char-

acter traits – generosity. Holidays – Christmas. Illness. Trains. Transportation.

This year's garden ill. by Mary Szilagyi. Bradbury, 1984. ISBN 0-02-777970-X Subj: Gardens, gardening.

Tulip sees America ill. by Lisa Desimini. Blue Sky, 1998. ISBN 0-590-84744-9 Subj: Activities – traveling. Animals – dogs. Automobiles.

The whales ill. by author. Blue Sky, 1996. ISBN 0-590-58285-2 Subj: Animals – whales. Sea and seashore.

When I was young in the mountains ill. by Diane Goode. Dutton, 1982. ISBN 0-525-42525-X Subj: Caldecott award honor books. Family life.

S. J. H. *see* Hale, Sarah Josepha Buell

Sabraw, John. *I wouldn't be scared* ill. by author. Watts, 1989. ISBN 0-531-08418-3 Subj: Emotions – fear. Imagination. Monsters.

Sabuda, Robert. *ABC Disney* ill. by author. Disney Pr., 1998. ISBN 0-7868-3132-4 Subj: ABC books. Format, unusual – toy and movable books.

Sabuda, Robert James. *The Blizzard's robe* ill. by author. Atheneum, 1999. ISBN 0-689-31988-6 Subj: Activities – sewing. Foreign lands – Arctic. Mythical creatures.

The Christmas alphabet ill. by author. Orchard, 1994. ISBN 0-531-06857-9 Subj: ABC books. Format, unusual – toy and movable books. Holidays – Christmas.

The movable Mother Goose ill. by author. Little Simon, 1999. ISBN 0-689-81192-6 Subj: Animals. Format, unusual – toy and movable books. Insects. Nursery rhymes.

The mummy's tomb ill. by author. Western, 1994. ISBN 0-307-17627-4 Subj: Animals – mice. Foreign lands – Egypt. Format, unusual – toy and movable books. Rhyming text.

St. Valentine ill. by author. Macmillan, 1993. ISBN 0-689-31762-X Subj: Holidays – Valentine's Day. Religion.

Tutankhamen's gift ill. by author. Atheneum, 1994. ISBN 0-689-31818-9 Subj: Foreign lands – Egypt. Gifts. Royalty – pharaohs.

Sachar, Louis. *Monkey soup* ill. by Cat Bowman Smith. Knopf, 1992. ISBN 0-679-90297-X Subj: Family life – fathers. Illness. Toys.

Sachs, Marilyn. *Fleet-footed Florence* ill. by Charles Robinson. Doubleday, 1981. ISBN 0-385-12746-4

Subj: Behavior – wishing. Magic. Sports – baseball.

Matt's mitt ill. by Hilary Knight. Doubleday, 1975. ISBN 0-385-00266-1 Subj: Sports – baseball.

Sackett, Elisabeth. *Danger on the African grassland* ill. by Martin Camm. Little, 1991. ISBN 0-316-76596-1 Subj: Animals – endangered animals. Animals – rhinoceros. Foreign lands – Africa.

Danger on the Arctic ice ill. by Martin Camm. Little, 1991. ISBN 0-316-76598-8 Subj: Animals – endangered animals. Animals – seals. Foreign lands – Arctic.

Saddler, Allen. *The Archery contest* ill. by Joe Wright. Oxford Univ. Pr., 1983. ISBN 0-19-279760-3 Subj: Humor. Magic. Royalty. Sports.

The king gets fit ill. by Joe Wright. Oxford Univ. Pr., 1983. ISBN 0-19-279761-1 Subj: Humor. Royalty – kings.

Sadie. *see* Williams, Sarah

Sadler, Catherine Edwards. *A duckling is born* (Isenbart, Hans-Heinrich)

A flamingo is born (Zoll, Max Alfred)

Sadler, Marilyn. *Alistair in outer space* ill. by Roger Bollen. Prentice-Hall, 1984. ISBN 0-13-022369-7 Subj: Libraries. Space and space ships.

Alistair's elephant ill. by Roger Bollen. Prentice-Hall, 1983. ISBN 0-13-022756-0 Subj: Animals – elephants. Behavior – misbehavior.

Alistair's time machine ill. by Roger Bollen. Prentice-Hall, 1986. ISBN 0-317-39621-8 Subj: Machines. School. Science. Space and space ships. Time.

Elizabeth, Larry, and Ed ill. by Roger Bollen. Simon & Schuster, 1992. ISBN 0671759566 Subj: Animals. Ecology. Friendship. Reptiles – alligators, crocodiles.

It's not easy being a bunny ill. by Roger Bollen. Random House, 1983. ISBN 0-394-96102-1 Subj: Animals – rabbits. Behavior – dissatisfaction. Self-concept.

Sadu, Itah. *Christopher changes his name* ill. by Roy Candy. Firefly, 1998. ISBN 1-55209-216-X Subj: Ethnic groups in the U.S. – African Americans. Names.

Safran, Sheri. *The musical cherub* ill. by Pete Bowman; paper engineering by David Hawcock. Tango, 1995. ISBN 1-8570-7128-X Subj: Angels. Careers – shepherds. Format, unusual – toy and movable books. Music. Religion – Nativity.

The painted cherub ill. by Pete Bowman; paper engineering by David Hawcock. Simon & Schuster, 1995. ISBN 0-689-80334-6 Subj: Angels. Format, unusual – toy and movable books.

Sage, Alison. *Rumpelstiltskin* (Grimm, Jacob)

Teddy bears at the seaside (Gretz, Susanna)

Teddy bears cure a cold (Gretz, Susanna)

Teddy bears stay indoors (Gretz, Susanna)

Teddy bears take the train (Gretz, Susanna)

Teddybears cookbook (Gretz, Susanna)

Sage, Angie. *Happy baby* (Sage, Chris)

Monkeys in the jungle ill. by author. Dutton, 1989. ISBN 0-525-44466-1 Subj: Animals. Jungle. Rhyming text.

Sleepy baby (Sage, Chris)

Sage, Chris. *Happy baby* by Chris and Angie Sage; ill. by Angie Sage. Dial, 1990. ISBN 0-8037-0883-1 Subj: Babies. Format, unusual – board books.

Sleepy baby by Chris and Angie Sage; ill. by Angie Sage. Dial, 1990. ISBN 0-8037-0888-2 Subj: Babies. Format, unusual – board books. Sleep.

That's mine, that's yours ill. by Angie Sage. Viking, 1991. ISBN 0-670-83746-6 Subj: Activities. Behavior – sharing. Family life – sisters.

The trouble with babies ill. by Angie Sage. Viking, 1990. ISBN 0-670-82392-9 Subj: Babies. Sibling rivalry.

Sage, James. *The boy and the dove* photos by Robert Doisneau. Workman, 1978. ISBN 0-89480-030-2 Subj: Birds – doves. Theater.

Coyote makes man ill. by Britta Teckentrup. Simon & Schuster, 1995. ISBN 0-689-80011-8 Subj: Animals – coyotes. Creation. Folk and fairy tales. Indians of North America – Crow.

The little band ill. by Keiko Narahashi. Macmillan, 1991. ISBN 0-689-50516-7 Subj: Ethnic groups in the U.S. Music.

To sleep ill. by Warwick Hutton. Macmillan, 1990. ISBN 0-689-50497-7 Subj: Bedtime. Dreams. Sleep.

Sage, Juniper. *see* Brown, Margaret Wise

Sage, Juniper. *see* Hurd, Edith Thacher

Sage, Michael. *Dippy dos and don'ts* by Michael Sage and Arnold Spilka; ill. by Arnold Spilka. Viking, 1967. Subj: Humor. Rhyming text.

If you talked to a boar ill. by Arnold Spilka. Lippincott, 1960. Subj: Humor. Language.

Sahagun, Bernardino de. *Spirit child: a story of the Nativity* trans. from Aztec by John Bierhorst; ill. by Barbara Cooney. Morrow, 1984. ISBN 0-688-02610-9 Subj: Folk and fairy tales. Foreign lands – Mexico. Holidays – Christmas. Religion – Nativity.

St. George, Judith. *The Halloween pumpkin smasher* ill. by Margot Tomes. Putnam, 1978. ISBN 0-399-20617-5 Subj: Animals – raccoons. Holidays – Halloween. Imagination – imaginary friends.

So you want to be president? ill. by David Small. Philomel, 2000. ISBN 0-399-23407-1 Subj: Caldecott award books. U.S. history.

St. Germain, Sharon. *The terrible fight* ill. by Deborah Zemke. Houghton Mifflin, 1990. ISBN 0-395-50069-9 Subj: Behavior – fighting, arguing. Friendship.

Saint James, Synthia. *The gifts of Kwanzaa* ill. by author. Albert Whitman, 1994. ISBN 0-8075-2907-9 Subj: Ethnic groups in the U.S. – African Americans. Gifts. Holidays – Kwanzaa.

Sunday ill. by author. Albert Whitman, 1996. ISBN 0-8075-7658-1 Subj: Ethnic groups in the U.S. – African Americans. Family life – grandparents. Multiple births – twins.

St. Pierre, Wendy. *Henry finds a home* ill. by Barbara Eidlitz. Firefly, 1981. ISBN 0-919984-05-3 Subj: Children as authors. Reptiles – turtles, tortoises.

Sakai, Kimiko. *Sachiko means happiness* ill. by Tomie Arai. Children's Book Pr., 1990. ISBN 0-89239-065-4 Subj: Ethnic groups in the U.S. – Japanese Americans. Family life – grandmothers. Illness – Alzheimer's. Old age.

Salariya, David. *From caterpillar to butterfly* (Legg, Gerald)

From egg to chicken (Legg, Gerald)

From seed to sunflower (Legg, Gerald)

From tadpole to frog (Legg, Gerald)

Salazar, Violet. *Squares are not bad* ill. by Harlow Rockwell. Golden Pr., 1967. Subj: Concepts – shape.

Saleh, Harold J. *Even tiny ants must sleep* ill. by Jerry Pinkney. McGraw-Hill, 1967. Subj: Animals. Poetry. Sleep.

Salt, Jane. *See and say picture word book* ill. by Sarah Pooley. Random House, 1989. ISBN 0-679-90099-3 Subj: Language.

Salter, Heidi. *Taddy McFinley and the great grey grimly* ill. by author. Landmark Editions, 1989. ISBN 0-933849-21-4 Subj: Children as authors. Children as illustrators. Family life – grandfathers. Imagination. Monsters.

Salter, Mary Jo. *The moon comes home* ill. by Stacey Schuett. Knopf, 1989. ISBN 0-394-99983-5 Subj: Activities – traveling. Moon. Night.

Saltzberg, Barney. *Cromwell* ill. by author. Atheneum, 1986. ISBN 0-689-31282-2 Subj: Animals – dogs. Humor.

The Flying Garbanzos ill. by author. Crown, 1998. ISBN 0-517-70979-1 Subj: Birthdays. Careers – acrobats. Food.

It must have been the wind ill. by author. HarperCollins, 1982. ISBN 0-06-025177-8 Subj: Bedtime. Noise, sounds. Weather – wind.

Phoebe and the spelling bee ill. by author. Hyperion, 1996. ISBN 0-7868-2114-0 Subj: Behavior – lying. Contests. Friendship. School.

Soccer mom from outer space ill. by author. Crown, 2000. ISBN 0-517-80064-0 Subj: Clothing – costumes. Family life – mothers. Sports – soccer.

The yawn ill. by author. Atheneum, 1985. ISBN 0-689-31073-0 Subj: Behavior – imitation. Wordless.

Saltzman, David. *The jester has lost his jingle* ill. by David Saltzman; afterword by Maurice Sendak. Jester Co., 1995. ISBN 0-9644563-0-3 Subj: Character traits – optimism. Clowns, jesters. Middle Ages. Rhyming text.

Salus, Naomi Panush. *My daddy's mustache* ill. by Tomie de Paola. Doubleday, 1979. ISBN 0-385-13189-5 Subj: Character traits – appearance.

Sampson, Michael R. *Adam, Adam, what do you see?* (Martin, Bill [William Ivan])

The little squeegy bug (Martin, Bill [William Ivan])

Rock it, sock it, number line (Martin, Bill [William Ivan])

Swish! (Martin, Bill [William Ivan])

Samson, Suzanne M. *Fairy dusters and blazing stars* ill. by Preston Neel. Roberts Rinehart, 1994. ISBN 1-879373-81-5 Subj: Flowers. Science.

Samton, Sheila White. *Amazing Aunt Agatha* ill. by Yvette Banek. Raintree, 1990. ISBN 0-8172-3575-2 Subj: ABC books. Ethnic groups in the U.S. – African Americans.

Beside the bay ill. by author. Putnam, 1987. ISBN 0-399-21420-8 Subj: Rhyming text. Sea and seashore.

Frogs in clogs ill. by author. Crown, 1995. ISBN 0-517-59875-2 Subj: Animals – pigs. Clothing. Frogs and toads. Insects. Rhyming text.

Jenny's journey ill. by author. Viking, 1991. ISBN 0-670-83490-4 Subj: Boats, ships. Friendship. Imagination.

Moon to sun ill. by author. Boyds Mills, 1991. ISBN 1-878093-13-4 Subj: Counting, numbers.

On the river ill. by author. Boyds Mills, 1991. ISBN 1-878093-14-2 Subj: Activities – picnicking. Counting, numbers.

Ten tiny monsters ill. by author. Crown, 1997. ISBN 0-517-70942-2 Subj: Animals. Counting, numbers. Monsters. Rhyming text.

The world from my window ill. by author. Crown, 1985. ISBN 0-517-55645-6 Subj: Counting, numbers. Rhyming text.

Samuels, Barbara. *Aloha, Dolores* ill. by author. DK, 2000. ISBN 0-7894-2508-4 Subj: Activities – vacationing. Animals – cats. Contests. Family life – sisters. Hawaii.

Duncan and Dolores ill. by author. Bradbury, 1986. ISBN 0-02-778210-7 Subj: Activities. Animals – cats. Family life – sisters. Humor.

Faye and Dolores ill. by author. Bradbury, 1985. ISBN 0-02-778120-8 Subj: Emotions – love. Sibling rivalry.

Happy birthday, Dolores ill. by author. Watts, 1989. ISBN 0-531-08391-8 Subj: Birthdays. Parties.

What's so great about Cindy Snappleby? ill. by author. Watts, 1992. ISBN 0-531-08579-1 Subj: Family life – sisters. Frogs and toads. Sibling rivalry.

Samuels, Vyanne. *Carry go bring come* ill. by Jennifer Northway. Macmillan, 1989. ISBN 0-02-778121-6 Subj: Ethnic groups in the U.S. – African Americans. Family life. Weddings.

San Diego Zoological Society. *Families* photos by Ron Garrison and F. D. Schmidt of the Zoological Society of San Diego; captions ed. by Georgeanne Irvine. Heian Intl., 1983. ISBN 0-89346-218-7 Subj: Animals. Zoos.

A visit to the zoo photos by Ron Garrison and F. D. Schmidt of the Zoological Society of San Diego; captions ed. by Georgeanne Irvine. Heian Intl., 1983. ISBN 0-89346-219-5 Subj: Animals. Zoos.

San José, Christine. *Sleeping Beauty* ill. by Dominic Catalano. Boyds Mills, 1997. ISBN 1-56397-636-6 Subj: Animals – dormice. Fairies. Folk and fairy tales.

Sánchez, Enrique O. *Saturday market* (Grossman, Patricia)

Sanchez, Jose Louis Garcia. *Kangaroo* by Jose Louis Garcia Sanchez and Miguel Angel Pacheco; ill. by Nella Bosnia. H P Books, 1983. ISBN 0-89586-286-7 Subj: Animals – kangaroos.

Sandberg, Inger. *Come on out, Daddy!* by Inger and Lasse Sandberg; ill. by Lasse Sandberg. Delacorte, 1971. Translation of Pappa, kom ut. Subj: Activities – working. Careers. Family life – fathers.

Dusty wants to borrow everything ill. by Lasse Sandberg. Farrar, 1988. ISBN 91-29-58782-4 Subj: Character traits – curiosity. Family life – grandparents.

Dusty wants to help trans. from Swedish by Judy A. Mauver; ill. by Lasse Sandberg. Farrar, 1987. ISBN 91-29-58336-5 Subj: Behavior – misbehavior. Family life – grandfathers.

Little Anna saved by Inger and Lasse Sandberg; ill. by Lasse Sandberg. Lothrop, 1965. Subj: Games.

Little ghost Godfry by Inger and Lasse Sandberg; trans. by Nancy S. Leupold; ill. by Lasse Sandberg. Delacorte, 1968. Subj: Ghosts.

Nicholas' favorite pet by Inger and Lasse Sandberg; ill. by Lasse Sandberg. Delacorte, 1969. Translation of Niklas' önskedjur. Subj: Animals. Animals – dogs. Birthdays. Pets.

Nicholas' red day by Inger and Lasse Sandberg; ill. by authors. Delacorte, 1964. Subj: Behavior – misbehavior. Concepts – color. Illness.

Sandberg, Lasse. *Come on out, Daddy!* (Sandberg, Inger)

Little Anna saved (Sandberg, Inger)

Little ghost Godfry (Sandberg, Inger)

Nicholas' favorite pet (Sandberg, Inger)

Nicholas' red day (Sandberg, Inger)

Sandburg, Carl (Charles August). *The Huckabuck family and how they raised popcorn in Nebraska and quit and came back* ill. by David Small. Farrar, 1999. The text was originally published in 1923 by Harcourt, Brace & Company in the book Rootabaga stories by Carl Sandburg. ISBN 0-374-33511-7 Subj: Careers – farmers. Farms. Humor.

The wedding procession of the rag doll and the broom handle and who was in it ill. by Harriet Pincus. Harcourt, 1978, c1922. ISBN 0-15-294930-5 Subj: Toys. Toys – dolls. Weddings.

Sandburg, Helga. *Anna and the baby buzzard* ill. by Brinton Turkle. Dutton, 1970. ISBN 0-525-25769-1 Subj: Birds – buzzards. Character traits – kindness to animals.

Sandeman, Anna. *Skin, teeth, and hair* ill. by Ian Thompson. Copper Beech, 1996. ISBN 0-7613-0489-4 Subj: Anatomy – skin. Hair. Science. Teeth.

Sanders, Eve. *What's your name?* (Sanders, Marilyn)

Sanders, Marilyn. *What's your name?* photos by Marilyn Sanders; text by Eve Sanders. Holiday, 1995. ISBN 0-8234-1209-1 Subj: ABC books. Names.

Sanders, Scott R. (Scott Russell). *Crawdad Creek* ill. by Robert Hynes. National Geographic, 1999. ISBN 0-7922-7097-5 Subj: Ecology. Family life – brothers and sisters. Rivers.

A place called Freedom ill. by Thomas B. Allen. Atheneum, 1997. ISBN 0-689-80470-9 Subj: Character traits – freedom. Ethnic groups in the U.S. – African Americans. Slavery. U.S. history – frontier and pioneer life.

Warm as wool ill. by Helen Cogancherry. Bradbury, 1992. ISBN 0-02-778139-9 Subj: Animals – sheep. Clothing. U.S. history – frontier and pioneer life.

Sanderson, Ruth. *The enchanted wood* ill. by author. Little, 1991. ISBN 0-316-77018-3 Subj: Folk and fairy tales. Royalty – princes.

Papa Gatto ill. by author. Little, 1995. ISBN 0-316-77073-6 Subj: Animals – cats. Behavior – greed. Folk and fairy tales. Foreign lands – Italy. Royalty – princes.

Sandin, Joan. *Boo and Baa at sea* (Landström, Olof)

Boo and Baa in a party mood (Landström, Olof)

Boo and Baa in windy weather (Landström, Olof)

Boo and Baa on a cleaning spree (Landström, Olof)

Who's scaring Alfie Atkins? (Bergström, Gunilla)

Sandman, Rochel. *Perfect porridge* ill. by Chana Zakashansky-Zverev. Hachai, 2000. ISBN 0-922613-92-3 Subj: Character traits – generosity. Food. Foreign lands – Uzbekistan. Immigrants. War.

Sandved, Kjell Bloch. *The butterfly alphabet* ill. by author. Scholastic, 1996. ISBN 0-590-48003-0 Subj: ABC books. Insects – butterflies, caterpillars. Insects – moths.

Sanfield, Steve. *Bit by bit* ill. by Susan Gaber. Philomel, 1995. ISBN 0-399-22736-9 Subj: Careers – tailors. Clothing. Cumulative tales. Folk and fairy tales. Jewish culture.

The girl who wanted a song ill. by Stephen T. Johnson. Harcourt, 1996. ISBN 0-15-200969-8 Subj: Birds – geese. Emotions – loneliness. Orphans. Songs.

The great turtle drive ill. by Dirk Zimmer. Knopf, 1996. ISBN 0-679-95834-7 Subj: Cowboys. Reptiles – turtles, tortoises.

Just rewards, or, Who is that man in the moon and what's he doing up there anyway? ill. by Emily Lisker. Orchard, 1996. ISBN 0-531-08885-5 Subj: Behavior – greed. Character traits – selfishness. Folk and fairy tales. Foreign lands – China. Moon.

Snow ill. by Jeanette Winter. Philomel, 1995. ISBN 0-399-22751-2 Subj: Rhyming text. Weather – snow.

Sanford, Doris. *David has AIDS* ill. by Graci Evans. Multnomah, 1989. ISBN 0-88070-299-0 Subj: Death. Emotions – grief. Illness.

Sanromán, Susana. *Señora Reganona* ill. by author. Douglas & McIntyre, 1998. ISBN 0-88899-320-X Subj: Bedtime. Emotions – fear. Foreign lands – Mexico. Friendship. Night.

Sansevere, John R. *Ooey gooey* (Farber, Erica)

Sansone, Adele. *The little green goose* ill. by Alan Marks; trans. by J. Alison James. North-South, 1999. ISBN 0-7358-1072-9 Subj: Birds – geese. Character traits – being different. Dinosaurs. Family life.

San Souci, Daniel. *In the moonlight mist: a Korean tale* ill. by Eujin Kim Neilan. Boyds Mills, 1999. ISBN 1-56397-754-0 Subj: Animals – deer. Family life. Folk and fairy tales. Foreign lands – Korea. Magic.

San Souci, Robert D. *The boy and the ghost* ill. by J. Brian Pinkney. Simon & Schuster, 1989. ISBN 0-671-67176-6 Subj: Ethnic groups in the U.S. – African Americans. Ghosts. Homes, houses.

The brave little tailor (Grimm, Jacob)

Brave Margaret: an Irish adventure ill. by Sally Wern Comport. Simon & Schuster, 1999. ISBN 0-689-81072-5 Subj: Boats, ships. Folk and fairy tales. Foreign lands – Ireland. Giants. Sea and seashore. Sex roles.

Callie Ann and Mistah Bear ill. by Don Daily. Dial, 1999. ISBN 0-8037-1768-7 Subj: Character traits – cleverness. Ethnic groups in the U.S. – African Americans. Folk and fairy tales.

Cendrillon: a Caribbean Cinderella ill. by Brian Pinkney. Simon & Schuster, 1998. ISBN 0-689-80668-X Subj: Folk and fairy tales. Foreign lands – Caribbean Islands.

The enchanted tapestry ill. by László Gál. Dial, 1987. ISBN 0-8037-0306-6 Subj: Activities – weaving. Behavior – greed. Character traits – bravery. Family life – brothers. Folk and fairy tales. Foreign lands – China.

The faithful friend ill. by J. Brian Pinkney. Simon & Schuster, 1995. ISBN 0-02-786131-7 Subj: Caldecott award honor books. Folk and fairy tales. Foreign lands – Caribbean Islands. Foreign lands – Martinique.

Feathertop: based on the tale by Nathaniel Hawthorne; ill. by reteller. Doubleday, 1992. ISBN 0-385-42045-5 Subj: Behavior – trickery. Magic. Scarecrows. Witches.

The firebird (The firebird)

The hired hand: an African-American folktale ill. by Jerry Pinkney. Dial, 1997. ISBN 0-8037-1297-9 Subj: Activities – working. Character traits – laziness. Ethnic groups in the U.S. – African Americans. Folk and fairy tales. Magic.

The Hobyahs ill. by Alexi Natchev. Doubleday, 1994. ISBN 0-385-30934-1 Subj: Animals – dogs. Folk and fairy tales. Foreign lands – England. Monsters. Rhyming text.

The house in the sky ill. by Wil Clay. Dial, 1996. ISBN 0-8037-1285-5 Subj: Folk and fairy tales. Foreign lands – Caribbean Islands. Homes, houses.

The legend of Scarface ill. by Daniel San Souci. Doubleday, 1987. ISBN 0-385-15874-2 Subj: Folk and fairy tales. Indians of North America – Blackfoot. Indians of North America – Siksika.

The legend of Sleepy Hollow adapt. by Robert D. San Souci; ill. by Daniel San Souci. Doubleday, 1986. Based on the story by Washington Irving. ISBN 0-385-23397-3 Subj: Folk and fairy tales. Holidays – Halloween.

Nicholas Pipe ill. by David Shannon. Dial, 1997. ISBN 0-8037-1765-2 Subj: Careers – fishermen. Emotions – love. Folk and fairy tales. Mythical creatures – mermaids, mermen. Sea and seashore.

Pedro and the monkey ill. by Michael Hays. Morrow, 1996. ISBN 0-688-13743-1 Subj: Animals – monkeys. Folk and fairy tales. Foreign lands – Philippines. Monsters.

The red heels ill. by Gary Kelley. Dial, 1995. ISBN 0-8037-1134-4 Subj: Careers – shoemakers. Folk and fairy tales. Magic. Witches.

The samurai's daughter ill. by Stephen T. Johnson. Dial, 1992. ISBN 0-8037-1136-0 Subj: Character traits – bravery. Family life – fathers. Folk and fairy tales. Foreign lands – Japan.

The secret of the stones ill. by James Ransome. Fogelman, 2000. ISBN 0-8037-1640-0 Subj: Ethnic groups in the U.S. – African Americans. Folk and fairy tales. Magic. Orphans.

Six foolish fishermen ill. by Doug Kennedy. Hyperion, 2000. ISBN 0-7868-2335-6 Subj: Character traits – foolishness. Sports – fishing.

The six swans (Grimm, Jacob)

The snow wife ill. by Stephen T. Johnson. Dial, 1993. ISBN 0-8037-1410-6 Subj: Behavior – secrets. Folk and fairy tales. Foreign lands – Japan.

Song of Sedna ill. by Daniel San Souci. Doubleday, 1981. ISBN 0-385-15866-1 Subj: Eskimos. Folk and fairy tales.

Sootface: an Ojibwa Cinderella story ill. by author. Delacorte, 1994. ISBN 0-385-31202-4 Subj: Character traits – meanness. Family life – sisters. Folk and fairy tales. Indians of North America – Ojibwa.

Sukey and the mermaid ill. by J. Brian Pinkney. Four Winds, 1992. ISBN 0-02-778141-0 Subj: Ethnic groups in the U.S. – African Americans. Folk and fairy tales. Mythical creatures – mermaids, mermen.

The talking eggs ill. by Jerry Pinkney. Dial, 1989. ISBN 0-8037-0619-7 Subj: Caldecott award honor books. Character traits – kindness. Eggs. Folk and fairy tales. Magic.

Two bear cubs: a Miwok legend from California's Yosemite Valley ill. by Daniel San Souci. Yosemite Assoc., 1997. ISBN 0-939666-87-1 Subj: Animals. Animals – bears. Animals – worms. Folk and fairy tales. Indians of North America – Miwok.

A weave of words ill. by Raúl Colón. Orchard, 1997. ISBN 0-531-33053-2 Subj: Activities – weaving. Folk and fairy tales. Foreign lands – Armenia. Royalty – kings. Royalty – queens. Sex roles.

The white cat ill. by Gennady Spirin. Watts, 1990. ISBN 0-531-08409-4 Subj: Animals – cats. Folk and fairy tales. Magic. Royalty.

Sant, Laurent Sauveur. *Dinosaurs* ill. by author. Wonder Books, 1971. Subj: Dinosaurs.

Santacruz, Daniel. *In . . . out: a Disney book of opposites = Dentro fuera: un libro Disney de opuestos* (Duerrstein, Richard)

One Mickey Mouse: a Disney book of numbers = Un Ratón Mickey: un libro Disney de números (Duerrstein, Richard)

Santore, Charles. *A stowaway on Noah's Ark* ill. by Charles Santore. Random House, 2000. ISBN 0-679-98820-3 Subj: Animals. Animals – mice. Behavior – hiding. Boats, ships. Religion – Noah.

William the Curious: Knight of the Water Lilies ill. by author. Random House, 1997. ISBN 0-679-98742-8 Subj: Ecology. Folk and fairy tales. Frogs and toads. Royalty – kings.

Santoro, Christopher. *Book of shapes* ill. by author. Dutton, 1979. ISBN 0-525-69406-4 Subj: Concepts – shape.

Santoro, Scott. *Isaac the Ice Cream Truck* ill. by author. Holt, 1999. ISBN 0-8050-5296-8 Subj: Careers – firefighters. Trucks.

Santos, Joyce Audy Dos. *see* Dos Santos, Joyce Audy

Sapphire, Paula. *The toddler's potty book* (Allison, Alida)

Sara. *Across town* ill. by author. Watts, 1991. ISBN 0-531-08532-5 Subj: Animals – cats. City. Wordless.

The rabbit, the fox, and the wolf ill. by author. Watts, 1991. ISBN 0-531-08553-8 Subj: Animals – foxes. Animals – rabbits. Animals – wolves. Wordless.

Sardegna, Jill. *K is for kiss good night* ill. by Michael Hayes. Doubleday, 1994. ISBN 0-385-31044-7 Subj: ABC books. Bedtime.

The roly-poly spider ill. by Tedd Arnold. Scholastic, 1994. ISBN 0-590-47119-8 Subj: Insects. Rhyming text. Spiders.

Sargent, Susan. *My favorite place* by Susan Sargent and Donna Aaron Wirt; ill. by Allan Eitzen. Abingdon, 1983. ISBN 0-687-27538-5 Subj: Handicaps – blindness. Senses – seeing.

Sarnoff, Jane. *That's not fair* ill. by Reynold Ruffins. Scribners, 1980. ISBN 0-684-16714-X Subj: Behavior – dissatisfaction. Family life. Sibling rivalry.

Sarrazin, Johan. *Tootle* ill. by Aislin. Tundra, 1984. ISBN 0-88776-168-2 Subj: Animals – dogs. Behavior – misbehavior.

Sarton, May. *Punch's secret* ill. by Howard Knotts. HarperCollins, 1974. ISBN 0-06-025192-1 Subj: Emotions – loneliness. Friendship.

A walk through the woods ill. by Kazue Mizumura. HarperCollins, 1976. ISBN 0-06-025190-5 Subj: Activities – walking. Nature. Poetry.

Sasaki, Isao. *Snow* ill. by author. Viking, 1982. ISBN 0-670-65364-0 Subj: Trains. Weather – snow. Wordless.

Sasso, Sandy Eisenberg. *For heaven's sake* ill. by Kathryn Kunz Finney. Jewish Lights, 1999. ISBN 1-58023-054-7 Subj: Family life – grandmothers. Friendship. Religion.

God's paintbrush ill. by Annette C. Compton. Jewish Lights, 1992. ISBN 1-879045-22-2 Subj: Religion.

In God's name ill. by Phoebe Stone. Jewish Lights, 1994. ISBN 1-879045-26-5 Subj: Names. Religion.

A prayer for the earth: the story of Naamah ill. by Bethanne Andersen. Jewish Lights, 1996. ISBN 1-879045-60-5 Subj: Animals. Boats, ships. Religion – Noah. Weather – floods. Weather – rain.

Sathre, Vivian. *Carnival time* ill. by Kazu. Simon & Schuster, 1992. ISBN 0-671-76963-4 Subj: Fairs.

On Grandpa's farm ill. by Anne Hunter. Houghton Mifflin, 1997. ISBN 0-395-76506-4 Subj: Activities – working. Family life – grandfathers. Farms.

Sato, Satoru. *I wish I had a big, big tree* trans. from Japanese by Hitomi Jitodai and Carol Eisman; ill. by Tsutomu Murakami. Lothrop, 1989. ISBN 0-688-07304-2 Subj: Activities – playing. Imagination. Trees.

Satterfield, Barbara. *The story dance* ill. by Fran Gregory. Fairview, 1997. ISBN 1-57749-022-3 Subj: Activities – dancing. Family life – grandmothers. Memories, memory.

Sattgast, L. J. *Look what God made* ill. by Janet McDonnell. Chariot Books, 1994. ISBN 0-7814-0184-4 Subj: Creation. Religion.

Sattler, Helen Roney. *No place for a goat* ill. by Bari Weissman. Elsevier-Nelson, 1981. ISBN 0-525-66723-7 Subj: Animals – goats. Homes, houses.

Train whistles ill. by Giulio Maestro. Rev. ed. Lothrop, 1985. ISBN 0-688-03980-4 Subj: Language. Trains.

Sauer, Julia Lina. *Mike's house* ill. by Don Freeman. Viking, 1954. Subj: Behavior – lost. City. Libraries. Weather – snow.

Saul, Carol P. *Barn cat* ill. by Mary Azarian. Little, 1998. ISBN 0-316-76113-3 Subj: Animals – cats. Counting, numbers. Rhyming text.

Peter's song ill. by Diane de Groat. Simon & Schuster, 1992. ISBN 0-671-73812-7 Subj: Activities – singing. Animals – pigs. Friendship. Frogs and toads.

Saunders, Dave. *Snowtime* by Dave and Julie Saunders; ill. by Dave Saunders. Bradbury, 1991. ISBN 0-02-781075-5 Subj: Animals. Birds – ducks. Birds – geese. Weather – snow.

Ten times better ill. by author. Cavendish, 2001. ISBN 0-7614-5070-X Subj: Animals. Counting, numbers. Format, unusual – toy and movable books. Rhyming text.

Saunders, Julie. *Snowtime* (Saunders, Dave)

Saunders, Susan. *Charles Rat's picnic* ill. by Robert Byrd. Dutton, 1983. ISBN 0-525-44067-4 Subj: Activities – picnicking. Animals – armadillos. Animals – rats. Friendship.

Fish fry ill. by S. D. Schindler. Viking, 1982. ISBN 0-670-31664-4 Subj: Activities – picnicking.

The golden goose (Grimm, Jacob)

A sniff in time ill. by Michael Mariano. Macmillan, 1982. ISBN 0-689-30890-6 Subj: Magic. Senses – smelling. Wizards.

Wales' tale ill. by Marilyn Hirsh. Viking, 1980. ISBN 0-670-74870-6 Subj: Animals – dogs.

Sautai, Raoul. *Bees* (Bees)

Native Americans (Native Americans)

Whales (Whales)

Savage, Kathleen. *Bear hunt* (Siewert, Margaret)

Savage, Stephen. *Making tracks* ill. by author. Dutton, 1992. ISBN 0-525-67353-9 Subj: Animals. Format, unusual – toy and movable books.

Savageau, Cheryl. *Muskrat will be swimming* ill. by Robert Hynes. Northland, 1996. ISBN 0-87358-604-2 Subj: Animals – muskrats. Family life – grandfathers. Folk and fairy tales. Indians of North America – Seneca. Self-concept.

Saville, Lynn. *Horses in the circus ring* ill. by author. Dutton, 1989. ISBN 0-525-44417-3 Subj: Animals – horses, ponies. Circus.

Sawicki, Norma Jean. *The little red house* ill. by Toni Goffe. Lothrop, 1989. ISBN 0-688-07892-3 Subj: Concepts – color. Toys.

Something for mom ill. by Martha Weston. Lothrop, 1987. ISBN 0-688-05590-7 Subj: Birthdays. Family life – mothers.

Sawyer, Jean. *Our village shop* ill. by Faith Jaques. Putnam, 1984. ISBN 0-399-21023-7 Subj: Stores.

Sawyer, Ruth. *The Christmas Anna angel* ill. by Kate Seredy. Viking, 1944. Subj: Angels. Caldecott award honor books. Holidays – Christmas.

Journey cake, ho! ill. by Robert McCloskey. Viking, 1953. ISBN 0-670-40943-X Subj: Caldecott award honor books. Cumulative tales. Folk and fairy tales. Poverty.

The remarkable Christmas of the cobbler's sons ill. by Barbara Cooney. Viking, 1994. ISBN 0-670-84922-7 Subj: Behavior – sharing. Folk and fairy tales. Foreign lands – Tyrol. Holidays – Christmas. Royalty – kings.

Saxe, John Godfrey. *The blind men and the elephant* ill. by Paul Galdone. McGraw-Hill, 1963. Subj: Animals – elephants. Handicaps – blindness. Senses – seeing.

Elephant? (Balian, Lorna)

Saxon, Charles D. *Don't worry about Poopsie* ill. by author. Dodd, 1958. Subj: Animals – dogs. Behavior – lost.

Saxon, Gladys Relyea. *see* Seyton, Marion

Saxon, Victoria. *Disney's Pooh's grand adventure: the search for Christopher Robin* (Henderson, Kathy)

Say, Allen. *Allison* ill. by author. Houghton Mifflin, 1997. ISBN 0-395-85895-X Subj: Adoption. Animals – cats. Behavior – misbehavior. Emotions. Family life.

The bicycle man ill. by author. Houghton Mifflin, 1982. ISBN 0-395-32254-5 Subj: Foreign lands – Japan. Sports – bicycling.

Grandfather's journey ill. by author. Houghton Mifflin, 1993. ISBN 0-395-57035-2 Subj: Activities – traveling. Caldecott award honor books. Ethnic groups in the U.S. – Japanese Americans. Family life. Family life – grandfathers. Foreign lands – Japan.

Once under the cherry blossom tree: an old Japanese tale ill. by author. HarperCollins, 1974. ISBN 0-06-025217-0 Subj: Folk and fairy tales. Foreign lands – Japan.

A river dream ill. by author. Houghton Mifflin, 1988. ISBN 0-395-48294-1 Subj: Dreams. Family life. Illness. Sports – fishing.

Tree of cranes ill. by author. Houghton Mifflin, 1991. ISBN 0-395-52024-X Subj: Family life – mothers. Foreign lands – Japan. Holidays – Christmas.

Sayre, April Pulley. *Home at last: a song of migration* ill. by Alix Berenzy. Holt, 1998. ISBN 0-8050-5154-6 Subj: Animals. Migration.

If you should hear a honey guide ill. by S. D. Schindler. Houghton Mifflin, 1995. ISBN 0-395-71545-8 Subj: Animals. Birds. Foreign lands – Africa. Insects – bees.

Splish! splash! animal baths ill. by author. Millbrook, 2000. ISBN 0-7613-1821-6 Subj: Activities – bathing. Animals.

Turtle, turtle, watch out! ill. by Lee Christiansen. Orchard, 2000. ISBN 0-531-33285-3 Subj: Character traits – kindness to animals. Migration. Reptiles – turtles, tortoises.

Sazer, Nina. *What do you think I saw? a nonsense number book* ill. by Lois Ehlert. Pantheon, 1976. ISBN 0-394-93182-3 Subj: Counting, numbers. Humor. Rhyming text.

Scamell, Ragnhild. *Solo plus one* ill. by Elizabeth Martland. Little, 1992. ISBN 0-316-77242-9 Subj: Animals – cats. Birds – ducks. Eggs.

Who likes Wolfie? ill. by Tim Warnes. Little, 1995. ISBN 0-316-77243-7 Subj: Animals – wolves. Birds. Emotions – loneliness. Self-concept. Teeth.

Scarry, Huck. *Huck Scarry's steam train journey* ill. by author. Collins-World, 1979. ISBN 0-529-05550-3 Subj: Trains.

Looking into the Middle Ages ill. by author. HarperCollins, 1985. ISBN 0-06-025224-3 Subj: Format, unusual – toy and movable books. Knights. Middle Ages.

On the road ill. by author. Putnam, 1981. ISBN 0-399-61183-5 Subj: Automobiles.

Scarry, Richard. *Egg in the hole* ill. by author. Golden Pr., 1967. ISBN 0-307-12030-9 Subj: Birds – chickens. Eggs. Format, unusual.

The great big car and truck book ill. by author. Golden Pr., 1976. ISBN 0-307-10473-7 Subj: Automobiles. Trucks.

Is this the house of Mistress Mouse? ill. by author. Golden Pr., 1964. ISBN 0-307-12029-5 Subj: Animals. Homes, houses.

Mr. Frumble's worst day ever ill. by author. Random House, 1992. ISBN 0-679-81616-X Subj: Animals – pigs. Behavior – bad day.

My first word book ill. by author. Random House, 1986. ISBN 0-394-88016-1 Subj: Activities – picnicking. Format, unusual – board books.

Pie rats ahoy! ill. by author. Random House, 1994. ISBN 0-679-94760-4 Subj: Animals. Boats, ships. Food. Pirates.

Pig Will and Pig Won't: a book of manners ill. by author. Random House, 1984. ISBN 0-394-96585-X Subj: Animals – pigs. Behavior.

Pig Will and Pig Won't ill. by author. Random House, 1990. ISBN 0-679-80067-0 Subj: Animals – pigs. Behavior. Format, unusual.

Richard Scarry's ABC word book ill. by author. Random House, 1971. ISBN 0-394-92339-1 Subj: ABC books.

Richard Scarry's animal nursery tales ill. by author. Golden Pr., 1975. ISBN 0-307-66810-X Subj: Animals. Folk and fairy tales. Nursery rhymes.

Richard Scarry's best Christmas book ever! ill. by author. Random House, 1981. ISBN 0-394-94936-6 Subj: Holidays – Christmas.

Richard Scarry's best counting book ever! ill. by author. Random House, 1975. ISBN 0-394-92924-1 Subj: Counting, numbers.

Richard Scarry's best first book ever! ill. by author. Random House, 1979. ISBN 0-394-94250-7 Subj: Concepts. Days of the week, months of the year.

Richard Scarry's biggest word book ever! ill. by author. Random House, 1985. ISBN 0-394-87374-2 Subj: Dictionaries. Format, unusual. Language.

Richard Scarry's busiest people ever ill. by author. Random House, 1976. ISBN 0-394-93293-5 Subj: Careers.

Richard Scarry's busy houses ill. by author. Random House, 1981. ISBN 0-394-84937-X Subj: Animals – worms. Format, unusual – board books. Homes, houses.

Richard Scarry's great big mystery book ill. by author. Random House, 1969. ISBN 0-394-92431-2 Subj: Animals. Crime. Stores.

Richard Scarry's hop aboard! Here we go! ill. by author. Golden Pr., 1972. Subj: Transportation.

Richard Scarry's Lowly Worm word book ill. by author. Random House, 1981. ISBN 0-394-84728-8 Subj: Format, unusual – board books.

Richard Scarry's mix or match storybook ill. by author. Random House, 1979. ISBN 0-394-84150-6 Subj: Animals. Format, unusual – toy and movable books.

Richard Scarry's Peasant Pig and the terrible dragon ill. by author. Random House, 1980. Subj: Animals – pigs. Character traits – bravery. Dragons. Middle Ages.

Richard Scarry's please and thank you book ill. by author. Random House, 1973. ISBN 0-394-92681-1 Subj: Etiquette.

Richard Scarry's Postman Pig and his busy neighbors ill. by author. Random House, 1978. ISBN 0-394-93898-4 Subj: Animals. Careers. Careers – postal workers. City. Post office.

Richard Scarry's storybook dictionary ill. by author. Golden Pr., 1966. ISBN 0-307-65548-2 Subj: Dictionaries.

Schaaf, Peter. *An apartment house close up* photos by author. Four Winds, 1980. ISBN 0-590-07670-1 Subj: Homes, houses.

The violin close up photos by author. Four Winds, 1980. ISBN 0-590-07655-8 Subj: Music.

Schachner, Judith Byron. *The Grannyman* ill. by author. Dutton, 1999. ISBN 0-525-46122-1 Subj: Animals – cats. Character traits – responsibility. Old age.

Schackburg, Richard. *Yankee Doodle* ill. by Ed Emberley. Prentice-Hall, 1965. Subj: Music. Songs. U.S. history.

Schade, Susan. *Toad on the road* (Buller, Jon)

Schaefer, Carole Lexa. *The copper tin cup* ill. by Stan Fellows. Candlewick, 1999. ISBN 0-7636-0471-2 Subj: Family life. Memories, memory.

Down in the woods at sleepytime ill. by Vanessa Cabban. Candlewick, 2000. ISBN 0-7636-0843-2 Subj: Animals. Bedtime. Dreams. Family life – mothers. Forest, woods.

Snow pumpkin ill. by Pierr Morgan. Crown, 2000. ISBN 0-517-80016-0 Subj: Activities – playing. Ethnic groups in the U.S. Snowmen. Weather – snow.

Sometimes moon ill. by Pierr Morgan. Crown, 1999. ISBN 0-517-70981-3 Subj: Moon.

Under the midsummer sky ill. by Pat Geddes. Putnam, 1994. ISBN 03-99-21858-0 Subj: Character traits – kindness. Folk and fairy tales. Foreign lands – Sweden. Holidays. Scarecrows.

Schaefer, Charles E. *Cat's got your tongue?* ill. by Judith Friedman. Gareth Stevens, 1993. ISBN 0-8368-0930-0 Subj: Character traits – shyness. Emotions – fear. School – first day.

Schaefer, Jackie Jasina. *Miranda's day to dance* ill. by author. Four Winds, 1994. ISBN 0-02-781111-5 Subj: Activities – dancing. Animals. Counting, numbers. Food. Foreign lands – South America.

Schaefer, Lola M. *This is the sunflower* ill. by Donald Crews. Greenwillow, 2000. ISBN 0-688-16414-5 Subj: Cumulative tales. Flowers. Nature. Plants. Rhyming text. Seeds.

Tugboats ill. with photos. Bridgestone, 2000. ISBN 0-7368-0505-2 Subj: Boats, ships.

Schaeffer, Cornelia. *The Holy Night: the story of the first Christmas* (Jüchen, Aurel von)

Schaffer, Libor. *Arthur sets sail* ill. by Agnès Mathieu. Holt, 1987. ISBN 0-8050-0489-0 Subj: Animals – aardvarks. Animals – pigs. Boats, ships. Character traits – appearance.

Schaffer, Marion. *I love my cat!* ill. by Kathy Vanderlinden. Kids Can Pr., 1981. ISBN 0-919964-26-5 Subj: Animals – cats. Foreign languages. Pets.

Schami, Rafik. *Albert and Lila* ill. by Els Cools and Oliver Streich; trans. by Anthea Bell. North-South, 1999. ISBN 0-7358-1183-0 Subj: Animals – foxes. Animals – pigs. Birds – chickens. Character traits – individuality. Prejudice.

The crow who stood on his beak ill. by Els Cools and Oliver Streich; trans. by Anthea Bell. North-South, 1996. ISBN 1-55858-528-1 Subj: Birds – crows. Birds – peacocks, peahens. Character traits – individuality.

Fatima and the dream thief ill. by Els Cools and Oliver Streich; trans. by Anthea Bell. North-South, 1996. ISBN 1-55858-654-7 Subj: Dreams. Folk and fairy tales. Giants.

Schanzer, Rosalyn. *In the synagogue* ill. by author. Kar-Ben Copies, 1991. ISBN 0-929371-60-7 Subj: Format, unusual – board books. Jewish culture. Religion.

Schären, Beatrix. *Tillo* trans. by Gwen Marsh; ill. by author. Addison-Wesley, 1974. Subj: Birds – owls.

Scharer, Niko. *Emily's house* ill. by Joanne Fitzgerald. Firefly, 1991. ISBN 0-88899-111-8 Subj: Animals. Homes, houses. Noise, sounds. Rhyming text.

Schatell, Brian. *Farmer Goff and his turkey Sam* ill. by author. Lippincott, 1982. ISBN 0-397-31983-5 Subj: Behavior – misbehavior. Birds – turkeys. Fairs.

The McGoonys have a party ill. by author. Lippincott, 1985. ISBN 0-397-32134-4 Subj: Behavior – forgetfulness. Behavior – misunderstanding. Handicaps.

Midge and Fred ill. by author. Lippincott, 1983. ISBN 0-397-32047-7 Subj: Fish. Humor.

Sam's no dummy, Farmer Goff ill. by author. Lippincott, 1984. ISBN 0-397-32062-0 Subj: Birds – turkeys. Character traits – cleverness.

Schatschneider, Lori Ann. *Song of Chirimia: La Musica de la Chirimia* (Volkmer, Jane Anne)

Schatz, Letta. *The extraordinary tug-of-war* ill. by John Burningham. Follett, 1968. Subj: Animals. Character traits – cleverness. Folk and fairy tales. Foreign lands – Africa.

Whiskers, my cat ill. by Paul Galdone. McGraw-Hill, 1967. Subj: Animals – cats.

Schecter, Ellen. *The flower of Sheba* (Orgel, Doris)

Scheer, Julian. *Rain makes applesauce* by Julian Scheer and Marvin Bileck; ill. by Marvin Bileck. Holiday, 1964. ISBN 0-8234-0091-3 Subj: Caldecott award honor books. Humor. Weather – rain.

Scheffler, Ursel. *Be brave, little lion!* ill. and trans. by Ruth Scholte van Mast. North-South, 2000. ISBN 0-7358-1265-9 Subj: Animals – lions. Character traits – bravery. Emotions – fear. Family life. Foreign lands – Africa.

Stop your crowing, Kasimir! ill. by Silke Brix-Henker. Carolrhoda, 1988. ISBN 0-87614-323-0 Subj: Birds – chickens. Communities, neighborhoods. Country. Noise, sounds.

Taking care of Sister Bear ill. by Ulises Wensell. Doubleday, 1999. ISBN 0-385-32660-2 Subj: Animals – bears. Babies. Behavior – lost. Family life – brothers and sisters.

A walk in the rain trans. by Andrea Mernan; ill. by Ulises Wensell. Putnam, 1986. ISBN 0-399-21267-1 Subj: Family life – grandmothers. Family life – grandparents. Weather – rain.

Who has time for Little Bear? ill. by Ulises Wensell. Doubleday, 1998. ISBN 0-385-32536-3 Subj: Animals – bears. Family life. Friendship.

Scheffrin-Falk, Gladys. *Another celebrated dancing bear* ill. by Barbara Garrison. Scribners, 1991. ISBN 0-684-19164-4 Subj: Activities – dancing. Animals – bears. Circus. Friendship.

Scheidl, Gerda Marie. *Can we help you, Saint Nicholas?* trans. by Rosemary Lanning; ill. by Jean-Pierre Corderoc'h. North-South, 1992. ISBN 1-55858-155-3 Subj: Animals. Forest, woods. Holidays – Christmas.

The moon man tr. and adapt. by J. Alison James; ill. by Józef Wilkon. North-South, 1994. ISBN 1-55858-272-X Subj: Art. Moon.

Pickle and Patch ill. by Jean-Pierre Corderoc'h; trans. by Rosemary Lanning. North-South, 1994. ISBN 1-55858-270-3 Subj: Animals – dogs. Animals – horses, ponies. Farms. Friendship.

Scheller, Melanie. *My grandfather's hat* ill. by Keiko Narahashi. Macmillan, 1992. ISBN 0-689-50540-X Subj: Clothing – hats. Death. Emotions – grief. Family life – grandfathers.

Schenk, Esther M. *Christmas time* ill. by Vera Stone Norman. Follett, 1931. Subj: Holidays – Christmas.

Schepp, Steven. *How babies are made* (Andry, Andrew C.)

Schermbrucker, Reviva. *Charlie's house* ill. by Niki Daly. Viking, 1991. ISBN 0-670-84024-6 Subj: Family life. Foreign lands – South Africa. Homes, houses. Poverty.

Schermer, Judith. *Mouse in house* ill. by author. Houghton Mifflin, 1979. ISBN 0-395-27801-5 Subj: Animals – mice. Family life. Problem solving.

Schertle, Alice. *Advice for a frog and other poems* ill. by Norman Green. Lothrop, 1995. ISBN 0-688-13487-4 Subj: Animals. Animals – endangered animals. Frogs and toads. Poetry.

Bill and the google-eyed goblins ill. by Patricia Coombs. Lothrop, 1987. ISBN 0-688-06702-6 Subj: Activities – dancing. Holidays – Halloween. Mythical creatures – goblins.

Down the road ill. by E. B. Lewis. Browndeer, 1995. ISBN 0-15-276622-7 Subj: Country. Eggs. Ethnic groups in the U.S. – African Americans. Family life.

Goodnight, Hattie, my dearie, my dove ill. by Linda Strauss Edwards. Lothrop, 1985. ISBN 0-688-03934-0 Subj: Bedtime. Counting, numbers. Toys.

The gorilla in the hall ill. by Paul Galdone. Lothrop, 1977. ISBN 0-688-51781-1 Subj: Animals – gorillas. Character traits – bravery. Emotions – fear.

Hob Goblin and the skeleton ill. by Katherine Coville. Lothrop, 1982. ISBN 0-688-00282-X Subj: Holidays – Halloween. Mythical creatures – trolls.

How now, brown cow? ill. by Amanda Schaffer. Browndeer, 1994. ISBN 0-15-276648-0 Subj: Animals – bulls, cows. Poetry.

I am the cat ill. by Mark Buehner. Lothrop, 1999. ISBN 0-688-13154-9 Subj: Animals – cats. Poetry.

In my treehouse ill. by Meredith Dunham. Lothrop, 1983. ISBN 0-688-01639-1 Subj: Behavior – solitude. Homes, houses. Trees.

Jeremy Bean's St. Patrick's Day ill. by Linda Shute. Lothrop, 1987. ISBN 0-688-04814-5 Subj: Behavior – hiding. Character traits – being different. Holidays – St. Patrick's Day. Parties. School.

Keepers ill. by Ted Rand. Lothrop, 1996. ISBN 0-688-11635-3 Subj: Poetry.

Little Frog's song ill. by Leonard Everett Fisher. HarperCollins, 1992. ISBN 0-06-020060-X Subj: Behavior – lost. Frogs and toads.

Maisie ill. by Lydia Dabcovich. Lothrop, 1995. ISBN 0-688-09311-6 Subj: Behavior – growing up. Family life – grandmothers. Farms.

My two feet ill. by Meredith Dunham. Lothrop, 1985. ISBN 0-688-02677-X Subj: Anatomy – feet.

That Olive! ill. by Cindy Wheeler. Lothrop, 1986. ISBN 0-688-04091-8 Subj: Animals – cats. Behavior – hiding.

That's what I thought ill. by John Wallner. HarperCollins, 1990. ISBN 0-06-025205-7 Subj: Character traits – questioning. Family life.

Witch Hazel ill. by Margot Tomes. HarperCollins, 1991. ISBN 0-06-025141-7 Subj: Family life – brothers. Moon. Plants. Scarecrows.

Schick, Alice. *Just this once* by Alice and Joel Schick; ill. by Joel Schick. Lippincott, 1978. ISBN 0-397-31803-0 Subj: Animals – wolves. Pets.

Schick, Eleanor. *Art lessons* ill. by author. Greenwillow, 1987. ISBN 0-688-05121-9 Subj: Art.

City green ill. by author. Macmillan, 1974. ISBN 0-02-781170-0 Subj: City. Poetry.

City in the winter ill. by author. Macmillan, 1970. Subj: City. Family life – only child. Seasons – winter. Weather – snow. Weather – wind.

I have another language: the language is dance ill. by author. Macmillan, 1992. ISBN 0-02-781209-X Subj: Activities – dancing.

The little school at Cottonwood Corners ill. by author. HarperCollins, 1965. Subj: Caldecott award honor books. School. Wordless.

Making friends ill. by author. Macmillan, 1969. Subj: Friendship. Wordless.

Mama ill. by author. Cavendish, 2000. ISBN 0-7614-5060-2 Subj: Death. Emotions – grief. Family life – mothers. Illness. Memories, memory.

My Navajo sister ill. by author. Simon & Schuster, 1996. ISBN 0-02-781155-7 Subj: Friendship. Indians of North America – Navajo.

Navajo ABC (Tapahonso, Luci)

One summer night ill. by author. Greenwillow, 1977. Subj: City. Music. Seasons – summer.

Peggy's new brother ill. by author. Macmillan, 1970. Subj: Babies. Emotions – envy, jealousy. Family life – new sibling. Sibling rivalry.

Peter and Mr. Brandon ill. by Donald Carrick. Macmillan, 1973. Subj: Activities – babysitting. City.

A piano for Julie ill. by author. Greenwillow, 1984. Subj: Family life. Music.

A surprise in the forest ill. by author. HarperCollins, 1964. Subj: Animals. Eggs. Forest, woods.

Schick, Joel. *Just this once* (Schick, Alice)

Schiller, Barbara. *The white rat's tale* ill. by Adrienne Adams. Holt, 1967. Subj: Animals – rats. Folk and fairy tales. Foreign lands – France. Royalty.

Schilling, Betty. *Two kittens are born: from birth to two months* photos by author. Holt, 1980. Subj: Animals – cats. Birth. Science.

Schindel, John. *Busy penguins* by John Schindel and Jonathan Chester; ill. with photos. Tricycle, 2000. ISBN 1-58246-016-7 Subj: Activities. Birds – penguins. Format, unusual – board books. Rhyming text.

Dear Daddy ill. by Dorothy Donohue. Albert Whitman, 1995. ISBN 0-8075-1531-0 Subj: Behavior – needing someone. Divorce. Family life – fathers. Letters, cards.

Frog face, my little sister and me photos by Janet Delaney. Holt, 1998. ISBN 0-8050-5546-0 Subj: Family life – new sibling. Family life – sisters.

Who are you? ill. by James Watts. Macmillan, 1991. ISBN 0-689-50523-X Subj: Animals – bears. Bedtime. Parties.

Schindler, Regina. *The bear's cave* trans. from German by Christopher Franceschelli; ill. by Sita Jucker. Dutton, 1990. ISBN 0-525-44553-6 Subj: Animals. Behavior – boasting. Seasons – winter.

Schlein, Miriam. *The amazing Mr. Pelgrew* ill. by Harvey Weiss. Abelard-Schuman, 1957. Subj: Careers – police officers.

Big talk ill. by Joan Auclair. Rev. ed. Bradbury, 1990. ISBN 0-02-781231-6 Subj: Animals – kangaroos. Behavior – boasting.

Big talk ill. by Laura Lydecker. Albert Whitman, 1988. ISBN 0-8075-0729-6 Subj: Animals – kangaroos. Behavior – boasting.

Billy, the littlest one ill. by Lucy Hawkinson. Albert Whitman, 1966. Subj: Behavior – growing up. Character traits – smallness. Family life.

Deer in the snow ill. by Leonard P. Kessler. Abelard-Schuman, 1956. Subj: Animals – deer. Character traits – kindness to animals. Seasons – winter. Weather – snow.

Elephant herd ill. by Symeon Shimin. Addison-Wesley, 1954. Subj: Animals – elephants.

Fast is not a ladybug ill. by Leonard P. Kessler. Addison-Wesley, 1953. Subj: Concepts – speed. Insects – ladybugs.

The four little foxes ill. by Louis Quintanilla. Addison-Wesley, 1953. Subj: Animals – foxes.

Go with the sun ill. by Symeon Shimin. Addison-Wesley, 1952. Subj: Family life – grandfathers. Seasons – winter.

Heavy is a hippopotamus ill. by Leonard P. Kessler. Addison-Wesley, 1954. Subj: Concepts – weight.

Here comes night ill. by Harvey Weiss. Albert Whitman, 1957. Subj: Night.

Herman McGregor's world ill. by Harvey Weiss. Albert Whitman, 1959. Subj: Behavior – growing up. World.

Home, the tale of a mouse ill. by E. Harper Johnson. Abelard-Schuman, 1958. Subj: Animals – mice.

It's about time ill. by Leonard P. Kessler. Addison-Wesley, 1955. Subj: Time.

Laurie's new brother ill. by Elizabeth Donald. Abelard-Schuman, 1961. Subj: Babies. Family life – new sibling. Sibling rivalry.

Little Rabbit, the high jumper ill. by Theresa Sherman. Addison-Wesley, 1957. Subj: Animals – rabbits.

Little Red Nose ill. by Roger Antoine Duvoisin. Abelard-Schuman, 1955. Subj: Seasons – spring.

Lucky porcupine! ill. by Martha Weston. Four Winds, 1980. Subj: Animals – porcupines. Science.

My family ill. by Harvey Weiss. Abelard-Schuman, 1960. Subj: Family life.

My house ill. by Joe Lasker. Albert Whitman, 1971. Subj: Family life. Homes, houses. Moving.

The pile of junk ill. by Harvey Weiss. Abelard-Schuman, 1962. Subj: Character traits – practicality. Values.

Shapes ill. by Sam Berman. Addison-Wesley, 1952. Subj: Concepts – shape.

Sleep safe, little whale: a lullaby ill. by Peter Sis. Greenwillow, 1997. ISBN 0-688-14757-7 Subj: Animals. Animals – whales. Bedtime. Format, unusual – toy and movable books. Lullabies.

Something for now, something for later ill. by Leonard Weisgard. HarperCollins, 1956. Subj: Farms.

The sun looks down ill. by Abner Graboff. Abelard-Schuman, 1954. Subj: Sun.

The sun, the wind, the sea and the rain ill. by Joe Lasker. Abelard-Schuman, 1960. Subj: Sea and seashore. Sun. Weather. Weather – rain. Weather – wind.

That's not Goldie! ill. by Susan Gough Magurn. Simon & Schuster, 1990. ISBN 0-671-70005-7 Subj: Fish. Pets.

What's wrong with being a skunk? ill. by Ray Cruz. Four Winds, 1974. Subj: Animals – skunks. Science.

When will the world be mine? the story of a snowshoe rabbit ill. by Jean Charlot. Addison-Wesley, 1953. Subj: Behavior – growing up. Caldecott award honor books.

Schmeltz, Susan Alton. *Pets I wouldn't pick* ill. by Ellen Appleby. Parents, 1982. Subj: Pets. Rhyming text.

Schmid, Eleonore. *Farm animals* ill. by author. Holt, 1986. ISBN 0-03-008032-0 Subj: Animals. Farms. Format, unusual – board books.

The living earth ill. by author. North-South, 1994. ISBN 1-55858-299-1 Subj: Earth. Ecology.

The squirrel and the moon trans. by Rosemary Lanning; ill. by author. North-South, 1996. ISBN 1-55858-531-1 Subj: Animals – squirrels. Moon. Trees.

The water's journey ill. by author. North-South, 1990. ISBN 1-55858-013-1 Subj: Rivers. Science. Water. Weather – snow.

Schmidt, Eric von. *The young man who wouldn't hoe corn* ill. by author. Houghton Mifflin, 1964. Subj: Character traits – laziness. Farms. Humor.

Schneider, Antonie. *The birthday bear* ill. by Uli Waas; trans. by J. Alison James. North-South, 1996. ISBN 1-55858-656-3 Subj: Animals – bears. Birthdays. Family life – grandparents.

Good-bye, Vivi! ill. by Maja Dusíková; trans. by J. Alison James. North-South, 1998. ISBN 1-55858-986-4 Subj: Birds – canaries. Death. Family life – grandmothers.

Luke the Lionhearted ill. by Cristina Kadmon; trans. by J. Alison James. North-South, 1998. ISBN 1-55858-977-5 Subj: Animals – lions. Behavior – lost. Behavior – running away. Zoos.

Schneider, Christine M. *Picky Mrs. Pickle* ill. by author. Walker, 1999. ISBN 0-8027-8703-7 Subj: Food. Rhyming text. Self-concept.

Schneider, Elisa. *The merry-go-round dog* ill. by author. Knopf, 1988. ISBN 0-394-99069-2 Subj: Animals – dogs. Merry-go-rounds.

Schneider, Herman. *Follow the sunset* by Herman and Nina Schneider; ill. by Lucille Corcos. Doubleday, 1952. Subj: Science. Sun. World.

Schneider, Howie. *The amazing Amos and the greatest couch on earth* (Seligson, Susan)

Amos ahoy: a couch adventure on land and sea (Seligson, Susan)

Amos camps out: a couch adventure in the woods (Seligson, Susan)

Amos: the story of an old dog and his couch (Seligson, Susan)

No dogs allowed ill. by author. Putnam, 1995. ISBN 0-399-22612-5 Subj: Activities – traveling. Activities – vacationing. Animals – dogs. Hotels.

Schneider, Nina. *Follow the sunset* (Schneider, Herman)

While Susie sleeps ill. by Dagmar Wilson. Addison-Wesley, 1948. Subj: Bedtime. Night. Sleep.

Schnitter, Jane. *William is my brother* ill. by Gerald Kruck. Perspectives Pr., 1991. ISBN 0-944934-03-X Subj: Adoption. Family life – brothers.

Schnur, Steven. *Autumn: an alphabet acrostic* ill. by Leslie Evans. Clarion, 1997. ISBN 0-395-77043-2 Subj: ABC books. Poetry. Seasons – fall.

Night lights ill. by Stacey Schuett. Frances Foster, 2000. ISBN 0-374-35522-3 Subj: Counting, numbers. Lights. Night. Rhyming text.

Spring thaw ill. by Stacey Schuett. Viking, 2000. ISBN 0-670-87961-4 Subj: Farms. Nature. Seasons – spring.

The tie man's miracle ill. by Stephen T. Johnson. Morrow, 1995. ISBN 0-688-13463-7 Subj: Character traits – kindness. Clothing. Holidays – Hanukkah. Holocaust. Jewish culture.

Schoberle, Ceile. *Beyond the Milky Way* ill. by author. Crown, 1986. ISBN 0-517-55716-9 Subj: Imagination. Science. Sky. Space and space ships.

Schoen, Mark. *Bellybuttons are navels* ill. by M. J. Quay. Focus International, 1990. ISBN 0-87975-585-7 Subj: Anatomy.

Schoenherr, John. *The barn* ill. by author. Little, 1968. Subj: Animals – mice. Animals – skunks. Barns. Birds – owls. Farms.

Bear ill. by author. Putnam, 1991. ISBN 0-399-22177-8 Subj: Alaska. Animals – bears. Nature.

Rebel ill. by author. Putnam, 1995. ISBN 0-399-22727-X Subj: Birds – geese. Character traits – curiosity. Family life. Lakes, ponds.

Scholey, Arthur. *Baboushka* ill. by Ray Burrows. Good News, 1983. ISBN 0-89107-281-0 Subj: Music. Religion. Royalty. Toys.

Scholte van Mast, Ruth. *Be brave, little lion!* (Scheffler, Ursel)

Schomp, Virginia. *If you were a . . . pilot* ill. by author. Benchmark, 1999. ISBN 0-7614-0919-X Subj: Activities – flying. Careers – airplane pilots. Transportation.

If you were a . . . teacher ill. by author. Benchmark, 1999. ISBN 0-7614-0916-5 Subj: Careers – teachers. School.

Schongut, Emanuel. *Look kitten* ill. by author. Simon & Schuster, 1983. Subj: Animals.

Schories, Pat. *Mouse around* ill. by author. Farrar, 1991. ISBN 0-374-35080-9 Subj: Activities – traveling. Animals – mice. Circular tales. Wordless.

Schotter, Richard. *There's a dragon about* by Richard and Roni Schotter; ill. by R. W. Alley. Orchard, 1994. ISBN 0-531-08708-5 Subj: Dragons. Rhyming text.

Schotter, Roni. *Bunny's night out* ill. by Margot Apple. Little, 1989. ISBN 0-316-77465-0 Subj: Animals – rabbits. Bedtime. Night.

Captain Bob sets sail ill. by Joe Cepeda. Atheneum, 2000. ISBN 0-689-82081-X Subj: Activities – bathing. Imagination. Pirates.

Captain Snap and the children of Vinegar Lane ill. by Marcia Sewall. Watts, 1989. ISBN 0-531-08397-7 Subj: Character traits – being different. Character traits – generosity. Character traits – kindness.

Dreamland ill. by Kevin Hawkes. Orchard, 1996. ISBN 0-531-08858-8 Subj: Careers – tailors. Character traits – individuality. Imagination.

Hanukkah! ill. by Marylin Hafner. Little, 1990. ISBN 0-316-77466-9 Subj: Holidays – Hanukkah. Jewish culture. Religion.

Nothing ever happens on 90th Street ill. by Kyrsten Brooker. Orchard, 1997. ISBN 0-531-08886-3 Subj: Activities – writing. Careers – writers. City.

Passover magic ill. by Marylin Hafner. Little, 1995. ISBN 0-316-77468-5 Subj: Holidays – Passover. Jewish culture. Religion.

Purim play ill. by Marylin Hafner. Little, 1998. ISBN 0-316-77518-5 Subj: Holidays – Purim. Jewish culture. Religion. Theater.

That extraordinary pig of Paris ill. by Dominic Catalano. Philomel, 1994. ISBN 0-399-22023-2 Subj: Animals – pigs. Food. Foreign lands – France. Foreign languages.

There's a dragon about (Schotter, Richard)

Schrecker, Judie. *Santa's new reindeer* ill. by Daniel Rodriguez. E.M. Pr., 1996. ISBN 1-880664-18-6 Subj: Animals. Animals – reindeer. Holidays – Christmas. Santa Claus.

Schreiber, Georges. *Bambino goes home* ill. by author. Viking, 1959. Subj: Clowns, jesters. Friendship.

Bambino the clown ill. by author. Viking, 1947. Subj: Animals – sea lions. Caldecott award honor books. Clowns, jesters.

Professor Bull's umbrella (Lipkind, William)

Schreier, Joshua. *Luigi's all-night parking lot* ill. by author. Dutton, 1990. ISBN 0-525-44626-5 Subj: Bedtime. Imagination. Toys.

Schrier, Jeffrey. *On the wings of eagles: an Ethiopian boy's story* ill. by author. Millbrook, 1998. ISBN 0-7613-0004-X Subj: Ethnic groups in the U.S. – African Americans. Foreign lands – Africa. Foreign lands – Ethiopia. Imagination. Jewish culture. Religion.

Schroder, William. *Pea soup and serpents* ill. by author. Lothrop, 1977. ISBN 0-688-51785-4 Subj: Monsters. Mythical creatures. Weather – fog.

Schroeder, Alan. *Ragtime Tumpie* ill. by Bernie Fuchs. Little, 1989. ISBN 0-316-77497-9 Subj: Activities – dancing. Ethnic groups in the U.S. – African Americans.

The stone lion ill. by Todd L. W. Doney. Scribners, 1994. ISBN 0-684-19578-X Subj: Behavior – greed. Character traits – honesty. Character traits – kindness. Character traits – selfishness. Folk and fairy tales. Foreign lands – Tibet.

Schroeder, Binette. *Laura* ill. by author; trans. by Rosemary Lanning. North-South, 1999. ISBN 0-7358-1171-7 Subj: Rhyming text. Self-concept. Toys – bears.

Ra ta ta tam: the strange story of a little engine (Nickl, Peter)

Tuffa and her friends ill. by author. Dial, 1983. ISBN 0-8037-9894-6 Subj: Animals – dogs. Format, unusual – board books. Friendship.

Tuffa and the bone ill. by author. Dial, 1983. ISBN 0-8037-9893-8 Subj: Animals – dogs. Format, unusual – board books.

Tuffa and the ducks ill. by author. Dial, 1983. ISBN 0-8037-9892-X Subj: Animals – dogs. Birds – ducks. Format, unusual – board books.

Tuffa and the picnic ill. by author. Dial, 1983. ISBN 0-8037-9896-2 Subj: Activities – picnicking. Animals – dogs. Behavior – misbehavior. Format, unusual – board books.

Tuffa and the snow ill. by author. Dial, 1983. ISBN 0-8037-9895-4 Subj: Animals – dogs. Format, unusual – board books. Weather – snow.

Schroeder, Glen W. *At the zoo* (Colonius, Lillian)

Schubert, Dieter. *Bear's eggs* (Schubert, Ingrid)

Little big feet (Schubert, Ingrid)

The magic bubble trip (Schubert, Ingrid)

There's a crocodile under my bed! (Schubert, Ingrid)

Where's my monkey? ill. by author. Dial, 1987. ISBN 0-8037-0069-5 Subj: Animals – monkeys. Behavior – losing things. Behavior – needing someone. Wordless.

Schubert, Ingrid. *Bear's eggs* written and ill. by Ingrid and Dieter Schubert. Front Street, 1999. ISBN 1-886910-46-4 Subj: Animals – bears. Animals – hedgehogs. Birds – geese. Eggs.

Little big feet by Ingrid and Dieter Schubert; trans. from Dutch by Amy Gelman; ill. by authors. Carolrhoda, 1990. ISBN 0-87614-426-1 Subj: Anatomy – feet. Witches.

The magic bubble trip by Ingrid and Dieter Schubert; ill. by authors. Kane/Miller, 1985. ISBN 0-916291-02-2 Subj: Bubbles. Foreign lands – Holland. Frogs and toads.

There's a crocodile under my bed! by Ingrid and Dieter Schubert; ill. by authors. McGraw-Hill, 1981. ISBN 0-07-055614-8 Subj: Bedtime. Furniture – beds. Reptiles – alligators, crocodiles.

Schuchman, Joan. *Two places to sleep* ill. by Jim LaMarche. Carolrhoda, 1979. ISBN 0-87614-108-4 Subj: Divorce. Family life.

Schuett, Stacey. *Somewhere in the world right now* ill. by author. Knopf, 1995. ISBN 0-679-96537-8 Subj: Geography. Time. World.

Schulman, Janet. *The big hello* ill. by Lillian Hoban. Greenwillow, 1976. ISBN 0-688-84036-1 Subj: Friendship. Moving. Toys – dolls.

Camp Kee Wee's secret weapon ill. by Marylin Hafner. Greenwillow, 1979. ISBN 0-688-84185-6 Subj: Camps, camping. Sports – baseball.

The great big dummy ill. by Lillian Hoban. Greenwillow, 1979. ISBN 0-688-84208-9 Subj: Animals – dogs. Friendship. Toys – dolls.

Jungles (Wood, John Norris)

Schulson, Rachel Ellenberg. *Guns . . . what you should know* ill. by Mary Jones. Albert Whitman, 1997. ISBN 0-8075-3093-X Subj: Safety. Weapons.

Schulz, Charles M. *Bon voyage, Charlie Brown (and don't come back!!)* ill. by author. Random House, 1980. ISBN 0-394-84415-7 Subj: Activities – traveling. Foreign lands.

The Charlie Brown dictionary based on the rainbow dictionary by Wendell W. Wright; asst. by Helene Laird; ill. by author. Random House, 1973. ISBN 0-394-93041-X Subj: Dictionaries.

Life is a circus, Charlie Brown ill. by author. Random House, 1981. ISBN 0-394-94826-2 Subj: Circus.

Snoopy's facts and fun book about boats ill. by author. Random House, 1979. ISBN 0-394-94171-3 Subj: Animals – dogs. Boats, ships.

Snoopy's facts and fun book about farms ill. by author. Random House, 1980. ISBN 0-394-94300-7 Subj: Animals – dogs. Farms.

Snoopy's facts and fun book about houses ill. by author. Random House, 1979. ISBN 0-394-94151-9 Subj: Animals – dogs. Homes, houses.

Snoopy's facts and fun book about nature ill. by author. Random House, 1979. ISBN 0-394-94299-X Subj: Animals – dogs. Nature. Science.

Snoopy's facts and fun book about planes ill. by author. Random House, 1979. ISBN 0-394-94172-1 Subj: Airplanes, airports. Animals – dogs.

Snoopy's facts and fun book about seashores ill. by author. Random House, 1979. ISBN 0-394-94298-1 Subj: Animals – dogs. Sea and seashore.

Snoopy's facts and fun book about seasons ill. by author. Random House, 1979. ISBN 0-394-94173-X Subj: Animals – dogs. Seasons.

Snoopy's facts and fun book about trucks ill. by author. Random House, 1979. ISBN 0-394-94273-6 Subj: Animals – dogs. Trucks.

You're the greatest, Charlie Brown ill. by author. Random House, 1979. ISBN 0-394-94260-4 Subj: Sports – Olympics.

Schulz, Walter A. *Will and Orv* ill. by Janet Schulz. Carolrhoda, 1991. ISBN 0-87614-669-8 Subj: Activities – flying. Airplanes, airports. U.S. history.

Schumacher, Claire. *Alto and Tango* ill. by author. Morrow, 1984. ISBN 0-688-02740-7 Subj: Birds. Fish. Friendship. Sea and seashore.

Brave Lily ill. by author. Morrow, 1985. ISBN 0-688-04963-X Subj: Character traits – bravery. Family life. Frogs and toads.

King of the zoo ill. by author. Morrow, 1985. ISBN 0-688-04132-9 Subj: Animals. Behavior – misbehavior. Friendship. Zoos.

Nutty's birthday ill. by author. Morrow, 1986. ISBN 0-688-06496-5 Subj: Activities – flying. Animals. Animals – squirrels. Birthdays.

Nutty's Christmas ill. by author. Morrow, 1984. ISBN 0-688-03852-2 Subj: Animals – squirrels. Holidays – Christmas.

Tim and Jim ill. by author. Dodd, 1987. ISBN 0-396-09040-0 Subj: Animals. Behavior – lost. Friendship.

Tommy the winner ill. by author. HarperCollins, 1991. ISBN 0-06-026905-7 Subj: Animals – mice. Letters, cards.

Schumaker, Ward. *Dance!* ill. by author. Harcourt, 1996. ISBN 0-15-200046-1 Subj: Activities – dancing. Animals. Rhyming text.

In my garden ill. by author. Chronicle, 2000. ISBN 0-8118-2689-9 Subj: Counting, numbers. Gardens, gardening.

Schur, Maxine Rose. *Day of delight* ill. by J. Brian Pinkney. Dial, 1994. ISBN 0-8037-1414-9 Subj: Foreign lands – Ethiopia. Jewish culture. Religion.

Schurr, Cathleen. *The long and the short of it* ill. by Dorothy Maas. Vanguard, 1950. Subj: Problem solving.

Schwalje, Marjory. *Mr. Angelo* ill. by Abner Graboff. Abelard-Schuman, 1960. Subj: Activities – cooking. Food. Humor.

Schwartz, Alvin. *All of our noses are here and other stories* ill. by Karen Ann Weinhaus. HarperCollins, 1985. ISBN 0-06-025288-X Subj: Folk and fairy tales. Humor.

Schwartz, Amy. *Annabelle Swift, kindergartner* ill. by author. Orchard, 1988. ISBN 0-531-08337-3 Subj: Character traits – pride. School – first day. Sibling rivalry.

Bea and Mr. Jones ill. by author. Bradbury, 1982. ISBN 0-87888-202-2 Subj: Behavior – imitation. Family life – fathers.

Begin at the beginning ill. by author. Harper-Collins, 1983. ISBN 0-06-025228-6 Subj: Behavior – growing up.

Camper of the week ill. by author. Watts, 1991. ISBN 0-531-08542-2 Subj: Behavior – misbehavior. Camps, camping. Friendship.

Her Majesty, Aunt Essie ill. by author. Bradbury, 1984. ISBN 0-02-781450-5 Subj: Behavior – boasting. Family life – aunts, uncles. Royalty.

How to catch an elephant ill. by author. DK, 1999. ISBN 0-7894-2579-3 Subj: Animals – elephants.

The lady who put salt in her coffee (Hale, Lucretia)

Mrs. Moskowitz and the Sabbath candlesticks ill. by author. Jewish Publication Society, 1983. ISBN 0-8276-0231-6 Subj: Jewish culture. Religion.

Oma and Bobo ill. by author. Bradbury, 1987. ISBN 0-02-781500-5 Subj: Animals – dogs. Family life – grandmothers.

Some babies ill. by author. Orchard, 2000. ISBN 0-531-33287-X Subj: Activities – storytelling. Bedtime. Family life.

A teeny, tiny baby ill. by author. Orchard, 1994. ISBN 0-531-08668-2 Subj: Babies. City.

Yossel Zissel and the wisdom of Chelm ill. by author. Jewish Publication Society, 1988. ISBN 0-8276-0258-8 Subj: Character traits – foolishness. Folk and fairy tales. Jewish culture.

Schwartz, David M. *How much is a million?* ill. by Steven Kellogg. Lothrop, 1985. ISBN 0-688-04050-0 Subj: Concepts – size. Counting, numbers.

If you hopped like a frog ill. by James Warhola. Scholastic, 1999. ISBN 0-590-09857-8 Subj: Animals. Concepts. Counting, numbers. Picture puzzles. Science.

Sugargrandpa ill. by Bert Dodson. Lothrop, 1991. ISBN 0-688-09899-1 Subj: Family life – grandfathers. Foreign lands – Sweden. Old age. Sports – bicycling. Sports – racing.

Schwartz, Delmore. *"I am Cherry Alive," the little girl sang* ill. by Barbara Cooney. HarperCollins, 1979. ISBN 0-06-025244-8 Subj: Poetry.

Schwartz, Ellen. *Mr. Belinsky's bagels* ill. by Stefan Czernecki. Charlesbridge, 1998. ISBN 0-8810-6256-1 Subj: Careers – bakers. Food.

Schwartz, Henry. *Albert goes Hollywood* ill. by Amy Schwartz. Watts, 1992. ISBN 0-531-08580-5 Subj: Dinosaurs. Pets. Theater.

How I captured a dinosaur ill. by Amy Schwartz. Watts, 1989. ISBN 0-531-08370-5 Subj: Camps, camping. Dinosaurs. Pets.

Schwartz, Lynne Sharon. *The four questions* ill. by Ori Sherman. Dial, 1989. ISBN 0-8037-0601-4 Subj: Holidays – Passover. Jewish culture. Religion.

Schwartz, Mary. *Spiffen: a tale of a tidy pig* ill. by Lynn Munsinger. Albert Whitman, 1988. ISBN 0-8075-7580-1 Subj: Animals – pigs. Character traits – cleanliness.

Schwartz, Roslyn. *The mole sisters and the piece of moss* ill. by author. Annick, 1999. ISBN 1-55037-583-0 Subj: Animals – moles. Character traits – helpfulness. Character traits – optimism. Family life – sisters.

The mole sisters and the rainy day ill. by author. Annick, 1999. ISBN 1-55037-611-X Subj: Animals – moles. Family life – sisters. Sports – swimming. Weather – rain.

Rose and Dorothy ill. by author. Watts, 1991. ISBN 0-531-08518-X Subj: Animals – elephants. Animals – mice. Friendship.

Schweiger-Dmi'el, Itzhak. *Hanna's Sabbath dress* ill. by Ora Eitan. Simon & Schuster, 1996. ISBN 0-689-80517-9 Subj: Character traits – helpfulness. Clothing – dresses. Folk and fairy tales. Jewish culture. Religion.

Schweitzer, Iris. *Hilda's restful chair* ill. by author. Atheneum, 1982. ISBN 0-689-50230-3 Subj: Animals. Friendship. Furniture – chairs.

Schweninger, Ann. *Autumn days* ill. by author. Viking, 1991. ISBN 0-670-82758-4 Subj: Animals – dogs. Seasons – fall.

Birthday wishes ill. by author. Viking, 1986. ISBN 0-670-80742-7 Subj: Animals – rabbits. Behavior – wishing. Birthdays. Parties.

Christmas secrets ill. by author. Viking, 1984. ISBN 0-670-22109-0 Subj: Animals – rabbits. Holidays – Christmas.

Halloween surprises ill. by author. Viking, 1984. ISBN 0-670-35935-1 Subj: Animals – rabbits. Holidays – Halloween.

The hunt for rabbit's galosh ill. by Kay Chorao. Doubleday, 1976. ISBN 0-385-00274-2 Subj: Animals – rabbits. Behavior – forgetfulness. Holidays – Valentine's Day.

The man in the moon as he sails the sky and other moon verse ill. by author. Dodd, 1979. ISBN 0-396-07741-2 Subj: Moon. Poetry.

Off to school! ill. by author. Viking, 1987. ISBN 0-670-81447-4 Subj: Animals – rabbits. School – first day.

Summertime ill. by author. Viking, 1992. ISBN 0-670-83610-9 Subj: Activities. Animals – dogs. Family life. Nature. Sea and seashore. Seasons – summer. Weather.

Valentine friends ill. by author. Viking, 1988. ISBN 0-670-81448-2 Subj: Animals – rabbits. Family life. Holidays – Valentine's Day.

Wintertime ill. by author. Viking, 1990. ISBN 0-670-83420-3 Subj: Animals – dogs. Seasons – winter.

Scieszka, Jon. *The book that Jack wrote* ill. by Daniel Adel. Viking, 1994. ISBN 0-670-84330-X Subj: Cumulative tales. Nursery rhymes.

The frog prince, continued ill. by Steve Johnson. Viking, 1991. ISBN 0-670-83421-1 Subj: Folk and fairy tales. Frogs and toads. Royalty – princes. Royalty – princesses. Witches.

The Stinky Cheese Man and other fairly stupid tales by Jon Scieszka and Lane Smith; ill. by Lane Smith. Viking, 1992. ISBN 0-670-84487-X Subj: Caldecott award honor books. Folk and fairy tales.

The true story of the three little pigs by A. Wolf, as told to Jon Scieszka ill. by Lane Smith. Viking, 1989. ISBN 0-670-82759-2 Subj: Animals – pigs. Animals – wolves. Folk and fairy tales.

Scoppetone, Sandra. *Bang, bang, you're dead* (Fitzhugh, Louise)

Scott, Ann Herbert. *Big Cowboy Western* ill. by Richard Lewis. Lothrop, 1965. Subj: Clothing. Cowboys. Ethnic groups in the U.S. – African Americans. Imagination. U.S. history – frontier and pioneer life.

Grandmother's chair ill. by Meg Kelleher Aubrey. Houghton Mifflin, 1990. ISBN 0-395-52001-0 Subj: Family life – grandmothers. Furniture – chairs.

Hi! ill. by Glo Coalson. Philomel, 1994. ISBN 0-399-21964-1 Subj: Behavior – unnoticed, unseen. Post office.

Let's catch a monster ill. by H. Tom Hall. Lothrop, 1967. Subj: City. Ethnic groups in the U.S. – African Americans. Holidays – Halloween.

On mother's lap ill. by Glo Coalson. Rev. ed. Houghton Mifflin, 1992. ISBN 0-395-58920-7 Subj: Behavior – needing someone. Emotions – love. Eskimos. Family life. Family life – mothers. Sibling rivalry.

One good horse ill. by Lynn Sweat. Greenwillow, 1990. ISBN 0-688-09147-4 Subj: Counting, numbers. Cowboys.

Sam ill. by Symeon Shimin. McGraw-Hill, 1992, c1967. ISBN 0-399-22104-2 Subj: Behavior – needing someone. Ethnic groups in the U.S. – African Americans. Family life.

Someday rider ill. by Ronald Himler. Houghton Mifflin, 1989. ISBN 0-89919-792-2 Subj: Animals – horses, ponies. Behavior – growing up. Cowboys.

Scott, C. Anne (Cynthia Anne). *Old Jake's skirts* ill. by David Slonim. Northland, 1998. ISBN 0-8735-8615-8 Subj: Behavior – losing things. Careers – farmers. Clothing. Farms.

Scott, Cora Annett. *see* Annett, Cora

Scott, Elaine. *Friends!* photos by Margaret Miller. Atheneum, 2000. ISBN 0-689-82105-0 Subj: Friendship.

Scott, Frances Gruse. *How many kids are hiding on my block?* (Merrill, Jean)

Scott, Geoffrey. *Memorial Day* ill. by Peter E. Hanson. Carolrhoda, 1983. ISBN 0-87614-219-6 Subj: Holidays – Memorial Day. Memories, memory.

Scott, Lesbia. *I sing a song of the saints of God* ill. by Judith Gwyn Brown. Seabury Pr., 1981. An ill. version of Lesbia Scott's hymn, "I sing a song of the saints of God" written in 1929. ISBN 0-8164-2339-3 Subj: Music. Religion. Songs.

Scott, Natalie (Anderson). *Firebrand, push your hair out of your eyes* ill. by Sandra Smith. Carolrhoda, 1969. ISBN 0-8761-4005-3 Subj: Character traits – appearance. Hair.

Scott, Rochelle. *Colors, colors all around* ill. by Leonard P. Kessler. Grosset, 1965. Subj: Concepts – color.

Scott, Sally. *Little Wiener* ill. by Beth Krush. Harcourt, 1951. Subj: Animals – dogs.

The magic horse ill. by adapt. Greenwillow, 1985. Retold and adapted from "The Ebony Horse," a story from The Arabian Nights tr. by Sir Richard Burton. ISBN 0-688-05898-1 Subj: Folk and fairy tales. Foreign lands. Magic. Royalty. Wizards.

There was Timmy! ill. by Beth Krush. Harcourt, 1957. Subj: Animals – dogs.

The three wonderful beggars ill. by author. Greenwillow, 1988. ISBN 0-688-06657-7 Subj: Careers – beggars. Folk and fairy tales.

Scott, William R. *This is the milk that Jack drank* adapt. from Mother Goose; ill. by Charles Green Shaw. Addison-Wesley, 1944. Subj: Cumulative tales.

Scribner, Charles. *The devil's bridge: a legend* retold by Charles Scribner, Jr.; ill. by Evaline Ness. Scribners, 1978. ISBN 0-684-15034-4 Subj: Devil. Folk and fairy tales. Foreign lands – France.

Hansel and Gretel (Grimm, Jacob)

Scruggs, Afi. *Jump rope magic* ill. by David Diaz. Blue Sky, 2000. ISBN 0-590-69327-1 Subj: Activities – jumping. Ethnic groups in the U.S. – African Americans. Games. Noise, sounds. Rhyming text.

Scruton, Clive. *Bubble and squeak* ill. by author. Random House, 1985. ISBN 0-394-87101-4 Subj: Animals – mice. Birds – ducks. Friendship.

Circus cow ill. by author. Random House, 1985. ISBN 0-394-87102-2 Subj: Animals – bulls, cows. Character traits – foolishness.

Mary's pets ill. by author. Lothrop, 1989. ISBN 0-688-08520-2 Subj: Animals. Format, unusual. Games. Pets. Rhyming text.

Pig in the air ill. by author. Random House, 1985. ISBN 0-394-87103-0 Subj: Activities – flying. Animals – pigs.

Scaredy cat ill. by author. Random House, 1985. ISBN 0-394-87014-X Subj: Animals – cats. Emotions – fear.

Scuderi, Lucia. *To fly* ill. by author. Kane/Miller, 1998. ISBN 0-916291-79-0 Subj: Activities – flying. Behavior – growing up. Birds. Family life. Format, unusual – toy and movable books.

Scullard, Sue. *Miss Fanshawe and the great dragon adventure* ill. by author. St. Martin's, 1987. ISBN 0-312-00510-5 Subj: Dragons. Format, unusual.

The Sea World alphabet book concept by Sally and Alan Sloan. Sea World Pr., 1979. ISBN 0-15-004037-7 Subj: ABC books. Sea and seashore.

Seabrook, Elizabeth. *Cabbages and kings* ill. by Jamie Wyeth. Viking, 1997. ISBN 0-670-87462-0 Subj: Friendship. Gardens, gardening. Plants.

Seabrooke, Brenda. *The best burglar alarm* ill. by Loretta Lustig. Morrow, 1978. ISBN 0-688-32165-8 Subj: Crime. Pets.

The swan's gift ill. by Wenhai Ma. Candlewick, 1995. ISBN 1-56402-360-5 Subj: Birds – swans. Family life. Farms. Folk and fairy tales. Food. Gifts. Poverty.

Seaside poems collected by Jill Bennett; ill. by Nick Sharratt. Oxford, 1998. ISBN 0-19-276173-0 Subj: Poetry. Sea and seashore.

Sedges, John. *see* Buck, Pearl S. (Pearl Sydenstricker)

See the dinosaurs ill. by Roma Bishop. Simon & Schuster, 1993. ISBN 0-671-88308-9 Subj: Dinosaurs. Format, unusual – toy and movable books.

Seeber, Dorothea P. *A pup just for me . . . A boy just for me* ill. by Ed Young. Philomel, 2000. ISBN 0-399-23403-9 Subj: Animals – dogs. Behavior – needing someone. Pets.

Seed, Jenny. *Ntombi's song* ill. by Anno Berry. Beacon, 1989. ISBN 0-8070-8318-6 Subj: Character traits – confidence. Foreign lands – South Africa.

Seeger, Charles Louis. *The foolish frog* (Seeger, Pete)

Seeger, Pete. *Abiyoyo* ill. by Michael Hays. Macmillan, 1986. ISBN 0-02-781490-4 Subj: Folk and fairy tales. Magic. Monsters.

The foolish frog by Pete Seeger and Charles Louis Seeger; ill. by Miloslav Jágr; adapt. and designed from Firebird Film by Gene Deitch. Macmillan, 1973. ISBN 0-02-781480-7 Subj: Cumulative tales. Folk and fairy tales. Frogs and toads. Music. Songs.

Segal, Lore. *All the way home* ill. by James Marshall. Farrar, 1973. Subj: Cumulative tales.

The bear and the kingbird (Grimm, Jacob)

The story of old Mrs. Brubeck and how she looked for trouble and where she found him ill. by Marcia Sewall. Pantheon, 1981. ISBN 0-394-94039-3 Subj: Behavior – worrying. Problem solving.

Tell me a Mitzi ill. by Harriet Pincus. Farrar, 1970. ISBN 0-374-37392-2 Subj: Family life. Jewish culture.

Tell me a Trudy ill. by Rosemary Wells. Farrar, 1977. ISBN 0-3743-7395-7 Subj: Family life. Jewish culture.

Segal, Sheila. *Joshua's dream* ill. by Jana Paiss. UAHC Pr., 1985. ISBN 0-8074-0272-9 Subj: Foreign lands – Israel. Jewish culture.

Seguin-Fontes, Marthe. *The cat's surprise* adapt. by Sandra Beris; ill. by author. Larousse, 1983. ISBN 0-88332-322-2 Subj: Animals – cats.

A wedding book adapt. by Sandra Beris; ill. by author. Larousse, 1983. ISBN 0-88332-321-4 Subj: Activities – photographing. Weddings.

Seibert, Patricia. *Mush! across Alaska in the world's longest sled-dog race* ill. by Jan Davey Ellis. Millbrook, 1992. ISBN 1-56294-705-2 Subj: Alaska. Animals – dogs. Sports – racing. Sports – sledding.

Seibold, J. Otto. *Mr. Lunch borrows a canoe* by J. Otto Seibold and Vivian Walsh; ill. by J. Otto Seibold. Viking, 1994. ISBN 0-670-85661-4 Subj: Animals – dogs. Boats, ships. Foreign lands – Italy.

Mr. Lunch takes a plane ride by J. Otto Seibold and Vivian Walsh; ill. by J. Otto Seibold. Viking, 1993. ISBN 0-670-84775-5 Subj: Activities – flying. Airplanes, airports. Transportation.

Penguin dreams by J. Otto Seibold and Vivian Walsh; ill. by J. Otto Seibold. Chronicle, 1999. ISBN 0-8118-2558-2 Subj: Activities – flying. Birds – penguins. Dreams. Foreign lands – Antarctic. Rhyming text.

Seiden, Art. *Trucks* ill. by Art Seiden. Platt, 1983. ISBN 0-448-40873-2 Subj: Trucks.

Seidler, Rosalie. *Grumpus and the Venetian cat* ill. by author. Atheneum, 1964. Subj: Animals – cats. Animals – mice. Birds. Foreign lands – Italy.

Seidler, Tor. *The steadfast tin soldier* (Andersen, H. C. [Hans Christian])

Seignobosc, Françoise. *The big rain* ill. by author. Scribners, 1961. Subj: Animals. Farms. Foreign lands – France. Weather – rain.

Biquette, the white goat ill. by author. Scribners, 1953. Subj: Animals – goats. Foreign lands – France. Illness.

Chouchou ill. by author. Scribners, 1958. Subj: Animals – donkeys. Foreign lands – France.

Jeanne-Marie at the fair ill. by author. Scribners, 1959. Subj: Fairs. Foreign lands – France.

Jeanne-Marie counts her sheep ill. by author. Scribners, 1951. Subj: Behavior – wishing. Counting, numbers. Foreign lands – France.

Jeanne-Marie in gay Paris ill. by author. Scribners, 1956. Subj: Character traits. Foreign lands – France.

Minou ill. by author. Scribners, 1962. Subj: Animals – cats. Behavior – lost. Foreign lands – France.

Noël for Jeanne-Marie ill. by author. Scribners, 1953. Subj: Foreign lands – France. Holidays – Christmas.

Small-Trot ill. by author. Scribners, 1952. Subj: Animals – mice. Circus.

Springtime for Jeanne-Marie ill. by author. Scribners, 1955. Subj: Animals – goats. Behavior – lost. Birds – ducks. Foreign lands – France. Seasons – spring.

The story of Colette ill. by author. Hale, 1940. Subj: Animals. Emotions – loneliness. Pets.

The thank-you book ill. by author. Scribners, 1947. Subj: Etiquette. Religion.

The things I like ill. by author. Scribners, 1960. Subj: Participation.

What do you want to be? ill. by author. Scribners, 1957. Subj: Careers. Character traits – ambition.

What time is it, Jeanne-Marie? ill. by author. Scribners, 1963. Subj: Time.

Seix, Victoria. *Cubs* (Landa, Norbert)

Puppies (Landa, Norbert)

Selberg, Ingrid. *Nature's hidden world* ill. by Andrew Miller. Putnam, 1984. ISBN 0-399-20973-5 Subj: Animals. Format, unusual – toy and movable books. Plants. Riddles. Science.

Selby, Jennifer. *Beach bunny* ill. by author. Harcourt, 1996. ISBN 0-15-200840-3 Subj: Animals – rabbits. Family life – mothers. Sea and seashore.

Selden, George. *The mice, the monks and the Christmas tree* ill. by Jan Balet. Macmillan, 1963. Subj: Animals – mice. Holidays – Christmas.

Sparrow socks ill. by Peter Lippman. HarperCollins, 1965. Subj: Birds – sparrows. Clothing – socks.

Selig, Sylvie. *Kangaroo* ill. by author. Merrimack, 1980. ISBN 0-224-01746-2 Subj: Animals – kangaroos. Wordless.

Ten what? a mystery counting book (Hoban, Russell)

Seligman, Dorothy Halle. *Run away home* ill. by Christine Hoffmann. Golden Gate, 1969. Subj: Behavior – running away. Family life.

Seligson, Susan. *The amazing Amos and the greatest couch on earth* by Susan Seligson and Howie Schneider; ill. by Howie Schneider. Little, 1989. ISBN 0-316-78033-2 Subj: Animals – dogs. Circus. Furniture – couches, sofas. Humor. Imagination.

Amos ahoy: a couch adventure on land and sea by Susan Seligson and Howie Schneider; ill. by Howie Schneider. Little, 1990. ISBN 0-316-77403-0 Subj: Animals – dogs. Furniture – couches, sofas. Imagination.

Amos camps out: a couch adventure in the woods by Susan Seligson and Howie Schneider; ill. by Howie Schneider. Little, 1992. ISBN 0-316-77402-2 Subj: Animals – dogs. Camps, camping. Forest, woods. Furniture – couches, sofas.

Amos: the story of an old dog and his couch by Susan Seligson and Howie Schneider; ill. by Howie Schneider. Little, 1987. ISBN 0-316-77404-9 Subj:

Animals – dogs. Furniture – couches, sofas. Humor. Imagination. Old age.

Selkowe, Valrie M. *Spring green* ill. by Jeni Bassett. Lothrop, 1985. ISBN 0-688-04056-X Subj: Animals. Concepts – color. Parties. Seasons – spring.

Sellers, Ronnie. *My first day at school* ill. by Patti Stren. Caedmon, 1985. ISBN 0-89845-373-9 Subj: Rhyming text. School – first day.

Selsam, Millicent E. *All kinds of babies* ill. by Symeon Shimin. Four Winds, 1967. Subj: Animals. Science.

Egg to chick ill. by Barbara Wolff. Rev. ed. Harper-Collins, 1970. ISBN 0-06-025290-1 Subj: Birds – chickens. Birth. Eggs. Science.

A first look at bird nests by Millicent E. Selsam and Joyce Hunt; ill. by Harriett Springer. Walker, 1985. ISBN 0-8027-6565-3 Subj: Birds. Science.

A first look at caterpillars by Millicent E. Selsam and Joyce Hunt; ill. by Harriett Springer. Walker, 1987. ISBN 0-8027-6702-8 Subj: Insects – butterflies, caterpillars. Metamorphosis. Science.

A first look at cats by Millicent E. Selsam and Joyce Hunt; ill. by Harriett Springer. Walker, 1981. ISBN 0-8027-6399-5 Subj: Animals – cats. Science.

A first look at dinosaurs by Millicent E. Selsam and Joyce Hunt; ill. by Harriett Springer. Walker, 1982. ISBN 0-8027-6456-8 Subj: Dinosaurs.

A first look at dogs by Millicent E. Selsam and Joyce Hunt; ill. by Harriett Springer. Walker, 1981. ISBN 0-8027-6409-6 Subj: Animals – dogs. Animals – foxes. Animals – wolves.

A first look at flowers by Millicent E. Selsam and Joyce Hunt; ill. by Harriett Springer. Walker, 1977. ISBN 0-8027-6282-4 Subj: Flowers. Science.

A first look at kangaroos, koalas and other animals with pouches by Millicent E. Selsam and Joyce Hunt; ill. by Harriett Springer. Walker, 1985. ISBN 0-8027-6579-3 Subj: Animals. Science.

A first look at monkeys by Millicent E. Selsam and Joyce Hunt; ill. by Harriett Springer. Walker, 1979. ISBN 0-8027-6359-6 Subj: Animals – gorillas. Animals – monkeys. Science.

A first look at owls, eagles and other hunters of the sky by Millicent E. Selsam and Joyce Hunt; ill. by Harriett Springer. Walker, 1986. ISBN 0-8027-6642-0 Subj: Birds. Science.

A first look at rocks by Millicent E. Selsam and Joyce Hunt; ill. by Harriett Springer. Walker, 1984. ISBN 0-8027-6531-9 Subj: Rocks. Science.

A first look at seashells by Millicent E. Selsam and Joyce Hunt; ill. by Harriett Springer. Walker, 1983. ISBN 0-8027-6503-3 Subj: Animals. Science. Sea and seashore.

A first look at sharks by Millicent E. Selsam and Joyce Hunt; ill. by Harriett Springer. Walker, 1979. ISBN 0-8027-6373-1 Subj: Fish – sharks. Science.

A first look at spiders by Millicent E. Selsam and Joyce Hunt; ill. by Harriett Springer. Walker, 1983. ISBN 0-8027-6481-9 Subj: Science. Spiders.

A first look at the world of plants by Millicent E. Selsam and Joyce Hunt; ill. by Harriett Springer. Walker, 1978. ISBN 0-8027-6299-9 Subj: Plants. Science.

A first look at whales by Millicent E. Selsam and Joyce Hunt; ill. by Harriett Springer. Walker, 1980. ISBN 0-8027-6388-X Subj: Animals – whales. Science.

Hidden animals ill. by David Shapiro. Harper-Collins, 1969. First pub. in 1947. ISBN 0-06-025282-0 Subj: Animals.

How kittens grow photos by Esther Bubley. Four Winds, 1975. ISBN 0-590-07409-1 Subj: Animals – cats. Science.

How puppies grow photos by Esther Bubley. Four Winds, 1971. Subj: Animals – dogs. Science.

How to be a nature detective ill. by Marlene Hill Donnelly. HarperCollins, 1995. ISBN 0-06-023448-2 Subj: Animals. Nature.

Is this a baby dinosaur? and other science picture puzzles ill. with photos. HarperCollins, 1972. ISBN 0-06-025303-7 Subj: Games. Science.

Keep looking! by Millicent E. Selsam and Joyce Hunt; ill. by Normand Chartier. Macmillan, 1988. ISBN 0-02-781840-3 Subj: Animals. Farms. Seasons – winter.

More potatoes! ill. by Ben Shecter. HarperCollins, 1972. ISBN 0-06-025323-1 Subj: Farms. Plants. School. Science.

Night animals ill. with photos. Four Winds, 1980. ISBN 0-590-07755-4 Subj: Animals. Night.

Sea monsters of long ago ill. by John Hamberger. Four Winds, 1978. ISBN 0-590-07567-5 Subj: Monsters. Sea and seashore.

Seeds and more seeds ill. by Tomi Ungerer. Harper-Collins, 1959. Subj: Plants. Science. Seeds.

Where do they go? Insects in winter ill. by Arabelle Wheatley. Scholastic, 1984. ISBN 0-02-778080-5 Subj: Insects. Science. Seasons – winter.

Selway, Martina. *Don't forget to write* ill. by author. Ideals, 1992. ISBN 0-8249-8543-5 Subj: Emotions. Family life – aunts, uncles. Family life – grandfathers. Farms. Letters, cards.

Greedyguts ill. by author. Hutchinson, 1990. ISBN 0-09-174151-3 Subj: Behavior – greed. Giants.

Selzer, Meyer. *Here comes the recycling truck!* photos by author. Albert Whitman, 1992. ISBN 0-8075-3235-5 Subj: Ecology. Trucks.

Seminario, José R. *This troll, that troll* (Inkpen, Mick)

Sendak, Maurice. *Alligators all around: an alphabet* ill. by author. HarperCollins, 1962. ISBN 0-06-

025530-7 Subj: ABC books. Reptiles – alligators, crocodiles.

Chicken soup with rice ill. by author. Harper-Collins, 1962. ISBN 0-06-025535-8 Subj: Days of the week, months of the year.

Hector Protector, and As I went over the water: two nursery rhymes ill. by author. HarperCollins, 1965. ISBN 0-06-025486-6 Subj: Nursery rhymes.

In the night kitchen ill. by author. HarperCollins, 1970. ISBN 0-06-026669-4 Subj: Caldecott award honor books. Dreams. Imagination.

The jester has lost his jingle (Saltzman, David)

Maurice Sendak's Really Rosie: starring the Nutshell Kids ill. by author; music by Carole King; design by Jane Byers Bierhorst. HarperCollins, 1976. ISBN 0-06-025537-4 Subj: Activities – playing. Music. Theater.

One was Johnny: a counting book ill. by author. HarperCollins, 1962. ISBN 0-06-025540-4 Subj: Counting, numbers.

Outside over there ill. by author. HarperCollins, 1981. ISBN 0-06-025524-2 Subj: Activities – babysitting. Babies. Caldecott award honor books. Mythical creatures – goblins.

Pierre: a cautionary tale in five chapters and a prologue ill. by author. HarperCollins, 1962. ISBN 0-06-118009-2 Subj: Behavior – indifference. Character traits – individuality. Humor. Rhyming text.

Seven little monsters ill. by author. HarperCollins, 1977. ISBN 0-06-025478-5 Subj: Counting, numbers. Monsters. Rhyming text.

The sign on Rosie's door ill. by author. Harper-Collins, 1960. ISBN 0-06-025506-4 Subj: Activities – playing. Imagination.

Some swell pup: or Are you sure you want a dog? by Maurice Sendak and Matthew Margolis; ill. by Maurice Sendak. Farrar, 1976. ISBN 0-374-46963-6 Subj: Animals – dogs. Pets.

Very far away ill. by author. HarperCollins, 1957. ISBN 0-06-025515-3 Subj: Animals. Behavior – needing someone. Behavior – running away.

Where the wild things are ill. by author. Harper-Collins, 1963. ISBN 0-06-025521-8 Subj: Behavior – misbehavior. Caldecott award books. Imagination. Monsters.

Senisi, Ellen B. *For my family, Love, Allie* photos by author. Albert Whitman, 1998. ISBN 0-8075-2539-1 Subj: Family life. Food. Marriage, interracial.

Hurray for pre-K! photos by author. Harper-Collins, 2000. ISBN 0-06-028897-3 Subj: Activities. Emotions. School.

Just kids: visiting a class for children with special needs ill. by author. Dutton, 1998. ISBN 0-525-45646-5 Subj: Handicaps. School.

Kindergarten kids ill. by author. Cartwheel, 1994. ISBN 0-590-47614-9 Subj: School.

Secrets ill. by author. Dutton, 1995. ISBN 0-525-45393-8 Subj: Behavior – secrets.

Serfozo, Mary. *Dirty Kurt* ill. by Nancy Poydar. Macmillan, 1992. ISBN 0-689-50537-X Subj: Behavior – carelessness. Character traits – cleanliness. Rhyming text.

Rain talk ill. by Keiko Narahashi. Macmillan, 1990. ISBN 0-689-50496-9 Subj: Noise, sounds. Weather – rain.

There's a square ill. by David A. Carter. Scholastic, 1996. ISBN 0-590-54426-8 Subj: Concepts – shape. Rhyming text.

Welcome Roberto! Bienvenido, Roberto! ill. by John Serfozo. Follett, 1969. ISBN 0-695-89225-8 Subj: Ethnic groups in the U.S. – Mexican Americans. Foreign languages.

What's what? a guessing game ill. by Keiko Narahashi. Margaret K. McElderry, 1996. ISBN 0-689-80653-1 Subj: Animals – dogs. Concepts – opposites. Ethnic groups in the U.S. – African Americans. Language.

Who said red? ill. by Keiko Narahashi. Macmillan, 1988. ISBN 0-689-50455-1 Subj: Concepts – color.

Who wants one? ill. by Keiko Narahashi. Macmillan, 1989. ISBN 0-689-50474-8 Subj: Counting, numbers. Rhyming text.

Serraillier, Anne. *Florina and the wild bird* (Chönz, Selina)

Serraillier, Ian. *Florina and the wild bird* (Chönz, Selina)

Suppose you met a witch ill. by Ed Emberley. Little, 1973. ISBN 0-316-78125-8 Subj: Rhyming text. Witches.

Service, Pamela F. *The wizard of wind and rock* ill. by Laura Marshall. Macmillan, 1990. ISBN 0-689-31600-3 Subj: Folk and fairy tales. Foreign lands – England. Wizards.

Sesame Street. *Ernie and Bert can . . . can you?* ill. by Michael J. Smollin. Random House, 1982. ISBN 0-394-85150-1 Subj: Format, unusual – board books. Puppets.

The Sesame Street book of letters created in cooperation with the Children's Television Workshop, producers of Sesame Street. Designed by Charles I. Miller and James J. Harvin. Preschool Pr., 1970. Subj: ABC books.

The Sesame Street book of numbers created in cooperation with the Children's Television Workshop, producers of Sesame Street. Designed by Charles I. Miller and James J. Harvin. Preschool Pr., 1970. Subj: Counting, numbers.

The Sesame Street book of people and things created in cooperation with the Children's Television Workshop, producers of Sesame Street. Designed by Charles I. Miller and James J. Harvin. Preschool Pr., 1970. Subj: Careers. Concepts. Emotions.

The Sesame Street book of shapes created in cooperation with the Children's Television Workshop, producers of Sesame Street. Designed by Charles I. Miller and James J. Harvin. Preschool Pr., 1970. Subj: Concepts – shape.

Sesame Street sign language fun ill. with photos. Random House, 1980. ISBN 0-394-94212-4 Subj: Language. Puppets.

Sesame Street word book ill. by Tom Leigh. Golden Pr., 1983. ISBN 0-307-65549-0 Subj: Language. Puppets.

Seuling, Barbara. *The teeny tiny woman: an old English ghost tale* ill. by author. Viking, 1976. ISBN 0-670-69505-X Subj: Folk and fairy tales. Foreign lands – England. Ghosts.

The triplets ill. by author. Houghton Mifflin, 1980. ISBN 0-395-29107-0 Subj: Character traits – individuality. Multiple births – triplets.

What kind of family is this? a book about step families ill. by Ellen Dolce. Childrens Pr., 1985. ISBN 0-307-62482-X Subj: Family life. Family life – step families. Sibling rivalry.

Winter lullaby ill. by Greg Newbold. Browndeer, 1997. ISBN 0-15-201403-9 Subj: Animals. Seasons – winter.

Seuss, Dr. *And to think that I saw it on Mulberry Street* ill. by author. Random House, 1989, c1937. ISBN 0-394-94494-1 Subj: Humor. Imagination. Rhyming text.

Bartholomew and the Oobleck ill. by author. Random House, 1949. ISBN 0-394-90075-8 Subj: Caldecott award honor books. Humor. Royalty.

The butter battle book ill. by author. Random House, 1984. ISBN 0-394-96580-9 Subj: Rhyming text. War.

The cat in the hat ill. by author. Random House, 1957. ISBN 0-394-90001-4 Subj: Animals – cats. Humor. Rhyming text.

The cat in the hat comes back! ill. by author. Random House, 1958. ISBN 0-394-90002-2 Subj: Animals – cats. Humor. Rhyming text.

The cat in the hat dictionary by the Cat himself and P. D. Eastman; ill. by Dr. Seuss. Random House, 1964. ISBN 0-394-91009-5 Subj: Dictionaries. Humor.

The cat's quizzer ill. by author. Random House, 1976. ISBN 0-394-93296-X Subj: Humor. Rhyming text. Riddles.

Come over to my house by Theo LeSeig; ill. by Richard Erdoes. Random House, 1966. ISBN 0-394-90044-8 Subj: Homes, houses. Rhyming text.

Did I ever tell you how high you can count? (Hayward, Linda)

Did I ever tell you how lucky you are? ill. by Richard Erdoes. Random House, 1973. ISBN 0-394-92719-2 Subj: Character traits – luck. Humor. Problem solving. Rhyming text.

Dr. Seuss's ABC ill. by author. Random House, 1963. ISBN 0-394-90030-8 Subj: ABC books. Humor. Rhyming text.

Dr. Seuss's sleep book ill. by author. Random House, 1962. ISBN 0-394-90091-X Subj: Humor. Rhyming text. Sleep.

The eye book ill. by Roy McKié. Random House, 1968. ISBN 0-394-91094-X Subj: Anatomy – eyes. Animals – rabbits. Rhyming text.

The foot book ill. by author. Random House, 1968. ISBN 0-394-90937-2 Subj: Anatomy – feet. Humor. Rhyming text.

Fox in socks ill. by author. Random House, 1965. ISBN 0-394-90038-3 Subj: Humor. Rhyming text.

Gerald McBoing Boing ill. by author; ed. by Kate Klimo. Random House, 2000. ISBN 0-679-99140-9 Subj: Communication. Concepts. Humor. Noise, sounds. Rhyming text. Senses.

A great day for up ill. by Quentin Blake. Random House, 1974. ISBN 0-394-92913-6 Subj: Concepts – up and down. Humor. Rhyming text.

Green eggs and ham ill. by author. Random House, 1960. ISBN 0-394-90016-2 Subj: Cumulative tales. Food. Humor. Rhyming text.

Happy birthday to you! ill. by author. Random House, 1959. ISBN 0-394-90076-6 Subj: Birthdays. Humor. Rhyming text.

Hooper Humperdink . . . ? Not him! ill. by Charles E. Martin. Random House, 1976. ISBN 0-394-93286-2 Subj: ABC books. Birthdays. Humor. Rhyming text.

Hop on Pop ill. by author. Random House, 1963. ISBN 0-394-90029-4 Subj: Humor. Rhyming text.

Horton hatches the egg ill. by author. Random House, 1940. ISBN 0-394-90077-4 Subj: Animals – elephants. Birds. Character traits – helpfulness. Eggs. Humor. Rhyming text.

Horton hears a Who! ill. by author. Random House, 1954. ISBN 0-394-90078-2 Subj: Animals – elephants. Character traits – kindness. Humor. Rhyming text.

How the Grinch stole Christmas ill. by author. Random House, 1957. ISBN 0-394-90079-0 Subj: Character traits – meanness. Holidays – Christmas. Humor. Rhyming text.

Hunches in bunches ill. by author. Random House, 1982. ISBN 0-394-95502-1 Subj: Problem solving. Rhyming text.

I am not going to get up today! ill. by James Stevenson. Random House, 1987. ISBN 0-394-99217-2 Subj: Humor. Rhyming text. Sleep.

I can add upside down! (Hayward, Linda)

I can draw it myself: by me, myself, with a little help from my friend Dr. Seuss ill. by author. Random House, 1987. ISBN 0-394-08009-7 Subj: Art. Character traits – individuality.

I can lick 30 tigers today and other stories ill. by author. Random House, 1969. ISBN 0-394-90094-X Subj: Animals – tigers. Humor. Rhyming text.

I can read with my eyes shut ill. by author. Random House, 1978. ISBN 0-394-93912-3 Subj: Activities – reading. Humor. Rhyming text.

I can write! a book by me, myself, with a little help from Theo LeSeig and Roy McKié ill. by Roy McKié. Random House, 1971. ISBN 0-679-84700-6 Subj: Activities – writing. Humor. Rhyming text.

I had trouble getting to Solla Sollew ill. by author. Random House, 1965. Subj: Activities – traveling. Humor. Rhyming text.

I wish that I had duck feet ill. by Barney Tobey. Random House, 1965. ISBN 0-394-90040-5 Subj: Behavior – wishing. Rhyming text.

If I ran the circus ill. by author. Random House, 1956. ISBN 0-394-90080-4 Subj: Circus. Humor. Rhyming text.

If I ran the zoo ill. by author. Random House, 1950. ISBN 0-394-90081-2 Subj: Caldecott award honor books. Humor. Rhyming text. Zoos.

In a people house ill. by Roy McKié. Random House, 1972. ISBN 0-394-92395-2 Subj: Homes, houses. Humor. Rhyming text.

The king's stilts ill. by author. Random House, 1939. ISBN 0-394-90082-0 Subj: Humor. Rhyming text. Royalty – kings. Toys.

The Lorax ill. by author. Random House, 1971. ISBN 0-394-92337-5 Subj: Ecology. Humor.

McElligot's pool ill. by author. Random House, 1947. ISBN 0-394-90083-9 Subj: Caldecott award honor books. Fish. Humor. Imagination. Rhyming text.

Marvin K. Mooney, will you please go now! ill. by author. Random House, 1972. ISBN 0-394-92490-8 Subj: Humor. Rhyming text.

Mr. Brown can moo! Can you? ill. by author. Random House, 1970. ISBN 0-394-80622-0 Subj: Animals. Humor. Noise, sounds. Participation. Rhyming text.

Oh say can you say? ill. by author. Random House, 1979. ISBN 0-394-94255-8 Subj: Humor. Imagination. Rhyming text.

Oh, the places you'll go! ill. by author. Random House, 1990. ISBN 0-679-90527-8 Subj: Self-concept.

Oh, the things you can count from 1-10 (Hayward, Linda)

Oh, the thinks you can think! ill. by author. Random House, 1975. ISBN 0-394-93129-7 Subj: Humor. Imagination. Rhyming text.

On beyond zebra ill. by author. Random House, 1955. ISBN 0-394-90084-7 Subj: Humor. Letters, cards. Rhyming text.

One fish, two fish, red fish, blue fish ill. by author. Random House, 1960. ISBN 0-606-04238-5 Subj: Fish. Humor. Rhyming text.

Please try to remember the first of Octember! ill. by Art Cumings. Random House, 1977. ISBN 0-394-93563-2 Subj: Behavior – wishing. Humor. Memories, memory. Rhyming text.

Scrambled eggs super! ill. by author. Random House, 1953. ISBN 0-394-90085-5 Subj: Food. Humor. Rhyming text.

The shape of me and other stuff ill. by author. Random House, 1973. ISBN 0-394-92687-0 Subj: Concepts – shape. Humor. Rhyming text.

The Sneetches, and other stories ill. by author. Random House, 1961. ISBN 0-394-90089-8 Subj: Emotions – fear. Humor. Rhyming text.

Ten apples up on top by Theo LeSieg; ill. by Roy McKié. Random House, 1961. ISBN 0-394-90019-7 Subj: Counting, numbers.

There's a wocket in my pocket ill. by author. Random House, 1974. ISBN 0-394-92920-9 Subj: Humor. Rhyming text.

Thidwick, the big-hearted moose ill. by author. Random House, 1948. ISBN 0-394-90086-3 Subj: Animals – moose. Birds. Humor. Rhyming text.

The tooth book ill. by Roy McKié. Random House, 1981. ISBN 0-394-94825-4 Subj: Health and fitness. Rhyming text. Teeth.

Wacky Wednesday ill. by George Booth. Random House, 1974. ISBN 0-394-92912-8 Subj: Humor. Participation. Rhyming text.

Wet foot, dry foot, low foot, high foot (Hayward, Linda)

Would you rather be a bullfrog? ill. by Roy McKié. Random House, 1975. ISBN 0-394-93128-9 Subj: Animals. Character traits – optimism. Frogs and toads.

Severn, Jeffrey. *George and his giant shadow* ill. by author. Chronicle, 1990. ISBN 0-87701-634-8 Subj: Animals. Shadows.

Severo, Emöke de Papp. *The good-hearted youngest brother: an Hungarian folktale* (The good-hearted youngest brother)

Sewall, Marcia. *Animal song* ill. by author. Little, 1988. ISBN 0-316-78191-6 Subj: Animals. Folk and fairy tales. Songs.

The cobbler's song ill. by author. Dutton, 1982. ISBN 0-525-44005-4 Subj: Behavior – worrying.

The Green Mist ill. by adapt. Houghton Mifflin, 1999. ISBN 0-395-90013-1 Subj: Folk and fairy tales. Foreign lands – England. Seasons – spring. Superstition.

The little wee tyke: an English folktale ill. by author. Atheneum, 1979. ISBN 0-689-30724-1 Subj: Animals – dogs. Folk and fairy tales. Foreign lands – England.

Ridin' that strawberry roan ill. by adapt. Viking, 1985. ISBN 0-670-80623-4 Subj: Animals – horses, ponies. Cowboys. Rhyming text. U.S. history – frontier and pioneer life.

The wee, wee mannie and the big, big coo: a Scottish folk tale ill. by author. Little, 1977. ISBN 0-316-78180-0 Subj: Animals – bulls, cows. Folk and fairy tales. Foreign lands – Scotland.

Sewell, Helen Moore. *Birthdays for Robin* ill. by author. Macmillan, 1943. Subj: Animals – dogs. Birthdays.

Blue barns ill. by author. Macmillan, 1933. Subj: Barns. Birds – ducks. Birds – geese. Farms.

Jimmy and Jemima ill. by author. Macmillan, 1940. Subj: Character traits – bravery. Sibling rivalry.

Ming and Mehitable ill. by author. Macmillan, 1936. Subj: Animals – dogs.

Peggy and the pony ill. by author. Oxford Univ. Pr., 1936. Subj: Animals – horses, ponies. Behavior – wishing.

Sexton, Anne. *Joey and the birthday present* (Kumin, Maxine W.)

Sexton, Gwain. *There once was a king* ill. by author. Scribners, 1959. Subj: Rhyming text. Royalty – kings.

Seymour, Dorothy Z. *The tent* ill. by Nancé Holman. Grosset, 1965. Subj: Cumulative tales.

Seymour, Peter S. *Animals in disguise* ill. by Jean Cassels Helmer. Macmillan, 1985. ISBN 0-02-782160-9 Subj: Animals. Format, unusual – toy and movable books.

How the weather works ill. by Sally Springer. Macmillan, 1984. ISBN 0-02-782110-2 Subj: Format, unusual – toy and movable books. Science. Weather.

Insects: a close-up look ill. by Jean Cassels Helmer. Macmillan, 1985. ISBN 0-02-782120-X Subj: Format, unusual – toy and movable books. Insects.

Pilots ill. by Norm Ingersoll. Lodestar, 1992. ISBN 0-525-67372-5 Subj: Airplanes, airports. Careers – airplane pilots. Format, unusual – toy and movable books.

The pop-up book of big trucks ill. by Chuck Murphy. Little, 1989. ISBN 0-316-78197-5 Subj: Format, unusual – toy and movable books. Trucks.

What lives in the sea? ill. by Pamela Johnson. Macmillan, 1985. ISBN 0-02-782170-6 Subj: Format, unusual – toy and movable books. Sea and seashore.

What's at the beach? ill. by David A. Carter. Holt, 1985. ISBN 0-03-002557-5 Subj: Monsters. Nature. Sea and seashore.

What's in the deep blue sea? ill. by David A. Carter. Holt, 1990. ISBN 0-8050-1449-7 Subj: Format, unusual – toy and movable books. Science. Sea and seashore.

What's in the prehistoric forest? ill. by David A. Carter. Holt, 1990. ISBN 0-8050-1450-0 Subj: Forest, woods. Format, unusual – toy and movable books. Science.

Seymour, Tres. *The gulls of the Edmund Fitzgerald* ill. by author. Orchard, 1996. ISBN 0-531-08859-6 Subj: Birds. Boats, ships. Lakes, ponds.

I love my buzzard ill. by S. D. Schindler. Orchard, 1994. ISBN 0-531-08669-0 Subj: Animals. Family life – mothers. Pets. Rhyming text.

Too quiet for these old bones ill. by Paul Brett Johnson. Orchard, 1997. ISBN 0-531-33052-4 Subj: Behavior – boredom. Family life – grandmothers. Noise, sounds. Rhyming text.

We played marbles ill. by Dan Andreasen. Orchard, 1998. ISBN 0-531-33074-5 Subj: Games. U.S. history. War.

Seyton, Marion. *The hole in the hill* ill. by Leonard W. Shortall. Follett, 1960. Subj: Cavemen. Family life.

Shakespeare, William. *Hamlet for kids* (Burdett, Lois)

Macbeth for kids (Burdett, Lois)

A midsummer night's dream for kids (Burdett, Lois)

Romeo and Juliet for kids (Burdett, Lois)

The tempest for kids (Burdett, Lois)

Twelfth night (Burdett, Lois)

Shalev, Meir. *My father always embarrasses me* trans. by Dagmar Herrmann; ill. by Yossi Abolafia. Wellington, 1990. ISBN 0-922984-02-6 Subj: Emotions – embarrassment. Family life – fathers.

Shalleck, Alan J. *Curious George and the dinosaur* (Curious George and the dinosaur)

Curious George goes to an ice cream shop (Curious George goes to an ice cream shop)

Curious George goes to school (Curious George goes to school)

Curious George goes to the dentist (Curious George goes to the dentist)

Shange, Ntozake. *Whitewash* ill. by Michael Sporn. Walker, 1997. ISBN 0-8027-8491-7 Subj: Ethnic groups in the U.S. – African Americans. Prejudice.

Shank, Ned. *The sanyasin's first day* ill. by Catherine Stock. Cavendish, 1998. ISBN 0-7614-5055-6 Subj: Careers. Foreign lands – India.

Shannon, David. *The amazing Christmas extravaganza* ill. by author. Blue Sky, 1995. ISBN 0-590-48090-1 Subj: Emotions – anger. Holidays – Christmas.

A bad case of stripes ill. by author. Blue Sky, 1998. ISBN 0-590-92997-6 Subj: Behavior. Character traits – individuality.

David goes to school ill. by author. Blue Sky, 1999. ISBN 0-590-48087-1 Subj: Behavior – misbehavior. School.

No, David! ill. by author. Blue Sky, 1998. ISBN 0-590-93002-8 Subj: Behavior – misbehavior. Caldecott award honor books.

The rain came down ill. by author. Blue Sky, 2000. ISBN 0-439-05021-9 Subj: Behavior. Behavior – misunderstanding. Weather – rain. Weather – rainbows.

Shannon, George. *April showers* ill. by José Aruego and Ariane Dewey. Greenwillow, 1995. ISBN 0-688-13122-0 Subj: Activities – dancing. Frogs and toads. Weather – rain.

Beanboy ill. by Peter Sis. Greenwillow, 1984. ISBN 0-688-03780-1 Subj: City. Cumulative tales. Humor.

Dancing the breeze ill. by Jacqueline Rogers. Macmillan, 1991. ISBN 0-02-782190-0 Subj: Activities – dancing. Family life – fathers. Flowers. Poetry.

Frog legs: a picture book of action verse ill. by Amit Trynan. Greenwillow, 2000. ISBN 0-688-17047-1 Subj: Frogs and toads. Poetry.

Heart to heart ill. by Steve Björkman. Houghton Mifflin, 1995. ISBN 0-395-72773-1 Subj: Animals – moles. Animals – squirrels. Friendship. Holidays – Valentine's Day.

Laughing all the way ill. by Meg McLean. Houghton Mifflin, 1992. ISBN 0-395-62473-8 Subj: Animals – bears. Behavior – bad day. Birds – ducks. Character traits – cleverness.

Lizard's home ill. by José Aruego and Ariane Dewey. Greenwillow, 1999. ISBN 0-688-16003-4 Subj: Character traits – cleverness. Homes, houses. Reptiles – lizards. Reptiles – snakes.

Lizard's song ill. by José Aruego and Ariane Dewey. Greenwillow, 1981. ISBN 0-688-84310-7 Subj: Animals – bears. Reptiles – lizards. Songs.

Oh, I love! ill. by Cheryl Harness. Bradbury, 1988. ISBN 0-02-782180-3 Subj: Cumulative tales. Folk and fairy tales. Poetry. Songs.

The Piney Woods peddler ill. by Nancy Tafuri. Greenwillow, 1982. ISBN 0-688-84304-2 Subj: Activities – trading. Folk and fairy tales.

Spring: a haiku story ill. by Malcah Zeldis. Greenwillow, 1996. ISBN 0-688-13889-6 Subj: Foreign lands – Japan. Poetry. Seasons – spring.

The surprise ill. by José Aruego and Ariane Dewey. Greenwillow, 1983. ISBN 0-688-02314-2 Subj: Animals – squirrels. Birthdays.

Tomorrow's alphabet ill. by Donald Crews. Greenwillow, 1995. ISBN 0-688-13505-6 Subj: ABC books. Concepts.

Shannon, Margaret. *Gullible's troubles* ill. by author. Houghton Mifflin, 1998. ISBN 0-395-83933-5 Subj: Animals – guinea pigs. Behavior – trickery. Family life. Monsters.

Shannon, Mark. *The acrobat and the angel* ill. by David Shannon. Putnam, 1999. ISBN 0-399-22918-3 Subj: Angels. Folk and fairy tales. Foreign lands – France. Illness. Middle Ages.

Gawain and the Green Knight ill. by David Shannon. Putnam, 1994. ISBN 0-399-22446-7 Subj: Folk and fairy tales. Foreign lands – England. Knights. Middle Ages. Monsters.

Shapes: *with Dib, Dab, and Dob.* DK, 1998. ISBN 0-7894-2913-6 Subj: Birds – ducks. Concepts – shape.

Shapiro, Arnold L. *Circle* ill. by Bari Weissman. Dial, 1992. ISBN 0-8037-1144-1 Subj: Concepts – shape. Format, unusual – toy and movable books.

Square ill. by Bari Weissman. Dial, 1992. ISBN 0-8037-1146-8 Subj: Activities – picnicking. Concepts – shape. Format, unusual – toy and movable books.

Triangles ill. by Bari Weissman. Dial, 1992. ISBN 0-8037-1147-6 Subj: Concepts – shape. Format, unusual – toy and movable books.

Who says that? ill. by Monica Wellington. Dutton, 1991. ISBN 0-525-44698-2 Subj: Animals. Noise, sounds. Rhyming text.

Shapp, Charles. *Let's find out about babies* (Shapp, Martha)

Let's find out about houses (Shapp, Martha)

Let's find out what's big and what's small (Shapp, Martha)

Shapp, Martha. *Let's find out about babies* by Martha and Charles Shapp and Sylvia Shepard; ill. by Jenny Williams. Watts, 1975. ISBN 0-531-00087-7 Subj: Babies. Science.

Let's find out about houses by Martha and Charles Shapp; ill. by Tomie de Paola. Watts, 1975. ISBN 0-531-00026-5 Subj: Homes, houses.

Let's find out what's big and what's small by Martha and Charles Shapp; ill. by Carol Nicklaus. Watts, 1975. ISBN 0-531-00005-2 Subj: Concepts – size.

Sharkey, Niamh. *The gigantic turnip* (Tolstoy, Aleksey Nikolayevich)

Sharmat, Andrew. *Smedge* ill. by Chris L. Demarest. Macmillan, 1989. ISBN 0-02-782261-3 Subj: Animals – dogs.

Sharmat, Marjorie Weinman. *Attila the angry* ill. by Lillian Hoban. Holiday, 1985. ISBN 0-8234-0545-1 Subj: Animals – squirrels. Emotions – anger.

Bartholomew the bossy ill. by Normand Chartier. Macmillan, 1984. ISBN 0-02-782520-5 Subj: Animals. Behavior – growing up. Friendship.

The best Valentine in the world ill. by Lilian Obligado. Holiday, 1982. ISBN 0-8234-0440-4 Subj: Animals – foxes. Holidays – Valentine's Day.

A big fat enormous lie ill. by David McPhail. Dutton, 1978. ISBN 0-525-26510-4 Subj: Behavior – lying.

Burton and Dudley ill. by Barbara Cooney. Holiday, 1975. ISBN 0-8234-0260-6 Subj: Activities – walking. Character traits – laziness. Friendship.

Gila monsters meet you at the airport ill. by Byron Barton. Macmillan, 1980. ISBN 0-02-782450-0 Subj: Behavior – misunderstanding. Moving.

Gladys told me to meet her here ill. by Edward Frascino. HarperCollins, 1970. ISBN 0-06-025550-1 Subj: Friendship.

Go to sleep, Nicholas Joe ill. by John Himmelman. HarperCollins, 1988. ISBN 0-06-025504-8 Subj: Bedtime. Family life.

Goodnight, Andrew. Goodnight, Craig ill. by Mary Chalmers. HarperCollins, 1969. Subj: Bedtime. Family life.

Grumley the grouch ill. by Kay Chorao. Holiday, 1980. ISBN 0-8234-0410-2 Subj: Behavior – dissatisfaction.

Helga high-up ill. by David Neuhaus. Scholastic, 1988. ISBN 0-590-40692-2 Subj: Anatomy. Animals – giraffes. Character traits – being different.

Hooray for Father's Day! ill. by John Wallner. Holiday, 1987. ISBN 0-8234-0637-7 Subj: Animals – mules. Holidays – Father's Day.

Hooray for Mother's Day! ill. by John Wallner. Holiday, 1986. ISBN 0-8234-0588-5 Subj: Birds – chickens. Holidays – Mother's Day.

I don't care ill. by Lillian Hoban. Macmillan, 1977. ISBN 0-02-782290-7 Subj: Behavior – indifference. Emotions – sadness. Ethnic groups in the U.S. – African Americans. Toys – balloons.

I want mama ill. by Emily Arnold McCully. HarperCollins, 1974. ISBN 0-06-025554-4 Subj: Family life – only child. Illness.

I'm not Oscar's friend any more ill. by Tony DeLuna. Dutton, 1975. Subj: Behavior – fighting, arguing. Emotions – anger. Friendship.

I'm Santa Claus and I'm famous ill. by Marylin Hafner. Holiday, 1990. ISBN 0-8234-0826-4 Subj: Careers. Holidays – Christmas. Santa Claus.

I'm terrific ill. by Kay Chorao. Holiday, 1977. ISBN 0-8234-0282-7 Subj: Animals – bears. Character traits – conceit. Character traits – pride. Self-concept.

I'm the best ill. by Will Hillenbrand. Holiday, 1991. ISBN 0-8234-0859-0 Subj: Animals – dogs. Pets.

Lucretia the unbearable ill. by Janet Stevens. Holiday, 1981. ISBN 0-8234-0395-5 Subj: Animals – bears. Behavior – worrying. Health and fitness.

Mitchell is moving ill. by José Aruego and Ariane Dewey. Macmillan, 1978. ISBN 0-02-782410-1 Subj: Dinosaurs. Friendship. Moving.

Mooch the messy ill. by Ben Shecter. HarperCollins, 1976. ISBN 0-06-025532-3 Subj: Animals – rats. Character traits – cleanliness.

My mother never listens to me ed. by Kathleen Tucker; ill. by Lynn Munsinger. Albert Whitman, 1984. ISBN 0-8075-5347-6 Subj: Activities – reading. Family life – mothers. Imagination.

Nate the Great ill. by Marc Simont. Coward, 1972. ISBN 0-698-30444-6 Subj: Careers – detectives. Food. Mystery stories.

Nate the Great and the fishy prize ill. by Marc Simont. Coward, 1985. ISBN 0-698-30745-3 Subj: Animals – dogs. Mystery stories. Pets.

Nate the Great and the lost list ill. by Marc Simont. Coward, 1975. ISBN 0-698-30593-0 Subj: Careers – detectives. Food. Mystery stories.

Nate the Great and the phony clue ill. by Marc Simont. Coward, 1977. ISBN 0-698-30650-3 Subj: Careers – detectives. Food. Mystery stories.

Nate the Great goes undercover ill. by Marc Simont. Coward, 1974. ISBN 0-698-30547-7 Subj: Careers – detectives. Food. Mystery stories.

The pizza monster by Marjorie and Mitchell Sharmat; ill. by Denise Brunkus. Delacorte, 1989. ISBN 0-385-29722-X Subj: Friendship. Monsters. Problem solving.

Rex ill. by Emily Arnold McCully. HarperCollins, 1967. Subj: Behavior – running away.

Rollo and Juliet . . . forever! ill. by Marylin Hafner. Doubleday, 1981. ISBN 0-385-15785-1 Subj: Behavior – fighting, arguing. Emotions – anger. Friendship.

Sasha the silly ill. by Janet Stevens. Holiday, 1984. ISBN 0-8234-0503-6 Subj: Animals – dogs. Character traits – vanity.

Scarlet Monster lives here ill. by Dennis Kendrick. HarperCollins, 1979. ISBN 0-06-025527-7 Subj: Behavior. Friendship. Monsters. Moving.

Sometimes mama and papa fight ill. by Kay Chorao. HarperCollins, 1980. ISBN 0-06-025612-5 Subj: Behavior – fighting, arguing. Family life.

Sophie and Gussie ill. by Lillian Hoban. Macmillan, 1973. Subj: Animals – squirrels. Friendship.

Taking care of Melvin ill. by Victoria Chess. Holiday, 1980. ISBN 0-8234-0368-8 Subj: Animals. Friendship. Self-concept.

Thornton, the worrier ill. by Kay Chorao. Holiday, 1978. ISBN 0-8234-0328-9 Subj: Animals – rabbits. Behavior – worrying.

The 329th friend ill. by Cyndy Szekeres. Four Winds, 1992. ISBN 0-02-782259-1 Subj: Animals. Animals – raccoons. Counting, numbers. Friendship. Self-concept.

The trip: and other Sophie and Gussie stories ill. by Lillian Hoban. Macmillan, 1976. ISBN 0-02-782300-8 Subj: Animals – squirrels. Behavior – losing things. Behavior – sharing. Clothing. Friendship.

Two ghosts on a bench ill. by Nola Langner. HarperCollins, 1982. ISBN 0-06-025519-6 Subj: Ghosts.

Walter the wolf ill. by Kelly Oechsli. Holiday, 1975. ISBN 0-8234-0253-3 Subj: Animals. Animals – wolves. Violence, nonviolence.

What are we going to do about Andrew? ill. by Ray Cruz. Macmillan, 1980. ISBN 0-02-782440-3 Subj: Character traits – individuality. Family life.

Sharmat, Mitchell. *Gregory, the terrible eater* ill. by José Aruego and Ariane Dewey. Four Winds, 1980. ISBN 0-590-07586-1 Subj: Animals – goats. Food.

The pizza monster (Sharmat, Marjorie Weinman)

The seven sloppy days of Phineas Pig ill. by Sue Truesdell. Harcourt, 1983. ISBN 0-15-272936-4 Subj: Animals – pigs. Character traits – cleanliness.

Sherman is a slowpoke ill. by David Neuhaus. Scholastic, 1988. ISBN 0-590-40938-7 Subj: Animals – sloths. Character traits – individuality. School – first day.

Sharon, Mary Bruce. *Scenes from childhood* ill. by author. Dutton, 1978. ISBN 0-525-38820-6 Subj: Art. Careers – artists.

Sharp, N. L. *Today I'm going fishing with my dad* ill. by Chris L. Demarest. Boyds Mills, 1993. ISBN 1-56397-107-0 Subj: Family life – fathers. Sports – fishing.

Sharpe, Sara. *Gardener George goes to town* ill. by Susan Moxley. HarperCollins, 1982. ISBN 0-06-025620-6 Subj: Gardens, gardening.

Sharr, Christine. *Homes* ill. by author. Wonder Books, 1971. ISBN 0-448-06372-7 Subj: Family life. Homes, houses.

Sharratt, Nick. *The green queen* ill. by author. Candlewick, 1992. ISBN 1-56402-093-2 Subj: Concepts – color. Royalty – queens.

I look like this ill. by author. Candlewick, 1992. ISBN 1-56402-016-9 Subj: Emotions. Format, unusual. Games.

Ketchup on your cornflakes? a wacky mix and match book ill. by author. Scholastic, 1997. ISBN 0-590-93106-7 Subj: Food. Format, unusual – toy and movable books.

Look what I found! ill. by author. Candlewick, 1992. ISBN 1-56402-017-7 Subj: Format, unusual. Sea and seashore.

Machine poems (Bennett, Jill)

Monday run-day ill. by author. Candlewick, 1992. ISBN 1-56402-092-4 Subj: Animals – dogs. Days of the week, months of the year. Rhyming text.

Mrs. Pirate ill. by author. Candlewick, 1994. ISBN 1-56402-249-8 Subj: Activities – traveling. Pirates. Rhyming text. Sea and seashore.

Rocket countdown ill. by author. Candlewick, 1995. ISBN 1-56402-622-1 Subj: Counting, numbers. Format, unusual – toy and movable books. Space and space ships.

Snazzy aunties ill. by author. Candlewick, 1994. ISBN 1-56402-214-5 Subj: Family life – aunts, uncles. Rhyming text.

The time it took Tom by Nick Sharratt and Stephen Tucker; ill. by Nick Sharratt. Little Tiger, 2000. ISBN 1-888444-63-0 Subj: Activities – painting. Behavior – misbehavior. Time.

Shavick, Andrea. *You'll grow soon, Alex* ill. by Russell Ayto. Walker, 2000. ISBN 0-8027-8736-3 Subj: Behavior – growing up.

Shaw, Alison. *Until I saw the sea* sel. and ill. by Alison Shaw. Holt, 1995. ISBN 0-8050-2755-6 Subj: Poetry. Sea and seashore.

Shaw, Charles Green. *The blue guess book* ill. by author. Addison-Wesley, 1942. Subj: Games.

The guess book ill. by author. Addison-Wesley, 1941. Subj: Games.

It looked like spilt milk ill. by author. HarperCollins, 1947. ISBN 0-06-025565-X Subj: Concepts – shape. Games. Imagination. Participation. Sky. Weather – clouds.

Shaw, Evelyn S. *Alligator* ill. by Frances Zweifel. HarperCollins, 1972. ISBN 0-06-025557-9 Subj: Reptiles – alligators, crocodiles. Science.

Fish out of school ill. by Ralph Carpenter. HarperCollins, 1970. Subj: Fish. Science. Sea and seashore.

Nest of wood ducks ill. by Cherryl Pape. HarperCollins, 1976. ISBN 0-06-025592-7 Subj: Birds – ducks. Science.

Octopus ill. by Ralph Carpentier. HarperCollins, 1971. ISBN 0-06-025558-7 Subj: Octopuses. Science. Sea and seashore.

Sea otters ill. by Cherryl Pape. HarperCollins, 1980. ISBN 0-06-025614-1 Subj: Animals – otters. Science.

Shaw, Nancy (Nancy E.). *Sheep in a jeep* ill. by Margot Apple. Houghton Mifflin, 1986. ISBN 0-395-41105-X Subj: Animals – sheep. Rhyming text.

Sheep in a shop ill. by Margot Apple. Houghton Mifflin, 1991. ISBN 0-395-53681-2 Subj: Animals – sheep. Rhyming text. Shopping.

Sheep on a ship ill. by Margot Apple. Houghton Mifflin, 1989. ISBN 0-395-48160-0 Subj: Animals – sheep. Boats, ships. Rhyming text.

Sheep out to eat ill. by Margot Apple. Houghton Mifflin, 1992. ISBN 0-395-61128-8 Subj: Animals – sheep. Food. Rhyming text.

Sheep take a hike ill. by Margot Apple. Houghton Mifflin, 1994. ISBN 0-395-68394-7 Subj: Animals – sheep. Rhyming text. Sports – hiking.

Sheep trick or treat ill. by Margot Apple. Houghton Mifflin, 1997. ISBN 0-395-84168-2 Subj: Animals – sheep. Holidays – Halloween. Rhyming text.

Shaw, Richard. *The kitten in the pumpkin patch* ill. by Jacqueline Kahane. Warne, 1973. ISBN 0-72-326099-0 Subj: Animals – cats. Holidays – Halloween. Witches.

Shay, Arthur. *What happens when you go to the hospital* ill. by author. Reilly & Lee, 1969. Subj: Hospitals. Illness.

Shea, Pegi Deitz. *Bungalow fungalow* ill. by Elizabeth Sayles. Houghton Mifflin, 1991. ISBN 0-395-55387-3 Subj: Activities – vacationing. Poetry. Sea and seashore.

I see me! ill. by Lucia Washburn. HarperFestival, 2000. ISBN 0-694-01278-5 Subj: Babies. Family life. Format, unusual – board books. Rhyming text.

New moon ill. by Cathryn Falwell. Boyds Mills, 1996. ISBN 1-56397-410-X Subj: Ethnic groups in the U.S. – Hispanic Americans. Family life – brothers and sisters. Moon.

The whispering cloth ill. by Anita Riggio; stitched by You Yang. Caroline House, 1995. ISBN 1-56397-134-8 Subj: Activities – sewing. Ethnic groups in the U.S. – Hmong Americans. Family life – grandmothers. Foreign lands – Thailand. War.

Shearer, Marilyn J. *The crown of fools: based on: The tortoise and the hare* ill. by author. Lauren Ashley & Joshua Storybooks, 1993. ISBN 1-879567-19-9 Subj: Character traits – perseverance. Folk and fairy tales. Reptiles – turtles, tortoises. Sports – racing.

I like to play ill. by Tom Roberts. Lauren Ashley & Joshua Storybooks, 1993. ISBN 0-685-30097-8 Subj: Activities – playing.

The Nubian princess ill. by Larry Walker. Lauren Ashley & Joshua Storybooks, 1993. ISBN 0-685-30091-9 Subj: Royalty – princesses.

The original three little pigs re-told (The three little pigs)

Sheather, Allan. *Neptune's nursery* (Toft, Kim Michelle)

One less fish (Toft, Kim Michelle)

Shecter, Ben. *The big stew* ill. by author. Harper-Collins, 1991. ISBN 0-06-025610-9 Subj: Activities – cooking. Food. Witches.

Conrad's castle ill. by author. HarperCollins, 1967. Subj: Imagination.

The discontented mother ill. by author. Harcourt, 1980. ISBN 0-15-223574-4 Subj: Behavior – wishing.

Emily, girl witch of New York ill. by author. Dial, 1963. Subj: City. Homes, houses. Magic. Progress. Witches.

Grandma remembers ill. by author. HarperCollins, 1989. ISBN 0-06-025618-4 Subj: Family life – grandmothers. Memories, memory. Moving.

Hester the jester ill. by author. HarperCollins, 1977. ISBN 0-06-025600-1 Subj: Character traits – ambition. Clowns, jesters.

If I had a ship ill. by author. Doubleday, 1970. Subj: Boats, ships. Character traits – generosity. Emotions – love. Imagination.

Partouche plants a seed ill. by author. HarperCollins, 1966. Subj: Animals – pigs. Foreign lands – France. Gardens, gardening. Plants. Seeds.

The stocking child ill. by author. HarperCollins, 1976. ISBN 0-06-025594-3 Subj: Senses – seeing. Toys – dolls.

Sheehan, Angela. *The beaver* ill. by Graham Allen. Watts, 1979. ISBN 0-531-09151-1 Subj: Animals – beavers. Science.

The duck ill. by Maurice Pledger and Bernard Robinson. Warwick Pr., 1979. ISBN 0-531-09074-4 Subj: Birds – ducks. Science.

The otter ill. by Bernard Robinson. Warwick Pr., 1979. ISBN 0-531-09109-0 Subj: Animals – otters. Science.

The penguin ill. by Trevor Boyer. Watts, 1979. ISBN 0-531-09153-8 Subj: Birds – penguins. Science.

Sheehan, Patty. *Shadow and the ready time* ill. by Itoko Maeno. Advocacy Pr., 1994. ISBN 0-911655-13-1 Subj: Animals – wolves. Behavior – growing up.

Shefelman, Janice Jordan. *A peddler's dream* ill. by Tom Shefelman. Houghton Mifflin, 1992. ISBN 0-395-60904-6 Subj: Careers – peddlers. Careers – storekeepers. Character traits – ambition. Ethnic groups in the U.S. – Lebanese Americans.

Victoria House ill. by Tom Shefelman. Harcourt, 1988. ISBN 0-15-200630-3 Subj: Homes, houses. Moving.

Sheffield, Margaret. *Before you were born* ill. by Sheila Bewley. Knopf, 1984. ISBN 0-394-53734-3 Subj: Babies. Birth. Science.

Where do babies come from? ill. by Sheila Bewley. Knopf, 1973. ISBN 0-394-48482-7 Subj: Babies. Birth. Science.

Shelby, Anne. *Homeplace* ill. by Wendy Anderson Halperin. Orchard, 1995. ISBN 0-531-08732-8 Subj: Family life. Family life – grandmothers.

Potluck ill. by Irene Trivas. Watts, 1991. ISBN 0-531-08519-8 Subj: ABC books. Ethnic groups in the U.S. Food.

The someday house ill. by Rosanne Litzinger. Orchard, 1996. ISBN 0-531-08860-X Subj: Homes, houses. Imagination.

We keep a store ill. by John Ward. Watts, 1990. ISBN 0-531-08456-6 Subj: Careers – storekeepers. Ethnic groups in the U.S. – African Americans. Family life. Stores.

Sheldon, Aure. *Of cobblers and kings* ill. by Don Leake. Parents, 1978. ISBN 0-8193-0832-3 Subj: Careers – shoemakers. Character traits – cleverness.

Sheldon, Dyan. *Love, your bear, Pete* ill. by Tania Hurt-Newton. Candlewick, 1994. ISBN 1-56402-332-X Subj: Activities – traveling. Family life – mothers. Foreign lands. Toys – bears.

Under the moon ill. by Gary Blythe. Dial, 1994. ISBN 0-8037-1670-2 Subj: Dreams. Indians of North America – Sioux.

Unicorn dreams ill. by Neil Reed. Dial, 1997. ISBN 0-8037-2284-2 Subj: Imagination. Mythical creatures – unicorns. School.

The whales' song ill. by Gary Blythe. Dial, 1991. ISBN 0-8037-0972-2 Subj: Animals – whales. Character traits – kindness to animals. Family life – grandmothers.

Shepard, Aaron. *The baker's dozen* ill. by Wendy Edelson. Atheneum, 1995. ISBN 0-689-80298-6 Subj: Careers – bakers. Character traits – generosity. Folk and fairy tales.

The crystal heart: a Vietnamese legend ill. by Joseph Daniel Fiedler. Atheneum, 1998. ISBN 0-689-81551-4 Subj: Folk and fairy tales. Foreign lands – Vietnam.

Forty fortunes: a tale of Iran ill. by Alisher Dianov. Clarion, 1999. ISBN 0-395-81133-3 Subj: Careers – fortune tellers. Folk and fairy tales. Foreign lands – Iran.

The gifts of Wali Dad ill. by Daniel San Souci. Atheneum, 1995. ISBN 0-684-19445-7 Subj: Behavior – wishing. Folk and fairy tales. Foreign lands – India. Foreign lands – Pakistan. Gifts.

The sea king's daughter ill. by Gennady Spirin. Atheneum, 1997. ISBN 0-689-80759-7 Subj: Careers – musicians. Folk and fairy tales. Foreign lands – Russia. Mythical creatures. Sea and seashore.

Shepard, E. H. (Ernest Howard). *Winnie-the-Pooh's ABC* ill. by author; inspired by A. A. Milne. Dutton, 1995. ISBN 0-525-45365-2 Subj: ABC books. Toys.

Shepard, Steve. *Elvis Hornbill, international business bird* ill. by author. Holt, 1991. ISBN 0-8050-1617-1 Subj: Birds – hornbills. Careers. Family life – fathers. Foreign lands – Africa.

Shepard, Sylvia. *Let's find out about babies* (Shapp, Martha)

Sheppard, Jeff. *The right number of elephants* ill. by Felicia Bond. HarperCollins, 1990. ISBN 0-06-025616-8 Subj: Animals – elephants. Counting, numbers.

Splash, splash ill. by Dennis Panek. Macmillan, 1994. ISBN 0-02-782455-1 Subj: Animals. Noise, sounds. Rhyming text. Water.

Shepperson, Rob. *The sandman* ill. by author. Farrar, 1990. ISBN 0-374-36405-2 Subj: Bedtime. Dreams. Mythical creatures – sandman. Sleep.

Sherman, Eileen Bluestone. *The odd potato: a Chanukah story* ill. by Katherine Janus Kahn. Kar-Ben Copies, 1984. ISBN 0-930494-36-9 Subj: Family life. Holidays – Hanukkah. Jewish culture.

Sherman, Elizabeth. *see* Friskey, Margaret (Margaret Richards)

Sherman, Ivan. *I am a giant* ill. by author. Harcourt, 1975. ISBN 0-15-237983-5 Subj: Giants. Imagination.

I do not like it when my friend comes to visit ill. by author. Harcourt, 1973. ISBN 0-15-238000-0 Subj: Behavior – sharing. Etiquette. Friendship.

Walking talking words ill. by author. Harcourt, 1980. ISBN 0-05-294511-3 Subj: Language. Poetry.

Sherman, Josepha. *Vassilisa the wise: a tale of medieval Russia* ill. by Daniel San Souci. Harcourt, 1988. ISBN 0-15-293240-2 Subj: Folk and fairy tales. Foreign lands – Russia. Royalty – princes.

Sherman, Nancy. *Gwendolyn and the weathercock* ill. by Edward Sorel. Golden Pr., 1961. Subj: Birds – chickens. Farms. Rhyming text. Weather – rain.

Gwendolyn the miracle hen ill. by Edward Sorel. Western, 1961. Subj: Birds – chickens. Dragons. Rhyming text.

Sherrow, Victoria. *There goes the ghost* ill. by Megan Lloyd. HarperCollins, 1985. ISBN 0-06-025510-2 Subj: Behavior – misbehavior. Ghosts. Homes, houses. Moving.

Wilbur waits ill. by James Watts. HarperCollins, 1990. ISBN 0-06-025484-X Subj: Birthdays. Friendship. Toys. Weather.

Shi, Zhang Xiu. *Monkey and the white bone demon* trans. by Ye Ping Kuei; rev. by Jill Morris; ill. by Lin Zheng and others. Viking, 1984. Adapt. from the 16th century novel, The pilgrimage to the west, by Wu Cheng En. ISBN 0-670-48574-8 Subj: Animals – monkeys. Folk and fairy tales. Foreign lands – China.

Shibano, Tamizo. *The old man who made the trees bloom* by Hanasaka Jijii; retold by Tamizo Shibano; trans. by D. T. Ooka; ill. by Bunshu Iguchi. Heian Intl., 1985. ISBN 0-89346-247-0 Subj: Animals – dogs. Behavior – greed. Character traits – kindness. Character traits – meanness.

Shiefman, Vicky. *Sunday potatoes, Monday potatoes* ill. by Louise August. Simon & Schuster, 1994. ISBN 0-671-86596-X Subj: Activities – cooking. Days of the week, months of the year. Family life. Food. Poverty.

Shields, Carol Diggory. *Colors* ill. by Svjetlan Junakovic. Handprint Books, 2000. ISBN 1-929766-04-1 Subj: Animals. Concepts – color. Format, unusual – toy and movable books. Rhyming text. Riddles.

Day by day a week goes round ill. by True Kelley. Dutton, 1998. ISBN 0-525-45457-8 Subj: Activities. Days of the week, months of the year. Rhyming text.

I am really a princess ill. by Paul Meisel. Dutton, 1993. ISBN 0-525-45138-2 Subj: Behavior – imitation. Character traits – vanity. Family life. Imagination. Royalty – princesses. Self-concept.

I wish my brother was a dog ill. by Paul Meisel. Dutton, 1997. ISBN 0-525-45464-0 Subj: Animals – dogs. Babies. Behavior – wishing. Emotions – anger. Family life – brothers. Family life – new sibling. Sibling rivalry.

Lucky pennies and hot chocolate ill. by Hiroe Nakata. Dutton, 2000. ISBN 0-525-46450-6 Subj: Family life – grandfathers.

Lunch money and other poems about school ill. by Paul Meisel. Dutton, 1995. ISBN 0-525-45345-8 Subj: Poetry. School.

Martian rock ill. by Scott Nash. Candlewick, 2000. ISBN 0-7636-0598-0 Subj: Aliens. Birds – penguins. Plants. Rhyming text. Space and space ships.

Month by month a year goes round ill. by True Kelley. Dutton, 1998. ISBN 0-525-45458-6 Subj: Days of the week, months of the year. Rhyming text. Seasons.

Saturday night at the dinosaur stomp ill. by Scott Nash. Candlewick, 1997. ISBN 1-56402-693-0 Subj: Activities – dancing. Dinosaurs. Rhyming text.

Shimin, Symeon. *I wish there were two of me* ill. by author. Warne, 1976. ISBN 0-723-26128-8 Subj: Behavior – wishing. Dreams. Imagination.

A special birthday ill. by author. McGraw-Hill, 1976. ISBN 0-07-056902-9 Subj: Birthdays. Wordless.

Shine, Deborah. *The little engine that could pudgy word book* ill. by Christina Ong. Putnam, 1988. ISBN 0-448-19054-0 Subj: Character traits – perseverance. Format, unusual – board books. Trains.

Shipton, Jonathan. *Busy! Busy! Busy!* ill. by Michael Foreman. Delacorte, 1991. ISBN 0-385-30306-8 Subj: Activities – working. Emotions – love. Family life – mothers.

How to be a happy hippo ill. by Sally Percy. Little Tiger, 1999. ISBN 1-888444-61-4 Subj: Animals – hippopotamuses. Family life – fathers.

In the night ill. by Gill Scriven. Little, 1992. ISBN 0-316-78586-5 Subj: Bedtime. Night.

No biting, horrible crocodile! ill. by Claudio Muñoz. Western, 1995. ISBN 0-307-17521-9 Subj: Behavior – bullying. Reptiles – alligators, crocodiles. School.

What if? ill. by Barbara Nascimbeni. Dial, 1999. ISBN 0-8037-2390-3 Subj: Imagination. Self-concept.

Shire, Ellen. *The mystery at number seven, Rue Petite* ill. by author. Random House, 1978. ISBN 0-394-93664-7 Subj: Character traits – bravery. Crime. Mystery stories.

Shirotani, Hideo. *Let's eat = Vamos a comer* ill. by author. Little Simon, 1992. ISBN 0-671-76927-8 Subj: Food. Foreign languages. Format, unusual – board books.

Let's play ill. by author. Little & Woods, 1991. ISBN 1-5618-0044-9 Subj: Activities – playing. Format, unusual – board books.

Let's take a walk = Vamos a caminar ill. by author. Little Simon, 1992. ISBN 0-671-76929-4 Subj: Activities – walking. Foreign languages. Format, unusual – board books.

Opposites ill. by author. Little & Woods, 1991. ISBN 1-5618-0041-4 Subj: Concepts – opposites.

Sounds ill. by author. Little & Woods, 1991. ISBN 1-5618-0042-2 Subj: Noise, sounds. Senses – hearing.

What color? = Qué color? ill. by author. Little Simon, 1992. ISBN 0-671-76930-8 Subj: Concepts – color. Foreign languages. Format, unusual – board books.

Shles, Larry. *Moths and mothers, feathers and fathers: a story about a tiny owl named Squib* ill. by author. Houghton Mifflin, 1984. ISBN 0-395-36695-X Subj: Birds – owls. Character traits – being different.

Shohet, Marti. *Market days* concept and ill. by Marti Shohet; text by Madhur Jaffrey. BridgeWater, 1995. ISBN 0-8167-3504-2 Subj: Activities – cooking. Foreign lands. Shopping.

Shopping ill. by Roser Capdevila. Firefly, 1986. ISBN 0-920303-43-9 Subj: Format, unusual – toy and movable books. Shopping. Wordless.

Short, Mayo. *Andy and the wild ducks* ill. by Paul M. Souza. Melmont, 1959. Subj: Animals. Ecology. Farms.

Shortall, Leonard W. *Andy, the dog walker* ill. by author. Morrow, 1968. Subj: Animals – dogs. Behavior – lost.

One way: a trip with traffic signs ill. by author. Prentice-Hall, 1975. ISBN 0-13-636142-0 Subj: Holidays – Fourth of July. Rhyming text. Safety. Traffic, traffic signs.

Tod on the tugboat ill. by author. Morrow, 1971. Subj: Boats, ships.

Tony's first dive ill. by author. Morrow, 1972. Subj: Emotions – fear. Sports – swimming.

Shostak, Myra. *Rainbow candles: a Chanukah counting book* ill. by Katherine Janus Kahn. Kar-Ben Copies, 1986. ISBN 0-930494-59-8 Subj: Counting, numbers. Format, unusual – board books. Holidays – Hanukkah. Jewish culture.

Shoten, Fukuinkan. *Elephant blue* (Nakano, Hirotaka)

Shott, Steve (Stephen). *Bathtime* photos by author. Dutton, 1991. ISBN 0-525-44754-7 Subj: Activities – bathing. Format, unusual – board books.

Look at me photos by author. Dutton, 1991. ISBN 0-525-44755-5 Subj: Anatomy. Format, unusual – board books. Self-concept.

Mealtime photos by author. Dutton, 1991. ISBN 0-525-44756-3 Subj: Food. Format, unusual – board books.

Playtime photos by author. Dutton, 1991. ISBN 0-525-44757-1 Subj: Activities – playing. Format, unusual – board books.

Shotwell, Nathaniel. *see* Dodge, Mary Mapes

Showalter, Jean B. *The donkey ride* ill. by Tomi Ungerer. Doubleday, 1967. Subj: Animals – donkeys. Folk and fairy tales. Humor.

Showers, Kay Sperry. *Before you were a baby* (Showers, Paul)

Showers, Paul. *Before you were a baby* by Paul Showers and Kay Sperry Showers; ill. by Ingrid Fetz. Crowell, 1968. ISBN 0-690-12882-7 Subj: Babies. Birth. Science.

Columbus Day ill. by Ed Emberley. Crowell, 1965. ISBN 0-690-19982-1 Subj: Holidays – Columbus Day. U.S. history.

A drop of blood ill. by Don Madden. Rev. ed. HarperCollins, 1989. ISBN 0-690-04717-7 Subj: Anatomy. Science.

Ears are for hearing ill. by Holly Keller. Harper-Collins, 1990. ISBN 0-690-04720-7 Subj: Anatomy – ears. Science. Senses – hearing.

How you talk ill. by Megan Lloyd. Rev. ed. Harper-Collins, 1992. ISBN 0-06-022768-0 Subj: Anatomy. Communication. Language.

The listening walk ill. by Aliki. Rev. ed. Harper-Collins, 1991. ISBN 0-06-021638-7 Subj: Activities – walking. Noise, sounds. Senses – hearing.

Look at your eyes ill. by True Kelley. Rev. ed. HarperCollins, 1992. ISBN 0-06-020188-6 Subj: Anatomy – eyes. Ethnic groups in the U.S. – African Americans. Science. Senses – seeing.

No measles, no mumps for me ill. by Harriett Barton. Crowell, 1980. ISBN 0-690-04018-0 Subj: Illness – mumps. Science.

Sleep is for everyone ill. by Wendy Watson. Harper-Collins, 1997. ISBN 0-06-025393-2 Subj: Animals. Bedtime. Dreams. Health and fitness. Science. Sleep.

Where does the garbage go? ill. by Randy Chewning. Rev. ed. HarperCollins, 1994. ISBN 0-06-021057-5 Subj: Careers – sanitation workers. Ecology. Science.

You can't make a move without your muscles ill. by Harriett Barton. Crowell, 1982. ISBN 0-690-04185-3 Subj: Anatomy. Science.

Your skin and mine ill. by Kathleen Kuchera. Rev. ed. HarperCollins, 1991. ISBN 0-06-022523-8 Subj: Anatomy – skin. Ethnic groups in the U.S. – African Americans.

Shub, Elizabeth. *The Bremen town musicians* (Grimm, Jacob)

Clever Kate (Grimm, Jacob)

Dear Sarah (Borchers, Elisabeth)

Dragon Franz text by Josef Guggenmos; adapt. by Elizabeth Shub; ill. by Ursula Konopka. Greenwillow, 1976. Orig. pub. in German under the title Franz, der Drache. ISBN 0-688-84077-9 Subj: Character traits – being different. Concepts – color. Dragons.

The emperor's plum tree (Nikly, Michelle)

The fisherman and his wife (Grimm, Jacob)

Jorinda and Joringel (Grimm, Jacob)

Seeing is believing ill. by Rachel Isadora. Greenwillow, 1979. ISBN 0-688-84211-9 Subj: Folk and fairy tales. Mythical creatures – leprechauns.

Sir Ribbeck of Ribbeck of Havelland (Fontane, Theodor)

The twelve dancing princesses (Grimm, Jacob)

Why Noah chose the dove (Singer, Isaac Bashevis)

Shulevitz, Uri. *Dawn* ill. by author. Farrar, 1974. ISBN 0-374-31707-0 Subj: Camps, camping. Family life – grandfathers. Morning. Sun.

The magician adapt. from the Yiddish of Isaac Loeb Peretz by Uri Shulevitz; ill. by adapt. Macmillan, 1985, c1973. ISBN 0-02-782770-4 Subj: Holidays. Jewish culture – Passover. Magic. Religion.

One Monday morning ill. by author. Aladdin, 1986, c1967. ISBN 0-684-13195-1 Subj: City. Days of the week, months of the year. Imagination. Royalty.

Rain rain rivers ill. by author. Farrar, 1969. ISBN 0-374-36171-1 Subj: Rhyming text. Weather – rain.

Snow ill. by author. Farrar, 1998. ISBN 0-374-37092-3 Subj: Caldecott award honor books. City. Nature. Weather – snow.

The treasure ill. by author. Farrar, 1978. ISBN 0-374-37740-5 Subj: Caldecott award honor books. Dreams. Folk and fairy tales.

What is a wise bird like you doing in a silly tale like this? ill. by author. Farrar, 2000. ISBN 0-3743-8300-6 Subj: Birds. Character traits – freedom. Royalty – emperors. Tall tales.

Shulman, Milton. *Prep, the little pigeon of Trafalgar Square* ill. by Dale Maxey. Random House, 1964. Subj: Birds – pigeons. Foreign lands – England.

Shute, Linda. *Clever Tom and the leprechaun* ill. by author. Lothrop, 1988. ISBN 0-688-07489-8 Subj: Folk and fairy tales. Mythical creatures – leprechauns.

Halloween party ill. by author. Lothrop, 1994. ISBN 0-688-11715-5 Subj: Holidays – Halloween. Parties. Rhyming text. Witches.

Momotaro, the peach boy ill. by author. Lothrop, 1986. ISBN 0-688-05864-7 Subj: Behavior – fighting, arguing. Character traits – bravery. Devil. Folk and fairy tales. Foreign lands – Japan.

Shuttlesworth, Dorothy Edwards. *ABC of buses* ill. by Leonard W. Shortall. Doubleday, 1965. Subj: ABC books. Buses.

Shyer, Marlene Fanta. *Here I am, an only child* ill. by Donald Carrick. Scribners, 1985. ISBN 0-684-18296-3 Subj: Family life – only child.

Stepdog ill. by Judith Schermer. Scribners, 1983. ISBN 0-684-17998-9 Subj: Animals – dogs. Emotions – envy, jealousy. Family life.

Sibbick, John. *Creatures of long ago: dinosaurs* ill. by John Sibbick; written by Peggy D. Winston. National Geographic, 1988. ISBN 0-87044-723-8 Subj: Dinosaurs. Format, unusual – toy and movable books.

Siberell, Anne. *A journey to paradise* ill. by author. Holt, 1990. ISBN 0-8050-1212-5 Subj: Folk and fairy tales. Foreign lands – India.

Whale in the sky ill. by author. Dutton, 1982. ISBN 0-525-44021-6 Subj: Animals – whales. Folk and fairy tales. Indians of North America.

Sicotte, Virginia. *A riot of quiet* ill. by Edward Ardizzone. Holt, 1969. ISBN 0-03-061289-5 Subj: Imagination. Noise, sounds. Poetry.

Siddals, Mary McKenna. *I'll play with you* ill. by David Wisniewski. Clarion, 2000. ISBN 0-395-90373-4 Subj: Activities – playing. Nature.

Millions of snowflakes ill. by Elizabeth Sayles. Clarion, 1998. ISBN 0-395-71531-8 Subj: Rhyming text. Weather – snow.

Tell me a season ill. by Petra Mathers. Clarion, 1997. ISBN 0-395-71021-9 Subj: Concepts – color. Rhyming text. Seasons.

Siddiqui, Ashraf. *Bhombal Dass, the uncle of lion: a tale from Pakistan* ill. by Thomas Arthur Hamil.

Macmillan, 1959. Subj: Animals – goats. Animals – lions. Character traits – cleverness. Folk and fairy tales. Foreign lands – Pakistan.

Siebert, Diane. *Heartland* ill. by Wendell Minor. HarperCollins, 1989. ISBN 0-690-04732-0 Subj: Poetry. U.S. history.

Mojave ill. by Wendell Minor. HarperCollins, 1988. ISBN 0-690-04569-7 Subj: Desert. Poetry.

Plane song ill. by Vincent Nasta. HarperCollins, 1993. ISBN 0-06-021467-8 Subj: Airplanes, airports. Rhyming text.

Sierra ill. by Wendell Minor. HarperCollins, 1991. ISBN 0-06-021640-9 Subj: Nature. Poetry.

Train song ill. by Mike Wimmer. HarperCollins, 1990. ISBN 0-690-04728-2 Subj: Rhyming text. Trains.

Truck song ill. by Byron Barton. Crowell, 1984. ISBN 0-690-04411-9 Subj: Rhyming text. Trucks.

Siegelson, Kim L. *In the time of the drums* ill. by Brian Pinkney. Hyperion, 1999. ISBN 0-7868-2386-0 Subj: Character traits – freedom. Ethnic groups in the U.S. – African Americans. Slavery.

Siekkinen, Raija. *Mister King* trans. from Finnish by Tim Steffa; ill. by Hannu Taina. Carolrhoda, 1987. ISBN 0-87614-315-X Subj: Animals – cats. Emotions – loneliness. Royalty – kings.

Siepmann, Jane. *The lion on Scott Street* ill. by Clement Hurd. Walck, 1952. Subj: Animals – lions. Imagination.

Sierra, Judy. *The beautiful butterfly* ill. by Victoria Chess. Clarion, 2000. ISBN 0-395-90015-8 Subj: Animals – mice. Folk and fairy tales. Foreign lands – Spain. Insects – butterflies, caterpillars. Royalty – kings.

The gift of the crocodile: a Cinderella story ill. by Reynold Ruffins. Simon & Schuster, 2000. ISBN 0-689-82188-3 Subj: Fairies. Family life – step families. Folk and fairy tales. Foreign lands – Indonesia. Reptiles – alligators, crocodiles.

The house that Drac built ill. by Will Hillenbrand. Harcourt, 1995. ISBN 0-15-200015-1 Subj: Cumulative tales. Holidays – Halloween. Homes, houses. Monsters. Rhyming text.

Tasty baby belly buttons ill. by Meilo So. Knopf, 1998. ISBN 0-679-99369-X Subj: Folk and fairy tales. Foreign lands – Japan. Mythical creatures – ogres. Sex roles.

There's a zoo in room 22 ill. by Barney Saltzberg. Harcourt, 2000. ISBN 0-15-202033-0 Subj: ABC books. Animals. Pets. Rhyming text. School.

Wiley and the Hairy Man ill. by J. Brian Pinkney. Lodestar, 1996. ISBN 0-525-67477-2 Subj: Character traits – cleverness. Ethnic groups in the U.S. – African Americans. Folk and fairy tales. Monsters.

Sieveking, Anthea. *Mary had a little lamb and other animal rhymes* photos by author. Barron's, 1991.

ISBN 0-8120-6217-5 Subj: Format, unusual – board books. Nursery rhymes.

Polly put the kettle on and other play rhymes photos by author. Barron's, 1991. ISBN 0-8120-6218-3 Subj: Format, unusual – board books. Nursery rhymes.

Rub-a-dub-dub and other splashy rhymes photos by author. Barron's, 1991. ISBN 0-8120-6219-1 Subj: Format, unusual – board books. Nursery rhymes.

Twinkle, twinkle, little star and other bedtime rhymes photos by author. Barron's, 1991. ISBN 0-8120-6220-5 Subj: Format, unusual – board books. Nursery rhymes.

What color? photos by author. Dial, 1991. ISBN 0-8037-0909-9 Subj: Concepts – color.

Siewert, Margaret. *Bear hunt* by Margaret Siewert and Kathleen Savage; ill. by Leonard W. Shortall. Prentice-Hall, 1976. ISBN 0-13-072660-5 Subj: Animals – bears. Games. Participation. Toys – bears.

Sikundar, Sylvia. *Forest singer* ill. by Alison Astill. Barefoot, 1999. ISBN 1-902283-60-0 Subj: Activities – singing. Dwarfs, midgets. Foreign lands – Africa. Forest, woods.

Silsbe, Brenda. *Just one more color* ill. by Shawn Steffler. Firefly, 1991. ISBN 1-55037-133-9 Subj: Activities – painting. Concepts – color. Homes, houses.

Silver, Jody. *Isadora* ill. by author. Doubleday, 1981. ISBN 0-385-17099-8 Subj: Animals – donkeys. Clothing.

Silverman, Erica. *Fixing the crack of dawn* ill. by Sandra Spiedel. BridgeWater, 1994. ISBN 0-8167-3458-5 Subj: Desert. Family life. Morning.

Follow the leader ill. by G. Brian Karas. Farrar, 2000. ISBN 0-374-32423-9 Subj: Activities – playing. Bedtime. Family life – brothers. Rhyming text.

Gittel's hands ill. by Deborah Nourse Lattimore. BridgeWater, 1996. ISBN 0-8167-3798-3 Subj: Character traits – kindness. Character traits – meanness. Holidays – Passover. Jewish culture. Religion.

The Halloween house ill. by Jon Agee. Farrar, 1997. ISBN 0-374-16768-0 Subj: Counting, numbers. Ghosts. Holidays – Halloween. Monsters. Rhyming text. Witches.

Mrs. Peachtree and the Eighth Avenue cat ill. by Ellen Beier. Macmillan, 1994. ISBN 0-02-782684-8 Subj: Animals – cats. City.

On Grandma's roof ill. by Deborah Kogan Ray. Macmillan, 1990. ISBN 0-02-782681-3 Subj: City. Family life – grandmothers. Homes, houses.

On the morn of Mayfest ill. by Marla Frazee. Simon & Schuster, 1998. ISBN 0-689-80674-4 Subj: Cumulative tales. Holidays – May Day. Parades. Rhyming text. Seasons – spring.

Warm in winter ill. by Michael J. Deraney. Macmillan, 1989. ISBN 0-02-782661-9 Subj: Animals – badgers. Animals – rabbits. Friendship. Seasons. Seasons – winter.

Silverman, Maida. *Bunny's ABC* ill. by Ellen Blonder. Grosset, 1986. ISBN 0-448-01464-5 Subj: ABC books. Animals – rabbits. Format, unusual – board books.

Dinosaur babies ill. by Carol Inouye. Simon & Schuster, 1988. ISBN 0-671-65897-2 Subj: Dinosaurs. Science.

Ladybug's color book ill. by Nancy Duell. Grosset, 1986. ISBN 0-448-01461-0 Subj: Concepts – color. Format, unusual – board books. Insects – ladybugs.

The magic well ill. by Manuel Boix. Simon & Schuster, 1989. ISBN 0-617-67885-X Subj: Emotions – love. Fairies. Family life – mothers. Magic. Royalty – queens.

Mouse's shape book ill. by Frederic Marvin. Grosset, 1986. ISBN 0-448-01463-7 Subj: Animals – mice. Concepts – shape. Format, unusual – board books.

My first book of Jewish holidays ill. by Barbara Garrison. Dial, 1994. ISBN 0-0837-1428-9 Subj: Holidays. Jewish culture. Religion.

Silverman, Martin. *My tooth is loose* ill. by Amy Aitken. Viking, 1992. ISBN 0-670-83862-4 Subj: Teeth.

Silverstein, Shel. *A giraffe and a half* ill. by author. HarperCollins, 1964. ISBN 0-06-025656-7 Subj: Cumulative tales. Humor. Rhyming text.

The giving tree ill. by author. HarperCollins, 1964. ISBN 0-06-024419-4 Subj: Character traits – generosity. Rhyming text.

The missing piece ill. by author. HarperCollins, 1976. ISBN 0-06-025672-9 Subj: Character traits – individuality. Concepts – shape.

Simmie, Lois. *Mister got to go/No cats allowed* ill. by Cynthia Nugent. Chronicle, 1996. ISBN 0-8118-1457-2 Subj: Animals – cats. Hotels. Weather – rain. Weather – storms.

Simmonds, Posy. *The chocolate wedding* ill. by author. Knopf, 1991. ISBN 0-679-91447-1 Subj: Behavior – boasting. Behavior – misbehavior. Dreams. Weddings.

Fred ill. by author. Knopf, 1988. ISBN 0-394-98627-X Subj: Animals – cats. Death. Emotions – grief.

Lulu and the flying babies ill. by author. Knopf, 1988. ISBN 0-394-99597-X Subj: Family life – fathers. Imagination. Museums. Weather – snow.

Simmons, Al. *Counting feathers* ill. by author. Longstreet, 1997. ISBN 1-56352-440-6 Subj: Birds. Counting, numbers.

Simmons, Jane. *Come along, Daisy!* ill. by author. Little, 1998. ISBN 0-316-79790-1 Subj: Behavior – lost. Birds – ducks. Family life. Nature.

Daisy and the egg ill. by author. Little, 1998. ISBN 0-316-79747-2 Subj: Birds – ducks. Eggs. Family life – brothers and sisters. Family life – new sibling.

Daisy says Coo! ill. by author. Little, 2000. ISBN 0-316-79764-2 Subj: Animals. Birds – ducks. Format, unusual – board books. Noise, sounds.

Daisy's day out ill. by author. Little, 2000. ISBN 0-316-79763-4 Subj: Birds – ducks. Format, unusual – board books. Noise, sounds.

Daisy's favorite things ill. by author. Little, 1999. ISBN 0-316-79762-6 Subj: Animals. Birds – ducks. Format, unusual – board books. Night. Rhyming text.

Ebb and Flo and the greedy gulls ill. by author. Margaret K. McElderry, 2000. ISBN 0-689-82484-X Subj: Animals – dogs. Behavior – misunderstanding. Birds – seagulls. Sea and seashore.

Go to sleep, Daisy ill. by author. Little, 1999. ISBN 0-316-79761-8 Subj: Bedtime. Birds – ducks. Dreams. Noise, sounds. Sleep.

Simmons, Steven J. *Alice and Greta: a tale of two witches* ill. by Cyd Moore. Charlesbridge, 1997. ISBN 0-8810-6974-4 Subj: Character traits – kindness. Character traits – meanness. Magic. Witches.

Alice and Greta's color magic ill. by Cyd Moore. Knopf, 2001. ISBN 0-375-81245-8 Subj: Behavior – misbehavior. Concepts – color. Magic. Witches.

Greta's revenge ill. by Cyd Moore. Crown, 1999. ISBN 0-517-80051-9 Subj: Behavior – misbehavior. Magic. Witches.

Simmons-Lynch, Julie. *Tom* (Torres, Daniel)

Simms, Laura. *The bone man: a Native American Modoc tale* ill. by Michael McCurdy. Hyperion, 1997. ISBN 0-7868-2074-8 Subj: Creation. Folk and fairy tales. Indians of North America – Modoc. Monsters. Weather – rain.

Moon and Otter and Frog ill. by Clifford Brycelea. Hyperion, 1995. ISBN 0-7868-2022-5 Subj: Animals – otters. Folk and fairy tales. Frogs and toads. Indians of North America – Modoc. Moon.

Rotten teeth ill. by David Catrow. Houghton Mifflin, 1998. ISBN 0-395-82850-3 Subj: Activities – storytelling. School. Teeth.

The squeaky door ill. by Sylvie Wickstrom. Crown, 1991. ISBN 0-517-57584-1 Subj: Bedtime. Cumulative tales. Emotions – fear. Folk and fairy tales. Noise, sounds.

Simon, Carly. *Amy the dancing bear* ill. by Margot Datz. Doubleday, 1989. ISBN 0-385-26721-5 Subj: Activities – dancing. Animals – bears.

Midnight farm ill. by David Delamare. Simon & Schuster, 1997. ISBN 0-689-81237-X Subj: Animals. Bedtime. Dreams. Farms. Islands. Multiple births – twins. Plants.

Simon, Charnan. *The good bad day* photos by Dorothy Handelman. Millbrook, 1998. ISBN 0-7613-2017-2 Subj: Behavior – bad day. Illness.

Mud! ill. by Dorothy Handelman. Millbrook, 1999. ISBN 0-7613-2051-2 Subj: Activities – playing. Rhyming text.

Show-and-tell Sam ill. by Gary Bialke. Childrens Pr., 1998. ISBN 0-516-20945-0 Subj: Animals – dogs. School.

Simon, Francesca. *But what does the hippopotamus say?* ill. by Helen Floate. Harcourt, 1994. ISBN 0-15-200029-1 Subj: Animals. Noise, sounds. Rhyming text.

Calling all toddlers ill. by Susan Winter. Orchard, 1999. ISBN 0-531-30120-6 Subj: Activities – playing. Rhyming text.

Camels don't ski ill. by Ailie Busby. Levinson Books, 1999. ISBN 1-899607-59-5 Subj: Animals – camels. Behavior – dissatisfaction. Seasons – winter. Sports – skiing.

Spider school ill. by Peta Coplans. Dial, 1996. ISBN 0-8037-1975-2 Subj: Behavior – bad day. Dreams. School. Spiders.

Toddler time ill. by Susan Winter. Orchard, 2000. ISBN 0-531-30251-2 Subj: Activities. Poetry.

The Topsy-Turvies ill. by Karen Ludlow. Dial, 1996. ISBN 0-8037-1969-8 Subj: Activities – babysitting. Character traits – being different. Family life.

Simon, Howard. *If you were an eel, how would you feel?* (Simon, Mina Lewiton)

Simon, Mina Lewiton. *If you were an eel, how would you feel?* by Mina and Howard Simon; ill. by Howard Simon. Follett, 1963. Subj: Animals.

Is anyone here? ill. by Howard Simon. Atheneum, 1967. Subj: Rhyming text. Sea and seashore.

Simon, Norma. *All kinds of children* ill. by Diane Paterson. Albert Whitman, 1999. ISBN 0-8075-0281-2 Subj: Character traits – individuality. Self-concept.

All kinds of families ill. by Joe Lasker. Albert Whitman, 1976. ISBN 0-8075-0282-0 Subj: Family life.

Cats do, dogs don't ill. by Dora Leder. Albert Whitman, 1986. ISBN 0-8075-1102-1 Subj: Animals – cats. Animals – dogs. Pets.

The daddy days ill. by Abner Graboff. Abelard-Schuman, 1958. Subj: Divorce. Family life – fathers.

How do I feel? ill. by Joe Lasker. Albert Whitman, 1970. ISBN 0-8075-3414-5 Subj: Emotions. Family life. Multiple births – twins.

I am not a crybaby! ill. by Helen Cogancherry. Albert Whitman, 1988. ISBN 0-8075-3447-1 Subj: Emotions. Ethnic groups in the U.S.

I know what I like ill. by Dora Leder. Albert Whitman, 1971. ISBN 0-8075-3507-9 Subj: Character traits – individuality.

I was so mad! ill. by Dora Leder. Albert Whitman, 1974. ISBN 0-8075-3520-6 Subj: Emotions – anger.

I wish I had my father ill. by Arieh Zeldich. Albert Whitman, 1983. ISBN 0-8075-3522-2 Subj: Behavior – wishing. Family life – fathers. Holidays – Father's Day.

I'm busy, too ill. by Dora Leder. Albert Whitman, 1980. ISBN 0-8075-3464-1 Subj: Activities. Activities – working. School.

Mama cat's year ill. by Dora Leder. Albert Whitman, 1991. ISBN 0-8075-4958-4 Subj: Animals – cats. Pets. Seasons.

Oh, that cat! ill. by Dora Leder. Albert Whitman, 1986. ISBN 0-8075-5919-9 Subj: Animals – cats. Family life. Pets.

The saddest time ill. by Jacqueline Rogers. Albert Whitman, 1986. ISBN 0-8075-7203-9 Subj: Death. Emotions – grief.

The story of Hanukkah ill. by Leonid Gore. HarperCollins, 1997. ISBN 0-06-027420-4 Subj: Holidays – Hanukkah. Jewish culture. Religion.

The story of Passover ill. by Erika Weihs. HarperCollins, 1997. ISBN 0-06-027063-2 Subj: Holidays – Passover. Jewish culture. Religion.

The wet world ill. by Jane Miller. Lippincott, 1954. Subj: Weather – rain.

The wet world ill. by Alexi Natchev. Candlewick, 1995. ISBN 1-56402-190-4 Subj: Weather – rain.

What do I do? ill. by Joe Lasker. Albert Whitman, 1969. ISBN 0-8075-8822-9 Subj: Activities. Character traits – helpfulness. City. Ethnic groups in the U.S. – Puerto Rican Americans. School.

What do I say? ill. by Joe Lasker. Albert Whitman, 1967. ISBN 0-8075-8826-1 Subj: Ethnic groups in the U.S. Ethnic groups in the U.S. – Puerto Rican Americans. Family life. Foreign languages. Participation. School.

Where does my cat sleep? ill. by Dora Leder. Albert Whitman, 1982. ISBN 0-8075-8926-8 Subj: Animals – cats. Sleep.

Why am I different? ill. by Dora Leder. Albert Whitman, 1976. ISBN 0-8075-9075-6 Subj: Character traits – being different. Character traits – individuality. Self-concept.

Simon, Paul. *At the zoo* ill. by Valerie Michaut. Doubleday, 1991. ISBN 0-385-41906-6 Subj: Animals. Songs. Zoos.

Simon, Seymour. *Animal fact - animal fable* ill. by Diane de Groat. Crown, 1979. ISBN 0-517-53474-6 Subj: Animals.

Beneath your feet ill. by Daniel Nevins. Walker, 1977. ISBN 0-8027-6293-X Subj: Earth. Science.

Icebergs and glaciers ill. with photos. Morrow, 1987. ISBN 0-688-06187-7 Subj: Nature. Science.

The largest dinosaurs ill. by Pamela Carroll. Macmillan, 1986. ISBN 0-02-782910-3 Subj: Dinosaurs.

Seymour Simon's book of trucks ill. by author. HarperCollins, 2000. ISBN 0-06-028481-1 Subj: Transportation. Trucks.

Shadow magic ill. by Stella Ormai. Lothrop, 1985. ISBN 0-688-02682-6 Subj: Shadows.

The smallest dinosaurs ill. by Anthony Rao. Crown, 1982. ISBN 0-517-54425-3 Subj: Dinosaurs.

Simon, Sidney B. *The armadillo who had no shell* ill. by Walter Lorraine. Norton, 1966. Subj: Animals – armadillos. Character traits – being different.

Henry, the uncatchable mouse ill. by Nola Langner. Norton, 1964. Subj: Animals – mice. Character traits – cleverness.

Simons, Traute. *Paulino* trans. by Ebbitt Cutler; ill. by Susi Bohdal. Tundra, 1978. ISBN 0-88776-110-0 Subj: Dreams. Toys.

Simont, Marc. *The goose that almost got cooked* ill. by author. Scholastic, 1997. ISBN 0-590-69075-2 Subj: Activities – flying. Birds – geese. Character traits – individuality. Farms.

How come elephants? ill. by author. HarperCollins, 1965. Subj: Animals – elephants. Character traits – questioning.

The Lieutenant Colonel and the gypsy (García Lorca, Federico)

Simple gifts: *a Shaker hymn* ill. by Chris Raschka. Holt, 1998. ISBN 0-8050-5143-0 Subj: Animals. Birds. Forest, woods. Music. Songs.

Simple Simon. *The adventures of Simple Simon* ill. by Chris Conover. Farrar, 1987. ISBN 0-374-36921-6 Subj: Nursery rhymes.

The history of Simple Simon ill. by Paul Galdone. McGraw-Hill, 1966. The version used in this book was published in London in 1840 by A. Park. Subj: Nursery rhymes.

Simple Simon ill. by Rodney Peppé. Holt, 1973. ISBN 0-03-091462-0 Subj: Nursery rhymes.

Simpson, Bert. *Rise and shine* (Raffi)

Simpson, Bonnie. *Rise and shine* (Raffi)

Simpson, Gretchen Dow. *Gretchen's ABC* ill. by author. HarperCollins, 1991. ISBN 0-06-025646-X Subj: ABC books. Art.

Sing, Rachel. *Chinese New Year's dragon* ill. by Shao Wei Liu. Modern Curriculum, 1992. ISBN 0-81362-238-7 Subj: Ethnic groups in the U.S. – Chinese Americans. Family life. Holidays – Chinese New Year.

Singer, Isaac Bashevis. *Why Noah chose the dove* trans. by Elizabeth Shub; ill. by Eric Carle. Farrar, 1974. ISBN 0-374-38420-7 Subj: Animals. Birds – doves. Boats, ships. Religion – Noah. Weather – floods. Weather – rain. Weather – rainbows.

Singer, Marilyn. *All we needed to say: poems about school from Tanya and Sophie* ill. by Lorna Clark. Atheneum, 1996. ISBN 0-689-80667-1 Subj: Friendship. Poetry. School.

Archer Armadillo's secret room ill. by Beth Weiner Lipson. Macmillan, 1985. ISBN 0-02-782700-3 Subj: Animals – armadillos. Behavior – running away. Moving.

Chester, the out-of-work dog ill. by Cat Bowman Smith. Holt, 1992. ISBN 0-8050-1828-X Subj: Activities – working. Animals – dogs. Behavior – lost.

The dog who insisted he wasn't ill. by Kelly Oechsli. Dutton, 1976. ISBN 0-525-28815-5 Subj: Animals – dogs. Character traits – individuality. Humor.

In the palace of the Ocean King ill. by Ted Rand. Atheneum, 1995. ISBN 0-689-31755-7 Subj: Emotions – sadness. Ethnic groups in the U.S. – African Americans. Family life – fathers.

The maiden on the moor ill. by Troy Howell. Morrow, 1995. ISBN 0-688-08675-6 Subj: Character traits – kindness. Folk and fairy tales. Middle Ages. Songs.

Minnie's Yom Kippur birthday ill. by Ruth Rosner. HarperCollins, 1989. ISBN 0-06-025847-0 Subj: Birthdays. Holidays – Yom Kippur. Jewish culture. Religion.

The Morgans' dream ill. by Gary Drake. Holt, 1995. ISBN 0-8050-3004-2 Subj: Dreams. Family life. Poetry.

Nine o'clock lullaby ill. by Frané Lessac. HarperCollins, 1991. ISBN 0-06-025648-6 Subj: Foreign lands. Time.

The one and only me ill. by Nicole Rubel. HarperFestival, 2000. ISBN 0-694-01279-3 Subj: Anatomy. Character traits – individuality. Family life.

Pickle plan ill. by Steven Kellogg. Dutton, 1978. ISBN 0-525-37021-8 Subj: Behavior – needing someone. Character traits – individuality.

Solomon sneezes ill. by Brian Floca. HarperCollins, 1999. ISBN 0-694-01748-5 Subj: Humor. Rhyming text.

Turtle in July ill. by Jerry Pinkney. Macmillan, 1989. ISBN 0-02-782881-6 Subj: Animals. Days of the week, months of the year. Nature. Poetry.

Will you take me to town on strawberry day? ill. by Trinka Hakes Noble. HarperCollins, 1981. ISBN 0-06-025738-5 Subj: Fairs. Music. Songs.

Singh, Jacquelin. *Fat Gopal* ill. by Demi. Harcourt, 1984. ISBN 0-05-227372-7 Subj: Character traits – cleverness. Foreign lands – India. Problem solving. Rhyming text.

Siomades, Lorianne. *The itsy bitsy spider* ill. by author. Boyds Mills, 1999. ISBN 1-56397-727-3 Subj: Character traits – persistence. Nursery rhymes. Spiders.

Kangaroo and cricket ill. by author. Boyds Mills, 1999. ISBN 1-56397-780-X Subj: Activities. Animals. Rhyming text.

My box of color ill. by author. Boyds Mills, 1998. ISBN 1-56397-711-7 Subj: Animals. Concepts – color.

A place to bloom ill. by author. Boyds Mills, 1997. ISBN 1-56397-656-0 Subj: Behavior – sharing. Earth. Ecology. Rhyming text.

Three little kittens ill. by reteller. Boyds Mills, 2000. ISBN 1-56397-845-8 Subj: Animals – cats. Animals – mice. Behavior – losing things. Clothing – gloves, mittens. Nursery rhymes.

Sipiera, Paul P. *I can be a geologist* ill. with photos. Childrens Pr., 1986. ISBN 0-516-01897-3 Subj: Careers – geologists.

Siracusa, Catherine. *No mail for Mitchell* ill. by author. McKay, 1990. ISBN 0-679-90476-X Subj: Animals. Careers – postal workers. Illness. Letters, cards.

Sirois, Allen. *Dinosaur dress up* ill. by Janet Street. Morrow, 1992. ISBN 0-688-10460-6 Subj: Clothing. Dinosaurs.

Sis, Peter. *Beach ball* ill. by author. Greenwillow, 1990. ISBN 0-688-09182-2 Subj: Concepts. Sea and seashore.

Dinosaur! ill. by author. Greenwillow, 2000. ISBN 0-688-17049-8 Subj: Dinosaurs. Imagination. Wordless.

Fire truck ill. by author. Greenwillow, 1998. ISBN 0-688-15878-1 Subj: Careers – firefighters. Counting, numbers. Format, unusual – toy and movable books. Trucks.

Going up! ill. by author. Greenwillow, 1989. ISBN 0-688-08125-8 Subj: Birthdays. Concepts – color. Counting, numbers. Elevators, escalators.

Higgledy-Piggledy: verses and pictures (Livingston, Myra Cohn)

Madlenka ill. by author. Frances Foster, 2000. ISBN 0-374-39969-7 Subj: Behavior – growing up. Foreign lands. Imagination. Teeth.

An ocean world ill. by author. Greenwillow, 1992. ISBN 0-688-09068-0 Subj: Animals – whales. Sea and seashore. Wordless.

Rainbow Rhino ill. by author. Knopf, 1987. ISBN 0-394-99009-9 Subj: Animals – rhinoceros. Birds. Friendship.

Ship ahoy! ill. by author. Greenwillow, 1999. ISBN 0-688-16644-X Subj: Boats, ships. Imagination. Monsters. Sea and seashore. Wordless.

Starry messenger ill. by author. Farrar, 1996. ISBN 0-374-37191-1 Subj: Astronomy. Caldecott award honor books. Space and space ships. Stars.

Trucks, trucks, trucks ill. by author. Greenwillow, 1999. ISBN 0-688-16276-2 Subj: Format, unusual – toy and movable books. Trucks.

Waving ill. by author. Greenwillow, 1988. ISBN 0-688-07160-0 Subj: Counting, numbers.

Sitomer, Harry. *How did numbers begin?* (Sitomer, Mindel)

Sitomer, Mindel. *How did numbers begin?* by Mindel and Harry Sitomer; ill. by Richard Cuffari. Crowell, 1976. ISBN 0-690-00794-9 Subj: Counting, numbers.

Sivulich, Sandra Stroner. *I'm going on a bear hunt* ill. by Glen Rounds. Dutton, 1973. ISBN 0-525-32535-2 Subj: Animals – bears. Games. Participation.

Sizes: *with Dib, Dab, and Dob.* DK, 1998. ISBN 0-7894-2915-2 Subj: Birds – ducks. Concepts – size.

Skaar, Grace Marion. *Nothing but (cats) and all about (dogs)* ill. by author. Addison-Wesley, 1947. Subj: Animals – cats. Animals – dogs.

The very little dog: and, The smart little kitty by Grace Marion Skaar and Louise Phinney Woodcock; ill. by Grace Marion Skaar and Lucienne Bloch. Addison-Wesley, 1967. Subj: Animals – cats. Animals – dogs.

What do the animals say? ill. by author. Addison-Wesley, 1968. 1950 ed. published under title: What do they say! Subj: Animals. Noise, sounds. Participation.

Skipper, Mervyn. *The fooling of King Alexander* ill. by Gaynor Chapman. Atheneum, 1967. Originally published in The white man's garden, by Mervyn Skipper. London, Mathews, 1931. Subj: Foreign lands – China. Royalty – kings.

Skofield, James. *All wet! All wet!* ill. by Diane Stanley. HarperCollins, 1984. ISBN 0-06-025752-0 Subj: Weather – rain.

Crow moon, worm moon ill. by Joyce Powzyk. Four Winds, 1990. ISBN 0-02-782915-4 Subj: Animals. Moon. Nature. Poetry. Seasons – spring.

Snow country ill. by Laura Jean Allen. Harper-Collins, 1983. ISBN 0-06-025787-3 Subj: Family life – grandparents. Farms. Weather – snow.

Skolsky, Mindy Warshaw. *Hannah and the whistling tea kettle* ill. by Diane Palmisciano. DK, 2000. ISBN 0-7894-2602-1 Subj: Crime. Family life – grandparents. Gifts. Noise, sounds. Stores.

Skorpen, Liesel Moak. *All the Lassies* ill. by Bruce Martin Scott. Dial, 1970. Subj: Animals. Animals – dogs. Character traits – perseverance. Cumulative tales. Family life – only child. Participation. Pets.

Charles ill. by Martha G. Alexander. Harper-Collins, 1971. ISBN 0-06-025712-1 Subj: Behavior – needing someone. Toys – bears.

Elizabeth ill. by Martha G. Alexander. Harper-Collins, 1970. Subj: Toys – dolls.

His mother's dog ill. by M. E. Mullin. Harper-Collins, 1978. ISBN 0-06-025723-7 Subj: Animals – dogs. Emotions – envy, jealousy. Family life. Sibling rivalry.

If I had a lion ill. by Ursula Landshoff. Harper-Collins, 1967. Subj: Animals – lions. Imagination.

Old Arthur ill. by Wallace Tripp. HarperCollins, 1972. ISBN 0-06-025715-6 Subj: Animals – dogs. Old age.

Outside my window ill. by Mercer Mayer. Harper-Collins, 1968. Subj: Animals – bears. Bedtime.

We were tired of living in a house ill. by Joe Cepeda. Putnam, 1999. ISBN 0-399-23016-5 Subj: Activities – painting. Cumulative tales. Family life – brothers and sisters. Homes, houses.

Skulavik, Mary Alys. *Bert* ill. by Zofia Kostyrko. Walker, 1990. ISBN 0-8027-6963-2 Subj: Computers. Family life. Self-concept.

Skurzynski, Gloria. *Here comes the mail* ill. by author. Bradbury, 1992. ISBN 0-02-782916-2 Subj: Careers – postal workers. Letters, cards. Post office.

Martin by himself ill. by Lynn Munsinger. Houghton Mifflin, 1979. ISBN 0-395-28271-3 Subj: Activities – working. Emotions – loneliness. Family life – mothers.

Skutina, Vladimir. *Nobody has time for me* trans. by Dagmar Herrmann; ill. by Marie-Jose Sacre. Wellington, 1991. ISBN 0-922984-07-7 Subj: Time.

Skwarek, Skip. *The horrors of Howling Hall* art by Compass Production Staff. Dial, 1992. ISBN 0-8037-1185-9 Subj: Format, unusual – toy and movable books. Ghosts. Rhyming text.

Mystery of Maggoty Mill art by Compass Production Staff. Dial, 1992. ISBN 0-8037-1186-7 Subj: Format, unusual – toy and movable books. Ghosts. Monsters.

Slangerup, Erik Jon. *Dirt Boy* ill. by John Manders. Albert Whitman, 2000. ISBN 0-8075-4424-8 Subj: Activities – bathing. Behavior – running away. Family life – mothers. Health and fitness.

Slate, Joseph. *Lonely Lula cat* ill. by Bruce Degen. HarperCollins, 1985. ISBN 0-06-025807-1 Subj: Animals – cats. Emotions – loneliness. Friendship.

The mean, clean, giant canoe machine ill. by Lynn Munsinger. Crowell, 1983. ISBN 0-690-04294-9 Subj: Activities – bathing. Animals – pigs. Witches.

Miss Bindergarten gets ready for kindergarten ill. by Ashley Wolff. Dutton, 1996. ISBN 0-525-45446-2 Subj: ABC books. Animals. School – first day.

The secret stars ill. by Felipe Dávalos. Cavendish, 1998. ISBN 0-7614-5027-0 Subj: Ethnic groups in the U.S. – Hispanic Americans. Family life – grandmothers. Royalty – kings. Stars.

The star rocker ill. by Dirk Zimmer. HarperCollins, 1982. ISBN 0-06-025749-0 Subj: Bedtime. Lullabies. Stars.

Story time for Little Porcupine ill. by Jacqueline Rogers. Cavendish, 2001. ISBN 0-7614-5073-4 Subj: Activities – storytelling. Animals – porcupines. Creation. Family life – fathers. Folk and fairy tales. Sun.

Who is coming to our house? ill. by Ashley Wolff. Putnam, 1988. ISBN 0-399-21537-9 Subj: Animals. Animals – mice. Religion. Rhyming text.

Slater, Teddy. *The cow that could tap dance* ill. by Sandra Forrest. Silver Pr., 1991. ISBN 0-671-70408-7 Subj: Behavior – boasting. Character traits – questioning.

The emperor's nightingale (Andersen, H. C. [Hans Christian])

The fabulous fish from Lake Wiggawalla ill. by Laura Rankin. Silver Pr., 1991. ISBN 0-671-70409-5 Subj: Activities – traveling. Behavior – boasting.

Jan and Dan and the super dads ill. by Sandra Forrest. Silver Pr., 1991. ISBN 0-671-70410-9 Subj: Family life – fathers.

Slavin, Bill. *The cat came back* ill. by adapt. Albert Whitman, 1992. ISBN 0807510971 Subj: Activities – traveling. Animals – cats. Music. Songs.

Slawski, Wolfgang. *Captain Jonathan sails the sea* ill. by author; trans. by Rosemary Lanning. North-South, 1997. ISBN 1-55858-814-0 Subj: Boats, ships. Character traits – helpfulness. Sailors. Sea and seashore.

Sleator, William. *The angry moon* ill. by Blair Lent. Little, 1970. ISBN 0-316-78737-5 Subj: Caldecott award honor books. Folk and fairy tales. Indians of North America – Tlingit. Moon.

That's silly ill. by Lawrence DiFiori. Dutton, 1981. ISBN 0-525-40981-5 Subj: Imagination. Magic.

Sleep, baby, sleep: *an old cradle song* ill. by Trudi Oberhänsli. Atheneum, 1967. Includes melody with words. Subj: Lullabies.

Slepian, Jan. *Emily just in time* ill. by Glo Coalson. Philomel, 1998. ISBN 0-399-23043-2 Subj: Behavior – growing up. Emotions – fear. Family life – grandmothers.

The hungry thing returns ill. by Richard E. Martin. Scholastic, 1990. ISBN 0-590-42890-X Subj: Food. Rhyming text.

Lost moose ill. by Ted Lewin. Philomel, 1995. ISBN 0-399-22749-0 Subj: Animals – babies. Animals – moose. Babies. Behavior – lost.

Sloan, Alan. *The Sea World alphabet book* (The Sea World alphabet book)

Sloan, Carolyn. *Carter is a painter's cat* ill. by Fritz Wegner. Simon & Schuster, 1971. ISBN 0-671-65172-2 Subj: Animals – cats. Careers – artists.

Sloan, Sally. *The Sea World alphabet book* (The Sea World alphabet book)

Sloat, Robert. *Rib-ticklers* (Sloat, Teri)

Sloat, Teri. *Farmer Brown goes round and round* ill. by Nadine Bernard Westcott. DK, 1999. ISBN 0-7894-2512-2 Subj: Animals. Farms. Noise, sounds. Rhyming text. Weather – tornadoes.

Farmer Brown shears his sheep: a yarn about wool ill. by Nadine Bernard Westcott. DK, 2000. ISBN 0-7894-2637-4 Subj: Animals – sheep. Farms. Rhyming text.

From letter to letter ill. by author. Dutton, 1989. ISBN 0-525-44518-8 Subj: ABC books.

Patty's pumpkin patch ill. by author. Putnam, 1999. ISBN 0-399-23010-6 Subj: ABC books. Rhyming text.

Rib-ticklers by Teri and Robert Sloat; ill. by authors. Lothrop, 1995. ISBN 0-688-12520-4 Subj: Animals. Riddles.

There was an old lady who swallowed a trout ill. by Reynold Ruffins. Holt, 1998. ISBN 0-8050-4294-6 Subj: Animals. Cumulative tales. Fish. Folk and fairy tales. Humor. Rhyming text.

The thing that bothered Farmer Brown ill. by Nadine Bernard Westcott. Orchard, 1995. ISBN 0-531-08733-6 Subj: Animals. Careers – farmers. Insects – mosquitoes. Night. Noise, sounds. Rhyming text. Sleep.

Slobodkin, Louis. *Clear the track for Michael's magic train* ill. by author. Macmillan, 1945. Subj: Family life. Imagination. Rhyming text. Trains.

Colette and the princess ill. by author. Dutton, 1965. Subj: Animals – cats. Folk and fairy tales. Foreign lands – France. Noise, sounds. Royalty – princesses.

Dinny and Danny ill. by author. Macmillan, 1951. Subj: Cavemen. Character traits – helpfulness. Dinosaurs. Friendship.

Friendly animals ill. by author. Vanguard, 1944. Subj: Animals. Rhyming text.

Hustle and bustle ill. by author. Macmillan, 1962. Subj: Animals – hippopotamuses. Behavior – fighting, arguing.

The late cuckoo ill. by author. Vanguard, 1962. Subj: Clocks, watches. Time.

Magic Michael ill. by author. Macmillan, 1944. Subj: Family life. Imagination. Magic. Self-concept.

Melvin, the moose child ill. by author. Vanguard, 1967, c1957. Subj: Animals. Animals – moose. Forest, woods.

Millions and millions and millions ill. by author. Vanguard, 1955. Subj: Character traits – individuality. Rhyming text.

Moon Blossom and the golden penny ill. by author. Vanguard, 1963. ISBN 0-8149-0399-1 Subj: Foreign lands – China. Money.

One is good, but two are better ill. by author. Vanguard, 1956. Subj: Rhyming text.

Our friendly friends ill. by author. Vanguard, 1951. Subj: Animals.

The polka-dot goat ill. by author. Macmillan, 1964. Subj: Animals – goats. Foreign lands – India.

The seaweed hat ill. by author. Macmillan, 1947. Subj: Rhyming text. Sea and seashore.

Thank you - you're welcome ill. by author. Vanguard, 1957. Subj: Etiquette.

Trick or treat ill. by author. Macmillan, 1959. Subj: Holidays – Halloween.

Up high and down low ill. by author. Macmillan, 1960. Subj: Animals – goats. Animals – sheep. Concepts – up and down. Rhyming text.

Wide-awake owl ill. by author. Macmillan, 1958. Subj: Birds – owls. Music. Sleep. Songs.

Yasu and the strangers ill. by author. Macmillan, 1965. Subj: Behavior – lost. Foreign lands – Japan.

Slobodkina, Esphyr. *Billy, the condominium cat* ill. by author. Addison-Wesley, 1980. ISBN 0-201-09204-2 Subj: Animals – cats. Old age.

Boris and his balalaika ill. by Vladimir Bobri. Abelard-Schuman, 1964. Subj: Foreign lands – Russia.

Caps for sale ill. by author. Addison-Wesley, 1940. ISBN 0-06-025778-4 Subj: Animals – monkeys. Careers – peddlers. Clothing – hats. Humor. Participation.

Pezzo the peddler and the circus elephant ill. by author. Abelard-Schuman, 1967. Subj: Animals – elephants. Careers – peddlers. Circus. Clothing. Humor. Parades. Participation.

Pezzo the peddler and the thirteen silly thieves ill. by author. Abelard-Schuman, 1970. ISBN 0-200-71675-1 Subj: Careers – peddlers. Clothing. Crime. Humor. Participation.

Pinky and the petunias ill. by author. Abelard-Schuman, 1959. Based on a story by Tamara Schildkraut. Subj: Animals – cats. Flowers.

The wonderful feast ill. by author. Greenwillow, 1993. ISBN 0-688-12349-X Subj: Animals. Animals – horses, ponies. Farms. Food.

Slocum, Rosalie. *Breakfast with the clowns* ill. by author. Viking, 1937. Subj: Circus. Clowns, jesters. Food.

Slote, Elizabeth. *Nelly's garden* ill. by author. Morrow, 1991. ISBN 0-688-10014-7 Subj: Dragons. Flowers. Gardens, gardening.

Slovenz-Low, Madeline. *Lion dancer: Ernie Wan's Chinese new year* (Waters, Kate)

Slyder, Ingrid. *The Fabulous Flying Fandinis* ill. by author. Cobblehill, 1996. ISBN 0-525-65212-4 Subj: Character traits – being different. Circus. Family life.

Small, David. *Eulalie and the hopping head* ill. by author. Macmillan, 1982. ISBN 0-02-786010-8 Subj: Animals – foxes. Character traits – kindness. Frogs and toads.

George Washington's cows ill. by author. Farrar, 1994. ISBN 0-374-32535-9 Subj: Animals. Rhyming text. U.S. history.

Imogene's antlers ill. by author. Crown, 1985. ISBN 0-517-55564-6 Subj: Animals. Character traits – appearance.

Paper John ill. by author. Farrar, 1987. ISBN 0-374-35738-2 Subj: Behavior – misbehavior. Character traits – cleverness. Emotions – anger. Mythical creatures. Paper.

Ruby Mae has something to say ill. by author. Crown, 1992. ISBN 0-517-58249-X Subj: Handicaps. Language. Machines.

Small, Ernest. *see* Lent, Blair

Small, Terry. *The legend of William Tell* ill. by author. Bantam, 1991. ISBN 0-553-07031-2 Subj: Character traits – bravery. Folk and fairy tales. Poetry.

A small treasury of Christmas poems and prayers ill. by Susan Spellman. Boyds Mills, 1997. ISBN 1-56397-680-3 Subj: Holidays – Christmas. Poetry. Religion – Nativity.

A small treasury of Easter poems and prayers ill. by Susan Spellman. Boyds Mills, 1997. ISBN 1-56397-647-1 Subj: Holidays – Easter. Poetry. Religion.

Smalley, Gary. *Mooki's secret* (Gibson, Kari Smalley)

Smallman, Clare. *Outside in* ill. by Edwina Riddell. Barron's, 1986. ISBN 0-8120-5760-0 Subj: Anatomy. Format, unusual – toy and movable books.

Smalls-Hector, Irene. *Because you're lucky* ill. by Michael Hays. Little, 1997. ISBN 0-316-79867-3 Subj: Behavior – sharing. Emotions – envy, jealousy. Ethnic groups in the U.S. – African Americans. Family life – cousins. Friendship.

Beginning school ill. by Toni Goffe. Silver Pr., 1996. ISBN 0-382-39328-7 Subj: Ethnic groups in the U.S. – African Americans. School – first day.

Irene and the big, fine nickel ill. by Tyrone Geter. Little, 1991. ISBN 0-316-79871-1 Subj: City. Communities, neighborhoods. Ethnic groups in the U.S. – African Americans. Family life. Money.

Irene Jennie and the Christmas masquerade ill. by Melodye Rosales. Little, 1996. ISBN 0-316-79878-9 Subj: Ethnic groups in the U.S. – African Americans. Holidays – Christmas. Slavery.

Jenny Reen and the Jack Muh Lantern ill. by Keinyo White. Atheneum, 1996. ISBN 0-689-31875-8 Subj: Ethnic groups in the U.S. – African Americans. Holidays – Halloween. Slavery. U.S. history.

Jonathan and his mommy ill. by Michael Hays. Little, 1992. ISBN 0-316-79870-3 Subj: Activities – walking. City. Communities, neighborhoods. Ethnic groups in the U.S. – African Americans. Family life – mothers.

Kevin and his dad ill. by Michael Hays. Little, 1999. ISBN 0-316-79899-1 Subj: Ethnic groups in the U.S. – African Americans. Family life – fathers. Rhyming text.

Louise's gift: or What did she give me that for? ill. by Colin Bootman. Little, 1996. ISBN 0-316-79877-0 Subj: Ethnic groups in the U.S. – African Americans. Family life. Gifts. Self-concept.

Smaridge, Norah. *Peter's tent* ill. by Brinton Turkle. Viking, 1965. Subj: Friendship.

Watch out! ill. by Susan Perl. Abingdon, 1965. Subj: Safety.

You know better than that ill. by Susan Perl. Abingdon, 1973. ISBN 0-687-46744-6 Subj: Etiquette. Poetry.

Smart, Christopher. *For I will consider my cat Jeoffry* ill. by Emily Arnold McCully. Atheneum, 1984. ISBN 0-689-31026-9 Subj: Animals – cats. Poetry.

Smath, Jerry. *But no elephants* ill. by author. Parents, 1979. ISBN 0-8193-1008-5 Subj: Animals – elephants. Pets.

Elephant goes to school ill. by author. Parents, 1984. ISBN 0-8193-1126-X Subj: Animals – elephants. School.

A hat so simple ill. by author. BridgeWater, 1993. ISBN 0-8167-3016-4 Subj: Clothing – hats. Reptiles – alligators, crocodiles. Rhyming text.

Mr. Digby's bad day by Jerry and Valerie Smath; ill. by authors. Simon & Schuster, 1989. ISBN 0-671-67802-7 Subj: Behavior – bad day. Umbrellas. Weather – rain.

Smath, Valerie. *Mr. Digby's bad day* (Smath, Jerry)

Smee, Nicola. *Finish the story, dad* ill. by author. Simon & Schuster, 1991. ISBN 0-671-74478-X Subj: Bedtime. Dreams. Family life – fathers.

The Tusk Fairy ill. by author. BridgeWater, 1994. ISBN 0-8167-3311-2 Subj: Activities – knitting. Fairies. Family life – grandmothers. Toys.

Smith, Barry. *A child's guide to bad behavior* ill. by author. Houghton Mifflin, 1991. ISBN 0-395-57435-8 Subj: Behavior – misbehavior. Etiquette. Family life.

Cumberland Road ill. by author. Houghton Mifflin, 1989. ISBN 0-395-51739-7 Subj: Behavior – losing things. Communities, neighborhoods.

The first voyage of Christopher Columbus ill. by author. Viking, 1992. ISBN 0-670-84051-3 Subj: Activities – traveling. Boats, ships. U.S. history.

Grandma Rabbitty's visit ill. by author. DK, 1999. ISBN 0-7894-4839-4 Subj: Animals – rabbits. Family life – grandmothers. Noise, sounds.

Minnie and Ginger ill. by author. Crown, 1991. ISBN 0-517-58253-8 Subj: Family life. Foreign lands – England. Old age. Weddings.

Tom and Annie go shopping ill. by author. Houghton Mifflin, 1989. ISBN 0-395-51738-9 Subj: Shopping.

Smith, Bozena. *The enchanted book: a tale from Krakow* (Porazinska, Janina)

Smith, Cara Lockhart. *Twenty-six rabbits run riot* ill. by author. Little, 1990. ISBN 0-316-80185-2 Subj: Animals – rabbits. Behavior – lost. Behavior – misbehavior.

Smith, Catriona Mary. *The long dive* (Smith, Raymond Kenneth)

The long slide (Smith, Raymond Kenneth)

Smith, Cynthia Leitich. *Jingle dancer* ill. by Cornelius Van Wright and Ying-Hwa Hu. Morrow, 2000. ISBN 0-688-16242-8 Subj: Activities – dancing. Family life. Indians of North America.

Smith, Donald. *Farm numbers: a counting book* ill. by author. Abelard-Schuman, 1970. ISBN 0-20-071635-2 Subj: Counting, numbers. Farms.

Who's wearing my baseball cap? ill. by author. Dial, 1987. ISBN 0-8037-0396-1 Subj: Animals. Clothing – hats. Format, unusual – board books. Problem solving.

Who's wearing my bow tie? ill. by author. Dial, 1987. ISBN 0-8037-0395-3 Subj: Animals. Clothing. Format, unusual – board books. Problem solving.

Who's wearing my sneakers? ill. by author. Dial, 1987. ISBN 0-8037-0398-8 Subj: Animals. Clothing – shoes. Format, unusual – board books. Problem solving.

Who's wearing my sunglasses? ill. by author. Dial, 1987. ISBN 0-8037-0399-6 Subj: Animals. Format, unusual – board books. Glasses. Problem solving.

Smith, Edward Biko. *A lullaby for Daddy* ill. by Susan Anderson. Africa World, 1994. ISBN 0-86543-403-4 Subj: Bedtime. Ethnic groups in the U.S. – African Americans. Family life. Lullabies. Music.

Smith, Elmer Boyd. *The story of Noah's ark* ill. by author. Houghton Mifflin, 1904. Subj: Boats, ships. Religion – Noah. Weather – floods. Weather – rain. Weather – rainbows.

Smith, Henry Lee. *Frog fun* (Stratemeyer, Clara Georgeanna)

Pepper (Stratemeyer, Clara Georgeanna)

Tuggy (Stratemeyer, Clara Georgeanna)

Smith, Janice Lee. *The monster in the third dresser drawer and other stories about Adam Joshua* ill. by Dick Gackenbach. HarperCollins, 1981. ISBN 0-06-025739-3 Subj: Behavior – misbehavior. Emotions – fear. Monsters.

Wizard and Wart in trouble ill. by Paul Meisel. HarperCollins, 1998. ISBN 0-06-027762-9 Subj: Animals. Magic. Wizards.

Smith, Jean Shannon. *Scooter and the magic star* (Gardner, Mercedes)

Smith, Jim. *The frog band and Durrington Dormouse* ill. by author. Little, 1977. ISBN 0-316-80155-0 Subj: Animals – mice. Frogs and toads.

The frog band and the onion seller ill. by author. Little, 1976. ISBN 0-316-80006-6 Subj: Animals. Frogs and toads. Humor. Problem solving.

The frog band and the owlnapper ill. by author. Little, 1981. ISBN 0-316-80163-1 Subj: Animals. Birds – owls. Frogs and toads. Humor.

Nimbus the explorer ill. by author. Little, 1981. ISBN 0-316-80168-2 Subj: Animals. Dinosaurs. Imagination. Jungle.

Smith, Lane. *The big pets* ill. by author. Viking, 1991. ISBN 0-670-83378-9 Subj: Animals. Dreams. Pets.

Flying Jake ill. by author. Macmillan, 1988. ISBN 0-02-785830-8 Subj: Activities – flying. Birds. Wordless.

Glasses . . . who needs 'em? ill. by author. Viking, 1991. ISBN 0-670-84160-9 Subj: Glasses. Senses – seeing.

The Stinky Cheese Man and other fairly stupid tales (Scieszka, Jon)

Smith, Lucia B. *A special kind of sister* ill. by Chuck Hall. Holt, 1979. ISBN 0-03-047121-4 Subj: Family life. Handicaps. Sibling rivalry.

Smith, Maggie. *Dear Daisy, get well soon* ill. by author. Crown, 2000. ISBN 0-517-80073-X Subj: Counting, numbers. Days of the week, months of the year. Family life – mothers. Friendship. Illness – chicken pox. Toys.

Smith, Maggie (Margaret C.). *Counting our way to Maine* ill. by author. Orchard, 1995. ISBN 0-531-08734-4 Subj: Activities – traveling. Counting, numbers.

My grandma's chair ill. by author. Lothrop, 1992. ISBN 0-688-10664-1 Subj: Family life – grandmothers. Furniture – chairs. Imagination.

Noly Poly Rabbit Tail and me ill. by author. Lothrop, 1990. ISBN 0-688-09571-2 Subj: Friendship. Toys – dolls.

There's a witch under the stairs ill. by author. Lothrop, 1991. ISBN 0-688-09885-1 Subj: Emotions – fear. Imagination. Witches.

This is your garden ill. by author. Crown, 1998. ISBN 0-517-70993-7 Subj: Gardens, gardening.

Smith, Mary. *Long ago elf* by Mary and Robert Alan Smith; ill. by authors. Follett, 1968. Subj: Mythical creatures – elves. Mythical creatures – gnomes.

Smith, Mavis. *Circles* ill. by author. Little, 1991. ISBN 1-55782-366-9 Subj: Concepts – shape. Concepts – size.

Fred, is that you? ill. by author. Little, 1992. ISBN 0-316-80241-7 Subj: Animals. Birds – ducks. Format, unusual – toy and movable books. Rhyming text.

Good night, Jessie! (Ziefert, Harriet)

A snake mistake ill. by author. HarperCollins, 1991. ISBN 0-06-026909-X Subj: Behavior – trickery. Eggs. Farms. Reptiles – snakes.

Smith, Peter. *Jenny's baby brother* ill. by Bob Graham. Viking, 1984. ISBN 0-670-40636-8 Subj: Babies. Family life – new sibling. Sibling rivalry.

Smith, Peter Dallas. *see* Dallas-Smith, Peter

Smith, Raymond Kenneth. *The long dive* by Raymond Kenneth and Catriona Mary Smith; ill. by authors. Atheneum, 1978. ISBN 0-689-30672-5 Subj: Sea and seashore. Toys.

The long slide by Raymond Kenneth and Catriona Mary Smith; ill. by authors. Atheneum, 1977. ISBN 0-689-30576-1 Subj: Toys.

Smith, Robert Alan. *Long ago elf* (Smith, Mary)

Smith, Robert Paul. *Jack Mack* ill. by Erik Blegvad. Coward, 1960. Subj: Humor. Tongue twisters.

Nothingatall, nothingatall, nothingatall ill. by Alan E. Cober. HarperCollins, 1965. Subj: Bedtime.

When I am big ill. by Lillian Hoban. HarperCollins, 1965. Subj: Behavior – growing up.

Smith, Rodger. *This old man: a musical counting book* (Ross, Tony)

The very good dinosaur (Inkpen, Mick)

Smith, Roger. *The empty island* ill. by author. Interlink, 1991. ISBN 0-940793-69-5 Subj: Islands.

How the animals saved the ark and put two and two together ill. by author. Simon & Schuster, 1989. ISBN 0-671-66560-X Subj: Animals. Boats, ships. Religion – Noah. Weather – floods. Weather – rain.

Runners, sliders, bouncers, climbers (Bantock, Nick)

Smith. Rosie. *Captain Pajamas* (Whatley, Bruce)

Smith, Theresa Kalab. *The fog is secret* ill. by author. Prentice-Hall, 1966. Subj: Sea and seashore. Weather – fog.

Smith, Wendy. *The lonely, only mouse* ill. by author. Viking, 1986. ISBN 0-670-81251-X Subj: Animals – mice. Behavior – sharing. Emotions – loneliness. Family life – only child.

Say hello, Tilly ill. by author. Bantam, 1991. ISBN 0-553-07160-2 Subj: Animals – bears. Birthdays. Character traits – shyness.

Twice mice ill. by author. Carolrhoda, 1989. ISBN 0-87614-371-0 Subj: Animals – mice. Emotions. Family life. Sibling rivalry.

Smith, William Jay. *Around my room* ill. by Erik Blegvad. Farrar, 2000. ISBN 0-374-30406-8 Subj: Poetry.

Birds and beasts ill. by Jacques Hnizdovsky. Godine, 1990. ISBN 0-87923-865-8 Subj: Animals. Birds. Poetry.

Children of the forest (Beskow, Elsa Maartman)

Puptents and pebbles: nonsense ABC ill. by Juliet Kepes. Little, 1959. Subj: ABC books. Humor. Poetry.

The sun is up by William Jay Smith and Carol Ra; ill. by Jane Chambless Wright. Boyds Mills, 1996. ISBN 1-56397-029-5 Subj: Days of the week, months of the year. Poetry. Seasons.

The telephone (Chukovskii, Kornei Ivanovich)

Smith-Ayala, Emilie. *Marisol and the yellow messenger* ill. by Sami Suomalainen. Firefly, 1994. ISBN 1-55037-973-9 Subj: Death. Emotions – grief. Family life – fathers. Foreign lands – Canada. Foreign lands – South America.

Smith-Moore, J. J. *Sally Small* ill. by author. Price Stern Sloan, 1989. ISBN 0-8431-2360-5 Subj: Concepts – shape. Concepts – size. Dreams. Rhyming text.

Smucker, Anna Egan. *No star nights* ill. by Steve Johnson. Knopf, 1989. ISBN 0-394-99925-8 Subj: City. Machines.

Smucker, Barbara Claasen. *Selina and the bear paw quilt* ill. by Janet Wilson. Crown, 1996. ISBN 0-517-70904-X Subj: Ethnic groups in the U.S. – Amish. Family life – grandmothers. Foreign lands – Canada. Quilts. U.S. history. War.

Smyth, Gwenda. *A pet for Mrs. Arbuckle* ill. by Ann James. Crown, 1981. ISBN 0-517-55434-8 Subj: Activities – traveling. Animals – cats. Pets.

Snape, Charles. *Frog odyssey* (Snape, Juliet)

Snape, Juliet. *Frog odyssey* by Juliet and Charles Snape; ill. by authors. Simon & Schuster, 1992. ISBN 0-671-74741-X Subj: Ecology. Frogs and toads. Moving.

Sneed, Brad. *Lucky Russell* ill. by author. Putnam, 1992. ISBN 0-399-22329-0 Subj: Animals. Animals – cats. Farms. Pets.

Snell, Nigel. *A bird in hand . . . a child's guide to sayings* ill. by author. David & Charles, 1987. ISBN 0-241-11815-8 Subj: Language.

Sneve, Virginia Driving Hawk. *The Cherokees* ill. by Ronald Himler. Holiday, 1996. ISBN 0-8234-1214-8 Subj: Creation. Folk and fairy tales. Indians of North America – Cherokee. U.S. history.

The Nez Perce ill. by Ronald Himler. Holiday, 1994. ISBN 0-8234-1090-0 Subj: Creation. Indians of North America – Nez Perce. U.S. history.

Sniff, Mr. *see* Abisch, Roz

Snihura, Ulana. *I miss Franklin P. Shuckles* ill. by Leanne Franson. Annick, 1998. ISBN 1-55037-517-2 Subj: Friendship.

Snoopy on wheels ill. by Charles M. Schulz. Random House, 1983. ISBN 0-394-85630-9 Subj: Animals – dogs. Birds. Toys. Wheels.

Snow, Alan. *Cluck!* ill. by author. Bantam, 1994. ISBN 0-553-09764-4 Subj: Birds – chickens. Farms. Format, unusual – board books. Noise, sounds.

The monster book of ABC sounds ill. by author. Dial, 1991. ISBN 0-8037-0935-8 Subj: ABC books. Animals – rats. Monsters. Noise, sounds. Rhyming text.

My first atlas ill. by author. Troll, 1992. ISBN 0-8167-2517-9 Subj: World.

My first dictionary ill. by author. Troll, 1992. ISBN 0-8167-2515-2 Subj: Language.

Oink! ill. by author. Bantam, 1994. ISBN 0-553-09765-2 Subj: Animals – pigs. Farms. Format, unusual – board books. Noise, sounds.

Quack! ill. by author. Bantam, 1994. ISBN 0-553-09762-8 Subj: Birds – ducks. Farms. Format, unusual – board books. Noise, sounds.

The truth about cats ill. by author. Little, 1996. ISBN 0-316-80282-4 Subj: Animals – cats. Space and space ships.

Woof! ill. by author. Bantam, 1994. ISBN 0-553-09763-6 Subj: Animals – dogs. Farms. Format, unusual – board books. Noise, sounds.

Snow, Pegeen. *Mrs. Periwinkle's groceries* ill. by Jerry Warshaw. Childrens Pr., 1981. ISBN 0-516-03558-4 Subj: Character traits – helpfulness. Cumulative tales. Old age.

A pet for Pat ill. by Tom Dunnington. Childrens Pr., 1984. ISBN 0-516-02049-8 Subj: Pets. Rhyming text.

Snyder, Anne. *The old man and the mule* ill. by Mila Lazarevich. Holt, 1978. ISBN 0-03-022571-X Subj: Animals – mules. Character traits – meanness.

Snyder, Dianne. *The boy of the three-year nap* ill. by Allen Say. Houghton Mifflin, 1988. ISBN 0-395-44090-4 Subj: Behavior – trickery. Caldecott award honor books. Character traits – laziness. Folk and fairy tales.

Snyder, Dick. *One day at the zoo* photos by author. Scribners, 1960. Subj: Animals. Animals – koalas. Zoos.

Talk to me tiger photos by author; foreword by George H. Pournelle. Golden Gate, 1965. Subj: Animals. Zoos.

Snyder, Margaret. *I know an old lady* (Little old lady who swallowed a fly)

Snyder, Zilpha Keatley. *The changing maze* ill. by Charles Mikolaycak. Macmillan, 1985. ISBN 0-02-785900-2 Subj: Animals – sheep. Folk and fairy tales. Magic. Wizards.

Come on, Patsy ill. by Margot Zemach. Atheneum, 1982. ISBN 0-689-30892-2 Subj: Activities – playing. Behavior – growing up. Friendship.

So, Meilo. *The emperor and the nightingale* (Andersen, H. C. [Hans Christian])

Sobat, Vera. *Little Bear and the big fight* (Langreuter, Jutta)

Little Bear brushes his teeth (Langreuter, Jutta)

Little Bear goes to kindergarten (Langreuter, Jutta)

Sobol, Harriet Langsam. *A book of vegetables* photos by Patricia Agre. Dodd, 1984. ISBN 0-396-08450-8 Subj: Food. Gardens, gardening.

Clowns photos by Patricia Agre. Coward, 1982. ISBN 0-698-20558-8 Subj: Clowns, jesters.

Jeff's hospital book photos by Patricia Agre. Walck, 1975. ISBN 0-8098-1229-0 Subj: Hospitals.

We don't look like our mom and dad photos by Patricia Agre. Coward, 1984. ISBN 0-698-20608-8 Subj: Adoption. Ethnic groups in the U.S. Family life.

Sohi, Morteza E. *Look what I did with a leaf!* ill. by author. Walker, 1993. ISBN 0-8027-8216-7 Subj: Activities – making things. Nature.

Sokolinsky, Martin. *Threadbear* (Gallaz, Christophe)

Solbert, Ronni (Romaine G.). *Emily Emerson's moon* (Merrill, Jean)

Solomon, Chuck. *Moving up from kindergarten to first grade* photos by author. Crown, 1989. ISBN 0-517-57286-9 Subj: Behavior – growing up. School.

Solomon, Joan. *A present for Mum* photos by Joan and Ryan Solomon. Hamish Hamilton, 1982. ISBN 0-241-10553-6 Subj: Foreign lands – England. Shopping. Stores.

Solotareff, Grégoire. *Don't call me little bunny* ill. by author. Farrar, 1988. ISBN 0-374-35012-4 Subj: Animals – rabbits. Behavior – misbehavior. Crime. Prisons.

Never trust an ogre ill. by author. Greenwillow, 1988. ISBN 0-688-07741-2 Subj: Animals. Behavior – greed. Mythical creatures – ogres.

The ogre and the frog king ill. by author. Greenwillow, 1988. ISBN 0-688-07079-5 Subj: Frogs and toads. Monsters. Mythical creatures – ogres.

Somme, Lauritz. *The penguin family book* by Lauritz Somme and Sybille Kalas; trans. by Patricia Crampton; ill. with photos. Picture Book Studio, 1988. ISBN 0-88708-057-X Subj: Birds – penguins.

Sommers, Tish. *Bert and the broken teapot* ill. by Diane Dawson Hearn. Childrens Pr., 1985. ISBN 0-307-62114-6 Subj: Behavior – carelessness. Friendship.

Sonberg, Lynn. *A horse named Paris* ill. by Ken Robbins. Bradbury, 1986. ISBN 0-02-786260-7 Subj: Animals – horses, ponies.

Sondergaard, Arensa. *Biddy and the ducks* by Arensa Sondergaard and Mary M. Reed; ill. by Doris Henderson and Marion Henderson. Heath, 1941. Subj: Birds – chickens. Birds – ducks.

Sondheimer, Ilse. *The boy who could make his mother stop yelling* ill. by Dee deRosa. Rainbow Pr., 1982. ISBN 0-943156-00-9 Subj: Behavior – bad day. Family life – mothers.

The magic of Pomme ill. by Dee deRosa. Rainbow, 1990. ISBN 0-943156-02-5 Subj: Food. Magic. Problem solving.

The song of the Three Holy Children ill. by Pauline Baynes. Holt, 1986. The text of this edition is taken from The Book of Common Prayer, 1662. ISBN 0-8050-0134-4 Subj: Nature. Religion. Songs.

Sonneborn, Ruth A. *Friday night is papa night* ill. by Emily Arnold McCully. Viking, 1970. ISBN 0-670-32938-X Subj: City. Ethnic groups in the U.S. – Puerto Rican Americans. Family life – fathers. Poverty.

I love Gram ill. by Leo Carty. Viking, 1971. ISBN 0-670-39064-X Subj: City. Family life – grandmothers. Hospitals. Illness. Old age.

Lollipop's party ill. by Brinton Turkle. Viking, 1967. Subj: City. Emotions – loneliness. Ethnic groups in the U.S. – Puerto Rican Americans.

Seven in a bed ill. by Don Freeman. Viking, 1968. Subj: Ethnic groups in the U.S. – Puerto Rican Americans. Family life. Poverty. Sleep.

Sonnenschein, Harriet. *Harold's hideaway thumb* ill. by Jürg Obrist. Simon & Schuster, 1991. ISBN 0-671-73568-3 Subj: Animals – rabbits. Behavior – growing up. Thumb sucking.

Harold's runaway nose ill. by Jürg Obrist. Simon & Schuster, 1989. ISBN 0-671-66912-5 Subj: Animals – rabbits. Behavior – losing things. Illness.

Sopko, Eugen. *Townsfolk and countryfolk* ill. by author. Faber, 1982. ISBN 0-051-12515-8 Subj: City. Country. Foreign lands – Europe.

Sorensen, Henri. *New Hope* ill. by author. Lothrop, 1995. ISBN 0-688-13926-4 Subj: Activities – traveling. Family life. U.S. history – frontier and pioneer life.

Sorine, Stephanie Riva. *Our ballet class* photos by Daniel S. Sorine. Knopf, 1981. ISBN 0-394-94821-1 Subj: Activities – dancing. Ballet.

Soto, Gary. *Chato and the party animals* ill. by Susan Guevara. Putnam, 2000. ISBN 0-399-23159-5 Subj: Animals – cats. Birthdays. Parties.

Chato's kitchen ill. by Susan Guevara. Putnam, 1995. ISBN 0-399-22658-3 Subj: Animals – cats. Animals – dogs. Animals – mice. City. Food. Foreign languages.

The old man and his door ill. by Joe Cepeda. Putnam, 1996. ISBN 0-399-22700-8 Subj: Character traits – helpfulness. Ethnic groups in the U.S. – Mexican Americans. Food. Foreign lands. Parties. Senses – hearing.

Snapshots from the wedding ill. by Stephanie Garcia. Putnam, 1997. ISBN 0-399-22808-X Subj: Ethnic groups in the U.S. – Mexican Americans. Family life. Weddings.

Too many tamales ill. by Ed Martinez. Putnam, 1993. ISBN 0-399-22146-8 Subj: Ethnic groups in the U.S. – Mexican Americans. Food. Foreign languages. Holidays – Christmas.

Sotzek, Hannelore. *A koala is not a bear!* by Hannelore Sotzek and Bobbie Kalman; ill. with photos and drawings. Crabtree, 1997. ISBN 0-8650-5739-7 Subj: Animals – koalas.

Souhami, Jessica. *The leopard's drum: an Asante tale from West Africa* ill. by author. Little, 1995. ISBN 0-316-80466-5 Subj: Animals – leopards. Folk and fairy tales. Foreign lands – Africa.

No dinner! the story of the old woman and the pumpkin ill. by author. Cavendish, 2000. ISBN 0-7614-5059-9 Subj: Animals. Animals – wolves. Behavior – trickery. Folk and fairy tales. Foreign lands – India.

Old MacDonald had a farm (Old MacDonald had a farm)

Rama and the demon king ill. by reteller. DK, 1997. ISBN 0-7894-2450-9 Subj: Animals – monkeys. Folk and fairy tales. Foreign lands – India. Royalty – kings. Royalty – princes.

Southey, Robert. *The cataract of Lodore* ill. by Mordicai Gerstein. Dial, 1991. ISBN 0-8037-1026-7 Subj: Foreign lands – England. Poetry. Water.

Sowden, Henry. *The grand old Duke of York* photos by author. Trafalgar Square, 1989. ISBN 0-575-04081-5 Subj: Poetry. Toys – soldiers.

Sowler, Sandie. *Amazing animal disguises* ill. by Ruth Lindsay and Jane Gedye and with photos by Jerry Young. Knopf, 1992. ISBN 0-679-92768-9 Subj: Animals. Behavior – hiding.

Amazing armored animals photos by Jerry Young and Jane Burton. Knopf, 1992. ISBN 0-679-92767-0 Subj: Animals.

Soya, Kiyoshi. *A house of leaves* ill. by Akiko Hayashi. Putnam, 1987. ISBN 0-399-21422-4 Subj: Insects. Weather – rain.

Spagnoli, Cathy. *Judge Rabbit and the tree spirit* (Wall, Lina Mao)

Nine-in-one Grr! Grr! (Xiong, Blia)

Spalding, Andrea. *Me and Mr. Mah* ill. by author. Orca, 1999. ISBN 1-55143-168-8 Subj: Flowers. Friendship. Gardens, gardening. Memories, memory. Old age.

Sarah May and the new red dress ill. by Janet Wilson. Orca, 1998. ISBN 1-55143-117-3 Subj: Clothing – dresses. Family life – grandmothers. Memories, memory. Old age.

Spang, Günter. *Clelia and the little mermaid* ill. by Pepperl Ott. Abelard-Schuman, 1967. Translation of Clelia und die kleine Wassernixe. Subj: Emotions – loneliness. Foreign lands – Germany. Friendship. Mythical creatures – mermaids, mermen.

Spangenburg, Judith Dunn. *see* Dunn, Judy

Spanner, Helmut. *I am a little cat* trans. from German by Robert Kimber; ill. by author. Barron's, 1983. ISBN 0-8120-5513-6 Subj: Animals – cats. Format, unusual – board books.

Speare, Jean. *A candle for Christmas* ill. by Ann Blades. Macmillan, 1987. ISBN 0-689-50417-9 Subj: Family life. Foreign lands – Canada. Holidays – Christmas. Indians of North America.

Speed, Toby. *Brave potatoes* ill. by Barry Root. Putnam, 2000. ISBN 0-399-23158-7 Subj: Activities – cooking. Fairs. Plants.

Hattie baked a wedding cake ill. by Cathi Hepworth. Putnam, 1994. ISBN 0-399-22342-8 Subj: Activities – cooking. Food. Weddings.

Two cool cows ill. by Barry Root. Putnam, 1995. ISBN 0-399-22647-8 Subj: Animals – bulls, cows. Moon. Rhyming text.

Watervoices ill. by Julie Downing. Putnam, 1998. ISBN 0-399-22631-1 Subj: Humor. Nature. Poetry. Riddles. Water.

Spelman, Cornelia. *Mama and Daddy Bear's divorce* ill. by Kathy Parkinson. Albert Whitman, 1998. ISBN 0-8075-5221-6 Subj: Animals – bears. Divorce. Emotions.

When I feel angry ill. by Nancy Cote. Albert Whitman, 2000. ISBN 0-8075-8888-1 Subj: Animals – rabbits. Behavior. Emotions – anger.

Your body belongs to you ill. by Teri Weidner. Albert Whitman, 1997. ISBN 0-8075-9474-1 Subj: Child abuse. Health and fitness. Safety.

Spence, Robert, III. *Clickety clack* ill. by Margaret Spengler. Viking, 1999. ISBN 0-670-87946-0 Subj: Animals. Noise, sounds. Rhyming text. Trains.

Spencer, Zane. *Bright Fawn and me* (Leech, Jay)

Spetter, Jung-Hee. *Lily and Trooper's fall* ill. by author. Front Street, 1998. ISBN 1-886910-38-3 Subj: Activities – playing. Animals – dogs. Seasons – fall.

Lily and Trooper's spring ill. by author. Front Street, 1998. ISBN 1-886910-36-7 Subj: Activities – picnicking. Activities – playing. Animals – dogs. Seasons – spring.

Lily and Trooper's summer ill. by author. Front Street, 1998. ISBN 1-886910-37-5 Subj: Activities – playing. Animals – dogs. Seasons – summer.

Lily and Trooper's winter ill. by author. Front Street, 1998. ISBN 1-886910-39-1 Subj: Activities. Animals – dogs. Seasons – winter. Weather – rain. Weather – snow.

Spiegel, Doris. *Danny and Company 92* ill. by author. Coward, 1945. Subj: Careers – firefighters. Fire.

Spiegelman, Art. *I'm a dog!* ill. by author. Harper-Collins, 1997. ISBN 0-06-027320-8 Subj: Animals – dogs. Format, unusual – toy and movable books. Magic.

Spier, Peter. *Bill's service station* ill. by author. Doubleday, 1981. ISBN 0-385-15727-4 Subj: Automobiles. Format, unusual – board books.

The Book of Jonah (Bible. Old Testament. Jonah)

Bored - nothing to do! ill. by author. Doubleday, 1978. ISBN 0-385-13178-X Subj: Airplanes, airports. Behavior – boredom. Humor.

Crash! bang! boom! ill. by author. Doubleday, 1972. ISBN 0-385-26569-7 Subj: Noise, sounds. Parades. Participation.

Dreams ill. by author. Doubleday, 1986. ISBN 0-385-19336-X Subj: Dreams. Sky. Weather – clouds. Wordless.

The Erie Canal ill. by author. Doubleday, 1970. ISBN 0-385-05452-1 Subj: Folk and fairy tales. Music. Songs. U.S. history.

Fast-slow, high-low: a book of opposites ill. by author. Doubleday, 1972. ISBN 0-385-06781-X Subj: Concepts – opposites. Concepts – speed.

Firehouse ill. by author. Doubleday, 1981. ISBN 0-385-15728-2 Subj: Careers – firefighters. Format, unusual – board books.

Food market ill. by author. Doubleday, 1981. ISBN 0-385-15731-2 Subj: Food. Format, unusual – board books. Shopping. Stores.

Gobble, growl, grunt ill. by author. Doubleday, 1971. ISBN 0-385-24094-5 Subj: Animals. Noise, sounds. Participation.

The legend of New Amsterdam ill. by author. Doubleday, 1979. ISBN 0-385-13180-1 Subj: Folk and fairy tales. U.S. history.

Little cats ill. by author. Doubleday, 1984. ISBN 0-385-18197-3 Subj: Animals – cats. Format, unusual – board books.

Little dogs ill. by author. Doubleday, 1984. ISBN 0-385-18196-5 Subj: Animals – dogs. Format, unusual – board books.

Little ducks ill. by author. Doubleday, 1984. ISBN 0-385-18199-X Subj: Birds – ducks. Format, unusual – board books.

Little rabbits ill. by author. Doubleday, 1984. ISBN 0-385-18198-1 Subj: Animals – rabbits. Format, unusual – board books.

My school ill. by author. Doubleday, 1981. ISBN 0-385-15732-0 Subj: Format, unusual – board books. School.

Noah's ark ill. by author. Doubleday, 1977. Includes P. Spier's translation of The flood, by Jacobus Revius. ISBN 0-385-12730-8 Subj: Animals. Boats, ships. Caldecott award books. Religion – Noah. Rhyming text. Weather – floods. Weather – rain. Wordless.

Oh, were they ever happy! ill. by author. Doubleday, 1978. ISBN 0-385-13176-3 Subj: Activities – painting. Concepts – color. Humor.

People ill. by author. Doubleday, 1980. ISBN 0-385-13182-8 Subj: World.

The pet store ill. by author. Doubleday, 1981. ISBN 0-385-15730-4 Subj: Animals. Format, unusual – board books. Pets. Stores.

Peter Spier's Christmas! ill. by author. Doubleday, 1983. ISBN 0-385-13183-6 Subj: Holidays – Christmas.

Peter Spier's circus! ill. by author. Doubleday, 1992. ISBN 0-385-41970-8 Subj: Circus.

Peter Spier's rain ill. by author. Doubleday, 1982. ISBN 0-385-15485-2 Subj: Weather – rain. Wordless.

The toy shop ill. by author. Doubleday, 1981. ISBN 0-385-15729-0 Subj: Format, unusual – board books. Stores. Toys.

We the people: the Constitution of the United States of America ill. by author. Doubleday, 1987. ISBN 0-385-23789-8 Subj: U.S. history.

Spilka, Arnold. *Dippy dos and don'ts* (Sage, Michael)

A lion I can do without ill. by author. Walck, 1964. Subj: Humor. Rhyming text.

Little birds don't cry ill. by author. Viking, 1965. Subj: Animals. Rhyming text.

A rumbudgin of nonsense ill. by author. Scribners, 1970. Subj: Humor. Poetry.

Spinelli, Eileen. *Coming through the blizzard* ill. by Jenny Tylden-Wright. Simon & Schuster, 1999. ISBN 0-689-81490-9 Subj: Holidays – Christmas. Weather – blizzards.

Night shift daddy ill. by Melissa Iwai. Hyperion, 2000. ISBN 0-7868-2424-7 Subj: Activities – working. Family life – fathers. Night.

Somebody loves you, Mr. Hatch ill. by Paul Yalowitz. Aladdin, 1994. ISBN 0-689-71872-1 Subj: Behavior – mistakes. Careers – postal workers. Communities, neighborhoods. Emotions – loneliness. Friendship. Holidays – Valentine's Day.

Thanksgiving at Tappletons' ill. by Maryann Cocca-Leffler. Addison-Wesley, 1982. ISBN 0-201-15892-2 Subj: Behavior – sharing. Family life. Holidays – Thanksgiving. Humor.

When Mama comes home tonight ill. by Jane Dyer. Simon & Schuster, 1998. ISBN 0-689-81065-2 Subj: Bedtime. Family life – mothers. Rhyming text.

Where is the night train going? ill. by Cyd Moore. Boyds Mills, 1996. ISBN 1-56397-171-2 Subj: Bedtime. Dreams. Poetry. Sleep.

Spinner, Stephanie. *The adventures of Pinocchio* (Collodi, Carlo)

The pirates of Tarnoonga (Weiss, Ellen)

Spohn, David. *Nate's treasure* ill. by author. Lothrop, 1991. ISBN 0-688-10091-0 Subj: Anatomy – skeletons. Animals. Death. Seasons.

Starry night ill. by author. Lothrop, 1992. ISBN 0-688-11171-8 Subj: Camps, camping. Family life – brothers. Family life – fathers. Night.

Winter wood ill. by author. Lothrop, 1991. ISBN 0-688-10094-5 Subj: Family life – fathers. Forest, woods. Seasons – winter.

Spohn, Kate. *Clementine's winter wardrobe* ill. by author. Watts, 1989. ISBN 0-531-08441-8 Subj: Animals – cats. Clothing.

Introducing Fanny ill. by author. Watts, 1991. ISBN 0-531-08520-1 Subj: Food. Friendship.

Piglet's bath ill. by author. Random House, 1998. ISBN 0-679-88677-X Subj: Activities – bathing. Animals – pigs. Format, unusual – board books.

Ruth's bake shop ill. by author. Watts, 1990. ISBN 0-531-08489-2 Subj: Activities – cooking. Octopuses.

Spooner, J. B. *The story of the little Black Dog* ill. by Terre Lamb Seeley. Arcade, 1994. ISBN 1-55970-239-7 Subj: Animals – dogs. Boats, ships. Pets. Sea and seashore.

Spooner, Michael. *Old Meshikee and the little crabs: an Ojibwe story* retold by Michael Spooner and Lolita Taylor; ill. by John Hart. Holt, 1996. ISBN 0-8050-3487-0 Subj: Crustaceans. Folk and fairy tales. Indians of North America – Ojibwa. Noise, sounds. Reptiles – turtles, tortoises.

Spriggs, Ruth. *The fables of Æsop* (Æsop)

Frank Baber's Mother Goose (Mother Goose)

Springer, Margaret. *A royal ball* ill. by Tom O'Sullivan. Boyds Mills, 1992. ISBN 1-878093-64-9 Subj: Folk and fairy tales. Parties. Pets. Royalty – princes. Royalty – princesses.

Springer, Nancy. *Music of their hooves* ill. by Sandy Rabinowitz. Boyds Mills, 1994. ISBN 1563971828 Subj: Animals – horses, ponies. Poetry.

Springer, Sally. *Let's make latkes* ill. by author. Kar-Ben Copies, 1991. ISBN 0-929371-58-5 Subj: Food. Format, unusual – board books. Jewish culture. Religion.

Springstubb, Tricia. *The magic guinea pig* ill. by Bari Weissman. Morrow, 1982. ISBN 0-688-01152-7 Subj: Behavior – mistakes. Witches.

Spurr, Elizabeth. *The biggest birthday cake in the world* ill. by Rosanne Litzinger. Harcourt, 1991. ISBN 0-15-207150-4 Subj: Behavior – sharing. Birthdays. Food. Parties.

The gumdrop tree ill. by Julia Gorton. Hyperion, 1994. ISBN 0-7868-2004-7 Subj: Gardens, gardening. Trees.

The long, long letter ill. by David Catrow. Hyperion, 1996. ISBN 0-7868-2100-0 Subj: Activities – writing. Emotions – loneliness. Family life – aunts, uncles. Family life – mothers. Letters, cards. Tall tales.

Mrs. Minetta's car pool ill. by Blanche Sims. Atheneum, 1985. ISBN 0-689-31103-6 Subj: Activities – flying. Automobiles. School.

The squire's bride: *a Norwegian folk tale* orig. told by P. C. Asbjørnsen; ill. by Marcia Sewall. Atheneum, 1975. ISBN 0-689-30463-3 Subj: Folk and fairy tales. Foreign lands – Norway. Weddings.

S-Ringi, Kjell. *see* Ringi, Kjell (Arne Sorensen)

Staake, Bob. *My little ABC book* ill. by author. Little Simon, 1998. ISBN 0-689-81659-6 Subj: ABC books. Format, unusual – board books.

My little 1 2 3 book ill. by author. Little Simon, 1998. ISBN 0-689-81660-X Subj: Counting, numbers. Format, unusual – board books.

Stacy, Joel. *see* Dodge, Mary Mapes

Stadler, John. *Animal café* ill. by author. Bradbury, 1980. ISBN 0-87888-166-2 Subj: Animals. Behavior – greed. Food. Restaurants.

The ballad of Wilbur and the moose ill. by author. Warner, 1990. ISBN 1-55782-047-3 Subj: Animals – moose. Animals – pigs. Cowboys. U.S. history – frontier and pioneer life.

Cat is back at bat ill. by author. Dutton, 1991. ISBN 0-525-44762-8 Subj: Animals. Rhyming text.

The cats of Mrs. Calamari ill. by author. Orchard, 1997. ISBN 0-531-33020-6 Subj: Animals – cats. Animals – dogs. City. Glasses. Weddings.

Gorman and the treasure chest ill. by author. Bradbury, 1984. ISBN 0-02-786650-5 Subj: Animals. Behavior – sharing.

Hector, the accordion-nosed dog ill. by author. Macmillan, 1987. ISBN 0-02-786680-7 Subj: Animals – dogs. Music.

Hooray for snail! ill. by author. Crowell, 1984. ISBN 0-06-443075-8 Subj: Animals – snails. Sports – baseball.

One seal ill. by author. Orchard, 1999. ISBN 0-531-33195-4 Subj: Animals. Behavior – losing things. Kites. Sea and seashore.

Ready, set, go! ill. by author. HarperCollins, 1996. ISBN 0-06-024947-1 Subj: Animals – dogs. Self-concept. Sports – ice skating.

Snail saves the day ill. by author. Crowell, 1985. ISBN 0-690-04469-0 Subj: Animals – snails. Sports – football.

Three cheers for hippo! ill. by author. Crowell, 1987. ISBN 0-690-04670-7 Subj: Activities – flying. Animals – hippopotamuses.

Stafford, Kay. *Ling Tang and the lucky cricket* ill. by Louise Zibold. McGraw-Hill, 1944. Subj: Character traits – luck. Foreign lands – China.

Stafford, Kim Robert. *We got here together* ill. by Debra Frasier. Harcourt, 1994. ISBN 0-15-294891-0 Subj: Family life – fathers. Nature. Sea and seashore. Water.

Stafford, William. *The animal that drank up sound* ill. by Debra Frasier. Harcourt, 1992. ISBN 0-15-203563-X Subj: Animals. Insects – crickets. Noise, sounds. Seasons – spring. Seasons – winter.

Stage, Mads. *The greedy blackbird* ill. by author. John Godon Burke, 1981. ISBN 0-222-00808-3 Subj: Behavior – greed. Behavior – sharing. Birds.

The lonely squirrel ill. by author. John Godon Burke, 1980. ISBN 0-222-00738-9 Subj: Animals – squirrels. Emotions – loneliness.

Staines, Bill. *All God's critters got a place in the choir* ill. by Margot Zemach. Dutton, 1989. ISBN 0-525-44469-6 Subj: Animals. Farms. Music. Songs.

Stalder, Valerie. *Even the devil is afraid of a shrew: a folktale of Lapland* adapt. by Ray Brocket; ill. by Richard Eric Brown. Addison-Wesley, 1972. ISBN 0-20-107188-6 Subj: Behavior – nagging. Devil. Folk and fairy tales. Foreign lands – Lapland.

Stamaty, Mark Alan. *Minnie Maloney and Macaroni* ill. by author. Dial, 1976. ISBN 0-8037-5589-9 Subj: Food. Humor.

Standiford, Natalie. *Dollhouse mouse* ill. by Denise Fleming. Random House, 1989. ISBN 0-394-99935-5 Subj: Animals – mice. Sky.

The headless horseman retold by Natalie Standford; ill. by Donald Cook. Random House, 1992. Based on 'The legend of Sleepy Hollow' by Washington Irving. ISBN 0-679-91241-X Subj: Ghosts. Holidays – Halloween.

Standon, Anna. *Little duck lost* by Anna and Edward Cyril Standon; ill. by Edward Cyril Standon. Delacorte, 1965. Subj: Behavior – lost. Birds – ducks. Eggs. Family life – mothers.

The singing rhinoceros ill. by Edward Cyril Standon. Coward, 1963. Subj: Animals – rhinoceros.

Three little cats by Anna and Edward Cyril Standon; ill. by authors. Delacorte, 1964. ISBN 0-87459-000-3 Subj: Activities – playing. Animals – cats. Behavior – misbehavior. Foreign languages.

Standon, Edward Cyril. *Little duck lost* (Standon, Anna)

Three little cats (Standon, Anna)

Stanek, Muriel. *All alone after school* ill. by Ruth Rosner. Albert Whitman, 1985. ISBN 0-8075-0278-2 Subj: Character traits – bravery. Emotions – loneliness. Family life – mothers.

Left, right, left, right! ill. by Lucy Hawkinson. Albert Whitman, 1969. ISBN 0-8075-4421-3 Subj: Concepts – left and right. Emotions – embarrassment.

My little foster sister ill. by Judith Cheng. Albert Whitman, 1981. ISBN 0-8075-5365-4 Subj: Adoption. Behavior – sharing. Sibling rivalry.

One, two, three for fun ill. by Seymour Fleishman. Albert Whitman, 1967. Subj: Counting, numbers. Ethnic groups in the U.S.

Stang, Judit. *see* Varga, Judy

Stanhope, Lavinia. *see* Schlein, Miriam

Stanley, Diane. *Birdsong lullaby* ill. by author. Morrow, 1985. ISBN 0-688-05805-1 Subj: Birds. Imagination. Lullabies. Night. Sleep.

Captain Whiz-Bang ill. by author. Morrow, 1987. ISBN 0-688-06227-X Subj: Animals – cats. Behavior – growing up.

The conversation club ill. by author. Macmillan, 1983. ISBN 0-02-786740-4 Subj: Animals – mice. Clubs, gangs. Communication. Noise, sounds.

A country tale ill. by author. Four Winds, 1985. ISBN 0-02-786780-3 Subj: Animals – cats. Behavior – seeking better things. City. Country. Friendship.

The good-luck pencil ill. by Bruce Degen. Macmillan, 1986. ISBN 0-02-786800-1 Subj: Character traits – luck. Magic. School.

Siegfried ill. by John Sandford. Bantam, 1991. ISBN 0-553-07022-3 Subj: Animals – cats. Clocks, watches. Emotions – envy, jealousy.

Stanley, John. *It's nice to be little* ill. by Jean Tamburine. Rand McNally, 1965. Subj: Character traits – smallness.

Stanley, Sanna. *Monkey Sunday* ill. by author. Farrar, 1998. ISBN 0-374-35018-3 Subj: Animals. Animals – monkeys. Family life – fathers. Foreign lands – Africa. Holidays.

The rains are coming ill. by author. Greenwillow, 1993. ISBN 0-688-10949-7 Subj: Weather – rain.

Stanovich, Betty Jo. *Big boy, little boy* ill. by Virginia Wright-Frierson. Lothrop, 1984. ISBN 0-688-03808-5 Subj: Family life – grandmothers.

Hedgehog adventures ill. by Chris L. Demarest. Lothrop, 1983. ISBN 0-688-01669-3 Subj: Animals – groundhogs. Animals – hedgehogs. Character traits – loyalty.

Stan-Padilla, Viento. *Dream Feather* ill. by author. Atheneum, 1980. ISBN 0-89742-035-7 Subj: Folk and fairy tales. Indians of North America. Religion.

Stansfield, Ian. *The legend of the whale* ill. by author. Godine, 1986. ISBN 0-87923-628-0 Subj: Animals – whales. Folk and fairy tales.

Stanton, Elizabeth. *Sometimes I like to cry* by Elizabeth and Henry Stanton; ill. by Richard Leyden. Albert Whitman, 1978. ISBN 0-8075-7537-2 Subj: Emotions.

The very messy room by Elizabeth and Henry Stanton; ill. by Richard Leyden. Albert Whitman, 1978. ISBN 0-8075-5077-9 Subj: Character traits – cleanliness. Family life.

Stanton, Henry. *Sometimes I like to cry* (Stanton, Elizabeth)

The very messy room (Stanton, Elizabeth)

Stanton, Jessie. *The taxi that hurried* (Mitchell, Lucy Sprague)

Stapler, Sarah. *Cordellia, dance!* ill. by author. Dial, 1990. ISBN 0-8037-0793-2 Subj: Activities – dancing. Character traits – being different. Reptiles – alligators, crocodiles.

Spruce the moose cuts loose ill. by author. Putnam, 1992. ISBN 0-399-21861-0 Subj: Animals – moose. Birthdays. Parties.

Trilby's trumpet ill. by author. HarperCollins, 1988. ISBN 0-06-025827-6 Subj: Animals – bears. Format, unusual – toy and movable books. Music. Noise, sounds. Sibling rivalry.

Starbird, Kaye. *The covered bridge house and other poems* ill. by Jim Arnosky. Four Winds, 1979. ISBN 0-590-07544-6 Subj: Poetry.

Starret, William. *see* McClintock, Marshall

Staub, Leslie. *Bless this house* ill. by author. Harcourt, 2000. ISBN 0-15-201984-7 Subj: Animals. Bedtime. Earth. Ecology. Lullabies.

Staunton, Ted. *Taking care of Crumley* ill. by Tina Holdcroft. Kids Can Pr., 1984. ISBN 0-919964-75-3 Subj: Behavior – bullying. School.

Steadman, Ralph. *The bridge* ill. by author. Collins, 1974, c1972. ISBN 0-0019-5068-1 Subj: Behavior – fighting, arguing. Bridges. Friendship.

The little red computer ill. by author. McGraw-Hill, 1969. Subj: Computers. Space and space ships.

Stecher, Miriam B. *Daddy and Ben together* photos by Alice Kandell. Lothrop, 1981. ISBN 0-688-00736-8 Subj: Family life – fathers.

Max, the music-maker by Miriam B. Stecher and Alice Kandell; photos by Alice Kandell. Lothrop, 1980. ISBN 0-688-50958-X Subj: Music. Science.

Steel, Barry. *Greek cities* ill. by Bernard Long. Watts, 1990. ISBN 0-531-18326-2 Subj: City. Foreign lands – Greece.

Steel, Danielle. *Freddie's first night away* ill. by Jacqueline Rogers. Dell, 1992. ISBN 0-440-40574-2 Subj: Friendship. Sleep. Sleepovers.

Freddie's trip ill. by Jacqueline Rogers. Dell, 1992. ISBN 0440405734 Subj: Activities – traveling. Activities – vacationing. Automobiles. Family life.

Martha's best friend ill. by Jacqueline Rogers. Delacorte, 1989. ISBN 0-385-29801-3 Subj: Friendship.

Martha's new daddy ill. by Jacqueline Rogers. Delacorte, 1989. ISBN 0-385-29799-8 Subj: Divorce. Family life. Family life – step families.

Martha's new school ill. by Jacqueline Rogers. Delacorte, 1989. ISBN 0-385-29800-5 Subj: Friendship. Moving. School – first day.

Max and the baby sitter ill. by Jacqueline Rogers. Delacorte, 1989. ISBN 0-385-29796-3 Subj: Activities – babysitting. Animals – cats. Emotions – fear. Family life. Problem solving.

Max's daddy goes to the hospital ill. by Jacqueline Rogers. Delacorte, 1989. ISBN 0-385-29797-1 Subj: Careers – firefighters. Family life – fathers. Hospitals. Illness.

Max's new baby ill. by Jacqueline Rogers. Delacorte, 1989. ISBN 0-385-29798-X Subj: Babies. Family life – new sibling. Multiple births – twins. Sibling rivalry.

Steele, Mary Quintard Govan. *see* Gage, Wilson

Steele, Philip. *The blue whale* ill. by Ian Jackson. Kingfisher, 1994. ISBN 1-85697-509-6 Subj: Animals – endangered animals. Animals – whales.

The giant panda ill. by John Butler. Kingfisher, 1994. ISBN 1-85697-511-8 Subj: Animals – endangered animals. Animals – pandas.

Steelsmith, Shari. *When you're mad and you know it* (Crary, Elizabeth)

Steer, Dougald. *Just one more story* ill. by Elisabeth Moseng. Dutton, 1999. ISBN 0-525-46215-5 Subj:

Activities – reading. Animals – pigs. Bedtime. Folk and fairy tales. Format, unusual.

Steers, Billy. *Tractor Mac* ill. by author. Golden Books, 1999. ISBN 0-307-10224-6 Subj: Animals – horses, ponies. Farms. Self-concept. Tractors.

Steffa, Tim. *Mister King* (Siekkinen, Raija)

The nighttime book (Kunnas, Mauri)

One spooky night and other scary stories (Kunnas, Mauri)

Twelve gifts for Santa Claus (Kunnas, Mauri)

Steger, Hans-Ulrich. *Traveling to Tripiti* trans. by Elizabeth D. Crawford; ill. by author. Harcourt, 1967. Subj: Activities – traveling. Cumulative tales. Toys. Toys – bears.

Stehr, Frédéric. *Quack-quack* ill. by author. Farrar, 1987. ISBN 0-374-36161-4 Subj: Animals. Behavior – needing someone. Birds – ducks. Family life – mothers.

Steig, Jeanne. *Consider the lemming* ill. by William Steig. Farrar, 1988. ISBN 0-374-31536-1 Subj: Animals – lemmings. Poetry.

Steig, William. *Abel's Island* ill. by author. Farrar, 1976. ISBN 0-374-30010-0 Subj: Animals – mice. Islands.

The amazing bone ill. by author. Farrar, 1976. ISBN 0-374-30248-0 Subj: Animals – pigs. Caldecott award honor books. Magic.

The bad speller ill. by author. Windmill, 1970. ISBN 0-671-66526-X Subj: Games. Language.

Brave Irene ill. by author. Farrar, 1986. ISBN 0-374-30947-7 Subj: Character traits – bravery. Character traits – perseverance. Seasons – winter. Weather – snow. Weather – storms.

Caleb and Kate ill. by author. Farrar, 1977. ISBN 0-374-31016-5 Subj: Animals – dogs. Magic. Witches.

Doctor De Soto ill. by author. Farrar, 1982. ISBN 0-374-31803-4 Subj: Animals – foxes. Animals – mice. Character traits – cleverness.

Doctor De Soto goes to Africa ill. by author. HarperCollins, 1992. ISBN 0-06-205003-6 Subj: Animals – elephants. Animals – mice. Careers – dentists. Foreign lands – Africa.

An eye for elephants ill. by author. Windmill, 1970. ISBN 0-8780-7002-8 Subj: Animals – elephants. Poetry.

Farmer Palmer's wagon ride ill. by author. Farrar, 1974. ISBN 0-374-32288-0 Subj: Animals – donkeys. Animals – pigs. Humor.

Gorky rises ill. by author. Farrar, 1980. ISBN 0-374-31752-1 Subj: Frogs and toads. Magic.

Pete's a pizza ill. by author. HarperCollins, 1998. ISBN 0-06-205157-1 Subj: Activities – playing. Family life – fathers. Food. Games. Imagination.

Roland, the minstrel pig ill. by author. Simon & Schuster, 1988, c1968. ISBN 0-671-66841-2 Subj: Animals – foxes. Animals – pigs. Music. Royalty.

Rotten island ill. by author. Rev. ed. of The bad island issued in 1969. Godine, 1984. ISBN 0-87923-526-8 Subj: Flowers. Islands. Monsters.

Solomon the rusty nail ill. by author. Farrar, 1985. ISBN 0-374-37131-8 Subj: Animals – cats. Animals – rabbits. Behavior – trickery. Magic.

Spinky sulks ill. by author. Farrar, 1988. ISBN 0-374-38321-9 Subj: Character traits – stubbornness. Emotions – happiness. Family life.

Sylvester and the magic pebble ill. by author. Little Simon, 1995, c1969. ISBN 0-689-80417-2 Subj: Animals. Animals – donkeys. Caldecott award books. Family life. Magic.

Tiffky Doofky ill. by author. Farrar, 1987. ISBN 0-374-37542-9 Subj: Animals – dogs. Careers – sanitation workers. Emotions – love. Magic.

Toby, where are you? ill. by author. HarperCollins, 1997. ISBN 0-06-205082-6 Subj: Activities – playing. Animals. Behavior – hiding. Family life.

The toy brother ill. by author. HarperCollins, 1996. ISBN 0-06-205079-6 Subj: Family life – brothers. Middle Ages. Science. Sibling rivalry.

Wizzil ill. by author. Farrar, 2000. ISBN 0-374-38466-5 Subj: Birds – parakeets, parrots. Careers – farmers. Character traits – kindness. Witches.

Yellow and pink ill. by author. Farrar, 1984. ISBN 0-374-38670-6 Subj: Toys – dolls.

The Zabajaba Jungle ill. by author. Farrar, 1987. ISBN 0-374-38790-7 Subj: Dreams. Jungle.

Zeke Pippin ill. by author. HarperCollins, 1994. ISBN 0-06-205076-1 Subj: Animals – pigs. Behavior – running away. Magic. Music.

Stein, Sara Bonnett. *About dying: an open family book for parents and children together* by Sara Bonnett Stein, in cooperation with Gilbert W. Kliman [et al.]; photos by Dick Frank; graphic design by Michael Goldberg. Walker, 1974. ISBN 0-8027-6170-0 Subj: Death. Emotions – grief.

About handicaps: an open family book for parents and children together by Sara Bonnett Stein, in cooperation with Gilbert W. Kliman [et al.]; photos by Dick Frank; graphic design by Michael Goldberg. Walker, 1974. ISBN 0-8027-6174-7 Subj: Handicaps.

The adopted one: an open family book for parents and children together Thomas R. Holman, consultant; photos by Erika Stone. Walker, 1979. ISBN 0-8027-6347-2 Subj: Adoption. Family life.

Cat ill. by Manuel Garcia. Harcourt, 1985. ISBN 0-15-215150-8 Subj: Animals – cats. Science.

A child goes to school photos by Don Connors. Doubleday, 1978. ISBN 0-385-12953-X Subj: School – first day.

A hospital story: an open family book for parents and children together photos by Doris Pinney; graphic design by Michel Goldberg. Walker, 1974. ISBN 0-8027-6173-9 Subj: Careers – doctors. Careers – nurses. Hospitals. Illness.

Mouse ill. by Manuel Garcia. Harcourt, 1985. ISBN 0-15-256021-1 Subj: Animals – mice. Science.

Oh, baby! photos by Holly Anne Shelowitz. Walker, 1993. ISBN 0-8027-8262-0 Subj: Babies. Family life.

On divorce: an open family book for parents and children together Thomas R. Holman, consultant; photos by Erika Stone. Walker, 1979. ISBN 0-8027-6345-6 Subj: Divorce. Family life.

That new baby: an open family book for parents and children together by Sara Bonnett Stein, in cooperation with Gilbert W. Kliman [et al.]; photos by Dick Frank; graphic design by Michael Goldberg. Walker, 1974. ISBN 0-8027-6175-5 Subj: Babies. Family life.

Stein, Stephanie. *Lucy's feet* ill. by Kathryn A. Imler. Perspectives Pr., 1992. ISBN 0-944934-05-6 Subj: Adoption. Emotions – anger. Sibling rivalry.

Steiner, Barbara (Annette). *But not Stanleigh* photos by George and Ruth Cloven. Childrens Pr., 1980. ISBN 0-516-03454-5 Subj: Animals – raccoons.

The whale brother ill. by Gretchen Will Mayo. Walker, 1988. ISBN 0-8027-6805-9 Subj: Animals – whales. Art. Eskimos. Sea and seashore.

Steiner, Charlotte. *ABC* ill. by author. Watts, 1946. Subj: ABC books.

Birthdays are for everyone ill. by author. Doubleday, 1964. Subj: Birthdays.

The climbing book by Charlotte Steiner and Mary Burlingham; ill. by Charlotte Steiner. Vanguard, 1943. Subj: Format, unusual. Holidays – Christmas.

Daddy comes home ill. by author. Doubleday, 1944. Subj: Family life. Family life – fathers.

Five little finger playmates ill. by author. Grosset, 1951. Subj: Counting, numbers. Games. Participation.

A friend is "Amie" ill. by author. Knopf, 1956. Subj: Foreign languages. Friendship.

Kiki and Muffy ill. by author. Doubleday, 1943. Subj: Animals – cats. Family life – grandmothers.

Kiki is an actress ill. by author. Doubleday, 1958. Subj: Theater.

Kiki's play house ill. by author. Doubleday, 1962. Subj: Activities – playing.

Listen to my seashell ill. by author. Knopf, 1959. Subj: Noise, sounds. Sea and seashore.

Look what Tracy found ill. by author. Knopf, 1972. ISBN 0-394-92305-7 Subj: Activities – playing. Imagination.

Lulu ill. by author. Doubleday, 1939. Subj: Animals – dogs. Imagination – imaginary friends.

My bunny feels soft ill. by author. Knopf, 1958. Subj: Animals – rabbits.

My slippers are red ill. by author. Knopf, 1958. Subj: Concepts – color.

Pete and Peter ill. by author. Doubleday, 1941. Subj: Animals – dogs. Sports – hunting.

Pete's puppets ill. by author. Doubleday, 1952. Subj: Puppets.

Polka Dot ill. by author. Doubleday, 1947. Subj: Pets.

Red Ridinghood's little lamb ill. by author. Knopf, 1964. Subj: Animals – sheep. Games. Mythical creatures.

The sleepy quilt ill. by author. Doubleday, 1947. Subj: Bedtime. Quilts.

What's the hurry, Harry? ill. by author. Lothrop, 1968. Subj: Behavior – hurrying. Character traits – patience.

Steiner, Joan (Joan Catherine). *Look-alikes* photos by Thomas Lindley. Little, 1998. ISBN 0-316-81255-2 Subj: Picture puzzles. Rhyming text.

Look-alikes, Jr. photos by Thomas Lindley. Little, 1999. ISBN 0-316-81307-9 Subj: Picture puzzles. Rhyming text.

Steiner, Jörg. *The bear who wanted to be a bear* from an idea by Frank Tashlin; ill. by Jörg Müller. Atheneum, 1977. ISBN 0-689-50079-3 Subj: Animals – bears. Progress. Stores.

Rabbit Island ill. by Jörg Müller. Harcourt, 1978. ISBN 0-15-265034-2 Subj: Animals – rabbits. Character traits – freedom.

Steinmetz, Leon. *Clocks in the woods* ill. by author. HarperCollins, 1979. ISBN 0-06-025650-8 Subj: Animals. Clocks, watches. Time.

Stemp, Robin. *Guy and the flowering plum tree* ill. by Carolyn Dinan. Atheneum, 1981. ISBN 0-689-50188-9 Subj: Imagination. Trees.

Stemple, Adam. *Jane Yolen's Old MacDonald songbook* (Yolen, Jane)

The lap-time song and play book (Yolen, Jane)

Stenmark, Victoria. *The singing chick* ill. by Randy Cecil. Holt, 1999. ISBN 0-8050-5255-0 Subj: Activities – singing. Animals. Birds – chickens.

Stephens, Helen. *I'm too busy* ill. by author. DK, 1999. ISBN 0-7894-2606-4 Subj: Animals – cats. Format, unusual – board books.

What about me? ill. by author. DK, 1999. ISBN 0-7894-4840-8 Subj: Animals – cats. Emotions – envy, jealousy. Ethnic groups in the U.S. – African Americans. Friendship.

Stephens, Karen. *Jumping* ill. by George Wiggins. Grosset, 1965. ISBN 0-448-04949-X Subj: Activities – jumping.

Stephenson, Dorothy. *How to scare a lion* ill. by John E. Johnson. Follett, 1965. Subj: Animals – lions. Illness.

The night it rained toys ill. by John E. Johnson. Follett, 1963. Subj: Holidays – Christmas. Poetry. Royalty. Toys.

Stepto, Michele. *Snuggle Piggy and the magic blanket* ill. by John Himmelman. Dutton, 1987. ISBN 0-525-44308-8 Subj: Animals – pigs. Family life. Night.

Steptoe, John. *Baby says* ill. by author. Lothrop, 1988. ISBN 0-688-07424-3 Subj: Activities – playing. Babies. Sibling rivalry.

Birthday ill. by author. Holt, 1972. ISBN 0-0309-1308-X Subj: Birthdays. Ethnic groups in the U.S. – African Americans.

Creativity ill. by Earl B. Lewis. Clarion, 1997. ISBN 0-395-68706-3 Subj: Ethnic groups in the U.S. – African Americans. Ethnic groups in the U.S. – Puerto Rican Americans. Friendship. School.

Daddy is a monster . . . sometimes ill. by author. Lippincott, 1980. ISBN 0-397-31893-6 Subj: Family life – fathers. Monsters.

Jeffrey Bear cleans up his act ill. by author. Lothrop, 1983. ISBN 0-688-01642-1 Subj: Animals – bears. School.

Mufaro's beautiful daughters: an African tale ill. by author. Lothrop, 1987. ISBN 0-688-04046-2 Subj: Caldecott award honor books. Character traits – kindness. Character traits – meanness. Folk and fairy tales. Foreign lands – Africa. Royalty – kings.

My special best words ill. by author. Viking, 1974. ISBN 0-670-50118-2 Subj: Ethnic groups in the U.S. – African Americans. Family life. Language.

Stevie ill. by author. HarperCollins, 1969. ISBN 0-06-025764-4 Subj: Ethnic groups in the U.S. – African Americans. Friendship.

The story of jumping mouse: a Native American legend ill. by author. Lothrop, 1984. ISBN 0-688-01903-X Subj: Animals – mice. Caldecott award honor books. Folk and fairy tales. Frogs and toads. Magic.

Uptown ill. by author. HarperCollins, 1970. Subj: City. Ethnic groups in the U.S. – African Americans. Poverty.

Sterling, Helen. *see* Hoke, Helen L.

Stern, Elsie-Jean. *Wee Robin's Christmas song* ill. by Elsie McKean. Nelson, 1945. Subj: Birds – robins. Holidays – Christmas. Music. Songs.

Stern, Maggie. *Acorn magic* ill. by Donna Ruff. Greenwillow, 1998. ISBN 0-688-15699-1 Subj: Animals. Animals – moose. Camps, camping.

The missing sunflowers ill. by Donna Ruff. Greenwillow, 1997. ISBN 0-688-14873-5 Subj: Animals – squirrels. Flowers. Mystery stories. Plants.

Stern, Mark. *It's a dog's life* ill. by author. Atheneum, 1978. ISBN 0-689-30643-1 Subj: Animals – dogs. Character traits – freedom.

Stern, Peter. *Floyd, a cat's story* ill. by author. HarperCollins, 1982. ISBN 0-06-025779-2 Subj: Animals – cats.

Max the dragon ill. by author. Crown, 1990. ISBN 0-517-57588-4 Subj: Animals – mice. Dragons. Monsters.

Stern, Ronnie. *Pop's secret* (Townsend, Maryann)

Stern, Simon. *Mrs. Vinegar* ill. by author. Prentice-Hall, 1979. ISBN 0-13-604488-3 Subj: Homes, houses.

Vasily and the dragon: an epic Russian fairy tale ill. by author. Merrimack, 1983. ISBN 0-7207-1331-5 Subj: Dragons. Folk and fairy tales. Foreign lands – Russia.

Steven, Kenneth C. *The bearer of gifts* ill. by Lily Moon. Dial, 1998. ISBN 0-8037-2374-1 Subj: Careers – woodcarvers. Gifts. Holidays – Christmas. Santa Claus.

Stevens, Bryna. *Borrowed feathers and other fables* ill. by Freire Wright and Michael Foreman. Random House, 1978. ISBN 0-394-83622-7 Subj: Folk and fairy tales.

Handel and the famous sword swallower of Halle ill. by Ruth Tietjen Councell. Putnam, 1990. ISBN 0-399-21548-4 Subj: Family life – fathers. Music.

Stevens, Carla. *Hooray for pig!* ill. by Rainey Bennett. Seabury Pr., 1974. ISBN 0-8164-3114-0 Subj: Animals. Animals – pigs. Sports – swimming.

Pig and the blue flag ill. by Rainey Bennett. Seabury Pr., 1977. ISBN 0-8164-3192-2 Subj: Animals. Animals – pigs. School. Sports – gymnastics.

Stories from a snowy meadow ill. by Eve Rice. Seabury Pr., 1976. ISBN 0-8164-3161-2 Subj: Animals. Character traits – kindness. Death. Friendship.

Stevens, Cat. *Teaser and the firecat* ill. by author. Four Winds, 1974. ISBN 0-590-07372-9 Subj: Animals – cats. Foreign languages. Imagination. Moon. Night.

Stevens, Harry. *Fat mouse* ill. by author. Viking, 1987. ISBN 0-670-80529-7 Subj: Animals. Animals – mice. Circular tales. Format, unusual – board books.

Parrot told snake ill. by author. Viking, 1987. ISBN 0-670-80530-0 Subj: Animals. Behavior – gossip. Format, unusual – board books.

Stevens, Jan Romero. *Twelve lizards leaping: a new Twelve days of Christmas* ill. by Christine Mau. Rising Moon, 1999. ISBN 0-8735-8744-8 Subj: Cumulative tales. Holidays – Christmas. Music. Religion. Songs.

Stevens, Janet. *Androcles and the lion* (Æsop)

Animal fair adapt. and ill. by Janet Stevens. Holiday, 1981. ISBN 0-8234-0388-2 Subj: Animals. Dreams. Fairs. Poetry.

The Bremen town musicians (Grimm, Jacob)

Cook-a-doodle-doo! by Janet Stevens and Susan Stevens Crummel; ill. by Janet Stevens. Harcourt, 1999. ISBN 0-15-201924-3 Subj: Activities – cooking. Animals. Birds – chickens. Food.

The emperor's new clothes (Andersen, H. C. [Hans Christian])

Goldilocks and the three bears (The three bears)

It's perfectly true! (Andersen, H. C. [Hans Christian])

My big dog by Janet Stevens and Susan Stevens Crummel; ill. by Janet Stevens. Golden Books, 1999. ISBN 0-307-10220-3 Subj: Animals – cats. Animals – dogs. Behavior – running away. Friendship.

Old bag of bones ill. by author. Holiday, 1996. ISBN 0-8234-1215-6 Subj: Animals. Animals – coyotes. Folk and fairy tales. Indians of North America – Shoshone. Old age.

The princess and the pea (Andersen, H. C. [Hans Christian])

The three billy goats Gruff (Asbjørnsen, P. C. [Peter Christen])

Tops and bottoms ill. by author. Harcourt, 1995. ISBN 0-15-292851-0 Subj: Animals – bears. Animals – rabbits. Behavior – trickery. Caldecott award honor books. Character traits – cleverness. Folk and fairy tales. Gardens, gardening.

The tortoise and the hare: an Æsop fable (Æsop)

The town mouse and the country mouse (Æsop)

Stevens, Kathleen. *Aunt Skilly and the stranger* ill. by Robert Andrew Parker. Ticknor & Fields, 1994. ISBN 0-395-68712-8 Subj: Birds – geese. Country. Crime. Quilts.

The beast in the bathtub ill. by Ray Bowler. Gareth Stevens, 1985. ISBN 0-918831-15-6 Subj: Activities – bathing. Bedtime. Monsters.

Stevens, Margaret (Dean). *When grandpa died* ill. by Kenneth Ualand. Childrens Pr., 1979. ISBN 0-516-02025-0 Subj: Death. Emotions – grief. Family life – grandfathers.

Stevens, Susanna. *The changeling* (Lagerlöf, Selma)

Stevenson, Drew. *The ballad of Penelope Lou . . . and me* ill. by Marcia Sewall. Crossing Pr., 1978. ISBN 0-89594-004-3 Subj: Character traits – bravery. Emotions – fear. Rhyming text. Sailors.

Stevenson, Harvey. *Big scary wolf* ill. by author. Clarion, 1997. ISBN 0-395-74213-7 Subj: Animals – wolves. Bedtime. Emotions – fear. Noise, sounds.

Grandpa's house ill. by author. Hyperion, 1994. ISBN 1-56282-589-5 Subj: Activities – traveling. Family life – grandfathers. Seasons – summer.

Stevenson, James. *All aboard!* ill. by author. Greenwillow, 1995. ISBN 0-688-12439-9 Subj: Activities – traveling. Animals – mice. Fairs. Trains.

Are we almost there? ill. by author. Greenwillow, 1985. ISBN 0-688-04239-2 Subj: Activities – traveling. Animals – dogs. Behavior – fighting, arguing.

Brr! ill. by author. Greenwillow, 1991. ISBN 0-688-09211-X Subj: Family life – grandfathers. Seasons – winter.

Clams can't sing ill. by author. Greenwillow, 1980. ISBN 0-688-84280-1 Subj: Animals. Music. Noise, sounds. Sea and seashore.

"Could be worse!" ill. by author. Greenwillow, 1977. ISBN 0-688-84075-2 Subj: Family life. Family life – grandfathers. Farms. Monsters.

Don't make me laugh ill. by author. Farrar, 1999. ISBN 0-374-31827-1 Subj: Animals. Behavior. Humor.

Emma ill. by author. Greenwillow, 1985. ISBN 0-688-04021-7 Subj: Behavior – trickery. Witches.

Fried feathers for Thanksgiving ill. by author. Greenwillow, 1986. ISBN 0-688-06676-3 Subj: Behavior – trickery. Character traits – meanness. Witches.

Fun, no fun ill. by author. Greenwillow, 1994. ISBN 0-688-11674-4 Subj: Careers – artists. Careers – writers. Concepts – opposites. Emotions.

Grandpa's great city tour: an alphabet book ill. by author. Greenwillow, 1983. ISBN 0-688-02324-X Subj: ABC books. Activities – flying. City. Family life – grandfathers. Wordless.

Grandpa's too-good garden ill. by author. Greenwillow, 1989. ISBN 0-688-08486-9 Subj: Family life – grandfathers. Gardens, gardening.

The great big especially beautiful Easter egg ill. by author. Greenwillow, 1983. ISBN 0-688-01791-6 Subj: Eggs. Family life – grandfathers.

Happy Valentine's Day, Emma! ill. by author. Greenwillow, 1987. ISBN 0-688-07358-1 Subj: Animals. Character traits – meanness. Holidays – Valentine's Day. Humor. Witches.

Heat wave at Mud Flat ill. by author. Greenwillow, 1997. ISBN 0-688-14206-0 Subj: Animals. Weather. Weather – rain.

Higher on the door ill. by author. Greenwillow, 1987. ISBN 0-688-06637-2 Subj: Behavior – growing up. Family life – grandparents.

Howard ill. by author. Greenwillow, 1980. ISBN 0-688-84255-0 Subj: Behavior – lost. Birds – ducks. Friendship.

I meant to tell you ill. by author. Greenwillow, 1996. ISBN 0-688-14178-1 Subj: Behavior – growing up. Careers – artists. Careers – writers. Family life – daughters. Family life – fathers.

July ill. by author. Greenwillow, 1990. ISBN 0-688-08823-6 Subj: Family life – grandparents. Sea and seashore. Seasons – summer.

Mr. Hacker ill. by author. Greenwillow, 1990. ISBN 0-688-09217-9 Subj: Animals. Emotions – loneliness. Pets.

Monty ill. by author. Greenwillow, 1992. ISBN 0-688-11241-2 Subj: Animals – rabbits. Birds – ducks. Frogs and toads. Reptiles – alligators, crocodiles.

The most amazing dinosaur ill. by author. Greenwillow, 2000. ISBN 0-688-16433-1 Subj: Anatomy – skeletons. Animals. Animals – rats. Dinosaurs. Museums.

National worm day ill. by author. Greenwillow, 1990. ISBN 0-688-08772-8 Subj: Animals. Friendship.

No friends ill. by author. Greenwillow, 1986. ISBN 0-688-06507-4 Subj: Family life – grandfathers. Friendship. Moving.

No need for Monty ill. by author. Greenwillow, 1987. ISBN 0-688-07084-1 Subj: Animals. Reptiles – alligators, crocodiles. Transportation.

Quick! Turn the page! ill. by author. Greenwillow, 1990. ISBN 0-688-09309-4 Subj: Problem solving.

Rolling Rose ill. by author. Greenwillow, 1992. ISBN 0-688-10675-7 Subj: Activities. Activities – walking. Babies.

Sam the Zamboni man ill. by Harvey Stevenson. Greenwillow, 1998. ISBN 0-688-14485-3 Subj: Careers. Family life – fathers. Machines. Sports – hockey. Sports – ice skating.

The Sea View Hotel ill. by author. Greenwillow, 1978. ISBN 0-688-84168-6 Subj: Activities – vacationing. Animals – mice. Hotels.

The stowaway ill. by author. Greenwillow, 1990. ISBN 0-688-08620-9 Subj: Animals – mice. Boats, ships. Friendship.

That dreadful day ill. by author. Greenwillow, 1985. ISBN 0-688-04036-5 Subj: Family life – grandfathers. School – first day.

That terrible Halloween night ill. by author. Greenwillow, 1980. ISBN 0-688-94281-X Subj: Family life – grandfathers. Holidays – Halloween.

That's exactly the way it wasn't ill. by author. Greenwillow, 1991. ISBN 0-688-09869-X Subj: Family life – brothers. Family life – grandfathers. Sibling rivalry.

There's nothing to do! ill. by author. Greenwillow, 1986. ISBN 0-688-04699-1 Subj: Behavior – boredom. Family life – grandfathers.

A village full of valentines ill. by author. Greenwillow, 1995. ISBN 0-688-13603-6 Subj: Animals. Holidays – Valentine's Day.

We can't sleep ill. by author. Greenwillow, 1982. ISBN 0-688-01214-0 Subj: Animals. Bedtime. Family life – grandfathers. Sleep.

What's under my bed? ill. by author. Greenwillow, 1983. ISBN 0-688-02327-4 Subj: Bedtime. Emotions – fear. Family life – grandfathers. Furniture – beds.

When I was nine ill. by author. Greenwillow, 1986. ISBN 0-688-05943-0 Subj: Family life.

Which one is Whitney? ill. by author. Greenwillow, 1990. ISBN 0-688-09062-1 Subj: Animals. Fish. Sea and seashore.

Wilfred the rat ill. by author. Greenwillow, 1977. ISBN 0-688-84103-1 Subj: Animals – chipmunks. Animals – rats. Animals – squirrels. Friendship.

Will you please feed our cat? ill. by author. Greenwillow, 1987. ISBN 0-688-06848-0 Subj: Character traits – helpfulness. Family life – grandfathers. Pets.

Winston, Newton, Elton, and Ed ill. by author. Greenwillow, 1978. ISBN 0-688-84152-X Subj: Animals – walruses. Birds – penguins. Sibling rivalry.

The wish card ran out! ill. by author. Greenwillow, 1981. ISBN 0-688-84305-0 Subj: Behavior – wishing.

Worse than the worst ill. by author. Greenwillow, 1994. ISBN 0-688-12250-7 Subj: Animals – dogs. Behavior – misbehavior. Family life – aunts, uncles.

Worse than Willy! ill. by author. Greenwillow, 1984. ISBN 0-688-02597-8 Subj: Babies. Family life – grandfathers. Family life – new sibling. Imagination. Sibling rivalry.

The worst person in the world ill. by author. Greenwillow, 1978. ISBN 0-688-84127-9 Subj: Friendship.

The worst person in the world at Crab Beach ill. by author. Greenwillow, 1988. ISBN 0-688-07299-2 Subj: Friendship. Humor.

The worst person's Christmas ill. by author. Greenwillow, 1991. ISBN 0-688-10211-5 Subj: Character traits – meanness. Holidays – Christmas.

Yard sale ill. by author. Greenwillow, 1996. ISBN 0-688-14127-7 Subj: Animals. Garage sales, rummage sales.

Yuck! ill. by author. Greenwillow, 1984. ISBN 0-688-03830-1 Subj: Magic. Witches.

Stevenson, Jocelyn. *Jim Henson's Muppets at sea* ill. by Graham Thompson. Random House, 1980. ISBN 0-394-84571-4 Subj: Boats, ships. Puppets. Sea and seashore.

Red and the pumpkins ill. by Kelly Oechsli. Holt, 1983. ISBN 0-03-068679-2 Subj: Food. Imagination. Puppets.

Stevenson, Robert Louis. *Block city* ill. by Ashley Wolff. Dutton, 1988. ISBN 0-525-44399-1 Subj: Imagination. Poetry. Sea and seashore. Toys.

A child's garden of verses ill. by Erik Blegvad. Random House, 1978. ISBN 0-394-93739-2 Subj: Poetry.

A child's garden of verses ill. by Pelagie Doane. Doubleday, 1942. Subj: Poetry.

A child's garden of verses ill., selected and arranged by Cooper Edens. DK, 1997. ISBN 0-7894-2068-6 Subj: Poetry.

A child's garden of verses ill. by Toni Frissell. U.S. Camera, 1944. Subj: Poetry.

A child's garden of verses ill. by Diane Goode. Morrow, 1998. ISBN 0-688-14584-1 Subj: Poetry.

A child's garden of verses ill. by Joan Hassall. HarperCollins, 1986. ISBN 0-87226-051-8 Subj: Poetry.

A child's garden of verses ill. by Joanna Isles. Abrams, 1994. ISBN 0-8109-3196-6 Subj: Poetry.

A child's garden of verses ill. by Thomas Kinkade; comp. by June Ford. Tommy Nelson, 1999. ISBN 0-8499-5869-5 Subj: Poetry.

A child's garden of verses ill. by Thea Kliros. Dover, 1992. ISBN 0-486-27301-6 Subj: Poetry.

A child's garden of verses ill. by Charles Robinson. Mainstream: Waterstone's, 1990. Reproduced from the 1896 edition. ISBN 1-85158-391-2 Subj: Poetry.

A child's garden of verses ill. by Jessie Willcox Smith. Children's Classics, 1995. ISBN 0-517-12397-5 Subj: Poetry.

A child's garden of verses ill. by Tasha Tudor. Simon & Schuster, 1999. ISBN 0-689-81882-3 Subj: Poetry.

The moon ill. by Denise Saldutti. HarperCollins, 1984. ISBN 0-06-025789-X Subj: Family life. Moon. Night. Poetry. Sports – fishing.

Where go the boats? ill. by Max Grover. Browndeer, 1998. ISBN 0-15-201711-9 Subj: Activities – playing. Poetry.

Stevenson, Suçie. *Christmas eve* ill. by author. Putnam, 1988. ISBN 0-399-21667-7 Subj: Animals – rabbits. Family life – sisters. Holidays – Christmas. Sibling rivalry.

Do I have to take Violet? ill. by author. Dodd, 1987. ISBN 0-396-08921-6 Subj: Activities – playing. Animals – rabbits. Sibling rivalry.

I forgot ill. by author. Watts, 1988. ISBN 0-531-08344-6 Subj: Animals. Behavior – forgetfulness. Birthdays.

Jessica the blue streak ill. by author. Watts, 1989. ISBN 0-531-08398-5 Subj: Animals – dogs. Behavior – misbehavior. Family life – fathers. Pets.

The princess and the pea (Andersen, H. C. [Hans Christian])

The twelve dancing princesses (Grimm, Jacob)

Stewart, Anne. *The ugly duckling* (Andersen, H. C. [Hans Christian])

Stewart, Charles P. *Dinosaurs and other creatures of long ago* (Stewart, Frances Todd)

Stewart, Dana. *Friends from Galilee: a Bible-times visit with Micah and Hannah* ill. by Kathy A. Couri. Standard, 1994. ISBN 0-7847-0003-6 Subj: Family life. Foreign lands – Galilee. Foreign lands – Palestine.

Stewart, Elizabeth Laing. *The lion twins* photos by Marlin and Carol Morse Perkins. Atheneum, 1964. Subj: Animals – lions. Multiple births – twins.

Stewart, Frances Todd. *Dinosaurs and other creatures of long ago* by Frances Todd Stewart and Charles P. Stewart, III; ill. by Forest Rogers and Kathy Borland. HarperCollins, 1988. ISBN 0-694-00229-1 Subj: Dinosaurs.

Stewart, Paul. *The birthday presents* ill. by Chris Riddell. HarperCollins, 2000. ISBN 0-06-028279-7 Subj: Animals – hedgehogs. Animals – rabbits. Behavior – sharing. Birthdays. Gifts.

A little bit of winter ill. by Chris Riddell. HarperCollins, 1999. ISBN 0-06-028278-9 Subj: Animals – hedgehogs. Animals – rabbits. Friendship. Hibernation. Seasons – winter.

Stewart, Robert S. *The daddy book* ill. by Don Madden. American Heritage, 1972. ISBN 0-07-061348-6 Subj: Careers. Family life – fathers.

Stewart, Sarah. *The gardener* ill. by David Small. Farrar, 1997. ISBN 0-374-32517-0 Subj: Caldecott award honor books. Careers – bakers. Family life – aunts, uncles. Gardens, gardening. Letters, cards. U.S. history.

The library ill. by David Small. Farrar, 1995. ISBN 0-374-34388-8 Subj: Activities – reading. Libraries. Rhyming text.

The money tree ill. by David Small. Farrar, 1991. ISBN 0-374-35014-0 Subj: Money. Seasons. Trees.

Stewig, John Warren. *Clever Gretchen* ill. by Patricia Wittmann. Cavendish, 2000. ISBN 0-7614-5066-1 Subj: Character traits – cleverness. Devil. Folk and fairy tales. Magic.

The fisherman and his wife (Grimm, Jacob)

King Midas ill. by Omar Rayyan. Holiday, 1999. ISBN 0-8234-1423-X Subj: Behavior – greed. Folk and fairy tales. Foreign lands – Greece. Royalty – kings.

Stone soup ill. by Margot Tomes. Holiday, 1991. ISBN 0-8234-0863-9 Subj: Character traits – cleverness. Folk and fairy tales. Food.

Stickland, Henrietta. *Dinosaur roar!* (Stickland, Paul)

Stickland, Paul. *A child's book of things* ill. by author. Watts, 1990. ISBN 0-531-08506-6 Subj: Activities. Family life.

Dinosaur roar! by Paul and Henrietta Stickland; ill. by Paul Stickland. Dutton, 1994. ISBN 0-525-45276-1 Subj: Concepts – opposites. Dinosaurs. Rhyming text.

Dinosaur stomp! ill. by author. Dutton, 1996. ISBN 0-525-45591-4 Subj: Activities – dancing. Dinosaurs. Format, unusual – toy and movable books. Rhyming text.

Machines as big as monsters ill. by author. Random House, 1989. ISBN 0-394-93913-1 Subj: Concepts – size. Machines.

Ten terrible dinosaurs ill. by author. Dutton, 1997. ISBN 0-525-45905-7 Subj: Counting, numbers. Dinosaurs. Rhyming text.

Truck jam ill. by author. Ragged Bears, 2000. ISBN 1-929927-03-7 Subj: Format, unusual – toy and movable books. Transportation. Trucks.

Stier, Catherine. *If I were president* ill. by DyAnne DiSalvo-Ryan. Albert Whitman, 1999. ISBN 0-8075-3541-9 Subj: U.S. history.

Stiles, Martha Bennett. *Island magic* ill. by Daniel San Souci. Atheneum, 1999. ISBN 0-689-80588-8 Subj: Family life – grandfathers. Islands. Nature.

Stiles, Norman. *I'll miss you, Mr. Hooper* ill. by Joseph Mathieu. Random House, 1984. ISBN 0-394-96600-7 Subj: Death. Emotions – grief. Puppets.

The Sesame Street ABC storybook (Moss, Jeffrey)

Still, James. *Jack and the wonder beans* ill. by Margot Tomes. Putnam, 1977. ISBN 0-399-20498-9 Subj: Folk and fairy tales. Giants.

Stillerman, Marci. *Nine spoons* ill. by Pesach Gerber. Hachai, 1998. ISBN 0-922613-84-2 Subj: Holidays – Hanukkah. Holocaust. Jewish culture. Religion. War.

Stillwell, Fred. *The airplane alphabet book* (Pallotta, Jerry)

Stilz, Carol Curtis. *Grandma Buffalo, May, and me* ill. by Constance R. Bergum. Sasquatch, 1995. ISBN 1-57061-015-0 Subj: Animals – buffaloes. Family life – grandmothers. U.S. history – frontier and pioneer life.

Kirsty's kite ill. by Gwen Harrison. Albatross, 1988. ISBN 0-86760-089-6 Subj: Death. Emotions – grief. Family life – grandfathers. Family life – mothers. Kites.

Stimson, Joan. *Big Panda, Little Panda* ill. by Meg Rutherford. Barron's, 1994. ISBN 0-8120-6404-6 Subj: Animals – pandas. Babies. Behavior – growing up. Family life – brothers and sisters. Family life – mothers. Family life – new sibling.

Stinchecum, Amanda Mayer. *All about scabs* (Yagya, Genichiro)

The gas we pass: the story of farts (Cho, Shinta)

Girl from the snow country (Hidaka, Masako)

Grandpa's town (Nomura, Takaaki)

Stine, Jovial Bob. *Pork and beans: play date* ill. by José Aruego and Ariane Dewey. Scholastic, 1989. ISBN 0-590-41579-4 Subj: Activities – playing. Animals – pigs. Games. Sibling rivalry.

Stinson, Kathy. *The bare naked book* ill. by Heather Collins. Firefly, 1986. ISBN 0-920303-52-8 Subj: Anatomy.

The dressed up book ill. by Heather Collins. Firefly, 1990. ISBN 1-55037-104-5 Subj: Activities – playing. Clothing. Imagination.

Mom and dad don't live together any more ill. by Nancy Lou Reynolds. Firefly, 1984. ISBN 0-920236-92-8 Subj: Divorce.

Red is best ill. by Robin Baird Lewis. Firefly, 1982. ISBN 0-920236-24-3 Subj: Concepts – color.

Teddy Rabbit ill. by Stéphane Poulin. Firefly, 1988. ISBN 1-55037-017-0 Subj: Toys. Trains.

Those green things ill. by Mary McLoughlin. Firefly, 1985. ISBN 0-920303-40-4 Subj: Imagination.

Stites, Clara. *The ugly duckling* (Andersen, H. C. [Hans Christian])

Stobbs, Joanna. *One sun, two eyes, and a million stars* by Joanna and William Stobbs; ill. by authors. Merrimack, 1983. ISBN 0-19-279747-6 Subj: Counting, numbers.

Stobbs, William. *Animal pictures* ill. by author. Bodley Head, 1982. ISBN 0-370-30341-5 Subj: Animals. Wordless.

A car called beetle ill. by author. Merrimack, 1979. ISBN 0-370-11144-3 Subj: Automobiles.

The hare and the frogs (Æsop)

Jack and the beanstalk (Jack and the beanstalk)

The little red hen (The little red hen)

One sun, two eyes, and a million stars (Stobbs, Joanna)

There's a hole in my bucket ill. by author. Merrimack, 1983. ISBN 0-19-279755-7 Subj: Seasons – summer. Songs.

This little piggy ill. by author. Bodley Head, 1981. ISBN 0-370-30428-4 Subj: Animals – pigs. Counting, numbers. Nursery rhymes. Rhyming text.

Stock, Catherine. *Alexander's midnight snack: a little elephant's ABC* ill. by author. Clarion, 1988. ISBN 0-89919-512-1 Subj: ABC books. Animals – elephants. Bedtime. Food.

The birthday present ill. by author. Bradbury, 1991. ISBN 0-02-788401-5 Subj: Birthdays. Parties.

Christmas time ill. by author. Bradbury, 1990. ISBN 0-02-788403-1 Subj: Family life – fathers. Holidays – Christmas.

Easter surprise ill. by author. Bradbury, 1991. ISBN 0-02-788371-X Subj: Family life – mothers. Holidays – Easter.

Emma's dragon hunt ill. by author. Lothrop, 1984. ISBN 0-688-02698-2 Subj: Dragons. Family life – grandfathers.

Halloween monster ill. by author. Bradbury, 1990. ISBN 0-02-788404-X Subj: Activities. Emotions – fear. Holidays – Halloween.

An island summer ill. by author. Lothrop, 1999. ISBN 0-688-12781-9 Subj: Islands. Seasons – summer.

Sampson the Christmas cat ill. by author. Putnam, 1984. ISBN 0-399-21002-4 Subj: Animals – cats. Holidays – Christmas.

Secret Valentine ill. by author. Bradbury, 1991. ISBN 0-02-788372-8 Subj: Character traits – kindness. Holidays – Valentine's Day.

Sophie's bucket ill. by author. Lothrop, 1985. ISBN 0-688-04225-2 Subj: Family life. Sea and seashore.

Sophie's knapsack ill. by author. Lothrop, 1988. ISBN 0-688-06458-2 Subj: Camps, camping. Family life.

Thanksgiving treat ill. by author. Bradbury, 1990. ISBN 0-02-788402-3 Subj: Family life – grandfathers. Holidays – Thanksgiving.

Stockdale, Susan. *Some sleep standing up* ill. by author. Simon & Schuster, 1997. ISBN 0-689-80509-8 Subj: Animals. Cumulative tales. Sleep.

Stoddard, Sandol. *Bedtime for bear* ill. by Lynn Munsinger. Houghton Mifflin, 1985. ISBN 0-395-38811-2 Subj: Animals – bears. Bedtime. Rhyming text.

Bedtime mouse ill. by Lynn Munsinger. Houghton Mifflin, 1981. ISBN 0-395-31609-X Subj: Animals. Animals – mice. Bedtime. Cumulative tales. Rhyming text.

Curl up small ill. by Trina Schart Hyman. Houghton Mifflin, 1964. Subj: Concepts – shape. Concepts – size. Family life. Imagination.

My very own special particular private and personal cat ill. by Remy Charlip. Houghton Mifflin, 1963. Subj: Animals – cats. Pets. Rhyming text.

The thinking book ill. by Ivan Chermayeff. Little, 1960. Subj: Family life. Imagination.

Turtle time ill. by Lynn Munsinger. Houghton Mifflin, 1995. ISBN 0-395-56754-8 Subj: Bedtime. Pets. Reptiles – turtles, tortoises. Rhyming text.

Stoeke, Janet Morgan. *A hat for Minerva Louise* ill. by author. Dutton, 1994. ISBN 0-525-45328-8 Subj: Behavior – misunderstanding. Birds – chickens. Clothing.

Hide and seek ill. by author. Dutton, 1999. ISBN 0-525-46189-2 Subj: Animals. Behavior – hiding. Birds – chickens. Farms. Format, unusual – board books. Games.

Minerva Louise ill. by author. Dutton, 1988. ISBN 0-525-44374-6 Subj: Behavior – misunderstanding. Birds – chickens.

Minerva Louise at school ill. by author. Dutton, 1996. ISBN 0-525-45494-2 Subj: Behavior – misunderstanding. Birds – chickens. School.

Minerva Louise at the fair ill. by author. Dutton, 2000. ISBN 0-525-46439-5 Subj: Behavior – mistakes. Birds – chickens. Fairs.

Stojic, Manya. *Rain* ill. by author. Crown, 2000. ISBN 0-517-80086-1 Subj: Animals. Cumulative tales. Foreign lands – Africa. Weather – rain.

Stoker, Wayne. *I can be a welder* (Lillegard, Dee)

Stolz, Mary Slattery. *Storm in the night* ill. by Pat Cummings. HarperCollins, 1988. ISBN 0-06-025912-4 Subj: Ethnic groups in the U.S. – African Americans. Family life – grandfathers. Night. Weather – storms.

Zekmet, the stone carver: a tale of Ancient Egypt ill. by Deborah Nourse Lattimore. Harcourt, 1988. ISBN 0-15-299961-2 Subj: Activities – working. Foreign lands – Egypt.

Stone, A. Harris. *The last free bird* ill. by Sheila Heins. Prentice-Hall, 1967. Subj: Birds. Ecology.

Stone, Bernard. *The charge of the mouse brigade* by Bernard Stone with Alice Low; ill. by Tony Ross. Pantheon, 1980. ISBN 0-394-84390-8 Subj: Animals – cats. Animals – mice. War.

Emergency mouse ill. by Ralph Steadman. Prentice-Hall, 1978. ISBN 0-13-274555-0 Subj: Animals – mice. Hospitals.

Stone, Beth. *Do you have a secret? how to get help for scary secrets* (Russell, Pamela)

Stone, Jon. *Big Bird in China* photos by Victor DiNapoli. Random House, 1983. ISBN 0-394-95645-1 Subj: Foreign lands – China. Puppets.

Stone, Kazuko G. *Goodnight Twinklegator* ill. by author. Scholastic, 1990. ISBN 0-590-43183-8 Subj: Bedtime. Imagination. Night. Reptiles – alligators, crocodiles. Sky. Stars.

Stone, Marti. *The singing fir tree* ill. by Barry Root. Putnam, 1992. ISBN 0-399-22207-3 Subj: Folk and fairy tales. Foreign lands – Switzerland. Trees.

Stone, Phoebe. *Go away, Shelley Boo!* ill. by author. Little, 1999. ISBN 0-316-81677-9 Subj: Friendship. Imagination.

What night do the angels wander? ill. by author. Little, 1998. ISBN 0-316-81439-3 Subj: Angels. Holidays – Christmas. Rhyming text.

When the Wind Bears go dancing ill. by author. Little, 1997. ISBN 0-316-81701-5 Subj: Nature. Weather – storms. Weather – wind.

Stone, Rosetta. *Because a little bug went ka-choo!* ill. by Michael K. Frith. Random House, 1975. ISBN 0-394-93130-0 Subj: Cumulative tales. Humor. Insects. Rhyming text.

Stonehouse, Bernard. *Kangaroos* ill. with photos. Raintree, 1978. ISBN 0-8172-1079-2 Subj: Animals – kangaroos.

Storm, Theodor. *Little Hobbin* trans. from German by Anthea Bell; ill. by Lisbeth Zwerger. North-South, 1995. ISBN 1-55858-461-7 Subj: Activities – traveling. Bedtime. Dreams. Folk and fairy tales. Furniture – beds. Moon. Sun.

Little John (Orgel, Doris)

Storr, Catherine (Cole). *Clever Polly and the stupid wolf* ill. by Marjorie-Ann Watts. Faber, 1979. ISBN 0-571-18011-6 Subj: Animals – wolves. Character traits – cleverness.

Hugo and his grandma ill. by Nita Sowter. Merrimack, 1980. ISBN 0-85122-136-X Subj: Activities – knitting. Family life – grandmothers.

King Midas ill. by Mike Codd. Raintree, 1985. ISBN 0-8172-2112-3 Subj: Behavior – greed. Behavior – wishing. Royalty – kings.

Rip Van Winkle (Irving, Washington)

Robin Hood ill. by Chris Collingwood. Raintree, 1984. ISBN 0-8172-2109-3 Subj: Foreign lands – England. Forest, woods. Middle Ages.

Stortz, Diane M. *Barnaby Mouse, detective, and the mystery of the big book* ill. by Patrick Girouard. Standard, 1994. ISBN 0-7847-0004-4 Subj: Activities – reading. Animals – mice. Careers – detectives. Mystery stories. Religion.

Stott, Dorothy. *Little Duck's bicycle ride* ill. by author. Dutton, 1991. ISBN 0-525-44728-8 Subj: Birds – ducks. Farms. Sports – bicycling.

Too much ill. by author. Dutton, 1990. ISBN 0-525-44569-2 Subj: Birds – ducks. Sports – swimming.

Stott, Rowena. *The hedgehog feast* ill. by Edith Holden. Dutton, 1978. ISBN 0-525-61580-2 Subj: Animals – hedgehogs. Hibernation. Parties.

Stover, Jo Ann. *If everybody did* ill. by author. McKay, 1960. ISBN 0-89084-487-9 Subj: Behavior. Etiquette. Rhyming text.

Why? Because ill. by author. McKay, 1961. Subj: Character traits – questioning.

Strachan, Geoffrey. *3 X 3: Three by three* (Krüss, James)

Strahl, Rudi. *Sandman in the lighthouse* tr. and adapt. by Anthea Bell; ill. by Eberhard Binder. Childrens Pr., 1967, 1969. Subj: Bedtime. Light-houses. Mythical creatures – sandman. Sea and seashore.

Straight, Susan. *Bear E. Bear* ill. by Marisabina Russo. Hyperion, 1995. ISBN 1-56282-527-5 Subj: Ethnic groups in the U.S. – African Americans. Family life. Laundry. Toys – bears.

Straker, Joan Ann. *Animals that live in the sea* ill. with photos. National Geographic, 1979. ISBN 0-8704-4264-3 Subj: Sea and seashore.

Strand, Keith. *Grandfather's Christmas tree* ill. by Thomas Locker. Silver Whistle, 1999. ISBN 0-15-201821-2 Subj: Birds – geese. Character traits – kindness to animals. Holidays – Christmas. U.S. history – frontier and pioneer life.

Strand, Mark. *The night book* ill. by William Pène Du Bois. Crown, 1985. ISBN 0-517-55047-4 Subj: Emotions – fear. Night.

The planet of lost things ill. by William Pène du Bois. Crown, 1983. ISBN 0-517-54184-X Subj: Bedtime. Dreams. Noise, sounds.

Strange, Florence. *Rock-a-bye whale: a story of the birth of a humpback whale* ill. by author. Manzanita, 1977. ISBN 0-931644-08-3 Subj: Animals – whales. Science.

Stratemeyer, Clara Georgeanna. *Frog fun* by Clara G. Stratemeyer and Henry Lee Smith, Jr.; ill. by Lucy Hawkinson. HarperCollins, 1963. Subj: Frogs and toads.

Pepper by Clara G. Stratemeyer and Henry Lee Smith, Jr. Benziger, 1971. Subj: Animals. Animals – cats.

Tuggy by Clara Georgeanna Stratemeyer and Henry Lee Smith, Jr. HarperCollins, 1971. Subj: Animals – dogs. Frogs and toads.

Strathdee, Jean. *The house that grew* ill. by Jessica Wallace. Oxford Univ. Pr., 1980. ISBN 0-19-558041-9 Subj: Family life. Homes, houses. Moving.

Strauss, Gwen. *The night shimmy* ill. by Anthony Browne. Knopf, 1992. ISBN 0-679-92384-5 Subj: Behavior – needing someone. Dreams. Friendship. Imagination – imaginary friends. Kites.

Trail of stones ill. by Anthony Browne. Knopf, 1990. ISBN 0-679-90582-0 Subj: Emotions. Folk and fairy tales. Poetry.

Strauss, Susan. *When woman became the sea: a Costa Rican creation myth* ill. by Cristina Acosta. Beyond Words, 1998. ISBN 1-885223-85-4 Subj: Creation. Folk and fairy tales. Foreign lands – Costa Rica. Sea and seashore.

Streatfield, Noel. *Sleepy Nicholas* (Brande, Marlie)

Street, Pat. *There's a frog in my throat: 312 animal sayings from the horse's mouth* (Leedy, Loreen)

Stren, Patti. *Hug me* ill. by author. HarperCollins, 1977. ISBN 0-06-026081-5 Subj: Animals – porcupines. Emotions – loneliness.

Mountain Rose ill. by author. Dutton, 1982. ISBN 0-525-35228-7 Subj: Character traits – appearance. Self-concept. Sports – wrestling.

Strete, Craig Kee. *Big thunder magic* ill. by Craig McFarland Brown. Greenwillow, 1990. ISBN 0-688-08854-6 Subj: Animals – sheep. Friendship. Indians of North America – Pueblo.

How the Indians bought the farm by Craig Kee Strete and Michelle Netten Chacon; ill. by Francisco X. Mora. Greenwillow, 1996. ISBN 0-688-14131-5 Subj: Animals. Behavior – trickery. Farms. Indians of North America.

The lost boy and the monster ill. by Steve Johnson and Lou Fancher. Putnam, 1999. ISBN 0-399-22922-1 Subj: Animals. Character traits – kindness to animals. Folk and fairy tales. Indians of North America – Southwest. Monsters. Reptiles – snakes.

They thought they saw him ill. by José Aruego and Ariane Dewey. Greenwillow, 1996. ISBN 0-688-14195-1 Subj: Concepts – color. Reptiles – lizards.

Strickland, Tessa. *Please, Mr. Crocodile!* (Please, Mr. Crocodile!)

Strom, Maria Diaz. *Rainbow Joe and me* ill. by author. Lee & Low, 1999. ISBN 1-880000-93-8 Subj: Concepts – color. Ethnic groups in the U.S. – African Americans. Friendship. Handicaps – blindness. Music.

Strong, Stacie. *Runners, sliders, bouncers, climbers* (Bantock, Nick)

Stroud, Bettye. *Down home at Miss Dessa's* ill. by Felicia Marshall. Lee & Low, 1996. ISBN 1-880000-39-3 Subj: Character traits – kindness. Ethnic groups in the U.S. – African Americans. Family life – sisters. Illness. Old age. Seasons – summer.

Stroud, Virginia A. *A walk to the Great Mystery* ill. by author. Dial, 1995. ISBN 0-8037-1637-0 Subj: Family life – grandmothers. Indians of North America – Cherokee. Nature.

Stroyer, Poul. *It's a deal* ill. by author. Astor-Honor, 1960. Subj: Activities – trading. Humor.

Strub, Susanne. *Lulu goes swimming* ill. by author. Viking, 1990. ISBN 0-670-83460-2 Subj: Behavior – growing up. Dreams. Sports – swimming.

Lulu on her bike ill. by author. Viking, 1990. ISBN 0-670-83461-0 Subj: Behavior – growing up. Dreams. Sports – bicycling.

Struppi ill. by Ingrid Graichen. Imported Pubs., 1983. ISBN 0-8285-2583-8 Subj: Animals. Format, unusual – board books. Wordless.

Stuart, Chad. *The Ballymara flood* ill. by George Booth. Harcourt, 1996. ISBN 0-15-205698-X Subj: Activities – bathing. Foreign lands – Ireland. Rhyming text. Weather – floods.

Stuart, Mary. *see* Graham, Mary Stuart Campbell

Stuart-Clark, Christopher. *Bright star shining: poems for Christmas* (Bright star shining)

Stubbs, Joanna. *Happy Bear's day* ill. by author. Elsevier-Dutton, 1979. ISBN 0-233-96999-3 Subj: Animals – bears. Behavior – solitude.

With cat's eyes you'll never be scared of the dark ill. by author. Dutton, 1983. ISBN 0-233-97485-7 Subj: Emotions – fear. Magic. Night.

Sturges, Philemon. *I love trucks!* ill. by Shari Halpern. HarperCollins, 1999. ISBN 0-06-027819-6 Subj: Careers – truck drivers. Rhyming text. Trucks.

The Little Red Hen makes a pizza (The little red hen)

Marushka and the Month Brothers: a folktale (Vojtech, Anna)

Ten flashing fireflies ill. by Anna Vojtech. North-South, 1995. ISBN 1-55858-421-8 Subj: Counting, numbers. Insects – fireflies. Night. Rhyming text.

What's that sound, Woolly Bear? ill. by Joan Paley. Little, 1996. ISBN 0-316-82021-0 Subj: Insects. Insects – butterflies, caterpillars. Insects – moths. Metamorphosis. Noise, sounds.

Who took the cookies from the cookie jar? (Lass, Bonnie)

Sturgis, Matthew. *Tosca's surprise* ill. by Anne Mortimer. Dial, 1991. ISBN 0-8037-0946-3 Subj: Animals – cats.

Sturtzel, Howard A. *see* Annixter, Paul

Sturtzel, Jane Levington. *see* Annixter, Jane

Stutson, Caroline. *By the light of the Halloween moon* ill. by Kevin Hawkes. Lothrop, 1993. ISBN 0-688-12046-6 Subj: Cumulative tales. Holidays – Halloween. Rhyming text.

Cowpokes ill. by Daniel San Souci. Lee & Shepard, 1999. ISBN 0-688-13974-4 Subj: Cowboys. Rhyming text.

Prairie primer A to Z ill. by Susan Condie Lamb. Dutton, 1996. ISBN 0-525-45163-3 Subj: ABC books. Family life. Farms. Rhyming text. U.S. history – frontier and pioneer life.

Stuve-Bodeen, Stephanie. *Elizabeti's doll* ill. by Christy Hale. Lee & Low, 1998. ISBN 1-880000-70-9 Subj: Emotions – love. Foreign lands – Tanzania. Imagination. Rocks. Toys – dolls.

Mama Elizabeti ill. by Christy Hale. Lee & Low, 2000. ISBN 1-58430-002-7 Subj: Babies. Family life – brothers. Family life – new sibling. Foreign lands – Tanzania.

We'll paint the octopus red ill. by Pam DeVito. Woodbine House, 1998. ISBN 1-890627-06-2 Subj: Family life – brothers and sisters. Handicaps – Down syndrome.

Stynes, Barbara White. *Walking with mama* ill. by author. Dawn Pub., 1997. ISBN 1-883220-56-4 Subj: Activities – walking. Family life – mothers.

Suba, Susanne. *The monkeys and the pedlar* ill. by author. Viking, 1970. ISBN 0-670-48655-8 Subj: Animals – monkeys. Careers – peddlers. Humor.

Suben, Eric. *Pigeon takes a trip* ill. by Tiziana Zanetti; graphic design by Giorgio Vanetti. Golden Books, 1984. ISBN 0-307-17103-5 Subj: Activities – traveling. Birds – pigeons. Format, unusual – board books.

Suen, Anastasia. *Delivery* ill. by Wade Zahares. Viking, 1999. ISBN 0-670-88455-3 Subj: Rhyming text. Transportation.

Window music ill. by Wade Zahares. Viking, 1998. ISBN 0-670-87287-3 Subj: Activities – trading. Family life – mothers. Rhyming text. Trains.

Suetake, Kunihiro. *Red dragonfly on my shoulder* (Cassedy, Sylvia)

Sueyoshi, Akiko. *Ladybird on a bicycle* ill. by Viv Allbright. Faber, 1983. ISBN 0-571-11802-X Subj: Insects – ladybugs. Sports – bicycling.

Sugar snow adapt. from the Little house books by Laura Ingalls Wilder; ill. by Doris Ettlinger. HarperCollins, 1998. ISBN 0-06-025933-7 Subj: Careers – farmers. U.S. history – frontier and pioneer life.

Sugita, Yutaka. *The flower family* ill. by author. McGraw-Hill, 1975. ISBN 0-07-061769-4 Subj: Flowers. Plants. Science.

Good night 1, 2, 3 ill. by author. Scroll Pr., 1971. ISBN 0-87592-022-5 Subj: Bedtime. Counting, numbers. Sleep.

Helena the unhappy hippopotamus ill. by author. McGraw-Hill, 1972. ISBN 0-07-061763-5 Subj: Animals – hippopotamuses. Behavior – needing someone. Emotions – loneliness. Emotions – sadness. Friendship.

My friend Little John and me ill. by author. McGraw-Hill, 1972. ISBN 0-07-062458-5 Subj: Animals – dogs. Wordless.

Suhl, Yuri. *The Purim goat* ill. by Kaethe Zemach. Four Winds, 1980. ISBN 0-590-07658-2 Subj: Animals – goats. Character traits – helpfulness. Holidays – Purim.

Simon Boom gives a wedding ill. by Margot Zemach. Four Winds, 1972. Subj: Cumulative tales. Humor. Jewish culture. Weddings.

Sullivan, Charles. *Numbers at play* ill. by author. Rizzoli, 1992. ISBN 0-8478-1501-3 Subj: Art. Counting, numbers. Rhyming text.

Sullivan, Silky. *Grandpa was a cowboy* ill. by Bert Dodson. Orchard, 1996. ISBN 0-531-08861-8 Subj: Cowboys. Family life – aunts, uncles. Family life – grandfathers. Old age. Orphans.

Sumiko. *Kittymouse* ill. by author. Harcourt, 1979. ISBN 0-15-243028-8 Subj: Animals – cats. Animals – mice.

Summers, Kate. *Milly and Tilly: the story of a town mouse and a country mouse* ill. by Maggie Kneen. Dutton, 1997. ISBN 0-525-45801-8 Subj: Animals – mice. City. Country. Folk and fairy tales.

Milly's wedding ill. by Maggie Kneen. Dutton, 1999. ISBN 0-525-46046-2 Subj: Animals – mice. Emotions – love. Weddings.

Summers, Susan. *The fourth wise man* based on the story by Henry Van Dyke; ill. by Jackie Morris. Dial, 1998. ISBN 0-8037-2312-1 Subj: Religion – Nativity.

Sundgaard, Arnold. *The bear who loved Puccini* ill. by Dominic Catalano. Putnam, 1992. ISBN 0-399-22135-2 Subj: Activities – singing. Animals – bears.

Jethro's difficult dinosaur ill. by Stanley Mack. Pantheon, 1977. ISBN 0-394-93391-X Subj: Dinosaurs. Eggs. Humor. Rhyming text.

The lamb and the butterfly ill. by Eric Carle. Watts, 1988. ISBN 0-531-08379-9 Subj: Animals – sheep. Character traits – freedom. Insects – butterflies, caterpillars.

Meet Jack Appleknocker ill. by Sheila White Samton. Putnam, 1988. ISBN 0-399-21472-0 Subj: Imagination.

Sundvall, Viveca. *Mimi and the biscuit factory* trans. from Swedish by Eris Bibb; ill. by Eva Eriksson. Farrar, 1989. ISBN 9-12-959142-2 Subj: Careers – bakers. Foreign lands – Sweden. School. Teeth.

Super, Gretchen. *Family traditions* ill. by Kees de Kiefte. Twenty-first Century, 1992. ISBN 0-8050-2218-X Subj: Etiquette. Family life.

Sisters and brothers ill. by Kees de Kiefte. Twenty-first Century, 1992. ISBN 0-8050-2219-8 Subj: Family life. Family life – brothers and sisters. Sibling rivalry.

The Superman mix or match storybook ill. by Ross Andru and Joe Orlando. Random House, 1979. ISBN 0-394-84211-1 Subj: Format, unusual – toy and movable books.

Supraner, Robyn. *Giggly-wiggly, snickety-snick* ill. by Stan Tusan. Parents, 1978. ISBN 0-8193-0855-2 Subj: Concepts.

Sam Sunday and the mystery at the Ocean Beach Hotel ill. by Will Hillenbrand. Viking, 1996. ISBN 0-670-84797-6 Subj: Animals. Birthdays. Careers – detectives. Friendship. Hotels. Mystery stories.

Would you rather be a tiger? ill. by Barbara Cooney. Houghton Mifflin, 1973. ISBN 0-395-15495-2 Subj:

Behavior. Imagination. Rhyming text. Self-concept.

Supree, Burton. *Harlequin and the gift of many colors* (Charlip, Remy)

"Mother, mother I feel sick" (Charlip, Remy)

Surany, Anico. *Kati and Kormos* ill. by Leonard Everett Fisher. Holiday, 1966. Subj: Animals – dogs. Emotions – loneliness. Foreign lands – Hungary.

Ride the cold wind ill. by Leonard Everett Fisher. Putnam, 1964. Subj: Boats, ships. Foreign lands – South America. Sports – fishing.

Surat, Michele Maria. *Angel child, dragon child* ill. by Vo-Dinh Mai. Raintree, 1983. ISBN 0-940742-12-8 Subj: Ethnic groups in the U.S. – Vietnamese Americans. School.

Sussman, Susan. *Hippo thunder* ill. by John C. Wallner. Albert Whitman, 1982. ISBN 0-8075-3307-6 Subj: Bedtime. Emotions. Weather – thunder.

Sutcliff, Rosemary. *The minstrel and the dragon pup* ill. by Emma Chichester Clark. Candlewick, 1993. ISBN 1-56402-098-3 Subj: Dragons. Eggs.

Suteev, V. (Vladimir). *The adventures of Snowwoman* (Arnold, Katya)

Meow! (Arnold, Katya)

Three kittens (Ginsburg, Mirra)

Sutherland, Colleen. *Jason goes to show-and-tell* ill. by Linda Weller. Boyds Mills, 1992. ISBN 1-878093-89-4 Subj: Behavior – forgetfulness. Character traits – orderliness. Clothing. Cumulative tales. School. Seasons – winter. Toys – bears.

Sutherland, Harry A. *Dad's car wash* ill. by Maxie Chambliss. Atheneum, 1988. ISBN 0-689-31335-7 Subj: Activities – bathing. Bedtime. Imagination.

Sutton, Elizabeth Henning. *A pony for keeps* ill. by Mary Brant Gamma. Thomasson-Grant, 1991. ISBN 0-934738-77-7 Subj: Animals – horses, ponies. Birthdays.

Sutton, Eve. *My cat likes to hide in boxes* ill. by Lynley Dodd. Parents, 1973. ISBN 0-8193-0753-X Subj: Animals – cats. Cumulative tales. Participation. Rhyming text.

Sutton, Jane. *What should a hippo wear?* ill. by Lynn Munsinger. Houghton Mifflin, 1979. ISBN 0-395-27800-7 Subj: Activities – dancing. Animals. Animals – hippopotamuses. Clothing.

Svend Otto S (Svend Otto Sorensen). *The giant fish and other stories* trans. from Danish by Joan Tate; ill. by author. Larousse, 1982. ISBN 0-88332-287-0 Subj: Behavior – growing up. Foreign lands.

Taxi dog ill. by author. Parents, 1978. ISBN 0-8193-0916-8 Subj: Animals – dogs. Behavior – running away. Careers – taxi drivers.

The three billy goats Gruff (Asbjørnsen, P. C. [Peter Christen])

Svendsen, Carol. *Hulda* ill. by Julius Svendsen. Houghton Mifflin, 1974. ISBN 0-395-19497-0 Subj: Behavior. Mythical creatures – trolls. Rhyming text.

Swados, Elizabeth. *Lullaby* ill. by Faith Hubley. HarperCollins, 1980. ISBN 0-06-026085-8 Subj: Bedtime. Lullabies.

Swain, Ruth Freeman. *Bedtime!* ill. by Cat Bowman Smith. Holiday, 1999. ISBN 0-8234-1444-2 Subj: Bedtime. Behavior. Furniture – beds. Sleep.

Swamp, Jake. *Giving thanks* ill. by Erwin Printup, Jr. Lee & Low, 1995. ISBN 1-880000-15-6 Subj: Ecology. Indians of North America – Mohawk. Nature. Religion.

Swan, Donald. *The hippopotamus song: a muddy love story* (Flanders, Michael)

Swan flyway: the tundra swan ill. by Jo-Ellen Bosson. Soundprints Pr., 1993. ISBN 0-92448-395-4 Subj: Birds – swans. Migration.

Swann, Brian. *A basket full of white eggs: riddle-poems* ill. by Ponder Goembel. Watts, 1988. ISBN 0-531-08334-9 Subj: Poetry. Proverbs. Riddles.

The house with no door: African riddle-poems ill. by Ashley Bryan. Harcourt, 1998. ISBN 0-15-200805-5 Subj: Folk and fairy tales. Foreign lands – Africa. Poetry. Riddles.

Swanson, June. *Summit up* ill. by Susan Slattery Burke. Lerner, 1994. ISBN 0-8225-2342-6 Subj: Mountains. Riddles.

Swanson-Natsues, Lyn. *Days of adventure* ill. by Joy Dunn Keenan. Mondo, 1996. ISBN 1-57255-160-7 Subj: Activities – playing. Ethnic groups in the U.S. – African Americans. Ethnic groups in the U.S. – Asian Americans. Imagination.

Swartz, Leslie. *A first Passover* ill. by Jacqueline Chwast. Modern Curriculum, 1992. ISBN 0-8136-2305-7 Subj: Holidays – Passover. Jewish culture.

Swartz, Nancy Sohn. *In our image: God's first creatures* ill. by Melanie Hall. Jewish Lights, 1998. ISBN 1-879045-99-0 Subj: Animals. Behavior – sharing. Creation. Religion.

Sweeney, Jacqueline. *Katie and the night noises* ill. by Arden Johnson. BridgeWater, 1993. ISBN 0-816-73014-8 Subj: Bedtime. Imagination. Noise, sounds. Rhyming text.

Sweet, Melissa. *Fiddle-i-fee* ill. by adapt. Little, 1992. ISBN 0-316-82516-6 Subj: Animals. Cumulative tales. Farms. Music. Songs.

Sweeten, Sami. *Wolf* ill. by author. Albert Whitman, 1994. ISBN 0-8075-9160-2 Subj: Animals – wolves.

Sweetland, Nancy. *God's quiet things* ill. by Rick Stevens. Eerdmans, 1994. ISBN 0-8028-5082-0 Subj: Behavior – solitude. Nature. Rhyming text.

Swendson, Patsy. *The potluck adventures of Mrs. Marmalade* by Patsy Swendson and Debbie Little; ill. by authors. Eakin Pr., 1989. ISBN 0-89015-718-9 Subj: Activities – cooking. Animals. Animals – possums.

Swift, Hildegarde Hoyt. *The little red lighthouse and the great gray bridge* by Hildegarde H. Swift and Lynd Ward; ill. by Lynd Ward. Harcourt, 1942. Subj: Boats, ships. Bridges. Lighthouses.

Swinburne, Stephen R. *Guess whose shadow?* ill. by author. Boyds Mills, 1999. ISBN 1-56397-724-9 Subj: Activities – photographing. Lights. Shadows.

Swallows in the birdhouse ill. by Robin Brickman. Millbrook, 1996. ISBN 1-56294-182-8 Subj: Activities – making things. Birds – swallows. Homes, houses.

Water for one, water for everyone: a counting book of African animals ill. by Melinda Levine. Millbrook, 1998. ISBN 0-7613-0269-7 Subj: Animals. Counting, numbers. Foreign lands – Africa.

What's a pair? What's a dozen? ill. by author. Boyds Mills, 2000. ISBN 1-56397-827-X Subj: Concepts. Counting, numbers.

What's opposite? ill. by author. Boyds Mills, 2000. ISBN 1-56397-881-4 Subj: Concepts – opposites.

Switzer, Robert E. *My friend the babysitter* (Watson, Jane Werner)

My friend the dentist (Watson, Jane Werner)

My friend the doctor (Watson, Jane Werner)

Sometimes a family has to move (Watson, Jane Werner)

Sometimes a family has to split up (Watson, Jane Werner)

Sometimes I get angry (Watson, Jane Werner)

Sometimes I'm afraid (Watson, Jane Werner)

Sometimes I'm jealous (Watson, Jane Werner)

Swope, Sam. *The Araboolies of Liberty Street* ill. by Barry Root. Crown, 1989. ISBN 0-517-57411-X Subj: Behavior. Communities, neighborhoods.

Gotta go! Gotta go! ill. by Sue Riddle. Farrar, 2000. ISBN 0-374-32757-2 Subj: Foreign lands – Mexico. Insects – butterflies, caterpillars. Migration.

Sykes, Julie. *Dora's eggs* ill. by Jane Chapman. Little Tiger, 1997. ISBN 1-888444-09-6 Subj: Animals. Birds – chickens. Birth. Eggs. Farms.

Hurry, Santa! ill. by Tim Warnes. Little Tiger, 1998. ISBN 1-888444-37-1 Subj: Behavior – tardiness. Holidays – Christmas. Santa Claus.

I don't want to take a bath! ill. by Tim Warnes. Little Tiger, 1997. ISBN 1-888444-20-7 Subj: Activities – bathing. Animals. Animals – tigers. Behavior – running away. Family life – mothers.

Little Tiger's big surprise ill. by Tim Warnes. Little Tiger, 1999. ISBN 1-888444-52-5 Subj: Animals – tigers. Emotions – anger. Emotions – envy, jealousy. Family life – new sibling.

Robbie Rabbit and the little ones ill. by Catherine Walters. Little Tiger, 1996. ISBN 1-888444-01-0 Subj: Activities – babysitting. Animals – rabbits. Behavior – misbehavior. Games.

Smudge ill. by Jane Chapman. Little Tiger, 1998. ISBN 1-888444-44-4 Subj: Animals. Animals – dogs. Weather – rain.

This and that ill. by Tanya Linch. Farrar, 1996. ISBN 0-374-37492-9 Subj: Animals – cats. Birth. Farms.

Syme, Daniel B. *I'm growing* (Bogot, Howard)

Szekeres, Cyndy. *Cyndy Szekeres' counting book, 1 to 10* ill. by author. Golden Pr., 1984. ISBN 0-307-12141-0 Subj: Animals – mice. Counting, numbers.

Cyndy Szekeres' learn to count, funny bunnies ill. by author. Scholastic, 2000. ISBN 0-439-14994-0 Subj: Animals – rabbits. Counting, numbers. Format, unusual – board books. Rhyming text.

Good night, Sammy ill. by author. Western, 1991. ISBN 0-307-12238-7 Subj: Animals – foxes. Format, unusual – board books. Sleep.

Hide-and-seek duck ill. by author. Western, 1991. ISBN 0-307-12235-2 Subj: Animals – rabbits. Behavior – hiding. Birds – ducks. Format, unusual – board books.

I can count 100 bunnies, and so can you! ill. by author. Scholastic, 1998. ISBN 0-590-38361-2 Subj: Animals – rabbits. Counting, numbers.

Ladybug, ladybug, where are you? ill. by author. Western, 1991. ISBN 0-307-62340-8 Subj: Activities – picnicking. Animals – mice. Insects – ladybugs.

Long ago ill. by author. McGraw-Hill, 1977. ISBN 0-07-062665-0 Subj: Animals. Pilgrims. U.S. history.

The mouse that Jack built ill. by author. Scholastic, 1997. ISBN 0-590-69197-X Subj: Animals – mice. Clothing. Cumulative tales. Seasons – winter.

Nothing-to-do puppy ill. by author. Western, 1991. ISBN 0-307-12237-9 Subj: Animals – dogs. Format, unusual – board books.

Suppertime for Frieda Fuzzypaws ill. by author. Western, 1991. ISBN 0-307-12234-4 Subj: Animals – cats. Behavior – trickery. Food. Format, unusual – board books.

Toby! ill. by author. Little Simon, 2000. ISBN 0-689-82645-1 Subj: Animals – mice. Behavior – boredom.

Szilagyi, Mary. *Thunderstorm* ill. by author. Bradbury, 1985. ISBN 0-02-788580-1 Subj: Emotions – fear. Pets. Weather – storms. Weather – thunder.

Taback, Simms. *Joseph had a little overcoat* ill. by author. Viking, 1999. ISBN 0-670-87855-3 Subj: Caldecott award books. Clothing – coats.

On our way to the barn (Ziefert, Harriet)

On our way to the forest (Ziefert, Harriet)

On our way to the water (Ziefert, Harriet)

On our way to the zoo (Ziefert, Harriet)

There was an old lady who swallowed a fly (Little old lady who swallowed a fly)

Tabberner, Jeffrey. *The endless party* (Delessert, Etienne)

Taber, Anthony. *Cats' eyes* ill. by author. Dutton, 1978. ISBN 0-525-07814-2 Subj: Animals – cats. Old age.

Taberski, Sharon. *Morning, noon, and night* ill. by Nancy Doniger. Mondo, 1996. ISBN 1-57255-128-3 Subj: Activities. Emotions. Poetry.

Tabler, Judith. *The new puppy* ill. by Pat Sustendal. Random House, 1986. ISBN 0-394-88038-2 Subj: Animals – dogs. Format, unusual – board books. Pets. Toys.

Tabor, Nancy (Maria Grande). *Bottles break* ill. by author. Charlesbridge, 1998. ISBN 0-8810-6317-7 Subj: Behavior. Careers – teachers. Family life – mothers. Illness – alcoholism.

Taborin, Glorina. *Norman Rockwell's counting book* (Rockwell, Norman)

Tafuri, Nancy. *All year long* ill. by author. Greenwillow, 1983. ISBN 0-688-01416-X Subj: Days of the week, months of the year.

The ball bounced ill. by author. Greenwillow, 1989. ISBN 0-688-07871-0 Subj: Babies. Toys – balls.

The barn party ill. by author. Greenwillow, 1995. ISBN 0-688-04617-7 Subj: Animals. Barns. Birthdays. Parties.

The brass ring ill. by author. Greenwillow, 1996. ISBN 0-688-14169-2 Subj: Activities – vacationing. Concepts – shape. Concepts – size.

Counting to Christmas ill. by author. Scholastic, 1998. ISBN 0-590-27143-1 Subj: Activities – making things. Animals. Counting, numbers. Holidays – Christmas.

Do not disturb ill. by author. Greenwillow, 1987. ISBN 0-688-06542-2 Subj: Activities. Animals. Camps, camping. Family life. Night. Noise, sounds. Wordless.

Early morning in the barn ill. by author. Greenwillow, 1983. ISBN 0-688-02329-0 Subj: Farms. Morning. Wordless.

Follow me! ill. by author. Greenwillow, 1990. ISBN 0-688-08774-4 Subj: Animals – sea lions. Crustaceans.

Have you seen my duckling? ill. by author. Greenwillow, 1984. ISBN 0-688-02798-9 Subj: Birds – ducks. Caldecott award honor books. Character traits – individuality.

I love you, little one ill. by author. Scholastic, 1997. ISBN 0-590-92159-2 Subj: Animals. Animals – babies. Emotions – love. Family life – mothers.

In a red house ill. by author. Greenwillow, 1987. ISBN 0-688-07185-6 Subj: Concepts – color. Format, unusual – board books. Toys.

Junglewalk ill. by author. Greenwillow, 1988. ISBN 0-688-07183-X Subj: Animals. Dreams. Imagination. Jungle. Wordless.

My friends ill. by author. Greenwillow, 1987. ISBN 0-688-07187-2 Subj: Animals. Babies. Format, unusual – board books. Friendship.

One wet jacket ill. by author. Greenwillow, 1988. ISBN 0-688-07465-0 Subj: Clothing – coats. Format, unusual – board books.

Rabbit's morning ill. by author. Greenwillow, 1985. ISBN 0-688-04064-0 Subj: Animals. Animals – rabbits. Wordless.

Snowy flowy blowy ill. by author. Scholastic, 1999. ISBN 0-590-18973-5 Subj: Days of the week, months of the year. Rhyming text. Seasons.

This is the farmer ill. by author. Greenwillow, 1994. ISBN 0-688-09469-4 Subj: Animals. Careers – farmers. Cumulative tales. Farms.

Two new sneakers ill. by author. Greenwillow, 1988. ISBN 0-688-07462-6 Subj: Clothing – shoes. Format, unusual – board books.

What the sun sees / What the moon sees ill. by author. Greenwillow, 1997. ISBN 0-688-14493-4 Subj: Bedtime. Dreams. Format, unusual. Moon. Nature. Night. Sun.

Where we sleep ill. by author. Greenwillow, 1987. ISBN 0-688-07189-9 Subj: Animals. Format, unusual – board books. Sleep.

Who's counting? ill. by author. Greenwillow, 1986. ISBN 0-688-06131-1 Subj: Animals. Animals – dogs. Counting, numbers. Farms.

Will you be my friend? ill. by author. Scholastic, 2000. ISBN 0-590-63782-7 Subj: Animals – rabbits. Birds. Friendship. Weather – storms.

Tagore, Rabindranath. *Paper boats* ill. by Grayce Bochak. Boyds Mills, 1992. ISBN 1-878093-12-6 Subj: Boats, ships. Paper. Poetry. Toys.

Taha, Karen T. *A gift for Tia Rose* ill. by Dee deRosa. Dillon, 1986. ISBN 0-87518-306-9 Subj: Death. Ethnic groups in the U.S. – Mexican Americans. Family life. Friendship. Gifts.

Tait, Nancy. *I'm deaf and it's okay* (Aseltine, Lorraine)

Takamado no Miya Hisako. *Katie and the dreameater* by Her Imperial Highness Princess Takamado; ill. by Brian Wildsmith. Oxford Univ. Pr., 1996. ISBN 0-19-279005-6 Subj: Bedtime. Dreams. Mythical creatures. Night. Sleep.

Takao, Yuko. *A winter concert* ill. by author. Millbrook, 1997. ISBN 0-7613-0301-4 Subj: Animals. Animals – mice. Concepts – color. Music. Seasons – winter.

Takeshita, Fumiko. *The park bench* trans. by Ruth A. Kanagy; ill. by Mamoru Suzuki. Kane/Miller, 1988. ISBN 0-916291-15-4 Subj: Activities. Foreign lands – Japan. Foreign languages. Parks.

Takihara, Koji. *Rolli* ill. by author. Picture Book Studio, 1988. ISBN 0-88708-058-8 Subj: Animals – moles. Seeds.

Talbot, John. *Pins and needles* ill. by author. Dial, 1992. ISBN 0-8037-0942-0 Subj: Animals – elephants. Animals – mice. Problem solving.

Talbott, Hudson. *Going Hollywood! A dinosaur's dream* ill. by author. Crown, 1989. ISBN 0-517-57309-1 Subj: Dinosaurs. Friendship. Self-concept.

Tallarico, Tony. *At home* ill. by author. Tuffy Books, 1984. ISBN 0-89828-055-9 Subj: Family life. Homes, houses.

Talley, Carol. *Clarissa* ill. by Itoko Maeno. MarshMedia, 1992. From a story by Penelope C. Paine. ISBN 1-55942-014-6 Subj: Animals – bulls, cows. Fairs. Farms. Self-concept.

Talley, Linda. *Jackson's plan* ill. by Andra Chase. MarshMedia, 1998. ISBN 1-55942-104-5 Subj: Activities – photographing. Animals. Frogs and toads. Swamps.

Tallon, Robert. *Latouse my moose* ill. by author. Knopf, 1983. ISBN 0-394-96017-3 Subj: Animals – dogs. Pets.

Talus, Taylor. *The adventures of the three colors* (Tison, Annette)

Animal hide-and-seek (Tison, Annette)

Inside and outside (Tison, Annette)

Tamar, Erika. *Donnatalee: a mermaid adventure* ill. by Barbara Lambase. Harcourt, 1998. ISBN 0-15-200386-X Subj: Imagination. Mythical creatures – mermaids, mermen. Sea and seashore. Seasons – summer.

The garden of happiness ill. by Barbara Lambase. Harcourt, 1996. ISBN 0-15-230582-3 Subj: Activi-

ties – painting. City. Communities, neighborhoods. Flowers. Gardens, gardening.

Tamburine, Jean. *I think I will go to the hospital* ill. by author. Abingdon, 1965. Subj: Hospitals.

Tan, Amy. *The Chinese Siamese cat* ill. by Gretchen Schields. Macmillan, 1994. ISBN 0-02-788835-5 Subj: Animals – cats. Foreign lands – China.

The moon lady ill. by Gretchen Schields. Macmillan, 1992. ISBN 0-02-788830-4 Subj: Behavior – wishing. Family life – grandmothers. Folk and fairy tales. Foreign lands – China. Moon.

Tan, Pierre Le. *see* Le-Tan, Pierre

Tanaka, Beatrice. *The chase: a Kutenai Indian tale* ill. by Michel Gay. Crown, 1991. ISBN 0-517-58624-X Subj: Animals. Cumulative tales. Folk and fairy tales. Indians of North America – Kutenai.

Tanaka, Hideyuki. *The happy dog* ill. by author. Atheneum, 1983. ISBN 0-689-50259-1 Subj: Animals – dogs. Wordless.

Tangvald, Christine Harder. *The best thing about Christmas* ill. by Judy Hand. Standard, 1990 (1998 printing). ISBN 0-7847-0850-9 Subj: Holidays – Christmas. Religion – Nativity.

Hey, Mr. Angel! ill. by Jeff Carnehl. Concordia, 1998. ISBN 0-570-05058-8 Subj: Angels. Holidays – Christmas. Religion – Nativity. Rhyming text. Theater.

Mom and dad don't live together anymore ill. by Benton Mahan. Cook, 1988. ISBN 1-55513-502-1 Subj: Divorce.

The Rinky Dinky Donkey ill. by Kathleen Estes. Standard, 1995. ISBN 0-7847-0168-7 Subj: Animals – donkeys. Concepts – size. Religion – Nativity.

Taniuchi, Kota. *Trolley* ill. by author. Watts, 1969. ISBN 0-531-01937-3 Subj: Cable cars, trolleys. Imagination.

Tapahonso, Luci. *Navajo ABC* by Luci Tapahonso and Eleanor Schick; ill. by Eleanor Schick. Macmillan, 1995. ISBN 0-689-80316-8 Subj: ABC books. Indians of North America – Navajo. Language.

Tapio, Pat Decker. *The lady who saw the good side of everything* ill. by Paul Galdone. Seabury Pr., 1975. ISBN 0-8164-3145-0 Subj: Activities – traveling. Animals – cats. Character traits – optimism. Emotions – happiness. Humor. Weather – floods. Weather – rain.

Tarbescu, Edith. *Annushka's voyage* ill. by Lydia Dabcovich. Clarion, 1998. ISBN 0-395-64366-X Subj: Ethnic groups in the U.S. – Russian Americans. Family life – fathers. Family life – sisters. Immigrants. Jewish culture. Religion.

The boy who stuck out his tongue: a Yiddish folk tale ill. by Judith Christine Mills. Barefoot, 2000. ISBN

1-84148-067-3 Subj: Character traits – stubbornness. Folk and fairy tales. Jewish culture.

Tarpley, Natasha. *I love my hair!* ill. by E. B. Lewis. Little, 1997. ISBN 0-316-52275-9 Subj: Ethnic groups in the U.S. – African Americans. Family life – mothers. Hair.

Tarrant, Graham. *Rabbits* ill. by Tonny King. Putnam, 1984. ISBN 0-399-21005-9 Subj: Animals – rabbits. Format, unusual.

Tarrant, Margaret. *Fairy tales* ill. with photos. Crowell, 1978. ISBN 0-690-03920-4 Subj: Folk and fairy tales.

The Margaret Tarrant nursery rhyme book ill. by author. Merrimack, 1986. ISBN 0-00-183732-X Subj: Nursery rhymes.

Tarsky, Sue. *The busy building book* ill. by Alex Ayliffe. Putnam, 1998. ISBN 0-399-23137-4 Subj: Buildings.

Tate, Joan. *A Christmas book* (A Christmas book)

The giant fish and other stories (Svend Otto S [Svend Otto Sorensen])

Tate, Suzanne. *Crabby's water wish* ill. by James Melvin. Nags Head Art, 1991. ISBN 1-878405-04-7 Subj: Ecology. Sea and seashore.

Tatham, Campbell. *see* Elting, Mary

Taublieb, Paul. *Giff the scaredy bear* (Gifford, Kathie Lee)

Giff's big game (Gifford, Kathie Lee)

Moochie's surprise (Gifford, Kathie Lee)

Taulbert, Clifton L. *Little Cliff and the porch people* ill. by E. B. Lewis. Dial, 1999. ISBN 0-8037-2175-7 Subj: Communities, neighborhoods. Ethnic groups in the U.S. – African Americans. Family life. Food. Friendship. Magic.

Tax, Meredith. *Families* ill. by Marylin Hafner. Little, 1981. ISBN 0-316-83240-5 Subj: Family life.

Taylor, Alice. *A child's treasury of Irish rhymes* ill. by Nicola Emoe. Barefoot, 1999. ISBN 1-902283-18-X Subj: Foreign lands – Ireland. Nursery rhymes.

Taylor, Anelise. *Lights on, lights off* ill. by author. Oxford Univ. Pr., 1988. ISBN 0-19-279843-X Subj: Emotions – fear. Night.

Taylor, Ann. *Baby dance* ill. by Marjorie van Heerden. HarperFestival, 1999. ISBN 0-694-01206-8 Subj: Activities – dancing. Activities – singing. Babies. Ethnic groups in the U.S. – African Americans. Family life – fathers. Format, unusual – board books.

Taylor, Edgar. *King Grisly-Beard* (Grimm, Jacob)

Taylor, Harriet Peck. *Coyote and the laughing butterflies* ill. by author. Macmillan, 1995. ISBN 0-02-

788846-0 Subj: Animals – coyotes. Indians of North America. Insects – butterflies, caterpillars. Lakes, ponds.

Two days in May ill. by Leyla Torres. Farrar, 1999. ISBN 0-374-37988-2 Subj: Animals. Animals – deer. City. Seasons – spring.

Ulaq and the northern lights ill. by author. Farrar, 1998. ISBN 0-374-38063-5 Subj: Animals. Animals – foxes. Foreign lands – Arctic.

Taylor, Jane. *Twinkle, twinkle, little star* ill. by Michael Hague. Morrow, 1992. ISBN 0-688-11169-6 Subj: Fairies. Nursery rhymes. Sky. Songs. Stars.

Taylor, John Edward. *Petrosinella: a Neapolitan Rapunzel* (Basile, Giambattista)

Taylor, Judy. *Dudley and the monster* ill. by Peter Cross. Putnam, 1986. ISBN 0-399-21329-5 Subj: Animals – mice. Monsters. Seasons – spring.

Dudley and the strawberry shake ill. by Peter Cross. Putnam, 1987. ISBN 0-399-21330-9 Subj: Animals – mice. Food.

Dudley goes flying ill. by Peter Cross. Putnam, 1986. ISBN 0-399-21328-7 Subj: Activities – flying. Animals – mice.

Dudley in a jam ill. by Peter Cross. Putnam, 1987. ISBN 0-399-21331-7 Subj: Animals – mice. Food.

Sophie and Jack ill. by Susan Gantner. Putnam, 1983. ISBN 0-399-20947-6 Subj: Activities – picnicking. Animals – hippopotamuses. Family life.

Sophie and Jack help out ill. by Susan Gantner. Putnam, 1984. ISBN 0-399-21059-8 Subj: Animals – hippopotamuses. Gardens, gardening. Weather – storms.

Taylor, Kim. *Frog* [written and ed. by Angela Royston] photos by Kim Taylor and Jane Burton. Dutton, 1991. ISBN 0-525-67345-8 Subj: Birth. Format, unusual – board books. Frogs and toads.

Too fast to see photos by author. Delacorte, 1991. ISBN 0-385-30219-3 Subj: Nature.

Too small to see photos by author. Delacorte, 1991. ISBN 0-385-30221-5 Subj: Nature.

Taylor, Livingston. *Pajamas* by Livingston and Maggie Taylor; ill. by Tim Bowers. Harcourt, 1988. ISBN 0-15-200564-1 Subj: Bedtime. Lullabies.

Taylor, Lolita. *Old Meshikee and the little crabs: an Ojibwe story* (Spooner, Michael)

Taylor, Maggie. *Pajamas* (Taylor, Livingston)

Taylor, Mark. *The bold fisherman* ill. by Graham Booth. Golden Gate, 1967. Subj: Folk and fairy tales. Music. Sea and seashore. Songs. Sports – fishing.

The case of the missing kittens ill. by Graham Booth. Atheneum, 1978. ISBN 0-689-30627-X Subj: Animals – cats. Animals – dogs. Behavior – lost. Mystery stories.

Henry explores the jungle ill. by Graham Booth. Atheneum, 1968. Subj: Animals – tigers. Character traits – bravery. Circus. Seasons – summer.

Henry explores the mountains ill. by Graham Booth. Atheneum, 1975. ISBN 0-689-30461-7 Subj: Character traits – bravery. Fire. Helicopters. Seasons – fall.

Henry the castaway ill. by Graham Booth. Atheneum, 1972. ISBN 0-689-30070-0 Subj: Behavior – lost. Boats, ships. Seasons – spring. Weather – rain.

Henry the explorer ill. by Graham Booth. Atheneum, 1988, c1966. ISBN 0-316-83384-3 Subj: Animals – bears. Behavior – lost. Character traits – bravery. Seasons – winter.

"Lamb," said the lion, "I am here." ill. by Anne Siberell. Golden Gate, 1971. ISBN 0-8746-4182-9 Subj: Animals. Religion.

Old Blue, you good dog you ill. by Gene Holtan. Golden Gate, 1970. ISBN 0-8746-4142-X Subj: Animals – dogs. Animals – possums. Folk and fairy tales. Friendship. Games. Music. Old age. Songs.

Taylor, Scott. *Dinosaur James* ill. by author. Morrow, 1990. ISBN 0-688-08577-6 Subj: Behavior – bullying. Dinosaurs. Rhyming text.

Taylor, Shirley. *The cross in the egg* ill. by Wendell E. Hall. August House, 1999. ISBN 0-8748-3549-6 Subj: Animals – rabbits. Eggs. Holidays – Easter. Religion.

Taylor, Sydney. *The dog who came to dinner* ill. by John E. Johnson. Follett, 1966. Subj: Animals – dogs. Ethnic groups in the U.S. – African Americans.

Mr. Barney's beard ill. by Charles Geer. Follett, 1961. Subj: Birds. Character traits – laziness.

Tazewell, Charles. *The littlest angel* ill. by Paul Micich. Ideals, 1991. ISBN 0-8249-8516-8 Subj: Angels. Holidays – Christmas.

Teague, Mark. *Baby tamer* ill. by author. Scholastic, 1997. ISBN 0-590-67712-8 Subj: Activities – babysitting. Behavior. Circus. Ethnic groups in the U.S. – African Americans.

The Lost and found ill. by author. Scholastic, 1998. ISBN 0-590-84619-1 Subj: Behavior – losing things. Imagination. School.

One Halloween night ill. by author. Scholastic, 1999. ISBN 0-590-63803-3 Subj: Holidays – Halloween. Magic.

Pigsty ill. by author. Scholastic, 1994. ISBN 0-590-45915-5 Subj: Animals – pigs. Character traits – cleanliness. Character traits – orderliness.

The secret shortcut ill. by author. Scholastic, 1996. ISBN 0-590-67714-4 Subj: Behavior – tardiness. School.

The trouble with the Johnsons ill. by author. Scholastic, 1989. ISBN 0-590-42394-0 Subj: Animals – cats. Dinosaurs. Moving.

Teasdale, Sara. *Christmas carol* ill. by Dale Gottlieb. Holt, 1993. ISBN 0-8050-2695-9 Subj: Holidays – Christmas. Poetry.

Tedesco, Donna. *Do you know how much I love you?* ill. by author. Bradbury, 1994. ISBN 0-02-789120-8 Subj: Emotions – love. Family life.

Tejima, Keizaburo. *The bears' autumn* trans. from Japanese by Susan Matsui; ill. by author. Green Tiger Pr., 1986. ISBN 0-88138-080-6 Subj: Animals – bears. Seasons – fall.

Fox's dream ill. by author. Philomel, 1987. ISBN 0-399-21455-0 Subj: Animals – foxes. Dreams. Forest, woods. Seasons – winter.

Ho-limlim ill. by author. Putnam, 1990. ISBN 0-399-22156-5 Subj: Animals – rabbits. Foreign lands – Japan. Old age.

Owl lake ill. by author. Philomel, 1987. ISBN 0-399-21426-7 Subj: Birds – owls. Family life. Nature. Night.

Swan sky ill. by author. Putnam, 1988. ISBN 0-399-21547-6 Subj: Birds – swans. Death.

Woodpecker forest ill. by author. Putnam, 1989. ISBN 0-399-21618-9 Subj: Birds – woodpeckers. Forest, woods. Nature.

Teleki, Geza. *Aerial apes: gibbons of Asia* by Geza Teleki and others; ill. with photos. Coward, 1979. ISBN 0-698-20477-8 Subj: Animals – monkeys.

Telephones ill. by Christine Sharr. Wonder Books, 1971. Subj: Communication. Telephone.

Tellenbach, Margrit Haubensak. *see* Haubensak-Tellenbach, Margrit

Tempest, Peter. *The tale of a hero nobody knows* (Marshak, S. [Samuil])

Temple, Charles A. *Train* ill. by Larry Johnson. Houghton Mifflin, 1996. ISBN 0-395-69826-X Subj: Ethnic groups in the U.S. – African Americans. Rhyming text. Trains. Transportation.

Temple, Frances. *Tiger soup* ill. by author. Orchard, 1994. ISBN 0-531-08709-3 Subj: Animals – monkeys. Animals – tigers. Behavior – trickery. Folk and fairy tales. Foreign lands – Jamaica. Spiders.

Tennyson, Alfred, Baron. *The brook* ill. by Charles Micucci. Orchard, 1994. ISBN 0-531-08704-2 Subj: Farms. Foreign lands – England. Poetry. Rivers.

Tennyson, Noel. *The lady's chair and the ottoman* ill. by author. Lothrop, 1987. ISBN 0-688-04098-5 Subj: Behavior – needing someone. Furniture – chairs.

Tensen, Ruth M. *Come to the zoo!* Reilly, 1948. Subj: Animals. Zoos.

Tessler, Stephanie Gordon. *Francis, the earthquake dog* (Enderle, Judith (Ann) Ross)

The good-for-something dragon (Enderle, Judith (Ann) Ross)

Nell Nugget and the cow caper (Enderle, Judith (Ann) Ross)

A pile of pigs (Enderle, Judith (Ann) Ross)

Six creepy sheep (Enderle, Judith (Ann) Ross)

Six sandy sheep (Enderle, Judith (Ann) Ross)

Six snowy sheep (Enderle, Judith (Ann) Ross)

Upstairs (Enderle, Judith (Ann) Ross)

What would Mama do? (Enderle, Judith (Ann) Ross)

Where are you, little Zack? (Enderle, Judith (Ann) Ross)

Testa, Fulvio. *The ideal home* ill. by author. Harper-Collins, 1986. ISBN 0-87226-055-0 Subj: Homes, houses.

If you look around ill. by author. Dial, 1983. ISBN 0-8037-0003-2 Subj: Concepts – shape.

If you take a paintbrush: a book of colors ill. by author. Dial, 1983. ISBN 0-8037-3829-3 Subj: Concepts – color.

If you take a pencil ill. by author. Dial, 1982. ISBN 0-8037-4023-9 Subj: Counting, numbers.

The land where the ice cream grows story and ill. by Fulvio Testa; told by Anthony Burgess. Doubleday, 1979. ISBN 0-510-00045-2 Subj: Food. Imagination.

A long trip to Z ill. by author. Harcourt, 1997. ISBN 0-15-201610-4 Subj: ABC books.

Never satisfied ill. by author. North-South, 1988. ISBN 3-85539-009-6 Subj: Behavior – dissatisfaction.

The paper airplane ill. by author. Holt, 1988. ISBN 0-8050-0743-1 Subj: Activities – flying. Airplanes, airports. Paper.

Wolf's favor ill. by author. Dial, 1986. ISBN 0-8037-0244-2 Subj: Animals. Character traits – generosity.

Tester, Sylvia Root. *Chase!* ill. by author. Childrens Pr., 1980. ISBN 0-516-06439-8 Subj: Animals.

Never monkey with a monkey: a book of homographic homophones ill. by John Keely. Childrens Pr., 1977. ISBN 0-913778-90-7 Subj: Language.

Parade! ill. by author. Childrens Pr., 1980. ISBN 0-516-06441-X Subj: Circus.

A visit to the zoo photos by author. Childrens Pr., 1987. ISBN 0-516-01494-3 Subj: Animals. Zoos.

What did you say? a book of homophones ill. by John Keely. Childrens Pr., 1977. ISBN 0-913778-91-5 Subj: Language.

Tether, Graham. *The hair book* ill. by Roy McKié. Random House, 1979. ISBN 0-3948-3665-0 Subj: Hair. Rhyming text.

Skunk and possum ill. by Lucinda McQueen. Houghton Mifflin, 1979. ISBN 0-395-28270-5 Subj: Activities – picnicking. Animals – possums. Animals – skunks. Friendship.

Tettelbaum, Michael. *The cave of the lost Fraggle* ill. by Peter Elwell. Holt, 1985. ISBN 0-03-004554-1 Subj: Caves. Character traits – pride. Puppets.

Tews, Susan. *Lizard sees the world* ill. by George Crespo. Clarion, 1997. ISBN 0-395-72662-X Subj: Activities – traveling. Animals. Reptiles – lizards.

Thacher, Edith. *see* Hurd, Edith Thacher

Thaler, Mike. *Hippo lemonade* ill. by Maxie Chambliss. HarperCollins, 1986. ISBN 0-06-026162-5 Subj: Animals. Animals – hippopotamuses. Behavior – wishing.

It's me, hippo! ill. by Maxie Chambliss. HarperCollins, 1983. ISBN 0-06-026154-4 Subj: Animals. Animals – hippopotamuses. Friendship.

Madge's magic show ill. by Carol Nicklaus. Watts, 1978. ISBN 0-531-01450-9 Subj: Magic.

Moonkey ill. by Giulio Maestro. HarperCollins, 1981. ISBN 0-06-026125-0 Subj: Animals – monkeys. Friendship. Moon.

My puppy ill. by Madeleine Fishman. HarperCollins, 1980. ISBN 0-06-026079-3 Subj: Animals – dogs. Imagination – imaginary friends. Pets.

Owley ill. by David Wiesner. HarperCollins, 1982. ISBN 0-06-026152-8 Subj: Birds – owls. Character traits – questioning. Family life – mothers.

Pack 109 ill. by Normand Chartier. Dutton, 1988. ISBN 0-525-44393-2 Subj: Animals. Clubs, gangs. Humor.

There's a hippopotamus under my bed ill. by Ray Cruz. Watts, 1977. ISBN 0-531-01318-9 Subj: Animals – hippopotamuses. Furniture – beds.

What could a hippopotamus be? ill. by Robert Grossman. Simon & Schuster, 1990. ISBN 0-671-70847-3 Subj: Animals – hippopotamuses. Careers.

The yellow brick toad: funny frog cartoons, riddles, and silly stories ill. by author. Doubleday, 1978. ISBN 0-385-14255-2 Subj: Humor. Riddles.

Tharlet, Eve. *Little pig, big trouble* trans. by Andrew Clements; ill. by author. Picture Book Studio, 1989. Translation of: Henri, le petit cochon bleu. ISBN 0-88708-073-1 Subj: Animals – pigs. Behavior – misbehavior. Friendship.

Thaxter, Celia. *Celia's island journal* adapt. and ill. by Loretta Krupinski. Little, 1992. Adapt. of:

Among the Isles of Shoals. ISBN 0-316-83921-3 Subj: Islands. Lighthouses. Sea and seashore.

Thayer, Ernest Lawrence. *Casey at the bat: a ballad of the Republic, sung in the year 1888* ill. by Christopher Bing. Handprint Books, 2000. ISBN 1-929766-00-9 Subj: Caldecott award honor books. Poetry. Sports – baseball.

Casey at the bat ill. by Gerald Fitzgerald. Atheneum, 1995. ISBN 0-689-31945-2 Subj: Poetry. Sports – baseball.

Casey at the bat: a ballad of the Republic, sung in the year 1888 ill. by Patricia Polacco. Putnam, 1988. ISBN 0-399-21585-9 Subj: Poetry. Sports – baseball.

Thayer, Jane. *Andy and his fine friends* ill. by Meg Wohlberg. Morrow, 1960. Subj: Animals. Imagination – imaginary friends.

Andy and the runaway horse ill. by Meg Wohlberg. Morrow, 1963. Subj: Animals – horses, ponies. Traffic, traffic signs.

Andy and the wild worm ill. by Beatrice Darwin. Morrow, 1973, 1954. ISBN 0-688-30061-8 Subj: Animals – worms. Imagination.

The cat that joined the club ill. by Seymour Fleishman. Morrow, 1967. Subj: Animals – cats.

The clever raccoon ill. by Holly Keller. Morrow, 1981. ISBN 0-688-00239-0 Subj: Animals – raccoons. Behavior – trickery.

Gus and the baby ghost ill. by Seymour Fleishman. Morrow, 1972. Subj: Babies. Ghosts. Museums.

Gus loved his happy home ill. by Seymour Fleishman. Shoe String Pr., 1989. ISBN 0-208-02249-X Subj: Ghosts. Kites.

Gus was a friendly ghost ill. by Seymour Fleishman. Morrow, 1962. Subj: Friendship. Ghosts.

Gus was a gorgeous ghost ill. by Seymour Fleishman. Morrow, 1978. ISBN 0-688-32133-X Subj: Clothing. Ghosts. Holidays – Halloween.

Gus was a real dumb ghost ill. by Joyce Audy dos Santos. Morrow, 1982. ISBN 0-688-01443-7 Subj: Ghosts. School.

The horse with the Easter bonnet ill. by Jay Hyde Barnum. Morrow, 1953. Subj: Animals – horses, ponies. Clothing – hats. Holidays – Easter.

I like trains ill. by George Fonseca. HarperCollins, 1965. Subj: Trains. Transportation.

Mr. Turtle's magic glasses ill. by Mamoru Funai. Morrow, 1971. Subj: Behavior – boredom. Glasses. Magic. Reptiles – turtles, tortoises. Senses – seeing.

The popcorn dragon ill. by Jay Hyde Barnum. Morrow, 1953. Subj: Dragons. Food. Friendship.

The popcorn dragon ill. by Lisa McCue. Morrow, 1989. ISBN 0-688-08876-7 Subj: Dragons. Food. Friendship.

The puppy who wanted a boy ill. by Seymour Fleishman. Morrow, 1958. ISBN 0-688-31631-X Subj: Animals – dogs. Holidays – Christmas.

The puppy who wanted a boy ill. by Lisa McCue. Morrow, 1986. ISBN 0-688-05945-7 Subj: Animals – dogs. Holidays – Christmas.

Quiet on account of dinosaur ill. by Seymour Fleishman. Mulberry, 1988. ISBN 0-688-08292-0 Subj: Dinosaurs. Noise, sounds.

What's a ghost going to do? ill. by Seymour Fleishman. Morrow, 1966. Subj: Ghosts. Homes, houses. Problem solving.

Thayer, Mike. *In the middle of the puddle* ill. by Bruce Degen. HarperCollins, 1988. ISBN 0-06-026054-8 Subj: Frogs and toads. Reptiles – turtles, tortoises. Weather – rain.

Thelen, Gerda. *The toy maker: how a tree becomes a toy village* retold by Louise F. Encking; ill. by Fritz Kukenthal. Albert Whitman, 1935. Subj: Activities – making things. Toys. Trees.

Theobalds, Prue. *The teddy bears' Christmas* (Kennedy, Jimmy)

Theroux, Phyllis. *Serefina under the circumstances* ill. by Marjorie Priceman. Greenwillow, 1999. ISBN 0-688-15942-7 Subj: Behavior – secrets. Birthdays. Family life – grandmothers. Imagination.

They followed a bright star ill. by Ulises Wensell; based on a poem by Joan Alavedra. Putnam, 1994. ISBN 0-399-22706-7 Subj: Religion – Nativity. Stars.

Thiele, Bob. *What a wonderful world* (Weiss, George [George David])

Thiele, Colin. *Farmer Schulz's ducks* ill. by Mary Milton. HarperCollins, 1988. ISBN 0-06-026183-8 Subj: Birds – ducks. Farms. Foreign lands – Australia.

Thiesing, Lisa. *Me and you: a mother-daughter album* ill. by author. Hyperion, 1998. ISBN 0-7868-2338-0 Subj: Family life – daughters. Family life – mothers.

Thoburn, Tina. *A B See* (Ogle, Lucille)

I hear (Ogle, Lucille)

Thomas, Abigail. *Pearl paints* ill. by Margaret Hewitt. Holt, 1994. ISBN 0-8050-2976-1 Subj: Activities – painting. Art. Careers – artists.

Thomas, Art. *Merry-go-rounds* ill. by George Overlie. Carolrhoda, 1981. ISBN 0-87614-168-8 Subj: Merry-go-rounds.

Thomas, Frances. *The Bear and Mr. Bear* ill. by Ruth Brown. Dutton, 1995. ISBN 0-525-45362-8 Subj: Animals – bears. Character traits – kindness to animals.

What if? by Frances Thomas and Ross Collins; ill. by Ross Collins. Hyperion, 1998. ISBN 0-7868-0482-3 Subj: Family life – mothers. Imagination. Monsters.

Thomas, Ianthe. *Lordy, Aunt Hattie* ill. by Thomas di Grazia. HarperCollins, 1973. ISBN 0-06-026115-3 Subj: Ethnic groups in the U.S. – African Americans. Family life – aunts, uncles. Seasons – summer.

Walk home tired, Billy Jenkins ill. by Thomas di Grazia. HarperCollins, 1974. ISBN 0-06-026109-9 Subj: Activities – walking. City. Ethnic groups in the U.S. – African Americans. Imagination.

Willie blows a mean horn ill. by Ann Toulmin-Rothe. HarperCollins, 1981. ISBN 0-06-026107-2 Subj: Family life – fathers. Music.

Thomas, Iolette. *Janine and the new baby* ill. by Jennifer Northway. Dutton, 1987. ISBN 0-233-97916-6 Subj: Babies. Family life – new sibling. Sibling rivalry.

Thomas, Jane Resh. *Celebration!* ill. by Raúl Colón. Hyperion, 1997. ISBN 0-7868-2160-4 Subj: Activities – picnicking. Ethnic groups in the U.S. – African Americans. Family life. Holidays – Fourth of July.

Lights on the river ill. by Michael Dooling. Hyperion, 1994. ISBN 0-7868-2003-9 Subj: Careers – migrant workers. Emotions. Ethnic groups in the U.S. – Mexican Americans. Family life. Farms. Poverty.

Saying good-bye to grandma ill. by Marcia Sewall. Clarion, 1988. ISBN 0-89919-645-4 Subj: Death. Emotions – grief. Family life – grandmothers.

Scaredy dog ill. by Marilyn Mets. Hyperion, 1996. ISBN 0-7868-0278-2 Subj: Animals – dogs. Character traits – kindness to animals. Character traits – perseverance. Family life – mothers. Pets.

Wheels ill. by Emily Arnold McCully. Ticknor & Fields, 1986. ISBN 0-89919-410-9 Subj: Sports – bicycling.

Thomas, Joyce Carol. *Brown honey in broomwheat tea* ill. by Floyd Cooper. HarperCollins, 1993. ISBN 0-06-021088-5 Subj: Ethnic groups in the U.S. – African Americans. Poetry.

Cherish me ill. by Nneka Bennett. HarperFestival, 1998. ISBN 0-694-01097-9 Subj: Character traits – individuality. Ethnic groups in the U.S. – African Americans. Poetry.

Gingerbread days ill. by Floyd Cooper. HarperCollins, 1995. ISBN 0-06-023472-5 Subj: Days of the week, months of the year. Ethnic groups in the U.S. – African Americans. Folk and fairy tales. Poetry.

You are my perfect baby ill. by Nneka Bennett. HarperCollins, 1999. ISBN 0-694-01096-0 Subj: Babies. Ethnic groups in the U.S. – African Americans. Family life – new sibling.

Thomas, Karen. *The good thing . . . the bad thing* ill. by Yaroslava. Prentice-Hall, 1979. ISBN 0-13-360354-7 Subj: Behavior.

Thomas, Kathy. *The angel's quest* ill. by Jacqueline Seitz. Living Flame Pr., 1983. ISBN 0-914544-99-3 Subj: Angels. Character traits – perseverance. Orphans. Religion.

Thomas, Naturi. *Uh-oh! It's Mama's birthday!* ill. by Keinyo White. Albert Whitman, 1997. ISBN 0-8075-8268-9 Subj: Birthdays. Ethnic groups in the U.S. – African Americans. Family life – mothers. Gifts.

Thomas, Pat (1959-). *My family's changing* ill. by Lesley Harker. Barron's, 1999. ISBN 0-7641-0995-2 Subj: Divorce. Family life.

Thomas, Patricia. *The one and only, super-duper, golly-whopper, jim-dandy, really-handy clock-tock-stopper* ill. by John O'Brien. Lothrop, 1990. ISBN 0-688-09341-8 Subj: Animals – porcupines. Animals – rabbits. Clocks, watches. Noise, sounds. Rhyming text.

"Stand back," said the elephant, "I'm going to sneeze!" ill. by Wallace Tripp. Lothrop, 1971. ISBN 0-688-09339-6 Subj: Animals. Humor. Rhyming text.

"There are rocks in my socks!" said the ox to the fox ill. by Mordicai Gerstein. Lothrop, 1979. ISBN 0-688-51851-6 Subj: Animals – bulls, cows. Animals – foxes. Problem solving. Rhyming text.

Thomas, Shelley Moore. *Good night, Good Knight* ill. by Jennifer Plecas. Dutton, 2000. ISBN 0-525-46326-7 Subj: Bedtime. Dragons. Knights. Magic. Royalty.

Putting the world to sleep ill. by Bonnie Christensen. Houghton Mifflin, 1995. ISBN 0-395-71283-1 Subj: Bedtime. Cumulative tales. Night. Rhyming text.

Somewhere today: a book of peace photos by Eric Futran. Albert Whitman, 1998. ISBN 0-8075-7546-1 Subj: Character traits – helpfulness.

Thomas, Valerie. *Winnie flies again* (Paul, Korky)

Winnie in winter (Paul, Korky)

Thomas's big railway pop-up book ill. by Owain Bell; paper engineering by David Hawcock. Random House, 1992. ISBN 0-679-83465-6 Subj: Format, unusual – toy and movable books. Trains.

Thomassie, Tynia. *Cajun through and through* ill. by Andrew Glass. Little, 2000. ISBN 0-316-84189-7 Subj: Family life – cousins.

Feliciana Feydra LeRoux: a Cajun tall tale ill. by Cat Bowman Smith. Little, 1995. ISBN 0-316-84125-0 Subj: Reptiles – alligators, crocodiles.

Thompson, Brenda. *Famous planes* by Brenda Thompson and Rosemary Giesen; ill. by Andrew Martin and Rosemary Giesen. Lerner, 1977. ISBN 0-8225-1354-4 Subj: Airplanes, airports.

Pirates by Brenda Thompson and Rosemary Giesen; ill. by Simon Stern and Rosemary Giesen. Lerner, 1977. ISBN 0-8225-1359-5 Subj: Pirates.

The winds that blow by Brenda Thompson and Cynthia Overbeck; ill. by Simon Stern and Rosemary Giesen. Lerner, 1977. ISBN 0-8225-1366-8 Subj: Concepts – measurement. Sea and seashore. Weather – wind.

Thompson, Carol. *Baby days* ill. by author. Macmillan, 1991. ISBN 0-02-789325-1 Subj: Activities. Babies. Rhyming text.

Piggy goes to bed ill. by author. Candlewick, 1998. ISBN 0-7636-0428-3 Subj: Animals – pigs. Furniture.

Time ill. by author. Delacorte, 1989. ISBN 0-385-29765-3 Subj: Animals – bears. Clocks, watches. Time.

Thompson, Colin (Colin Edward). *Unknown* ill. by Anna Pignataro. Walker, 2000. ISBN 0-8027-8731-2 Subj: Animals – dogs. Behavior – needing someone. Fire.

Thompson, Elizabeth. *The true book of time* (Ziner, Feenie)

Thompson, George Selden. *see* Selden, George

Thompson, Harwood. *The witch's cat* ill. by Quentin Blake. Addison-Wesley, 1971. ISBN 0-20-107574-1 Subj: Animals – cats. Folk and fairy tales. Foreign lands – England. Witches.

Thompson, Kathleen. *Paul Revere* (Gleiter, Jan)

Sacagawea (Gleiter, Jan)

Thompson, Lauren. *Mouse's first Christmas* ill. by Buket Erdogan. Simon & Schuster, 1999. ISBN 0-689-82325-8 Subj: Animals – mice. Holidays – Christmas.

Mouse's first Halloween ill. by author. Simon & Schuster, 2000. ISBN 0-689-83176-5 Subj: Animals – mice. Holidays – Halloween.

Thompson, Mary. *Gran's bees* ill. by Donna Peterson. Millbrook, 1996. ISBN 1-56294-652-8 Subj: Family life – grandmothers. Farms. Insects – bees.

Thompson, Richard. *Effie's bath* ill. by Eugenie Fernandes. Firefly, 1989. ISBN 1-55037-055-3 Subj: Activities – bathing. Friendship. Imagination.

Foo ill. by Eugenie Fernandes. Firefly, 1988. ISBN 1-55037-005-7 Subj: Emotions – love. Family life.

Gurgle, bubble, splash ill. by Eugenie Fernandes. Firefly, 1989. ISBN 1-55037-029-4 Subj: Family life. Imagination. Sea and seashore.

I have to see this ill. by Eugenie Fernandes. Firefly, 1988. ISBN 1-55037-015-4 Subj: Activities – walking. Family life – fathers. Night.

Jenny's neighbours ill. by Kathryn E. Shoemaker. Firefly, 1987. ISBN 0-920303-73-0 Subj: Activities – playing. Friendship. Imagination.

Jesse on the night train ill. by Eugenie Fernandes. Firefly, 1990. ISBN 1-55037-093-6 Subj: Imagination. Night. Trains.

Sky full of babies ill. by Eugenie Fernandes. Firefly, 1987. ISBN 0-920303-93-5 Subj: Family life. Imagination. Space and space ships.

Thompson, Susan L. *Diary of a monarch butterfly* graphic design by Sas Colby; ill. by Judy LaMotte. Walker, 1976. ISBN 0-8027-6267-0 Subj: Insects – butterflies, caterpillars. Metamorphosis. Science.

One more thing, dad ill. by Dora Leder. Albert Whitman, 1980. ISBN 0-8075-6095-2 Subj: Counting, numbers.

Thompson, Vivian Laubach. *Camp-in-the-yard* ill. by Brinton Turkle. Holiday, 1961. Subj: Camps, camping. Multiple births – twins. Problem solving.

The horse that liked sandwiches ill. by Aliki. Putnam, 1962. Subj: Animals – horses, ponies. Food.

Thomson, Pat. *Beware of the aunts!* ill. by Emma Chichester Clark. Macmillan, 1992. ISBN 0-689-50538-8 Subj: Character traits – individuality. Family life – aunts, uncles.

Rhymes around the day ill. by Jan Ormerod. Lothrop, 1983. ISBN 0-688-02074-7 Subj: Family life. Nursery rhymes.

Thomson, Peggy. *The brave little tailor* (Grimm, Jacob)

The king has horse's ears ill. by David Small. Simon & Schuster, 1988. ISBN 0-671-64953-1 Subj: Behavior – secrets. Character traits – appearance. Royalty – kings.

Thomson, Ruth. *Drawing* ill. by author. Childrens Pr., 1994. ISBN 0-516-07989-1 Subj: Activities – drawing. Art.

Eyes ill. by Mike Galletly. Watts, 1988. ISBN 0-531-10549-0 Subj: Anatomy – eyes. Senses – seeing.

My bear: I can . . . can you? ill. by Ian Beck. Dial, 1985. ISBN 0-8037-0110-1 Subj: Activities. Rhyming text. Toys – bears.

My bear: I like . . . do you? ill. by Ian Beck. Dial, 1985. ISBN 0-8037-0105-5 Subj: Rhyming text. Toys – bears.

Painting ill. by author. Childrens Pr., 1994. ISBN 0-516-07990-5 Subj: Activities – painting. Art.

Peabody all at sea ill. by Ken Kirkwood. Lothrop, 1978. ISBN 0-688-51862-1 Subj: Activities – vacationing. Animals – dogs. Boats, ships. Careers – detectives. Crime. Mystery stories.

Peabody's first case ill. by Ken Kirkwood. Lothrop, 1978. ISBN 0-688-51861-3 Subj: Animals – dogs. Careers – detectives. Crime. Mystery stories.

Printing ill. by author. Childrens Pr., 1994. ISBN 0-516-07992-1 Subj: Activities – making things. Art.

The Rainforest Indians ill. by author. Childrens Pr., 1996. ISBN 0-516-08074-1 Subj: Activities – making things. Foreign lands – South America. Forest, woods. Indians of South America – Yanomamo.

Thong, Roseanne. *Round is a mooncake* ill. by Grace Lin. Chronicle, 2000. ISBN 0-8118-2676-7 Subj: Concepts – shape. Ethnic groups in the U.S. – Chinese Americans.

Thoreau, Henry D. *What befell at Mrs. Brooks's* ill. by George Overlie. Lerner, 1974. ISBN 0-8225-0284-4 Subj: Behavior – hurrying.

Thorne, Ian. *see* May, Julian

Thorne, Jenny. *Adam and Eve* ill. by author. Aladdin, 1989. ISBN 0-689-71305-3 Subj: Religion.

Jonah and the whale ill. by author. Aladdin, 1989. ISBN 0-689-71307-X Subj: Animals – whales. Religion – Jonah.

My uncle ill. by author. Atheneum, 1982. ISBN 0-689-50233-8 Subj: Activities. Dreams. Family life – aunts, uncles. Sports – fishing.

Noah's ark ill. by author. Aladdin, 1989. ISBN 0-689-71306-1 Subj: Animals. Boats, ships. Religion – Noah. Weather – floods. Weather – rain. Weather – rainbows.

The walls of Jericho ill. by author. Aladdin, 1989. ISBN 0-689-71308-8 Subj: Religion.

Thornhill, Jan. *A tree in a forest* ill. by author. Simon & Schuster, 1992. ISBN 0-671-75901-9 Subj: Ecology. Foreign lands – Canada. Forest, woods. Trees.

Wild in the city ill. by author. Sierra Club, 1996. ISBN 0-87156-910-8 Subj: Animals. Animals – cats. Birds. City. Ecology. Night.

Wildlife ABC ill. by author. Simon & Schuster, 1990. ISBN 0-671-67925-2 Subj: ABC books. Animals. Nature.

The wildlife 1-2-3 ill. by author. Simon & Schuster, 1989. ISBN 0-671-67926-0 Subj: Animals. Counting, numbers. Nature.

Threadgall, Colin. *Proud rooster and the fox* ill. by author. Morrow, 1992. ISBN 0-688-11124-6 Subj: Animals – foxes. Birds – chickens. Character traits – cleverness. Farms.

The three bears. *Goldilocks* adapt. and ill. by Janice Russell. Boyds Mills, 1997. ISBN 1-56397-430-4 Subj: Animals – bears. Folk and fairy tales.

Goldilocks retold by Dom DeLuise; ill. by Christopher Santoro. Simon & Schuster, 1992. ISBN 0-671-74690-1 Subj: Animals – bears. Folk and fairy tales.

Goldilocks and the three bears retold and ill. by H. Amery. E D C, 1988. ISBN 0-88110-318-7 Subj: Animals – bears. Folk and fairy tales.

Goldilocks and the three bears retold by Marcia Leonard; ill. by Yvette Banek. Silver Pr., 1990. ISBN 0-671-69346-8 Subj: Animals – bears. Folk and fairy tales.

Goldilocks and the three bears retold and ill. by Jan Brett. Dodd, 1987. ISBN 0-396-08925-9 Subj: Animals – bears. Folk and fairy tales.

Goldilocks and the three bears adapt. and ill. by Lorinda Bryan Cauley. Putnam, 1981. ISBN 0-399-20794-5 Subj: Animals – bears. Folk and fairy tales.

Goldilocks and the three bears ill. by Jane Dyer. Grosset, 1984. ISBN 0-448-10213-7 Subj: Animals – bears. Folk and fairy tales. Format, unusual – board books.

Goldilocks and the three bears adapt. by Armand Eisen; ill. by Lynn Bywaters Ferris. Knopf, 1987. ISBN 0-394-55882-0 Subj: Animals – bears. Folk and fairy tales.

Goldilocks and the three bears adapt. by Linda Hayward; ill. by Madelaine Gill Linden. Random House, 1988. ISBN 0-394-89637-8 (package) Subj: Animals – bears. Folk and fairy tales. Format, unusual. Rebuses.

Goldilocks and the three bears retold and ill. by David McPhail. Scholastic, 1995. ISBN 0-590-48117-7 Subj: Animals – bears. Folk and fairy tales.

Goldilocks and the three bears adapt. and ill. by James Marshall. Dial, 1988. ISBN 0-8037-0543-3 Subj: Animals – bears. Caldecott award honor books. Folk and fairy tales.

Goldilocks and the three bears retold by Harriet Ziefert; ill. by Laura Rader. Putnam, 1981. ISBN 0-688-13258-8 Subj: Animals – bears. Folk and fairy tales.

Goldilocks and the three bears retold and ill. by Tony Ross. Overlook Pr., 1992. ISBN 0-87951-453-1 Subj: Animals – bears. Folk and fairy tales.

Goldilocks and the three bears retold and ill. by Janet Stevens. Holiday, 1985. ISBN 0-8234-0608-3 Subj: Animals – bears. Folk and fairy tales.

Goldilocks and the three bears adapt. and ill. by Bernadette Watts. Knopf, 1985. ISBN 0-03-005737-X Subj: Animals – bears. Folk and fairy tales.

Goldilocks and the three bears retold by Betty Miles; ill. by Bari Weissman. Simon & Schuster, 1998. ISBN 0-689-81787-8 Subj: Animals – bears. Folk and fairy tales.

The story of the three bears ill. by L. Leslie Brooke. Warne, 1934. Subj: Animals – bears. Folk and fairy tales.

The story of the three bears ill. by William Stobbs. McGraw-Hill, 1965. Subj: Animals – bears. Folk and fairy tales.

The three bears (Hillert, Margaret)

The three bears adapt. and ill. by Byron Barton. HarperCollins, 1991. ISBN 0-06-020424-9 Subj: Animals – bears. Folk and fairy tales.

The three bears ill. by Paul Galdone. Seabury Pr., 1972. Subj: Animals – bears. Folk and fairy tales.

The three bears adapt. by Kathleen N. Daly; ill. by Feodor Rojankovsky. Golden Pr., 1967. Subj: Animals – bears. Folk and fairy tales.

The three bears ill. by Robin Spowart. Knopf, 1987. ISBN 0-394-98862-0 Subj: Animals – bears. Folk and fairy tales.

The three little pigs. *The original three little pigs retold* adapt. by Marilyn J. Shearer; ill. by Jonathan Smith. Lauren Ashley & Joshua Storybooks, 1990. ISBN 0-685-33065-6 Subj: Animals – pigs. Animals – wolves. Character traits – cleverness. Folk and fairy tales.

The story of the three little pigs ill. by L. Leslie Brooke. Warne, 1934. Subj: Animals – pigs. Animals – wolves. Character traits – cleverness. Folk and fairy tales.

The story of the three little pigs ill. by William Stobbs. McGraw-Hill, 1965. Subj: Animals – pigs. Animals – wolves. Character traits – cleverness. Folk and fairy tales.

Three little pigs. Facsimile ed. Bragdon, 1987. Reprint of 1924 ed. ISBN 0-916410-38-2 Subj: Animals – pigs. Animals – wolves. Character traits – cleverness. Folk and fairy tales.

The three little pigs retold and ill. by Val Biro. Oxford Univ. Pr., 1991. ISBN 0-19-279880-4 Subj: Animals – pigs. Animals – wolves. Character traits – cleverness. Folk and fairy tales. Format, unusual – board books.

The three little pigs retold and ill. by Gavin Bishop. Scholastic, 1990. ISBN 0-590-43358-X Subj: Animals – pigs. Animals – wolves. Character traits – cleverness. Folk and fairy tales.

The three little pigs ill. by Erik Blegvad. Atheneum, 1980. ISBN 0-689-50139-0 Subj: Animals – pigs. Animals – wolves. Character traits – cleverness. Rhyming text.

The three little pigs adapt. and ill. by Caroline Bucknall. Dial, 1987. ISBN 0-8037-0100-4 Subj: Animals – pigs. Animals – wolves. Character traits – cleverness. Folk and fairy tales. Rhyming text.

The three little pigs retold by H. Amery; ill. by Stephen Cartwright. E D C, 1987. ISBN 0-88110-293-8 Subj: Animals – pigs. Animals – wolves. Character traits – cleverness. Folk and fairy tales.

The three little pigs ill. by Lorinda Bryan Cauley. Putnam, 1980. ISBN 0-399-20733-3 Subj: Animals – pigs. Animals – wolves. Character traits – cleverness. Folk and fairy tales.

The three little pigs tr. and adapt. by Elizabeth D. Crawford; ill. by Jean Claverie. North-South, 1989. ISBN 1-55858-004-2 Subj: Animals – pigs. Animals – wolves. Character traits – cleverness. Folk and fairy tales.

The three little pigs retold by Marcia Leonard; ill. by Doug Cushman. Silver Pr., 1990. ISBN 0-671-69345-X Subj: Animals – pigs. Animals – wolves. Character traits – cleverness. Folk and fairy tales. Picture puzzles.

The three little pigs: in verse ill. by William Pène Du Bois. Viking, 1962. Subj: Animals – pigs. Animals – wolves. Character traits – cleverness. Folk and fairy tales. Rhyming text.

The three little pigs ill. by Paul Galdone. Seabury Pr., 1970. Subj: Animals – pigs. Animals – wolves. Character traits – cleverness. Folk and fairy tales.

The three little pigs adapt. by Linda Hayward; ill. by Madelaine Gill. Random House, 1988. ISBN 0-394-89637-8 (package) Subj: Animals – pigs. Animals – wolves. Character traits – cleverness. Folk and fairy tales. Rebuses.

The three little pigs retold and ill. by Steven Kellogg. Morrow, 1997. ISBN 0-688-08732-9 Subj: Animals – pigs. Animals – wolves. Character traits – cleverness. Family life – mothers. Folk and fairy tales.

The three little pigs retold and ill. by David McPhail. Scholastic, 1995. ISBN 0-590-48118-5 Subj: Animals – pigs. Animals – wolves. Character traits – cleverness. Folk and fairy tales.

The three little pigs retold and ill. by James Marshall. Dial, 1989. ISBN 0-8037-0594-8 Subj: Animals – pigs. Animals – wolves. Character traits – cleverness. Folk and fairy tales.

The three little pigs by Betty Miles; ill. by Paul Meisel. Simon & Schuster, 1998. ISBN 0-689-81788-6 Subj: Animals – pigs. Animals – wolves. Character traits – cleverness. Folk and fairy tales.

The three little pigs ill. by Rodney Peppé. Lothrop, 1980. ISBN 0-688-51923-7 Subj: Animals – pigs. Animals – wolves. Character traits – cleverness. Folk and fairy tales.

The three little pigs ill. by Edda Reinl. Picture Book Studio, 1983. ISBN 0-907234-32-1 Subj: Animals – pigs. Animals – wolves. Character traits – cleverness. Folk and fairy tales.

The three little pigs ill. by John Wallner. Viking, 1987. ISBN 0-670-81707-4 Subj: Animals – pigs. Animals – wolves. Character traits – cleverness. Folk and fairy tales. Format, unusual – toy and movable books.

The three little pigs retold by Margaret Hillert; ill. by Irma Wilde. Follett, 1963. Subj: Animals – pigs. Animals – wolves. Character traits – cleverness. Folk and fairy tales.

The three little pigs: an old story ill. by Margot Zemach. Farrar, 1988. ISBN 0-374-37527-5 Subj: Animals – pigs. Animals – wolves. Character traits – cleverness. Folk and fairy tales.

The three little pigs and the big bad wolf retold and ill. by Glen Rounds. Holiday, 1992. ISBN 0-8234-0923-6 Subj: Animals – pigs. Animals – wolves. Character traits – cleverness. Folk and fairy tales. Rhyming text.

The three little pigs and the fox adapt. by William H. Hooks; ill. by S. D. Schindler. Macmillan, 1989. ISBN 0-02-744431-7 Subj: Animals – foxes. Animals – pigs. Birds – chickens. Character traits – cleverness. Folk and fairy tales.

The three pigs ill. by Tony Ross. Pantheon, 1983. ISBN 0-394-96143-9 Subj: Animals – pigs. Animals – wolves. Character traits – cleverness. Folk and fairy tales.

Who's at the door? adapt. and ill. by Jonathan Allen. Tambourine, 1993. ISBN 0-688-12257-4 Subj: Animals – pigs. Animals – wolves. Character traits – cleverness. Disguises. Folk and fairy tales. Format, unusual – toy and movable books.

Thurber, James. *The great Quillow* ill. by Steven Kellogg. Harcourt, 1994. ISBN 0-15-232544-1 Subj: Careers – toy makers. Character traits – being different. Character traits – cleverness. Giants. Toys.

Many moons ill. by Marc Simont. Harcourt, 1990. ISBN 0-15-251872-X Subj: Clowns, jesters. Illness. Moon. Royalty – princesses.

Many moons ill. by Louis Slobodkin. Harcourt, 1943. ISBN 0-15-251873-8 Subj: Caldecott award books. Clowns, jesters. Illness. Moon. Royalty – princesses.

Thury, Frederick. *The last straw* ill. by Vlasta Van Kampen. Charlesbridge, 1999. ISBN 0-88106-152-2 Subj: Animals – camels. Gifts. Holidays – Christmas. Religion – Nativity.

Thuswaldner, Werner. *Æsop's fables* (Æsop)

Thwaite, Ann. *The day with the Duke* ill. by George Him. World, 1969. Subj: Games.

Thwaites, Lyndsay. *Super Adam and Rosie Wonder* ill. by author. André Deutsch, 1983. ISBN 0-233-97532-2 Subj: Activities – playing. Family life.

Tibo, Gilles. *Simon and the snowflakes* ill. by author. Tundra, 1988. ISBN 0-88776-218-2 Subj: Friendship. Stars. Weather – snow.

Tidd, Louise Vitellaro. *The best pet yet* photos by Dorothy Handelman. Millbrook, 1998. ISBN 0-7613-2006-7 Subj: Animals. Animals – rabbits. Pets.

I'll do it later photos by Dorothy Handelman. Millbrook, 1999. ISBN 0-7613-2066-0 Subj: Behavior – tardiness. School.

Tierney, Hanne. *Where's your baby brother, Becky Bunting?* ill. by Paula Winter. Doubleday, 1979. ISBN 0-385-08654-7 Subj: Behavior – misbehavior. Family life. Sibling rivalry.

Tilden, Ruth. *Freddie works out* ill. by author. Hyperion, 1995. ISBN 0-7868-0108-5 Subj: Format, unusual – toy and movable books. Frogs and toads. Health and fitness.

Sophie's dance class ill. by author. Hyperion, 1996. ISBN 0-7868-0239-1 Subj: Activities – dancing. Ballet. Format, unusual – toy and movable books.

Tildes, Phyllis Limbacher. *Animals in camouflage* ill. by author. Charlesbridge, 2000. ISBN 0-88106-120-4 Subj: Animals. Disguises. Picture puzzles.

Baby animals black and white ill. by author. Charlesbridge, 1998. ISBN 0-88106-313-4 Subj: Animals – babies. Format, unusual – board books. Wordless.

The magic babushka ill. by author. Charlesbridge, 1998. ISBN 0-88106-840-3 Subj: Eggs. Folk and fairy tales. Holidays – Easter.

Tiller, Ruth. *Cats vanish slowly* ill. by Laura L. Seeley. Peachtree, 1995. ISBN 1-56145-106-1 Subj: Animals – cats. Farms. Poetry.

The Timbertoes 1 2 3 counting book by the editors of Highlights for Children; ill. by Judith A. Hunt. Boyds Mills, 1997. ISBN 1-56397-627-7 Subj: Counting, numbers. Puppets.

The Timbertoes ABC alphabet book by the editors of Highlights for Children; ill. by Judith A. Hunt. Boyds Mills, 1997. ISBN 1-56397-604-8 Subj: ABC books. Puppets.

Timlock, Jason. *Basil, the loneliest boy* ill. by Brett Colquhoun. Viking, 1990. ISBN 0-670-83125-5 Subj: Emotions – loneliness.

Timmermans, Felix. *A gift from Saint Nicholas* adapt. by Carole Kismaric; ill. by Charles Mikolaycak. Holiday, 1988. ISBN 0-8234-0674-1 Subj: Character traits – generosity. Gifts. Holidays – Christmas.

Tinkelman, Murray. *Cowgirl* ill. by author. Greenwillow, 1984. ISBN 0-688-02883-7 Subj: Animals – horses, ponies. Sports.

Tippett, James Sterling. *Counting the days* ill. by Elizabeth Tyler Wolcott. HarperCollins, 1940. Subj: Holidays – Christmas. Rhyming text.

Tison, Annette. *The adventures of the three colors* by Annette Tison and Talus Taylor. Collins-World, 1971. Subj: Concepts – color. Format, unusual.

Animal hide-and-seek by Annette Tison and Talus Taylor; ill. by authors. Collins-World, 1972. ISBN 0-529-04543-5 Subj: Activities – photographing. Animals. Format, unusual. Games. Insects.

Animals in color magic ill. by author. Merrill, 1980. ISBN 0-675-01046-2 Subj: Animals. Format, unusual.

Inside and outside by Annette Tison and Taylor Talus. Collins-World, 1972. ISBN 9-06-151014-7 Subj: Format, unusual. Homes, houses.

Titherington, Jeanne. *Baby's boat* ill. by author. Greenwillow, 1992. ISBN 0-688-08556-3 Subj: Babies. Bedtime. Boats, ships. Lullabies. Sea and seashore.

Baby's boat, a board book ill. by author. 1st Tupelo board book ed. Tupelo, 1998. ISBN 0-688-15979-6 Subj: Babies. Bedtime. Boats, ships. Format, unusual – board books. Lullabies. Sea and seashore.

Big world, small world ill. by author. Greenwillow, 1985. ISBN 0-688-04023-3 Subj: Concepts – perspective. Family life – mothers. Self-concept.

A child's prayer ill. by author. Greenwillow, 1989. ISBN 0-688-08318-8 Subj: Bedtime. Religion.

A place for Ben ill. by author. Greenwillow, 1987. ISBN 0-688-06494-9 Subj: Babies. Emotions – loneliness. Family life – brothers. Family life – new sibling.

Pumpkin pumpkin ill. by author. Greenwillow, 1985. ISBN 0-688-50696-1 Subj: Gardens, gardening. Holidays – Halloween.

Where are you going, Emma? ill. by author. Greenwillow, 1988. ISBN 0-688-07082-5 Subj: Behavior – lost. Family life – grandfathers.

Titus, Eve. *Anatole* ill. by Paul Galdone. McGraw-Hill, 1957. Subj: Animals – mice. Caldecott award honor books. Foreign lands – France.

Anatole and the cat ill. by Paul Galdone. McGraw-Hill, 1957. Subj: Animals – cats. Animals – mice. Caldecott award honor books. Character traits – bravery. Foreign lands – France. Problem solving.

Anatole and the piano ill. by Paul Galdone. McGraw-Hill, 1966. Subj: Animals – mice. Foreign lands – France. Music.

Anatole and the Pied Piper ill. by Paul Galdone. McGraw-Hill, 1979. ISBN 0-07-064897-2 Subj: Animals – mice. Foreign lands – France. Music. Problem solving.

Anatole and the poodle ill. by Paul Galdone. McGraw-Hill, 1965. Subj: Animals – dogs. Animals – mice. Foreign lands – France. Problem solving.

Anatole and the robot ill. by Paul Galdone. McGraw-Hill, 1960. Subj: Animals – mice. Foreign lands – France. Problem solving. Robots.

Anatole and the thirty thieves ill. by Paul Galdone. McGraw-Hill, 1969. Subj: Animals – mice. Crime. Foreign lands – France. Problem solving.

Anatole and the toyshop ill. by Paul Galdone. McGraw-Hill, 1970. Subj: Animals – mice. Foreign lands – France. Problem solving. Toys.

Anatole in Italy ill. by Paul Galdone. McGraw-Hill, 1973. ISBN 0-07-064899-9 Subj: Animals – mice. Foreign lands – Italy. Problem solving.

Anatole over Paris ill. by Paul Galdone. McGraw-Hill, 1961. Subj: Activities – flying. Animals – mice. Foreign lands – France. Kites.

The kitten who couldn't purr ill. by Amrei Fechner. Morrow, 1991. ISBN 0-688-09364-7 Subj: Animals. Animals – cats. Noise, sounds.

Tobias, Tobi. *At the beach* ill. by Gloria Singer. McKay, 1978. ISBN 0-679-20447-4 Subj: Activities – vacationing. Family life. Sea and seashore.

Chasing the goblins away ill. by Victor G. Ambrus. Warne, 1977. ISBN 0-7232-6144-X Subj: Bedtime. Mythical creatures – goblins. Night. Sleep.

The dawdlewalk ill. by Jeanette Swofford. Carolrhoda, 1983. ISBN 0-87614-190-4 Subj: Activities – walking.

A day off ill. by Ray Cruz. Putnam, 1973. ISBN 0-399-60762-5 Subj: Family life. Illness.

Jane wishing ill. by Trina Schart Hyman. Viking, 1977. ISBN 0-670-40565-5 Subj: Behavior – wishing. Emotions – happiness. Family life. Humor. Self-concept.

Moving day ill. by William Pène du Bois. Knopf, 1976. ISBN 0-394-93115-7 Subj: Emotions. Moving. Toys – bears.

The quitting deal ill. by Trina Schart Hyman. Viking, 1975. ISBN 0-670-58582-3 Subj: Family life – mothers. Thumb sucking.

Tobias catches trout (Hertz, Ole)

Tobias goes ice fishing (Hertz, Ole)

Tobias goes seal hunting (Hertz, Ole)

Tobias has a birthday (Hertz, Ole)

A world of words: an ABC of quotations ill. by Peter Malone. Lothrop, 1997. ISBN 0-688-12130-6 Subj: ABC books. Language. Poetry.

Tobola, Deborah. *The big buck adventure* (Gill, Shelley)

Todaro, John. *Phillip the flower-eating phoenix* by John Todaro and Barbara Ellen; ill. by John Todaro. Abelard-Schuman, 1961. Subj: Mythical creatures – phoenix.

Todd, Kathleen. *Snow* ill. by author. Addison-Wesley, 1982. ISBN 0-201-16280-6 Subj: Activities – playing. Family life. Weather – snow.

Todd, Sarah Manning. *see* Freeman, Jean Todd

Toft, Kim Michelle. *Neptune's nursery* Kim Michelle Toft and Allan Sheather; ill. by Kim Michelle Toft. Charlesbridge, 2000. ISBN 1-57091-391-9 Subj: Animals. Picture puzzles. Rhyming text. Science. Sea and seashore.

One less fish Kim Michelle Toft and Allan Sheather; ill. by Kim Michelle Toft. Charlesbridge, 1998. ISBN 0-88106-322-3 Subj: Counting, numbers. Fish. Picture puzzles. Rhyming text.

Tokuda, Wendy. *Humphrey the lost whale: a true story* by Wendy Tokuda and Richard Hall; ill. by Hanako Wakiyama. Heian Intl., 1986. ISBN 0-89346-270-5 Subj: Animals – whales. Behavior – lost. Behavior – needing someone. Sea and seashore.

Tolhurst, Marilyn. *Somebody and the three Blairs* ill. by Simone Abel. Watts, 1991. ISBN 0-531-08478-7 Subj: Animals – bears. Folk and fairy tales.

Tolkien, Baillie. *The Father Christmas letters* (Tolkien, J. R. R. [John Ronald Reuel])

Tolkien, J. R. R. (John Ronald Reuel). *The Father Christmas letters* ed. by Baillie Tolkien; ill. by author. Houghton Mifflin, 1977. ISBN 0-395-24981-3 Subj: Communication. Holidays – Christmas.

Tolstoy, Aleksey Nikolayevich. *The gigantic turnip* by Aleksei Tolstoy and Niamh Sharkey; ill. by Niamh Sharkey. Barefoot, 1999. ISBN 1-902283-12-0 Subj: Cumulative tales. Farms. Folk and fairy tales. Foreign lands – Russia. Plants. Problem solving.

The great big enormous turnip ill. by Helen Oxenbury. Watts, 1968. Subj: Animals. Cumulative tales. Farms. Folk and fairy tales. Foreign lands – Russia. Plants. Problem solving.

Shoemaker Martin trans. from Russian by Michael Hale; adapt. by Brigitte Hanhart; ill. by Bernadette Watts. Holt, 1986. ISBN 0-8050-0040-2 Subj: Character traits – generosity. Character traits – kindness. Religion.

Tom Thumb. *Dick Bruna's Tom Thumb* (Bruna, Dick)

Grimm Tom Thumb by Jacob and Wilhelm Grimm; trans. by Anthea Bell; ill. by Svend Otto S. Larousse, 1976. Translation of Tommeliden. ISBN 0-8833-2043-6 Subj: Folk and fairy tales. Little people.

Tom Thumb ill. by L. Leslie Brooke. Warne, 1904. Subj: Folk and fairy tales. Little people.

Tom Thumb adapt. by Margaret Hillert; ill. by Dennis Hockerman. Follett, 1982. ISBN 0-695-41542-5 Subj: Folk and fairy tales. Little people.

Tom Thumb by the Brothers Grimm; ill. by Felix Hoffmann. Atheneum, 1973. Translation of Der Daumling. ISBN 0-689-30318-1 Subj: Folk and fairy tales. Little people.

Tom Thumb: a tale adapt. and ill. by Lidia Postma. Schocken, 1983. Based on a tale by Charles Perrault. ISBN 0-8052-3855-7 Subj: Folk and fairy tales. Little people.

Tom Thumb adapt. and ill. by Richard Jesse Watson. Harcourt, 1989. ISBN 0-15-289280-X Subj: Folk and fairy tales. Little people.

Tom Thumb ill. by William Wiesner. Walck, 1974. ISBN 0-8098-1215-0 Subj: Folk and fairy tales. Little people.

Tom Tit Tot. *Tom Tit Tot: an English folk tale* ill. by Evaline Ness. Scribners, 1965. Subj: Caldecott award honor books. Folk and fairy tales. Magic. Names.

Tomchek, Ann Heinrichs. *I can be a chef.* Childrens Pr., 1985. ISBN 0-516-01886-8 Subj: Activities – cooking. Careers – chefs, cooks.

Tomfool. *see* Farjeon, Eleanor

Tomkins, Jasper. *The catalog* ill. by author. Green Tiger Pr., 1981. ISBN 0-914676-54-7 Subj: Animals. Humor.

Tomlinson, Theresa. *Little stowaway* ill. by Jane Browne. Julia MacRae Books, 1998. ISBN 1-85681-691-5 Subj: Activities – traveling. Careers – fishermen. Sea and seashore.

Tompert, Ann. *Badger on his own* ill. by Diane de Groat. Crown, 1978. ISBN 0-517-53226-3 Subj: Animals – badgers. Birds – owls.

A carol for Christmas ill. by Laura Kelly. Macmillan, 1994. ISBN 0-02-789402-9 Subj: Animals – mice. Foreign lands – Austria. Holidays – Christmas. Songs.

Charlotte and Charles ill. by John Wallner. Crown, 1979. ISBN 0-517-53660-9 Subj: Giants. Middle Ages.

Grandfather Tang's story ill. by Robert Andrew Parker. Crown, 1990. ISBN 0-517-57272-9 Subj: Animals – foxes. Family life – grandfathers. Foreign lands – China.

The hungry black bag ill. by Jacqueline Chwast. Houghton Mifflin, 1999. ISBN 0-395-89418-2 Subj: Animals. Animals – goats. Behavior – greed. Behavior – stealing. Crime. Farms.

The jade horse, the cricket, and the peach stone ill. by Winson Trang. Boyds Mills, 1996. ISBN 1-56397-239-5 Subj: Folk and fairy tales. Foreign lands – China. Royalty – emperors.

Just a little bit ill. by Lynn Munsinger. Houghton Mifflin, 1993. ISBN 0-395-51527-0 Subj: Activities – playing. Animals – elephants. Animals – mice. Concepts. Cumulative tales.

Little Fox goes to the end of the world ill. by John Wallner. Crown, 1976. ISBN 0-517-52600-X Subj: Animals – foxes. Imagination.

Little Otter remembers and other stories ill. by John Wallner. Crown, 1977. ISBN 0-517-52751-0 Subj: Animals – otters. Family life – mothers. Memories, memory.

Nothing sticks like a shadow ill. by Lynn Munsinger. Houghton Mifflin, 1984. ISBN 0-395-35391-2 Subj: Animals – groundhogs. Animals – rabbits. Holidays – Groundhog Day. Shadows.

Saint Nicholas ill. by Michael Garland. Boyds Mills, 2000. ISBN 1-56397-844-X Subj: Folk and fairy tales. Religion. Santa Claus.

Savina, the gypsy dancer ill. by Dennis Nolan. Macmillan, 1991. ISBN 0-02-789205-0 Subj: Activities – dancing. Gypsies.

The silver whistle ill. by Beth Peck. Macmillan, 1988. ISBN 0-02-789160-7 Subj: Foreign lands – Mexico. Holidays – Christmas.

The Tzar's bird ill. by Robert Rayevsky. Macmillan, 1990. ISBN 0-02-789401-0 Subj: Emotions – fear. Foreign lands – Russia. Royalty.

Will you come back for me? ill. by Robin Kramer. Albert Whitman, 1988. ISBN 0-8075-9112-2 Subj: Behavior – needing someone. Dreams. Emotions – fear. School – first day.

Topek, Susan Remick. *A costume for Noah* ill. by Sally Springer. Kar-Ben Copies, 1995. ISBN 0-929371-91-7 Subj: Clothing. Family life – brothers and sisters. Family life – new sibling. Holidays – Purim. Jewish culture. School.

Shalom, Shabbat: a book for havdalah ill. by Shelly S. Ephraim. Kar-Ben Copies, 1998. ISBN 1-58013-010-0 Subj: Format, unusual – board books. Jewish culture. Religion. Senses.

Tord, Bijou Le. *see* Le Tord, Bijou

Torgersen, Don Arthur. *The girl who tricked the troll* ill. by Tom Dunnington. Childrens Pr., 1978. ISBN 0-516-03465-0 Subj: Farms. Mythical creatures – trolls.

The troll who lived in the lake ill. by Tom Dunnington. Childrens Pr., 1978. ISBN 0-516-03631-9 Subj: Ecology. Mythical creatures – trolls.

Tornborg, Pat. *The Sesame Street cookbook* ill. by Robert Dennis. Platt, 1978. ISBN 0-448-13035-1 Subj: Activities – cooking. Puppets.

Tornqvist, Rita. *The Christmas carp* trans. from Swedish by Greta Kilburn; ill. by Marit Tornqvist. Farrar, 1990. ISBN 91-29-59784-6 Subj: Behavior – wishing. Family life. Holidays – Christmas.

Torre, Betty L. *The luminous pearl* ill. by Carol Inouye. Watts, 1990. ISBN 0-531-08490-6 Subj: Character traits – honesty. Character traits – kindness. Dragons. Folk and fairy tales. Foreign lands – China. Royalty.

Torres, Daniel. *Tom* ill. by author; English adapt. by Julie Simmons-Lynch. Viking, 1996. ISBN 0-670-86665-2 Subj: City. Dinosaurs. Friendship.

Torres, Leyla. *Liliana's grandmothers* ill. by author. Farrar, 1998. ISBN 0-374-35105-8 Subj: Family life – grandmothers. Foreign lands – Latin America. Quilts.

Saturday sancocho ill. by author. Farrar, 1995. ISBN 0-374-36418-4 Subj: Activities – cooking. Activities – trading. Family life – grandmothers. Food. Foreign lands – Colombia.

Tortillas and lullabies = Tortillas y cancioncitas ill. by "Corazones Valientes"; trans. by Rebecca Hart. Greenwillow, 1998. ISBN 0-688-14629-5 Subj: Family life. Foreign lands – Central America. Foreign languages.

Towle, Faith M. *The magic cooking pot: a folktale of India* ill. by author. Houghton Mifflin, 1975. ISBN 0-395-20273-6 Subj: Folk and fairy tales. Food. Foreign lands – India. Magic.

Townley, Roderick. *Paul and Sebastian* (Escudie, René)

Townsend, Anita. *The kangaroo* ill. by Michael Atkinson. Watts, 1979. ISBN 0-531-09152-X Subj: Animals – kangaroos. Science.

Townsend, Kenneth. *Felix, the bald-headed lion* ill. by author. Delacorte, 1967. Subj: Animals – lions. Clothing. Emotions – embarrassment. Hair.

Townsend, Maryann. *Pop's secret* by Maryann Townsend and Ronnie Stern; ill. with photos. Addison-Wesley, 1980. ISBN 0-201-07707-8 Subj: Death. Emotions – grief. Family life – grandfathers.

Townson, Hazel. *Terrible Tuesday* ill. by Tony Ross. Morrow, 1986. ISBN 0-688-06244-X Subj: Emotions – fear. Family life. Imagination.

What on earth . . . ? ill. by Mary Rees. Little, 1991. ISBN 0-316-85138-8 Subj: Activities – playing. Family life – fathers. Imagination.

Toye, William. *Fire stealer* photos by Elizabeth Cleaver. Oxford Univ. Pr., 1988. ISBN 0-19-540515-3 Subj: Folk and fairy tales. Indians of North America – Algonquian.

How summer came to Canada photos by Elizabeth Cleaver. Walck, 1969. ISBN 0-8098-1153-7 Subj: Folk and fairy tales. Foreign lands – Canada. Indians of North America – Micmac. Seasons – summer. Seasons – winter.

The loon's necklace photos by Elizabeth Cleaver. Oxford Univ. Pr., 1988. ISBN 0-19-540278-2 Subj: Folk and fairy tales. Foreign lands – Canada. Indians of North America.

The mountain goats of Temlaham photos by Elizabeth Cleaver. Walck, 1969. ISBN 0-8098-1154-5 Subj: Folk and fairy tales. Foreign lands – Canada. Indians of North America – Tsimshian.

Trains created by Gallimard Jeunesse and James Prunier; ill. by James Prunier; American text by Wendy Barish. Scholastic, 1998. ISBN 0-590-38156-3 Subj: Trains.

Trân-Khánh-Tuyê. *The little weaver of Thái-Yên Village* trans. from Vietnamese by Christopher N. H. Jenkins and author; ill. by Nancy Hom. Children's Book Pr., 1987. ISBN 0-89239-030-1 Subj: Activities – weaving. Foreign lands – Vietnam. Language.

Trapani, Iza. *How much is that doggie in the window?* ill. by author; words and music by Bob Merrill. Gareth Stevens, 1999. ISBN 0-8368-2486-5 Subj: Animals – dogs. Family life. Pets. Songs.

The itsy bitsy spider ill. by author. Gareth Stevens, 1996. ISBN 0-8368-1550-5 Subj: Character traits – persistence. Music. Nursery rhymes. Songs. Spiders.

Mary had a little lamb ill. by author. Whispering Coyote, 1998. ISBN 1-58089-009-1 Subj: Animals – sheep. Behavior – misbehavior. Music. Nursery rhymes. Songs.

Mary had a little lamb (Hale, Sarah Josepha Buell)

Row, row, row your boat ill. by author. Whispering Coyote, 1999. ISBN 1-58089-022-9 Subj: Animals. Animals – bears. Boats, ships. Family life. Pets. Rhyming text. Weather – storms.

What am I? ill. by author. Whispering Coyote, 1992. ISBN 1-879085-76-3 Subj: Animals. Games. Rhyming text.

Tredez, Alain. *see* Trez, Alain

Tredez, Denise. *see* Trez, Denise

Treherne, Katie Thamer. *The little mermaid* (Andersen, H. C. [Hans Christian])

Trent, Robbie. *The first Christmas* ill. by Marc Simont. HarperCollins, 1990, c1948. Subj: Holidays – Christmas. Religion – Nativity. Rhyming text.

Trenter, Anna. *Little Bear's Christmas* (Landa, Norbert)

Tresselt, Alvin R. *Autumn harvest* ill. by Roger Antoine Duvoisin. Lothrop, 1951. ISBN 0-688-51155-4 Subj: Holidays – Thanksgiving. Seasons – fall.

The beaver pond ill. by Roger Antoine Duvoisin. Lothrop, 1970. Subj: Animals – beavers. Ecology.

The dead tree ill. by Charles Robinson. Parents, 1972. ISBN 0-819-30564-2 Subj: Ecology. Trees.

The fisherman under the sea (Matsutani, Miyoko)

Follow the wind ill. by Roger Antoine Duvoisin. Lothrop, 1950. Subj: Rhyming text. Weather – wind.

Frog in the well ill. by Roger Antoine Duvoisin. Lothrop, 1958. Subj: Frogs and toads.

The gift of the tree ill. by Henri Sorensen. Lothrop, 1992. Original title: The dead tree. ISBN 0-688-10685-4 Subj: Ecology. Forest, woods. Trees.

Hi, Mister Robin ill. by Roger Antoine Duvoisin. Lothrop, 1950. ISBN 0-688-51168-6 Subj: Birds – robins. Family life. Seasons – spring.

Hide and seek fog ill. by Roger Antoine Duvoisin. Lothrop, 1965. ISBN 0-688-51169-4 Subj: Caldecott award honor books. Sea and seashore. Weather – fog.

How far is far? ill. by Ward Brackett. Parents, 1964. Subj: Concepts – distance. Science.

I saw the sea come in ill. by Roger Antoine Duvoisin. Lothrop, 1954. Subj: Behavior – solitude. Sea and seashore.

It's time now! ill. by Roger Antoine Duvoisin. Lothrop, 1969. Subj: City. Seasons.

Johnny Maple-Leaf ill. by Roger Antoine Duvoisin. Lothrop, 1948. Subj: Seasons. Seasons – fall. Trees.

The mitten: an old Ukrainian folktale ill. by Yaroslava. Lothrop, 1989, c1964. Adapt. by Alvin Tresselt from the version by E. Rachev. ISBN 0-606-04277-6 Subj: Animals. Folk and fairy tales. Foreign lands – Ukraine.

The rabbit story ill. by Carolyn Ewing. Lothrop, 1989. ISBN 0-688-08651-9 Subj: Animals – rabbits.

Rabbit story ill. by Leonard Weisgard. Lothrop, 1957. Subj: Animals – rabbits.

Rain drop splash ill. by Leonard Weisgard. Lothrop, 1946. ISBN 0-688-51165-1 Subj: Caldecott award honor books. Cumulative tales. Science. Weather – rain.

Smallest elephant in the world ill. by Milton Glaser. Knopf, 1959. ISBN 0-394-90763-9 Subj: Animals – elephants. Character traits – smallness. Circus.

Sun up ill. by Roger Antoine Duvoisin. Lothrop, 1949. Subj: Farms. Sun. Weather.

Sun up ill. by Henri Sorensen. Lothrop, 1991. ISBN 0-688-08657-8 Subj: Farms. Sun. Weather.

Wake up, city! ill. by Carolyn Ewing. Lothrop, 1989. ISBN 0-688-08653-5 Subj: City. Morning.

Wake up, farm! ill. by Roger Antoine Duvoisin. Lothrop, 1955. ISBN 0-688-51162-7 Subj: Animals. Farms. Morning. Noise, sounds.

Wake up, farm! ill. by Carolyn Ewing. Lothrop, 1991. ISBN 0-688-08655-1 Subj: Animals. Farms. Morning. Noise, sounds.

What did you leave behind? ill. by Roger Antoine Duvoisin. Lothrop, 1978. ISBN 0-688-51829-X Subj: Emotions.

White snow, bright snow ill. by Roger Antoine Duvoisin. Lothrop, 1988, c1947. ISBN 0-688-51161-9 Subj: Caldecott award books. Weather – snow.

The wind and Peter ill. by Garry McKenzie. Oxford Univ. Pr., 1948. Subj: Weather – wind.

The witch's magic cloth (Matsutani, Miyoko)

The world in the candy egg ill. by Roger Antoine Duvoisin. Lothrop, 1967. Subj: Eggs. Holidays – Easter. Magic.

Trevelyan, Kathy. *Don't be surprised!* ill. by Haydn Cornner. Dial, 1997. ISBN 0-8037-2282-6 Subj: Activities – traveling. Dragons. Format, unusual – toy and movable books. Magic.

Trez, Alain. *Good night, Veronica* (Trez, Denise)

The little knight's dragon (Trez, Denise)

Maila and the flying carpet (Trez, Denise)

Rabbit country (Trez, Denise)

The royal hiccups (Trez, Denise)

Trez, Denise. *Good night, Veronica* by Denise and Alain Trez; trans. by Douglas McKee; ill. by authors. Viking, 1968. Subj: Bedtime. Dreams. Sleep.

The little knight's dragon by Denise and Alain Trez; ill. by authors. Collins-World, 1963. Subj: Dragons. Knights.

Maila and the flying carpet by Denise and Alain Trez; trans. by Douglas McKee; ill. by authors. Viking, 1969. ISBN 0-670-45107-X Subj: Activities – flying. Foreign lands – India. Magic. Royalty.

Rabbit country by Denise and Alain Trez; ill. by authors. Viking, 1966. Subj: Animals – rabbits.

The royal hiccups by Denise and Alain Trez; trans. by Douglas McKee; ill. by authors. Viking, 1965. Subj: Emotions – fear. Illness. Royalty.

Trimble, Marcia. *Malinda Martha and her stepping stones* ill. by Susi Grell. Images Pr., 1999. ISBN 1-891577-72-7 Subj: Activities – playing. Rocks. Sea and seashore.

Trimble, Patti. *Lost!* ill. by Daniel Moreton. Harcourt, 2000. ISBN 0-15-202667-3 Subj: Behavior – lost. Insects – ants.

What day is it? ill. by Daniel Moreton. Harcourt, 2000. ISBN 0-15-202500-6 Subj: Birthdays. Friendship. Insects – ants. Parties.

Trimby, Elisa. *Mr. Plum's paradise* ill. by author. Lothrop, 1977. ISBN 0-688-51797-8 Subj: City. Gardens, gardening.

Trinca, Rod. *One woolly wombat* by Rod Trinca and Kerry Argent; ill. by Kerry Argent. Kane/Miller, 1985. ISBN 0-916291-00-6 Subj: Animals. Counting, numbers. Foreign lands – Australia.

Tripp, Paul. *The strawman who smiled by mistake* ill. by Wendy Watson. Doubleday, 1967. Subj: Emotions – happiness. Farms. Friendship. Scarecrows.

Tripp, Valerie. *Happy, happy Mother's Day* ill. by Sandra Kalthoff Martin. Childrens Pr., 1989. ISBN 0-516-01521-4 Subj: Animals. Holidays – Mother's Day. Rhyming text.

Sillyhen's big surprise ill. by Sandra Kalthoff Martin. Childrens Pr., 1989. ISBN 0-516-01522-2 Subj: Birds – chickens. Rhyming text.

Tripp, Wallace. *My Uncle Podger* ill. by author. Little, 1975. Based on a passage from Three men in a boat (to say nothing of the dog) by Jerome Klapka Jerome. ISBN 0-316-46180-6 Subj: Animals – rabbits. Family life – aunts, uncles. Humor.

The tale of a pig: a caucasian folktale adapt. and ill. by Wallace Tripp. McGraw-Hill, 1968. Subj: Animals – pigs. Folk and fairy tales.

Trist, Glenda. *A child's book of prayers* ill. with photos. DK, 1999. ISBN 0-7894-3976-X Subj: Religion.

Trivas, Irene. *Annie . . . Anya: a month in Moscow* ill. by author. Watts, 1992. ISBN 0-531-08602-X Subj: Foreign lands – Russia. Friendship.

Emma's Christmas ill. by author. Watts, 1988. ISBN 0-531-08380-2 Subj: Holidays – Christmas. Songs. Weddings.

Trosclair. *Cajun night before Christmas* ed. by Howard Jacobs; ill. by James Rice. Pelican, 1992. ISBN 0-88289-940-6 Subj: Cumulative tales. Ethnic groups in the U.S. – Acadians. Holidays – Christmas. Poetry. Reptiles – alligators, crocodiles. Santa Claus.

Trottier, Maxine. *Dreamstones* ill. by Stella East. Stoddart Kids, 1999. ISBN 0-7737-3191-1 Subj: Animals. Bedtime. Behavior – lost. Dreams. Foreign lands – Arctic. Indians of North America – Inuit.

Flags ill. by Paul Morin. Stoddart Kids, 1999. ISBN 0-7737-3136-9 Subj: Ethnic groups in the U.S. – Japanese Americans. Gardens, gardening. Plants. U.S. history. War.

Prairie willow ill. by Laura Fernandez and Rick Jacobson. Stoddart Kids, 1998. ISBN 0-7737-3067-2 Subj: Careers – farmers. Death. Dreams. Emotions – grief. Family life. Foreign lands – Canada. Trees.

A safe place ill. by Judith Friedman. Albert Whitman, 1997. ISBN 0-8075-7212-8 Subj: Child abuse. Family life – fathers. Family life – mothers. Safety.

The tiny kite of Eddie Wing ill. by Al Van Mil. Kane/Miller, 1996. ISBN 0-916291-66-9 Subj: Ethnic groups in the U.S. – Chinese Americans. Imagination. Kites.

The walking stick ill. by Annouchka G. Galouchko. Stoddart, 1999. ISBN 0-7737-3101-6 Subj: Ethnic groups in the U.S. – Vietnamese Americans. Immigrants. Religion.

Troughton, Joanna. *How rabbit stole the fire* ill. by adapt. HarperCollins, 1986. ISBN 0-87226-040-2 Subj: Animals – rabbits. Fire. Folk and fairy tales. Indians of North America.

How the birds changed their feathers: a South American Indian folk tale ill. by adapt. HarperCollins, 1986. ISBN 0-87226-080-1 Subj: Birds. Concepts – color. Folk and fairy tales. Foreign lands – South America.

Make-believe tales ill. by reteller. Peter Bedrick, 1991. ISBN 0-87226-451-3 Subj: Animals. Folk and fairy tales. Foreign lands – Burma.

Mouse-Deer's market ill. by adapt. HarperCollins, 1984. ISBN 0-911745-63-7 Subj: Animals. Animals – deer. Character traits – cleverness.

The quail's egg: a folk tale from Sri Lanka ill. by author. Peter Bedrick, 1988. ISBN 0-87226-185-9 Subj: Birds – quail. Cumulative tales. Eggs. Folk and fairy tales. Foreign lands – Sri Lanka.

Tortoise's dream: an African folk tale ill. by adapt. HarperCollins, 1986. ISBN 0-87226-039-9 Subj: Dreams. Folk and fairy tales. Foreign lands – Africa. Reptiles – turtles, tortoises.

What made Tiddalik laugh: an Australian Aborigine folk tale ill. by adapt. HarperCollins, 1986. ISBN 0-87226-081-X Subj: Folk and fairy tales. Foreign lands – Australia. Frogs and toads.

Who will be the sun? ill. by adapt. HarperCollins, 1986. ISBN 0-87226-038-0 Subj: Creation. Folk and fairy tales. Indians of North America – Kutenai. Sun.

Trucks ill. with photos. Macmillan, 1991. ISBN 0-689-71405-X Subj: Transportation. Trucks.

Trumbull, Suzanne. *Upside-downers: more pictures to stretch the imagination* (Anno, Mitsumasa)

Tryon, Leslie. *Albert's alphabet* ill. by author. Atheneum, 1991. ISBN 0-689-31642-9 Subj: ABC books. Activities – making things. Birds – ducks. School.

Albert's birthday ill. by author. Atheneum, 1999. ISBN 0-689-82296-0 Subj: Animals. Birds – ducks. Birthdays. Parties.

Albert's Christmas ill. by author. Atheneum, 1997. ISBN 0-689-81034-2 Subj: Animals. Birds – ducks. Holidays – Christmas. Rhyming text. Santa Claus.

Albert's Halloween: the case of the stolen pumpkins ill. by author. Atheneum, 1998. ISBN 0-689-81136-5 Subj: Animals. Birds – ducks. Careers – detectives. Holidays – Halloween. Mystery stories.

Albert's play ill. by author. Atheneum, 1992. ISBN 0-689-31525-2 Subj: Animals. Rhyming text. Theater.

Tseng, Grace. *White tiger, blue serpent* ill. by Jean and Mou-sien Tseng. Lothrop, 1999. ISBN 0-688-12516-6 Subj: Activities – weaving. Animals – tigers. Folk and fairy tales. Foreign lands – China. Magic. Reptiles – snakes.

Tsow, Ming. *A day with Ling* photos by Christopher Cormack. Hamish Hamilton, 1983. ISBN 0-241-10828-4 Subj: Family life.

Tsubakiyama, Margaret (Holloway). *Mei-Mei loves the morning* ill. by Cornelius Van Wright and Ying-Hwa Hu. Albert Whitman, 1999. ISBN 0-8075-5039-6 Subj: Family life – grandparents. Foreign lands – China. Health and fitness – exercise.

Tsultim, Yeshe. *The mouse king: a story from Tibet* ill. by Kusho Ralla. Penguin, 1979. ISBN 0-14-030804-0 Subj: Animals – mice. Folk and fairy tales. Foreign lands – Tibet.

Tsutsui, Yoriko. *Anna in charge* ill. by Akiko Hayashi. Viking, 1989. ISBN 0-670-81672-8 Subj: Activities – babysitting. Behavior – lost. Emotions – fear. Family life.

Anna's secret friend ill. by Akiko Hayashi. Viking, 1987. ISBN 0-670-81670-1 Subj: Family life. Friendship. Moving.

Before the picnic ill. by Akiko Hayashi. Putnam, 1987. ISBN 0-399-21458-5 Subj: Activities – picnicking. Family life.

Tuber, Joel. *The steadfast tin soldier* (Andersen, H. C. [Hans Christian])

The ugly duckling (Andersen, H. C. [Hans Christian])

Tucker, Kathleen. *The little bear who forgot* (Chevalier, Christa)

My mother never listens to me (Sharmat, Marjorie Weinman)

Tucker, Kathy. *Do cowboys ride bikes?* ill. by Nadine Bernard Westcott. Albert Whitman, 1997. ISBN 0-8075-1693-7 Subj: Character traits – questioning. Country. Cowboys. Rhyming text.

Do knights take naps? ill. by Nick Sharratt. Albert Whitman, 2000. ISBN 0-8075-1695-3 Subj: Knights. Middle Ages. Rhyming text. Sleep.

Do pirates take baths? ill. by Nadine Bernard Westcott. Albert Whitman, 1994. ISBN 0-8075-1696-1 Subj: Pirates. Rhyming text. Sea and seashore.

Tucker, Kiyoko. *The boy and the bird* (Fujita, Tamao)

Tucker, Nicholas. *Mother Goose abroad: nursery rhymes* ill. by Trevor Stubley. Crowell, 1974. ISBN 0-2410-2464-1 Subj: Nursery rhymes.

Tucker, Sian. *A is for astronaut* ill. by author. Orchard, 1995. ISBN 1-852138-19-X Subj: ABC books. Format, unusual – toy and movable books.

At home ill. by author. Simon & Schuster, 1991. ISBN 0-671-73399-0 Subj: Babies. Family life. Format, unusual – board books.

Going out ill. by author. Simon & Schuster, 1991. ISBN 0-671-73397-4 Subj: Babies. Format, unusual – board books. Nature.

My clothes ill. by author. Simon & Schuster, 1991. ISBN 0-671-73396-6 Subj: Babies. Clothing. Format, unusual – board books.

My toys ill. by author. Simon & Schuster, 1991. ISBN 0-671-73398-2 Subj: Babies. Format, unusual – board books. Toys.

Tucker, Stephen. *The time it took Tom* (Sharratt, Nick)

Tudor, Bethany. *Samuel's tree house* ill. by author. Collins-World, 1979. ISBN 0-529-05522-8 Subj: Birds – ducks. Friendship. Homes, houses. Toys. Trees.

Skiddycock Pond ill. by author. Lippincott, 1965. Subj: Birds – ducks. Boats, ships.

Tudor, Tasha. *Around the year* ill. by author. Walck, 1957. Subj: Days of the week, months of the year. Poetry. Seasons.

Corgiville fair ill. by author. Crowell, 1971. ISBN 0-690-21791-9 Subj: Animals – goats. Fairs. Mythical creatures – trolls.

The doll's Christmas ill. by author. Simon & Schuster, 1999. ISBN 0-689-82809-8 Subj: Holidays – Christmas. Parties. Toys – dolls.

Junior's tune ill. by author. Holiday, 1980. ISBN 0-8234-0411-0 Subj: Music. Sibling rivalry.

Mildred and the mummy ill. by author. Holiday, 1980. ISBN 0-8234-0372-6 Subj: Libraries.

Miss Kiss and the nasty beast ill. by author. Holiday, 1979. ISBN 0-8234-0355-6 Subj: Emotions – love.

More prayers ill. by author. McKay, 1967. ISBN 0-8098-1954-6 Subj: Religion.

1 is one ill. by author. Walck, 1956. ISBN 0-02-688535-2 Subj: Caldecott award honor books. Counting, numbers.

Snow before Christmas ill. by author. Oxford Univ. Pr., 1941. Subj: Holidays – Christmas. Seasons – winter. Weather – snow.

A tale for Easter ill. by author. Random House, 1989, c1941. ISBN 0-394-94404-6 Subj: Dreams. Holidays – Easter.

Tufts, Mary L. *The wee kitten who sucked her thumb* ill. by Lucinda McQueen. Platt & Munk, 1986. ISBN 0-448-19076-1 Subj: Animals. Animals – cats. Thumb sucking.

Tullet, Hervé. *Night / day* ill. by author. Little, 1999. ISBN 0-316-84244-3 Subj: Concepts – opposites. Format, unusual – toy and movable books. Language.

Tulloch, Richard. *Danny in the toybox* ill. by Armin Greder. Scholastic, 1990. ISBN 0-8689-6610-X Subj: Behavior – hiding. Emotions – anger. Family life.

Stories from our house ill. by Julie Vivas. Cambridge Univ. Pr., 1987. ISBN 0-521-33485-3 Subj: Family life. Humor.

Tulloch, Shirley. *Who made me?* ill. by Cathie Felstead. Augsburg, 2000. ISBN 0-8066-4045-6 Subj: Animals. Foreign lands – Africa. Religion.

Tune, Suelyn Ching. *How Maui slowed the sun* ill. by Robin Yoko Burningham. Univ. of Hawaii Pr., 1988. ISBN 0-8248-1083-X Subj: Folk and fairy tales. Hawaii. Magic.

Tunnell, Michael O. *Halloween pie* ill. by Kevin O'Malley. Lothrop, 1999. ISBN 0-688-16805-1 Subj: Food. Holidays. Magic. Monsters. Witches.

Mailing May ill. by Ted Rand. Greenwillow, 1997. ISBN 0-688-12879-3 Subj: Careers – postal workers. Family life – grandparents. Trains. Transportation. U.S. history.

Turbak, Gary. *Mountain animals in danger* ill. by Lawrence Ormsby. Northland, 1994. ISBN 0-87358-573-9 Subj: Animals – endangered animals.

Ocean animals in danger ill. by Lawrence Ormsby. Northland, 1994. ISBN 0-87358-574-7 Subj: Animals – endangered animals. Sea and seashore.

Türk, Hanne. *Goodnight Max* ill. by author. Firefly, 1983. ISBN 0-907234-39-9 Subj: Animals – mice. Bedtime. Wordless.

Happy birthday Max ill. by author. Alphabet Pr., 1984. ISBN 0-907234-42-2 Subj: Animals – mice. Birthdays. Wordless.

Max packs ill. by author. Alphabet Pr., 1984. ISBN 0-907234-40-2 Subj: Activities – traveling. Animals – mice. Wordless.

Max the artlover ill. by author. Alphabet Pr., 1983. ISBN 0-907234-25-9 Subj: Animals – mice. Art. Wordless.

Max versus the cube ill. by author. Alphabet Pr., 1982. Subj: Animals – mice. Problem solving. Riddles. Wordless.

Merry Christmas Max ill. by author. Firefly, 1983. ISBN 0-907234-37-2 Subj: Animals – mice. Holidays – Christmas. Wordless.

Rainy day Max ill. by author. Alphabet Pr., 1983. ISBN 0-907234-24-0 Subj: Activities – walking. Animals – mice. Weather – rain. Wordless.

Raking leaves with Max ill. by author. Firefly, 1983. ISBN 0-907234-38-0 Subj: Activities – working. Animals – mice. Wordless.

The rope skips Max ill. by author. Alphabet Pr., 1982. Subj: Activities. Animals – mice. Wordless.

Snapshot Max ill. by author. Alphabet Pr., 1984. ISBN 0-907234-41-2 Subj: Activities – photographing. Animals – mice. Wordless.

A surprise for Max ill. by author. Alphabet Pr., 1982. ISBN 0-907234-18-6 Subj: Animals – mice. Problem solving. Wordless.

Turkel, Pauline. *see* Kesselman, Judi R.

Turkle, Brinton. *The adventures of Obadiah* ill. by author. Viking, 1977. ISBN 0-670-10614-3 Subj: Behavior – lying. Character traits – honesty. Ethnic groups in the U.S. – Amish. U.S. history.

Deep in the forest ill. by author. Dutton, 1976. ISBN 0-525-28617-9 Subj: Animals – bears. Folk and fairy tales. Wordless.

Do not open ill. by author. Dutton, 1981. ISBN 0-525-28785-X Subj: Animals – cats. Behavior – trickery. Behavior – wishing. Monsters. Sea and seashore.

The magic of Millicent Musgrave ill. by author. Viking, 1967. Subj: Magic.

Obadiah the Bold story and pictures by Brinton Turkle. Viking, 1965. ISBN 0-14-050233-5 Subj: Activities – playing. Behavior – growing up. Ethnic groups in the U.S. – Amish. Sea and seashore. U.S. history.

Rachel and Obadiah ill. by author. Dutton, 1978. ISBN 0-525-38020-5 Subj: Behavior – sharing. Ethnic groups in the U.S. – Amish. Money. Sibling rivalry.

The sky dog ill. by author. Viking, 1969. ISBN 0-670-65049-8 Subj: Animals – dogs. Imagination. Sea and seashore. Weather – clouds.

Thy friend, Obadiah ill. by author. Viking, 1969. ISBN 0-670-71229-9 Subj: Birds – seagulls. Caldecott award honor books. Character traits – kindness to animals. Ethnic groups in the U.S. – Amish. Seasons – winter. U.S. history.

Turnage, Sheila. *Trout the magnificent* ill. by Janet Stevens. Harcourt, 1984. ISBN 0-15-290962-1 Subj: Behavior – dissatisfaction. Fish. Self-concept.

Turnbull, Ann. *Rob goes a-hunting* ill. by Denise Teasdale. Watts, 1990. ISBN 0-531-08477-9 Subj: Animals – dogs. Behavior – lost. Sports – hunting.

The sand horse ill. by Michael Foreman. Atheneum, 1989. ISBN 0-689-31581-3 Subj: Careers – artists. Sand. Sea and seashore.

The tapestry cats ill. by Carol Morley. Little, 1992. ISBN 0-316-85626-6 Subj: Animals – cats. Behavior – wishing. Birthdays. Fairies. Royalty – princesses. Royalty – queens.

Too tired ill. by Emma Chichester Clark. Harcourt, 1994. ISBN 0-15-200549-8 Subj: Animals. Animals – sloths. Religion – Noah. Weather – floods. Weather – rain.

Turner, Ann Warren. *Angel hide and seek* ill. by Lois Ehlert. HarperCollins, 1998. ISBN 0-06-027086-1 Subj: Angels. Picture puzzles. Religion. Rhyming text.

The Christmas house ill. by Nancy Edwards Calder. HarperCollins, 1994. ISBN 0-06-023429-6 Subj: Family life. Holidays – Christmas. Homes, houses. Poetry.

Dakota dugout ill. by Ronald Himler. Macmillan, 1985. ISBN 0-02-789700-1 Subj: Farms. U.S. history – frontier and pioneer life.

Dust for dinner ill. by Robert Barrett. HarperCollins, 1995. ISBN 0-06-023377-X Subj: Farms. Moving. Poverty. U.S. history.

Hedgehog for breakfast ill. by Lisa McCue. Macmillan, 1989. ISBN 0-02-789241-7 Subj: Animals – foxes. Animals – hedgehogs. Behavior – misunderstanding.

Let's be animals ill. by Rick Brown. HarperFestival, 1998. ISBN 0-694-01154-1 Subj: Activities – playing. Animals. Imagination.

Nettie's trip south ill. by Ronald Himler. Macmillan, 1987. ISBN 0-02-789240-9 Subj: Activities – traveling. Behavior – disbelief. Ethnic groups in the U.S. – African Americans. Family life.

Red flower goes West ill. by Dennis Nolan. Hyperion, 1999. ISBN 0-7868-2253-8 Subj: Family life. Flowers. U.S. history – frontier and pioneer life.

Secrets from the dollhouse ill. by Raúl Colón. HarperCollins, 2000. ISBN 0-06-024567-0 Subj: Poetry. Toys – dolls.

Shaker hearts ill. by Wendell Minor. HarperCollins, 1997. ISBN 0-06-025370-3 Subj: Religion. Rhyming text. U.S. history.

Stars for Sarah ill. by Mary Teichman. HarperCollins, 1991. ISBN 0-06-026187-0 Subj: Family life – mothers. Moving.

Through moon and stars and night skies ill. by James Graham Hale. HarperCollins, 1990. ISBN 0-06-026190-0 Subj: Adoption.

Tickle a pickle ill. by Karen Ann Weinhaus. Macmillan, 1986. ISBN 0-02-789280-8 Subj: Poetry.

Turner, Charles. *The turtle and the moon* ill. by Melissa Bay Mathis. Dutton, 1991. ISBN 0-525-44659-1 Subj: Activities – playing. Moon. Reptiles – turtles, tortoises.

Turner, Ethel. *Walking to school* ill. by Peter Gouldthorpe. Watts, 1989. ISBN 0-531-08399-3 Subj: Activities – walking. Emotions. Foreign lands – Australia. Poetry. School – first day.

Turner, Gwenda. *Colors* ill. by author. Viking, 1990. ISBN 0-670-82552-2 Subj: Concepts – color.

Once upon a time ill. by author. Viking, 1990. ISBN 0-670-82551-4 Subj: Family life. Time.

Over on the farm ill. by author. Viking, 1994. ISBN 0-670-85437-9 Subj: Animals. Counting, numbers. Farms. Foreign lands – New Zealand. Rhyming text.

Playbook ill. by author. Viking, 1986. ISBN 0-670-80660-9 Subj: School.

Shapes ill. by author. Viking, 1991. ISBN 0-670-83744-X Subj: Concepts – shape.

Turner, Josie. *see* Crawford, Phyllis

Turner, Nancy Byrd. *When young Melissa sweeps* ill. by Debrah Santini. Peachtree, 1998. ISBN 1-56145-157-6 Subj: Activities – dancing. Activities – working. Poetry.

Turner, Priscilla. *Among the odds and evens* ill. by Whitney Turner. Farrar, 1999. ISBN 0-374-30343-6 Subj: ABC books. Counting, numbers. Etiquette.

Turska, Krystyna. *The magician of Cracow* ill. by author. Greenwillow, 1975. ISBN 0-688-84010-8 Subj: Character traits – ambition. Devil. Folk and fairy tales. Foreign lands – Poland. Magic. Moon.

The woodcutter's duck ill. by author. Macmillan, 1972. Subj: Birds – ducks. Character traits – kindness to animals. Folk and fairy tales. Foreign lands – Poland. Frogs and toads.

Tusa, Tricia. *Bunnies in my head* ill. by author and young patients at the M.D. Anderson Cancer Center in Houston, Texas. Univ. of Texas M. D. Anderson Cancer Center, 1998. ISBN 0-9664551-8-

5 Subj: Art. Children as illustrators. Illness – cancer. Imagination.

Camilla's new hairdo ill. by author. Farrar, 1991. ISBN 0-374-31021-1 Subj: Character traits – individuality. Hair. Imagination. Problem solving.

Chicken ill. by author. Macmillan, 1986. ISBN 0-02-789320-0 Subj: Behavior – misunderstanding. Birds – chickens. Pets. Self-concept.

Libby's new glasses ill. by author. Holiday, 1984. ISBN 0-8234-0523-0 Subj: Glasses. Self-concept. Senses – seeing.

Maebelle's suitcase ill. by author. Macmillan, 1987. ISBN 0-02-789250-6 Subj: Birds. Clothing. Old age.

Miranda ill. by author. Macmillan, 1985. ISBN 0-02-789520-3 Subj: Character traits – stubbornness. Music.

Sherman and Pearl ill. by author. Macmillan, 1989. ISBN 0-02-789542-4 Subj: Progress. Roads.

Sisters ill. by author. Crown, 1995. ISBN 0-517-70033-6 Subj: Behavior – fighting, arguing. Food. Sibling rivalry.

Stay away from the junkyard! ill. by author. Macmillan, 1988. ISBN 0-02-789541-6 Subj: Art. Behavior – collecting things.

Tutt, Kay Cunningham. *And now we call him Santa Claus* ill. by author. Lothrop, 1963. Subj: Holidays – Christmas. Santa Claus.

Twain, Mark. *The prince and the pauper* (Mayer, Marianna)

The twelve days of Christmas.. English folk song.
Brian Wildsmith's The twelve days of Christmas ill. by Brian Wildsmith. Watts, 1972. ISBN 0-531-01555-6 Subj: Cumulative tales. Holidays – Christmas. Music. Songs.

Jack Kent's twelve days of Christmas ill. by Jack Kent. Parents, 1973. ISBN 0-819-30697-5 Subj: Cumulative tales. Holidays – Christmas. Humor. Music. Songs.

The twelve days of Christmas ill. by Jan Brett. Dodd, 1986. ISBN 0-396-08821-X Subj: Cumulative tales. Holidays – Christmas. Music. Songs.

The twelve days of Christmas ill. by Ilonka Karasz. HarperCollins, 1949. Subj: Cumulative tales. Holidays – Christmas. Music. Songs.

The twelve days of Christmas ill. by Ilse Plume. HarperCollins, 1990. ISBN 0-06-024738-X Subj: Cumulative tales. Holidays – Christmas. Music. Songs.

The twelve days of Christmas ill. by Erika Schneider. Alphabet Pr., 1984. ISBN 0-907234-62-3 Subj: Cumulative tales. Format, unusual. Holidays – Christmas. Music. Songs.

The twelve days of Christmas ill. by Vladimir Vagin. HarperCollins, 1998. ISBN 0-06-028399-8 Subj: Cumulative tales. Holidays – Christmas. Music. Songs.

The twelve days of Christmas ill. by Sophie Windham. Putnam, 1986. ISBN 0-399-21327-9 Subj: Cumulative tales. Holidays – Christmas. Music. Songs.

Twinem, Neecy. *Changing colors* ill. by author. Charlesbridge, 1996. ISBN 0-88106-941-8 Subj: Animals. Farms. Problem solving.

High in the trees ill. by author. Charlesbridge, 1996. ISBN 0-88106-940-X Subj: Animals. Problem solving.

In the air ill. by author. Charlesbridge, 1997. ISBN 0-88106-943-4 Subj: Animals. Birds. Format, unusual – board books. Picture puzzles.

Twining, Edith. *Sandman* ill. by author. Doubleday, 1991. ISBN 0-385-41259-2 Subj: Bedtime. Boats, ships. Dreams. Mythical creatures – sandman. Sleep.

Tworkov, Jack. *The camel who took a walk* ill. by Roger Antoine Duvoisin. Aladdin, 1951. ISBN 0-525-27393-X Subj: Activities – walking. Animals. Animals – camels. Animals – tigers. Cumulative tales. Morning.

Tyers, Jenny. *When it is night and when it is day* ill. by author. Houghton Mifflin, 1996. ISBN 0-395-71546-6 Subj: Animals. Night. Noise, sounds.

Tyler, Linda Wagner. *After Christmas tree* ill. by Susan Davis. Viking, 1990. ISBN 0-670-83045-3 Subj: Character traits – kindness to animals. Holidays – Christmas.

The sick-in-bed birthday book ill. by Susan Davis. Viking, 1988. ISBN 0-670-81823-2 Subj: Animals – pigs. Birthdays. Illness.

Waiting for mom ill. by Susan Davis. Viking, 1987. ISBN 0-670-81408-3 Subj: Animals – hippopotamuses. Behavior – worrying. Family life – mothers. School.

When daddy comes home ill. by Susan Davis. Viking, 1986. ISBN 0-670-80301-4 Subj: Animals – hippopotamuses. Family life – fathers.

Tyrrell, Anne. *Elizabeth Jane gets dressed* ill. by Caroline Castle. Barron's, 1987. ISBN 0-8120-5775-9 Subj: Clothing. Days of the week, months of the year. Rhyming text. Toys.

Mary Ann always can ill. by Caroline Castle. Barron's, 1988. ISBN 0-8120-5939-5 Subj: Character traits – individuality. Rhyming text. Sibling rivalry.

Tzannes, Robin. *Sanji and the baker* ill. by Korky Paul. Oxford Univ. Pr., 1998. ISBN 0-19-279960-6 Subj: Activities – cooking. Activities – traveling. Careers – bakers.

Uchida, Yoshiko. *The bracelet* ill. by Joanna Yardley. Philomel, 1993. ISBN 0-399-22503-X Subj: Ethnic groups in the U.S. – Japanese Americans. Friendship. Slavery. U.S. history.

The magic purse ill. by Keiko Narahashi. Margaret K. McElderry, 1993. ISBN 0-689-50559-0 Subj: Character traits – bravery. Folk and fairy tales. Foreign lands – Japan.

Sumi's prize ill. by Kazue Mizumura. Scribners, 1964. Subj: Character traits – ambition. Foreign lands – Japan. Kites.

Sumi's special happening ill. by Kazue Mizumura. Scribners, 1966. Subj: Birthdays. Foreign lands – Japan. Old age.

The two foolish cats ill. by Margot Zemach. Macmillan, 1987. ISBN 0-689-50397-0 Subj: Animals – cats. Folk and fairy tales. Food.

The wise old woman ill. by Martin Springett. Margaret K. McElderry, 1994. ISBN 0-689-50582-5 Subj: Folk and fairy tales. Foreign lands – Japan. Old age.

Udry, Janice May. *Alfred* ill. by Judith S. Roth. Albert Whitman, 1960. Subj: Animals – dogs. Behavior – animals, dislike of. Emotions – fear.

Emily's autumn ill. by Erik Blegvad. Albert Whitman, 1969. ISBN 0-8075-1998-7 Subj: Farms. Seasons – fall. Toys – dolls.

How I faded away ill. by Monica De Bruyn. Albert Whitman, 1976. ISBN 0-8075-3416-1 Subj: Behavior – unnoticed, unseen. Emotions – embarrassment. Self-concept.

Is Susan here? ill. by Peter Edwards. Abelard-Schuman, 1962. Subj: Animals. Character traits – helpfulness. Family life – mothers. Imagination.

Is Susan here? ill. by Karen Gundersheimer. Newly ill. ed. HarperCollins, 1993. ISBN 0-06-026143-9 Subj: Animals. Character traits – helpfulness. Family life – mothers. Imagination.

Let's be enemies ill. by Maurice Sendak. Harper-Collins, 1961. ISBN 0-06-026131-5 Subj: Behavior – fighting, arguing. Emotions – hate. Friendship.

Mary Ann's mud day ill. by Martha G. Alexander. HarperCollins, 1967. Subj: Activities – playing. Ethnic groups in the U.S. – African Americans.

Mary Jo's grandmother ill. by Eleanor Mill. Albert Whitman, 1970. ISBN 0-8075-4984-3 Subj: Ethnic groups in the U.S. – African Americans. Family life – grandmothers. Illness. Seasons – winter. Weather – snow.

The mean mouse and other mean stories ill. by Ed Young. HarperCollins, 1962. Subj: Character traits – meanness.

The moon jumpers ill. by Maurice Sendak. Harper-Collins, 1959. ISBN 0-06-026145-5 Subj: Caldecott award honor books. Moon. Twilight.

"Oh no, cat!" ill. by Mary Chalmers. Coward, 1976. ISBN 0-698-30620-1 Subj: Animals – cats. Pets.

Theodore's parents ill. by Adrienne Adams. Lothrop, 1958. Subj: Adoption. Family life.

Thump and Plunk ill. by Geoffrey Hayes. Newly ill. ed. HarperCollins, 2000. ISBN 0-06-028528-1 Subj: Behavior – fighting, arguing. Birds – ducks. Family life – mothers. Sibling rivalry. Toys – dolls.

Thump and Plunk ill. by Ann Schweninger. HarperCollins, 1981. ISBN 0-06-026150-1 Subj: Animals – mice. Behavior – fighting, arguing. Family life – mothers. Sibling rivalry. Toys – dolls.

A tree is nice ill. by Marc Simont. HarperCollins, 1956. ISBN 0-06-026156-0 Subj: Caldecott award books. Poetry. Seasons. Trees.

What Mary Jo shared ill. by Eleanor Mill. Albert Whitman, 1966. ISBN 0-8075-8842-3 Subj: Character traits – shyness. Ethnic groups in the U.S. Ethnic groups in the U.S. – African Americans. Family life – fathers. School.

What Mary Jo wanted ill. by Eleanor Mill. Albert Whitman, 1968. Subj: Animals – dogs. Ethnic groups in the U.S. – African Americans. Family life. Pets.

Ueno, Noriko. *Elephant buttons* ill. by author. HarperCollins, 1973. ISBN 0-06-026161-7 Subj: Animals. Circular tales. Concepts – in and out. Concepts – size. Games. Humor. Participation. Wordless.

Uff, Caroline. *Hello, Lulu* ill. by author. Walker, 1999. ISBN 0-8027-8712-6 Subj: Clothing – shoes. Family life. Friendship. Pets.

Lulu's busy day ill. by author. Walker, 2000. ISBN 0-8027-8716-9 Subj: Activities. Family life.

Uhlberg, Myron. *Flying over Brooklyn* ill. by Gerald Fitzgerald. Peachtree, 1999. ISBN 1-56145-194-0 Subj: Activities – flying. U.S. history. Weather – snow.

Mad Dog McGraw ill. by Lydia Monks. Putnam, 2000. ISBN 0-399-23308-3 Subj: Animals – dogs. Problem solving.

Uhlig, Elizabeth. *Dog and cat* (Alcantara, Ricardo)

Ulmer, Wendy K. *A campfire for cowboy Billy* ill. by Kenneth J. Spengler. Northland, 1997. ISBN 0-8735-8681-6 Subj: Cowboys. Emotions – grief. Family life – grandfathers. Imagination.

Ulrich, George. *The spook matinee: and other scary poems for kids* ill. by author. Delacorte, 1992. ISBN 0-385-30552-4 Subj: Humor. Poetry.

Umansky, Kay. *You can swim, Jim* by Kaye Umansky and Margaret Chamberlain; ill. by Margaret Chamberlain. Bodley Head, 1997. ISBN 0-370-32452-8 Subj: Poetry. Sports – swimming.

Umezawa, Rui. *Aiko's flowers* ill. by Yuji Ando. Tundra, 1999. ISBN 0-8877-6465-7 Subj: Flowers.

Uncle Gus. *see* Rey, H. A. (Hans Augusto)

Underhill, Liz. *The lucky coin* ill. by Liz Underhill; text by Margaret Greaves. Stewart, Tabori & Chang, 1989. ISBN 1-55670-129-2 Subj: Animals. Character traits – luck. Format, unusual – toy and movable books. Money.

Ungerer, Jean Thomas. *see* Ungerer, Tomi

Ungerer, Tomi. *Adelaide* ill. by author. TomiCo, 1999. ISBN 1-57098-296-1 Subj: Activities – flying. Activities – traveling. Animals – kangaroos. Foreign lands – France.

The beast of Monsieur Racine ill. by author. Farrar, 1971. ISBN 0-374-30640-0 Subj: Behavior – trickery. Foreign lands – France. Humor. Monsters.

Christmas eve at the Mellops ill. by author. Harper-Collins, 1960. ISBN 1-57098-227-9 Subj: Animals – pigs. Holidays – Christmas.

Crictor ill. by author. HarperCollins, 1958. ISBN 0-06-026181-1 Subj: Humor. Reptiles – snakes.

Emile ill. by author. HarperCollins, 1960. ISBN 0-440-40593-9 Subj: Humor. Octopuses.

Flix ill. by author. Roberts Rinehart, 1998. ISBN 1-57098-161-2 Subj: Animals – cats. Animals – dogs. Prejudice.

The hat ill. by author. Parents, 1970. ISBN 0-8193-0378-X Subj: Clothing – hats. Foreign lands – Italy. Magic. Weather – wind.

The Mellops go diving for treasure ill. by author. HarperCollins, 1957. Subj: Animals – pigs. Sea and seashore. Sports – skin diving.

The Mellops go flying ill. by author. HarperCollins, 1957. Subj: Activities – flying. Airplanes, airports. Animals – pigs.

The Mellops go spelunking ill. by author. Harper-Collins, 1963. Subj: Animals – pigs. Caves. Character traits – perseverance.

The Mellops strike oil ill. by author. HarperCollins, 1958. Subj: Animals – pigs. Fire. Oil.

Moon man ill. by author. HarperCollins, 1967. ISBN 0-06-026235-4 Subj: Moon. Space and space ships.

No kiss for mother ill. by author. HarperCollins, 1973. ISBN 0-06-026237-0 Subj: Animals – cats. Family life – mothers.

One, two, where's my shoe? ill. by author. Harper-Collins, 1964. Subj: Games. Wordless.

Orlando, the brave vulture ill. by author. Harper-Collins, 1966. Subj: Birds – vultures. Desert. Foreign lands – Mexico.

Rufus ill. by author. HarperCollins, 1961. Subj: Animals – bats.

Snail, where are you? ill. by author. HarperCollins, 1962. Subj: Animals – snails. Games. Wordless.

The three robbers ill. by author. Atheneum, 1962. Subj: Crime. Orphans.

Tortoni Tremelo the cursed musician ill. by author. Roberts Rinehart, 1998. ISBN 1-57098-226-0 Subj: Careers – musicians. Magic. Music.

Warwick's 3 bottles (Hodeir, André)

Zeralda's ogre ill. by author. HarperCollins, 1967. Subj: Activities – cooking. Character traits – kindness. Giants. Monsters. Mythical creatures – ogres.

Unobagha, Uzoamaka Chinyelu. *Off to the sweet shores of Africa and other talking drum rhymes* ill. by Julia Cairns. Chronicle, 2000. ISBN 0-8118-2378-4 Subj: Foreign lands – Africa. Poetry.

Untermeyer, Louis. *The kitten who barked* ill. by Lilian Obligado. Golden Pr., 1962. Subj: Animals – cats. Animals – dogs.

Unwin, Pippa. *The great zoo hunt!* ill. by author. Doubleday, 1990. ISBN 0-385-41107-3 Subj: Animals. Behavior – hiding. Zoos.

Tomcat takes a walk ill. by author. Andersen, 1998. ISBN 0-86264-705-3 Subj: Animals – cats. Foreign lands – England.

Updike, David. *An autumn tale* ill. by Robert Andrew Parker. Pippin Pr., 1988. ISBN 0-945912-02-1 Subj: Imagination. Night. Seasons – fall.

A winter's journey ill. by Robert Andrew Parker. Prentice-Hall, 1985. ISBN 0-13-961566-0 Subj: Animals – dogs. Dreams. Family life. Weather – snow.

Updike, John. *A helpful alphabet of friendly objects* ill. by David Updike. Knopf, 1995. ISBN 0-679-94324-2 Subj: Poetry.

Upham, Elizabeth. *Little brown bear loses his clothes* ill. by Normand Chartier. Platt, 1978. ISBN 0-448-46523-X Subj: Animals – bears. Behavior – losing things.

Upper, Jonathan. *Spin's really wild Africa tour* ill. by Barbara Gibson. National Geographic, 1996. ISBN 0-7922-3501-0 Subj: Animals. Desert. Foreign lands – Africa. Jungle.

Upton, Pat. *Who does this job?* ill. by Matt Novak. Boyds Mills, 1991. ISBN 1-878093-20-7 Subj: Careers.

Who lives in the woods? ill. by Karen Lee Schmidt. Boyds Mills, 1991. ISBN 1-878093-19-3 Subj: Animals. Forest, woods.

Usher, Margo Scegge. *see* McHargue, Georgess

Ushinskii, K. D. (Konstantin Dmitrievich). *How a shirt grew in the field* (Rudolph, Marguerita)

Uttley, Alice Jane. *see* Uttley, Alison

Uttley, Alison. *The Christmas box* ill. by Graham Percy. Faber, 1989. ISBN 0-571-15264-7 Subj: Animals – pigs. Holidays – Christmas.

Sam Pig and the dragon ill. by Graham Percy. Faber, 1989. ISBN 0-571-15294-5 Subj: Animals – pigs. Dragons.

Sam Pig and the hurdy-gurdy man ill. by Graham Percy. Faber, 1989. ISBN 0-571-15076-4 Subj: Animals – pigs. Music.

Sam Pig and the wind ill. by Graham Percy. Faber, 1989. ISBN 0-571-15295-3 Subj: Animals – pigs. Clothing – pants. Weather – wind.

Utton, Peter. *Jennifer's room* ill. by author. Orchard, 1995. ISBN 0-531-06842-0 Subj: Imagination.

The witch's hand ill. by author. Farrar, 1989. ISBN 0-374-38463-0 Subj: Family life. Witches.

Uysal, Ahmet E. *New patches for old: a Turkish folktale* (Walker, Barbara K. [Barbara Kerlin])

Va, Leong. *A letter to the king* trans. from Norwegian by James Anderson; ill. by author. HarperCollins, 1991. ISBN 0-06-020070-7 Subj: Character traits – bravery. Character traits – loyalty. Folk and fairy tales. Foreign lands – China. Foreign languages. Royalty – kings.

Vaës, Alain. *The porcelain pepper pot* ill. by author. Puffin, 1987, c1982. ISBN 0-14-050727-2 Subj: Activities – picnicking. Emotions – love. Farms.

The wild hamster ill. by author. Little, 1985. ISBN 0-316-89504-0 Subj: Animals – hamsters. Pets.

Vagin, Vladimir Vasil'evich. *Dear brother* (Asch, Frank)

The enormous carrot ill. by reteller. Scholastic, 1998. ISBN 0-590-45491-9 Subj: Animals. Cumulative tales. Farms. Folk and fairy tales. Foreign lands – Russia. Plants. Problem solving.

The flower faerie (Asch, Frank)

Here comes the cat! by Vladimir Vagin and Frank Asch; ill. by authors. Scholastic, 1989. ISBN 0-590-41859-9 Subj: Animals – cats. Animals – mice. Foreign languages.

Insects from outer space (Asch, Frank)

The nutcracker ballet (Hoffmann, E. T. A.)

Peter and the wolf (Prokofiev, Sergei Sergeievitch)

Vail, Rachel. *Over the moon* ill. by Scott Nash. Orchard, 1998. ISBN 0-531-33068-0 Subj: Animals. Moon. Nursery rhymes. Theater.

Vainio, Pirkko. *The Christmas angel* ill. by Pirkko Vainio; trans. by Anthea Bell. North-South, 1995. ISBN 1-55858-500-1 Subj: Angels. Holidays – Christmas. Homeless. Music. Poverty.

The dream house ill. by author; trans. by J. Alison James. North-South, 1997. ISBN 1-55858-750-0 Subj: Activities – making things. Animals – cats. Homes, houses. Magic. Weather – storms.

Valderrama, Candido A. *Mister North Wind* (De Posadas Mane, Carmen)

Valens, Amy. *Jesse's day care* ill. by Richard Eric Brown. Houghton Mifflin, 1990. ISBN 0-395-53357-0 Subj: Activities – working. Family life – mothers. School.

Valens, Evans G. *Wingfin and Topple* ill. by Clement Hurd. Collins-World, 1962. Subj: Activities – flying. Fish.

Valentine, Johnny. *The duke who outlawed jelly beans and other stories* ill. by Lynette Schmidt. Alyson Wonderland, 1991. ISBN 1-55583-199-0 Subj: Folk and fairy tales.

One dad, two dads, brown dad, blue dads ill. by Melody Sarecky. Alyson Wonderland, 1994. ISBN 1-55583-253-9 Subj: Ethnic groups in the U.S. Family life – fathers. Prejudice.

Valeri, M. Eulalia. *Hansel and Gretel* (Grimm, Jacob)

Sleeping Beauty (Grimm, Jacob)

The ugly duckling (Andersen, H. C. [Hans Christian])

Valfre, Edward. *Backseat buckaroo* ill. by author. Thomasson-Grant, 1995. ISBN 1-56566-078-1 Subj: Activities – traveling. Imagination.

Vacationers from outer space ill. by author. Chronicle, 1997. ISBN 0-8118-1717-2 Subj: Activities – vacationing. Aliens. Imagination.

Valgardson, W. D. *Winter rescue* ill. by Ange Zhang. Margaret K. McElderry, 1995. ISBN 0-689-80094-0 Subj: Family life – grandfathers. Foreign lands – Canada. Holidays – Christmas. Lakes, ponds. Seasons – winter. Sports – fishing.

Van Allsburg, Chris. *Bad day at Riverbend* ill. by author. Houghton Mifflin, 1995. ISBN 0-395-67347-X Subj: Activities – drawing. Imagination.

The garden of Abdul Gasazi ill. by author. Houghton Mifflin, 1979. ISBN 0-395-27804-X Subj: Animals – dogs. Behavior – misbehavior. Caldecott award honor books. Imagination. Magic.

Jumanji ill. by author. Houghton Mifflin, 1981. ISBN 0-395-30448-2 Subj: Caldecott award books. Games. Imagination. Jungle.

The mysteries of Harris Burdick ill. by author. Houghton Mifflin, 1984. ISBN 0-395-35393-9 Subj: Imagination.

The polar express ill. by author. Houghton Mifflin, 1985. ISBN 0-395-38949-6 Subj: Caldecott award books. Holidays – Christmas. Imagination. Night. Santa Claus. Trains.

The stranger ill. by author. Houghton Mifflin, 1986. ISBN 0-395-42331-7 Subj: Behavior – forgetfulness. Country. Seasons – fall.

Two bad ants ill. by author. Houghton Mifflin, 1988. ISBN 0-395-48668-8 Subj: Homes, houses. Insects – ants.

The widow's broom ill. by author. Houghton Mifflin, 1992. ISBN 0-395-64051-2 Subj: Magic. Prejudice. Witches.

The wreck of the Zephyr ill. by author. Houghton Mifflin, 1983. ISBN 0-395-33075-0 Subj: Boats, ships. Sailors. Weather – storms.

The Z was zapped ill. by author. Houghton Mifflin, 1987. ISBN 0-395-44612-0 Subj: ABC books.

Van Camp, Richard. *What's the most beautiful thing you know about horses?* ill. George Littlechild. Children's Book Pr., 1998. ISBN 0-89239-154-5 Subj: Animals – horses, ponies. Foreign lands – Canada. Indians of North America.

Van Caster, Nancy. *An alligator lives in Benjamin's house* ill. by Dale Gottlieb. Putnam, 1990. ISBN 0-399-21489-5 Subj: Animals. Behavior – imitation. Family life. Imagination.

Vance, Eleanor Graham. *Jonathan* ill. by Albert John Pucci. Follett, 1966. Subj: Character traits – questioning. Poetry. Weather.

Van den Berg, Marinus. *The three birds: a story for children about the loss of a loved one* ill. by Sandra Ireland. Gareth Stevens, 1994. ISBN 0-8368-1072-4 Subj: Birds. Death. Emotions – grief. Illness – cancer.

Van den Honert, Dorry. *Demi the baby sitter* ill. by Meg Wohlberg. Morrow, 1961. Subj: Activities – babysitting. Animals – dogs.

Van der Beek, Deborah. *Alice's blue cloth* ill. by author. Putnam, 1989. ISBN 0-399-21622-7 Subj: Birthdays. Family life.

Superbabe! ill. by author. Putnam, 1988. ISBN 0-399-21507-7 Subj: Babies. Family life. Parks. Rhyming text. Sibling rivalry.

VanderKlipp, Michael A. *Joy to the world! a Christmas counting book* ill. by Nancy Munger. Zondervan, 1998. ISBN 0-310-97660-X Subj: Counting, numbers. Format, unusual – board books. Religion – Nativity. Rhyming text.

Van der Meer, Atie. *Oh Lord!* (Van der Meer, Ron)

Pigs at home (Van der Meer, Ron)

Van der Meer, Ron. *Babette Cole's beastly birthday book* (Cole, Babette)

Funny hats ill. by Atie van der Meer. Random House, 1992. ISBN 0-679-82850-8 Subj: Clothing – hats. Counting, numbers. Format, unusual – toy and movable books.

Oh Lord! by Ron and Atie van der Meer; ill. by authors. Crown, 1980. ISBN 0-517-54006-1 Subj: Humor. Religion.

Pigs at home by Ron and Atie Van der Meer; ill. by authors. Atheneum, 1988. ISBN 0-689-71232-4 Subj: Animals – pigs. Format, unusual – toy and movable books.

Sailing ships (McGowan, Alan)

Van Dyke, Henry. *The fourth wise man* (Summers, Susan)

Van Emst, Charlotte. *Little Rabbit's big day* ill. by author. Little, 1990. ISBN 0-316-89623-3 Subj: Animals – rabbits. Concepts – size.

Van Fleet, Matthew. *Fuzzy yellow ducklings* ill. by author. Dial, 1995. ISBN 0-8037-1759-8 Subj: Animals. Birds. Concepts – color. Concepts – shape. Format, unusual – toy and movable books.

One yellow lion ill. by author. Dial, 1992. ISBN 0-8037-1099-2 Subj: Animals. Concepts – color. Counting, numbers. Format, unusual – toy and movable books.

Spotted yellow frogs ill. by author. Dial, 1998. ISBN 0-8037-2350-4 Subj: Animals. Concepts – color. Concepts – shape. Format, unusual – toy and movable books.

Van Gelder, Richard George. *Animals in winter* (Bancroft, Henrietta)

Van Haeringen, Annemarie. *The cats' tale* ill. by author. Oxford Univ. Pr., 1989. ISBN 0-19-279819-7 Subj: Animals – cats. Family life – grandparents. Gardens, gardening. Giants.

Van Horn, Grace. *Little red rooster* ill. by Sheila Perry. Abelard-Schuman, 1961. Subj: Birds – chickens. Farms.

Van Horn, William. *Harry Hoyle's giant jumping bean* ill. by author. Atheneum, 1978. ISBN 0-689-30636-9 Subj: Animals – cats. Animals – pack rats. Behavior – collecting things.

Twitchtoe, the beastfinder ill. by author. Atheneum, 1978. ISBN 0-689-30670-9 Subj: Problem solving.

Van Laan, Nancy. *The big fat worm* ill. by Marisabina Russo. Knopf, 1987. ISBN 0-394-98763-2 Subj: Animals. Birds. Circular tales.

La boda: a Mexican wedding celebration ill. by Andrea Arroyo. Little, 1996. ISBN 0-316-89626-8 Subj: Foreign lands – Mexico. Foreign languages. Indians of North America – Zapotec. Weddings.

The legend of El Dorado story and ill. by Beatriz A. Vidal; adapt. by Nancy Van Laan. Knopf, 1991. ISBN 0-679-90136-1 Subj: Folk and fairy tales. Foreign lands – South America. Indians of South America. Royalty – kings.

Little baby Bobby ill. by Laura Cornell. Knopf, 1997. ISBN 0-679-94922-4 Subj: Behavior – running away. Humor. Rhyming text. Toys – bears.

Little Fish lost ill. by Jane Conteh-Morgan. Atheneum, 1998. ISBN 0-689-81331-7 Subj: Animals. Family life – mothers. Fish. Foreign lands – Africa. Rhyming text.

The magic bean tree ill. by Beatriz Vidal. Houghton Mifflin, 1998. ISBN 0-395-82746-9 Subj: Folk and fairy tales. Foreign lands – Argentina. Indians of South America – Quechua.

Mama rocks, Papa sings ill. by Roberta Smith. Knopf, 1995. ISBN 0-679-94016-2 Subj: Activities – babysitting. Babies. Counting, numbers. Cumulative tales. Foreign lands – Haiti. Rhyming text.

A mouse in my house ill. by Marjorie Priceman. Knopf, 1990. ISBN 0-679-90043-8 Subj: Animals. Behavior. Rhyming text.

People, people, everywhere ill. by Nadine Bernard Westcott. Knopf, 1992. ISBN 0-679-91063-8 Subj: Activities. City. Rhyming text.

Possum come a-knocking ill. by George Booth. Knopf, 1990. ISBN 0-394-92206-9 Subj: Animals – possums. Cumulative tales. Family life. Rhyming text.

Rainbow crow ill. by Beatriz A. Vidal. Knopf, 1989. ISBN 0-394-99577-5 Subj: Birds – crows. Concepts – color. Creation. Fire. Folk and fairy tales. Indians of North America – Lenape.

Round and round again ill. by Nadine Bernard Westcott. Hyperion, 1994. ISBN 0-7868-2005-5 Subj: Ecology. Rhyming text.

Shingebiss: an Ojibwe legend ill. by Betsy Bowen. Houghton Mifflin, 1997. ISBN 0-316-89627-6 Subj: Birds – ducks. Folk and fairy tales. Indians of North America – Ojibwa. Seasons – winter.

Sleep, sleep, sleep ill. by Holly Meade. Little, 1995. ISBN 0-316-89732-9 Subj: Animals. Foreign lands. Foreign languages. Lullabies. Sleep.

So say the little monkeys ill. by Yumi Heo. Atheneum, 1998. ISBN 0-689-81038-5 Subj: Animals – monkeys. Folk and fairy tales. Foreign lands – Brazil. Rhyming text.

This is the hat ill. by Holly Meade. Hyperion, 1995. ISBN 0-7868-1030-0 Subj: Animals. Circular tales. Clothing – hats. Rhyming text.

A tree for me ill. by Sheila White Samton. Knopf, 2000. ISBN 0-679-99384-3 Subj: Animals. Counting, numbers. Rhyming text. Trees.

When winter comes: a lullaby ill. by Susan Gaber. Atheneum, 2000. ISBN 0-689-81778-9 Subj: Animals. Lullabies. Seasons – winter.

Van Leeuwen, Jean. *Across the wide dark sea: the Mayflower journey* ill. by Thomas B. Allen. Dial, 1995. ISBN 0-8037-1167-0 Subj: Activities – traveling. Boats, ships. Pilgrims. Religion. U.S. history.

The emperor's new clothes (Andersen, H. C. [Hans Christian])

Going west ill. by Thomas B. Allen. Dial, 1992. ISBN 0-8037-1028-3 Subj: Family life. Moving. U.S. history – frontier and pioneer life.

More tales of Oliver Pig ill. by Arnold Lobel. Dial, 1981. ISBN 0-8037-8714-6 Subj: Animals – pigs. Family life.

Nothing here but trees ill. by Phil Boatwright. Dial, 1998. ISBN 0-8037-2180-3 Subj: Careers – farmers. Trees. U.S. history – frontier and pioneer life.

The strange adventures of Blue Dog ill. by Marco Ventura. Dial, 1999. ISBN 0-8037-1878-0 Subj: Animals – dogs. Farms. Toys.

The tickle stories ill. by Mary Whyte. Dial, 1998. ISBN 0-8037-2049-1 Subj: Activities – storytelling. Bedtime. Family life. Family life – grandfathers.

Too hot for ice cream ill. by Martha G. Alexander. Dial, 1974. ISBN 0-8037-6077-9 Subj: Behavior – bad day. Sports – swimming. Weather.

Touch the sky summer ill. by Dan Andreasen. Dial, 1997. ISBN 0-8037-1820-9 Subj: Activities – vacationing. Family life. Family life – grandparents. Lakes, ponds. Seasons – summer.

Van Liew Foster, Doris. *see* Foster, Doris Van Liew

Van Nutt, Julia. *The monster in the shadows* ill. by Robert Van Nutt. Doubleday, 2000. ISBN 0-385-32565-7 Subj: Crime. Monsters. Shadows.

The mystery of Mineral Gorge ill. by Robert Van Nutt. Doubleday, 1998. ISBN 0-385-32562-2 Subj: Animals – pigs. Mystery stories.

Pignapped! ill. by Robert Van Nutt. Doubleday, 2000. ISBN 0-385-32559-2 Subj: Animals – pigs. Character traits – foolishness. Museums.

Pumpkins from the sky? ill. by Robert Van Nutt. Doubleday, 1999. ISBN 0-385-32568-1 Subj: Animals – pigs. Fairs. Weather – storms.

Van Rynbach, Iris. *Five little pumpkins* ill. by author. Boyds Mills, 1995. ISBN 1-56397-452-5 Subj: Holidays – Halloween. Plants. Rhyming text.

The soup stone adapt. and ill. by Iris Van Rynbach. Greenwillow, 1988. ISBN 0-688-07255-0 Subj:

Careers – military. Character traits – cleverness. Folk and fairy tales. Food.

Van Stockum, Hilda. *A day on skates: the story of a Dutch picnic* ill. by author. Bethlehem Books, 1994, c1934. ISBN 1-883937-00-0 Subj: Activities – picnicking. Foreign lands – Holland. Sports – ice skating.

Van Vorst, M. L. *A Norse lullaby* ill. by Margot Tomes. Lothrop, 1988. ISBN 0-688-05813-2 Subj: Animals. Lullabies. Poetry. Seasons – winter. Sleep.

Van West, Patricia E. *The crab man* ill. by Cedric Lucas. Turtle Books, 1998. ISBN 1-890515-08-6 Subj: Character traits – kindness to animals. Crustaceans. Foreign lands – Jamaica.

Van Woerkom, Dorothy. *Alexandra the rock-eater: an old Rumanian tale retold* ill. by Rosekrans Hoffman. Knopf, 1978. ISBN 0-394-93536-5 Subj: Dragons. Family life. Folk and fairy tales. Food. Foreign lands.

Becky and the bear ill. by Margot Tomes. Putnam, 1975. ISBN 0-399-60924-5 Subj: Animals – bears. Character traits – bravery. U.S. history – frontier and pioneer life.

Donkey Ysabel ill. by Normand Chartier. Macmillan, 1978. ISBN 0-02-791280-9 Subj: Animals – donkeys. Humor.

Harry and Shelburt ill. by Erick Ingraham. Macmillan, 1977. ISBN 0-02-791290-6 Subj: Animals – rabbits. Friendship. Reptiles – turtles, tortoises. Sports – racing.

Hidden messages ill. by Lynne Cherry. Crown, 1980. ISBN 0-517-53520-3 Subj: Communication. Insects. Science.

The queen who couldn't bake gingerbread ill. by Paul Galdone. Knopf, 1975. ISBN 0-394-93033-9 Subj: Folk and fairy tales. Foreign lands – Germany. Humor. Royalty – queens.

The rat, the ox and the zodiac: a Chinese legend ill. by Errol Le Cain. Crown, 1976. ISBN 0-517-51849-X Subj: Animals. Animals – rats. Character traits – cleverness. Folk and fairy tales. Foreign lands – China. Zodiac.

Sea frog, city frog ill. by José Aruego and Ariane Dewey. Macmillan, 1975. ISBN 0-02-791300-7 Subj: Folk and fairy tales. Foreign lands – Japan. Frogs and toads.

Something to crow about ill. by Paul Harvey. Albert Whitman, 1982. ISBN 0-8075-7534-8 Subj: Birds – chickens. Family life – fathers.

Varekamp, Marjolein. *Little Sam takes a bath* ill. by author. Watts, 1991. ISBN 0-531-05944-8 Subj: Activities – bathing. Animals – pigs. Format, unusual – toy and movable books.

Varga, Judy. *Circus cannonball* ill. by author. Morrow, 1975. ISBN 0-688-32026-0 Subj: Circus.

Janko's wish ill. by author. Morrow, 1969. Subj: Behavior – wishing. Foreign lands – Hungary. Magic. Weddings.

The mare's egg ill. by author. Morrow, 1972. Subj: Animals – foxes. Behavior – trickery. Folk and fairy tales. Foreign lands – Russia.

Miss Lollipop's lion ill. by author. Morrow, 1963. Subj: Animals – lions. Circus. Pets.

The monster behind Black Rock ill. by author. Morrow, 1971. Subj: Animals. Behavior – gossip. Cumulative tales.

Varley, Dimitry. *The whirly bird* ill. by Feodor Rojankovsky. Knopf, 1961. Subj: Birds. Character traits – kindness to animals.

Varley, Susan. *Badger's parting gifts* ill. by author. Lothrop, 1984. ISBN 0-688-02703-2 Subj: Animals – badgers. Death. Friendship. Gifts.

Vasiliu, Mircea. *A day at the beach* ill. by author. Random House, 1978. ISBN 0-394-93475-X Subj: Activities – playing. Family life. Sand. Science. Sea and seashore.

Everything is somewhere ill. by author. John Day, 1970. Subj: Religion.

What's happening? ill. by author. John Day, 1970. Subj: Activities. City.

Vathanaprida, Supaporn. *The girl who wore too much* (MacDonald, Margaret Read)

Vaughan, Marcia Kapok. *Abbie against the storm* ill. by Bill Farnsworth. Beyond Words, 1999. ISBN 1-58270-007-9 Subj: Lighthouses. Sea and seashore. U.S. history.

The dancing dragon ill. by Stanley Wong Hoo Foon. Mondo, 1996. ISBN 1-57255-134-8 Subj: Dragons. Ethnic groups in the U.S. – Chinese Americans. Format, unusual. Holidays – Chinese New Year. Rhyming text.

The lemonade stand ill. by Thomas Payne. Grosset, 1999. ISBN 0-448-41977-7 Subj: Animals. Humor. Money.

The Sea-Breeze Hotel by Marcia Kapok Vaughn and Patricia Mullins; ill. by Patricia Mullins. HarperCollins, 1992. ISBN 0-06-020504-0 Subj: Hotels. Kites. Weather – wind.

Snap! ill. by Sascha Hutchinson. Scholastic, 1996. ISBN 0-590-60377-9 Subj: Animals. Animals – kangaroos. Reptiles – alligators, crocodiles.

Whistling Dixie ill. by Barry Moser. HarperCollins, 1995. ISBN 0-06-021029-X Subj: Animals. Pets.

Wombat stew ill. by Pamela Lofts. Silver Burdett, 1986. ISBN 0-382-09211-2 Subj: Animals. Foreign lands – Australia. Music. Songs.

Vaughn, Jenny. *On the moon* ed. by Jenny Vaughn; Angela Grunsell, consultant; ill. by Tessa Barwick and Elsa Godfrey. Watts, 1983. ISBN 0-531-04631-1 Subj: Moon. Space and space ships. U.S. history.

Veldkamp, Tjibbe. *22 orphans* ill. Philip Hopman. Kane/Miller, 1998. ISBN 0-916291-81-2 Subj: Activities – playing. Behavior – misbehavior.

Velthuijs, Max. *Crocodile's masterpiece* ill. by author. Farrar, 1992. ISBN 0-374-31658-9 Subj: Animals – elephants. Careers – artists. Imagination. Reptiles – alligators, crocodiles.

Frog and the birdsong ill. by author. Farrar, 1991. ISBN 0-374-32467-0 Subj: Animals. Death. Frogs and toads.

Frog in love trans. from Dutch by Anthea Bell; ill. by author. Farrar, 1989. ISBN 0-374-32465-4 Subj: Birds – ducks. Emotions – love. Frogs and toads.

Frog is a hero ill. by author. Andersen, 1995. ISBN 0-86264-601-4 Subj: Animals. Friendship. Frogs and toads. Weather – floods.

Frog is frightened ill. by author. Tambourine, 1995. ISBN 0-688-14203-6 Subj: Animals. Bedtime. Birds. Friendship. Frogs and toads. Noise, sounds.

Little Man finds a home ill. by author. Holt, 1985. ISBN 0-03-005734-5 Subj: Homes, houses. Weather – rain.

Little Man to the rescue ill. by author. Holt, 1986. ISBN 0-8050-0036-4 Subj: Animals – rabbits. Character traits – kindness to animals. Emotions – envy, jealousy. Frogs and toads.

Little Man's lucky day trans. from German by Rosemary Lanning; ill. by author. Holt, 1986. ISBN 0-03-005847-3 Subj: Character traits – luck.

The painter and the bird trans. by Ray Broekel; ill. by author. Addison-Wesley, 1975. Translation of Der Maler und der Vogel. ISBN 0-20-108082-6 Subj: Birds. Careers – artists. Imagination.

Venable, Alan. *The checker players* ill. by Byron Barton. Lippincott, 1973. ISBN 0-397-31479-5 Subj: Animals – bears. Behavior – fighting, arguing. Boats, ships. Friendship. Games. Reptiles – alligators, crocodiles.

Venino, Suzanne. *Animals helping people* ill. with photos. National Geographic, 1983. ISBN 0-87044-493-X Subj: Animals. Character traits – helpfulness.

Ventura, Marisa. *The painter's trick* (Ventura, Piero)

Ventura, Piero. *The painter's trick* by Piero and Marisa Ventura; ill. by Marisa Ventura. Random House, 1977. ISBN 0-394-93320-6 Subj: Careers – artists.

Venturo, Betty Lou Baker. *see* Baker, Betty

Verboven, Agnes. *Ducks like to swim* ill. by Anne Westerduin. Orchard, 1997. ISBN 0-531-30054-4 Subj: Animals. Birds – ducks. Farms. Noise, sounds. Water. Weather – rain.

Verdet, Andre. *All about time* created by Gallimard Jeunesse and Andre Verdet; ill. by Céline Bour-Chollet, Daniel Moignot, and Donald Grant. Scholastic, 1995. ISBN 0-590-42795-4 Subj: Clocks, watches. Days of the week, months of the year. Format, unusual – toy and movable books. Seasons. Time.

Verdi, Giuseppe. *Aïda* (Price, Leontyne)

VerDorn, Bethea. *Day breaks* ill. by Thomas Graham. Arcade, 1992. ISBN 1-55970-187-0 Subj: Animals. Friendship. Morning.

Moon glows ill. by Thomas Graham. Arcade, 1990. ISBN 1-55970-073-4 Subj: Animals. Moon. Night. Rhyming text.

Vernon, Adele. *The riddle* ill. by Robert Rayevsky and Vladimir Radunsky. Dodd, 1987. ISBN 0-396-08920-8 Subj: Folk and fairy tales. Foreign lands – Spain. Royalty.

Vernon, Tannis. *Little Pig and the blue-green sea* ill. by author. Crown, 1986. ISBN 0-517-56118-2 Subj: Animals – pigs. Behavior – running away. Boats, ships. Sea and seashore.

Vesey, A. *Merry Christmas, Thomas!* ill. by author. Little, 1986. ISBN 0-87113-096-3 Subj: Animals – cats. Family life. Holidays – Christmas.

The princess and the frog ill. by author. Little, 1985. ISBN 0-87113-038-6 Subj: Character traits – willfulness. Folk and fairy tales. Frogs and toads. Royalty – princesses.

Vessel, Matthew F. *My goldfish* (Wong, Herbert H.)

My ladybug (Wong, Herbert H.)

My plant (Wong, Herbert H.)

Our caterpillars (Wong, Herbert H.)

Our earthworms (Wong, Herbert H.)

Our tree (Wong, Herbert H.)

Vevers, Gwynne. *Animal homes* ill. by Wendy Bramall. Merrimack, 1982. ISBN 0-370-30245-1 Subj: Animals. Homes, houses.

Animal parents ill. by Colin Threadgall. Merrimack, 1982. ISBN 0-370-30172-2 Subj: Animals. Family life.

Animals of the dark ill. by Wendy Bramall. Merrimack, 1982. ISBN 0-370-30331-8 Subj: Animals. Night.

Animals that store food ill. by Joyce Bee. Merrimack, 1982. ISBN 0-370-30330-X Subj: Animals. Food.

Animals that travel ill. by Matthew Hillier. Merrimack, 1982. ISBN 0-370-30399-7 Subj: Activities – traveling. Animals.

Vidal, Beatriz A. *The legend of El Dorado* (Van Laan, Nancy)

Vidaure, Morris. *The invisible hunters* (Rohmer, Harriet)

Vieira, Linda. *The ever-living tree* ill. by Christopher Canyon. Walker, 1994. ISBN 0-8027-8278-7 Subj: Trees. U.S. history.

Vigna, Judith. *Anyhow, I'm glad I tried* ill. by author. Albert Whitman, 1978. ISBN 0-8075-0378-9 Subj: Behavior – misbehavior. Character traits – kindness. School.

Boot weather ed. by Ann Fay; ill. by author. Albert Whitman, 1988. ISBN 0-8075-0837-3 Subj: Activities – playing. Clothing – shoes. Imagination. Seasons – winter. Weather.

Couldn't we have a turtle instead? ill. by author. Albert Whitman, 1975. ISBN 0-8075-1312-1 Subj: Animals. Babies. Emotions – envy, jealousy. Family life – mothers. Family life – new sibling.

Daddy's new baby ill. by author. Albert Whitman, 1982. ISBN 0-8075-1435-7 Subj: Divorce. Family life – fathers. Sibling rivalry.

Everyone goes as a pumpkin ill. by author. Albert Whitman, 1977. ISBN 0-8075-2186-8 Subj: Family life – grandmothers. Holidays – Halloween.

Grandma without me ill. by author. Albert Whitman, 1984. ISBN 0-8075-3030-1 Subj: Divorce. Family life – grandmothers.

The hiding house ill. by author. Albert Whitman, 1979. ISBN 0-8075-3275-4 Subj: Behavior – hiding. Behavior – sharing. Friendship.

I wish my daddy didn't drink so much ed. by Ann Fay; ill. by author. Albert Whitman, 1988. ISBN 0-8075-3523-0 Subj: Behavior – wishing. Family life – fathers. Illness.

Mommy and me by ourselves again ill. by author. Albert Whitman, 1987. ISBN 0-8075-5232-1 Subj: Behavior – needing someone. Birthdays. Family life – mothers.

My two uncles ill. by author. Albert Whitman, 1995. ISBN 0-8075-5507-X Subj: Birthdays. Family life – aunts, uncles. Family life – grandfathers. Homosexuality.

Nobody wants a nuclear war ill. by author. Albert Whitman, 1986. ISBN 0-8075-5739-0 Subj: Emotions – fear. Family life. War.

Saying goodbye to daddy ill. by author. Albert Whitman, 1990. ISBN 0-8075-7253-5 Subj: Death. Emotions. Emotions – grief. Family life – fathers.

She's not my real mother ill. by author. Albert Whitman, 1980. ISBN 0-8075-7340-X Subj: Behavior – misbehavior. Divorce. Family life.

Villarejo, Mary. *The art fair* ill. by author. Knopf, 1960. Subj: Art.

The tiger hunt ill. by author. Knopf, 1959. Subj: Activities – photographing. Animals. Animals – tigers. Foreign lands – India.

Villoldo, Alberto. *The first story ever told* (Jendresen, Erik)

Skeleton woman ill. by Yoshi. Simon & Schuster, 1995. ISBN 0-689-80279-X Subj: Anatomy – skeletons. Eskimos. Folk and fairy tales. Indians of North America – Aleuts.

Vincent, Gabrielle. *Bravo, Ernest and Celestine!* ill. by author. Greenwillow, 1982. ISBN 0-688-00858-5 Subj: Animals – bears. Animals – mice. Behavior – sharing. Money. Music.

Breakfast time, Ernest and Celestine ill. by author. Greenwillow, 1985. ISBN 0-688-04555-3 Subj: Animals – bears. Animals – mice. Behavior – misbehavior. Friendship. Wordless.

Ernest and Celestine ill. by author. Greenwillow, 1982. ISBN 0-688-00856-9 Subj: Animals – bears. Animals – mice. Toys.

Ernest and Celestine at the circus ill. by author. Greenwillow, 1989. ISBN 0-688-08685-3 Subj: Animals – bears. Animals – mice. Circus.

Ernest and Celestine's patchwork quilt ill. by author. Greenwillow, 1985. ISBN 0-688-04577-X Subj: Animals – bears. Animals – mice. Behavior – sharing. Friendship. Quilts. Wordless.

Ernest and Celestine's picnic ill. by author. Morrow, 1988, 1982. ISBN 0-688-07809-5 Subj: Activities – picnicking. Animals – bears. Animals – mice. Weather – rain.

Merry Christmas, Ernest and Celestine ill. by author. Greenwillow, 1984. ISBN 0-688-02606-0 Subj: Animals – bears. Animals – mice. Friendship. Holidays – Christmas. Parties.

Smile, Ernest and Celestine ill. by author. Greenwillow, 1982. ISBN 0-688-01249-3 Subj: Activities – photographing. Animals – bears. Animals – mice.

Where are you, Ernest and Celestine? ill. by author. Greenwillow, 1986. ISBN 0-688-06235-0 Subj: Animals – bears. Animals – mice. Behavior – lost. Museums.

Vinson, Pauline. *Willie goes to the seashore* ill. by author. Macmillan, 1954. Subj: Animals – mice. Sea and seashore.

Viorst, Judith. *Alexander and the terrible, horrible, no good, very bad day* ill. by Ray Cruz. Aladdin, 1987, c1972. ISBN 0-689-71173-5 Subj: Behavior – bad day. Family life.

Alexander, who used to be rich last Sunday ill. by Ray Cruz. Atheneum, 1978. ISBN 0-689-30602-4 Subj: Money.

Alexander, who's not (Do you hear me? I mean it!) going to move ill. by Robin Preiss-Glasser. Atheneum, 1995. ISBN 0-689-31958-4 Subj: Character traits – stubbornness. Family life. Moving.

The Alphabet from Z to A: (with much confusion on the way) ill. by Richard Hull. Atheneum, 1994. ISBN 0-689-31768-9 Subj: ABC books. Games. Language. Poetry.

The good-bye book ill. by Kay Chorao. Atheneum, 1988. ISBN 0-689-31308-X Subj: Activities – babysitting. Activities – reading. Imagination.

I'll fix Anthony ill. by Arnold Lobel. Harper-Collins, 1988, c1969. ISBN 0-689-71202-2 Subj: Family life. Sibling rivalry.

My mama says there aren't any zombies, ghosts, vampires, creatures, demons, monsters, fiends, goblins, or things ill. by Kay Chorao. Atheneum, 1973. ISBN 0-689-30102-2 Subj: Bedtime. Emotions – fear. Family life – mothers. Imagination. Monsters.

Rosie and Michael ill. by Lorna Tomei. Atheneum, 1974. ISBN 0-689-30418-8 Subj: Friendship.

Sunday morning ill. by Hilary Knight. Harper-Collins, 1986, c1968. ISBN 0-689-70447-X Subj: Activities – playing. Family life. Humor.

The tenth good thing about Barney ill. by Erik Blegvad. Atheneum, 1987, c1971. ISBN 0-689-71203-0 Subj: Animals – cats. Careers – doctors. Death. Emotions – grief. Pets.

Try it again, Sam: safety when you walk ill. by Paul Galdone. Lothrop, 1970. Subj: Activities – walking. Character traits – individuality. Safety.

Vipont, Charles. *see* Foulds, Elfrida Vipont

Vipont, Elfrida. *see* Foulds, Elfrida Vipont

A visit to a pond ill. with photos. Imported Pubs., 1983. ISBN 0-8285-2360-6 Subj: Animals. Format, unusual – board books. Wordless.

Vizurraga, Susan. *Our old house* ill. by Leslie Baker. Holt, 1997. ISBN 0-8050-3911-2 Subj: Homes, houses. Memories, memory.

Voake, Charlotte. *First things first: a baby's companion* ill. by author. Little, 1988. ISBN 0-316-90510-0 Subj: Activities. Poetry.

Ginger ill. by author. Candlewick, 1997. ISBN 0-7636-0108-X Subj: Animals – cats. Behavior – running away. Emotions – envy, jealousy.

Here comes the train ill. by author. Candlewick, 1998. ISBN 0-7636-0438-0 Subj: Family life. Trains.

Mr. Davies and the baby ill. by author. Candlewick, 1996. ISBN 1-56402-390-7 Subj: Animals – dogs. Babies. Family life.

Mrs. Goose's baby ill. by author. Little, 1989. ISBN 0-316-90511-9 Subj: Adoption. Birds – chickens. Birds – geese. Character traits – being different.

Tom's cat ill. by author. Lippincott, 1986. ISBN 0-397-32195-3 Subj: Animals – cats. Noise, sounds.

Voce, Louise. *Over in the meadow* ill. by author. Candlewick, 1994. ISBN 1-56402-428-8 Subj: Animals. Counting, numbers. Nursery rhymes.

Vogel, Carole Garbuny. *The dangers of strangers* by Carole Garbuny Vogel and Kathryn Allen Goldner; ill. by Lynette Schmidt. Dillon, 1983. ISBN 0-87418-253-4 Subj: Behavior – talking to strangers. Safety.

Vogel, Ilse-Margret. *The don't be scared book: scares, remedies and pictures* ill. by author. Atheneum,

1964. Subj: Emotions – fear. Imagination. Rhyming text.

Voigt, Hannelore. *Not now, Sara!* ill. by Olivier Corthésy and Nicolas Fossati; trans. by J. Alison James. North-South, 1995. ISBN 1-55858-394-7 Subj: Activities – painting. Art. Family life.

Vojtech, Anna. *Marushka and the Month Brothers: a folktale* retold by Anna Vojtech and Philemon Sturges; ill. by Anna Vojtech. North-South, 1996. ISBN 1-55858-629-6 Subj: Days of the week, months of the year. Family life – step families. Folk and fairy tales. Foreign lands – Czechoslovakia. Mythical creatures.

Volkmer, Jane Anne. *Song of Chirimia: La Musica de la Chirimia* trans. by Lori Ann Schatschneider; ill. by adapt. Carolrhoda, 1990. ISBN 0-87614-423-7 Subj: Folk and fairy tales. Foreign lands – Mexico. Foreign languages. Indians of Central America – Maya. Religion.

Von Hippel, Ursula. *The craziest Halloween* ill. by author. Coward, 1957. Subj: Holidays – Halloween.

Von Jüchen, Aurel. *see* Jüchen, Aurel von

Von Königslöw, Andrea. *see* Wayne-von-Königslöw, Andrea

Vozar, David. *M. C. Turtle and the hip hop hare: a nursery rap* ill. by Betsy Lewin. Doubleday, 1995. ISBN 0-385-32157-0 Subj: Animals. Animals – rabbits. Reptiles – turtles, tortoises. Rhyming text. Sports – racing.

Yo, hungry wolf! a nursery rap ill. by Betsy Lewin. Doubleday, 1993. ISBN 0-385-30452-8 Subj: Animals – wolves. Folk and fairy tales. Rhyming text.

Vreeken, Elizabeth. *The boy who would not say his name* ill. by Leonard W. Shortall. Follett, 1959. Subj: Behavior – lost. Careers – police officers. Imagination. Names.

Henry ill. by Polly Jackson. Follett, 1961. Subj: Animals – mice. Pets.

One day everything went wrong ill. by Leonard W. Shortall. Follett, 1966. Subj: Behavior – bad day.

Vries, Anke de. *My elephant can do almost anything* ill. by Ilja Walraven. Front Street, 1996. ISBN 1-886910-06-5 Subj: Animals – elephants. Imagination – imaginary friends. Pets.

Vulliamy, Clara. *Bang and shout* ill. by author. Candlewick, 1994. ISBN 1-56402-409-1 Subj: Activities – playing. Babies. Format, unusual – board books. Games. Rhyming text.

Blue hat, red coat ill. by author. Candlewick, 1994. ISBN 1-56402-361-3 Subj: Babies. Clothing. Format, unusual – board books. Rhyming text.

Boo baby boo! ill. by author. Candlewick, 1994. ISBN 1-56402-388-5 Subj: Activities – playing. Babies.

Format, unusual – board books. Games. Rhyming text.

Ellen and Penguin and the new baby ill. by author. Candlewick, 1996. ISBN 1-56402-697-3 Subj: Babies. Family life – brothers. Family life – mothers. Family life – new sibling. Toys.

Good night, baby ill. by author. Candlewick, 1996. ISBN 1-56402-817-8 Subj: Babies. Bedtime. Family life. Format, unusual – board books. Rhyming text. Sleep.

Wide awake ill. by author. Candlewick, 1996. ISBN 1-56402-816-X Subj: Activities. Family life. Format, unusual – board books. Rhyming text.

Yum yum ill. by author. Candlewick, 1994. ISBN 1-56402-408-3 Subj: Animals. Babies. Food. Format, unusual – board books. Rhyming text.

Vullo, Vera. *About things you find at the beach* ill. by author. Benchmark, 1999. ISBN 0-7614-0851-7 Subj: Sea and seashore.

Vyner, Sue. *The stolen egg* ill. by Tim Vyner. Viking, 1992. ISBN 0-670-84460-8 Subj: Birds. Circular tales. Eggs. Reptiles. Science.

Wabbes, Marie. *Good night, Little Rabbit* ill. by author. Little, 1987. ISBN 0-871-13127-7 Subj: Animals – rabbits. Bedtime.

Happy birthday, Little Rabbit ill. by author. Little, 1987. ISBN 0-87113-129-3 Subj: Animals – rabbits. Birthdays.

It's snowing, Little Rabbit ill. by author. Little, 1987. ISBN 0-87113-128-5 Subj: Animals – rabbits. Seasons – winter. Weather – snow.

Little Rabbit's garden ill. by author. Little, 1987. ISBN 0-871-13126-9 Subj: Animals – rabbits. Gardens, gardening.

Rose is hungry ill. by author. Messner, 1988. Subj: Animals – pigs. Food.

Rose is muddy ill. by author. Messner, 1988. ISBN 0-671-66610-X Subj: Animals – pigs. Character traits – cleanliness.

Rose's bath ill. by author. Messner, 1988. ISBN 0-671-66612-6 Subj: Activities – bathing. Animals – pigs. Toys.

Rose's picture ill. by author. Messner, 1988. ISBN 0-671-66613-4 Subj: Activities – painting. Animals – pigs. Art.

Waber, Bernard. *An anteater named Arthur* ill. by author. Houghton Mifflin, 1967. ISBN 0-395-20336-8 Subj: ABC books. Animals – anteaters.

Bearsie Bear and the surprise sleepover party ill. by author. Houghton Mifflin, 1997. ISBN 0-395-86450-X Subj: Animals. Bedtime. Seasons – winter. Sleepovers.

Bernard ill. by author. Houghton Mifflin, 1982. ISBN 0-395-31865-3 Subj: Animals – dogs. Behavior – running away. Behavior – sharing.

But names will never hurt me ill. by author. Houghton Mifflin, 1976. ISBN 0-395-24383-1 Subj: Behavior – name calling. Names.

Do you see a mouse? ill. by author. Houghton Mifflin, 1995. ISBN 0-395-72292-6 Subj: Animals – mice. Behavior – disbelief. Hotels. Puzzles.

Funny, funny Lyle ill. by author. Houghton Mifflin, 1987. ISBN 0-395-43619-2 Subj: Behavior – misunderstanding. Family life. Reptiles – alligators, crocodiles.

Gina ill. by author. Houghton Mifflin, 1995. ISBN 0-395-74279-X Subj: Emotions – loneliness. Friendship. Moving. Rhyming text. Sports – baseball.

How to go about laying an egg ill. by author. Houghton Mifflin, 1963. Subj: Birds – chickens. Eggs. Humor.

I was all thumbs ill. by author. Houghton Mifflin, 1975. ISBN 0-395-21404-1 Subj: Octopuses. Sea and seashore.

Ira says goodbye ill. by author. Houghton Mifflin, 1988. ISBN 0-395-48315-8 Subj: Emotions. Friendship. Moving.

Ira sleeps over ill. by author. Houghton Mifflin, 1972. ISBN 0-395-13893-0 Subj: Activities – playing. Bedtime. Friendship. Sleep. Toys – bears.

A lion named Shirley Williamson ill. by author. Houghton Mifflin, 1996. ISBN 0-395-80979-7 Subj: Animals – lions. Behavior – running away. Flowers. Names. Zoos.

Lorenzo ill. by author. Houghton Mifflin, 1961. Subj: Character traits – curiosity. Fish.

Lovable Lyle ill. by author. Houghton Mifflin, 1969. ISBN 0-395-25378-0 Subj: Friendship. Reptiles – alligators, crocodiles.

Lyle and the birthday party ill. by author. Houghton Mifflin, 1966. ISBN 0-395-15080-9 Subj: Birthdays. Emotions – envy, jealousy. Reptiles – alligators, crocodiles.

Lyle at Christmas ill. by author. Houghton Mifflin, 1998. ISBN 0-395-91304-7 Subj: Animals – cats. Holidays – Christmas. Reptiles – alligators, crocodiles.

Lyle at the office ill. by author. Houghton Mifflin, 1994. ISBN 0-395-70563-0 Subj: Activities – working. Reptiles – alligators, crocodiles.

Lyle finds his mother ill. by author. Houghton Mifflin, 1974. ISBN 0-395-19489-X Subj: Family life – mothers. Reptiles – alligators, crocodiles.

Lyle, Lyle Crocodile ill. by author. Houghton Mifflin, 1965. ISBN 0-395-13720-9 Subj: Character traits – helpfulness. Reptiles – alligators, crocodiles.

Mice on my mind ill. by author. Houghton Mifflin, 1977. ISBN 0-395-25935-5 Subj: Animals – cats. Animals – mice.

The mouse that snored ill. by author. Houghton Mifflin, 2000. ISBN 0-395-97518-2 Subj: Animals – mice. Noise, sounds. Rhyming text.

Nobody is perfick ill. by author. Houghton Mifflin, 1971. ISBN 0-395-12582-0 Subj: Behavior – mistakes. Friendship. Humor.

Rich cat, poor cat ill. by author. Houghton Mifflin, 1963. ISBN 0-590-43091-2 Subj: Animals – cats.

The snake: a very long story ill. by author. Houghton Mifflin, 1978. ISBN 0-395-27157-6 Subj: Format, unusual. Reptiles – snakes.

"You look ridiculous," said the rhinoceros to the hippopotamus ill. by author. Houghton Mifflin, 1979. ISBN 0-395-07156-9 Subj: Animals. Animals – hippopotamuses. Character traits – individuality. Self-concept.

You're a little kid with a big heart ill. by author. Houghton Mifflin, 1980. ISBN 0-395-29163-1 Subj: Behavior – growing up. Behavior – wishing. Magic.

Waboose, Jan Bourdeau. *Firedancers* ill. by C. J. Taylor. Stoddart, 2000. ISBN 0-7737-3138-5 Subj: Activities – dancing. Family life – grandparents. Indians of North America – Ojibwa. Night.

Morning on the lake ill. by Karen Reczuch. Kids Can Pr., 1998. ISBN 1-55074-373-2 Subj: Family life – fathers. Indians of North America – Ojibwa. Nature.

Waddell, Martin. *Alice the artist* ill. by Jonathan Langley. Dutton, 1988. ISBN 0-525-44385-1 Subj: Art. Careers – artists.

Amy said ill. by Charlotte Voake. Little, 1990. ISBN 0-316-91636-6 Subj: Behavior – misbehavior. Family life – grandmothers.

The big big sea ill. by Jennifer Eachus. Candlewick, 1994. ISBN 1-56402-066-5 Subj: Family life – mothers. Night. Sea and seashore.

Can't you sleep, Little Bear? ill. by Barbara Firth. Candlewick, 1992. ISBN 1-56402-007-X Subj: Animals – bears. Bedtime. Emotions – fear. Family life – fathers. Night. Sleep.

Farmer Duck ill. by Helen Oxenbury. Candlewick, 1992. ISBN 1-56402-009-6 Subj: Animals. Birds – ducks. Careers – farmers. Character traits – helpfulness. Farms.

Good job, Little Bear! ill. by Barbara Firth. Candlewick, 1999. ISBN 0-7636-0736-3 Subj: Animals – bears. Character traits – confidence. Character traits – helpfulness.

Grandma's Bill ill. by Jane Johnson. Watts, 1991. ISBN 0-531-08523-6 Subj: Family life – grandparents.

The happy hedgehog band ill. by Jill Barton. Candlewick, 1992. ISBN 1-56402-011-8 Subj: Animals. Animals – hedgehogs. Music.

The hidden house ill. by Angela Barrett. Candlewick, 1997. ISBN 0-7636-0335-X Subj: Emotions – loneliness. Homes, houses. Toys – dolls.

Let's go home, Little Bear ill. by Barbara Firth. Candlewick, 1993. ISBN 1-56402-131-9 Subj: Animals – bears. Emotions – fear. Family life – fathers. Forest, woods. Noise, sounds.

Mimi and the dream house ill. by Leo Hartas. Candlewick, 1998. ISBN 0-7636-0587-5 Subj: Animals – mice. Dreams. Family life. Homes, houses.

Mimi and the picnic ill. by Leo Hartas. Candlewick, 1996. ISBN 0-7636-0588-3 Subj: Activities – picnicking. Animals – mice.

Mimi's Christmas ill. by Leo Hartas. Candlewick, 1997. ISBN 0-7636-0413-5 Subj: Animals – mice. Behavior – worrying. Family life. Holidays – Christmas.

My great grandpa ill. by Dom Mansell. Putnam, 1990. ISBN 0-399-22155-7 Subj: Family life – great-grandparents. Handicaps – physical handicaps. Rhyming text.

Night night Cuddly Bear ill. by Penny Dale. Candlewick, 2000. ISBN 0-7636-1195-6 Subj: Animals – bears. Bedtime. Family life. Toys – bears.

Once there were giants ill. by Penny Dale. Delacorte, 1989. ISBN 0-385-29806-4 Subj: Behavior – growing up. Family life.

Owl babies ill. by Patrick Benson. Candlewick, 1992. ISBN 1-56402-101-7 Subj: Birds – owls. Emotions – fear. Family life – mothers. Night.

Owl babies, a board book ill. by Patrick Benson. Candlewick, 1996. ISBN 1-56402-965-4 Subj: Emotions – fear. Family life – mothers. Format, unusual – board books. Night.

The park in the dark ill. by Barbara Firth. Lothrop, 1989. ISBN 0-688-08517-2 Subj: Emotions – fear. Night. Parks. Rhyming text. Toys.

The pig in the pond ill. by Jill Barton. Candlewick, 1992. ISBN 1-56402-050-9 Subj: Animals. Animals – pigs. Careers – farmers. Cumulative tales. Lakes, ponds. Sports – swimming.

Rosie's babies ill. by Penny Dale. Candlewick, 1999. ISBN 0-7636-0718-5 Subj: Family life – mothers. Family life – new sibling. Toys.

Sailor Bear ill. by Virginia Austin. Candlewick, 1992. ISBN 1-56402-040-1 Subj: Behavior – lost. Boats, ships. Sailors. Sea and seashore. Toys – bears.

Sam Vole and his brothers ill. by Barbara Firth. Candlewick, 1992. ISBN 1-56402-082-7 Subj: Animals – mice. Emotions – loneliness. Family life – brothers. Sibling rivalry.

Small Bear lost ill. by Virginia Austin. Candlewick, 1996. ISBN 1-56402-871-2 Subj: Activities – traveling. Behavior – lost. Toys – bears.

Squeak-a-lot ill. by Virginia Miller. Greenwillow, 1991. ISBN 0-688-10245-X Subj: Activities – playing. Animals – mice. Noise, sounds.

The tough princess ill. by Patrick Benson. Putnam, 1987. ISBN 0-399-21380-5 Subj: Fairies. Folk and fairy tales. Royalty – princesses.

The toymaker ill. by Terry Milne. Candlewick, 1992. ISBN 1-56402-103-3 Subj: Careers – toy makers. Emotions – love. Family life – fathers. Illness. Toys – dolls.

We love them ill. by Barbara Firth. Lothrop, 1990. ISBN 0-688-09332-9 Subj: Animals – dogs. Animals – rabbits. Friendship.

When the teddy bears came ill. by Penny Dale. Candlewick, 1995. ISBN 1-56402-529-2 Subj: Babies. Family life – brothers and sisters. Family life – new sibling. Toys – bears.

Who do you love? ill. by Camilla Ashforth. Candlewick, 1999. ISBN 0-7636-0586-7 Subj: Animals – cats. Bedtime. Emotions – love.

Yum, yum, yummy ill. by John Bendall-Brunello. Candlewick, 1998. ISBN 0-7636-0477-1 Subj: Animals – bears. Behavior – bullying. Behavior – greed. Family life – mothers. Food.

Wade, Alan. *I'm flying!* ill. by Petra Mathers. Knopf, 1990. ISBN 0-394-94510-7 Subj: Activities – ballooning.

Wade, Anne. *A promise is for keeping* ill. by Jon Petersson. Childrens Pr., 1979. ISBN 0-516-02024-2 Subj: Friendship.

Wade, Barrie. *Little monster* ill. by Katinka Kew. Lothrop, 1990. ISBN 0-688-09597-6 Subj: Behavior – misbehavior. Emotions – love. Family life.

Wadhams, Margaret. *Anna* ill. by Michael Charlton. Salem House, 1987. ISBN 0-370-30612-0 Subj: Character traits – being different. Illness.

Wadsworth, Ginger. *One tiger growls: a counting book of animal sounds* ill. by James M. Needham. Charlesbridge, 1999. ISBN 0-88106-273-1 Subj: Animals. Counting, numbers. Noise, sounds.

Tomorrow is Daddy's birthday ill. by Maxie Chambliss. Caroline House, 1994. ISBN 1-56397-042-2 Subj: Behavior – secrets. Birthdays. Family life – fathers.

Wadsworth, Olive A. *Over in the meadow: a counting-out rhyme* ill. by Mary Maki Rae. Viking, 1985. ISBN 0-670-53276-2 Subj: Counting, numbers. Nursery rhymes.

Waechter, Friedrich Karl. *Three is company* trans. by Harry Allard; ill. by author. Doubleday, 1980. ISBN 0-385-14633-7 Subj: Animals – pigs. Birds. Fish. Friendship.

Wagener, Gerda. *Leo the lion* trans. from German by Nina Ignatowicz; ill. by Reinhard Michl. HarperCollins, 1991. ISBN 0-06-021657-3 Subj: Animals – lions. Emotions – loneliness.

Waggoner, Karen. *Dad Gummit and Ma Foot* ill. by Anita Riggio. Watts, 1990. ISBN 0-531-08491-4 Subj: Behavior – fighting, arguing. Family life.

The lemonade babysitter ill. by Dorothy Donohue. Little, 1992. ISBN 0-316-91711-7 Subj: Activities – babysitting. Behavior. Old age.

Wagner, Elaine Knox. *see* Knox-Wagner, Elaine

Wagner, Jenny. *Amy's monster* ill. by Terry Denton. Viking, 1991. ISBN 0-670-82748-7 Subj: Behavior – bullying. Family life – cousins. Monsters. Multiple births – twins. Seasons – summer.

Aranea: a story about a spider ill. by Ron Brooks. Bradbury, 1978. ISBN 0-87888-138-7 Subj: Spiders. Weather – rain.

The bunyip of Berkeley's Creek ill. by Ron Brooks. Bradbury, 1977. ISBN 0-87888-122-0 Subj: Foreign lands – Australia. Monsters. Mythical creatures.

John Brown, Rose and the midnight cat ill. by Ron Brooks. Bradbury, 1978. ISBN 0-8788-8120-4 Subj: Animals – cats. Animals – dogs.

Wagner, Karen. *Bravo, Mildred and Ed!* ill. by Janet Pedersen. Walker, 2000. ISBN 0-8027-8735-5 Subj: Animals – mice. Character traits – confidence. Friendship.

Chocolate chip cookies ill. by Leah Palmer Preiss. Holt, 1990. ISBN 0-8050-1268-0 Subj: Activities – cooking. Family life. Multiple births – twins.

A friend like Ed ill. by Janet Pedersen. Walker, 1998. ISBN 0-8027-8663-4 Subj: Animals – mice. Concepts – opposites. Friendship.

Silly Fred ill. by Normand Chartier. Macmillan, 1989. ISBN 0-02-792280-4 Subj: Animals. Animals – pigs. Self-concept.

Wahl, Jan. *The adventures of Underwater Dog* ill. by Tim Bowers. Putnam, 1989. ISBN 0-448-09313-8 Subj: Animals – dogs. Crime. Sea and seashore.

Button eye's orange ill. by Wendy Watson. Warne, 1980. ISBN 0-7232-6188-1 Subj: Handicaps. Toys.

Cabbage moon ill. by Adrienne Adams. Holt, 1965. Subj: Humor. Moon. Royalty.

Carrot nose ill. by James Marshall. Farrar, 1978. ISBN 0-374-31122-6 Subj: Animals – rabbits.

Doctor Rabbit's foundling ill. by Cyndy Szekeres. Pantheon, 1977. ISBN 0-394-93275-7 Subj: Animals – rabbits. Careers – doctors. Frogs and toads.

Dracula's cat ill. by Kay Chorao. Prentice-Hall, 1978. ISBN 0-13-218933-X Subj: Animals – cats. Monsters.

Dracula's cat and Frankenstein's dog ill. by Kay Chorao. Simon & Schuster, 1990. ISBN 0-671-

70820-1 Subj: Animals – cats. Animals – dogs. Format, unusual. Monsters. Pets.

The field mouse and the dinosaur named Sue ill. by Bob Doucet. Scholastic, 2000. ISBN 0-439-09984-6 Subj: Animals – mice. Dinosaurs. Museums.

The fishermen ill. by Emily Arnold McCully. Norton, 1969. Subj: Family life – grandfathers. Sports – fishing.

The five in the forest ill. by Erik Blegvad. Follett, 1974. ISBN 0-695-40446-6 Subj: Animals – rabbits. Eggs. Forest, woods. Holidays – Easter.

Follow me cried Bee ill. by John Wallner. Crown, 1976. ISBN 0-517-52353-1 Subj: Cumulative tales. Insects – bees. Rhyming text. Weather – rain.

Frankenstein's dog ill. by Kay Chorao. Prentice-Hall, 1977. ISBN 0-13-330522-8 Subj: Animals – dogs. Monsters.

Hello, elephant ill. by Edward Ardizzone. Holt, 1964. Subj: Animals – elephants.

Humphrey's bear ill. by William Joyce. Holt, 1987. ISBN 0-8050-0332-0 Subj: Bedtime. Dreams. Toys – bears.

I met a dinosaur ill. by Chris Sheban. Harcourt, 1997. ISBN 0-15-201644-9 Subj: Dinosaurs. Imagination. Museums. Rhyming text.

"I remember," cried Grandma Pinky ill. by Arden Johnson. BridgeWater, 1994. ISBN 0-8167-3456-9 Subj: Animals – polar bears. Behavior – forgetfulness. Family life – grandmothers. Memories, memory. Old age.

Jamie's tiger ill. by Tomie de Paola. Harcourt, 1978. ISBN 0-15-239500-8 Subj: Handicaps – deafness. Illness. Senses – hearing. Toys.

Little Eight John ill. by Wil Clay. Dutton, 1992. ISBN 0-525-67367-9 Subj: Behavior – misbehavior. Folk and fairy tales.

Little Johnny Buttermilk ill. by Jennifer Mazzucco. August House, 1999. ISBN 0-87483-559-3 Subj: Behavior. Character traits – cleverness. Folk and fairy tales. Foreign lands – England. Witches.

Mabel ran away with the toys ill. by Liza Woodruff. Whispering Coyote, 2000. ISBN 1-58089-059-8 Subj: Babies. Behavior – running away. Emotions – envy, jealousy. Family life – new sibling. Sibling rivalry.

Mrs. Owl and Mr. Pig ill. by Eileen Christelow. Dutton, 1991. ISBN 0-525-67311-3 Subj: Animals – pigs. Behavior – sharing. Birds – owls. Character traits.

The Muffletumps ill. by Edward Ardizzone. Holt, 1966. Subj: Toys – dolls.

The Muffletumps' Christmas party ill. by Cyndy Szekeres. Follett, 1975. ISBN 0-695-40617-5 Subj: Holidays – Christmas. Toys – dolls.

The Muffletumps' Halloween scare ill. by Cyndy Szekeres. Follett, 1977. ISBN 0-695-40754-6 Subj: Toys – dolls.

My cat Ginger ill. by Naava. Tambourine, 1992. ISBN 0-688-10723-0 Subj: Animals – cats. Imagination. Nature. Night. Pets.

Old Hippo's Easter egg ill. by Lorinda Bryan Cauley. Harcourt, 1980. ISBN 0-15-257835-8 Subj: Animals – hippopotamuses. Animals – mice. Birds – ducks. Emotions – love. Family life.

Once when the world was green ill. by Fabricio Vandenbroeck. Tricycle, 1996. ISBN 1-883672-12-0 Subj: Ecology. Family life – fathers. Indians of Central America – Maya.

Peter and the troll baby ill. by Erik Blegvad. Golden Pr., 1984. ISBN 0-307-16525-6 Subj: Activities – babysitting. Mythical creatures – trolls. Sibling rivalry.

Pleasant Fieldmouse ill. by Maurice Sendak. HarperCollins, 1964. Subj: Animals. Animals – mice.

Pleasant Fieldmouse's Halloween party ill. by Wallace Tripp. Putnam, 1974. ISBN 0-399-60885-0 Subj: Animals. Animals – mice. Holidays – Halloween.

Push Kitty ill. by Garth Williams. HarperCollins, 1968. Subj: Activities – playing. Animals – cats.

Rabbits on roller skates! ill. by David Allender. Crown, 1986. ISBN 0-517-55935-8 Subj: Animals – rabbits. Rhyming text. Sports – roller skating.

The singing geese ill. by Sterling Brown. Lodestar, 1998. ISBN 0-525-67499-3 Subj: Activities – singing. Birds – geese. Ethnic groups in the U.S. – African Americans. Tall tales.

The sleepytime book ill. by Arden Johnson. Morrow, 1992. ISBN 0-688-10276-X Subj: Animals. Babies. Bedtime. Night. Rhyming text. Sleep.

Sylvester Bear overslept ill. by Lee Lorenz. Parents, 1979. ISBN 0-8193-1003-4 Subj: Animals – bears. Circus. Family life. Sleep.

Tiger watch ill. by Charles Mikolaycak. Harcourt, 1982. ISBN 0-15-287674-X Subj: Animals – tigers. Death. Foreign lands – India. Sports – hunting.

The toy circus ill. by Tim Bowers. Harcourt, 1986. ISBN 0-15-200609-5 Subj: Circus. Dreams. Sleep. Toys.

The woman with the eggs (Andersen, H. C. [Hans Christian])

Wahl, Mats. *Grandfather's laika* ill. by Tord Nygren. Carolrhoda, 1990. ISBN 0-87614-434-2 Subj: Animals – dogs. Death. Emotions – grief. Family life – grandfathers. Pets.

Wahl, Robert. *Pyxx* ill. by author. Price Stern Sloan, 1989. ISBN 0-8431-2347-8 Subj: Behavior. Imagination.

Waite, Judy. *Mouse, look out!* ill. by Norma Burgin. Dutton, 1998. ISBN 0-525-42031-2 Subj: Animals – cats. Animals – dogs. Animals – mice. Homes, houses. Rhyming text.

Waite, Michael P. *Jojofu* ill. by Yoriko Ito. Lothrop, 1996. ISBN 0-688-13661-3 Subj: Animals – dogs. Character traits – loyalty. Folk and fairy tales. Foreign lands – Japan.

Wakefield, Joyce. *Ask a silly question* ill. by Mike Venezia. Childrens Pr., 1979. ISBN 0-516-03408-1 Subj: Rhyming text. Riddles.

From where you are ill. by Tom Dunnington. Childrens Pr., 1978. ISBN 0-516-03460-X Subj: Concepts – perspective. Rhyming text.

Walbrecker, Dirk. *Benny's hat* ill. by Hans Poppel. Atomium, 1991. ISBN 1-56182-028-8 Subj: Clothing – hats.

Waldman, Sarah. *Light: the first seven days* ill. by Neil Waldman. Harcourt, 1993. ISBN 0-15-220870-4 Subj: Children as authors. Creation. Religion.

Waldron, Jan L. *Angel Pig and the hidden Christmas* ill. by David M. McPhail. Dutton, 2000. ISBN 0-525-45744-5 Subj: Animals – pigs. Holidays – Christmas. Rhyming text.

John Pig's Halloween ill. by David M. McPhail. Dutton, 1998. ISBN 0-525-45941-3 Subj: Animals – pigs. Emotions – fear. Holidays – Halloween. Monsters. Parties. Rhyming text.

Waldron, Kathleen Cook. *Loon Lake fishing derby* ill. by Dean Griffiths. Orca, 1999. ISBN 1-55143-142-4 Subj: Animals – squirrels. Sports – fishing.

Walker, Alice. *Finding the green stone* ill. by Catherine Deeter. Harcourt, 1991. ISBN 0-15-227538-X Subj: Behavior. Character traits. Ethnic groups in the U.S. – African Americans. Rocks.

To hell with dying ill. by Catherine Deeter. Harcourt, 1987. ISBN 0-15-289075-0 Subj: Death. Ethnic groups in the U.S. – African Americans. Friendship.

Walker, Barbara K. (Barbara Kerlin). *New patches for old: a Turkish folktale* retold by Barbara K. Walker and Ahmet E. Uysal; ill. by Harold Berson. Parents, 1974. ISBN 0-8193-0714-9 Subj: Behavior – mistakes. Folk and fairy tales.

Pigs and pirates: a Greek tale ill. by Harold Berson. White, 1969. Subj: Animals – pigs. Foreign lands – Greece. Pirates.

Teeny-Tiny and the witch-woman ill. by Michael Foreman. Pantheon, 1975. ISBN 0-394-93088-6 Subj: Character traits – cleverness. Foreign lands – Turkey. Witches.

Walker, David. *The sleeping beauty* (Perrault, Charles)

Walker, Jane. *Ten little penguins* ill. by author. Bantam, 1995. ISBN 0-553-09768-7 Subj: Birds – penguins. Counting, numbers. Format, unusual – toy and movable books.

Walker, Richard. *Jack and the beanstalk* (Jack and the beanstalk)

Wall, Lina Mao. *Judge Rabbit and the tree spirit* adapt. by Cathy Spagnoli; ill. by Nancy Hom. Children's Book Pr., 1991. ISBN 0-89239-071-9 Subj: Character traits – vanity. Folk and fairy tales. Foreign lands – Cambodia. Language.

Wallace, Barbara Brooks. *Argyle* ill. by John Sandford. Abingdon, 1987. ISBN 0-687-01724-6 Subj: Animals – sheep. Character traits – being different.

Wallace, Daisy. *Fairy poems* ill. by Trina Schart Hyman. Holiday, 1980. ISBN 0-8234-0371-8 Subj: Fairies. Poetry.

Ghost poems ill. by Tomie de Paola. Holiday, 1979. ISBN 0-8234-0344-0 Subj: Ghosts. Night. Poetry.

Giant poems ill. by Margot Tomes. Holiday, 1978. ISBN 0-8234-0326-2 Subj: Giants. Poetry.

Monster poems (Monster poems)

Witch poems (Witch poems)

Wallace, Ian. *Chin Chiang and the dragon's dance* ill. by author. Atheneum, 1984. ISBN 0-689-50299-0 Subj: Emotions – fear. Ethnic groups in the U.S. – Chinese Americans. Family life – grandfathers. Holidays – Chinese New Year.

Morgan the magnificent ill. by author. Macmillan, 1988. ISBN 0-689-50441-1 Subj: Angels. Behavior – misbehavior. Circus.

The sparrow's song ill. by author. Viking, 1987. ISBN 0-670-81453-9 Subj: Behavior – misbehavior. Birds – sparrows. Character traits – kindness to animals. Death.

Wallace, John. *Building a house with Mr. Bumble* ill. by author. Candlewick, 1996. ISBN 0-7636-0074-1 Subj: Activities – making things. Animals. Homes, houses. Insects – bees. Tools.

Little Bean's friend ill. by author. HarperFestival, 1997. ISBN 0-694-00973-3 Subj: Activities – playing. Animals – dogs. Behavior – losing things. Family life.

Tiny Rabbit goes to a birthday party ill. by author. Holiday, 2000. ISBN 0-8234-1489-2 Subj: Animals – rabbits. Birthdays. Gifts. Parties.

Wallace, Karen. *Bears in the forest* ill. by Barbara Firth. Candlewick, 1994. ISBN 1-56402-336-2 Subj: Animals – bears. Forest, woods. Nature.

Big machines ill. with photos. DK, 2000. ISBN 0-7894-5412-2 Subj: Careers – construction workers. Machines. Trucks.

City pig ill. by Lydia Monks. Orchard, 2000. ISBN 0-531-30252-0 Subj: Activities – vacationing. Animals – pigs. City.

Imagine you are a tiger ill. by Peter Melnyczuk. Holt, 1996. ISBN 0-8050-4636-4 Subj: Animals – tigers. Behavior – growing up. Imagination.

My hen is dancing ill. by Anita Jeram. Candlewick, 1994. ISBN 1-56402-303-6 Subj: Birds – chickens.

Red fox ill. by Peter Melnyczuk. Candlewick, 1994. ISBN 1-56402-422-9 Subj: Animals – foxes.

Scarlette Beane ill. by Jon Berkeley. Dial, 2000. ISBN 0-8037-2475-6 Subj: Food. Gardens, gardening. Magic. Nature. Plants.

Wallace, Nancy Elizabeth. *Apples, apples, apples* ill. by author. Winslow, 2000. ISBN 1-890817-19-8 Subj: Activities – cooking. Animals – rabbits. Family life. Farms. Music. Songs.

Paperwhite ill. by author. Houghton Mifflin, 2000. ISBN 0-618-04283-0 Subj: Animals – rabbits. Flowers. Friendship. Gardens, gardening. Plants. Seasons – spring.

Rabbit's bedtime ill. by author. Houghton Mifflin, 1999. ISBN 0-395-98266-9 Subj: Animals – rabbits. Bedtime. Rhyming text.

Snow ill. by author. Western, 1995. ISBN 0-307-17562-6 Subj: Animals – rabbits. Family life – grandfathers. Weather – snow.

Tell-a-bunny ill. by author. Winslow, 2000. ISBN 1-890817-29-5 Subj: Animals – rabbits. Birthdays. Parties.

Wallace-Brodeur, Ruth. *Goodbye, Mitch* ill. by Kathy Mitter. Albert Whitman, 1995. ISBN 0-8075-2996-6 Subj: Animals – cats. Death. Emotions – grief. Pets.

Home by five ill. by Mark Graham. Margaret K. McElderry, 1992. ISBN 0-689-50509-4 Subj: Behavior – tardiness. City. Family life. Sports – ice skating.

Wallas, Ada. *Clean Peter and the children of Grubbylea* (Adelborg, Ottilia)

Waller, Barrett. *New feet for old* ill. by Harvey Stevenson. Four Winds, 1992. ISBN 0-02-792371-1 Subj: Anatomy – feet. Behavior – dissatisfaction. Careers – peddlers.

Wallis, Diz. *Battle of the beasts: a tale of epic proportions from the brothers Grimm* retold and ill. by Diz Wallis. Ragged Bears, 2000. ISBN 1-929927-15-0 Subj: Animals. Behavior – fighting, arguing. Birds. Folk and fairy tales.

Pip's adventure ill. by author. Boyds Mills, 1991. ISBN 1-878093-43-6 Subj: Activities – cooking. Animals – cats. Animals – mice.

Wallis, Lisa. *Island child* ill. by Deborah Haeffele. Dutton, 1992. ISBN 0-525-67324-5 Subj: Family life. Islands.

Wallner, Alexandra. *An Alcott family Christmas* ill. by author. Holiday, 1996. ISBN 0-8234-1265-2 Subj: Behavior – sharing. Character traits – generosity. Family life. Holidays – Christmas.

Beatrix Potter ill. by author. Holiday, 1995. ISBN 0-8234-1181-8 Subj: Activities – drawing. Animals. Art. Careers – writers. Emotions – loneliness. Imagination.

Betsy Ross ill. by author. Holiday, 1994. ISBN 0-8234-1071-4 Subj: Activities – sewing. U.S. history.

The first air voyage in the United States: the story of Jean-Pierre Blanchard ill. by author. Holiday, 1996. ISBN 0-8234-1224-5 Subj: Activities – ballooning. Animals – dogs. U.S. history.

Munch ill. by author. Crown, 1976. ISBN 0-517-52459-7 Subj: Food. Poetry.

Sergio and the hurricane ill. by author. Holt, 2000. ISBN 0-8050-6203-3 Subj: Family life. Foreign lands – Puerto Rico. Islands. Weather – hurricanes.

Wallner, John C. *Look and find* ill. by author. Putnam, 1988. ISBN 0-448-19068-0 Subj: Concepts. Counting, numbers. Format, unusual – toy and movable books. Picture puzzles.

Old MacDonald had a farm: a musical pop-up book ill. by author. Dutton, 1986. ISBN 0-525-44279-0 Subj: Animals. Cumulative tales. Farms. Format, unusual – toy and movable books. Music. Songs.

Sleeping Beauty (Grimm, Jacob)

Wallwork, Amanda. *Find the fish that looks like this: a hide-and-seek animal book* ill. by author. Puffin, 1997. ISBN 0-14-055909-4 Subj: Animals. Concepts – color. Concepts – shape. Concepts – size. Picture puzzles.

Walsh, Ellen Stoll. *For Pete's sake* ill. by author. Harcourt, 1998. ISBN 0-15-200324-X Subj: Birds – flamingos. Character traits – being different. Character traits – individuality. Reptiles – alligators, crocodiles.

Jack's tale ill. by author. Harcourt, 1997. ISBN 0-15-200323-1 Subj: Activities – storytelling. Careers – authors. Character traits – cleverness. Folk and fairy tales. Frogs and toads. Mythical creatures – trolls. Royalty – princesses.

Mouse count ill. by author. Harcourt, 1991. ISBN 0-15-256023-8 Subj: Animals – mice. Counting, numbers. Reptiles – snakes.

Mouse magic ill. by author. Harcourt, 2000. ISBN 0-15-200326-6 Subj: Animals – mice. Concepts – color. Magic. Wizards.

Mouse paint ill. by author. Harcourt, 1989. ISBN 0-15-256025-4 Subj: Activities – painting. Animals – mice. Behavior – hiding. Concepts – color.

Pip's magic ill. by author. Harcourt, 1994. ISBN 0-15-292850-2 Subj: Animals. Emotions – fear. Magic. Night. Reptiles – salamanders.

Two too much ill. by Pat Cummings. Bradbury, 1990. ISBN 0-02-792290-1 Subj: Emotions. Ethnic groups in the U.S. – African Americans. Family life – brothers and sisters.

You silly goose ill. by author. Harcourt, 1992. ISBN 0-15-299865-9 Subj: Animals – foxes. Animals – mice. Birds – geese.

Walsh, Grahame L. *Didane the koala* ill. by John Morrison. Univ. of Queensland Pr., 1986. ISBN 0-7022-1889-8 Subj: Animals – koalas. Folk and fairy tales. Foreign lands – Australia.

The goori goori bird ill. by John Morrison. Univ. of Queensland Pr., 1986. ISBN 0-7022-1777-8 Subj: Birds. Folk and fairy tales. Foreign lands – Australia.

Walsh, Jill Paton. *Connie came to play* ill. by Stephen Lambert. Viking, 1996. ISBN 0-670-86210-X Subj: Activities – playing. Behavior – sharing. Imagination.

Lost and found ill. by Mary Rayner. André Deutsch, 1985. ISBN 0-233-97672-8 Subj: Behavior – losing things. Character traits – luck. Family life – grandfathers.

Pepi and the secret names ill. by Fiona French. Lothrop, 1995. ISBN 0-688-13428-9 Subj: Activities – painting. Animals. Careers – artists. Folk and fairy tales. Foreign lands – Egypt. Hieroglyphics. Names.

When Grandma came ill. by Sophy Williams. Viking, 1992. ISBN 0-670-83581-1 Subj: Family life – grandmothers.

When I was little like you ill. by Stephen Lambert. Viking, 1997. ISBN 0-670-87608-9 Subj: Family life – grandmothers. Memories, memory.

Walsh, Joanna. *What if?* ill. by author. Jonathan Cape, 2000. ISBN 0-224-04752-3 Subj: Imagination.

Walsh, Melanie. *Do donkeys dance?* ill. by author. Houghton Mifflin, 2000. ISBN 0-618-00330-4 Subj: Activities. Animals. Nature.

Do monkeys tweet? ill. by author. Houghton Mifflin, 1997. ISBN 0-395-85081-9 Subj: Animals. Noise, sounds.

Hide and sleep ill. by author. DK, 1999. ISBN 0-7894-4820-3 Subj: Bedtime. Behavior – hiding. Games.

Ned's rainbow ill. by author. DK, 2000. ISBN 0-7894-5623-0 Subj: Activities – painting. Weather – rainbows.

Walsh, Vivian. *Mr. Lunch borrows a canoe* (Seibold, J. Otto)

Mr. Lunch takes a plane ride (Seibold, J. Otto)

Penguin dreams (Seibold, J. Otto)

Walt Disney Productions. *In . . . out: a Disney book of opposites = Dentro fuera: un libro Disney de opuestos* (Duerrstein, Richard)

Mickey is happy: a Disney book of feelings (Duerrstein, Richard)

One Mickey Mouse: a Disney book of numbers = Un Ratón Mickey: un libro Disney de números (Duerrstein, Richard)

Tod and Copper. Random House, 1981. ISBN 0-394-94819-X Subj: Animals – dogs. Animals – foxes.

Tod and Vixey. Random House, 1981. ISBN 0-394-94904-8 Subj: Animals – dogs. Animals – foxes.

Walt Disney's Snow White and the seven dwarfs. Viking, 1979. ISBN 0-670-65381-0 Subj: Dwarfs, midgets. Emotions – envy, jealousy. Folk and fairy tales. Magic. Witches.

Walt Disney's The adventures of Mr. Toad. Random House, 1981. ISBN 0-394-94818-1 Subj: Animals – moles. Animals – rats. Frogs and toads.

Walter, Mildred Pitts. *Brother to the wind* ill. by Leo and Diane Dillon. Lothrop, 1985. ISBN 0-688-03811-5 Subj: Activities – flying. Foreign lands – Africa.

Darkness ill. by Marcia Jameson. Simon & Schuster, 1995. ISBN 0-689-80305-2 Subj: Night. Shadows.

My mama needs me ill. by Pat Cummings. Lothrop, 1983. ISBN 0-688-01671-5 Subj: Emotions – loneliness. Ethnic groups in the U.S. – African Americans. Family life.

Ty's one-man band ill. by Margot Tomes. Four Winds, 1980. ISBN 0-02-792300-2 Subj: Folk and fairy tales. Music.

Walter, Villiam Christian. *see* Andersen, H. C. (Hans Christian)

Walter, Virginia. *"Hi, pizza man!"* ill. by Ponder Goembel. Orchard, 1995. ISBN 0-531-08735-2 Subj: Animals. Noise, sounds.

Walters, Catherine. *Are you there, Baby Bear?* ill. by author. Dutton, 1999. ISBN 0-525-46161-2 Subj: Animals – babies. Animals – bears. Family life – new sibling. Multiple births – twins.

When will it be spring? ill. by author. Dutton, 1998. ISBN 0-525-45881-6 Subj: Animals – bears. Character traits – patience. Family life – mothers. Hibernation. Nature. Seasons – spring. Seasons – winter.

Walters, Marguerite. *The city-country ABC: My alphabet walk in the country, and My alphabet ride in the city* ill. by Ib Spang Olsen. Doubleday, 1966. The two stories are bound dos-à-dos. Subj: ABC books. City. Country. Format, unusual.

Walters, Virginia. *Are we there yet, Daddy?* ill. by S. D. Schindler. Viking, 1999. ISBN 0-670-87402-7 Subj: Activities – traveling. Automobiles. Family life – fathers. Maps. Rhyming text.

Walton, Ann. *Dumb clucks! jokes about chickens* (Walton, Rick)

Something's fishy! jokes about sea creatures (Walton, Rick)

Walton, Rick. *Dance, pioneer, dance!* ill. by Brad Teare. Deseret Book, 1997. ISBN 1-57345-243-2

Subj: Activities – dancing. U.S. history – frontier and pioneer life.

Dumb clucks! jokes about chickens by Rick and Ann Walton; ill. by Joan Hanson. Lerner, 1987. ISBN 0-8225-0991-1 Subj: Birds – chickens. Riddles.

How many, how many, how many ill. by Cynthia Jabar. Candlewick, 1993. ISBN 1-56402-062-2 Subj: Counting, numbers. Nursery rhymes. Riddles.

Little dogs say "Rough!" ill. by Henry Cole. Putnam, 2000. ISBN 0-399-23228-1 Subj: Animals. Noise, sounds. Rhyming text.

My two hands, my two feet ill. by Julia Gorton. Putnam, 2000. ISBN 0-399-23338-5 Subj: Anatomy – feet. Anatomy – hands. Communication.

Noah's square dance ill. by Thor Wickstrom. Lothrop, 1995. ISBN 0-688-11187-4 Subj: Activities – dancing. Animals. Boats, ships. Religion – Noah. Rhyming text. Weather – floods. Weather – rain.

One more bunny ill. by Paige Miglio. Lothrop, 2000. ISBN 0-688-16848-5 Subj: Animals – rabbits. Counting, numbers.

So many bunnies ill. by Paige Miglio. Lothrop, 1998. ISBN 0-688-13657-5 Subj: ABC books. Counting, numbers. Rhyming text. Sleep.

Something's fishy! jokes about sea creatures by Rick and Ann Walton; ill. by Joan Hanson. Lerner, 1987. ISBN 0-8225-0993-8 Subj: Fish. Riddles.

Walty, Margaret. *Rock-a-bye baby: lullabies for bedtime* ill. by author. Barefoot, 1998. ISBN 1-902283-03-1 Subj: Bedtime. Lullabies. Music.

Wan, Manyee. *Lao Lao of Dragon Mountain* (Bateson-Hill, Margaret)

Wandelmaier, Roy. *Clouds* ill. by John Jones. Troll, 1985. ISBN 0-8167-0338-8 Subj: Weather – clouds. Weather – rain.

Stars ill. by Irene Trivas. Troll, 1985. ISBN 0-8167-0339-6 Subj: Science. Stars.

Wang, Mary Lewis. *The ant and the dove* (Æsop)

Wang, Rosalind C. *The fourth question* ill. by Ju-Hong Chen. Holiday, 1991. ISBN 0-8234-0855-8 Subj: Character traits – generosity. Folk and fairy tales. Foreign lands – China.

The treasure chest ill. by Will Hillenbrand. Holiday, 1995. ISBN 0-8234-1114-1 Subj: Character traits – generosity. Folk and fairy tales. Foreign lands – China. Magic.

Wang, Xing Chu. *China's bravest girl: the legend of Hua Mu Lan* (Chin, Charlie)

Warbler, J. M. see Cocagnac, A. M. (Augustin Maurice)

Warburton, Nick. *Mr. Tite's belongings* ill. by Alex Ayliffe. Viking, 1992. ISBN 0-670-84155-2 Subj: Character traits – selfishness.

Ward, Andrew. *Baby bear and the long sleep* ill. by John Walsh. Little, 1980. ISBN 0-316-92197-1 Subj: Animals – bears. Hibernation. Seasons – winter.

Ward, Cindy. *Cookie's week* ill. by Tomie de Paola. Putnam, 1988. ISBN 0-399-21498-4 Subj: Animals – cats. Behavior – misbehavior. Days of the week, months of the year.

Ward, Heather Patricia. *I promise I'll find you* ill. by Sheila McGraw. Firefly, 1994. ISBN 1-895565-40-5 Subj: Behavior – lost. Emotions – love. Family life – mothers. Rhyming text.

Ward, Helen. *The golden pear* ill. by author. Ideals, 1991. ISBN 0-8249-8471-4 Subj: Folk and fairy tales. Friendship.

The hare and the tortoise (Æsop)

The king of the birds ill. by author. Millbrook, 1997. ISBN 0-7613-0288-3 Subj: Activities – flying. Birds. Character traits – cleverness. Royalty – kings.

The moonrat and the white turtle ill. by author. Ideals, 1990. ISBN 0-8249-8467-6 Subj: Character traits – selfishness. Moon. Pirates. Reptiles – turtles, tortoises.

Ward, Jennifer. *Somewhere in the ocean* by Jennifer Ward and T. J. Marsh; ill. by Ken Spengler. Rising Moon, 2000. ISBN 0-87358-748-0 Subj: Animals – babies. Counting, numbers. Rhyming text. Sea and seashore.

Way out in the desert (Marsh, T. J.)

Ward, Leila. *I am eyes, ni macho* ill. by Nonny Hogrogian. Greenwillow, 1978. ISBN 0-688-84161-9 Subj: Foreign lands – Africa. Nature.

Ward, Lynd. *The biggest bear* ill. by author. Houghton Mifflin, 1952. Subj: Animals – bears. Caldecott award books. Character traits – kindness to animals. Foreign lands – Canada. Pets.

The little red lighthouse and the great gray bridge (Swift, Hildegarde Hoyt)

Nic of the woods ill. by author. Houghton Mifflin, 1965. Subj: Animals. Animals – dogs. Foreign lands – Canada. Forest, woods.

The silver pony ill. by author. Houghton Mifflin, 1973. ISBN 0-395-14753-0 Subj: Animals – horses, ponies. Dreams. Wordless.

Ward, May McNeer. see McNeer, May Yonge

Ward, Nanda Weedon. *The black sombrero* ill. by Lynd Ward. Ariel, 1952. Subj: Animals. Clothing – hats. Cowboys.

The elephant that ga-lumped by Nanda Weedon Ward and Robert Haynes; ill. by Robert Haynes. Ariel, 1959. Subj: Animals. Animals – elephants. Foreign lands – India.

Ward, Nick. *Farmer George and the fieldmice* ill. by author. Pavilion, 1999. ISBN 1-86205-203-4 Subj:

Animals. Animals – mice. Careers – farmers. Farms. Homes, houses. Machines.

Farmer George and the lost chick ill. by author. Pavilion, 1999. ISBN 1-86205-412-6 Subj: Animals. Behavior – lost. Birds – chickens. Careers – farmers. Farms.

Giant. Oxford Univ. Pr., 1983. ISBN 0-19-278201-0 Subj: Behavior – misbehavior. Giants. Toys.

Ward, Sally G. *Charlie and Grandma* ill. by author. Scholastic, 1986. ISBN 0-590-33954-0 Subj: Behavior – misbehavior. Family life – grandmothers.

Molly and Grandpa ill. by author. Scholastic, 1986. ISBN 0-590-33955-9 Subj: Character traits – persistence. Family life – grandfathers. Food.

Punky goes fishing ill. by author. Dutton, 1991. ISBN 0-525-44681-8 Subj: Family life – grandfathers. Sports – fishing.

What goes around comes around ill. by author. Doubleday, 1991. ISBN 0-385-41223-1 Subj: Character traits – generosity. Communities, neighborhoods. Family life – grandmothers.

Wardlaw, Lee. *Bow-wow birthday* ill. by Arden Johnson-Petrov. Boyds Mills, 1998. ISBN 1-56397-489-4 Subj: Animals – dogs. Birthdays. Family life – grandfathers. Parties.

Saturday night jamboree ill. by Barry Root. Dial, 2000. ISBN 0-8037-2189-7 Subj: Activities – babysitting. Activities – dancing. Family life.

The tales of Grandpa Cat ill. by Ronald Searle. Dial, 1994. ISBN 0-8037-1512-9 Subj: Animals – cats. Family life – grandparents.

Warner, Sunny. *Madison finds a line* ill. by author. Houghton Mifflin, 1999. ISBN 0-395-88508-6 Subj: Activities – dancing. Animals – cats. Imagination. Insects. Music. Rhyming text.

The magic sewing machine ill. by author. Houghton Mifflin, 1997. ISBN 0-395-82747-7 Subj: Activities – sewing. Family life – brothers and sisters. Orphans.

Warnick, Elsa. *Bedtime* ill. by author. Browndeer, 1998. ISBN 0-15-201471-3 Subj: Activities. Bedtime.

Warren, Cathy. *Fred's first day* ill. by Pat Cummings. Lothrop, 1984. ISBN 0-688-03814-X Subj: Friendship. School – first day.

Saturday belongs to Sara ill. by DyAnne DiSalvo-Ryan. Bradbury, 1988. ISBN 0-02-792491-2 Subj: Character traits – kindness. Family life – mothers.

Springtime bears ill. by Pat Cummings. Lothrop, 1987. ISBN 0-688-05906-6 Subj: Animals – bears. Behavior – hiding. Seasons – spring.

The ten-alarm camp-out ill. by Steven Kellogg. Lothrop, 1983. ISBN 0-688-02128-X Subj: Camps, camping. Counting, numbers.

Warren, Elizabeth. *see* Supraner, Robyn

Warren, Robert. *I'm sorry* (McBratney, Sam)

Warren, Vic. *Buffalo* (Midge, Tiffany)

Warshofsky, Isaac. *see* Singer, Isaac Bashevis

Washington, Donna L. *The story of Kwanzaa* ill. by Stephen Taylor. HarperCollins, 1996. ISBN 0-06-024819-X Subj: Ethnic groups in the U.S. – African Americans. Holidays – Kwanzaa. U.S. history.

Wasmuth, Eleanor. *An alligator day* ill. by author. Grosset, 1983. ISBN 0-448-21703-1 Subj: Activities – playing. Reptiles – alligators, crocodiles.

The picnic basket ill. by author. Grosset, 1983. ISBN 0-448-21704-X Subj: Activities – picnicking. Food. Reptiles – alligators, crocodiles.

Wasserberg, Esther. *Grandmother dear* (Finfer, Celentha)

Wasson, Valentina Pavlovna. *The chosen baby* ill. by Glo Coalson. 3rd ed. HarperCollins, 1977. ISBN 0-397-31738-7 Subj: Adoption.

Watanabe, Shigeo. *Daddy, play with me!* ill. by Yasuo Ohtomo. Putnam, 1985. ISBN 0-399-21211-6 Subj: Activities – playing. Animals – bears. Family life – fathers.

How do I put it on? ill. by Yasuo Ohtomo. Putnam, 1979. ISBN 0-529-05557-0 Subj: Animals – bears. Clothing. Participation.

I can build a house! ill. by Yasuo Ohtomo. Philomel, 1983. ISBN 0-399-20950-6 Subj: Activities – playing. Animals – bears. Character traits – perseverance. Homes, houses.

I can ride it! ill. by Yasuo Ohtomo. Putnam, 1982. ISBN 0-399-61194-0 Subj: Activities – playing. Animals – bears. Character traits – perseverance.

I can take a bath! ill. by Yasuo Ohtomo. Putnam, 1987. ISBN 0-399-21362-7 Subj: Activities – bathing. Animals – bears. Family life – fathers.

I can take a walk! ill. by Yasuo Ohtomo. Putnam, 1984. ISBN 0-399-21044-X Subj: Activities – walking. Animals – bears.

Ice cream is falling! ill. by Yasuo Ohtomo. Putnam, 1989. ISBN 0-399-21550-6 Subj: Animals – bears. Seasons – winter. Weather – snow.

I'm the king of the castle! ill. by Yasuo Ohtomo. Putnam, 1982. ISBN 0-399-61195-9 Subj: Activities – playing. Animals – bears. Sand.

It's my birthday ill. by Yasuo Ohtomo. Putnam, 1988. ISBN 0-399-21492-5 Subj: Animals – bears. Birthdays. Family life – grandparents.

Let's go swimming ill. by Yasuo, Ohtomo. Putnam, 1990. ISBN 0-399-21896-3 Subj: Animals – bears. Family life – fathers. Sports – swimming.

What a good lunch! ill. by Yasuo Ohtomo. Collins-World, 1980. ISBN 0-529-05580-5 Subj: Animals – bears. Food. Humor.

Where's my daddy? ill. by Yasuo Ohtomo. Philomel, 1982. ISBN 0-399-20899-2 Subj: Animals – bears. Behavior – lost. Character traits – perseverance. Family life – fathers.

Watanabe, Yuichi. *Wally the whale who loved balloons* trans. from Japanese by D. T. Ooka; ill. by author. Heian Intl., 1982. ISBN 0-89346-150-4 Subj: Animals – whales. Behavior – misbehavior. Toys – balloons.

Waters, Fiona. *The selfish giant* (Wilde, Oscar)

Waters, Kate. *Lion dancer: Ernie Wan's Chinese new year* by Kate Waters and Madeline Slovenz-Low; photos by Martha Cooper. Scholastic, 1990. ISBN 0-590-43046-7 Subj: Activities – dancing. Ethnic groups in the U.S. – Chinese Americans. Holidays – Chinese New Year.

Waters, Tony. *Sailor's bride* ill. by author. Doubleday, 1991. ISBN 0-385-41441-2 Subj: Animals – mice. Behavior – lost. Boats, ships. Sailors. Sea and seashore.

Waterton, Betty. *Orff, 27 dragons (and a snarkel)* ill. by Karen Kulyk. Firefly, 1984. ISBN 0-920303-02-1 Subj: Activities – flying. Character traits – perseverance. Dragons. Dreams.

Pettranella ill. by Ann Blades. Vanguard, 1981. ISBN 0-8149-0844-6 Subj: Family life – grandmothers. Foreign lands – Canada. Seasons – spring.

A salmon for Simon ill. by Ann Blades. Atheneum, 1980. ISBN 0-689-50169-2 Subj: Character traits – kindness to animals. Sports – fishing.

Watkins, Hope (Brister). *The cunning fox and other tales* ill. by Henry C. Pitz. Knopf, 1943. Subj: Animals. Folk and fairy tales.

Watkins, Sherrin. *White Bead Ceremony* ill. by Kim Doner. Council Oak Books, 1994. ISBN 0-933031-92-0 Subj: Family life – grandmothers. Indians of North America – Shawnee. Names.

Watson, Carol. *Æsop's fables* (Æsop)

Opposites ill. by David Higham. Usborne, 1983. ISBN 0-86020-758-7 Subj: Concepts – opposites.

Rabbit by Carol Watson and Jane Burton; ill. by Jane Burton. Rooster Books, 1994. ISBN 0-553-09547-1 Subj: Animals – rabbits. Format, unusual – board books.

Shapes ill. by David Higham. Usborne, 1983. ISBN 0-86020-759-5 Subj: Concepts – shape.

Sizes ill. by David Higham. Usborne, 1983. ISBN 0-86020-760-9 Subj: Concepts – size.

Watson, Claire. *Big creatures from the past* ill. by Robert Cremins; design and paper engineering by Keith Moseley. Putnam, 1990. ISBN 0-399-22159-X Subj: Dinosaurs. Format, unusual – toy and movable books.

Watson, Clyde. *Applebet: an ABC* ill. by Wendy Watson. Farrar, 1982. ISBN 0-374-30384-3 Subj: ABC books. Fairs. Rhyming text.

Catch me and kiss me and say it again ill. by Wendy Watson. Collins-World, 1978. ISBN 0-529-05438-8 Subj: Family life. Poetry.

Father Fox's feast of songs ill. by Wendy Watson. Putnam, 1983. ISBN 0-399-20928-X Subj: Animals – foxes. Music. Poetry.

Fisherman lullabies ed. and ill. by Wendy Watson; music by Clyde Watson. Collins-World, 1968. Subj: Bedtime. Lullabies. Music.

Hickory stick rag ill. by Wendy Watson. Crowell, 1976. ISBN 0-690-00960-7 Subj: Activities – picnicking. Humor. Rhyming text. School.

How Brown Mouse kept Christmas ill. by Wendy Watson. Farrar, 1980. ISBN 0-374-33494-3 Subj: Animals – mice. Holidays – Christmas.

Love's a sweet ill. by Wendy Watson. Viking, 1998. ISBN 0-670-83453-X Subj: Emotions – love. Poetry.

Midnight moon ill. by Susanna Natti. Collins-World, 1979. ISBN 0-529-05527-9 Subj: Activities – flying. Bedtime. Imagination. Moon.

Tom Fox and the apple pie ill. by Wendy Watson. Crowell, 1972. ISBN 0-690-82784-9 Subj: Animals – foxes. Behavior – sharing. Fairs. Food.

Valentine foxes ill. by Wendy Watson. Watts, 1988. ISBN 0-531-08400-0 Subj: Animals – foxes. Family life. Food. Holidays – Valentine's Day.

Watson, Esther (Pearl). *The adventures of Jules and Gertie* ill. by author. Harcourt, 1999. ISBN 0-15-201975-8 Subj: Animals – horses, ponies. Cowboys. Humor.

Watson, Jane Werner. *My friend the babysitter* by Jane Werner Watson, Robert E. Switzer and J. Cotter Hirschberg; ill. by Hilde Hoffmann. Golden Pr., 1971. Subj: Activities – babysitting.

My friend the dentist by Jane Werner Watson, Robert E. Switzer and J. Cotter Hirschberg; ill. by Cat Bowman Smith. Crown, 1987. ISBN 0-517-56485-X Subj: Careers – dentists. Health and fitness.

My friend the doctor by Jane Werner Watson, Robert E. Switzer and J. Cotter Hirschberg; ill. by Cat Bowman Smith. Crown, 1987. ISBN 0-517-56485-8 Subj: Careers – doctors. Health and fitness.

Sometimes a family has to move by Jane Werner Watson, Robert E. Switzer and J. Cotter Hirschberg; ill. by Cat Bowman Smith. Crown, 1988. ISBN 0-517-56593-5 Subj: Family life. Moving.

Sometimes a family has to split up by Jane Werner Watson, Robert E. Switzer and J. Cotter Hirschberg; ill. by Cat Bowman Smith. Crown, 1988. ISBN 0-517-56811-X Subj: Divorce. Family life.

Sometimes I get angry by Jane Werner Watson, Robert E. Switzer and J. Cotter Hirschberg; ill. by

Irene Trivas. Crown, 1986. ISBN 0-517-56088-7 Subj: Emotions – anger.

Sometimes I'm afraid by Jane Werner Watson, Robert E. Switzer and J. Cotter Hirschberg; ill. by Irene Trivas. Crown, 1986. ISBN 0-517-56087-9 Subj: Emotions – fear.

Sometimes I'm jealous by Jane Werner Watson, Robert E. Switzer and J. Cotter Hirschberg; ill. by Irene Trivas. Crown, 1986. ISBN 0-517-56062-3 Subj: Emotions – envy, jealousy.

Which is the witch? ill. by Victoria Chess. Pantheon, 1979. ISBN 0-394-93978-6 Subj: Holidays – Halloween. Witches.

Watson, John. *We're the noisy dinosaurs!* ill. by author. Candlewick, 1992. ISBN 1-56402-089-4 Subj: Dinosaurs. Noise, sounds.

Watson, Mary. *The butterfly seeds* ill. by author. Tambourine, 1995. ISBN 0-688-14133-1 Subj: Activities – traveling. Ethnic groups in the U.S. Family life – grandparents. Insects – butterflies, caterpillars. Memories, memory. Seeds.

Watson, Nancy Dingman. *The birthday goat* ill. by Wendy Watson. Crowell, 1974. ISBN 0-690-00146-0 Subj: Animals – goats. Birthdays. Crime. Fairs.

Sugar on snow ill. by Aldren Auld Watson. Viking, 1964. Subj: Food. Weather – snow.

Tommy's mommy's fish ill. by Aldren Auld Watson. Viking, 1971. ISBN 0-670-71926-9 Subj: Birthdays. Family life – mothers. Sports – fishing.

Tommy's mommy's fish ill. by Thomas Aldren Dingman Watson. Viking, 1996. ISBN 0-670-85681-9 Subj: Birthdays. Family life – mothers. Sports – fishing.

What does A begin with? ill. by Aldren Auld Watson. Knopf, 1956. Subj: ABC books. Farms.

What is one? ill. by Aldren Auld Watson. Knopf, 1954. Subj: Counting, numbers. Farms.

When is tomorrow? ill. by Aldren Auld Watson. Knopf, 1955. Subj: Sea and seashore. Time.

Watson, Pauline. *Curley Cat baby-sits* ill. by Lorinda Bryan Cauley. Harcourt, 1977. ISBN 0-15-221110-1 Subj: Activities – babysitting. Animals – cats.

Days with Daddy ill. by Joanne Scribner. Prentice-Hall, 1977. ISBN 0-13-196907-2 Subj: Family life. Family life – fathers.

The walking coat ill. by Tomie de Paola. Walker, 1980. ISBN 0-8027-6351-0 Subj: Clothing – coats.

Wriggles, the little wishing pig ill. by Paul Galdone. Seabury Pr., 1978. ISBN 0-8164-3216-3 Subj: Animals – pigs. Behavior – wishing. Monsters.

Watson, Richard Jesse. *Tom Thumb* (Tom Thumb)

Watson, Wendy. *Boo! It's Halloween* ill. by author. Clarion, 1992. ISBN 0-395-53628-6 Subj: Family life. Holidays – Halloween.

The bunnies' Christmas eve ill. by author. Putnam, 1983. ISBN 0-399-20968-9 Subj: Animals – rabbits. Format, unusual – toy and movable books. Holidays – Christmas.

Fisherman lullabies (Watson, Clyde)

Happy Easter day! ill. by author. Clarion, 1993. ISBN 0-395-53629-4 Subj: Animals – cats. Family life. Holidays – Easter.

Has winter come? ill. by author. Collins-World, 1978. ISBN 0-529-05441-8 Subj: Animals – groundhogs. Hibernation. Seasons – winter.

Hurray for the Fourth of July ill. by author. Houghton Mifflin, 1992. ISBN 0-395-53627-8 Subj: Family life. Holidays – Fourth of July. Poetry.

Lollipop ill. by author. Crowell, 1976. ISBN 0-690-00768-X Subj: Animals – rabbits. Behavior – misbehavior.

Moving ill. by author. Crowell, 1978. ISBN 0-690-01327-2 Subj: Moving.

Tales for a winter's eve ill. by author. Farrar, 1988. ISBN 0-374-37373-6 Subj: Animals – foxes. Illness. Seasons – winter.

Thanksgiving at our house ill. by author. Houghton Mifflin, 1991. ISBN 0-395-53626-X Subj: Family life. Holidays – Thanksgiving. Nursery rhymes.

A Valentine for you ill. by author. Houghton Mifflin, 1991. ISBN 0-395-53625-1 Subj: Emotions – love. Holidays – Valentine's Day. Poetry.

Wattenberg, Jane. *Henny-Penny* (Chicken Little)

Mrs. Mustard's baby faces photos by author. Chronicle, 1989. ISBN 0-87701-659-3 Subj: Babies. Format, unusual.

Watts, Barrie. *Apple tree* photos by author. Silver Burdett, 1987. ISBN 0-382-09436-0 Subj: Nature. Science. Trees.

Bird's nest photos by author. Silver Burdett, 1987. ISBN 0-382-09439-5 Subj: Animals. Birds. Science.

Butterfly and caterpillar photos by author. Silver Burdett, 1986. ISBN 0-382-09282-1 Subj: Insects – butterflies, caterpillars. Metamorphosis. Science.

Dandelion photos by author. Silver Burdett, 1987. ISBN 0-382-09438-7 Subj: Plants. Science.

Duck [written and ed. by Angela Royston] photos by author. Dutton, 1991. ISBN 0-525-67346-6 Subj: Birds – ducks. Birth. Format, unusual – board books.

Hamster photos by author. Silver Burdett, 1986. ISBN 0-382-09281-3 Subj: Animals – hamsters. Science.

Ladybug photos by author. Silver Burdett, 1987. ISBN 0-382-09437-9 Subj: Insects – ladybugs. Science.

Mouse photos by Barrie Watts; written by Angela Royston and ill. by Rowan Clifford. Lodestar,

1992. ISBN 0-525-67357-1 Subj: Animals – mice. Behavior – growing up.

Mushrooms photos by author. Silver Burdett, 1986. ISBN 0-382-09287-2 Subj: Plants. Science.

Rabbit [written and ed. by Angela Royston] ill. by Rowan Clifford; photos by author. Dutton, 1992. ISBN 0-525-67356-3 Subj: Animals – rabbits. Birth. Format, unusual. Science.

Tomato photos and ill. by author. Silver Burdett, 1990. ISBN 0-382-24008-1 Subj: Gardens, gardening. Plants. Science.

Watts, Bernadett. *The town mouse and the country mouse: an Æsop fable* (Æsop)

Watts, Bernadette. *The Christmas bird* ill. by author. North-South, 1996. ISBN 1-55858-603-2 Subj: Activities – whistling. Birds. Holidays – Christmas. Religion – Nativity.

David's waiting day ill. by author. Prentice-Hall, 1978. ISBN 0-13-197178-6 Subj: Babies. Family life – new sibling.

The elves and the shoemaker (Grimm, Jacob)

The fir tree (Andersen, H. C. [Hans Christian])

Goldilocks and the three bears (The three bears)

Green is beautiful (Rogers, Margaret)

Harvey Hare, postman extraordinaire ill. by author. North-South, 1997. ISBN 1-55858-688-1 Subj: Animals – rabbits. Careers – postal workers. Gifts.

Harvey Hare's Christmas ill. by author. North-South, 1999. ISBN 0-7358-1059-1 Subj: Animals. Animals – rabbits. Careers – postal workers. Holidays – Christmas.

The lion and the mouse (Æsop)

Rapunzel (Grimm, Jacob)

St. Francis and the proud crow ill. by author. Watts, 1988. ISBN 0-531-08358-6 Subj: Behavior – seeking better things. Folk and fairy tales.

Snow White and Rose Red (Grimm, Jacob)

Tattercoats ill. by author. North-South, 1989. ISBN 1-55858-002-6 Subj: Gardens, gardening. Scarecrows. Seasons. Weather.

The ugly duckling (Andersen, H. C. [Hans Christian])

Watts, Jeri Hanel. *Keepers* ill. by Felicia Marshall. Lee & Low, 1997. ISBN 1-880000-58-X Subj: Activities – storytelling. Ethnic groups in the U.S. – African Americans. Family life – grandmothers. Old age.

Watts, Mabel (Pizzey). *The day it rained watermelons* ill. by Lee Albertson. Lantern Pr., 1964. Subj: Behavior – indifference.

Something for you, something for me ill. by Abner Graboff. Abelard-Schuman, 1960. Subj: Activities – trading. Behavior – sharing.

Weeks and weeks ill. by Abner Graboff. Abelard-Schuman, 1962. Subj: Activities – photographing.

Watts, Marjorie-Ann. *Crocodile medicine* ill. by author. Warne, 1978. ISBN 0-7232-6154-7 Subj: Behavior – boredom. Hospitals. Illness. Reptiles – alligators, crocodiles.

Crocodile plaster ill. by author. Dutton, 1984. ISBN 0-233-96962-4 Subj: Hospitals. Illness. Reptiles – alligators, crocodiles.

Zebra goes to school ill. by author. Elsevier-Dutton, 1981. ISBN 0-233-97241-2 Subj: Imagination – imaginary friends. School – first day.

Waxman, Stephanie. *What is a girl? What is a boy?* photos by author. HarperCollins, 1989. ISBN 0-690-04711-8 Subj: Anatomy. Behavior – growing up. Character traits – individuality.

Wayland, April Halprin. *To Rabbittown* ill. by Robin Spowart. Scholastic, 1989. ISBN 0-590-40852-6 Subj: Animals – rabbits. Imagination. Pets.

Wayne-von-Königslöw, Andrea. *Bing and Chutney* ill. by author. Annick, 1999. ISBN 1-55037-609-8 Subj: Activities – cooking. Activities – dancing. Animals – elephants. Animals – pigs. Friendship.

That's my baby? ill. by author. Firefly, 1986. ISBN 0-920303-56-0 Subj: Babies. Family life. Sibling rivalry. Toys.

We wish you a merry Christmas: *a traditional Christmas carol* ill. by Tracey Campbell Pearson. Dial, 1983. ISBN 0-8037-9400-2 Subj: Behavior – misbehavior. Holidays – Christmas. Songs.

Weary, Ogdred. *see* Gorey, Edward (St. John)

Weatherby, Meredith. *Upside-downers: more pictures to stretch the imagination* (Anno, Mitsumasa)

Weatherford, Carole Boston. *Juneteenth jamboree* ill. by Yvonne Buchanan. Lee & Low, 1995. ISBN 1-880000-18-0 Subj: Ethnic groups in the U.S. – African Americans. Holidays – Juneteenth. Slavery. U.S. history.

Weatherill, Stephen. *The very first Lucy Goose book* ill. by author. Prentice-Hall, 1987. ISBN 0-13-941410-X Subj: Birds. Birds – geese. Humor.

Webb, Angela. *Talkabout air* photos by Chris Fairclough. Watts, 1987. ISBN 0-531-10369-2 Subj: Science.

Talkabout light photos by Chris Fairclough. Watts, 1988. ISBN 0-531-10455-9 Subj: Concepts. Science.

Talkabout reflections photos by Chris Fairclough. Watts, 1988. ISBN 0-531-10457-5 Subj: Concepts. Science.

Talkabout sand photos by Chris Fairclough. Watts, 1987. ISBN 0-531-10370-6 Subj: Sand. Science.

Talkabout soil photos by Chris Fairclough. Watts, 1987. ISBN 0-531-10371-4 Subj: Science.

Talkabout sound photos by Chris Fairclough. Watts, 1988. ISBN 0-531-10456-7 Subj: Concepts. Noise, sounds. Science.

Talkabout water photos by Chris Fairclough. Watts, 1987. ISBN 0-531-10372-2 Subj: Science.

Webb, Clifford. *The story of Noah* ill. by author. Warne, 1932. Subj: Animals. Boats, ships. Religion – Noah. Weather – floods. Weather – rain. Weather – rainbows.

Webb, Denise. *The same sun was in the sky* ill. by Walter Porter. Northland, 1994. ISBN 0-87358-602-6 Subj: Family life – grandfathers. Indians of North America – Hohokam. Petroglyphs.

Weber, Alfons. *Elizabeth gets well* ill. by Jacqueline Blass. Crowell, 1970. Translation of Elisabeth wird gesund. ISBN 0-690-25839-9 Subj: Hospitals. Illness.

Weedn, Flavia. *The elephant prince* by Flavia Weedn and Lisa Weedn Gilbert; ill. by Flavia Weedn. Hyperion, 1995. ISBN 0-7683-2052-6 Subj: Animals – elephants. Character traits – perseverance. Folk and fairy tales. Foreign lands – Scandinavia.

The enchanted tree by Flavia Weedn and Lisa Weedn Gilbert; ill. by Flavia Weedn. Hyperion, 1995. ISBN 0-7868-0120-4 Subj: Animals – giraffes. Character traits – being different. Folk and fairy tales. Self-concept. Trees.

The giant's garden by Flavia Weedn and Lisa Weedn Gilbert; ill. by Flavia Weedn. Hyperion, 1995. Based on: The selfish giant by Oscar Wilde. ISBN 0-7868-0121-2 Subj: Character traits – kindness. Character traits – selfishness. Folk and fairy tales. Gardens, gardening. Giants. Seasons – spring.

The little snow bear by Flavia Weedn and Lisa Weedn Gilbert; ill. by Flavia Weedn. Hyperion, 1995. ISBN 0-7868-0044-5 Subj: Animals – bears. Friendship. Snowmen.

The magic cap by Flavia Weedn and Lisa Weedn Gilbert; ill. by Flavia Weedn. Hyperion, 1995. ISBN 0-7868-0119-0 Subj: Clothing – hats. Folk and fairy tales. Foreign lands – Sweden. Magic.

The moon maiden by Flavia Weedn and Lisa Weedn Gilbert; ill. by Flavia Weedn. Hyperion, 1995. ISBN 0-7868-0045-3 Subj: Folk and fairy tales. Foreign lands – Japan. Insects – fireflies. Moon.

The ragged peddler by Flavia Weedn and Lisa Weedn Gilbert; ill. by Flavia Weedn. Hyperion, 1995. ISBN 0-7868-0046-1 Subj: Behavior – dissatisfaction. Emotions – happiness. Folk and fairy tales. Foreign lands – Middle East. Jewish culture.

The star gift by Flavia Weedn and Lisa Weedn Gilbert; ill. by Flavia Weedn. Hyperion, 1995. ISBN 0-7868-0122-0 Subj: Family life. Folk and fairy tales. Gifts. Orphans. Stars.

The weekend ill. by Roser Capdevila. Firefly, 1986. ISBN 0-920303-44-7 Subj: Activities – picnicking. Country. Sea and seashore.

Weeks, Sarah. *Crocodile smile* ill. by Lois Ehlert. HarperCollins, 1994. ISBN 0-06-022867-9 Subj: Animals. Animals – endangered animals. Music. Songs.

Drip, drop ill. by Jane Manning. HarperCollins, 2000. ISBN 0-06-028524-9 Subj: Animals – mice. Homes, houses. Rhyming text. Weather – rain.

Happy birthday, Frankie ill. by Warren Linn. Laura Geringer, 1999. ISBN 0-06-028522-2 Subj: Birthdays. Humor. Monsters.

Mrs. McNosh and the great big squash ill. by Nadine Bernard Westcott. Laura Geringer, 2000. ISBN 0-694-01202-5 Subj: Gardens, gardening. Homes, houses. Plants. Rhyming text.

Mrs. McNosh hangs up her wash ill. by Nadine Bernard Westcott. Laura Geringer, 1998. ISBN 0-694-01076-6 Subj: Humor. Laundry.

Noodles ill. by David A. Carter. HarperCollins, 1996. ISBN 0-694-00842-7 Subj: Food. Format, unusual – toy and movable books.

Splish splash ill. by Ashley Wolff. HarperCollins, 1999. ISBN 0-06-027893-5 Subj: Activities – bathing. Animals. Fish. Rhyming text.

Weelen, Guy. *The little red train* ill. by Mamoru Funai. Lothrop, 1966. Subj: Foreign lands – France. Trains.

Wegen, Ron. *The balloon trip* ill. by author. Houghton Mifflin, 1981. ISBN 0-395-30370-2 Subj: Activities – ballooning. Family life. Wordless.

Billy Gorilla ill. by author. Lothrop, 1983. ISBN 0-688-01986-2 Subj: Behavior – trickery. Holidays – April Fools' Day.

The Halloween costume party ill. by author. Houghton Mifflin, 1983. ISBN 0-89919-184-3 Subj: Holidays – Halloween. Parties.

Sand castle ill. by author. Greenwillow, 1977. ISBN 0-688-84033-7 Subj: Sea and seashore.

Sky dragon ill. by author. Greenwillow, 1982. ISBN 0-688-01146-2 Subj: Weather – clouds.

Where can the animals go? ill. by author. Greenwillow, 1978. ISBN 0-688-84137-6 Subj: Animals. Ecology.

Weidt, Maryann N. *Daddy played music for the cows* ill. by Henri Sorensen. Lothrop, 1995. ISBN 0-688-10058-9 Subj: Animals – bulls, cows. Farms. Music.

Weihs, Erika. *Count the cats* ill. by author. Doubleday, 1976. ISBN 0-385-11088-X Subj: Animals – cats. Counting, numbers.

Weil, Ann. *Animal families* ill. by Roger Vernam. Childrens Pr., 1956. Subj: Animals.

Weil, Lisl. *The candy egg bunny* ill. by author. Holiday, 1975. ISBN 0-823-40250-9 Subj: Animals – rabbits. Holidays – Easter. Witches.

Gertie and Gus ill. by author. Parents, 1977. ISBN 0-8193-0912-5 Subj: Careers – fishermen. Family life.

Gillie and the flattering fox ill. by author. Atheneum, 1978. ISBN 0-689-30637-7 Subj: Animals – foxes. Birds – chickens. Friendship.

Let's go to the circus ill. by author. Holiday, 1988. ISBN 0-8234-0693-8 Subj: Circus.

Let's go to the library ill. by author. Holiday, 1990. ISBN 0-8234-0529-9 Subj: Libraries.

Let's go to the museum ill. by author. Holiday, 1989. ISBN 0-8234-0784-5 Subj: Museums.

The magic of music ill. by author. Holiday, 1989. ISBN 0-8234-0735-7 Subj: Music.

Mother Goose picture riddles: a book of rebuses ill. by author. Holiday, 1981. ISBN 0-5234-0393-9 Subj: Nursery rhymes. Rebuses.

Owl and other scrambles ill. by author. Dutton, 1980. ISBN 0-525-36527-3 Subj: Games. Participation.

Pandora's box ill. by adapt. Atheneum, 1986. ISBN 0-689-31216-4 Subj: Character traits – curiosity. Folk and fairy tales.

Santa Claus around the world ill. by author. Holiday, 1987. ISBN 0-8234-0665-2 Subj: Holidays – Christmas. Santa Claus.

To sail a ship of treasures ill. by author. Atheneum, 1984. ISBN 0-689-31059-5 Subj: Behavior – collecting things.

Weilerstein, Sadie Rose. *The best of K'tonton* ill. by Marilyn Hirsh. Jewish Publication Society, 1980. ISBN 0-8276-0184-0 Subj: Jewish culture.

K'tonton's Yom Kippur kitten ill. by Joe Boddy. Jewish Publication Society, 1995. ISBN 0-8276-0541-2 Subj: Animals – cats. Behavior – misbehavior. Holidays – Yom Kippur. Jewish culture. Religion.

Weinberg, Florence. *Grandmother dear* (Finfer, Celentha)

Weinberg, Lawrence. *The Forgetful Bears* ill. by Paula Winter. Houghton Mifflin, 1982. ISBN 0-89919-068-5 Subj: Animals – bears. Behavior – forgetfulness.

The Forgetful Bears meet Mr. Memory ill. by author. Scholastic, 1987. ISBN 0-590-40781-3 Subj: Animals – bears. Animals – elephants. Behavior – forgetfulness. Memories, memory.

Weir, Alison. *Peter, good night* ill. by Deborah Kogan Ray. Dutton, 1989. ISBN 0-525-44464-5 Subj: Bedtime. Night. Sleep.

Weir, Bob. *Panther dream* by Bob and Wendy Weir; ill. by Wendy Weir. Walt Disney, 1991. ISBN 1-56282-075-3 Subj: Food. Foreign lands – Africa. Forest, woods.

Weir, Wendy. *Panther dream* (Weir, Bob)

Weird pet poems comp. by Dilys Evans; ill. by Jacqueline Rogers. Simon & Schuster, 1997. ISBN 0-689-80734-1 Subj: Animals. Pets. Poetry.

Weisgard, Leonard. *The funny bunny factory* ill. by author. Grosset, 1950. Subj: Animals – rabbits. Holidays – Easter.

Mr. Peaceable paints ill. by author. Scribners, 1956. Subj: Activities – painting. Careers – artists.

Silly Willy Nilly ill. by author. Scribners, 1953. Subj: Animals – elephants. Behavior – forgetfulness.

Who dreams of cheese? ill. by author. Scribners, 1950. Subj: Behavior – wishing. Dreams. Sleep.

Weiss, Ellen. *Clara the fortune-telling chicken* ill. by author. Dutton, 1978. ISBN 0-525-61576-8 Subj: Animals – sheep. Birds – chickens. Careers – fortune tellers. Seasons – winter.

For every child, a better world (Gikow, Louise)

Millicent Maybe ill. by author. Watts, 1979. ISBN 0-531-02299-4 Subj: Reptiles – alligators, crocodiles.

Mokey's birthday present ill. by Elizabeth Miles. Holt, 1985. ISBN 0-03-004559-2 Subj: Birthdays. Friendship. Puppets.

Pigs in space ill. by Alastair Graham. Random House, 1983. ISBN 0-394-85730-5 Subj: Animals – pigs. Puppets. Space and space ships.

The pirates of Tarnoonga ed. by Stephanie Spinner; ill. by Bunny Carter. Random House, 1986. ISBN 0-394-87926-0 Subj: Pirates.

Telephone time: a first book of telephone do's and don'ts ill. by Hilary Knight. Random House, 1986. ISBN 0-394-98252-5 Subj: Etiquette. Telephone.

You are the star of a Muppet adventure ill. by Benjamin Alexander. Random House, 1983. ISBN 0-394-85623-6 Subj: Puppets.

Weiss, George (George David). *What a wonderful world* by George David Weiss and Bob Thiele; ill. by Ashley Bryan. Atheneum, 1995. ISBN 0-689-80087-8 Subj: Nature. Poetry. Puppets. Songs.

Weiss, Harvey. *My closet full of hats* ill. by author. Abelard-Schuman, 1962. Subj: Clothing – hats.

The sooner hound: a tale from American folklore ill. by author. Putnam, 1959. Subj: Animals – dogs. Careers – firefighters. Folk and fairy tales.

Weiss, Leatie. *Funny feet!* ill. by Ellen Weiss. Watts, 1978. ISBN 0-531-01348-0 Subj: Anatomy – feet. Birds – penguins. Clothing – shoes.

My teacher sleeps in school ill. by Ellen Weiss. Warne, 1984. ISBN 0-7232-6253-5 Subj: Animals – elephants. Careers – teachers. School.

Weiss, Miriam. *see* Schlein, Miriam

Weiss, Monica. *Mmmm . . . cookies!* ill. by Rosemary Berlin. Troll, 1992. ISBN 0-8167-2486-6 Subj: Counting, numbers. Food. Frogs and toads.

Weiss, Nicki. *Barney is big* ill. by author. Greenwillow, 1988. ISBN 0-688-07587-8 Subj: Behavior – growing up. Family life. School – first day.

Battle day at Camp Delmont ill. by author. Greenwillow, 1985. ISBN 0-688-04307-0 Subj: Camps, camping. Friendship.

Dog boy cap skate ill. by author. Greenwillow, 1989. ISBN 0-688-08276-9 Subj: Animals. Sports – ice skating.

A family story ill. by author. Greenwillow, 1987. ISBN 0-688-06505-8 Subj: Family life – sisters. Friendship.

If you're happy and you know it ill. by author. Greenwillow, 1987. ISBN 0-688-06444-2 Subj: Folk and fairy tales. Music. Songs.

Maude and Sally ill. by author. Greenwillow, 1983. ISBN 0-688-01638-3 Subj: Friendship.

On a hot, hot day ill. by author. Putnam, 1992. ISBN 0-399-22119-0 Subj: Activities. Ethnic groups in the U.S. – Hispanic Americans. Family life – mothers. Seasons.

Princess Pearl ill. by author. Greenwillow, 1986. ISBN 0-688-05895-7 Subj: Family life – sisters. Sibling rivalry.

Sun sand sea sail ill. by author. Greenwillow, 1989. ISBN 0-688-08271-8 Subj: Family life. Rhyming text. Sea and seashore.

Waiting ill. by author. Greenwillow, 1981. ISBN 0-688-00603-5 Subj: Character traits – patience.

Weekend at Muskrat Lake ill. by author. Greenwillow, 1984. ISBN 0-688-03768-2 Subj: Activities – vacationing. Family life.

Where does the brown bear go? ill. by author. Greenwillow, 1989. ISBN 0-688-07863-X Subj: Animals. Bedtime. Night. Sleep. Toys.

Where does the brown bear go? A board book ill. by author. Tupelo, 1998. ISBN 0-688-16388-2 Subj: Animals. Bedtime. Format, unusual – board books. Night. Sleep. Toys.

The world turns round and round ill. by author. Greenwillow, 2000. ISBN 0-688-17214-8 Subj: Clothing. Ethnic groups in the U.S. Rhyming text. World.

Weissmann, Joe. *Hickory dickory duck: a book of very funny rhymes and picture puzzles* (Patterson, Pat)

Weitzman, Elizabeth. *Let's talk about when a parent dies* ill. by author. Rosen, 1996. ISBN 0-8239-2309-6 Subj: Death. Emotions – grief. Family life.

Let's talk about when someone you love has Alzheimer's disease ill. by author. Rosen, 1996. ISBN 0-8239-2306-1 Subj: Family life. Illness – Alzheimer's.

Weitzman, Jacqueline Preiss. *You can't take a balloon into the Metropolitan Museum* ill. by Robin Preiss Glasser. Dial, 1998. ISBN 0-8037-2302-4 Subj: Art. City. Family life – grandmothers. Museums. Toys – balloons. Wordless.

You can't take a balloon into the National Gallery ill. by Robin Preiss Glasser. Dial, 2000. ISBN 0-8037-2303-2 Subj: Art. City. Family life – grandmothers. Museums. Picture puzzles. Toys – balloons. Wordless.

Welber, Robert. *Goodbye, hello* ill. by Cyndy Szekeres. Pantheon, 1974. ISBN 0-394-92770-2 Subj: Animals. Behavior – growing up. Rhyming text.

Song of the seasons ill. by Deborah Kogan Ray. Pantheon, 1973. ISBN 0-394-92413-4 Subj: Seasons.

Welch, Martha McKeen. *Will that wake mother?* photos by author. Dodd, 1982. ISBN 0-396-08090-1 Subj: Animals – cats.

Welch, Willy. *Dancing with Daddy* ill. by Liza Woodruff. Whispering Coyote, 1999. ISBN 1-58089-020-2 Subj: Activities – dancing. Animals. Family life – fathers. Rhyming text. Trees.

Grumpy Bunnies ill. by Tammie Lyon. Charlesbridge, 2000. ISBN 1-58089-053-9 Subj: Animals – rabbits. Rhyming text. School.

Playing right field ill. by Marc Simont. Scholastic, 1995. ISBN 0-590-48298-X Subj: Songs. Sports – baseball.

Weller, Frances Ward. *The angel of Mill Street* ill. by Robert J. Blake. Philomel, 1998. ISBN 0-399-23133-1 Subj: Accidents. Angels. Animals – dogs. Careers – musicians. Ethnic groups in the U.S. – Irish Americans. Holidays – Christmas. Weather – snow.

The closet gorilla ill. by Cat Bowman Smith. Macmillan, 1991. ISBN 0-02-792531-5 Subj: Animals – gorillas. Family life – aunts, uncles. Holidays – Halloween.

Madaket Millie ill. by Marcia Sewall. Philomel, 1997. ISBN 0-399-22785-7 Subj: Character traits – helpfulness. Character traits – perseverance. Sea and seashore. U.S. history.

Matthew Wheelock's wall ill. by Ted Lewin. Macmillan, 1992. ISBN 0-02-792612-5 Subj: Activities – making things. Rocks.

Riptide ill. by Robert J. Blake. Putnam, 1990. ISBN 0-399-21675-8 Subj: Animals – dogs. Sea and seashore.

Wellington, Anne. *Apple pie* ill. by Nita Sowter. Prentice-Hall, 1978. ISBN 0-13-038745-2 Subj: Seasons.

Wellington, Monica. *All my little ducklings* ill. by author. Dutton, 1989. ISBN 0-525-44459-9 Subj: Activities. Birds – ducks.

Baby at home ill. by author. Dutton, 1997. ISBN 0-525-45640-6 Subj: Babies. Format, unusual – board books. Homes, houses.

Baby in a buggy ill. by author. Dutton, 1995. ISBN 0-525-45295-8 Subj: Babies. Format, unusual – board books.

Baby in a car ill. by author. Dutton, 1995. ISBN 0-525-45296-6 Subj: Babies. Format, unusual – board books.

Bunny's first snowflake ill. by author. Dutton, 2000. ISBN 0-525-46464-6 Subj: Animals. Animals – rabbits. Format, unusual – board books. Seasons – winter. Weather – snow.

Bunny's rainbow day ill. by author. Dutton, 1999. ISBN 0-525-46047-0 Subj: Animals. Animals – rabbits. Format, unusual – board books. Weather – rain. Weather – rainbows. Weather – storms.

Mr. Cookie Baker ill. by author. Dutton, 1992. ISBN 0-525-44965-5 Subj: Activities – cooking. Careers – chefs, cooks. Food.

Night city by Monica Wellington, with Andrew Kupfer; ill. by Monica Wellington. Dutton, 1998. ISBN 0-525-45948-0 Subj: Activities. Animals – cats. Animals – mice. City. Night.

Night rabbits ill. by author. Dutton, 1995. ISBN 0-525-45335-0 Subj: Animals – rabbits. Night. Weather – storms.

The sheep follow ill. by author. Dutton, 1992. ISBN 0-525-44837-3 Subj: Animals – dogs. Animals – sheep. Careers – shepherds. Farms.

Squeaking of art, the mice go to the museum ill. by author. Dutton, 2000. ISBN 0-525-46165-5 Subj: Animals – cats. Animals – mice. Art. Museums.

Wells, H. G. (Herbert George). *The adventures of Tommy* ill. by author. Knopf, 1967. Subj: Animals – elephants. Character traits – bravery. Character traits – kindness.

Wells, Joel. *The manger mouse: what she saw and did and got on the very first Christmas* ill. by Annette Boarini Anderson. Thomas More, 1990. ISBN 0-8834-7255-4 Subj: Animals – mice. Holidays – Christmas. Religion – Nativity.

Wells, Rosemary. *Abdul* ill. by author. Dial, 1986. ISBN 0-8037-4462-5 Subj: Animals – camels. Animals – horses, ponies. Character traits – being different.

The bear went over the mountain ill. by author. Scholastic, 1998. ISBN 0-590-02910-X Subj: Animals – bears. Mountains. Songs.

Bingo ill. by author. Scholastic, 1999. ISBN 0-590-02913-4 Subj: Animals – dogs. Format, unusual – board books. Music. Songs.

Bunny cakes ill. by author. Dial, 1997. ISBN 0-8037-2144-7 Subj: Activities – cooking. Animals – rabbits. Family life – brothers and sisters. Family life – grandmothers.

Bunny money ill. by author. HarperCollins, 1997. ISBN 0-06-027258-9 Subj: Animals – rabbits. Family life – brothers and sisters. Family life – grandmothers. Money.

Don't spill it again, James ill. by author. Dial, 1990. ISBN 0-8037-2118-8 Subj: Animals – foxes. Rhyming text. Trains. Weather – rain.

Emily's first 100 days of school ill. by author. Hyperion, 2000. ISBN 0-7868-2443-3 Subj: Animals – rabbits. Counting, numbers. School – first day.

First tomato ill. by author. Dial, 1992. ISBN 0-8037-1175-1 Subj: Animals – rabbits. Gardens, gardening. Rhyming text. School.

The fisherman and his wife (Grimm, Jacob)

Forest of dreams by Rosemary Wells and Susan Jeffers; ill. by Susan Jeffers. Dial, 1988. ISBN 0-8037-0570-0 Subj: Nature. Seasons – spring. Seasons – winter.

Fritz and the mess fairy ill. by author. Dial, 1991. ISBN 0-8037-0983-8 Subj: Animals – skunks. Behavior – misbehavior. Character traits – cleanliness. Fairies.

Good night, Fred ill. by author. Dial, 1981. ISBN 0-8037-2992-8 Subj: Behavior – misbehavior. Imagination. Sibling rivalry.

Goodnight Max ill. by author. Viking, 2000. ISBN 0-670-88707-2 Subj: Bedtime. Family life – brothers and sisters. Format, unusual – toy and movable books.

Hazel's amazing mother ill. by author. Dial, 1985. ISBN 0-8037-0210-8 Subj: Animals. Animals – badgers. Behavior – misbehavior. Family life – mothers.

Hooray for Max ill. by author. Dial, 1986. ISBN 0-8037-0202-7 Subj: Animals – rabbits. Format, unusual – board books.

The island light ill. by author. Dial, 1992. ISBN 0-8037-1178-6 Subj: Animals – rabbits. Family life – fathers. Illness. Lighthouses.

The itsy-bitsy spider ill. by author. Scholastic, 1998. ISBN 0-590-02911-8 Subj: Birds – ducks. Format, unusual – board books. Songs. Spiders.

The language of doves ill. by Greg Shed. Dial, 1996. ISBN 0-8037-1471-8 Subj: Birds – doves. Birds – pigeons. Death. Family life – grandfathers. War.

A lion for Lewis ill. by author. Dial, 1982. ISBN 0-8037-4686-5 Subj: Activities – playing. Imagination.

The little lame prince ill. by author. Dial, 1990. ISBN 0-8037-0789-4 Subj: Animals – pigs. Behavior – greed. Folk and fairy tales. Handicaps – physical handicaps. Royalty – princes.

Lucy comes to stay ill. by Mark Graham. Dial, 1994. ISBN 0-8037-1214-6 Subj: Animals – dogs. Pets.

McDuff and the baby ill. by Susan Jeffers. Hyperion, 1997. ISBN 0-7868-2258-9 Subj: Animals – dogs. Babies. Family life.

McDuff comes home ill. by Susan Jeffers. Hyperion, 1997. ISBN 0-7868-2259-7 Subj: Animals – dogs. Behavior – lost.

McDuff moves in ill. by Susan Jeffers. Hyperion, 1997. ISBN 0-7868-2257-0 Subj: Animals – dogs. Behavior – needing someone.

McDuff's new friend ill. by Susan Jeffers. Hyperion, 1998. ISBN 0-7868-2337-2 Subj: Animals – dogs. Holidays – Christmas. Santa Claus.

Max and Ruby's Midas ill. by author. Dial, 1995. ISBN 0-8037-1783-0 Subj: Animals – rabbits. Behavior – greed. Family life – brothers and sisters. Food.

Max cleans up ill. by author. Viking, 2000. ISBN 0-670-89218-1 Subj: Animals – rabbits. Babies. Character traits – cleanliness. Family life – brothers and sisters.

Max's bath ill. by author. Dial, 1985. ISBN 0-8037-0162-4 Subj: Activities – bathing. Animals – rabbits. Format, unusual – board books.

Max's bedtime ill. by author. Dial, 1985. ISBN 0-8037-0160-8 Subj: Animals – rabbits. Bedtime. Format, unusual – board books. Sibling rivalry. Toys.

Max's birthday ill. by author. Dial, 1985. ISBN 0-8037-0163-2 Subj: Animals – rabbits. Birthdays. Format, unusual – board books. Toys.

Max's breakfast ill. by author. Dial, 1998. ISBN 0-8037-2273-7 Subj: Animals – rabbits. Character traits – patience. Format, unusual – board books. Sibling rivalry.

Max's chocolate chicken ill. by author. Dial, 1999. ISBN 0-8037-2351-2 Subj: Animals – rabbits. Holidays – Easter. Seasons – spring. Sibling rivalry.

Max's Christmas ill. by author. Dial, 1986. ISBN 0-8037-0290-6 Subj: Animals – rabbits. Holidays – Christmas. Santa Claus.

Max's dragon shirt ill. by author. Dial, 1991. ISBN 0-8037-0945-5 Subj: Activities – babysitting. Animals – rabbits. Behavior – lost. Clothing. Family life – brothers and sisters. Stores.

Max's first word ill. by author. Dial, 1979. ISBN 0-8037-6066-3 Subj: Animals – rabbits. Format, unusual – board books. Language.

Max's new suit ill. by author. Dial, 1979. ISBN 0-8037-6065-5 Subj: Animals – rabbits. Clothing. Format, unusual – board books.

Max's ride ill. by author. Dial, 1979. ISBN 0-8037-6069-8 Subj: Animals – rabbits. Format, unusual – board books. Language.

Max's toys: a counting book ill. by author. Dial, 1979. ISBN 0-8037-6068-X Subj: Animals – rabbits. Counting, numbers. Format, unusual – board books. Toys.

Morris's disappearing bag ill. by author. Viking, 1999. ISBN 0-670-88721-8 Subj: Animals – rabbits. Gifts. Holidays – Christmas.

Moss pillows ill. by author. Dial, 1992. ISBN 0-8037-1177-8 Subj: Animals – rabbits. Family life. Forest, woods. Rhyming text.

Night sounds, morning colors ill. by David McPhail. Dial, 1994. ISBN 0-8037-1302-9 Subj: Activities. Family life. Seasons. Senses.

Noisy Nora ill. by author. Dial, 1997. ISBN 0-8037-1835-7 Subj: Animals – mice. Behavior – needing someone. Rhyming text.

Old MacDonald (Old MacDonald had a farm)

Peabody ill. by author. Dial, 1983. ISBN 0-8037-0005-9 Subj: Sibling rivalry. Toys – dolls.

Read to your bunny ill. by author. Scholastic, 1998. ISBN 0-590-30284-1 Subj: Activities – reading. Animals – rabbits. Rhyming text.

Shy Charles ill. by author. Dial, 1988. ISBN 0-8037-0564-6 Subj: Activities – babysitting. Animals – mice. Character traits – individuality. Family life. Rhyming text.

Stanley and Rhoda ill. by author. Dial, 1978. ISBN 0-8037-8249-7 Subj: Activities – babysitting. Animals – mice. Sibling rivalry.

Timothy goes to school ill. by author. Dial, 1981. ISBN 0-8037-8949-1 Subj: Animals – raccoons. Behavior – growing up. School – first day.

Unfortunately Harriet ill. by author. Dial, 1972. ISBN 0-8037-9169-0 Subj: Behavior – bad day.

Yoko ill. by author. Hyperion, 1998. ISBN 0-7868-2345-3 Subj: Animals – cats. Animals – raccoons. Food. Prejudice. School.

Wells, Ruth. *The farmer and the poor god* ill. by Yoshi. Simon & Schuster, 1996. ISBN 0-689-80214-5 Subj: Character traits – laziness. Clothing – shoes. Folk and fairy tales. Foreign lands – Japan. Poverty.

Wells, Tony. *Allsorts* ill. by author. Macmillan, 1988. ISBN 0-689-71185-9 Subj: Concepts – color. Concepts – shape. Games.

Puzzle doubles ill. by author. Macmillan, 1988. ISBN 0-689-71186-7 Subj: Concepts – color. Concepts – size. Games.

Wen, George. *The little Christmas soldier* (Dedieu, Thierry)

Uglypuss (Gregoire, Caroline)

Wende, Philip. *Bird boy* ill. by author. Cowles, 1970. ISBN 0-40-214201-2 Subj: Activities – flying. Dreams.

Weninger, Brigitte. *The elf's hat* ill. by John A. Rowe; trans. by J. Alison James. North-South, 2000. ISBN 0-7358-1255-1 Subj: Animals. Clothing – hats. Cumulative tales. Fairies. Insects – fleas. Rhyming text.

Good-bye, daddy! ill. by Alan Marks. North-South, 1995. ISBN 1-55858-383-1 Subj: Divorce. Emotions. Family life – fathers. Toys – bears.

Happy birthday, Davy ill. by Eve Tharlet; trans. by Rosemary Lanning. North-South, 2000. ISBN 0-7358-1346-9 Subj: Animals – rabbits. Birthdays. Parties.

A Letter to Santa Claus ill. by Anne Möller. North-South, 2000. ISBN 0-7358-1360-4 Subj: Holidays – Christmas. Letters, cards. Santa Claus.

Lumina: a story for the dark time of the year ill. by Julie Wintz-Litty; trans. by Anthea Bell. North-South, 1997. ISBN 1-55858-791-8 Subj: Holidays – Christmas. Homeless. Lights. Orphans.

Merry Christmas, Davy! ill. by Eve Tharlet; trans. by Rosemary Lanning. North-South, 1998. ISBN 1-55858-981-3 Subj: Animals. Animals – rabbits. Behavior – sharing. Holidays – Christmas.

What's the matter, Davy? trans. by Rosemary Lanning; ill. by Eve Tharlet. North-South, 1998. ISBN 1-55858-900-7 Subj: Animals – rabbits. Behavior – losing things. Toys.

Why are you fighting, Davy? ill. by Eve Tharlet; trans. by Rosemary Lanning. North-South, 1999. ISBN 0-7358-1074-5 Subj: Animals – rabbits. Behavior – fighting, arguing. Character traits – individuality. Friendship.

Will you mind the baby, Davy? ill. by Eve Tharlet; trans. by Rosemary Lanning. North-South, 1997. ISBN 1-55858-732-2 Subj: Activities – babysitting. Animals – rabbits. Babies. Family life – new sibling.

Wenning, Elisabeth. *The Christmas mouse* ill. by Barbara Remington. Holt, [1983] 1959. ISBN 0-03-015066-3 Subj: Animals – mice. Foreign lands – Austria. Holidays – Christmas. Music. Songs.

Werner, Jane. *see* Watson, Jane Werner

Wersba, Barbara. *Amanda dreaming* ill. by Mercer Mayer. Atheneum, 1973. ISBN 0-689-30073-5 Subj: Dreams. Sleep.

Do tigers ever bite kings? ill. by Mario Rivoli. Atheneum, 1966. Subj: Animals – tigers. Character traits – kindness to animals. Poetry. Royalty – kings.

West, Colin. *Go tell it to the toucan* ill. by author. Bantam, 1990. ISBN 0-553-05889-4 Subj: Animals. Birthdays. Cumulative tales. Parties.

Have you seen the crocodile? ill. by author. Lippincott, 1986. ISBN 0-397-32172-4 Subj: Birds. Cumulative tales. Reptiles – alligators, crocodiles.

I brought my love a tabby cat ill. by Caroline Anstey. Chronicle, 1988. ISBN 0-87701-518-X Subj: Animals. Careers – tailors. Clothing. Weddings.

The king of Kennelwick castle ill. by Anne Dalton. Lippincott, 1987. ISBN 0-397-32197-X Subj: Cumulative tales. Royalty – kings.

The king's toothache ill. by Anne Dalton. Lippincott, 1988. ISBN 0-397-32252-6 Subj: Cumulative tales. Illness. Rhyming text. Royalty – kings. Teeth.

A moment in rhyme ill. by Julie Banyard. Dial, 1987. ISBN 0-8037-0259-0 Subj: Poetry.

One day in the jungle ill. by author. Candlewick, 1995. ISBN 1-56402-646-9 Subj: Animals. Cumulative tales. Jungle. Noise, sounds.

"Only joking!" laughed the lobster ill. by author. Candlewick, 1995. ISBN 1-56402-647-7 Subj: Crustaceans. Fish – sharks.

"Pardon?" said the giraffe ill. by author. Lippincott, 1986. ISBN 0-397-32173-2 Subj: Animals. Character traits – persistence. Frogs and toads.

West, Emily. *see* Payne, Emmy

West, Ian. *Silas, the first pig to fly* ill. by author. Grosset, 1977. ISBN 0-448-14288-0 Subj: Activities – flying. Animals – pigs.

West, James. *see* Withers, Carl

West, Judy. *Have you got my purr?* ill. by Tim Warnes. Dutton, 2000. ISBN 0-525-46390-9 Subj: Animals. Animals – cats. Behavior – losing things. Noise, sounds.

West, Keith. *Little Pig's special day* ill. by author. Putnam, 1991. ISBN 0-399-22209-X Subj: Animals – pigs. Babies. Family life – new sibling.

West, Kipling. *A rattle of bones: a Halloween book of collective nouns* ill. by author. Orchard, 1999. ISBN 0-531-33196-2 Subj: Holidays – Halloween. Language. Rhyming text.

Westcott, Nadine Bernard. *Getting up* ill. by author. Little, 1987. ISBN 0-316-93131-4 Subj: Family life. Morning.

The giant vegetable garden ill. by author. Little, 1981. ISBN 0-316-93129-2 Subj: Activities – picnicking. Gardens, gardening.

Going to bed ill. by author. Little, 1987. ISBN 0-316-93132-2 Subj: Bedtime. Family life. Night. Toys.

I know an old lady who swallowed a fly (Little old lady who swallowed a fly)

The lady with the alligator purse ill. by author. Little, 1988. ISBN 0-316-93135-7 Subj: Games. Humor. Poetry.

Peanut butter and jelly: a play rhyme ill. by author. Dutton, 1987. ISBN 0-525-44317-7 Subj: Animals – elephants. Careers – bakers. Family life. Food. Rhyming text.

Skip to my Lou ill. by adapt. Little, 1989. ISBN 0-316-93137-3 Subj: Farms. Folk and fairy tales. Music. Songs.

There's a hole in the bucket ill. by adapt. Harper-Collins, 1990. ISBN 0-06-026423-3 Subj: Animals. Farms. Music. Songs.

Westell, Kerry. *Amanda's book* ill. by Ruth Ohi. Firefly, 1991. ISBN 1-55037-185-1 Subj: Animals – cats. Behavior – collecting things. Imagination.

Westerberg, Christine. *The cap that mother made* ill. by adapt. Prentice-Hall, 1977. ISBN 0-13-113365-9

Subj: Clothing – hats. Folk and fairy tales. Foreign lands – Sweden.

Westman, Barbara. *Dancing dogs: Charlotte and Emilio at the circus* ill. by author. HarperCollins, 1991. ISBN 0-06-022460-6 Subj: Activities – dancing. Animals – dogs. Circus.

The day before Christmas: a story of Charlotte and Emilio ill. by author. HarperCollins, 1990. ISBN 0-06-026429-2 Subj: Animals – dogs. Holidays – Christmas.

Weston, Martha. *Bad baby brother* ill. by author. Clarion, 1997. ISBN 0-395-72103-2 Subj: Babies. Emotions. Family life – new sibling.

Bea's four bears ill. by author. Houghton Mifflin, 1992. ISBN 0-395-57791-8 Subj: Activities – picnicking. Behavior – sharing. Counting, numbers. Toys – bears.

Peony's rainbow ill. by author. Lothrop, 1981. ISBN 0-688-00541-1 Subj: Animals – pigs. Weather – rainbows.

Space guys! ill. by author. Holiday, 2000. ISBN 0-8234-1487-6 Subj: Aliens. Night. Rhyming text. Space and space ships.

Tuck in the pool ill. by author. Clarion, 1995. ISBN 0-395-65479-3 Subj: Animals – pigs. Emotions – fear. Sports – swimming.

Westwood, Jennifer. *Going to Squintum's: a foxy folktale* ill. by Fiona French. Dial, 1985. ISBN 0-8037-0015-6 Subj: Animals – foxes. Character traits – cleverness. Folk and fairy tales.

The Star Child (Wilde, Oscar)

Wethered, Peggy. *Touchdown Mars! an ABC adventure* by Peggy Wethered and Ken Edgett; ill. by Michael Chesworth. Putnam, 2000. ISBN 0-399-23214-1 Subj: ABC books. Animals – cats. Planets. Space and space ships.

Wetterer, Margaret. *Kate Shelley and the midnight express* ill. by Karen Ritz. Carolrhoda, 1990. ISBN 0-87614-425-3 Subj: Character traits – bravery. Trains. U.S. history.

Patrick and the fairy thief ill. by Enrico Arno. Atheneum, 1980. ISBN 0-689-50160-0 Subj: Character traits – cleverness. Fairies. Family life – mothers.

Wettlin, Margaret. *In the van* (Marshak, S. [Samuil])

Wexler, Jerome (LeRoy). *Find the hidden insect* (Cole, Joanna)

Flowers, fruits, seeds photos by author. Prentice-Hall, 1988. ISBN 0-13-322397-3 Subj: Plants. Science.

Wonderful pussy willows photos by author. Dutton, 1992. ISBN 0-525-44867-5 Subj: Plants. Science.

Wezel, Peter. *The good bird* ill. by author. HarperCollins, 1964. Subj: Behavior – sharing. Birds. Fish. Wordless.

The naughty bird ill. by author. Follett, 1967. Translation of Der freche Vogel Figaro. Subj: Animals – cats. Birds. Wordless.

Whales created by Gallimard Jeunesse, Ute Fuhr and Raoul Sautai; ill. by Ute Fuhr and Raoul Sautai. Scholastic, 1993. ISBN 0-590-47130-9 Subj: Animals – whales. Format, unusual – toy and movable books.

Wharton, Thomas. *Hildegard sings* ill. by author. Farrar, 1991. ISBN 0-374-33242-8 Subj: Animals – hippopotamuses. Emotions – fear. Theater.

What a morning! *the Christmas story in Black spirituals* sel. and ed. by John M. Langstaff; ill. by Ashley Bryan; musical arrangements by John Andrew Ross. Margaret K. McElderry, 1987. ISBN 0-689-50422-5 Subj: Holidays – Christmas. Music. Religion. Songs.

What do babies do? ill. with photos. Random House, 1985. ISBN 0-394-87279-7 Subj: Babies. Format, unusual – board books.

What do toddlers do? ill. with photos. Random House, 1985. ISBN 0-394-87280-0 Subj: Babies. Format, unusual – board books.

What do you feed your donkey on? *rhymes from a Belfast childhood* col. by Colette O'Hare; ill. by Jenny Rodwell. Collins-World, 1978. ISBN 0-00183-734-6 Subj: Foreign lands – Ireland. Nursery rhymes.

What we do ill. by Roser Capdevila. Firefly, 1986. ISBN 0-920303-46-3 Subj: Activities.

Whatley, Bruce. *Captain Pajamas* by Bruce Whatley and Rosie Smith; ill. by Bruce Whatley. HarperCollins, 1999. ISBN 0-06-026614-7 Subj: Aliens. Animals – dogs. Imagination. Night. Sleep.

That magnetic dog ill. by author. HarperCollins, 1999. ISBN 0-207-18420-8 Subj: Animals – dogs. Pets. Rhyming text.

Wheeler, Cindy. *Marmalade's Christmas present* ill. by author. Knopf, 1984. ISBN 0-394-96794-1 Subj: Animals – cats. Holidays – Christmas.

Marmalade's nap ill. by author. Knopf, 1983. ISBN 0-394-95022-4 Subj: Animals – cats. Noise, sounds. Sleep.

Marmalade's picnic ill. by author. Knopf, 1983. ISBN 0-394-95023-2 Subj: Activities – picnicking. Animals – cats.

Marmalade's snowy day ill. by author. Knopf, 1982. ISBN 0-394-95025-9 Subj: Animals – cats. Weather – snow.

Marmalade's yellow leaf ill. by author. Knopf, 1982. ISBN 0-394-95024-0 Subj: Animals – cats. Seasons – fall.

More simple signs ill. by author. Viking, 1998. ISBN 0-670-87477-9 Subj: Communication. Handicaps – blindness. Language.

Rose ill. by author. Knopf, 1985. ISBN 0-394-96233-8 Subj: Animals – pigs. Farms.

Simple signs ill. by author. Viking, 1995. ISBN 0-670-86282-7 Subj: Communication. Handicaps – deafness. Language.

Wheeler, M. J. (Mary Jane). *First came the Indians* ill. by James Houston. Atheneum, 1983. ISBN 0-689-50258-3 Subj: Indians of North America.

Wheeler, Opal. *Sing in praise: a collection of the best loved hymns* ill. by Marjorie Torrey. Dutton, 1946. Subj: Caldecott award honor books. Music. Religion. Songs.

Sing Mother Goose ill. by Marjorie Torrey; music by Opal Wheeler. Dutton, 1945. Subj: Caldecott award honor books. Music. Nursery rhymes. Songs.

Wheeler, William A. (Adolphus). *Mother Goose's melodies: or, songs for the nursery* (Mother Goose)

Wheeling, Lynn. *When you fly* ill. by author. Little, 1967. Subj: Activities – flying. Airplanes, airports. Poetry.

Whelan, Gloria. *Bringing the farmhouse home* ill. by Jada Rowland. Simon & Schuster, 1992. ISBN 0-671-74984-6 Subj: Death. Family life. Family life – grandmothers. Quilts.

A week of raccoons ill. by Lynn Munsinger. Knopf, 1988. ISBN 0-394-98396-3 Subj: Animals – raccoons.

Whippo, Walt. *Little white duck* lyrics by Walt Whippo; music by Bernard Zaritzky; ill. by Joan Paley. Little, 2000. ISBN 0-316-03227-1 Subj: Animals. Birds – ducks. Music. Songs. Theater.

Whishaw, Iona. *Henry and the cow problem* ill. by Chum McLeod. Firefly, 1992. ISBN 1-55037-375-7 Subj: Animals – bulls, cows. Bedtime. Emotions – fear.

Whitcher, Susan. *The key to the cupboard* ill. by Andrew Glass. Farrar, 1997. ISBN 0-374-34127-3 Subj: Imagination. Magic. Witches. Wizards.

Something for everyone ill. by Barbara Lehman. Farrar, 1995. ISBN 0-374-37138-5 Subj: Activities – traveling. Family life – aunts, uncles. Friendship. Moving.

Whitcomb, Mary E. *Odd Velvet* ill. by Tara Calahan King. Chronicle, 1998. ISBN 0-8118-2004-1 Subj: Character traits – being different. School.

White, Carolyn. *Whuppity Stoorie* ill. by S. D. Schindler. Putnam, 1997. ISBN 0-399-22903-5 Subj: Animals – pigs. Folk and fairy tales. Foreign lands – Scotland. Names. Witches.

White Deer of Autumn. *The great change* ill. by Carol Grigg. Beyond Words, 1992. ISBN 0-941831-79-5 Subj: Death. Family life – grandfathers. Indians of North America.

White, Florence Meiman. *How to lose your lunch money* ill. by Chris Jenkyns. Ritchie, 1970. Subj: Behavior – losing things. Behavior – misbehavior. School.

White, Kathryn (Kathryn Ivy). *When they fight* ill. by Cliff Wright. Winslow, 2000. ISBN 1-890817-46-5 Subj: Behavior – fighting, arguing. Family life.

White, Linda Arms. *Comes a wind* ill. by Tom Curry. DK, 2000. ISBN 0-7894-2601-3 Subj: Birthdays. Contests. Family life – brothers. Family life – mothers. Tall tales. Weather – wind.

Too many pumpkins ill. by Megan Lloyd. Holiday, 1996. ISBN 0-8234-1245-8 Subj: Behavior – dissatisfaction. Food. Friendship.

White, Paul. *Janet at school* photos by Jeremy Finlay. Crowell, 1978. ISBN 0-381-99557-7 Subj: Handicaps. School.

Whiteley, Opal Stanley. *Only Opal: the diary of a young girl* by Opal Whiteley; sel. and adapt. by Jane Boulton; ill. by Barbara Cooney. Philomel, 1994. An adapt. of: The story of Opal. ISBN 0-399-21990-0 Subj: Family life. Poetry. U.S. history – frontier and pioneer life.

Whiteside, Karen. *Lullaby of the wind* ill. by Kazue Mizumura. HarperCollins, 1984. ISBN 0-06-026412-8 Subj: Bedtime. Lullabies. Sleep. Weather – wind.

Whitethorne, Baje. *Sunpainters* ill. by author. Northland, 1994. ISBN 0-87358-587-9 Subj: Folk and fairy tales. Indians of North America – Navajo. Sun.

Whitfield, Susan. *The animals of the Chinese zodiac* ill. by Philippa-Alys Browne. Crocodile Books, 1998. ISBN 1-56656-236-8 Subj: Animals. Foreign lands – China.

Whitlock, Susan Love. *Donovan scares the monsters* ill. by Yossi Abolafia. Greenwillow, 1987. ISBN 0-688-06439-6 Subj: Family life – grandmothers. Monsters.

Whitman, Candace. *The night is like an animal* ill. by author. Farrar, 1995. ISBN 0-374-35521-5 Subj: Bedtime. Night. Rhyming text.

Now it is morning ill. by author. Farrar, 1999. ISBN 0-374-35527-4 Subj: Morning.

Whitmore, Adam. *Max in America* ill. by Janice Poltrick Donato. Silver Burdett, 1986. ISBN 0-382-09244-9 Subj: Animals – cats. Character traits – being different.

Max in Australia ill. by Janice Poltrick Donato. Silver Burdett, 1986. ISBN 0-382-09246-5 Subj: Animals – cats. Character traits – being different. Foreign lands – Australia.

Max in India ill. by Janice Poltrick Donato. Silver Burdett, 1986. ISBN 0-382-09245-7 Subj: Animals – cats. Character traits – being different. Foreign lands – India.

Max leaves home ill. by Janice Poltrick Donato. Silver Burdett, 1986. ISBN 0-382-09243-0 Subj: Animals – cats. Behavior – running away. Character traits – being different.

Whitney, Alex. *Once a bright red tiger* ill. by Charles Robinson. Walck, 1973. ISBN 0-8098-1212-6 Subj: Animals – tigers. Character traits – pride.

Whitney, Alma Marshak. *Just awful* ill. by Lillian Hoban. Addison-Wesley, 1971. ISBN 0-20-108625-5 Subj: Careers – nurses. Illness. School.

Leave Herbert alone ill. by David McPhail. Addison-Wesley, 1972. ISBN 0-201-08623-9 Subj: Animals – cats. Character traits – kindness to animals.

Whitney, Dorothy B. *Creatures of an exceptional kind* ill. by author. Humanics, 1989. ISBN 0-89334-127-4 Subj: Animals. Character traits – individuality. Handicaps.

Whitney, Thomas P. *The Month-Brothers: a Slavic tale* (Marshak, S. [Samuil])

Whittier, John Greenleaf. *Barbara Frietchie* ill. by Paul Galdone. Crowell, 1965. ISBN 0-690-11532-6 Subj: Character traits – loyalty. U.S. history. War.

Whittington, Mary K. *Carmina, come dance!* ill. by Michael McDermott. Macmillan, 1989. ISBN 0-689-31554-6 Subj: Activities – dancing. Family life – great-grandparents. Imagination. Music.

The patchwork lady ill. by Jane Dyer. Harcourt, 1991. ISBN 0-15-259580-5 Subj: Birthdays. Quilts.

Winter's child ill. by Sue Ellen Brown. Atheneum, 1992. ISBN 0-689-31685-2 Subj: Seasons – spring. Seasons – winter.

Whittle, Emily. *Sailor cats* ill. by Jeri Burdick. Green Tiger Pr., 1993. ISBN 0-671-79933-9 Subj: Animals – cats. Sailors. Sea and seashore. Sports – sailing.

Whybrow, Ian. *A baby for Grace* ill. by Christian Birmingham. Kingfisher, 1998. ISBN 0-7534-5142-5 Subj: Babies. Family life – new sibling. Family life – sisters.

Harry and the snow king ill. by Adrian Reynolds. Levinson Books, 1997. ISBN 1-899607-85-4 Subj: Family life. Seasons – winter. Snowmen. Weather – snow.

Parcel for Stanley ill. by Sally Hobson. Levinson Books, 1997. ISBN 1-899607-53-6 Subj: Animals. Animals – bulls, cows. Animals – cats. Animals – rabbits. Birds – ducks. Magic. Rhyming text.

Quacky quack-quack! ill. by Russell Ayto. Four Winds, 1991. ISBN 0-02-792741-5 Subj: Animals. Circular tales. Noise, sounds. Rhyming text.

Sammy and the dinosaurs ill. by Adrian Reynolds. Orchard, 1999. ISBN 0-531-30207-5 Subj: Behavior – losing things. Dinosaurs. Imagination.

Wick, Walter. *I spy Christmas: a book of picture riddles* by Walter Wick and Jean Marzollo; photos by Walter Wick. Scholastic, 1992. ISBN 0-590-45846-9

Subj: Holidays – Christmas. Picture puzzles. Rhyming text. Riddles.

I spy extreme challenger: a book of picture riddles by Walter Wick and Jean Marzollo; photos by Walter Wick. Scholastic, 2000. ISBN 0-439-19900-X Subj: Picture puzzles. Rhyming text. Riddles.

I spy fantasy: a book of picture riddles by Walter Wick and Jean Marzollo; photos by Walter Wick. Scholastic, 1994. ISBN 0-590-46295-4 Subj: Imagination. Picture puzzles. Rhyming text. Riddles.

I spy gold challenger! a book of picture riddles by Walter Wick and Jean Marzollo; photos by Walter Wick. Scholastic, 1998. ISBN 0-590-04296-3 Subj: Picture puzzles. Rhyming text. Riddles.

I spy school days photos by Walter Wick; riddles by Jean Marzollo. Scholastic, 1995. ISBN 0-590-48135-5 Subj: Picture puzzles. Rhyming text. Riddles. School.

I spy spooky night: a book of picture riddles by Walter Wick and Jean Marzollo; photos by Walter Wick. Scholastic, 1996. ISBN 0-590-48137-1 Subj: Ghosts. Holidays – Halloween. Picture puzzles. Rhyming text. Riddles.

I spy super challenger! by Walter Wick and Jean Marzollo; photos by Walter Wick. Scholastic, 1997. ISBN 0-590-34128-6 Subj: Picture puzzles. Rhyming text. Riddles.

I spy treasure hunt by Walter Wick and Jean Marzollo; photos by Walter Wick. Scholastic, 1999. ISBN 0-439-04244-5 Subj: Mystery stories. Picture puzzles. Pirates. Rhyming text. Riddles.

Wickings, Ruth. *The story of the Nativity* (McCaughrean, Geraldine)

Wickstrom, Sylvie (Sylvie Kantrovitz). *Mothers can't get sick* ill. by author. Crown, 1989. ISBN 0-517-57181-1 Subj: Birthdays. Family life. Family life – mothers. Illness.

Turkey on the loose! ill. by author. Dial, 1990. ISBN 0-8037-0820-3 Subj: Birds – turkeys.

Widdecombe Fair: *an old English folk song* ill. by Christine Price. Warne, 1968. Subj: Fairs. Folk and fairy tales. Foreign lands – England. Music. Songs.

Widerberg, Siv. *The boy and the dog* trans. from Swedish by Richard E. Fisher; ill. by Jens Ahlbom. Farrar, 1991. ISBN 91-29-59926-1 Subj: Animals – dogs. Emotions – fear.

Widman, Christine. *Housekeeper of the wind* ill. by Lisa Desimini. HarperCollins, 1990. ISBN 0-06-026468-3 Subj: Behavior – fighting, arguing. Careers – housekeepers. Emotions – anger. Weather – wind.

The star grazers ill. by Robin Spowart. HarperCollins, 1989. ISBN 0-06-026473-X Subj: Animals – sheep. Stars.

Wiencirz, Gerlinde. *Peter and the wolf* (Prokofiev, Sergei Sergeievitch)

Wiener, Lori. *Be a friend: children who live with HIV speak* art and writing comp. by Lori Weiner and others. Albert Whitman, 1994. ISBN 0-8075-0590-0 Subj: Children as authors. Children as illustrators. Illness – AIDS.

Wiese, Kurt. *The cunning turtle* ill. by author. Viking, 1956. Subj: Reptiles – turtles, tortoises.

The dog, the fox and the fleas ill. by author. McKay, 1953. Subj: Animals – dogs. Animals – foxes. Insects – fleas.

Fish in the air ill. by author. Viking, 1948. Subj: Caldecott award honor books. Foreign lands – China. Humor. Kites.

The five Chinese brothers (Bishop, Claire Huchet)

Happy Easter ill. by author. Viking, 1952. Subj: Animals – rabbits. Holidays – Easter.

The story about Ping (Flack, Marjorie)

You can write Chinese ill. by author. Viking, 1945. Subj: Caldecott award honor books. Foreign languages.

Wiesmüller, Dieter. *The adventures of Marco and Polo* ill. by author; trans. from German by Beate Peter. Walker, 2000. ISBN 0-8027-8729-0 Subj: Activities – traveling. Animals – monkeys. Birds – penguins.

Wiesner, David. *Free fall* ill. by author. Lothrop, 1988. ISBN 0-688-05584-2 Subj: Activities – reading. Bedtime. Caldecott award honor books. Dragons. Dreams. Wordless.

Hurricane ill. by author. Houghton Mifflin, 1990. ISBN 0-395-54382-7 Subj: Family life – brothers and sisters. Imagination. Weather – storms.

The loathsome dragon by David Wiesner and Kim Kahng; ill. by David Wiesner. Putnam, 1987. ISBN 0-399-21407-0 Subj: Dragons. Folk and fairy tales. Magic. Royalty.

Sector 7 ill. by author. Clarion, 1999. ISBN 0-395-74656-6 Subj: Caldecott award honor books. School. Weather – clouds. Wordless.

Tuesday ill. by author. Houghton Mifflin, 1991. ISBN 0-395-55113-7 Subj: Activities – flying. Caldecott award books. Frogs and toads. Magic. Night.

Wiesner, William. *Happy-Go-Lucky: a Norwegian tale* ill. by author. Seabury Pr., 1970. Subj: Character traits – optimism. Cumulative tales. Farms. Foreign lands – Norway. Humor.

Noah's ark ill. by author. Dutton, 1966. Subj: Animals. Boats, ships. Religion – Noah. Weather – floods. Weather – rain.

Tops ill. by author. Viking, 1969. ISBN 0-670-72089-5 Subj: Friendship. Giants. Violence, nonviolence.

The Tower of Babel ill. by author. Viking, 1968. Based on the book of Genesis and on commentaries . . . in the book Hebrew myths by Robert Graves and Raphael Patai. Subj: Language. Religion.

Turnabout: a Norwegian tale ill. by author. Seabury Pr., 1972. This text has been adapted from the version of Edouard Laboulaye. ISBN 0-8164-3083-7 Subj: Behavior – dissatisfaction. Foreign lands – Norway. Humor.

Wijngaard, Juan. *Bear* ill. by author. Crown, 1991. ISBN 0-517-58201-5 Subj: Animals – bears. Format, unusual – board books.

Cat ill. by author. Crown, 1991. ISBN 0-517-58202-3 Subj: Animals – cats. Format, unusual – board books.

Dog ill. by author. Crown, 1991. ISBN 0-517-58203-1 Subj: Animals – dogs. Format, unusual – board books.

Duck ill. by author. Crown, 1991. ISBN 0-517-58204-X Subj: Birds – ducks. Format, unusual – board books.

The Nativity ill. by author. Candlewick, 1996. ISBN 1-56402-981-6 Subj: Holidays – Christmas. Religion – Nativity.

Wikland, Ilon. *Christmas in noisy village* (Lindgren, Astrid)

Wikler, Linda. *see* Berkowitz, Linda

Wikler, Madeline. *All about Hanukkah* (Groner, Judyth Saypol)

All about Sukkot (Groner, Judyth Saypol)

Let's build a Sukkah by Madeline Wikler and Judyth Groner; ill. by Katherine Janus Kahn. Kar-Ben Copies, 1986. ISBN 0-930494-58-X Subj: Format, unusual – board books. Holidays. Jewish culture.

My first seder by Madeline Wikler and Judyth Groner; ill. by Katherine Janus Kahn. Kar-Ben Copies, 1986. ISBN 0-930494-61-X Subj: Food. Format, unusual – board books. Holidays – Passover. Jewish culture.

My very own Jewish community (Groner, Judyth Saypol)

The Purim parade by Madeline Wikler and Judyth Groner; ill. by Katherine Janus Kahn. Kar-Ben Copies, 1986. ISBN 0-930494-60-1 Subj: Format, unusual – board books. Holidays – Purim. Jewish culture.

Thank you, God! a Jewish child's book of prayers (Groner, Judyth Saypol)

Where is the Afikomen? (Groner, Judyth Saypol)

Wilbur, Richard. *The disappearing alphabet* ill. by David Diaz. Harcourt, 1998. ISBN 0-15-201470-5 Subj: ABC books. Poetry.

Runaway opposites ill. by Henrik Drescher. Harcourt, 1995. ISBN 0-15-258722-5 Subj: Concepts – opposites. Poetry.

Wilcox, Cathy. *Enzo the Wonderfish* ill. by author. Ticknor & Fields, 1994. ISBN 0-395-68382-3 Subj: Fish. Pets.

Wilcox, Daniel. *The Sesame Street ABC storybook* (Moss, Jeffrey)

Wild, Jocelyn. *The bears' ABC book* (Wild, Robin)

The bears' counting book (Wild, Robin)

Florence and Eric take the cake ill. by author. Dial, 1987. ISBN 0-8037-0305-8 Subj: Animals – sheep. Behavior – misunderstanding. Family life.

Little Pig and the big bad wolf (Wild, Robin)

Spot's dogs and the alley cats (Wild, Robin)

Wild, Margaret. *Big cat dreaming* ill. by Anne Spudvilas. Annick, 1997. ISBN 1-55037-493-1 Subj: Animals – cats. Animals – dogs. Family life – grandmothers.

Going home ill. by Wayne Harris. Scholastic, 1994. ISBN 0-590-47958-X Subj: Activities – traveling. Dreams. Hospitals.

Let the celebrations begin! ill. by Julie Vivas. Watts, 1991. ISBN 0-531-08537-6 Subj: Toys. War.

Mr. Nick's knitting ill. by Dee Huxley. Harcourt, 1989. ISBN 0-15-200518-8 Subj: Activities – knitting. Friendship. Hospitals. Illness.

My dearest dinosaur ill. by Donna Rawlins. Orchard, 1992. ISBN 0-531-08603-8 Subj: Dinosaurs. Family life.

Old Pig ill. by Ron Brooks. Dial, 1996. ISBN 0-8037-1917-5 Subj: Animals – pigs. Death. Family life – grandmothers. Old age.

Our granny ill. by Julie Vivas. Ticknor & Fields, 1994. ISBN 0-395-67023-3 Subj: Family life – grandmothers.

The queen's holiday ill. by Sue O'Loughlin. Orchard, 1992. ISBN 0-531-08573-2 Subj: Royalty – queens. Sea and seashore.

Remember me ill. by Dee Huxley. Albert Whitman, 1995. ISBN 0-8075-6934-8 Subj: Behavior – forgetfulness. Family life – grandmothers. Memories, memory. Old age.

Rosie and Tortoise ill. by Ron Brooks. DK, 1999. ISBN 0-7894-2630-7 Subj: Animals – rabbits. Family life – new sibling.

Thank you, Santa ill. by Kerry Argent. Scholastic, 1992. ISBN 0-590-45805-1 Subj: Animals – polar bears. Foreign lands – Arctic. Foreign lands – Australia. Holidays – Christmas. Letters, cards.

Toby ill. by Noela Young. Ticknor & Fields, 1994. ISBN 0-395-67024-1 Subj: Animals – dogs. Behavior – misbehavior. Death. Emotions. Family life – brothers and sisters.

Tom goes to kindergarten ill. by David Legge. Albert Whitman, 2000. ISBN 0-8075-8012-0 Subj: Animals – pandas. Family life. School – first day.

The very best of friends ill. by Julie Vivas. Harcourt, 1990. ISBN 0-15-200625-7 Subj: Animals – cats. Death. Farms. Friendship.

Wild, Robin. *The bears' ABC book* by Robin and Jocelyn Wild; ill. by authors. Lippincott, 1978. ISBN 0-397-31767-0 Subj: ABC books. Animals – bears.

The bears' counting book by Robin and Jocelyn Wild; ill. by authors. Lippincott, 1978. ISBN 0-397-31808-1 Subj: Animals – bears. Counting, numbers.

Little Pig and the big bad wolf by Robin and Jocelyn Wild; ill. by authors. Coward, 1972. Subj: Animals – pigs. Animals – wolves. Character traits – cleverness. Rhyming text.

Spot's dogs and the alley cats by Robin and Jocelyn Wild; ill. by authors. Lippincott, 1979. ISBN 0-397-31841-3 Subj: Animals – cats. Animals – dogs. Behavior – trickery.

Wilde, Oscar. *Fairy tales of Oscar Wilde: The selfish giant, and The star child* adapt. and ill. by P. Craig Russell. NBM, 1992. Vol. 1. ISBN 1-56163-056-X Subj: Character traits – kindness. Character traits – selfishness. Folk and fairy tales. Gardens, gardening. Giants. Seasons – spring.

The giant's garden (Weedn, Flavia)

The happy prince ill. by Jane Ray. Dutton, 1995. ISBN 0-525-45367-9 Subj: City. Folk and fairy tales. Poverty. Royalty – kings.

The selfish giant ill. by S. Saelig Gallagher. Putnam, 1995. ISBN 0-399-22448-3 Subj: Character traits – kindness. Character traits – selfishness. Folk and fairy tales. Gardens, gardening. Giants. Seasons – spring.

The selfish giant ill. by Dom Mansell. Prentice-Hall, 1986. ISBN 0-13-803586-5 Subj: Character traits – kindness. Character traits – selfishness. Folk and fairy tales. Gardens, gardening. Giants. Seasons – spring.

The selfish giant retold by Fiona Waters; ill. by Fabian Negrin. Knopf, 2000. ISBN 0-375-90319-4 Subj: Character traits – kindness. Character traits – selfishness. Folk and fairy tales. Gardens, gardening. Giants. Seasons – spring.

The selfish giant ill. by Lisbeth Zwerger. Alphabet Pr., 1984. ISBN 0-907234-30-5 Subj: Character traits – kindness. Character traits – selfishness. Folk and fairy tales. Gardens, gardening. Giants. Seasons – spring.

The Star Child abridged by Jennifer Westwood; ill. by Fiona French. Four Winds, 1979. An abridged version of one chapter from the author's A house of Pomegranates. ISBN 0-590-07641-8 Subj: Character traits – pride. Character traits – selfishness. Folk and fairy tales.

Wilder, Laura Ingalls. *A farmer boy birthday* (A farmer boy birthday)

Going to town ill. by Renée Graef. HarperCollins, 1994. ISBN 0-06-023013-4 Subj: City. Family life – sisters. U.S. history – frontier and pioneer life.

Laura Ingalls Wilder's fairy poems intro. and comp. by Stephen W. Hines; ill. by Richard Hull. Doubleday, 1998. ISBN 0-385-32533-9 Subj: Fairies. Poetry.

My little house songbook ill. by Holly Jones. HarperCollins, 1995. ISBN 0-06-024295-7 Subj: Music. Songs. U.S. history – frontier and pioneer life.

Sugar snow (Sugar snow)

Wilds, Kazumi Inose. *Hajime in the North Woods* ill. by author. Little, 1994. ISBN 1-55970-240-0 Subj: Animals. Babies. Forest, woods.

Wildsmith, Brian. *Animal games* ill. by author. Oxford Univ. Pr., 1980. ISBN 0-19-279731-X Subj: Animals. Games.

Animal homes ill. by author. Oxford Univ. Pr., 1980. ISBN 0-19-279732-8 Subj: Animals. Homes, houses.

Animal shapes ill. by author. Oxford Univ. Pr., 1980. ISBN 0-19-279733-6 Subj: Animals. Concepts – shape.

Animal tricks ill. by author. Oxford Univ. Pr., 1980. ISBN 0-19-279743-3 Subj: Animals. Rhyming text.

Bear's adventure ill. by author. Pantheon, 1982. ISBN 0-394-95295-2 Subj: Activities – ballooning. Animals – bears.

The Bremen town band (Grimm, Jacob)

Brian Wildsmith 1 2 3 ill. by author. Millbrook, 1995. ISBN 1-56294-905-5 Subj: Concepts – shape. Counting, numbers.

Brian Wildsmith's birds ill. by author. Watts, 1967. Subj: Birds.

Brian Wildsmith's circus ill. by author. Watts, 1970. ISBN 0-531-01541-6 Subj: Circus.

Brian Wildsmith's puzzles ill. by author. Millbrook, 1996. ISBN 0-761-30052-X Subj: Games.

Carousel ill. by author. Knopf, 1988. ISBN 0-394-91937-8 Subj: Dreams. Fairs. Illness. Merry-go-rounds.

A Christmas story ill. by author. Eerdmans, 1998. ISBN 0-8028-5173-8 Subj: Animals – donkeys. Holidays – Christmas. Religion – Nativity.

The Easter story ill. by author. Knopf, 1994. ISBN 0-679-84727-8 Subj: Holidays – Easter. Religion.

Fishes ill. by author. Watts, 1968. Subj: Fish.

Give a dog a bone ill. by author. Pantheon, 1985. ISBN 0-394-97709-2 Subj: Animals – dogs. Format, unusual.

Goat's trail ill. by author. Knopf, 1986. ISBN 0-394-98276-2 Subj: Animals. Animals – goats. Cumulative tales. Format, unusual. Noise, sounds.

Hunter and his dog ill. by author. Oxford Univ. Pr., 1979. ISBN 0-19-279725-5 Subj: Animals – dogs. Character traits – kindness to animals. Sports – hunting.

Joseph ill. by author. Eerdmans, 1997. ISBN 0-8028-5161-4 Subj: Religion.

The lazy bear ill. by author. Watts, 1974. ISBN 0-531-01559-9 Subj: Animals – bears. Character traits – laziness. Friendship.

The little wood duck ill. by author. Watts, 1972. ISBN 0-19-279686-0 Subj: Birds – ducks.

The miller, the boy and the donkey (La Fontaine, Jean de)

The owl and the woodpecker ill. by author. Watts, 1971. ISBN 0-19-279676-3 Subj: Birds – owls. Birds – woodpeckers. Character traits – compromising.

Pelican ill. by author. Pantheon, 1983. ISBN 0-394-95668-0 Subj: Birds – pelicans. Format, unusual. Sports – fishing.

Professor Noah's spaceship ill. by author. Oxford Univ. Pr., 1980. ISBN 0-19-279741-7 Subj: Animals. Ecology. Space and space ships.

Python's party ill. by author. Watts, 1975. ISBN 0-531-02808-9 Subj: Animals. Behavior – trickery. Reptiles – snakes.

Seasons ill. by author. Oxford Univ. Pr., 1980. ISBN 0-19-279730-1 Subj: Nature. Seasons.

The true cross ill. by author. Oxford Univ. Pr., 1985, 1977. ISBN 0-19-279718-2 Subj: Folk and fairy tales. Religion.

What the moon saw ill. by author. Oxford Univ. Pr., 1978. ISBN 0-19-279724-7 Subj: Animals. Concepts – opposites. Language. Moon. Sun.

Wild animals ill. by author. Watts, 1967. ISBN 0-19-272103-8 Subj: Animals.

Wilhelm, Hans. *Bunny trouble* ill. by author. Scholastic, 1991. ISBN 0-590-63153-5 Subj: Animals – rabbits.

A cool kid - like me! ill. by author. Crown, 1990. ISBN 0-517-57822-0 Subj: Character traits – confidence. Family life – grandmothers. Toys – bears.

Don't cut my hair ill. by author. Scholastic, 1997. ISBN 0-590-30700-2 Subj: Animals – dogs. Hair.

I lost my tooth! ill. by author. Scholastic, 1999. ISBN 0-590-64230-8 Subj: Animals – dogs. Behavior – growing up. Problem solving. Teeth.

I'll always love you ill. by author. Crown, 1985. ISBN 0-517-55648-0 Subj: Animals – dogs. Death. Emotions – grief. Pets.

It's too windy! ill. by author. Scholastic, 2000. ISBN 0-439-10849-7 Subj: Animals – dogs. Babies. Family life. Weather – wind.

Let's be friends again! ill. by author. Crown, 1986. ISBN 0-517-56252-9 Subj: Emotions – anger. Family life – sisters. Friendship.

More bunny trouble ill. by author. Scholastic, 1989. ISBN 0-590-41589-1 Subj: Animals – foxes. Animals – rabbits. Eggs. Family life – brothers. Family life – sisters. Holidays – Easter.

A new home, a new friend ill. by author. Random House, 1985. ISBN 0-394-97226-0 Subj: Animals – dogs. Family life. Friendship. Moving.

Oh, what a mess ill. by author. Crown, 1988. ISBN 0-517-56909-4 Subj: Animals – pigs. Character traits – cleanliness.

Schnitzel's first Christmas ill. by author. Simon & Schuster, 1991. ISBN 0-671-74494-1 Subj: Animals – dogs. Behavior – needing someone. Holidays – Christmas. Santa Claus.

Tyrone the horrible ill. by author. Scholastic, 1988. ISBN 0-590-41471-2 Subj: Behavior – bullying. Dinosaurs.

Wilkes, Angela. *The big book of dinosaurs* ill. by author. DK, 1994. ISBN 1-56458-718-5 Subj: Dinosaurs.

My first word book ill. by author. New ed. DK, 1999. ISBN 0-7894-3977-8 Subj: Dictionaries. Language.

See how I grow ill. with photos. DK, 1994. ISBN 1-56458-464-X Subj: Babies. Behavior – growing up.

Wilkes, Larry. *The king's egg dance* ill. by author. Carolrhoda, 1990. ISBN 0-87614-446-6 Subj: Activities – dancing. Eggs. Royalty – kings.

Wilkin, Refna. *Just one apple* (Janosch)

Wilkins, Mary Huiskamp Calhoun. *see* Calhoun, Mary

Wilkinson, Sylvia. *Automobiles* ill. with photos. Childrens Pr., 1982. ISBN 0-516-01608-3 Subj: Automobiles.

I can be a race car driver ill. with photos. Childrens Pr., 1986. ISBN 0-516-01898-1 Subj: Automobiles. Careers – race car drivers. Sports – racing.

Wilkon, Józef. *Lullaby for a newborn king* by Józef Wilkon and Hermann Moers; trans. from German by Rosemary Lanning; ill. by Józef Wilkon. North-South, 1991. ISBN 1-55858-123-5 Subj: Holidays – Christmas. Lullabies. Religion.

Wilkon, Piotr. *The brave little kittens* trans. by Helen Graves; ill. by Józef Wilkon. North-South, 1991. ISBN 1-55858-103-0 Subj: Animals – cats. Character traits – bravery.

Rosie the cool cat ill. by Józef Wilkon. Viking, 1991. ISBN 0-670-83707-5 Subj: Animals – cats. Behavior – running away. Character traits – being different.

Wilkowski, Susan. *Baby's Bris* ill. by Judith Friedman. Kar-Ben Copies, 1999. ISBN 1-58013-052-6 Subj: Babies. Family life – brothers and sisters. Jewish culture. Names. Religion.

Will. *see* Lipkind, William

Willard, Barbara. *To London! To London!* ill. by Antony Maitland. Weybright & Talley, 1968. Subj: Foreign lands – England.

Willard, Nancy. *The high rise glorious skittle skat roarious sky pie angel food cake* ill. by Richard Jesse Watson. Harcourt, 1990. ISBN 0-15-234332-6 Subj: Activities – cooking. Angels. Birthdays. Family life – mothers.

The marzipan moon ill. by Marcia Sewell. Harcourt, 1981. ISBN 0-15-252962-4 Subj: Behavior – wishing. Birthdays. Food. Magic.

The mountains of quilt ill. by Tomie de Paola. Harcourt, 1987. ISBN 0-15-256010-6 Subj: Dreams. Family life – grandmothers. Magic. Quilts.

Night story ill. by Ilse Plume. Harcourt, 1986. ISBN 0-15-257348-8 Subj: Dreams. Night. Rhyming text.

The nightgown of the sullen moon ill. by David McPhail. Harcourt, 1983. ISBN 0-15-257429-8 Subj: Moon. Night.

Pish posh, said Hieronymous Bosch ill. by Leo and Diane Dillon. Harcourt, 1991. ISBN 0-15-262210-1 Subj: Careers – artists. Poetry.

Shadow story ill. by David Diaz. Harcourt, 1999. ISBN 0-15-201638-4 Subj: Folk and fairy tales. Mythical creatures – ogres. Orphans. Shadows.

Simple pictures are best ill. by Tomie de Paola. Harcourt, 1978. ISBN 0-15-682625-9 Subj: Activities – photographing. Humor.

The tale I told Sasha ill. by David Christiana. Little, 1999. ISBN 0-316-94115-8 Subj: Family life – mothers. Imagination.

A visit to William Blake's inn: poems for innocent and experienced travelers ill. by Alice and Martin Provensen. Harcourt, 1981. ISBN 0-15-293822-2 Subj: Caldecott award honor books. Imagination. Poetry.

The voyage of the Ludgate Hill: travels with Robert Louis Stevenson ill. by Alice and Martin Provensen. Harcourt, 1987. ISBN 0-15-294464-8 Subj: Activities – traveling. Animals. Boats, ships. Poetry. Sea and seashore. Weather – storms.

The well-mannered balloon ill. by Haig and Regina Shekerjian. Harcourt, 1991. ISBN 0-15-294986-0 Subj: Behavior – misbehavior. Night. Toys – balloons.

Willey, Margaret. *Thanksgiving with me* ill. by Lloyd Bloom. Laura Geringer, 1998. ISBN 0-06-027114-0 Subj: Family life – aunts, uncles. Holidays – Thanksgiving. Rhyming text.

Willhoite, Michael. *Daddy's roommate* ill. by author. Alyson Wonderland, 1990. ISBN 1-55583-178-8 Subj: Divorce. Family life – fathers. Homosexuality.

Williams, Arlene. *Dragon soup* ill. by Sally J. Smith. H.J. Kramer, 1996. ISBN 0-915811-63-4 Subj: Behavior – fighting, arguing. Dragons. Folk and fairy tales. Food.

Williams, Barbara. *Albert's toothache* ill. by Kay Chorao. Dutton, 1974. ISBN 0-525-25368-8 Subj: Illness. Reptiles – turtles, tortoises. Teeth.

Chester Chipmunk's Thanksgiving ill. by Kay Chorao. Dutton, 1974. ISBN 0-525-27655-6 Subj: Animals – chipmunks. Holidays – Thanksgiving.

Donna Jean's disaster ill. by Margot Apple. Albert Whitman, 1986. ISBN 0-8075-1682-1 Subj: Family life. Poetry. School. Self-concept. Sibling rivalry.

Hello, dandelions! photos by author. Holt, 1979. ISBN 0-03-048326-3 Subj: Flowers. Plants.

I know a salesperson ill. by Frank E. Aloise. Putnam, 1978. ISBN 0-399-61118-5 Subj: Careers. Stores.

If he's my brother ill. by Tomie de Paola. Harvey House, 1976. ISBN 0-8178-5422-3 Subj: Character traits – questioning. Family life.

Jeremy isn't hungry ill. by Martha G. Alexander. Dutton, 1978. ISBN 0-525-32760-6 Subj: Activities – babysitting. Babies. Humor.

Kevin's grandma ill. by Kay Chorao. Dutton, 1975. ISBN 0-525-33115-8 Subj: Family life – grandmothers. Friendship.

So what if I'm a sore loser? ill. by Linda Strauss Edwards. Harcourt, 1981. ISBN 0-15-277260-X Subj: Character traits – conceit. Family life.

Someday, said Mitchell ill. by Kay Chorao. Dutton, 1976. ISBN 0-525-39580-6 Subj: Behavior – wishing. Character traits – helpfulness. Character traits – smallness. Emotions – happiness.

Whatever happened to Beverly Bigler's birthday? ill. by Emily Arnold McCully. Harcourt, 1979. ISBN 0-15-295286-1 Subj: Behavior – misbehavior. Birthdays. Weddings.

Williams, Charles. *see* Collier, James Lincoln

Williams, David. *Walking to the creek* ill. by Thomas B. Allen. Knopf, 1990. ISBN 0-394-90598-9 Subj: Activities – walking. Country. Nature.

Williams, Garth. *The big golden animal ABC* ill. by author. Simon & Schuster, 1957. First published under the title: The golden animal A.B.C. Subj: ABC books. Animals.

The chicken book ill. by author. Delacorte, 1970. ISBN 0-385-30110-3 Subj: Birds – chickens. Counting, numbers. Nursery rhymes.

The rabbits' wedding ill. by author. HarperCollins, 1958. ISBN 0-06-026496-9 Subj: Animals – rabbits. Weddings.

Williams, Gweneira Maureen. *Timid Timothy, the kitten who learned to be brave* ill. by Leonard Weisgard. Addison-Wesley, 1944. Subj: Emotions – fear. Food. Science.

Williams, Jay. *The city witch and the country witch* ill. by Ed Renfro. Macmillan, 1979. ISBN 0-02-793050-5 Subj: Activities – vacationing. City. Country. Witches.

Everyone knows what a dragon looks like ill. by Mercer Mayer. Four Winds, 1976. ISBN 0-590-07284-6 Subj: Dragons. Foreign lands – China.

I wish I had another name by Jay Williams and Winifred Lubell; ill. by authors. Atheneum, 1962. Subj: Names. Rhyming text.

The practical princess ill. by Friso Henstra. Parents, 1969. Subj: Folk and fairy tales. Royalty – princesses.

School for sillies ill. by Friso Henstra. Parents, 1969. Subj: Character traits – cleverness. Humor. Royalty.

The surprising things Maui did ill. by Charles Mikolaycak. Four Winds, 1980. ISBN 0-590-07553-5 Subj: Folk and fairy tales. Hawaii.

Williams, Jenny (Jennifer). *Here's a ball for baby: finger rhymes for young children* ill. by author. Dial, 1987. ISBN 0-8037-0388-0 Subj: Nursery rhymes.

One, two, buckle my shoe: counting rhymes for young children ill. by author. Dial, 1987. ISBN 0-8037-0390-2 Subj: Counting, numbers. Nursery rhymes.

Playtime 1 2 3 ill. by author. Dial, 1992. ISBN 0-8037-1077-1 Subj: Activities. Counting, numbers. Rhyming text.

Ride a cockhorse: animal rhymes for young children ill. by author. Dial, 1987. ISBN 0-8037-0389-9 Subj: Animals. Nursery rhymes.

Ring around a rosy: action rhymes for young children ill. by author. Dial, 1987. ISBN 0-8037-0391-0 Subj: Games. Nursery rhymes.

A wet Monday (Edwards, Dorothy)

Williams, Julie Stewart. *And the birds appeared* ill. by Robin Yoko Burningham. Univ. of Hawaii Pr., 1988. ISBN 0-8248-1194-1 Subj: Birds. Folk and fairy tales. Hawaii.

Williams, Karen Lynn. *Galimoto* ill. by Catherine Stock. Lothrop, 1990. ISBN 0-688-08790-6 Subj: Foreign lands – Africa. Toys.

Painted dreams ill. by Catherine Stock. Lothrop, 1998. ISBN 0-688-13902-7 Subj: Activities – painting. Foreign lands – Haiti. Problem solving.

Tap-tap ill. by Catherine Stock. Clarion, 1994. ISBN 0-395-65617-6 Subj: Clothing – hats. Family life – mothers. Foreign lands – Haiti. Stores. Trucks.

When Africa was home ill. by Floyd Cooper. Watts, 1991. ISBN 0-531-08525-2 Subj: Family life. Foreign lands – Africa. Friendship.

Williams, Laura E. *ABC kids* ill. by author. Philomel, 2000. ISBN 0-399-23370-9 Subj: ABC books.

The long silk strand ill. by Grayce Bochak. Boyds Mills, 1995. ISBN 1-56397-236-0 Subj: Death. Family life – grandmothers. Folk and fairy tales. Foreign lands – Japan.

Torch fishing with the sun ill. by Fabricio Vandenbroeck. Boyds Mills, 1999. ISBN 1-56397-685-4 Subj: Careers – fishermen. Family life – grandfathers. Folk and fairy tales. Hawaii. Night. Sun.

Williams, Leslie. *A bear in the air* ill. by Carme Solé Vendrell. Stemmer House, 1980. ISBN 0-916144-54-2 Subj: Animals – bears. Weather – clouds. Weather – rainbows.

Williams, Linda. *The little old lady who was not afraid of anything* ill. by Megan Lloyd. Crowell, 1986. ISBN 0-690-04586-7 Subj: Cumulative tales. Emotions – fear. Scarecrows.

Williams, Marcia. *The first Christmas* ill. by author. Random House, 1988. ISBN 0-394-80434-1 Subj: Holidays – Christmas. Religion – Nativity.

Jonah and the whale ill. by author. Random House, 1989. ISBN 0-394-92345-6 Subj: Animals – whales. Religion – Jonah.

Joseph and his magnificent coat of many colors ill. by author. Candlewick, 1992. ISBN 1-56402-019-3 Subj: Clothing – coats. Religion.

Not a worry in the world ill. by author. Crown, 1991. ISBN 0-517-58156-6 Subj: Behavior – worrying. Family life.

Williams, Margery. *see* Bianco, Margery Williams

Williams, Sam. *The baby's word book* ill. by author. Greenwillow, 1999, c1993. ISBN 0-688-16834-5 Subj: Activities. Babies. Dictionaries.

Williams, Sarah. *Ride a cock-horse* ill. by Ian Beck. Oxford Univ. Pr., 1987. ISBN 0-19-279831-6 Subj: Nursery rhymes.

Williams, Sherley Anne. *Girls together* ill. by Synthia Saint James. Harcourt, 1999. ISBN 0-15-230982-9 Subj: Activities – playing. City. Ethnic groups in the U.S. – African Americans. Friendship.

Working cotton ill. by Carole M. Byard. Harcourt, 1992. ISBN 0-15-299624-9 Subj: Activities – working. Caldecott award honor books. Careers – migrant workers. Ethnic groups in the U.S. – African Americans. Family life.

Williams, Sheron. *And in the beginning . . .* ill. by Robert Roth. Atheneum, 1992. ISBN 0-689-31650-X Subj: Creation. Folk and fairy tales. Foreign lands – Africa.

Williams, Sophy. *Nana's garden* ill. by author. Viking, 1994. ISBN 0-670-85287-2 Subj: Activities – playing. Family life – grandmothers. Gardens, gardening. Ghosts.

Williams, Sue. *I went walking* ill. by Julie Vivas. Harcourt, 1990. ISBN 0-15-200471-8 Subj: Activities – walking. Animals. Concepts – color. Rhyming text.

Let's go visiting ill. by Julie Vivas. Harcourt, 1998. ISBN 0-15-201823-9 Subj: Animals. Counting, numbers. Pets. Rhyming text.

Williams, Susan. *Poppy's first year* ill. by author. Macmillan, 1989. ISBN 0-02-793031-9 Subj: Babies. Family life – brothers and sisters.

Williams, Suzanne. *Library Lil* ill. by Steven Kellogg. Dial, 1997. ISBN 0-8037-1698-2 Subj: Activities – reading. Careers – librarians. Tall tales.

Mommy doesn't know my name ill. by Andrew Shachat. Houghton Mifflin, 1990. ISBN 0-395-54228-6 Subj: Family life – mothers. Names.

My dog never says please ill. by Tedd Arnold. Dial, 1997. ISBN 0-8037-1681-8 Subj: Animals – dogs. Behavior – wishing. Family life.

Williams, Terry Tempest. *Between cattails* ill. by Peter Parnall. Scribners, 1985. ISBN 0-684-18309-9 Subj: Ecology. Rhyming text.

Williams, Vera B. *A chair for my mother* ill. by author. Greenwillow, 1982. ISBN 0-688-00915-8 Subj: Behavior – seeking better things. Caldecott award honor books. Family life. Furniture – chairs.

Cherries and cherry pits ill. by author. Greenwillow, 1986. ISBN 0-688-05146-4 Subj: Art. Ethnic groups in the U.S. – African Americans. Imagination.

"More more more," said the baby ill. by author. Greenwillow, 1991. ISBN 0-688-09174-1 Subj: Babies. Caldecott award honor books. Ethnic groups in the U.S. Family life.

Music, music for everyone ill. by author. Greenwillow, 1984. ISBN 0-688-20604-4 Subj: Family life. Family life – grandmothers. Illness. Music.

Something special for me ill. by author. Greenwillow, 1983. ISBN 0-688-01807-6 Subj: Birthdays. Family life. Gifts.

Three days on a river in a red canoe ill. by author. Greenwillow, 1981. ISBN 0-688-84307-7 Subj: Boats, ships. Camps, camping.

Williams-Garcia, Rita. *Catching the wild waiyuuzee* ill. by Mike Reed. Simon & Schuster, 2000. ISBN 0-689-82601-X Subj: Ethnic groups in the U.S. – African Americans. Hair. Imagination.

Williamson, Hamilton. *Little elephant* ill. by Berta and Elmer Hader. Doubleday, 1930. Subj: Animals – elephants.

Monkey tale ill. by Berta and Elmer Hader. Doubleday, 1929. Subj: Animals – monkeys.

Williamson, Mel. *Walk on!* by Mel Williamson and George Ford; ill. by authors. Third Pr., 1972. ISBN 0-8938-8042-6 Subj: City. Ethnic groups in the U.S. – African Americans.

Williamson, Stan. *The no-bark dog* ill. by Tom O'Sullivan. Follett, 1962. Subj: Animals – dogs. Ethnic groups in the U.S. – African Americans.

Willington, Monica. *Seasons of swans* ill. by author. Dutton, 1990. ISBN 0-525-44621-4 Subj: Birds – swans. Birth. Nature.

Willis, Jeanne. *The boy who lost his bellybutton* ill. by Tony Ross. DK, 2000. ISBN 0-7894-6164-1 Subj: Anatomy. Animals. Animals – dogs. Jungle. Reptiles – alligators, crocodiles.

Earth mobiles as explained by Professor Xargle ill. by Tony Ross. Dutton, 1992. ISBN 0-525-44892-6 Subj: Activities – traveling. Space and space ships. Transportation.

Earth tigerlets as explained by Professor Xargle ill. by Tony Ross. Dutton, 1991. ISBN 0-525-44732-6 Subj: Animals – cats. Space and space ships.

Earthlets as explained by Professor Xargle ill. by Tony Ross. Dutton, 1989. ISBN 0-525-44465-3 Subj: Babies. Space and space ships.

The long blue blazer ill. by Susan Varley. Dutton, 1988. ISBN 0-525-44381-9 Subj: Aliens. Character traits – being different. School. Space and space ships.

The monster bed ill. by Susan Varley. Lothrop, 1987. ISBN 0-688-06805-7 Subj: Bedtime. Emotions – fear. Furniture – beds. Monsters. Rhyming text.

The monster storm ill. by Susan Varley. Lothrop, 1995. ISBN 0-688-13785-7 Subj: Emotions – fear. Monsters. Rhyming text. Weather – storms.

Sloth's shoes ill. by Tony Ross. Kane/Miller, 1998. ISBN 0-916291-78-2 Subj: Animals. Animals – sloths. Behavior – tardiness. Birthdays. Rhyming text.

The tale of Georgie Grub ill. by Margaret Chamberlain. Holt, 1982. ISBN 0-03-061222-5 Subj: Activities – bathing. Character traits – cleanliness.

What did I look like when I was a baby? ill. by Tony Ross. Putnam, 2000. ISBN 0-399-23595-7 Subj: Babies. Behavior – growing up. Character traits – appearance.

Willis, Val. *The mystery in the bottle* ill. by John Shelley. Farrar, 1991. ISBN 0-374-35194-5 Subj: Format, unusual – board books. Mythical creatures. School.

The secret in the matchbox ill. by John Shelley. Farrar, 1988. ISBN 0-374-36603-9 Subj: Behavior – secrets. Dragons. School.

Silly little chick ill. by Judy Brook. Dutton, 1989. ISBN 0-233-98307-4 Subj: Behavior – growing up. Birds – chickens. Farms.

Willoughby, Elaine Macmann. *Boris and the monsters* ill. by Lynn Munsinger. Houghton Mifflin, 1980. ISBN 0-395-29067-8 Subj: Animals – dogs. Monsters.

Wilner, Isabel. *The baby's game book* ill. by Sam Williams. Greenwillow, 2000. ISBN 0-688-15916-8 Subj: Babies. Family life. Games.

A garden alphabet ill. by Ashley Wolff. Dutton, 1991. ISBN 0-525-44731-8 Subj: ABC books. Animals. Gardens, gardening. Rhyming text.

Wilson, April. *April Wilson's magpie magic* ill. by author. Dial, 1999. ISBN 0-8037-2354-7 Subj: Activities – drawing. Birds – magpies. Concepts – color. Concepts – shape. Concepts – size. Wordless.

Wilson, Barbara Ker. *ABC et = and 123* ill. by Gisèle Daigle. Fitzhenry & Whiteside, 1981. ISBN 0-88878-165-2 Subj: ABC books. Counting, numbers. Foreign languages.

The turtle and the island ill. by Frané Lessac. Lippincott, 1990. ISBN 0-397-32439-1 Subj: Folk and fairy tales. Foreign lands – New Guinea. Islands. Reptiles – turtles, tortoises.

Wilson, Beth P. *Jenny* ill. by Dolores Johnson. Macmillan, 1990. ISBN 0-02-793120-X Subj: Ethnic groups in the U.S. – African Americans. Family life – grandmothers.

Wilson, Bob. *Stanley Bagshaw and the twenty-two ton whale* ill. by author. David & Charles, 1984. ISBN 0-241-10812-8 Subj: Animals – whales. Sports – fishing.

Wilson, Christopher Bernard. *Hobnob* ill. by William Wiesner. Viking, 1968. Subj: Behavior – sharing.

Wilson, Dorminster. *Mother scorpion country* (Rohmer, Harriet)

Wilson, Hazel Hutchins. *see* Hutchins, H. J. (Hazel J.)

Wilson, Joyce Lancaster. *Tobi* ill. by Anne Thiess. Funk & Wagnalls, 1968. Subj: Animals – cats.

Wilson, Julia. *Becky* ill. by John Wilson. Crowell, 1966. Subj: Character traits – honesty. Ethnic groups in the U.S. – African Americans. Toys – dolls.

Wilson, Lynn. *Baby whale* ill. by author. Putnam, 1991. ISBN 0-448-40073-1 Subj: Animals – whales.

Wilson, Margaret. *The dog show* (Gray, Nigel)

Wilson, Robina Beckles. *Merry Christmas! children at Christmastime around the world* ill. by Satomi Ichikawa. Putnam, 1983. ISBN 0-399-20921-2 Subj: Holidays – Christmas.

Wilson, Ron. *Mice* ill. with photos. Global Lib. Mktg. Serv., 1984. ISBN 0-7136-2388-8 Subj: Animals – mice. Nature. Science.

Wilson, Sarah. *Beware the dragons!* ill. by author. HarperCollins, 1985. ISBN 0-06-026509-4 Subj: Dragons. Folk and fairy tales. Weather – storms.

The day that Henry cleaned his room ill. by author. Simon & Schuster, 1990. ISBN 0-671-69202-X Subj: Character traits – cleanliness.

Good zap, little grog ill. by Susan Meddaugh. Candlewick, 1995. ISBN 1-56402-286-2 Subj: Family life. Names. Rhyming text.

June is a tune that jumps on a stair ill. by author. Simon & Schuster, 1992. ISBN 0-671-73919-0 Subj: Poetry.

Love and kisses ill. by Melissa Sweet. Candlewick, 1999. ISBN 1-56402-792-9 Subj: Animals. Emotions – love. Rhyming text.

Muskrat, muskrat, eat your peas! ill. by author. Simon & Schuster, 1989. ISBN 0-671-67515-X Subj: Animals – muskrats. Family life. Food.

Uncle Albert's flying birthday ill. by author. Simon & Schuster, 1991. ISBN 0-671-72793-1 Subj: Activities – bathing. Birthdays. Parties.

Wilson, Toña. *The cook and the king* (Brusca, María Cristina)

When jaguars ate the moon: and other stories about animals and plants of the Americas (Brusca, María Cristina)

Wilson-Kelly, Becky. *Mother Grumpy's dog biscuits* ill. by author. Holt, 1990. ISBN 0-8050-1287-7 Subj: Activities – cooking. Animals – dogs. Character traits. Food.

Wilson-Max, Ken. *Big blue engine* ill. by author. Scholastic, 1996. ISBN 0-590-89801-9 Subj: Format, unusual – toy and movable books. Trains.

Big red fire truck ill. by author. Scholastic, 1997. ISBN 0-590-10082-3 Subj: Careers – firefighters. Fire. Format, unusual – toy and movable books.

Faraha means happy: a book of Swahili words ill. by author. Hyperion, 2000. ISBN 0-7868-2480-8 Subj: Foreign lands – Kenya. Foreign languages.

Halala means welcome: a book of Zulu words ill. by author. Hyperion, 1998. ISBN 0-7868-0914-9 Subj: Foreign lands – South Africa. Foreign languages.

Little red plane ill. by author. Scholastic, 1995. ISBN 0-590-43008-4 Subj: Airplanes, airports. Format, unusual – toy and movable books.

Max loves sunflowers ill. by author. Hyperion, 1998. ISBN 0-7868-0413-0 Subj: Flowers. Format, unusual – toy and movable books. Plants. Science.

Wake up; Sleep tight ill. by author. Scholastic, 1998. ISBN 0-590-76779-8 Subj: Format, unusual. Time.

Winch, Madeleine. *Come by chance* ill. by author. Crown, 1990. ISBN 0-517-57667-8 Subj: Animals. Homes, houses. Seasons – winter.

Windham, Sophie. *Down in the marvelous deep* ill. by author. Scholastic, 1994. ISBN 0-590-20898-5 Subj: Poetry. Sea and seashore.

Noah's ark ill. by author. Putnam, 1989. ISBN 0-399-21564-6 Subj: Animals. Boats, ships. Food. Format, unusual. Religion – Noah. Weather – floods. Weather – rain.

Wing, Natasha. *Jalapeño bagels* ill. by Robert Casilla. Atheneum, 1996. ISBN 0-02-793077-7 Subj: Ethnic groups in the U.S. Family life. Food. School.

Winkleman, Katherine K. *Firehouse* ill. by John S. Winkleman. Walker, 1994. ISBN 0-8027-8317-1 Subj: Careers – firefighters. Trucks.

Winn, Chris. *Archie's acrobats* ill. by author. Trafalgar Square, 1990. ISBN 0-575-04481-0 Subj: Activities. Circus.

Helping ill. by author. Holt, 1986. ISBN 0-8050-0064-X Subj: Activities. Format, unusual – board books.

Holiday ill. by author. Holt, 1986. ISBN 0-8050-0067-4 Subj: Format, unusual – board books. Holidays.

My day ill. by author. Holt, 1986. ISBN 0-8050-0066-6 Subj: Family life. Format, unusual – board books. Shopping.

Playing ill. by author. Holt, 1986. ISBN 0-8050-0065-8 Subj: Activities – playing. Format, unusual – board books.

Winston, Clara. *Thumbelina* (Andersen, H. C. [Hans Christian])

Winston, Peggy D. *Creatures of long ago: dinosaurs* (Sibbick, John)

Winston, Richard. *Thumbelina* (Andersen, H. C. [Hans Christian])

Winter, Jeanette. *The Christmas tree ship* ill. by author. Philomel, 1994. ISBN 0-399-22693-1 Subj: Boats, ships. Holidays – Christmas. Trees. U.S. history.

Cowboy Charlie ill. by author. Harcourt, 1995. ISBN 0-15-200857-8 Subj: Activities – playing. Art. Careers – artists. Cowboys. U.S. history – frontier and pioneer life.

Follow the drinking gourd ill. by author. Dragonfly Books, 1992. ISBN 0-679-81997-5 Subj: Ethnic groups in the U.S. – African Americans. Sailors. Slavery. Stars. U.S. history.

The girl and the moon man: a Siberian folktale ill. by author. Pantheon, 1984. ISBN 0-394-96326-1 Subj: Animals. Folk and fairy tales. Foreign lands – Russia. Moon. Music.

The house that Jack built (The house that Jack built)

Winter, Jonah. *Diego* ill. by Jeanette Winter. Knopf, 1991. ISBN 0-679-91987-2 Subj: Art. Careers – artists. Foreign languages.

Winter, Paula. *The bear and the fly* ill. by author. Crown, 1976. ISBN 0-517-52605-0 Subj: Animals – bears. Insects – flies. Wordless.

Sir Andrew ill. by author. Crown, 1980. ISBN 0-517-53911-X Subj: Animals – donkeys. Character traits – vanity. Wordless.

Winter, Susan. *A baby just like me* ill. by author. DK, 1994. ISBN 1-56458-668-5 Subj: Babies. Emotions – envy, jealousy. Family life – new sibling. Family life – sisters. Sibling rivalry.

My shadow ill. by author. Doubleday, 1994. ISBN 0-385-31066-8 Subj: Shadows.

Winteringham, Victoria. *Penguin day* ill. by author. HarperCollins, 1982. ISBN 0-06-026514-0 Subj: Activities. Birds – penguins.

Winters, Kay. *The teeny tiny ghost* ill. by Lynn Munsinger. HarperCollins, 1997. ISBN 0-06-027358-5 Subj: Emotions – fear. Ghosts. Holidays – Halloween.

Tiger trail ill. by Laura Regan. Simon & Schuster, 2000. ISBN 0-689-82323-1 Subj: Animals – tigers. Behavior – growing up. Nature.

Whooo's haunting the teeny tiny ghost? ill. by Lynn Munsinger. HarperCollins, 1999. ISBN 0-06-027359-3 Subj: Emotions – fear. Ghosts. Holidays – Halloween.

Wolf watch ill. by Laura Regan. Simon & Schuster, 1997. ISBN 0-689-80218-8 Subj: Animals. Animals – wolves. Behavior – growing up. Nature. Rhyming text.

Winthrop, Elizabeth. *As the crow flies* ill. by Joan Sandin. Clarion, 1998. ISBN 0-395-77612-0 Subj: Divorce. Family life – fathers.

Bear and Mrs. Duck ill. by Patience Brewster. Holiday, 1988. ISBN 0-8234-0687-3 Subj: Activities – babysitting. Animals – bears. Birds – ducks.

Bear and Roly-Poly ill. by Patience Brewster. Holiday, 1996. ISBN 0-8234-1197-4 Subj: Activities – babysitting. Family life – brothers and sisters. Toys.

Bear's Christmas surprise ill. by Patience Brewster. Holiday, 1991. ISBN 0-8234-0888-4 Subj: Activities – babysitting. Animals – bears. Birds – ducks. Holidays – Christmas.

The Best Friends Club ill. by Martha Weston. Lothrop, 1989. ISBN 0-688-07583-5 Subj: Character traits – selfishness. Clubs, gangs. Friendship.

Bunk beds ill. by Ronald Himler. HarperCollins, 1972. ISBN 0-06-026532-9 Subj: Activities – playing. Bedtime. Family life. Furniture – beds. Imagination.

A child is born: the Christmas story adapt. from the New Testament; ill. by Charles Mikolaycak. Holiday, 1983. ISBN 0-8234-0472-2 Subj: Holidays – Christmas. Religion – Nativity.

He is risen: the Easter story ill. by Charles Mikolaycak. Holiday, 1985. ISBN 0-8234-0547-8 Subj: Holidays – Easter. Religion.

I think he likes me ill. by Denise Saldutti. HarperCollins, 1980. ISBN 0-06-026552-3 Subj: Family life. Sibling rivalry.

I'm the Boss! ill. by Mary Morgan. Holiday, 1994. ISBN 0-8234-1113-3 Subj: Animals – dogs. Character traits – assertiveness. Family life.

Katharine's doll ill. by Marylin Hafner. Dutton, 1983. ISBN 0-525-44061-5 Subj: Friendship. Toys – dolls.

The little humpbacked horse ill. by Alexander Koshkin. Clarion, 1997. ISBN 0-395-65361-4 Subj: Animals – horses, ponies. Character traits – cleverness. Folk and fairy tales. Foreign lands – Russia. Royalty – tsars.

Lizzie and Harold ill. by Martha Weston. Lothrop, 1986. ISBN 0-688-02712-1 Subj: Friendship.

Maggie and the monster ill. by Tomie de Paola. Holiday, 1987. ISBN 0-8234-0639-2 Subj: Bedtime. Monsters. Problem solving.

Potbellied possums ill. by Barbara McClintock. Holiday, 1977. ISBN 0-8234-0289-4 Subj: Animals – possums. Emotions – fear. Food. Night.

Shoes ill. by William Joyce. HarperCollins, 1986. ISBN 0-06-026592-2 Subj: Clothing – shoes. Rhyming text.

Sledding ill. by Sarah Wilson. HarperCollins, 1989. ISBN 0-06-026566-3 Subj: Rhyming text. Sports – sledding.

Sloppy kisses ill. by Anne Burgess. Macmillan, 1980. ISBN 0-02-793210-9 Subj: Animals – pigs. Friendship.

That's mine ill. by Emily Arnold McCully. Holiday, 1977. ISBN 0-8234-0308-4 Subj: Activities – playing. Behavior – fighting, arguing. Behavior – greed. Behavior – sharing. Sibling rivalry. Toys – blocks.

Tough Eddie ill. by Lillian Hoban. Dutton, 1985. ISBN 0-525-44364-6 Subj: Character traits – pride. Gender roles. School.

Vasilissa the beautiful ill. by Alexander Koshkin. HarperCollins, 1991. ISBN 0-06-021663-8 Subj: Folk and fairy tales. Foreign lands – Russia. Royalty. Toys – dolls. Witches.

A very noisy girl ill. by Ellen Weiss. Holiday, 1991. ISBN 0-8234-0858-2 Subj: Family life – mothers. Imagination. Noise, sounds.

Winton, Tim. *The deep* ill. by Karen Louise. Tricycle, 2000. ISBN 1-58246-024-8 Subj: Animals – dolphins. Emotions – fear. Nature. Sea and seashore. Sports – swimming.

Wirt, Donna Aaron. *My favorite place* (Sargent, Susan)

Wirth, Beverly. *Margie and me* ill. by Karen Ann Weinhaus. Four Winds, 1983. ISBN 0-590-07870-4 Subj: Animals – dogs. Pets.

Wisbeski, Dorothy Gross. *Pícaro, a pet otter* ill. by Edna Miller. Hawthorn, 1971. Subj: Animals – otters. Pets.

Wise, Fred. *A you're adorable* (Lippman, Sidney)

Wiseman, Bernard. *Christmas with Morris and Borris* ill. by author. Little, 1983. ISBN 0-316-94855-1 Subj: Animals – bears. Animals – moose. Holidays – Christmas.

Doctor Duck and Nurse Swan ill. by author. Dutton, 1984. ISBN 0-525-44095-X Subj: Animals. Problem solving.

Don't make fun! ill. by author. Houghton Mifflin, 1982. ISBN 0-395-32086-0 Subj: Animals – pigs. Behavior – misbehavior.

Little new kangaroo ill. by Robert Lopshire. Macmillan, 1973. ISBN 0-02-793220-6 Subj: Animals. Animals – kangaroos. Foreign lands – Russia. Rhyming text.

Morris and Boris at the circus ill. by author. HarperCollins, 1988. ISBN 0-06-026478-0 Subj: Animals – bears. Animals – moose. Circus.

Morris has a birthday party! ill. by author. Little, 1983. ISBN 0-316-94854-3 Subj: Animals – bears. Animals – moose. Behavior – misunderstanding. Parties.

Morris the moose ill. by author. Rev. ed. HarperCollins, 1989. ISBN 0-06-026476-4 Subj: Animals – bulls, cows. Animals – moose. Behavior – misunderstanding.

Oscar is a mama ill. by author. Garrard, 1980. ISBN 0-8116-6081-8 Subj: Animals – bulls, cows. Toys – dolls.

Tails are not for painting ill. by author. Garrard, 1980. ISBN 0-8116-6078-8 Subj: Animals. Behavior – mistakes. Humor. School.

Wishinsky, Frieda. *Oonga boonga* ill. by Suçie Stevenson. Little, 1990. ISBN 0-316-94872-1 Subj: Babies. Family life – brothers and sisters.

Oonga boonga ill. by Carol Thompson. New ed. Dutton, 1998. ISBN 0-525-46095-0 Subj: Babies. Family life – brothers and sisters.

Wisniewski, David. *Elfwyn's saga* ill. by author. Lothrop, 1990. ISBN 0-688-09590-9 Subj: Folk and fairy tales. Foreign lands – Iceland. Handicaps – blindness. Magic.

Golem ill. by author. Clarion, 1996. ISBN 0-395-72618-2 Subj: Caldecott award honor books. Folk and fairy tales. Foreign lands – Czechoslovakia. Jewish culture. Mythical creatures.

Rain player ill. by author. Houghton Mifflin, 1991. ISBN 0-395-55112-9 Subj: Foreign lands – Central America. Foreign lands – Mexico. Games. Indians of Central America – Maya.

Sundiata: lion king of Mali ill. by author. Clarion, 1992. ISBN 0-395-61302-7 Subj: Folk and fairy tales. Foreign lands – Mali. Handicaps. Royalty – kings.

Tough cookie ill. by author. Lothrop, 1999. ISBN 0-688-15338-0 Subj: Food. Humor.

The warrior and the wise man ill. by author. Lothrop, 1989. ISBN 0-688-07890-7 Subj: Folk and fairy tales. Foreign lands – Japan. Multiple births – twins. Royalty.

Witch poems ed. by Daisy Wallace; ill. by Trina Schart Hyman. Holiday, 1976. ISBN 0-8234-0281-9 Subj: Poetry. Witches.

Withers, Carl. *The tale of a black cat* ill. by Alan E. Cober. Holt, 1966. Subj: Animals – cats. Games.

The wild ducks and the goose ill. by Alan E. Cober. Holt, 1968. Subj: Birds – ducks. Games. Sports – hunting.

Wittbold, Maureen. *Mending Peter's heart* ill. by Larry Salk. Portunus Pub., 1995. ISBN 0-9641330-2-4 Subj: Animals – dogs. Death. Emotions – grief. Friendship. Pets.

Wittels, Harriet. *Things I hate!* by Harriet Wittels and Joan Greisman; ill. by Jerry McConnel. Behavioral, 1973. ISBN 0-8770-5096-1 Subj: Behavior. Emotions. Rhyming text.

Wittington, Mary K. *Troll games* ill. by Betsy Day. Macmillan, 1991. ISBN 0-689-31630-5 Subj: Games. Mythical creatures – trolls. Night.

Wittman, Sally. *The boy who hated Valentine's Day* ill. by Chaya M. Burstein. HarperCollins, 1987. ISBN 0-06-026594-9 Subj: Character traits – kindness. Friendship. Holidays – Valentine's Day. School.

Pelly and Peak ill. by author. HarperCollins, 1978. ISBN 0-06-026560-4 Subj: Birds – peacocks, peahens. Birds – pelicans. Friendship.

Plenty of Pelly and Peak ill. by author. HarperCollins, 1980. ISBN 0-06-026563-9 Subj: Birds – peacocks, peahens. Birds – pelicans. Friendship.

A special trade ill. by Karen Gundersheimer. HarperCollins, 1978. ISBN 0-06-026554-X Subj: Behavior – growing up. Friendship. Old age.

The wonderful Mrs. Trumbly ill. by Margot Apple. HarperCollins, 1982. ISBN 0-06-026512-4 Subj: Friendship. School. Weddings.

Wittmann, Patricia. *Buffalo Thunder* ill. by Bert Dodson. Cavendish, 1997. ISBN 0-7614-5001-7 Subj: Animals – buffaloes. Family life. U.S. history – frontier and pioneer life.

Go ask Giorgio! ill. by Will Hillenbrand. Macmillan, 1992. ISBN 0-02-793221-4 Subj: Activities – working. Careers. Character traits – helpfulness. Clothing – hats.

Wodge, Dreary. *see* Gorey, Edward (St. John)

Wohl, Lauren L. *Matzoh mouse* ill. by Pamela Keavney. HarperCollins, 1991. ISBN 0-06-026581-7 Subj: Family life. Holidays – Passover. Jewish culture. Religion.

Wojciechowski, Susan. *The best Halloween of all* ill. by Susan Meddaugh. 2nd ed. Candlewick, 1998. ISBN 0-7636-0458-5 Subj: Clothing – costumes. Holidays – Halloween.

The Christmas miracle of Jonathan Toomey ill. by P. J. Lynch. Candlewick, 1995. ISBN 1-56402-320-6 Subj: Careers – woodcarvers. Friendship. Holidays – Christmas. Religion.

Wojtowycz, David. *Animal antics from 1 to 10* ill. by author. Holiday, 2000. ISBN 0-8234-1552-X Subj: Animals. Counting, numbers. Hotels.

David Wojtowycz presents Animal ABC ill. by author. David & Charles, 2000. ISBN 1-86233-107-3 Subj: ABC books. Animals.

Wolcott, Patty. *Double-decker, double-decker, double-decker bus* ill. by Bob Barner. Addison-Wesley, 1980. ISBN 0-201-08735-9 Subj: Buses. Friendship.

Eeeeeek! ill. by Ned Delaney. Random House, 1991. ISBN 0-679-91929-5 Subj: Animals. Sleep. Sports – hunting.

Wold, Jo Anne. *Tell them my name is Amanda* ed. by Caroline Rubin; ill. by Dennis Hockerman. Albert Whitman, 1977. ISBN 0-8075-7768-5 Subj: Character traits – shyness. Names. Problem solving. Self-concept.

Well! Why didn't you say so? ill. by Unada. Albert Whitman, 1975. ISBN 0-8075-8724-9 Subj: Animals – dogs. Behavior – lost. Behavior – misunderstanding. City.

Wolde, Gunilla. *Betsy and Peter are different* ill. by author. Random House, 1979. Translation of Annorlunda Emma och Per. ISBN 0-394-94210-8 Subj: Family life. Friendship.

Betsy and the chicken pox ill. by author. Random House, 1976. Translation of Emmas lillebror ar sjuk. ISBN 0-394-83328-7 Subj: Behavior – needing someone. Illness. Sibling rivalry.

Betsy and the doctor ill. by author. Random House, 1978. Translation of Emma hos doktorn. ISBN 0-394-95382-7 Subj: Careers – doctors. Hospitals. Illness.

Betsy and the vacuum cleaner ill. by author. Random House, 1979. ISBN 0-394-94209-4 Subj: Family life. Machines.

Betsy's first day at nursery school ill. by author. Random House, 1976. Translation of Emmas första dag på dagis. ISBN 0-394-95381-9 Subj: School – first day.

Betsy's fixing day ill. by author. Random House, 1978. ISBN 0-394-93781-3 Subj: Character traits – helpfulness. Family life.

This is Betsy ill. by author. Random House, 1975. Translation of Emma tvärtimot. ISBN 0-394-93161-0 Subj: Emotions. Family life.

Wolf, Ann. *The rabbit and the turtle* ill. by author. Wonder Books, 1965. Subj: Animals – rabbits. Folk and fairy tales. Reptiles – turtles, tortoises.

Wolf, Bernard. *Adam Smith goes to school* photos by author. Lippincott, 1978. ISBN 0-397-31764-6 Subj: School – first day.

Anna's silent world photos by author. Lippincott, 1977. ISBN 0-397-31739-5 Subj: Handicaps – deafness. Senses – hearing.

Don't feel sorry for Paul photos by author. Lippincott, 1974. ISBN 0-397-31588-0 Subj: Handicaps.

Michael and the dentist photos by author. Four Winds, 1980. ISBN 0-590-07637-X Subj: Careers – dentists. Emotions – fear. Teeth.

Wolf, Gita. *The very hungry lion* adapt. and ill. by Indrapramit Roy. Firefly, 1996. ISBN 1-55037-461-3 Subj: Animals – lions. Behavior – trickery. Character traits – laziness. Folk and fairy tales. Foreign lands – India.

Wolf, Jake. *Daddy, could I have an elephant?* ill. by Marylin Hafner. Greenwillow, 1996. ISBN 0-688-13295-2 Subj: Animals. Family life – fathers. Pets.

Wolf, Janet. *Adelaide to Zeke* ill. by author. HarperCollins, 1987. ISBN 0-06-026598-1 Subj: ABC books. Names.

The best present is me ill. by author. HarperCollins, 1984. ISBN 0-06-026584-1 Subj: Art. Family life – grandmothers.

The rosy fat magenta radish ill. by author. Little, 1990. ISBN 0-316-95045-9 Subj: Gardens, gardening.

Wolf, Sallie. *Peter's trucks* ill. by Cat Bowman Smith. Albert Whitman, 1992. ISBN 0-8075-6519-9 Subj: Circular tales. Rhyming text. Trucks.

Wolf, Susan. *The adventures of Albert, the running bear* (Isenberg, Barbara)

Albert the running bear gets the jitters (Isenberg, Barbara)

Wolf, Winfried. *The Easter bunny* ill. by Agnès Mathieu. Dial, 1986. ISBN 0-8037-0239-6 Subj: Animals – rabbits. Holidays – Easter.

Wolfe, Art. *Northwest animal babies* by Art Wolfe and Andrea Helman; photos by Art Wolf. Sasquatch, 1998. ISBN 1-57061-144-0 Subj: Animals – babies.

1, 2, 3 moose photos by author; text by Andrea Helman. Sasquatch, 1996. ISBN 1-57061-078-9 Subj: Animals. Counting, numbers.

Wolfe, Robert L. *The truck book* photos by author. Carolrhoda, 1981. ISBN 0-87614-125-4 Subj: Trucks.

Wolff, Ashley. *The bells of London* ill. by author. Dodd, 1985. ISBN 0-396-08485-0 Subj: Birds – doves. Emotions – sadness. Foreign lands – England. Songs.

Only the cat saw ill. by author. Dodd, 1985. ISBN 0-396-08727-2 Subj: Animals – cats. Family life. Night.

Stella and Roy go camping ill. by author. Dutton, 1999. ISBN 0-525-45864-6 Subj: Camps, camping. Family life. Sibling rivalry.

A year of beasts ill. by author. Dutton, 1986. ISBN 0-525-44240-5 Subj: Animals. Days of the week, months of the year. Farms.

A year of birds ill. by author. Dodd, 1984. ISBN 0-396-08313-7 Subj: Birds. Days of the week, months of the year. Seasons.

Wolff, Ferida. *The emperor's garden* ill. by Kathy Osborn. Tambourine, 1994. ISBN 0-688-11652-3 Subj: Behavior – sharing. Folk and fairy tales. Foreign lands – China. Gardens, gardening. Royalty – emperors.

On Halloween night by Ferida Wolff and Dolores Kozielski; ill. by Dolores Avendaño. Tambourine, 1994. ISBN 0-688-12973-0 Subj: Counting, numbers. Holidays – Halloween. Rhyming text. Witches.

The woodcutter's coat ill. by Anne Wilsdorf. Little, 1992. ISBN 0-316-95048-3 Subj: Circular tales. Clothing – coats. Crime.

Wolff, Patricia Rae. *The toll-bridge troll* ill. by Kimberly Bulcken Root. Browndeer, 1998. ISBN 0-15-277665-6 Subj: Mythical creatures – trolls. Riddles. School.

Wolff, Robert Jay. *Feeling blue* ill. by author. Scribners, 1968. Subj: Concepts – color.

Hello, yellow! ill. by author. Scribners, 1968. Subj: Concepts – color.

Seeing red ill. by author. Scribners, 1968. Subj: Concepts – color.

Wolfson, Margaret. *Turtle songs* ill. by Karla Sachi. Beyond Words, 1999. ISBN 1-885223-95-1 Subj: Folk and fairy tales. Foreign lands – Fiji. Reptiles – turtles, tortoises. Royalty – princesses. Sea and seashore.

Wolkstein, Diane. *The banza: a Haitian story* ill. by Marc Brown. Dial, 1981. ISBN 0-8037-0429-1 Subj: Animals – goats. Animals – tigers. Character traits – bravery. Folk and fairy tales. Music.

Bouki dances the Kokioko: a comical tale from Haiti ill. by Jesse Sweetwater. Harcourt, 1997. ISBN 0-15-200034-8 Subj: Activities – dancing. Behavior – trickery. Folk and fairy tales. Foreign lands – Haiti. Royalty – kings.

The cool ride in the sky ill. by Paul Galdone. Knopf, 1973. ISBN 0-394-92489-4 Subj: Activities – flying. Animals – monkeys. Birds – buzzards. Birds – vul-

tures. Character traits – cleverness. Folk and fairy tales.

The glass mountain (Grimm, Jacob)

The legend of Sleepy Hollow ill. by R. W. Alley. Morrow, 1987. Based on the story by Washington Irving. ISBN 0-688-06533-3 Subj: Folk and fairy tales. Ghosts. Holidays – Halloween. Humor.

Little Mouse's painting ill. by Maryjane Begin. Morrow, 1992. ISBN 0-688-07610-6 Subj: Animals. Animals – mice. Careers – artists. Friendship.

The magic wings: a tale from China ill. by Robert Andrew Parker. Dutton, 1983. ISBN 0-525-44062-3 Subj: Activities – flying. Behavior – wishing. Cumulative tales. Folk and fairy tales. Foreign lands – China. Seasons – spring.

Oom razoom; or, Go I know not where, Bring back I know not what ill. by Dennis McDermott. Morrow, 1991. ISBN 0-688-09417-1 Subj: Folk and fairy tales. Foreign lands – Russia. Magic.

Step by step ill. by Jos. A. Smith. Morrow, 1994. ISBN 0-688-10316-2 Subj: Friendship. Insects – ants. Insects – grasshoppers.

White wave: a Chinese tale ill. by Ed Young. Crowell, 1979. ISBN 0-690-03894-1 Subj: Folk and fairy tales. Foreign lands – China.

Wolman, Bernice. *Taking turns* ill. by Catherine Stock. Atheneum, 1992. ISBN 0-689-31677-1 Subj: Poetry.

Wolski, Slawomir. *Tiger cat* trans. by Elizabeth D. Crawford; ill. by Józef Wilkon. Holt, 1988. ISBN 0-8050-0741-5 Subj: Animals – tigers. Pets.

Wondriska, William. *Mr. Brown and Mr. Gray* ill. by author. Holt, 1968. Subj: Animals – pigs. Emotions – happiness. Money.

Puff ill. by author. Pantheon, 1960. Subj: Self-concept. Trains.

The stop ill. by author. Holt, 1972. ISBN 0-03-091982-7 Subj: Animals – horses, ponies. Character traits – kindness to animals. Desert. Emotions – fear. Indians of North America. Weather – storms.

The tomato patch ill. by author. Holt, 1964. Subj: Plants. Violence, nonviolence. Weapons.

Wong, Herbert H. *My goldfish* by Herbert H. Wong and Matthew F. Vessel; ill. by Arvis L. Stewart. Addison-Wesley, 1969. Subj: Fish. Pets. Science.

My ladybug by Herbert H. Wong and Matthew F. Vessel; ill. by Marie Nonast Bohlen. Addison-Wesley, 1969. Subj: Insects – ladybugs. Science.

My plant by Herbert H. Wong and Matthew F. Vessel; ill. by Richard Cuffari. Addison-Wesley, 1976. ISBN 0-201-08760-X Subj: Plants. Science.

Our caterpillars by Herbert H. Wong and Matthew F. Vessel; ill. by Arvis L. Stewart. Addison-Wesley, 1977. ISBN 0-201-08764-2 Subj: Insects – butterflies, caterpillars. Metamorphosis. Science.

Our earthworms by Herbert H. Wong and Matthew F. Vessel; ill. by Bill Davis. Addison-Wesley, 1977. ISBN 0-201-08766-9 Subj: Animals – worms. Science.

Our tree by Herbert H. Wong and Matthew F. Vessel; ill. by Kenneth Longtemps. Addison-Wesley, 1969. Subj: Science. Trees.

Wong, Janet S. *Buzz* ill. by Margaret Chodos-Irvine. Harcourt, 2000. ISBN 0-15-201923-5 Subj: Family life. Insects – bees. Noise, sounds.

This next New Year ill. by Yangsook Choi. Frances Foster, 2000. ISBN 0-374-35503-7 Subj: Ethnic groups in the U.S. Family life. Holidays – Chinese New Year.

Wood, A. J. *Amazing animals* ill. by Helen Ward. Boyds Mills, 1991. ISBN 1-878093-46-0 Subj: Animals.

Beautiful birds ill. by Helen Ward. Boyds Mills, 1991. ISBN 1-878093-47-9 Subj: Birds.

Look! The ultimate spot-the-difference book ill. by April Wilson. Dial, 1990. ISBN 0-8037-0925-0 Subj: Concepts. Games. Wordless.

Wood, Audrey. *The Bunyans* ill. by David Shannon. Blue Sky, 1996. ISBN 0-590-48089-8 Subj: Mythical creatures. Nature. Tall tales. U.S. history – frontier and pioneer life.

The Christmas adventure of Space Elf Sam ill. by Bruce Robert Wood. Blue Sky, 1998. ISBN 0-590-03143-0 Subj: Aliens. Holidays – Christmas. Santa Claus. Space and space ships.

Elbert's bad word ill. by author. Harcourt, 1988. ISBN 0-15-225320-3 Subj: Behavior – misbehavior. Family life. Language.

The flying dragon room ill. by Mark Teague. Blue Sky, 1996. ISBN 0-590-48193-2 Subj: Activities – making things. Imagination. Magic.

Heckedy Peg ill. by Don Wood. Harcourt, 1987. ISBN 0-15-233678-8 Subj: Behavior – talking to strangers. Character traits – cleverness. Days of the week, months of the year. Folk and fairy tales. Food. Witches.

Jubal's wish ill. by Don Wood. Blue Sky, 2000. ISBN 0-439-16964-X Subj: Behavior – wishing. Friendship. Frogs and toads. Reptiles – lizards.

King Bidgood's in the bathtub ill. by Don Wood. Harcourt, 1985. ISBN 0-15-242730-9 Subj: Activities. Activities – bathing. Caldecott award honor books. Humor. Royalty – kings.

Little Penguin's tale ill. by author. Harcourt, 1989. ISBN 0-15-246475-1 Subj: Activities – dancing. Animals. Animals – whales. Birds. Birds – penguins. Foreign lands – Antarctic.

Moonflute ill. by Don Wood. Harcourt, 1986. ISBN 0-15-255337-1 Subj: Bedtime. Moon. Night. Sleep.

The napping house ill. by Don Wood. Harcourt, 1984. ISBN 0-15-256708-9 Subj: Animals. Cumulative tales. Family life – grandmothers. Rhyming text. Sleep.

The napping house wakes up ill. by Don Wood. Harcourt, 1994. ISBN 0-15-200890-X Subj: Animals. Family life – grandmothers. Format, unusual – toy and movable books. Insects – fleas. Rhyming text. Sleep.

Oh my baby bear! ill. by author. Harcourt, 1990. ISBN 0-15-257698-3 Subj: Animals – bears. Bedtime. Behavior – growing up.

Piggies (Wood, David)

The rainbow bridge ill. by Robert Florczak. Harcourt, 1995. ISBN 0-15-265475-5 Subj: Animals – dolphins. Creation. Folk and fairy tales. Indians of North America – Chumash.

Silly Sally ill. by author. Harcourt, 1992. ISBN 0-15-274428-2 Subj: Activities – traveling. Animals. Cumulative tales. Rhyming text.

Sweet dream pie ill. by Mark Teague. Blue Sky, 1998. ISBN 0-590-96204-3 Subj: Bedtime. Dreams.

The Tickleoctopus ill. by Don Wood. Harcourt, 1994. ISBN 0-15-287000-8 Subj: Activities – playing. Cavemen. Family life. Mythical creatures.

Weird parents ill. by author. Dial, 1990. ISBN 0-8037-0649-9 Subj: Character traits – being different. Emotions – embarrassment. Family life.

Wood, David. *Happy birthday, Mouse!* (Fowler, Richard)

Piggies by Don and Audrey Wood; ill. by Don Wood. Harcourt, 1991. ISBN 0-15-256341-5 Subj: Animals – pigs. Games.

Silly spider! ill. by Richard Fowler. Harcourt, 1998. ISBN 0-15-201842-5 Subj: Format, unusual – toy and movable books. Spiders.

Wood, Douglas. *Grandad's prayers of the earth* ill. by P. J. Lynch. Candlewick, 1999. ISBN 0-7636-0660-X Subj: Death. Emotions – grief. Family life – grandfathers. Nature.

Making the world ill. by Yoshi and Hibiki Miyazaki. Simon & Schuster, 1998. ISBN 0-689-81358-9 Subj: Creation. Nature. World.

Northwoods cradle song ill. by Lisa Desimini. Simon & Schuster, 1996. ISBN 0-689-80503-9 Subj: Ethnic groups in the U.S. – Amish. Family life – mothers. Forest, woods. Indians of North America. Lullabies. Night. Poetry.

Old Turtle ill. by Cheng-Khee Chee. Pfeifer-Hamilton, 1991. ISBN 0-938586-48-3 Subj: Animals. Ecology. Religion.

Rabbit and the moon ill. by Leslie Baker. Muppet Pr., 1986. ISBN 0-689-80769-4 Subj: Animals – rabbits. Folk and fairy tales. Indians of North America – Cree. Moon.

What dads can't do ill. by Doug Cushman. Simon & Schuster, 2000. ISBN 0-689-82620-6 Subj: Family life – fathers.

What moms can't do ill. by Doug Cushman. Simon & Schuster, 2000. ISBN 0-689-83358-X Subj: Family life – mothers.

Wood, Jakki. *Across the big blue sea* ill. by author. National Geographic, 1998. ISBN 0-7922-7308-7 Subj: Animals. Boats, ships. Nature. Sea and seashore.

Dads are such fun ill. by Rog Bonner. Simon & Schuster, 1992. ISBN 0-671-75342-8 Subj: Activities – playing. Animals. Family life – fathers.

Fiddle-i-fee ill. by author. Bradbury, 1994. ISBN 0-02-793396-2 Subj: Animals. Cumulative tales. Music. Noise, sounds.

Moo moo, brown cow ill. by Rog Bonner. Harcourt, 1992. ISBN 0-15-200533-1 Subj: Animals. Animals – cats. Concepts – color. Counting, numbers. Farms.

One bear with bees in his hair ill. by author. Dutton, 1991. ISBN 0-525-44695-8 Subj: Animals – bears. Counting, numbers. Rhyming text.

Wood, Jenny. *The animal kingdom* ill. by Andrew Bale. Macmillan, 1992. ISBN 0-02-793395-4 Subj: Animals. Nature.

Wood, John Norris. *Jungles* ed. by Janet Schulman; ill. by Kevin Dean. Knopf, 1987. ISBN 0-394-87802-7 Subj: Animals. Behavior – hiding. Format, unusual. Jungle.

Oceans ill. by Mark Harrison. Knopf, 1985. ISBN 0-394-87583-4 Subj: Behavior – hiding. Fish. Format, unusual. Sea and seashore.

Wood, Joyce. *Grandmother Lucy goes on a picnic* ill. by Frank Francis. Collins-World, 1976. ISBN 0-529-05288-1 Subj: Activities – picnicking. Activities – walking. Family life – grandmothers.

Grandmother Lucy in her garden ill. by Frank Francis. Collins-World, 1975. ISBN 0-529-05239-3 Subj: Family life – grandmothers. Foreign lands – England. Seasons. Seasons – spring.

Wood, Leslie. *A dog called Mischief* ill. by author. Oxford Univ. Pr., 1997. ISBN 0-19-849014-3 Subj: Animals – dogs. Behavior – hiding things. Food.

Wood, Nancy C. *Little wrangler* ill. by Myron Wood. Doubleday, 1966. Subj: Cowboys.

Wood, Tim. *Gymnastics* photos by Chris Fairclough. Watts, 1989. ISBN 0-531-10826-0 Subj: Sports – gymnastics.

Motor racing ill. by Chris Fairclough. Watts, 1989. ISBN 0-531-10828-7 Subj: Automobiles. Sports – racing.

Motorcycling ill. by Chris Fairclough. Watts, 1989. ISBN 0-531-10827-9 Subj: Sports – racing.

Woodcock, Louise Phinney. *The very little dog: and, The smart little kitty* (Skaar, Grace Marion)

Wooding, Sharon L. *Arthur's Christmas wish* ill. by author. Atheneum, 1986. ISBN 0-689-31211-3 Subj: Animals – mice. Behavior – wishing. Holidays – Christmas.

The painter's cat ill. by author. Putnam, 1994. ISBN 0-399-22414-9 Subj: Animals – cats. Art. Behavior – running away. Careers – artists.

Woodman, Allen. *The bear who came to stay* by Allen Woodman and David Kirby; ill. by Harvey Stevenson. Bradbury, 1994. ISBN 0-02-793397-0 Subj: Animals – bears. Family life. Forest, woods.

Cows are going to Paris (Kirby, David K.)

Woodruff, Elvira. *Can you guess where we're going?* ill. by Cynthia Fisher. Holiday, 1998. ISBN 0-8234-1387-X Subj: Family life – grandfathers. Libraries.

The memory coat ill. by Michael Dooling. Scholastic, 1999. ISBN 0-590-67717-9 Subj: Clothing – coats. Ethnic groups in the U.S. – Russian Americans. Immigration. Jewish culture. Memories, memory.

Mrs. McCloskey's monkeys ill. by Jill Kastner. Scholastic, 1991. ISBN 0-590-41233-7 Subj: Animals – monkeys. Behavior – misbehavior. Family life – brothers. Zoos.

Show and tell ill. by Denise Brunkus. Holiday, 1991. ISBN 0-8234-0883-3 Subj: Bubbles. Magic. School.

Tubtime ill. by Suçie Stevenson. Holiday, 1990. ISBN 0-8234-0777-2 Subj: Activities – bathing. Bubbles. Family life – brothers and sisters. Imagination.

The wing shop ill. by Stephen Gammell. Holiday, 1991. ISBN 0-8234-0825-6 Subj: Activities – flying. Moving.

Woodson, Jacqueline. *We had a picnic this Sunday past* ill. by Diane Greenseid. Hyperion, 1997. ISBN 0-7868-2192-2 Subj: Activities – picnicking. Ethnic groups in the U.S. – African Americans. Family life.

Woodtor, Dee. *Big meeting* ill. by Dolores Johnson. Atheneum, 1996. ISBN 0-689-31993-9 Subj: Activities – traveling. Ethnic groups in the U.S. – African Americans. Family life – aunts, uncles. Family life – grandparents. Religion. Seasons – summer.

Woodworth, Viki. *Fairy tale jokes* ill. by author. Child's World, 1993. ISBN 0-89565-862-3 Subj: Folk and fairy tales. Riddles.

Woolaver, Lance. *Christmas with the rural mail* ill. by Maud Lewis. Nimbus Pub., 1981. ISBN 0-920852-04-1 Subj: Foreign lands – Canada. Holidays – Christmas. Poetry.

From Ben Loman to the sea ill. by Maud Lewis. Nimbus Pub., 1981. ISBN 0-920852-05-X Subj: Behavior – running away. Poetry. Sea and seashore. Seasons – spring.

Wooldridge, Connie Nordhielm. *Wicked Jack* ill. by Will Hillenbrand. Holiday, 1995. ISBN 0-8234-1101-X Subj: Behavior – wishing. Character traits – meanness. Devil. Folk and fairy tales.

Woolf, Virginia. *Nurse Lugton's curtain* ill. by Julie Vivas. Harcourt, 1982. ISBN 0-15-200545-5 Subj: Activities – sewing. Animals. Careers – nurses. Imagination. Sleep.

Woolley, Catherine. *see* Thayer, Jane

Worley, Daryl. *Billy and the attic adventure* ill. by John Daab. Tyke Corp., 1989. ISBN 0-924067-00-4 Subj: Family life – fathers. Homes, houses.

Wormell, Christopher. *Blue Rabbit and friends* ill. by author. Fogelman, 2000. ISBN 0-8037-2499-3 Subj: Animals. Animals – rabbits. Friendship. Homes, houses.

Wormell, Mary. *Hilda Hen's happy birthday* ill. by author. Harcourt, 1995. ISBN 0-15-200299-5 Subj: Animals. Birds – chickens. Birthdays. Farms.

Hilda Hen's search ill. by author. Harcourt, 1994. ISBN 0-15-200069-0 Subj: Birds – chickens. Eggs. Farms.

Why not? ill. by author. Farrar, 2000. ISBN 0-374-38422-3 Subj: Animals. Animals – babies. Animals – cats. Character traits – questioning. Farms.

Worth, Bonnie. *Peter Cottontail's surprise* ill. by Greg Hildebrandt. Unicorn Publishing House, 1985. ISBN 0-88101-015-4 Subj: Animals – rabbits. Birthdays. Parties. Seasons – spring.

Worth, Valerie. *At Christmastime* ill. by Antonio Frasconi. HarperCollins, 1992. ISBN 0-06-205020-6 Subj: Holidays. Holidays – Christmas. Poetry.

Worthington, Joan. *Teddy bear farmer* (Worthington, Phoebe)

Worthington, Phoebe. *Teddy bear baker* by Phoebe and Selby Worthington; ill. by authors. Warne, 1980. ISBN 0-7232-2339-4 Subj: Careers – bakers. Foreign lands – England. Toys – bears.

Teddy bear coalman: a story for the very young by Phoebe and Selby Worthington; ill. by authors. Warne, 1980. ISBN 0-7232-2052-2 Subj: Foreign lands – England. Toys – bears.

Teddy bear farmer by Phoebe and Joan Worthington; ill. by authors. Viking, 1985. ISBN 0-670-80342-1 Subj: Animals. Farms. Toys – bears.

Worthington, Selby. *Teddy bear baker* (Worthington, Phoebe)

Teddy bear coalman: a story for the very young (Worthington, Phoebe)

Worthy, Judith. *Eyes* ill. by Beba Hall. Doubleday, 1989. ISBN 0-385-24966-7 Subj: Anatomy – eyes. Animals.

Wouters, Anne. *This book is for us* ill. by author. Dutton, 1992. ISBN 0-525-44882-9 Subj: Animals – moles. Animals – polar bears. Night. Wordless.

This book is too small ill. by author. Dutton, 1992. ISBN 0-525-44881-0 Subj: Animals – moles. Animals – polar bears. Wordless.

Woychuk, Denis. *The other side of the wall* ill. by Kim Howard. Lothrop, 1991. ISBN 0-688-09895-9 Subj: Animals – hippopotamuses. Animals – mice. Emotions – love. Middle Ages.

Pirates ill. by Kim Howard. Lothrop, 1992. ISBN 0-688-10337-5 Subj: Animals – hippopotamuses. Animals – mice. Pirates.

Wright, Betty Ren. *The cat next door* ill. by Gail Owens. Holiday, 1991. ISBN 0-8234-0896-5 Subj: Animals – cats. Death. Emotions – grief. Family life – grandmothers.

Pet detectives! ill. by Kevin O'Malley. BridgeWater, 1999. ISBN 0-8167-4952-3 Subj: Animals – cats. Animals – dogs. Crime. Rhyming text.

Wright, Cliff. *Santa's ark* ill. by author. Millbrook, 1997. ISBN 0-7613-0314-6 Subj: Animals – babies. Animals – reindeer. Holidays – Christmas. Santa Claus.

Wright, Courtni Crump. *Journey to freedom* ill. by Gershom Griffith. Holiday, 1994. ISBN 0-8234-1096-X Subj: Character traits – freedom. Ethnic groups in the U.S. – African Americans. Slavery. U.S. history.

Jumping the broom ill. by Gershom Griffith. Holiday, 1994. ISBN 0-8234-1042-0 Subj: Ethnic groups in the U.S. – African Americans. Slavery. U.S. history. Weddings.

Wagon train: a family goes west in 1865 ill. by Gershom Griffith. Holiday, 1995. ISBN 0-8234-1152-4 Subj: Activities – traveling. Ethnic groups in the U.S. – African Americans. U.S. history – frontier and pioneer life.

Wright, Dare. *The doll and the kitten* photos by author. Doubleday, 1960. Subj: Animals – cats. Toys – bears. Toys – dolls.

Edith and Midnight photos by author. Doubleday, 1978. ISBN 0-385-14156-4 Subj: Toys – bears. Toys – dolls.

Edith and Mr. Bear photos by author. Random House, 1964. Subj: Behavior – running away. Toys – bears. Toys – dolls.

Edith and the duckling photos by author. Doubleday, 1981. ISBN 0-385-17101-3 Subj: Birds – ducks. Eggs. Toys – bears. Toys – dolls.

The lonely doll photos by author. Houghton Mifflin, 1998. ISBN 0-395-90112-X Subj: Emotions – loneliness. Toys – bears. Toys – dolls.

The lonely doll learns a lesson photos by author. Random House, 1961. Subj: Animals – cats. Pets. Toys – bears. Toys – dolls.

Look at a calf photos by author. Random House, 1974. ISBN 0-394-92776-1 Subj: Animals – bulls, cows. Farms.

Look at a colt photos by author. Random House, 1969. Subj: Animals – horses, ponies. Farms.

Look at a kitten photos by author. Random House, 1975. ISBN 0-394-93123-8 Subj: Animals – cats.

Wright, Freire. *Beauty and the beast* ill. by adapt. David & Charles, 1985. ISBN 0-7182-6091-0 Subj: Character traits – appearance. Character traits – loyalty. Emotions – love. Folk and fairy tales. Magic.

Wright, Jill. *The old woman and the jar of ums* ill. by Glen Rounds. Putnam, 1990. ISBN 0-399-21736-3 Subj: Behavior – misbehavior. Magic.

The old woman and the Willy Nilly Man ill. by Glen Rounds. Putnam, 1987. ISBN 0-399-21355-4 Subj: Activities – dancing. Behavior – trickery. Clothing. Folk and fairy tales. Humor.

Wright, Joan Richards. *Bugs* (Parker, Nancy Winslow)

Wright, Josephine Lord. *Cotton Cat and Martha Mouse* ill. by John E. Johnson. Dutton, 1966. Subj: Animals – cats. Animals – mice. Behavior – sharing. Poetry.

Wright, Lillian. *Hearing* ill. by author. Raintree, 1995. ISBN 0-8114-5516-5 Subj: Senses – hearing.

Seeing ill. by author. Raintree, 1995. ISBN 0-8114-5515-7 Subj: Senses – seeing.

Smelling and tasting ill. by author. Raintree, 1995. ISBN 0-8114-5518-1 Subj: Senses – smelling. Senses – tasting.

Touching ill. by author. Raintree, 1995. ISBN 0-8114-5517-3 Subj: Senses – touching.

Wright, Martin. *Granny Stickleback* (Moore, John)

Wright, Sue (Sue M.). *The Christmas path: a legend of the luminarias* ill. by David Wenzel. Scholastic, 1998. ISBN 0-590-04709-4 Subj: Folk and fairy tales. Holidays – Christmas. Lights. Religion – Nativity.

Wundrow, Deanna. *Jungle drum* cut-paper ill. by Susan Swan. Millbrook, 1999. ISBN 0-7613-1270-6 Subj: Animals. Jungle. Noise, sounds.

Wyeth, Sharon Dennis. *Always my dad* ill. by Raúl Colón. Knopf, 1995. ISBN 0-679-93447-2 Subj: Behavior – needing someone. Country. Ethnic groups in the U.S. – African Americans. Family life – fathers. Family life – grandparents.

Something beautiful ill. by Chris K. Soentpiet. Doubleday, 1998. ISBN 0-385-32239-9 Subj: City. Communities, neighborhoods. Ethnic groups in the U.S. – African Americans.

Wyler, Rose. *Puddles and ponds* ill. by Steven James Petruccio. Messner, 1990. ISBN 0-671-66348-8 Subj: Animals. Nature. Science. Water.

Raindrops and rainbows ill. by Steven James Petruccio. Messner, 1989. ISBN 0-671-66346-1 Subj: Science. Weather – rain. Weather – rainbows.

The starry sky ill. by Steven James Petruccio. Messner, 1989. ISBN 0-671-66345-3 Subj: Earth. Science. Sky. Stars.

Wyllie, Stephen. *Dinner with fox* ill. by Korky Paul. Dial, 1990. ISBN 0-8037-0796-7 Subj: Animals – foxes. Animals – wolves. Food. Format, unusual – toy and movable books.

Ghost train ill. by Brian Lee. Dial, 1992. ISBN 0-8037-1163-8 Subj: Format, unusual. Ghosts. Trains.

The great race ill. by Anni Axworthy. Harper-Collins, 1987. ISBN 0-694-00126-0 Subj: Animals. Format, unusual. Rebuses. Sports – racing.

Snappity snap ill. by Maureen Roffey. Harper-Collins, 1989. ISBN 0-06-026630-9 Subj: Activities – photographing. Animals. Counting, numbers. Format, unusual – toy and movable books.

White Rabbit builds a dream house ill. by Anni Axworthy. Ideals, 1990. ISBN 0-8249-8363-7 Subj: Animals – rabbits. Format, unusual. Homes, houses.

Wyndham, Robert. *The Chinese Mother Goose rhymes* (Mother Goose)

Wynne-Jones, Tim. *Builder of the moon* ill. by Ian Wallace. Macmillan, 1989. ISBN 0-689-50472-1 Subj: Moon. Problem solving. Space and space ships. Toys – blocks.

The hour of the frog ill. by Catharine O'Neill. Little, 1990. ISBN 0-316-96309-7 Subj: Frogs and toads. Night. Noise, sounds.

Zoom upstream ill. by Eric Beddows. Harper-Collins, 1994. ISBN 0-06-022978-0 Subj: Animals – cats. Foreign lands – Egypt.

Wynot, Jillian. *The Mother's Day sandwich* ill. by Maxie Chambliss. Watts, 1990. ISBN 0-531-08457-4 Subj: Family life – mothers. Food. Holidays – Mother's Day.

Wyse, Lois. *How to take your grandmother to the museum* by Lois Wyse and Molly Rose Goldman; ill. by Marie-Louise Gay. Workman, [pub. in association with the] American Museum of Natural History, c1998 1998. ISBN 0-7611-0990-0 Subj: Family life – grandmothers. Museums.

Two guppies, a turtle and Aunt Edna ill. by Roger Coast. Collins-World, 1966. Subj: Family life – aunts, uncles. Fish. Problem solving. Reptiles – turtles, tortoises. Telephone.

Xiong, Blia. *Nine-in-one Grr! Grr!* adapt. by Cathy Spagnoli; ill. by Nancy Hom. Childrens Pr., 1989. ISBN 0-89239-048-4 Subj: Animals – tigers. Folk and fairy tales. Foreign lands – Laos.

Yabuki, Seiji. *I love the morning* ill. by author. Collins-World, 1969. Subj: Emotions – happiness. Morning.

Yabuuchi, Masayuki. *Animals sleeping* ill. by author. Putnam, 1983. ISBN 0-399-20983-2 Subj: Animals. Science. Sleep.

Whose baby? ill. by author. Putnam, 1985. ISBN 0-399-21210-8 Subj: Animals.

Whose footprints? ill. by author. Putnam, 1985. ISBN 0-399-21209-4 Subj: Animals.

Yaccarino, Dan. *Deep in the jungle* ill. by author. Atheneum, 2000. ISBN 0-689-82235-9 Subj: Animals. Animals – lions. Behavior – dissatisfaction. Circus.

Good night, Mr. Night ill. by author. Harcourt, 1997. ISBN 0-15-201319-9 Subj: Bedtime. Dreams. Night.

If I had a robot ill. by author. Viking, 1996. ISBN 0-670-86936-8 Subj: Behavior. Family life. Robots.

An octopus followed me home ill. by author. Viking, 1997. ISBN 0-670-87401-9 Subj: Animals. Octopuses. Pets.

Zoom! Zoom! Zoom! I'm off to the moon! ill. by author. Scholastic, 1997. ISBN 0-590-95610-8 Subj: Moon. Rhyming text. Space and space ships.

Yacowitz, Caryn. *The jade stone* ill. by Ju-Hong Chen. Holiday, 1992. ISBN 0-8234-0919-8 Subj: Careers – artists. Folk and fairy tales. Foreign lands – China. Royalty – emperors.

Pumpkin fiesta ill. by Joe Cepeda. HarperCollins, 1998. ISBN 0-06-027659-2 Subj: Fairs. Foreign lands – Mexico. Gardens, gardening. Plants.

Yaffe, Alan. *The magic meatballs* ill. by Karen Born Andersen. Dial, 1979. ISBN 0-8037-5140-0 Subj: Behavior – dissatisfaction. Family life. Magic.

Yagawa, Sumiko. *The crane wife* trans. from Japanese by Katherine Paterson; ill. by Suekichi Akaba. Morrow, 1982. ISBN 0-688-00496-2 Subj: Activities – weaving. Birds – cranes. Character traits – kindness to animals. Folk and fairy tales. Foreign lands – Japan.

Yagelski, Robert. *The day the lifting bridge stuck* ill. by Jennifer Beck Harris. Bradbury, 1992. ISBN 0-02-793595-7 Subj: Bridges. Machines. Problem solving. Traffic, traffic signs.

Yagya, Genichiro. *All about scabs* ill. by author; trans. by Amanda Mayer Stinchecum. Kane/Miller, 1998. ISBN 0-916291-82-0 Subj: Health and fitness. Hygiene.

Yamaguchi, Tohr. *Two crabs and the moonlight* ill. by Marianne Yamaguchi. Holt, 1965. Subj: Crustaceans. Moon.

Yamashita, Haruo. *Mice at the beach* ill. by Kazuo Iwamura. Morrow, 1987. ISBN 0-688-07064-7 Subj: Animals – mice. Family life. Safety. Sea and seashore.

Yardley, Joanna. *The red ball* ill. by author. Harcourt, 1991. ISBN 0-15-200894-2 Subj: Family life. Imagination. Toys – balls.

Yardley, Thompson. *Buy now, pay later* ill. by author. Millbrook, 1992. ISBN 1-56294-149-6 Subj: Ecology. Money. Shopping.

Yardumian, Miryam. *see* Miryam

Yaroshevskaya, Kim. *Little Kim's doll* ill. by Luc Melanson. Douglas & McIntyre, 1999. ISBN 0-88899-353-6 Subj: Birthdays. Foreign lands – Russia. Sex roles. Toys – dolls.

Yashima, Mitsu. *Momo's kitten* ill. by Taro Yashima. Viking, 1961. Subj: Animals – cats. Ethnic groups in the U.S. – Japanese Americans.

Plenty to watch ill. by Taro Yashima. Viking, 1954. Subj: Foreign lands – Japan.

Yashima, Taro. *Crow boy* ill. by author. Viking, 1955. ISBN 0-670-24931-9 Subj: Caldecott award honor books. Character traits – shyness. Emotions – loneliness. Foreign lands – Japan. School.

Momo's kitten (Yashima, Mitsu)

Seashore story ill. by author. Viking, 1967. Subj: Caldecott award honor books. Folk and fairy tales. Reptiles – turtles, tortoises. Sea and seashore.

Umbrella ill. by author. Viking, 1958. ISBN 0-670-73858-1 Subj: Birthdays. Caldecott award honor books. City. Ethnic groups in the U.S. – Japanese Americans. Umbrellas. Weather – rain.

The village tree ill. by author. Viking, 1972, c1953. ISBN 0-670-05072-5 Subj: Foreign lands – Japan. Seasons – summer. Trees.

The youngest one ill. by author. Viking, 1962. Subj: Character traits – shyness. Ethnic groups in the U.S. – Japanese Americans. Friendship.

Yates, Irene. *All about color* ill. by Jill Newton. Benchmark, 1998. ISBN 0-761-40514-3 Subj: Concepts – color.

All about pattern ill. by Jill Newton. Benchmark, 1998. ISBN 0-761-40517-8 Subj: Concepts – shape.

All about shape ill. by Jill Newton. Benchmark, 1998. ISBN 0-761-40515-1 Subj: Concepts – shape.

All about touch ill. by Jill Newton. Benchmark, 1998. ISBN 0-761-40516-X Subj: Senses – touching.

Ybáñez, Terry. *Hairs = Pelitos* (Cisneros, Sandra)

Ye Pin Kwei. *Monkey creates havoc in heaven* (P'an, Ts'ai-ying)

Ye, Ting-xing. *Share the sky* ill. by Suzane Langlois. Annick, 1999. ISBN 1-55037-579-2 Subj: Ethnic groups in the U.S. – Chinese Americans. Family life – grandfathers. Foreign lands – China. Kites.

Three monks, no water ill. by Harvey Chan. Annick, 1997. ISBN 1-55037-443-5 Subj: Activities – working. Folk and fairy tales. Foreign lands – China.

Yee, Brenda Shannon. *Sand castle* ill. by Thea Kliros. Greenwillow, 1999. ISBN 0-688-16194-4 Subj: Castles. Cumulative tales. Sand. Sea and seashore.

Yee, Patrick. *Baby bear* ill. by author. Viking, 1993. ISBN 0-670-85288-0 Subj: Animals – bears. Format, unusual – board books.

Baby lion ill. by author. Viking, 1993. ISBN 0-670-85289-9 Subj: Animals – lions. Format, unusual – board books.

Baby monkey ill. by author. Viking, 1993. ISBN 0-670-85290-2 Subj: Animals – monkeys. Format, unusual – board books.

Baby penguin ill. by author. Viking, 1993. ISBN 0-670-85291-0 Subj: Birds – penguins. Foreign lands – Antarctic. Format, unusual – board books.

Bedtime for Rosie Rabbit ill. by Patrick Yee; text by Lucy Coats. Simon & Schuster, 1996. ISBN 0-689-80716-3 Subj: Animals – rabbits. Bedtime. Format, unusual – toy and movable books.

Let's go ill. by author. Viking, 1995. ISBN 0-670-85937-0 Subj: Food. Format, unusual – board books.

Let's make friends ill. by author. Viking, 1995. ISBN 0-670-85940-0 Subj: Format, unusual – board books. Friendship.

Let's play ill. by author. Viking, 1995. ISBN 0-670-85939-7 Subj: Activities – playing. Format, unusual – board books.

Little Buddy meets Bobo ill. by author. Viking, 1993. ISBN 0-670-84803-4 Subj: Animals – elephants.

Animals – rabbits. Format, unusual – toy and movable books.

Rosie Rabbit's colors ill. by author. Little Simon, 1998. ISBN 0-689-81842-4 Subj: Animals – rabbits. Concepts – color. Format, unusual – board books.

Rosie Rabbit's numbers ill. by author. Little Simon, 1998. ISBN 0-689-81843-2 Subj: Animals – rabbits. Counting, numbers. Format, unusual – board books.

Rosie Rabbit's opposites ill. by author. Little Simon, 1998. ISBN 0-689-81844-0 Subj: Animals – rabbits. Concepts – opposites. Format, unusual – board books.

Rosie Rabbit's shapes ill. by author. Simon & Schuster, 1998. ISBN 0-689-81845-9 Subj: Animals – rabbits. Concepts – shape. Format, unusual – board books.

Winter rabbit ill. by author. Viking, 1994. ISBN 0-670-85353-6 Subj: Animals – rabbits. Snowmen.

Yee, Paul. *The boy in the attic* ill. by Gu Xiong. Douglas & McIntyre, 1998. ISBN 0-88899-330-7 Subj: Friendship. Ghosts. Insects – butterflies, caterpillars.

Let's eat ill. by author. Viking, 1995. ISBN 0-670-85938-9 Subj: Activities – traveling. Format, unusual – board books. Transportation.

Roses sing on new snow ill. by Harvey Chan. Macmillan, 1992. ISBN 0-02-793622-8 Subj: Activities – cooking. Ethnic groups in the U.S. – Chinese Americans.

Yee, Wong Herbert. *Big black bear* ill. by author. Houghton Mifflin, 1993. ISBN 0-395-66359-8 Subj: Animals – bears. Behavior – misbehavior. Etiquette. Rhyming text.

A drop of rain ill. by author. Houghton Mifflin, 1995. ISBN 0-395-71549-0 Subj: Babies. Behavior – mistakes. Ethnic groups in the U.S. – Chinese Americans. Rhyming text. Weather – rain.

Eek! There's a mouse in the house ill. by author. Houghton Mifflin, 1992. ISBN 0-395-62303-0 Subj: Animals. Cumulative tales. Homes, houses. Rhyming text.

Fireman Small ill. by author. Houghton Mifflin, 1994. ISBN 0-395-68987-2 Subj: Animals. Animals – pigs. Careers – firefighters. Fire. Rhyming text.

Fireman Small, fire down below ill. by author. Houghton Mifflin, 2001. ISBN 0-618-00707-5 Subj: Animals. Animals – pigs. Careers – firefighters. Fire. Hotels. Rhyming text.

Fireman Small to the rescue ill. by author. Houghton Mifflin, 1998. ISBN 0-395-88122-6 Subj: Animals. Animals – pigs. Careers – farmers. Careers – firefighters. Fire. Rhyming text.

Hamburger Heaven ill. by author. Houghton Mifflin, 1999. ISBN 0-395-87548-X Subj: Activities – working. Animals. Animals – pigs. Food. Restaurants.

Mrs. Brown went to town ill. by author. Houghton Mifflin, 1996. ISBN 0-395-75282-5 Subj: Animals. Homes, houses. Rhyming text.

The Officers' Ball ill. by author. Houghton Mifflin, 1997. ISBN 0-395-81182-1 Subj: Activities – dancing. Animals. Animals – hippopotamuses. Careers – police officers. Crime. Rhyming text.

Yektai, Niki. *Bears at the beach* ill. by author. Millbrook, 1996. ISBN 0-7613-0022-8 Subj: Animals – bears. Counting, numbers. Sea and seashore.

Bears in pairs ill. by Diane de Groat. Bradbury, 1987. ISBN 0-02-793691-0 Subj: Animals – bears. Concepts. Rhyming text.

Hi bears, bye bears ill. by Diane de Groat. Watts, 1990. ISBN 0-531-08458-2 Subj: Rhyming text. Toys – bears.

What's missing? ill. by Susannah Ryan. Clarion, 1987. ISBN 0-89919-510-5 Subj: Games. Problem solving.

Yen, Clara. *Why rat comes first* ill. by Hideo C. Yoshida. Children's Book Pr., 1991. ISBN 0-89239-072-7 Subj: Animals. Foreign lands – China. Royalty. Zodiac.

Yenne, Bill. *Joshua and the battle of Jericho* ill. by reteller. Nelson, 1994. ISBN 0-7852-8331-5 Subj: Religion. War.

Yeoman, John. *The bear's water picnic* ill. by Quentin Blake. Atheneum, 1987, 1970. ISBN 0-689-31386-1 Subj: Activities – picnicking. Animals – bears. Animals – hedgehogs. Animals – pigs. Animals – squirrels. Frogs and toads.

Mouse trouble ill. by Quentin Blake. Collier, 1976, c1972. ISBN 0-02-045610-7 Subj: Animals – cats. Animals – mice. Friendship. Windmills.

Old Mother Hubbard's dog dresses up ill. by Quentin Blake. Houghton Mifflin, 1990. ISBN 0-394-53358-9 Subj: Animals – dogs. Clothing. Rhyming text.

Old Mother Hubbard's dog learns to play ill. by Quentin Blake. Houghton Mifflin, 1990. ISBN 0-395-53360-0 Subj: Animals – dogs. Music. Rhyming text.

Old Mother Hubbard's dog needs a doctor ill. by Quentin Blake. Houghton Mifflin, 1990. ISBN 0-395-53359-7 Subj: Animals – dogs. Rhyming text.

Old Mother Hubbard's dog takes up sport ill. by Quentin Blake. Houghton Mifflin, 1990. ISBN 0-395-53361-9 Subj: Animals – dogs. Rhyming text. Sports.

Our village ill. by Quentin Blake. Atheneum, 1988. ISBN 0-689-31451-5 Subj: Communities, neighborhoods. Poetry.

The wild washerwomen: a new folk tale ill. by Quentin Blake. Crown, 1986, c1979. ISBN 0-517-56255-3 Subj: Activities – working. Behavior – misbehavior. Folk and fairy tales.

The young performing horse ill. by Quentin Blake. Parents, 1979. ISBN 0-8193-0971-0 Subj: Animals – horses, ponies. Multiple births – twins. Theater.

Yeomans, Thomas. *For every child a star: a Christmas story* ill. by Tomie de Paola. Holiday, 1986. ISBN 0-8234-0526-5 Subj: Holidays – Christmas. Night. Stars.

Yep, Laurence. *The city of dragons* ill. by Jean and Mou-Sien Tseng. Scholastic, 1995. ISBN 0-590-47865-6 Subj: Anatomy – faces. Behavior – running away. Character traits – appearance. Character traits – being different. Giants.

Dragon prince ill. by Kam Mak. HarperCollins, 1997. ISBN 0-06-024393-7 Subj: Dragons. Emotions – envy, jealousy. Family life – sisters. Folk and fairy tales. Foreign lands – China. Sibling rivalry.

The junior thunder lord ill. by Robert Van Nutt. BridgeWater, 1994. ISBN 0-8167-3454-2 Subj: Character traits – generosity. Character traits – kindness. Folk and fairy tales. Foreign lands – China. Weather – droughts. Weather – rain.

The Khan's daughter ill. by Jean and Mou-Sien Tseng. Scholastic, 1997,. ISBN 0-590-48389-7 Subj: Folk and fairy tales. Foreign lands – Mongolia. Monsters. Royalty – khans. Weddings.

The man who tricked a ghost ill. by Isadore Seltzer. BridgeWater, 1993. ISBN 0-816-73030-X Subj: Behavior – trickery. Foreign lands – China. Ghosts. Middle Ages.

The shell woman and the king ill. by Yang Ming-Yi. Dial, 1993. ISBN 0-8037-1394-0 Subj: Folk and fairy tales. Foreign lands – China. Magic. Royalty – kings.

Tiger woman ill. by Robert Roth. BridgeWater, 1994. ISBN 0-8167-3464-X Subj: Animals. Behavior – greed. Character traits – selfishness. Folk and fairy tales. Foreign lands – China. Rhyming text.

Yerxa, Leo. *A fish tale, or, The little one that got away* ill. by author. Douglas & McIntyre, 1995. ISBN 0-88899-247-5 Subj: Behavior – trickery. Fish. Sports – fishing.

Last leaf first snowflake to fall ill. by author. Orchard, 1994. ISBN 0-531-08674-7 Subj: Indians of North America – Nishnawbe. Nature. Poetry. Seasons – fall. Seasons – winter. Weather – snow.

Yezback, Steven A. *Pumpkinseeds* ill. by Mozelle Thompson. Bobbs-Merrill, 1969. Subj: Behavior – solitude. City. Ethnic groups in the U.S. – African Americans.

Yezerski, Thomas. *Queen of the world* ill. by author. Farrar, 2000. ISBN 0-374-36165-7 Subj: Birthdays. Family life – mothers. Family life – sisters. Sibling rivalry.

Together in Pinecone Patch ill. by author. Farrar, 1998. ISBN 0-374-37647-6 Subj: Emotions – love. Ethnic groups in the U.S. – Irish Americans. Ethnic groups in the U.S. – Polish Americans. Immigrants. Prejudice. Weddings.

Yim, Natasha. *Otto's rainy day* ill. by Pamela R. Levy. Talewinds, 2000. ISBN 1-57091-400-1 Subj: Activities – playing. Family life – mothers. Weather – rain.

Ylla. *Animal babies* by Ylla and Arthur S. Gregor; ill. by Ylla. HarperCollins, 1959. Designed by Luc Bouchage. Subj: Animals.

I'll show you cats by Ylla and Crosby Newell Bonsall; ill. by Ylla. HarperCollins, 1964. Planned by Charles Rado; designed by Luc Bouchage. Subj: Animals – cats.

Listen, listen! (Bonsall, Crosby Newell)

The little elephant by Ylla and Arthur S. Gregor; ill. by Ylla. HarperCollins, 1956. Designed by Luc Bouchage. Subj: Animals – elephants.

Look who's talking by Ylla and Crosby Newell Bonsall; ill. by Ylla. HarperCollins, 1962. Planned by Charles Rado; designed by Luc Bouchage. Subj: Birds – ostriches. Zoos.

Polar bear brothers by Ylla and Crosby Newell Bonsall; ill. by Ylla. HarperCollins, 1960. Designed by Luc Bouchage. Subj: Animals – polar bears.

Two little bears ill. by author. HarperCollins, 1954. Subj: Animals – bears. Behavior – lost.

Yoaker, Harry. *The view* by Harry Yoaker and Simon Henwood; ill. by Simon Henwood. Dial, 1992. ISBN 0-8037-1105-0 Subj: Communities, neighborhoods. Homes, houses.

Yolen, Jane. *All in the woodland early: an ABC book* ill. by Jane Breskin Zalben; music and lyrics by author. Collins-World, 1980. ISBN 0-529-05509-0 Subj: ABC books. Forest, woods.

All those secrets of the world ill. by Leslie A. Baker. Little, 1991. ISBN 0-316-96891-9 Subj: Concepts – perspective. Family life – fathers. War.

Alphabestiary: animal poems from A to Z (Alphabestiary)

Baby Bear's bedtime book ill. by Jane Dyer. Harcourt, 1990. ISBN 0-15-205120-1 Subj: Activities – babysitting. Animals – bears. Bedtime.

Before the storm ill. by Georgia Pugh. Boyds Mills, 1995. ISBN 1-56397-240-9 Subj: Activities – playing. Seasons – summer. Weather – storms.

Beneath the ghost moon ill. by Laurel Molk. Little, 1994. ISBN 0-316-96892-7 Subj: Animals – mice. Character traits – bravery. Holidays – Halloween. Rhyming text.

Bird watch: a book of poetry ill. by Ted Lewin. Philomel, 1990. ISBN 0-399-21612-X Subj: Birds. Poetry.

Child of faerie, child of earth ill. by Jane Dyer. Little, 1997. ISBN 0-316-96897-8 Subj: Fairies. Folk and fairy tales. Holidays – Halloween. Poetry.

Dragon night and other lullabies ill. by Demi. Methuen, 1980. ISBN 0-416-30711-6 Subj: Animals. Bedtime. Lullabies. Sleep.

Eeny, meeny, miney mole ill. by Kathryn Brown. Harcourt, 1992. ISBN 0-15-225350-5 Subj: Animals – moles. Character traits – curiosity.

Elfabet ill. by Lauren Mills. Little, 1989. ISBN 0-316-96900-1 Subj: ABC books. Activities. Mythical creatures – elves.

The emperor and the kite ill. by Ed Young. Philomel, 1988, c1967. ISBN 0-399-21499-2 Subj: Caldecott award honor books. Character traits – smallness. Family life – fathers. Foreign lands – China. Kites. Royalty – emperors.

The giant's farm ill. by Tomie de Paola. Seabury Pr., 1977. ISBN 0-8164-3193-0 Subj: Farms. Giants.

The giants go camping ill. by Tomie de Paola. Seabury Pr., 1979. ISBN 0-8164-3223-6 Subj: Camps, camping. Giants.

The girl in the golden bower ill. by Jane Dyer. Little, 1994. ISBN 0-316-96894-3 Subj: Folk and fairy tales. Orphans. Witches.

The girl who loved the wind ill. by Ed Young. Crowell, 1972. ISBN 0-690-33100-2 Subj: Behavior – running away. Weather – wind.

Greyling ill. by David Ray. Putnam, 1991. ISBN 0-399-22262-6 Subj: Animals – seals. Careers – fishermen. Folk and fairy tales. Foreign lands – Scotland. Mythical creatures.

How beastly! ill. by James Marshall. Boyds Mills, 1994. ISBN 1-56397-086-4 Subj: Animals. Poetry.

An invitation to the butterfly ball: a counting rhyme ill. by Jane Breskin Zalben. Parents, 1976. ISBN 0-819-30800-5 Subj: Animals. Counting, numbers. Rhyming text.

Jane Yolen's Old MacDonald songbook musical arrangements by Adam Stemple; ill. by Rosekrans Hoffman. Boyds Mills, 1994. ISBN 1-56397-281-6 Subj: Animals. Cumulative tales. Farms. Music. Songs.

King Long Shanks ill. by Victoria Chess. Harcourt, 1998. ISBN 0-15-200013-5 Subj: Character traits – pride. Character traits – vanity. Clothing. Folk and fairy tales. Frogs and toads. Imagination. Royalty – kings.

The lap-time song and play book musical arrangements by Adam Stemple; ill. by Margot Tomes. Harcourt, 1989. ISBN 0-15-243588-3 Subj: Games. Music. Nursery rhymes. Songs.

Letting Swift River go ill. by Barbara Cooney. Little, 1992. ISBN 0-316-96899-4 Subj: Country. U.S. history. Water.

Little Mouse and Elephant ill. by John Segal. Simon & Schuster, 1996. ISBN 0-689-80493-8 Subj: Animals – mice. Behavior – boasting. Folk and fairy tales. Foreign lands – Turkey. Self-concept.

The lullaby songbook ill. by Charles Mikolaycak; scores by Adam Stemple. Harcourt, 1986. ISBN 0-15-249903-2 Subj: Bedtime. Lullabies. Music.

Milkweed days photos by Gabriel Amadeus Cooney. Crowell, 1976. ISBN 0-690-01140-7 Subj: Seasons – summer.

Miz Berlin walks ill. by Floyd Cooper. Philomel, 1997. ISBN 0-399-22938-8 Subj: Activities – storytelling. Activities – walking. Ethnic groups in the U.S. – African Americans. Old age.

Moon ball ill. by Greg Couch. Simon & Schuster, 1999. ISBN 0-689-81095-4 Subj: Bedtime. Dreams. Space and space ships. Sports – baseball.

The musicians of Bremen (Grimm, Jacob)

No bath tonight ill. by Nancy Winslow Parker. Crowell, 1978. ISBN 0-690-03882-8 Subj: Activities – bathing. Days of the week, months of the year. Family life – grandmothers.

Nocturne ill. by Anne Hunter. Harcourt, 1997. ISBN 0-15-201458-6 Subj: Animals. Animals – dogs. Family life – mothers. Night. Poetry.

Off we go! ill. by Laurel Molk. Little, 2000. ISBN 0-316-90228-4 Subj: Animals – babies. Family life – grandparents. Rhyming text.

Old Dame Counterpane ill. by Ruth Tietjen Councell. Philomel, 1994. ISBN 0-399-22686-9 Subj: Activities – sewing. Counting, numbers. Creation. Quilts. Rhyming text.

Owl moon ill. by John Schoenherr. Philomel, 1987. ISBN 0-399-21457-7 Subj: Birds – owls. Caldecott award books. Family life – fathers. Forest, woods. Night.

Pegasus, the flying horse ill. by Ming Li. Dutton, 1998. ISBN 0-525-65244-2 Subj: Character traits – vanity. Folk and fairy tales. Mythical creatures. Mythical creatures – Pegasus.

Picnic with Piggins ill. by Jane Dyer. Harcourt, 1988. ISBN 0-15-261534-2 Subj: Activities – picnicking. Animals. Animals – pigs. Birthdays.

Piggins ill. by Jane Dyer. Harcourt, 1987. ISBN 0-15-261685-3 Subj: Animals. Animals – pigs. Behavior – stealing. Parties. Problem solving.

Raising Yoder's barn ill. by Bernie Fuchs. Little, 1998. ISBN 0-316-96887-0 Subj: Barns. Communities, neighborhoods. Ethnic groups in the U.S. – Amish. Farms.

Ring of earth: a child's book of seasons ill. by John Wallner. Harcourt, 1986. ISBN 0-15-267140-4 Subj: Poetry. Seasons.

The seeing stick ill. by Remy Charlip and Demetra Maraslis. Crowell, 1977. ISBN 0-690-00596-2 Subj: Foreign lands – China. Handicaps – blindness. Royalty. Senses – seeing.

Sky dogs ill. by Barry Moser. Harcourt, 1990. ISBN 0-15-275480-6 Subj: Animals – horses, ponies. Folk and fairy tales. Indians of North America – Blackfoot. Indians of North America – Siksika.

The sleeping beauty (Grimm, Jacob)

Snow, snow: winter poems for children ill. by Jason Stemple. Wordsong, 1998. ISBN 1-56397-721-4 Subj: Poetry. Seasons – winter. Weather – snow.

Spider Jane ill. by Stefen Bernath. Coward, 1978. ISBN 0-698-30696-1 Subj: Behavior – sharing. Birds. Insects – flies. Spiders.

Street rhymes around the world ill. by 17 international artists. Boyds Mills, 1992. ISBN 1-878093-53-3 Subj: Counting, numbers. Foreign lands. Foreign languages. Games. Nursery rhymes.

The three bears holiday rhyme book ill. by Jane Dyer. Harcourt, 1995. ISBN 0-15-200932-9 Subj: Animals – bears. Holidays. Poetry.

The three bears rhyme book ill. by Jane Dyer. Harcourt, 1987. ISBN 0-15-286386-9 Subj: Animals – bears. Folk and fairy tales. Poetry.

Welcome to the icehouse ill. by Laura Regan. Putnam, 1998. ISBN 0-399-23011-4 Subj: Animals. Foreign lands – Arctic. Nature. Science. Seasons.

Welcome to the sea of sand ill. by Laura Regan. Putnam, 1996. ISBN 0-399-22765-2 Subj: Animals. Desert. Ecology. Plants. Poetry.

Wings ill. by Dennis Nolan. Harcourt, 1992. ISBN 0-15-297850-X Subj: Activities – flying. Mythical creatures. Royalty – princes.

Yorinks, Arthur. *Bravo, Minski* ill. by Richard Egielski. Farrar, 1988. ISBN 0-374-30951-5 Subj: Behavior – seeking better things. Problem solving.

Christmas in July ill. by Richard Egielski. HarperCollins, 1991. ISBN 0-06-020257-2 Subj: Behavior – losing things. Clothing. Holidays – Christmas. Santa Claus.

Company's coming ill. by David Small. Crown, 1988. ISBN 0-517-56751-2 Subj: Behavior – misunderstanding. Humor. Space and space ships.

Harry and Lulu ill. by Martin Matje. Hyperion, 1999. ISBN 0-7868-2276-7 Subj: Animals – dogs. Emotions – anger. Emotions – love. Foreign lands – France. Imagination. Toys.

Hey, Al ill. by Richard Egielski. Farrar, 1986. ISBN 0-374-33060-3 Subj: Animals – dogs. Behavior – running away. Caldecott award books. Dreams. Imagination.

Louis the fish ill. by Richard Egielski. Farrar, 1980. ISBN 0-374-34658-5 Subj: Careers – butchers. Fish. Imagination.

The Miami giant ill. by Maurice Sendak. HarperCollins, 1995. ISBN 0-06-205069-9 Subj: Careers – explorers. Foreign lands – Italy. Giants. Jewish culture.

Oh, brother ill. by Richard Egielski. Farrar, 1989. ISBN 0-374-35599-1 Subj: Behavior – fighting, arguing. Careers – tailors. Family life – brothers. Multiple births – twins. Orphans.

Ugh ill. by Richard Egielski. Farrar, 1990. ISBN 0-374-38028-7 Subj: Family life – brothers. Sibling rivalry. Sports – bicycling.

Whitefish Will rides again ill. by Mort Drucker. HarperCollins, 1994. ISBN 0-06-205037-0 Subj: Careers – sheriffs. U.S. history – frontier and pioneer life.

Yoshi. *One, two, three* ill. by author. Picture Book Studio, 1991. ISBN 0-88708-159-2 Subj: Counting, numbers.

Who's hiding here? ill. by author. Picture Book Studio, 1987. ISBN 0-88708-041-3 Subj: Animals. Format, unusual – toy and movable books. Rhyming text.

Yoshida, Toshi. *Elephant crossing* ill. by author. Putnam, 1989. ISBN 0-399-21745-2 Subj: Animals. Animals – elephants. Foreign lands – Africa.

Rhinoceros mother ill. by author. Putnam, 1991. Original title: Quarrel. ISBN 0-399-22270-7 Subj: Animals. Animals – rhinoceros. Birds. Foreign lands – Africa. Nature.

Young lions ill. by author. Putnam, 1989. ISBN 0-399-21546-8 Subj: Animals – lions. Behavior – growing up. Foreign lands – Africa.

You and me: *poems of friendship* sel. and ill. by Salley Mavor. Orchard, 1997. ISBN 0-531-33045-1 Subj: Friendship. Poetry.

You can name 100 trucks! ill. by Randy Chewning. Scholastic, 1994. ISBN 0-590-46302-0 Subj: Format, unusual – board books. Trucks.

Youldon, Gillian. *Colors* ill. by author. Watts, 1979. ISBN 0-531-00439-2 Subj: Concepts – color. Format, unusual – toy and movable books.

Counting ill. by James Hodgson. Watts, 1980. ISBN 0-531-02142-4 Subj: Counting, numbers. Format, unusual.

Numbers ill. by author. Watts, 1979. ISBN 0-531-00440-6 Subj: Counting, numbers. Format, unusual – toy and movable books.

Shapes ill. by author. Watts, 1979. ISBN 0-531-00441-4 Subj: Concepts – shape. Format, unusual.

Sizes ill. by author. Watts, 1979. ISBN 0-531-00442-2 Subj: Concepts – size. Format, unusual.

Young animals in the zoo ill. with photos. Imported Pubs., 1983. ISBN 0-8285-2211-1 Subj: Animals. Format, unusual – board books. Wordless.

Young domestic animals ill. with photos. Imported Pubs., 1983. ISBN 0-8285-2428-9 Subj: Animals. Format, unusual – board books. Wordless.

Young, Ed (Edward). *Cat and Rat* ill. by author. Holt, 1995. ISBN 0-8050-2977-X Subj: Animals – cats. Animals – rats. Folk and fairy tales. Foreign lands – China. Royalty – emperors. Zodiac.

Donkey trouble ill. by author. Atheneum, 1995. ISBN 0-689-31854-5 Subj: Animals – donkeys.

Behavior – misunderstanding. Desert. Folk and fairy tales. Stores.

High on a hill: a book of Chinese riddles ill. by the selector. Collins-World, 1980. ISBN 0-529-05554-6 Subj: Folk and fairy tales. Foreign lands – China. Riddles.

Little Plum ill. by author. Philomel, 1994. ISBN 0-399-22683-4 Subj: Character traits – cleverness. Character traits – smallness. Folk and fairy tales. Foreign lands – China.

Lon Po Po: a Red Riding Hood story from China ill. by author. Putnam, 1989. ISBN 0-399-21619-7 Subj: Animals – wolves. Caldecott award books. Folk and fairy tales. Foreign lands – China.

The lost horse ill. by author. Silver Whistle, 1998. ISBN 0-15-201016-5 Subj: Animals – horses, ponies. Folk and fairy tales. Foreign lands – China. Weather – storms.

Monkey King ill. by author. HarperCollins, 2001. ISBN 0-06-027950-8 Subj: Animals – monkeys. Behavior – trickery. Foreign lands – China.

Mouse match ill. by author. Silver Whistle, 1997. ISBN 0-15-201453-5 Subj: Animals – mice. Family life – fathers. Foreign lands – China. Format, unusual. Weddings.

Night visitors ill. by author. Philomel, 1995. ISBN 0-399-22731-8 Subj: Dreams. Folk and fairy tales. Foreign lands – China. Insects – ants.

The rooster's horns: a Chinese puppet play to make and perform by Ed Young and Hilary Beckett; ill. by Ed Young. Collins-World, 1978. ISBN 0-529-05447-7 Subj: Folk and fairy tales. Foreign lands – China. Puppets.

Seven blind mice ill. by author. Putnam, 1992. ISBN 0-399-22261-8 Subj: Animals – elephants. Animals – mice. Caldecott award honor books. Days of the week, months of the year. Foreign lands – India. Handicaps – blindness. Senses – seeing.

The terrible Nung Gwama: a Chinese folktale ill. by author. Collins-World, 1978. ISBN 0-529-05445-0 Subj: Character traits – cleverness. Folk and fairy tales. Foreign lands – China. Monsters.

Up a tree ill. by author. HarperCollins, 1983. ISBN 0-06-026814-X Subj: Animals – cats. Trees. Wordless.

Young, Evelyn. *The tale of Tai* ill. by author. Oxford Univ. Pr., 1940. Subj: Behavior – lost. Foreign lands – China. Holidays – Chinese New Year.

Wu and Lu and Li ill. by author. Walck, 1959, c1939. Subj: Family life. Foreign lands – China.

Young, Helen. *A throne for Sesame* ill. by Shirley Hughes. Elsevier-Dutton, 1979. ISBN 0-233-96871-7 Subj: Behavior – growing up.

Young, James. *Everyone loves the moon* ill. by author. Little, 1992. ISBN 0-316-97130-8 Subj: Animals – possums. Animals – raccoons. Moon. Rhyming text. Weddings.

A million chameleons ill. by author. Little, 1990. ISBN 0-316-97129-4 Subj: Concepts – color. Rhyming text.

Penelope and the pirates ill. by author. Arcade, 1990. ISBN 1-55970-074-2 Subj: Animals – cats. Boats, ships. Pirates.

Young, Miriam Burt. *If I drove a bus* ill. by Robert M. Quackenbush. Lothrop, 1973. Subj: Buses. Careers – bus drivers. Transportation.

If I drove a car ill. by Robert M. Quackenbush. Lothrop, 1971. Subj: Automobiles. Transportation.

If I drove a tractor ill. by Robert M. Quackenbush. Lothrop, 1973. ISBN 0-688-50041-2 Subj: Tractors.

If I drove a train ill. by Robert M. Quackenbush. Lothrop, 1972. Subj: Trains. Transportation.

If I drove a truck ill. by Robert M. Quackenbush. Lothrop, 1967. Subj: Careers – truck drivers. Transportation. Trucks.

If I flew a plane ill. by Robert M. Quackenbush. Lothrop, 1970. Subj: Activities – flying. Airplanes, airports. Careers – airplane pilots. Transportation.

If I rode a horse ill. by Robert M. Quackenbush. Lothrop, 1973. ISBN 0-6885-0042-0 Subj: Animals – horses, ponies.

If I rode an elephant ill. by Robert M. Quackenbush. Lothrop, 1974. ISBN 0-688-51589-4 Subj: Animals – elephants.

If I sailed a boat ill. by Robert M. Quackenbush. Lothrop, 1971. Subj: Boats, ships.

Jellybeans for breakfast ill. by Beverly Komoda. Parents, 1968. Subj: Activities – playing. Imagination.

Miss Suzy's Easter surprise ill. by Arnold Lobel. Parents, 1972. ISBN 0-819-30556-1 Subj: Animals – squirrels. Holidays – Easter.

Please don't feed Horace ill. by Abner Graboff. Dial, 1961. Subj: Animals – hippopotamuses. Zoos.

The sugar mouse cake ill. by Margaret Bloy Graham. Scribners, 1964. Subj: Activities – cooking. Animals – mice. Careers – bakers. Food. Royalty.

Young, Ruth. *Daisy's taxi* ill. by Marcia Sewall. Watts, 1991. ISBN 0-531-08521-X Subj: Boats, ships. Concepts – opposites. Sea and seashore.

Golden Bear ill. by Rachel Isadora. Viking, 1992. ISBN 0-670-82577-8 Subj: Ethnic groups in the U.S. – African Americans. Friendship. Imagination. Rhyming text. Toys – bears.

My baby-sitter ill. by author. Viking, 1987. ISBN 0-670-81305-2 Subj: Activities – babysitting.

My blanket ill. by author. Viking, 1987. ISBN 0-670-81306-0 Subj: Babies.

My potty chair ill. by author. Viking, 1987. ISBN 0-670-81307-9 Subj: Behavior – growing up. Toilet training.

The new baby ill. by author. Viking, 1987. ISBN 0-670-81304-4 Subj: Babies. Family life – new sibling. Sibling rivalry.

A trip to Mars ill. by Maryann Cocca-Leffler. Watts, 1990. ISBN 0-531-08492-2 Subj: Imagination. Space and space ships.

Who says moo? ill. by Lisa Campbell Ernst. Viking, 1994. ISBN 0-670-85162-0 Subj: Animals. Character traits – questioning. Noise, sounds. Riddles.

Youngs, Betty. *Pink pigs in mud: a color book* ill. by author. Merrimack, 1985. ISBN 0-370-30344-X Subj: Animals. Concepts – color.

Youngs, Betty Ferrell. *One panda: an animal counting book* ill. by author. Merrimack, 1985. ISBN 0-370-30150-1 Subj: Animals. Counting, numbers.

Yudell, Lynn Deena. *Make a face* ill. by author. Little, 1970. Subj: Anatomy – faces. Emotions. Games. Participation.

Yulya. *Bears are sleeping* ill. by Nonny Hogrogian. Scribners, 1967. Subj: Animals – bears. Hibernation. Music. Sleep. Songs.

Zabar, Abbie. *Fifty-five friends* ill. by author. Hyperion, 1994. ISBN 0-7868-2017-9 Subj: Animals. Counting, numbers. Cumulative tales. Friendship.

Zacharias, Thomas. *But where is the green parrot?* by Thomas and Wanda Zacharias; ill. by Wanda Zacharias. Delacorte, 1968. Translation of Und wo ist der grüne Papagei? Subj: Birds – parakeets, parrots. Concepts – color. Games.

Zacharias, Wanda. *But where is the green parrot?* (Zacharias, Thomas)

Zadrzynska, Ewa. *The Peaceable Kingdom* ill. by Tomek Olbinski; painting from the Brooklyn Museum. M.M. Art Books, 1993. ISBN 0-9638904-0-9 Subj: Animals. Art. Museums.

Zaffo, George J. *Big book of real fire engines* text by Elizabeth Cameron; ill. by author. Grosset, 1964, c1950. Subj: Careers – firefighters.

The book of real airplanes ill. by author. Grosset, 1966. Subj: Airplanes, airports. Helicopters. Transportation.

The giant book of things in space ill. by author. Doubleday, 1969. Subj: Space and space ships.

The giant nursery book of things that go: fire engines, trains, boats, trucks, airplanes ill. by author. Doubleday, 1959. Subj: Airplanes, airports. Boats, ships. Transportation. Trucks.

The giant nursery book of things that work ill. by author. Doubleday, 1967. Subj: Machines. Tools. Transportation.

Zager, Karen. *Bubbles* ill. by author. Price Stern Sloan, 1988. ISBN 0-8431-1873-3 Subj: Bubbles. Format, unusual – toy and movable books. Wordless.

Zagone, Theresa. *No nap for me* ill. by Lillian Hoban. Dutton, 1978. ISBN 0-525-35982-6 Subj: Behavior – growing up. Sleep.

Zagwÿn, Deborah Turney. *Apple batter* ill. by author. Tricycle, 1999. ISBN 1-883672-92-9 Subj: Family life. Food. Sports – baseball.

Papa's latkes ill. by author. Holt, 1994. ISBN 0-8050-3099-9 Subj: Family life – fathers. Food. Holidays – Hanukkah. Jewish culture. Religion.

The pumpkin blanket ill. by author. Celestial Arts, 1990. ISBN 0-89087-637-1 Subj: Behavior – growing up. Foreign lands – Canada. Gardens, gardening. Quilts.

Turtle spring ill. by author. Tricycle, 1998. ISBN 1-883672-53-8 Subj: Family life – new sibling. Hibernation. Reptiles – turtles, tortoises. Seasons.

The winter gift ill. by author. Tricycle, 2000. ISBN 1-883672-93-7 Subj: Family life – grandmothers. Holidays – Christmas. Memories, memory. Moving.

Zakhoder, Boris Vladimirovich. *The good stepmother* adapt. by Marguerita Rudolph; ill. by Darcy May. Simon & Schuster, 1992. ISBN 0-671-68270-9 Subj: Character traits – cleverness. Family life – step families. Foreign lands – Russia. Royalty – princesses.

How a piglet crashed the Christmas party trans. by Marguerita Rudolph; ill. by Kurt Werth. Lothrop, 1971. Subj: Animals – pigs. Holidays – Christmas.

Rosachok trans. by Marguerita Rudolph; ill. by Yaroslava. Lothrop, 1970. Translation of Rusachok. ISBN 0-688-51113-9 Subj: Animals – rabbits. Behavior – dissatisfaction. Character traits – optimism. Frogs and toads.

Zalben, Jane Breskin. *Basil and Hillary* ill. by author. Macmillan, 1975. ISBN 0-02-793720-8 Subj: Animals. Animals – pigs. Farms.

Beni's first Chanukah ill. by author. Holt, 1988. ISBN 0-8050-0479-3 Subj: Animals – bears. Family life. Friendship. Holidays – Hanukkah. Jewish culture.

Beni's first wedding ill. by author. Holt, 1998. ISBN 0-8050-4846-4 Subj: Animals – bears. Family life. Jewish culture. Weddings.

Buster gets braces ill. by author. Holt, 1992. ISBN 0-8050-1682-1 Subj: Careers – dentists. Dinosaurs. Family life – brothers and sisters. Sibling rivalry. Teeth.

Happy Passover, Rosie ill. by author. Holt, 1990. ISBN 0-8050-1221-4 Subj: Animals – bears. Family life. Holidays – Passover. Jewish culture. Religion.

Leo and Blossom's Sukkah ill. by author. Holt, 1990. ISBN 0-8050-1226-5 Subj: Animals – bears. Family life. Holidays – Sukkot. Jewish culture. Religion.

Miss Violet's shining day ill. by author. Boyds Mills, 1995. ISBN 1-56397-234-4 Subj: Animals – rabbits. Character traits – shyness. Music.

Norton's nighttime ill. by author. Collins-World, 1979. ISBN 0-529-05431-0 Subj: Animals. Bedtime. Forest, woods. Night. Noise, sounds.

Oliver and Alison's week ill. by Emily Arnold McCully. Farrar, 1980. ISBN 0-374-35535-8 Subj: Activities. Friendship.

Pearl plants a tree ill. by author. Simon & Schuster, 1995. ISBN 0-689-80034-7 Subj: Animals – sheep. Family life – grandfathers. Gardens, gardening. Trees.

Pearl's eight days of Chanukah ill. by author. Simon & Schuster, 1998. ISBN 0-689-81488-7 Subj: Animals – sheep. Holidays – Hanukkah. Jewish culture. Religion.

Pearl's marigolds for grandpa ill. by author. Simon & Schuster, 1997. ISBN 0-689-80448-2 Subj: Animals – sheep. Death. Emotions – grief. Family life – grandfathers. Memories, memory.

A perfect nose for Ralph ill. by John Wallner. Putnam, 1980. ISBN 0-399-61154-1 Subj: Emotions – love. Toys – bears.

Zallinger, Peter. *Dinosaurs* ill. by author. Random House, 1977. ISBN 0-394-83485-2 Subj: Dinosaurs. Science.

Zamorano, Ana. *Let's eat!* ill. by Julie Vivas. Scholastic, 1997. ISBN 0-590-13444-2 Subj: Family life. Food. Foreign lands – Spain. Health and fitness.

Zander, Hans. *My blue chair* ill. by author. Firefly, 1985. ISBN 0-920303-16-1 Subj: Behavior – losing things. Furniture – chairs.

Zarin, Cynthia. *Rose and Sebastian* ill. by Sarah Durham. Houghton Mifflin, 1997. ISBN 0-395-75920-X Subj: City. Communities, neighborhoods. Emotions – fear. Friendship. Noise, sounds.

What do you see when you shut your eyes? ill. by Sarah Durham. Houghton Mifflin, 1998. ISBN 0-395-76507-2 Subj: Ethnic groups in the U.S. Imagination. Rhyming text. Senses.

Zarins, Joyce Audy. *see* Dos Santos, Joyce Audy

Zaritzky, Bernard. *Little white duck* (Whippo, Walt)

Zaslavsky, Claudia. *Count on your fingers African style* ill. by Jerry Pinkney. Crowell, 1980. ISBN 0-690-03865-8 Subj: Counting, numbers. Foreign lands – Africa.

Zero! Is it something? Is it nothing? ill. by Jeni Bassett. Watts, 1989. ISBN 0-531-10693-4 Subj: Concepts. Counting, numbers.

Zekauskas, Felicia. *The magic hockey stick* (Maloney, Peter)

Redbird at Rockefeller Center (Maloney, Peter)

Zeldis, Malcah. *Eve and her sisters: women of the Old Testament* (McDonough, Yona Zeldis)

Zelinsky, Paul O. *The lion and the stoat* ill. by author. Greenwillow, 1984. ISBN 0-688-02563-3 Subj: Animals – lions. Animals – weasels. Art. Friendship.

The maid and the mouse and the odd-shaped house ill. by author. Dodd, 1981. ISBN 0-396-07938-5 Subj: Animals – mice. Folk and fairy tales. Homes, houses.

Rapunzel (Grimm, Jacob)

Rumpelstiltskin (Grimm, Jacob)

The wheels on the bus ill. by adapt. Dutton, 1990. ISBN 0-525-44644-3 Subj: Buses. Family life – grandmothers. Format, unusual – toy and movable books. Music. Songs.

Zelver, Patricia. *The wonderful Towers of Watts* ill. by Frané Lessac. Tambourine, 1994. ISBN 0-688-12650-2 Subj: Art. Behavior – collecting things. Buildings.

Zemach, Harve. *Duffy and the devil: a Cornish tale* ill. by Margot Zemach. Farrar, 1973. ISBN 0-374-31887-5 Subj: Caldecott award books. Devil. Folk and fairy tales. Foreign lands – England.

The judge: an untrue tale ill. by Margot Zemach. Farrar, 1969. ISBN 0-374-33960-0 Subj: Caldecott award honor books. Careers – judges. Monsters. Rhyming text.

Mommy, buy me a China doll: adapt. from an Ozark children's song ill. by Margot Zemach. Follett, 1966. ISBN 0-374-35005-1 Subj: Music. Songs. Toys – dolls.

Nail soup: a Swedish folk tale ill. by Margot Zemach. Follett, 1964. Subj: Character traits – cleverness. Folk and fairy tales. Foreign lands – Sweden.

The tricks of Master Dabble ill. by Margot Zemach. Holt, 1965. Subj: Behavior – trickery. Humor. Royalty.

Zemach, Kaethe. *The beautiful rat* ill. by author. Four Winds, 1979. ISBN 0-590-07584-5 Subj: Animals – rats. Folk and fairy tales.

The character in the book ill. by author. HarperCollins, 1998. ISBN 0-06-205060-5 Subj: Activities – reading.

The funny dream ill. by author. Greenwillow, 1988. ISBN 0-688-07501-0 Subj: Dreams. Family life.

Zemach, Margot. *It could always be worse: a Yiddish folk tale* ill. by author. Farrar, 1976. ISBN 0-374-33650-4 Subj: Caldecott award honor books. Folk and fairy tales. Humor. Jewish culture. Problem solving.

Jake and Honeybunch go to heaven ill. by author. Farrar, 1982. ISBN 0-374-33652-0 Subj: Animals – mules. Behavior – misbehavior. Ethnic groups in the U.S. – African Americans. Folk and fairy tales.

The little red hen: an old story (The little red hen)

The little tiny woman ill. by author. Bobbs-Merrill, 1965. Subj: Folk and fairy tales. Ghosts.

The three wishes: an old story adapt. and ill. by Margot Zemach. Farrar, 1986. ISBN 0-374-37529-1 Subj: Behavior – wishing. Character traits – foolishness. Folk and fairy tales.

To Hilda for helping ill. by author. Farrar, 1977. ISBN 0-374-37663-8 Subj: Character traits – helpfulness. Emotions – envy, jealousy. Family life.

Zemach-Barsin, Kaethe. *see* Zemach, Kaethe

Zeman, Ludmila. *The first red maple leaf* ill. by author. Tundra, 1997. ISBN 0-88776-372-3 Subj: Birds – geese. Creation. Foreign lands – Canada. Indians of North America. Mythical creatures. Seasons.

Sinbad: from the tales of the Thousand and one nights ill. by author. Tundra, 1999. ISBN 0-88776-460-6 Subj: Folk and fairy tales. Foreign lands – Arabia. Sailors. Sea and seashore.

Zemke, Deborah. *The shadow of Matilda Hunt* ill. by author. Houghton Mifflin, 1991. ISBN 0-395-55334-2 Subj: Behavior – misbehavior. Imagination – imaginary friends. Shadows.

The way it happened ill. by author. Houghton Mifflin, 1988. ISBN 0-395-47984-3 Subj: Behavior – misunderstanding. Behavior – secrets.

Zhang, Song Nan. *The ballad of Mulan* ill. by reteller. Pan Asian Publications, 1998. ISBN 1-57227-056-X Subj: Foreign lands – China. Sex roles. War.

The five heavenly emperors and other Chinese myths from the creation ill. by author. Tundra, 1994. ISBN 0-88776-338-3 Subj: Creation. Folk and fairy tales. Foreign lands – China.

Ziefert, Harriet. *All clean!* ill. by Henrik Drescher. HarperCollins, 1986. ISBN 0-694-00100-7 Subj: Animals.

All gone! ill. by Henrik Drescher. HarperCollins, 1986. ISBN 0-694-00098-1 Subj: Animals.

Animal music ill. by Donald Saaf. Houghton Mifflin, 1999. ISBN 0-395-95294-8 Subj: Animals. Music. Rhyming text.

Animals of the Bible ill. by Letizia Galli. Doubleday, 1995. ISBN 0-385-32084-1 Subj: Animals. Format, unusual – toy and movable books. Religion.

Baby Ben's bow-wow book ill. by Norman Gorbaty. Random House, 1984. ISBN 0-394-86821-8 Subj: Animals. Babies. Format, unusual – board books.

Baby Ben's busy book ill. by Norman Gorbaty. Random House, 1984. ISBN 0-394-86819-6 Subj: Activities. Babies. Format, unusual – board books.

Baby Ben's go-go book ill. by Norman Gorbaty. Random House, 1984. ISBN 0-394-86820-X Subj: Activities – playing. Babies. Format, unusual – board books. Toys.

Baby Ben's noisy book ill. by Norman Gorbaty. Random House, 1984. ISBN 0-394-86822-6 Subj: Activities. Babies. Format, unusual – board books.

Bear all year ill. by Arnold Lobel. HarperCollins, 1986. ISBN 0-694-00087-6 Subj: Animals – bears. Format, unusual – toy and movable books. Games. Seasons.

Bear gets dressed ill. by Arnold Lobel. HarperCollins, 1986. ISBN 0-694-00086-8 Subj: Animals – bears. Clothing. Format, unusual – toy and movable books. Games.

Bear goes shopping ill. by Arnold Lobel. HarperCollins, 1986. ISBN 0-694-00085-X Subj: Animals – bears. Format, unusual – toy and movable books. Games. Shopping.

Bear's busy morning ill. by Arnold Lobel. HarperCollins, 1986. ISBN 0-694-00084-1 Subj: Activities. Animals – bears. Format, unusual – toy and movable books. Games.

Before I was born ill. by Rufus Coes. Knopf, 1989. ISBN 0-394-95128-X Subj: Activities – making things. Babies. Family life. Quilts.

Breakfast time! by Harriet Ziefert and Lisa Campbell Ernst; ill. by Lisa Campbell Ernst. Viking, 1988. ISBN 0-670-81579-9 Subj: Animals – rabbits. Babies. Food.

Bye-bye, daddy! by Harriet Ziefert and Lisa Campbell Ernst; ill. by Lisa Campbell Ernst. Viking, 1988. ISBN 0-670-81581-0 Subj: Animals – rabbits. Babies.

A car trip for mole and mouse ill. by David Prebenna. Viking, 1991. ISBN 0-670-83858-6 Subj: Activities – traveling. Animals – mice. Animals – moles. Automobiles.

Chocolate mud cake ill. by Karen Gundersheimer. HarperCollins, 1988. ISBN 0-06-026892-1 Subj: Family life – grandparents.

Clara Ann Cookie ill. by Emily Bolam. Houghton Mifflin, 1999. ISBN 0-395-92324-7 Subj: Clothing. Family life – mothers. Rhyming text.

Clara Ann Cookie go to bed! ill. by Emily Bolam. Houghton Mifflin, 2000. ISBN 0-395-97381-3 Subj: Bedtime. Rhyming text. Toys – bears.

A clean house for Mole and Mouse ill. by David Prebenna. Viking, 1988. ISBN 0-670-82032-6 Subj: Animals – mice. Animals – moles. Character traits – cleanliness.

Cock-a-doodle-doo! ill. by Henrik Drescher. Harper-Collins, 1986. ISBN 0-694-00099-X Subj: Animals.

Come out, Jessie! ill. by Mavis Smith. Harper-Collins, 1991. ISBN 0-06-107414-4 Subj: Activities – playing. Toys.

Cow in the house ill. by Emily Bolam. Viking, 1997. ISBN 0-670-86779-9 Subj: Animals. Animals – bulls, cows. Folk and fairy tales. Homes, houses. Noise, sounds. Sleep.

Daddies are for catching fireflies ill. by Cynthia Jabar. Puffin, 1999. ISBN 0-14-056553-1 Subj: Family life. Format, unusual – toy and movable books.

Dancing ill. by Laura Rader. HarperCollins, 1991. ISBN 0-06-107422-5 Subj: Activities – dancing. Animals. Ballet. Format, unusual – toy and movable books.

A dozen dogs: a read-and-count story ill. by Carol Nicklaus. Random House, 1985. ISBN 0-394-96935-9 Subj: Animals – dogs. Counting, numbers. Sea and seashore.

Elemenopeo ill. by Donald Saaf. Houghton Mifflin, 1998. ISBN 0-395-90493-5 Subj: Activities – painting. Animals – cats.

First He made the sun ill. by Todd McKie. Putnam, 2000. ISBN 0-399-23199-4 Subj: Creation. Religion. Rhyming text.

First Night ill. by S. D. Schindler. Putnam, 1999. ISBN 0-399-23120-X Subj: Holidays – New Year's. Parades. Rhyming text.

Getting ready for new baby ill. by Laura Rader. HarperCollins, 1990. ISBN 0-06-026897-2 Subj: Babies. Emotions – envy, jealousy. Family life – new sibling. Science. Sibling rivalry.

The gingerbread boy (The gingerbread boy)

Goldilocks and the three bears (The three bears)

Good luck, bad luck ill. by Lillie James. Viking, 1991. ISBN 0-670-84275-3 Subj: Character traits – luck.

Good morning, sun! by Harriet Ziefert and Lisa Campbell Ernst; ill. by Lisa Campbell Ernst. Viking, 1988. ISBN 0-670-81578-0 Subj: Animals – rabbits. Babies. Morning.

Good night everyone! ill. by Andrea Baruffi. Little, 1988. ISBN 0-316-98756-5 Subj: Bedtime. Sleep. Toys.

Good night, Jessie! by Harriet Ziefert and Mavis Smith; ill. by Mavis Smith. Random House, 1987. ISBN 0-394-89193-7 Subj: Behavior – losing things. Family life. Sea and seashore.

Happy birthday, Grandpa! ill. by Sidney Levitt. HarperCollins, 1988. ISBN 0-694-00242-9 Subj: Animals. Animals – rabbits. Birthdays. Family life – grandfathers.

Happy Easter, Grandma! ill. by Sidney Levitt. HarperCollins, 1988. ISBN 0-694-00225-9 Subj: Animals – rabbits. Birds. Eggs. Holidays – Easter.

Harry takes a bath ill. by Mavis Smith. Viking, 1987. ISBN 0-670-81721-X Subj: Activities – bathing. Animals – hippopotamuses.

Hats off for the Fourth of July! ill. by Gustaf Miller. Viking, 2000. ISBN 0-670-89118-5 Subj: Clothing – hats. Holidays – Fourth of July. Rhyming text.

Henny Penny (Chicken Little)

Hurry up, Jessie! ill. by Mavis Smith. Random House, 1987. ISBN 0-394-89194-5 Subj: Character traits – cleanliness. Night.

I swapped my dog ill. by Emily Bolam. Houghton Mifflin, 1998. ISBN 0-395-89159-0 Subj: Animals. Animals – dogs. Cumulative tales. Farms. Rhyming text.

I want to sleep in your bed! ill. by Mavis Smith. HarperCollins, 1990. ISBN 0-06-026895-6 Subj: Bedtime. Family life. Sleep.

I won't go to bed! ill. by Andrea Baruffi. Little, 1987. ISBN 0-316-98768-9 Subj: Bedtime.

Jason's bus ride ill. by Simms Taback. Viking, 1987. ISBN 0-670-81718-X Subj: Buses.

Keeping daddy awake on the way home from the beach ill. by Seymour Chwast. HarperCollins, 1986. ISBN 0-694-00080-9 Subj: Activities – traveling. Family life. Sea and seashore.

Let's get dressed! by Harriet Ziefert and Lisa Campbell Ernst; ill. by Lisa Campbell Ernst. Viking, 1988. ISBN 0-670-81580-2 Subj: Animals – rabbits. Babies. Clothing.

Let's go! Piggety Pig ill. by David Prebenna. Little, 1986. ISBN 0-316-98760-3 Subj: Animals – mice. Animals – pigs. Concepts – opposites.

Lewis the fire fighter ill. by Carol Nicklaus. Random House, 1986. ISBN 0-394-97618-5 Subj: Activities – playing. Fire. Imagination.

Listen! Piggety Pig ill. by David Prebenna. Little, 1986. ISBN 0-316-98761-1 Subj: Animals. Noise, sounds.

The little red hen (The little red hen)

Little Red Riding Hood ill. by Emily Bolam. Viking, 2000. ISBN 0-670-88389-1 Subj: Animals – wolves. Behavior – talking to strangers. Family life – grandmothers. Folk and fairy tales.

Math riddles ill. by Andrea Baruffi. Viking, 1997. Subj: Counting, numbers. Humor. Riddles.

Me, too! Me, too! ill. by Karen Gundersheimer. HarperCollins, 1988. ISBN 0-06-026893-X Subj: Behavior – sharing.

Mike and Tony: best friends ill. by Catherine Siracusa. Viking, 1987. ISBN 0-670-81719-8 Subj: Friendship.

Mommies are for counting stars ill. by Cynthia Jabar. Penguin Putnam, 1999. ISBN 0-14-056552-3 Subj:

Family life – mothers. Format, unusual – toy and movable books.

Moonride by Harriet Ziefert and Seymour Chwast; ill. by Seymour Chwast. Houghton Mifflin, 2000. ISBN 0-618-00229-4 Subj: Bedtime. Dreams. Moon. Night.

Mother Goose math ill. by Emily Bolam. Viking, 1997. ISBN 0-670-87569-4 Subj: Counting, numbers. Nursery rhymes.

My getting-ready-for-school book ill. by Mavis Smith. Random House, 1989. ISBN 0-394-82248-X Subj: Concepts. Format, unusual – board books.

My sister says nothing ever happens when we go sailing ill. by Seymour Chwast. HarperCollins, 1986. ISBN 0-694-00081-7 Subj: Boats, ships. Family life.

A new coat for Anna ill. by Anita Lobel. Knopf, 1988. ISBN 0-394-97426-3 Subj: Clothing – coats. Family life. War.

A new house for Mole and Mouse ill. by Mavis Smith. Viking, 1987. ISBN 0-670-81720-1 Subj: Animals – mice. Animals – moles. Homes, houses. Moving.

Nicky upstairs and down ill. by Richard Eric Brown. Viking, 1987. ISBN 0-670-81717-1 Subj: Animals – cats.

Nicky's Christmas surprise ill. by Richard Eric Brown. Penguin, 1985. ISBN 0-14-050555-5 Subj: Animals – cats. Farms. Holidays – Christmas.

Nicky's friends ill. by Richard Eric Brown. Viking, 1986. ISBN 0-670-81298-6 Subj: Animals – cats. Farms. Format, unusual – board books. Friendship.

No more! Piggety Pig ill. by David Prebenna. Little, 1986. ISBN 0-316-98763-8 Subj: Animals – mice. Animals – pigs. Concepts – color.

No, no, Nicky! ill. by Richard Eric Brown. Viking, 1986. ISBN 0-670-81297-8 Subj: Animals – cats. Format, unusual – board books. Safety.

Oh, what a noisy farm! ill. by Emily Bolam. Tambourine, 1995. ISBN 0-688-13261-8 Subj: Animals. Farms. Noise, sounds.

On our way to the barn by Harriet Ziefert and Simms Taback; ill. by Simms Taback. HarperCollins, 1985. ISBN 0-06-026877-8 Subj: Animals. Farms. Format, unusual – board books. Noise, sounds. Rhyming text.

On our way to the forest by Harriet Ziefert and Simms Taback; ill. by Simms Taback. HarperCollins, 1985. ISBN 0-06-026878-6 Subj: Forest, woods. Format, unusual – board books. Noise, sounds. Rhyming text.

On our way to the water by Harriet Ziefert and Simms Taback; ill. by Simms Taback. HarperCollins, 1985. ISBN 0-06-026879-4 Subj: Format, unusual – board books. Noise, sounds. Rhyming text.

On our way to the zoo by Harriet Ziefert and Simms Taback; ill. by Simms Taback. HarperCollins, 1985. ISBN 0-06-026880-8 Subj: Animals. Format, unusual – board books. Noise, sounds. Rhyming text. Zoos.

People of the Bible ill. by author. Doubleday, 1996. ISBN 0-553-09766-0 Subj: Format, unusual – toy and movable books. Religion.

Piggety Pig from morn 'til night ill. by David Prebenna. Little, 1986. ISBN 0-316-98764-6 Subj: Activities. Animals – pigs.

A polar bear can swim: what animals can and cannot do ill. by Emily Bolam. Viking, 1998. ISBN 0-670-88056-6 Subj: Activities. Animals. Circular tales.

The princess and the pea (Andersen, H. C. [Hans Christian])

Pumpkin Pie ill. by Donald Dreifuss. Houghton Mifflin, 2000. ISBN 0-618-04883-9 Subj: Animals – goats. Fairs. Farms.

Pushkin meets the bundle ill. by Donald Saaf. Atheneum, 1998. ISBN 0-689-81413-5 Subj: Animals – dogs. Babies. Family life.

Pushkin minds the bundle ill. by Donald Saaf. Atheneum, 2000. ISBN 0-689-83216-8 Subj: Activities – vacationing. Animals – dogs. Babies. Family life.

Rabbit and Hare divide an apple ill. by Emily Bolam. Viking, 1998. ISBN 0-670-87790-5 Subj: Animals – rabbits. Behavior – sharing. Concepts. Counting, numbers. Food.

Run! Run! ill. by Henrik Drescher. HarperCollins, 1986. ISBN 0-694-00097-3 Subj: Animals.

Sam and Lucy ill. by Claire Schumacher. HarperCollins, 1992. ISBN 0-06-026974-X Subj: Animals – dogs. Behavior – running away.

Sarah's questions ill. by Susan Bonners. Lothrop, 1986. ISBN 0-688-05615-6 Subj: Character traits – questioning. Family life – mothers. Nature.

Say good night! ill. by Catherine Siracusa. Viking, 1987. ISBN 0-670-81722-8 Subj: Bedtime. Morning. Night. Sleep.

Sleepy dog ill. by Norman Gorbaty. Random House, 1984. ISBN 0-394-96877-8 Subj: Animals – dogs. Sleep.

Strike four! ill. by Mavis Smith. Viking, 1988. ISBN 0-670-82033-4 Subj: Activities – playing. Behavior – misbehavior. Family life.

Surprise! ill. by Mary Morgan. Viking, 1988. ISBN 0-670-82036-9 Subj: Birthdays. Family life – mothers. Food.

Talk, baby! ill. by Emily Bolam. Holt, 1999. ISBN 0-8050-6144-4 Subj: Activities – talking. Babies. Family life – new sibling. Format, unusual – toy and movable books.

The three billy goats Gruff (Asbjørnsen, P. C. [Peter Christen])

Train song ill. by Donald Saaf. Orchard, 2000. ISBN 0-531-30204-0 Subj: Rhyming text. Trains.

The turnip ill. by Laura Rader. Viking, 1996. ISBN 0-670-86053-0 Subj: Cumulative tales. Farms. Folk and fairy tales. Foreign lands – Russia. Plants. Problem solving.

Two little witches ill. by Simms Taback. Candlewick, 1996. ISBN 1-56402-621-3 Subj: Counting, numbers. Holidays – Halloween. Witches.

Waiting for baby ill. by Emily Bolam. Holt, 1998. ISBN 0-8050-5929-6 Subj: Babies. Family life – new sibling.

Wee G. ill. by Donald Saaf. Atheneum, 1997. ISBN 0-689-81064-4 Subj: Animals – cats. Behavior – lost.

When daddy had the chicken pox ill. by Lionel Kalish. HarperCollins, 1991. ISBN 0-06-026907-3 Subj: Family life – fathers. Illness.

When I first came to this land ill. by Simms Taback. Putnam, 1998. ISBN 0-399-23044-0 Subj: Cumulative tales. Folk and fairy tales. Immigrants. Poverty. Songs.

Where's daddy's car? ill. by Andrea Baruffi. HarperCollins, 1992. ISBN 0-694-00378-6 Subj: Automobiles. Format, unusual – toy and movable books.

Where's mommy's truck? ill. by Andrea Baruffi. HarperCollins, 1992. ISBN 0-694-00377-8 Subj: Family life – mothers. Format, unusual – toy and movable books. Trucks.

Where's the cat? ill. by Arnold Lobel. HarperCollins, 1987. ISBN 0-694-00185-6 Subj: Animals – cats. Behavior – hiding. Format, unusual. Format, unusual – board books.

Where's the dog? ill. by Arnold Lobel. HarperCollins, 1987. ISBN 0-694-00184-8 Subj: Animals – dogs. Behavior – hiding. Format, unusual. Format, unusual – board books.

Where's the guinea pig? ill. by Arnold Lobel. HarperCollins, 1987. ISBN 0-694-00182-1 Subj: Animals – guinea pigs. Behavior – hiding. Format, unusual. Format, unusual – board books.

Where's the turtle? ill. by Arnold Lobel. HarperCollins, 1987. ISBN 0-694-00183-X Subj: Behavior – hiding. Format, unusual. Format, unusual – board books. Reptiles – turtles, tortoises.

Who can boo the loudest? ill. by Claire Schumacher. HarperCollins, 1990. ISBN 0-06-026899-9 Subj: Ghosts. Moon.

With love from Grandma ill. by Deborah Kogan Ray. Viking, 1989. ISBN 0-670-83004-6 Subj: Activities – knitting. Emotions – love. Family life – grandmothers.

Ziegler, Sandra. *A visit to the bakery* photos by author. Childrens Pr., 1987. ISBN 0-516-01495-1 Subj: Careers – bakers.

Ziegler, Ursina. *Squaps the moonling* trans. by Barbara Kowall Gollob; ill. by Sita Jucker. Atheneum, 1969. Translation of Squaps, der Mondling. Subj: Aliens. Moon. Space and space ships.

Zijlstra, Tjerk. *Benny and his geese* ill. by Ivo de Weerd. McGraw-Hill, 1975. Translation of Bennie en zijn ganzen. ISBN 0-07-072825-9 Subj: Birds – geese. Folk and fairy tales. Wizards.

Zimelman, Nathan. *The great adventure of Wo Ti* ill. by Julie Downing. Macmillan, 1992. ISBN 0-02-793731-3 Subj: Animals – cats. Behavior – trickery. Fish. Foreign lands – China.

How the second grade got $8,205.50 to visit the Statue of Liberty ill. by Bill Slavin. Albert Whitman, 1992. ISBN 0-8075-3431-5 Subj: Activities. Money. School.

If I were strong enough . . . ill. by Diane Paterson. Abingdon, 1982. ISBN 0-687-18670-6 Subj: Behavior – growing up. Family life.

Mean Murgatroyd and the ten cats ill. by Tony Auth. Dutton, 1984. ISBN 0-525-44116-6 Subj: Animals – cats. Animals – dogs. Character traits – meanness.

Once when I was five ill. by Carol Rogers. Steck-Vaughn, 1967. Subj: Birthdays. Imagination.

Positively no pets allowed ill. by Pamela Johnson. Dutton, 1980. ISBN 0-525-37560-0 Subj: Animals – gorillas. Pets.

The star of Melvin ill. by Olivier Dunrea. Macmillan, 1987. ISBN 0-02-793750-X Subj: Angels. Holidays – Christmas. Stars.

To sing a song as big as Ireland ill. by Joseph Low. Follett, 1967. Subj: Behavior – wishing. Foreign lands – Ireland. Holidays – St. Patrick's Day. Music. Mythical creatures.

Treed by a pride of irate lions ill. by Toni Goffe. Little, 1990. ISBN 0-316-98802-2 Subj: Animals – lions. Family life – fathers. Foreign lands – Africa.

Walls are to be walked ill. by Donald Carrick. Dutton, 1977. ISBN 0-525-42175-0 Subj: Activities – playing.

Zimmer, Dirk. *The trick-or-treat trap* ill. by author. HarperCollins, 1982. ISBN 0-06-026861-1 Subj: Holidays – Halloween. Parties. Witches.

Zimmerman, Andrea Griffing. *Trashy town* by Andrea Zimmerman and David Clemesha; ill. by Dan Yaccarino. HarperCollins, 1999. ISBN 0-06-027140-X Subj: Careers – sanitation workers. City.

Yetta, the trickster ill. by Harold Berson. Seabury Pr., 1978. ISBN 0-8164-3218-X Subj: Foreign lands – Russia. Humor.

Zimmerman, Baruch. *A Japanese fairy tale* (Iké, Jane Hori)

Zimmermann, H. Werner (Heinz Werner). *Alphonse knows . . . a circle is not a Valentine* ill. by author. Oxford Univ. Pr., 1991. ISBN 0-19-540744-X Subj: Concepts – shape. Holidays – Valentine's Day. Wizards.

Alphonse knows . . . the colour of spring ill. by author. Oxford Univ. Pr., 1991. ISBN 0-19-540743-1 Subj: Seasons – spring. Wizards.

Alphonse knows . . . twelve months make a year ill. by author. Oxford Univ. Pr., 1990. ISBN 0-19-540798-9 Subj: Animals – mice. Days of the week, months of the year. Seasons. Wizards.

Alphonse knows . . . zero is not enough ill. by author. Oxford Univ. Pr., 1990. ISBN 0-19-540797-0 Subj: Counting, numbers. Wizards.

Zimnik, Reiner. *The bear on the motorcycle* trans. by Cornelia Schaeffer; ill. by author. Atheneum, 1963. Translation of Der bär auf dem motorrad. Subj: Animals – bears. Behavior – running away. Circus. Motorcycles.

The proud circus horse ill. by author. Pantheon, 1957. Subj: Animals – horses, ponies. Behavior – running away. Character traits – pride. Circus.

Zindel, Paul. *I love my mother* ill. by John Melo. HarperCollins, 1975. ISBN 0-06-026836-0 Subj: Emotions – loneliness. Emotions – love. Family life – mothers.

Ziner, Feenie. *Counting carnival* by Feenie Ziner and Paul Galdone; ill. by Paul Galdone. Coward, 1962. Subj: Activities – playing. Counting, numbers. Cumulative tales. Ethnic groups in the U.S. – African Americans. Parades. Poetry.

The true book of time by Feenie Ziner and Elizabeth Thompson; ill. by Katherine Evans. Childrens Pr., 1956. Subj: Time.

Zinnemann-Hope, Pam. *Find your coat, Ned* ill. by Kady MacDonald Denton. Macmillan, 1988. ISBN 0-689-50426-9 Subj: Behavior – losing things. Clothing – coats. Pets. Weather – rain.

Let's go shopping, Ned ill. by Kady MacDonald Denton. Macmillan, 1987. ISBN 0-689-50416-0 Subj: Shopping.

Let's play ball, Ned ill. by Kady MacDonald Denton. Macmillan, 1988. ISBN 0-689-50427-6 Subj: Activities – playing. Family life.

Time for bed, Ned ill. by Kady MacDonald Denton. Macmillan, 1987. ISBN 0-689-50415-2 Subj: Bedtime. Family life – mothers.

Zion, Gene. *All falling down* ill. by Margaret Bloy Graham. HarperCollins, 1951. Subj: Caldecott award honor books. Concepts – up and down.

Dear garbage man ill. by Margaret Bloy Graham. HarperCollins, 1957. Subj: Careers – sanitation workers. City.

Harry, the dirty dog ill. by Margaret Bloy Graham. HarperCollins, 1956. Subj: Activities – bathing. Animals – dogs. Behavior – running away.

Hide and seek day ill. by Margaret Bloy Graham. HarperCollins, 1954. Subj: Behavior – hiding. City. Games.

Jeffie's party ill. by Margaret Bloy Graham. Harper-Collins, 1957. Subj: Games. Parties.

The meanest squirrel I ever met ill. by Margaret Bloy Graham. Scribners, 1962. Subj: Animals – squirrels. Character traits – meanness. Friendship. Holidays – Thanksgiving.

No roses for Harry ill. by Margaret Bloy Graham. HarperCollins, 1958. ISBN 0-06-026891-3 Subj: Animals – dogs. Clothing.

The plant sitter ill. by Margaret Bloy Graham. HarperCollins, 1959. ISBN 0-06-443012-X Subj: Plants.

Really spring ill. by Margaret Bloy Graham. HarperCollins, 1956. Subj: Seasons – spring.

The summer snowman ill. by Margaret Bloy Graham. HarperCollins, 1955. Subj: Holidays – Fourth of July. Seasons – summer. Snowmen. Weather – snow.

Zirbes, Laura. *How many bears?* ill. by E. Harper Johnson. Putnam, 1960. Subj: Animals – bears. Counting, numbers.

Zirkel, Lynn. *The shell dragon* ill. by Peter Bowman. Oxford Univ. Pr., 1989. ISBN 0-19-279838-3 Subj: Birds. Dragons.

Zoehfeld, Kathleen Weidner. *Great white shark, ruler of the sea* ill. by Steven James Petruccio. Soundprints Pr., 1995. ISBN 1-56899-122-3 Subj: Fish – sharks. Sea and seashore.

How mountains are made ill. by James Graham Hale. HarperCollins, 1995. ISBN 0-06-024510-7 Subj: Earth. Mountains. Science.

What lives in a shell? ill. by Helen Davie. Harper-Collins, 1994. ISBN 0-06-022999-3 Subj: Animals. Science. Sea and seashore.

What's alive? ill. by Nadine Bernard Westcott. HarperCollins, 1995. ISBN 0-06-023444-X Subj: Animals. Plants. Science.

Zola, Meguido. *The dream of promise: a folktale in Hebrew and English* ill. by Ruben Zellermayer. Kids Can Pr., 1981. ISBN 0-919964-31-1 Subj: Folk and fairy tales. Foreign languages. Jewish culture. Self-concept.

Only the best ill. by Valerie Littlewood. Watts, 1982. ISBN 0-531-04066-6 Subj: Emotions – love. Family life – fathers.

Zoll, Max Alfred. *Animal babies* trans. by Violetta Castillo; ed. by Hanns Reich; ill. by author. Hill & Wang, 1971. Translation of Tierkinder. ISBN 0-8090-2001-7 Subj: Animals.

A flamingo is born trans. by Catherine Edwards Sadler; photos by Winifried Noack. Putnam, 1978. ISBN 0-399-20632-9 Subj: Birds – flamingos. Science.

Zolotow, Charlotte (Shapiro). *The beautiful Christmas tree* ill. by Yan Nacimbene. Haughton, 1999.

ISBN 0-395-91365-9 Subj: Holidays – Christmas. Trees.

Big sister and little sister ill. by Martha G. Alexander. HarperCollins, 1966. ISBN 0-06-026926-X Subj: Behavior – running away. Family life.

The bunny who found Easter ill. by Helen Craig. Houghton Mifflin, 1998. ISBN 0-395-86265-5 Subj: Animals – rabbits. Emotions – loneliness. Holidays – Easter.

But not Billy ill. by Kay Chorao. HarperCollins, 1983. ISBN 0-06-026964-2 Subj: Babies. Behavior – growing up.

Do you know what I'll do? ill. by Javaka Steptoe. HarperCollins, 2000. ISBN 0-06-027880-3 Subj: Babies. Behavior – growing up. Emotions – love. Ethnic groups in the U.S. – African Americans. Family life.

Flocks of birds ill. by Ruth Lercher Bornstein. Crowell, 1981. ISBN 0-690-04113-6 Subj: Bedtime. Birds.

The hating book ill. by Ben Shecter. Harper-Collins, 1969. ISBN 0-06-443197-5 Subj: Behavior – gossip. Emotions – hate. Friendship.

Hold my hand ill. by Thomas di Grazia. Harper-Collins, 1972. ISBN 0-06-026952-9 Subj: Friendship. Weather – snow.

I have a horse of my own ill. by Yoko Mitsuhashi. Crowell, 1980. ISBN 0-690-04047-4 Subj: Animals – horses, ponies. Dreams. Night.

I know a lady ill. by James Stevenson. Greenwillow, 1984. ISBN 0-688-03837-9 Subj: Character traits – kindness. Old age.

I like to be little ill. by Erik Blegvad. HarperCollins, 1987. ISBN 0-690-04674-X Subj: Behavior – growing up. Family life – mothers.

If it weren't for you ill. by Ben Shecter. Harper-Collins, 1966. ISBN 0-06-026943-X Subj: Family life. Sibling rivalry.

In my garden ill. by Roger Antoine Duvoisin. Lothrop, 1960. Subj: Plants. Seasons.

It's not fair ill. by William Pène Du Bois. Harper-Collins, 1976. ISBN 0-06-026935-9 Subj: Behavior – dissatisfaction. Emotions – envy, jealousy. Family life.

Janey ill. by Ronald Himler. HarperCollins, 1973. ISBN 0-06-026928-6 Subj: Emotions – loneliness. Friendship. Moving.

May I visit? ill. by Erik Blegvad. HarperCollins, 1976. ISBN 0-06-026933-2 Subj: Behavior – growing up. Emotions – love. Family life.

Mr. Rabbit and the lovely present ill. by Maurice Sendak. HarperCollins, 1962. ISBN 0-06-026946-4 Subj: Animals – rabbits. Birthdays. Caldecott award honor books. Concepts – color. Family life – mothers. Holidays – Easter.

The moon was the best ill. by Tana Hoban. Greenwillow, 1993. ISBN 0-688-09941-6 Subj: Moon.

My friend John ill. by Ben Shecter. HarperCollins, 1968. ISBN 0-06-026948-0 Subj: Friendship.

My grandson Lew ill. by William Pène Du Bois. HarperCollins, 1974. ISBN 0-06-026961-8 Subj: Death. Emotions – grief. Family life. Family life – grandfathers.

The new friend ill. by Emily Arnold McCully. Crowell, 1981. ISBN 0-690-04087-3 Subj: Behavior – sharing. Friendship.

The old dog ill. by James Ransome. HarperCollins, 1995. ISBN 0-06-024412-7 Subj: Animals – dogs. Death. Emotions – grief. Ethnic groups in the U.S. – African Americans. Pets.

One step, two . . . ill. by Roger Antoine Duvoisin. Lothrop, 1955. Subj: Activities – walking. City. Counting, numbers.

Over and over ill. by Garth Williams. HarperCollins, 1957. ISBN 0-06-026956-1 Subj: Holidays. Time.

The park book ill. by Hans Augusto Rey. HarperCollins, 1944. ISBN 0-06-026973-1 Subj: Activities – playing. City. Parks.

The poodle who barked at the wind ill. by Roger Antoine Duvoisin. Lothrop, 1964. Subj: Animals – dogs. Noise, sounds. Pets.

The quarreling book ill. by Arnold Lobel. HarperCollins, 1963. ISBN 0-06-026976-6 Subj: Behavior – fighting, arguing. Cumulative tales. Emotions – anger. Weather – rain.

The quiet mother and the noisy little boy ill. by Marc Simont. HarperCollins, 1989. ISBN 0-06-026979-0 Subj: Family life. Noise, sounds.

River winding ill. by Kazue Mizumura. Crowell, 1978. ISBN 0-690-03867-4 Subj: Poetry.

A rose, a bridge, and a wild black horse ill. by Robin Spowart. HarperCollins, 1987. ISBN 0-06-026939-1 Subj: Emotions – love. Family life.

Say it! ill. by James Stevenson. Greenwillow, 1980. Subj: Activities – walking. Emotions – love. Family life – mothers. Nature. Seasons – fall.

The seashore book ill. by Wendell Minor. HarperCollins, 1992. ISBN 0-06-020214-9 Subj: Family life – mothers. Imagination. Sea and seashore.

The sky was blue ill. by Garth Williams. HarperCollins, 1963. ISBN 0-06-027001-2 Subj: Emotions – love. Family life.

The sleepy book ill. by Vladimir Bobri. Lothrop, 1958. Subj: Animals. Bedtime. Sleep.

The sleepy book ill. by Ilse Plume. Rev. ed. HarperCollins, 1988. ISBN 0-06-026968-5 Subj: Animals. Bedtime. Sleep.

Some things go together ill. by Ashley Wolff. Newly illustrated ed. HarperFestival, 1999. ISBN 0-694-01197-5 Subj: Emotions – love. Family life. Poetry.

Someday ill. by Arnold Lobel. HarperCollins, 1965. ISBN 0-06-027016-0 Subj: Behavior – wishing. Dreams.

Someone new ill. by Erik Blegvad. HarperCollins, 1978. ISBN 0-06-027018-7 Subj: Behavior – growing up. Family life.

Something is going to happen ill. by Catherine Stock. HarperCollins, 1988. ISBN 0-06-027029-2 Subj: Morning. Weather – snow.

The song ill. by Nancy Tafuri. Greenwillow, 1982. ISBN 0-688-00817-8 Subj: Nature. Seasons. Songs.

The storm book ill. by Margaret Bloy Graham. HarperCollins, 1952. ISBN 0-06-027026-8 Subj: Caldecott award honor books. Emotions – fear. Weather. Weather – rain. Weather – rainbows.

Summer is . . . ill. by Ruth Lercher Bornstein. Crowell, 1983. ISBN 0-690-04304-X Subj: Rhyming text. Seasons – summer.

The summer night ill. by Ben Shecter. HarperCollins, 1974. Published in 1958 under the title The night when mother was away. ISBN 0-06-026960-X Subj: Activities – walking. Bedtime. Family life. Family life – fathers.

This quiet lady ill. by Anita Lobel. Greenwillow, 1992. ISBN 0-688-09306-X Subj: Family life – mothers.

Three funny friends ill. by Mary Chalmers. HarperCollins, 1961. Subj: Emotions – loneliness. Friendship. Imagination – imaginary friends.

A tiger called Thomas ill. by Catherine Stock. Lothrop, 1988. ISBN 0-688-06697-6 Subj: Character traits – shyness. Emotions – loneliness. Holidays – Halloween.

A tiger called Thomas ill. by Kurt Werth. Lothrop, 1963. Subj: Character traits – shyness. Emotions – loneliness. Holidays – Halloween.

Timothy too! ill. by Ruth Robbins. Houghton Mifflin, 1986. ISBN 0-395-39378-7 Subj: Friendship. Sibling rivalry.

The unfriendly book ill. by William Pène Du Bois. HarperCollins, 1975. ISBN 0-06-026931-6 Subj: Behavior – fighting, arguing. Friendship.

Wake up and goodnight ill. by Pamela Paparone. HarperCollins, 1998. ISBN 0-694-01032-4 Subj: Activities. Animals. Bedtime. Circular tales. Dreams. Format, unusual. Morning. Night.

When I have a son ill. by Hilary Knight. HarperCollins, 1967. ISBN 0-06-027051-9 Subj: Behavior – growing up. Family life. Imagination.

When the wind stops ill. by Stefano Vitale. HarperCollins, 1995. ISBN 0-06-026972-3 Subj: Bedtime. Nature. Night. Weather – wind.

The white marble ill. by Lilian Obligado. Abelard-Schuman, 1963. Subj: Activities – playing. Friendship. Night.

Who is Ben? ill. by Kathryn Jacobi. HarperCollins, 1997. ISBN 0-06-027352-6 Subj: Bedtime. Dreams. Night.

William's doll ill. by William Pène Du Bois. HarperCollins, 1972. ISBN 0-06-027048-9 Subj: Family life. Family life – grandmothers. Toys – dolls.

Zoo animals ill. with photos. Imported Pubs., 1983. Subj: Animals. Format, unusual – board books. Wordless.

Zoo animals ill. with photos and drawings. Macmillan, 1991. ISBN 0-689-71406-8 Subj: Animals. Nature.

Zusman, Evelyn. *The Passover parrot* ill. by Katherine Janus Kahn. Kar-Ben Copies, 1984. ISBN 0-930494-29-6 Subj: Birds – parakeets, parrots. Family life. Holidays – Passover. Jewish culture.

Zweifel, Frances W. *Animal baby-sitters* ill. by Irene Brady. Morrow, 1981. ISBN 0-688-00444-X Subj: Activities – babysitting. Animals. Nature.

Bony ill. by Whitney Darrow, Jr. HarperCollins, 1977. ISBN 0-06-027071-3 Subj: Animals – squirrels. Pets.

The Make-Something Club ill. by Ann Schweninger. Viking, 1994. ISBN 0-670-82361-9 Subj: Activities – cooking. Activities – making things. Animals – raccoons. Animals – squirrels. Food.

Zwetchkenbaum, G. *The Peanuts shape circus puzzle book* ill. by author. Scholastic, 1983. ISBN 0-590-32905-7 Subj: Concepts – shape. Riddles.

The Peanuts sleepy time puzzle book ill. by author. Scholastic, 1983. ISBN 0-590-32906-5 Subj: Riddles. Sleep.

The Snoopy farm puzzle book ill. by author. Scholastic, 1983. ISBN 0-590-32907-3 Subj: Farms. Riddles.

Snoopy safari puzzle book ill. by author. Scholastic, 1983. ISBN 0-590-32908-1 Subj: Riddles.

Title Index

Titles appear in alphabetical sequence with the author's name in parentheses, followed by the page number of the full listing in the Bibliographic Guide. For identical title listings, the illustrator's name is given to further identify the version. In the case of variant titles, both the original and differing titles are listed.

A

B

C

D

E

F

G

H

I

J

K

M

N

O

Q

R

T

U

V

Y

Z

Illustrator Index

Illustrators appear alphabetically in bold-face followed by their titles. Names in parentheses are authors of the titles when different from the illustrator. Page numbers refer to the full listing in the Bibliographic Guide.

A

Candy, Roy. *Christopher changes his name* (Sadu, Itah), 1184

Canning, Kate. *A painted tale,* 706

Cannon, Annie. *The bat in the boot,* 706
Whistle home (Honeycutt, Natalie), 914
You hold me and I'll hold you (Carson, Jo), 713

Cannon, Beth. *Why worry?* (Kimmel, Eric A.), 962

Cannon, Janell. *Stellaluna,* 706
Stellaluna: a pop-up book and mobile, 706
Trupp, 706
Verdi, 706

Cannon, Karen. *A special place for Charlee* (Morehead, Debby), 1082

Canyon, Christopher. *The ever-living tree* (Vieira, Linda), 1270
The tree in the ancient forest (Reed-Jones, Carol), 1159

Caparn, Rhys. *Down the mountain* (Bartlett, Margaret Farrington), 635

Capdevila, Roser. *At the farm* (At the farm), 620
City (City), 729
Let's count (Ballart, Elisabet), 629
Our house (Our house), 1119
Shopping (Shopping), 1211
The weekend (The weekend), 1284
What we do (What we do), 1290

Capek, Jindra. *The most beautiful song* (Bolliger, Max), 664

Capelle, Erika Dietzsch *see* Dietzsch-Capelle, Erika

Caple, Kathy. *The biggest nose,* 706
The coolest place in town, 706
Fox and bear, 706
Harry's smile, 706
Inspector Aardvark and the perfect cake, 707
The purse, 707
Starring Hillary, 707
The wimp, 707

Caputo, Robert. *More than just pets,* 707

Carey, Joanna. *Clara's dancing feet* (Richardson, Jean), 1163

Carigiet, Alois. *Anton the goatherd,* 707
A bell for Ursli (Chönz, Selina), 725
Florina and the wild bird (Chönz, Selina), 725
The pear tree, the birch tree and the barberry bush, 707
The snowstorm (Chönz, Selina), 725

Carle, Eric. *Brown bear, brown bear, what do you see?* (Martin, Bill [William Ivan]), 1053
Chip has many brothers (Baumann, Hans), 638
Do bears have mothers too? (Fisher, Aileen Lucia), 809
Do you want to be my friend? 707
Does a kangaroo have a mother, too? 707
Dragons dragons and other creatures that never were, 707
Draw me a star, 707
The foolish tortoise (Buckley, Richard), 692
From head to toe, 707
Gravity at work and play (Engelbrektson, Sune), 797
The greedy python (Buckley, Richard), 692
The grouchy ladybug, 707
Have you seen my cat? 708
Hello, red fox, 708
The hole in the dike (Green, Norma B.), 851
A house for Hermit Crab, 708
I see a song, 708

The lamb and the butterfly (Sundgaard, Arnold), 1240
Little cloud, 708
Little cloud, a board book, 708
The mixed-up chameleon, 708
The mountain that loved a bird (McLerran, Alice), 1038
My apron, 708
My very first book of colors, 708
My very first book of food, 708
My very first book of growth, 708
My very first book of heads and tails, 708
My very first book of homes, 708
My very first book of motion, 708
My very first book of numbers, 708
My very first book of shapes, 708
My very first book of sounds, 708
My very first book of tools, 708
My very first book of touch, 708
My very first book of words, 708
1, 2, 3 to the zoo, 708
Pancakes, pancakes, 708
Papa, please get the moon for me, 708
Polar bear, polar bear, what do you hear? (Martin, Bill [William Ivan]), 1053
The rooster who set out to see the world, 708
Rooster's off to see the world, 708
The secret birthday message, 708
The sun is a star (Engelbrektson, Sune), 797
The tiny seed, 708
Today is Monday, 708
Twelve tales from Æsop, 708
The very busy spider, 708
The very clumsy click beetle, 708
The very hungry caterpillar, 708
The very lonely firefly, 708
The very quiet cricket, 708
Walter the baker, 708
Watch out! A giant! 708
Why Noah chose the dove (Singer, Isaac Bashevis), 1217

Carling, Amelia Lau. *Mama and Papa have a store,* 709

Carlson, Nancy L. *ABC, I like me!* 709
Arnie and the new kid, 709
Arnie and the skateboard gang, 709
Arnie and the stolen markers, 709
Arnie goes to camp, 709
Baby and the bear (Pearson, Susan), 1129
Bunnies and their hobbies, 709
Bunnies and their sports, 709
Harriet and the garden, 709
Harriet and the roller coaster, 709
Harriet and Walt, 709
Harriet's Halloween candy, 709
Harriet's recital, 709
How to lose all your friends, 709
I like me, 709
It's going to be perfect, 709
Lenore's big break (Pearson, Susan), 1129
Life is fun, 709
Look out kindergarten, here I come! 709
Louanne Pig in making the team, 709
Louanne Pig in the mysterious valentine, 709
Louanne Pig in the perfect family, 709
Loudmouth George and the big race, 709
Loudmouth George and the cornet, 709
Loudmouth George and the fishing trip, 709

Cassouto, Lynne. *Seven days of creation* (Aronow, Sara), 616

Castilla, Julia Mercedes. *Family / familia* (Bertrand, Diane Gonzales), 652

Castle, Caroline. *Elizabeth Jane gets dressed* (Tyrrell, Anne), 1262
Mary Ann always can (Tyrrell, Anne), 1262

Caswell, Helen Rayburn. *God must like to laugh*, 716
Parable of the good Samaritan, 716

Catalano, Dominic. *The bear who loved Puccini* (Sundgaard, Arnold), 1240
Bernard's bath (Goodman, Joan Elizabeth), 846
Bernard's nap (Goodman, Joan Elizabeth), 846
The frog went a-courting (A frog he would a-wooing go [folk-song]), 821
Rabbit surprise (Houck, Eric L.), 917
Rise and shine! (Carlstrom, Nancy White), 711
Sleeping Beauty (San José, Christine), 1186
That extraordinary pig of Paris (Schotter, Roni), 1195

Catalanotto, Peter. *All I see* (Rylant, Cynthia), 1182
Book (Lyon, George Ella), 1024
The catspring somersault flying one-handed flip-flop (Kiser, SuAnn), 965
Cecil's story (Lyon, George Ella), 1024
Christmas always . . ., 716
Circle of thanks (Fowler, Susi Gregg), 816
Dad and me, 716
Dark cloud strong breeze (Patron, Susan), 1127
A day at damp camp (Lyon, George Ella), 1024
Dreamplace (Lyon, George Ella), 1024
Dylan's day out, 716
The longest wait (Bradby, Marie), 671
Mama is a miner (Lyon, George Ella), 1024
Mr. Mumble, 716
My house has stars (McDonald, Megan), 1031
The painter, 716
The Rolling Store (Johnson, Angela), 941
Who came down that road? (Lyon, George Ella), 1024

Catania, Tom. *The grizzly bear with the golden ears* (George, Jean Craighead), 831

Catrow, David. *Cesar's amazing journey* (Policoff, Stephen Phillip), 1142
The emperor's old clothes (Lasky, Kathryn), 987
Good cats/Bad cats (Ghigna, Charles), 834
Good dogs/Bad dogs (Ghigna, Charles), 834
The long, long letter (Spurr, Elizabeth), 1227
Rotten teeth (Simms, Laura), 1215
That's good! that's bad! (Cuyler, Margery), 756
There was an old witch (Reeves, Howard W.), 1159
Westward ho, Carlotta! (Fleming, Candace), 811
Why Lapin's ears are long and other stories of the Louisiana bayou (Doucet, Sharon Arms), 781

Cauley, Lorinda Bryan. *The animal kids*, 717
The bake-off, 717
The beginning of the armadillos (Kipling, Rudyard), 964
Clancy's coat (Bunting, Eve [Anne Evelyn]), 694
Clap your hands, 717
The cock, the mouse and the little red hen (The little red hen), 1012
Curley Cat baby-sits (Watson, Pauline), 1282
The elephant's child (Kipling, Rudyard), 964
Goldilocks and the three bears (The three bears), 1251
The goodnight circle (Lesser, Carolyn), 997

The goose and the golden coins, 717
The house of five bears (Jameson, Cynthia), 936
If you say so, Claude (Nixon, Joan Lowery), 1106
Jack and the beanstalk (Jack and the beanstalk), 933
Little grey rabbit (Bowden, Joan Chase), 669
Old Hippo's Easter egg (Wahl, Jan), 1275
Old MacDonald had a farm (Old MacDonald had a farm), 1113
The owl and the pussycat (Lear, Edward), 990
The pancake boy (The gingerbread boy), 838
Pease porridge hot, 717
Puss in boots (Perrault, Charles), 1133
Rabbits' search for a little house (Kwitz, Mary DeBall), 981
Small Bear solves a mystery (Holl, Adelaide), 913
Three blind mice (Ivimey, John William), 932
The three little kittens (Mother Goose), 1092
The three little pigs (The three little pigs), 1252
The town mouse and the country mouse (Æsop), 589
Treasure hunt, 717
The trouble with Tyrannosaurus Rex, 717
The ugly duckling (Andersen, H. C. [Hans Christian]), 605
Where's Henrietta's hen? (Freschet, Berniece), 820

Cazet, Denys. *Are there any questions?* 717
Big shoe, little shoe, 717
Born in the gravy, 717
Christmas moon, 717
Daydreams, 718
December 24th, 718
The duck with squeaky feet, 718
A fish in his pocket, 718
Frosted glass, 718
Good morning, Maxine! 718
Great-Uncle Felix, 718
I'm not sleepy, 718
Lucky me, 718
Mother night, 718
Mud baths for everyone, 718
Never spit on your shoes, 718
Night lights, 718
Nothing at all, 718
Saturday, 718
Sunday, 718
Where can Daniel be? (Komaiko, Leah), 969
You make the angels cry, 718

Cecil, Randy. *Dusty Locks and the three bears* (Lowell, Susan), 1021
Little Red Cowboy Hat (Lowell, Susan), 1021
The runaway tortilla (Kimmel, Eric A.), 962
The singing chick (Stenmark, Victoria), 1231

Cellini, Eva. *Let's walk up the wall* (Johnson, Ryerson), 943

Cellini, Joseph. *Little apes* (Conklin, Gladys), 741

Censoni, Robert. *Benjamin's balloon* (Quin-Harkin, Janet), 1153

Centola, Tom. *Siren in the night* (Aylesworth, Jim), 622

Cepeda, Joe. *Captain Bob sets sail* (Schotter, Roni), 1195
Gracias, the Thanksgiving turkey (Cowley, Joy), 748
Koi and the kola nuts (Aardema, Verna), 583
The old man and his door (Soto, Gary), 1225
Pumpkin fiesta (Yacowitz, Caryn), 1309
We were tired of living in a house (Skorpen, Liesel Moak), 1218

Two lonely ducks, 789
Veronica, 789
Veronica and the birthday present, 789
Veronica's smile, 789
Wake up, farm! (Tresselt, Alvin R.), 1257
The web in the grass (Freschet, Berniece), 820
What did you leave behind? (Tresselt, Alvin R.), 1257
Which is the best place? (Ginsburg, Mirra), 839
White snow, bright snow (Tresselt, Alvin R.), 1257
The wishing well in the woods (Friedrich, Priscilla), 821
Wobble the witch cat (Calhoun, Mary), 704
The world in the candy egg (Tresselt, Alvin R.), 1257
Dwyer, Mindy. *Coyote in love,* 789
Dyer, Jane. *Baby Bear's bedtime book* (Yolen, Jane), 1312
Child of faerie, child of earth (Yolen, Jane), 1312
The girl in the golden bower (Yolen, Jane), 1312
Goldilocks and the three bears (The three bears), 1251
If anything ever goes wrong at the zoo (Hendrick, Mary Jean), 892
The patchwork lady (Whittington, Mary K.), 1292
Picnic with Piggins (Yolen, Jane), 1313
Piggins (Yolen, Jane), 1313
The snow speaks (Carlstrom, Nancy White), 711
The three bears holiday rhyme book (Yolen, Jane), 1313
The three bears rhyme book (Yolen, Jane), 1313
Time for bed (Fox, Mem), 816
When Mama comes home tonight (Spinelli, Eileen), 1227
Dyke, John. *The magician who lived on the mountain* (Green, Marion), 851
Pigwig, 789
Pigwig and the pirates, 789
Dypold, Pat. *One cow coughs* (Loomis, Christine), 1019
Dzierzawska, Malgorzata. *Little Mouse's rescue* (Chottin, Ariane), 726

E

Eachus, Jennifer. *The big big sea* (Waddell, Martin), 1273
Daddy, will you miss me? (McCormick, Wendy), 1027
Good-bye, Papa (Leavy, Una), 991
I'm sorry (McBratney, Sam), 1025
In the middle of the night (Henderson, Kathy), 891
Eagle, Ellen. *Gypsy's cleaning day,* 789
Someday with my father (Buckley, Helen Elizabeth), 692
Earle, Olive L. *Squirrels in the garden,* 789
Earle, Vana. *Animal tales from Ireland* (Cormack, M. Grant), 745
Easmon, Carol. *Amoko and Efua Bear* (Appiah, Sonia), 611
East, Stella. *Dreamstones* (Trottier, Maxine), 1258
Eastman, P. D. (Philip D.). *The alphabet book,* 790
Are you my mother? 790
Flap your wings, 790
Go, dog, go! 790

I'll teach my dog 100 words (Frith, Michael K.), 821
Robert the rose horse (Heilbroner, Joan), 888
Sam and the firefly, 790
Snow (McKié, Roy), 1035
Eaton, John. *Fairy tales* (Cummings, E. E. [Edward Estlin]), 753
Eaton, Su. *Punch and Judy in the rain,* 790
Eaton, Tom. *Doghouse for sale* (Pape, D. L. [Donna Lugg]), 1123
Steven and the green turtle (Cromie, William J.), 752
Where is my little Joey? (Pape, D. L. [Donna Lugg]), 1123
Ebborn, Caroline. *How the leopard got his spots* (Kipling, Rudyard), 964
Ebel, Alex. *The moon* (Asimov, Isaac), 620
Eberbach, Andrea. *Willie the slowpoke* (Greydanus, Rose), 856
Eccles, Jane. *Maxwell's birthday,* 790
Eckart, Frances. *I want to be a carpenter* (Greene, Carla), 852
Eckert, Horst *see* Janosch
Edelson, Wendy. *The baker's dozen* (Shepard, Aaron), 1210
Billy goats Gruff (Asbjørnsen, P. C. [Peter Christen]), 617
Edens, Cooper. *The prince of the rabbits* (Meroux, Felix), 1066
Edman, Polly. *Red thread riddles* (Jensen, Virginia Allen), 939
Eduar, Gilles. *Dream journey,* 791
Jooka saves the day, 791
Edwards, Gunvor. *Snuffle to the rescue* (Beresford, Elisabeth), 649
Edwards, Linda Strauss. *The downtown day,* 791
Goodnight, Hattie, my dearie, my dove (Schertle, Alice), 1192
So what if I'm a sore loser? (Williams, Barbara), 1297
Edwards, Mark. *The sand children* (Dunbar, Joyce), 786
Edwards, Michelle. *Alef-bet,* 791
And Sunday makes seven (Baden, Robert), 624
A baker's portrait, 791
Chicken Man, 791
Dora's book, 791
Eve and Smithy, 791
Edwards, Peter. *Is Susan here?* (Udry, Janice May), 1263
Egan, Tim. *The blunder of the Rogues,* 792
Chestnut Cove, 792
Distant Feathers, 792
Friday night at Hodges' café, 792
Metropolitan cow, 792
Egielski, Richard. *Bravo, Minski* (Yorinks, Arthur), 1313
Buz, 792
Call me Ahnighito (Conrad, Pam), 741
Christmas in July (Yorinks, Arthur), 1313
Fire! Fire! said Mrs. McGuire (Martin, Bill [William Ivan]), 1053
The gingerbread boy (The gingerbread boy), 838
Hey, Al (Yorinks, Arthur), 1313
Jazper, 792
The little father (Burgess, Gelett), 696

F

Gobbato, Imero. *Barney the Beard* (Bunting, Eve [Anne Evelyn]), 694
Tops and bottoms (Conger, Lesley), 741

Gobhai, Mehlli. *Lakshmi, the water buffalo who wouldn't,* 841
Usha, the mouse-maiden, 841

Goble, Paul. *Adopted by the eagles,* 841
Beyond the ridge, 841
Buffalo woman, 841
Crow chief, 841
Death of the iron horse, 841
The dream wolf, 841
The friendly wolf, 841
The gift of the sacred dog, 841
The girl who loved wild horses, 841
The great race of the birds and animals, 841
Her seven brothers, 841
I sing for the animals, 841
Iktomi and the berries, 841
Iktomi and the boulder, 841
Iktomi and the buffalo skull, 841
Iktomi and the buzzard, 841
Iktomi and the coyote, 841
Iktomi and the ducks, 841
The legend of the White Buffalo Woman, 842
The lost children, 842
Love flute, 842
Remaking the earth, 842
The return of the buffaloes, 842
Star boy, 842

Godard, Alex. *Idora,* 842

Godfrey, Elsa. *On the moon* (Vaughn, Jenny), 1268

Godkin, Celia. *What about ladybugs?* 842

Godon, Ingrid. *Curious kids go to preschool* (Antoine, Héloïse), 611

Godt, John. *Listen for the bus* (McMahon, Patricia), 1038

Goembel, Ponder. *A basket full of white eggs* (Swann, Brian), 1241
"Hi, pizza man!" (Walter, Virginia), 1278
The night Iguana left home (McDonald, Megan), 1031

Goennel, Heidi. *The circus,* 842
Colors, 842
Heidi's zoo, 842
I pretend, 842
If I were a penguin . . ., 842
In just-spring (Cummings, E. E. [Edward Estlin]), 753
It's my birthday, 842
My day, 842
My dog, 842
Odds and evens, 842
Seasons, 842
Sometimes I like to be alone, 842
When I grow up . . ., 842
While I am little, 842

Goetzl, Robert F. *Many nations* (Bruchac, Joseph), 688

Goffe, Toni. *Beginning school* (Smalls-Hector, Irene), 1220
Clap your hands (Hayes, Sarah), 885
Ice cream at the castle (Love, Ann), 1020
The knight who was afraid to fight (Hazen, Barbara Shook), 887
Little boy soup (Harrison, David Lee), 878
The little red house (Sawicki, Norma Jean), 1189

Miss Fannie's hat (Karon, Jan), 951
Mother Halverson's new cat (Aylesworth, Jim), 622
The prince who wrote a letter (Love, Ann), 1020
Rocks in my pocket (Harshman, Marc), 878
The story of creation, 842
Toby's animal rescue service, 842
Treed by a pride of irate lions (Zimelman, Nathan), 1321

Goffin, Josse. *The Christmas story,* 842
Oh! 842
Silent Christmas, 842
Who is the boss? 842
Yes, 842

Goffstein, M. B. (Marilyn Brooke). *Across the sea,* 842
An actor, 842
An artist, 842
Artists' helpers enjoy the evening, 842
Family scrapbook, 843
Fish for supper, 843
A house, a home, 843
Laughing latkes, 843
A little Schubert, 843
Me and my captain, 843
My Noah's ark, 843
Natural history, 843
Neighbors, 843
Our prairie home, 843
Our snowman, 843
School of names, 843
Sleepy people, 843
A writer, 843

Gohman, Vera. *Word Bird's spring words* (Moncure, Jane Belk), 1078
Word Bird's winter words (Moncure, Jane Belk), 1078

Gold, Caroline. *The crooked apple tree* (Houghton, Eric), 917

Gold, Ethel. *A very special sister* (Levi, Dorothy Hoffman), 999

Goldberg, Barry. *Merry Christmas, Rugrats!* (Richards, Kitty), 1163

Goldberg, Grace. *Jungle life* (Nayer, Judy), 1100
Night animals (Nayer, Judy), 1100
Reptiles (Nayer, Judy), 1100
Sea creatures (Nayer, Judy), 1100

Goldin, David. *Lost cat* (Hardy, Tad), 876

Golding, Kim. *Alphababies,* 843

Goldman, Dara. *There's no such thing!* 843

Goldman, Susan. *Cousins are special,* 843
Grandma is somebody special, 843

Goldsborough, June. *An alphabet book* (Chase, Catherine), 722
Dolphins and porpoises (Gordon, Sharon), 847
It happened on Thursday (Delton, Judy), 767
Who am I? (Raebeck, Lois), 1155

Gold-Vukson, Marji. *The colors of my Jewish Year,* 844

Golembe, Carla. *Annabelle's big move,* 844
Why the sky is far away (Gerson, Mary-Joan), 833
The woman in the moon (Rattigan, Jama Kim), 1157

Goloshapov, Sergei. *The six servants* (Grimm, Jacob), 862

Gomboli, Mario. *Look inside a house,* 844
Look inside a ship, 844

Gomi, Taro. *The big book of boxes,* 844
Bus stop, 844

Coco can't wait! 844
The crocodile and the dentist, 844
First comes Harry, 844
Guess what? 844
Guess who? 844
Hi, butterfly! 844
My friends, 844
Santa through the window, 844
Seeing, saying, doing, playing, 844
Spring is here, 844
Toot! 844
Where's the fish? 844
Who ate it? 844
Who hid it? 844
Gon, Adriano. *Good night, sleep tight* (Lively, Penelope), 1013
Gonzales, Edward. *Farolitos for Abuelo* (Anaya, Rudolfo A.), 601
Gonzales, Tomás. *I can use tools* (Kesselman, Judi R.), 958
Gonzalez, Maya Christina. *From the bellybutton of the moon and other summer poems / poems = Del ombligo de la luna y otros poemas de verano / poemas* (Alarcón, Francisco X), 592
Goodall, John S. *The adventures of Paddy Pork,* 845
The ballooning adventures of Paddy Pork, 845
Creepy castle, 845
An Edwardian Christmas, 845
An Edwardian summer, 845
Great days of a country house, 845
Jacko, 845
Little Red Riding Hood (Grimm, Jacob), 860
The midnight adventures of Kelly, Dot and Esmeralda, 845
Naughty Nancy, 845
Naughty Nancy goes to school, 845
Paddy goes traveling, 845
Paddy Pork, 845
Paddy Pork's holiday, 845
Paddy to the rescue, 845
Paddy under water, 845
Paddy's evening out, 845
Paddy's new hat, 845
Puss in boots (Perrault, Charles), 1133
Shrewbettina's birthday, 845
The story of a castle, 845
The story of a farm, 845
The story of a main street, 845
The story of an English village, 845
The surprise picnic, 845
Goode, Diane. *The adventures of Pinocchio* (Collodi, Carlo), 740
A child's garden of verses (Stevenson, Robert Louis), 1235
Christmas carols (Christmas carols), 728
Cinderella (Perrault, Charles), 1133
The Diane Goode book of American folk tales and songs (Durell, Ann), 788
Diane Goode's book of silly stories & songs, 845
The dinosaur's new clothes, 845
The dream eater (Garrison, Christian), 829
The fir tree (Andersen, H. C. [Hans Christian]), 603
The good-hearted youngest brother (The good-hearted youngest brother), 844
The house Gobbaleen (Alexander, Lloyd), 593
I go with my family to Grandma's (Levinson, Riki), 1000

I hear a noise, 845
The little book of cats (The little book of cats), 1011
The little book of farm friends, 845
The Little book of mice (The Little book of mice), 1011
The Little book of pigs (The Little book of pigs), 1011
Little pieces of the west wind (Garrison, Christian), 829
Mama's perfect present, 845
Peter Pan (Barrie, J. M. [James M.]), 634
The unicorn and the plow (Moeri, Louise), 1076
Watch the stars come out (Levinson, Riki), 1000
When I was young in the mountains (Rylant, Cynthia), 1183
Where's our mama? 845
Goodell, Jon. *Little Salt Lick and the Sun King* (Armstrong, Jennifer), 614
Mice are nice (Ghigna, Charles), 834
A mouse called Wolf (King-Smith, Dick), 963
One winter night (Kimmel, Eric A.), 962
Goodenow, Earle. *The last camel,* 846
The owl who hated the dark, 846
Gooding, Beverley. *The friendly fox* (Koralek, Jenny), 970
King Gorboduc's fabulous zoo (Boswell, Stephen), 668
Once there were no pandas (Greaves, Margaret), 850
The open road (Grahame, Kenneth), 849
Goodman, Joan Elizabeth. *The gingerbread boy* (The gingerbread boy), 838
Goodman, Vivienne. *Guess what?* (Fox, Mem), 816
Goor, Nancy. *All kinds of feet* (Goor, Ron), 846
In the driver's seat (Goor, Ron), 846
Shadows (Goor, Ron), 846
Signs (Goor, Ron), 846
Goor, Ron. *All kinds of feet,* 846
In the driver's seat, 846
Shadows, 846
Signs, 846
Goor, Ronald *see* Goor, Ron
Gorbachev, Valeri. *The Fool of the world and the flying ship,* 846
Little Bunny's sleepless night (Roth, Carol), 1176
Nicky and the big, bad wolves, 846
So much in common (Jacobs, Laurie A.), 935
What if? (Hulme, Joy N.), 922
Where is the apple pie? 846
Young Mouse and Elephant (Farris, Pamela J.), 803
Gorbaty, Norman. *Baby Ben's bow-wow book* (Ziefert, Harriet), 1318
Baby Ben's busy book (Ziefert, Harriet), 1318
Baby Ben's go-go book (Ziefert, Harriet), 1318
Baby Ben's noisy book (Ziefert, Harriet), 1318
Beep! Beep! I'm a jeep (Haus, Felice), 881
Get up and go, little dinosaur! 846
I did it! (Ross, Anna), 1175
I have to go (Ross, Anna), 1175
Naptime (Ross, Anna), 1175
Otto the cat (Herman, Gail), 894
Say the magic word, please (Ross, Anna), 1175
Sleepy dog (Ziefert, Harriet), 1320
Tow truck, 846
What a hungry puppy! (Herman, Gail), 894

J

L

The sleeping beauty (Grimm, Jacob), 862
A special trick, 1061
Terrible troll, 1061
There's a nightmare in my closet, 1061
There's an alligator under my bed, 1061
There's something in my attic, 1061
This is my family (Mayer, Gina), 1060
Two moral tales, 1061
What do you do with a kangaroo? 1061
You're the scaredy cat, 1061
Mayhew, James. *The boy and the cloth of dreams*
(Koralek, Jenny), 970
Katie and the dinosaurs, 1062
Katie and the Mona Lisa, 1062
Katie meets the Impressionists, 1062
Maynard, Barbara. *Fraidy cat* (Barrows, Marjorie
Wescott), 634
Mayo, Diana. *Daniel in the lions' den* (Bible. Old
Testament. Daniel), 654
Mayo, Gretchen Will. *Change* (Greene, Laura), 853
Help (Greene, Laura), 853
The whale brother (Steiner, Barbara [Annette]),
1231
Maze, Deborah. *Edmund and the White Witch*
(Edmund and the White Witch), 791
Lucy steps through the wardrobe (Lucy steps
through the wardrobe), 1021
Mazzola, Frank. *Counting is for the birds*, 1062
The crayon counting book (Ryan, Pam Muñoz),
1181
Mazzucco, Jennifer. *Little Johnny Buttermilk* (Wahl,
Jan), 1275
Meade, Holly. *Boss of the plains* (Carlson, Laurie
M.), 709
Cocoa ice (Appelbaum, Diana Karter), 611
Hush! (Ho, Minfong), 905
John Willy and Freddy McGee, 1063
Sleep, sleep, sleep (Van Laan, Nancy), 1267
Small green snake (Gray, Libba Moore), 850
This is the hat (Van Laan, Nancy), 1267
Meadway, Clifford. *Let's look at tractors* (Rickard,
Graham), 1163
Meddaugh, Susan. *Amanda's perfect hair* (Milstein,
Linda Breiner), 1073
Beast, 1063
The best Halloween of all (Wojciechowski, Susan),
1303
The best place, 1063
Bimwili and the Zimwi (Aardema, Verna), 583
Cinderella's rat, 1063
Five little piggies (Martin, David), 1054
Good zap, little grog (Wilson, Sarah), 1300
Hog-eye, 1063
In the haunted house (Bunting, Eve [Anne Evelyn]), 695
Martha and Skits, 1063
Martha blah blah, 1063
Martha calling, 1063
Martha speaks, 1063
Martha walks the dog, 1063
Maude and Claude go abroad, 1063
No nap (Bunting, Eve [Anne Evelyn]), 695
A perfect Father's Day (Bunting, Eve [Anne Evelyn]), 695
The silver bear (Marzollo, Jean), 1057
Too short Fred, 1063
Tree of birds, 1063
Two ways to count to ten (Dee, Ruby), 764

The witches' supermarket, 1063
Medearis, Angela Shelf. *Picking peas for a penny*,
1063
Medina, Nina. *Have you ever noticed that rabbits don't
sing?* 1064
Mednikov, Vera. *Count your way through Russia*
(Haskins, Jim [James]), 880
Meer, Atie Van der *see* Van der Meer, Atie
Meer, Ron Van der *see* Van der Meer, Ron
Meeuwissen, Tony. *Remarkable animals*, 1064
Megale, Marina. *Baby and I can play* (Hendrickson,
Karen), 892
Fun with toddlers (Hendrickson, Karen), 892
Safety zone (Meyer, Linda D.), 1067
Meier, David Scott. *Ellsworth and Millicent* (Alexander, Sue), 594
What's wrong now, Millicent? (Alexander, Sue),
595
Meisel, Paul. *And that's what happened to little Lucy*
(Davidson, Jill A.), 761
A cake all for me! (Beil, Karen Magnuson), 641
Engine, engine, number nine (Calmenson,
Stephanie), 704
The Fixits (Mazer, Anne), 1062
Go away, dog (Lexau, Joan M.), 1004
Howard and the sitter surprise (Paton, Priscilla),
1127
I am really a princess (Shields, Carol Diggory),
1211
I wish my brother was a dog (Shields, Carol Diggory), 1211
Lunch money and other poems about school (Shields,
Carol Diggory), 1211
Mr. Baseball (Hooks, William H.), 914
Mr. Dinosaur (Hooks, William H.), 914
Mr. Monster (Hooks, William H.), 914
The three little pigs (The three little pigs), 1252
Wizard and Wart in trouble (Smith, Janice Lee),
1222
Your insides (Cole, Joanna), 738
Mekibel, Shoshana. *Here come the Purim players!*
(Cohen, Barbara), 734
Melanson, Luc. *Little Kim's doll* (Yaroshevskaya,
Kim), 1309
Melcher, Mary. *Mommy, who does God love?* 1064
Peekaboo bunny (Capucilli, Alyssa Satin), 707
Melle, Gerta. *The cats' party* (Redies, Rainer), 1158
Melling, David. *Gerda the goose* (Oram, Hiawyn),
1116
Melmon, Deborah . *Hello Peter = Bonjour, Rémy*
(Morris, Ann), 1085
Melnyczuk, Peter. *Imagine you are a tiger* (Wallace,
Karen), 1276
Red fox (Wallace, Karen), 1277
Sleeping Nanna (Crossley-Holland, Kevin), 752
While shepherds watched (Fleetwood, Jenni), 811
Melo, John. *I love my mother* (Zindel, Paul), 1321
Meloni, Maria Teresa. *Rosie's ballet slippers* (Hampshire, Susan), 874
Melvin, James. *Crabby's water wish* (Tate, Suzanne),
1245
Mendelson, S. T. *Stupid Emilien*, 1065
Mendez, Consuelo. *Atariba and Niguayona*
(Rohmer, Harriet), 1171
Mendoza, George. *The alphabet boat*, 1065
Merrick, Patrick. *Easter bunnies*, 1066

Q

R

A colt named mischief, 1154
Music of their hooves (Springer, Nancy), 1227
What's happening to Daisy? 1154
Racioppo, Larry. *Halloween,* 1154
Rackham, Arthur. *Mother Goose* (Mother Goose), 1090
Mother Goose nursery rhymes (Watts, 1969; reprint of 1913 ed.) (Mother Goose), 1090
Mother Goose nursery rhymes (Viking, 1975) (Mother Goose), 1090
Radcliffe, Theresa. *The snow leopard,* 1154
Rader, Laura. *A book of friends* (Ross, Dave [David]), 1175
A book of hugs (Ross, Dave [David]), 1175
A book of kisses (Ross, Dave [David]), 1175
Dancing (Ziefert, Harriet), 1318
Getting ready for new baby (Ziefert, Harriet), 1318
Goldilocks and the three bears (The three bears), 1251
The three billy goats Gruff (Asbjørnsen, P. C. [Peter Christen]), 617
The turnip (Ziefert, Harriet), 1320
When I am big (Packard, Mary), 1121
Radford, Derek. *Building machines and what they do,* 1154
Cargo machines and what they do, 1154
Harry at the garage, 1154
Harry builds a house, 1154
Radin, Chari. *Everything's changing - It's pesach!* (Auerbach, Julie Jaslow), 620
Radunsky, Vladimir. *An Edward Lear alphabet* (Lear, Edward), 990
Hail to mail (Marshak, S. [Samuil]), 1051
Maestro plays (Martin, Bill [William Ivan]), 1053
The pup grew up! (Marshak, S. [Samuil]), 1051
The riddle (Vernon, Adele), 1269
Square, triangle, round, skinny (Radunsky, Eugenia), 1154
The story of a boy named Will, who went sledding down the hill (Kharms, Daniil), 960
Telephone (Chukovskii, Kornei Ivanovich), 728
Yucka Drucka Droni (Radunsky, Eugenia), 1155
Radzinski, Kandy. *Lullaby* (Aragon, Jane Chelsea), 612
Rae, Mary Maki. *The farmer in the dell* (The farmer in the dell), 803
Little chicks' mothers and all the others (Lüton, Mildred), 1023
Over in the meadow (Wadsworth, Olive A.), 1274
Ragins, Charles. *Anna's Athabaskan summer* (Griese, Arnold A.), 856
Raglin, Tim. *The birthday ABC* (Metaxas, Eric), 1067
Deputy Dan and the bank robbers (Rosenbloom, Joseph), 1175
The elephant's child (Kipling, Rudyard), 964
How the camel got his hump (Kipling, Rudyard), 964
Uncle Mugsy and the terrible twins of Christmas (Metaxas, Eric), 1067
Raglus, Jeff. *Schnorky the wave puncher,* 1155
Rahn, Joan Elma. *Holes,* 1155
Raible, Alton. *Rolling the cheese* (Miles, Miska), 1069
Raine, Patricia. *Orange cheeks* (O'Callahan, Jay), 1111
Raines, Antony Groves *see* Groves-Raines, Antony

Rakoncay, Frank. *Shapes, sides, curves and corners* (Podendorf, Illa), 1141
Ralla, Kusho. *The mouse king* (Tsultim, Yeshe), 1259
Ramel, Charlotte. *The bake-a-cake book* (Meijer, Marie), 1064
My sister Lotta and me (Dahlbäck-Lutteman, Helena), 757
Ramos, Mario. *Orson* (Rascal), 1156
Ramsey, Marcy Dunn. *The friendship garden* (Medearis, Angela Shelf), 1063
Ramsey, Ted. *Katie did!* (Galbraith, Kathryn Osebold), 824
Rand, Paul. *Little 1* (Rand, Ann), 1155
Sparkle and spin (Rand, Ann), 1155
Rand, Ted. *Aloha, Salty!* (Rand, Gloria), 1155
Baby in a basket (Rand, Gloria), 1155
Barn dance! (Martin, Bill [William Ivan]), 1053
The bear that heard crying (Kinsey-Warnock, Natalie), 963
The cabin key (Rand, Gloria), 1155
Country crossing (Aylesworth, Jim), 622
Don't forget (Lakin, Pat [Patricia]), 983
Here are my hands (Martin, Bill [William Ivan]), 1053
The hornbean tree and other poems (Norman, Charles), 1108
The hullabaloo ABC (Cleary, Beverly), 730
In the palace of the Ocean King (Singer, Marilyn), 1217
The jumblies (Lear, Edward), 990
Keepers (Schertle, Alice), 1192
Knots on a counting rope (Martin, Bill [William Ivan]), 1053
A little excitement (Harshman, Marc), 878
Mailing May (Tunnell, Michael O.), 1260
Mama and me and the Model-T (Gibbons, Faye), 834
Mountain wedding (Gibbons, Faye), 834
My buddy (Osofsky, Audrey), 1118
My father's boat (Garland, Sherry), 829
Night tree (Bunting, Eve [Anne Evelyn]), 695
Once when I was scared (Pittman, Helena Clare), 1140
The owl who became the moon (London, Jonathan), 1018
Prince William (Rand, Gloria), 1155
Salt hands (Aragon, Jane Chelsea), 612
Salty dog (Rand, Gloria), 1155
Salty sails north (Rand, Gloria), 1155
Salty takes off (Rand, Gloria), 1155
Secret place (Bunting, Eve [Anne Evelyn]), 695
The sun, the wind and the rain (Peters, Lisa Westberg), 1134
Up and down on the merry-go-round (Martin, Bill [William Ivan]), 1054
The walloping window blind (Carryl, Charles E. [Charles Edward]), 713
Water's way (Peters, Lisa Westberg), 1134
Whiffle Squeek (Cohen, Caron Lee), 734
White Dynamite and Curly Kidd (Martin, Bill [William Ivan]), 1054
The wild horses of Sweetbriar (Kinsey-Warnock, Natalie), 963
Willie takes a hike (Rand, Gloria), 1155
With a dog like that, a kid like me . . . (Rosen, Michael J. [1954-]), 1174
Raney, Ken. *Stick horse,* 1155

Reidel, Marlene. *Jacob and the robbers,* 1159
Reidy, Kathleen. *Alphabet sheep* (Mendoza, George), 1065
    Silly sheep and other sheepish rhymes (Mendoza, George), 1065
Reifel, Bruce. *Babette Cole's ponies* (Cole, Babette), 735
    Dad (Cole, Babette), 736
Reilly, Jack. *You are what you are* (McLenighan, Valjean), 1038
Reiner, Traudl. *Me and Clara and Baldwin the pony* (Inkiow, Dimiter), 928
    Me and Clara and Casimir the cat (Inkiow, Dimiter), 928
    Me and Clara and Snuffy the dog (Inkiow, Dimiter), 928
    Me and my sister Clara (Inkiow, Dimiter), 928
Reiner, Walter. *Me and Clara and Baldwin the pony* (Inkiow, Dimiter), 928
    Me and Clara and Casimir the cat (Inkiow, Dimiter), 928
    Me and Clara and Snuffy the dog (Inkiow, Dimiter), 928
    Me and my sister Clara (Inkiow, Dimiter), 928
Reinl, Edda. *The little snake,* 1159
    Mother hen (McCrea, Lilian), 1028
    The three little pigs (The three little pigs), 1252
Reisberg, Mira. *Just like home = Como en mi tierra* (Miller, Elizabeth I.), 1070
    Leaving for America (Bresnick-Perry, Roslyn), 675
Reisberg, Veg. *Baby Rattlesnake* (Ata, Te), 620
    Elinda who danced in the sky (Moroney, Lynn), 1084
Reiser, Lynn. *Any kind of dog,* 1159
    Bedtime cat, 1159
    Best friends think alike, 1159
    Cherry pies and lullabies, 1160
    Christmas counting, 1160
    Dog and cat, 1160
    Earthdance, 1160
    Little clam, 1160
    Night thunder and the Queen of the Wild Horses, 1160
    The surprise family, 1160
    Two mice in three fables, 1160
Reisman, Celia. *Jeremy and the ghost* (Charlton, Elizabeth), 721
Reiss, John J. *Colors,* 1160
    Numbers, 1160
    Shapes, 1160
Reiss, Susan. *Feet* (Chase, Catherine), 722
Reitveld, Jane Klatt. *Monkey island,* 1160
Remington, Barbara. *The Christmas mouse* (Wenning, Elisabeth), 1289
Remington, Frederic. *My very first book of cowboy songs* (Moon, Dolly M.), 1079
Remkiewicz, Frank. *Ants can't dance* (Jackson, Ellen B.), 934
    Froggy gets dressed (London, Jonathan), 1017
    Froggy goes to bed (London, Jonathan), 1017
    Froggy goes to school (London, Jonathan), 1017
    Froggy learns to swim (London, Jonathan), 1017
    Froggy plays soccer (London, Jonathan), 1017
    Froggy's first Christmas (London, Jonathan), 1017
    Froggy's first kiss (London, Jonathan), 1017
    Froggy's Halloween (London, Jonathan), 1017
    Greedyanna, 1160

I love Saturday (Giff, Patricia Reilly), 836
Incredible Ned (Maynard, Bill), 1062
Just enough carrots (Murphy, Stuart J.), 1097
The last time I saw Harris, 1160
Let's go, Froggy! (London, Jonathan), 1017
Little Red Monkey (London, Jonathan), 1017
Piggy and Dad (Martin, David), 1055
Quiet, Wyatt! (Maynard, Bill), 1062
Rabbit's pajama party (Murphy, Stuart J.), 1097
Renfro, Ed. *The city witch and the country witch* (Williams, Jay), 1297
Resko, John. *The snowplow that tried to go south* (Retan, Walter), 1160
Ressmeyer, Roger. *Astronaut to zodiac,* 1160
Rettich, Margret. *The voyage of the jolly boat,* 1160
Rex, Michael. *Crunch munch* (London, Jonathan), 1017
    My fire engine, 1160
    Snuggle wuggle (London, Jonathan), 1018
    Sunrise (Pittman, Helena Clare), 1140
    Who builds? 1160
    Who digs? 1160
    Wiggle, waggle (London, Jonathan), 1018
Rey, H. A. (Hans Augusto). *Anybody at home?* 1161
    Billy's picture (Rey, Margret [Margret Elisabeth Waldstein]), 1161
    Cecily G and the nine monkeys, 1161
    Curious George, 1161
    Curious George flies a kite (Rey, Margret [Margret Elisabeth Waldstein]), 1161
    Curious George gets a medal, 1161
    Curious George goes to the hospital (Rey, Margret [Margret Elisabeth Waldstein]), 1162
    Curious George learns the alphabet, 1161
    Curious George rides a bike, 1161
    Curious George takes a job, 1161
    Don't frighten the lion (Brown, Margaret Wise), 684
    Elizabite, 1161
    Elizabite, adventures of a carnivorous plant, 1161
    Feed the animals, 1161
    How do you get there? 1161
    Humpty Dumpty and other Mother Goose songs, 1161
    Katy no-pocket (Payne, Emmy), 1128
    Look for the letters, 1161
    The original Curious George, 1161
    The park book (Zolotow, Charlotte [Shapiro]), 1323
    Pretzel (Rey, Margret [Margret Elisabeth Waldstein]), 1162
    Pretzel and the puppies (Rey, Margret [Margret Elisabeth Waldstein]), 1162
    See the circus, 1161
    Spotty (Rey, Margret [Margret Elisabeth Waldstein]), 1162
    Tit for tat, 1161
    Where's my baby? 1161
Reyna, Marilyn De *see* Hafner, Marylin
Reynolds, Adrian. *Baby loves* (Lawrence, Michael [Michael C.]), 989
    Harry and the snow king (Whybrow, Ian), 1292
    Sammy and the dinosaurs (Whybrow, Ian), 1292
    Silly Goose and Dizzy Duck play hide-and-seek (Grindley, Sally), 865
Reynolds, Jan. *Amazon,* 1162
    Down under, 1162
    Far north, 1162
    Himalaya, 1162

Sorel, Edward. *The goings on at Little Wishful* (Miller, Warren), 1072
  Gwendolyn and the weathercock (Sherman, Nancy), 1210
  Gwendolyn the miracle hen (Sherman, Nancy), 1210
  Pablo paints a picture (Miller, Warren), 1072
Sorensen, Henri. *A book about God* (Fitch, Florence Mary), 810
  Daddy played music for the cows (Weidt, Maryann N.), 1284
  Deep river (Moore, Elaine), 1080
  Footprints and shadows (Dodd, Anne Westcott), 778
  The gift of the tree (Tresselt, Alvin R.), 1257
  Grandaddy's highway (Diller, Harriett), 777
  Hurricane! (London, Jonathan), 1017
  I love you as much . . . (Melmed, Laura Krauss), 1065
  Jumbo's lullaby (Melmed, Laura Krauss), 1065
  Mommy's lap (Horowitz, Ruth), 917
  My grandfather's house (Coville, Bruce), 747
  New Hope, 1225
  Prince Nautilus (Melmed, Laura Krauss), 1065
  River day (Mason, Jane B.), 1057
  Sun up (Tresselt, Alvin R.), 1257
  What does the rain play? (Carlstrom, Nancy White), 711
  When the rain stops (Cole, Sheila), 738
Sorine, Daniel S. *Our ballet class* (Sorine, Stephanie Riva), 1225
Souci, Daniel San *see* San Souci, Daniel
Souhami, Jessica. *The leopard's drum*, 1225
  No dinner! 1225
  Old MacDonald had a farm (Old MacDonald had a farm), 1113
  Rama and the demon king, 1225
Sours, Michael. *Howard and Gracie's luncheonette* (Kroll, Steven), 976
Souza, Diana. *Heather has two mommies* (Newman, Lesléa), 1103
Souza, Paul M. *Andy and the wild ducks* (Short, Mayo), 1211
Sowden, Henry. *The grand old Duke of York*, 1225
Sowter, Nita. *Apple pie* (Wellington, Anne), 1286
  Hey diddle diddle (Mother Goose), 1089
  Hugo and his grandma (Storr, Catherine [Cole]), 1238
  Little Boy Blue (Mother Goose), 1089
Spalding, Andrea. *Me and Mr. Mah*, 1225
Spangler, Noel. *Colors* (Allington, Richard L.), 599
  Measuring (Allington, Richard L.), 599
  Tasting (Allington, Richard L.), 600
Spanner, Helmut. *I am a little cat*, 1225
Spear, Laurinda. *The fisherman and his wife* (Grimm, Jacob), 859
Spearing, Craig. *Prairie dog pioneers* (Harper, Jo), 877
Spector, Joel. *Perseus* (Mayer, Marianna), 1060
Speidel, Sandra. *Clap clap!* (Helldorfer, M. C. [Mary Claire]), 889
  Coconut kind of day (Joseph, Lynn), 947
  Evan's corner (Hill, Elizabeth Starr), 898
  My mama sings (Peterson, Jeanne Whitehouse), 1135
Speirs, John. *A fair bear share* (Murphy, Stuart J.), 1097

The magic school bus plants seeds (Relf, Patricia), 1160
Spellman, Susan. *The little drummer boy* (Quattrocki, Carolyn), 1153
  A small treasury of Christmas poems and prayers (A small treasury of Christmas poems and prayers), 1220
  A small treasury of Easter poems and prayers (A small treasury of Easter poems and prayers), 1220
Spengler, Kenneth. *A campfire for cowboy Billy* (Ulmer, Wendy K.), 1263
  How Jackrabbit got his very long ears (Irbinskas, Heather), 930
  Somewhere in the ocean (Ward, Jennifer), 1279
  Way out in the desert (Marsh, T. J.), 1050
Spengler, Margaret. *Clickety clack* (Spence, Robert, III.), 1226
Sperling, Thomas. *Columbus Day* (DeRubertis, Barbara), 774
Spetter, Jung-Hee. *Just a minute* (Kranendonk, Anke), 971
  Lily and Trooper's fall, 1226
  Lily and Trooper's spring, 1226
  Lily and Trooper's summer, 1226
  Lily and Trooper's winter, 1226
Spiedel, Sandra. *Fixing the crack of dawn* (Silverman, Erica), 1214
Spiegel, Doris. *Danny and Company 92*, 1226
Spiegelman, Art. *I'm a dog!* 1226
Spier, Peter. *Bill's service station*, 1226
  The Book of Jonah (Bible. Old Testament. Jonah), 654
  Bored - nothing to do! 1226
  The cow who fell in the canal (Krasilovsky, Phyllis), 971
  Crash! bang! boom! 1226
  Dreams, 1226
  The Erie Canal, 1226
  Fast-slow, high-low, 1226
  Firehouse, 1226
  Food market, 1226
  The fox went out on a chilly night (The fox went out on a chilly night), 817
  Gobble, growl, grunt, 1226
  Hurrah, we're outward bound! (Mother Goose), 1089
  The legend of New Amsterdam, 1226
  Little cats, 1226
  Little dogs, 1226
  Little ducks, 1226
  Little rabbits, 1226
  London Bridge is falling down (Mother Goose), 1090
  My school, 1226
  Noah's ark, 1226
  Oh, were they ever happy! 1226
  People, 1226
  The pet store, 1226
  Peter Spier's Christmas! 1226
  Peter Spier's circus! 1226
  Peter Spier's rain, 1226
  The Star-Spangled Banner (Key, Francis Scott), 959
  To market! To market! (Mother Goose), 1092
  The toy shop, 1226
  We the people, 1226

T

Taylor, Bridget Starr. *Harry McNairy, Tooth Fairy* (Alper, Ann Fitzerald), 600

Taylor, C. J. (Carrie J.). *Firedancers* (Waboose, Jan Bourdeau), 1273

Taylor, Cheryl Munro. *Camel caravan* (Roberts, Bethany), 1165
Coconut mon (Milstein, Linda Breiner), 1073
Snug (Hanson, Mary Elizabeth), 876
Song and dance (Hopkins, Lee Bennett), 916

Taylor, Elizabeth Watson. *The animals who changed their colors* (Allamand, Pascale), 597

Taylor, Harriet Peck. *Coyote and the laughing butterflies*, 1245
Ulaq and the northern lights, 1245

Taylor, Jody. *The old witch and the ghost parade* (DeLage, Ida), 766

Taylor, Kim. *Buffy the barn owl* (Burton, Jane), 699
Butterfly (Ling, Mary), 1008
Chester the chick (Burton, Jane), 699
Dabble the duckling (Burton, Jane), 699
Dazy the guinea pig (Burton, Jane), 699
The egg (Burton, Robert), 700
Freckles the rabbit (Burton, Jane), 699
Frog, 1245
Ginger the kitten (Burton, Jane), 699
Too fast to see, 1245
Too small to see, 1245
Trill the fox cub (Burton, Jane), 699

Taylor, Liba. *Mazal-Tov* (Patterson, José), 1127

Taylor, Martin. *Good night, a pop-up lullaby* (Pienkowski, Jan), 1137

Taylor, Michael C. *The sing-song of old man kangaroo* (Kipling, Rudyard), 964

Taylor, Myke. *Some bugs glow in the dark* (Llewellyn, Claire), 1014
Spiders have fangs (Llewellyn, Claire), 1014

Taylor, Scott. *Dinosaur James*, 1246
Fiesta! (Behrens, June), 641

Taylor, Stephen. *The story of Kwanzaa* (Washington, Donna L.), 1280

Taylor, Tamar. *How Georgina drove the car very carefully from Boston to New York* (Bate, Lucy), 637

Teague, Mark. *Baby tamer*, 1246
The flying dragon room (Wood, Audrey), 1305
How do Dinosaurs say goodnight? (Damjan, Mischa), 759
The iguana brothers, a perfect day (Johnston, Tony), 944
The Lost and found, 1246
No moon, no milk! (Babcock, Chris), 623
One Halloween night, 1246
Pigsty, 1246
The secret shortcut, 1246
Sweet dream pie (Wood, Audrey), 1305
The trouble with the Johnsons, 1246

Teare, Brad. *Dance, pioneer, dance!* (Walton, Rick), 1278

Teasdale, Denise. *Mrs. Mary Malarky's seven cats* (Hindley, Judy), 901
Rob goes a-hunting (Turnbull, Ann), 1261
Walter's magic wand (Houghton, Eric), 917

Teason, James. *Science* (Allington, Richard L.), 599

Teckentrup, Britta. *Coyote makes man* (Sage, James), 1184

Tedesco, Donna. *Do you know how much I love you?* 1246

Tegg, Simon. *Jetliners* (Richards, Jon), 1163

Teichman, Mary. *Color* (Rossetti, Christina Georgina), 1176
Stars for Sarah (Turner, Ann Warren), 1261

Tejima, Keizaburo. *The bears' autumn*, 1246
Fox's dream, 1246
Ho-limlim, 1246
Owl lake, 1246
Swan sky, 1246
Woodpecker forest, 1246

Temple, Frances. *Tiger soup*, 1246

Tenggren, Gustaf. *Mother Goose* (Mother Goose), 1090
The night before Christmas (Moore, Clement C.), 1080
Thumbelina (Andersen, H. C. [Hans Christian]), 605

Tenniel, John. *The nursery "Alice"* (Carroll, Lewis), 713

Tenny, Eric. *Lions and tigers* (Pluckrose, Henry Arthur), 1141

Tennyson, Noel. *The lady's chair and the ottoman*, 1246

Terrett, Paul. *A man and his hat* (Parr, Letitia), 1126

Testa, Fulvio. *The butterfly collector* (Lewis, Naomi), 1002
The ideal home, 1247
If you look around, 1247
If you take a paintbrush, 1247
If you take a pencil, 1247
The land where the ice cream grows, 1247
Leaves (Lewis, Naomi), 1002
A long trip to Z, 1247
Never satisfied, 1247
The paper airplane (Baumann, Kurt), 638
The paper airplane, 1247
Wolf's favor, 1247

Tester, Sylvia Root. *Chase!* 1247
Parade! 1247
A visit to the zoo, 1247

Thaler, Mike. *The yellow brick toad*, 1247

Thaler, Shmuel. *Pumpkin circle* (Levenson, George), 999

Thamer, Katie. *The black horse* (Mayer, Marianna), 1060

Tharlet, Eve. *The brave little tailor* (Grimm, Jacob), 858
Dizzy from fools (Miller, M. L.), 1070
Happy birthday, Davy (Weninger, Brigitte), 1288
Jack in luck (Grimm, Jacob), 860
Little pig, big trouble, 1247
Merry Christmas, Davy! (Weninger, Brigitte), 1289
The princess and the pea (Andersen, H. C. [Hans Christian]), 604
What's the matter, Davy? (Weninger, Brigitte), 1289
Why are you fighting, Davy? (Weninger, Brigitte), 1289
Will you mind the baby, Davy? (Weninger, Brigitte), 1289
The wishing table (Grimm, Jacob), 863

Thatcher, Frances. *Percival's party* (Hynard, Julia), 926
Snowy the rabbit (Hynard, Stephen), 926
Snuffles' house (Faunce-Brown, Daphne), 805

U

V

X

Y

Z

GAYLORD